Allison Prites, '59
Eastern Baptist Seminary,
Philadelphia 31, Pa.

ANALYTICAL HEBREW AND CHALDEE

LEXICON.

THE ANALYTICAL
HEBREW AND CHALDEE LEXICON:

CONSISTING OF

AN ALPHABETICAL ARRANGEMENT OF EVERY WORD AND
INFLECTION CONTAINED IN THE OLD TESTAMENT
SCRIPTURES, PRECISELY AS THEY OCCUR
IN THE SACRED TEXT, WITH A

GRAMMATICAL ANALYSIS OF EACH WORD, AND LEXICOGRAPHICAL
ILLUSTRATION OF THE MEANINGS.

A COMPLETE SERIES OF HEBREW AND CHALDEE PARADIGMS,
WITH GRAMMATICAL REMARKS AND EXPLANATIONS.

BY B. DAVIDSON,

AUTHOR OF THE SYRIAC AND CHALDEE READING LESSONS, AND JOINT AUTHOR OF THE ELEMENTARY
ARABIC GRAMMAR AND READING LESSONS, ETC.

SAMUEL BAGSTER AND SONS LIMITED
80 WIGMORE STREET, LONDON, W1
NEW YORK: HARPER AND BROTHERS

Printed in Great Britain
by T. and A. Constable Ltd., Hopetoun Street,
Printers to the University of Edinburgh

1956

PREFACE.

OF the several languages which constitute the group commonly designated the Shemitic Family, as those spoken by the descendants of Shem, two have always held the foremost place of interest and importance, namely, the Hebrew and the Chaldee. This distinction is owing to the fact of their being the channel through which the Divine Revelation was imparted directly to the chosen people of Israel, to show them the way of salvation and prepare them for the coming of that Just One to whom the Law of Moses, the Prophets, and the Psalms, successively bore their continuous witness as the Saviour of mankind.

The study of the "Oracles of God" in their original form never relaxed among the favoured people to whom they had been committed, but continued to be jealously treasured when, on their rejection of the Gospel, it was preached to the Gentiles, and the Scriptures transferred to European language. Few, however, among the doctors of the early Christian Church, were learned in the Hebrew tongue; through the mediæval ages the Old Testament of their Bible was the Septuagint Greek Version in the East, and the Latin Vulgate in the West of Europe, until, on the Revival of Learning in the fifteenth century, this among other branches of knowledge began to be increased, Christian Hebraists to flourish, Grammars and Lexicons to be issued in abundance. Eminent among lexicographers were Pagninus, the Buxtorfs, Simonis, and others, who retained the Etymological arrangement of words in vogue among the Jews, according to derivation from their verbal roots.

After them the renowned Gesenius adopted the Alphabetical arrangement of Nouns and Particles, by which a great facility was afforded to students, who often experienced a difficulty in tracing their Radical derivation. Other famous Hebraists, as Lee and Fürst, followed the Alphabetical example set by Gesenius, and the result has been that in modern times the knowledge of Hebrew has greatly advanced, both in Universities and Collegiate Schools, and also among those who, without the advantage of professorial instruction, study for themselves.

A still further step, however, remained to be taken for the benefit of these. Not only the derivation of Nouns, but the inflections of Verbs also, and the combinatio‎ of Particles, are often difficult to a beginner, and to such as for want of leisure cannot acquire or afterwards retain for themselves the mastery of all the Hebrew forms as they could wish. Accordingly, the ANALYTICAL HEBREW AND CHALDEE LEXICON has been compiled, in which every separate word of the Old Testament original, in every variety of conformation, is exhibited in its Alphabetical place, accompanied with a full grammatical Analysis of its composition, the indication of its root, and its English meaning after the best authorities. The utility of such a work is obvious. and can hardly be overrated. To augment its value, a complete Series of Paradigms, both of Nouns and Verbs, with explanatory remarks, is prefixed.

Although the primary design of this Lexicon has been to supply the learner wit‎ the utmost possible assistance, it is no less serviceable for permanent use by those who have attained a scholarly proficiency in the study of the Hebrew and Chaldee Scriptures.

THE CONTENTS.

PAGE

OBJECT AND PLAN vii
LIST OF ABBREVIATIONS x

GRAMMATICAL OBSERVATIONS, WITH TABLES OF PARADIGMS OF THE HEBREW LANGUAGE.

SECTION   I.   The Personal Pronoun . . . (TABLE A) 9
                   The Separate Pronoun 10
    II.   The Verbal Suffix 10
    III.   Suffixes to the Noun in the Singular 12
    IV.   Suffixes to the Noun in the Plural 12
    V.   Suffixes attached to the Prefix Prepositions לְ and בְּ, the Conjunction כְּ, אֵת (Sign of the Accusative) and the Prepositions מִן and עַם 13
    VI.   Unusual Conjugations 15
    VII.   Quadriliterals 17
    VIII.   Regular Verb—KAL . . . (TABLE B, p. 15) . . 17
    IX.   Niphal 20
    X.   Piel and Pual 21
    XI.   Hiphil and Hophal 22
    XII.   Hithpael 24
    XIII.   Verb Pe Guttural . . . . (TABLE C, p. 25) . . 26
    XIV.   Ayin Guttural . . . . (TABLE D, p. 25) . 28
    XV.   Lamed Guttural . . . . (TABLE E, p. 26) . 29
    XVI.   Regular Verb with Suffixes . . . (TABLE F, p. 29) . 30
    XVII.   Irregular Verbs—Pe Nun . . (TABLE G, p. 32) . 33
    XVIII.   Ayin doubled . . (TABLE H) . . . 34
    XIX.   Pe Aleph . . (TABLE I) . . . 39
    XX.   Pe Yod . . (TABLE K) . . . 41
    XXI.   Ayin Vav . . (TABLE L, p. 44) . . 45
    XXII.   Ayin Yod . . (Ditto) . 47
    XXIII.   Lamed Aleph . . (TABLE M) . . 48
    XXIV.   Lamed He . . (TABLE N, p. 50) . 51
    XXV.   Verbs doubly Anomalous 54
    XXVI.   Nouns derived from the Regular Verb 55
    XXVII.   Irregular Verbs 56
    XXVIII.   The Vowel-changes of Nouns 57
    XXIX.   On the Declension of the Masculine Nouns in General (TABLE O, pp. 59, 60) . 58

THE CONTENTS.

PAG

SECTION XXX. First Declension of the Masculines 61
XXXI. Second Declension of the Masculines 62
XXXII. Third Declension of the Masculines 63
XXXIII. Fourth Declension of the Masculines 64
XXXIV. Fifth Declension of the Masculines 64
XXXV. Sixth Declension of the Masculines 65
XXXVI. Seventh Declension of the Masculines 68
XXXVII. Eighth Declension of the Masculines 69
XXXVIII. Ninth Declension of the Masculines 70
XXXIX. Vowel-changes in the Formation of **Feminine Nouns** . 71
XL. On the Declension of the Feminine Nouns in General . **(TABLE O, p. 60)** 73
XLI. Tenth Declension, or the *First* of the Feminines . . . 73
XLII. Eleventh Declension, or the *Second* of the Feminines . . . 73
XLIII. Twelfth Declension, or the *Third* of the Feminines . . . 74
XLIV. Thirteenth Declension, or the *Fourth* of the Feminines . . 75
XLV. Irregular Nouns 76

OF THE CHALDEE LANGUAGE.

The Personal Pronoun . . . . **(TABLE P)** . 78
XLVI. On the Suffixes to Nouns Singular and Plural 78
XLVII. On the Regular Verb . . . . . **(TABLE Q, p. 79)** . 80
XLVIII. Unfrequent Conjugations 80
XLIX. Verbs with Gutturals 81
L. On the Regular Verb with Suffixes . . . **(TABLE R, p. 81)** . 82
TABLE T. Verbs Ayin doubled 82
LI. On Verbs Pe Nun . . . . . . **(TABLE S, p. 82)** . 83
LII. On Verbs Pe Yod (and Pe Vav) . . . **(TABLE U)** . . 83
LIII. Verbs Pe Aleph 83
LIV. On Verbs Ayin Vav (and Ayin Yod) . . . **(TABLE V)** . 84
LV. On Verbs Lamed Aleph (and Lamed He) . . **(TABLE W, p. 85)** . 86
LVI. Verbs doubly Anomalous 86
TABLE X. Declension of Masculine and Feminine Nouns . . . 87
LVII. First Declension of Masculines 88
LVIII. Second Declension of Masculines 88
LIX. Third Declension of Masculines 88
LX. Fourth Declension of Masculines 89
LXI. Fifth Declension of Masculines 89
LXII. Sixth Declension of Masculines 89
LXIII. Seventh Declension of Masculines 89
LXIV. Eighth Declension, or the *First* of Feminines 89
LXV. Ninth Declension, or the *Second* of Feminines 89
LXVI. Tenth Declension, or the *Third* of Feminines 89
LXVII. Eleventh Declension, or the *Fourth* of Feminines . . . 89
LXVIII. Irregular Nouns 90

THE ANALYTICAL HEBREW AND CHALDEE LEXICON, Containing the Alphabetical
Arrangement of the Words of the Entire Hebrew Scriptures, with parsing Analysis
and Lexicography . . . . . . **I. to DCCLXXXIV**

THE OBJECT AND PLAN

OF THIS

LEXICON.

FROM what has been briefly stated in the Preface, it will sufficiently appear that this Work is intended, not so much to teach the first principles of Hebrew Grammar, as to provide the Student who has already begun to read a little (ever so little) with the means of making *speedy and sure after progress.* Its object is to assist him in his practice of the Sacred Text, by enabling him to apply the Rules he has learned, and may be learning; and, by supplying him with the Analysis of every single word in the entire language, under every form it can assume, it promises him exemption from the tedium and disappointment of uncertainty in his investigations.

Experience has shown that multitudes of Hebrew students, after having overcome the first difficulties under the instruction of a living Teacher, abandon further study for lack of a Guide through the yet untrodden intricacies of the Language. Our aim has been to provide a permanent Instructor, to succeed the living Teacher in his function of solving the difficulties of the inquiring Student; and we have endeavoured neither to mislead by imperfect information, nor to disappoint by suppressing the explanation of apparently trifling matters.

As an ANALYTICAL LEXICON, this work embraces especially the ETYMOLOGY and SIGNIFICATION of WORDS.

The following summary will exhibit the mode of treatment adopted :—

THE ETYMOLOGY OF WORDS.

I. The entire body of Words, contained in the Hebrew Scriptures, exactly as they are found in the Text, have been thrown into Alphabetical order : so that each, accompanied by its prefixes, suffixes, and under every modification of form, may be immediately found by an alphabetical reference.

II. Each word thus arranged is concisely and fully *parsed*, its composition is explained, and its simple form and root given.

III. Whenever the form of the word analysed agrees with the Tables of Paradigms, a plain but full statement of the nature of the word has been considered sufficient; but where any peculiar difficulty or irregularity exists, reference has also been made to the section of the Grammatical Introduction in which the deviation is explained.

IV To provide standards of inflexion and comparison, a complete series of PARADIGMS of the Verbs, Pronouns, and Nouns, of both the Hebrew and Chaldee languages, has been prepared.

V. These Tables are accompanied with Explanations and Remarks, which account for every deviation from the Tables, and comprise a COLLECTION OF EVERY SINGLE EXCEPTIONAL CASE. In the body of the work, these *Explanations* are indicated by reference to their number.

VI Every form that happens to occur but once in the Bible has its reference to the passage given at the foot of the page. To this we have attended in the minutest difference of the forms, in order to increase the references, so valuable to the beginner who has no Concordance When, however, the form is especially peculiar, more than one reference is given.

 ⁎ It is an interesting and important fact, that this collection of citations constitutes a Concordance of more than three-fourths of the forms of the Language.

VII. The place of the Accent is throughout indicated by a pependicular line (‚) under the tone-syllable, except when the form is affected by a pausal accent, where (.) is used to indicate the tone-syllable; while the absence of pausal accent and influence are marked with (‚).

VIII. Kamets Hhattuph (ŏ) is distinguished from the long Kamets (ā) by this sign (ₒ). But this is used only in the forms analysed, in the leading forms of the derivatives under their respective roots, and in those forms where its use requires particular notice.

THE SIGNIFICATION OR LEXICOGRAPHY OF WORDS.

IX. A full explanation of the various meanings of the words will be found under their respective Roots in their alphabetical place.

X. In preparing the Lexicography, Gesenius has been chiefly relied on for definitions; but the works of Dr. Lee, Winer, Biesenthal, Fürst, and others, have been compared throughout.

XI. In addition to the various significations of each root, a Synoptical List of all the words derived from each is given, to aid the student in remembering the connection between the root and its derivatives.

BENJAMIN DAVIDSON.

LIST OF ABBREVIATIONS

IN THE WORK.

abs. st.	absolute state	genit.	genitive	part.	participle
acc.	accent, accusative	gent.	gentile & gentilic	patronym.	patronymi
a. & act.	active	gutt.	guttural	perh.	perhaps
adj.	adjective	Hiph.	Hiphil	pers.	person
adv.	adverb	Hithpa.	Hithpael	Pi.	Piël
anom.	anomaly & anomalous	Hithpal.	Hithpalel	Pil.	Pilel
ap. & apoc.	apocopated	Hithpol.	Hithpolel	pl.	plural
Aph.	Aphel	Hoph.	Hophal	Pol.	Polal & Polel
aphær.	aphæresis	Hothp.	Hothpael	Polp	Polpal
Arab.	Arabic	i. q.	id quod	preced.	preceding
art.	article	id.	idem	pref.	prefix
bef.	before	imp.	imperative	prep.	preposition
c. & com.	common	impl.	implied	pret.	preterite
causat.	causative	inf. & infin.	infinitive	prim.	primary
Ch. & Chald.	Chaldee	interrog.	interrogative	pr. n. m	proper name, mas
coll.	collated	intrans.	intransitive		culine
collect.	collectively	irr. & irreg.	irregular	prob.	probably
comp.	compare	Ithpe.	Ithpeel	pron. demon.	demonstrative pro-
compd.	compounded	Ishtaph.	Ishtaphal		noun
compos.	composition	K.	Keri	pron. relat.	relative pronoun
concr.	concrete	Kh. & Kheth.	Khethiv	prop.	properly
conj.	conjunction & con-	l. c.	loco citato	prosth.	prosthetic
	junctive	lab.	labial	Pu.	Pual
const.	construed	lett.	letter	Pul.	Pulal
constr.	construct	loc.	local	q. v.	quod vide
contr.	contracted	m. & masc.	masculine	R.	Root
conv.	conversive	Mak.	Makkeph	Seg. n	Segolate noun
cop.	copulative	metaph.	metaphorically	Shaph.	Shaphel
d. & dec.	declension	meton.	metonymy & meto-	sc.	scilicet
Dag.	Dagesh		nymically	Sept.	Septuagint
def. & defect.	defective	monos.	monosyllable & mo-	suff.	suffix
demon.	demonstrative		nosyllabic	s. & sing.	singular
denom.	denominative	n. f. s.	noun, feminine, sin-	Talm.	Talmud
deriv.	derivative		gular	term.	termination
dist.	distinctive	n. m. s.	noun, masculine, sin-	Tiph.	Tiphal
du.	dual　[tically.		gular	trop.	tropically
emph.	emphatic & empha-	n. m. p.	noun, masculine, plu-	ult.	ultimate
Eng. vers.	English version		ral	Vulg.	Vulgate
epenth.	epenthetic	Niph.	Niphal	§ & rem.	refers to the Paradigms
Ethiop.	Ethiopic	Nith.	Nithpael		and remarks at the
euph.	euphony	numb. card.	cardinal number		commencement of
f. & fem.	feminine	obsol.	obsolete		the work
f.	for	p. & pass.	passive	1 p., 2 p.,	1 pers. & 2 pers., &c., 1st
foll.	following	Pa.	Pael		or 2nd person
fr.	from	Pal.	Palel	3 p. s. m.	3rd person singular
fut.	future	parad.	paradigm		masculine, &c.
gen.	gender	parag.	paragogic		

ᵃ, ᵇ, or ᶜ, &c. after any word, refers to the passage at the foot of the page.

׀, ׀, ׀, or ׀, placed before any word indicates that such word occurs only with this conjunction.

׀, ׀, ׀, or ׀, placed before any word indicates that such word occurs with and without this conjunction.

(This sign divides the explanation of the word's prefix from the analysis of the word itself.

[ ] inclose forms which do not actually occur in the Scriptures.

TABLES OF PARADIGMS

OF

THE HEBREW LANGUAGE,

WITH

REMARKS AND OCCASIONAL EXPLANATIONS.

SECTION I.—THE PERSONAL PRONOUN

TABLE A.	THE PERSONAL PRONOUN.				
SEPARATE PRONOUN.	**VERBAL SUFFIX.**		**NOMINAL SUFFIX.**		
	A. SIMPLE FORM.	**B.** WITH נ EPENTHETIC.	**A.** SUFF. TO NOUNS SINGULAR.	**B.** TO NOUNS PLURAL AND DUAL.	
Singular.					
1. *com.* אָנֹכִי, in pause אָנֹכִי; אֲנִי, in pause אָנִי; אֲנִי } *I.*	־ֵנִי; ־ַנִי; נִי *me.*	־ַנִּי, ־ַנִּי *me.*	־ִי *my.*	־ַי *my.*	
2. { *m.* (אַתָּ) אַתָּה, in pause אַתָּה; *f.* אַתְּ (אַתִּי) prop. אַתִּי; (אַתִּי) in p. אָתְּ } *thou.*	ךָ, in pause ־ֶךָ } *thee.* ; ־ְךָ ; ־ָךְ ; ־ֵךְ *thee.*	־ֶ֫ךָּ *thee.* not found.	ךָ, in pause ־ֶ֫ךָ } *thy.* ; ־ָ֫ךְ, ךְ *thy.*	־ֶי֫ךָ } *thy.* ; ־ַ֫יִךְ *thy.*	
3. { *m.* הוּא *he.*	־ֵהוּ, ־ֵ֫הוּ; וֹ, הוּ, ־ֹ, וֹ; (־ֹמוֹ) } *him.*	(נּוֹ, ־ֶ֫נּוּ) *him.*	הוּ, וֹ, ־ֹ; הוּ, וֹ *his.*	־ָיו, ־ֵ֫יהוּ *his.*	
{ *f.* הִיא *she.*	הָ; ־ָהּ; ־ֶ֫הָ *her.*	־ֶ֫נָּה *her.*	הָ; ־ָהּ; ־ֶ֫הָ *her.*	־ֶ֫יהָ *her.*	
Plural.					
1. *com.* (נַחְנוּ) אֲנַ֫חְנוּ, (אֲנוּ) } *we.*	נוּ; ־ֵ֫נוּ; ־ָ֫נוּ (*nos*) *us.*	־ֵ֫נּוּ *us.*	נוּ; ־ֵ֫נוּ; *our.*	־ֵ֫ינוּ *our.*	
2. { *m.* אַתֶּם *f.* אַתֶּ֫נָה, אַתֵּן } *ye.*	כֶם } ; כֶן *you.*	not found.	כֶם ; כֶן } *your.*	־ֵיכֶם ; ־ֵיכֶן } *your.*	
3. { *m.* הֵ֫מָּה, הֵם } *they.*	־ָם, ם, ־ֵם, ־ֶם, ; ־ֹמוֹ, ־ֵ֫מוֹ, ־ָ֫מוֹ (*eos*) } *them.*	not found.	־ָ֫מוֹ, ־ָם; הֶם } *their.*	־ֵ֫ימוֹ, ־ֵיהֶם } *their.*	
{ *f.* הֵ֫נָּה, הֵן }	־ָן, ן; ־ֵן, ־ֶן; ־ֶ֫נָה (*eas*) } *them.*		־ָן, הֶן, ־ֶן *their.*	־ֵ֫יהֶן *their.*	

SECTION I.—THE SEPARATE PRONOUN. (Table A).

REMARKS.

1. *First Person Singular.*

אָנֹכִי is the ancient and full form, of which אֲנִי is an abbreviation, and from the latter are formed the suffixes attached to nouns, verbs, &c.

2. *Second Person Singular.*

Instead of Dagesh forte in אַתָּה, אַתְּ (pl. אַתֶּם), the kindred dialects have נ before ת (Chald. & Arab. אַנְתְּ), which, however, is not the original form, but ת alone is the characteristic consonant.*

אַתְּ without ה occurs only in 1 Sa. 24. 19 ; Ps. 6. 4 ; Job 1. 10 ; Ec. 7. 22 ; Ne. 9. 6 ; it is, however, in each place corrected in the Keri. The *feminine* form אַתִּי in Ju. 17. 2 ; 1 Ki. 14. 2 ; 2 Ki. 4. 16, 23 ; 8. 1 ; Je. 4. 30 ; Eze. 36. 13, was originally pronounced אַתִּי (with the feminine designation ־ִי, probably from הִיא she, properly *thou she*, comp. תִּקְטְלִי) as in the Syriac and the vulgar Arabic. The pointing with Sheva is agreeably to the Keri אַתְּ, because the Jewish critics, as it appears, did not recognise the form אַתִּי. The same final ' appears likewise in the unfrequent form of the suffix ־ֵכִי, ־ֵיכִי.

3. *Third Person Singular.*

The masculine הוּא is of common gender in the Pentateuch, and signifies also *she* (which is expressed by הִיא only eleven times, viz., Ge. 14. 2 ; 20. 5 ; 38. 25 ; Le. 2. 15 ; 11. 39 ; 13. 10, 21 ; 16. 31 ; 21. 9 ; Nu. 5. 13). The punctuators, however, either from want of appreciating such an idiom, or for the sake of distinction, whenever הוּא stands in the text for הִיא, give it the appropriate pointing of this form, (הִוא), and require it to be read הִיא. It is, however,

to be sounded rather according to the old form הוּא. Besides the Pentateuch, הוּא occurs also in 1 Ki. 17. 15 ; Job 31. 11 ; Is. 30. 33.

4. *First Person Plural.*

אֲנַחְנוּ is manifestly the plural of אָנֹכִי, with the exchange of כ for ח, as אֲנוּ is of אֲנִי. The form אֲנוּ, from which the suffixes (נו, ־ֵנוּ, ־ָנוּ) are derived, is found only in Je. 42. 6, Khethib. The Masorites, however, did not recognize so unusual a form, and instead of it put אֲנַחְנוּ, which, indeed, some MSS. and editions have even as the reading of the text itself. Nevertheless, אֲנוּ appears also in the Rabbinical. The abbreviated form נַחְנוּ is found only six times, viz., Ge. 42. 11 ; Ex. 16. 7, 8 ; Nu. 32. 32 ; 2 Sa. 17. 12 ; La. 3. 42.

5. *Second Person Plural.*

אַתֵּן & אַתֶּם are blunted forms of אַתּוּם (Arab. *antum*, Chald. אַתּוּן, a form which lies at the foundation of some verbal inflexions, comp. the preterite with suffix), and אַתֵּין, the full final vowel giving place to the obtuse sound of *e*, somewhat in the manner of the third person (הֵם). אַתֵּן is found only once, Eze. 34. 31 (where another reading is אַתֶּם) ; and אַתֵּנָה (for which some MSS. have also אַתֵּנָּה) occurs only in Ge. 31. 6 ; Eze. 13. 11, 20 ; 34. 17.

6. *Third Person Plural.*

הֵם & הֵן are got from הוּא and הִיא in the same manner as אַתֶּם from אַתָּה. The ־ֵה in both forms (ה *paragogic*) has a *demonstrative* force.

SECTION II.—THE VERBAL SUFFIX.† (Table A).

REMARKS.

1. *First Person Singular*

Has this peculiarity, that the union vowel of the form נִי־ is invariably *Pattah*, though in an open syllable we expect *Kamets*, as in ־ָנוּ, ־ָהוּ ; but this

Kamets is found only in pause, e. g. Ex. 5. 22. For נִי־, the full form נִי־ is found with the *fut.* in 1 Ki. 2. 24, Kheth. For ־ֶנִּי see Ps. 118. 18 ; Ge. 30. 6 ; with the *fut.* Job 7. 14 ; 9. 34 ; ־ֵנִי Je. 50. 44.

---

* Comp. Sansc. *toa* ; Egypt. *entok*, fem. *ento* ; ancient and modern Pers. *tu* ; Greek τυ (συ) ; Germ. *tu*, *du* [Engl. *thou*], see Gesenius's Heb. Gram. § 33, note.

† Just as the separate suffixes stand for the nominative, so the inseparable, when appended to verbs, stand for the accusative, and but rarely for the dative, as with intransitive verbs. Particles having the force of a verb, or where the substantive verb must be supplied, take the verbal suffixes. As, הִנְנִי *behold me !* but on the contrary אֵינֶנּוּ he (is) *not*, עוֹדֶנּוּ *he (is) yet*, where the nominative is designated by the same suffix. The suffixes are but seldom employed with prepositions. Comp. § 3, note.

2. Second Person Singular.

The pausal form for the masculine, ךָ‎, commonly found with the verbs ל״א‎ & ל״ה‎ (Is. 30. 19; Je. 23. 37; Eze. 28. 15), is seldom attached to other verbs (Is. 55. 5; De. 28. 24, 45), but ךָ‎ is the more usual form (Is. 43. 5; 44. 2; Ps. 30. 13); the reverse, however, obtains when appended to the particles.

Unfrequent forms are, כָה‎ 1 Ki. 18. 44, and כָּה‎ Pr. 2. 11. אֲמָסָאֵךְ‎ Ho. 4. 6 is probably pointed incorrectly for אֲמָסָאֵךְ‎, a Syriac form of the suffix, which occurs a few times in the Codex Sam. (Ge. 22. 26.)

The form ךְ‎ for the *feminine* is unusual with the verb (Is. 54. 6), as is also כִי‎ when appended to the *preterite*, and ךְ‎, the tone being thrown back (Is. 47. 10, comp. Is. 60. 7). ־ֵכִי‎, כִי‎ (as in the Syriac) are frequently found in the later Psalms, comp. Ps. 137. 6.

3. Third Person Singular.

The forms נּוּ‎, ־ָנָה‎ occur frequently, and are most common in pause, comp. Ps. 65. 10; Job 5. 27; 41. 2. The two forms (viz., with and without epenth. נ‎) are found in immediate succession in Is. 26. 5, יַשְׁפִּילֶנָּה עַד אֶרֶץ‎ *he casts her down, casts her down to the earth.* The first word ought, doubtless, to conclude the first hemistich, though the accents decide differently.

־ָהּ‎ is frequently written without Mappik, comp. וַתַּחְמְרָה‎ Ex. 2. 3; הֶעָסְדָה‎ Ex. 9. 18; שָׁמְרָה‎ Amos 1. 11 (the best mode of explaining the latter passage).

־ָנָה‎ is of common occurrence.

4. First Person Plural.

In Is. 85. 7, several MSS. and editions have ־ֵינוּ‎ instead of ־ֵנוּ‎.

For this suffix the Chaldee uses the form נָא‎. Some discover such a Chaldaism in תִּקְרֶאנָה‎ Ex. 1. 10, for תִּקְרֶאנוּ‎ (*she befalls us*). But נָה‎ here may be regarded as the afformative of the fut. 3 pers. pl. fem. agreeing with מִלְחָמָה‎, which follows it, in a col-

lective sense (*wars*).* The Samaritan text indeed has such a Chaldaism in De. 32. 3, where לֵאלֹהֵינָה‎ stands for לֵאלֹהֵינוּ‎, and in Nu. 16. 13.

5. Third Person Plural.

That the forms of מוֹ‎ belong exclusively to the poetical style, may be seen from the examples in Noldius, Concordd. Particul. ed. Tympe, pp. 438, 498, 563, 564. But comp. § 5. No. 2, note. In Ex. 15. 5, occurs יְכַסְיֻמוּ‎ with ו‎ which is found nowhere else. This is, however, the common form in the Ethiopic.

For the suffix ן‎ (fem.), ם‎ is frequently substituted (prob. to prevent its being mistaken for the paragogic Nun), so that the distinction between masc. and fem. entirely ceases: e. g. וַיְגָרְשׁוּם‎ *and they drove them* (the daughters) *away*, Ex. 2. 17; וַיַּאַסְרוּם‎ *and they tied them* (the kine), 1 Sa. 6. 10. Comp. Ge. 26. 15; Nu. 17. 3, 4; Jos. 4. 8; Ho. 2. 14; Pr. 6. 21. Just the reverse is found in the word יְדַעְתִּין‎ Is. 48. 7, where ן‎ stands for ם‎.

6. The tone invariably rests on the union vowel, or, in the absence of this, on the last syllable of the word. כֶם‎, כֶן‎ and הֶם‎, הֶן‎ are excepted, and are therefore called *grave*, the others *light* suffixes.

7. The participles and infinitives may take either the verbal, or nominal suffixes. The participle is but slightly affected by their difference, as עֹשֵׂנִי‎ *he who created me*, Job 32. 22, and עֹשִׂי‎ *my creator;* רֹאֲנִי‎ Is. 47. 10, comp. Is. 28. 4. With the infinitive, however, they effect a change in the signification. E. g. קָרְאִי‎ *my calling*, Ps. 141. 1, פָּקְדִי‎ *my visiting*, Je. 32. 5; but לְהָרְגֵנִי‎ *to slay me*, Ex. 2. 14, לְעָזְרֵנִי‎ *to help me*, 1 Ch. 12. 17. In the first examples, the suffix denotes the genitive, in the latter the accusative. A single exception is found in Eze. 47. 7, בְּשׁוּבֵנִי‎ *in my returning*, for בְּשׁוּבִי‎.

---

* In the same manner may be explained in Job 17. 16, תֵּרַדְנָה‎, as agreeing with תִּקְוֹתִי‎ (collect. *expectations*) of the preceding verse; in Is. 28. 3, תֵּרָמַסְנָה‎, instead of agreeing with the subject עֲטֶרֶת‎, agrees with the instrumental רַגְלַיִם‎; and so in Ju. 5. 26, תִּשְׁלַחְנָה‎, agrees with the accusative יָדָהּ‎ (collect. *her hands*), comp. Ge. 27. 39; 31. 8; Is. 18. 5, where the verb, instead of agreeing with the subject, agrees with the predicate. Moreover, תִּשְׁלַחְנָה‎ Ob. 13, may refer to the people addressed there, in the feminine. Hence several grammarians and commentators have been induced to observe, that the plural form of the future, תִּקְטֹלְנָה‎, frequently stands for the singular תִּקְטֹל‎, which, indeed, suits well the several passages.

SECTION III.—SUFFIXES TO THE NOUN IN THE SINGULAR.* (TABLE A).

REMARKS.

1. When the *First Person* ־ִי is to be appended to a noun terminatng in ־ִי, one Yod is dropped, as גּוֹיִ my people, Zep. 2. 9, for גּוֹיִי .

־ִי has the tone, which it loses when the word following is either monosyllabic, or dissyllabic, having the tone on the first syllable (Milêl); e. g. אֲחֹתִי אָתְּ (thou art my sister) Ge. 12. 13; כֹּחִי עַתָּה Jos. 14. 11, comp. Ge. 20. 2, 5; 26. 7, 9; 49. 3; Je. 2. 27; 31. 9; 2 Sa. 23. 17; Job 19. 25; 20. 2; Ps. 140. 7.

2. *Second Person Singular.*

Unfrequent forms: masc. כַּפְּכָה (thy hand) Ps. 139. 5, חֵלְכָה (thy host) Ps. 10. 14, but see the analysis of this form in the alphabetical order. Fem. ־ֵיךְ Eze. 5. 12; ־ֵךְ (like the suffix of the verb) for ־ֵךְ, Eze. 23. 28; ־ֵכִי Je. 11. 15; Ps. 103. 3.

3. *Third Person Singular.*

The form ה for וֹ seems to belong to an older orthography. It is generally corrected in the Keri, as in Ge. 49. 11 (twice); Ex. 22. 26; Le. 23. 13; 2 Ki. 19. 23; 20. 13; but is not corrected in Je. 2. 21; Eze. 20. 40.

־ָה is also found without Mappik, as in Nu. 15. 28 (Job 31. 22): so that even אָ־ is substituted for it in Eze. 36. 5, אֱדוֹם כֻּלָּא (Edom, the whole of her) for כֻּלָּה.

The forms ־ֵהוּ and ־ֶהָ are usually attached to nouns ending in ־ֶה, e. g. מַרְאֶה (sight)—מַרְאֵהוּ, מַרְאֶהָ; שָׂדֶה (field)—שָׂדֵהוּ; עָלֶה (leaf)—עָלֵהוּ ; and so with רֵעַ מֵרֵעַ for רֵעֶה, מֵרֵעֶהָ (friend). With other words they are seldom used, as לְמִינֵהוּ Ge. 1. 12, comp. Ju. 19. 24; Na. 1. 13; Job 25. 3.

4. *First Person Plural.*

The form ־ֵנוּ (like the suff. of the verb) instead of ־ֵנוּ, must be regarded as an exception, as Job 22. 20; Ru. 3. 2, comp. No. 2.

5. *Second and Third Person Plural.*

Anomalous and unfrequent forms are : 2 pers. ־ְכֶנָה Eze. 23. 48 (comp. Eze. 13. 20); 3 pers. masc ־ֵהֶם 2 Sa. 23. 6, for ־ֶהֶם (whence contr. ־ֵם); fem. ־ְהֶנָה 1 Ki. 7. 37; ־ְנָה e. g. כֻּלָּנָה Ge. 42. 36; Pr. 31. 29; בְּאָנָה Ru. 1. 19; Je. 8. 7; לִדְתָנָה Job 39. 2; לְבִנְנָה Ge. 21. 29; ־ֶנָה Ge. 41. 21; ־ֶהֶן and ־ֶהֶן e. g. מַלְכָּתָן Eze. 13. 17, פִּתְחֶהֶן Is. 3. 1

SECTION IV.—SUFFIXES TO THE NOUN IN THE PLURAL (TABLE A).

REMARKS.

1. The ' which distinguishes these suffixes, is occasionally omitted in most of the persons; e. g. דְּרָכֶךָ (similar to the pausal form of the singular) for דְּרָכֶיךָ thy ways, Ex. 33. 13; Ps. 119. 37; Jos. 1. 8; רֵעֵהוּ for רֵעֵיהוּ his friends, Job 42. 10; 1 Sa. 30. 26; אֲשֻׁרֵהוּ for אֲשֻׁרֵיהוּ his felicities, Pr. 29. 18; חֶלְבְּמוֹ their fat, Ge. 4. 4; גּוֹיֵהֶם their nations, Ge. 10. 5; after their kinds, Ge. 1. 21; לִבְבָהֶן their hearts, Na. 2. 8. This is most frequent in suffixes of the 3 pers. sing. masc., ־ָיו, which is very often, and in all the copies alike, written ־ָו, but the Keri almost always substitutes the common form ־ָיו. The word יַחְדָּו (together, properly *his unions*) is alone excepted, in which the Keri has made no change, probably because וֹ was not regarded as a suffix. יַחְדָּיו occurs only in Je. 46. 12, 21; 49. 3.

2. Although ־ַי, or the ' prefixed to these suffixes, is, doubtless, originally the plural termination of the masculine, they are yet regularly attached to the feminine plural וֹת also; as קוֹלוֹתַי my voices, קוֹלוֹתֶיךָ thy voices. It is hence to be regarded as an exception, when these suffixes are occasionally found appended to וֹת without this '. As, עֵדְוֹתִי my testimonies, Ps. 132. 12; מַכֹּתְךָ thy strokes, De. 28. 59; אֲחִיוֹתָךְ thy sisters, Ex. 16. 52; אֲבוֹתָם their fathers, Ex. 4. 5; אוֹתוֹתָם their signs, Ps. 74. 4; עַצְּבוֹתָם their pains, Ps. 16. 4; צָרוֹתָם their distresses, Ps. 34. 18.

3. These suffixes with ' are found, on the other hand, also with forms of the *singular*; as, תְּהִלָּתֶךָ thy praise, Ps. 9. 15; שִׂנְאָתֶיךָ thy hatred, Eze. 35. 11; בְּנִיָּתֶיךָ thy building, Eze. 16. 31; הִנֻּרוֹתֵיכֶם your dis-

---

* The suffixes appended to the noun properly stand for the genitive, as סוּסִי *the horse of me*, i. e. my horse. The prepositions, being originally substantives, take likewise these suffixes with a few exceptions (as בַּעֲרֵנִי, תַּחְתֵּנִי) comp. § 2, note.

persion, Eze. 6. 8. To these may be added חֲמִישִׁתִי Le. 5. 24, as it has, at least, the signification of the singular, *his fifth part*.

4. *Second Person Singular.*

Yod in ־ִיךְ is furtive (like that in בַּיִת for בַּיְת), and the original form ־ְךָ is found in the Syriac and Chaldee. The feminine in these dialects is ــِكِ، ־ֵכִי, and so it is likewise in the Hebrew, by a Syriacism, as in Ps. 103. 3, 4, 5; 116. 7, and in Kheth. 2 Ki. 4. 3, 7. ־ֵיךְ Ec. 10. 17, is formed in imitation of the singular ־ְךָ. The suffix in מַלְאָבְכֵה (*her messengers*) Nah. 2. 14, can hardly be accounted for; other codices read ־ְכֵה and ־ְכֵה.

5. *Third Person Singular.*

The poetic ־ֵיהוּ is formed in imitation of the singular ־ֵהוּ, e. g. Job 24. 23; Na. 2. 4.—וְהִי in תִּנְמוּלוֹהִי Ps. 116. 12, is strictly a Chaldee form. For ־ֵיהָ is found הָא in Eze. 41. 15, comp. Chald. ־ָהָא *her*. Here we meet, finally, with an epenthetic נ, viz. in מָעֻנֶיהָ Is. 23. 11, for מָעֻנֶיהָ *her fortresses*.

6. For the poetic form ־ֵימוֹ, comp. De. 32. 37; Job 20. 23; 22. 2; 27. 23; Ps. 11. 7. Some of the older grammarians* observe, that this form stands occasionally also for the singular. Kimchi (incorrectly) assigns as a reason, that this form exhibits both characteristics of the plural and of the singular. But though it cannot be denied that in the passages cited above (De. 32. 37 excepted) this suffix has reference to nouns singular, nevertheless, those nouns being collectives, do not lose their plural signification. Another instance is in Ps. 11. 7, where פָּנֵימוֹ as referring to יְהֹוָה may be regarded as a *Pluralis majestatis* But were this form even to be admitted as strictly a singular, e. g. in Ps. 11. 7, we should then have to suppose it a misuse arising from its frequent occurrence in connection with collective nouns. The passages (Lu. 2. 4; Jo. 19. 27; Ac. 1. 20, from the Ethiopic version) cited by Lud. de Dieu (Crit. Sacra, p. 226, on Is. 53. 6), seem at all events to prove, that the suffix וֹמוּ, answering to the Hebrew ־ֵימוֹ, does in the Ethiopic stand for the singular.†

Other unfrequent forms are, ־ֵיהֵמָה Eze. 40. 16, ־ֵיהֵנָה Eze. 1. 11; ־ֵיכֵמָה Eze. 13. 20.

SECTION V.

Suffixes attached to the Prefix Prepositions לְ and בְּ, the Conjunction כְּ, אֵת (Sign of the Accusative) and the Prepositions מִן and עַם.‡

(a) לְ *to*, sign of the dative.

			Sing.		Plur.	
1.	c.	לִי	. . *to me.*	לָנוּ	. . *to us.*
2.	{ m. { f.	לְךָ, in pause לָךְ לָךְ	} *to thee.*	לָכֶם לָכֶן	. . *to you.*
3.	{ m. { f.	לוֹ, (לָמוֹ comp. r. 2) *to him.* לָהּ *to her.*		לָהֶם, poet. לָמוֹ לָהֶן	} *to them.*

(b) בְּ *in*

			Sing.		Plur.	
1.	c.	בִּי	. . *in me.*	בָּנוּ	*in us*
2.	{ m. { f.	בְּךָ, in p. בָּךְ בָּךְ	} *in thee*	בָּכֶם	} *in you.*
3.	{ m. { f.	בּוֹ *in him.* בָּהּ *in her.*		בָּם בָּהֶן, בָּהֵן	} *in them*

(c) כְּ *as* (for which also כְּמוֹ, כְּמוֹ).

			Sing.		Plur.	
1.	c.	כָּמוֹנִי	. . *as I.*	כָּמוֹנוּ	. . *as we.*
	{ m. { f.	כָּמוֹךָ ——	} *as thou.*	כְּמוֹכֶם seldom כָּכֶם	} *as ye.*
3.	{ m. { f.	כָּמוֹהוּ כָּמוֹהָ	*as he.* *as she.*	כְּמוֹהֶם, כָּהֶם כָּהֵם	} *as they.*

(d) אֵת (sign of the accusative).

			Sing.		Plur.	
1.	c.	אוֹתִי, אֹתִי	. *me.*	אֹתָנוּ	*us.*
2.	{ m. { f.	אֹתְךָ, in p. אֹתָךְ אֹתָךְ	} *thee.*	אֶתְכֶם אֶתְכֶן	} *you.*
3.	{ m. { f.	אֹתוֹ אֹתָהּ	*him.* *her.*	אֹתָם אֹתָן	} *them*

---

* Kimchii Michlol, fol. 266, comp. l' Empereur on M. Kimchii, ὁδοιπορια, p. 243; Noldii Concordd. Partic. pp. 904, 916.

† We have given this remark of Gesenius in full, chiefly on account of his admission with regard to the use of this suffix in the Ethiopic, which is important, and may assist in the explanation of the form לָמוֹ in the following §, rem. 2.

‡ We exhibit these in particular, because of some peculiar forms they take when connected with the suffixes.

(e) מִן *from* (for which also מִמֶּן, properly, *a part*).   (f) עִם *with*.

		Sing.		Plur.		Sing.		Plur.	
1.	c.	מִמֶּנִּי, poet. מִנִּי, מֶנִּי	*from me.*	מִמֶּנּוּ	*from us.*	עִמִּי	*with me.*	עִמָּנוּ	*with us.*
2.	m.	מִמְּךָ, in pause מִמֶּךָּ } *from thee.*		מִכֶּם } *from you.*		עִמְּךָ, in p. עִמָּךְ } *with thee.*		עִמָּכֶם } *with you.*	
	f.	מִמֵּךְ }		מִכֶּן }		עִמָּךְ }			
3.	m.	מִמֶּנּוּ, poet. מֶנְהוּ, מֶנְהוּ	*from him.*	מֵהֶם, poet. מִנְהֶם } *from them.*		עִמּוֹ	*with him.*	עִמָּהֶם, עִמָּם } *with them.*	
	f.	מִמֶּנָּה	*from her.*	מֵהֶן }		עִמָּהּ	*with her.*		

REMARKS.

I. On the Suffixes with לְ.

1. Instead of לוֹ the form לֹא is found several times (according to the Masora on Nu. chap. 11, 21 times) in Kheth., e. g. Ex. 21. 8; Le. 11. 21; 1 Sa. 2. 3, &c.

2. As regards the form לָמוֹ, grammarians maintain that it is also a singular, i. q. לוֹ, because it often agrees with nouns singular. Those singulars, however, are all collectives, and can therefore not serve as a proof. The examples are, Ge. 9. 26 (where it refers to שֵׁם, i. e. the descendants of Shem); Ps. 28. 8 (where it refers to the people of ver. 9, and hence some copies read לְעַמּוֹ); Ps. 73. 10 (also in reference to עַם); Is. 44. 15 (in reference to אֵל and פֶּסֶל, which may likewise be taken in a collective sense); and finally Is. 53. 8. Though the subject of this last chapter is throughout given in the singular, yet the change to the plural form in ver. 8 is fully accounted for, when the *servant of God* (chap. 51. 13, like 42. 1, and 49. 3, 6) is considered to stand collectively for *the prophets*, which to me seems quite evident. Some copies have in Is. 44. 15 and 53. 8, לוֹ, which is an exegetical gloss. (Gesenius.)*

3. Unfrequent forms are:—2 pers. masc. לְכָה Ge. 27. 37; 2 pers. pl. fem. לָכֵנָה Eze. 13. 18 (לָכֶן) does not occur at all). לָהֵן Ru. 1. 13, is different from לָהֶן, and signifies *therefore*, as in the Chaldee.

II. On the Suffixes with אֵת.

4. The forms in the paradigm are the usual ones; unfrequent forms are:—2 pers. masc. אוֹתְכָה (in pause) Ex. 29. 35, אֶתְכֶם Jos. 23. 15, אֹתְהֶם Ge. 32. 1, אֹתָם Eze. 23. 45; fem. אוֹתְהֶן Eze. 23. 47, אֹתְנָה Ex. 35. 26.

III. On the Suffixes with מִן.

5. מִנִּי (*from me*) must not be confounded with מִנִּי where ' is paragogic.

6. מִמֶּנּוּ *from him* (for מִמֶּנְהוּ), and מִמֶּנּוּ *from us* (for מִמֶּנֶּנוּ) can only be distinguished by the context.

7. The pronouns הֵמָּה and הֵנָּה often retain their full form after the prepositions, as, בָּהֵמָּה Ex. 36. 1; Hab. 1. 16; כָּהֵמָּה Je. 36. 32; לָהֵמָּה Je. 14. 16; מֵהֵמָּה Ec. 12. 12; Je. 10. 2; fem. בָּהֵנָּה Le. 5. 22; Nu 13. 19; כָּהֵנָּה Ge. 41. 19; לָהֵנָּה Eze. 1. 5, 23; 42. 9; מֵהֵנָּה Le. 4. 2.

---

* But if there were even no other passage to establish the use of לָמוֹ in the singular, the passages Is. 53. 8, and 44. 15 alone might have been sufficient for this purpose: the former, where throughout the chapter only the singular appears, and the latter, where the plural does not at all suit the sense, and the writer himself explains it in the same connection by לוֹ in ver. 17. Comp. Hengstenberg's "Christology of the Old Testament," p. 523 of Prof. Keith's translation. In confirmation of this we may add the facts, that some copies do really read לוֹ instead of לָמוֹ in both passages, and that the form אִמוֹ in the Ethiopic, answering to the Hebrew יָמוֹ־, is used in that version for the singular, as Gesenius himself admits (comp. § 5. rem. 6). When we, moreover, consider that this poetic syllable, which never receives the tone as a suffix, almost everywhere occurs in pause, or, which amounts to the same thing, stands with a word preceding the pause (comp. De. 32. 27; Ps. 11. 7; Job 20. 23; and Lehrgeb. § 52, 4 anm. 1 in reference to Jos. 3. 9; De. 32. 37, comp. Is. 21. 14; Ps. 4. 3, comp. also below, § 24. rem. 5), its specific use in the poetical books, appears to be, that it takes the place of other forms, which must necessarily have the tone upon the ultimate, to suit the pause, the tendency of which is to throw the tone back upon the penultimate. Thus לָמוֹ which occurs 55 times, is everywhere in pause, except three times (Ps. 66. 7, 119. 165; Job 24. 17) before the word in pause, most probably for לָהֶם or לוֹ, which, the former with grave suffix and the latter as a monosyllable, never can change the tone. Nor is it improbable that the מ of לָמוֹ in the singular is merely epenthetic, as in כָּמוֹנִי, comp. the poetical forms בְּמוֹ, כְּמוֹ, לְמוֹ, as independent words formed from the prefixes בְּ, כְּ, לְ, and the syllable מוֹ.

TABLE B.　REGULAR VERB.

	KAL.		NIPHAL.	PIEL.	PUAL.	HIPHIL.	HOPHAL.	HITHPAEL.
Pret. 3. m.	קָטַל	כָּבֵד	נִקְטַל	קִטֵּל	קֻטַּל	הִקְטִיל	הָקְטַל	הִתְקַטֵּל
3. f.	קָטְלָה	כָּבְדָה	נִקְטְלָה	קִטְּלָה	קֻטְּלָה	הִקְטִילָה	הָקְטְלָה	הִתְקַטְּלָה
2. m.	קָטַלְתָּ	כָּבַדְתָּ	נִקְטַלְתָּ	קִטַּלְתָּ	קֻטַּלְתָּ	הִקְטַלְתָּ	הָקְטַלְתָּ	הִתְקַטַּלְתָּ
2. f.	קָטַלְתְּ	כָּבַדְתְּ	נִקְטַלְתְּ	קִטַּלְתְּ	קֻטַּלְתְּ	הִקְטַלְתְּ	הָקְטַלְתְּ	הִתְקַטַּלְתְּ
1. c.	קָטַלְתִּי	כָּבַדְתִּי	נִקְטַלְתִּי	קִטַּלְתִּי	קֻטַּלְתִּי	הִקְטַלְתִּי	הָקְטַלְתִּי	הִתְקַטַּלְתִּי
Plur. 3. c.	קָטְלוּ	כָּבְדוּ	נִקְטְלוּ	קִטְּלוּ	קֻטְּלוּ	הִקְטִילוּ	הָקְטְלוּ	הִתְקַטְּלוּ
2. m.	קְטַלְתֶּם	כְּבַדְתֶּם	נִקְטַלְתֶּם	קִטַּלְתֶּם	קֻטַּלְתֶּם	הִקְטַלְתֶּם	הָקְטַלְתֶּם	הִתְקַטַּלְתֶּם
2. f.	קְטַלְתֶּן	כְּבַדְתֶּן	נִקְטַלְתֶּן	קִטַּלְתֶּן	קֻטַּלְתֶּן	הִקְטַלְתֶּן	הָקְטַלְתֶּן	הִתְקַטַּלְתֶּן
1. c.	קָטַלְנוּ	כָּבַדְנוּ	נִקְטַלְנוּ	קִטַּלְנוּ	קֻטַּלְנוּ	הִקְטַלְנוּ	הָקְטַלְנוּ	הִתְקַטַּלְנוּ
Inf. absol.	קָטוֹל		הִקָּטֹל, נִקְטֹל	קַטֹּל	קֻטֹּל	הַקְטֵיל		
constr.	קְטֹל		הִקָּטֵל	קַטֵּל	קֻטַּל	הַקְטִיל	הָקְטֵל	הִתְקַטֵּל
Imp. m.	קְטֹל	כְּבַד	הִקָּטֵל	קַטֵּל		הַקְטֵל		הִתְקַטֵּל
f.	קִטְלִי	כִּבְדִי	הִקָּטְלִי	קַטְּלִי	wanting	הַקְטִילִי	wanting	הִתְקַטְּלִי
Plur. m.	קִטְלוּ	כִּבְדוּ	הִקָּטְלוּ	קַטְּלוּ		הַקְטִילוּ		הִתְקַטְּלוּ
f.	קְטֹלְנָה	כְּבַדְנָה	הִקָּטַלְנָה	קַטֵּלְנָה		הַקְטֵלְנָה		הִתְקַטֵּלְנָה
Fut. 3. m.	יִקְטֹל	יִכְבַּד	יִקָּטֵל	יְקַטֵּל	יְקֻטַּל	יַקְטִיל	יָקְטַל	יִתְקַטֵּל
3. f.	תִּקְטֹל	תִּכְבַּד	תִּקָּטֵל	תְּקַטֵּל	תְּקֻטַּל	תַּקְטִיל	תָּקְטַל	תִּתְקַטֵּל
2. m.	תִּקְטֹל	תִּכְבַּד	תִּקָּטֵל	תְּקַטֵּל	תְּקֻטַּל	תַּקְטִיל	תָּקְטַל	תִּתְקַטֵּל
2. f.	תִּקְטְלִי	תִּכְבְּדִי	תִּקָּטְלִי	תְּקַטְּלִי	תְּקֻטְּלִי	תַּקְטִילִי	תָּקְטְלִי	תִּתְקַטְּלִי
1. c.	אֶקְטֹל	אֶכְבַּד	אֶקָּטֵל	אֲקַטֵּל	אֲקֻטַּל	אַקְטִיל	אָקְטַל	אֶתְקַטֵּל
Plur. 3. m.	יִקְטְלוּ	יִכְבְּדוּ	יִקָּטְלוּ	יְקַטְּלוּ	יְקֻטְּלוּ	יַקְטִילוּ	יָקְטְלוּ	יִתְקַטְּלוּ
3. f.	תִּקְטֹלְנָה	תִּכְבַּדְנָה	תִּקָּטַלְנָה	תְּקַטֵּלְנָה	תְּקֻטַּלְנָה	תַּקְטֵלְנָה	תָּקְטַלְנָה	תִּתְקַטֵּלְנָה
2. m.	תִּקְטְלוּ	תִּכְבְּדוּ	תִּקָּטְלוּ	תְּקַטְּלוּ	תְּקֻטְּלוּ	תַּקְטִילוּ	תָּקְטְלוּ	תִּתְקַטְּלוּ
2. f.	תִּקְטֹלְנָה	תִּכְבַּדְנָה	תִּקָּטַלְנָה	תְּקַטֵּלְנָה	תְּקֻטַּלְנָה	תַּקְטֵלְנָה	תָּקְטַלְנָה	תִּתְקַטֵּלְנָה
1. c.	נִקְטֹל	נִכְבַּד	נִקָּטֵל	נְקַטֵּל	נְקֻטַּל	נַקְטִיל	נָקְטַל	נִתְקַטֵּל
Fut. apoc.						יַקְטֵל		
Part. act.	קֹטֵל		נִקְטָל	מְקַטֵּל	מְקֻטָּל	מַקְטִיל	מָקְטָל	מִתְקַטֵּל
pass.	קָטוּל							

SECTION VI.—UNUSUAL CONJUGATIONS.

Besides the five usual forms of conjugation exhibited in the preceding paradigm (viz. Kal, Niphal, Piel and Pual, Hiphil and Hophal, Hithpael), there are other unusual forms, which, although they occur but seldom in the regular verb, are, nevertheless, usual in certain classes of the irregular verb. Of the latter conjugations some are connected in form with Piel, and are made by the doubling or repetition of one or more radical letters, or by the insertion of a long vowel. i. e. by changes within the root itself:

2**

others are analogous to Hiphil, and are formed by the addition of prefix letters or syllables. To the former class, besides a Passive distinguished by the more obscure vowels in the final syllable, belongs also a reflective form with the prefix הִתְ after the analogy of Hithpael.

Those which are analogous to Piel, and which follow it in their inflexion are :—

1. *Poel*; as קוֹטֵל, reflexive הִתְקוֹטֵל, fut. יְקוֹטֵל, part. מְקוֹטֵל, fut. pass. יְקוֹטַל. In the regular verb it occurs very seldom. Examples are:—מְשֹׁפְטִי *my judge,* Job 9. 15 ; יוֹדַעְתִּי *I have appointed,* 1 Sa. 21. 3 ; שֹׁרֵשׁ *to take root,* Is. 40. 24, denom. from שֹׁרֶשׁ *root.* In verbs ע"ע it is far more frequent; e. g. חוֹנֵן, סוֹבֵב, הוֹלֵל. Its signification is mostly analogous to Piel.

2. *Pilel, Pulal, Hithpalel*; as קְטָלַל and קְטֵלֵל, pass. קְטְלַל, reflexive הִתְקַטְלֵל (the last radical letter being repeated). In the regular verb, the following are the only examples :—נִפְלָל Eze. 28. 23, i. q. נָפַל *to fall ;* צִמְתָתֻנִי *it has consumed me,* Ps. 119. 139, Ps. 88. 17, which probably is to be read *צִמְתְתֻנִי (from צָמַת) *they consume me* (Dagesh in both instances is euphonic) ; with guttural שַׁאֲנַן *to be at rest,* רַעֲנַן *to be green* ; pass. אֻמְלַל *to be withered.* It is more frequent in verbs ע"ו, where it takes the place of Piel and Hithpael.

3. *Pealal,* as קְטַלְטַל (the two last letters being repeated) used especially of slight motions repeated in quick succession ; e. g. סְחַרְחַר *to go about with quick motion,* hence of the heart, *to beat quick, to palpitate,* Ps. 38. 11, from סָחַר *to go about,* pass. (Poalal) חֳמַרְמַר *to ferment with violence, to make a rumbling sound,* La. 1. 20.

4. *Pilpel,* formed from a *biliteral root* by doubling both radical letters, as כִּלְכֵּל, כּוּל ; סִבְסֵב, סָבַב. This

also is used of motion rapidly repeated, e. g. צִפְצֵף *to chirp,* צִלְצֵל *to tinkle,* גִּרְגֵּר *to gargle,* עִפְעֵף *to flutter* (from עוּף *to fly*) ; reflex. הִתְגַּלְגֵּל *to roll oneself down.*

With Hiph. are connected :—

5. *Tiphel,* as תִּקְטֵל, with תִ prefixed ; e. g. תִּרְגֵּל *to teach one to walk, to lead,* denom. from רֶגֶל *a foot* ; תַּחֲרָה, fut. יִתַחֲרָה *to emulate,* Je. 12. 5 ; 22. 15 (from חָרָה *to be ardent, eager*).

6. *Shaphel,* as שַׁקְטֵל frequent in the Syriac ; e. g. שַׁלְהֵב *to burn,* from לַהַב. In the Hebrew it is found only in the noun שַׁלְהֶבֶת *flame.*

Forms of which single examples occur :—

7. קְטֶלַט, pass. קְטֻלַט ; as מְחֻסְפָּס *scaled off, having the form of scales,* Ex. 16. 14, from חָשַׂף=חָסַף *to peel, to scale.*

8. קְטַקַל, as זַרְזִיף Ps. 72. 6, *a violent rain,* from זָרַף.

9. קְטַקְטַל (the two first letters repeated) a passive, only יָפְיָפִיתָ *thou art fair,* Ps. 45. 3, from יָפָה.

10. נִתְקַטֵּל (frequent in the Rabbinic) a form compounded of Niph. and Hiph., found in the examples נִתֻּסְּרוּ for נִתְוַסְּרוּ *they permit themselves to be admonished,* Eze. 23. 48 ; נְכַּפֶּר De. 21. 8 ; נִשְׁתַּוָה Pr. 27. 15.†

11. קְטוֹטֵל, in הַצוֹצֵר *to blow the trumpet,* from הָצַר. The participle מחצצרים occurs 1 Ch. 15. 24 ; 2 Ch. 5. 13 ; 7. 6 ; 13. 14 ; 29. 28 in Kheth., and is doubtless to be read מְהַצֹצְרִים ; but the Keri invariably rejects one צ, pointing it either as Hiph. or Piel, מְהַצְרִים or מַהֲצְרִים.

---

* The supposition that תְתוּ stands for תְּתוּ may be founded upon the principle, that the feeble subordinate sound of *vocal Sheva* often conforms to the following proper vowel of the syllable, e. g. סְדֹם, LXX Σοδόμ, Sodom ; שְׁלֹמֹה Σολομών, Solomon (Lehrg. § 14. Gram. § 10. 2).

† The form נִגְאֲלוּ La. 4. 14, is supposed to be likewise a compound, viz. of Niph. and Pual (גֹּאֲלוּ and נִגְאֲלוּ), in which form Gesenius discovers a passive of Niphal. Passives of Hithpael are : הִתְפָּקְדוּ for הִתְפַּקְּדוּ Nu. 1. 47 , 2. 33 ; הֻטַּמָּא for הִתְטַמָּא, De. 24. 4 ; הֻכַּבֵּס Le. 13. 55, 56 ; הֻדַּשׁ Is. 34. 6. Lehrg. § 71. 4.

SECTION VII.—QUADRILITERALS.

The few verbs of this kind are formed after the analogy of Piel. The following are all the examples which occur:—

Pret. פִּרְשֵׂז *he spread out*, Job 26. 9 (with Pattahh under the first syllable, as in the Chaldee).

Fut. יְחַרְסְמֶנָּה *he will devour it*, Ps. 80. 14

Pass. רַטֲפַשׁ *to become green*, Job 33. 25.

Part. מְכֻרְבָּל *girded*, 1 Ch. 15. 27.

SECTION VIII.—REGULAR VERB. (TABLE B.)

REMARKS.

I. On the Preterite of Kal.

1. The verbs of *middle O* (as קָטֹן)* retain this Hholem in the 2nd and 1st persons, as יָכֹלְתִּי *I am able*, Ge. 30. 8; Ju. 8. 3; Ps. 40. 13; יָגֹרְתִּי, יָגֹרְתָּ *thou wast, I was, afraid*. De. 28. 60; 9. 19; קָטֹנְתִּי *I am small*, Ge. 32. 11; יָקֹשְׁתִּי *I lay snares*, Je. 50. 24. This and the usual form (*middle A*) are found together in Ge. 43. 14, כַּאֲשֶׁר שָׁכֹלְתִּי שָׁכָלְתִּי *as I am bereaved, I am bereaved*. In those cases, however, where (according to rem. 7) the tone is shifted to the ultimate, viz. in the 2nd pers. pl., before suffixes, and Vav conversive of the preterite, Hholem is shortened to Kamets Hhatuph; as וְיָכָלְתָּ *and thou shalt be able*, Ex. 18. 23, יָכָלְתִּי Ps. 13. 5.

The verbs *middle E* generally lose the sound (ֵ) in their inflexion, e. g. חָפֵץ, חָפֵצָה (like קָטַל, קָטֵל), and this original vowel appears again only:—

(*a*) in the 3 pers. sing. and pl. standing in pause, as גָּבֵרוּ *they are strong*, 2 Sa. 1. 23; דָּבֵקָה *she cleaves*, Job 29. 10; דָּבֵקוּ Job 41. 15. Several verbs, properly *middle E*, have Pattahh in the 3 pers. when not in pause, and the E sound appears again only *in pause*; e. g. דָּבַק, גָּבַר, comp. שָׁכֵן Ex. 40. 35; Jos. 22. 19, *in pause* שָׁכֵן De. 33. 12, 20; Ju. 5. 17 (comp. in Piel גָּדַל, in pause גָּדֵל).†

(*b*) In forms with the tone on the ultimate, in which case (ֵ) is shortened into (ֶ) or (ִ), as, שְׁאֶלְתֶּם *ye have asked*, 1 Sa. 12. 13; 25. 5; וִירִשְׁתֶּם *and thou shalt succeed them in possession*, De. 19. 1; וִירִשְׁתָּ De. 30. 5; יְלִדְתִּיךָ *I have begotten thee*, Ps. 2. 7;

שְׁאֵלְתִּיו 1 Sa. 1. 20, שְׁאִלְתִּיהוּ Ju. 13. 6, comp. Je. 2. 27; 15. 10; Nu. 11. 12; Jos. 1. 15.‡

2. In some instances the 3 pers. has (ַ) in the second syllable, although not in pause; as, שָׁפַט *he judged*, 1 Sa. 7. 17, גָּזַל *he robbed*, Eze. 18. 12,§ שָׁגַג *he erred*, Le. 5. 18.

3. *Third Person Feminine.* ת‑, the usual form in the Syriac and Arabic, is sometimes used also in the Hebrew; as, אָזְלַת De. 32. 36. Another Aramaic termination is ‑א in Eze. 31. 5.

An example with *euphonic Dagesh*, in pause, is נָשָׁתָּה (for נָשָׁתָה) *she dries up*, Is. 41. 17.

4. *Third Person Plural.* The form וּא (with parag. א), usual in the Arabic, is found in the Hebrew; as הָלְכוּא Jos. 10. 24.

It is but seldom that parag. ן is appended to the preterite; as, יָדְעוּן De. 8. 3, 16. Examples with *euphonic Dagesh*, in pause, are:—חָדֵלּוּ Ju. 5. 7; 1 Sa. 2. 5 (where, however, MSS. vary); נָתַנּוּ Eze. 27. 19.

5. *Second Person Singular.* Besides the common form תָּ for the masculine, the full form תָּה also occurs; e. g. בָּנִתָה Mal. 2. 14, זָקַנְתָּה Jos. 13. 1.

2 pers. fem. As was observed above (§ 1. rem. 2), that besides the pronoun אַתְּ, there occurs another form אַתִּי in Kheth., so it should be remembered in this affirmative derived from it, there occurs, besides תְּ, also the form תִּי in Kheth., e. g. הָלַכְתִּי Je. 31. 21,

---

* The common form of the 3 pers. pret. has, in the final syllable of the ground-form, either *A* (Pattahh), *E* (Tseri pure), or *O* (Hholem pure),—as מָלַךְ *to reign*, חָמֵץ *to be sour*, יָכֹל *to be able*,—which are found likewise in the irregular verb, e. g. מֵת (for מָוַת) *to die*, אוֹר (for אָוֹר) *to be light, bright*. For the sake of brevity, these are called, after the example of the Arabic grammarians, verbs *middle A*, *middle E*, and *middle O*. The two latter are usual in *intransitive* verbs, e. g. זָקֵן *to be old*, קָטֹן *to be small* (Lehrg. § 66. 3).

† It is better, however, to view these as two different forms of the same verb, comp. the Lexicon.

‡ This shortening, however, into (ֶ) & (ִ) may properly be from *Pattahh*, occasioned by the removal of the tone to the next following syllable, comp. יֶרְכֶם for יַרְכֶם, מִדּוֹ for מַדּוֹ from מַד, comp. especially § 11. rem. 1; so that there is no need to suppose here a ground-form *middle E*, as שָׁאַל, יֵרֵשׁ, יָלַד.

§ Nevertheless, Zakeph-katon may in this instance have the force of a pausal accent.

comp. Eze. **16. 13**, which is to be read הֲלַכְתִּי. In such instances the Keri אתי the note יָתִיר (abundat ʾ), and in thus rejecting ʾ the vowel points are suited accordingly.

6. *Second Person Plural Feminine.* Instead of תֶּן, the form תֶּנָה is used in Am. **4. 3**, corresponding to a similar form of the pronoun, § 1. rem. 5.

7. In combination with the afformatives תָּ, תִּי, נוּ the tone is on the penultima, and the word is said to be *Milél* (above), but with the other afformatives the tone is on the ultimate, and the word is said to be *Milra* (below). The tone, however, is shifted, (a) by *conversive Vav* of the preterite from the penultima to the ultimate (comp. § 18. rem. 1), e. g. וּפָקַדְתָּ *and thou shalt visit*, Job 5. 24, וּפָקַדְתִּי Ex. 32. 34, except in pause, comp. however, De. 8. 6 ; (b) by the suffixes, comp. the table of the verb with suffixes ; (c) by the *pause* in several of the persons from the ultimate to the penultima, where the original vowel, if it has fallen away, is likewise restored, as קָטַלְתְּ, מָלְאוּ, קָטְלוּ, קָטְלָה, &c.; the tone, however, remains fixed with the grave afformatives, as קְטַלְתֶּם.

II. On the Infinitive of Kal.

8. There is but one form for the *inf. abs.* which is קָטוֹל (with Hholem impure). The Hholem is found written either *in full,* or *defectively* (קָטֹל); the former, however, is the original.

9. For the *inf. constr.* the usual form is קְטֹל (with Hholem pure), besides which there is also an unusual form קְטַל, as שְׁכַב *to lie down*, Ge. 34. 7; 2 Ki. 14. 22; שְׁפַל *to be humbled*, Pr. 16. 19 ; Ec. 12. 4. That they are strictly *Segolate* forms is seen from their inflexion (שְׁכְבִי, קָטְלִי), which perfectly agrees with the declension of the *Segolates* (קְטֶל or קְטֹל; קַטַל or קַטֶל) comp. § 35. rem. 10.

10. The various infinitive forms, which occur as *verbal nouns*, will be enumerated farther on (§ 26). Here belong only such as are really construed as infinitives. They are :—

(a) קַטְלָה, קָטְלָה and קִטְלָה, as feminine forms from קְטֹל ; e. g. לְגָבְהָה *to be lifted up*, Zep. 3. 11; לְטָמְאָה *to become unclean*, Le. 15. 32 ; לְחֶמְלָה *to*

have compassion, Eze. 16. 5 ; לְמָשְׁחָה *to anoint*, Ex. 29. 29 ; לְרָחְצָה *to wash*, Ex. 30. 18 ; לְקָרְבָה *to draw near*, Ex. 36. 2 ; לְקִרְאַת, instead of which by *Syriasm*, לְקָרְאַת *to meet* (i. e. *against*). Moreover, יִרְאָה *to fear*, De. 4. 10, and שִׂנְאָה *to hate*, De. 1. 27, occur construed as infinitives, but are besides, more usually *verbal* nouns. Forms like חָזְקָה, אַשְׁמָה, are produced by the effect of the gutturals.

(b) With a preformative מ, as in the Syriac and Chaldee, as מִגְרַשׁ *to drive*, Eze. 36. 5 ; מִקְרָא *to convoke*, Nu. 10. 2; so likewise in some verbs of פ נ, as מַשָּׂא for מַנְשָׂא *to carry*, Nu. 4. 24; מַסַּע *to remove*, De. 10. 11.*

(c) Other examples are יֵשַׁע Hab. 3. 13, אָפֻדָּה Ex. 28. 8, which may, however, be regarded as *verbal nouns.**

(d) דָּרִיושׁ Ezr. 10. 16, for דְּרֹשׁ is quite anomalous. (Gesenius, in his Thesaurus, is inclined to regard it as an *inf. Piel*, for דָּרֹושׁ, comp. דָּלִיו Pr. 26. 7, for דְּלֹו.)

III. On the Imperative of Kal.

11. The verbs which have *A* in the second syllable of the future retain the same also in the imperative ; as שְׁכַב *lie down*, 2 Sa. 13. 5 ; Eze. 4. 4 ; לְבַשׁ *put on*, 1 Ki. 22. 30 ; שְׁלַם *be peaceable*, Job 22. 20.

With parag. ָה the form קְטֹל becomes קָטְלָה, the form קְטַל becomes קָטְלָה ; as, שָׁמְרָה *watch over* (from שְׁמֹר) Ps. 25. 20, זָכְרָה *remember* (from זְכֹר) 2 Ch. 6. 42 ; שִׁכְבָה *lie down*, Ge. 39. 12, מִכְרָה *sell*, Ge. 25. 31, נִצְּרָה (with euphonic Dagesh) from נְצֹר *to keep*, Ps. 141. 3.†

12. The form קִטְלִי, קִטְלוּ is more directly derived from קְטַל than קְטֹל, and is chiefly found with imperatives of the first form, e. g. שִׁכְבִי, לְבִשִׁי, though also with those of the latter form. The form קְטֹלִי however, is comparatively unfrequent ; as, מָלְכִי *reign*, Ju. 9. 10, 12 ; עָלְזִי *rejoice*, Zep. 3. 14 ; קָרְחִי *make bald*, Mi. 1. 16 ; מָשְׁכוּ *draw*, Eze. 32. 20 (but also מִשְׁכוּ Ex. 12. 21) ; with composite Sheva, קָסְמִי *use enchantment*, 1 Sa. 28. 8, Keri. Segol is found only with gutturals (§ 13. rem. 3).

In pause the long *O* or *A* returns again ; as, שְׁפֹטוּ *judge ye*, Zec. 7. 9. Such forms, however, are found also without pause, as Da. 9. 19, with which the following may be classed : רָגְזָה—פְּשֹׁטָה וְעֹרָה *tremble —strip thyself and make thee bare*, Is. 32. 11, and according to some, also חֲגֹרָה (*gird thyself*) which immediately follows in this passage.

---

* The infinitives of *b* and *c*, on account of their small number, must, in the Lexicon, be sought for among the nouns.

† The *lengthened imperative* or *imp. parag.* is, as may be seen from a comparison of the references given above, expressive of *wish* and *entreaty* ; and is often *emphatic*, as קוּם *stand up*, קוּמָה *up!* (comp. rem. 13, and § 11. rem. 5).

In some instances Hholem has been retained in the inflexion according to Kheth.; as צְרוּפָה *try*, Ps. 26. 2, מְלוּכָה *reign*, Ju. 9. 8, קְסוֹמִי *use enchantment*, 1 Sa. 28. 8, where the Keri has invariably cancelled וֹ.

IV. Oɴ ᴛʜᴇ Fᴜᴛᴜʀᴇ ᴏғ Kᴀʟ.

13. The Hholem in the second syllable of the future is almost exclusively confined to the *transitive verbs* (middle *A*); while the verbs middle *E* and *O* (קָטֵל, קָטֹל) have regularly Pattahh in the future; e. g. גָּדֵל, fut. יִגְדַּל *to be great*, כָּבֵד, fut. יִכְבַּד *to be honoured*; קָטֹן, fut. יִקְטַן *to be small*, שָׁכֵל, fut. יִשְׁכַּל *to be childless*. In several verbs, however, this difference of form exists only in the future, so that the future *O* stands for the transitive, and the future *A* for the intransitive signification; as קָצַר *to cut off*, *to reap* (Le. 25.5; De. 24. 19, &c.), future *A*, *to be cut*, i. e. *to be short* (Ju. 10. 16; 16. 16); חָרַשׁ, future *O*, *to cut, to plough*, future *A*, *to be dumb*, (properly, *to be blunted*); חָלַשׁ, future *O*, *to subdue*, Ex. 17. 13, future *A*, *to be subdued*, Job 14. 10; כָּרַם *to overlay, cover*, fut. *A* intrans. ver. 8. In a few instances the difference in the signification is of another character; e. g. יָגֹז *he shall cut* (*eat*), Is. 9. 19, יָגַז trop. *he shall decide*, Job 22. 28; חָבַשׁ fut. *O*, *to saddle*, fut. *A* and *O*, *to bind up*, Job 5. 18; Eze. 34. 16; עָרַב fut. *O*, *to be surety for*, עָרַב fut. *A*, *to be sweet*.

Very frequently both occur without any difference of signification; as יִשְׁבַּת (Le. 26. 35) and יִשְׁבֹּת (ver. 34) *he shall rest*; טָרַף, future *O* (Ps. 7. 3; Ho. 5. 14), and future *A* (Ge. 49. 27), *to tear*; נָדַר fut. *O* (Nu. 6. 21; De. 12. 17, &c.), and fut. *A* (Ge. 28. 20, &c.), *to vow*; נָשַׁךְ fut. *O*, Ec. 10. 11, and fut. *A*, Pr. 23. 22, *to bite*; בָּגַד fut. *O*, Mal. 2. 15, fut. *A*, ver. 10. *to be treacherous*.

With parag. ה, the form אֶקְטֹל becomes אֶקְטְלָה. This (so called) *lengthened future* (comp. note to rem. 11) is usually attached to the 1 pers. sing. and pl., and is found in all classes of the regular and irregular verbs, except in the *passives*, and has the tone, wherever it is taken, by the afformatives וּ and ־ִי, and hence affects in precisely the same manner the final vowel of the ground-form, e. g. Kal אֶשְׁמְרָה, Piel נְנַתְּקָה Ps. 2. 3; but Hiph. אַזְכִּירָה.*

It is, however, sometimes found attached to other persons, as the second and third, comp. Is. 5. 19; Eze. 23. 20; Ps. 20. 4. The form ־ֶה is also sometimes found instead of ־ָה, as אֶקְרָאֶה 1 Sa. 28. 15, יְדַשְׁנֶה Ps. 20. 4.

14. In the forms in which, according to the paradigm, Hholem is dropped, something of the O sound seems to have been expressed in the time when the Hebrew was a living language. Thus the vowel of the last syllable is constantly retained in the Arabic, and is lost only in the vulgar dialect. Traces of this are observable, (*a*) in the old *matres lectionis*, which the Keri has cancelled:—וָאֶשְׁקוֹלָה *and I weighed*, Ezr. 8. 25, אֶשְׁקוֹטָה *I will rest*, Is. 18. 4, יִכְשׁוֹלוּ *they stumble*, Pr. 4. 16; (*b*) where the vowel remains and is pointed וֹ, being considered shorter than וּ; as יִשְׁפּוֹטוּ *they shall judge*, Ex. 18. 26, תַּעֲבוֹרִי *thou shalt pass on*, Ru. 2. 8, תִּשְׁמוֹרֵם *thou shalt observe them*, Pr. 14. 3; (*c*) in (ֳ) which the punctuators have occasionally substituted for simple Sheva, e. g. וָאֶשְׁקֳלָה and אֶשְׁקֳטָה in the Keri of the passages quoted above, comp. Ezr. 8. 26; Je. 32. 9; אֶשֳּׁקָה *I might kiss*, 1 Ki. 19. 20, אָפֳרֵם Ho. 10. 10; comp. Is. 27. 3; 62. 2; Eze. 35. 6.

15. The vowel of the last syllable is regularly restored again *in pause*, with which it receives the tone. Pattahh is then lengthened into Kamets, e. g. תִּקְטֹל, יִלְכֹּדוּ, תִּלְבָּשִׁי.

16. For the 3 pers. pl. fem. תִּקְטֹלְנָה, the form יִקְטֹלְנָה is substituted, in three instances, to distinguish it from the 2 pers., viz. יַעֲמֹדְנָה *they shall arise*, Da. 8. 22, comp. Ge. 30. 38; 1 Sa. 6. 12. The parag. ה in נָה, both for the masc. and fem. is often dropped, so that only וּן remain; e. g. תְּבֻשָׁן Ge. 33. 6.

A single anomaly is וַתְּגְבְּהֶינָה, Eze. 16. 50, for תִּגְבַּהְנָה (comp. Verb *Ain gutt.*) where ־ְי is inserted after the manner of verbs עי and עע.

17. To the forms ending in וּ or ־ִי a parag. ן is often appended, most frequently at the end of a period, where the vowel of the second syllable is restored, though this vowel does not (as in No. 15) receive the tone; e. g. תִּשְׁמְעוּן יִרְגָּזוּן Ex. 15. 14, De. 1. 17, comp. Ps. 104. 9, 22, 28, 29; Joel 3. 1; Ex. 9. 29. For instances of this *without pause* comp. Ru. 2. 8, 9; Ps. 4. 3; but the vowel is then more frequently not restored, comp. Hab. 3. 7; Ps. 104. 28, 29, De. 8. 20; Ex. 4. 9.

V. Oɴ ᴛʜᴇ Iɴғɪɴɪᴛɪᴠᴇ, Iᴍᴘᴇʀғᴇᴄᴛ, ᴀɴᴅ Fᴜᴛᴜʀᴇ ᴏғ Kᴀʟ.

18. Hholem of the *inf. constr.* and *fut.*, being a

---

* The *future parag.* expresses excitement (in the sing., *of oneself*, in the pl., *of one another*), determination, wish, entreaty &c., e. g. אֲנִילָה וְאֶשְׂמְחָה *let me be glad and rejoice!* Ps. 31. 8; נֵלְכָה *let us go!* Ge. 22. 5 (comp. § 11. rem. 6).

pure vowel, is in most instances written without וֹ. The full form occurs most frequently in pause or in the later books, comp. תְּקָצוֹר Le. 25. 5, לִבְלוֹם Ps. 32. 9, תְּבְגּוֹד Is. 48. 8, אֶסְגּוֹד Is. 44. 19.

Before Makkeph, Hholem is changed into Kamets-hhatuph, as:—דְּרָשׁ־נָא לִשְׁאָל־לוֹ 2 Sa. 8. 10; Ps. 78. 18, Je. 21. 2, תְּנְבָּל־בָּה Zec. 9. 2. Where וֹ stands in the text, it is cancelled in the Keri, so that it remains only in the Kheth.; e.g. לנאול־לו Ru. 4. 6 Kh. (Keri לִגְאָל־לוֹ), כתוב־לך Eze. 24. 2 Kh. (Keri כְּתָב־לָךְ), אכתוב־לו Ho. 8. 12 Kh. (Keri אֶכְתָּב־לוֹ).

VI. On the Participle of Kal.

19. קוֹטֵל is the regular participle of the verbs middle _A_, like קָטַל. The Hholem is _impure_, and ought, therefore, to be written _fully_; it is, however, more frequently written _defectively_, not only before an accession at the end, but even in the ground form, קֹטֵל.

Like the noun, it often has parag. וֹ appended to the construct state; as שֹׁכְנִי סְנֶה _the inhabitant of the_ thorn-bush, De. 33. 16, הֹפְכִי הַצוּר _who changes the rock_, Ps. 114. 8, יֹשְׁבִי בַּשָּׁמַיִם _who dwells in heaven_, Ps. 123. 1, אֹסְרִי לַגֶּפֶן _who binds to the vine_, Ge. 49. 11, עֹזְבִי הַצֹּאן Zec. 11. 17.

In its inflexion it differs in nothing from the noun (comp. dec. 7), and by the same analogy is formed the feminine; only that it must be noticed, that the feminine form קֹטֶלֶת (with gutt. שֹׁמַעַת) is here more frequent than קֹטְלָה.

When the tone is thrown back on account of a word, with the tone on the _penultima_, following it, Segol is substituted in the final syllable, as in Is. 41. 7, הֹלֶם פָּעַם _who smites the anvil_.

An unfrequent form is תוֹמִיךְ _upholding_, Ps. 16. 5, for תֹּמֵךְ; הִנְנִי יֹסֵף _behold I am adding_, Is. 29. 14; 38. 5.*

20. The participles of the verbs middle _E_ and _O_ do not differ in form from the preterite; as מָלֵא _he is full_, and _full_; יָשֵׁן _he slept_, and _sleeping_; יָגֹר _he was afraid_, and _fearing_. Where these forms do not occur as participles, they are at least _verbal adjectives_.†

SECTION IX.—NIPHAL.

REMARKS.

1. _Preterite._ There is no positive proof for the existence of preterites like נִקְטַל נִקְטֵל, corresponding to קָטַל קָטֵל, of the Kal (comp. § 8. rem. 1, note), in addition to the form נִקְטַל; for נֶחְתּוֹם Est. 8. 8, נַעֲתוֹר 1 Ch. 5. 20, נַהֲפוֹךְ Est. 9. 1, usually regarded as such preterites, are properly _infinitives abs._

With regard to the tone and its changes, the remarks already made upon Kal (§ 8. rem. 7) are also applicable to Niphal.

2. The first _inf. abs._ (נִקְטֹל), connects itself, in form, with the preterite, to which it bears the same relation as קָטוֹל to קָטַל, and is the only infinitive of this kind. Examples are—נִלְחֹם _warring_, Ju. 11. 25, נִכְסֹף _longing_, Ge. 31. 30, נִשְׁאֹל _asking for oneself_, 1 Sa. 20. 6, נִשְׁלֹח _sending_, Est. 3. 13. Examples for the second form are—הִנָּתֹן Je. 32. 4, הֵאָכֹל Le. 7. 18, once אִדָּרֹשׁ _being inquired of_, Eze. 14. 3, which is quite an Arabic form. The construct form is but seldom used instead of the absolute, e. g. הִשָּׁמֵר De. 4. 26. In Ps. 68. 3, כְּהִנְדֹּף עָשָׁן תִּנְדֹּף _as smoke is driven away thou drivest_ (them) _away_, the form הִנְדֹּף, as the construct of הִנָּדֵף, is chosen instead of הִנָּדֵף, probably for its agreement of sound with the following תִּנְדֹּף.

3. The _infinitive, imperative,_ or _future_, in those persons which have no afformatives, when immediately followed by a word of one syllable, have the tone commonly drawn back to the penultima, and the final syllable having lost the tone receives Segol instead of Tseri; as יִכָּשֵׁל בָּה Ec. 7. 26, יִלָּכֶד בָּה Eze. 33. 12, תִּכָּתֶב זֹאת Ps. 102. 19, וַיֵּעָתֶר לוֹ Ge. 25. 21; 2 Ch. 33. 13, יֵחָלֶק אוֹר Job 38. 24; so in the _inf._ לְהִסָּתֶר שָׁם Job 34. 22; in the _imp._ הִלָּחֶם בּוֹ Ju. 9. 38. In some words, however, this form with the retracted tone has become the usual one; e. g. הִשָּׁמֶר Ex. 23. 21, and with _conversive Vav_, וַיִּלָּחֶם Nu. 21. 23; Jos. 24. 9; Ju. 9. 39; 1 Sa. 14. 47; וַיִּנָּגֶף 1 Sa. 4. 2, 10; 2 Sa. 2. 17; 2 Ki. 14. 12.

4. In a similar case, Pattahh is sometimes, though but seldom, put for Tseri, as תֵּעָזַב אֶרֶץ Job 18. 4; it is, however, more frequently found with distinctive

---

* This form is, however, not universally acknowledged as a participle. Thus is תוֹמִיךְ regarded as fut. of Hiph. _thou makest wide, glorious_, from יָמַךְ, Arab. _amplus fuit_ (Schult., instit. ad fundam. 1 Hebr. p. 298). יֹסֵף is likewise taken as Hiph. with אֲשֶׁר supplied, and rendered, _I am he who shall add_.

† This is indeed true in principle; we find it, however, more convenient to class even the participle cited here, among the adjectives where they will be found in the Lexicon.

accents, e. g. וַיִּגָּמַל *he was weaned*, Ge. 21. 8; וַיִּנָּפֵשׁ *he was refreshed*, Ex. 31. 17; יֵאָמֵר *it is said*, Ge. 10. 9; Nu. 21. 14; וַיֵּאָמֶר Jos. 2. 9, וַיֵּאָנֵשׁ *he became sick*, 2 Sa. 12. 15. In the 2 and 3 pers. pl. the form with Pattahh is more common than that with Tseri, not only in pause (as תִּשָּׁגַלְנָה Zec. 14. 2, תֵּרַמַסְנָה Is. 28. 3), and with gutturals or ר (as תִּנָּחֵרְנָה Is. 65. 17, תִּפָּתַחְנָה Is. 35. 5), but even in the absence of either of these, e. g. תֵּאָכַלְנָה Je. 24. 2.

5. The fut. 1 pers. sing. has frequently also Hhirek

under the preformative, as אִשָּׁבֵעַ *I swear*, Ge. 21. 24, אִדָּרֵשׁ Eze. 14. 3, comp. Ge. 19. 20; 1 Sa. 20. 29; 27. 1; Job 1. 15, 16, 17; Is. 1. 24, &c.

6. When the prepositions בְּ, כְּ, לְ, are to be prefixed to the infinitive the ה is frequently contracted, but not so frequently as in the Hiphil; e. g. בַּכָּשְׁלוֹ for בְּהִכָּשְׁלוֹ Pr. 24. 17. This contraction, however, is more usually with verbs of *first guttural*, as בֵּעָטֵף for בְּהֵעָטֵף La. 2. 11, comp. Eze. 26. 15; Is. 1. 12, &c.

SECTION X.—PIEL AND PUAL.
REMARKS.

I. On Piel.

1. The *pret.* of Piel has frequently (ֵ) in the final syllable instead of (ִ); e. g. אִבַּד 2 Ki. 21. 3; La. 2. 9; especially before a Makkeph and in the *middle of a period*, whereas in the end of a period (ִ) is preferred, e. g. לִמַּד־דַּעַת *he teaches wisdom*, Ec. 12. 9, וּמִלַּט־הוּא אֶת־הָעִיר *he delivered the city*, Ec. 9. 15, comp. Eze. 33. 5, וְהוּא נִזְהָר נַפְשׁוֹ מִלֵּט *he who is warned saves his life*. See גֻּדַּל Is. 49. 21, and גֻּדַּל Jos. 4. 14; Est. 3. 1.

A few verbs, of which the following are all the examples, have (ֶ) in the final syllable—וְכִבֶּס *and he shall wash*, Le. 13. 6, 34; 14. 8, 9, &c. (comp. כִּבֶּס Ge. 49. 11; 2 Sa. 19. 25); וְכִפֶּר *and he shall atone*, Le. 4. 20, 26, 31, &c.; דִּבֶּר *he spoke*, frequently דִּבֵּר at the end of a period.

A single instance of (ַ) in the first syllable in the manner of Aramaic and Arabic, is found in Ge. 41. 51, נַשַּׁנִי אֱלֹהִים וגו' *God makes me forget*, which is occasioned by a play upon the name מְנַשֶּׁה.

2. *Infinitive*. The distinguishing form of the inf. abs. is יַסֹּר Ps. 118. 18, קַנֹּא 1 Ki. 19. 10, רַפֹּא Ex. 21. 19; and in the same relation is נַאֵץ 2 Sa. 12. 14.

The latter form, which resembles the 3 pers. pret., is found also in Le. 14. 43 as an inf. constr. אַחַר חִלֵּץ *after drawing out*. Here, it is true, אֲשֶׁר or כִּי may be supplied, and אַחַר taken as a conjunctive, *after one has drawn out*; see, however, the remarks on Hiph. § 11. rem. 4.

Somewhat more frequent are here the forms with the feminine termination—זַמְּרָה *to sing*, Ps. 147. 1; יַסְּרָה *to chasten*, Le. 26. 18; צִדְקָתֵךְ *thy justifying* (comp. § 8. rem. 10) Eze. 16. 52.

3. An *imperative* with Pattahh in the final syllable is פַּלֵּט Ps. 55. 10.

4. The *inf. imp.* and *fut.*, when followed by a Makkeph, or a word which has the tone on the penultima, take generally (ֶ) in the final syllable, e. g. דַּבֶּר־עֶשֶׁק Is. 59. 13; Je. 9. 4; קַדֶּשׁ־לִי Ex. 13. 2; וּבַקֶּשׁ־לוֹ Is. 40. 20; and so, moreover, with *Vav conversive*, e. g. וַתְּגָרֶשׁ Jos. 24. 12.

Instead of תְּקֻפַּלְנָה the form also with Pattahh in the second syllable is found, as תְּרַטַּשְׁנָה, Is. 13. 18.

The following are examples with parag. ן—יְהַלֵּכוּן Ps. 104. 10, יְחַלּוּן Is. 51. 5, comp. Kal § 8. rem. 17.

II. On Pual.

5. The less frequent form of Pual, with Kamets-hhatuph instead of Kibbuts, is found in the following examples—מָאָדָּם *dyed red*, Na. 2. 4; יָחָבְרָךְ *he is joined to thee*, Ps. 94. 20 (beside יֻחַבָּר Ec. 9. 4); כֻּרָּת *he is cut off*, Eze. 16. 4; and in the regular syllables of some irregular verbs, as שָׁדְּדָה *she is desolate*, Na. 3. 7 (usually שֻׁדַּד, שֻׁדְּדָה); כָּלּוּ *they are at an end*, Ps. 72. 20, כֻּסּוּ *they are covered*, Ps. 80. 11; Pr. 24. 31.

It is merely an orthographical variation when Shurek takes the place of Kibbuts, as יֻלַּד, in pause יוּלַד Ju. 13. 8; 18. 29; Job 5. 7 (which may also be taken for Hophal, comp. הֻגַּדְתָּ Eze. 16. 4); זוּנָּה *fornication is committed*, Eze. 16. 34; מָאוּגָּל *spun*, Eze. 27. 19; הוּלְּלוּ *they were praised*, Ps. 78. 63, comp. also Ec. 9. 12.

6. The participle of Pual occurs sometimes without the prefix מְ; it is then distinguished, like the part. of Niph., by the Kamets only in the last syllable; as לֻקָּח for מְלֻקָּח *taken away*, 2 Ki. 2. 10; *the* הַהֻלָּלָה* *praised*, Eze. 26. 17; לֹא נֻחָמָה *not comforted*, Is. 54. 11; לֹא רֻחָמָה *not pitied*, Ho. 1. 6, 8; יֻקָּשִׁים or יוּקְשִׁים *ensnared*, Ec. 9. 12; מֻמְרָט for מֹרָט Eze. 21. 15, 16.

* This and the two next following examples are to be taken rather as preterites, in consequence of their having the tone retracted to the penultima by the pause accent, which is hardly ever to be met with in participles and adjectives.

III. IN GENERAL.

7. In those forms of Piel and Pual, which have Sheva under the radical letter, the characteristic Dagesh is often dropped; e. g. שְׁלָחָה for שִׁלְּחָה *she stretched out*, Eze. 17. 7, שִׁלְחוּ Ps. 74. 7; תְּבֻקְשִׁי *thou shalt be sought*, Eze. 26. 21; though in most instances it is inserted.

The absence of this Dagesh is sometimes intimated (*a*) by the lengthening of the preceding vowel, e. g. יַחֲלֵקֶם for יְחַלְּקֵם 1 Ch. 23. 6; (*b*) by a Hhatuph under the letter which was to have had the Dagesh, e. g. לָקֳחָה for לֻקְּחָה Ge. 2. 23. comp. Ju. 16. 16.

SECTION XI.—HIPHAL AND HOPHAL.

REMARKS.

I. ON HIPHIL.

1. The characteristic ־ִי impure of the final syllable is only retained in the 3 *pers.* preterite of Hiph. (in the participle also, but with some exceptions) so as not to have another form with Tseri. In the imp. inf. and fut. there exists also a form with Tseri in the final syllable, which however differs from the other in signification, as the following remarks will show.

Forms in the *preterite* deviating from the paradigm are, (*a*) with (ֶ) under ה, e. g. הִכָּלַמְנוּ *we are ashamed*, 1 Sa. 25. 7, which is still more usual in verbs ל״ה, e. g. הִסְפָּדָה, הִגְלָה, הֶחֱלָאָה; (*b*) with א, as in the Aramaic; אֶנְאַלְתִּי *I have polluted*, Is. 63. 3; (*c*) with (ֶ) in the 2 and 3 pers., however only with suffix, as הִשְׁאִלְתִּיהוּ 1 Sa. 1. 28.

2. The *inf. absol.* has generally Tseri with or without Yod; as הַשְׁכֵּם *to rise up early*, Je. 7. 13, and הַשְׁכֵּים Je. 44. 4, &c.; הַשְׁמֵד *destroying*, Is. 14. 23, and הַשְׁמֵיד Am. 9. 8; הַשְׁלֵךְ *casting*, Je. 22. 19; הַקְטֵיר *burning incense*, 1 Ki. 9. 25; הַעֲנֵיק Ne. 7. 3: De. 15. 14, &c.

A form with א, by Chaldaism, is אַשְׁכֵּים Je. 25. 3. As such may be taken אַבְרֵךְ Ge. 41. 42, viz. as an *inf. abs.* for the imperative, *bow the knee*, if regarded according to Hebrew etymology.

When followed by Makkeph the inf. takes Segol, as הַכֶּר־פָּנִים Pr. 24. 23; 28. 21.

Unfrequent exceptions are, when the form with *Tseri* occurs for the *inf. constr.*, as הַנְחֵל De. 32. 8, comp. ch. 26. 12; Da. 11. 35, and the form with ־ִי for the *inf. abs.* Jos. 7. 7.

3. When the prepositions בְּ, כְּ, לְ are prefixed to the inf. constr. generally no contraction takes place, and the form remains בְּהַקְטִיל, לְהַקְטִיל, &c., differing

in this respect from the future, where יַקְטִיל stands for יְהַקְטִיל. There are, however, some few exceptions; e. g. לְשְׁמִיד *to destroy*, Is. 23. 11; לַשְׁבִּית *to put an end to*, Am. 8. 4; לְלְבֵּן *to make white*, Da. 11. 35; לַאֲדִיב Nu. 5. 22; *to cause to languish*, 1 Sa. 2. 33; לַעְשֵׂר, בַּעְשֵׂר *to pay tithes*, Ne. 10. 39; De. 26. 12, comp. Ex. 13. 21; Ps. 78. 17, and in Kheth., as לַעְזִיר 2 Sa. 18. 3, for which the Keri has לַעֲזוֹר; לַגִּיד 2 Ki. 9. 15.

4. *Infinitives* not differing in form from the *preterite*, are more frequent here than in Piel (§ 10. rem. 2); e. g. עַד הִשְׁאִיר 2 Ki. 3. 25; לְמַעַן הַרְגִּיעַ וְהִרְגּוּ Je. 50. 34; יָגֵן יְהֹוָה־גָּנוֹן וְהִצִּיל פָּסֹחַ וְהִמְלִיט Is. 31. 5. These examples may yet be doubted, as they can be regarded as real preterites, and the prepositions before them as mere conjunctions (for עַד אֲשֶׁר (לְמַעַן אֲשֶׁר; there are, however, others which must be recognised as infinitives, e. g. הַשְׁמִידָךְ De. 7. 24; moreover אַחֲרֵי הַקְצוֹת אֶת־הַבַּיִת *after the scraping of the house*, Le. 14. 43 (where the ending וֹת of the verb ל״ה decides for the inf.)

5. In the *imp.* the leading form (הַקְטִיל) does not occur at all;* instead of it are employed the shortened and lengthened forms, הַקְטֵל and הַקְטִילָה (§ 8. rem. 13); e. g. הַשְׁמֵן *make fat*, Is. 6. 10; הַקְשֵׁב *attend*, Job 33. 31; הַקְשִׁיבָה Ps. 5. 3; 17. 1; הַצְלַח *prosper*, 1 Ki. 22. 12, 15, and הַצְלִיחָה Ps. 118. 25 (nowhere הַצְלִיחַ); הַבֵּט *look*, Job 35. 5, and הַבִּיטָה La. 1. 11; הַגֵּד *tell*, 1 Sa. 25. 11; הַבְדֵּל *separate*, Is. 56. 3; הַקְשִׁיבָה *hearken*.

Before Makkeph (־) is changed into (ֶ), as הַסְכֶּן־נָא Job 22. 21; הַבֶּט־נָא Ge. 15. 5.

6. In the future, the more usual form is that with Tseri for the *shortened future*, and has in general the

---

* This remains, however, the ground-form whenever the suffixes are added, as הַשְׁמִיעֵנִי Ps. 143. 8, and is analogous to the forms with the afformatives having a union vowel, as הַקְטִילִי, הַקְטִילוּ.

signification of the subjunctive, similar to the length-ened future (§ 8. rem. 13), with some modification occasioned by the difference of person.   It is found—

(a) In the expression of command and wish; e. g. יִכָּרֵת *may be cut off*, Ps. 12. 4 ; 109. 15 (comp. יַכְרִית *he shall cut off*, De. 12. 29 ; 19. 1 ; 1 Ki. 14. 14); יֹסֵף *may he add, may he increase*, Ge. 30. 24 ; Le. 5. 16, 24 ; 27. 31 ; Nu. 5. 7 ; 22. 19 ; De. 1. 11 (comp. יֹסִיף Jos. 23. 13 ; 2 Sa. 14. 10); תּוֹצֵא *let her bring forth* (comp. תּוֹצִיא Is. 61. 11 ; Hag. 1. 11); יַפְקֵד *let him appoint*, Ge. 41. 34 ; Est. 2. 3 (יַפְקִיד Is. 10. 28); יַשֵּׂג *let him overtake*, Ps. 7. 6 ; תֹּאבֵל Eze. 3. 3 ; תּוֹחֵל 1 Sa. 10. 8, &c.

(b) More usually in the expression of prohibition with אַל ; e. g. אַל־תַּסְתֵּר *hide not*, Ps. 27. 9 ; 69. 18 ; 102. 3 ; 119. 19 (comp. תַּסְתִּיר Ps. 13. 2 ; 44. 25); אַל־תַּשְׁחֵת *destroy not*, De. 9. 26 ; Ps. 57. 1, &c. ; אַל־תַּסְגֵּר *shut not up*, Ob. 14 ; תַּצֵּל *deliver not*, Ps. 119. 43 (comp. 1 Sa. 30. 8); אַל־תַּפֵּל *let not fail*, Est. 6. 10 (comp. Pr. 1. 14); אַל־תַּבֵּט *look not*, 1 Sa. 16. 7 ; אַל־יַאֲמֵן *let him not trust*, Job 15. 31 ; אַל יוֹתֵר *let him not leave*, Ex. 16. 19 ; see also Pr. 30. 10 ; Ob. 12.

(c) Less frequently with a וְ preceding it, expressive of the conjunction *that, in order that*, as in Ju. 14. 15, *entice thy husband* וְיַגֶּד־לָנוּ *that he declare to us*, and so Job 11. 6 ; 12. 7 ; Je. 42. 3 ; וְיַצֵּל *that he deliver*, 1 Sa. 7. 3.

(d) With a negation, e. g. לֹא־תֹסֵף *she shall not continue*, Ge. 4. 12, comp. Job 40. 32 (27); לֹא אֹסֵף De. 18. 16 ; Ho. 9. 15 ; אַל תּוֹתֵר *thou shalt not have the pre-eminence*, Ge. 49. 4 ; see also Is. 13. 20.

(e) After *conversive Vav;* the first person, how-ever, is excepted, which generally retains the form with ֘י ; e. g. וָאַשְׁמִיד *and I destroyed*, Am. 2. 9 ; וָאַשְׁלִיךְ *and I cast*, Zec. 11. 13 ; וָאַגִּיד *and I told*, Is. 48. 5 ; וָאַמְלִיךְ *and I made king*, 1 Sa. 12. 1 ; וָאַסְתִּיר *and I hid*, Eze. 39. 23, 24.   It is likewise so pointed when י is omitted in the text—וָאַעְשִׁר *and I enriched*, Zec. 11. 5 ; וָאַחְבִּא *and I hid*, 1 Ki. 18. 13 ; וָאַצִּל *and I delivered*, Jos. 24. 10 ; Ju. 6. 9 ; 1 Sa. 10. 18.

Exceptions where יַקְטֵל is used for the plain *future* (or *present*), are only found with the poets, e. g. יַשְׁלֵךְ *he casts*, Job 15. 33 ; 27. 22 ; יַמְטֵר *he causes to rain*, Job 20. 23 ; Ps. 11. 6 ; see also Job 18. 9 ; 34. 29 ; 37. 4 ; 40. 9, 19 ; Ps. 25. 9 ; 2 Sa. 22. 14 ; 1 Sa. 2. 10 ; Mi. 3. 4.   Also with somewhat later authors, e. g. יַדְבֵּק *he shall make to cleave*, De. 28. 21 ; יֹלֵךְ *he shall lead*, De. 28. 36 ; אָז יַקְהֵל *then he assembled*, 1 Ki. 8. 1,

for which 2 Ch. 5. 2 אָז יַקְהִיל (doubtless *to be read* יַקְהִיל); וְאַחֲזֻק *and I shall lay hold*, Is. 42. 6.

7. Before Makkeph this Tseri of the shortened future becomes Segol; e. g. וַיַּחֲזֶק־בּוֹ *and he laid hold upon him*, Ju. 19. 4 ; וַיִּגַּשׁ־לוֹ *and he drew near to him*, Ge. 27. 25 ; וַנַּגֶּד־לוֹ *and we told him*, Ge. 43. 7.   In pause it occurs with Pattahh—וַיִּגַּשׁ Ju. 6. 19.   In the plural Tseri is sometimes entirely dropped, as is the case with the *e* of the final syllable in the Aramaic—וַיַּדְרְכוּ for וַיַּדְרִיכוּ *and they bent* (the bow), Je. 9. 2 ; וַיִּרְדְּפוּ *and they pursued*, 1 Sa. 14. 22 ; 31. 2

8. In the participle the form with (ִ) seldom occurs in the singular, see however מַסְתֵּר for מַסְתִּיר *hiding*, Is. 53. 3, and in the fem. מַכְרֶבֶת Nu. 5. 15, מַצֶּרֶת Est. 2. 20.   Hence are the plurals מַחְלְמִים *dreaming*, Je. 29. 8, מַעְזְרִים *helping*, 2 Ch. 28. 23, מַהְלְכִים *leading (leaders)*, Zec. 3. 7, comp. the Chaldee מַהְלְכִין Da. 3. 25 ; 4. 34.

9. The tone in Hiph. differs from that of the rest of the conjugations, inasmuch as it does not rest upon the afformatives ִי and ֫י in the pret., imp. and fut.   In the pret. however, they receive the tone by *conversive Vav;* וְהִבְדִּילָה *and she shall divide*, Ex. 26. 33, but is retained in וְהִגִּידָה *and she told*, 2 Sa. 17. 17

II. On Hophal.

10. Besides the form with Kamets-Hhatuph given in the paradigm, there is another with Kibbuts equally frequent, and often in one and the same verb, e. g. הֻשְׁלַךְ *he is cast*, Da. 8. 11, הָשְׁלַכְתָּ Is. 14. 19, הֻשְׁלַכְתִּי Ps. 22. 11, fut. יֻשְׁלַךְ Is. 34. 3, Eze. 16. 5, part. מֻשְׁלָךְ 2 Sa. 20. 21 ; הֻשְׁכַּב *to be laid*, Eze. 32. 32, imp. הֻשְׁכְּבָה ver. 19 ; הָפְקַד *to be appointed*, Je. 6. 6, part. מֻפְקָדִים 2 Ch. 34. 10 ; תֻּקְטַר *to be burned*, Le. 6. 15, part. מֻקְטָר Mal. 1. 11.

11. The *inf. abs.* is distinguished by (ָ) in the final syllable, e. g. הָחְתֵּל *to be swaddled*, Eze. 16. 4 ; הָגֵּר Jos. 9. 24.   Of the *inf. constr.* as given in the paradigm, there happens to occur no example in the regular verb.

12. Of the *participle* there occurs, in Eze. 46. 22, the uncontracted form מְהֻקְצָעוֹת for מְקֻצָּעוֹת.   This form occurs likewise in the fut. of the verbs פ״י, as יוּדָה for יֻדָּה (comp. § 20. rem. 10\).

SECTION XII.—HITHPAEL.

REMARKS.

1. The *preterite*, as in Piel, has frequently also *Pattahh* in the final syllable, e. g. הִתְחַזַּק *to show oneself courageous*, 2 Ch. 13. 7 ; 15. 8. This vowel occurs also in the future and imperative, as יִתְחַכַּם *he thinks himself wise*, Ec. 7. 16 ; הִתְעַנַּג *delight thyself*, Ps. 37. 4 ; הִתְקַדַּשׁ *sanctify thyself*, Jos. 3. 5, comp. 1 Ki. 20. 22. In pause these forms take Kamets, as pret. הִתְאַזָּר *he girded himself*, Ps. 93. 1 ; fut. יִתְאַבָּל *he mourns*, Eze. 7. 12. 27, יִתְאַדָּם *it sparkles*, Pr. 23. 31.

2. The *preterite* with conversive Vav has sometimes *Hhirek* instead of *Pattahh* in the penultima which has lost the tone, as וְהִתְגַּדִּלְתִּי וְהִתְקַדִּשְׁתִּי *I will show myself great and holy*, Eze. 38. 23 ; וְהִתְקַדִּשְׁתֶּם *and ye shall show yourself holy*, Le. 11. 44 ; 20. 7, comp. in Kal the form יְלִדְתִּיךָ (§ 8. rem. 1 b).

3. The Syriac form with אֶת occurs in 2 Ch. 20. 35, אֶתְחַבַּר for הִתְחַבַּר *he joined himself*.

Note. The ת of the syllable הִתְ suffers the following

changes :—(*a*) when the first radical of the verb is a sibilant (ס, צ, שׁ) it changes place with ת, as הִשְׁתַּמֵּר for הִתְשַׁמֵּר, הִסְתַּבֵּל for הִתְסַבֵּל ; צ causes, moreover, a change of ת into the more nearly related ט, as הִצְטַדֵּק for הִצְתַּדֵּק ; (*b*) before ד, ז, ט, & ת it is assimilated, e. g. הַדַּבֵּר from דָּבַר, הִנַּכּוּ from זָכָה Is. 1. 16, הִטַּהֵר, הִתַּמֵּם ; sometimes also before נ & כ, as הַנַּבֵּא, elsewhere הִתְנַבֵּא ; וַתִּכּוֹנֵן for הִתְכּוֹנֵן.

4. Forms followed by Makkeph are :—הִתְהַלֶּךְ־נֹחַ *Noah walked*, Ge. 6. 9 ; יִתְעַלֶּם־שָׁלֶג *the snow hides itself*, Job 6. 16 ; with parag. ן, הִתְהַלָּכוּן *they walk*, Ps. 12. 9 (comp. Kal fut. § 8. rem. 17) ; with parag. ה, אֶתְהַלְּכָה *I will walk*, Ps. 119. 45 (comp. Kal § 8. rem. 13).

5. In forms, in which the middle radical has Sheva, so that Dagesh may be dropped (§ 10. rem. 7), this latter is sometimes compensated by lengthening (◌ֵ) into (◌ֵ), as הִתְפָּקְדוּ for הִתְפַּקְדוּ, Ju. 20. 15, and from habit of the punctuator, also in the sing. יִתְפָּקֵד (for יִתְפַּקֵד) Ju. 21. 9.*

---

* Some have adopted here another conjugation הִתְקַאטֵל.

TABLES OF THE VERBS WITH GUTTURALS.

	TABLE C. VERB PE GUTTURAL.				TABLE D. VERB AYIN GUTTURAL.				
	KAL.	NIPHAL.	HIPHIL.	HOPHAL.	KAL.	NIPHAL.	PIEL.	PUAL.	HITHPAEL.
PRET. 3. m.	עָמַד	נֶעֱמַד	הֶעֱמִיד	הָעֳמַד	שָׁחַט	נִשְׁחַט	בֵּרֵךְ	בֹּרַךְ	הִתְבָּרֵךְ
3. f.	עָמְדָה	נֶעֶמְדָה	הֶעֱמִידָה	הָעֳמְדָה	שָׁחֲטָה	נִשְׁחֲטָה	בֵּרְכָה	בֹּרְכָה	הִתְבָּרְכָה
2. m.	עָמַדְתָּ	נֶעֱמַדְתָּ	הֶעֱמַדְתָּ	הָעֳמַדְתָּ	שָׁחַטְתָּ	נִשְׁחַטְתָּ	בֵּרַכְתָּ	בֹּרַכְתָּ	הִתְבָּרַכְתָּ
2. f.	עָמַדְתְּ	נֶעֱמַדְתְּ	הֶעֱמַדְתְּ	הָעֳמַדְתְּ	שָׁחַטְתְּ	נִשְׁחַטְתְּ	בֵּרַכְתְּ	בֹּרַכְתְּ	הִתְבָּרַכְתְּ
1. c.	עָמַדְתִּי	נֶעֱמַדְתִּי	הֶעֱמַדְתִּי	הָעֳמַדְתִּי	שָׁחַטְתִּי	נִשְׁחַטְתִּי	בֵּרַכְתִּי	בֹּרַכְתִּי	הִתְבָּרַכְתִּי
Plur. 3. c.	עָמְדוּ	נֶעֶמְדוּ	הֶעֱמִידוּ	הָעֳמְדוּ	שָׁחֲטוּ	נִשְׁחֲטוּ	בֵּרְכוּ	בֹּרְכוּ	הִתְבָּרְכוּ
2. m.	עֲמַדְתֶּם	נֶעֱמַדְתֶּם	הֶעֱמַדְתֶּם	הָעֳמַדְתֶּם	שְׁחַטְתֶּם	נִשְׁחַטְתֶּם	בֵּרַכְתֶּם	בֹּרַכְתֶּם	הִתְבָּרַכְתֶּם
2. f.	עֲמַדְתֶּן	נֶעֱמַדְתֶּן	הֶעֱמַדְתֶּן	הָעֳמַדְתֶּן	שְׁחַטְתֶּן	נִשְׁחַטְתֶּן	בֵּרַכְתֶּן	בֹּרַכְתֶּן	הִתְבָּרַכְתֶּן
1. c.	עָמַדְנוּ	נֶעֱמַדְנוּ	הֶעֱמַדְנוּ	הָעֳמַדְנוּ	שָׁחַטְנוּ	נִשְׁחַטְנוּ	בֵּרַכְנוּ	בֹּרַכְנוּ	הִתְבָּרַכְנוּ
INF. absol.	עָמוֹד	נַעֲמוֹד	הַעֲמִיד		שָׁחוֹט	נִשְׁחוֹט	בָּרוֹךְ		
constr.	עֲמֹד	הֵעָמֵד	הַעֲמִיד	הָעֳמַד	שְׁחֹט	הִשָּׁחֵט	בָּרֵךְ	בֹּרַךְ	הִתְבָּרֵךְ
IMP. m.	עֲמֹד　חֲזַק	הֵעָמֵד	הַעֲמֵד	הָעֳמַד	שְׁחַט	הִשָּׁחֵט	בָּרֵךְ		הִתְבָּרֵךְ
f.	עִמְדִי　חִזְקִי	הֵעָמְדִי	הַעֲמִידִי		שַׁחֲטִי	הִשָּׁחֲטִי	בָּרְכִי		הִתְבָּרְכִי
Plur. m.	עִמְדוּ　חִזְקוּ	הֵעָמְדוּ	הַעֲמִידוּ	wanting	שַׁחֲטוּ	הִשָּׁחֲטוּ	בָּרְכוּ	wanting.	הִתְבָּרְכוּ
f.	עֲמֹדְנָה　חֲזַקְנָה	הֵעָמַדְנָה	הַעֲמֵדְנָה		שְׁחַטְנָה	הִשָּׁחַטְנָה	בָּרֵכְנָה		הִתְבָּרֵכְנָה
FUT. 3. m.	יַעֲמֹד	יֵחָזַק　יֵעָמֵד	יַעֲמִיד	יָעֳמַד	יִשְׁחַט	יִשָּׁחֵט	יְבָרֵךְ	יְבֹרַךְ	יִתְבָּרֵךְ
3. f.	תַּעֲמֹד	תֵּחָזַק　תֵּעָמֵד	תַּעֲמִיד	תָּעֳמַד	תִּשְׁחַט	תִּשָּׁחֵט	תְּבָרֵךְ	תְּבֹרַךְ	תִּתְבָּרֵךְ
2. m.	תַּעֲמֹד	תֵּחָזַק　תֵּעָמֵד	תַּעֲמִיד	תָּעֳמַד	תִּשְׁחַט	תִּשָּׁחֵט	תְּבָרֵךְ	תְּבֹרַךְ	תִּתְבָּרֵךְ
2. f.	תַּעַמְדִי	תֵּחָזְקִי	תַּעֲמִידִי	תָּעֳמְדִי	תִּשְׁחֲטִי	תִּשָּׁחֲטִי	תְּבָרְכִי	תְּבֹרְכִי	תִּתְבָּרְכִי
1. c.	אֶעֱמֹד	אֶחֱזַק	אַעֲמִיד	אָעֳמַד	אֶשְׁחַט	אֶשָּׁחֵט	אֲבָרֵךְ	אֲבֹרַךְ	אֶתְבָּרֵךְ
Plur. 3. m.	יַעַמְדוּ	יֵחָזְקוּ	יַעֲמִידוּ	יָעֳמְדוּ	יִשְׁחֲטוּ	יִשָּׁחֲטוּ	יְבָרְכוּ	יְבֹרְכוּ	יִתְבָּרְכוּ
3. f.	תַּעֲמֹדְנָה	תֵּחֱזַקְנָה	תַּעֲמֵדְנָה	תָּעֳמַדְנָה	תִּשְׁחַטְנָה	תִּשָּׁחַטְנָה	תְּבָרַכְנָה	תְּבֹרַכְנָה	תִּתְבָּרַכְנָה
2. m.	תַּעַמְדוּ	תֵּחָזְקוּ	תַּעֲמִידוּ	תָּעֳמְדוּ	תִּשְׁחֲטוּ	תִּשָּׁחֲטוּ	תְּבָרְכוּ	תְּבֹרְכוּ	תִּתְבָּרְכוּ
2. f.	תַּעֲמֹדְנָה	תֵּחֱזַקְנָה	תַּעֲמֵדְנָה	תָּעֳמַדְנָה	תִּשְׁחַטְנָה	תִּשָּׁחַטְנָה	תְּבָרַכְנָה	תְּבֹרַכְנָה	תִּתְבָּרַכְנָה
1. c.	נַעֲמֹד	נֵחֱזַק	נַעֲמִיד	נָעֳמַד	נִשְׁחַט	נִשָּׁחֵט	נְבָרֵךְ	נְבֹרַךְ	נִתְבָּרֵךְ
FUT. apoc.			יַעֲמֵד						
PART. act.	עֹמֵד	נֶעֱמָד	מַעֲמִיד	מָעֳמָד	שֹׁחֵט	נִשְׁחָט	מְבָרֵךְ	מְבֹרָךְ	מִתְבָּרֵךְ
pass.	עָמוּד				שָׁחוּט				

TABLE E. VERB LAMEDH GUTTURAL.

	KAL.	NIPHAL.	PIEL.	PUAL.	HIPHIL.	HOPHAL.	HITHPAEL.
PRET. 3. m.	שָׁלַח	נִשְׁלַח	שִׁלַּח	שֻׁלַּח	הִשְׁלִיחַ	הָשְׁלַח	הִשְׁתַּלַּח
3. f.	שָׁלְחָה	נִשְׁלְחָה	שִׁלְּחָה	שֻׁלְּחָה	הִשְׁלִיחָה	הָשְׁלְחָה	הִשְׁתַּלְּחָה
2. m.	שָׁלַחְתָּ	נִשְׁלַחְתָּ	שִׁלַּחְתָּ	שֻׁלַּחְתָּ	הִשְׁלַחְתָּ	הָשְׁלַחְתָּ	הִשְׁתַּלַּחְתָּ
2. f.	שָׁלַחַתְּ	נִשְׁלַחַתְּ	שִׁלַּחַתְּ	שֻׁלַּחַתְּ	הִשְׁלַחַתְּ	הָשְׁלַחַתְּ	הִשְׁתַּלַּחַתְּ
1. c.	שָׁלַחְתִּי	נִשְׁלַחְתִּי	שִׁלַּחְתִּי	שֻׁלַּחְתִּי	הִשְׁלַחְתִּי	הָשְׁלַחְתִּי	הִשְׁתַּלַּחְתִּי
Plur. 3. c.	שָׁלְחוּ	נִשְׁלְחוּ	שִׁלְּחוּ	שֻׁלְּחוּ	הִשְׁלִיחוּ	הָשְׁלְחוּ	הִשְׁתַּלְּחוּ
2. m.	שְׁלַחְתֶּם	נִשְׁלַחְתֶּם	שִׁלַּחְתֶּם	שֻׁלַּחְתֶּם	הִשְׁלַחְתֶּם	הָשְׁלַחְתֶּם	הִשְׁתַּלַּחְתֶּם
2. f.	שְׁלַחְתֶּן	נִשְׁלַחְתֶּן	שִׁלַּחְתֶּן	שֻׁלַּחְתֶּן	הִשְׁלַחְתֶּן	הָשְׁלַחְתֶּן	הִשְׁתַּלַּחְתֶּן
1. c.	שָׁלַחְנוּ	נִשְׁלַחְנוּ	שִׁלַּחְנוּ	שֻׁלַּחְנוּ	הִשְׁלַחְנוּ	הָשְׁלַחְנוּ	הִשְׁתַּלַּחְנוּ
INF. absol.	שָׁלוֹחַ	נִשְׁלֹחַ	שַׁלֵּחַ		הַשְׁלֵחַ		
constr.	שְׁלֹחַ	הִשָּׁלַח	שַׁלַּח	שֻׁלַּח	הַשְׁלִיחַ	הָשְׁלַח	הִשְׁתַּלֵּחַ
IMP. m.	שְׁלַח	הִשָּׁלַח	שַׁלַּח		הַשְׁלַח		הִשְׁתַּלַּח
f.	שִׁלְחִי	הִשָּׁלְחִי	שַׁלְּחִי	wanting	הַשְׁלִיחִי	wanting	הִשְׁתַּלְּחִי
Plur. m.	שִׁלְחוּ	הִשָּׁלְחוּ	שַׁלְּחוּ		הַשְׁלִיחוּ		הִשְׁתַּלְּחוּ
f.	שְׁלַחְנָה	הִשָּׁלַחְנָה	שַׁלַּחְנָה		הַשְׁלַחְנָה		הִשְׁתַּלַּחְנָה
FUT. 3. m.	יִשְׁלַח	יִשָּׁלַח	יְשַׁלַּח	יְשֻׁלַּח	יַשְׁלִיחַ	יָשְׁלַח	יִשְׁתַּלַּח
3. f.	תִּשְׁלַח	תִּשָּׁלַח	תְּשַׁלַּח	תְּשֻׁלַּח	תַּשְׁלִיחַ	תָּשְׁלַח	תִּשְׁתַּלַּח
2. m.	תִּשְׁלַח	תִּשָּׁלַח	תְּשַׁלַּח	תְּשֻׁלַּח	תַּשְׁלִיחַ	תָּשְׁלַח	תִּשְׁתַּלַּח
2. f.	תִּשְׁלְחִי	תִּשָּׁלְחִי	תְּשַׁלְּחִי	תְּשֻׁלְּחִי	תַּשְׁלִיחִי	תָּשְׁלְחִי	תִּשְׁתַּלְּחִי
1. c.	אֶשְׁלַח	אֶשָּׁלַח	אֲשַׁלַּח	אֲשֻׁלַּח	אַשְׁלִיחַ	אָשְׁלַח	אֶשְׁתַּלַּח
Plur. 3. m.	יִשְׁלְחוּ	יִשָּׁלְחוּ	יְשַׁלְּחוּ	יְשֻׁלְּחוּ	יַשְׁלִיחוּ	יָשְׁלְחוּ	יִשְׁתַּלְּחוּ
3. f.	תִּשְׁלַחְנָה	תִּשָּׁלַחְנָה	תְּשַׁלַּחְנָה	תְּשֻׁלַּחְנָה	תַּשְׁלַחְנָה	תָּשְׁלַחְנָה	תִּשְׁתַּלַּחְנָה
2. m.	תִּשְׁלְחוּ	תִּשָּׁלְחוּ	תְּשַׁלְּחוּ	תְּשֻׁלְּחוּ	תַּשְׁלִיחוּ	תָּשְׁלְחוּ	תִּשְׁתַּלְּחוּ
2. f.	תִּשְׁלַחְנָה	תִּשָּׁלַחְנָה	תְּשַׁלַּחְנָה	תְּשֻׁלַּחְנָה	תַּשְׁלַחְנָה	תָּשְׁלַחְנָה	תִּשְׁתַּלַּחְנָה
1. c.	נִשְׁלַח	נִשָּׁלַח	נְשַׁלַּח	נְשֻׁלַּח	נַשְׁלִיחַ	נָשְׁלַח	נִשְׁתַּלַּח
FUT. apoc.					יַשְׁלַח		
PART. act.	שֹׁלֵחַ	נִשְׁלָח	מְשַׁלֵּחַ	מְשֻׁלָּח	מַשְׁלִיחַ	מָשְׁלָח	מִשְׁתַּלֵּחַ
pass.	שָׁלוּחַ						

SECTION XIII.—VERB PE GUTTURAL. (TABLE C.)

REMARKS.

I. ON KAL.

1. In the *preterite* no other deviation exists except הֱיִיתֶם (with Hhateph-Segol) *ye are*, Job 6. 21, and the same word with simple Sheva וְהָיִיתֶם Ge. 3. 5 (comp. rem. 13).

2. In the verbs פ״א the *inf. constr.* takes (ֱ) under the first letter, as אֱכֹל especially with the prefixes, בֶּאֱחֹז, לֶאֱחֹז *to seize*, כֶּאֱסֹף, לֶאֱסֹף *to collect*, Is. 17. 5; 2 Ki. 5. 7; לֶאֱכֹל Ge. 24. 33, and * בַּאֲכֹל Nu. 26.10. With simple Sheva לֶאְסֹר (for לֶאֱסֹר) *to bind*, Ps. 105. 22. With the feminine termination:—אַשְׁמָה *to become guilty*, Le. 5. 26, אַהֲבָה *to love*, De. 10. 12; 11. 22; חָזְקָה, whence בְּחֶזְקָתוֹ *when he gained strength*, 2 Ch. 12. 1; 26. 16.

3. *Imperative.* In the verbs פ״א the first letter takes (ֱ), as אֱזֹר *gird on*, Job 38. 3, אֱחֹז *lay hold*, Ex. 4. 4, אֱסֹף *collect*, Nu. 21. 16; אֱהַב *love*, Ho. 3. 1. The rest of the persons have generally the regular form, only in a few instances Segol is retained, e. g. אֶסְפָה *collect*, Nu. 11. 16, עֶרְכָה *order*, Job 33. 5, חֶשְׂפִּי *make bare*, Is. 47. 2, which more especially happens when the second radical is likewise a guttural, אֶהֱבוּ Ps. 31. 24, אֱחֻזוּ Ca. 2. 15, אֶחֱזוּ Ru. 3. 15.

4. The **form** of the *future* exhibited in the paradigm is that of the verbs *fut. O*, as יַחֲלֹם *to dream*, יַעֲבֹד *to serve*, יַעֲבֹר *to pass over*, יַעֲרֹךְ *to set in order*. The verbs *fut. A* take Segol under the preformatives, as יֶאֱבַל *to mourn*, יֶחֱזַק *to be strong*, יֶחֱרַד *to tremble*, יֶעֱרַב *to be sweet.* Less frequently do verbs *fut. O* occur with Segol, as יֶאֱסֹף *to collect*, יֶחְשֹׂף *to make bare*, and once in pause יֶחְדָּל Job 10. 20 (elsewhere יֶחְדָּל). Both futures, like יֶחֱזַק & יַעֲמֹד, are found in one and the same verb (with or without a difference of signification), as in חָבַשׁ *to bind*, חָלַשׁ *to be weak*, חָרַשׁ *to cut*, חָפֵץ *to delight in*, עָרַב (§ 8. rem. 18). Moreover, יַהֲלֹךְ *to go*, תְּהֲלַךְ (*grassari*) for תֵּהֲלַךְ (comp. rem. 12) Ex. 9. 23; Ps. 73. 9.

Examples with afformatives are: — יַהַרְגוּ, יַהַרְגוּ; אַהֲרָגָה (*to kill*), יַהֲפֹךְ, יַהַפְכוּ (*to turn*); יֶחֱזַק, יֶחֱזְקוּ; יֶחֱרַד, יֶחֶרְדוּ (*to tremble*).

5. Other verbs have very constantly simple Sheva under the guttural; but in the same relation as mentioned above. This is most frequently the case with ח, as יַחְגֹּר (for יַחֲגֹר) *to gird on*, יַחְמֹל *to pity*, יַחְשֹׁב *to think*; יֶחְדַּל *to cease*, יֶחְכַּם *to be wise.* The persons with afformatives remain quite regular, as יֶחְדְּלוּ, יַחְגְּרוּ. Less frequently are both forms found in the same verb, e. g. יֶאֱהַב Pr. 3. 12, and יֶאֱהַב Pr.

15. 9, 12, and especially **when the** leading form has composite Sheva; but **with** the afformatives and suffixes, simple Sheva is introduced, as יַחֲבֹשׁ, but יַחְבְּשׁוּ 1 Ki. 13. 13, יַחְבְּשֵׁהוּ Ho. 6. 1; יַחֲבֹל De. 24. 6, pl. יַחְבְּלוּ Job 24. 3; יַחֲלֹק, pl. יַחְלְקוּ Jos. 14. 5; so also יַעֲבֹר, pl. יַעַבְרוּ, but נַעְבְּרָה, נַעֲבֹרָה.

6. Since the punctuation (ַ-ֲ), (ֲ-) is considered shorter than (ַ-ְ), (ֱ-), the former is sometimes used where the **form** is augmented by afformatives, suffixes, &c., while the leading form has the latter punctuation. E. g. יֶאֱסֹף (*to collect*), but תַּאַסְפוּ, יַאַסְפוּ, and so with suffix; יֶאֱסֹר (*to bind*), with suff. יַאַסְרֵהוּ, &c.; יֶחֱסַר (*to want*), pl. יַחְסְרוּ Ps. 34. 11; Eze. 4. 17. According to the same principle we find יַחְפְּרוּ (*to blush*), Ps. 35. 4, 26, in pause יֶחְפָּרוּ Ps. 34. 6; Job 6. 20; יַחְפְּצוּ, in pause יֶחְפָּצוּ (comp. rem. on Niph. and Hiph.).

II. On Niphal.

7. *Preterite.* Besides the form exhibited in the paradigm there is another with simple Sheva, as נֶאְשַׁם (*to be guilty*), נֶהְדַּר (*to be glorified*). The shorter (ֶ-ְ) is introduced only with the augmentation at the end of the participle, as נֶעְלָם *hid*, Ec. 12. 14, but on the contrary, נַעֲלָמָה Na. 3. 11, and נַעֲלָמִים Ps. 26. 4; so נֶחֱרָבוֹת *waste*, Eze. 30. 7; a single exception is נֶעֱרָץ *terrible*, Ps. 89. 8. A few infinitives absol. formed according to the preterite (§ 9. rem. 1) have likewise this *a*, as נַחֲפוֹךְ.†

8. The *future* is once written *fully* תֵּעָשֶׂה for תֵּעָשֶׂה Ex. 35. 31. In a few instances Segol is found instead of Tseri, e. g. בְּהֶהָרֵג (for בְּהֵהָרֵג, בְּהֵהָרֵג) Eze. 26. 15, and so likewise in a few earlier editions in Eze. 43. 18; Job 19. 7.

III. On Hiphil and Hophal.

9. The forms with (ֶ-ֱ) in the preterite, and (ֲ-) in the infinitive, imperative and future, as exhibited in the paradigm, are as regular here as in the non-guttural verb the forms with (ִ-) and (ַ-) to which they correspond; only that here occurs also the form with simple Sheva, as הֶחְסִיר, fut. יַחְסִיר *shall cause to want*; מַחְפִּיר *causing shame.*

10. In the *preterite*, the punctuation is remarkably

---

* Pattahh is found here (as the shorter form, comp. rem. 6) because the tone is forcibly thrown forward, בַּאֲכֹל הָאֵשׁ. For the same reason they wrote אֲמַרְתֶּם not אֱמַרְתֶּם.

† There are, however, preterites as well as participles (in the leading form) of verbs ל״ה and ל״א which have this (ֲ-); (ֱ-) as עֲשִׂיתִי Ps. 38. 7; Is. 21. 3; נַעֲלָה Nu. 9. 21; 10. 11; נַעֲנֶה Is. 53. 7; נַעֲנֵיתִי Ps. 119. 107; נַעֲשֶׂה Le. 7. 9; נַעֲשׂוּ Le. 18. 30, but also נֶעֶשְׂתָה Nu. 15. 24; נַחְבֵּאת Ge. 31. 27; נַחְבְּתֶם Jos. 2. 16.

affected by the *conversive Vav*, since the tone connected with it changes (ִ.ַו) into the shorter (ְ.ֶ.ַ). E. g. וְהַחֲרַמְתִּי *I have devoted*, 1 Sa. 15. 20; and *I shall devote*, Nu. 21. 2; Mi. 4. 13; וְהַחֲרַמְתָּה 1 Sa. 15. 18, וְהַחֲרַמְתֶּם 1 Sa. 15. 3; הֶעֱמַדְתָּ *thou hast appointed*, Ne. 6. 7; Ps. 31. 9; וְהַעֲמַדְתָּ *and thou shalt appoint*, Nu. 3. 6; 8. 13; 27. 19; Eze. 29. 7; הֶעֱבַרְתִּי *I caused to pass*, Zec. 3. 4; וְהַעֲבַרְתָּ *and I shall cause to pass*, Je. 15. 14; וְהַעֲבַרְתָּ Ex. 13. 12; Le. 25. 9; Nu. 27. 7; Eze. 5. 1; הֶאֱכַלְתִּי Ex. 16. 32; וְהַאֲכַלְתִּי Is. 49. 26; וְהַאֲבַדְתִּי & הֶאֱבַדְתִּי &c. The like change is effected by the *conversive Vav* even in the 3rd person, comp. הֶאֱזִין *he hearkened*, De. 1. 45, and וְהַאֲזִין *and he shall hearken*, Ps. 77. 2.*

11. Of *Hophal* only a few instances occur with simple and composite Sheva under the guttural, as הָהְפַּךְ, fut. יָחֳרַם, part. מֶעֳמָד.

12. In the *part. of Hiph.* (ַ.ִי) is sometimes changed into (ַ.ֵי), and in Hoph. (ַ.ִי) into (ָ.ֳ), prolonging the short vowel which was sustained by Metheg, e. g. הֶעֳבַרְתָּ (elsewhere הֶעֱבַרְתָּ) Jos. 7. 7; הֵעֳלָה Hab. 1. 15 (elsewhere הֶעֱלָה); הֵעֳלָה Na. 2. 8, and that often, for

הֵעֳלָה. Comp. in Kal תֶּחֱלַד for תֶּחְבַּד (§ 13. rem. 4), Ex. 9. 23; Ps. 73. 9; but—Note, on the contrary, (ִי.ַו) is put for (ִי.ַ) in אַחֲרִי (Piel for אַחֲרוּ) Ju. 5. 28; יַחֲמוּ Ge. 30. 39; יֶחֱמַתְנִי Ps. 51. 73.

IV. In General.

13. A few verbs ל״ה with Pe guttural differ from the above inasmuch as their ה & ח are not at all treated as gutturals, viz. הָיָה *to be* (except the pret., see rem. 1), fut. יִהְיֶה, with prepositions לִהְיוֹת, Niph. נִהְיָה; so also חָיָה *to live*, pret. וִחְיִיתֶם Eze. 37. 5, 6, inf. לִחְיוֹת, imp. with copulative Vav, וֶחְיוּ, fut. יִחְיֶה. Only in a few examples the guttural character is retained (viz. when the guttural begins the word), as הֶיֹת, הָיָה, Eze. 21. 15. The same analogy is observed in the apocopated future וַיְחַן, יְחַן (otherwise וַיַּחַר & יַחֲנֶה).

14. The letter ר as first radical comes within this anomaly only in the *inf.* and *fut. of Niph.*, e. g. יֵרָאֶה *he is seen*. The unusual form with Pattahh under the preformative is found only in the apocopated fut. וַיֵּרָא, and in Hiph. וְהִרְאֵתִי Na. 3. 5, with conversive Vav, otherwise הֵרָאָה & יֵרָאֶה.

SECTION XIV.—VERB AYIN GUTTURAL. (Table D.)

REMARKS IN GENERAL.

1. In *Piel*, *Pual* and *Hithpael*, Dagesh forte of the middle radical letter is lost, but in the greater number of examples, particularly before ה, ח & ע, the preceding vowel remains short, and the guttural has *Dagesh forte implicitum*, or Dagesh forte implied, e. g. Piel נִהֵג *to lead*, נִחֵם *to comfort*, בֵּעֵר *to destroy*, inf. צַחֵק *to mock*, fut. יְטַהֵר *to cleanse*, part. מְטַהֵר; Pual רֻחַץ *to be washed*; Hithpa. הִטַּהֲרוּ. Before א the vowel is commonly prolonged (but comp. יְנָאֵץ, נִאֵץ, Pu. רָאוּ Job 33. 21), and always before ר.

2. In *Pi.* and *Hiph.* the tone is sometimes drawn back to the penultima, and Tseri of the final syllable is shortened to Segol, viz. :—

(a) When a monosyllabic word, or one with the tone on the penultima follows, e. g. לְשָׁרֶת שָׁם *to minister there*, De. 17. 12 (otherwise לְשָׁרֵת); בְּנוּ בִּי לְצַחֶק *to mock me* or *us*, Ge. 39. 14, 17; בָּה בִּי כָּחֶשׁ *he*

denies *him, her*, Job 8. 18; Le. 5. 22, comp. כָּחֶשׁ Le. 5. 21, בָּה יְכַחֶשׁ Ho. 9. 2, but וַתְּכַחֶשׁ Ge. 18. 15; יֶחֱרָף צָר *shall the adversary reproach*, Ps. 74. 10, but וַיְחָרֵף 2 Sa. 21. 21.

(b) After conversive Vav, as וַיְבָרֶךְ אוֹתָם *and he blessed them*, Ge. 1. 22, 28; 2. 3; 5. 2 (without a tone syllable following it); וַיְגָרֶשׁ *and he drove away*, Ex. 10. 11; De. 33. 27, &c.; וַיְשָׁרֶת אֹתוֹ *and he scared him*, Ge. 39. 4; וַתִּתְפָּעֶם רוּחוֹ *and his spirit was troubled*, Da. 2. 1. The (ֵ) is, however, retained in both these cases, especially in the latter, e. g. וַיְמָאֵן *and he refused*, Ge. 48. 19; Nu. 20. 21, וַיְמָהֵר *and he made haste*, Ge. 18. 6, 7.

3. In the *Hithpa.*, when the second radical takes Kamets on account of the pause, the preceding syllable takes (ָ) instead of (ַ) or (ֶ). E. g. הִטַּהָרוּ *cleanse yourselves*, Nu. 8. 7; הִנָּחָמְתִּי Eze. 5. 13.

---

* As an exception of this rule must be regarded הַחֲיִתֶם (for הֶחֱיִתֶם) Ju. 6. 14.

REMARKS.

1. In the *inf.* and *fut.* of Niphal, and in the *pret.*, *inf.* and *fut.* of Piel, the form with (ָ) is employed at the beginning and in the middle of a period (with conjunctive accent), that with (ַ) and furtive Pattahh is used at the end of a period (with distinctive accent). E. g. Niph. הִכָּנַע 2 Ch. 33. 23, but on the contrary לְהִבָּקֵעַ Eze. 30. 16; fut. יִגְרַע Nu. 27. 4; 36. 4; comp. יִגְרְעָ chap. 36. 3; יִגְרַע Na. 1. 14, but יִגָּרֵעַ Le. 11. 37; De. 21. 4. Piel pret. פִּתָּה Job 30. 11, and פִּתָּךְ chap. 12. 18; גֵּרַע 2 Ch. 34. 7, and גֵּרַע ver. 4;

inf. בַּלַּע Hab. 1. 13; Nu. 4. 20, comp. בַּלַּע La. 2. 8; שַׁלַּח Ex. 5. 2; 7. 14, and שַׁלַּח chap. ־ 27; 9. 2; fut. יְבַקַּע Hab. 3. 9; Ps. 78. 15; Ge. 22. 3, comp. יְבַקַּע Eze. 13. 11; 2 Ki. 8. 12; יְנַקַּח & יְנַקַּח Le. 14. 9; אֲבַלַּע 2 Sa. 20. 20, comp. אֲבַלַּע Is. 19. 3.

2. The *participle of Niphal* must be supposed to admit of another form like נִשְׁלָח, which loses (ָ) before an accession at the end (comp. dec. 7); hence נִדְחוּ 2 Sa. 14. 13, נִדְחֲכֶם Ne. 1. 9 (comp. § 23. rem. 6).

REGULAR VERB WITH SUFFIXES

TABLE F. REGULAR VERB WITH SUFFIXES.										
SUFFIXES for	1 Sing.	2 Sing. m.	2 Sing. f.	3 Sing. m.	3 Sing. f.	1 Plur.	2 Plur. m.	2 Plur. f.	3 Plur. m.	3 Plur. f.
PRET. Kal. 3. m.	קְטָלַנִי	קְטָלְךָ	קְטָלֵךְ	קְטָלְהוּ קְטָלוֹ	קְטָלָהּ	קְטָלָנוּ	קְטַלְכֶם	קְטַלְכֶן	קְטָלָם	קְטָלָן
3. f.	קְטָלַתְנִי	קְטָלָתֶךָ	קְטָלָתֶךְ	קְטָלַתְהוּ קְטָלַתּוּ	קְטָלַתָּה	קְטָלַתְנוּ	קְטָלַתְכֶם	קְטָלַתְכֶן	קְטָלָתַם	קְטָלָתַן
2. m.	קְטַלְתַּנִי קְטַלְתֵּנִי	—	—	קְטַלְתָּהוּ קְטַלְתּוֹ	קְטַלְתָּהּ	קְטַלְתָּנוּ	—	—	קְטַלְתָּם	קְטַלְתָּן
2. f.	קְטַלְתִּינִי	—	—	קְטַלְתִּיהוּ קְטַלְתִּיו	קְטַלְתִּיהָ	קְטַלְתִּינוּ	—	—	קְטַלְתִּים	קְטַלְתִּין
1. c.	—	קְטַלְתִּיךָ	קְטַלְתִּיךְ	קְטַלְתִּיו	קְטַלְתִּיהָ	—	קְטַלְתִּיכֶם	קְטַלְתִּיכֶן	קְטַלְתִּים	קְטַלְתִּין
Plur. 3. c.	קְטָלוּנִי	קְטָלוּךָ	קְטָלוּךְ	קְטָלוּהוּ	קְטָלוּהָ	קְטָלוּנוּ	קְטָלוּכֶם	קְטָלוּכֶן	קְטָלוּם	קְטָלוּן
2. m.	קְטַלְתּוּנִי	—	—	קְטַלְתּוּהוּ	קְטַלְתּוּהָ	קְטַלְתּוּנוּ	—	—	קְטַלְתּוּם	קְטַלְתּוּן
1. c.	—	קְטַלְנוּךָ	קְטַלְנוּךְ	קְטַלְנוּהוּ	קְטַלְנוּהָ	—	קְטַלְנוּכֶם	קְטַלְנוּכֶן	קְטַלְנוּם	קְטַלְנוּן
INF. Kal.	קָטְלִי קָטְלֵנִי	קָטְלְךָ קָטְלֶךָ	קָטְלֵךְ	קָטְלוֹ	קָטְלָהּ	קָטְלֵנוּ	קָטְלְכֶם קָטְלְכֶם	קָטְלְכֶן	קָטְלָם	קָטְלָן
Imp. Kal.	קָטְלֵנִי	—	קָטְלֵהוּ	קָטְלָה קָטְלֵהוּ		קָטְלֵנוּ	—	—	קָטְלֵם	—
FUT. Kal. 3. m.	יִקְטְלֵנִי	יִקְטָלְךָ	יִקְטְלֵךְ	יִקְטְלֵהוּ	יִקְטְלֶהָ יִקְטְלָהּ	יִקְטְלֵנוּ	יִקְטָלְכֶם	יִקְטָלְכֶן	יִקְטְלֵם	יִקְטְלֵן
3. m. with Nun epenthet.	יִקְטְלֵנִי	יִקְטְלֶךָ	—	יִקְטְלֶנּוּ	יִקְטְלֶנָּה	יִקְטְלֶנּוּ	—	—	—	—
Plur. 3. m.	יִקְטְלוּנִי	יִקְטְלוּךָ	יִקְטְלוּךְ	יִקְטְלוּהוּ	יִקְטְלוּהָ	יִקְטְלוּנוּ	יִקְטְלוּכֶם	יִקְטְלוּכֶן	יִקְטְלוּם	יִקְטְלוּן
PRET. Piel.	קִטְּלַנִי	קִטְּלְךָ	קִטְּלֵךְ	קִטְּלוֹ	קִטְּלָהּ	קִטְּלָנוּ	קִטֶּלְכֶם	קִטֶּלְכֶן	קִטְּלָם	קִטְּלָן

3*

SECTION XVI.—REGULAR VERB WITH SUFFIXES. (Table F.)

REMARKS.

I. On the Preterite of Kal.

1. Third Person Masculine. In the verbs *middle E* (§ 8. rem. 1) this characteristic vowel remains also before the suffix, as אֲהֵבְךָ De. 7. 13; 15. 16; 23. 6, from אָהֵב; לְבֵשָׁהּ Le. 16. 4; שְׂנֵאָהּ De. 24. 3.

2. Third Person Feminine. The form קְטָלַת designating the *fem.* has a twofold peculiarity—(*a*) it takes the suffixes which form a syllable by themselves (נִי, הוּ, הָ, נוּ, כֶם, כֶן) without a union-vowel, though itself ends with a consonant; (*b*) with the rest of the suffixes it indeed takes the union-vowel, but the tone is drawn back to the penultima, so that they appear in the shortened form ־ֶךָ, ־ָךְ, ־ַתַם, ־ַתֶן. E. g. אֲהֵבָתֶךָ *she loves thee*, Ru. 4. 15; שֻׁבְּבֶתְךָ *it has perverted thee*, Is. 47. 10; שְׂרָפָתַם *she burns them*, Is. 47. 14; אֲכָלָתַם *it consumes them*, Ho. 2. 14; גְּנָבָתַם *she had stolen them*, Ge. 31. 32; נְצָרָתַם *it observes them*, Ps. 119. 129; מְצָאָתַם *it befell them*, Ex. 18. 8; but on the contrary עֲנָקַתְמוֹ Ps. 73. 6.

3. In the suffix of the third person a kind of contraction takes place, which may be compared with the form ־ֶנּוּ for ־ֶהְנוּ, viz. ־תְהוּ contr. ־תּוּ, and ־תָהּ contracted from ־תְהָ. In the masculine both occur, the contracted and uncontracted form, as גְּמָלָתְהוּ *she shows him*, Pr. 31. 12; גְּמָלַתּוּ *she weaned him*, 1 Sa. 1. 24; סְמָכַתְהוּ Is. 59. 16, comp. Ge. 37. 20; 1 Sa. 18. 28, and גְּנָבַתּוּ Job 21. 18, comp. Ru. 4. 15. With the suffix of the feminine only the contracted form exists, אֲחָזַתָּה Je. 49. 24; Is. 34. 17. For ־ְתָךְ, ־ְתָנוּ, ־תַנִי the pause exhibits ־תָנִי &c., e. g. אֲכָלַתָּנִי Ps. 69. 10; מְצָאָתְנוּ Nu. 20. 14; Ca. 8. 5 (where חִבְּלָתֶךָ in the first member of the sentence is so pointed for the sake of consonance).

4. The *Second Person Masculine* assumes in all cases the form קְטַלְתָּ, wherefore the suffix has no union-vowel, except with the suffix of the 1 and 2 pers. sing. masc., where sometimes קְטַלְתְּ appears as the ground-form, and so to it is attached the suffix (־ִי, ־וֹ) by its union-vowel. Hence חֲקַרְתָּנִי *thou searchest me*, Ps. 139. 1; חֲזַקְתָּנִי *thou hast overcome me*, Je. 20. 7 (elsewhere, however, עֲזַבְתָּנִי Ps. 22. 2); אֲסַפְתּוֹ *thou gatherest him*, 2 Ki. 5, 6, comp. Nu. 23. 27; Ps. 89. 44; Hab. 1. 12 (elsewhere also כְּפַרְתָּה Eze. 43. 20).

5. Second Person Feminine. All the forms exhibited in the paradigm assume the ground-form קְטַלְתִּי, so that the suffix has no union-vowel. ־ִי is often written defectively, as יְלִדְתִּנִי *thou hast borne me*, Je. 15. 10; comp. Ca. 4. 9; 1 Sa. 19. 17. The form קְטַלְתְּ, however, occurs also with suffixes which have the union-vowel, as יְלִדְתָּנוּ *thou hast brought us forth*, Je. 2. 27; Jos. 2. 17; Ca. 5. 9 (for (׳) in the final syllable comp. § 8. rem. 1 b).

6. All the *persons of the plural* follow one rule, as all the verbal forms end here alike in וּ, and the suffixes have therefore no union-vowel. These are frequently written *defectively*, as דְּרַשְׁנֻהוּ 1 Ch. 13. 3, which, of course, is immaterial.

II. On the Infinitive of Kal.

7. The shortened form קְטָל is found most frequently before the suffixes כֶם & כֶן, אֲכָלְכֶם *your eating*, Ge. 3. 5, אֲמָרְכֶם *your saying*, Mal. 1. 7; somewhat less frequent are forms like עָבְרְכֶם De. 27. 4; Le. 23. 22. The same inconstancy is found before the suff. ךָ, e. g. עָבְרְךָ *thy passing over*, De. 29. 11; שָׁמְעֲךָ *thy hearing*, 2 Ki. 22. 19; but also עָמְדְךָ Ob. 11; אֲכָלְךָ Ge. 2. 17. There is also a form קָצְרְךָ Le. 23. 22, which agrees with קָצְרְכֶם in the same verse.

8. When the middle letter is a guttural it takes (־ֲ) instead of simple Sheva, e. g. בָּחֳרִי *my choosing*, Eze. 20. 5; אָהֳבָם *their loving*, Ho. 9. 10; and in the 2 pers., Kamets-Hhatuph, as מָאָסְכֶם Is. 30. 12, and so also (with ר) קָרָבְכֶם De. 20. 2.

9. An anomalous form, otherwise found with guttural (comp. § 13. rem. 12) is מֹצַאֲכֶם for מְצָאֲכֶם Ge. 32. 20. In the same way some explain the form בּוֹשַׁסְכֶם for בֶּשַׁסְכֶם Am. 5. 11; this, however, may be regarded as a form of Poel (§ 6. No. 1).

10. The inf. קְטֹל assumes with suffix the form קָטְל (comp. § 35. rem. 10), also קְטָל, with כֶם only the form קְטָל is used. As פְּתְחִי *my opening*, Eze. 37. 13; בִּקְעָם *their cleaving*, Am. 1. 13; לְשָׁמְנוּ *to hinder him*, Zec. 3. 1; רָקְעֲךָ *thy stamping*, Eze. 25. 6; לְחָנֶנְכֶם *to be gracious to you*, Is. 30. 18. With the middle guttural לְפַעֲמוֹ *to drive him on*, Ju. 13. 25.

III. On the Imperative of Kal.

11. Examples are—זָכְרֵנִי *remember me*, Je. 15. 15; רָדְפֵהוּ *pursue him*, Ps. 34. 15; כָּתְבֵם *write them*, Pr. 3. 3; נִצְּרֵהָ (with euphonic Dagesh) *preserve them*, Pr. 4. 13, or (in the other form of the suffix) like כָּתְבָה Is. 30. 8.

When a guttural happens to be in the final syllable, the vowel of the final syllable is retained and lengthened to Kamets, as שְׁמָעֵנִי *hear me*, Ge. 23. 11; שְׁמָעֶנָּה *hear it*, Job 5. 27; אֱהָבֶהָ *love her*, Pr. 4. 6. *Plur.* שְׁמָעוּנִי *hear me*, Ge. 23. 8; שְׁאָלֻנִי *ask me*, Is. 45. 11.

IV. On the Future of Kal.

12. The verbs future *A* (§ 8. rem. 13), to which belong all those with 2nd and 3rd radical guttural, retain this A-sound in the sing. and pl., and besides, lengthen Pattahh to Kamets; e. g. יִלְבָּשֵׁנִי *he will clothe me*, Job 29. 14; יִלְבָּשֵׁם Ex. 29. 30, comp. Ca. 5. 3; יִשְׁכָּבֶנָּה De. 28. 30; יִשְׁמָעֵנִי Ex. 6. 12; אֶהֱבֶנִי Ge. 29. 32, comp. also Job 22. 27; Je. 42. 5. *Plur.* יְגָאֲלוּהוּ *they pollute him*, Job 3. 5; יִבְעָלוּךְ Is. 62. 5; יִמְצָאֻהוּ Job 20. 8, &c. An example, where this is not the case, is וָאֶנְעֲלֵךְ *and I shod thee*, Eze. 16. 10.

A few examples are already given above (§ 8. rem. 14) in which there are some traces left of the O-sound, either by (ָ) or וֹ, in the final syllable before suffix.

13. Besides the union-vowel, there is another mode of connecting the suffix with the verbal form, by means of an inserted נ or the syllable ־ַנְ, ־ֶנְ, ־ֶנָּ, commonly called epenthetic Nun. It is found only with the future before the suffix of the singular, and usually in pause. E. g. יְכַבְּדַנִי *he will honour me*, Ps. 50. 23; אֶתְּקֶנְךָ *I will pluck thee*, Je. 22. 24; יַעַבְרֶנְהוּ

he passes over it, Je. 5. 22; יְבָרֲכֶנְהוּ *he will bless him*, Ps. 72. 15, comp. De. 32. 10; Ex. 15. 2. This נ is for the most part assimilated to the suffix, and hence the separate form of the suffixes with epenthetic Nun in the paradigm.

14. By a Syriacism, the suffixes are sometimes attached, without a union-vowel, to the form יִקְטְלוּן with the paragogic Nun. E. g. יִקְרָאֻנִי *they shall call me*, Pr. 1. 28; יִמְצָאֻנְנִי ibid.; יְשַׁבְּחוּנְךָ *they shall praise thee*, Ps. 63. 4; יְשָׁרְתוּנְךָ *they shall serve thee*, Is. 60. 7, 10; יַעַבְרֻנְהוּ *it shall pass it*, Je. 5. 22; יִלְכְּדוּנוֹ *they shall take him*, Pr. 5. 22; יִמְצָאֻנְהָ *they shall find her*, Je. 2. 24. With a union-vowel occurs יְדַכְּאוּנַנִּי *they crush me*, Job 19. 2, for which Athias's bible reads יְדַכְּאֻנִּי more consistently with analogy.

V. On Piel and Hiphil with Suffix.

15. Examples of Piel are—*Pret.* קִבֶּצֵךְ *he gathers thee*, De. 30. 3; בֵּרַכְךָ *he blesses thee*, De. 2. 7. *Inf.* רַחֶמְכֶם *your pitying*, Is. 30. 18; פָּרֶשְׂכֶם *your spreading out*, Is. 1. 15; שַׁחֶתְכֶם *your destroying*, Eze. 5. 16. *Fut.* יְקַבֶּצְךָ *he will gather thee*, De. 30. 4; אֲחַלֶּלֵךְ *I will pollute thee*, Eze. 28. 16; אֹסֶפְךָ *I will gather thee*, 2 Ki. 22. 20; אֲאַמֶּצְכֶם *I will strengthen you*, Job 16. 5. *Part.* מְקַדִּשְׁכֶם *who sanctifies you*, Ex. 31. 13.

The same is observed in Poel, e. g. אֲרוֹמִמְךָ *I will extol thee*, Is. 25. 1.

In a few instances Tseri has been retained, even before ךְ, as אֲשַׁלֵּחֲךָ *I will send thee*, Ge. 31. 27; מְשַׁלֵּחֶךָ Je. 28. 16; תְּכַבְּדֵךְ *she will honour thee*, Pr. 4. 8.

16. The only example, in which the form of Tseri is assumed in Hiph. before suffix (by a Syriacism) is יַעְשִׁירֶנּוּ for יַעֲשִׁירֶנּוּ *he will enrich him*, 1 Sa. 17. 25.*

---

* Here, however, must be added וַיְכֻנְנֶךָ for וַיְכֹנְנֶךָ De. 32. 7; יֹשִׁיעֲכֶם for יוֹשִׁיעֲכֶם Is. 35. 4.

TABLE G. VERB PE NUN (פ״ן).

		KAL.	NIPHAL.	HIPHIL.	HOPHAL.
PRET	3. m.	נָגַשׁ	נִגַּשׁ	הִגִּישׁ	הֻגַּשׁ
	3. f.		נִגְּשָׁה	הִגִּישָׁה	הֻגְּשָׁה
	2. m.		נִגַּשְׁתָּ	הִגַּשְׁתָּ	הֻגַּשְׁתָּ
	2. f.		נִגַּשְׁתְּ	הִגַּשְׁתְּ	הֻגַּשְׁתְּ
	1. c.	regular	נִגַּשְׁתִּי	הִגַּשְׁתִּי	הֻגַּשְׁתִּי
Plur.	3. c.		נִגְּשׁוּ	הִגִּישׁוּ	הֻגְּשׁוּ
	2. m.		נִגַּשְׁתֶּם	הִגַּשְׁתֶּם	הֻגַּשְׁתֶּם
	2. f.		נִגַּשְׁתֶּן	הִגַּשְׁתֶּן	הֻגַּשְׁתֶּן
	1. c.		נִגַּשְׁנוּ	הִגַּשְׁנוּ	הֻגַּשְׁנוּ
INF.	absol.	נָגוֹשׁ	הִנָּגֹשׁ	הַגֵּישׁ	הֻגֵּשׁ
	constr	גֶּשֶׁת	הִנָּגֵשׁ	הַגִּישׁ	
IMP.	m.	גַּשׁ	הִנָּגֵשׁ	הַגֵּשׁ	
	f.	גְּשִׁי	הִנָּגְשִׁי	הַגִּישִׁי	wanting
Plur.	m.	גְּשׁוּ	הִנָּגְשׁוּ	הַגִּישׁוּ	
	f.	גַּשְׁנָה	הִנָּגַשְׁנָה	הַגֵּשְׁנָה	
FUT.	3. m.	יִגַּשׁ	יִגָּגֵשׁ	יַגִּישׁ	יֻגַּשׁ
	3. f.	תִּגַּשׁ		תַּגִּישׁ	תֻּגַּשׁ
	2. m.	תִּגַּשׁ		תַּגִּישׁ	תֻּגַּשׁ
	2. f.	תִּגְּשִׁי		תַּגִּישִׁי	תֻּגְּשִׁי
	1. c.	אֶגַּשׁ	regular	אַגִּישׁ	אֻגַּשׁ
Plur.	3. m.	יִגְּשׁוּ		יַגִּישׁוּ	יֻגְּשׁוּ
	3. f.	תִּגַּשְׁנָה		תַּגֵּשְׁנָה	תֻּגַּשְׁנָה
	2. m.	תִּגְּשׁוּ		תַּגִּישׁוּ	תֻּגְּשׁוּ
	2. f.	תִּגַּשְׁנָה		תַּגֵּשְׁנָה	תֻּגַּשְׁנָה
	1. c.	נִגַּשׁ		נַגִּישׁ	נֻגַּשׁ
FUT.	apoc.			יַגֵּשׁ	
PART.	act.	נֹגֵשׁ	נִגָּשׁ	מַגִּישׁ	מֻגַּשׁ
	pass.	נָגוּשׁ			

SECTION XVII.—VERBS פ״ן.

REMARKS.

I. On Kal.

1. *Inf. constr.* In some instances both the full, regular, and the defective forms are found in one and the same verb, in others the irregular only are in use. E. g. נָגַע *to touch*, Ge. 20. 6, with suff. נָגְעוֹ Le. 15. 23, but also נַעַת 2 Sa. 14. 10; נְטֹעַ *to plant*, Is. 51. 16; Je. 1. 10, but also טַעַת Ec. 3. 2; נְתֹן Ge. 38. 9; Nu. 20. 21, along with תֵּת for תְּנֹת. Examples without the defective forms are—נְצֹר *to preserve*, Pr. 2. 8, נְבֹל *to fade*, Is. 34. 4; נְקֹם *to avenge*, Eze. 24. 8; 25. 12. An example of the inf. with suff. is גִּשְׁתּוֹ Ge. 33. 3.

2. In the *imp.* the defective form has *Pattahh* as well as Tseri and Hholem, comp. גַּשׁ 2 Sa. 1. 15; גְּשׁ Ge. 19. 9; גְּשָׁה Ru. 2. 14; גֹּשׁוּ Jos. 3. 9; 1 Sa. 14. 38. Other examples are—שַׁל *put off*, Ex. 3. 5; תֵּן *give*, Ge. 14. 21.

These forms frequently take parag. הׇ, and then the vowel is lost; e. g. תְּנָה *give*; גְּשָׁה *draw near*, &c. (comp. § 8. rem. 11).

Examples of the full regular form are—נְטֹשׁ *leave*, Pr. 17. 14; נִדְרוּ *vow ye*, Ps. 76. 12; נִטְעוּ *plant ye*, 2 Ki. 19. 29.

3. *Future.* Examples of the full regular form occur even in verbs not Ayin-guttural,* but invariably only when the contracted form is likewise found in use; as תִּנָּגְשׂוּ Is. 58. 3, and יִנֹּשׁ De. 15. 2 (*to oppress*); תִּנְדֹּף Ps. 68. 3, and יִדֹּף Ps. 1. 4 (*to drive*); יִנְטֹר Je. 3. 5, and יִטֹּר Ps. 103. 9 (*to preserve*); יִנְצֹר Ps 78. 7; 140. 2; 61. 8, and יִצֹּר (*to preserve*); יִנְקֹב Job 40. 24, and יִקֹּב Le. 24. 11 (*to bore through*).

The vowel *Pattahh* in the final syllable is found only in a few other verbs besides נָגַשׁ of the paradigm; e. g. יִשַּׁל De. 28. 40, יִשַּׁק Ge. 41. 40; the *future O*, however, occurs most frequently. Future E occurs only in the verb נָתַן.

II. On Niphal.

4. Since Piel has sometimes also Pattahh in the second syllable (§ 10. rem. 1), it follows that the pret. of Niph. and Piel are occasionally similar in form,

and can only be distinguished by the context. E g. נָחַת (*to descend*), Niph. in Ps. 38. 3, and Piel in Ps. 18. 35; 65. 11; נָקַם (*to be avenged*) Niph. in 1 Sa. 14. 24, and Piel in 2 Ki. 9. 7; Je. 51. 36; and so נִשָּׂא (*to be borne*) comp. Ex. 25. 28, and 1 Ki. 9. 11. With regard to נִשָּׁא Is. 3. 5, it is doubtful whether it is Piel or Niph., since the construction admits of either.

5. The only example of an *inf. absol.* is נָגוֹף Ju. 20. 39.

III. On Hiphil and Hophal.

6. In a very few instances only is נ retained in Hiphil, as לְהַנְתִּיךְ *to pour out*, Eze. 22. 20; לְנַפֵּל *to cause to fall*, Nu. 5. 22; with gutturals, as וַיַּנְעִלוּם *and they shod them*, 2 Ch. 28. 15, הִנְחַלְתִּי *I have given for an inheritance*, Je. 3. 18.

7. In Hophal, the form with *Kibbuts* is general, and the only exception is הֻנְתְּקוּ *they were drawn away*, Ju. 20. 31.

IV. In General.

8. The anomalies of the verbs פ״ן are also in part exhibited in the verb לָקַח, in which ל is treated like the *Nun* of these verbs. Hence *imp.* קַח (seldom לְקַח, as Ex. 29. 1), קָחוּ, קָחָה, קְחִי (seldom לְקְחִי, as 1 Ki. 17. 11); *fut.* יִקַּח; *inf. abs.* לָקוֹחַ, *constr.* קַחַת (once קְחַת 2 Ki. 12. 9), with *suff.* קַחְתִּי; *Hoph. fut.* יֻקַּח; but *Niph.* always like נִלְקַח.

Some of the old grammarians (as Buxtorf Thes. Gramm. p. 154) derive נִתְּעוּ *they are broken out*, (spoken of the teeth), Job 4. 10, from לָתַע, and combine it with מַלְתָּעוֹת. The Nun, however, in this word is perfectly certain, so that נָתַע is the same as נָתַץ, and the verb with Lamed is to be rejected.

9. The verb נָתַן (*to give*) has this peculiarity, that the final Nun is likewise assimilated, at least so in the *pret.* and *inf.* of Kal. Hence נָתַתָּ, נָתַתִּי, נְתַתֶּם; *inf.* תֵּת for תְּנֵת, with *suff.* תִּתִּי, &c. תִּתָּה 2 Sa. 22. 44, is by aphæresis for נָתַתָּה of the parallel passage, Ps. 18. 44.

---

* Most of the verbs Ayin-guttural are perfectly regular, as יַנְחַל יֵנָאֵץ.

TABLE H. VERB AYIN DOUBLED (ע״ע). § 66.

	KAL	NIPHAL	HIPHIL	HOPHAL	POEL	POAL
Pret. 3. m.	סַב	נָסַב	הֵסֵב	הוּסַב	סוֹבֵב	סוֹבַב
3. f.	סַבָּה	נָסַבָּה	הֵסַבָּה	הוּסַבָּה	סוֹבְבָה	סוֹבְבָה
2. m.	סַבּוֹתָ	נְסַבּוֹתָ	הֲסִבּוֹתָ	הוּסַבּוֹתָ	סוֹבַבְתָּ	סוֹבַבְתָּ
2. f.	סַבּוֹת	נְסַבּוֹת	הֲסִבּוֹת	הוּסַבּוֹת	סוֹבַבְתְּ	סוֹבַבְתְּ
1. c.	סַבּוֹתִי	נְסַבּוֹתִי	הֲסִבּוֹתִי	הוּסַבּוֹתִי	סוֹבַבְתִּי	סוֹבַבְתִּי
Plur. 3. c.	סַבּוּ	נָסַבּוּ	הֵסַבּוּ	הוּסַבּוּ	סוֹבְבוּ	סוֹבְבוּ
2. m.	סַבּוֹתֶם	נְסַבּוֹתֶם	הֲסִבּוֹתֶם	הוּסַבּוֹתֶם	סוֹבַבְתֶּם	סוֹבַבְתֶּם
2. f.	סַבּוֹתֶן	נְסַבּוֹתֶן	הֲסִבּוֹתֶן	הוּסַבּוֹתֶן	סוֹבַבְתֶּן	סוֹבַבְתֶּן
1. c.	סַבּוֹנוּ	נְסַבּוֹנוּ	הֲסִבּוֹנוּ	הוּסַבּוֹנוּ	סוֹבַבְנוּ	סוֹבַבְנוּ
Inf. absol.	סָבוֹב	הִסּוֹב	הָסֵב	הוּסֵב	סוֹבֵב	סוֹבֵב
constr.	סֹב	הִסֵּב	הָסֵב			
Imp. m.	סֹב	הִסֵּב	הָסֵב		סוֹבֵב	
f.	סֹבִּי	הִסָּבִּי	הָסֵבִּי	*wanting*	סוֹבְבִי	*wanting*
Plur. m.	סֹבּוּ	הִסָּבּוּ	הָסֵבּוּ		סוֹבְבוּ	
f.	סֻבֶּינָה	הִסָּבֶּינָה	הֲסִבֶּינָה		סוֹבֵבְנָה	
Fut. 3. m.	יָסֹב יִסֹּב	יִסַּב	יָסֵב	(יָסַב) יוּסַב	(יְסַבֵּב) יְסוֹבֵב	יְסוֹבַב
3. f.	תָּסֹב תִּסֹּב	תִּסַּב	תָּסֵב	תּוּסַב	תְּסוֹבֵב	תְּסוֹבַב
2. m.	תָּסֹב תִּסֹּב	תִּסַּב	תָּסֵב	תּוּסַב	תְּסוֹבֵב	תְּסוֹבַב
2. f.	תָּסֹבִּי תִּסְבִּי	תִּסַּבִּי	תָּסֵבִּי	תּוּסַבִּי	תְּסוֹבְבִי	תְּסוֹבְבִי
1. c.	אָסֹב אָסֵב	אֶסַּב	אָסֵב	אוּסַב	אֲסוֹבֵב	אֲסוֹבַב
Plur. 3. m.	יָסֹבּוּ יִסְבוּ	יִסַּבּוּ	יָסֵבּוּ	יוּסַבּוּ	יְסוֹבְבוּ	יְסוֹבְבוּ
3. f.	תְּסֻבֶּינָה תִּסֹּבְנָה	תִּסַּבֶּינָה	תְּסֻבֶּינָה	תּוּסַבֶּינָה	תְּסוֹבֵבְנָה	תְּסוֹבַבְנָה
2. m.	תָּסֹבּוּ תִּסְבוּ	תִּסַּבּוּ	תָּסֵבּוּ	תּוּסַבּוּ	תְּסוֹבְבוּ	תְּסוֹבְבוּ
2. f.	תְּסֻבֶּינָה תִּסֹּבְנָה	תִּסַּבֶּינָה	תְּסֻבֶּינָה	תּוּסַבֶּינָה	תְּסוֹבַבְנָה	תְּסוֹבַבְנָה
1. c.	נָסֹב נִסֹּב	נִסַּב	נָסֵב	נוּסַב	נְסוֹבֵב	נְסוֹבַב
Fut. *with Vav conv.*	וַיָּסָב		וַיָּסַב			
Part. act.	סוֹבֵב	נָסָב	מֵסֵב	מוּסָב	מְסוֹבֵב	מְסוֹבָב
pass.	סָבוּב					

SECTION XVIII.—VERBS ע״ע

REMARKS.

I. On Kal.

1. In the pret. there occur a few examples of *middle O* (according to יָכֹל, § 8. rem. 1), as רֹמוּ *they are lifted up*, Job 24. 24 (for רָמְמוּ); רֹבּוּ *they shoot arrows*, Ge. 49. 23 (for רָבְבוּ), by which form it is distinguished from רַבּוּ *they are many*.

Examples, in which the geminate letter is a guttural, are—וָאָרֹתִי and I curse, Mal. 2. 2; שַׁחוֹתִי I was bowed down, Ps. 35. 14; צָחוּ they are bright, La. 4. 7 (the two last with dag. forte implied, comp. § 14. rem. 1).

When conversive Vav is prefixed to the preterite, the tone is shifted from the penultima to the ultimate (comp. § 8. rem. 7); e. g. וְחַדּוּ and they shall be quick, Hab. 1. 8; וְרַבָּה and she will be great, Is. 6. 12. The tone is, however, also found upon the ultimate without any apparent cause; as רַבּוּ Ps. 3. 2; קַלּוּ Je. 4. 13; זַמּוּ Job 15. 15; דַּלּוּ Is. 38. 14; שַׁתּוּ Ps. 73. 9; רַכּוּ Ps. 55. 22; שַׁחוּ Hab. 3. 6, and in the first person, דַּלּוֹתִי Ps. 116. 6; חַמּוֹתִי Is. 44. 16; שַׁנּוֹתִי De. 32. 41.

2. *Hholem* of the *inf.*, *imp.* and *fut.* (יָסֹב, סֹב, answering to יִקְטֹל, קְטֹל, from which they originated), being a pure vowel, is written *defectively*. There are, however, some few exceptions, especially in the later orthography; e. g. inf. לָבוֹז to plunder, Est. 3. 13; 8. 11; imp. גּוֹל Ps. 37. 5 (comp. גֹּל Ps. 22. 9), דּוֹמִּי be silent, stand still, Jos. 10. 12; Ps. 37. 7; Ps. 62. 6; צוֹר bind together, Is. 8. 16; קוֹשּׁוּ gather, Zep. 2. 1; fut. יָעוֹז he becomes powerful, Da. 11. 12; יָנוֹדוּ they gather themselves together, Ps. 94. 21; וַיָּבוֹל and he gave fodder, Ju. 19. 21 Khethib, (Keri וַיָּבָל).

3. The common form of the *inf.*, סֹב, is shortened before Makkeph into סָב־, e. g. רָן־ to shout, Job 38. 7; with suff. like בְּחֻקּוֹ when he established, Pr. 8. 27.

Other verbs have the form סַב (according to שְׁכַב), e. g. שַׁח to bow down, Je. 5. 26; לָרַד to lay to the ground, Is. 45. 1; with suff. בְּשַׁגָּם because they have erred, Ge. 6. 3; לְבָרָם to select them, Ec. 3. 18; הַל (from הָלַל) his shining, Job 29. 3.

A form with the fem. designation (comp. § 8. rem. 10) is רֹעָה to break (from רָעַע) Is. 24. 19, used as an inf. absol. Here belong doubtless also the forms שַׁמּוֹת to lay waste, Eze. 36. 3; חַנּוֹת to be gracious, Ps. 77. 10; חַלּוֹתִי my being wounded, Ps. 77. 11; זַמּוֹתִי my thinking, Ps. 17. 3; all of which, according to their occurrence, must be taken as infinitives of the verbs זָמַם, חָלַל, חָנַן, שָׁמֵם, and can only be regarded as original plurals, after the form שַׁךְ, fem. שַׁכָּה.

4. Besides the form סֹב of the *imp.*, there is

another with *Pattahh*, גֹל *roll*, Ps. 119. 22; with parag. ה, as אָרָה (for אֲרָה) *curse*, Nu. 22. 6.*

Before suffixes the tone is shifted to the afformative, and the vowel before dagesh is shortened from Hholem to Kamets-hhatuph; e. g. סָלֻּיהָ *cast her up*, Je. 50. 26; but sometimes also without suffix, e. g. גֻּזּיִ *shear*, Je. 7. 29; רָנּיִ *shout*, Zec. 2. 14; רָנּוּ Is. 44. 23; Je. 31. 7; חָגּיִ *keep a festival*, Na. 2. 1.

Before parag. ה the tone remains, hence עֻזָּה *be strong*, Ps. 68. 29. קָבְנוֹ *curse him*, Nu. 23. 13, has epenthetic Nun before the suffixes.

5. When the *future* receives conversive Vav, the tone is drawn back to the penultima, and Hholem is changed into Kamets-hhatuph, וַיְגַל *and he shaved*, Job 1. 20, וַיָּסָב *and he compassed*, Ju. 11. 18, וַיָּהָם *and he troubled*, Ex. 14. 24; but in pause וַיָּהֹם 2 Sa 22. 15 Keri. (The form here is precisely the same as in the verbs ע"י).

The same change of Hholem takes place, when the tone is shifted to the afformatives at the addition of suffixes, e. g. יְחָנֵּנוּ *may he be gracious unto us*, Ps. 67. 2; 123. 2; תְּחָגֻּהוּ *ye shall solemnize it*, Ex. 12. 14; יַשֵּׁדֵם *he shall destroy them*, Pr. 11. 3 Keri; or Kibbuts is chosen instead, e. g. יְחֻנַּנִי Ge. 27. 12; יְחֻנֶּךָּ, יְחֻנַּנִּי *he will be gracious to thee, him*, Nu. 6. 25; Is. 27. 11.

In יָחְנְךָ *he will be gracious unto thee*, there is a transposition of the vowels, for יְחָנְךָ.

6. The *future A* (comp. § 8. rem. 13) of these verbs, which are often mistaken for an anomalous form of Niph., has Tseri under the preformative. The examples which occur of these are—יֵמַר *it is bitter*, Is. 24. 9 (from מָרַר); וְאֵקַל *and I am despised*, Ge. 16. 5; תֵּקַל ver. 4; יֵקַלּוּ from קָלַל; יֵחַם *it is hot*, De. 19. 6; Eze. 24. 11; יֵחַמּוּ Ho. 7. 7 (from חָמַם), along with יְחָם Is. 44. 16; אֵיתַם *I am blameless*, Ps 19. 14 (along with יִתֹּם of a different signification) with Yod as a *mater lectionis*, which, however, is omitted in several MSS.

As a *future A*, with Kamets under the preformative, may be regarded יָחַד *it is sharpened*, Pr. 27. 17 (יַחַד in the second member is to be taken as a Chaldaizing fut. of Hiph. for יֵחַד comp. rem. 14).

---

* This view is grounded upon the supposition that the Kamets under א of the form אָרָה in the last verse is lengthened from Pattahh. The form קָבָה־לִּי, however, which is found in the same chapter, ver. 17, being an analogous form (from קָבַב), proves this vowel to be Kamets-hhatuph, shortened from Hholem on account of the loss of the accent before Makkeph. It is also to be observed that the form קָבָה has unnecessarily been derived by some from נָקַב, for נָקְבָה=נָקְבָה.

II. On Niphal.

7. Besides the usual form with Pattahh in the second syllable, as exhibited in the paradigm, there are two others to be met with throughout the whole of this conjugation, with Tseri and Hholem (like קָטֵל, קָטֵל, קָטַל).

Examples with Tseri :—

Pret. נָקֵל *it is a light thing*, 2 Ki. 20. 10; Is. 49. 6 (along with נָקַל 2 Ki. 3. 18). נָמֵס *it faints*, Ps. 22. 15; נָסֵבָּה *she is turned*, Eze. 26. 2.

Inf. הִמֵּס *to melt*, Ps. 68. 3, הֵחֵל *to be polluted*, Eze. 20. 9, 14; with suff. הֵחַלּוֹ Le. 21. 15.

Fut. תֵּחֵל *she is polluted*, Le. 21. 9, which, however, may also be taken as a fut. of Hiph., *she begins*.

Part. נָמֵס *dissolved, refuse*, 1 Sa. 15. 9.

Examples with Hholem :—

Pret. נָגֹלּוּ *they are rolled together*, Is. 34. 4, נָגֹזּוּ *they are cut off*, Na. 1. 12; נָבֹזּוּ *they are spoiled*, Am. 3. 11; נָרֹץ *he is broken*, Eze. 29. 7; נָקֹטּוּ *they loathe themselves*, Eze. 6. 9.

Inf. abs. twice in Is. 24. 3, הִבּוֹק תִּבּוֹק הָאָרֶץ וְהִבּוֹז תִּבּוֹז *the land shall be emptied and spoiled.*

Imp. הֵרֹמּוּ *rise up*, Nu. 17. 10.

Fut. תֵּרֹץ *thou art broken*, Eze. 29. 7; תִּדֹּמִּי *thou shalt be cut off*, Je. 48. 2 (along with יִדַּמּוּ 1 Sa. 2. 9); יֵרֹמּוּ *they are raised up*, Eze. 10. 17.

Note. Since the fut. of Kal may likewise have dag. forte in the first radical (according to the analogy of the Chaldee, see rem. 14), and since the last syllable may in both conjugations have either the vowel A or E, it follows that in some forms it may become doubtful as to whether they are to be taken as Kal or Niphal. Thus, tor instance, יִתֹּם has been taken as the fut. of Niphal; but this and its plural יִתַּמּוּ differ in signification from יִתַּמּוּ, which latter is undoubtedly Niphal, so that the former must be taken as Kal.

8. In the preterite and participle there occurs, besides the usual form with Kamets under the preformative, another with Hhirek and Tseri, especially when the first radical happens to be a guttural, as נֵחַל *he was profaned* (from חָלַל); נֵחַן *he is pitied* (from חָנַן). These forms may be explained in a twofold manner; either that the usual form of Niphal, נִקְטַל, is here at the foundation, so that נֵחַל tands for נִחְלַל, like נָסַב, for נִסְבַּב, or they are Chal-

daizing forms referred to below (rem. 14). The latter seems the most suitable explanation, (a) because that Chaldaizing formation is found in all the conjugations besides Niphal, and were probably not wanting in this; (b) because the doubling of the last radical before the afformatives is omitted in these as well as in the Chaldaizing forms referred to below.

9. The future 1 pers. אֶכַּף *I bow down*, Mi. 6. 6, stands for אֶכַּף comp. § 9. rem. 5.

III. Hiphil.

10. Instead of Tseri, in the final syllable of Hiphil, the vowel Pattahh is frequently found throughout the whole of this conjugation, not only when one radical happens to be a guttural, as in הֵמַר *he has embittered*, Job 27. 2; הֵרַךְ *he has intimidated*, Job 23. 16; inf. הָבַר *to cleanse*, Je. 4. 11, and in pause, as הֵתַן *he cuts off*, Is. 18. 5,† but even in the absence of these accidents, as pret. הֵדַק *he stamped small*, 2 Ki. 23. 15; הֵקַל *he made light*, Is. 8. 23; הֵמַסּוּ *they intimidated*, De. 1. 28, הֵסַבּוּ 1 Sa. 5. 10; הֵשַׁמּוּ Je. 10. 25; 2 Sa. 20. 18; inf. הָדַק *to beat in pieces*, 2 Ch. 34. 7; part. מֵצַל *shading*, Eze. 31. 3.

11. In the *future* the accent is drawn back to the penultima, on account of which Tseri is shortened to Segol, (a) after conversive Vav, as וַיָּגֶל *and he rolled down*, Ge. 29. 10; וַיָּסֶךְ *and he covered*, Job 38. 8; (b) before a monosyllabic word, as יָסֶךְ לְךָ Ps. 91. 4.

With gutturals Pattahh is used instead of Segol, as יָצַר־לֹו *he straitens him*, 1 Ki. 8. 37; אַל תָּצַר De. 2. 9. An example with suffix is יְסָבֵּנִי Eze. 47. 2.

IV. In General.

12. The verbs עַ״ע are closely related to the verbs עַ״ו, as appears from the similarity in their conjugations, which are parallel throughout. In form the verb עַ״ע is generally shorter than the other (comp. הָקֵם and יָקוּם, הָסֵב and יָסֹב). In some cases they have precisely the same form, as in the fut. convers. of Kal and Hiphil, in Hophal, &c. On account of this relation they have sometimes borrowed forms from each other. Thus, for instance,

(a) Kal inf. לָבֻּר for לָבֹּר *to search out*, Ec. 9. 1. With suffix בְּחֻקּוֹ for בְּחֻקּוֹ Pr. 8. 29. Fut. יָרֹנּוּ *he shouts* for יָרֹן Pr. 29. 6; יָרֻץ *he breaks*, for יָרֹץ Is. 42. 4.

(b) Hiph. inf. הֲתִימְךָ* for הֲתִמְּךָ *thy ceasing*, Is. 33. 1

---

† This last only assumes the form as if from תֵּן, but is to be derived from תִּן q. v.

* The forms, however, as הֲתִימְךָ, אֲדִיכֶם, יְחִיתַן, find their analogy in nouns in which, instead of sharpening the syllable

Fut. אֲדִקֵּם* for אֲדַקֵּם *I beat them small*, 2 Sa.
22. 43; יָשֵׁם Je. 49. 20, and נָשֵׁים Nu. 21. 30, *he, she
shall lay waste* (for which comp. rem. 14), from
שָׁמַם; וַתָּרָץ* *and she broke*, Ju. 9. 53; יְחִיתַן *he
terrifies them*, for יְחִתַּן*, Hab. 2. 17. This is frequently the case in the Chald. e. g. אָעֵילוּ Aph. of
עֲלַל Ca. 2. 5. Targ.

13. Besides the contracted defective forms hitherto
treated upon, there are also found, especially in certain conjugations and tenses, others which are quite
regular, as :—

Kal pret. דָּלְלוּ *they languish*, Is. 19. 6, also דַּלּוּ Job
28. 4; גָּלְלוּ *they roll*, Ge. 29. 3, 8, but גַּלּוֹתִי Jos. 5. 9;
זַמֹּתִי *I devise*, Zec. 8. 14, 15, and זַמּוֹתִי Ps. 17. 3.
Thus it is with בָּזַז *to plunder*, מָדַד *to measure*, שָׁדַד
to spoil, שָׁלַל *to rob*, &c.
Inf. סָבַב Nu. 21. 4, and סֹב De. 2. 3, so גָּזֹז, שָׁדֹד; with
suff. חֲנַנְכֶם *your pitying*, Is. 30. 18.
Imp. חָנְנֵנִי (like קָטְלֵנִי) *have mercy upon me*, Ps. 9. 14,
elsewhere חָנֵּנִי Ps. 4. 2; 6. 3; שָׁדְּדוּ *spoil ye*, Je.
49. 28, for שָׁדֹּדוּ.
Fut. יָחֹן *he will have mercy*, Am. 5. 15. With suff.
יְשָׁדְדֵם *he shall spoil them*, Je. 5. 6, but also יְשָׁדֵּם
Pr. 11. 3.
Hiph. pret. הִרְנִין, fut. יַרְנִין (*to shout*) is nowhere found
written defectively; וְהַחֲתַתִּי *and I break*, Je. 49. 37
(but also הַחְתֹּתָ *thou hast broken*, Is. 9. 3). Inf.
הַשְׁמֵם *laying waste*, Mi. 6. 13. Part. מְשַׁמִּים
astonished, Eze. 3. 15.

V. Chaldaisms.

14. In a great number of these verbs the vowel of
the preformative in Kal, Niphal, Hiphil, and Hophal
is a short instead of a long vowel, and Dag. forte is
inserted in the next (first radical) letter. This formation is general in the Chaldee, as Peal fut. יִדֹּק for
יִדַק (from דְּקַק); Aph. pret. אַדֵּק for אָדֵק, Heb.
הֵדֵק, fut. יַדֵּק for יָדֵק. That this Dagesh in the first
radical is a compensation for the one omitted in the
second radical, is evident from the forms with af-

formatives in which the Dagesh is wanting in the
second radical, as יִדְקוּ, אֲדִקוּ, יַדְקוּ.
Examples in the Hebrew are :—

Kal fut. יִסֹּב and יָסֹב (from סָבַב); יָדֹם, pl. יָדֹמּוּ (from
דָּמַם); יִשֹּׁם *shall be established*, 1 Ki. 9. 8, but pl.
יִשֹּׁמּוּ Ps. 40. 16; so יִקֹּד, pl. יִקְדוּ (*to bow down*)
from קָדַד. Examples of *fut. A* are יִתַּמּוּ Ps. 102. 28;
יִמַּלּוּ Job 24. 24; Ps. 37. 2; with Kibbuts in the
final syllable, תֻּתַּם Eze. 24. 11 (comp. the forms with
וּ in the regular verb, § 8. rem. 14).
Niph. pret. נָחַל *he is polluted*, Eze. 25. 3; נָחַר *he is
burned*, Ps. 69. 4; 102. 4 (but also נִחַר Je. 6. 29),
pl. נָחֲרוּ Ca. 1. 6; נָחַת *he is broken, terrified*, Mal. 2. 5;
נֵחַנְתָּ *thou art to be pitied*, Je. 22. 23. Part. נָאָרִים
cursed, Mal. 3. 9; נֶחָמִים *inflamed*, Is. 57. 5 (without
Dagesh as in יִתַּמּוּ above).
Hiph. fut. וַיִּסֹּב Ex. 13. 18; תַּתַּם Job 22. 3; יָחַל Nu.
30. 3; and אַחֵל *shall be profaned* (with Dag. forte impl.
in ח) to distinguish it from יָחֵל, אָחֵל *to begin*; pl.
וַיַּכְּתוּ *and they destroyed*, De. 1. 44, with suff.
וַיַּכְּתוּם† Nu. 14. 45; וַיָּסֵבּוּ† Ju. 18. 23; 1 Sa. 5. 8.§
Hophal יֻכַּת Is. 24. 12, with Shurek יוּסַב Is. 28. 27;
יוּשַׁד Ho. 10. 14; תּוּשַׁד Is. 33. 1; הֻשַּׁם Le. 26. 34
(Dagesh is here incorrectly omitted in several copies);
pl. הֻכְּמוּ† Job 4. 20; Je. 46. 5.

15. We have seen from the preceding examples,
that in the future of the Chaldee form the Dagesh
of the third radical, together with the preceding
vowel, is omitted before afformatives. Of the same
omission in the Hebrew form there are unquestion-
able examples :—

Kal fut. נָבְלָה Ge. 11. 7, *let us confound*, for נָבֹלָּה (from
בָּלַל, with parag. ה); יָזְמוּ Ge. 11. 6, *they will devise*,
for יָזֹמּוּ (from זָמַם).
Niph. pret. נְסַבָּה for נָסַבָּה *she turned round*, Eze. 41. 7;
וְנָבְקָה for וְנָבַקָּה *and she shall be made empty*, Is. 19. 3;
fut. נָדְמָה for נָדַמָּה (1 pers. pl. with parag. ה)
Je. 8. 14, *let us perish*. This last, however, is best
taken as Kal fut. (see No. 14), *and let us be quiet.‡*

---

by Dagesh forte in the final consonant, the vowel is prolonged by the insertion of a vowel letter, as מוֹרִנִים 1 Ch. 21. 23, for
מֹרְנִים 2 Sa. 24. 22, and פִּלַּגְשׁ and פִּלֶּגֶשׁ, קִימֹשׁ and קִמֹּשׁ, &c.—וַתָּרָץ may be thus pointed only to distinguish it from וַתָּרֶץ
Hiph. of רוּץ.

† The forms marked with † are the only examples in which the geminates have retained Dagesh in the lengthened form.

§ Here may also be added as examples for pret. and inf. of Hiph. הַחִלּוֹת *thou hast begun*, De. 3. 24; 2. 31; הַחְתֹּתָ *thou
hast broken*, Is. 9. 3; inf. הַחִלָּם *their beginning*, Ge. 11. 6, in which Pattahh under the preformative seems to indicate a Dag.
forte implicit.

‡ In the examples given above both the Dagesh and the preceding vowel are omitted. In other examples the vowel is
retained, and even prolonged by the pause, as יַחְקֹּ for יַחֹקּוּ Job 19. 23; יָדְמוּ 1 Sa. 2. 9, for יָדֹמּוּ; חָיָה *she lives*, Ex. 1. 16

16. In the Chaldee, both the epenthetic וֹ and ־ֵי in those forms in which the Hebrew has them, and the Dagesh in the last radical, are omitted. The like formation is also found in the Hebrew, by way of exception, especially in those forms which have likewise the Chaldaism of No. 14. E. g.

> Kal pret. תַּמֹּנוּ *we are consumed*, Ps. 64. 7, for תַּמּוֹנוּ; fut. תְּצַלְנָה *they tingle*, Je. 19.3; תְּפַמֹּקְנָה *they consume away*, Zec. 14. 12. The two last, however, may be Niphal.
>
> Niph. pret. נֵחַלְתְּ (Dag. forte impl.) *thou art polluted*, Eze. 22. 16; נֵחַנְתְּ *thou art to be pitied*, Je. 22. 23.

Instead of the epenthetic וֹ there is (ֻ) put in נְשַׁדֻּנוּ Mi. 2. 4, for נְשַׁדּוֹנוּ *we are destroyed*.

17. In the Aramaic, the verbs ע״ע borrow several forms from the verbs ע״א. An example of this kind in the Hebrew is שֹׁאֲסַיִךְ (as it ought to be pointed) *those that spoil thee*, Je. 30. 16, in Khethib for שֹׁסַיִךְ.

> *Note.* Other examples referred to in the Lehrgebäude (§ 103, 17) and by other grammarians are—
>
> Niph. fut. יִמָּאֵס *it melts*, for יִמַּס, Job 7. 5; pl. יִמָּאֲסוּ, Ps. 58. 8.

Hiph. fut. תְּכָאִיבוּ 2 Ki. 3. 19, *ye shall mar*, for יַכְבִּיבוּ from כבב Syr. and Arab. *to injure*, part. מַמְרִיר for מֵמִיר *causing pain*, Eze. 28. 24, fen.. מַמְאֶרֶת Le. 13. 51, 52. A similar example is the noun צְאֵלִים Job 40. 21, for צְלָלִים *shades, shady trees*.

But this is unnecessary, since all these forms may be derived immediately from roots ע״א, as כָּאַב, מָאַס, צָאַל, מָאַר, as kindred roots of מסס, כָּבַב, מָסַס, &c.

18. In the Piel, Pual, and Hithpael these verbs are without any contraction. There is, however, one form which seems to be inflected like the Chaldee, Ithpeel or Ittaphal, viz. תִּתַּבָּר 2 Sa. 22. 27, *thou showest thyself pure*, for תִּתְבָּרַר of the parallel passage in Ps. 18. 27. In the Chaldee, the Ithpeel (passive of Kal) would be אִתְבַּר, fut. יִתְבַּר, Ittaphal (passive of Hiphil) אִתַּבַּר, precisely like the above form.* This shorter form seems to be chosen for the sake of harmony with the immediately preceding תִּתַּמָּם Ps. 18. 26. A more difficult form is תִּתְפַּל ver. 27, which, according to the context, must necessarily be derived from פָּתַל. This difficulty can only be solved by supposing that תִּתְפַּתַּל (contr. תִּתְפַּל) is a transposition for תִּתְפַּתֵּל.

---

for חָיָה. Some of the like forms, however, occur without being in pause, as הָעֻזָּה for הָעֻזֶּה Pr. 7. 13; נְחֻמִּים Is. 57. 5, for נְחֻמִים; comp. also תְּרַנֶּגָה Ps. 71. 23, for תְּרַנֵּנָה (to avoid the concurrence of four Nuns), and תֶּעֱגֵנָה Ru. 1. 13, for תֵּעָגֵנָה.

* i. e. only as regards the preformatives תִּתְ; but as regards the second syllable, תִּתַּבָּר must then be supposed to stand for תִּתְבַּר, comp. הִתְפָּקֵד for הִתְפַּקֵּד § 12 rem. 5.

TABLE I. VERB PE ALEPH (פ"א).				
		KAL.	NIPHAL.	HIPHIL.	HOPHAL.

		KAL.	NIPHAL.	HIPHIL.	HOPHAL.
Pret.	3. m.	אָכַל	נֶאֱכַל	הֶאֱכִיל	הָאֳכַל
	3. f.				
	2. m.				
	2. f.				
	1. c.		Like the Verb *Pe guttural*, in Paradigm C.		
Plur. 3. c.					
	2. m.				
	2. f.				
	1. c.				
Inf.	absol.	אָכוֹל	הֵאָכֵל		
	constr.	אֲכֹל	הֵאָכֵל	הַאֲכִיל	הָאֳכַל
Imp.	m.	אֱכֹל	הֵאָכֵל	הַאֲכֵל	
	f.	אִכְלִי			
Plur. m.		אִכְלוּ	ETC.	ETC.	wanting.
	f.	אֱכֹלְנָה			
Fut.	3. m.	יֹאכַל	יֵאָכֵל	יַאֲכִיל	יָאֳכַל
	3. f.	תֹּאכַל			
	2. m.	תֹּאכַל			
	2. f.	תֹּאכְלִי	ETC.	ETC.	ETC.
	1. c.	אֹכַל			
Plur. 3. m.		יֹאכְלוּ			
	3. f.	תֹּאכֵלְנָה			
	2. m.	תֹּאכְלוּ			
	2. f.	תֹּאכֵלְנָה			
	1. c.	נֹאכַל			
Fut. *with Vav conv.*		וַיֹּאכַל,	וַיֹּאמֶר		
Part.	act.	אֹכֵל	נֶאֱכָל	מַאֲכִיל	מָאֳכָל
	pass.	אָכוּל			

SECTION XIX.—VERBS פ"א. (TABLE I.)

REMARKS.

I. On Fut. of Kal.

1. The relation between *Tseri* and *Pattahh* in the final syllable is the same here as in the Piel pret. of the regular verb (§ 10. rem. 1), and in several forms of the verb with gutturals (§ 15. rem. 1). That with Tseri seems, however, to be the original

and here the peculiar form. Examples are—יֹאבַד Job 3. 3, and יֹאבֵד Job 20. 7; תֹּאבַד De. 22. 3, comp. תֹּאבֵד Job 8. 13; Ps. 1. 6; תֹּאכַל Ge. 2. 16, comp. תֹּאכֵל ver. 17, and so constantly יֹאמַר and יֹאמֵר. The form with Tseri appears also in the plural, where this vowel is again introduced on account of the *pause*; e. g. יֹאכֵלוּ De. 18. 1, 8, comp. וְאֹכֵלָה *that I may eat*, Ge. 27. 4.

2. With *conversive Vav*, the tone is drawn back to the penultima, e. g. וַיֹּאכַל *and he ate*, Ge. 25. 34; 31. 15; וַיֹּאמֶר *and he spoke* (where Tseri of the final syllable is shortened to Segol). But the tone is retained,

    (a) Where the word stands at the end of a period, hence with a distinctive accent; e. g. וַיֹּאכַל Ge. 27. 25, וַיֹּאמֶר Ge. 14. 19; Ex. 2. 14.

    (b) In the first person; e. g. וָאֹמַר Ge. 20. 13; 24. 39; וָאֹכַל Ge. 27. 33. This is precisely the case with the verbs ע"ו in the first person.

The tone may, moreover, be drawn back on account of a monosyllabic word following it; e. g. יֹאבַד יוֹם Job 3. 3.

3. Examples, in which א becomes quiescent in *Tseri*, are—תֵּאתֶה *she shall come*, Mi. 4. 8; אֵהַב *I will love*, Pr. 8. 17 (along with אֹהַב, Mal. 1. 2); וַיֵּתֵא *and he came*, De. 33. 21 (for יֶאֱתֶה from אָתָה); תֵּזְלִי for תֶּאֱזְלִי (from אָזַל) *she goes away.** In וַיֵּאת *and he came*, Is. 41. 25, the א is indeed quiescent after *Pattahh*, but it is only so on account of being apocopated for יֶאֱתֶה, and properly stands for וַיֵּאת, and the vowel already in the syllable is retained.

4. Both forms (viz. the one in which א is quiescent, and the other in which it is moveable) are found also in one and the same verb; as וַתֹּאחֵז *and it takes hold*, De. 32. 41, also תֶּאֱחֹז; אֹסְפָה Mi. 4. 6; וַיֶּסֶף 2 Sa. 6. 1; תֹּסֵף Ps. 104. 29, but also יֶאֱסֹף; אֹהַב and אֱהַב (comp. rem. 3), also יֶאֱהַב. An example with a full Hholem is הַאֹכֵל (*do I eat?*) Ps. 50. 13; several MSS., however, have it without ו.

5. א which is regularly omitted in the first pers. fut., is also omitted in the following instances, יִמְרוּךָ for יֹאמְרוּךָ Ps. 139. 20; תֹּמְרוּ 2 Sa. 19. 14;

וַתֹּפֵהוּ *and she baked it*, 1 Sa. 28. 24; תֹּבֶא for תֹּאבֶה *she is willing*, Pr. 1. 10.

II. On the Inf. and Imp. of Kal.

6. In the *inf.* א is quiescent only in the frequent form לֵאמֹר for לֶאֱמֹר, but is otherwise moveable, as בֶּאֱמֹר De. 4. 10; כֶּאֱמֹר Jos. 6. 8. In the imp. the Aramaic punctuation is often introduced, as אֵפוּ for אֱפוּ Ex. 16. 23; אֵתָיוּ for אֱתָיוּ Is. 21. 12; 56. 9, 13

III. On the Pret. of Niphal.

7. The only example is נֹאחַז *he has taken possession of*, Jos. 22. 9, along with the part. נֶאֱחָז *held*, Ge. 22. 13.

IV. On Hiphil and Hophal.

8. In the *inf.*, *imp.*, and *fut.* of *Hiphil*, א is sometimes quiescent after *Hholem*, *Tseri*, and *Kamets*, and then it is altogether omitted.

Inf. הָכִיל for הַאֲכִיל *to eat*, Eze. 21. 33.

Imp. הֵתָיוּ for הַאֲתָיוּ *bring* (from אָתָה), Is. 21. 14 Je 12. 9.

Fut. (a) with Hholem, as אוֹכִיל *I feed*, Ho. 11. 4, אֹצְרָה for אַאֲצְרָה (comp. § 11. rem. 7) = אַאֲצִירָה *make treasures*, Ne. 13. 13; אֹבִידָה *I will destroy*, Je. 46. 8; אֹסְפֵךְ 1 Sa. 15. 6; וַיֹּחֵר 2 Sa. 20. 5. In the Chald. and Syr. this is the usual form, e. g אוֹכֵל; so in the Hebrew ו is likewise sometimes substituted for א.

(b) With Kamets, as וַיַּאְצֶל *he separated*, Nu. 11. 25, אָזִין for אַאֲזִין *I hearken*, Job 32. 11; וַיָּרֶב for וַיַּאְרֵב *and he set an ambush*, 1 Sa. 15. 5.

Part. מֵזִין for מַאֲזִין *hearkening*, Pr. 17. 4.

9. In Hophal יֻכְלוּ Eze. 42. 5, stands for יֻאְכְלוּ *they are cut off*, i. e. become shorter. In the Chaldee of Daniel—as the Targums have no Hophal— there occurs a Hophal in the form הוּבַד Da. 7. 11.

V. On Piel.

10. There are a few anomalous forms in Piel in which א is not quiescent, but entirely dropped with its preceding Sheva, so that the preformative takes ts place in the punctuation: viz. וַתַּזְרֵנִי *and thou girdest me*, 2 Sa. 22. 40, for וַתְּאַזְּרֵנִי in the parallel passage, Ps. 18. 40; וַאֲבַדֶּךָ for וָאֲאַבֶּדְךָ *and I destroy thee*, Eze. 28. 16; מַלְּפֵנוּ for מְאַלְּפֵנוּ *our teacher*, Job 35. 11; יַהֵל for יְאַהֵל *shall pitch his tent*, Is. 13. 20.

---

* The Tseri, however, in these forms is not the original vowel of the preformative, but is introduced in consequence of a contraction from the form in which א is moveable, so תָּאתָה for תֵּאתֶה, comp. לֶאֱמֹר for לֵאמֹר לֵאלֹהִים for לֵאלֹהִים

TABLE K. VERB PE YOD פ"י (orig. פ"ו).					Properly Pe Yod (פ"י).	
	KAL.	NIPHAL.	HIPHIL.	HOPHAL.	KAL.	HIPHIL.
Pret. 3. m.	יָשַׁב	נוֹשַׁב	הוֹשִׁיב	הוּשַׁב	יָטַב	הֵיטִיב
3. f.		נוֹשְׁבָה	הוֹשִׁיבָה	הוּשְׁבָה		הֵיטִיבָה
2. m.		נוֹשַׁבְתָּ	הוֹשַׁבְתָּ	הוּשַׁבְתָּ		הֵיטַבְתָּ
2. f.		נוֹשַׁבְתְּ	הוֹשַׁבְתְּ	הוּשַׁבְתְּ		הֵיטַבְתְּ
1. c.	regular	נוֹשַׁבְתִּי	הוֹשַׁבְתִּי	הוּשַׁבְתִּי	regular	הֵיטַבְתִּי
Plur. 3. c.		נוֹשְׁבוּ	הוֹשִׁיבוּ	הוּשְׁבוּ		הֵיטִיבוּ
2. m.		נוֹשַׁבְתֶּם	הוֹשַׁבְתֶּם	הוּשַׁבְתֶּם		הֵיטַבְתֶּם
2. f.		נוֹשַׁבְתֶּן	הוֹשַׁבְתֶּן	הוּשַׁבְתֶּן		הֵיטַבְתֶּן
1. c.		נוֹשַׁבְנוּ	הוֹשַׁבְנוּ	הוּשַׁבְנוּ		הֵיטַבְנוּ
Inf. absol.	יָשׁוֹב		הוֹשֵׁב, הוֹשִׁיב		יָטוֹב	הֵיטֵב
constr.	יְסֹד, שֶׁבֶת	הִוָּשֵׁב	הוֹשִׁיב	הוּשַׁב	יְטֹב	הֵיטִיב
Imp. m.	שֵׁב	יְרַשׁ	הִוָּשֵׁב	הוֹשֵׁב		יְטַב	הֵיטֵב
f.	שְׁבִי	יְרַשִׁי	הִוָּשְׁבִי	הוֹשִׁיבִי		יְטִבִי	הֵיטִיבִי
Plur. m.	שְׁבוּ	יְרַשׁוּ	הִוָּשְׁבוּ	הוֹשִׁיבוּ	wanting	יְטְבוּ	הֵיטִיבוּ
f.	שֵׁבְנָה	יְרַשְׁנָה	הִוָּשֵׁבְנָה	הוֹשֵׁבְנָה		יְטַבְנָה	הֵיטֵבְנָה
Fut. 3. m.	יֵשֵׁב	יִירַשׁ	יִוָּשֵׁב	יוֹשִׁיב	יוּשַׁב	יִיטַב	יֵיטִיב
3. f.	תֵּשֵׁב	תִּירַשׁ	תִּוָּשֵׁב	תּוֹשִׁיב	תּוּשַׁב	תִּיטַב	תֵּיטִיב
2. m.	תֵּשֵׁב	תִּירַשׁ	תִּוָּשֵׁב	תּוֹשִׁיב	תּוּשַׁב	תִּיטַב	תֵּיטִיב
2. f.	תֵּשְׁבִי	תִּירְשִׁי	תִּוָּשְׁבִי	תּוֹשִׁיבִי	תּוּשְׁבִי	תִּיטְבִי	תֵּיטִיבִי
1. c.	אֵשֵׁב	אִירַשׁ	אִוָּשֵׁב	אוֹשִׁיב	אוּשַׁב	אִיטַב	אֵיטִיב
Plur. 3. m.	יֵשְׁבוּ	יִירְשׁוּ	יִוָּשְׁבוּ	יוֹשִׁיבוּ	יוּשְׁבוּ	יִיטְבוּ	יֵיטִיבוּ
3. f.	תֵּשַׁבְנָה	תִּירַשְׁנָה	תִּוָּשַׁבְנָה	תּוֹשֵׁבְנָה	תּוּשַׁבְנָה	תִּיטַבְנָה	תֵּיטֵבְנָה
2. m.	תֵּשְׁבוּ	תִּירְשׁוּ	תִּוָּשְׁבוּ	תּוֹשִׁיבוּ	תּוּשְׁבוּ	תִּיטְבוּ	תֵּיטִיבוּ
2. f.	תֵּשַׁבְנָה	תִּירַשְׁנָה	תִּוָּשַׁבְנָה	תּוֹשֵׁבְנָה	תּוּשַׁבְנָה	תִּיטַבְנָה	תֵּיטֵבְנָה
1. c.	נֵשֵׁב	נִירַשׁ	נִוָּשֵׁב	נוֹשִׁיב	נוּשַׁב	נִיטַב	נֵיטִיב
Fut. apoc.				יֹשֵׁב			יֵיטֵב
Fut. with Vav conv.	וַיֵּשֶׁב			וַיּוֹשֶׁב		וַיִּיטַב, וַיָּקָם	וַיֵּיטֶב
Part. act.	יֹשֵׁב	נוֹשָׁב	מוֹשִׁיב	מוּשָׁב		יֹטֵב	מֵיטִיב
pass.	יָשׁוּב					יָטוֹב	

SECTION XX.—VERBS פ"י. (Table K.)

EXPLANATORY.

1. The Hebrew verbs פ"י are divided into three principal classes; the distinction of which is not manifest in the ground-form, but in the inflexion and derivation. By far the greater number are :—

(a) Verbs originally פ״ו, which in the Arabic are written with ו in the ground-form, e. g. יָלַד, Arab. ולד, יָרַד, Arab. ורד. In the Hebrew, the radical Vav appears only in the conjugations Niphal, Hiphil, and Hophal, but so that in the pret. and part. of Niphal it becomes quiescent in Hholem, and in the Hophal in Shurek, as נוֹשַׁב for נְוֹשַׁב, הֹשִׁיב for הֹושִׁיב, הוּשַׁב for הֻוֹשַׁב. In the inf., imp. and future of Niphal, the Vav remains a consonant, and the inflexion is regular, as יִוָּשֵׁב, הִוָּשֵׁב; and so likewise in the Hithpael of some verbs, יָדַע, יָכַח, יָרָה, from הִתְוַדָּה, הִתְוַכַּח, הִתְוַדַּע.

(b) Verbs originally פ״י, which are the same in the Arabic. In the Hiphil the original Yod is retained quiescent in Tseri, as הֵימִן, הֵינִיק, הֵילִיל, הֵיטִיב, and is but seldom moveable, e. g. מַיְמִינִים who use the right hand, 1 Ch. 12. 2; יַיְשִׁירוּ they are upright, Pr. 4. 25; comp. הַיָּשָׁר Ps. 5. 9, Keri.

(c) A few verbs, the Yod of which is assimilated like נ in verbs פ״נ, e. g. יָצַע Hiph. הִצִּיעַ.

REMARKS.

On the first class or verbs originally פ״י.

I. KAL.

1. In the *fut. imp.* and *inf. constr.* of Kal there is a twofold form. About half the number of these verbs have the *fut. E.* Hence fut. יֵישֵׁב, contracted יֵשֵׁב, but written, without exception, *defectively*; imp. שֵׁב (by *aphæresis*) for יְשֵׁב; inf. שֶׁבֶת for יְשֶׁבֶת (with the fem. termination ת‍, to distinguish it from the imp. The other half have *fut. A,* and retain Yod quiescent in Hhirek, as יִירַשׁ, imp. יְרַשׁ, inf. יְסֹד *to lay the foundation,* Is. 51. 16; יְבֹשׁ *to be dry,* Is. 27. 11. To the first mode of inflexion belong, for instance, יָלַד *to bear;* יָלַךְ *to go;* יָצָא *to go out;* יָרַד *to go down;* יָשַׁב *to sit.*

Those of the latter class take *Pattahh* instead of Tseri in the final syllable when it has guttural or ר; e. g. יָדַע, imp. דַּע, inf. דַּעַת (from יָדַע *to know*); הַב, pl. הָבוּ *give* (from יָהַב); יֵקַר Ps. 72. 14 (from יָקַר *to be precious*); יֵקַר, however, in Is. 10. 16, is an instance with Pattahh where the syllable does not contain a guttural.

2. In some verbs the full forms occur along with the defective, as יִיקַד De. 32. 22, and יֵקַד Is. 10. 16 (from יָקַד *to burn*); יִיקַר 1 Sa. 18. 30, and יֵקַר Ps. 72. 14 (from יָקַר *to be precious*); imp. רֵשׁ 1 Ki. 21. 15, רַשׁ De. 2. 24, 31, but also יְרַשׁ, in pause with ה parag. יְרָשָׁה De. 33. 23; צַק 2 Ki. 4. 41, and יְצֹק Eze. 24. 3 (from יָצַק *to pour out*); יָרַד Ju. 5. 13, and frequently רֵד (from יָרַד *to go down*).

A full form with Tseri is exhibited in יֵיקַר Ps. 72. 14, and אֵילְכָה *I will go,* Mi. 1. 8.

The form יִירַשׁ is frequently written *defectively,* but this is not an essential difference; e. g. וַיִּרָא 1 Sa. 18. 12; יִרְאוּ (with Metheg) 2 Ki. 17. 28; יְבַשׁ Job 8. 12, pl. יָבְשׁוּ Job 12. 15.

3. The *inf.* of Kal, without the radical Yod, has very seldom the masculine form like דַּע *to know,* Job 32. 6, 10, or the feminine termination ת‍, like לֵדָה

to bear, 2 Ki. 19. 3; רְדָה *to go down,* Ge. 46. 3. With suffix the form שֶׁבֶת is used, as שִׁבְתִּי, רִדְתִּי (from רֶדֶת). With guttural the latter takes the form ת‍ instead of ת‍; e. g. דֵּעַת. Examples for the full form of the infinitive with the feminine termination are, יְבֹשֶׁת *to become dry,* Ge. 8. 7; יְכֹלֶת *to be able,* Nu. 14. 16 (comp. § 8. rem. 1). With prepositions are, לִיסוֹד *to lay the foundation,* Is. 51. 16; לִרֹא *to fear,* for לִירֹא 1 Sa. 18. 29.

The defective *imperative* has frequently parag. ה, as רְדָה *go down,* Ge. 45. 9; לְכָה *go;* instead of which also לֵךְ Nu. 23. 13; Ju. 19. 13; once דְּעֶה Pr. 24. 14, for דְּעָה, comp. § 8. rem. 11.

4. The *future* יֵשֵׁב has, in some cases, the accent drawn back to the penultima, when the final syllable takes Segol instead of Tseri.

(a) *Before monosyllabic words,* or immediately preceding another tone-syllable, e. g. אֵלְכָה־לִּי *let me go,* Ca. 4. 6; יֵשֶׁב־בָּהּ *he dwells therein,* Job 22. 8; תֵּרֶד אֵשׁ *fire descends,* 2 Ki. 1. 10, 12.

(b) *After conversive Vav,* as וַיֵּשֶׁב, וַיֵּרֶד, וַיֵּלֶךְ. The tone, however, is in this case retained (1) in the first person, as וָאֵלֵךְ, וָאֵרֵד, וָאֵשֵׁב, and (2) in pause, as וַיֵּשֵׁב.

Pattahh instead of *Tseri* is found in this defective form, as noticed above (rem. 1), only by concurrence with a guttural, and besides also in pause; e. g. וַיֵּלַךְ *and he disappears,* Job 27. 21; וַיֵּלַךְ *and he went,* Ge. 24. 61; 25. 34; Nu. 12. 9, &c.

II. NIPHAL.

5. In the *pret.* and *part.* there are a few examples where ו is quiescent in Shurek, as נוּגֵי Zep. 3. 18, and נוּגוֹת *mourning,* La. 1. 4; נוּלְדוּ (with euphonic Dagesh) *they were born,* 1 Ch. 3. 5; 20. 8.

6. In two instances moveable ׳ occurs instead of moveable ו, and that in verbs which are undoubtedly פ״י, viz. יִיָּרֶה *he shall be shot through,* Ex. 19. 13, and וַיְיַחֶל *and he waited,* Ge. 8. 12 (pret. נוֹחַל, Hiph. הוֹחִיל).

7. The fut. 1 pers. takes here invariably *Hhirek* under the preformative, as אֵלֵךְ (not אוּלֵךְ) Job. 3. 3, comp. Pr. 30. 9; Eze. 20. 5; 2 Sa. 22. 4; Ps. 18. 4; 119. 117; Je. 17. 4; 1 Ki. 19. 10.

III. PIEL.

8. The only deviation to be met with in Piel is, that in a few examples the radical Yod is dropped after the preformative, and the latter adopts its punctuation, as is the case in verbs פ"א (§ 19. rem. 10): as וַיְבַּשֵּׁהוּ for וַיְיַבְּשֵׁהוּ *and he dries it up*, Na. 1. 14; וַיַּדּוּ for וַיְיַדּוּ *and they threw*, La. 3. 5, 3; וַיַּנֶּה *and he afflicted*, La. 3. 33; וַיִּשְׁרֵם 2 Ch. 32. 30, Khethib for וַיְיַשְּׁרֵם.

IV. HIPHIL AND HOPHAL.

9. The apocopated form of the future, יוֹשֵׁב, has the tone drawn back to the penultima, and the final syllable takes Segol (comp. rem. 4)—

(*a*) *Before another tone-syllable*, as יוֹסֵף לֶקַח *he shall add knowledge*, Pr. 1. 5.

(*b*) *After conversive Vav*, as וַיּוֹלֶךְ *and he led*, Ex. 14. 21; וַיּוֹלֶד *and he begat*, Ge. 5. 3; 4. 6; but not in the first person, as וָאוֹלֵךְ Le. 26. 13. The tone-less helping Segol is omitted, and even Sheva put instead, in אַל־תּוֹסְףְ *add not*, Pr. 30. 6, for תּוֹסֵף (comp. the nominal form קֹשְׁטְ for קֹשֶׁט).

10. Almost peculiar to these verbs is the uncontracted form of the Hiph. fut. in which ה is retained: as, יְהוֹשִׁיעַ *he will save*, 1 Sa. 17. 47; Ps. 116. 6; יְהוֹדֶה *he shall praise*, Ne. 11. 17; אֲהוֹדֶנּוּ *I shall praise him*, Ps. 28. 7 (comp. § 11. rem. 12).

11. Vav may also be omitted, as וַיֵּלֶךְ 2 Ki. 6. 19; 25. 20.

12. In Hophal הוֹדַע appears in Le. 4. 23 for הוּדַע.

V. HITHPAEL.

13. The only deviating form in Hithp. is תֵּתַצַּב Ex. 2. 4, for תִּתְיַצַּב *and she placed herself*. The omission of the radical Yod here is analagous to the cases in Piel (rem. 8), and the omission of the first radical א in the Chaldee; e. g. אִתְּמַר for אִתְאֲמַר.

On the second class or verbs properly פ"י.

14. The number of the verbs really belonging to this class is very limited. They are properly only the verbs יָצַר, יָנַק, יָלַל, יָטַב. Along with these some single forms occur of real פ"ו, and *vice versâ*; viz. הַיֵּצֵא *bring forth*, Ge. 8. 17, Keri, for Khethib הוֹצֵא (which is the common form); אֲיַסִּרֵם *I will chastise them*, Ho. 7. 12 (along with Niph. נוֹסַר and the noun מוּסָר); הֵילִיכִי *bring*, Ex. 2. 9 (elsewhere always הוֹלִיךְ); הוֹשֵׁר Ps. 5. 9 Khethib, but יְשִׁירוּ Pr. 4. 25; and תֵּיטְבִי Na. 3. 8, for תִּיטְבִי.

15. Some forms of the *Hiphil* are sometimes written *defectively*; e. g. הֵמִין, הֵטִיב for הֵימִין, הֵיטִיב. There is an uncontracted form also of this class in Is. 52. 5, where יְהֵילִילוּ stands for יְיֵלִילוּ *they howl* (comp. rem. 10).

A few forms of Hiph. fut. have occasioned much difficulty to grammarians, viz. יֵיטִיב for יֵיטִיב Job 24. 21; יְיֵלִיל Is. 15. 2; 16. 7; יְיֵלִילוּ Ho. 7. 14; Je. 48. 31, and constantly so in this verb (excepting אֵילִילָה Mi. 1. 8), to which another example of Kal fut. is added, viz. יֵדַע *he knows*, for יֵדַע Ps. 138. 6. The oldest grammarians regard ' as changed from the characteristic ה, so that יְיֵלִיל stands for יְהֵלִיל. This seems of all others the best explanation, only that it does not suit יֵדַע, which cannot be Hiphil.

On the third class, or verbs פ"י, whose Yod is assimilated.

16. Yod in these verbs does not remain quiescent, but is assimilated like נ in the verbs פ"ן. Some verbs belong exclusively to this class; e. g. יָצַע, Hiph. הִצִּיעַ, Hoph. fut. יֻצַּע, derivative מַצָּע; יָצַת, Hiph. הִצִּית. Others have two forms; one in which Yod is assimilated, and another in which it is quiescent; e. g. יָצַק, fut. יִצֹּק *he shall pour*, Le. 14. 26, and וַיִּצֶק 1 Ki. 22. 35, Hoph. part. מֻצָק Job 11. 15; יָצַר fut. יִצְּרֵהוּ *he fashions it*, Is. 44. 12; אֶצָּרְךָ Je. 1. 5 Keri, but also וַיִּיצֶר.

The same assimilation takes place in some Chaldee verbs, e. g. יְכַל, fut. יִכַּל; יְדַע, fut. יִדַּע; but so that Dagesh is again resolved in Nun, as יִנְדַּע for יֵדַע.

17. The *future O* of the verbs פ"י is only to be met with in this class, as יִצֹּר, יִצֹּק, יִפֹּר.

	TABLE L. VERB AYIN VAV (ע״ו).						AYIN YOD (ע״י).	
	KAL.	NIPHAL.	HIPHIL.	HOPHAL.	PILEL.	PULAL.	KAL.	NIPHAL.
PRET. 3. m.	קָם	נָקוֹם *	הֵקִים	הוּקַם	קוֹמֵם	קוֹמַם	בָּן	בִּין	נָבוֹן
3. f.	קָמָה	נָקוֹמָה	הֵקִימָה	הוּקְמָה	קוֹמְמָה	קוֹמֲמָה	בָּנָה	בִּינָה	נָבוֹנָה
2. m.	קַמְתָּ	נָקוּמוֹתָ	הֲקִימוֹתָ	הוּקַמְתָּ	קוֹמַמְתָּ	קוֹמַמְתָּ	בַּנְתָּ	בִּינוֹתָ	נְבוּנוֹתָ
2. f.	קַמְתְּ	נָקוּמוֹת	הֲקִימוֹת	הוּקַמְתְּ	קוֹמַמְתְּ	קוֹמַמְתְּ	בַּנְתְּ	בִּינוֹת	נְבוּנוֹת
1. c.	קַמְתִּי	נָקוּמוֹתִי	הֲקִימוֹתִי	הוּקַמְתִּי	קוֹמַמְתִּי	קוֹמַמְתִּי	בַּנְתִּי	בִּינוֹתִי	נְבוּנוֹתִי
Plur. 3. c.	קָמוּ	נָקוֹמוּ	הֵקִימוּ	הוּקְמוּ	קוֹמְמוּ	קוֹמֲמוּ	בָּנוּ	בִּינוּ	נָבוֹנוּ
2. m.	קַמְתֶּם	נְקוּמוֹתֶם	הֲקִימוֹתֶם	הוּקַמְתֶּם	קוֹמַמְתֶּם	קוֹמַמְתֶּם	בַּנְתֶּם	בִּינוֹתֶם	נְבוּנוֹתֶם
2. f.	קַמְתֶּן	נְקוּמוֹתֶן	הֲקִימוֹתֶן	הוּקַמְתֶּן	קוֹמַמְתֶּן	קוֹמַמְתֶּן	בַּנְתֶּן	בִּינוֹתֶן	נְבוּנוֹתֶן
1. c.	קַמְנוּ	נָקוּמוֹנוּ	הֲקִימוֹנוּ	הוּקַמְנוּ	קוֹמַמְנוּ	קוֹמַמְנוּ	בַּנּוּ	בִּינוֹנוּ	נְבוֹנוּ
INF. absol.	קוֹם	הִקּוֹם	הָקֵם, הֲקֵם				בּוֹן		הִבּוֹן
constr.	קוּם	הִקּוֹם	הָקִים	הוּקַם	קוֹמֵם	קוֹמֵם	בִּין		הִבּוֹן
IMP. m.	קוּם	הִקּוֹם	הָקֵם		קוֹמֵם		בִּין		הִבּוֹן
f.	קוּמִי	הִקּוֹמִי	הָקִימִי	wanting	קוֹמְמִי	wanting	בִּינִי	as	הָקּוֹם
Plur. m.	קוּמוּ	הִקּוֹמוּ	הָקִימוּ		קוֹמְמוּ		בִּינוּ		
f.	קֹמְנָה	הִקּוֹמְנָה	הֲקֵמְנָה		קוֹמֵמְנָה				——
FUT. 3. m.	יָקוּם	יִקּוֹם	יָקִים	יוּקַם	יְקוֹמֵם	יְקוֹמַם	יָבִין		יִבּוֹן
3. f.	תָּקוּם	תִּקּוֹם	תָּקִים	תּוּקַם	תְּקוֹמֵם	תְּקוֹמַם	תָּבִין	as	יָקּוֹם
2. m.	תָּקוּם	תִּקּוֹם	תָּקִים	תּוּקַם	תְּקוֹמֵם	תְּקוֹמַם	תָּבִין		
2. f.	תָּקוּמִי	תִּקּוֹמִי	תָּקִימִי	תּוּקְמִי	תְּקוֹמְמִי	תְּקוֹמְמִי	תָּבִינִי		
1. c.	אָקוּם	אֶקּוֹם	אָקִים	אוּקַם	אֲקוֹמֵם	אֲקוֹמַם	אָבִין		
Plur. 3. m.	יָקוּמוּ	יִקּוֹמוּ	יָקִימוּ	יוּקְמוּ	יְקוֹמְמוּ	יְקוֹמֲמוּ	יָבִינוּ		
3. f.	תְּקוּמֶינָה	תִּקּוֹמְנָה	תָּקֵמְנָה	תּוּקַמְנָה	תְּקוֹמֵמְנָה	תְּקוֹמַמְנָה	תְּבִינֶינָה		
2. m.	תָּקוּמוּ	תִּקּוֹמוּ	תָּקִימוּ	תּוּקְמוּ	תְּקוֹמְמוּ	תְּקוֹמְמוּ	תָּבִינוּ		
2. f.	תְּקוּמֶינָה	תִּקּוֹמְנָה	תָּקֵמְנָה	תּוּקַמְנָה	תְּקוֹמֵמְנָה	תְּקוֹמַמְנָה	תְּבִינֶינָה		
1. c.	נָקוּם	נִקּוֹם	נָקִים	נוּקַם	נְקוֹמֵם	נְקוֹמַם	נָבִין		
FUT. apoc.	יָקֹם		יָקֵם				יָבֵן		
FUT. with ו conv.	וַיָּקָם, וַיָּקָם		וַיָּקֶם				וַיָּבֶן		
									נָבֵבָן
PART. act.	קָם, קָֽם	נָקוֹם	מֵקִים	מוּקַם	מְקוֹמֵם	מְקוֹמָם	בָּן		נָבוֹן
pass.	קוּם						בּוּן		

* The few instances of *Piel* and *Hithp.* from ע״ו are עוֹד, חָיֵב, קִיֵּם, הִצְטַיֵּד.

SECTION XXI.—VERBS ע״ו. (TABLE L.)

REMARKS.

I. Pret. and Part. of Kal.

1. We class these two forms together, on account of their similarity in these verbs. The form of the paradigm, in which the pret. is *middle A* (קוּם, contr. קָם), is very seldom written *in full*. Examples, however, are—קָאַם *he arises*, Ho. 10. 14; part. שָׁאטִים *despising*, Eze. 28. 24, 26; fem. שָׁאטוּת Eze. 16. 57; and in the adjective, as לָאט *secretly*, Ju. 4. 21; רָאשׁ *poor*, Pr. 10. 4; 13. 23. Here must be referred the form כָּאֲרִי Ps. 22. 17, which, according to the present punctuation, seems to stand for כָּאֲרִים, or, with a slight change of the vowels, for כָּאֲרִי, in both cases from כּוּר. Two codices read כארו, in the preterite, for כָּרוּ.*

2. In the intransitive verbs *middle E* and *O*, which in the regular verb have likewise the pret. and part. alike (§ 8. rem. 20), the latter are formed like מֵת (for מִית from מָוֵת) אוֹר (from אָוֹר). Examples are:—

Pret. מֵתָה *she died*, Ex. 7. 21; מֵתוּ Ex. 4. 19, 2 pers. מַתָּה Eze. 28. 8; פֹּשְׁתֶּם Mal. 3. 20, from פּוּשׁ, 3 pers. pret. פָּשׁ; בּוֹשׁ, 2 and 1 pers. בֹּשְׁתָּ, בֹּשְׁנוּ *thou art, we are, ashamed*; אוֹר, pl. אוֹרוּ *they are enlightened*, 1 Sa. 14. 29; טֹבוּ *they are good*, Nu. 24. 5; זֹרוּ *they are estranged*, Ps. 58. 4 (also זֹרוּ), *they are pressed out*, Is. 1. 6. בָּאוּ Je. 27. 18 is the only example in this verb, elsewhere always בָּאוּ.

Part. עֵר *waking*, Ca. 5. 2; לָנִים *lodging*, Ne. 13. 21; and written in *full* גֵּרִים *stranger*, 2 Ch. 2. 16. With *O*, קוֹמִים *arising*, 2 Ki. 16. 7 (also קָמִים); בּוֹשִׁים *being ashamed*, Eze. 32. 30.

The part. fem. קָמָה is distinguished from the pret. 3 pers. fem. קָמָה by the tone.

II. Inf., Imp. and Fut. of Kal.

3. In some verbs the ו of the *inf., constr., imp.* and *fut.* is always quiescent in Hholem, as אוֹר *to be light*, בּוֹא *to come*, בּוֹשׁ *to be ashamed*; in all the rest it is quiescent in Shurek only, like קוּם. Both forms are found also in one and the same verb, as דּוּשׁ *to thresh*, imp. דּוֹשִׁי Mi. 4. 13; inf. מוֹט *to totter*, Ps. 46. 3, fut. יָמוּט. חוּס *to spare*, has a double fut. יָחוּס and יָחֹם; the latter, however, seems everywhere to be the apocopated future (but written *in full* contrary to

rule). Those, however, with ו have regularly ו in the inf. abs., and apocopated fut. and imp.

4. Examples of the *inf. abs.* are—גּוֹר יָגוּר *dwelling he shall dwell*, Is. 54. 15; מוֹת תְּמוּתוּן *dying ye shall die*, Ge. 3. 4; קוֹם יָקוּמוּ *arising they shall arise*, Je. 44. 29; נוֹחַ Est. 9. 16, &c. Here belongs likewise the adv. עוֹד properly *repeating*.

5. There are also some examples of the *imp.* with Kibbuts, as מֻת *die*, De. 32. 50; קֻם לָךְ *get thee up*, Jos 7. 10; שֻׁב *return*, Ex. 4. 19; רֻץ *run*, 2 Ki. 4. 26 This form is certainly to be regarded as an apocopated imperative, and not as accidently written *defectively*, since Kibbuts is found also in the future besides the form with defective Hholem (comp. rem. 7).

Lengthened imperatives are שׁוּבָה קוּמָה (comp. § 8. rem. 11).

6. In one verb alone the preformatives of the future have Tseri, viz. יֵבֹשׁ (for יִבוֹשׁ), strictly after the form יַקְטֹל.

7. The *apocopated future* is יָקֹם, very seldom יָקֻם, or in full יָקוֹם; e. g. תָּמֹת *may she die*, Nu. 23. 10; Ju. 16. 30; יָשֹׁב *let him return*, Ju. 7. 3; יָרֹם *let him be exalted*, 2 Sa. 22. 47; אַל יָשֹׁב *let him not return*, Ps. 74. 21; וְיָמֹת *that he may die*, 1 Ki. 21. 10. Examples of the full orthography (יָקוֹם) are very frequent in the verb חוּם, besides which there are also single instances found in other verbs, as וַיָּצוֹם *and he fasted*, 1 Ki. 21. 27; וַתָּמוֹג *and she melted away*, Am. 9. 5; moreover a few times in Khethib, where, in the Keri, Vav is cancelled, as וַתָּלשׁ *and she kneaded*, 2 Sa. 13. 8; וַיָּשׁוֹב *and he returned*, Eze. 18. 28. In both these last instances we are doubtless to sound it ו and not ו.

8. When the tone of the *apocopated future* is drawn back to the penultima, Hholem is shortened to Kamets-hhatuph, יָקָם. This takes place—

(*a*) *Before monosyllabic words*, as יָקָם לָךְ Job 22. 28; frequently with Makkeph (which otherwise is not usual in the like combination); e. g. שָׁב־נָא 2 Sa. 19. 38; Da. 9. 16; תָּשָׁב־נָא 1 Ki. 17. 21.

---

* This is likewise the reading of the Masora on Nu. 24. 9 . comp. Prof. Lee's Heb. Lex. under כּוּר.

(b) After *conversive Vav*, as וַיָּקָם, וַיָּמָת. In pause, however, the tone remains on the ultimate, as וַיָּמֹת, וַיָּקָם, comp. Ge. 11. 28, 32, with ch. 5. 5, 8. The *first person* of the *future* forms another exception, which generally retains the full form after *conversive Vav* (§ 11. rem. 6); e. g. וָאָקוּם 2 Ch. 6. 10; Ne. 2. 12; 4. 8; Da. 8. 27.

9. When the first or last letter of the monosyllabic root is a guttural or ר, the *apocopated future with conversive Vav* may take *Pattahh* in the final syllable; e. g. וַיָּסַר *and he turned aside*, Ru. 4. 1; וַיָּזַר *and he wringed out*, Ju. 6. 38; וַיָּנַח *and he rested*, Ex. 10. 14; וַיִּעַף *and he became weary*, Ju. 4. 21.

10. For the *fut.* 2 and 3 *pers. pl.*, the form given in the paradigm (תְּקוּמֶינָה) is the usual one; e. g. תְּשׁוּבֶינָה Eze. 16. 55, comp. Is. 54. 10; 60. 8; Zec. 1. 17; 13. 7; there occurs, however, also a form like תְּשֹׁבְן besides תְּשׁוּבֶינָה in Eze. 16. 55, and תָּבֹאנָה Est. 4. 4; 1 Sa. 10. 17 in Keri.

III. Niphal.

11. In the *preterite* occurs the form נֵעוֹר for נָעוֹר (according to נִקְטֹל) Zec. 2. 17, which corresponds to the Kal fut. יֵבוֹשׁ (comp. rem. 6). This, however, may be compared with the form נְמוֹל and referred to the Chaldee or Rabbinic punctuation of *rem.* 24.

12. The ו is sometimes retained in those forms in which, according to the paradigm, it is to be changed to ו on account of the accession at the end. Thus נְפוֹצוֹתֶם (for נְפוּצוֹתֶם) *ye are dispersed*, Eze. 11. 17; 20. 41; נְקֹטֹתֶם Eze. 20. 43. The ו is, on the other hand, inserted contrary to the paradigm in the inf. כְּהִדּוֹשׁ Is. 25. 10, and part. נְבוֹכִים Ex. 14. 3 (comp. § 32. rem. 5).

IV. Hiphil.

13. *Preterite.* Besides the forms with epenthetic ו, there are others without it, after the form הֵקַמְתָּ (הִקְטַלְתָּ); e. g. הֵנַפְתָּ *thou liftest up*, Ex. 20. 25, besides הֲנִיפוֹתִי Job 31. 21; הֵבֵאתִי (according to הֲבֵאוֹתִי) Ge. 27. 12, besides הֲבֵאוֹתִי Eze. 38. 16 (comp. Je. 25. 13); הֵטַלְתִּי *I cast*, Je. 16. 13. The ו is especially omitted in verbs ל"ת and ל"ן before the afformatives with ת and נ, as הֵמַתִּי, הֵמַתָּה, pl. הֲמַתֶּם,

with suff. הֲמִיתִיהָ Ho. 2. 5; הָכֵנּוּ *we prepare*, 2 Ch. 29. 19, besides הֲכִינוֹנוּ 1 Ch. 29. 16.

There is, on the other hand, epenthetic יְ instead of ו in the fut. תְּהִימֶנָה for תְּהִימֶינָה Mi. 2. 12.* (The change of תְּהִי from תָּהֵי is occasioned by the shifting of the tone, comp. the pret. הֲקִימוֹתִי, הֲקִימֹתָ, but imp. הֲקֵמְנָה).

14. Less important deviations from the paradigm are :—

(a) Forms like הֲרֵמֹת (for הֲרִימֹת) Nu. 31. 28, especially before suffix הֲקֵמֹתוֹ 2 Ki. 9. 2 (comp. 1 Ki. 8. 34; Ex. 19. 23; Ca. 3. 4 Keri); and written *fully* הֲשִׁיבוֹתָם 2 Ch. 6. 25. (b) With *Segol* instead of *Pattahh* under the preformatives, as הֲמֵיבוֹתָ 1 Ki. 8. 18; הֲבֵישׁוֹתָ Ps. 44. 8; הֲקֵיצוֹתִי Ps. 139. 18; comp. also rem. 24.

15. Of the *inf.* there once occurs a Chaldee form with the fem. termination, viz. הֲנָפָה (with impure Kamets) for הָנִיף Is. 30. 28 (comp. הֲזָדָה Da. 5. 20), from נוף.

16. In the *imp.* the shortened and lengthened form הָקֵם, הָקִימָה have wholly supplanted the regular form הָקִים.†

17. The *apocopated future* has the form יָקֵם. Examples are, וְיָרֵם *that he take up*, Nu. 17. 2; יָסַר *let him take away*, Job 9. 34; וְיָסַר *that he may remove*, Ex. 10. 17; Nu. 21. 7. As the poetic future and present, יָעֵר Da. 11. 25; יָפֵץ Job 38. 24; יָרֵם 1 Sa. 2. 10.

18. When the tone is drawn back, the final syllable takes *Segol* instead of *Tseri*, as (after a negation) אַל־תָּשֵׁב *turn not away*, 1 Ki. 2. 20, or after *conversive Vav*, וַיָּרֶם, וַיָּפֶץ &c. The 1 pers., however, forms an exception here as in Kal (rem. 8), as וָאָשִׁיב Ne. 2. 20; 6. 4; וָאָעִיד vers. 13, 15, besides וָאָעֵד Je. 32. 10; וָאָקִים Am. 2. 11.

19. When one of the letters is a guttural or ר the final syllable takes *Pattahh*, as in Kal (rem. 9), and the context must decide between Kal and Hiphil, as וַיָּסַר *and he removed*, Ge. 8. 13; וַיָּנַח *and he gave rest*, Jos. 21. 42.

V. Pilel, Pulal and Hithpalel.

20. In the *Hithpal* the final syllable has some-

---

* The form נָה for יְנָה is found also in תְּמוּתֶנָה Zec. 13. 19, תְּפוּצֶנָה Zec. 1. 17, but not in all MSS. and editions (comp. § 24. rem. 6).

† This, however, remains the ground-form whenever the suffixes are added, as הֲקִימוֹ Je. 23. 20; 30. 24; comp. § 11. rem. 5.

times also *Pattahh*, as in the Hithpa. of the regular verb (§ 12. rem. 1), and hence Kamets in pause, as pret. הִתְבּוֹנֵן Is. 1. 3; מִתְקוֹמְמָה Job 20. 27; imp. הִתְרוֹעֵעַ Ps. 60. 10; fut. תִּתְמוֹגֵג Ps. 107. 26, comp. Ps. 119. 158; 139. 21; 58. 8.

21. The form וַיְכֻנְנֵנוּ *he has prepared us*, Job 31. 15, stands for וַיְכוֹנְנֵנוּ (from יְכוֹנֵן) the first Nun being compensated for by Dagesh, and וֹ having lost the tone is shortened to וּ (comp. Niph. נָקוֹם, 2 pers. נְקוּמוֹת). The omission of Dagesh in the נ of the suffix seems to be designed for avoiding the concurrence of too many Nuns.

VI. In General.

22. On account of the intimate relation between verbs עי״ and עע״ (see above § 18. rem. 12), some of the former class borrow forms from the latter, as Kal pret. בַּז *he despised* for בָּז (from בּוז), Zec. 4. 10; מַח *he besmeared*, for מָח, Is. 44. 18.

23. The verbs whose middle radical is a moveable Vav are, in respect to this letter, quite regular. They are, however, comparatively few. E. g. חָוַר,

fut. יֶחֱוָר *to be white*; גָּוַע, fut. יִגְוַע *to die*; רָוַח, fut. יִרְוַח *to be wide*, Pu. מְרֻוָּח; צָוַח, fut. יִצְוַח *to cry*; עָוַל, Pi. עִוֵּל *to act perversely*; עָוַר, Pi. עִוֵּר *to blind*; and several others which are also לי״ה, as בָּוָה, חָוָה, הָוָה, קָוָה, לָוָה &c.

24. The verbs עי״ have also this in common with the verbs עע״ (§ 18. rem. 14) that some forms take Dagesh forte in the first radical letter like the verbs פי״ן, and the preformative takes a short vowel instead of the long, which is more usual in the Chaldee and Rabbinic; e. g. יַלִּינוּ, מַלִּינִים Ex. 16. 7, 8; Nu. 14. 27 (from לוּן *to murmur*); יַלִּיזוּ *they depart* (from לוּז); מַסִּית, יַסִּית along with הֵסִית, יָסִית (*to stimulate*); Niph. נִמּוֹל *he was circumcised*, Ge. 17. 26, 27; 34. 22 (from מוּל); with gutt. נֵעוֹר Zec. 2. 17 (comp. rem. 11). In the same way may be explained הַעִירוֹתִי Is. 41. 25; הַעִדֹתִי Je. 11. 7 (with Dagesh forte implicit) for הַעֵדֹתִי. Here belong, moreover, some forms of verbs *Pe guttural* with *Dagesh forte implicit*, as Kal fut. וַתַּחַשׁ for וַתָּחֹשׁ *and she hastened* (from חוּשׁ) Job 31. 5; וַתָּעַט, וַיָּעַט 1 Sa. 15. 19, and 14. 32 Keri, from עוּט or עִיט *to rush upon*.

SECTION XXII.—ON THE VERBS עי״. (Table L.)

REMARKS

1. In the *preterite* some verbs have both the forms exhibited in the paradigm, as בִּינֹתִי Da. 9. 2; בַּנְתָּה Ps. 139. 2; רִיבוֹתָ *thou contendest*, Job 33. 13; רַבְתָּה La. 3. 58; דִּיגוּם *they fish them*, Je. 16. 16. The participle exhibits here also two forms, as בָּז *middle A*, and לֵנִים *middle E*, Ne. 13. 21 (comp. § 21. rem. 2).

2. Examples of the *inf. abs.* are—רֹב *striving*, Ju. 11. 25; Job 40. 2; שֹׂת *putting*, Is. 22. 7; also רִיב Je. 50. 34.

3. Examples of the *apocopated fut.* are—(*a*) יָרֵב *let him plead*, 1 Sa. 24. 16; יֵשֵׁם *may he give*, 1 Sa. 2. 20; יָגֵל *may he rejoice*, Ps. 13. 6; אַל יָרֵב Ho. 4. 4. (*b*) וַיָּבֶן *that he may observe*, Je. 9. 11; Ho. 14. 10. (*c*) As a positive future of poesy, as יָשֵׁם *he shall put*, Job 33. 11; 24. 25; Ps. 107. 33 (comp. § 11. rem. 6). With the retracted tone the final syllable

takes Segol (*a*) before a *monosyllabic word*, as יָרֶב לוֹ Ju. 6. 31, 32; (*b*) after אַל, as אַל תֵּלֶן 2 Sa. 17. 16; (*c*) with *conversive Vav*, as וַיָּבֶן, וַיָּשֶׂם.

Pattahh occurs instead of *Tseri* (*a*) on account of a *guttural*, as יָרַח *he may smell*, 1 Sa. 26. 19; (*b*) in *pause*, as אַל תָּלַן Ju. 19. 20; תָּלַן Job 17. 2.

II. Niphal.

4. נָזִיד *pottage* (properly *sodden*), Ge. 25. 29, from זִיד, is the only example in which Yod is retained in Niphal. (There is at least no trace of a root זִיד-נָזַד).

III. Hiphil.

5. The *fut.* of Hiph. can be distinguished from the fut. of Kal by the signification only; e. g. יָבִין *he understands*; Hiph. תְּבִינֵם *he gives them understanding*, Job 32. 8.

4**

TABLE M. VERB LAMED ALEPH (ל״א).

		KAL.	NIPHAL.	PIEL.	PUAL.	HIPHIL.	HOPHAL.	HITHPAEL.
PRET. 3. m.		מָצָא	נִמְצָא	מִצֵּא	מֻצָּא	הִמְצִיא	הָמְצָא	הִתְמַצֵּא
3. f.		מָצְאָה	נִמְצְאָה	מִצְּאָה	מֻצְּאָה	הִמְצִיאָה	הָמְצְאָה	הִתְמַצְּאָה
2. m.		מָצָאתָ	נִמְצֵאתָ	מִצֵּאתָ	מֻצֵּאתָ	הִמְצֵאתָ	הָמְצֵאתָ	הִתְמַצֵּאתָ
2. f.		מָצָאת	נִמְצֵאת	מִצֵּאת	מֻצֵּאת	הִמְצֵאת	הָמְצֵאת	הִתְמַצֵּאת
1. c.		מָצָאתִי	נִמְצֵאתִי	מִצֵּאתִי	מֻצֵּאתִי	הִמְצֵאתִי	הָמְצֵאתִי	הִתְמַצֵּאתִי
Plur. 3. c.		מָצְאוּ	נִמְצְאוּ	מִצְּאוּ	מֻצְּאוּ	הִמְצִיאוּ	הָמְצְאוּ	הִתְמַצְּאוּ
2. m.		מְצָאתֶם	נִמְצֵאתֶם	מִצֵּאתֶם	מֻצֵּאתֶם	הִמְצֵאתֶם	הָמְצֵאתֶם	הִתְמַצֵּאתֶם
2. f.		מְצָאתֶן	נִמְצֵאתֶן	מִצֵּאתֶן	מֻצֵּאתֶן	הִמְצֵאתֶן	הָמְצֵאתֶן	הִתְמַצֵּאתֶן
1. c.		מָצָאנוּ	נִמְצֵאנוּ	מִצֵּאנוּ	מֻצֵּאנוּ	הִמְצֵאנוּ	הָמְצֵאנוּ	הִתְמַצֵּאנוּ
INF. absol.		מָצוֹא	נִמְצֹא	מַצֵּא		הַמְצֵא		
constr		מְצֹא	הִמָּצֵא	מַצֵּא	מֻצָּא	הַמְצִיא	הָמְצָא	הִתְמַצֵּא
IMP. m.		מְצָא	הִמָּצֵא	מַצֵּא		הַמְצֵא		הִתְמַצֵּא
f.		מִצְאִי	הִמָּצְאִי	מַצְּאִי		הַמְצִיאִי		הִתְמַצְּאִי
Plur. m.		מִצְאוּ	הִמָּצְאוּ	מַצְּאוּ	wanting	הַמְצִיאוּ	wanting	הִתְמַצְּאוּ
f.		מְצֶאנָה	הִמָּצֶאנָה	מַצֶּאנָה		הַמְצֶאנָה		הִתְמַצֶּאנָה
FUT. 3. m.		יִמְצָא	יִמָּצֵא	יְמַצֵּא	יְמֻצָּא	יַמְצִיא	יָמְצָא	יִתְמַצֵּא
3. f.		תִּמְצָא	תִּמָּצֵא	תְּמַצֵּא	תְּמֻצָּא	תַּמְצִיא	תָּמְצָא	תִּתְמַצֵּא
2. m.		תִּמְצָא	תִּמָּצֵא	תְּמַצֵּא	תְּמֻצָּא	תַּמְצִיא	תָּמְצָא	תִּתְמַצֵּא
2. f.		תִּמְצְאִי	תִּמָּצְאִי	תְּמַצְּאִי	תְּמֻצְּאִי	תַּמְצִיאִי	תָּמְצְאִי	תִּתְמַצְּאִי
1. c.		אֶמְצָא	אֶמָּצֵא	אֲמַצֵּא	אֲמֻצָּא	אַמְצִיא	אָמְצָא	אֶתְמַצֵּא
Plur. 3. m.		יִמְצְאוּ	יִמָּצְאוּ	יְמַצְּאוּ	יְמֻצְּאוּ	יַמְצִיאוּ	יָמְצְאוּ	יִתְמַצְּאוּ
3. f.		תִּמְצֶאנָה	תִּמָּצֶאנָה	תְּמַצֶּאנָה	תְּמֻצֶּאנָה	תַּמְצֶאנָה	תָּמְצֶאנָה	תִּתְמַצֶּאנָה
2. m.		תִּמְצְאוּ	תִּמָּצְאוּ	תְּמַצְּאוּ	תְּמֻצְּאוּ	תַּמְצִיאוּ	תָּמְצְאוּ	תִּתְמַצְּאוּ
2. f.		תִּמְצֶאנָה	תִּמָּצֶאנָה	תְּמַצֶּאנָה	תְּמֻצֶּאנָה	תַּמְצֶאנָה	תָּמְצֶאנָה	תִּתְמַצֶּאנָה
1. c.		נִמְצָא	נִמָּצֵא	נְמַצֵּא	נְמֻצָּא	נַמְצִיא	נָמְצָא	נִתְמַצֵּא
FUT. apoc. (Jussive)						יַמְצֵא		
PART. act.		מֹצֵא	נִמְצָא	מְמַצֵּא	מְמֻצָּא	מַמְצִיא	מָמְצָא	מִתְמַצֵּא
pass.		מָצוּא						

SECTION XXIII.—ON THE VERBS ל״א. (TABLE M.)

REMARKS.

I. KAL.

1. The verbs *middle E*, like יָרֵא, retain *Tseri* throughout the rest of the persons, as יָרֵאתָ *thou didst fear*; מָלֵאתִי *I have filled*. The 3 pers. fem. assumes sometimes the Aramaic form, as קָרָאת Is. 7. 14; and so in Niph. נִפְלָאת Ps. 118. 23; in Hoph. הֻבָאת Ge.

33. 11. There are also examples where א is omitted, מָצָתִי Nu. 11. 11; יָצָתִי Job 1. 21; מִלְתִי Job 32. 18.

2. Forms of the *infinitive* deviating from the paradigm are—(*a*) like מְצָאָה, חֲטָאָה, יְרָאָה, also לְקְרֹאת* by Syriacism for לְקְרֹאת (constr. of קְרִאָה); (*b*) מְלֹאת for מַלֹּאת (after יְכֹלֶת) Le. 12. 4; קְרֹאת *to call*, Ju. 8. 1; שְׂנֹאת *to hate*, Pr. 8. 13; (*c*) מַשֹּׂאוּת *to carry*, Eze. 17. 9, for מַשָּׂאֵת.

א is omitted in חֲטוֹ Ge. 20. 6.

3. In the *imperative* there is an anomalous form, יְראוּ *fear ye*, Ps. 34. 10 (comp. נִרְפְּאוּ Niph. Eze. 47. 8), where א is passed over in the pronunciation. The punctuators have given to this word the character of ל״ה probably to distinguish it from יִרְאוּ *they shall see*.

A striking anomaly is presented in צְאֶינָה וּרְאֶינָה *go out and see*, Ca. 3. 11, where the first word stands for צֶּאנָה, comp. the fut. תִּשֶּׁאינָה Eze. 23. 49. The epenthetic ־ֶ is as anomalous here as it is in the regular verb § 8. rem. 16, only that here it is chosen for the sake of consonance with רְאֶינָה.

4. The *part. fem.* is commonly, by contraction, מֹצֵאת, seldom with the Syriac punctuation מֹצֵאת for מֹצֵאת, Ca. 8. 10; 1 Ki. 10. 22; and defective יֹצֵת De. 28. 57.

In the *masculine* a Syriac punctuation is introduced in חֹטְאִים for חֹטָאִים *sinners*, 1 Sa. 14. 33; בֹּרְאָם for בֹּרְאָם Ne. 6. 8.

II. Niphal.

5. In a few instances א is omitted, as נִטְמֵתֶם *ye are polluted*, Le. 11. 43; נֶחְבֵּתֶם *ye have hid yourself*, Jos. 2. 16. In the 3 pers. fem. the same kind of contraction is found as in Kal (rem. 1), as נִפְלָאת Ps. 118. 23; †נִפְלָאת De. 30. 11; נִטְמָאת Nu. 5. 20; Eze. 23. 30.

6. In the *participle* there are traces of a form like נִמְצָא, viz. in the plurals נִמְצָאִים Est. 1. 5; 4. 16; נִטְמָאִים Eze. 20. 30; נֶחְבָּאִים Jos. 10. 17 (comp. § 15. rem. 2, and dec. 7).

III. Hiphil.

7. Anomalous forms are הָחֱטִי 2 Ki. 13. 6; inf. הַחֲטִיא, הַחֲטִיא Je. 32. 35, for הַחֲטִי.

IV. In General.

8. In addition to the anomalous forms exhibited above there are others, the irregularity of which consists in assuming forms of verbs ל״ה. The ל״א and ל״ה of the Hebrew form but one class in the Aramaic. The Syriac has א only, and the Chaldee has א and ה promiscuously forming but one class. In the Hebrew this is either peculiar to certain verbs, and the two exist as distinct verbs ל״א and ל״ה, and as such occupy separate places in the Lexicon, e. g. קָרָא and קָרָה *to meet*, פָּלָא and פָּלָה *to be distinguished*, &c., or in the real ל״א there occur some isolated forms which borrow either the punctuation only or the inflexion altogether from ל״ה; comp. the following remarks.

9. Examples of such verbs, where א is retained, and only the punctuation of ל״ה is adopted, are—כָּלֵאתִי *I have refrained*, Ps. 119. 101; part. מֹצֶה, חֹטֶא Ec. 7. 26; 8. 12; Piel מִלֵּה *he accomplished*, Je. 51. 34; דִּכָּה Ps. 143. 3; רְפָאתִי *I heal*, 2 Ki. 2. 21; fut. יִמָּה *he swallows*, Job 39. 24; inf. מַלֹּאוּת 2 Ch. 36. 21; מַלֹּאת Ex. 31. 5; Hithp. הַמִּתְנַבְּאוֹת Eze. 13. 17; Hiph. הִפְלָא Is. 28. 29; De. 28. 59; הֶחְבְּאָתָה *she concealed* (with ה parag.), Jos. 6. 17.

10. In the following examples there is, on the contrary, the punctuation of ל״א retained, and ה only is adopted. Kal imp. רְפָה for רְפָא *heal*, Ps. 60. 4; נְשָׂה for נְשָׂא, נְשָׂא Ps. 4. 7. Niph. inf. abs. נֶחְבָּה Je. 49. 10, constr. הֵחָבֵה *to hide oneself*, 1 Ki. 22. 25; הֵרָפֵה Je. 19. 11. Piel יְמַלֶּה *he shall fill*, Job 8. 21.

11. Finally, forms which are entirely inflected after ל״ה—צָמֵת *thou art thirsty*, Ru. 2. 9; מָלוּ for מָלְאוּ *they are full*, Eze. 28. 16; כָּלוּ for כָּלְאוּ 1 Sa. 6. 10; נָשׂוּא Ps. 139. 20 (with parag. א § 8. rem. 4), for נָשׂוּ, נָשְׂאוּ; fut. תִּרְפֶּינָה Job 5. 18; part. fem. יֹצֵא for יֹצֵאת, יֹצְאָה Ec. 10. 5; pass. נָשׂוּי Ps. 32. 1. Niph. נִבֵּיתָ *thou hast prophesied*, Je. 26. 9; נִטְמִינוּ *we are polluted*, Job 18. 3; נִרְפְּתָה Je. 51. 9; fut. (perhaps) יִמָּצוּ *they are found*, Ps. 73. 10; יִנָּשׂוּא Je. 10. 5 (with parag. א). Piel יְרַפּוּ Je. 8. 11. Hithp. הִתְנַבִּיתָ 1 Sa. 10. 6; הִתְנַבּוֹת 1 Sa. 10. 6. Hiph. הִמְצִיתָך 2 Sa. 3. 8; part. מַקְנֶה for מַקְנִיא Eze. 8. 3.

---

* Comp. חֹטָאִים for חֹטְאִים rem. 4.   † This, however, must be taken as a participle, comp. rem. 4.

TABLE N. VERB LAMED HE (ל״ח)

	KAL.	NIPHAL.	PIEL.	PUAL.	HIPHIL.	HOPHAL.	HITHPAEL.
Pret. 3. m.	גָּלָה	נִגְלָה	גִּלָּה	גֻּלָּה	הִגְלָה	הָגְלָה	הִתְגַּלָּה
3. f.	גָּלְתָה	נִגְלְתָה	גִּלְּתָה	גֻּלְּתָה	הִגְלְתָה	הָגְלְתָה	הִתְגַּלְּתָה
2. m.	גָּלִיתָ	נִגְלֵיתָ	גִּלִּיתָ	גֻּלֵּיתָ	הִגְלֵיתָ	הָגְלֵיתָ	הִתְגַּלֵּיתָ
2. f.	גָּלִית	נִגְלֵית	גִּלִּית	גֻּלֵּית	הִגְלֵית	הָגְלֵית	הִתְגַּלֵּית
1. c.	גָּלִיתִי	נִגְלֵיתִי	גִּלִּיתִי	גֻּלֵּיתִי	הִגְלֵיתִי	הָגְלֵיתִי	הִתְגַּלֵּיתִי
Plur. 3. c.	גָּלוּ	נִגְלוּ	גִּלּוּ	גֻּלּוּ	הִגְלוּ	הָגְלוּ	הִתְגַּלּוּ
2. m.	גְּלִיתֶם	נִגְלֵיתֶם	גִּלִּיתֶם	גֻּלֵּיתֶם	הִגְלֵיתֶם	הָגְלֵיתֶם	הִתְגַּלֵּיתֶם
2. f.	גְּלִיתֶן	נִגְלֵיתֶן	גִּלִּיתֶן	גֻּלֵּיתֶן	הִגְלֵיתֶן	הָגְלֵיתֶן	הִתְגַּלֵּיתֶן
1. c.	גָּלִינוּ	נִגְלֵינוּ	גִּלִּינוּ	גֻּלֵּינוּ	הִגְלֵינוּ	הָגְלֵינוּ	הִתְגַּלֵּינוּ
Inf. absol.	גָּלֹה	נִגְלֹה	גַּלֹּה	גֻּלֹּה	הַגְלֵה	הָגְלֵה	הִתְגַּלֹּה
constr.	גְּלוֹת	הִגָּלוֹת	גַּלּוֹת	גֻּלּוֹת	הַגְלוֹת	הָגְלוֹת	הִתְגַּלּוֹת
Imp. m.	גְּלֵה	הִגָּלֵה	גַּלֵּה		הַגְלֵה		הִתְגַּלֵּה
f.	גְּלִי	הִגָּלִי	גַּלִּי	*wanting*	הַגְלִי	*wanting*	הִתְגַּלִּי
Plur. m.	גְּלוּ	הִגָּלוּ	גַּלּוּ		הַגְלוּ		הִתְגַּלּוּ
f.	גְּלֶינָה	הִגָּלֶינָה	גַּלֶּינָה		הַגְלֶינָה		הִתְגַּלֶּינָה
Fut. 3. m.	יִגְלֶה	יִגָּלֶה	יְגַלֶּה	יְגֻלֶּה	יַגְלֶה	יָגְלֶה	יִתְגַּלֶּה
3. f.	תִּגְלֶה	תִּגָּלֶה	תְּגַלֶּה	תְּגֻלֶּה	תַּגְלֶה	תָּגְלֶה	תִּתְגַּלֶּה
2. m.	תִּגְלֶה	תִּגָּלֶה	תְּגַלֶּה	תְּגֻלֶּה	תַּגְלֶה	תָּגְלֶה	תִּתְגַּלֶּה
2. f.	תִּגְלִי	תִּגָּלִי	תְּגַלִּי	תְּגֻלִּי	תַּגְלִי	תָּגְלִי	תִּתְגַּלִּי
1. c.	אֶגְלֶה	אֶגָּלֶה	אֲגַלֶּה	אֲגֻלֶּה	אַגְלֶה	אָגְלֶה	אֶתְגַּלֶּה
Plur. 3. m.	יִגְלוּ	יִגָּלוּ	יְגַלּוּ	יְגֻלּוּ	יַגְלוּ	יָגְלוּ	יִתְגַּלּוּ
3. f.	תִּגְלֶינָה	תִּגָּלֶינָה	תְּגַלֶּינָה	תְּגֻלֶּינָה	תַּגְלֶינָה	תָּגְלֶינָה	תִּתְגַּלֶּינָה
2. m.	תִּגְלוּ	תִּגָּלוּ	תְּגַלּוּ	תְּגֻלּוּ	תַּגְלוּ	תָּגְלוּ	תִּתְגַּלּוּ
2. f.	תִּגְלֶינָה	תִּגָּלֶינָה	תְּגַלֶּינָה	תְּגֻלֶּינָה	תַּגְלֶינָה	תָּגְלֶינָה	תִּתְגַּלֶּינָה
1. c.	נִגְלֶה	נִגָּלֶה	נְגַלֶּה	נְגֻלֶּה	נַגְלֶה	נָגְלֶה	נִתְגַּלֶּה
Fut. apoc.	יִגֶל	יִגָּל	יְגַל		יַגֶל		יִתְגַּל
Part. act.	גֹּלֶה	נִגְלֶה	מְגַלֶּה	מְגֻלֶּה	מַגְלֶה	מָגְלֶה	מִתְגַּלֶּה
pass.	גָּלוּי						

SECTION XXIV.—VERBS ל״ה. (Table N.)

REMARKS.

I. Kal.

1. Instead of the *pret.* 3 fem. גָּלְתָה, there occurs an Aramaic form like גְּלָת properly for גָּלְיַת,* after the form קְטָלַת, comp. § 8. rem. 3, and § 23. rem. 1, hence גְּלָאת, גְּלָת); e. g. עָשָׂת *she brings forth*, Le. 25. 21. The like inflexion is found in Hiphil and Hophal (see rem. 14).

2. The *inf. abs.* assumes also the form גָּלֹו, which probably stands for גָּלֹו (galov) with the radical ו (properly from the root גָּלַו*), and hence is derived the form גְּלֹות for גָּלֹת constr. st. E. g. רָאֹו *seeing*, Ge. 26. 28; בְּכֹו *weeping*, Is. 30. 19. As the *inf. constr.* occurs also, though seldom, a form like קְנֹה *to buy*, Pr. 16. 16; עָשֹׂה Ge. 50. 20; רְאֹו Ge. 48. 11; and, on the other hand, as the *inf. abs.* the form שָׁתֹות Is. 22. 13; רָאֹות Is. 42. 20 Keri. Another *inf. constr.* is רַאֲנָה *to see*, Eze. 28. 17 (like אַהֲבָה, comp. § 8. rem. 10, and § 13. rem 2).

3. The *apocope* of the *future* occasions the following changes :—

(a) The first radical letter most commonly receives the auxiliary vowel *Segol*, or, when the middle radical is a guttural, *Pattahh*, e. g. יֶגֶל for יִגְל; וַיֵּשַׁע *and he looked* (from יָשָׁע), וַיֶּמַח *and he destroyed* (from מָחָה).

(b) The *Hhirek* of the preformative is also sometimes lengthened into *Tseri* (because it is brought into an open syllable); the two forms, however, are commonly found in one and the same verb, as וַיִּפֶן *and he turned himself*, Ex. 2. 12; but in the 1 & 2 pers. וָאֵפֶן De. 9. 15; וַתֵּפֶן De. 2. 1; תֵּפֶן De. 9. 27; יֵרֶב and וַיִּרֶב *he was multiplied*, but also וַתֵּרֶב; the latter form occurs in תֵּתַע וַתֵּתַע Ge. 21. 14; Pr. 7. 25 (from תָּעָה); וַתֵּכַהּ Job 17. 7 (from כָּהָה); (וַתֵּמְלָא) Ge. 47. 13 (from לָהָה).

(c) In both these cases Segol is sometimes omitted, especially when the middle letter is an aspirate, as וַיִּשְׁבְּ *and he took captive*, Nu. 21. 1; וַיִּפְתְּ *and he persuaded*, Job 31. 27; וַיֵּבְךְּ וַתֵּבְךְּ *and he, she wept*; וַיַּרְדְּ Nu. 24. 19; אַל יֵשְׁטְ Pr. 7. 25 (comp. § 11.

r. 6). The verb רָאָה has the two forms, יֵרָא, תֵּרָא, וַתֵּרָא, and with conv. Vav also וַיַּרְא (the latter with Pattahh on account of ר).

(d) Examples of verbs which are *Pe guttural* as well as *Lamed He*: וַיַּעַן, וַיַּעַשׂ, and in pause אֶחֱזֶה *I see* (from חָזָה), Job 23. 9; וַיַּחַל *and he was sick*, 2 Ki. 1. 2 (from חָלָה). Sometimes, however, the punctuation of the first syllable is not affected by the guttural, as וַיַּחַר *and it was kindled* (from חָרָה), וַיַּחַן *and he encamped*, וַיַּחַד *and he rejoiced*.

(e) The verbs הָיָה *to be*, and חָיָה *to live*, which would properly have in the fut. apoc. יְהִי, יְחִי, change these forms into יְהִי and יְחִי (like the derivative פְּרִי for פַּרְיְ, § 27. V). Another example is תֵּשִׁי. De. 32. 18 (in pause for תֶּשִׁי, comp. § 35. r. 14), if directly derived from שָׁיָה. A perfectly Syriac form is יֶהֱוֵא Ec. 11. 3, for יִהְוֶה, ap. יְהוּ (from הָוָה *to be*).

4. In the *part. act.* the *fem.* frequently assumes the form of גֹּלְיָה, evidently from a masc. גֹּלִי for גֹּלִיְ* (after the form תֹּמִיךְ, see § 8. r. 19). E. g. פֹּרִיָּה *fruitful*, Ps. 128. 3; בֹּכִיָּה *weeping*, La. 1. 16; צֹפִיָּה *watching*, Pr. 31. 27; הֹמִיָּה *making a noise*, Pr. 7. 11; pl. אֹתִיּוֹת *coming, future things*, Is. 41. 23. (This is not to be confounded with the form גֹּלְיָה of rem. 5.)

The *part. pass.* is sometimes without י, as עָשֹׂ for עָשׂוּי (properly for עָשׂוּו, with moveable Vav*) *made*, Job 41. 25; צָפוּ for צָפוּו Job 15. 22; hence the pl. fem. עָשׂוֹת Is. 3. 16; נְטוּוֹת 1 Sa. 25. 18, in the Khethib; in the Keri, however, it is נְטִיּוֹת, עֲשׂיּוֹת; the form גָּלֹו, as it appears, was not recognised by the Masorites.

5. The original י* is sometimes retained and usually preceded by (ִ) before the afformatives beginning with a vowel, especially where, for any reason, emphasis rests upon the word, as in pause, or before pause, and before Nun parag. of the future. Pret. חָסָיוּ בֹו *they take refuge in him*, De. 32. 37; before pause, חָסָיָה Ps. 57. 2; נָטָיוּ Ps. 73. 2; imp. אִם תִּבְעָיוּן Is. 21. 12; Fut. יִשְׁלָיוּ Job 12. 6; יֶרְבְּיוּן Is. 21. 12; בְּעָיוּ שֻׁבוּ אֵתָיוּ

---

* The verbs ל״ה, like those of פ״י, properly embrace two different classes of the irregular verbs, viz. ל״י and ל״ו, which in Arabic are perfectly distinguished from each other, being actually written with י and ו. But in Hebrew the original י and ו have passed over into a feeble ה, in all those forms which end with the third radical, and which hence appear as verbs ל״ה as גָּלָה for גָּלַי, שָׁלָה for שָׁלַו (Ges. Gram. § 74).

De. 8. 13; יִרְוָיֻן Ps. 36. 9; in pause, יִשְׁתָּיוּן Ps. 78. 44, יֶחֱסָיוּן Ps. 36. 8; comp. Is. 26. 11; 41. 5; Job 3. 25, with ה parag. אֶהֱמָיָה *I mourn*, Ps. 77. 4. Part. עֹטְיָה *covered*, Ca. 1. 7.

6. A variation from the form תִּגְלֶינָה is תִּרְאֶנָּה Mi. 7. 10, תַּעֲנֶנָּה Ju. 5. 29, the termination of which must not be confounded with the suffix of the same form. Comp. § 21. rem. 13.

7. The ־ֶ, ־ֶי of the second syllable is but seldom written *defectively*, e. g. הָיִתָ for הָיִיתָ 2 Sa. 15. 33; בָּנִתִי 1 Ki. 8. 44; תַּעֲשֶׂנָה Job 5. 12.

II. NIPHAL.

8. In the *pret.* occurs also the form נַגְלִינוּ (instead of נִגְלִינוּ) 1 Sa. 14. 8; נִפְּתָ Ge. 24. 8. In pause is נְטָיו Nu. 24. 6, comp. rem. 5.

9. An anomalous form of the *inf. abs.* is נִגְלוֹת 2 Sa. 6. 20; כְּהִגָּלוֹת נִגְלוֹת אַחַד הָרֵקִים lit. *as uncovering uncovers himself one of the vain fellows;* where the second inf. is to be regarded as pleonastic, and this form is probably chosen to agree in sound with the termination of the preceding הִגָּלוֹת, comp. also rem. 2.

Another inf. abs., with the termination ־ֹה (which occurs also in Hiph.), is נֵחֹבָּה *to hide oneself*, Je. 49. 10, instead of נֵחָבֹה.

10. The *apocope* of the *future* occasions here no further changes, e. g. וָאֶפֵּת *and I was persuaded*, Je. 20. 7; וַיִּקַּר *and he met*, Nu. 23. 16. There is, however, יִמַּח Ps. 109. 13; וַיִּמַּח Ge. 7. 23, for יִמָּחֶה (from מָחָה).

III. PIEL.

11. In the *pret.* the second syllable has Hhirek in the greater number of examples, as דִּמִּיתִי, קִוִּיתִי, which is therefore adopted in the paradigm.

12. The *fut. apoc.* loses the Dagesh forte of the second radical, e. g. וַיְצַו *and he commanded;* יְקַו *let him look for*, Job 3. 9. Hithp. וַיִּתְגַּל *and he uncovered himself*, Ge. 9. 21. In but few instances the vowel is lengthened, as וַיְתָו, *and he made marks*, 1 Sa. 21. 14; יִתְאָו *he desires*, Ps. 45. 12.

The *apocope* occurs also in the *imp.* of Piel and Hithp., as דַם for דַּמֵּה *be silent*, Am. 6. 10; הִתְחָל *feign thyself sick*, 2 Sa. 13. 5; with ר as the second radical הִתְנַּר (for עֻנָּה = הִתְנַּרָה) De. 2. 24.

13. Examples where the original י has been retained (comp. rem. 5): imp. דַּלְיוּ* prop. *draw off*, i. e. *take away*, Pr. 26. 7. Fut. תְּדַמְיוּנִי Is. 40. 25; יְכַסְיוּמוּ *they cover them*, Ex. 15. 5; אַרְוֶךָ by transp. for אֶרְוֵךָ *I will water thee*, Is. 16. 9.

IV. HIPHIL.

14. In the *pret.* the forms הִגְלִיתָ and הִגְלִתָ are about equally common; before suffixes the latter is used as being somewhat shorter than the other.

For the 3 pers. fem. there occurs also the Aramaic form of ־ת (as in Kal), e. g. הִרְצָת Le. 26. 34; הֶגְלָאת Eze. 24. 12. Hoph. הָגְלָת Je. 13. 19.

15. The Tseri of the *inf. abs.* is the regular vowel (as הַגְלֵה), to this corresponds the inf. abs. of Hoph., as הָפְדֵּה Le. 19. 20 (comp. rem. 20).

The verb רָבָה *to be much* or *many*, has three forms of the infinitive, viz. הַרְבֵּה *much* (used adverbially), הַרְבָּה used when the inf. is pleonastic, and הַרְבּוֹת the inf. constr.

16. The *fut. apoc.* either remains a monosyllabic like יֵרְדְּ *that he may have dominion over*, Is. 41. 2; יַפְתְּ *may he enlarge*, Ge. 9. 27, or it takes the helping vowel as in יֶגֶל for which, however, is invariably substituted the form יַגֶל (comp. § 35. No. 1), as וַיֶּגֶל 2 Ki. 18. 11; יֶפֶר *he makes fruitful*, Ps. 105. 24. Examples with gutturals: וַיַּתַע *he made to err*, 2 Ch. 33. 9; אַל תֶּמַח Ne. 13. 14; when the first radical is a guttural, like וַיֶּעַל, יַעַל Eze. 14. 7; Nu. 23. 2. The latter forms can be distinguished from the *fut. Kal* only by the context.

17. The *imp. apoc.* has invariably the auxiliary vowel, hence הֶרֶב *increase*, for הַרְבְּ; הֶרֶף *let alone*, for הַרְפֵּה, הַרְףְּ De. 9. 14; הַעַל for הַעֲלֵה, Ex. 33. 12.

18. In the Aramaic the *preterite* (as in all conjugations) terminates in ־ִי, the *fut.* in ־ֵה. The form with ־ִי is found also in the Hebrew with the pret. and future. Pret. הֶחֱלִי for הֶחֱלָה *he made sick*

---

* This seems the only way of accounting for this form, if derived from דָּלָה. Prof. Lee, who takes it as the *pret.* of Kal, does not sufficiently account for the form; for we should then expect דָּלְיוּ. Gesenius has finally declared himself in favour of the Rabbinic opinion, that דַּלְיוּ stands for דְּלָלוּ, comp. his Man. and Thes. under דָּלַל.

Is. 53. 10; pl. הִמְסִיו *they caused to faint*, Jos. 14. 8 (which is quite Aramaic, comp. רְמִיו Da. 3. 21; הֵיתִיו Da. 5. 3). Fut. וַתִּמְזֵנִי Je. 3. 6; תָּמְחִי Je. 18. 23, for תִּמְחֶה (masc.).

V. ARAMAISMS.

19. In the same manner as the verbs ל״א have occasionally some forms inflected after the analogy of ל״ה (§ 23. rem. 8—11), so it happens, *vice versâ*, that the latter borrow forms from the former, though not so frequently, according to the following division :—

(*a*) The ה is retained and the punctuation alone of ל״א is adopted, e. g. Kal fut. אֶשְׁעָה *I will have respect to*, for אֶשְׁעֶה, Ps. 119. 117; תִּכְלָה for תִּכְלֶה 1 Ki. 17. 14, comp. Da. 10. 14. Niph. part. יוֹם נַחְלָה, for נַחְלֶה *a grievous day*, Is. 17. 11,* and defective אָתָנוּ *we come*, Je. 3. 22.

(*b*) The א is adopted and the punctuation of ל״ה is retained, e. g. Kal pret. רָצָאתִי *I delight*, Eze. 43. 27; fut. יִשְׁנָא *it is changed*, La. 4. 1; וַיֶּחֱלָא *he became sick*, 2 Ch. 16. 12; inf. נְשֹׁא for נְשֹׁה, *to forget*, Je. 23. 39. Piel שִׁנָּא 2 Ki. 25. 29. Pual יְשֻׁנֶּא Ec. 8. 1. Comp. also וַיֹּראוּ הַמֹּראִים *and the archers shot*, 2 Sa. 11. 24.

(*c*) The consonant and the vowels of ל״א are adopted, as תְּלָאוּם *they hanged them*, 2 Sa. 21. 12; יַפְרִיא for יַפְרֶה *he is fruitful*, Ho. 13. 15. (But here we may suppose roots תָּלָא and פָּרָא i. q. תָּלָה and פָּרָה, comp. Gesenius' Manuale.)

20. In the Aramaic, where the verbs ל״א and ל״ה flow into one another, both classes terminate, in the fut. and part. of all the conjugations, in the Syriac in ָא־, in the Chald. in ִי־. As intimations of this mode of formation we are to regard those forms of the inf., imp. and fut. in ֵה־, less frequently ָא־ and ֵי־, which are found in Hebrew also. Inf. הֱיֵה Eze. 21. 15. Imp. הֱוֵא *be thou*, Job 37. 6. Fut. תִּהְיֶה Je. 17. 17; תֹּבֵא for תֹּאבֶה *thou wilt*, Pr. 1. 10; וַיֵּתֵא for וַיֶּאֱתָה *he came*, De. 33. 21. Piel inf. עַנֵּה Ex.

22. 22; imp. כַּלֵּה 1 Sa. 3. 12; 2 Ch. 24. 10; חַפִּי Ho. 6. 9; fut. תְּגַלֵּה Le. 18. 7. Hiph. (comp. rem. 15). Hoph. הָפְדֵה Le. 19. 20.

VI. FORMS WITH SUFFIXES.

21. The annexing of the suffixes to the verbs ל״ה occasions various changes, viz. :—

(*a*) In all the forms which end in ה, the ה is dropped with the preceding vowel. E. g. עָנַנִי *he answered me*, Ps. 118. 5, צִוְּךָ *he has commanded thee*, De. 6. 17;† קָנֶךָ *he has bought thee*, De. 32. 6; fut. יַעַנְךָ Ps. 20. 2. Piel אַכְלְךָ for אֲכַלֶּךָ *I consume thee*, Ex. 33. 3 (comp. Chald. מָנִי for מַנִּי Ezr. 7. 25). Hiph. הֶעֱלָךְ Ne. 9. 18; seldom fut. like יִתְךָ *he shall take thee away*, Ps. 52. 7.

(*b*) Very seldom does ֵי־ take the place of ֶה־, ֵה־, as חַיֵּיהוּ *revive it*, Hab. 3. 2; יְחַיֵּנוּ Ho. 6. 2; הַכֵּינִי *smite me*, 1 Ki. 20. 35; אַמְאִיהֶם (Hiph. fut. from פָּאָה) De. 32. 26, perhaps also נֹטֵיהֶם Is. 42. 5, in reference to Jehovah, which may be regarded as a plural.

(*c*) The *pret*. 3 pers. sing. fem. takes invariably the form נָּלָת. E. g. רָאָתֶךָ Job 33. 4; עֲשָׂתְנִי Job 42. 5; צִוַּתָּה Zec. 5. 4; כְּלַתּוּ for כָּלְתָה Ps. 44. 16; כְּסָתְנִי Ru. 3. 6; הֶעֱלָתָם Jos. 2. 6.

VII. PILEL (comp. § 6. No. 2).

22. This conjugation with its reflexion occurs in three verbs ל״ה, where the third radical, which the conjugation requires to be doubled, appears under the form וֹ, as

נָאָה (*to be comely*) in Kal not used, Pil. נַאֲוָה, contracted נָאוָה, pl. נָאווּ Ca. 1. 5; 2. 14. Deriv. adj. נָאוֶה.

מָחָה, in Kal not used, Pil. part. מְטַחֲוֵי קֶשֶׁת *archers*, Ge. 21. 16.

שָׁחָה *to bow down* (usual in Kal and Hiph.), Pil. שַׁחֲוָה hence Hithpal. הִשְׁתַּחֲוָה (comp. § 9 & 12. rem. 3), fut. יִשְׁתַּחֲוֶה, apoc. יִשְׁתַּחוּ for יִשְׁתַּחַו (analogous with יְהִי for יִהְיֶה). Inf. Chald. הִשְׁתַּחֲוָיָה 2 Ki. 5. 18.

---

* Unless we prefer to take נַחְלָה (with Gesenius, comp. his Manuale) as a substantive, and render *day of possession*, i. e. day of harvest.

† The form ־ךָ for the masc. *thy*, which is seldom found with other verbs (§ 2. rem 2), is here somewhat more usual, e. g. עָנָךְ Is. 30. 19; Je. 23. 37.

SECTION XXV.—VERBS DOUBLY ANOMALOUS.

1. Such is the designation of verbs which have **two** radical letters affected by the anomalies which are exhibited in the paradigms of irregular verbs. These verbs exhibit no new changes; and even in cases where two anomalies might occur, usage must teach whether the verb is actually subject to both or but one of them, or, as it sometimes happens, to neither.

Thus from נָדַד (*to flee*) are formed יִדֹּד Na. 3. 7; יַדֹּד Ge. 31. 40 (after the analogy of verb פ״צ); Hiph. הַנַּד (after ע״ע); Hoph. הֻנַּד, but fut. יֻדַּד (after פ״ן).

Thus the verbs פ״ן and ע״ו, as נוד, נוע, are irregular only in respect to the middle radical letter, not in respect to the Nun.

2. The following are examples of doubly anomalous verbs, and of difficult forms derived from them :—

(*a*) Verbs פ״ן and ל״א, as

נָשָׂא (*to bear, carry*) Kal imp. שָׂא; inf. constr. שְׂאֵת (for שְׂאֵאת), also שֵׂאת, with suff. שְׂאֵתִי; fut. תִּשֶּׂנָה (for תִּשְׂאֶנָה) Ru. 1. 14.

נָשָׁא (*to deceive*) Hiph. fut. יַשִּׁי (for יַשִּׁיא) Ps. 55. 16 Keri.

(*b*) Verbs פ״ן and ל״ה :

נָטָה (*to bow, incline*) Kal fut. יִטֶּה, apoc. יֵט Zep. 2. 12; fem. תֵּט Ps. 4. 5, 27; Hiph. imp. הַטֵּה, apoc. הַט Ps. 17. 6; fut. יַטֶּה, apoc. וַיֵּט 2 Sa. 19. 15; 1 pers. אַט Job 23. 11; וָאַט Je. 15. 6; 2 pers. אַל תַּט Ps. 27. 9; with suff. יַטֶּךָ.

נָכָה (*to smite*) Hiph. הִכָּה; inf. הַכּוֹת; imp. הַכֵּה, apoc. הַךְ Ex. 8. 12; fut. יַכֶּה, apoc. יַךְ Ho. 14. 6; 1 pers. וָאַךְ Ex. 9. 15, with suff. יַכּוּ 2 Sa. 14. 6; יַכֶּכָּה Ps. 121. 6.

נָזָה (*to sprinkle*) Kal fut. apoc. יֵז Is. 63. 3; וַיֵּז 2 Ki. 9. 33. Hiph. fut. apoc. וַיַּז Le. 8. 11, 30.

(*c*) Verbs פ״א and ל״ה, as

אָתָה (*to come*) Kal pret. אָתָנוּ Je. 3. 22; imp. אֱתָיוּ (for אֱתָיְוּ, אֵתוּ, אֱתָיוּ, § 19. rem. 6, & § 24. rem. 5) Is. 21. 12; 56. 9; fut. וַיֵּתָא (for וַיֶּאְתָה, § 19. rem. 3) De. 33. 21; apoc. וַיֵּאת (for וַיֶּאֱתֶה, וַיֶּאְתָה § 19. rem. 3). Hiph. imp. הֵתָיוּ (for הֶאֱתָיוּ, § 19. rem. 8) Is. 21. 14.

אָלָה (*to swear*) Hiph. fut. ap. וַיֹּאֶל (from יַאֲלֶה, § 24. rem. 3) 1 Sa. 14. 24.

אָפָה (*to bake*) Kal imp. אֱפוּ (for אֶאֱפוּ § 19. rem. 6) Ex. 16. 23; וַתֹּאפֵהוּ (for וַתֶּאֱפֵהוּ § 19. r. 5) 1 Sa. 28. 24.

(*d*) Verbs פ״י and ל״א, as

יָצָא (*to go out*) Kal inf. צֵאת (for צְאֵת, comp. § 23 rem. 4) ; imp. צֵא, Hiph. הוֹצִיא.

(*e*) Verbs פ״י and ל״ה :

יָדָה (*to throw*, Hiph. *to confess*) Piel fut. וַיַּדּוּ (for וַיַּיְדוּ § 20. rem. 8) La. 3. 53. Hiph. fut. אוֹדֶךָ, with suff. אוֹדֶךָ Ps. 35. 18; אוֹדְךָ Ps. 30. 13, and ה retained יְהוֹדֶךָ (§ 20. rem. 10).

יָנָה (*to oppress*) Kal fut. with suff. יוֹנֵם Ps. 74. 8. Hiph. הוֹנָה fut. with suff. תּוֹנֵנוּ De. 23. 17; part מוֹנַיִךְ Is. 49. 26.

יָפָה (*to be fair*) Kal fut. apoc. וַיְּיִף (fr. יִיְפֶה) Eze. 31. 7. Unusual conj. Pu. יָפְיָפִיתָ Ps. 45. 3, see § 6. No. 9.

יָרָה (*to throw*, Hiph. *to show, instruct*) Kal imp. יְרוּ; inf. יְרוֹת; fut. with suff. יִירָם Nu. 21. 30. Hiph. הוֹרָה; inf. הוֹרוֹת; fut. יוֹרֶה, apoc. וַיּוֹר 2 Ki. 13. 17, with suff. תּוֹרֵךְ Ps. 45. 5; Job 12. 7, 8; יֹרֻנוּ Ps. 25. 12.

(*f*) Verbs ע״ו and ל״א, as

בּוֹא (*to come*) Kal pret. בָּא, pl. בָּאנוּ 1 Sa. 25. 8 ; inf. בּוֹא ; fut. יָבוֹא, once וַיָּבֹא 1 Ki. 2. 12 Kheth. Hiph. הֵבִיא, 2 pers. הֵבֵאתָ ; fut. יָבִיא, 1 pers. אָבִי for אָבִיא 1 Ki. 21. 29 ; Mi. 1. 15 ; imp. הָבֵא once הָבִי Ru. 3. 15.

נוּא Hiph. הֵנִיא (*to withhold, refuse*) fut. יָנִי for יָנִיא Ps. 141. 5.

(*g*) One verb ע״ע and ע״י is

חָיָה=חַיּ (*to live*) only in the pret. חַי, in such connection where it cannot be the adj. חַי (*living*), e.g. Ge. 5. 5 ; 11. 12, 14 ; 25. 7.

REM. A few other anomalies must be mentioned here, which are occasioned by the verbs ל״ן and ל״ת, of which ן and ת are assimilated with the afformatives. Such are : לַנּוּ Ju. 19. 13, for לַנְנוּ (from לון) ; from מות (*to die*), מַתָּה מַתִּי *thou diest, I die*, Eze. 28. 8, for מַתְתָּה מַתְתִּי Ge. 19. 19. Pil. מוֹתַתִּי *I put to death* 2 Sa. 1. 16. Hiph. הֵמַתָּ הֵמַתָּה *thou puttest, he put to death*, with suff. הֲמִיתִיו 1 Sa. 17. 35, with the *mater lexionis* in Kheth., for הֲמִתִּיו Keri.

Finally, the anomaly of the verb יָלַד, viz. יְלֹד, inf. לֶדֶת, contracted לַת 1 Sa. 4. 19.

SECTION XXVI.—NOUNS DERIVED FROM THE REGULAR VERB.

We distinguish here—

I. Forms originally Participles, and Participial Nouns, from Kal.

1. קָטָל, *fem.* קְטָלָה the most simple participial form of verbs *middle A* (comp. § 8. r. 1); in use as a participle only in verbs ע״י (e. g. קָם for קָוַם). It is most frequently employed as an adjective expressing *quality*, as חָכָם *wise*, חָדָשׁ *new*, יָקָר *precious*, יָשָׁר *straight*, נָבָל *foolish*. It occurs, however, also as an infinitive form (No. 12).

2. קָטֵל, *fem.* קְטֵלָה, seldom קְטֶלֶת. Part. of verbs *middle E* (§ 8. r. 1), is likewise the form of adjectives of quality, e. g. זָקֵן *old, old man*, יָבֵשׁ *dry*. The Tseri is sometimes *immutable*, and the form is then related to No. 5, e. g. אָבֵל *mourning* (in other dialects אביל), *fem.* גְּזֵלָה *that which is plundered*.

3. קָטֹל and קָטוֹל (with Hholem *immutable*), *fem.* קְטֹלָה, Part. of verbs *middle O*; e. g. יָגֹר *fearing*, יָקֹשׁ *fowler*; then frequently as an adjective, even when no preterite with Hholem is found, as גָּדוֹל *great*, רָחוֹק *far*, עָשׁוֹק=עָשֵׁק *oppressor* (comp. No. 21).

4. קֹטֵל, קֹטֶל, *fem.* קֹטֶלֶת, קֹטְלָה, the usual participial form of transitive verbs; e. g. אֹיֵב *enemy*, יוֹנֵק *suckling*, hence of the instrument by which the action is performed, as חֹרֵשׁ *a cutting instrument, a tool*. A feminine with collective signification is אֹרְחָה *caravan*.

5. קָטוּל and קָטִיל passive participles of Kal, the latter (Chaldaizing) form employed rather as a substantive, like the Greek verbals in τός, e. g. אָסוּר *imprisoned*, מָשׁוּחַ *anointed*, אָסִיר *prisoner*, מָשִׁיחַ *one anointed*.

In intransitive verbs, also with an active signification, as צָעִיר *small*, עָצוּם *strong*. Some words of this form indicate the *time* of the action, as קָצִיר *time of harvest*, חָרִישׁ *time of ploughing*. The feminines and the plurals are apt to take the abstract signification, as יְשׁוּעָה *deliverance* (*the being delivered*), חֲנֻטִים *the act of embalming*.

6. קַטָּל (Arab. פַטָּאל) with Kamets *immutable* in the Arabic, the usual intensive form of the participle, hence in the Hebrew expresses what is habitual,

e. g. נַגָּח *apt to butt*, חַטָּא *sinner* (different from חֹטֵא *sinning*), גַּנָּב *thief*; so of occupation, trades, e. g. טַבָּח *cook*, חָרָשׁ (for חַרָּשׁ) *smith*. Here, again, the feminine often takes the abstract signification, as חַטָּאת (for חַטָּאַת) *sinfulness, sin*. Such intensive forms are also the three following.

7. קַטּוּל and קַטִּיל, of which forms are most adjectives in the Chaldee, צַדִּיק *righteous*, אַבִּיר *strong*, חַנּוּן *compassionate*. In Hebrew from intransitive verbs alone.

8. קָטוֹל, as יְסוֹר *censurer*, שִׁכּוֹר *one drunken*, נִבּוֹר *strong one, hero*; rarely in a passive sense, יִלּוֹד *born*, אִיּוֹב *proper name* (*persecuted*).

9. קִטֵּל indicates very great intensity, often excessive, so as to become a fault and a defect; e. g. קֵרֵחַ, *bald-headed*, אִלֵּם *dumb*, עִוֵּר *blind*, פִּסֵּחַ *lame*, חֵרֵשׁ *deaf*. The abstract signification is found in the feminine, as עִוֶּרֶת *blindness*.

II. Forms which were originally infinitives of Kal.*

10. קְטֹל, קְטָל, קְטֵל (with *mutable* vowels) the simplest forms of the infinitive, of which the first and last are employed in the verb (§ 8. rem. 9). They seldom occur as nominal forms, e. g. גְּבַר *man*, פְּאָר *ornament*, צְחֹק *laughter*. Instead of these, the three following—

11. קֶטֶל, קֵטֶל, קֹטֶל, called Segolate forms, are the more frequent; e. g. מֶלֶךְ *king* (for מַלְךְ, מַלֶךְ), סֵפֶר (for סִפְר) *book*, קֹדֶשׁ (for קֻדְשׁ) *holiness*. These have the characteristic vowel in the first syllable, and the auxiliary vowel Segol in the second. When the second or third radical letter is a guttural, *Pattahh* is used instead of *Segol*, as זֶרַע *seed*, נֶצַח *eternity*, פֹּעַל *work*. Examples of feminines: מַלְכָּה *queen*, יִרְאָה *fear*, עֶזְרָה *help*, חָכְמָה *wisdom*.

In masculines as well as feminines the *abstract* is the prevailing signification, and is the original one even in cases where the *concrete* occurs; e. g. מֶלֶךְ and מַלְכָּה *prop. royalty*; נַעַר † *a youth* (*prop. the season of youth*, comp. in Eng. *youth* and *a youth*); בַּעַר *brutish* (*prop. brutishness*). For the abstract in such cases another form is employed, as מַלְכוּת *royalty*, נֹעַר *youth*.

---

* All these forms are found, *mutatis mutandis*, in the Arabic as infinitives, or the so called *nomina actionis*.

† As there is a tendency to employ abstract terms for names of offices, e. g. פֶּחָה *governor* (prop. *office of governor*, comp. the English *lordship*).

12. קְטָל, like No. 1, and קְטֵל, *fem.* קְטָלָה, often from verbs *middle E*, with the abstract signification, e. g. רָעֵב *hunger*, אָשָׁם *guilt*, along with the concretes of the form No. 2 (רָעֵב *hungry*, אָשֵׁם *guilty*), very frequent in the feminine, as צְדָקָה *righteousness*.

13. קְטֹל (for קְטָאל, קְטֹל, (for קְטִיל), קָטִיל, קָטוֹל, קָטוּל, with an *immutable* vowel between the second and third radical, as כְּתָב *book*, כְּאָב *pain*, שָׁבִיל *way*, חֲלוֹם *dream*, זְבוּל *habitation;* sometimes also with prosthetic Aleph as אַכְזָב (prop. *deception*), *deceitful stream,* i. e. whose waters fail in the summer; אֶפְרֹחַ *brood*. The corresponding feminines will suggest themselves; but the forms קְטִילָה, קְטוּלָה coincide with the feminines of No. 5.

14. מִקְטָל, the Chaldee form of the infinitive, e. g. מִשְׁפָּט *judgment*. Related forms are מִזְמוֹר *song*, מַחְמָד *desire*, מַלְקוֹחַ *booty*, מְלָאכָה *kingdom*, מַשְׂכֹּרֶת *wages*. This form indicates, not only the action itself, but also often the place of the action, as מִזְבֵּחַ *altar*, מִדְבָּר *a place of driving,* i. e. to which cattle are driven, whence *a desert*.

15. קִטָּלוֹן, קִטָּלָן, and other similar forms with the terminations וֹן & ־ָן, which are generally appended to the Segolates, as חֶשְׁבּוֹן *reckoning* (from חָשַׁב), קָרְבָּן *offering* (immediately from קֹרֶב); but there are also forms like זִכָּרוֹן *remembrance*.

16. With the feminine termination וּת appended to the Segolate form, e. g. רְפָאוּת *healing*. In the Syriac this is the usual termination of the infinitive. The ת is properly the sign of the feminine, and the masculine form would be רְפָא (like עִבְרִי, עִבְרִית).

III. *Participles of the derived conjugations.*

17. From Niph. נִקְטָל, as נִפְלָאוֹת *wonders*.

18. 19. From *Piel* and *Hiph.;* e. g. מְזַמֶּרֶת *snuffers*, מַזְמֵרָה *pruning-knife*.

20. From *Poel*, as חוֹתָם *signet-ring*, prop. *that which seals*.

21. From *Pil.*, קְטֹל, *fem.* קְטֹלָה; and 22. קְטַלָל for the most part adjectives of colour, as אָדֹם *fem.* אֲדֻמָּה *red*, רַעֲנָן *green*.

23. קְטַלְטַל, קְטַלְטֹל, adjectives with a *diminutive* signification, as אֲדַמְדָּם *reddish*, שְׁחַרְחֹר *blackish;* hence in a contemptuous sense (like *miser*, *misellus*), as אֲסַפְסֻף *collected rabble* (with the passive form, for אָסוּף).

IV. *Infinitives of the derived conjugations.*

24. From Niph., as נִפְתּוּלִים *struggles*.

25. From *Piel*, like נַפֵּץ *dispersion*, more frequently in the fem., as בַּקָּשָׁה *request*, with Kamets *immutable*.

26. קַטּוֹל, and 27. תַּקְטִיל, תַּקְטוּל, likewise infinitives of *Piel* (the latter very common in the Arabic); e. g. חִבּוּק *folding of the hands*, תַּגְמוּל *benefit*, תַּכְרִיךְ *mantle*.

28. From *Hiph.*, like אַזְכָּרָה *remembrance-offering*, הַשְׁמָעוּת *annunciation* (with Kamets *immutable*), an Aramaic infinitive.

29. From *Hithpa.* הִתְיַחֵשׂ *register*.

30. From *Poel*, like הוֹלֵלָה *folly*, and 31. like קִיטוֹר *smoke*, the latter form common in Arabic.

32. From *Pil.*, אֲפֻדָּה *a putting on*, and 33, נַאֲפוּף *adultery*.

34. פְּקַחְקוֹחַ *opening*, inf. of No. 23.

35. שְׁקַטֵל, e. g. שַׁלְהֶבֶת *flame* (comp. § 7. No. 6).

36. Quadriliterals, like סָלְעָם *locust*.

SECTION XXVII.—NOUNS DERIVED FROM THE IRREGULAR VERBS.

The formation of these is perfectly analagous to that of the regular verb, and whatever is differently modified is caused merely by the peculiar structure of these verbs. We shall therefore follow the preceding order, and exhibit such verbs and forms only in which the irregularity has been of some important influence.

I. FROM VERBS פ״ן.

Connected with the *infinitive* of Kal 14. מַתָּן *gift*,

מַגֵּפָה *overthrow;* of Hiph. 28. הַצָּלָה *deliverance*. The noun מַדָּע *knowledge* from יָדַע; comp. § 20. 16.

II. FROM VERBS ע״ע.

From the *part.* of Kal—1. תָּם *upright* (like קְטֵל) more frequently with *Pattahh* (to indicate the sharpening of the syllable), דַּל *abject*, רַב *much*, fem. דַּלָּה, תַּמָּה. 2. מֵחַ *fat*. From the inf. 10. 11. בַּז *booty*, חֵן *favour*, חֹק *law*, fem. מִלָּה *word*, חֻקָּה *law*. 14. מָעוֹז *fastness* מֵסַב *that which surrounds anything,* fem.

מְגִלָּה *roll*. The form מֵסַב sometimes, by retraction of the tone, becomes a Segolate form, as מֵמֶר *bitterness*, מֹרֶךְ *timidity* (from רָכַךְ). 22. קַלְקַל *contemned*, עֲרוֹר *naked* (a collateral form of Pilpel). 27. תְּהִלָּה *praise*, תְּפִלָּה *prayer*, with the Segolate form also תֶּמֶס *a melting away* (from מָסַס), תֹּרֶן *mast* (from רָנַן *to shout*). From the unfrequent conjugation Pilpel (§ 6. No. 4), גַּלְגַּל *wheel*, from גָּלַל *to roll*.

III. From Verbs פ"וֹ and פ"י.

The *participial* forms are regular. Forms originally *infinitives* are—10. דֵּעַ, fem. דֵּעָה, דַּעַת *knowledge*, עֵצָה *counsel*. 13. סוֹד for יְסוֹד *divan*. 14. מוֹרָא *fear*, מוֹקֵשׁ *snare*, מוֹלֶדֶת *birth*, מוּסָר *punishment*; and from a verb properly פ"י, מֵיטָב *the best*. 27. תּוֹשָׁב *inhabitant*, תּוֹלֶדֶת *generation*, תֵּימָן *the south*.

IV. From Verbs ע"וֹ and ע"י.

Participles: 1. זָר *foreign*. 2. גֵּר *stranger*, עֵדָה *a witness, testimony*. 3. טוֹב *good*, טוֹבָה *what is good*. *Infinitives:* 11. the different Segolate forms, as מָוֶת *death*, and בַּיִת *house*, קוֹל *voice*, רוּחַ *spirit*, and in the fem. בֹּשֶׁת, עוֹלָה. 14. מָקוֹם *place*, מָנוֹחַ, fem. מְנוּחָה *rest*, also מִשּׁוֹט *oar* (from שׁוּט). 27. תְּבוּנָה *intelligence*, תְּעוּדָה *testimony*, תָּמִיד *continuance*. 28. הֲנָחָה *rest*.

> Rem. A וֹ in one of these nouns is not sufficient warrant to limit its derivation to ע"וֹ, nor is י sufficient to limit it to ע"י, since each of these classes sometimes borrow forms from the other, e. g. תְּבוּנָה from בִּין.

V. From Verbs ל"ה.

Participles: 2. יָפֶה *fair*, קָשֶׁה *hard*, fem. יָפָה, קָשָׁה.

Some lose ה‑, as תְּוֹ *sign*, for תְּוָה. 4. רֹאֶה *seer*, fem. עֹלָה *burnt-offering*. 5. כָּסוּי *covering*, נָקִי *pure*, עָנִי *poor*. Originally *infinitives:* 11. the Segolates in different forms, not often with ה retained, as בְּכֶה *a weeping*, רֵעֶה *friend*, חֹזֶה, רֹאֶה *vision, revelation*, commonly without it, as רֵעַ (for רְעֶה), or with the original י or וֹ, which then becomes quiescent in Hhirek (comp. on יְהִי § 24. rem. 3), e. g. פְּרִי *fruit*, חֳלִי *sickness*, בֹּהוּ *waste*, and in the masc. seldom *moveable*, as קָצוּ *end*, but always in the fem. עֲנָוָה *humility*, לִוְיָה *garland*. 13. סְתָו *winter*, שְׁתִי fem. שְׁתִיָּה *a drinking*, fem. מְנָת (for מְנָאת, מְנָאָת) *part*, חֲצוֹת *the midst*, שְׁבוּת *captivity*. 14. מִקְנָה *possessions*, מַרְאֶה *appearance*; fem. מִצְוָה *command*. Apocopated form מַעַל for מַעֲלֶה. 15. קִנְיָן *wealth*, כִּלָּיוֹן *destruction*. 27. תַּבְנִית *structure*, תַּרְבּוּת *brood*, also perh. תֶּבֶן (for תִּבְנֶה) *straw*. 28. אֶשֶׁךְ *testicle*, for אַשְׁכָה from שָׁכָה.

VI. From Doubly Anomalous Verbs.

We exhibit only some cases of special difficulty:—

1. From פ"ן and ל"א שֵׂת for שְׂאֵת, from נָשָׂא.
2. From פ"י and ל"ה תּוֹרָה *precept, law*, מוֹפֵת *sign*, perh. from יָפָה; but see the analysis.
3. From ע"א and ל"ה שֵׂת Nu.24.17, from שָׁאָה for שְׂאֵת.
4. From ע"ו and ל"ה אִי *island*, from אָוָה *to dwell*, for אֲנִי; אוֹת *sign*, for אָוָה from אָוָה; קַו *cord*, from קָוָה; תָּא *chamber*, for תָּו from תָּוָה *to dwell*, גּוֹי *people*, from גָּוָה.

> The root is also often obscured by contraction of Nun, Daleth, He, e. g. גַּת *wine-press*, for גַּנַת; אַף *anger*, for אֶנֶף; יַנֶּפֶת (from יָנַף); זוּ for זְהַר *brightness*, זֶה for זְהֶה (from זָהָה); אַדְרֶת *coulter*, for אַדֶרֶת.

SECTION XXVIII.—THE VOWEL-CHANGES OF NOUNS.*

1. The consideration of the *cases* of the noun does not belong to this part of Hebrew Grammar,† but to the syntax, because the cases do not at all affect the inflexion of the noun, as they are merely indicated by prepositions without any change of the *form* of the word itself. On the contrary, the connection of the noun with suffixes—with the feminine, dual and plural terminations—or with a noun following in the genitive, produces numerous changes in its form, and thus originates another species of declension. The theory of this peculiar, but important, system of inflexion can be displayed conspicuously only by a full exhibition of paradigms, inasmuch as the term declension is used in Hebrew Grammar, with a meaning differing considerably from that it bears in the Grammar of the Greek and Latin languages.‡

---

* The adjective entirely agrees in form with the substantive, so that in treating of the declension of nouns, adjectives are included.

† This work having especially the etymology of words alone for its object.

‡ In these latter, the term *declension* (κλίσις) properly denotes the variation of the ground-form by cases (casus, πτώσεις). We may, however, be permitted to retain the term *declension*, though it does not properly express the mode of inflexion of Hebrew nouns just as the term *conjugation* is employed, though not in its ordinary sense (Gesen. Gram. 78. 2).

These vowel-changes are caused (*a*) by a noun following in the genitive ; (*b*) by the suffixes ; (*c*) by the dual and plural terminations ; to which is added, again, the effect of a genitive following, or suffix.

2. The tone in all these cases is moved forward more or less, or even thrown upon the following word. We here distinguish three cases, viz. :—

(*a*) *When the tone is moved forward only one place.* This is the case when the appendage to the noun is either monosyllabic, or at least has the tone on the penultima, and likewise begins with a vowel. Such are (1) the terminations for the plural and dual (‍יִם‍ֹ; ‍ַיִם‍, ‍וֹת‍); (2) the light suffixes for the singular nouns (‍כֶם‍, ‍ָם‍; ‍ֶנִי‍; ‍וֹ‍, ‍ָךְ‍, ‍ֶךָ‍, ‍ָהּ‍, ‍ָה‍, ‍ְךָ‍; ‍ִי‍; ‍מוֹ‍); (3) the light suffixes for the plural nouns (‍ֵ‍ךָ‍, ‍ַיִךְ‍, ‍יו‍, ‍ֶיהָ‍, ‍יָה‍; ‍ֵנוּ‍, ‍ֵ‍ימוֹ‍). In this case, generally, only one of two mutable vowels in the noun is dropped, e. g. from דָּבָר—דְּבָרִים, דְּבָרִי; in a few forms the second only is dropped, e. g. אֹיֵב—אֹיְבִים, or the ground-form of the word, which, in the leading form, has undergone some change, appears again, as from מֶלֶךְ (for מַלְכִּי)—מַלְכִּי.

(*b*) *When the tone is moved forward two places,* as in the plural *constr. st.,* and when the *grave* suffixes are appended to the plural (‍ֵיכֶם‍, ‍ֵיהֶם‍, ‍ֵיהֶן‍, ‍ֵיהֶן‍).

In this case both vowels, if mutable, are dropped, as דִּבְרֵי הָעָם *words of the people* ; דִּבְרֵיכֶם *your words,* דִּבְרֵיהֶם *their words.*

(*c*) When the suffix begins with a consonant without a union-vowel, and forms a syllable by itself, as the suffixes of the singular, as ‍ךָ‍, ‍הֶן‍, ‍הֶם‍, ‍כֶן‍, ‍כֶם‍ (more commonly ‍כֶם‍, ‍‍ךְ‍). Of these the first is a light suffix, and regularly affects the tone in just the same manner, as ‍ָךְ‍, וֹ, e. g. זְקֵנְךָ, דְּבָרְךָ, דָּמְךָ. The others are grave suffixes, and have more effect in shortening the vowels, as דְּבַרְכֶם, &c. A similar effect is seen in the *constr. st.* of the singular number, as חֲצַר הַבַּיִת ; דְּבַר אֱלֹהִים (from חָצֵר).

The application of these three cases to the different forms of the masculine noun is exhibited in the nine paradigms of the *Masculines* given below, to which also the necessary explanations are subjoined. For the sake of brevity, we will use the terms *first, second, third, &c. declension.*

3. In the formation of the Feminine from the Masculine, by appending the termination ‍ָה‍, the same change of vowels is introduced as in No. 2 (*a*), since the tone is moved forward in the very same proportion as shown there. The vowel-change is somewhat different when the second feminine termination ‍ָת‍ is appended. Both will be shown in § 39.

SECTION XXIX.—ON THE DECLENSION OF THE MASCULINE NOUNS IN GENERAL.

1. The following paradigms exhibit—of each noun—the *absolute* and *construct state* in the sing., plur., and dual, and the singular and plural forms with *light* and *grave* suffixes. To render this subject easier, it should be noticed that :

(*a*) The shortening of the vowels is the same in the dual and the plural, except in the sixth declension, where the dual is more shortened than the plural, e. g. pl. מְלָכִים, but du. רַגְלַיִם.

(*b*) In the plural, *light suffixes* are, without exception, attached to the *absolute,* and *grave suffixes* to the *constr.* state, e. g. דְּבָרִים, דְּבָרֵי; דְּבָרֵיכֶם.

2. According to the nine paradigms of the masculines alluded to, are also declined those feminine and common nouns which are without a distinctive feminine termination, e. g. אֶבֶן *stone,* חֶרֶב *sword,* except that in most cases they take in the plural the ending וֹת, which remains unchanged in the constr. st. and before suffixes.

3. The changes of the vowels generally affect the two last syllables, and in a very few instances only the third from the end is affected (comp. § 31. r. 3). Changes of consonants occur in the ninth declension alone.

TABLE O. DECLENSION OF MASCULINE NOUNS.

I., **II.**, **III.**, **IV.**, **V.**, **VI.**

Row labels (reading down each section):
- Sing. absol.
- constr.
- light suff.
- grave suff.
- Plur. absol.
- constr.
- light suff.
- grave suff.
- Dual absol.
- constr.

Glosses by section and sub-column:

I. a. (horse) — b. (hero)

II. a. (blood) — b. (eternity)

III. a. (overseer) — b. (interpreter) — c. (remembrance)

IV. a. (word) — b. (heart) — c. (wise) — d. (hair)

V. a. (old) (shoulder) — b. (snow) — c. (heel) (court)

Additional dual/plural glosses: (hands), (pair of tongs), (two weeks), (two days), (myriads, own), (wings)

VI. a. (king) (feet) / (grave) (knees) — b. (book) — c. (sanctuary) (ring) — d. (a youth) (shoe) — e. (perpetuity) — f. (work) (noon) — g. (death) — h. (olive) (eyes) — i. (fruit) (gazelles) — k. (sickness)

DECLENSION OF MASCULINE NOUNS—continued.

	VII. a. (name)	VII. b. (enemy)	VII. c. (altar)	VIII. a. (sea)	VIII. b. (mother)	VIII. c. (statute)	VIII. d. (much)	VIII. e. (garments)	VIII. f. (Levite)	IX. a. (seer)	IX. b. (held)
Sing. absol.											
constr.											
light suff.											
grave suff.											
Plur. absol.											
constr.											
light suff.											
grave suff.											
Dual absol.		(balances)		(hands)	(teeth)						
constr.											

DECLENSION OF FEMININE NOUNS.

	(I.) X.* a. (virgin)	(I.) X.* b. (year)	(I.) X.* c. (righteousness)	(II.) XI.* a. (queen)	(II.) XI.* b. (corners / sleep)	(II.) XI.* c.	(III.) XII.* a. (garment)	(III.) XII.* b. (reproach / double embroidery)	(III.) XII.* c. (waste)	(III.) XII.* d. (maid)	(III.) XII.* e. (enclosure / mistress)	(IV.) XIII.* a. (slothfulness)	(IV.) XIII.* b. (wife)	(IV.) XIII.* c. (cymbals / coat / double fetters)
Sing. absol.														
constr.														
light suff.														
grave suff.														
Plur. absol.														
constr.														
light suff.														
grave suff.														
Dual absol.	(two cubits)	(lips)			(corners)		(sides)							
constr.														

* See note to the heading of § 41.

SECTION XXX.—FIRST DECLENSION OF THE MASCULINES. (Table O.)

EXPLANATORY.

1. In this declension the noun itself undergoes no change of vowels before the suffixes, and stands, as an indeclinable, merely for comparison with the others. It is, however, important to know the various forms which are thus indeclinable.

2. To this paradigm belong all nouns whose vowels are immutable,* e. g. (according to the note given below, No. 1) עִיר city, קוֹל voice, לְבוּשׁ garment, זְרוֹעַ arm; (No. 2) קָם, part. of קוּם arising, גָּר, part. of גּוּר, stranger, נֵר (for נִיר) lamp, כְּתָב (כְּתָאב) book; (No. 3) גִּבּוֹר hero, צַדִּיק righteous, מַלְכוּת kingdom, אֶבְיוֹן poor, מַשְׁחִית destruction; (No. 4) פָּרָשׁ for פָּרָשׁ horseman.

3. The vowels (ָ) and (ֵ) occasion here peculiar difficulty, as it often cannot be determined, at first sight, whether they are pure or impure, or whether a Dagesh is omitted in the form (comp. note No. 2). There is, however, no difficulty in forms like קָם, גֵּר, as soon as we are aware of their derivation from קוּם, גּוּר, from which it becomes evident that they stand for גֵּיר, קָאם (§ 21. rem. 1); in קַטָּל, קְטָל, the general formation of nouns that (ָ) is impure, and therefore

immutable (§ 25. No. 6); but with regard to forms like כְּאָב pain, פָּרָשׁ horseman, it can be known only from the existing inflexions (as, constr. state כְּאֵבִי, פָּרְשֵׁי) that they stand for כְּאִיב, פָּרָשׁ, since there are also words of the like forms in which the vowels are pure, and therefore mutable.

4. Hence, of the classes of verbal nouns (of § 26), the following belong to this declension:

(a) Of the derivatives from the regular verb, the forms of No. 6. חַטָּא sinner, פֶּחָר (for פַּחָר) potter, פָּרָשׁ (for פָּרָשׁ) horseman, חַנּוּן compassionate, צַדִּיק righteous; 8. גִּבּוֹר hero; 13. כְּתָב book, כְּאָב pain (though the forms קְטֹל, קְטָל occur also with pure vowels, and are inflected according to dec. 6. § 35. rem. 10); 14. מִזְמוֹר song, מַלְבּוּשׁ garment; 15. שִׁלְטוֹן government, חֶסְרוֹן want; 16. גְּבוּלֹת border, &c.; 19. מַשְׁחִית destruction; 26. הַבּוּג a folding, זֵרוּעַ (for זֵרוּעַ) herbs; 27. תַּלְמִיד, תַּנְמוּל.

(b) Of the derivatives from the irregular verbs (of § 27), II. 16. סֻכּוֹת tabernacle; 27. תַּעֲלוּל action; IV. 13. סוּד; בּוּל; 14. מִישׁוֹר; 28. תִּירוֹשׁ; V. 1. קָם; 2. גֵּר; 3. 5. 8; VIII. 13. שְׁבוּת, שְׁבִית, מְנָת; 15. רַעְיוֹן; 16. גָּלוּת (note, with Kamets impure).

REMARKS.

1. That Kamets is impure, and therefore immutable, in the form קְטָל, is sufficiently evident from a comparison with the Arab. קְטָאל, and also from many examples where it remains unchanged in the declension, e. g. חַטָּא Am. 9. 10, comp. אַבְרֵיכֶם their husbandmen, Is. 61. 5. The punctuators, however, have sometimes from neglect shortened this Kamets. E. g. דַּיַּן אַלְמָנוֹת judge of the widows, Ps. 68. 6, חָרָשׁ smith, constr. state חָרָשׁ Ex. 28. 11; Is. 44. 12, 13, פָּרָשׁ, constr. state פָּרָשׁ Eze. 26. 10. Moreover, צַוָּאר (which even in the Hebrew is written in full), pl. constr. צַוְּארֵי. This plural, however, must doubtless be derived from a feminine צַוָּארָת, with the pl. termination ־ִים (comp. שַׁבָּלָת, pl. שִׁבֳּלִים), according to the 4th declension of the feminines.

2. Of the form קָטוּל there occurs also an example which changes Hholem, viz. צִפּוֹר (a small bird, sparrow), pl. צִפֳּרִים Le. 14. 4, 49; Ec. 9. 12; Is. 31. 5. Here, however, the plural appears to be derived from a sing. fem. צִפֹּרֶת, Hholem of which is pure, comp. קְטוֹר, fem. קְטֹרֶת with suff. קְטָרְתִּי (§ 39. No. 4 d), as in צַוָּאר, comp. rem. 1.

3. As regards the forms of No. 15 (of § 26), we might reasonably expect the Kamets to be impure in שִׁלְטָן, קֻרְבָּן, since in the Arabic they assume the form like קֻרְבָּאן. The punctuators, however, have seldom attended to it, and have usually shortened that Kamets. E. g. אָבְדָן, constr. אָבְדַן destruction, Est. 8. 6; שִׁלְטָן Nu. 4. 7; קָרְבָּן

---

* Immutable vowels are: 1. Those in which their homogeneous vowel is quiescent, as ־ָא; ־ֵי; וֹ, וּ, e. g. רֹאשׁ, הֵיכָל, זְבוּל, קוֹל, פָּקִיד. These are sometimes written defectively, which, however, is not an essential shortening.

2. Those which must originally have been written in full, but from which the vowel letter has been omitted; hence called impure (vocalis impuræ). E. g. רֹשׁ for רֹאשׁ, מָשִׁחַ for מָשִׁיחַ, קֹלֹת for קוֹלֹת, זְבֻל for זְבוּל. Whether a vowel is thus made impure, can be known only from etymology, flexion, and comparison of the kindred dialects. The cases are noticed in the grammars and lexicons.

3. A short vowel in a sharpened syllable followed by Dagesh forte, as נֵּב, גִּבּוֹר; also a short vowel in a compound syllable, when another such syllable immediately follows, e. g. מִדְבָּר, מִשְׁכָּל, אֶבְיוֹן, מַלְכוּת.

4. Vowels after which a Dagesh forte has been omitted on account of a guttural. E. g. חָרָשׁ for חַרָּשׁ, אֲחִים for אַחִים, חָרָשׁ for חַרָּשׁ.

Le. 2. 1; קָרְבְּנֵיהֶם Le. 7. 38 (but where several MSS. have קֻרְבָּנֵיהֶם).

4. Among the indeclinables here, there are yet a few with וֹ in the final syllable, which they change to וּ before suffixes and in the plural. E. g. מַחְסוֹר *want*, pl. מַחְסֹרֶיךָ Pr. 24. 34 (according to some

copies); שָׁפוֹט, pl. שְׁפוֹטִים Eze. 23. 10; מַטְמוֹן, pl. מַטְמוֹנִים, but constr. מַטְמֹנֵי Is. 45. 3, comp. § 32 rem. 5.

5. Several forms which belong here will be noticed also among the exceptions of the following declension.

SECTION XXXI.—SECOND DECLENSION OF THE MASCULINES. (TABLE O.)

EXPLANATORY.

1. To this declension belong all nouns which have a *pure changeable Kamets* in their final syllable, and are either monosyllabic or have their preceding vowels immutable. E. g. יָד *hand*, הֵיכָל *palace*, מִיכָל *little water*, אוֹצָר *treasure*, מוּסָר *chastisement*, מִשְׁמָר *custody*, &c., comp. § 26. Nos. 14, 20; § 27. III. 14, 27. Here belong also the plurals, נָשִׁים *women*, יָמִים *days*, the particle עַל *above*, constr. state עַל *upon*, pl. constr. עֲלֵי, with suff. עֲלֵיכֶם עָלָיו.

2. The vowel-change consists simply in this, that

(*a*) In the *constr.* state and before the *grave suffixes* of the *singular* (ָ) is changed into (ַ);

(*b*) This (ָ) is altogether dropped in the *constr.* state, and before the *grave suffixes* in the plural.

3. There are nouns which resemble in form the above examples, but which have an *impure* Kamets in their final syllable, and therefore do not belong to this declension, comp. § 30. No. 4. Other exceptions are contained in the following remarks.

REMARKS.

1. Certain nouns of the form מַקְטָל have Kamets *impure* in their final syllable, especially derivatives from the irregular verbs. E. g. מַעֲבָדֵיהֶם *their works*, Job 34. 25; מַטָּעֵי כֶרֶם *plantings of a vineyard*, Mi. 1. 6; מוֹרָשֵׁי לְבָבִי *possessions of my heart*, Job 17. 11, comp. מוֹרָשֵׁיהֶם Ob. 17; מַתָּן אָדָם *gift of a man*, Pr. 18. 18. This is especially the case in the derivatives from verbs לא׳ (where י seems to have some hold upon the vowel Kamets), as מִקְרָאֵי *assemblies*, Le. 23. 2, 4, 37; מוֹצָא *goings out*, Ps. 65. 9; מוֹצָאֵיהֶם Nu. 33. 2, and so צֶאֱצָאֵי *shoots*, Is. 48. 19. Comp. Is. 61. 9; Job 21. 8.

Kamets is, moreover, immutable in תּוֹשָׁב *inhabitant*, whence תּוֹשָׁבִי 1 Ki. 17. 1, to which there is a corresponding form in the Arabic תִּפְעָאל.

2. In the word יָם Kamets has been retained even before Makkeph, e. g. always יָם־הַמֶּלַח *salt-sea*; יָם כִּנֶּרֶת *sea Chinereth*, i. e. Genesareth; except in the combination יַם־סוּף *sea of reeds*. (Notwithstanding the constancy of this punctuation, no ground can be assigned for the difference.) There are, moreover, found in the constr. st. the forms אוּלָם *porch, portico*, Eze. 40. 7; פִּתְגָם *word*, Est. 1. 20. without changing Kamets.

3. With the suffix כֶם, יָד becomes יֶדְכֶם (for יַדְכֶם,) Ge. 9. 2; דָּם becomes דִּמְכֶם Ge. 9. 5 (because the forms (ְ) and (ִ) are shorter than (ַ), comp. אֲכָלְךָ for אֲכָלְךָ, מַדּוֹ for מָדּוֹ). An instance of regular formation before כֶם, though terminating with א (comp. rem. 1), is מוֹרַאֲכֶם *fear of you*, Is. 8. 13.

The form like נֶחְבָּאִים, נִטְמָאִים is doubtless the plural of a Niph. part. with (ָ) in the final syllable, from נֶחְבָּא, נִטְמָא comp. § 23. rem. 6.

4. For מִבְטָח with suff. מִבְטַחוֹ, pl. מִבְטָחִים see below § 37. rem. 7.

5. The few words with *Pattahh* in the ultimate, preceded by an immutable syllable (comp. § 30. No. 2. note), follow the analogy of this declension in their inflexion, as far as regards the suffixes and the plural. They are, אֶצְבַּע *finger*, with suff. אֶצְבָּעוֹ, pl. אֶצְבָּעוֹת; אַרְבַּע *four*, pl. אַרְבָּעִים *forty*; שַׁד dual שָׁדַיִם *breasts*; כּוֹבַע *helmet*, pl. כּוֹבָעִים. The latter noun is written with the tone on the ultimate, כּוֹבַע, in Eze. 27. 10; but כּוֹבַע in 1 Sa. 17. 5; Is. 59. 17, according to which it is a Segolate form written, by way of exception, with a full Hholem. The first form, however, is favoured by the fact that וֹ is retained in the plural, which is inconsistent with the Segolate forms.

SECTION XXXII.—THIRD DECLENSION OF THE MASCULINES. (Table O.)
EXPLANATORY.

1. This declension embraces all nouns which have an *immutable vowel* in the final syllable, and *mutable Kamets* or *Tseri* in the penultima, as פָּקִיד, or some other syllables may precede, as כִּלָּיוֹן. Of the derivatives from the regular verb (§ 26) belong here those of No. 3. קָדוֹשׁ *holy*, גָּדוֹל *great*; No. 5. עָצוּם *mighty*, פָּקִיד *officer*; No. 15. רְעָבוֹן *famine*, עֵרָבוֹן (for עֶרְבוֹן) *pledge*, זִכָּרוֹן *remembrance*. Of the derivatives from the irregular verbs (§ 27), from פ״א, as אֵזוֹר *girdle*, אֱמוּן *faithfulness*; from ע״י No. 14. מָקוֹם *place*; No. 27. תָּמִיד *continuance*; moreover, the participles of Hiphil, as מֵלִיץ, מֵשִׁיב, מֵקִים. From ל״ה No. 15. הָמוֹן *multitude*, גִּלָּיוֹן *roll*. The primitives and denominatives follow the same analogy.

2. The vowel-change here consists in this, that Kamets (or Tseri) of the penultima is dropped in all the forms, except the absol. state of the singular. In the forms like כִּלָּיוֹן, זִכָּרוֹן, Dagesh of the middle radical is likewise dropped, and the first two syllables are combined into one, as כִּלָּיוֹן, זִכָּרוֹן. Another combination of the letters is effected in פֵּרָזוֹן, with suff. פֵּרָזוֹנוֹ, with guttural רְעָבוֹן, constr. רַעֲבוֹן (for רְעָבוֹן).

3. Here also are to be distinguished nouns which resemble the above forms, but which have *impure* Kamets, and as such do not belong here, as בָּרִיחַ (for בְּרִיחַ) *fugitive*, עָרִיץ (for עֲרִיץ) *tyrant*, חָרוּץ (for חֲרוּץ) *diligent* (according to § 26. No. 7), and the derivatives of ל״ה of the form גָּלוּת, חָזוּת, the Kamets of which is likewise *impure*.

REMARKS.

1. Of the forms קָטִיל, קָטוֹל, קָטוּל (§ 26. Nos. 3 & 4) there are some few words in which Kamets is *impure*. E. g. שָׁלִישׁ *charioteer*, pl. שָׁלִישִׁים Ex. 14. 7, with suff. שָׁלִישׁוֹ, שָׁלִישָׁיו 2 Ki. 15. 25; Ex. 15. 4; שָׁבוּעַ *week*, pl. שָׁבֻעוֹת, שָׁבֻעִים Da. 9. 24, 25, with suff. שְׁבֻעֹתֵיכֶם Nu. 28. 26 (though also שָׁבֻעוֹת Je. 5. 24; Eze. 45. 21), and in the Gentilic nouns יְמִינִי, מְכִירִי Nu. 26. 12, 29; comp. 2 Sa. 20. 26, instead of which we would expect מָכִירִי, יָמִינִי.

2. With regard to some words with middle guttural, the punctuators seem to have disagreed among themselves, as to whether they belong to the form קָטִיל or קְטִיל, i. e. whether Kamets is to be changed or not. Hence inconsistencies like the following: בָּרִיחִים *fugitives*, Is. 43. 14 (from בָּרִיחַ); but, on the contrary, בְּרִיחֶיהָ Is. 15. 5; סָרִים *eunuch*, constr. state סָרִיס Ge. 37. 36, pl. סָרִיסִים 2 Ki. 9. 32, constr. state סָרִיסֵי Est. 2. 21, and סָרִיסֵי Ge. 40. 7, with suff. סָרִיסָיו Ge. 40. 2; פָּרִיץ *violent*, constr. state פְּרִיץ Is. 35. 9, but pl. פָּרִיצִים Je. 7. 11; פְּרִיצֵי Da. 11. 14.

3. Some nouns of the form זִכָּרוֹן, when shortened, take Segol instead of Hhirek. Thus, חִזָּיוֹן *vision*, constr. state חֶזְיוֹן Job 33. 15, pl. חֶזְיֹנוֹת Job 4. 13; עִשָּׂרוֹן *tenth deal* (dry measure), pl. עֶשְׂרֹנִים Ex. 29. 40; Le. 14. 10. This is doubtless the effect of the first letter which is a guttural (§ 35. rem. 6), though עִצָּבוֹן has the constr. state עֶצְבוֹן, and חִשָּׁבוֹן the pl. חִשְּׁבֹנוֹת.

4. In the forms like אֵזוֹר, אֵבוּס where, on account of א, Tseri stands, by Syriacism, for (ֶ) (comp. § 19. r. 6), it is retained also in the constr. state, because the same cause continues to exist here as in the abs.

state, as אֵבוּס בְּעָלָיו Is. 1. 3; אֵטוּן מִצְרַיִם Pr. 7. 16; אֵפוֹד בַּד 1 Sa. 2. 18; but, in the plural, where the shorter (ֲ) is to be introduced, the Syriacism is no longer employed; hence אֲבוּסִים *cribs*, Job 39. 9; אֲסוּרִים *bands*, Ju. 15. 14; also אֲמוּנִים *faithful*, Ps. 31. 24.*

5. In several nouns of the form מָקוֹם, especially such as are derived from verbs ע״י, ו, is changed to ו in the shortening. E. g. מָנוֹחַ *rest*, pl. מְנוּחִים; מָנוֹס *flight*, with suff. מְנוּסִי; מָעוֹן *habitation*, pl. מְעוּנִים; מָגוֹר *fear*, pl. מְגוּרִים; מָצוֹר, with suff. מְצוּרֶךָ, as there exists no ground-form with Kibbuts for any of these forms. This is moreover the case in the adj. מָתוֹק of which the pl. is מְתוּקִים (comp. § 39. No. 3. r. 1).

6. Among the derivatives from ע״י there are a few of the form לָצוֹן (from לוּץ) in which Kamets is shortened, contrary to analogy (comp. § 30. Nos. 2 & 3), as זָדוֹן *arrogance*, constr. זְדוֹן Ob. 3, with suff. זְדֹנְךָ 1 Sa. 17. 28; שָׂשׂוֹן *joy*, constr. שְׂשׂוֹן Ps. 51. 14, from זִיד or זוּד and שׂוּשׂ. The vowel-change here gives them the character of derivatives from (as it were) שָׂשָׂה, שָׂדָה.

7. In some few instances *Hholem* of the form קָטוֹל (§ 26. No. 3) is treated as a *pure* vowel, and is shortened to *Kamets-hhatuph*, as שְׁלָשׁ־אֵלֶּה *these three*, Ex. 21. 11; גְּדָל Ps. 145. 8; Na. 1. 3 Keri; טְהָר־ Job 17. 9; Pr. 22. 11 Keri. Still more striking is the kind of shortening in הֲמָנְכֶם Eze. 5. 7, for הֲמֹנְכֶם *your noise*. Comp. also קְנָמָד Ex. 30. 23, from קִנָּמוֹן *cinnamon*.

8. מָדוֹן *contention*, (from דִּין or דּוּן) has the pl. מְדָנִים with moveable Vav, comp. § 35. rem. 13.

* Comp. § 13. rem 2, note; also rem. 7 and 9

SECTION XXXIII.—FOURTH DECLENSION OF THE MASCULINES. (TABLE O.)

EXPLANATORY.

1. This declension embraces nouns of two syllables, either with *Kamets pure* in both, or *Tseri pure* in the first and *Kamets* in the second. Here belong only the derivatives from the regular verb (§ 26. Nos. 1 & 2), as זָהָב *gold*, זָנָב *tail*, שֵׁכָר *strong drink*, and with gutturals, אָשָׁם *guilt*, רָעָב *famine*, שָׂבָע *satiety*, שֵׂעָר *hair*, עֵנָב *cluster of grapes*.

2. The vowel-change in this declension consists in this, that

(*a*) Kamets or Tseri of the first syllable is always dropped, except in the ground-form;

(*b*) in the constr. st. sing., and before the suffix כֶם, (ָ) of the final syllable is changed to (ַ);

(*c*) in the plural, Kamets is altogether dropped in the constr. st. and before the *grave* suffixes, and the two Shevas, now coming to stand under the first two radicals (דְּבָ), are combined in one syllable by Hhirek, with a guttural by Pattahh, hence שְׂעָרֵי, חַכְמֵי, דִּבְרֵי, E. g. עָפָר *dust*, pl. constr. עַפְרוֹת; עָנָו *afflicted*, pl constr. עֲנָוֵי, &c.

3. For some exceptions like חָרָשׁ *smith*, פָּרָשׁ *horseman*, see § 30. No. 4, also rem. 1.

REMARKS.

1. In the pl. constr. there is *Pattahh* found under the first radical, even where there is no guttural, e. g. כָּנָף *wing*, du. constr. כַּנְפֵי; זָנָב *tail*, pl. constr. זַנְבוֹת; צֵלָע *rib*, pl. constr. צַלְעוֹת. On the contrary, *Hhirek* is found also under guttural instead of *Pattahh*, as עָמֹק *deep*, Is. 33. 19, from עָמֵק; עִנְבֵי *grapes*, De. 32. 32 (with euphonic Dagesh for עַנְבֵי); חִזְקֵי *strong*, Eze. 2. 4; 3. 7, from חָזָק.

2. This class of nouns derived from לֵ״א retain in the constr. st. the (ָ), in which א is quiescent, as צָבָא *host*, constr. צְבָא; צָמָא *thirst*, constr. צְמָא.

3. For a few nouns of this class (קְטָל and קֵטָל.), the Segolate form is used in the constr. st. and before suffixes (comp. dec. 5). E. g. עָשָׁן *smoke*, constr. עֲשַׁן and עֶשֶׁן; עָנָף *branch*, with suff. עֲנַפְכֶם Eze. 36. 8; צֵלָע *rib*, constr. צְלַע and צֶלַע (Milêl), with suff. צַלְעִי. The case is reversed in חֶדֶר *chamber*, with suff חֲדָרוֹ, but constr. חֲדַר (as if from חָדָר).

SECTION XXXIV.—FIFTH DECLENSION OF THE MASCULINES. (TABLE O.)

1. This declension embraces nouns of two syllables, which have *Tseri pure* in the final, and *Kamets* in the preceding syllable, hence chiefly derivations of the regular verb only of No. 2 (§ 26). The two forms exhibited in the paradigm differ only with respect to the first radical when a guttural.

2. This declension is very similar to the preceding, as regards the vowel-change, and is properly a mere variation of the same. In this the *Tseri* of the final syllable is treated like final *Kamets* in the foregoing, except that the form קְטֵל, which might be expected in the constr. st., occurs but very seldom (see, however, לְבֶן *white*, Ge. 49. 12; אֲבֶל *mourning*, Ps. 35. 14), and instead of it the forms like either that of זָקֵן or כָּתֵף are used. According to the latter form are inflected, גָּדֵר, constr. גֶּדֶר *wall*; יָרֵךְ, constr. יֶרֶךְ *hip*; גָּזֵל, constr. גֶּזֶל *robbery, any thing taken by violence*; אָרֵךְ, constr. אֶרֶךְ *long*; to the first belong יָתֵד, constr. יֶתֶד *peg, pin*; קָצֵר, constr. קֶצֶר *short*, &c. Both forms appear in כָּבֵד *heavy*, constr. כְּבַד Ex. 4. 10, and כְּבֵד Is. 1. 4; עָרֵל *uncircumcised*, constr. עֲרַל Ex. 6. 12, 30 and עֲרֵל Eze. 44. 9.

REMARKS.

1. The nouns of this form derived from לֵ״א retain *Tseri* in the constr. st., e g. מָלֵא, מְלֵא; טָמֵא, טְמֵא; יָרֵא, יְרֵא (§ 33. rem. 2); this, however, is not confined to forms with א merely, comp. יָוֵן *mire*, constr. יְוֵן Ps. 69. 3; עָקֵב *heel*, constr. עֲקֵב Ge. 25. 26; יָפֵחַ *puffing out*, constr. יְפֵחַ Ps. 27. 12; finally, חָמֵשׁ *five*, constr. חֲמֵשׁ.

2. Some nouns retain *Tseri* in the pl. constr. st., e. g. יָשֵׁן *sleeping*, constr. יְשֵׁנֵי Da. 12. 2; אָבֵל *mourning*, אֲבֵלֵי Is. 61. 3; שָׂמֵחַ *joyful*, שְׂמֵחֵי Ps. 35. 26 (but also שִׂמְחֵי Is. 24. 7); שָׁכֵחַ *forgetful*, שְׁכֵחֵי Ps. 9. 18; חָפֵץ *delighting*, חֲפֵצֵי Ps. 40. 15; 70. 3.

3. אָבֵל *(grassy place)* remains entirely unchanged in the pr. names אָבֵל מְחוֹלָה Ju. 7. 22, אָבֵל הַשִּׁטִּים 11. 33, &c.; comp. also כָּתֵף פְּלִשְׁתִּים Is. 11. 14.

4. *Hhirek* under the first radical when a guttural, like עִקְּבֵי in paradigm *c*, is a mere exception; it occurs in Ca. 1. 8, and with euphonic Dagesh, עִקְּבֵי Ge. 49. 17; Ju. 5. 22; for the like Dagesh, comp. עַצְּבֵכֶם Is. 58. 3. from עָצֵב. (This, however, may be derived from עֶצֶב in the sense of *labour*.)

SECTION XXXV.—SIXTH DECLENSION OF THE MASCULINES. (TABLE O.)

EXPLANATORY.

1. This declension embraces the large class of nouns denominated *Segolate forms*, i. e. those dissyllabic nouns which have the tone and characteristic vowels in the first, and an auxiliary Segol (with guttural Pattahh) in the second syllable. The characteristic vowel may be either A, E, or O ; hence the following forms :—

(a) From the regular verb, like מֶלֶךְ for מַלְךְ, סֵפֶר, קֹדֶשׁ ; (b) with gutturals, like נַעַר, נֶצַח, פֹּעַל ; (c) from the verb ע״וּ, like חַיִל, מָוֶת, or שׁוֹר for שׁוֹר (§ 27. IV) ; (d) from verbs ל״ה, like אֲרִי, לֶחִי, חֳלִי (§ 27. V). They are closely related to the forms like קֶטֶל, שֶׁכֶב, שֶׁכֶם (§ 26. No. 10), which in the Aramaean occupy the place of the Hebrew Segolates.

2. The peculiarity in their inflexion is as follows :—

(a) In the constr. st. the form remains unchanged, with the exception of חַיִל מָוֶת, in which וּ and י become quiescent.

(b) Before the suffixes the original monosyllabic form is introduced, which they have in the Arabic (מֶלֶךְ, קֹדֶשׁ, סֵפֶר or סֵפֶר), hence סִפְרִי, מַלְכִּי, &c. This is likewise the case in the constr. st. of the plural and dual.

(c) The plural is not formed immediately from the Segolate form of the singular, but from the kindred form מֶלֶךְ, סֵפֶר, קֹדֶשׁ or קֹדֶשׁ, which they have in the Aramaean, hence סְפָרִים, מְלָכִים, so that Pattahh, which in this case would stand in an open syllable, is changed into Kamets, like שָׁד dual שָׁדַיִם (§ 31. rem. 5).

REMARKS.

I. On the form מֶלֶךְ (& נַעַר).

1. In the form of two Segols, like מֶלֶךְ, the first *generally* stands for Pattahh (מַלְךְ), and this again for the monosyllabic מַלְךְ. The latter form is the Arabic, which the Arabian usually pronounces *mĕlk*, and the vulgar even *mĕlĕk*. The Hebrew language exhibits this original form in the word גַּיְא *a valley*, and the proper name אַרְד Ge. 46. 21 ; Nu. 26. 40. The Greek translators of the Old Testament have also sometimes expressed this form in the same way, e. g. קֶרֶן Aqu & Symm. καρν Job 42. 14 ; חָרָשׁ αρς Is. 17. 9.

2. In a few words only the original *a*, as (־ִ & (־ֶ), appears already in the ground-form, viz., (a) in the nouns which have a guttural for their second radical, as נַעַל, נַעַר, בַּעַל ; (b) in the derivatives from ע״וּ, as חַיִל, מָוֶת ; (c) in the contracted forms like אַף from אֶנֶף *wrath*, בַּת from בֶּנֶת ; (d) in the word הָאָרֶץ, but only with the article (for הָאָרֶץ) ; (e) in pause, as כָּרֶם, כָּלֶד, and with paragogic ה, אַרְצָה *to the ground*.

3. There is, however, a considerable number of nouns of this form, in which, seemingly, the first Segol does not stand for Pattahh or Kamets, but for *Tseri*, as לֶדֶת for לֶדֶת, קֹטֶלֶת for קֹטֶלֶת. These, though similar to the preceding in the ground-form, are nevertheless inflected like the form סֵפֶר (to which they originally belong) with *Hhirek*, seldom *Segol*, in the first syllable. An example of this kind is presented in the paradigm קֶבֶר.

Nouns inflected in this manner with *Hhirek*, the ground-form being קָטֶל not קֵטֶל, are the following : בֶּגֶד *garment*, בֶּטֶן *belly*, בֶּרֶךְ *knee*, גֶּוַע *stem*, גֶּשֶׁם *rain*, גֶּרֶשׂ *something pounded*, דֶּגֶל *banner*, דֶּשֶׁן *fat*, זֶבַח *sacrifice*, טֶבַח *slaughter*, יֶתֶר *string*, כֶּלֶא *confinement*, לֶקַח *doctrine*, מֶתֶג *bridle*, נֶגַע *stroke*, נֶזֶם *ring*, נֶטַע *planting*, נֶשֶׁר *eagle*, נֶשֶׁף *twilight*, פֶּגֶר *carcase*, פֶּלֶךְ *district*, פֶּסֶל *image*, צֶדֶק *righteousness*, צֶמַח *sprout*, קֶרֶב *midst*, קֶשֶׁר *conspiracy*, רֶכֶב *chariot*, רֶסֶן *bridle*, רֶשֶׁף *flame*, שֶׁקֶר *falsehood*, שֶׁמֶשׁ *sun*. In others this characteristic of the word becomes apparent in its change to the feminine, e. g. גֶּבַע fem. גִּבְעָה *hill*. With Segol in the first syllable are inflected חֶלֶד *life-time*, נֶגֶב (with ה parag. נֶגְבָּה) *south*, נֶגֶר *before*, נֶכֶד *progeny*.

4. Sometimes both forms (like מַלְכִּי and בְּגְדִי) are found with one ground-form like קָטֶל, e. g. יֶלֶד *child*, hence יַלְדִי Is. 57. 4, and יַלְדִי Ho. 1. 2 (fem. יַלְדָּה) ; חֶדֶר *chamber*, with suff. חַדְרִי, but with ה parag. חַדְרָה pl. constr. חַדְרֵי ; הֶבֶל *vanity*, with suff. הֶבְלִי, but pl. constr. הַבְלֵי ; חֶבֶל *band*, pl. חָבָלִי, but with pref. בְּ always בְּחַבְלֵי Is. 5. 18 ; Job 36. 8. So likewise in the change to the feminine, as כֶּבֶשׂ *lamb*, fem. כַּבְשָׂה and כִּבְשָׂה.

5. When the third radical is a guttural, the pointing is like that of זֶרַע *seed*, פֶּתַח *door*, סֶלַע *rock*, פֶּסַח *passover*, when the second is a guttural, like that of נַעַר (parad. d). The cases, however, are but rare where the punctuation is not affected by the guttural, e. g. לֶחֶם *bread* רֶחֶם (but also רַחַם) *womb*. In the

word כְּנָעֶנֶיהָ *her merchants*, Is. 23. 8, from כְּנַעַן, the Sheva coming, in the plural, to stand under נ is combined into one syllable with the Sheva under כְּ (for כְּנַעֲנֶיהָ). כְּנַעַן stands for כְּנַעֲנִי *Canaanite*, which latter is used for *a merchant* in general.

Nouns of the form נַעַר are often found with simple Sheva, in those combinations where the latter exhibits a composite Sheva, as יַעֲרֵי for יַעֲרֵי from יַעַר *wood, forest* (comp. § 13. rem. 5).

II. ON THE FORM סֵפֶר (& נֵצַח).

6. The nouns of the form סֵפֶר (seldom in the monosyllabic form like גֶּרֶד, חֵטְא) are all inflected according to the paradigm, e. g. סֵתֶר *covering*, שֵׁבֶט *rod*, נֵדֶר *vow*; those, however, with the first radical guttural, take nearly all of them *Segol* instead of *Hhirek* in the first syllable, as אֵבֶר *pinion*, with suff. אֶבְרוֹ, חֵלֶב *fat*, חֵלֶק *part*, חֵפֶץ *delight*, חֵרֶם *net*, עֵבֶר *country on the other side*, עֵגֶל *calf*, עֵדֶר *flock*, עֵזֶר *help*, עֵרֶךְ *valuation*. There are, however, some few with guttural which retain *Hhirek*, as חֵקֶר *searching*, עֵמֶק *valley*, pl. constr. חִקְרֵי, עִמְקֵי. The noun יֵשַׁע *salvation* has both forms, יִשְׁעֶךָ 2 Sa. 22. 36, and יֵשַׁע Ps. 85. 8.

חֵטְא *sin*, has in the pl. constr. חֲטָאֵי 2 Ki. 10. 29; Am. 9. 10, with suff. חֲטָאֵיכֶם Is. 1. 18, where (ָ) is retained on account of א (comp. § 30. rem. 1).

7. Some few Segolates of the forms נֵצַח, זֶרַע, have their constr. state like זֶרַע Nu. 11. 7, as שֶׁבַע *seven*, and תֵּשַׁע *nine*, constr. שֶׁבַע and תֵּשַׁע, so likewise in the proper name יְשַׁעְיָהוּ (for יֵשַׁע יָהוּ) *salvation of the Lord*. The same analogy follows חֶדֶר *chamber*, in the constr. state חֲדַר.

III. ON THE FORM קֹדֶשׁ (& פֹּעַל).

8. The form קֹדֶשׁ takes sometimes *Kibbuts* in the inflexion before suffix, as סֻבְכוֹ *thicket*, Is. 4. 7, גֻּדְלֵ *greatness*, גֻּדְלוֹ Ps. 150. 2 (also קֻמְץ, גֻּדְלוֹ) *handful*, קֻמְצוֹ.

Those with the middle letter guttural like פֹּעַל take sometimes, though not often, simple Sheva under the guttural, as בָּאְשׁוֹ *his stink*, Joel ii. 20; רָחְבּוֹ *his breadth*, Ex. 25. 10. In some instances the vowels ־ָ are put instead of ־ֳ, as פָּעֳלוֹ for פָּעֳלוֹ *his work*, Is. 1. 31; תָּאֳרוֹ *his visage*, Is. 52. 14, for תָּאֳרוֹ 1 Sa. 28. 14.

With the suffix ךְ the form becomes פָּעֳלְךָ Is. 45. 9; Hab. 3. 2, אָהֳלְךָ (*thy tent*), Ps. 61. 5, and even so

without the influence of a guttural, as קָטְבְךָ Ho 13. 14, from קֶטֶב *destruction*; the usual form, however, is like קָדְשְׁךָ, קָדְשָׁם. (The same form is found under the infinitive, § 16. rem. 7—9.)

9. The plural with *Hhateph-Kamets* under the first letter is found (besides קְדָשִׁים of the parad.) only in חֳדָשִׁים *months*, from חֹדֶשׁ, and אֳרָחוֹת *ways*, from אֹרַח, but everywhere else with simple Sheva (like in the plural of מֶלֶךְ, סֵפֶר); as בְּקָרִים, בֹּקֶר *mornings*; סְבָכִים, סֹבֶךְ *thickets*; גְּרָנוֹת, גֹּרֶן *threshing-floors*; שְׁעָלִים, שֹׁעַל *hollow hands*; קְמָצִים, קֹמֶץ *handfuls*; כְּפָרִים, כֹּפֶר *cyprus flowers*; רְמָחִים, רֹמַח *spears*; רְתָמִים, רֹתֶם *genista*; פְּעָלִים, פֹּעַל *actions*; and so probably כְּמָרִים *idol-priests*, from an obsolete כֹּמֶר*.

Kamets-Hhatuph (instead of *Hhateph-Kamets*) under the first radical occurs in שֳׁרָשִׁים (*shŏrashim*) and קֳדָשִׁים (so usually with the article, but without it, קְדָשִׁים, according to the paradigm).

The noun אֹהֶל (*tent*) has by Syriacism pl. אֹהָלִים for אֳהָלִים, whence אֹהָלָיו, אֹהָלָךְ for אֳהָלֶיךָ, אֳהָלְךָ, but again, אֹרַח אֶהֳלֵכֶם, אָהֳלֵי also makes אָרַח also makes אָרְחֹתַי, אָרְחֹתָיו. בֹּהֶן *thumb*, has for its plural בְּהֹנוֹת, so that, instead of קֹטֶל, the parallel form קְטֹל is used.

IV. ON THE FORMS קְטֹל, קְטֵל, קְטַל.

10. The Chaldee has, instead of the forms מֶלֶךְ, סֵפֶר, the corresponding forms מְלַךְ, מְלֵךְ, מְלֹךְ, with the vowel between the last two radicals. Examples of this kind are found also in the Hebrew, which agree with the Segolates in the inflexion: they are, however, of too rare occurrence for a paradigm and general rule to be given for them. They are:— דְּבַשׁ *honey*, with suff. דִּבְשִׁי; גֶּבֶר i. q. גֶּבֶר *man*; שְׁכֶם *shoulder*, in pause שֶׁכֶם Ps. 21. 13, with suff. שִׁכְמִי, with ה parag. שֶׁכְמָה (*to Shechem*) Ho. 6. 9; בְּאֵר *cistern*, pl. בְּאֵרוֹת, constr. בְּאֵרֹת; פְּאֵר *head-dress*, pl. פְּאֵרִים, constr. פַּאֲרֵי (also, on the contrary, פַּאֲרֵיכֶם Eze. 24. 23); הֶבֶל *vanity*, Eze. 1. 2; 12. 8; בְּאֹשׁ *ill-savour*, with suff. בָּאְשׁוֹ Joel 2. 20.

Here belong also the infinitives of Kal of the form קְטֹל, קְטֵל, for the inflexion of which see § 16. rem. 7—10.

For שְׂלָו *quails*, pl. שַׂלְוִים, see below, rem. 16.

V. ON THE FORMS בַּיִת, מָוֶת.

11. Of the form מָוֶת are the following nouns:— אָוֶן *adversity*, with suff. אוֹנִי, pl. אוֹנִים; תָּוֶךְ *midst*,

---

*Hence it is, that some have in the pl. constr. the form קָדְשֵׁי instead of קָדְשֵׁי, viz. סֹבֶךְ, pl. סְבָכִים: סִבְכֵי; pl. שֶׁקֶת, constr. שְׁקָתוֹת, so that there is no *necessity* to suppose other ground-forms, like שֶׁקֶת סֻבֶךְ.

constr. תּוֹךְ, with suff. תּוֹכִי; and the monosyllabic
שָׁוְא *nothingness*. The only instance without the
contraction is עֹל, constr. עֹל, with suff. עֻלּוֹ Eze.
18. 26; 33. 13. The plurals אוֹנִים, מוֹתִים (not מָתִים,
אֳנִים, which one would naturally expect here; comp.
סְפָרִים, מְלָכִים) are the only instances which occur of
this form, which properly is a contraction of the
shortened form אֳנִים, מָוְתִים (rem. 16).

12. Of the form זַיִת are, אַיִל *ram*, לַיִל *night*,
צַיִד *hunting*. A few others have ־ָ instead of ־ַ before
suffix, e. g. עַיִר *foal*, עֵירֹה Ge. 49. 11; שַׁיִת *thorns*, שִׁיתוֹ
Is. 10. 17; לַיִל *night*, pl. לֵילוֹת, but derivative לַיְלָה.
The plural is generally contracted, as in the paradigm. There are, however, some instances with
moveable Yod in the plural, as חֲיָלִים *forces*, עֲיָנוֹת
fountains (from עַיִן), but dual עֵינַיִם), עֲיָרִים *foals*. Here
belongs also גַּיְא, pl. גֵּיָאוֹת Khethib (see under the
irreg. nouns, § 45). Compare the following remark.

13. It has already been noticed, § 27. No. 11, of
the verbs עו"י, that nouns of the form קוֹל, קֻל, קִיל
may likewise be *originally* Segolate forms, for קֹל,
קֵל. As such they are inflected, at least in the plural,
like the Segolates, so that ו and י may again become
moveable. E. g. שׁוֹר, pl. שְׁוָרִים *oxen*; חוֹחַ *thorn*, pl.
חוֹחִים 2 Ch. 33. 11, and חֲוָחִים 1 Sa. 13. 6; דּוּד, pl.
דְּוָדִים *pots*; שׁוּק, pl. שְׁוָקִים *streets*.

VI. On the Forms חֳלִי, פְּרִי.

14. For the origin of this form see § 27. No. 11,
of the verbs ל"ה. Nouns of this form may also be
properly divided into three classes, likewise distinguished by the sounds *A, E,* and *O,* e. g. לְחִי, אֲרִי;
חֳלִי, in pause חֵלִי), לָחִי, אֲרִי), חֹלִי, with suff. אַרְיֵה,
חֲלָיִי, in the plural and dual אֲרָיִים, לְחָיַיִם, חֳלָיִים.
Those of the second class have almost always *Hhirek*
before suffixes which begin with a vowel, and *Segol*
before ךְ: e. g. פְּרִי, פִּרְיוֹ Le. 19. 23; Ps. 1. 3; פֶּרְיְךָ
Ho. 14. 9; שְׁבִי *captivity*, שִׁבְיוֹ De. 21. 10; שֶׁבְיְךָ Ju.
5. 12; מְרִי *rebellion*, מִרְיָם Ne. 9. 17; מֶרְיְךָ De. 31. 27,
and so כֶּלְיְךָ *thy vessel*, De. 23. 25; תֶּלְיְךָ *thy quiver*, Ge.
27. 3. Before the suffixes כֶם, כֶן, הֶם, הֶן, the ground-
form usually remains unchanged, as פֶּרְיְהֶם Am. 9. 14;
שִׁבְיְכֶם Je. 29. 28; שֶׁבְיָם Nu. 31. 19 (otherwise פִּרְיָם
שִׁבְיָם), comp. however פֶּרְיָם Eze. 36. 8.

Examples in which the first radical is a guttural:
חֲלִי *necklace*; עֲדִי *ornament*, with suff. עֶדְיוֹ; עֱלִי *pestle*; with the middle guttural, לְחִי *jaw-bone*, with suff.
לֶחְיוֹ Job 40. 26; לֶחְיָה La. 1. 2.

15. Examples of the plural, according to the para-
digm: אֲרִי *lion*, pl. אֲרָיוֹת, אֲרָיִים; גְּדִי *kid*, pl. גְּדָיִים;
צְבִי *gazelle*, pl. צְבָיִים 2 Sa. 2. 18; פֶּתִי *simple*, pl.
פְּתָיִים. On account, however, of the preceding characteristic Kamets, the third radical י is often changed
into ה. Hence חֲלִי, pl. חֲלָאִים *necklaces*; לְבִי, pl.
לְבָאוֹת, לְבָאִים *lions, lionesses*; and צְבִי, פֶּתִי take, besides
the form *exhibited* in the paradigm, also that of צְבָאִים
1 Ch. 12. 8, and צְבָאוֹת Ca. 2. 7, פְּתָאִים Pr. 1. 4.*
The dual לְחָיַיִם, as given in the paradigm, corresponds to the form of the plural, though the greater
shortening, as לֶחָיַיִם, לְחָיַיִם, would have been expected
here.
The interchange of י and א is doubtless the reason
why Kamets remains immutable in גְּדָיַי Ge. 27. 9, 16,
and לְחָיַי Is. 30. 28 (instead of גְּדָיַי, לְחָיַי) they resemble the form חֲטָאִי (see rem. 6). For the form לְחָיֵהֶם
your cheeks, Ho. 11. 4, an abs. לְחָיִים must oe supposed, like כְּלִי, כֵּלִים (see irreg. nouns, § 45).

VII. In General.

16. Some few plurals of this class deviate from
the general formation in this, that in the abs. state
and before light suffixes the greater shortening is
introduced, which otherwise is used only in the
constr. state. Such are, עֶשְׂרִים *twenty* (not עֲשָׂרִים,
from עֶשֶׂר *ten*); שִׁבְעִים *seventy* (from שֶׁבַע *seven*);
תִּשְׁעִים *ninety* (from תֵּשַׁע *nine*); בָּטְנִים *pistacia-nuts*
(comp. the Arab. بطم); פִּילַגְשִׁים *concubines* (from
פִּילֶגֶשׁ); שַׂלְוִים *quails* (from שְׂלָו, שְׂלָו); דְּלָיָו *his buckets*,
Nu. 24. 7 (from דְּלִי, for דְּלָיָו; אֲשֶׁרָיו, אֲשֶׁרֵהוּ
thine, his happiness (i. e. happiness to thee, him);
עַל אָפְנָיו *at a suitable season*, Pr. 25. 11; שִׁקְמִים *sycamore trees*, הָבְנִים *ebony*. The singulars אֹפֶן, אֲשֶׁר,
הֹבֶן,† שֶׁקֶם are merely supposed forms, and do not
really occur.

17. In the pl. constr. a euphonic Dagesh is often
inserted in the letter which has Sheva, e. g. (*a*) of
the form מֶלֶךְ there is חַלְּקֵי for חַלְקֵי; (*b*) of the form
סֵפֶר there are שַׁבְּלֵי, עִצְּבוֹת; (*c*) of the form קֹדֶשׁ,

---

* In a similar manner may be accounted for the plurals דּוּדָאִים *mandrakes*, לוּלָאוֹת *winding stairs*, viz. probably from lost
singulars לוּלַי, דּוּדַי, with the Aramaean adjective termination ־ַי, hence דּוּדַי signifies properly *pertaining to love*, from
דּוֹד=דַּי *love*. The plural which was to have been דּוּדָיִים is become דּוּדָאִים, similar to the Chaldee קַדְמַי, emph. קַדְמָאָה.
† In the Mishna (tract. Kilaim. No 8, ed. Surenh.) is found the sing. שִׁקְמָה.

סְבָלוֹ, also שְׁקָתוֹת in which Dagesh is omitted and compensated by composite Sheva under the following letter, comp. כִּנְרוֹת and וַתֶּאֱלַצְהוּ and וַתְּאַלְצֵהוּ, עַנֵּנִי for עַנֵּנִי; comp. also אֲמָרוֹת, רְטֵפֵשׁ יִצְחָק, which forms are to be regarded as if they had euphonic Dagesh in *syllaba brevi* (Lehrg. § 15. 4, lit. *c*).

18. The paragogic ה effects no further change in the form of these words than that the auxiliary Segol becomes Sheva. Hence אֶרֶץ, אַרְצָה (rem. 2); קֶדֶם and קֵדְמָה *towards the east*; אֹהֶל, אֹהֱלָה *into the tent*; גֹּרֶן, גֹּרְנָה *to the threshing-floor*, Mi. 4. 2; מוֹתָה *death*, לַיְלָה *night*, from מֵת לַיִל. שְׁכֶם becomes שְׁכְמָה (rem. 10).

SECTION XXXVI.—SEVENTH DECLENSION OF THE MASCULINES. (TABLE O.)
EXPLANATORY.

1. To this declension belong nouns which have Tseri *pure* in their final syllable, and are either monosyllabic or have their preceding vowels immutable. It accordingly embraces participles in Kal (§ 26. No. 4); those in Piel and Hithpael, and other words of a similar form, e. g. כֹּהֵן *priest*, עֹרֵב *raven* (also the Chaldee שָׂהֵד *witness*, Job 16. 19); to which must be added of the verbal nouns from the regular verb (§ 26) No. 9. קֵטֵל; No. 14. the forms מִסְפֵּד; מַכְתֵּשׁ: No. 25. קֵטֵל; and the primitives of the like forms, as כִּסֵּא *throne*, מַקֵּל *staff*, or pluriliterals, as צְפַרְדֵּעַ *frog*. Nouns derived from verbs פ"י, as מוֹעֵד *time*; and those from verbs ל"ה, as בֵּן *son*. The verbal nouns, however, of No. 19 do not belong to this declension, e. g. מַקְהֵל, pl. מַקְהֵלִים.

2. This declension is characterised by the following peculiarities:

(*a*) Most of the words of this class do not change at all in the constr. state of the singular, e. g. שֵׁם, אֹיֵב, in others Tseri is changed into Pattahh, e. g. מִזְבֵּחַ, מִזְבַּח.

(*b*) In all the forms, other than the ground-form of the singular, the vowel of the final syllable is entirely lost, except the monosyllabic words which retain Tseri in the plural abs. e. g. שֵׁמוֹת.

(*c*) In the singular, where two Shevas would occur together before the suffixes ךָ, כֶם, בֶן, they are combined into one syllable by Hhirek, e. g. אֹיִבְךָ. אֹיִבְכֶם.

For the numerous deviations see the remarks.

REMARKS.

1. The words in which (ֵ) is changed to (ֶ) are, besides the one given in the paradigm, מַעֲשֵׂר *tenth*, מִסְפֵּד *lamentation*, מַקֵּל *staff* (constr מַקֵּל Ge. 30. 37, and מַקֵּל Je. 1. 11), and in participles of Kal and Piel of the verbs with guttural, e. g. שֹׁמֵעַ Le. 11. 7, and without guttural in אֹבֵד עֵצוֹת *of corrupt counsel*, De. 32. 28.

It is, moreover, to be observed, that some nouns of the form מַקְטֵל have for their constr. state מִקְטַל; e. g. מַפְתֵּחַ *key*, constr. מִפְתַּח; מַרְבֵּץ *place of lying down*, constr. מִרְבַּץ; מַשְׁבֵּר *matrix*, constr. מִשְׁבַּר; מַרְזֵחַ *cry*, constr. מִרְזַח; מַשְׁחֵת *destruction*, constr. מַשְׁחַת; מִשְׁעֵן *stay*, constr. מִשְׁעַן; this last, however, may be referred to the ground-form מַשְׁעֵן which actually occurs.

2. Some monosyllabic words *retain Tseri* in the singular before the *light suffixes*, e. g. גֵּוִי *back*, גֵּוּ Is. 50. 6; גֵּוִי Is. 38. 17; עֵץ *wood*, עֵצִי, עֵצְךָ; רֵעַ *knowledge*, דֵּעִי Job 33. 6, 10; רֵעַ *companion, friend*, also *thought*, רֵעִי Ps. 139. 2; רֵעֶךָ Le. 19. 18. Those monosyllabic words are, of course, excepted which from the nature of their derivation have Tseri *impure*, e. g. the participles of ע"י, as מֵת *dead*, גֵּר *stranger*, אֵל *God* (from אול).

3. Before the suffixes ךָ, כֶם, כֶן some of these nouns take Segol, as מַקֶּלְכֶם *your staff*, Ex. 12. 11; יֵשְׁךָ *thou art* (as a particle belongs also to this declension); אֶשְׁכֶם *your fire*, Is. 50. 11 (with gutturals they take Pattahh, as אֹהַבְךָ 2 Ch. 20. 7; שֹׂנַאֲךָ Ex. 23. 5); on the contrary, however, with Sheva is כִּסְאֲךָ 2 Sa. 7. 16; Ps. 45. 7; 89. 5; 93. 2 (for כִּסְאֶךָ, comp. § 10. r. 7, not כִּסְאֲךָ, from כִּסֵּא); others have immutable Tseri, as אַבְנֵטְךָ *thy girdle*, Is. 22. 21.

Changes of (ֵ) into (ֶ) occur only in the words בֵּן constr. בֶּן *son*, six times, the form שֶׁם from שֵׁם; עֵת *time*, constr. עֵת, but also עֶת־ Le. 15. 25; Hag. 1. 2.

4. In the *plural abs.* all the monosyllabic words retain Tseri, e. g. עֵץ *wood*, pl. abs. עֵצִים, constr. עֲצֵי; דֵּעַ *knowledge*, pl. דֵּעִים; du. רֵחַיִם *hand-mill*. There are, however, several plurisyllabic nouns which follow the same analogy, e. g. שְׁלֵשִׁים, רִבֵּעִים *descendants of the third, fourth generation*; שׁוֹמֵמוֹת *desolations*, Da. 9. 26; and quadriliterals, עֲטַלֵּפִים *bats*, סַנְוֵרִים *blindness*, פַּרְדֵּסִים *parks*, אַבְנֵטִים *girdles*; מֵעִים *friend, intestines*, retain Tseri even before the *grave suffixes*; רֵעֵיכֶם Ps. 28. 3; מֵעֵיהֶם Eze. 7. 19 (but also מֵעַי). These examples are better regarded as so many irregularities than *forma dagessanda*, according to which רֵעַ is to be supposed to stand for רֶעֶה, רֵעֶה; מֵעִים for מֵעַיִם.

5. The analogy of these nouns is followed also in several nouns which have *Pattahh* in the final syllable, and are derived from verbs לה׳, or, at least, they assume a similar form, and are consequently of the same origin as the form בֵּן, שֵׁם. They are בַּר son, with suff. בְּרִי Pr. 31. 2 (from בְּרָא=בְּרָה); זֵן, pl. זְנִים kind; מְתִים men, from a lost singular מַת, Ethiopic מת (with the sixth vowel) man, husband.

Here is to be noticed also other nouns with *Pattahh*, in which this vowel is substituted for *Tseri* on account of a guttural, e. g. הִכָּנַע (for הִכָּנֵעַ Niph. inf.), with suff. הִכָּנְעוֹ 2 Ch. 12. 12.

6. There are a few nouns ending with *Hholem pure*, in which this vowel is dropped like Tseri in this declension, as קָדְקֹד *crown of the head*, with suff. קָדְקֳדוֹ; אֶשְׁכֹּל *cluster*, pl. אֶשְׁכֹּלוֹת; צִפֹּר *bird*, pl. constr. צִפֳּרֵי, though the two last may be derived from a fem. צִפֹּרֶת, אֶשְׁכֹּלֶת (according to § 30. rem. 2). In the same manner the punctuators have inflected the original plural בָּמֹות *heights*, viz. בָּמֳתֵי, בָּמֳתִים (bamŏthim, bamŏthai).

7. תֵּבֵל is without vowel-change, prob. for תֵּיבֵל from יָבַל.

SECTION XXXVII.—EIGHTH DECLENSION OF THE MASCULINES. (Table O.)
EXPLANATORY.

1. This declension embraces nouns which double the final consonant whenever a suffformative is added at the end, e. g. יָם *sea*, pl. יַמִּים; אֵם *mother*, pl. אִמֹּות. This reduplication lies doubtless already in the character of the ground-form יָם itself, only that, according to a rule of Hebrew orthography, no such reduplication is to be expressed at the end of the word.*

2. According to the original form with Dagesh, the forms mentioned above would have had short vowels (כַּל, אַם, יַם), but having lost the sharpening, they are changed into long vowels, יָם, אֵם, כֹּל.† When the sharpening is now again introduced, by an accession at the end, the long vowel is again shortened, viz., Kamets into Pattahh, Tseri into Hhirek, Hholem (and Shurek) into Kibbuts. Pattahh is either retained or attenuated to Hhirek.

In the *constr. st.* of the singular, the vowel-change depends upon the general character of the form, e. g. עַם, constr. עַם (according to the second declension), but on the contrary אֵם, constr. אֵם (according to the seventh declension).

If the word is of more than one syllable, the penultimate vowel conforms to the principles which regulate the vowel-changes, as אֹופָן pl. אֹופַנִּים; גַּלְגַּל pl. גַּלְגַּלִּים, where the first syllable is immutable (according to the second declension), but on the other hand גָּמָל pl. גְּמַלִּים, constr. גְּמַלֵּי (according to the fourth declension).

3. This reduplication of the final radical is found, however, in nouns of the most heterogeneous forms; and whether or not a noun is to be inflected according to the scheme mentioned above, can seldom be known from the ground-form, though its etymology will generally decide. Etymology refers to this declension the following classes of nouns:—

(a) All the derivatives of the verbs עע׳ (§ 27. II), in which the geminate terminates the word,‡ e. g. תָּם, רַב, No. 10. גַּן, חֵן, חֹק, No. 14. מֵסַב, מָעֹוז, מָנֵן, and the primitives which follow the same analogy, יָם *sea*, אֵשׁ *fare*, גַּג *roof*.

(b) Many contracted forms in which נ is assimilated in the final letter. E. g. אַף (for אַנְף, אַנֶף) *wrath*, with suff. אַפִּי; בַּת (for בְּנֶת) *daughter*, with suff. בִּתִּי; תֵּת (for תֵּנֶת) *to give*, תִּתִּי; אֱמֶת (for אֲמֶנֶת) *truth*, אֲמִתִּי; חֵךְ (Arab. חנך) *palate*, חִכִּי; עֵז (Arab. עזז) *goat*, pl. עִזִּים.

(c) Derivatives from the regular verb (§ 26) of the following forms: No. 1. עָצָב *idol*, pl. עֲצַבִּים, עֲצַבֵּי; קָטָן *small*, fem. קְטַנָּה. No. 5. חָרֻל *nettle*, pl. חֲרֻלִּים; No. 6. שַׁבָּת *sabbath*, with suff. שַׁבַּתֹּו. No. 10. זְמָן *time*, לִשָׁד *juice*, אֶשְׁנָב *window-lattice*, אַשְׁמַנִּים *darkness*. No. 14. מַחְשָׁךְ *darkness*, מַחְמָד *loveliness*, מִשְׁגָּב *height*, מִשְׁמָן *fatness*, מְשֻׁבָּה *destruction*, מַאֲמִין *strength*, &c. No. 20. אֹופָן *wheel*. No. 21. אָדֹם *red*, pl. אֲדֻמִּים; נָקֹד *spotted*, pl. נְקֻדִּים. No. 22. שַׁאֲנָן *quiet*, pl. שַׁאֲנַנִּים. No. 34. גִּבְנֹן, pl. גִּבְנֻנִּים *summits*. Finally, several quadriliterals, as עַקְרָב *scorpion*, pl. עַקְרַבִּים; חַרְטֹם *magician*, pl. חַרְטֻמִּים; גַּרְזֶן *axe*, with suff. גַּרְזַנִּי. Primitives of the forms mentioned are, גָּמָל *camel*, שָׁפָן *coney*, מֹורַג *threshing instrument*, pl. מֹורַגִּים.

4. Here also are to be noticed other derivatives from irregular verbs of the following forms: (a) like עָנִי *afflicted*, pl. עֲנִיִּים, for עֲנִיִים (after the form קָטִיל); (b) אִי *island*, pl. אִיִּים; עִי *heap*, pl. עִיִּים, for עֳוָיִים (the geminate Yod properly stands for וֹי); קָו *cord*, with suff. קַוָּם (from קוה, קָו, properly for קָוְו). Finally, several patronymic and gentilic nouns terminating in ־ִי, as לֵוִי, pl. לְוִיִּים, כּוּשִׁי, pl. כּוּשִׁיִּים (on the contrary יְהוּדִי has the pl. יְהוּדִים *Jews*).

---

* Comp. אַף *anger* for אַנְף, (aff) אַנֶף, וַיֵּצְא for וַיֵּצֵא (y'tzavv) &c.

† Comp. בְּרַךְ for בֵּרַךְ, בֵּרְךְ for בֵּרֶךְ, בֹּרַךְ for בֹּרַךְ, יָעַל for יַעַל.

‡ In others, where the geminate stands in the middle, as חַלֹּון, מְנֻעָה, the reduplication has already been effected on account of the terminations ־ָה, ון.

REMARKS.

1. **Some nouns of the form** אָם take *Pattahh* before the accession, as כַּן *pedestal*, with suff. כַּנּוֹ (from כֵּן); עֵת *time*, with suff. עִתִּי, but with ה parag. עַתָּה *at this time, now*.

2. The nouns of the form חֹק generally have *Makkeph* in the *constr. st.*, and thence *Kamets-hhatuph* for their vowel, e. g. כֹּל *all*, כָּל־; רֹב *multitude*, רָב־; עֹז *strength*, עָז־.

Before the suffixes which begin with a vowel, *Kamets-hhatuph* occurs also, though but seldom, as עָזִּי Ex. 15. 2; Ps. 118. 14; but more frequently before the suffixes ךָ, כֶם, בָן, as עָזְּךָ Ex. 15. 13; Ps. 21. 2 (also עֻזְּךָ Ps. 63. 3), where, however, *Kibbuts* is not unfrequent, e. g. כֻּלְּכֶם.

Instead of Kibbuts, *Shurek plene* is sometimes found, as עוּזֵּנוּ Ps. 81. 2, comp. § 10. rem. 5.

3. According to paradigm כַּד (lett. e) are inflected, סַף *threshold*, pl. סִפִּים; פַּת *morsel*, pl. פִּתִּים; בַּז *spoil*, גַּלְגַּל *wheel*, מֹרַג *threshing instrument*, חַת *fear*; מֵסַב *divan*, with suff. מְסִבּוֹ. מוֹרִגִים 1 Ch. 21. 23, is written *in full* for מֹרִגִים from מֹרַג.

Nouns having *Segol* in the final syllable follow the same analogy, בַּרְזֶל, בַּרְזִלּוֹ; גֶּרֶן, גָּרְנוֹ, &c. All others with *Pattahh* retain this vowel in the inflexion.

4. Some of the derivatives from ע״ע, with the preformative מ (from No. 14) do not shorten Kamets under מ, e. g. מָעוֹז *fortress*, pl. מָעֻזִּים; מָסָךְ *covering*, constr. מְסַךְ; מָגֵן *shield*, with suff. מָגִנִּי, pl. מָגִנִּים.

5. Some few nouns are, in different passages, inflected either with or without Dagesh, which in some instances may be ascribed to a mere inconsistency of the punctuators. E. g. אֵת *ploughshare*, whence אִתּוֹ, אִתִּים 1 Sa. 13. 20, 21 (in several MSS. even אִתּים, אִיתּוֹ), but also אִתִּים Is. 2. 4; Joel 4. 10; מַעֲדַנִּים *dainties*, Je. 51. 34, and מַעֲדַנִּים Pr. 29. 17; Ge. 49. 20, comp. מַעֲדַנּוֹת Job 38. 31; נִכְבָּדִים *honourable*, Nu. 22. 15, with suff. נִכְבְּדֵיהֶם Ps. 149. 8, but also נִכְבַּדֵּי Is. 23. 8, 9; Pr. 8. 24; נִכְבַּדֶּיהָ Na. 3. 10; כַּרְמֶל *fruitful field* (also pr. name), with suff. כַּרְמִלּוֹ 2 Ki. 19. 23, but gentile noun כַּרְמְלִי 1 Sa. 30. 5; 2 Sa. 23. 35. Especially fluctuating in the inflexion is ־ִי in the patronymic and gentilic nouns, as יְהוּדִי, pl. יְהוּדִיִּים and יְהוּדִים.

In some cases the signification is affected by this difference of inflexion, עֲרֻמִּים *naked* (from עָרוֹם), Job 22. 6, and עֲרוּמִים *wise*, Job 5. 12; so also the particle אֵת, whence אוֹתִי *me*, and אִתִּי *with me*.

6. The noun חַי *living, life*, from חָיַי is inflected in the same manner, e. g. pl. חַיִּים, fem. חָיָה, with this difference, that it is contracted in the constr. state of the singular to חֵי. So also דַּי *sufficient*, constr. דֵּי, with suff. דַּיוֹ דַּיִי.

7. When the geminate letter is a guttural or ר, the omission of the Dagesh is compensated by lengthening the preceding vowel. E. g. שַׂר *prince*, with suff. שָׂרוֹ (for שַׂרּוֹ), pl. שָׂרִים, but with grave suff. שָׂרְכֶם. There are, however, a few exceptions as regards ר, e. g. שָׁרֵּךְ *thy navel*, Eze. 16. 4, from שֹׁר. Others have the so called *Dagesh forte implicit.*, e. g. לַח *fresh* pl. לַחִים (for לַחִּים); אָח *brother*, pl. אַחִים; מִבְטָח with suff. מִבְטַחוֹ, pl. מִבְטַחִים.

SECTION XXXVIII.—NINTH DECLENSION OF THE MASCULINES. (Table O.)

EXPLANATORY.

1. This declension comprises derivatives from verbs ל״ה (§ 27. V) which terminate in ־ֶה, as No. 2. יָפֶה *beautiful*; No. 4. רֹאֶה *seer*; No. 11. קֵצֶה *end*; רֵעֶה *friend*; No. 14. מַרְאֶה *appearance*; from Pilel נָאוֶה *comely* (§ 24. rem. 22); finally, the primitives analogous to the above, as שָׂדֶה *field*.

2. The first syllable is treated according to the nature of its form; ־ֶה, however, undergoes the following changes:—

  (*a*) In the constr. state of the singular it becomes ה־ֵ.

  (*b*) Before any of the afformatives it is entirely dropped.

REMARKS.

1. The original termination ־ִי for which ה־ֶ is substituted* is often restored, and affects the inflexion of the word. Thus, with suff. מְכַפָּיִךְ (sing. *thy covering*, which might also be expressed by מְכַסֵּךְ),

---

* As יִגְלֶה prop. for יִגְלִי, מַרְאֶה for מַרְאִי, comp. שָׂדֶה, poet. שָׂדַי, Gesen. gram. § 42. 2; comp. also above, § 24. r. 4 & 4.

Is. 14. 11 ; מְקָנֶיךָ Is. 30. 23 ; מַרְאַיִךְ (almost universally, though erroneously, taken for the plural), Ca. 2. 14 ; מַרְאֵיהֶם, מַרְאָיו Da. 1. 15 ; Eze. 1. 5. In the plural מְמָחַיִם from מֶמַח for מְמָחֵי Pual part , Is. 25. 6 (Ges. Gram. § 90. 9).

2. To this declension is properly to be referred the plural שָׁמַיִם (from a singular שָׁמֶי, comp. rem. 1), constr. שְׁמֵי, with suff. שָׁמֶיךָ. The form שָׁמַיִם is only an apparent dual, but is a plural in fact, on account of the final י, like גּוֹי which makes the plural גּוֹיִם (not גּוֹיִים), מֵי pl. מַיִם, which latter has likewise the dual form, comp. Lehrg. p. 537.

3. In a few instances הָ is retained even before a genitive, e. g. רֵעֶה הַמֶּלֶךְ friend of the king, 1 Ki. 4. 5; מִשְׁנֵה שִׁבָּרוֹן double destruction, Je. 17. 18.

SECTION XXXIX.—VOWEL-CHANGES IN THE FORMATION OF FEMININE NOUNS.

EXPLANATORY.

1. A substantive or adjective feminine is formed from its corresponding masculine, by appending either of the two terminations הָ and ֶת (with gutturals ַת). Where the one or the other termination is used, and how the masculine is thereby modified, especially with respect to the vowels, has already become evident from the examples given in § 26 and 27, being everywhere accompanied by the corresponding feminine forms; a closer consideration, however, of the general analogy of this formation is still necessary in this place.

2. The termination הָ is more general than ֶת (ַת), since, in most cases, the latter occurs only in connection with the other, and is commonly used for the constr. state, because ת with Pattahh or Segol affords a convenient transition to the following word. E. g. מִשְׁפָּחָה and מַמְלָכָה kingdom, מַמְלֶכֶת and מִשְׁפַּחַת family, אַשְׁמֻרָה and אַשְׁמֹרֶת night-watch, the latter invariably as the constr. state. With the participles, however, and certain infinitives, the termination ֶת is, on the contrary, more commonly in use, e. g. קֹטֶלֶת is more frequent than קֹטְלָה, לֶדֶת more frequent than לֵדָה. In like manner the feminine of nouns terminating in ִי is seldom ִיָה, but frequently ִית (for ֶיֶת). The latter termination, however, is very seldom appended to words which have a quiescent letter, especially ִי, וּ, in the final syllable, e. g. צַדִּיק, עָצוּם.

3. The termination הָ appended to a masculine noun affects the tone of the word, and consequently its vowel, in the same manner as the light suffixes beginning with a vowel (§ 28. No. 21). The following are examples of the formation of feminines in the several declensions :—

Decl.	masc.		fem.	
1.	סוּס	horse	סוּסָה	mare
	תַּחְתּוֹן		תַּחְתּוֹנָה	lower
2.	מוֹצָא		מוֹצָאָה	origin
3.	גָּדוֹל		גְּדוֹלָה	great
	עָצוּם		עֲצוּמָה	mighty
	בָּרִיא		בְּרִיאָה	fat
	מֵקִים		מְקִימָה	raising
4.	נָקָם		נְקָמָה	vengeance
5.	זָקֵן	old man	זְקֵנָה	old woman
6.	מֶלֶךְ	king	מַלְכָּה	queen
	גֶּבַע		גִּבְעָה	hill
	אֹמֶר		אָמְרָה	word
	עֵגֶל	vitulus	עֶגְלָה	vitula
	אֹכֶל		אָכְלָה	food
	חֹזֶק		חָזְקָה	strength
	עָוֶל		עַוְלָה	wrong
	צַיִד	hunting	צֵידָה	game, provision
7.	אֹרַח	traveller	אֹרְחָה	caravan
	מוֹקֵד		מוֹקְדָה	burning
	רֵעַ		דֵּעָה	knowledge
8.	תָּם		תַּמָּה	innocent
	נֵץ		נִצָּה	flower
	כֵּן		כַּנָּה	pedestal
	חֹק		חֻקָּה	law
	בַּז		בִּזָּה	spoil
	גַּן		גַּנָּה	garden
	שַׂר	prince	שָׂרָה	princess
9.	יָפֶה		יָפָה	fair
	מַרְאֶה		מַרְאָה	appearance.

REMARKS.*

On Declension 3.

1. In some few words וּ of the final syllable is changed in the feminine into יּ (comp. § 32. rem. 5). E. g. מָתוֹק sweet, fem. מְתוּקָה; מָלוֹן lodging, fem.

---

* The reader, when directed to the remarks of this section, should bear in mind that there are other remarks, besides these after No. 4.

מָנוֹחַ‎ ;מְלֹאנָה‎ rest, fem. מְנוּחָה‎ ; מָנוֹס‎ flight, fem. מְנוּסָה‎ ;
מָצוֹר‎ fortress, fem. מְצוּרָה‎ .

2. An example of *Kamets pure* in the first syllable
is בְּנוֹדָה‎ Je. 3. 7, 10, comp. § 32. rem. 1.

On Declensions 4 & 5.

3. The forms קְטָל‎ and קְטֵל‎ have sometimes feminines which seem to be derived from *Segolate forms*,
which, from their close relation, is quite natural.
E. g. יָעֵל‎, fem. יַעֲלָה‎ (not יַעֲלָה‎) *wild goat*, יָעֵן‎, fem.
יַעֲנָה‎ *ostrich*; יָרֵךְ‎, fem. יְרֵכָה‎ *thigh*;* שֵׂעָר‎, fem. שַׂעֲרָה‎
hair.

On Declension 7.

4. *Tseri* of the final syllable is even more frequently retained here than in the accession of the
suffixes (§ 36. rem. 4). As עֵץ‎ *wood*, fem. עֵצָה‎ (collect.); מַשְׁעֵן‎ *stay*, fem. מַשְׁעֵנָה‎ ; especially so with
the participles, as בֹּגְדָה‎ *treacherous*, Je. 3. 8, 11 ; יֹלֵדָה‎
bearing, Is. 21. 3 ; נֹצְרָה‎ *watching*, Ca. 1. 6 ; סֹרֵרָה‎
rebellious, Ho. 4. 16 ; זוֹלְלָה‎ *despised*, La. 1. 11 ; אֹכְלָה‎
eating, Is. 30. 30 (but also אֹכְלָה‎ De. 4. 24) ; בֹּעֵרָה‎
burning, Is. 34. 9 (but בֹּעֵרָה‎ ch. 30. 33) ; שֹׁמֵמָה‎ *desolate*, Is. 54. 1 ; שֹׁקֵקָה‎ *eager*, Ps. 107. 9 ; Piel מְשַׁכֵּלָה‎
miscarrying, Ex. 23. 26 ; מְכַשֵּׁפָה‎ *sorceress*, Ex. 22. 17 ;
מְרַקְּדָה‎ *dancing*, Na. 3. 2 ; Hithp. מִתְנַכֵּרָה‎ *feigning a
stranger*, 1 Ki. 14. 5, 6.

4. The penultimate vowel is affected in the same manner
(No. 3) when the feminine termination תְ‎ (תַ‎) is employed,
e. g. עֲטָרָה‎, עֲטֶרֶת‎ *crown* (from masc. עֶטֶר‎) ; עֹקָר‎ *barren*, fem.
עֲקֶרֶת‎ ; חָבֵר‎ *companion*, fem. חֲבֶרֶת‎ ; but remains immutable

in declensions 2 and 7, as חוֹתָם‎ fem. חוֹתֶמֶת‎, קְטָל‎ fem.
קְטֶלֶת‎. The final vowel is also affected in several ways, viz.:—

  (*a*) *Kamets* and *Pattahh* are both changed to *Segol*
    (like מֶלֶךְ‎ for מֶלֶךְ‎, מָלָךְ‎), e. g. מִשְׁעָן‎ *staff*, fem.
    מִשְׁעֶנֶת‎.

  (*b*) *Tseri* is retained in some words, in others it is
    changed to *Segol*, e. g. חָמֵשׁ‎ *five*, fem. חֲמֵשֶׁת‎ ; נֶדֶר‎
    wall fem. גְּדֵרֶת‎ ; inf. לֵד‎ *to bear*, fem. לֶדֶת‎.

  (*c*) תַ‎, employed when a word ends with a guttural,
    changes the preceding *Kamets* or *Tseri* to *Pattahh*, as
    מוֹדָע‎ fem. מוֹדַעַת‎ *acquaintance*; דֵּעַ‎ fem. דַּעַת‎
    knowledge; נֹחַ‎ *rest*, נַחַת‎ (perhaps from masculines
    נַח‎, שֹׁחַ‎).

  (*d*) In the few examples which admit of this ter-
    mination, though they have an *immutable* vowel
    (א‎, יִ‎, וֹ‎, וּ‎) in the final syllable (comp. No. 2),
    this vowel is exchanged for its corresponding mutable
    one, as אִישׁ‎, fem. אֵשֶׁת‎ (for אִישֶׁת‎) ; שַׁלִּיט‎, fem.
    שַׁלֶּטֶת‎ *imperious*, Eze. 16. 30 ; מַקְטִיל‎, fem. מַקְטֶלֶת‎
    (§ 11. rem. 8) ; גְּבִיר‎ *master*, fem. גְּבֶרֶת‎ (but also
    גְּבִירָה‎) ; בּוֹשׁ‎ *shame*, fem. בֹּשֶׁת‎ (with suff. בָּשְׁתִּי‎).
    אֲשְׁמוּרָה‎ and נְחוּשָׁה‎, שָׁלוֹשׁ‎, fem. נְחֹשֶׁת‎ *brass*; שְׁלֹשֶׁת‎, fem. שָׁלוֹשׁ‎,
    and אַשְׁמֹרֶת‎ *night-watch* (from a masc. אַשְׁמוּר‎; in
    תְּשׁוּמֶת‎ however, in Le. 5. 21, וּ‎ has remained un-
    changed, and so in the pr. name תַּנְחוּמֶת‎ 2 Ki. 25. 23,
    Je. 40. 8.

The like feminines most probably existed from צַוָּאר‎
  and צִפּוֹר‎, viz. צַוָּארֶת‎, צִפֹּרֶת‎, which accounts for
  the plurals צַוָּארִים‎ and צִפֳּרִים‎ § 30. rem. 1 & 2. This gives
  rise to another three Segolate forms for the declension of the feminines, like קֹדֶשׁ‎, סֵפֶר‎, מֶלֶךְ‎, viz.
  בֹּשֶׁת‎, אֵשֶׁת‎, קְטֶלֶת‎.

When the word terminates in a quiescent vowel-letter,
  the *Segol*, as a toneless vowel, is entirely dropped,
  hence חַטָּאת‎ *sin*, for חַטֶּאֶת‎ (from חָטָא‎), עִבְרִית‎ for
  עִבְרִיֶּת‎.

REMARKS.†

I. On the Termination תַ‎.

1. This termination is not generally appended to
masculine nouns of the eighth declension which have
the final letter doubled, but where this does take
place, the reduplication of the last radical is omitted.
E. g. אֲדַמְדָּם‎ *reddish*, pl. אֲדַמְדַּמִּים‎ Le. 14. 37, but
fem. אֲדַמְדֶּמֶת‎ Le. 13. 19 ; קַשְׂקַשִּׂים‎ *scales*, 1 Sa. 17. 5,
but fem. sing. קַשְׂקֶשֶׂת‎, whence the plural קַשְׂקְשׂוֹת‎ Eze.
29. 4. The same analogy exists in the feminines
of the patronymics, gentilics, and ordinals terminating in יִ‎, which are inflected יָה‎, and יִת‎ by

solving the reduplication. E. g. מוֹאָבִיָּה‎ Ru. 4. 5,
and מוֹאָבִית‎ 2 Ch. 24. 26, *a Moabitish woman*; אֲרַמִּיָּה‎
Syrian woman 1 Ch. 7. 14, and אֲרָמִית‎ *in the Syrian
language*, 2 Ki. 18. 26 ; שְׁלִישִׁיָּה‎ Is. 15. 5, and שְׁלִישִׁית‎
third; and in like manner the cardinal numerals
חֲמִשָּׁה‎ and חֲמֵשֶׁת‎ *five*, שִׁשָּׁה‎ and שֵׁשֶׁת‎ *six*.‡

2. Where the Hebrew has the Segolate termina-
tion (ֶֶ), the Aramaean has usually (ְַ), as מֶלֶךְ‎ מְלַךְ‎.
The like Syriacism is found here in the feminine termination, as מִשָּׂאת‎ for שְׂאֵת‎ *to bear*; שְׂאָת‎ for

---

* In this word, however, there appears to be a twofold derivation, viz. יְרֵכָה‎ (with suff. יַרְכָתוֹ‎, du. יַרְכָתַיִם‎) from יָרֵךְ‎; and
יַרְכָּה‎ (whence du. יַרְכְּתֵי‎) from the Segolate form יֶרֶךְ‎, the constr. of יֶרֶךְ‎.

† For other remarks in this section see above, after No. 3.

‡ This accounts for the plural termination יוֹת‎ used for the nouns of יִת‎, as עִבְרִית‎ pl. עִבְרִיּוֹת‎, namely, an original
form of יָה‎ must likewise be supposed as the ground-form, comp. Ges. Lehrg. § 124. 3.

gift; מִצְאֶת for מָצָאת *finding,* invariably, as it appears, when the last radical is א.

3. The reverse of the inflexion just mentioned is that of the Arabic, which has (ִ־) instead of (ֵ֖) as מִלְךָ for מֶלֶךָ. A similar form in the Hebrew is יֹלַדְתְּ *bearing,* for יֹלֶדֶת Ge. 16. 11; Ju. 13. 5.

II. IN GENERAL.

4. The vowels are shortened in the same manner when the formative syllables יִ־, וֹ, יִ־, וּת are ap-

pended, as when the termination הָ־ is appended, which affords the explanation for the vowel-changes of § 26. Nos. 15, 16, &c.

5. Finally, it is to be observed that, since there are not masculines extant for every feminine, it is often doubtful to which class a certain feminine is to be referred. Thus, for instance, there is an entire want of masculine forms corresponding to the feminines of וּת; there can, however, be no doubt that they must have ended in וֹ.

SECTION XL.—ON THE DECLENSION OF THE FEMININE NOUNS IN GENERAL

The declension of these nouns is much more simple than that of the masculines, since the addition of the feminine termination has already occasioned a shortening of the vowels. In the plural no distinction is made between the *light* and

grave suffixes, both being appended to the *constr.* state. The inflexion of the feminine nouns is best exhibited in four declensions (comp. the note to the following section).

SECTION XLI.—TENTH DECLENSION, OR THE *FIRST* OF THE FEMININES.* (TABLE O.)
EXPLANATORY.

1. This declension, like the first of the masculines, has no vowel-change, and is inserted merely for the sake of comparison.

2. After what has been said, it is hardly necessary to point out the nouns belonging to this declension, viz. the feminines terminating in הָ־ from the masc. dec. 3. גְּדוֹלָה, 7. קְטֻלָּה, 8. חֻקָּה, בִּצָּה, תַּמָּה.

SECTION XLII.—ELEVENTH DECLENSION, OR THE *SECOND* OF THE FEMININES. (TABLE O.)
EXPLANATORY.

1. To this declension belong those nouns which have a pure *Kamets* or *Tseri* before the feminine termination הָ־. Such are the following derivatives from the regular verb (§ 26), the feminine forms of Nos. 1. as נְבָלָה *foolish,* חֲכָמָה *wise;* 2. לְבֵנָה *brick;* 4. תּוֹעֵבָה *abomination;* 12. נְקָמָה *vengeance;* 14. מַמְלָכָה *kingdom,* מַצֵּבָה *pillar;* 17. נִפְלָאָה *wonder;* also the following derivatives from the regular verbs (§ 27) are, e. g. from פ"ו, Nos. 10. עֵצָה *counsel,* חֵמָה *wrath;* 14. מוֹעֵצָה *counsel;* from ל"ה, Nos. 2. יָפָה *fair;* 11. בְּרֵה *pit;* 12. בַּלָּה *destruction;* consequently the feminine forms from dec. 2, 4, 5, 9.

2. This inflexion is analogous to that of the second declen-

sion of the masculines, whether the vowel is *Kamets* or *Tseri.* When Sheva precedes the terminations הָ־, הֶ־, as in paradigm c, the two Shevas of the shortened form (צְדְקַת) are combined in one syllable, צִדְקַת.

3. The following are regular exceptions, in which (ָ) and (ֵ) are *immutable,* either as being *impure* vowels, or as standing in sharpened syllables with Dagesh, *syllaba dagessanda :*—
Of the derivatives from the regular verb (§ 26), the feminine forms of Nos. 6. יַבָּשָׁה *dry land;* 13. חֲשֵׁכָה (for חֲשִׁיכָה) *darkness,* and several others; בַּקָּשָׁה *request,* נֶאָצָה *reproach,*† פְּרָשָׁה (for פַּרְשָׁה) *exposition;* 28. אַזְכָּרָה *memorial;* also from פ"ו, as הַצָּלָה *deliverance,* הַכָּרָה *a knowing;* and so all the

---

* Gesenius gives two separate tables: one for the masculines, consisting of nine declensions, and another for the feminines, consisting of four. For the sake of convenience, we have given both in one table, making together *thirteen* declensions; here, however, in the explanations, where they must necessarily be kept distinct, we have in this manner contrived to point out both orders.

† נֶאָצָה with Dagesh forte implicit. for נַאְצָה, *Pattahh* is changed to *Segol* before the *guttural* with *Kamets,* comp. אֵם § 45, also § 37. rem. 7 and § 14. rem. 3.

feminines whose geminate letter is a guttural, on account of which it cannot be doubled, and are therefore preceded by (ָ) or (ֶ); e. g. (§ 27) Nos. 1. צָרָה *enemy* (from צַר), רָעָה *evil* (from רַע), בָּרָה *pure* (from בַּר); 2. גָּרָה *rumination* (from גָּרַר); 14. מְאֵרָה *curse* (from אָרַר), מְגֵרָה *a saw* (from גָּרַד).

so also derivatives from ע"י and ע"י (whose Kamets and Tseri are invariably *impure*), as Nos. 1. זָרָה *strange*, בָּמָה *height*; 2. עֵדָה *witness*; and finally, derivatives from ל"א, No. 2. מְלֵאָה *full*, טְמֵאָה *unclean*.

REMARKS.

I. ON THE FORM WITH ָה.

1. Forms of parad. c, when their first or second letter is a guttural, take in the shortened form either (-) or (ֶ); e. g. חֲכָמָה *wise*, pl. c. חַכְמוֹת; עֲגָלָה *waggon*, with suff. עֶגְלָתוֹ; זַעֲקָה *cry*, constr. זַעֲקַת.

2. In a small number of derivatives from ל"ה Kamets of the penultima is immutable, as תְּלָאָה *travail* (from לָאָה), אָלָה *aqueduct* (from עָלָה), אָלָה *oath*, with suff. אָלָתִי, אָלָתוֹ Ge. 24. 41; De. 29. 11; מָנָה *portion*, whence מְנוֹתֶיהָ Est. 2. 9 (but sing. constr. מְנָת Je. 13. 25); הָרָה *pregnant*, whence הָרוֹתֶיהָ 2 Ki. 15. 16; הָרוֹתֵיהֶם 2 Ki. 8. 12 (but sing. constr. הֲרַת Je. 20. 17); יָפֶה *fair*, with suff. יָפָתִי Ca. 2. 10, 13 (elsewhere constr. יְפַת, pl. יָפוֹת).

3. An irregularity similar to the preceding is found in the word קְעָרָה *dish*, of which the pl. constr. is קַעֲרוֹת, and yet with suff. קַעֲרוֹתָי.

II. ON THE FORM WITH ָה.

4. By far the greater number of this class of nouns retain the Tseri in the inflexion, and but few occur with *mutable Tseri* besides those given in No. 1 of this section, viz., אֲשֵׁרָה *outpouring*, pl. constr. אֲשֵׁרוֹת; שְׂדֵמָה *field*, pl. constr. שְׂדֵמוֹת; בְּהֵמָה *cattle*, constr. בְּהֵמַת, pl. בְּהֵמוֹת; comp. also שְׁאֵלָה, with suff. שְׁאֵלָתִי. With *immutable Tseri* are, אֲבֵדָה *something lost*, גְּזֵלָה *robbery*, אֲפֵלָה *darkness*, בְּרֵכָה *pool*, גְּנֵבָה *something stolen*, מְרֵרָה *gall*, שְׂרֵפָה *burning*, תְּאֵנָה *fig*; from (§ 26) No. 14. מַהְפֵּכָה *overthrow*, מַגֵּפָה *plague*, &c. With some nouns both the contracted and uncontracted forms are found to consist together, as

נְבֵלָה *dead body*, whence נְבֵלָתִי, but constr. נִבְלַת, with suff. נִבְלָתוֹ Le. 5. 2; De. 21. 3; שְׁאֵלָה *request*, whence שְׁאֵלָתִי 1 Sa. 1. 27, and שְׁאֵלָתִי Job 6. 8; גְּדֵרָה *wall*, pl. גְּדֵרוֹת 1 Sa. 24. 4, but pl. with suff. גְּדֵרוֹתָיו Ps. 89. 41.

III. IN GENERAL.

5. Several nouns of both the foregoing forms take in the constr. st., and before suffixes, the secondary Segolate form ֶ-ת, ַ-ת, a case similar to that of the masculines (§ 34. No. 2), as the following examples show:—

מַמְלָכָה *kingdom*,	constr.	מַמְלֶכֶת	with suff.	מַמְלַכְתִּי
מִשְׁפָּחָה *family*	"	מִשְׁפַּחַת	"	מִשְׁפַּחְתִּי
מְלָאכָה *work*	"	מְלֶאכֶת	"	מְלַאכְתְּךָ
מֶרְכָּבָה *chariot*	"	מֶרְכֶּבֶת	"	מֶרְכַּבְתּוֹ
מֶמְשָׁלָה *government*	"	מֶמְשֶׁלֶת	"	מֶמְשַׁלְתּוֹ
מִלְחָמָה *war*	"	. . . . .	"	מִלְחַמְתִּי
תִּפְאָרָה *ornament*	"	תִּפְאֶרֶת	"	תִּפְאַרְתּוֹ

Comp. also עֲטָרָה, constr. עֲטֶרֶת *crown*; דְּבֵלָה, constr. דְּבֶלֶת *a lump of figs*; נֶחֱרָצָה *determined*, constr. נֶחֱרֶצֶת; גְּבִירָה *mistress*, constr. גְּבֶרֶת; לֶהָבָה *flame*, constr. לֶהֶבֶת; אַיָּלָה *hind*, constr. אַיֶּלֶת; בְּהֵמָה *cattle*, with suff. בְּהֶמְתְּךָ, בְּהֶמְתֵּנוּ, and of the numerals אַרְבָּעָה constr. אַרְבַּעַת *four*, עֲשָׂרָה constr. עֲשֶׂרֶת *ten*.

Several of these, e. g. תִּפְאֶרֶת, אַיֶּלֶת, occur also in the absolute state, which is sufficient warrant that the Segolate is a ground-form; the latter, however, is so frequently used as the construct in connection with the form ָה, that constructs like אַיֶּלֶת, תִּפְאֶרֶת do not occur any longer.

SECTION XLIII.—TWELFTH DECLENSION, OR THE *THIRD* OF THE FEMININES. (TABLE O.)

1. To this declension belong the feminines derived from the Segolate form of the regular verb (§ 26. No. 11), or of the irregular verbs, as long as this form is unaffected by the irregularity, e. g. from פ"י, as יַלְדָּה *maiden*, and ל"ה, as שַׁלְוָה *rest*, רַעְיָה *companion*; hence the feminines from the masculine forms of declension 6.

2. The inflexion is analogous to that of the masculines, and is especially distinguished by the peculiar formation of the plural, for which see explanation § 35. No. 2 c.

3. There are other nouns resembling this in form, but as they are not feminines derived from the Segolate forms, they do not belong to this declension, especially derivatives from ל"ה like מִצְוָה *commandment* (from צָוָה), מִרְמָה *deceit*, &c., which form their plural without any vowel-change מִצְוֹת, מִרְמוֹת.

REMARK.

There are a few words which deviate from the paradigm, in having their middle Vav *moveable* in the ground-form, but *quiescent* in the shortening;

as עַוְלָה *wickedness*, with ה parag. עֹלָתָה Job 5. 16, pl. עֹלוֹת Ps. 58. 3; 64. 7; לֹוְיָה *garland*, pl. לֹיוֹת 1 Ki. 7. 29, 30, 36.

SECTION XLIV.—THIRTEENTH DECLENSION, OR THE *FOURTH* OF THE FEMININES. (TABLE O.)

1. To this declension belong the feminines formed by the addition of the feminine termination ־ֶת or ־ַת (§ 39. Nos. 2 & 3). They are properly Segolate forms, and as such correspond in the inflexion to the masculine Segolates.

2. Their inflexion is,

(a) In the singular, in every respect the same as that of the masculines. There is, therefore, no change of vowels in the constr. state, and before the suffixes Segol of the penultima is changed to *Pattahh* (and *Hhirik*), *Tseri* to *Hhirik*, *Hholem pure* to *Kamets-hhatuph*, like in קֹדֶשׁ, סֵפֶר, (נֶקֶר) מֶלֶךְ.

(b) In the plural there exists this peculiarity, that the

vowel preceding the final Segol (or Pattahh) is dropped even in the absolute state; the form ־ֶת, however, either leaves some trace behind in the vowel (ְ־), as שִׁבֹּלֶת, pl. שִׁבֳּלִים, as in the paradigm, or is entirely dropped, as גֻּלְגֹּלֶת, pl. גֻּלְגְּלוֹת.

These vowels are invariably *pure* and mutable, viz. (ּ־)ּ (־ֹ)ֹ (־) *pure*. The entire rejection of these vowels in the inflexion will be easier understood, if it is borne in mind that the terminations (ֶ־ת)ת, (ֶ־ת)ת, ־ַת, are also elsewhere interchanged with (־ָ), (ּ־ֹ), ־ֹ (comp. § 26. Nos. 10 & 11, & § 35. rem. 10). Here also may be adduced as an instance, מַשְׂאֵת for מַשְׂאָת, pl. מַשְׂאוֹת.

REMARKS.

I. On the Sing. with Suffix.

1. According to the paradigm, the form ending in ־ַת takes, before suffixes, in some words, Pattahh; in others, Hhirik. This, however, is not merely arbitrary, but depends upon the origin of the form. If the masculine from which it is derived terminates in (־ַ) or (־), as is the case with most of them, the *Pattahh* appears in the inflexion of the feminine; but if the masculine terminates in (־ֵ) or ־ֹ, the feminine takes *Hhirik* (comp. § 35. rem. 3). Thus the following are inflected :—

With *Pattahh*, e. g. מִשְׁמֶרֶת *custody* (from מִשְׁמָר), דֶּלֶת *door* (from דַּל), comp. the examples given in § 42. rem. 5).

With *Hhirik*, all the infinitives of the verbs פ"י, e. g. שֶׁבֶת *to dwell* (masc. שֵׁב), with suff. שִׁבְתִּי; רֶדֶת *to descend* (masc. רֵד), רִדְתִּי; לֶדֶת *to bear*, לִדְתִּי; in the same manner גְּבֶרֶת *mistress* (masc. גְּבִיר), with suff. גְּבִרְתִּי; מֵינֶקֶת *nurse* (masc. מֵינִיק), מֵנִקְתּוֹ; זֶפֶת *pitch* (masc. Chald. זֵפֶא, זֶפֶת), זִפְתִּי; אֱמֶנֶת contracted אָמֶת *thrust* (masc. אָמֵן), with suff. אֲמִתּוֹ; בַּת contr. from בְּנַת *daughter* (masc. בֵּן), with suff. בִּתּוֹ for בִּנְתּוֹ.

There are, comparatively, but few examples in which the punctuation does not conform to the origin of the form. Such are, e. g. יוֹנֶקֶת *sprout* (masc. יוֹנֵק), יוֹנַקְתּוֹ, and so אִגֶּרֶת *letter*, אִוֶּלֶת *folly*, מַצֵּבָה *pillar*, which have Pattahh, though (according

to § 26. No. 9) we must suppose them derived from masc. מַצֵּב, אִוֵּל, אִגֵּר (for which comp. מַצֵּבָה). There occurs, moreover, שִׁבְתִּי *my dwelling*. Ps. 23. 6, which elsewhere is שֶׁבְתִּי, comp. Ps. 27. 4.

2. Of the form (ֶ־ת), the shortening is constantly Hhirik, e. g. אֵשֶׁת, אִשְׁתִּי.

3. The forms ־ֶת and ־ַת, which have commonly (־) and (־) in the shortening, occur also with *Segol*, but almost exclusively before the suffix, ךְ, e. g. אֶשְׁתְּךָ *thy wife*, Ps. 128. 3; otherwise, אִשְׁתְּ, אִשְׁתּוֹ; and even אִשְׁתְּךָ Ge. 6. 18; Am. 7. 17; חֲבֶרֶת *companion*, חֲבֶרְתָּהּ Mal. 2. 14; בְּהֶמָת, בְּהֶמְתְּךָ Le. 19.19; 25. 7; but also בְּהֶמְתֵּנוּ Nu. 32. 26; Ne. 9. 37. So, finally, לֶכֶת *to go*, with all the suffixes, לַכְתִּי, לַכְתָּם, לָכְתּוֹ, לָכְתְּךָ.

4. The form ־ַת, besides its inflexion given in the paradigm, is in certain words also inflected with *Kibbuts*. Here, however, like in rem. 1, reference must be made to the origin of the form, viz. where the masculine has originally וֹ, the feminine takes *Kamets-hhatuph*; but *Kibbuts* when the masculine has וּ. E. g. בֹּשֶׁת *shame* (from בּוֹשׁ), with suff. בֻּשְׁתִּי; גֻּלְגֹּלֶת *skull* (as if from גֻּלְגֹּל), with suff. גֻּלְגָּלְתִּי; שְׁלֹשֶׁת *three* (from שָׁלֹשׁ), with suff. שְׁלָשְׁתְּכֶם; but נְחֹשֶׁת

brass (masc. נְחוּשׁ, comp. the other form נְחוּשָׁה), with suff. נְחָשְׁתִּי; and so מַשְׂכֹּרֶת מַתְכֹּנֶת wages, measure, מַחֲלֹקֶת division, may be derived from forms like מַשְׁבּוּר. An exception is נָחָשְׁתִּי La. 3. 7.

II. ON THE FORM OF THE PLURAL.

5. The characteristic of the inflexion of the plural, which is the rejection of the vowel preceding the final syllable, may be seen in numerous examples, as אִגֶּרֶת, pl. אִגְּרוֹת letters; יוֹנֶקֶת, pl. יוֹנְקוֹת sprouts; מַחֲלֹקֶת, pl. מַחְלְקוֹת divisions; גֻּלְגֹּלֶת, pl. גֻּלְגְּלוֹת skulls; and with (מ) צִפֳּרִים birds (from a fem. צִפֹּרֶת). Several nouns, however, of this class, borrow their plural from the coexisting fem. form הָ-, הֶ- (though this form does not actually occur), so that the vowel of

the original masculine appears again in full. Such are:— כֹּתֶרֶת chapiter (from כֹּתֶר), pl. כֹּתָרוֹת; מַאֲכֶלֶת knife (as if from מַאֲכָל), pl. מַאֲכָלוֹת; תּוֹכַחַת reproof, pl. תּוֹכָחוֹת (as if from תּוֹכָחָה); טַבַּעַת ring, pl. טַבָּעוֹת (as if from טַבָּעָה); מִשְׁפַּחַת family, pl. מִשְׁפָּחוֹת; מִקְלַעַת carved work; מֵינֶקֶת nurse, pl מֵינִיקוֹת (as if from מֵינִיקָה); מַחֲרֶשֶׁת, pl. מַחֲרֵשׁוֹת ploughshares. A few, however, of the form הֶ- occur likewise with the pl. -וֹת, e. g. עַשְׁתֹּרֶת Astarte, pl. עַשְׁתָּרוֹת; בַּצֹּרֶת draught, pl. בַּצָּרוֹת. Thus the plurals אַרְמְנוֹת palaces, אֶשְׁכֹּלוֹת clusters, should probably be derived from singulars אַרְמֶנֶת, אֶשְׁכֹּלֶת, though only the masculines אַרְמוֹן, אֶשְׁכּוֹל occur.

Here belongs, moreover, חַטָּאת sin, for חַטָּאַת, pl. חַטָּאוֹת.

SECTION XLV.—IRREGULAR NOUNS.

There are several anomalous forms of inflexion chiefly occurring in single examples only, or, at the most, in very few. Most of these irregularities of inflexion consist in the derivation of the *constr. state*, or of the *plural*, not from the absolute state of the singular, but from another wholly different form.

These irregularities require the more attention, because, as in all languages, the words which they affect are those in most common use. And though most of these nouns are primitives, they nevertheless follow the analogy of verbal nouns without even their roots occurring as verbs. They follow here in alphabetical order:—

אָב, *father*, for אָבֶה; as if from אָבָה (like a derivative from a verb לִ'ה § 27. V. No. 2); constr. state אֲבִי (like a Segolate form from לִ'ה No. 11); with light suff. אָבִי, with grave suff. אֲבִיהֶם, אֲבִיכֶם, אָבִינוּ, אָבִיךָ, אָבִיךְ (from אָב). Plur. אָבוֹת (with fem. termination).

> The regular form of the constr. state, viz. אַב, occurs only in Ge. 17. 4, 5, in order to bring in the etymology of אַבְרָהָם, as in the like cases rare forms are often introduced. This form occurs also besides in several proper names, e. g. אַבְנֵר, אַבְשָׁלוֹם. The Chald. and Arab. form אֲבִי is found, according to Khethib, in the proper name אֲבוּגַיִל 1 Sa. 25. 18.

אָח, *brother*, constr. אֲחִי with suff. אָחִיךָ, אָחִיו, אֲחִיכֶם, plur constr. אֲחֵי, אֲחֵיכֶם. All these forms follow the analogy of verbs לִ'ה, as if אָח stood for אָחֶה, from אָחָה, comp. the preceding אָב. But the plur. abs. is אַחִים with *Dag. forte implicit.* (comp. § 37. r. 7), as if from אַחַח, hence אַחַי, &c. But אָחִיו, אֶחָי for אֲחִיו, אֲחָיֶה אַחֶיךָ, אֶחָי, where Segol takes the place of Pattahh before the guttural ח with Kamets (חָ), comp. הֶחָזוֹן for הַחָזוֹן. כַּחֵשׁ for כָּחָשׁ כֶּחָשׁ.

אֶחָד, *one* (for אַחָד, with *Dag. forte implicit.*, comp. the preceding אָח), constr. state אַחַד, fem. אַחַת for אַחַדְתְּ, אַחְדַּת, in pause אֶחָת (for אַחַת comp. אֶחָיו above). In one instance, Eze. 33. 30, it takes the form חַד by aphaeresis. Pl. masc. אֲחָדִים as if from אֶחָד or אַחַד.

אָחוֹת, *sister* (contr. for אֲחֹוֶת from a masculine for אָחוּ comp. חֲצוֹת § 27. V. No. 13, & § 24. rem. 2). Plur. only with suff. אֲחִיֹתַי, אַחְיוֹתַי (from a sing. אַחְיָה fem. of אֲחִי), also אַחְוֹתַיִךְ (as if from a sing. fem. from אָח אָחָה).

אַחֵר, *another*, fem. אַחֶרֶת (with *Dag. forte implicit.*); but plur. אֲחֵרִים, אֲחֵרוֹת, as if from a form אָחֵר (after dec. V).

אִישׁ *man*, a softened form from אֱנָשׁ; in the plural it has very seldom אִישִׁים, the usual form being אֲנָשִׁים (from אֱנָשׁ) constr. אַנְשֵׁי. Comp. אִשָּׁה.

---

* This is true as far as the use of these forms is concerned; but it seems more natural to class together אִישִׁים with אִישׁ, אֲנָשִׁים with אֱנָשׁ; so that there remains the only one irregularity, that the plural of אֱנָשׁ is used for אֱנוֹשׁ. This is the order we have followed in this work, and have accordingly adopted two roots אֱנָשׁ, and אִישׁ, the latter being secondary, and softened from the former. Under אֱנָשׁ we have put אִשָּׁה for אֲנָשָׁה, plur. נָשִׁים. Under אִישׁ we have put אֵשֶׁת for אִשֶּׁת (§ 39. 4. d).

אָמָה maid-servant, plur. (with ה inserted) אֲמָהוֹת, אֲמָהֹת. Comp. in Chaldee אֲבָהָן fathers.

אִשָּׁה woman (for אִנְשָׁה fem. from אֱנָשׁ), plur. נָשִׁים by aphaeresis for אֲנָשִׁים. For אֵשֶׁת see the note under אִישׁ above.

בַּיִת house, constr. בֵּית, plur. בָּתִּים, with light suff. בָּתָּיו, but with grave suff. בָּתֵּיהֶם, בָּתֵּיכֶם (with Metheg). The root of this word is doubtful. It is usually derived from בּוּת, to pass the night, and the plur. בָּתִּים for בָּתָתִים from a sing. בֹּתֶת (after the form בֹּשֶׁת from בּוֹשׁ). Or בַּיִת is supposed to be a softened form from בֶּנֶת (like אִישׁ for אֱנָשׁ) derived from בָּנָה to build; plur. בָּתִּים (bottim) for בָּנְתִּים from another sing. בֹּנֶת. For this plural form comp. § 35. rem. 16.

בֵּן son (for בֶּנֶה from בָּנָה), constr. state בֶּן, seldom בָּן, once בְּנִי, and finally בְּנוֹ. With suff. בְּנִי, בִּנְךָ; plur. בָּנִים (as if from בָּן, for בָּנָה), constr. state בְּנֵי.

בַּת daughter (for בֶּנֶת, fem. from בֵּן), with suff. בִּתִּי (for בִּנְתִּי), plur. בָּנוֹת (from the sing. בָּנָה comp. בָּנִים sons, pl. of בֵּן), constr. state בְּנוֹת.

גַּיְא fully, גַּיְא valley. The Khethib נִיאוֹת, 2 Ki. 2. 16, ought, doubtless, to be pointed גֵּיאוֹת, which is the regular plural (§ 35. rem. 12); but it is often transposed גְּאָיוֹת.

חָם stepfather, with suff. חָמִיךָ, and חָמוֹת stepmother, comp. אָח brother, אָחוֹת sister.

יוֹם day, with suff. יוֹמִי, dual יוֹמַיִם. Plur. יָמִים by Chaldaism (as if from יָם for יָמָה) constr. יְמֵי and poet. יְמוֹת.

כְּלִי vessel, plur. כֵּלִים (as if from כֶּלֶה, כֵּל).

כְּנָת associate, prop. for כְּנָאת, כְּנָאַת (§ 39. No. 4), plur. with suff. כְּנָוֹתָיו. As if from כְּנָנָה, comp. מְנָת.

מַיִם plur. water, constr. state מֵי, and also מֵימֵי, with suff. מֵימֵיכֶם. The last two are regular plural forms from מַיִם regarded as a singular, like בַּיִת.

מְנָת portion (from מָנָה), for מְנָאת, whence plur. מְנָאוֹת and מְנָיוֹת (both with (ָ) pure).

This inflexion is best accounted for in the following manner:—the form מְנָאת=מְנָת is derived from a masc. מְנָא, which stands for מְנִי (after the form כְּתָב § 26. No. 13). Hence מְנָאת for מְנָיַת, מְנָיִת. Whence the plural, but not immediately from the form ת—ָ, but from מְנָאָה, מְנָיָה, according to § 44. rem. 5, as the termination ת—ָ would lose the preceding long vowel.

עִיר city, plur. עֲיָרִים (according to § 35. rem. 12), only Ju 10. 4, elsewhere עָרִים. This might indeed be taken as a contraction from עֲיָרִים; but better from עָר = עִיר, which still occurs in the proper names, e. g. עָר מוֹאָב.

עַם, with distinctive accent and with the article עָם, people, plur. עַמִּים, but also by Aramaism עֲמָמִים, עַמְמֵי (as if from a Segolate form עֲמָם).

פֶּה mouth (prop. for פֶּאֶה, comp. שֶׂה), constr. state פִּי (for פְּאִי), with suff. פִּי (my mouth), פִּיו, פִּיךָ, &c. Plur פִּים, also פִּיּוֹת. Fem. פֵּיָה from פֶּיָה.

פֶּחָה governor, for פַּחָה (with Dag. forte implicit.), comp. אָחִיו under אָח), plur. פַּחוֹת, with suff. פַּחֲוֹתָיהָ, but constr. state פַּחֲווֹת, like the Chald. פַּחֲוָתָא. The sing. with suff. is פֶּחָם Ne. 5. 14, as if from פֶּחָ.

רֹאשׁ head (for רְאֹשׁ Segolate form), plur. רָאשִׁים (for אֲשִׁים once with suff. רָאשָׁיו.

שֶׂה sheep or goat, for שָׂיֶה (like פֶּה), constr. state שֵׂה, with suff. שְׂיוֹ and שְׂיָהוּ.

6*

CHALDEE PARADIGMS.

Since the Biblical Chaldee occupies only a few chapters, viz. Ezr. 4. 8; 6. 18; 7. 12—26; Da. 2. 4—7. 21; Je. 10. 11, it needs hardly to be noticed, that but an exceedingly small number of examples can be found in the Bible itself applicable to the Chaldee paradigms. But it must be remarked, that were we, agreeably to the purpose of this work, to form paradigms for the Biblical portion alone, they would not only be incomplete, but they would likewise, in a measure, misrepresent its true Chaldee character, because this portion is so replete with Hebraisms. We give, accordingly, the paradigms as they are found in Winer's Chaldee Grammar, but confine our remarks to the occurrences of the Biblical portion.

TABLE P. THE PERSONAL PRONOUN.

SEPARATE PRONOUN.		VERBAL SUFFIX.		NOMINAL SUFFIX.			
				A. SUFFIXES TO NOUNS SINGULAR.		B. SUFFIXES TO NOUNS PLURAL.	
Singular.							
1. com.	אֲנָה, אֲנָא . . . . *I.*	נִי, ־ַנִי . . . . *me.*		־ִי . . . . *my.*		־ַי . . . . *my.*	
2. com.	אַתְּ, אַנְתְּ, אַנְתָּה *thou*	־ָךְ, ־ָךְ } *thee.*		־ָךְ } *thy.*		־ָךְ, ־ָיךְ } *thy*	
2. f.		־ִיךְ, ־ַךְ, ־ֵךְ, ־ֵיךְ		־ֵךְ, (־ֵיךְ)		־ַיִכִי, ־ֵיךְ	
3. { m.	הוּא . . . . *he.*	־ֵהּ, ־ֵיהּ, (וְהִי, הִי) *him.*		־ֵהּ . . . *his.*		־ וֹהִי *his*	
{ f.	הִיא . . . . *she.*	־ַהּ, הָא . . . *her.*		־ַהּ (in Bibl. Ch. ־ַהּ) *her.*		־ַהָא, (־ַיהָ Da. 7. 7, 19) } *her.*	
Plural.							
1. com.	נַחְנָא, אֲנַחְנָא . . . *we.*	נָא; ־ַנָא . . . *us.*		־ַנָא . . . . *our.*		־ַיְנָא . . . . *our.*	
2. { m.	אַתּוּן, אַנְתּוּן } *ye.*	כְוֹן } *you.*		(כְוֹם, כְוֹן) } *your.*		־ֵיכוֹן } *your.*	
{ f.	אַתֵּין, אַנְתֵּין	כֵן		כֵן		־ֵיכֵן	
3. { m.	הִמּוֹ, הִמּוֹן, הִמּוֹן, הִנּוּן, אִנּוּן } *they.*	־ֻנּוֹן; נוֹן } *them.*		(הוֹם) הוֹן } *their.*		־ֵיהֹם } *their.*	
{ f.	הֵנֵּין, אִנֵּין	־ֵן; נֵן		הֵן, הֵין		־ֵיהֵן	

SECTION XLVI.*—ON THE SUFFIXES TO NOUNS SINGULAR AND PLURAL.
REMARKS.

I. ON THE SUFFIX TO NOUNS SINGULAR.

1. Instead of ־ֵהּ there is twice found ־ָא in פִּשְׁרֵא *its interpretation*, Da. 4. 15; 5. 8 Kheth., but which is not recognised by the Masorites, who give ־ֵהּ in the Keri.

Appended to the words אָח, אָב, which before suffix become אֲבִי, &c., the suffixes of the 2nd and 3rd pers sing. take the forms ־ָךְ, ־הִי, ־הָא; which forms do not elsewhere occur (in the Bible) as nominal suffixes. E. g. אֲבוּךְ Da. 5. 11, 18; אֲבוּהִי Da. 5. 2.

2. The same forms are attached to prepositions

---

* We continue the sections from the Hebrew to the Chaldee, for the sake of convenience to the reader (especially such as are originally plural nouns) and to signs of cases, בְּ, לִי, בִּי, יָת, &c.; as, יָתֵהּ, לִי, בִּי, יָת, &c.

II. On the Suffix to Nouns Plural.

3. These suffixes are regularly appended, however, only to plurals masculine. Feminines frequently take the singular suff. יִ־, ־ֶהָ, &c. E. g. יַרְבָתֵהּ *his sides*; Da. 2. 32; שֶׁנְלָתֵהּ וּלְחֵנָתֵהּ *his wives*

and his concubines, Da. 5. 2; כְּנָוָתְהֹן *their companies.* מַחְלְקָתְהוֹן, פְּלֻנָּתְהוֹן Ezr. 4. 17; 6. 18.

4. The suffix יִ־ךְ frequently appears abbreviated ךְ־; e. g. רֶעְיוֹנָךְ Da. 5. 10, comp. Da. 2. 29.

5. Prepositions, which are originally plural nouns, take the suffixes of plur. nouns; e. g. קָדְמֵי, קָדְמוֹהִי, עֲלֵיהוֹן, עֲלוֹהִי.

TABLE G. REGULAR VERB.

		PEAL.	ITHPEAL.	PAEL.	ITHPAAL.	APHEL.	ITTAPHAL.
Pret.	3. m.	קְטַל	אִתְקְטֵל	קַטֵּל	אִתְקַטַּל	אַקְטֵל	אִתַּקְטַל
	3. f.	קִטְלַת	אִתְקְטִלַת	קַטִּלַת	אִתְקַטְּלַת	אַקְטִלַת	אִתַּקְטַלַת
	2. m.	קְטַלְתְּ	אִתְקְטֵלְתְּ	קַטֵּלְתָּא, קַטֵּלְתְּ	אִתְקַטַּלְתְּ	אַקְטֵלְתָּא, אַקְטֵלְתְּ	אִתַּקְטַלְתְּ
	2. f.	קְטַלְתְּ	אִתְקְטֵלְתְּ	קַטֵּלְתְּ	אִתְקַטַּלְתְּ	אַקְטֵלְתְּ	אִתַּקְטַלְתְּ
	1. c.	קְטַלֵת	אִתְקְטֵלֵת	קַטֵּלֵת	אִתְקַטַּלֵת	אַקְטֵלֵת	אִתַּקְטַלֵת
Plur.	3. m.	קְטַלוּ	אִתְקְטִלוּ	קַטִּלוּ	אִתְקַטַּלוּ	אַקְטִלוּ	אִתַּקְטַלוּ
	3. f.	קְטַלָא	אִתְקְטִלָא	קַטִּלָא	אִתְקַטַּלָא	אַקְטִלָא	אִתַּקְטַלָא
	2. m.	קְטַלְתּוּן	אִתְקְטֵלְתּוּן	קַטִּלְתּוּן	אִתְקַטַּלְתּוּן	אַקְטֵלְתּוּן	אִתַּקְטַלְתּוּן
	2. f.	קְטַלְתֵּן	אִתְקְטֵלְתֵּן	קַטִּלְתֵּן	אִתְקַטַּלְתֵּן	אַקְטֵלְתֵּן	אִתַּקְטַלְתֵּן
	1. c.	קְטַלְנָא	אִתְקְטֵלְנָא	קַטִּלְנָא	אִתְקַטַּלְנָא	אַקְטֵלְנָא	אִתַּקְטַלְנָא
Inf		מִקְטַל	אִתְקְטָלָא	קַטָּלָא	אִתְקַטָּלָא	אַקְטָלָא	אִתַּקְטָלָא
Imp.	2. m.	קְטֵל	אִתְקְטֵל	קַטֵּל	אִתְקַטַּל	אַקְטֵל	אִתַּקְטַל
	2. f.	קְטֵלִי	אִתְקְטֵלִי	קַטֵּלִי	אִתְקַטַּלִי	אַקְטֵלִי	אִתַּקְטַלִי
Plur.	2. m.	קְטֵלוּ	אִתְקְטֵלוּ	קַטִּלוּ	אִתְקַטַּלוּ	אַקְטִלוּ	אִתַּקְטַלוּ
	2. f.	קְטֵלְנָא	אִתְקְטֵלְנָא	קַטִּלְנָא	אִתְקַטַּלְנָא	אַקְטֵלְנָא	אִתַּקְטַלְנָא
Fut.	3. m.	יִקְטֵל	יִתְקְטֵל	יְקַטֵּל	יִתְקַטַּל	יַקְטֵל	יִתַּקְטַל
	3. f.	תִּקְטֵל	תִּתְקְטֵל	תְּקַטֵּל	תִּתְקַטַּל	תַּקְטֵל	תִּתַּקְטַל
	2. m.	תִּקְטֵל	תִּתְקְטֵל	תְּקַטֵּל	תִּתְקַטַּל	תַּקְטֵל	תִּתַּקְטַל
	2. f.	תִּקְטְלִין	תִּתְקַטְלִין	תְּקַטְּלִין	תִּתְקַטְּלִין	תַּקְטְלִין	תִּתַּקְטְלִין
	1. c.	אֶקְטֵל	אֶתְקְטֵל	אֲקַטֵּל	אֶתְקַטַּל	אַקְטֵל	אִתַּקְטַל
Plur.	3. m.	יִקְטְלוּן	יִתְקַטְלוּן	יְקַטְּלוּן	יִתְקַטְּלוּן	יַקְטְלוּן	יִתַּקְטְלוּן
	3. f.	יִקְטְלָן	יִתְקַטְלָן	יְקַטְּלָן	יִתְקַטְּלָן	יַקְטְלָן	יִתַּקְטְלָן
	2. m.	תִּקְטְלוּן	תִּתְקַטְלוּן	תְּקַטְּלוּן	תִּתְקַטְּלוּן	תַּקְטְלוּן	תִּתַּקְטְלוּן
	2. f.	תִּקְטְלָן	תִּתְקַטְלָן	תְּקַטְּלָן	תִּתְקַטְּלָן	תַּקְטְלָן	תִּתַּקְטְלָן
	1. c.	נִקְטֵל	נִתְקְטֵל	נְקַטֵּל	נִתְקַטַּל	נַקְטֵל	נִתַּקְטַל
1. Part. {	m.	קָטֵל	מִתְקְטֵל	מְקַטֵּל	מִתְקַטַּל	מַקְטֵל	מִתַּקְטַל
	f.	קָטְלָא	מִתְקַטְלָא	מְקַטְּלָא	מִתְקַטְּלָא	מַקְטְלָא	מִתַּקְטְלָא
2. Part. {	m.	קְטִיל		מְקַטַּל		מַקְטַל	
	f.	קְטִילָא		מְקַטְּלָא		מַקְטְלָא	

SECTION XLVII.—ON THE REGULAR VERB. (TABLE Q.)

I. GENERAL REMARKS.

1. Forms with (..) often take (.) instead ; e. g.

   (a) Part. act. of Peal, נְחֵת Da. 4. 10, 20 ; יָכֵל Da. 3. 17 ; 4. 34.

   (b) Pret. of Ithpeel, אִתְרְחִצוּ Da. 3. 28.

   (c) Pret. of Pael, קַטֵּל Da. 3. 22, בָּרֵךְ Da. 2. 19.

   (d) The part. pass. sometimes, though seldom, appears in a contracted form, like קְטֵל, as תְּקֵל Da. 7. 25.

2. Preterite. Instead of the affirmative תְּ for the 2 pers. masc., sometimes appears תָּ, by a Hebraism, e. g. יְדַעְתָּ Da. 5. 22 ; רְשַׁמְתָּ Da. 6. 13, 14 ; Pael שַׁכַּחְתָּ Da. 5. 13 ; and even the full form חֲזַיְתָה Da. 2. 41.

3. Future. The 3 pers. pl. masc. takes sometimes the termination וּ instead of וּן, as יָחִיטוּ Ezr. 4. 12.

4. In those conjugations in which א is preformative, ה is generally used instead in the Biblical Chaldee. E. g. Ithpeel, הִתְרְחִצוּ Da. 3. 28, for אִתְרְחִצוּ (comp. No. 1) ; Ithpael, הִתְנַדַּבוּ Ezr. 7. 15 ; Aphel, הַכְרִזוּ Da. 5. 29 ; so in the fut. and part., even after the characteristic prefix, as יְהַשְׁפֵּל Da. 7. 24 ; מְהַקְרְבִין Ezr. 6. 10. Comp. also note to Table T.

5. Infinitive. The Biblical Chaldee has everywhere אָ‑ָ instead of הָ‑ָ of the Targums, a termination of all infinitives excepting Peal. E. g. הוֹבָדָה Da. 2. 12 (Aph. of אֲבַד) ; קַטָּלָה ver. 14 ; בַּקָּרָה Ezr. 7. 14 ; הַשְׁכָּחָה Da. 6. 5. Once, however, occurs לְהַשְׁנָיָא Ezr. 6. 12.

II. ON THE SEVERAL CONJUGATIONS.

6. Peal. (a) Some verbs, especially such as are intransitive, take (..), (.), or even ‑ֵ as the characteristic vowel of the preterite ; e. g. בְּאֵשׁ to be evil, מְאָב to be good, יְתֵב to sit, עֲשִׁית to think. These vowels remain in those persons, where (‑) is usually retained ;

e. g. שְׁאֵלְנָא we asked, Ezr. 5. 9 ; סְלִקוּ they went up, Ezr. 4. 12. The 3 pers. sing. fem. also retains its vowel, as בְּטֵלַת it ceased, Ezr. 4. 24.

   (b) The future has also in the final syllable (‑) instead of (‑), as תִּלְבַּשׁ thou shalt be clothed, Da. 5. 16.

7. Ithpeel. The preformative sometimes takes אֶת instead of אִת, Da. 7. 15. The final syllable takes (.) instead of (..), תִּשְׁתְּבִב Da. 2. 44, comp. No. 1.

8. Pael. As in Hebrew, Dagesh forte is sometimes omitted when the middle radical has Sheva, comp. § 10. rem. 7.

9. Aphel. Hiphil (and pass., Hoph.) sometimes takes the place of Aphel in the Biblical Chaldee ; comp. No. 4.

10. Ittaphal. The place of this conjugation, which occurs very seldom anywhere, is supplied in the Biblical Chaldee, by Hophal. E. g. Ezr. 4. 15 ; Da. 4. 33 ; 7. 11. There occurs, however, one form of this conjugation, usually taken for Ithpeel, viz. יִתְּזִין Da. 4. 9, fut. of זוּן ; but comp. § 54. rem. 3.

III. PERSONAL INFLEXION OF THE PARTICIPLE PEIL.

11. In the Biblical Chaldee a kind of Preterite passive tense is in use, formed by appending the afformatives of the Preterite to the participle Peil It takes the place of Ithpeel.*

	3 m.	3 f.	2 m.	2 f.	1 c.
Sing.	קְטִיל	קְטִילַת	קְטִילְתָּ, קְטִילְתְּ		קְטִילֵת
Plur.	קְטִילוּ	קְטִילָא	קְטִילְתּוּן	קְטִילְתֵּן	קְטִילְנָא

E. g. תְּקִילְתָּא Da. 5. 27, יְהִיבַת ver. 28 ; comp. ver. 30 ; 7. 4 ; 6. 11 ; יְהִיבוּ Ezr. 5. 14.

SECTION XLVIII.—UNFREQUENT CONJUGATIONS

As in Hebrew, there are here certain unfrequent conjugations, some of which are confined to particular classes of irregular verbs.

   (a) Poel and Ithpoal, especially in verbs עע ; the characteristics are the same as in the Hebrew. E. g. מְסוֹבְלִין Ezr. 6. 3.

   (b) Palel and Ithpalel in verbs עוי ; e. g. רוֹמֵם Da. 4. 34, הִתְרוֹמַם (for אִתְ) Da. 5. 23

   (c) Shaphel and Ishtaphal ; e. g. שַׁכְלֵל Ezr. 4. 12 ; יִשְׁתַּכְלֵל Ezr. 4. 13 ; שֵׁיצִיא Ezr. 6. 15, is Shaphel from יְצָא.

   (d) Altogether peculiar is the verb שֵׁיזִיב (שֵׁיזִב) Da. 3. 28. Fut. יְשֵׁיזִב ver. 17. Inf. שֵׁיזָבוּת ibid. Part. מְשֵׁיזִב Da. 6. 28. Passive אִשְׁתֵּיזִיב in the Targum Ge. 32. 30.

---

* In the Targums both participles are inflected by the addition of pronominal fragments, which forms there the present tense ; as קָטֵלְנָא I slay, קְטִילְנָא I am slain.

SECTION XLIX.—VERBS WITH GUTTURALS.

1. The gutturals (א, ה, ח, ע, and in part ר) present the same peculiarities as in Hebrew. It will be sufficient, therefore, to give examples of the most important forms.

2. *Verbs Pe guttural.* Peal pret. עֲבַד f. עֲבַדְת 1 c. עֲבָדֵת; imp. עֲבַד, עֲבֵד; inf. מֶעְבַּד, מֶחֱדַר (comp. § 13 rem. 1, 2, 3, 4); fut. יֶחֱזוֹר, יֶעְרַק (§ 139. 4); participles עֲבֵד, עֲבִיד. Ithpeel אִתְעֲבַד, אִתְעֲבֵד. Pael pret. עַבֵּד; fut. יְעַבֵּד. Ithpaal אִתְעַבַּד. Aphel pret. אַעְבֵּד, אַחְסִן, אַחְרִיב; fut. יַחֲלִיף, יַחְפֵּס; part. מַחֲלֵף.

3. *Verbs Ayin guttural.* Peal pret. בְּחַן, בָּחַן; imp. בְּחַן; inf. מִבְחַן; fut. יִבְחַן; part. בָּחֵן, בְּחִין. Ithpeel אִתְבְּחַן, אִתְבְּחִין. Pael חָרֵשׁ. Aphel אַבְחֵן.

4. *Verbs Lamed guttural.* Peal pret. שְׁכַח, שְׁכַחַת; imp. שְׁכַח, שְׁכַחִי; fut. יִשְׁכַּח, יִשְׁלַח; part. שְׁכַח, שְׁכִיחַ. Ithpeel אִשְׁתְּכַח, fem. אִשְׁתַּכְחַת. Pael pret. שַׁכַּח; fut. יְשַׁכַּח. Ithpaal אִשְׁתַּכַּח. Aphel אַשְׁכַּח, אַשְׁכִּיחַ, 1st pers. אַשְׁכַּחַת.

Rem. 1. *Verbs Lamed guttural* have the pret. 3 pers. sing. fem. sometimes terminating in (ַ־ַ) with the tone on the penultima, of which there is no example in the Bible (comp. Targ. אֲמֶרֶת Ge. 30. 16), though there are some without gutt., as אֲמֶרֶת Da. 5. 10; אִתְגְּזֶרֶת Da. 2. 45; הַדֶּקֶת Da. 2. 34, 45 (from דְּקַק).

2. Instead of שְׁמְעֵת (1 pers. com.) Da. 5. 14, Buxtorf, and after him Dr. Fürst, in his Concordance, give the form שְׁמֶעֵת Da. 5. 16, but we cannot tell on what authority.

3. When the first radical takes a composite Sheva, verbs פ"א and פ"ה have (ַ־ַ), as אֲמַרוּ Da. 2. 9; verbs פ"ח and פ"ע take generally (ַ־ַ).

4. Forms like חָסִין Da. 7. 22, belong not to Aphel but to Hiphel, and are Hebraisms.

TABLE R. REGULAR VERB WITH SUFFIXES.

Suffixes for	1 Sing.	2 Sing. m.	2 Sing. f.	3 Sing. m.	3 Sing. f.	1 Plur.	2 Plur. m.	2 Plur. f.	3 Plur. m.	3 Plur. f.
Pret.										
Peal 3. m.	קַטְלַנִי	קַטְלָךְ	קַטְלֵךְ	קַטְלֵהּ	קַטְלַהּ	קַטְלַנָא	קַטְלְכוֹן	קַטְלְכֵן	קַטְלְנוּן / קַטְלִנּוּן	קַטְלַנִּן
3. f.	קַטְלַתְנִי	קַטְלָתָּךְ	קַטְלָתֵךְ	קַטְלָתֵּהּ	קַטְלָתַּהּ	קַטְלָתְנָא	קַטְלַתְכוֹן	קַטְלַתְכֵן	קַטְלָתְּנוּן	קַטְלָתְּנֵן
2. m.	קַטְלְתַּנִי	—	—	קַטְלְתֵּהּ	קַטְלְתַּהּ	קַטְלְתַּנָא	—	—	קַטְלְתּוּן	קַטְלְתַּנֵּן
2. f.	קַטְלְתִּינִי	—	—	קַטְלְתִּיהִי	קַטְלְתִּיהָ	קַטְלְתִּינָא	—	—	קַטְלְתִּינוּן	קַטְלְתִּינֵן
1. c.	—	קַטְלְתָּךְ	קַטְלְתֵּךְ	קַטְלְתֵּיהּ	קַטְלְתַּהּ	—	קַטְלִתְּכוֹן	קַטְלְתְּכֵן	קַטְלְתּוּן	קַטְלְתַּן
Plur. 3. c.	קַטְלוּנִי	קַטְלוּךְ	קַטְלוּךְ	קַטְלוּהִי	קַטְלוּהָ	קַטְלוּנָא	קַטְלוּנְכוֹן	קַטְלוּנְכֵן	קַטְלוּנּוּן	קַטְלוּנֵּן
2. m.	קַטְלְתּוּנִי	—	—	קַטְלְתּוּנֵהּ	קַטְלְתּוּנַהּ	קַטְלְתּוּנָא	—	—	קַטְלְתּוּנּוּן	קַטְלְתּוּנֵּן
1. c.	—	קַטְלְנָךְ	קַטְלְנָךְ	קַטְלְנָהִי	קַטְלְנָהָא	קַטְלְנָנָא	קַטְלְנוּן	קַטְלְנְכֵן	קַטְלְנָנּוּן	קַטְלְנָנֵּן
Inf.										
Peal	מִקְטְלִי	מִקְטְלָךְ	מִקְטְלֵךְ	מִקְטְלֵהּ	מִקְטְלַהּ	מִקְטְלָנָא	מִקְטְלְכוֹן	מִקְטְלַבֵּן	מִקְטְלְהוֹן	מִקְטְלְהֵין
Imp.										
Peal m.	קַטְלַנִי			קַטְלֵהּ	קַטְלַהּ	קַטְלַנָא	—	—	קַטְלַנּוּן	קַטְלַנֵּן
f.	קַטְלִינִי	—	—	קַטְלִיהִי	קַטְלִיהָ	קַטְלִינָא	—	—	קַטְלִינוּן	קַטְלִינֵן
Plur. m.	קַטְלוּנִי	—	—	קַטְלוּהִי	קַטְלוּהּ	קַטְלוּנָא	—	—	קַטְלוּנוּן	קַטְלוּנֵּן
Fut.										
Peal 3. m.	יִקְטְלַנִי	יִקְטְלִנָּךְ	יִקְטְלִנֵּךְ	יִקְטְלִנֵּהּ	יִקְטְלִנַּהּ	יִקְטְלַנָא	יִקְטְלִנְכוֹן	יִקְטְלִנְכֵן	יִקְטְלִנּוּן	יִקְטְלִנָּן
Plur. 3. m.	יִקְטְלוּנַנִי	יִקְטְלוּנָּךְ	יִקְטְלוּנֵּךְ	יִקְטְלוּנֵּהּ	יִקְטְלוּנַהּ	יִקְטְלוּנַנָא	יִקְטְלוּנְכוֹן	יִקְטְלוּנְכֵן	יִקְטְלוּנּוּן	יִקְטְלוּנָּן

SECTION L.—ON THE REGULAR VERB WITH SUFFIXES.

REMARK.

An epenthetic ן is frequently inserted between the verb and the suffix. This occurs as the prevailing usage in the *fut.* and *imp.*, less frequently in the pret., and still less frequently in the inf. In the Biblical Chaldee examples are only found with the future. Once the union-vowel is (ֶ) instead of (ִ), יִשְׁאֲלֶנְכוֹן Ezr. 7. 21.

TABLE S. VERBS פ״נ.					TABLE T. VERBS ע״ע.*			
		PEAL.	APHEL.	ITTAPHAL.			PEAL.	APHEL.	ITTAPHAL.
Pret.	3. *m.*	נְפַק	אַפֵּק	אִתַּפַּק	**Pret.**	3. *m.*	דַּק	אַדֵּק	אִתַּדַּק
	3. *f.*	נֶפְקַת	אַפְּקַת	אִתַּפְּקַת		3. *f.*	דַּקַּת	אַדְּקַת	אִתַּדְּקַת
	2. *m.*	נְפַקְתָּ	אַפֵּקְתָּ	אִתַּפְּקְתָּ		2. *m.*	דְּקַתְּא, דַּקְתְּ	אַדֵּקְתָּ	אִתַּדְּקְתָּ
	2. *f.*	נְפַקְתְּ	אַפֵּקְתְּ	אִתַּפְּקְתְּ		2. *f.*	דְּקַתְּ	אַדֵּקְתְּ	אִתַּדְּקְתְּ
	1. *c.*	נְפַקֵת	אַפֵּקֵת	אִתַּפְּקֵת		1. *c.*	דַּקֵת	אַדֵּקֵת	אִתַּדְּקֵת
Plur.	3. *m.*	נְפַקוּ	אַפְּקוּ	אִתַּפְּקוּ	*Plur.*	3. *m.*	דַּקּוּ	אַדְּקוּ	אִתַּדְּקוּ
	3. *f.*	נְפַקָא	אַפְּקָא	אִתַּפְּקָא		3. *f.*	דַּקָּא	אַדְּקָא	אִתַּדְּקָא
	2. *m.*	נְפַקְתּוּן	אַפֵּקְתּוּן	אִתַּפְּקְתּוּן		2. *m.*	דַּקְתּוּן	אַדְּקְתּוּן	אִתַּדְּקְתּוּן
	2. *f.*	נְפַקְתֵּן	אַפֵּקְתֵּן	אִתַּפְּקְתֵּן		2. *f.*	דַּקְתֵּן	אַדְּקְתֵּן	אִתַּדְּקְתֵּן
	1. *c.*	נְפַקְנָא	אַפֵּקְנָא	אִתַּפְּקְנָא		1. *c.*	דַּקְנָא	אַדְּקְנָא	אִתַּדְּקְנָא
Inf.		מִפַּק	אַפָּקָא	אִתַּפָּקָא	**Inf.**		מִדַּק	אַדָּקָא	אִתַּדָּקָא
Imp.	*m.*	פֵּק, פַּק	אַפֵּק	אִתַּפַּק	**Imp.**	2. *m.*	דֵּק	אַדֵּק	אִתַּדַּק
	f.	פֵּקִי	אַפֵּקִי	אִתַּפַּקִי		2. *f.*	דֵּקִי	אַדֵּקִי	אִתַּדַּקִי
Plur.	*m.*	פֵּקוּ, פַּקוּ	אַפֵּקוּ	אִתַּפַּקוּ	*Plur.*	2. *m.*	דֵּקוּ	אַדֵּקוּ	אִתַּדַּקוּ
	f.	פֵּקְנָא	אַפֵּקְנָא	אִתַּפַּקְנָא		2. *f.*	דֵּקְנָא	אַדֵּקְנָא	אִתַּדַּקְנָא
Fut.	3. *m.*	יַפֵּק, יִפַּק	יַפֵּק	יִתַּפַּק	**Fut.**	3. *m.*	יְדֵּק	יַדֵּק	יִתַּדַּק
	3. *f.*	תֵּפֵּק, תִּפַּק	תַּפֵּק	תִּתַּפַּק		3. *f.*	תְּדֵּק	תַּדֵּק	תִּתַּדַּק
	2. *m.*	תֵּפֵּק, תִּפַּק	תַּפֵּק	תִּתַּפַּק		2. *m.*	תְּדֵּק	תַּדֵּק	תִּתַּדַּק
	2. *f.*	תֵּפְּקִין	תַּפְּקִין	תִּתַּפְּקִין		2. *f.*	תְּדְּקִין	תַּדְּקִין	תִּתַּדְּקִין
	1. *c.*	אֶפֵּק, אַפֵּק	אַפֵּק	אֶתַּפַּק		1. *c.*	אֶדֵּק	אַדֵּק	אֶתַּדַּק
Plur.	3. *m.*	יַפְּקוּן	יַפְּקוּן	יִתַּפְּקוּן	*Plur.*	3. *m.*	יְדְּקוּן	יַדְּקוּן	יִתַּדְּקוּן
	3. *f.*	יַפְּקָן	יַפְּקָן	יִתַּפְּקָן		3. *f.*	יְדְּקָן	יַדְּקָן	יִתַּדְּקָן
	2. *m.*	תֵּפְּקוּן	תַּפְּקוּן	תִּתַּפְּקוּן		2. *m.*	תְּדְּקוּן	תַּדְּקוּן	תִּתַּדְּקוּן
	2. *f.*	תֵּפְּקָן	תַּפְּקָן	תִּתַּפְּקָן		2. *f.*	תְּדְּקָן	תַּדְּקָן	תִּתַּדְּקָן
	1. *c.*	נֵפֵּק, נִפַּק	נַפֵּק	נִתַּפַּק		1. *c.*	נְדֵּק	נַדֵּק	נִתַּדַּק
1. Part.	*m.*	נָפֵק	מַפֵּק	מִתַּפַּק	**1. Part.**	*m.*	דָּקֵק	מַדֵּק	מִתַּדֵּק
	f.	נָפְקָא	מַפְּקָא	מִתַּפְּקָא		*f.*	דָּקְקָא	מַדְּקָא	מִתַּדְּקָא
2. Part.	*m.*	נְפִיק	מַפַּק		**2. Part.**	*m.*	דְּקִיק	מַדַּק	
	f.	נְפִיקָא	מַפְּקָא			*f.*	דְּקִיקָא	מַדְּקָא	

* All that may be remarked here is, (*a*) that the *Dagesh forte* is sometimes resolved in נ, as הַנְעַל Da. 2. 25; comp. Da. 4. 3 (for הֶעַל, הַעֵל, comp. § 52. rem. 2); (*b*) that several Hebraisms occur, as Aph. הַדֵּקוּ Da. 6. 25; הַעֵלְנִי Da. 2. 24; Hoph. הֵעַל, הֻעֲלוּ Da. 5. 13, 15 (comp. § 47. rem. 4 & 9).

SECTION LI.—ON VERBS PE NUN.

REMARKS.

1. Some verbs of this class are inflected regularly, e. g. תִּנְתֵּן Ezr. 7. 20; יִנְתֵּן Da. 2. 16; הַנְפֵּק Ezr. 5. 14. This is especially the case when the second radical is a guttural, of which, in the Bible, we have the only example in Hophal of נְחַת, viz. הָנְחַת Da. 5. 20. But this verb is defective throughout Aphel, as תַּחֵת Ezr. 6. 5; מְהַחֲתִין Ezr. 6. 1 (with *Dag. forte impl.* comp. § 14. rem. 1); but the imp. is אֲחֵת Ezr.

5. 15, for אַחֵת, probably to distinguish it from the 1st pers. fut.

2. In the Targums, the verb נְתַן takes (..) in the future as its characteristic vowel, e. g. אֶתֵּן Ex. 25. 16 Instead of this, the Biblical Chaldee exhibits the full form יִנְתֵּן, תִּנְתּוּן Ezr. 4. 13; 7. 20. Once (with Makkeph) יִנְתֶּן־ Da. 2. 16.

SECTION LII.—ON VERBS PE YOD (AND PE VAV).

TABLE U.	VERBS פ״י.	VERBS פ״ו	
PAEL.	Preter. 3. p.	יָלִיד, יְלַד	יָלְדַת, יְלִידַת
	1. p.	etc. יְלִידַת	etc. יָלְדֵת
	Imper.	הַב	(תֵּב) תֵּב
	Inf.	מֵילַד	
	Fut.	יֵילַד	
	Part.	יָלֵיד, יָלַד	
ITHPEEL.	Pret.	אִתְיְלַד (אִתְיְלִיד) אִתְיְדַע	
PAEL.	Pret.	יַלֵּד	יַטֵּב
	Fut.	יְיַלֵּד	יֵיטֵב
ITHPAAL.	Pret.	אִתְיַלַּד	
APHEL.	Pret.	אוֹלִיד	אִיטִיב
	Fut.	יוֹלִיד	יֵיטִיב

REMARKS.

1. As in Hebrew there are three classes of verbs, viz., (1) verbs originally פ״ו; (2) verbs properly פ״י; and (3) those in which י is not treated as a quiescent, but is *assimilated* like the נ of verbs פ״ן.

2. For the inflexion of the first and second classes see parad.* They assimilate their first radical to the following letter in the *inf.* and *fut. Peal,* and in *Aphel;* so that they are in those forms entirely analogous to verbs פ״ן. Of this class all the occurring examples in the Biblical Chaldee are:—יְדַע *to know;* where, however, Dagesh is always resolved in נ as fut. תִּנְדַּע Da. 2. 30; 4. 22, 23, 29; אֶנְדַּע Da. 2. 9, for אֶדַּע תֵּדַּע (comp. note to Table T); יְכֵל *to be able;* fut. יִכַּל Da. 3. 29; תֻּכּוּל Da. 5. 16, Keri; יָצֵב Aph. inf. יַצָּבָא Da. 7. 19, formed after Hiphil with the termination ־ָא.

SECTION LIII.—VERBS PE ALEPH.

1. A few verbs פ״א are treated not only as gutturals, but at the same time as quiescents, viz., אֲמַר, אֲבַד, אֲתָא, אֲכַל. The א of these verbs, in the fut. and inf. Peal, is quiescent in (..), e. g. יֵאכַל, and sometimes even changed in י, as מֵימַר, יֵיבַד (in the Biblical Chaldee defective, comp. inf. מֵתָא, מֵמַר (and מֵאמַר), from אֲמַר, אֲתָא). Throughout Aphel it be-

comes וֹ as הוֹבָדָה, הְהוֹבַד. An instance of Hophal is הוּבַד Da. 7. 11.

REM. 1. The form of the imp. אֱזֵל Ezr. 5. 15, stands with Makkeph, where it has lost the tone, for אֲזֵל, as Syriacism for אֲזֵל, comp. § 19. rem. 3 & 6.

2. For the verb אֲתָא see the doubly anomalous verbs, section 25.

---

* The ה of Aphel is frequently retained in the future, as תְּהוֹדַע Da. 2. 5, comp. § 53. No. 1.

TABLE V. VERBS עי׳.

		PEAL.	ITHPEAL.	PAEL.	ITHPAAL.	APHEL.	ITTAPHAL.	POEL.	ITHPOAL.
PRET.	3. m.	קָם	אִתְּקִם	קַיֵּם	אִתְקַיַּם	אֲקִים	אִתְּקִים	קוֹמֵם	אִתְּקוֹמֵם
	3. f.	קָמַת	אִתְּקִמַת	קַיְּמַת	אִתְקַיְּמַת	אֲקִימַת, אֲקִימַת	אִתְּקִימַת	קוֹמֵמַת	אִתְּקוֹמֵמַת
	2. m.	קָמְתָּ, קַמְתְּ	קָמְתְּ אִתְּקִמְתְּ	קַיֵּמְתְּ	אִתְקַיַּמְתְּ	אֲקִימְתְּ, אֲקִימְתְּ	אִתְּקִימְתְּ	קוֹמֵמְתָּ	אִתְּקוֹמֵמְתְּ
	2. f.	קָמְתְּ	אִתְּקִמְתְּ	קַיֵּמְתְּ	אִתְקַיַּמְתְּ	אֲקִימְתְּ	אִתְּקִימְתְּ	קוֹמֵמְתְּ	אִתְּקוֹמֵמְתְּ
	1. c.	קָמֵת	אִתְּקִמֵת	קַיֵּמֵת	אִתְקַיַּמֵת	אֲקִימֵת, אֲקִימֵת	אִתְּקִימֵת	קוֹמֵמֵת	אִתְּקוֹמֵמֵת
Plur.	3. m.	קָמוּ	אִתְּקִמוּ	קַיְּמוּ	אִתְקַיַּמוּ	אֲקִימוּ	אִתְּקִימוּ	קוֹמֵמוּ	אִתְּקוֹמֵמוּ
	3. f.	קָמָא	אִתְּקִמָא	קַיְּמָא	אִתְקַיַּמָא	אֲקִימָא	אִתְּקִימָא	קוֹמֵמָא	אִתְּקוֹמֵמָא
	2. m.	קַמְתּוּן, קַמְתּוּן	אִתְּקִמְתּוּן	קַיֵּמְתּוּן	אִתְקַיַּמְתּוּן	אֲקִימְתּוּן	אִתְּקִימְתּוּן	קוֹמֵמְתּוּן	אִתְּקוֹמֵמְתּוּן
	2. f.	קַמְתֵּן, קַמְתֵּן	אִתְּקִמְתֵּן	קַיֵּמְתֵּן	אִתְקַיַּמְתֵּן	אֲקִימְתֵּן	אִתְּקִימְתֵּן	קוֹמֵמְתֵּן	אִתְּקוֹמֵמְתֵּן
	1. c.	קָמְנָא, קַמְנָא	אִתְּקִמְנָא	קַיֵּמְנָא	אִתְקַיַּמְנָא	אֲקִימְנָא	אִתְּקִימְנָא	קוֹמֵמְנָא	אִתְּקוֹמֵמְנָא
INF.		מְקָם (מְקוּם)	אִתְּקָמָא	קַיָּמָא	אִתְקַיָּמָא	אֲקָמָא	אִתְּקָמָא	קוֹמָמָא	אִתְּקוֹמָמָא
IMP.	2. m.	קוּם	אִתְּקִם	קַיֵּם	אִתְקַיַּם	אֲקִים	אִתְּקִים	קוֹמֵם	אִתְּקוֹמֵם
	2. f.	קוּמִי	אִתְּקִמִי	קַיְּמִי	אִתְקַיַּמִי	אֲקִימִי	אִתְּקִימִי	קוֹמֵמִי	אִתְּקוֹמֵמִי
Plur.	2. m.	קוּמוּ	אִתְּקִמוּ	קַיְּמוּ	אִתְקַיַּמוּ	אֲקִימוּ	אִתְּקִימוּ	קוֹמֵמוּ	אִתְּקוֹמֵמוּ
	2. f.	קוּמְנָא	אִתְּקִמְנָא	קַיְּמְנָא	אִתְקַיַּמְנָא	אֲקִימְנָא	אִתְּקִימְנָא	קוֹמֵמְנָא	אִתְּקוֹמֵמְנָא
FUT.	3. m.	יְקוּם	יִתְּקִם	יְקַיֵּם	יִתְקַיַּם	יְקִים	יִתְּקִים	יְקוֹמֵם	יִתְּקוֹמֵם
	3. f.	תְּקוּם	תִּתְּקִם	תְּקַיֵּם	תִּתְקַיַּם	תְּקִים	תִּתְּקִים	תְּקוֹמֵם	תִּתְּקוֹמֵם
	2. m.	תְּקוּם	תִּתְּקִם	תְּקַיֵּם	תִּתְקַיַּם	תְּקִים	תִּתְּקִים	תְּקוֹמֵם	תִּתְּקוֹמֵם
	2. f.	תְּקוּמִין	תִּתְּקִמִין	תְּקַיְּמִין	תִּתְקַיַּמִין	תְּקִימִין	תִּתְּקִימִין	תְּקוֹמֵמִין	תִּתְּקוֹמֵמִין
	1. c.	אֲקוּם	אִתְּקִם	אֲקַיֵּם	אִתְקַיַּם	אֲקִים	אִתְּקִים	אֲקוֹמֵם	אִתְּקוֹמֵם
Plur.	3. m.	יְקוּמוּן	יִתְּקִמוּן	יְקַיְּמוּן	יִתְקַיַּמוּן	יְקִימוּן	יִתְּקִימוּן	יְקוֹמֵמוּן	יִתְּקוֹמֵמוּן
	3. f.	יְקוּמָן	יִתְּקִמָן	יְקַיְּמָן	יִתְקַיַּמָן	יְקִימָן	יִתְּקִימָן	יְקוֹמֵמָן	יִתְּקוֹמֵמָן
	2. m.	תְּקוּמוּן	תִּתְּקִמוּן	תְּקַיְּמוּן	תִּתְקַיַּמוּן	תְּקִימוּן	תִּתְּקִימוּן	תְּקוֹמֵמוּן	תִּתְּקוֹמֵמוּן
	2. f.	תְּקוּמָן	תִּתְּקִמָן	תְּקַיְּמָן	תִּתְקַיַּמָן	תְּקִימָן	תִּתְּקִימָן	תְּקוֹמֵמָן	תִּתְּקוֹמֵמָן
	1. c.	נְקוּם	נִתְּקִם	נְקַיֵּם	נִתְקַיַּם	נְקִים	נִתְּקִים	נְקוֹמֵם	נִתְּקוֹמֵם
1. Part.	m.	קָאֵם, קָיֵם	מִתְּקִם	מְקַיֵּם	מִתְקַיַּם	מְקִים	מִתְּקִים	מְקוֹמֵם	מִתְּקוֹמֵם
	f.	קָיְמָא	מִתְּקִמָא	מְקַיְּמָא	מִתְקַיְּמָא	מְקִימָא	מִתְּקִימָא	מְקוֹמְמָא	מִתְּקוֹמְמָא
2. Part.	m.	קִים		מְקַיַּם		מְקָם		מְקוֹמַם	
	f.	קִימָא		מְקַיְּמָא		מְקָמָא		מְקוֹמְמָא	

SECTION LIV.—ON VERBS AYIN VAV (AND AYIN YOD).
REMARKS.

1. Peal future. Instead of the form יְקוּם there also occurs the contracted form יְהָךְ Ezr. 5. 5; 6. 5, from הוּךְ.

2. The second participle (Peil) takes also, like the inf., the form קוּם, from which a new pret. passive is formed, thus שְׂמַת (3 p. f.) Da. 6. 18, comp. § 47. r. 11.

3. Ithpeel. Besides the form אִתְּקִם with (ִ) under the first radical, there are also instances in the Targums of the form אִתְּקִים, comp. Je. 33. 22; Ge. 38. 26, to which may also be reckoned יְתָּדוּן Da. 4. 9; but comp. § 47. rem. 10.

4. Aphel. Instead of the characteristic ־ִ, some

times ־' is used, as הָקִים Da. 3. 2, 3, 5, 7 ; 6. 2, comp. Da. 3. 18, and in the 1st pers. with (ָ) under the last radical, הֲקִימֵת Da. 3. 14.

HEBRAISMS.

5. Hebraisms, besides the constant use of ה for א, are :—*Peal* pret. שָׁמַּת Da. 3. 10, for שָׂמֵת. *Aphel*

pret. הֲקֵימְתָּ Da. 3. 18 ; fut. תֶּסַּף Da. 2. 44 ; for תֹּסִיף, יָחִיט Ezr. 4. 12 ; part. מָרִים Da. 5. 19.

6. Examples of verbs inflected like עי׳ are only רם Da. 5. 20, which, however, may be the part. Peil pret., comp. No. 2, and § 47. rem. 11. Imp. שִׂימוּ Ezr. 4. 21 ; part. pass. שִׂים Da. 3. 29 ; 4. 3, &c.

TABLE W. VERB ל״א.

	PEAL.	ITHPAEL.	PAEL.	ITHPAAL.	APHEL.	ITTAPHAL.
PRET. 3. m.	גְּלָא (סְגָא) (סְגִי)	אִתְגְּלִי (ֵ)	גַּלִּי	אִתְגַּלִּי (ֵ)	אַגְלִי (ֵ)	אִתַּגְלִי
3. f.	גְּלָת ,סְגִיאַת(סְגָאת)סְגִיאַת(ְ־יאַת)אִתְגְּלִיאַת	אִתְגְּלִיאַת	גַּלִּיאַת, גַּלִּת	אִתְגַּלִּת	אַגְלִיאַת(ְ־יאַת)אַגְלִת	אִתַּגְלִיאַת(ְ־יאַת)
2. m.	גְּלִיתָ ,גְּלָת	סְגִיתָ	אִתְגְּלִיתָ	גַּלִּיתָ (ְ־יתָ)	אִתְגַּלִּיתָ	אַגְלִיתָ (ְ־יתָ)	אִתַּגְלִית
2. f.	גְּלִית ,גְּלָת צְבִית, סְגִית	אִתְגְּלִית	גַּלִּית	אִתְגַּלִּית	אַגְלִית (ְ־ית)	אִתַּגְלִית
1. c.	גְּלִיתִי ,גְּלֵת	סְגִיתִי	אִתְגְּלִיתִי	גַּלִּיתִי ,גַּלֵּת	אִתְגַּלִּיתִי	אַגְלִיתִי	אִתַּגְלִיתִי
Plur. 3. m.	גְּלוֹ סְנִיו, סְנִיאוּ(ְ־יאוּ)	אִתְגְּלִיו (ְ־יאוּ)	גַּלִּיו (ְ־יאוּ) ,גַּלִּיאוּ	אִתְגַּלִּיו (ְ־יאוּ)	אַגְלִיו (ְ־יאוּ)	אִתַּגְלִיו
3. f.	גְּלָאָה	סְגִיאָה	אִתְגְּלִיאָה	גַּלִּיאָה	אִתְגַּלִּיאָה (ְ־יאָה)	אַגְלִיאָה (ְ־יאָה)	אִתַּגְלִיאָה
2. m.	גְּלִיתוּן	סְגִיתוּן	אִתְגְּלִיתוּן גַּלִּיתוּן	אִתְגַּלִּיתוּן	אַגְלִיתוּן	אִתַּגְלִיתוּן
2. f.	גְּלִיתֶן	סְגִיתֶן	אִתְגְּלִיתֶן גַּלִּיתֶן	אִתְגַּלִּיתֶן	אַגְלִיתֶן	אִתַּגְלִיתֶן
1. c.	גְּלֵינָא	סְגֵינָא	אִתְגְּלֵינָא ,גַּלֵּינָא	אִתְגַּלֵּינָא	אַגְלֵינָא	אִתַּגְלֵינָא
IMP.	סְגֵלָא (מִגְלֵיהּ ,מִגְלָא)	אִתְגְּלָאָה	גַּלָּאָה	אַגְלָיָה ,אַגְלָאָה אִתַּגְלָאָה		אִתַּגְלָאָה
IMP. m.	גְּלִי (גְּלָא) ,גְּלִי	אִתְגְּלָא	גַּלִּי ,גַּלִּי	אִתְגַּלָּא	אַגְלִי (ֵ)	אִתַּגְלִי
f.	גְּלָא ,גְּלִי	אִתְגְּלָא	גַּלָּא	אִתְגַּלָּא	אַגְלָא	אִתַּגְלָא
Plur. m.	גְּלוֹ	אִתְגְּלוֹ	גַּלּוֹ	אִתְגַּלּוֹ	אַגְלוֹ	אִתַּגְלוֹ
f.	גְּלָאָה ,גְּלָן	אִתְגְּלָנָא	גַּלָּא	אִתְגַּלָּנָא	אַגְלִינָא	אִתַּגְלִינָא
FUT. 3. m.	יִגְלֵא (ְ־י)	יִתְגְּלֵי (ֵ־א)	יְגַלֵּי (ֵ־א)	יִתְגַּלֵּי (ֵ־א)	יַגְלֵי (ֵ־א)	יִתַּגְלֵא (ְ־י)
3. f.	תִּגְלֵא (ְ־י)	תִּתְגְּלֵי (ֵ־א)	תְּגַלֵּי (ֵ־א)	תִּתְגַּלֵּי (ֵ־א)	תַּגְלֵי (ֵ־א)	תִּתַּגְלֵא (ְ־י)
2. m.	תִּגְלֵא (ְ־י)	תִּתְגְּלֵי (ֵ־א)	תְּגַלֵּי (ֵ־א)	תִּתְגַּלֵּי (ֵ־א)	תַּגְלֵי (ֵ־א)	תִּתַּגְלֵא (ְ־י)
2. f.	תִּגְלֵין	תִּתְגְּלֵין	תְּגַלֵּין	תִּתְגַּלֵּין	תַּגְלֵין	תִּתַּגְלֵין
1. c.	אֶגְלֵא (ְ־י)	אֶתְגְּלֵי (ֵ־א)	אֲגַלֵּי (ֵ־א)	אֶתְגַּלֵּי (ֵ־א)	אַגְלֵי (ֵ־א)	אֶתַּגְלֵא (ְ־י)
Plur. 3. m.	יִגְלוֹן	יִתְגְּלוֹן	יְגַלּוֹן	יִתְגַּלּוֹן	יַגְלוֹן	יִתַּגְלוֹן
3. f.	יִגְלְיָן	יִתְגְּלְיָן	יְגַלְּיָן	יִתְגַּלְּיָן	יַגְלְיָן	יִתַּגְלְיָן
2. m.	תִּגְלוֹן	תִּתְגְּלוֹן	תְּגַלּוֹן	תִּתְגַּלּוֹן	תַּגְלוֹן	תִּתַּגְלוֹן
2. f.	תִּגְלְיָן	תִּתְגְּלְיָן	תְּגַלְּיָן	תִּתְגַּלְּיָן	תַּגְלְיָן	תִּתַּגְלְיָן
1. c.	נִגְלֵא (ְ־י)	נִתְגְּלֵי (ֵ־א)	נְגַלֵּי (ֵ־א)	נִתְגַּלֵּי (ֵ־א)	נַגְלֵי (ֵ־א)	נִתַּגְלֵא (ְ־י)
1. Pt. m.	גָּלֵא ,גָּלֵי	מִתְגְּלֵי	מְגַלֵּי (ֵ־א)	מִתְגַּלֵּי (ֵ־א)	מַגְלֵי (ֵ־א)	מִתַּגְלֵא
f.	גָּלְיָא	מִתְגַּלְיָא	מְגַלְיָא	מִתְגַּלְיָא	מַגְלְיָא	מִתַּגְלְיָא
2. Pt. m.	גָּלֵא ,גָּלֵי		מְגַלַּי		מַגְלַי	
f.	גָּלְיָא		מְגַלְּיָא		מַגְלְיָא	

SECTION LV.—ON VERBS LAMED ALEPH (AND LAMED HE*).

REMARKS.

1. *Pret.* The 3 pers. sing. fem. Peal appears sometimes in the full orthography, as מְלָאת Da. 2. 35. It takes, however, also (־ַ) instead of (־ָ), as הֲנַת Da. 2. 35; מְטָת Da. 4. 19. The 2 pers. sing. masc. is also written *fully*, terminating in ־ָה, as חֲזַיְתָה Da. 2. 41. Instead of ־ִי in the 1 pers. sing. there is ־ִ in צְבִית Da. 7. 19. The 3 pers. pl. masc. sometimes follows the analogy of the other derived conjugations (Ithpe., Pa., &c.), as רְמִיו Da. 3. 21. An example with prosthetic א is אִשְׁתִּיו Da. 5. 3, 4.

2. *Future.* The 3 pers. sing. masc. terminates also in ־ֵ in יִתְקְרֵי Da. 5. 12. The 3 pers. pl. takes also the termination וֹן instead of וֹ, as יְהַעֲדוֹן Da. 7. 26.

3. The *infinitive* of *Peal* takes sometimes the termination א־, in the Biblical Chaldee, as יִצְבָּא Da. 7. 19; more usually ־ָה, as לְמִבְנְיָה Ezr. 5. 9; and in the other conjugations ־ָיָה, e. g. Da. 2. 10; 5. 2.

4. *Part. Peil.* In some instances the first radical takes composite Sheva, though a non-guttural, as קְרִי Ezr. 4. 18, 23; גֱּלִי Da. 2. 30, and גֱּלִי ver. 19.

SECTION LVI.—VERBS DOUBLY ANOMALOUS (Comp. § 25).

1. פ"נ and ל"א:—נְשָׂא. Imp שָׂא Ezr. 5. 15.

2. פ"א and ל"א:—אֲתָא, אֲנָא. *Peal inf.* מֵתָא Da. 3. 2; מֵזֵה Da. 3. 19, by syncope for מֵאֲתָא, &c.; *Part. pass.* אֲזֵה Da. 3. 22; by Syriacism for אֲזֵה (comp. § 53. rem. 1). *Aphel,* pret. 3 pers. sing. masc. הַיְתִי Da. 5. 13; 3 pers.

plur. הַיְתִיו Da. 5. 3; (comp. inf. הַיְתָיָה Da. 5. 2). Altogether peculiar are the anomalies of Hophal, 3 pers. fem. הֵיתָיִת Da. 6. 18; 3 pers. plur. masc. הֵיתָיוּ Da. 3. 13.

3. פ"י and ל"א. Only יְדָא, *Aph.* Part. מְהוֹדֵא Da. 2. 23, and מוֹדֵא 6. 11.

---

^ In the Biblical Chaldee ה is promiscuously used instead of א, comp. § 46. rem. 4, & § 54. rem. 5.

TABLE X. DECLENSION OF MASCULINE NOUNS.

	I. a.	I. b.	II. a.	II. b.	III. a.	III. b.	III. c.	III. d.
Sing. absol.	טוּר (mount)	אִילָן (tree)	עָלַם (eternity)	כָּהֵן (priest)	מֶלֶךְ (king)	זְמַן (time)	חֵלֶם (dream)	עַיִן (eye)
constr.	טוּר	אִילָן	עָלַם	כָּהֵן	מְלֶךְ	זְמַן	חֵלֶם	עֵין
emphat.	טוּרָא	אִילָנָא	עָלְמָא	כַּהֲנָא	מַלְכָּא	זִמְנָא	חֶלְמָא	עֵינָא (עַיְנָא)
with suff. {	טוּרֵהּ	אִילָנֵהּ	עָלְמֵהּ	כַּהֲנֵהּ	מַלְכֵּהּ	זִמְנֵהּ	חֶלְמֵהּ	עֵינֵהּ (עַיְנֵהּ)
	טוּרְכוֹן	אִילָנְכוֹן	עָלְמְכוֹן	כַּהֲנְכוֹן	מַלְכְּכוֹן	זִמְנְכוֹן	חֶלְמְכוֹן	עֵינְכוֹן
Plur. absol.	טוּרִין	אִילָנִין	עָלְמִין	כַּהֲנִין	מַלְכִין	זִמְנִין	חֶלְמִין	עֵינִין
constr.	טוּרֵי	אִילָנֵי	עָלְמֵי	כַּהֲנֵי	מַלְכֵי	זִמְנֵי	חֶלְמֵי	עֵינֵי (עַיְנֵי)
emphat.	טוּרַיָּא	אִילָנַיָּא	עָלְמַיָּא	כַּהֲנַיָּא	מַלְכַיָּא	זִמְנַיָּא	חֶלְמַיָּא	עֵינַיָּא (עַיְנַיָּא)
with suff. {	טוּרוֹהִי	אִילָנוֹהִי	עָלְמוֹהִי	כַּהֲנוֹהִי	מַלְכוֹהִי	זִמְנוֹהִי	חֶלְמוֹהִי	עֵינוֹהִי (עַיְנוֹהִי)
	טוּרֵיכוֹן	אִילָנֵיכוֹן	עָלְמֵיכוֹן	כַּהֲנֵיכוֹן	מַלְכֵּיכוֹן	זִמְנֵיכוֹן	חֶלְמֵיכוֹן	עֵינֵיכוֹן (עַיְנֵיכוֹן)

	IV	V. a.	V. b.	V. c.	VI. a.	VI. b.	VII.
Sing. absol.	מִתְקְטֵל (murderer)	גַּב (back)	עֵז (goat)	אֹם (people)	גָּלֵא (revealer)	מַגְלֵי	קַדְמַי (first)
constr.	מִתְקְטֵל	גַּב	עֵז	אֹם	גָּלֵא	מַגְלֵי	קַדְמֵי
emphat.	מִתְקַטְלָא	גַּבָּא	עִזָּא	אִמָּא	גָּלְיָא	מַגְלְיָא	קַדְמָאָה
with suff.	מִתְקַטְלֵהּ	גַּבֵּהּ	עִזֵּהּ	אִמֵּהּ	גָּלְיֵהּ	מַגְלְיֵהּ	קַדְמָאֵהּ
Plur. absol.	מִתְקַטְלִין	גַּבִּין	עִזִּין	אִמִּין	גָּלַיִן	מַגְלַיִן	קַדְמָאִין
constr.	מִתְקַטְלֵי	גַּבֵּי	עִזֵּי	אִמֵּי	גָּלַי	מַגְלֵי	קַדְמָאֵי
emphat.	מִתְקַטְלַיָּא	גַּבַּיָּא	עִזַּיָּא	אִמַּיָּא	גָּלַיָּא	מַגְלַיָּא	קַדְמָאֵי
with suff.	מִתְקַטְלֵיכוֹן	גַּבֵּיכוֹן	עִזֵּיכוֹן	אִמֵּיכוֹן	גָּלֵיכוֹן	מַגְלֵיכוֹן	קַדְמָאֵיכוֹן

DECLENSION OF FEMININE NOUNS.

	(A) VIII.* a.	(A) VIII.* b.	(A) VIII.* c.	(B) IX.*	(C) X.*	(D) XI.*
Sing. absol.	מְדִינָא (province)	מַשְׁרִי (army)	מַלְכּוּ (kingdom)	אַרְמְלָא (widow)	גָּלְיָא (discoverer)	קַדְמָאָה (first)
constr.	מְדִינַת	מַשְׁרִית	מַלְכוּת	אַרְמְלַת	גָּלְיַת	קַדְמָאַת
emphat.	מְדִינְתָּא	מַשְׁרִיתָא	מַלְכוּתָא	אַרְמַלְתָּא	גָּלִיתָא	קַדְמָיְתָא
with suff. {	מְדִינְתֵּהּ	מַשְׁרִיתֵהּ	מַלְכוּתֵהּ	אַרְמַלְתֵּהּ	גָּלִיתֵהּ	קַדְמָיְתֵהּ
	מְדִינָתְהוֹן	מַשְׁרִיתְהוֹן	מַלְכוּתְהוֹן	אַרְמְלָתְהוֹן		קַדְמָיָתְהוֹן
Plur. absol.	מְדִינָן	מַשְׁרִין	מַלְכְּוָן	אַרְמְלָן	גָּלְיָן	קַדְמָאָן
constr.	מְדִינָת	מַשְׁרְיָת	מַלְכְוָת	אַרְמְלָת	גָּלְיָת	קַדְמָאָת
emphat.	מְדִינָתָא	מַשְׁרְיָתָא	מַלְכְוָתָא	אַרְמְלָתָא	גָּלְיָתָא	קַדְמָיָתָא
with suff.	מְדִינָתְהוֹן	מַשְׁרְיָתְהוֹן	מַלְכְוָתְהוֹן	אַרְמְלָתְהוֹן	גָּלְיָתְהוֹן	קַדְמָיָתְהוֹן

SECTION LVII.—FIRST DECLENSION OF MASCULINES.
EXPLANATORY.

This declension includes all nouns, which have all their vowels immutable. It comprehends,

(a) Nouns which have ‫ִי‬, ‫ֵ‬, ‫וֹ‬ or ‫וּ‬ before their final consonant, e. g. ‫דִּין‬ *judgment,* ‫יוֹם‬ *day,* ‫אַתּוּן‬ *furnace.*

(b) Those which have ‫ַ‬ in their final syllable; as ‫טָב‬ *good,* ‫גַּנָּב‬ *thief.* There are, however, a few of those which change ‫ַ‬ to ‫ָ‬, compare the following remark.

REMARK.

Nouns with ‫ָ‬ in the ultimate are chiefly of six classes :—

(1) Nouns derived from ‫ע״וּ‬, e. g. ‫קָל‬, ‫דָּר‬ (Heb. ‫דּוֹר‬, ‫קוֹל‬) ;

(2) Nouns of the form ‫כְּתָב‬ ‫שְׁלָם‬ (Heb. ‫שָׁלוֹם‬) ;

(3) Nouns of the form ‫קְטָל‬ (Arab. ‫קַטָאל‬, and also in the Heb. with ‫ַ‬ *impure*) ;

(4) Nouns like ‫קְטֵל‬ (also in the Heb. with ‫ַ‬ *impure*).

(5) Nouns which have the formative ending ‫ָן‬, e. g. ‫קָרְבָּן‬ (Arab. ‫קרבאן‬).

(6) Nouns of the form ‫קוֹטֵל‬, e.g. ‫אוֹצָר‬, ‫עוֹבֵד‬. They have a twofold inflexion :—

(a) The first three of these classes retain ‫ָ‬ in all the inflexions, and consequently belong regularly to Declension 1.

(b) Nouns of the fourth, fifth, and sixth classes sometimes take ‫ָ‬ instead of ‫ַ‬ in the constr. sing., and before the suffixes ‫כוֹן‬ and ‫הוֹן‬. Elsewhere ‫ַ‬ is retained. The punctuation of these nouns is, however, variable; and as they present no other irregularity, they may better be regarded as exceptions from Declension 1, than as forming a separate declension.

SECTION LVIII.—SECOND DECLENSION OF MASCULINES.
EXPLANATORY

The second declension embraces nouns with final ‫ֵ‬ or ‫ֶ‬, either monosyllabic, as ‫יַד‬, ‫שֵׁם‬, or having the preceding vowels immutable, as ‫מִסְפֵּד‬, ‫עָדְרַע‬, ‫קָטֵל‬, ‫עָלֵם‬. These vowels are dropped before suffixes beginning with a vowel.

Rem. 1. The forms like ‫קַטְלִין‬ for ‫קָטְלִין‬, pl. of ‫קָטֵל‬ (part. act.), must be attributed to the variable vocal-ization of the Chaldee; as ‫פַּרְסִין‬ Da. 5. 25 ; ‫חַשְׁחָן‬ for ‫חָשְׁחָן‬ (plur. fem. of ‫חָשַׁח‬) Ezr. 6. 9.

2. To this paradigm belongs also ‫פַּרְזֶל‬, emph. st. ‫פַּרְזְלָא‬

3. Before ‫כוֹן‬ and ‫הוֹן‬, monosyllables, as in Hebrew, take ‫ֵ‬, ‫ַ‬, or ‫ְ‬ ; e. g. ‫יְדְכוֹן‬, ‫דְּמֵהוֹן‬

SECTION LIX.—THIRD DECLENSION OF MASCULINES.

This declension embraces all nouns which correspond to the Segolate forms in the Hebrew. They may either be written with two vowels (the second of which is always considered an auxiliary vowel), as ‫חֵלֶם‬, ‫מֶלֶךְ‬ (almost exclusively in the Biblical Chaldee), ‫קֹדֶשׁ‬, ‫בַּיִת‬ ; or with only *one* vowel between the last two consonants, as ‫סְפַר‬, ‫מְלַךְ‬. They are inflected, however, for the most part, as in Hebrew; except,

(a) In the plural absol. the forms ‫מֶלֶךְ‬ and ‫סְפַר‬ become, as they do in most other inflexions ‫מַלְךָ‬ and ‫סִפְר‬.

(b) The form ‫קֹדֶשׁ‬ either follows the analogy of the Hebrew, as ‫תָּקְפָּא‬ Da. 2. 37, or takes ‫ָ‬, as ‫כָּתְלִיָּא‬ Ezr. 5. 8.

(c) In the form ‫בַּיִת‬, the ‫י‬ often remains moveable in the inflexion, as ‫עֵינֵי‬ Da. 7. 8 ; ‫עֵינַי‬ Da. 4. 31 ; ‫בֵּיתָא‬ Ezr. 5. 3 ; ‫בַּיְתֵהּ‬ Da. 5. 23.

(d) The forms ‫מֶלֶךְ‬ and ‫סְפַר‬, in the course of inflexion, usually take ‫ִ‬, ‫ֻ‬, or rarely ‫ְ‬, under their first radical.

Nouns having gutturals for their first or second radical, naturally take ‫ַ‬, as ‫מַעַם‬, ‫עֲבַד‬, ‫עַבְדָּא‬, ‫מַעְמָא‬

SECTION LX.—FOURTH DECLENSION OF MASCULINES.

The fourth declension comprehends those nouns in which the vowel of the final syllable falls away in the course of inflexion, and the third consonant from the end receives then, ָ (.) or ֶ (_). To this declension belong the participles of Ithpeel.

SECTION LXI.—FIFTH DECLENSION OF MASCULINES.

The fifth declension embraces those nouns which double the final consonant when they receive any accession. They are mostly monosyllables derived from verbs ע״ע. The long vowels (..) and וֹ are changed in the course of inflexion into the corresponding short vowels. In some nouns (_) becomes (.), as גַּלְגַּל, גַּלְגְּלִין Da. 7. 9.

> Rem. כֹּל has in the emph. st. כֹּלָּא, &c. with the tone on the penultima (Da. 2. 40); but with suff. כָּלְּהוֹן Da. 2. 38; 7. 19.

SECTION LXII.—SIXTH DECLENSION OF MASCULINES.

The sixth declension includes nouns, participles, and infinitives, derived from verbs ל״א (ל״ה) and terminating in ָא (ָה), ֵי, ֵי, ֵי, e. g. גְּלָא, מִתְגְּלֵי, מַגְלֵי, בְּכֵי. The general rule is, that י appears in the course of declension, as the third radical, displacing א in forms like גְּלָא. That י is joined to the suffix throughout the singular, and thus becomes moveable; in forms like רְבִי, בְּכִי a short vowel is pronounced under the first radical. The termination יִן of the plural absol. is sometimes contracted into יֵ. In the constr. and emph. plur. no trace of the radical י remains.

SECTION LXIII.—SEVENTH DECLENSION OF MASCULINES.

Here belong nouns which terminate in the formative syllable ַי (ָאִי). They are mostly *gentilic* or *patronymic nouns*, or *ordinal numerals*. They all have this in common, (a) that in the course of inflexion their final י is changed into א, which is likewise *moveable*, and commences the following syllable. As a consequence, (_) is here changed into (ָ). (b) The plur. emph. terminates in ַיֵ, agreeing in form with the construct.

Exceptions from b : כַּשְׂדָּיֵא Da. 2. 5; תִּפְתָּיֵא Da. 3. 2, 3; יְהוּדָיֵא Da. 3. 8; Ezr. 4. 12, 23; 5. 1, 5.

SECTION LXIV.—EIGHTH DECLENSION OR *FIRST* OF FEMININES.

This declension includes all invariable feminines, i. e. all nouns with the feminine terminations, ָא, ָה, ִי, and וּ, the final syllable of which commences with only one consonant; as בְּמָא, עֵצָא, בּוּרָא, מְנָלָא, מַרְבִּי, גְּזֵרָה, סְנִירוּ, טָבוּ.

SECTION LXV.—NINTH DECLENSION, OR THE *SECOND* OF FEMININES.

This declension embraces all those feminines the final syllable of which commences with two consonants, as שְׂפָא *lip*; אִצְטְלִי *a robe*; זְכוּ *purity*.

(a) Nouns in ָא, to avoid, in the emph. and suff. states, two consonants with sheva under each in immediate succession, as שְׂפְתָא, אַרְמְלְתָא, &c., a short vowel must necessarily be supplied for the first of these. The supplied vowel is *Hhirek* or *Pattahh* (the latter with gutturals); more rarely Segol; e. g. חֶמְתָא, חֲמָא, אֲמְתָא, אֲמָא, שִׂפְתָא, שְׂפָא.

(b) The forms in ִי and וּ are regular in the singular (like Dec. VIII). In the plural, as becomes necessary, they also take a supplied vowel, *Hhirek* or *Pattahh*.

SECTION LXVI.—TENTH DECLENSION, OR THE *THIRD* OF FEMININES.

This declension includes all feminines in יָא (derived from לי"א) which have a consonant without a vowel immediately preceding this termination, as מַנְלְיָא, גַּלְיָא. In the sing. emph. and suff. states, | this consonant takes the supplied vowel Hhirek (for the cause stated in the preceding section), so that ' becomes quiescent in it.

SECTION LXVII.—ELEVENTH DECLENSION, OR THE *FOURTH* OF FEMININES

Here belong feminines in יָ־אָה derived from masculines in יָ־ (Dec. VII). In the emphatic state and before suffixes, א is changed in *moveable* ', though ordinal numerals take also יָ־ or יָ־; e. g. רְבִיעֵתָא, קַדְמֵיתָא (but רְבִיעָיתָא Da. 7. 19). In the plural absol. and constr. the usual forms are קַדְמָאָת, קַדְמָאָן.

REM. When feminine nouns are formed from masculines by adding the terminations יָ־אָ, ו or יָ־, the changes in the ground-form are precisely the same as those which appear in the emph. state of masculines. E. g. מַלְכָּא and מַלְכוּת; מֶלֶךְ, עוּלְמָא; עוּלַם צִדְיָא, צָדִי.

SECTION LXVIII.—IRREGULAR NOUNS (Comp. § 45).

אַב *father*, with suff. אָבִי, but also אֲבוּךְ, אֲבוּהִי (from אֲבוּ as if from R. אָבָה comp. Heb. אָב § 45. rem). Plur. with suff. אֲבָהָתָנָא, אֲבָהָתָךְ, אֲבָהָתִי from the abs. אֲבָהָן (as if from a sing. אֲבָהָא).

אָח *brother*, plur. with suff. אֶחָיךְ Ezr. 7. 18, by Hebraism (comp. אָח § 45), for אֲחִיךְ, from אֲחֵי=אֲחוּ R. אחה.

אֱנָשׁ *man*, emph. state אֲנָשָׁא, אֲנָשָׁא, but also אֲנֹשָׁא Khethib (as if from אֱנוֹשׁ). Plur. (by Hebraism) אֲנָשִׁים.

אֲרִי *lion*, plur. emph. אַרְיְוָתָא, from the absolute אַרְיָוָן (as if from a sing. אַרְיֵה, comp. Dec. VIII).

בַּיִת *house*, emph. בֵּיתָא, בַּיְתָה, constr. בֵּית, with suff. בֵּיתִי

and בַּיְתָה (comp. Dec. III, c), but plur. with suff. בָּתֵּיכֹן from בָּתִּין (comp. Heb. בַּיִת § 45).

נְבִיא *prophet*, emph. state נְבִיאָה (for נְבִיאָא, נְבִיָּא). Plur. emph. נְבִיאַיָּא with א in otio, for נְבִיָּיא (as if from as absolute נְבִיִּין).

עַם *people*, emph. state עַמָּא, but pl. emph. עַמְמַיָּא (comp Heb. עַם § 45).

רֵאשׁ *head*, emph. state רֵאשָׁה, with suff. רֵישֵׁהּ. Plur. רֵאשִׁין, but with suff. רֵאשֵׁהֶם (as if from רֵאשׁ).

שֵׁם *name*, but with suff. שְׁמֵהּ (from שֵׁם, comp. Dec. II). Plur. constr. שְׁמָהָת, with suff. שְׁמָהָתְהֶם (as if from שְׁמָהָא).

THE ANALYTICAL
HEBREW AND CHALDEE
LEXICON.

LEXICON.

א

אֹזֶר Piel fut. 1 pers. s. [אֲאַזֶּר], suff. 2 s. m. (§ 16. r. 15)

אֶלְפְּךָ Piel fut. 1 pers. sing. [אֲאַלֶּף], suff. 2 pers. sing. masc. (§ 16. rem. 15); ן before (–ְֶ). אלף

אַאֲמִין Hiph. fut. 1 pers. sing.   .   .   .   אמן

אֲאַמִּצְכֶם Piel fut. 1 s. [אֲאַמֵּץ], suff. 2 pl. m. (§ 16. r. 15) אמץ

אֶאֱסֹף Kal fut. 1 pers. sing.   .   .   .   אסף

אָאֹר Kal fut. 1 pers. sing. .   .   .   .   ארר

אַאֲרִיךְ Hiph. fut. 1 pers. sing. .   .   .   ארך

אָב [ן] masc. irreg. (§ 45).—I. *father.*—II. *forefather, ancestor.*—III. *author, inventor.*—IV. *father,* as an honorary appellation to priests and prophets in the character of teachers.—Hence, V. an *adviser.* Ge. 45. 8.

אַב Ch. masc. irreg. (§ 68), i. q. Heb. אָב *father.*

Proper names compounded with : אֲבִי, אֲבוּ, אֲבִ, אַב.

אֲבוּנַיִל Khethib, 1 Sa. 25. 18, for the usual אֲבִינַיִל q. v.

אֲבִי fem. mother of Hezekiah, also called אֲבִיָה, compare 2 Ki. 18. 2 with 2 Ch. 29. 1.

אֲבִי־עַלְבּוֹן (*father of strength,* i. e. *strong,* עלב collated with the Arab. *to be strong*) masc. one of David's heroes, called also אֲבִיאֵל, compare 2 Sa. 23. 31 with 1 Ch. 11. 32.

אֲבִיאֵל (*father of strength,* i.e. *strong*) masc.—I. grandfather of Saul, called also נֵר, compare 1 Sa. 9. 1 with 1 Ch. 9. 39.—II. one of David's heroes, compare the preceding.

אֲבִיאָסָף (*father of gathering,* i.e. *gatherer*) masc. a Korahite, called also אֶבְיָסָף, compare Ex. 6. 24 with 1 Ch. 6. 8.

אב

אֲבִיגַיִל (*father of exultation,* i. e. *exulting,* גַּיִל i. q. גִּיל) fem.—I. wife of David; before of Nabal.—II. sister of David, called also אֲבִינַיִל, compare 1 Ch. 2. 16 with 2 Sa. 17. 25.

אֲבִידָן (*father of the judge,* see דָּן) masc. chief of the tribe of Benjamin.

אֲבִידָע (*father of knowledge,* i. e. *knowing,* R. יָדַע) masc. a son of Midian.

אֲבִיָּה, אֲבִיָּהוּ (whose *father is the Lord,* see יָהּ) name of several persons, especially—I. of the second son of Samuel.—II. of a king of Judah, son of Rehoboam, called also אֲבִים, compare 2 Ch. 13. 1 with 1 Ki. 14. 31.—III. of the wife of Hezron, 1 Ch. 2. 24.

אֲבִיהוּא (whose *father is He,* viz. God) masc. a son of Aaron.

אֲבִיהוּד (*father of glory,* הוּד i.q. הוֹד) m. 1 Ch. 8. 3.

אֲבִיחַיִל (perhaps for אֲבִיחַיִל) fem.—I. wife of Rehoboam.—II. wife of Abishur, 1 Ch. 2. 29.

אֲבִיחַיִל (*father of valour,* i. e. *valiant*) masc.—I. a Levite.—II. a Gadite.—III. father of Esther.

אֲבִיטוּב (*father of goodness*) masc. a Benjaminite, 1 Ch. 8. 11.

אֲבִיטַל (*father of dew*) fem. wife of David.

אֲבִימָאֵל (*father of fatness,* מאל Arab *to be fat*) masc. a son of Joktan.

אֲבִימֶלֶךְ (*father of the king*) masc.—I. name of several Philistine kings.—II. son of Gideon.—III. 1 Ch. 18. 16, for אֲחִימֶלֶךְ 2 Sa. 8. 17.

אֲבִינָדָב (*noble father,* see נָדָב) masc. name of several men, especially—I. of a son of Jesse.—II. of a son of Saul.

---

a Is. 45. 5.   *b* Job 33. 33.   *c* Job 9. 16.   *d* Job 16. 5.   *e* Mi. 2. 12.   *f* Ge. 12. 3.

2

אֲבִינֹעַם (*father of pleasantness*) m. father of Barak.

אֲבִינֵר (*father of light*) masc. Saul's commander-in-chief; elsewhere אַבְנֵר.

אֲבִיעֶזֶר (*father of help*) masc.—I. son of Gilead.—Patronymic אֲבִי הָעֶזְרִי. An abridged form is אִיעֶזֶר, Nu. 26. 30, and patronymic אִיעֶזְרִי.—II. one of David's heroes.

אֲבִירָם (*father of height*, רָם from רום) masc.—I. one of the conspirators against Moses, Nu. 16. 1.—II. son of Hiel restorer of Jericho, 1 Ki. 16. 34.

אֲבִישָׁג (*father of error*, R. שָׁגַג) fem. a concubine of David.

אֲבִישׁוּעַ (*father of prosperity*, R. יָשַׁע or שׁוּעַ) masc.—I. a Benjaminite, son of Bela.—II. a son of Phinehas, 1 Ch. 5. 30.

אֲבִישׁוּר (*father of song*, שׁוּר i. q. שִׁיר) a man of the posterity of Judah.

אֲבִישַׁי (*father of gift*, compare שַׁי) masc. a brother of Joab, also called אַבְשַׁי, 2 Sa. 10. 10; 1 Ch. 2. 16.

אֲבִישָׁלוֹם (*father of peace*) masc. father-in-law of Rehoboam, called also אַבְשָׁלוֹם, compare 1 Ki. 15. 2 with 2 Ch. 11. 20.

אֶבְיָתָר (*father of abundance*) masc. a son of Abimelech the priest.

אַבְנֵר (*father of light*) masc. Saul's commander-in-chief, also called אֲבִינֵר q. v.

אַבְרָהָם (*father of a great multitude*, lit. *father great of* (i. e. as to) *multitude*, for אַב רַב הָם see הָם, R. הָמָה) masc. the Father and founder of the Hebrews, called אַבְרָם (*father of height*) before the covenant by circumcision, Ge. 17. 5.

אַבְשָׁלוֹם (*father of peace*) masc. third son of David, famous for his rebellion against his father.

אָב id. construct state . . . אב

אָבָא defect. for אָבִיא (q. v.) . . . בוא

וָאָבֹא Kal fut. 1 pers. sing.; וָ for וְ conversive . . . בוא

אָבֹאָה id. with paragogic ה . . . בוא

וָאָבֵאם defect. for אָבִיאֵם (q. v.) . . . בוא

אָבֵב in the Heb. not used; Chald. Pa. אַבֵּב *to bear fruit*.

אֵב masc. dec. 8 b, *greenness, verdure*. אִבֵּי הַנָּחַל *green herbs of the valley*. Ca. 6. 11.

אֵב Ch. *fruit*, with suff. אִנְבֵּהּ for אִבֵּהּ Dag. forte resolved in Nun, (compare § 52. rem. 2) Da. 4. 9.

אָבִיב masc. *green ears of corn*. חֹדֶשׁ הָאָבִיב *month of green ears*, viz. the month in which the

---

earing of the barley took place, beginning with the new moon of April.

אַבְנִיל } pr. name masc. defect. for אֲבִינַיִל q. v. } אב
אֲבִינַיִל }

אַבַגְתָא ‡ pr. name of a Persian eunuch. Est. 1. 10.

אָבַד fut. יֹאבַד-I. *to stray, wander, be lost.*—II. *to perish* const. with לְ and מִן of the person. Piel I. *to caus to stray, to disperse.*—II. *to cause to perish, to destroy.* Hiph. הֶאֱבִיד fut. once, אֹבִידָה (q. v.) causat. o Kal i. q. Piel.

אֲבַד Chald. *to perish.* Aph. *to destroy.* Hoph *to be destroyed.*

אֹבֵד masc. *destruction, ruin.* Nu. 24. 20, 24.

אֲבֵדָה fem. dec. 10.—I. *something lost.*—II. i. q אֲבַדּוֹן Pr. 27. 20. Khethib.

אֲבַדּוֹן masc.—I. *destruction.*—II. *place of destruction, abyss.*

אָבְדָן, אַבְדָן masc. *destruction, ruin.* Est. 8. 6; 9. 5

אָבַד } Kal preter. 3 pers. sing. masc. (com- } אבד
אָבַד } pare § 8. rem. 2) . . . }

אַבֵּד ‡ וְ Piel infin. construct used for the absolute אבד

אָבֹד Kal infin. absolute . . . אבד

אֲבֹד id. infin. construct . . . אבד

אַבֵּד ‡ וְ Piel pret. 3 pers. sing. masc. (§ 10. rem. 1) אבד

אֹבֵד construct of the following (§ 36. rem. 1) אבד

אֹבֵד Kal part. act. sing. masc. dec. 7 b. אבד

אֹבֵד † noun masc. sing. . . . אבד

אָבְדָה Kal preter. 3 pers. sing. fem. for אֲבֵדָה . אבד

אֲבֵדֹה וְ Kh. אֲבֵדָה (q.v.), K. אֲבַדּוֹן (q.v.); וְ bef. אבד
אֲבֵדָה noun fem. sing. dec. 10. . . . אבד

אָבְדָה וְ Kal preter. 3 pers. sing. fem. . אבד

אָבְדוּ ‡ } id. preter. 3 pers. pl. (§ 8. rem. 7) } אבד
אָבְדוּ }

אֲבַדּוֹן וְ noun masc. sing.; וְ before אבד

אֹבְדוֹת Kal part. act. fem., pl. of אֹבֶדֶת dec. 13 a אבד

אַבְדִּילָה וְ Hiph. fut. 1 pers. s. with parag. ה; וְ f. וְ conv. בדל

אַבֶּדְךָ וְ contr. from [אֲאַבֶּדְךָ] Piel fut. 1 pers. sing.
[אֲאַבֵּד] suff. 2 pers. sing. m.; וְ f. וְ conv. אבד

אָבְדְךָ ‡ Kal inf., suff. 2 pers. sing. m. (§ 16. rem. 7) אבד

אֲבֹדְךָ ‡ id. id. in pause for [אָבְדְךָ] . . . אבד

אָבְדְכֶם id., suff. 2 pers. pl. masc. . . . אבד

אַבְדִּיל ‡ וְ for [אַבְדִּיל] Hiph. fut. 1 pers. s.; וְ f. וְ conv. בדל

אַבְּדֵם Kal infin., suff. 3 pers. pl. masc. אבד

אִבַּדְם Piel pret. 3 p. s. m. (אִבַּד) suff. 3 pl. m. (§ 16. r. 15) אבד

אַבְדָן וְ noun masc. sing. . . . אבד

אָבַדְנוּ ‡ } Kal preter. 1 pers. pl. (§ 8. rem. 7) } אבד
אֲבַדְנוּ }

---

* Ge. 17. 5.   ᵈ De. 12. 2.   ᶠ De. 32. 28.   ᵏ Je. 48. 36.   ᵐ Ezr. 8. 24.   ᵗ De. 28. 22.   ˣ Le. 20. 26.   ᵇ 2 Ki. 13. 7.   ʸ Nu. 17. 27.
ᵇ Ju. 15. 1.   ᵉ De. 7. 20.   ʰ Nu. 24. 20, 24.   ᵖ Pr. 15. 11.   ⁿ Eze. 28. 16.   ᵘ Jos. 23. 13.   ᶻ Est. 9. 5.   ᵏ Nu. 17. 27.
ᶜ Hos. 29. 28.   ᶠ Je. 51. 55.   Pr. 27. 20.   ⁿ Je. 50. 6.   ᵖ De. 28. 20.   ʳ Ge. 24. 42.   ᵗᵇ 1. 12.

"ן id., suff. 3 pers. pl. masc.; ן id.	אֲבֹתֵיהֶם	אב
id., suff. 3 pers. sing. masc.	אֲבוֹתָי	אב
id., suff. 2 pers. sing. masc.	אֲבוֹתֶיךָ	אב
"ן id., suff. 2 pers. pl. masc.; ן before (-.)	וַאֲבוֹתֵיכֶם	אב
ן id., suff. 1 pers. pl.; ן id.	אֲבוֹתֵינוּ	אב
ן id., suff. 3 pers. pl. masc. (§ 4. rem. 2); ן id.	אֲבוֹתָם	אב
Kal fut. 1 pers. sing. [אֶבְחָן], suff. 2 p. sing. m.	אֶבְחַנְךָ	בחן
ן Kal fut. 1 pers. sing.; ן for ן conv.	אֶבְחַר	בחר
id. with paragogic ה	אֶבְחֲרָה	בחר
id., suff. 3 pers. sing. masc. (§ 16. rem. 12)	אֶבְחֲרֵהוּ	בחר

אָבָה Root not used, whence אֲבֵחָה fem. only Eze. 21. 20, אִבְחַת חֶרֶב *threatening of the sword*, i. e. the threatening sword. Prof. Lee, *resting, remaining*.

} Kal fut. 1 pers. sing. (§ 8. rem. 15) }	אֶבְטְחָה / אֶבְטַח	בטח
n. m. s., suff. 1 pers. sing. from [אָב] dec. 2a.	אַבִּי	אבה
ן n. m. s., suff. 1 p. s. from אָב irr. (§ 45)	אָבִי	אב
Kh. for אָבִיא Hiph. fut. 1 pers. sing. (§ 25, 2 f.)	אָבִי	בוא
Ch. n. m. s., suff. 1 p. s. from [אָב] irr. (§ 68)	אֲבִי	אב
ן n. masc. sing., construct of אָב irr. (§ 45); also pr. name fem., and in compos. as, אֲבִי עַלְבוֹן (אֲבִיעֶזֶר), and אֲבִי הָעֶזְרִי (see אֲבִיעֶזֶר)	אֲבִי	אב
ן Hiph. fut. 1 pers. sing.; ן for ן conv.	אָבִיא	בוא
ן id. with paragogic ה (Kh. אֲבִיאָה), Keri אָבִיא (q. v.)	אָבִיאָה	בוא
id., suff. 2 pers. sing. masc.	אֲבִיאֲךָ	בוא
pr. name masc.	אֲבִיאֵל	אב
ן Hiph. fut. 1 s., suff. 3 p. pl. m.; ן for ן conv	אֲבִיאֵם	בוא
id., suff. 3 pers. sing. fem.	אֲבִיאֶנָּה	בוא
id., suff. 3 pers. sing. masc.	אֲבִיאֶנּוּ	בוא
ן pr. name masc.; ן before (-.)	אֲבִיאָסָף	אב
noun masc. sing.	אָבִיב	אבב
} pr. name fem.; ן before (-.) }	אֲבִיגַיִל / אֲבִיגַיִל	אב
id. by contraction	אֲבִיגַל	אב
Hiph. fut. 1 pers. s. with paragogic ה (§ 19. r. 8)	אֲבִידָה	אבד
pr. name masc.	אֲבִידָן / וַאֲבִידָע	אב
ן n. m. s., suff. 3 p. sing. f. from אָב irr. (§ 45)	אֲבִיָּה	אב
ן pr. name masc. or (1 Ch. 2. 24) fem.	אֲבִיָּה	אב
n. m. s., suff. 3 p. sing. m. from אָב irr. (§ 45)	אֲבִיהוּ	אב
masc. & אֲבִיהוּא ן masc., וַאֲבִיהוּד masc., אֲבִיהַיִל fem., pr. names	אֲבִיהוּא	אב
ן noun masc. sing., suff. 3 pers. pl. masc. from אָב irreg. (§ 45); ן before (-.)	אֲבִיהֶם	אב
id., suff. 3 pers. pl. fem.	אֲבִיהֶן	אב
ן id., suff. 3 pers. sing. masc.	אָבִיו	אב

noun fem. sing., construct of אֲבֵדָה dec. 10	אֲבֵדֶת	אבד
Kal preter. 2 pers. sing. masc.	אָבַדְתָּ	אבד
id. preter. 2 pers. sing. fem.	אָבַדְתְּ	אבד
Piel preter. 2 pers. sing. masc.	אִבַּדְתָּ	אבד
} Kal preter. 1 pers. sing. (§ 8. rem. 7) }	אָבַדְתִּי / אָבַדְתִּי	אבד
Piel preter. 1 pers. sing.	אִבַּדְתִּי	אבד
ן id.; acc. shifted to ult. by conv. ן	וָאֹבְדָה	אבד
ן Kal preter. 2 pers. pl. masc.; ן for ן conv.	אֲבַדְתֶּם	אבד
ן Piel preter. 2 pers. pl. masc.	אִבַּדְתֶּם	אבד

אָבָד fut. יֹאבֶה *to be willing, inclined, desirous.* Is followed by an infin. with or without pref. לְ.

אַבֶּה masc. *reed, bulrush,* אֳנִיּוֹת אֵבֶה *vessels of reed,* probably *the papyrus,* only Job 9. 26.

אָב masc. *desire,* Job 34. 36, according to the Targum.

אֱבוֹי *poverty, misery,* only Pr. 23. 29.

אֶבְיוֹן adj. dec. 1 b.—prop. *wishing, desiring,* hence —I. *poor, needy.*—II. *miserable, wretched.*

אֲבִיּוֹנָה fem. *desire,* only Ec. 12. 5.

noun masc. sing.	אֲבֵהָ	אבה
Niph. fut. 1 pers. sing.	אֶבָּהֵל	בהל
Ch. n. m. pl., suff. 1 p. s. fr. [אָב] irr. (§ 68)	אֲבָהָתִי	אב
Ch. id., suff. 2 pers. sing. masc.	אֲבָהָתָךְ	אב
Ch. id., suff. 1 pers. pl.	אֲבָהָתַנָא	אב
Kal pret. 3 pers. pl.	אָבוּ	אבה
ן Kal fut. 1 pers. sing.; ן for ן conv.	אָבוֹא	בוא
Kal pret. 3 pers. pl. for אָבוּ (§ 8. rem. 4)	אָבוֹא	אבה
ן Kal fut. 1 pers. sing. with paragogic ה	אָבוֹאָה	בוא
Kh., אֲבִינֵגִיל K. (q. v.)	אֲבוֹנֵגִיל	אב
Ch. n. m. s., suff. 3 p. s. m. fr. [אָב] irr. (§ 68)	אֲבוֹהִי	אב
noun masc. sing. (after the form קָטוּל)	אֲבוֹי	אבה
Ch. n.m.s., suff. 2 p. s. m. from [אָב] irr. (§ 68)	אֲבוּךְ	אב
Kal part. pass. sing. masc.	אָבוּס	אבס
ן Kal fut. 1 pers. sing.	וְאָבוּס	בוס
noun masc. sing. dec. 3 b.	אֵבוּס	אבס
Kal part. pass. masc., pl. of אָבוּס dec. 3 a.	אֲבוּסִים	אבס
noun masc. sing., suff. 2 pers. sing. masc. for [סְךָ] from אֵבוּס dec. 3 b.	אֲבוּסֶךָ	אבס
Kal fut. 1 pers. sing., suff. 3 pers. sing. masc.	אֲבוּסֶנּוּ	בוס
Kal fut. 1 pers. sing. (§ 21. rem. 6)	אֲבֹאֵשׁ	באש
id. with paragogic ה	אֲבֹאֵשָׁה	באש
n. m. with pl. fem. term. from אָב irr. (§ 45)	אָבוֹת	אב
ן id., construct state; ן before (-.)	אֲבוֹת	אב
} id., suff. 1 pers. sing. ן before (-.) }	אֲבוֹתַי / אֲבוֹתַי	אב

---

a Nu. 21. 29.   b Je. 15. 7.   d Da. 2. 23.   k Da. 5. 2.   l 1 Ki. 5. 3.   o 2 Ch. 32. 13.   r Job 34. 36.   u Ca. 8. 2.   x Je. 46. 8.
c Eze. 26. 17.   Eze. 6. 3.   Exr. 4. 15.   Da. 19. 4.   Job 39. 9.   Je. 19. 4.   Da. 5. 13.   Zec. 10. 10.   Nu. 13. 14.
Ps. 9. 6.   g Job 9. 26.   Exr. 5. 12.   Is. 63. 6.   Ps. 81. 8.   Jos. 24. 8.   Is. 44. 1.   Ge. 42. 3.
Ea. 4. 16.   Job 23. 15.   Is. 28. 12.   Is. 14. 25.   Je. 44. 21.

אֶבְיוֹן   וֹ׀ adj. masc. sing. dec. 1 b. · אבה

אֶבְיוֹנֵי־   ו׀ id. pl., construct state . · אבה

אֶבְיוֹנֶיהָ   id. pl., suff. 3 pers. sing. fem.   אבה

אֶבְיוֹנִים   ו׀ id. pl., absolute state . · אבה

אֲבִיחַיִל · אֲבִיהַיִל   } pr. name masc., or (2 Ch. 11. 18) fem. . } אב

אַבִּיט   ו׀ Hiph. fut. 1 pers. sing. . · נבט

אַבִּיטָה   ו׀ id. with paragogic ה · נבט

אֲבִיטוּב   masc., אֲבִיטָל fem., pr. names . — אב

אָבִיךָ   ו׀ n. m. s., suff. 2 p. s. m. from אָב irr. (§ 45) אב

אָבִיךְ   id., suff. 2 pers. sing. fem. . — אב

אֲבִיכֶם   id., suff. 2 pers. pl. masc. . — אב

אֲבִיכֶן   ן׀ id., suff. 2 pers. pl. fem.; ו before ‿ . אב

אֲבִיָּם   pr. name masc., see אֲבִיָּהוּ . — אב

אֹבִים   Kal part. masc., pl. of [אֹבֶה] dec. 9 a. אבה

אֲבִימָאֵל · אֲבִימֶלֶךְ   ו׀ and ן׀ pr. names masc. אב

אָבִין   Kal fut. 1 pers. sing. . · בין

אֲבִינָדָב   ו׀ pr. name masc.; ו before ‿ אב

אָבִינָה   וֹ׀, ן׀, Kal fut. 1 p.s. with parag. ה; ו for וַ conv. בין

אָבִינוּ   n. m. s., suff. 1 pers. pl. from אָב irr. (§ 45) אב

אֲבִיעֵי־   construct of the following . · אבה

אֶבְיֹנִים   adj. masc., pl. of אֶבְיוֹן dec. 1 b. . אבה

אֶבְיֹנְךָ   id. sing., suff. 2 pers. sing. masc. . אבה

אֲבִיעֶזֶר   אֲבִיסָף · אֲבִיגֵר (see אֲבִיאָסָף) pr. names masc. אב

אַבִּיעָה   Hiph. fut. 1 pers. sing. with paragogic ה נבע

אֲבִיעֶזֶר   pr. name masc. . · אב

אַבִּיר   adj. masc. sing. dec. 1 b. . · אבר

אָבִיר   noun masc. sing., constr. of [אָבִיר] dec. 3 a. אבר

אַבִּירַי   adj. m. pl., suff. 1 pers. sing. from אַבִּיר dec. 1 b. אבר

אַבִּירֵי   id. pl., construct state . · אבר

אַבִּירָיו   id. pl., suff. 3 pers. sing. masc. . אבר

אַבִּירֶיךָ   id. pl., suff. 2 pers. sing. masc. . אבר

אַבִּירִים   id. pl., absolute state . · אבר

אֲבִירָם   נ׀ masc. & אֲבִישׁוּעַ נ׀ fem. & נ׀ masc. & אֲבִישַׁג נ׀ masc. & אֲבִישׁוּר נ׀ masc. & אֲבִישַׁי נ׀ masc. & אֲבִישָׁלוֹם masc., pr. names אב

אָבִיתִי   Kal pret. 1 pers. sing. . · אבה

אֲבִיתֶם   id. pret. 2 pers. pl. masc. . · אבה

אֶבְיָתָר   ו׀ pr. name masc. . · אב

אָבַךְ   Hith. only Is. 9. 17, וַיִּתְאַבְּכוּ גֵּאוּת עָשָׁן they shall roll or swell up in the mounting up of smoke.

אֶבְכֶּה   ו׀, ן׀ Kal. fut. 1 pers. sing.; ו for וַ conv. . בכה

אָבֵל   ו׀ fut. יֶאֱבַל to mourn; with עַל of the pers. mourned over. Hiph. to cause to mourn. Hithp. i. q. Kal. אָבֵל adj. dec. 5 c (§ 34, 2 & r. 2), mourning.

מִצְרָיִם (mourning of Egypt) pr. name of a place near Jordan, Ge. 50. 11.

אֵבֶל m. dec. 6 b (§ 35. r. 6) mourning, lamentation.

אָבֵל   Root not used. Arab. to be moist, sc. with the moisture of grass; hence Syr. יְבַל grass.

אָבֵל grassy place, meadow, 1 Sa. 6. 18, where the Sept. and Syr. express אֶבֶן, comp. vv. 14, 15. Hence the following pr. names.—I. אָבֵל בֵּית־מַעֲכָה Abel near Beth Maacha, a city in the north of Palestine, eastward of Jordan, not far from Antilibanus, in the tribe of Manasseh, called also אָבֵל־מַיִם, comp. 1 Ki. 15. 20 with 2 Ch. 16. 4, and perhaps simply אָבֵל 1 Sa. 6. 18, see above.—II. אָבֵל הַשִּׁטִּים (Acacia-meadow) a place in the land of Moab, Nu. 33. 49.—III. אָבֵל כְּרָמִים (meadow of vineyards) a village of the Ammonites on the other side of Jordan Ju. 11. 33.—IV. אָבֵל מְחוֹלָה (meadow of dancing) a village in the land of Issachar, the birth-place of the prophet Elisha.

אוֹבִיל (chief of the camels, coll. with the Arab.) pr. name of an Ishmaelite who had the charge of David's camels, 1 Ch. 27. 30.

אָבָל   adv. . · בלה

אָבָל adj. masc. sing. dec. 5 c. (§ 34. 2, & rem. 2), also pr. name in composition as א׳ הַשִּׁטִּים א׳, בֵּית מַעֲכָה, &c. . · אבל

אֵבֶל   ו׀ noun masc. sing. dec. 6. (§ 35. rem. 6) . אבל

אָבֵלָה pr. name of a place (אָבֵל) with local ה אבל

אָבְלָה Kal pret. 3 sing. fem. . · אבל

אָבְלוּ   ו׀ id. pret. 3 pers. pl. . · אבל

אֲבֵלוֹת   adj. pl. fem. from אָבֵל masc. . אבל

אַבְלִיגָה   ו׀ Hiph. fut. 1 sing. with paragogic ה בלג

אֲבֵלִים   adj. m., pl. of אָבֵל dec. 5 c. (§ 34, 2 & r. 2) אבל

אֶבְלְךָ   n. m. s., suff. 2 p. s. from אֵבֶל dec. 6. (§ 35. r. 6) אבל

אֶבְלָם   id., suff. 3 pers. pl. masc. . אבל

אֲבַלַּע · אֲבַלְּעָה   } Piel fut. 1 pers. sing. (§ 15. rem. 1) } בלע

אֶבֶן   com. (mostly fem.) with suff. אַבְנוֹ dec. 6 a.—I. a stone, generally; אֶבֶן הַשָּׂדֶה the common stone of the field; אֶבֶן יָד a stone which may be thrown with the hand; אַבְנֵי בָרָד hail-stones; אַבְנֵי אֵשׁ shining-stones; לֵב הָאֶבֶן obdurate heart.—II. precious stone, gem, also fully, אֶבֶן יְקָרָה.—III. rock, Ge. 49. 24.—IV. weight; אֶבֶן וָאֶבֶן diverse

---

ᵃ Is. 29. 19.   ᵈ 2 Sa. 17. 8.   ᶠ Job 23. 5.   ʰ Ex. 23. 6.   ᵏ Je. 46. 15.   ᵐ Am. 8. 8.   Joel 1. 9.   ᵗ Is. 69. 20.   ᵛ 2 Sa. 20. 20.

ᵇ Ps. 132. 15   ᵉ Eze. 3. 7.   ᵍ Ex. 23. 11.   ⁱ La. 1. 15.   ˡ Is. 16. 9.   ⁿ Mi. 1. 8.   ᵖ La. 1. 4.   Je. 31. 13.   ˣ Is. 19. 3.

ᶜ Is. 65. 5.

weights; אַבְנֵי כִים weights of (i. e. carried in) the bag.—V. plummet, Is. 34. 11. אַבְנֵי תֹהוּ stones of desolations; i. e. minutely measured off for desolation.—VI. pr. names; a. אֶבֶן הָאָזֶל (stone of departure), a stone not far from Jerusalem, 1 Sa. 20. 19. b. אֶבֶן הַזֹּחֶלֶת (smooth stone, coll. with Chald. and Arab.) a stone near Jerusalem, 1 Ki. 1. 9. c. אֶבֶן עֵזֶר (stone of help), a stone set up by Samuel.

אֶבֶן Chald. emph. אַבְנָא dec. 3a—a stone.

אֲבֵנָה 2 Ki. 5. 12. Kheth. in Keri אֲמָנָה q. v.

אֶבֶן masc. only in dual אֲבָנַיִם.—I. potter's wheel, Je. 18. 3.—II. Ex. 1. 16. where it is doubtful what it refers to; according to Kimchi, the seat or stool of a woman in labour.

אָבֶן }
אֶבֶן } (וְ), (וְ) } noun com. (suff. אַבְנוּ) dec. 6a. Chald. 3a; for וְ see letter ו.

אַבְנָא וְ Chald. n. m. s. emph. of אֶבֶן dec. 3a. (§ 59)

אֲבֵנָה Kh., אֲמָנָה K. (q. v.)

אֶבְנֶה וְ, וְ Kal fut. 1 pers. sing.; וְ for וְ conv.

אֶבָּנֶה וְ Niph. fut. 1 pers. sing. (§ 10. rem. 5).

אַבְנוּ noun com. sing., suff. 3 pers. sing. masc. from אֶבֶן dec. 6a

אַבְנֵט וְ noun, masc. sing. dec. 1b. (§ 36. No. 1)

אַבְנֵטֶךָ וְ id., suff. 2 pers. sing. masc.

אַבְנֵטִים id. pl., absolute state

אַבְנֵי וְ noun com. pl. construct from אֶבֶן dec. 6a.

אֲבָנֶיהָ id. pl., suff. 3 pers. sing. fem.

אַבְנֵיהֶם id. pl., suff. 3 pers. pl. masc.

אֲבָנֵינוּ id. pl., suff. 3 pers. sing. masc.

אֲבָנַיִךְ וְ id. pl., suff. 2 pers. sing. fem.; וְ before (־)

אֲבָנִים וְ id. pl., absolute state; וְ id.

אֶבְנֶךָ Kal fut. 1 pers. sing. (אֶבְנֶה), suff., 2 pers. sing. fem. (§ 24. rem. 21)

אֶבְנֶנָּה וְ id., suff. 3 pers. sing. fem. (§ 2. rem. 3)

אַבְנֵר וְ pr. name masc.

[אָבַס] to feed, or fatten cattle.

אֵבוּס (by Syriasm for אָבוּס) masc. pl. אֲבוּסִים a crib or stall in which animals are fed.

מַאֲבוּס masc. dec. 1b, barn, granary, Je. 50. 26.

אֶבְעָא Chald. Peal fut. 1 pers. sing. R. בְּעָא see בעה

אֲבַעְבֻּעֹת n. f., pl. of [עֲעָה] from [בַּעְבּוּעַ] & א prosth.

אֶבֶץ וְ for אֶבֶן (perhaps tin, i. q. Chald. אֲבָצָא) pr. n. of a city in the tribe of Issachar, Jos. 19. 20.

אִבְצָן (labour, i. q. Chald. אוּבְצָן) pr. n. of a judge of Israel, Ju. 12. 8, 10.

אָבָק masc. dec. 4c.—fine dust, different to עָפָר thick and heavy dust. Niph. denom. to wrestle, prop. to dust each other by wrestling, Ge. 32. 25, 26.

אֲבָקָה fem. only in the construct אַבְקַת (§ 42. rem. 1), powder, aromatic powder, Ca. 3. 6.

אֲבַק id. construct state

אֲבַקָם id., suff. 3 pl. masc.

אֲבַקֵּר Piel fut. 1 pers. sing.

אֲבַקֵּשׁ וְ Piel fut. 1 pers. sing.; וְ for וְ conv.

אֲבַקֶּשׁ־ id. with Mak. (§ 10. rem. 4)

אֲבַקְשָׁה וְ id. with parag. ה (§ 10. r. 7), וְ for וְ conv.

אֲבַקְשֶׁהוּ וְ id. with suff. 3 pers. sing. masc.; וְ id.

אֲבַקְשֶׁנּוּ id., suff. 3 pers. sing. masc.

אַבְקַת noun fem. sing., constr. of [אֲבָקָה] dec. 11c. (§ 42. rem. 1)

אָבַר Kal, not used, in the deriv. to be strong. Hiph. to fly, soar, Job 39. 26.

אָבִיר m. dec. 3a—the mighty one, spoken of God

אַבִּיר adj. dec. 1b.—I. strong, mighty, brave אַבִּירֵי לֵב stout-hearted; אַבִּירֵי בָשָׁן strong ones (i.e bulls) of Bashan.—II. nobles, princes; אַבִּיר הָרֹעִים chief of the shepherds.

אֵבֶר masc. wing-feather, pinion.

אֶבְרָה fem. with suff. אֶבְרָתוֹ (no pl. absolute) id.

אָבַר noun masc. sing.

אֶבְרָה noun fem. sing. (no pl. absolute)

אֶבְרַח וְ Kal fut. 1 pers. sing.; וְ for וְ conv.

אַבְרָהָם וְ pr. name masc.

אַבְרוֹתֶיהָ וְ n. f. pl, suff. 3 pers. s. f. from אֶבְרָה (q. v.)

אֶבְרַח Kal fut. 1 pers. sing. for [אֶאֱבְרָה]

אַבְרִיחֶהָ וְ Hiph. fut. 1 pers. sing. suff. 3 pers. sing. masc.; וְ for וְ conv.

אֲבָרֵךְ וְ Piel fut. 1 pers. sing.; וְ for וְ conv.

אַבְרֵךְ noun masc. formed like אַבְנֵט; or a Syriasm for הַבְרֵךְ Hiph. inf.

אֲבָרְכָה וְ Piel fut. 1 pers. s. with parag. ה; וְ bef. (־)

אֲבָרְכֶהוּ וְ id. with suff. 3 pers. sing. masc.; וְ for

אֲבָרְכֵהוּ וְ וְ conversive; וְ before (־)

אֲבָרֶכְךָ וְ id., suff. 2 pers. sing. masc. (§ 16. rem.

אֲבָרֶכְךָ וְ 15 & 13. § 2. rem. 3); וְ before (־)

אֲבָרְכֶכָּה וְ id. id. (§ 2. rem. 2); וְ id.

אֲבָרְכֵם וְ id., suff. 3 pers. pl. masc.; וְ id.

אַבְרָם וְ pr. n. masc. see אַבְרָהָם

אֶבְרָתוֹ n. f. s., suff. 3 p. s. m. fr אֶבְרָה (no pl. abs.)

אֲבֹשָׁה defect for אֲבוֹשָׁה (q. v.)

a 1 Ch. 21. 22.   f Ex. 28. 40.   l Je. 31. 4.   q Na. 1. 3.   v Da. 8. 15.   c 2 Sa. 13. 6, 10.   i Ge. 41. 43.   n Ps. 145. 2.   r Nu. 6. 27.
b Ge. 16. 2.   g Ne. 3. 35.   m Ne. 2. 5.   r Eze. 26. 10.   y Ps. 37. 36.   d Ps. 68. 14.   k Ps. 34. 2.   o Ge. 26. 3.   s Ge. 48. 9.
Ge. 30. 3.   h Is. 54. 11.   n Da. 7. 16.   s Eze. 34. 12.   z Pr. 23. 35.   e Ps. 139. 7.   l Ge. 27. 33.   p Ge. 12. 2.   t Ge. 32. 11.
c 2 Ki. 3. 25.   i Eze. 26. 12.   o Ex. 9. 9, 19.   t Eze. 22. 30.   a Ca. 3. 6.   f Ne. 13. 28.   m Is. 51. 2.   q Ge. 27. 7.   u Je. 17. 18.
Is. 22. 21.   k 1 Ch. 22. 14.   p De. 28. 24.   u Ru. 3. 1.   b Job 39. 13.   g Ge. 24. 48.

אַבְשַׁי ׳וְ (אֲבִישַׁי see), אַבְשָׁלוֹם ׳וְ pr. n. אב

אֲבַשְּׂרָה Piel fut. 1 p.s. with parag. ה; וְ before (-) for וּ · בשׂר

אָבֹת for אָבוֹת noun masc. with pl. fem. term. from אָב irreg. (§ 45) . אב

אֲבֹתַי / אֲבוֹתַי } id., suff. 1 pers. sing. . } אב

אֲבֹתֵיהֶם ׳וְ id., suff. 3 pers. pl. masc.; וְ bef. (-) . אב

אֲבֹתָיו id., suff. 3 pers. sing. masc. . . אב

אֲבֹתֶיךָ וְ id., suff. 2 pers. sing. masc.; וְ before (-) . אב

אֲבֹתֵיכֶם ׳וְ id., suff. 2 pers. pl. masc.; וְ id. . אב

אֲבֹתֵינוּ ׳וְ id., suff. 1 pers. pl.; וְ id. . אב

אֲבֹתָם id., suff. 3 pers. pl. masc. (§ 4. rem. 2) . אב

אַגָּא (fugitive coll. with the Arab.) pr. name masc. 2 Sam. 23. 11.

אֶגְאַל Kal fut. 1 pers. sing. for [אֶגְאָל] . . גאל

אֶגְאָלֵם id., suff. 3 pers. pl. masc. (§ 16. rem. 12) . גאל

אֶגְאַלְתִּי in pause for [אֶגְאָלְתִּי] Chaldaism for [הִגְאַלְתִּי] Hiph. pret. 1 pers. sing. · גאל

אֲגַג / אֲגָג } pr. name of Amalekitish kings. אגג Arab. to burn.

אֲגָגִי gent. name of Haman.

אָגַד Heb. not used. Chald. to bind together.

אֲגֻדָּה fem. dec. 10.—I. bands, knots, Is. 58. 6.—II. bundle, bunch, Ex. 12. 22.—III. band of men, troop, 2 Sam. 2. 25.—IV. vault of heaven, Am. 9. 6.

אַגִּד ׳וְ defect. for אַגִּיד (q. v.) . . נגד

אֲגֻדּוֹת noun fem., pl. of אֲגֻדָּה dec. 10 . אגד

אַגְדִּיל Hiph. fut. 1 pers. sing. . גדל

אַגְדִּל Kal fut. 1 pers. sing. . גדל

אֲגַדְּלוֹ וְ Piel fut. 1 pers. sing. with parag. ה; וְ bef. (-) גדל

אֲגַדְּלֶנּוּ וְ id., suff. 3 pers. sing. masc.; וְ id. גדל

אֲגַדֵּעַ Piel fut. 1 pers. s. for [אֲגַדֵּעַ] (§ 15. rem. 1) גדע

אֶגְדַּע וְ Kal fut. 1 pers. sing.; וְ for וּ conversive גדע

אֲגֻדַּת noun fem. sing., construct of אֲגֻדָּה dec. 10 אגד

אֲגֻדָּתוֹ וְ id. with suff. 3 pers. sing. masc.; וְ before (-) אגד

אֱגוֹז a nut, Cant. 6. 11. Arab. جوز, Syr. ܓܘܙܐ.

אֶגְוַע / אֶגֹּעַ ׳וְ } Kal fut. 1 pers. sing. . } נוע

אֶגּוֹף Kal fut. 1 pers. sing. . . נגף

אֶגּוּר Kal fut. 1 pers. sing. . . נור

אֶגּוּר pr. name masc. . . . אגר

אֶגּוּרָה Kal fut. 1 pers. sing. with parag. ה נור

אַגִּיד ׳וְ Hiph. fut. 1 pers. sing.; וְ for וּ conv. נגד

אַגִּידָה ׳וְ id. with paragogic ה . נגד

אַגִּדֶנּוּ id. with suff. 3 pers. sing. masc. (§ 2. rem. 3) נגד

אַגִּילָה Kal fut. 1 pers. sing. with parag. ה נִיל

אָגַל Heb. not used. Arab. to flow together, be collected.

אֵגֶל masc. only in pl. constr. אֶגְלֵי טַל reservoirs, or drops of dew, Job 38. 28.

אֶגְלַיִם (two ponds) pr. name of a village in the territory of Moab, Is. 15. 8.

אֲגַלֶּה Piel fut. 1 pers. sing. . . . גלה

אֶגְלֶה Kal fut. 1 pers. sing. . . . גלה

אֶגְלֵי n. masc. pl. constr. fr. [אֵגֶל] dec. 6 (§ 35. r. 6) אגל

אֶגְלַיִם pr. name of a place . . אגל

אָגַם Heb. not used. Arab. to be hot, to be warm, stagnant of water; Chald. (אֲגַם) to be pained, grieved.

אֲגַם masc. with dist. acc. אֲגָם Is. 35. 7, pl. constr. אַגְמֵי dec. 6. (§ 35. rem. 10.), abs. אֲגַמִּים dec. 8 b.—I. pool, marsh.—II. marshy, reedy place, Jer. 51. 32.

אָגֵם adj. dec. 5 c. only pl. constr. אַגְמֵי, Is. 19. 10.

אַגְמוֹן masc.—I. caldron, Job 41. 13.—II. reed, bulrush.—III. rope of rushes, Is. 40. 25.

אֲגַם n. masc. sing. dec. 6. (§ 35. r. 10) but pl. אֲגַמִּים אגם

אַגְמוֹן וְ noun masc. sing. . . אגם

אַגְמֵי ׳וְ noun masc. pl. const. of אֲגַם (q.v.) . אגם

אַגְמֵי adj. masc. pl. construct from [אָגֵם] dec. 5 c. אגם

אַגְמֵיהֶם n.masc. pl., suff. 3 pers.pl.masc. fr. אֲגַם (q v.) אגם

אֲגַמִּים וְ id. pl. absolute dec. 8 a; וְ before (-) . אגם

אַגְמֹן ׳וְ noun masc. sing. . . . אגם

אָגֵן Root not used, whence אַגָּן masc.dec. 2 b. bason, bowl.

אַגַּן noun masc. sing. construct of [אַגָּן] dec. 1 b. (comp. § 30. Nos. 3. 4. & rem. 1) . אגן

אֶגֹּף וְ Kal fut. 1 sing. וְ for וּ conversive . נגף

אַנְפֶּיהָ n. m. pl., suff. 3 pers. s. fem. fr. [אַף] dec. 8 a. נפף

אַנְפָּיו id., suff. 3 pers. sing. fem. . נפף

אַנְפֶּיךָ id., suff. 2 pers. sing. masc. . . נפף

[אָגַר] to gather, collect.

אָגוּר (collected) pr. name of a wise man, the son of Jakeh, Prov. 30. 1.

אֲגוֹרָה f. only constr. אֲגוֹרַת, a small coin, 1 Sa. 2. 36.

אִגֶּרֶת fem. dec. 13 a.—letter, epistle, edict.

אִגְּרַת fem. dec. 9.—epistle.

אֹגֵר Kal part. act. sing. masc. . . אגר

אִגְּרָא Chald. noun fem. sing. dec. 9. . אגר

אָגְרָה Kal preter. 3 pers. sing. fem. . . אגר

אִגְּרוֹת noun fem., pl. of אִגֶּרֶת dec. 13 a. אגר

אֲגַרְטְלֵי noun masc. pl. construct from אֲגַרְטֵל bason, charger. Its etymology is not defined.

אֶגְרַע ׳וְ Kal fut. 1 pers. sing.; וְ for וּ conv. . גרע

a 2 Sa. 18. 19.   f Is. 65. 3.   l Ge. 41. 40.   q Ex. 12. 22.   v De. 32. 27.   a Job 38. 28.   e Ex. 7. 19.   f Jos. 24. 5.   k Pr. 6. 8.
b 1 Ch. 9. 19.   g Je. 42. 21, etc.   m Ge. 12. 2.   r Am. 9. 6.   w Ps. 61. 5.   y Ps. 114. 8.   c Job 40. 26.   g Eze. 38. 6.   l Ezr. 1. 9.
c Ru. 4. 4.   i Is. 58. 6.   n Ps. 69. 31.   s Job 10. 18.   x Job 31. 37.   b Is. 14. 23.   d Job 41. 12.   h Pr. 10. 5.   m Eze. 5. 11.
d Ho. 13. 14.   k Eze. 24. 9.   o Zec. 11. 10, 14.   u Ps. 89. 4.   t Ru. 4. 4.   c Is. 19. 10.   e Ca. 7. 3.   i Ezr. 4. 8.   n Eze. 16. 27.

אֶגְרֹשׁ	(נ') Piel fut. 1 pers. sing.; ן id. . . . גרש
אֲגָרֲשֵׁם	id., suff. 3 pers. pl. masc. . . . גרש
אֲגָרֲשֶׁנּוּ	('ה) id., suff. 3 pers. sing. masc.; ן before (-ְ) גרש
אִגֶּרֶת	(נ') noun fem. sing. dec. 13a. . . . אנר
אִגַּרְתָּא	Chald. noun fem. sing., emph. of אִגְּרָא dec. 9. אנר
אִגְּרֹתֵיהֶם	n. fem. pl., suff. 3 pers. pl.m.fr. אִגֶּרֶת dec.13a. אנר
אֵד	ן noun masc. sing. dec. 1a. . . . אוד
אָדַב	Kal not used, Hiph. *to languish, faint,* 1 Sa. 2. 33.
אֶדְאַג	Kal fut. 1 pers. sing. . . . דאנ
אַדְבְּאֵל	ן (*miracle of God,* coll. with the Arab.; or *finger of God,* Chald. אַדְבְּעָא *finger*) pr. name of a son of Ishmael, Gen. 25. 13.
אַדְבִּיק	Hiph. fut. 1 pers. sing. . . . דבק
אֲדַבֵּר	(נ', ה) Piel fut. 1 pers. sing. (§ 10. rem. 4); ן for ו *cop.,* ן for . *conversive*
אֲדַבְּרָה / אֲדַבְּרָה	(ה', נ') id. with paragogic ה; ן ו id.
אָדַד	Heb. not used, i. q. הדד Arab. *to befall* any one, as a misfortune.

אֲדַד pr. name of an Edomite, 1 Ki. 11. 17; called also הֲדַד ver. 14.

אַדּוֹ pr. name masc. Ez. 8. 17.

אַדָּן pr. n. masc. Ez. 2. 59; called אַדּוֹן Neh. 7. 61.

אֶדֶד	pr. name masc. . . . אדד
אֶתְדַּדֶּה	Hithp. fut. 1 pers. sing. contr. for [אֶתְדַּדֶּה] דדה
אֶדַּדֵּם	id. with suff. 3 pers. masc. pl. . . דדה
אַדּוּ	pr. name masc. . . . אדר
אֱדוֹם	ן pr. name of a man or nation; ן before (ם) אדם
אֱדוֹם	ן written *fully* for אֱדֹם (q. v.) אדם
אֲדוֹמִים	gent. noun masc., pl. of אֲדוֹמִי from אֱדוֹם אדם
אָדוֹן	noun masc. sing. dec. 3a. . . דון
אַדּוֹן	pr. name masc. . . . אדר
אֲדוֹן	noun masc. sing., construct of אָדוֹן dec. 3a. דון
אֲדֹנַי	id. pl. spoken only of God, elsewhere אֲדֹנָי (q.v.) דון
אֲדוֹנֶיהָ	id. pl. with suff. 3 pers. sing fem. דון
אֲדוֹנִיָּה	pr. name masc. . . . דון
אֲדוֹנֵיהֶם	n. m. pl., suff. 3 pers. pl. m. fr. אָדוֹן dec. 3a. דון
אֲדוֹנָיו	id. pl. absolute state . . . דון
אֲדוֹרַיִם	pr. name of a place . . . אדר
אֲדוֹשׁ	Kal inf. absolute . . . אדש
אֵדוֹת	defect. for אוֹדוֹת noun fem. pl. . אוד
אֹדוֹתַי	id. with suff. 1 pers. pl. . . אוד
אֹדוֹתֶךָ	id. with suff. 2 pers. s. masc. . אוד
אַדִּיהֶם	Hiph. fut. 1 pers. sing., suff. 3 pers. pl. masc. נדה
אֱדַיִן	(נ') Chald. adv. *then, at that time;* בֵּאדַיִן id.; מִן אֱדַיִן *since that time.*

	אַ–ר
אַדִּיר	adj. masc. sing. dec. 1 b . אדר
אַדִּירוֹ	id., suff. 3 pers. sing. masc אדר
אַדִּירֵי	(נ') id. pl., construct state אדר
אַדִּירֵיהֶם	(נ', ו') id. pl., suff. 3 pers. pl. masc. אדר
אַדִּירָיו	id. pl., suff. 3 pers. sing. masc. אדר
אַדִּירֶךָ	id. pl., suff. 2 pers. sing. masc. אדר
אַדִּירִים / אַדִּרִים	} id. pl., absolute state } אדר
אֲדַלֶּן־	with Mak. for [אֲדַלֵּן] Piel fut. 1 pers. sing. דלן
אֲדַלְיָא	pr. n. of a son of Haman, Est. 9.8. As a Pers. name Gesenius conjectures, *heart* or *eagle*

[אָדַם] *to be red, ruddy.*—Pu. part. *made,* or *dyed red.*—Hiph. *to be red,* Is. 1. 18.—Hithp. *to be red, sparkling,* Prov. 23. 31.

אָדָם masc. (has no pl. number)—I. *a man,* human being irrespective of sex; more frequently collect. *men,* for which also is used בְּנֵי אָדָם *sons of man;* בֶּן אָדָם *son of man,* i. e. weak and mortal man; פֶּרֶא אָדָם *wild ass of a man,* i. e. a wild man, Ge. 16. 12; in the construct (without change of vowels) אָדָם בְּלִיַּעַל *a man of worthlessness,* Prov. 6. 12.—II. *a man,* not a woman, i. q. אִישׁ, Eccl. 7. 28.—III. pr. name—(a.) of the first man, 1 Ch. 1. 1.—(b.) of a city near Jordan.

אָדֹם, אָדוֹם adj. pl. אֲדֻמִּים dec. 8c. (§ 37. Nos. 2 & 3) fem. אֲדֻמָּה *red, ruddy,* or *a reddish brown,* comp. § 26. No. 23.

אֱדֹם, אֱדוֹם pr. name.—I. of the elder son of Isaac, Ge. 25. 30, usually called עֵשָׂו.—II. *Edomite,* collect. *Edomites;* fully בְּנֵי אֱדֹם בַּת אֱדֹם; also as the name of the country *Idumea.* Gent. n. אֱדֹמִי *Edomite,* fem. אֲדֹמִית *Edomitish woman,* pl. אֲדֹמִיּוֹת comp. § 39. No. 4. rem. 1, note.

אֹדֶם masc. *a ruby,* or *cornelian.* Sept. Vulg. *Sardius.*

אֲדַמְדֶּמֶת, fem. אֲדַמְדָּמֶת pl. אֲדַמְדַּמּוֹת (§ 39. No. 4. rem. 1), adj. *reddish,* comp. § ?. No. 23.

אֲדָמָה fem. dec. 11c. (§ 42. rem. 1).—I. *ground, soil, land.*—II. *land, region, country.*—III. pr. name of a city in the tribe of Naphtali, Jos. 19. 36.

אַדְמָה pr. name of a city destroyed with Sodom and Gomorrah.

אַדְמִי (*human*) pr. name of a city in the tribe of Naphtali, Jos. 19. 33.

אַדְמוֹנִי, אַדְמֹנִי adj. *red-haired.*

אַדְמָתָא pr. n. of a Persian nobleman, Est. 1. 14.

a Ju. 2. 3.   d Ex. 23. 29, 30.   f Ne. 6. 17.   i Eze. 3. 26.   m Ca. 5. 10.   p Ps. 123. 2.   s Jos. 14. 6.   v Je. 30. 21.   y Na. 2. 6.
b Ju. 6. 9.   e Nu. 22. 6.   g Ge. 2. 6.   k Eze. 2. 1.   n Ju. 13. 18.   q Mal. 1. 6.   t Jos. 14. 6.   w Ps. 16. 3.   z Na. 3. 13.
c Ho. 9. 15.   h Es. 9. 29   h Ps. 38. 19.   l Da. 10. 16.   o Ju. 19. 26.   r Is. 28. 28.   u Exr. 5. 5.   x Ne. 10. 30.
Is. 38. 15.   gg Ps. 42. 5.   hh Zec. 11. 2.

דָּם (for אֲדָם) m. dec. 2 a.—I. *blood*; אָכַל עַל־דָּם *to eat* (flesh) *with the blood*; דָּם נָקִי *innocent blood*; but דָּם נָקִי *blood of the innocent.*—II. *blood-shed, blood-guiltiness*; אֵין לוֹ דָּם *he is not guilty of blood*; in the plural, אִישׁ דָּמִים, עִיר דָּמִים *bloody man, city*; דָּמָיו בּוֹ *his blood is upon him*, is guilty of his own blood.—III. *blood of grapes, wine.*

אָדָם וְ noun masc. sing., also pr. name . . אדם
אָדֹם adj. m. s., pl. אֲדֻמִּים dec. 8 c. (§ 37. Nos. 2 & 3) אדם
אֶאֱדֹם־ וְ Kal fut. 1 pers. s. (§ 18. r. 14); וְ for וְ conv. דמם
אֹבֵד see עֹבֵד אָדֹם . . . עבד
אָדֹם noun masc. sing. . . . . אדם
אֲדַמְדָּם adj. masc. sing. (§ 39. 4. rem. 1) . . אדם
אֲדַמְדֶּמֶת in pause for אֲדַמְדֶּמֶת (q. v.) . . אדם
אֲדַמְדַּמֹּת pl. of the following . . . אדם
אֲדַמְדֶּמֶת adj. fem. sing. from אֲדַמְדָּם m. (§ 39. 4. rem. 1) אדם
אֲדָמָה וְ noun fem. sing. dec. 11 c. (§ 42 rem. 1), also pr. name; וְ before (־ַ) . . אדם
אֲדַמֶּה Piel fut. 1 pers. sing. . . . דמה
אֲדָמָה וְ pr. name of a place . . . אדם
אֲדֻמָּה adj. fem. s. from אָדֹם m. (§ 39. No. 3. parad.) אדם
אֲדַמֶּה contr. for [אֶתְדַּמֶּה], Hithp. fut. 1 pers. sing. דמה
אָדְמוּ Kal pret. 3 pers. pl. . . . אדם
אַדְמוֹנִי adj. masc. sing. . . . . אדם
אֲדָמוֹת noun fem. pl. absolute from אֲדָמָה dec. 11 c. אדם
אַדְמִי וְ pr. name of a place; וְ before (־ַ) אדם
אַדְמִי gent. noun masc. from אֱדוֹם . . אדם
אֲדָמִיִּם id. pl. dec. 8. . . . . אדם
אֲדָמִים see מַעֲלַת אֲדֻמִּים . . עלה
אֲדֻמִּים adj. masc., pl. of אָדֹם dec. 8 c. (§ 37. Nos. 2 & 3) אדם
אַדְמִית gent. noun fem., pl. of אֲדֹמִית (§ 39. No. 4. rem. 1) from אַדְמִי masc. (q. v.) . אדם
אַדְמֹנִי וְ adj. masc. sing. . . אדם
אַדְמַת n. f. s., constr. of אֲדָמָה dec. 11 c. (§ 42. r. 1) אדם
אַדְמָתָא pr. name masc. . . . . אדם
אַדְמָתָהּ noun fem. sing., suff. 3 pers. sing. fem. from אֲדָמָה dec. 11 c. (§ 42. rem. 1) . . אדם
אַדְמָתוֹ id., suff. 3 pers. sing. masc. . . אדם
אַדְמָתִי id., suff. 1 pers. sing. . . . אדם
אַדְמָתְךָ / אַדְמָתֶךָ } id., suff. 2 pers. sing. masc. . } אדם
אַדְמַתְכֶם id., suff. 2 pers. pl. masc. . . אדם
אַדְמָתָם id., suff. 3 pers. pl. masc. . . אדם
אַדְמָתֵנוּ וְ id., suff. 1 pers. pl. . . אדם

[אֶדֶן] masc. in pause אָדֶן dec. 6 a.—I. *base of a column.*—II. *trop. foundation*, Job 38. 6.

אַדָּן pr. name masc. . . . . אדד
אַדֹנָו Kheth. for אֲדֹנָיו (q. v.) . . . דון
אַדֹנֵי noun masc. pl. constr. from [אָדֹן] dec. 6 a. . אדן
אֲדֹנָי noun pl. *the Lord*, spoken of God, different from אֲדֹנַי pl. with suff. (q. v.) . . דון
אֲדֹנָי וְ id. contracted for [וַאֲדֹנָי] . . דון
אֲדֹנַי noun m. pl., suff. 1 pers. s. from אָדֹן dec. 3 a. דון
אֲדֹנֵי־ id. pl. construct state; וְ bef. (־ַ) . דון
אֲדֹנַי id. s., suff. 1 pers. s., with pref. for [וַאֲדֹנַי]; אֲדֹנַי וְ also pr. name in compos. as אֲדֹנִי־בֶזֶק &c. } דון
אֲדֹנֶיהָ n. m. pl., suff. 3 pers. s. fem. fr. [אָדֹן] dec. 6 a. אדן
אֲדֹנֶיהָ n. m. pl., suff. 3 pers. s. f. from אָדֹן dec. 3 a. דון
אֲדֹנִיָּה וְ & אֲדֹנִיָּהוּ וְ pr. names masc. . . דון
אֲדֹנֵיהֶם וְ n. m. pl., suff. 3 pers. pl. m. fr. [אָדֹן] dec. 6 a. אדן
אֲדֹנֵיהֶם n. m. pl., suff. 3 pers. pl. m. fr. אָדֹן dec. 3 a. דון
אֲדֹנָיו וְ noun masc. pl., suff. 3 pers. sing. masc. from [אָדֹן] dec. 6 a.; וְ before (־ַ) אדן
אֲדֹנָיו n. m. pl., suff. 3 pers. s. m. from אָדֹן dec. 3 a. דון
אֲדֹנֶיךָ id., suff. 2 pers. sing. masc. . דון
אֲדֹנַיִךְ id. suff. 2 pers. sing. fem. . . דון
אֲדֹנֵיכֶם id., suff. 2 pers. pl. masc. . . דון
אֲדֹנִים noun masc., pl. of [אָדֹן] dec. 6 a. אדן
אֲדֹנִים noun masc., pl. of אָדֹן dec. 3 a. דון
אֲדֹנֵינוּ וְ id. with suff. 1 pers. pl.; וְ before (־ַ) דון
אֲדֹנִיקָם, וַאֲדֹנִירָם pr. names masc. . . דון
אֲדֹנֵנוּ n. m. s., suff. 1 pers. pl. from אָדֹן dec. 3 a. דון

אֵדַע אֵדַע וְ } Kal fut. 1 pers. sing.; וְ for וְ conv. } ידע
אֶדְעָה וְ Kh. אֶדַע q. v., K. אֶדְעָה (q. v.) . ידע
אֵדְעָה אֵדְעָה וְ } Kal fut. 1 pers. sing. with paragogic ה; וְ for וְ conv. } ידע
אֵדָעֲךָ וְ, וְ id. with suff. 2 p. s. m. (§ 16. r. 12); וְ id. ידע
אַדְבְּקֶם Hiph. fut. 1 pers. sing. [אֶדְבֵּק], suff. 3 pers. pl. masc. (§ 18. rem. 11) . . דבק

אָדַר Niph. *to become glorious*, Ex. 15. 6, 11.—Hiph. *to make honourable, glorious*, Is. 42. 21.

אֲדוֹרַיִם pr. name of a city of Judah, 2 Chr. 11. 9 Its etymology is uncertain. Gesenius, *two princes* or *two mounds*; others derive it from דּוּר, *two dwellings.*

אַדִּיר adj. m. dec. 1 b.—I. *great, mighty.*—II. *noble, excellent*; hence—III. *prince.*

אֶדֶר pr. name of a Benjaminite, 1 Chr. 8. 3. see also חֲצַר אַדָּר

אֲדָר the twelfth month of the Hebrew year, beginning with the new moon of March, and ending with that of April. The etymology is uncertain. Chald. id. Ezr. 6. 15.

a Job 31. 34.   c Le. 13. 19.   e Le. 13. 24. 43.   h La. 4. 7.   l Sa. 17. 42.   f Pr. 30. 10.   n 1 Sa. 16. 16.   p Ge. 18. 21.   r Ex. 33. 13. 17.
b Le. 13. 42, 49.   d Le. 14. 37.   f Is. 14. 13.   k Ps. 49. 12.   k Am. 5. 2.   m De. 10. 17.   o Ru. 4. 4.   q Je. 11. 18.   s 2 Sa. 22. 45.
bb Nu. 19. 2.   dd Ge. 47. 18, 19.   ff Ne. 13. 10

אַדִּר masc.—I. *cloak, mantle*, Mi. 2.8.—II. *greatness, splendour*, Zec. 11.13.

אַדֶּרֶת fem. with suff. אַדַּרְתּוֹ dec. 13a.—I. *cloak, mantle.*—II. *magnificence.*

אֲדַרְגָּזְרִין Chald. *chief judges*, Da. 3.2,3. From אֲדַר *greatness*, and גְּזְרִין part. of גְּזַר q. v.

אֲדַרְמֶלֶךְ (*splendour of the king*, contracted from אֶדֶר הַמֶּלֶךְ) pr. n.—I. of an idol, 2 Ki. 17.31.—II. of a son of Sennacherib, 2 Ki. 19.37.

אַדָּר pr. name masc.   אדר

אֲדָר name of a month   אדר

אֶדֶר noun masc. sing.   אדר

אֲדַרְגָּזְרַיָּא Chald. n. masc. pl. emph. from [גְּזַר] dec. 2 b.   אדר

אַדְרָה pr. name of a place [אַדָּר] with parag. ה   אדר

אֶדְרוֹשׁ Kal fut. 1 pers. sing. (comp. § 8. rem. 18)   דרש

אָדְרַזְדָּא Chald. adv. *quickly, diligently*, Ezr. 7.23.

אַדְרֵי Chald. n. m. pl. constr. from [אַדָּר] dec. 2a.   נדר

אַדְרִיכֶם Hiph. fut. 1 pers. sing., suff. 2 pers. pl. masc.   דרך

אֶדְרְכֶם וְ Kal fut. 1 pers. s. [אֶדְרֹךְ], suff. 3 pers. pl. m.   דרך

אֲדַרְכְּנִים *darics*, a Persian gold coin, see also דַּרְכְּמוֹנ׳   אדר

אַדְרָם וְ pr. name, see אֲדֹנִירָם   דון

אַדְרַמֶּלֶךְ וְ pr. name masc.   אדר

אַדְרָעִי וְ pr. name of a place for [אֶדְרֶעִי]   דרע

אֶדְרֹשׁ Kal fut. 1 pers. sing.   דרש

אֶדָּרֵשׁ Niph. fut. 1 pers. sing. (§ 10. rem. 5)   דרש

אֶדְרְשָׁה וְ Kal fut. 1 pers. s. (אֶדְרֹשׁ) with parag. ה   דרש

אֶדְרְשֶׁנּוּ id. with suff. 3 pers. sing. masc. (§ 2. rem. 3)   דרש

אַדְרָת } noun fem. sing. dec. 13a.   אדר
אַדֶּרֶת

אַדַּרְתּוֹ id., suff. 3 pers. sing. masc.   אדר

אַדַּרְתָּם id., suff. 3 pers. pl. masc.   אדר

[אֲדֹשׁ] *to thresh*, once, Is. 28.28.

אָהַב, אָהֵב fut. יֶאֱהַב, יֶאֱהָב, 1 pers. אֹהַב, אֵהַב, אֹהֵב.—I. *to love*, with the acc., rarely with לְ and בְּ; part. אֹהֵב *friend.*—II. *to love to do* anything, followed by an infin. with לְ.—Niph. part. *lovely, amiable*, 2 Sa. 1.23.—Pi. part. *a lover.*

אַהַב masc. only pl. אֲהָבִים.—I. *amours, loves*, Ho. 8.9.—II. *loveliness*, Pr. 5.19.

אֹהַב m. only pl. אֹהָבִים *amours, loves*, Pr. 7.18.

אַהֲבָה fem.—I. infin. of the verb אָהַב e. g. לְאַהֲבָה אֶת־שֵׁם יְהֹוָה *to love the name of the Lord.*—II. subst. *love, beloved.*—III. adv. *delightfully*, Ca. 3.10.

אֹהַב Kal fut. 1 r. s. in pause for [אֶאֱהַב] (§ 19. r. 3)   אהב

אֱהַב־ id. imp. sing. masc.   אהב

אֹהַב וְ id. fut. 1 pers. sing. ; וְ for וָ conv.   אהב

אֹהֵב וְ id. part. act. sing. masc. dec. 7 b.   אהב

אַהֲבָה וְ (prop. inf. § 8. rem. 10. & 13. rem. 2) noun fem. only in the sing. (§ 26. No. 11)   אהב

אֲהֵבָהּ Kal pret. 3 pers. sing. masc. (אָהַב), suff. 3 pers. sing. fem. (§ 16. rem. 1)   אהב

אֱהֵבֶהָ id. imp. 3 p. s. m. (אֱהַב), suff. 3 p. s. f. (§ 16. r. 11)   אהב

אֹהֲבֶנּוּ וְ id. fut. 1 pers. sing. (אֹהַב), suff. 3 pers. sing. masc. (§ 16. rem. 12) ; וְ for וָ   אהב

אֲהֵבוּ id. pret. 3 pers. pl.   אהב

אֲהֵבוּ id. pret. 3 pers. s. m. (אָהַב), suff. 3 pers. s. m.   אהב

אֶהֱבוּ } id. imp. pl. masc. (§ 8. rem. 12) } אהב
וְאֶהֱבוּ

אֹהֲבוּ וְ id. part. act. s. m. (אֹהֵב) suff. 3 s. m. dec. 7 b.   אהב

אֲהֵבוּךָ id. pret. 3 p. pl. (s. אָהַב), suff. 2 p. s. m.   אהב

אֲהֵבוּם id. id., suff. 3 pers. pl. masc.   אהב

אֹהֲבַי id. part. act. pl. m., suff. 1 pers. s. dec. 7 b.   אהב

אֹהֲבֵי וְ id. id. pl., construct state   אהב

אֹהֲבִי וְ id. id. sing., suff. 1 pers. sing.   אהב

אֹהֲבֶיהָ Kh. אֹהֲבֶיהָ q. v., K. אֹהֲבַי (q. v.)   אהב

אֹהֲבֶיהָ Kal part. act. pl. m., suff. 3 pers. s. f. dec. 7 b.   אהב

אֹהֲבָיו וְ id., suff. 3 pers. sing. masc.   אהב

אֹהֲבֶיךָ id., suff 2 pers. sing. masc.   אהב

אֹהֲבָיִךְ id., suff. 2 pers. sing. fem. for [בָיִךְ]   אהב

אֲהָבִים noun masc., pl. of [אַהַב] dec. 6 d.   אהב

אֹהֲבִים Kal part. act. pl. masc., from אֹהֵב dec. 7 b.   אהב

אֲהֵבַךְ וְ id. preter. 3 pers. sing. masc. (אָהַב), suff. 2 pers. sing. m. (§ 16. r. 1) ; וְ for וָ conv.   אהב

אֹהַבְךָ id. part. act. sing. masc. (אֹהֵב), suff. 2 pers. sing. masc., dec. 7 b. (§ 36. rem. 3)   אהב

אֲהֵבֶם וְ id. fut. 1 pers. s. (אֹהַב), suff. 3 pers. pl. masc. ; וְ for וָ conv.   אהב

אַהֲבַת וְ n. fem. sing., construct of אַהֲבָה (q. v.)   אהב

אֲהֻבַת Kal part. pass. sing. fem., construct of אֲהוּבָה dec. 10, from אָהוּב masc.   אהב

אֹהֶבֶת id. part. act. sing., fem. of אֹהֵב   אהב

אָהַבְתָּ id. preter. 2 pers. sing. masc.   אהב

אָהַבְתָּ וְ id. id., acc. shifted by conv. וְ (§ 8. rem. 7)   אהב

אָהַבְתְּ id. preter. 2 pers. sing. fem.   אהב

אֲהֵבְתִּהוּ id. pret. 3 pers. s. f., suff. 3 p. s. m. (§ 16. r. 1)   אהב

אַהֲבָתִי n. f. s. with suff. 1 pers. s. from אַהֲבָה (q. v.)   אהב

אָהַבְתִּי } Kal preter. 1 pers. sing. (§ 8. rem. 7) } אהב
אָהֵבְתִּי

אֹהַבְתִּי id. part. act. s. f. (אֹהֶבֶת) with parag. י, dec. 13 a.   אהב

אֲהַבְתִּיךְ id. pret. 1 pers. sing., suff. 2 pers. sing. masc.   אהב

a Da. 3.2,3. | d 1 Ch. 29.7. | g Ese. 17.8. | m Mal. 1.2. | p Zec. 8.19. | s Je. 8.2. | v Ju. 5.31. | f 2 Ch. 20.7. | k Ge. 25.28.
b Ese. 20.40. | e Ese. 32.18. | h Zec. 11.3. | n Pr. 15.17. | q Ps. 31.24. | t Is. 41.8. | w Ps. 122.6. | g Ho. 14.5. | l 1 Sa. 13.28.
c Is. 42.16. | f 1 Sa. 28.7. | i Pr. 8.17. | o Pr. 4.6. | r Am. 5.15. | u Pr. 8.17. | x Ps. 119.167. | h Ho. 3.1. | m Ho. 10.11.
d Is. 63.5. | g Ge. 9.5. | Ho. 3.1. | Ho. 11.1. | Pr. 13.24. | Pr. 18.21. | De. 7.13. | De. 13.4. | Ho. 3.1. | n Is. 43.4.

אֲהַבְתִּיךְ Kal preter. 1 pers. sing., suff. 2 pers. sing. fem. אהב

אֲהַבָתֵךְ n. f. s., suff. 2 pers. s. m. from אַהֲבָה (q. v.) אהב

אֲהֵבְתְּ Kal pret. 3 p. s. f., suff. 2 p. s. t. (§ 16. r. 2) אהב

אַהֲבָתָם n. f. s., suff. 3 pers. pl. m. from אַהֲבָה (q. v.) אהב

אֲהַבְתֶּם וְ' Kal preter. 2 pers. pl. masc.; וְ before (‑) אהב

אֲהַבְתָּנוּ id. preter. 2 pers. sing. masc., suff. 1 pers. pl. אהב

אֲהַבְתָּנִי id. with suff. 1 pers. sing. אהב

אֶהְגֶּה Kal fut. 1 pers. sing. (§ 13. rem. 5) הגה

אֹהַד וְ' pr. name of a son of Simeon, Ge. 46. 10. The etymology is uncertain; coll. with the Samar. *portion*. According to Gesenius, *union*, אֹהַד i. q. אֶחָד.

אֵהוּד (by Syr. for אֱהוּד) pr. name of a judge in Israel.

אֲהָהּ interj. expressive of grief, *ah! alas!*

אַהֲוָא pr. name of a country and a river. Ezr. 8. 21, 31.

אֹהֵב וְ' Kal part. p. sing. masc. אהב

אֹהֲבָה id. fem. (§ 38. No. 3. dec. 3) dec. 10. אהב

אֵהוּד וְ' pr. name masc. אהד

אֲהוֹדֶנּוּ Hiph. fut. 1 pers. sing., suff. 3 pers. sing. masc. (§ 20. rem. 10. § 25. No. 2e). ידה

אֲהוֹדְעִנֵּהּ Chald. Aph. fut. 1 pers. sing., suff. 3 pers. sing. masc. (§ 47. rem. 4, compare 53. 1) ידע

אֱהִי i. q. אַיֵּה *where!* Ho. 13. 10. Others take it as an interj. expressive of derision, *ha!*

אֱהִי וְ' apocopated for the following (§ 24. r. 3) היה

אֶהְיֶה וְ', וָ' Kal fut. 1 pers. sing.; וָ for וְ conv. היה

אֲהִימָה וְ' Hiph. fut. 1 pers. sing. with paragogic ה הום

אָהַל i. q. הָלַל, only Hiph. *to shine*, Job 25. 5. See also the following article.

אֹהֶל וְ' masc. dec. 6, with suff. אָהֳלֶךְ, אָהֳלִי (§ 35. r. 8), with ה paragogic אָהֱלָה, pl. אֹהָלִים (rem. 9).— I. *tent, tabernacle, dwelling*.—II. pr. name of a son of Zerubbabel. 1 Ch. 3. 20.

אָהַל *to pitch a tent, to live in tents*. Piel id. Is. 13. 20.

אָהֳלָהּ (*her tent*, for אָהֱלָהּ, see § 3. rem. 3) an allegorical name given to Samaria by Ezekiel, 23. 4, sq.

אָהֳלִיאָב (*tent of* (his) *father*) pr. name of an artificer employed in the work of the tabernacle.

אָהֳלִיבָה (*my tent* (is) *in her*, בָּהּ for בָּהּ, see § 3. rem. 3) an allegorical name given to Jerusalem by Ezekiel, 23. 4.

אָהֳלִיבָמָה (*tent of the high place*) pr. name of a wife of Esau. Ge. 36. 2, 14.

אֹהֱלָה pr. name fem. אהל

אָהֳלֹה noun masc. sing., suff. 3 pers. sing. masc. from אֹהֶל (§ 35. rem. 9) אהל

אָהֳלוֹ id., with suff. 3 pers. sing. masc. אהל

אָהֳלוֹת וְ' noun pl. fem. see אֹהָלִים אהל

אָהֳלֵי n. masc. pl., constr. from אֹהֶל (§ 35. rem. 9) אהל

אָהֳלִי id. sing., suff. 1 pers. sing. אהל

אָהֳלַי id. pl., suff. 1 pers. sing. (note א) אהל

אָהֳלִיאָב m., וְ' אָהֳלִיבָמָה f., וְ' f., pr. n. m. אהל

אָהֳלֵיהֶם וְ' noun masc. pl., suff. 3 pers. pl. masc. from אֹהֶל (§ 35. rem. 9) אהל

אָהֳלֶךָ id. pl., suff. 2 pers. sing. masc. (note א) אהל

אָהֳלֵיכֶם id. pl., suff. 2 pers. pl. masc. אהל

אֲהָלִים masc. pl. and אֲהָלוֹת fem. pl. *lign-aloes*, or *aloes wood*, a perfumed wood.

אֹהָלִים וְ' noun masc., pl. of אֹהֶל, dec. 6. (note א, § 35. rem. 9) אהל

אֶהֱלָךְ id. sing., suff. 2 pers. sing. masc. for [אֶהֳלְךָ] אהל

אֵהֵלֵךְ Piel fut. 1 pers. sing. הלך

אֶהֳלֵךְ n. m. s., suff. 2 pers. s. f. from אֹהֶל (q. v.) אהל

אֵלֵךְ Kal fut. 1 pers. sing. הלך

אֲהַלֵּל Piel fut. 1 pers. sing. הלל

וַאֲהַלְלָה id. with parag. ה; לְ for לְ, (§ 10. rem. 7) הלל

אֲהַלֶּלְךָ id., suff. 2 pers. sing. masc. for [אֲהַלֶּלְךָ] (§ 2. rem. 3. and 16. rem. 15) הלל

אֲהַלְלֶנּוּ id. with suff. 3 pers. sing. masc. הלל

אֶהֱמֶה וְ' Kal fut. 1 pers. sing. המה

אֶהֱמַיָּה וְ' id. (§ 24. rem. 5) המה

אֶהְפֹּךְ Kal fut. 1 pers. sing. (§ 13. rem. 5) הפך

אֶהֱרֹג Kal fut. 1 pers. sing. הרג

אֶהֶרְגָה וְ' id. with paragogic ה (§ 13. rem. 4). הרג

אֶהַרְגֶהוּ וְ' id., suff. 3 pers. s. m.; וְ for וָ conv. הרג

אֶהֱרוֹן *fully* for אֶהֱרֹג (q. v.) הרג

אֶהֱרֹס Kal fut. 1 pers. sing. הרס

אַהֲרֹן וְ' pr. name of the brother of Moses, and the first high-priest.

אֶהֱרֹם Kal fut. 1 pers. sing. הרס

אוֹ conj.—I. *or, either*; אוֹ—אוֹ *whether—or*. II. *or else*.—III. *if, but if*: יָמִים אוֹ עָשׂוֹר *some days, if it were perhaps ten*, i. e. about ten days.

אוּאֵל וְ' pr. name of a man. Ezr. 10. 34. Simonis, *strength of God*, for אוּל אֵל; Gesenius, perhaps *will of God*, for אָו אֵל see R. אָוָה.

אוֹב Root not used; whence, אוֹב masc. pl. אֹבוֹת.—I. *leathern bottle*, Job 32. 19.—II. *a spirit of divina-*

a 2 Sa. 1. 26.   d De. 10. 19.   k Ne. 13. 26.   h Da. 5. 17.   n Ju. 6. 5.   f Pr. 7. 17.   f Ps. 77. 4.   s Am. 9. 1.   z Am. 2. 3.
b Eu. 4. 15.   e Mal. 1 2.   h De. 21. 15.   i Ps. 55. 3.   o Nu. 24. 5.   r Is. 54. 2.   u Zep. 3. 9.   y Ge. 27. 41.   c Mal. 1. 4.
c Am. 4. 5.   f Ju. 14. 16.   i Ps. 28. 7.   m Je. 4. 20.   p Jos. 22. 8.   t Ps. 55. 18.   uu Ps. 145. 2.   yy Ps. 109. 30.

tion, or *necromancy*.—III. *necromancer, one who calls up spirits to learn of them the future.*

אֹבֹת (*water skins*) pr. name of a station of the Israelites in the wilderness.

אוֹב	noun masc. sing. dec. 1 a.	אוב
אֹבֵד	Kal part. act. sing *m*asc. dec. 7 b.	אבד
אוֹבִיל	pr. name masc.	אבל
אוֹבִילֵם	Hiph. fut. 1 pers. sing., suff. 3 pers. pl. masc.	יבל
אוֹבִישׁ	Hiph. fut. 1 pers. sing.	יבש
אוֹבִלָה	[for אוֹבֵל] Hoph. fut. 1 pers. sing.	יבל
אוּבְלִי	n. masc. sing., construct of בֵל' dec. 2 b.	יבל

אוּד Root not used; Arab.—I. *to bend, to turn, to sur-round.*—II. *to be strong.*

אֵד masc. dec. 1 a., *mist, vapour,* the exhalations arising from, and surrounding, the earth.

אוּד masc. dec. 1 a., *a wooden poker,* for turning or stirring the fire, Is. 7.4; hence, *a fire-brand.*

אֹדוֹת pl. fem. dec. 10, *causes,* (prop. *turnings,* compare גַּלָל, סִבָּה, Eng. *circumstances*), עַל אוֹדוֹת *for the causes,* i. e. on account of; עַל אוֹדוֹתַי *on my account.*

אֵיד m. dec. 1 a., *straitness, calamity, destruction.*

מְאֹד masc. dec. 1 a.—I. *might, power, excess;* בִּמְאֹד מְאֹד *in excess of excess,* i. e. *very exceed-ingly;* עַד לִמְאֹד עַד מְאֹד *even to excess, till* (it amounted) *to excess, exceedingly.*—II. adv. *exceed-ingly;* מְאֹד מְאֹד *very exceedingly;* טוֹב מְאֹד *very good;* נִמְצָא מְאֹד *he is very present;* הֵרֶד מְאֹד *go down quickly.*

אוּד	noun masc. sing. dec. 1 a.	אוד
אוֹדֶה	'(ו) Hiph. fut. 1 pers. sing. (§ 25. No. 2 e)	ידה
אוֹדִיעַ	Hiph. fut. 1 pers. sing.	ידע
אוֹדִיעָה	id. with paragogic ה	ידע
אוֹדִיעֲךָ	id., suff. 2 pers. sing. masc.	ידע
אוֹדִיעֵם	id., suff. 3 pers. pl. masc.	ידע
אוֹדְךָ	'(ו) Hiph. fut. 1 pers. sing. (אוֹדֶה), suff. 2 p.	ידה
אוֹדֶךָ	'(ו) sing. masc. (§ 25. No. 2 e. & § 2. r. 3)	
אוֹדֶנּוּ	id., suff. 3 pers. sing. masc., (§ 2. rem. 3)	ידה
אֵדְעָה	ן' Kal fut. 1 pers. sing. (§ 20. rem. 7); ן before gutt. for ו conversive	ידע
אוֹדֹת	noun pl. fem. from the form [אוד]	אוד

1. אָוָה Kal, not used. Arab. *to bend, inflect,* also *turn aside, take lodgings, dwell.* Pi. *to desire, to long for.* Hithp.—I. *id.*—II. *to take for a dwelling.*

אַו masc. *desire.* Pr. 31. 4. Khethib.

אַוָּה fem. dec. 10.—I. *desire, longing.*—II. *lust.*

אֲוִי (*desire*) pr. name of a king of Midian.

אִי masc. (for אֱוִי) pl. אִיִּים (§ 37. No. 4) *habit-able earth* or *land, coast, sea-coast, island.* See also אִי R. אוה II

מַאֲוַי masc. only, pl. מַאֲוַיִּים *desires.* Ps. 140. 9.

תַּאֲוָה fem. dec. 10.—I. *desire, appetite, lust.*—II. *object of desire, a delight.*

II אָוָה Root not used. Arab. *to howl.*

אוֹי I. *wailing.*—II. interj. *wo! alas!* expressive of grief.—III. *ho!* expressive of threatening.

אוֹיָה id. *alas!* Ps. 120. 5.

אִי masc. (for אֱוִי)—I. *jackal,* only in the plural, אִיִּים—II. interj. *wo! alas!* אִי לוֹ *wo to him,* Ec. 4. 10.

אַיָּה fem.—I. the name of a bird of prey, Sept. and Vulg. *vulture; kite.*—II. pr. name of a man.

III. אָוָה Root not used; supposed to signify, *to mark, describe with a mark.*

אוֹת (for אָוֶת) com. dec. 1 a., pl. אֹתוֹת—I. *mark, memorial, warning.*—II. *sign, portent, miracle.*

אָת Chald. masc. id.

אִוָּה	Piel preter. 3 pers. sing. masc.	אוה
אוֹהֵב	Kal part. act. sing. masc. dec. 7 b.	אהב
אוּנַי	pr. name of a man. Ne. 3. 25. אוּן Arab. *quick.*	
אוּזָל	pr. name masc.	אזל
אוֹחִילָה	(Kh. ?) אוֹחֲגִלָה K. אוֹחִילָה Hiph. fut. 1 pers. s. ה parag. in form from יָחַל in sense fr.	חול
אוֹחִיל	Hiph. fut. 1 pers. sing.	יחל
אוֹחִילָה	id., with paragogic ה	יחל
אוֹי	interj.	אוה
אֱוַי	pr. name masc.	אוה
אוֹיֵב	ן' Kal part. act. sing. masc. dec. 7 b.	איב
אוֹיְבִי	} id. pl., suff. 1 pers. sing.	} איב
אוֹיְבַי		
אוֹיְבֵי	id. pl., construct state	איב
אוֹיְבִי	id. sing., suff. 1 pers. sing. Hiph.	איב
אוֹיְבֵיהֶם	id. pl., suff. 3 pers. pl. masc.	איב
אוֹיְבָיו	id. pl., suff. 3 pers. sing. masc.	איב
אוֹיְבֶיךָ	id. pl., suff. 2 pers. sing. masc.	איב
אוֹיִבֵךְ	id. id. (Kh. אוֹיְבָיִךְ); K. אוֹיְבָךְ (q. v.)	איב
אוֹיְבֵיכֶם	id. pl., suff. 2 pers. pl. masc.	איב
אוֹיְבִים	id. pl., absolute state	איב
אוֹיְבֵינוּ	id. pl., suff. 1 pers. pl.	איב
אוֹיִבֵךְ	id. sing., suff. 2 pers. sing. masc.	איב
אוֹיַבְנוּ	id., sing., suff. 1 pers. pl.	איב
אוֹיָה	interj.	אוה
אֱוִיל	ן' noun masc. sing., dec. 1 a.; also pr. name in compos. אֱ' מְרֹדַךְ; ן before (ר)	אול

a Je. 31. 9.   c Da. 8. 2.   e Ps. 138. 2.   g Ps. 118. 28.   Ge. 21. 11.   i Pr. 27. 6.   m Mi. 7. 7.   p 1 Ki. 21. 20.   r Ps. 127. 5.
b Job 10. 19.   d Zec. 3. 2.   f Ps. 34. 4.   h Eze. 20. 5.   k Ps. 132. 12.   n Je. 4. 19.   Ps. 102. 9.   q Pr. 24. 17.   s Pr. 24. 12.
ib Je. 16. 21.   Ju. 16. 23. 24.

אֱוִילִים‎ רֶ n. masc., pl. of אֱוִיל‎ dec. 1a.; ן‎ id.   אול

אֲוִיתִיהָ‎ Piel preter. 1 pers. sing., suff. 3 pers. sing. fem.   אוה

אֲוִיתִךָ‎ id. with suff. 2 pers. sing. masc. for [תִיךָ‎]   אוה

אוֹכִיחַ‎ Hiph. fut. 1 pers. sing.   יכח

אוֹכִיחֲךָ‎ / אוֹכִיחֲךָ‎ } id., suff. 2 pers. sing. masc.   יכח

אוֹכִיל‎ [for אֹאכִיל‎] Hiph. fut. 1 pers. s. (§ 19. r. 8)   אכל

אֹכֵל‎ Kal part. act. sing. masc. dec. 7b.   אכל

אוּכַל‎ / אוּכַל‎ } Hoph. fut. 1 pers. sing.   יכל

אוֹכְלָה‎ Kal part. act. fem. for [אֹכְלָה‎]   אכל

אוֹכְלָתִי‎ id. pl. m., suff. 3 pers. s. f. from אוֹכֵל‎ dec. 7b.   אכל

אֵלֵד‎ Niph. fut. 1 pers. sing. (§ 20. rem. 7); Milêl before monos. for [אִוָּלֵד‎]   ילד

אָוַל‎ Root not used; i. q. יָאַל‎ to be foolish.

אֱוִיל‎ masc. dec. 1a., a fool, by implication an impious wicked person.

אֱוִילִי‎ adj. foolish, Zec. 11. 15.

אֱוִיל מְרֹדַךְ‎ pr. name of a king of Babylon, successor of Nebuchadnezzar. See מְרֹדַךְ‎ the name of a Babylonian idol; the fool of Merodach, perhaps so called by the Jews by way of opprobrium for, the wise of Merodach.

אִוֶּלֶת‎ f. with suff. אִוַּלְתִּי‎ dec. 13a., folly, impiety.

אוּל‎ & אַיִל‎ Root not used,—Arab.—I. to be the first, chief.—II. to be strong.

אוּל‎ masc. dec. 1a.—I. prince, chief, 2 Ki. 24. 15. Kh.—II. body, Ps. 73. 4.

אוּלַי‎ pr. name of a river flowing by Susa in Persia, Da. 8. 2. See also analyt. order.

אֵלָם, אוּלָם‎ masc., pl. אֵילַמִּים‎.—I. vestibule, porch.—II. pr. name of a man. Note.—Some editions have also the form אֻלָם‎.

אַיִל‎ masc. dec. 6h.—I. ram.—II. a certain ornament over doors or windows.

אַיָּל‎ com. a stag, hart, or deer, also fem. hind.

אַיָּלָה‎ fem. dec. 11a., hind or female deer.

אַיֶּלֶת‎ fem. id. אַיֶּלֶת הַשַּׁחַר‎ hind of the morning, in the heading of Ps. 22, to designate the subject of the Psalm.

אַיָּלוֹן‎ (belonging to deer, deer-field), pr. name of a city in the tribe of Dan, and another in the tribe of Zebulun.

אֱיָל‎ masc. strength, force, Ps. 88. 5.

אֱיָלוּת‎ fem. id., Ps. 22. 20.

אַיִל‎ masc. dec. 1a.—I. the mighty, noble.—II. applied to strong trees, as the oak, the pine, or terebinth, &c.

אֵילִם‎ pr. name of a station of the Israelites in the wilderness.

אֵילוֹן‎ (oak).—I. pr. name of several men.—II. of a city in the tribe of Dan.

אֵילוֹת, אֵילַת‎ pr. name of a sea-coast town in Idumea.

אֵילָם‎ only pl. אֵילַמִּים‎, אֵלַמּוֹת‎ vestibules, porticos.

אִילָן‎ Chald. masc. dec. 1., a tree.

אֵל‎ masc. dec. 1a.—I. strong, mighty man, hero.—II. power, יֶשׁ־לְאֵל יָדִי‎ it is in the power of my hand.—III. God, the Mighty One.—IV. a supposititious god, an idol.

אֵלִיָּהוּ‎, אֵלִיָּה‎ (my God is the Lord), pr. name of the celebrated prophet, Elijah, during the reign of Ahab, king of Israel, and likewise of two other but obscure persons.

לָאֵל‎ (to God, sc. dedicated), pr. name masc. Nu. 3. 24.

אֵלָא‎ (i. q. אֵלָה‎ terebinth), pr. name masc. 1 Ki. 4. 18.

אֵלָה‎ fem.—I. terebinth.—II. pr. name of one of the dukes of Idumea.—III. of a king of Israel, son of Baasha, and others.

אֵלוֹן‎ masc. dec. 1b.—I. oak, others, terebinth.—II. pr. name masc. Ge. 46. 14.

אוּלַי‎ Kh., אֻלַי‎ K. noun masc. pl. construct from אוּל‎ or אַיִל‎   אול

אוּלַי‎ pr. name of a river, for [אֻלַי‎]   אול

אוּלַי‎ (compounded of אוֹ=אוּ, and לַי‎ i. q. לֹא‎ compare לוּלֵי‎) adv.—I. if not, unless.—II. perhaps, peradventure.

אֱוִילִי‎ for [אֱוִילִי‎] adj. masc. sing.   אול

אוֹלִיד‎ Hiph. fut. 1 pers. sing.   ילד

אוֹלִיךְ‎ Hiph. fut. 1 pers. sing.   ילד

אוֹלִיכָה‎ ן‎ id. with paragogic ה‎   ילד

אוֹלִיכֵם‎ id., suff. 3 pers. pl. masc.   ילד

אֱוִילִם‎ def. for אֱוִילִים‎ n. masc., pl. of אֱוִיל‎ dec. 1a.   אול

אֹלֵךְ‎ ן‎ apoc. for אוֹלִיךְ‎ (q. v.); ן‎ for וַ‎ conversive   ילד

אוּלָם‎ pr. name masc.   אול

אוּלָם‎ n. m. s., suff. 3 pers. pl. m. from [אוּל‎] dec. 1a.   אול

אוּלָם‎ ן‎ noun masc. sing., pl. c. אֻלַמֵּי‎ dec. 8a.   אול

אוּלָם‎ ן‎ (compounded of אוֹ=אוּ, and לָם‎ Arab. not) adv. prop. whether not, i. q. but perhaps, but.

אִוֶּלֶת‎ ן‎ n. fem. sing. dec. 13a. (see the following)   אול

אול dec. 13 a. אֻלַּת n. f. s., suff. 3 pers. s. m. from אֻלָּתוֹ

אול id., suff. 1 pers. sing. . . . אֻלָּתִי

אמר 'וְ pr. name masc. . . . אוֹמַר

אמר Kal fut. 1 pers. sing.; 'וְ for 'וַ conversive אוֹמַר

אמר id part. act. sing. masc. dec. 7 b. . אוֹמֵר

אמר id. fut. 1 pers. sing. with paragogic ה אוֹמְרָה

אָוֶן Heb. not used, in the derivatives.—I. *to be nothing, to be light, easy.*—II. *to be strong.*

אָוֶן masc. dec. 6 h.—I. *nothingness, falsehood, vanity.*—II. *idol, idols;* בֵּית אָוֶן *house of idols;* בִּקְעַת אָוֶן *valley of idols,* Am. 1. 5.—III. *wickedness, iniquity;* מְתֵי אָוֶן *wicked men;* פֹּעֲלֵי אָוֶן *workers of iniquity.*—IV. *adversity, calamity, sorrow.*

אוֹן masc. dec. 1 a.—I. *power, strength, vigour,* רֵאשִׁית הָאוֹן *beginning of strength,* i. e. first-born. —II. *wealth, riches.*—III. pr. name masc. Nu. 16. 1. —IV. אֹן & אוֹן (sun), *Heliopolis,* an Egyptian city.

אוֹנוֹ (*strong,* for אוֹנוֹן) pr. name of a city in Benjamin.

אוֹנָם (id.) pr. name of a man.

אוֹנָן (id.) pr. name of a son of Judah.

אַיִן masc. dec. 6 i., construct אֵין.—I. *nothingness,* Is. 40. 23.—II. as an adv. *not,* including the idea of the subst. verb *to be* (compare יֵשׁ); אֵין אִישׁ *there is no man,* אֵין פּוֹתֵר *there was none interpreting;* אָדָם אַיִן *there was no man,* לֵב־אַיִן *there is no heart;* אֵין לָבוֹא *it is not to enter,* i. e. none dare enter, אֵין עֲרוֹךְ *there is no comparing,* i. e. cannot be compared; אֵין דָּבָר מְאוּמָה *nothing;* אֵין כֹּל *nothing at all.*—III. If a personal pronoun is the subject of the proposition, the particle takes the verbal suffixes, אֵינֶנִּי *I am,* or *was not, shall not be,* אֵינֶנּוּ, אֵינֶנָּה, אֵינְךָ, &c.—IV. When followed by the dative, אֵין לִי *there is not to me,* i. e. *I have not,* אֵין לָהֶם *they have not.*—V. Combined with prepositions; בְּאֵין (a) *without,* (b) *before there was,* were, Pr. 8. 24; כְּאֵין (a) *as nothing,* (b) *almost.* Ps. 73. 2; לְאֵין (a) *to him who has not,* (b) *that there should be no,* &c.; מֵאֵין (a) *so as not to be,* יֹשֵׁב *so that there shall be no inhabitants,* Is. 5. 9; Je. 34. 22. (b) *because there is not;* מֵאֵין מַיִם *for want of water,* Is. 50. 2.

אִין i. q. אַיִן. 1 Sa. 21. 9.

תְּאָנִים masc. pl., *vanity, falsehood,* Ez. 24. 12.

און אֹ֫וֶן 'וְ n. m. s. dec. 6 g; also pr. n.; 'וַ see lett. ו

און אוֹן 'וֹ noun masc. sing. dec. 1 a; also pr. n. m. .

און וְ pr. name of a place . . . אוֹנוֹ

און וְ n. m. s. from אוֹן, or אָוֶן, (q. v.), אוֹנִי

און noun masc. sing. from אוֹן, dec. 1 a. אוֹנִי

און Kh. אוֹנִיּוֹת, K. אֳנִיּוֹת, noun fem., pl. of אֳנִיּוֹת אֳנִיָּה or (הוֹמִיָּה participial form like) אנה

און noun masc., pl. of אוֹן dec. 1 a. . אוֹנִים

און noun masc., pl. of אָוֶן dec. 6 g. . אוֹנִים

און id. sing., suff. 2 pers. sing. fem. . אוֹנֵךְ

און id. sing., suff. 3 pers. pl. masc. . אוֹנָם

און n. m. s., suff. 3 pers. pl. m. from אוֹן dec. 1 a. אוֹנָם

און 'וְ pr. name masc. . . . אוֹנָם

און 'וְ pr. name masc. . . . אוֹנָן

יסף Hiph. fut. 1 pers. sing. . . אוֹסִיף

יסף ap. for the preceding . . אוֹסֵף

יסר וְ Niph. fut. 1 pers. s. (§ 20. r. 7); 'וַ for 'וְ conv. אִוָּסֵר

יעד Niph. fut. 1 pers. sing. (§ 20. rem. 7) אִוָּעֵד

אוּפָן pr. name of a country rich in gold, the situation of which is not known.

אפר אוֹפִיר pr. name of a region . . .

אפר אוֹפִירָה id. with paragogic ה .

אפן אוֹפָן noun masc. sing.; pl. אֳפַנִּים dec. 8. אופן וְ (§ 37. No. 2)

אפן אוֹפַנָּי id. pl., construct state

אפן אוֹפַנֵּיהֶם id. pl., suff. 3 pers. pl. masc.

אפן אוֹפַנִּים id. pl., absolute state

אפר אוֹפֵר defect. for אוֹפִיר (q. v.)

[אוּץ] I. *to be narrow.* Jos. 17. 15.—II. trans. *to press on, to urge.*—III. *to urge oneself, to hasten;* const. with מִן *to hasten away.* Je. 17. 16. Hiph. *to press on, urge,* const. with בְּ.

יצא וְ defect. for אוֹצִיא (q. v.) . .

יצא וְ Kh. אוֹצִיאָה Hiph. fut. 1 pers. sing. R. יצא; צוה K. אֲצַוֶּה (q. v.) . .

יצא וְ Hiph. fut. 1 pers. sing.; 'וַ for 'וְ conv. אוֹצִיא

יצא id. with paragogic ה . אוֹצִיאָה

יצא וְ id. with suff. 3 pers. pl. masc.; 'וַ for 'וְ אוֹצִיאֵם

אצר noun masc. sing., dec. 2 b. אוֹצָר

אצר id. construct state . אוֹצַר

אצר וְ Hiph. fut. 1 pers. sing. with paragogic ה, for אוֹצְרָה [אַאֲצִירָה] (§ 19. r. 8. & § 11. r. 7); 'וַ for 'וְ

אצר noun masc. sing., suff. 3 pers. sing. masc. from אוֹצָר dec. 2 b. אוֹצְרוֹ

אצר וְ id. pl., absolute state . אוֹצָרוֹת

אצר 'וֹ id. pl., construct state . אוֹצְרוֹת

אצר id. pl., suff. 2 pers. sing. masc. אוֹצְרוֹתֶיךָ

אצר 'וֹ id. pl., suff. 3 pers. pl. masc. אוֹצְרוֹתָם

a Ps. 38. 6.   c Job 40. 16.   f Pr. 11. 7;—   g Je. 4. 14.   h Ho. 9. 15.   i 1 Ki. 7. 30.   t Eze. 28. 18.   o Pr. 21. 20.   y Je. 17. 3.
b Ps. 42. 10.   d 2 Ch. 8. 18.   & perhaps   k Ps. 94. 23.   l Je. 31. 18.   r Ezr. 8. 17.   n Ne. 13. 13.   z Is. 38. 6.
d Ho. 12. 8.   Ho. 9. 4.   Ps. 105. 36.   m Na. 3. 2.   Eze. 10. 9.   Eze. 20. 10.   x 2 Ch. 33. 27.

אוֹצָרֹת• noun m. with pl. f. term. from אוֹצָר dec. 2b.   אצר

אוֹצְרֹתֶיהָ• id. pl., suff. 3 pers. sing. fem. . אצר

אוֹצְרֹתֶיךָ• id. pl., suff. 2 pers. sing. masc. . אצר

אוֹקִיר• Hiph. fut. 1 pers. sing. . . . יקר

אוֹר (§ 21. rem. 2) *to become light, to shine, to be enlightened,* and impers. *it is light.* Niph. *to become bright.* Part. *glorious.* Hiph.—I. *to give light, to enlighten, illuminate.* Meton. *to cheer, enliven,* const. with הֵאִיר פָּנִים אֶל פ'; אֶת, לְ, בְּ, עַל, אֶל *to cause one's face to shine upon any one, to be propitious to him.*—II. *to kindle.*

אוֹר masc. dec. 1a—I. *light, lightning, luminary.* —II. Meton. *prosperity.*—III. *knowledge.*

אוּר m. dec. 1a—I. *fire.*—II. *light;* אוּר אֵשׁ *the light of fire;* הָאֻרִים וְהַתֻּמִּים *light,* i. e. *revelation and truth,* the Urim and Thummim worn by the high-priest.—III. pr. name masc. 1 Ch. 11. 35.— IV. pr. name of a city in Chaldea, fully אוּר כַּשְׂדִּים *Ur of the Chaldeans,* the native place of Abraham.

אוֹרָה fem. dec. 10.—I. *light,* Ps. 139. 12.—II. *prosperity,* Est. 8. 16.—III. *herbs.*

אוּרִי (*shining*) pr. name of several men.

אוּרִיאֵל (*light of God*) pr. n. of two different men.

אוּרִיָּה (*light of the Lord*) pr. name —I. of the husband of Bath-sheba, afterwards the wife of David. —II. of a priest in the time of Ahaz and Isaiah.

אוּרִיָּהוּ (id.) pr. name of a prophet, contemporary with Jeremiah. Je. 26. 20. sq.

יָאִיר (*he shall enlighten*) pr. name.—I. of a son of Manasseh, Nu. 32. 41.—II. of a judge of Israel, Ju. 10. 3.—Patronym. יָאִירִי, 2 Sa. 20. 26.—III. Est. 2. 5.

מָאוֹר masc. dec. 3a, pl. מְאֹרִים, מְאֹרוֹת.—I. *light, luminary,* the sun, the moon; מְנוֹרַת הַמָּאוֹר *the candlestick* in the tabernacle.—II. *the candlestick.* Ex. 25. 6.

מְאוּרָה fem. only construct מְאוּרַת *a hole, viper's den,* Is. 11. 8.

אוֹר• פ', ‹' Kal pret. 3 pers. sing. masc. (§ 21. rem. 2); וְ see lett. וֹ . . אור

אוֹר וְ', פ' noun masc. sing. dec. 1a; וְ id.   אור

אוֹר noun masc. sing. dec. 1a; also pr. name . אור

אֹרֵב וְ' Kal part. act. sing. masc. dec. 7b. . ארב

אוֹרִדְךָ• וְ Hiph. fut. 1 pers. sing., suff. 2 pers. sing. m.   ירד

אוֹרָה• noun fem. sing. . . . אור

אוֹרֶה• Hiph. fut. 1 pers. sing. . . ירה

אוֹרֵהוּ n. m. s. suff. 3 pers. s. masc. from אוֹר dec. 1 a   אור

אוֹרוֹ וְ' id., suff. 3 pers. sing. masc. . אור

אוֹרוּ• Kal pret. 3 pers. pl. (§ 21. rem. 2) . אור

אוֹרוּ• *fully for* אֹרוּ Kal imp. pl. masc. . ארר

אוֹרִי mm Kal imp. sing. fem. (§ 21. rem. 2)   אור

אוֹרִי• noun m. s., suff. 1 pers. s. from אוֹר dec. 1 a.   אור

אוּרִי, וְ' אוּרִיאֵל pr. names masc. . אור

אוֹרִיד וְ Hiph. fut. 1 pers. sing. . ירד

אוֹרִידְךָ id., suff. 2 pers. sing. masc. . ירד

אוֹרִידֵם id., suff. 3 pers. pl. masc. . ירד

אוּרִיָּה וְ' אוּרִיָּהוּ pr. names masc. . אור

אוֹרֶיךָ• וְ noun masc. pl., suff. 2 pers. sing. masc. from אור dec. 1 a. . . אור

אוֹרִים• noun masc., pl. of אוֹר dec. 1 a.   אור

אוֹרִישׁ• Hiph. fut. 1 pers. sing. . ירשׁ

אוֹרִישֵׁם id., suff. 3 pers. pl. masc. . ירשׁ

אוֹרְךָ } noun masc. sing., suff. 2 pers. sing. masc. } אור
אוֹרְךָ• } *from* אוֹר dec. 1 a. }

אוֹרֶךָ• } Hiph. fut. 1 pers. sing. (אֹרֶה), suff. 2 pers. sing. masc. (§ 25. No. 2e. § 24. rem. 21)   ירה

אוֹרֵךְ• noun masc. sing., suff. 2 pers. sing. fem. from אוֹר dec. 1 a.   אור

אוֹרָם id., suff. 3 pers. pl. masc. . אור

אִוָּרֵשׁ• Niph. fut. 1 pers. sing. (§ 20. rem. 7)   רשׁ

אוֹרִשֶׁנּוּ וְ Hiph. fut. 1 pers. sing., suff. 3 pers. sing. masc. (§ 2. rem. 3)   ירשׁ

אֹרֹת• noun pl. fem. from אוֹרָה or אוֹר . אור

אוֹשִׁיבְךָ• Hiph. fut. 1 pers. sing., suff. 2 pers. s. masc.   ישׁב

אוֹשִׁיעַ Hiph. fut. 1 pers. sing. . ישׁע

אוֹשִׁיעָה וְ id., with paragogic ה; וְ for וַ   ישׁע

אוֹשִׁיעֵךְ• id., suff. 2 pers. sing. fem. . ישׁע

אוֹשִׁיעֵם• id., suff. 3 pers. pl. masc. . ישׁע

אִוָּשֵׁעַ וְ' Niph. fut. 1 pers. sing. (§ 20. rem. 7) for [אִוָּשֵׁעָ] (§ 15. rem. 1)   ישׁע

אִוָּשֵׁעָה• וְ id. with paragogic ה for [אִוָּשֵׁעָ]   ישׁע

אֲוַשֵּׁר• Kh. אֹשֵּׁר, K. אֲיַשֵּׁר Hiph. or Piel fut. 1 p. s.   ישׁר

אוֹת or אָוֹת. Niph. *to consent, to agree to* any one.

אַוַּת noun fem. sing., construct of [אַוָּה] dec. 10.   אוה

אוֹת noun com. sing. dec. 1 a. . אוה

אִוְּתָה Piel pret. 3 pers. sing. fem. . אוה

אֹתָהּ וְ' as if [אוֹת] with suff. 3 pers. sing. fem., see אֵת sign of the accus. (§ 5. parad.)   את

אֹתָהֶם id., suff. 3 pers. pl. masc. . את

אֹתָהֶן• id., suff. 3 pers. pl. fem. . את

אֹתוֹ id., suff. 3 pers. sing. masc. . את

אוֹתִי וְ' id., suff. 1 pers. sing. . את

---

a Je. 51. 12.   d Ge. 44. 3.   g Ezr. 8. 31.   k Job 37. 3.   o De. 33. 8.   r Ps. 42. 3.   u Nu. 14. 12.   z 2 Ki. 6. 27.   Is. 45. 2.
b Je. 50. 37.   e 1 Sa. 29. 10.   h 1 Sa. 30. 15.   l Est. 8. 16.   p Ps. 136. 7.   s Ps. 82. 8.   v Ho. 1. 7.   Esc. 43. 45.
c Je. 15. 13.   f Pr. 4. 18.   i Est. 8. 16.   m Ju. 5. 23.   q Ex. 34. 24.   t Is. 60. 1.   w Je. 17. 14.   Is. 45. 2.
Is. 13. 12.   Is. 5. 30.   Job 25. 3.   Ps. 27. 1.   Jos. 13. 6.   Pr. 30. 9.   Ju. 12. 12.   Ps. 119. 117.   Is. 60. 1.

אֱנִיתִים	Piel pret. 1 pers. sing [אֱנִיתִי], suff. 3 p. s. f.	אוה
אוֹתִירִי	Hiph. fut. 1 pers. sing. . . .	יתר
אוֹתְךָ	as if [אות] with suff. 2 pers. sing. masc., see אֵת sign of the accus. (§ 5. parad.) .	את
אוֹתָךְ	id., suff. 2 pers. sing. fem., or אוֹתָךְ in pause 2 pers. sing. masc.	את
אוֹתְכֶם	id., suff. 2 pers. pl. masc. . . .	את
אוֹתָם	'} id., suff. 3 pers. pl. masc. . . .	את
אוֹתָנָה	id., suff. 3 pers. pl. fem. (§ 5. rem. 4) .	את
אוֹתָנוּ	'} id., suff. 1 pers. pl.	את
אוֹתֵר	'} Niph. fut. 1 pers. s. (§ 20. r. 7); '} for '} conv.	יתר
אוֹתֹת	noun masc., pl. of אות (q. v.) dec. 1 a.	אוה
אוֹתֹתָם	id., suff. 3 pers. pl. masc. (§ 4. rem. 2)	אוה

אָז '} adv. *then, at that time,* referring either to past or future time. מֵאָז & מִן־אָז prop. *from then,* hence—I. *from ancient times, from old.* —II. *from the time, since.*

אֲזַי adv. *then, at that time,* Ps. 124. 3, 4, 5.

אָזָה, אֲזָא Chald. *to kindle.*

אֵזֹב Root not used, whence

אֵזוֹב, אֵזֹב masc. *hyssop*

אֶזְבַּי (perh. *dwarf*) pr. name, masc. 1 Ch. 11. 37.

אֶזְבַּח	Kal fut. 1 pers. sing. . .	זבח
אֲזַבֵּחַ	Piel fut. 1 pers. sing. . .	זבח
אֶזְבְּחָה	'} id. with paragogic ה . .	זבח
אֹזְבִּי	pr. name masc. for אֵזְבַּי	אזב

[אֲזַד] אֲזַדָּא Chald. *to go away, depart,* only Da. 2. 5, 8, part. f. for אֲזַד from אָזַד masc. (§ 67 rem.)

אַזְדָּא Chald. see the preced. R.

אֲזָה	Ch. Peal part. pass. s. m. (§ 56. No. 2. § 23. r. 8)	אזא
אָזוֹב	'} noun masc. sing. . . .	אזב
אָזוּר	Kal part. pass. sing. masc. . .	אזר
אֵזוֹר	'} noun masc. sing. . . .	אזר
אֲזַי	adv. . . .	אז
אַאֲזִין	for [אַאֲזִין] Hiph. fut. 1 pers. sing. (§ 19. r. 8)	אזן
אַזְכִּיר	Hiph. fut. 1 pers. sing. . .	זכר
אֶזְכֹּר	Kheth id., K. אֶזְכּוֹר Kal fut. 1 pers. sing.	זכר
אַזְכִּירָה	Hiph. fut. 1 pers. sing. with parag. ה .	זכר
אֶזְכֹּר	'} Kal fut. 1 pers. sing. (§ 8. rem. 18); '} for '} conv.	זכר
אֶזְכְּרָה	id. with paragogic ה . . .	זכר
אֶזְכָּרְךָ	id., suff. 2 pers. sing. masc.	זכר
אֶזְכְּרֵכִי	id., suff. 2 pers. sing. fem. (§ 2. rem. 2)	זכר
אֶזְכְּרֶנּוּ	id., suff. 3 pers. sing. masc.	זכר
אַזְכָּרָתָהּ	n. f. s., suff. 3 pers. s. f. from זכר dec. 10.	זכר

אֲזָל	*to go away, to depart,* Pu. part. מְאֻזָּל for מְאֻזָּל *something spun,* Talm. אֻזְלָה *weaver.*	
אֲזַל	Chald. id. *to go away, to depart*	
אֱזֹל	*departure,* see אֶבֶן	
אוּזָל	pr. name masc. Ge. 10. 27.	
אזל	Chald. Peal pret. 3 pers. sing. masc. .	אזל
אֱזֶל	Chald. Peal imp. sing. masc. with Mak. for [אֲזֵל] by Syr. for [אֲזֵל]	אזל
אֹזֵל	'} Kal part. act. sing. masc.	אזל
אֲזַלוּ	Chald. Peal 3 pers. pl. masc. .	אזל
אָזְלוּ	Kal pret. 3 pers. pl. . .	אזל
אַזְלָא	Chald. Peal preter. 1 pers. sing. .	אזל
אָזְלַת	Kal preter. 3 pers. fem. sing.; Milêl before monos. for [אָזְלַת=אֲזָלָה § 8. rem. 3] .	אזל
אֲזַמֵּר	Piel fut. 1 pers. sing. . .	זמר
אֲזַמְּרָה	נ'/} id. with paragogic ה; '} before (-) .	זמר
אֲזַמֶּרְךָ	נ'} id., suff. 2 pers. sing. masc. (§ 16. rem. 15, and § 2. rem. 3); '} id. .	זמר

I. אָזַן Kal not used. Hiph. denom. of אֹזֶן, *to give ear, to listen, to attend,* const. with לְ, אֶל, עַד, עַל.

II. אָזַן Kal not used. Pi. *to weigh,* trop. *to consider,* Ec. 12. 9.

אָזֵן masc. dec. 5 c, *a kind of instrument or weapon,* only De. 23. 14, Chald. אֲזַן *to be armed.*

אֹזֶן fem. dec. 6 c, *the ear,* בְּאָזְנֵי פ' *in the ears,* i. e. in the hearing *of any one.*

אָזְנִי (*hearing well*) pr. name masc. Nu. 26. 16.

אֲזַנְיָה (whom *the Lord hears*) pr. n. m. Ne. 10. 10.

אֻזֵּן שֶׁאֱרָה pr. name of a city built by Sherah, 1 Ch. 7. 24.

אַזְנוֹת־תָּבוֹר (*ears,* i. e. summits *of Tabor*) pr. name of a city, Jos. 19. 34.

יַאֲזַנְיָה (whom *the Lord hears*) pr. name of two different men.

יַאֲזַנְיָהוּ (id.) pr. name masc. 2 Ki. 25. 23, called יֹונְיָה, יֹונְיָהוּ Je. 40. 8; 42. 1.

מֹאזְנַיִם dual (of מֹאזֵן dec. 7 b) *balances, a balance* מֹאזְנַיָּא Chald. id. only emph. בְּמֹאזַנְיָא, Da. 5. 27

אָזַן	'} Piel pret. 3 pers. sing. masc. .	אזן
אֹזֶן	'} noun fem. sing. dec. 6 c.	אזן
אֻזֵּן	pr. name, see אֻזֵּן שֶׁאֱרָה	אזן
אָזְנוֹ	Kh. אָזְנוֹ q. v., K. אָזְנִי (q. v.)	אזן
אָזְנוֹ	n. fem. s., suff. 3 pers. s. m. from אֹזֶן dec. 6 c.	אזן
אַזְנוֹת	pr. name, see אַזְנוֹת תָּבוֹר	אזן

a Ps. 132. 14.   c 1 Ki. 19. 10. 14.   e Ps. 27. 6.   g 2 Ki. 1. 8.   i Ex. 6. 5.   l Le. 2. 2. 9.   n Ezr. 4. 23.   p Ps. 57. 8.   r Ec. 12. 9.
b Eze. 39. 28.   d Ps. 74. 4.   f Da. 3. 22.   h Job 32. 11.   k Je. 31. 34.   m 1 Sa. 9. 7.   o Job 14. 11.   q Ps. 57. 10.   s Ps. 18. 15.
c Jo. 23. 15.   f Ps. 116. 17.   g Nu. 19. 6.   i Ps. 77. 12.   k Ps. 42. 7.   n Ezr. 5. 15.   o Ezr. 5. 8.   q Ps. 108. 4.   t 1 Sa. 22. 17.
d Eze. 34. 21.   h 2 Ch. 28. 23.   i 2 Ki. 1. 8.   j Ps. 45. 18.   l Ps. 137. 6.   o Pr. 20. 14.   p De. 32. 36.   q Ps. 138. 1.

אָזְנָי֖ noun fem. dual, suff. 1 pers. sing. from אֹזֶן dec. 6 c.   אזן

אָזְנִי id. sing., suff. 1 pers. sing.   אזן

אָזְנַי ן id. dual, construct state   אזן

אֲזַנְיָה pr. name masc. .   אזן

אָזְנֵיהֶם 'ן noun fem. dual, suff. 3 pers. pl. masc. from אֹזֶן dec. 6 c.   אזן

אָזְנָיו 'ן id. dual, suff. 3 pers. sing. masc. .   אזן

אָזְנֶיךָ 'ן id. dual, suff. 2 pers. sing. masc.   אזן

אָזְנַיִךְ / אָזְנַיִךְ ן id. dual, suff. 2 pers. sing. fem.   אזן

אָזְנַיִם / אָזְנַיִם ן id. dual, absolute state .   אזן

אָזְנְךָ for [אָזְנְךָ] noun masc. sing., suff. 2 pers. sing. masc. from [אֹזֶן] dec. 5 c.   אזן

אָזְנֶךָ defect. for אָזְנֶיךָ q. v., or in pause for the foll.   אזן

אָזְנֵךְ noun f. s., suff. 2 p. s. m. from אֹזֶן, dec. 6 c.   אזן

אָזְנֵךְ id., suff. 2 pers. sing. fem.   אזן

אָזְנְכֶם id., suff. 2 pers. pl. masc. .   אזן

אָזְנָם id., suff. 3 pers. pl. masc.   אזן

אֶזְעַם Kal fut. 1 pers. sing. .   זעם

אֶזְעַק / וָאֶזְעַק ן Kal fut. 1 pers. sing. (§ 8. rem. 15); ן for ו conversive .   זעק

[אָזַר] I. *to bind, gird about*, spoken of a girdle, a garment, and trop. of strength.—II. *to gird up*, spoken of the loins. Niph. *to be girded.* Pi. *to gird*, with a double acc. of the person, and of the girdle. Hithp. *to gird oneself.*

אֵזוֹר (Syriacism for אֱזוֹר) m.—I. *girdle, belt.*—II. *fetters.*

אֱזָר Kal imp. sing. masc. with Mak. for [אֱזֹר] (§ 8. rem. 18) .   אזר

אֲזָרֶה Piel fut. 1 pers. sing. for [אֲזָרֶה] .   זרה

אֵזָֽרוּ Kal pret. 3 pers. pl.   אזר

אֲזָרֵם ן Kal fut. 1 pers. sing. [אֲזָרֶה], suff. 3 pers. pl. masc. (§ 24. rem. 21); ן for ו conv.   זרה

אֶזְרְעָה Kal fut. 1 pers. sing. with paragogic ה   זרע

אֶזְרֹעִי ן noun fem. sing., suff. 1 pers. s. from אֶזְרוֹעַ dec. 1 b.   זרע

אֶזְרְעֵם ן Kal fut. 1 pers. sing. [אֶזְרַע], suff. 3 pers. pl. masc. (§ 16. rem. 12)   זרע

אָח 'ן, 'ן masc. irreg. (§ 45).—I. *brother.*—II. *relative, kinsman.*—III. *countryman.*—IV. *friend.*—V. *fellow*, used both of persons and things; אִישׁ אֶל אָחִיו *one towards another.*

אַח Chald. *brother*, Ezr. 7. 18.

אַחְאָב (*brother of the father*) pr. name—I. of a king of Israel.—II. of a false prophet, Je. 29. 21, called אֶחָב v. 22.

אַחְבָּן (*brother of the wise* בֵּן from בִּין) pr. name masc. 1 Ch. 2. 29.

אֲחוּמַי (*brother of water*) pr. name m. 1 Ch. 4. 2.

אֲחִי (*brother*, comp. אֲבִי) pr. name of a man.

אֲחִיאָם (*brother of the mother, uncle* אֵם i. q. אֵם) pr. name of a man.

אֲחִיָּה (*friend of the Lord*) pr. name of several men, especially—I. of a priest in the time of Saul 1 Sa. 14. 3, 18.—II. of a prophet in the time of Jeroboam, called also אֲחִיָּהוּ

אֲחִיהוּד (*friend of the Jews*, for אֲחִי יְהוּד) pr name masc. Nu. 34. 27.

אֲחִיוֹ (*brotherly*, for אֲחִיוֹן) pr. name of several men.

אֲחִיחֻד (*brother of union*, for אֲחִי יַחֻד) pr. name masc. 1 Ch. 8. 7.

אֲחִיטוּב (*brother of goodness*) pr. name of several men.

אֲחִילוּד (*brother of Lud*) pr. name of the father of Jehoshaphat.

אֲחִימוֹת (*father of death*) pr. name m. 1 Ch. 6. 10.

אֲחִימֶלֶךְ (*brother of the king*) pr. name—I. of a priest and friend of David put to death by Saul.—II. of a high-priest in the time of David.

אֲחִימָן (*the brother's likeness*, כָּמוֹ root מוּן) pr. name—I. one of the Anakims.—II. 1 Ch. 9. 17.

אֲחִימַעַץ (*brother of anger*) pr. name masc.—I. 1 Sa. 14. 50.—II. son of Zadok the high-priest in the time of David.

אַחְיָן (*brotherly*) pr. name masc. 1 Ch. 7. 19.

אֲחִינָדָב (*noble* or *liberal brother*) pr. name masc. 1 Ki. 4. 14.

אֲחִינֹעַם (*brother of pleasantness*) pr. name fem.—I. of a wife of Saul, 1 Sa. 14. 50.—II. of a wife of David, comp. 1 Sa. 25. 43.

אֲחִיסָמָךְ (*brother of support*) pr. name of a man.

אֲחִיעֶזֶר (*brother of help*) pr. name—I. of a chief of the tribe of Dan.—II. of an ally of David, 1 Ch. 12. 3.

אֲחִיקָם (*the rising brother*, קָם part. of קוּם) pr. name of a man.

אֲחִירָם (*exalted brother* רָם part. of רוּם) pr. name masc. Nu. 26. 38. Patronym. אֲחִירָמִי ibid.

אֲחִירַע (*unfortunate brother*, i. e. *unfortunate*) name of a chief of the tribe of Naphtali.

אֲחִישַׁחַר (*brother of the morning*) pr. name masc. 1 Ch. 7. 10.

אֲחִישָׁר (*brother of the singer,* שָׁר *part. of* שִׁיר) pr. name masc. 1 Ki. 4. 6.

אֲחִיתֹפֶל (*brother of folly*) pr. name of a courtier of David and conspirator with Absalom.

אַחֲוָה fem. *brotherhood,* Zec. 11. 14.

אָחוֹת fem. irreg. (§ 45).—I. *sister.*—II. *relative, kinswoman.*—III. *countrywoman,* Nu. 25. 18.—IV. *an ally.*—V. *fellow,* of persons and things, אֶל אִשָּׁה *one to another.* אֲחוֹתָהּ

אָח interj. expressive of grief, *ah! alas!*

אֹחַ m., only pl. אֹחִים, a kind of *howling* animals. Is. 13. 21.

אַחַד apocopated for אֶחָד

אַחְאָב 'ו pr. name masc.   אח

אֶחָבֵא ו for [אֵחָבֵא] Niph. fut. 1 pers. sing.; ו for · ו conversive   חבא

אַחְבִּיא ו for [אַחְבִּיא] Hiph. fut. 1 pers. sing.; ו id.   חבא

אַחְבִּירָה Hiph. fut. 1 pers. sing. with paragogic ה   חבר

אֶחְבֹּל Kal fut. 1 pers. sing.   חבל

אַחְבָּן pr. name masc.   אח

אֶחְבֹּשׁ Kal fut. 1 pers. sing. (§ 13. rem. 4, 5)   חבש

אַחְבְּשָׁה id. with paragogic ה   חבש

אֶחְבָּשְׁךָ ו id., suff. 2 pers. sing. fem.; ו for · ו conv.   חבש

אֶחָד ו irr. constr. אַחַד; fem. אַחַת *and in pause* אֶחָת (§ 45).—I. *one.*—II. *first,* only in the enumerating of time, where the cardinal stands for the ordinal, בְּאֶחָד לַחֹדֶשׁ *on the first* (day) *of the month;* שְׁנַת אַחַת *the first year.*—III. *some one, any one;* אֶחָד הָעָם *one of the people,* אֶחָד מֵאֶחָיו *one of his brethren,* אֶחָד לֹא *no one.* Hence—IV. as the indef. art., אַיִל אֶחָד *a ram,* נָבִיא אֶחָד *a prophet, a certain prophet.*—V. אֶחָד-אֶחָד *one-another;* אִישׁ אֶחָד אֶחָד *one man from each tribe.*—V. כְּאֶחָד *as one, together, at once.*—VI. fem. אַחַת, בְּאַחַת *one time, once;* (a) בְּאַחַת *at once.*—Pl. אֲחָדִים *the same;* (b) *joined into one;* (c) *a few.*

אָחַד Hithpa. *to unite oneself,* Eze. 21. 21.

אֵחוּד (*union*) pr. name masc., called also אֲחִי, comp. 1 Ch. 8. 6, with Ge. 46. 21.

אַח (apocopated for אֶחָד) *one.* Eze. 18. 10.

חַד Eze. 33. 30, by Chaldaism for אֶחָד *one.*

חַד Ch. emph. חֲדָה, חֲדָא—I. *one.*—II. *first.*—

III. חַד שִׁבְעָה עַל דִּי *seven times more.*—IV. יַחְדָּה *at the same time, together.*

אַחַד ו id. construct state · אחד
אֲחָדִים id. pl., absolute state · אחד
אֶחְדָּל Kal fut. 1 pers. sing. for [אֶחְדָּל] (§ 13. r. 5)   חדל
אֶחְדְּלָה ו id. with paragogic ה (§ 13. rem. 5) · חדל
אָחוּ grass, reeds, bulrushes, an Egyptian word.
אֶחֱוֵא Ch. Pael fut. 1 pers. sing. · חוא
אֵחוּד pr. name, masc. · אחד
אֲחֹדָה Kal fut. 1 pers. sing. with paragogic ה   חוד
אֲחַוֶּה Piel fut. 1 pers. sing. · חוה
אֹחֵז Kal part. p. sing. masc. dec. 3 a. · אחז
אֲחוּזִים id. pl. absolute state. *Eze. 41. 6, 6.   אחז
אָחוֹז ו pr. name, masc.; ו before (‐ָ)   אחז
אַחֲוָיַת ו Chald. noun fem. sing., constr. of [אַחֲוָיָה] dec. 8 a.   חוה
אֲחַוֶּךָ ו Piel fut. 1 pers. sing. [אֲחַוֶּה] suff. 2 pers. sing. masc. (§ 2. rem. 3); ו for · ו conv.   חוה
אַחוּמַי pr. name masc. · אח
אָחוּס Kal fut. 1 pers. sing.   חוס
אָחוֹר ו noun masc. sing. dec. 3 a., used also as an adv.   אחר
אָחוֹת n. fem. sing. contr. for [אֲחֹתֵת] irr. (§ 45)   אח
אֲחוֹת ו id. construct state; ו before (‐ָ)   אח
אֲחוֹתָהּ id., suff. 3 pers. sing. fem.   אח
אַחֲוָתִי ו noun fem. sing., suff. 1 pers. s. from [אַחֲוָה] dec. 10 (§ 43. rem. 3)   חוה
אֲחוֹתַי n. f. pl., suff. 1 pers. s.; Kh. אֲחוֹתַי as if from a sing. [אָחָה], K. אֲחִיוֹתַי as if from [אֲחִיָה] see אָחוֹת irr. § 45   אח
אֲחוֹתִי id. sing., suff. 1 pers. sing. · אח
אֲחוֹתָיִךְ ו id. pl., suff. 2 pers. sing. fem. as if from a sing. [אָחָה]; ו before (‐ָ)   אח
אֲחוֹתֵךְ ו id. sing., suff. 2 pers. sing. fem.; ו id.   אח
אֲחוֹתָךְ id. sing., suff. 2 pers. sing. masc.   אח
אֲחוֹתָם id. sing., suff. 3 pers. pl. masc.   אח
אֲחוֹתֵנוּ id. sing., suff. 1 pers pl.   אח

אָחַז ו fut. יֶאֱחֹז and יֹאחֵז.—I. *to seize,* construed with acc. and בְּ.—II. *to take, catch,* in hunting.—III. *to hold,* const. with בְּ; אֹחֲזֵי חֶרֶב *holding the sword.* —IV. *to join.*—V. *to shut up, close.* Ne. 7. 3.— VI. *to cover, overlay.* 1 Ki. 6. 10.—VII. *to draw out by lot.* Niph.—I. *to be caught.* Ec. 9. 12 — II. *to be held.* Ge. 22. 13.—III. *to take or have possession.* Pi. *to shut up.* Job 26. 9. Hoph. *to be joined, fastened.*

---

a Eze. 6. 11; & 21. 20.   b Eze. 18. 10.   c Ge. 3. 10.   d 1 Ki. 18. 13.   e Job 16. 4.   f Job 34. 31.   g Eze. 34. 16.   h 2 Sa. 19. 27.   i Eze. 16. 10.   k Ge. 37. 9.   l Job 16. 6.   m Job 8. 11.   n Da. 2. 24.   o Ju. 14. 12.   p Job 32, 10. 17.   q Est. 1. 6.   r Da. 5. 12.   s Job 36. 2.   t Job 15. 17.   u Job 13. 17.   v Jos. 2. 13.   x Eze.16.51,61.   y Eze. 16. 55.   z Eze.16.46,46.   a Lc. 18. 9, 11.   b Ge. 34. 13.

אָחָז (*possessor*) pr. name —I. of a king of Judah.
—II. of another person, compare 1 Ch. 8. 35.

אֲחֻזָּה fem. dec. 10, *possession*.

אֲחַזְוַי pr. name masc. Ne. 11. 13, called יַחְזֵרָה in 1 Ch. 9. 12.

אֲחַזְיָה, אֲחַזְיָהוּ (whom *the Lord holds*) pr. name —I. of a son of Ahab king of Israel.—II. of a son of Joram king of Judah.

אֲחֻזָּם (*their possession*) pr. name m. 1 Ch. 4. 6.

אֲחֻזַּת (*possession*) pr. name masc. Ge. 26. 26.

אֹחֵז [*a*] Kal fut. 1 pers. sing. for [אֶחֱזֹ] apoc. for אֶחֱזֶה, אֶחֱזָה . . . . חזה

אָחָז ן pr. name masc. . . . . אחז

אֱחֹז Kal inf. construct . . . . אחז

אֱחֹז ן id. imp. sing. masc. ; ן before (וְ) . אחז

אָחֻז [*c*] id. part. pass. sing. masc. dec. 3a. . אחז

אֹחֵז id. part. act. sing. masc. . . . אחז

אֹחֵז ן id. fut. 1 pers. sing. ; ן for ן conv. . אחז

אָחֲזָה id. preter. 3 pers. sing. fem. . . אחז

אֲחֻזָּה ן noun fem. sing. dec. 10 ; ן before (־ַ) אחז

אֶחֱזֶה [*g*] ן Kal fut. 1 pers. sing. ; ן for ן conv. חזה

אֶחֱזֶה ן [*h*] Kal fut. 1 pers. sing. with parag. ה ; id. חזה

אֲחָזוּ id. preter. 3 pers. pl. . . . אחז

אֶחֱזוּ [*i*]
אֶחֱזוּ ן } id. imp. pl. masc. (§ 8. rem. 12) ; } אחז
אֶחֱזוּ ן } ן before (וְ) }

אֲחָזוּנִי id. preter. 3 pers. pl., suff. 1 pers. sing. אחז

אֲחֻזַּם pr. name masc. . . . . אחז

אֹחֲזֵי [*k*] Kal part. p. pl. construct from אָחוּז dec. 3a ; Milêl before penacute, (חֶרֶב) . . . אחז

אֶחֱזִי [*m*] ן id. imp. sing. fem. (§ 13. rem. 3, & § 8. r. 12) אחז

אֲחֻזָּה, אֲחַזְיָה ן אָחָז ן, id. אֲחַזְיָהוּ ן pr. names masc. אחז

אֲחָזַנִי [*n*] Kal preter. 3 pers. sing. masc., suff. 1 pers. sing. אחז

אַחֲזִיק [*o*] ן Hiph. fut. 1 pers. sing., ap. for [אַחֲזִיק] (§ 11. rem. 6) . . . . . . חזק

אֲחַזֵּק Piel fut. 1 pers. sing. . . . חזק

אֲחַזְּקֶנּוּ id., suff. 3 pers. sing. masc. . . חזק

אֲחֻזַּת ן noun fem. sing., construct of עָה' dec. 10 ; ן before (־ַ) . . . . . . אחז

אָחָז ן pr. name masc. ; ן id. . . . אחז

אֹחֶזֶת [*p*] Kal part. act. s. fem., from אָחַז m.(§ 8. r. 19) אחז

אָחַזְתָּ Kal preter. 2 pers. sing. masc. . . אחז

אֲחָזַתָּה [*q*] id. preter. 3 pers. sing. f., suff. 3 pers. sing. f. אחז

אֲחֻזָּתוֹ noun fem. sing., suff. 3 pers. sing. masc. from אֲחֻזָּה dec. 10 . . . . . אחז

אֲחַזְתִּיו [*r*] Kal preter. 1 pers. sing., suff. 3 pers. sing. m. אחז

אֲחֻזָּתְךָ [*s*] ן noun fem. sing., suff. 2 pers. sing. masc. from אֲחֻזָּה dec. 10 ; ן before (־ַ) אחז

אֲחֻזַּתְכֶם id., suff. 2 pers. pl. masc. . . . אחז

אֲחָזָתַם [*t*] Kal preter. 3 pers. sing. fem., suff. 3 pers. pl. masc. (§ 16. rem. 2) . . . . . אחז

אֲחֻזָּתָם ן noun fem. sing., suff. 3 pers. pl. masc. from אֲחֻזָּה dec. 10 . . . . . . אחז

אֲחָזָתְנִי [*u*] Kal preter. 3 pers. sing. fem., suff. 1 pers. sing. אחז

אָחַח Root not used ; Arab. *to be warm, hot.*

אָח masc. *fire-pot* or *pan*, for warming rooms. Jer. 36. 22, 23.

אֲחוֹחַ pr. name masc. 1 Ch. 8. 4, for which v. 7 אֲחִיָּה.—Patronym. אֲחֹחִי 2 Sa. 23. 9, 28.

אֲחִי pr. name masc. Ge. 46. 21.

אֶחֱטָא [*v*] Kal fut. 1 pers. sing. . . . חטא

אֲחִטוּב defect. for אֲחִיטוּב (q. v.) . . . אח

אֶחֱטָם [*w*] for [אֶחֱטֹם] Kal fut. 1 pers. sing. . חטם

אֲחַסְּנֶנָּה [*x*] for [אֲחַסְּנֶנָּה] Piel fut. 1 pers. sing., suff. 3 pers. sing. fem. . . . . . חטא

אַחַי ן noun masc. pl., suff. 1 pers. sing. [for אֶחָי], from אָח irr. (§ 45) . . . אח

אֲחֵי id. pl., construct state . . . . אח

אָחִי id. sing., suff. 1 pers. sing. . . אח

אֲחִי ן id. sing., construct state ; also pr. n. m. . אח

אָחִי in pause for אֶחָי (§ 45) . . . אח

אֲחִי pr. name masc. see אָחוֹת . . . אחה

אֲחִיאָם pr. name masc. . . . . אח

אֲחִידָן [*z*] Chald. noun fem., pl. of [אֲחִידָא] dec. 8a. . חוד

אֲחַיֶּה ן [*b*] Piel fut. 1 pers. sing. ; ן for ן . חיה

אַחְיָה noun masc. pl., suff. 3 pers. sing. fem.[for אֲחֶיהָ] from אָח irr. (§ 45) . . . אח

אֲחִיָּה ן pr. name masc. ; ן before (־ַ) . אח

אָחִיהָ noun masc. sing., suff. 3 pers. sing. fem. from אָח irr. (§ 45) . . . . . אח

אֲחַיֶּה ן Kal fut. 1 pers. sing. . . . חיה

אָחִיהוּ noun masc. sing., suff. 3 pers. sing. masc. from אָח irr. (§ 45) . . . . . אח

אֲחִיהוּד, אֲחִיהֻד ן pr. names masc. . אח

אֲחֵיהֶם ן noun masc. pl., suff. 3 pers. pl. masc. from אָח irr. (§ 45) ; ן before (־ַ) . . אח

אֲחִיהֶם id. sing., suff. 3 pers. pl. masc. . . אח

אָחִיו ן id. sing., suff. 3 pers. sing. masc. . . אח

אֶחָיו ן id. pl., suff. 3 pers. s. m. [for אָחָיו § 45] אח

אֲחִיו ן pr. name masc. . . . . אח

אַחְיֹתֵךְ [*d*] noun fem. pl., suff. 2 pers. sing. f. as if from [אֲחִיָּה] see אָחוֹת irreg. (§ 45, for suff. see § 4. rem. 2)

אֲחִיטוּב, אֲחִיטֻב ן & pr. names masc. . אח

a Job 23. 9.   *c* Ju. 20. 6.   *f* 2 Sa. 4. 10.   *k* Is. 21. 3.   *r* Is. 42. 6.   *x* Ca. 3. 4.   *b* Ps. 119. 53.   *e* Ge. 31. 39.   *k* Je. 48. 11.
b 1 Ki. 6. 6.   *f* Eze. 44. 28.   *g* Job 18. 20.   *l* Ca. 3. 8.   *s* Is. 22. 21.   *p* Ps. 2. 8.   *c* Ps. 119. 11.   *f* Ge. 14. 13.   *l* De. 32. 39.
c 1 Ch. 24. 6.   *c* Pr. 24. 32.   *k* Ca. 2. 15.   *n* Ru. 3. 15.   *t* Ge. 25. 26.   *q* Ps. 48. 7.   *d* Is. 42. 9.   *g* Da. 5. 12.   Eze. 16. 39.
d 2 Ch. 25. 5.   *d* Ca. 7. 9.   *i* Ne. 7. 3.   *o* 2 Sa. 1. 9.   *w* Je. 49. 34.

אַחֶיךָ	וֹ' noun masc. pl., suff. 2 pers. sing. masc.[for אַחֶיךָ] from אָח irreg. (§ 45) . .	אח
אָחִיךָ	id. sing., suff. 2 pers. sing. masc. .	אח
אַחַיִךְ	id. pl., suff. 2 pers. sing. fem. for [אַחַיִךְ § 45]	אח
אָחִיךְ	id. sing., suff. 2 pers. sing. fem. .	אח
אֲחַיִךְ	Chald. noun masc. pl., suff. 2 pers. sing. masc. [from אָח § 68]	אח
אֲחֵיכֶם	וֹ' noun masc. pl., suff. 2 pers. pl. masc. from אָח irreg. (§ 45); וֹ bef. (-:)	אח
אֲחִיכֶם	id. sing., suff. 2 pers. pl. masc. .	אח
אֹחִילָה	def. for אֹל, Hiph. fut. 1 pers. s. with parag. ה	יחל
אֲחִילוּד	pr. name masc. .	
אַחִים	וֹ' noun m. pl. for [אַחִים] from אָח irr. (§ 45) . .	אח
אֹחִים	noun masc., pl. of [אֹחַ] dec. 1 a, see אוֹ interj.	
אֲחִימוֹת	אֲחִימַעַץ ,וֹ' & אֲחִימָן ,נ' & אֲחִימֶלֶךְ ,נ' and אֲחִימַעַץ & ,אֶחְוָן ,אֲחִינָדָב	אח
אַחִיט	noun masc. pl., suff. 1 pers. pl. [for אַחֵינוּ] from אָח irreg. (§ 45) .	אח
אָחִינוּ	וֹ' id. sing., with suff. 1 pers. pl.	אח
	אֲחִיקָם, אֲחִיסָמָךְ, אֲחִיעֶזֶר, אֲחִירַע ,נ' & pr. names masc. .	אח
אַחִישָׁה	Hiph. fut. 1 pers. sing. with paragogic ה	חוש
אֲחִישַׁחַר	וֹ' pr. name masc.; וֹ before (-:)	
אֲחִישֶׁנָּה	Hiph. fut. 1 pers. sing. [אָחִישׁ], suff. 3 pers. sing. fem. (§ 2. rem. 3) . .	חוש
אֲחִישָׁר	וֹ' pr. name masc.; וֹ before (-:)	
אֲחִיתֵיכֶם	וֹ' noun fem. pl., suff. 3 pers. pl. masc. as if from [אֲחִיָּה] see אָחוֹת irreg. (§ 45)	אח
אֲחִיתָיו	id. with suff. 3 pers. sing. masc. .	אח
אֲחִיתֹפֶל	נ' pr. name masc.; וֹ before (-:)	אח
אֶחְכְּמָה	for [כְמָה], Kal fut. 1 pers. s. with parag. ה	חכם
אָחֵל	Hiph. fut. 1 pers. sing. . .	חלל
אָחֵל	id.; Dag. impl. [for אָהֵל], Ch. form (§ 18. r. 14)	חלל
אֵחֵל	[for אֶהֵל] Niph. fut. 1 pers. sing.; וֹ before gutt. for וֹ conv. . .	חלל
אַחְלָב	pr. name of a place	חלב
אַחֲלַי	אַחֲלֵי, adv. expressive of wish, O that!	
אָחֳלָי	for אָחֳלַי pr. name masc. and fem.	
אֲאַחַלֵּל	וֹ' Piel fut. 1 pers. sing.; וֹ for וֹ	חלל
אֲחַלֶּךָ	וֹ' id., suff. 2 pers. sing. masc.; וֹ for וֹ conv.	חלל
אַחְלָמָה	וֹ noun masc. sing. [אֲחָלָם] with paragogic ה	חלם
אֲחַלְּצָה	וֹ' Piel fut. 1 pers. sing. with parag. ה; וֹ for וֹ	חלץ
אֲחַלְּצֵהוּ	id., suff. 3 pers. sing. masc.	חלץ
אֲחַלְּצֶךָ, אֲחַלְּצֶךָּ	id., suff. 2 pers. sing. masc. (§ 2. rem. 3); וֹ for וֹ conv.	חלץ

אֲחַלֵּק	Piel fut. 1 pers. sing. (§ 10. rem. 4) .	חלק
אַחַלְקָה	id. with paragogic ה . . .	חלק
אֲחַלְּקֵם	id., suff. 3 pers. pl. masc. . .	חלק
וְאֶחְמְדֵם	Kal fut. 1 pers. sing. [וְאֶחְמֹד], suff. 3 pers. pl. masc. (§ 13. rem. 5), וֹ for וֹ conv.	חמד
אֶחְמוֹל, אֶחְמֹל	Kal fut. 1 pers. sing. (§ 13. rem. 5); נ' וֹ id. . . .	חמל
[אַחְמְתָא]	pr. name Ecbatana, the metropolis of Media, Ezr. 6. 2.	
אָחֹן	Kal fut. 1 pers. sing. . .	חנן
אֲחַסְבַּי	pr. name masc. . . .	חסה
אֶחֱסֶה	Kal fut. 1 pers. sing. . . .	חסה
אַחְסֹר	for [חְסַר] Kal fut. 1 pers. sing. (§ 13. rem. 5)	חסר
אֶחְפָּץ	in pause for [חְפָּץ], and	חפץ
אֶחְפֹּץ	Kal fut. 1 pers. sing. (§ 13. rem. 4, 5) .	חפץ
וְאֶחְפְּרָה	וֹ' Kal fut. 1 pers. s. (§ 13. r. 5); וֹ for וֹ conv.	חפר
אֲחַפֵּשׂ	Piel fut. 1 pers. sing. . .	חפש
אֶחְקֹר	Kal fut. 1 pers. sing. . .	חקר
אֶחְקְרֶהוּ	id., suff. 3 pers. sing. masc. . .	חקר

[אָחַר] to stay, tarry, Ge. 32. 5. Pi.—I. to retard, hinder.—II. intrans. to stay long, to linger, constr. with עַל.

אַחֵר I. adj. irr. (§ 45) another; אֱלֹהִים אֲחֵרִים other i. e. strange gods; שָׁנָה אַחֶרֶת next year.—II. pr. name masc. 1 Ch. 7. 12.

אַחַר I. prep. behind, after; הָלַךְ אַחַר פְּ' to go after, to follow any one; מֵאַחַר עָלוֹת from behind, i. e. from following the ewes.—II. of time, after, אַ' הַדְּבָרִים הָאֵלֶּה after these things.—III. adv. of time, afterwards, then.—IV. conj. after that, and fully אַחַר אֲשֶׁר id.—Pl., construct אַחֲרֵי, with suff. אַחֲרֵיכֶם, אַחֲרַי, &c.—I. the hinder part, 2 Sa. 2. 23.—II. prep. of place, after, behind any one.—III. of time, after, after that; אַחֲרֵי אֲשֶׁר after that; אַחֲרֵי כֵן, afterwards.—IV. מֵאַחֲרֵי from after, i. e. from going after, hence מֵאַחֲרֵי כֵן afterwards; עַל, אֶל אַחֲרֵי after, behind.

אַחַר Chald. id. only in the phrase אַחֲרֵי דְנָה after this, Da. 2. 29, 45, and with suff. 7. 24.

אָחוֹר masc. dec. 3 a.—I. the hinder side, back part.—II. the west.—III. adv. מֵאָחוֹר, לְאָחוֹר, בְּאָחוֹר behind; לְאָחוֹר hereafter.

אַחֲרוֹן adj.—I. hinder; hence, western.—II. following, future, pl. אַחֲרֹנִים posterity.—III. last, compare Is. 44. 6; fem. אַחֲרֹנָה, בָּאַחֲרֹנָה, לָאַחֲרֹנָה last, the last.

ᵃ Jos. 2. 18.	ᵉ Ge. 44. 26.	ⁱ 1 Ch. 2. 16.	ᵐ Eze. 39. 7.	ʳ Eze. 28. 16.	ᵛ Ps. 81. 8.	ᶻ Ge. 49. 7.	ᵉᵉ Eze. 36. 21.	ʰ Je. 13. 7.
ᵇ Ezr. 7. 18.	ᶠ Ps. 55. 9.	ʲ Job 42. 11.	ⁿ Ps. 7. 5.	ˢ Ps. 91. 15.	ʷ Ex. 15. 9.	ᵃᵃ Jos. 7. 21.	ᶠᶠ Is. 30. 12.	ⁱ 1 Sa. 20. 12.
ᶜ 2 Sa. 18. 14.	ᵍ Is. 60. 22.	ᵏ De. 2. 25; &	ᵒ Ps. 119. 5.	ᵗ Eze. 9. 10.	ˣ Is. 53. 12.	ᵇᵇ Job 13. 3.	ᵍᵍ Is. 43. 28; Ps. 89. 35.	ᵏ Job 29. 16.
ᵈ Is. 13. 21	ʰ Job 1. 4.	Jos. 3. 7.	ᵖ 2 Ki. 5. 2.	ᵘ Ps. 56. 5.	ᵞ 1 Ch. 26. 9. 11.	ᵈᵈ Ec. 7. 23.	ⁱⁱ Ps. 23. 1.	

אֲחַרְחַה (*after the brother*, for אֲחַרְאָה) pr. name masc. 1 Ch. 8. 1.

אֲחַרְחֵל (*behind the wall*) pr. name m. 1 Ch. 4. 8.

אָחֳרִי Chald. adj. fem. *another*.

אָחֳרֵין Chald. adj. *last*, preceded by עַד, *at last*, Da. 4. 5. Kheth.

אַחֲרִית fem. dec. 1 b.—I. *the last*, or *uttermost part*, Ps. 139. 9.—II. *the latter time*, אַחֲרִית הַיָּמִים *the latter days*, אַחֲרִית הַשָּׁנָה *the end of the year*.—III. *posterity*.

אַחֲרִית Chald. fem. i. q. Hebr. No. II.

אָחֳרָן Chald. masc. *another*.

אֲחֹרַנִּית adv. *backwards*.

אַחַר וְ [for אָחַר] adv. and prep. . . אחר
אַחַר pr. name masc. . . . . אחר
אַחֵר וְ adj. masc. sing. irr., pl. אֲחֵרִים (§ 45) אחר
אֵחַר for [אָחַר] Piel pret. 3 pers. sing. masc. אחר
אֹחַר וְ for [אֶאֱחַר] Kal fut. 1 pers. s. (§ 19. r. 3) אחר
אַחֲרִב וְ
אַחֲרִבִי וְ } Hiph. fut. 1 pers. sing. (§ 13. rem. 9) חרב
אַחֲרָו וְ Kheth for K. אַחֲרָיו (q. v.) . אחר
אֵחֲרוּ for [אֶאֶחֱרוּ] Piel pret. 3 pers. pl. (§ 13. r. 12) אחר
אַחֲרוֹן וְ adj. masc. sing. dec. 1 b. . . אחר
אַחֲרוֹת adj. fem., pl. of אַחֶרֶת, from אַחֵר masc. irr. (§ 45) אחר
אַחֲרַח וְ, אֲחַרְחֵל pr. names masc. . . אחר
אַחֲרִי
אַחֲרַי } prep., pl. with suff. 1 pers. sing. from אַחַר
אַחֲרֵי וְ id. pl., construct state . . . אחר
אַחֲרַי noun masc. pl., suff. 1 pers. sing. for [אַחֲרַי] from אָחוֹר dec. 3 a אחר
אַחֲרֵי id. pl., construct state . . . אחר
אַחֲרִי וְ Chald. adj. f. s. by apocope for [אַחֲרִית] אחר
אַחֲרִיב Hiph. fut. 1 pers. sing. . . חרב
אַחֲרֶיהָ וְ prep., pl. with suff. 3 pers. sing. fem. from אַחַר
אַחֲרֵיהֶם וְ id., suff. 3 p. pl. masc. . . אחר
אַחֲרֵיהֶם noun masc. pl., suff. 3 pers. pl. masc. from [אָחוֹר] dec. 3 a אחר
אַחֲרֵיהֶן prep., pl. with suff. 3 pers. pl. fem. from אַחַר
אַחֲרֵיהֹן Chald. id., suff. 3 pers. pl. masc. . אחר
אַחֲרָיו וְ Heb. id., suff. 3 pers. sing. masc. . אחר
אַחֲרַיִךְ id., suff. 2 pers. sing. fem. . . אחר
אַחֲרֶיךָ וְ id., suff. 2 pers. sing. masc. . . אחר
אַחֲרֵיכֶם id., suff. 2 pers. pl. masc. . . אחר
אֲחֵרִים adj. masc., pl. of אַחֵר irr. (§ 45) . אחר
אָחֳרִין id. with Chald. term. . . . אחר

אָחֳרִין Chald., Keri רֵין adj. sing. masc. . . אחר
אַחֲרֵינוּ prep., pl. with suff. 1 pers. pl. from אַחַר אחר
אַחֲרִישׁ Hiph. fut. 1 pers. sing. . . . חרש
אַחֲרִית וְ noun fem. sing. dec. 1 b . . . אחר
אַחֲרִיתָהּ וְ id., suff. 3 pers. sing. fem. . . אחר
אַחֲרִיתוֹ וְ id., suff. 3 pers. sing. masc. . . אחר
אַחֲרִיתִי id., suff. 1 pers. sing. . . . אחר
אַחֲרִיתְךָ וְ id., suff. 2 pers. sing. masc. . . אחר
אַחֲרִיתֵךְ וְ id., suff. 2 pers. sing. fem. . . אחר
אַחֲרִיתְכֶן וְ id., suff. 2 pers. pl. fem. . . אחר
אַחֲרִיתָם וְ id., suff. 3 pers pl. masc. . . אחר
אַחֲרִיתָן id., suff. 3 pers. pl. fem. . . אחר
אַחֲרִיתֵנוּ id., suff. 1 pers. pl. . . . אחר
אַחֲרָן וְ Chald. adj. masc. sing. . . . אחר
אַחֲרֹנִים adj. masc., pl. of אַחֲרוֹן, dec. 1 b אחר
אַחֲרֹנִית adv., a fem. form from a masc. [אַחֲרֹנִי] אחר
אַחֲרֵשׁ for [רֵישׁ] Hiph. fut. 1 pers. sing. . חרש
אַחֶרֶת adj. fem. sing. from אַחֵר masc. (q. v.) אחר
אֲחַשְּׁבָה וְ Piel fut. 1 pers. sing. with parag. ה ; וְ for חשׁב
[אֲחַשְׁדַּרְפְּן] only in the pl., *chief satraps*, officers of the Persian court, Chald. id.
אֲחַשְׁדַּרְפְּנֵי id. pl., construct state.
אֲחַשְׁדַּרְפְּנַיָּא וְ Chald. id. pl., emph. st.; וְ before (־ַ)
אֶחֱשֶׂה Kal fut. 1 pers. sing. . . . חשׂה
אֲחַשְׁוֵרוֹשׁ pr. name of several kings of Persia and Media.
אֶחְשֹׁךְ וְ Kal fut. 1 pers. s. (§ 13. r. 5); וְ for וֹ conv. חשׁך
אֶחְשָׁךְ id. with Mak. (§ 8. rem. 18) חשׁך
אֲחַשְׁרֵשׁ Kh. for אֲחַשְׁוֵרוֹשׁ q. v.
[אֲחַשְׁתָּרִי] only with the art., pr. name m. of Persian origin.
[אֲחַשְׁתְּרָן] only in the pl. תְּרָנִים, *mules*, Est. 8. 10, 14, a word of Persian origin.
אַחַת וְ [for אַחְדְתְּ=אֲחֶדֶת] card. num., fem. of אֶחָד (§ 45) . . . אחד
אַחֵת Chald. Aph. imp. sing. masc. (§ 51. No. 1) נחת
אַחַת [for אַחְתְּ] in pause for אֲחַת f. of אֶחָד (§ 45) אחר
אֲחֹתָהּ noun fem. sing. with suff. 3 pers sing. fem. from אָחוֹת irr. (§ 45) . . אח
אֶאֱחָתָה Kal fut. 1 pers. sing. [אָחַת § 18. rem. 6] with paragogic ה חתת
אֲחֹתוֹ וְ noun fem. sing., suff. 3 pers. sing. masc. from אָחוֹת irr. (§ 45) וְ before (־ַ) אח
אֲחֹתִי id. with suff. 1 pers. sing.; וְ id. . אח
אַחְתְּךָ Hiph. fut. 1 pers. sing. [אָחַת], suff. 2 pers. sing. masc. (§ 18. rem. 11) חתת
אֲחֹתָם noun fem. sing., suff. 3 pers. pl. masc. from אָחוֹת irr. (§ 45) . . אח

a Ge. 34. 19.   c Ju. 5. 28.   e Ex. 26. 12.   g Eze. 16. 34.   i Nu. 23. 10.   l De. 32. 20.   o Je. 4. 19.   q Job 7. 11.   t 1 Ch. 7. 12.
b Ge. 32. 5.   d Job 19. 25.   f Da. 7. 20.   h Job 31. 10.   k Job 8. 7.   m Ps. 73. 16.   r Est. 3. 12.   s Ezr. 5. 15.   u Job 17. 14.
2 Ki. 19. 24.   Is. 43. 10.   2 Ch. 11. 20.   Da. 4. 5.   Eze. 23. 25.   Is. 41. 22.   Je. 17. 18.   Je. 1. 17.
Is. 37. 25.   Ex. 33. 23.   Da. 7. 24.   Ec. 10. 13.   Am. 4. 2.   Je. 12. 4.   Ge. 20. 6.

אֶחְתָּם* וְ Kal fut. 1 p. s. (§ 13. r. 5); וְ for וַ conv.   חתם

אֲחֹתֵנוּ n. f. s., suff. 1 pers. pl. from אָחוֹת irr. (§ 45)   אח

אֶחְתְּרִ* וְ Kal fut. 1 pers. sing. (§ 13. rem. 5); וְ
for וַ conv.   .   .   .   .   חתר

אַט
אַטּ* } ap. for אָטָּה (q. v.); וְ for וַ conv.   נטה
וְ, וַיַּ*

אַט adv.   .   .   .   .   .   אטט

אָטָד* masc.—I. blackthorn; rhamnus paliurus of Linn.—
II. pr. name of a place beyond Jordan, Ge. 50. 10, 11.

אֶטְבְּעָה* Kal fut. 1 pers. sing. [אֶטְבַּע] with paragogic
ה for [בְּעָ' § 8. rem. 15]   .   .   נבע

אַטֶּה Hiph. fut. 1 pers. sing. (§ 25. 2 b)   .   נטה

אֲטַהֵר* Piel (dag. forte impl. § 14. r. 1) fut. 1 pers. s.   טהר

אֶטְהָר* וְ Kal fut. 1 pers. sing. for [הַר' § 8. rem. 15]   טהר

אֵטוּן masc. a kind of Egyptian thread, or linen,
Prov. 7. 16. The word is probably of
Egyptian origin.

אֶטּוֹר* Kal fut. 1 pers. sing. (§ 17. rem. 3)   נטר

אטט Root not used; Arab. to utter a gentle sound, to
murmur.

אַט masc. pl. אִטִּים dec. 8 e.—I. necromancer,
only Is. 19. 3.—II. gentleness, softness, hence adv.
gently, slowly, 1 Ki. 21. 27, and with pref. לָאַט,
לָאַט; לְאִטִּי at my ease, convenience.

אַטִּילֵךְ* for [לְךָ] Hiph. fut. 1 p. s., suff. 2 p. s. m.   טול

[אָטַם] to shut, to close, Hiph. id. Ps. 58. 5.
אֹטֵם Kal part. act. sing. masc.   .   אטם

אֲטַמֵּא* וְ Piel fut. 1 pers. sing.; וְ for וַ conv.   טמא

אֲטֻמוֹת* Kal part. p. fem., pl. of [אָטוּמָה] dec. 10   אטם

אֲטֻמִים* id. masc., pl. of [אָטוּם] dec. 3 a   .   אטם

אֶטְמְנֶהוּ* וְ Kal fut. 1 pers. sing. [אֶטְמֹן], suff. 3 pers.
sing. masc.; וְ for וַ conv.   .   .   טמן

אֶטְנְפֵם* Piel fut. 1 pers. sing., suff. 3 pers. pl. masc.   טנף

אֶטְעָם* Kal fut. 1 pers. sing.   .   .   טעם

אַטִּף* for [אָטִיף] Hiph. fut. 1 pers. sing.   .   נטף

[אָטַר] fut. תֶּאְטָר, to shut, to close, Ps. 69. 16.
אָטֵר (lame?) pr. name masc.
אִטֵּר adj. prop. shut up, bound, impotent, אִטֵּר
יַד יְמִינוֹ having his right hand bound, i. e. being
left-handed.

אֶטְרֹף* Kal fut. 1 pers. sing.   .   .   טרף

[אַי] construct אֵי (§ 37. rem. 6) adv. of interrog. where?

with suff. אַיֶּכָּה where art thou? אַיּוֹ where is he?
אַיָּם where are they? With adverbs and pronouns,
אֵי זֶה which? what? where? whither? אֵי מִזֶּה
whence? from what? אֵי לָזֹאת on what account?
wherefore? Je. 5. 7.—With parag. ה, אַיֵּה where?
אֵיךְ (for the next אֵיכָה q. v.) how? Also as
an exclamation of grief, how!
אֵיכָה (from אֵי, אַי, and כֹּה כָה i. q. כֹּה so) where?
how? As an exclamation of grief, ah, how!
אֵיכֹה where? 2 Ki. 6. 13, where Keri has אֵיכוֹ
אֵיכָכָה how? compare כָּכָה.
אַיִן adv. of interrog. (where?) only in the form
מֵאַיִן whence?
אֵיפֹה where? how? comp. פֹּה.
אָן (contr. from אַיִן אֵין) where? מֵאָן whence? 2 Ki.
5. 25. in Kheth; עַד־אָן until when? how long?
Job 8. 2. With parag. ה, אָנָה whither? where?
עַד אָנָה how long? אָנָה וָאָנָה hither and thither,
1 Ki. 2. 36, 42.

אִי* וְ noun masc. sing., pl. אִיִּים, dec. 8. (§ 37,
No. 4. a); or interj.   .   .   .   אוה

אִי* i. q. אֵין, אַיִן, not, Job 22. 30. Hence the
name אִי־כָבוֹד (inglorious, others where
is the glory, i. q. אֵי־כָבוֹד) 1 Sa. 4. 20,
compare also אִיזָבֶל.

[אָיַב] to hate, to be an enemy, Ex. 23. 22. Part. אֹיֵב
as a subst. dec. 7 b, adversary, enemy. Fem.
אֹיֶבֶת id.
אֵיבָה fem. dec. 10, enmity.
אִיּוֹב (persecuted) pr. name, Job, the patriarch.

אֹיֵב Kal part. act. sing. masc. dec. 7 b.   .   איב

אֵיבָה* וְ noun fem. sing dec. 10.   .   .   איב

אֹיְבוֹ Kal part. act. sing. masc., suff. 3 pers. sing.
masc. from אֹיֵב dec. 7 b.   .   .   איב

אֹיְבַי
אֹיְבָי } id. pl., suff. 1 pers. sing.   .   איב

אֹיְבֵי* וְ id. pl., construct state   .   .   איב

אֹיְבִי id. sing., suff. 1 pers. sing.   .   .   איב

אֹיְבֶיהָ id. pl., suff. 3 pers. sing. fem.   .   איב

אֹיְבֵיהֶם id. pl., suff. 3 pers. pl. masc.   .   .   איב

אֹיְבָיו* וְ id. pl., suff. 3 pers. sing. masc.   .   איב

אֹיְבֶיךָ id. pl., suff. 2 pers. sing. masc.   .   איב

אֹיְבֵיךְ*
אֹיְבַיִךְ } id. pl., suff. 2 pers. sing. fem.   .   איב

אֹיְבֶיךָ id. pl., (Kh. אֹיְבֶיךָ), suff. 2 pers. sing. masc.
K. אֹיְבֶךָ (q. v.)   .   .   איב

• Je. 22. 19.   d Ho. 11. 4.   f Ps. 58. 10.   k Je. 3. 12.   n 1 Ki. 6. 4.   r 2 Sa. 3. 35.   t Ec. 4. 10.   u Ge. 3. 15.   y Mt. 4. 10.
Eze. 8. 8.   e Je. 15. 6.   g Ps. 69. 15.   l Eze. 32. 4.   o Je. 13. 5.   • Mi. 2. 11.   •• Nu. 35. 22.   • Ps. 37. 20.   • La. 2. 18.
Job 22. 11.   f 1 Ki. 21. 27.   i Eze. 36. 25.   m Eze. 20. 26.   p Ca. 5. 3.   ~ Ps. 51. 9.

אֹיְבֵיכֶם	Kal part. act. pl. m., suff. 2 pl. m. fr. אֹיֵב d. 7 b.	איב
אֹיְבֵינוּ	'} id. pl., suff. 1 pers. pl.	איב
אֹיִבְךָ	id. s., suff. 2 p. s. m. in pause for אֹיִבְךָ (q. v.)	איב
אֹיִבֵךְ	id. sing., suff. 2 pers. sing. fem.	איב
אֹיִבְךָ	id. sing., suff. 2 pers. sing. masc.	איב
אֹיְבֵנוּ	id. sing., suff. 1 pers. sing.	איב
אֵיבֹשׁ	Kal fut. 1 pers. sing. for [בֹּשׁ] (§ 8. rem. 15)	יבש
אֵיבַת	noun fem. sing. construct of בָה dec. 10.	איב
אֹיַבְתִּי	Kal pret. 1 pers. sing.; acc. shifted by conv. } (§ 8. rem. 7)	איב
אֹיֶבֶת	id. part. act. sing. fem. [אֹיֶבֶת] with paragogic ' (§ 9. rem. 19)	איב
אִיגַּע	Kal fut. 1 pers. sing. for [גַּע] (§ 8. rem. 15)	יגע
אֵיד	'} noun masc. sing. dec. 1 a.	אוד
אֵידוֹ	id., suff. 3 pers. sing. masc.	אוד
אֵידִי	id., suff. 1 pers. sing.	אוד
אֵידְךָ	id., suff. 2 pers. sing. masc. for [אֵידְךָ]	אוד
אֵידְכֶם	'} id., suff. 2 pers. pl. masc.	אוד
אֵידָם	id., suff. 3 pers. pl. masc.	אוד
אַיָּה	noun fem. sing.; also pr. name masc.	אוה
אַיֵּה	'} interrog. adv. [אַי], with paragogic ה construct אַי (q. v.)	אי
אַיּוֹ	'} id., suff. 3 pers. sing. m. dec. 8 d. (§ 37. r. 6)	אי
אַיּוֹ	Kh. אַיּוֹ q. v., K. אַיֵּה (q. v.)	אי
אִיּוֹב	'} pr. name masc.	איב
אִיזֶבֶל	} pr. n. f. (non-inhabited) comp. אִי & R. (זְבַל)	
אִיזָבֶל	} pr. n. f. the wife of Ahab king of Israel.	
אֲיַחֵל	Piel (dag. f. impl. § 14. r. 1) fut. 1 pers. s.	יחל
אֲיַחֲלָה	'} id. with paragogic ה; } for }	יחל
אֵיטִיב	Hiph. fut. 1 pers. sing.	יטב
אֵיטִיבָה	'} id. with paragogic ה	יטב
אֵיֵי	'} construct of the following	אוה
אִיִּים	'} noun masc., pl. of אִי dec. 8. (§ 37. No. 4 a)	אוה
אֵיךְ	'} interrog. adv.	אי
אֵיכָה	interr. adv. [אַי], suff. 2 pers. sing. masc. dec. 8 d. (§ 37. rem. 6)	אי
אֵיכָה	interrog. adv.	אי
אֵיכֹה	id. Kh. אֵיכָה K. אֵיכוֹ	אי
אֵיכְכָה	'} interrog. adv.	אי
אַיִל	noun masc. sing. dec. 1 b.	אול
אַיִל	'}, '} noun masc. sing. dec. 6 h; } see lett. ו	אול
אֵיל	id., construct state	אול
אַיִל	noun masc. sing.	אול
אֵילָה	noun fem. sing. (§ 42. rem. 5)	אול
אֵילוֹ	'} Kh. for [אֵילָיו § 4. rem. 1], noun masc. pl., suff. 3 pers. sing. m. from אַיִל dec. 6 h.	אול

אַיָּלוֹן	'} pr. name of a place	אול
אֵילוֹן	'} pr. name of a man or place	אול
אַיָּלוֹת	noun fem., pl. of אַיָּלָה dec. 10. (§ 42. rem. 5)	אול
אֵילוֹת	pr. name of a place	אול
אֱלוּתִי	noun fem. sing., suff. 1 pers. sing. from [לוּת] dec. 1 b.	אול
אֵילֵי	'} n. m. pl. constr. fr. אַיִל dec. 6 h., or אֵילֵי	אול
אֵילִיל	Hiph. fut. 1 pers. sing. (§ 20. rem. 15)	ילל
אֵילִילָה	'} Hiph. fut. 1 pers. sing. with parag. ה	ילל
אֵילִים	'} noun masc., pl. of אַיִל dec. 6 h.	אול
אֵילְכָה	Kal fut. 1 pers. sing. with parag. ה	ילך
אֵילִם	pr. name of a place	אול
אֵילִם	'} defect. for אֵילִים (q. v.)	אול
אֵילִמָה	pr. name of a place (אֵילָם) with loc. ה	אול
אֵילַמּוֹ	} noun masc. pl., suff. 3 pers. sing. masc. from אֵלָם dec. 8 a. for [לָמוֹ § 4. rem. 1]	אול
אֵילָן	pr. name masc. see אֵילוֹן	אול
אִילָן	Chald. noun masc. sing. dec. 1 b.	אול
אִילָנָא	Chald. id., emph. st.	אול
אַיָּלֹנָה	pr. name of a place (אַיָּלוֹן) with loc. ה	אול
אֵילַת	noun fem. sing. construct of אַיָּלָה; but as abs. Je. 14. 5 (§ 42. rem. 5)	אול
אֵילַת	pr. name of a place, see אֵילוֹת	אול

אַיִם   Root not used; Chald. Pa. *to terrify.*

אָיֹם	adj. *terrible*, fem. אֲיֻמָּה	
אֵימִים	or אֵמִים masc. pl. אֵימִים.—I. *terror, dread.* —II. *idols,* Je. 50. 38.—III. pr. name of the original inhabitants of Moab.	
אֵימָה	fem. dec. 10, *terror, dread.*	

אַיָם	interrog. adv. [אַי], suff. 3 pers. pl. masc. dec. 8 d. (§ 37. rem. 6)	אי
אָיֹם	adj. masc. sing.	אים
אֵימָה	noun fem. sing. dec. 10.	אים
אֲיֻמָּה	adj. fem. sing. from אָיֹם masc. (§ 39. No. 3)	אים
אֵימוֹת	'} noun fem., pl. of אֵימָה dec. 10.	אים
אֵימְנָה	'} Hiph. fut. 1 pers. sing. with paragogic ה	ימן
אֵימַת	noun fem. sing., construct of אֵימָה dec. 10.	אים
אֵימָתָה	id. with paragogic ה	אים
אֵימָתִי	id., suff. 1 pers. sing.	אים
אֵימָתְךָ	'} id., suff. 2 pers. sing. masc.	אים
אֵימַתְכֶם	id., suff. 2 pers. pl. masc.	אים
אַיִן	'} (prim. subst.) used as an adv.; for }	אין
אַיִן	'} see lett. ו	
אַיִן	'} adv. i. q. אַיִן	אין

אֵין ן adv., prop. construct of אֵין dec. 6 h. . אין

אֵינֵימוֹ ן id. pl., suff. 3 pers. pl. masc. . אין

אֵינְךָ ן id sing., suff. 2 pers. sing. masc. . אין

אֵינֵךְ ן id sing., suff. 2 pers. sing. fem. . אין

אֵינְכֶם id., suff. 2 pers. pl. masc. . אין

אֵינָם ן id., suff. 3 pers. pl. masc. . אין

אֵינֶנָּה id., (verbal) suff. 3 pers. sing. fem. . אין

אֵינֶנּוּ ן id., (verbal) suff. 3 pers. s. m. or 1 pers. pl. אין

אֵינֶנִּי ן id., (verbal) suff. 1 pers. sing. . אין

אִינַק Kal fut. 1 pers. sing. for [אֵינַק § 8. rem. 15] ינק

אֵסִירֵם Hiph. fut. 1 pers. sing., suff. 3 pers. pl. masc. יסר
  (§ 20. rem. 14) . . . .

אֲיַסֵּר Piel fut. 1 pers. sing. . . יסר

אִיעָר contr. for אֲבִיעָר (q. v.) . . אב

אִיעָצָה Kal fut. 1 pers. sing. with paragogic ה יעץ

אִיעָצְךָ id., suff. 2 pers. sing. masc. (§ 16. rem. 12) יעץ

אִיעָצֵךְ id., suff. 2 pers. sing. fem. . יעץ

אֵיפָה ן fem. dec. 10, an Ephah, a corn measure.

אֵיפֹה ן interrog. adv. . . . אי

אֵיפַת ן noun fem. sing., construct of אֵיפָה dec. 10. איף

אִיקֵץ ן for [אֵיקֵץ] Kal fut. 1 pers. sing. (§ 8. יקץ
  rem. 15); ן for ו conv.

אִירָא ן Kal fut. 1 pers. sing.; ן id. . ירא

אִירָאֶנּוּ id., suff. 3 pers. sing. masc. (§ 2. rem. 3) ירא

אִירָשֶׁנָּה Kal fut. 1 pers. sing., suff. 3 pers. sing. fem. ירש
  (§ 2. rem. 3) . . .

אִישׁ ן, ן masc. dec. 1 a.—I. man, Lat. vir, with reference to strength; hence as denoting sex, a male, of the human species or brutes.—II. husband.—III. man, as opposed to God, to animals, Lat. homo.—IV. used before other nouns to denote the qualities or qualifications of men; אִישׁ אֱמֶת a faithful man; אִישׁ אָוֶן a wicked man; אִישׁ תֹּאַר a handsome man; אִישׁ מִלְחָמָה a warrior.—V. any one, any person.—VI. each, every one; אִישׁ אִישׁ every one; אִישׁ וָאִישׁ each and every one. Plur. only occurs three times, more frequently is אֲנָשִׁים, see אֱנוֹשׁ (comp. § 45.)

אִישׁ denom. Hithpal. הִתְאֹשֵׁשׁ to show oneself a man, Is. 46. 8.

אִישׁ־בֹּשֶׁת (man of shame) pr. name of a son of Saul; also called אֶשְׁבַּעַל (man of Baal.)

אִישְׁהוֹד (man of glory) pr. name of a man, 1 Ch. 7. 18.

אִישׁוֹן masc. prop. dimin. the little man, the small image of a person as seen in the eye.—I.

אִישׁוֹן בַּת עַיִן the pupil of the eye.—II. Metaph. the middle, followed by לַיְלָה, חֹשֶׁךְ midnight, midst of darkness.

אֵשֶׁת fem. dec. 13 b.—I. woman; female (of animals,) Ge. 7. 2.—II. wife; אֵשֶׁת אָב father's wife, a stepmother. It is used as the construct of אִשָּׁה q. v.

אֶשְׁתּוֹן (womanish) pr. name m. 1 Ch. 4. 11, 12.

אִישָּׁהּ ן id. with suff. 3 pers. sing. fem. איש

אִישְׁהוֹד pr. name masc. . . . . איש

אִישׁוֹ noun masc. sing., suff. 3 pers. sing. masc. from אִישׁ dec. 1 a. (but see § 45) איש

אִישִׁי ן pr. name masc., see יִשַׁי . ישה

אִישִׁי noun masc. sing., suff. 1 pers. sing. from אִישׁ dec. 1 a. (but see § 45) איש

אִישִׁים id. pl., absolute state . . איש

אִישֵׁךְ id. sing., suff. 2 pers. sing. fem. איש

אִישִׂימָה ן Kal fut. 1 pers. s. with parag. ה, Kh. R. שִׂם K. אָשִׂימָה R. שִׂים see שׂום

אִישַׁן אִישָׁן } Kal fut. 1 pers. sing. (§ 8. rem. 15) ישן

אִישְׁנָה ן id. with parag. ה, for [וָאִישְׁנָה § 8. rem. 15]; ן for ו conv. ישן

אֲאַשֵּׁר Piel fut. 1 pers. sing. . . . ישר

אִיתוֹהִי Chald. the following with suff. 3 pers. s. m.

אִיתַי Chald. i. q. Heb. יֵשׁ there is; with the suff. of the pl. אִיתָיִךְ thou art; אִיתוֹהִי he is; אִיתַנָא we are; אִיתֵיכוֹן ye are. Hence the two following names.

אִיתַי pr. name of a man, 1 Ch. 11. 31, for which אִתַּי 2 Sa. 23. 29.

אִיתִיאֵל (there is a God) pr. name of a man, Pr. 30. 1.

אִיתֵיכוֹן Chald. adv. (אִיתַי) with suff. 2 pers. pl. m.

אִיתָּם־ Kal fut. 1 pers. sing., for [אֶתַּם, § 18. rem. 6] . . . . תמם

אִיתָמָר ן pr. name masc. . . . . אוה

אֵיתָן ן adj. or subst. masc. sing. (no vowel change); also pr. name . . . יתן

אִיתַנָא Chald. adv. (אִיתַי) with suff. 1 pers. pl. .

אֵיתָנִים ן noun masc., pl. of אֵיתָן (no vowel change) יתן

אַךְ ן adv.—I. only; אַךְ הַפַּעַם only this once; אַךְ חֹשֶׁךְ darkness only; i. e. nothing but darkness.—II. only, but.—III. only now, just now.—IV. surely, certainly.

אַךְ־ ן Hiph. fut. 1 pers. sing., ap. for אַכֶּה (§ 25. No. 2 b); ן for ו conv. נכה

אֲכַבֵּד Piel fut. 1 pers. sing. . . . כבד

אֶכְבַּד	וְ] Niph. fut. 1 pers. sing.	כבד
אֶכְבְּדָה	וְ] id., (Kh. אֶכָּבֵד), K. אֶכְבְּדָה (q. v.)	כבד
אֲכַבְּדָה	וַ] Piel fut. 1 pers. sing. with parag. ה; וְ] for וַ]	כבד
אִכָּבְדָה	וְ] Niph. fut. 1 pers. sing. with parag. ה (§ 10. rem. 5). 2 Sa. 6. 22.	כבד
אֲכַבְּדֶהוּ	וַ] Piel fut. 1 pers. sing., suff. 3 pers. sing. masc.; וְ] for וַ]	כבד
אֲכַבֶּדְךָ	id., suff. 2 pers. sing. masc.	כבד
אֶכֶּד	] pr. name of a city, Ge. 10. 10; supposed to signify *fortress*, i. q. אָכַד עקד, אָנַד to *bind*, to *strengthen*.	
אַכֶּה	s וַ] וְ] Hiph. fut. 1 pers. sing. (§ 25. No. 2 b); וְ] for וַ] conv.	נכה
אַכֵּהוּ	וְ] id., suff. 3 pers. sing. masc.	נכה
אָכוֹל	Kal inf. absolute	אכל
אֲכוֹלָה	וְ] id. imp. sing. masc.; וַ] bef.	אכל
אֲכֹלוּ	וְ] Kh. אָכוֹל Kal inf. absolute, K. אִכְלוּ (q. v.)	אכל
אֲכַזֵּב	Piel fut. 1 pers. sing.	כזב
אַכְזָב	adj. masc. sing.	כזב
אַכְזִיב	] pr. name of a place	כזב
אַכְזִיבָה	id. with loc. ה	כזב
אַכְזָר	adj. masc. sing	כזר
אַכְזָרִי	id. with the adj. term. יָ־	כזר
אַכְזְרִיּוּת	noun fem. sing., formed from the preceding	כזר
אֲאַחֵד	Piel (dag. f. impl. § 14. r. 1) fut. 1 pers. sing.	כחד
אַכְחִיד	וַ] Hiph. fut. 1 pers. sing.; וְ] for וַ] conv.	כחד
אָכִין	Hiph. fut. 1 pers. sing.	כון
אָכִינָה	id. with paragogic ה	כון
אַכִּיר	Hiph. fut. 1 pers. sing.	נכר
אַכִּירָה	וָ] id. with parag. ה; וָ] for וַ] conv.	נכר
אָכִישׁ	pr. name of a king of the Philistines.	
אַכֶּכָּה	Hiph. fut. 1 pers. sing. (אַכֶּה § 25. No. 2), suff. 2 pers. sing. masc. (§ 2. rem. 2)	נכה

אָכַל (§ 19. rem. 1. and 2.)—I. *to eat, to eat up*, const. with acc., בְּ, לְ, מִן.—II. *to devour, to consume*, const. with בְּ.—III. *to enjoy*, const. with בְּ.—IV. יֹאכְלוּ אַתִּיקִים *the columns occupied*, Eze. 42. 5. *Niph. to be eaten*; also *to be fit for food*. *Pi. to consume*, Job 20. 26. *Pu. to be consumed. Hiph.*—I. *to give to eat, to feed.*—II. *to cause to consume*, Eze. 21. 33. *Hoph.* (§ 19. rem. 9.)

קְרַץ Ch. (§ 53.) id., comp. אָכַל.

אֹכֶל masc. dec. 6 c.—I. *an eating, the act of eating.*—II. *food.*

אָכְלָה fem. *food, meat.*

אֲכִילָה	fem. id.	
מַאֲכָל	masc. dec. 2 b, *food*; עֵץ מַאֲכָל *fruit-tree*	
צֹאן מַאֲכָל	*flock of* (i. e. slaughtered for) *food*.	
מַאֲכָלֹת	fem. pl. (§ 44. rem. 5) *a knife* both for eating and slaughtering.	
מַאֲכֹלֶת	fem. *food*, trop. for fire, Is. 9. 4, 18.	
מַאֲכֹלֶת	fem. *food*. 1 Ki. 5. 25.	
אָכַל אָכֵל	וְ] וַ] Kal pret. 3 pers. sing. masc. (§ 8. rem. 7)	אכל
אֲכַל	וַ] Piel fut. 1 pers. sing., ap. for אֲכַלֶּה; for וְ] conv.	כלה
אָכֹל	וְ] Kal inf. abs.	אכל
אֲכֹל אֱכָל	} id. inf. constr. (§ 8. rem. 18)	אכל
אֱכֹל אֱכָל	וֶ] id. imp. sing. masc. (§ 8. rem. 18); וְ] before (יֶ)	אכל
אֹכַל אֹכֵל	וְ] וַ] id. fut. 1 pers. sing. (§ 19. r. 1); וָ] for וַ] conv.	אכל
אֹכֵל	וְ] id. part. act. sing. masc. dec. 7 b	אכל
אֹכֶל	noun masc. sing. dec. 6 c.	אכל
אֻכָּל	Pual part. sing. masc. for מַאֲכָל [§ 10. r. 6]	אכל
אֻכָל	] pr. name masc. Prov. 30. 1.	
אֶכְלָא	Kal fut. 1 pers. sing.	כלא
אֹכְלָה	וְ] in pause for אָכְלָה q. v. (§ 8. rem. 7)	אכל
אֲכָלָה	וַ] Kal pret. 3 pers. sing. masc., suff. 3 pers. sing. fem.; וַ] for וְ] conv.	אכל
אֲכַלֶּה	וַ] Piel fut. 1 pers. sing.; וְ] for וַ]	כלה
אָכְלָה	וְ] Kal pret. 3 pers. sing. fem.	אכל
אָכְלָה	Chald. Peal part. act. sing. fem. from [אֲכַל] masc.	אכל
אָכְלָה	Kal inf. const. (§ 8. rem. 10)	אכל
אָכְלָה	וְ] id. imp. sing. masc. with paragogic ה (§ 8. rem. 11)	אכל
אֹכְלָה	id. part. act., fem. of אֹכֵל (§ 8. rem. 19)	אכל
אֹכְלָה	וְ] וַ] id. fut. 1 pers. sing. with parag. ה (§ 19. r. 1); וָ] for וַ] conv.	אכל
אֲכָלֻהוּ	וַ] id. pret. 3 pers. pl., suff. 3 pers. sing. masc.; וַ] for וְ] conv.	אכל
אִכְלֻהוּ	id imp. pl. masc., suff. 3 pers. sing. masc., [for אִכְלוּהוּ]	אכל
אֲכָלוֹ	וַ] id. pret. 3 pers. sing. masc., suff. 3 pers. sing. masc.; וַ] for וְ] conv.	אכל
אֹכְלוּ	in pause for אָכְלוּ q. v. (§ 8. rem. 7)	אכל
אֲכַלוּ	וַ] Ch. Peal pret. 3 pers. pl. masc.; וַ] bef. (יֶ)	אכל
אָכְלוּ	וְ] Kal pret. 3 pers. pl. masc.	אכל

a Le. 10. 3.   f Ps. 91. 15.   l Is. 37. 30.   q 1 Ch. 23. 5.   v De. 12. 23.   a Is. 44. 19.   h Eze. 19. 14.   m Ge. 27. 19.   r Ex. 16. 25.
b Is. 49. 5.   g Je. 40. 15.   m Je. 15. 18.   r Ne. 6. 12.   y Ge. 3. 11.   b Ge. 3. 12, 13.   i Ho. 11. 6.   n De. 12. 20.   s 2 Sa. 9. 10.
c Hag. 1. 8.   h Ne. 13. 25.   n Pr. 27. 4.   s 2 Sa. 2. 22.   z Am. 7. 12.   c Ec. 4. 5.   k De. 14. 21.   o Ge. 27. 25.   t Eze. 22. 25.
d Ps. 86. 12.   i Is. 57. 17.   o Job 27. 11.   t Ge. 27. 10.   a Job 31. 17.   d Ex. 3. 2.   l Da. 7. 7, 19.   p Eze. 3. 3.   u Da. 6. 25.
Ex. 14. 4, 17.   k 1 Sa. 28. 22.   p Zec. 11. 8.   Eze. 43. 8.   b Ge. 27. 33.   e Ps. 40. 10.   =1 Sa. 1. 9.   q Ge. 27. 4.   w Da. 3. 8.

וְאֹכְלוּ / נ אַכְּלוּ } id. imp. pl. masc. (§ 8. rem. 12) . אכל

אֹכְלוּ id. inf.; or noun masc. with suff. 3 pers. sing. masc. from אֹכֶל dec. 6c. . אכל

אָכְלוּ Pual pret. 3 pers. pl. masc. . אכל

אֲכָלֻהָ Kal imp. pl. masc., suff. 3 pers. sing. fem. אכל

וַיֹּאכְלוּם id. pret. 3 pers. pl. with suff. 3 pers. pl. masc.; ו for וּ conv. . אכל

אֲכֻלִי Chald. Peal imp. sing. fem. . אכל

וְאֹכְלֵי Kal part. act. pl. constr. masc. from אֹכֵל dec. 7b . אכל

וְאֹכְלָיו id. pl., suff. 3 pers. sing. masc. אכל

אֹכְלַיִךְ id. pl., suff. 2 pers. sing. fem. . אכל

וְאֹכְלִים id. pl., abs. st. . אכל

אֲכָלְךָ Kal inf. with suff. 2 pers sing. masc. from אָכַל . אכל

אֲכָלֵךְ Piel fut. 1 pers. sing. (אֲכַלֶּה), suff. 2 pers. sing. masc. (§ 24. rem. 21a. & § 10. r. 7) כלה

אֲכָלְךָ for לְךָ, noun masc. sing., suff. 2 pers. sing. masc. from אֹכֶל dec. 6c . אכל

אֲכַלְכֵּל Pilpel fut. 1 pers. sing. (§ 6. No. 4) . כול

אֲכַלְכְּלֵם id., suff. 3 pers. pl. masc.; ו for וּ conv. כול

אֲכָלְכֶם Kal inf., suff. 2 pers. pl. masc. (§ 16. r. 7) . אכל

אָכְלָם noun masc. sing. with suff. 3 pers. pl. masc. from אֹכֶל dec. 6c. . אכל

וָאֲכַלֵּם Piel fut. 1 pers.s. (אֲכַלֶּה), suff.3 pers. pl. masc. (§ 24. r. 21a); ו for וּ, ו for וַ conv. כלה

וָאֹכְלֵם Kal fut. 1 pers. sing., suff. 3 pers. pl. masc.; ו id. אנל

וָאֲכַלְנֻהוּ id. pret. 1 pers. pl., suff. 3 pers. sing. masc.; ו for וּ . אכל

אֲכָלָנוּ id. pret. 3 pers. sing. masc., suff. (Ku. נ K. נִי) 1 pers. pl. or sing. אכל

אֲכָלָנוּ id. pret. 1 pers. pl. . אכל

אֲכָלַנִי id. pret. 3 pers. sing. masc., suff. 1 pers. sing. . אכל

אֲכַלְתָּ / אֲכַלְתָּ } id. pret. 2 pers. sing. masc. (§ 8. rem. 7) אכל

אֲכַלְתָּ id. id.; acc. shifted by conv. ו (§ 8. r. 7) . אכל

אֲכַלְתְּ id. pret. 2 pers. sing. fem. . אכל

אֹכְלֵת / אֹכָלֶת } id. part. act. sing. fem. . אכל

אֲכָלָתְהוּ / אֲכָלָתְהוּ } id. pret. 3 pers. sing. fem. with suff. 3 pers. sing. masc. אכל

אֲכָלַתָּי id. pret. 2 pers. sing. fem. Kh. תִּי, K. תְּ (§ 8. rem. 5) . אכל

אֲכַלְתִּי / וְ } id. pret. 1 pers. sing. (§ 8. rem. 7) . אכל

אֲכָלַתָּךְ id. pret. 3 pers. sing. f., suff. 2 pers. sing. m. . אכל

אֲכָלָתַם נ id. id., suff. 3 pers. pl. masc.; ו for וּ conv. אכל

אֲכַלְתֶּם וְנ id. pret. 2 pers. pl. masc.; נ id. . אכל

אֲכָלַתְנִי id. pret. 3 pers. sing. fem., suff. 1 pers. sing. [for לְתַנִי] . אכל

אָכֵן adv. . . כון

אֲכַנֶּה Piel fut. 1 pers. sing. . כנה

אַכֶּנּוּ Hiph. fut. 1 pers. sing. (אַכֶּה § 25, No. 2 b), suff. 3 pers. sing. masc. . נכה

אַכְנִיעַ Hiph. fut. 1 pers. sing. . כנע

אֲכַנְּךָ Piel fut. 1 pers. sing. (אֲכַנֶּה), suff. 2 pers. sing. masc. (§ 24. rem. 21) . כנה

וְאֲכַסֶּה Piel fut. 1 pers. sing.; ו for וּ conv. . כסה

אֲכַסֵּךְ id., suff. 2 pers. sing. fem. (§ 24. rem. 21); ו id. . כסה

אֲכַסֶּנּוּ id., suff. 3 pers. sing. masc. . כסה

אַכְעִיסֵם Hiph. fut. 1 pers. sing., suff. 3 pers. pl. masc. . כעס

אֶכְעַס Kal fut. 1 pers. sing. . כעס

אָכַף *to bow down*, cogn. כָּפַף, hence *to compel*, Pr.16.26. אָכֶף masc. i. q. כַּף *the palm of the hand*, only with suff. אַכְפִּי, Job 33. 7.

אֶכֹּף Niph. fut. 1 pers. sing. . כפף

אַכְפִּי noun masc. sing. with suff. 1 pers. sing. from [אֶכֶף] dec. 6a . אכף

אֲכַפֵּר Piel fut. 1 pers. sing. . כפר

אֲכַפְּרָה id. with paragogic ה . כפר

אָכַר Root not used; Arab. *to dig*, whence אִכָּר masc. dec. 1b (§ 30. rem. 1) *ploughman, husbandman.*

אֶכְרֶהָ Kal fut. 1 pers. s., suff. 3 pers. s. fem. with euph. dag. for [אֶכְרֶהָ]; ו for וּ conv. . כרה

אֶכְרוֹת Kal fut. 1 pers. sing. . כרת

אֶכְרֹת id.; Kh. רוֹת, K. רַת with Mak. (§ 8. r. 18) כרת

אִכָּרֵיכֶם noun masc. pl., suff. 2 pers. pl. masc. from אִכָּר dec. 1b . אכר

אִכָּרִים id. pl., absolute state . אכר

וְאַכְרִית Hiph. fut. 1 pers. sing.; ו for וּ conv. . כרת

וְאֶכְרְעָה Kal fut. 1 pers. sing. [אֶכְרַע] with parag. ה; ו id. . כרע

וְאֶכְרֹת Kal fut. 1 pers. sing. . כרת

a Is. 55. 1.   g Le. 19. 8.   n Ge. 50. 21.   t Je. 15. 16.   z Ge. 3. 11.   d Eze. 16. 13.   i Is. 45. 4.   o De. 32. 21.   t Ho. 3. 2.
b Le. 10. 12.   h Je. 30. 16.   o 1 Ki. 18. 13.   u 1 Ki. 17. 12.   a Eze. 28. 18.   e Pr. 23. 8.   k Is. 46. 8.   p Eze. 16. 42.   u Jos. 9. 7.
c Je. 50. 7.   i Am. 6. 4.   p Ge. 3. 5.   v Je. 51. 34.   b Ps. 69. 10.   f Eze. 18. 8.   l Eze. 16. 8.   q Mic. 6. 6.   v Is. 61. 5.
d Ob. 1. 18.   k Ge. 2. 17.   q Ex. 32. 10.   w Ru. 2. 14.   c Ps. 81. 15.   g Job 32. 21, 22.   m Eze. 16. 10.   r Job 33. 7.   w 1 Ch. 17. 8.
e Da. 7. 5.   l Ex. 33. 3.   r 2 Sa. 22. 39.   x Je. 19. 43.   h Eze. 15. 5.   n Eze. 32. 7.   s 2 Sa. 21. 3.   x Ezr. 9. 5.
f Da. 11. 6.   m Le. 25. 37.   s Ho. 13. 8.   y Ge. 31. 40.

אֶכְרְתָה֯ וֽ Hiph. fut. 1 pers. sing. with parag. ה;   כרת
    וֽ for וֽ conv. . . . .

אֶכְרְתָה֯ וֽ Kal fut. 1 pers. sing. (אֶכְרֹת) with parag. ה   כרת

אַכְשֵׁף וֽ pr. name of a place . . . כשף

אֹכַּת֯ וֽ Kal fut. 1 pers. sing., for [אֹכֹת § 18.   כתת
    rem. 14]; וֽ for וֽ conv. . .

אֶכְתָּב֯ וֽ, וֽ Kal fut. 1 pers. sing.; וֽ id. .   כתב

אֶכְתֲבֶנָּה֯ id., suff. 3 pers.sing.fem. (§ 8. r. 14, & § 2. r.3)   כתב

אֶכְתּוֹב֯ Kh. תּוֹב', K. תֲּב Kal. fut. 1 pers. sing   כתב
    (§ 8. rem. 18.)

אֵל   (only 1 Ch. 20. 8. elsewhere (הָאֵל) and אֵלֶּה pron.
pl. com., *these*, used as the pl. of זֶה and זֹאת.—
Chald. id.

   אֵלַּיָן and אֵלֶּךְ Chald. id.

אֱל וֽ noun m. s. dec. 1 a., or def. of אֱיל (q.v.)   אול

אַל וֽ adv. of negation . . . אלל

אֶל וֽ more frequently אֶל, prop. constr. of אֵל
(following the analogy of לֵה, as if for אֱלֶה comp.
§ 27, V. § 36. rem. 2, 3, 4, hence) pl. constr. אֱלֵי,
with suff. אֵלַי, אֵלֶיךָ, אֵלָיו, אֲלֵיהֶם, once אֵלֵיהֶם,
poet. אֱלֵימוֹ, prep. expressing, in general, motion
or direction towards any thing, whether physically
or intellectually, but also a state of rest attained
to, equivalent to עַל.—I. *to*, sign of the dative
case, like לְ.—II. *to, towards*.—III. *about, concerning*.—IV. *for, on account of*.—V. *in, into*.—VI.
denoting rest, *at, on, near; among; through, by*.—
VII. with other particles its force is sometimes
entirely lost, אֶל־מֵחוּץ לְ, אֶל־אַחֲרַי *behind me*;
without; אֶל־תַּחַת יָדִי *under my hand*, 1 Sa. 21. 5;
אֶל־מִן *out of*, Job 5. 5.

אֵלָא pr. name masc. . . . אול

אַלְבֵּן Hiph. fut. 1 pers. sing. . . לבן

אַלְבִּישׁ Hiph. fut. 1 pers. sing. . . לבש

אַלְבִּשֶׁךָ וֽ id., suff. 2 pers. sing. fem.; וֽ for וֽ conv.   לבש

אַלְבִּשֶׁנָּה Kal fut. 1 pers. sing. [וְאַלְבָּשׁ], suff. 3 pers.
    sing. fem. (§ 16. rem. 12, & § 2. rem. 3)   לבש

אֶלְגָּבִישׁ noun masc. sing. . . . נבש

אַלְגּוּמִּים וֽ noun pl. masc., see אַלְמֻגִּים.

אֵלֵד וֽ Kal fut. 1 pers. sing.; וֽ for וֽ conv   ילד

אֶלְדָּד וֽאֶלְדָּעָה pr. names masc. . . אלה

אָלָה Root not used; Arab. *to worship, to adore*.
   אֱלֹהַּ masc. dec. 1; sing. and pl. (אֱלֹהִים).—I.
God, the true God, especially with the art. הָאֱלֹהִים.

—II. applied *to false gods*, or *idols*.—III. applied to
angels, Ps. 8. 6. אֱלֹהִים in the sense of the singular,
spoken of God, is followed by the verb or adj.
in the singular very rarely in the plural; comp.
Ge. 20. 13; 1 Sa. 17. 26; 2 Sa. 7. 23.

אֱלָהּ Chald. masc. dec. 1 a, *God*.

I. אָלָה denom. of אֵל (R. אוּל) prop. *to invoke God*.—I. *to
swear*.—II. *to curse*, Ju. 17. 2.—III. *to howl*, cogn.
יָלַל, אָלַל. Hiph. *to cause to swear*.

אָלָה fem. dec. 10. with suff. אָלָתִי.—I. *oath*, especially a covenant made by an oath.—II. *imprecation, curse, cursing*; שְׁבֻעַת הָאָלָה *an oath of
imprecation*, i. e. joined with cursing; הָיָה לְאָלָה
to be for a curse; נָתַן לְאָלָה *to give over unto
cursing*; לִשְׁאוֹל בְּאָלָה נַפְשׁוֹ *to wish a curse for
his soul*.

תַּאֲלָה fem. dec. 10, *curse*, La. 3. 65.

אֵל (with tseri pure) and אֱלִי in composition
with the following pr. names i. q. אֵל *God*, R. אוּל.

אֶלְדָּד (whom *God loves*, R. דוּד) pr. name masc.
Nu. 11. 26, 27.

אֶלְדָּעָה (whom *God calls*, דעא Arab. *to call*), pr.
name masc. Ge. 25. 4.

אֶלְזָבָד (whom *God has given*) pr. name masc.

אֶלְחָנָן (whom *God favours*) pr. name of one of
David's heroes.

אֱלִיאָב (*God is his father*) pr. name of several
men, especially—I. of a chief of the tribe of Zebulun.—II. of a brother of David.

אֱלִיאֵל (*God is his strength*) pr. name of several
men, especially—I. of a hero of David.—II. of a chief
of the tribe of Manasseh.—III. of a chief of the
tribe of Benjamin.

אֱלִיאָתָה (to whom *God comes*) pr. name masc.
1 Ch. 25. 4, called ver. 27 אֱלִיָּתָה (Simonis, *lamentation* from אלה).

אֶלְיָדָד (whom *God loves*, comp. אֶלְדָּד) pr. name
of a chief of Benjamin, Nu. 34. 21.

אֶלְיָדָע (whom *God knows*) pr. name of several
men, especially of a son of David, 2 Sa. 5. 16, for
which בְּעֶלְיָדָע 1 Ch. 14. 7.

אֵלִיָּהוּ (*God is He*, i. e. the Lord) pr. name
masc., see the following.

אֵלִיָּהוּא (id.) pr. name of several men, especially
of one of Job's friends, written also אֱלִיהוּ.

אֶלְיַחְבָּא (*God will hide* (protect) him) pr. name
of one of David's heroes, 2 Sa. 23. 32.

אֱלִיהׇרַף (*God is his recompense* חרף Arab. *to recompense*) pr. name masc. 1 Ki. 4. 3.

אֱלִימֶלֶךְ (*God is his king*) pr. name of the father-in-law of Ruth.

אֶלְיָסָף (*whom God has added*) pr. name masc.—I. of a chief of the tribe of Gad.—II. Nu. 3. 24.

אֱלִיעֶזֶר (*God is his help*) pr. name of several men, especially—I. of a servant of Abraham.—II. of the second son of Moses.

אֱלִיעֵינַי (*God is mine eye*, i. e. directs me) pr. name masc. 1 Ch. 8. 20.

אֱלִיעָם (*God's people*) pr. name masc.—I. 2 Sa. 11. 3, for which עַמִּיאֵל 1 Ch. 3. 5.—II. 2 Sa. 23. 34.

אֱלִיפַז (*God is strength*, or *precious*, R. פזז) pr. name masc.—I. of a son of Esau.—II. of a friend of Job.

אֱלִיפָל (*whom God judges*, R. פלל) pr. name masc. 1 Ch. 11. 35.

אֱלִיפְלֵהוּ (*whom God distinguishes*) pr. name masc. 1 Ch. 15. 18, 21.

אֱלִיפֶלֶט, אֱלִיפָלֶט (*God is his deliverance*) pr. name of various men.

אֱלִיצוּר (*God is his rock*) pr. name masc.

אֱלִיצָפָן, אֶלְצָפָן (*whom God protects*) pr. name masc.

אֱלִיקָא (*God's congregation*, comp. קָא, אֱלִיעָם for קָהָא Chald. *to congregate*) pr. name masc. 2 Sa. 23. 25.

אֶלְיָקִים (*God establishes* him) pr. name masc.—I. of a prefect of the palace under King Hezekiah.—II. of a king of Judah, afterwards changed to יְהוֹיָקִים.—III. Ne. 12. 41.

אֱלִישֶׁבַע (*God is her oath*) pr. name fem. Ex. 6. 23.

אֱלִישׁוּעַ (*God is his salvation*) pr. name of a son of David.

אֶלְיָשִׁיב (*God will restore*) pr. name of various men.

אֱלִישָׁמָע (*whom God hears*) pr. name masc.—I. of a son of David.—II. of a son of Ammihud, a chief of Ephraim.—III. of the grandfather of Ishmael who slew Gedaliah, comp. 2 Ki. 25. 25.—IV. of a priest in the time of Jehoshaphat, 2 Ch. 17. 8.—V. 1 Ch. 2. 41.

אֱלִישָׁע (*God is his salvation*, for אֵלִי יֵשַׁע) pr. name masc. prophet and successor of Elijah.

אֱלִישָׁפָט (*whom God judges*) pr. name masc. 2 Ch. 23. 1.

אֶלְנַעַם (*God is his delight*) pr. name masc. 1 Ch. 11. 46.

אֶלְנָתָן (*whom God has given*, i. e. given of God) pr. name masc.—I. of the grandfather of King Jehoiakim.—II. Ezr. 8. 16.

אֶלְעָד (apoc. for אֶלְעָדָה q. v.) pr. name masc. 1 Ch. 7. 21.

אֶלְעָדָה (*whom God adorns*) pr. name masc. 1 Ch. 7. 20.

אֶלְעוּזַי (*God my strength* or *praise*, for עֻזִּי R. עזז) pr. name masc. 1 Ch. 12. 5.

אֶלְעָזָר (*whom God helpeth*) pr. name of various men.

אֶלְעָלֵה, אֶלְעָלֵא (*God ascending*) pr. name of a town in the tribe of Reuben.

אֶלְעָשָׂה (*God has done it!*) pr. name of various men.

(פְּעֻלָּה) אֶלְפַּעַל (*God of recompense*, comp. פֹּעַל) pr. name of a man.

אֶלְקָנָה (*whom God created*) pr. name of various men, especially—I. of a son of Korah.—II. of the father of Samuel.

אֶלְתּוֹלַד (*God of posterity*, see תּוֹלֵד R. ילד) pr. name of a city.

אֶלְתְּקֵה, אֶלְתְּקֵא (*God of worship*, תקא Arab. *to fear*) pr. name of a city in the tribe of Dan.

אֶלְתְּקֹן (*God is its establishment*) pr. name of a city in the tribe of Judah, Jos. 15. 59.

II. אלה Arab. *to be stout, fat*, cogn. אגל.

אַלְיָה fem. the large *tail* of the eastern sheep.

אָלָה	noun fem. sing. dec. 10. (§ 42. rem. 2) . אלה
אָלֹה	Kal infin. absolute . . . . אלה
אֵלֶּה	Chald. Kh. אֵלֶּה, K. אֵל pron. demon. pl. . אל
אֱלוֹן	noun fem. sing.; also proper name masc. אול
אֱלָהּ	Chald. noun masc. sing. dec. 1a. . . אלה
אֵל	pron. demon. pl. ccm. gen. . . . אל
אַלָּה	noun masc. sing. dec. 1a. . . . אלה
אֱלָהָא, אֱלָהָא	Chald. n. m. s., emph. of אֱלָהּ dec. 1a; with pref. contr. [for וְאֶלָהָא] . אלה
אֱלָהֵהּ	Chald. id., suff. 3 pers. sing. masc. . אלה
אֱלָהֲהוֹן	Chald. id., suff. 3 pers. pl. masc. . אלה
אֱלָהֲהֹם	Chald. id., suff. 3 pers. pl. masc., ם by Hebraism for ן . . . . אלה
אֱלָהִי	Chald. id., suff. 1 pers. sing. . . אלה
אֱלֹהָי	in pause for אֱלֹהַי (q. v.) . . . אלה

אֱלֹהֵי   'וַ id. contracted [for וַיֵ']   אלה

אֱלֹהַי   } noun m. pl., suff. 1 pers. s. from אֱלֹוהַ   אלה
אֱלֹהָי   } dec. 1 a; with pref. contr. [for וַיֵ']

אֱלֹהֵי   } id. pl., construct state; with pref. id.   אלה
אֱלֹהֵי

אֱלָהַיָּא   Chald. noun masc. pl. emph from אֱלָה dec. 1 a.   אלה

אֱלֹהֶיהָ   noun masc. pl., suff. 3 pers. sing. fem. from אֱלֹוהַ dec. 1 a.   אלה

אֱלֹהֵיהֶם   } id., suff. 3 pers. pl. masc.; with pref. contr. [for וַיֵ']   אלה
אֱלֹהֵיהֶם

אֱלֹהֵיהֶן   id., suff. 3 pers. pl. fem.   אלה

אֱלֹהֵיו   } id., suff. 3 pers. sing. masc.; with pref. con. [for וַיֵ']   אלה
אֱלֹהֵיו

אֱלֹהֶיךָ   id., suff. 2 pers. sing. masc.   אלה

אֱלֹהַיִךְ   } id., suff. 2 pers. sing. fem.   אלה
אֱלֹהָיִךְ

אֱלֹהֵיךְ   'וַ id. id.; contracted [for וַיֵ']   אלה

אֱלֹהֵיךָ   id., suff., Kh. הָיֵ q. v., K. הִים (q. v.)   אלה

אֱלֹהֵיכֶם   id., suff. 2 pers. pl. masc.   אלה

הִים   } id. pl., absolute state; with pref. contr.   אלה
הִים   } [for וַיֵ']

אֱלֹהֵימוֹ   id., suff. 3 pers. pl. masc.   אלה

אֱלָהִין   Chald. noun masc. pl. abs. from אֱלָה dec. 1 a.   אלה

אֱלֹהֵינוּ   } noun m. pl., suff. 1 pers. pl. from אֱלֹוהַ dec. 1 a.; with pref. contr. [for וַיֵ']   אלה
אֱלֹהֵינוּ

אֱלָהָךְ   Chald. noun masc. sing., suff. 2 pers. sing. masc. from אֱלָה dec. 1 a.   אלה

אֱלָהֲכוֹן   Chald. id., suff. 2 pers. pl. masc.   אלה

אֱלָהֲכֹם   Chald. id., suff. 2 pers. pl. masc., ם by Hebraism for ן   אלה

אֲלֵהֶם   'וַ for אֲלֵי', prep. (אֶל), with pl. suff. 3 pers. pl. masc.   אל

אֲלֵהֶן   id., suff. 3 pers. pl. fem.   אל

אֱלָהֲנָא   Chald. noun masc. sing., suff. 1 pers. pl. from אֱלָה dec. 1 a.   אלה

אֲלוּ   ן Chald. i. q. אֲרוּ see! behold!

אִלּוּ   ן conj. (contr. from אִם־לֹא) if, though.

אֵלוֹ   Kh., for K. אֵלָיו (q. v.)   אל

אֵלוֹ   'וַ Kh. id.; noun masc. pl., suff. 3 pers. sing. masc. from אַיִל dec. 6 h.   אול

אֱלֹוהַ   'מ noun masc. sing. dec. 1 a; ן before (־)   אלה

אֱלֹהַי   } id. pl. with suff. 1 pers. sing.   אלה
אֱלֹהָי

אֱלִיל   Kh. אֲלֻל, K. אֱלִיל noun masc. sing. dec. 1 a; ן before (־)   אלל

אַלּוֹן   'ן noun masc. sing. dec. 1 b; also pr. name masc.   אלל

אֵלוֹן   'ן noun masc. sing. dec. 1 b; also pr. name m.   אול

אַלּוֹנֵי   noun masc. pl. construct from אַלּוֹן dec. 1 b.   אלל

אֵלוֹנֵי   noun masc. pl. construct from אֵלוֹן dec. 1 b.   אול

אַלּוֹנִים   noun masc. pl. absolute from אַלּוֹן dec. 1 b.   אלל

אַלּוּף   noun masc. sing. dec. 1 b.   אלף

אַלּוּפֵי   id. pl., construct state.   אלף

אַלּוּפִי   id. sing., suff. 1 pers. sing.   אלף

אַלּוּפֵיהֶם   id. pl., suff. 3 pers. pl. masc.   אלף

אַלּוּפֵינוּ   id. pl., suff. 1 pers. pl.   אלף

אָלוֹת   n.f., pl. of אָלָה d. 10 (§ 42. r. 2), or Kal inf. con.   אלה

אֶלְזָבָד   pr. name masc.   אלה

אָלַח   Niph. to be corrupt, in a moral sense.

אֶלְחַם   Kal fut. 1 pers. sing.   לחם

אֶלְחָנָן   pr. name masc.   אלה

אֵלַי   } prep. (אֶל) with pl. suff. 1 pers. sing.   אל
אֵלָי

אֵלֵי   id. pl., construct state.   אל

אֵילִי   noun masc. sing., suff. 1 pers. sing from אֵיל dec. 1 a.   אול

אֱלִי   Kal imp. sing. fem.   אלה

אֱלִי   defect. for אוּלִי adv.   אול

אֶלְיָדָע, אֶלְיָדָד, אֶלְיָאתָה   'ב, & אֱלִיאֵל   'ן, & אֱלִיאָב pr. names masc.; ן before (־)   אלה

אֵלֶיהָ   prep. (אֶל) with pl. suff. 3 pers. sing. fem.   אל

אֵלִיָּה   'ו, & אֵלִיָּהוּ pr. names masc.   אול

אֵלִיהוּ   'ב, & אֱלִיהוּא 'ן pr. names masc.; ן before (־)   אלה

אֵלֶיהֶם   'ב prep. (אֶל) with pl. suff. 3 pers. pl. masc.   אל
(towards the Lord are mine eyes, compare אֶל יְהוָה R. הוה) contr. אֵלִיוֹעֵינַי pr. name of various men.

אֱלֵיהֶם   noun masc. pl., suff. 3 pers. pl. masc. from אַיִל dec. 1 a.   איל

אֱלֵיהֶמָּה   noun masc. pl., suff. 3 pers. pl. masc. from אַיִל dec. 6 h. (§ 4. rem. 6)   איל

אֲלֵיהֶן   prep. (אֶל) with pl. suff. 3 pers. pl. fem.   אל

אֵלָיו   'ו id., suff. 3 pers. sing. masc.   אל

Je. 10. 11.   1 Ki. 1. 47.   Ezr. 7. 17, 18.   Da. 3. 17.   Ps. 143. 10.   Is. 44. 14.   Ps. 55. 14.   Joel 1. 8.   Eze. 31. 14.
Ju. 2. 3.   De. 32. 37.   Le. 17. 8.   Eze. 40. 29, 33.   Ps. 145. 1.   De. 11. 30.   Ge. 36. 19.   Ge. 24. 29.   Eze. 40. 16.
2 Sa. 7. 23.   Da. 2. 47.   Ex. 1. 19.   Job 24. 12.   Je. 14. 14.   Eze. 27. 6.   Ps. 141. 4.   2 Sa. 20. 3.   De. 24. 15
Ho. 4. 12.   Ps. 144. 14.   De. 29. 20.   Ho. 10. 4.

אֱלִיעֵינִי
אֶלְיוֹעֵנַי } pr. name masc., see אֶלְיְהוֹעֵינַי.

אֶלְיָחְבָּא, אֶלְיָחְרָף pr. names masc. . . . אלה

אֵלֶיךָ { prep. (אֶל) with pl. suff. 2 pers. sing. masc. אל

אֵלַיִךְ
וְאֵלַיִךְ } id. with suff. 2 pers. sing. fem. . אל

אֲלֵיכֶם id., suff. 2 pers. pl. masc. . . אל

אֱלִילֵי [וְ] n. masc. pl. construct from אֱלִיל dec. 1 a. אלל

אֱלִילִים
אֱלִילִם } id. pl., absolute state . . . אלל

אֵילִים noun masc., pl. of אַיִל or אֵיל dec. 6 h. or 1 a. אול

אֲלֵיהֶם prep. (אֶל) with pl. suff. 3 pers. pl. masc. . אל

אֱלִימֶלֶךְ pr. name masc. . . . . אלה

אֵלִין Kal fut. 1 pers. sing. R. לִין see . . לון

אִלֵּין Chald. pron. demon. pl. com. gen. . . אל

אֵלֵינוּ prep. (אֶל) with pl. suff. 1 pers. pl. . אל

אֱלִיפָז, אֱלִיעָם, וַאֱלִיעֵינַי נ׳, & אֱלִישָׁע, & אֱלִיסָף
& וַאֱלִיפֶלֶט, וַאֱלִיפְלֵהוּ, אֱלִיפָל, אֱלִיפָז,
אֶלְיָקָא, אֶלְיָסָבָן, אֱלִיצוּר נ׳, & אֱלִיפֶלֶט,
אֱלִישֶׁבַע אֱלְיָקִים (fem.), pr. names masc. אלה

אֱלִישָׁה pr. name of a region . . . אלש

נ׳ & אֱלִישָׁע נ׳, & אֱלִישָׁמָע וְ׳, & אֱלִישִׁיב נ׳,
אֱלִישָׁפָט pr. names masc. . . . אלה

אָלִית Kal preter. 2 pers. sing. fem. . . אלה

אֵלֵךְ, וְ
וְאֵלֵךְ וְ׳ & } Kal fut. 1 pers. sing. (§ 20. rem. 4); וָ for וְ conv. } ילך

אֵלֶךְ id.; Milêl before monos. . . . ילך

אִלֵּךְ Chald. pron. demon. pl. . . . אל

אֶלְכֹּד Kal fut. 1 pers. sing. . . . לכד

אֵלְכָה וְ]
אֵלְכָה } Kal fut. 1 pers. sing. with paragogic ה . ילך

אֲלֵכֶם def. [for אֵלַי] prep. (אֶל) with pl. suff. 2 pers. sing. masc. . . . . אל

אָלַל Root not used, in the deriv.—I. to be nothing.—II. to howl, cogn. יָלַל.—III. to be strong, cogn. אוּל.

אַל prop. subst. nothing, Job 24. 25.—Adv.—I. abs. nay! not so! אַל בְּנֹתַי nay, or not so, my daughters!—II. conj. that not; especially before the future, to express prohibition and dehortation; אַל יֵצֵא אִישׁ let no man go out; אַל אֵבוֹשָׁה let me not be ashamed; but rarely like

לֹא, as אַל יֶחֱרַשׁ he will not be silent, Ps. 50. 3 —III. once before a pret. interrogatively, 1 Sa. 27. 10.

אַל Chald. i. q. Heb. No. II.

אֵלָה fem terebinth, others, an oak, Jos. 24. 26.

אֵלוֹן masc. dec. 1 b.—I. an oak.—II. pr. name masc., 1 Ch. 4. 37.

אֱלוּל masc.—I. i. q. אֱלִיל, vanity, Je. 14. 14. Kheth.—II. Elul, the sixth month of the Hebrew year, answering nearly to our September, Ne. 6. 15. Its etymology is uncertain.

אֱלִיל masc. dec. 1 a.—I. adj. nought, vain, hence, pl. idols —II. vanity.

אֲלַי interj. expressive of grief, wo! alas!

אַלַּמֶּלֶךְ (the king's oak for אֵל הַמֶּלֶךְ, comp. fem. אֵלָה) pr. name of a place in the tribe of Asher, Jos. 19. 26.

אֱלִי def. for אֱלִיל noun masc. sing., dec. 1 a. . אלל

אֲלַי interj. . . . . אלל

אָלַם Kal not used, in the deriv. to bind. Niph.—I. to be dumb.—II. to be silent. Pi. to bind, as sheaves, Ge. 37. 7.

אֹלֶם masc. silence, Ps. 58. 2; is there indeed silence (when) ye ought to decree justice (though contrary to the accents), Ps. 56. 1; correctly Gesenius, the silent dove among strangers, designating the subject of the Psalm.

אִלֵּם masc. dec. 7 b, adj. dumb.

אֲלֻמָּה fem. dec. 10. pl. ־ים & ־וֹת, a sheaf of corn

אַלְמָן masc. adj forsaken, widowed, Je. 51. 5.

אַלְמֹן masc. widowhood, Is. 47. 9.

אַלְמָנָה fem. dec. 11 b.—I. a widow.—II. desolate places, Is. 13. 22.

אַלְמָנוּת fem. dec. 3 a, widowhood.

אַלְמֹנִי some one, a certain one, always joined with פְּלֹנִי.

אֵלֶם noun masc. sing. . . . . אלם

אִלֵּם adj. masc. sing. dec. 7 b. . . . אלם

אֵלֶם [וְ] not in all copies, for אוּלָם (q. v.) . אול

אֵלָם [וְ] accord. to some copies אֵלֶם for אוּלָם (q. v.) אול

אַלְמֻגִּים pl. almug-trees, a kind of precious wood, by some supposed to be the red sandal-wood. It is also found by transposition אַלְגּוּמִּים.

אֶלְמַד Kal fut. 1 pers. sing. . . . . למד

אֲלַמְּדָה	Piel fut. 1 pers. sing. with parag. ה .	למד
וֽאֶלְמְדָה	Kal fut. 1 pers. sing. (אֶלְמַד) with parag. ה	למד
אֲלַמֶּדְכֶם	Piel fut. 1 pers. sing., suff. 2 pers. pl. masc.	למד
אֲלַמְּדֵם	id., suff. 3 pers. pl. masc. . .	למד
וְאֵלַמּוֹ	noun masc. pl., suff. 3 pers. pl. masc. (§ 4. rem. 1) from [אֵילָם] dec. 8a.	אול
אַלְמוֹדָד	pr. name of a son of Joktan.	
אֵלַמּוֹת	n. m. with pl. fem. term. from אֵילָם dec. 8a.	אול
וְאֵלַמֵּי	noun masc. pl. constr. from אוּלָם dec. 8a.	אול
אֵלַמִּים	noun fem. with pl. masc. term. from אֲלֻמָּה dec. 10.	אלם
אִלְּמִים	adj. masc., pl. of אִלֵּם dec. 7b.	אלם
אַלַּמֶּלֶךְ	pr. name of a place . . .	אלל
אַלְמָן	adj. masc. sing. . . .	אלם
וְאַלְמֹן	noun masc. sing. . . .	אלם
אַלְמָנָה	noun fem. sing. dec. 11a. .	אלם
אַלְמָנוֹת	id. pl., absolute state . .	אלם
אַלְמְנוּת	noun fem. sing., constr. of [מָנוֹת] dec. 3c.	אלם
אַלְמְנֻתָהּ	id., suff. 3 pers. sing. fem.	אלם
אַלְמְנוֹתָו	noun fem. pl., suff. (K. תָיו, § 4. rem. 1) 3 pers. sing. masc. from מָנָה dec. 11a.	אלם
אַלְמְנוֹתֶיהָ	id., suff. 3 pers. sing. fem.	אלם
אַלְמְנוֹתָיו	id., suff. 3 pers. sing. masc.	אלם
וְאַלְמְנוֹתָיו	id., suff. 2 pers. sing. masc.	אלם
אַלְמְנוּתַיִךְ	noun fem. pl., suff. 2 pers. sing. fem. from [מָנוֹת] dec. 3a. . .	אלם
אַלְמֹנִי	adj. masc. sing. . . .	אלם
וְאַלְמְנֹתָיו	defect for אַלְמְנוֹתָיו (q. v.)	אלם
אַלְמָתִי	noun fem. sing., suff. 1 pers. sing. from [אֲלֻמָּה] dec. 10.	אלם
אֲלֻמֹּתָיו	id. pl., suff. 3 pers. sing. masc.	אלם
אֲלֻמֹּתֵיכֶם	id. pl., suff. 2 pers. pl. masc.	אלם
אִלֵּן	Chald. elsewhere אִלֵּין pron. demon. pl. com.	אל
אֶלְנַעַם	for אֶלְנָתָן & נַעַם pr. names masc. .	אלה
אֶלָּסָר	pr. name of a city, Ge. 14. 1, 9.	
אֶלְעָה	Kal fut. 1 pers. sing.	לעה
אֶלְעָד	אֶלְצָלָה, אֶלְעָלָא, אֶלְעָזָר, אֶלְעוּזַי, וֶאֶלְעָדָה, אֶלְעָשָׂה pr. names masc. . .	אלה
[אָלַף]	fut. תֶּאֱלַף (§ 13. rem. 5), to learn, only Pr. 22. 25. In the deriv. and prim. to accustom oneself, to become familiar; to join together, to associate, Pi. to teach.	

Hiph. denom. from אֶלֶף, to bring forth thousands

אַלּוּף adj. masc. dec. 1b.—I. tame, gentle, Je. 11. 19.—II. familiar, friend.—III. ox, bullock, Ps. 144. 14.—IV. head of a family or tribe.

אֶלֶף masc. dec. 6a. with suff. אַלְפִּי.—I. thousand; אֶלֶף אֲלָפִים a hundred thousand; אַלְפֵי רְבָבָה thousands of myriads.—II. family, as a subdivision of a tribe.—III. pl. oxen, comp. אַלּוּף.—IV. pr. name of a city, Jos. 18. 28.

אֶלֶף, אֲלַף (by Hebraism, Da. 7. 10.) Chald. masc. dec. 3a. thousand.

אֲלַף	Chald. noun masc. sing. dec. 3a. .	אלף
וֶאֱלֶף, אֱלֶף	noun m. sing. dec. 6a. (with suff. (אַלְפִּי); , see lett. ו	אלף
אַלְפָּא	Chald. noun m. sing., emph. of אֲלַף, dec. 3a.	אלף
אַלְפֵי	noun masc., pl. constr. from אֶלֶף dec. 6a. .	אלף
אַלְפִּי	id. sing., suff. 1 pers. sing.	אלף
אַלֻּפֵי	noun masc. pl. constr. from אַלּוּף dec. 1b.	אלף
אַלֻּפֶיךָ	noun masc. pl., suff. 2 pers. sing. masc. from אֶלֶף (q. v.) . .	אלף
אֲלָפִים וַ	id. pl. absolute state; וַ before (?)	אלף
אַלֻּפִים	noun masc., pl. of אַלּוּף dec. 1b. .	אלף
אַלְפַּיִם וְאַלְפַּיִם	noun masc., dual of אֶלֶף dec. 6a.	אלף
אֲלָפִים	Chald. by Hebraism for Keri אֲפִין pl. of אֲלַף (q. v.)	אלף
וֶאֶלְפַּעַל & אֶלְפָּעַל	for פֶלֶט (see אֱלִיפֶלֶט, אֶלְפֶּלֶט) pr. names masc. . .	אלה

אָלַץ Pi. to urge, press, Ju. 16. 16.

אֶלְצָפָן וַ pr. name masc. see אֱלִיצָפָן . . אלה

אַלְקוּם Pr. 30. 31. מֶלֶךְ אַלְקוּם עִמּוֹ a king against whom there is no rising up (from אַל not, and קוּם). Most of the moderns, a king with whom is the people, i. e. surrounded by his people, (אַל the Arab. art. and קוּם Arab. people). Prof. Lee, a king (having) provision with him (coll. with the Arab. לקם).

אֶלָּקַח Niph. fut. 1 pers. sing. . . לקח

וַאֲלַקְּטָה Piel fut. 1 pers. sing. with parag. ה (§ 10 rem. 7); וַ for וְ . . . לקט

אֶלְקָנָה וְ pr. name masc. . . . אלה

אֶלְקֹשִׁי gent. noun Elkoshite, spoken of the prophet Nahum, from a place אֶלְקֹשׁ, Na. 1. 1.

a Ps. 51. 15.	c Eze. 40. 21.	i Je. 51. 5.	m Ge. 38. 14, 19.	r Is. 44. 4.	u Da. 6. 7.	b Da. 5. 1.	f Je. 13. 21.	l 2 Ki. 2. 2.
b Ps. 119. 73.	f Eze. 40. 30.	k Is. 47. 9.	n Je. 15. 8.	o Ge. 37. 7.	v Pr. 1. 26.	e Da. 5. 1.	g Ju. 6. 15.	m Ru. 2. 7.
c Ps. 34. 12.	g Eze. 41. 15.	l Je. 18. 21.	p Eze. 22. 25.	p Ps. 126. 7.	w Da. 5. 1.	d Zec. 12. 5, 6.	h Da. 7. 10.	n Ru. 2. 2.
d Ps. 132. 12.	h Ge. 37. 7.		q 2 Sa. 20. 3.	q Je. 49. 11.	Ge. 37. 7.	Exr. 2. 69.	Ps. 8. 5.	

אָלָשׁ Root not used, whence

אֶלָּשׁ (according to the Talmud, *a crowd of people*) pr. name of a station in the wilderness, Nu. 33. 13.

אֱלָשָׁה pr. name of a region situated on the Mediterranean.

אֱלָתוֹ‎ noun fem. sing., suff. 3 pers. sing. masc. from אֵלָה dec. 10. (§ 42. rem. 2) . . . אלה

אֶלְתּוֹלַד‎ ‎} pr. name of a place . . . אלה

אֱלָתִי‎ noun fem. sing., suff. 1 pers. sing. from אֵלָה dec. 10. (§ 42. rem. 2) . . . אלה

אֶלְתְּקָא‎
אֶלְתְּקֵה‎ ‎} pr. name of a place . . . אלה

אֶלְתְּקֹן‎ } pr. name of a place . . . אלה

אֵם fem. dec. 8 b.—I. *mother*.—II. *grandmother*.—III. *mother-city* or *metropolis*.—IV. metaph. of a nation, also of the earth, Job 1. 21.—V. אֵם הַדֶּרֶךְ *mother* (i. e. head) *of the way*, i. e. a place whence two ways diverge.

אַמָּה fem. dec. 10.—I. *the fore-arm, cubitus*, prop. *the mother of the arm*; whence—II. *a cubit*, a measure; אַרְבַּע בָּאַמָּה *four by the cubit*, i. e. four cubits.—III. *mother-city*, or *metropolis*, 2 Sa. 8. 1.—IV. *basis* or *pedestal*, Is. 6. 4.—V. pr. name of a hill, 2 Sa. 2. 24.

אַמָּה Chald. fem. pl. אַמִּין, *a cubit*.

אִם ‎} mostly אִם.—I. conj. *if, supposing, that*; אִם—אִם *whether—or*; אִם in swearing is properly conditional, *if*, as in 1 Sa. 3. 17, *God do so to thee, and more so, if thou*, &c.; but the form of imprecation is elsewhere omitted, and it is conveniently rendered by a negation, *not*, and אִם לֹא by an affirmative.—II. *though, although*.—III. adv. *when*, referring either to time past or future; עַד אִם *till when, till that*.—IV. *surely, truly.*— V. interrog. i. q. הֲ *if? whether?* הַ—אִם, אִם—אִם *whether—or?* and without interrog. in an indirect inquiry.—VI. הַאִם i. q. הֲלֹא *is not?*—VII. אִם־לֹא *if not, unless*, compare also No. 1.

אֶמְאַס Kal fut. 1 pers. sing. . . . מאס

אֶמְאָסְךָ‎ } id., suff. 2 pers. sing. masc. (§ 2. rem. 2); ‎} for וַ conv. . . . מאס

אֲמַגֶּנְךָ Piel fut. 1 pers. sing., suff. 2 pers. sing. masc. . . . מגן

אֲמֹדֵד Piel fut. 1 pers. sing. . . . מדד

אָמָה ‎} fem. irr. (§ 45) *a maid-servant, handmaid, servant.* בֶּן־אָמָה

אַמָּה ‎} noun fem. sing. dec. 10. . . . אם

אַמָּה ‎} noun fem. sing., suff. 3 pers. sing. fem. from אֵם dec. 8 b. . . . אם

אַמַּיָּא Chald. noun fem. sing., pl. emph. אמם

אַמְהוֹת noun fem. pl., constr. of אֲמָהוֹת from אָמָה, irr. (§ 45) . . . אמה

אֲמָהָתִי id., suff. 1 pers. sing. . . . אמה

אַמְהָתֶיהָ id., suff. 3 pers. sing. fem. . . . אמה

אַמְהֹתֵיהֶם id., suff. 3 pers. pl. masc. . . . אמה

אַמְהֹתָיו id., suff. 3 pers. sing. masc. . . . אמה

אַמְהֹתֵיכֶם ‎} id., suff. 2 pers. pl. masc. . . . אמה

אִמּוֹ ‎} noun fem. sing., suff. 3 pers. sing. masc. from אֵם dec. 8 b. . . . אם

אָמוּט Niph. fut. 1 pers. sing. . . . מוט

אָמוֹן noun masc. sing., also pr. name . . . אמן

אֱמוּנָה ‎} noun fem. sing dec. 10; ‎} before (וַ) . . . אמן

אֱמוּנוֹת pl. of the preceding . . . אמן

אֱמוּנֵי Kal part. p. pl. masc. constr. from [אָמַן] dec. 3 a. . . . אמן

אֱמוּנִים id. pl. abs.; or noun masc., pl. of [אָמוּן] dec. 3 b. . . . אמן

אֱמוּנַת noun fem. sing., constr. of נָה dec. 10. . . . אמן

אֱמוּנָתוֹ ‎} id., suff. 3 pers. sing. masc.; ‎} before (וַ) . . . אמן

אֱמוּנָתִי ‎} id., suff. 1 pers. sing.; ‎} id. . . . אמן

אֱמוּנָתֶךָ‎
אֱמוּנָתְךָ ‎} id., suff. 2 pers. sing. masc.; ‎} before (וַ) . . . אמן

אָמוֹץ pr. name masc. . . . אמץ

אָמוֹר Kal inf. abs. . . . אמר

אַמּוֹת ‎} noun fem., pl. of אַמָּה dec. 10. . . . אם

אָמוּת Kal fut. 1 pers. sing. . . . מות

אַמּוֹת Kh. אַמּוֹת q. v., K. מֵאוֹת (q. v.) . . . מאה

אֲמָהוֹת noun fem., pl. of אָמָה dec. 10. . . . אמם

אָמוּתָה Kal fut. 1 pers. sing. with parag. ה . . . מות

אֶמְחֶה ‎} Kal fut. 1 pers. sing. . . . מחה

אֶמְחָנּוּ id., suff. 3 pers. sing. masc. . . . מחה

אֶמְחָצֵם ‎} Kal fut. 1 pers. sing., suff. 3 pers. sing. masc. (§ 16. rem. 12); ‎} for וַ conv. . . . מחץ

אַמְטִיר Hiph. fut. 1 pers. sing. . . . מטר

אָמִי pr. name masc., see אָמוֹן . . . אמן

אִמִּי ‎} n. fem. sing., suff. 1 pers. sing. from אֵם dec. 8 b. . . . אם

אַמַּיָּא Chald. noun fem. with pl. (emph.) masc. term. from אָמָה . . . אמם

אֲמִידְ noun masc. pl. with suff. 2 pers. sing. masc. from [אִים or אַיָּם] . . . אים

---

a Eze. 17. 16.   e Ex. 21. 32.   i Job 19. 15.   m De. 12. 12.   p Pr. 28. 20.   s Ps. 100. 5.   x 2 Ch. 6. 13.   b Ge. 46. 30.   Ps. 18. 39.
b Eze. 17. 19.   f Le. 25. 44.   k Da. 3. 29.   n Na. 2. 8.   q 2 Sa. 20. 19.   t Ps. 98. 3.   y Eze. 42. 16.   c De. 9. 14.   z 2 Sa. 22. 39.
c Ho. 4. 6.   g Da. 3. 29.   l Ge. 20. 17.   o Ps. 119. 75, 138.   r Is. 33. 6.   u Ps. 89. 25.   z Nu. 25. 15.   d Ex. 32. 33.   f Ps. 86. 16.
d Ho. 11. 3.   h 2 Sa. 6. 20.

אֲמִילֵם• Hiph. fut. 1 pers. sing. [אָמִיל], suff. **3 pers.** pl. masc. . . . . . מול

אֵמִים• noun masc. pl. abs. def. for אֵימִים (q. v.); also pr. name . . . . אים

אֲמִין Chald. noun fem., with pl. masc. term. from [אֲמָה] . . . . . אם

אַמִּיץ ־וְ adj. masc. sing. . . . אמץ

אֲמִיר noun masc. sing. . . . אמר

אֲמִיר• Hiph. fut. 1 pers. sing. . . מור

אֲמִישׁ Hiph. fut. 1 pers. sing. . . מוש

אֲמִית• Hiph. fut. 1 pers. sing. . . מות

אֲמִיתְךָ } id., suff. 2 pers. sing. masc. . מות
אֲמִיתֶךָ•

אֲמִיתֵךְ• id., suff. 2 pers. sing. fem. . מות

אֲמָךְ ־וְ } noun fem. sing., suff. 2 pers. sing.
אִמֵּךְ ־וְ } masc. from אֵם dec. 8 b. } אם
אִמֵּךְ ־וְ id., suff. 2 pers. sing. fem. . אם
אִמְּכֶם id., suff. 2 pers. pl. masc. . אם
אִמְּכֶן id., suff. 2 pers. pl. fem. . אם

[אָמַל] to languish, to be sick, Eze. 16. 30. Pul. (§ 6. No. 2) to languish, to droop, to waste away.

אֲמֵלָל adj. masc. feeble, only pl. אֲמֵלָלִים Ne.3.34.

אֻמְלָל adj. masc. languishing, wasting, Ps. 6. 3.

אֲמַלֵּא ־נָ Piel fut. 1 pers. sing.; וְ for וָ   מלא

אֲמַלְאָה• Niph. fut. 1 pers. sing. with paragogic ה (§ 9. rem. 5) . . . מלא

אֲמַלְאֵהוּ• וְ Piel fut. 1 pers. sing., suff. 3 pers. sing. masc. (§ 10. rem. 7); וְ for וָ   מלא

אֲמֻלָה• Kal part. p. sing. fem. from [אָמוּל] masc. . אמל

אֲמַלּוֹט• Kal fut. 1 pers. sing. . . . מלך

אֲמַלֵּט ־וְ Piel fut. 1 pers. sing.; וְ for וָ   מלט

אֶמָּלֵט• Niph. fut. 1 pers. sing. (§ 9. rem. 5)   מלט

אֲמַלְּטָה ־הָ id. with paragogic ה; וְ for וַ conversive   מלט

אֲמַלֶּטְךָ• Piel fut. 1 pers. sing., suff. 2 pers. sing. masc.   מלט

אֲמַלִּיךְ• וָ Hiph. fut. 1 pers. sing.; וְ for וָ conversive   מלך

אֲמְלֹךְ• Kal fut. 1 pers. sing. . . מלך

אֻמְלָל } Pulal preter. 3 pers. sing. masc.; adj.
אֻמְלָל ־וְ } Ps. 6. 3, (§ 6. No. 2) } אמל

אֻמְלְלָה } id. preter. 3 pers. sing. fem. (§ 8. rem. 7)
אֻמְלָלָה }

אֻמְלְלוּ } id. preter. 3 pers. pl.
אֻמְלָלוּ• }

אָמַם Root not used, Arab. to be related, cogn. עָמַם.

אָמָם (union?) 1. name of a city in the tribe of Judah, Jos. 15. 26.

אֹם masc. dec. 8 c. i. q. אֻמָּה, Ps. 117. 1

אֻמָּה fem. dec. 10. people, nation.

אֻמָּה Chald. pl. emph. אֻמַּיָּא id.

אִמָּם• noun fem. sing., suff. 3 pers. pl. masc. from אֵם dec. 8 b. . . . אם

[אָמַן] I. to stay, to support, La. 4. 5.—II. to nurse, to bring up; part. אֹמֵן, nursing-father, foster-father.—III. intrans. to be firm, true, faithful Niph.—I. to be borne, Is. 60. 4.—II. to be firm established, sure.—III. to be true, faithful. Hiph. —I. to trust, confide, believe in, rely upon, const. with בְּ, לְ.—II. for הֵימִין to turn to the right, Is. 30. 21.

אֲמַן Chald. Aph. to confide in; part. pass. true, faithful.

אָמוֹן masc.—I. Pr. 8. 30, foster-child. Prof. Lee, constant, unwearying. Others, artificer.— II. for הָמוֹן multitude, Je. 52. 15.—III. pr. name of various persons, especially of a king of Judah. Amon of Ne. 7. 59, is also called אָמִי Ezr. 2. 57.—IV. pr. name of an Egyptian idol Je. 46. 25.

אֵמוּן masc. (by Syriasm for אֱמוֹן), faithfulness, truth, De. 32. 20. Pl. אֵמֻנִים id. Ps. 31. 24.

אֱמוּנָה fem. dec. 10.—I. steadiness, Ex. 17. 12. —II. truth, Is. 33. 6.—III. faithfulness.

אֲמִינוֹן (faithful) pr. name i. q. אַמְנוֹן q. v.

אָמָּן masc. artificer, Ca. 7. 2.

אָמֵן masc.—I. truth, Is. 65. 16.—II. adv. Amen, so be it.

אֹמֶן masc. truth, faithfulness, Is. 25. 1.

אֲמָנָה fem.—I. covenant, Ne. 10. 1.—II. fixed allowance, Ne. 11. 23.—II. pr. name of a river and the region near Damascus.

אֲמֵנָה fem. a beam, lintel, 2 Ki. 18. 16.

אֹמְנָה fem.—I. education, nursing, Est. 2. 20.— II. adv. truly, indeed.

אַמְנוֹן (faithful) pr. name.—I. the eldest son of David, called אֲמִינוֹן 2 Sa. 13. 20.—II. 1 Ch. 4. 20.

אָמְנָם, אֻמְנָם adv. verily, truly, indeed, כִּי true that, it is true that.

אֱמֶת fem. (for אֱמֶנֶת) with suff. אֲמִתּוֹ (§ 37 No. 3).—I. firmness, stability.—II. faithfulness, fidelity.—III. truth, as opposed to falsehood.

---

a.118.10,11,12.   b Ho. 4.7.   f 1 Ki. 2.8.   k Ge. 37.10.   o Eze. 26.2.   r Eze. 20.33.   t 1 Sa. 27.1.   v 1 Sa. 12.1.   a Ho. 4.3.
Job 20. 25.   c Job 23. 13.   g 1 Sa. 19.17.   l Eze. 16.45.   p Ps. 81.11.   s Job 29.12.   u Job 1.15.   w 1 Ki. 1.5.   b Ho.2.7.
Is. 17.6.   d De. 32.39.   i Pr. 23.25.   m Ex. 31.3.   n Eze. 16.30.   q Is. 46.4.   z Je. 39.18.   cc Je.14.2.

אֲמִתַּי (*veracious*), pr. name of the father of the prophet Jonah.

הֵימָן (*faithful* for מְהֵימָן) pr. name of two different men.

מְהוּגְמָן (*faithful*), pr. name of a Persian eunuch. Est. 1. 10.

אֹמֶן noun masc. sing. . . . . . אמן

אָמֵן 'וְ subst. and adv. . . . . אמן

אָמוֹן pr. name masc. . . . . אמן

אָמֹנִי defect. for [אָמוֹן] noun masc. sing. dec. 3 b. אמן

אֹמֵן Kal part. act. sing. masc. dec. 7 b.   אמן

אֹמְן noun masc. sing. . . . . אמן

אֲמָנָה 'וְ noun fem. sing.; also pr. name, וְ before (דָ) אמן

אֻמְנָה noun fem. sing. . . . . אמן

אַמְנוֹן pr. name masc. . . . . אמן

אֹמְנַיִךְ Kal part. act. pl. masc., suff. 2 pers. sing. fem. from אֹמֵן dec. 7 b. . . אמן

אֳמָנִים noun masc., pl. of אֹמֶן dec. 3 b.   אמן

אָמְנָם
אֻמְנָם } adv.; from אֹמֶן with the term. ם‎ָ‎ אמן

אַמְנוֹן pr. name masc. . . . . אמן

וָאָמְנַע 'וְ Kal fut. 1 pers. sing.; וְ for וְ conv. מנע

אֲמֻנָתוֹ noun fem. sing., suff. 3 pers. sing. masc. from אֲמוּנָה dec. 10. . . . אמן

אֹמַנְתּוֹ Kal part. act. sing. fem. (אֹמֶנֶת) suff. 3 pers. sing. masc. dec. 13 a. (§ 8. rem. 19) אמן

אַמְסֶה Hiph. fut. 1 pers. sing. . . מסה

אָמְעַד [for עָד § 8. rem. 15], Kal fut. 1 pers. sing. . . . . מעד

[אָמֵץ] *to be strong, courageous.* Pi.—I. *to strengthen, make strong; to encourage.*—II. *to repair, restore.* —III. *to harden,* spoken of the heart. Hiph. *to strengthen, confirm.* Hithp. *to strengthen one-self, to take courage.*

אָמִיץ adj. *strong, powerful.*

אָמוֹץ (*strong*) pr. name of the father of the prophet Isaiah.

אָמֹץ adj. masc., only pl. אֲמֻצִּים (§ 32. rem. 5), *active, fleet,* or *vigorous.*

אֹמֶץ masc. *strength,* Job 17. 9.

אַמְצָה fem. id. Zec. 12. 5.

אַמְצִי (*strong*) pr. name masc.

אֲמַצְיָה (*whom the Lord strengthens*) pr. name of several men, especially,—I. of a king of Judah, also called אֲמַצְיָהוּ.—II. of an idolatrous priest. Am. 7. 10, sq.

מַאֲמָץ masc. only pl. c. מַאֲמַצֵּי *powers, forces,* Job 36. 19.

אַמֵּץ Piel imp. sing. masc. . . . אמץ

אַמֵּץ 'וְ defect. for אַמֵּיץ (q. v.) . . אמץ

אֱמַץ וַ
אֱמָץ וַ } Kal imp. sing. masc. (§ 8. rem. 11 & 12); וַ before (קָ) אמץ

אַמֵּץ וְ Piel fut. 3 pers. sing. masc. . אמץ

אֹמֶץ noun masc. sing. . . . אמץ

אֶמְצָא 'וְ Kal fut. 1 pers. sing.; וְ for וְ conv. מצא

אֶמְצָאֵהוּ 'וְ id., suff. 3 pers. sing. masc.   מצא

אֶמְצָאֲךָ
וְאֶמְצָאֲךָ } id., suff. 2 pers. sing. masc.; וְ for וְ conv. מצא

אֶמְצָה noun fem. sing. . . . אמץ

אַמְּצֵהוּ Piel imp. s. m. (אַמֵּץ), suff. 3 pers. s. m. אמן

אַמְּצוּ [for אַמְּצוּ] Piel imp. pl. masc. . אמץ

אָמְצוּ Kal preter. 3 pers. pl. . . אמץ

אִמְצוּ וְ id. imp. pl. masc. . . . אמץ

אַמְצִי pr. name masc. . . . אמץ

אֲמַצְיָה
אֲמַצְיָהוּ } pr. name masc.; וְ before (קָ) אמץ

אֲמַצְתִּיךָ Piel pret. 1 pers. sing., suff. 2 pers. sing. m. אמץ

אַמִּיצִים adj. masc., pl. of אַמִּיץ dec. 8 c. (§ 37. No. 2) אמץ

אִמַּצְתָּ
אִמַּצְתָּה } Piel pret. 2 pers. sing. masc. (§ 8. rem. 5) אמץ

אָמַר fut. יֹאמַר, וַיֹּאמֶר, with conjunctive accent (§ 19. rem. 2 & 1.)—I. *to say, declare,* (different from דִּבֶּר *to speak*) mostly followed by the words spoken, constr. with אֶל, לְ before the person *to* or *of* whom any thing is said, and rarely with an acc. comp. Ge. 43. 27, De. 1. 39, Ps. 139. 20.—II. *to command.*—III. *to think,* either followed by בְּלֵב, לְלֵב or not. Niph.—I. *to be said,* constr. with אֶל, לְ; impers. *it is said, on dit.*—II. *to be called,* constr. with לְ. Hiph. *to cause to say, promise,* De. 26. 17, 18. Hithp. *to peak of oneself, to boast oneself,* Ps. 94. 4.

אֲמַר Chald. (§ 53. No. 1. & § 49. rem. 1.)—I. *to say.*—II. *to command.*

אָמִיר masc., English version, *bough, branch.* Others, *top, summit,* lit. something prominent, manifest; or simply from the idea of *height,* supposed to be contained in the root. Prof. Lee, the *pod* which contains the fruit of the palm tree.

אֹמֶר masc. dec. 6 b.—I. *word, discourse.*—II. *appointment, declaration,* Job 20. 29.

---

a Ca. 7. 2.	e Ne. 10. 1.	i Ge. 18. 13.	= 2 Sa. 4. 4.	p Na. 2. 2.	s Job 17. 9.	v Ca. 8. 1.	d De. 3. 26.
b De. 32. 20.	f Ne. 11. 23.	k Ese. 31. 15.	n Ps. 6. 7.	q 2 Sa. 15. 12.	t Ne. 7. 5.	y Pr. 7. 15.	e Je. 35. 3.
c Mat. 3. 7.	g Is. 49. 23.	l 1 Sa. 26. 23.	o Ps. 26. 1.	r De. 2. 30.	u Job 23. 3.	z Zec. 12. 5.	f Is. 41. 19.
d Is. 20. 4.	h Is. 26. 2.						

z Zec. 6. 3.   g Ps. 80. 19.   h Ps. 63. 16.

4

אִמְרָה & אֶמְרָה fem. dec. 12 b. *word, saying, discourse.*

אִמַּר Chald. only pl. אִמְּרִין *lambs.*

אָמִיר (*loquacious*, others, *tall*, comp.) (אָמִיר) pr. name of two different men.

אֹמֶר m.—I. *word, saying, discourse.*—II. *thing, matter,* Job 22. 28.

אֹמֵר (*eloquent,* others, *tall,* comp. אָמִיר) pr. name of a man.

אֱמֹרִי gent. noun *Amorite,* collect. *Amorites,* a Canaanitish people. Simonis conjectures its signification to be *mountaineer,* comp. אָמִיר.

אִמְרִי (*eloquent*) pr. name of two different men.

אֲמַרְיָה, אֲמַרְיָהוּ (*whom* the Lord *promised*) pr. name of several men, especially of two high-priests.

מַאֲמָר masc. only constr. מַאֲמַר *edict, command.*

מֵאמַר Chald. masc. id.

אָמַר } Kal pret. 3 pers. sing. masc. (compare }
אָמֵר } § 8. rem. 7) . . . . }

אָמַר וַ} Chald. Peal part. act. sing. masc. dec. 2 a. (§ 49. No. 4)

אֲמַר וַ Ch. id. pret. 3 pers. sing. masc.; וַ before (‑ְ)

אֱמֹר Kh. אָמַר q. v., K. אָמְרוּ (q. v.) .

אָמֹר Kal inf. abs. . . . . .

אֱמָר־ id. inf. constr., with Mak. for אֱמֹר (§ 8. r. 18)

אֱמָר־ id. imp. sing. masc. with Mak. for אֱמֹר (§ 8. rem. 13) וַ before (‑ְ)

אֱמַר }
אֱמַר } Chald. Peal imp. sing. masc. (§ 49. No. 2)

אֱמֹר Kal inf. constr. or imp. sing. masc. .

אֹמֶר וַ pr. name masc. . . . .

אֹמַר ‑וַ, ‑וָ, Kal fut. 1 pers. sing. (§ 19. rem. 2 & 1); וָ for וַ conv. .

אֹמֵר id. part. act. sing. masc. dec. 7 b.

אֹמֶר noun masc. sing. . . . .

אָמְרָה וַ Kal pret. 3 pers. sing. fem.

אֹמְרָה ‑וָ, ‑וָ; id. fut. 1 pers. sing. with parag. ה; וָ for וַ conv. . . .

אֲמַרוּ Chald. Peal pret. 3 pers. pl. masc. (§ 49. No. 2)

אָמְרוּ וַ Kal pret. 3 pers. pl. .

אֱמַרוּ Chald. Peal imp. pl. masc. (§ 49. No. 2) .

אִמְרוֹ noun masc. sing., suff. 3 pers. sing. masc. from [אֹמֶר] dec. 6 b. . . .

אִמְרוּ וַ Kal imp. pl. masc. . . .

אֲמָרוֹת noun fem., pl. of [אִמְרָה] dec. 12 b. .

אֲמָרוֹת id. pl., construct state . . אמר

אֹמְרָה ‑וָ Kal fut. 1 pers. sing. with parag. ה; וָ for וַ conversive . . . מרט

אֹמְרֵם id., suff. 3 pers. pl. masc.; וָ id. . מרט

אֲמָרַי } noun masc. pl., suff. 1 pers. sing. from }
אֲמָרָי } [אֹמֶר] dec. 6 b. . . . } אמר

אִמְרִי gent. noun masc. . . . אמר

אִמְרֵי noun masc. pl. constr. from [אֹמֶר] dec. 6 b. אמר

אִמְרִי pr. name masc. . . . . אמר

אִמְרִי Kal imp. sing. fem. . . . אמר

אָמְרִי Kal inf., suff. 1 pers. sing. . אמר

אֲמָרֶיהָ noun masc. pl., suff. 3 pers. sing. fem. from [אֹמֶר] dec. 6 b. . . . אמר

אֲמַרְיָה }
אֲמַרְיָהוּ } pr. name masc.; וָ before (‑ְ) . אמר

אֲמָרָיו noun masc. pl., suff. 3 pers. sing. masc. from [אֹמֶר] dec. 6 b. . . . אמר

אִמְרֵיכֶם id., suff. 2 pers. pl. masc. . אמר

אֲמָרִים id. pl., absolute state . . אמר

אֹמְרִים וָ Kal part. act. masc., pl. of אֹמֵר dec. 7 b. . אמר

אָמְרִין וַ Chald. Peal part. act. masc., pl. of אֲמַר dec. 2 a. (§ 49. No. 4) אמר

אִמְּרִין וַ Chald. noun masc., pl. of [אִמַּר] dec. 2 b. אמר

אִמְרֵךָ Kal inf., suff. 2 pers. sing. masc., (§ 16. r. 7) אמר

אִמְרֵךְ id., suff. 2 pers. sing. fem. . . אמר

אִמְרֵכֶם id., suff. 2 pers. pl. masc. comp. אֲמָרְךָ . אמר

אֲמַרְנָא Chald. Peal pret. 1 pers. pl. (§ 49. No. 2) אמר

אָמַרְנוּ וַ Kal pret. 1 pers. pl. . . . אמר

אַמְרָפֶל וַ pr. name of a king of Shinar in the time of Abraham, Ge. 14. 1, 9.

אֲמָרֵר Piel fut. 1 pers. sing. [for אֲאַמְרֵר] . מרר

אָמַרְתָּ }
אָמַרְתְּ } Kal pret. 2 pers. sing. masc. (§ 8. r. 7) אמר

אָמַרְתָּ וַ id. id.; acc. shifted by conv. וָ (§ 8. rem. 7) אמר

אָמַרְתְּ וַ id. pret. 2 pers. sing. fem. . אמר

אַמְרֵת Chald. Peal pret. 1 pers. sing. (§ 49. No. 2) אמר

אַמְרַת וַ Chald. id. pret. 3 pers. sing. fem. (§ 49. No. 2. and rem. 1); וָ before (‑ְ) אמר

אִמְרַת noun fem. sing. constr. of [אִמְרָה] dec. 12 b. אמר

אֹמְרֶת Kal part. act. sing. fem. (§ 8. rem. 19) אמר

אֲמָרֹת id. id. pl. dec. 13 a. . . . אמר

אִמְרָתוֹ noun fem. sing., suff. 3 pers. sing. masc. [from אֶמְרָה] . . . . אמר

אִמְרָתוֹ noun fem. sing., suff. 3 pers. sing. masc. from [אִמְרָה] dec. 12 b. . . . אמר

אָמַרְתִּי }
אָמַרְתִּי } Kal pret. 1 pers. sing. (§ 8. rem. 7) אמר

• 1 Sa. 13. 19.   d Eze. 13. 15.   g Da. 4. 23.   k Ps. 12. 7.   n Ne. 13. 25.   r Eze. 35. 10.   t Is. 22. 4.   y Je. 36. 22.   • Ps. 147. 15.
b Pr. 25. 7.   e Pr. 28. 24.   h Da. 2. 9.   i Ps. 12. 7.   o Is. 41. 26.   s Je. 23. 33.   u Da. 4. 5.   z La. 2. 17.   • Ps. 40. 11.
c Da. 2. 4.   f Ge. 46. 31.   i Job 20. 29.   m Ezr. 9. 3.   p Ezr. 6. 9.   q Ezr. 5. 4.   x Da. 5. 10.

אָמַרְתִּי וְ } Kal pret. 1 pers. s.; acc. shifted by conv. ו (§ 8. rem. 7)	אמר
אִמְרָתִי noun fem. sing., suff. 1 pers. sing. from [אִמְרָה] dec. 12 b. . . .	אמר
אִמְרָתֶךָ / אִמְרָתְךָ } id., suff. 2 pers. sing. masc.	אמר
אִמְרָתֵךְ id., suff. 2 pers. sing. fem. . .	אמר
אֲמַרְתֶּם וַ Kal pret. 2 pers. pl. masc.; ו for conv. ו	אמר
אֶמֶשׁ / אָמֶשׁ } prop. past night—I. adv. *last night, yesterday.*—II. *night, darkness,* Job 30. 3.	
אֲמָשְׁךָ וַ Kal fut. 1 pers. sing. [אָמוּשׁ], suff. 2 pers. sing. masc.; ו for ו .	מוש
אֶמְשְׁכֵט Kal fut. 1 pers. sing., suff. 3 pers. pl. masc.	משך
אֶמְשֹׁל Kal fut. 1 pers. sing.	משל
אָמֵת וּ } for אָמוּת, Kal fut. 1 pers. sing. (compare § 28. rem. 7) . .	מות
אַמַּת noun fem. sing., constr. of אַמָּה dec. 10.	אם
אַמֹּת pl. of the preceding . . .	אם
אֲמָת וַ } noun fem. sing., contr. [for אֲמֶנֶת], with suff. אֲמִתּוֹ (§ 37. No. 3) . .	אמן
אֲמָתָהּ noun fem. sing., suff. 3 pers. sing. fem. from אָמָה irr. (§ 45) . .	אמה
אֲמָתוֹ וַ id., suff. 3 pers. sing. masc.; ו before (‑:)	אמה
אֲמִתּוֹ וַ noun fem. sing., suff. 3 pers. sing. masc. from אֱמֶת (q. v.); ו id. .	אמן
אֲמִתוֹ וּ noun fem. sing., suff. 3 pers. sing. masc. from אֵימָה dec. 10. .	אים
אַמְתַּחַת noun fem. sing. dec. 13 a. .	מתח
אַמְתְּחֹת id., pl. . . .	מתח
אַמְתַּחְתּוֹ id. sing., suff. 3 pers. sing. masc.	מתח
אַמְתְּחֹתֵיכֶם id. pl., suff. 2 pers. pl. masc.	מתח
אַמְתְּחֹתֵינוּ id. pl., suff. 1 pers. pl.	מתח
אֲמָתִי noun fem. sing., suff. 1 pers. sing. from אָמָה irr. (§ 45) . .	אמה
אֲמִתַּי pr. name masc. . .	אמן
אַמָּתַיִם וַ noun fem., dual of אַמָּה dec. 10.	אם
אֲמֹתֵינוּ n. fem. pl., suff. 1 pers. pl. from אֵם dec. 8 b.	אם
אֲמָתֶךָ בַּ / נַ } noun fem. sing., suff. 2 pers. sing. masc. from אָמָה irr. (§ 45); ו bef. (‑:) }	אמה
אֲמִתְּךָ בַּ } noun fem. sing., suff. 2 pers. sing. masc. from אֱמֶת (q. v.); ו id. }	אמן
אֲמֹתָם noun fem. pl., suff. 3 pers. pl. masc. from אֵם dec. 8 b. .	אם
אֲמָתְנִי וַ Ch. adj. masc. sing. by apoc. [for אֲמָתְנִית]	מתן
אֲמִתְתָהוּ וַ Pilel fut. 1 pers. sing., suff. 3 pers. sing. masc.; ו for ו.	מות
אֵן interrog. adv. . . .	אי

אֹן pr. name for און	און
אָנָּא (*anna,* with double accent except Ps. 118. 25. before a penacute) interj. of entreaty, *I pray,* &c.; also written אָנָּה.	
אֲנָא Ch. pers. pron. sing. com. *I,* also written אֲנָה	
אַנְבֵּהּ וְ Ch. [for אַבֵּהּ], n. m. s. with suff. 3 p. s. m. from אַב dec. 5 b. (comp. § 52. rem. 2)	אבב
אַנְדַּע וְ Chald. Peal fut. 1 pers. sing. [for אֶדַּע] (§ 52. rem. 2)	ידע

I. [אָנָה] *to sigh, to mourn.*
אֲנִיָּה fem. *mourning, sorrow.*
תַּאֲנִיָּה fem. id.
אֲנִיעָם (*mourning of the people*) pr. name masc. 1 Ch. 7. 19.

II. אָנָה Kal not used, Arab. *to meet; to be in good time.* Pi. *to cause to come, or happen,* Ex. 21. 13. Pu. *to befall* any one. Hithp. *to seek occasion against* any one, const. with ל, 2 Ki. 5. 7.
אֳנִי masc. *ship,* collect. *ships, a fleet.*
אֳנִיָּה fem. dec. 10. *a ship.*
אֳנִיּה fem. id. 2 Ch. 8. 18. Kheth.
תַּאֲנָה fem. dec. 10. *sexual impulse,* Je. 2. 24.
תֹּאֲנָה fem. *occasion, cause,* Ju. 14. 4.
תַּאֲנַת שִׁלֹה (*approach to Shiloh*) pr. name of a place in Ephraim, Jos. 16. 6.

אָנָה i. q. אָנָּא (q. v.) . . .	אנא
אָנָה וְ, וְ, interrog. adv. (אָן) with parag. ה; ו see lett. ו .	אי
אֲנָה וַ Chald. for אֲנָא (q. v.) . .	אנא
אָנָה adv. (אָן) with parag. ה . .	אי
אִנָּה Piel pret. 3 pers. sing. masc. .	אנה
אֶנְהָגֵךְ Kal fut. 1 pers. sing. [אֶנְהַג], suff. 2 pers. sing. masc. (§ 16. rem. 12) .	נהג
אָנוּ וְ Kal pret. 3 pers. pl. . .	אנה
אֹנוֹ noun masc. sing., suff. 3 pers. sing. masc. from אוֹן or אָנֶן dec. 1. or 6 g.	און
אוֹנוֹ וְ pr. name of a place . . .	און
אֲנִיחֶנּוּ וְ Hiph. fut. 1 pers. sing., suff. 3 pers. sing. m.	נוח
אָנוּחַ Kal fut. 1 pers. sing.	נוח
אִנּוּן Chald. pron. pers. pl. masc. *they,* fem. אִנִּין	
אֲנוּסָה Kal fut. 1 pers. sing. with parag. ה .	נוס
אֲנִיעֶךָ [Kh. אָנוּ], [K. אָנִי], Kal or Hiph. fut. 1 pers. sing., suff. 2 pers. sing. masc.	נוע
אָנוּשׁ Kal part. pass. sing. masc. .	אנש

a Is. 29. 4, 4.   d Ju. 8. 23.   g Ex. 2. 5.   l Ge. 44. 2.   o Ge. 30. 3.   r Ps. 71. 22.   u Da. 4. 11.   x Ex. 21. 13.   a Hab. 3. 16.
b Ge. 31. 42.   f 2 Sa. 19. 28.   h Ps. 91. 4.   m Ge. 44. 1.   p Job 31. 13.   s Da. 7. 7.   v Da. 4. 9, 18.   b Ca. 8. 3.   y Ex. 14. 25.
c Ge. 27. 21.   i Je. 51. 13.   j Job 9. 34.   n Ge. 43. 12.   q La. 5. 3.   t 2 Sa. 1. 10.   w Da. 2. 9.   z Ex. 15. 2.   s Sa. 15. 20.
d Ho. 11. 4.

אֱנוֹשׁ noun masc. sing., pl. אֲנָשִׁים irr. (comp. אִישׁ
§ 45) ; also pr. name . . . אנש

אֲנוֹשָׁא Chald. Kh. אֲנָשָׁא as if from אֱנָשׁ, K.
אֲנָשָׁא q. v. (§ 68) . . . אנש

אֶאֱנוֹשָׁה וְ Kal fut. 1 pers. sing. witl. parag. ה ; ו for
וְ conv. . . . נוש

אֲנוּשָׁה Kal part. pass. sing. fem. from אֱנוֹשׁ masc. . נש

אָנַח Niph. to sigh, const. with מִן עַל.
אֲנָחָה fem. dec. 11 c. suff. אַנְחָתִי (§ 42. rem. 1)
sighing, sigh.

אֲנָחָה וְ noun fem. sing. dec. 11 c. (§ 42. rem. 1) ;
וְ before (-ָ) . . . אנח

אַנִּחֶהוּ וְ Hiph. fut. 1 pers. sing., suff. 3 pers. sing. m. נחח

אֲנַחֵם Niph. fut. 1 pers. sing. . . suff. נחם

אֲנַחֲמֵךְ וְ Piel (§ 14. rem. 1) fut. 1 pers. sing., suff.
2 pers. sing. fem. ; וְ for וְ . . נחם

אֲנַחֶמְכֶם id., suff. 2 pers. pl. masc. (§ 16. rem. 15) נחם

אֲנַחְנָא
אֲנַחְנָה } Chald. pron. pers. 1 pers. com. we.

אֲנַחֶנָּה Hiph. fut. 1 pers. sing., suff. 3 pers. sing. fem.
(§ 24. rem. 21) . . . . נחח

אֲנַחְנוּ
נַ אֲנַחְנוּ } pers. pron. 1 pl. com. we, by aphæresis
נַחְנוּ.

אֲנָחֲרַת וְ pr. name of a city belonging to the tribe
of Issachar, Jos. 19. 19.

אֲנַחְתָּה noun fem. sing. (אֲנָחָה) with paragogic ה
dec. 11 c. (§ 42. rem. 1)

אֲנַחְתִּי וְ id., suff. 1 pers. sing. . . אנח

אֲנַחְתֵי id. pl., suff. 1 pers. sing. . . אנח

אֲנִי
נ אֲנִי } pers. pron. 1 pers. sing. com. I, i. q. אָנֹכִי

אֳנִי (vo-ŏnee'), noun masc. sing.; וְ before (-ָ)
for וְ . . . אנה

אֲנִיָּה וְ noun fem. sing.; וְ before (-ָ) . אנה

אֳנִיָּה noun fem. sing. dec. 10. . . אנה

אֳנִיּוֹת (vo-ŏniy-') id. pl.; וְ before (-ָ) for וְ . אנה

אֲנִין Chald. fem. of אִנּוּן (q. v.)

אֲנִיעָה וְ Hiph. fut. 1 pers. sing with paragogic ה . נוע

אֶאֱנָעֵם וְ pr. name masc. . . . אנה

אֲנִינֹת noun fem., pl. of אֲנִיָּה dec. 10. . אנה

אֲנָךְ masc.—I. lead.—II. plummet, Am. 7. 7, 8.

אָנֹכִי וְ pers. pron. 1 pers. sing. com. I, whence the
shorter form אֲנִי.

אָנַן. Hithpo. to complain, murmur.

[אָנַם] to urge, compel, only part. אֹנֵם, Est. 1. 8.
אֲנַם Chald. to trouble, only part. אֲנֵם, Da. 4. 6.

אֲנַסֶּה Piel fut. 1 pers. sing. . . נסה

אֲנַסֶּכָה Piel fut. 1 pers. sing., suff. 2 pers. sing. masc.
(§ 2. rem. 2) . . . נסה

אֲנַסֶּנּוּ id., suff. 3 pers. sing. masc. . נסה

אֶאֱנַעֲלֵךְ וְ Kal fut. 1 pers. sing., suff. 2 pers. sing. fem.
(§ 16. rem. 12); וְ for וְ conv. . נעל

אֶאֱנָעֵר וְ Niph. fut. 1 pers. sing. (§ 9. rem. 5) . נער

[אָנַף] to breathe through the nose, snort; hence to be
angry, construed with בְּ. Hithp. to be or become
angry.

אֲנַף Chald. masc. dec. 3 a. face, comp. אַף.

אֲנָפָה fem. an unclean bird, according to
Bochart, a species of eagle.

אַף (for אֲנַף=אָנַף) masc. with suff. אַפִּי dec. 8 d.
(§ 37. No. 3).—I. nose.—II. anger, אַף בַּעַל
אִישׁ אַף an angry man. Dual אַפַּיִם.—I. the
nostrils.—II. meton. face, countenance; אַפַּיִם
אַרְצָה the face to the ground; לְאַפִּי at the face
of, before.—III. two persons, אַפַּיִם אַחַת מָנָה a
portion of two persons, i. e. a double portion.—
IV. anger; אֶרֶךְ אַ slow to anger, קְצַר אַ quick
to anger, impatient.

אַנְפּוֹהִי Chald. noun masc. pl., suff. 3 pers. sing.
masc. from [אֲנַף] dec. 3 a. . . אנף

אָנַפְתָּ Kal pret. 2 pers. sing. masc. . אנף

אָנַפְתָּ וְ id.; acc. shifted by conv. וְ (§ 8. rem. 7) אנף

אֶאֱנָּצְלָה Niph. fut. 1 p. sing. with parag. ה (§ 9. r. 5) נצל

אָנַק fut. יֶאֱנַק to groan. Niph. to moan, lament.
אֲנָקָה fem. construct אֶנְקַת (§ 42. rem. 1).—I.
a groaning, lamentation.—II. a kind of lizard
Le. 11. 30.

אֲנָקָה וְ noun fem. sing., dec. 11 c. construct אֶנְקַת
(§ 42. rem. 1) . . . אנק

אֲנַקֶּךָ Piel fut. 1 pers. sing., suff. 2 pers. sing.
masc. (§ 24. rem. 21. & § 2. rem. 1) נקה

אֶאֱנָקְמָה וְ Niph. fut. 1 pers. sing. with paragugic ה
(§ 9. rem. 5) . . . נקם

אֶנְקַת noun fem. sing., const. of אֲנָקָה dec. 11 c.
(§ 42. rem. 1) . . . אנק

[אָנַשׁ] only in part. pass. in Kal.—I. incurable, mortal.—
II. trop. grievous, sorrowful, of pain, of a day;
malignant, of the human heart.

---

a Da. 4. 13, 14.   d Is. 57. 18.   g Is. 66. 13.   i Is. 21. 2.   n 1 Ki. 9. 26.   p Da. 7. 17.   r Ec. 2. 1.   t Eze. 16. 10.   v Ps. 69. 15.
b Ps. 69. 21.   e Is. 51. 19.   h Esr. 4. 16.   l Ps. 38. 10.   o Is. 60. 9.   q Job 18. 4.   s Ex. 16. 4.   u Ju. 16. 20.   y Mal. 2. 15.
c Is. 35. 10.   f La. 2. 13.   i Job 31. 18.   m La. 1. 22.   Ge. 49. 13.

אֱנ֫וֹשׁ masc. (see אִישׁ § 45).—I. *man, mankind.*
—II. *the common people.*—Pl. אֲנָשִׁים, construct
אַנְשֵׁי, with suff. אֲנָשָׁי, *men,* commonly used for
אִישִׁים the plural of אִישׁ.—III. pr. name masc.
grandson of Adam.

אֲנָשׁ, אֱנָשׁ Chald. masc. irr. (§ 68) *man, mankind.*
אִשָּׁה f. irr. (§ 45) pl. נָשִׁים.—I. *woman, female;*
אִשָּׁה פִּלֶגֶשׁ *a concubine;* אִשָּׁה אַלְמָנָה *a widow.*
II. *wife.*—III. *every one;* אִ־רְעוּת אִ־אָחוֹת
one-another. Comp. also אֵשֶׁת under אִישׁ.

אֱנֹשׁ	ו defect. for אֱנוֹשׁ (q. v.) . . .	אנש
אֱנָשׁ, וֶאֱנָשׁ	Chald. noun masc. sing. (§ 68) ; ו before (ֶ) . .	אנש
אֲנָשָׁא, אֱנָשָׁא	Chald. id., emph. state . . .	אנש
אֱנָשֵׁא	Niph. fut. 1 pers. sing. . . .	נשא
אֲנָשַׁי	noun masc. pl., suff. 1 pers. sing. [as if from אֱנוֹשׁ], see אֱנוֹשׁ (& אִישׁ § 45)	אנש
אַנְשֵׁי	ו id. pl., construct state . .	אנש
אֲנָשֶׁיהָ	id. pl., suff. 3 pers. sing. fem.	אנש
אַנְשֵׁיהֶם	ו id. with suff. 3 pers. pl. masc. .	אנש
אַנְשֵׁיהֶן	id. pl., suff. 3 pers. pl. fem.	אנש
אֲנָשָׁיו	ו id. pl., suff. 3 pers. sing. m.; ו before (ֶ)	אנש
אֲנָשֶׁיךָ	ו id. pl., suff. 2 pers. sing. masc.; ו id.	אנש
אֲנָשִׁים	ו id. pl., absolute state, Chald. Da. 4. 14.	אנש
אֲנָשֵׁינוּ	id. pl., suff. 1 pers. pl. .	אנש
אַנְתְּ, וְאַנְתְּ	Kheth. אַנְתָּה Chald. pers. pron. 2 pers. s. masc. *thou.* For ב comp. § 1. r. 2.	
אַנְתּוּן	אַנְתּוּן Chald. pl. of the preceding, *you, ye,* Da. 2. 8.	

אַתָּה (for אַנְתָּה but compare § 1. rem. 2)
thou, in pause אָתָּה.

אַתְּ *thou,* f., in Kh. אַתִּי, read אַתִּי (§ 1. r. 2)
אַתֶּם *you, ye,* fem. אַתֶּן, with parag. ה, אַתֵּנָה.

אֲנַתְּחֶהָ	ו Piel fut. 1 p. s., suff. 3 p. s. fem.; ו for ו	נתח
אֲנַתֵּק	Piel fut. 1 pers. sing. . .	נתק
אָסָא	ו pr. name masc. . . .	אסה
אֲסוֹבְבָה	ו Pilel fut. 1 p. s. with parag. ה; ו bef. (ֶ) Ps. 26. 6.	סבב
אֶסְבֹּל	Kal fut. 1 pers. sing. .	סבל
אֶסְגּוֹד	Kal fut. 1 pers. sing. (§ 8. rem. 18)	סגד

אָסָה *Root not used,* coll. with the Arab. اسو *to be hurt,*
injured, and trans. *to hurt, injure.*

אָסָא (*injurious*) pr. name.—I. of a king of
Judah, son of Abijam, grandson of Rehoboam.—
II. 1 Ch. 9. 16.

אָסוֹן masc. *hurt, injury, mischief.*

אֲסוֹבְבָה	ו Pilel fut. 1 pers. sing. with paragogic ה ; ו for ו	סבב
אָסוּךְ	noun masc. sing. . . .	סוך
אָסוֹן	noun masc. sing. . .	אסה
אָסוֹר	Kal inf. absolute . . .	אסר
אָסוּר	Kal fut. 1 pers. sing. . .	סור
אָסוּר	Kal part. p. sing. masc. dec. 3 a.	אסר
אֲסוּרֵי	Kh. אֲסוּרֵי id. pl. constr., K. אֲסִירֵי (q. v.)	אסר
אֲסוּרָיו	noun masc. pl., suff. 3 pers. sing. masc. from אָסוֹר dec. 3 b.	אסר
אֲסוּרִים	id. pl. abs. (Ec. 7. 26); or pl. of אָסוּר (q. v.)	אסר
אַסְפִּיד	Hiph. fut. 1 pers. sing. . .	נסך
אֹסִיף	defect. for אוֹ, Hiph. fut. 1 pers. sing. .	יסף
אֲסִיפֵם	Hiph. fut. 1 pers. sing., suff. 3 pers. pl. m.	סוף
אָסִיר	ו & ו Hiph. fut. 1 pers. s.; ו for ו conv.	סור
אָסִיר	noun masc. sing. dec. 3 a. . .	אסר
אַסִּיר	ו noun masc. sing.; also pr. name masc. .	אסר
אָסִירָה	ו Hiph. fut. 1 pers. sing. with paragogic ה	סור
אֲסִירֵי	noun masc. pl. construct from אָסִיר dec. 3 a.	אסר
אֲסִירָיו	id., suff. 3 pers. sing. masc.	אסר
אֲסִירַיִךְ	id., suff. 2 pers. sing. fem.	אסר
אֲסִירִים	id. pl., absolute state	אסר
אֶסֹּכֵךְ	ו Kal fut. 1 pers. sing. [אֶסֹּךְ], suff. 2 pers. sing. fem.; ו for ו conv.	סוך
אֲסַלְדָה	ו Piel fut. 1 pers. sing. with paragogic ה; ו for ו	סלד
אֶסְלוֹחַ, אֶסְלַח	ו Kal fut. 1 pers. sing.; Kh. אֶסְלוֹחַ (§ 8. rem. 18)	סלח

אָסָם masc. only in the pl. אֲסָמֶיךָ *thy storehouses,*
Pr. 3. 10, compare De. 28. 8.

אַסְנָה (*thorn-bush,* compare סְנֶה) pr. name masc.
Ezr. 2. 50.

אֹסְנַפַּר pr. name of an Assyrian general, Ezr. 4. 10.

אָסְנַת pr. name of the wife of Joseph, daughter of
the priest Potiphar. Coll. with the Egyptian by Gesenius it signifies, *belonging to*
Neith, the Minerva of the Egyptians.

אֶסְעָרֵם ו Piel fut. 1 pers. sing., suff. 3 pers. pl. m.,
by Syriasm for סָעַר (compare § 19. rem. 6) — סער

אָסַף ו—I. *to collect, to gather, to assemble,* const. with
אֶל, עַל, *to designate the person or place to or in*
which.—II. *to take, or, receive to oneself.*—III. *to*
take in, to draw back, as the hand.—IV. *to take*
away; hence, *to destroy.*—V. *to gather in, or up,*

Da. 6. 8, 13.   d 1 Sa. 23. 12.   g 1 Sa. 28. 1.   k Ju. 20. 6.   n 2 Ki. 4. 2.   q Ju. 15. 14.   t Is. 10. 13.   w Eze. 16. 9.   z Je. 5. 7.
Da. 2. 10.   e Jos. 10. 2.   h Je. 44. 19.   l Is. 46. 4, 4.   o Ju. 16. 11.   r Ps. 16. 4.   u Eze. 16. 56.   x Job 6. 10.   aa Zec. 7. 14.
Is. 33. 10.   f Eze. 16. 45.   i Ezr. 7. 25.   m Is. 44. 19.   p Ge. 39. 20.   s Je. 8. 13.   v Zec. 9. 11.   y Je. 17. 9.   bb Ca. 8. 2.

as the rear does an army. Niph. pass. of Kal No. I. II. IV. constr. with עַל, לְ, אֶל. Pi.—I. i. q. Kal No. I. Is. 62. 9.—II. to receive, as a guest, Ju. 19. 15, 18.—III. i. q. Kal No. V.—Pu. to be gathered. Hithp. to be gathered together, Deut. 33. 5.

אָסָף (collector) pr. name of several men, especially of a Levite and chief singer of David.

אָסֻף only in pl. אֲסֻפִּים (§ 37. No. 3c) stores, storehouses.

אֹסֶף masc. dec. 6c. ingathering, harvest of fruits.

אָסִיף masc. id. Ex. 23. 16; 34. 22.

אֲסֵפָה fem. gathering, collection, Is. 24. 22.

אֲסֻפָּה fem. assembly, a council, Ec. 12. 11.

אֲסַפְסֻף masc. mixed multitude, Nu. 11. 4.

אָסָף	‌ pr. name masc.	אסף
אָסִף	Hiph. fut. 1 pers. sing., ap. for אָסִיף	סוף
אֱסֹף	Kal inf. abs.	אסף
אֱסֹף	id. imp. sing. masc. . . .	אסף
אֹסֵף	Hiph. fut. 1 pers. sing. ap. for אוֹסִיף	יסף
אֹסֵף	noun masc. sing. . . .	אסף
אֹסֵף	defect for אוֹסִיף Hiph. fut. 1 pers. sing.	יסף
אֻסַּף	‌ Pual pret. 3 pers. sing. masc.	אסף
אֶסְפְּרָה	Kal fut. 1 pers. sing. with parag. ה	ספר
אֲסֵפָה	noun fem. sing. . . .	אסף
אֹסִפָה	Hiph. fut. 1 pers. sing. . .	ספה
אֶסָּפֶה	Niph. fut. 1 pers. sing. . .	ספה
אָסְפָה	Kal imp. sing. masc. with parag. ה (§ 13. r. 3)	אסף
אֶסְפָה	id. fut. 1 pers. sing. [אֹסֵף] with parag. ה (§ 19. rem. 4)	אסף
אֹסִפָה	‌ Hiph. fut. 1 pers. sing. (אוֹסִיף) with parag. ה	יסף
אָסְפוּ	‌ Kal pret. 3 pers. plur.	אסף
אִסְפוּ	id. imp. pl. masc.	אסף
אֻסְּפוּ	‌ Pual pret. 3 pers. pl.	אסף
אֲסֻפּוֹת	noun fem., pl. of [אֲסֻפָּה] dec. 10.	אסף
אֹסְפֵי	Kal part. p. pl. construct masc. fr. [אָסוּף] dec. 3 a.	אסף
אִסְפִי	id. imp. sing. fem.	אסף
אָסְפְךָ	id. fut. 1 pers. sing. [אֹסֵף] suff. 2 pers. sing. masc. (§ 19. rem. 4)	אסף
אֹסִפְךָ	id. part. act. sing. masc. with suff. 2 pers. sing. masc. from אֹסֵף dec. 7 b.	אסף
אֹסְפָם	id. id. with suff. 3 pers. pl. masc.	אסף
אֲסַפֵּר	‌ Piel fut. 1 pers. sing.; ‌ for ‌	ספר
אֲסַפְּרָה	‌ id. with parag. ה; ‌ id.	ספר
אֲסַפְּרֵם	Kal fut. 1 pers. sing., suff. 3 pers. pl. masc.	ספר
אָסְפַּרְנָא	Ch. adv. diligently, comp. Ez. 5. 8; 6. 8; 7. 17.	

אֲסַפְּרֶנָּה	Piel fut. 1 pers. sing., suff. 3 pers. sing. fem. (§ 2. rem. 3)	ספר
אָסַפְתָּ	Kal pret. 2 pers. sing. masc. . .	אסף
אָסַפְתְּ	‌ id.; acc. shifted by conv. ‌ (§ 8. rem. 7)	אסף
אַסְפָּתָא	pr. name of a son of Haman, Est. 9. 7.	
אֲסַפְתָּה	‌ Kal pret. 2 pers. sing. masc. (§ 8. r. 5. & 7	אסף
אֲסַפְתּוֹ	‌ id. with suff. 3 pers. sing. m.; ‌ for ‌ conv	אסף
אָסַפְתִּי }	id. pret. 1 pers. sing. (§ 8. rem. 7) .	אסף
אֲסַפְתִּי }		
אָסַפְתִּי	‌ id.; acc. shifted by conv. ‌ (§ 8. rem. 7)	אסף
אֶסֹּף	Kal fut. 1 pers. sing. . . .	נסם

[אָסַר] I. to bind.—II. to put in bonds, to fetter; part. אָסוּר captive, prisoner.—III. to bind, tie, fasten to any thing, const. with בְּ, לְ; whence, to harness a chariot, with acc.—IV. אָסַר אִסָּר עַל נַפְשׁוֹ to bind an oath upon oneself, i. e. bind oneself by an oath Niph. to be bound, Ju. 16. 6, 13; to be imprisoned. Pu. to be reduced to bondage.

אָסִיר masc. dec. 3a, captive, prisoner.

אַסִּיר masc. I. id.—II. pr. name masc.

אֱסָר m. dec. 2b, obligation, or vow of abstinence.

אֵסָר masc. dec. 1a, id.

אֱסָר Chald. dec. 1a, an interdict, Da. 6. 8, 13. sq.

אָסוּר masc. dec. 3b, bond, fetter; בֵּית הָאֵסוּר prison.

אֱסוּר Chald. masc. dec. 1a, id.

מֹסֶרֶת (for מַאֲסֹרֶת) bond, obligation, Ez. 20. 37.

מוֹסֵר (for מַאֲסֹר) masc. dec. 7b, pl. וֹת & ־ים, bands, bonds, fetters.

מֹסֵר De. 10. 6, and מֹסֵרָה Nu. 33. 30. (bands) pr. name of a station of the Israelites in the wilderness.

אַסֻּר	pr. name masc. for אָסִיר	אסר
אֱסֹר	Kal inf. abs.	אסר
אֵסַר־חַדֹּן }	pr. name of a king of Assyria, son of	
אֵסַר־חַדֹּן }	Sennacherib.	
אֱסָר	Chald. noun masc. sing. dec. 1b.	אסר
אֱסָר	Chald. id. construct state	אסר
אֱסֹר	Kal imp. sing. masc.	אסר
אִסָּר	noun masc. sing. dec. 2b.	אסר
אֲסָרָא	‌ Chald. noun masc. sing., emph. of אֱסָר dec. 1 b; ‌ before (־ָ)	אסר
אָסְרָה	‌ Kal pret. 3 pers. sing. fem.	אסר
אָסֻרָה	Kal fut. 1 pers. sing. with parag. ה for אָסוּרָה	סור
אֶסְרָהּ	‌ noun masc. sing., suff. 3 pers. sing. fem. from [אֱסָר] dec. 1. (§ 30. No. 3) ‌ bef. (־ָ)	אסר

a Zep. 1. 2, 3.   d 1 Sa. 27. 1.   Ec. 12. 11.   n 2 Ki. 22. 20; &   Ps. 118. 17.   m Ps. 145. 6.   Ps. 139. 5.   1 Ki. 18. 44.   h Nu. 30. 4.
a Mi. 1. 8.   f Nu. 11. 16.   Ese. 34. 29.   2 Ch. 34. 28.   r Ps. 85. 4.   Ju. 18. 25.   Da. 6. 8; 13. 16.   Da. 6. 9, 14.   Ex. 3. 3.
c Is. 24. 22.   g Mi. 4. 6.   l Je. 10. 17.   Ps. 39. 7.   Ps. 66. 16.   Ju. 18. 25.   Da. 6. 8.   g Da. 6. 10.   Nu. 30. 5.
d De. 32. 23.   h 2 Sa. 12. 8.   1 Sa. 15. 6.   Ps. 22. 18.   f Ps. 139. 18.   Is. 10. 14.   Da. 6. 12.

אֶסְרֶהָ	id. pl., suff. 3 pers. sing. fem. for אֲסָרֶיהָ	אסר
אִסְרוּ	Kal imp. pl. masc.	אסר
אֻסְּרוּ / אֻסָּֽרוּ	} Pual pret. 3 pers. pl. masc. (comp. § 8. rem. 7)	אסר
אֲסָרֽוּךָ	נ Kal pret. 3 pers. pl., suff. 2 pers. sing. masc.; נ for וֹ	אסר
אֲסֻרוֹת	id. part. p. fem., pl. of [אָסוּרָה] dec. 10.	אסר
אֹסְרִי	id. part. act. sing. m. with parag. י (§ 8. r. 19)	אסר
אֲסָרֶיהָ	נ noun masc. pl., suff. 3 pers. sing. fem. from אֶסָר dec. 1 a. (§ 30. No. 3)	אסר
אֲסָרָם	Kal pret. 3 pers. sing. masc., suff. 3 pers. pl. masc.	אסר
אֶסְרֵם	וְ Kal fut. 1 pers. sing., suff. 3 pers. pl. masc. (§ 20. rem. 16. & § 8. rem. 14)	יסר
אֲסַרְנֻהוּ	נ Kal pret. 1 pers. plur., suff. 3 pers. sing. masc.; נ for וֹ conv.	אסר
אֲסַרְתֶּם	נ id. pret. 2 pers. pl. masc.; נ id.	אסר
אַסְתִּיר	נ״ Hiph. fut. 1 pers. sing.; נ for וֹ conv.	סתר
אַסְתִּירָה	id. with parag. ה	סתר
אֶסָּתֵר	נ״ Niph. fut. 1 pers. sing.	סתר
אֶסָּתֵר	נ״ (star, Pers. sitareh) pr. name fem. foster-daughter of Mordecai, afterwards wife of Ahasuerus and queen of Persia.	
אָע	נ״ Chald. masc. dec. 1. i. q. Heb. עֵץ wood.	
אָעָא	Chald. id., emph. st.	
אֶעֱבֹד	Kal fut. 1 pers. sing.	עבד
אֶעֶבְדָךְ	id., suff. 2 pers. sing. masc.	עבד
אֶעֱבוֹר	Kh. Kal fut. 1 p. s. R. עבר; K. אֶעֱבֹר (q.v.)	עבר
אֶעֱבֹר	וֹ Kal fut. 1 pers. sing. (§ 8. rem. 19); נ for וֹ conv.	עבר
אַעֲבִיר	Hiph. fut. 1 pers. sing.	עבר
אֶעֱבֹר	נ Kal fut. 1 pers. sing.; נ for וֹ conv.	עבר
אֶעְבְּרָה / אֶעְבְּרָה	} id. with parag. ה (§ 8. rem. 15); נ id.	עבר
אָעֵד	נ ap. for אָעִיד (q.v.)	עוד
אֶעֶדֵּךְ	נ Kal fut. 1 pers. sing. [אֶעְדֶּה], suff. 2 pers. sing. fem. (§ 24. rem. 21); נ for וֹ conv.	עדה
אָעוֹדֵךְ	Kh. ’אָעֵ, K. ’אָעֵ, Kal or Hiph. fut. 1 pers. sing., suff. 2 pers. sing. fem.	עוד
אָעוּפָה	Kal fut. 1 pers. sing. with parag. ה	עוף
אֶעֱזֹב	Kal fut. 1 pers. sing.	עזב
אֶעֶזְבָה	נ id. with parag. ה	עזב
אֶעֶזְבֶךָ / אֶעֶזְבֶךָ	} id., suff. 2 pers. sing. masc. (§ 2. rem. 3)	עזב
אֶעֶזְבֵם	id., suff. 3 pers. pl. masc.	עזב
אָעִיד	נ Hiph. fut. 1 pers. sing.; נ for וֹ conv.	עוד

עֵידָה	נ, נ״ id. with paragogic ה; נ id.	עוד
אוֹעִיל	Hiph. fut. 1 pers. sing. [for אֹעִיל]	יעל
אָעִירָה	Hiph. fut. 1 pers. sing. with parag. ה	עור
אַעַל	נ Kal (De. 10. 3) or Hiph. (Nu. 23. 4) fut. 1 pers. sing. ap. for אֶעֱלֶה or אַעֲלֶה (§ 24. rem. 3 & 15); נ for וֹ conv.	עלה
אַעֲלֶה	נ Hiph. fut. 1 pers. sing.; נ id.	עלה
אֶעֱלֶה	Kal fut. 1 pers. sing.	עלה
אֶעְלֹזָה	fully, for אֶעֶלְזָה q. v. (§ 8. rem. 14)	עלז
אֶעֶלְזִי	נ Kal fut. 1 pers. s. (§ 13. r. 5); נ for וֹ conv.	עלז
אֶעֶלְזָה	id. with parag. ה in pause [for אֶעֶלְזָה]	עלז
אַעֲלִים	נ״ Hiph. fut. 1 pers. sing. (§ 13. rem. 9)	עלם
אַעַלְךָ	Hiph. fut. 1 pers. sing. (אַעֲלֶה), suff. 2 pers. sing. masc. (§ 24. rem. 21)	עלה
אֶעֶלְצָה	נ Kal fut. 1 pers. sing. with paragogic ה	עלץ
אֶעֱמֹד	נ Kal fut. 1 pers. sing.; נ for וֹ conv.	עמד
אֶעֶמְדָה	id. with parag. ה in pause [for אֶעְמְדָה] (§ 8. rem. 15)	עמד
אַעֲמִידֵם	נ the following with suff. 3 pers. pl. masc.	עמד
אַעֲמִיד	נ Hiph. fut. 1 pers. sing.; נ for וֹ conv.	עמד
אַעֲמִידָה	נ id. with parag. ה; נ id.	עמד
אַעַן	נ Kal fut. 1 p.s., ap. for אֶעֱנֶה (§ 24. r. 3); נ id.	ענה
אֶעֶנְדֶנּוּ	Kal fut. 1 pers. sing., suff. 3 pers. sing. masc.	ענד
אֶעֱנֶה / וָאַעַן	} Kal fut. 1 pers sing.	ענה
אֵעָנֶה	Niph. fut. 1 pers. sing.	ענה
אֲעַנֶּה	נ with א quiescent [for וָאֲעַנֶּה] Piel fut. 1 p.s.	ענה
אֶעֶנְהֵגוּ	נ Kal fut. 1 pers. sing., suff. 3 pers. sing. masc.	ענה
אֲעַנֵּךְ	Piel fut. 1 p.s., suff. 2 p.s. fem. (§ 24. r. 21)	ענה
אֶעֶנְךָ / אֶעֶנְךָ / נ״	} Kal fut. 1 p. s. (אֶעֱנֶה), suff. 2 p. s. m. (§ 24. rem. 21. & § 2. rem. 3)	ענה
אֶעֶנֵם	נ״ id., suff. 3 pers. pl. masc.	ענה
אֶעֶנֶנּוּ	id., suff. 3 pers. sing. masc. (§ 2. rem. 3)	ענה
אֶעֶצֹר	Kal fut. 1 pers. sing. (§ 13. rem. 5)	עצר
אֶעֶרְבֶנּוּ	Kal fut. 1 pers. sing., suff. 3 pers. sing. masc.	ערב
אֶעֱרֹץ	Kal fut. 1 pers. sing. (§ 8. rem. 19)	ערץ
אֶעֱרֹךְ	Kal fut. 1 pers. sing., (§ 8. rem. 19)	ערך
אֶעֶרְכָה	נ״ id. with parag. ה	ערך
אַעַשׂ	נ ap. for the following (§ 24. rem. 3)	עשה
אֶעֱשֶׂה	נ, נ, Kal fut. 1 pers. sing.; נ for וֹ conv.	עשה
אֶעֶשְׂךָ	נ״ id., suff. 2 pers. sing. masc.	עשה
אֶעֱשֶׂנָּה	id., suff. 3 pers. sing. fem. (§ 2. rem. 3)	עשה
אַעְשִׁר	נ with quiescent א and def. [for וָאַעֲשִׁיר] Hiph. fut. 1 pers. sing.	עשר
אֲעַשְּׂרֶנּוּ	Piel fut. 1 pers. sing., suff. 3 pers. sing. masc.	עשר

a Nu. 30. 8.   b Is. 22. 3.   c Is. 22. 3.   Eze. 3. 25.   2 Sa. 3. 34.   f Ge. 49. 11.   g Nu. 30. 6, 15.

h Job 36. 13.   i Ho. 10. 10.   k Ju. 16. 5.   l Da. 5. 4, 23.   m 1 Sa. 6. 7.   n Eze. 39. 23, 24.   o De. 32. 20.   p Ps. 55. 13.

q Ezr. 6. 4, 11.   r Ezr. 5. 8.   s La. 2. 13.   t 2 Sa. 16. 19.   u Ge. 29. 18.   v Je. 2. 20.   w Ju. 12. b.

x Eze. 16. 11.   y Job 35. 3.   z 1 Ki. 6. 13.   a Je. 9. 1.   b Ge. 28. 15.   c Is. 41. 17.

d Ne. 13. 15.   e Ne. 13. 21.   f Hab. 3. 18.   g Je. 15. 17.   h Ne. 13. 15.   i Is. 1. 15.   k 1 Sa. 12. 3.

l Ge. 46. 4.   m Ps. 9. 3.   n 2 Sa. 1. 10.   o Hab. 3. 1.   p Ps. 81. 8.   q Job 31. 36.   r Job 32. 17.

s Job 19. 7.   t 1 Ki. 11. 39.   u Ps. 91. 15.   v Na. 1. 12.   w Ge. 43. 9.   x Job 31. 34.   y Je. 33. 3.   Is. 41. 17.

z Zec. 10. 6.   a Job 9. 14, 32.   b 2 Ch. 7. 13.   c Ge. 12. 2.   d Job 31. 34.   e Ps. 5. 4.

f Job 23. 4.   g Ps. 50. 21.   h Eze. 35. 6.   i Ge. 12. 2.   k Zec. 11. 5.   l Ge. 28. 22.

אַעְתִּיר   Hiph. fut. 1 pers. sing. (§ 13. rem. 9)   עתר

אַף   } noun masc. sing. dec. 8 d. contr. [for
אַף   }   אָנַף § 37. No. 3]   אנף
אַף   }

אַף   } conj. *also, moreover, indeed, yea*; אַף כִּי (a)
how much more, how much less; (b) *yea
more, yea furthermore;* נֶתַ] אַף כִּי אָמַר
is it even so, that (God) *has said?* Ge. 3. :

אַף   } Chald. *also,* Da. 6. 23.

אֶפְאֵיהֶם   Hiph. fut. 1 pers. sing. [אֶפְאֶה], suff. 3 pers.
pl. masc. (§ 24. rem. 21)   פאה

אֲפָאֵר   Piel fut. 1 pers. sing.   פאר

אֶפְגַּע   Kal fut. 1 pers. sing.   פגע

אֶפְגְּשֵׁם   Kal fut. 1 pers. sing., suff. 3 pers. pl. masc.   פגשׁ

[אָפַד]   *to gird on, put on,* const. with לְ of the person and
בְּ of the thing.

אֵפֹד, אֵפוֹד, אֵפֹד masc.—!. *ephod,* especially that of
the high-priest, a kind of short coat without sleeves
girded on over all the garments.—II. perhaps *an
idol dressed in an ephod.*—III. pr. name masc.
Nu. 34. 23.

אֲפֻדָּה fem. dec. 10.—I. *a putting on* of the
ephod.—II. *a vestment in which idols were dressed,*
Is. 30. 22.

אֵפֹד   noun m. s., defect for אֵפוֹד; also pr. name   אפד

אֶפְדֶּה   Kal fut. 1 pers. sing.   פדה

אֶפְדֵּם   id., suff. 3 pers. pl. masc. (§ 24. rem. 21)   פדה

אַפֶּדְנוֹ   noun masc. sing., suff. 3 pers. sing. masc. from
[אַפֶּדֶן] dec. 6 a.   פדן

אָפַדְתָּ   } Kal pret. 2 pers. sing. masc.; acc. shifted
   } to ult. by conv. ן (§ 8. rem. 7)   אפד

אֲפֻדָּת   noun fem. sing., constr. of [דָּה] dec. 10.   אפד

אֲפֻדָּתוֹ   id., suff. 3 pers. sing. masc.   אפד

אָפָה   } *to bake;* part. אֹפֶה dec. 9 a. *baker.* Niph. *to
be baked.*

מַאֲפֶה masc. *a baking, something baked,* Le. 2. 4.
תֻּפִינִים masc. pl. *bakings, baked pieces,* Le. 6. 14.

אַפֶּה   noun masc. sing., suff. 3 pers. sing. fem. from
אַף (q. v.) dec. 8 d.   אנף

אֹפֶה   Kal part. act. sing. masc. dec. 9 a.   אפה

אֹפֵהֶם   id., suff. 3 pers. pl. masc.   אפה

אָפוּ   } id. pret. 3 pers. pl.   אפה

אַפּוֹ   noun masc. sing., suff. 3 pers. sing. masc.
from אַף (q. v.) dec. 8 d.   אנף

אֱפוּ   Kal imp. pl. masc. by Syriacism [for אֵפוּ
§ 19. rem. 6].   אפה

אֵפוֹ   } adv. *now, then,* אַיֵּה אֵפוֹא *where now?*
אֵפוֹא   } מָה אֵי who, *what then?* לְכָה אֵי
come on now! אִם כֵּן אֵי *if then it be so;*
דְּעוּ אֵי *know then!*

אֵפוֹד   } noun masc. sing. Ex. 28. 4.   אפד

אֶפְנֶה   Kal fut. 1 pers. sing. with parag. ה   פון

אֶפְחַד   } Kal fut. 1 pers. sing. (§ 8. rem. 15)   פחד
אֶפְחָד   }

אַפִּי   } noun masc. sing., suff. 1 pers. sing. from
אַף (q. v.) dec. 8 d.   אנף

אַפֶּיהָ   id. du., suff. 3 pers. sing. fem.   אנף

אַפָּיו   id. du., suff. 3 pers. sing. masc.   אנף

אָפִיחַ   Hiph. fut. 1 pers. sing.   פוח

אָפִיחַ   pr. name masc. 1 Sa. 9. 1. אָפַח perhaps i. q.
פוח *to breathe.*

אַפֶּיךָ   noun masc. pl., suff. 2 pers. sing. masc. from
אַף (q. v.) dec. 8 d.   אנף

אַפִּיל   Hiph. fut. 1 pers. sing.   נפל

אֲפִילֹת   adj. fem. pl., from [אָפִיל] masc.   אפל

אַפַּיִם   } noun masc., du. of אַף (q. v.) dec. 8 d.;
אַפָּיִם   } also pr. name masc.   אנף

אַפֵּינוּ   id., suff. 1 pers. pl.   אנף

אָפִיץ   } Hiph. fut. 1 pers. sing.; ן for נ conv   פוץ

אֲפִיצֵם   } id., suff. 3 pers. pl. masc.; ן for נ   פוץ

אָפִיק   pr. name of a place, see אָפֵק.   אפק

אֲפִיקֵי   adj. and subst. m. pl. constr. from אָפִיק dec. 3 a   אפק

אֲפִיקֵיו   id., (subst.) pl., suff. 3 pers. sing. masc.   אפק

אֲפִיקֶךָ   id. id., suff. 2 pers. sing. masc.   אפק

אֲפִיקִים   id. id. pl., absolute state   אפק

אָפִיר   Hiph. fut. 1 pers., as if from פוּר, see   פרר

אָפִיתָ   } Kal pret. 2 pers. sing. masc.; acc. shifted
   } to ult. by conv. ן (§ 8. rem. 7)   אפה

אָפִיתִי   id. pret. 1 pers. sing.   אפה

אַפָּךְ   } noun masc. sing., suff. 2 pers. sing. masc. }
אַפֶּךָ   } from אַף (q. v.) dec. 8 d. } אנף

אַפֵּךְ   id., suff. 2 pers. sing. fem.   אנף

אָפֵל   Root not used, Arab. *to set, go down,* as the sun.
אָפִיל adj., f. אֲפִילָה, *late,* as to growth, Ex. 9.32.
אָפֵל adj. masc. *dark, obscure,* Am. 5. 20.
אֲפֵלָה fem. *darkness, thick darkness.*
אֹפֶל masc. *thick darkness;* trop. *misfortune.*
מַאֲפֵל masc. *darkness,* Jos. 24. 7.
מַאְפֵלְיָה *great darkness,* comp. of the preceding
and יָה, lit. *darkness of the Lord,* Je. 2. 31.

אָפֵל   } adj. masc. sing.   אפל

אַפֵּל   } Kal fut. 1 p. s. (§ 17. r. 3); ן for נ conv.   נפל

a Ex. 8. 5.   c Ho. 13. 8.   e Ex. 29. 5.   g Ge. 24. 47.   i Exr. 3. 22.   k 2 Sa. 14. 4.   m La. 4. 20.   o Is. 8. 7.   q Le. 24. 5.
b De. 32. 26.   d Ex. 28. 15.   f Is. 30. 22.   h Ge. 40. 17.   j Ex. 16. 23.   l Eze. 21. 36.   n Na. 1. 3.   p Eze. 35. 3.   r Is. 44. 19.
c Is. 60. 7.   g Ex. 13. 15.   g Ge. 19. 3.   p Ho. 7. 6.   s Ps. 58. 16.   Ex. 9. 32.   Eze. 36. 19.   Job 12. 21.   Am. 5. 20.
d Is. 47. 3.   h Da. 11. 45.   i Is. 44. 15.   t Le. 26. 26.   u Job 23. 15.   1 Sa. 1. 5.   Je. 13. 17.   Ps. 89. 34.   1 Ch. 21. 13.

אָפֵל noun masc. sing. . . . . אפל

אֲפֵלָה◦ noun fem. sing. dec. 10; וַ before (־ֶ). אפל

אֹפְלָה Kal fut. 1 pers. sing. with parag. ה (§ 8. rem. 15); וָ for וְ . . } נפל
וָאֹפְלָה

אֲפַלְּטָה Piel fut. 1 p. s. [אֲפַלֵּט] with parag. ה; וַ for } פלט
וָאֲפַלְּטָה id., suff. 3 pers. sing. masc.; וָ id.

אֲפַלֵּל וָ pr. name masc. . . . . פלל

אֲפֵלָתְךָ noun fem. sing., suff. 2 pers. sing. masc. from אֲפֵלָה dec. 10; וָ id. . אפל

אַפָּם noun masc. sing., suff. 3 pers. sing. masc. from אַף (q. v.) dec. 8d. . אנף

אָפַן Root not used, prob. cogn. with פָּנָה, to turn, revolve.

אֹפָן & אוֹפַן masc. dec. 8. pl. אוֹפַנִּים, a wheel.

אֹפֶן masc. season, comp. תְּקוּפָה; only אָפְנָיו (for אָפְנָיו § 35. rem. 16) Pr. 25. 11.

אֵפֶן ap. for אֵפָנֶה q. v. (§ 24. rem. 3); וָ for וְ } פנה conversive

אֹפֶן noun masc. sing. constr. dec. 8. (§ 37. No. 2) אפן

אֶפְנֶה◦ וָ Kal fut. 1 pers. sing. . . . פנה

אָפְנָיו noun masc. pl., suff. 3 pers. sing. masc. from [אֹפֶן] dec. 6c. (§ 35. rem. 16) . אפן

אָפֵס to cease, fail, have an end.

אֶפֶס masc. dec. 6a.—I. end, extremity.—II. dual אַפְסַיִם two extremities, i. e. the soles or ankles of the feet, Eze. 47. 3.—III. adv. (a) no more; none besides, and so with paragogic Yod אַפְסִי; (b) not, non; בְּאֶפֶס without; (c) nothing; מֵאֶפֶס of nothing; בְּאֶפֶס for nothing; (d) nothing but, only; אֶפֶס כִּי prop. only that, except, unless.

אֶפֶס דַּמִּים pr. name of a town in the tribe of Judah, 1 Sa. 17. 1, for which פַּס דַּמִּים 1 Ch. 11. 13.

אֶפֶס noun m. s., (pl. c. אַפְסֵי) dec. 6a. (also as an adv.), and pr. name in אֶפֶס דַּמִּים } אפס
אֶפֶס וָ

אַפְסִי וָ noun masc. s. (אֶפֶס dec. 6a) with parag. י as an adv. . . . . . אפס

אַפְסֵי id. pl., construct state . . . . אפס

אֲפָסִים id. dual, absolute state [for אַפְסַיִם] . אפס

אֶפְסֹל◦ וָ Kal fut. 1 pers. sing.; וָ for וְ conv. פסל

אָפַע Root not used, prob. cogn with פָּאָה, פָּעָה to breathe; whence—

אֶפַע masc. breath, nothingness, vanity, Is. 41. 24.

אֶפְעֶה◦ Kal fut. 1 pers. sing. . . . פעה

אֲפֶעָה noun masc. sing. . . . . אפע

אֶפְעַל Kal fut. 1 pers. sing. . . . . פעל

[אָפַף] to surround, encompass.

אֲפָפוּ Kal preter. 3 pers. pl. . . . . אפף

אֲפָפוּנִי id. with suff. 1 pers. sing. . . אפף
אֲפָפֻנִי

אָפַק Kal not used, coll. with the Arab. the ideas of motion and force, or strength, are ascribed to it. Hithp. prop. to put force upon oneself.—I. to restrain oneself.—II. to constrain oneself to act, 1 Sa. 13. 12.

אָפֵק (fortress) pr. name.—I. of a town in the tribe of Asher, also called אֲפִיק comp. Jos. 19. 30 with Ju. 1. 31.—II. of a city in the tribe of Issachar.

אֲפֵקָה (fortress) pr. name of a town in the mountains of Judah, Jos. 15. 53.

אָפִיק masc. dec. 3 a.—I. adj. mighty, eminent, Job 12. 21.—II. the boss of a shield, Job 41. 7.—III. brook, torrent; also applied to the bed of a brook or stream, a channel; hence,—IV. Metaph. a tube, spoken of the bones of the Behemoth.

אֲפֵק וָ pr. name of a place . . . אפק

אֶפְקֹד◦ וָ(ָ) Kal fut. 1 pers. sing. (§ 8. rem. 18);
וָאֶפְקֹד־ וָ for וְ conversive } פקד

אֲפֵקָה וָ pr. name of a place; וָ before (־ֶ). אפק

אֶפְקוֹד Kal fut. 1 pers. sing. (§ 8. rem. 18) . פקד

אֶפְקַח Kal fut. 1 pers sing. . . . . פקח

אַפְקִיד Hiph. fut. 1 pers. sing. . . . פקד

אֲפִקִים◦ וָ defect. for אֲפִיקִים (q. v.) . . . אפס

אָפַר Root not used, Arab. to be light, fleet.

אֵפֶר masc.—I. ashes.—II. anything worthless.

אֲפֵר masc. a kind of head-band, turban, from אָפַר i. q. עָפַר to cover. According to others it is by transposition for פְּאֵר a tiara, crown.

אֶפְרַיִם (double fruitfulness, double fruit, with the signification of פָּרָה, comp. Ge. 41. 52; Ho. 13. 15.)—I. pr. name of the second son of Joseph.—II. of the tribe descended from him, afterwards the chief tribe of the kingdom of Israel.

אֶפְרָת, אֶפְרָתָה (fertility, comp. אֶפְרַיִם) pr. name.—I. of a city in the tribe of Judah, called also Bethlehem.—II. i. q. אֶפְרַיִם, Ps. 132. 6.—III. of the wife of Caleb.

a Ex. 10. 22.   d Job 25. 7.   f Is. 58. 10.   g Ge. 24. 49.   k Eze. 47. 3.   m Is. 42. 14.   o 2 Sa. 22. 5.   r Je. 9. 8.   s Ps. 31. 6.
b 2 Sa. 24. 14.   c Ps. 91. 14.   g Ex. 14. 25.   h Pr. 25. 11.   Da. 10. 3.   n Ps. 40. 13.   p Le. 18. 25.   t Zec. 12. 4.   t Eze. 32. 6.
Ch. 21. 13.

אֶפְרָתִי gent. noun.—I. an Ephrathite.—II. an Ephraimite, comp. אֶפְרָת No. II.

אוֹפִיר pr. name of a place celebrated for its gold.

אֶפֶּר Hiph. fut. 1 pers. sing. . . . . . פרר

אֶפֶר וְ noun masc. sing.; for וְ see letter ו . אפר

אֶפְרשׁ Kal fut. 1 pers. sing. (§ 8. rem. 18) . פרשׂ

אֶפְרֹחוֹ וְ noun masc. pl., suff. 3 pers. sing. masc. (§ 4. rem. 1) from [אֶפְרֹחַ] dec. 1 b. . פרח

אֶפְרֹחֶיהָ id. pl. with suff. 3 pers. sing. fem. . פרח

אֶפְרֹחִים id. pl., absolute state . . . . . פרח

אֶפְרְיוֹן noun masc. sing. . . . . . . פרה

אֶפְרַיִם
אֶפְרָיִם וְ pr. name of a man and a **country** . אפר

אֲפָרְסָיָא Chald. pr. name of a people . . . פרס

אֲפָרְסְכָיֵא Chald. pr. name of a people . . . פרס

וַאֲפָרְסַתְכָיֵא Chald. pr. name of a people; וְ before (הַ‍) פרס

אֶפְרַע Kal fut. 1 pers. sing. . . . . פרע

אֶפְרֹשׂ וְ Kal fut. 1 pers. sing.; וְ for ־ conv. . פרשׂ

אֶפְרְשָׂה וְ id. with paragogic ה; וְ id. . . פרשׂ

אֶפְרָת
אֶפְרָתָה } pr. name of a place and a woman . אפר

אֶפְרָתִי gent. noun from the preceding . . אפר

אֶפְרָתִים id. pl. absolute . . . . . אפר

אַפְשִׁיטֶמֶנָּה Hiph. fut. 1 pers. sing., suff. 3 pers. sing. f. פשׁט

אֶפְשְׂעָה Kal fut. 1 pers. s. with parag. ה (§ 8 r. 14) פשׂע

וָאֶפֶּת Niph. fut. 1 pers. sing. ap. [for אֶפָּתֶה § 24. rem. 10]; וְ for ־ conv. . . פתה

אֶפְתַּח
אֶפְתָּח } Kal fut. 1 pers. sing. (§ 8. rem. 15);
וְ‍ } וְ for וְ conversive } פתה

אֲפַתֶּה [for אֶפְתֶּה] Piel fut. 1 pers sing. (§ 15. r. 1) פתה

אֶפְתְּחָה Kal fut. 1 pers. sing. with paragogic ה . פתה

אַפְּתֹם וְ Chald. adv. at last, Ezr. 4. 13.

אֲפַתֶּנּוּ Piel fut. 1 pers. s., suff. 3 p. s. m. (§ 2. r. 3) פתה

אָץ וְ Kal pret. 3 pers. sing. m.; or part. dec. 1 a. אוץ

אֵצֵא וְ Kal fut. 1 pers. sing.; וְ for וְ conv. . יצא

אֵצְאָה וְ & וְ‍י id. with paragogic ה; וְ id. . יצא

אֶצְבּוֹן pr. name.—I. Ge. 4. 16.—II. 1 Ch. 7. 7.

אֶצְבַּע noun fem. sing., comp. dec. 2 b. (§ 31. r. 5) צבע

אֶצְבְּעוֹ id., suff. 3 pers. sing. masc. . . . צבע

אֶצְבָּעוֹת id. pl., absolute state . . . . צבע

אֶצְבְּעוֹת וְ id. pl., construct state . . . . צבע

אֶצְבְּעוֹ זִי id. pl., suff. 1 pers. pl. . . . צבע

אֶצְבְּעוֹתֵיכֶם וְ id. pl., suff. 2 pers. pl. masc. . . צבע

אֶצְבְּעָן Chald. noun fem., pl. of אֶצְבַּע dec. 2 a. צבע

אֶצְבְּעָת וְ Chald. id. pl., construct state . . . צבע

אֶצְבְּעֹת וְ noun fem., pl. of אֶצְבַּע (q. v.) . . צבע

אֶצְבְּעָתָא וְ Chald. noun f. pl. emph. of אֶצְבַּע dec. 2 a. צבע

אֶצְבְּעֹתֵי וְ noun f. pl. suff. 1 p. pl. from אֶצְבַּע (q. v.) צבע

אֶצְבְּעֹתָיו וְ‍י id., suff. 3 pers. sing. masc. . . צבע

אֶצְבְּעֹתֶיךָ id., suff. 2 pers. sing. masc. . . . צבע

אַצְדִּיק Hiph. fut. 1 pers sing. . . . . צדק

אֶצְדָּק
אֶצְדָּק } Kal fut. 1 pers. sing. (§ 8. rem. 15) צדק

אֲצַו וְ apoc. for the following . . . . צוה

אֲצַוֶּה וְ Piel fut. 1 pers. sing.; וְ for וַ . . צוה

אֲצַוֶּנּוּ
אֲצַוֶּנּוּ } id. with suff., in pause without נ epenth. &
id. with suff. in pause with נ epenth., for : } צוה

אֲצַוְּךָ id. with suff. 2 p. s. m. (§ 24. r. 21. & § 2. r. 2) צוה

אָצוּם Kal fut. 1 pers. sing. . . . . צום

אֲצַוֶּנּוּ וְ‍י Piel fut. 1 pers. sing. (אֲצַוֶּה), suff. 3 pers. sing. masc. (§ 24. r. 21. & § 2. r. 3); וְ for צוה

אָצוּרְךָ Kh. אֲצוּרְךָ from צוּר; K. אֶצָּרְךָ Kal fut. 1 pers. sing., suff. 2 pers. s. m. (§ 20. r. 16) יצר

אָצִינָה Hiph. fut. 1 p. s. with parag. ה (§ 20. r. 16) יצנ

אַצִּיל וְ‍י Hiph. fut. 1 pers. sing.; וְ for וְ conv. . נצל

אֲצִילָה noun fem. sing. dec. 10. . . . אצל

אַצִּילוֹת pl. of the preceding . . . . אצל

אֲצִילֵי noun masc. pl. constr. of [אָצִיל] dec. 1 b. אצל

אֲצִילֵי noun masc., pl. constr. of [אַצִּיל] dec. 3 a. אצל

אַצִּילְךָ Hiph. fut. 1 pers. sing., suff. 2 pers. sing. masc. נצל

אָצִים Kal part. act. masc., pl. of אָץ dec. 1 a. אוץ

אַצִּיעָה וְ Hiph. fut. 1 p. s. with parag. ה (§ 20. r. 16) יצע

אֲצִיתֶנָּה Hiph. fut. 1 pers. sing., suff. 3 pers. sing. fem. צות

[אָצַל] I. to hold back, withhold, const. with מִן.—II. to reserve, const. with לְ. Niph. to be contracted, Eze. 42. 6.—Hiph. to withhold, const. with מִן, Nu. 11. 25.

אָצִיל masc. dec. 3 a. prop. adj. set aside, select; secluded.—I. nobleman, Ex. 24. 11.—II. remote part, Is. 41. 9.

אַצִּיל masc. dec. 1 b. pl. ־ים and ־וֹת, juncture, joint, אַצִּילֵי יָדַיִם the wrists, which others take to be the armpits, taking יַד for the whole arm.

אָצֵל (noble, see אָצִיל) pr. name—I. of a man, in pause אָצַל.—II. of a town near Jerusalem, Zec. 14. 5.

אֵצֶל masc. dec. 6. (§ 35. rem. 6).—I. the side.— II. prep. by, near.

אֲצַלְיָהוּ (whom the Lord has reserved) pr. name masc. 2 Ch. 34. 8.

אָצָל
אָצֵל } pr. name of a man and of a place אצל

a Ju. 2. 1.   e Eze. 24. 14.   k Je. 20. 7.   l 2 Ch. 1. 10.   s Is. 59. 3.   z Ca. 5. 5.   1 Ki. 11. 38.   t Ge. 33. 15.   z Eze. 13. 18.
b Ho. 7. 12.   f Ex. 9. 29.   Job 31. 32.   m Ne. 2. 13.   t Da. 5. 5.   l 1 Ch. 20. 6.   a Je. 1. 7.   r Zec. 11. 6.   a Ex. 24. 11.
c Job 39. 30.   g Eze. 16. 8.   n Eze. 3. 2.   p Je. 52. 21.   u Da. 2. 42.   m Job 13. 18.   b Est. 4. 16.   s 1 Sa. 10. 18.   b Ex. 5. 13.
d Ps. 84. 4.   h Ezr. 9. 5.   o Is. 45. 1.   q 2 Sa. 21. 20.   v 2 Sa. 21. 20.   n Job 9. 20.   c De. 31. 14.   t Eze. 41. 8.   c Ps. 139. 8.
De. 22. 6.   i Ho. 2. 5   p Ps. 78. 2.   r Ps. 144. 1.   w Da. 2. 41.   o De. 3. 18.   d Je. 1. 5.   u Je. 38. 12.   d Is. 27. 4.
f Ca. 3. 9.   j Is. 27. 4.   Eze. 3. 23.

אֶצֶל‎ defect for אֵצִיל (q. v.) — נצל

אֵצֶל‎ (prim. a subst.) prep. dec. 6. (§ 35. rem. 6) — אצל

אֶצְלָהּ‎ id., suff. 3 pers. sing. fem. — אצל

אֶצְלָה‎ Kal fut. 1 pers. sing. — צלה

אֶצְלוֹ‎ prep., suff. 3 pers. sing. masc. from אֵצֶל (q. v.) — אצל

אֶצְלִי‎ id., suff. 1 pers. sing. — אצל

אֲצַלְיָהוּ‎ pr. name masc. — אצל

אֶצְלָם‎ prep., suff. 3 pers. pl. masc. from אֵצֶל (q. v.) — אצל

אָצַלְתָּ‎ Kal pret. 2 pers. sing. masc. — אצל

אָצַלְתִּי‎ id. pret. 1 pers. sing. — אצל

אֶצְלְתִּי‎ id. id.; acc. shifted by conv. וְ (§ 8. rem. 7) — אצל

אֹצֶם‎ pr. name masc. 1 Ch. 2. 15, 25.

אַצְמִיחַ‎ Hiph. fut. 1 pers. sing. — צמח

אַצְמִית‎ Hiph. fut. 1 pers. sing. — צמת

אַצְמִיתֵם‎ id., suff. 3 pers. pl. masc. — צמת

אַצְעָדָה‎ noun fem. sing., pl. עֲדוֹת — צעד

אֶצְעַק‎ Kal fut. 1 pers. sing. — צעק

אֶצְעָקָה‎ id. with parag. ה, in pause [for עָקָה §8.r.15] — צעק

אֲצַפֶּה‎ Piel fut. 1 pers. sing.; וְ for וָ — צפה

אֲצַפְצֵף‎ Pilpel (§ 6. No. 4) fut. 1 pers. sing. — צפף

אֶצְעַק‎ / אֶצְעַק‎ } Kal fut. 1 pers. sing. (§ 20. r. 16. § 8. r. 18) — יצק

[אָצַר]‎ to lay up, treasure up, Niph. pass. Is. 23. 18. Hiph. to appoint as treasurer, Ne. 13. 13.

אוֹצָר‎ masc. dec. 2 b. pl. אוֹצָרוֹת.—I. store, treasure.—II. store-house, treasury.

אֵצֶר‎ (treasure) pr. name masc. Ge. 36. 21, 30.

אֶצֹּר‎ Kal fut. 1 pers. sing. — נצר

אֶצְּרֶהָ‎ / אֶצְּרָה‎ } id. with parag. ה (§ 8. rem. 15) — נצר

אָצְרוּ‎ Kal pret. 3 pers. pl. — אצר

אוֹצָרוֹת‎ noun masc. with pl. (abs.) fem. term. from אוֹצָר dec. 2 b. — אצר

אוֹצְרוֹת‎ id. pl., construct state — אצר

אֶצָּרְךָ‎ Kal fut. 1 pers. sing. (אֶצֹּר), suff. 2 pers. sing. masc. (R. יצר § 20. r. 16) or — נצר

אֶצֳּרֶנָּה‎ id., suff. 3 pers. sing. fem. — נצר

אֶצֳּרֶנָּה‎ id. id. (§ 8. rem. 14) — נצר

אֶצְרֹף‎ Kal fut. 1 pers. sing. — צרף

אֶצְרְפֶנָּה‎ id., suff. 3 pers. sing. fem. — צרף

אוֹצְרֹתֵיהֶם‎ noun masc. with pl. fem. term. and suff. 3 pers. pl. masc. from אוֹצָר dec. 2 b. — אצר

אַצְתִּי‎ Kal pret. 1 pers. sing. — אוץ

אֶקֹּב‎ Kal fut. 1 pers. sing. — נקב

אֲקַבֵּץ‎ Piel fut. 1 pers. sing. — קבץ

אֶקְבֹּץ‎ Kal fut. 1 pers. sing. — קבץ

אֲקַבְּצָה‎ Piel fut. 1 p. s. with parag. ה [for אֲקַבְּצָה] — קבץ

אֶקְבְּצָה‎ וְ, וָ, Kal fut. 1 s. with parag. ה; וְ for וָ conv. — קבץ

אֲקַבֶּצְךָ‎ Piel fut. 1 pers. sing. id., suff. 2 pers. sing. fem. — קבץ

אֲקַבֶּצְךָ‎ id., suff. 2 pers. sing. masc. (§ 2. rem. 2) — קבץ

אֲקַבְּצֵם‎ וְ, וָ, id., suff. 3 p. pl. m.; וְ for וָ for וָ conv. — קבץ

אֶקְבְּצֵם‎ וְ Kal fut. 1 p. s., suff. 3 p. pl. m.; וְ id. — קבץ

אֶקָּבֵר‎ Niph. fut. 1 pers. sing. — קבר

אֶקְבְּרָה‎ Kal fut. 1 pers. sing. with parag. ה — קבר

אֶקְבְּרֶהָ‎ id., suff. 3 pers. sing. fem.; וְ for וָ conv. — קבר

אֶקֹּד‎ Kal fut. 1 p. s. [for אָקֹד § 14. r. 18]; וְ id. — קדד

אָקְדָּח‎ noun masc. sing. — קדח

אַקְדִּיר‎ Hiph. fut. 1 pers. sing.; וְ for וָ conv. — קדר

אַקְדִּירֵם‎ id., suff. 3 pers. pl. masc. — קדר

אֲקַדֵּם‎ Piel fut. 1 pers. sing. — קדם

אֲקַדֵּשׁ‎ Piel fut. 1 pers. sing. — קדש

אֶקָּדֵשׁ‎ Niph. fut. 1 pers. sing. — קדש

אַקּוֹ‎ m. a sort of wild goat or gazelle, De. 14. 5.

אָקוֹב‎ Kal fut. 1 pers. sing. (§ 17. rem. 3 & § 8. rem. 18); וְ for וָ conv. — נקב

אֲקַוֶּה‎ וָ, וְ, Piel fut. 1 p. s.; וְ for וָ, וָ for וָ conv. — קוה

אָקוּט‎ Kal fut. 1 pers. sing. — קוט

אָקוּם‎ וְ Kal fut. 1 pers. sing.; וְ for וָ conv. — קום

אָקוּמָה‎ וְ id. with parag. ה — קום

אֲקוֹמֵם‎ Pilel fut. 1 pers. sing. — קום

אֶקַּח‎ / אֶקָּח‎ } Kal fut. 1 pers. sing. (§ 8. rem. 15. & § 17. rem. 8); וְ for וָ conv. } — לקח

אֶקְחָה‎ וְ, ה, id. with parag. ה (for אֶקְחָה comp. § 10. rem. 7); וְ id. — לקח

אֶקָּחֶנּוּ‎ id., suff. 3 pers. sing. masc. (§ 16. rem. 12) — לקח

אֶקָּחֲךָ‎ id., suff. 2 pers. sing. masc. (§ 16. rem. 12) — לקח

אֶקָּחֵם‎ id., suff. 3 p. pl. m. (§ 16. r. 12); וְ for וָ conv. — לקח

אֶקְטֹף‎ Kal fut. 1 pers. sing. — קטף

אָקִים‎ וְ Hiph. fut. 1 pers. sing.; וְ for וָ conv. — קום

אֲקִימָה‎ וְ Piel fut. 1 pers. sing. with parag. ה [for אֲקִימָה]; וְ id. — קום

אֲקִים‎ Chald. Aph. pret. 3 pers. s., suff. 3 pers. s. m. — קום

אָקִיץ‎ Hiph. fut. 1 pers. sing. — קוץ

אֶקֹּל‎ וְ Kal fut. 1 p. s. (§ 18. r. 6); וְ for וָ conv. — קלל

אֲקַלְלֵם‎ וְ Piel fut. 1 p. s., suff. 3 p. pl. m. (§ 10. r. 7); וְ id. — קלל

אָקֹם‎ וְ Kal fut. 1 pers. sing. for אָקוּם (but comp. § 21. rem. 7); וְ id. — קום

אֶקְנֶה‎ וְ Kal fut. 1 pers. sing.; וְ id. — קנה

᷍ Pr. 7. 12.   ᵏ 9 Sa. 22. 41.   ᵖ Is. 44. 3.   ᵛ Is. 27. 3.   ˣ Mi. 4. 6.   ᶜ Ge. 48. 7.   ᵉ Le. 10. 3.   ʰ Is. 44. 26.   Eze. 17. 22.
ᵇ Is. 44. 19.   Nu. 31. 50.   ᵠ Is. 44. 3.   Is. 1. 25.   2 Sa. 3. 21.   ᵍ Ge. 24. 48.   Job 5. 3.   Ho. 13. 11.   Am. 2. 11.
ᶜ Ge. 37. 36.   2 Sa. 1. 10.   ʳ Ps. 119. 69.   Ju. 7. 4.   Is. 54. 7.   Is. 54. 12.   Job 17. 14.   Is. 56. 12.   Ps. 119. 106.
ᵈ Ez. 2. 12.   ⁱ Job 19. 7.   ˢ Ps. 119. 145.   Pr. 8. 21.   Zec. 10. 8.   Eze. 31. 15.   Ps. 52. 11.   Ge. 18. 5.   Da. 3. 1.
ᵉ Nu. 11. 17.   ʲ Ps. 119. 34. 115.   Je. 17. 16.   Ne. 13. 11.   Exr. 8. 15.   Eze. 32. 8.   Ps. 69. 21.   Zec. 11. 15.   Pr. 23. 35.
ᶠ Ps. 101. 5, 8.   Mi. 7. 7.   Is. 42. 6; 49. 8.   Nu. 23. 8.   Mi. 6. 6.   Ps. 95. 10.   2 Ki. 6. 13.   Ge. 16. 5.
ᵍ Ps. 18. 41.   Is. 33. 14.   Ps. 119. 33.   Eze. 22. 20.   Ru. 1. 17.   Ex. 29. 44.   2 Sa. 17. 1.   Ios. 7. 21.   Ne. 13. 35.
ʰ Is. 43. 5.

אֶקְנִיאֵם	Hiph. fut. 1 pers. sing., suff. 3 pers. pl. masc.	קנא
אָקֵץ	Kal fut. 1 pers. sing. for [אָקוּץ], but comp. § 21. rem. 7]; ו for ו conv.	קוץ
אֶקְצוֹף / אֶקְצָף	Kal fut. 1 pers. sing. (§ 8. rem. 18)	קצף
אֶקְרָא	Kal fut. 1 pers. sing.; ו for ו conv.	קרא
אֶקְרֵא	Chald. Peal fut. 1 pers. sing.	קרא
אֶקְרָאָה	Kal fut. with parag. ה; ו for ו conv.	קרא
אֶקְרָאֶךָ	id., suff. 2 pers. sing. masc. (§ 2. rem. 3)	קרא
אֶקְרַב	Kal fut. 1 p. s. (§ 8. r. 13); ו for ו conv.	קרב
אֲקָרֶבְנּוּ	Piel fut. 1 p. s., suff. 3 p. s. m. (§ 2. r. 3.)	קרב
אֶקְרֶה	Niph. fut. 1 pers. sing. (§ 10. rem. 5)	קרה
אֶקְרַע / וָאֶקְרַע	Kal fut. 1 pers. sing. (§ 8. rem. 15); ו for ו conv.	קרע
אֶקְרָעֶנָּה	id., suff. 3 pers. sing. f. (§ 10. r. 5. § 2. r. 3)	קרע
אֶקְשֶׁה	Hiph. fut. 1 pers. sing.	קשה
אֶרָא	pr. name masc.; ו before (-)	ארה
אֵרָא	ap. for אֶרְאֶה (q. v.) § 24. r. 10; ו for ו conversive	ראה
אֵרֶא & וָ	ap. for אֶרְאֶה (q. v.) § 24. r. 3c; ו id.	ראה
אֵרָאֶה	Niph. fut. 1 pers. sing.	ראה
אֶרְאֶה	Kh. אֶרְאֶה q. v., K. אֵרָא (q. v.).	ראה
אֶרְאֶה וָ & וָ	Kal fut. 1 pers. sing.; ו for ו conv.	ראה
אַרְאֶהוּ	Hiph. fut. 1 pers. sing., suff. 3 pers. sing. masc. (§ 24. rem. 21)	ראה
אַרְאֶךָ	id., suff. 2 pers. sing. masc.	ראה
אֶרְאֶךָ	Kal fut. 1 pers. s., suff. 2 p. s. m. (§ 2. r. 3)	ראה
אֶרְאֵךְ	id., suff. 2 pers. sing. s. f.; ו for ו conv.	ראה
אֲרָאֵל	noun masc. sing. compound of אֵל & אֲרִי	ארה
אַרְאֵלִי וָ	pr. name masc.	ארה
אֶרְאֶלָּם	noun masc. sing. [אֶרְאֵל], suff. 3 pers. pl. m.	ארה
אֶרְאֵם	Kal fut. 1 p. s., suff. 3 p. pl. m. (§ 24. r. 21)	ראה
אַרְאֶנּוּ	Hiph. fut. 1 p. s., suff. 3 p. s. m. (§ 24. r. 21)	ראה
אֶרְאֶנּוּ וָ	Kal fut. 1 p. s., suff. 3 p. s. m (§ 24. r. 21)	ראה

אָרַב וָ to lie in wait or ambush, const. with עַל, ל, and acc.; part. אוֹרֵב a lier-in-wait, collect. liers-in-wait, an ambush. Pi. i. q. Kal, const. with עַל; abs. Ju. 9. 25. Hiph. to place an ambush, 1 Sa. 15. 5.

אֲרָב (ambush) pr. name of a city in the mountains of Judah, Jos. 15. 52, gent. n. אַרְבִּי, 2 Sa. 23. 35.

אֶרֶב masc.—I. a lying-in-wait, Job 38. 40.—II. a place of lying-in-wait, a lair of wild beasts, Job 37. 8.

אֹרֶב masc. dec. 6c. fraud, plot, Je. 9. 7.

אֲרֻבָּה fem. dec. 12c. id. only in pl. constr אֲרֻבּוֹת, Is. 25. 11.

אֲרֻבָּה fem. dec. 10. a kind of net-work or wicker-work, to guard various apertures, and applied to—I. a window, Ec. 12. 3.—II. a pigeon-house, Is. 60. 8.—III. a chimney, Ho. 13. 3.—IV. Meton. of the visible heavens.

מַאֲרָב masc. dec. 2b.—I. a place of ambush.—II. persons in an ambush, 2 Ch. 13. 13.

אֲרָב	pr. name of a place	ארב
אֲרָב	for [אֶרֶב] noun masc. sing. (§ 35. rem. 2)	ארב
אַרְבֶּה וָ	Hiph. fut. 1 pers. sing., Kh. אֶרֶב ap. K. ; ו for ו conv.	רבה
אֱרֹב וָ / אֱרָב־	Kal imp. sing. masc. (§ 8. rem. 18); ו before (v:)	ארב
אֹרֵב וָ	id. part. act. sing. masc. dec. 7b.	ארב
אַרְבֵּאל	pr. name, see בֵּית אַרְבֵּאל	בית
אַרְבָּה	noun masc. sing.	רבה
אַרְבֶּה וָ	Hiph. fut. 1 pers. sing.	רבה
אַרְבֶּהוּ וָ	id., suff. 3 pers. sing. masc. (§ 24. rem. 21)	רבה
אַרְבּוּ	Kal preter. 3 pers. pl.	ארב
אָרְבּוֹ	n. m. s., suff. 3 p. s. m. from אֶרֶב dec. 6c.	ארב
אֲרֻבּוֹת	noun fem. pl. constr. from [אֲרֻבָּה] dec. 12c.	ארב
אֲרֻבּוֹת	noun fem., pl. of אֲרֻבָּה dec. 10.	ארב
אֹרְבִים	Kal part. act. masc., pl. of אֹרֵב dec. 7b.	ארב
אַרְבִּיצֵם	Hiph. fut. 1 pers. sing., suff. 3 pers. pl. masc.	רבץ
אַרְבַּע / אַרְבַּע	num. card. fem. (§ 31. rem. 5)	רבע
אַרְבָּעָה וָ	id. masc., constr. אַרְבַּעַת (§ 42. rem. 5).	רבע
אַרְבְּעָה וָ	Chald. num. card. masc.	רבע
אַרְבָּעִים וָ	num. card. com., pl. of אַרְבַּע (§ 31. r. 3)	רבע
אַרְבַּעַת	Kh. בַּעַת q. v., K. בַּע (q. v.).	רבע
אַרְבַּעַת וָ	num. card. m., constr. of אַרְבָּעָה (§ 42. r. 5)	רבע
אַרְבַּעְתַּיִם	id., dual (of בַּעַת comp. dec. 13a), for בַּע תַּיִם	רבע
אַרְבַּעְתָּם	id. sing., suff. 3 pers. sing. masc.	רבע
אֲרֻבֹת וָ	defec. for אֲרֻבּוֹת q. v.; ו before (-)	ארב
אָרַבְתִּי	Kal pret. 1 pers. sing. [for אָרַבְתִּי § 8. r. 7]	ארב
אֲרֻבֹתֵיהֶם	n. f. pl., suff. 3 p. pl. m. from אֲרֻבָּה d. 10.	ארב
אֲרַבְתֶּם וָ	Kal pret. 2 pers. pl. masc.; ו for ו	ארב

[אָרַג] I. to plait the hair, Ju. 16. 13.—II. to weave, אֹרֵג weaving, a weaver.

אֶרֶג masc. I. texture, web, Ju. 16. 14.—II. weaver's shuttle, Job 7. 6.

אֹרֶג	noun masc. sing. [for אֶרֶג § 35. r. 2]	ארג
אֹרֵג וָ	Kal. part. act. sing. masc. dec. 7b.	ארג

a De. 32. 21.   e 1 Sa. 28. 15.   k Ho. 13. 8.   p Is. 41. 28.   u Eze. 16. 6, 8.   z De. 19. 11.   e Ge. 17. 2.   k Da. 7. 6.   o Is. 60. 8.
b Le. 20. 23.   f Job 31. 37.   l 1 Ki. 14. 3.   q Ps. 42. 3.   v 2 Sa. 23. 20.   a Jos. 24. 3.   f Is. 51. 2.   l Eze. 7. 2.   p Ju. 21. 20.
c Is. 57. 14.   g Nu. 23. 15.   m 1 Ki. 11. 12.   r Jos. 7. 21.   w Is. 33. 7.   b Ju. 9. 32.   g Je. 9. 7.   m Is. 25. 11.   q Job 7. 6.
d Da. 5. 17.   h 1 Ki. 11. 12.   n Ex. 7. 3.   s Ps. 91. 16.   x Je. 18. 17.   c Je. 9. 7.   h 2 Sa. 15. 6.   n Job 11. 9.   r Ex. 35. 35.
i 1 Ki. 11. 11.   o Ez. 6. 3.   t Ju. 4. 22.   y Ge. 45. 28.   d Ju. 20. 33.   i Da. 1. 17.   s 2 Ki. 3. 14.

אַרְגֹּב   pr. name of a region . . . רגב

אַרְגָּוָן   *purple,* i.q. אַרְגָּמָן, only 2 Ch. 2.6, and Chald.
emph. אַרְגְּוָנָא Da. 5. 7, 16, 29.

אֹרְגֹות   Kal part. act. pl. f. from אָרַג m. (§ 8. r. 19) ארג

אֶאֱרֹג   Kal fut. 1 pers. sing. [for גֹ' § 8. rem. 15] רגן

אַרְגִּיעַ   Hiph. fut. 1 pers. sing. . . . רגן

אֹרְגִים   Kal part. act. masc., pl. of אֹרֵג dec. 7 b. ארג

אַרְגִּיעַ   Hiph. fut. 1 pers. sing. . . . רגע

אַרְגִּיעָה   id. with parag. ה . . . . רגע

אַרְגָּמָן   *purple, reddish purple,* both of the colour
itself and clothes dyed with purple. The
etymology is uncertain.

אָרַד   Root not used, perhaps i.q. עָרַד *to flee;* in the
Chald. אַרְדָּא *mushroom.* Whence—
אַרְדְּ (*mushroom ?*) pr. name of a son or grandson of Benjamin, Ge. 46. 21; Nu. 26 40. called
אַדָּר 1 Ch. 8. 3. Gent. n. אַרְדִּי.
אָרֹוד (*flight,* or perhaps i.q. עָרֹוד *wild ass*) pr.
name masc. Nu. 26. 17. Gent. n. אֲרֹודִי Ge. 46. 16.
אַרְדֹּון (*fugitive*) pr. name masc. 1 Ch. 2. 18.
אֲרִידַי (*strong,* coll. with the Pers.) pr. name of
a son of Haman, Est. 9. 9.
אֲרִידָתָא (id.) pr. name of a son of Haman,
Est. 9. 8.

אֵרֵד   Kal fut. 1 pers. sing.; וָ for וְ conv. ירד

אֵרְדָה   id. with paragogic ה . . . ירד

אֶרְדֹּוף   Kal fut. 1 pers. sing. (§ 8. rem. 18) רדף

אַרְדַּי   pr. name masc. for אֲרִידַי ארד

אֶרְדֹּף   Kal fut. 1 pers. sing. . . . רדף

אֶרְדְּפָה   id. with paragogic ה . . . רדף

[אָרָה]   I. *to pull,* or *pluck off,* Ps. 80. 13.—II. *to gather,*
Ca. 5. 1.
אַרְאָ (*lion,* comp. אֲרִי) pr. name masc. 1 Ch. 7.38.
אֻרְוָה (for אֲרֻוָה, fem. of אֲרִי, pl. abs. אֻרָוֹת for
אֻרְוֹת, constr. אֻרְוֹת comp. dec. 12c) and אַרְיֵה,
fem. *a stall, a stable.*
אָרֹון   com. dec. 3 a.—I. *ark, chest.*—II. *coffin,*
Ge. 50. 26.
אֲרִי   masc. dec. 6. pl. אֲרָיִים and אֲרָיֹות, *lion.*
אַרְיֵה   i.q. אֲרִי, with parag. ה *a lion.*
אַרְיֵה   Chald. id. irr. comp. § 68.
אֲרִיאֵל   masc. prop. *a lion of God,* hence—I. *a
hero,* applied also to the altar of burnt-offering,
Eze. 43. 15, 16. and Jerusalem, Is. 29. 1, 2.—II. pr.
name masc. Ezr. 8. 16.

אֲרְאֵל   contr. from the preceding, *a hero,* only
with suff. אֶרְאֵלָּם, Is. 33. 7.

אַרְאֵלִי   (*hero*) pr. name masc. Ge. 46. 16.

אַרְיֹוךְ   (*lion-like,* the syllable אַךְ being an adj
term. in the Pers., Gesenius) pr. name—I. a king
of Ellasar, Ge. 14. 1, 9.—II. a Chaldean, Da. 2. 14.

אֲרִיסַי   (*lion-like,* Pers. סַם, סַה *like*) pr. name
of a son of Haman, Est. 9. 9.

אֲרֵה   Kal imp. sing. masc., [אַר] with parag. ה [for
אַרֵה § 18. rem. 4] ארר

אֲרוּ   Chald. *lo, behold !* Da. 7. 2, 5, 6, 7, 13.

אָרוּ   Kal pret. 3 pers. pl. (§ 21. rem. 2) . אור

אָרוּ   Kal imp. pl. m. from [אֹר] sing., comp. אֲרֵה ארר

אֲרוֹד   pr. name of a place . . . . רוד

אֲרֹודִי   gent. noun from אֲרֹוד ארד

אֲרוּהָ   Kal pret. 3 pers. pl., suff. 3 pers. sing. fem. ארה

אֲרוּכָה   noun fem. sing. dec. 10. ארך

אָרוּם   Kal fut. 1 pers. sing. . . . רום

אֲרוֹמִים   Kh., for אֲדֹומִים K., see אֱדֹום . אדם

אֲרוֹמַם   [for אֶתְרֹו] Hithpal fut. 1 pers. s. (§ 21. r. 20) רום

אֲרוֹמִמְךָ   Pilel fut. 1 pers. sing., suff. 2 pers. sing.
אֲרוֹמִמְךָ   masc. (§ 2. rem. 3) . . . רום

אֲרוֹן   noun com., constr. of אֲרֹון dec. 3 a; וַ bef. ארה

אַרְנָה   pr. name masc. ארן

אֲרוּץ   Kal fut. 1 p. s. (2 Sa. 22. 30, perh. R. רצץ) רוץ

אֲרוּצָה   וָ id. with paragogic ה רוץ

אֲרוּצֵם   Kh. אֲרִיצֵם Kal fut. with suff. R. רצץ (§18.r.12)
K. אֲרִיצֵם Hiph. fut. 1 p.s. with suff. 3 p. pl. m. רוץ

אָרֹור   Kal inf. abs. . . . . . ארר

אָרוּר   id. part. p. sing. masc. dec. 3 a. ארר

אֲרוּרָה   id. id. fem. ארר

אֲרוּרִים   id. id. pl. masc. ארר

אֲרָוֹת   noun fem., pl. of [אֻרְוָה] q. v. . ארה

אֻרְוֹת   id. pl., construct state . . . ארה

אֲרוֹתִי   Kal pret. 1 pers. sing. [for אָרֹותִי; acc.
shifted by conv. וָ) (§ 8. rem. 7) ארר

אֲרֹותִיהָ   id., suff. 3 pers. sing. fem. ארר

[אָרַז]   *to be firm, fast,* only in part. pass. Eze. 27. 24.
אֶרֶז   masc. dec. 6 a. (pl. c. אַרְזֵי) *cedar.*
אַרְזָה   fem. *cedar wainscot,* Zep. 2. 14.
מָרֹוז   (built *of cedar* for מְאָרֹוז) pr. name of a
town in Palestine, Ju. 5. 23.
אֶרֶז   noun masc. sing., (pl. c. אַרְזֵי § 35.
אֶרֶז   rem. 1, 2) dec. 6a; for וָ see lett. וֹ ארז
אַרְזָה   noun fem. sing. . . . . ארז
אַרְזֵי   noun masc. pl. constr. from אֶרֶז dec. 6a. ארז

a 2 Ki. 23. 7.   d Is. 19. 9.   g Ps. 18. 38.   i 1 Sa. 14. 29.   n Ps. 46. 11, 11.   r 2 Sa. 18. 19.   v Ju. 5. 23.   z 1 Ki. 5. 6.   k 1 Ki. 6. 18.
b Hos. 3. 16.   e Is. 51. 4.   h 2 Sa. 22. 38.   l Ju. 5. 23.   o Is. 33. 10.   s 2 Ki. 4. 22.   w Ge. 3. 17.   a Mal. 2. 2.   c Zep. 2. 14.
c Is. 13. 12.   f Ge. 18. 21.   i 2 Sa. 17. 1.   m Ps. 80. 13.   p Ps. 118. 28.   t Je. 50. 44.   x 2 Ch. 32. 28.   b 1 Ki. 7. 11.

אַרְזָיו id. pl., suff. 3 pers. sing. masc. . ארז

אַרְזֶיךָ id. pl., suff. 2 pers. sing. masc. . ארז

אֲרָזִים וְ' id. pl., absolute state; וְ before ‏(־)‏ ארז

אֲרֻזִים וְ Kal part. pass. pl. of [אָרוּז] dec. 3a; וְ id. ארז

אָרַח וְ *to go, to be on the way*, Job 34. 8; part. אֹרֵחַ *a way-farer, traveller.*

אָרַח (*wanderer*) pr. name masc.

אֹרַח com. dec. 6c. pl. אֳרָחוֹת constr. and with suff. אָרְחוֹת, by Syr. אֻרְחֹתַי (§ 35. rem. 5 & 9).— I. *way, road, path.*—II. *manner, mode.*—III. poet. for אֹרֵחַ *traveller*, Job 31. 32.

אֹרַח Chald. id. dec. 3c. pl. אָרְחָן.

אֹרְחָה fem. dec. 10. *a company of travellers, a caravan.*

אֲרֻחָה fem. dec. 10.—I. *appointed portion.*—II. *portion, generally*, Pr. 15. 17.

אֶרַח pr. name masc. . ארח

אֹרַח וְ' noun com. sing. dec. 6. pl. אֳרָחוֹת *more under the Root* . ארח

אֹרְחָה noun fem. sing. dec. 10. . ארח

אָרְחוֹ n. com. s., suff. 3 pers. s. m. from אֹרַח (q. v.) ארח

אֳרָחוֹת id. pl., absolute state . ארח

אֹרְחוֹת noun fem., pl. of [אֹרְחָה] dec. 10. . ארח

אָרְחוֹת וְ' noun com. pl. constr. from אֹרַח (q. v.) ארח

אָרְחֹתֶיךָ id., suff. 2 pers. sing. masc. (א § 35. r. 9) ארח

אָרְחֹתָם id., suff. 3 pers. pl. masc. (א ibid.) ארח

אָרְחִי id. sing., suff. 1 pers. sing. . ארח

אֹרְחִים Kal part. act. masc., pl. of אֹרֵחַ dec. 7b. ארח

אַרְחִיק Hiph. fut. 1 pers. sing. . רחק

אֲרֻחָתְךָ [for חָזָה] noun com. sing., suff. 2 pers. sing. masc. from אֹרַח dec. 6c. (more under R.) ארח

אֲרַחֵם Piel fut. 1 pers. sing. (§ 14. rem. 1) רחם

אֶרְחָמְךָ Kal fut. 1 pers. s. [אֶרְחָם], suff. 2 pers. s. m. רחם

אֲרַחֲמֶנּוּ Piel fut. 1 p. s., suff. 3 p. s. m. (§ 14. r. 1) רחם

אֶרְחַץ וְ' Kal fut. 1 pers. sing.; וְ for וְ conv. רחץ

אֶרְחָצֵךְ וְ id., suff. 2 pers. sing.fem. (§ 16.r.12); וְ id. רחץ

אֹרַחַת noun fem. sing. constr. of [חָזָה] dec. 10. ארח

אֲרֻחַת noun fem. sing., constr. of [חָזָה] dec. 10. ארח

אָרְחָתְךָ וְ Chald. noun com. pl. [אָרְחָן], suff. 3 pers. sing. masc., comp. Heb. אֹרַח ‏.‏ ארח

אֲרֻחָתוֹ וְ noun fem. sing., suff. 3 pers. sing. masc. from אֲרֻחָה dec. 10; וְ before ‏(־)‏ ‏.‏ ארח

אָרְחֹתָיו noun com., pl., suff. 3 pers. sing. masc. from אֹרַח q. v. (א § 35. rem. 9) . ארו

אָרְחֹתַי id., suff. 1 pers. sing. [for אָרְחֹתַי] . ארח

אָרְחֹתֵיהֶם id., suff. 3 pers. pl. masc. . ארח

אָרְחָתֶיךָ id., suff. 2 pers. sing. masc. (א § 35. rem. 9) ארח

אָרְחָתְךָ Chald. id. pl. with suff. 2 pers. s. m. dec. 3 e. ארח

אֲרִי noun masc. sing. dec. 6i. (§ 35. rem. 14) ארה

אֲרִי pr. name masc. for אוּרִי . אור

אֲרִיאֵל noun masc. sing. compound of אֵל & אֲרִי ארה

אָרִיב וְ' Kal fut. 1 pers. sing.; וְ for וְ conv. ריב

אָרִיבָה וְ id. with parag. ה; וְ id. ריב

אָרִיד Hiph. fut. 1 pers. sing. . רוד

אֲרִידִי pr. name masc. . ארד

אֲרִידָתָא pr. name masc. . ארד

אַרְיֵה Kh. אַרְיֵה q. v., K. אֲרִי (q. v.) ארה

אַרְיֵה וְ' n.m.s., from אֲרִי with parag. ה (§35.r.14) ארה

אֲרִיוֶךָ Piel fut. 1 pers. s. [אָרִיוֶה from pret. רִיוָה, like קִיֵּם from קוּם] with suff. 3 p. s. f., rad. ה changed to וְ, comp. רָאֲוָה from רָאָה. Or it may stand by transp. for אַרְגִּיעֶךָ (§ 24. r. 13) רוה

אַרְיוֹךְ וְ' pr. name masc. . ארה

אֲרָיוֹת n. masc. with pl. fem. term. from אֲרִי (q. v.) ארה

אֲרָיוֹת noun fem., pl. of [אַרְיֵה] dec. 10. . ארה

אַרְיָוָתָא Chald. noun masc. with pl. fem. term., emph. st. from אַרְיֵה irr. (§ 68) . ארה

אָרִיחַ Hiph. fut. 1 pers. sing. . רוח

אֲרִיךְ Chald. Peal part. pass. sing. . ארך

אֲרָיִים noun masc., pl. of אֲרִי dec. 6i. . ארה

אָרִים Hiph. fut. 1 pers. sing. . רום

אֲרִיסַי pr. name masc. . ארה

אֲרִיצֵנּוּ Hiph. fut. 1 p.s. [אָרִיץ], suff. 3 p.s.m. (§2.r.3) רוץ

אָרִיק Hiph. fut. 1 pers. sing. . רוק

אֲרִיקֵם id., suff. 3 pers. pl. masc. . רוק

אָרִיתִי Kal pret. 1 pers. sing. . ארה

[אָרַךְ] *to be* or *become long*, spoken of boughs (Eze. 31. 5), and of time; אָרְכוּ לוֹ שָׁם הַיָּמִים *he had been there a long time*. Hiph.—I. *to make long, to prolong*, הַאֲרִיךְ יָמִי פ' *to prolong one's life.*—II. *to defer*, הַאֲרִיךְ אַפּוֹ *to defer one's anger, to be patient.*— III. intrans. *to be long*, 1 Ki. 8. 8; יַאֲרִיכוּ יָמָיו *his days are long*, i. e. *lives long.*

אֲרַךְ Chald. only part. pass. *meet, fit*, Ezr. 4. 14.

אָרֵךְ masc. adj. only fem. אֲרֻכָּה (§ 39. No. 3. dec. 8. & § 26. III. No. 22) *long*, of space and time.

אֹרֶךְ masc.—I. *length*, Eze. 17. 3, אֹרֶךְ הָאֵבֶר *length of wing* for the concrete *long-winged.*—II. *slowness, tardiness*, אֹרֶךְ אַפַּיִם *slowness of anger*, i. e. *forbearance*, Je. 15. 15, elsewhere in this phrase and אֹרֶךְ רוּחַ (slowness of spirit) for the concrete *patient, long-suffering*, spoken of God or men.—

a Je. 22. 7.   e Je. 40. 5.   i Ps. 25. 4.   m Ps. 18. 2.   p Eze. 16. 9.   r Pr. 2. 15.   t Ps. 55. 3.   v 2 Ch. 9. 25.   x Je. 49. 19.
b Is. 9. 9.   f Ps. 119. 9.   k Je. 9. 1.   n Je. 31. 20.   q Da. 4. 34.   s La. 3. 10.   u 1 Ki. 10. 20.   y Ps. 18. 43.
c Eze. 27. 24.   g Is. 21. 13.   l Ps. 44. 19.   o Ps. 73. 13.   r Ne. 13. 25.   t Is. 16. 9.   w Ezr. 4. 14.   z Ca. 5. 1.
d Job 34. 8.   h Pr. 2. 29.   ll Ju. 5. 6.   oo Ge. 37. 25.   q Pr. 22. 25.

III. pr. name of a city of Babylonia, Ge. 10. 10. Gent. noun אַרְכִּי.

אֹרֶךְ masc. dec. 6 c. *length*, of time and space, אֹרֶךְ אַפַּיִם *forbearance*, comp. אָרֵךְ.

אַרְכָּא & אַרְכָה Chald. fem. *length, duration*, Da. 4. 24 ; 7. 12.

אֲרוּכָה, אֲרֻכָה fem. dec. 10. (prop. prolongation) *a repairing, restoring, healing.*

אַרְכְּוָי Chald. gent. noun from אֶרֶךְ q. v. pl. אַרְכְּוָי Kheth' אַרְכְּוָא K. (§ 63) Ezr. 4. 9.

אֶרֶךְ '(noun masc. sing.; also pr. name of a place
אֶרֶךְ '(noun masc. sing. dec. 6 c.
אֶרְכַּב (Kal fut. 1 pers. sing.
אֻרְכְּבָתָא (Chald. noun fem. sing., suff. 3 pers. sing. masc. from [אַרְכֻּבָּא] dec. 8 a.
אַרְכָּא
אַרְכָה (} Chald. noun fem. sing.
defect. for אֲרוּכָה, noun fem. sing. dec. 10.
אֲרֻכָּה adj. fem. sing. fr. [אָרֵךְ] masc. (§ 37. No. 3. & § 39. rem. 3. dec. 8)
אָרְכָּהּ n. m. s., suff. 3 pers. s. f. from אֹרֶךְ dec. 6 c.
אָרְכוּ Kal pret. 3 pers. pl.
אָרְכוֹ '(n. m. s., suff. 3 pers. s. m. from אֹרֶךְ dec. 6 c.
אַרְכְּוָי Chald. gent. noun pl. Kh. (more under R.)
אַרְכִּיב Hiph. fut. 1 pers. sing.
אָרְכָּם n. m. s., suff. 3 p. pl. m. from אֹרֶךְ dec. 6 c.
אֲרֻכַת noun fem. sing., constr. of אֲרוּכָה dec. 10.
אֲרֻכָתְךָ '(id., suff. 2 pers. sing. masc.; וַ before (ָ֯)

אָרַם Root not used, i. q. רוּם, רָמַם, רָאַם, &c. *to be high*, whence

אֲרוּמָה (*lofty*) pr. name of a city near Sichem, Ju. 9. 41, called רוּמָה 2 Ki. 23. 36.

אֲרָם, constr. אֲרַם (*high*) pr. name.—I. son of Kamuel and grandson of Nahor, Ge. 22. 21, but according to chap. 10. 22, he was a son of Shem.—II. 1 Ch. 7. 34.—III. *Aramea, Syria*, the whole region between Phenicia, the Taurus, Tigris and Palestine; the principal part is, אֲרַם דַּמֶּשֶׂק *Syria of Damascus*, the territory of and round Damascus; אֲרַם נַהֲרַיִם *Syria of the two rivers*, i. e. Mesopotamia, also called פַּדַּן אֲרָם *plain of Syria*, and שְׂדֵה אֲרָם *field of Syria.*

אֲרַמִּי gent. noun *Aramean, Syrian*, fem. אֲרַמִּיָה; pl. אֲרַמִּים.

אֲרָמִית (formed of the preceding, see § 39. No. 4. rem. 1) adv. *in the language of Syria, in Syriac.*

אַרְמוֹן masc. pl. constr. אַרְמְנוֹת [as if from אַרְמֹנֶת § 44. rem. 5], *castle, palace.*

אַרְמֹנִי (*palastine*) pr. name of a son of Saul, 2 Sa. 21. 8.

אֲרָם '(noun masc. sing. (q. v.)
אֲרַמִּי gent. noun from אֲרָם
אֲרַמִּים id. pl. absolute
אֲרָמִית adv. from the gentilic n. אֲרַמִּי (§ 39. No. 4. r. 1)
אֲרֹמְמֶנְהוּ וַ Piel fut. 1 pers. sing. with epenth. נ (§ 16. r. 13) and suff. 3 pers. sing. masc.; וַ for דוֹם
אַרְמְנוֹת noun masc. with pl. fem. term. const. [as if from אַרְמֹנֶת § 44. r. 5] see אַרְמוֹן
אַרְמְנוֹתֶיהָ id. with suff. 3 pers. sing. fem.
אַרְמְנוֹתַיִךְ '' id., suff. 2 pers. sing. fem. for תַיִךְ'
אַרְמֹנִי pr. name masc.
אַרְמְנֹתֶיהָ noun masc. with fem. term. and suff. 3 pers. sing. fem. from אַרְמוֹן (q. v.)
אַרְמְנֹתָיו '(id., suff. 3 pers. sing. masc.
אֶרְמְסֵם '(Kal fut. 1 pers. sing. [אָרַמ], suff. 3 pers. pl. masc.

אָרַן Root not used, Arab. *to be active, nimble.*

אֹרֶן (*wild goat*, Syriac ארנא id.) pr. n. of a man.

אֹרֶן masc.—I. a kind of tree, supposed to be the *mountain ash*, Vulg. *pinus*, Is. 44. 14. Its connexion with the Root is uncertain.—II. pr. name masc. 1 Ch. 2. 25.

אֲרָן (*nimble*) pr. name masc. 1 Ch. 3. 21.

אָרְנָן (id.) pr. name of a Jebusite, on the site of whose threshing-floor Solomon built the temple, 1 Ch. 21. 15 ; 2 Ch. 3. 1.

אֲרַוְנָה pr. name, stands for אָרְנָן in 2 Sa. 24. 20, sq. which is called in v. 16, אֲוַרְנָה Kheth., in v. 18, אֲרַנְיָה Kheth.

אֶרֶן וַ pr. name masc.; וַ before (ָ֯)
אֲרֹן noun masc. sing. constr. of אָרוֹן dec. 3 a.
אֶרֶן '(noun masc. sing.; also pr. name
[אַרְנֶבֶת] f. *hare*; only with the art. Le. 11. 6; De. 14. 7.
אַרְנוֹן pr. name of a river
אֲרַנְיָה pr. name masc., K. אֲרוֹנָה
אֲרַנֵּן '(Piel fut. 1 pers. sing.
אֹרֶן pr. name masc.
אַרְנִין [for עַיִן] Hiph. fut. 1 pers. sing.
אַרְנֹן pr. name of a river for אַרְנוֹן
אֲרַן '(pr. name masc.

אָרַע Chald. only in the emph. st. אַרְעָא (dec. 3 a).—I.

the earth, i.q. Heb. אֶרֶץ.—II. adv. low, inferior, Da. 2. 39.

אַרְעִית Chald. fem. (prop. constr. of אַרְעִי, comp. dec. 8b) the bottom, Da. 6. 25.

אֶרַע Hiph. fut. 1 pers. sing. (§ 18. rem. 11)   רעע

אַרְעָא Chald. Kh. אַרְעָא, K. אֲרַע adv.   ארע

אַרְעָא b) Chald. noun f. s. emph. of [אֲרַע] dec. 3a.   ארע

אֶרְעַב Kal fut. 1 pers. sing.   רעב

אֶרְעֶה c) Kal fut. 1 pers. sing.; וְ for וַ conv.   רעה

אֶרְעֶנָּה id., suff. 3 pers. sing. fem. (§ 24. rem. 21)   רעה

אֵרָפֵא d) Niph. fut. 1 pers. sing.   רפא

אֶרְפָּא e) Kal fut. 1 pers. sing.   רפא

אֶרְפָּאֵהוּ id., suff. 3 pers. sing. masc.   רפא

אֶרְפָּאֵךְ id., suff. 2 pers. sing. fem.   רפא

אַרְפַּד f) pr. name of a region   רפד

אַרְפֶּה Hiph. fut. 1 p. s., suff. 3 p. s. f. (§ 24. r. 21)   רפה

אֶרְפָּא g) Kal fut. 1 pers. sing. (§ 23. rem. 10)   רפא

אַרְפְּךָ Hiph. fut. 1 pers. sing. [אַרְפֶּה], suff. 2 pers. sing. masc. (§ 24. rem. 21)   רפה

אַרְפַּכְשַׁד h) pr. name of the third son of Shem.

אַרְפֶּנּוּ Hiph. fut. 1 pers. sing. [אַרְפֶּה], suff. 3 pers sing. masc. (§ 24. rem. 21, & § 2. rem. 3)   רפה

אֶרֶץ fem. rarely masc. dec. 6a. with the art. הָאָרֶץ, with suff. אַרְצִי.—I. the earth, opp. to שָׁמַיִם.—II. earth, land, opposed to יָם.—III. land, ground.—IV. land, country. Pl. אֲרָצוֹת lands, countries, especially Gentile countries.

אַרְצָא pr. name of a man, 1 Ki. 16. 9.

אֶרֶץ } i) noun fem. sing. dec. 6a. (§ 35. rem. 2);
 אֶרֶץ } for וֹ see lett. ו   ארץ

אָרוּץ k) Kal fut. 1 p. s. (perhaps from רוץ § 18. r. 12)   רוץ

אַרְצָא pr. name masc.   ארץ

אַרְצָה / אַרְצָה } noun f. s. (אֶרֶץ), with parag. ה dec. 6a.   ארץ

אַרְצָהּ id., suff. 3 pers. sing. fem.   ארץ

אָרוּצָה Kal fut. 1 pers. sing. with parag. ה for אָרוּצָה   רוץ

אֶרְצֶה l) Kal fut. 1 pers. sing.   רצה

אַרְצוֹ noun f. s., suff. 3 p. s. m. from אֶרֶץ dec. 6a.   ארץ

אֲרָצוֹת id. pl. absolute state   ארץ

אַרְצוֹת id. pl. constr. state   ארץ

אֶרְצֶה Niph. fut. 1 pers. sing. [for צֶה § 15. rem. 1]   רצה

אַרְצִי noun f. s., suff. 1 pers. s. from אֶרֶץ dec. 6a.   ארץ

אַרְצְךָ / אַרְצְךָ } id., suff. 2 pers. sing. masc.   ארץ

אַרְצֵךְ id., suff. 2 pers. sing. fem.   ארץ

אַרְצְכֶם id., suff. 2 pers. pl. masc.   ארץ

אַרְצָם id., suff. 3 pers. pl. masc.   ארץ

אֶרְצֵם Kal fut. 1 pers. sing. (אֶרְצֶה), suff. 3 pers. pl. masc. (§ 24. rem. 21)   רצה

אַרְצֵנוּ וְ noun f. s., suff. 1 p. pl. from אֶרֶץ dec. 6a.   ארץ

אַרְקָא Chald. only emph. st. אַרְקָא (dec. 3a) Je. 10 11. the earth.

אַרְקָעֵם Kal fut. 1 pers. sing. [אֶרְקַע], suff. 3 pers. pl. masc. (§ 16. rem. 12)   רקע

[אָרַר] to curse, execrate. Niph. to be cursed, Mal. 3. 9. Pi.—I. to curse, Ge. 5. 29.—II. to bring on a curse, Nu. 5. 18, 19. sq. Hoph. to be cursed, Nu. 22. 6. מְאֵרָה fem. dec. 10. curse, execration.

אֲרַרְתִּהָ Piel pret. 1 pers. sing., suff. 3 pers. sing. fem.   ארר

אֲרָרָט / אֲרָרַט } pr. name of a province in Armenia, upon whose mountains the ark of Noah rested.

אֹרְרֵי Kal part. act. m., pl. c. from [אָרַר] dec. 7b.   ארר

אֹרְרֶיךָ id. pl., suff. 2 pers. s. m. (ךָ anom. for ךָ)   ארר

אָרַשׂ Pi. to betroth; the price paid for a wife is put with בְּ. Pu. to be betrothed.

אָרַשׁ Root not used, Arab. to desire. אֲרֶשֶׁת fem. desire, request, Ps. 21. 3.

אֵרַשׂ Piel pret. 3 pers. sing. masc. (§ 10. rem. 1)   ארש

אֹרָשָׂה Pual pret. 3 pers. sing. fem. [for אֹרְשָׂה]   ארש

אֶרְשַׁע Kal fut. 1 pers. sing. [for אֶרְשַׁע § 8. rem. 15]   רשע

אֶרֶשֶׁת וְ noun fem. sing.; וְ before (־)   ארש

אֵרַשְׂתִּי Piel pret. 1 pers. sing.   ארש

אֵרַשְׂתִּיךְ id., suff. 2 pers. sing. masc.   ארש

אֹרֶת noun m., with pl. f. term. from אוֹר dec. 1a.

אַרְתַּחְשַׁשְׁתָּא / אַרְתַּחְשַׁשְׁתָּא / אַרְתַּחְשַׁסְתָּא } Artaxerxes pr. name of several Persian kings.

אֵשׁ וְ com. dec. 8b.—I. fire; used of lightning, of the sun, and trop. of anger.—II. shining brightness, Na. 2. 4; אַבְנֵי אֵשׁ stones of fire, glittering gems, Ez. 28. 14, 16.

אֵשׁ Chald. emph. אֶשָּׁא, id. Da. 7. 11.

אִשֶּׁה f. fire, only in Kheth. (מֵ אֶשָּׁתָם) Je. 6. 29.

אִשֶּׁה masc. dec. 9a. an offering made by fire.—I. a burnt-offering.—II. incense-offering.

אֵשׁ i.q. יֵשׁ there is, there are, comp. Ch. אִית.

אֶשָּׁא Chald. noun masc. sing. emph. of אֵשׁ dec. 8b.

אֶשָּׂא וְ, וָ, Kal fut. 1 pers. sing.; וָ for וַ conv.   נשא

a Da. 2. 39.   e Eze. 34. 16.   i Je. 30. 17.   n Ps. 18. 30.   r Pr. 22. 13.   u Ps. 85. 13.   y Job 3. 8.   c De. 20. 7.   f Ho. 2. 21, 23.
b Exr. 5. 11.   f Je. 17. 14.   k Je. 3. 22.   o Is. 8. 23.   s Is. 62. 4.   x 2 Sa. 22. 43.   z Ge. 5. 29.   d Ps. 21. 3.   g 2 Ki. 4. 29.
c Ps. 50. 12.   g 2 Ch. 7. 14.   l Jos. 1. 5.   p 2 Sa. 18. 22.   t Esc. 20. 46.   y Ge. 5. 29.   a Nu. 24. 9.   e Sa. 3. 14.   h Da. 7. 11.
d Zec. 11. 7, 7.   h Is. 57. 18.   m Ca. 3. 4.   q Hag. 1. 8.

אֶשְׁאָב Kal fut. 1 pers. s. [for אֶשְׁאַב § 8. rem. 15] שׁאב

אַשְׁאִיר Hiph. fut. 1 pers. sing. . . . שׁאר

אֶשְׁאַל וְ] Kal fut. 1 pers. sing.; וָ] for וְ] conv. . שׁאל

אֶשְׁאֲלָה id. with paragogic ה . . . . שׁאל

אֶשְׁאָלְךָ וְ] id., suff. 2 pers. sing. m. (§ 16. rem. 12) שׁאל

אֶשְׁאָלֵם וְ] & וָ] id., suff. 3 pers. pl. masc. (§ 16. rem. 12); וָ] for וְ] . . . שׁאל

אֶשְׁאָנֶנּוּ וְ] Kal fut. 1 pers. sing., suff. 3 pers. sing. masc. (§ 2. rem. 3) . . . נשׁא

אֶשְׁאַף וְ] Kal fut. 1 pers. sing. . . . שׁאף

אֶשְׁאָפָה וְ] id. with paragogic ה, [for אֶשְׁאַף § 8. rem. 15]; וָ] for וְ] conv. . . . שׁאף

אָשֵׁב ap. for אָשִׁיב (q. v.) . . . שׁוב

אָשֵׁב defect. for אָשׁוּב (q. v.) . . . שׁוב

אֵשֵׁב וְ] & וָ] Kal fut. 1 pers. sing.; וָ] for וְ] conv. ישׁב

אֵשְׁבָה וְ] & וָ] id. with parag. ה (§ 8. rem. 15); ישׁב

אֵשְׁבָה וָ] id. . . ישׁב

אֶשְׁבֹּר Kal fut. 1 pers. sing. (§ 8. rem. 18) . שׁבר

אַשְׁבִּיעַ Hiph. fut. 1 pers. sing. . . . שׁבע

אַשְׁבִּיעֶהוּ id., suff. 3 pers. sing. masc. . שׁבע

אַשְׁבִּיעֲךָ Hiph. fut. 1 pers. sing. with suff. 2 p. s. m. שׁבע

אַשְׁבִּיעֶךָ Hiph. fut. 1 pers. sing. with suff. 2 pers. sing. masc. (for עֶךָ § 2. rem. 3) . שׁבע

אַשְׁבִּיעֵם וָ] Hiph. fut. 1 pers. sing., suff. 3 pers. pl. masc.; וָ] for וְ] conv. . . . שׁבע

אַשְׁבִּיר Hiph. fut. 1 pers. sing. . . . שׁבר

אַשְׁבִּיתָהּ Hiph. fut. 1 pers. sing. with paragogic ה . שׁבת

אַשְׁבֵּל וָ] pr. name of a son of Benjamin. Patronym. אַשְׁבֵּלִי, Nu. 26. 38.

אַשְׁבָּן וָ] pr. name masc. Ge. 36. 26.

אֶשְׁבַּע pr. name. masc. . . . שׁבע

אַשְׁבִּעַ וָ] Hiph. fut. 1 pers. sing.; וָ] for וְ] conv. שׁבע

אֶשְׁבַּע Kal fut. 1 pers. sing. . שׁבע

אֶשָּׁבַע וָ] Niph. fut. 1 pers. sing.; וָ] for וְ] conv.
אֶשָּׁבֵעַ וָ] (§ 9. rem. 5. & § 15. rem. 1). } שׁבע

אֶשְׁבְּעָה Kal fut. 1 pers. sing. with paragogic ה שׁבע

אֶשְׁבַּעַל for בַּעַל pr. name masc. see אִישׁ־בּשֶׁת אישׁ

אֲשַׁבֵּר Piel fut. 1 pers. sing. . . . שׁבר

אֶשְׁבֹּר וָ] Kal fut. 1 pers. sing.; וָ] for וְ] conv. שׁבר

אֲשַׁבְּרָה וָ] Piel fut. 1 pers. sing. with parag. ה. שׁבר

אֲשַׁבְּרֵם וָ] id., suff. 3 pers. pl. masc.; וָ] id. שׁבר

אֲשַׁבְּרֵהוּ Piel fut. 1 pers. sing., suff. 3 pers. sing. m. שׁבר

אֶשְׁגֶּה וָ] Kal fut. 1 pers. sing.; וָ] for וְ] conv. שׁנה

אֶשֶׁד Root not used; Chald. and Syr. to pour out.
אֶשֶׁד a pouring out, Nu. 21. 15, אֶשֶׁד הַנְּחָלִים

i. e. places where the torrents from the mountains are poured out or flow down into the valleys and plains below, q. d. ravines. (Gesenius.)

אֲשֵׁדָה fem. dec. 11c. (§ 42. rem. 1. & 4) a low place or ravine, at the foot of a mountain, see the preceding.

אֶשֶׁד וָ] noun masc. sing. . . . אשׁד

אַשְׁדּוֹד pr. name of a place . . . שׁדד

אַשְׁדּוֹדָה id. with local ה . . . שׁדד

אַשְׁדּוֹדִיּוֹת gent. noun pl. fem. from אַשְׁדּוֹד, Kh. דּוֹדִיּוֹת Kr. דּוֹדִיּוֹת . . . . שׁדד

אַשְׁדּוֹדִים id. pl. masc. . . . שׁדד

אַשְׁדּוֹדִית adv. from a gent. noun אַשְׁדּוֹד=אַשְׁדּוֹדִי . שׁדד

אַשְׁדֹּת וָ] noun fem. pl. constr. of אֲשֵׁדוֹת from
אַשְׁדֹּת [דָה] sing. dec. 11c. (§ 42. No. 1) } אשׁד

אָשָׁה Root not used; i. q. אֲשֵׁשׁ to found; Arab. to neat.
אָשְׁיָה fem. foundation, only pl. with suff. אֲשׁוּיֹתֶיהָ, Je. 50. 15 Keri, but Kheth. אָשׁוּיֶהָ from אָשׁוּיָה.

יֹאשִׁיָּה (whom the Lord heals) pr. name masc. Zec. 6. 10.

יֹאשִׁיָּהוּ (id.) pr. name of a king of Judah.

אִשָּׁה וָ] noun fem. sing. dec. 10. (compare § 45) . אנשׁ

אֵשֶׁת constr. of the foll. . . . אישׁ

אִישׁ וָ] noun masc. sing. dec. 9a. . . . אישׁ

אִישׁוֹ n. com. s., suff. 3 p. s. m. from אֵשׁ dec. 8b. אישׁ

אָשׁוֹב Kh. אָשִׁיב q. v., K. אָשִׁיב (q. v.) . . שׁוב

אָשׁוּב וָ] & וָ] Kal fut. 1 pers. sing.; וָ] for וְ] conv. שׁוב

אָשׁוּבָה וָ] id. with paragogic ה . . . שׁוב

אַשְׁוֶה וָ] Hiph. fut. 1 pers. sing. . . . שׁוה

אֶשְׁוֶה וָ] Kal fut. 1 pers. sing. . . שׁוה

אֶשְׁוֹהִי וָ] Chald. noun masc. pl., suff. 3 pers. sing. m. from אֵשׁ dec. 5c. . . . אשׁשׁ

אָשׂוֹחֵחַ Pilel fut. 1 pers. sing. for חֵחַ [§ 15. rem. 1] שׂיח

אָשׁוּתָיִךְ Kh. אָשׁוּיתִי, K. אָשׁוּיֹתַי, noun fem. with suff. [from אָשׁיָה or אֲשׁוּיָה] . . . . אשׁה

אָשׂוֹם Kal inf. absolute . . . אשׂם

אֶשְׁוֵּעַ וָ] Piel fut. 1 pers. sing. (§ 15. rem. 1);
אֲשַׁוֵּעַ וָ] וָ] for וְ] . . . } שׁוע

אֲשַׁוֵּעָה וָ] id. id. with parag. ה; וָ] for וְ] conv. שׁוע

אָשׁוּר וָ] Kal fut. 1 pers. sing. . . . שׁור

אַשּׁוּר וָ] pr. name of a man, people and country . אשׁר

אַשּׁוּרָה pr. name of a country (אַשּׁוּר) with loc. ה אשׁר

אַשּׁוּרִים gent. noun, pl. of אַשּׁוּרִי . . . שׁור

a Ge. 24. 19, 44.	k Ne. 1. 2.	m Jos. 14. 7.	r Ho. 2. 20.	y Ne. 5. 12.	d Ge. 21. 24.	i Ps. 91. 14.	o Le. 22. 22.	t Ps. 143. 5.
b Is. 7. 12.	l Job 31. 36.	n Zec. 6. 1.	s Ps. 132. 15.	z Is. 66. 9.	e Ps. 17. 15.	l 1 Sa. 26. 21.	p Zec. 1. 3.	u Je. 50. 15.
c Ge. 24. 47.	Je. 10. 19.	o 1 Sa. 27. 5.	t Ps. 91. 16.	a De. 32. 26.	La. 2. 13.	q Nu. 21. 15.	La. 2. 13.	x Eze. 25. 12.
Ju. 8. 24.	Is. 42. 14.	p Exr. 9. 3.	u Ge. 24. 3.	b Je. 5. 7.	h Job 29. 17.	Jos. 12. 3.	Is. 40. 25.	y La. 3. 8.
d Job 38. 3; 40. 7.	f Ps. 119. 131.	Is. 49. 20.	p Ps. 81. 17.	Pr. 30. 7.	c De. 9. 17.	Jos. 13. 20.	Exr. 6. 3.	z Ho. 13. 7.
Is. 41. 28.	Ps. 140							

5

Form	Description	Root
אֲשׁוּרֶנּוּ וְ	[a] ו (וְ) Kal fut. 1 p.s. (אָשׁוּר), suff. 3 p.s.m.; ו for וְ	שׁוּר
אֶשְׁחֶה	[b] Hiph. fut. 1 pers. sing.	שׁחה
אַשְׁחוּר	pr. name masc.	שׁחר
אֶשְׁחַט	Kal fut. 1 pers. sing.; ו for וְ conv.	שׁחט
אַשְׁחִית	Hiph. fut. 1 pers. sing.	שׁחת
וָאֶשְׁחָתֶךָ	id., suff. 2 pers. sing. fem.; ו for וְ conv.	שׁחת
אַשְׁחִיתָם	id., suff. 3 pers. pl. masc.	שׁחת
אֶשְׂחָק / אֶצְחָק	} Kal fut. 1 pers. sing. (§ 8. rem. 15)	שׂחק
וְאֶשְׂחָקֵם	ו Kal fut. 1 pers. sing. [אֶשְׂחָק], suff. 3 pers. pl. masc. (§ 16. rem. 12)	שׂחק
אֲשַׁחֲרֶךָ	Piel fut. 1 pers. sing., suff. 2 pers. sing. masc. (§ 14. rem. 1. & § 2. rem. 2)	שׁחר
וְאֶשְׁטֹף	ו Kal fut. 1 pers. sing.; ו for וְ conv.	שׁטף
אִשֵּׁי	noun masc., pl. constr. from אִשֶּׁה dec. 9a.	אשׁ
אִשַּׁיָּא	[k] ו Chald. n. m., pl. emph. from [אֵשׁ] dec. 5c.	אשׁ
אָשִׁיב	ו & וְ Hiph. fut. 1 pers. s.; ו for וְ conv.	שׁוּב
אָשִׁיבָה	ו & וְ id. with paragogic ה; ו id.	שׁוּב
אֲשִׁיבְךָ / וַאֲשִׁיבְךָ	} id., suff. 2 pers. sing. masc. (§ 3. r. 2); ו for וְ	שׁוּב
אֲשִׁיבֶנָּה	id., suff. 3 pers. sing. fem. (§ 2 rem. 3)	שׁוּב
אֲשִׁיבֶנּוּ	id., suff. 3 pers. sing. masc.	שׁוּב
אַשִּׁיג	Hiph. fut. 1 pers. sing.	נשׂג
אַשִּׁיגֵם	id., suff. 3 pers. pl. masc.	נשׂג
אָשִׂיחַ	Kal fut. 1 pers. sing.	שׂיח
אָשִׂיחָה	וְ id. with paragogic ה	שׂיח
אָשִׂים	ו & וְ Kal fut. 1 p.s.; ו for וְ; R. שׂים see	שׂום
אֲשִׁימָא	pr. name of an idol of the city of Hamath, 2 Ki. 17. 30.	
אָשִׂימָה	[uu] ו & וְ Kal fut. 1 pers. s. with parag. ה; ו for וְ; R. שׂום see	שׂום
אֲשִׂימְךָ	id., suff. 2 pers. sing. masc.	שׂום
אֲשִׂימֵךְ	id., suff. 2 pers. sing. fem.	שׂום
אֲשִׂימֵם	id., suff. 3 pers. pl. masc.	שׂום
אֲשִׂימֶנָּה	[cc] id., suff. 3 pers. sing. fem. (§ 2 rem. 3)	שׂום
אֲשִׂימֶנּוּ	id., suff. 3 pers. sing. masc. (id.)	שׂום
אָשִׁיר	Kal fut. 1 pers. sing.	שׁיר
אָשִׁירָה	id. with paragogic ה	שׁיר
אֲשֵׁירָה	noun fem. sing. dec. 10.	אשׁר
אֲשֵׁירֵיהֶם	id. pl. with masc. term. and suff. 3 pers. pl. masc.; ו before (–)	אשׁר
אֲשֵׁירֶיךָ	id., suff. 2 pers. sing. masc.	אשׁר
אָשִׁישׁ	Kal fut. 1 pers. sing. R. שׁושׁ see	שׁושׁ
אֲשִׁישָׁה	ו noun fem. sing. dec. 10; ו before (–)	אשׁשׁ
אֲשִׁישֵׁי	id., with pl. masc. term., construct state	אשׁשׁ
אָשִׁית	Kal fut. 1 pers. sing.	שׁית
אֲשִׁיתֵהוּ	ו id., suff. 3 pers. sing. masc.; ו for וְ	שׁית
אֲשִׁיתְךָ	id., suff. 2 pers. sing. masc.	שׁית
אֲשִׁיתֵךְ	id., suff. 2 pers. sing. fem.	שׁית
אֶשֶׁךְ	[for אֶשֶׁךְ § 35. r. 2] m. testicles, Le. 21. 20.	
אֶשְׁכַּב	[h] Kal fut. 1 pers. sing. [for כַּב § 8. rem. 16]	שׁכב
אֶשְׁכְּבָה	id. with paragogic ה	שׁכב
אֶשְׁכֹּל	pr. name of a place, see אֶשְׁכֹּל	שׁכל
אֶשְׁכּוֹל	[i] וְ n.m., pl. אֶשְׁכֹּלוֹת, כֻּלוֹת, & אֶשׁ (§ 44. r. 5)	שׁכל
אֶשְׁכּוֹן	[k] ו n. m. Kal fut. 1 pers. sing. (§ 8. rem. 18)	שׁכן
אֶשְׁכַּח	Kal fut. 1 pers. sing.	שׁכח
אֶשְׁכָּחָה	[m] id. with paragogic ה	שׁכח
אֶשְׁכָּחֵךְ	id., suff. 2 pers. sing. fem. (§ 16. rem. 12)	שׁכח
אַשְׁכִּילָה	Hiph. fut. 1 pers. sing. with paragogic ה	שׁכל
אַשְׂכִּילְךָ	id., suff. 2 pers. sing. masc.	שׁכל
אֶשְׁכָּם	[p] by Chaldaism for הַשְׁכֵּם (q.v.) § 11. rem. 2.	שׁכם
אַשְׂכִּיר	[q] Hiph. fut. 1 pers. sing.	שׁכר
אֶשְׁכֹּל	Kal fut. 1 pers. sing.	שׁכל
אֶשְׁכֹּל	noun masc. sing., pl. אֶשְׁכֹּלוֹת, כֻּלֹת & אֶשׁ (§ 44. rem. 5); also pr. name masc.	שׁכל
אֶשְׁתַּכְלְלוּ	Chald., Kh. אֶשְׁתַּכְלְלוּ [for אֶשְׁתַּכְלְלוּ] Ishtaph., K. שַׁכְלְלוּ Shaph., pret. 3 p. pl. m. (§ 48. 1)	כלל
אַשְׁכְּלַת	noun pl. fem., as if from אֶשְׁכְּלַת (comp. dec. 13. § 44. rem. 5) see אֶשְׁכֹּל	שׁכל
אַשְׁכְּלָתֶיהָ	id. with suff. 3 pers. sing. fem.	שׁכל
אֶשְׁכֶּם	[x] noun com. sing., suff. 2 pers. pl. masc. from אֵשׁ dec. 8b. (§ 36. rem. 3)	אשׁ
אֶשְׁכָּן	[y] Kal fut. 1 pers. sing. for כֵּן (§ 8. rem. 18).	שׁכן
אֲשַׁכְּנָה	ו Piel fut. 1 pers. s. with parag. ה; ו for וְ	שׁכן
אֶשְׁכְּנָה / אֶשְׁכְּנָה	} [b] ו Kal fut. 1 pers. sing. with paragogic ה (§ 8. rem. 15)	שׁכן
אַשְׁכְּנַז	ו pr. name of a son of Gomer, Ge. 10.3, and a province called after him.	
אֶשְׁכָּר	[c] noun masc. sing. (no vowel change)	שׁכר
אֶשְׁכָּרְךָ	id., suff. 2 pers. sing. fem.	שׁכר
אֲשַׁכְּרֵם	[e] ו Piel fut. 1 p.s., suff. 3 p. pl. m.; ו for וְ	שׁכר
אֵשֶׁל	[pp] masc. the tamarisk, a middle-sized prickly tree.	
אֲשַׁלַּח	[f] ו Piel fut 1 pers. sing.; ו for וְ	שׁלח
אֶשְׁלְחָה / אֶשְׁלַח	[g] } [h] ו & וְ Kal fut. 1 pers. sing. (§ 8. rem. 15); ו for וְ conv.	שׁלח
אֲשַׁלֵּחַ	[i] Piel fut. 1 pers. sing. [for לֵחַ § 15. rem. 1]	שׁלח
אֲשַׁלְּחֶהָ	[k] ו id., suff. 3 pers. sing. fem.; ו for וְ	שׁלח
אֲשַׁלְּחָה	id. with paragogic ה; ו id.	שׁלח
וָאֲשַׁלְּחָה	ו & וְ Kal fut. 1 p.s. with parag. ה; ו for וְ conv.	שׁלח

---

a Ho. 14. 9.   e Eze. 16. 9.   h Nu. 23. 20.   n Ezr. 8. 17.   s Ho. 3. 1.   v Is. 57. 15.   y De. 32. 42.   Eze. 43. 7.   Is. 63. 6.
b Ps. 6. 7.   Exr. 5. 16.   Ex. 15. 9.   Je. 6. 8.   Is. 5. 6.   Job 29. 25.   Ge. 27. 45.   Je. 7. 3.   Zec. 8. 10.
c Ge. 40. 11.   Eze. 4. 12.   Ps. 18. 38.   1 Ki. 5. 23.   Je. 22. 6.   Job 9. 27.   Ezr. 4. 12.   Ps. 55. 7.   Is. 42. 19.
Je. 15. 6.   1 Sa. 12. 3.   Ps. 119. 78.   Ps. 59. 17.   Je. 3. 19.   Ps. 101. 2.   De. 32. 32.   Ps. 139. 9.   2 Ki. 6. 13.
2 Ch. 12. 7.   Job 40. 4.   Je. 10. 4.   2 Ki. 17. 16.   Job 7. 21.   Ps. 32. 8.   Ge. 40. 10.   Ps. 72. 10.   Ex. 5. 2.
Pr. 1. 26.   Job 35. 4.   Ge. 44. 21.   Is. 61. 10.   Nu. 13. 23.   Is. 50. 1.   Ge. 40. 10.   Eze. 27. 15.   Ju. 20. 6.
g Job 29. 24.   Je. 15. 19.   uu De. 17. 14.   Eze. 21. 32.   Mic. 5. 13.   Je. 21. 33.

אֲשַׁלְּחֶ֫נּוּ ן Piel fut. 1 pers. s., suff. 3 p. s. m. ; ן id. שלח

אֲשַׁלְּחֲךָ id. (ו'), suff. 2 pers. sing. m. (§ 2. rem. 2) ;) שלח
אֲשַׁלֵּחֵ֫ךָ ון') ן for ן . . . . }

אֲשַׁלַּחַ֫ךְ ן Kal fut. 1 pers. sing. (אֲשַׁלַּח), suff. 2 p. שלח
sing. masc. (§ 16. rem. 12) .

אֲשַׁלְּחֵם ן id., suff. 3 pers. pl. masc. שלח

אֲשַׁלְּחֶ֫נּוּ) Piel fut. 1 pers. s., suff. 3 p. s. m. (§ 2. r. 3) שלח

אַשְׁלִיךְ s'ן Hiph. fut. 1 pers. sing. . . שלך

אַשְׁלִ֫יכָה) id. with paragogic ה ; ן for ן conversive שלך

אַשְׁלִךְ) id. defect. for אַשְׁלִיךְ q. v. ; ן id. . שלך

אַשְׁלִכֵ֫הוּ) id., suff. 3 pers. sing. masc. ;) id. . שלך

אַשְׁלִכֶם') id., suff. 3 pers. pl. masc. ;) id. . שלך

אֲשַׁלֵּם) Piel fut. 1 pers. sing. . . שלם

אֲשַׁלְּמָה
אֲשַׁלְּמֶ֫נָּה b) id. with paragogic ה; (comp. § 8. rem.
15) ; ן for ן . } שלם

אָשַׁם, אָשֵׁם ן ן—I. to be or become guilty, to transgress,
with ל of the person against whom, and ל, בְּ of
the thing in which.—II. to feel one's guilt.—III.
to bear one's guilt, suffer punishment.—IV. to be
laid waste, i. q. שָׁמֵם יָשֵׁם, Eze. 6. 6. Niph. to be
destroyed, Joel 1. 18. Hiph. to bring the con-
sequences of sin upon any one, Ps. 5. 11.

אָשָׁם masc. dec. 4 c.—I. guilt.—II. damage.—
III. a sacrifice for guilt, trespass-offering.

אָשֵׁם adj. masc. dec. 5 c. guilty.

אַשְׁמָה fem. dec. 12 a.—I. prop. inf. (§ 8. rem.
10), לְאַשְׁמָה בָהּ to trespass therein.—II. guilt,
trespass.—III. trespass-offering, Le. 5. 24.

אָשָׁם noun masc. sing. dec. 4 c. . . אשם

אָשֹׁם) defect. for אָשִׂים (q. v.) . . שום

אָשֹׁם p Kal inf. absolute, compare אָשׂוֹם אשם

אֶשֹּׁם q Kal fut. 1 p. s. from שׁמם (§ 18. r. 14), or נשם

אֲשַׁמָּ֫י r ן n. com. s., suff. 3 pl. m. from אַשׁ dec. 8 b. אש

אַשְׂמְאִ֫ילָה) Hiph. fut. 1 pers. sing. with paragogic ה שמאל

אָשְׁמָה) Kal pret. 3 pers. sing. fem. . . אשם

אָשֹׂ֫מָה u') defect. for אָשִׂ֫ימָה (q. v.) . . שום

אָשְׁמוּ) Kal pret. 3 p. pl. [for אָשְׁמוּ § 8. rem. 1] אשם

אַשְׁמָה) noun fem. sing. dec. 12 a. . . אשם

אֲשָׁמוֹ) n. m. s., suff. 3 p. s. m. from אָשָׁם dec. 4 c. אשם

אֶשְׁמֹר־ Kh. מוֹר', K. מֹר' Kal fut. 1 p. s. (§ 8. r. 18) שמר

אַשְׁמֻרָה) noun fem. s., constr. אַשְׁמֹ֫רֶת, pl אַשְׁמֻרֹת
(§ 39. No. 4) . . . . . שמר

אֲשָׁמוֹת noun fem., pl. abs. from אַשְׁמָה dec. 12 a אשם

אֲשָׁמוֹתַי) id. with suff. 1 pers. sing. . אשם

אֶשְׂמַח Kal fut. 1 pers. sing. . . . שמח

אֶשְׂמְחָה c') id. with parag. ה . . . שמח

אַשְׁמִיד d') Hiph. fut. 1 pers. sing. ;) for) conv. שמד

אַשְׁמִידְךָ id., suff. 2 pers. sing. masc. . . שמד

אַשְׁמִידֵם) נ',) id., suff. 3 pers. pl. m. ;) for) conv. שמד

אֲשֵׁמִים g) adj. m., pl. of אָשֵׁם dec. 5 c ;) before (־ֵ) אשם

אַשְׁמִיעַ) Hiph. fut. 1 pers. sing. . . שמע

אַשְׁמִיעֲךָ k') id., suff. 2 pers. sing. masc. שמע

אַשְׁמִיעֵם cc) id., suff. 3 pers. pl. masc. . שמע

אַשְׁמָם l) n. m. s., suff. 3 pers. pl. m. from אַשׁ dec. 4 c. אש

אַשְׁמֵם m) Hiph. fut. 1 p. s. [אָשֵׁם], suff. 3 pers. pl. m. שמם

אָשֵׂם n) defect. for אָשִׂ֫ים q. v. ;) for) שום

אֶשְׁמַע o(ן) Kal fut. 1 pers. sing. (§ 8. rem. 15) ;
אֶשְׁמַע (ן) for) conv. } שמע

אֶשְׁמָעָה p', q') id. with parag. ה ;) id. . שמע

אֶשְׁמָעֵם r') defect. for אַשְׁמִיעֵם (q. v.) . שמע

אֶשְׁמֹר) Kal fut. 1 pers. sing. . . שמר

אֶשְׁמְרָה
אֶשְׁמֹ֫רָה } id. with parag. ה (§ 8. rem. 15) ;
)) for) conv. . . . } שמר

אַשְׁמֻרוֹת noun fem., pl. of אַשְׁמֻרָה, sing. const.
אַשְׁמֹ֫רֶת (§ 39. No. 4) . . . . שמר

אֶשְׁמְרֶ֫נָּה) Kal. future, 1 p. s. (אֶשְׁמֹר), suff. 3 p. s. f. שמר

אָשַׁמְתָּ s') Kal pret. 2 p. s. m. [for וְאָשַׁמְתָּ § 8. r. 7] אשם

אָשַׁמְתְּ t') id. pret. 2 pers. sing. fem. . אשם

אַשְׁמַת v') noun fem. sing., const. of מָה' dec. 12 a. אשם

אַשְׁמָתוֹ) id., suff. 3 pers. sing. masc. . אשם

אַשְׁמָתָם b') id., suff. 3 pers. pl. masc. . אשם

אַשְׁמָתֵ֫נוּ d'( ) id., suff. 1 pers. pl. . . אשם

אֶשְׂנָא e') Kal fut. 1 pers. sing. . . שנא

אֶשְׁנַבִּ֫י f') n. masc. sing., suff. 1 pers. sing. from אֶשְׁנָב'
dec. 8 a. (§ 37. No. 3) . . . שנב

אֲשַׁנֶּה g') Piel fut. 1 pers. sing. . . שנה

אֶשְׁנָה) (fortified) pr. name of two cities in the tribe
of Judah, Jos. 15. 33, 43 ; from אָשׁן Arab.
to be strong, to which Root Pr. 20. 20, (Keri)
is referred.

אִישַׁן h) Kal fut. 1 pers. sing. . . שנה

אֶשְׁעָה i) Kal fut. 1 pers. sing. [for עָה' § 24. r. 18] שעה

אֶשָּׁעֵן) Niph. fut. 1 pers. sing. . . שען

אֶשְׁעָן) pr. name of a place . . שען

אָשַׁף) Root not used ; Syr. to use enchantment, perhaps
primarily to cover.

---

a Ps. 81. 13.
b Ge. 32. 27.
c Ge. 31. 27.
d 1 Sa. 9. 26.
e Jos. 18. 4.
f Is. 10. 6.
g Zec. 11. 13.

k Ne. 13. 8.
l De. 9. 21.
m Ex. 32. 24.
n De. 9. 17.
o Jon. 2. 10.
p Pr. 20. 22.
q 1 Sa. 28. 22.

o Ps. 41. 11.
p Le. 5. 19.
q Is. 42. 14.
r Is. 66. 24.
s Ps. 69. 6.
t Ps. 9. 3.

d Le. 4. 13.
e Am. 2. 9.
f Eze. 25. 7.
g De. 9. 14.
h Ge. 42. 21.
i Je. 18. 2.

d Am. 2. 9.
Eze. 25. 7.
De. 9. 14.
Ps. 89. 29.
Ps. 90. 4.
2 Ch. 28. 10.

k 1 Sa. 9. 27.
Nu. 18. 9.
Eze. 20. 26.
De. 1. 13.
Ezr. 10. 19.

r Da. 8. 13.
De. 4. 10.
Ps. 59. 10.
Ps. 119. 55.
Ps. 119. 34.
2 Ch. 28. 13.
Ezr. 9. 6.

y Eze. 22. 4.
Ezr. 10. 10.
Le. 5. 24.
Ezr. 10. 19.
Pr. 30. 10.

z Ps. 139. 21.
Pr. 7. 6.
Ps. 89. 35.
1 Sa. 26. 8.
Ps. 119. 117.
Ju. 16. 28.

5 *

אָשֵׁף Chald. dec. 2b (prop. participle), *an enchanter, magician.*

אַשָּׁף masc. id. pl. אַשָּׁפִים; Chald. Da. 2. 2.

אַשְׁפָּה fem. (no pl.) *a quiver,* בְּנֵי אַ׳ *sons of the quiver, i. e. arrows.*

אשף	אַשְׁפָּה noun fem. sing. dec. 10.
שפט	אֶשְׁפּוֹט Kal fut. 1 pers. sing. (§ 8. rem. 18)
שפך	אֶשְׁפּוֹךְ Kal fut. 1 pers. sing. (§ 8. rem. 18)
שפט	אֶשְׁפֹּט Kal fut. 1 pers. sing.
שפט	אֶשְׁפְּטָה Niph. fut. 1 pers. sing. (א § 10. rem. 5)
שפט	וְ אִשָּׁפְטָה id. with parag. ה
שפט	אֶשְׁפְּטֵךְ Kal fut. 1 pers. sing. (אֶשְׁפֹּט), suff. 2 pers. sing. masc. [for פְטֵךְ]
שפט	אֶשְׁפְּטֵם id., suff. 3 pers. pl. masc.
אשף	אָשְׁפַיָּא Chald. noun m. pl. emph. from [אָשֵׁף] dec.2b.
שפל	אַשְׁפִּיל׳ Hiph. fut. 1 pers. sing.
אשף	אָשְׁפִין Chald. noun m. pl. abs. from [אָשֵׁף] dec.2b.
שפך	אֶשְׁפֹּךְ׳ Kal fut. 1 pers. sing.; וְ for וַ conv.
שפך	וְ אֶשְׁפְּכָה id. with parag. ה
	[אַשְׁפְּנַז] pr. name of one of the eunuchs of Nebuchadnezzar, Da. 1.3.
שפר	וְ אֶשְׁפָּר noun masc. sing.
שפה	אֶשְׁפַּתּוֹ noun f. s., suff. 3 p. s. m. from פֶּה׳ dec.10.
שפת	אַשְׁפַּתּוֹת noun pl. f., from a sing. אַשְׁפָּתָה or אַשְׁפֹּת (comp. § 37. No. 3)
שקד	אֶשְׁקֹד Kal fut. 1 pers. sing.
שקה	וְ אַשְׁקֶה Hiph. fut. 1 pers. sing.; וְ for וַ conv.
נשק	אֶשְׁקָה Kal fut. 1 pers. sing. [אֶשֹּׁק] with parag. ה (§ 8. rem. 14)
שקט	וְ אֶשְׁקוֹט Kal fut. 1 pers. sing. (§ 8. rem. 18)
שקט	אֶשְׁקוֹטָה id. with parag. ה, Kh. אֶשְׁקוֹטָה, K. (§ 8. rem. 14)
שקל	אֶשְׁקוֹל Kal fut. 1 pers. sing. (§ 8. rem. 18)
שקל	וְ אֶשְׁקֹלָה id. with parag. ה Kh. אֶשְׁקוֹלָה, K. (§ 8. rem. 14); וְ for וַ conv.
שקע	אַשְׁקִיעַ Hiph. fut. 1 pers. sing
שקה	אַשְׁקֵךְ Hiph. fut. 1 pers. sing. (אַשְׁקֶה), suff. 2 pers. sing. masc. (§ 24. rem. 21)
נשק	אֶשָּׁקֵךְ Kal fut.1 p.s. [אֶשֹּׁק], suff.2 p.s.m. (§16.r.12)
שקל	אֶשְׁקֹל וְ Kal fut. 1 pers. sing.; וְ for וַ conv.
שקל	אֶשְׁקְלָה וְ id. with parag. ה (§ 8. rem. 14); וְ id.
שקל	אֶשְׁקְלָה׳ id. id., [as if from אֶשְׁקָל]
שקל	וְ אֶשְׁקְלוֹן pr. name of a place
שקה	אַשְׁקֶנָּה Hiph. fut. 1 pers. sing. (אַשְׁקֶה), suff. 3 pers. sing. fem. (§ 2. rem. 3, & § 24. rem. 21)
שקר	אֲשַׁקֵּר Piel fut. 1 pers. sing.

אָשַׁר Root not used, probably i. q. אָסַר *to bind.*

אַשְׂרָאֵל (*whom God has bound*) pr. name masc. 1 Ch. 4. 16.

אֲשַׂרְאֵל (*vow of God*) pr. name masc. Patronym. אֲשַׂרְאֵלִי Nu. 26. 31.

[אָשַׁר] *to go straight on,* Pr. 9. 6. Pi.—I. *to guide, direct aright.*—II. *to pronounce happy, to call blessed.* Pu.—I. *to be guided,* Is. 9. 15.—II. *to be made or pronounced happy, blessed.*

אָשֵׁר (*happy, blessed*) pr. name—I. a son of Jacob, from whom came the tribe of *Asher.* Gent. n. אָשֵׁרִי Ju. 1. 32.—II. of a city near Sichem, Jos. 17. 7.

אֲשֵׁרָה, אֲשֵׁירָה fem. dec. 10. pl. ות & ־ים. English version after the Sept. and Vulg. "grove." Modern interpreters, *fortune, goddess of fortune,* put for the image of Astarte, and in the pl. *images.* Prof. Lee conjectures, *shrine, shrines.*

אֹשֶׁר masc. *happiness, blessedness;* only in pl. constr. in the character of an interj. אַשְׁרֵי הָאִישׁ *O the happiness of the man!* With suff. אַשְׁרֶיךָ *happy art thou!* אַשְׁרֵהוּ, אַשְׁרָיו, for אַשְׁרֶיךָ, &c. see § 35. rem. 16, for הוּ־, § 3. rem. 1, 5.

אֹשֶׁר masc. dec. 6 c. *happiness,* Ge. 30. 13.

אָשׁוּר or אָשׁוּר fem. dec. 1 or 3 a.—I. *step, going.*—II. *wood of the box-tree,* Eze. 27. 6.

אַשּׁוּר fem.—I. *step,* Job 31. 7.—II. pr. name *Assyria, the Assyrian empire.*

אַשּׁוּרִי pr. name of an Arabian tribe, Ge. 25. 3. called אַשּׁוּרִי 2 Sa. 2. 9.

אֲשַׂרְאֵלָה (*upright towards God*) pr. name masc. 1 Ch. 25. 2. written also יְשַׂרְאֵלָה v. 14.

אָשַׁרְנָא Chald. masc. *a wall,* Ezr. 5. 3.

תְּאַשּׁוּר masc. *the box-tree.*

אשר	וְ אָשֵׁר pr. name of a man and a place
אשר	וְ אַשֵּׁר Piel imp. sing. masc.
אשר	וְ אֲשֶׁר —I. relat. pron. of both genders and numbers, *who, which;* often including the pers. pronoun, *he which, she which, what, that which;* וַאֲשֶׁר תָּאֹר *and he whom thou cursest,* אֲ׳ אָכְלוּ הַנְּעָרִים *that which the young men have eaten;* especially after prepositions, לַאֲשֶׁר *to him who, to them who,* אֶת־אֲשֶׁר *him who, that which,* מֵאֲשֶׁר *from or of that which;* when the prep. refers to place, בַּאֲשֶׁר *where,* see No. IV.—II. לַאֲשֶׁר *whither,*

a Eze. 20. 36.   d Eze. 7. 27   g La. 4. 5.   k Je. 25. 17.   n Job 3. 18.   q Ezr. 8. 25.   t Ca. 5. 1.   y Je. 32. 9.   B Ps. 89. 34.
b 1 Sa. 12. 7.   e Is. 13. 11.   Je. 31. 38.   l 1 Ki. 19. 20.   o Is. 18. 4.   r Eze. 32. 14.   u Je. 32. 10.   z Is. 27. 3.   h Pr. 23. 19.
c Eze. 35. 11.   f Ps. 42. 5.   Ge. 24. 14, 46.   m Is. 62. 1.   p Est. 3. 9.   s Ca. 8. 1.   x Ezr. 8. 26

note of the relative before adverbs and pronouns; אֲשֶׁר מִשָּׁם *where;* אֲשֶׁר הוּא חַי *whence;* אֲשֶׁר בּוֹ *which liveth;* אֲשֶׁר לוֹ *to whom;* אֲשֶׁר אֶת־עָפָר *in whom;* אֲשֶׁר לְשֹׁנוֹ *whose tongue;* אֲשֶׁר אֹתִי *which dust,* acc. בְּחַרְתִּיךָ *me, whom;* אֲשֶׁר לְ *thee whom I have chosen.*—III. circumscribing the genitive, שִׁיר הַשִּׁירִים אֲשֶׁר לִשְׁלֹמֹה *the song of songs of Solomon,* i. e. Solomon's Song of Songs.—IV. conj. (a) *that, to the end that;* (b) *because, because that;* (c) *if, that if;* (d) *when;* (e) *of place, where;* (f) with prefixes, בַּאֲשֶׁר *in that, because,* see also No. I.;— כַּאֲשֶׁר *according to, as; as if; because; when;*— מֵאֲשֶׁר *since,* see also No. I.

אָשֵׁר, K. וַאֲשֵׁב (q. v.) ישב

pr. name of a people, for אַשּׁוּר . אשר

pr. name masc.; ן before (-ֶ) . אשר

pr. name masc.; ן id. . אשר

noun fem. sing. dec. 10. . אשר

noun m. pl., suff. 3 pers. s. m. [from אֲשֶׁר dec. 6 a. for אֲשֵׁרֵיהוּ § 35. r. 16, & § 4. r. 1] אשר

Piel imp. pl. masc. . אשר

Kal imp. pl. masc. . אשר

Piel pret. 3 pers. pl. . אשר

id. pret. 3 pers. pl., suff. 1 pers. sing. אשר

noun fem., pl. of רָה, dec. 10. . אשר

noun masc. pl. const. [from אֲשֶׁר dec. 6 a. § 35. rem. 16] אשר

noun masc. pl., suff. 1 pers. sing. [from אָשׁוּר or אֲשׁוּר dec. 1 or 3 a.] אשר

noun m. s., suff. 1 p. s. [from אַשּׁוּר dec. 1 b.] אשר

pr. name masc. . אשר

noun fem. with pl. masc. term. and suff. 3 pers. pl. masc. from אֲשֵׁרָה dec. 10. אשר

id. with suff. 3 pers. pl. masc. . אשר

noun masc. pl., suff. 3 pers. sing. masc. [from אֲשֶׁר dec 6a. for אֲשֵׁרָיו § 35. rem. 16] . אשר

noun m. pl. with suff. 3 pers. s. m. see אֲשֵׁרָיו אשר

noun masc. pl., suff. 2 pers. sing. masc. [from אֲשֶׁר dec. 6a. for אֲשֵׁרֶיךָ § 35. rem. 16] אשר

id., suff. 2 pers. sing. fem. [for אֲשָׁרַיִךְ]; id. אשר

id., suff. 3 pers. pl. masc. . אשר

n. f. with pl. m. term. from אֲשֵׁרָה dec. 10. אשר

pr. name of a people, pl. of אַשּׁוּרִי אשר

noun m. s., suff. 1 p. pl. from אַשּׁוּר dec. 1 b אשר

noun m. sing., suff. 1 pers. pl. (see אֲשֵׁרִי) אשר

אֲשַׁרְנָא Chald. noun masc. sing. . אשר

אֶשְׂרֹף Kal fut. 1 pers. sing.; ן for ־ְ conv. שׂרף

אֶשְׁרְקָה Kal fut. 1 pers. sing. with parag. ה . שׁרק

אָשַׁשׁ Root not used; Arab. *to found, make firm.*
אָשִׁישׁ masc. dec. 3 a. *foundation,* Is. 16. 7.
אֲשִׁישָׁה fem. dec. 10. pl. וֹת & ־ִים, *cake.*

אֵשְׁתְּ ap. for אֶשְׁתֶּה q.v. (§ 24. r. 3); ן for ־ְ conv. שׁתה

אֵשֶׁת noun fem. sing. abs. and const. dec. 13 b. (see אִשָּׁה § 45) . אישׁ

אֵשֶׁת noun fem., pl. of אִשָּׁה dec. 10. (§ 45) . אנשׁ

אֶשְׁתָּאוֹל / אֶשְׁתָּאֹל pr. name of a place . שׁאל

אֶשְׁתַּדּוּר Chald. noun masc. sing. . שׁדר

אֶשְׁתֶּה Kal fut. 1 pers. sing. . שׁתה

אֶשְׁתּוֹ noun fem. sing., suff. 3 pers. sing. m. from אֵשֶׁת dec. 13 c. (see אִשָּׁה § 45) . אישׁ

אֶשְׁתּוֹלְלוּ [for אֶתְשׁוֹלְלוּ by Syriacism for הִתְשׁ § 12. rem. 3] Hithpo. pret. 3 pers. pl. . שׁלל

אֶשְׁתּוֹמַם Chald. [for אֶתְשׁוֹמַם] Ithpo. pret. 3 pers. s. masc. (comp. § 21. rem. 20) . שׁמם

אֶשְׁתּוֹמֵם ן, וֵ Hithpoel, fut. 1 p. s.; ן for ־ְ conv. שׁמם

אֶשְׁתּוֹן pr. name masc. . אישׁ

אֶשְׁתּוֹנַן [for אֶתְשׁוֹנַן] Hithpal. fut. 1 pers. sing. (comp. § 21. rem. 20) . שׁנן

אֶשְׁתַּחֲוֶה וֵ, ן, Hithpal. fut. 1 pers. s. [for הִתְשׁ § 24. r. 25, & § 6. No. 2]; ן for ־ְ conv. שׁחה

אִשְׁתִּי noun fem. sing., suff. 1 pers. sing. from אֵשֶׁת dec. 13 b. (see אִשָּׁה § 45) . אישׁ

אֶשְׁתִּיו Chald. Peal pret. 3 pers. pl. masc. with prosth. א [for שְׁתִיו § 55. rem. 1] . שׁתא

אֶשְׁתְּךָ / אֶשְׁתֶּךָ / אֶשְׁתְּךָ noun fem. sing., suff. 2 pers. sing. masc. from אֵשֶׁת dec. 13 c. (§ 45, & 44. r. 3) . אישׁ

אֶשְׁתְּלֶנּוּ Kal fut. 1 pers. sing. [אֶשְׁתֹּל], suff. 3 pers. sing. masc. (§ 8. rem. 14, & § 2. rem. 3) שׁתל

אֶשְׁתְּמֹעַ, אֶשְׁתְּמוֹעַ, וֵ, ן, pr. name of a place . שׁמע

אֶשְׁתַּמֵּר [for אֶתְשׁמֵּר] Hith. fut. 1 pers. s.; ן for ־ַ שׁמר

אֶשְׁתַּמְּרָה id. with parag. ה . שׁמר

אֶשְׁתֶנּוּ Kal fut. 1 pers. sing. (אָשִׁית), suff. 3 pers. sing. masc. (§ 2. rem. 3) R. שׁית see שׁות

אֶשְׁתַּנִּי Chald. [for אֶתְשׁ] Ithpa. pret. 3 pers. sing. masc., K. נִּי; Kh. נַּו or נַּו 3 pers. pl. m. שׁנא

אֶשְׁתַּעְשַׁע [for אֶתְשׁ] Hithpalp. fut. 1 pers. sing. (§ 6. No. 4) שׁעע

ᵃ Eze. 3. 15.   ᶠ Ge. 30. 13.   ⁱ Ex. 34. 13.   ʳ Ps. 17. 11.   ᵘ Ge. 24. 46.   ᵇ Da. 4. 16.   ˡ 1 Sa. 15. 25.   ᵖ Ps. 128. 3.   ᵗ 1 Ki. 11. 34.
ᵇ Pr. 29. 18.   ᵍ 2 Ch. 33. 3.   ᵏ Ps. 17. 5.   ˢ Ps. 37. 31.   ᵛ Ezr. 5. 3.   ᶜ Is. 63. 5.   ᵐ Ge. 24. 43.   ᵍ Eze. 17. 23.   ᵖ Da. 3. 19.
ᶜ Is. 1. 17.   ʰ Ps. 17. 5.   ˡ Ec. 10. 17.   ᵗ Ezr. 4. 15, 19.   ʷ Da. 8. 27.   ᵈ Da. 5. 4.   ⁿ Ps. 18. 24.   ʳ Ps. 119. 16.
ᵈ Pr. 9. 6.   ⁱ Job 31. 7.   ᵐ Is. 32. 20.   ᵗ De. 9. 21.   Ps. 76. 6.   ᵉ Da. 5. 5.   ᵒ 2 Sa. 22. 24.   ˢ Ps. 119. 16.
ᵉ Mal. 3. 12.   ʲ 1 Ki. 14. 15.   ᵖ Is. 27. 9.   ᵗ Zec. 10. 8.   Ps. 73. 21.   ᵗ Ps. 119. 47.

I. [אֵת] masc. with suff. אִתּוֹ, pl. אִתִּים & אֵתִים (§ ᴣ7. rem. 5) *ploughshare.*

II. אֵת, אֶת־ sign of—I. the accusative.—II. the nominative with verbs passive and neuter; יִקָּרֵא אֶת־שְׁמֶךָ *thy name shall be called,* יֻתַּן אֶת־הָאָרֶץ *let the land be given;* אַל יֵרַע אֶת־הַדָּבָר *let the thing not displease.* With suff. אֹתִי, אֹתִי, אֶתְכֶם see § 5. For מֵאוֹתִי see the following.

III. אֵת, אֶת־ with suff. אִתִּי, אִתְּךָ, אִתָּךְ, אִתָּךְ fem. &c. prep.—I. *with, by, near.*—II. *with, in company with.*—III. *towards.*—IV. מֵאֵת prop. *from with,* i. e. *from,* מֵאִתִּי *from me,* מֵאִתְּךָ *from thee,* &c.; but also מֵאוֹתְךָ, מֵאוֹתִי.

    אִתִּי (*near*) pr. name—I. 2 Sa. 15. 19; 18. 2.—II. 2 Sa. 23. 29, written also אִיתַי q. v.

אַתְּ, אַתָּ, אַתְּ Kh., K. אַתָּה pron. pers. 2 pers. sing. masc. אנת

id. 2 pers. sing. fem. . . . אנת

אָתָא Kal pret. 3 pers. s. m. for אָתָה (§ 24. r. 18) אתה

אָתָא Chald. Peal pret. 3 pers. sing. masc. see אתה

אֶתְאַבְּלָה Hith. fut. 1 pers. s. with parag. ה; וְ for וָ } אבל

אֶתְאַפֵּק Hith. fut. 1 pers. sing. (§ 12. rem. 1); וְ for וָ conv. . . . } אפק

אֶתְבּוֹנֵן, אֶתְבֹּנָן Hithpal. fut. 1 pers. sing. (§ 21. rem. 20); וְ for וָ conv. . . . } בין

אֶתְבַּעַל (*with Baal*) pr. name of a king of Sidon, 1 Ki. 16. 31.

אֶתְגְּזָרֶת Chald. Ithpe. pret. 3 pers. s. fem. (§ 49. r. 1) נזר

אָתָה, אָתָא וְ (§ 24. rem. 18. & 20, & § 25. No. 2c) *to come,* const. with עַד, לְ of the pers. to whom; part. אוֹתִיּוֹת (§ 24. rem. 4) *things to come.*

    אֲתָה Chald. (§ 55. rem. 1 note. & § 56. No. 2) *to come,* const. with עַל of the pers. Aph. *to cause to come, to bring.*

    אֵיתוֹן masc. *entrance,* Eze. 40. 15. Keri.

אַתָּה וְ pers. pron. 2 pers. sing. masc.; for } אנת

אַתָּה וְ, וְ וְ see lett. ו }

אֲתָה Ch. Peal pret. 3 pers. s. m. (§ 55. r. 1 note) אתה

אָתֵה Chald. id. part. act. sing. masc. (id.) . אתה

אִתָּהּ prep. (אֵת) with suff. 3 pers. sing. fem. . את

אֹתָהּ וְ prop. [אוֹת] sign of the accus. with suff. 3 pers. sing. fem. see אֵת (§ 5) . . את

אֶתְהַלֵּךְ Hith. fut. 1 pers. sing. . . הלך

אֶתְהַלְּכָה וְ id. with parag. ה . . הלך

אֶתְהֶם (אֵת), sign of the accus. with suff. 3 pers. pl. masc. (§ 5) . . . את

אֶתְהֶן וְ id. with suff. 3 pers. pl. fem. . את

אֲתוֹ Ch. Peal pret. 3 p. pl. m. R. אתָא see אתה

אֹתוֹ noun m. s., suff. 3 p. s. m. from אֵת (q. v.) את

אֱתוֹ וְ Chald. id. imp. pl. masc.; וְ before (וַ); R. אתָא see . . . . אתה

אִתּוֹ וְ prep. (אֵת) with suff. 3 pers sing. masc. את

אֹתוֹ וְ prop. [אוֹת] sign of the accus. with suff. 3 pers. sing. masc. see אֵת (§ 5) . . את

אֶתְוַדֶּה וְ Hith. fut. 1 p.s. (§20.No.1); וְ for וָ conv. ידה

אֶתְוַדַּע [for יֵדַע] Hith. fut. 1 pers. sing. (§ 20. No. 1) ידע

אֲתוֹהִי Chald. noun masc. pl., suff. 3 pers. sing. masc. from [אֵת] dec. 1 a. . . . אוה

אֶתּוּן Chald. noun com. sing. dec. 1 a. [for אֶתְנוּן] תנן

אַתּוּנָא וְ Chald. id. emph. st. . . . תנן

אֲתוֹנוֹת noun fem., pl. of אָתוֹן dec. 3 a. . אתן

אַתּוּקֵיהָא וְ Kh. אַתּי, K. אַתּי, noun m. pl., suff. 3 pers. s. f. (§ 4. r. 5) [from אַתּוּק or אַתִּיק q. v.] אתק

אֶתֹּשׁ Kal fut. 1 pers. sing. . . . נתש

אֹתוֹת noun com., pl. of אוֹת dec. 1 a. . . אוה

אֹתוֹתַי id., suff. 3 pers. sing. masc. . . אוה

אֹתוֹתֵינוּ id., suff. 1 pers. pl. . . . אוה

אֶתְחַבֵּר for הִתְ (§ 12. rem. 3) Hith. pret. 3 pers. sing. masc. (§ 12. rem. 1) . . . חבר

אֶתְחַנַּן וְ Hith. fut. 1 pers. sing. [for עֵן § 12. r. 1] חנן

אֶתְחַנָּן id. before Mak. [for הַחַן] . . . חנן

אַתִּי in pause for the following . . . }

אַתִּי וְ Kh. אַתִּי, K. אַתְּ pers. pron. 2 pers. sing. fem. (§ 1. rem. 2) } אנת

אִתַּי pr. name masc. . . . . . את

אִתִּי prep. (אֵת) with suff. 1 pers. sing. . . את

אֹתִי וְ prop. [אוֹת] sign of the accus. with suff. 1 pers. sing. see אֵת (§ 5) . . . את

אַתַּיָּא Chald. noun m. pl. emph. from [אֵת] dec. 1 a. אוה

אֱתָיוּ Kal imp. pl. masc.; [for אֱתָיוּ § 1ꝰ. rem. 6, § 25. No. 2, & § 24. rem. 5] . . . אתה

אֹתִיּוֹת וְ Kal part. act. pl. fem., as if from a masc. [אֹתִי] § 24. rem. 4, & § 39. No. 2] . אתה

אֶתְכֶם noun m. pl., suff. 2 p. pl. m. from אֵת (q.v.) את

אֲתִין Chald. noun masc., pl. of [אֵת] dec. 1 a. . אוה

אִתְעֲטוּ Chald. Ithpa. pret. 3 pers. pl. masc. . יעט

אֶתְיַצְּבָה וְ Hith. fut. 1 pers. sing. . . . יצב

אַתִּיק noun masc. sing. dec. 1 b. . . . אתק

אַתִּיקִים id. pl., absolute state . . . אתק

אִתָּךְ prep. (אֵת) with suff. 2 pers. sing. fem., or in pause for the following . . . את

ᵃ Is. 21. 12.   ᵉ 1 Sa. 13. 12.   ⁱ Is. 21. 12.   ᵐ Ps. 119. 45.   ʳ Da. 3. 26.   ᵛ Da. 3. 6, 11, 15,   ᶻ Ps. 74. 9.   ᵈ Da. 3. 32.   ᵍ Da. 6. 8.

ᵇ Ezr. 5. 16.   ᶠ 1 Ki. 3. 21.   ᵏ 2 Ki. 9. 25.   ⁿ Le. 20. 14.   ˢ Da. 3. 4.   17, 21, 23, 26.   ʷ 2 Ch. 20. 35.   ˢ Is. 44. 7.   ʰ Hab. 2. 1.

ᶜ Ne. 1. 4.   ᵍ Da. 2. 45.   ˡ Da. 7. 13.   ᵒ Ezr. 4. 12.   ᵖ Nu. 12. 6.   ˣ Da. 3. 22.   ᵃ De. 3. 23.   ᵇ Joel 4. 10.   ⁱ Eze. 4ꝰ. 3, ᴣ.

ᵈ Is. 42. 14.   ʰ De. 33. 2.   ᵍ Le. 10. 17.   ᵠ 1 Sa. 13. 20.   ᵠ Da. 3. 33.   ʸ Ese. 41. 15.   ᶜ Job 19. 16.   ᵇ Da. 6. 28.   ᵐ Eze. 42. 5.

אַתְּךָ — prep. (אֵת) with suff. 2 pers. sing. masc. — את

אֹתְךָ [וְ] — prop. [אוֹת] sign of the accus. (see אֵת § 5), suff. 2 pers. sing. fem., or in pause for : — את

אֹתָךְ / אֹתְכָה / אֹתְכָה — id., suff. 2 pers. sing. masc. (§ 5. rem. 4) — את

אֶתְכֶם [וְ] — id., suff. 2 pers. pl. masc. strictly from אֵת

אֶתְכֶם [וְ] — prep. (אֵת) with suff. 2 pers. pl. masc. — את

אֶתְכְּרִיַּת — Chald. Ithpe. pret. 3 pers. sing. fem. — כרא

אַתֶּם [וְ] — pers. pron. 2 pers. pl. masc. see אַתָּה — אנת

אֹתָם [וְ] — prep. (אֵת) with suff. 3 pers. pl. masc. — את

אֹתָם [וְ] — prop. [אוֹת] sign of the accus. with suff. 3 pers. pl. masc. see אֵת (§ 5) — את

אֶתְמוֹל / אֶתְמוּל [וְ] — adv.; תְּמוֹל with prosth. א — תמל

אֶתְמַד־ — Kal fut. 1 p. s. before Mak. [for מֹד § 8.r.18] — תמד

אֶתְמַלְּטָה [וְ] — Hithp. fut. 1 pers. sing.; [וְ] for וַ conv. — מלט

אֶתְמַשְׁלָה [וְ] — Hithp. fut. 1 pers. sing.; [וְ] id. — משל

אָתַן — Root not used; Arab. *to step slowly.* אָתוֹן fem. dec. 3 a. *she-ass.*

אֵיתָן — (prim. adj.) noun masc. sing. dec. 1. for אֵיתָן — יתן

אַתֵּן [וְ] — pers. pron. 2 pers. pl. fem. see אַתָּה — אנת

אֶתֵּן / אֶתֶּן [וְ, נְ] — Kal fut. 1 pers. sing. (§ 17. rem. 2 & 3); [וְ] for וַ conv. — נתן

אֹתָן — prop. [אוֹת] sign of the accus. with suff. 3 pers. sing. fem. see אֵת (§ 5) — את

אֶתְנָה [וְ] — for אֶתֵּן q. v. (§ 1. rem. 5) — אנת

אֶתְּנָה / אֶתְּנָה — Kal fut. 1 p. s. with parag. ה (comp.) [וְ, נְ] § 8.r.15, § 17.r.3); [וְ] for וַ conv. — נתן

אֶתְּנֶנָּה [וְ] — id. with suff. 3 pers. sing. fem. — נתן

אֶתְנָה — noun fem. sing., [תְּנָה] with prosth. א — תנה

אֹתָנָה — for אֹתָן q. v. (§ 5. rem. 4) — את

אֶתְּנֶנָּהוּ ['וְ] — Kal fut. 1 pers. sing., suff. 3 pers. s. m. — נתן

אֶתְנַהֲלָה — Hithp. fut. 1 pers. sing. with paragogic ה (§ 14. rem. 1) — נהל

אֲתָנוּ — Kal pret. 1 pers. pl. R. אָתָא (§ 24. rem. 18) — אתה

אֲתֹנוֹ — noun fem. sing., suff. 3 pers. sing. masc. from אָתוֹן dec. 3a. — אתן

אֹתָנוּ ['וְ] — prep. (אֵת) with suff. 1 pers. pl. — את

אֹתָנוּ — prop. [אוֹת], sign of the accus. with suff. 1 p. pl. see אֵת (§ 5) — את

אֲתֹנוֹת — noun fem., pl. of אָתוֹן dec. 3a. — אתן

אֶתְנַחֵם [וְ] — Hithp. fut. 1 pers. sing. (§ 14. r. 1 & 3); [וְ] for וַ conv. — נחם

אֶתְנִי — pr. name masc. — תנה

אֶתְנֶךָ — noun masc. sing., suff. 2 pers. sing. masc. from אֶתְנַן dec. 3a. — אתן

אֶתֶּנְךָ [וְ, נְ] — Kal fut. 1 pers. sing., suff. 2 pers. sing. masc. (§ 17. rem. 3); [וְ] for וַ conv. — נתן

אֶתְּנֵךְ [וְ, נְ] — id., suff. 2 pers. sing. fem.; [וְ] id. — נתן

אֶתֶּנְכֶם [וְ] — id., suff. 3 pers. pl. masc.; [וְ] id. — נתן

אֶתְנַן [וְ] — with dist. acc. for the foll.; also pr. name m. — תנה

אֶתְנַן [וְ] — noun masc. sing dec. 8d. — תנה

אֶתְנַנָּה [וְ] — id., suff. 3 pers. sing. fem. — תנה

אֶתְּנֶנָּה [וְ] — Kal fut. 1 p. s., suff. 3 p.s.f.; [וְ] for וַ conv. — נתן

אֶתְּנֶנּוּ [וְ] — id., suff. 3 pers. sing. masc. — נתן

אֶתְנַנֶּיהָ — noun masc. pl., suff. 3 pers. sing. fem. from אֶתְנַן dec. 8d. — תנה

אֶתְנַפֵּל [וְ] — Hithp. fut. 1 pers. sing.; [וְ] for וַ conv. — נפל

אֲתֹנֹת [וְ] — noun f., pl. of אָתוֹן dec. 3 a.; [וְ] before (ֽ) — אתן

אֶתְעַבָּה [וְ] — [for אֶתְעַבָּה] Piel fut. 1 pers. sing. with paragogic ה (§ 14. rem. 1) [וְ] id. — תעב

אֶתְעֲקָרוּ — Chald. Ith. pret. 3 pers. pl., Kh. קרו masc. (by Hebraism), K. קרה fem. — עקר

אֶתְפָּאֵר — Hithp. fut. 1 pers. sing. [for פָּאַר § 12. r. 1] — פאר

אֶתְפַּלֵּל — in pause [for פָּלַל § 12. rem. 1]

אֶתְפַּלֵּל [וְ] & [וְ] — Hithp. fut. 1 p. s.; [וְ] for וַ conv. — פלל

אֶתְפַּלְלָה [וְ] — id. with paragogic ה; [וְ] id. — פלל

אֶתְפֹּשׂ [וְ] — Kal fut. 1 pers. sing.; [וְ] id. — תפש

אֶתֵּץ [וְ] — Kal fut. 1 pers. sing. (§ 17. rem. 3) — נתץ

אָתַק — Root not used; whence perhaps אַתִּיק masc. dec. 1 b. an obscure term in architecture, Sept. *peristyle,* Vulg. *portico.* In Kheth. אַתּוּק, Eze. 41. 15.

אֶתְקוֹטֵט — Hithpal. fut. 1 pers. s. [for קֹט § 21. r. 20] — קוט

אֶתְקוֹטְטָה [וְ] — id. with parag. ה [for קוֹמְטָה]; [וְ] for וַ conv. — קוט

אֶתְקָנְךָ — Kal fut. 1 pers. s. with epenth. נ (§ 16. r. 13) and suff. 2 pers. sing. masc. — נתק

אֲתַר — Chald. masc. dec. 3 a.—I. *place;* אֲתַר דִּי *in the place where.*—II. prep. בָּאֲתַר (for בַּאֲתַר) *after,* Da. 7. 6, 7, בָּתְרָךְ *after thee,* Da. 2. 39. אֲתָרִים (*places*) pr. name of a place in the south of Palestine, Nu. 21. 1.

אַתְרֵהּ — Chald. id., suff. 3 pers. sing. masc. — אתר

אַתַּרְגּוּ — Chald. Aph. imp. pl. masc. — נתר

אֶתְרוֹעֵעַ — Hithpal. fut. 1 pers. sing. [for עֵעַ] — רוע

אֹתֹת — noun com. gen., pl. of אוֹת dec. 1 a. — אוה

אֹתֹתַי — id., suff. 1 pers. sing. — אוה

אֹתֹתָיו — id., suff. 3 pers. sing. masc. — אוה

אֹתֹתָם [וְ] — id., suff. 3 pers. pl. masc. (§ 4. rem. 2) — אוה

---

a Ge. 12. 12.   g Job 19. 20.   m Eze. 16. 54.   t Eze. 31. 11.   b Eze. 5. 14.   2 Ch. 7. 20.   Da. 7. 8.   r De. 9. 17.   y Da. 4. 11.

b Ex. 29. 35.   h Job 30. 19.   Eze. 13. 20.   Eze. 16. 34.   c Ge. 33. 14.   Mi. 1. 7.   Is. 49. 3.   Ju. 8. 9.   Ps. 108. 10.

c Nu. 22. 33.   i Job 33. 19.   1 Ki. 14. 8.   Je. 3. 22.   Is. 23. 18.   De. 9. 18, 25.   Ps. 5. 3.   Ps. 139. 21.   Ne. 9. 10.

d Mi. 2. 8.   k Eze. 34. 31.   Ho. 2. 14.   Ju. 15. 2.   Nu. 22. 30, 32.   Ge. 12. 16.   1 Sa. 7. 5.   Ps. 119. 158.   De. 11. 3.

Is. 42. 1.   Je. 3. 19.   Ex. 35. 26.   Nu. 22. 30. 32.   Ju. 20. 28.   Da. 9. 4.   Ps. 119. 163.   Je. 22. 24.   Job 41. 22.

s. 89. 28.   Eze. 26. 21.   Eze. 16. 27.

ב

בְּ everywhere with Sheva except in the following cases :—בְּ before a word beginning with Sheva, as בְּבִשֵׂר for בִּבְשֵׂר, בֶּ, בַּ, בָּ before the composites (בָּאֲדֹנָי for בַּאֲדֹנָי), as בַּעֲמָל, (and contr. עֵד,, בַּ֫—; בַּ חֲרִי, (בֵּאלֹהֵי for בַּאֲלֹהֵי), בֶּ אֱמֹר, (contr. בֵּאלֹהֵי for בַּאֲלֹהֵי), בָּ, when displacing the art. ה (q. v.), as בַּדָּם for בְּהַדָּם, בָּאָרֶץ for בְּהָאָרֶץ, בֶּחָלָל for בְּהֶחָלָל ;—בָּ rarely before the tone-syllable, as בָּהֶם, בָּזֶה. For בְ with suffixes see § 5.

Prep.—I. of place and time, in, within, among, and rarely after verbs of motion, into.—II. noting nearness, at, near, by, on, before, (in the presence of), and of motion, to, unto, upon, against ; for, of price and exchange ; for, on account of, because of.—III. noting accompaniment and instrument, with, by, through.—IV. after verbs often lost in the translation, as וַיִּגְעַר־בּוֹ and he rebuked him, Ge. 37. 10, comp. v. 11.—V. prefixed to the inf. of verbs, in or when.

בָּא ¹ Kal pret. 3 pers. sing. masc.; ¹ before lab.   בוא

בָּא ¹ id. part. act. s. m. dec. 1 a ; for ¹ see lett. ¹   בוא

בֹּא ¹ id. inf. abs. and const. (§ 21. No. 2) ; ¹ id.   בוא

בֹּא ³ id. imp. sing. masc.; ¹ before lab.   בוא

בְּאָבְדִי ¹ pref. בַּ before (־) X Kal inf. constr.; ¹ id.   אבד

בַּאֲבַדּוֹן ¹ pref. בַּ for בַּה, ·בַּה X noun masc. sing.   אבד

בְּאָבְדָם ¹ pref. בַּ X Kal inf. with suff. 3 pers. pl. m.; ¹ bef. (:) . . . .   אבד

בְּאֵבֶן ¹ pref. id. X noun m. s., constr. of [אֶבֶן] dec. 2 a.   אבן

בְּאָבוּ ¹ pref. id. X n.m.s., suff. 3 p.s.m. fr. [אָב] dec. 8 b.   אבב

בַּאֲבוֹתֵיכֶם ¹ pref. בַּ before (־) X noun m. with pl. f. term. and suff. 2 p. pl. m. from אָב irr. (§ 45)   אב

בַּאֲבֵי ¹ pref. בַּ X n. m. pl. constr. from [אָב] dec. 8 b.   אבב

בַּאֲבִיגַיִל ¹ pref. בַּ before (־) X pr. name fem. .   אב

בַּאֲבִימֶלֶךְ ¹ pref. id. X pr. name masc. . .   אב

בַּאֲבִירָם ¹ pref. id. X pr. name masc. . .   אב

בְּאָבֵל ¹ pref. בָּ X pr. name of a place .   אבל

בְּאָבֵלָה ¹ pref. id. X id. with parag. ה id.   אבל

בְּאֶבֶן ¹ pref. }   for בַּה, ·בַּה { noun f. s. (suff.
בָּאֶבֶן ¹ pref. }   { (אַבְנוֹ) d. 6 a;   אבן
בָּאֶבֶן ³ pref. בָּ q. v.   } ¹ before labial

בְּאַבְנֵט ¹ pref. בַּ for בַּה, ·בַּה } noun masc. sing. dec. }   בנט
בָּאַבְנֵט ¹ pref. בָּ q. v.   } 1 b; ¹ before (:) . }

בָּאַבְנֵי ¹ pref. בָּ X noun fem. with pl. masc. term., constr. st. from אֶבֶן dec. 6 a. . .   אבן

בָּאֲבָנִים ¹ pref. בָּ for בַּה, ·בַּה X id.pl.abs.st.; ¹ bef. lab.   אבן

בְּאַבְרָם ¹ pref. בַּ X pr. name masc., see אַבְרָהָם   אב

בְּאֶבְרָתוֹ ¹ pref. id. X noun fem. sing., suff. 3 pers. sing. masc. from אֶבְרָה (no pl. absolute) .   אבר

בְּאַבְשָׁלוֹם ¹ pref. id. X pr. name masc. .   אב

בְּאָבֵת ¹ pref. id. X pr. name of a place .   אוב

בַּאֲבֹתֶיךָ ¹ pref. בַּ before (־) X noun masc. with pl. fem. term. and suff. 2 p. s. m. from אָב irr. (§ 45)   אב

בַּאֲבֹתֵיכֶם ¹ pref. id. X id. pl., suff. 2 p. pl. m.; ¹ bef. lab.   אב

בַּאֲנֹת ¹ pref. בַּ for בַּה, ·בַּה X noun masc. with pl. fem. term. from אֵגֵן dec. 1. (§ 30. rem. 1)   אגן

בַּאֲגְרוֹף ¹ pref. בַּ X noun masc. sing. .   נרף

בָּאִגְּרוֹת ¹ pref. בַּ for בַּה, ·בַּה X n.f.,pl. of אִגֶּרֶת dec. 13 a.   אגר

בְּאֶגְרֹף ¹ pref. בַּ X noun masc. sing. . .   נרף

בֶּאֱדוֹם ¹ pref. בֶּ X pr. name of a people and country   אדם

בֶּאֱדַיִן Chald. pref. בֶּ, contr. for בֶּאֱדַיִן, adv. .   אדין

בָּאַדִּיר ¹ pref. בָּ X adj. masc. sing. dec. 1 b.   אדר

בָּאָדָם ⁵ pref. בָּ from בַּה, ·בַּה } n. m. s.; also (Jos.
בָּאָדָם ¹ pref. בָּ q. v.   } 3. 16) pr. name } אדם
    of a place ; ¹ before labial . }

בֶּאֱדָם ¹ pref. בֶּ before (־־) X pr. name of a people .   אדם

בָּאֲדָמָה ¹ pref. בָּ bef. (־־) X n. f. s. dec. 11 c. (§ 42. r. 1)   אדם

בָּאֲדֹנָי ¹ pref. בָּ, contr. for בַּאֲדֹנָי X noun masc. pl. the name of God, different from עַ¹, pl. suff.   דון

בָּאֲדֹנָי ¹ pref. בָּ id. X noun masc. sing., suff. 1 pers. sing. for אָדוֹן dec. 3 a. . .   דון

בְּאַדְרַע Chald. pref. בְּ X noun com. sing. .   דרע

בְּאֶדְרֶעִי ¹ pref. id. X pr. n. of a place [for אֶדְרֶעִי]; ¹ bef. (:)   דרע

בְּאַדַּרְתּוֹ ¹ pref. id. X noun fem. sing., suff. 3 pers. sing. masc. from אַדֶּרֶת dec. 13 a.   אדר

בָּאָה ⁴ Kh. בָּאָה q. v., K. בָּא (q. v.) .   בוא
בָּאָה Kal part. act. s. fem. dec. 10, from בָּא masc.   בוא

בָּאָה ¹ id. pret. 3 pers. sing. fem.; ¹ for ¹ conv.   בוא

בֹּאָה ¹ ¹ id. imp. sing. masc. with parag. ה (§ 25. No. 2); for ¹ see lett. ¹ . .   בוא

בְּאַהֲבָה ⁵ pref. בַּ for בַּה, ·בַּה X noun fem. s. (no pl.)   אהב

בַּאֲהָבִים ⁶ pref. בַּ before (־־) for בַּ X noun masc., pl. [of אֹהַב dec. 6. § 35. rem. 9] . .   אהב

בְּאַהֲבַת ¹ pref. בַּ X noun f. s. constr. of אַהֲבָה (no pl.)   אהב

בְּאַהֲבָתָהּ ¹ pref. id. X id., suff. 3 pers. sing. fem. .   אהב

בְּאַהֲבָתוֹ ¹ pref. id. X id., suff. 3 pers. sing. masc. .   אהב

ᵃ Est. 5. 14.   ᵉ Est. 8. 6.   ⁱ 1 Sa. 17. 50.   ᵐ Jos. 10. 11.   ʳ Ex. 24. 6.   ᵘ Is. 10. 34.   ˣ Ezr. 4. 23.   ᵈ Je. 43. 11.   ʰ Ca. 8. 7.
ᵇ Pr. 11. 10.   ᶠ Job 8. 12.   ᵏ Da. 11. 33.   ⁿ Ps. 91. 4.   ˢ Is. 58. 4.   ᵛ Is. 32. 20.   ʸ 1 Ki. 19. 13.   ᵉ 1 Ki. 13. 7.   ⁱ Pr. 7. 18.
ᶜ Ps. 88. 12.   ᵍ Je. 11. 7.   ˡ Le. 8. 7.   º De. 10. 15.   ᵗ 2 Ch. 30. 6.   ʷ Pr. 28. 2.   ᶻ Je. 15. 9.   ᶠ 1 Sa. 30. 21.   ᵏ Pr 5. 19.
ᵈ Pr. 28. 28.   ʰ Ca. 6. 11.   ᵐ Le. 16. 4.   ᵖ 1 Sa. 12. 15.   ᵠ Ex. 21. 18.

בָּאֹהֶל	pref. בְּ for ־בְּ, ־בַּה noun m. sing. dec. 6.	אהל
בָאֹהֶל	־וֹ pref. בָּ q. v. (§ 35. r. 9) ꜟ before lab.	אהל
בְּאָהֳלוֹ	pref. בְ)(id., suff. 3 pers. sing. masc.	אהל
בְּאָהֳלֵי	pref. id.)(id. pl., construct state	אהל
בְּאָהֳלֵיהֶם	pref. id.)(id. pl., suff. 3 pers. pl. masc.	אהל
בְּאֹהָלֶיךָ	pref. id.)(id. pl., suff. 2 p. s. m. (א § 35. r. 9)	אהל
בְאָהֳלֵיכֶם	pref. id.)(id. pl., suff. 2 pers. pl. masc.	אהל
בְּאֹהָלִים	pref. בָּ before (־) for בְּ)(id. pl., abs. st.	אהל
בְּאָהֳלֶךָ בְּאָהֳלֶךָ	} pref. בְּ)(id. sing., suff. 2 pers. sing. masc.	אהל
בְּאַהֲרֹן	ꜟ pref. id.)(pr. name masc.; ꜟ before (־)	אהר
בָּאוּ	־וֹ, ־וּ, Kal pret. 3 p. pl.; ꜟ for וָ, וַ see lett. וְ	בוא
בֹּאוֹ	id. inf. (בּוֹא) suff. 3 pers. sing. masc. dec. 1 a. (§ 25. No. 2)	בוא
בֹּאוּ	־וֹ, ־וּ, id. imp. (or pret. Je. 27. 18. § 21. r. 2) pl. masc.; ꜟ for וָ, וַ see lett. וְ	בוא
בָּאוֹב	pref. בָּ for ־בְּ, ־בְּה)(noun m. s. dec. 1 a.	אוב
בְּאוּלָם	pref. id.)(noun m. s., pl. c. ־אֻלַּמֵּי, dec. 8 a.	אול
בְּאִוַּלְתּוֹ	pref. בְּ)(noun fem. sing., suff. 3 pers. sing. masc. from אִוֶּלֶת dec. 13 a.	אול
בְּאוֹנוֹ	ꜟ pref. id.)(noun masc. sing., suff. 3 pers. sing. masc. from אוֹן dec. 1 a.; ꜟ before (־)	און
בְּאוֹפַנִּים	pref. בְּ for ־בְּה, אֹפָן)(noun masc., pl. of אוֹפָן dec. 8 d. (§ 37. rem. 2 & 3)	אפן
בְּאוֹצְרוֹת	pref. בְּ)(noun masc. with pl. fem. term., abs. st. from אוֹצָר dec. 2 b.	אצר
בְּאוֹצְרוֹת	ꜟ pref. id.)(id. const. st.; ꜟ before (־)	אצר
בְּאוֹצְרוֹתֶיךָ	pref. id.)(id., suff. 2 pers. sing. masc.	אצר
בְּאוֹצְרוֹתֶיךְ	ꜟ pref. id.)(id., suff. 2 pers. s. f.; ꜟ bef. (־)	אצר
בְּאוֹצְרֹתֵינוּ	pref. id.)(id., suff. 1 pers. pl. [for ־תַי]	אצר
בְּאוֹצְרֹתָיו	pref. id.)(id., suff. 3 pers. sing. masc.	אצר
בָּאוֹר	pref. בְּ for ־בְּה, ־בְּה)(noun m. s. dec. 1 a.	אור
בְאוֹר	pref. id.)(noun masc. sing. dec. 1 a.	אור
בְּאֻר	pref. בְּ)(noun masc. sing. dec. 1 a.	אור
בְּאוּר	pref. id.)(n. m. s. dec. 1 a; also pr. n. of a place	אור
בְּאוּרִים	pref. בְּ for ־בְּה, ־בְּה)(id. pl., abs. st.	אור
בְּאוֹרְךָ	pref. id.)(n. m. s., suff. 2 p. s. m. fr. אוֹר dec. 1 a.	אור
בָּאוּשָׁתָא	ꜟ Ch. adj. fem. s., emph. of בָּאוּשָׁא dec. 8 a. fr. בָּאוּשׁ masc. § 67. rem.]; ꜟ bef. labial	באשׁ
בָּאוֹת	־וֹ Kal part. act. fem., pl. of בָּאָה dec. 10, from בָּא masc.; ꜟ id.	בוא
בְּאַוַּת	pref. בְּ)(n. f. s., constr. of [אַוָּה] dec. 10.	אוה
בְאַוָּתִי	pref. id.)(id., suff. 1 pers. sing.	אוה
בְּאֵזוֹב בְּאֵזוֹב	ꜟ pref. בְּ for ־בְּה, ־בְּה } noun masc. sing. pref. בְּ q. v.	אזב

בְּאָזְנוֹ	pref. בְּ)(n. f. s., suff. 3 p.s.m.fr. אֹזֶן dec. 6 c.	אזן
בְּאָזְנִי בְּאָזְנִי	} pref. id.)(id. du. suff. 1 pers. sing.	אזן
בְּאָזְנֵי	ꜟ pref. id.)(id. du., constr. st.; ꜟ before (־)	אזן
בְּאָזְנֵיהֶם	pref. id.)(id. du., suff. 3 pers. pl. masc.	אזן
בְּאָזְנֵינוּ	ꜟ pref. id.)(id. du., suff. 3 p. s. m.; ꜟ bef. (־)	אזן
בְּאָזְנֵךְ	pref. id.)(id. du., suff. 2 pers. sing. fem.	אזן
בְּאָזְנֶךָ	ꜟ pref. id.)(id. du., suff. 2 p. s. m.; ꜟ bef. (־)	אזן
בְּאָזְנֵיכֶם	pref. id.)(id. du., suff. 2 pers. pl. masc.	אזן
בְּאָזְנֵינוּ	pref. id.)(id. du., suff. 1 pers. pl.	אזן
בָּאֻקִּים	pref. בְּ, contr. from אֹקֶ, בָּאֳ, בְּהָאֳ)(noun masc. pl. of [אֹקֶ] dec. 8 b.	זקק
בְּאֶזְרֹעַ	ꜟ pref. בְּ)(noun com. s. dec. 1 b; ꜟ bef. (־)	זרע
בָּאֶזְרָח	pref. בָּ for ־בְּה, ־בְּה)(n. m. s. dec. 2 b.	זרח
בְּאֶזְרַח	ꜟ pref. בְּ)(id., construct state; ꜟ bef. (־)	זרח
בַּאֲחַד	Kh. בְּאֶחָד q. v., K. בְּאַחַת (q. v.)	אחר
בְּאַחַד	pref. בְּ)(constr. of the following	אחר
בְּאֶחָד	־וֹ pref. id.)(num. card. masc. irr. (§ 45)	אחר
בְּאַחוּ	pref. בְּ, for ־בְּה, ־בְּה)(noun fem. sing.	אחו
בְּאָחוֹרִי	pref. בְּ)(noun masc. sing. dec. 3 a.	אחר
בֶּאֱחֹז	pref. בְּ bef. (־־))(Kal inf. constr.	אחז
בְּאֲחֻזָּתוֹ	pref. בַּ before (־))(noun fem. sing., suff. 3 pers. sing. masc. from אֲחֻזָּה dec. 10.	אחז
בַּאֲחֻזָּתָם	pref. id.)(id., suff. 3 pers. pl. masc.	אחז
בְּאָחִיהוּ	pref. בְּ)(noun masc. sing., suff. 3 pers. sing. masc. from אָח irr. (§ 45)	אח
בְּאָחִיו	־וֹ ꜟ pref. id.)(id., suff. 3 p. s. m.; ꜟ bef. (־)	אח
בְּאֶחָיו	pref. id.)(id. pl., suff. 3 pers. sing. masc., (as if from אָח R. אחה see § 45)	אח
בְּאָחִיךָ	pref. id.)(id. sing., suff. 2 pers. sing. masc.	אח
בַּאֲחֵיכֶם	ꜟ pref. בַּ before (־))(id. pl., suff. 2 pers. pl. masc. comp. בְּאֶחָי; ꜟ before labial	אח
בָּאֲחַמְתָא	pref. בְּ)(pr. name of a place, see אַחְמְתָא	
בָּאַחֲרֹנָה	pref. בְּ for ־בְּה, ־בְּה)(adj. f. s. fr. אַחֲרוֹן masc.	אחר
בְּאַחֲרֵי	pref. id.)(n. m. pl. constr. from אַחַר (q. v.)	אחר
בְּאַחֲרִית	ꜟ pref. id.)(noun fem. s. dec. 1 b; ꜟ bef. (־)	אחר
בְּאַחֲרִיתָהּ	pref. id.)(id., suff. 3 pers. sing. fem.	אחר
בְּאַחֲרִיתוֹ	ꜟ pref. id.)(id., suff. 3 p. s. m.; ꜟ bef. (־)	אחר
בְּאַחֲרִיתֶךָ	pref. id.)(id., suff. 2 p. s. m. [for אַחֲרִיתְךָ]	אחר
בָּאַחֲרֹנָה	defect. for בְּאַחֲרוֹנָה (q. v.)	אחר
בְּאַחַת	־וֹ pref. בְּ)(num. card., [for אַחֲדַת], fem. of אֶחָד irr. (§ 45); ꜟ before (־)	אחר
בְּאָחַת	pref. id.)(id. in pause (comp. בְּאָחִיו under אָח § 45)	אחר
בְּאַחֻתָהּ	־וֹ pref. בַּ bef. (־))(noun fem. sing., suff. 3 pers. sing. fem. from אָחוֹת irr. (§ 45)	אח

ᵃ Ge. 31. 33, 33.   ᶠ Ho. 12. 4.   ᵏ Je. 48. 7.   ᵖ Ps. 36. 10.   ᵘ Le. 14. 52.   ᶜ Je. 32. 21.   ʰ Ge. 41. 2, 18.   ᵐ Ex. 32. 29.   ᵗ Pr. 25. 8.
ᵇ De. 1. 27.   ᵍ Eze. 1. 20, 21.   ˡ Job 33. 28.   ᑫ Ps. 51. 9.   ᵛ Pr. 29. 11.   ᵈ Le. 17. 15.   ⁱ Ps. 56. 1.   ⁿ Le. 25. 46.   ᵘ Je. 17. 11.
ᶜ Ps. 61. 5.   ʰ Ps. 33. 7.   ᵐ Eze. 5. 2.   ʳ Is. 50. 11.   ʷ De. 15. 17. Is. 6. 10.   ᵉ Ex. 12. 19.   ʲ 2 Ki. 14. 14.   ᵒ 2 Sa. 2. 26.   ᵛ Je. 10. 8.
ᵈ Ec. 8. 10.   ⁱ 2 Ki. 14. 14.   ⁿ Is. 50. 11.   ˢ Je. 2. 24.   ˣ Is. 49. 20.   ᶠ Ca. 4. 9.   ᵏ 1 Ch. 9. 2.   ᵖ 2 Sa. 2. 23.   ʷ Pr. 28. 13.
ᵉ 1 Ki. 7. 19.   ʲ Eze. 28. 4.   ᵒ 1 Sa. 28. 6.   ᵗ Ho. 10. 10.   ʸ Je. 40. 1.   ᵍ Ezr. 7. 9.   ˡ Job 41. 9.   ᑫ Da. 8. 23.   ᵛ Ge. 30. 1.

בָּאִי	Kal part. act. pl. constr. from בָּא dec. 1 a.	בוא
בָּאִי	id. inf. (בּוֹא), suff. 1 p. s. dec. 1 a. (§ 25. No. 2)	בוא
בָּאִי	id. imp. sing. fem.; ו bef. labial	בוא
בְּאִיבָה	pref. בְּ ✗ noun fem. sing. dec. 10.	איב
בְּאִיבִי	ו pref. id. ✗ the foll. with suff. 1 p. s.; ו bef.	איב
בְּאֹיְבַי	pref. id. ✗ Kal part. act. pl. constr. masc. from אֹיֵב dec. 7 b.	איב
בְּאֵידְכֶם	pref. id. ✗ n. m. s., suff. 2 p. pl. m. fr. אֵיד d. 1 a.	אוד
בָּאֶיהָ	Kal part. act. pl. m., suff. 3 p. s. f. fr. בָּא dec. 1 a.	בוא
בְּאִיּוֹב	pref. בְּ ✗ pr. name masc.	איב
בָּאֵי	pref. id ✗ constr. of the following: Is. 24. 15.	
בָּאִיִּים	pref. בְּ, for בְּהָ ✗ בְּהָ ✗ noun masc., pl. of אִי dec. 8. (§ 37. No. 4)	אוה
בָּאַיִל	pref. id. ✗ noun m. s. dec. 6 h. (§ 35. r. 12)	אול
בָּאֵיל	pref. בְּ ✗ id., construct state	אול
בְּאֵילֹה	pref. id. ✗ pr. name of a place	אול
בְּאַיָּלוֹת	pref. id. ✗ n. f., pl. of אַיֶּלֶת or אַיָּלָה (§ 42. r. 5)	אול
בְּאֵילִים	pref. id. ✗ noun masc., pl. of אַיִל dec. 6 h.	אול
בְּאֵילִם	ו pref. id. ✗ pr. name of a place; ו bef. lab.	אול
בָּאִים	ו Kal part. act. m., pl. of בָּא dec. 1 a; ו id.	בוא
בְּאֵימָה	pref. בְּ ✗ noun fem. sing. dec. 10.	אים
בְּאֵימִים	ו pref. בְּ for בְּהָ ✗ בְּהָ ✗ noun masc. pl. of [אֵים, or אַיִם]; ו bef. lab.	אים
בְּאַיִן	וׁ pref. בְּ ✗ adv., prop. noun masc. sing., constr. of אַיִן dec. 6 h; ו id.	און
בְּאִישׁ	pref. בְּ, f. בְּהָ ✗ noun masc. s. dec. 1. } pref. בְּ q. v. (comp. § 45) }	איש
בְּאִישָׁהּ	pref. id. ✗ id., suff. 3 pers. sing. fem.	איש
בְּאִישׁוֹן	Kh. בָּאִישׁוֹן see the following, K. בָּאִשׁוֹן, pref. בְּ ✗ noun masc. sing. R.	אשן
בְּאִישׁוֹן	pref. בְּ ✗ noun masc. sing.	איש
בְּאִיתָן	pref. id. ✗ noun m. sing. (no vowel change)	יתן
בִּיאַךְ	ו Kh. וּבָאַךְ (q. v. ?), K. יְבִאַךְ, defect. for יְבִיאַךְ (q. v.)	בוא
בָּאֲךָ / בֹּאֲךָ	וׁ Kal inf. (בּוֹא), suff. 2 pers. sing. masc. dec. 1 a. (§ 25. No. 2); ו bef. lab. }	בוא
בֹּאֲכָה	id. for בֹּאֲךָ (§ 3. rem. 2)	בוא
בְּאָכְלָ	pref. בְּ bef. ✗ Kal inf. constr.	אכל
בְּאָכְלֹ	pref. בְּ for בְּהָ ✗ בְּהָ ✗ Kal part. act. s. m. d. 7 b.	אכל
בְּאָכְלִ	pref. בְּ ✗ noun masc. sing. dec. 6 c.	אכל
בְּאָכְלֵי	pref. id. ✗ Kal part. act. pl. constr. masc. from אֹכֵל dec. 7 b.	אכל
בְּאָכָלְכֶם	pref. בְּ bef. ✗ Kal inf., suff. 2 pers. pl. m.	אכל
בְּאָכְלָם	pref. בְּ ✗ id., suff. 3 pers. pl. masc.	אכל
בְּאָכְלֵנוּ	pref. id. ✗ id., suff. 1 pers. pl.	אכל

בֹּאֲכֶם	Kal inf. (בּוֹא), suff. 2 pers. pl. masc. dec. 1 a. (§ 25. No. 2)	בוא
בְּאֵל	pref. בְּ ✗ noun masc. sing. dec. 1 a.	אול
בְּאֵלָה	pref. בְּ, for בְּהָ ✗ noun fem. sing.	אול
בָּאֵלֶּה	pref. id. bef. tone-syl. s. ✗ pron. demon. pl. com.	אל
בְּאֵלָה	pref. בְּ ✗ noun fem. sing. dec. 10. (§ 42. r. 2)	אלה
בָּאֵלֶּה	וׁ pref. id. ✗ pron. demon. pl. com.; ו bef.	אל
בַּאלָהּ	Chald. pref. בְּ contr. [for בָּאֵ] ✗ noun masc. sing., suff. 3 pers. sing. masc. אֱלָהּ dec. 1 a.	אלה
בֵּאלֹהַי	וׁ pref. id. ✗ noun masc. pl., suff. 1 pers. sing. from אֱלוֹהַּ dec. 1; ו bef. lab.	אלה
בֵּאלֹהֵי	וׁ pref. id. ✗ id., construct state; ו id.	אלה
בֵּאלֹהֶיהָ	pref. id. ✗ id., suff. 3 pers. sing. fem.	אלה
בֵּאלֹהֵיהֶם	ו pref. id. ✗ id., suff. 3 pers. pl. m.; ו bef. lab.	אלה
בֵּאלֹהָיו	וׁ pref. id. ✗ id., suff. 3 pers. s. m.; ו id.	אלה
בֵּאלֹהֶיךָ	וׁ pref. id. ✗ id., suff. 2 pers. sing. masc.	אלה
בֵּאלֹהֵיכֶם	pref. id. ✗ id., suff. 2 pers. pl. masc.	אלה
בֵּאלֹהִים	pref. בְּהַ for בְּהָ, בְּהֶ	אלה
בֵּאלֹהִים	pref. בְּ, [for בָּאֵ] } id. pl., absolute st.	
בֵּאלֹהֵינוּ	pref. id. ✗ id., suff. 1 pers. pl.	אלה
בְּאַלּוּף	pref. בְּ ✗ noun masc. sing. dec. 1 a.	אלף
בְּאַלּוּשׁ	pref. id. ✗ pr. name of a place.	אלש
בֶּאֱלִילִים	pref. בְּ for בְּהָ ✗ בְּהָ ✗ n. m., pl. of אֱלִיל d. 1 a.	אלל
בֵּאלִים / בְּאֵלִם	} pref. id. ✗ noun masc., pl. of אֵל dec. 1 a.	אול
בְּאֻלָם	ו pref. בְּ ✗ n. m. s. for אוּלָם q. v.; ו bef.	אול
בְּאַלְמְנוֹתָיו	pref. id. ✗ noun fem. pl., suff. 3 pers. sing. masc. from אַלְמָנָה dec. 11 a.	אלם
בְּאַלּוֹנֵי	pref. id. ✗ n. m. pl. constr. from אַלּוֹן dec. 1 b.	אול
בְּאֶלֶף	pref. id. ✗ noun m. s., (suff. אַלְפִי) dec. 6 a.	אלף
בְּאַלְפוֹ	pref. בְּ before ✗ id. pl., suff. 3 pers. sing. masc., K. פָּיו (§ 4. rem. 1)	אלף
בְּאַלְפֵי	pref. בְּ ✗ id. pl., construct state	אלף
בְּאֶלְתוֹ	וׁ pref. id. ✗ n. f. s., suff. 3 p. s. m.; ו bef.	אלה
בֹּאָם	Kal inf. (בּוֹא), suff. 3 p. pl. m. d. 1 a. (§ 25. No.)	בוא
בְּאָמָה	pref. בְּ for בְּהָ ✗ בְּהָ ✗ noun fem. sing. dec. 10.	אם
בַּאֲמָהּ	pref. בְּ ✗ n. f. s., suff. 3 p. s. f. fr. אָם d. 8 b.	אם
בֶּאֱמוּנָה	pref. בְּ bef. ✗ noun fem. sing. dec. 10.	אמן
בֶּאֱמוּנָתוֹ	pref. id. ✗ id., suff. 3 pers. sing. masc.	אמן
בֶּאֱמוּנָתִי	pref. id. ✗ id., suff. 1 pers. sing.	אמן
בֶּאֱמוּנָתְךָ	pref. id. ✗ id., suff. 2 pers. s. m. [for נָתֶךָ]	אמן
בֶּאֱמוּנָתָם	pref. id. ✗ id., suff. 3 pers. pl. masc.	אמן
בְּאַמּוֹת	pref. בְּ for בְּהָ ✗ בְּהָ ✗ n. f., pl. of אַמָּה d. 10.	ם
בְּאַמְכֶם	pref. id. ✗ n. f. s., suff. 2 p. pl. m. fr. אָם d. 8 b.	אם

ᵃ Nu. 35. 21.   ᶠ Eze. 40. 38.   ˡ Pr. 20. 20.   ᵠ Nu. 26. 10.   ᵛ Ex. 6. 3.   ᶜ Is. 48. 1.   ᶦ Jos. 24. 27.   ᵐ Eze. 40. 39.   ᵖ Ps. 89. 34.
ᵇ Ps. 54. 9.   ᵍ Esr. 3. 3.   ᵐ Je. 50. 38.   ʳ Ge. 49. 24.   ʸ 2 Sa. 18. 9, 10.   ᵈ Ho. 14. 1.   ʲ Mi. 7. 5.   ⁿ Is. 13. 22.   ᵠ Ps. 89. 50.
ᶜ Pr. 1. 26.   ʰ Je. 50. 38.   ⁿ Pr. 7. 9.   ˢ La. 1. 15.   ᶻ Nu. 26. 64.   ᵉ Nu. 33. 4.   ᵏ Ps. 97. 7.   ᵒ De. 29. 11.   ʳ Eze. 43. 13.
ᵈ Pr. 2. 19.   ᶦ Pr. 26. 20.   ᵒ Ex. 13. 11.   ᵗ Nu. 15. 19.   ᵃ Da. 6. 24.   ᶠ Is. 8. 21.   ˡ Is. 57. 5.   ᵖ Mi. 7. 6.   ˢ Ho. 2. 4.
ᵉ Da. 5. 7.   ᵏ Nu. 5. 27.   ᵖ 1 Ki. 2. 13.   ᵘ Ex. 16. 3.   ᵇ Ps. 18. 30.   ᵍ Ho. 12. 7.   ᵐ Ex. 15. 11.

בָּאֲמָנָה defect. for בָּאֱמוּנָה (q. v.) — אמן

בָּאֳמְנָה• pref. בְּ ✕ noun fem. sing. — אמן

בָּאֲמֻנָתְךָי pref. בְּ bef. (ֶּ) ✕ noun fem. sing., suff. 2 pers. sing. masc. from אֲמוּנָה dec. 10. — אמן

בָּאַמְּצוֹי pref. בְּ ✕ (Piel inf. (אַמֵּץ), suff. 3 p. s. m. d. 7 b. — אמץ

בָּאֲמַצְיָהּ pref. בְּ bef. (ֶ) ✕ pr. name masc. — אמץ

בָּאֱמֹר pref. בְּ bef. (ֶ) ✕ Kal inf. constr. — אמר

בָּאֹמְרֵי pref. בְּ ✕ n. m. pl. constr. fr. [אֹמֶר] dec. 6 b. — אמר

בָּאָמְרִיּ pref. id. ✕ Kal inf., suff. 1 p. s.; וּ bef. (ַ) — אמר

בְּאָמְרֵיכֶם וּ pref. id. ✕ noun masc. pl., suff. 2 pers. pl. masc. from [אֹמֶר] dec. 6 b.; וּ id. — אמר

בָּאֹמְרִים pref. id. ✕ Kal part. act. m., pl. of אֹמֵר d. 7 b. — אמר

בָּאָמָרְכֶם pref. בְּ bef. ✕ id. inf., suff. 2 pers. pl. m. — אמר

בָּאָמְרָם pref. בְּ ✕ id id., suff. 3 pers. pl. masc. — אמר

בָּאִמְרָתֶךָי pref. id. ✕ noun fem. sing., suff. 2 pers. sing. masc. from [אִמְרָה] dec. 12 b. [for רָתְךָ] — אמר

בָּאֲמַתּ׳ pref. id. ✕ noun f. s., constr. of אָמָה dec. 10. — אם

בָּאֱמֶת ׳ pref. בְּ before (ֶ) ✕ noun fem. sing. (suff. אֲמִתּוֹ) dec. 6 b. [for אֲמִנָת]; וּ bef. lab. — אמן

בָּאֲמִתַּחַת• pref. בְּ ✕ noun f. s. dec. 13 a. (§ 44. No. 1) — מתח

בָּאֲמִתַּחְתִּי pref. id. ✕ id., suff. 1 pers. sing. — מתח

בָּאֲמִתְּחֹתֵיכֶם• pref. id. ✕ id., suff. 2 pers. pl. masc. — מתח

בָּאֲמִתְּחֹתֵינוּ• pref. id. ✕ id., suff. 1 pers. pl. — מתח

בָּאֲמִתְּךָ } pref. בְּ before (ֶ) ✕ noun fem. sing., suff. 2 p. s. m. from אֱמֶת (q. v.) dec. 8 b. } — אמן
בָּאֲמִתְּךָי }

בָּאֲנָהּ Kal inf. (בּוֹא), suff. 3 p. pl. fem. (§ 4. r. 5) d. 1 a. — בוא

בָּאנוּ וּ id. pret. 1 pers. pl. (§ 25. 2); וּ bef. lab. — בוא

בָּאֵנוּי id. inf. (בּוֹא), suff. 1 pers. pl. dec. 1 a. — בוא

בָּאֱנוֹשׁ pref. בְּ bef. (ֶ) ✕ n. m. s. (comp. אִישׁ § 45) — אנש

בָּאֲנָחָהּ pref. בְּ for בְּהָ, בְּהַ ✕ n. f. s. d. 11 c. (§ 42. r. 1) — אנח

בָּאֲנָחָתִי pref. בְּ ✕ id. with suff. 1 pers. sing. — אנח

בָּאֳנִיּ pref. בְּ before (ֳ) ✕ noun masc. sing. — אנה

בָּאֳנִיּי pref. בְּ ✕ (n.m.s., suff. 1 p. s. from אֹן dec. 1 a. — און

בָּאֲנִיָּהּ pref. בְּ for בְּהָ, בְּהַ ✕ noun fem. sing. dec. 10. — אנה

בָּאֳנִיּוֹת וּ pref. בְּ before (ֳ) ✕ id. pl.; וּ bef. lab. — אנה

בָּאֲנָקֹ pref. בְּ bef. (ֶ) ✕ Kal inf. constr. — אנק

בָּאֱנוֹשֵׁיוּ pref. בְּ ✕ constr. of the foll.; וּ bef. (ַ) — אנש

בָּאֲנָשִׁים pref. בְּ for בְּהָ, בְּהַ ✕ n. m. pl., as if from } — אנש
בָּאֲנָשִׁיםּ pref. בְּ before (ֶ) ✕ ✕ [אֱנָשׁ] d. 6, see אֲנוֹשׁ }

בָּאֲסוּרֹ וּ Ch. pref. בְּ bef. (ֶ) ✕ n.m.s. d. 1 a; וּ bef. lab. — אסר

בָּאֲסָמֶיךָי pref. בְּ bef. (ֶ) ✕ noun masc. pl., suff. 2 pers. sing. masc. [from אָסָם] — אסם

בָּאֹסְפֵיּ pref. id. ✕ noun masc. pl. constr. [from אָסִף dec. 8 c. § 37. No. 3.] — אסף

בָּאָסְפְּךָ pref. בְּ ✕ Kal inf., suff. 2 pers. sing. masc. — אסף

בָּאָסְפְּכֶם pref. id. ✕ id., suff. 2 pers. pl. masc. — אסף

בָּאָסְרָם pref. id. ✕ Kal inf., suff. 3 pers. pl. masc. — אסר

בָּאַף pref.=בְּ (בְּהַ, בְּהָ) ✕ noun masc. sing. dec. 8 d; וּ pref. בְּ q. v. for [אַנְף]; וּ bef. (ַ) — אנף

בָּאַפּוֹ pref. id. ✕ id., suff. 3 pers. sing. masc. — אנף

בָּאַפִּי pref. id. ✕ id., suff. 1 pers. sing. — אנף

בָּאַפָּיו pref. id. ✕ id. du., suff. 3 pers. sing. masc. — אנף

בָּאַפַּיִםּ pref. id. ✕ id. du., absolute state — אנף

בָּאֲפִיקִיםּ pref. בְּ for בְּהָ, בְּהַ ✕ n.m.,pl. of [אָפִיק] d. 3 a. — אפק

בָּאַפְּךָ } pref. בְּ ✕ noun masc. sing., suff. 2 pers. sing. masc. from אַף dec. 8 d. } — אנף
בָּאַפֶּךָ }

בָּאַפְּכֶםי וּ pref. id. ✕ id., suff. 2 p. pl. m.; וּ bef. (ַ) — אנף

בָּאֹפֶלּ pref. בְּ for בְּהָ, בְּהַ ✕ noun masc. sing. — אפל

בָּאֲפֵלָה pref. id. ✕ noun fem. sing. dec. 10. (§ 42. r. 4) — אפל

בָּאֲפֵלוֹת • pref. בְּ before (ַ) ✕ id. pl. — אפל

בָּאַפָּם pref. בְּ ✕ noun masc. sing., with suff. 3 pers. pl. masc. from אַף dec. 8 d. — אנף

בָּאָפֵס וּ pref. id. ✕ noun masc. sing., as an adv. also pr. name masc.; אֶפֶס דַּמִּים; וּ bef. labial — אפס

בָּאֲפֵק pref. בְּ before (ַ) ✕ pr. name of a place — אפק

בָּאֵפֶרּ pref. בְּ for בְּהָ, בְּהַ ✕ noun masc. sing. — אפר

בָּאֵפֶר pref. id. ✕ noun masc. sing. — אפר

בָּאֶפְרַיִם וּ pref. בְּ ✕ pr. name of a tribe; וּ before (ֶ) — אפר

בָּאֶפְרָתָה pref. id. ✕ pr. name of a place — אפר

בָּאֶצְבַּע pref. בְּ ✕ noun fem. sing. dec. 2 b. (§ 31. r. 5) — צבע

בָּאֶצְבָּעוֹ pref. id. ✕ id., suff. 3 pers. sing. masc. — צבע

בָּאֶצְבָּעֶךָ pref. id. ✕ id., suff. 2 pers. sing. m., [for בַּעֵךָ] — צבע

בָּאֶצְבְּעֹתָיוי pref. id. ✕ id. pl., suff. 3 pers. sing. masc. — צבע

בָּאֹצָרוֹת וּ pref. id. ✕ noun masc. with pl. fem. term., constr. state from אוֹצָר dec. 2 b; וּ before (ִ) — אצר

בָּאֹצְרֹתַיּ pref. id. ✕ id., suff. 1 pers. sing [for תַי] — אצר

בָּאֹצְרֹתֶיהָי pref. id. ✕ id., suff. 3 pers. sing. fem. — אצר

בָּאַר Kal not used; Pi.—I. to engrave, as upon a tablet Hab. 2. 2.—II. to expound, explain.

בְּאֵר fem. with suff. בְּאֵרְךָ, pl. בְּאֵרוֹת, constr בְּאֵרֹת (§ 35. rem. 10).—I. a well, cistern.—II. pit.—III. pr. name of a station of the Israelites in the desert, probably the same which is called בְּאֵר אֵלִים (well of heroes) in Is. 15. 8.—IV. a place in Judah, Ju. 9. 21.

בְּאֵר לַחַי רֹאִי pr. name of the well where the angel appeared to Hagar. The etymology according to Ge. 16. 14 is, "well of life of vision," i. e. life retained notwithstanding the vision of God. רֹאִי in pause for רָאִי=רֳאִי (comp. § 35. rem. 14) probably to avoid the concurrence of this accent with that of the preceding לַחַי.

* Est. 2. 20.   f Ps. 122. 1.   ⁱ Ge. 42. 28.   ᵖ 2 Sa. 17. 12.   ᵘ Jon. 1. 5.   ˣ Da. 4. 12, 20.   ᵏ La. 3. 43; Is. 11. 6.   ⁿ Ps. 91. 6.   ᵗ Pr. 6. 13.
ᵇ Ps. 143. 1.   ᵍ Ps. 119, 133, 143.   ᵐ Ge. 43. 23.   q Ex. 10. 26.   ʸ Da. 11. 40.   c De. 28. 8.   ᶦ Da. 11. 20.   ᵒ Is. 59. 9.   ʳ 2 Ki. 16. 8.
ᶜ Pr. 8. 28.   ʰ De. 3. 11.   ⁿ Ge. 43. 18, 22.   ʳ Ps. 31. 11.   ᶻ Ne. 12. 25.   ᵈ Ezе. 26. 15.   ᵏ Eze. 34. 13.   ᵖ Ge. 49. 6.   ˢ 2 Ki. 20. 15.
ᵈ Eze. 33. 14.   ⁱ Jos. 24. 14.   ᵒ Ps. 54. 7.   ᵏ 1 Ki. 9. 27.   ᵃ Le. 23. 39.   ᵉ 2 Sa. 2. 31.   Am. 4. 10.   ᵖ 1 Ki. 20. 38.   t Je. 49. 4.
ᵉ Job 33. 14.   ᵏ Ge. 44. 12.   ᵖ Je. 8. 7.   ᵒ De. 26. 14.   ᵇ 1 Sa. 17. 12.   ᵍ Ho. 10. 10.

בְּאֵר שֶׁבַע (*well of oath*) pr. name of a city in the tribe of Judah, afterwards of Simeon.

בְּאֵרָא (*well*) pr. name masc. 1 Ch. 7. 37.

בְּאֵרָה (*id.*) pr. name masc. 1 Ch. 5. 6.

בְּאֵרוֹת (*wells*) pr. name of a city in the tribe of Benjamin. Gent. noun בְּאֵרֹתִי and contr. בֵּרֹתִי.

בְּאֵרוֹת בְּנֵי יַעֲקָן (*wells of the sons of Jaakan*) pr. name of a station of the Israelites in the desert. De. 10. 6, called בְּנֵי יַעֲקָן in Nu. 33. 31.

בְּאֵרִי (*belonging to a well*) pr. name.—I. the father of Hosea, Ho. 1. 1.—II. father-in-law of Esau, Ge. 26. 34.

בֹּאר masc. pl. בֹּארוֹת i. q. בּוֹר *a cistern*.

בּוֹר (for בְּאֹר=בֹּאר) masc. dec. 1 a. pl. בֹּרוֹת.—I. *pit*.—II. *cistern*.—III. *dungeon* or *prison*; בֵּית הַבּוֹר *prison-house*.—IV. *grave, sepulchre*.

בּוֹר הַסִּרָה (*cistern of departure*) pr. name of a place, 2 Sa. 3. 26.

בְּאֵיר i. q. בְּאֵר *a cistern*, Je. 6. 7, Keri.

בֵּרִי (for בְּאֵרִי q. v.) pr. name masc. 1 Ch. 7. 36.

בֵּרוֹתָה ,בֵּרוֹתַי (*my well*) pr. name of a city between Damascus and Hamath, Eze. 47. 16; 2 Sa. 8. 8.

בָּאֵר [b] Piel inf.; ↓ before labial . . . . באר

בָּאֵר [c] id. pret. 3 pers. sing. masc. . . באר

בְּאֵר [d] noun fem.sing. (§ 35. r. 10); ↓ before labial באר

בְּאֵרָא ↓ pr. name masc.; ↓ before (ִ) . . . באר

בְּאַרְבָּה pref. בָּ, for בְּהָ, בְּהַ (noun masc. sing. . רבה

בְּאַרְבּוֹת [f] pref. id. (noun fem., pl. of אֲרֻבָּה dec. 10; also pr. name of a place . . . . ארב

בְּאַרְבָּם pref. בָּ (noun masc. sing. suff. 3 pers. pl. masc. from [אֹרֶב] dec. 6c. . . . . ארב

בְּאַרְבַּע [g] pref.id.(num. card.f.(§ 30.r.5); ↓ before (ִ) רבע

בְּאַרְבָּעָה [h] pref.id.(id.m.constr.(§ 42.r.5); ↓ id. רבע

בְּאַרְבָּעִים pref.id. (id. pl. com. (§ 30. rem. 5) . רבע

בְּאַרְבַּעַת pref.id.(id.s.m., constr. of אַרְבָּעָה (§ 42.r.5) רבע

בְּאַרְגָּז ↓ pref. id. (n. m. s.; ↓ before labial, see R. ארג/'

בְּאַרְגָּז pref. בָּ (for בְּהָ, בְּהַ; noun masc. sing. רגז

בְּאַרְגָּמָן ↓ pref. id. (id. noun masc. sing.; ↓ id. ארג/'

בְּאֵרָה pr. name masc. . . . . . . באר

בְּאֵרָה pr. name of a place (בְּאֵר) with local ה . באר

בְּאַרְמָה pref. בָּ [for בְּ'] (pr. name of a place . ארם

בְּאַרוֹן pref. id. (noun masc. sing. dec. 3a. . ארה

בְּאֵרֹן [k] pref. בָּ before (ִ) (id., construct state . ארה

בְּאֵרוֹת ↓ pr. name of a place . . . . . . באר

בְּאֵרוֹת [l] noun m.with pl. fem. term. from בְּאֵר, dec. 1a. באר

בָּאָרֶז [p] pref. בָּ for בְּהָ, בְּהַ (noun masc. sing.),] ארז
בָּאָרֶז [q] pl. c. אַרְזֵי dec. 6a. (§ 35. rem. 2) }

בָּאֲרָזֶיךָ pref. בָּ before (ִ) (id. pl. with suff. 2 p. s. m. ארז

בָּאֲרָזִים pref. בָּ for בְּהָ, בְּהַ (id. pl., absolute state ארז

בָּאֹרַח pref. בָּ (noun com. sing. dec. 6c. . ארח

בְּאֹרְחֹתָיו pref. id.(id. pl., suff. 3 p. s. m. (א § 35. r. 9) ארח

בְּאֵרִי pr. name masc. . . . . . . באר

בָּאוֹרִים pref. בָּ for בְּהָ, בְּהַ (n. m., pl. of אוֹר dec. 1a. אור

בָּאֹרֶךְ pref. id. (noun masc. sing. dec. 6c. . ארך

בְּאָרְכִּי pref. בָּ (noun masc. sing., suff. 2 pers. sing. masc. from בָּאֵר dec. 1 & 6. (§ 35. rem. 10) באר

בָּאֹרֶךְ pref. id. (noun masc. sing. dec. 6c. . ארך

בַּאֲרָם pref. בָּ before (ִ) (pr. name of a people and region . . . . ארם

בְּאַרָם pref. id. (pr. name of a region . . ארם

בְּאַרְמוֹן pref. id. (noun masc. sing. (§ 37. rem. 6) ארם

בְּאַרְמְנוֹתֶיהָ pref. id. (id. pl., suff. 3 pers. sing. fem. as if from [אַרְמֹנֶת § 44. rem. 5] . ארם

בְּאַרְמְנוֹתֵיהֶם pref. id. (id. pl., suff. 3 pers. pl. masc. ארם

בְּאַרְמְנוֹתָיִךְ pref. id. (id. pl., suff. 2 pers. sing. masc. ארם

בְּאַרְמְנוֹתֵינוּ pref. id. (id. pl., suff. 1 pers. pl. ארם

בְּאַרְנֹן pref. id. (pr. name of a region . רנן

בְּאַרְעָא [r] Chald. pref. id. (noun fem. sing., emph. of [אֲרַע] dec. 3a; ↓ before lab. ארע

בָּאָרֶץ [s] pref. בָּ for בְּהָ, בְּהַ (noun fem. sing., (suff.] ארץ
בְּאֶרֶץ [t] pref. בָּ q. v. (אַרְצִי) dec. 6a; ↓ id. }

בְּאַרְצוֹ pref. id. (id., suff. 3 pers. sing. masc. ארץ

בַּאֲרָצוֹת pref. בָּ for בְּהָ, בְּהַ (id. pl., absolute state] ארץ
בָּאֲרָצוֹת pref. בָּ before (ִ) (}

בְּאַרְצוֹת [b] pref. בָּ (id. pl., construct state . . ארץ

בְּאַרְצִי pref. id. (id. sing., suff. 1 pers. sing. ארץ

בְּאַרְצְךָ pref. id. (id. sing., suff. 2 pers. sing. masc.] ארץ
בְּאַרְצֶךָ }

בְּאַרְצֵךְ pref. id. (id. sing., suff. 2 pers. sing. fem. ארץ

בְּאַרְצְכֶם [d] pref. id. (id. s., suff. 2 p. pl. m.; ↓ before (ִ) ארץ

בְּאַרְצָם pref. id. (id. sing., suff. 3 pers. pl. masc. ארץ

בְּאַרְצֵנוּ pref. id. (id. sing., suff. 1 pers. pl. ארץ

בְּאַרְצֹת pref. id. (id. pl., construct state . . ארץ

בְּאַרְצֹתָם pref. id. (id. pl., suff. 3 pers. pl. masc. . ארץ

בְּאֵרֹת [e] noun fem., pl. constr. from בָּאֵר, dec. 1a. באר

בְּאֵרֹת [g] id. pl. constr., dec. 6. (§ 35. rem. 10) באר

בָּאַשׁ [h] ↓ *to stink*. Niph. metaph. *to become odious* to any one, const. with בְּ, אֶת of pers. Hiph.—I. *to cause to stink*, Ec. 10. 1.—II. metaph. *to make loathsome, odious*, const. with בְּ.—III. intrans. *to stink*, metaph. *to be odious*, 1 Sa. 27. 12.—IV. *to act*

a De. 27. 8.	e Ex. 10. 12.	Exe. 46. 22.	u 1 Sa. 6. 19.	r Zec. 11. 1.	n 2 Ki. 15. 25.
b Hab. 2. 2.	f Ec. 12. 3.	k 2 Ch. 2. 6.	m Je. 2. 13.	s Is. 24. 14.	o Ps. 48. 4.
c De. 1. 5.	g Ho. 7. 6.	l 1 Sa. 6. 8.	p Je. 22. 14, 15.	t Pr. 5. 15.	y Am. 3. 10.
d Pr. 23. 27.	h Est. 9. 13.		q 2 Ch. 2. 13.		1 Ki. 7. 3, 7.
				z Ps. 122. 7.	s Is. 60. 18.	f Ge. 26. 18.
				a Da. 6. 28.	e Le. 22. 24.	g Ge. 14. 10.
				b Ps. 116. 9.	Le. 26. 36, 39.	h Ex. 7. 18

badly, wickedly, Pr. 13.5. Hithp. *to make oneself odious*, const. with עַם, 1 Ch. 19.6.

בְּאֵשׁ Chald. *to be evil*, only Da. 6.15, const. with עַל, *to be displeased at*.

בְּאֹשׁ masc. with suff. בָּאְשׁוֹ (§ 35. r. 10) *stench*.

בְּאֻשִׁים masc. pl. *bad, unripe or sour grapes*, Is. 5.2, 4.

בְּאִישׁ Chald. masc. adj. (§ 67. rem.) *bad, wicked*, Ezr. 4.12.

בָּאְשָׁה fem. *a bad plant, weed*, Job 31.40.

אֵשׁ ‹ בְּאֵשׁ ‹ pref. בְּ for בְּהַ, בְּהָ [n. com. sing. dec. } בְּאֵשׁ ‹ pref. בְּ } 8 b; ‹ before lab. }

שְׁדַד בְּאַשְׁדּוֹד ‹ pref. id. [pr. name of a place; ‹ id.

אֶשֶׁד בְּאַשְׁדוֹת ‹ pref. בְּ for בְּהַ, בְּהָ [n. fem., pl. of אֲשֵׁדָה dec. 11 c. (§ 42. rem. 4); ‹ id.

אֲנָשׁ בְּאִשָּׁה ‹ noun fem. s. dec. 10. (comp. § 45); ‹ id.

בְּאֵשׁ בְּאִשָּׁה noun fem. sing.

בָּאְשׁוֹ noun masc. sing., suff. 3 pers. sing. masc. from בְּאֹשׁ dec. 6. (§ 35. rem. 10)

אַשּׁוּר בְּאַשּׁוּר ‹ pref. בְּ [pr. name of a country; ‹ before

בְּאֵשׁ בְּאִישִׁים noun masc. pl.

אִשָּׁה בְּאִישִׁישׁוֹת pref. בְּ for בְּהַ, בְּהָ [n.f., pl.of אֲשִׁישָׁה dec.10.

שְׁכֵּל בְּאֶשְׁכֹּל pref. id. [noun masc. sing., pl. אֲשְׁכֹּלוֹת (§ 36. rem. 6. & § 44. rem. 5).

אֵשׁ בְּאִשָּׁם n.m.s., suff. 3 pl.m.from בְּאֵשׁdec.6.(§35.r.10)

אָשָׁם בְּאַשְׁמָה pref. בְּ [noun fem. sing. dec. 12 a.

אָשָׁם בְּאַשְׁמָיו pref. בְּ before (–) [noun masc. pl., suff. 3 pers. sing. masc. from אָשָׁם dec. 4 c.

שָׁמַן בְּאַשְׁמַנִּים pref. בְּ for בְּהַ, בְּהָ [n.m., pl.of [אַשְׁמָן] dec. 8 a.

שָׁמַר בְּאַשְׁמֻרוֹת pref. בְּ [noun fem., pl. of אַשְׁמוּרָה dec. 10.

שָׁמַר בְּאַשְׁמֹרֶת pref. id. [id. s., constr. st. (§ 39. No. 3. rem. 4)

אָשָׁם בְּאַשְׁמַת pref. id. [n. f. s., constr. of אַשְׁמָה dec. 12 a.

אָשָׁם בְּאַשְׁמָתֵינוּ pref. id. [id. suff. 1 pers. pl. (for ‹ see § 4.r.3)

אָשָׁם בְּאַשְׁמָתָם pref. id. [id., suff. 3 pers. pl. masc.

אָשָׁם בְּאַשְׁמָתֵנוּ ‹ pref. id. [id., suff. 1 pers. pl.; ‹ before (–)

אָשֵׁף בְּאַשְׁפָּתוֹ pref. id. [noun fem. sing., suff. 3 pers. sing. masc. from אַשְׁפָּה (no vowel change)

אֲשֶׁר בַּאֲשֶׁר ‹ pref. בְּ before (–) [pron. relat. and conj.

אָשֵׁר בְּאָשֵׁר ‹ pref. בְּ [pr. name of a tribe; ‹ before (–)

אֲשׁוּר בַּאֲשׁוּרוֹ pref. בְּ before (–) [noun masc. sing., suff. 3 pers. sing. masc. from [אֲשׁוּר] dec. 3 a.

אֲשֵׁר בְּאָשְׁרִי pref.בְּ [n.m.s., suff. 1 p.s.from [אֲשֵׁר] dec.6 c.

אִישׁ בְּאֵשֶׁת ‹ pref. id. [noun f. s. dec. 13 c; ‹ before (–)

אִישׁ בְּאִישְׁתּוֹ ‹ pref. id. [id., suff. 3 pers. sing. m.; ‹ id.

שְׁמַע בְּאֶשְׁתְּמֹעַ pref. id. [pr. name of a place.

בּוֹא בָּאת ‹ Kal pret. 2 p.s.m. (§ 25. No. 2.f.); ‹ bef.lab.

בוא ‹ בָּאת ‹ } Kal pret. 2 pers. sing. fem. ; ‹ id.
בוא ‹ בָּאתְ ‹ }

בוא בָּאתָה id. pret. 2 pers. s. m. for בָּאתָ (§ 8. rem. 5)

אוֹת בָּאֹתוֹת ‹ ‹ pref. בְּ [noun com., pl. of אוֹת dec. 1 a. [for אֹת]; ‹ before lab.

בוא בָּאתִי ‹ Kal pret. 1 pers. sing. (§ 29. rem. 2); ‹ id.

בוא בָּאתֶם ‹ id. pret. 2 pers. pl. masc.; ‹ id.

יַתַּם בָּאתֶם pref. בְּ [pr. name of a place

בוא בָּאתְנוּ ‹ Kal pret. 3 pers. sing. fem., suff. 1 pers. pl.

אָתַר בָּאֲתַר Chald. pref. בְּ [contr. (בְּאֲתַר] [noun m. s.

אוֹת בָּאֹתֹת defect. for בָּאוֹתֹת (q. v.)

בוא בְּבֹא ‹ pref. בְּ [Kal inf. constr. (§ 21.r.2); ‹ bef. (–)

בוא בְּבֹאָה pref. בְּ for בְּהָ [noun fem. sing.

בוא בְּבֹאָה‹ pref. בְּ [Kal inf. (בּוֹא) with parag. ה (§21.r.2)

בוא בְּבֹאָה ‹ pref. id. [id. with suff. 3 p. s. f.; ‹ bef.

בוא בְּבֹאוֹ ‹ pref. id. [id. with suff. 3 pers. s. m.; ‹ id.

בוא בְּבֹאִי pref. id. [id., suff. 1 pers. sing.

בוא בְּבֹאֲךָ ‹ }
בוא בְּבֹאֶךָ ‹ } pref. id. [id., suff. 2 pers. sing. masc.

בוא בְּבֹאֲכֶם pref. id. [id., suff. 2 pers. pl. masc.

בוא בְּבֹאָם pref. id. [id., suff. 3 pers. pl. masc.

בוא בְּבֹאָן pref. id. [id., suff. 3 pers. pl. fem.

באר בִּבְאֵר ‹ pref. בְּ bef. (–) [pr. n. in compos. בְּאֵר שֶׁבַע

בלל בְּבָבֶל pref. בְּ [pr. name of a city and country

בוב בְּבָבַת pref. id. [noun f. s., constr. of [בָּבָה] d.10.

בנד בְּבֶגֶד ‹ pref. בְּ for בְּהָ [in pause as if from [בֶּגֶד] § 25. rem. 2.]

בנד בְּבֶגֶד pref. id. } noun masc. sing. (with suff. בְּבִגְדִי
בנד בְּבֶגֶד pref בְּ } dec. 6 a.

בנד בְּבִגְדוֹ pref.id. [id., Ge.39.12(inf.Ex.21.8)suff.3 p.s.m.

בנד בְּבִגְדֵנוּ pref. id. [id. pl.suff. 3 p.pl.m.K. [בְּדָיו] (§4.r.1)

בנד בְּבִגְדֵי pref. id. [id. pl., constr. st.

בנד בְּבִגְדֵיהֶם pref. id. [id. pl., suff. 3 pers. pl. masc.

בנד בְּבִגְדָיו pref. id. [id. pl., suff. 3 pers. sing. masc.

בנד בִּבְגָדִים pref. בְּ for בְּהָ [id. pl., absolute state

בדד בְּבַד pref. בְּ [noun masc. sing. dec. 8 d.

בהל בְּבֶהִילוּ Chald. pref. בְּ before (–) [noun fem. sing.

בהל בְּבֶהָלָה pref. בְּ for בְּהָ [n. f. s. dec. 10. (§ 42. No. 3)

בהם בִּבְהֵמָה ‹ pref. id. } noun f. s. dec. 11 (§ 42.
בהם בַּבְּהֵמָה *‹ pref.בְּ bef. (–) } r.5); ‹ bef.lab.*Ezr. 1.4

בהם בַּבְּהֵמוֹת ‹ pref. id. [id. pl., constr. st. (comp. § 42. r. 1)

בהם בְּבֶהֱמַת ‹ pref. id. [id. sing., constr. state (comp. id.)

בהם בִּבְהֶמְתְּךָ ‹ pref. בְּ bef. (–) [id. sing., suff. 2 pers. sing. masc. [from בֶּהֱמָת dec. 13. see § 44. r. 3]

בהם בִּבְהֶמְתֵּנוּ ‹ pref. id. [id. sing., suff. 1 pers. pl. see the preceding; ‹ bef. labial

a 2 Sa. 23.7.   g Is. 5.2, 4.   m Is. 59.10.   t Is. 49.2.   b 2 Sa. 3.7.   g Eze. 8.5.   m Zec. 2.12.   r Eze. 44.19.   y Ps. 78.33.
b Zep. 1.18.   h Ca. 2.5.   n Ps. 63.7.   p Job 23.11.   c Je. 32.21.   k 1 Ki. 14.12.   n 1 Sa. 19.13.   s 2 Ki. 2.12.   z Mi. 5.7.
c Jos. 12.8.   i Is. 65.8.   o Ge. 30.13.   q Ezr. 9.15.   d De. 26.8.   l 2 Sa. 3.13.   o Le. 13.47, 47.   t 1 Ki. 1.1.   a Nu. 3.41.
d Ho. 12.13.   k Is. 34.3   p Am. 8.14.   r Ge. 2.24.   e De. 28.6, 19.   m 2 Sa. 1.11.   p Ex. 30.34.   u De. 7.14.
e Job 31.40.   l Ezr. 9.7.   q 2 Ch. 24.18.   s Ge. 26.11.   f Ge. 30.39.   n Eze. 27.29.   q Ezr. 4.23.   x Ne. 9.37.
f Joel 2.20.   m Ps. 68.22.   r Ezr. 9.13.   u 2 Sa. 14.5.   g Da. 7.6, 7.

בַּבַּהֶרֶת֙ pref. בַּ for בְּהַ ✕ noun fem. sing., pl. בֶּהָרוֹת (§ 42. No. 3, & § 44. rem. 5) . . . בהר

בְּבוֹא ׳ pref. בְּ ✕ Kal inf. constr. dec. 1. (§ 21. rem. 2) ; ׳ bef. (:) . . . . בוא

בְּבוֹאוֹ pref. id. ✕ id., suff. 3 pers. sing. masc. . בוא

בְּבוֹאָם pref. id. ✕ id., suff. 3 pers. pl. masc. . בוא

בְּבוֹאָן׳ pref. id. ✕ id., suff. 3 pers. pl. fem. . בוא

בַּבּוּץ׳ ׳ pref. בַּ for בְּהַ ✕ noun m. s. ; ׳ bef. labial בוץ

בַּבֻּר pref. id.׳ noun masc. sing. dec. 1, for בְּבוֹר׳ pref. בַּ q.v. ⎫ בְּאֵר q.v.; but Job 9. 30, see R. ⎬ ברד

בַּבִּזָּה ׳ pref. בַּ f. בְּהַ ⎫ noun sing. fem. ✕ id. בז
בַּבִּזָּה׳ ׳ pref. בַּ q. v. ⎭

בַּבֶּזֶק ⎫ pref. id. ✕ pr. name of a place (§ 35. r. 2) בזק
בַּבָּזֶק ⎭

בַּבְּחֻרִים pref. id. ✕ pr. name of a place . . בחר

בַּבִּטְחָה׳ ׳ pref. id. ✕ noun sing. fem. ; ׳ bef. (:) . בטח

בַּבֶּטֶן pref. בַּ for בְּהַ ⎫ noun fem. sing. (suff. בְּטָנִי)
בַּבֶּטֶן pref. בְּ q. v. ⎬ dec. 6a. . . בטן

בְּבִטְנָהּ pref. id. ✕ id., suff. 3 pers. sing. fem. . בטן

בְּבִטְנֵנוּ pref. id. ✕ id., suff. 3 pers. sing. masc. . בטן

בְּבִטְנְךָ׳ pref. id. ✕ id., suff. 2 pers. sing. masc. [for בֶּטֶן] בטן

בְּבִטְנֵךְ׳ pref. id. ✕ id., suff. 2 pers. sing. fem. . בטן

בְּבִי [for בְּבַי] pr. name masc. etymon not known.

בְּבֵין׳ pref. בְּ ✕ prep., prop. constr. of בַּיִן d. 6 h. בין

בַּבִּינָה׳ pref. בַּ for בְּהַ ✕ noun fem. sing. dec. 10. בין

בְּבִירְתָא׳ Ch. pref. בְּ ✕ n. f. s., emph. of בִּירָא d. 8 a. ביר

בַּבַּיִת ⎫ pref. בַּ f. בְּהַ ⎫
בַּבַּיִת ⎬ ⎬ noun masc. sing. irr. (§ 45) בית
בְּבַיִת ⎭ pref. בְּ q. v. ⎭

בְּבֵית ׳ pref. id. ✕ id. constr. st. Heb. & Ch. (§ 68), also pr. n. in compos. בְּבֵית־אֵל, &c.; ׳ bef. (:) . בית

בַּבֵּית Kh. בַּבַּיִת, K. בֵּית (q. v.) . . . בית

בְּבֵיתָהּ׳ pref. בְּ ✕ noun masc. sing., suff. 3 pers. sing. fem., from בַּיִת irr. (§ 45) . . . בית

בְּבֵיתוֹ׳ pref. id. ✕ id., suff. 3 pers. s. m. ; ׳ bef. (:) בית

בְּבֵיתִי׳ pref. id. ✕ id., suff. 1 pers. sing. Heb. and Chald. (§ 68) ; ׳ id. . . . . בית

בְּבֵיתְךָ ⎫ pref. id. ✕ id., suff. 2 pers. sing. masc. בית
בְּבֵיתָךְ ⎭

בְּבִכוֹרֵיהֶם׳ pref. בְּ bef. (:) ✕ noun masc. pl., suff. 3 pers. pl. masc. from בְּכוֹר dec. 1 a. בכר

בַּבְּכִי׳ pref. בַּ for בְּהַ ⎫ noun masc. sing. dec. 6 i.
בְּבֶכִי׳ ׳ pref. בְּ bef. (:) ⎬ (§ 35. r. 14); ׳ bef. lab. בכה

בְּבִכֹרוֹ׳ pref. id. ✕ noun masc. sing. dec. 1 a. . בכר

בִּבְכֹרוֹ׳ pref. id. ✕ id., suff. 3 pers. sing. masc. . בכר

בָּבֶל׳ ׳ pr. name of a city and province ; ׳ bef. lab. בבל

בְּבָלָה id. with parag. ה . . . . בלל

בִּבְלָהָה ׳ pref. בְּ ✕ pr. name fem. ; ׳ bef. (:) בלה

בִּבְלִי pref. בְּ bef. (:) ✕ (prop. subst.) adv. בלה

בַּבְלָיֵא Chald. pr. name of a people, pl. emph. [from § 63] בלל

בְּבַלַּע׳ pref. בְּ ✕ Piel inf. constr. . . . בלע

בַּבָּמָה pref. בַּ for בְּהַ ✕ noun fem. sing. dec. 10. בום

בַּבָּמוֹת pref. id. ✕ id. pl. . . . . בום

בְּבָמוֹתֵ͏ימוֹ pref. בְּ ✕ id. pl., suff. 3 pers. pl. m. (§ 4. r. 2) בום

בַּבֵּן׳ pref. id. ✕ noun m. s. constr. of בֵּן irr. (§ 45) בנה

בִּבְנָהּ׳ ׳ pref. בְּ bef. (:) ✕ id., suff. 3 p. s. f.; ׳ bef. lab. בנה

בִּבְנוֹ pref. id. ✕ id., suff. 3 pers. sing. masc. . בנה

בִּבְנוֹת׳ ׳ pref. id. ✕ Kal inf. constr. ; ׳ bef. lab. בנה

בַּבָּנוֹת pref. id. ✕ noun fem. pl., constr. of בָּנוֹת see בַּת irr. (§ 45) . . . . . בנה

בִּבְנוֹתֶיהָ ׳ pref. id. ✕ id., suff. 3 pers. s. f.; ׳ bef. lab. בנה

בִּבְנוֹתַיִךְ׳ pref. id. ✕ Kal inf. (בְּנוֹת), suff. 2 p.s.f. for תֵךְ בנה

בִּבְנוֹתְכֶם׳ pref. id. ✕ id., suff. 2 pers. pl. masc. בנה

בִּבְנוֹתֵ͏נוּ׳ ׳ pref. id. ✕ noun fem. pl. (בָּנוֹת), suff. 1 pers. pl. see בַּת irr. (§ 45) ; ׳ bef. labial בנה

בִּבְנֵי ׳ pref. id. ✕ n. m. pl., constr. of בָּנִים, see בֵּן irr. (§45); also pr. n. in compos. בִּבְנֵי יַעֲקָן; ׳ id. בנה

בִּבְנֶיהָ ׳ pref. בְּ ✕ id. pl., suff. 3 pers. s. f.; ׳ id. בנה

בִּבְנָיו׳ pref. id. ✕ id., pl. suff. 3 pers. sing. masc. בנה

בְּבָנֶיךָ׳ ׳ pref. id. ✕ id. pl., suff. 2 p. s. m.; ׳ bef. (:) בנה

בַּבָּנִים pref. בַּ for בְּהַ ✕ id. pl., absolute state בנה

בְּבִנְיָמִן׳ pref. בְּ ✕ pr. name of a tribe, see בִּנְיָמִן בנה

בְּבָנֵ͏ינוּ pref. בְּ ✕ noun masc. pl. (בָּנִים), suff. 1 pers. pl., see בֵּן irr. (§ 45) . . . . בנה

בִּבְנֹתֶ͏יהָ ׳ pref. בְּ bef. (:) ✕ noun fem. pl. (בָּנוֹת), suff. 3 pers. sing. fem. see בַּת irr (§ 45) בנה

בִּבְנֹתְכֶם׳ pref. id. ✕ Kal inf. (בְּנוֹת), suff. 2 pers. pl. m. בנה

בַּבַּעַל ⎫ pref. בַּ for בְּהַ ✕ n. m. s. dec. 6 d, also pr.
בַּבָּעַל ⎬ name in compos. as בְּבַעַל הָמוֹן, &c. בעל

בִּבְעָלָ͏יו׳ pref. בְּ bef. (:) ✕ id. pl., suff. 3 pers. s. m. בעל

בַּבֵּץ׳ pref. בְּ for בְּהַ ✕ noun masc. sing. . . בצץ

בְּבִצְעוֹ׳ pref. בְּ ✕ n. m. s., (suff. בִּצְעוֹ) d. 6 a (§ 35. r. 5) בצע

בְּבָצְרָה pref. id. ✕ pr. name of a place . . בצר

בַּבִּקְעָה pref. בַּ for בְּהַ ✕ noun fem. sing. dec. 12 b. בקע

בְּבִקְעַת pref. בְּ ✕ id., construct state . . בקע

בַּבֹּקֶר׳ pref. בַּ for בְּהַ ✕ n. m. s. d. 4 a; ׳ bef. lab. בקר

בְּבֹקֶר׳ pref. id. ✕ n. m. s. d. 6 c. (§ 35. r. 9); ׳ id. בקר

בַּבְּקָרִים pref. id. ✕ noun masc., pl. of בָּקָר dec. 4 a. . בקר

בִּבְקָרְךָ׳ pref. בְּ bef. (:) ✕ id. sing., suff. 2 pers. s. m. בקר

בִּבְקַרְכֶם׳ ׳ pref. id. ✕ id., suff. 3 pers. pl. m.; ׳ bef. lab. בקר

בִּבְקָרֵנוּ׳ ׳ pref. id. ✕ id., suff. 1 pers. pl.; ׳ id. . בקר

ᵃ Le. 13. 25, 26.   ᵈ Da. 11. 33.   ᵍ Job 39. 17.   ᵏ Ps. 136. 10.   ⁿ Ps. 78. 58.
ᵇ Eze. 42. 12.   ᵉ Is. 30. 15.   ʰ Exr. 6. 2.   ˡ Joel 2. 12.   ᵒ De. 28. 56.   ᵗ De. 15. 19.
² Ch. 2. 13.   ᶠ Pr. 22. 18.   ⁱ Pr. 7. 11.   ᵐ De. 15. 19.   ᵖ Ex. 32. 29.   ˢ Ho. 5. 6.
ᶜ Je. 38. 6.   ᶠ Ge. 25. 23.   ʲ Jos. 6. 26.   ᵐ Ex. 17. 17.   ᵗ 1 Sa. 16. 1.
ᵏ Ps. 88. 7.   ⁱ Is. 44. 4.   ᵏ Is. 3. 7.   ᵐ Hab. 1. 13.   ᵤ Eze. 16. 31.
ᶜ Jos. 22. 16.   ᵍ Ex. 13. 13.   ˡ Jos. 22. 19.   ᵖ 1 Ch. 12. 40.
ᵈ 2 Ch. 21. 14.   ʰ Ex. 10. 9.   ᵐ Ex. 21. 29.   ᵗ De. 15. 19.
ᵉ De. 28. 57.   ⁱ Ne. 11. 28.   ᵐ Je. 38. 22.   ˢ Is. 33. 15.
ᵖ Pr. 17. 2.   ᵘ Am. 6. 12.   ᵗ Ex. 10. 9.

בְּבַקֶשָׁתִי	pref. בְּ (n. f. s., suff. 1 p. s. from בַּקָּשָׁה d. 10.	בקש
בַּבָּר	pref. בְּ for בְּה (noun masc. sing. [for בַּר]	ברר
בְּבֹרִי	pref. בְּ (noun masc. sing. dec. 1 a.	ברר
בַּבָּרֶד	pref. בְּ for בְּה (noun m. s.; ו bef. lab.	ברד
בַּבְּארוֹת	ו pref. id. (noun masc. with pl. fem. term. from בּוֹר dec. 1 ; ו id.	באר
בְּבָרוּתִי	pref. בְּ (noun f. s., suff. 1 pers. sing. d. 1 b.	ברה
בְּבַרְזֶל	* ו pref. בַּ f. (בְּה) noun masc. sing.; ו before labial, *2 Ch. 2. 6	ברזל
בַּבְרֹחַ	pref. בְּ bef. (:) (Kal inf. constr.	ברח
בְּבָרְחוֹ	pref. בְּ (id., suff. 3 pers. sing. masc.	ברח
בְּבָרְחִי	pref. id. (id., suff. 1 pers. sing.	ברח
בְּבָרְחֲךָ	pref. id. (id., suff. 2 pers. sing. masc.	ברח
בַּבְּרִית	pref. בְּ for בְּה } noun fem. sing. dec. 1 a.	ברה
בַּבְּרִית	pref. בְּ bef. (:) }	
בִּבְרִיתוֹ	pref. id. (id., suff. 3 pers. sing. masc.	ברה
בִּבְרִיתִי	pref. id. (id., suff. 1 pers. sing.	ברה
בִּבְרִיתֶךָ	pref. id. (id., suff. 2 pers. s. m. [for בְּרִיתְךָ]	ברה
בִּבְרָכָה	pref. id. (noun fem. sing. dec. 11 c.	ברך
בְּבָרְכוֹ	pref. בְּ (Piel inf. (בָּרֵךְ), suff. 3 pers. sing. masc. [for בָּרְכוֹ dec. 7 b.]	ברך
בְּבִרְכַּת	pref. id. (n. f. s., constr. of בְּרָכָה dec. 11 c.	ברך
בַּבְּשָׂמִים	pref. בַּ for בְּה (noun m., pl. of בֶּשֶׂם dec. 6.	בשׂם
בַּבָּשָׁן	ו pref. id. (pr. name of a region ; ו bef. lab.	בשׁן
בַּבָּשָׂר	pref. id. (noun masc. sing. 4 c.	בשׂר
בִּבְשַׂר	pref. בְּ bef. (:) (id., construct state	בשׂר
בִּבְשָׂרָהּ	pref. id. (id., suff. 3 pers. sing. fem.	בשׂר
בִּבְשָׂרִי	ו pref. id. (id., suff. 1 pers. sing. ; ו bef. lab.	בשׂר
בִּבְשַׂרְכֶם	pref. id. (id., suff. 2 pers. pl. masc.	בשׂר
בִּבְשָׂרָם	ו pref. id. (id., suff. 3 pers. pl. m. ; ו bef. lab.	בשׂר
בְּבֹשֶׁת	ו pref. בְּ (noun fem. sing. dec. 13 c. (§ 39. No. 4. d.) ; ו id.	בוֹשׁ
בְּבָשְׁתֵּנוּ	pref. id. (id., suff. 1 pers. pl.	בוֹשׁ
בְּבַת	pref. id. (noun fem. sing. irr. (§ 43)	בנה
בְּבִתָּהּ	ו pref. id. (id., suff. 3 pers. sing. fem. comp. dec. 8 e ; ו bef. (:)	בנה
בִּבְתוּאֵל	ו pref. בְּ bef. (:) (pr. name of a place, see בְּתוּאֵל ; ו id.	בתואל
בִּבְתוּלֶיהָ	pref. בְּ bef. (:) (noun masc. pl., suff. 3 pers. sing. fem. [from בְּתוּל dec. 1 a.]	בתל
בְּבָתֵּי	ו pref. בְּ (noun masc. pl., constr. of בָּתִּים, see בַּיִת irr. (§ 45) ; ו bef.	בית
בְּבָתֵּיהֶם	ו pref. id. (id. pl., suff. 3 pers. pl. masc.	בית
בְּבָתֵּיךֶם	ו pref. id. (id. pl., suff. 2 p. pl. m. ; ו bef.	בית
בְּבָתֵּיכֶם	pref. id. (id. pl., suff. 2 pers. pl. masc.	בית
בַּבָּתִּים	pref. בַּ for בְּה (id. pl., absolute state	בית

בְּבִתְּכֶם	pref. בְּ (noun fem. sing., suff. 2 pers. pl. masc. from בַּת irr. (§ 45)	בנה
[בַּג]	food, only Eze. 25. 7. Kheth. (K. בַּז) found besides in the compound פַּתְבָּג q. v.	
בִּגְאָוָה	pref. id. (noun fem. sing. (no vowel change)	גאה
בִּגְאוֹן	pref. בְּ bef. (:) (n. m. s., constr. of גָּאוֹן d. 3 a.	גאה
בִּגְאוֹנָם	pref. id. (id., suff. 3 pers. pl. masc.	גאה
בְּגַאֲוַת	pref. בְּ (noun fem. sing., constr. of גַּאֲוָה (no vowel change)	גאה
בְּגֵאוּת	pref. id. (noun fem. sing.	גאה
בִּגְאוֹנָתוֹ	ו pref. id. (noun fem. sing., suff. 3 pers. sing. masc. from גַּאֲוָה (q. v.) ; ו bef. (:)	גאה
בְּגָב	pref. id. (pr. name of a place	גוב
בְּגַבָּהּ	pref. id. (noun masc. sing. dec. 6 c. (§ 35. r. 5)	נבה
בְּגַבְהוֹ	pref. id. (id., suff. 3 pers. sing. masc.	נבה
בְּגָבְהָם	pref. id. (id., suff. 3 pers. pl. masc.	נבה
בִּגְבוּל	pref. בְּ bef. (:) (noun masc. sing. dec. 1 a.	גבל
בִּגְבוּלֶךָ	pref. id. (id. pl., suff. 2 pers. s. m. [for לֶךָ]	גבל
בִּגְבוּלָם	pref. id. (id. sing., suff. 3 pers. pl. masc.	גבל
בִּגְבוּלֵנוּ	pref. id. (id. sing., suff. 1 pers. pl.	גבל
בְּגִבּוֹר	pref. בְּ (noun masc. sing. dec. 1 b.	גבר
בִּגְבוּרָה	pref. בְּ bef. (:) (noun fem. sing. dec. 10.	גבר
בִּגְבוּרוֹת	pref. id. (id. pl.	גבר
בַּגִּבּוֹרִים	pref. בַּ for בְּה (noun m., pl. of גִּבּוֹר dec. 1 b.	גבר
בִּגְבוּרַת	pref. בְּ bef. (:) (noun fem. sing., constr. of dec. 10.	גבר
בִּגְבוּרֹת	pref. id. (id. pl.	גבר
בִּגְבוּרָתוֹ	pref. id. (id. sing., suff. 3 pers. sing. masc.	גבר
בִּגְבוּרֹתָיו	pref. id. (id. pl., suff. 3 pers. sing. masc.	גבר
בִּגְבוּרָתְךָ	ו pref. id. (id. s., suff. 2 p. s. m. ; ו bef. lab.	יבר
בִּגְבוּרָתָם	pref. id. (id. sing., suff. 3 pers. pl. masc.	גבר
בַּגִּבַּחַת	pref. בַּ for בְּה (noun fem. sing. dec. 13 a.	נבח
בְּגַבַּחְתּוֹ	pref. בְּ (id., suff. 3 pers. sing. masc.	נבח
בִּגְבָלוֹ	pref. בְּ bef. (:) (noun masc. sing., suff. 3 pers. sing. masc. from גְּבוּל dec. 1 a.	גבל
[בִּגְבֻלְךָ=גְבֻלֶךָ]	pref. id. (id., suff. 2 p. s. m. [for גְבֻלֶךָ]	גבל
בִּגְבֻלֹת	pref. id. (noun fem., pl. of [גְּבֻלָה] dec. 10.	גבל
בְּגֶבַע	pref. בְּ (pr. name of a place	גבע
בַּגִּבְעָה	pref. בַּ for בְּה (pr. name of a place	גבע
בִּגְבְעוֹן	ו pref. בְּ (pr. name of a place ; ו bef. (:)	גבע
בְּגִבְעַת	pref. בְּ (n. f. s., constr. of גִּבְעָה dec. 12 b, also pr. name בְּגִבְעַת בִּנְיָמִן	גבע
בִּגְבָרוֹת	pref. בְּ bef. (:) (n. fem., pl. of גְּבוּרָה d. 10.	גבר
בִּגְבַרְתּוֹ	pref. id. (id. sing., suff. 3 pers. sing. masc.	גבר
בִּגְבְּתוֹן	pref. id. (pr. name of a place	גבת

a Est. 7. 3.   f Ps. 69. 22.   k Ps. 78. 37.   o Est. 2. 12.   s Je. 3. 25.   w Ge. 34. 8.   a Eze. 31. 14.   e Ps. 147. 10.   i Le. 13. 42.
b Job 39. 4.   g Pr. 27. 17.   l Is. 56. 4. 6.   p Le. 15. 7.   t De. 28. 56.   x Ps. 59. 13.   b Is. 60. 18.   f Ps. 90. 10.   k Ex. 10. 4.
c Job 22. 30.   h Jos. 22. 8.   m Ps. 44. 18.   q Le. 21. 13.   u Ps. 10. 2.   y Ps. 10. 2.   c 1 Ch. 6. 39.   g Ps. 150. 2.   l N 1. 32. 33.
d Ps. 78. 47.   i 1 Sa. 23. 6.   n Ps. 109. 17.   r Job 10. 20.   v Is. 42. 22.   z Ps. 46. 4.   d Mi. 5. 5.   h Ps. 54. 3.   m Ps. 71. 16.
Hag. 2. 17.   j 1 Ki. 3. 7   o Ge. 28. 6.   s Le. 21. 5.   v De. 19. 1.   a De. 33. 26.   e Je. 46. 12.   i Eze. 32. 29.   n Ju. 4. 31.
e 1 Sa. 13. 6.   * Ge. 35. 1.   * Pr. 11. 11.   r Esr. 9. 7.   * Ex. 8. 17.   * 2 Ch. 32. 26.   f Ps. 20. 7.

[בָּגַד] *to act covertly, to deal falsely, treacherously,* const. absol. also with מִן, oftener with בְּ ; part. בּוֹגֵד *treacherous person.*

בָּגוֹד adj. only fem. בָּגוֹדָה (Kamets impure, § 39. No. 3. rem. 2) *treacherous,* Je. 3. 7, 10.

בֶּגֶד masc. with suff. בִּגְדִי dec. 6a. (but in pause בָּגֶד § 35. rem. 2 & 4)—I. *a covering, wrapper.*—II. *cloak, garment.*—III. *faithlessness, treachery,* Je. 12. 1.—IV. *rapine, violence,* Is. 24. 16.

בְּגָדוֹת fem. pl. *treachery,* Zeph. 3. 4.

בְּגַד⟩ Kh. בָּגַד (pref. בְּ) n. m.; K. בָּא גַד (q. v.) } בוא נדד

בָּגֶד in pause, as if from [בֶּגֶד § 35. r. 2] and בְּגָד⟩ n. m. s. (suff. בִּגְדִי) dec. 6a ; �907 bef. lab. } בנד

בֹּגְדִי Kal part. act. sing. masc. dec. 7b. .   בנד

בָּגְדָה id. pret. 3 pers. sing. fem. .   בנד

בֹּגְדָה⟩ id. part. act. s. f. fr. בֹּגֵד m. (§ 39. No. 3. r. 4)   בנד

בָּגְדוּ בָּגָדוּ } id. pret. 3 pers. pl. (§ 8. rem. 7)   בנד

בִּגְדוֹ n. m. s., suff. 3 pers. s. m. from בֶּגֶד dec. 6a.   בנד

בְּגֵדוּד⟩ pref. בְּ for בָּה) noun masc. sing. dec. 1a.   נדד

בְּגָדוֹל⟩ pref. id.) adj. masc. sing. dec. 3a.   נדל

בְּגָדוֹת⟩ noun fem. pl. .   .   .   בנד

בְּגָדַי n. m. pl., suff. 1 p. s. from בֶּגֶד d. 6. (§ 35. r. 3)   בנד

בִּגְדֵי⟩ id. pl., construct state ; ﬗ bef. lab.   בנד

בִּגְדִי id. sing., suff. 1 pers. sing. .   בנד

בְּגֵדִי⟩ pref. בְּ bef. (:)) noun masc. sing. dec. 6i.   נדה

בֹּגְדֵי⟩ Kal part act. pl. constr. m. from בֹּגֵד d. 7b.   בנד

בְּגָדֶיהָ noun m. pl., suff. 3 pers. s. f. from בֶּגֶד d. 6a.   בנד

בִּגְדֵיהֶם id. pl., suff. 3 pers. pl. masc.   בנד

בִּגְדָיו⟩ id. pl., suff. 3 pers. sing. masc. ; ﬗ bef. (:)   בנד

בְּגָדֶיךָ⟩ בְּגָדַיִךְ⟩ } id. pl., suff. 2 pers. sing. fem. .   בנד

בִּגְדֶיךָ⟩ id. pl., suff. 2 pers. sing. masc. ; ﬗ bef. lab.   בנד

בִּגְדֵיכֶם⟩ id. pl., suff. 2 pers. pl. masc. ; ﬗ id.   בנד

בְּגָדִים⟩ id. pl., absolute state ; ﬗ id.   בנד

בֹּגְדִים Kal part. act. masc., pl. of בֹּגֵד dec. 7b.   בנד

בְּגָדֵינוּ⟩ n. m. pl., suff. 1 pers. pl. from בֶּגֶד dec. 6a.   בנד

בְּגָדֹל⟩ pref. בְּ bef. (:)) n. m. s., constr. of גָּדֹל d.3a.   נדל

בְּגָדֹל⟩ ﬗ pref. בְּ) noun masc. sing. dec. 6c ; ﬗ bef. (:)   נדל

בְּגָדְלוֹ⟩ pref. id.) id., suff. 3 pers. sing. masc.   נדל

בִּגְדֹלוֹת⟩ pref. בְּ bef. (:)) adj. fem., pl. of גְּדוֹלָה dec. 10, from גָּדֹל masc.   נדל

בְּגָדְלֶךָ⟩ pref. בְּ) n. m. s., suff. 2 p. s. m. fr. גֹּדֶל d. 6c.   נדל

בְּגִדְרוֹת⟩ pref. בְּ for בָּה) noun fem., pl. of גְּדֵרָה dec. 11c. (§ 42. rem. 4)   נדר

בְּגַדְתָּ Kal pret. 2 pers. sing. masc. (§ 8. rem. 5) .   בנד

בָּגַדְתִּי id. pret. 1 pers. sing. [for בָּגַדְתִּי § 8. r. 7]   בנד

בִּגְדֹתֶיךָ noun masc. with pl. fem. term. and suff. 2 pers. sing. masc. from בֶּגֶד dec. 6a.   בנד

בִּגְדְתֶּם Kal pret. 2 pers. pl. masc. .   בנד

בִּגְוֵּ⟩ Ch. pref. בְּ) noun masc. sing., constr. of בְּגוֹא⟩ ﬗ irr. (§ 68) *Da. 7. 15. . } נוה

בָּגוֹב pr. name of a place .   .   נוב

בָּגוֹד Kal inf. abs. .   .   בנד

בְּגוֹדָה⟩ adj. fem. s. [from בָּגוֹד m. § 39. No. 3. r. 2]   בנד

בְּגֵוַּהּ⟩ Ch. pref. בְּ) noun masc. sing., suff. 3 בְּגֵוַּהּ⟩ pers. sing. fem. from גֵּו irr. (§ 68) } נוה

בְּגֵוֵהּ⟩ Ch. pref. id.) id., suff. 3 pers. sing. masc.   נוה

בְּגֵוָהּ⟩ Chald. pref. id.) noun fem. sing. .   נאה

בַּגְוַי⟩ בִּגְוָי⟩ } pr. name masc. etymon doubtful.

בְּגוֹי⟩ pref. בְּ) noun masc. sing. dec. 1a. .   נוה

בִּגְוֹיהֶם⟩ pref. id.) id. pl., suff. 3 p. pl. m. (§ 4. r. 1)   נוה

בַּגּוֹיִם⟩ ﬗ pref. בְּ f. [בָּה) id. pl., absolute state   נוה

בְּגוֹיִם⟩ pref. בְּ q. v. }   נוה

בְּגוֹיַת⟩ pref. בְּ bef. (:)) n. f. s., constr. of גְּוִיָּה d. 10.   נוה

בִּגְוִיָּתָם⟩ pref. id.) id., suff. 3 pers. pl. masc.   נוה

בְּגוֹלָה⟩ ﬗ pref. בְּ for בָּה) noun fem. sing.; ﬗ bef. lab.   נלה

בְּגֹעַ⟩ pref. בְּ bef. (:)) Kal inf. constr.   נוע

בִּגְעֹר⟩ pref. בְּ) pr. name in compos. בְּגַר־בַּעַל   נדר

בְּגֹדֶל⟩ pref. בְּ f. [בָּה)   } בַּגֹּדֶל⟩ pref. בְּ q. v. } noun masc. sing. dec. 2b.   נדל

בְּגֹדֶל⟩ pref. id.) id., construct state .   נדל

בִּגְדֹלוֹת⟩ pref. id.) id. pl., absolute state .   נדל

בְּגָדְלֶךָ⟩ pref. id.) id. s., suff. 2 p. s. m. [for גֹּדֶל⟩   נדל

בְּגוּנָּה⟩ pref. בְּ for בָּה) noun fem. sing. dec. 10.   נזז

בִּגְזֹז⟩ pref. בְּ bef. (:)) Kal inf. constr.   נזז

בְּגֵזִית⟩ pref. בְּ) noun fem. sing. .   נזה

בְּגֵזֶל⟩ ﬗ pref. id.) noun masc. sing. .   נזל

בַּגֶּגֶר⟩ בַּגֶּגֶר⟩ } pref. id.) pr. name of a place (§ 35. r. 2)   נדר

בְּגֵזֵרַת⟩ pref. בְּ bef. (:)) n. f. s., constr. of גְּזֵרָה d. 10.   נזר

בְּגִחוֹן⟩ pref. בְּ) pr. name of a stream .   ניח

בַּגִּיא⟩ pref. בְּ for בָּה) noun com. sing. irr. (§ 45)   ניא

בְּגֵי⟩ ﬗ pref. בְּ) id., constr. st. (§ 37. r. 6); ﬗ bef. (:)   ניא

בַּגַּיְא⟩ בַּגָּיְא⟩ } pref. בְּ for בָּה) noun com. sing. irr. (§ 45)   ניא

בְּגֵיא⟩ pref. בְּ) id., construct state (§ 37. rem. 6)   ניא

בְּגִיד⟩ pref. id.) noun masc. sing. dec. 1a.   ניד

בְּגִיחוֹ⟩ pref. id.) Kal inf., suff. 3 pers. sing. masc.   ניח

בַּגּוֹיִם⟩ Kheth., but Keri בַּגּוֹיִם (q. v.)   נוה

ᵃ Ge. 30. 11.   ʰ Zep. 3. 4.   ⁱ Is. 63. 2.   ᵠ Ps. 131. 1.   ᵘ Je. 3. 7, 10.   ᶜ De. 15. 6.   ʰ Jos. 14. 2.   ᵐ La. 3. 9.   ᵖ Jos. 19. 27.
ᵇ Pr. 22. 12.   ᶠ Esr. 9. 3, 5.   ᵐ Le. 10. 6.   ʳ Mal. 2. 14.   ᵛ Ezr. 4. 15.   ᵈ Ju. 14. 8.   ⁱ 1 Ch. 24. 5.   ⁿ Le. 5. 21.   ᵠ De. 3. 29.
ᶜ Js. 3. 8.   ᵍ Ju. 15. 1.   ⁿ Ne. 4. 17.   ˢ Ps. 73. 15.   ʷ Ezr. 6. 2.   ᵉ Na. 3. 3.   ᵏ Ju. 1. 3.   ᵒ Ps. 62. 11.   ʳ Ge. 32. 13.
ᵈ Job 29. 25.   ʰ Ese. 23. 26.   ᵒ Ex. 15. 16.   ᵗ Ps. 45. 9.   ˣ Ezr. 5. 7.   ᶠ Je. 48. 11.   ˡ Ju. 6. 39.   ᵖ Da. 4. 14.   ˢ Job 38. 8.
ᵉ Ge. 44. 12.   ⁱ Ese. 16. 39.   ᵖ Ese. 31. 7.   ᵘ Da. 3. 25; 4.7.   ʸ Da. 4. 34.   ᵍ Nu. 20. 3.   ⁻¹ Sa. 25. 2.   ᵠ De. 34. 6.   ᵗ Ps. 79. 10.

Hebrew	Gloss	Root
בְּגָרֶב	pref. id.)(noun masc. sing.;)(id.	נרב
בִּגְרוֹן	pref. בְּ)(noun masc. sing. dec. 3a.	נרה
בִּגְרוֹנָם	pref. בְּ bef. (.;))(id., suff. 3 pers. pl. masc.	נרה
בְּגָרֻת	pref. בְּ)(noun fem. sing.	נור
בַּגֶּזֶן	pref. בַּ for בְּהַ)(noun masc. sing.	נרז
בְּגֹרָלִי	pref. בְּ)(n. m. s., suff. 1 p. s. fr. גּוֹרָל d. 2b.	נרל
בַּגֹּרֶן	pref. בַּ f.)(בְּהַ	
בַּגֹּרֶן	pref. בַּ q. v.)(noun fem. sing. dec. 6c.	נרן
בְּגֶרֶר	pref. בְּ bef. (.;))(pr. name of a place	נרר
בִּגְשׁוּר	pref. id.)(pr. name of a place, see גְּשׁוּר	
בְּגִשְׁמְהוֹן	Ch. pref. בְּ)(noun masc. sing., suff. 3 pers. pl. masc. [from גֶּשֶׁם dec. 3. § 59]	נשׁם
בְּגֶשֶׁת	pref. id.)(Kal inf. constr. dec. 13a.	נגשׁ
בְּגִשְׁתָּם	pref. id.)(id., suff. 3 pers. pl. masc.	נגשׁ
בַּגַּת	pref. בַּ f.)(בְּהַ	
בְּגַת	pref. בְּ q. v.)(noun fem. sing. dec. 6e.	נת
בִּגְתָא	pr. name of a eunuch of Ahasuerus, Est. 1. 10.	
בִּגְתָן	pr. name of a eunuch of Ahasuerus,	
בִּגְתָנָא	Est. 2. 21; 6. 2.	
בַּד	noun masc. sing. dec. 8d.	בדד
בָּד		
בָּדָא	to devise, feign.	
בִּדְאָנָה	pref. בְּ bef. (.;))(noun fem. s.;)(bef. lab.	דאן
בַּדַּבִּיר	pref. בַּ for בְּהַ)(noun masc. sing.	דבר
בַּדָּבָר	pref. id.)(noun m. s. dec. 4a.;)(bef. lab.	דבר
בַּדָּבָר	pref. בַּ for בְּהַ)(noun masc. sing. dec. 6a. (§ 35. r. 2);)(bef. lab.	דבר
בִּדְבַר	pref. בְּ)(noun masc. sing. dec. 4a.	דבר
בְּדַבֵּר	pref. id.)(Piel inf. constr. d. 7b;)(bef. (.;)	דבר
בִּדְבַר	pref. id.)(noun masc. sing. dec. 6a.	דבר
בִּדְבַר	pref. בְּ bef. (.;))(noun masc. sing., constr. of דְּבַר dec. 4a;)(bef. lab.	דבר
בְּדַבְּרוֹ	pref. בְּ)(Piel inf. (דַּבֵּר), suff. 3 pers. sing. masc. dec. 7b;)(id.	דבר
בִּדְבָרְךָ	pref. בְּ bef. (.;))(noun masc. sing., suff. 3 pers. sing. masc. from דָּבָר dec. 4a.	דבר
בְּדַבְּרִי	pref. בְּ)(Piel inf. (דַּבֵּר), suff. 1 pers. sing. dec. 7b;)(bef. (.;)	דבר
בְּדִבְרֵי	pref. id.)(n. m. pl. constr. from דָּבָר d. 4a.	דבר
בִּדְבָרַי	pref. בְּ bef. (.;))(id. pl., suff. 1 pers. sing.	דבר
בִּדְבָרֶיהָ	pref. id.)(id. pl., suff. 3 pers. sing. fem.	דבר
בִּדְבָרָיו	pref. id.)(id. pl., suff. 3 pers. sing. masc.	דבר
בִּדְבָרֶיךָ	pref. id.)(id. pl., suff. 2 pers. sing. masc.	דבר
בִּדְבָרֶיךָ	pref. id.)(id. id. (Kh. בִּדְבָרֶיךָ), K. בִּדְבָרָךְ sing. with suff. 2 pers. sing. masc.	דבר

Hebrew	Gloss	Root
בַּגִּלְבֹּעַ	pref. בַּ for בְּהַ)(pr. name of a place	נלל
בַּגַּלְגַּל	pref. id.)(noun m. s. dec. 8d. (§ 37. No. 2)	נלל
בַּגִּלְגָּל	pref. id.)(pr. name of a place	נלל
בְּגִלּוּלֵי	pref. בְּ)(noun masc. pl. constr. from [גִּלּוּל] d. 1b;)(bef. (:.)	נלל
בְּגִלּוּלֵיהֶם	pref. id.)(id. pl., suff. 3 pers. pl. masc.;)(id.	נלל
בְּגִלּוּלָיו	pref. id.)(id. pl., suff. 3 pers. sing. masc.	נלל
בְּגִלּוּלַיִךְ	pref. id.)(id. pl., suff. 2 p. s. f.;)(bef. (:.)	נלל
בְּגִלּוּלֵיכֶם	pref. id.)(id. pl., suff. 2 pers. pl. m.;)(id.	נלל
בְּגַלֹּמִי	pref. בְּ bef. (.;))(n.m.pl.constr.fr.[גָּלֹם] d.1a.	נלם
בְּגַלֹּתוֹ	pref. בְּ, contr. for בְּהַגְלוֹתוֹ, Hiph. inf., suff. 3 pers. sing. masc. (§ 11. rem. 3)	נלה
בְּגַלְּחוֹ	pref. בְּ)(Piel inf. [גַּלַּח], suff. 3 pers. sing. masc.;)(before (.;)	נלח
בַּגָּלִיל	pref. בַּ for בְּהַ)(pr. name of a region	נלל
בִּגְלַל	pref. בְּ bef. (.;))(prep.; prop. noun masc. constr. of גָּלָל dec. 4c;)(id.	נלל
בִּגְלָלַי	pref. בְּ)(n.m.pl.constr.fr.[גָּלָל]d.6.(§35.r.3.)	נלל
בְּגָלְלְךָ	pref. בְּ bef. (.;))(noun masc. sing., suff. 2 pers. sing. masc. from גָּלָל dec. 4a.	נלל
בְּגָלְלֵךְ	pref. id.)(id., suff. 2 pers. sing. fem.	נלל
בִּגְלַלְכֶם	pref. id.)(id., suff. 2 pers. pl. masc.	נלל
בַּגִּלְעָד	pref. בַּ f.)(בְּהַ	
בְּגִלְעָד	pref. בְּ q. v.)(pr. name of a region, see גִּלְעָד	
בַּגְּמַלִּים	pref. בַּ for בְּהַ)(noun masc., pl. of גָּמָל dec. 8a. (§ 37. rem. 2)	נמל
בַּגָּן	pref. id.)(	
בְּגַן	pref. בְּ)(noun com. sing. dec. 8d.	ננן
בְּגַנְבִים	pref. id.)(noun m. s. dec. 1b. (§ 30. No. 3)	ננב
בִּגְנֵבָתוֹ	pref. בְּ bef. (.;))(noun fem. sing., suff. 3 pers. sing. masc. from גְּנֵבָה dec. 10.	ננב
בַּגַּנּוֹת	pref. בַּ for בְּהַ)(noun f., pl. of גַּנָּה dec. 10.	ננן
בְּגִנְזֵי	pref. בְּ)(noun masc. pl. constr. from [גֶּנֶז] dec. 6b;)(bef. (:.)	ננז
בַּגַּנִּים	pref. בַּ for בְּהַ)(n. com., pl. of גַּן dec. 8d.	ננן
בְּגַעַל	pref. בְּ)(noun masc. sing.	נעל
בְּגַעֲרַת	pref. בְּ)(n.f.s.,constr.of גְּעָרָה d.11c.(§42.r.1)	נער
בְּגַעֲרָתִי	pref. id.)(id., suff. 1 pers. sing.	נער
בְּגַפּוֹ	pref. id.)(noun masc. sing., suff. 3 pers. sing. masc. from [גַּף] dec. 8d.	נפף
בַּגֶּפֶן	pref. בַּ for בְּהַ)(noun com. sing., (suff. גַּפְנִי) dec. 6a;)(bef. labial.	נפן
בַּגְּפָנִים	pref. id.)(id. pl., absolute state	נפן
בַּגּוּר	pref. id.)(noun m. s. dec. 1a.;)(bef. lab.	נור

a Ps. 77. 19.   g Je. 27. 20.   n Ex. 9. 3.   t Eze. 27. 24.   z Ge. 40. 10.   f Je. 41. 17.   m Ju. 6. 11.   s Je. 14. 12.   x Eze. 8. 27.
b Eze. 20. 7.   h 2 Sa. 14. 26.   o 1 Ch. 12. 40.   u Eze. 16. 5.   a Hab. 3. 17.   g De. 19. 5.   n Is. 63. 2.   t Is. 32. 7.   y Eze. 3. 4.
c 2 Ki. 21. 11.   i De. 18. 12.   p Ge. 3. 8, 10.   v Eze. 12. 19.   b Ex. 12. 19.   h Ju. 1. 3.   o 1 Ki. 12. 33.   u 2 Ch. 8. 13.   z Ju. 16. 16.
d Eze. 22. 4.   k Eze. 4. 12.   q Je. 48. 27.   w Is. 52. 2.   c Le. 17. 15.   i Ju. 6. 37.   p Eze. 12. 19.   v Eze. 9. 15.   a Da. 10. 12.
e Eze. 20. 39.   Ge. 30. 27.   r Is. 50. 2.   x Ex. 22. 2.   d Ex. 21. 3, 4.   k Is. 9. 15.   q Da. 3. 27.   w Ex. 19. 9.   b 1 Ki. 13. 36.
f Eze. 27. 24.   Ge 12. 13.   s Is. 65. 3.   y Je. 8. 13.   e De. 28. 27.   l Nu. 8. 19.   r Je. 21. 9.

6

בְּדִבְרֵיכֶם   pref. בְּ)(id. pl., suff. 2 pers. pl. masc.   דבר

בַּדְּבָרִים   pref. בַּ for בְּהַ)(} id. pl., absolute state .   דבר

בִּדְבָרִים   pref. בִּ bef. (.:) }   דבר

בִּדְבָרְךָ   pref. בְּ)(Kal inf., suff. 2 p. s. m. [for דְבָר]   דבר

בְּדָבְרְךָ   pref. בְּ bef. (.:))(noun m. sing., suff. 2 pers. sing. masc. [for בִּדְבָרְךָ] from דָּבָר dec. 4 a.   דבר

בְּדַבֶּרְכֶם   pref. בְּ)(Piel inf. (דַּבֵּר), suff. 2 pers. pl. masc. dec. 7 b. (§ 36. rem. 3) .   דבר

בְּדַבְּרָם   pref. id.)(id., suff. 3 pers. pl. masc. .   דבר

בִּדְבַשׁ   pref. בִּ bef. (.:))([for בִּדְבַשׁ] noun m. sing. dec. 6. (§ 35. rem. 10) .   דבש

בְּדַבָּשֶׁת   pref. בְּ)(pr. name of a place, for דַּבָּשֶׁת   דבש

בְּדִגְנַת   pref. בְּ bef. (.:))(n. f. s., constr. of דְּגָנָה d. 11 a.   דגה

[בָּדַד]   I. to be separate, solitary, only part. בּוֹדֵד solitary.—II. in the deriv. to devise, feign, comp. בָּטָא, בָּדָא, see בַּד below.

   בַּד masc. prop. separation, only as an adv. לְבַדָד and בָּדָד solitary, alone.

   בְּדַד (separation) pr. name masc. Ge. 36. 35.

   בַּד masc. dec. 8 d.—I. a part.—II. pl. בַּדִּים parts of a body, members, limbs.—III. branches.—IV. staves, poles; metaph. princes, Ho. 11. 6.—V. בַּד fine linen, pl. linen garments.—VI. pl. lies, comp. בַּד No. II.—VII. לְבַד separately, alone; לְבַדִּי, &c. I, thou, he alone; לְבַדְּךָ לְבַדּוֹ, and מִלְּבַד besides; לְבַד עַל, Eze. 1. 6, and אֲשֶׁר מִלְּבַד Nu. 6. 21. besides that which.

בָּדָד   adv. . . . .   בדד

בְּדַד   pr. name masc. . . .   בדד

בְּדֻגְוֹד   pref. בַּ for בְּהַ)(noun masc. sing. pl. דֻּגְוֹדִים & דֹּנְדִים (§ 35. rem. 13) .   דוד

בְּדוֹד   pref. בְּ)(pr. name masc. .   דוד

בְּדֹגְדָאִי   pref. id.)(n. m. pl. constr. [from דּוּגָי § 35. r. 15]   דוד

בַּדּוּגִים   pref. בַּ for בְּהַ)(noun m., pl. of דּוּד d. 1 a.   דוד

בַּדּוֹדִים   pref. id.)(id. pl. abs. (§ 35. r. 13); bef. labial   דוד

בְּדָוִד   pref. בְּ)(pr. name masc. .   דוד

בַּדּוּר   pref. בַּ f. בְּהַ } noun masc. sing. dec. 1 a.

בְּדוֹר   pref. בְּ q. v. }   דור

בַּדֵּי   noun masc. pl. constr. from בַּד dec. 8 d.   בדד

בְּדֵי   pref. בְּ)(prep., prop. subst. masc. constr. of דַּי dec. 8 d. (§ 37. rem. 6) .   די

בְּדִיבֹן   pref. id.)(pr. name of a place .   דוב

בַּדָּיו   noun m. pl., suff 3 pers. s. f. from בַּד d. 8 d.   בדד

בְּדָיָה   (perh. for בְּאָד יָהּ in the strength of the Lord, comp. R. אוד) pr. name m. Ezr. 10. 35.

בַּדָּיו   noun m. pl., suff. 3 pers. s. m. from בַּד d. 8 d.   בדד

בַּדְּיוֹ   pref. בַּ for בְּהַ)(noun masc. sing.   דיה

בַּדָּיִךְ   noun m. pl., suff. 2 pers. s. m. from בַּד d. 8 d.   בדד

בְּדִיל   noun masc. sing. dec. 1 a; before (.:)   בדל

בְּדִילָיִךְ   id. pl., suff. 2 pers. s. f. [for לָיִךְ], Is. 1. 25.   בדל

בַּדִּים   noun masc., pl. of בַּד dec. 8 d.   בדד

בְּדִינָה   pref. בְּ)(pr. name fem. .   דין

בְּדִישׁוֹ   pref. id.)(Kal inf. [דִּישׁ], suff. 3 pers. sing. masc. dec. 1 a. .   רישׁ

בָּדַל   Niph. I. to be separated, with מִן from to be chosen out, with לְ to any thing.—II. to depart, with מִן of the place and אֶל of the person. Hiph. I. to separate, to make a division, const. with בֵּין.—II to distinguish, const. with בֵּין, בֵּין-לְבֵין, וּבֵין-בֵּין.—III. to separate, select, with מִן, מֵעַל, לְ.

   בֶּדֶל masc. d. 4 a, part, portion, only, Am. 3. 12.

   בְּדִיל masc. dec. 1 a, tin.

   מִבְדָּלָה fem. separation, separate place, Jos. 16. 9.

   בְּדֹלַח masc. Eng. vers., after most of the ancient interpreters, bdellium, a transparent gum; the Arab., and so the Rabbies and Bochart, pearls.

בְּדֶל   noun masc. sing., constr. of [בֶּדֶל] dec. 4 a. .   בדל

בַּדַּלְקַת   pref. בַּ for בְּהַ)(noun f. s.; before lab.   דלק

בַּדֶּלֶת   pref. בַּ for בְּהַ)(noun fem. sing. see דֶּלֶת.   דלה

בְּדַלְתּוֹ   pref. בְּ)(id., suff. 3 pers. sing. masc.   דלה

בְּדַלְתוֹת   pref. id.)(id. pl., constr. of דְּלָתוֹת (§ 44. rem. 5), ת treated as if radical .   דלה

בִּדְלָתָיִם   pref. בִּ bef. (.:))(n. f., du. of [דֶּלֶת] d. 11 a.   דלה

בַּדָּם   pref. בַּ f. בְּהַ } noun m. s. d. 2 b.)(bef. (.:)   אדם

בַּדָּם   pref. בַּ }

בְּדַם   pref. id.)(id., constr. state; id. .   אדם

בִּדְמוּת   pref. בְּ bef. (.:))(noun fem. sing. dec. 1 a.   דמה

בִּדְמוּתוֹ   pref. id.)(id., suff. 3 pers. sing. masc.   דמה

בְּדָמִי   pref. בְּ)(noun masc. sing., suff. 1 pers. sing. from דָּם dec. 2 a.   אדם

בְּדָמֵי   pref. בְּ before (.:))(id. pl., constr. state .   אדם

בִּדְמִי   pref. id.)(noun masc. sing. .   רמה

בְּדָמַיִךְ   pref. בְּ)(noun masc. pl., suff. 2 pers.

בְּדָמַיִךְ   } sing. fem. from דָּם dec. 2 b   אדם

בְּדָמִים   pref. בְּ for בְּהַ } id. pl., absolute state .   אדם

בְּדָמִים   pref. בְּ q. v. }

בְּדָמְךָ   pref. id.)(id. s., suff. 2 pers. sing. fem. .   אדם

בְּדָמְךָ   pref. id.)(noun masc. sing., suff. 2 pers. sing. masc. [from דָּם]   רמה

בְּדִמְעָה   pref. id.)(noun fem. sing. dec. 12 b.   מע

a Mal. 2. 17. | c Ex. 16. 31. | 2 Ch. 35. 13. | e Job 11. 3. | r Am. 3. 12. | 2 Ki. 12. 10. | k Ge. 49. 11. | l Is. 38. 10. | Eze. 19. 10.
b Ps. 51. 6. | d Ge. 1. 26, 28. | Ge. 7. 1. | Eze. 27. 12. | De. 28. 22. | Ju. 16. 3. | Ge. 5. 1. | Eze. 16. 6. | Ps. 126. 5.
Ps. 119. 42. | 1 Sa. 3. 14. | Eze. 19. 14. | Eze. 22. 18, 20. | 2 Ki. 6. 52. | Job 33. 8. | Ge. 5. 3. | Eze. 16. 6. | 2 Ki. 14.
De. 5. 25. | Ge. 30. 16. | Je. 36. 18. | De. 25. 4. | De. 15. 17. | Eze. 33. 22. | Pa. 30. 10. | Ps. 106. 38.

בְּדִמְעוֹת֙ pref. בְּ f. בְּהַ(...) id. pl., absolute state . רמע
בְּדִמְעוֹת pref. בְּ bef. (ָ))
בְּדִמְעָתִי pref. בְּ)(id. sing., suff. 1 pers. sing. . רמע
בְּדַמֶּשֶׂק }
בְּדַמֶּשֶׂק } pref. id.)(pr. name of a place . דמשק
וּ בְדַמֶּשֶׂק pref. בְּ bef. (ַ))(noun m. s.; וּ bef. lab. דמשק
בְּדָן pref. בְּ)(proper name of a place . דין
בְּדָן (for בֶּן־דָּן Danite, comp. בֶּן־דָּר) proper name, masc.—I. 1 Sa. 12. 11.—II. 1 Ch. 7. 17.
בְּדַנְיֵאל pref. בְּ)(pr. name masc. . . דין
בְּדַעַת } pref. id.)(noun fem. sing. dec. 13 a. } ידע
וּ בְדַעַת } (§ 44. No. 1); וּ before (ַ) . }
בְּדַעְתּוֹ pref. id.)(id., suff. 3 pers. sing. masc. . ידע
בְּדִבְקָה pref. id.)(pr. name of a place . דפק
[בָּדַק] Arab. *to tear, rend*, in Heb. only as denom. of בֶּדֶק *to repair a breach*, 2 Ch. 34. 10.
    בֶּדֶק masc. dec. 6 a, with suff. בִּדְקֵךְ *a breach, rupture*, in a building.
בֶּדֶק in pause; Seg. n. as if from [בֶּדֶק] }
בִּדְק noun m. sing. dec. 6 a. (see the following) } ברק
בִּדְקֵךְ id., suff. 2 pers. sing. fem. . . ברק
בִּדְקַר (for בֶּן־דֶּקֶר *son of stabbing*, i. e. *stabber*, comp. בֶּן־דָּד) pr. name masc., 2 Ki. 9. 25.
[בְּדַר] Chald. Pa. *to scatter*, Da. 4. 11.
בְּדֹר pref. בְּ)(noun masc. sing. for דּוֹר . דור
וּ בַדַּרוּ וּ Ch. Pael pret. 3 pers. pl. m.; וּ bef. labial בדר
בְּדָרוֹם pref. בְּ for בְּהַ)(noun masc. sing. [for דָּרוֹם] דרר
בְּדֶרֶךְ pref. בְּ f. בְּהַ(...) }
בְּדֶרֶךְ וּ pref. id.)(noun com. sing., (suff. דַּרְכִּי) } דרך
בְּדֶרֶךְ וּ pref. בְּ q. v.)(dec. 6 a; וּ before labial }
וּ בְדֶרֶךְ וּ pref. id. }
בְּדַרְכוֹ וּ pref. id.)(id. s. with suff. 3 pers. s. m.; וּ id. דרך
בְּדַרְכָו pref. בְּ bef. (ָ))(id. pl., suff. 3 pers. sing. masc. (for כָּיו § 4. rem. 1) . . דרך
בְּדַרְכֵי וּ pref. בְּ)(id. pl., constr. state; וּ bef. (ָ) דרך
בְּדַרְכֵי pref. בְּ before (ַ))(id. pl., suff. 1 pers. sing. דרך
בְּדַרְכֵיכֶם pref. בְּ)(id. pl., suff. 3 pers. pl. masc. . דרך
בְּדַרְכֵיכֶן pref. בְּ)(id. pl., suff. 3 pers. pl. fem. . דרך
בְּדַרְכָיו pref. בְּ bef. (ַ))(id. pl., suff. 3 pers. sing. m. דרך
בְּדַרְכֶיךָ pref. id.)(id. pl., suff. 2 pers. sing. masc. דרך
בְּדַרְכְּךָ pref. id.)(id. sing., suff. 2 pers. sing. masc. דרך
בְּדַרְכְּךָ pref. בְּ before (ַ))(id. pl., suff. 2 pers. sing. masc. for דְּרָכֶיךָ (§ 4. rem. 1) . דרך
בְּדַרְכָּם pref. בְּ)(id. sing., suff. 3 pers. pl. masc. דרך

בְּדַרְמֶשֶׂק pref. id.)(pr. name of a place . דמשק
בְּדֹרֹתָיו pref. id.)(noun m. with pl. fem. term. and suff. 3 pers. sing. masc. from דּוֹר dec. 1 a.
בַּדָּשֶׁן pref. בְּ for בְּהַ)(n. m. s., (pl. c. דְּשֵׁנֵי) d. 6 a. רשן
בְּדָת Ch. pref. בְּ)(noun fem. s. (constr.) d. 1 b. רת
בְּדָת Chald. pref. id.)(id. construct state . רת
בְּדָתָא Ch. pref. בְּ)(n. m. s., emph. of [דָּתָא] d. 3 b. רתא
בְּדָתָה Chald. pref. id.)(id. by Hebraism . רתא
בְּדָתֵי pref. id.)(n. f. s. dec. 1 a. (but constr. דָּת) רת
בְּדֹתָן pref. id.)(pr. name of a place, see דֹּתָן
בָּהּ ו pref. prep. בְּ with suff. 3 pers. s. fem. (§ 5) ב
בַּהּ Chald. id. with suff. 3 pers. sing. masc. ב
בָּהּ Kh. בַּהּ q. v., K. בּוֹ q. v. . כ
בְּהֵאָבְקוֹ pref. בְּ)(Niph. inf. [הֵאָבֵק], suff. 3 p. s. m. d. 7 b אבק
בְּהַאֲרִיךְ ו pref. id.)(Hiph. inf. constr.; וּ before (ַ) ארך
בַּהֲבִיאִי pref. בְּ before (ַ))(Hiph. inf. (הָבִיא), suff. 1 pers. sing., dec. 3 a. . . בוא
בְּהִתְיָאֲבֶכֶם pref. id.)(id., suff. 2 pers. pl. masc. בוא
בְּהַבִּיטִי pref. בְּ)(Hiph. inf., suff. 1 p. sing., dec. 1 b. נבט
בְּהֶבֶל pref. בְּ for בְּהַ)(n. m. s. dec. 6 a. (§ 35. r. 4) הבל
בְּהַבְלֵי pref. בְּ)(id. pl., construct state . הבל
בְּהַבְלֵיהֶם pref. id.)(id. pl., suff. 3 pers. pl. masc. הבל
בְּהִבָּנֹתוֹ pref. id.)(Niph. inf., suff. 3 p. s. m., dec. 1 b. בנה
בְּהִבָּרְאָם pref. id.)(Niph. inf. [הִבָּרֵא], suff. 3 pers. pl. masc., dec. 7 b. . . ברא
בְּהַגְיֹנִי pref. בְּ bef. (ַ))(noun masc. sing., suff. 1 p. sing. from [הִגָּיֹן] dec. 3 a. . . הגג
וּ בְהַגִּיעַ וּ pref. בְּ)(Hiph. inf. constr. dec. 1 b; וּ bef. (ַ) נגע
בְּהַגְלוֹת pref. id.)(Hiph. inf. construct dec. 1 a. נלח
בְּהִגָּלוֹת pref. id.)(Niph. inf. construct נלה
בְּהַגְלוֹתִי pref. id.)(Hiph. inf., suff. 1 pers. s. dec. 1 b. נלה
בְּהֲדַדְעֶזֶר pref. בְּ before (ַ))(pr. name masc. הדד
בְּהָדְפוֹ pref. id.)(Kal inf. construct הדף
בֶּהָדָר pref. בְּ for בְּהַ בְּהַ)(noun m. sing. dec. 4 c. הדר
בְּהַדְרִי pref. id.)(id., suff. 1 pers. sing. הדר
בְּהַדְרֵי pref. בְּ)(id. pl., construct state . הדר
בַּהֲדָרֶךָ pref. הַ art. & בְּ)(n. com. s., (suff. דְּרְכִּי) dec. 6 a. דרך
בְּהַדְרֶעֶזֶר pref. בְּ bef. (ַ))(pr. name m., see הֲדַדְעֶזֶר הדד
בְּהַדְרַת pref. בְּ)(noun fem. sing. constr. [of הֲדָרָה dec. 11 c, § 42. rem. 1] . . הדר
בָּהָה Root not used; Arab. בהו *to be void.* Hence—
בֹּהוּ וּ (for בֹּהֶו) masc. *emptiness*.
וּ בְהוֹלֵדֹת pref. בְּ)(Hiph. inf. constr. (§ 25. No. 2); וּ before (ַ) . . . . ידה
בְּהוֹלִד pref. id.)(Niph. inf. constr., bef. monos. for הֹלֵּד ילר

ᵃ La. 2. 11.   ᵈ 2 Ki. 12. 6.   ᵍ 1 Sa. 15. 18.   ᵏ Ps. 119. 37.   ° Da. 4. 12.   ˢ Nu. 9. 22.   ᵛ 1 Ki. 6. 7, 7.   ᶻ Eze. 21. 22.   ᵉ Ps. 119. 6.
ᵇ Ps. 80. 6.   ᵉ Eze. 27. 9, 37.   ʰ Eze. 46. 8.   ˡ Eze. 36. 17.   ᵖ Da. 4. 20.   ᵗ Nu. 9. 19.   ʷ Ge. 2. 4.   ᵃ Eze. 39. 28.   ᵇ Ne. 9. 19.
ᶜ Ps. 6. 7.   ᶠ Ps. 90. 1.   ⁱ 1 Sa. 8. 3.   ᵐ Ge. 6. 9.   ᵍ Est. 1. 19.   ᵘ Eze. 44. 7.   ˣ Ps. 55. 4.   ᵇ De. 9. 4.   ᶜ Is. 34. 11.
Am. 3. 12.   ᵏ Da. 4. 20, 21.   ⁱ 2 Ch. 21. 12.   ⁿ Is. 55. 2.   ʳ Je. 17. 24.   Ps. 119. 6.   ʸ Est. 2. 12, 15.   ᵈ Ps. 26. 4.   ᵈ Exr. 9. 11.
Pr. 13. 16.   Ec. 11. 5.   Eze. 16. 47.   Exr. 7. 14.   Ge. 32. 28.   Ec. 6. 4.   1 Ch. 5. 41.   Eze. 16. 14.   Ge. 21. 5.
Job 34. 35.   Je. 6. 23.   Ho. 10. 13.
6*

בְּהוֹלְלִים   pref. בְּ for בְּהַ ✕ Kal part. act. masc., pl. of [חוֹלֵל] dec. 7 b.   הלל

בְּהוֹן   Chald. pref. prep. בְּ with suff. 3 p. pl. masc.   ב

בְּהִוָּסְדָם   pref. בְּ ✕ Niph. inf. [הִוָּסֵד], suff. 3 p.s.m., dec. 7b.   יסד

בְּהוֹצִיאוֹ   pref. id. ✕ Hiph. inf., suff. 3 p. s. m., dec. 1 b.   יצא

בְּהוֹצִיאִי   pref. id. ✕ id., suff. 1 pers. sing.   יצא

בְּהוֹצִיאֲךָ   pref. id. ✕ id., suff. 2 pers. sing. masc.   יצא

בְּהוֹצִיאָם   pref. id. ✕ id., suff. 3 pers. pl. m.; וּ bef. (ː)   יצא

בְּהוֹרִידִי   pref. id. ✕ Hiph. inf. (הוֹרִיד), suff.1 p.s., dec. 1 b.   ירד

בְּהוֹשֵׁעַ   pref. id. ✕ pr. name masc.   ישע

בְּהַוַּת   pref. id. ✕ noun fem. sing., constr. of [הַוָּה] dec. 10; וּ before (ː)   הוה

בְּהַוָּתוֹ   pref. id. ✕ id., suff. 3 pers. sing. masc.   הוה

בְּהִזָּרוֹתֵיכֶם   pref. id. ✕ Niph. inf. [הִזָּרוֹת], suff. 2 pers. pl. masc., dec. 1 b. contrary to rule, for הִזָּרוֹתֵיכֶם; comp. בִּזְנוּתַיִךְ, Eze. 16. 31.   זרה

בְּהֵחָבֵא   pref. id. ✕ Niph. inf. construct   הבא

בְּהֵחָפְזָם   pref. id. ✕ Kh. בְּהֵחָפְזָם, Niph. inf. [הֵחָפֵז], dec.7b], K. בְּחָפְזָם Kal inf., suff. 3 p. pl. m.   חפז

בַּהַט   masc. a species of marble, only Est. 1. 6.

בִּהְיוֹת   pref. בְּ bef. (ː) ✕ Kal inf. constr. (הֱיוֹת § 13. rem. 13, comp. rem. 1 and 2)   היה

בִּהְיוֹתוֹ   pref. id. ✕ id., suff. 3 pers. sing. masc.   היה

בִּהְיוֹתֵךְ   pref. id. ✕ id., suff. 2 pers. sing. fem.   היה

בִּהְיוֹתְכֶם   pref. id. ✕ id., suff. 2 pers. pl. masc.   היה

בִּהְיוֹתָם   pref. id. ✕ id., suff. 3 pers. pl. masc.   היה

בִּהְיוֹתֵנוּ   pref. id. ✕ id., suff. 1 pers. pl.   היה

בְּהֵיטִיבוֹ   pref. בְּ ✕ Hiph. inf., suff. 3 pers. sing. masc.   יטב

בְּהֵיכַל   pref. בְּ for בְּהַ ✕ noun masc. sing., dec. 2 b.   היכל

בְּהֵיכָל   pref. בְּ ✕ id.; construct state   היכל

בְּהֵיכְלָא   Chald. pref. id. ✕ n.m., emph. of [הֵיכָל] dec.2 a.   היכל

בְּהֵיכְלוֹ   וּ pref. id. ✕ noun masc. sing., suff. 3 pers. sing. masc. from הֵיכָל dec. 2 b; וּ bef. (ː)   היכל

בְּהֵיכְלֵי   pref. id. ✕ id. pl., construct state   היכל

בְּהֵיכְלִי   Chald. pref. id. ✕ noun masc. sing., suff. 1 p. sing. from הֵיכָל dec. 2 a.   היכל

בְּהִיר   adj. masc. sing.   בהר

בִּהְיוֹת   pref. בְּ before (ː) ✕ Kal inf. constr. dec.1a, comp. בִּהְיוֹת   חיה

בִּהְיוֹתוֹ   pref. id. ✕ id., suff. 3 pers. sing. masc.   היה

בְּהִכָּבְדִי   pref. בְּ ✕ Niph.inf. [הִכָּבֵד], suff.1 p.s., dec.7b.   כבד

בְּהַכּוֹתִי   pref. id. ✕ Hiph. inf., suff. 1 pers. s., dec. 1 b, (§ 25. No. 2)   נכה

בְּהָכִין   pref. בְּ with the relat. art. for בְּהַ (comp. 2 Ch. 29. 36); Hiph. pret. 3 pers. sing. m.   כון

בַּהֲכִינוֹ   pref. בַּ before (ː) ✕ Hiph. inf. (הָכִין), suff. 3 pers. sing. masc., dec. 3 a.   כון

בְּהַכְלִים   pref. בְּ ✕ Hiph. inf. construct .   כלם

בְּהִכָּנְעוֹ   וּ pref. id. ✕ Niph. inf. הִכָּנֵע (§ 36. rem. 5) suff. 3 pers. sing. masc.; וּ before (ː)   כנע

בְּהַכְרִית   } pref. id. ✕ Hiph. inf. construct dec. 1 b.   כרת
בְּהַכְרִתוֹ   }

בְּהִכָּרֵת   pref. id. ✕ Niph. inf. construct   כרת

בְּהִכָּשְׁלָם   וּ pref. id. ✕ Niph. inf. [הִכָּשֵׁל], suff. 3 pers. pl. masc., dec. 7 b ; וּ before (ː)   כשל

בְּהַכֹּתִי   pref.id. ✕ Hiph. inf., suff. 1 pers.s. (§ 25. No. 2)   נכה

בָּהַל   Niph.—I. to be agitated, terrified, amazed.—II. to hasten, with לְ after Pr. 28. 22.—III. to be ruined. Pi.—I. to terrify, confound.—II. to cause to hurry, hasten, const. acc., בְּ, עַל.—Pu. part. hurried, hastened. Hiph. i. q. Piel.

    בְּהַל   Chald. Ithpe.inf. haste. Pa. to terrify, alarm בֶּהֱלָה fem., pl. בֶּהָלוֹת fear, terror.

    בְּהִילוּ   Chald. fem. haste, Ezr. 4. 23.

בֶּהָלָה   noun f. s. dec. 10. (§ 42. No. 3 comp. note)   בהל

בְּהִלּוֹ   pref. בְּ ✕ Kal inf. [הָל § 18. rem. 3], suff. 3 p. sing. masc. dec. 8 e.   הלל

בֶּהָלוֹת   וּ n. f. pl. abs. from [בֶּהָלָה] (q. v.); וּ bef. lab.   בהל

בְּהִלָּחֲמוֹ   pref. בְּ ✕ Niph. inf. [הִלָּחֵם], suff. 3 pers. sing. masc., dec. 7 b.   לחם

בַּהֲלִיכוֹתָם   pref. בַּ bef. (ː) ✕ Kh. כוֹתָם noun f. pl., K. כָתָם sing. with suff. from הֲלִיכָה dec.10. הלך

בְּהַלֵּל   וּ pref. בְּ ✕ Piel inf. constr.; וּ before (ː)   הלל

בָּהַם   Root not used; Arab. to be dumb.

    בְּהֵמָה   fem. constr. בֶּהֱמַת, pl. בְּהֵמוֹת, constr. בֶּהֱמוֹת (comp. § 42. rem. 4) sing. with suff. בְּהֶמְתּוֹ (as if from בְּהֶמֶת § 42. rem. 5).—I. cattle.—II wild beast. By the plural, in Job 40. 15, some stupendous quadruped is understood, according to some the hippopotamus, others, the elephant.

בָּהֶם   וּ pref.prep. בְּ with suff. 3 p.pl.m. (§ 5); וּ id.   ב

בֹהֶם   pref. בְּ ✕ pr. name of a region .   המה

בְּהֵמָּה   pref. בְּ q. v. ✕ pron. pers. 3 pl. masc. with paragogic ה (§ 5. rem. 7)   הם

בְּהֵמָה   וּ n. f. s. dec.11. (§ 42. r. 4 & 5); וּ bef.   בהם

בְּהִמּוֹל   pref. בְּ ✕ Niph. inf. construct, dec. 1 b.   מול

בַּהֲמוֹן   pref. בַּ before (ː) ✕ construct of the following   המה

בְּהֲמוֹן   pref. בְּ for בְּהַ ✕ noun masc. s. dec. 3 a.   המה

בֶּהֱמוֹת   construct of the following .   בהם

---

a Ps. 73. 3.   f Ps. 52. 9.   l 1 Sa. 35. 15.   p Da. 4. 1.   t Eze. 32. 15.   z 2 Ch. 12. 12.   d Da.11. 34.   h Je. 15. 8.   m Mal. 2. 17.
b Ps. 31. 14.   g Eze. 6. 8.   m Ex. 30. 7.   q Job 37. 21.   u 2 Ch. 1. 4.   a 1 Ki. 18. 4.   e Ex. 12. 13.   i 2 Ki. 8. 29.   n Ge. 37. 22.
c 2 Ch. 34. 14.   h Da. 10. 7.   n Ezr. 5. 15.   r Ex. 19. 16.   v Pr. 8. 27.   b 1 Sa. 20. 15.   f Le. 26. 16.   k Na. 2. 6.   Je. 51. 42.
d Eze. 31. 16.   i 2 Ki. 7. 15.   o Ps. 29. 9.   s Ex. 14 18.   y Pr. 25. 8.   Ps. 37. 34.   g Job 29. 3.   l 2 Ch. 5. 12.   o Ec. 5. 9.
e Pr. 11. 6.   k Eze. 16. 22.

בְּהֵמוֹת	n.f. pl. abs. from בְּהֵמָה dec. 11 c. (§ 42. r. 4 & 5)	בהם
בְּהָמֵר	pref. בְּ)(Hiph. inf. construct .	מור
בְּהִמֹּלוֹ	pref. id.)(Niph. inf., suff. 3 p. s. m. dec. 1 b.	מול
בְּהִמָּצְאוֹ	pref. id.)(Niph. inf. (הִמָּצֵא), suff. 3 pers. sing. masc. dec. 7 b.	מצא
בְּהַמְרוֹתָם	פ pref. id.)(Hiph. int., suff. 3 p. pl. m.; ל bef. (:)	מרה
בֶּהֱמַת	n.f.s., constr. of בְּהֵמָה dec. 11 c. (§ 42. r. 4 & 5)	בהם
בְּהֶמְתּ	id. pl., absolute state	בהם
בֶּהֱמְתָּהּ	פ/ id. sing., suff. 3 p. s. f. [from בְּהֶמְתָּ]; ל bef. (:)	בהם
בֶּהֱמְתּוֹ	id. sing., suff. 3 pers. sing. masc.	בהם
בֶּהֶמְתְּךָ	פ/ id. sing., suff. 2 pers. sing. m.; ל bef. (:)	בהם
בֶּהֶמְתֶּךָ		
בֶּהֶמְתְּכֶם	פ/ id. sing., suff. 2 pers. pl. masc.; ל id.	בהם
בֶּהֶמְתָּם	פ/ id. sing., suff. 3 pers. pl. masc.; ל id.	בהם
בֶּהֶמְתֵּנוּ	פ/ id. sing., suff. 1 pers. pl.; ל id.	בהם

בֹּהֶן Root not used ; Arab. *to shut up.*

בֹּהֶן masc., pl. בְּהֹנוֹת (as if from בָּהַן § 35. rem. 9).—I. *the thumb.*—II. *the great toe.*

בֹּהַן (*thumb*) pr. name of a son of Reuben; whence אֶבֶן־בֹּהַן, the name of a place in Judah, Jos. 15. 6; 18. 17.

בָּהֶן	pref. בְּ, see lett. בְּ)(pron. pers. pl., fem. of הֵם	הם
בָּהֶן	pref. prep. בְּ with suff. 3 pers. sing. fem. (§ 5)	ב
בֹּהַן	pr. name of a place	בהן
בֹּהֶן	noun fem. sing., pl. בְּהֹנוֹת (§ 35. rem. 9) .	בהן
בְּהִבָּאוֹ	pref. בְּ)(Niph. inf. (הִבָּנֵא), suff. 3 p.s.m., d. 7 b.	נבא
בְּהִנָּבְאֹתוֹ	pref. id.)(id. [from הִנָּבְאוֹת § 23. rem. 9)	נבא
בְּהִנָּגֵף	pref. id.)(Niph. inf. construct	נגף
בְּהֵנָּה	pref. בְּ, see lett. בְּ)(pron. pers. pl. fem. with parag. ה, from הֵם masc.	הם
בְּהֹנוֹת	noun fem., pl. of בֹּהֶן (§ 35. rem. 9)	בהן
בְּהַנְחֵל	pref. בְּ)(Hiph. inf. constr. for הַנְחִיל (§ 11. r. 2)	נחל
בְּהָנִיחַ	pref. id.)(Hiph. inf. construct dec. 3 a.	נוח
בְּהִנָּשֵׂא	פ pref. id.)(Niph. inf. constr. d. 7 b.; ל bef. (:)	נשא
בְּהִנָּשְׂאָם	פ pref. id.)(id., suff. 3 pers. pl. masc.; ל id.	נשא
בְּהַעֲבִיר	pref. id.)(Hiph. inf. construct dec. 1 b.	עבר
בְּהַעֲוֹתוֹ	pref. id.)(Hiph. inf., suff. 3 p. s. m. dec. 1 b.	עוה
בְּהַעֲטִיף	פ pref. id.)(Hiph. inf. construct; ל before	עטף
בְּהַעֲלוֹת	pref. id.)(Hiph inf. construct dec. 1 b.	עלה
בְּהַעֲלֹתְ	פ/ pref. id.)(Niph. inf. constr. d. 1 b.; ל bef.	עלה
בְּהַעֲלוֹתִי	פ pref. id.)(foll. with suff. 1 pers. sing.; ן id.	עלה
בְּהַעֲלֹת	פ pref. id.)(Hiph. inf. constr. dec. 1 b.; ל id.	עלה
בְּהֵעָלֹת	פ pref. id.)(Niph. inf. with suff. 3 pers. sing. masc. dec. 1 b; ל id.	עלה
בְּהַעֲלֹתְךָ	pref. id.)(Hiph. inf., suff. 2 p. s. m. dec. 1 b.	עלה

בְּהֵעָצֵר	pref. id.)(Niph. inf. construct	עצר
בְּהַפִּילְכֶם	פ Hiph. inf., suff. 2 p. pl. m. d. 1 b.; ל bef. (:)	נפל
בְּהָפִיצִי	pref. בְּ bef. (ָ))(Hiph. inf. [הָפִיץ], suff. 1 p. s. d. 3 a.	פוץ
בְּהֶפֵּך	pref. id.)(Kal inf. construct .	הפך
בְּהַפְרִידוֹ	pref. בְּ)(Hiph. inf., suff. 3 p. s. m. dec. 1 b.	פרד
בְּהַצֹּתוֹ	pref. id.)(Hiph. inf., suff. 3 p. s. m. dec. 1 b.	נצה
בְּהַצֹּתָם	pref. id.)(id., suff. 3 p. pl. m. (§ 25. No. 2)	נצה

בָּהַק Root not used; Arab. *to be white, shining.* Hence—

בֹּהַק masc. only Le. 13. 39, a kind of harmless *leprosy*, consisting of dull whitish spots.

בְּהִקָּבֵץ	פ/ pref. בְּ)(Niph. inf. construct ; ל bef. (:)	קבץ
בְּהִקָּדְשִׁי	pref. id.)(Niph. inf. [הִקָּדֵשׁ], suff. 1 p. s. d. 7 b.	קדש
בְּהַקְהִיל	פ pref. id.)(Hiph. inf. constr.; ל before (:)	קהל
בְּהִקָּהֲלָ	pref. id.)(Niph. inf. construct	קהל
בְּהָקִיץ	pref. id.)(Hiph. inf. construct	קוץ
בְּהַקְצִיף	pref. id.)(Hiph. inf. construct	קצף
בְּהַקְרִיבָם	pref. id.)(Hiph. inf. (הַקְרִיב) suff. 3 p. pl. m. d. 1 b.	קרב
בְּהַקְרִיבְכֶם	pref. id.)(id., suff. 3 pers. pl. masc.	קרב
בְּהַקְרִיבָם	pref. id.)(id., suff. 3 pers. pl. masc.	קרב
בְּהִקָּשֹׁתָהּ	pref. id.)(Hiph. inf., suff. 3 p. s. f. dec. 1 b.	קשה

בָּהַר Root not used ; Arab. *to shine.*

בַּהֶרֶת fem., pl. בֶּהָרֹת (§ 42. No. 3 note, and § 44. rem. 5) *a shining, whitish scurf*, sinking in the skin and having white hair.

בָּהִיר masc. adj. *bright, shining*, Job 37. 21.

בָּהָר	פ/ pref. בְּ. f. [בְּהָ] noun m. s. dec. 8. (§ 37	הר
בָּהָר	פ/ pref. בְּ q. v. rem. 7); ל before (:)	הר
בָּהָר	pref. id.)(pr. name of a mountain	הר
בְּהֵרָאֹתוֹ	pref. id.)(Niph. inf., suff. 3 p. s. m. dec. 1 b.	ראה
בְּהַרְאֹתוֹ	pref. id.)(Hiph. inf., suff. 3 p. s. m. dec. 1 b.	ראה
בַּהֲרֹג	pref. בַּ before (ָ))(Kal inf. construct	הרג
בְּהֵהָרֵג	pref. בְּ [for בְּהֵהָרֵג], Niph. inf. constr. (§ 13. rem. 8)	הרג
בַּהֲרוּגִים	pref. בַּ before (ָ))(Kal part. pass. masc., pl. of [הָרוּג] dec. 3 a.	הרג
בֶּהָרֵי	פ/ל pref. בְּ)(noun masc. pl. constr. [for הַרֵי from הַר dec. 8. (§ 37. rem. 7); ל bef. (:)	הר
בַּהֲרִיחוֹ	pref. בַּ bef. (:))(Hiph. inf. [הָרִיחַ], suff. 3 pers. sing. masc. dec. 3 a.	רוח
בֶּהָרִים	pref. בְּ for בְּהָ, בְּהָ)(noun m. [for הָרִים, pl. of הַר dec. 8. (§ 37. rem. 7)	הרר
בַּהֲרִימְכֶם	pref. בַּ before (ָ))(Hiph. inf. [הָרִים], suff. 2 pers. pl. masc. dec. 3 a.	רום
בְּהָרִיעַ	pref. בְּ)(Hiph. inf. constr.	רוע

ᵃ Ps. 46. 3. | ᵍ Ex. 20. 10. | ᵐ Zec. 13. 3. | ᵗ Eze. 1. 19. | ˣ Eze. 37. 13. | ᵇ Ge. 19. 29. | ⁿ Nu. 10. 7. | ᵏ Nu. 26. 61. | ⁿ Eze. 37. 9.
ᵇ Ge. 17. 24, 25. | ʰ Le. 26. 22. | ⁿ Zec. 13. 4. | ᵘ Eze. 1. 21. | ʸ Ex. 30. 8. | ᵈ De. 32. 8. | ˡ Nu. 17. 7. | ᵐ Ge. 35. 17. | ʳ Eze. 34. 14.
ᶜ Is. 55. 6. | ⁱ 2 Ki. 3. 17. | ᵒ 1 Ki. 8. 33. | ᵛ 2 Sa. 7. 14. | ᶻ Nu. 9. 22. | ᵉ Nu. 26. 9. | ᵐ Ps. 17. 15. | ⁿ Mal. 3. 2. | ˢ Ju. 16. 9.
ᵈ Job 17. 2. | ⁱ Ps. 107. 38. | ᵖ Ju. 1. 6, 7. | ʷ Ge. 30. 42. | ᵃ Nu. 8. 2. | ᶠ Nu. 26. 9. | ⁿ Zec. 3. 14. | ᵒ Est. 1. 6. | ᵗ Nu. 18. 30, 32.
ᵉ De. 32. 3a. | ᵏ Nu. 33. 38. | ᵠ De. 32. 8. | ᵂ Jer. 37. 11. | ᵇ Eze. 45. 1. | ᵍ Ps. 102. 23. | ᵖ Est. 2. 8, 19. | ⁿ Eze. 26. 15. | ᵘ 2 Ch. 13. 15.
ᶠ Jos. 8. 3. | ˡ Ne. 10. 37. | ʳ De. 25. 19. | ᵉ Ex. 40. 36. | ᶜ Eze. 12. 15.

בְּהַרְרֵי   pref. בְּ)(n. m. pl. constr. from [הָרָר] d. 4 c.   הרר

בְּהַרְרָם   pref. id.)(id., suff. 3 pers. pl. masc.   הרר

בַּהֶרֶת   noun fem. sing. see the following   בהר

בֶּהָרֹת   id. pl. absolute (§ 42. No. 3. & § 44. rem. 5)   בהר

בְּהַשְׁבִּיעַ   pref. בְּ)(Hiph. inf. construct   שבע

בְּהַשָּׂדֶה   Kh. בְּהַשָּׂדֶה preff. הַ & בְּ, K. contr. שׂדה, q.v.   שׂדה

בְּהַשְׂכִּיל   pref. בְּ)(Hiph. inf. absolute as subst.   שׂכל

בְּהַשְׂכִּיל   וּ pref. id.)(id. inf. constr.; וּ before labial   שׂכל

בְּהַשְׁמֵהּ   pref. בְּ)(הַשְׁמָה (comp. יָחְדָּו for יַחְדָּו) Hoph. inf. construct (§ 18. rem. 14)   שׁמם

בְּהַשָּׁמַיִם   preff. הַ art. & בְּ)(n. m. pl. [of שָׁמַי § 38. r. 2)   שׁמה

בְּהִשָּׁמַע   pref. בְּ)(Niph. inf. construct   שׁמע

בְּהִשָּׁעֶנְךָ   וּ pref. id.)(Niph. inf. (הִשָּׁעֵן), suff. 2 pers. sing. masc., dec. 7 b; וּ before   שׁען

בְּהִשָּׁעֲנָם   וּ pref. id.)(id., suff. 3 pers. pl. masc.; וּ id.   שׁען

בְּהִשָּׁפֵט   pref. id.)(Niph. inf. constr. dec. 7 b.   שׁפט

בְּהִשָּׁפְטוֹ   pref. id.)(id., suff. 3 pers. sing. masc.   שׁפט

בְּהַשְׁקֵט   } pref. id.)(Hiph. inf. constr. (§ 11. r. 2)   שׁקט

בְּהִשְׁתַּחֲוָיָתִי   pref. id.)(a Chald. form of Hithpal. inf. [הִשְׁתַּחֲוָיָה § 47. r. 5] and suff. 1 p. s.   שׁחה

בְּהִשְׁתַּפֵּךְ   pref. id.)(Hithpa. inf. constr. [for הִתְשַׁפֵּךְ]   שׁפך

בְּהִתְאַסֵּף   pref. id.)(Hithpa. inf. constr.   אסף

בְּהִתְבַּהֲלָה   וּ Ch. pref. id.)(Ithpe. inf. (§ 47. rem. 5)   בהל

בְּהִתְנַגְלוֹת   pref. id.)(Hithpa. inf. constr.   נלה

בְּהִתְהַלֶּכְךָ   pref. id.)(Hithpa. inf. (הִתְהַלֵּךְ), suff. 2 pers. sing. masc. dec. 7 b. (§ 16. r. 15. & § 36. r. 3)   הלך

בְּהִתְוַדְּעַ   pref. id.)(Hithpa. inf. constr. (§ 20. rem. 1)   ידע

בְּהִתְחַבֶּרְךָ   pref. id.)(Hithpa. inf. [הִתְחַבֵּר], suff. 2 pers. sing. masc. d. 7 b. (§ 16. r. 15. & § 36. r. 3)   חבר

בְּהִתְחַנְנוֹ   pref. id.)(Hithpa. inf. [הִתְחַנֵּן], suff. 3 pers. sing. masc. dec. 7 b. (§ 10. rem. 7)   חנן

בְּהִתְיַחֵשׂ   pref. id.)(Hithpa. inf. constr. d. 7 b. (§ 14. r. 1)   יחשׂ

בְּהִתְנַדֵּב   pref. id.)(Hithpa. inf. constr. dec. 7 b.   נדב

בְּהִתְנַשְּׂאָא   pref. id.)(Hithpa. inf. constr.   נשׂא

בְּהִתְעַטֵּף   pref. id.)(Hithpa. inf. constr. dec. 7 b.   עטף

בְּהִתְעַטְּפָם   pref. id.)(id., suff. 3 pers. pl. masc.   עטף

בְּהִתְפַּלְלוֹ   pref. id.)(Hithpa. inf. (הִתְפַּלֵּל), suff. 3 pers. sing. masc. dec. 7 b. (§ 10. rem. 7)   פלל

בוֹ   וּ pref. prep. בְּ with suff. 3 pers. s. m. (§ 5)   ב

בּוֹא   fut. יָבוֹא (§ 21. r. 2, 3. & § 25. No. 2 f).—I. to enter, come or go in, const. with בְּ, אֶל, לְ, also acc.; בָּא הַשֶּׁמֶשׁ the sun went down; צֵאת וָבוֹא to go out and come in, i. e. to manage one's affairs, with לִפְנֵי הָעָם to go before, lead on a people;

בּוֹא   בְּ to have intercourse with, Jo. 23. 7, 12; בּוֹא בְמִשְׁפָּט עִם to enter into judgment with, i. e. to arraign; בּוֹא בִבְרִית to enter into a covenant, i. e. to engage in it; בּוֹא בְדָמִים to enter into blood-shed, i. e. commit it; בּוֹא בַיָּמִים to advance in years; בּוֹא אֶל, עַל אִשָּׁה to have connection with a woman.—II. to come, const. with אֶל, עַל, עַד of pers. or place, unto, with בְּ with any thing. —III. rarely i. q. הָלַךְ to go. Hiph. I.—to cause to come in, to lead, bring in.—II. to cause to come, to lead, bring. Hoph. pass. of Hiph.

בָּאָה   fem. entrance, Eze. 8. 5.

מָבוֹא   masc. dec. 3 a.—I. an entering, Eze. 26. 10.—II. entrance, place of entering; מְבוֹא הַשֶּׁמֶשׁ place of sunset, the west.

מוֹבָא   masc. (no vowel change) entrance, only Eze. 43. 11, and Keri 2 Sam. 3. 25.

תְּבוּאָה   fem. dec. 10.—I. a coming in, being stored up, Ps. 107. 37.—II. income, profit.—III. produce, fruit; trop. result, Prov. 18. 20.

בּוֹא   Kal inf. or imp. sing. masc. (§ 21. rem. 2)   בוא

בּוֹא   וּ id. inf. dec. 1 a; for וּ see lett. וּ   בוא

בּוֹאוֹ   id. id., suff. 3 pers. sing. masc.   בוא

בּוֹאִי   id. id., suff. 1 pers. sing.   בוא

בּוֹאִי   וּ id. imp. sing. fem.; וּ bef. labial   בוא

בּוֹאֲךָ   } id. inf., suff. 2 pers. s. m. d. 1 a; וּ id.   בוא

בּוֹאֶנָה   id. inf., suff. 3 pers. pl. fem. (§ 3. rem. 5)   בוא

בּוּב   to be hollow, whence the forms נָבוּב, נְבוּב are supposed to be Niph., but see נָבַב.

בָּבָה   fem. only in the constr. בָּבַת (Kamets impure, comp. § 30. No. 2) Zech. 2. 12, apple of the eye, pupil. Talm. בִּיב hollow place, Arab. בָּאב gate.

בּוֹגֵד   וּ Kal part. act. s. m. dec. 7 b; וּ bef. labial   בגד

בּוֹגְדִים   וּ id. pl., absolute state; וּ id.   בגד

בּוֹדְאָם   Kal part. act. sing. masc., suff. 3 pers. pl. masc. [for בּוֹדְאָם § 23. rem. 4]   בדא

בּוֹדֵד   Kal part. act. sing. masc.   בדד

[בּוּז]   to despise, contemn.

בּוּז   masc.—I. contempt.—II. pr. name of the second son of Nahor, Ge. 22. 21, and of a people in Arabia Deserta, Je. 25. 23. Gent. noun בּוּזִי Job 32. 2.—III. pr. name masc. 1 Ch. 5. 14.

בּוּזָה   fem. object of contempt, Ne. 3. 36.

a Ge. 14. 6.   f Pr. 21. 11.   l 2 Ch. 16. 8.   p Job 37. 17.   u Da. 6. 20.   z 2 Ch. 20. 37.   d Pr. 30. 32.   h Mal. 3. 2.   l Is. 37. 28.
b Le. 13. 38, 39.   g Le. 26. 43.   m Eze. 29. 7.   q 2 Ki. 5. 18.   v Pr. 18. 2.   a Ge. 42. 21.   e La. 2. 12.   i 1 Sa. 10. 8.   m Ps. 121. 8.
c 1 Sa. 14. 27.   h Ps. 36. 6.   n 2 Ch. 22. 8.   r La. 2. 12.   w De. 33. 5.   b 1 Ch. 5. 7   f Job 42. 10.   k 2 Sa. 13. 11.   n Is. 33. 1.
d 2 Ki. 7. 12.   i Est. 2. 8.   o Is. 30. 15.   s Pr. 6. 22.   x Ge. 45. 1.   c Ju. 5. 2.   g 2 Ch. 18. 29.   l Ca. 4. 16.   o Ne. 6. 8.
e Job 34. 35.   k 2 Ch. 16. 7.   oo Ruth 1. 19.

בּוּזִי pr. name of the father of the prophet Eze- kiel, Eze. 1. 3.

בּוֹז   Kal inf. abs.   בוז

בָּז   *b/ᵍ* & ן noun masc. sing. also pr. name; ᵍ bef. labial, for ן see lett. ו   בוז

בּוֹזֶה   Kal part. act. sing. masc. dec. 9a.   בזה

בּוּזָה   noun fem. sing.   בוז

בּוֹזֵהוּ   Kal part. act. s. m. (בּוֹזֶה), suff. 3 p. s. m. d. 9a.   בזה

בּוֹזֵי   id. pl., constr. state   בזה

בּוּזִי   pr. name masc.   בוז

בֻזוֹת   ᵍ pl. of בּוּזָה q. v. ᵍ before labial .   בזה

בּוֹזְנַי   pr. name, see שְׁתַר בּוֹזְנַי   שתר

בּוֹטֶה   Kal part. act. sing. masc.   בטה

בּוֹטֵחַ   ᵍ Kal part. act. sing. masc. dec. 7b; ᵍ bef. lab.   בטה

בִּנִּי   pr. name masc. Ne. 11. 18.

בּוּךְ.   Niph. part. *perplexed, confused.*

מְבוּכָה   fem. dec. 10. *perplexity, confusion.*

בּוֹכֶה   ᵍ Kal part. act. sing. masc. dec. 9a.   בכה

בּוֹכִיָה   id. fem. (§ 24. rem. 4)   בכה

בּוֹכִים   id. pl. absolute masc.   בכה

בּוּל   noun masc. sing.   יבל

בּוֹלֵם   ᵍ Kal part. act. sing. masc.; ᵍ bef. labial .   בלם

בּוֹלְקָהּ   ᵍ Kal part. act. sing. masc. [בּוֹלֵק], suff. 3 pers. sing. fem. dec. 7b; ᵍ id.   בלק

בּוֹם   Root not used; probably *to be high,* Syr. בִּים *a raised place, a pulpit.*

בָּמָה   f. dec. 10. (pl. c. בָּמוֹתֵי Kh. with double plural, בָּמֳתֵי K. see § 36. r. 6).—I. *high place, hill, hillock,* usually *dedicated to religious worship,* whether true or false; בָּתֵּי הַבָּמוֹת *houses* or *temples erected upon high places;* כֹּהֲנֵי הַבָּמוֹת *idolatrous priests.* Metaph. spoken of *the waves* of the sea, Job 9. 8; of *the clouds,* Is. 14. 14.— II. *height, strong place.*

בָּמוֹת *(heights)* and בָּמוֹת בַּעַל *(heights of Baal)* pr. name of a town in Moab on the river Arnon.

בּוּנָה   ᵍ *(discretion)* fr. בּוּן i. q. בִּין) pr. n. m. 1Ch. 2. 25.

בּוֹנֶה   Kal part. act. sing. masc. dec. 9a.   בנה

בּוֹנֵה   id., constr. state   בנה

בֻּנִּי   pr. name masc., see בָּנִי   בנה

בּוֹנָיו   Kal part. act. pl., suff. 3 p. s. m. fr. בּוֹנֶה d. 9a.   בנה

בּוֹנִים   ᵍ id. pl., absolute state   בנה

[בּוּס]   *to trample upon, tread under foot.*   Pil. *to tread*

down, (profane). Hoph. part. *trodden under foot,* Is. 14. 19. Hithpal. part. id. Eze. 16. 6, 22.

בֻּסִי   *(trampler)* pr. name of a man.

יְבוּס   *(place trodden down)* the ancient name of Jerusalem. Gent. n. יְבוּסִי.

מְבוּסָה   fem. *a treading down.*

תְּבוּסָה   fem. dec. 10a. *a treading down, destruc- tion,* 2 Ch. 22. 7.

בֹּסִים   Kal part. act. pl. masc. (§ 21. rem. 2)   בוס

בֹּסְסוּ   Pilel pret. 3 pers. pl.   בוס

בּוּעַ   Root not used; Chald. *to boil, to swell up.*

אֲבַעְבֻּעֹת   fem. *blains, pustules,* Ex. 9. 9, 10.

בּוּץ   Root not used; Arab. *to be white, shining.*

בּוּץ   masc. *fine linen, byssus.*

בֵּיצָה   (Chald. בֵּיעָה & בֵּיצָה) fem. dec. 10. only pl. בֵּצִים *eggs.*

בֵּצַי   *(white)* pr. name of a man.

בּוֹץ   ᵍ noun masc. sing.; ᵍ before labial .   בוץ

בּוֹצֵעַ   Kal part. act. sing. masc.   בצע

בּוֹצֵץ   pr. name of a rock   בצץ

בּוּק   Root not used; i. q. בָּקַק *to empty.*

בּוּקָה   fem. *emptiness, devastation,* Na. 2. 11.

מְבוּקָה   fem. *emptiness,* Na. 2. 11.

בּוּקָה   noun fem. sing.   בוק

בּוֹקֵעַ   Kal part. act. sing. masc.   בקע

בּוֹקֵק   Kal part. act. sing. masc. dec. 7b.   בקק

בּוֹקֵר   noun masc. sing.   בקר

[בּוּר]   cogn. בָּרַר *to examine, prove,* Eccl. 9. 1.

בּוֹר   Kh. בּוֹר q. v., K. בַּיר noun masc. sing. . .   באר

בּוֹר   ᵍ noun masc. sing. dec. 1a.   באר

בּוֹרֵא   ᵍ Kal part. act. s. m. dec. 7b; ᵍ bef. labial   ברא

בּוֹרְאֶיךָ   id. pl., suff. 2 pers. sing. masc.   ברא

בּוֹרוֹ   noun m. s., suff. 3 pers. s. m. fr. בּוֹר d. 1a.   באר

בּוֹשׁ   (§ 21. r. 2, 3, 6)—I. *to be ashamed,* const. with מִן. —II. *to be disappointed, to be confused, perplexed.* Pil. *to delay.* Hiph. *to make ashamed, cause shame, disgrace.* Hithpal. *to be ashamed.*

בּוּשָׁה   fem. *shame, ignominy.*

בָּשְׁנָה   fem. *shame,* Hos. 10. 6.

בֹּשֶׁת   fem. dec. 13c. (§ 39. No. 4d)—I. *shame, confusion.*—II. *ignominy.*—III. *an idol.*

מְבֻשִׁים   m. d. 3a., only in pl. *secret parts,* De. 25. 11.

ᵃ Ca. 8. 7.	ᵈ Pr. 14. 2.	ᵍ Pr. 12. 18.	ᵏ Job 40. 29.	ⁿ Ps. 147. 2.	ʳ Zec. 10. 5.	ᵘ Na. 2. 11.	ˣ Je. 6. 7.	ᵃᵃ Ec. 12. 1.
ᵇ Job 31. 34.	ᵉ Mal. 1. 6.	ʰ 2 Sa. 15. 30.	ˡ Am. 7. 14.	ᵒ Ps. 127. 1.	ˢ Is. 63. 18.	ᵛ Am. 7. 14.	ʸ Le. 11. 26.	ᵇᵇ Is. 33. 16.
ᶜ Ne. 3. 36.	ᶠ 2 Ch. 36. 16.	ⁱ La. 1. 16.	ᵐ Is. 24. 1.	ᵖ Ne. 4. 12.				

בּוֹשׁ	Kal inf., or pret. 3 pers. s. m. (§ 21. r. 2) בוש
בּוֹשָׁה	ᵃ id. pret. 3 pers. sing. fem.; ᵃ bef. labial בוש
בּוּשָׁה	noun fem. sing. . . . . בוש
בּוֹשׁוּ	Kal imp. pl. m., or pret. 3 pers. pl. (§21.r.2) בוש
בּוֹשִׁי	id. imp. sing. fem. . . . בוש
בּוֹשִׁים	id. part. act. sing. masc. (§ 21. rem. 2) . בוש
בֹּשְׁכֶם	Poel inf. [בּוֹשׁ § 6. No. 1], suff. 2 p. pl. m.
	[for בּשְׁכֶם or בָּשְׁכֶם comp. § 16.r. 15] בשׁ

[בּוּת] Ch. *to pass the night*, Da. 6. 19. Hence commonly derived בַּיִת *a house*, q. v.

בָּז	Kal part. act. sing. masc. . . בוז
בָּז	Kal pret. 3 p. s. m. (as if fr. בּוֹז § 21. r. 22) בוז
בַּז	noun masc. sing. dec. 8 e. . . בוז

[בָּזָא] i. q. בָּזַז *to spoil*, Is. 18. 2, 7. Others, i. q. בָּזַע *to cleave, divide.*

בָּזְאוּ	Kal pret. 3 pers. pl. . . . בזא
בָּזֹאת	ᵃ pref. בְּ for בְּ } pron. demon. fem. s., see זה
בָּזֹאת	pref. בְּ q. v. }
בִּזְבֻּלָן	} pref. בְּ bef. (:) X pr. n. of a tribe; ᵃ bef. lab. זבל
בִּזְבֻלוּן	}
בְּזֶבַח	pref. בְּ for בְּה } noun masc.sing., (suff. [זִבְחִי])
בַּזָּבַח	pref. בְּ q. v. } dec. 6a. (§ 35. rem. 5) זבח
בְּזָבְחוֹ	pref. id. X Kal inf., suff. 3 pers. sing. masc. זבח
בְּזִבְחִי	pref. id. X noun masc.sing., suff. 1 pers. sing.
	from זֶבַח dec. 6a. (§ 35. rem. 5) . זבח
בִּזְבָחֵינוּ	ᵃ pref. בְּ bef. (:) X id. pl., suff. 1 pers. pl.;
	ᵃ before labial זבח
בְּזָדוֹן	pref. בְּ X noun masc.sing. d. 3a. (§ 32. r. 6) זוד

בָּזָה ᵃⁱ *to despise, contemn*, const. with acc., לְ, עַל. Niph. part. *despised.* Hiph. *to render contemptible*, Est. 1. 17.

   בָּזֶה adj. masc. dec. 3 a, *despised*, Is. 49. 7.

   בִּזָּיוֹן masc. *contempt*, Est. 1. 18.

   בִּזְיוֹתְיָה (*contempt of the Lord*) pr. name of a town in Judah, Jos. 15. 28.

   נִבְזָה *contemptible*, 1 Sa. 15. 9, Niph. part. denom. of a subst. מִבְזָה.

בָּזֶה	ᵃⁱ pref. בְּ, see בְּ } pron. demon. sing.
בַּזֶּה	pref. בְּ for בְּה } masc.; ᵃ bef. labial זה
בִּזָּה	noun masc. sing. . . . בזז
בִּזָּהּ	noun m. s., suff. 3 pers. sing. f. fr. בַּז d. 8e. בזז
בַּזָּהָב	ᵃ pref. בְּ f. בְּה } n. m. s. d. 4a; ᵃ bef. laoial זהב
בְּזָהָב	ᵃ pref. בְּ q. v. }

בָּזוּג	Kal pret. 3 pers. sing. masc. . . בזז
בָּזֹּגוּ	Kal imp. pl. masc. . . . בזז
בְּזוֹבְלִי	pref. בְּ X n. m. s., suff. 3 p. s. m. fr. זוב d. 1 a. זוב
בָּזוּז	Kal part. pass. sing. masc. . . בזז
בָּזוּי	Kal part. pass. sing. masc. dec. 3 a. בזה
בְּזוּי	ᵃ id., constr. state ; ᵃ bef. lab. . בזה
בְּזוּיָה	id., fem. of בָּזוּי . . . בזה
בַּזּוּנָה	pref. בְּ for בְּה X Kal part. pass. sing. fem.
	dec. 10. [from זוּנָה masc.] . . זנה
בַּזּוֹנוּ	Kal pret. 1 pers. pl. . . . בזז

ᵃ בָּזַז ᵃ (§ 18. rem. 13) *to take as a prey, to spoil, plunder.* Niph. *to be spoiled.* Pu. id. Jer. 50. 37.

   בַּז masc. dec. 8 e. *prey, spoil, booty*; הָיָה לָבַז *to become a prey*; נָתַן לָבַז *to give as a prey, to be spoiled.*

   בִּזָּה fem. *prey, booty.*

   בִּגְתָא (*prey* for בִּזְתָא) pr. name of a eunuch of Ahasuerus, Est. 1. 10.

בָּזְזוּ	} Kal pret. 3 pers. pl. (§ 18. r. 13. & § 8. }
בָּזָזוּ	} r. 7) בָּזַזוּ anom. for בָּזְזוּ; ᵃ bef. lab. בזז
בָּזֹזוּ	}
בֻּזְזוּ	ᵃ Pual pret. 3 p. pl. [for בָּזְזוּ comp. § 8. r. 7] בזז
בְּזָזוּם	ᵃ Kal pret. 3 p. pl., suff. 3 p. pl. m.; ᵃ bef.lab. בזז
בֹּזְזֵיהֶם	id. part. act. masc., pl. of [בֹּזֵז] dec. 7 b. . בזז
בֹּזְזַיִךְ	id. pl., suff. 2 pers. sing. fem. בזז
בֹּזְזִים	id. pl., absolute state . . . בזז
בַּזֹּנוּ	Kal pret. 1 pers. pl. . . . בזז
בֹּזַי	ᵃ Kal part. act. pl. masc., suff. 1 pers. pl. fr.
	בֹּזֶה dec. 9 a ; ᵃ id. . . . בזה
בִּזָּיוֹן	noun masc. sing. . . . בזה
בִּזְיוֹתְיָה	ᵃ pr. name of a place . . . בזה
בִּזָּיוֹן	Kal pret. 1 pers. sing. . . . בזה
בְּזִיקוֹת	ᵃ pref. בְּ X noun pl. fem. for זִקּוֹת (comp.
	§ 18. r. 12 note) from a sing. [זֵק for זֶנֶק] זנק
בָּזִית	Kal pret. 2 pers. sing. fem. . . בזה
בָּזִיתָ	ᵃ id. pret. 2 pers. sing. masc. . בזה
בְּזָכְרֵנוּ	pref. בְּ X Kal inf., suff. 1 pers. pl. . זכר
בְּזֹלְלֵי	pref.id. X Kal part.pl.constr.m.from זָלַל d.7b. זלל
בְּזִמָּה	pref. id. X noun. fem. sing. dec. 10. זמם
בְּזִמַּגְיֵהֶם	pref. בְּ bef. (:) X noun masc. pl., suff. 3 pers.
	pl. masc. from זְמָן dec. 8 a. . . זמן
בִּזְמִירוֹת	pref. id. X n.m.with pl.f.term.from זָמִיר d.1a. זמר
בְּזָנְבוֹ	pref.id. X n.m.s.,suff.3 p.s.m.from זָנָב d.4a. זנב
בִּזְנוּנֶיהָ	pref.id. X n.m.pl.,suff.3 p.s.f. [from זָנוּן d.1a.] זנה
בִּזְנוּתַיִךְ	pref.id. X n. f. pl.,suff. 2 p.s.f.from זָנוּת d.1a. זנה

ᵃ Is. 24. 23.   ᶠ 2 Ch. 19. 2.   ⁱ Jos. 22. 27.   ᵍ Da. 11. 38.   ᵖ Ps. 22. 6.   ⁿ Nu. 31. 9.   ᵏ Je. 30. 16.   ᵐ Mal. 1. 6.   ᵗ Est. 9. 31.
ᵇ Eze. 32. 30.   ᵍ 1 Sa. 16. 3, 5.   ᵏ Eze. 17. 18.   ʳ Pr. 1. 7.   ᵍ Ec. 9. 16.   ᵒ Nu. 31. 53.   ˡ 2 Ch. 20. 25.   ⁿ Is. 50. 11.   ᵖ Ps. 95. 2.
ᶜ Am. 5. 11.   ʰ 1 Sa. 3. 14.   ˡ Est. 2. 13.   ˢ Na. 2. 10.   ᵇ Joel 4. 3.   ᵖ Je. 50. 37.   ᵐ De. 2. 35.   ᵒ 2 Sa. 12. 9.   ᵠ Ex. 4. 4.
ᵈ Zec. 4. 10.   ⁱ 1 Sa. 15. 12.   ᵐ 1 Sa. 21. 11.   ᵗ Le. 15. 3.   ᶜ De. 3. 7.   ᵍ Je. 20. 5.   ⁱ 1 Sa. 2. 30.   ᵖ Ps. 137. 1.   ʳ Na. 3. 4.
ᵉ Is. 18. 2, 7.   ⁱ 1 Sa. 2. 29.   ⁿ Eze. 29. 19.   ᵘ Is. 42. 22.   ᵈ Eze. 29. 19.   ᵍ Eze. 39. 10.   ᵐ Est. 1. 18.   ᵗ Pr. 23. 20.   ˢ Je. 3. 2.

בִּנֹתֶךָ*	pret. id.)(Kal inf. [זְנוֹת] suff. 2 pers. s. f.	זנה
בִּזְנוּתָם*	pref. id.)(n.f.s., suff. 3 p. pl.m. from זְנוּת d.1 a.	זנה
בְּזַעַם	pref. id.)(noun masc. sing. dec. 6 d.	זעם
בְּזַעַף	pref. id.)(noun masc. sing. dec. 6 d.	זעף
בְּזַעֲפוֹ*	)(Kal inf., suff. 3 p. s. m. (§ 16. r. 10);)(bef. (י)	זעף
בִּזְעָקֵךְ*	pref. id.)(Kal inf., suff. 2 p. s. f. (§ 16. r. 10)	זעק
בְּזַעַת	pref. id.)(n. f. s., construct of [זֵעָה] dec. 10.	יזע
בַּזֹּפֶת*	)(pref. בְּ for בַּה for זֶפֶת, n. f. s.;)(bef. lab.	זפת

בָּזָק Root not used; Syr. and Chald. *to scatter.*

    בָּזָק masc. *lightning,* Eze. I. 14.

    בֶּזֶק (*lightning*) pr. name of a Canaanitish city.

בֶּן	pr. name, see אֲדֹנִי בֶזֶק	דון
בַּזְּקֵנִים	pref. בְּ f. בַּה	
בִּזְקֵנִים*	pref. בְּ q. v.	noun masc. pl. [of זֵק dec. 8 b.]	זקק
בַּזָּקֵן*	pref. בְּ for בַּה)(adj. masc. sing. dec. 5 a.	זקן
בְּזָקֵן*	pref. בְּ)(noun com. sing. dec. 4 a.	זקן
בִּזְקַן*	pref. id.)(id. construct state	זקן
בִּזְקְנוֹ*	pref. id.)(id., suff. 3 pers. sing. masc.	זקן
בִּזְקֵנֵינוּ*	)(adj. pl. masc., suff. 1 pers. pl. from זָקֵן dec. 5 a.;)(before labial	זקן

[בָּזַר] *to scatter, disperse,* Da. II. 24. Pi. id. Ps. 68. 31.

בִּזֵּר*	Piel pret. 3 pers. sing. masc.	בזר
בְּזֹרֶה*	pref. בְּ)(Kal part. s. f. dec. 10. from זָר masc.	זור
בִּזְרוֹעַ*	)(pref. בְּ bef. (י))(n. com. s. d. 1 a;)(bef. lab.	זרע
בִּזְרֹעִי*	)(pref. id.)(id., suff. 1 pers. sing.;)(id.	זרע
בְּזֹרִים*	pref. בְּ)(Kal part. act. m. pl. of זָר dec. 1 a.	זור
בְּזֶרַע*	pref. בְּ bef. (י))(n. m. s., constr. of זֶרַע (§ 35. r. 7)	זרע
בִּזְרֹעַ*	)(defect. for בִּזְרוֹעַ q. v.	זרע
בְּזַרְעוֹ*	pref. בְּ)(noun masc. sing., suff. 3 pers. sing. masc. from זֶרַע dec. 6 a. (§ 35. rem. 7)	זרע
בִּזְרֹעוֹ*	pref. בְּ bef. (י))(noun com. sing., suff. 3 pers. sing. masc. from זְרֹעַ dec. 1 a.	זרע
בְּזַרְעֲךָ*	)(pref. בְּ)(noun masc. sing., suff. 2 pers. sing. masc. from זֶרַע dec. 6 a.;)(bef. lab.	
בִּזְרֹעֲךָ*	)(pref. בְּ bef. (י))(noun com. sing., suff. 2 p. sing. masc. from זְרֹעַ dec. 1 a.;)(id.	זרע
בְּזַרְעָם*	pref. בְּ)(noun masc. sing., suff. 3 pers. pl. masc. from זֶרַע dec. 6 a. (§ 35. rem. 7)	זרע
בְּזָרֵת*	pref. בְּ for בַּה)(noun fem. sing.	זרה
בִּזְתָא*	pr. name masc.	בזז
בְּזִתַנִי*	Kal pret. 2 pers. s. m. (בָּזִיתָ), suff. 1 p. s.	בזה
בְּחָבוֹר*	)(pr. name of a river;)(before (י)	חבר
בְּחֻבִּי*	pref. בְּ)(n. m. s., suff. 1 p. s. [from חֹב dec. 8 c.]	חבב

בַּחֲבֵל*	pref. בַּ f. (בָּה f. בַּה))(noun m. sing. dec. 6 a. (§ 35.	
בְּחֶבֶל*	)(pref. בְּ q. v. rem. 4);)(before lab.	חבל
בְּחַבְלֵי*	)(pref. id.)(id. pl., construct state ;)(id.	חבל
בַּחֲבֻלֶיהָ*	pref. בַּ bef. (-:))(noun masc. pl., suff. 3 pers. sing. fem. from חֶבֶל dec. 6. (§ 35. rem. 6)	חבל
בַּחֲבָלִים*	pref. בַּ)(n. m. pl. of חֶבֶל dec. 6. (§ 35. r. 4)	חבל
בְּחֶבְרוֹן*	pref. בְּ)(pr. name of a place	חבר
בַּחֲבָרֶיךָ*	pref. בַּ for בַּה)(noun masc. pl., suff. 2 p. sing. fem. from חָבֵר dec. 6 a.	חבר
בַּחֲבֶרֶת*	pref. בַּ for בַּה)(noun fem. sing. for [חֹבֶרֶת]	חבר
בַּחֲבֻרָתוֹ*	)(pref. בַּ bef. (-:))(noun fem. sing. with suff. 3 p. s. m. from [חַבּוּרָה] dec. 10;)(bef. lab.	חבר
בַּחַג*	pref. בַּ for בַּה, בַּה)(noun masc. sing. dec. 8 a.	חגג
בְּחַג*	)(pref. בְּ)(id. construct state;)(before (י)	חגג
בְּחַגְוֵי*	pref. id.)(noun masc. pl. constr. [of חֲגָוִים]	חגה
בַּחַגִּים*	)(pref. בַּ for בַּה)(noun masc., pl. of חָג dec. 8 a;)(before labial	חגג
בְּחַגֶּךָ*	pref. בְּ)(id. sing., suff. 2 p. s. m. [for חַגְּךָ]	חגג
בַּחֲגֹרְתוֹ*	pref. בַּ bef. (-:))(n. f. s., const. of חֲגֹרָה d. 10.	חגר
בְּחֶדְוָה*	Chald. noun fem. sing.	חדה
בַּחֲדַר*	)(pref. בַּ bef. (-:))(constr. of the foll. (§ 33. r. 3)	חדר
בְּחֶדֶר*	pref. בְּ for בַּה	
בַּחֲדָר*	pref. בַּ f. בָּה, בַּה &	noun masc. s. dec. 6.
בְּחֶדֶר*	pref. בְּ q. v. & ה	(§ 35. rem. 4)	חדר
בְּחַדְרֵי*	)(pref. id.)(id. pl., const. state;)(bef. (י)	חדר
בְּחַדְרֶיךָ*	pref. בְּ bef. (-:))(id. pl., suff. 2 pers. sing. m.	חדר
בֶּחָדָשׁ*	)(pref. בְּ f. בָּה)(noun masc. sing. dec. 6 c.	
בֶּחֹדֶשׁ*	pref. בְּ q. v.	חדש
בְּחָדְשָׁהּ*	pref. id.)(id., suff. 3 pers. sing. fem.	חדש
בְּחָדְשׁוֹ*	)(pref. id.)(id., suff. 3 pers. sing. masc.	חדש
בֶּחֳדָשִׁים*	)(pref. בְּ for בָּה, בַּה)(id. pl., abs. st.;)(bef. lab.	חדש
בַּחוֹחַ*	)(pref. בְּ)(n. m. sing. d. 1 a. & 6;)(bef. lab.	חוח
בַּחוֹחִים*	)(pref. בַּ for בָּה)(id. pl. absolute (§ 35.	
בַּהוֹחִים*	)(rem. 13);)(id.	חוח
בַּחוּל*	pref. id.)(noun masc. sing.	חול
בַּחוֹמָה*	)(pref. id.	noun f. s. dec. 10,)(bef. lab.
בְּחוֹמָה*	pref. בְּ	חמה
בְּחוֹמַת*	)(pref. id.)(id., construct state;)(id.	חמה
בְּחוֹמֹת*	)(pref. id.)(id. pl.	חמה
בְּחוֹמֹתַי*	)(pref. id.)(id. pl., suff. 1 pers. sing.;)(id.	חמה
בָּחוּן*	adj. masc. sing.	בחן
בְּחוֹף*	)(pref. בְּ)(noun masc. s. (for חֹף);)(bef. (י)	חפף
בַּחוּץ*	pref. בַּ for בָּה)(noun masc. sing. dec. 1 a.	חוץ
בַּחוּצוֹת*	pref. id.	id. pl. with fem. term.;)(bef. (י)
בְּחוּצוֹת*	)(pref. בְּ	חוץ

a. Eze. 23. 30.   g. Ps. 149. 8.   l. Ps. 68. 31.   r. De. 4. 37.   b. Job 31. 33.   h. Is. 53. 5.   n. Ex. 7. 28.   u. Job 40. 26.   z. 2 Ch. 27. 3.
b. Eze. 43. 7.   h. Is. 3. 5.   m. Is. 40. 11.   s. Ps. 78. 55.   c. Eze. 45. 17.   o. Ju. 16. 9.   v. 1 Sa. 13. 6.   a. Ne. 2. 13.
c. 2 Ch. 26. 19.   i. Le. 13. 29.   n. Je. 27. 5.   t. Ge. 23. 14.   d. Eze. 46. 11.   p. Ju. 16. 12.   y. 2 Ch. 33. 11.   b. Is. 56. 5.
d. Is. 57. 13.   k. 2 Sa. 20. 9.   o. De. 32. 16.   u. Pr. 5. 22.   e. De. 16. 14.   q. Ex. 2. 12.   z. Je. 6. 27.
e. Ge. 3. 19.   l. 1 Sa. 17. 34.   p. Da. 2. 43.   v. 1s. 40. 12.   f. 1 Ki. 2. 5.   r. Is. 26. 20.   a. Jos. 2. 15.   c. De. 1. 7.
f. Ex. 2. 3.   m. Ex. 10. 9.   q. De. 5. 15.   w. 2 Sa. 12. 16.   g. Ex. 26. 4, 10.   s. Ezr. 6. 16.   b. Je. 2. 24.   d. Is. 30. 13.   e. Je. 7. 17.   f. Job 40. 25

בְּחוּצוֹתֶיהָ	pref. id.)(id. pl., suff. 3 pers. sing. fem. .	חוץ
בְּחוּצוֹתֵינוּ	pref. id.)(id. pl., suff. 1 pers. pl.	חוץ
בְּחֻצֹת	pref. id.)(id. pl., defect. for חוצות	חוץ
בְּחוּצֹתָיו	pref. id.)(id. pl., suff. 3 pers. s. m. Is. 15. 3.	חוץ
בְּחֻקּוֹ	pref. id.)(Kal inf., suff. 3 pers. sing. masc., for חֻקֹּו (§ 18. rem. 12)	חקק
בְּחֻקֵּי	pref. id.)(noun masc. pl. constr. (for חֻקֵּי § 37. rem. 2) from חֹק dec. 8 c.	חקק
בָּחוֹר*	)(Kal inf. absolute;)(before lab. *Is. 7. 15, 16.	בחר
בָּחוּר	)(id. part. pass. sing. masc. dec. 3 a;)(id.	בחר
בָּחוּר	n. m. s. [for בָּחֻר], pl. בַּחוּרִים (dag. for impl.)	בחר
בְּחוּרוֹתֶיךָ	noun f. pl. (בְּחוּרוֹת), suff. 2 p. s. m. dec. 10.	בחר
בַּחוּרַי / בַּחוּרִי	noun masc. pl., suff. 1 pers. sing. from בָּחוּר (q. v.);)(before lab.	בחר
בַּחוּרֵי	)(id. pl., construct state;)(id.	בחר
בַּחוּרֵי	Kal part. pass. pl. constr. m. from בָּחוּר d. 3 a.	בחר
בַּחוּרֶיהָ	n. m. pl., suff. 3 p. s. f. from בָּחוּר [for בַּחֻר]	בחר
בַּחוּרֵיהֶם	id. pl., suff. 3 pers. pl. masc.	בחר
בַּחוּרָיו	)(id. pl., suff. 3 pers. sing. masc.;)(bef. lab.	בחר
בַּחוּרֵיכֶם	id. pl., suff. 2 pers. pl. masc.	בחר
בַּחוּרִים	)(id. pl., abs. state, also pr. name;)(bef. lab.	בחר
בֶּחָרִים	pref. בַּ for בְּהַ)(n. m., pl. of [חֹר] dec. 1 a.	חור
בַּחֲזָוָא	Chald. pref. בַּ)(n. m. s., emph. of [חֲזָו] dec. 3 c.	חזא
בְּחֶזְוֵי	Chald. pref. id.)(id. pl. construct state .	חזא
בְּחֶזְוִי	Chald. pref. id.)(id. sing., suff. 1 pers. sing.	חזא
בַּחֲזוֹן	pref. בַּ bef. (־))(construct of the following :	חזה
בְּחֵזֶה	pref. בְּ f. בָּה, בָּה)(noun masc. sing. dec. 3 a.	חזה
בַּחֲזֶה	pref. בַּ q. v. & ה	חזה
בַּחֲזוֹת	pref. בַּ before (־))(Kal inf. construct	חזה
בֶּחָזוֹת	)(pref. id.)(noun masc. sing. construct [of חָזוֹת dec. 3 a.];)(before lab.	חזה
בֶּחָזָק	pref. בֶּ)(adj. m. s. dec. 4 c. (§ 33. rem. 1)	חזק
בְּחֹזֶק	pref. בְּ)(noun masc. sing. dec. 6 c.	חזק
בְּחָזְקָה	)(pref. id.)(noun fem. sing.;)(before (־)	חזק
בְּחָזְקֵנוּ	pref. id.)(n. m. s., suff. 1 p. pl. from חֹזֶק d. 6 c.	חזק
בְּחֶזְקַת	pref. id.)(noun fem. sing., constr. of חֶזְקָה (no vowel change)	חזק
בַּחַיִּים	pref. בַּ for בְּהַ)(noun masc., pl. of חָי § 37. rem. 7. (as if from a Root עע) see	חוח
בְּחֵטְא	)(pref. בְּ)(n. m. s. d. 6. (§ 35. r. 6);)(bef. (־)	חטא
בְּחֶטְאָה	pref. id.)(id., suff. 3 pers. s. f. (for ה without Mak. § 3. rem. 3)	חטא
בְּחֶטְאוֹ	pref. id.)(id., suff. 3 pers. sing. masc.	חטא
בְּחַטֹּאות	)(pref. id.)(n. f. pl. [for חַטָּאוֹת comp. § 23. No. 4] construct of חַטָּאוֹת, from חַטָּאת (§ 39. No. 4 d. & 44. rem. 5)	חטא
בְּחַטֹּאותֶיךָ	pref. id.)(id. pl., suff. 2 pers. sing. masc.	חטא
בְּחַטֹּאותֵינוּ	pref. id.)(id. pl., suff. 1 pers. pl.	חטא
בַּחַטָּאִים	pref. בַּ for בְּהַ)(n. m., pl. of [חַטָּא] d. 1 b.	חטא
בְּחַטָּאֵנוּ	pref. בְּ bef. (־))(noun masc. pl., suff. 1 pers. pl. from חֵטְא dec. 6. (§ 35. rem. 6)	חטא
בְּחַטָּאת	pref. בְּ)(noun f. s. (§ 39. No. 4 d. & 44. r. 5)	חטא
בְּחַטֹּאת	pref. id.)(id. pl. construct state [for חַטָּאוֹת comp. § 23. rem. 4]	חטא
בְּחַטָּאתוֹ	)(pref. id.)(id. sing., suff. 3 p. s. m.;)(bef. (:)	חטא
בְּחַטֹּאתָיו	)(pref. id.)(id. pl., with suff. (Kh.), בְּחַטֹּאתֹו K. (q. v.);)(id.	חטא
בְּחַטֹּאתַיִךְ	pref. id.)(id. pl., suff. 2 pers. sing. fem.	חטא
בְּחַטֹּאתָם	pref. id.)(id. pl., suff. 3 pers. pl. masc.	חטא
בְּחֶטְּי	pref. id.)(noun masc. with pl. fem. term., construct state from חִטָּה	חטה
בְּחֵי	pref. id.)(adj. m. s. constr. of חַי d. 8 d. (§ 37. r. 6)	חיי
בְּחִידוֹת / בְּחִידֹת	)(pref. id.)(noun fem., pl. of חִידָה dec. 10.	חוד
בְּחִיָּה	)(pref. בַּ for בְּהַ)(n. f. s. dec. 10;)(bef. lab.	חיי
בְּחִיָּו	Kh., for K. בְּחִיָּיו (q. v. & § 4. rem. 1)	חיי
בְּחַיַּי / בְּחַיָּי	pref. בְּ)(noun masc. pl., suff. 1 pers. sing. from חַי dec. 8 d. (§ 37. rem. 6)	חיי
בְּחַיֶּיהָ	)(pref. id.)(id. pl., suff. 3 pers. sing. fem.	חיי
בְּחַיֵּיהֶם	)(pref. id.)(id. pl., suff. 3 pers. pl. masc.	חיי
בְּחַיָּיו	)(pref. id.)(id. pl., suff. 3 pers. sing. masc.	חיי
בְּחַיֶּיךָ	)(pref. id.)(id. pl., suff. 2 pers. sing. masc.	חיי
בַּחַיִּים	pref. בַּ for בְּהַ)(id. pl., absolute state	חיי
בַּחַיִּין	)(pref. id.)(id. pl., absolute state, Chald. form	חיי
בְּחַיִּין	Chald. pref. בְּ)(adj. m., pl. of חַי dec. 5 a.	חיי
בְּחַיִל / בְּחָיִל	)(pref. id.)(noun masc. sing. dec. 6 h. (§ 35. rem. 12), Chald. dec. 3 d.	חול
בְּחֵיל	pref. id.)(id., construct st. Chald. Da. 4. 32.	חול
בְּחֵילַהּ	Chald. pref. id.)(id., suff. 3 pers. sing. fem.	חול
בְּחֵילָה	pref. id.)(noun fem. sing.	חול
בְּחֵילוֹ	pref. id.)(noun masc. sing., suff. 3 pers. sing. masc. from חַיִל dec. 6 h. (§ 35. rem. 12)	חול
בְּחֵילְךָ / בְּחֵילֶךָ	)(pref. id.)(id., suff. 2 pers. sing. masc.	חול
בְּחֵילֵךְ	pref. id.)(id., suff. 2 pers. sing. fem.	חול
בַּחֲנִינוּ	Kh. בַּחֲנִינוּ, K. בָּחֳנֵינוּ, noun masc. pl. with suff. from [חֹנֶן or בָּחַן]	בחן
בְּחִיצוֹן	)(pref. בַּ for בְּהַ)(adj. masc. sing.;)(bef. lab.	חוץ
בַּחֵיק	pref. id.	חוק
בְּחֵיק / בְּחֵיק	pref. בְּ)(noun masc. sing. dec. 1 a.	חוק
בְּחֵיקָהּ	)(pref. id.)(id., suff. 3 pers. sing. fem.	חוק

a Ps. 144. 12.   d Is. 31. 3.   g Ps. 89. 20.   i Is. 8. 11.   n Ne. 9. 37.   q 1 Ki. 16. 26.   t 2 Sa. 18. 18.   w Da. 3. 4.   z Ps. 59. 12.
b 2 Sa. 1. 20.   e Is. 40. 30.   Eze. 21. 34.   Eze. 19. 4, 9.   Pr. 25. 16.   Eze. 16. 52.   Ge. 27. 46.   Da. 3. 20.   Is. 23. 13.
c Pr. 3. 29.   f Is. 42. 22.   h 2 Ch. 9. 29.   k Ps. 51. 7.   o Da. 9. 16.   Eze. 27. 17.   Le. 18. 18.   x Job 6. 10.   Eze. 41. 17.
Eze. 20. 18.   g Da. 2. 19.   Is. 40. 10.   Nu. 15. 28.   Je. 17. 3.   Da. 12. 7.   De. 28. 66.   Ob. 1. 13.   Pr. 16. 33.
La. 1. 15.   i Da. 7. 2.   Eze. 34. 4.   Mi. 1. 5.   2 Ki. 24. 3.   Nu. 12. 8.   Job 24. 22.   Eze. 28. 5.   Ec. 7. 9.
Ps. 78. 31.   2 Ch. 32. 32.   Am. 6. 13.   Is. 43. 24.   Eze. 3. 20.   Ge. 7. 21.   Da. 7. 12.   Ec. 11. 9.

Word	Description	Root
בְּחֻקִּי	‹ pref. id)(id., suff. 3 pers. sing. masc.	חוק
בְּחֻקִּי	pref. id.)(id., suff. 1 pers. sing.	חוק
בְּחֻקֶּךָ	pref. id.)(id., suff. 2 pers. s. m. [for וְחֻקֶּךָ]	חוק
בָּחִיר	adj. masc. sing., constr. of [בָּחִיר] dec. 3a.	בחר
בְּחִירוֹ	id., suff. 3 pers. sing. masc.	בחר
בְּחִירַי / בְּחִירָי	} id. pl., suff. 1 pers. sing.	בחר
בְּחִירִי	id. sing., suff. 1 pers. sing.	בחר
בְּחִירָיו	id. pl., suff. 3 pers. sing. masc.	בחר
בְּחִירֶיךָ	id. pl., suff. 2 pers. sing. masc.	בחר
בְּחַיַּת	pref. בְּ)(noun fem. s., constr. of חַיָּה d. 10.	חיה
בְּחַכָּה	pref. id.)(noun fem. sing.	חנך
בְּחִכִּי	pref. id.)(n. m. s., suff. 1 p. s. fr. חֵךְ d. 8b.	חנך
בְּחָכְמָה	pref. בְּ for בְּהַ } n. f. s. (no vowel change);	חכם
בְּחָכְמָה	pref. בְּ q. v. & ה Chald. (Da. 2. 30) d. 8a. }	חכם
בְּחָכְמָתָהּ	pref. id.)(id., suff. 3 pers. sing. fem.	חכם
בְּחָכְמָתוֹ	pref. id.)(id., suff. 3 pers. sing. masc.	חכם
בְּחָכְמָתִי	‹ pref. id.)(id., suff. 1 pers. sing.; ‹ bef. (:)	חכם
בְּחָכְמָתְךָ	pref. id.)(id., suff. 2 pers. sing. masc.	חכם

[בָּחַל] I. as in Syr. *to loathe*, with בְּ, Zec. 11. 8.—II. as in Arab. *to be greedy*, only Pu. part. *greedily gotten*, Prov. 20. 21. Kheth.

Word	Description	Root
בְּחֶלְי / בְּחֶלִי	pref. בְּ f. בְּהַ } pref. בְּ q. v. } noun masc. sing. dec. 1a.	חול
בְּחֵלֶב	pref. בְּ bef. (־:))(n.m.s., constr. of [חָלָב] d.5c.	חלב
בְּחֶלֶב	pref. בְּ for בְּהַ)(noun masc. sing. dec. 4c.	חלב
בְּחֶלְבּוֹ	pref. בְּ)(noun masc. sing., suff. 3 pers. sing. masc. from חֶלֶב dec. 6. (§ 35. rem. 6)	חלב
בַּחֲלָבֵי	pref. id.)(id. pl., construct state	חלב
בָּחֲלָה	Kal pret. 3 pers. sing. fem.	בחל
בַּחֲלוֹם	pref. בַּ bef. (־:))(noun masc. sing. dec. 1a.	חלם
בַּחֲלוֹמִי	pref. id.)(id., suff. 1 pers. sing. Ge. 40 9,16.	חלם
בַּחֲלוֹמֹתָם	pref. id.)(id. pl., suff. 3 pers. pl. masc.	חלם
בְּחַלּוֹן / בְּחַלּוֹן	pref. בְּ f. בְּהַ } pref. בְּ q. v. } noun com. sing. dec. 1a.	חלל
בַּחֲלוֹנֵינוּ	pref. id.)(id. pl., suff. 1 pers. pl.	חלל
בַּחֲלוֹתָם	pref. בַּ bef. (־:))(Kal inf., suff. 3 p. pl. m. d. 1b.	חלה
בְּחֶלְחָה	pref. id.)(pr. name of a province	חלח
בְּחַלְיוֹ	pref. בְּ)(n. m. s., suff. 3 p. s. m. fr. חֲלִי d. 6k.	חלה
בֶּחֳלָיִים	pref. בַּ bef. (־:))(id. pl. absolute state	חלה
בְּחַלִּיל	pref. בַּ for בְּהַ)(בְּהָ)(noun masc. sing. dec. 3a.	חלל
בַּחֲלַל	pref. בַּ bef. (־:))(constr. of the following	חלל
בֶּחָלָל	pref. בַּ for בְּהַ)(בְּהָ)(adj. masc. sing. dec. 4c.	חלל

Word	Description	Root
בְּחַלְּלוֹ	‹ pref. בְּ)(Piel inf. (חַלֵּל), suff. 3 pers sing. masc. dec. 7v; ‹ bef. (:)	חלל
בַּחֲלָלִים	pref. בַּ bef. (־:))(noun m., pl. of חָלָל d. 3a.	חלל
בַּחֲלֹם	pref. id.)(noun masc. sing. dec. 1a.	חלם
בַּחֲלֹמוֹת	pref. id.)(id. pl. with fem. term.	חלם
בַּחֲלֹמִי	pref. id.)(id. sing., suff. 1 pers. sing.	חלם
בַּחֲלָמִישׁ	pref. בְּ for בְּהַ)(noun masc. sing. dec. 3c.	חלם
בְּחֶלְקַ	pref. בְּ)(noun masc. sing. dec. 6b. (§ 35.r.6.)	חלק
בְּחֶלְקָה	pref. בְּ for בְּהַ)(noun fem. sing. dec. 12b.	חלק
בַּחֲלָקוֹת	pref. בְּ bef. (־:))(id. pl. absolute state	חלק
בַּחֲלָקוֹת	pref. id.)(noun fem., pl. of [חֲלֻקָּה] dec. 10.	חלק
בְּחֶלְקֵי	pref. בְּ)(noun masc. pl. constr. from חֵלֶק with dag. euph. (§ 35. rem. 17)	חלק
בַּחֲלַקְלַקּוֹת	pref. בְּ bef. (־:))(n. pl. fem. [from חֲלַקְלַק]	חלק
בְּחֶלְקָם	pref. בְּ)(Piel inf. [חַלֵּק], suff. 3 p. pl. m. d. 7b.	חלק
בְּחֶלְקַת	pref. id.)(noun f. s., constr. of חֶלְקָה d. 12b.	חלק
בְּחַלֹּתוֹ	pref. בְּ bef.)(Kal inf., suff. 3 p. s. m. d. 1a.	חלה
בְּחֹם	pref. בְּ)(noun masc. sing.	חמם
בַּחֲמָא	by Chaldaism for בְּחֵמָה (q. v.)	יחם
בַּחֲמֻדוֹת	‹ pref. בְּ bef. (־:))(noun fem. pl.; ‹ bef. lab.	חמד
בַּחֲמָה	‹ pref. בְּ)(noun fem. sing. dec. 11b; ‹ id.	יחם
בַּחֲמָה	pref. id.)(noun s. fem. by syncope for חֲמָאָה	חמא
בְּחֻמּוֹ	pref. id.)(Kal inf. (חֹם), suff. 3 p. s. m. d. 8c.	חמם
בַּחֲמוּדְרוֹ	pref. בְּ bef. (־:))(Kal part. pass. [חָמוּד], suff 3 pers. sing. masc. dec 3a.	חמד
בַּחֲמוֹרִים	pref. id.)(noun masc., pl. of חֲמוֹר dec. 1a.	חמר
בַּחֲמוֹתָיִךְ	pref. בְּ)(n.m.pl., suff. 2 p.s.m. fr. חוֹמָה d.10.	חמה
בַּחֲמִישִׁי	pref. בְּ for בְּהַ)(num. ord. sing. masc.	חמש
בְּחֶמְלַת	pref. בְּ)(noun fem. sing., constr. of חֶמְלָה	חמל
בְּחֶמְלָתוֹ	‹ pref. id.)(id., suff. 3 pers. s. m.; ‹ bef. (:)	חמל
בְּחֻמָּם	pref.id.)(Kal inf. (חֹם), suff.3 pers.pl.m. d.8c.	חמם
בְּחֵמֶץ	pref. בְּ for בְּהַ)(noun masc. sing.	חמץ
בְּחֵמָר	‹ pref. בְּ bef. (־:))(n. m. s. d 1a; ‹ bef. lab.	חמר
בַּחֹמֶר	pref. בְּ for בְּהַ)(noun masc. sing. *Ex. 2. 3.	חמר
בַּחֹמֶר / בֶּחֹמֶר	pref. id. } pref. בְּ })(noun masc. sing. *Na. 3. 14.	חמר
בַּחֲמֹרִים	‹ pref. בְּ bef. (־:))(noun masc., pl. of חֲמוֹר dec. 1a; ‹ bef. lab.	חמר
בַּחֲמֵשׁ	pref. id.)(num. card. sing. fem. constr. of חָמֵשׁ (§ 34. rem. 1)	חמש
בַּחֲמֵשׁ	‹ pref. id.)(id. masc., constr. חֲמֵשֶׁת	חמש
בַּחֲמִשִׁי	pref. בְּ for בְּהַ)(num. ord. m. s. from חָמֵשׁ	חמש
בַּחֲמִשִּׁים	pref. בְּ bef. (־:))(num. card. com., pl. of חָמֵשׁ	חמש חמש
בַּחֲמַת	pref. id.)(pr. name of a place	חמת

a 2 Sa. 21. 6.   d Job 53. 2.   h Ca. 5. 12.   l Je. 9. 20.   q 1 Ki. 1. 40.   u Is. 57. 6.   x Job 29. 6.   f Zec. 7. 5.   n De. 22. 10.
b Ps. 106. 23.   e 2 Sa. 20. 22.   i Job 15. 27.   m Ps. 35. 13.   r Ge. 41. 17, 22.   Da. 11. 21, 34.   y Job 6. 17.   g Ge. 19. 14.   Ex. 1. 14.
c Is. 65. 22.   Is. 10. 13.   k 2 Ch. 29. 35.   2 Ch. 21. 15.   s Job 28. 9.   Is. 9. 2.   z Job 20. 20.   Is. 65. 9.   Ge. 47. 17.
Ps. 106. 5.   Eze. 23. 4.   Zec. 11. 8.   Is. 30. 29.   t Is. 38. 9.   1 Ch. 12. 40.   Je. 51. 39.   Eze. 45. 2.
Is. 65. 9.   2 Sa. 20. 15.   Je. 23. 27.   Nu. 19. 16.   f Ps. 73. 18.   Da. 11. 44.   Eze. 26. 9.   Ru. 2. 14.   Eze. 20. 2.
Ho. 4. 3.   1 Ki. 21. 23.   Pr. 7. 6.   1 Ch. 5. 1.   Da. 11. 32.   Da. 11. 38.

בְּחֵמַת pref. id.)(n. f s., constr. of חֵמָה dec. 11 b.   יחם

בַּחֲמָתָהּ pref. id.)(noun fem. sing., suff. 3 pers. sing. fem. from [חָמוֹת] dec. 3 a.   חם

בַּחֲמָתוֹ pref. id.)(noun fem. sing., suff. 3 pers. sing. masc. from חֵמָה dec. 11 b; בּ bef. lab.   יחם

בַּחֲמָתִי pref. id.)(id., suff. 1 pers. sing.; בּ id.   יחם

בַּחֲמָתֶךָ pref. id.)(id., suff. 2 pers. sing. masc.; בּ id.   יחם

[בָּחַן] to try, prove, test. Niph. to be tried. Pu. id. Eze. 21. 18, but see בָּחַן.

בַּחַן masc. watch-tower, Is. 32. 14.

בֹּחַן masc. proof, trial, Is. 28. 16, to which some refer also Eze. 21. 18, see the verb.

בֹּחֵן masc. adj. trier, assayer of metals, Je. 6. 27.

בָּחוּן (after the form קָטוּל) a watch-tower, Is. 23. 13 Keri, בָּחִין Kheth.

בֹּחַן ן noun masc. sing.; for ן see lett. ו

בָּחַן noun masc. sing.

בֹּחֵן Kal part. act. sing. masc.; בּ bef. labial

בָּחֲנוּ id. pret. 3 pers. pl.

בְּחָנוּנִי id. id., suff. 1 pers. sing.

בְּחָנוּנִי id. imp. [בָּחַן], pl. masc., suff. 1 pers. sing. (§ 16. rem. 11); בּ bef. lab.

בְּחָנִית pref. בּ bef.)(n. fem. sing. d. 1 a; בּ id.

בַּחֲנִיתוֹ pref. id.)(id., suff. 3 pers. sing. masc.

בַּחֲנֻכַּת בּ pref. id.)(noun fem. sing., constr. of חֲנֻכָּה dec. 10; בּ bef. lab.

בַּחֲמָל pref. בּ for בְּהַ)(noun masc. sing.

בְּחָנֵנִי Kal pret. 3 pers. sing. masc., suff. 1 pers. sing.

בְּחָנֵנִי id. imp. s. m., [בָּחַן], suff. 1 p. s. (§ 16. r. 11)

בַּחֲנַף pref. בּ)(noun m. pl. constr. from חֵנֶף d. 5 c.

בָּחַנְתָּ Kal pret. 2 pers. sing. masc.

בָּחַנְתְּ id. id.; acc. shifted by ו (bef. lab. for ו) conv. (§ 8. rem. 7)

בְּחָנֹת בּ pref. בּ bef.)(Kal inf. constr.; בּ bef. lab.

בַּחֲנֻתִים בּ Kal pret. 1 pers. s., suff. 3 pers. pl. m.; בּ id.

בַּחֲנַתֶּנוּ id. pret. 2 pers. sing. masc., suff. 1 pers. pl.

בַּחֶסֶד pref. בּ for בְּהַ)(noun m. sing., (suff. חַסְדְּ)

בְּחֶסֶד בּ pref. בּ q. v. dec. 6 a; בּ bef.

בְּחַסְדֶּךָ pref. id.)(id., suff. 2 pers. s. m.; בּ id.

בַּחֲסָדֶךָ

בְּחֶסְפָּא Chald. pref. בּ bef.)(noun m. s. dec. 3 a.

בַּחֲסַר pref. id.)(adj. masc. sing. constr. of חָסֵר d.5 c.

בְּחֶסֶר pref. בּ)(noun masc. sing.

בַּחֶסֶר pref. id.)(noun masc. sing.; בּ bef.

בְּחָפְזִי pref. id.)(Kal inf., suff. 3 pers. sing. fem.

בְּחִפָּזוֹן pref. id.)(noun masc. sing.

בְּחָפְנִי pref. id.)(Kal inf., suff. 1 pers. sing.

בְּחָפְנָיו pref. id.)(n. m. du., suff. 3 p. s. m. fr. [חֹפֶן] d. 6 c.

בְּחֵפֶץ pref. id.)(noun masc. sing. dec. 6 b. (§ 35. r. 6)

בְּחָצוֹר pref. id.)(pr. name of a place

בַּחֲצֹת בּ noun masc. with pl. fem. term. def. for חֲצֹת from חֹץ dec. 1 a; בּ bef.

בְּחֶצִי pref. בּ bef.)(noun masc. sing. dec. 6 i.

בְּחֶצִי pref. בּ for בְּהַ (§ 35. rem. 14)

בַּחִצִּים בּ pref. id.)(noun masc., pl. of חֵץ dec. 8 b;

בַּחִצִּים בּ pref. בּ)(בּ bef. lab.

בְּחָצֵן pref. id.)(noun masc. sing. dec. 6 c.

בַּחֵץ pref. בּ for בְּהַ)(noun masc. sing. dec. 4 c.

בַּחֲצַצוֹן pref. בּ)(pr. name of a place, see חַצְצוֹן תָּמָר

בְּחַצְרוֹת pref. בּ bef.)(n. f., pl. of חֲצֵרָה d. 10.

בַּחֲצֵרֹת

בֶּחָצֵר pref. בּ bef.)(constr. of the following; also pr. name in compos. as בַּחֲצַר סוּסִים

בְּחָצֵר pref. בּ for בְּהַ)(noun com. sing. dec. 5 c.

בַּחֲצֵרוֹ pref. בּ bef.)(id., suff. 3 pers. sing. masc.

בַּחֲצֵרוֹת pref. id.)(id., pl. abs. st. and pr. name of a place

בְּחַצְרוֹת בּ pref. בּ)(id., constr. st. fem. term.

בְּחַצְרֵי pref. id.)(id. pl. constr. masc. term.

בְּחַצְרֵיהֶם pref. id.)(id., pl., suff. 3 pers. pl. masc.

בַּחֲצֵרֶיךָ pref. בּ bef.)(id. pl., suff. 2 pers. sing. masc.

בַּחֲצֵרִים pref. id.)(id. pl. masc., as a pr. name of a place

בְּחַצְרֹתֵיהֶם בּ pref. בּ)(id. pl. fem., suff. 3 pers. pl. m.

בַּחֵק pref. בּ for בְּהַ)(noun m. sing. for חֵיק d. 1 a.

בְּחֻקּוֹ pref. בּ)(noun masc. sing. dec. 8 c.

בְּחֻקּוֹת pref. id.)(noun fem., pl. of חֻקָּה dec. 10.

בְּחֻקּוֹתַי pref. id.)(id. with suff. 1 pers. sing.

בְּחֵיקִי pref. id.)(n. m. s., suff. 1 pers. s. fr. חֵיק d. 1 a.

בְּחֻקַּי pref. id.,)(n. m. pl., suff. 1 p. s. fr. חֹק d. 6 c.

בְּחֻקָּיו pref. id.)(id., suff. 3 pers. sing. masc.

בְּחֻקֶּיךָ pref. id.)(id., suff. 2 pers. sing. masc.

בְּחֹקֶר pref. id.)(noun masc. sing. d. 6 b; בּ bef.

בְּחֻקֹּת pref. id.)(noun fem., pl. of חֻקָּה dec. 10.

בְּחֻקֹּתַי בּ pref. id.)(id., suff. 1 pers. sing.; בּ bef.

בְּחֻקֹּתֵיהֶם בּ pref. id.)(id., suff. 3 pers. pl. masc.; בּ id.

בְּחֻקֹּתָיו בּ pref. id.)(id., suff. 3 pers. sing. masc.; בּ id.

בְּחֻקֹּתֶיךָ pref. id.)(id., suff. 2 pers. sing. masc.

בָּחַר I. to prove, examine (so in the Syr Job 34. 3; Is. 48. 10; and 2 Ch. 34. 6. Kheth.—II. to choose, elect, select, const. with acc., בּ, לְ, once עַל, with

a Mi. 7. 6.	f Mal. 3. 15.	l Job 23. 10.	q Ps. 143. 12.	v De. 28. 48.	z Eze. 39. 9.	h Ne. 13. 7.	m Pr. 8. 27.	t Je. 44. 10.
b Est. 7. 7.	g Ps. 95. 9.	k Ps. 35. 16.	r Da. 2. 41, 43.	w 2 Sa. 4. 4.	i Is. 49. 22.	o Ps. 84. 11.	n Job 19. 27.	u Le. 18. 3.
c De. 29. 22.	h Mal. 3. 10.	l Ps. 17. 3.	s Pr. 10. 21.	x Pr. 30. 4.	j La. 3. 16.	p De. 2. 23.	p 1 Ki. 8. 61.	v Je. 44. 23.
d Ps. 6. 2.	i Ne. 12. 27.	n Nu. 1. 51.	o Job 30. 3.	y Pr. 31. 13.	k 2 Sa. 17. 18.	q Ne. 8. 16.	r Job 38. 16.	w Ps. 119. 16.
e Is. 32. 14.	j Ps. 78. 47.	p Ps. 66. 10.	u De. 28. 57.	z 1 Ch. 12. 2.	g Ne. 8. 16.	— Pr. 21. 14.	s Le. 20. 23.	

מֵן *to be better than.* Niph. part. *chosen, choice, excellent,* with לְ *by;* with מִן *more.*

בָּחוּר (for בַּחוּר) masc., pl. בַּחוּרִים (dag. forte implied), *a youth,* prop. *choice for vigour and activity.*

בַּחֻרִים (*place of youths*) pr. name of a town in the tribe of Judah, Gent. n. בַּחֲרוּמִי, 1 Ch. 11. 33. and transp. בַּרְחֻמִי, 2 Sa. 23. 31.

בְּחֻרִים masc. pl. (prop. from a sing. § 26. No. 13) *youth, youthful age,* see the prec. Nu. 11. 28.

בְּחֻרוֹת fem. pl. id. Ec. 11. 9; 12. 1.

בָּחִיר masc. dec. 3 a, *chosen, elect.*

יִבְחָר (whom He *chooses*) pr. name of a son of David.

מִבְחָר masc. dec. 2 b.—I. *choice, best.*—II. pr. name masc. 1 Ch. 11. 38.

מִבְחוֹר masc. id. 2 Ki. 3. 19; 19. 23.

בָּחַר׳ Kal pret. 3 pers. sing. m. for בָּחַר (§ 8. r. 7) — בחר

בָּחֹר׳ id. inf. absolute; ᵃ bef. labial — בחר

בְּחַר id. imp. sing. masc. — בחר

בְּחַרְבֹתֵיהֶם Kh. בָּחַר בָּתֵּיהֶם q.v.; K. בְּחַר בָּתֵּיהֶם, pref. בְּ ✗ noun fem. pl., suff. 3 pers. pl. masc. from חֶרֶב dec. 6 a. — חרב

בָּחֹר pref. בְ ✗ pr.n. in compos., see הֹר הָהָר under R. נגד — בחר

בֹּחֵר Kal part. act. sing. masc. — בחר

בַּחֶרֶב׳ pref. בַּ f. בָּה ⎫
בֶּחֶרֶב pref. בֶּ f. בָּה, בֶּה ⎬ noun fem. s. (suff. חַרְבִּי) dec. 6 a; ᵃ bef. (:)
בְּחֶרֶב׳ pref. בְּ q.v. & ה ⎭

בְּחֹרֶב׳ pref. id. ✗ pr. name of a place; ᵇ bef. (:) — חרב

בֶּחָרְבָּה pref. בֶּ for בָּה, bef. הָ for בָּה ✗ noun f. s. — חרב

בְּחָרְבּוֹ׳ ᵉ pref. בְּ ✗ noun fem. sing., suff. 3 pers. sing. masc. from חֶרֶב dec. 6 a. — חרב

בְּחַרְבוֹנֵי pref. id. ✗ noun masc. pl. c. [from חַרְבוֹן d. 3 c. § 32. No. 2]; Milêl before monos. — חרב

בֶּחֳרָבוֹת׳ pref. בֶּ for בָּה ✗ n. f. pl. abs. fr. חֶרֶב d. 6 a. — חרב

בְּחָרְבוֹת pref. בְּ bef. (־) ✗ n. f. pl. abs. fr. חָרְבָּה d. 12 c. — חרב

בְּחָרְבוֹת pref. בְּ ✗ noun fem. pl., constr. of חַרְבוֹת from חֶרֶב dec. 6 a. — חרב

בֶּחֳרָבוֹת׳ pref. בֶּ for בָּה ✗ noun fem. pl. abs. from חָרְבָּה dec. 12 c. — חרב

בְּחַרְבוֹתָיו׳ pref. בְּ ✗ noun fem. pl., suff. 3 pers. sing. masc. from חֶרֶב dec. 6 a. — חרב

בְּחַרְבוֹתָם pref. id. ✗ id. pl., suff. 3 pers. pl. masc. — חרב

בְּחַרְבִּי׳ pref. id. ✗ id. sing., suff. 1 pers. sing. — חרב

בְּחַרְבְּךָ pref. id. ✗ id. sing., suff. 2 pers. sing. masc. — חרב

בְּחַרְבָּם׳ pref. id. ✗ id. sing. 3 pers. pl. masc. — חרב

בְּחַרְדָּה pref. בְּ bef. (־:) ✗ pr. name of a place — חרד

בָּחֲרוּ ⎫
בְּחֲרוּ׳ ⎬ Kal pret. 3 pers. pl. (§ 8. r. 7); ᵇ bef. lab — בחר
בַּחֲרוּ׳ ⎭

בַּחֲרוּ id. imp. pl. masc. — בחר

בַּחֲרוּזִים pref. בַּ bef. (־:) ✗ noun masc. pl. [of חָרוּז] — חרז

בְּחֲרוֹן pref. id. ✗ noun m. s., constr. of חָרוֹן d. 3 a. — חרה

בַּחֲרוֹנוֹ pref. id. ✗ id., suff. 3 pers. s. m.; ᵇ bef. lab. — חרה

בַּחֲרוּץ pref. בַּ for בָּה, bef. הָ for בָּה ✗ n. m. s. d. 3 a. — חרץ

בַּחֲרוּת pref. בַּ, bef. (־:) ✗ Kal inf. constr. — חרה

בַּחֲרוּתֶיךָ׳ noun f. pl. [בְּחֻרוֹת], suff. 2 pers. sing. m. — בחר

בְּחַרְחֻר׳ ᵇ pref. בְּ ✗ noun masc. sing.; ᵃ bef. (:) — חרר

בַּחֶרֶט pref. בַּ for בָּה ⎫
בְּחֶרֶט pref. בְּ q.v. ⎬ noun masc. sing. — חרט

בַּחַרְטֻמָּם׳ pref. בַּ for בָּה ✗ noun masc. pl. [of חַרְטֹם dec. 8 c. § 37. No. 4] — חרט

בַּחֲרִי pref. בַּ bef. (־:) ✗ noun masc. sing. — חרה

בַּחֲרִי Kal inf., suff. 1 pers. sing. (§ 16. rem. 8) — בחר

בַּחֲרִיהָ noun masc. pl., suff. 3 pers. sing. fem. (dag. forte impl. in ה) from בָּחוּר [for בַּחוּר] — בחר

בַּחֲרִיהֶם׳ id. with suff. 3 pers. pl. masc. ✗ ᵇ bef. lab. — בחר

בַּחֲרִיהֶן pref. בְּ ✗ n. m. pl., suff. 3 p. pl.f.fr. חוֹר d. 1 a. — חור

בַּחֲרִים pr. name of a place — בחר

בַּחֲרִים׳ ᵇ defect. for בַּחוּרִים (q.v.) — בחר

בַּחֲרִיצֵי׳ ᵇ pref. בְּ ✗ noun masc. pl. const. fr. [חָרִיץ] dec. 3 a; ᵇ bef. labial — חרץ

בֶּחָרִישׁ pref. בְּ for בָּה, bef. הָ for בָּה ✗ n. m. s. d. 3 a. — חרש

בַּחֵרֶם pref. בַּ for בָּה ✗ noun m. s. d. 6 (§ 35. r. 6) — חרם

בְּחֶרְמָה׳ ᵇ pref. בְּ ✗ pr. name of a place — חרם

בְּחֶרְמוֹ׳ pref. id. ✗ id., suff. 3 pers. sing. masc. — חרם

בְּחֶרְמִי pref. id. ✗ id., suff. 1 pers. sing. — חרם

בְּחָרָן pref. id. ✗ pr. name of a place — חרר

בַּחֵרֶם׳ ᵇ pref. בְּ for בָּה, bef. הָ for בָּה ✗ noun m. sing., for חֵרֶם dec. 6 a. (§ 35. r. 1); ᵇ bef. labial — חרם

בַּחֲרֹף׳ ᵇ pref. בְּ for בָּה bef. הָ for בָּה ✗ n. m. s. dec. 6 c; ᵇ id. — חרף

בְּחֶרְפָּה׳ᵇ pref. בְּ ✗ noun fem. sing. dec. 12 b; ᵇ id. — חרף

בְּחָרְפָם pref. id. ✗ Piel inf. חָרֵף suff. 3 pers. pl. m. — חרף

בַּחֲרֻצוֹת׳ pref. בַּ bef. (־:) ✗ adj. pl. fem. from חָרוּץ m. — חרץ

בַּחֲרִיצֵי׳ ᵇ defect. for בַּחֲרִיצֵי (q.v.) — חרץ

בַּחֲרָשָׁה׳ pref. בַּ for בָּה ✗ noun masc. sing. (חֹרֶשׁ) with parag. ה dec. 6 c. (§ 35. rem. 18) — חרש

בַּחֲרָשִׁים׳ ᵇ pref. בַּ for בָּה, bef. הָ for בָּה ✗ id. pl. abs.; ᵇ bef. labial — חרש

בְּחֲרֹשֶׁת׳ ᵇ pref. בְּ bef. (־:) ✗ noun fem. sing., also pr. name, see חֲ הַגּוֹיִם — חרש

בָּחַרְתָּ ⎫
בְּחַרְתָּ ⎬ Kal pret. 2 pers. sing. masc. (§ 8. rem. 7) — בחר

ᵃ Ps. 78. 67.   ᶠ Is. 27. 1.   ⁱ Eze. 33. 27.   ᵍ Is. 56. 4.   ᵖ Ps. 124. 3.   ᵘ Ex. 9. 11.   ᵏ Je. 31. 13.   ᵐ De. 28. 27.   ʳ Am. 1. 3.
ᵇ 1 Sa. 2. 28.   ᵍ Is. 66. 16.   ᵏ Eze. 26. 9.   ᵗ Ca. 1. 10.   ᵠ Ec. 12. 1.   ᵛ Eze. 20. 5.   ˡ 1 Ch. 20. 3.   ⁿ Zec. 14. 8.   ˢ 3 Sa. 12. 31.
ᶜ 2 Ch. 34. 6.   ʰ Ps. 32. 4.   ˡ Ge. 48. 22.   ᵐ Na. 1. 6.   ʳ De. 28. 22.   ʷ Ex. 32. 4.   ᵐ Je. 51. 3.   ᵒ Ne. 1. 3.   ᵗ 1 Sa. 23. 15, 15.
ᵈ Sa. 20. 30.   ᵉ 1 Ki. 18. 26.   ᵐ Ps. 44. 4.   ⁿ Ps. 2. 5.   ˢ Is. 8. 1.   ᶻ 2 Ki. 8. 12.   ᵖ Eze. 32. 3.   ᵖ 2 Sa. 23. 9.   ᵘ 2 Ch. 27. 4.
ᵉ De. 28. 22.   ʲ Eze. 32. 13.   ʰ Is. 66. 3.   ᵒ Is. 28. 27.   ᵗ Zec. 14. 12.   ʸ Ex. 34. 21.

בָחַרְתָּ	id. id. acc. shifted by ו (bef. labial for ו) conv. (§ 8. r. 7)	בחר
בָּחַרְתִּי בָּחַרְתִּי	id. pret. 1 pers. sing.; ו bef. labial	בחר
בְּחַרְתִּיךָ	id. id., suff. 2 pers. sing. masc.	בחר
בְּחַרְתֶּם	id. pret. 2 pers. pl. masc.	בחר
בְּחָשָׁב	pref. בְּ ✗ noun masc. sing.	חשב
בְּחֶשְׁבּוֹן	pref. id. ✗ pr. name of a place	חבש
בַּחֲשׁוֹכָא	Chald. pref. בְּ bef. (־) ✗ noun masc. sing., emph. of [חֲשׁוֹךְ] dec. 1 a.	חשך
בַּחֹשֶׁךְ	ו pref. בְּ for בְּה ✗ n. m. s. d. 6 c; ו bef. lab.	חשך
בַּחֲשֵׁכָה	pref. בְּ bef. (־) ✗ noun fem. sing. dec. 10.	חשך
בְּחַשְׁמֹנָה	pref. בְּ ✗ pr. name of a place	חשם
בְּחֹשֶׁן	pref. id. ✗ noun masc. sing.	חשן
בְּחָתִיתָם	pref. id. ✗ n. f. s., suff. 3 p. pl. m. from חִתִּית d. 1 b.	חתת
בְּחֹתָמוֹ	pref. id. ✗ noun masc. sing., suff. 3 pers. sing. masc. from חוֹתָם [no vowel change]	חתם

בָּטָא Pi. to utter, or talk rashly, or unadvisedly, comp. בָּטָה.

מִבְטָא masc. rash utterance, Nu. 30. 7, 9.

בַּטַּבָּעֹת	pref. בְּ for בְּה ✗ pl. abs. from the following:	טבע
בְּטַבַּעַת	pref. בְּ ✗ noun fem. sing. (§ 4. rem. 5).	טבע
בְּטַבְּעֹת	pref. id. ✗ id. pl., construct state	טבע

בָּטָה i. q. בָּטָא, only part. בֹּטֶה an idle talker, Pr. 12. 18.

בְּטָהוֹר	pref. בְּ for בְּה ✗ adj. m. s. d. 3 a (§ 32. r. 7)	טהר
בְּטָהֳרָתוֹ	pref. בְּ ✗ n. f. s., suff. 3 p. s. m. from [טָהֳרָה] (no pl.)	טהר
בְּטוֹב בְּטוֹב	pref. בְּ for בְּה ✗ adj. and subst. masc. sing.} pref. בְּ q. v. dec. 1 a. }	טוב
בְּטוּב	ו pref. id. ✗ noun m. s. dec. 1 a; ו before (־)	טוב
בְּטוֹבָה	pref. בְּ for בְּה ✗ noun fem. sing. dec. 10.	טוב
בְּטוּבְךָ	ו pref. בְּ ✗ noun masc. sing., suff. 2 pers. sing. masc. from טוּב dec. 1 a; ו before (־)	טוב
בְּטוֹבַת	pref. id. ✗ noun f. s., constr. of טוֹבָה dec. 10.	טוב
בְּטוֹבָתָהּ	pref. id. ✗ id., suff. 2 pers. sing. masc.	טוב
בָּטוֹחַ	Kal inf. absolute	בטח
בָּטוּחַ	id. part. pass. sing. masc.	בטח

בָּטַח prop. to cling to, comp. Hiph., hence—I. to rely upon, trust, confide in, const. with בְּ, אֶל, עַל.—II. abs. to be confident, secure, in a good and bad sense. Hiph.—I. to cause to cling to or hang upon, Ps. 22. 10.—II. to cause to trust, confide, with עַל, אֶל.

בֶּטַח masc.—I. trust, confidence, security; לְבֶטַח and בֶּטַח confidently, securely, safely.—II. pr. name

of a city in Syria, 2 Sa. 8. 8, for which טִבְחַת 1 Ch. 18. 8.

בִּטְחָה fem. confidence, Is. 30. 15.

בִּטָּחוֹן masc. confidence, hope.

בַּטֻּחוֹת fem. pl. security, tranquillity, Job 12. 6.

אֲבַטִּיחַ masc. melon, by transp. from טבח Arab. to cook, ripen, Nu. 11. 5.

מִבְטָח masc. with suff. מִבְטַחִי dec. 2 b, but also מִבְטַחִי (§ 37. rem. 7) trust, confidence, security meton. object of confidence.

בָּטַח	Kal preter. 3 pers. sing. masc. for בָּטַח (comp. § 8. rem. 1 and 7)	בטח
בָּטַח	defect. for בָּטוּחַ (q. v.).	בטח
בֶּטַח	ו noun masc. sing.; for ו see letter ו.	בטח
בְּטַח	ו Kal imp. sing. masc.; ו before labial	בטח
בֹּטֵחַ	ו id. part. act. sing. masc. dec. 7 b; ו id.	בטח
בָּטְחָה	id. pret. 3 pers. sing. f. [for בָּטְחָה § 8. r. 7]	בטח
בָּטְחוּ	id. preter. 3 pers. pl.	בטח
בִּטְחוּ	ו id. imp. pl. masc.; ו before labial	בטח
בִּטָּחוֹן	noun masc. sing.	בטח
בַּטּוּחוֹת	pref. בְּ for בְּה ✗ noun fem. pl. [of טוּחָה]	טוח
בַטֻּחוֹת	noun fem. pl. [of בַּטֻּחָה]; ו before labial	בטח
בַּטֻּחוֹת	Kal part. act. f., pl. of בֹּטְחָה d. 10. from בֹּטֵחַ m.	בטח
בַּטְּחִים	ו pref. בְּ for בְּה ✗ Kal part. act. masc., pl. of [טָח] dec. 1 a; ו before labial	טוח
בֹּטְחִים	Kal part. act. masc., pl. of [בֹּטֵחַ] dec. 7 b.	בטח
בְּטָחֶךָ	Kal inf. [בְּטָח], suff. 2 p. s. m. (§ 16. r. 10)	בטח
בָּטַחְנוּ	id. pret. 1 pers. pl. [for בָּטַחְנוּ § 8. rem. 7]	בטח
בָּטַחְתָּ בָּטָחְתָּ	id. pret. 2 pers. sing. masc. (§ 8 rem. 7) }	בטח
בָּטַחְתְּ	ו id. id.; acc. shifted by ו (before labial for ו) conversive (§ 8. rem. 7)	בטח
בָּטַחְתִּי בָּטָחְתִּי	id. pret. 1 pers. sing. (§ 8. rem. 7) }	בטח
בַּטִּיט	pref. בְּ for בְּה } pref. בְּ q. v. } noun masc. sing.	טוא
בְּטִיט		
בְּטִירֹתָם	ו pref. בְּ ✗ noun fem. pl., suff. 3 pers. pl. masc. from [טִירָה] dec. 10; ו before (־)	טור

בָּטֵל to cease, rest from, Ec. 12. 3.

בְּטֵל Chald. (§ 47. rem. 6) id. Ezr. 4. 24. Pa. to cause to cease, to hinder.

בְּטֵל	ו Chald. pref. בְּ ✗ noun m. s.; ו before labial	טלל
בְּטֵלָא	Chald. Peal part. act. fem. [of בָּטֵל m.]	בטל
בַּטְּלָאִים	pref. בְּ for בְּה ✗ pr. name of a place, see טְלִי	טלה
בְּטֵלוּ	ו Kal pret. 3 pers. pl.; ו before labial	בטל

a De. 38. 19.   e Ec. 6. 4, 4.   i 1 Ki. 21. 8.   n De. 28. 47.   r Ps. 106. 5.   v Ps. 112. 7.   z Ps. 4. 6.   f Je. 48. 7.   k Da. 4. 12, 20.
b 2 Ch. 7. 12.   f Ps. 83. 5.   k Ex. 25. 15.   o Job 21. 25.   s Ps. 68. 11.   w Is. 32. 17.   a Ec. 9. 4.   g Job 11. 18.   l Ezr. 4. 24.
c Is. 41. 8, 9.   f Ex. 26. 29.   l Le. 15. 8.   p Ne. 9. 25.   t Is. 59. 4.   x Ps. 37. 5.   b Job 12. 6.   h Zec. 10. 5.   m Ec. 12. 3.
d Da. 2. 21.   h Exo. 32. 29.   m Le. 14. 32.   q Ne. 9. 35.   u Is. 26. 3.   y Zep. 3. 2.   c Eze. 18. 15.   i Ge. 25. 16.   nn Job 38. 36.

בטל   Chald. Pael pret. 3 p.pl. m. (§ 47.r.1); יₐ id.   בְּטֵלוּ

בטל   Chald. Peal pret. 3 pers. sing. f. Ezr. 4. 24.   בְּטֵלַת

טמא   pref. בְּ)(adj. m. sing. dec. 5 a. (§ 34. rem. 1)   בְּטָמֵא

טמא   pref. id.)(Piel inf. (טַמֵּא), suff. 2 pers. pl. masc. dec. 7 b. (§ 36. rem. 2)   בְּטַמְּאָכֶם

טמא   pref. id.)(id., suff. 3 pers. pl. masc.   בְּטַמְּאָם

טמא   pref. id.)(noun f. s., constr. of טֻמְאָה d. 10.   בְּטֻמְאַת

טמא   pref. id.)(id., suff. 2 pers. sing. masc.   בְּטֻמְאָתְךָ

טמא   pref. id.)(id., suff. 3 pers. pl. masc.   בְּטֻמְאָתָם

טמן   pref. בְּ for בַּה)(Kal part. pass. sing. masc.   בַּטָּמוּן

בֶּטֶן m/f, feminine, dec. 6 a. (with suff. בִּטְנִי).—I. *belly.*—II. *womb*; פְּרִי בֶטֶן *fruit of the womb*, i. e. offspring; בַּר בִּטְנִי *mine own son*; בְּנֵי בִטְנִי *mine own children*.—III. *the inmost part*, spoken of the heart, the mind, also of שְׁאוֹל.—IV. *a protuberance* in a column, 1 Ki. 7. 20.—V. pr. name of a town in Asher, Jos. 19. 25.

בֶּטֶן masc. only pl. בָּטְנִים (§ 35. rem. 16) *pistachio nuts*, Ge. 43. 11.

בָּטְנִים (*pistachio nuts*) pr. name of a town in Gad, Jos. 13. 26.

בטן   for בֶּטֶן Seg. n. as if from [בֶּטֶן § 35. r. 2]

טנא   pref. בְּ for בַּה)(n. m. s. (suff. טַנְאֲךָ) d. 6 a.   בְּטַנְאֲךָ

בטן   noun f. s., suff. 3 pers. s. f. from בֶּטֶן d. 6 a.   בִּטְנָהּ

בטן   id., suff. 3 pers. sing. masc.   בִּטְנוֹ

בטן   יₐ id., suff. 1 pers. sing.; ı bef. labial   בִּטְנִי

בטן   ı pr. name of a place; ı id.   בְּטֹנִים

בטן   noun masc. pl. [of בֶּטֶן § 35. r. 16]   בָּטְנִים

בטן   noun fem., suff. 2 pers. s. m. fr. בֶּטֶן d. 6 a.   בִּטְנְךָ

בטן   id., suff. 2 pers. sing. fem.   בִּטְנֵךְ

בטן   יₐ id., suff. 3 pers. pl. masc.; ı bef. labial   בִּטְנָם

בטן   id., suff. 1 pers. pl.   בִּטְנֵנוּ

טעם   Chald. pref. בְּ bef. (:))(noun m. s. d. 3 a.   בְּטַעַם

טפף   pref. בְּ for בַּה)(noun m. s. for טַף d. 8 d.   בַּטָּף

טרם   Kh. בְּטֶרוֹם pref. בְּ)(adv., K. בְּטֶרֶם (q.v.)   בְּטְרוֹם

טרם   יₐ pref. בְּ)(adv.; ı bef. (:)   בְּטֶרֶם

I   particle of entreaty; always with אֲדֹנִי, אֲדֹנָי   *pray my Lord.* It is supposed to be contr. from בְּעִי *entreaty.* R. בָּעָה.   בִּי

ב   pref. prep. בְּ with suff. 1 pers. sing. (§ 5)   בִּי

יאר   pref. בְּ for בַּה)(noun masc. sing. d. 1 a.   בִּיאֹר / בַּיְאֹר

יאר   pref. id.)(id. pl. absolute   בַּיְאֹרִים

יבל   יₐ pref. id.)(noun m. s. d. 7 b; ı bef. lab.   בַּיֹּבֵל

יבש   pref בְּ)(pr. name of a place   בְּיָבֵשׁ

יבש   pref. בְּ [for בְּיָבֵשׁ, בְּיָ]; Kal inf. constr.   בִּיבֹשׁ

יבש   pref. בְּ for בָּה)(noun fem. sing.   בַּיַּבָּשָׁה

יבש   pref. בְּ)(pr. name of a place, ה parag.   בִּיבֵשָׁה

יבש   pref. בְּ for בָּה)(noun f. s. for יַבֶּשֶׁת   בַּיַּבֶּשֶׁת

ינה   pref. בְּ)(noun masc. sing. dec. 3 a.   בְּיָגֹון

יד   ı pref. id.)(noun com. s. d. 2 a; ı bef. (:)   בְּיָד

יד   ı pref. id.)(id., constr. st. (Ch. d. 2 a); ı id.   בְּיַד

יד   pref. id.)(id., suff. 3 pers. sing. fem.   בְּיָדָהּ

יד   Chald. pref. בְּ [for בְּיָדָהּ, בְּיָ]; noun fem. sing., suff. 3 pers. sing. fem. from יַד d. 2 a.   בִּידַהּ

יד   Chald. pref. בְּ)(id., suff. 3 pers. pl. masc.   בִּידְהֹם

יד   ı pref. בְּ)(noun com. sing., suff. 3 pers. sing. masc. from יַד dec. 2 a; ı bef. (:)   בְּיָדֹו

יד   pref. id.)(id., suff. 1 pers. sing.   בְּיָדִי

יד   pref. בְּ [for בְּיָדִי, בְּיָ])(id. du., constr. st.   בִּידֵי

יד   pref. בְּ)(id. du., suff. 3 pers. sing. fem.   בִּידֶיהָ

יד   pref. בְּ [f. בְּיָ, בְּיָדֵי])(id. du., suff. 3 p.pl.m.   בִּידֵיהֶם

יד   pref. id.)(id. du., suff. 3 pers. pl. fem.   בִּידֵיהֶן

יד   ı pref. בְּ)(id. du., suff. 3 pers. s. m.; ı bef. (:)   בְּיָדָיו

יד   pref. בְּ)(id. du., suff. 2 masc. (Kh. בְּיָדֶיךָ), K. בְּיָדֶךָ q.v.   בִּידֶיךָ

יד   ı pref. בְּ [for בְּיָ, בְּיָדֵי])(id. du. with suff. 2 pers. pl. masc.; ı bef. labial   בִּידֵיכֶם

יד   pref. בְּ)(id. du., absolute state   בְּיָדַיִם

יד   Chald. pref. בְּ [for בְּיָ, בְּיָדֵי]; noun fem., du. of יַד dec. 2 a.   בִּידַיִן

יד   pref. בְּ)(noun com. sing., suff. 2 pers. sing. masc. from יַד dec. 2 a; ı bef. (:)   בְּיָדְךָ / בְּיָדֶךָ

יד   pref. id.)(id., suff. 2 pers. sing. fem.   בְּיָדֵךְ

יד   Chald. pref. בְּ [for בְּיָדְךָ, בְּיָ]; noun fem sing., suff. 2 pers. sing. m. from יַד d. 2 a.   בִּידָךְ

ד   pref. בְּ)(noun com. sing., suff. 2 pers. pl. masc. from יַד dec. 2 a. (§ 31. rem. 2)   בְּיֶדְכֶם

יד   pref. id.)(id., suff. 2 pers. pl. fem.   בְּיֶדְכֶן

יד   pref. id.)(id., suff. 3 pers. pl. masc.   בְּיָדָם

יד   pref. id.)(id., suff. 1 pers. pl.   בְּיָדֵנוּ

הוה   pref. id.)(abbrev. from יְהֹוָה (q.v.).   בְּיָהּ

ידה   pref. בְּ, for [בְּיֶהוּד]; pr. name of a country   בִּיהוּד

ידה   ı pref. id.)(pr. name of a tribe and country   בִּיהוּדָה

הוה   ı pref. בְּ)(the most sacred name of God, with the vowels of (בַּ)אֲדֹנָי contr. בַּאדֹנָי, יהוה   בַּיהוָה

ידה   pref. בְּ, [for בִּיהוּדִי])(gent. n. m. fr. יהודה   בִּיהוּדִי

ידה   pref. בְּ for בָּה)(id. pl., Kh. דִים, K. דִּים   בַּיהוּדִים

הוה   pref. בְּ, [for בִּיהֹו])(pr. name masc.   בִּיהֹונָתָן

יסף   pref. id.; pr. name masc.   בִּיהֹוסֵף

הוה   pref. id.)(pr. name masc.   בִּיהֹושֻׁעַ

יהץ   pref. בְּ)(pr. name of a place   בִּיהְצָה

הוה   pref. id.)(pr. name masc.   בִּיוֹאָב

ᵃ Ezr. 5. 5.   ᵉ Le. 18. 28.   ʲ Pr. 13. 25.   ᵐ Ge. 43. 11.   ᵖ Da. 5. 2.   ʳ Le. 25. 31.   ˢ Ezr. 5. 8.   ᵛ 2 Ch. 6. 4.   ᵈ Pr. 30. 28.
ᵇ Ezr. 4. 23.   ᶠ Le. 15. 31.   ᵏ De. 26. 2.   Job 15. 35.   ᵖ Ru. 3. 14.   Is. 27. 11.   Eze. 23, 37, 45.   Jos. 10. 8.   Da. 2. 34, 35.
ᶜ Ezr. 4. 24.   ᵍ Ese. 24. 13.   ˡ Ps. 31. 10.   Ps. 44. 26.   Na. 3. 8.   Ex. 4. 9.   Ex. 17. 12.   Je. 44. 25.   Eze. 13. 21.
ᵈ De. 26. 14.   ʰ Job 40. 13.   ᵘ Nu. 31. 17.

בְּיוֹם	pref. בְּ f. בְּהַ
בְּיוֹם	pref. בְּ q. v. } n. com. s. irr. (§ 45); וּ bef. (:)

יוֹם

בְּיוֹמָא Chald. pref. id.)(id., emph. st.   יוֹם

בְּיוֹמוֹ pref. id.)(id., suff. 3 pers. sing. masc.   יוֹם

בְּיוֹמֵי Ch. pref. id.)(id. pl., constr. st., וּ bef. (:)   יוֹם

בְּיוֹמֵיהוֹן Ch. pref. id.)(id. pl., suff. 3 p. pl. m.; וּ id.   יוֹם

בְּיוֹמָם pref. id.)(id. sing., suff. 3 pers. pl. masc.   יוֹם

בְּיֵין pref. בְּ [for בְּיֵ, בְּיֵין]; noun masc. sing., constr. of יַיִן dec. 5a. (§ 34. rem. 1)   יין

בְּיוֹנָתָן pref. בְּ)(pr. name masc., see יְהוֹנָתָן   הוה

בְּיוֹשְׁבֵי pref. id.)(Kal part. act. pl. constr. masc. from יָשַׁב dec. 7b.; וּ bef. (:)   ישׁב

בְּיֶזַע pref. בְּ for בְּהַ)(noun masc. sing. for [יֶזַע]   יזע

בְּיִזְרְעֶאל pref. בְּ)(pr. name of a place   זרע

בְּיָטְבָתָה pref. id.)(pr. name of a place   יטב

בְּיַיִן	} pref. בְּ for בְּהַ
בַּיַּיִן	} noun m.s.dec.6h; וּ bef. lab.
בְּיַיִן	pref. בְּ q. v.

יין

בְּיַיִן pref. id.)(id. construct state; וּ id.   יין

בְּיֶלֶד pref. בְּ for בְּהַ)(n. m. s. (pl. c. יַלְדֵי) d. 6a.   ילד

בְּיַלְדוּתֶךָ pref. בְּ)(n. f. s., suff. 2 p.s.m.fr. יַלְדוּת d. 1b.   ילד

בְּיַלְדֵי pref. id.)(noun masc. pl. constr. from יֶלֶד dec. 6a.; וּ bef. (:)   ילד

בְּיִלְדֵי defect. for בְּיִלִידֵי (q. v.)   ילד

בְּיַלֶּדְכֶן pref. בְּ)(Piel inf. [יַלֵּד], suff. 2 pers. pl. masc. dec. 7b. (§ 16. rem. 15)   ילד

בְּילִידֵי pref. בְּ [for בְּיְ, בְּיִ], noun masc. pl. constr. from [יָלִיד] dec. 3a.   ילד

בְּיַלְקוּט pref. בְּ for בְּהַ)(noun masc. s.; וּ bef. lab.   לקט

בַּיָּם pref. בְּ for בְּהַ)(noun masc. sing. dec. 8a.   ים

בְּיָם pref. בְּ)(id., construct state   ים

בְּיָמַי	} pref. id.)(n. com. pl., suff. 1 p. s. [as if
בְיָמַי	} from יָם [יֵם] see יוֹם (§ 45)

יוֹם

בְּיְמֵי pref. בְּ [for בְּיְ, בְּיֵמֵי])(id. pl., constr. st.   יוֹם

בִּימֵיהֶם pref. id.)(id. pl., suff. 3 pers. pl. masc.   יוֹם

בְּיָמָיו pref. id.)(id. pl., suff. 3 pers. sing. masc.   יוֹם

בְּיָמֶיךָ pref. id.)(id. pl., suff. 2 pers. sing. masc.   יוֹם

בִּימֵיכֶם pref. בְּ [for בְּיְ, בְּיֵמֵי])(id.pl.,suff.2 p.pl.m.   יוֹם

בַּיָּמִים	pref. בְּ f. בְּהַ)(id., absolute state
בְּיָמִים	pref. בְּ q. v.

יוֹם

בַּיָּמִים pref. בְּ for בְּהַ)(noun masc., pl. of יָם dec. 8a.   ים

בְּיָמִין Kh. בְּיָמִין, K. מְיָמִין (pref. בְּ or מְ) n.m.s.d.3a.   ימן

בִּימִין pref. בְּ [for בְּיְ, בְּיָמִין])(id., construct state   ימן

בִּימִינָהּ pref. בְּ)(id., suff. 3 pers. sing. fem.   ימן

בִּימִינוֹ pref. id.)(id., suff. 3 pers. sing. masc.   ימן

בִּימִינִי pref. id.)(id., suff. 1 pers. sing.   ימן

בִּימִינֶךָ	} pref. id.)(id., suff. 2 pers. sing. masc.
בִּימִינְךָ	

ימן

בִּין, בּוּן I. *to distinguish, discern.*—II. *to mark, attend.*—III. *to understand, know;* const. with עַל, לְ, אֶל.—IV. abs. *to have understanding, be intelligent, wise.* Niph. i. q. Kal No. IV.; part. נָבוֹן *intelligent, discreet, knowing,* Pil. *to make to discern, to instruct,* De. 32. 10. Hiph. I. *to cause to understand, to explain, to teach.*—II. i. q. Kal No. I. II. III. const. with בְּ, אֶל, לְ; part. מֵבִין *intelligent, wise.* Hithpal. I. *to mark, attend to;* const. with עַד, עַל, בְּ, אֶל.—II. *to understand,* Job 26. 14.—III. *to be wise,* Ps. 119. 100.

בֵּין dec. 6h.—I. *interval, midst,* אִישׁ הַבֵּנַיִם *a middle man, umpire,* 1 Sa. 17. 4.—II. prep. *between, betwixt;* and *within,* of space and time. בֵּין—לְ, בֵּין—לְבֵין, בֵּין—וּבֵין *between—and,* sometimes also *whither—or;* אֶל־בֵּינוֹת and אֶל־בֵּין *between, among,* with motion implied; בְּבֵין *as among,* Is. 44. 4; עַל־בֵּין and מִבֵּינוֹת לְ *from between, out of;* מִבֵּין *among,* with motion implied.

בֵּין Chald. *between,* Da. 7. 5, 8.

בִּינָה fem. dec. 10, *understanding, intelligence, discernment, prudence.*

בִּינָה Chald. id. Da. 2. 21.

יָבִין (*whom He knows*) pr. name—I. of two Canaanitish kings.—II. Ju. 4. 2; Ps. 83. 10.

מְבוֹנִים masc. pl. *wisdom,* for concr. *wise teachers,* 2 Ch. 25. 3 Kheth.; Keri מְבִינִים.

תָּבוּן masc. d. 3a, *understanding, prudence,* Ho. 13. 2.

תְּבוּנָה fem. dec. 10. id.; also *intelligent words, or speeches,* Job 32. 11.

תּוּבְנָה id. Job 26. 12. Kheth.

בִּין וּ prep.; prop. constr. of [בַּיִן] dec. 6h.   בין

בִּין וּ Kal inf.abs. or imp.s.m. & pret. Da.10.1; וּ bef. lab.   בין

בִּינָה id. imp. sing. masc. with parag. ה   בין

בִּינָה וּ noun masc. sing. dec. 10; וּ bef. lab.   בין

בֵּינוֹ וּ prep. בֵּין [prop. from בַּיִן dec. 6h] with pl. suff. 3 pers. sing. masc. (§ 4. rem. 1)   בין

בֵּינוֹ id. sing., suff. 3 pers. sing. masc.   בין

בִּינוּ Kal imp. pl. masc.   בין

בֵּינוֹת prep.; pl. fem. of בֵּין, constr. of [בַּיִן] d. 6h.   בין

בִּינוֹת noun fem., pl. of בִּינָה dec. 10.   בין

בֵּינוֹתֵינוּ prep. בֵּין [prop. from בַּיִן dec. 6h] with pl. fem., suff. 1 pers. pl.   בין

---

a Da. 6. 11.   f 2 Ch. 20. 23.   l Eze. 27. 18.   p Is. 2. 6.   t 1 Sa. 17. 40.   x Je. 16. 9.   d Ki. 12. 10.   h Ps. 17. 7.   n Jos. 8. 11.
b Da. 5. 11.   g Eze. 44. 18.   m Da. 1. 8.   q 2 Sa. 21. 18.   u Ps. 116. 2.   y Ju. 18. 1.   e Is. 41. 10.   i Ps. 16. 11.   o Jos. 3. 4.
c Da. 2. 44.   h Est. 1. 10.   n Ge. 42. 22.   r Ex. 1. 16.   v Ps. 44. 2.   z Eze. 38. 17.   f Pr. 3. 16.   k Pr. 23. 1.   p Eze. 10. 3. 7.
d Ne. 9. 19.   i De. 14. 26.   o Ec. 11. 9.   s 2 Sa. 21. 16.   w 1 Ki. 11. 12.   a Da. 11. 20.   g Is. 44. 20.   l Ps. 5. 2.   p Is. 27. 11.
e Ps. 69. 3.   k Pr. 9. 5.

בִּינִי   id. sing. suff. 1 pers. sing. . . .   בין

בְּינֵיהוֹן   Chald. id. pl. masc. suff. 3 pers. pl. Kh. 'הוֹן masc., K. הֵן fem.   בין

בֵּינֵיהֶם   id. pl. masc., suff. 3 pers. pl. m.; ‍ bef. lab.   בין

בֵּינֵיכֶם   id. pl. masc., suff. 2 pers. sing. masc.; ‍ id.   בין

dd בֵּינֵיכֶם   id. pl. masc., suff. 2 pers. sing. masc.; ‍ id.   בין

בֵּינֵינוּ   id. pl. masc., suff. 1 pers. pl.   בין

בֵּינֶךְ   id. sing., suff. 2 pers. sing. fem.; ‍ bef. lab.   בין

kh בֵּינֶךָ / בֵּינֶךָ } id. sing., suff. 2 pers. sing. m.; ‍ bef. lab.   בין

בֵּינֵיכֶם   defect. for בֵּינֵיכֶם (q. v.) . . .   בין

בִּינַת   fl noun f. s., constr. of בִּינָה d. 10; ‍ bef. lab.   בין

בִּינַתִי   Kal pret. 1 pers. sing. . . .   בין

בֵּינֹתֵינוּ   prep. בֵּין [prop. from בַּין dec. 6h] with pl. fem. term. suff. 1 pers. pl.   בין

בִּינָתְךָ   noun f. sing., suff. 2 pers. s. m. fr. בִּינָה d. 10.   בין

בִּינַתְכֶם   id., suff. 2 pers. pl. masc.; ‍ bef. lab.   בין

בֵּינֹתָם   prep. בֵּין [prop. from בַּין dec. 6h] with pl. fem. term. suff. 3 pers. pl. masc. (§ 4. rem. 2)   בין

qq בִּיסְדוֹ   pref. בְּ)(Kal inf., suff. 3 pers. sing. masc.   יסד

uu בִּיסְדִי   pref. id.)(id., suff. 1 pers. sing.   יסד

בִּיעָרִים   pref. בַּ for בָּה Kh. 'יְעָרִים, noun masc., pl. [of יְעוֹר]; K. יְעָרִים, pl. of יַעַר dec. 6a.   יער

בִּיעֶזֶר   pref. בְּ)(pr. name of a place . . .   עזר

בִּיעַן   ‍ pref. id.)(prop. subst. used as a conj.   ענה

בִּיעַף   pref. בְּ [for בִּיעָף, 'בְּ]; noun masc. sing.   יעף

בִּיעֲקֹב   pref. בְּ)(pr. name masc. . . .   עקב

בִּיעַר / בִּיעַר } pref. בַּ for בָּה } noun masc. sing. dec. 6d. בִּיעַר   pref. בְּ q. v.   יער

בִּיעֲרָהּ   pref. id.)(id., suff. 3 pers. s. fem. (§ 35. r. 5)   יער

בִּיעֲרַת   pref. id.)(noun fem. sing., constr. of [יַעֲרָה comp. § 35. rem. 5] .   יער

בִּיפְיוֹ   pref. בְּ)(n. m. s., suff. 3 p. s.m. fr. [יְפִי] d. 6k.   יפה

בִּיפְיֵךְ   pref. id.)(id., suff. 2 pers. sing. m. [for יָפְיֵךְ]   יפה

בִּיפְיֵךְ   pref. id.)(id., suff. 2 pers. sing. fem.   יפה

בִּיצְחָק   pref. id.)(pr. name masc. . . .   צחק

בִּיצֵי   noun fem. with pl. masc. term., constr. st., from [בֵּיצָה] dec. 10.   בוץ

בֵּיצֶיהָ   id. pl., suff. 3 pers. sing. fem.   בוץ

בֵּיצִים   id. pl., absolute state   בוץ

בִּיצְקָתוֹ   pref. בְּ, [for 'בְּ, בִּיצְ]; noun fem. sing., suff. 3 pers. sing. masc. from [יְצָקָה] dec. 10.   יצק

aa בִּיקֶב   pref. בְּ)(noun masc. sing. (pl. c. [יִקְבֵי] d. 6a.   יקב

בִּיקָבִים   pref. בַּ for בָּה)(id. pl. absolute state   יקב

בִּיקַבְאֵל   ‍ pref. בְּ [for 'יְקַב]; pr. name of a place; ‍ bef. lab. . . . .   קבץ

בִּיקָר   pref. בְּ [for בִּיקָר, 'בְּ])(noun m. s. d. 1a.   יקר

בִּיקָרוֹ   pref. id.)(id. with suff. 3 pers. sing. masc.   יקר

בִּיקְרוֹתֶיךָ   pref. id., contr. for בִּיקְרוֹתֶיךָ)(adj. pl. fem. (constr. יְקָרוֹת dag. euph.), suff. 2 pers. sing. fem. from יְקָרָה dec. 11c. from יָקָר m.   יקר

a בִּירְאָה   pref. בְּ)(noun fem. sing. (no pl.)   ירא

בִּירְאַת   ‍ pref. id.)(id., construct state; ‍ bef.   ירא

בִּירְאָתְךָ   pref. id.)(id., suff. 2 pers. s. m., for יִרְאָתְךָ   ירא

בִּירְדֵּן   pref. בְּ for בְּה)(pr. name of a river .   ירד

בִּירָה fem. I. *castle, palace*.—II. *the temple*, 1 Ch. 29. 1. 19

בִּירָא Chald. dec. 8a. id. Ezr. 6. 2.

בִּירָנִית fem. only pl. בִּירָנִיוֹת (§ 39. No. 4. r. 1, note) *palaces*.

‍ בִּירוּשָׁלָה
‍ בִּירוּשָׁלַיִם
‍ בִּירוּשָׁלֵם
‍ בִּירוּשָׁלֵם } pref. בְּ)(pr. name of a place; ‍ bef. lab.   ‍דה

בִּירֶחַ   pref. בְּ)(noun masc. sing., dec. 6a. (pl. con. יַרְחֵי § 35. rem. 5) . . .   ירח

בִּירִיחוֹ
בִּירִיחוֹ } pref. בְּ [for 'בְּ]; pr. name of a place   רוח

בִּירִיעָה   pref. בַּ for בְּה)(noun fem. sing. dec. 10.   ירע

בִּירִיעֹת   pref. בְּ [for בִּירִי, 'בְּ])(id. pl.   דע

בִּירְכָתַיִם   pref. בְּ)(noun fem. sing. du. constr. [fr. יֶרֶךְ=יַרְכָה § 39. No. 3. rem. 3]   ירך

בַּירְכָתַיִם   pref. בַּ for בְּה)(n. f., du. of [יַרְכָה] d. 11c. K. בַּירְכָתַיִם id.; Kh. 'כָתַם sing. with suff. 3 pers. pl. masc. .   ירך

‍ בִּירְמוּת   pref. בְּ)(pr. name of a place; ‍ bef. (:)   ירם

בִּירְמְיָהוּ   pref. בְּ)(noun masc. sing. . . .   רמה

בִּירָנִיוֹת   noun fem. pl. [of בִּירָנִית § 39, No. 4. rem. 1]   ביר

בַּיֶּרֶק   pref. בַּ for בְּה)(noun m. sing.; ‍ bef. lab.   ירק

בִּירַקְרַק   pref. בְּ [for 'בְּ, בִּירַק]; noun masc. sing.   ירק

בִּישֵׁב   pref. בְּ)(Kal part. act. sing. masc. dec. 7b.   ישב

בִּישְׁבֵי   ‍ pref. id.)(id. pl., construct state; ‍ bef. (:)   ישב

h בִּישׁוּעָה   pref. בְּ [for 'בְּ, בִּישׁוּ])(noun fem. sing. d. 10.   ישע

בִּישׁוּעָתוֹ   pref. id.)(id., suff. 3 pers. sing. masc.   ישע

בִּישׁוּעָתִי   pref. id.)(id., suff. 1 pers. sing. .   ישע

בִּישׁוּעָתֶךָ
‍ בִּישֻׁעָתְךָ } pref. id.)(id., suff. 2 pers. sing. masc.; ‍ before labial   ישע

בִּישִׁימוֹן   pref. id.)(noun masc. sing. . . .   ישם

בִּישִׁישִׁים   pref. id.)(noun m., pl. of יָשִׁישׁ dec. 3a.   ישש

בִּישַׁע   pref. בְּ)(n. m. s., d. 6a. (suff. יִשְׁעִי § 35. r. 5)   ישע

בִּישֵׁר   ‍ pref. id.)(noun m. sing. dec. 6c.; ‍ bef. lab.   ישר

בִּישְׂרָאֵל   ‍ pref. id.)(pr. name of a people; ‍ id.   שהר

בִּישְׁרוּ   pref. id.)(n. m. s., suff. 3 p. s.m. fr. יֹשֶׁר d. 6c.   ישר

a Da. 7. 8.	e Pr. 30. 2.	i De. 4. 6.	m 2 Sa. 18. 6.	r Eze. 16. 14, 15.	u Is. 16. 10.	z Pr. 16. 6.	f Ps. 68. 14.	k Ps. 21. 2.
b Eze. 43. 8.	f Is. 29. 14.	k Eze. 34. 25.	n Je. 21. 14.	s Is. 59. 5.	v Ps. 49. 13, 21.	c Ps. 5. 8.	g Ge. 34. 30.	l Job 12. 12.
c Ru. 1. 17.	g Da. 9. 2.	l Eze. 36. 3.	o 1 Sa. 14. 27.	t Job 39. 14.	w Ps. 45. 10.	d Ex. 26 12.	h Ps. 149. 4.	m Pr. 14. 2.
d Is. 59. 2.	h Ju. 22. 34.	mm Da. 9. 21.	p 1 Ki. 7. 24.	u Ps. 2. 11.	x Ju. 7. 25.	e Eze. 46. 19.	i Ps. 91. 16.	

7

בֵּיתָה   *b 'ג* Chald. noun masc. sing. (for בַּיְתָא), emph. of בַּיִת irr. (§ 68) ; ג bef. labial .   בית

בַּיְתֵהּ   'ג Chald. id., suff. 3 per. sing. masc. ; ג id.   בית

בֵּיתָהּ   'ג noun masc. sing., suff. 3 pers. sing. fem. from בַּיִת irr. (§ 45) .   בית

בֵּיתָה   id., constr. state with paragogic ה   בית

בֵּיתוֹ   'ג id., suff. 3 pers. sing. masc. ; ג bef. labial   בית

בֵּיתִי   'ג id., suff. 1 pers. sing., ג id.   בית

בֵּיתְךָ   }   'ג id., suff. 2 pers. sing. masc. ; ג id.   בית
בֵּיתֶךָ   }

בֵּיתֵךְ   'ג id., suff. 2 pers. sing. fem. ; ג id.   בית

בֵּיתְכֶם   'ג id., suff. 2 pers. pl. masc. ; ג id.   בית

בֵּיתָם   id., suff. 3 pers. pl. masc.   בית

בִּיתָן   noun masc., constr. of [בִּיתָן] dec. 2 b.   בית

בְּיֶתֶר   pref. בְּ)(pr. name of a place   יתר

בְּיִתְרוֹ   *h 'ג* pref. id.)(noun masc. sing., (suff. יִתְרוֹ) dec. 6 a ; ג bef. (:)   יתר

בָּךְ   pref. prep. בְּ with suff. 2 pers. sing. fem. (§ 5)   ב

בְּךָ   [בָּךְ]   id., with suff. 2 pers. sing. masc. (§ 5) ;   ב

בָּךְ   'ג ג bef. (:), for ו see וְ .   }

בָּכָא Root not used ; i. q. בָּכָה *to weep.*

בָּכָא masc. dec. 4 a.—I. *a weeping*, only as a pr. name עֵמֶק הַבָּכָא (*valley of weeping*), a valley in Palestine, Ps. 84. 7.—II. the name of a *shrub* distilling a white sort of acrid gum.

בְּכָאִים   noun masc., pl. of בָּכָא dec. 4 a.   בכא

בִּכְבֵּד   pref. בְּ for בְּהַ)(noun masc. sing. dec. 5 a.   כבד

בִּכְבֵּדִי   pref. בְּ bef. (:))(noun masc. sing., suff. 1 pers. sing. from כָּבוֹד dec. 3 a .   כבד

בְּכֹבֶדֶת   pref. id.)(noun fem. sing.   כבד

בִּכְבוֹד   pref. בְּ)(noun masc. sing. dec. 3 a.   כבד

בִּכְבוֹדוֹ   pref. בְּ bef. (:))(id., suff. 3 pers. sing. masc.   כבד

בִּכְבוֹדָם   'ג pref. id.)(id., suff. 3 pers. pl. m. ; ג bef. lab.   כבד

בְּכַבֶּדְתְךָ   pref. בְּ)(Piel inf., suff. 2 pers. s. m., dec. 1 b.   כבה

בְּכַבֶּל   pref. בְּ for בְּהַ)(noun masc. sing. dec. 6 a.   כבל

בְּכַבְלֵי   pref. בְּ)(id. pl., constr. st.   כבל

בַּכְּבָרָה   pref. בְּ for בְּהַ)(noun fem. sing. .   כבר

בַּכְּבָשִׂים   pref. id.)(noun masc., pl. of כֶּבֶשׂ dec. 6 a.   כבש

בַּכַּד   pref. id.)(noun com. sing. dec. 8 d.   כדד

בָּכָה I. *to weep.*—II. *to mourn, lament ;* const. with acc., לְ, עַל, אֶל. Pi. *to mourn, deplore,* const. acc., עַל

בָּכֶה masc. *a weeping,* Ezr. 10. 1.

בְּכִי masc. dec. 6 i.—I. *a weeping, lamentation.*—II. *a dropping* or *trickling* of water, Job 28. 11.

בֹּכִים (*weepers*) pr. name of a place near Gilgal, Ju. 2. 1, 5.

בְּכוֹת   fem. *a weeping, mourning,* Ge. 35. 8.

בְּכִית   fem. dec. 1 a, id. Ge. 50. 4.

בָּכֹה   'ג Kal inf. abs. ; ג bef. lab.   בכה

בְּכָה   'ג 'ג pref. prep. בְּ with suff. 2 p. s. m. (§ 5) ; ג id.   ב

בֶּכֶה   'ג noun masc. sing. .   בכה

בָּכֹה   pref. בְּ)(adv. Je. 41. 6.   כה

בֹּכֶה   'ג Kal part. act. sing. masc. dec. 9 a ; ג bef. lab.   בכה

בַּכֹּהֲנִי   pref. בְּ)(n. m. pl. constr. from כֹּהֵן dec. 7 b.   כהן

בְּכֹהֲנָיו   pref. id.)(id. pl., suff. 3 pers. sing. masc.   כהן

בַּכֹּהֲנִים   'ג pref. בְּ for בְּהַ)(id. pl., abs. st. ; ג bef. lab.   כהן

בָּכוֹ   'ג Kal inf. abs. (§ 24. rem. 2) ; ג id. .   בכה

בָּכוּ   'ג 'ג id. pret. 3 pers. pl. ; ג id. .   בכה

בְּכוּ   'ג 'ג id. imp. pl. masc. ; ג id. .   בכה

בְּכוֹבָעִים   'ג pref. בְּ)(noun masc., pl. of כּוֹבַע dec. 2. (§ 31. rem. 5) .   כבע

בַּכּוֹכָבִים   'ג pref. בְּ for בְּהַ)(n. m., pl. of כּוֹכָב dec. 2 b.   כבב

בְּכוֹר   noun masc. sing. dec. 1.   כבר

בְּכוֹר   pref. בְּ)(pr. name in compos. כּוֹר עָשָׁן   כבר

בִּכּוֹר   *h* pref. id.)(noun masc. sing.   כבר

בְּכוֹרָה   'ג noun fem. sing. .   בכר

בְּכוֹרוֹ   n. m. s., suff. 3 pers. s. m. from בְּכוֹר dec. 1 a.   בכר

בְּכוֹרֵי   id. pl., constr. state   בכר

בְּכוֹרִי   id. sing., suff. 1 pers. sing.   בכר

בִּכּוּרֵי   *h 'ג* noun masc. pl. const. from [בִּכּוּר] dec. 1 b ; ג bef. lab.   בכר

בִּכּוּרֶיךָ   'ג id. pl., suff. 2 pers. sing. masc.   בכר

בִּכּוּרִים   'ג id. pl., absolute state   בכר

בְּכוֹרַת   pr. name masc.   בכר

בְּכוּשׁ   pref. בְּ)(pr. name of a country   כוש

בַּפּוֹשָׁרוֹת   *m* pref. בְּ for בְּהַ)(noun fem. pl. [of פּוֹשָׁרָה]   כשר

בָּכוּת   noun fem. sing.   בכה

בְּכַזֶּבְכֶם   'ג pref. בְּ)(Piel inf. [כַּזֵּב], suff. 2 p. pl. m. d. 7 b.   כזב

בְּכָזִיב   pref. בְּ bef. (:))(pr. name of a place   כזב

בְּכֹחַ   pref. בְּ f. [בְּהַ]   }   noun masc. sing. dec. 1 a.   כחח
בַּכֹּחַ   pref. בְּ q. v.   }

בְּכֹחוֹ   'ג pref. id.)(id., suff. 3 pers. sing. masc.   כחח

בְּכֹחִי   'ג pref. id.)(id., suff. 1 pers. sing. .   כחח

בְּכֹחֲךָ   'ג pref. id.)(id., suff. 2 pers. sing. masc.   כחח

בְּכַחַשׁ   'ג pref. id.)(noun masc. sing. dec. 6 d.   כחש

בְּכַחֲשֵׁיהֶם   'ג pref. id.)(id. pl., suff. 3 p. pl. m. ; ג bef. (:)   כחש

בֶּכִי   }   noun m. s. dec. 6 i (§ 35. rem. 14) ; ג id.   בכה
בְּכִי   'ג }

בַּכִּידוֹן   pref. בְּ for בְּהַ   }   noun masc. sing. ; ג id.   כיד
בְּכִידוֹן   'ג pref. בְּ q. v.   }

בְּכִיּוֹר   pref. בְּ for בְּהַ)(noun masc. sing. dec. 1 b.   כור

a Ezr. 6. 15.   *f* Est. 1. 15.   *l* Eze. 21. 26.   *p* Ps. 149. 8.   *v* Ezr. 10. 1.   *aa* Eze. 27. 31.   *ff* Is. 48. 10.   *ll* Ge. 35. 8.   *rr* Est. 4. 3.
b Ezr. 5. 12.   *g* Jos. 23. 12.   *m* Ex. 29. 43.   *q* Am. 9. 9.   *w* 1 Sa. 22. 17.   *bb* Je. 22. 10.   *gg* Mi. 7. 1.   *mm* Eze. 13. 19.   *ss* Jos. 8. 18, 12, 24.
c Jos. 2. 19.   *h* De. 28. 54.   *n* Ex. 14. 25.   *r* Nu. 15. 11.   *x* Ps. 99. 6.   *cc* Joel 1. 5.   *hh* Ne. 10. 36.   *nn* Je. 27. 5.   *tt* 1 Sa. 17. 45.
d 2 Ki. 8. 1.   *i* Nu. 21. 7.   *o* Is. 61. 6.   *s* 1 Ki. 17. 12.   *y* Ezr. 8. 15.   *dd* Je. 46. 4.   *ii* Le. 2. 14.   *oo* Ho. 12. 1.   *uu* 1 Sa. 2. 14.
Nu. 18. 31.   *k* 2 Sa. 5. 23.   *p* Ps. 105. 18.   *t* Ex. 7. 29.   *z* Je. 50. 4.   *ee* Is. 47. 13.   *kk* Ps. 68. 7.   *pp* Ho. 7. 3.   *vv* Eze. 32. 7.

7*

בִּכְיִי	noun m. s., suff. 1 pers. s. from בְּכִי dec. 6 i.	בכה
בֹּכִים	Kal part. act. m., pl. of בֹּכֶה d. 9 a. (also) pr. n.	בכה
בְּכֶינָה	id. imp. pl. fem.	בכה
בָּכִינוּ	id. pret. 1 pers. pl.	בכה
בַּכִּים	pref. בְּ for בְּהַ)(Kh. כִּים q. v., K. כּוּם (q. v.)	כום
בְּכִים	‖ pref. בְּ)(noun m. sing. dec. 1 a; ‖ bef. (ָ)	כום
בְּכִיסְךָ	pref. id.)(id., suff. 2 pers. sing. masc.	כום
בַּכִּישׁוֹר	pref. בְּ for בְּהַ)(noun masc. sing.	כשר
בְּכִיתוֹ	n. fem. s., suff. 3 p. s. m. from [בְּכִית] dec. 1 a.	בכה
בָּכִיתִי	Kal pret. 1 pers. sing.	בכה
בְּכִיתֶם	id. pret. 2 pers. pl. masc.	בכה
בְּכֶכֶר	pref. בְּ)(noun m. s., constr. of כִּכָּר dec. 2 b.	כרר
בְּכִכְּרַיִם	pref. id.)(id. dual, in the constr. for כִּכָּרַיִם	כרר
בַּכֹּל / בַּכָּל / בַּכֹּל	pref. בְּ for בְּהַ)(noun masc. sing. dec. 8 c; ‖ bef. (ָ) ‖ pref. בְּ q. v.	כלל
בְּכֶלֶב	pref. id.)(pr. name in compos. כָּלֵב אֶפְ׳	כלב
בְּכָלְהוֹן	Chald. pref. id.)(noun masc. sing., suff. 3 pers. pl. masc. (§ 61. rem.)	כלל
בִּכְלוֹת	pref. בְּ bef. (ָ))(Kal inf. constr.	כלה
בְּכַלּוֹתִי	pref. בְּ)(Piel inf., suff. 1 pers. sing. dec. 1 b.	כלה
בְּכַלּוֹתְךָ	pref. id.)(id., suff. 2 pers. sing. masc.	כלה
בְּכֶלַח	pref. id.)(noun masc. sing.	כלה
בִּכְלִי / בַּכְלִי	pref. בְּ for בְּהַ)(noun masc. sing. irr. (§ 45. & § 35. rem. 14)	כלה
בִּכְלֵי	‖ pref. בְּ bef. (ָ))(id. pl., constr. st.; ‖ bef. lab.	כלה
בַּכְלִי	‖ pref. id.)(id. sing., absolute state; ‖ id.	כלה
בִּכְלֵיהֶם	pref. id.)(id. pl., suff. 3 pers. pl. masc.	כלה
בְּכֵלָיו	‖ pref. id.)(id. pl., suff. 3 p. s. m.; ‖ bef. (ָ)	כלה
בִּכְלֵיכֶם	pref. id. bef. (ָ))(id. pl., suff. 2 pers. pl. m.	כלה
בַּכֵּלִים	pref. בְּ for בְּהַ)(id. pl., absolute state	כלה
בְּכִלְיֹתַי	pref. בְּ)(n. f. pl., suff. 1 p.s. fr. [כִּלְיָה] d. 12 b.	כלה
בְּכֻלָּם	pref. id.)(n. m. s., suff. 3 p. pl. m. fr. כֹּל (q.v.)	כלל
בַּכְּלִמָּה	pref. בְּ for בְּהַ)(noun fem. sing. dec. 10.	כלם
בָּכֶם	pref. prep. בְּ with suff. 2 pers. pl. m. (§ 5)	ב
בְּכֵן	‖ pref. בְּ)(adv.; ‖ bef. (ָ)	כון
בַּכְּבוֹר / בִּכְבוֹר	pref. בְּ f. בְּהַ)(noun masc. sing. d. 1 b; ‖ id. ‖ pref. בְּ q. v.	כנר
בְּכִמְעֲנִי	pref. בְּ for בְּהַ)(gent. n. fr. כְּמָן	כנע
בְּכַנְף	pref. בְּ bef. (ָ))(n. f. s., constr. of כָּנָף d. 4 a.	כנף
בִּכְנָפוֹ	pref. id.)(id., suff. 3 pers. sing. masc.	כנף
בְּכַנְפוֹת	pref. id.)(id. pl., constr. state (§ 33. rem. 1)	כנף
בְּכַנְפֵיהָ	pref. בְּ bef. (ָ))(id. du., suff. 3 pers. sing. f.	כנף
בְּכַנְפֵיהֶם	pref. id.)(id. du., suff. 3 pers. pl. m. (§33.r.1)	כנף

בִּכְנָפָיו	pref. בְּ bef. (ָ))(id. du., suff. 3 pers. s. m.	כנף
בִּכְנָפֶיךָ	pref. id.)(id. du., suff. 2 pers. sing. masc.	כנף
בִּכְנָפֶיךָ	pref. id.)(id. du., suff. 2 pers. sing. masc.	כנף
בְּכִנֹּרוֹת	‖ pref. בְּ)(noun masc. with pl. fem. term. from כִּנּוֹר dec. 1 b; ‖ before (ָ)	כנר
בַּכֶּסֶה	pref. בְּ for בְּהַ)(noun masc. s. [for כֶּסֶא]	כסא
בַּכְּסִילִים	pref. id.)(noun masc., pl. of כְּסִיל dec. 1 a.	כסל
בְּכִסְלֵו	pref. בְּ)(name of a month, see כִּסְלֵו *Zec. 7. 1.	כסל
בִּכְסָלֶךָ	pref. id.)(noun masc. sing., suff. 2 pers. sing. masc. from כֶּסֶל dec. 6 a.	כסל
בַּכֶּסֶף / בְּכֶסֶף / בְּכָסֶף / בְּכֶסֶף	pref. בְּ f. בְּהַ)(/ pref. בְּ q. v. — noun masc. sing. dec. 6 a. (§ 35. rem. 2); ‖ bef. lab.	כסף
בְּכַסְפָּא	Chald. pref. id.)(noun masc. sing., emph. of כְּסַף dec. 3 a.	כסף
בִּכְסִפְיָא	pref. id.)(pr. name of a place	כסף
בְּכַעַס	pref. id.)(noun masc. sing. dec. 6 d.	כעס
בְּכַעְסוֹ	pref. id.)(id., suff. 3 pers. sing. masc.	כעס
בַּכַּף / בְּכַף	pref. בְּ f. בְּהַ)(/ pref. בְּ q.v. — noun fem. sing. dec. 8 d.	כפף
בְּכַפּוֹ	pref. id.)(id., suff. 3 pers. sing. masc.	כפף
בְּכַפִּי / בְּכַפַּי	pref. id.)(id. du., suff. 1 p. s.; ‖ Der. (ָ)	כפף
בְּכַפִּי	pref. id.)(id. sing., suff. 1 pers. sing.	כפף
בְּכַפֵּיהֶם	pref. id.)(id. du., suff. 3 pers. pl. masc.	כפף
בַּכַּפִּים	‖ pref. בְּ for בְּהַ)(n. m. pl. [of כַּף]; ‖ bef. lab.	כף
בַּכְּפֹר	Kh. בְּכַפֹּר q. v., K. בַּכֹּר (q. v.)	כפף
בְּכַפְּךָ	pref. בְּ)(n. f. s., suff. 2 p.s. m. fr. כַּף d. 8 d.	כף
בַּכְּפֶל	pref. id.)(noun masc. s. (du. [כִּפְלַיִם]) d. 6 a.	כפל
בַּכָּפָן	‖ pref. id.)(noun masc. sing.; ‖ bef. (ָ)	כפן
בַּכְּפָר	pref. בְּ for בְּהַ)(noun masc. sing. dec. 6 c.	כפר
בְּכַפְּרִי	pref. בְּ)(Piel inf. (כַּפֵּר), suff. 1 pers. s. d. 7 b.	כפר
בַּכְּפָרִים	‖ pref. בְּ for בְּהַ)(n. m., pl. of [כָּפָר] d. 4 a.	כפר
בַּכְּפִירִים	pref. id.)(noun masc., pl. of כְּפִיר dec. 1 a.	כפר
בְּכַפֶּרְךָ	pref. בְּ)(Piel inf. (כַּפֵּר), suff. 2 pers. sing. masc. dec. 7 b. (§ 16. rem. 15)	כפר
בְּכַפְתֹּרֶיהָ	pref. id.)(noun masc. pl., suff. 3 pers. sing. fem. from כַּפְתֹּר dec. 1 b	כפתר

בָּכַר   Kal not used; Arab. *to be early.* Pi—1. *to bear early fruit,* Eze. 47. 12.—II. *to constitute* (one) *first-born,* De. 21. 16.

בֶּכֶר   masc. dec. 6 b, *a young camel,* Is. 60. 6.

ᵃ Ps. 6.9.   ᵇ Pr. 31. 19.   ᶜ Pr. 5. 11.   ᵈ 1 Ki. 19. 21.   ᵉ Is. 45. 16.   ᶠ Eze. 5. 3.   ᵍ Ps. 31. 10.   ʰ Je. 4. 29.   ⁱ Eze. 16. 63.

ᵏ 2 Sa. 1. 24.   ˡ Ge. 50. 4.   ᵐ Eze. 5. 13.   ⁿ Jos. 7. 11.   ᵒ Ge. 31. 27.   ᵖ Ps. 81. 4.   ᵠ 1 Ki. 15. 30.   ʳ Eze. 29. 7.   ˢ Ca. 7. 12.

ᵗ Ps. 137. 1.   ᵘ Job 30. 25.   ᵛ Eze. 43. 23.   ʷ Nu. 4. 16.   ˣ Hag. 2. 12.   ʸ Pr. 3. 26.   ᶻ Eze. 21. 16.   ᵃ Eze. 6. 11.   ᵇ 1 Ch. 27. 25.

ᶜ Pr. 23. 31.   ᵈ Nu. 11. 18.   ᵉ Job 5. 26.   ᶠ 1 Ch. 23. 5   ᵍ Job 38. 13.   ʰ Is. 48. 10.   ⁱ 1 Ch. 12. 17.   ᵏ Job 41. 5.   ˡ Ne. 6. 2.

ᵐ Mi. 6. 11.   ⁿ 1 Ki. 16. 24.   ᵒ 1 Sa. 21. 6.   ᵖ La. 3. 13.   ᵠ Le. 1. 17.   ʳ Da. 11. 38.   ˢ 1 Ch. 12. 2.   ᵗ Job 30. 3.   ᵘ Ex. 29. 36.

ᵛ De. 25. 13.   ʷ Da. 2. 38.   ˣ 1 Ki. 17. 10   ʸ Ec. 11. 8.   ᶻ Je. 2. 34.   ᵃ Ezr. 7. 17.   ᵇ Job 31. 7.   ᶜ Ge. 6. 14.   ᵈ Zep. 2. 14.

בֶּכֶר (*young camel*) pr. name.—I. of a son of Ephraim, Nu. 26. 35. Gent. n. בַּכְרִי ibid.—II. of a son of Benjamin, Ge. 46. 21.

בִּכְרָה fem. *a young she-camel*, Je. 2. 23.

בִּכְרִי (*juvenile*) pr. name masc. 2 Sa. 20. 1.

בִּכּוּר masc. dec. 1 b. *first-fruit*, in the sing. only Is. 28. 4; יוֹם הַבִּכּוּרִים *the feast of the first-fruits, Pentecost.*

בַּכּוּרָה, בִּכּוּרָה (Je. 24. 2) f. *the early fig*, Ho. 9. 10; Mi. 7. 1.

בְּכוֹר masc. dec. 1 a.—*the first-born, firstling*, both of man and beast; בְּכוֹרֵי דַלִּים *the first-born of the poor*, i.e. *the poorest*; בְּכוֹר מָוֶת *mortal disease.*

בְּכֹרָה, בְּכוֹרָה fem. dec. 10.—I. *first-born, firstling* both of man and beast.—II. *earlier birth, primogeniture*; מִשְׁפַּט הַבְּכֹרָה *birth-right.*

בְּכֹרַת (*primogeniture*) pr. name m. 1 Sa. 9. 1.

בְּכִיר masc. adj., only fem. *first-born daughter.*

בְּכֹרוֹ (for בְּכֹר הוּא *he is the first-born*) pr. n. m.

בֶּכֶר in pause for בֶּכֶר (q. v.) . . בכר

בְּכַר pref. בְּ ✗ noun masc. sing. d. 8. (§ 37. r. 7) בכר

בֶּכֶר ן pr. name masc.; for ן see lett. . בכר

בְּכֹר noun masc. sing. dec. 1 a. for בְּכוֹר בכר

בְּכֹרָה noun fem. sing. dec. 10. for בְּכוֹרָה בכר

בִּכְרָה noun fem. sing. . . . בכר

בְּכֹרוֹ noun m. s., suff. 3 pers. s. m. fr. בְּכוֹר d. 1 a. בכר

בִּכְרוּ proper name masc. . . . בכר

בְּכֹרוֹת noun fem., pl. of בְּכוֹרָה dec. 10. . בכר

בְּכֹרִי noun m. s., suff. 1 pers. sing. fr. בְּכוֹר d. 1 a. בכר

בִּכְרֵי noun masc. pl. constr. from [בֶּכֶר] dec. 6 b. בכר

בִּכְרִי pr. name of a man.

בְּכֹרִים pref. בְּ ✗ n. m. pl. [f. כָּרִים] fr. כַּר d. 8. (§ 37. r. 7) כרר

בְּכֹרְךָ } n. m. s., suff. 2 pers. s. m. fr. בְּכוֹר d. 1 a. בכר
בְּכֹרֶךָ }

בְּכַרְכְּמִישׁ } pref. בְּ ✗ pr. name of a place . כרד
בְּכַרְכְּמִישׁ }

בַּכֶּרֶם pref. בַּ for בְּהַ ✗ noun f. pl.; ו bef. labial כרד

בִּכְרָמוֹת pref. בְּ ✗ n. m. s. d. 6 a. (see the foll.); ו bef. כרם
בַּכְרָמִים

בַּכְרָמִים pref. id. ✗ id pl., constr. state

בַּכַּרְמִיל pref. בַּ f. בְּהַ ✗ n. m. s.; ו bef. lab. see כַּרְמֶל

בַּכְרָמִים pref. id. ✗ noun masc., pl. of כֶּרֶם, (suff. כַּרְמִי) dec. 6 a.; ו id.

בַּכַּרְמֶל pref. id. ן noun masc. sing. dec. 8 b. (§ 37.
בְּכַרְמֶל בְּ pref. } rem. 5) also pr. name; ו id.

בִּכְרֹת pref. בְּ bef. (:) ✗ Kal inf. constr. with Mak. for כְּרֹת (§ 8. rem. 18) . . כרת

בְּכֹרֹת ו adj. fem., pl. of בְּכוֹרָה dec. 10; ו bef. (:) בכר

בְּכֹרָתוֹ noun f. s., suff. 3 pers. s. m. fr. בְּכוֹרָה d. 10. בכר

בְּכֹרָתִי id. id., suff. 1 pers. sing. . . בכר

בְּכָרְתִי pref. בְּ ✗ Kal inf., suff. 1 pers. sing. . כרת

בְּכֹרָתְךָ noun f. s., suff. 2 pers. s. m. fr. בְּכוֹרָה d. 10. בכר

בַּכְּשָׂבִים pref. בְּ f. בְּהַ ✗ noun m., pl. of כֶּשֶׂב d. 6 a. כשׂב

בַּכָּשִׁיל pref. בְּ ✗ noun masc. sing כשׁל

בְּהִכָּשְׁלוֹ ו pref. בְּ [for בְּהִכָּשְׁלוֹ § 10. r. 6]; Niph. inf.
[הִכָּשֵׁל], 3 pers. s. m. d. 7 b; ו bef. lab. כשׁל

בְּכִשְׁפֶיהָ pref. בְּ bef. (:) ✗ noun masc. pl., suff. 3 pers. sing. fem. from [כֶּשֶׁף] dec. 6. כשׁף

בְּכִשְׁרוֹן ו pref. בְּ ✗ noun masc. s.; ו bef. lab. כשׁר

בִּכְתָב ו pref. בְּ bef. (:) ✗ noun m. s. d. 1 a; ו id. כתב

בְּכָתְבוֹ pref. בְּ ✗ Kal inf., suff. 3 pers. sing. masc. כתב

בַּכְּתֻבִים pref. בַּ for בְּהַ ✗ id. pt. p. m., pl. of כָּתוּב d. 3 a. כתב

בְּכָתְבָהּ ו Kal pret. 3 pers. sing. fem.; ו bef. labial כתה

בְּכָתוֹב pref. בְּ bef. (:) ✗ Kal inf. constr. . כתב

בְּכָתְלַיָּא Chald. pref. בְּ ✗ noun masc. pl. emph. [from כֹּתֶל § 59 b] . . . . כתל

בְּכֶתֶם pref. id. ✗ noun masc. sing. . . כתם

בְּכֻתֳנֹתָם pref. בְּ ✗ noun fem. pl., suff. 3 pers. pl. masc. [from כֻּתֹּנֶת dec. 13 c. § 44. No. 2] . כתן

בַּכָּתֵף pref. בַּ for בְּהַ ✗ } noun f. s. dec. 5 b; ו bef. (:) כתף
בְּכָתֵף ו pref. בְּ q. v. }

בְּכֻתֳּתָם pref. בְּ bef. (:) ✗ id., suff. 3 pers. pl. masc. כתף

בְּכֶתֶר pref. בְּ ✗ noun masc. sing. . . כתר

בַּל Chald. masc. *the heart*, Da. 6. 15.

בַּל ו adv.; ו before labial . . . בלה

בֵּל proper name of an idol . . . בעל

בְּלֹא pref. בְּ ✗ adv. . . . . לא

בַּלְאֲדָן pr. name masc. . . . בעל

בַּלְאֵט pref. בַּ for בְּהַ ✗ prop. Kal part., with the pref. as an adv. . . . לוט

בַּלְאֻמִּים pref. id. ✗ noun masc., pl. of לְאֹם dec. 8 c. לאם

בְּלֵב ו pref. בְּ ✗ n. masc. sing. dec. 8 b. (comp.
בְּלֶב § 36. rem. 3); ו bef. (:) } לבב

בִּלְבַב ו pref. id. ✗ noun masc. sing. dec. 4 b; ו id. לבב

בִּלְבַב pref. בְּ bef. (:) ✗ id., construct state לבב

בִּלְבָבָהּ pref. id. ✗ id., suff. 3 pers. sing. fem. . לבב

בִּלְבָבוֹ ו pref. id. ✗ id., suff. 3 p. s. m.; ו bef. lab. לבב

בִּלְבָבִי pref. id. ✗ id., suff. 1 pers. sing. . לבב

בִּלְבָבֶךָ } pref. id. ✗ id., suff. 2 p. s. m.; ו bef. lab. לבב
בִּלְבָבְךָ }

בִּלְבָבֵךְ pref. id. ✗ id., suff. 2 pers. sing. fem. . לבב

בִּלְבַבְכֶם pref. id. ✗ id., suff. 2 pers. pl. masc. . לבב

a Ge. 31. 34.   f Eze. 27. 21.   k Ca. 1. 14.   p Is. 32. 16.   u Ge. 25. 31.   z Ec. 2. 21.   e De. 21. 13.   i Is. 11. 14.   t Ju. 4. 21.
b Ge 25. 32.   g Ge. 27. 32.   l Is. 66. 20.   q 1 Sa. 22. 8.   v Ps. 74. 6.   a Eze. 13. 9.   f Ps. 87. 6.   k Jon. 2. 4.
c Je. 2. 23.   h Is. 1. 8.   m Ju. 21. 20.   r Ge. 27. 36.   w Je. 45. 1.   b Ezr. 5. 8.   g 1 Ch. 15. 15.   l Da. 8. 25.
d Ne. 10. 37.   i Is. 16. 10.   n 1 Sa. 24. 12.   s Pr. 24. 17.   x Na. 3. 4.   c Nu. 11. 26.   h Le. 10. 5.   m De. 30. 14.
e Is. 60. 6.

בִּלְבָבָם   pref. id.)(id., suff. 3 pers. pl. masc.   .   לבב

בִּלְבָּה   pref. בְּ)(noun masc. sing., suff 3 pers. sing. fem. from לֵב dec. 8 b.   .   .   לבב

בִּלְבָבוֹ   pref. id.)(id., suff. 3 pers. sing. masc.   לבב

בִּלְבוֹנָה   pref. בְּ bef. (:))(noun fem. sing. dec. 10.   .   לבן

בִּלְבוּשׁ   pref. id.)(noun masc. sing. dec. 1 a.   .   לבש

בִּלְבוּשׁוֹ   pref. id.)(id., suff. 3 pers. sing. masc.   לבש

בִּלְבוּחָם   pref. בְּ)(noun fem., pl. of [לְבָּה] dec. 10.   לבב

בִּלְבִּי   pref. id.)(noun masc. sing., suff. 1 pers. sing. from לֵב dec. 8 b, Chald. dec. 5 b.   .   לבב

בִּלְבָבְךָ   pref. id.)(id., suff. 2 pers. sing. m., for לִבְבְךָ   לבב

בִּלְבָבֵךְ   pref. id.)(id., suff. 2 pers. sing. fem.   לבב

בִּלְבָבְכֶם   pref. id.)(id., suff. 3 pers. pl. masc.   לבב

בִּלְבָן   pref. id.)(pr. name masc.   .   .   לבן

בִּלְבָנָה   pref. id.)(pr. name of a place   .   לבן

בַּלְּבָנוֹן   pref. בְּ for בְּהַ)(pr. n. of a region; ₁ bef. lab.   לבן

בַּלְּבֵנִים   pref. בְּ bef. (:))(n. fem. with pl. m. term. from לְבֵנָה d. 11 c. (§ 42. r. 4); ₁ bef. lab.   לבן

בִּלְבֻשֵׁיהֶם   pref. id.)(noun masc. pl., suff. 3 pers. pl. masc. from לְבוּשׁ dec. 1 a.   .   לבש

בְּלַבַּת   pref. בְּ)(noun fem. sing., constr. of [לַבָּה] contr. for [לְהָבָה]   .   .   להב

בָּלַג   Kal not used; Arab. to open; to shine; hence Hiph.—I. to open, or cause to break out, upon, with עַל, Am. 5. 9.—II. to make cheerful, to enliven, with פָּנִים the face, also without it, to be cheerful, glad.

בִּלְגָּה   (joy) pr. name masc. Ne. 12. 5, 18, written בִּלְגַּי chap. 10. 9.

מַבְלִיגִית   fem. exhilaration, cheerfulness, Je. 8. 18.

בִּלְגָּה   pr. name masc.   .   .   .   בלג

בִּלְגַּי   pr. name masc.   .   .   .   בלג

בִּלְדַּד   (for בֶּן־לָדַד son of strife, לדד Arab. to strive, see בְּלָשָׁן) pr. n. of a friend of Job; ₁ bef. lab.

בְּלֶדֶת   pref. בְּ)(Kal inf. constr. dec. 13 b.   .   ילד

בְּלִדְתָּהּ   pref. id.)(id., suff. 3 pers. sing. fem.   ילד

בִּלָּה   Pi. to harass, trouble, Ezr. 4. 4. Keri.

בַּלָּהָה   fem. dec. 11 a.—I. terror.—II. calamity.

בִּלְהָה   (feebleness) pr. name—I. of a hand-maid of Rachel.—II. of a place in the tribe of Simeon, 1 Ch. 4. 29, comp. בַּעֲלָה.

בִּלְהָן   (feeble) pr. name masc.—I. Ge. 36. 27.—II. 1 Ch. 7. 10.

[בָּלָה]   I. to grow old.—II. to waste away.   Pi. to cause to waste away, to consume.

בַּלָּא   Pa. to destroy, Da. 7. 25.

בָּלֶה   masc. dec. 9, adj., fem. בָּלָה; old, worn out.

בָּלָה   pr. name of a place, Jos. 19. 3, for בַּלְהָה q.v.

בְּלוֹ   Chald. masc. custom, tax.

בְּלֹאי & בְּלוֹי   masc. only pl. com. (like פְּתָיִים for פְּתָאִים) old clothes, rags.

בַּל   adv.—I. not.—II. nothing.

בְּלִי   masc.—I. consumption, destruction, Is. 38. 17. —II. want, only adverbially, not; without; בִּבְלִי, לִבְלִי without; מִבְּלִי because not; lit. from want of; עַד בְּלִי as long as, lit. until the wanting of; עַל בְּלִי because not, Ge. 31. 20.

בְּלִימָה   (compounded of בְּלִי & מָה not any thing) nothing, Job 26. 7.

בְּלִיַּעַל   (compounded of בְּלִי without, and יַעַל use).—I. worthlessness.—II. wickedness, אִישׁ בְּ a wicked man; also ellipt. without אִישׁ.—III. injury, destruction.

בִּלְעֲדֵי   (compounded of בַּל not, and עֲדֵי to, R. עָדָה), also בַּלְעֲדֵי, with suff. בַּלְעֲדַי, בִּלְעֲדֶיךָ.—I. not, or nothing to, as far as regards Ge. 14. 24; 41. 16.—II. besides, without.

בֵּלֶת, with suff. בִּלְתֶּךָ, בִּלְתִּי only Ho. 13. 4, & 1 Sa. 2. 2, elsewhere בִּלְתִּי with parag. Yod.—I. adv. not, 1 Sa. 20. 26.—II. without, besides.—III. conj. besides that; except that, unless; בִּלְתִּי אִם unless it be that; לְבִלְתִּי chiefly as the negation before an inf. (בִלְתִּי לֶאֱכֹל for לְבִלְתִּי אֱכֹל not to, so that not; מִבִּלְתִּי because not; עַד בִּלְתִּי until not; so long as.

אֲבָל   adv.—I. nay indeed, nay rather.—II. truly, certainly.—III. but, yet, nevertheless.

תַּבְלִית   fem. dec. 1 b, destruction, Is. 10. 25.

בָּלָה   ₁ pr. name of a place, contr. for בַּלְהָה; ₁ bef.lab.   בלה

בִּלָּה   Piel pret. 3 pers. sing. masc.   .   .   בלה

בְּלַהַב   pref. בְּ)(noun masc. sing. dec. 6 d.   .   להב

בְּלֶהָבָה   ₁ pref. id.)(n. fem. sing. dec. 11 a ; ₁ bef. (:)   להב

בְּלַהֲבֵי   pref. id.)(n. m. pl. constr. from לַהַב dec. 6 d.   להב

בַּלָּהָה   noun fem. sing. dec. 11 a.   בלה

בִּלְהָה   pr. name fem.   .   .   בלה

בַּלָּהוֹת   noun fem. pl., of בַּלָּהָה dec. 11 a.   בלה

בַּלָּהוֹת   id. pl., construct state   .   .   בלה

בְּלַהֲטֵיהֶם   pref. בְּ)(noun masc. pl. with suff. for לַהֲטֵיהֶם (comp. Ex. 7. 22). R. לוט, or from לַהַט.   להט

בלהן	pr. name masc. . . . . בלה
בלהו	Kal pret. 3 pers. pl. . . . . בלה
בלהו	Chald. noun masc. sing. . . בלה
בלו	pref. בְּ ‖ pr.n. in compos., see לֹא דָבָר, לוֹ דָבָר
בלוא	pref. בְּ ‖ adv. more frequently לֹא'; ‖ bef., לא
for בְּלוֹאֵי, בְּלוֹאֵי like פְּתָאִים for פְּתַיִם (§35.r.15) בלה
בלוז	pref. בְּ ‖ pr. name of a place . . לוז
בלוט	pref. id. ‖ pr. name masc. . . לוט
בלוי	‖ noun masc. pl. constr. [for בְּלוֹיֵי from comp. § 3. rem. 1]; ‖ bef. . . בלה
בלוים	pref. בְּ for בְּהַ ‖ patronym., pl. of לֵוִי dec. 8f. לוה
בלול	Kal part. pass. sing. masc. . . בלל
בלולה	id. fem. dec. 10. . . . בלל
בלולים	‖ pref. בְּ ‖ noun m., pl. of [לוּל]; ‖ bef. לול
בלולת	Kal part. pass. fem., pl. of בְּלוּלָה dec.10. from בָּלַל masc. בלל
בלות	adj. fem., pl. of בָּלָה, fr. [בָּלֶה] masc. בלה
בלחמו	pref. בְּ bef. ‖ noun masc. sing., suff. 3 pers. sing. masc. from [לָחוּם] לחם
בלחי	pref. בְּ for בְּהַ ‖ pr. name of a place, for לֶחִי (§ 35. rem. 14) לחה
בלחי	pref. בְּ bef. ‖ noun masc. sing. dec. 6 i. (§ 35. rem. 14. & 15) . . לחה
בלחייך	pref. id. ‖ id. du. (לְחָיַיִם) with suff. 2 p. s. m. לחה
בלחם, בלחם, בלחם	pref. בְּ for בְּהַ ‖ noun com. sing. dec. 6a; ‖ bef. lab pref. בְּ q. v. לחם
בלחמו	pref. id. ‖ id., suff. 3 pers. sing. masc. . לחם
בלחמי	pref. id. ‖ id., suff. 1 pers. sing. . לחם
בלחמך	pref. id. ‖ id., suff. 2 pers. s. m. from לחם'לַחְמְ
בלחי, בלחץ	pref. בְּ f. בְּהַ ‖ noun masc. sing. dec. 6d. pref. בְּ q. v. לחץ
בלט	pref. בְּ for בְּהַ ‖ prop. Kal part., with the pref. as an adv. . לוט
בלטיהם	pref. בְּ ‖ id. as a subst. pl., suff. 3 pers. pl. m. לוט
בלטשאצר, בלטשאצר	pr. name given to Daniel at the court of Nebuchadnezzar.
בלי	Kh. בלי q. v., K. בַּל q. v. . . בלה
בלי	noun masc. sing. (Is. 38. 17), otherwise adv. בלה
בלי	pref. בְּ for בְּהַ ‖ Kh. לֵיל noun masc. sing. dec. 6h, K. בַּלַּיְלָה (q.v.) ליל
בלי	pref. בְּ ‖ id., constr. state . . ליל
בלי	noun masc. sing. dec. 1a. בלל

בלילה, בלילה	pref. בְּ f. בַּהַ ‖ noun m. s. לַיִל d. 6h) with parag. ה; ‖ bef. lab. ליל
בלילה	pref. בְּ q. v.
בלילו	noun m. s., suff. 3 pers. s. m. fr. בְּלִיל d. 1a. בלל
בלילות	pref. בְּ for בְּהַ ‖ noun masc. with pl. fem. term. from לַיִל dec. 6h. . . ליל
בליליא	Chald. pref. בְּ ‖ noun m. s. emph., [fr. לֵילְ] ליל
בלים	adj. masc., pl. of [בָּלֶה] dec. 9b. בלה
בלימה	compound of בְּלִי & מָה see בלה
בליעל, בליעל	noun m. s., compound of בְּלִי & יַעַל see בלה
בלכת	‖ pref. בְּ ‖ Kal inf. constr. dec. 13. (§ 44. rem. 3) ; ‖ bef. ילך
בלכתו	pref. id. ‖ id., suff. 3 pers. sing. masc. . ילך
בלכתך	‖ pref. id. ‖ id., suff. 2 pers. s. m.; ‖ bef. ילך
בלכתם	‖ pref. id. ‖ id., suff. 3 pers. pl. masc.; ‖ id. ילך
בלכתן	pref. id. ‖ id., suff. 3 pers. pl. fem. . [ילך]

בָּלַל I. to suffuse, Ps. 92. 3.—II. to mingle, mix, confound.—III. to give fodder, Ju. 19. 21, denom. of בְּלִיל. Hithpo. to mix oneself, to be mixed, Ho. 7.8. בָּבֶל (for בַּלְבֵּל confusion) Babylon; also used for the kingdom of Babylon, Babylonia.

בַּבְלַי Chald. only pl. emph. בָּבְלָיֵא Babylonians, Ezr. 4. 9.

בְּלִיל masc. dec. 1a, mixed provender, fodder.

תֶּבֶל masc. mixture or confusion of species by bestiality, or of relation by incest.

תְּבַלֻּל masc. son... disorder or blemish in the eye, Le. 21. 20.

בַּלְאֹת pref. בְּ for בְּהַ ‖ noun pl. fem. defect. [for לֻלְאֹת fr. לוּלִי comp. § 35. r. 15, note] ליל

[בָּלַם] to bind, to bridle, Ps. 32. 9.

בלמדי pref. בְּ ‖ Kal inf., suff. 1 pers. sing. למד

בלמדי pref. id. ‖ adj. masc. pl., suff. 1 pers. sing. fr. לָמֵד dec. 1 b. . . למד

[בָּלַס] to pluck or gather figs, Am. 7. 14.

בָּלַע I. to swallow.—II. to consume, to destroy. Niph. to be swallowed up, lost. Pi. i. q. Kal. Pu. to be destroyed, to perish. Hithpa. id.
בֶּלַע m. d. 6a.(§35.r.5) with suff. בִּלְעִי—I. a thing swallowed, Je. 51. 44.—II. destruction, Ps. 52. 6.—

Is. 55. 1.   1 Ki 6. 8.   Ge. 47. 19.   Pr. 9. 5.   Ho. 9. 16.   Is. 28. 19.   Job 26. 7.   Ex. 26. 11.   Is. 8. 16.
Je. 38. 12.   Jos. 9. 5.   Le. 8. 32.   Ju. 13. 16.   Is. 15. 1.   Da. 5. 30.   2 Ch. 24. 25.   Ps. 119. 7.   Job 20. 15.
Je. 38. 11, 11.   Job 20. 23.   Ne. 5. 15.   Job 36. 15.   Is. 30. 24.   Jos. 9. 4.   Ge. 11. 9.   Ju. 15. 16, 16.   Eze. 1. 9, 12, 17.

III. pr. name (a) of a city near the Dead sea. Gent. n. בַּלְעִי ; (b) of a man.

בִּלְעָם (for בָּלַע עָם *wasting of the people*) pr. name.—I. of the prophet Balaam.—II. of a city in Manasseh, called also יִבְלְעָם (for יִבְלַע עָם

בָּלַע [for בֶּלַע] noun m. s., (suff. בִּלְעוֹ) dec. 6a. — בלע

בַּלַּע Piel imp. sing. masc. — בלע

בֶּלַע pr. name of a man and city — בלע

בָּלַע id. pret. 3 pers. sing. masc.; bef. labial — בלע

בִּלְעֲגֵי pref. בְּ X adj. pl. const. masc. fr. [לָעֵג] d. 5. — לעג

בִּלְעָדַי } the following with suff. 1 pers. sing.
בִּלְעָדֵי }

adv., in form pl. constr., compound of בַּל & עַד see — בלה

בִּלְעָדֶיךָ id. with suff. 2 pers. sing. m.; bef. lab. — בלה

בִּלְעָה Kal pret. 3 pers. sing. fem.; bef. lab. — בלה

בִּלְעוֹ noun masc. sing., suff. 3 pers. sing. masc. fr. [בֶּלַע] dec. 6a. (§ 35. rem. 5) — בלע

בִּלְעוּ Piel pret. 3 p. pl. [for בִּלְּעוּ comp. § 8. r. 7] — בלע

בְּלָעוּנוּ Kal pret. 3 pers. pl., suff. 1 pers. pl. — בלע

בַּלְּעִי id. inf. [בַּלַּע], suff. 1 pers. sing. (§ 16. r. 10) — בלע

בִּלְעֲךָ pref. בְּ X noun masc. sing., suff. 2 pers. sing. m. [for לְעֲךָ fr. לֹעַ] — לוע

בִּלְעָם pr. name masc.; bef. lab. — בלע

בְּלָעֵנוּ Kal pret. 3 pers. sing. masc., suff., Kh. עָנוּ 1 pers. pl., K. עָנִי 1 pers. sing. — בלע

בִּלַּעְנוּ Piel pret. 1 p. pl. [for בִּלַּעְנוּ comp. § 8. r. 7] — בלע

בִּלְּעָנֻהוּ id., suff. 3 pers. sing. masc. — בלע

בַּלַּפִּדִים } pref. בְּ for בְּהַ X noun masc., pl. of [לַפִּיד] dec. 1b. — לפד
בַּלַּפִּידִים }

[בָּלַק] to empty out, make waste, Is. 24. 1. Pu. to be made waste, Na. 2. 11. Hence

בָּלָק (empty) pr. name of a king of Moab in the time of Moses — בלק

בֵּלְשַׁאצַּר pr. name of the last of the Chaldean kings, written בֵּלְאשַׁצַּר in Da. 7. 1.

בַּלָּשׁוֹן pref. בְּ for בְּהַ } noun com. s. d. 3a; bef. (:) — לשן
בְּלָשׁוֹן pref. בְּ q. v. }

בִּלְשׁוֹן pref. בְּ bef. (:) X id., constr. state — לשן

בִּלְשׁוֹנוֹ pref. id. X id., suff. 3 pers. sing. masc. — לשן

בִּלְשׁוֹנִי pref. id. X id., suff. 1 pers. sing. — לשן

בִּלְשׁוֹנָם pref. id. X id., suff. 3 p. pl. m.; bef. lab. — לשן

בַּלִּשְׁכֹת pref. בְּ for בְּהַ X noun fem. pl. abs. from לִשְׁכָּה dec. 12b. — לשך

בַּלִּשְׁכַּת pref. בְּ X id. sing., constr. state — לשך

בַּלְשָׁכֹת pref. id. X id. pl., constr. state — לשך

בִּלְשָׁן (for בֶּן־לָשֹׁן son of tongue, i. e. *eloquent*, comp. בִּמְהָל) pr. name of a man.

בָּלְתָה Kal pret. 3 pers. sing. fem. — בלה

בָּלִתִי Kal pret. 1 pers. sing. — בלל

בְּלֹתִי Kal inf. [בְּלוֹת], suff. 1 pers. sing. — בלה

בִּלְתִּי adv. and prep., בְּלֶת with parag. ' — בלה

בִּלְתִּי prep. [בְּלֶת] with suff. 1 pers. sing. — בלה

בִּלְתְּךָ id., suff. 2 pers. sing. masc., [for בִּלְתְּךָ] — בלה

בָּם pref. prep. בְּ with suff. 3 pers. pl. m. (§ 5); bef. lab. — ב

בִּמְאֹד pref. בְּ bef. (:) X adv. — אוד

בִּמְאָה pref. בְּ X noun fem sing. dec. 11b. — מאה

בִּמְאֹזְנֵי pref. id. X n. m. du. constr. fr. [מֹאזֵן] d. 7b. — אזן

בְּמֹאזְנַיָּא Chald. pref. id. X id. du., emph. state — אזן

בְּמֹאזְנַיִם } pref. id. X id. du., abs. state — אזן
בְּמֹאזְנָיִם }

בְּמַאֲרָב pref. id. X n. m. s., constr. of [מַאֲרָב] d. 2b. — ארב

בַּמְּאֵרָה pref. בְּ for בְּהַ X noun f. s. dec. 10. (§ 42. r. 3) — ארר

בַּמְּבוֹא pref. id. X noun masc. sing. dec. 3a. — בוא

בְּמִבְחַר pref. בְּ X n. m. s., constr. of [מִבְחַר] d. 2b. — בחר

בְּמִבְטָחֶיךָ pref. id. X noun masc. pl., suff. 2 pers. sing. masc. fr. [מִבְטָח] dec. 2b. (§ 37. rem. 7) — בטח

בַּמֵּבִין pref. id. X Hiph. part. sing. masc. — בין

בְּמִבְצָרֶיהָ pref. id. X noun masc. pl., suff. 3 pers. sing. fem. fr. מִבְצָר dec. 2b. — בצר

בְּמִבְצָרִים pref. id. X id. pl., abs. state — בצר

בִּמְבַקְשֵׁי pref. בְּ bef. (:) X Piel part. pl. constr. masc. dec. 7b. (comp. § 10. rem. 7) — בקש

בִּמְבֻשָּׁיו pref. id. X noun masc. pl., suff. 3 pers. sing. masc. from [מְבוּשׁ] dec. 3a. — בוש

בְּמִגְדּוֹל pref. בְּ X pr. name of a place — גדל

בַּמִּגְדָּלוֹת pref. בְּ for בְּהַ X noun masc. with pl. fem. term. from מִגְדָּל dec. 2b.; bef. lab. — גדל

בְּמִגְדְּלוֹתַיִךְ pref. בְּ X id. pl., suff. 2 pers. sing. fem. — גדל

בַּמִּגְדָּנוֹת pref. בְּ for בְּהַ X noun fem. pl.; bef. lab. — מגד

בִּמְגוֹן pref. בְּ X pr. name of a region — גון

בִּמְגוֹרָה pref. בְּ for בְּהַ X noun fem. sing. dec. 10. — גור

בִּמְגוּרָיו pref. בְּ bef. (:) X noun masc. pl., suff. 3 pers. sing. masc. from [מָגוֹר] dec. 3a. — גור

בִּמְגוּרָם pref. id. X id. pl., suff. 3 pers. pl. masc. — גור

a Ps. 52. 6.   f Job 34. 32.   l Ps. 124. 3.   q Ps. 35. 25.   Pr. 21. 6.   z Ge. 18. 12.   e Ps. 10. 8.   k Is. 34. 13.   o Eze. 27. 11.
b Ps. 55. 10.   g Ge. 41. 44.   m Job 7. 19.   r Ju. 7. 20.   v Ps. 78. 36.   a Ho. 13. 4.   f Mal. 3. 9.   l Nu. 13. 19.   p Ezr. 1. 6.
c Is. 25. 7.   h Nu. 16. 30.   n Pr. 23. 2.   s Ju. 15. 5.   w 1 Ch. 9. 33.   b 1 Sa. 2. 2.   g Ge. 23. 6.   m Est. 9. 2.   q Hag. 2. 19.
d Is. 28. 11.   i Je. 51. 44.   o Je. 51. 34.   t Je. 18. 12.   x Eze. 44. 19.   c Je. 2. 37.   h De. 25. 11.   n 1 Ch. 27. 25.   r Job 18. 19.
e Ge. 14. 24.   k Is. 3. 12.   p La. 2. 16.   u Je. 18. 11.   y Ps. 92. 11.   d Da. 5. 27.   i Pr. 17. 10.   s Ps. 55. 16.

בְּמֹעֲצוֹתֵיהֶם֙ — pref. id.)(noun fem. pl., suff. 3 pers. pl. masc. from [מוֹעֵצָה] dec. 11b . . יען

בְּמוֹפְתִים — pref. id.)(noun masc., pl. of מוֹפֵת dec. 7b; bef. . יפת

בְּמוּצָק — pref. id.)(noun masc. sing. for מוּצָק . צוק

בְּמוֹקְשִׁים — pref. id.)(noun masc., pl. of מוֹקֵשׁ dec. 7b. יקש

בְּמוֹרָא — pref. id.)(noun masc. sing. dec. 1b. (§ 31. rem. 1 & 3); bef. lab. ירא

בְּמוֹרָאִים — pref. id.)(id. pl., absolute state; id. . ירא

בַּמּוֹרָד — pref. בַּ f. בְּהַ)(
בְּמוֹרָד — pref. בַּ q. v.)(} noun masc. sing. dec. 2b. דד

בְּמוֹרָד — pref. id.)(id. construct state . ירד

בְּמוֹשָׁב — pref. id.)(noun masc.sing., constr. of מוֹשָׁב dec. 2b; bef. . ישב

בְּמוֹשְׁבֹתָם֙ — pref. id.)(id. pl., suff. 3 pers. pl. masc. ישב

בַּמָּוֶת — pref. בַּ for בְּהַ)(noun masc. sing. dec. 6g. מות

בָּמוֹת — n.f., pl.of בָּמָה d. 10, also pr. name; bef.lab. בום

בְּמוֹת — pref. בְּ)(n.m.s., constr. of מָוֶת dec.6g; id. מות

בְּמוֹתוֹ — pref. id.)(id., suff. 3 pers. sing. masc. מות

בָּמוֹתַי — noun fem. pl. suff. 1 pers. s. from בָּמָה dec. 10. בום

בָּמֳתֵי — id.constr.st., Kh. בָּמוֹתֵי, K. בָּמֳתֵי, (§ 36.r.6) בום

בְּמוֹתִי — pref. בְּ)(n.m.s., suff. 1 p.s. fr. מָוֶת dec. 6g. מות

בָּמוֹתֵימוֹ — n. fem. pl., suff. 3 p.s.m. from בָּמָה dec. 10. בום

בָּמוֹתֶיךָ — id. pl., suff. 2 pers. sing. masc. בום

בָּמוֹתֵיכֶם֙ — id. pl., suff. 2 pers. pl. masc. בום

בָּמוֹתֵימוֹ — id. pl., suff. 3 pers. pl. masc. בום

בָּמוֹתָם — id. pl., suff. 3 pers. pl. masc. (§ 4. rem. 2) בום

בְּמוֹתָם — pref. בְּ)(noun masc. sing., suff. 3 pers. pl. masc. from מָוֶת dec. 6g; bef. . מות

בַּמִּזְבֵּחַ — pref. בַּ for בְּהַ)(noun masc. sing. dec. 7c. זבח

בְּמִזְמוֹת — pref. בַּ bef.)(n. fem., pl. of מְזִמָּה dec. 10. זמם

בַּמִּזְמֹרוֹת — pref. בַּ for בְּהַ)(n.fem., pl. [מַזְמֵרָה] dec. 11b. זמר

בַּמִּזְרֶה֙ — pref. id. }
בְּמִזְרֶה — pref. בְּ } noun masc. sing.; bef. lab. זרה

בְּמִזְרְקֵי — pref. id.)(n. m. pl. constr. fr. מִזְרָק dec. 2b. זרק

בַּמַּחֲבֶרֶת —
בְּמַחְבֶּרֶת — } pref. בַּ for בְּהַ)(noun fem. sing. dec. 13a. חבר

בַּמַּחֲנֶה — pref. id.)(noun fem. sing.; bef. lab. חון

בְּמָחוֹל — pref. בְּ)(noun masc. sing. dec. 3a. חול

בִּמְחוֹל — pref. בַּ bef.)(id., construct state . חול

בַּמַּחֲזֶה — pref. בַּ for בְּהַ)(noun masc. sing. dec. 9a. חזה

בִּמְחִיר — pref. בַּ bef.)(noun masc. sing. dec. 1a. מחר

בְּמַחֲרֵיהֶם֙ — pref. id.)(id. pl., suff. 3 pers. pl. masc. מחר

בְּמַחֲלָה — pref. בְּ)(n. m. s. constr. of [מַחֲלָה] dec. 9a. חלה

בְּמַחֲלוֹת — pref. בַּ bef.)(noun fem., pl. of [מַחֲלָה] dec. 10; bef. lab. חלל

בִּמְגִזְרוֹת — pref. בְּ)(noun fem. pl. constr. from [מַגְזֵרָה] dec. 11b; bef. . גזר

בַּמְּגֻלָּה — pref. בַּ for בְּהַ)(noun fem. sing. dec. 10. נלל

בִּמְגִלַּת — pref. בַּ bef.)(id., construct state נלל

בַּמַּגֵּפָה — pref. בַּ f. בְּהַ)(
בְּמַגֵּפָה — pref. בַּ q. v.)(} noun fem. sing. dec. 10. נגף

בַּמִּגְרָה — pref. בַּ for בְּהַ)(n. fem. s. dec. 10. (§ 42. r. 3) נרר

בַּמִּגְרָות — pref. id.)(id. pl.; bef. lab. נרר

בַּמִּגְרוֹן — pref. בַּ)(pr. name of a place . מגר

בַּמִּדְבָּר — pref. בַּ for בְּהַ)(noun m. s. dec. 2b; id. דבר

בְּמִדְבַּר — pref. בַּ)(id., construct state . דבר

בַּמִּדָּה — pref. בַּ f. בְּהַ)(
בְּמִדָּה — pref. בַּ q. v.)(} noun fem. sing. dec. 10. מדד

בְּמָדַי — pref. id.)(pr. name of a region, see מָדַי

בְּמִדְיָן — pref. id.)(pr. name of a region R. see דין

בַּמְּדִינָה — pref. בַּ for בְּהַ)(n. fem. s. dec. 10. R. see דין

בַּמְּדִינוֹת — pref. בַּ for בְּהַ }
בַּמְּדִינוֹת — pref. בַּ bef. } id. pl. דון

בִּמְדִינַת — Ch. pref. id.)(n.f.s., constr. of [מְדִינָא] d. 8a. דון

בְּמַדְלֵכָה — pref. בַּ for בְּהַ)(noun fem. sing. . דוך

בְּמַדָּעֲךָ — pref. בְּ)(n. m. s., suff. 2 pers. s. m. from מַדָּע ידע

בְּמִדְרָשׁ — pref. id.)(n. m. s., constr. of [מִדְרָשׁ] dec. 2b. דרש

בָּמָה — noun fem. sing. dec. 10. (pl. c. [בָּמֳתֵי]). בום

בַּמֶּה — pref. בַּ for בְּהַ)(pron.interrog. in pause (2 Ki. 22.21; 2 Ch.18.20), and bef. the gutt. א & ה מה

בַּמֶּה — pref. id.)(pron. interrog. bef. non-gutt., and
בַּמֶה — pref. בְּ)(once (2 Ch. 7.21) bef. ע } מה

בִּמְהֹל — comp. for בֶּן־מָהֹל circumcised, i.q. מהל מול (for בַּעֲלִים) pr. name masc. 1 Ch. 7.33.

בְּמַהֲלֻכוֹת — pref. id.)(noun fem. pl. . המר

בְּמַהֵר — pref. id.)(noun masc. sing. . מהר

בִּמְהֵרָה — pref. בַּ bef.)(noun fem. sing. . מהר

בְּמוֹ — pref. בְּ with the parag. syllable, מוֹ q. v.

בְּמוֹאָב — pref. בַּ)(pr. name of a people and country, see מוֹאָב; bef.

בַּמּוֹט — pref. בַּ for בְּהַ)(noun masc. sing. dec. 1a. מוט

בְּמוֹט — pref. בַּ)(Kal inf. constr.; bef. . מוט

בַּמּוֹסֵר — pref. בַּ for בְּהַ)(noun masc. sing. dec. 2b. יסר

בְּמוֹעֲדוֹ — pref. בַּ)(n.m.s., suff. 3 p. s. m. fr. מוֹעֵד d. 7b. יעד

בְּמוֹעֲדָיו — pref. id.)(id. pl., suff. 3 pers. sing. fem. יעד

בְּמוֹעֲדֵי — pref. id.)(noun masc. pl., suff. 3 pers. sing. masc. from [מוֹעֵד] dec. 2b. יעד

בְּמוֹעֲדֵיכֶם — pref. id.)(noun masc. pl., suff. 2 pers. pl. masc. from מוֹעֵד dec. 7b; bef. lab. יעד

בְּמוֹעֲדִים — pref. בַּ for בְּהַ)(id. pl., abs. state; id. יעד

בְּמוֹעֲדָם — pref. בְּ)(id. sing., suff. 3 pers. pl. masc. יעד

a 2 Sa. 12.31.   d Est. 2.16.   g Ec. 3.22.   k Ps. 46.3.   o Eze. 46.9, 11.   s Jos. 7.5.   w 2 Ch. 32.12.   a Is. 18.5.   e Je. 31.4.
b Je. 36.6.   e Da. 3.1, 30.   h Ps. 140.11.   l Pr. 4.13.   p Le. 23.14.   t Mi. 1.4.   x 2 Sa. 1.19, 25.   b Is. 30.24.   f Ge. 15.1.
c Ps. 40.8.   f Nu. 11.8.   i 1 Sa. 18.25.   m Ps. 81.13.   q Nu. 31.10.   u De. 33.29.   y Je. 15.7.   c Ps. 44.13.
d Eze. 24.16.   g Ec. 10.20.   k Ec. 4.12.   n Eze. 36.38.   r Est. 2.7.   v 2 Sa. 1.23.   z Is. 44.13.   d 2 Ch. 21.15.
e 1 Ch. 20.3.   h 2 Ch. 13.22.   l Nu. 13.23.   o Job 37.10.   s 1 Ki. 13.31.   w Ps. 10.2.   a Je. 2.19.
f La 1.1.   i 2 Sa. 21.3.   m Ps. 38.17.   p Nu. 29.39.   t Job 40.24.   x Ps. 102.   b Je. 32.21.   Eze. 6.3.
Nu. 10.10.   De. 4.34.   Job 28.25.

Hebrew	Description	Root
בְּמַחֹלות / בִּמְחֹלת	pref. בְּ for בְּהַ (noun fem., pl. of [מְחֹלָה] dec. 10; וּ bef. lab. — pref. בְּ bef. (:)	חול
בְּמַחֲלָיִים	pref. בְּ (noun masc., pl. of [מַחֲלִי] dec. 1b.	חלה
בְּמַחְלְקות	pref. id. (noun fem., pl. of מַחֲלֹקֶת dec. 13c.	חלק
בְּמַחְלְקותֵיהֶם	pref. id. (id. pl., suff. 3 pers. pl. masc.	חלק
בְּמַחְלְקותֵיכֶם	pref. id. (id. pl., suff. 2 pers. pl. masc.	חלק
בְּמַחְלְקותָם	pref. id. (id. pl., suff. 3 pers. pl. m. (§ 4 r.2)	חלק
בְּמַחְלְקתְהון	Chald. pref. id. (noun fem. pl., suff. 3 pers. pl. masc. from [מַחְלְקָא] dec. 9a.	חלק
בְּמָחֹלַת וּ	pref. בְּ bef. (:) (n. fem., pl. of [מְחֹלָה] d.10.	חול
בְּמַחֲזֵן	Chald. pref. בְּ (Peal inf. (dag. forte impl.in) חנן	חנן
בַּמַּחֲנֶה	pref. בְּ for בְּהַ (noun com. sing. dec. 9a.	חנה
בְּמַחֲנֵה	pref. בְּ (id., construct state	חנה
בְּמַחֲנות	pref. בְּ for בְּהַ (id. pl. fem.	חנה
בְּמַחֲנַיִם	pref. בְּ (pr. name of a place	חנה
בִּמְחֹקֵק	pref. בְּ bef. (:) (Poel part. sing. m. dec. 7b.	חקק
בְּמַחְשָׁךְ	pref. בְּ (noun masc. sing. dec. 8a.	חשך
בְּמַחֲשַׁכִּים	pref. id. (id. pl. absolute	חשך
בַּמַּחְתֶּרֶת	pref. בְּ for בְּהַ (noun fem. sing.	חתר
בְּמַטְמָא	pref. בְּ (noun masc. sing.	טוא
בַּמַּטֶּה	pref. בְּ for בְּהַ (noun masc. sing. dec. 9a.	נטה
בַּמַּטֶּה	pref. id. (noun fem. sing. dec. 10.	נטה
בְּמַטֵּהוּ	pref. בְּ (n.m.s., suff. 3 p.s.m.fr. מַטֶּה dec.9a.	נטה
בַּמֹּטות	pref. בְּ for בְּהַ (n. fem., pl. of מוֹטָה dec. 10.	מוט
בְּמַטָּיו	pref. בְּ (n. m. pl., suff. 3 p.s.m.fr. מַטֶּה dec.9a.	נטה
בְּמַטְּךָ	pref. id. (id. s., suff. 2 pers. s. m. [for מַטֶּךָ]	נטה
בְּמִי	Kh. בְּמוֹ q. v., K. בְּמֵי q. v.	מי
בְּמֵי	pref. בְּ (noun masc. pl., constr. of מַיִם, [sing. מֵי § 38. rem. 2. & § 45]	מי
בְּמֵי	pref. id. (pron. interrog.	מי
בְּמוֹ	Kh. בְּמֵי q. v., K. בְּמוֹ q. v.	מי
בְּמֵיטַב	pref. בְּ (n. m. s., constr. of [מֵיטָב] dec.2b.	יטב
בְּמַיִם / בַּמַּיִם / בְּמַיִם	pref. בְּ f. בְּהַ (n. m., pl. [of מֵי § 38.r.2. & 45]; וּ bef. lab. — pref. בְּ q. v.	מי
בַּמִּישׁור	pref. בְּ f. בְּהַ (	ישר
בְּמִישׁור	pref. בְּ q. v. (noun m. sing.; וּ bef. lab.	ישר
בְּמִישׁר	pref. בְּ for בְּהַ	ישר
בְּמֵישָׁרִים	pref. בְּ (noun masc. pl., also as an adv.	ישר
בְּמֵיתָרֵיךָ	pref. id. (noun masc. pl., suff. 2 pers. sing. masc. from [מֵיתָר] dec. 2b.	יתר
בְּמַכְאוֹב	pref. id. (noun masc. sing. dec. 1b.	כאב
בְּמַכֹּנָה	pref. בְּ for בְּהַ (noun fem. sing. dec. 10.	כוה
בַּמְּכֹנָה	pref. id. (noun fem. sing. dec. 10.	כון
בִּמְכֹונֵי	pref. בְּ bef. (:) (n. m. pl. constr. fr. מָכון d.3a.	כון

Hebrew	Description	Root
בְּמַכְלֻלִים	pref. בְּ (n. m. masc. pl. [of [מַכְלוּל]	כלל
בְּמִכְמַנֵּי	pref. id. (n. ... pl. constr. from [מִכְמָן] d.8a.	כמן
בְּמִכְמָרָיו	pref. id. (noun masc., pl., suff. 3 pers. sing. masc. from [מִכְמֹר] dec. 1b.	כמר
בְּמִכְמַרְתּו	pref. id. (noun fem. sing., suff. 3 pers. sing. masc. from מִכְמֶרֶת dec. 13a.	כמר
בְּמִכְמָשׁ	pref. id. (pr. name of a place, see מִכְמָס	כמס
בְּמִבְנֶה וּ	pref. בְּ bef. (:) (pr. name of a place; וּ bef.	כון
בְּמִכְסֵה	pref. בְּ (n. m. s., constr. of מִכְסֶה dec. 9a.	כסה
בְּמִכְסַת	pref. id. (noun fem.sing., constr. [of [מִכְסָה], from מֶכֶס masc.	כסס
בַּמַּכְפֵּלָה	pref. בְּ for בְּהַ (pr. name of a region	כפל
בַּמְכַשְּׁפִים	pref. id. (Piel part. m., pl. of מְכַשֵּׁף dec. 7b.	כשף
בְּמִכְתָּב	pref. בְּ (noun masc. sing. dec. 2b.	כתב
בְּמִכְתַּב וּ	pref. id. (id., construct state; וּ bef. lab.	כתב
בַּמַּכְתֵּשׁ	pref. בְּ for בְּהַ (noun masc. sing.	כתש
בְּמִכְתָּבו	pref. בְּ bef. (:) (noun fem. sing., suff. 3 pers. sing. masc. from [מִכְתָּה] dec. 10.	כתת
בִּמְלֹאות	pref. id. (Kal inf. constr. [for מְלֹא=מְלֹאת § 23. rem. 2. 4. & 9]	מלא
בַּמְּלָאכָה	pref. בְּ for בְּהַ (n. fem. s. see under the R.	לאך
בְּמַלְאֲכות	pref. id. (n. f. s., constr. of [מַלְאֲכות] d.3a.	לאך
בְּמַלְאֲכֵי	pref. id. (n.m.pl. constr. from מַלְאָךְ dec. 2b.	לאך
בְּמַלְאָכָיו וּ	pref. id. (id., suff. 3 pers. s. m.; וּ bef. lab.	לאך
בְּמַלְאֶכֶת / בְּמַלְאֶכֶת	pref. בְּ for בְּהַ (noun fem. sing., constr. of מְלָאכָה (§ 42. rem. 5) — pref. בְּ bef. (:)	לאך
בִּמְלַאכְתּו	pref. id. (id., suff. 3 pers. sing. masc.	לאך
בִּמְלֹאת וּ	pref. id. (Kal inf. constr. (see [בִּמְלֹאות]; וּ bef. lab.	מלא
בִּמְלֹאתָם	pref. בְּ (noun fem. pl., suff. 3 pers. pl. masc. from [מְלוֹאָה] dec. 10.	מלא
בַּמַּלְבֵּן	pref. בְּ for בְּהַ (noun masc. sing.	לבן
בְּמֹלָדָה וּ	pref. בְּ (pr. name of a place; וּ bef.	ילד
בִּמְלֹאות וּ	pref. בְּ bef. (:) (Kal inf. constr., see בִּמְלֹאות; וּ bef. lab.	מלא
בִּמְלֹואָתָם	pref. בְּ (n. fem. pl., suff. fr. [מְלוֹאָה] dec. 10.	מלא
בַּמָּלון	pref. בְּ for בְּהַ (noun masc. sing. dec. 3a.	לון
בַּמֶּלַח	pref. id. (n. masc. sing. (segolate § 35. r. 5)	מלח
בַּמִּלְחָמָה / בְּמִלְחָמָה וּ	pref. id. (noun fem. sing. dec. 11a. (comp.) — pref. בְּ (§ 42. rem. 5); וּ bef. (:)	לחם
בְּמִלְחֲמות וּ	pref. id. (id. pl., construct state; וּ id.	לחם
בַּמֶּלֶט	pref. בְּ for בְּהַ (noun masc. sing.	מלט
בְּמִלִּים / בְּמִלִּין	pref. בְּ (noun fem. with pl. masc. term. — pref. id. from מִלָּה dec. 10.	מלל

a Ju. 11.34.   g Ezr. 6.18.   l Is. 14.23.   t Ge. 47.6,11.   b Ps. 141.10.   h Is. 30.14.   o 2 Ch. 13.10.   y Ex. 28.20.
b 2 Ch. 24.25.   h Ex. 15.20.   l 1 Ch. 15.15.   v Le. 13.25.   c Hab. 1.15.   i Job 20.22.   p Le. 12.6.   z Le. 2.13.
c 2 Ch. 31.15.   i Da. 4.24.   m 2 Ch. 26.10.   w 1 Ki. 7.32.   d Ex. 12.4.   k Hag. 1.13.   q Ex. 39.13.   a Da. 11.20.
d 2 Ch. 31.17.   k Zec. 14.5.   n Mal. 2.6.   x Is. 18.4.   e Eze. 27.24.   l 2 Ch. 36.16.   r Je. 43.9.   b Is. 30.3.
e 2 Ch. 35.4.   l Nu. 21.18.   o Ex. 8.1.   y Jos. 20.8.   f Da. 11.43.   m Job 4.18.   s 2 Sa. 12.31. Je. 43.9.   c Je. 34.32.
f 2 Ch. 8.14.   m Is. 29.15.   p Job 9.30. Is. 25.10.   z Ps. 21.13. Job 33.19.   g Pr. 27.22.   n Mal. 3.3.   t Est. 1.5.

בְּמַעֲנְעִים | ו pref. בְּ bef. (:) ✗ noun m. pl. [for מְנַעֲנְעִים fr. נַעֲ מְנַעֲנַע § 36. r. 5] ; ו bef. labial | נוע

בַּמְּנֹרָה | ו pref. בְּ for בְּהַ ✗ noun fem. s. dec. 10; ו id. | נור

בְּמִסַבּוֹ | pref. בְּ bef. (:) ✗ noun masc. sing., suff. 3 p. s. m. fr. מֵסַב d. 8 e. (§ 37. No. 2, & r. 3) | סבב

בַּמַּסָּה | pref. בְּ f. בְּהַ } pr. name of a place; ו bef. (:) | נסה
בְּמַסָּה | ו ref. בְּ q. v.

בְּמִסְגֶּרֶת | pref. id. ✗ noun fem. sing. | סבן

בַּמְסִלָּה | pref. בְּ f. בְּהַ } noun fem. sing. dec. 10. | סלל
בִּמְסִלָּה | pref. בְּ bf. (:)

בִּמְסִלּוֹת | pref. בְּ for בְּהַ ✗ id. pl. | סלל

בִּמְסִלּוֹתָם | pref. בְּ bef. (:) ✗ id. pl., suff. 3 pers. pl. m. | סלל

בִּמְסִלַּת | pref. id. ✗ id. sing., constr. state | סלל

בִּמְסִלָּתוֹ | pref. id. ✗ id. sing., suff. 3 pers. sing. masc. | סלל

בְּמִסְמְרוֹת | pref. בְּ ✗ noun masc. with pl. fem. term. fr. [מַסְמֵר] dec. 7 b. | סמר

בְּמַסְמְרִים | pref. id. ✗ id. with pl. masc. term. | סמר

בְּמִסְפֵּד | pref. id. ✗ noun masc. sing. dec. 7 c. (§ 36. rem. 1); ו bef. (:) | ספד

בְּמִסְפָּר | ו pref. id. ✗ noun masc. sing. dec. 2 b ; ו id. | ספר

בְמִסְפָּר | ו pref. id. ✗ id., constr. state | ספר

בְּמִסְפָּרָם | pref. id. ✗ id., suff. 3 pers. pl. masc. | ספר

בְּמֹסֵרוֹת | pref. id. ✗ pr. name of a place, see מוֹסֵר | אסר

בְּמֹסְרָם | ו pref. id. ✗ noun masc. sing., suff. 3 pers. pl. masc. fr. [מֹסֵר] ; ו bef. (:) | יסר

בְּמַאֲסֶרֶת | pref. id. ✗ noun fem. sing. [for מַאֲסֶרֶת | אסר

בְּמַסֹּת | pref. id. ✗ noun fem., pl. of מַסָּה dec. 10. | נסה

בְּמִסְתָּר | pref. בְּ for בְּהַ ✗ noun masc. sing. dec. 2 b. | סתר

בַּמִּסְתָּרִים | pref. id. } id. pl., absolute state | סתר
בְּמִסְתָּרִים | pref. בְּ

בְּמַעֲבֶה | pref. id. ✗ n. m. s., constr. of [מַעֲבֶה] d. 9 b. | עבה

בַּמַּעְגָּל | pref. בְּ for בְּהַ ✗ noun masc. sing. dec. 2 b. | עגל

בְּמַעְגְּלוֹתֶיךָ | pref. בְּ ✗ noun fem. pl., suff. 2 pers. sing. masc. fr. מַעְגָּלָה dec. 11 a. | עגל

בְּמַעְגְּלוֹתָם | pref. id. ✗ id. pl., suff. 3 pers. pl. masc. | עגל

בְּמַעְגְּלֵי | pref. id. ✗ n. m. pl. constr. fr. מַעְגָּל d. 2 b. | עגל

בְּמַעְגְּלֹתָם | pref. id. ✗ noun fem. pl., suff. 3 pers. pl. masc. fr. מַעְגָּלָה dec. 11 a. | עגל

בְּמַעֲמָד | pref. id. ✗ noun masc. sing. dec. 7 b. | יעד

בְּמַעֲמָדוֹ | pref. id. ✗ id., suff. 3 pers. sing. masc. | יעד

בְּמַעֲמָדֵיכֶם | pref. id. ✗ id. pl., suff. 2 pers. pl. masc. | יעד

בַּמַּעְדֵּר | pref. בְּ for בְּהַ ✗ noun masc. sing. | עדר

בְּמָעֹז | pref. בְּ ✗ noun masc. s. (suff. מָעֻזּוֹ) dec. 8 c. | עזז

בְּמָעוֹן | pref. id. ✗ pr. name of a place | עון

בִּמְעוֹן | pref. בְּ bef. (:) ✗ noun masc. sing., constr. of מָעוֹן dec. 3 a. | עון

בִּמְלִיצֵי | pref. בְּ bef. (:) ✗ Hiph. part. pl. constr masc. from מֵלִיץ dec. 3 b. | לוץ

בַּמֶּלֶךְ | pref. בְּ for בְּהַ } noun masc. sing. dec. 6 a. | מלך
בְּמֶלֶךְ | pref. בְּ q. v.

בְּמְלֹךְ | Kh. בִּמְלֹךְ, K. מִמְלֹךְ; pref. בְּ or ✗ Kal inf. constr. | מלך

בַּמַּלְכָּה | pref. בְּ for בְּהַ ✗ noun fem. sing. dec. 12 a. | מלך

בְּמַלְכּוֹ | pref. בְּ ✗ noun masc. sing., suff. 3 pers. sing. masc. fr. מֶלֶךְ dec. 6 a. | מלך

בְּמַלְכוּ | pref. id ✗ Kal inf., suff. 3 pers. sing. masc. | מלך

בַּמַּלְכוּת | pref. בְּ f. בְּהַ ✗ n. f. s. d. 1 b. Ch. constr. of | מלך
בְּמַלְכוּת | ו pref. בְּ q. v. ✗ מַלְכוּ dec. 8 c ; ו bef. (:)

בְּמַלְכוּתָא | Ch. pref. id. ✗ n. f. s., emph. of מַלְכוּ d. 8 c. | מלך

בְּמַלְכוּתוֹ | pref. id. ✗ noun fem. sing., suff. 3 pers. sing. masc. fr. מַלְכוּת dec. 1 b. | מלך

בְּמַלְכוּתִי | Chald. pref. id. ✗ noun fem. sing., suff. 1 pers. sing. fr. מַלְכוּ dec. 8 c. | מלך

בְּמַלְכוּתִי | ו pref. id. ✗ noun fem. sing., suff. 1 pers. sing. fr. מַלְכוּת dec. 1 b.; ו bef. (:) | מלך

בְּמַלְכוּתְךָ | Chald. pref. id. ✗ noun fem. sing., suff. 2 pers. sing. masc. fr. מַלְכוּ dec. 8 c. | מלך

בְּמַלְכוּתָם | pref. id. ✗ noun fem. sing., suff. 3 pers. pl masc. fr. מַלְכוּת dec. 1 b. | מלך

בַּמְּלָכִים | pref. בְּ for בְּהַ ✗ noun m., pl. of מֶלֶךְ dec. 6 a. | מלך

בְּמַלְכֵי | ו pref. בְּ ✗ id. pl., constr. st.; ו bef. | מלך

בְּמַלְכָּם | pref. id. ✗ id. sing., suff. 3 pers. pl. masc. | מלך

בְּמַלְכָּן | pref. בְּ for בְּהַ ✗ Kh. perh. מַלְכָּן (i. q. מַלְכָּם the name of an idol, and meton. for the temple); K. מַלְכָּן, noun masc. sing. | לבן

בְּמַלְמַד | pref. בְּ ✗ n. m. s., constr. of [מַלְמָד] d. 2 b. | למד

בְּמַלְקָחַיִם | pref. id. ✗ noun masc., du. of [מֶלְקָח] d. 2 b. | לקח

בַּמַּמְלָכָה | pref. בְּ f. בְּהַ } noun fem. sing. (§ 42. rem. 5) | מלך
בְּמַמְלָכָה | pref. בְּ q. v.

בִּמְנָאֲפִים | ו pref. בְּ for בְּהַ ✗ Piel part. masc., pl. of מְנָאֵף dec. 7 b.; ו bef. labial | נאף

בִּמְנוּחֹת | ו pref. בְּ bef. (:) ✗ noun fem., pl. of מְנוּחָה dec. 10; ו id. | נוח

בִּמְנוּסָה | ו pref. id. ✗ noun fem. sing. dec. 10; ו id. | נוס

בַּמִּנְחָה | pref. בְּ f. בְּהַ } noun f. s. d. 12 b; ו bef. (:) | מנח
בְּמִנְחָה | ו pref. בְּ q. v.

בְּמִנְחַת | ו pref. id. ✗ id., constr. state; ו id. | מנח

בְּמִנְחָתִי | ו pref. id. ✗ id., suff. 1 pers. sing.; ו id. | מנח

בַּמִּנִּים | pref. id. ✗ noun m., pl. of [מֵן] dec. 8 b. | מנן

בְּמִנַשֶּׁה | pref. בְּ bef. (:) ✗ pr. name of a tribe | נשה

בִּמְנַעֲמֵיהֶם | pref. בְּ ✗ noun masc. pl., suff. 3 pers. pl. masc. fr. [מַנְעָם] dec. 8 a. | נעם

---

a 2 Ch. 32. 31.   d Da. 5. 11.   m Is. 6. 6.   Is. 52. 12.   p Ps. 150. 4.   q 1 Sa. 6. 12.   t Is. 41. 7.   x De. 4. 34.   Is. 59. 8.
b 2 Ki. 23. 33.   i Ne. 9. 35.   n Am. 9. 8.   o Ge. 32. 21.   r Ps. 141. 4.   u Ju. 20. 31, 45.   y Joel 2. 12.   z 1 Ki. 7. 46.   De. 31. 10.
c Est. 1. 15.   f 1 Sa. 14. 47.   Is. 19. 2.   1 Sa. 6. 5.   s 2 Sa. 6. 5.   Is. 59. 7.   1 Ch. 9. 28.   Pr. 26. 5, 7.   Nu. 15. 3.
Is. 8. 21.   k 2 Sa. 12. 31.   Mal. 3. 5.   Ezr. 9. 5.   Ca. 1. 12.   Job 33. 16.   Ps. 17. 5.   Is. 7. 25.
Ezr. 7. 13.   Ju. 3. 31.   Is. 32. 18.   1 Sa. 2. 29.   De. 8. 9.   Je. 10. 4.   Eze. 20. 37.   Pr. 2. 15.   Ps. 68. 6.
1 Ch. 17. 14.   Nu. 9. 3, 7. 13.

בִּמְעוֹנֹת — pref. בְּ for בָּה)(noun f., pl. מְעֹנָה dec. 10. — עון

בִּמְעוֹנֹתֶיהָ — וּ pref. בְּ bef. (ְ))(id. pl., suff. 3 pers. sing. fem.; וּ bef. labial — עון

בִּמְעוֹנֹתֵינוּ — pref. id.)(id. pl., suff. 1 pers. pl. — עון

בִּמְעֻזִּי — pref. בְּ)(noun masc. sing., suff. 1 pers. sing. fr. מָעֹז dec. 8c (§ 37. rem. 4) — עזז

בִּמְעַט / בִּמְעַט- — pref. בְּ bef. (ְ))(noun masc. sing. d. 8d — מעט

בִּמְעָיַ — pref. בְּ)(noun masc. pl., suff. 1 pers. sing. fr. [מֵעֶה] dec. 7a. (§ 36. rem. 4) — מע

בִּמְעֵי — pref. בְּ bef. (ְ))(id. pl., constr. state — מע

בִּמְעָיָו — pref. בְּ)(id. pl., suff. 3 pers. sing. masc. — מע

בִּמְעַיִךְ — pref. id.)(id. pl., suff. 2 pers. sing. fem. — מע

בִּמְעִיל — pref. בְּ bef. (ְ))(noun masc. sing. dec. 1a. — מעל

בַּמַּעַל / בְּמַעַל — pref. בַּ f. בָּה)(/ pref. בְּ q. v. } noun masc. sing. dec. 6d. — מעל

בְּמַעַל — pref. id.)(noun masc. sing. — מעל

בַּמַּעֲלָה — pref. בַּ for בָּה)(noun masc. sing. dec. 9a. — עלה

בְּמַעֲלֵה — pref. בְּ)(id., constr. state — עלה

בְּמַעֲלוֹ — pref. id.)(n. m. s. or inf., suff. 3 s. m. fr. מַעַל d. 6d. — מעל

בַּמַּעֲלוֹת / בְּמַעֲלוֹת — pref. בַּ f. בָּה)(noun fem., pl. of מַעֲלָה / pref. בְּ q. v. dec. 10; וּ bef. (ְ) — עלה

בְּמַעַלְלֵיהֶם — pref. id.)(noun masc. pl., suff. 3 pers. pl. masc. [for מַעַלְלֵי] from מַעֲלָל dec. 2b. — עלל

בְּמַעַלְלָיו — pref. id.)(id. pl., suff. 3 pers. sing. masc. — עלל

בְּמַעַלְלָם — pref. id.)(n. m. s. or inf., suff. 3 pl. m. fr. מַעַל d. 6d. — מעל

בְּמַעֲלֹת — pref. id.)(noun fem., pl. of מַעֲלָה dec. 10. — עלה

בְּמַעֲלֹתָו — pref. id.)(id. pl., 3 pers. sing. masc. (K. תָיו § 4. rem. 1) — עלה

בְּמַעֲמַקֵּי — pref. id.)(n. m. pl. constr. from [מַעֲמָק] d. 8a. — עמק

בְּמַעֲנֵה — pref. id.)(n. m. s., constr. of מַעֲנֶה dec. 9b. — ענה

בְּמַעֲצָד — pref. בְּ for בָּה)(noun masc. sing. — עצד

בְּמֹעֲצוֹת — pref. id.)(noun m., pl. of [מוֹעֵצָה] dec. 11b. — יעץ

בְּמֹעֲצוֹתָם — pref. id.)(id. pl., suff. 3 pers. pl. masc. — יעץ

בְּמַעֲרָבֵךְ — pref. id.)(noun masc. sing., suff. 2 pers. sing. fem. from [מַעֲרָב] dec. 2b. — ערב

בַּמְּעָרָה — pref. בַּ for בָּה)(noun fem. sing. dec. 10. — עור

בַּמְּעָרוֹת / בַּמְּעָרוֹת — וּ pref. id. } id. pl. / pref. בַּ bef. (ְ) — עור

בְּמַעֲרָכָה — pref. בְּ for בָּה)(noun fem. sing. dec. 11a. — ערך

בְּמַעֲרָצָה — pref. בְּ)(noun fem. sing. — ערץ

בִּמְעָרַת — pref. בְּ bef. (ְ))(n. f. s., constr. of מְעָרָה d. 10. — עור

בְּמַעֲשֵׂה — pref. בְּ)(n. m. s., constr. of מַעֲשֶׂה dec. 9a. — עשה

בְּמַעֲשֵׂי — pref. id.)(id. pl., construct state — עשה

בְּמַעֲשֵׂיהֶם — pref. id.)(id. pl., suff. 3 pers. pl. masc. — עשה

בְּמַעֲשָׂיו — pref. id.)(id. pl., suff. 3 pers. sing. masc. — עשה

בְּמַעֲשַׂיִךְ — pref. id.)(id. pl., suff. 2 pers. sing. fem. — עשה

בְּמַעֲשֵׂינוּ — pref. id.)(id. pl., suff. 1 pers. pl. — עשה

בַּמַּפְגִּיעַ — pref. id.)(Hiph. part. sing. masc. — פגע

בְּמַפַּלְתָּם — pref. id.)(noun fem. sing., suff. 3 pers. pl. masc. from מַפֶּלֶת dec. 13a. — פל

בְּמִפְקַד — pref. id.)(n. m. s., constr. of [מִפְקָד] d. 2b. — פקד

בַּמֹּפְתִים — וּ pref. בַּ for בָּה)(noun masc., pl. of מוֹפֵת dec. 7b; וּ bef. lab. — יפת

בְּמָצְאֲכֶם — pref. בְּ)(Kal inf., suff. 2 pers. pl. masc. [for מָצְאֲכֶם=מְצָאֲכֶם § 16. rem. 9] — מצא

בַּמָּצָר — pref. בַּ for בָּה)(noun masc. sing. dec. 1a. — צור

בַּמְצָדָה — pref. id.)(noun fem. sing. dec. 10. — צוד

בַּמְצָדוֹת — pref. id.)(noun masc. with pl. fem. term. from מָצָד dec. 1a. — צוד

בִּמְצָדוֹת — pref. id.)(noun fem., pl. of [מְצוֹדָה] dec. 10. — צוד

בִּמְצָדוֹת — pref. בְּ bef. (ְ))(n. masc., pl. of מְצָד dec. 1a. — צוד

בַּמְּצוּדָה — pref. בְּ for בָּה)(noun fem. sing. dec. 10. — צוד

בִּמְצוֹדָתֹה — pref. בְּ bef. (ְ))(noun fem. sing. dec. 10. — צוד

בִּמְצוֹדָתִי — pref. id.)(n.f.s., suff. 1 p.s.fr. [מְצוֹדָה] d. 10. — צוד

בִּמְצֻוָּה — וּ pref. בְּ for בָּה)(n. fem. s. dec. 10; וּ bef. lab. — צוה

בִּמְצֻלָּה — pref. בְּ bef. (ְ))(noun fem. sing. dec. 10. — צול

בִּמְצוּלֹת — pref. id.)(id. pl. — צול

בִּמְצוֹלֹת — pref. id.)(noun fem., pl. of [מְצוֹלָה] dec. 10. — צול

בְּמָצוֹק — וּ pref. בְּ)(noun masc. sing.; וּ bef. (ְ) — צוק

בַּמָּצוֹר / בְּמָצוֹר — pref. בַּ f. בָּה)(/ pref. בְּ q. v. } n. m. s. dec. 3a. (§ 32. rem. 5) — צור

בִּמְצוֹת — וּ pref. בְּ for בָּה)(n.f., pl. of מַצָּה d. 10; וּ bef. lab. — מצץ

בְּמִצְוַת — pref. id.)(n. fem. s., constr. of מִצְוָה dec. 10. — צוה

בְּמִצְוֹתָיו — וּ pref. id.)(id. pl., suff. 3 p.s.m.; וּ bef. (ְ) — צוה

בְּמִצְוֹתֶיךָ — pref. id.)(id. pl., suff. 2 pers. sing. masc. — צוה

בְּמִצְחוֹ — pref. id.)(n. m. s., suff. 3 p. s. m. fr. מֵצַח d. 6e. — מצח

בִּמְצֻלָה — pref. בְּ for בָּה)(n. fem. s. (for מְצוּלָה) d. 10. — צול

בִּמְצֻלֹת — pref. בְּ bef. (ְ))(noun fem., pl. of מְצֻלָה dec. 10. — צול

בַּמְצַלֵּחַ — pref. בְּ)(Hiph. part. sing. masc. — צלח

בַּמְצִלְתַּיִם / בִּמְצִלְתַּיִם / בִּמְצִלְתַּיִם — pref. בַּ for בָּה)(/ וּ pref. בְּ bef. (ְ) / וּ pref. id. } n.fem., du. of [מְצֵלֶת] d. 13c. (comp. § 39. No. 4. rem. 1); וּ bef. lab. — צלל

בְּמִצְנֶפֶת — וּ pref. בְּ)(noun fem. sing.; וּ id. — צנף

בְּמִצְעָדָיו — pref. id.)(noun masc. pl., suff. 3 pers. sing. masc. from [מִצְעָד] dec. 2b. — צעד

בְּמִצְעָר — pref. id.)(n. m. s., constr. of מִצְעָר dec. 2b. — צער

בְּמִצְפָּה — pref. בְּ for בָּה)(pr. name of a place — צפה

בְּמִצְקָתוֹ — pref. id.)(noun fem. sing., suff. 3 pers. sing. masc. from [מְצֻקֶת] dec. 13a. — יצק

---

a Job 38. 40.   h Jon. 2. 1.   o Ne. 12. 37.   u Eze. 40. 6.   Eze. 33. 27.   Job 36. 32.   Eze. 19. 9.   Mic. 7. 19.   Ps. 88. 7.
b Job 37. 8.   Nu. 5. 22.   Eze. 40. 49.   Pr. 15. 23.   Is. 2. 19.   Pr. 29. 16.   1 Sa. 24. 1.   Ju. 6. 21.   Ps. 37. 7.
c Je. 21. 13.   1 Ch. 15. 27   Eze. 40. 22.   Je. 16. 16.   Is. 10. 33.   De. 26. 8.   Ec. 9. 12.   Ps. 112. 1.   Le. 10. 6.
d Is. 27. 5.   Ezr. 9. 2.   Ps. 106. 29.   Mi. 6. 16.   Ge. 50. 13.   Ge. 32. 20.   Eze. 12. 13.   2 Ch. 17. 4.   Da. 11. 43.
e 1 Sa. 14. 6.   Jos. 22. 22.   Pr. 20. 17.   Eze. 27. 19.   1 Ch. 11. 7.   2 Ch. 31. 21.   Ps. 119. 47, 66.   2 Ch. 24. 24.
f Da. 11. 23.   Ne. 8. 6.   Ex. 20. 26.   1 Sa. 13. 6.   2 Sa. 5. 9.   Ps. 107. 24.   Zec. 1. 8.   2 Ch. 4. 3.
g Ruth 1. 11.

בְּמִצְרַיִם	pref. בְּ) pr. name of a country	מצר
בְּמִצְרַיִם		
בַּמַּקְּבוֹת	ו pref. בַּ f. [בָּה] noun fem., pl. of [מַקֶּבָה];	נקב
בְּמַקְּבוֹת	ו pref. בְּ q. v. ו bef. lab.	
בְּמַקְּדָה	pref. id.) pr. name of a place	נקד
בְּמִקְדַּשׁ	pref. id.) n. m. s., constr. of מִקְדָּשׁ dec. 2 b.	קדש
בְּמִקְדָּשׁוֹ	pref. id.) id., suff. 3 pers. sing. masc.	קדש
בְּמִקְדָּשִׁי	pref. id.) id., suff. 1 pers. sing.	קדש
בְּמַקְהֵלוֹת	pref. id.) noun pl. fem. and masc. [from מַקְהֵל § 36. No. 1]	קהל
בְּמַקְהֵלִים		
בְּמַקְהֵלֹת	pref. id.) pr. name of a place	קהל
בַּמָּקוֹם	ו pref. בַּ f. [בָּה] noun com. sing. dec. 3 a;	קום
בְּמָקוֹם	ו pref. בְּ q. v.	
בִּמְקוֹם	ו pref. בְּ bef. (:)) id. constr. state; ו id.	קום
בִּמְקוֹמוֹ	pref. id.) id., suff. 3 pers. sing. masc.	קום
בִּמְקוֹמֵנוּ	pref. id.) id., suff. 1 pers. pl.	קום
בַּמַּקֵּל	pref. בַּ for [בָּה]) n. m. s. dec. 7 b. (§ 36. r. 1)	מקל
בְּמַקֵּל	ו pref. בְּ) id., constr. st.; ו bef. (:)	מקל
בַּמַּקְלוֹת	pref. בַּ for [בָּה]) id. pl. [for מַקְלוֹת comp. § 10. rem. 7]	מקל
בְּמַקְלִי	pref. בְּ) id. sing., suff. 1 p. s. [for מַקְלִי comp. id.]	מקל
בִּמְקֹם	pref. id.) noun com. sing. dec. 3 a.	קום
בִּמְקֹמוֹ	pref. בְּ bef. (:)) id., suff. 3 pers. sing. masc.	קום
בַּמִּקְנֶה	pref. בְּ f. [בָּה] noun m. s. dec. 9 a; ו bef. (:)	קנה
בְּמִקְנֶה	ו pref. בְּ	
בְּמִקְנֶה	ו pref. id.) id., constr. st.; ו id.	קנה
בְּמִקְנֵיכֶם	pref. id.) id. pl., suff. 2 pers. pl. masc.	קנה
בְּמִקְנֶךָ	pref. id.) sing., suff. 2 pers. sing. masc.	קנה
בְּמִקְצָץ	pref. id.) pr. name of a place	קצץ
בְּמִקְצֹעַ	pref. id.) noun masc. sing. dec. 1 b.	קצע
בַּמַּקְצֻעוֹת	pref. בַּ for [בָּה]) n. fem., pl. of [מַקְצֻעָה] d. 10.	קצע
בַּמִּקְרָא	pref. id.) noun m. sing. dec. 1 b. (§ 31. r. 1)	קרא
בְּמִקְשָׁה	pref. בְּ) noun fem. sing., [for מִקְשָׁאָה]	קשא
בְּמֹר	pref. id.) noun masc. sing. dec. 8. (§ 37. r. 7)	מרר
בְּמִקְרָא	ו pref. id.) n. m. s. d. 1 b. (§ 31. r. 1. & 2); ו bef. (:)	ירא
בַּמַּרְאָה	pref. בַּ for [בָּה]) noun fem. sing. dec. 10.	ראה
בַּמַּרְאֶה	pref. id.) noun masc. sing. dec. 9 a.	ראה
בְּמַרְאֹת	pref. בְּ) noun fem., pl. of מַרְאָה dec. 10.	ראה
בְּמַרְאֵי	ו pref. id.) Kh. מַרְאֵי, K. מַרְאֵה n. m. pl. or sing. constr. from מַרְאֵה dec. 9 a.	ראה
בְּמַרְאֹת	pref. id.) noun fem., pl. of מַרְאָה dec. 10.	ראה
בְּמַרְבִּית	ו pref. id.) noun fem. s. dec. 1 b; ו bef. (:)	רבה
בְּמַרְגְּמָה	ו pref. id.) noun fem. sing.	רגם
בְּמֶרֶד	ו pref. id.) noun masc. sing.	מרד
בְּמֹרְדֵי	ו pref. id.) Kal part. pl. constr. masc. from [מוֹרֵד] dec. 7 b.	מרד

בְּמָרְדְּכַי	pref. id.) pr. name masc., see מָרְדְּכַי	מרד
בְּמָרָה	pref. id.) pr. name of a fountain	מרר
בַּמָּרוֹם	pref. בַּ for [בָּה]) noun masc. sing. dec. 3 a.	רום
בְּמָרוֹם	pref. בְּ bef. (:)) id., construct state	רום
בִּמְרוֹמָיו	pref. id.) id. pl., suff. 3 pers. sing. masc.	רום
בַּמְּרוֹמִים	pref. בַּ for [בָּה]) id. pl., absolute state	רום
בַּמְּרוֹרִים	pref. id.) noun masc., pl. of [מָרוֹר] dec. 3 a.	מרר
בְּמֶרְחָב	pref. id.) noun masc. sing. dec. 2 b.	רחב
בַּמֶּרְחַקִּים	ו pref. id.) n.m., pl. of מֶרְחָק d. 8 a; ו bef. lab.	רחק
בַּמַּרְחֶשֶׁת	pref. id.) noun fem. sing.	רחש
בִּמְרִיבַת	pref. בְּ bef. (:)) n.f.s., constr. of מְרִיבָה d. 10.	ריב
בִּמְרִיֵם	pref. בְּ) n. m. s., suff. 3 p. pl. m. fr. מְרִי d. 6 i.	מרה
בִּמְרִירוּת	ו pref. בְּ bef. (:)) noun fem. sing.; ו bef. lab.	מרר
בַּמֶּרְכָּבָה	ו pref. בַּ for [בָּה]) n. fem. s. (§ 42. r. 5); ו id.	רכב
בְּמֶרְכֶּבֶת	pref. id.) id. construct state	רכב
בְּמֶרְכַּבְתּוֹ	pref. id.) id., suff. 3 pers. sing. masc.	רכב
בְּמַרְבַּלְתֵּךְ	pref. id.) noun fem. sing., suff. 2 pers. sing. fem. from [מַרְבֶּלֶת] dec. 13 c.	רבל
בְּמִרְמָה	ו pref. id.) n. fem. sing. dec. 10; ו bef. lab.	רמה
בְּמִרְעֶה	pref. id.) noun masc. sing. dec. 9 b.	רעה
בַּמְּרֵעִים	pref. בַּ for [בָּה]) Hiph. part. masc., pl. of [מֵרַע for מֵרֵעַ] dec. 3 b.	רעע
בִּמְרֻצֹתָם	pref. בְּ bef. (:)) Kh. צוֹתָם, K. צֹתָם, pl. or sing. with suff. 3 pers. pl. m. from [מְרוּצָה]	רוץ
בַּמַּרְצֵעַ	pref. בַּ for [בָּה]) noun masc. sing.	רצע
בְּמֶרְקַחַת	pref. בְּ) noun fem. sing.	רקח
בַּמַּשָּׂא	pref. בַּ f. [בָּה]) noun m. s. d. 1 a. (§ 31. r. 1)	נשא
בְּמַשָּׂא	pref. בְּ q. v.	נשא
בְּמַשְׁאוֹן	pref. id.) noun masc. sing.	נשא
בְּמִשְׁאֲרוֹתֶיךָ	ו pref. id.) noun fem. pl., suff. 2 pers. s. m. fr. [מִשְׁאֶרֶת] d. 13 a; ו bef. (:)	שאר
בְּמִשְׁבָּר	pref. id.) noun masc. sing., constr. of מַשְׁבֵּר (§. 36. rem. 1)	שבר
בְּמִשְׁבְּתָם	pref. id.) noun masc. pl., suff. 3 pers. pl. masc. fr. מוֹשָׁב dec. 2 b.	ישב
בְּמֹשֶׁה	ו pref. id.) pr. name masc.; ו bef. (:)	משה
בִּמְשֹׁךְ	pref. בְּ bef. (:)) Kal inf. constr.	משך
בִּמְשׁוֹרָה	ו pref. בְּ f. [בָּה]) noun fem. sing.; ו bef. lab.	שור
בִּמְשׁוֹרָה	pref. בְּ bef. (:)	
בִּמְשִׁיחַ	pref. id.) noun m. s., constr. of מָשִׁיחַ d. 3 a.	משח
בִּמְשִׁיחָי	pref. id.) id. pl., suff. 1 pers. sing. for מְשִׁיחַי	משח
בַּמֹּשֵׁךְ	pref. בַּ) Kal part. act. sing. masc. dec. 7 b.	משך
בִּמְשֹׁךְ	pref. בְּ bef. (:)) id. inf. constr.	משך
בְּמִשְׁכָּב	pref. בְּ for [בָּה]) noun masc. sing. dec. 2 b.	שכב
בְּמִשְׁכָּבָהּ	pref. id.) id., suff. 3 pers. sing. fem.	שכב
בְּמִשְׁכָּבוֹ	pref. id.) id., suff. 3 pers. sing. masc	שכב

* Is. 44. 12. ^{a} Ge. 29. 26. ^{p} Jos. 22. 8. ^{u} Ne. 8. 8. ^{d} Pr. 26. 8. ^{k} Zec. 10. 9. ^{q} Ge. 41. 43. ^{y} Ex. 21. 6. ^{s} Ex. 10. 23.

Je. 10. 4. ^{b} Nu. 22. 27. ^{q} Ge. 47. 17. ^{v} Is. 1. 8.   · Jos. 22. 22.   · Le. 7. 9. ^{r} 1 Sa. 8. 11. ^{z} 2 Ch. 16. 14. ^{t} Le. 19. 35.

^{c} Ps. 96. 6. ^{c} Ge. 39. 9. ^{r} Ge. 47. 16. ^{w} De. 26. 8. ^{e} Job 24. 13. ^{m} Nu. 27. 14. ^{s} Eze. 27. 24. ^{a} 1 Ch. 15. 22. ^{u} Eze. 4. 11, 16.

Eze. 44.7,8,11. ^{d} Ge. 32. 11. ^{s} Ex. 9. 3. ^{x} Ec. 11. 9. ^{t} Je. 31. 12. ^{n} Ne. 9. 17. ^{t} Ho. 12. 1. ^{b} Pr. 26. 26. ^{v} Am. 9. 13.

Ps. 68. 27. ^{e} Ex. 29. 31.   Eze. 46. 21. ^{y} Ex. 38. 8. ^{f} Job 25. 2. ^{o} Eze. 21. 11. ^{u} Eze. 34. 14. ^{c} Ex. 7. 28. ^{w} 2 Ch. 16. 14.

Ps. 26. 12. ^{f} 1 Ch. 16. 27.   · Is. 44. 13. ^{z} Le. 25. 37. ^{g} La. 3. 15. ^{p} Zec. 6. 2, 3, 3. ^{v} Jer. 8. 6. ^{d} Ho. 13. 13. ^{x} Le. 15. 21.

Hag 2. 9. ^{g} Ge. 13. 2.

בְּמָשְׁכוֹ — pref. בְּ)(Kal inf., suff. 3 pers. sing. masc. . משך

בְּמַשְׂכִּיּוֹת — pref. id.)(n. f., pl. of (§ 39. No. 4. r. 1) . שכה

בְּמִשְׁכָּן — ‎ pref. id.)(noun masc. sing. d. 2 b; ‎ bef. (:) . שכן

בְּמִשְׁכְּנוֹת — ‎ id. pl. fem., constr. state; ‎ id. . שכן

בְּמַשְׂכֻּרְתִּי — pref. id.)(noun fem. sing., suff. 3 pers. sing. masc. fr. מַשְׂכִּית dec. 1 b. . שכה

בְּמָשָׁל — pref. id.)(noun masc. sing. dec. 4 a. משל

בִּמְשֹׁל — ‎ pref. בְּ bef. (:))(Kal inf. constr. ‎ bef. lab. משל

בְּשִׁמְמַנֵּי — ‎ pref. בְּ)(noun masc. pl. constr. fr. [מִשְׁמָן] dec. 8 a; ‎ id. . שמן

בְּמִשְׁמַנֵּיהֶם — pref. id.)(id., suff. 3 pers. pl. masc. . שמן

בְּמִשְׁמַנַּיו — pref. id.)(id., suff. 3 pers. sing. masc. . שמן

בַּמִּשְׁמָר / בְּמִשְׁמָר — pref. בַּ f. [בְּהַ] / pref. בְּ q. v. } noun masc. sing. dec. 2 b. . שמר

בְּמִשְׁמַר — pref. id.)(id., constr. state . שמר

בְּמִשְׁמָרוֹ — pref. id.)(id., suff. 3 pers. sing. masc. . שמר

בְּמִשְׁמְרוֹתֵיהֶם / בְּמִשְׁמְרוֹתָם — pref. id.)(noun f. pl., suff. 3 pers. pl. m. fr. מִשְׁמֶרֶת d. 13 a. (§ 4. r. 2) } שמר

בְּמִשְׁמָרָיו — ‎ pref. בְּ)(noun masc. pl., suff. 3 pers. sing. masc. fr. מִשְׁמָר dec. 2 b; ‎ bef. (:) . שמר

בְּמִשְׁמֶרֶת — pref. id.)(noun fem. sing. dec. 13 a, pl. מִשְׁמָרוֹת (§ 44. rem. 5) . שמר

בְּמִשְׁמַרְתָּם — pref. id.)(id. pl., suff. 3 p. pl. m. (§ 4. r. 2) שמר

בַּמִּשְׁנֶה — pref. בַּ for [בְּהַ])(noun masc. sing. dec. 9 a. שנה

בְּמִשְׁעוֹל — pref. בְּ)(noun masc. sing. שעל

בְּמִשְׁעֵנֹתָם — pref. id.)(noun fem. pl., suff. 3 pers. pl. m. fr. מִשְׁעֶנֶת dec. 13 a. שען

בְּמִשְׁפְּחוֹתֵיהֶם / בְּמִשְׁפְּחוֹתָם — pref. id.)(noun fem. pl., suff. 3 pers. pl. masc. fr. מִשְׁפַּחַת, constr. of פְּחָה (§ 42. r. 5. & § 4. r. 2) } שפח

בְּמִשְׁפַּחְתּוֹ — ‎ pref. id.)(id. s., suff. 3 p. s. m.; ‎ bef. (:) . שפח

בַּמִּשְׁפָּט / בְּמִשְׁפָּט — pref. בַּ for [בְּהַ] noun masc. sing. dec. 2 b; / pref. בְּ q. v. } ‎ bef. (:) . שפט

בְּמִשְׁפַּט — pref. id.)(id., constr. state . שפט

בְּמִשְׁפָּטַי — ‎ pref. id.)(id. pl., suff. 1 pers. s.; ‎ bef. (:) . שפט

בְּמִשְׁפְּטֵיהֶם — ‎ pref. id.)(id. pl., suff. 3 p. pl. m.; ‎ id. . שפט

בְּמִשְׁפָּטֶיךָ — ‎ pref. id.)(id. pl., suff. 2 pers. s. m.; ‎ id. . שפט

בְּמִשְׁקוֹל — pref. id.)(noun masc. sing. שקל

בַּמִּשְׁקָל / בְּמִשְׁקָל — pref. בַּ f. [בְּהַ] / pref. בְּ q. v. } noun masc. sing. dec. 2 b. . שקל

בְּמִשְׁקַל — pref. id.)(id., constr. state . שקל

בְּמִשְׁקָלוֹ — pref. id.)(id., suff. 3 pers. sing. masc. . שקל

בְּמִשְׂרְפוֹת — ‎ pref. id.)(noun f. pl. constr. fr. [מִשְׂרָפָה] dec. 11 a; ‎ bef. (:) . שרף

בְּמִשְׁתֵּה — pref. id.)(noun masc. sing., constr. of מִשְׁתֶּה dec. 9 a. שתה

בַּמֵּת — pref. בַּ for [בְּהַ])(Kal part. sing. masc. d. 1 a. מות

בְּמֵת — pref. בַּ q. v. מות

בְּמִתְנֵי / בְּמָתְנָי — pref. id.)(n. m. s., (suff. מָתְנַי) d. 6 a. מתן

בְּמָתְנוֹ — pref. id.)(noun masc. sing., suff. 3 pers. s. m. fr. מֹתֶן dec. 6 g. מות

בְּמוֹתַי — noun fem. pl., suff. 1 pers. s. fr. בָּמָה d. 10. בום

בְּמֹתֵי — id. pl. constr. [fr. בָּמֹתֵים § 4. r. 2. & § 36. r. 6] בום

בְּמֵתֵי — pref. בְּ bef. (:))(noun masc. pl. constr. [fr. מֵת § 36. r. 5.] מתה

בָּמֹתָיו — noun f. pl., suff. 3 pers. s. m. fr. בָּמָה d. 10. בום

בְּמוֹתָיו — pref. בְּ)(noun masc. pl., suff. 3 pers. sing. masc. fr. מָוֶת dec. 6 g. מות

בָּמֹתֶיךָ — noun f. pl., suff. 2 pers. s. m. fr. בָּמָה d. 10. בום

בְּמוֹתֵיכֶם — id. pl., suff. 2 pers. pl. masc. . בום

בַּמֵּתִים — pref. בַּ for [בְּהַ])(Kal part. m., pl. of מֵת d. 1 a. מות

בְּמַתְכֻּנְתָּהּ — pref. בְּ)(noun fem. sing., suff. 3 pers. sing. fem. fr. מַתְכֹּנֶת dec. 13 c. תכן

בְמַתְכֻּנְתּוֹ — ‎ pref. id.)(id., suff. 3 p. s. m.; ‎ bef. (:) . תכן

בְּמֹתָם — pref. id.)(noun masc. sing., suff. 3 pers. pl. masc. fr. מָוֶת dec. 6 g. מות

בְּמַתְּנוֹתֵיכֶם — pref. id.)(noun fem. pl., suff. 2 pers. pl. masc. fr. מַתָּנָה dec. 11 a. נתן

בְּמַתְּנוֹתָם — pref. id.)(id. pl., suff. 2 p. pl. m. (§ 4. r. 2) נתן

בְּמַתְּנֵיהֶם — pref. id.)(noun masc., du, suff. 3 pers. pl. masc. fr. [מֹתֶן] dec. 6 c. מתן

בְּמָתְנָיו — pref. id.)(id. du., suff. 3 pers. sing. masc. מתן

בְּמָתְנֵינוּ — pref. id.)(id. du., suff. 1 pers. pl. מתן

בְּמִתְקָה — pref. id.)(pr. name of a place מתק

בְּמַתַּת — pref. id.)(noun fem. sing., [for מַתָּנָת] נתן

בֵּן — Kh. בֵּן q. v., K. בַּת (q. v.). . כנה

בֵּן — ‎ n. m. s. irr. (§ 45), also pr. n. m.; ‎ bef. lab. בנה

בֶּן — ‎ id., constr. state (§ 36. r. 3), also pr. name in compos. as בֶּן־אוֹנִי, &c. . בנה

בֶּן — ‎ id. constr. state; ‎ id. בנה

בִּנְא — pref. בְּ)(pr. n. of a place, see נא

בִּנְאָדָד — pref. id.)(n. m. s., suff. 2 p. s. m. fr. נֹאד d. 1 a. נאד

בִּנְאוֹת — pref. בְּ bef. (:))(noun fem. pl. constr. fr. [נָאָה] dec. 11 a. נאה

בְּנֶאֱמָנֵי — pref. בְּ)(Niph. part. pl. constr. [for נֶאֱמָנֵי] fr. נֶאֱמָן dec. 2 b. אמן

בִּנְב — pref. id.)(pr. name of a place נבה

בִּנְבִיאֵי — ‎ defect. for בִּנְבִיאֵי q. v. נבא

בְּנַבוּאַת — Ch. pref. בְּ bef. (:))(noun fem. sing., constr. of נְבוּאָה dec. 8 a. נבא

בִּנְבִיאֵי — ‎ pref. בְּ)(noun m. s. dec. 3 a; ‎ bef. lab. נבא

בִּנְבִיאֵי — ‎ pref. בְּ bef. (:))(id. pl. constr. state נבא

a Ps. 10. 9. f Pr. 29. 2. k 2 Ch. 31. 17. p Nu. 21. 18. u Eze. 23. 24. z Je. 34. 5. e Je. 17. 3. k Eze. 20. 26. p Ps. 101. 6.
b Pr. 25. 11. g Da. 11. 24. l 2 Ch. 31. 16. q 1 Ch. 6. 45. v Eze. 7. 27. a Nu. 19. 18. l Le. 26. 30. z 2 Ch. 11. 18. q Je. 23. 14.
c 2 Sa. 7. 6. h Ps. 78. 31. m Ne. 13. 14. r 1 Ch. 4. 38. w Ne. 9. 29. b Nu. 19. 11, 13, 16. m Ps. 88. 6. a Jon. 4. 10. r Ge. 6. 14.
d Is. 32. 18. i Is. 10. 16. n Nu. 4. 27. s Le. 20. 5. x Eze. 4. 10. c Ps. 32. 9. n Ex. 30. 37. b Ps. 56. 9. s Ho. 12. 14, 14.
e Pr. 18. 11. j Ge. 40. 4. o Nu. 8. 26. t Ho. 2. 21. y 1 Ch. 28. 15. d 2 Sa. 22. 34. o Ex. 30. 32. c Ps. 23. 2. t Je. 23. 13.
f Ps. 78. 2. k Ne. 7. 3. o Nu. 22. 24. t Nu. 27. 21. z Ge. 43. 21. e Is. 53. 9. o Eze. 20. 39. aa Pr. 25. 14.

בִּנְבִיאֵי	pref. id.)(id. pl., suff. 1 pers. sing.	נבא
בִּנְבִיאָיו	pref. id.)(id. pl., suff. 3 pers. sing. masc.	נבא
בַּנְּבִיאִים, בִּנְבִיאִם	pref. בְּ for בְּהַ)(id. pl., absolute state	נבא
בִּנְבֵל, בִּנְבְלֵי	pref. בְּ)(noun masc. sing., pl. constr. dec. 6 b. & a.	נבל
בִּנְבָלִים	pref. בְּ bef. (ְ))(id. pl., abs. st.; id.	נבל
בְּנִבְלַת	pref. בְּ)(noun fem. sing., constr. of נְבֵלָה dec. 11. (§ 42. rem. 4)	נבל
בְּנִבְלָתָהּ	pref. id.)(id., suff. 3 pers. sing. fem.	נבל
בְּנִבְלָתָם	pref. id.)(id., suff. 3 pers. pl. masc.	נבל
בַּנֶּגֶב	pref. בַּ f.(בְּהַ)(noun masc. sing. dec. 6.	נגב
בְּנֶגֶב	pref. בְּ q.v. (§ 35. rem. 3)	נגב
בְּנֶגְבָּה	pref. בְּ for בְּהַ)(id. with parag. ה	נגב
בְּנֶגְהָא	Ch. pref. בְּ)(noun masc. sing., emph. of נֹגַהּ dec. 3 e.	נגה
בִּנְגִינוֹת	pref. בְּ bef. (ְ))(n. f., pl. of [נְגִינָה] d. 10.	נגן
בִּנְגִינוֹתַי	pref. id.)(id. pl., suff. 1 pers. sing. for תַי	נגן
בִּנְגִינֹת	defect. for נְגִינוֹת (q.v.)	נגן
בַּנֶּגַע	pref. בַּ f.(בְּהַ)(noun masc. sing. (d. 6 a. pl.	נגע
בְּנֶגַע	pref. בְּ q.v. constr. נִגְעֵי § 35. r. 5)	נגע
בְּנֶגְעוֹ	pref. id.)(Kal inf., suff. 3 pers. sing. masc.	נגע
בְּנֶגְעִי	pref. id.)(constr. of the following	נגע
בִּנְגָעִים	pref. בְּ bef. (ְ))(noun masc., pl. of נֶגַע dec. 6 a. (§ 35. rem. 5), bef. labial	נגע
בְּנָגְפוֹ	pref. בְּ)(Kal inf., suff. 3 pers. sing. masc.	נגף
בְּנֹגְשֵׂיהֶם	pref. id.)(Kal part. act. pl. masc., suff. 3 pers. pl. masc. fr. נֹגֵשׂ dec. 7 b.	נגש
בִּנְדָבָה	pref. בְּ bef. (ְ))(noun fem. sing. dec. 11 c.	נדב
בִּנְדִיבִים	pref. id.)(noun masc., pl. of נָדִיב dec. 3 a.	נדב
בְּנִדַּת	pref. בְּ)(noun fem. sing. dec. 10.	נדד
בְּנִדָּתָהּ	pref. id.)(id., suff. 3 pers. sing. fem.	נדד

בָּנָה I. *to build*, *to construct*, as a house, temple, &c. The materials of which something is built is mostly put in the acc. but rarely with בְּ; the place where, with בְּ, עַל.—II. *to repair, restore*.—III. metaph. *to establish, prosper*; בָּנָה בַּיִת לְ *to build a house to* or *for* any one, to give him posterity, or increase his family. Niph.—I. pass. of Kal Nos. I. & II.—II. *to be built up*, i. e. obtain children, spoken of a woman, Ge. 16. 2.

בְּנָא, בְּנָה Chald. *to build*. Ithpe. *to be built*.

בֵּן masc. irr. (§ 45).—I. *a son*; also used for *child*; בֶּן זָכָר *male-child*.—II. *foster-son*; hence applied to *pupils*.—III. *descendant*, as *a grandson*, &c. בְּנֵי בָנִים *grandsons*; בְּנֵי יִשְׂרָאֵל *Israelites*;

בְּנֵי עַמּוֹן *Ammonites*; applied to the inhabitants of a country בְּנֵי צִיּוֹן *inhabitants of Zion*.—IV. metaph. בֶּן מָוֶת *son of death*, i. e. one worthy of or destined for death; בִּן הַכּוֹת *worthy of stripes*, בֶּן חַיִל *son of strength*, i. e. warrior; בֶּן בְּלִיַּעַל *son of wickedness*, i. e. a wicked man; בֶּן עַוְלָה *son of perverseness*, i. e. a perverse man; בֶּן עֳנִי *son of affliction*, i. e. afflicted.—V. with a genit. of time, בֶּן שָׁנָה *son of a year*, i. e. a year old; בֶּן שְׁמוֹנִים שָׁנָה *eighty years old*; בֶּן לַיְלָה *a night old*.—VI. the young of brutes; בֶּן אֲתֹנוֹ *son of the ass*, i. e. foal; בֶּן יוֹנָה *young dove*; applied to plants, בֶּן פֹּרָת *a twig of a fruitful t...*—VII. pr. name masc. 1 Ch. 15. 18.

בֵּן Chald. masc. dec. 2 b, *son*.

בֶּן אוֹנִי (*son of my sorrow*) pr. name given to Benjamin by his mother, Ge. 35. 18.

בֶּן הֲדַד (*son of Hadad*, an Assyrian idol) pr. name of the kings of Damascus.

בֶּן חַיִל (*son of strength*) pr. name of a man, 2 Ch. 17. 7.

בֶּן חָנָן (*son of the gracious*) pr. name of a man, 1 Ch. 4. 20.

בִּן יָמִין (*son of my right hand*) pr. name masc of two different persons.

בִּנּוּי (*building*) pr. name masc. of several persons.

בְּנֵי בְרַק (*sons of Berak*, i. e. of lightning) pr. name of a town in the tribe of Dan, Jos. 19. 45.

בְּאֵרוֹת בְּ׳ יַעֲקָן pr. name of a place, see בְּ׳.

בָּנִי (*built up*) pr. name masc. of several persons.

בֻּנִּי (*built up*) pr. name of two different men.

בְּנָיָה (whom *the Lord built up*) pr. name masc. of several persons.

בְּנָיָהוּ (id.) pr. name masc. of several persons.

בִּנְיָה fem. *a building*, Eze. 41. 13.

בִּנְיָמִן, בִּנְיָמִין (*son of my right hand*) pr. name of Benjamin the youngest son of Jacob, and the tribe descended from him. Gent. n. בֶּן יְמִינִי, אִישׁ יְמִינִי, בֶּן הַיְמִינִי, and ellipt. יְמִינִי *Benjaminite*.

בִּנְיָן masc. *a building*. In Chald. id. only emph. בִּנְיָנָא Ezr. 5. 4.

בְּנִינוּ (*our son*, from Seg. בְּנִי) pr. name masc Ne. 10. 14.

בַּת fem. irr. (§ 45).—I. *daughter*.—II. *foster-daughter*.—III. *a female descendant*; בְּנוֹת יִשְׂרָאֵל *the daughters of Israel*, i. e. Hebrew women; בְּנוֹת הַפְּלִשְׁתִּים *Philistine women*; and applied to the inhabitants of a place, בְּנוֹת צִיּוֹן *the daughters*,

a 1 Ch. 16. 22.   c Ps. 33. 2.   e Le. 11. 24, 27. 36.   g Jos. 15. 21.   i Hab. 3. 19.   l De. 24. 8.   n 2 Sa. 7. 14.   p Ex. 12. 27.   Le. 1. 19,

b 1 Sa. 19. 24.   d Le. 11. 39.   Ju. 1. 16.   h Dr. 6. 20.   k Le. 13. 2.   m Le. 15. 23.   Ps. 89. 33.   r Is. 14. 2.   20. 32.

female inhabitants, of Zion; in the sing. collect. for בַּת־צִיּוֹן *daughter of Zion* for the inhabitants in general, so בַּת־עַמִּי *Tyrians*; בַּת־צֹר *my country people*.—IV. with the genit. of time, בַּת־תִּשְׁעִים שָׁנָה *a woman ninety years old*.—V. metaph. בַּת־עַיִן *daughter of the eye*, i. e. *the pupil*; בְּנוֹת הַשִּׁיר *daughters of song*, i. e. *songstresses*; applied to the produce of animals, trees, and places; בַּת הַיַעֲנָה *the female ostrich*; pl. בָּנוֹת *branches*, Gen. 49. 22; by *daughters*, when spoken of a city, are understood the *small towns* and *villages* dependent upon it.

בַּת־רַבִּים (*daughter of many*) pr. name of a gate in Heshbon, Ca. 7. 5.

בַּת־שֶׁבַע (*daughter of oath*) pr. name of the wife of Uriah, afterwards of David, mother of Solomon.

בִּתְיָה (*daughter*, i. e. *worshipper of the Lord*) pr. name fem. 1 Ch. 4. 18.

יַבְנֶה (which *He causes to be built*) pr. name of a town of the Philistines.

יַבְנְאֵל (which *God causes to be built*) pr. name of a town—I. in the tribe of Judah, Jos. 15. 11.— II. in Naphtali, Jos. 19. 33.

יִבְנְיָה (whom *the Lord will build up*) pr. name masc. 1 Ch. 9. 8.

יִבְנִיָּה (id.) pr. name masc. 1 Ch. 9. 8.

מִבְנֶה masc. dec. 9, *a building*, Eze. 40. 2.

מִבְנַּי (*built up*) pr. name of a warrior of David, 2 Sa. 23. 27, elsewhere סִבְּכַי q. v.

תִּבְנִי (for תִּבְנְיָה *building of the Lord*) pr. name masc. 1 Ki. 16. 21, 22.

תַּבְנִית fem. dec. 1 b.—I. *model*.—II. *form, resemblance*.—III. *building*.

בָּנֹה Kal inf. abs.   .   .   .   .   .   בנה
בָּנָהּ pref. בְּ ✗ n.m.s., suff. 3 p.s.f.fr. בֵּן irr. (§ 45)   בנה
בְּנֵה Chald. Peal part. pass. sing. masc.   .   בנה
בְּנֵה Kal imp. sing. masc.   .   .   .   בנה
בֹּנֶה id. part. act. sing. masc. dec. 9 a.   .   בנה
בְּנָהִי Chald. Peal pret. 3 p. s. m., suff. 3 p. s. m.   בנה
בַּנְּהָר[a] pref. בַּ for בְּהַ ✗ noun masc. sing. dec. 4 a.   נהר
בִּנְהַר pref. בְּ bef. (:) ✗ id., construct state   .   נהר
בִנְהָרוֹת[b] pref. בַּ for בְּהַ ✗ id. pl. f., abs. st.; וּ bef. lab.   נהר
בַּנְּהָרִים pref. id. ✗ id. pl. masc., absolute state   .   נהר
בְּנַהֲרֹתֶיךָ[c] pref. בְּ ✗ id. pl. fem., suff. 2 pers. sing. masc.   נהר
בְּנוֹ[d] Kh. for בְּנָיו (q. v. § 4. rem. 1)   .   בנה
בָּנוּ[e] Kal pret. 3 pers. pl.; וּ bef. lab.   .   בנה
בָּנוּ[f] Kal pret. 1 pers. pl. for בָּאנוּ (§ 25. No. 2. f.)   בוא

בָּנוּ pref. prep. בְּ with suff. 1 pers. pl. (§ 5)   ב
בְּנוֹ Kh. בָּנוֹ q. v., K. בְּנִי (q. v.)   בנה
בְּנוֹ[g] noun m. s., suff. 3 p. s. m. or (Nu. 24. 3, 15) with וּ parag. from בֵּן irr. (§ 45); וּ bef. (:)   בנה
בְּנוֹ[h] Chald. Peal pret. 3 pers. pl. masc.; וּ id.   בנה
בְּנוֹ[i] Kal imp. pl. masc.; וּ id.   .   .   בנה
בְּנֹוֶה pref. בְּ ✗ noun masc. sing. dec. 9 b.   .   נוה
בִּנְוֵה pref. בְּ bef. (:) ✗ id., construct state   .   נוה
בְּנוֹהוּ Kal pret. 3 pers. pl., suff. 3 pers. sing. masc.   בנה
בְּנוֹהִי[k] Chald. n. m. pl., suff. 3 p. s. m. fr. בֵּן d. 2 t   בנה
בָּנוּי[l] Kal part. pass. sing. masc. dec. 3 a.   .   בנה
בָּנוּי[m] pr. name masc.; וּ bef. lab.   .   .   בנה
בְּנוּיִם[n] Kal part. pass. [for בְּנוּיִים comp. § 3. rem. 1] from בָּנוּי dec. 3 a.   .   .   בנה
בְּנוֹית pref. בְּ ✗ Kh. נְוִית, K. נְיוֹת pr. name of a place   נוה
בְּנוּסָם pref. id. ✗ Kal inf. (נוּס), suff. 3 p. pl. m. d. 1 a.   נוס
בָּנוֹת[o] noun fem. pl. [as if from בָּנָה dec. 11 a] see בַּת irr. (§ 45); וּ bef. lab.   .   בנה
בָּנוֹת[p] id., construct state; or Kal inf. constr.; וּ id.   בנה
בְּנוֹתַי[q] id., suff. 1 pers. sing.; וּ id.   .   בנה
בְּנוֹתֶיהָ id., suff. 3 pers. sing. fem.; וּ id.   בנה
בְּנוֹתֵיהֶם id., suff. 3 pers. pl. masc.; וּ id.   בנה
בְּנוֹתָיו id., suff. 3 pers. sing. masc.; וּ id. .   בנה
בְּנוֹתַיִךְ[r] } id., suff. 2 pers. sing. fem.; וּ bef. lab.   בנה
בְּנוֹתָיִךְ[r] }
בְּנוֹתֶיךָ[s] id., suff. 2 pers. sing. masc.; וּ id.   בנה
בְּנוֹתֵיכֶם[t] id., suff. 2 pers. pl. masc.; וּ id.   בנה
בְּנוֹתֵינוּ[u] id., suff. 1 pers. pl.; וּ id.   .   בנה
בַּנּוֹתָר[v] pref. בַּ for בְּהַ ✗ Niph. part. sing. masc.   יתר
בְּנֵזֶק[w] pref. בְּ ✗ noun masc. sing.   .   .   נזק
בְּנֻחֹה[x] pref. id. ✗ Kal inf. (נוּחַ), suff. 3 pers. sing. masc.; וּ bef. lab.   .   .   .   נוח

בַּנַּחַל
בַּנָּחַל }pref. בַּ f. בְּהַ } noun masc. sing. dec. 6 c.   נחל
בְּנַחַל }
בִּנְחַל pref. בְּ q. v.
בַּנַּחֲלָה pref. בַּ f. בְּהַ } noun fem. sing. 12 d.   נחל
בְּנַחֲלָה pref. בְּ q. v. }
בְּנַחֲלֵי pref. id. ✗ constr. of the following: .   נחל
בַּנְּחָלִים[y] pref. בַּ for בְּהַ ✗ noun masc., pl. of נַחַל dec. 6 d; וּ bef. lab.   .   .   נחל
בְּנַחֲלַת pref. בְּ ✗ n. fem. s., constr. of נַחֲלָה dec. 12 d.   נחל
בְּנַחֲלָתוֹ[z] pref. id. ✗ id., suff. 3 pers. s. m.; וּ bef. lab.   נחל
בְּנַחֲלָתְךָ[a] } pref. id. ✗ id., suff. 2 pers. sing. masc.   נחל
בְּנַחֲלָתֶךָ[b] }
בְּנַחֲלַתְכֶם[c] pref. id. ✗ id., suff. 2 pers. pl. masc.   נחל
בְּנַחֲלָתָם pref. id. ✗ id. sing., suff. 3 pers. pl. masc.   נחל

---

[a] 1 Ki. 8. 13.   [e] Hab. 3. 8.   [i] 1 Ch. 22. 7.   [m] Ca. 4. 4.   [p] Eze. 16. 48.   [s] Ps. 144. 12.   [w] Est. 7. 4.   [y] Is. 7. 19.   [z] Ps. 79. 1.
[b] Esr. 5. 11.   [f] Eze. 32. 2.   [k] Ezr. 6. 14.   [n] Ne. 7. 4.   [q] Ge. 31. 31.   [t] 2 Ch. 29. 9.   [x] Nu. 10. 36.   [A] Le. 11. 9. 10.   [B] De. 19. 14
[c] Ezr. 5. 11.   [g] Da. 11. 10.   [l] Ne. 3. 13.   [o] Is. 43. 6.   [r] 2 Ki. 4. 7.   [u] Je. 12. 14.   Ps. 78. 62.   [f] Nu. 18. 26.
Ps. 66. 6.   [d] 1 Sa. 25.

בְּנַחֶמְךָ · pref. בְּ χ Piel inf. (נֵחֶם § 14. rem. 1), suff. 2 pers. sing. masc. dec. 7 b .   נחם

בַּנְחֹשֶׁת ⁾ pref. בַּ for בְּהַ χ noun fem. sing. dec. 13 c;   נחש
בִּנְחֹשֶׁת ⁾ pref. בְּ bef. (.:) ⁾ bef. lab. .

בִּנְחֻשְׁתַּיִם pref. בְּ for בְּהַ χ id. dual, abs. st. (comp. § 35. r. 8)   נחש

בְּנַחַת ⁵ pref. בְּ χ noun fem. sing. .   נוח

בָּנַט Root not used; probably *to bind*, comp. Pers. *bando*, Germ. and Eng. *band.*

אַבְנֵט masc. dec. 1 b, *a girdle* worn by the priests.

בְּנָטֵנִי ⁷ pref. בְּ bef. (.:) χ Kal inf. constr., suff. 1 pers. sing. dec. 1 a . . . . נטה

בָּנַי ⎫ noun m. pl. (בָּנִים), suff. 1 pers. sing. ⎫   בנה
בָּנַי ⎬ irr. of בֵּן (§ 45); ⁾ bef. lab. ⎭
בָּנִי ⎭ ⁾ pr. name masc.; ⁾ id.   בנה

בָּנִי Kh. בָּנַי q. v., K. בֵּן (q. v.)   בנה

בְּנֵי ⁾ n. m. pl., constr. of בָּנִים irr. of בֵּן (§ 45); also pr. name in compos. as בְּנֵי־בְרַק &c.   בנה

בְּנִי ⁾ id. sing. construct state (Ge. 49. 11), or with suff. 1 pers. sing.; ⁾ bef. lab. .   בנה

בֹּנַי ⁾⁾ Kal part. pl. constr. m. fr. בָּנָה d. 9 a; ⁾ id.   בנה

בֻּנִּי ⁾ pr. name masc. . . . .   בנה

בָּנֶיהָ ¹¹ noun masc. pl. (בָּנִים), suff. 3 pers. sing. fem. irr. of בֵּן (§ 45); ⁾ bef. lab.   בנה

בְּנָיָה ⁾ pr. name masc.; ⁾ id. . .   בנה

בְּנָיָהוּ ⁾ pr. name masc.; ⁾ id. . .   בנה

בְּנֵיהֶוֹת Ch. n. m. pl., suff. 3 pers. pl. m. from בֵּן d. 2 b   בנה

בְּנֵיהֶם ⁾ id. pl., suff. 3 pers. pl. masc.; ⁾ bef. (.:)   בנה

בְּנֵיהֶם־ pref. בְּ χ noun masc. sing., suff. 3 pers. pl. masc. [from נִי for נְהִי] .   נהה

בְּנֵיהֶן ⁾¹ noun masc. pl. (בָּנִים), suff. 3 pers. pl. fem. irr. of בֵּן (§ 45); ⁾ bef. lab. .   בנה

בָּנָיו ⁾ id. pl., suff. 3 pers. sing. masc.; ⁾ id.   בנה

בָּנַיִךְ ⎫ id., suff. 2 pers. sing. fem. .   בנה
בָּנַיִךְ ⎭

בָּנֶיךָ ⁾ id., suff. 2 pers. sing. masc.; ⁾ bef. lab. .   בנה

בֹּנָיִךְ ⁾ Kal part. act. pl. masc., suff. 2 pers. sing. fem. from בָּנָה dec. 9 a .   בנה

בָּנַיְכִי noun masc. pl. (בָּנִים), suff. 2 pers. sing. fem. Kh. בָּנַיְכִי (§ 4. r. 4) K. בָּנַיִךְ, see בֵּן (§ 45)   בנה

בְּנֵיכֶם ⁾ id. pl., suff. 2 pers. pl. masc.; ⁾ bef. lab. .   בנה

בָּנִים ⁾ id. pl. absolute state; ⁾ id. .   בנה

בִּנְיָמִין ⎫ pr. name masc.; ⁾ id. . .   בנה
בִּנְיָמִן ⎬
בְּנַיִן ⁾ Chald. Peal part. act. masc., pl. of [בְּנָא] dec. 6 a; ⁾ id. see . .   בנה

בִּנְיָן ⁾ noun masc. sing. . . . .   בנה

בִּנְיָנָא Chald. id., emph. state dec. 1 a   בנה

בָּנֵינוּ ⁴⁾ noun masc. pl. (בָּנִים), suff. 1 pers. pl., irr. of בֵּן (§ 45); ⁾ bef. lab. .   בנה

בָּנִינוּ ⁾ Kal pret. 1 pers. pl.; ⁾ id.   בנה

בֵּינֵינוּ ⁾⁴ defect. for בֵּינֵינוּ (q. v.) .   בין

בְּנִינוּ ⁾ pr. name masc. . . .   בנה

בְּנִינְוֵה pref. בְּ χ pr. name of a place, see נִינְוֵה .

בָּנִיתָ ⁾⁵ Kal pret. 2 pers. sing. masc.; ⁾ bef. lab.   בנה

בָּנִיתָ id. pret., Kh. בָּנִית 2 p. s. m., K. בָּנִיתִי 1 p. s.   בנה

בָּנִית ⁵ id. pret. 2 pers. sing. fem.   בנה

בְּנִיתַהּ Chald. Peal pret. 1 p. s., suff. 3 p. s. fem., see   בנה

בָּנִיתִי ⁴⁾ Kal pret. 1 pers. sing.; ⁾ bef. lab.   בנה

בְּנִיתִיהָ ⁾ id. id., suff. 3 pers. sing. fem.; ⁾ id.   בנה

בְּנִיתִים ᵍᵍ id. id., suff. 3 pers. pl. masc.; ⁾ id.   בנה

בְּנִיתֶם ⁾ id. pret. 2 pers. pl. masc.   בנה

בָּנֵךְ in pause for בְּנֵךְ (q. v.) . .   בנה

בְּנֵךְ ⁾¹ noun masc. sing., suff. 2 pers. sing. fem. from בֵּן irr. (§ 45); ⁾ bef. lab. .   בנה

בִּנְךָ ⁾ id., suff. 2 pers. sing. masc.; ⁾ id.   בנה

בְּנִכְבָּר pref. בְּ for בְּהַ χ Niph. part. sing. masc. dec. 2 & 8 (§ 37. rem. 5)   כבד

בִּנְכְלֵיהֶם] pref. בְּ [n. m. pl., suff. 3 p. pl. m. fr. נֵכֶל] d. 6 b   נכל

בִּנְכָסִים pref. בְּ bef. (.:) χ noun m., pl. of [נֶכֶס] dec. 6 a   נכס

בְּנֻגֵּנוּ noun m. s., suff. 1 pers. pl. from בֵּן irr. (§ 45)   ינח

בְּנַם Chald. *to be angry*, Da. 2. 12.

בִּנְסָכִים ⁴ pref. בְּ for בְּהַ χ noun masc., pl. of נֶסֶךְ dec. 6 b; ⁾ bef. lab. . . .   נסך

בִּנְסֹעַ ⁷⁾ pref. בְּ bef. (.:) χ Kal inf. constr.; ⁾ id.   נסע

בְּנָסְעָם pref. בְּ χ id., suff. 3 pers. pl. masc. .   נסע

בִּנְעָא ⎫ pr. name of a man, 1 Ch. 8. 37; 9. 43.
בִּנְעָה ⎭

בִּנְעוּרַיִן" pref. בְּ bef. (.:) χ noun masc. pl., suff. 3 pers. sing. fem. from [נָעוּר] dec. 1 a .   נער

בִּנְעוּרֵיהֶם‟ pref. id. χ id., suff. 3 pers. pl. masc.   נער

בִּנְעוּרֵיהֶן pref. id. χ id., suff. 3 pers. pl. fem.   נער

בִּנְעוּרָיו ⁾ pref. id. χ id., suff. 3 pers. sing. masc.   נער

בַּנְּעִימִים pref. בַּ for בְּהַ χ adj. m., pl. of נָעִים dec. 3 a   נעם

בְּנַעֲלוֹ⁵ ⁾ pref. בְּ χ noun masc. sing., suff. 3 pers. sing. masc. from נַעַל dec. 6 d; ⁾ bef. lab.   נעל

בַּנְּעָלִים pref. בַּ for בְּהַ χ id. pl., absolute state   נעל

בִּנְעַם‟ pref. בְּ χ noun masc. sing. . .   נעם

בַּנַּעַר‟ ⁾ pref. בַּ for בְּהַ χ noun masc. sing. dec. 6 d   נער

בְּנַעַר ⁾ pref. id. χ noun masc. sing.   נער

בִּנְעָרוֹת ⁵ pref. בְּ χ noun f. pl. constr. fr. נַעֲרָה d. 12 d   ער

a Eze. 16. 54.   f 2 Ki. 23. 10.   i Da. 6. 25.   ² 2 Ki. 4. 7.   ⁿ Ne. 2. 18, 20.   ᵖ Da. 4. 27.   t Jos. 22. 8.   * Ps. 144. 12.   r Ps. 27. 4.
b Jos. 22. 6.   g Ge. 49. 11.   ⁴ Eze. 27. 32.   s Ezr. 5. 11.   o Jos. 22. 25, 27.   q Am. 9. 11.   De. 21. 20.   ² Eze. 23. 3.   ² 2 Sa. 13. 12.
c Ec. 9. 17.   ⁴ 1 Ki. 5. 32.   ⁴ 1 Ki. 5. 33.   ³ Eze. 23. 37.   ⁾ De. 6. 10.   ¹ Ch. 29. 35.   k La. 3. 27.   ⁴ 1 Ki. 3. 9.   ⁴ Job 36. 14.
e Pr. 7. 5.   ¹ 1 Ki. 5. 33.   ¹ Esc. 4. 4.   ⁴ Eze. 16. 45.   ¹ Is. 3. 5.   ¹ 1 Ki. 8. 48.   ¹ Nu. 1. 51.   ¹ 1 Ki. 1. 21.   ⁴ Ru. 2. 23.
¹ 1 Sa. 12. 2.   ⁴ 1 Ki. 16. 45.   ⁴ Eze. 27. 4.   ⁴ 2 Ch. 29. 9.   ⁾ Ise. 16. 25.   ᵐ Nu. 25. 18.   ⁿ Eze. 23. 8.   ⁴ Je. 24. 6.

8

בִּנְעָרֵי	pref. בְּ ✕ noun m. pl. constr. fr. נַעַר d. 6 d.	נער
בִּנְעָרֶיהָ	pref. בְּ bef. (:) ✕ noun masc. pl., suff. 3 pers. sing. fem. fr. [נְעוּר] dec. 1 a.	נער
בַּנְּעָרִים	וּ pref. בְּ for בְּהַ ✕ noun masc., pl. of נַעַר dec. 6 d; וּ bef. labial	נער
בִּנְעָרֵינוּ	pref. בְּ bef. (:) ✕ id. pl., suff. 1 pers. pl.	נער
בְּנֹף	וּ pref. בְּ ✕ pr. n. of a place, see נֹף; וּ bef. (:)	
בִּנְפוֹת	וּ pref. id. ✕ noun f., pl. of [נָפָה] d. 10; וּ id.	נוף
בְּנִפְךָ	pref. id. ✕ noun masc. sing.	נפך
בִּנְפֹל	pref. בְּ bef. (:) ✕ Kal inf. constr.	נפל
בִּנְפְלָאוֹת	וּ pref. בְּ ✕ Niph. part. pl. abs. fr. [נִפְלָאָה] dec. 11 a, fr. נָפְלָא masc.	פלא
בְּנִפְלְאֹתֶיךָ	pref. id. ✕ id. pl., suff. 2 pers. sing. masc.	פלא
בְּנִפְלְאֹתָיו	pref. id. ✕ id. pl., suff. 3 pers. sing. masc.	פלא
בַּנֹּפְלִים	pref. בְּ for בְּהַ ✕ Kal part. act. masc., pl. of נֹפֵל dec. 7 b.	נפל
בַּנֶּפֶשׁ	pref. id. } noun com. sing., (suff. נַפְשִׁי)	נפש
בְּנֶפֶשׁ	וּ pref. בְּ dec. 6 a; וּ bef. (:) }	נפש
בְּנַפְשׁוֹ	וּ pref. id. ✕ id., suff. 3 pers. sing. m.; וּ id.	נפש
בְּנַפְשׁוֹ	pref. id. ✕ id., suff., Kh. נַפְשׁוֹ 3 pers. sing. masc. K. נַפְשִׁי 1 pers. sing.	נפש
בְּנַפְשֹׁתֵיכֶם	pref. id. ✕ id. pl., suff. 2 pers. pl. masc.	נפש
בְּנַפְשֹׁתָם	pref. id. ✕ id. pl., suff. 3 pers. pl. m. (§ 4. r. 2)	נפש
בְּנַפְשִׁי	וּ pref. id. ✕ id. s., suff. 1 pers. s.; וּ bef.	נפש
בְּנַפְשְׁךָ	pref. id. ✕ id. sing., suff. 2 pers. sing. fem.	נפש
בְּנַפְשָׁם	pref. id. ✕ id. sing., suff. 3 pers. pl. masc.	נפש
בְּנַפְשֵׁנוּ	pref. id. ✕ id. sing., suff. 1 pers. pl.	נפש
בְּנַפְשֹׁתָם	pref. id. ✕ id. pl., suff. 3 pers. pl. m. (§ 4. r. 2)	נפש
בְּנֶפַת	pref. id. ✕ noun f. s., constr. of [נָפָה] d. 10.	נוף
בְּנַפְתָּלִי	וּ pref. id. ✕ pr. name of a tribe	פתל
בַּנֹּצְרִים	וּ pref. בַּ for בְּהַ ✕ Kal part. p. masc., pl. of נָצוּר dec. 3 a; וּ bef. lab.	נצר
בְּנִצָּתָהּ	pref. בְּ ✕ noun fem. sing., suff. 3 pers. sing. fem. fr. [נִצָּה] dec. 10.	יצא
בְּנָקְבוֹ	pref. id. ✕ Kal inf., suff. 3 pers. sing. masc.	נקב
בַּנְּקָדִים	pref. בְּ for בְּהַ ✕ noun m., pl. of נָקֹד d. 7 b.	נקד
בִּנְקֹר	pref. בְּ bef. (:) ✕ Kal inf. constr.	נקר
בְּנָקִיק	pref. id. ✕ noun masc. sing. dec. 1 a.	נקק
בְּנִקָּיוֹן	pref. בְּ ✕ noun masc. sing. dec. 3 c.	נקה
בְּנִקְיוֹן	וּ pref. id. ✕ id., constr. state; וּ bef. labial	נקה
בִּנְקִיקֵי	וּ pref. בְּ bef. (:) ✕ noun masc. pl. constr. fr. נָקִיק dec. 1 a; וּ id.	נקק
בְּנָקְם	pref. id. ✕ Kal inf. constr.	נקם
בְּנִקְמָתָהּ	pref. id. ✕ noun fem. sing. dec. 11 c.	נקם
בִּנְקָרוֹת	pref. בְּ ✕ noun fem., pl. of [נְקָרָה] dec. 11 c.	נער
בְּנִקְרַת	pref. id. ✕ id. sing., constr. state	נקר

בַּנְּגֵרוֹת	pref. בְּ for בְּהַ ✕ noun masc. with pl. f. term. fr. נֵר dec. 1 a.	נור
בְּנָשְׂאִי	pref. בְּ ✕ Kal inf., suff. 1 pers. sing.	נשא
בַּנִּשְׁבָּעִים	וּ pref. בְּ f. בְּהַ ✕ Niph. part. pl. m.; וּ bef. lab.	שבע
בְּנִשְׁךְ	וּ pref. בְּ ✕ the following with suff. 2 pers. sing. masc.; וּ bef. labial	אנש
בַּנָּשִׁים	pref. בְּ for בְּהַ ✕ noun fem. with pl. masc. term. see אִשָּׁה in (§ 45)	אנש
בַּנֶּשֶׁף	pref. id. }	
בְּנֶשֶׁף	pref. בְּ } noun masc. sing. (§ 35. rem. 2)	נשף
בַּנֶּשֶׁף	pref. id. }	
בַּנֶּשֶׁף	pref. בְּ f. בְּהַ } noun masc. sing., (suff.	נשף
בַּנֶּשֶׁף	pref. בְּ q. v. } נִשְׁפּוֹ) dec. 6 a.	
בַּנֶּשֶׁק	pref. בְּ f. בְּהַ } noun masc. sing.	נשק
בְּנֶשֶׁק	pref. בְּ q. v. }	
בָּנְתָה	Kal pret. 3 pers. sing. fem.	בנה
בִּנְתָה	Kal pret. 2 pers. sing. masc. (§ 8. rem. 5)	בין
בָּנִיתָה	Kal pret. 2 pers. sing. masc. (§ 8. rem. 5)	בנה
בְּנֹתַי	noun fem. pl. (בָּנוֹת), suff. 1 pers. sing. irr. of בַּת (§ 45)	בנה
בִּנְתִיב	pref. בְּ bef. (:) ✕ noun masc. sing., constr. of נָתִיב dec. 3 a.	נתב
בִּנְתִיבוֹת	pref. id. ✕ noun fem., pl. of נְתִיבָה dec. 10.	נתב
בִּנְתִיבֹתֶיהָ	pref. id. ✕ id. pl., suff. 3 pers. sing. fem.	נתב
בִּנְתִיבֹתָיו	pref. id. ✕ id. pl., suff. 3 pers. sing. masc.	נתב
בְּנֹתֶיהָ	וּ noun fem. pl. (בָּנוֹת), suff. 3 pers. sing. fem., irr. of בַּת (§ 45); וּ bef. (:)	בנה
בְּנֹתֵיהֶם	וּ id. pl., suff. 3 pers. pl. masc.	בנה
בְּנֹתָיו	וּ id. pl., suff. 3 pers. sing. masc.	בנה
בְּנֹתַיִךְ	וּ id. pl., suff. 2 pers. sing. fem.	בנה
בְּנֹתֶיךָ	וּ id. pl., suff. 2 pers. sing. masc.	בנה
בְּנֹתֵיכֶם	וּ id. pl., suff. 2 pers. pl. masc.	בנה
בְּנֹתֵינוּ	וּ id. pl., suff. 1 pers. pl.	בנה
בְּנֹתָם	id. pl., suff. 3 pers. pl. masc. (§ 4. rem. 2)	בנה
בַּנֶּתֶר	pref. בְּ for בְּהַ ✕ noun masc. sing.	נתר
בִּסְאָה	pref. בְּ ✕ noun fem. sing.	סאה
בְּסֹבְאֵי	pref. id. ✕ Kal part. act. pl. constr. masc. from סָבָא dec. 7 b.	סבא
בִּסְבִיבָיו	וּ pref. בְּ bef. (:) ✕ noun masc. pl. constr. from סָבִיב dec. 3 a.; וּ bef. labial	סבב
בַּסְּבַךְ	pref. בְּ for בְּהַ ✕ noun masc. sing.	סבך
בִּסְבָךְ	pref. בְּ bef. (:) ✕ n. m. s. with mak. [for סְבַךְ]	סבך
בִּסְבְכֵי	pref. id. ✕ noun masc. pl. constr. [for סִבְכֵי] without metheg fr. סְבַךְ dec. 6 b; or perhaps from סֹבֶךְ § 35. rem. 10]	סבך
בַּסֵּבֶל	pref. בְּ for בְּהַ ✕ noun masc. sing.	סבל

a 1 Ki. 20. 14.   e Ps. 131. 1.   i Est. 4. 13.   m Le. 1. 16.   q Is. 7. 19.   u Ps. 28. 2.   y Eze. 39. 9.   c Pr. 7. 25.   g Pr. 23. 20.
b Nu. 30. 4, 17.   f Ps. 119. 27.   k Ps. 106. 15.   n Le. 24. 16.   r Eze. 25. 12.   v Mal. 3. 5.   z Ps. 139. 2.   d Job 24. 13.   h Ge. 22. 13.
c Job 1. 16.   g Ps. 78. 32.   l La. 5. 9.   o Am. 1. 1.   s 2 Ch. 21. 14.   w Is. 2. 21.   a Eze. 18. 8, 13.   e Ge. 34. 21.   i Nu. 74. 5.
d Ex. 10. 9.   h 1 Ch. 28. 9.   Nu. 17. 5.   p 1 Sa. 11. 2.   t Is. 2. 21.   x Pr. 7. 9.   b Ps. 119. 35.   f Je. 2. 22.   k Is. 9. 17.
Jos. 11. 2.   2 Sa. 18. 13.   Is. 30. 28.   Je. 13. 4.   Ex. 33. 22.   Is. 42. 16.   Is. 27. 8.   Ne. 4. 11.
Eze. 27. 16.   1 Sa. 2. 35.   Is. 85. 4.   Ge. 20. 5.   Zep. 1. 12.   Eze. 39. 10.

בְּסִבְלֹתָם	pref. בְּ)(noun fem. pl., suff. 3 pers. pl. masc. [§ 4. rem. 2; from [סִבְלָה or סְבָלָה	סבל
בַּסָּד	pref. בְּ for בַּה)(noun masc. sing.	סדד
בְּסָדִים‹	pref. בְּ)(noun masc. sing., suff. 3 pers. pl. masc. from סוֹד dec. 1 a.	יסד
בִּסְדֹם	pref. בְּ bef. (:))(pr. name of a place	סדם
בַּסּוּגַר‹	pref. בְּ for בַּה)(noun masc. sing.	סגר
בִּיסוֹד‹	pref. בְּ)(noun masc. sing. d. 1 a. [for [יְסוֹד	יסד
בְּסוֹדִי‹	pref. id.)(id., suff. 1 pers. sing.	יסד
בְּסוֹדְיָה	pr. name masc.	יסד
בְּסוּסֿ‹	pref. id.)(noun masc. sing. dec. 1 a.	סוס
בְּסוּסֹו‹	pref. id.)(id. pl., suff. 3 p. s. m. (§ 4. r. 1)	סוס
בַּסּוּסִים‹	‹ pref. בְּ f. בַּה)(id. pl., absolute state; ‹	סוס
בְּסוּסִים‹	pref. בְּ q. v. bef. labial	
בַּסּוּף‹	pref. בְּ for בַּה)(noun masc. sing.	סוף
בְּסוּףֿ‹	pref. בְּ)(noun masc. sing. dec. 1 a.	סוף
בְּסוּפָה	pref. בְּ)(noun fem. sing. dec. 10.	סוף
בְּסִי‹ בְּסַי	pr. name masc.	בוס
בְּסוּפָתֵךְ‹	‹ pref. בְּ)(noun fem., suff. 2 pers. sing. masc. fr. סוּפָה dec. 10; ‹ bef. labial	סוף
בַּסִּיר	pref. בְּ for בַּה)(noun com. sing. dec. 1 a.	סיר
בַּסִּירוֹת‹	pref. id. ‹ id. pl. fem.	סיר
בְּסִירֹות‹	pref. בְּ ‹	סיר
בַּסִּירִים‹	pref. בְּ for בַּה)(id. pl. masc.	סיר
בַּסָּךְ‹	pref. id.)(noun masc. sing.	סכך
בַּסֻּכָּה‹	pref. id. ‹	סכך
בְּסֻכָּה‹	pref. בְּ ‹ noun fem. sing. dec. 10.	סכך
בְּסֻכֹּה‹	pref. id.)(noun masc. sing., suff. 3 pers. sing. masc. (§ 3. rem. 3) fr. [סֹךְ] dec. 8 c.	סכך
בַּסֻּכֹּות‹	pref. בְּ for בַּה)(noun f., pl. of סֻכָּה d. 10.	סכך
בְּסִכְלוּת‹	pref. בְּ)(noun fem. sing.	סכל
בְּסֻכֹּת	pref. בְּ for בַּה)(noun f., pl. of סֻכָּה dec. 10.	סכך
בְּסֻכֹּת	pref. בְּ)(pr. name of a place	סכך
בַּסֶּלַע‹ בַּסֶּלַע‹ בְּסֶלַע‹	}pref. בְּ f. בַּה {noun masc. sing. dec. 8 d; ‹ bef. lab.	סלל
בְּסַלְכָה‹	‹ pref. id.)(pr. name of a place ; ‹ id.	סלך
בַּסֶּלַע‹ בְּסֶלַע‹	pref. בְּ f. בַּה {noun masc. s., (suff. [סַלְעִי]) dec. 6 a. (§ 35. rem. 5)	סלע
בַּסְּלָעִים‹	‹ pref. בְּ for בַּה)(id. pl., abs. st.; ‹ bef. lab.	סלע
בְּסֹמְכֵי‹	pref. בְּ)(Kal part. act. pl. constr. masc. from סָמַךְ dec. 7 b.	סמך
בַּסַּנְוֵרִים‹	pref. בְּ for בַּה)(noun masc., pl. of [סַנְוֵר]	סנור
בִּסְנַסִּנָּיו‹	pref. בְּ)(noun masc. pl., suff. 3 pers. sing. masc. from [סַנְסָן] dec. 8 e.	סנן

בְּסָסוּ	Pilel pret. 3 pers. pl. Je. 12. 10.	בוס
בִּסְעִיף‹	pref. בְּ bef. (:))(noun masc. sing. dec. 1 a.	סעף
בִּסְעִפַּי‹	‹ pref. id.)(id. pl., constr. st.; ‹ bef. labial	סעף
בִּסְעַפֶּיהָ	pref. id.)(id. pl., suff. 3 pers. sing. masc.	סעף
בְּסַעֲפֹתָיו‹	pref. id.)(noun fem. pl., suff. 3 pers. sing. masc. from [סְעַפָּה] dec. 10.	סעף
בְּסַעַר‹	pref. בְּ)(noun masc. sing. dec. 6 d.	סער
בַּסְּעָרָה‹	pref. בְּ for בַּה)(noun fem. sing.	סער
בִּסְעָרָה‹	pref. id.)(noun fem. sing. dec. 11 c. (§ 42. r. 1)	סער
בְּסַעֲרֹות‹	pref. בְּ)(id. pl., construct state	סער
בְּסַעְרֶךָ‹	pref. id.)(noun masc. sing., suff. 2 pers. sing. masc. [for [סַעֲרֶךָ], from סַעַר dec. 6 d.	סער
בַּסַּף‹ בַּסַּף‹ בְּסַף‹	}pref. בְּ f. בַּה {noun masc. sing. dec. 8 e.	ספף
בַּסִּפְּכִים‹	pref. בְּ q. v.	
בַּסַּפִּים‹	pref. בְּ for בַּה)(id. pl., absolute state	ספף
בַּסַּפִּירִים‹	pref. id.)(noun masc., pl. of סַפִּיר dec. 1 b.	ספר
בְּסַפֵּל‹	pref. id.)(noun masc. sing.	ספל
בַּסֵּפֶר‹ בְּסֵפֶר‹	pref. בְּ for בַּה {noun masc. sing. dec. 6 b. pref. בְּ q. v.	ספר
בְּסִפְרָא‹	Chald. pref. בְּ bef. (:))(noun m. s. dec. 3 b.	ספר
בִּסְפָרָד‹	pref. id.)(pr. name of a region	ספרד
בַּסְּפָרִים‹	pref. בְּ for בַּה)(n. m., pl. of סֵפֶר dec. 6 b.	ספר
בְּסִפְרָתְךָ‹	pref. בְּ)(n. f. s., suff. 2 p. s. m. [for [סִפְרָתְךָ] fr. סְפֹרָה	ספר
בָּסַר	Root not used ; Arab. *to do any thing too soon* ; also *to look sour*.
	בֹּסֶר m. d. 6 b, coll. *unripe, sour grapes*, Job 15.33 Also	
בֹּסֶר‹	‹ noun masc. i. q. בֹּסֶר ; ‹ bef. lab.	בסר
בְּסׇרְבַּלֵּיהֹון‹	Chald. pref. בְּ)(noun masc. pl., suff. 3 pers. pl. masc. from [סַרְבָּל] dec. 1 a.	סרבל
בְּסִרְיֹו‹	n. m. s., suff. 3 p. s. m. from [בֶּסֶר] dec. 6 b.	בסר
בְּסִרְיֹנֹו‹	pref. בְּ)(noun masc. sing., suff. 3 pers. sing. masc. from [סִרְיֹן] dec. 1 b. see שׂרה	שׂרה
בְּסׇתֻם‹	‹ pref. id.)(Kal part. pass. sing. masc. for סָתוּם dec. 3 a.; ‹ bef. (:)	סתם
בַּסֵּתֶר‹	pref. בְּ for בַּה)(seg. n. in pause [as if from סָתֶר=סֵתֶר § 35. rem. 2] see the following:	סתר
בַּסֵּתֶר‹ בְּסֵתֶר‹	pref. id. {noun masc. sing. dec. 6 b. pref. בְּ	סתר
בְּעֵא‹	Chald. Peal part. act. sing. masc. dec. 6 a.	בעא
בְּעָא‹	‹ Chald. Peal pret. 3 pers. s. m.; ‹ bef. (:)	בעא
בְּעָב‹	pref. בְּ)(noun masc. sing., constr. of עָב, as if from עָבָה, see עָב R.	עוב
בַּעֲבֹדָה‹	pref. בְּ for בַּה)(noun fem. sing. dec. 10.	עבד

ᵃ Ge. 49. 6.	ᵉ Ex. 2. 3.	ⁱ Ps. 42. 5.	ᵐ Ge. 40. 17.	ᵖ Ju. 15. 8.	ᵗ 2 Ki. 2. 1.
ᵇ Eze. 19. 9.	ᶠ 2 Ch. 20. 16.	ʲ Job 38. 40.	ⁿ Eze. 31. 6.	ᵠ Ju. 20. 47; 21. 13.	ᵘ 2 Ki. 2. 1.
ᶜ Je. 23. 22.	ᵍ Ps. 83. 16.	ᵏ Ps. 31. 21.	ᵒ Ec. 2. 3.	ʳ Is. 17. 6.	ᵛ Zec. 9. 14.
ᵈ Eze. 26. 7.	ʰ 1 Ch. 35. 13.	ˡ Am. 4. 2.	ᵖ 1 Sa. 21. 9.	ˢ Eze. 31. 6.	ʷ Ps. 83. 16.
ᵉ 2 Ki. 5. 9.					
ᶠ Ho. 1. 7.	ⁱ Ho. 2. 8.		Ju. 6. 19.		Am. 1. 14.

-ᵏ 1 Ki. 14. 17.   -ᵖ Ps. 56. 9.   ᵘ Ps. 51. 8.
-ᵖ 1 Ch. 9. 26.   ᵠ Is. 18. 5.   ˣ Da. 3. 21.
ᵘ Is. 54. 11.   ʸ Is. 5. 4.   ᶻ Da. 2. 49.
ᵛ Ju. 5. 25.   ᶻ Job 15. 33.   Da. 2. 16.
ᵉ Ezr. 4. 15.   Je. 51. 3.   Ex. 19. 9.

ᴤ*

בְּעָבְדוֹ   pref. בְּ)(n. m. s., suff. 3 p. s. m. fr. עֶבֶד d. 6a.   עבד

בְּעָבְדִי   pref. id.)(id., suff. 1 pers. sing.   עבד

בַּעֲבָדָיו   pref. בַּ bef. (־))(id. pl., suff. 3 pers. sing. m.   עבד

בַּעֲבָדֶיךָ   ﬣ pref. id.)(id. pl., suff. 2 p. s. m.; ﬣ bef. lab.   עבד

בְּעַבְדְּךָ } pref. בְּ)(id. sing., suff. 2 pers. sing. masc.   עבד
בַּעֲבָדֶךָ }

בַּעֲבֹדַת   pref. בַּ bef. (־))(n. f. s., constr. of עֲבוֹדָה d. 10.   עבד

בַּעֲבֹדָתָם   pref. id.)(id., suff. 3 pers. pl. masc.   עבד

בַּעֲבֹדָתֵנוּ   ﬣ pref. בַּ)(n. f. s., suff. 1 p. s. fr. [עֲבֹדוֹת] d. 10.   עבד

בַּעֲבוּר   ﬣ pref. בַּ bef. (־))(prep. and conj.; ﬣ bef. lab.   עבר

בַּעֲבוּרָהּ   pref. id.)(id., suff. 3 pers. sing. fem.   עבר

בַּעֲבוּרִי   pref. id.)(id., suff. 1 pers. sing.   עבר

בַּעֲבוּרְךָ   pref. id.)(id., suff. 2 pers. s. m. [for עַבוּרְךָ]   עבר

בַּעֲבוּרֵךְ   pref. id.)(id., suff. 2 pers. sing. fem.   עבר

בַּעֲבוּרָם   pref. id.)(id., suff. 3 pers. pl. masc.   עבר

בַּעֲבֹטוֹ   pref. id.)(n. m. s., suff. 3 p. s. m. fr. עֲבֹט d. 1 a.   עבט

בְּעֶבִי   pref. id.)(noun masc. sing.   עבה

בְּעָבָיו   pref. בְּ)(the following with suff. 3 pers. s. m.   עוב

בֶּעָבִים } pref. בֶּ f. בְּהֶ, בַּ)(noun m., pl. of עָב d. 1 a.   עוב
בְּעָבִים }

בְּעֵבֶר   Chald. pref. בְּ bef. (־))(noun masc. sing.   עבר

בַּעֲבֹר   pref. id.)(Kal inf. constr.   עבר

בַּעֲבֻר   defect. for בַּעֲבוּר (q. v.)   עבר

בְּעֵבֶר   pref. בְּ)(noun masc. sing. dec. 6. (§ 35. r. 6)   עבר

בְּעֵבֶר   Kh. בְּעֵבֶר q. v., K. מֵעֵבֶר (q. v.)   עבר

בְּעֶבְרָה   pref. בְּ)(noun fem. sing. dec. 12 b.   עבר

בְּעָבְרוֹ   pref. id.)(Kal inf., suff. 3 pers. sing. masc.   עבר

בְּעַבְרוֹת   pref. id.)(n. fem. pl., constr. from עֶבְרָה d. 12 a.   עבר

בְּעַבְרוֹת   pref. id.)(Kh. constr. of עֶבְרָה q. v., K. בַּעֲרָבוֹת (q. v.)   עבר

בְּעִבְרִי   pref. id.)(n. m. pl. constr. fr. עֵבֶר d. 6. (§ 35. r. 6)   עבר

בְּעָבְרֶךָ   pref. id.)(Kal inf., suff. 2 pers. s. m. for עָבְרְךָ   עבר

בְּעֶבְרְכֶם   pref. id.)(id., suff. 2 pers. pl. masc.   עבר

בְּעַבְרֹנָה   pref. id.)(pr. name of a place   עבר

בְּעֶבְרַת   pref. id.)(n. fem. s., constr. of עֶבְרָה d. 12 b.   עבר

בְּעֶבְרָתוֹ   pref. id.)(id., suff. 3 pers. sing. masc.   עבר

בְּעֶבְרָתִי   pref. id.)(id., suff. 1 pers. sing.   עבר

בְּעֶבְרָתֶךָ   pref. id.)(id., suff. 2 pers. sing. m. [for רָתְךָ]   עבר

בְּעַבְתֹתוֹ   pref. בַּ for בְּהַ)(noun com. with pl. fem. term. from עֲבֹת dec. 1 a.   עבת

בַּעֲבֹתִים   pref. id.)(id. pl. masc.   עבת

בַּעֲנָלָה } pref. בַּ f. בְּהַ, בְּהָ)(noun fem. sing. dec. 11 c.
בָּעֲנָלָה } pref. בָּ before (־) (§ 42. rem. 1).

בַּעֲנָלוֹת   pref. id.)(id. pl., absolute state

בַּעֲנְלֵי   pref. בָּ)(noun masc. pl. constr. from עֵנֶל dec. 6. (§ 35. rem. 6)

בַּעֲנָלִים   pref. בַּ bef. (־))(id. pl. absolute state   ענל

בְּעֶנְלָתִי   pref. בְּ)(n. f. s., suff. 1 p. s. from עֶנְלָה d. 12 b.   ענל

בַּעַד   Root not used; Arab. to be distant. Hence

בַּעַד   ﬣ, [and בְּעַד] dec. 6 d. (§ 35. rem. 10) prep.—I. after, behind, about; מִבַּעַד לְ behind.—II. about, round about, and especially after the verbs of shutting up, &c.—III. for, in behalf of.

בְּעַד   ﬥ pref. בְּ)(prop. inf., used as an adv.   עוד

בַּעֲדָהּ   prep. [בַּעַד] dec. 6 d] with suff. 3 pers. s. fem.   בעד

בְּעֶדְרָהּ   pref. בְּ for בְּהַ, בְּהָ)(n. fem. s. dec. 11 b.   יעד

בַּעֲדוֹ   prep. [בַּעַד] with suff. 3 pers. sing. masc.   בעד

בְּעֶדְוֹתָיו   ﬣ pref. בְּ)(noun fem. pl., suff. 3 pers. s. m. from עֵדוּת (comp. Ch. dec. 8 c.); ﬣ bef. (:)   עוד

בְּעֵדֹתֶיךָ   ﬣ pref. id.)(id., suff. 2 pers. sing. m.; ﬣ id.   עוד

בַּעֲדִי   pref. בַּ bef. (־))(noun masc. sing., (suff. עֶדְיוֹ) dec. 6 i. (§ 35. rem. 14)   עדה

בַּעֲדִי   prep. [בַּעַד] dec. 6 d] with suff. 1 pers. sing.   בעד

בַּעֲדֵינוּ   id. pl., suff. 1 pers. pl.   בעד

בַּעֲדֵךְ   id. sing., suff. 2 pers. sing. fem.   בעד

בַּעֲדְךָ } id. sing., suff. 2 pers. sing. masc.   בעד
בַּעֲדֶךָ }

בַּעַדְכֶם   id. sing., suff. 2 pers. pl. masc.   בעד

בַּעֲדָם   id. sing., suff. 3 pers. pl. masc.   בעד

בְּעֶדֶן   pref. בְּ)(pr. name of a place   עדן

בְּעֶדְנָא   Chald. pref. id.)(n. m. s., emph. of עֶדַן dec. 1 b.   עדד

בַּעֲדֶנּוּ   prep. [בַּעַד] dec. 6 d] with suff. 1 pers. pl.   בעד

בַּעֲדֵנִי   id. with suff. 1 pers. sing.   בעד

בְּעֹדֵף   pref. בְּ for בְּהַ, בְּהָ)(Kal part. s. m. d. 7 b.   עדף

בְּעֵדֶר   pref. id.)(noun masc. sing. dec. 6. (§ 35. r. 6)   עדר

בְּעֶדְרוֹ   pref. בְּ)(id., suff. 3 pers. sing. masc.   עדר

בַּעֲדָרֵי   pref. id.)(id. pl., construct state   עדר

בַּעֲדַת   pref. בַּ bef. (־))(n. f. s., constr. of עֵדָה dec. 11 b   יעד

בְּעֵדֹתֶיךָ   pref. בְּ)(n. f. pl., suff. 2 p. s. m. fr. עֵדָה d. 10.   עוד

בַּעֲדָתָם   pref. בַּ bef. (־))(noun fem. sing., suff. 3 pers. sing. fem. from עֵדָה dec. 11 b.   יעד

בָּעָה   I. to make to swell, boil up, Is. 64. 1.—II. to seek, ask, request. Niph. I. to swell out, Is. 30. 13.—II. to be sought out, Obad. 6.

בְּעָא   Chald.—I. to seek, search after, const. with acc.—II. to ask, request, with מִן קֳדָם, מִן. Pa. to search after, with לְ.

בָּעוּ   fem. dec. 8 c. petition, Da. 6. 8, 14.

בָּעִי   masc. prayer, Job 30. 24; comp. בִּי.

בָּעֵה   ﬣ Chald. Peal part. act. s. m. [for בָּעֵא § 62] d. 6 a.   בעה

ª Nu. 12. 8.   ᵇ 1 Ch. 24. 3.   ᶜ Ezr. 9. 8.   ᵈ Ezr. 9. 9.   ᵉ Ge. 12. 16.

ᶠ 1 Sa. 23. 10.   ᵍ Ge. 3. 17.   ʰ Ge. 12. 13.   ⁱ De. 24. 12.   ʲ Job 26. 8.

ᵏ Ps. 147. 8.   ˡ Ex. 33. 22.   ᵐ Ge. 27. 10, 31.   ⁿ Jos. 24. 15.   ᵒ Is. 14. 6.

ᵖ Ps. 7. 7.   ᵠ 2 Sa. 15. 28.   ʳ De. 27. 3.   ˢ La. 2. 2.   ᵗ Ho. 13. 11.

ᵘ Ps. 90. 9.   ᵛ Ho. 11. 4.   ʷ Mi. 6. 6.   ˣ Ju. 14. 18.   ʸ Je. 15. 9.   ᶻ Ge. 46. 5.

ª Ps. 68. 34.   ᵇ Ps. 119. 31.   ᶜ Eze. 16. 7.   ᵈ Am. 9. 10.   ᵉ Ex. 34. 31.

ᵈ Je. 44. 23.   ᵉ Da. 3. 5, 15.   ᶠ Ps. 139. 11.   ᵍ Ex. 26. 13.   ʰ 2 Ki. 4. 4.

ⁱ Is. 26. 20.   ʲ Da. 6. 12.   ᵏ Ps. 119. 46.   ˡ Ex. 26. 13.   ᵐ Je. 31. 24.

ⁿ Mal. 1. 14.   ᵒ Mi. 5. 7.   ᵖ Ps. 119. 46.   ᵠ Ps. 106. 19.   ʳ Da. 6. 12.

בְעוֹ	₄ Chald. id. pret. 3 p. pl. m. R. בְּעָא; ₄ bef. (:) . . . בעה
בָעוּ	Chald. noun fem. sing. dec. 8c. . . . בעה
בְעוֹד	₄ pref. בְּ)(adv. dec. 1a; ₄ bef. (:) . . . עוד
בְעוֹדָהּ	pref. id.)(id., suff. 3 pers. sing. fem. . עוד
בְעוֹדִי	pref. id.)(id., suff. 1 pers. sing. . . עוד
בְעוֹדֶנּוּ	pref. id.)(id., (verbal) suff. 3 p.s.m. (§ 2.note) . עוד
בְעוֹדֶנִּי	pref. id.)(id., (verbal) suff. 1 p.s. (§ 2.note) עוד
בְעָוֹן	pref. בְּ)(noun masc. sing. dec. 3a. . עוה
בָעֹז	pref.בְּ f.בְּהָ,בְהָ } noun m.s., for עֹז dec. 8c. עזז
בְעֹז	pref. בְּ q.v. }
בְּעֹל	pref. id.)(noun masc. sing. (§ 35. rem. 11) עול
בְּעֹל	pref. id.)(noun masc. sing. for עֹל dec. 8c. עלל
בְּעֹלָה	pref. id.)(noun fem. sing. . . עול
בְּעוֹלָה	pref. id.)(noun fem., contr. for עוֹלָה R. עול (Is. 61.8); or for עֹלָה (q.v.) . עלה
בְּעֹלָה	Kal part. p. sing. fem. dec. 10, from [בָּעֹל] m. בעל
בְּעֻלְוֹ	₄ pref. בְּ)(noun m. sing., suff. 3 pers. sing. masc. from עֹל (§ 35. rem. 11); ₄ bef. lab. עול
בְּעֹלוֹת	pref. id.)(noun fem., pl. of עוֹלָה dec. 10. עלה
בְּעוֹלָתָהּ	pref. id.)(n. fem. sing. (עוֹלָה) with parag. ה עול
בְּעֹן	pref. בַּ bef. (-:))(constr. for the following: עוה
בְּעֹון	pref. בְּ for בְּהַ)(noun masc. sing. dec. 3a. עוה
בְּעֹונָהּ	pref. בַּ bef. (-:))(id., suff. 3 pers. sing. fem. עוה
בְּעֹונוֹ	pref. id.)(id., suff. 3 pers. sing. masc. . עוה
בַּעֲוֹנוֹת	₄ pref. id.)(id. pl. fem. term.; ₄ bef. lab. עוה
בַּעֲוֹנַי	pref. id.)(id. sing., suff. 1 pers. sing. . עוה
בְּעֵינַי	Kh. בָּעֵינַי (pref. בָּ), in pause for עֵנַי R. ענה; K. בְּעֵינַי, עַיִן with suff. 1 pers. sing. . עין
בַּעֲוֹנֶךָ	pref. בַּ bef. (-:))(noun masc. sing., suff. 2 pers. sing. masc. from עָוֹן dec. 3a. עוה
בַּעֲוֹנָם	pref. id.)(id., suff. 3 pers. pl. masc. . עוה
בַּעֲוֹנֹתֵיךָ	pref. id.)(id. pl. fem., suff. 2 pers. sing. m. עוה
בַּעֲוֹנֹתֵינוּ	pref. id.)(id. pl., suff. 1 pers. pl.; ₄ id. עוה
בַּעֲוֹנֹתֵיכֶם	pref. id.)(id. pl., suff. 2 pers. pl. masc. עוה
בָּעוֹף	₄ pref.בְּ f.בְּהָ,בְּהָ } noun masc. sing.; ₄ } עוף
בְּעוֹף	₄ pref. בְּ q.v. } bef. (:) }
בְּעוֹפְפִי	pref. id.)(Pilel inf. [עוֹפֵף], suff. 1 pers. sing. dec. 7b. עוף
בָּעוֹר	pref.בְּ f.בְּהָ,בְּהָ } noun masc. sing. dec. 1a. } עור
בְּעוֹר	pref. בְּ q.v. }
בְּעוֹר	pr. name masc. . . . . בער
בַּעֲוֹרֹן	pref. בַּ for בְּהָ } noun masc. sing. } עור
בְּעֹורֹן	₄ pref. בְּ q.v. }
בְּעוֹרִי	pref. id.)(noun masc. sing. dec. 1a. . עור
בְּעוּתַהּ	Ch. noun fem. sing., suff. 3 pers. sing. masc. from בְּעוּ dec. 8c. . . בעה

בְּעוּתַי	noun fem. pl. constr. from [בְּעוּת] dec. 1b. בעת
בְּעוּתֶיךָ	id. p.., suff. 2 pers. sing. masc. . . בעת
בְּעֹז	pref. בְּ)(noun masc. sing. dec. 8c. . עזז
בֹּעַז	₄ (alacrity) pr. name—I. of the husband of Ruth.—II. of a pillar in Solomon's temple.
בְּעַזָּא	pref. בְּ)(pr. name masc. . . . עזז
בְּעֶזְבוֹנַיִךְ	pref. id.)(noun masc. pl., suff. 2 pers. sing. }
בְּעִזְבוֹנַיִךְ	fem. from עִזָּבוֹן dec. 3c. } עזב
בְּעָזְבְכֶם	pref. בַּ bef. (-:))(Kal inf., suff. 2 p. pl. m. עזב
בְּעָזְבָם	pref. בְּ)(id., suff. 3 pers. pl. masc. . עזב
בְּעֶזָּה	pref. id.)(pr. name of a place . עזז
בְּעַזָּה	pref. id.)(pr. name masc. . . עזז
בְּעֻזּוֹ	pref. id.)(noun masc. sing., suff. 3 pers. sing. masc. fr. עֹז dec. 8c. עזז
בַּעֲזוֹז	pref. בַּ bef. (-:))(Kal inf. constr. . עזז
בְּעֵזִים	₄ pref. בְּ for בְּהַ, בְּהָ)(noun fem., pl. of עֵז dec. 8b; ₄ bef. labial עזז
בְּעֻזֶּךָ	pref. בְּ)(noun m. s., with suff. 2 p. s. }
בְּעֻזָּךְ	masc. from עֹז dec. 8 c. (§ 37. rem. 2) } עזז
בְּעֶזְקַת	₄ Ch. pref. id.)(noun fem. sing., constr. of עִזְקָא dec. 8a; ₄ bef. (:) . עזק
בְּעֶזְקָתֵהּ	Ch. pref. id.)(id., suff. 3 pers. sing. masc. עזק
בְּעֶזְר	pref. בְּ bef. (ֶ:))(Kal inf. constr. . עזר
בְּעֶזְרוֹ	pref. בְּ)(noun masc. sing., suff. 1 pers. sing. from עֵזֶר dec. 6. (§ 35. rem. 6) עזר
בְּעֶזְרִי	pref. id.)(id., suff. 1 pers. sing. . עזר
בְּעֹזְרַי	pref. id.)(Kal part. act. pl., suff. 1 pers. sing. from עֵזֶר dec. 7b. עזר
בְּעֶזְרֶךָ	pref. id.)(noun sing. masc., suff. 2 pers. sing. masc. [for עֶזְרָךְ] from עֵזֶר (§ 3. r. 6) עזר
בְּעֶזְרָתִי	pref. id.)(noun fem. sing., suff. 1 pers. sing. from עֶזְרָה (no pl. absolute) . עזר
בְּעֶזְרָתֵךְ	pref. id.)(id., suff. 2 pers. sing. fem. עזר
בָּעַט	I. to kick, kick up, Deu. 32. 15.—II. to kick, spurn at, with בְּ 1 Sa. 2. 29.
בַּעַט	pref. בַּ)(noun masc. sing. . . עוט
בַּעֲטֹף	pref. בַּ bef. (-:))(Kal inf. constr. . עטף
בֵּהֵעָטֵף	pref. בְּ, [for בְּהֵעָטֵף], Niph. inf. constr. (§ 10. rem. 6) . . עטף
בַּעֲטָרָה	pref. בַּ for בְּהָ)(noun fem. sing., constr. עֲטֶרֶת (§ 42. rem. 5) . עטר
בְּעִי	pref. id.)(pr. name of a place עוה
בְּעִי	n. m. s. R. בעה, or pref. בְּ, עִי n. m. s. R. עוה
בְּעוּ	Kal imp. pl. masc. (§ 24. rem. 5) עוה
בְּעַיֵ	pref. בְּ)(n. m. pl. constr. pr. n., עַיֵי הָעֲבָרִים עוה

---

a Da. 2. 13.   g Ps. 51. 7.   n Eze. 33. 13.   t Ps. 31. 11.   z Eze. 32. 10.   g Ps. 88. 17.   n Ps. 78. 26.   t 1 Ch. 15. 26.   Ps. 61. 3.
b Da. 6. 8.   h Pr. 24. 5.   o Ps. 125. 3.   u 2 Sa. 16. 12.   a Zec. 12. 4.   h Pr. 8. 28.   o Ps. 146. 5.   u Ex. 18. 4.   La. 2. 11.
c Is. 7. 8.   i Pr. 31. 17.   p Is. 59. 3.   v Ho. 14. 2.   b De. 28. 28.   i Eze. 27. 16.   p Le. 22. 19.   v Ps. 118. 7.   Ca. 3. 11.
d Is. 28. 4.   k Eze. 28. 18.   q Je. 51. 6.   w Is. 43. 24.   c Job 19. 20.   k Ps. 21. 14.   q Ps. 118. 7.   w Ex. 18. 4.   Job 30. 24.
e Ge. 25. 6.   l De. 21. 3.   r Le. 26. 39.   x Ezr. 9. 7.   d Da. 6. 14.   l Da. 6. 18.   r Ps. 35. 2.   x Da. 6. 18.   Is. 21. 12.
f De. 31. 27.   m Eze. 18. 26.   s Da. 9. 16.   y Le. 20. 25.   e 1 Ki. 18. 18.   f 2 Ch. 28. 6.   s Na. 3. 9.

בְּעֵילָם pref. בְּ)(pr. name of a province, see עֵילָם

בְּעַם for עַם, pref. בַּ bef. (־ַ))(n. m. s. constr. עם

בָּעֵן Ch. Peal part. act. m., pl. R. בְּעָא see בְּעָא, d. 6a. בעה

בְּעֵן pref. בְּ, f. בָּהּ, בְּהֵ, noun com. sing. dec.) עין
בְּעֵן id pref. בְּ q. v.) 6 h., also p n.; bef. lab.
בְּעֵן pref. id.)(id., constr. state, also pr. name
    in compos. as דֹּאר עֵין &c. . . . עין

בְּעֵנָא Ch. Peal pret. 1 pers. pl. R. בְּעָא see בעה

בְּעֵנוּ Kh. for בְּעֵינוּ Keri (q. v. § 4. rem. 1) עין

בְּעֵינִי pref. בְּ)(noun com. sing., suff. 3 pers. sing.
    masc. from עֵין dec. 6h. . . . עין

בְּעֵינֵי
בְּעֵינַי } pref. id.)(id., du., suff. 1 pers. sing. . עין

בְּעֵינֵי id pref. id.)(id. du., constr. state; bef. lab. עין
בְּעֵינֶיהָ pref. id)(id. du., suff. 3 pers. sing. fem. . עין
בְּעֵינֵיהֶם pref. id.)(id. du., suff. 3 pers. pl. masc. עין
בְּעֵינֵיהֶן pref. id.)(id. du., suff. 3 pers. pl. fem. . עין
בְּעֵינָיו pref. id.)(id. du., suff. 3 pers. sing. masc. עין
בְּעֵינָיִךְ
בְּעֵינַיִךְ } pref. id.)(id. du., suff. 2 pers. sing. fem. עין
בְּעֵינֶיךָ pref. id.)(id. du., suff. 2 pers. sing. masc. עין
בְּעֵינֵיכֶם pref. id.)(id. du., suff. 2 pers. pl. masc. עין
בָּעֵינָיִם pref. בָּ for בְּהָ, בְּהֵ)(id. du. abs. st. pr. n. עין
בְּעֵינֵינוּ pref. בְּ)(id. du., suff. 1 pers. pl. . עין
בְּעֵינֶךָ defect. for בְּעֵינֶיךָ (q. v.) . . עין
בָּעִיר for בְּהָעִיר pref. בְּ)(n. m. with the art. R. עיר
    q.v.; or, better (הָעִיר) Hiph. inf. constr. עור
בַּעֵיר pref. בְּ, f. בְּהֵ, noun fem. sing. irr.)
בְּעִיר pref. בְּ q. v.) (§ 45) עור
בְּעִיר pref. id.)(noun masc. sing. . . עיר
בְּעִירֹה noun masc. sing., suff. 3 pers. sing. masc.
    from [בְּעִיר] dec. 1 a. . . . בער

בְּעִירוֹ id pref. בְּ)(noun fem. sing., suff. 3 pers.
    sing. masc. from עִיר irr. (§ 45); bef. (־ִ) עור
בְּעִירִי pref. id.)(id., suff. 1 pers. sing. . עור
בְּעִירְכֶם noun masc. sing., suff. 2 pers. pl. masc.
    from [בְּעִיר] dec. 1 a. . . בער

בְּעִירָם id., suff. 3 pers. pl. masc.; bef. (־ִ) בער
בְּעֵרִים pref. בְּ)(noun masc. sing. dec. 8c; id. ערם
בְּעִירֵנוּ noun masc. sing., suff. 1 pers. pl. from
    [בְּעִיר] dec. 1a.; id. בער

בְּעֹכְרַי pref. בְּ)(Kal part. act. pl., suff. 1 pers.
    sing. from עֹכֵר dec. 7 b. . . . עכר

בָּעַל I. to have dominion, be lord over, possess any
thing.—II. to become a husband of any one, to
marry a wife; part. pl. בְּעָלַיִךְ thy (sc. God's) hus-

band; pass. fem. בְּעֻלָה and בְּעוּלָה one
married.—III. to disdain, despise, const. with בְּ.
Niph. to be married.

בַּעַל masc. dec. 6 d.—I. lord, possessor, owner,
and sometimes pl. majest. בְּעָלִים lord, &c.—II.
husband.—III. from the idea of possessor various
phrases are formed, as בַּעַל שְׁכֶם inhabitants of
Shechem, Shechemites; בַּעַל הַקְּרָנַיִם having two
horns; בַּעַל כְּנָפַיִם winged; בַּעַל הַחֲלֹמוֹת the
dreamer; בַּעַל בְּרִית confederate; בַּעַל דְּבָרִים one
having a law-suit.—IV. הַבַּעַל pr. name Baal,
the tutelary god of the Phenicians; in pl. image
of Baal. He was worshipped also under the
following names, as בַּעַל בְּרִית lord of covenant;
בַּעַל פְּעוֹר, בַּעַל זְבוּב fly-god, fly-destroyer; see
פְּעוֹר.—V. pr. name of a town on the borders
of Simeon, 1 Ch. 4. 33, probably the same as
בַּעֲלַת בְּאֵר Jos. 19. 8.—VI. compounded in the
names of towns: בַּעַל גָּד (Baal of fortune) a town
at the foot of Hermon, Jos. 11. 17.—בַּעַל חָמוֹן
(place of multitude) at the foot of Lebanon,
Cant. 8. 11.—בַּעַל חָצוֹר (having a village) a town
in the tribe of Benjamin, 2 Sa. 13. 23 near mount Hermon.—בַּעַל מְעוֹן (place of dwelling) in the tribe of Reuben, see בֵּית מְ.—בַּעַל
פְּרָצִים (place of defeats) where David routed the
Philistines, comp. 2 Sa. 5. 20.—בַּעַל צְפוֹן (place
of Typhon, a divinity) a town in Egypt near the
Red sea.—בַּעַל שָׁלִשָׁה place in the district of
Shalishah, 2 Ki. 4. 42, comp. 1 Sa. 9. 4.—בַּעַל תָּמָר
(place of palms) not far from Gibeah, Ju. 20. 33.
—VII. בַּעַל pr. name masc. of two different persons.—בַּעַל חָנָן (lord of grace) pr. name (a) of a
king of Edom; (b) 1 Ch. 27. 28.

בְּעֵל Ch. masc. lord, Ez. 4. 8, 9, 17, see מְעֵם.

בַּעֲלָה fem.—I. a mistress, comp. אוֹב; בַּעֲלַת
כְּשָׁפִים a sorceress.—II. pr. name (a) of a city in the
north of Judah, called also קִרְיַת יְעָרִים & קִרְיַת בַּעַל
(b) another in the south of Judah, Jos. 15. 29,
perhaps the same as בָּלָה, בִּלְהָה.

בַּעֲלוֹת pr. name of a city in the tribe of Judah,
Jos. 15. 24.

בַּעֲלַת pr. name of a city in the tribe of Dan.
For בַּעֲלַת בְּאֵר see בַּעַל No. VI.

בְּעֶלְיָדָע (whom the Lord knows) pr. name of a
son of David, 1 Ch. 14. 7, called אֱלְיָדָע 2 Sa. 5. 16.

a Is. 11. 15. d Da. 2. 23. g Est. 1. 17. k De. 15. 18. m Ho. 11. 9. i 1 Sa. 28. 3. r Ge. 45. 17. t De. 28. 48. x Ju. 11. 35.
b Da. 6. 5. c Le. 21. 20. f Ge. 16. 6. i Ps. 73. 20. n Ex. 22. 4. p 2 Sa. 19. 38. s Nu. 20. 11. v Nu. 20. 4. z Mal. 2. 11.
c 1 Sa. 29. 1. f Ge. 16. 4, 5. i 1 Sa. 1. 22.

בְּעַלְיָה (whose *lord is the Lord*) pr. name masc. 1 Ch. 12. 5.

בֵּל (contr. from בַּעַל i. q. בַּעַל) pr. name of the god of the Babylonians.

בַּלְאֲדָן (whose *lord is Baal*) pr. name of a king of Babylon, father of Merodach-Baladan, 2 Ki. 20. 12.

בַּעַל n. m. s. d. 6d, also pr. n. of an idol, and in compos., as בַּעַל בְּרִית &c. . . . . . בעל

בַּעַל Ch, noun masc. sing. . . . . . בעל

בַּעֲלָא pref. בְ)(noun masc. sing. dec. 8c. . עלל

בַּעֲלָה pr. name of a place . . . . . . בעל

בַּעֲלָה noun masc. sing., suff. 3 pers. sing. fem. dec. 6d. [for בַּעֲלָהּ § 35. rem. 5] . . בעל

בְּעָלָהּ נ Kal pret. 3 pers. sing. masc., suff. 3 pers. sing. fem.; נ bef. labial . . . . בעל

בְּעָלוּ id. pret. 3 pers. pl. . . . . בעל

בְּעָלוּנוּ id. id., suff. 1 pers. pl. . . . . . בעל

בַּעֲלוֹת pref. בַ bef. (־))(Kal inf. constr. . . עלה

בַּעֲלוֹת Kh. i. q. prec.; K. בַּעֲלוֹת (q. v.) . עלה

בַּעֲלוֹת נ pr. name of a place; נ bef. . . . בעל

בַּעֲלוֹת pref. בַ)(noun fem., pl. of עֹלָה dec. 10. עלה

בַּעֲלוֹתָהּ pref. בַ bef. (־))(Kal inf., suff. 3 pers. sing. fem. dec. 1a. . . . . . . עלה

בַּעֲלוֹתוֹ pref. id.)(id., suff. 3 pers. sing. masc. . עלה

בַּעֲלוֹתַיִן pref. בַ)(noun fem. pl., suff. 1 pers. pl. from עֹלָה dec. 10. . . . עלה

בַּעֲלוֹתָם pref. בַ bef. (־))(Kal inf., suff. 3 p. pl. m. d. 1a. עלה

בַּעֲלָטָה pref. בַ for בְּהַ)(noun fem. sing. . עלט

בַּעֲלֵי נ n. m. pl. constr. fr. בַּעַל d. 6d; נ bef. lab. בעל

בַּעֲלִי id. sing. with suff. 1 pers. sing. . . . בעל

בַּעֲלִי pref. בַ for בְּהַ)(noun masc. sing. . עלה

בַּעֲלְיָדָע נ pr. name masc.; נ bef. (־) . . . . בעל

בַּעֲלְיָה נ pr. name masc.; נ id. . . . . . בעל

בְּעָלֶיהָ noun m. pl., suff. 3 p. s. f. fr. בַּעַל dec. 6d. בעל

בַּעֲלֵיהֶן id., suff. 3 pers. pl. fem. . . . . . בעל

בַּעֲלָיו id., suff. 3 pers. sing. masc. . . . . בעל

בַּעֲלִיָּה pref. בַ)(adj. masc. sing. dec. 1b. . עלה

בֹּעֲלַיִךְ Kal part. act. pl., suff. 2 p. s. f. fr. [בַּעַל] dec. 7b בעל

בַּעֲלִיל pref. בַ bef. (־))(noun masc. sing. . עלל

בַּעֲלִילוֹתַי נ pref. id.)(noun fem. pl., suff. 2 pers. sing. masc. from עֲלִילָה dec. 10; נ bef. labial עלל

בַּעֲלִילוֹת נ pref. id.)(id., suff. 3 pers. pl. masc.; נ id. עלל

בְּעֵלִים [for בְּנֵי עֵלִים son of exultation, R. עלם comp. [בַּעֲנָא] pr. name of a king of the Ammonites, Je. 40. 14.

בַּעֲלִית pref. id.)(n. f. sing., constr. of עֲלִיָּה d. 10. עלה

בַּעֲלִיָּתָהּ Ch. pref. בַ)(noun fem. sing., suff. 3 pers. sing. masc. from [עֲלִי] dec. 8c. . . עלה

בַּעֲלִיָּתוֹ pref. בַ bef. (־))(noun fem. sing., suff. 3 pers. sing. masc. from עֲלִיָּה dec. 10. . עלה

בַּעַלְמָה pref. בַ)(noun fem. sing. dec. 12a. עלם

בַּעַלְמֹן pref. id.)(pr. name of a place, עַלְמֹן דִּבְלָתַיִם with parag. ה Nu. 33. 46. . . . עלם

בַּעֲלֹץ pref. בַ bef. (־))(Kal inf. constr. . עלץ

בַּעֲלָת נ pr. name of a place; נ bef. labial. בעל

בַּעֲלַת noun fem. sing., constr. of [בַּעֲלָה], also pr. name in compos. בַּעֲלַת בְּאֵר . . בעל

בֹּעֲלַת Kal part. p. fem., constr. of בְּעוּלָה, [from בָּעוּל masc.] . . . . . . בעל

בַּעֲלָתָה pr. name of a place (בַּעֲלָת) with loc. ה . בעל

בְּעָלְתָהּ נ Kal pret. 2 pers. sing. masc., suff. 3 pers. sing. fem.; נ bef. labial . . . . בעל

בַּעֲלֹתוֹ pref. בַ bef. (־))(Kal inf. (עֲלוֹת), suff. 3 pers. sing. masc. dec. 1a. . . . . עלה

בָּעַלְתִּי Kal pret. 1 pers. sing. . . . . . בעל

בַּעֲלֹתִי pref. בַ bef. (־))(Kal inf., suff. 1 p. s. d. 1a. עלה

בַּעֲלֹתְךָ pref. id.)(id., suff. 2 pers. sing. masc. עלה

בְּעַם pref. בְ, בְּהַ)(noun com. s. d. 8, pl. irr. עמם

בָּעַם נ pref. בַ q. v. (§ 45); נ bef. (־:) עמם

בְּעַמֻד נ defect. for עַמּוּד (q. v.). . . . עמד

בַּעֲמֹד pref. בַ)(Kal inf., suff. 3 pers. sing. masc. עמד

בְּעָמְדָם נ pref. id.)(id., suff. 3 p. pl. m.; נ bef. (־:) עמד

בְּעַמּוֹ pref. id.)(noun com. sing., suff. 3 pers. sing. masc. from עַם or עָם dec. 8. (§ 45) עמם

בְּעַמּוּד נ pref. id.)(noun m. s. d. 1b; נ bef. lab. עמד

בַּעֲמֵי pref. id.)(noun com. pl. constr. from עַם or עָם dec. 8. (§ 45) . . . . עמם

בְּעַמִּי pref. id.)(id. sing., suff. 1 pers. sing. עמם

בַּעֲמָיו pref. id.)(id. pl., suff. 3 pers. sing. masc. עמם

בַּעֲמֶיךָ pref. id.)(id. pl., suff. 2 pers. sing. masc. עמם

בָּעַמִּים pref. בַ f. בְּהַ)(id. pl. abs עמם

בַּעֲמִיר pref. בַ)(noun masc. sing. . . . עמר

בַּעֲמִיתוֹ pref. בַ bef. (־))(noun fem. sing., suff. 3 pers. sing. masc. from [עָמִית] dec. 3a. עמה

בְּעַמֶּךָ נ pref. בַ)(noun com. s., suff. 2 pers. sing. masc. from עַם or עָם dec. 8. (§ 45) עמם

בַּעֲמָל pref. בַ bef. (־))(constr. for the following עמל

בֶּעָמָל נ pref. בַ for בְּהַ)(noun masc. sing. dec. 4c; נ bef. labial . . . . . ל

בַּעֲמָלוֹ pref. בַ bef. (־))(id., suff. 3 pers. sing. masc. עמל

בַּעֲמָלְךָ נ pref. id.)(id., suff. 2 p. s. m.; נ bef. lab. עמל

a Ezr. 4. 8, 9, 17.   f Jos. 4. 18; 6. 15.   k Jos. 22. 27.   r Est. 1. 17.   z Ps. 77. 15.   a Pr. 30. 19.   e De. 9. 9.   g Ge. 41. 46.   l Ex. 22. 27.
b Je. 27. 8, 11, 12.   g 1 Sa. 15. 22.   l 2 Sa. 1. 6.   s Ps. 73. 11.   a Eze. 36. 17.   e Pr. 28. 12.   h Ex. 34. 24.   h Eze. 1. 21.   m Ps. 107. 12.
c De. 24. 1.   h 1 Sa. 2. 19.   m Ho. 2. 18.   t Is. 54. 5.   b Da. 6. 11.   e De. 21. 13.   i Eze. 17. 9.   l Ezr. 9. 2, 14.   n Ec. 2. 11.
d 1 Ch. 4. 22.   i Ju. 11. 13.   n Pr. 27. 22.   u Ps. 12. 7.   c 2 Ki. 1. 2.   d 1 Sa. 15. 2.   f Nu. 14. 14.   l Zec. 12. 6.   e Ec. 9. 9.
Is. 26. 13.   k Ju. 3. 9.

Hebrew	Description	Root
בַּעֲמָלָם	pref. id. ✕ id., suff. 3 pers. pl. masc.	עמל
בַּעֲמָלֵק	pref. id. ✕ pr. name of a people	עמלק
בַּעֲמָמֶיךָ	pref. id. ✕ noun com. pl., suff. 2 pers. sing. masc. irr. of עַם (§ 45)	עמם
בְּעֵמֶק / בַּעֲמֶק	׳i pref. בַ f. בְּהַ ,בָּה ✕ noun masc. sing. dec. 6b; ׳i bef. lab.	עמק
בְּעִמְקֵי	pref. id. ✕ id. pl., construct state	עמק
בַּעֲמָקִים / בַּעֲמָקִים׳	pref. בַ f. בְּהָ ,בָּה ✕ id. pl., absolute state	עמק
בָּעֳמֵר	pref. בָ for בְּהַ ,בָּה ✕ noun masc. sing. dec. 6c.	עמר
בָּעֳמָרִים	pref. id. ✕ id. pl. absolute state	עמר
בְּעֹן	׳i pr. name see בֵּית בַּעַל מְעוֹן under	בית
בֶּעֳנָא / בַּעֲנָה	[for בֶּן־עָנָא son of affliction R. ענה, see בְּשָׁלֵם] pr. name m. of several persons.	
בְּעׇנִי	pref. בָ bef. (ָ) ✕ n. m. s. (constr. st.) d. 6k.	ענה
בְּעָנְיוֹ	pref. id. ✕ id., suff. 3 pers. sing. masc.	ענה
בְּעׇנְיִי	pref. id. ✕ id., suff. 1 pers. sing.	ענה
בְּעִנְיַן	pref. id. ✕ noun m. s., constr. of עִנְיָן dec. 2b.	ענה
בָּעָנָן	׳i pref. בָ for בְּהַ ,בָּה ✕ n. m. s. d. 4c; ׳i bef. lab.	ענן
בְּעַנּוֹתֵנִי	pref. בַ ✕ Piel inf. [עַנּוֹת], suff. 1 pers. sing. dec. 7b. [for עַנֵּן comp. § 10. rem. 7]	ענן
בַּעֲנָפוֹהִי׳	׳i Ch. pr. בַ ✕ n.m. pl., suff. 3 m. s. [fr. עֲנָף] d. 3a.	ענף
בַּעֲנָקִים	pref. בַ for בְּהַ ,בָּה ✕ pr. name of a people, pl. of עֲנָק	ענק
בַּעֲנֹשׁ־	pref. בַ bef. (ָ) ✕ Kal inf. c., for עֲנֹשׁ (§ 8. r. 18)	ענשׁ
בְּעַנָתוֹת / בְּעַנְתֹת	} pref. id. ✕ pr. name of a place.	ענה
בְּעֹפֶל	pref. בָ for בְּהַ ,בָּה: ✕ pr. name of a place	עפל
בָּעֳפָלִים	׳i K. בַּטְּחֹרִים, pref. בַ, n. m. pl. R. טְחַר; Kh. בָּעֳפָלִים, pref. בָ, pl. of עֹפֶל dec. 6c.	עפל
בְּעַפְעַפָּי	pref. בַ ✕ n. m. du. constr. fr. [עַפְעַף] dec. 8d.	עוף
בְּעַפְעַפֶּיהָ	pref. בַ ✕ id., suff. 3 pers. sing. fem.	עוף
בֶּעָפָר	׳i pref. בַ for בְּהַ ,בָּה ✕ noun m. s. dec. 4c.	עפר
בְּעׇפְרָה	pref. בַ ✕ pr. name of a place	עפר
בְּעֶפְרוֹן	pref. id. ✕ pr. name masc.	עפר
בְּעֶפְרָת	pref. id. ✕ pr. name of a place, constr. of עֶפְרָה	עפר
בָּעֵץ / בָעֵץ׳	׳i pref. בָ f. בְּהָ ,בָּה ✕ noun masc. sing. dec. 7a. ׳i pref. בָ q. v. (§ 36. rem. 2)	עצה
בְּעֶצֶב	pref. id. ✕ noun masc. sing., dec. 6a.	עצב
בְּעֹצֶב	pref. id. ✕ noun masc. sing. dec. 6c.	עצב
בְּעֶצְבוֹן	pref. id. ✕ noun masc. sing. dec. 3c.	עצב
בְּעַצְבַּת	׳i pref. id. ✕ noun fem. sing. constr., [as if from עַצְבָה] see עֶצֶב ׳i bef. lab.	עצב
בְּעֵצָה	pref. id. ✕ noun fem. sing. dec. 11b.	יעץ
בְּעֵצוֹ	pref. id. ✕ noun masc. sing., suff. 3 pers. sing. masc. from עֵץ dec. 7a. (§ 36. rem. 2)	עצה

Hebrew	Description	Root
בַּעֲצוּמָיו	pref. בַ bef. (ָ) ✕ noun masc. pl. (עֲצוּמִים), suff. 3 pers. sing. masc.	עצם
בְּעֵצִי	׳i pref. בָ bef. (ָ) ✕ noun masc. pl. constr. from עֵץ dec. 7a. (§ 36. rem. 2); ׳i bef. lab.	עצה
בְּעֶצְיוֹן	pref. בָ ✕ pr. name in compos. עֶצְיוֹן גֶּבֶר	עצה
בָּעֵצִים	׳i pref. בָ f. בְּהָ ,בָּה ✕ noun masc. pl. abs. fr.	עצה
בְּעֵצִים׳	pref. בָ q. v. עֵץ dec. 7a; ׳i bef. lab.	עצה
בְּעֶצְיוֹן	pr. name defect. for עֶצְיוֹן (q. v.)	עצה
בְּעֶצְלָתַיִם׳	pref. בַ bef. (ָ) ✕ n. fem., dual of עַצְלָת d. 13a.	עצל
בְּעַצְמִי	׳i pref. בַ for בְּהָ n. f. s., (suff. עַצְמִי) dec. 6a,	עצם
בְּעֶצֶם	pref. בָ q. v. also pr. n. of a place; ׳i bef.	עצם
בְּעֹצֶם	pref. id. ✕ noun masc. sing. dec. 6c.	עצם
בְּעַצְמוֹת	׳i pref. בַ bef. (ָ) ✕ noun fem. pl. abs. from עֶצֶם dec. 6a. (comp. the following)	עצם
בְּעַצְמוֹת׳	pref. id. ✕ id. pl., construct state	עצם
בְּעַצְמוֹתַי	pref. id. ✕ id. pl., suff. 1 pers. sing.	עצם
בְּעַצְמוֹתָיו	pref. id. ✕ id. pl., suff. 3 pers. sing. masc.	עצם
בְּעַצְמַי	pref. בָ bef. (ָ) ✕ id. pl. m., suff. 1 pers. sing.	עצם
בְּעַצְמַת׳	pref. בָ ✕ n. fem. s. constr. [of עָצְמָה; no pl.]	עצם
בְּעַצְמֹתַי / בְּעַצְמֹתָי׳	} pref. בָ ✕ noun fem. pl., suff. 1 pers. sing. from עֶצֶם dec. 6a.	עצם
בְּעַצְרֹתֵיכֶם	pref. id. ✕ n. f. pl., suff. 2 pers. pl. masc. from עֲצָרָה dec. 11c. (§ 42. rem. 1)	עצר
בַּעֲצַת	pref. בַ bef. (ָ) ✕ n. f. s., constr. of עֵצָה d. 11b.	יעץ
בַּעֲצָתְךָ	pref. id. ✕ id., suff. 2 pers. sing. masc.	יעץ
בַּעֲצָתָם	pref. id. ✕ id., suff. 3 pers. pl. masc.	יעץ
בְּעֹקֶב־	pref. id. ✕ constr. of the following (§ 34. r. 1)	עקב
בְּעֵקֶב־	pref. בָ ✕ noun masc. sing. dec. 5. (§ 35. r. 4)	עקב
בְּעֶקְבָה	pref. id. ✕ noun sing. fem.	עקב
בְּעִקְּבֵי׳	pref. id. ✕ n. m. pl. constr. fr. עָקֵב d. 5. (§ 35. r. 4)	עקב
בָּעֲקְרַבִּים	pref. בָ for בְּהָ ,בָּה ✕ n. m., pl. of עַקְרָב d. 8a.	עקרב

בָּעַר I. to consume, burn up with fire; metaph. of anger, const. mostly with בְּ.—II. intrans. to burn.—III. denom. of בְּעִיר, to be brutish, part. בֹּעֲרִים brutish זen. Niph. to become brutish. Pi.—I. to feed עpon, to consume, as a field, vineyard, with בְּ.— II. to consume with fire; to kindle, to set on fire, with בְּ.—III. to remove, to destroy, with מִן, אַחֲרֵי. Pu. to be kindled, to burn. Hiph.—I. to feed upon.— II. to consume with fire; to kindle, to set on fire, with בְּ.—III. to remove, destroy.

בַּעַר masc. stupid, brutish.

בַּעְרָא (stupid) pr. name fem. 1 Ch. 8. 8.

בְּעֵרָה fem. a burning, Ex. 22. 5.

בְּעוֹר (torch) pr. name—I. of the father of Balaam. —II. of the father of Bela king of the Edomites.

a Ec. 4. 9.	f 1 Ch. 27. 29.	l Ec. 5. 13.	r De. 28. 27.	x Le. 14. 52.	∂ Ho. 4. 12.	λ Job 30. 21.	ρ Je. 20. 9.	φ Ge. 25. 26.
b Ju. 5. 14.	g Ex. 16. 18.	m De. 1. 33.	s Job 3. 16.	y Ge. 3. 16.	e Ps. 10. 10.	μ Job 10. 11.	σ La. 1. 13.	χ Job 18. 9.
c Jos. 13. 27.	h Ruth 2. 7.	n Ge. 9. 14.	t Pr. 6. 25.	z 1 Ch. 4. 9.	ζ Zec. 12. 6.	ν 2 Ki. 13. 21.	τ Am. 3. 21.	ψ 2 Ki. 10. 19.
d Pr. 9. 18.	i 1 Sa. 1. 11.	o Pr. 21. 11.	u Job 14. 8.	α Ge. 3. 17.	η Ec. 10. 10.	ξ Ps. 42. 11.	υ Ps. 73. 24.	ω Ca. 1. 8.
e Je. 49. 4.	k Job 36. 15.	p 1 Sa. 5. 6, 12.	v Eze. 15. 6.	β Pr. 15. 13.	θ Nu. 19. 18.	ο Is. 47. 9.	ππ Da. 4. 9, 10.	

בְּעִיר masc. dec. 1 b.—I. *beasts, cattle*, generally, collect.—II. *beasts* of burden.

תַּבְעֵרָה (*burning*) pr. name of a place in the desert.

בָּעַר } בֹּעַר }	noun masc. sing.; ן see ן	בער
בָּעֵר	Piel inf. constr.	בער
בָּעָר	pref. בְּ) pr. name of a place .	עור
בֹּעֵר	pr. name masc. for בְּעוֹר	בער
בִּעֵר	⁴ Pi. (dag. forte impl. § 14.r.1) pret. 3 p.s. m.	בער
בֹּעֵר	Kal part. act. sing. dec. 7 b.	בער
בְּעָרָא	pr. name fem.	בער
בְּעָרָב } בַּעֲרָב }	pref. בַּ bef. (־־)) pr. name of a country	ערב
בְּעֶרֶב	in pause for בְּעֶרֶב (q. v.) . .	ערב
בְּעֶרֶב⁴	pref. בְּ for בְּהַ ; בְּהֵ) noun masc. sing. .	ערב
בָּעֶרֶב	⁴ pref. id.) noun masc. sing., (du. עֲרָבִּים) dec. 6 a; ⁴ bef. lab. . . .	ערב
בְּעֵרֶב	pref. בְּ) noun masc. sing. .	ערב
בַּעֲרָב⁴	pref. id.) noun m. sing. (du. עֲרָבִים) dec. 6 a.	ערב
בָּעֲרָבָה	⁴ pref. בַּ for בְּהַ ; בְּהֵ) noun fem. sing. dec. 11 c. (§ 42. rem. 1); ⁴ bef. lab. .	ערב
בָּעֲרָבוֹת⁴	pref. id.) id. pl., absolute state .	ערב
בְּעַרְבוֹת	pref. בְּ) id. pl., construct state .	ערב
בָּעַרְבִים	pref. בַּ for בְּהַ ; בְּהֵ) gent. noun masc., pl. of עַרְבִי, from עֲרָב . .	ערב
בַּעֲרָבִים⁴	pref. בַּ for בְּהַ) Kal part. act. m., pl. of עֹרֵב d. 7 b.	ערב
בְּעַרְבֹת	pref. בְּ) noun fem. pl. constr. from עֲרָבָה dec. 11 c. (§ 42. rem. 1) . .	ערב
בָּעֲרָה	⁴ Kal pret. 3 pers. sing. fem.; ⁴ bef. lab. .	בער
בֹּעֵרָה⁴ בֹּעֲרָה }	id. part. act., sing. fem. from בֹּעֵר masc. (§ 39. No. 3. rem. 4) . . }	בער
בָּעֲרוּ⁴	⁴ id. pret. 3 pers. pl.; ⁴ bef. lab. .	בער
בִּעֲרוּ⁴	⁴ Piel(dag. forte impl.§14.r.1)pret.3 p.pl.; ⁴ id.	בער
בְּעֵרוֹ	pref. בְּ) n. m. s., suff. 3 p. s. m. fr. עוֹר d. 1 a.	עור
בְּעַרְעֵר	pref. בַּ bef. (־־)) pr. name of a place	ערר
בַעֲרֹעֵר	⁴ pref. בְּ) pr. n. of a place, see עֲרוֹעֵר ; ⁴ bef. (꞉)	ערר
בְּעֵרָצוֹן	pref. בְּ bef. (־־)) noun masc. sing. .	ערץ
בֹּעֲרוֹת	Kal part. act. fem., pl. of בָּעֲרָה or בֹּעֵרָת [from בֹּעֵר masc.]	בער
בְּעָרֵי	⁴ pref. בְּ) noun fem. pl. constr. of עָרִים irr. of עִיר (§ 45); ⁴ bef. (꞉) .	עור
בְּעָרֶיהָ	pref. id.) id. pl., suff. 3 pers. sing. fem.	עור
בְּעָרֵיהֶם	pref. id.) id. pl., suff. 3 pers. pl. masc. .	עור
בְּעָרָיו⁴	⁴ pref. id.) id. pl., suff. 3 p. s. m.; ⁴ bef. (꞉)	עור
בְּעָרֵיכֶם	pref. id.) id. pl., suff. 2 pers. pl. masc. .	עור
בֶּעָרִים	pref. בֶּ for בְּהֶ ; בְּהָ) id. pl., absolute state	עור

בֹּעֲרִים	Kal part. act. masc., pl. of בֹּעֵר dec. 7 b. .	בער
בְּעֵינִיגוּ⁴	pref. בְּ) noun fem. pl. (עֵרִים), suff. 1 pers. pl., irr. of עִיר (§ 45) . .	עור
בָּעֲרִיפֶיהָ	pref. בַּ bef. (־־)) noun masc. pl., suff. 3 pers. sing. fem. from [עֲרִיף] dec. 1 a. .	ערף
בְּעָרְכְּךָ } בְּעֶרְכְּךָ }	pref. בְּ) noun masc. sing., suff. 2 pers. sing. m. from עֵרֶךְ dec. 6. (§ 35. r. 6) }	ערד
בְּעָרְלָה	pref. id.) noun fem. sing. dec. 12 c.	ערל
בְּעָרְמָה	pref. id.) noun fem. sing. .	ערם
בְּעָרְמָם⁼	pref. id.) n. m. s., suff. 3 p. pl. m. fr. [עֲרָם] d. 6 c.	ערם
בָּעֹר	defect for עֲרוֹעֵר (q. v.) . .	ערר
בְּעָרְפּ⁴	pref. בְּ) noun masc. sing. dec. 6 c.	ערף
בְּעָרְפִּי	pref. id.) id., suff. 1 pers. sing .	ערף
בְּעַרְפֶּל⁴	pref. בְּ f. בְּהַ ; בְּהֵ } noun masc. sing. .	ערף
בָּעַרְפֶּל	pref. בַּ bef. (־־) } .	ערף
בִּעַרְתָּ	Piel (dag. forte impl. § 14. r. 1) pret. 2 p. s. m.	בער
בִּעַרְתָּ⁴	⁴ id. id.; acc. shifted by conv. ⁴ (bef. lab.)	בער
בֹּעֶרֶת⁴	Kal part. act. sing. fem. dec. 13, from בֹּעֵר m.	בער
בִּעַרְתִּי	Piel (dag. forte impl. § 14. r. 1) pret. 1 pers. s.	בער
בִּעַרְתִּי⁴	⁴ id. id.; acc. shifted by conv. ⁴ (bef. lab.)	בער
בִּעַרְתִּיהָ	id. id. with suff. 3 pers. sing. fem.	בער
בִּעַרְתֶּם	id. pret. 2 pers. pl. masc. .	בער
בַּעְשָׁא	pr. name of a king of Israel.	
בְּעֶשֶׂב	Chald. pref. בַּ bef. (־־)) noun m. s. dec. 3 b.	עשב
בְּעֵשֶׂב⁴	⁴ pref. בְּ) n. m. s. d. 6. (§ 35. r. 6); ⁴ bef. lab.	עשב
בֶּעָשׂוֹר⁴	⁴³ pref. בֶּ for בְּהֶ ; בְּהָ) noun masc. sing.	עשׂר
בַּעֲשׂוֹת	pref. בַּ bef. (־־)) Kal inf. constr. dec. 1 a.	עשׂה
בַּעֲשׂוֹתִי	pref. id.) id., suff. 1 pers. sing. .	עשׂה
בַּעֲשׂוֹתְךָ⁴	pref. id.) id., suff. 2 pers. sing. masc.	עשׂה
בַּעֲשׂוֹתֵךְ⁴	pref. id.) id., suff. 2 pers. sing. fem.	עשׂה
בְּעֹשֵׂי	pref. בְּ) Kal part. pl. constr. m. fr. עֹשֶׂה d. 9 a.	עשׂה
בַּעֲשֵׂיָה	(perhaps for מַעֲשֵׂיָה *work of the Lord*) pr. name masc. 1 Ch. 6. 25.	
בְּעֹשָׂיו⁼	pref. id.) Kal part. pl. masc., suff. 3 pers. sing. masc. from עֹשֶׂה dec. 9 a. .	עשׂה
בָּעֲשִׂירִי⁼	pref. בָּ for בְּהָ ; בְּהֵ) adj. ord. sing. masc.	עשׂר
בְּעֶשֶׁן	pref. בְּ f. בְּהַ ; בְּהֵ } noun masc. sing. dec. 4 c.	עשׁן
בֶּעָשָׁן⁼	pref. בֶּ q. v. }	
בְּעֶשֶׂק⁼	pref. בְּ f. בְּהַ } noun masc. sing.	עשׂק
בֶּעָשֶׂק	pref. בֶּ q. v. }	
בְּעֹשְׂקֵי⁼	⁴ pref. id.) Kal part. act. pl. constr. masc. from עשׁק dec. 7 b. .	עשׁק
בַּעֲשֵׂר	[for בְּהַעֲשֵׂר] pref. בְּ; Hiph. inf.constr. (§ 11. rem. 3. & § 13. rem. 9. also 1, 2) .	עשׂר
בָּעֹשֶׁר⁼	pref. בָּ for בְּהָ ; בְּהֵ) noun masc. sing. .	עשׁר
בְּעָשְׂרוֹ	pref. בְּ) n. m. s., suff. 3 p. s. m. fr. עֹשֶׂר d. 6 c.	עשׂר
בַּעֲשִׂרִי	defect. for בָּעֲשִׂירִי (q. v.) . .	עשׂר

ᵃ Pr. 12. 1.   ᵉ Pr. 7. 9.   ⁱ Eze. 39. 9, 9.   ᵖ Je. 31. 23.   ᵘ Job 5. 13.   ᵇ 2 Ch. 19. 3.   ᵉ Ex. 10. 15.   ˡ Eze. 16. 30.   ᵖ Eze. 22. 7, 12.
ᵇ Ps. 49. 11.   ᶠ Ps. 68. 5.   ᵏ Le. 13 18, 24.   ᵍ Ezr. 10. 14.   ᵛ Ge. 49. 8.   ᶜ Je. 20. 9.   ᵐ Nu. 29. 7.   ᵐ Ps. 149. 2.   ᵛ Mal. 3. 5.
ᶜ Le. 13. 49, 51,   ᵍ Pr. 22. 26.   ˡ Job 36. 6.   ʳ Is. 5. 30.   ʷ Job 16. 12.   ᵈ De. 26. 13, 14.   ⁿ Eze. 23. 21.   ⁿ Ge. 8. 5.   ʷ Ne. 10. 39.
53, 57.   ʰ Is. 30. 33.   ᵐ Eze. 1. 13.   ˢ Le. 27. 27, 27.   ˣ 1 Ki. 8. 12.   ᵉ Eze. 21. 4.   ᵒ Is. 64. 2.   ᵖ Ps. 102. 4.   ˣ Ex. 12. 8.
ᵈ Le. 13. 48.   Is 1. 31.   2 Ki. 17. 24.   Je. 9. 24.   ᵗ 2 Ch. 6. 1.   ᶠ Da. 4. 12.

בְּעֶשְׂרִים pref. בְּ)(n.m. card. com. gen., pl. of עֲשָׂרָה see עֶשֶׂר . . עשר

בַּעֲשֹׂתָהּ pref. בַּ bef. (_))(Kal inf. (עֲשׂוֹת) suff. 3 pers. sing. fem. dec. 1a . . עשה

בַּעֲשֹׂתוֹ pref. id.)(id., suff. 3 pers. sing. masc. עשה

בַּעֲשְׁתֵּי pref. בְּ)(n.m pl. constr. from עֶשֶׁת dec. 6a. עשת

בְּעֶשְׁתְּרָה (for בֵּית עַשְׁתְּרָה *temple of Astarte*) pr. name of a Levitical city in Manasseh, Jos. 21.27. called עַשְׁתָּרוֹת 1 Ch. 6. 56.

בְּעַשְׁתְּרוֹת } pref. בְּ)(pr. name of a place, see עַשְׁתָּרֶת
בְּעַשְׁתְּרֹת }

בְּעַשְׁתְּרֹת pref. id.)(pr. name in compos. עַשְׁתְּרֹת קַרְנַיִם see עַשְׁתָּרֶת.

בָּעַת Niph. *to be terrified*, const. with מִפְּנֵי. Pi.—I. *to terrify, alarm.*—II. *to come upon suddenly*, 1 Sa.16.14.
בְּעָתָה fem. *terror.*
בְּעוּתִים masc. pl. (of בִּעוּת dec. 1b) *terrors.*

בָּעֵת / pref. בְּ f. בָּהּ, בְּהָ } noun com. sing. dec. } עדה
בָּעֵת / pref. בְּ (q.v.) } 8b; בְּ bef. (:) }

בָּעֵתָה noun fem. sing. . . . בעת

בְּעִתָּהּ pref. בְּ)(noun com. sing., suff. 3 pers. sing. fem. from עֵת dec. 8b. עדה

בִּעֲתֻהוּ Piel (dag. forte impl. § 14. rem. 1) pret. 3 pers. pl., suff. 3 pers. sing. masc. [for בִּעֲתוּהוּ] בעת

בְּעִתּוֹ pref. בְּ)(noun com. sing., suff. 3 pers. sing. masc. from עֵת dec. 8b. עדה

בְּעִתִּים / pref. בְּ f. בָּהּ, בְּהָ } id. pl., absolute state; } עדה
בָּעִתִּים pref. בְּ q.v. } בְּ bef. lab. }

בְּעִתְּךָ pref. בְּ bef. (_))(pr. name of a place עתך

בְּעִתָּם pref. בְּ)(id. sing., suff. 3 pers. sing. masc. עדה

בִּעֲתַתּוּ / Piel pret. 3 pers. sing. fem. [בִּעֲתָה § 14. rem. 1], suff. 3 pers. s. m. [for בִּעֲתַתְהוּ] בעת

בִּעֲתַתְנִי / id., suff. 1 pers. sing. [for בִּעֲתַתְנִי] בעת

בִּפְאַת / pref. בְּ bef. (:))(noun fem. sing., constr. of פֵּאָה dec. 11b. פאה

בִּפְגֹעוֹ / pref. בְּ)(Kal inf. (פְּגֹעַ), suff. 3 pers. sing. masc. (§ 16. rem. 10) פגע

בְּפִגְרֵי / pref. id.)(noun masc. pl. constr. from פֶּגֶר dec. 6a; בְּ bef. (:) פגר

בְּפַדֶּן pref. id.)(pr. name in compos. פַּדַּן אֲרָם פדן

בְּפָה pref. id.)(noun masc. sing. [for פֵּאָה § 45] פאה

בְּפוּךְ pref. בְּ for בְּהַ)(noun masc. sing. פוך

בִּפְגֹּלָן pref. בְּ)(pr. name of a place פון

בְּפָז pref. בְּ for בְּהַ)(noun masc. sing. פז

בַּפָּח pref. id.)(for פַּח, n.m.s., pl. פַּחִים (§ 37.r.7) פח

בְּפַחַד pref. בְּ)(noun masc. sing. dec. 6d. פחד

בְּפַחֲזוּתָם / pref. id.)(noun fem. sing., suff. 3 pers. pl. masc. from [פַּחֲזוּת] dec. 1; בְּ oef. lab. פחז

בַּפֶּחָם / pref. בַּ for בְּהַ)(noun masc. sing. פחם

בִּפְאִי / pref. בְּ)(n. m. s. constr., or with suff. 1 p. s. [for פְּאִי] from פֶּה irr. (§ 45); בְּ bef. (_) פאה

בְּפִיד pref. id.)(noun masc. sing. dec. 1a. פיד

בְּפִידוֹ pref. id.)(id., suff. 3 pers. sing. masc. פיד

בְּפִיהָ pref. id.)(noun masc. sing., suff. 3 pers. sing. fem. from פֶּה irr. (§ 45) פאה

בְּפִיהוּ pref. id.)(id., suff. 3 pers. sing. masc. פאה

בְּפִיהֶם pref. id.)(id., suff. 3 pers. pl. masc. פאה

בְּפִיו pref. id.)(id., suff. 3 pers. sing. masc. פאה

בְּפִיךָ pref. id.)(id., suff. 2 pers. sing. masc. פאה

בְּפִיךְ pref. id.)(id., suff. 2 pers. sing. fem. פאה

בְּפִיכֶם pref. id.)(id., suff. 2 pers. pl. masc. פאה

בְּפִילַגְשׁוֹ / pref. id.)(noun fem. sing., suff. 3 pers. sing. masc. from פִּילֶגֶשׁ dec. 6a. (§ 35. rem. 16) פלגש

בְּפִילַגְשִׁי / pref. id.)(id., suff. 1 pers. sing. פלגש

בְּפִימוֹ / pref. id.)(noun masc. sing., suff. 3 pers. pl. from פֶּה irr. (§ 45) פאה

בִּפְלַגּוֹת pref. בְּ bef. (:))(n. fem., pl. of [פְּלַגָּה] d. 10. פלג

בִּפְלַגָּתְהוֹן Chald. pref. id.)(noun fem. pl., suff. 3 pers. pl. masc. from [פְּלַגָּה] dec. 8a. פלג

בַּפֶּלֶךְ pref. בַּ for בְּהַ)(n.m.s., [suff. פַּלְחוֹ] d. 6a. פלך

בִּפְלִילִים pref. בְּ bef. (:))(n.m., pl. of [פָּלִיל] d. 3a. פלל

בַּפֶּלֶס pref. בַּ for בְּהַ)(noun masc. sing. פלס

בַּפְּלִשְׁתִּים / pref. id.)(gent. noun masc., pl. of פְּלֶשֶׁת from פלש

בְּפֻם Chald. pref. בְּ)(noun masc. sing. dec. 3c. פום

בְּפֻמַּהּ / Chald. pref. id.)(id., suff. 3 pers. sing. fem. פום

בִּפְנוֹתָם / pref. בְּ bef. (:))(Kal inf. (פְּנוֹת), suff. 3 pers. pl. masc. dec. 1a. פנה

בְּפָנַי / pref. בְּ)(noun masc. pl., suff. 1 pers. sing. from [פָּנֶה] dec. 9b. פנה

בְּפָנֵי / pref. בְּ bef. (:))(id. pl., constr. state פנה

בְּפָנֶיהָ pref. בְּ)(id. pl., suff. 3 pers. sing. fem. פנה

בִּפְנֵיהֶם pref. בְּ bef. (:))(id. pl., suff. 3 pers. pl. m. פנה

בְּפָנָיו pref. id.)(id. pl., suff. 3 pers. sing. masc. פנה

בְּפָנֶיךָ pref. id.)(id. pl., suff. 2 pers. sing. masc. פנה

בִּפְנֵיכֶם pref. בְּ bef. (:))(id. pl., suff. 2 pers. pl. masc. פנה

בְּפָנִים pref. בְּ)(id. pl., absolute state פנה

בִּפְנִימִי / pref. בְּ for בְּהַ)(adj. masc. sing. dec. 1a. פנם

בַּפַּס pref. id.)(pr. n. of a place, see אָפֵס דַּמִּים

בִּפְסִילֶיהֶם / pref. בְּ bef. (:))(noun masc. pl., suff. 3 pers. pl. masc. from [פָּסִיל] dec. 3a. פסל

בַּפֶּסֶל pref. בַּ for בְּהַ)(for פֶּסֶל noun masc. sing. פסל

a Le. 4. 27.   f 1 Sa. 16. 14.   i Is. 66. 24.   q Ge. 31. 53.   b Job 31. 29.   u Ju. 20. 6.   c Ex. 21. 22.   h Eze. 29. 16.   l De. 5. 4.
k Is. 60. 22.   l Is. 21. 4.   i Eze. 43. 7.   n Je. 23. 32.   f Job 30. 24.   v Ps. 58. 7.   d Is. 40. 12.   k Job 16. 8.   m Eze. 41. 17.
t Job 18. 11.   m Am. 3. 12.   n Pr. 11. 9.   o Is. 44. 12.   r Eze. 16. 56.   w Ezr. 6. 18.   o Da. 4. 28.   l Eze. 42. 12.   n Ps. 78. 58.
c Da. 11. 6.   h Nu. 35. 19, 21.   f La. 4. 2.   p Pr. 11. 11.   s Ju. 19. 25, 29.   g 2 Sa. 3. 29.   p Da. 7. 5.   m Nu. 12 14.   o Is. 42. 17.
Ne. 13. 31.

בְּפִסְלֵיהֶם — defect. for בְּפְסִילֵיהֶם (q. v.) — פסל

בְּפָעֳלוֹ — pref. בְ χ noun masc. sing. dec. 6f. — פעל

בְּפָעֳלְךָ — pref. id. χ id., suff. 2 pers. s. m., for פָּעֳלְךָ — פעל

בְּפָעֳלָם — pref. id. χ id., suff. 3 pers. pl. masc. — פעל

בְּפַעַם } בְּפָעַם — pref. בְ for בְּהַ } pref. בְ q. v. — noun fem. sing. dec. 6 d. — פעם

בִּפְקֹד — pref. בְ bef. (:) χ Kal inf. constr. — פקד

בְּפִקְדוֹן — pref. בְ χ noun masc. sing. — פקד

בְּפִקֻּדֶיךָ } בְּפִקּוּדֶיךָ — pref. בְ χ noun masc. pl., suff. 2 pers. sing. masc. [פִּקּוּד] dec. 1 b. — פקד

בְּפַר } בְּפָר — pref. בְ for בְּהַ } noun masc. sing. pl. פָּרִים — pref. בְ q. v. (§ 37. rem. 7) — פרר

בִּפְרָדִים — ו pref. בְ for בְּהַ χ noun masc., pl. of פָּרָד (suff. פְּרָדוֹ) dec. 6a; ו bef. labial — פרד

בַּפְרוּר — pref. id. χ noun masc. sing. — פרר

בַּפַּרְוָרִים — pref. id. χ noun m., pl. of פַּרְבָּר, see פַּרְבָּר

בִּפְרָזִי — ו pref. id. χ pr. n. of a people; ו bef. labial — פרז

בִּפְרֹחַ — pref. בְ bef. (:) χ Kal inf. constr. — פרח

בִּפְרִי — ו pref. id. χ noun masc. s. d. 6i; ו bef. lab. — פרה

בְּפִרְיוֹ — pref. בְ χ id., suff. 3 pers. sing. masc. — פרה

בִּפְרָים — pref. id. χ noun m., pl. of פַר (§ 37. r. 7) — פרר

בְּפִרְכֶךָ } בְּפִרְכֶּךָ — pref. בְ χ noun masc. sing. (§ 35. r. 2) — פרך

בִּפְרָסוֹת — pref. id. χ noun fem., pl. of פַּרְסָה dec. 12a. — פרס

בִּפְרֹעַ — pref. בְ bef. (:) χ Kal inf. constr. — פרע

בְּפַרְעֹה — pref. בְ χ pr. name masc., see פַּרְעֹה — פרע

בְּפַרְעָתוֹן — pref. id. χ pr. name of a place — פרע

בְּפֶרֶץ — pref. בְ for בְּהַ χ noun masc. sing. (pl. with suff. פְּרָצֵיהֶם) dec. 6a. — פרץ

בְּפִרְצוֹת — pref. id. χ id. pl., absolute state — פרץ

בְּפָרֵשׁ — pref. בְ χ Piel inf. constr. — פרשׁ

בִּפְרָשָׁיו — ו pref. id. χ noun masc. pl., suff. 3 pers. sing. m. fr. פָּרָשׁ dec. 1b. (§ 30. r. 1); ו bef. (:) — פרשׁ

בְּפָרָשִׁים — ו pref. id. χ id. pl., absolute state; ו id. — פרשׁ

בְּפָרֶשְׁכֶם — ו pref. id. χ Piel inf. (פָּרֵשׁ) suff. 2 pers. pl. masc. dec. 7 b; ו id. — פרשׁ

בִּפְרָת — pref. בְ bef. (:) χ pr. name of a river — פרת

בַּפּוּשׁ — pref. בְ for בְּהַ χ noun masc. sing. — פושׁ

בְּפֶשַׁע } בְּפִשְׁעַ — pref. בְ χ noun masc. sing., d. 6a. (suff. פִּשְׁעִי) dec. 6 a. § 35. rem. 5) — פשׁע

בְּפִשְׁעֵיכֶם — ו pref. id. χ id. pl., suff. 2 p. pl. m.; ו bef. (:) — פשׁע

בְּפִשְׁתִּי — pref. id. χ constr. of the following — פשׁת

בְּפִשְׁתִּים — pref. בְ for בְּהַ χ noun fem. with pl. masc. term. fr. פִּשְׁתָּה dec. 10. — פשׁת

בַּפְּתָאִים — pref. id. χ n. m., pl. of פֶּתִי d. 6i. (§35.r.15) — פתה

בְּפִתְאֹם — pref. בְ χ adv. for פִּתְאֹם — פתע

בְּפִתְגָּן — pref. id. χ n. m. s., constr. of [פִּתְגָּן] d. 2b. — פתגן

בִּפְתוּחֵי — ו pref. בְ bef. (:) χ noun masc. pl. constr. fr. [פִּתּוּחֹת] dec. 1 a; ו bef. labial — פתח

בַּפֶּתַח } בְּפֶּתַח } בְּפֶתַח — pref. בְ f. בְּהַ } pref. בְ q. v. — noun masc. sing., d. 6a. (suff. פִּתְחוֹ § 35. r. 5) — פתח

בְּפִתְחֵי — ו pref. id. χ id. pl., constr. state; ו bef. (:) — פתח

בְּפִתְחִי — ו pref. id. χ Kal inf. [פָּתַח], suff. 1 pers. sing. (§ 35. rem. 5) — פתח

בְּפִתְחֶיהָ — pref. בְ bef. (:) χ noun masc. pl., suff. 3 pers. sing. fem. (see בְּפֶתַח) — פתח

בִּפְתִיל — pref. id. χ n. m. s., constr. of פָּתִיל d. 3a. — פתל

בִּפְתָע — pref. בְ χ prop. masc. n., used as an adv. — פתע

בְּפַתְרוֹם — pref. id. χ pr. name of a region, see פַּתְרוֹם

בַּצֹּאן } בְּצֹאן — ו pref. בְ f. בְּהַ } pref. בְ q. v. — noun masc. sing. dec. 1a. — צאן

בְּצֹאנֶךָ } בְּצֹאנְךָ — pref. id. χ id., suff. 2 pers. sing. masc.; ו bef. labial — צאן

בְּצֹאנְכֶם — pref. id. χ id., suff. 3 pers. pl. masc. — צאן

בְּצֹאנֵנוּ — pref. id. χ id., suff. 1 pers. pl. — צאן

בְּצֵאת — pref. id. χ Kal inf. constr. [for צָאֵת § 25. No. 2, comp. § 23. rem. 2 & 4] — צא

בְּצֵאתוֹ — ו pref. id. χ id., suff. 3 pers. s. m.; ו bef. (:) — יצא

בְּצֵאתְנוּ — noun fem. pl., suff. 3 pers. sing. masc., for [בָּצוֹתָיו] from בֵּצָה dec. 10. — בצץ

בְּצֵאתִי — pref. בְ χ Kal inf. with suff. 1 p. s. comp. בְּצֵאת — יצא

בְּצֵאתְךָ } בְּצֵאתְךָ — pref. id. χ id., suff. 2 pers. sing. masc. — יצא

בְּצֵאתְכֶם — pref. id. χ id., suff. 2 pers. pl. masc. — יצא

בְּצֵאתָם — ו pref. id. χ id., suff. 3 p. pl. m.; ו bef. lab. — יצא

בַּצָּבָא — pref. בְ for בְּהַ χ n. m. s. d. 4a. (§ 34. r. 2) — צבא

בְּצִבְאוֹת — pref. id. χ bef. (:) χ noun masc. with pl. fem. term. from צְבִי dec. 6i. (§ 35. rem. 15) — צבה

בְּצִבְאוֹתֵינוּ } בְּצִבְאֹתֵינוּ — pref. בְ χ n. m., with pl. fem. term. & suff. 1 pers. pl. from צָבָא dec. 4a. — צבא

בַּצְּבִים — ו pref. בְ for בְּהַ χ noun masc., pl. of צָב dec. 8a; ו bef. labial — צבב

בְּצַד — pref. בְ χ noun masc. sing. dec. 8e. — צדד

בְּצִדָּהּ — pref. בְ χ id., suff. 3 pers. sing. fem. — צדד

בְּצִידָה — pref. בְ bef. (:) χ noun fem. sing. — צדה

בְּצִדֵּיכֶם — pref. בְ χ noun masc. pl., suff. 2 pers. pl. masc. from צַד dec. 8e. — צדד

בְּצִדְקִי } בְּצֶדֶק — pref. בְ f. בְּהַ } pref. בְ q. v. — noun masc. sing., suff. צִדְקִי dec. 6a. — צדק

בִּצְדָקָה — Chald. pref. id. χ noun fem. sing. — צדק

a Je. 8. 19.   f Ps. 119. 78.   l 1 Sa. 1. 24.   r Ps. 68. 15.   a Is. 50. 1.   Eze. 33. 30.   s Ho. 5. 6.   v Is. 66. 20.
b Ps. 9. 17.   g Ps. 119. 15.   Eze. 34. 4.   Joel 2. 4.   Jos. 2. 6.   Eze. 37. 13.   Ex. 10. 9.   Ge. 6. 16.
c Ps. 92. 5.   Eze. 43. 22.   m Le. 25. 53.   Is. 1. 15.   b Le. 13. 52.   Mi. 5. 5.   Eze. 47. 11.   Nu. 35. 20.
d Job 24. 5.   h 2 Ki. 23. 11.   n Eze. 26. 11.   Job 35. 15.   Pr. 7. 7.   1 Ki. 14. 6.   Ge. 31. 41.   De. 23. 5, etc.   Pr. 25. 5.
Ex. 30. 12, 12.   i Ps. 92. 8.   Ju. 5. 2.   Da. 8. 12.   2 Ch. 29. 36.   Pr. 1. 21.   De. 15. 19.   Ps. 108. 12.   Da. 4. 24.
Le. 5. 21.   Ca. 8. 11.   Eze. 13. 5.

בְּצִדְקָתְ׳ | pref. בְּ bef. (ִ)) (n. f. s. d. 11c; וֹ bef. lab. | צדק
בְּצִדְקוֹ | pref. בְּ) (noun masc. sing., suff. 3 pers. sing. masc. from צֶדֶק dec. 6a . . | צדק
בְּצִדְקָתוֹ | pref. id.) (noun fem. sing., suff. 3 pers. sing. masc. from צְדָקָה dec. 11c . . | צדק
בְּצִדְקָתִי | pref. id.) (id., suff. 1 pers. sing. . . | צדק
בְּצִדְקָתְךָ֫ | pref. id.) (id., suff. 2 pers. sing. masc.; | צדק
בְּצִדְקָתֶ֫ךָ | וֹ וֹ וֹ bef. labial . . }
בְּצִדְקָתֵךְ | pref. id.) (Piel inf. [צַדֵּקַת § 10. r. 2], suff. 2 pers. sing. fem. dec. 13b . . | צדק
בְּצִדְקָתָם | pref. id.) (noun fem. sing., suff. 3 pers. pl. masc. from צְדָקָה dec. 11c . . | צדק
בְּצָה | וֹ noun fem. sing. dec. 10; וֹ bef. labial . | בצץ
בַּצָּהֳרַ֫יִם | pref. בַּ for בְּהַ) (noun fem., du. of צֹהַר | צהר
בַּצֳּהֳרַ֫יִם | dec. 6f. (§ 35. rem. 9. & 16) }
בְּצוּאר | pref. בְּ) (n. m. s. d. 2b. (comp. § 30. r. 1) | צור
בְּצַוָּארוֹ | pref. id.) (id., suff. 3 pers. sing. masc. | צור
בְּצַוְּארֵי׳ | pref. id.) (id. pl., constr. state . | צור
בַּצּוֹם | pref. בַּ for בְּהַ) (noun masc. sing. dec. 1; וֹ | צום
בְּצוֹם | וֹ pref. בְּ q. v. } bef. (ִ) . . | צום
בְּצ֫וֹעֵר | pref. id.) (pr. name of a place | צער
בְּצוֹק׳ | וֹ pref. id.) (noun masc. sing.; וֹ bef. (ִ) | צוק
בַּצּוּר | pref. בַּ for בְּהַ | צור
בְּצוּר | וֹ pref. בְּ q. v. } noun masc. s. d. 1a; וֹ id. | צור
בְּצוּרָה | Kal part. pass. s. f. d. 10, [from בָּצוּר m.] | בצר
בַּצֻּרוֹת׳ | pref. בַּ for בְּהַ) (noun masc. with pl. fem. term. from צור dec. 1a . . | צור
בְּצֻרוֹת׳ | Kal part. pass. fem., pl. of בְּצוּרָה d. 10 | בצר
בְּצֻרֹת׳ | וֹ [from בָּצוּר masc.]; וֹ bef. (ִ) } | בצר
בְּצַוֹּת׳ | pref. בְּ) (Kal inf. const. dec. 1b. | צוה
בְּצַוֹּתוֹ׳ | pref. id.) (id., suff. 3 pers. sing. masc. | צוה
בְּצַחֲחַיִּם | pref. בַּ for בְּהַ) (adj. masc. Kh. חַיִּים׳, K. חָיִי׳ [pl. of צָחִיחַ] . | צחח
בְּצַחְצָחוֹת | pref. בְּ) (noun fem. pl. [of צַחְצָחָה] . | צחח
בְּצֵעִי | for בֶּצֵי׳ pr. name masc. . | בוץ
בַּצִּיָּה׳ | pref. בַּ for בְּהַ) (noun fem. sing. dec. 10. | ציה
בַּצִּיּוֹן | pref. בְּ) (noun masc. sing. . | ציה
בְּצִיּוֹן | pref. id.) (pr. name of a place | ציה
בַּצִּיּוֹת׳ | pref. בַּ for בְּהַ) (noun fem., pl. of צִיָּה d. 10. | ציה
בְּצִים׳ | pref. id.) (noun m., pl. of צִי (comp. § 3. r. 1) | ציה
בְּצִיצָתְ׳ | pref. בְּ) (noun fem. sing. . | צוץ
בְּצִיר | וֹ׳ noun masc. sing. dec. 3a; וֹ bef. lab. | בצר
בְּצִירֵךְ׳ | id. with suff. 2 pers. sing. fem. . | בצר

בְּצֵל | Root not used; Arab. to strip, peel.
    בְּצֵל masc. only pl. בְּצָלִים onions Nu. 11. 5.

בַּצְלוּת (nakedness) pr. name masc. Ezr. 2. 52, called בַּצְלִית Ne. 7. 54.
בְּצֵל׳ | pref. בַּ for בְּהַ } noun masc. sing. dec. 8b; | צלל
בְּצֵל | וֹ pref. בְּ q. v. } וֹ bef. (ִ) . . | צלל
בְּצַלְאֵל | וֹ pref. id.) (pr. name masc. . . | צלל
בְּצִלָּה׳ | pref. id.) (n. m. s., suff. 3 p. s. fem. fr. צֵל d. 8b. | צלל
בְּצִלּוֹ | וֹ׳ pref. id.) (id., suff. 3 pers. sing. masc. | צלל
בַּצְלוּת | pr. name masc. . . . | בצל
בַּצַּלַּ֫חַת | pref. בַּ for בְּהַ) (noun fem. sing. . | צלח
בַּצְלָחוֹת׳ | וֹ pref. id.) (n. fem. pl. [of צְלָחָה]; וֹ bef. lab. | צלח
בְּצִלִּי׳ | pref. בְּ) (n. m. s., suff. 1 p. s. from צֵל d. 8b. | צלל
בַּצְלִית | pr. name masc., see בַּצְלוּת | צלל
בְּצֶ֫לֶם | pref. בְּ) (noun m. s. dec. 6a. (see the foll.) | צלם
בְּצַלְמוֹ | pref. id.) (id., suff. 3 pers. sing. masc. | צלם
בְּצַלְמוֹן | pref. id.) (pr. name of a mountain . | צלם
בְּצַלְמָ֫וֶת׳ | pref. id.) (n. f. s., compound of צֵל and מָ֫וֶת | צלל
בְּצַלְמֹ֫נָה | pref. id.) (pr. name of a place . | צלם
בְּצַלְמֵ֫נוּ׳ | pref. id.) (n. m. s., suff. 1 p. pl. fr. צֶ֫לֶם d. 6a. | צלם
בְּצֵ֫לַע | pref. id.) (n. fem. s., constr. of צֵ֫לָע dec. 4c. (§ 33. No. 2. r. 3); also pr. name of a place | צלע
בְּצַלְעוֹת׳ | pref. id.) (id. pl., construct state . | צלע
בְּצַלְעִי׳ | וֹ pref. id.) (noun m. sing., suff. 1 pers. sing. from צֵ֫לָע dec. 6a. (§ 35. rem. 5); וֹ bef. (ִ) | צלע
בְּצַלְצַח | pref. id.) (pr. name of a place . | צלל
בְּצִלְצַל׳ | pref. id.) (noun m. s. [for צְלַצַל, constr. of צַלְצַל] for צֵל comp. d. 4, & 12c; וֹ bef. (ִ) | צלל
בְּצִלְצָלֵי׳ | pref.id.) (id.pl.,constr.st.; (for צֵל comp.§36.r.5) | צלל
בְּצִלְצְלִים׳ | וֹ pref. id.) (id. pl., absolute state; וֹ bef. (ִ) | צלל
בְּצָמָא | pref. בַּ for בְּהַ } noun m. sing. dec. 4a; וֹ id. | צמא
בְּצָמָא | וֹ pref. בְּ q. v. } | צמא
בְּצַמְרֵ׳ | pref. בַּ for בְּהַ) (n. m. s. (suff. צַמְרִי) d. 6a. | צמר
בְּצִנָּה׳ | pref. בְּ) (noun fem. sing. dec. 10. . | צנן
בַּצִּנּוֹר׳ | pref. בַּ for בְּהַ) (noun masc. sing. dec. 1b. | צנר
בְּצִנּוֹת׳ | pref. בְּ) (noun fem., pl. of צִנָּה dec. 10. | צנן

בָּצַע I. to break, or cut off, to break in pieces. In Joel 2. 8, perhaps intrans., or the word course is to be implied.—II. to spoil, plunder; hence to acquire unjust gain. Pi.—I. to cut off, (as the weaver his web from the loom Is. 38. 12)—II. to defraud, Eze. 22. 12.—III. to finish, complete. Hence

בֶּ֫צַע | m. d. 6a. (with suff. בִּצְעוֹ § 35. r. 5. & 3. 2). —I. plunder, unjust gain.—II. gain, profit in general | בצע
בֶּ֫צַע | }

Hebrew	Definition	Root
בְּצֹעַ	Kal inf. constr.	בצע
בָּצַע	Piel pret. 3 pers. sing. masc.	בצע
בֹּצֵעַ	Kal part. act. sing. masc.; ו bef. lab.	בצע
בְּצַעְדְּךָ	pref. בְּ)(Kal inf. [צְעַד], suff. 2 pers. sing. masc. (§ 16. rem. 10)	צעד
בְצָעוֹ	n.m.s., suff. 3 p.s.m.fr. בֶּצַע d. 6a. (§ 35. r.5)	בצע
בַּצְעִיף	pref. בַּ for בְּהַ)(noun masc. sing. dec. 3a.	צעף
בִּצְעִירוֹ	ו pref. בְּ bef. (:) adj. masc. sing., suff. 3 pers. sing. masc. from צָעִיר dec. 3a; ו bef. lab.	צער
בְצֶעְךָ	noun masc. sing., suff. 2 pers. sing. masc. [for עֶצַע from בֶּצַע dec. 6a. (§ 35. rem. 5)	בצע
בִּצְעֵךְ	id., suff. 2 pers. sing. fem.	בצע
בִּצְעָם	id., suff. 3 pers. pl. masc.	בצע
בִצְעָם	ו Kal imp. sing. masc. [בְּצַע], suff. 3 pers. pl. masc. [for בְּצָעֵם] § 16. rem. 11; ו bef. lab.	בצע
בְּצֹעַן	pref. בְּ)(pr. name of a place	צען
בְּצַעֲנִים Kh.} בְּצַעֲנַיִם K.}	pref. id.)(pr. name of a place	צען
בַּצָּפוֹן	pref. בַּ for בְּהַ)(noun masc. sing. dec. 3a.	צפן
בַּצַּפַּחַת	pref. id.)(noun fem. sing. צַפַּחַת	צפח
בְּצִפִּיָתֵנוּ	pref. בְּ)(n.fem.s.,suff.1 p.pl.fr. צִפִּיָה d. 10.	צפה
בַּצִּפֳּרִים	ו pref. id.)(noun com. sing. (pl. צִפֳּרִים § 30. rem. 1); ו before labial	צפר
בַּצְפַרְדְּעִים	pref. בַּ for בְּהַ)(n.com.,pl.of צְפַרְדֵּעַ d.7 b.	צפרדע
בְּצִפָּרֶן	pref. בְּ)(noun masc. sing. dec. 6c.	צפר

בָּצַץ Root not used; Arab. *to flow slowly, trickle.*
   בִּץ masc. *mire, mud,* Jer. 38. 22.
   בִּצָּה fem. *a marsh, fen*; pl. with suff. בִּצֹּאתָיו for בִּצּוֹתָיו.
   בּוֹצֵץ (*shining,* בצץ Arab. *to shine* comp. בּוּץ) pr. name of a rock near Gibeah, 1 Sa. 14. 4.

בָּצֵק *to swell,* spoken of the feet.
   בָּצֵק masc. dec. 5a, *dough.*
   בָּצְקַת (*elevation*) pr. name of a city in the tribe of Judah.

Hebrew	Definition	Root
בָּצֵק	noun masc. sing. dec. 5a.	בצק
בָּצְקָה	Kal pret. 3 p. s. fem. [for בָּצְקָה § 8. r. 1. & 7]	בצק
בָּצְקוּ	id. pret. 3 pers. pl. [for בָּצְקוּ see prec.]	בצק
בְּצֵקוֹ	n.m.s., suff. 3 pers. s. m. from בָּצֵק dec. 5a.	בצק
בְּצַקְלֹן	ו pref. בְּ)(pr. name of a place; ו bef. (:)	צקלן
בְּצִקְלֹנוֹ	pref. id.)(noun masc. sing., suff. 3 pers. sing. masc. from [צִקְלוֹן] dec. 1 b.	צקל
בִּצְקֶת	pref. id.)(Kal inf. constr.	יצק
בְּצָקַת	ו pr. name of a place; ו bef. lab.	בצק

[בָּצַר] I. *to cut off.*—II. *to prune the vine.*—III. *to gather the vintage;* part. בֹּצֵר *a vintager,* metaph. of a destructive enemy.—IV. part. pass. בָּצוּר *inaccessible, fortified, strong,* access to it being *cut off*; metaph. *incomprehensible,* Je. 33. 3. Niph. *to be cut off, restrained,* with מִן. Pi. *to make inaccessible, to fortify.*

   בָּצִיר masc. dec. 3a.—I. *vintage.*—II. adj. *fortified* (comp. R. No. IV.) Zec. 11. 2. Keri.
   בֶּצֶר masc. *gold,* Job 36. 19.
   בֶּצֶר masc. dec. 6, in pause בָּצֶר.—I. *gold.*—II. pr. name of a city in the tribe of Reuben.—III pr. name masc. 1 Ch. 7. 37.
   בָּצְרָה fem.—I. *fold for cattle,* Mic. 2. 12.—II. pr. name of the capital of Edom.
   בִּצָּרוֹן masc. *fortress, strong-hold,* Zec. 9. 12.
   בַּצָּרוֹת fem. pl. בַּצָּרוֹת (§ 44. rem. 5) *withholding of rain, drought.*
   מִבְצָר masc. dec. 2b. pl. ־ים & ־וֹת.—I. *fortification;* עִיר מִבְצָר *a fortified city.*—II. pr. name of a prince of the Edomites, Ge. 36. 42.

Hebrew	Definition	Root
בַּצָּר בֶּצֶר	pref. בַּ for בְּהַ)(noun masc. sing. pl. צָרִים (§ 37. rem. 7)	צרר
בֵּצֶר	noun masc. sing. for [בֶּצֶר] dec. 6a.	בצר
בָּצֶר	noun masc. sing. [for בֶּצֶר]	בצר
בַּצָּר	pref. בְּ)(noun m. sing., pl. צָרִים (§ 37. r. 7)	צרר
בֶּצֶר	pr. name of a man and a place	בצר
בַּצְרָה	perhaps noun fem. sing., (after the form קְלָסָה, בַּקָּשָׁה)	בצר
בַּצָּרָה	pref. בַּ for בְּהַ)(n.fem.s.d.10. [for צָרָה] fr.	צרר
בְּצָרָה	ו pref. בְּ q.v.)(צָר m. § 37. r. 7; ו bef. (:)	צרר
בָּצְרָה	noun fem. sing. (Mic. 2. 12); also pr. name	בצר
בִּצְרוֹר	pref. בְּ bef. (:))(noun masc. sing. dec. 1a.	צרר
בְּצָרוֹת	pref. בְּ)(noun fem., pl. of צָרָה dec. 10.	צרר
בְּצֻרוֹת	ו Kal part. pass. fem., pl. of בְּצוּרָה dec. 10. [from בָּצוּר masc.]	בצר
בַּצְּרִיחִים	ו pref. בַּ for בְּהַ)(noun masc., pl. of [צְרִיחַ] dec. 3a.; ו bef. lab.	צרח
בְּצָרָיו	pref. בְּ)(noun masc. pl., suff. 3 pers. sing. masc. from צַר (§ 37. rem. 7)	צרר
בְּצָרֶיךָ	n. m. pl., suff. 2 p. s. m. from [בֶּצֶר] dec. 6.	בצר
בֹּצְרִים	Kal part. act. m., pl. of [בֹּצֵר] dec. 7 b.	בצר
בְּצָרַת	noun fem. sing., (comp. בַּצָּרָה)	בצר
בְצָרֹת	ו defect. for בְּצֻרוֹת (q. v.)	בצר
בְּצָרָתָה	pref. בַּ for בְּהַ)(n.f.s. צָרָה q.v.) with ה parag.	צרר
בַּקְבּוּק	pr. name masc.	בקק
בִּקְבוּרָה	pref. בְּ bef. (:))(noun fem. sing. dec. 10.	קבר

ᵃ Eze. 22. 27.   ᵈ Ge. 38. 14.   ᶠ Ec. 11. 3.   ᵏ Ex. 7. 27.   ʳ Ex. 12. 34.   ᵘ Job 22. 24.   ᵇ Ps. 91. 15   ᵉ Ps. 112. 8.   ʰ De. 3. 5; 9. 1
ᵇ La. 2. 17.   ᵉ Jos. 6. 26.   ᶢ 1 Ki. 17. 12.   ˡ Je. 17. 1.   ˢ 2 Ki. 4. 42.   ᵛ Ne. 9. 37   ᶜ Job 22. 25.   ᶠ Ps. 120. 1.
ᶜ Ps. 10. 3.   ᶠ Je. 22. 17.   ⁱ La. 4. 17.   ᵐ De. 8. 4.   ᵗ Job 38. 38.   ʷ Job 7. 11.   ᵈ 1 Sa. 13. 6.   ᵍ Is. 14. 20.
ᵈ Is. 57. 17   ᵉ Am. 9. 1.   ᵐ Le. 14. 52.   ⁿ Ne. 9. 21.   ᵖ Ps. 4. 2.   ˣ Ps. 10. 3.   ᵉ Je. 17. 8.

בְּקַבְּצִי[a]	pref. בְּ)(Piel inf. (קַבֵּץ), suff. 1 p. s. d. 7 b.	קבץ
בַּקְבֻּק[b]	noun masc. sing.)(וּ bef. lab.	בקק
בָּקְבֻּקְיָה	וּ pr. name masc.; וּ id.	בקק
בַּקְבֻּקַּר	וּ pr. name masc.; וּ id.	בקק
בַּקֶּבֶר[c] } בְּקֶבֶר } בַּקָּבֶר[d] } בְּקָבֶר }	pref. בְּ f. בָּה } noun masc. sing. dec. 6 a. (§ 35. rem. 2; but with pref. בַּ q. v. } suff. קִבְרוֹ)	קבר
בְּקִבְרוֹ[e]	pref. id.)(id., suff. 3 pers. sing. masc.	קבר
בְּקִבְרוֹת	וּ pref. id.)(id. pl. constr. fem.	קבר
בְּקִבְרִי[f]	pref. id.)(id. sing., suff. 1 pers. sing.	קבר
בַּקְּבָרִים	pref. בַּ for בָּה)(id. pl., absolute state	קבר
בְּקִבְרֹת	וּ pref. בְּ)(pr. name in compos. קִבְרֹת הַתַּאֲוָה	קבר
בְּקִבְרָתוֹ	pref. בְּ bef. (.))(noun fem. sing., suff. 3 pers. sing. m. from קְבוּרָה dec. 10.	קבר
בְּקִבְרֹתָיו[g]	pref. בְּ)(noun masc. with pl. fem. term. and suff. 3 pers. sing. masc. from קֶבֶר dec. 6 a.	קבר
בְּקִבְרָתָם	pref. בְּ bef. (.))(noun f. sing., suff. 3 pers. pl. masc. from קְבוּרָה dec. 10.	קבר
בַּקְּדֵחַת[h]	וּ pref. בַּ for בָּה)(noun fem. sing.; וּ bef. lab.	קדח
בִּקְדֹשׁ	pref. בְּ bef. (.))(adj. m. s., constr. of קָדֹשׁ d. 3 a.	קדש
בַּקֹּדֶשׁ } בְּקֹדֶשׁ }	pref. בַּ for בָּה } pref. בְּ q. v. } noun masc. sing. dec. 6 c.	קדש
בְּקָדֵשׁ	pref. id.)(pr. name of a place, also in compos. קָדֵשׁ בַּרְנֵעַ	קדש
בְּקָדְשׁוֹ	pref. id.)(noun masc. sing, suff. 3 pers. sing. masc. from קֹדֶשׁ dec. 6 c.	קדש
בִּקְדֹשָׁיו[i]	pref. בְּ bef. (.))(adj. pl. masc., suff. 3 pers. sing. masc. (§ 4. rem. 1) from קָדֹשׁ dec. 3 a.	קדש
בְּקָדְשִׁי[k]	pref. בְּ)(n. m. s., suff. 1 p. s. fr. קֹדֶשׁ d. 6 c.	קדש
בַּקֳּדָשִׁים[l]	pref. בַּ for בָּה)(n. masc. pl. of קָדֹשׁ dec. 5 a.	קדש
בְּקָדָשִׁים	pref. id.)(noun masc., pl. of קֹדֶשׁ dec. 6 c.	קדש
בַּקָּהֵל } בְּקָהֵל } בִּקְהַל }	pref. id. בְּ pref. } noun m. sing. dec. 4 a.; וּ bef. lab. וּ pref. בְּ bef. (.))(id., constr. st.; וּ id.	קהל
בִּקְהָלָם	pref. id.)(id., suff. 3 pers. pl. masc.	קהל
בְּקֵהֵלָתָה	pref. id.)(pr. name of a place	קהל
בַּקֵּו[m]	pref. בַּ for בָּה)(n. m. s. d. 8 a. (§ 37. No. 4)	קוה
בְּקוֹל[n]	וּ pref. בְּ)(noun m. sing. dec. 1 a.; וּ bef. (.)	קול
בְּקוֹלֹה	pref. id.)(id., suff. 3 pers. sing. fem.	קול
בְּקוֹלוֹ[o]	וּ pref. id.)(id., suff. 3 pers. s. m.; וּ bef. (.)	קול
בְּקוֹלִי[p]	וּ pref. id.)(id., suff. 1 pers. sing.; וּ id.	קול
בְּקוֹלֵךְ	pref. id.)(id., suff. 2 pers. sing. fem.	קול
בְּקוֹלֶךָ	pref. id.)(id., suff. 2 pers. sing. m. for קוֹלָךְ	קול
בְּקוֹלָם	pref. id.)(id., suff. 3 pers. pl. masc.	קול
בְּקוֹלֵנוּ	pref. id.)(id., suff. 1 pers. pl.	קול
בְּקוּם[q]	וּ pref. id.)(Kal inf. constr.; וּ bef. lab.	קום
בְּקוֹמָה[r]	וּ pref. id.)(noun fem. sing. dec. 10.	קום
בְּקוּמֹה[s]	וּ pref. id.)(Kal inf., suff. 3 p. f. s. d. 1 a; וּ bef. lab.	קום
בְּקוּמוֹ	pref. id.)(id., suff. 3 pers. sing. masc.	קום
בְּקוּמֶךָ	pref. id.)(id., suff. 2 pers. sing. masc. [for וּ bef. (.) ; קוּמָךְ]	קום
בְּקוֹמָתָם[t]	pref. id.)(noun fem. sing., suff. 3 pers. pl. masc. from קוֹמָה dec. 10.	קום
בַּקֹּצֵר[u]	pref. בַּ for בָּה)(Kal part. act. s. m. d. 7 b.	קצר
בְּקַחְתּוֹ	pref. בְּ)(Kal inf. קַחַת (§ 17. rem. 8), suff. 3 pers. sing. masc. dec. 13 a. (§ 44. No. 1)	לקח
בְּקַחְתְּךָ[x]	pref. id.)(id., suff. 2 pers. sing. fem.	לקח
בַּקָּטֹן	וּ pref. בַּ for בָּה)(adj. m. s., d. 3 a; וּ bef. lab.	קטן
בְּקִי	וּ pr. name masc.	בקק
בְּקִיאוֹ	pref. בְּ)(noun masc. sing., suff. 3 pers. sing. masc. from קִיא dec. 1 a.	קוא
בְּקִיָּהוּ	pr. name masc.	בקק
בְּקִיטוֹר[y]	pref. בְּ)(noun masc. sing.	קטר
בְּקִינוֹתֵיהֶם[z]	pref. id.)(noun fem. pl., suff. 3 pers. pl. masc. from קִינָה dec. 10.	קון
בְּקִיעֵי	noun masc. pl. constr. of [בָּקִיעַ] dec. 1 a.	בקע
בַּקַּיִץ	pref. בַּ for בָּה)(noun masc. sing. 6 h.	קוץ
בַּקִּיר בְּקִיר	וּ pref. id. } pref. בַּ q. v. } noun masc. sing. dec. 1 a.; וּ bef. labial }	קיר
בְּקִירוֹת בְּקִירֹת[aa]	} pref. id.)(id. pl. fem.	קיר
בְּקָל[bb]	Ch. pref. id.)(noun masc. sing.	קול
בְּקֹלָהּ[cc]	pref. id.)(noun masc. sing., suff. 3 pers. sing. fem. from קוֹל dec. 1 a.	קול
בְּקֹלוֹ[dd]	וּ pref. id.)(id., suff. 3 p. s. m.; וּ bef. lab.	קול
בְּקָלוֹן	pref. id.)(noun masc. sing. dec. 3 a.	קלה
בַּקְּלַחַת	pref. בַּ for בָּה)(noun fem. sing.	קלה
בְּקֹלִי	pref. בְּ)(n. m. s., suff. 1 p. s. fr. קוֹל d. 1 a.	קול
בְּקֹלֶךָ[ee]	pref. id.)(id., suff. 2 pers. s. m., for קוֹלָךְ	קול
בְּקֹלְכֶם	pref. id.)(id., suff. 2 pers. pl. masc.	קול
בְּקַלְלוֹ[ff]	pref. id.)(Piel inf. (קַלֵּל § 10. rem. 7), suff. 3 pers. sing. masc. dec. 7 b.	קלל
בְּקֹלֵנוּ[gg]	pref. id.)(noun masc. sing., suff. 1 pers. pl from קוֹל dec. 1 a.	קול
בַּקֶּלַע[hh]	pref. בַּ for בָּה)(n. m. s., (suff. קַלְעוֹ) d. 6 a.	קלע
בְּקָמָה	pref. id.)(noun fem. sing. dec. 10.	קום
בְּקָמֹן	pref. בְּ)(pr. name of a place	קום
בְּקֹמֹה[ii]	וּ defect. for בְּקוֹמָה (q. v.)	קום
בְּקָמוֹת	pref. בְּ)(noun fem., pl. of קָמָה dec. 10.	קום

a Eze. 28. 25.	d De. 9. 22.	k Job 15. 15.	t Ge. 49. 6.	b Pr. 28. 12.	g Am. 9. 13.	m Is. 22. 9.	r De. 13. 5.	y De. 21. 20.
b Je. 19. 1.	e Ge. 50. 5.	l Ps. 89. 36.	u Is. 34. 17.	c Eze. 31. 10.	h Eze. 16. 61.	n 1 Ki. 6. 6.	s Ho. 4. 7.	z 1 Sa. 17. 52.
c 1 Ki. 14. 3.	f Is. 65. 4.	m Job 36. 14.	x Jos. 24. 24.	d Ge. 19. 33.	i Ge. 44. 12.	o Le. 14. 37, 39.	t 1 Sa. 2. 14.	aa De. 16. 9
Nu. 19. 16.	g 2 Ch. 16. 14.	Le. 22. 4.	y Je. 3. 13.	Is. 2. 19, 21.	Da. 6. 21.	p 1 Sa. 2. 14.	Ge. 19. 35.
Nu. 19. 16.	Ge. 47. 30.	Eze. 17. 17.	z 1 Sa. 25. 35.	Eze. 31. 14.	2 Ch. 35. 25.	Ge. 21. 12.	bb 3 Sa. 16. 7.	cc 1u. 15. 5.
1 Ki. 13. 30.	De. 28. 22.	Eze. 23. 24.	3 Sa. 12. 18.					

בְּקָמֵיהֶם֮ pref. בְּ)(Kal part. pl. masc., suff. 3 pers. pl. masc. from קָם dec. 1 a.   קום

בַּקָּמִים pref. בַּ for בְּהַ)(id. pl., absolute state   קום

בְּקִמְצוֹ pref. בְּ)(noun masc. sing., suff. 3 pers. sing. masc. fr. [קֹמֶץ] dec. 6 c. (§ 35. r. 8)   קמץ

בְּקָמַת pref. id.)(noun f. s. constr. of קָמָה d. 10.   קום

בְּקַנְאוֹ pref. id.)(Piel inf. [קַנֵּא], suff. 3 pers. sing. masc. dec. 7 b. (comp. § 10. rem. 7)   קנא

בְּקַנֹּאתוֹ pref. id.)(id. [קַנֹּאת § 23. r. 2 & 9], suff. 3 p. s. m.   קנא

בְּקִנְאָתִי pref. id.)(noun sing. fem., suff. 1 pers. sing. fr. קִנְאָה dec. 12 b; ׳ before (:)   קנא

בַּקָּנֶה pref. בַּ f. בְּהַ
בְּקָנֶה pref. בְּ q. v. } noun masc. sing. dec. 9 b.   קנה

בִּקְנֵה pref. id. bef. (:))(id. constr. state   קנה

בְּקָסְם־ pref. id.)(Kal inf. constr., with Mak. [for קְסֹם § 8. rem. 18]   קסם

בָּקַע I. *to cleave, divide*; const. with בְּ *to break through.* — II. *to break* or *lay open*, as a fortified city; hence *to break open* or *hatch eggs*, Is. 34. 15. — III. *to rip open* a woman with child, Am. 1. 13. Niph. — I. *to be cleft, to divide itself.* — II. *to be opened, laid open; to be hatched*, comp. Kal No. II. Pi. — I. i. q. Kal Nos. I. II. III. — II. *to rend, tear in pieces*, as wild beasts. Pu. pass. of Pi. — Hiph. I. i. q. Kal No. II. — II. with אֶל *to break through* to any one, 2 Ki. 3. 26. Hoph. pass. of Hiph. No. I. Je. 39. 2. Hithp. *to be cleft, rent.*

בֶּקַע masc. *half a shekel.*

בִּקְעָה f. dec. 12 b, *a valley;* also used for a *low plain.*

בִּקְעָא Ch. fem. dec. 8 a, id. Da. 3. 1.

בָּקִיעַ masc. dec. 1, *fissure, cleft.*

בֶּקַע noun masc. sing.   בקע

בָּקַע Piel pret. 3 pers. s. m. [for בִּקַּע § 15. r. 1]   בקע

בֹּקֵעַ ׳ Kal part. act. sing. masc.; ׳ bef. lab.   בקע

בִּקְעָה noun fem. sing. dec. 12 b.   בקע

בִּקְעוּ Piel pret. 3 p. pl. [for בִּקְעוּ comp. § 8. r. 7]   בקע

בָּקְעָה ׳ Kal pret. 3 pers. sing. fem.; ׳ bef. lab.   בקע

בִּקְעֵהוּ ׳ id. imp. sing. masc. [בְּקַע], suff. 3 pers. sing. masc. (§ 16. rem. 11) ׳ id.   בקע

בְּקָעוֹת noun fem. pl. absolute from בִּקְעָה dec. 12 b.   בקע

בְּקַעְלָה pref. בְּ bef. (:))(pr. n. of a place, see קְעִילָה

בְּקִיעִם noun masc., pl. of [בָּקִיעַ] dec. 1 a.   בקע

בִּקְעָם Kal inf. [בְּקַע], suff. 3 p. pl. m. (§ 16. r. 10)   בקע

בָּקַעְתָּ id. pret. 2 pers. sing. masc.   בקע

בָּקַעְתָּ ׳ id. id.; ac. shifted by conv. ׳, bef. lab. for ׳ (§ 8. r. 7)   בקע

בְּקָעֹת ׳ noun fem., pl. abs. of בִּקְעָה dec. 12 b; ׳ id.   בקע

בִּקְעַת noun fem. sing., constr. of בִּקְעָה dec. 12 b.   בקע

בְּקַעְתִּי ׳ Piel pret. 1 pers. sing.; acc. shifted to ult. by conv. ׳, bef. labial for ׳ (§ 8. rem. 7)   בקע

בְּקֵצֶה ׳ pref. בְּ bef. (:))(noun masc. sing., constr. of קָצֶה dec. 9 b; ׳ bef. lab.   קצה

בְּקָצְהוּ pref. בְּ)(id., suff. 3 pers. sing. masc.   קצה

בַּקָּצִיר ׳ pref. בַּ for בְּהַ)(noun masc. sing. dec. 3 a; ׳ bef. labial   קצר

בִּקְצִירִי ׳ pref. בְּ bef. (:))(id., suff. 1 pers. sing.   קצר

בַּקֶּצֶף ׳ pref. בְּ)(noun masc. sing. dec. 6 a (see the following); ׳ bef. (:)   קצף

בְּקִצְפִּי ׳ pref. id.)(id., suff. 1 pers. sing.   קצף

בְּקָצְפְּךָ ׳ pref. id.)(id., suff. 2 p. s. m. (§ 35. r. 3 & 4)   קצף

בְּקָצְרְךָ ׳ pref. id.)(Kal inf., suff. 2 pers. sing. masc. [for קָצְרְךָ § 16. rem. 7, comp. § 35. rem. 8]   קצר

בְּקָצְרְכֶם ׳ pref. id.)(id., suff. 2 p. pl. m.; ׳ bef. lab.   קצר

בָּקַק I. *to empty, make empty*, as a land of its inhabitants, *to depopulate*; of counsel, *to empty, pour out*, deprive one of it. — II. *to pour itself out*, of a tree, גֶּפֶן בּוֹקֵק *spreading* or *luxuriant vine*, Ho. 10. 1. Niph. pass. of Kal No. 1. Po. i. q. Kal *to make empty*, Je. 51. 2.

בַּקְבּוּק masc. I. *a bottle.* — II. pr. name of a man, Ezr. 2. 51; Neh. 7. 53.

בַּקְבֻּקְיָה (*profusion of the Lord*) pr. name of a man.

בַּקְבַּקַּר (for בַּקְבַּק הָר *profusion of the mountain*) pr. name masc. 1 Ch. 9. 15.

בֻּקִּי (for בֻּקִּיָהוּ q. v.) pr. name of two different men.

בֻּקִּיָּהוּ (*profusion of the Lord*) pr. name of a man, 1 Ch. 25. 4, 13.

יַבֹּק (*effusion*) pr. name of a stream flowing into the Jordan.

בְּקָקוּם ׳ Kal pret. 3 pers. pl., suff. 3 pers. pl. masc.   בקק

בּוֹקְקִים ׳ id. part. act. masc., pl. of בּוֹקֵק dec. 7 b.   בקק

בָּקַר Kal not used; in the deriv. *to plough; to break forth* (as light); *to search.* Pi. — I. *to search, look after.* — II. *to consider, observe.* — III. *to take care of*, const. with acc. בְּ, לְ — בֵּין. לְ.

בְּקַר Ch. Pa. *to search, examine.* Ithpe. pass. Ezr. 5. 17.

בָּקָר com. dec. 4 a, coll. *oxen*, without distinction of sex; חֶמְאַת בָּ׳ *milk of kine*, בָּ׳ עָלוֹת *milch cows*; בֶּן־בָּקָר *a calf*, עֵגֶל בֶּן־בָּ׳ id.; rarely pl בְּקָרִים *oxen.*

^a Ex. 32. 25.   ^d De. 23. 26.   ^g Eze. 38. 19.   ^k Ps. 141. 7.   ⁿ Is. 34. 15.   ^q Am. 1. 13.   ^t Ps. 19. 5.   ^v Job 29. 19   ^x Le 23. 22.
^b Ps. 92. 12.   ^e Nu. 25. 11.   ^h Eze. 21. 34.   ^l Ge. 11. 2.   ^o Ex. 14. 16.   ^r Eze. 29. 7.   ^u Ex. 19. 12.   ^w Is. 60. 10.   ^y Na. 2. 3.
^c Le. 6. 8.   ^f 2 Sa. 21. 2.   ⁱ Ps. 78. 13.   ^m Is. 59. 5.   ^p Am. 6. 11.   ^s Eze. 13. 13.   ^t Ex. 34. 21.   ^w Ps. 38. 2.   ^z Na. 2. 2.
De. 11. 11.

בֹּקֵר masc. *herdsman*, Am. 7. 14.

בֹּקֶר masc. pl. בְּקָרִים (§ 35. rem. 9)—I. *the dawn, morning* (prop. *day-break*); לַבֹּקֶר בַּבֹּקֶר *in the morning*; בַּבֹּקֶר בַּבֹּקֶר, לַבְּקָרִים *every morning*.—II. *the morrow*, adv. *to-morrow*; לַבֹּקֶר *early soon*, Ps. 49. 15.

בַּקָּרָה fem. dec. 10. (§ 42. No. 3) *a looking after, curing*, Eze. 34. 12.

בִּקֹּרֶת fem. *chastisement*, Lev. 19. 20, from the idea of *searching, visiting*, comp. פְּקֻדָּה, פָּקַד.

בקר	בָּקָר ⸿ noun com. sing. dec. 4 a; ⸿ bef. labial
בקר	בְּקַר- id. constr. state
בקר	בְּקָרִ⸿, ⸿ noun m. s. d. 6 c. § 35. r. 9; ⸿ bef. lab.
קרא	בִּקְרֹא pref. בְּ bef. (:) ⟩(Kal inf. constr.
קרא	בְּקָרְאִי pref. בְּ ⟩(id. inf. with suff. 1 pers. sing.
קרא	בְּקֹרְאֵי- pref. id. ⟩(id. part. act. pl. constr. masc. fr. קֹרֵא dec. 7 b.
קרב	בִּקְרָב- pref. בְּ for בְּהַ ⟩(noun masc. sing. dec. 1 a.
קרב	בְּקֶרֶב ⸿ pref. בְּ ⟩(n. m. s. (suff. קִרְבִּי) d. 6 a; ⸿ bef. (:)
קרב	בִּקְרֹב- pref. בְּ bef. (:) ⟩(Kal inf. constr. (§ 8. r. 18)
קרב	בְּקִרְבָּהּ pref. בְּ ⟩(n. m. s., suff. 3 p. s. f. fr. קֶרֶב d. 6 a.
קרב	בְּקִרְבּוֹ ⸿ pref. id. ⟩(id., suff. 3 pers. s. m.; ⸿ bef.
קרב	בְּקִרְבִּי pref. id. ⟩(id., suff. 1 pers. sing.
קרב	בִּקְרֹבַי- pref. בְּ bef. (:) ⟩(adj. masc. pl., suff. 1 pers. sing. from קָרוֹב dec. 3 a.
קרב	בְּקִרְבְּךָ pref. בְּ ⟩(noun masc. sing., suff. 2 pers. sing. masc. from קֶרֶב dec. 6 a.
קרב	בְּקִרְבֵּךְ pref. id. ⟩(id., suff. 2 pers. sing. fem.
קרב	בְּקִרְבְּכֶם pref. id. ⟩(id., suff. 2 pers. pl. masc.
קרב	בְּקִרְבָּם ⸿ pref. id. ⟩(id., suff. 3 p. pl. m.; ⸿ bef. (:)
קרב	בְּקִרְבֵּנוּ pref. id. ⟩(id., suff. 1 pers. pl.
קרדם	בְּקָרְבָתָם- pref. id. ⟩(Kal inf., [קָרְבָה] § 8. rem. 10] suff. 3 pers. pl. m.; ⸿ bef. lab.
קרדם	בְּקַרְדֻּמוֹת- pref. id. ⟩(noun masc. with pl. fem. term. from [קַרְדֹּם] dec. 8 c; ⸿ id.
קרד	בַּקָּרָה- pref. בְּ for בְּהַ ⟩(noun fem. sing. d. 10. [for § 37. rem. 7] from קָרֶה masc.
קרב	בְּקָרוֹב- pref. בְּ ⟩(prop. adj. with the pref. as an adv.
קרח	בַּקָּרַחַת- pref. בְּ for בְּהַ ⟩(n. f. s. d. 13 a (§ 44. No. 1.)
קרח	בְּקָרַחְתּוֹ pref. בְּ ⟩(id., suff. 3 pers. sing. masc.
בקר	בְּקַרוּ ⸿ Ch. Pael pret. 3 pers. pl. masc.; ⸿ bef. lab.
קרה	בְּקָרִי pref. בְּ ⟩(n. m. s. [for קְרִי § 35. r 14]
קרה	בְּקָרְיָה Ch. pref. id. ⟩(noun fem. sing. dec. 8 a.
בקר	בְּקָרִים- noun com., pl. of בָּקָר dec. 4 a.
בקר	בְּקָרֵינוּ id. pl., suff. 1 pers. pl.

קרה	בְּקִרְיַת pref. בְּ ⟩(noun fem. sing., constr. of קִרְיָה d. 10, also pr. n. in compos., as קִרְיַת אַרְבַּע &c.
בקר	בְּקָרְךָ⸿ ⸿ pref. בְּ ⟩(noun com. sing., suff. 2 pers. sing. masc. fr. בָּקָר d. 4 a; ⸿ bef. (:)
בקר	בְּקַרְכֶם⸿ pref. id. ⟩(id., suff. 2 pers. pl. masc.; ⸿ id.
בקר	בְּקָרָם ⸿ pref. id. ⟩(id., suff. 3 p. pl. m.; ⸿ id.
קרן	בְּקֶרֶן pref. id. ⟩(noun fem. sing., (suff. קַרְנִי) d. 6 a.
קרן	בְּקַרְנָא⸿ Ch. pref. id. ⟩(id., emph. state dec. 3 a.
קרן	בְּקַרְנוֹת pref. id. ⟩(id. pl., constr. of קָרְנוֹת
קרן	בְּקַרְנַיָּא⸿ Ch. pref. id. ⟩(id. du., emph. state dec. 3 a.
קרן	בְּקַרְנָיו⸿ pref. id. ⟩(id. du., suff. 3 pers. sing. masc.
קרו	בְּקַרְנֵיכֶם⸿ pref. id. ⟩(id. du., suff. 2 p. pl. m.; ⸿ bef. (:)
קרם	בַּקְּרָסִים pref. בְּ for בְּהַ ⟩(noun masc. pl. (constr. קַרְסֵי) from קֶרֶס dec. 6 a.
קרע	בְּקָרְעַי⸿ ⸿ pref. בְּ ⟩(Kal inf., suff. 1 pers. s.; ⸿ bef. (:)
קרקע	בְּקַרְקַע pref. id. ⟩(noun masc. sing.
קור	בַּקְּרֹקֹר pref. בְּ for בְּהַ ⟩(pr. name of a place
בקר	בִּקֹּרֶת⸿ noun fem. sing.
בקר	בְּקַרְתִּים ⸿ Piel pret. 1 p. s., suff. 3 p. pl. m.; ⸿ bef. lab.

בִּקֵּשׁ ⸿ Pi. I. *to seek*, with acc., *to seek after*, with לְ; בִּקֵּשׁ אֶת־יְהוָה *to seek the Lord*, to apply to him by acts of worship, or to apply for an oracle; בִּקֵּשׁ נֶפֶשׁ פְּ *to seek the life of* any, i. e. to endeavour to kill him; בִּקֵּשׁ רָעַת פְּ *to seek one's hurt*.—II. *to require, demand*, with acc.; מִיַּד, מִן *of, at the hand of* any one.—III. *to ask, request*, with acc. of the thing and מִן of pers.; with עַל *to supplicate for.* Pu. *to be sought*.

בַּקָּשָׁה fem. d. 10. (§ 42. No. 3) *request, petition*

בקש	בַּקֵּשׁ⸿ Piel imp. sing. m., inf. Ec. 7. 25; ⸿ bef. lab.
בקש	בִּקֵּשׁ- id. pret. 3 pers. masc. for בִּקֵּשׁ
בקש	בִּקְשָׁה id. pret. 3 pers. sing. fem. (§ 10. rem. 7)
בקש	בִּקְשָׁהוּ id. pret. 3 p. pl. (בִּקְשׁוּ), suff. 3 p. s. m. (§ 10. r. 7)
בקש	בַּקְּשׁוּ ⸿ id. imp. pl. masc.; ⸿ bef. lab.
בקש	בִּקְשׁוּ ⸿ id. pret. 3 pers. pl. (§ 10. rem. 7) ; ⸿ id.
בקש	בַּקְּשׁוּנִי- id. imp. pl. masc., suff. 1 pers. sing.
בקש	בִּקְשׁוּנִי- id. pret. 3 p. pl. (בִּקְשׁוּ) § 10. r. 7), suff. 1 p. s.
קשה	בְּקַשְׁתֹתֵיךָ pref. בְּ ⟩(noun fem. pl., suff. 2 pers. sing. m. from מַשְׁקֶת d. 13 a. (§ 39. No. 4. r. 1;
קשר	בַּקֹּשְׁרִים pref. בְּ for בְּהַ ⟩(Kal part. act. masc., pl. of [קֹשֵׁר] dec. 7 b.
קוש	בַּקֶּשֶׁת / בְּקֶשֶׁת / בְּקֶשֶׁת pref. id. / pref. בְּ ⟩(n. com. s., with suff. קַשְׁתִּי, pl. קְשָׁתוֹת, constr. קַשְׁתוֹת, ת treated as if radical, comp. dec. 6 a.

• Nu. 7. 88.   ⸿ 2 Sa. 17. 11.   ⸿ Ps. 62. 5.   ⸿ Eze. 11. 3.   ⸿ 2 Ch. 4. 3.   ⸿ Ex. 10. 24.   ⸿ Eze. 34. 21.   ⸿ 1 Sa. 20. 16.   ⸿ Is. 65. 1.
⸿ Ex. 16. 7.   ⸿ Pr. 14. 33.   ⸿ Le. 16. 1.   ⸿ Le. 13. 42.   ⸿ Ne. 10. 37.   ⸿ Da. 7. 8.   ⸿ Ezr. 9. 5.   ⸿ Ecc. 7. 25.   ⸿ Eze. 29. 1. 4.
⸿ Ps. 55. 18.   ⸿ Ps. 27. 2.   ⸿ Ex. 40. 32.   ⸿ Le. 13. 43, 55.   ⸿ Ex. 20. 24.   ⸿ Da. 7. 8.   ⸿ Le. 19. 20.   ⸿ Je. 5. 1.   ⸿ 2 Sa. 15. 31.
⸿ Je. 36. 13.   ⸿ 2 Sa. 15. 5.   ⸿ Je. 46. 22.   ⸿ Ezr. 4. 10.   ⸿ Je. 5. 17.   ⸿ Ge. 22. 13.   ⸿ Eze. 34. 11.   ⸿ Is. 45. 19.   ⸿ Is. 7. 24.
⸿ Ps. 99. 6.   ⸿ Le. 10. 3.   ⸿ Job 24. 7.   ⸿ Pr. 14. 6.

בְּקַשְׁתּוֹ noun fem. sing., suff. 3 pers. sing. masc. from [בַּקָּשָׁה] dec. 10. (§ 42. No. 3) . . בקש

בְּקַשְׁתִּי ¹ id., suff. 1 pers. sing.; ¹ bef. lab. בקש

בִּקַּשְׁתִּי Piel pret. 1 pers. sing. . . בקש

בְּקַשְׁתִּי ¹ pref. בְּ ⟩⟨ noun com. sing., suff. 1 pers. sing. (see [בֶּקֶשֶׁת]; ¹ bef. (ְ) . . קוש

בִּקַּשְׁתִּיהוּ Piel pret. 1 pers. sing., suff. 3 pers. sing. masc. בקש

בִּקַּשְׁתִּיו id. id., suff. 3 pers. sing. masc. . . בקש

בְּקַשָׁתֵךְ noun fem. sing., suff. 2 pers. sing. fem. from [בַּקָּשָׁה] dec. 10 (§ 42. No. 3) . . בקש

בְּקַשְׁתְּךָ ⟩ pref. בְּ ⟩⟨ noun com. sing., suff. 2 pers.
בְּקַשְׁתְּךָ ⟨ sing. masc. (see [בֶּקֶשֶׁת]); ¹ bef. lab.⟩ קוש

בִּקַּשְׁתֶּם ¹ Piel pret. 2 pers. pl. masc.; ¹ id. בקש

בִּקְשָׁתַם ¹ id. pret. 3 pers. sing. fem. suff. 3 pers. pl. masc. (§ 10. rem. 7. & 16. rem. 2); ¹ id. בקש

בָּקַתִּי ¹¹ Kal pret. 1 pers. sing.; ¹ id. בקק

בַּר
בָּר ⟩ noun masc. sing.; adj. Pr. 14. 4. . . ברר

בַּר noun masc. sing., dec. 2 a. (§ 36. rem. 5) ברא

בַּר ¹ adj. masc. sing. (pl. constr. בָּרֵי § 37. rem. 7); ¹ before labial . . . . ברר

בֹּר ¹ noun masc. sing. dec. 1 a. (for בְּאֵר, בּוֹר) באר

בָּרָא ¹/¹ to create, form, make. Niph.—I. to be created. —II. to be born. Pi.—I. to cut, cut down.—II. to form, fashion. Hiph. to feed, fatten.

    בֵּן masc. with suff. בְּרִי (§ 36. rem. 5) a son.

    בַּר Chald. masc. dec. 2 a.—I. son.—II. grandson, Ezr. 5. 1.

    בָּרִיא masc. dec. 3 a. adj. fem. בְּרִיאָה dec. 10.— fat, fattened.

    בְּרִיאָה fem. a new, wonderful thing, Nu. 16. 30.

    בְּרָאיָה (whom the Lord created) pr. name masc. 1 Ch. 8. 21.

בָּרָא Chald. noun masc. sing. [for בַּרָּא] emph. of [בַּר] (comp. § 37. r. 7) . . . ברר

בָּרֵא ¹ Piel imp. sing. masc. . . . ברא

בָּרֹא ¹ id. inf. abs.; ¹ bef. lab. . . ברא

בְּרֹא Kal inf. constr. . . . ברא

בְּרָא ¹ id. imp. sing. masc. . . . ברא

בֹּרֵא ¹ id. part. act. sing. masc. dec. 7 b.; ¹ bef. lab. ברא

בְּרֹאדַךְ pr. name see מְרֹאדַךְ

בִּרְאֹה pref. בְּ for בְּהַ, בְּהֶ ⟩⟨ Kal part. act. s. m. d. 9 a. ראה

בְּרָאָהּ Kal pret. 3 pers. sing. m., suff. 3 pers. sing. fem. ראה

בְּרִאָה ᵖᵖ adj. fem. for בְּרִיאָה, from בָּרִיא masc. . ברא

בְּרְאוֹת ¹⁹ pref. בְּ bef. (ְ) ⟩⟨ Kal inf. const. d. 1 a.; ¹ bef. lab. ראה

בְּרֹאוֹתָם pref. id. ⟩⟨ id., suff. 3 pers. pl. masc. ראה

בְּרֹאִי pr. name see בֵּית בְּרָאִי under בֵּית . . בית

בְּרָאיָה ¹ pr. name masc.; ¹ bef. (ְ) . . ברא

בְּרִאִים adj. masc., pl. of בָּרִיא dec. 3 a. . . ברא

בֹּרַאֲךָ Kal part. act. sing., suff. 2 pers. sing. masc. from בָּרָא dec. 7 b. (§ 36. rem. 3) . ברא

בְּרָאָם id. pret. 3 pers. sing. masc., suff. 3 pers. pl. m. ברא

בְּרָאָנוּ id. id. suff. 1 pers. pl. . . ברא

בְּרֹאשׁ pref. בְּ f. בְּהַ (בְּהֶ) ⟩⟨ noun masc. sing. irr.⟩
בְּרֹאשׁ ¹ pref. בְּ q. v. ⟨ (§ 45); ¹ bef. (ְ) ⟩ ראש

בְּרֹאשָׁהּ pref. id. ⟩⟨ id., suff. 3 pers. sing. fem. . ראש

בְּרֵאשֵׁהּ Chald. pref. id. ⟩⟨ noun masc. s., suff. 3 pers. sing. masc. from רֵאשׁ dec. 1. . . ראש

בְּרָאשֵׁהֹם Ch. pref. id. ⟩⟨ id., suff. 3 pers. pl. m. (§ 68) ראש

בְּרֹאשׁוֹ pref. id. ⟩⟨ noun masc. sing., suff. 3 pers. sing. masc. from רֹאשׁ irr. (§ 45) . . ראש

בָּרִאשׁוֹן pref. בְּ for בְּהַ, בְּהֶ ⟩⟨ adj. masc. sing. dec. 1 b. ראש

בָּרִאשׁוֹנָה pref. id. ⟩⟨ id. fem. dec. 10. . . ראש

בְּרָאשֵׁי ¹ pref. בְּ ⟩⟨ noun masc. pl. constr. from רֹאשׁ irr. (§ 45); ¹ bef. (ְ) . . . ראש

בְּרָאשֵׁיהֶם pref. id. ⟩⟨ id. pl., suff. 3 pers. pl. masc. ראש

בְּרָאשֵׁיכֶם pref. id. ⟩⟨ id. pl., suff. 2 pers. pl. masc. . ראש

בְּרָאשֵׁינוּ ¹ pref. id. ⟩⟨ id. pl., suff. 1 pers. pl. . ראש

בְּרֵאשִׁית pref. id. ⟩⟨ noun fem. sing. dec. 1 b. . ראש

בְּרֹאשִׁתָהּ pref. id. ⟩⟨ id., suff. 3 pers. sing. fem. . ראש

בְּרֹאשְׁךָ pref. id. ⟩⟨ noun masc. sing., suff. 2 pers. sing. masc. from רֹאשׁ irr. (§ 45) . . ראש

בְּרֹאשְׁךָ pref. id. ⟩⟨ id., suff. 2 pers. sing. fem. . ראש

בְּרֹאשְׁכֶם pref. id. ⟩⟨ id., suff. 2 pers. pl. masc. . ראש

בְּרֹאשָׁם pref. id. ⟩⟨ id., suff. 3 pers. pl. masc. . ראש

בָּרִאשֹׁן ¹¹ pref. בְּ for בְּהַ, בְּהֶ ⟩⟨ adj. m. sing. dec. 1 b. ראש

בָּרִאשֹׁנָה pref. id. ⟩⟨ id. fem. dec. 10. . . ראש

בְּרֹאשֵׁנוּ pref. בְּ ⟩⟨ noun masc. sing., suff. 1 pers. pl. from רֹאשׁ irr. (§ 45) . . . ראש

בָּרִאשֹׁנִים pref. בְּ for בְּהַ, בְּהֶ ⟩⟨ adj. m., pl. of רִאשׁוֹן d. 1 b. ראש

בָּרָאתָ Kal pret. 2 pers. sing. masc. . . ברא

בְּרֵאתָ ¹ Piel pret. 2 pers. sing. masc.; acc. shifted by conv. ¹, bef. lab. for ¹ (§ 8. rem. 7) . ברא

בְּרֵאתוֹ ¹ id. with suff. 3 pers. sing. masc.; ¹ bef. lab. ברא

בְּרֹאתוֹ pref. בְּ bef. (ְ) ⟩⟨ Kal inf. (רְאוֹת) with suff. 3 pers. sing. masc. dec. 1 a. . . ראה

בָּרָאתִי Kal pret. 1 pers. sing. . . ברא

בִּרְאֹתִי pref. בְּ bef. (ְ) ⟩⟨ Kal inf. (רְאוֹת), suff. 1 p. s. ראה

בְּרָאתִיו Kal pret. 1 pers. sing., suff. 3 pers. sing. masc. ברא

בְּרָאתָם id. pret. 2 pers. sing. masc., suff. 3 pers. pl. m. ברא

בִּרְאֹתָם pref. בְּ bef. (ְ) ⟩⟨ Kal inf. (רְאוֹת), suff. 3 pers. pl. masc. dec. 1 a. . . . ראה

בְּרָב ¹ pref. בְּ ⟩⟨ adj. masc. sing. dec. 8 d. . רבב

ᵃ Ezr. 7. 6.	ᶜ Ca. 5. 6.	ⁱ Ho. 2. 9.	ᵍ Eze. 23. 47.	ᵏ 2 Ch. 12. 7.	ᵒ Mal. 2. 10.	ᵗ 1 Ch. 12. 19.	ᵘ Ex. 12. 18.	ʸ Jos. 17. 18.
ᵇ Est. 5. 8.	ᵈ Ca. 3. 1, 2.	ᵐ Je. 19. 7.	ʰ Ge. 5. 1.	ˡ 1 Sa. 17. 24.	ᵖ Est. 2. 17.	ᵗ Ho. 9. 10.	ᵛ 2 Sa. 21. 9.	ᶻ Da. 8. 2, 15.
ᶜ Est. 5. 7.	ᵉ Jos. 24. 12.	ⁿ Ex. 21. 53.	ⁱ Ps. 51. 12.	ᵐ 1 Ki. 5. 3.	ᵠ Da. 7. 20.	ˢ Eze. 16. 12.	ʷ Ps. 89. 48.	ᵖᵖ Ps. 89. 13.
ᵈ Ps. 44. 7.	ᶠ 2 Ki. 6. 22.	ᵒ Is. 4. 5.	ⁱ Am. 4. 13.	ⁿ Is. 43. 1.	ʳ Ezr. 5. 10.	ᵗ Joel 4. 4, 7.	ˣ Jos. 17. 15.	ᶜᶜ 1 Sa. 14. 6.
ᵉ Ge. 48. 22		ᵖ Eze. 34. 4.	ᶠ Eze. 21. 24, 24.	ⁱ Is. 28. 7.	ᵍ Ge. 5. 2.	ᶠ De. 1. 13.	ᵘ Je. 19. 7.	ʷʷ Hab. 1. 16.	

9

בְּרָב	pref. בְּ)(noun masc. sing. dec. 8c. (§ 37. rem. 2) ; וּ bef. (:)	רבב
בְּרַב־		
בְּרִבְבוֹת	pref. id.)(n. fem. pl. constr. from רְבָבָה d. 11 c.	רבב
בְּרִבְבֹתוֹ	pref. id.)(id. pl., suff. 3 pers. sing. masc. (§ 4. rem. 1)	רבב
בְּרִבְבֹתָיו		
בְּרֻבָּה	pref. id.)(pr. name of a place	רבב
בְּרִבוֹת	pref. בְּ bef. (:))(Kal inf. constr.	רבה
בְּרִבִיבִים	pref. id.)(noun masc. pl.	רבב
בְּרַבִּים	pref. בְּ f. בָּה)(adj. masc., pl. of רַב dec. 8 d.	רבב
בְּרַבִּים	pref. בְּ q. v.	
בִּרְבִיעִי	pref. בְּ for בָּה)(בָּה)(adj. ord. masc.	רבע
בְּרִבְלָה	pref. בְּ)(pr. name of a place	רבל
בְּרִבְלָתָה	pref. id.)(id. with parag. ה	רבל
בְּרִבָם	pref. בְּ)(noun masc., pl. of רִיב dec. 1 a.	ריב
בִּרְבִיעִית	pref. בְּ bef. (:))(adj. ord., fem. of רְבִיעִי	רבע
בְּרָבְרִים	וּ noun masc. pl. ; וּ before labial	ברר
בְּרַבַּת	pref. בְּ)(pr. name of a place, constr. of רַבָּה	רבב
בְּרֹגֶז	pref. id.)(noun masc. sing. dec. 6 c.	רגז
בִּרְגֶז	Chald. pref. בְּ bef. (:))(noun masc. sing.	רגז
בְּרָגְזָה	pref. בְּ)(noun fem. sing.	רגז
בְּרֶגֶל	pref. id.)(n. fem. sing. dec. 6 a. (§ 35. r. 2)	רגל
בְּרַגְלֵי		
בְּרַגְלוֹ	pref. id.)(id. du., suff. 3 p. s. m. (§ 4. r. 2)	רגל
בְּרַגְלוֹ	pref. id.)(id. sing., suff. 3 pers. sing. masc.	רגל
בְּרַגְלִי	pref. id.)(id. dual, suff. 1 pers. sing.	רגל
בְּרַגְלַי		
בְּרַגְלֵי	pref. id.)(id. du., construct state	רגל
בְּרַגְלֵיהּ	Chald. pref. id.)(id. du., suff. 3 pers. sing. fem. (§ 46. parad.)	רגל
בְּרַגְלֵיהֶם	וּ pref. id.)(id. du., suff. 3 p. pl. m.; וּ bef. (:)	רגל
בְּרַגְלָיו	pref. id.)(id. du., suff. 3 pers. sing. masc.	רגל
בְּרַגְלֶךָ	pref. id.)(id. du., suff. 2 pers. sing. masc.	רגל
בְּרַגְלֵיכֶם	pref. id.)(id. du., suff. 2 pers. pl. masc.	רגל
בְּרַגְלַיִם	pref. id.)(id. du., absolute state	רגל
בְּרַגְלְךָ	pref. id.)(id. sing., suff. 2 pers. sing. masc.	רגל
בְּרֶגַע	וּ pref. id.)(noun masc. sing. dec. 6. (§ 35. rem. 5) ; וּ bef. (:)	רגע
בְּרֶגֶשׁ	pref. id.)(noun m. s. [for רֶגֶשׁ § 35. rem. 2]	רגש
בָּרָד	וּ to hail, Is. 32. 19.	

בָּרָד masc. adj. only pl. בְּרֻדִּים (§ 8. No. 9)
spotted. Also the two following—

בָּרָד	וּ masc. *hail*; אַבְנֵי בָרָד *hail-stones,* i. q. *hail*	ברד
בָּרָד	(*hail*) pr. name—I. of a place in the desert of Shur.—II. of a man, 1 Ch. 7. 20.	ברד
בֶּרֶד		

בְּרֻדִּים	וּ adj. masc., pl. of [בָּרֹד] dec. 8 c. (§ 37. No. 3) ; וּ bef. (:)	ברד
בְּרָדְפִי	pref. בְּ)(Kal part. act. pl. masc., suff. 1 pers. sing. from רָדַף dec. 7 b.	רדף
בְּרָדְפָם	pref. id.)(id. inf., suff. 3 pers. pl. masc.	רדף
בְּרֶדֶת	וּ pref. id.)(Kal inf. constr. d. 13 b. (§ 44. r. 1)	ירד
בְּרִדְתּוֹ	pref. id.)(id., suff. 3 pers. sing. masc.	רד
בְּרִדְתִּי	pref. id.)(id., suff. 1 pers. sing.	רד

בָּרָה prop. *to cut,* i. q. Pi. of בָּרָא ; hence—I. *to eat*—II. *to choose, select,* 1 Sa. 17. 8. Pi. *to eat,* La. 4. 10, but see בָּרוֹת. Hiph. *to give to eat.*

בָּרוֹת fem. (after the form אָחוֹת) *food,* La. 4. 10, but see Pi. above.

בָּרוּת fem. dec. 1 b. id. Ps. 69. 22.

בְּרִי only fem.—בְּרִיָה—I. adj. *fat,* Eze. 34. 20.—II. subs. *food.*

בְּרִית fem. dec. 1 a.—I. *agreement, league, covenant* (from the idea of cutting, comp. כָּרַת), see also בַּעַל Nos. III., IV.—II. *sign of the covenant,* i. e. circumcision ; מַלְאַךְ הַבְּרִית *the angel of the covenant,* the Messiah, comp. Jud. 2. 1. Ro. 15. 8.

בָּרָה	adj. fem. sing. for [בָּרָה § 37. rem. 7] from בַּר m. (also pr. name in compos. see בַּיִת)	ברר
בְּרֵהּ	Ch. noun m. s., suff. 3 p. s. m. from בַּר d. 2 b.	ברא
בְּרָהֲטִים	pref. בְּ for בָּה, בְּהָ ; בְּהָ)(n.m., pl. of רַהַט d. 6 d.	רהט
בְּרוּ	Kal imp. pl. masc.	ברה
בְּרוֹ	noun m. s., suff. 3 pers. s. m. from בּוֹר d. 1 a.	באר
בָּרוֹחַ	Kal inf. absolute	ברח
בָּרוּחַ	pref. בְּ for בָּה)(n. com. s. dec. 1 a ; וּ bef. (ו)	רוח
בְּרוּחַ	וּ pref. בְּ q. v.	רוח
בְּרוּחוֹ	pref. id.)(id., suff. 3 pers. sing. masc.	רוח
בְּרוּחִי	pref. id.)(id., suff. 1 pers. sing.	רוח
בְּרוּחֲךָ	pref. id.)(id., suff. 2 pers. sing. masc.	רוח
בְּרוּחֲכֶם	pref. id.)(id., suff. 2 pers. pl. masc.	רוח
בָּרוּךְ	Kal inf. abs. or [for בָּרֹךְ] Piel inf. abs. (§ 10. r. 2)	רך
בָּרוּךְ	וּ id. part. pass. sing. masc. dec. 3 a ; also pr. name masc. ; וּ bef. lab.	ברך
בְּרוּךְ	id., construct state	ברך
בְּרוּכָה	וּ id. fem. ; וּ bef. (:)	ברך
בְּרוּכֵי	id. pl. const. masc. dec. 3 a.	ברך
בְּרוּכִים	id. pl., absolute state	ברך
בְּרוֹמִים	noun masc. pl. [of בְּרוֹם]	ברם
בְּרוֹמָם	וּ pref. בְּ)(Kal inf. [of רוֹם § 21. rem. 3], suff. 3 pers. pl. masc.	רום
בְּרֹק	Kal imp. sing. masc.	ברק

• Mi. 6. 7.   ∫ Nu. 15. 4.   ‖ Pr. 6. 13.   ∥ Is. 3. 16.   ‴ Zec. 6. 3.   ° Ex. 34. 29.   † 2 Ki. 18. 31.   ‡ Jos. 24. 10.   ♭ Ps. 115. 15.

ᵇ 1 Sa. 18. 7.   ∫ 1 Ki. 5. 3.   = 2 Sa. 15. 18.   Is. 54. 7.   ƒ Ge. 31. 10, 12.   ♭ Ps. 30. 10.   ʰ Job 27. 22.   ≈ Ruth 3. 10.   ᵍ Eze. 27. 24.

Ps. 65. 11.   ♭ Da. 3. 13.   ᵐ Nu. 20. 19.   Job 21. 13.   ♭ Ps. 119. 84.   ♭ 2 Sa. 12. 17.   ♭ 1 Sa. 25. 33.   ♭ Eze. 10. 17.

Ps. 55. 19.   ♭ Eze. 12. 18.   ″ 1 Sa. 25. 27.   ♭ Ps. 55. 15.   ♭ De. 11. 4.   ♭ Is. 33. 19.   ♭ Mal. 2. 15, 16.   Is. 65. 23.   Ps. 144. 6.

ᵈ Job 31. 13.   ♭ De. 19. 21.   ° Da. 7. 7   ″ Is. 33. 19.   ♭ Nu. 11. 9.   ~ Eze. 1. 1.

בָּרוּר Kal part. pass. sing. masc. dec. 3a. . ברר
בְּרוּרָה id. fem. dec. 10. . ברר
בְּרוּרִים id. pl. masc., dec. 3a. . ברר
בְּרוֹשׁ noun masc. sing. dec. 1a. . ברש
בְּרוֹשָׁיו id. pl., suff. 3 pers. sing. masc. . ברש
בְּרוֹשִׁים id. pl., absolute state . ברש
בֵּרוֹת noun m. with pl. fem. term. from בּוֹר dec. 1a. באר
בֵּרוֹתָה pr. name of a place . באר
בָּרוֹתִי Kal pret. 1 pers.sing. [for בָּרוֹתִי]; ו bef.lab. ברר
בְּרוֹתִים n.m.,pl.of [בְּרוֹת] i.q. בְּרוֹשׁ cypress,Cant.1.17.
Kh. בְּרוֹזוֹת, K. בְּרוֹזַת pr. name fem. 1 Ch. 7.31. בְּרַז Chald. *to pierce.*

בַּרְזֶל ו masc.—I. *iron*; metaph. of a thing *hard, inflexible.*—II. *instrument of iron.*

בַּרְזִלַּי / בַּרְזִלָּי (of iron, austere) pr. name—I. of an intimate friend of David.—II. Ezr. 2. 61.

בָּרַח I. *to pass* or *shoot along,* as a bar Ex. 36. 33.—II. *to flee* constr. with לְ, אֶל of the place *whither,* מִפְּנֵי, מֵאֵת, מִן *from whom,* אַחֲרֵי *after whom* one *flees;* בְּרַח לְךָ *flee, get away,* Hiph.—I. i. q. Kal No. 1.—II. *to cause to flee, put to flight.*
בָּרַח, בָּרִחַ masc. dec. 1b, (for בָּרִיחַ)—I. *fleeing, fugitive.*—II. pr. name masc. 1 Ch. 3. 22.
בְּרִיחַ masc. dec. 1a.—I. *bar, cross-bar.*—II. *bar, bolt.*—III. *fugitive,* Is. 15. 5.
מִבְרָח masc. dec. 2b, *fugitives,* Eze. 17. 21.

בָּרָח adj. masc. sing. dec. 1b. [for בָּרִיחַ] . ברח
בְּרַח Kal imp. sing. masc. . ברח
בֹּרֵחַ id. part. act. sing. masc. . ברח
בִּרְחַב pref. בְּ for בְּהַ } noun masc. sing. dec. 6f. רחב
בְּרֹחַב pref. בְּ q. v. } רחב
בִּרְחֹב pref. בְּ bef. (:))(noun fem. sing. dec. 1a. . רחב
בִּרְחָבָה pref. בְּ for בְּהַ, בְּהָ)(adj. fem. s. from רָחָב m. רחב
בִּרְחֹבוֹת / בִּרְחֹבוֹת pref. id. } noun fem., pl. of רְחוֹב dec.
pref. בְּ bef. (:) } 1a ; ו bef. lab. רחב
בִּרְחֹבֹתֶיהָ pref. id.)(id. pl., suff. 3 pers. s. fem.; ו id. רחב
בִּרְחֹבֹתֵינוּ pref. id.)(id. pl., suff. 1 pers. pl. . רחב
בָּרְחוּ / בָּרֵחוּ } Kal pret. 3 pers. pl. (§ 8. rem. 7) ברח
בִּרְחוּ id. imp. pl. masc. . ברח
בִּרְחוֹב pref. בְּ f. בְּהָ, בְּהַ, } noun fem. sing. dec. 1a;
בִּרְחֹב pref. בְּ bef. (:) } ו bef. lab. רחב
בִּרְחוֹבֹתֶיהָ pref. id.)(id. pl., suff. 3 pers. sing. fem. רחב
בְּרָחֹק pref. בְּ)((prop. adj.) noun m. sing. dec. 3a. רחק

בְּרִיחֶהָ n. m. pl., suff. 3 p. s. fem. from בְּרִיחַ d. 1a. ברח
בְּרַחֲמִים pret. בְּ for בְּהַ, בְּהַ)(noun masc. dual, see רח
בְּרָחֵל pref. בְּ)(pr. name fem. רחל
בְּרַחֲמָם pref.בְּ for בְּהַ, בְּהַ)(n.m.s.(suff. רַחֲמָה),d.6a. רחם
בְּרַחֲמֶיךָ ו pref. בְּ)(the following with suff. 2 p. s. m. רחם
בְּרַחֲמִים ו pref. id.)(noun fem. pl. [for רַחֲמִים § 35. rem. 16. from רַחַם; ו bef. (:) רחם
בִּרְחֹץ pref. בְּ bef. (:))(Kal inf. constr. . רחץ
בְּרַחַת pref. בָּ for בְּהַ, בְּהַ)(noun fem. sing. . רוח
בֹּרַחַת Kal part. act. fem. of בֹּרֵחַ (§ 8. rem. 19) ברח
בְּרִי noun masc. sing., either from R. ברה, or pref. בְּ & רִי (for רְוִי) R. רוה
בְּרִי n. m. s., suff. 1 pers. s. from בַּר (§ 36. r. 5) ברא
בְּרִי ו pr. name masc.; ו before labial באר
בְּרִיא ו/ב adj. masc. sing. dec. 3a ; ו id. . ברא
בְּרִיאָה noun fem. sing. . ברא
בְּרִיאוֹת adj. fem., pl. of בְּרִיאָה d. 10, from בָּרִיא m. ברא
בְּרִיאֵי ו id. m. pl. constr. from בָּרִיא d. 3a; ו bef. (:) ברא
בְּרִיאֹת / defect. for בְּרִיאוֹת q. v.; ו id. ברא
בְּרִיב pref. בְּ)(noun masc. sing. dec. 1a. . ריב
בְּרִיבוֹ pref. id.)(id., suff. 3 pers. sing. masc. ריב
בִּרְיָה adj. fem. sing. from [בָּרִי] masc. . ברה
בְּרִיחַ ו pr. name masc.; ו before labial ברה
בְּרִיחַ pref. בְּ)(noun masc. sing. dec. 1a. . רוח
בְּרִיחַ ו noun masc. sing. dec. 1a ; ו before (:) ברח
בְּרִיחֶהָ id. pl., suff. 3 pers. sing. fem. for בְּרִיחֶיהָ (according to some copies) ברח
בְּרִיחַו id. pl., suff. 3 pers. s. m. for בְּרִיחָיו (§ 4. r. 2) ברח
בְּרִיחֵי ו id. pl., construct state ; ו before (:) ברח
בְּרִיחֶיהָ id. pl., suff. 3 pers. sing. fem. ברח
בְּרִיחָיו ו id. pl., suff. 3 pers. sing. masc.; ו bef. (:) ברח
בְּרִיחֶיךָ id. pl., suff. 2 pers. sing. fem. [for חֶיךָ] ברח
בְּרִיחִים noun masc. pl. [of בְּרִיחַ for בָּרִיחַ] dec. 1b. ברח
בְּרִיחִם ו } noun masc., pl. of בְּרִיחַ dec. 1a; ו bef. (:)
בְּרִיחֶם } ברח
בְּרִיךְ Chald. Peal part. pass. sing. masc. . בר
בְּרִיעָה ו pr.name—I. of a son of Ephraim 1 Ch.7.31, in which passage the signification is defined to be, *in calamity,* רָעָה from (רוֹע).—II. masc. Ge. 46.17.—III. 1 Ch. 8.13.—IV. 1 Ch. 23.10.—Patronym. from No. II בְּרִיעִי Nu. 26.44.
בְּרִיר pref. בְּ)(noun masc. sing. dec. 1a. רור
בְּרִית noun fem. sing. . ברת
בְּרִית ו noun fem. sing. dec. 1a ; ו bef. (:) ברה
בְּרִיתוֹ ו/ב id., suff. 3 pers. sing. masc.; ו id. ברה
בְּרִיתִי ו/ב id., suff. 1 pers. sing.; ו id. ברה

* Zep. 3.9.   f Ps. 119.45.   l Ne. 8.16,16   p Job 31.15.   u Is. 30.24.   y Ps. 73.4.   d Ge. 41.2.   h Ex. 40.18.   m Da. 3.22.
* 1 Ch. 7.40.   g Ca. 3.2.   m Je. 5.1.   q Ne. 9.19.   v Nu. 16.30.   z Nu. 16.30.   e Pr. 31.2.   i Na. 3.13.   n Job 6.6.
* Eze. 20.38.   h Is. 22.3.   n Ps. 10.1.   r Ne. 9.31.   w Ge. 41.5,18.   a Pr. 18.6.   f Ju. 3.17.   k Is. 43.14.   o Je. 3.22.
* Eze. 48.15.   i Job 9.25.   o Jon. 2.7.   s Zec. 1.16.   x Da. 1.15.   b Eze. 34.20.   l 2 Ch. 14.6.   p Ps. 25.14.
Ju. 19.17.   k Is. 48.20.   t Job 29.6.   aa Is. 37.24.   c Is. 15.5.

9*

בְּרִיתֵךְ id., suff. 2 pers. sing. fem. . . ברה

בְּרִיתֶךָ
בְּרִיתְךָ } id., suff. 2 pers. sing. masc.; וּ bef. (:)   ברה

בְּרִיתְכֶם id., suff. 2 pers. pl. masc. . . ברה

[בָּרַךְ] I. *to bend the knee, to kneel.*—II. *to worship, to bless,* בָּרוּךְ יְהוָֹה *blessed be the Lord.* Niph. *to be blessed.* Pi.—I. *to praise, adore, bless* God, const. with acc., לְ.—II. *to bless, to pronounce a blessing upon any one,* of men towards men.—III. meton. by a euphemism, *to curse* God, comp. Job 1. 5, 11. —IV. *to salute, greet.* Pu. pass. of Pi. Nos. I. II. Hiph. *to make to kneel* Ge. 24. 11 ; perhaps *to bend the knee* 41. 43. Hithp. *to be blessed,* with בְ *in* or *through* whom ; reflex. De. 29. 18.

בְּרַךְ Chald.—I. *to kneel.*—II. *to bless.* Pa. *to bless, praise.*

בֶּרֶךְ fem. dec. 6 a, (du. בִּרְכַּיִם) *knee.*

בֶּרֶךְ Chald. dec. 3 b, id. Da. 6. 11.

בְּרָכָה once בֶּרֱכָה fem. dec. 11 c.—I. *a blessing,* either an ascription of praise to God, or *blessing received of God.*—II. *gift, present.*—III. *peace.*— IV. pr. name, (a) of a valley 2 Ch. 20. 26 ; (b) masc. 1 Ch. 12. 3.

בְּרֵכָה fem. dec 10, *a pool of water.*

בָּרוּךְ (*blessed*) pr. name of the companion of Jeremiah and various other men.

בֶּרֶכְאֵל (whom *God has blessed*) pr. name masc. Job 32. 2, 6. Other MSS. read בָּרַכְאֵל.

בֶּרֶכְיָה (whom *the Lord has blessed,* for יְבֶרֶכְיָה) pr. name masc.—I. of a son of Zerubabel, 1 Ch. 3. 20.—II. ib. 9. 16.—III. Ne. 3. 4, 30.

בֶּרֶכְיָהוּ (id.) pr. name masc.—I. of the father of the prophet Zechariah, Zec. 1. 7, but בֶּרֶכְיָה ver. 1. —II. 1 Ch. 6. 24.—III. 2 Ch. 28. 12.

יְבֶרֶכְיָהוּ (*the Lord blesses* him!) pr. name m. Is. 8. 2.

בָּרֵךְ Chald. Peal part. act. sing. masc.   ברך

בָּרֵךְ Piel inf. or imp. sing. masc.   ברך

בָּרֵךְ id. imp. sing. masc.; וּ before labial   ברך

בָּרֵךְ Ch. Pael pret. 3 pers. sing. masc. (§ 47. r. 1) ברך

בֵּרַךְ
בֵּרֵךְ } Piel pret. 3 pers. sing. masc. (§ 10. rem. 1) ; וּ before labial } ברך

בֶּרֶךְ noun fem. sing. (du. בִּרְכַּיִם) dec. 6 a. ברך

בֶּרֶכְאֵל pr. name masc.   ברך

בְּרָכָב
בְּרֶכָב } pref. בְ f. (בְּרָ) noun masc. sing., (suff.) pref. בְ q.v. } (רִכְבִּי) d. 6 a; וּ bef. (:) } רכב

בְּרִכָּב K. בְּרַכָב q.v.; Kh. בְּרִכָּב pref. בְ, Kal inf. constr. רכב

בְּרִכְבּוֹ pref. בְ χ noun masc. sing., suff. 3 pers. sing. masc. from רֶכֶב dec. 6 a ; וּ bef. (:) רכב

בְּרִכְבֵי pref. id. χ id. pl., constr. state   רכב

בְּרָכָה noun fem. sing. dec. 11 c, also pr. name masc.; וּ before labial . רך

בָּרְכוּ
בָּרֲכוּ } Piel imp. pl. masc.; וּ id.   רך

בֵּרֲכוּ
בֵּרְכוּ } id. pret. 3 pers. sing. masc. (בֵּרֵךְ), suff. 3 pers. sing. masc. } ברך

בֵּרֲכוּ id. pret. 3 pers. pl.; וּ bef. labial   ברך

בִּרְכוֹ noun fem. du., suff. 3 pers. sing. masc. (§ 4. rem. 2) fr. בֶּרֶךְ dec. 6 a.   ברך

בִּרְכוֹהִי Ch. id. du., suff. 3 pers. sing. masc.   ברך

בֵּרְכוּנִי Piel pret. 3 pers. pl., suff. 1 pers. sing. ברך

בַּבְרֹשׁ pref. בְ for בְּהָ (בְּהָ) noun masc. sing. dec. 1 a. רכשׁ
בַּבְרֹשׁ pref. בְ bef. (:) }

בְּרָכוֹת noun fem. pl. abs. fr. בְּרָכָה dec. 11 c. ברך

בְּרָכוֹת noun fem. pl. of בְּרֵכָה dec. 10.   ברך

בִּרְכוֹת noun fem. pl. constr. fr. בְּרָכָה dec. 11 c. ברך

בִּרְכוֹתֵיכֶם id. pl., suff. 2 pers. pl. masc. ברך

בָּרֲכִי Piel imp. sing. fem.   ברך

בִּרְכַּי noun fem. du., suff. 1 pers. s. fr. בֶּרֶךְ d. 6 a. ברך

בִּרְכֵּי id. du., constr. state . ברך

בֶּרֶכְיָה וּ pr. name masc.; וּ bef. labial ברך

בִּרְכֶּיהָ noun f. du., suff. 3 pers. s. f. fr. בֶּרֶךְ d. 6 a. ברך

בֶּרֶכְיָהוּ pr. name masc.   ברך

בִּרְכֵּיהֶם noun f. pl., suff. 3 pers. pl. m. fr. בֶּרֶךְ d. 6 a. ברך

בִּרְכָּיו id. du., suff. 3 pers. sing. masc.   ברך

בְּרֻכִים Kal part. pass. m., pl. of בָּרוּךְ dec. 3 a. ברך

בִּרְכַּיִם
בִּרְכָּיִם } noun fem., du. of בֶּרֶךְ dec. 6 a; וּ before labial } ברך

בֵּרַכְךָ
בֵּרֶכְךָ } Piel pret. 3 pers. sing. m. (בֵּרֵךְ), suff. 2 pers. sing. m. (§ 2. r. 2); וּ bef. lab. } ברך

בִּרְכַּל pref. בְ χ pr. name of a place   כל

בְּרִכַלָּתְךָ pref. בְ bef. (:) χ noun fem. sing., suff. 2 pers. sing. masc. fr. [רְכֻלָּה] dec. 10. רכל

בֵּרַכְנוּ Piel pret. 1 pers. sing.   ברך

בֵּרַכְנוּכֶם id. id., suff. 2 pers. pl. masc.   ברך

בָּרֲכֵנִי id. imp. sing. masc. (בָּרֵךְ), suff. 1 pers. sing. ברך

בֵּרֲכַנִי id. pret. 3 pers. s. m. (בֵּרֵךְ), suff. 1 pers. s. ברך

בִּרְכָשׁ defect. for בִּרְכוּשׁ (q.v.)   רכשׁ

בָּרְכֵת Ch. Pael pret. 1 pers. sing.   ברך

בֵּרַכְתָּ Piel pret. 2 pers. sing. masc.   ברך

בֵּרַכְתְּ id. acc. shifted by conv. וּ, bef. lab. for וּ; (§ 8. rem. 7) . . . ברך

a Zec. 9. 11.   f Ps. 10. 3.   k Eze. 26. 7.   o Pr. 11. 26.   t 2 Ch. 20. 26.   y Job 31. 20.   c Mal. 2. 2.   g Eze. 23. 5.   Jos. 17. 14.
b De. 33. 9.   g Nu. 23. 20.   l Is. 45. 23.   p Ju. 19. 23.   u 2 Ki. 5. 9.   z Job 1. 5.   d Ezr. 1. 6.   h Ge. 50. 23.   Ge. 15. 14.
c Is. 28. 18.   h Is. 45. 23.   m 2 Ki. 5. 9.   q 2 Sa. 21. 3.   w 1 Ki. 18. 42.   a Da. 11. 23.   Ju. 7. 6.   Ps. 129. 8.   Da. 4. 31.
d Da. 6. 11.   i Is. 66. 20.   n Ca. 1. 9.   r 1 Ch 26. 5.   x Da. 6. 11.   b Ps. 21. 4.   f De. 24. 13.   Ge. 27. 34, 38.   Da. 8. 16.
e Da. 2. 19.   #Is. 28. 18.   s Ps. 134. 2.

בִּרְכַּת	noun fem. sing., constr. of בְּרָכָה dec. 10.	ברך
בִּרְכַּת	noun fem. sing., constr. of בְּרָכָה dec. 11c.	ברך
בִּרְכֹת	id. pl., constr. state . . .	ברך
בֵּרַכְתִּי	Piel pret. 1 pers. sing.	ברך
בֵּרַכְתִּי	⁴ id. acc. shifted by conv. ו, bef. lab., (§ 8. r. 7)	ברך
בִּרְכָתִי	ᵉⁱ noun fem. sing., suff. 1 pers. sing. from בְּרָכָה dec. 11c; ו bef. lab. .	ברך
בֵּרַכְתִּיהָ	ⁱ Piel pret. 1 pers. s., suff. 3 pers. s. f.; ⁱ id.	ברך
בֵּרַכְתִּיךָ	ⁱ id., suff. 2 pers. sing. masc.; ⁱ id.	ברך
בִּרְכָתֶךָ	noun f. s., suff. 2 pers. s. m. fr. בְּרָכָה d. 11c	ברך
בֵּרַכְתֶּם	ⁱ Piel pret. 2 pers. pl. masc.; ⁱ bef. lab.	ברך
בֵּרַכְתַּנִי	id. pret. 2 pers. sing. masc., suff. 1 pers. s.	ברך

בְּרֹם   Root not used; Arab. *to twist threads together.*

בְּרֹמִים masc. pl. *cloth interwoven with various colours,* Eze. 27. 24.

בְּרַם   Ch. adv. *but, yet, nevertheless.*

בְּרָמָה	pref. בְּ for בְּהַ, בְּהָ)(pr. name of a place	רום
בְּרָמוֹת	pref. בְּ)(pr. name of a place . .	רום
בְּרֻמַח	ˢ ⁱ pref. בְּ)(noun masc. sing. dec. 6c; (§ 35. rem. 5) ⁱ bef. lab. . .	רמח
בְּרֻמָחִים	ⁱʰ pref. בְּ for בְּהַ, בְּהָ)(id. pl., abs. state (§ 35. rem. 9); ⁱ id. .	רמח
בְּרִמּוֹן	pref. בְּ)(pr. name רִמּוֹן פֶּרֶץ	רמם
בִּרְד־	ˡ pref. בְּ)(Kal inf. constr., with mak. [for רֹן § 18. rem. 3]	רנן
בְּרִנָּה	pref. id.)(noun fem. sing. dec. 10.	רנן
בְּרַנְנָה	pref. בְּ bef. (ְ))(noun fem. sing. dec. 11c.	רנן
בִּרְנֵעַ	pr. name, see קָדֵשׁ בַּרְנֵעַ under	קדש
בְּרִסָּה	pref. בְּ)(pr. name of a place . .	רסם
בֶּרַע	pref. בְּ f. בְּהָ, הָ (for רַע) adj. & subst. m.	רעע
בֶּרַע	pref. בְּ q. v. dec. 8. (§ 37. rem. 7)	
בֶּרַע	(*gift;* coll. Arab.) pr. name of a king of Sodom, Ge. 14. 2.	
בְּרֵעַּ	pref. בְּ)(noun masc. sing. dec. ı. (§ 36. r. 4)	רעע
בְּרֵעַּ	pref. id.)(noun masc. sing. . .	רעע
בִּרְעֹב	ⁱ pref. בְּ f. בְּהָ, בְּהַ (בְּהָ) noun masc. sing. dec.	רעב
בְּרָעָב	pref. בְּ q. v. 4a; ⁱ bef. labial	
בְּרָעֵדָה	pref. בְּ bef. (ְ))(noun fem. sing. .	רעד
בְּרָעָה	pref. בְּ f. בְּהָ, בְּהָ (בְּהָ) no ᵘʰ fem. sing. dec. 10.	רעע
בְּרָעָה	pref. בְּ q. v [f. (רָעָה) fr. רַע m.	
בְּרִעָה	ⁱ defect. f רָעָה q. v.	
בְּרֵעֵהוּ	pref. בְּ)(noun masc. sing., suff. 3 pers. sing. masc. fr. רֵעַ dec. 1a.	רוע
בְּרֵעֵהוּ	pref. id.)(noun masc. sing., suff. 3 pers. sing. masc. fr. רֵ dec. 1. (§ 36. rem. 4)	רעה

בְּרֵעוֹת	pref. בְּ)(noun fem., pl. of רָעָה dec. 10, fr. רַע masc. (§ 37. rem. 7)	רעע
בְּרַעְיוֹתֵיהֶם	pref. id.)(id. pl., suff. 3 pers. pl. masc.	רעע
בְּרַעְיוֹן	ⁱ pref. id.)(noun masc. sing.; ⁱ bef. (ְ)	רעה
בְּרֵעֶךָ / בְּרֵעֶךָ	pref. id.)(noun masc. sing., suff. 2 pers. sing. masc. fr. רֵעַ dec. 1. (§ 36. rem. 4)	רעה
בְּרַעַם	pref. id.)(noun masc. sing. dec. 6d. .	רעם
בְּרַעַשׁ / בְּרַעַשׁ	pref. בְּ f. בְּהַ, בְּהָ)(noun masc. sing. dec. 6d; ⁱ bef. (ְ)	רעש
בְּרַעְתּוֹ	pref. id.)(noun fem. sing., suff. 1 pers. sing. fr. רָעָה dec. 10, fr. רַע masc. (§ 37. r. 7)	רעע
בְּרַעְתוֹ	pref. בְּ bef. (ְ))(Kal inf., suff. 3 p. s. m. d. 1a.	רעה
בְּרַעְתִּי	pref. בְּ)(noun fem. sing., suff. 1 pers. sing. fr. רָעָה dec. 10, fr. רַע masc. (§ 37. r. 7)	רעע
בְּרָעָתֶךָ	pref. id.)(id., suff. 2 pers. s. m. for רָעָתֶךָ	רעע
בְּרָעָתֵךְ	ᵈⁱ pref. id.)(id., suff. 2 pers. s. f.; ⁱ bef. (ְ)	רעע
בְּרָעָתָם	ᶠⁱ pref. id.)(id., suff. 3 pers. pl. m.; ⁱ id.	רעע
בְּרֹפְאִים	ˢ pref. בְּ for בְּהַ, בְּהָ)(Kal part. act. masc., pl. of רֹפֵא dec. 7b. .	רפא
בְּרֻפִידִים / בְּרִפִידִים	pref. בְּ bef. (ְ))(pr. name of a place .	רפד
בְּרִפָתִים	ⁱ pref. בְּ for בְּהָ, בְּהָ)([n. m.], pl. of רֶפֶת d. 6.	רפת
בְּרָצוֹן	pref. בְּ bef. (ְ))(noun masc. sing., constr. of רָצוֹן dec. 3a. .	רצה
בִּרְצוֹנוֹ	pref. id.)(id., suff. 3 pers. sing. masc.	רצה
בִּרְצוֹנִי	ⁱ pref. id.)(id., suff. 1 pers. sing.; ⁱ bef. lab.	רצה
בִּרְצוֹנֶךָ	ᵐⁱ pref. id.)(id., suff. 2 pers. sing. m.; ⁱ id.	רצה
בִּרְצוֹת	ⁿ pref. id.)(Kal inf. constr. dec. 1a.	רצה
בִּרְצוֹתִי	ᵒⁱ pref. id.)(id., suff. 1 pers. sing.	רצה
בְּרֶצַח	pref. בְּ)(noun masc. sing.	רצח
בְּרַצֵּי	ᵖⁱ pref. id.)(n. m. pl. constr. fr. [רַץ] dec. 8d.	רצץ
בִּרְצֹנָם	ⁱ pref. בְּ bef. (ְ))(noun masc. sing., suff. 3 pers. pl. masc. fr. רָצוֹן dec. 3c.; ⁱ bef. lab.	רצה
בִּרְצֹתוֹ	ᵘⁱ pref. id.)(Kal inf. (רְצוֹת), suff. 3 p. s. m. d. 1.	רצה

בָּרַק   *to lighten, send forth lightning,* Ps. 144. 6.

בָּרָק masc. dec. 4a.—I. *lightning.*—II. *glitter of a sword,* Job 20. 25.—III. pr. name of an Israelitish captain who with Deborah defeated the Canaanites, Jud. 4. 6, &c.

בָּרֶקֶת, בָּרְקַת fem., *a species of gem,* supposed to be the *emerald.*

בַּרְקָן masc. only pl. בַּרְקָנִים *threshing wagons,* or *sledges* furnished underneath with pointed stones (prob. *fire-stones*) which were drawn over the grain. Symm. τρίβολοι *briers.*

ᵃ Ge. 17. 20.   ᶠ Ge. 32. 27.   ˡ Ps. 100. 2.   ᵖ Ps. 88. 4.   ᵘ Is. 29. 6.   ᵉ Nu. 11. 15.   ᵏ Ho. 7. 3.   ⁱ Ps. 106. 4.   ⁿ Pr. 16. 7.

ᵇ Ge. 17. 16.   ᵍ Eze. 39. 9.   ᵐ Ne. 4. 15.   ᵠ Ps. 141. 5.   ¹ Ki. 19. 11.   ᶠ Sa. 16. 8.   ˡ Ps. 94. 23.   ² Ch. 16. 12.   ⁱ Ch. 29. 2.

Is. 44. 3.   ʰ Ne. 4. 15.   Ec. 7. 3.   Ec. 2. 22.   ᶜ Is. 29. 6.   Is. 47. 10.   Is. 60. 10.   Ps. 63. 31.

ᶜ Ge. 17. 16.   ⁱ Ki. 18. 28.   Ps. 2. 11.   Pr. 24. 23.   ᵈ Ge. 36. 24.   Je. 3. 2.   Hab. 3. 17.   Pa. 89. 18.   Ge. 49. 6.

Ex. 12. 32.   ᵏ Job 38. 7.   ᵖ Ex. 32. 17.   Job 34. 9.

בְּרָק noun masc. sing. dec. 4a, also pr. name masc.; ‡ bef. (:) . . . . . . ברק

בְּרָק ‡ id., constr. st.; (also pr. name see בֶּן R. (בָּנָה); ‡ id. . . . . ברק

בַּרְקוֹם pr. n. m. Ezr. 2. 53; Ne. 7. 55; etym. uncertain.

בְּרָקָיו noun m. pl., suff. 3 p. s. m. fr בָּרָק d. 4a. ברק

בְּרָקִים ‡ id. pl., absolute state; ‡ bef. (:) . ברק

בִּרְקִיעַ pref. בְּ bef. (:) χ noun masc. sing., constr. of רָקִיעַ dec. 3a. . . . . . רקע

בְּרִקְמָה pref. בְּ χ noun fem. sing. dec. 12b. . רקם

בָּרֶקֶת ‡ noun fem. sing.; ‡ bef. lab. . . ברק

בָּרֶקֶת ‡ noun fem. sing.; ‡ id. . . . . ברק

בְּרִקְתוֹ pref. בְּ χ noun fem. sing., suff. 3 pers. sing. masc. from רָקָה dec. 10. . . רקק

בָּרַר I. *to separate*, with מִן Eze. 20. 38; hence, *to select, choose out*.—II. *to purge, purify;* only part. בָּרוּר *pure, chaste*.—III. *to examine, prove.* Niph. *to purify oneself;* part. נָבָר *pure*, morally. Pi. *to purify*, Da. 11. 35. Hiph.—I. *to cleanse, clear*, as corn.—II. *to polish, furbish* a sword. Hithpa. *to be purified*, Da. 12. 10 ; *to show oneself pure*, morally.

בַּר masc. בָּרָה fem. (§ 37. r. 7) adj.—I. *chosen, beloved*, Ca. 6. 9.—II. *pure, clear;* also *pure* in a moral sense.—III. *empty*, Pr. 14. 4.

בַּר, בָּר masc.—I. *corn, grain*, purified from the chaff; also of growing corn, Ps. 65. 14.—II. *open fields, country*, Job 39. 4.

בַּר Ch. masc. emph. בָּרָא (for בַּרָא § 37. r. 7) *open fields, country*.

בֹּר masc. d. 1a.—I. *cleanness, purity.*—II. *soap.*

בֹּרִית fem. *soap*, Je. 2. 22 ; Mal. 3. 2.

בָּרְבֻּרִים masc. pl. 1 Ki. 5. 3, Vulg. *birds, fowls;* Kimchi, *capons;* Gesenius *geese*, from their whiteness; Prof. Lee, *choice beasts*.

בְּרֻרוֹת Kal part. pass. f., pl. בְּרוּרָה d. 10, fr. בָּרַר m. ברר

בְּרוֹשׁ Root not used; signification uncertain.

בְּרוֹשׁ masc. dec. 1, *fir-tree.* Gesenius, Lee, *cypress.*—II. *any thing made of that wood*, as *a lance*, Nah. 2. 4 ; *musical instrument*, 2 Sa. 6. 5.

בְּרוֹשָׁיו noun m. pl., suff. 3 p. s. m. fr. בְּרוֹשׁ d. 1a. ברש

בְּרֹשִׁים pref. בְּ χ Kal part. act. m., pl. of רָשׁ d. 1a. רוש

בְּרֶשַׁע pref. id. χ n. m. s. d. 6a. (suff. רִשְׁעוֹ; § 35. r. 5) (for בֶּן־רֶשַׁע *son of wickedness*, comp. בִּשְׁלָם) pr. name of a king of Gomorrah, Ge. 14. 2. רשע

בְּרִשְׁעוֹ pref. בְּ χ id., suff. 3 pers. sing. masc. fr. רֶשַׁע dec. 6a. (§ 35. rem. 5) . . רשע

בָּרְשָׁעִים pref. בְּ for בְּהָ χ adj. m., pl. of רָשָׁע d. 4a. רשע

בְּרִשְׁעַת pref. id. χ noun fem. s., constr. of רִשְׁעָה (no pl.) ; ‡ bef. (:) . . . רשע

בְּרִשְׁעָתוֹ ‡ pref. id. χ id. suff. 3 pers. s. masc.; ‡ id. רשע

בֶּרֶשֶׁת pref. id. χ noun fem. sing. dec. 13a. . ירש

בְּרִשְׁתּוֹ pref. id. χ id., suff. 3 pers. sing. masc. ירש

בְּרַתִּיקוֹת pref. id. χ n. f. pl. Kh. רַתִּיקוֹת, K. רתק

בָּרֹת ‡ n. m. with pl. f. term. fr. בּוֹר d. 1; ‡ bef. lab. באר

בְּרִתְמָה pref. בְּ χ pr. name of a place . . רתם

בָּשׁ ‡ Kal pret. 3 p. s. m. (§ 21. r. 2) ; ‡ bef. lab. בוש

בְּשַׁאֲנַנְתִּי pref. בְּ χ noun fem. sing., suff. 1 pers. sing. from שַׁאֲנָה dec. 11c. (§ 42. rem. 1) שאן

בִּשְׁאוֹל pref. בְּ bef. (:) χ noun masc. sing. . שאל

בְּשָׁאוֹן pref. בְּ χ noun masc. sing. dec. 3a. . שאה

בִּשְׁאָט pref. בְּ bef. (:) χ noun masc. sing. . שאט

בְּשֶׁאֱלָתִי pref. id. χ noun fem. sing., suff. 1 pers. sing. from שְׁאֵלָה dec. 10 & 11, (§ 42. rem. 4) שאל

בִּשְׁאָר pref. id. χ noun masc. sing. . . . שאר

בִּשְׁאָר Ch. pref. id. χ n. m. s., constr. of שְׁאָר d. 1a. שאר

בִּשְׂאֵת pref. בְּ for בְּהָ χ noun f. s. (§ 39. No. 4. r. 2) נשא

בִּשְׂאֵת ‡ pref. בְּ bef. (:) χ Kal inf. constr. (§ 25. No. 2. § 39. No. 4. rem. 2) dec. 1a; ‡ bef. lab. נשא

בְּשׁוּבוֹ pref. בְּ χ Kal inf. (שׁוּב), suff. 3 p. s. m. d. 1a. שוב

בִּשְׁבוּעָה ‡ pref. בְּ bef. (:) χ noun f. s. d. 10; ‡ bef. lab. שבע

בְּשֵׁבֶט pref. בְּ for בְּהָ χ Seg. n. in pause as if for שֵׁבֶט=שָׁבֶט § 35. r. 2], but see the foll. . שבט

בְּשֵׁבֶט pref. id. ⎫ noun com. sing. dec. 6b; ‡ שבט

בְּשֵׁבֶט ‡‡ pref. בְּ ⎭ bef. lab. . . . . שבט

בְּשִׁבְטֵי pref. id. χ id. pl., constr. state . . שבט

בְּשִׁבְטָיו pref. בְּ bef. (:) χ id. pl., suff. 3 pers. s. m. שבט

בְּשִׁבְטְךָ pref. בְּ χ id. s., suff. 2 pers. s. m. for שִׁבְטְךָ שבט

בְּשִׁבְיִ ⎫
בִּשְׁבִי ⎬ pref. בְּ for בְּהָ ⎫ n. m. s. d. 6i. (§ 35. r. 14) שׁבה
בִּשְׁבִי ‡‡ pref. בְּ bef. (:) ⎭

בְּשִׁבְיָה pref. בְּ for בְּהָ χ noun fem. sing. . שבה

בַּשְּׁבִיעִי ‡ pref. id. χ adj. ordin. m.; ‡ bef. lab. שבע

בַּשְּׁבִיתָא pref. id. χ noun fem. sing. dec. 1a. . שבה

בַּשִּׁבֳּלִים pref. id. χ noun fem. with pl. masc. term. from שִׁבֹּלֶת (§ 44. rem. 2) שבל

בְּשֶׁבַע ‡‡ pref. בְּ χ num. card. fem. (constr. שֶׁבַע § 35. rem. 7) ; ‡ bef. (:) . . שבע

בְּשִׁבְעַת ‡‡ pref. id. χ id. fem., constr. שִׁבְעַת ; ‡ id. שבע

בִּשְׁבֻעָה pref. בְּ bef. (:) χ noun fem. sing., constr. of שְׁבוּעָה dec. 10. שבע

כִּשְׁבְעַיִם	pref. בְּ ✗ num. card. com. pl. of שֶׁבַע (§35. r. 16) . שבע
בִּשְׁבִעֵתᵃ	ᵇ' pref. בַּ for בְּהַ ✗ adj. ordin., fem. of שְׁבִיעִי ; ᵇ bef. lab. . שבע
בִּשְׁבֻעַת	pref. בְּ bef. (ִ:) ✗ n. f. s., constr. of שְׁבֻעָה d. 10. שבע
בִּשְׁבֻעֹתֵיכֶם	pref. בְּ ✗ noun masc. pl. fem., suff. 2 pers. pl. masc. from שָׁבֻעַ (§ 32. rem. 1) . שבע
בַּשֶּׁבֶר	pref. בַּ for בְּהַ ✗ noun masc. sing. (suff.)
בְּשִׁבְרֵ	pref. בְּ q. v. } (שִׁבְרִי) dec. 6a. שבר
בִּשְׁבָרוֹן	pref. id. ✗ n. m. s., constr. of שִׁבָּרוֹן dec. 3c. שבר
בְּשִׁבְרִי	pref. id. ✗ Kal inf. [שְׁבֹר], suff. 1 pers. sing. 16. rem 10) . שבר
בַּשַּׁבָּת	pref. בַּ for בְּהַ ✗ noun com. sing. dec. 8a, (but pl. שַׁבָּתוֹת constr.) . שבת
בַּשַּׁבָּתᵇ	pref. id. ✗ in pause seg. as if for שֶׁבֶת=שַׁבָּת (§ 32. rem. 2) but see the following : ישב
בְּשִׁבְתְּᵇ	pref. id. } Kal inf. and subst. fem. (suff.)
בְּשִׁבְתְּ	pref. בְּ } (שִׁבְתִּי) dec. 13 a. ישב
בְּשִׁבְתּוֹ	pref. id. ✗ n. com. s., suff. 3 p. s. m. (see בַּשֶּׁבֶת) שבת
בְּשִׁבְתּוֹ	pref. id. ✗ Kal inf. (שֶׁבֶת), suff. 3 pers. sing. masc. dec. 13 a. . ישב
◄ בַּשַּׁבָּתוֹתᵇ	ᵇ' pref. בַּ for בְּהַ ✗ noun com. pl. abs. (see בַּשַּׁבָּת); ᵇ bef. lab. שבת
בְּשִׁבְתִּיᵇ	pref. בְּ ✗ Kal inf. (שֶׁבֶת), suff. 1 p. s. d. 13 a. ישב
בְּשִׁבְתְּךָ	pref. id., suff. 2 pers. sing. masc. ישב
בְּשִׁבְתְּכֶם	pref. id., suff. 2 pers. pl. masc. ישב
בְּשִׁבְתָּם	pref. id., suff. 3 pers. pl. masc. . ישב
בְּשִׁבְתֵּנוּᵇ	pref. id., suff. 1 pers. pl. ישב
בְּשִׁבְתְּכֶם	pref. id. ✗ noun com. pl., suff. 2 pers. pl. masc. (see בַּשֶּׁבֶת) . שבת
בְּשִׂגְּנָה	pref. בְּ q. v. bef. (ִ:) ✗ noun fem. sing. dec. 11c. שנג
בִּשְׂגוּבᵇ	ᵇ pref. id. ✗ pr. name m., Kh. שְׂגִיב, K. שְׂגוּב . שגב
בִּשְׁגַּםᵇ	preff. בְּ and שֶׁ with גַּם adv.; or, Kal inf. [שָׁגַג § 18. rem. 3] with suff. 3 pers. pl. masc. . שגג
בְּשִׁגְעוֹן	pref. בַּ f. בְּהַ }
בְּשִׁגָּעוֹן	pref. בְּ q. v. } noun masc. sing. . שגע
בַּשָּׂדֶה	ᵇ' pref. בַּ f. בְּהַ ✗ noun masc. sing. dec. 9 b;}
בַּשָּׂדֶה	pref. בְּ q. v. } ᵇ before labial . שדה
בַּשָּׂדֶה	pref. בְּ bef. (ִ:) ✗ id., construct state שדה
בִּשְׂדֵיᵇ	ᵇ' pref. id. ✗ id. pl., constr. st.; ᵇ bef. lab. שדה
בְּשָׂדְךָᵇ	} pref. id. ✗ id. sing., suff. 2 pers. sing. masc. שדה
בְּשָׂדְךָᵇ	} שדה
בְּשַׂדְמוֹתᵇ	pref. id. ✗ noun fem. pl. constr. from שְׁדֵמָה dec. 11. (§ 42. rem. 4) . שדם
בַּשִּׁדָּפוֹן	ᵇ' pref. בַּ for בְּהַ ✗ noun masc. sing. . שדף
בִּשְׂדֹתָם	pref. בְּ bef. (ִ:) ✗ noun masc. pl., suff. 3 pers. pl. masc. from שָׂדֶה dec. 9 a. שדה

בִּשָׂה	pref. בְּ ✗ noun com. sing. irr (§ 45) . שׂיה
בְּשֹׁהַם	pref. id. ✗ noun masc. ᵇing. . שהם
בַּשָּׁוְאᵏᵏ	pref. בַּ for בְּהַ ✗ noun masc. sing., K. שָׁוְא שוא
בְּשׁוּ	ᵇ', ᵇ' Kal pret. 3 pers. pl. (§ 21. rem. 2); ᵇ bef. lab., for וַ see lett. ו . בוש
בִּשְׂאֹאᵇ	pref. בְּ ✗ Kal inf. constr. for נְשֹׂא (§ 17. r. 1) נשא
בִּשְׂאָהᵍ	pref. id. ✗ noun fem. sing. dec. 10. . שאה
בְּשׁוּב	ᵇ' pref. id. ✗ Kal inf. constr.; ᵇ bef. (ִ:) שוב
בְּשׁוֹבְבִיᵇ	pref. id. ✗ Pilel inf. (שׁוֹבֵב), suff. 1 p. s. d. 7 b. שבב
בִּשְׁוָהᵇ	pref. id. ✗ noun fem. sing. . שוב
בְּשׁוּבוֹᵇ	pref. id. ✗ Kal inf. (שׁוּב), suff. 3 pers. s. m. שוב
בְּשׁוּבִי	pref. id., suff. 1 pers. sing. . שוב
בְּשׁוּבְכֶםᵍ	pref. id., suff. 2 pers. pl. masc. . שוב
בְּשׁוּבֵנוּᵐ	pref. id., suff. 1 pers. pl. . שוב
בְּשָׁוֵה	pref. id. ✗ pr. name in compos. שָׁוֵה קִרְיָתַיִם שוה
בְּשׁוֹטᵇ	pref. id. ✗ noun masc. sing. dec. 1 a. שוט
בַּשּׁוֹטִים	pref. בַּ for בְּהַ ✗ id. pl. abs. . שוט
בְּשׁוּלֶיהָᵇ	pref. בְּ ✗ n. m. pl., suff. s. fem. fr. [שׁוּל] d. 1. שול
בַּשּׁוּלַמִּית	pref. בַּ for בְּהַ ✗ gent. noun fem. . שלם
בְּשׂוּם	pref. בְּ ✗ Kal inf. constr. dec. 1 a. שׂים
בְּשׂוּמוֹ	pref. id., suff. 3 pers. sing. masc. . שׂום
בְּשׂוּמִי	pref. id., suff. 1 pers. sing. . שׂום
בְּשׁוּנֵם	pref. id. ✗ pr. name of a place . שׁאן
בְּשַׁוְּעוֹᵇ	ᵇ pref. id. ✗ Piel inf. [שִׁוַּע], suff. 3 pers. sing. masc. dec. 7 b; ᵇ bef. (ִ:) . שוע
בְּשַׁוְּעִי	pref. id. ✗ id. with suff. 1 pers. sing. שוע
בַּשַּׁפֵּרᵇ	pref. בַּ f. בְּהַ }
בְּשׁוֹפֵרᵇ	pref. בְּ q. v. } noun masc. sing. dec. 2b. שפר
בַּשּׁוֹפָרוֹתᵇ	ᵇ' pref. בַּ f. בְּהַ }
בְּשֹׁפָרוֹתᵇ	ᵇ' pref. בְּ q. v. } id. pl., abs. state; ᵇ bef. (ִ:) שפר
בַּשּׁוֹק	pref. בַּ for בְּהַ ✗ noun masc. sing. (pl. שׁוֹקִים § 35. rem. 13) . שׁוק
בְּשֹׁקֵי	pref. בְּ ✗ n. fem. pl. constr. from שׁוֹק d. 1 a. שׁוק
בַּשּׁוֹקִיםᵐ	pref. בַּ for בְּהַ ✗ noun masc., pl. of שׁוֹק (§ 35. rem. 13) שׁוק
בְּשׁוֹרֵᵇ	pref. בְּ ✗ noun masc. sing. dec. 1 a. (pl. שְׁוָרִים § 35. rem. 13) . שׁור
בְּשׁוֹרָה	noun fem. sing. . . כשׁר
בְּשׁוּרֵיᵇ	pref. בְּ ✗ noun masc. pl., suff. 1 pers. pl. from [שׁוּר] dec. 1 a. שׁור
בְּשׁוּרִיᵇ	pref. id. ✗ Kal inf. [שׁוּר], suff. 1 pers. sing. שׁור
בְּשׁוֹרְרָיᵇ	pref. id. ✗ Kal part. act. pl., suff. 1 pers. sing. from [שׁוֹרֵר] dec. 7 b. שׁרר
בְּשׁוּשָׁן	} pref. id. ✗ pr. name of a place ; ᵇ bef. (ִ:) שׁוש
בְּשׁוּשָׁן	ᵇ' } שׁוש
בַּשּׁוֹשַׁנִּים	pref. בַּ for בְּהַ ✗ noun m., pl. of שׁוֹשָׁן d. 8 a שׁוש

ᵃ De. 10. 22.	ᵍ La. 4. 10.	ᵏ Eze. 45. 17.	ᵖ Ge. 6. 3.	ᵘ De. 11. 15.	ᶠ Ps. 89. 10.	2 Ch. 30. 9.	⁑ Ps. 22. 25.	⁎ De. 22. 10.
ᵇ 1 Ki. 18. 44.	ᵉ Eze. 21. 11.	ˡ 2 Sa. 15. 8.	ᵠ 2 Ki. 23. 4.	ᵛ Ps. 35. 8.	ᵍ Eze. 47. 7.	ᶻ Is. 27. 13.	⁎ 2 Ch. 15. 14.	⁂ 2 Sa. 18. 25, 27
ᶜ Ex. 21. 2.	ᵈ 2 Sa. 23. 7.	ᵐ Le. 26. 35.	ʳ Ge. 39. 5.	ʷ Eze. 39. 27.	ʰ Job 5. 21.	ᵃ 2 Ch. 15. 14.	⁎ Ca. 3. 2.	⁎ Ps. 92. 12.
ᵈ Nu. 5. 21.	ᵉ Eze. 23. 8.	ⁿ Eze. 39. 26.	ˢ Pr. 23. 10.	ˣ Ne. 11. 25.	ⁱ Is. 30. 15.	ᵇ La. 1. 9.	⁎ Ps. 147. 10.	⁎ Ho. 9. 12.
ᵉ Nu. 26. 28.	ᶠ Pr. 31. 23.	ᵒ Ex. 16. 3.	ᵗ De. 24. 19.	ʸ Job 28. 16.	ʲ Eze. 18. 23.	ᶜ Job 37. 15.	⁎ Ca. 3. 2.	⁎ Ps. 59. 11.
ᶠ Ge. 47. 14.	⁎ Eze. 46. 3.	⁎ Le. 26. 35.	⁑ Nu. 28. 26.	⁑ 2 Ki. 23. 4.	⁎ Job 15. 31.			

בַּשֹּׂחַד‎ pref. בַּ for בְּהַ‎ }
בְּשֹׂחַד‎ pref. בְּ q. v. } noun masc. sing. . שׂחד

בִּשְׂחֹק‎ pref. בְּ bef. (ְ))(Kal inf. constr. . שׂחק

בְּשִׂחֻתְוֹ‎ pref. id.)(noun fem. sing., suff. 3 pers. sing. masc. from [שְׂחוּת] dec. 1a. שׂחה

בְּשַׁחֲטָם‎ ٩ pref. בְּ)(Kal inf. [שְׁחַט], suff. 3 pers. pl. m. (§ 16. r. 10, comp. § 35. r. 10. & d. 6d. שׁחט

בַּשְּׁחִין‎ pref. בַּ for בְּהַ‎ }
בִּשְׁחִין‎ pref. בְּ bef. (ְ) } noun masc. sing. . שׁחן

בִּשְׁחִיתוֹתָם‎ pref. id.)(noun fem. pl., suff. 3 pers. pl. masc. from [שְׁחִית] dec. 1a. . שׁחה

בַּשַּׁחֶפֶת‎ pref. בַּ for בְּהַ‎)(noun fem. sing. . שׁחף

בַּשַּׂחַק‎ pref. id.)(noun masc. sing. dec. 6d. שׂחק

בִּשְׂחָק‎ pref. בְּ bef. (ְ))(noun masc. sing. שׂחק

בַּשְּׂחָקִים‎ pref. בַּ for בְּהַ‎)(n. m., pl. of שַׂחַק‎ dec. 6d. שׂחק

בַּשַּׁחַר‎ pref. id.)(noun masc. sing. dec. 6d. שׁחר

בַּשַּׁחַת‎ pref. id. }
בַּשַּׁחַת‎ pref. id. } noun fem. sing. dec. 13a. . שׁוח
בְּשַׁחַת‎ pref. בְּ }

בְּשַׁחֵת‎ pref. id.)(Piel inf. constr. (§ 14. rem. 1) שׁחת

בְּשַׁחֲתָם‎ pref. id.)(n. fem. sing., suff. 3 pers. pl. m. [for שַׁחֲתָם‎ comp. § 35. r. 5] from שַׁחַת‎ d. 13a. שׁוח

בַּשִּׁטִּים‎ pref. בַּ for בְּהַ‎)(pr. name of a place שׁטה

בַּשֶּׁטֶף‎ pref. id. }
בְּשֶׁטֶף‎ ٩ pref. בְּ } noun masc. sing.; ٩ bef. (ְ) שׁטף

בַּשִּׁיבָה‎ pref. id.)(noun fem. sing. dec. 10. שׁיב

בְּשִׂיבָתוֹ‎ pref. id.)(noun fem. sing., suff. 3 pers. sing. masc. from שֵׂיבָה‎ dec. 10. . . ישׁב

בַּשִּׂיד‎ pref. בַּ for בְּהַ‎)(noun masc. sing. . שׂיד

בְּשִׁיחוֹר‎ ٩ pref. בְּ)(pr. name of a river; ٩ bef. (ְ) שׁחר

בְּשִׂיחִי‎ pref. id.)(noun masc. sing., suff. 1 pers. sing. from שִׂיח‎ dec. 1a. . . שׂיח

בְּשִׁילֹה‎ }
בְּשִׁילוֹ‎ } pref. id.)(pr. name of a place . שׁלה

בַּשִּׁיר‎ pref. בַּ for בְּהַ‎ }
בְּשִׁירֵי‎ ٩ pref. בְּ q. v. } noun m. s. d. 1a; ٩ bef. (ְ) . שׁיר

בַּשִּׁירִים‎ ٩ pref. id.)(id. pl., absolute state; ٩ id. שׁיר

בְּשָׁכְבָּה‎ pref. id.)(Kal inf. (שְׁכַב), suff. 3 pers. sing. fem. (§ 16. rem. 10) שׁכב

בְּשִׁכְבוֹ‎ pref. id.)(id. (שְׁכַב), suff. 3 pers. sing. masc. שׁכב

בְּשָׁכְבְּךָ‎ ٩ pref. id.)(id. id., suff. 2 p. s. m.; ٩ bef. (ְ) שׁכב

בְּשֵׂכֶר‎ preff. בְּ & שׁ (q. v.))(adv. . . כבר

בְּשֶׂכוּ‎ pref. בְּ for בְּהַ‎)(pr. name of a place שׂכה

בַּשְּׂכוֹת‎ pref. בְּ)(noun fem., pl. of [שְׂכָּה] dec. 10. שׂכך

בַּשִּׂכְלָל‎ pref. id.)(noun m. sing., (suff. שִׂכְלוֹ) dec. 6a. שׂכל

בִּשְׁכֶם‎ pref. בְּ bef. (ְ))(pr. name of a place שׁכם

בִּשְׁכֹּן‎ pref. id.)(Kal inf. constr. שׁכן

בַּשֵּׂכָר‎ ٩ pref. בַּ for בְּהַ‎)(n. m. sing.; ٩ bef. lab. שׂכר

בִּשְׂכָרוֹ‎ pref. בְּ bef. (ְ))(n. m. s., suff. שְׂכָר‎ dec. 4a. שׂכר

בָּשַׁל‎ I. to boil intrans. Eze. 24. 5.—to ripen, become ripe, Joel 4. 13. Pi. to boil, cook, seethe. Pu. pass. of Pi.—Hiph. to ripen, bring to maturity, Ge. 40. 10. בָּשֵׁל‎ adj., fem. בְּשֵׁלָה‎ boiled, sodden, Ex. 12. 9; Nu. 6. 19.

מְבַשְׁלוֹת‎ fem. pl. (of מְבַשֶּׁלֶת‎ dec. 13) boilers Eze. 46. 23.

בָּשֵׁל‎ ٩ adj. masc. sing.; ٩ bef. lab. . . בשׁל

בַּשֵּׁל‎ ٩ Piel imp. sing. masc.; ٩ id. . . בשׁל

בְּשֶׁל‎ pref. בְּ)(particle made up of the preff. שׁ & ל see שׁ

בְּשֵׁלָה‎ adj. fem. sing. from בָּשֵׁל‎ masc. בשׁל

בְּשִׁלֹה‎ pref. בְּ)(pr. name of a place, see שִׁילֹה‎ . שׁלה

בֻּשְּׁלָה‎ Pual pret. 3 p. s. fem. [for בֻּשְּׁלָה‎ comp. § 8. r. 7] בשׁל

בִּשְּׁלוּ‎ Kal pret. 3 pers. pl. . בשׁל

בַּשְּׁלוּ‎ Piel imp. pl. masc; p. בַּשְׁלוּ‎ Ex. 16. 23. בשׁל

בְּשִׁלוֹ‎ pref. בְּ)(pr. name of a place, see שׁלה שׁלה

בִּשְּׁלוּ‎ ٩ Piel pret. 3 pers. pl.; ٩ bef. lab. בשׁל

בְּשִׁלְיָה‎ ٩ pref. בְּ)(n. fem. sing. (no pl. abs.); ٩ id. שׁלה

בְּשִׁלְיָנִי‎ pref. בְּ)(noun masc. sing., suff. 1 pers. sing. from [שֶׁלִי] dec. 6a. . . שׁלה

בַּשָּׁלוֹם‎ pref. בַּ for בְּהַ‎)((prim. adj.) noun masc. }
בְּשָׁלוֹם‎ ٩ pref. בְּ q. v. } s. dec. 3a; ٩ before (ְ) שׁלם

בַּשָּׁלוֹם‎ pref. בַּ for בְּהַ‎)(noun masc. sing. dec. 1b. שׁלם

בִּשְׁלוֹמָהּ‎ pref. בְּ bef. (ְ))(noun masc. sing., suff. 3 pers. sing. fem. from שָׁלוֹם‎ dec. 3a. . שׁלם

בִּשְׁלֹשְׁתָּהּ‎ pref. id.)(num. card. masc. (constr. שְׁלֹשֶׁת) from שָׁלֹשׁ‎ fem שׁלשׁ

בְּשִׁלְוֹתֶיךָ‎ pref. בְּ)(noun fem. pl., suff. 2 pers. sing. fem. from שַׁלְוָה‎ (no pl. abs.) שׁלה

בַּשָּׁלַח‎ pref. בַּ for בְּהַ‎)(n. m. s. for שָׁלַח‎ as if from שָׁלַח‎ (§ 35. rem. 2) but with suff. שִׁלְחוֹ‎ שׁלח

בְּשַׁלַּח‎ pref. בְּ)(Piel inf. constr. שׁלח

בְּשֶׁלַח‎ pref. id.)(n. m. s. (suff. שִׁלְחוֹ) § 35. r. 5) d. 6a. שׁלח

בִּשְׁלֹחַ‎ pref. בְּ bef. (ְ))(Kal inf. constr.; ٩ bef. lab. שׁלח

בְּשַׁלְּחָהּ‎ pref. בְּ)(Piel inf. [שַׁלַּח] suff. 3 pers. sing. fem. dec. 7b. (§ 36. rem. 5) . שׁלח

בְּשַׁלְחוֹ‎ pref. id.)(id. with suff. 3 pers. sing. masc. שׁלח

בְּשָׁלְחִי‎ pref. id.)(id., suff. 1 pers. sing. שׁלח

בְּשָׁלְחִי‎ pref. id.)(Kal inf., suff. 1 pers. sing. שׁלח

a Is. 33. 15.   f De. 28. 22.   m Eze. 19. 4, 8.   t 1 Ch. 13. 8.   b 1 Ch. 26. 14.   2 Ki. 4. 38.   n Da. 11. 21, 24.   t Je. 29. 7.   z De. 9. 23.
b Ju. 16. 27.   g Pr. 14. 13.   n Da. 9. 26.   s Ge. 19. 33, 35.   c Ge. 35. 22.   Ec. 8. 17.   o Da. 8. 25.   u Je. 22. 21.   a Is. 27. 8.
c Pr. 28. 10.   h Ho. 10. 15.   o Na. 1. 8.   r Ruth 3. 4.   d Is. 28. 7.   Nu. 6. 19.   p Ps. 30. 7.   v Job 33. 18.   b Eze. 31. 5.
d Eze. 23. 39.   Job 33. 28.   p 2 Sa. 19. 24.   q Pr. 6. 22.   e Ex. 22. 14.   Le. 6. 21.   q Is. 55. 12.   w Ex. 13. 17.   c Eze. 5. 16.
e Le. 13. 20.   De. 27. 2, 4.   q Ec. 2. 16.   Joel 4. 13.   f Eze. 24. 5.   Mi. 7. 3.   x Job 36. 12.   d Nu. 32. 8.
f La. 4. 20.   Ge. 19. 29.   Ps. 69. 31.   Job 40. 31.   g Ex. 12. 9.   Le. 8. 31.

בְּשַׁלַּחֲךָ‎ pref. בְּ)(Piel inf. with suff. 2 pers. **sing. m.** [strictly from the form שַׁלַּח instead of שָׁלַח, comp. § 16. rem. 15] . . . שלח

בְּשִׁלְיָ‎ pref. בְּ for בְּהַ)(n. m. s. [for שִׁלְיָ § 35. r. 14] . . שלה

בְּשֶׁלִי‎ pref. בְּ)(particle שֶׁל (from the preff. שֶׁ & לְ) with suff. 1 pers. sing. . . . . ש

בְּשִׁלְיָתָהּ‎ וּ pref. id.)(noun fem. sing. with suff. 3 pers. sing. fem. [from שִׁלְיָה]; וּ bef. (:) . . שלה

בְּשֶׁלִּישִׁי‎ pref. בְּ for בְּהַ)(adj. ordin. masc. . שלש

בְּשַׁלִּישִׁת‎ pref. id.)(id. fem. defect. for שִׁית . . שלש

בְּשַׁלֶּכֶת‎ pref. בְּ)(noun fem. sing. . . . שלך

בְּשָׁלָל‎ pref. בְּ for בְּהַ)(noun masc. sing. dec. 4 a. שלל

בְּשָׁלֵם‎ pref. בְּ)(pr. name of a place . . . שלם

בְּשָׁלֹם‎ defect. for בְּשָׁלוֹם (q. v.) . . . שלם

בְּשִׁלֵּם‎ Piel pret. 3 p. s. m. [בְּשָׁלֵם], suff. 3 p. pl. m. שלם (for בֶּן־שָׁלֵם son of peace, comp. בַּרְדְּקַר) pr. name masc. Ezr. 4. 7.

בְּשַׁלְמָה‎ pref. בְּ for בְּהַ } noun fem. sing. dec. 12 a. שלם
pref. בְּ q. v. }

בְּשַׁלְמֹה‎ pref. בְּ bef. (:))(pr. name masc. . . שלם

בְּשַׁלְמוֹת‎ וּ pref. בְּ bef. (:))(n. f., pl. of שַׂלְמָה d. 12 a שלם

בְּשַׁלְמִי‎ pref. בְּ)(compound of שֶׁל (see בְּשֶׁל) & מִי pron. interrog. . . . . . ש

בְּשַׁלְמָיו‎ pref. בְּ bef. (:))(adj. masc. pl., suff. 3 pers. sing. masc. from שָׁלֵם dec. 3 a. . שלם

בְּשַׁלְמֵינוּ‎ וּ pref. בְּ bef. (:))(noun masc. pl., suff. 1 pers. pl. from שָׁלֵם dec. 6 a.; וּ bef. lab. שלם

בְּשַׁלְמָתוֹ‎ pref. בְּ)(noun fem. sing., suff. 3 pers. sing. masc. from שַׂלְמָה dec. 12 a. . . שלם

בְּשָׁלִיט‎ pref. בְּ for בְּהַ)(noun masc. sing. defect. for שָׁלִישׁ dec. 1 b. (§ 32. rem. 1) . . שלש

בְּשָׁלִישׁ‎ pref. בְּ)(num. card. sing. fem. . . שלש

בְּשָׁלִשׁ‎ וּ pref. בְּ bef. (:))(id. constr. st.; וּ bef. lab. שלש

בְּשָׁלְשָׁה‎ pref. בְּ for בְּהַ } id. fem. (constr. שְׁלֹשֶׁת) שלש
בְּשָׁלֹשָׁה‎ pref. בְּ bef. (:) }

בְּשָׁלִשִׁים‎ וּ pref. בְּ)(noun masc., pl. of שָׁלִישׁ dec. 1 b. (§ 32. rem. 1); וּ bef. (:) . . . שלש

בְּשָׁלֹשִׁים‎ pref. בְּ for בְּהַ)(adj. ordin. m., pl. of שְׁלִישִׁי שלש
בְּשָׁלֹשִׁים‎ pref. id. } num. card. com., pl. of שָׁלֹשׁ שלש
בְּשָׁלֹשִׁים‎ pref. בְּ bef. }

בְּשָׁלֹשֶׁת‎ וּ pref. id.)(id. sing. masc., constr. of שְׁלֹשָׁה (§ 42. rem. 5); וּ bef. lab. . . שלש

בְּשָׁלַּחְתָּ‎ וּ Piel pret. 2 pers. sing. masc.; acc. shifted by conv. וּ, bef. lab. for וְ (§ 8. rem. 7) בשל

בָּשָׂם‎ Root not used; Chald. and Syr. *to be sweet, pleasant, fragrant.*

בָּשָׂם‎ masc. dec. 4 a, *the balsam-tree,* Ca. 5. 1.

בֹּשֶׂם & בֶּשֶׂם‎ masc. pl. בְּשָׂמִים.—I. *scent, odour of perfume.*—II. *perfumes themselves.*—III. *balsam-tree,* Ca. 5. 13; 6. 2.

בָּשְׂמַת‎ (*fragrant*) pr. name.—I. of a wife of Esau.—II. of a daughter of Solomon, 1 Ki. 4. 15.

יִבְשָׂם‎ (*pleasant*) pr. name masc. 1 Ch. 7. 2.

מִבְשָׂם‎ (*fragrance*) pr. name masc.—I. Ge. 25. 13.—II. 1 Ch. 4. 25.

בְּשֵׁם‎ noun masc. sing. dec. 6. . . . בשם

בַּשֵׁם‎ וּ pref. בַּ)(noun masc. s. d. 7 a; וּ bef. (:) . שם

בִּשֵׁם‎ Ch. pref. id.)(noun masc. sing. irr. (§ 68) שם

בַּשֵׁם‎ noun masc. sing. . . . . בשם

בִּשְׁמוֹאֵלָה‎ pref. בְּ bef. (:))(noun masc. sing., suff. 3 pers. sing. fem. from שְׁמוֹאֵל dec. 1 a. שמאל

בִּשְׁמוֹאֵלוּ‎ pref. id.)(id., suff. 3 pers. sing. masc. שמאל

בִּשְׁמוֹ‎ וּ pref. id.)(noun masc. sing., suff. 3 pers. sing. masc. from שֵׁם dec. 7 a; וּ bef. lab. שם

בִּשְׁמוֹנָה‎ וּ pref. id.)(num. card. fem.; וּ id. . שמן

בִּשְׁמוֹנִים‎ pref. id.)(id. pl. com. gen. (comp. dec. 9) שמן

בִּשְׁמוּעָה‎ pref. בְּ for בְּהַ)(noun fem. sing. dec. 10. שמע

בִּשְׁמוֹר‎ pref. בְּ bef. (:))(Kal inf. constr. (§ 8. r. 18) שמר

בִּשְׁמוֹת‎ pref. בְּ)(n. m. with pl. f. term., abs. fr. שֵׁם d. 7 a. שם

בִּשְׁמוֹתָם‎ pref. בְּ bef. (:))(id. with suff. 3 pers. pl. masc. שם

בְּשִׂמְחָה‎ pref. בְּ)(noun fem. sing. dec. 12 b. שמח

בְּשִׂמְחַת‎ pref. id.)(id., constr. state . . . שמח

בְּשִׂמְחֹת‎ pref. בְּ bef. (:))(id. pl., absolute state . שמח

בְּשִׂמְחָתוֹ‎ וּ pref. בְּ)(id. s., suff. 3 p. s. m.; וּ bef. (:) שמח

בְּשִׂמְחַתְכֶם‎ pref. id.)(id. sing., suff. 2 pers. pl. masc. שמח

בִּשְׁמִי‎ noun m. s., suff. 1 pers. s. fr. שֵׁם d. 4 a. בשם

בְּשָׁמַי‎ pref. בְּ bef. (:))(noun masc., pl., constr. of שָׁמַיִם [fr. sing. שָׁמַי comp. § 38. rem. 2] שמה

בִּשְׁמִי‎ וּ pref. id.)(noun masc. sing. with suff. 1 pers. sing. fr. שֵׁם dec. 7 a; וּ bef. lab. . שם

בִּשְׁמַיָּא‎ Ch. pref. id.)(noun masc. pl., emph. of בִּשְׁמֵי, comp. שְׁמַיִן . . . . שמה

בִּשְׁמָיו‎ noun m. pl., suff. 3 pers. s. m. fr. בָּשָׂם d. 6. בשם

בְּשָׂמִיכָה‎ pref. בְּ for בְּהַ)(noun fem. sing. see סמך

בַּשָׁמַיִם‎ pref. id.)(noun m. pl. [of שָׁמַי comp. שמה
בְּשָׁמַיִם‎ } § 38. rem. 1]

בְּשָׂמִים‎ וּ noun masc., pl. of בָּשָׂם dec. 6 a; וּ bef. (:) בשם

בְּשָׁמִיר‎ pref. בְּ)(pr. name of a place . . . שמר

בִּשְׁמֶךָ‎ וּ pref. id. } noun m. s., suff. 2 p. s. m. שם
בְּשִׁמְךָ‎ pref. בְּ bef. (:) } fr. שֵׁם d. 7 a; וּ bef.

a De. 15. 18. b 2 Sa. 3. 27. c De. 1. 12. d De. 28. 59. e Eze. 31. 1.
f 1 Sa. 3. 8. g Is. 6. 13. h Jos. 7. 21. i 1 Ki. 2. 5, 6. k 1 Ki. 19. 21.
l 1 Ki. 11. 30. m 1 Ki. 11. 29. n Jos. 22. 8. o Jon. 1. 7. p Ps. 55. 21.
q Jos. 22. 27. r De. 24. 13. s Is. 40. 12. t Is. 16. 14. u Ju. 7. 8.
v 1 Sa. 18. 6. w Pr. 3. 16. x 2 Ch. 35. 19. y 2 Ch. 34. 8. z Ex. 30. 23.
aa Ezr. 5. 1. bb Eze. 42. 3. cc Job 32. 3. dd Ps. 49. 12.
ee 1 Ki. 6. 1. ff Je. 51. 46. gg 2 Sa. 11. 16. hh Ps. 45. 16.
ii Pr. 14. 10. kk Is. 66. 5. ll Ca. 5. 1. mm Ps. 68. 34.
nn Ps. 89. 25. oo Da. 6. 28. pp Ca. 4. 16. qq Ju. 4. 18.

בִּשְׂמָכָה	pref. בְּ ✕ id. id. for שְׂמָךְ (comp. § 3. r. 2)	שם
בְּשִׂמְלָה	pref. בְּ for בְּהָ ✕ noun fem. sing. dec. 12b.	שמל
בְּשִׂמְלֹתָם	pref. בְּ ✕ id. pl., suff. 3 pers. pl. masc. .	שמל
בִּשְׁמָם	pref. בְּ bef. (:) noun masc. sing., suff. 3 pers pl. masc. from שֵׁם dec. 7a. .	שם
בְּשַׂמְמֹן	pref. בְּ ✕ noun masc. sing.; ﬨ bef. (:)	שמם
בַּשֶּׁמֶן / בְּשֶׁמֶן / בְּשָׁמֶן	{pref. בְּ f. בְּהָ ✕ noun masc. sing., dec. 6a. (with suff. שַׁמְנִי § 35.) pref. בְּ q. v. rem. 2)}	שמן
בִּשְׁמֹנָה	pref. בְּ bef. (:) ✕ masc. of the foll., (constr. שְׁמֹנַת)	שמן
בִּשְׁמֹנֶה	pref. id. ✕ num. card. fem.; ﬨ bef. labial	שמן
בִּשְׁמֹנִים	pref. id. ✕ id. pl. com. gen.	שמן
בִּשְׁמֹעַ	pref. id. ✕ Kal inf. construct	שמע
בְּשָׁמְעוֹ	pref. בְּ ✕ id., suff. 3 pers. sing. masc. .	שמע
בְּשָׁמְעוֹ	pref. id. ✕ id., suff. 3 p.s.m., K. בְּשָׁמְעוֹ (q.v.)	שמע
בְּשָׁמְעֶךָ	pref. id. ✕ id., suff. 2 p.s.m., K. בְּשָׁמְעֲךָ (q.v.)	שמע
בְּשָׁמְעֲךָ	pref. id. ✕ id., suff. 2 pers. sing. masc.	שמע
בְּשָׁמְעֲכֶם	pref. id. ✕ id., suff. 2 pers. pl. masc. .	שמע
בְּשָׁמְעָם	pref. id. ✕ id., suff. 3 pers. pl. masc.	שמע
בְּשֹׁמְרוֹן	pref. id. ✕ pr. name of a place	שמר
בְּשֹׁמְרָיִן	Chald. pref. id. ✕ pr. name of a place	שמר
בְּשָׁמְרָם	pref. id. ✕ Kal inf., suff. 3 pers. pl. masc.	שמר
בַּשֶּׁמֶשׁ	pref. בְּ f. בְּהָ ✕ n.com.s. (suff. שִׁמְשָׁךְ) dec.6a.	שמש
בְּשֵׁמֹת	pr. name, fem.; ﬨ before labial .	בשם
בְּשֵׁמֹת	pref. בְּ ✕ noun m.pl.abs.from שֵׁם d.7a. id.	שם
בִּשְׁמֹתָם	pref. בְּ before (:) ✕ id., suff 3 pers. pl. masc.	שם
בָּשָׁן	(light sandy soil, coll. with the Arab. Gesen.) pr. name of a region beyond Jordan, between Hermon and the brook of Jabbok. נִבְשָׁן (soft soil) pr. name of a place in the desert, Jos. 15. 62.	
בְּשֵׁן	pref. בְּ ✕ noun com. sing. dec. 8b.	שנן
בְּשִׂנְאָה	pref. id. ✕ noun fem. sing. (no pl.)	שנא
בְּשֹׂנְאַי	pref.id.✕Kal part.act.pl.,suff. 1 p.s.fr.שֵׂנָא d.7b.	שנא
בְּשֹׂנְאֵיהֶם	pref. id. ✕ id. pl., suff. 3 pers. pl. masc. .	שנא
בְּשִׂנְאַת	pref. id. ✕ n. f. s., constr. of שִׂנְאָה (no pl.)	שנא
בְּשָׁנָה	pref. בְּ f. בְּהָ ✕ noun fem. sing. dec. 11a.; pref. בְּ q. v. ﬨ before labial	שנה
בֹּשְׁנָה	noun fem. sing.	בוש
בֹּשְׁנוּ	Kal pret. 1 pers. sing. (§ 21. rem. 2)	בוש
בְּשַׁנּוֹתוֹ	pref. בְּ ✕ Piel inf., suff. 3 pers. sing. masc.	שנה
בַּשֵּׁנִי	pref. בְּ for בְּהָ ✕ adj. ord. masc. from שְׁנַיִם	שנה
בִּשְׁנֵי	pret. בְּ ✕ n. com. du., suff. 1 p. s. fr. שֵׁן dec. 8b.	שנן
בִּשְׁנֵי	pref. בְּ before (:) ✕ num. card. masc., constr. of שְׁנַיִם; ﬨ before labial .	שנה
בִּשְׁנֵי	pref. id. ✕ n. m. s., constr. of שְׁנֵי d.3a: ﬨ id.	שנה
בִּשְׁנֵיהֶם	pref. בְּ ✕ n. com. du., suff. 3 p.pl.m.fr. שֵׁן d.8b	שנן
בִּשְׁנֵינוּ	pref. id. ✕ id. du., suff. 3 pers. sing. masc.	שנן
בְּשָׁנִים	pref. בְּ for בְּהָ ✕ noun fem. with pl. fem. term. from שָׁנָה dec. 11a.	שנה
בִּשְׁנַיִם / בִּשְׁנָיִם	{pref. בְּ for בְּהָ / pref. בְּ bef.(:)} num. card. du. masc.	שנה
בִּשְׁנַיִם	pref. id. ✕ id., construct state only before עֶשֶׂר; ﬨ before labial	שנה
בִּשְׁנַת	pref. id. ✕ n.f.s., constr. of שָׁנָה d.11a; ﬨ id.	שנה
בִּשְׁנַת	Ch. pref. id. ✕ n. f. s., constr. of שָׁנָה dec. 8a.	שנה
בִּשְׁנָתְ	Kh. בִּשְׁנַת q. v., K. בַּשָּׁנָה (q. v.)	שנה
בָּשַׁם	Po. to trample upon, with עַל, Amos 5. 11.	
בְּשָׂעִיר	pref. בְּ ✕ pr. name of a region; ﬨ bef. (:)	שער
בְּשַׁעַלְבִּים	pref. id. ✕ pr. name of a place; ﬨ id.	שעל
בְּשַׁעֲלוֹ	pref. id. ✕ n.m.s., suff. 3 p.s.m. fr.שֹׁעַל d.6f.	שעל
בְּשַׁעֲלֵי	pref. id. ✕ n.m. pl. constr. from שֹׁעַל dec. 6d.	שעל
בִּשְׁעָפִים	pref. בְּ before (:) ✕ noun masc., pl. of שָׂעֵף dec. 8b. (§ 37. No. 3), see	סעף
בַּשַּׁעַר / בְּשַׁעַר	{pref. בְּ for בְּהָ / pref. בְּ q. v.} noun com sing. masc. dec. 6d.	שער
בְּשַׁעֲרָה	pref. בְּ bef. (:) ✕ noun fem. s.; ﬨ bef. lab.	שער
בְּשַׁעֲרֵי	pref. id. ✕ n. com. pl. constr. from שַׁעַר dec. 6d.	שער
בִּשְׁעָרֶיהָ	pref. בְּ bef. (:) ✕ id. pl., suff. 3 pers. sing. fem.	שער
בִּשְׁעָרַיִךְ	pref. id. ✕ id. pl., suff. 2 pers. sing. fem.	שער
בִּשְׁעָרֶיךָ	pref. id. ✕ id. pl., suff. 2 p.s.m.; ﬨ bef.lab.	שער
בִּשְׁעָרֵיכֶם	pref. בְּ ✕ id pl., suff. 2 pers. pl. masc. .	שער
בַּשְּׁעָרִים	pref. בְּ for בְּהָ ✕ id. pl., absolute state	שער
בַּשְּׁעָרַיִם	pref. בְּ ✕ id.du.pr.name of a place; ﬨ bef.	שער
בְּשִׂפָּה	pref. id. ✕ noun fem. sing. dec. 11a.	שפה
בְּשִׁפְחָתֵךְ	pref. id. ✕ noun fem. sing., suff. 2 pers. sing. masc. (for חָתֵךְ) from שִׁפְחָה dec. 12b. .	שפח
בִּשְׁפָטִים	pref. בְּ before (:) ✕ noun masc., pl. of שֶׁפֶט dec. 6; ﬨ before labial .	שפט
בְּשָׁפְטְךָ	pref. בְּ ✕ Kal inf., suff. 2 p. s. m. [for שָׁפְטְךָ]	שפט
בְּשָׁפְכְּךָ	pref. בְּ before (:) ✕ Kal inf. construct	שפך
בְּשָׁפְכְּךָ	pref. id. ✕ id. suff. 2 pers. sing. masc.	שפך
בְּשֵׁפֶל	pref. בְּ for בְּהָ ✕ noun masc. sing. dec. 6b.	שפל
בְּשֵׁפֶל	pref. בְּ bef. (:) ✕ adj.m.s., constr. of שָׁפָל d.4a.	שפל
בַּשְּׁפֵלָה	pref. בְּ for בְּהָ ✕ noun fem. sing.; ﬨ bef. lab.	שפל
בַּשְּׁפֵלָה	pref. id. ✕ noun fem. sing. dec. 10; ﬨ id.	שפל
בִּשְׁפְלוּת	pref. בְּ ✕ noun fem. sing.; ﬨ id.	שפל
בְּשִׂפְמוֹת	pref. id. ✕ pr. name of a place	שפם

---

a Je. 29. 25.   g 2 Ki. 6. 25.   n Ps. 19. 12.   t De. 1. 27.   z Le. 14. 52.   f Est. 9. 1.   l Job 9. 17.   q 2 Ki. 4. 16.   v Eze. 9. 8.
b Ex. 12. 34.   h Ex. 16. 8.   o Is. 38. 8.   u Ho. 10. 6.   a Mi. 3. 5.   g Je. 28. 1.   m Na. 1. 3.   r Ex. 7. 4.   w Ec. 10. 6.
c Ho. 2. 19.   i 1 Sa. 11. 6.   p Nu. 32. 38.   v Ps. 34. 1.   b Job 16. 9.   h Is. 40. 12.   n Je. 17. 27.   s Ex. 6. 6.   x Ec. 12. 4.
d Eze. 12. 19.   k 2 Sa. 5. 24.   q Nu. 4. 32.   w 1 Ch. 11. 21.   c Eze. 13. 19.   i De. 6. 9; 11. 20.   o Ps. 51. 6.   t Is. 32. 19.
e Eze. 4. 16.   l Jos. 6. 5.   r De. 19. 21.   x Job 13. 14.   d Job 4. 13.   k Ps. 22. 8.   p Eze. 17. 17.   u Ec. 10. 18.
f Je. 41. 15.   m 2 Ch. 20. 29.   s Ps. 118. 7.   y Job 42. 7.   e Ju. 15. 13.

בִּשְׂפָק   pref. בְּ)(noun m. s. [for שְׂפָק § 35. rem. 2]   שפק

בְּשִׂפְרִי   pref. בְּ for בְּהְ)(noun masc. sing. dec. 2 b.   שפר

בְּשַׁפְרְפָרָא   Ch. pref. בְּ bef.)(n.m.s. emph. [of שְׁפַרְפַּר]   שפר

בִּשְׂפָת   pref. id.)(n. f. s., constr. of שָׂפָה dec. 11 a.   שפה

בִּשְׂפָתוֹ   pref. id.)(id. du., suff. 3 pers. sing. masc., K. תָיו (§ 4. rem. 1)   שפה

בְּשִׂפְתוֹתֵיהֶם   pref. בְּ)(id. pl., suff. 3 pers. pl. masc.   שפה

בְּשִׂפְתוֹתֶיךָ   pref. id.)(id. pl., suff. 2 pers. sing. masc.   שפה

בְּשִׂפְתֵי   pref. id.)(id. du., construct state   שפה

בִּשְׂפָתַי   pref. בְּ before)(id. du., suff. 1 pers. sing.   שפה

בִּשְׂפָתָיו   pref. id.)(id. du., suff. 3 p. s. m.; ו bef. lab.   שפה

בִּשְׂפָתֶיךָ   pref. id.)(id. du., suff. 2 pers. sing. masc.   שפה

בִּשְׂפָתַיִם   pref. id.)(id. du., absolute state   שפה

בִּשְׂצֶף   pref. בְּ)(noun masc. sing.   שצף

בַּשֹּׁק   pref. בְּ for בְּהְ)(for שֹׁק noun m. s. dec. 8 d.   שקק

בְּשֹׁקוֹ   pref. בְּ)(id., suff. 3 pers. sing. masc.   שקק

בְּשִׁקּוּצֵיהֶם   pref. id.)(noun masc. pl., suff. 3 pers. pl. masc. from שִׁקּוּץ dec. 2 b; ו before   שקץ

בַּשְּׁקִים   pref. בְּ f. בְּהְ)(noun m., pl. of שַׂק dec. 6 d;   שקק

בִּשְׁקָקִים   ו pref. בְּ q.v. id.   שקק

בְּשִׁקֵּל   pref. id.)(noun m. s. (pl. c. שִׁקְלֵי), dec. 6 a.   שקל

בַּשֶּׁקֶר   pref. בְּ for בְּהְ)(noun masc. sing. for שֶׁקֶר as if from שָׁקַר (§ 35. rem. 2) but see the foll.   שקר

בְּשֶׁקֶר   ו pref. id.)(noun masc. sing. dec. 6 a. (see   שקר

בְּשָׁקֶר   pref. בְּ)(the foll.); ו before labial   שקר

בְּשִׁקְרֵיהֶם   pref. id.)(id. pl. suff. 3 pers. pl. masc.   שקר

בְּשִׁקֲתוֹת   pref. id.)(noun fem., pl. of [שֹׁקֶת]; (but comp. § 35. rem. 9, note)   שקה

בָּשַׂר.   Pi.—I. *to announce, declare.*—II. *to bring, tell good tidings.*—Hithp. *to receive good tidings*, 2 Sa. 18. 31.

בְּשׂוֹר (*cool, cold,* coll. with the Arab. Gesenius) pr. name of a torrent near Gaza, 1 Sa. 30. 9, 10, 21.

בְּשׂוֹרָה, בְּשֹׂרָה fem.—I. *good tidings, news.*—II. *reward for good tidings,* 2 Sa. 4. 10.

בָּשָׂר   ו masc. dec. 4 a.—I. *flesh.*—II. *body.*—III. כָּל־בָּשָׂר *all flesh,* i.e. all creatures or animate beings.—IV. *near relation, consanguinity.*—V. *the secret parts* (viri).

בְּשַׂר   Chald. m. dec. 3 b, i.q. Heb. בָּשָׂר Nos. I, III.

בְּשַׂר   ו n. m. s., constr. of בָּשָׂר dec. 4 a; ו bef.   בשר

בִּשְׂרֵי   Chald. noun masc. sing. dec. 3 b.   בשר

בִּשַּׂר   Piel pret. 3 pers. sing. masc. (§ 10. rem. 1)   בשר

בִּשְׂרָא   Chald. noun masc. s., emph. of בְּשַׂר dec. 3 b.   בשר

בִּשְׂרָד   pref. בְּ for בְּהְ)(noun masc. sing.   שרד

בָּשְׂרָהּ   noun m. s., suff. 3 pers. s. f. from בָּשָׂר dec. 4 a.   בשר

בְּשָׂרָה   noun fem. sing.   בשר

בַּשְּׂרוּ   Piel imp. pl. masc.   בשר

בְּשָׂרוֹ   ו noun masc. sing., suff. 3 pers. sing. masc. from בָּשָׂר dec. 4 a; ו before   בשר

בְּשָׂרוֹן   pref. בְּ for בְּהְ)(pr. name of a region   ישר

בְּשָׂרוֹתֶיהָ   pref. בְּ)(noun fem. pl., suff. 3 pers. sing. fem. from [שָׂרָה] dec. 10.   שור

בְּשָׂרִי   ו n. m. s., suff. 1 p. s. from בָּשָׂר dec. 4 a; ו bef.   בשר

בַּשְׂרִידִים   ו pref. בְּ for בְּהְ)(noun masc., pl. of שָׂרִיד dec. 3 a; ו before labial   שרד

בַּשָּׁרִים   pref. id.)(noun masc., pl. of שִׁיר dec. 1 a.   שיר

בַּשָּׂרִים   noun masc., pl. of בָּשָׂר dec. 4 a.   בשר

בַּשָּׂרִים   pref. בְּ)(noun masc., pl. of שַׂר (§ 37. r. 7)   שרר

בְּשִׁרִים   ו pref. id.)(noun masc., pl. of שִׁיר dec. 1 a.   שיר

בְּשִׁרִירוּת   pref. בְּ before)(noun fem. sing.   שרר

בְּשִׁרִירֵי   pref. id.)(adj. m. pl. constr. from [שָׁרִיר] d. 3 a.   שרר

בְּשָׂרְךָ   noun masc. sing., suff. 2 pers. sing. masc.; ו from בָּשָׂר dec. 4 a; ו before   בשר

בְּשַׂרְכֶם   ו id., suff. 2 pers. pl. masc.; ו id.   בשר

בִּשְׂרָם   ו id., suff. 3 pers. pl. masc.; ו id.   בשר

בְּשָׂרֵנוּ   id., suff. 1 pers. pl.   בשר

בִּשְׂרֵין   pref. בְּ for בְּהְ)(noun masc. sing.   שרר

בְּשָׁרְרוּת   defect. for בְּשָׁרִירוּת (q. v.)   שרר

בַּשַּׂרְשְׂרוֹת   pref. בְּ for בְּהְ)(n. f., pl. of [שַׁרְשְׂרָה] dec. 10.   שרר

בִּשַּׂרְתָּ   ו Piel pret. 2 pers. sing. masc.; acc. shifted by conv. ו, before labial for וְ (§ 8. rem. 7)   בשר

בִּשַּׂרְתִּי   id. pret. 1 pers. sing.   בשר

בְּשָׁרֵתָם   pref. בְּ)(Piel inf. (שָׁרֵת), suff. 3 p. pl. m. d. 7 b.   שרת

בְּשֵׁשׁ   ו pref. בְּ for בְּהְ)(noun masc. s.; ו bef. lab.   שש

בְּשֵׁשׁ   pref. בְּ)(num. card. fem.   שש

בִּשֵּׁשׁ   Pilel pret. 3 pers. sing. masc.   בוש

בְּשִׂשֹּׁן   pref. בְּ)(noun m. s. dec. 3 a. (§ 32. rem. 6)   שוש

בַּשִּׁשִּׁי   pref. בְּ for בְּהְ)(adj. ordin. masc. from שֵׁשׁ   שש

בְּשִׁשִּׁים   ו pref. בְּ)(num. card. com., pl. of שֵׁשׁ   שש

בַּשָּׁשָׂר   pref. בְּ for בְּהְ)(noun masc. sing. [for שָׂשָׂר   שש

בֹּשֶׁת   ו n. f. s. dec. 13 c. (§ 39. No. 4); ו bef. lab.   בוש

בֹּשְׁתְּ   ו Kal pret. 2 p. s. f. (§ 21. r. 2); for ו see lett. ו   בוש

בָּשְׁתִּי   ו noun f. s., suff. 1 pers. s. from בֹּשֶׁת (q. v.)   בוש

בְּשֶׁתִּי   pref. בְּ for בְּהְ   noun masc. sing.   שתה

בְּשִׁתִּי   pref. בְּ bef.)(

בִּשְׁתַּיִם   ו construct of בִּשְׁתַּיִם (q. v.)   שנה

בֹּשְׁתִּי   Kal pret. 1 pers. sing. (§ 21. rem. 2)   בוש

בִּשְׁתַּיִם   ו pref. בְּ before)(num. card., constr. שְׁתֵּי, fem. of שְׁנַיִם ; ו before labial   שנה

בִּשְׁתֵּים   pref. id.)(id., constr. state, only bef. עֲשָׂרָה   שנה

a Job 36. 18.   f Pr. 10. 13.   m Ne. 9. 1.   q Je. 20. 15.   v Joel 3. 5.   a Job 40. 16.   k Le. 11. 29.   p Eze. 16. 10.   u Ps. 69. 20.
b 2 Sa. 20. 22.   h Is. 29. 13.   n Is. 28. 15.   r Is. 44. 15.   w Pr. 25. 20.   b Ec. 5. 5.   l 2 Ch. 2. 16.   q 2 Ch. 12. 3.   v Le. 13. 48.
c Da. 6. 20.   i Le. 5. 4.   o Je. 23. 32.   s Nu. 19. 5.   x Pr. 14. 30.   c Ju. 8. 7.   m 2 Sa. 18. 20.   r Ps. 44. 16.   w Ju. 16. 3.
d Pr. 26. 24.   k Ge. 30. 38.   p Is. 54. 8.   t Je. 17. 16.   y Pr. 19. 10.   d Ju. 9. 2.   n Ps. 40. 10.   s Je. 2. 36.   x Eze. 43. 16.
e Ps. 59. 8.   l Is. 54. 8.   u Je. 5. 10.   z Ge. 31. 27.   Nu. 18. 18.   o Eze. 44. 17.   t Eze. 16. 63.   y 2 Ch. 34. 3.
f Pa. 45. 3.   n Ge. 42. 35.

בּֽשְׁתְּכֶם‹	noun fem. sing., suff. 2 pers. pl. masc. from בּשֶׁת dec. 13 c. (§ 39. No. 4) . . בוש
בְּשֶׁתָּם	id. with suff. 3 pers. pl. masc. . . בוש
בָּת‹	Chald. Peal pret. 3 pers. s. m.; ּו bef. lab. בות
בַּת‹	noun fem. sing. irr., pl. בָּנוֹת (§ 45); also pr. name in compos. as בַּת־רַבִּים, &c. בנה
בַּת‹	noun masc. sing. dec. 8 d. . . בתת
בַּתְּאֵנָה‹	pref. בְּ for בְּהַ } noun fem. sing. dec. 10. . תאן
בִּתְאֵנָה‹	pref. בְּ bef. (ְ) }
בַּתֵּבָה‹	pref. בְּ for בַּה)(noun fem. sing. dec. 10. תבה
בִּתְבוּאֹת‹	pref. id.)(noun fem., pl. of תְּבוּאָה dec. 10. בוא
בִּתְבוּאַת‹	ּו pref. בְּ bef. (ְ))(id. sing., constr. st.; ּו bef. lab. בוא
בִּתְבוּנָה	ּו pref. id.)(noun fem. sing. dec. 10; ּו id. בין
בִּתְבוּנוֹת	ּו pref. id.)(id. pl.; ּו id. בין
בִּתְבוּנָם‹	pref. id.)(n.m.s., suff.3 p.pl.m.fr.[תָּבוּן] d.3 a. בין
בִּתְבוּנָתוֹ	ּו pref. id.)(noun fem. sing., suff. 3 pers. sing. masc. from תְּבוּנָה dec. 10; ּו before lab. בין
בִּתְבוּנָתֶךָ	ּו pref. id.)(id., suff. 2 pers. sing. masc.; ּו id. בין
בְּתֵבֵל‹	pref. בְּ)(noun fem. sing. . . יבל
בְּתַבְנִית	pref. id.)(noun fem. sing. dec. 1 b. בנה
בְּתַבְנִיתָם‹	pref. id.)(id., suff. 3 pers. pl. masc. בנה
בְּתַבְעֵרָה	ּו pref. id.)(pr. name of a place; ּו before (ְ) בער
בְּתֵבֵץ‹	pref. id.)(pr. name of a place, see תֵּבֵץ .
בְּתִדְיָרָא‹	Ch. pref. בְּ bef. (ְ))(properly noun fem. s., with the pref. as an adv. . . דור
בָּתָה‹	noun fem. sing., as if fr. בּוּת or בָּתָה see בתת
בָּתָּהּ‹	ּו noun fem. sing., suff. 3 pers. sing. fem. from בַּת irr. (§ 45); ּו bef. lab. בנה
בַּתֹּהוּ‹	pref. בְּ for בְּהַ } noun masc. sing.; ּו bef. (ְ) . תהה
בְּתֹהוּ‹	ּו pref. בְּ q. v. }
בַּתְּהִלָּה‹	pref. בְּ bef. (ְ))(noun fem. sing. dec. 10. הלל
בִּתְהִלָּתֶךָ‹	pref. id.)(id., suff. 2 p. s. m. (for תְּהִלָּתֶךָ) הלל
בַּתְּהֹמוֹת‹	pref. בְּ for בְּהַ)(noun com. with pl. fem. term. from תְּהוֹם dec. 1 a. הום
בְּתַהְפֻּכוֹת‹	pref. בְּ)(noun fem., pl. of [תַּהְפּוּכָה] d. 10. הפך
בִּתּוֹ‹	ּו noun fem. sing. with suff. 3 pers. sing. masc. from בַּת irr. (§ 45); ּו bef. lab. בנה
בְּתוּאֵל	(for בְּתוּל אֵל set apart of God, comp. בָּתַל) pr. name.—I. of the father of Laban.—II. of a place in the tribe of Simeon, 1 Ch. 4. 30, called בָּתוּל Jos. 19. 4.
בְּתוֹדָה‹	pref. בְּ)(noun fem. sing. dec. 10. . ידה
בְּתוֹדוֹת‹	ּו pref. id.)(id. pl.; ּו bef. (ְ) ידה
בַּתָּוֶךְ‹	pref. בְּ for בְּהַ)(noun masc. sing. dec. 6 g. תוך
בְּתוֹךְ‹	ּו pref. id.)(id. const. state; ּו bef. (ְ) תוך
בְּתוֹכָהּ‹	pref. id.)(id., suff. 3 pers. sing. fem. תוך

בְּתוֹכֹה‹	pref. id.)(id., suff. 3 pers. sing. masc. תוך
בְּתוֹכֶהְנָה‹	pref. id.)(id., suff. 3 pers. pl. f. (§ 3. r. 5) תוך
בְּתוֹכוֹ	pref. id.)(id., suff. 3 pers. sing. masc. תוך
בְּתוֹכָחוֹת‹	pref. id.)(n. f., pl. abs. fr. תּוֹכַחַת (§ 44. r. 5) יכח
בְּתוֹכְחוֹת‹	pref. id.)(id. pl., constr. state . יכח
בְּתוֹכַחְתּוֹ‹	pref. id.)(id. sing., suff. 3 pers. sing. masc. (prop. fr. תּוֹכַחַת dec. 13 a) . . יכח
בְּתוֹכִי‹	pref. id.)(noun masc. sing., suff. 1 pers. sing. from תָּוֶךְ dec. 6 g. . . . תוך
בְּתוֹכֵךְ‹	pref. id.)(id., suff. 2 pers. sing. fem. } תוך
בְּתוֹכֵכִי‹	(§ 3. rem. 2) . . . }
בְּתוֹכְכֶם‹	pref. id.)(id. with suff. 2 pers. pl. masc. } תוך
בְּתוֹכֲכֶם‹	}
בְּתוֹכָם‹	pref. id.)(id., suff. 3 p. pl. m.; ּו bef. (ְ) תוך
בְּתוֹכֵנוּ	pref. בְּ)(id. with suff. 1 pers. pl. תוך
בְּתוּל‹	contr. for בְּתוּאֵל q. v.
בְּתוֹלַד‹	ּו pref. בְּ)(pr. name of a place; ּו bef. (ְ) ילד
בְּתוּלָה‹	ּו noun fem. sing. dec. 10; ּו bef. (ְ) . בתל
בְּתוּלוֹת‹	pl. of the prec. . . . בתל
בְּתוּלַי‹	noun m. pl., suff. 1 pers. s. fr. [בְּתוּל] d. 1 a. בתל
בְּתוּלַי‹	id. pl., constr. state . . . בתל
בְּתוּלֶיהָ	id. pl., suff. 3 pers. sing. fem. בתל
בְּתוּלֵיהֶן	id. pl., suff. 3 pers. pl. fem. בתל
בְּתוּלִים	id. pl., absolute state . . . בתל
בַּתּוֹלָעַת‹	ּו pref. בְּ)(noun fem. s. d. 13 a; ּו bef. (ְ) תלע
בְּתוּלַת‹	noun fem. sing., constr. of בְּתוּלָה dec. 10. בתל
בְּתוּלֹת‹	id. pl. of the prec. . . . בתל
בְּתוּלֹתַי	id. pl., suff. 1 pers. sing. . בתל
בִּתְלוֹתֶיהָ‹	id., suff. 3 pers. sing. fem. . בתל
בְּתוּלֹתָיו‹	ּו id., suff. 3 pers. sing. masc.; ּו bef. (ְ) בתל
בַּתֹּם‹	pref. בְּ for בְּהַ)(for תֹם, noun m. s. d. 8 c. תמם
בְּתוֹעֲבוֹתָם‹	pref. בְּ)(noun fem. pl., suff. 3 pers. pl. masc. (§ 4. rem. 2) fr. תּוֹעֵבָה dec. 11 b. תעב
בְּתוֹעֲבֹת‹	pref. id.)(id. pl., absolute state . תעב
בְּתוֹעֲבֹתֵיהֶם‹	pref. id.)(id. pl., suff. 3 pers. pl. masc. תעב
בַּתּוֹרָה‹	ּו pref. בְּ for בְּהַ)(n. f. s. d. 10; ּו bef. lab. ירה
בַּתּוֹרִים‹	pref. id.)(noun masc., pl. of תּוֹר dec. 1 a. תור
בְּתוֹרַת‹	pref. בְּ)(noun f. s. constr. of תּוֹרָה d. 10. ירה
בְּתוֹרָתוֹ‹	ּו pref. בְּ)(id., suff. 3 pers. s. m.; ּו bef. (ְ) ירה
בְּתוֹרָתִי‹	pref. id.)(id., suff. 1 pers. sing. . ירה
בְּתוֹרֹתָיו‹	pref. id.)(id. pl., suff. 3 pers. sing. masc. ירה
בִּתְזְנוּתַיִךְ‹	pref. בְּ)(noun fem. pl., suff. 2 pers. } זנה
בְּתַזְנוּתַיִךְ‹	sing. fem. from [תַּזְנוּת] dec. 1 b. . }
בְּתַזְנוּתָם‹	pref. id.)(id. sing., suff. 3 pers. pl. masc. זנה

ᵃ Is. 61. 7.   ᵍ Ge. 47. 24.   ᵐ Ps. 106. 20.   ˢ Ps. 100. 4.   ᵃ Ps. 39. 12.   ᶠ Nu. 16. 3.   ˡ Ex. 35. 35.   ᵍ Eze. 43. 8.   ᵐ Is. 42. 24.
ᵇ Da. 6. 19.   ʰ Pr. 15. 6.   ⁿ Ex. 25. 40.   ᵗ Pr. 2. 14.   ᵇ Eze. 25. 17.   ᵍ Ju. 11. 37.   ᵐ Ex. 38. 23.   ʰ De. 32. 16.   ⁿ Da. 9. 10.
ᶜ Eze. 45. 10.   ⁱ Ps. 78. 72.   ᵒ Da. 6. 17, 19.   ᵘ Ne. 12. 27.   ᶜ Pr. 3. 11.   ʰ De. 22. 15, 17.   ⁿ La. 1. 4.   ⁱ Ezr. 9. 11.   ᵒ Eze. 16. 33.
ᵈ Je. 8. 13.   ᵏ Ho. 13. 2.   ᵖ Is. 5. 6.   ᵛ Is. 5. 6.   ᵈ Ps. 143. 4.   ⁱ Eze. 48. 15, 21.   ᵒ Ps. 78. 63.   ᵏ 2 Ch. 31. 21.   ᵖ Eze. 16. 34, 36
ᵉ Ho. 9. 10.   ˡ Eze. 28. 4.   ᵠ Le. 18. 17.   ʷ Eze. 16. 53.   ᵉ Eze. 6. 7.   ᵏ Eze. 23. 8, ect.   ᵖ Eze. 23. 3.   ˡ Ca. 1. 10.   ᵠ Eze. 23. 17.
ᶠ Ge. 8. 1.   ᵐ Pr. 8. 31.   ʳ De. 32. 10.   ᵉ Eze. 23. 3.   ᶠ Pr. 10. 9.

בְּתַחְבֻּלֹתָו	pref. בְּ ✗ noun fem. pl., suff. 3 pers. pl. m. (§ 4. r. 2) from [תַּחְבּוּלָה] dec. 10.	חבל
בְּתַחְבֻּלוֹת	pref. id. ✗ id. pl., absolute st.; ו bef. (:)	חבל
בְּתַחֲלֻאִים	pref. בְּ ✗ noun m., pl. of [תַּחֲלוּא] d. 1 b.	חלא
בַּתְּחִלָּה	pref. בַּ for בְּהַ ✗ noun fem. sing. dec. 10.	חלל
בִּתְחִלַּת	pref. בְּ bef. (:) ✗ id., constr. state	חלל
בְּתַחֲנוּנִים	ו pref. בְּ ✗ noun masc., pl. of [תַּחֲנוּן] dec. 1b; ו bef. (:)	חנן
בְּתַחְפַּנְחֵס	ו pref. בְּ bef. (:) pr. name of a place, see תַּחְפַּנְחֵם	
בְּתַחְפַּנְחֵם	ו pref. בְּ q. v.	
בְּתָחַת	pref. id. ✗ pr. name of a place, for תַּחַת	תוח
בְּתַחְתִּיֹּות	pref. id. ✗ pl. of the following	תוח
בְּתַחְתִּיר	pref. id. ✗ adj. fem. sing. from [תַּחְתִּי] m.	תוח
בָּתֵּי	ו noun masc. pl., constr. of בָּתִּים irr. of בַּיִת (§ 45); ו before labial	בית
בִּתִּי	noun f. s., suff. 1 pers. s. fr. בַּת irr. (§45)	בנה
בִּתְיָה	pr. name fem.	בנה
בָּתֵּיהֶם	ו noun masc. pl. (בָּתִּים), suff. 3 pers. pl. masc. irr. of בַּיִת (§ 45); ו bef. labial	בית
בָּתֵּיהֶן	ו id., suff. 3 pers. pl. fem.; ו id.	בית
בָּתָּיו	ו id., suff. 3 pers. sing. masc.	בית
בָּתֵּךְ	id., suff. 2 pers. sing. fem.	בית
בָּתֵּיךָ	id., suff. 2 pers. sing. masc.	בית
בָּתֵּיכוֹן	ו Ch. id., suff. 2 pers. pl. masc.; ו bef. lab.	בית
בָּתֵּיכֶם	ו Heb. id., suff. 2 pers. pl. masc.; ו id.	בית
בָּתִּים	ו id. pl., absolute state; ו id.	בית
בָּתִּים	noun masc., pl. of בַּת dec. 8d.	בתת
בָּתֵּימוֹ	noun masc. pl. (בָּתִּים), suff. 3 pers. pl. masc. from בַּיִת, irr. (§ 45)	בית
בְּתֵימָן	pref. בְּ ✗ pr. name of a region	ימן
בַּתִּין	Chald. noun masc., pl. of בַּת dec. 5a.	בתת
בָּתֵּינוּ	ו noun masc. pl. (בָּתִּים), suff. 1 pers. pl. from בַּיִת irr. (§ 45); ו before labial	בות
בִּתֶּךָ / בִּתְּךָ	noun fem. sing., suff. 2 pers. sing. masc. from בַּת, irr. (§ 45); ו bef. lab.	בנה
בְּתוֹכְחוֹת	ו pref. בְּ ✗ noun fem. pl., constr. of תּוֹכָחוֹת from תּוֹכַחַת (§ 44. rem. 5); ו id.	יכח
בְּתוֹכְכֶם	pref. id. ✗ noun masc. sing., suff. 2 pers. pl. masc. from תָּוֶךְ dec. 6g.	תוך
בַּתְּכֵלֶת	pref. בַּ for בְּהַ ✗ noun fem. sing.	תכל
בְּתוֹכְכֶם	pref. בְּ ✗ noun masc. sing., suff. 3 pers. pl. masc. from תָּוֶךְ dec. 6g.	תוך

בְּתֻל Root not used; Arab. *to separate.*
בְּתוּלָה fem. dec. 10.—I. *a virgin.*—II. applied to cities and countries, comp. בַּת.

בְּתוּלִים	masc. pl. (of בָּתוּל) dec. 1a.—I. *virginity.*—II. *tokens of virginity,* De. 22. 14, 15, &c.	
בִּתְלָאשָׁר	pref. בְּ bef. (:) ✗ pr. n. of a region, see תְּלָאשָׁר	
בְּתוּלֹת	noun fem., pl. of בְּתוּלָה dec. 10.	בתל
בְּתַלְמֵי	pref. בְּ ✗ noun m. sing. (pl. c. תַּלְמֵי) dec. 6a. pr. name of a place; see תְּלָאשָׁר	תלם
בְּתוּלֹת	noun fem., pl. of בְּתוּלָה dec. 10.	בתל
בְּתָם	pref. בְּ ✗ bef. Mak. for תֹּם noun m. s. d. 8 c.	תמם
בַּתֻּמֶּיהוֹן	pref. בַּ for בְּהַ ✗ noun masc. sing. dec. 3c.	תמה
בִּתְמֵיהוֹן	ו pref. בְּ ✗ id. construct state; ו bef. (:)	תמה
בְּתֻמֹּו	pref. בְּ ✗ noun masc. sing., suff. 3 pers. sing. masc. from תֹּם dec. 8c.	תמם
בְּתֻמִּי	pref. id. ✗ id. with suff. 1 pers. sing.	תמם
בִּתְמִים	ו pref. בְּ ✗ adj. m. sing. dec. 3a; ו bef. (:)	תמם
בְּתִמְנַת	pref. id. ✗ pr. name in compos. תִּמְ חֶרֶם &c.	מנה
בְּתִמְנָתָה	pref. id. ✗ pr. name of a place, (תִּמְנַת) with paragogic ה	מנה
בְּתָמָר	pref. בְּ ✗ noun masc. sing. dec. 4a.	תמר
בְּתַמְרוּקֵי	ו pref. id. ✗ noun masc. pl. constr. from תַּמְרוּק dec. 1b; ו bef. (:)	מרק
בְּתִמְרָתוֹ	pref. id. ✗ noun fem. sing., suff. 3 pers. sing. masc. from תִּמָּרָה dec. 10.	תמם
בְּתִמְנָתֶךָ	pref. id. ✗ id., suff. 2 pers. s. m. [for תִּמְנָתְךָ]	תמם
בִּתְּנוּ	n. fem. s., suff. 1 pers. pl. from בַּת, irr. (§ 45)	בנה
בִּתְנוּמוֹת	pref. בְּ bef. (:) ✗ n. fem., pl. of תְּנוּמָה d. 10.	נום
בַּתַּנּוּר	pref. בַּ f. בְּהַ ✗	תנר
בְּתַנּוּר	pref. בַּ q. v. } noun masc. sing. 1b.	תנר
בְּתַנּוּרֶיךָ	ו pref. בְּ ✗ id. pl., suff. 2 p. s. m.; ו bef. (:)	תנר
בִּתְעוּת	pref. בְּ bef. (:) ✗ Kal inf. constr.	תעה
בַּתַּעֲלָה	pref. בְּ for בְּהַ ✗ noun fem. sing. dec. 10.	עלה
בְּתַעֲלוּלֵיהֶם	pref. בְּ ✗ noun masc. pl., suff. 3 pers. pl. masc. from [תַּעֲלוּל] dec. 1b.	עלל
בְּתַעֲלַת	pref. בְּ bef. (:) ✗ noun fem. sing., constr. of תְּעָלָה dec. 10.	עלה
בַּתַּעֲנוּגִים	pref. בְּ for בְּהַ ✗ noun m., pl. of תַּעֲנוּג d. 1b.	ענג
בְּתַעֲנָךְ	pref. בְּ ✗ pr. name of a place, see תַּעֲנָךְ	
בְּתַעַר	pref. בְּ ✗ n. m. s. comp. dec. 6d [for תַּעֲרָה]	ערה
בְּתַעְרָה	pref. בְּ ✗ id. suff. 3 pers. sing. masc. [for תַּעֲרָה comp. § 35. rem. 5].	ערה
בְּתֹף	pref. id. ✗ noun masc. sing. dec. 8c.	תפף
בַּתַּפּוּחִים	pref. בַּ for בְּהַ ✗ noun m., pl. of תַּפּוּחַ d. 1b.	נפח
בְּתֻפִּים	ו pref. בְּ ✗ n. m., pl. of תֹּף d. 8c; ו bef. (:)	תפף
בַּתְּפִלָּה	pref. בַּ for בְּהַ ✗ noun fem. sing. dec. 10.	פלל
בִּתְפִלַּת	pref. בְּ bef. (:) ✗ id., construct state	פלל
בְּתִפְשָׂם	pref. בְּ ✗ Kal inf., suff. 3 pers. pl. masc.	תפש
בְּתֹפֶת	ו pref. id. ✗ pr. name of a place; ו bef. (:)	תוף

a Job 37. 12. | f Ex. 19. 17. | l Da. 2. 5. | q Job 2. 1. | * De. 28. 28. | b Est. 2. 12. | f Job 33. 15. | t 1 Ki. 18. 38. | a Ca. 2. 5.
b Pr. 24. 6. | g Eze. 23. 47. | m Ps. 49. 12. | r Zec. 9. 17. | * Pr. 28. 6. | c Job 2. 3. | g Le. 7. 9. | s Is. 66. 4. | b Da. 9. 21.
c 2 Ch. 21. 19. | h 1 Ch. 28. 11. | n Ezr. 7. 22, 22. | s Job 39. 10. | * Ju. 9. 16, 19. | d Job 2. 9. | h Le. 26. 26. | * Ca. 7. 7. | c Ps. 80. 5.
d 2 Ch. 21. 19. | i Eze. 16. 41. | o Ne. 5. 3. | t La. 5. 11. | * Ca. 7. 9. | e Ge. 34. 17. | i Ex. 7. 28. | 2 Sa. 20. 8. | e Eze. 20. 7.
e Je. 31. 9. | k Ex. 10. 6. | p Eze. 5. 15. | u Zec. 12. 4.

בָּתַק Pi. *to cut, pierce,* only in the following form—

וּבִתְּקוּךָ[a] Piel pret. 3 p. pl., suff. 2 p. s. fem.; וּ bef. lab.   בתק

בִתְקוֹמְמֶיךָ[b] וּ pref. בְּ bef. (ּ) (noun masc. pl., suff. 2 pers. s. m. from [תְּקוֹמֵם] d. 7 b; וּ bef. lab.   קום

בַּתְּקוֹעַ[c] pref. בַּ for בְּהַ (noun masc. sing.   תקע

בִתְקוֹעַ[d] וּ pref. בְּ bef. (ּ) (pr. n. of a place; וּ bef. lab.   תקע

בְּתֶקַע[e] pref. בְּ (noun masc. sing.   תקע

בְּתֹקְעֵי[f] pref. id. (Kal part. act. m. pl. c. fr. תֹּקֵעַ d. 7 b.   תקע

בְּתֹקֶף[f] pref. id. (noun masc. sing. dec. 6 c.   תקף

בִּתְקָף[g] Chald. pref. בְּ bef. (ּ) (noun masc. sing., a better reading is בִּתְקָף   תקף

[בָּתַר] *to cut in pieces, to divide,* Ge. 15. 10. Pi. id. ibid.
בֶּתֶר m. dec. 6 a. (suff. בִּתְרוֹ, but in pause בָּתֶר § 35. r. 2).—I. *piece, part.*—II. *separation,* Ca. 2. 17.

בִּתְרוֹן (*section*) pr. name of a place on the Jordan, 2 Sa. 2. 29.

בָּתַר[a] Kal pret. 3 pers. s. m. [for בָּתַר § 8. rem. 7]   בתר

בִּתְרִי[b] noun masc. sing. for [בֶּתֶר § 35. rem. 2] dec. 6 a, but with suff. בִּתְרוֹ; also pr. name   בתר

וְתַרְבִּיתָ[a] וּ Kh. preff. בְ & וּ bef. lab.; K. וְתַרְבִּית n. f. s.   רבה

בִּתְרוֹ[b] noun masc. sing., suff. 3 pers. sing. masc. from [בֶּתֶר] dec. 6 a.   בתר

בִּתְרוּמַת[a] pref. בְּ bef. (ּ) (n. f., constr. of תְּרוּמָה d. 10.   רום

בִתְרוּעָה[a] וּ pref. id. (noun fem. sing. d. 10; וּ bef. lab.   רוע

בְּתֹרוֹתֶיךָ[a] וּ pref. בְּ (Kh. תֹרוֹתֶךָ, K. תֹרֹתֶךָ, n. fem. pl. or s., suff. 2 p. s. m. from תּוֹרָה d. 10; וּ id.   ירה

בְּתָרַח[a] pref. id. (pr. name of a place, for תֶּרַח   תרח

בְּתָרֵי[a] noun masc. pl. constr. from [בֶּתֶר] dec. 6 a.   בתר

בִּתְרָיו[b] id. pl., suff. 3 pers. sing. masc.   בתר

בְּאַתְרָךְ[c] Ch. [for בְּאַתְרָךְ] pref. בְּ; n. m. s., suff. 2 pers. s. m. from אֲתַר dec. 3 a; וּ bef. lab.   אתר

בִּתְרֻמָה[d] pref. בְּ (noun fem. sing.   רמה

בַּתְּרֻמִית[e] pref. בַּ for בְּהַ (noun fem. sing. dec. 1 b.   רמה

בִּתְרַע[f] Chald. pref. בְּ bef. (ּ) (noun masc. sing.   תרע

בִּתְרָפִים[g] pref. בְּ for בְּהַ (noun masc. pl.   תרף

בְּתִרְצָה[h] pref. בְּ (pr. name of a place.   רצה

בַּתִּרְשִׁישׁ[i] pref. בַּ for בְּהַ (noun masc. sing.   רשש

בְתֹרָתוֹ[j] וּ pref. בְּ (noun fem. sing. with suff. 3 pers. sing. masc. from תּוֹרָה dec. 10; וּ bef. lab.   ירה

בִּתְשֻׁמֶת[k] pref. בְּ bef. (ּ) (noun fem. sing.   ישום

בְּתִשְׁעָה[l] pref. בְּ (num. card. masc. from תֵּשַׁע fem.   תשע

בָּתַת Root not used; Arab. *to cut; to mark out, define.*

בַּת com. dec. 8 d, *bath,* a measure for liquids, the tenth part of an homer.

בַּת Chald. dec. 5 a, idem.

בָּתָּה fem. (for בַּתָּה) *excision, desolation,* Is. 5. 6.

בַּתָּה fem. dec. 10, *clefts, fissures,* Is. 7. 19.

בְּתֵת pref. בְּ (contr. for [תֵּנֶת § 17. r. 9], Kal inf. construct dec. 8 b.

בְּתִתּוֹ[a] pref. id. (id., suff. 3 pers. sing. masc.   נתן

בְּתִתִּי[b] pref. id. (id., suff. 1 pers. sing.   נתן

בְּתִתֵּךְ[c] וּ pref. id. (id., suff. 2 pers. s. fem.; וּ bef. (ּ)   נתן

בְּתִתְּךָ pref. id. (id., suff. 2 pers. sing. masc.   נתן

בְּתִתָּם[d] pref. id. (id., suff. 3 pers. pl. masc.   נתן

נ

גֵּא[a] adj. masc. sing. [for גֵּאֶה]   נאה

גָּאָה[b] I. *to grow up, to increase,* of a plant, of water.—II. *to be lifted, exalted, majestic.*

גֵּא adj. masc. *proud,* Is. 16. 6.

גֵּאֶה adj. masc. dec. 9 b. (§ 38. Nos. 1 & 2).—I. *lifted up, high.*—II. *proud, haughty.*

גֵּאָה fem. *pride, haughtiness,* Pr. 8. 13.

גֵּאוּת fem. (constr. גַּאֲוַת; no pl.)—I. *exaltation, majesty.*—II. *ornament, splendour.*—III. *pride, arrogance.*

גְּאוּאֵל (*majesty of God*) pr. name m. Nu. 13. 15.

גָּאוֹן masc. dec. 3 a.—I. *excellency, majesty.*—II. *ornament, splendour.*—III. *pride, arrogance.*

גֵּאוּת fem.—I. *a rising up, ascending,* Is. 9. 17.—

II. *majesty.*—III. *ornament, splendour.*—IV. *pride, arrogance.*

גֵּאֶיוֹן adj. masc. *proud,* Ps. 123. 4. Kheth; Keri
גֵּאֵי יוֹנִים *proud oppressors.*

גֵּוָה fem. (contr. for גֵּאֲוָה).—I. *exaltation,* Job 22. 29.—II. *pride, arrogance.*

גֵּוָה Chald. *pride,* Da. 4. 34.

גֵּאֹה[e] Kal inf. abs.   נאה

גֵּאָה[f] noun fem. sing.   נאה

גֵּאֶה adj. masc. sing. dec. 9 b. (§ 38. Nos. 1 & 2)   נאה

גָּאוּ[g] Kal pret. 3 pers. pl.   נאה

גְּאוּאֵל[h] pr. name masc.   נאה

גֵּאֲוָה[i] noun fem. sing. dec. 10.   נאה

גְּאוּלַי[j] Kal part. p. pl. masc., suff. 1 pers. sing., from [גָּאוּל] dec. 3 a.   נאל

---

a Eze. 16. 40.   c Pr. 22. 26.   i Ca. 2. 17.   n 2 Ch. 1b. 14.   j Da. 2. 39.   e Eze. 21. 26.   b Le. 20. 4.   b Is. 16. 6.   e Pr. 8. 13.
b Ps. 139. 21.   d Da. 11. 17.   k Pr. 25. 8.   o Ju. 9. 31.   c Ca. 5. 14.   c Eze. 16. 34.   c Ex. 15. 1, 21.   Eze. 47. 5.
c Eze. 7. 14.   e Da. 4. 27.   l Ge. 15. 10.   p Je. 34. 19.   d Je. 44. 23.   d Eze. 43. 3.   d Ex. 15. 1.   f Is. 62. 4.
d Ps. 150. 3.   f Ge. 15. 10.   m Le. 22. 12.   q Je. 34. 18.   Le. 5. 21.   Da. 2. 49.

נֹאֲלֵ id. pl., construct state . . . . נאל

וְנֹאֲלָיו } Kal part. act. pl. masc., suff. 3 pers. sing. masc. from נֹאַל dec. 7 b . נאל

נְּאוּלִים Kal part. act. masc. pl. of [נָּאוּל] dec. 3 a . נאל

נָּאוֹן noun masc. sing. dec. 3 a . נאה

נְּאוֹן id., construct state . . . . נאה

נְּאוֹנוֹ id., suff. 3 pers. sing. masc.; וֹ bef. (ּ) נאה

נְּאוֹנַיִךְ id. pl., suff. 2 pers. sing. fem. [for עֵנִיִךְ] . נאה

נְּאוֹנֶךָ } נְּאוֹנֵךְ } id., suff. 2 pers. sing. masc. נאה

נְּאוֹנָם id., suff. 3 pers. pl. masc. . נאה

נְּאֲוַת g וְ noun fem. sing., constr. of נַּאֲוָה (no pl.) נאה

נְּאֲוֹת noun fem. sing. נאה

נְּאֲוָתוֹ h וְ noun fem. sing. suff. 3 pers. sing. masc. from נַּאֲוָה (no pl.) . . . נאה

נְּאֲוָתִי id., suff. 1 pers. sing. נאה

נְּאֲוָתְךָ k id., suff. 2 pers. sing. masc. [for וָתְךָ] נאה

נְּאֲוָתֵךְ id., suff. 2 pers. sing. fem. נאה

נְּאֲיוֹת n. com. with pl. fem. term., irr. of נַיְא (§ 45) ניא

נֵּאִים adj. m., pl. of נָּאֶה d. 9 b. (§ 38. Nos. 1 & 2) נאה

I. נָּאַל *וְ* I. *to redeem, ransom, recover, by paying back the value for.*—II. *to retribute, to avenge;* part. נֹּאֵל *redeemer, avenger, nearest kinsman,* to whom was assigned the right of redemption and the duty of avenging the death of any one. Niph. *to be redeemed, ransomed.*

II. נָּאַל. Niph. *to be polluted, stained,* Zep. 3. 1. Pi. *to pollute,* Mal. 1. 7. Pu. *to be polluted,* Mal. 1. 7, 12. Hiph. *to soil, stain,* Is. 63. 3. Hithpa. *to defile oneself,* Da. 1. 8.

נֹּאֵל masc. *pollution,* only Ne. 13. 29. נֹּאֲלֵי comp. dec. 6 f.

נְּאֻלָּה fem. dec. 10.—I. *redemption, purchase.*—II. *duty, right of redemption.*—III. *price of redemption.*—IV. *thing redeemed,* Ru. 4. 6.—V. *relationship,* Eze. 11. 15.

יִנְאַל (*He* (God) *will redeem* him) pr. name of several men.

נָּאֹל Kal inf. abs. . . . . . נאל

נְּאַל } נְּאָל } id. imp. masc. sing. נאל

נֹּאֵל id. part. act. masc. sing. dec. 7 b. נאל

נְּאָלָהּ id. imp. m. s. (נְּאַל) suff. 3 p. s. f. (§ 16. r. 11) נאל

נְּאֻלָּה noun fem. sing. dec. 10. . נאל

נְּאָלוֹ וּ Kal pret. 3 pers. sing. masc., suff. 3 pers. sing. masc.; וֹ bef. (ּ) . . . נאל

נְּאָלוֹ *וְ* id. part. act. sing. masc. with suff. 3 pers. sing. masc. from נֹּאֵל dec. 7 b. . . נאל

נֹּאֲלֵי noun m. pl. constr. from [נֹּאֵל] comp. dec. 6 f. נאל

נֹּאֲלִי Kal part. act. sing. masc., suff. 1 pers. sing. from נֹּאֵל dec. 7 b. . . . נאל

נְּאָלְךָ × } נְּאָלֶךָ } id. s., suff. 2 pers. sing. m. (§ 36. rem. 3) נאל

נְּאָלֵךְ וְ id. id., suff. 2 pers. sing. fem. נאל

נְּאָלְכֶם id., suff. 2 pers. pl. masc. (§ 36. rem. 3) . נאל

נְּאָלָם Kal pret. 3 pers. sing. m., suff. 3 pers. pl. m. נאל

נֹּאֲלָם id. part. act. sing. masc., suff. 3 pers. pl. masc. from נֹּאֵל dec. 7 b. . . . נאל

נְּאָלָנוּ id. id., suff. 1 pers. pl. . . . . נאל

נְּאָלְנֻךְ d Piel pret. 1 pers. pl., suff. 2 pers. sing. masc. נאל

נְּאָלֵנִי *וְ* Kal imp. sing. masc. (נְּאַל), suff. 1 pers. sing. (§ 16. rem. 10); וְ bef. (ּ) . . . נאל

נְּאַלְתָּ *ו* } נְּאַלְתְּ } id. pret. 2 pers. sing. masc. (§ 8. rem. 7) נאל

נְּאֻלַּת g noun fem. sing., constr. of נְּאֻלָּה dec. 10. נאל

נְּאֻלָּתוֹ h id., suff. 3 pers. sing. masc. נאל

נְּאַלְתִּי *וְ* Kal pret. 1 pers. sing.; acc. shifted by conv. וְ (§ 8. rem. 7) . . . . . נאל

נְּאֻלָּתִי noun m. sing., suff. 1 p. s. from נְּאֻלָּה dec. 10. נאל

נְּאַלְתִּיךָ Kal pret. 1 pers. sing., suff. 2 pers. sing. m. נאל

נְּאַלְתִּיךְ *ו* id. id., suff. 2 pers. fem. sing.; וְ bef. (ּ) נאל

נְּאֻלָּתְךָ m n. f. s., suff. 2 p. s. m. [for וָתְךָ] fr. נְּאֻלָּה d. 10. נאל

נְּאוֹנוֹ n. m. sing., suff. 3 pers. s. m. from נָּאוֹן d. 3 a. נאה

נֶּגֶב p } noun masc. sing. dec. 8 d. . . נגב

נָּבָא Root not used; Arab. *to gather together.*

נֵּבֶא masc. dec. 6 a.—I. *cistern,* Is. 30. 14.—II. *marsh, pool,* Eze. 47. 11.

נֶּבֶא noun masc. sing., emph. of נֵּב dec. 5 c. נבב

נְּבָאָיו *ו* noun masc. pl., suff. 3 pers. sing. masc. from נֵּבֶא dec. 6; וְ bef. (ּ) . . נבא

נָּבַב Root not used; in the deriv.—I. i. q. כָּפַף *to be curved.*—II. i. q. יָנַב *to dig.*

נַּב masc. dec. 8 d. (pl. נַּבִּים, נֹת.)—I. *a back.*—II. *boss of a shield or buckler,* Job 15. 26.—III. *defence, mound,* Job 13. 12.—IV. *vault.*—V. *the*

a 1 Ki. 16. 11.   f Pr. 29. 23.   l Zep. 3. 11.   r Ruth 4. 6.   x Ne. 13. 29.   b Is. 54. 8.   f Ex. 15. 13.   k Ex. 6. 6.   s Is. 2. 10.
b Eze. 16. 56.   g Is. 13. 11.   m Eze. 31. 12.   s Ps. 69. 19.   y Job 19. 25.   e Is. 43. 14.   g Is. 25. 32.   k Ruth 4. 6.   t Eze. 16. 24.
c Is. 14. 11.   h Je. 48. 29.   n Le. 25. 25.   t Je. 31. 11.   z Is. 44. 24.   d Mal. 1. 7.   h Le. 25. 26, 29,   l Ruth 3. 13.   p Eze. 43. 13.
d Ex. 15. 7.   i Is. 13. 3.   o Le. 27. 18, 19, 31.   u Le. 25. 25.   aa Is. 48. 17.   Ps. 119. 154.   29, 51, 52.   m Eze. 11. 15.   q Eze. 47. 11.
e Zep. 2. 10.   k De. 33. 29.   p Ruth 4. 4.   w Is. 44. 6.   bb Pr. 8. 13.

rim or *curvature of a wheel.*—VI. *arch of the eye-brow,* Le. 14. 9.

גַּב Chald. masc. dec. 5 a, *back,* Da. 7. 6.

גֹּב Chald. masc. dec. 5 c, *pit, den.*

גַּבַּי (*tax-gatherer* Chald. גְּבָא *to raise a tax*) pr. name masc. Ne. 11. 8.

גִּבְּתוֹן (*hilly,* from a form גִּבְעָה i. q. Chald. גִּבְעָא *hill*) pr. name of a town of the Philistines in the tribe of Dan.

גָּבַהּ ['] I. *to be high, lofty.*—II. *to be lifted up, exalted.*—III. *to be proud, arrogant.* Hiph. *to make high, to raise;* הַמַּגְבִּיהִי לָשָׁבֶת *who maketh high to dwell,* i. e. dwelleth on high; יַגְבִּיהוּ עוּף *they fly on high.*

גָּבֵהַּ adj. masc. dec. 4 a, *high, lofty, proud.*

גָּבְהַ, גָּבוֹהַּ masc. dec. 3 a. (constr. גְּבָהּ), fem. d. 10. adj.—I. *high, tall.*—II. *proud, arrogant.*

גֹּבַהּ masc. dec. 6 c. (§ 35. rem. 5.)—I. *height.*—II. *majesty,* Job 40. 10.—III. *pride, arrogance;* גֹּבַהּ אַף *height of nose,* i. e. *insolence.*

גַּבְהוּת fem. *pride, arrogance,* Is. 2. 11, 17.

יַגְבְּהָה (*elevation*) pr. name of a town in the tribe of Gad.

גָּבֹהַּ adj. masc. sing. dec. 3 a. . . . נבה

גְּבֹהַּ id., construct state . . . נבה

גֹּבַהּ ['], [']' noun masc. sing. dec. 6 c. (§ 35. rem. 5); for ו see lett. ו . .   נבה

גְּבֹהַּ ['] adj. masc. sing., constr. of [גָּבֹהַּ] dec. 4 a; ו before (ִ) . . נבה

גָּבְהָא Kal pret. 3 pers. s. fem. [for גָּבְהָה § 8. r. 3.] . נבה

גְּבֹהָה adj. fem. sing. dec. 10, from גָּבֹהַּ masc. . נבה

גָּבְהוּ noun masc. sing. suff. 3 pers. sing. masc. from גֹּבַהּ dec. 6 c. (§ 35. rem. 5) . נבה

גָּבְהוּ Kal pret. 3 pers. pl. . . נבה

גַּבְהוּת noun fem. sing. . . נבה

גְּבֹהוֹת adj. fem., pl of גְּבֹהָה dec. 10, fr. גָּבֹהַּ masc. . נבה

גְּבֹהִי n. m., pl. constr. of גֹּבַהּ d. 6 c. (§ 35. r. 5) . נבה

גְּבֹהִים ['] adj. masc., pl. of גָּבֹהַּ dec. 3 a; ו bef. (ִ) . נבה

גַּבְּהֶם ['] noun m. pl. [for גַּבֵּיהֶם] suff. 3 pers. pl. masc. from גַּב dec. 8 d. . נבב

גָּבַהְתָּ Kal pret. 2 pers. sing. masc. . נבה

גְּבֹהַ ['] adj. masc. sing. dec. 3 a. . נבה

נֵבֶל ['] noun masc. sing. dec. 1 a; ו bef. (ִ) . נבל

גִּבְלָה ['] id., suff. 3 pers. sing. fem.; ו id. . נבל

גִּבְלוֹ id., suff. 3 pers. sing. masc. . נבל

גְּבֻלוֹת noun fem., pl. of [גְּבוּלָה] dec. 10. . נבל

גְּבֻלַי noun fem. s., suff. 1 pers. s. fr. גְּבוּל d. 1 a. . נבל

גְּבֻלֶיהָ id. pl., suff. 3 pers. sing. fem. . . נבל

גְּבֻלַיִךְ id. pl. suff. 2 pers. sing. fem. [for לָיִךְ] . נבל

גְּבֻלֶיךָ id. pl. with suff. 2 pers. sing. masc. . נבל

גְּבֻלְךָ } id. sing., suff. 2 pers. sing. masc. . נבל
גְּבֻלְ־ }

גְּבֻלֵךְ id. sing., suff. 2 pers. sing. fem. . נבל

גְּבֻלְכֶם id. sing., suff. 2 pers. pl. masc. . נבל

גְּבֻלָם id. sing., suff. 3 pers. pl. masc. . נבל

גְּבֻלָן id. sing., suff. 3 pers. fem. pl. . בל

גְּבֻלֹת noun fem., pl. of [גְּבוּלָה] dec. 10. . נבל

נִבּוֹר ['] adj. masc. sing. dec. 1 b. . נבר

גְּבוּרָה ['] noun fem. sing. dec. 10; ו bef. (ּ) . נבר

גְּבוּרוֹת pl. of the preced. . נבר

גִּבּוֹרַי adj. m. pl., suff. 1 pers. sing. fr. גִּבּוֹר d. 1 b. . נבר

גִּבּוֹרֵי [']' id. pl., constr. state . . נבר

גְּבוּרֹתֶיהָ id. pl., suff. 3 pers. sing. fem. . נבר

גִּבּוֹרֵיהוּ id. pl., suff. 3 pers. sing. masc. (§ 4. rem. 5) . נבר

גִּבּוֹרֵיהֶם ['] id. pl., suff. 3 pers. pl. masc. . נבר

גִּבּוֹרָיו id. pl., suff. 3 pers. sing. masc. . נבר

גִּבּוֹרֶיךָ id. pl., suff. 2 pers. sing. masc. . נבר

גִּבֹּרִים id. pl., absolute state . . נבר

גִּבֹּרָם ['] id. sing., suff. 3 pers. pl. masc. . נבר

גְּבוּרְתָּא ['] Ch. noun fem. sing., emph. of [גְּבוּרָא] dec. 8 a; ו bef. (ּ). . נבר

גְּבוּרָתוֹ ['] noun fem. sing., suff. 3 pers. s. m. from גְּבוּרָה dec. 10; ו id. . נבר

גְּבוּרֹתָו id. pl., suff. 3 pers. sing. masc. (§ 4. rem. 1) . נבר

גְּבוּרֹתַי id. sing., suff. 1 pers. sing. . נבר

גְּבוּרֹתָיו id. pl., suff. 3 pers. sing. masc. . נבר

גְּבוּרֹתֶיךָ ['] id. pl., suff. 2 pers. sing. masc.; ו bef. (ּ). . נבר

גְּבוּרָתֶךָ id. sing. with suff. 2 pers. sing. masc. for רָתְךָ . . נבר

גְּבוּרָתֵךְ ['] id. sing., suff. 2 pers. sing. fem.; ו bef. (ּ). . נבר

גְּבוּרָתְךָ ['] id. sing., suff. 2 pers. sing. masc.; ו id. . נבר

גְּבוּרָתְכֶם ['] id. sing., suff. 2 pers. pl. masc. . נבר

גְּבוּרָתָם [']' id. sing., suff. 3 pers. pl. masc.; ו bef. (ּ). . נבר

גָּבַח Root not used; Samar. *to be high,* used in the Arab. of the forehead.

גִּבֵּחַ masc. *bald in the forehead,* Le. 13. 41.

גַּבַּחַת fem. dec. 13 a.—I. *baldness in the forehead,* Le. 13. 42, 43.—II. trop. *bareness thread-bare,* Le. 13. 15.

גֶּבַח ['] noun masc. sing. . . נבח

גַּבַּי pr. name masc. . . נבב

גַּבֵּי ['] noun masc. pl. constr. from גַּב dec. 8 d. . נבב

* Is. 52. 13.   ' Eze. 31. 5.   ' Is. 5. 15.   " Ps. 138. 6.   Eze. 27. 4.   ' Is. 13. 3.   ' Je. 26. 21.   ' Je. 16. 21.   ' Is. 30. 15.
' 1 Sa. 16. 7.   Is. 2. 11, 17.   ' Ec. 5. 7.   ' Eze. 43. 13.   ' Ex. 7. 27.   ' 1 Ch. 11. 26.   ' Sa. 17. 51.   ' Ps. 145. 12.   ' Je. 23. 10.
' Job 40. 10.   ' Da. 8. 3.   ' Eze. 10. 12.   ' Jos. 1. 4.   ' Na. 2. 4.   ' Da. 2. 20, 23.   ' Is. 3. 25.   ' Le. 13. 41.
' Eze. 31. 3.   ' Job 11. 8.   ' Eze. 31. 10.   ' 1 Ch. 4. 10.   ' 1 Sa. 7. 14.   ' Je. 46. 5.   ' Job 26. 14.   ' Ps. 145. 11.   ' Jo. 15. 26.

גְּבַי id. sing., suff. 1 pers. sing. .   נבב

גֹּבַי defect. for גּוֹבַי n. m. pl. or collect. of גּוֹב   נוב

גַּבָּהּ Ch. K. גַּבָּהּ noun masc. sing., suff. 3 pers. sing. fem. from גַּב dec. 5 a.   נבב

גַּבֵּיהֶם noun. m. pl., suff. 3 pers. pl. m. fr. גַּב d. 8 d.   נבב

גַּבֵּיהֶן id., suff. 3 pers. pl. fem.   נבב

גַּבֵּיכֶם id., suff. 2 pers. pl. masc. .   נבב

גֵּבִים noun masc., pl. of [גֵּב] dec. 1 a, also pr. n.   נוב

גְּבִיעַ noun masc. sing., constr. of גָּבִיעַ dec. 3 a.   נבע

גְּבִיעִי id., suff. 1 pers. sing. .   נבע

גְּבִיעֶיהָ id. pl., suff. 3 pers. sing. fem. .   נבע

גְּבִיעִים id. pl. abs. state   נבע

גְּבִיר noun masc. sing. .   נבר

גָּבִישׁ } noun masc. sing.   נבש

גַּבֵּךְ noun m. s., suff. 2 pers. s. f. fr. גַּב d. 8 d.   נבב

גָּבַל I. to bound, limit.—II. to set a boundary.—III. with בְּ to border upon.

גְּבָל (mountain, coll. with the Arab.) pr. n. of a Phenician city, Eze. 27. 9.—Gent. n. גִּבְלִי 1 Ki. 5. 32.

גְּבָל (id.) pr. n. of a mountainous tract in the south of Idumea, Ps. 83. 8.

גְּבוּל, גְּבֻל masc. d. 1 a.—I. bound, limit, border.—II. a limited space, territory, margin, edge, Eze. 43. 13, 17.

גְּבֻלָה, גְּבוּלָה fem. dec. 10.—I. bound, border.—II. territory.

גַּבְלֻת f. a bordering, edging, Ex. 28. 22; 39, 15.

מִגְבָּלֹה fem. id. only מִגְבָּלֹת, Ex. 28. 14.

גְּבָל pr. name of a region .   נבל

גְּבָל pr. name of a place .   נבל

גְּבֻל defect. for גְּבוּל n. m. s. d. 1 a; ו bef. (:)   נבל

גָּבְלוּ Kal pret. 3 pers. pl. .   נבל

גְּבֻלוֹ noun m. s., suff. 3 p. s. m. fr. גְּבוּל d. 1 a.

גְּבֻלְךָ } id., suff. 2 pers. sing. masc.   נבל

גְּבֻלְכֶם id., suff. 2 pers. pl. masc. .   נבל

גְּבֻלֹת noun fem., pl. of [גְּבוּלָה] dec. 10.   נבל

גְּבֻלֹת noun fem. sing. [for גְּבֻלוֹת] .   נבל

גְּבֻלָתוֹ n. f. s., suff. 3 pers. s. m. fr. [גְּבוּלָה] d. 10.   נבל

גָּבֵן Root not used; Syr. to coagulate, to be condensed.

גְּבִינָה f. cheese, Job 10. 10. Also the two foll.

גִּבֵּן masc. hunchbacked, Lev. 21. 20. .   נבן

גַּבְנֻנִּים masc. pl. [of גַּבְנֹן dec. 8 c] heights, summits, Ps. 68. 16, 17.   נבן

גָּבַע Root not used; cogn. גָּבַב, גָּבַהּ, גָּבַה to be high.

גֶּבַע (hill, comp. גִּבְעָה) pr. name of a Levitical city in the tribe of Benjamin.

גִּבְעָא (id.) pr. name masc., 1 Ch. 2. 49.

גִּבְעָה fem. dec. 12 b.—I. a hill.—II. pr. name of a city in the tribe of Judah, Jos. 15. 57.—III. more frequently with the art. הַגִּבְעָה pr. name of a city in the tribe of Benjamin, more fully גִּבְעַת בְּנֵי ב׳, called also גִּבְעַת בִּנְיָמִין שָׁאוּל comp. 1 Sa. 11. 4, with 10. 26, as the birth-place of Saul, and גִּבְעַת הָאֱלֹהִים 1 Sa. 10. 5, comp. ver. 10. Gent. n. גִּבְעָתִי 1 Ch. 12. 3.—IV. גִּבְעַת פִּינְחָס pr. name of a city in the mount of Ephraim, Jos. 24. 33.

גִּבְעַת (hill) pr. name of a town in the tribe of Judah, Jos. 18. 28.

גִּבְעוֹן (hill-city) pr. name of a city in the tribe of Benjamin.—Gent. n. גִּבְעֹנִי.

גָּבִיעַ masc. dec. 3 a.—I. cup, goblet.—II. the cup or bell of a flower, as an ornament of the sacred candlestick.

מִגְבָּעָה fem. only pl. מִגְבָּעוֹת mitres or bonnets of the common priests, probably of a conic form.

גֶּבַע גֶּבַע } pr. n. of a place; (§ 35. r. 2) for ן see lett. ו   נבע

גִּבְעָא pr. name masc. .   נבע

גִּבְעָה noun fem. sing. dec. 12 b; also pr. name of a place .   נבע

גִּבְעוֹן pr. name of a man and a place .   נבע

גִּבְעֹנָה pr. name of a place (גִּבְעוֹן) with parag. ה   נבע

גְּבָעוֹת n. fem. pl. abs. fr. גִּבְעָה d. 12 b; ו bef. (ַ)   נבע

גִּבְעוֹת id. pl., constr. state .   נבע

גִּבְעֹתֶיךָ id. pl., suff. 2 pers. sing. masc.   נבע

גְּבִעִים noun masc., pl. of גָּבִיעַ dec. 3 a.   נבע

גִּבְעֹל only Ex. 9. 31, הַפִּשְׁתָּה גִּבְעֹל the flax was in the flower (comp. ל גָּבִיעַ, being added as in כַּרְמֶל, חֲרֹל). Luther: the flax had knots. But the word is probably made up of the two roots נבל and נבע.

גִּבְעֹנָה pr. name of a place (גִּבְעוֹן) with parag. ה .   נבע

גִּבְעַת noun fem. s., constr. of גִּבְעָה dec. 12. b, also in compos. with pr. n., as גִּבְעַת בִּנְיָמִין &c.   נבע

גִּבְעַת pr. name of a place .   נבע

גִּבְעֹת noun fem. pl. constr. of גִּבְעָה dec. 12 b.   נבע

גִּבְעָתָה pr. name of a place (גִּבְעָה) with parag. ה   נבע

גִּבְעָתָהּ n. f. s., suff. 3 pers. s. f. from גִּבְעָה dec. 12 b.   נבע

גִּבְעָתִי id., suff. 1 pers. sing.   נבע

* Ps. 129. 3.   d 1 Ki. 7. 35.   g Ge. 44. 2.   k Job 28. 18.   m De. 19. 14.   o De. 32. 8.   q Le. 21. 20.   s Is. 40. 4.   u Is. 31. 4.
b Am. 7. 1.   e Eze. 1. 18.   h Ge. 44. 2.   i Eze. 16. 31, 39.   n De. 11. 24.   p Is. 28. 25.   r Ps. 68. 16, 17.   t Eze. 35 8.   x Ese. 84. 26.
c Da. 7. 6.   f Job 13. 12.   Ge. 27. 29, 37.   ll Ex. 25. 34.

10

גָּבַר (pl. גָּבְרוּ, נַבְרוּ).—I. *to be* or *become strong, powerful, mighty,* constr. abs.; with מִן עַל *to be stronger than, to prevail against.*—II. *to increase,* of water; גָּבַר חַיִל *to increase in strength.* Pi. *to make strong, strengthen.* Hiph.—I. i. q. Kal No. I. constr. with לְ, Ps. 12. 5.—II. *to confirm,* Da. 9. 27. Hithp.—I. *to show oneself strong,* with עַל, Is. 42. 13.—II. *to behave oneself stoutly, insolently,* with אֶל against any one.

גֶּבֶר masc. dec. 6a.—I. *man,* i. q. אִישׁ.—II. *husband.*—III. *warlike-man, warrior.*—IV. *each, every one*; לִגְבָרִים גְבָרִים *man by man.*—V. pr. name masc., 1 Ki. 4. 19.

גְּבַר Chald. masc. *a man,* pl גֻּבְרִין, emph. גֻּבְרַיָּא (as if from a sing. גּוּבַר).

גֶּבֶר masc. id. Ps. 18. 26.

גִּבָּר Chald. dec. 1b.—I. *hero,* Da. 3. 20.—II. pr. name of a city, Ezr. 2. 20.

גִּבֹּר, גִּבּוֹר masc. dec. 1b.—I. adj. *strong, mighty, valiant.*—II. subst. *warrior, hero, chief;* גִּבּוֹר חַיִל *a valiant warrior, hero;* also *one mighty in wealth.*

גְּבוּרָה fem. dec. 10.—I. *strength, power, might.*—II. *valour, courage.*—III. *mighty acts.*

גְּבוּרְתָּא Chald. fem. id. only emph. (dec. 8a) Da. 2. 20, 23.

גְּבִיר masc. *master, lord,* Ge. 27. 29, 37.

גְּבִירָה fem. *mistress, lady, queen.*

גְּבֶרֶת fem. dec. 13, *mistress.*

גַּבְרִיאֵל (*man of God*) pr. name of an archangel.

גֶּבֶר in pause for גֶּבֶר (q. v.) . . . . נבר

גְּבַר Heb. and Chald. noun masc. sing. נבר

גֶּבֶר noun masc. s dec. 6a; also pr. name masc. נבר

גֶּבֶר pr. name of a place . . . נבר

גִּבֹּר (for גִּבּוֹר) adj. masc. sing. dec. 1b. נבר

גָּבְרוּ } Kal pret. 3 pers. pl. (§ 8. rem. 1) . נבר
גָּבְרוּ }

גֻּבְרֵי Chald. noun m., pl. constr. from [גְּבַר] dec. 1. נבר

גִּבֹּרֵי adj. masc. pl. constr. from גִּבּוֹר dec. 1b. נבר

גֻּבְרַיָּא Ch. n. m. pl. emph. [as if from גּוּבַר see גְּבַר נבר

גַּבְרִיאֵל pr. name masc. . . . נבר

גִּבֹּרֶיהָ } adj. m. pl., suff. 3 p. s. f. from גִּבּוֹר dec.1b. נבר

גִּבֹּרָיו } id., suff. 3 pers. sing. masc. . נבר

גְּבָרִים noun masc., pl. of גֶּבֶר dec. 6. נבר

גִּבֹּרִים adj. masc., pl. of גִּבּוֹר dec. 1b. נבר

גֻּבְרִין Chald. n. m. pl. abs. [as if from גּוּבַר see גְּבַר נבר

גְּבֶרֶת } noun fem. sing. dec. 13a. (see the foll.) . נבר
גְּבֶרֶת }

גְּבִרְתָּהּ id., suff. 3 pers. sing. fem. . . נבר

גִּבַּרְתִּי } Piel pret. 1 pers. sing. . . . נבר

גְּבִרְתִּי noun fem. s., suff. 1 p. s. from גְּבֶרֶת dec. 13a. נבר

גְּבוּרָתִי noun fem. s., suff. 1 p. s. from גְּבוּרָה dec.10. נבר

גִּבַּרְתִּים } Piel pret. 1 pers. sing., suff. 3 pers. pl. m. נבר

גְּבִרְתֵּךְ noun f. s., suff. 2 p. s. f. from גְּבֶרֶת dec. 13a. נבר

גָּבַשׁ Root not used; Arab. *to congeal;* Chald. גְּבַשׁ *to gather together.*

גָּבִישׁ masc. *crystal,* (prop. *ice*), Job 28. 18.

אֶלְגָּבִישׁ masc. *hail,* אֶל supposed to be i. q. אֵל the article in the Arab.

מַגְבִּישׁ (*gathering*) pr. name of a place or person, Ezr. 2. 30.

גַּבַּת noun m. with pl. fem. term. from גַּב dec. 8 d. נבב

נַבַּחְתָּם } id., suff. 3 pers. pl. masc. . . נבב

גִּבְּתוֹן pr. name of a place . . . נבב

גַּג masc. dec. 8 a.—I. *roof* of a house.—II. *top* of an altar.

גַּג id., construct state . . . . נג

גַּגּוֹ id., suff. 3 pers. sing. masc. . . נג

גַּגּוֹת id. pl. fem. . . . . נג

גַּגּוֹתֶיהָ id. pl., suff. 3 pers. sing. fem. . ע

גַּגּוֹתֵיהֶם } id. pl., suff. 3 pers. pl. masc. נג
גַּגֹּתֵיהֶם }

גָּד pr. name of a man and a tribe . . נדד

גָּד noun masc. sing. . . . . נדד

גְּדָבְרַיָּא Chald. noun masc. pl. emph. *treasurers,* Da. 3. 2, 3, comp. גִּזְבָּר.

גָּדַד prop. *to cut,* hence *to press upon,* with עַל Ps. 94. 21 Hithpo.—I. *to cut oneself, to make incisions.*—II. *to press* or *crowd together.*

גְּדַד Chald. *to cut* or *hew down,* Da. 4. 11, 20.

גָּד masc.—I. *good fortune.*—II. pr. name of a son of Jacob, and the tribe descended from him.— Gent. noun גָּדִי *Gadite.*

גַּד masc.—I. *coriander seed.*—II. (*fortuna,*) pr. name of an idol, Is. 65. 11.

גִּדְגָּד (*cleft, chink,*) pr. name of a station of the Israelites in the desert, De. 10. 7; called חֹר הַגִּדְגָּד (*cavern of the cleft,*) Nu. 33. 32.

גַּדָּה (*fortune*) see גַּד חָצַר.

גְּדוּד masc. dec. 1b. (pl. ־ים, ־וֹת.)—I. *a cutting,* Je. 48. 37.—II. *furrow,* Ps. 65. 11.—III. *troop,* or *detachment of an army.*

* Ex. 17. 11, 11.   d Da. 3. 22.   g Je. 41. 16.   i Is. 47. 7.   * Ge. 16. 4, etc.   n Ge. 16. 8.   p Ge. 16. 9.   r Eze. 1. 13.   t Je. 32. 29.
b 2 Sa. 1. 25.   e Je. 51. 57.   h Da. 3. 8, 12,   k Is. 47. 5.   m Zec. 10. 6.   o Zec. 10. 12.   q Le. 14. 9.   s Is. 15. 3.   u Je. 19. 12.
c Da. 3. 20.   f 2 Ch. 32. 3.   24, 25.   kk Is. 33. 13.

גַּדִּי.—I. gent. noun of גָּד q. v.—II. **pr. name** masc., 2 Ki. 15. 14.

גַּדִּי (*fortunate*) pr. name masc., Nu. 13. 11.

גַּדִּיאֵל (*fortune of God*) pr. name m., Nu. 13. 10.

מְגִדּוֹ, מְגִדּוֹן (*place of troops*) pr. name of a city of Manasseh situated within the borders of Issachar.

נְדֻדְתִּי noun masc. with pl. f. term. from גְּדוּד dec. 1 a. נדד

גָּדָה   Root not used ; Arab. *to pluck out*, or *off*   Syr. *to leap*.

גָּדָה fem. dec. 11 a, *banks of a river*.

גְּדִי masc. dec. 6 i, *a kid* ; גְּדִי עִזִּים *kid of the goats*.

גְּדִיָה fem. *banks of a river*, 1 Ch. 12. 15, Kheth.

גְּדִיָה fem. dec. 10, *a female kid*, Ca. 1. 8.

גַּדָּה	pr. name in compos. חֲצַר גַּדָּה	.	חצר
גֻּדּוּ	Chald. Peal imp. pl. masc. .	.	גדד
גְּדוּד	noun masc. sing. dec. 1 a. .	.	גדד
גְּדוּדֶהָ	id. pl., suff. 3 pers. s. fem. [for רֶיהָ]		גדד
גְּדוּדַי	id. pl. construct state ; ו before (:)		גדד
גְּדוּדָיו	id. pl., suff. 3 pers. s. masc. .		גדד
גְּדוּדִים	id. pl., absolute state . .	.	גדד
גָּדוֹל	adj. masc. sing. dec. 3 a. .	.	גדל
גְּדוֹל	id., construct state . .	.	גדל
גְּדוֹל	id. with Mak., Kh. גָּדוֹל K. (§ 32. r. 7)		גדל
גְּדוֹלָה	adj. f. s. dec. 10, from גָּדוֹל m.; ו bef. (:)		גדל
גְּדוּלָה	noun fem. sing. dec. 10 ; ו id.		גדל
גְּדוֹלֶיהָ	adj. m. pl., suff. 3 pers. s. f. from גָּדוֹל dec. 3 a.		גדל
גְּדוֹלִים	id. pl., absolute state . .		גדל
גְּדוֹלָם	id. sing., suff. 3 pers. pl. masc. .		גדל
גְּדוֹלֹת	id. fem., pl. of לָה dec. 10, from גָּדוֹל masc.		גדל
גְּדוּלָתוֹ	noun f. s., suff. 3 p. s. m. from לָה dec. 10.		גדל
גְּדוּעָה	Kal part. pass. sing. fem. .		גדע
גְּדוּפָה	noun fem. sing.; ו before (:)		גדף
גְּדוֹר	pr. name of a man and a place ; ו id.	.	גדר
גְּדוֹתָיו	n. f. pl., suff. 3 p. s. m. from [גָּדָה] dec. 11 a.		גדה
גְּדִי	pr. name masc., or patronym. of גָּד		גדד
גַּדִּי	pr. name masc. . .		גדד
גְּדִי	noun masc. sing. dec. 6 i; ו before (:)		גדה
גְּדִי	pr. name, see עֵין גְּדִי . .		עין
גַּדִּיאֵל	pr. name masc. . .		גדד
גְּדָיֵי	noun masc. pl., constr. from גְּדִי dec. 6 i.		גדה
גְּדָיִים	id. pl., absolute state . .	.	גדה
גָּדִישׁ	noun masc. sing. . .		גדש
גְּדֹתָיו	Kh. גְּדוֹתָיו [pl. of גָּדָה], K. גְּדֹתָיו (q. v.)		גדה
גְּדֹתָיו	noun fem. pl., suff. from [גָּדָה] dec. 10.		גדה

גָּדַל (with suff. גְּדָלַנִי, Job 31.18; fut. יִגְדַּל).—I. Arab.

& Syr. *to twist*, only in the deriv. גָּדִיל q. v.—II. *to be* or *become great, to grow.*—III. *to be great exalted.* Pi.—I. *to make great, to cause to grow* of hair, plants ; of children *to educate.*—II. *to exalt, to extol.* Pu. *to be brought up*, Ps. 144. 12. Hiph.—I. *to make great* ; הִגְדִּיל פֶּה *to boast* · הִ׳ חַסְדּוֹ עִם פּ׳ *to show one great kindness ;* with an inf. הִ׳ לַעֲשׂוֹת *to do great things ;* in a bad sense, *to act proudly,* and so ellipt. הִגְדִּיל with עַד הִגְדִּיל [לִבְכּוֹת] of the pers.; 1 Sa. 20. 41, *until he wept greatly ;* הִ׳ בְּפֶה *to boast.*—II. *to lift up,* Ps. 41. 10. Hithpa. *to show oneself great.*

גָּדֵל adj. masc. dec. 5 a, *becoming great,* Ge. 26.13; 1 Sa. 2. 26 ; *great,* Eze. 16. 26.

גָּדִיל masc. only pl. ־לִים.—I. *fringes,* De. 22. 12. —II. *platted chain-work,* 1 Ki. 7. 17.

גָּדוֹל masc. dec. 3 a. (with Mak. גְּדָל § 32. rem. 7), גְּדוֹלָה fem. dec. 10.—I. adj. *great,* in extent, number, quantity, age, dignity, &c. עוֹד הַיּוֹם גָּדוֹל *it is yet great [high] day,* i. e. early, (French *grand jour ;*) הַכֹּהֵן הַגָּדוֹל *the high-priest.*—II. subst. *greatness,* Ex. 15. 16 ; pl. גְּדֹלוֹת *great things.*

גְּדֻלָּה, גְּדוּלָה, גְּדֻלָה fem. dec. 10.—I. *great deed* or *act.*—II. *greatness, majesty, magnificence.*

גֹּדֶל masc. dec. 6 c. (suff. גָּדְל־, גָּדְלוֹ § 35. rem. 8).— I. *greatness.*—II. *majesty, magnificence.*—III. *pride.*

גִּדֵּל (*over-grown,* comp. § 26. No. 9) pr. name of two different men.

גְּדַלְיָהוּ, גְּדַלְיָה (*great is the Lord*) pr. name of several men, especially of the governor of Judea, appointed by Nebuchadnezzar.

גִּדַּלְתִּי (*I extol* Him) pr. name masc. 1 Ch. 25. 4, 29.

יִגְדַּלְיָהוּ (*the Lord be extolled*) pr. n. m. Je. 35. 4.

מִגְדָּל masc. dec. 2 b. (pl. ־ים, ־וֹת).—I. *tower.* —II. *pulpit,* Ne. 8. 4.—III. *bed* in a garden, Ca. 5. 13.—IV. in compos. with pr. names, as מִגְדַּל־אֵל (*tower of God*) a fortress in the tribe of Naphtali, Jos. 19. 38 ; מִגְדַּל־גָּד (*tower of God*) a town in the tribe of Judah, Jos. 15. 37 ; מִגְדַּל עֵדֶר (*tower of the flock*) a village near Bethlehem.

מִגְדּוֹל, מִגְדָּל masc.—I. *tower,* 2 Sa. 22. 51. Keri.—II. pr. name of a city in Egypt.

גָּדֵל	adj. masc. sing. dec. 5 a. .	.	גדל
גַּדֵּל	Piel inf. absolute . .	.	גדל
גָּדֵל	adj. masc. sing. for גָּדוֹל dec. 3 a.	.	גדל
גְּדָל	id., construct state . .	.	גדל
גִּדֵּל, גִּדְּלִי	Piel pret. 3 pers. sing. masc. (§ 10. rem. 1)		גדל

a Je. 48. 37.   d 2 Ki. 13. 20.   g Eze. 17. 3.   k Est. 6. 3.   o Est. 1. 4.   r Eze. 5. 15.   u Ge. 27. 9, 16.   y 1 Ch. 12. 15.   A Nu. 6. 5.
b Da. 4. 11, 20.   e Job 19. 12.   h Ec. 9. 12.   l Na. 3. 10.   p Is. 15. 2.   s 1 Sa. 16. 20.   v 1 Sa. 10. 3.   z Ca. 1. 8.   B Is. 49. 21.
c Ps. 65. 11.

10*

גָּדֵל   pr. name masc.   .   .   .   נדל

גֹּדֶל   noun masc. sing. dec. 6 c.   .   .   נדל

גָּדְלָה   Kal pret. 3 pers. sing. fem.   .   .   נדל

גְדֹלָה   adj. fem. s. dec. 10, from גָּדוֹל m.; ♭ bef. (:)   נדל

גִּדְּלָה   Piel pret. 3 p. s. f. [for גִּדְּלָה comp. § 8. r. 7]   נדל

גָּדְלוּ   Kal pret. 3 pers. pl.   .   .   .   נדל

גָּדְלוֹ   noun m. s., suff. 3 p. s. m. from גֹּדֶל dec. 6 c.   נדל

גַּדְּלוּ   Piel imp. pl. masc.   .   .   .   נדל

גִּדְּלוֹ   id. pret. 3 pers. sing. masc., suff. 3 pers. s. m.   נדל

גְּדֹלוּהוּ   for גְּדֹלוּ q. v. (§ 35. rem. 8)   .   נדל

גְּדֹלוֹת   Piel pret. 3 pers. pl., suff. 3 pers. sing. masc.   נדל

גְּדֹלוֹת   adj. fem., pl. of גְּדֹלָה dec. 10, from גָּדוֹל m.   נדל

גְּדֻלּוֹת   noun fem., pl. of גְּדֻלָּה dec. 10, see גְּדֻלָּה .   נדל

גְּדֻלּוֹתָיךָ   ♪ Kh. גְּדֻלֹתֶיךָ, K. גְּדֻלֹתְךָ noun fem. pl. or   s., suff. 2 p.s.m. from גְּדֻלָּה d.10; ♭ bef. (:)   נדל

גְּדֹלֵי   adj. masc. pl. construct from גָּדוֹל dec. 3 a.   נדל

גֹּדְלֵי   adj. masc. pl. construct from גֹּדֶל dec. 5 a.   נדל

גְּדַלְיָה   ♪ pr. name masc.; ♭ before (:)   .   נדל

גְּדַלְיָהוּ   ♪ pr. name masc.; ♭ id.   .   נדל

גְּדֹלָיו   ♪ adj. m. pl., suff. from גָּדוֹל dec. 3 a; ♭ id.   נדל

גְּדִלִים   noun masc., pl. of גָּדִיל dec. 3 a.   נדל

גְּדֹלִים   adj. masc., pl. of גָּדוֹל dec. 3 a.   נדל

גָּדְלֶךָ   n. m. s., suff. 2 pers. s. m. from גֹּדֶל dec. 6 c.   נדל

גַּדֶּלְךָ   Piel inf. (גַּדֵּל), suff. 2 pers. sing. masc.   (§ 15. rem. 16, & § 36. rem. 3)   נדל

גְּדָלַנִי   Kal pret. 3 pers. sing. masc. (גָּדֵל), suff.   1 pers. sing. (comp. § 8. rem. 1)   .   נדל

גָּדַלְתָּ   id. pret. 2 pers. sing. masc.   .   נדל

גְּדֻלַּת   noun f. s., constr. of לָּה׳ dec. 10, see גְּדֻלָּה   נדל

גְּדֹלֹת   adj. f., pl. of גְּדֹלָה dec. 10, from גָּדוֹל masc.   נדל

גִּדַּלְתּוֹ   Piel pret. 2 pers. sing. m., suff. 3 pers. s. m.   נדל

גִּדַּלְתִּי   id. pret. 1 pers. sing.   .   .   נדל

גְּדַלְתִּי   pr. name masc.   .   .   .   נדל

גִּדַּלְתִּי   ♪ Kal pret. 1 pers. sing.; acc. shifted to ult.   by conversive ♭ (§ 8. rem. 7)   .   נדל

גְּדֻלָּתִי   noun f. s., suff. 1 p. s. from גְּדֻלָּה see גְּדֻלָּה   נדל

גָּדַע   I. to cut off or down.—II. to cut or break asunder. Niph. to be cut off. Pi. to break, break in pieces. Pu. to be cut down, Is. 9. 9.

גִּדְעֹם   (a cutting down) pr. name of a town in the tribe of Benjamin, Ju. 20. 45.

גִּדְעוֹן   (cutter) pr. name of a judge in Israel, Ju. chap. 6—8.

גִּדְעֹנִי   (id.) pr. name masc. Nu. 1. 11; 2. 22.

גִּדַּע   } Piel pret. 3 pers. sing. masc. (§ 15. rem. 1)   נדע
גֻּדַּע

גֻּדְּעוּ   Pual pret. 3 p. pl. [for גֻּדְּעוּ comp. § 8. r. 7]   נדע

גִּדְעוֹן   ♭ pr. name masc.   .   .   נדע

גְּדֻעִים   Kal part. pass. pl. masc. from [גָּדוּעַ] dec. 3 a.   נדע

גָּדַעְתִּי   ♭ Kal pret. 1 pers. sing.; acc. shifted to ult.   by conversive ♭ (§ 8. rem. 7)   .   נדע

גִּדְעֹם   pr. name of a place   .   .   נדע

גִּדְעֹנִי   pr. name masc.   .   .   נדע

גָּדַף   Pi. to reproach, revile, blaspheme.

גִּדּוּף   masc. dec. 2 b, only pl. (וֹת, ־ים) reproaches.

גְּדוּפָה   fem. reproach, Eze. 5. 15.

גִּדְּפוּ   Piel pret. 3 pers. pl.   .   .   נדף

גִּדֻּפֵי   ♭ noun m. pl. constr. from [גִּדּוּף] dec. 1 b.   נדף

גִּדַּפְתָּ   ♭ Piel pret. 2 pers. sing. masc.   .   נדף

גָּדַר   to wall, fence up.

גָּדֵר   com. dec. 5 b.—I. wall, fence.—II. fenced place, Ezr. 9. 9.

גֶּדֶר   (wall) pr. name of a Canaanitish city, Jos. 12. 13; i. q. בֵּית גָּדֵר.

גְּדֵרָה   fem. dec. 11 c. (§ 42. rem. 4)—I. wall.— II. walled or fenced place; גִּדְרוֹת צֹאן sheep folds. —III. pr. name of a city in the tribe of Judah, Jos. 15. 36.   Gent. noun גְּדֵרָתִי, 1 Ch. 12. 4.

גְּדֶרֶת   fem. wall, fence, Eze. 42. 12.

גְּדֵרוֹת   (folds) pr. name of a town in the tribe of Judah.

גְּדֵרוֹתָיִם   (two folds) pr. name of a town in the tribe of Judah, Jos. 15. 36.

גְּדֵרִי   Gent. noun of בֵּית גָּדֵר q. v. 1 Ch. 27. 28.

גְּדוֹר   (wall) pr. n.—I. of a town in the tribe of Judah, Jos. 15. 58—II. of a man, 1 Ch. 8. 31; 9. 37.

גֶּדֶר   ♭ n. com. s. d. 5 b. (pr. n. in compos. see בֵּית)   נדר

גֶּדֶר   ♪ id. construct state; also pr. name   .   נדר

גֶּדֶר   pr. name masc.   .   .   נדר

גֹּדֵר   Kal part. act. sing. masc. dec. 7 b.   .   נדר

גְּדֵרָה   ♪♭ n. f. s. dec. 11 c. (§ 42. rem. 4); ♭ bef. (:)   נדר

גְּדֵרוֹ   ♭ noun m. s., suff. 3 p. s. m. from גָּדֵר dec. 5 b.   נדר

גְּדֵרוֹת   ♭ noun fem. pl. constr. from גְּדֵרָה dec. 11 c.   נדר

גְּדֵרֹת   ♪ id. pl. abs. pr. name of a place; ♭ before (:)   נדר

גְּדֵרֹתֶיהָ   noun m. pl., suff. 3 pers. s. f. from גָּדֵר dec. 5 b.   נדר

גְּדֵרֹתַיִךְ   id., suff. 2 pers. sing. fem. [for רַיִךְ׳]   נדר

גִּדְרֹת   ♪♭ noun fem. pl. constr. from גְּדֵרָה dec. 11 c.   (§ 42. rem. 4)   .   .   נדר

a Ne. 7. 4.   Ps. 150. 2.   c 2 Ki. 10. 6.   e De. 3. 24.   r Jon. 4. 10.   g 2 Ch. 34. 7.   i Zep. 2. 8.   l 1 Ch. 4. 23.   k Ps. 80. 13.
b Is. 51. 18.   f Eze. 31. 4.   d Eze. 16. 26.   Jos. 3. 7.   s Ecc. 1. 16.   h Is. 9. 9.   c Eze. 42. 10.   m Is. 5. 5.   l Mi. 7. 11.
c De. 5. 24.   1 Ch. 17. 21.   2 Ki. 10. 11.   p Job 31. 18.   t Ps. 71. 21.   d Pr. 24. 31.   1 Sa. 24. 4.   Nu. 32. 16.
d Ps. 34. 4.   h Ps. 145. 6.   m Jon. 3. 7.   r Est. 10. 2.   u La. 2. 3.   1 Sa. 2. 31.   Ho. 2. 8.   Zep. 2. 6.   Nu. 32. 36.

נְדֶרֶת *id. pl., absolute state; before (ֵ) . נדר

נָדַרְתִּי וְ Kal pret. 1 pers. sing.; acc. shifted to ult. by conversive וְ (§ 8. rem. 7) . נדר

גְּדֵרֹתָיו n. f. pl., suff. 3 p. s. m., from גְּדֵרָה (§ 42. r. 4) נדר

גְּדֵרֹתַיִם *pr. name of a place; before (ָ) . נדר

גָּדַשׁ Root not used; Chald. *to heap up.*

גָּדִישׁ masc.—I. *sepulchral mound,* Job 21. 32.— II. *stack of corn.*

גֹּה prob. for זֶה *this,* Eze. 47. 13.

[גָּהָה] *to heal, cure,* Ho. 5. 13. **Hence**

גֵּהָה fem. *healing, cure,* Pr. 17. 22. . נהה

[גָּהַר] *to bow, bend down oneself.*

גֵּו noun masc. sing. (§ 36. rem. 2) . נוה

גֵּוָא Chald. noun m. s., constr. of [גַּו] irr. (§ 45) נוה

גּוֹאֵל Kal part. act. sing. masc. dec. 7 b. . נאל

גֹּאֲלִי וְ id. with suff. 1 pers. sing. . נאל

[גּוּב] I. Arab. *to cut, cleave,* only in the derivv. **Hence** —II. *to plough,* 2 Ki. 25. 12, Kheth.

גֵּב masc. dec. 1 a.—I. *board, plank,* 1 Ki. 6. 9.— II. *well, cistern,* Je. 14. 3.—III. *locust,* Is. 33. 4.

גֵּבִים (*cisterns,* or *locusts*) pr. name of a place near Jerusalem, Is. 10. 31.

גֹּב masc.—I. *locust,* pl. or collect. גּוֹבַי, גֵּב *locust,* Am. 7. 1; Na. 3. 17.—II. pr. name of a place, 2 Sa. 21. 18, 19, otherwise unknown.

גּוֹבַי [for חֵבָי] noun masc. pl. or collect. [of גּוֹב] נוב

גּוֹג pr. name.—I. of a Reubenite, 1 Ch. 5. 4.—II. of a prince of the land of Magog.

מָגוֹג pr. name.—I. of a son of Japheth, Ge. 10. 2.—II. of an unknown region, perhaps *Scythia.*

[גּוּד] *to press upon,* cogn. גָּדַד.

גָּוָה & גָּוַו Root not used; cogn. גָּבַה, גָּבַב *to be rising, convex.*

גֵּו masc. dec. 8 e, *a back.*

גֵּו Chald. masc. irr. (§ 68).—I. *middle, midst.* —II. prep. *in, into.*

גֵּו masc. dec. 1 a.—I. *back.*—II. *middle, midst,* Job 20. 5.

גֵּוָה fem. *body,* Job 20. 25.

גְּוִיָּה fem. dec. 10.—I. *body, person.*—II. *dead body, corpse, carcase,* of men and animals.

גּוֹי masc. dec. 1 a. (with suff. גּוֹיִ; pl. גּוֹיִם § 3. rem. 1) prop. *a body of men,* hence—I. *a people, nation,* generally of foreign nations; but also of Israel, Is. 1. 4; Ge. 12. 2; in the pl. foreign, heathen nations.—II. metaph. applied to locusts, Joel 1. 6, to other animals, Zep. 2. 14.

גֵּוָה וְ noun fem. sing. [for גַּאֲוָה] . נאה

[גּוּז] *to pass over,* Ps. 90. 10; perhaps causat. Nu. 11. 31.

גּוֹזִי Kal part. act. s. m., suff. 1 p. s. fr. [גּוֹזֵה] d. 9 a. נזה

גּוֹזֵל Kal part. act. sing. masc. dec. 7 b. נזל

גּוֹזָל וְ noun masc. sing. dec. 2 b. נזל

גּוֹזָלָיו id. pl. with suff. 3 pers. sing. masc. . נזל

גּוֹזָן pr. name of a place . נזה

גֵּוִי n. m. s. with suff. 1 p. s. from גֵּו (§ 36. r. 2) נוה

גֵּוִי וְ noun masc. sing. dec. 1 a. נוה

גּוִֹי id. with suff. 1 pers. sing. (§ 3. rem. 1) . נוה

גְּוִיֹּת noun fem., pl. of גְּוִיָּה dec. 10. נוה

גְּוִיֵּי noun masc. pl. constr. of גּוֹי d. 1 a. (§ 3. r. 1) נוה

גּוֹיֵךְ id. sing., suff. 2 pers. sing. masc. [for גּוֹיְךָ] נוה

גּוֹיַיִךְ וְ id. sing. (Kh. ךְ), or pl. (K. גּוֹיַיִךְ), suff. 2 pers. sing. fem. נוה

גּוֹיִם וְ id., pl., absolute state . . נוה

גְּוִיַּת noun fem. sing. constr. of גְּוִיָּה dec. 10. נוה

גְּוִיֹּת id. pl. [for גְּוִיֹּות] . נוה

גְּוִיָּתוֹ וְ id. sing., suff. 3 pers. sing. masc.; וְ bef. (ָ) נוה

גְּוִיָּתֵיהֶם id. pl., suff. 3 pers. pl. masc. . . נוה

גְּוִיָּתֵיהֶנָּה id., suff. 3 pers. pl. fem. (§ 4. rem. 6) נוה

גְּוִיָּתֵינוּ id., suff. 1 pers. pl. . . נוה

גְּוִיָּתֵנוּ id. sing., suff. 1 pers. pl. . נוה

גֵּוְךָ n. m.s., suff. 2 p.s.m. [for גֵּוְךָ, from גֵּו] d. 8 d. נוה

גֵּוְךָ noun m. s., suff. 2 pers. sing. masc. from גֵּו נוה

גֵּוֵךְ n. m. s., suff. 2 pers. s. fem. fr. [גֵּו] dec. 8 d. נוה

גֵּוֵךְ noun masc. sing., suff. 2 pers. sing. fem. from גֵּו (§ 36. rem. 2) נוה

גּוֹזִל Kh. גּוֹל, K. גִּיל Kal inf. abs. . ניל

גֹּל Kal imp. sing. masc. for גֹּל . נלל

גֹּלָה n. f. s., or (Is. 49. 21) fem. of the foll. dec. 10. נלה

גֹּלָה Kal part. act. sing. masc. dec. 9 a. נלה

גּוֹלָן pr. name of a place . . נלה

גֻּלָּם n. m. s., suff. 3 pers. pl. m. from [גֹּל] dec. 8 d נוה

גּוֹמֶץ noun masc. sing. . . . נמץ

גּוּנִי וְ (*coloured,* Chald. גָּוַן *to colour, dye*) pr. name masc.—I. Ge. 46. 24, and patronym. Nu. 26. 48.—II. 1 Ch. 5. 15.

a Nu. 32. 24.   d Is. 59. 20.   f Ps. 71. 6.   m Is. 50. 6.   r Exe. 36. 13.   w 1 Sa. 31. 12.   b Exe. 1. 11.   f Is. 38. 17.   t Pr. 23. 24.
b Ps. 89. 41.   e Ps. 19. 15.   k Pr. 26. 24.   o Zep. 2. 9.   s Exe. 36. 14, 15.   x 1 Sa. 31. 10.   c Ne. 9. 37.   g Exe. 23. 35.   k Ps. 37. 5.
c Job 30. 5.   f Na. 3. 17.   l Ge. 15. 9.   p Ps. 110. 6.   t Zec. 8. 22.   y Da. 10. 6.   d Ge. 47. 18.   i Is. 51. 22.   Ne. 9. 26.
d Da. 3. 26.   c Job 33. 17.   m De. 32. 11.   q Ps. 106. 5.   v 1 Sa. 31. 12.   z Exe. 1. 23   c 1 Ki. 14. 9.   hh Ec. 10. 8.

גָּוַע *to expire, to die.*

נוע   גֹּוֵעַ Kal part. act. sing. masc.

נוע   גָּוְעוּ Kal pret. 3 pers. pl., [גָּוְעוּ § 8. rem. 7]

נוע   גָּוַעְנוּ id. pret. 1 pers. pl.

נער   גֹּוֵעַר Kal part. act. sing. masc.

גּוּף Kal not used; *to be hollow*, cogn. נָפַח, נָבַב. Hiph. *to shut*, Ne. 7. 3.

נוף   גּוּפָה fem. dec. 10, *dead body, corpse*, 1 Ch. 10. 12.

נוף   גּוּפַת noun fem. sing. constr. of [גּוּפָה] dec. 10.

נוף   גּוּפֹת pl. of the preceding.

[גּוּר] I. *to sojourn, dwell* for a time, as a stranger, const. with בְּ, עִם, acc. Part. גָּר *dwelling*; גָּרֵי בֵיתִי *sojourners of my house*, i. e. servants; גָּרַת בֵּיתָהּ *her inmate.*—II. *to fear,* with מִן, מִפְּנֵי.—III. *to congregate, come together,* with עַל, אֶת *against* any one. Hithpal.—I. *to sojourn,* 1 Ki. 17. 20.—II. *to congregate,* Ho. 7. 14.

גֵּר masc. dec. 1 a, *sojourner, stranger, foreigner.*

גֵּיר masc. id. only 2 Ch. 2. 16.

גֵּרוּת fem. *place of sojourning, dwelling*, Je. 41. 17.

גּוּר i. q. גּוֹר *lion's whelp*, only pl. גֹּרִים, גֹּרוֹת, Je. 51. 38; Na. 2. 13.

גּוֹר masc. dec. 1 a.—I. *a lion's whelp.*—II. *the whelp of a jackal*, La. 4. 3.—III. מַעֲלֵה־גוּר (*ascent of whelps*) pr. name of a place, 2 Ki. 9. 27.

גּוּר בַּעַל (*dwelling of Baal*) pr. name of a town in Arabia, 2 Ch. 26. 7.

יָגוּר (*He shall dwell* there) pr. name of a town in the tribe of Judah, Jos. 15. 21.

מָגוֹר masc. *fear, terror*; pl. La. 2. 22. (§ 32. rem. 5).

מָגוּר masc. dec. 3 a.—I. *sojourning.*—II. *dwelling, residence*, Ps. 55. 16.

מְגוֹרָה fem. dec. 10, *fear*, Pr. 10. 24.

מְגוּרָה fem. dec. 10.—I. *granary.*—II. *fear, terror.*

מַמְּגֻרָה fem. (denom. of מְגוּרָה) only pl., *garners, storehouses*, Joel 1. 17.

נור   גּוֹר Kal inf. absolute

נור   גוּר n. m. s. or pr. n. in compos. גּוּר בַּעַל, מַעֲלֵה גוּר

נור   גּוּר Kal imp. sing. masc.

נור   גּוּרוּ id. imp. pl. masc.

נור   גּוּרִי id. imp. sing. fem.

נור   גּוּרֶיהָ n. m. pl., suff. 3 pers. s. fem. fr. גּוֹר dec. 1 a.

נור   גּוּרֶיהָן id., suff. 3 pers. pl. fem.

נרל   גּוֹרָל noun masc. sing. dec. 2 b.

נרל   גּוֹרַל id. sing., construct state

נרל   גּוֹרָלוֹ id., suff. 3 pers. sing. masc.

נרל   גּוֹרָלוֹת id., pl. fem. term.

נרל   גּוֹרָלִי id. sing., suff. 1 pers. sing.

נרל   גּוֹרָלְךָ id., suff. 2 pers. sing. masc.

נרל   גּוֹרָלֵךְ id., suff. 2 pers. sing. fem.

נרל   גּוֹרָלָם id., suff. 3 pers. pl. masc.

נרה   גָּרוֹנְךָ וּ K. גְּרוֹנֶךָ noun masc. sing., suff. 2 pers. sing. fem., from גָּרוֹן dec. 3 a; וּ bef. (:).

נוז   גָּז Kal pret. 3 pers. sing. masc.

נזז   גֵּז noun masc. sing. dec. 8 b.

[גִּזְבָּר] masc. *treasurer*, Ezr. 1. 8, pl. גִּזְבָּרִין see the foll.

גִּזְבְּרַיָּא Ch. id. pl. emph. as if from [גִּזְבָּר] see גִּזְבָּר.

גָּזָה *to cut, cut off*, only part. Ps. 71. 6, for which comp. Eze. 16. 4.

גָּזִית fem. *a cutting, hewing*, hence אַבְנֵי גָ׳ and simply גָּזִית *hewn stones.*

גֹּזָן (for גִּיזֹה *quarry*) only in the Gen. n. 1 Ch. 11. 34, comp. the forms שִׁילֹה, שִׁילֹנִי, גִּילֹנִי, גֹּזָן (id. after the form גֹּלָן) pr. name of a region of Mesopotamia on the river Chaboras, whither Shalmaneser carried away part of the ten tribes.

נזל   גָּזוּל Kal part. pass. sing. masc.

[גָּזַז] *to shear, to cut off*, hair, wool, &c. Niph. *to be cut off*, Na. 1. 12.

גֵּז masc. dec. 8 b, prop. *a shearing, cutting*, hence—I. *the fleece.*—II. *young grass after mowing.*

גִּזָּה fem. dec. 10, *fleece*, Ju. 6. 37—40. Also

נזז   גָּזֵז (*barber*) pr. name masc. 1 Ch. 2. 46.

נזז   גֹּזֵז Kal part. act. sing. masc. dec. 7 b.

נזז   גֹּזְזֵי id. pl. construct state

נזז   גֹּזְזֶיהָ id. pl., suff. 3 pers. sing. fem.

נזז   גֹּזְזִים id. pl., absolute state

נזז   גָּזִּי, גֹּזִּי } id. imp. s. fem. (§ 18. r. 4); for וּ see וּ

נזז   גִּזֵּי noun masc. pl. constr. from גֵּז dec. 8 b.

נזה   גָּזִית noun fem. sing.

גָּזַל, גָּזֵל (§ 8. rem. 7).—I. *to strip off*, Mi. 3. 2.—II. *to pluck, snatch away.*—III. *to spoil, rob* any one. Niph. *to be taken away*, Pr. 4. 16.

---

a Ps. 88. 16.   d 1 Ch. 10. 12.   g Ge. 26. 3.   k 2 Ki. 8. 1.   n 1 Ch. 26. 14.   r Je. 2. 25.   t De. 28. 29.   y Is. 53. 7.   a Am. 7. 1.
b La. 1. 19.   e 1 Ch. 10. 12.   h Job 19. 29.   l Eze. 19. 2.   o Ps. 16. 5.   s Ps. 90. 10.   u 1 Sa. 25. 4.   z Je. 7. 29.   β Is. 9. 9.
c Na. 1. 4.   f Is. 54. 15.   Ps. 22. 24.   m La. 4. 3.   p Pr. 1. 14.   q Ezr. 7. 21.   x Ge. 38. 12.   z Mi. 1. 16.

גּוֹזָל masc. (no vowel change) *young pigeon*, Ge. 15. 9; De. 32. 11. Also the three following:

גָּזֵל masc. *rapine, plunder* . . . . גזל

גָּזֵל'וְ masc. id. Eze. 18. 18; Ecc. 5. 7. . . גזל

גְּזֵלָה'יּ fem. dec. 10, idem. . . . . גזל

גָּזְלוּ'וְ } Kal pret. 3 pers. pl. (§ 8. rem. 7) . גזל
גָּזְלוּ'וְ }

גְּזֵלוֹת'וְ noun fem., pl. of גְּזֵלָה dec. 10. . . גזל

גֹּזְלֵי'וְ Kal part. act. pl. constr. m. from גּוֹזֵל d. 7 b. גזל

גְּזֵלַת'פּ noun fem. sing., constr. of גְּזֵלָה dec. 10. . גזל

גָּזַלְתִּי'פ Kal pret. 1 pers. sing. . . . גזל

גָּזָם Root not used; Arab. *to cut, crop off.*

     גָּזָם masc. a species of *locust.* Also

גַּזָּם (*devourer*) pr. name m. Ezr. 2. 48; Ne. 7. 51. גזם

גָּזַע Root not used; Arab. *to cut down.*

     גֶּזַע masc. dec. 6a. (suff. גִּזְעוֹ; § 35. rem. 5) *stock* or *trunk* of a tree.

גִּזְעוֹ'וְ noun masc. sing., suff. 3 pers. sing. masc. from גֶּזַע (§ 35. rem. 5) dec. 6a. . . . גזע

גִּזְעָם'פ id., suff. 3 pers. pl. masc. . . . גזע

גָּזַר'וְ I. *to cut off* or *down,* 2 Ki. 6. 4.—II. *to cut in two parts, to divide.*—III. *to decide, decree.* Niph.—I. *to be cut off, separated,* with מִן—II. *to perish.*—III. *to be decided, decreed,* with עַל, Est. 2. 1.

     גְּזַר Chald. *to decide, decree,* part. גָּזְרִין *soothsayers.* Ithpe. *to be cut out,* Da. 2. 34, 45.

     גֶּזֶר masc. dec. 6a.—I. *piece, part.*—II. pr. name of a Levitical city on the west of mount Ephraim.

     גְּזֵרָה fem. *separation, solitude,* Le. 16. 22.

     גְּזֵרָא Ch. fem. d. 8a, *decision, decree,* Da. 4. 14, 21.

     גִּזְרָה fem. (no pl. abs.)—I. *form, figure* of a man, La. 4. 7.—II. *a separate place* or *side-chamber* in the temple, Eze. 42. 1, sq.

     גִּזְרִי'וְ pr. name of a people in the neighbourhood of Philistia, 1 Sa. 27. 8. Keri.

     מְגֵרָה fem. dec. 11 b, *axe,* 2 Sa. 12. 31.

גֶּזֶר } pr. name of a place (§ 35. rem. 2) . נזר
גָּזֵר }

גֶּזְרָה id. with loc. ה [for גְּזֵרָה] . . . נזר

גִּזְרָה'פ noun fem. sing. . . . . . נזר

גִּזְרוּ'וְ } Kal imp. pl. masc. (§ 8. rem. 12) . נזר
גָּזְרוּ'וְ }

גָּזְרַיָּא'וְ Ch. Peal part. act. pl. emph. m. fr. [גָּזַר] d. 2 b. נזר

גָּזְרִין Ch. id. pl., absolute state . . . נזר

גְּזֵרַת'פ וּ Ch. n. f., constr. of [גְּזֵרָא] d. 8a; וּ bef. (ּ:) נזר

גִּזְרָתָם'פ noun fem. sing., suff. 3 pers. pl. masc. from גִּזְרָה (no pl.) . . . . . נזר

גֻּנַּת'פ'וְ noun fem. sing. constr. of גִּנָּה dec. 10. . נזן

גָּחוֹן'וְ noun masc. sing. dec. 3a. . . . נחן

גִּיחוֹן pr. name of a stream see גִּיחוֹן . . . ניח

גַּחֲזִי'וְ pr. name masc., see גֵּיחֲזִי . . . . ניא

גֹּחִי'וְ Kal part. act. m., suff. 1 p. s. fr. [גּוֹחַ §21. r. 2] ניח

נְחִי'וְ וּ id. imp. sing. fem.; for וְ see lett. וְ . ניח

גָּחַל Root not used; Arab. *to burn.*

     גַּחֶלֶת fem. (of the form קַטֶּלֶת; dag. f. impl., with suff. גַּחַלְתִּי, pl. גֶּחָלִים (§ 42. No. 3 note) constr. גַּחֲלֵי, suff. גֶּחָלָיו) *coal, burning coal;* metaph. for *lightning.*

גֶּחָלֵי'וְ n. f. with pl. m. term. constr. st. fr. גַּחֶלֶת (q. v.) נחל

גַּחָלֶיהָ'וְ id. pl., suff. 3 pers. sing. fem. . . . נחל

גֶּחָלָיו'וְ id. pl., suff. 3 pers. sing. masc. . . . נחל

גֶּחָלִים id. pl., absolute state . . . . נחל

גַּחֶלֶת'פ id. sing. absolute state . . . . נחל

גַּחַלְתִּי'פ id. sing., suff. 1 pers. sing. . . . נחל

נַחַם pr. name of a son of Nahor, Ge. 22. 24.

גָּחַן Root not used; Syr. and Chald. *to incline, to bend.*

     גָּחוֹן masc. dec. 3a, *the belly* of any reptile.

גְּחֹנְךָ'פ noun m. s., suff. 2 pers. s. m. fr. גָּחוֹן d. 3a. נחן

גַּחַר } pr. name masc. Ezr. 2. 47; Ne. 7. 49.
גַּחַר }

גֵּי noun com. sing., constr. of גַּיְא irr. (§ 45) also in compos. with pr. n. as הָעֹבְרִים &c. ניא

גַּיְא Root not used; i. q. נוה Arab. *to flow together.*

     גַּיְא, גֵּי, גַּיְא, גֵּי com. irr. constr. גֵּיא and גֵּי pl. see § 46.—I. *valley, a low plain.*—II. pr. n. הַגַּיְא a station of the Israelites in mount Pisgah. —גֵּי בְנֵי הִנֹּם, גֵּי and גֵּיא בֶן־הִנֹּם (*valley of the son* or *sons of Hinnom*) a valley on the south-east quarter of Jerusalem, also called הַגַּיְא Je. 2. 23.— גֵּי חֲרָשִׁים (*valley of artists*) place in the borders of Judah. גֵּי יִפְתַּח־אֵל (*a valley God does open*) in the northern part of Zebulun, Jos. 19. 14, 27 —גֵּי מֶלַח (*valley of salt*) near the Dead sea.— גֵּי הָעֹבְרִים (*valley of passengers*) on the sea of Galilee, Eze. 39. 11.—גֵּי הַצֹּבְעִים (*valley of hyænas*) in the tribe of Benjamin, 1 Sa. 13. 18.—גֵּי צְפָתָה

---

* Eze. 18. 16.   d Eze. 22. 29.   g Is. 3. 14.   k Is. 40. 24.   o 1 Ki. 3. 26.   r La. 4. 7.   v Ps. 22. 10.   y Eze. 24. 11.   z 2 Sa. 14. 7.
b Ju. 21. 23.   e Eze. 18. 12.   h Ps. 69. 5.   l Hab. 3. 17.   p 1 Ki. 3. 25.   s Ju. 6. 37.   w Mi. 4. 10.   a Is. 44. 19.   c Ge. 3. 14.
c Mi. 2. 2.   f Mi. 3. 2.   i Job 14. 8.   m Le. 16. 22.   q Da. 4. 21.   t Le. 11. 42.   x Ps. 18. 13, 14.   b Is. 47. 14.

(*valley near Zephath*) **in the plains of Judah,** 2
Ch. 14. 9.

גִּיחֲזִי (*valley of vision*) and גֵּחֲזִי pr. name of
the servant of Elisha.

גַּיְא   noun com. sing. irr. (§ 45) . . .   גיא

גֵּיא   וְ' id. constr. state (abs. Zec. 14. 4), also in
compos. with pr. n. as גֵּיא מֶלַח &c. .   גיא

גֵּיא   id. absolute state . . . .   גיא

גֵּיאוֹתָיו   וְ' id. pl., suff. 2 pers. sing. masc. . .   גיא

גִּיד   Root not used; Arab. *to bind.*   Hence

גִּיד   וְ' m. d. 1 a, *sinew, nerve*; perhaps *band*, Is. 48. 4.   גיד

גִּידֵי   id. pl., constr. state . . . .   גיד

גִּידִים   וְ' id. pl., absolute state . . .   גיד

[גּיחַ] & גּוּחַ I. *to break* or *burst forth,* spoken of
water, of an infant from the womb.—II. trans. *to
bring forth.* Hiph. *to rush forth,* Ju. 20. 33.

גִּיחַ or גּוּחַ Ch. Aph. *to rush forth,* Da. 7. 2.—
Hence the two following—

גִּיחַ   (*a breaking forth*) pr. n. of a place, 2 Sa. 2. 24.   גיח

גִּיחוֹן   (*stream*) pr. name *Gihon*.—I. one of the four
rivers of Eden, Ge. 2. 13.—II. an aqueduct near
Jerusalem also called שִׁלֹחַ . . .   גיח

גִּיחֲזִי   pr. name masc. . . . .   גיא

גּוֹיִם   Kh. גּוֹיִם K. n. m., pl. of גּוֹי d. 1 a. (comp. § 3. r. 1)   גוה

[גּיל] & גּוּל prop. *to move in a circle,* hence *to exult,
rejoice*; perh. *to tremble,* Ho. 10. 5. Hence the
two following—

גִּיל   וְ', וָ' m. d. 1, prop. *a circle,* hence—I. *generation, age* (comp. דּוֹר) Da. 1. 10.—II.
exultation, rejoicing.

גִּילָה   fem. dec. 10, *exultation, rejoicing.*

גִּילוּ   וְ' Kal imp. pl. masc. . . .   גיל

גִּילִי   וְ' id. imp. sing. fem. . . .   גיל

גִּילִי   noun m. sing., suff. 1 pers. s. fr. גִּיל d. 1 a.   גיל

גִּילַת   noun fem. sing., constr. of גִּילָה dec. 10. .   גיל

גִּינַת   pr. name masc. . . . .   גנן

[גִּיר] masc. *burnt lime-stone,* Is. 27. 9; Chald. *plaster of
lime,* Da. 5. 5.

גִּירָא   Ch. id., emph. state . . . .   גיר

גִּישׁ   וְ' masc. *clod,* Job 7. 5, Kheth., גּוּשׁ Keri.

גִּישָׁן   וְ' pr. name masc. 1 Ch. 2. 47.

גַּל
גָּל } noun masc. sing. dec. 8 d. . .   נלל

גַּלֵּה   Piel imp. sing. masc. ap. [for גַּלֵּה] .   נלה

גַּל   Kal imp. sing. masc. (§ 18. rem. 4)   נלל

גַּל   Kal inf. or imp. sing. masc. .   נלל

גָּלֵא   וְ' Ch. Peal part. act. sing. m. R. גְּלָא see   נלה

גָּלַב Root not used; Arab. *to scrape, to shave.*

גַּלָּב   masc. d. 1 b. (§ 30. No. 3), *barber,* Eze. 5. 1.

גִּלְבֹּעַ   pr. name of a region . . .   נלל

גִּלְגָּל   pr. name of a place . . .   נלל

גַּלְגַּל   וְ' noun masc. sing. dec. 8 e. .   נלל

גַּלְגַּל   noun masc. sing., constr. of גַּל' dec. 2 b. .   נלל

גַּלְגְּלוֹתֵי   Ch. noun masc. pl., suff. 3 pers. sing. masc.
from גַּלְגַּל dec. 5. (§ 61) . . .   נלל

גַּלְגַּלָּיו   וְ' noun masc. pl., suff. 3 pers. sing. masc.
from גַּלְגַּל dec. 8 e . . . .   נלל

גֻּלְגָּלְתּוֹ   n. f. s., suff. 3 pers. s. m. fr. גֻּלְגֹּלֶת d. 13 c.   נלל

גִּלְגַּלְתִּיךָ   וְ' Pilp. pret. 1 p. s., suff. 2 p. s. m. (§ 6. No. 4)   נלל

[גֶּלֶד] masc. dec. 6 a, *skin;* only

גֶּלְדִּי   noun m. sing., suff. 1 pers. sing. [fr. גֶּלֶד]   נלד

גָּלָה I. *to make bare, open, to uncover;* גָּלָה אֹזֶן פְּ' *to
uncover the ear of any one,* i. e. *to inform him
privately;* בְּ' סוֹד *to disclose, reveal a secret.*—
II. *to lay bare,* a city or country, i. e. *to emigrate,
to go* or *be carried into captivity.*—III. trop. *to
pass away, disappear.* Niph. I. *to be uncovered.*—
II. *to be discovered, revealed.*—III. *to be carried
away,* Is. 38. 12. Pi. I. *to make naked, to uncover.*—II. with עֶרְוָה *to have carnal intercourse
with.*—III. *to disclose, reveal.* Pu. I. *to be uncovered,* Na. 2. 8.—II. part. *open, plain,* Pr. 27.
5. Hiph. *to lead away captive.* Hoph. pass.
Hithp. I. *to uncover oneself,* Ge. 9. 21.—II. *to disclose oneself,* Pr. 18. 2.

גְּלָא   Ch. *to reveal.* Aph. *to carry into captivity*

גִּלֹה   (*captivity*) pr. name of a city in the mountains of Judah.—Gent. n. גִּילוֹנִי 2 Sa. 15. 12.

גּוֹלָה   fem. dec. 10.—I. *captivity.*—II. *collect
captives, a company of exiles.*

גּוֹלָן   (*captivity*) pr. name of a city in Manasseh.

גָּלוּ   Ch. fem. dec. 8 c, *captivity.*

גָּלוּת   fem. dec. 1 b.—I. *captivity.*—II. *collect
captives.*

a 1 Sa. 17. 52.   d Ge. 32. 33.   g Eze. 37. 6, 8.   k Ps. 65. 13.   n Is. 49. 13.   q Da. 5. 5.   t Ps. 119. 22.   x Is. 28. 28.   a Is. 5. 28.
b Is. 40. 4.   e Is. 48. 4.   h Job 10. 11.   i Is. 65. 18.   o Ps. 43. 4.   r Ge. 31. 46.   u Da. 2. 22.   y Da. 7. 9.   c Je. 51. 25.
c Eze. 35. 8.   f Job 40. 17.   i Ge. 25. 23.   m Joel 2. 23.   p Is. 35. 2.   s Ps. 119. 18, 22.   w Da. 2. 29.   z Je. 47. 3.   d Job 16. 15.

גִּלָּיוֹן masc. dec. 3c.—I. *a tablet*, Is. 8. 1.—II. pl. *mirrors*, Is. 3. 23.

גָּלְיָת (*exile, captive*) **pr. name of the Philistine** giant slain by David.

יַגְלִי (*exiled*) **pr. name masc.** Nu. 34. 23.

גְלָא Ch. for גָּלָא (q. v.) . . . . נלה

גָּלֹה Kal inf. absolute . . . . נלה

נְגְלֵה id. imp. sing. masc.; ו bef. (:) . . נלה

גִּלָּה Piel pret. 3 pers. sing. masc. . . נלה

גָּלֶה pr. name of a place . . . נלה

גָּלָה fem. of the following . . . נלה

גֹּלֶה Kal part. act. sing. masc. dec. 9a. . נלה

גָּלָהּ noun masc. sing., suff. **3 pers. sing. fem.** from [גָּל] dec. 8c. . נלל

גָּלוּ Kal pret. 3 pers. pl. . . . נלל

גִּלּוּ Piel pret. 3 pers. pl. . . . נלה

גְּלוּ Kal imp. pl. masc. . . . נלל

גָּלוּי id. part. pass. sing. masc. dec. 3a. . נלה

נְגְלוֹי id. constr. state; ו bef. (:) . . נלה

גַּלְגַּלֵּי noun masc. pl. constr. from [גַּלְגַּל] dec. 1b. . נלל

גַּלְגִּלָּיה id. pl., suff. 3 pers. sing. fem.

גַּלְגִּלֵּיהֶם id., suff. 3 pers. pl. masc.

גַּלְגִּלֵּיהֶן id., suff. 3 pers. pl. fem.

גַּלְגִּלָּיו id., suff. 3 pers. sing. masc.

גַּלְגִּלֵּיכֶם id., suff. 2 pers. pl. masc.

גַּלְגִּלֵּיכֶן id., suff. 2 pers. pl. fem.

גַּלְגִּלִּים id. pl., absolute state

גֹּלָן Kh. גָּלָן, K. גּוֹלָן pr. name of a place . נלה

גָּלוּת noun fem. sing. dec. 1b. . . נלה

גְּלוֹת Kal inf. constr. . . . נלה

גָּלֻיוֹת noun fem., pl. of גָּלָה dec. 10. . נלל

גָּלוּתָא Ch. noun fem. sing. emph. of [גָּלוּ] dec. 8c. . נלא

גָּלוּתִי noun f. s., suff. 1 pers. s. fr. גָּלוּת d. 1b. . נלה

גָּלוֹתִי Kal pret. 1 pers. sing. . . נלל

גִּלַּח Pi.—I. *to shave*, the head, beard; intrans. *to shave oneself.*—II. trop. *to devastate*, Is. 7. 20. Pu. *to be shaven.* Hithpa. *to shave oneself.*

גִּלַּח ו Piel pret. 3 pers. sing. masc. . . נלח

גֻּלַּח Pual pret. 3 p. s. m. [for גֻּלַּח comp. §8.r.7] . נלח

גִּלְּחָה ו Piel pret. 3 pers. sing. fem. . . נלח

גִּלְּחוּ ו id. pret. 3 pers. s. m., suff. 3 pers. s. m. . נלח

גִּלַּחְתְּ id. pret. 1 pers. sing. . . נלח

גַּלִּי Piel imp. sing. fem. . . . נלה

גְּלִי
גְּלֵא } Ch. Peal part. pass. sing. m. R. גְּלָא see . נלה

גַּלֵּיהֶם noun m. pl., suff. 3 pers. pl. m. fr. גַּל d. 8d. . נלל

גַּלָּיו id. with suff. 3 pers. sing. masc. . . נלל

גִּלָּיוֹן noun masc. sing. dec. 3c. . . נלל

גַּלֵּיךְ ו noun m. pl., suff. 2 p. s. m. fr. גַּל d. 8d. . נלל

גְּלִיל noun masc. sing., constr. of גָּלִיל dec. 3a. . נלל

גְּלִילוֹת noun f., pl. of גְּלִילָה d. 10; also pr. name . נלל

גְּלִילֹת constr. of the following . . נלל

גַּלִּילִים noun masc. pl. absolute from גָּלִיל dec. 3a. . נלל

גֻּלִּים noun masc., pl. of גַּל dec. 8d, also pr. name of a place . נלל

גֹּלִים Kal part. act. masc., pl. of גָּלָה dec. 9a. . נלה

גָּלִיתָ ו id. pret. 2 pers. sing. masc. . . נלה

גַּלְיַת
גָּלְיָת } pr. name masc. . . . נלח

גָּלִית ו Piel pret. 2 pers. sing. fem. . . נלה

גָּלִתָה Kal pret. 2 pers. sing. masc. . . נלה

גָּלִיתִי ו id. pret. 1 pers. sing. . . נלה

גִּלִּיתִי
גִּלִּיתִי } Piel pret. 1 pers. sing. (§ 24. rem. 11) . נלה

גָּלִיתִי ו id.; acc. shifted to ult. by conv. ו (comp. § 8. rem. 7) . . . . נלה

[גָּלַל] I. *to roll*, e. g. stones.—II. metaph. with מֵעַל *to roll away, remove* from any one, e. g. reproach; גֹּל עַל אֶל יְהוָה *commit to the Lord*, as one's ways or works. Niph. נָגֹל—I. *to roll along*, Am. 5. 24.—II. *to be rolled together*, Is. 34. 4. Poal גּוֹלָל with בְּ *to be rolled about in*, Is. 9. 4. Hithpo.—I. i. q. Po. 2 Sa. 20. 12.—II. *to roll, rush in*, with עַל *upon* Ge. 43. 18. Pilp. גִּלְגֵּל (§ 6. No. 4) *to roll down* any one, with מִן, Je. 51. 25. Hithpalp. (§ 6. No. 4) i. q. Hithpo. Job 30. 14. Hiph. הֵגֵל *to roll away*, Ge. 29. 10.

גָּלָל masc. dec. 4a.—I. *dung*, 1 Ki. 14. 10.—II. prop. *circumstance, cause*, as a prep. בִּגְלַל *because of.*—III. pr. name masc. of two persons.

גְּלָל Ch. *heaviness, weight*; ו אֶבֶן *heavy stone.*

גֵּל masc. dec. 6. (suff. גֶּלְלוֹ § 35. r. 3) *dung.*

גִּלְלַי pr. name masc. Ne. 12. 36.

גִּלּוּל masc. dec. 1b, only in pl. *idols.*

גָּלִיל masc. dec. 3a.—I. adj. *rolling, turning,*

a Da. 2. 28.   e Is. 49. 21.   i Nu. 24. 4, 16.   n Is. 45. 13.   r 2 Sa. 14. 26.   v Da. 2. 30.   z Is. 8. 23.   d Eze. 12. 3.   f 2 Sa. 7. 26.
b Da. 2. 47.   f 1 Sa. 22. 8.   k Je. 50. 2.   o Jos. 5. 9.   s Ju. 16. 17.   w Is. 8. 1.   a Am. 6. 7.   e Is. 57. 8.   g 1 Sa. 20. 12, 13.
c Eze. 12. 3.   g Zec. 4. 2.   l Eze. 23. 37.   p Ju. 16. 22.   t Is. 47. 2.   x Job 38. 11.   b 1 Ch. 17. 25.   f Ruth 3. 4.   h Je. 49. 10.
d Le. 20. 18.   h Am. 1. 5.   m Eze. 23. 49.   q De. 21. 12.   u Da. 2. 19.

1 Ki. 6. 34.—II. *ring.*—III. *circuit, tract of country*; הַגָּלִילָה, הַגָּלִיל, a district with twenty towns in the tribe of Naphtali, *Galilee.*

גְּלִילָה fem. dec. 10, *circuit, region.*

גַּל masc. dec. 8 d.—I. *heap* of stones.—II. *spring, fountain.*—III. pl. *waves, billows.*

גִּלְבֹּעַ (*boiling fountain*, comp. בּוּעַ) pr. name of a mountain in the tribe of Issachar.

גַּלְעֵד (*heap of testimony*) pr. name of a heap of stones raised by Jacob and Laban, Ge. 31. 47, 48.

גֹּל masc. dec. 8 c, *an oil-bowl* or cup, Zec. 4. 2.

גֻּלָּה fem. dec. 10.—I. *spring, fountain.*—II. *an oil-bowl* or cup.—III. *bowl* or *globe*, as an ornament on the capitals of columns.

גַּלְגַּל masc. dec. 8 e.—I. *wheel.*—II. *whirlwind.*—III. *chaff.*

גַּלְגַּל Ch. masc. dec. 5. (§ 61), *wheel*, Da. 7. 9.

גִּלְגָּל masc.—I. *wheel*, Is. 28. 28.—II. pr. name of a place between Jericho and Jordan.

גֻּלְגֹּלֶת fem. dec. 13 c, *scull*; in counting men it is used for *head* or *poll.*

מְגִלָּה fem. d. 10, *volume, roll, book.* Chald. id.

גָּלָל וְ pr. name masc. . . . . נלל
גְּלָל Ch. noun masc. sing. . . . נלל
גֹּלֵל וְ Kal part. act. sing. masc. . נלל
נָלֲלוּ וְ id. pret. 3 pers. pl. [for גָּלֲלוּ] נלל
גַּלֲלֵי noun m. pl. constr. fr. [גָּלָל] d. 6. (§ 35. r. 3) נלל
גְּלָלַי pr. name masc. . . . . נלל
גַּלֲלֵיהֶם n. m. pl., suff. 3 p. pl. m. fr. [וְגָלֹּל] d. 1 b. נלל

[גָּלַם] *to wrap together*, 2 Ki. 2. 8.

גְּלוֹם masc. dec. 1 a, *mantle, cloak*, Eze. 27. 24.

גֹּלֶם masc. dec. 6 c, *embryo*, prop. *an unformed mass*, as it were wrapt up together, Ps. 139. 16.

גַּלְמוּד masc. adj.—I. *sterile barren.*—II. *famished.* Made up of נמר and נלל Arab. *to be hard.* (Gesen.)

נַלְמוּדָה וְ fem. of the prec.

גָּלְמִי noun m. s., suff. 1 pers. s. fr. [גֹּלֶם] d. 6 c. נלם

גָּלַע Hithpa. *to grow warm, become angry, irritated,* with בְּ of the thing or cause.

גָּלֵע pr. name of a place . . נלל

גִּלְעָד (*hard, rough*, coll. with the Arab.) pr. name.—I. of several men; especially a son of Machir grandson of Manasseh. Hence

patronym. גִּלְעָדִי.—II. with the **art.** הַגִּלְעָד a region beyond Jordan.

גִּלְעָדָה pr. name (גִּלְעָד II) with parag. ה

גִּלְעָדִים gent. noun, pl. of גִּלְעָדִי fr. גִּלְעָד q. v.

[גָּלַשׁ] prob. i. q. שָׁלַג *to be white*, hence *to shine*, Ca. 4. 1; 6. 5. Eng. Ver. "appear".

נָלֹת וְ noun fem. sing. dec. 1 b, for גָּלוּת . נלה
נָלַת noun fem. sing., constr. of גָּלָה dec. 10. . נלה
נָלֹת וְ pl. of the prec. . . . . נלל
גָּלְתָה Kal pret. 3 pers. sing. fem. . . נלה
גִּלְּתָה וְ Piel pret. 3 pers. sing. fem. . נלה
גֻּלְּתָה Pual pret. 3 pers. sing. fem. . נלה
גָּלִיתִי וְ Kal pret. 1 pers. sing.; acc. shifted to ult. by conv. וְ (comp. § 8. rem. 7) . ניל

נַם וְ conj. . . . . . . נמם

גָּמָא Pi. *to drink in, to swallow*, Job 39. 24. Hiph. *to give to drink*, Ge. 24. 17. Hence

גֹּמֶא וְ masc. *reed, paper reed, papyrus*; תֵּבַת גֹּמֶא *an ark of papyrus* . . . נמא

גֹּמֶד masc. a kind of *measure of length*, Ju. 3. 16.

גַּמָּדִים וְ masc., pl. *bold warriors*, Eze. 27. 11. נמד Arab. *to cut off*; Syr. *to be bold.* Others take it as a pr. name of a people.

גָּמוּל Kal part. p. masc. sing. dec. 3 a. (pr. name in compos. see בֵּית) . . . . נמל
גְּמוּל וְ noun masc. sing. dec. 1 a; וּ bef. (ָ) . נמל
גְּמוּלֵי Kal part. p. pl. constr. m. from גָּמוּל dec. 3 a. נמל
גְּמוּלָיו n. m. pl., suff. 3 pers. s. m. from גְּמוּל d. 1 a. נמל
גְּמֻלֵךְ id. sing., suff. 2 pers. sing. fem. נמל
גְּמוּלָם id. sing., suff. 3 pers. pl. masc. נמל
גִּמְזוֹ (*place of sycomores* Arab. גמיז Chald. גמזוז sycomore) pr. name of a town in the tribe of Judah, 2 Ch. 28. 18.

גְּמִיר Chald. Peal part. pass. sing. masc. . . מל

גָּמַל I. *to retribute, to recompense*, good or evil, with acc., עַל, לְ.—II. generally *to do, show* good or evil to any one.—III. *to mature, ripen* fruit; intrans *to become ripe.*—IV. *to wean* a child.

גָּמָל com dec. 8. (pl. גְּמַלִּים § 37. No. 2) *camel.*
גָּמוּל (*weaned*) pr. name masc. 1 Ch. 24. 17
גְּמוּל masc. dec. 1 a.—I. *retribution, recompense.*—II. any *act* done or shown to any one, good or evil

a Pr. 26. 27.   d De. 29. 16.   g Ob. 1. 20.   k La. 1. 3.   n Na. 2. 8.   p Is. 35. 7.   r Pr. 12. 14.   t Ps. 103. 2.   x Ps. 28. 4.
b Ge. 29. 3, 8.   e Is. 49. 21.   h Ec. 12. 6.   l Le. 20. 18.   o Is. 65. 19.   q Is. 11. 8.   s Is. 28. 9.   u Ps. 137. 8.   y Ezr. 7. 12.
c Eze. 4. 15.   f Ps. 139. 16.   i 1 Ki. 7. 41.   m Is. 26. 21.

גְּמוּלָה fem. dec. 10, *retribution, recompense*; especially *benefit*.

גְּמַלִּי (*camel-owner*) pr. name masc. Nu. 13. 12.

גַּמְלִיאֵל (*benefit of God*) pr. name masc.

תַּגְמוּל masc. dec. 1 b, *benefit, kindness*, Ps. 116. 12.

גָּמָל[a]	n. com. s., pl. גְּמַלִּים d. 8 a. (§ 37. Nos. 2 & 3)		נמל
גְּמֹל[b]	Kal imp. sing. masc.		נמל
גֹּמֵל	id. part. act. sing. masc. dec. 7 b. .		נמל
גָּמְלָהּ[c]	id. inf. with suff. 3 pers. sing. fem. .		נמל
גָּמְלוּ[d]	id. pret. 3 pers. pl.		נמל
גְּמֻלוֹ[e]	n. m. s., suff. 3 p. s. m. fr. גְּמוּל d. 1 a.; וּ bef. (:)		נמל
גְּמָלֻךְ	Kal pret. 3 pers. pl. with suff. 2 pers. sing. m.		נמל
גְּמֻלוֹת	noun fem., pl. of גְּמוּלָה dec. 10.		נמל
גְּמַלִּי	pr. name masc.		נמל
גַּמְלִיאֵל	pr. name masc.		נמל
גְּמֻלֵיהֶם[f]	noun com. pl., suff. 3 pers. pl. masc. from גָּמָל dec. 8 a. (§ 37. No. 2); וּ bef. (:)		נמל
גְּמַלָּיו	id. pl., suff. 3 pers. sing. masc.		נמל
גְּמַלֶּיךָ	id. pl., suff. 2 pers. sing. masc.		נמל
גְּמַלִּים	id. pl., absolute state; וּ bef. (:)		נמל
גֹמְלִים	Kal part. act. masc., pl. of גֹּמֵל dec. 7 b.		נמל
גָמְלֵךְ[g]	id. inf. with suff. 2 pers. sing. fem. .		נמל
גְּמָלֵךְ	id. pret. 3 pers. sing. m., suff. 2 pers. sing. m.		נמל
גְּמֻלְךָ	n. m. s., suff. 2 pers. s. m. from גְּמוּל d. 1 a.		נמל
גְּמֻלְכֶם	id., suff. 2 pers. pl. masc. .		נמל
גְּמָלָם[h]	Kal pret. 3 pers. sing. m., suff. 3 pers. pl. m.		נמל
גְּמַלְנוּ	id. pret. 1 pers. pl.		נמל
גְּמָלָנוּ[i]	id. pret. 3 pers. sing. masc., suff. 1 pers. pl.		נמל
גְּמָלַתְהוּ	id. pret. 3 pers. sing. fem., suff. 3 pers. sing. m.		נמל
גְּמָלַתּוּ[k]	id. id. with dag. euph. .		נמל
גְּמָלְתִּי	id. pret. 1 pers. sing.		נמל
גְּמַלְתִּיךָ	id. id., suff. 2 pers. sing. masc. .		נמל
גְּמַלְתִּנִי	id. pret. 2 pers. sing. masc., suff. 1 pers. sing.		נמל

גָּמַם Root not used; Arab. *to heap up, increase*; intrans. *to be heaped up.*

גַּם conj.—I. *also*; גַּם—גַּם *both—and*; הִיא גַּם *she also herself.* A pronoun repeated for the sake of emphasis has the nominative form though the preceding is in the oblique case בָּרֲכֵנִי גַם־אָנִי *bless me, me also*, Ge. 27. 34; אֶת־דָּמְךָ גַם־אָתָּה *thy blood, thine also*.—II. *yea, truly*, especially at the beginning of a sentence; גַּם־כִּי *although.*—III. *yet, nevertheless.*

מְגַמָּה fem. dec. 10, *troop, host*, Hab. 1. 9. Others *desire, longing.*

גָּמַן Root not used; Chald. *to dig.*

גּוּמֵץ masc. *a pit*, Ec. 10. 8.

גָּמַר—I. *to bring to an end, to complete*, with עַל, בַּעַד. II. intrans. *to come to an end, to fail.*

גְּמִר Ch. id. part. pass. *perfect, skilled*, Ezr. 7. 12.

גֹּמֶר (*perfection*) pr. name—I. of a son of Japheth, and applied to his posterity.—II. of the wife of the prophet Hosea, Ho. 1. 3.

גְּמַרְיָהוּ, גְּמַרְיָה (*whom the Lord makes perfect*) pr. name of two different men.

גֹּמֶר	pr. name of a man and a people . .		נמר
גֹּמֵר[l]	Kal part. act. sing. masc. . .		נמר
גְּמַרְיָה[m], גְּמַרְיָהוּ	pr. name masc.; וּ bef. (:) . .		נמר
גַּן	noun com. sing. dec. 8 d. . .		ננ

[גָּנַב] I. *to steal*; trop. *to carry away*, as a storm does the chaff.—II. *to deceive*, especially with לֵב. Niph. *to be stolen*, Ex. 22. 11. Pi. i. q. Kal. Pu.—I. *to be stolen.*—II. *to be brought secretly*, with אֶל of the person, Job 4. 12. Hithpa. *to steal oneself away*, 2 Sa. 19. 4.

גַּנָּב masc. dec. 1 b. (§ 30. rem. 3) *a thief.*

גְּנֵבָה fem. dec. 10, *a thing stolen*, Ex. 22. 2, 3.

גְּנֻבַת (*theft*) pr. name masc. 1 Ki. 11. 20.

גַּנָּב[n]	noun masc. sing. dec. 1 b. . . .		ננב
גָּנֹב[o]	Kal inf. abs.		ננב
גֹּנֵב[p]	id. part. act. sing. masc. . .		ננב
גֻּנָּב[q]	Pual pret. 3 pers. sing. masc.		ננב
גֻּנֹּב[r]	id. inf. abs.		ננב
גָּנְבוּ	Kal pret. 3 pers. pl. . . .		ננב
גְּנֵבוּךָ[s]	id., suff. 2 pers. s. masc.		ננב
גַּנָּבִים	noun masc., pl. of גַּנָּב dec. 1 b.		ננב
גָּנַבְתָּ[t]	Kal pret. 2 pers. sing. masc. .		ננב
גְּנֻבַת	pr. name masc. . . .		ננב
גְּנָבַתּוּ	id. Kal pret. 3 pers. s. fem., suff. 3 pers. s. m.		ננב
גָּנַבְתִּי	id. pret. 1 pers. sing.; acc. shifted to ult. by וּ conv. (§ 8. rem. 7) . .		ננב
גְּנֻבְתִי[u]	id. part. pass. fem. sing. [גְּנֻבָה] with parag. י (comp. § 8. rem. 19); וּ bef. (:)		ננב
גֻּנַּבְתִּי	Pual pret. 1 pers. sing. . .		ננב
גְּנָבָתַם	Kal pret. 3 pers. sing. fem., suff. 3 pers. pl. m.		ננב
גָּנוּב[v]	id. part. pass. sing. masc. dec. 3 a.		ננב

a Is. 21. 7, etc.	c Ge. 50. 17.	i Pr. 3. 30.	n Is. 63. 7.	r 1 Sa. 24. 18.	z Ex. 22. 11.	b Ex. 22. 6.	f Pr. 30. 9.	Ge. 40. 15.
b Ps. 119. 17.	f Ge. 24. 20.	h Ob. 1. 15.	o Pr. 31. 12.	s 1 Sa. 24. 18.	Ho. 4. 2.	c Ge. 40. 15.	g Ge. 31. 32.	
1 Sa. 1. 23.	g Ge. 24. 14, 46.	l Joel 4. 4, 7.	p 1 Sa. 1. 24.	t Ps. 57. 3.	De. 24. 7.	2 Sa. 19. 42.	i Ge. 31. 39.	l Ge. 30. 32.
Pr. 19. 17.	h 1 Sa. 1. 23.	m Ge. 50. 15.	q Ps. 7. 5.	u Ho. 7. 1.	Ex. 21. 16.	Ge. 31. 30.	kk Is. 3. 9.	u Is. 63. 7.

גְּנוּבִים[a]   id. id. pl., absolute state   .   גנב

גָּנֹן   Kal inf. abs.   .   .   .   גנן

גַּנּוֹת   noun fem., pl. of גַּנָּה dec. 10.   .   גנן

גָּנוֹתִי[b]   וֹ Kal pret. 1 pers. sing.; acc. shifted to ult.
    by conv. וֹ (comp. § 8. rem. 7)   גנן

גַּנּוֹתֵיכֶם[c]   n. fem. pl., suff. 2 pers. pl. m. from גַּנָּה d. 10. גנן

גָּנַן   Root not used ; to cover; to collect, cogn. כָּנַס.

   גְּנָז masc. only pl. com. גְּנָזִי, treasures; Eze.27.24.
   perhaps chests in which precious things are stored.

   גְּנַז Chald. masc. dec. 3 b, treasure.

   גִּנְזַךְ masc. dec. 8 d, treasury, 1 Ch. 28. 11.

גִּנְזֵי   noun masc. pl. constr. from [גֶּנֶז] dec. 6 a. .   גנז

גִּנְזֵי[d]   Chald. id. from [גְּנַז] dec. 3 b.   .   .   גנז

גִּנְזַיָּא   Chald. id. pl., emph. st.   .   .   גנז

גְּנָזַיִךְ[e]   וֹ n. m. pl., suff. 3 p. s. m. from [גֶּנֶז] d. 8.   גנז

גַּנִּי[f]   noun com. sing., suff. 1 pers. s. from גַּן d. 8 d.   גנן

גַּנִּים[g]   id. pl., absolute state   .   .   גנן

[גָּנַן]   prop. to cover, whence to protect, const. with אֶל,
    עַל.   Hiph. id. with בְּעַד, עַל.

   גַּן com. dec. 8 d, garden.

   גַּנָּה and גִּנָּה fem. dec. 10, id.

   גִּנְּבַת (garden for גַּנַּת dag. forte resolved in Yod)
   pr. name masc. 1 Ki. 16. 21, 22.

   גִּנְּתוֹן (gardener) pr. name masc., also written
   גִּנְּתוֹי comp. Ne. 12. 4, with ver. 16.

   מָגֵן masc. dec. 8 b, pl. מָגִנִּים וֹת (§ 37. rem. 4),
   shield; trop. prince.

   מְגִנָּה fem. dec. 10, with לֵב veiling, covering of
   the heart, La. 3. 65.

גַּנַּת   noun fem. sing., constr. of [גַּנָּה] dec. 10. .   גנן

גַּנָּתוֹ   n. fem. s., suff. 3 pers. s. m. from גַּנָּה d. 10.   גנן

גִּנְּתוֹי
גִּנְּתוֹן } pr. name masc.   גנן

גְּעַ[h]   וֹ Kal imp. sing. masc.   .   .   געע

[גָּעָה]   to low, as an ox or cow.

   גֹּעָה (lowing) pr. name of a place near Jerusalem, Je. 31. 39.

גָּעֹו   וֹ Kal inf. abs. (§ 24. rem. 2) .   .   געה

[גָּעַל]   to loathe, abhor.   Niph. to be cast away, 2 Sa. 1. 21.
   Hiph. to cast the young, i.e. suffer abortion, Job 21. 10.

   גַּעַל (loathing), pr. name masc. Ju. 9. 26, 28, 30.

   גֹּעַל masc. a loathing, Eze. 16. 5.

גַּעַל   pr. name masc.   .   .   .   געל

גָּעֲלָה   וֹ Kal pret. 3 pers sing. fem.   .   געל

גָּעֲלוּ[i]   id. pret. 3 pers. pl.   .   .   געל

גֹּעֶלֶת   id. part., act. sing. fem. (§ 8. rem. 19) .   געל

גְּעַלְתִּים[k]   id. pret. 1 pers. sing., suff. 3 pers. pl. masc.   געל

גָּעַר[l]   וֹ to rebuke, reprove, const. with בְּ.

   גְּעָרָה fem. dec. 11 c. (constr. גַּעֲרַת § 42. rem. 1)
   rebuke, reproof.

   מִגְעֶרֶת fem. rebuke, or curse, De. 28. 20.

גְּעַר   Kal imp. sing. masc.   .   .   געל

גֹּעֵר   id. part. act. sing. masc.   .   .   גער

גְּעָרָה   noun fem. sing. (constr. גַּעֲרַת) dec. 11 c.   גער

גָּעַרְתָּ   Kal pret. 2 pers. sing. masc.   .   גער

גַּעֲרַת   n. fem. s., constr. of גְּעָרָה d. 11 c. (§ 42. r. 1)   גער

גַּעֲרָתוֹ   וֹ id., suff. 3 pers. sing. masc.   .   גער

גָּעַרְתִּי[n]   וֹ Kal pret. 1 pers. sing.; acc. shifted to ult.
    by conv. וֹ (§ 8. rem. 7)   גער

גַּעֲרָתְךָ[o]   noun fem. sing., suff. 2 pers. sing. masc. from
   גְּעָרָה dec. 11 c. (§ 42. rem. 1)   .   גער

[גָּעַשׁ]   to shake, tremble.   Pu. to be shaken, Job 34. 20.
   Hithpa. to be moved, shaken, agitated.   Hithpo.
   to stagger, reel.

   גַּעַשׁ (quaking) pr. name of one of the mountains of Ephraim.

גַּעַשׁ   pr. name of a mountain [for גַּעַשׁ] .   געש

גָּעְתָה   pr. name of a place [גֹּעָה] with paragogic ה   געה

גַעְתָּם   וֹ pr. name masc.   .   .   .   גנע

גַּפֵּי   noun fem. pl. constr. from [גַּף] dec. 8 d. .   גפף

גַּפֶּיהָ[p]   Chald. K. גַּפֵּהּ, Kh. גַּפַּיהּ, noun fem. pl., suff.
   3 pers. sing. fem. from [גַּף] dec. 5 d. .   גפף

גַּפִּין[q]   וֹ Chald. id. pl., absolute state   .   גפף

גָּפַן   Root not used ; i. q. גָּבַן, כָּפַן to be bent, curved.
   Hence

גֶּפֶן
גָּפֶן } noun com. dec. 6 a, vine; שָׂדֶה גַּ׳
    וֹ, the wild vine   גפן

גַּפְנָהּ[r]   id., suff. 3 pers. sing. fem.   .   .   גפן

גַּפְנוֹ   id., suff. 3 pers. sing. masc.   .   .   גפן

גַּפְנִי[s]   id., suff. 1 pers. sing.   .   .   גפן

גַּפְנְךָ[t]   id., suff. 2 pers. sing. masc.   .   .   גפן

גַּפְנָם   id., suff. 3 pers. pl. masc.   .   .   גפן

גָּפַף   Root not used ; i. q. גָּבַב to be bent, curved.

   גַּף masc. dec. 8 d.—I. back, i. e. hillock, Pr. 9. 3.
   —II. body, person, only בְּנַפּוֹ by himself, alone,
   Ex. 21. 3, 4.

a Pr. 9. 17.	e Ezr. 7. 20.	i Job 8. 16.	m Eze. 16. 45.	q Is. 17. 13.	t Is. 66. 15.	v Pr. 9. 3.	z Da. 7. 4.	c Ho. 2. 14.
b Is. 31. 5.	f 1 Ch. 28. 11.	k Ps. 144. 5.	n Ps. 68. 31.		r Mal. 3. 11.	w Da. 7. 4.	a Da. 7. 4.	d Joel 1. 7.
c 2 Ki. 19. 34. etc.	g Ca. 4. 16.	l 1 Sa. 6. 12.	o Le. 26. 44		s Mal. 2. 3.	x Ps. 104. 7.	b Joel 2. 22.	e Je. 5. 17.
d Am. 4. 9.	h Ca. 4. 15.		m Ie. 26. 30.				y Da. 7. 6.	

גַּף Chald. fem. dec. 3 a, *wing*, Da. 7. 4, 6.

אָגַף masc. only pl. אֲגַפִּים, prop. *wings*, poet. for *armies, hosts*.

גֹּפֶר masc. the name of a tree; prob. the *pitch-pine*, Ge. 6. 14, נָפֶר i. q. כָּפַר *to cover over*.

נָפְרִית fem. *brimstone*.

נֵר '1 Kal pret. 3 pers. sing. masc., part. act.   נור

גֵּר '1 noun masc. sing. dec. 1 a.   נור

גֵּר defect. [for נִיר] noun masc. sing.   ניר

גֵּרָא '1 pr. name masc.   נרר

גָּרָב masc. *scurf, scurvy*.

גָּרֵב (*scurvied*) pr. name—I. masc. 2 Sa. 23. 38.— II. of a hill near Jerusalem, Je. 31. 39.

גַּרְגְּרִים noun masc. pl. [of גַּרְגַּר, § 36. rem. 5] .   נרר

גַּרְגְּרֹתֶיךָ noun fem. pl. [גַּרְגָּרֹת], suff. 2 pers. s. m.   נרר

[גִּרְגָּשִׁי] pr. name of a Canaanitish nation.

גָּרַד . Hithpa. *to scrape oneself*, Job 2. 8.

גָּרָה Kal not used; prob. to produce a *grating* sound, whence גָּרוֹן. Pi. *to excite, stir up* strife. Hithpa. *to excite oneself*, especially *to contention, war*; with בְּ *to contend with*.

גָּרוֹן noun dec. 3 a, *the throat*.

תִּגְרָה fem. dec. 10, *strife, contention*, Ps. 39. 11.

גֵּרָה '1 noun fem. sing. [for גִּרָה] .   נרר

גָּרוּ Kal pret. 3 pers. pl.   נור

גֵּרוֹ noun m. s., suff. 3 pers. s. m. from גֵּר dec. 1 a.   נור

גָּרוֹן noun masc. sing. dec. 3 a   נרה

גְּרוֹנִי id. suff. 1 pers. sing.   נרה

גְּרוֹנֶךָ id., suff. 2 pers. sing. masc.   נרה

גְּרוּשָׁה '1 Kal part. pass. s., fem. of [גָּרוּשׁ]; וּ bef.   נרש

גְּרוּשֹׁתָיו n. pl. fem., suff. 3 pers. s. m. from [גּוּר] d. 1 a.   נור

גָּרַז Niph. *to be cut off*, Ps. 31. 23.

גִּרְזִי (*inhabitant of a sterile land*) pr. name of a Canaanitish nation subdued by David, 1 Sa. 27. 8. Kheth., גִּזְרִי Keri. Also the two following—

גְּרִזִים always with הַר (*mount of the Gerisites*) pr. name of a mountain near Shechem in the tribe of Ephraim, opposite mount Ebal.

גַּרְזֶן masc. *an axe*.

גָּרֵי construct of the following

גָּרִים '1 Kal part. act. masc., pl. of גֵּר dec. 1 a.   נור

גֵּרִים noun masc., pl. of גֵּר dec. 1 a.   נור

גֵּרֶיךָ '1 id. sing., suff. 2 pers. sing. masc.   נור

גָּרַל Root not used ; Arab. *to be gritty, stony*.

גָּרָל adj. with Mak. גְּרָל *harsh angry*, Pr. 19. 19 Kheth., גָּדֵל Keri.

גּוֹרָל masc. dec. 2 b. (pl. גּוֹרָלוֹת).—I. *lot*, prop. the stone by which the lot was determined; הִפִּיל גּוֹרָל *to cast lots*, so also with the verbs עָלָה, יָצָא גּוֹרָל, נָתַן, הֵטִיל, הִשְׁלִיךְ, יָדַד, יָרָה גּוֹרָל *the lot fell*, constr. with עַל, אֶל, לְ of the person.—II. *lot, portion, inheritance*.

גֹּדֶל־ Kh., גָּדֵל K. adj. m. s., constr. of גֹּדֶל or גָּדֵל, with Mak. [for גֹּרֶל or גְּדֹל § 32. r. 7.]

גֹּרָלוֹת noun masc. with pl. fem. term., absolute state from גּוֹרָל dec. 2 b.   נרל

גֶּרֶם , גָּרַם (§ 35. rem. 2) masc. dec. 6 a.—I. *bone*.—II. *strength*, חֲמוֹר גָּרֶם *strong ass*, Ge. 49. 14.—III. *substance, body*, 2 Ki. 9. 13. אֶל־גֶּרֶם הַמַּעֲלוֹת *upon the steps themselves*, the very steps, comp. עֶצֶם Prof. Lee, *frame-work*.

גְּרַם Chald. masc. dec. 3 a, *bone*, Da. 6. 25.

גָּרַם *to gnaw a bone*, Zep. 3. 3, *they shall not gnaw* לַבֹּקֶר *in the morning*, i. e. they shall leave nothing to gnaw. Pi. id. Nu. 24, 8. Meton. of sherds, *to gnaw, lick them clean*, Eze. 23. 34.

גַּרְמִי (*bony*) pr. name, masc. 1 Ch. 4. 19.

גָּרְמוּ Kal pret. 3 pers. pl.   נרם

גַּרְמֵיהוֹן Chald. noun masc. pl., suff. 3 pers. pl. masc. from [גְּרַם] dec. 3 a.   נרם

גְּרָמָיו noun masc. pl., suff. 3 pers. sing. masc. from גֶּרֶם dec. 6.   נרם

גֹּרֶן fem. dec. 6 c, pl. גְּרָנוֹת, construct גָּרְנוֹת (נרן) Arab. *to make smooth, level*).—I. *a level place at the gate of the city*, the *forum* of the Hebrews, 1 Ki. 22. 10; 2 Ch. 18. 9.—II. *threshing-floor*. Meton. for the grain itself, Job 39. 12.

גֹּרְנָה id. with paragogic ה   נרן

גָּרְנֹת id. pl., construct state   נרן

גָּרְנִי id. sing., suff. 1 pers. sing.   נרן

גָּרְנְךָ '1 id. sing., suff. 2 pers. sing. masc.   נרן

גָּרְנָם noun masc. sing., suff. 3 pers. pl. masc. from גֹּרֶן dec. 3 a.   נרה

[גָּרַם] *to be broken, crushed*, Ps. 119. 20. Hiph. *to crush*, La. 3. 16.

גֶּרֶשׂ masc. dec. 6 a. (suff. גְּרִשִׂי,) *something crushed, bruised*, perhaps *corn*.

a Ia. 11. 6.   d Ex. 6. 4.   g Eze. 16. 11.   Na. 2. 13.   Job 19. 15.   n 2 Ki. 9. 13.   p Job 40. 18.   r Ho. 9. 1.   t Job 39. 12.
Ia. 17. 6.   e De. 1. 16.   h Le. 21. 7.   i De. 20. 19.   m Pr. 19. 19.   o Zep. 3. 3.   q Mi. 4. 12.   s Ia. 21. 10.   u Ps. 5. 10.
Le. 11. 26.   f Ps. 69. 4.   hh Is. 27. 9.   kk Is. 3. 16.   mm Da. 6. 25.

גֵּרְסָה Kal preter. 3 pers. sing. fem. • גרס

[גָּרַע] fut. יִגְרַע.—I. *to take away* the beard.—II. *to detract, to withhold*, construed with מִן ; *to reserve*, with אֶל.—II. *to diminish*, with acc. Niph. *to be detracted, diminished, lessened.* Pi. *to draw off*, Job 36. 27.

מִגְרָעוֹת fem. only pl. absolute *narrowed rests, rebatements*, in building, 1 Ki. 6. 6.

גְּרֻעָה Kal part. pass. sing. fem. from [גָּרוּעַ] masc. נרע

[גָּרַף] I. *to carry, sweep away*, Ju. 5. 21.—II. in the deriv. *to grasp, gripe*, Germ. *greifen.*

אֶגְרוֹף masc. *fist*, Ex. 21. 18 ; Is. 58. 4.

מְגְרָפָה fem. dec. 11a, *clod*, Joel 1. 17 ; so Gesenius and others before him. Prof. Lee, *furrow.*

גְּרָפָם Kal pret. 3 pers. s. m., suff. 3 pers. pl. masc. גרף

[גָּרַד] *to drag, draw away.* Niph.—I. *to be dragged, carried away*, so נִגְרוֹת Job 20. 28, which some derive from נֵגֶר.—II. *to ruminate, to chew the cud*, Le. 11. 7. Po. *to be sawed*, 1 Ki. 7. 9. Hithpo. *to sweep away with itself*, Je. 30. 23.

גֵּרָא (*grain* i. q. גֵּרָה) pr. name of several men, especially of a son of Benjamin, Ge. 46. 21.

גֵּרָה fem.—I. *the cud.*—II. *a grain, gerah*, a weight equal to the twentieth part of a shekel.

גְּרָר pr. name of a city of the Philistines, formerly the residence of their kings ; נַחַל גְּרָר *valley of Gerar*, Ge. 26. 17.

גַּרְגַּר masc. only pl. גַּרְגְּרִים (§ 36. rem. 5) *berries*, Is. 17. 6.

גַּרְגְּרוֹת fem. pl. (perhaps from a sing. גַּרְגֶּרֶת) *throat, neck.*

מְגְרָה fem. dec. 10, *a saw.*

גָּרֵד pr. name of a place • גרד

גְּרֵדָה id. with paragogic ה • גרד

[גָּרַשׁ] I. *to cast out* or *up*, Is. 57. 20 ; hence *to drive out, expel, divorce.*—II. *to plunder, spoil*, Eze. 36. 5. Pi. *to drive out, expel*, with מִן of the place. Niph.—I. *to be cast out.*—II. *to be agitated, tossed*, Is. 57. 20.

גֶּרֶשׁ masc. *produce, fruit*, De. 33. 14.

גְּרֻשָּׁה fem. dec. 10, *expulsion*, Eze. 45. 9.

גֵּרְשׁוֹן (*expulsion*) pr. name of a son of Levi. Patronym. גֵּרְשֻׁנִּי.

מִגְרָשׁ masc. dec. 2 b, pl. מִגְרָשִׁים, once מִגְרָשׁוֹת (prop. from מִגְרֶשֶׁת).—I. inf. see the root No. II. and analyt. order.—II. *pasture*, a place whither cattle is driven to graze.—III. *any lands surrounding* a city or *edifice.*

גָּרֵשׁ Piel inf. (Ge. 20. 10), or imp. sing. masc. • נרש

גֶּרֶשׁ noun masc. sing. • נרש

גֶּרְשׁ noun masc. sing., suff. גֶּרְשָׁהּ, dec. 6a, see • נרש

גֹּרֵשׁ Kal part. act. sing. masc. • נרש

גֵּרְשָׁה } Piel pret. 3 pers. sing. fem. • נרש

גֹּרְשׁוּ } Pual pret. 3 pers. pl. • נרש

גֵּרְשׁוֹם pr. name masc. see גֵּרְשֹׁם • נרש

גֵּרְשׁוֹן pr. name masc. • נרש

גֵּרְשֻׁנִי Piel pret. 3 pers. pl., suff. 1 pers. sing. • נרש

גֵּרְשֹׁם (*a stranger there*, see Ex. 2. 22, or *expulsion*. R. גֵּרֵשׁ) pr. name.—I. of a son of Moses by Zipporah.—II. of a son of Levi.—III. Ju. 18. 30.—IV. Ezr. 8. 2.

גֵּרַשְׁתָּ Pi. pret. 2 pers. sing. masc. • נרש

גֵּרַשְׁתִּי } id. pret. 1 pers. sing. ; acc. shifted by conv. ו (comp. § 8. rem. 7) • נרש

גֵּרַשְׁתִּיהוּ id. id., suff. 3 pers. sing. masc. • נרש

גֵּרַשְׁתִּיו } id. id., suff. 3 pers. sing. masc. • נרש

גֵּרַשְׁתְּכֶם n. fem. pl., suff. 2 pers. pl. m. fr. [גְּרֻשָּׁה] d. 10. • נרש

גֵּרַשְׁתְּמוֹ } Piel pret. 2 pers. sing. masc., suff. 3 pers. pl. • נרש

גַּרְתָּה Kal pret. 2 pers. sing. masc. (§ 8. rem. 5) • נור

גַּרְתִּי id. pret. 1 pers. sing. • נור

גְּשִׁי־ } Kal imp. sing. masc. (§ 17. rem. 2) • ננש

גְּשָׁה־ id. id. with paragogic ה • ננש

גְּשׁוּ } id. imp. pl. masc. (§ 17. rem. 2) ; ו bef. (1) • ננש

גְּשׁוּר (*bridge*, Chald. גִּשׁוּרָא) pr. name of a district in Syria ; whence gent. n. גְּשׁוּרִי *Geshurite*, —I. De. 3. 14 ; Jos. 12. 5, 13. 13 ; 1 Ch. 2. 23.—II Jos. 13. 2 ; 1 Sa. 27. 8.

גְּשֻׁרָה id. with paragogic ה.

גְּשִׁי id. imp. sing. fem. (§ 17. rem. 2) • ננש

גָּשַׁם Hiph. *to cause to rain*, Je. 14. 22.

גֶּשֶׁם masc. dec. 6 a. (pl. c. גִּשְׁמֵי, but in pause § 35. rem. 5).—I. *rain, heavy shower.*—II. pr. name masc., also called גַּשְׁמוּ comp. Ne. 6. 1, 2, with ver. 6.

גֹּשֶׁם masc. dec. 6c, id. Eze. 22. 24.

גֶּשֶׁם Ch. m. dec. 3, (suff. גִּשְׁמֵהּ, גִּשְׁמְהוֹן) *body* in pause, Seg. n. as if from גַּשָׁם (§ 35. rem. 5) נַּשָׁם

• Ps. 119. 20.   d De. 33. 14.   g Ex. 23. 28.   i 1 Sa. 26. 19.   l Ex. 33. 2.   n Nu. 22. 11.   p Ex. 23. 31.   r 2 Sa. 1. 15.   t Je. 46. 3.
• Je. 48. 37.   e Le. 2. 14.   h Ex. 12. 39.   k Ge. 4. 14.   m Es. 31. 11.   Eze. 45. 9.   q Ge. 21. 28.   s Ge. 19. 9.   u Ruth 2. 14.
• Ju. 5. 21.   f Ex. 34. 11.

גֶּשֶׁם ['] noun masc. sing. (pl. c. גִּשְׁמֵי) dec. 6 a ; also pr. name masc. . . . . נשם

גִּשְׁמֵהּ Chald. noun masc., suff. 3 pers. sing. fem. from [גֶּשֶׁם] dec. 3 b. . . . נשם

גִּשְׁמֵהּ Chald. id., suff. 3 pers. sing. masc. . נשם

גִּשְׁמָהּ noun masc. sing., suff. 3 pers. sing. fem. from [גֶּשֶׁם] dec. 6 c. (§ 35. rem. 8) . נשם

גַּשְׁמוּ ['] pr. name masc., see גֶּשֶׁם . . נשם

גִּשְׁמֵי noun masc. pl. construct from גֶּשֶׁם dec. 6 a. נשם

גִּשְׁמֵיהוֹן Chald. noun masc. pl. (Kh. גִּשְׁמֵיהוֹן) or sing. (K. גִּשְׁמְהוֹן), suff. 3 pers. pl. masc. from [גֶּשֶׁם] comp. dec. 3 c. . . . נשם

גִּשְׁמֵיהֶם n. m. pl., suff. 3 pers. pl. m. from גֶּשֶׁם dec. 6. נשם

גִּשְׁמֵיכֶם id. pl., suff. 2 pers. pl. masc. . נשם

גְּשָׁמִים id. pl., absolute state . . . . נשם

גֹּשֶׁן ['] pr. name.—I. of a region in Egypt inhabited by the Israelites during their bondage.—II. a city in the tribe of Judah.

גֹּשְׁנָה id. with paragogic ה

גִּשְׁפָּט ['] (flattery, coll. with the Syr.) pr. name masc. Ne. 11. 21.

גָּשַׁשׁ Pl. to feel, grope, Is. 59. 10.

גַּשְׁתּוֹ Kal inf. (גֶּשֶׁת) suff. 3 pers. sing. masc. dec. 13 a. . . . . . . נגש

גַּת ['] fem. dec. 8 e.—I. wine-press, or rather the vat, in which grapes were trodden.—II. pr. name—of a city of the Philistines, the birth-place of Goliah. —גַּת חֵפֶר (wine-press of the well) a city in Zebu-lun.—גַּת רִמּוֹן (press of the pomegranate) a city in the tribe of Dan, Jos. 19. 45.

גִּתִּי gent. noun from גַּת No. II.—Hence fem. גִּתִּית, the name of a musical instrument.

גִּתַּיִם (two wine-presses) pr. name of a city in the tribe of Benjamin, Ne. 11. 33.

גַּתָּה pr. name of a place (גַּת) with paragogic ה נת

גַּתָּה־חֵפֶר pr. name of a place (גַּת חֵפֶר) with parag. ה נת

גִּתּוֹת noun fem., pl. of גַּת dec. 8 e. . . . נת

גִּתַּיִם pr. name of a place [for גִּתַּיִם] . . נת

גִּתָּיְמָה id. with paragogic ה . . . . נית

גֶּתֶר ['] pr. name of a region in Syria, Ge. 10. 23.

ד

דָּא Chald. pron. demon. fem. this; דָּא לְדָא one against the other, together.

[דָּאַב] prop. to flow, melt; hence to pine away, to languish.
דְּאָבָה fem. anxiety, distress, Job 41. 14.
דְּאָבוֹן masc. dec. 3. (§ 32. rem. 2) languor, fainting, De. 28. 65.

דָּאֲבָה Kal pret. 3 pers. sing. fem. . . . דאב

דַּאֲבָה noun fem. sing. . . . . . דאב

דַּאֲבוֹן n. m. s., constr. of [דְּאָבוֹן] d. 3. (§ 32. r. 2) דאב

דָּאַג ['] to be anxious, uneasy, afraid, const. with acc., מִן, לְ.

דֹּאֵג (solicitous) pr. name of an Edomite, the chief of Saul's herdsmen, and betrayer of David and Ahimelech, also called דּוֹיֵג, comp. 1 Sa. 21. 8, with 22. 18, 22.

דְּאָגָה fem. anxiety, alarm, dread.

דְּאָגָה noun masc. sing., see דָּג . . . דנה

דֹּאֵג pr. name masc. . . . . . ראג

דֹּאֵג Kal part. act. sing. masc. dec. 7 b. . ראג

דֹּאֲגָה noun fem. sing. . . . . . ראג

דֹּאֲנִים Kal part. act. masc., pl. of דֹּאֵן dec. 7 b. . ראן

דֹּאַנְתְּ id. pret. 2 pers. sing. fem. . . . ראן

[דָּאָה] to fly.

דָּאָה fem. Le. 11. 14, the name of a bird, kite or glede, so Vulg. milvus.

דָּאֲנִין Ch. Kh. דָּאֲנִין, K. דְּאֲנִין Peal part. act. m. pl. [of דָּא dec. 1, or דֶּין dec. 2 b] . דון

דֹּאר pr. name of a place, see דוֹר . . דור

דָּאֲרֵי ['] Ch. constr. of the following . . דור

דָּאֲרִין Ch. Kh. דָּאֲרִין, K. דְּאֲרִין Peal part. act. m. pl. [of דָּאר dec. 1, or דָּיֵר dec. 2 b] . דור

דֹּב [',] noun masc. sing. dec. 8 c; for דֹּב see lett. ו . . . . . . רבב

דְּבָא Root not used; Arab. to rest; Chald. to cause to flow in, comp. דָּאַב דָּבַב.
דֹּבֶא masc. dec. 6 c, once De. 33. 25, rest, poet. for death; or affluence, resource, means.

דְּבָאֲךָ noun masc. sing., suff. 2 pers. sing. masc. [for דָּבְאֲךָ from דֹּבֶא] dec. 6 c. . . דבא

a Da. 7. 11.   d Da. 3. 28.   f Le. 26. 4.   h Ge. 33. 8.   k Job 41. 14.   m Je. 38. 19.   o Is. 57. 11.   r Da. 4. 32.   s Is. 11. 7.
b Ese. 22. 24.   e Ps. 105. 32.   g Ezr. 10. 13.   i Ne. 13. 15.   l De. 28. 65.   n Je. 42. 16.   p Ezr. 7. 25.   q Pr. 28. 15.   t De. 33. 25.
c Ese. 34. 25.   z Ne. 13. 16.

[דָּבַב] *to go softly, to creep along*, only of wine *to flow softly*, Ca. 7. 10.

דּוֹב דֹּב masc. dec. 8 c, *bear*.   Ch. id. Da. 7. 5.

דִּבָּה fem. dec. 10, *slander, evil report*.

דָּבָה Root not used; i. q. דָּבַב, דָּבָא *to flow*.

דִּבְיוֹן masc., only pl. דִּבְיוֹנִים 2 Ki. 6. 25, Keri, *doves' dung*; perhaps properly for דַּב יוֹנִים *what flows from pigeons*.

דֶּבֶּה noun fem. sing. dec. 10.   רבב

דְּבוֹרָה pr. name fem.; וּ bef. (ְ)   דבר

[דְּבַח] Ch. *to sacrifice*. Ezr. 6. 3, i. q. Heb. זָבַח.

דְּבַח Ch. m. d. 3 b, *a sacrifice*, Ezr. 6. 3.

מַדְבַּח masc. dec. 2 a, *altar*, Ezr. 7. 17.

דָּבְחִין Ch. Peal part. act. m., pl. of [דְּבַח] d. 2 a.   דבח

דִּבְחִין Ch. noun masc., pl. of [דְּבַח] dec. 2 b.   דבח

דֻּבִּים noun masc., pl. of דֹּב dec. 8 c. .   דבב

דְּבִיר noun masc. s., also pr. name; וּ bef. (ְ)   דבר

דָּבַק Root not used; i. q. דָּבַק *to cleave, adhere*.

נִדְבָּךְ Chald. masc. d. 1, *a row, layer of stones*, Ezr. 6. 4.

דָּבַל Root not used; Arab. *to press together*.

דְּבֵלָה fem., constr. דְּבֶלֶת (§ 42. rem. 5), pl. דְּבֵלִים, *a cake of dried figs*.

דִּבְלָה (*cake*) pr. name of a city in the northern borders of Palestine, Eze. 6. 14.

דִּבְלַיִם (*two cakes*) pr. name masc. Ho. 1. 3.

דִּבְלָתַיִם (id.) Nu. 33. 46, & בֵּית דִּ' Je. 48. 22, pr. name of a city in Moab.

דְּבֵלָה noun fem. sing., constr. דְּבֶלֶת (§ 42. r. 5)   דבל

דְּבֵלִים id. with pl. masc. term.   דבל

דִּבְלַיִם pr. name masc. . . .   דבל

דִּבְלַת noun fem. sing., constr. of דְּבֵלָה (§ 42. r. 5)   דבל

דִּבְלָתָה pr. name of a place (דִּבְלָה) with parag. ה   דבל

דִּבְלָתַיִם pr. name of a place . . .   דבל

דִּבְלָתָיְמָה id. with parag. ה   דבל

דָּבַק [also דָּבֵק comp. Job 29. 10; 41. 15]—I. *to cleave, adhere.*—II. *to reach, overtake*. Const. with בְּ, לְ, אֶל, אַחֲרֵי. Pu. *to cleave together*, with בְּ. Hiph. I. *to make adhere*.—II. *to follow close, to pursue*, with אַחֲרֵי.—III. *to overtake*; causat. De. 28. 21. Hoph. part. *cleave fast*, Ps. 22. 16.

דְּבַק Chald. *to adhere*, Da. 2. 43.

דָּבֵק m. d. 5 a, f. דְּבֵקָה, adj. *cleaving, adhering*.

דֶּבֶק masc. dec. 6 a.—I. *soldering* of metals, Is. 41. 7.—II. *a joint* in armour.

דָּבֵק adj. masc. sing. dec. 5 a. . .   דבק

דָּבְקָה Kal pret. 3 pers. sing. fem. (§ 8. rem. 1 a)   דבק
דְּבֵקָה }

דְּבֵקָה adj. fem. sing. from דָּבֵק masc. .   דבק

דָּבְקוּ Kal pret. 3 pers. pl. (§ 8. rem. 1) .   דבק
וּ' }

דָּבְקִין Ch. Peal part. act. m., pl. of [דְּבַק] d. 2 b.   דבק

דָּבַקְתִּי Kal pret. 1 pers. sing. .   דבק

דְּבַקְתֶּם וּ id. pret. 2 pers. pl. masc.; וּ bef. (ְ)   דבק

[דָּבַר] *to speak*; primarily *to range in order, to connect*; whence, in the derivatives, *to lead, guide, drive, to subdue, destroy*. Pi. I. *to speak*, const. with the acc. of that which is spoken, as דִּבֶּר דְּבָרִים *to speak words*; *to speak to* or *with* any one, with אֶל, לְ, עִם, (rarely) אֵת, בְּ; *concerning* any one, with בְּ, אֶל, עַל; *against* any one, with עַל, בְּ; *by* any one, with בְּ; דִּבֶּר עַל־לֵב פּ' *to speak kindly to* any one; דִּבֶּר אֶל־, עַל־לִבּוֹ *to speak to one's own heart*, i. e. *to think*; for which also דִּבֶּר טוֹבוֹת אֶת, אֶל־; בְּלִבּוֹ, עִם לִבּוֹ *to speak kindly with* any one; דִּבֶּר שָׁלוֹם עִם, אֶת *to speak friendly with* any one; דִּבֶּר מִשְׁפָּט עִם, אֶת *to litigate, contend with* any one; דִּבֶּר שִׁיר *to sing a song.*—II. *to destroy*, 2 Ch. 22. 10. Pu. *to be spoken*. Niph. *to speak together*, comp. נִלְחַם. Hiph. *to subdue*. Hithpa. *to speak with*; part. מְדַבֵּר (for מִתְדַּבֵּר) *speaking*.

דָּבָר masc. dec. 4 a.—I. *word, speech, command*; אִישׁ דְּבָרִים, בַּעַל *a man of words*, i. e. *eloquent man*; עֲשֶׂרֶת הַדְּבָרִים *the ten commandments.*—II. *thing, matter, affair*; דִּבְרֵי הַיָּמִים *chronicles*; דְּבַר יוֹם בְּיוֹמוֹ *the thing* (i. e. *duty*) *of the day in its day*; דִּבְרֵי הָאֲתֹנוֹת *the matter about the asses.* —III. *something*; אֵין דָּבָר, לֹא דָבָר *nothing*; כָּל־דָּבָר *every thing.*—IV. *cause, suit at law*; בַּעַל דְּבָרִים *one who has law-suits.*—V. *cause, reason*; עַל דְּבַר *because of*.

דֶּבֶר m. d. 6 a, (in pause דָּבֶר) *plague, pestilence*.

דִּבֶּר m., with Mak. דִּבֶּר־ *word*, Je. 5. 13; Ho. 1. 2.

דֹּבֶר m. d. 6 c, *pasture*, whither flocks are driven.

דַּבָּרָה fem. *words, sayings*, only De. 33. 3. יִשָּׂא מִדַּבְּרֹתֶיךָ *he shall receive of thy sayings*; but it may better be regarded as a participle of Hithp. *things spoken by thee*, i. e. *thy sayings, precepts*.

דְּבֵרָה fem. (no pl.) with parag. Yod דִּבְּרָתִי .—

I. *manner, mode, order,* Ps. 110. 4.—II. *cause, law-suit,* Job 5. 8.—III. *cause, reason;* עַל־דִּבְרַת *because of.*

דִּבְרָא Chald. fem. dec. 8 a, *cause, reason.*

דִּבְרִי (perhaps for דִּבְרְיָה *promise of the Lord,* דְּבָר=דְּבַר) pr. name masc. Le. 24. 11.

דָּבְרַת & דִּבְרַת, 1 Ch. 6. 57, (*pasture,* comp. דֹּבֶר) pr. name of a Levitical city in the tribe of Issachar, Jos. 19. 12; 21. 28.

דֹּבְרַת fem. dec. 13 a, *float, raft,* 1 Ki. 5. 23.

דְּבֹרָה, דְּבֹרָה fem. d. 10. (pl. דְּבֹרִים).—I. *a bee.* —II. pr. name of a prophetess who judged Israel.— III. pr. name of the nurse of Rebekah, Ge. 35. 8.

דְּבִיר masc.—I. *oracle, seat of the oracle,* that part of the temple from whence the Lord *spoke* and issued his orders and directions, and where the ark of the covenant was placed, comp. 1 Ki. 6. 19, also called *Holy of Holies.*—II. pr. name of the king of Eglon, Jos. 10. 3.—III. pr. name of a city in the tribe of Judah.

מִדְבָּר masc. d. 2 b.—I. *a large plain,* in which cattle are driven for pasture.—II. *a desert* or *wilderness.*—III. *speech,* Ca. 4. 3.

דָּבָר	Kh. = דְּבָר q. v., K. הַדָּבָר (q. v.) .	דבר
דָּבָר	וְ noun masc. sing. dec. 4 a.	דבר
דְּבַר	noun sing. masc. d. 6 a, for דָּבָר (§ 35. r. 2)	דבר
דַּבֵּר	וְ Piel inf., or imp. sing. masc.	דבר
דַּבֶּר	וְ id. with Mak.	דבר
דָּבֻר	Kal part. pass. sing. masc. [defect. for דָּבוּר]	דבר
דֶּבֶר	וְ, וְ noun masc. s. d. 6 a; for וְ see lett. ו	דבר
דְּבִיר	pr. name, see לוֹ דְּבָר	דבר
דְּבַר	וְ n. m. s., constr. of דָּבָר d. 4 a; וְ bef. (:)	דבר
דְּבִר	pr. name of a place, defect. for דְּבִיר	דבר
דִּבֶּר	Piel pret. 3 pers. sing. masc.	דבר
דִּבֵּר	וְ id. id. (§ 10. rem. 1) or *inf.* (§ 10. rem. 2); or perhaps *subst.* (Ho. 1. 2) .	דבר
דֹּבֵר	וְ Kal part. act. sing. masc. dec. 7 b.	דבר
דְּבִרָה	pr. name of a place (דְּבִיר) with parag. ה	דבר
דְּבֹרָה	pr. name fem.	דבר
דִּבְּרָה	Piel pret. 3 pers. sing. fem..	דבר
דַּבְּרוֹ	id. inf. (דַּבֵּר), suff. 3 pers. sing. masc. d. 7 b.	דבר
דַּבְּרוּ	וְ } id. imp. pl. masc. (comp. § 8. rem. 7)	דבר
דִּבְּרוּ	וְ }	
דְּבָרוֹ	noun m. s., suff. 3 pers. s. m. fr. דָּבָר d. 4 a.	דבר
דִּבְּרוֹ	Piel pret. 3 pers. sing. m., suff. 3 pers. s. m.	דבר
דִּבְּרוּ	וְ } id. pret. 3 pers. pl. (comp. § 8. rem. 7)	דבר
דִּבְּרוּ	וְ }	

דְּבֹרוֹת	noun fem., pl. of [דְּבֹרָה] dec. 13 .	דבר
דַּבְּרִי	Pi. imp. sing. fem. in pause for the foll. (comp. § 8. rem. 7) .	דבר
דַּבְּרִי	id. imp. sing. fem. (Ju. 5. 12); or inf. (דַּבֵּר) with suff. 1 pers. sing. dec. 7 b. .	דבר
דְּבָרַי	} noun masc. pl., suff. 1 pers. sing. for [דָּבָר] dec. 4 a ; וְ before (:) .	דבר
דְּבָרַי	}	
דְּבָרִי	id. sing., suff. 1 pers. sing. .	דבר
דִּבְרֵי	וְ } id. pl., construct state .	דבר
דִּבְרִי	pr. name masc. .	דבר
דֹּבְרֵי	Kal part. act. m. pl. constr. from דֹּבֵר d. 7 b.	דבר
דְּבָרֶיהָ	noun m. pl., suff. 3 p. s. fem. from דָּבָר d. 4 a.	דבר
דִּבְרֵיהֶם	id. pl., suff. 3 pers. pl. masc. .	דבר
דְּבָרָיו	וְ } id. id., suff. 3 pers. sing. masc.; וְ bef. (:)	דבר
דִּבְרוֹ	id. sing., suff. 3 pers. sing. masc. (K. דִּבְרוֹ), Kh. דִּבְרָיו (q. v.) .	דבר
דְּבָרַיִךְ	id. pl. with suff. 2 pers. sing. fem. [for רַיִךְ]	דבר
דְּבָרֶיךָ	וְ id. pl., suff. 2 pers. sing. masc.; וְ bef. (:)	דבר
דְּבָרֶיךָ	noun m. pl., suff. 2 p. s. m. from דָּבָר dec. 6 a.	דבר
	Kh. דְּבָרֶיךָ q. v., K. דְּבָרֶיךָ (q. v.)	דבר
דִּבְרֵיכֶם	n. m. pl., suff. 2 p. p. m. from דָּבָר d. 4 a.	דבר
דְּבָרִים	וְ id. pl., absolute state ; וְ before (:)	דבר
דְּבֹרִים	n. fem. with pl. m. term. from [דְּבֹרָה] dec. 10.	דבר
דֹּבְרִים	Kal part. act. masc., pl. of דֹּבֵר dec. 7 b.	דבר
דַּבֶּרְךָ	Piel inf. (דַּבֵּר), suff. 2 p. s. m. d. 7 b. (§ 16. r. 15)	דבר
דְּבָרְךָ	} noun masc. sing., suff. 2 pers. sing. masc. from דָּבָר dec. 4 a.	דבר
דְּבָרֶךָ	}	
דַּבֶּרְכֶם	Piel inf. (דַּבֵּר), suff. 2 p. pl. m. d. 7 b. (§ 16. r. 15)	דבר
דְּבָרֵנוּ	noun m. sing., suff. 1 pers. pl. fr. דָּבָר d. 4 a.	דבר
דִּבַּרְנוּ	Piel pret. 1 pers. pl.	דבר
דָּבְרַת, דִּבְרַת	pr. name of a place .	דבר
דִּבַּרְתָּ	Piel pret. 2 pers. sing. masc. .	דבר
דִּבַּרְתָּ	id. id.; acc. shifted to ult. by conv. וְ (§ 8. r. 7)	דבר
דִּבַּרְתְּ	וְ id. pret. 2 pers. sing. fem.	דבר
דִּבְרַת	noun fem., constr. of [דִּבְרָה; no vowel change]	דבר
דֹּבְרֹת	Kal part. act. pl. fem. from דֹּבֵר masc.	דבר
דִּבַּרְתִּי	Piel pret. 1 pers. sing.	דבר
דִּבַּרְתִּי	id. id.; acc. shifted to ult. by conv. וְ (§ 8. r. 7)	דבר
דִּבַּרְתְּ	id. pret. 2 pers. sing. fem., Kh. דִּבַּרְתִּי, K. דִּבַּרְתְּ (§ 8. rem. 5)	דבר
דִּבְרָתִי	noun fem. sing. with parag. י from [דִּבְרָה; no vowel change] .	דבר
דִּבְרָתִי	id. with suff. 1 pers. sing. .	דבר
דִּבַּרְתֶּם	וְ Piel pret. 2 pers. pl. masc. .	דבר

דְּבַשׁ וְ masc. dec. 6 b. (§ 35. rem. 10), *honey.*

יָדְבָּשׁ (*sweet as honey*) pr. name masc. 1 Ch. 4. 3.

a Je. 40. 3.	d Eze. 14. 21.	g De. 18. 21, 22.	i 1 Ki. 1. 14.	m Ho. 13. 14.	o Nu. 36. 5.	r Jos. 2. 14. 20.	s Nu. 27. 7.	w Ps. 110. 4.
Hab. 3. 5.	c Ge. 37. 4.	1 Ki. 5. 23.	2 Sa. 7. 28.	n Ju. 14. 8.	p Ex. 4. 10.	2 Sa. 14. 3.	t Je. 3. 5.	x Job 5. 8.
Pr. 25. 11.	f Ju. 19. 30.	i 2 Sa. 14. 12.						

11

דְּבַשׁ	ⁱ id. in pause; וּ bef. (:)
דִּבְשִׁי	id. with suff. 1 pers sing. · · דבש
דַּבֶּשֶׁת	fem.—I. the bunch or hump of a camel, Is. 30. 6.
	—II. pr. name of a place, Jos. 19. 11.
דִּבַּת	ᶜⁱ noun fem. sing. constr. of דִּבָּה dec. 10. דבב
דִּבָּתְךָ	וּ id., suff. 2 pers. sing. masc. · דבב
דִּבָּתָם	id., suff. 3 pers. pl. masc. · · דבב
דָּג	ⁿ noun masc. sing. dec. 2a. · · דנה

[דָּגָה] to multiply, be increased, Ge. 48. 16.

דָּג masc. dec. 2a, fish; once, with the mater lectionis, דָּאג Ne. 13. 16.

דָּגָה fem. dec. 11a, a fish; mostly collect. fish.

דָּגוֹן (large fish) pr. name of an idol of the Philistines worshipped at Ashdod.

דָּגָן masc. dec. 4a, corn, grain; meton. for bread, La. 2. 12.

דָּגָה	ᵉ noun fem. sing. dec. 11a. · · דנה
דָּגוּל	ᵇ Kal part. pass. sing. masc. · דגל
דָּגוֹן	pr. name of an idol (and pr. name in compos. with בֵּית q. v.) · · דנה
דְּגֵי	ⁿ n. m. pl. constr. from דָּג dec. 2a; וּ bef. (:) דנה
דָּגִים	id. pl., absolute state · · דנה

[דָּגַל] I. to be marked, signalized, Ca. 5. 10.—II. (denom. of דֶּגֶל) to set up a banner, Ps. 20. 6. Niph. to be furnished with banners, Ca. 6. 4, 10. Hence

דֶּגֶל masc. dec. 6a, flag banner, standard.

דִּגְלוֹ	וּ id., suff. 3 pers. sing. masc. · דגל
דָּגָן	וּ noun masc. sing. dec. 4a. · · דנה
דָּגֹן	pr. name, see בֵּית דָּגֹן, see. · בית
דְּגַן	וּ id. constr. state; וּ bef. (:) · דנה
דְּגָנִי	id., suff. 1 pers. sing. · · דנה
דְּגָנֶךָ / דְּגָנֶךָ	} id., suff. 2 pers. sing. masc. · דנה
דְּגָנֵךְ	id., suff. 2 pers. sing. fem. · דנה
דְּגָנָם	id., suff. 3 pers. pl. masc. · דנה

[דָּגַר] to hatch, brood over eggs.

דָּגַר	ⁿ Kal pret. 3 pers. sing. masc. [for דָּגַר § 8. r. 7] דנר
דָּגְרָה	וּ id. pret. 3 pers. sing. fem. · דנר
דְּגַת	ᵛ noun fem. sing., constr. of דָּגָה dec. 11a. דנה
דְּגָתָם	id., suff. 3 pers. pl. masc. · דנה

דַּד	masc. dec. 8d, the breast; only in the dual, breasts.
דֹּד	noun masc. sing. defect. for דּוֹד dec. 1a. דוד

[דָּדָה]. Hithpa. to proceed softly, gently, submissively.

דּוֹד דֹּדוֹ	n. m. s., suff. 3 pers. s. m. from דּוֹד dec. 1a. דוד
דֹּדִי	id., suff. 1 pers. sing. · דוד
דֹּדִי	pr. name masc. Kheth. דֹּדָי, K. · דוד
דֹּדֵי	noun masc. pl. constr. from [דַּד] dec. 8d. דד
דֹּדֶיהָ	id., suff. 3 pers. sing. fem. · דד
דֹּדֵיהֶן	noun m. pl., suff. 3 p. pl. fem. from דּוֹד d. 1a. דוד
דַּדַּיִךְ	n. m. pl., suff. 2 pers. s. fem. fr. [דַּד] d. 8d. דד
דֹּדַיִךְ	n. m. pl., suff. 2 pers. s. m. from דּוֹד dec. 1a. דוד
דֹּדַיִךְ	id., suff. 2 pers. sing. fem. · דוד
דֹּדִים	id. pl., absolute state · דוד
דֹּדְךָ	id. sing., suff. 2 pers. sing. masc. · דוד
דְּדָן	וּ pr. name of a people and a region in the north of Arabia.
דְּדָנָה	וּ id. with parag. ה; וּ bef. (:)
דְּדָנִים	וּ pr. name of a people descended from Javan, Ge. 10. 4, written רוֹדָנִים in 1 Ch. 1. 7.
דְּדָנִים	gen. n., pl. of דְּדָנִי from דְּדָן
דֹּדָתוֹ	n. fem. s., suff. 3 p. s. m. from [דּוֹדָה] d. 10. דוד
דֹּדָתְךָ	id., suff. 2 pers. sing. masc. · דוד

דְּהַב	ᶜⁱ Chald. masc. dec. 3a, i. q. Heb. זָהָב gold. מַדְהֵבָה fem. Is. 14. 4, gold-making, i. e. exactress of gold; others, place of gold.
דְּהַב	ᵈ id. in pause; וּ bef. (:) · · רהב
דַּהֲבָא / דַּהֲבָה	} Chald. id. emph. st.; וּ id. · רהב
דֶּהָוֵא	pr. name of a people who were colonised in Samaria, Ezr. 4. 9, Keri דָּהֲיֵא

[דָּהַם]. Niph. to be overwhelmed, overcome, Je. 14. 9.

[דָּהַר] to move quickly, spoken of a horse, to prance, Na. 3. 2.

דַּהֲרָה fem. only pl. דַּהֲרוֹת prancings, Ju. 5. 22

תִּדְהָר masc. the name of a tree; Vulg. ulmus the elm, Is. 41. 19; 60. 13.

דֹּהֵר	ᵍ Kal part. act. sing. masc. · יהר
דַּהֲרוֹת	ʰ noun fem., pl. of [דַּהֲרָה] · רהר
דֹּאן	pr. name masc., see דָּאג · ראן

[דּוּב] Hiph. to cause to waste, or pine away, Le. 26. 16.

דִּיבֹן (a pining, wasting away) pr. name—I. of a city in the borders of Moab built by the Gadites.—II. of a city in the tribe of Judah, Ne. 11. 25, called דִּימוֹנָה in Jos. 15. 22.

ᵃ 1 Sa. 14. 26.   ᵉ Ge. 37. 2.   ⁱ Job 40. 31.   ⁿ De. 11. 14.   ʳ Je. 32. 8, 9, 12.   ᵛ Nu. 36. 11.   ᶻ Ca. 4. 10, 10.   ᵉ Ezr. 7. 18.   ᶠ Ezr. 7. 18, etc
ᵇ Ca. 5. 1.   ᶠ Jon. 2. 1.   ᵏ Ca. 2. 4.   ° Is. 62. 8.   ˢ Eze. 23. 3, 8.   ʷ Eze. 23. 21.   ᵃ Je. 32. 7.   ᵉ Ezr. 7. 15.   ᵍ Na. 3. 2.
ᶜ Eze. 36. 3.   ᵍ De. 4. 18.   ˡ Ps. 78. 24.   ᵖ Is. 34. 15.   ᵗ Pr. 5. 19.   ˣ Ca. 1. 2, 4.   ᵇ Le. 18. 14.   ᵈ Da. 5. 23.   ʰ Ju. 5. 22.
ᵈ Pr. 25. 10.   ʰ Ca. 5. 10.   ᵐ Ho. 2. 11.   ᵠ Eze. 29. 4, 4, 5.   ᵘ Je. 17. 11.

דּוֹבֵב Kal part. act. sing. masc. . דבב

דּוֹבְרֵי Kal part. act. pl. c. masc. from דָּבַר dec. 7 b.

[דּוּג, דִּיג] to fish, Je. 16. 16.

דַּיָּג, דַּוָּג masc. dec. 1 b, fisher. Also

דּוּגָה fem. a fishing, Am. 4. 2, סִירוֹת דּוּגָה fishing-hooks דון

דָּגִים noun masc., pl. of [דָּג] dec. 1 a. . דון

דּוּד Root not used;—I. Syr. to disturb, agitate.—II. i. q. יָדַד to love.

דּוּד masc.—I. pot, boiler, or cauldron, pl. דְּוָדִים (§ 35. rem. 13).—II. basket, pl. דּוּדִים.

דּוֹד, דֹּד masc.—I. love, but only in the plural.—II. for concr. beloved, friend.—III. uncle, father's brother.

דָּוִיד, דָּוִד (beloved; passive form § 26. No. 5) pr. name of the son of Jesse, king of Israel.

דּוֹדָה, דֹּדָה fem. dec. 10, aunt.

דּוֹדוֹ (His, sc. God's, beloved, comp. דּוֹד) pr. name masc. of several persons.

דּוֹדָוָהוּ (love of the Lord, for דּוֹדִיָּהוּ) pr. name masc. 2 Ch. 20. 37.

דּוּדַי masc. only pl. דּוּדָאִים (§ 35. rem. 15 note). —I. baskets, comp. דּוּד, Je. 24. 1.—II. mandrakes, the apples of the Madragora (Atropa Mandragora of Linn.)

דּוֹדַי (beloved) pr. name masc. 1 Ch. 27. 4.

דָּוִד ן׳ pr. name masc. . . . דוד
דּוֹד noun masc. sing. dec. 1 a. . . דוד
דּוּדָאֵי constr. of the following : . דוד
דּוּדָאִים noun masc., pl. of [דּוּדַי § 35. rem. 15 note] דוד
דּוֹדָהּ noun masc. sing., suff. 3 pers. sing. fem. from דּוֹד dec. 1 a. . . . . דוד
דּוֹדוֹ id., suff. 3 pers. sing. masc. . דוד
דּוֹדוֹ pr. name masc. . . . . דוד
דּוֹדָוָהוּ pr. name masc. . . . דוד
דּוֹדַי pr. name masc. . . . דוד
דּוֹדַי n. m. pl., suff. 1 pers. sing., from דּוֹד d. 1 a. דוד
דּוֹדִי ן׳ id. sing., suff. 1 pers. sing. . דוד
דּוֹדִים id. pl., absolute state . . . דוד
דּוֹדֵךְ id. sing., suff. 2 pers. sing. fem. . דוד
דְּדָנִים ן׳ pr. name, see דְּדָנִים

[דָּוָה] to be languid, sick, in the verb only used of the female periodical sickness, Le. 12. 2.

דָּוֶה masc., דָּוָה fem. adj.—I. sick, specially of a woman in the menses.—II. sad, unhappy.

דְּוַי masc. sick, faint.

דְּוָי masc. pl. com. דְּוַי (comp. § 38. rem. 2).—I. sickness, Ps. 41. 4.—II. something sickening, loathsome, Job 6. 7.

מַדְוֶה masc. dec. 9a, sickness, disease.

דָּוָה fem. of the following . . . דוה
דָּוֶה adj. masc. sing. . . . . דוה

דּוּחַ Hiph. I. to cast out, expel, Je. 31. 54.—II. to cleanse, wash away.

דַּוָּי adj. masc. sing. . . . . דוה
דְּוָי noun masc. sing. [for דְּוַי] . . דוה
דּוּאֵג pr. name masc. for דֹּאֵג (q. v.) . ראג
דָּוִיד pr. name masc., see דָּוִד . דוד

[דּוּךְ] to pound, bray in a mortar, Nu. 11. 8.

מְדֹכָה fem. mortar, Nu. 11. 8.

[דּוּכִיפַת] fem. the name of an unclean bird; Vulg. upupa, the hoopoe, Le. 11. 19; De. 14. 18.

דּוּם Root not used, i. q. דָּמַם to be silent, still.

דּוּמָה fem.—I. silence, death. Meton. place of the dead, the grave.—II. pr. name of a tribe and district in Arabia.

דּוּמִיָּה fem.—I. silence, quietness, Ps. 22. 3; adv. silently, Ps. 39. 3.—II. silent resignation sc. to the will of God; Ps. 62. 2, לֵ נַפְשִׁי דּ׳ my soul is silent resignation, i. e. is perfectly resigned; Ps. 65. 2. לְךָ דֻמִיָּה תְהִלָּה to thee silent resignation is praise, i. e. redounds to thy praise, or is that by which thou art to be praised.

דּוּמָם masc.—I. silence, dumbness, Hab. 2. 19.— II. adv. in silence, silently.

דּוּם Kal imp. sing. masc. for דֹּם . . רמם
דּוּמָה׳ Kal part. act. sing. masc. . . רמה
דּוּמָה noun fem. sing. . . . . דום
דּוּמָה ן׳ pr. name of a tribe and region . דום
דּוּמִי׳ Kal imp. sing. fem. for דֹּמִּי . רמם
דּוּמִיָּה noun fem. sing. from [דּוּמִי] m. (§ 39. No. 2) דם
דּוּמָם ן׳ adv. with the term. ־ָם, comp. יוֹמָם, חִנָּם, &c. דום
דֹּמַמְתִּי ן׳ Poel pret. 1 pers. sing. . רמם
דּוּמֶשֶׂק pr. name, see דַּמֶּשֶׂק

[דּוּן] & [דִּין] pret. דָּן; imp. דִּין; fut. יָדִין & יָדוֹן.—I. to rule, govern, perhaps so in 1 Sa. 2. 10; Zec. 3. 7. —II. to judge.—III. to plead, defend the cause of any one.—IV. to judge, punish, with acc. בְּ.— V. to contend, strive, with עִם, Ec. 6. 10; Ge. 6. 3.

a Ca. 7. 16.   d Am. 4. 2.   g Ge. 30. 14.   k Ca. 7. 13.   l La. 5. 17.   i Ca. 2. 9.   m Ps. 62. 6.   n La. 3. 26.   o Ps. 131. 2.
b Ps. 63. 12.   e Eze. 47. 10.   f Ca. 8. 5.   h Ca. 5. 1.   k Ps. 41. 4.

11*

לֹא־יָדוֹן רוּחִי בָאָדָם לְעֹלָם *my spirit shall not always strive with man,* sc. in testifying against him, but judgment must ensue. Niph. *to contend, strive together,* 2 Sa. 19. 10.

דּוּן Chald. *to judge,* Ezr. 7. 25.

דּוּן masc. *judgment,* Job 19. 29, שַׁדּוּן K. *that there is a judgment,* Kh. שַׁדִּין.

דִּין masc. dec. 1 a.—I. *judgment.*—II. *cause for judgment :* עָשָׂה דִין דָּן דִּין *to defend a cause.*—III. *controversy, strife,* Pr. 22. 10.

דִּין Chald. masc. dec. 1 a.—I. *judgment.*—II. meton. *tribunal, court of judgment.*—III. *justice, right.*—IV. *punishment,* Ezr. 7. 26.

דַּיָּן masc. (construct דַּיַּן § 30 rem. 1.)—I. *a judge,* 1 Sa. 24. 16.—II. *defender,* Ps. 68. 6.; Chald. Ezr. 7. 25.

דִּינָה (*judged*) pr. name of the daughter of Jacob.

דִּינָיֵא Chald. masc. pl. pr. name of a people of Assyria, Ezr. 4. 9.

דָּן (*judge*) pr. name.—I. of a son of Jacob and the tribe descended from him. Gent. noun דָּנִי, *Danite.*—II. of a city in the north of Palestine, called also לֶשֶׁם & לַיִשׁ.

דָּנִיֵּאל, דָּנִיֵאל (*judge of God*) pr. name of the celebrated Hebrew prophet at the court of Babylon.

אָדוֹן masc. dec. 3 a, *master, lord.* Pl. אֲדֹנִים *lords ;* more frequently used as a Plur. excellentiæ, *lord ;* אֲדֹנֵי הָאָרֶץ *lord of the land ;* אֲדֹנִים קָשֶׁה *a hard master ;* אִם־אֲדֹנִים אָנִי *If I am Lord.* Note others derive this and the following word from אדן, whence is אֶרֶן *a base.*

אֲדֹנָי, once אֲדֹנִי (Ju. 13. 8) *Lord, the Lord,* exclusively applied to God. Grammarians disagree about the termination יָ—, which some regard as a pl. form for יִ— i. q. יִם—, to distinguish it from אֲדֹנַי *my lords ;* others, as the suff. of 1 pers. with pl. nouns, prop. denoting *my Lord,* the force of the possessive pronoun being neglected. Others again regard it as an adjective termination, whence אֲדֹנָי *ruling, governing,* and in the same way explain שַׁדַּי *Almighty.*

אֲדֹנִי־בֶזֶק (*lord of Bezek*) pr. name of a king of the Canaanitish city *Bezek,* Ju. 1. 5, 6, 7.

אֲדֹנִי־צֶדֶק (*lord of righteousness*) pr. name of a Canaanitish king of Jerusalem, Jos. 10. 1, 3.

אֲדֹנִיָּהוּ (*the Lord is my Lord*) pr. name.—I. of a son of David, called also אֲדֹנִיָּה, comp. 1 Ki. 1. 8,

with ver. 5.—II. 2 Ch. 1. 8.—III. Ne. 10. 17, called אֲדֹנִיקָם (*lord of the enemy,* part. of קוּם) in Ezr. 2. 13. Comp. Ezr. 8. 13 ; Ne. 7. 18.

אֲדֹנִירָם (*the Lord is exalted,* part. of רוּם) pr. name of an officer under David, called also אֲדֹרָם comp. 1 Ki. 4. 6, with 12. 18, and again הֲדֹרָם 2 Ch. 10. 18.

יָדוֹן (*He judges*) pr. name of a man, Ne. 3. 7.

מָדוֹן masc. pl. מְדוֹנִים or מְדָנִים, מִדְיָנִים (§ 32. rem. 8 & 35. rem. 13) only in Kheth.—I. *contention, strife ;* אִישׁ מָדוֹן *man of contention,* pass. i. e. a man contended with, Je. 15. 10. (see also R. מדה) ; Kh. אִישׁ מִדְיָנִים, אֵשֶׁת מִדְיָנִים act. *contentious man, woman ;* K. מִדְיָנִים.—II. *object of strife,* Ps. 80. 7. —III. pr. name of a city of the Canaanites.

מִדְיָן masc. dec. 2 b.—I. *contention, strife,* see the preceding.—II. pr. name of a son of Abraham by Keturah and the tribe descended from the same. —Gent. noun מִדְיָנִי, pl. ים—, fem. ית—, *Midianite.*

מְדִינָה fem. dec. 10, prop. *jurisdiction,* hence— I. *province.*—II. *region, country.*

מְדִינָא Chald. fem. dec. 8, id.

מְדָן masc.—I. *contention, strife,* only pl. מְדָנִים —II. pr. name of a son of Abraham by Keturah.

מְדָנִי gent. noun contr. for מִדְיָנִי (comp. מִדְיָן and מְדָן) *Midianite,* Ge. 37. 36, comp. ver. 28.

דּוֹנֵג* noun masc sing. . . . . רנג

דּוֹפֵק† Kal part. act. sing. masc. . . . דפק

[דּוּץ] *to leap, exult,* Job 41. 14.

דּוּק Root not used ; Chald. and Syr. *to look round, look out ;* Arab. conj. IV. *to surround.*

דָּיֵק masc. *watch-tower ;* but on account of the word סָבִיב with which it occurs, others understand it to signify, *a wall or line of circumvallation* LXX. περίτειχος *a surrounding wall.*

[דּוּר] I. *to dwell,* Ps. 84. 11.—II. in the deriv., according to the Arab., *to move in a circle, go round.*

דּוּר Chald. *to dwell.*

דּוּר masc.—I. *a circle,* Is. 29. 3.—II. *a ball,* Is. 22. 18.—III. *a round pile of bones,* Eze. 24. 5.

דֹּר, דּוֹר masc. dec. 1 a, pl. ים—, וֹת, prop. *revolution,* hence—I. *age, generation ;* דֹּר וָדוֹר *age and age,* i. e. for ever ; so likewise דּוֹר דּוֹרִים ; בְּכָל־דּוֹר וָדוֹר *throughout all ages or generations.* —So מִדֹּר דֹּר, עַד דֹּר וָדֹר, לָדֹר וָדֹר, לְדֹר דֹּר

* Ps. 68. 3.   b Ca. 5. 2.

II. *habitation*, Is. 38. 12; meton. for *sepulchre* Ps. 49. 20.—III. pr. name of a city, see נֹפָה.

דּוּרָא Chald. pr. name of a valley in Babylonia, Da. 3. 1.

מְדוֹר Chald. masc. dec. 1 a, *habitation*.

מְדֹר Chald. masc. dec. 1 a, id. Da. 2. 11.

מְדוּרָה fem. dec. 10, *pile of fuel*.

בִּתְדִירָא Chald. fem. *revolution*, hence *continually*, Da. 6. 17.

דּוֹר דֹּר, נָ' noun masc. sing. dec. 1 a; also pr. name for נָ' see lett. ו   .   דור

דּוּר noun masc. sing.   .   דור

דּוּרָא pr. name of a place.   .   דור

דּוֹרוֹ noun m. s., suff. 3 pers. s. m. from דּוֹר dec. a.   דור

דֹּרוֹת id. fem. with pl. term.   .   דור

דֹּרוֹתֵינוּ id. pl., suff. 1 pers. pl.   .   דור

דּוֹרִי id. sing., suff. 1 pers. sing.   .   דור

דֹּרִים id. pl., absolute state   .   דור

דֹּרֵךְ וְ Kal part. act. sing. masc. dec. 7 b.   דרך

דּוֹרֵשׁ Kal part. act. sing. masc. dec. 7 b.   דרש

[דּוּשׁ, דִּישׁ] I. to tread down, tread under foot.—II. to tread out corn, to thresh.—III. metaph. Am. 1. 3.

דּוּשׁ Chald. to thresh, Da. 7. 23.

דַּיִשׁ masc. *threshing-time*, Le. 26. 5.

דִּישׁוֹן masc.—I. a species of *gazelle* or *antelope*, De. 14. 5.—II. pr. name; (a) of a son of Seir and of a region called after his name; (b) of a grandson of Seir.

דִּישָׁן pr. name of the third son of Seir and a region called after him.

מְדוּשָׁה fem. dec. 10, *a threshing*, Is. 21. 10.

דּוּשִׁי וְ Kal imp. sing. fem.; for וְ see lett. ו   .   דוש

דּוּשָׁם id. inf. [דּוּשׁ], suff. 3 pers. sing. masc. dec. 1 a. דוש

דּוֹחָתָהּ Kal inf. [דּוֹח], suff. 3 pers. sing. fem. dec. 1 a. דוח

[דָּחָה] to push, thrust, drive; part. דְּחוּיָה *thrust down.* Niph. to be thrust down. Pu. id., Ps. 36. 13.

דַּחֲוָא Chald. fem. only pl. דַּחֲוָן Da. 6. 19, a sort of *musical instrument*.

דְּחִי masc. only in pause דֶּחִי (§ 35. rem. 14) *stumbling, falling.*

מִדְחֶה masc. *fall, ruin*, Pr. 26. 28.

דָּחֹה Kal inf. absolute   .   דחה

דֹּחֶה Kal part. act. sing. masc.   .   דחה

דֹּחוּ Pual pret. 3 pers. pl. [for דֻּחוּ]   רחה

דַּחֲוָן וְ Chald. noun masc., pl. of [דַּחֲוָא] d. 8 a. דחה

רְחוּפִים פ Kal part. p. pl. of [דָּחוּף] dec. 3 a; וּ bef. (?) דחף

דָּחַח Niph. to be thrust down, Je. 23. 12.

דְּחִיל Chald. Peal part. p. sing. masc.   .   דחל

דְּחִילָה Chald. fem. of the preceding   .   דחל

דְּחִיתַנִי Kal pret. 2 pers. sing. masc., suff. 1 pers. sing. דחה

[דְּחֵל] Chald. to fear, be afraid; part. pass. *fearful, terrible.* Pa. to terrify, Da. 4. 2.

דָחֲלִין וְ Ch. Peal part. act. m., pl. of [דְּחֵל] dec. 2 b. דחל

דֹּחַן וְ masc. *millet*, Eze. 4. 9.

[דָּחַף] to impel, urge, hasten. Niph. to urge oneself, to hasten.

מַדְחֵפָה fem. *ruin, destruction*, Ps. 140. 12.

[דָּחַק] to press upon; part. דֹּחֵק *oppressor.*

דֹּחֲקֵיהֶם וְ Kal part. act. pl., suff. 3 pers. pl. masc. from [דָּחַק] dec. 7 b.   .   דחק

דִּי וְ Chald.—I. relat. pron. *who, which, what*, i. q. Heb. אֲשֶׁר; דִּי אִנִּין *which* they i. e. which; דִּי מְדָרְהוֹן *whose dwelling*; דִּי תַמָּה *where.*— II. a sign of the genitive; after the emphatic state שַׁלִּיטָא דִּי מַלְכָּא *the captain of the king*; after the construct state, נְהַר דִּי נוּר *a stream of fire*; pleon. after suff. as שְׁמֵהּ דִּי אֱלָהָא for שֵׁם דִּי אֱלָהָא *the name of God.*—III. conj. *that*; *so that*; *because that*; כְּדִי *when*; מִן דִּי *from the time when, after*; עַד דִּי *until.*

דִּי זָהָב (of gold) pr. name of a place in the desert of Sinai, De. 1. 1.

דַּי [in pause for דָּי] noun m. dec. 8 d, constr. דֵּי (§ 37. rem. 6).—I. *sufficiency, what is sufficient*, hence adverbially, *enough*; דֵּי חָלָב *enough of milk*; דֵּי שֶׂה *as much as is sufficient for a lamb*; כְּדֵי גְאֻלָּתוֹ *sufficient for its redemption*; דַּיָּם, דַּיֶּךָ, *sufficient for thee, them.*—II. in the construct state it is sometimes affixed to the prepositions כְּ, בְּ, מִן, as כְּדֵי *for; whenever; as*; מִדֵּי *according to; as often as, whenever; from.* Etymo. doubtful.

דֵּי וְ id. construct state.   .   די

דִּיגוֹם וְ Kal pret. 3 pers. pl., suff. 3 pers. pl. masc. R. דִּין see   .   דון

---

a Eze. 24. 5.   d Jos. 22. 27.   g Mi. 4. 13.   k Ps. 118. 13.   n Da. 6. 19.   p Est. 8. 14.   Da. 7. 7, 19.   t Ju. 2. 18.   w Pr. 27. 27.
b Is. 53. 8.   e Is. 38. 12.   h Am. 1. 3.   i Ps. 35. 5.   o Est. 3. 15.   q Da. 2. 31.   s Ps. 118. 13.   u Mal. 3. 19.   x Je. 16. 16.
c Is. 51. 9.   f Job 9. 8.   i Le. 12. 2.   m Ps. 36. 13.

דִּיבֹן‎ דִּיבֹן‎ } pr. name of a place.   דוב

דִּיָּה‎ Root not used; prob. i. q. Chald. דְּהָא‎ *to be dark, obscure.*

   דַּיָּה‎ fem. dec. 10, *the black vulture.*

   דְּיוֹ‎ masc. *ink,* Je. 36. 18.

דַּיּוֹת‎ noun fem., pl. of דַּיָּה‎ dec. 10.   דיה

דַּיֶּךָ‎ noun masc. sing., suff. 2 pers. sing. masc.
   [for דַּיְךָ‎] from דַּי‎ dec. 8d. (§ 37. rem. 6)   די

דַּיָּם‎ id., suff. 3 pers. pl. masc.   די

דִּימוֹן‎ דִּימוֹנָה‎ } pr. name, see דִּיבוֹן‎   דוב

דַּיָּן‎ } noun m. s., constr. of [דַּיָּן‎] R. דִּין‎ see   דון

דִּין‎ } noun masc. sing. dec. 1 a; Chald.
   (Da. 4. 34) dec. 1; for ן‎ see lett. ו‎, see .   דון

דִּין‎ } Kal imp. sing. masc. R. דִּין‎ see   דון

דִּינָא‎ דִּינָה‎ } Chald. n. m. s. emph. of דִּין‎ dec. 1 a, see   דון

דִּינָה‎ pr. name fem. R. דִּין‎, see   דון

דִּינוּ‎ Kal imp. pl. masc. R. דִּין‎ see .   דון

דִּינִי‎ } noun m. s., suff. 1 p. s. fr. דִּין‎ d. 1 a, see   דין

דִּינָיֵא‎ Chald. pr. name of a people. R. דִּין‎ see   דון

דִּינִין‎ } Ch. noun m., pl. of דַּיָּן‎ d. 1 a.   דון

דִּינֶךָ‎ noun m. s., suff. 2 p. s. f. fr. דִּין‎ d. 1 a, see   דון

דִּיפַת‎ } pr. n. according to some copies, see רִיפַת‎   דון

דַּיֵק‎ noun masc. sing.   דוק

דַּיִשׁ‎ noun masc. sing. .   דוש

דִּישָׁן‎ } pr. name masc.   דוש

דִּישֹׁן‎ } noun masc. sing., also pr. name masc.   דוש

דָּךְ‎ Chald. pron. demon., fem. of דֵּךְ‎ .   דך

דַּךְ‎ דַּךְ‎ } adj. masc. sing. dec. 8 d; for ו‎ see lett. ו‎   דכך

דֵּךְ‎ Chald. pron. demon. masc. *this.* Fem. דָּךְ‎
   דִּכֵּן‎ Chald. i. q. דֵּךְ‎ *this.*

דָּכָא‎ Pi.—I. *to break in pieces, to bruise.*—II. *to trample upon.* Pu.—I. *to be broken, bruised.*—II. *to be contrite.* Niph. part. *broken, contrite,* Is. 57. 15. Hithp. הִדַּכָּא‎ (for הִתְדַּכָּא‎) *to be broken in pieces.* Hence

   דַּכָּא‎ adj. masc. pl. c. דַּכָּאֵי‎ (§ 30. rem. 1).—I. *bruised, crushed.*—II. *contrite, humble.*

דִּכָּא‎ Piel pret. 3 pers. sing. masc.   דכא

דַּכְּאוֹ‎ id. inf. [דַּכֵּא‎], suff. 3 pers. sing. m. d. 7 b.   דכא

דֻּכְּאוּ‎ Pual pret. 3 pers. pl.   דכא

דַּכְּאֵי‎ adj. m. pl. constr. fr. דַּכָּא‎ d. 2 b. (§ 30. r. 1)   דכא

דִּכֵּאתָ‎ Piel pret. 2 pers. sing. masc.   דכא

[דָּכָה‎] *to be bruised, crushed,* Ps. 10. 10. Niph. *to be broken, crushed;* of the heart, *to be contrite.* Pi. *to break in pieces.*

   דְּכִי‎ masc. dec. 6 k, *a beating, dashing,* Ps. 93. 3.

דָּכָה‎ ו‎ Kh. וְדָכָה‎, K. יִדְכֶּה‎ Kal pret. or fut. 3 pers. sing. masc.   רכה

דַּכּוּ‎ Kal pret. 3 pers. sing. masc.   דוך

דַּכָּיו‎ adj. m. pl., suff. 3 pers. s. m. fr. דַּךְ‎ d. 8 d.   דכך

דַּכָּים‎ noun masc. sing., suff. 3 pers. pl. masc. fr.
   [דְּכִי‎] dec. 6 k. .   דכה

דִּכִּיתָ‎ Piel pret. 2 pers. sing. masc.   דכה

דִּכִּיתָנוּ‎ id., suff. 1 pers. pl.   דכה

דָּכַךְ‎ Root not used; i. q. דָּכָה‎, דּוּךְ‎ q. v.

   דַּךְ‎ adj. masc. dec. 8 d, *afflicted, oppressed, poor;* Pr. 26. 28 יִשְׂנָא דַכָּיו‎ *hateth its afflicted,* i. e. those to whom it had caused affliction.

   דַּכָּה‎ fem. *a crushing, bruising,* De. 23. 2 פְּצוּעַ דַּכָּה‎ *mutilated by crushing.*

דְּכֵן‎ Chald. pron. demon. com. .   דך

[דְּכַר‎] Chald. Root not used in the Holy Scriptures; i. q. זָכַר‎ *to remember.*

   דְּכַר‎ Chald. masc. dec. 3 b, prop. i. q. זָכָר‎ *male,* only by way of eminence, *a ram.*

   דִּכְרוֹן‎ Ch. m. d. 1, *memorial, record,* Ezr. 6. 2.

   דָּכְרָן‎ Chald. masc. dec. 1, id. Ezr. 4. 15.

דִּכְרוֹנָה‎ Ch. n. m., emph. of [דִּכְרוֹן‎] dec. 1 a.   דכר

דִּכְרִין‎ } Chald. noun m., pl. of [דְּכַר‎] dec. 3 b.   דכר

דִּכְרַנְיָא‎ Ch. noun m. pl. emph. fr. [דָּכְרָן‎] dec. 1 b.   דכר

דַּל‎ דַּל‎ } adj. & subst. masc. sing. dec. 8 d; } דלל
דַּל‎ } for ו‎ see lett. ו‎ .
דְּלִי‎ noun masc. sing.   דלה

[דָּלַג‎] *to leap, skip,* Zep. 1. 9. Pi. id. const. with acc., עַל‎

דָּלָה‎ *to draw,* as water from a well. In the deriv. also *to hang down.* Pi. *to draw up,* as from a prison, *to deliver,* Ps. 30. 2.

   דַּל‎ masc. *door,* Ps. 141. 3, comp. דֶּלֶת‎ .

   דֶּלֶת‎ fem. dec. 11 a, *door, gate.* Du. דְּלָתַיִם‎, constr. דַּלְתֵי‎ *double doors, folding doors* or *gates* metaph. דַּלְתֵי שָׁמַיִם‎ *the doors of heaven* i. e. the clouds; דַּלְתֵי פָנִים‎ *the doors of the face,* i. e. the jaws. דֶּלֶת‎ fem. of דַּל‎ (§ 44. rem. 1) with suff. דַּלְתּוֹ‎ id.—Pl. דְּלָתוֹת‎, constr. דַּלְתוֹת‎ (ת‎ being treated as if radical, comp. קֶשֶׁת‎, also § 44. rem. 5)—I.

a Is. 34. 15.   e Est. 1. 13.   i Ezr. 7. 26.   m Je. 30. 13.   r Ps. 74. 21.   w Ps. 34. 19.   bb Ps. 93. 3.   f Ezr. 6. 9.   t Pr. 28. 11.
b Pr. 25. 16.   f Pr. 31. 9.   k Je. 21. 12.   n Le. 26. 5.   s Ps. 143. 3.   x Ps. 89. 11.   cc Ps. 51. 10.   g Ezr. 4. 15.   u Ps. 141. 3.
c Ps. 68. 6.   g Da. 7. 10.   l Ps. 9. 5.   o De. 14. 5.   t Is. 53. 10.   y Ps. 10. 10.   dd Ps. 44. 20.   h Zep. 3. 12.   v Ex. 2. 19.
d Job 36. 17.   h Da. 7. 22, 26.   m Ezr. 7. 25.   p Ps. 10. 18.   u Je. 44. 10.   z Nu. 11. 8.   Ezr. 6. 2.   aa Ps. 9. 5.   n Pr. 26. 28.

doors, gates.—II. *leaves* or *valves of gates.*—III. *leaves* or *columns* of a roll or book, Je. 36. 23.

דְּלִי masc. *bucket,* Is. 40. 15.

דְּלִי masc. id. Nu. 24. 7, see מִדָּלְיָו analyt. order.

דְּלָיָהוּ , דְּלָיָה (*whom the Lord has delivered*) pr. name m. of several persons.

דָּלִית f. only pl. דָּלִיּוֹת (§ 39, 4. rem. 1) *boughs, branches.*

דָּלֹה [a] Kal inf. abs. . . . . . דלה
דָּלּוּ [b] Kal pret. 3 pers. pl. . . . . דלל
דַּלּוֹנוּ [c] id. pret. 1 pers. pl. . . . דלל
דַּלּוֹת [cc] adj. fem., pl. of דַּלָּה dec. 10, from דַּל masc. דלל
דִּלּוֹתִי Piel pret. 1 pers. sing. . . . דלל

[דָּלַח] to *trouble* or *disturb* water by trampling in it, Eze. 32. 2, 13.

דְּלָיָה [d] pr. name masc.; ו bef. (:) . . דלה
דְּלָיָהוּ [d] pr. name masc.; ו id. . . . דלה
דְּלִיּוּ [e] Piel imp. pl. m., R. דלה (§ 24. r. 13 note) or דלל
דָּלִיּוֹתָיו [e] noun fem. pl., suff. 3 pers. sing. masc. [fr. דָּלִית § 39, 4. rem. 1] . . . דלה
דְּלִילָה pr. name fem. . . . . . דלל
דַּלִּים adj. masc., pl. of דַּל dec. 8 c. דלל
דַּלְיֹתָיו defect. for דָּלִיּוֹתָיו (q. v.) . . . דלה
דִּלִּיתָנִי Piel pret. 2 pers. sing. masc., suff. 1 pers. s. דלה

[דָּלַל] pret. דָּלְלוּ and דַּלּוּ (§ 18. rem. 13); imp. דְּלִיּוּ (but see § 24. r. 13 note).—I. to *hang down.*—II. to be *languid, be weakened, feeble.* Niph. to be *brought low, be reduced.*

דַּל m. pl. דַּלִּים , f. דַּלּוֹת adj. *low, weak, poor.*

דַּלָּה fem. dec. 10.—I. *thin thread,* spoken of the threads or thrums which tie the web to the weaver's beam, Is. 38. 12.—II. *hair* or *locks* of the head, Ca. 7. 6.—III. *lowness, weakness, poverty.*

דְּלִילָה (*languishing, languid*) pr. name fem. a paramour of Samson.

דָּלְלוּ [f] Kal pret. 3 pers. pl. . . . דלל

דִּלְעָן (*place of gourds,* Chald. דְּלַעַת a gourd) pr. name of a city in the tribe of Judah, Jos. 15. 38.

[דָּלַף] I. to *drop, drip,* Ec. 10. 18.—II. to *shed tears,* to *weep.*

דֶּלֶף masc. *rain-drop,* Pr. 19. 13; 27. 15.

דַּלְפוֹן (*weeper?*) pr. name of a son of Haman, Est. 9. 7.

יִדְלָף (*shedding tears*) pr. name of a son of Nahor, Ge. 22. 22.

דֶּלֶף [a] ו noun sing. masc. . . . . דלף
דָּלְפָה Kal pret. 3 pers. sing. fem. . . דלף
דַּלְפוֹן pr. name masc. . . . . . דלף

[דָּלַק] fut. יִדְלַק.—I. to *burn, consume,* const. with בְּ.—II. applied metaph. to the affections of the mind. Pr. 26. 23 שְׂפָתַיִם דֹּלְקִים *burning lips,* i. e. professing ardent love; to *burn with anguish,* Ps. 10. 2; const. with אַחֲרֵי to *pursue ardently.* Hiph. to *kindle, inflame.*

דְּלַק Chald. to *burn,* Da. 7. 9.

דַּלֶּקֶת fem. *burning fever,* De. 28. 22.

דָּלְקָא [a] Chald. Peal part. act. sing. masc. . דלק
דָּלְקוּ [b] ו Kal pret. 3 pers. pl. . . . דלק
דֹּלְקִים [c] Kal part. act. masc., pl. of [דָּלַק] dec. 7 b. דלק
דְּלָקֻנוּ [d] Kal pret. 3 pers. pl., suff. 1 pers. pl. דלק
דָּלַקְתָּ Kal pret. 2 pers. sing. masc. . . דלק
דַּלָּת [e] ו noun fem. sing., constr. of דַּלָּה dec. 10. דלל
דֶּלֶת noun fem. sing. (q. v.) . . . . דלה
דַּלְתוֹת id. pl., constr. of the foll. (§ 44. rem. 1) דלה
דְּלָתוֹת [g] ו id. pl. abs. st. (§ 44. r. 5) ת treated as if radical; ו bef. (:) . . . . דלה
דַּלְתוֹתֵיהֶם [h] ו id. pl., suff. 3 pers. pl. masc. . דלה
דַּלְתוֹתָיו [i] ו id. pl., suff. 3 pers. sing. masc. דלה
דַּלְתֵי [k] ו id. du., constr. of [דֶּלֶת] dec. 11 a. (for דַּ comp. § 44. rem. 1) . . . דלה
דְּלָתַי id. du., suff. 1 pers. sing. . . דלה
דְּלָתֶיהָ id. du., suff. 3 pers. sing. fem. . דלה
דְּלָתֶיךָ id. du., suff. 2 pers. sing. masc. . דלה
דְּלָתֶךָ id. du. (Kh. דְּלָתֶיךָ) K. דְּלָתְךָ sing., suff. 2 pers. sing. masc. . . . דלה
דְּלָתַיִם [l] ו id. du., absolute state; ו bef. (:) דלה
דְּלָתָיִם ו
דִּלְּתַחְתִּי id. pl., suff. 1 pers. sing. from דָּלַת (q. v.) דלה
דִּלְתֹתָיו id. pl., suff. 3 pers. sing. masc. . דלה
דָּם [m] ו noun masc. sing. d. 2 a; for ו see lett. ו אדם
דַּם ו id., constr. state . . . . אדם
דֹּם [n] Kal imp. sing. masc. . . . דמם

I. דָּמָה to be or *become like,* to *resemble,* const. with אֶל, לְ. Niph. to *become like,* to *resemble,* const. with בְּ,

---

a Ex. 2. 19.   d Eze. 17. 7.   g Is. 19. 6.   k Da. 7. 9.   n La. 4. 19.   q Ca. 7. 6.   t 2 Ch. 4. 22.   y Zec. 11. 1.   b Job 38. 10.
b Ps. 79. 8.   e 2 Sa. 3. 1.   h Pr. 27. 15.   Ob. 1. 18.   o Ge. 31. 36.   r Ca. 8. 9.   u 2 Ch. 3. 7.   z Is. 26. 20.   c Pr. 8. 34.
c Pr. 26. 7.   f Ps. 30. 2.   i Pr. 19. 13.   m Pr. 26. 23.   p 2 Ki. 24. 14.   s 2 Ch. 4. 9.   w Job 31. 32.   a Eze. 38. 11.   d Eze. 34. 17.
e Ge. 41. 19.   2 Ch. 4. 9.

also w'th acc. Pi.—I. *to liken, compare*, with אֶל, לְ.
— II. *to imagine think, meditate;* 2 Sa. 21. 5
דִּמָּה לָנוּ *meditated against us*, sc. destruction.
Hithp. fut. 1 pers. אֶדַּמֶּה (for אֶתְדַּמֶּה) *to become
like*, Is. 14. 14.

II [דָּמָה] I. *to be dumb, silent, quiet.*—II. meton. *to reduce to silence, to destroy.* Niph. *to be destroyed,
cut off.*

    דְּמָה Chald. *to be like, similar.*

    דָּם masc. *likeness, similitude,* so according to
some in Eze. 19. 10.

    דְּמוּת fem. dec. 1 a.—I. *similitude, likeness.*—II.
model, pattern, 2 Ki. 16. 10.—III. adv. *as, like,* Is.
13. 4; so כִּדְמוּת Ps. 58. 5.

    דֳּמִי, דְּמִי masc. *silence, quiet, rest.*

    דִּמְיוֹן masc. dec. 1 b, *likeness,* Ps. 17. 12.

דָּמָהּ	noun m. s., suff. 3 pers. s. fem. fr. דָּם d. 2 a.	אדם
דָּמֵהּ *a*	Ch. Peal part. act. sing. masc. (§ 47. rem. 4)	דמה
דְּמֵה *c*/*f*	Kal imp. sing. masc.; ¹ bef. (:)	דמה
דִּמָּה *d*	Piel pret. 3 pers. sing. masc.	דמה
דָּמוּ	¹/ n. m. s., suff. 3 pers. s. m. from דָּם d. 2 a.	אדם
דָּמוּ *g*	Kal pret. 3 pers. pl.	דמה
דָּמּוּ *h*	Kal pret. 3 pers. pl. [for דָּמְמוּ]	דמם
דִּמּוּ *i*	Piel pret. 3 pers. pl.	דמה
דֹּמּוּ *g*	¹/ Kal imp. pl. masc.	דמם
דְּמוּת *h*	¹/ noun fem. sing. dec. 1 a; ¹ bef. (:)	דמה
דְּמִי *i*/*k*	¹ Kal imp. sing. fem.; for ¹ see lett. ¹	דמם
דָּמִי	¹/¹ n. m. s., suff. 1 pers. s. from דָּם dec. 2 a.	אדם
דֳּמִי	noun masc. sing.	דמה
דְּמֵי	¹/ n. m., pl. constr. of דָּם dec. 2 a; ¹ bef. (:)	אדם
דָּמְיָה *l*	Chald. Peal part. sing. fem., of דְּמָה masc.	
	(§ 47. rem. 4)	דמה
דְּמֻנָה *m*	defect. for דּוּמִיָּה noun fem. sing.	דום
דָּמֶיהָ	n. m. pl., suff. 3 pers. s. fem. from דָּם d. 2 a.	אדם
דְּמֵיהֶם	id., suff. 3 pers. pl. masc.	אדם
דָּמָיו	¹/¹ id., suff. 3 pers. sing. masc.	אדם
דָּמֶיךָ	id. (Kh. דָּמֶיךָ), suff. 2 pers. sing. masc., K.	
	דָּמֶךָ (q. v.)	אדם
דָּמַיִךְ *n*	id., suff. 2 pers. sing. fem.	אדם
דַּמִּים	pr. name, see אֲפַס דַּמִּים	אפס
דָּמִים	¹/ noun masc., pl. of דָּם dec. 2 a.	אדם
דָּמִינוּ *o*	Kal pret. 1 pers. pl.	דמה
דִּמִּינוּ *p*	Piel pret. 1 pers. pl.	דמה
דִּמְיֹנוֹ	noun masc. sing., suff. 3 pers. sing. masc.	
	from [דִּמְיוֹן] dec. 1 b.	דמה
דָּמִיתָ	Kal pret. 2 pers. sing. masc.	דמה

דִּמִּיתָ *a*	Piel pret. 2 pers. sing. masc.	דמה
דָּמִיתִי *c*/¹	Kal pret. 1 pers. sing.	דמה
דִּמִּיתִי	Piel pret. 1 pers. sing.	דמה
דְּמִיתִיךְ *e*	id., suff. 2 pers. sing. fem.	דמה
דָּמְךָ	noun m. s., suff. 2 pers. s. m. from דָּם d. 2 a.	אדם
דָּמֶךָ	id., suff. 2 pers. sing. fem.	אדם
דִּמְכֶם *g*	id., suff. 2 pers. pl. masc.	אדם

[דָּמַם] fut. דֹּם pl. יִדְּמוּ (§ 18. rem. 14).—I. *to be dumb,
silent, quiet;* דֹּם לַיהוָה, לֵאלֹהִים *be silent toward
the Lord God,* i. e. submit quietly to Him.—II. *to
rest, cease, leave off.*—III. *to stand still,* Jos. 10.12,13.
Po. *to silence, quiet,* Ps. 131. 2. Hiph. *to reduce
to silence, to destroy, cut off,* Je. 8. 14. Niph. fut.
תִּדְּמִי, יִדַּמּוּ.—I. *to be destroyed, cut off, to perish.*—
II. *to be laid waste.*

    דְּמָמָה fem. *silence, stillness.*

    דֳּמָה fem. *destruction, desolation,* for concr. *deso-
late,* Eze. 27. 32. But it may be rendered with
Prof. Lee, כְּדָמָה בְּתוֹךְ הַיָּם *as silence in the midst
of the sea.*

דָּמָם *a*/¹	id., suff. 3 pers. pl. masc.	אדם
דְּמָמָה	noun fem. sing.	דמם

דֹּמֶן masc. *dung, manure.*

    דִּמְנָה (*dunghill*) pr. name of a town in the
tribe of Zebulun, Jos. 21. 35.

    מַדְמֵן (id.) pr. name of a town in Moab, Je. 48. 2.

    מַדְמֵנָה fem.—I. *dunghill,* Is. 25. 10.—II. pr.
name of a town in the tribe of Benjamin, Is. 10. 31.

    מַדְמַנָּה (*dunghill*) pr. name of a town in the
tribe of Judah, Jos. 15. 31.

דִּמְנָה	pr. name of a place	רמן

[דָּמַע] *to weep, shed tears,* Je. 13. 17.

    דֶּמַע masc. dec. 6 a. (§ 35. rem. 5) prop. *tear,*
collect. *tears;* metaph. for the *juice* of grapes and
olives, &c. Ex. 22. 28.

    דִּמְעָה fem. dec. 12 b, *tear,* collect. *tears.*

דָּמֹעַ *e*	¹ Kal inf. abs.	דמע
דִּמְעָה	noun fem. sing. dec. 12 b.	דמע
דִּמְעֲךָ *d*	¹ noun masc. sing., suff. 2 pers. sing masc.	
	from [דֶּמַע] dec. 6 a. (§ 35. rem. 5)	דמע
דִּמְעַת *e*	noun fem. sing., constr. of דִּמְעָה dec. 12 b.	דמע
דִּמְעָתָהּ	¹/ id., suff. 3 pers. sing. fem.	דמע
דִּמְעָתִי	id., suff. 1 pers. sing.	דמע
דִּמְעָתְךָ	id., suff. 2 pers. sing. masc. [for תְךָ]	דמע

a Da. 3. 25.	*c* Eze. 31. 8.	*i* Je. 51. 35.	ᵐ Ps. 65. 2.	*p* Eze. 16. 9.	*s* Ps. 17. 12.	*v* Ho. 4. 5.	*z* Ju. 9. 24.	*d* Ex. 22. 28.
b Ca. 2. 17.	*f* Ju. 20. 5.	*k* 2 Ki. 9. 7.	*n* Ho. 12. 15.	*q* Is. 9. 1.	*t* Eze. 31. 2, 18.	*w* Ca. 1. 9.	*a* Ps. 83. 11.	*e* Ec. 4. 1.
c Ca. 8. 14.	*g* Ps. 4. 5.	*l* Da. 7. 5.	*o* 2 Sa. 1. 16.	*r* Is. 48. 10.	*u* Ge. 9. 5.	*x* Ps. 50. 21.	*c* Je. 13. 17.	*f* La. 1. 2.
d 2 Sa. 21. 5.	*h* Je. 47. 6.				

דַּמֶּשֶׂק	} sometimes דַּרְמֶשֶׂק, דּוּמֶשֶׂק (Syriac orthography) pr. name—I. *Damascus*, the metropolis of Syria on the river Chrysorrhoas.—II. concrete for *Damascene*, Ge. 15. 2.	
דְּמֶשֶׁק	}	

דְּמֶשֶׁק (in many MSS. דַּמֶשֶׂק) *damask*, silk cloth made at Damascus, Am. 3. 12.

דָּמְתָה	Kal pret. 3 pers. sing. fem.	דמה
[דֵּן]	Chald. emph. דְּנָה pron. demonstr. com. gen. *this, that*; כְּדְנָה *like this, such*; *as this, thus*; עַל דְּנָה *thereupon, therefore*; אַחֲרֵי דְנָה *afterwards*.	
דָּן	} pr. name of a man and a tribe (see also לֵט. דָּן).	דון
דָּן	Kal pret. 3 p. s. m. (Je. 22. 16); or part. act.	דון
דָּנִיֵּאל	defect. for דָּנִיֵּאל (q. v.)	דון

דָּנַג Root not used; whence
דּוֹנַג masc. *wax*.

דַּנָּה	} pr. name of a town in the tribe of Judah, Jos. 15. 49.	
דְּנָה	} Chald. pron. demon. com. emph. of [דֵּן]	דן
דִּנְהָבָה	pr. name of a town in Edom, Ge. 36. 32; 1 Ch. 1. 43.	
דָּנוּ	Kal pret. 3 pers. pl.	דון
דָּנִיֵּאל	} pr. name masc.	דון
דָּנַנִּי	Kal pret. 3 p. sing. masc., suff. 1 pers. sing.	דון
דַּע, דַּע	} Kal, or (Da. 6. 16) Ch. Peal, imp. sing. masc. (§ 20. rem. 1)	ידע
דֵּעָה	noun fem. sing. dec. 10, from דֵּעַ masc.	ידע
דְּעָה	Kal imp. sing. masc. (דַּע) with parag. ה (§ 20. rem. 1 & 3)	ידע
דְּעֵהוּ	id., suff. 3 pers. sing. masc. (comp. § 16. r. 12)	ידע
דְּעוּ	} id. imp. pl. masc.; bef. (:)	ידע
דְּעוּאֵל	(invocation of God; דעה Arab. *to invoke*) pr. name masc., called also רְעוּאֵל, comp. Nu. 7. 42, with 2. 14.	
דֵּעוֹת	noun fem., pl. of דֵּעָה dec. 10.	ידע
דְּעִי	} Kal imp. sing. fem.; bef. (:)	ידע
דֵּעִי	noun masc. sing from דֵּעַ dec. 1 a. (§ 36. r. 2)	ידע
דֵּעִים	id. pl., absolute state	ידע

[דָּעַךְ] *to go out, be extinguished*, as a light; trop. *to be destroyed*. Niph. *to become extinct*, of water *to be dried up*, Job 6. 17. Pu. *to be quenched, destroyed*, Ps. 118. 12.

דָּעֲכוּ	Kal pret. 3 pers. pl.	דעך
דֹּעֲכוּ	Pual pret. 3 pers. pl.	דעך

דַּעַת	} Kal inf. constr. (§ 20. r. 3) or subst. fem. dec. 13 a; for דַּעַת see lett. ו	ידע
דֵּעַת	}	
דַּעְתִּי	id. inf., suff. 1 p. s. [for דַּעְתִּי comp. § 35. r. 5]	ידע
דַּעְתְּךָ	id. subst., suff. 2 pers. sing. masc.	ידע
דַּעְתֵּךְ	id. id., suff. 2 pers. sing. fem.	ידע
דַּעְתָּם	id. id., suff. 3 pers. pl. masc.	ידע

דָּפָה Root not used; Arab. *to thrust, push*. Hence
דֹּפִי [for דָּפִי § 35. rem. 14] *stroke, ruin, destruction*, Ps. 50. 20. . . . . דפה

[דָּפַק] I. *to beat, knock*, Ca. 5. 2.—II. *to drive, overdrive*, Ge. 33. 13. Hithp. *to knock*, Ju. 19. 22.
דָּפְקָה (*cattle-driving*) pr. name of a station of the Israelites in the desert, Nu. 33. 12.

דְּפָקוּם	} Kal pret. 3 pers. pl. with suff. 3 pers. pl. masc.; bef. (:)	דפק
דַּק, דָּק	} Kal pret. 3 pers. masc. or adj. masc. sing.	דקק
דַּקָּה	adj., fem. of the preceding	דקק
דָּקוּ	Chald. Peal pret. 3 pers. pl. masc. [for דַּקּוּ]	דקק
דַּקּוֹת	} adj. fem., pl. of דַּק d. 10, from דַּק masc.	דקק
דִּקְלָה	(i. q. Chald. דִּקְלָא *palm-tree*) pr. name of a district in Arabia, Ge. 10. 27.	

[דָּקַק] pret. דַּק, fut. יָדֹק.—I. *to beat or grind small*.—II. intrans. *to be beaten or ground small*, Ex. 32. 20; De. 9. 21. Hiph. הֵדַק *to beat small, break in pieces*; inf. הָדֵק adv. *very small, fine*, and so לְהָדֵק (§ 18. r. 10). Hoph. *to be ground small* Is. 28. 28.
דְּקַק Ch. *to be beaten, broken in pieces*, Da. 2. 35. Aph. הַדֵּק, fut. תַּדֵּק, תַּדִּק *to beat or grind small*.
דַּק, fem. דַּקָּה adj.—I. *small, thin, fine*, hence as a subst. *small dust*.—II. *slender, thin, withered*.
דֹּק masc. *thin, fine cloth*, Is. 40. 22.

[דָּקַר] *to thrust through, to pierce*. Niph. *to be thrust through*, Is. 13. 15. Pu. *to be thrust through*; metaph. by want, La. 4. 9.
דֶּקֶר (*a stabbing*) pr. name masc. 1 Ki. 4. 9.
מַדְקֵרָה (מַדְקָרָה or מַדְקְרוֹת) fem. pl. constr. (fr. *piercings of the sword*, Pr. 12. 18.

דֶּקֶר	pr. name masc.	דקר
דָּקְרוּ	Kal pret. 3 pers. pl. [for דְּקָרוּ § 8. r. 7]	דקר
דְּקָרֻהוּ	id. id., suff. 3 pers. sing. masc.; bef. (:)	דקר
דָּקְרֵנִי	} id. imp. sing. masc., suff. 1 pers. sing.	דקר
דְּקָרֻנִי	id. pret. 3 pers. pl., suff. 3 p. s. m.; bef. (:)	דקר

a Ca. 7. 8.   d Ge. 39. 6.   g Pr. 3. 6.   k Ps. 118. 12.   n Job 10. 7.   p Is. 44. 25.   s Da. 2. 35.   t Ge. 41. 3.   w Zec. 13. 3.
b Da. 5. 25.   e Ec. 11. 9.   h Job 37. 16.   l Ps. 119. 66.   o Is. 47. 10.   q Ge. 33. 13.   u Ge. 41. 6, 23.   x Zec. 13. 10.   y 1 Sa. 31. 4.
c Je. 5. 28.   f Pr. 24. 14.   i Is. 43. 17.   m De. 9. 24.

דקק   m. דַּק from d. 10, דַּקָּה pl., fem. adj. ן   דַּקַּת•

דור   Chald. noun masc. sing.   ן   דָּר

דרר   noun masc. sing.   ן   דָּר•

דור   defect. for דוֹר (q. v.)   ן   דָּר

דְּרָא   Root not used; Arab. *to excite evil.*

דְּרָאוֹן masc., constr. דְּרָאוֹן (§ 32. Nos. 1 & 2) *abhorrence, contempt,* Da. 12. 2. Also—

דֵּרָאוֹן (for דְּרָאוֹן) m. *abhorrence,* Is. 66. 24.

דְּרָב   Root not used; Arab. *to be pointed.*

דָּרְבֹנוֹת only in pl. *goads,* Ec. 12. 11. דָּרְבָן masc. *goad,* 1 Sa. 13. 21.

דְּרָג   Root not used; Arab. *to ascend by steps.*

מַדְרֵגָה fem. *steep place, precipice,* Ca. 2. 14; Eze. 38. 20.

דַּרְדַּע   (*pearl of wisdom;* דַּר Arab. *pearl*) pr. name masc. 1 Ki. 5. 11, called דָּרַע 1 Ch. 2. 6.

דרר   noun masc. sing.   ן   דַּרְדַּר

דרר   Kal part. pass. fem. sing. dec. 10, [from דָּרוּךְ masc.]   דְּרוּכָה•

דרר   noun masc. sing. [for דַּדּוּם]   ן   דָּרוֹם

דרר   noun masc. sing.; ן bef. (:)   ן   דָּרוֹר

דרש   Kal part. pass. fem. sing. (see the foll.)   דְּרוּשָׁה•

דרש   id. masc., pl. of דָּרוּשׁ dec. 3 a.   דְּרוּשִׁים•

דור   defect. for דוֹרוֹת (q. v.)   דֹּרוֹת

דָּרְיָוֶשׁ   pr name *Darius.*—I. *Darius the Mede,* i.e. *Cyaxares,* comp. Da. 6. 1.—II. *Darius Hystaspis, king of Persia,* comp. Hag. 1. 1. —III. *Darius Nothus, king of Persia,* Ne. 12. 22.

דָּרַךְ   ן ו'   fut. יִדְרֹךְ *to tread,* with the acc.; with עַל *to tread upon* any thing; with בְּ *to tread,* e. g. a *way;* hence *to tread in* or *upon, to enter;* with מִן *to tread forth, come forth, out of* a place; metaph. *to tread down* enemies; דָּרַךְ גַּת יַעֲקֹב *to tread the wine-press;* יַיִן דָּ, זַיִת, *to tread the grapes, the olives;* דָּ קֶשֶׁת *to bend the bow;* and meton. דָּ חִצִּים *to bend the arrows,* for, *the bow.* Hiph.—I. *to cause to tread, go, walk, to lead.*— II. i. q. Kal *to tread a way, to walk in it; to tread a threshing-floor;* metaph. *to tread* or *bend the tongue,* like a bow; *to tread down* enemies.

דֶּרֶךְ com. dec. 6 a, with suff. דַּרְכִּי (Du. דְּרָכַיִם

(דֶּרֶךְ).—I. *a going, way, journey,* as if אֵם; דֶּרֶךְ יוֹם *a day's journey;* עָשָׂה דָרֶךְ *to make one's way.*—II. *way, path;* דֶּרֶךְ הַמֶּלֶךְ *the king's high-way;* הָלַךְ דַּרְכּוֹ *to go one's way;* הָלַךְ דֶּרֶךְ כָּל־הָאָרֶץ *to go the way of all the earth,* i. e. *to die.* —III. *mode, manner, custom;* כְּדֶרֶךְ כָּל־הָאָרֶץ *after the manner of all the earth,* i. e. *all mankind.*

מִדְרָךְ masc. *place trodden upon, footing,* De. 2. 5.

דרך   דֶּרֶךְ ן, דֶּרֶךְ ן   n. com. sing. d. 6 a. (§ 35. r. 2) ; ן   ן ן', for ן see lett. ו

דרך   ן'   Kal part. act. sing. masc. dec. 7 b   דֹּרֵךְ•

דרך   Kal pret. 3 pers. sing. fem.   דָּרְכָה•

דרך   noun com. s., suff. 3 p. s. f. from דֶּרֶךְ d. 6 a.   דַּרְכָּהּ•

דרך   id., with suff., Kh. כוֹ' 3 pers. s. m., K. כִּי' 1 pers. sing.   דַּרְכּוֹ•

דרך   id. pl., suff. 3 p. sing. masc. K. כָיו' (§ 4. r. 1)   דְּרָכָו

דרך   Kal pret. 3 pers. pl.   ן'   דָּרְכוּ

דרך   ן'   n. com. s., suff. 3 p. s. m. from דֶּרֶךְ d. 6 a.   דַּרְכּוֹ

דרך   Kal part. pass. fem., pl. from דְּרוּכָה (q. v.)   דְּרֻכוֹת•

דרך   noun com. pl. constr. from דֶּרֶךְ dec. 6 a.   דַּרְכֵי•

דרך   id. sing., suff. 1 pers. sing.   דַּרְכִּי•

דרך   id. pl., suff. 1 pers. sing.   דְּרָכַי, דְּרָכָי

דרך   ן   Kal part. act. pl. constr. m. from דֹּרֵךְ s.   דֹּרְכֵי

דרך   n. com. pl., suff. 3 pers. s. f. from דֶּרֶךְ d. 6 a.   דְּרָכֶיהָ

דרך   id. pl., suff. 3 pers. pl. m.   דַּרְכֵיהֶם

דרך   ן'   id. pl., suff. 3 pers. sing. masc.; ו bef. (:)   דְּרָכָיו

דרך   id. pl., suff. 2 pers. sing. fem.   דְּרָכֶיךְ

דרך   ן'   id. pl., suff. 2 pers. sing. masc.; ו bef. (:)   דְּרָכֶיךָ

דרך   id. pl., suff. 2 pers. pl. masc.   דַּרְכֵיכֶם

דרך   id. dual, absolute state (as if from דֶּרֶךְ)   דְּרָכַיִם'

דרך   id. pl., absolute state   דְּרָכִים

דרך   Kal part. act. masc., pl. of דֹּרֵךְ dec. 7 b   דֹּרְכִים

דרך   noun com. pl., suff. 1 pers. pl. from דֶּרֶךְ d. 6 a.   דְּרָכֵינוּ•

דרך   id. sing., suff. 2 pers. sing. masc. for כְּךָ'   דִּרְכְּךָ•

דרך   id. sing., suff. 2 pers. sing. fem.   דִּרְכֵּךְ

דרך   id. pl., suff. 2 pers. s. masc. defect. for כֶיךְ'   דְּרָכֶךָ

דרך   id. sing., suff. 2 pers. pl. masc.   דַּרְכְּכֶם•

דרך   id. sing. suff., 3 pers. pl. masc.   דַּרְכָּם

דַּרְכְּמוֹנִים, דַּרְכְּמֹנִים   masc. pl. *darics, a Persian coin.*

דרך   n. com. s., suff. 1 pers. pl. from דֶּרֶךְ d. 6 a.   דָּרְכֵנוּ•

דרך   Kal pret. 2 pers. sing. masc.   דָּרַכְתָּ•

דרך   id. pret. 1 pers. sing.   דָּרַכְתִּי•

דַּרְמֶשֶׂק, דַּרְמֶשֶׂק   pr. name, see דַּמֶּשֶׂק.•

a Ge. 41. 4.   d De. 32. 25.   f Ps. 111. 2.   i Is. 59. 8.   m Job 28. 23.   p Ps. 37. 22.   t Pr. 31. 3.   u Ne. 13. 15.   y Ju. 18. 6.
b Est. 1. 6.   e Ps. 84. 4.   g Mi. 1. 3.   k Am. 4. 13.   2 Sa. 22. 33.   q Is. 5. 28.   Pr. 28. 6, 18.   x La. 3. 40.   Hab. 3. 15.
c Is. 21. 15.   f Is. 62. 12.   Is. 35. 8.   Jos. 14. 9.   r Ps. 37. 14.

[דְּרַע] Chald. i. q. Heb. זְרוֹעַ *the arm*, Da. 2. 32.

אֶדְרָע Chald. id. with prosthetic א Ezr. 4. 23.

אֶדְרֶעִי, in pause אֶדְרָעִי (*strong, mighty*; Simonis, for אֶדֶר רְעִי *large pasture*) pr. name.—I. of the metropolis of Bashan, afterwards belonging to the tribe of Manasseh.—II. of a town in the tribe of Naphtali, Jos. 19. 37.

דָּרַע וְ pr. name, for דְּרַע, see דַּרְדַּע

דְּרָעוֹהִי Chald. n. com. pl., suff. 3 pers. sing. masc. from [דְּרַע] dec. 1 a. . . . דרע

דַּרְקוֹן pr. name masc. Ezr. 2. 56.

דָּרַר Root not used; Arab. *to fly round*, cogn. דּוּר, *to radiate*; *to flow freely*.

דַּר m. Est. 1. 6, *pearl*; others, *mother of pearl*, or some kind of alabaster resembling it.

דְּרוֹר m.—I. *swallow*.—II. *a spontaneous flowing*, Eze. 30. 23.—III. *liberty*.

דָּרוֹם m. (for דָּרוּם) *the south*, the southern quarter. Poet. for *the south wind*, Job 37. 17.

דַּרְדַּר m. *brambles*; others, *weeds*, as growing luxuriantly.

דָּרַשׁ fut. יִדְרֹשׁ.—I. *to seek unto, visit* or *frequent*, e. g. a place, const. with the acc. of the place or person, with אֶל, לְ.—II. *to seek, search for*, with an acc. of the thing; with אַחַר *to seek after*.—III. *to ask, inquire*, especially *to inquire of* or *consult* an oracle, the Lord; *to inquire about* any thing, with acc., לְ; with עַל of the person of whom, and the thing *about* which inquiry is made (2 Ch. 31. 9); with מֵעִם, מֵאֵת, also בְּ of the person *through* whom God is consulted.—IV. *to ask for, demand back, require*, with the acc. of the thing and with דָּרַשׁ דָּם, מִיַּד, מֵעִם, מֵאֵת of person; מֵעִם, מִיַּד *to require the blood of any one*, i. e. to punish bloodshed.—V. *to seek, apply oneself unto, to promote*; דָּרַשׁ שָׁלוֹם פּ׳ *to promote the welfare of any one*; דָּרְשָׁה צֶמֶר *applieth herself to wool*; hence *to care for, regard*. Niph.—I. *to be sought for*, 1 Ch. 26. 31.—II. pass. of Kal No. III., with לְ.—III. pass. of Kal No. IV., Ge. 42. 22.

מִדְרָשׁ m. d. 2 b, *commentary*, 2 Ch. 13. 22 ; 24. 27.

דָּרֵשׁ Kal pret. 3 pers. s. m. for דָּרַשׁ (§ 8. r. 7) דרש

דָּרוֹשׁ id. inf. absolute . . . דרש

דְּרָשׁ id. imp. sing. masc. for דְּרֹשׁ (§ 8. rem. 18) דרש

דְּרֹשׁ id. inf. constr. . . . דרש

לֹרֵשׁ וְ	id. part. act. sing. masc. dec. 7 b.	דרש
דָּרְשָׁה	id. pret. 3 pers. sing. fem.	דרש
דְּרָשָׁהוּ	id. pret. 3 pers. pl., suff. 3 pers. sing. masc.	דרש
דָּרְשׁוּ וְדָרְשׁוּ	id. pret. 3 pers. pl. (§ 8. rem. 7)	דרש
דְּרָשׁוֹ	id. inf., suff. 3 pers. sing. masc.	דרש
דִּרְשׁוּ וְ	id. imp. pl. masc.	דרש
דְּרָשׁוּהָ וְ	id. pret. 3 p. pl., suff. 3 p. s. m.; bef. (:)	דרש
דְּרָשׁוּם	id. id., suff. 3 pers. pl. masc.	דרש
דְּרָשׁוּנִי	id. id., suff. 1 pers. pl.	דרש
דִּרְשׁוּנִי	id. imp. pl. masc., suff. 1 pers. sing.	דרש
דֹּרְשֵׁי וְ	id. part. act. pl. c. masc. from דֹּרֵשׁ d. 7 b.	דרש
דְּרָשָׁיו	id. id., suff. 3 pers. sing. masc.	דרש
דְּרָשֶׁךָ	id. id., suff. 2 pers. sing. masc.	דרש
דָּרְשֵׁנוּ	id. pret. 3 pers pl.	דרש
דְּרָשָׁהוּ	id. id., suff. 3 pers. sing. masc.	דרש
דָּרַשְׁתָּ	id. pret. 2 pers. sing. masc.	דרש
דָרַשְׁתָּ וְ	id. id.; acc. shifted by conv. וְ (§ 8. r. 7)	דרש
דְּרַשְׁתִּי דְּרַשְׁתִּי	id. pret. 1 pers. sing.	
דָרַשְׁתִּי וְ	id. id.; acc. shifted by conv. וְ (§ 8. r. 7)	דרש
דְּרַשְׁתִּיךָ	id. pret., suff. 2 pers. sing. masc.	דרש
דֹּרֹתֵיכֶם	noun masc. with pl. fem. term. and suff. 2 pers. pl. masc. from דּוֹר dec. 1 a.	דור
דֹּרֹתֵינוּ	id. with suff. 1 pers. pl.	דור
דָּשׁ	Kal pret. 3 pers. sing. masc.	דוש

[דָּשָׁא] to spring, sprout forth, Joel 2. 22. Hiph. *to send forth grass*, Ge. 1. 11.

דֶּשֶׁא masc. *tender grass, young herbage*.

דָּשָׁה	Kal part. fem. sing. [for דָּשָׁה from דָּשׁ masc.]	דוש
דָּשָׁא	noun masc. sing.	דשא
דָּשְׁאוּ	Kal pret. 3 pers. pl.	דשא

דָּשֵׁן וְ *to grow fat*, De. 31. 20. Pi.—I. *to make fat*, Pr. 15. 30.—II. *to anoint*, Ps. 23. 5.—III. *to regard as fat*, an offering, i. e. accept it, Ps. 20. 4.—IV. denom. of דֶּשֶׁן *to remove the ashes*. Pu. *to be made fat, be abundantly satisfied*. Hothpa. הִתְדַּשֵּׁן for הִתְדַּשֵּׁן (§ 6. No. 10 note) *to be besmeared with fat*, Is. 34. 6.

דָּשֵׁן adj. masc. dec. 5 a.—I. *fat*, of soil; of trees, *full of sap*.—II. *rich, opulent*, Ps. 22. 30.

דֶּשֶׁן masc. dec. 6 a. (with suff. דִּשְׁנִי).—I. *fatness, fat*; trop. *fertility*.—II. *ashes*, especially those from the victims consumed upon the altar.

דָּשֵׁן adj. masc. sing. dec. 5 a. דשן

a Da. 2. 32.   d Pr. 31. 13.   g Ps. 78. 34.   k Am. 5. 4.   m Ps. 9. 11.   o Eze. 34. 10, 11.   t Le. 23. 43.   v 1 Ch. 21. 20.   z Joel 2. 22.
b 2 Ch. 17. 4.   e Zep. 1. 6.   h Je. 8. 2.   i Ps. 69. 33.   n Ps. 24. 5.   p Ps. 119. 10.   r Jos. 22. 28.   w Je. 50. 11.   x Is. 30. 25.
c De. 22. 2   f 2 Ch. 26. 5.   Is. 65. 10   u 2 Ch. 14. 6

דֶּשֶׁן } noun masc. sing. dec. 6a. (§ 35. rem. 2, but comp. דִּשְׁאֵי); for וַ see lett. וַ   דשן

דִּישׁוֹן pr. name masc. for דִּישֹׁן   דוש

דִּשַּׁנּוּ Piel pref. 1 pers. pl.   דשן

דִּשְׁנֵי adj. masc. pl., constr. of דָּשֵׁן dec. 5a.   דשן

דִּשְׁנִי noun m. s., suff. 1 pers. s. from דֶּשֶׁן dec. 6a.   דשן

דְּשֵׁנִים adj. masc., pl. of דָּשֵׁן dec. 5a.   דשן

דִּשַּׁנְתָּ Piel pret. 2 pers. sing. masc.   דשן

דַּשְׁתִּי Kal. pret. 1 pers. sing.; acc. shifted to ult. by conv. וַ (§ 8. rem. 7.)   דוש

דָּת וְ׳ (דָּתְכוֹן) fem. dec. 1. (but also דַּת construct, and Heb. & Chald.—I. law, statute.—II. edict, decree. דְּתָבַר Chald. masc. judge or lawyer, pl. emph. דְּתָבְרַיָּא Da. 3. 2, 3.

[דִּתְאָ] Chald. masc. emph. דִּתְאָא tender grass, i. q. Heb דֶּשֶׁא Da. 4. 12, 20.

דָּתָא וְ׳ Chald. noun fem. emph. of דָּת dec. 1 b.   רת

דְּתָבְרַיָּא Chald. noun masc. pl. emph. of [דְּתָבַר]   רת

דָּתֵהוֹ וְ׳ noun fem. s., suff. 3 pers. s. m. fr. דָּת dec. 1 a.   רת

דָּתֵי Heb. & Chald. id. pl. onstruct state   רת

[דֹתַיִן] (two wells, Chald. דַּת a well) Ge. 37. 17, contracted דֹּתָן 2 Ki. 6. 13, pr. name of a place in the north of Samaria.

דֹּתָיְנָה id. with local ה

דָּתֵיהֶם׳ וְ׳ noun fem. pl., suff. 3 pers. pl. masc. from דָּת dec. 1 a.   רת

דַּתְכוֹן־ Chald. id. sing., suff. 2 pers. pl. m. dec. 1 b.   רת

דָּתָן וְ׳ pr. name of one of the conspirators with Korah

ה

הַ (followed by dag. forte) before letters not guttural, as הַסּוּס ; הָ (Pattah lengthened into Kamets) before the gutturals and ר; but invariably so before א and ר, as הָרֹאשׁ, הָרֶגֶל, הָאִישׁ, הָאָשָׁם ; before ה and ח only in the monosyllabic words, הָהָר, הָחַי Ge. 6. 19; (הָהָרָה), הָהֵם, (הָהֵמָּה, הָהֵנָּה) before ע not having kamets for its vowel, as הָעִיר, הָעֶבֶד, or having kamets in a monosyllabic, or dissyllabic word with the accent on the penult, as הָעָם, הָעַיִן ;—הַ (not followed by dag. forte) before ה and ח where dag. is said to be implied (dag. forte implicitum, occultum), as הַהֹלֵךְ, הַהוּא, הַעֹזְבִים, before ע only in הַחֲזִיר, הַחֶשֶׁךְ Pr. 2. 13, 17, הָעֲרֵקִי Ge. 10. 17, כָּעִוְרִים Is. 59. 10. in which the best copies agree ;—הֶ (dag. forte impl.) before a guttural having kamets, especially before ח, as הֶחֳרִי, הֶחָכָם ; before ה and ע only in polysyllabic words, as הֶהָרִים, הֶעָרִים, הֶעָנָן, הֶהָרִיוֹתְיָה ; the Hebrew article. I. prop. pron. demonstr. this; הַיּוֹם this day; הַפַּעַם this time.—II. for the definite article the.—III. for the indefinite article, a; הַיּוֹם on a day, once. Comp. our expression, " on a certain day; a certain man," in which there is both definiteness and indefiniteness.—IV. for the vocative; הַמֶּלֶךְ O king.—V. pron. relat. who, which, הַהֹלְכוּא who had gone, Jos. 10. 24; הָעֲלִיָּה that which is above her, 1 Sa. 9. 24.

הַ before letters not guttural; rarely followed by dag. forte, like the article, especially before sheva (comp. הַלְּבָן Ge. 17. 17, הַבִּתַּחַת 37. 32) ; הֶ before gutturals, as הָאֵלֶּה ; הָ before gutturals having kamets, as הֶחָזָק, הֶאָנֹכִי ; a sign of interrogation I. of direct interrogation ; Job 2. 3, הֲשַׂמְתָּ לִבְּךָ אֶל־עַבְדִּי אִיּוֹב hast thou considered my servant Job? —II. in indirect interrogation, whether ; De. 13. 4, to know הֲיִשְׁכֶם אֹהֲבִים אֶת־יְהוָֹה whether ye love the Lord.

הָא Chald. interj. lo ! behold ! Da. 3. 25.

הָא Heb. & Chald. id. Ge. 47. 23 ; Eze. 16. 43 ; Da. 2. 43.

הָאָב֗ pref. הָ for ׃הַ (noun masc. sing. irr. (§ 45)   אב

הָאֲבֵדָה׳ pref. id. (noun fem. sing. dec. 10.   אבד

הָאֹבְדוֹת׳ pref. id. (Kal part. act. fem. pl. from dec. 13a. (§ 8. rem. 19)   אבד

הָאֹבְדִים׳ pref. id. (id. masc., pl. of אֹבֵד dec. 7 b.   אבד

הָאֹבֶדֶת׳ pref. id. (id. fem. sing. dec. 13a.   אבד

הֶאֱבַדְתָּ וְ׳ } Hiph. pret. 2 pers. sing. masc.; acc. shifted
הֶאֱבַדְתְּ וְ׳ } by conv. וַ (§ 8. rem. 7, & § 13. rem. 10)   אבד

הֶאֱבַדְתִּי וְ׳ id. pret. 1 pers. sing.; acc. shifted to ult. by conv. וַ (comp. id.)   אבד

הֶאֱבַדְתִּיךָ וְ׳ id. id., suff. 2 pers. sing. masc. (comp. id.)   אבד

הֶאֱבַדְתִּיךְ וְ׳ id. id., suff. 2 pers. sing. fem. (comp. id.)   אבד

הֶאֱבַדְתָּם וְ׳ id. id. 2 pers. sing. masc., suff. 3 pers. pl. masc. (comp. id.)   אבד

a Ps. 65. 6.   d Ju. 9. 9.   g Ju. 8. 7.   k Est. 4. 11.   n Da. 2. 9.   q Le. 5. 23.   t Is. 27. 13.   w Job 14. 19.   z Zep. 2. 5.
b Nu. 4. 13.   e Ps. 92. 15.   h Da. 7. 25.   l Est. 3. 8.   o Eze. 18. 4, 20.   r 1 Sa. 9. 20.   u Eze. 34. 4, 16.   x Eze. 25. 7.   aa De. 9. 3.
Ps. 22. 30.   f Ps. 23. 5.   i Da. 3. 2, 3.

הָאָבוֹת	'ן pref. for הָ)(noun masc. with fem. term. from אָב irr. (§ 45) . . .	אב
הָאֹבוֹת	pref· id.)(noun masc. with pl. fem. term. from אוֹב dec. 1a.	אוב
הָאֲבַטִּחִים	pref. id.)(noun m., pl. of [אֲבַטִּיחַ] dec. 1a.	בטח
הָאָבִיב	pref. id.)(name of a month.	אבב
הַאֲבִידִ	Hiph. inf. construct . . .	אבד
הֶאֱבִידוֹ	ן id. pret. 3 pers. sing. masc.	אבד
הַאֲבִידוֹ	id. inf., suff. 3 pers. sing. masc. dec. 1 b.	אבד
הָאֶבְיוֹן	pref. הַ for הָ)(adj. noun m. s. dec. 1 b.	אבה
הָאֲבִיוֹנָה	pref. id.)(noun fem. sing.	אבה
הָאֶבְיוֹנִים	ן pref. id.)(adj. masc., pl. of אֶבְיוֹן dec. 1 a.	אבה
הַאֲבֶכָּה	pref. הַ interr. for הָ)(Kal fut. 1 pers. sing.	בכה
הָאֵבֶל	pref. הָ for הַ)(n. m. s. dec. 6 b. (§ 35. rem. 6)	אבל
הַיֹּבֵל	pref. id.)(noun masc. sing. dec. 2 b.	יבל
הֶאֱבַלְתִּי	Hiph. pret. 1 pers. sing.	אבל
הָאֶבֶן	'ן pref. הָ for הָ)(n. fem. s. (suff. אַבְנוֹ) dec. 6 a.	אבן
הָאַבְנֵט	pref. id.)(noun masc. sing. dec. 1 a.	בנט
הָאֲבָנִים	וֹן pref. id.)(noun fem., pl. from אֶבֶן (suff. אֲבָנוֹ) dec. 6 a. . . .	אבן
הָאָבְנַיִם	pref. id.)(noun fem., dual of [אֹבֶן] dec. 6 c.	אבן
הָאַבְרֵ־	pref. id.)(noun masc. sing.	אבר
הָאַגָּגִי	pref. id.)(gent. noun masc. from אֲגַג	אגג
הָאֲגַמִּים	pref. id.)(noun masc. pl. of אֲגַם dec. 8.	אגם
הָאֲגָנוֹת	pref. id.)(noun masc. with pl. fem. term. from אַגָּן dec. 1 b.	אגן
הָאִגֶּרֶת	pref. id.)(noun fem. sing. dec. 13 a.	אגר
הָאֲדֹמִי	pref. id.)(gent. noun masc. from אֱדוֹם	אדם
הָאָדוֹן	pref. id.)(noun masc. sing. dec. 3 a.	דון
הָאַדִּירִים	pref. id.)(adj. masc., pl. of אַדִּיר dec. 1 b.	אדר
הָאָדָם	'ן pref. id.)(noun. masc. sing. .	אדם
הָאָדֹם	pref. id.)(adj. masc. sing., pl. אֲדֻמִּים dec. 8 c. (§ 37. Nos. 2 & 3)	אדם
הָאֲדָמָה	'ן pref. id.)(n. fem. s. dec. 11 c. (§ 42. r. 1)	אדם
הָאֲדָמִי	pref. id.)(gent. noun masc. from אֲדָם	אדם
הָאָדֹן	pref. id.)(noun masc. sing. dec. 3 a.	דון
הָאֲדֹנִים	pref. id.)(id. pl. absolute	דון
הָאֲדֹנִים	ן pref. id.)(noun masc. pl. (constr. אֲדֹנֵי) from [אָדֹן] dec. 6 a.	אדן
הַאֵדַע	pref. הַ interr. הָ)(Kal fut. 1 pers. sing.	ידע
הָאַדְרֵשׁ	pref. id.)(Niph. inf. absolute [for הַהֵדָרֵשׁ]	דרש
הָאַדַּרְתְּ	pref. הָ for הַ)(n. fem. s. (suff. אַדַּרְתּוֹ) d. 13 a.	אדר
הָאַהֲבָה	pref. id.)(noun fem. sing. dec. 10.	אהב
הָאֲהוּבָה	pref. id.)(Kal part. pass. fem. from אָהוּב m.	אהב
הָאֱהָלֵי	Kheth. הָאֹהֵל q. v., Keri הָאֹהֱלָה (q. v.)	אלה
הָאֹהֶל	'ן pref. הָ for הַ)(n. m. s. d. 6. (§ 35. r. 9)	אהל

הָאֹהֱלָה	pref. id.)(id. with local הָ	אהל
הָאֹהֱלִי	pref. id.)(id., suff. 1 pers. sing.	אהל
הָאֲגוּדִים	pref. id.)(noun masc., pl. of אֲגוּד dec. 1 a.	אוד
הָאוֹיֵב	pref. id.)(Kal part. act. sing. masc. dec. 7 b.	איב
הָאֱוִיל	pref. id.)((prim. adj.), noun m. sing. dec. 1 a.	אול
הַאֹכַל	pref. הַ interr. for הָ)(Kal fut. 1 pers. sing.	אכל
הָאוּכַל	pref. id.)(Hoph. fut. 1 pers. sing.	יכל
הָאוּלָם	'ן pref. הָ for הָ)(noun masc. sing., dec. 8 a.	אול
הָאָוֶן	pref. id.)(noun masc. sing. dec. 6 g.	און
הָאוֹסִיף	} pref. הַ interr. for הָ)(Hiph. fut. 1 pers. s.	יסף
הָאוֹסֵף		
הָאוֹפִים	pref. הָ for הָ)(Kal part. act., pl. of אֹפֶה d. 9 a.	אפה
הָאוֹפָן	} pref. id.)(noun masc. sing. dec. 8 a & d.	אפן
הָאוֹפֶן		
הָאוֹפַנִּים	'ן pref. id.)(id. pl., absolute state	אפן
הָאוֹצָר	pref. id.)(noun masc. sing. dec. 2 b.	אצר
הָאֹצָרוֹת	pref. id.)(id. with pl. fem. term., constr. st.	אצר
הָאוֹר	'ן pref. id.)(noun masc. sing. dec. 1 a.	אור
הָאוֹרֵב	ן pref. id.)(Kal part. act., pl. of אוֹרֵב d. 7 b.	ארב
הָאוּרִים	pref. id.)(noun masc., pl. of [אוּר] dec. 1 a.	אור
הָאֲוַרְנָה	pref. id.)(Kh. אוֹרְנָה, K. אֲרַוְנָה pr. name m.	ארן
הָאוֹת	pref. id.)(noun com. sing. dec. 1 a.	אוה
הַאֹתִי	pref. הַ interr. for הָ)(as if from [אוֹת] with suff. 1 pers. sing., see אֵת sign of the accu.	את
הָאֵזֹב	} pref. הָ for הָ)(noun masc. sing.	אזב
הָאֵזוֹב		
הָאֵזוֹר	pref. id.)(noun masc. sing.	אזר
הֶאֱזִין	} Hiph. pret. 3 pers. sing. masc. (§ 13. r. 10)	אזן
הֶאֱזִין		
הַאֲזִינָה	id. imp. sing. masc. with parag. הַ	אזן
הַאֲזִינוּ	ן id. imp. pl. masc.	אזן
הֶאֱזִינוּ	id. pret. 3 pers. pl. masc.	אזן
הַאֲזִינִי	ן id. imp. sing. fem. (comp. § 13. rem. 10)	אזן
הַאֶזְכֶּה	pref. הַ interr.)(Kal fut. 1 pers. sing.	זכה
הָאָצֵל	pref. הָ for הָ)([for אֵצֶל] pr. name see אֶבֶן	אבן
הַאֲזֵנָּה	Hiph. imp. pl. fem. [for הַאֲזֵנָּה § 17. rem. 9. & § 25. rem.)	אזן
הָאָזְנִי	pref. הָ for הָ)(pr. name masc.	אזן
הֶאֱזִנִיחוּ	ן Hiph. pret. 3 pers. pl.; a mixed form from the Chald. אֲזִנִיחוּ, and Heb. הֶאֱזִנִיחוּ	זנח
הֶאֱזַנְתָּ	ן id. pret. 2 pers. sing. masc., acc. shifted to ult. by conv. ן (§ 8. rem. 7. & § 13. rem. 10)	אזן
הָאֲזֻקִּים	[for הָאֲזִקִּים] pref. הָ; noun masc. pl. of [אֲזֵק] dec. 8 b.	זקק
הָאֶזְרָח	pref. הָ for הָ)(noun masc. sing. dec. 2 b.	זרח
הָאֶזְרָחִי	pref. id.)(patronym. masc., from אֶזְרָח	זרח

ᵃ Nu. 11. 5.   ᶠ Is. 41. 17.   ᵏ Ex. 8. 1.   ᵖ Ex. 38. 17.   ᵗ 1 Ki. 7. 45.   ʸ Ps. 50. 13.   ᵈ Ge. 40. 2.   ᶠ Je. 5. 22.   ᵐ Is. 1. 2.
ᵇ 2 Ki. 10. 19.   ᵍ Zec. 7. 3.   ˡ Da. 8. 3, 6.   ᑫ Est. 9. 26.   ᵘ 2 Sa. 19. 36.   ᶻ Nu. 3. 25.   ʰ 1 Ki. 7. 32.   ᵍ Le. 14. 6, 51.   ⁿ Mi. 6. 11.
ᶜ Nu. 24. 19.   ʰ Is. 22. 24.   ᵐ Eze. 14. 3.   ʳ Jos. 7. 21.   ᵛ Ps. 125. 5.   ᵃ 1 Ch. 9. 26.   ⁱ 1 Ki. 5. 13.   ᵒ Is. 19. 6.
De. 28. 51.   ⁱ Ex. 31. 15.   ⁿ Ge. 4. 1.   ˢ Jos. 7. 24.   ʷ Is. 7. 4.   ᵇ Ge. 12. 2.   ᵏ Pr. 77. 2.   ᵖ Ex. 15. 26.
De. 15. 7, 9.   ⁱ Ex. 39. 29.   ᵒ Ge. 25. 30.   ᵗ De. 21. 15, 16.   ˣ Ju. 20. 23.   ᶜ Ju. 20. 28.   ˡ De. 1. 45.   ᑫ Je. 40. 4.
Ec. 12. 5.   ᵉ Eze. 17. 3.   ᵈ Jos. 8. 19.

הָאָח interj. of joy or scorn, aha !

הָאָח pref. הַ for הָ) noun fem. sing. . . אחה

הָאֶחָד Kh. הָאֶחָד q. v. K. אֶחָד (q. v.) . . אחד

הָאֶחָד וְ pref. הָ for הַ) num. card. masc. irr. (§ 45) אחד

הָאֲחֻוָה pref. id.) noun fem. sing. . . . אח

הָאֲחֻזִי pref. id.) Kal part. p. s. m. for אָחֻוֹ dec. 3a. אחז

הֵאָחֵזוּ וְ Niph. imp. pl. masc. . . . אחז

הָאֲחֻזוֹת pref. הָ for הַ) Kal part. pass. fem. pl. from
אָחֻוֹ masc. dag. f. euph. . . . אחז

הָאֲחֹחִי pref. id.) patronym. masc. from אָחֹחַ . אחח

הַאֶחְיֶה pref. הַ interr. for הֲ) Kal fut. 1 pers. sing. חיה

הָאֲחֻזְכֶם pref. id.) noun masc. pl., suff. 2 pers. pl.
masc. from אָח irr. (§ 45) . . . אח

הָאֲחִירָמִי pref. הָ for הַ) patronym. m. from אֲחִירָם (q.v.) אח

הָאַחֵר pref. id.) adj. masc. sing. irr. (§ 45) אחר

הָאַחֲרוֹן וְ pref. id.) adj. masc. sing. dec. 1 b. אחר

הָאַחֲרֹנִים וְ } pref. id.) id. pl. . . . אחר
הָאַחֲרֹנִים וְ }

הָאַחֶרֶת pref. id.) adj. fem. s. from אַחֵר m. irr. (§ 45) אחר

הָאֲחַשְׁדַּרְפְּנִים וְ pref. id.) noun masc. pl. of [פָּן] אחשדרפן

הָאֲחַשְׁתְּרִי pref. id.) pr. name masc. . . אחשת׳

הָאֲחַשְׁתְּרָנִים pref. id.) noun masc., pl. of [רָן] אחשתר׳

הָאַחַת וְ } pref. id.) num. card. fem. [for אַחֶרֶת]
הָאַחַת } from אֶחָד m. for (ת) comp. § 45)} אחר

הָאֵטֶר pref. id.) pr. name of a place . אטר

הָאֵטֶר pref. id.) noun masc. sing. . . אטר

הָאֲטָדִים pref. id.) noun masc., pl. of אָט dec. 8e. אטד

הָאֲטֻמוֹתִי pref. id.) Kal part. pass. pl. fem. from
[אָטֻם] masc. . . . אטם

הָאִי pref. id.) noun m. sing. dec. 8f. (§ 37. No. 4) אוה

הָאֹיֵב defect. for הָאוֹיֵב (q. v.) . . . איב

הָאָיָה pref. הַ for הָ) noun fem. sing. . . אוה

הָאִיִּים pref. id.) n. m., pl. of אִי dec. 8f. (§ 37. r. 4) איה

הָאַיִל pref. id.) noun masc. sing. dec. 1 b. . אול

הָאַיִל } pref. id.) noun masc. sing. dec. 6 h. . אול
הָאַיִל }

הָאֵילִים pref. id.) noun masc., pl. of אַיִל dec. 1 b. . אול

הָאֵילִם } pref. id.) noun masc., pl. of אַיִל dec. 6 h. . אול
הָאֵילִם }

הָאֵימִים pref. id.) pr. name of a people . אים

הַאַיִן pref. הַ interr. for הֲ) adv., prop., noun masc.
sing. constr. of אַיִן dec. 6 h. . . און

הָאַיִן pref. הָ for הַ) noun masc., pl. of אִי dec. 8f.
(§ 37. No. 4) . . . . אוה

הַאֵינְךָ pref. הַ interr. for הֲ) adv. (suff. 2 pers. sing.
masc. for אַיִן) dec. 6 h. . . . און

הָאֲבִיעֶזְרִי pref. הָ for הַ) patronym. m. from אֲבִיעֶזֶר (q.v.) אב

הָאֵיפָה pref. id.) noun fem. sing. dec. 10. . איף

הָאֵירוּ וְ Hiph. pret. 3 pers. sing. masc. . אור

הָאִירָה id. imp. sing. masc. with parag. ה . אור

הֵאִירָה id. pret. 3 pers. sing. fem. . . אור

הֵאִירוּ id. pret. 3 pers. pl. . . . אור

הָאִישׁ וְ noun masc. sing. dec. 1 a. . . איש

הַאִיתָךְ Chald. pref. הַ interr. for הֲ) adv., (אִיתַי)
with suff. 2 pers. sing. masc. . אית

הַאַכֶּה pref. הַ id.) Hiph. fut. 1 pers. sing. . נכה

הֶאָכוֹל pref. הָ interr. for הֲ, הַ) Kal inf. abs. . אכל

הָאֲכִילָה pref. הָ for הַ) noun fem. sing. . אכל

הַאֲכִילֵהוּ Hiph. imp. sing. masc., suff. 3 pers. sing. m. אכל

הַאֲכִילֵהוּ וְ id. imp. pl. masc., suff. 3 pers. sing. masc. אכל

הָאֹכֵל וְ pref. הָ for הַ) Kal part. act. s. m. d. 7 b. אכל

הָאֹכֶל pref. id.) noun masc. sing. dec. 6 c. אכל

הֵאָכֵל Niph. inf. abs. . . . אכל

הַאֲכִלֵהוּ וְ Hiph. imp. pl. masc., suff. 3 pers. sing. m. אכל

הָאֹכְלִים pref. הָ for הַ) Kal part. act. masc., pl. of
אֹכֵל dec. 7 b. . . . אכל

הָאֹכֶלֶת pref. id.) id. sing. fem. (§ 8. rem. 19) . אכל

הֶאֱכַלְתִּי } Hiph. pret. 1 pers. sing. (§ 13. r. 9 & 10) אכל
הֶאֱכַלְתִּי וְ }

הֶאֱכַלְתִּיךָ } id. id., suff. 2 pers. s. m. & fem. (§ 13.
הֶאֱכַלְתִּיךְ } rem. 9 & 10)} אכל

הֶאֱכַלְתִּים וְ } id. id., suff. 3 pers. pl. masc. (§ 13. r. 9 & 10) אכל

הֶאֱכַלְתֶּם id. pret. 2 pers. sing. masc., suff. 3 pers. pl. m. אכל

הָאָל וְ pref. הָ for הַ) noun masc. sing. dec. 1 a. אול

הָאֵל pref. id.) pron. demon. pl. com. . . אלה

הָאֵל pref. הַ interr. for הֲ) noun masc. sing. d. 1 a. אול

הָאֶל pref. id.) prep. see אֶל . . . אל

הָאַלְגּוּמִּים by transpos. for אַלְמֻגִּים q. v.

הָאֵלָה pref. הָ for הַ) noun fem. sing. dec. 10. אלה

הָאַלָּה pref. id.) noun fem. sing. . . אלל

הָאֵלָה pref. id.) pr. name of a valley . אול

הָאֵלָה pref. id.) noun fem. sing. . . אלה

הָאֵלֶּה pref. id.) pron. demon. pl. com. . אל

הַאֱלֹהֵי pref. הַ interr. for הֲ) constr. of the following אלה

הָאֱלֹהִים וְ pref. הָ for הַ) art.) noun masc., pl. of
הָאֱלֹהִים pref. הַ interr. for הֲ) אֱלוֹהַּ dec. 1 a. . אלה

הָאָלוֹן pref. הָ for הַ) noun masc. sing. dec. 1 b. אלל

הָאָלוֹת pref. id.) noun fem., pl. of אָלָה dec. 10. אלה

הָאֵלִי pref. id.) gent. noun, see בֵּית הָאֵלִי . בית

---

a Je. 36. 22, 23.   f 2 Ki. 8. 8, 9.   l Est. 8. 10, 14.   q Eze. 26. 18.   u Da. 2. 26.   z Pr. 25. 21.   e Is. 49. 26.   k 2 Ch. 9. 11.
b 1 Ki. 4. 7.   g Nu. 32. 6.   m Is. 19. 3.   r Je. 7. 17.   w 2 Ki. 6. 21.   a 2 Ch. 18. 26.   f Ps. 80. 6.   l Le. 23. 23.
c Zec. 11. 14.   h Is. 8. 23.   n Eze. 41. 16.   s Ex. 25. 37.   x 2 Sa. 19. 43.   b 1 Ki. 22. 27.   g Is. 5. 16.   m 2 Ki. 7. 5.
d Nu. 31. 47.   i Est. 8. 9.   o Je. 15. 11.   t 1 Ki. 19. 8.   y Ex. 16. 32.   c Is. 58. 14.   h Job 8. 3.   n Ge. 35. 2.
e Ec. 9. 12.   k Est. 9. 2.   p De. 12. 22.   d Je. 19. 9.   i Is. 36. 12.

Hebrew	Description	Root
הָאֵלָה	'וְ׳ pref. הָ for הַ)(noun fem. sing.	אלה
הָאֱלִיל	pref. id.)(noun masc. sing. dec. 1a.	אלל
הָאֱלִילִים׳ / הָאֱלִילִם׳	} 'וְ׳ pref. id.)(id. pl., absolute state	אלל
הָאֵילִים׳	pref. id.)(noun masc., pl. of אַיִל dec. 6h.	אול
הָאֵלֵד	pref. הַ interr. for הַ)(Kal fut. 1 pers. sing.	ילך
הָאֻלָם׳	pref. הָ for הַ)(noun masc. sing. dec. 8a.	אול
הָאַלְמֻגִּים׳	pref. id.)(noun masc. pl., see אַלְמֻגִּים	
הָאַלְמָנָה׳	'וְ׳ pref. id.)(noun fem. sing. dec. 11a.	אלם
הָאֵלֹנִי	pref. id.)(patronym. m. from אֵלוֹן	אול
הָאָלֶף׳ / הָאֶלֶף׳	} pref. id.)(noun m. s. d. 6a. (§ 35. r. 2)	אלף
הָאֲלָפִים	'וְ׳ pref. id.)(id. pl., absolute state	אלף
הָאֶלְקֹשׁ׳	pref. id.)(gent. noun masc., see אֶלְקֹשִׁי	
הָאָלֹת׳	'וְ׳ pref. id.)(n. f., pl. of אָלָה d.10. (§ 42. r. 2)	אלה
הָאֵם׳	'וְ׳ pref. id.)(noun fem. sing. dec. 8b.	אם
הַאִם	pref. הַ interr. for הֲ)(particle	אם
הָאָמָה	pref. הָ for הַ)(noun fem. sing. irr. (§ 45)	אמה
הָאַמָּה	'וְ׳ pref. id.)(noun fem. sing. dec. 10.	אמם
הָאֲמָהוֹת׳ / הָאֲמָהֹת׳	} pref. id.)(n. f. pl. abs. of אָמָה irr. (§ 45)	אמה
הָאָמוֹן׳	pref. id.)(noun masc. sing.	אמה
הָאֲמָנָה׳	'וְ׳ pref. id.)(noun fem. sing. dec.10.	אמן
הָאָמֻר׳	pref. הָ interr. for הַ)(Kal part. pass. s. m.	אמר
הָאֵמִים	pref. הָ for הַ)(pr. name of a people	אים
הָאֵמִים׳	pref. id.)(noun masc., pl. of אֹם dec. 6c.	אמם
הֶאֱמִן	Hiph. pret. 3 pers. sing. masc.	אמן
הַאֲמִינוּ׳	Hiph. imp. pl. masc.	אמן
הֶאֱמִינוּ	'וְ׳ Hiph. pret. 3 pers. pl.	אמן
הַאֲמִינוֹן	pref. הַ interr. bef. (_.))(pr. n. m., see אַמְנוֹן	אמן
הָאָמִיר׳	'וְ pref. הָ for הַ)(noun masc. sing.	אמר
הַאֲמִירְךָ׳	Hiph. pret. 3 pers. s. m., suff. 2 pers. s. m.	אמר
הָאֲמֵלָלִים	pref. הָ for הַ)(adj. masc., pl. of [אֲמֵלָל]	אמל
הָאֹמֵן׳	pref. id.)(Kal part. act. sing. masc.	אמן
הֶאֱמִן׳	'וְ Hiph pret. 3 pers. masc. sing.	אמן
הָאֲמֹנוֹת׳	pref. הָ for הַ)(n. f., pl. of [אָמְנָה] d.10.	אמן
הָאֲמֻנִים׳	pref. id.)(Kal part. p. masc., pl. of [אָמוּן] dec. 3a.	אמן
הָאֹמְנִים׳	'וְ׳ pref. id.)(id. part. act. m., pl. of אֹמֵן d. 7b.	אמן
הָאֻמְנָם	pref. הָ interr. for הַ)(adv. formed from אֹמֶן and the term. □ָ- .	אמן
הֶאֱמַנְתִּי׳ / הַאֲמַנְתִּי׳	} Hiph. pret. 1 pers. sing. (§ 8. rem. 7)	אמן
הֶאֱמַנְתֶּם	id. pret. 2 pers. pl. masc.	אמן
הָאֲמֻצִּים	'וְ pref. הָ for הַ)(adj. m., pl. of [אָמֹץ] dec. 8c. (§ 37. No. 3)	אמץ
הַאֲמֹר׳׳	pref. הַ interr. for הֲ)(Kal inf. constr.	אמר
הָאֹמֵר	pref. הָ for הַ)(id. part. act. masc. dec. 7b.	אמר
הֶאָמֹר׳	pref. הֶ interr. for הֲ,)(id. pret. 3 p. s. m.	אמר
הָאָמֹר׳	pref. id.)(id. inf. absolute	אמר
הָאֹמְרָה	pref. הָ for הַ)(id. part. act., f. of אֹמֵר m.	אמר
הָאֲמָרוֹת׳	pref. id.)(id. pl. d.10, or from אֲמֶרֶת d.13a.	אמר
הָאֱמֹרִי׳	'וְ׳ pref. id.)(gent. noun masc.	אמר
הָאֹמְרִים	pref. id.)(Kal part. m. pl. of אֹמֵר dec. 7b.	אמר
הֶאֱמַרְתָּ׳	Hiph. pret. 2 pers. sing. masc.	אמר
הָאֱמֶת	'וְ pref. הָ for הֶ)(noun f.s. (suff. אֲמִתּוֹ)	אמן
הַאֱמֶת׳	pref. הַ interr. for הֶ §37. No.3) d.13a.	
הָאֱנוֹשׁ׳	pref. id.)(noun masc. s. (comp. אִישׁ § 45)	אנש
הָאָנַח	Niph. inf. constr.	אנח
הָאֲנִי׳	pref. הַ interr. for הֲ)(pron. pers. 1 p. sing.	אני
הָאֳנִיָּה	'וְ pref. הָ art. for הָ)(noun fem. sing. d.10.	אנה
הָאָנֹכִי	pref. הַ interr. for הֲ,)(pron. pers. 1 p. s.	אנך
הָאֲנָפָה׳	'וְ pref. הָ for הַ)(noun fem. sing.	אנף
הָאָנֵק	Niph. inf. constr.	אנק
הָאֲנָקָה׳	'וְ pref. הָ for הַ)(noun fem. sing. dec. 11c.	אנק
הָאֲנָשִׁים	'וְ׳ n. m. pl., as if from אֲנוֹשׁ dec. 6, see אֱנֹשׁ	אנש
הָאָסוּר׳׳	pref. הָ for הַ)(noun masc. sing. dec. 3b.	אסר
הָאֲסוּרִים׳	pref. id.)(Kh. אֲסִירִים Kal part. p. pl. of אָסוּר d. 3a, K. אֲסִירִים (q. v.)	אסר
הָאָסִיף׳	pref. id.)(noun masc. sing.	אסף
הָאֲסִירִים׳	pref. id.)(Kh. אֲסֻרִים noun m., pl. of אָסִיר dec. 3a, K. אֲסֻרִים (q. v.)	אסר
הָאָסֻף׳	defect. for הָאָסִיף (q. v.)	אסף
הָאֹסֵף׳	pref. הָ for הַ)(Kal part. act. s. m. dec. 7b.	אסף
הָאָסֹף	'וְ Niph. inf. constr., or imp. sing. masc.	אסף
הָאָסֹף׳	id. inf. absolute	אסף
הָאָסְפוּ׳	id. imp. pl. masc.	אסף
הָאָסְפִי׳	id. imp. sing. fem.	אסף
הָאֲסֻפִּים׳	pref. הָ for הַ)(noun m., pl. of [אָסֹף] d.8c. (§ 37. No. 3)	אסף
הָאֲסַפְסֻף׳	'וְ pref. id., for הָאֲסַפְסֻף)(noun masc. sing.	אסף
הָאֵסְרוּ׳	Niph. imp. pl. masc.	אסר
הַאֲעֱלֶה	pref. הַ interr. for הֲ)(Kal fut. 1 pers. sing.	עלה
הָאַף׳ / הָאַף	} pref. הָ for הַ)(n.m. s. d.8d. (§ 37. No.3)	אנף
הַאַף	pref. הַ interr. for הֲ)(conj.	אף
הָאֵפֹד	pref. הָ for הַ)(noun masc. sing.	אפד
הָאֵיפָה	pref. id.)(noun masc. sing. d. 10, for אֵיפָה	איף
הָאֹפֶה׳	'וְ pref. id.)(Kal part. act. masc. sing. d. 9a.	אפה
הָאֵפוֹד	pref. id.)(noun masc. sing.	אפד

a Ex. 29. 22. b Zec. 11. 17, etc. c Is. 2. 18, & 19. 3. d Le. 19. 4. e Eze. 40. 49. f 1 Ki. 10. 12.

1 Ki. 17. 20. — 1 Sa. 17. 18. — Is. 30. 24. — Je. 52. 15. — Je. 7. 28. — Is. 11. 5. — De. 23. 6, 7. — De. 22. 2. — Ez. 26. 12.

2 Sa. 6. 22. — Ge. 31. 33. — Is. 17. 9. — De. 26. 18. — Ne. 3. 34. — Nu. 11. 12. — Ps. 117. 1. — Ge. 15. 6.

2 Ch. 20. 20, 20. — Ex. 4. 8. — La. 4. 5. — 2 Ki. 10. 1. — 2 Ki. 10. 5. — Ps. 119. 66. — Zec. 6. 7. — Job 34. 18.

2 Ki. 18. 16. — Job 34. 31. — Eze. 28. 9. — Am. 4. 1. — Le. 11. 19. — De. 14. 18. — Eze. 24. 17. — Lev. 11. 30. — Eze. 21. 11.

Is. 66. 9. — Jon. 1. 4. — De. 14. 18. — Ge. 42. 16. — Job 4. 17. — Ge. 39. 22.

Ex. 24. 23. — Ju. 16. 21, 25. — Ex. 23. 16. — Nu. 19. 10. — De. 22. 50. — 2 Sa. 17. 11. — Je. 37. 15.

Je. 47. 6. — 1 Ch. 26. 15. — Nu. 11. 4. — Ge. 42. 16. — Is. 3. 22.

Hebrew	Description	Root
הָאֹפִים	pref. id.)(Kal part. act. m., pl. of אֹפֶה d. 9a.	אפה
הַאֶפֶס	pref. הַ interr. for הֲ)(prop. subst. used adverbially	אפס
הָאֶפֶס	pref. הָ id. for הַ, הֲ)(Kal pret. 3 pers. s. m.	אפס
הָאֵפֶר	pref. הָ for ·הַ)(noun masc. sing.	אפר
הָאֵפֶר	pref. id.)(noun masc. sing.	אפר
הָאֶפְרֹחִים	pref. id.)(noun m., pl. of [אֶפְרֹחַ] d. 1b.	פרח
הָאֶפְרָתִי	pref. id. (interr.))(gent. noun masc.	אפר
הָאָצֵל	pref. id.)(pr. name, see בֵּית הָאָצֵל .	בית
הָאֲצֵרוֹת	pref. id.)(noun masc. with pl. fem. term., abs. from אוֹצָר dec. 2b.	אצר
הָאֹצְרִים	pref. id.)(Kal part. act. m., pl. of [אֹצֵר] d. 7b.	אצר
הַאֲקַדְּמֶנּוּ	pref. הַ interr. for הֲ)(Piel fut. 1 pers. sing., suff. 3 pers. sing. masc.	קדם
הָאֵר	)(Hiph. imp. sing. masc.	אור
הָאֲרִאֵל	ן pref. הָ for ·הַ)(K. אֲרִיאֵל noun m. sing.	ארה
הָאֲרִאֵלִי	)(pref. id.)(pr. name	ארה
הָאֹרֵב	)(prf. id.)(Kal part. act. sing. masc. dec. 7b.	ארב
הָאַרְבֶּה	pref. id.)(noun masc. sing.	רבה
הָאַרְבִּי	pref. id.)(gent. noun from אֲרָב	ארב
הָאֹרְבִים	pref. id.)(Kal part. act. m., pl. of אֹרֵב d. 7b.	ארב
הָאַרְבַּע	pref. id.)(pr. name, see קִרְיַת הָ under .	קרה
הָאַרְבָּעִים	pref. id.)(num. card. masc., pl. of אַרְבַּע (§ 31. rem. 5) .	רבע
הָאַרְגָּ	pref. id.)(noun masc. sing.	ארג
הָאַרְגֹּב	pref. id.)(pr. name of a region	רגב
הָאַרְגָּז	pref. id.)(noun masc. sing.	רגז
וְהָאַרְגָּמָן	pref. id.)(noun masc. sing. see אַרְגָּמָן.	
הָאֹרִד	pref. הָ interr. for הֲ)(Kal fut. 1 pers. sing.	ירד
הָאַרְדִּי	pref. הָ for ·הַ)(gent. noun from אַרְדְּ	ארד
הָאֲרוֹדִי	pref. id.)(gent. noun from אֲרוֹד	רוד
הָאֲרוֹדִי	pref. id.)(gent. noun from אֲרוֹד	ארד
הָאֲרוּרָה	pref. הָ for ·הַ)(Kal part. pass., f. of אָרוּר m.	ארר
הָאֶרֶז / הָאֶרֶז	pref. id.)(noun masc. sing., dec. 6a.} (§ 35. rem. 2)	ארז
הָאֲרָזִים	pref. id.)(id. pl., absolute state	ארז
הָאֹרֵחַ	pref. id.)(Kal part. act. sing. masc.	ארח
הָאֹרֵחַ	pref. הָ interr. for הֲ)(noun com. sing. d. 6. (§ 35. rem. 5 & 9)	ארח
הָאֲרִי	pref. הָ for ·הַ)(noun masc. sing. dec. 6i.	ארה
הָאַרְיֵה	ן pref. id.)(id. with parag. ה; also pr. n. m.	ארה
הָאֲרָיוֹת	pref. id.)(id. pl., absolute state	ארה
הָאֱרִיךְ	Hiph. pret. 3 pers. sing. masc.	ארך
הָאֱרִיכוּ	id. pret. 3 pers. pl.	ארך
הָאֲרִיכִי	id. imp. sing. fem.	ארך
הָאָרֹךְ	pref. הָ for ·הַ)(noun masc. sing. dec. 6c.	ארך
הָאַרְכִּי	pref. id.)(gent. noun from אֶרֶךְ	ארד
הָאֲרַמִּי	pref. id.)(gent. noun from אֲרָם . .	ארם
הָאֲרַמִּיָּה	pref. id.)(id. fem.	ארם
הָאָרוֹן	pref. id.)(noun com. sing. dec. 3a.	ארה
הַאֲרִכֵךְ	ן Hiph. fut. 2 pers. sing. masc.; acc. shifted by conv. (§ 8. rem. 7, & § 13. rem. 10)	ארך
הַאֲרַכְתִּי	ן id. pret. 1 pers. sing.; acc. id.	ארך
הַאֲרַכְתֶּם	ן id. pret. 2 pers. pl. masc.	ארך
הָאָרֹן	defect. for הָאָרוֹן (q. v.)	ארה
הָאַרְנֶבֶת	pref. הָ for הַ)(noun fem. sing.	רנב
הָאָרֶץ	וְ pref. id.)(noun fem. sing. with the art. for אֶרֶץ (§ 35. rem. 2) dec. 6a.	ארץ
הַאַרְצֶה	pref. הַ interr. for הֲ)(Kal fut. 1 pers. sing.	רצה
הָאֲרָצוֹת / הָאַרְצֹת	pref. הָ for ·הַ)(noun fem., pl. of אֶרֶץ (with suff. אַרְצִי) dec. 6a.	ארץ
הָאֲרָרִי	pref. id.)(gent. noun for (הָ)הֲרָרִי	הרר
הָאֵשׁ	ן pref. id.)(noun com. sing. dec. 8b.	אש
הָאֵשׁ	pref. הַ interr. for הֲ)(adv. used for the subst. verb	אש
הָאֶשְׁבְּלִי	pref. הָ for ·הַ)(patronym. from אַשְׁבֵּל q. v.	
הָאַשְׁדּוֹדִי	ן pref. id.)(gent. noun from אַשְׁדּוֹד .	שדד
הָאַשְׁדּוֹדִים	ן pref. id.)(id. pl.	שדד
הָאֲשֵׁרוֹת	ן pref. הָ for ·הַ)(noun masc. pl. abs. from [אֲשֵׁרָה] dec. 11c. (§ 42. rem. 4)	אשר
הָאִשָּׁה	ן pref. id.)(noun fem. sing. [for אֶנְשָׁה], dec. 10. (comp. § 45)	אנש
הָאִישׁה	pref. id.)(noun masc. sing. dec. 9a.	איש
הָאַשּׁוּרִי	pref. id.)(gent. noun, see אַשּׁוּרִי .	אשר
הַאֲשִׂיגֶנּוּ	pref. הַ interr. for הֲ)(Hiph. fut. 1 pers. sing., suff. 3 pers. sing. masc.	נשג
הָאֲשִׁימֵם	Hiph. imp. sing. masc., suff. 3 pers. pl. m.	אשם
הָאֶשְׁכֹּלוֹת	pref. הָ for ·הַ)(noun masc. s., pl. (§ 36. rem. 6)	שבל
הָאֵשֶׁל	pref. id.)(noun masc. sing.	אשל
הָאָשָׁם	ן pref. id.)(noun masc. sing. dec. 4c.	אשם
הָאַשְׁמֻרָת	pref. id.)(noun fem. sing.	שמר
הָאַשְׁנָב	pref. id.)(noun masc. sing. dec. 8a.	שנב
הָאֶשְׁפֹּות	pref. id.)(written fully for הָאַשְׁפֹּת (q. v.)	שפת
הָאַשְׁפִּים	pref. id.)(noun masc., pl. of אַשָׁף dec. 1b.	אשף
הָאַשְׁפֹּת	pref. id.)(noun m. s. fr. שְׁפֹת with prosth. א	שפת
הָאֶשְׁקְלוֹנִי	pref. id.)(gent. noun from אֶשְׁקְלוֹן .	שקל
הַאֲשֶׁר	pref. הַ interr. for הֲ)(pron. relat. com. .	אשר
הָאֲשֵׁרָה	וְ prefa הָ for ·הַ)(noun fem. sing. dec. 10.	אשר
הָאֲשֵׁרוֹת	ן pref. id.)(id. pl.	אשר
הָאֲשֵׁרִי	pref. id.)(gent. noun from אָשֵׁר	אשר
הָאֲשֵׁרִים	ן pref. id.)(id. with pl. fem. term.	אשר
הָאֶשְׁתָּאֻלִי	ן pref. id.)(gent. noun from אֶשְׁתָּאֹל	שאל
הָאָת	pref. id.)(defect. for הָאוֹת (q. v.)	אוה

---

a 2 Sa. 9. 3.   f Am. 3. 10.   k Ju. 16. 14.   p Ju. 19. 17.   u Pr. 19. 11.   z 1 Ki. 3. 14.   b Jos. 10. 40.   f Nu. 13. 24.   + Ne. 3. 14.
b Ps. 77. 9.   g Mi. 6. 6.   l 1 Sa. 6. 11, 15.   q Job 22. 15.   v Is. 54. 2.   a De. 5. 33.   c Nu. 28. 3.   g Ju. 7. 19.   + Da. 1. 14.
c 1 Ki. 20. 41.   h Eze. 43. 16.   m 1 Sa. 14. 37.   r 1 Ki. 13. 24, 28.   w 2 Ch. 3. 3, 4.   b Mal. 1. 13.   d 1 Sa. 30. 8.   h Ju. 5. 28.   2 Ki. 6. 13.
d De. 22. 6.   i Je. 51. 12.   n 2 Ki. 9. 34.   t 2 Ki. 17. 25, 26.   x De. 22. 7.   y Mi. 6. 10.   e Ps. 5. 11.   4 Ex. 39. 1.   n Ju. 6. 28.

Hebrew	Description	Root
הָאַתָּה	pref. הַ interr. for הָ)(pron. pers. 2 p. s. m.	אנת
הָאֵתוֹן	pref. הָ for הַ)(noun fem. sing. dec. 3 a.	אתן
הָאֵתֹות	pref. id.)(noun com., pl. of אֹות d. 1.	אוה
הַאֹתִי	pref. הַ interr. for הָ)(as if [אֹות] with suff. 1 pers. sing. (§ 5) see sign of the acc.	את
הָאֹתִיֹות	pref. הָ for הַ)(Kal part. act. fem. pl. [as if from אֹתִי masc. § 24. rem. 4]	אתה
הָאַתִּיקִי	)(pref. id.)(noun masc., pl. of אַתִּיק d. 1 b.	אתק
הָאַתֶּם	pref. הָ interr. for הַ)(pers. pron. 2 m. pl., from אַתֶּה sing.	אנת
הָאֶתֵּן	pref. הָ id.)(Kal fut. 1 pers. sing.	נתן
הָאֲתֹנֹות	)'(pref. הָ for הַ)(n. f., pl. of אָתֹון d. 3 a.	אתן
הָאֵתָנִים	)'(pref. id.)((prim. adj.) n. m., pl. of אֵיתָן d. 1	יתן
הָאֲתֹנֹת	defect. for הָאֲתֹנֹות (q. v.).	אתן
הָאֲתָרִים	pref. הָ for הַ)(pr. name of a place	אתר
הָאֹתֹת	)'(defect. for הָאֹתֹות (q. v.).	אוה
הַב	Kal, or (Da. 5. 17) Peal, imp. sing. masc.	יהב
הַב	)(see וָהַב under lett. ו	
הַבָּא	pref. הַ)(Kal pret. 3 pers. sing. masc.	בוא
הַבָּא	)'(pref. הַ)(id. part. sing. masc. dec. 1 a.	בוא
הָבֵא	)"(Hiph. imp. sing. masc.	בוא
הַבָּאָה	)'(pref. הַ)(Kal part. sing. fem. dec. 10.	בוא
הַבָּאֹות	pref. id.)(id. id. pl.	בוא
וַהֲבֵאֹותִי	)'(Hiph. pret. 1 pers. s. Kh. וַהֲבֵאֹותִי (comp. parad. קוּם), K. וְהֵבֵאתִי (§ 21. rem. 13)	בוא
וַהֲבֵאֹותִיךָ	)'(id. id., suff. 2 pers. sing. masc. ו bef. (ָ) for ו, conv.	בוא
וַהֲבֵאֹותָם	)'(id. pret. 2 pers. sing. masc., suff. 3 pers. pl. masc.; ו id.	בוא
הַבָּאִים	)'(pref. הַ)(Kal part. pl. m. fr. בָּא d. 1 a.	בוא
הַבְאִישׁ	Hiph. pret. 3 pers. sing. masc.	באש
הֹבְאִישׁ	Kh. הִבְאִישׁ q. v., K. הֹבִישׁ (q. v.)	יבש
הַבְאִישׁוּ	Hiph. pret. 3 pers. pl.	באש
הַבְּאֵר	pref. הַ)(noun fem. s. d. 1, but pl. בְּאֵרֹות (§ 35. rem. 10)	באר
הַבְּאֵרָה	pref. id.)(noun masc. s. d. 1 a. [for בְּאֵר]	באר
הַבְּאֵרֹת	pref. id.)(noun fem., pl. of בְּאֵר dec. 1 a, (pl. c. בְּאֵרֹות § 35. rem. 10)	באר
הַבְּאֵרֹתִי	pref. id.)(gent. noun from בְּאֵרֹות	באר
הַבְּאֵרֹתִי	pref. id.)(id. pl.	באר
הַבְאֵשׁ	Hiph. inf. absolute	באש
הִבְאַשְׁתֶּם	id. pret. 2 pers. pl. masc.	באש
הֵבֵאתָ	pref. הַ)(Kal pret. 2 p. s. m. (§ 25. No. 2 f)	בוא
הֵבֵאת	defect. for הֲבֵאֹות (q. v.).	בוא
הֵבֵאתָ	Hiph. pret. 2 pers. sing. masc. (§ 21. r. 13)	בוא
הֵבֵאתְ	)(id. id. acc. shifted by conv. ו (§ 8. r. 7)	בוא

Hebrew	Description	Root
הֻבָאת	Hoph. pret. 3 pers. fem. sing. (§ 25. No. 2 f)	בוא
הֲבֵאֹתָה	id. pret. 2 pers. s. m. (comp. id. & § 8. r. 5)	בוא
וַהֲבֵאֹתָה	)'(Hiph. pret. 2 pers. sing. masc. with suff. 3 p. s. fem. (§ 25. No. 2 f) ; ו for ו conv.	בוא
הֲבֵאֹתִיו	)'(id., suff. 3 pers. sing. masc.; ו id.	בוא
הֲבֵאֹתִי	id. pret. 1 pers. sing.	בוא
הֲבֵאֹתִי	)'(id. id.; acc. shifted by conv. ו (§ 8. r. 7)	בוא
הֲבֵאֹתִיהָ	id. id., suff. 3 pers. sing. fem.	בוא
הֲבֵאֹתִיו	id., suff. 3 pers. sing. masc. (see parad. קוּם)	בוא
הֲבֵאֹתִים	)'(id., suff. 3 pers. pl. masc.; ו for ו conv.	בוא
וַהֲבֵאֹתִים	)'((§ 25. No. 2 f)	בוא
הֲבֵאֹתָם	)'(id. pret. 2 pers. pl. m.; ו for ו conv.	בוא
הֲבֵאֹתָנוּ	id. pret. 2 pers. sing. masc., suff. 1 pers. pl.	בוא
הַבֶּגֶד	)'(pref. הַ)(noun m. s., (suff. בִּגְדִי) d. 6 a.	בגד
הַבְּגָדִים	pref. id.)(id. pl., absolute state	בגד
הַבַּד	pref. id.)(for בַּד noun masc. sing. dec. 8 d.	בדד
הַבְדִּיל	pref. id.)(noun masc. sing.	בדל
הִבְדִּיל	Hiph. pret. 3 pers. sing. masc.	בדל
הִבְדִּילָה	)'(id. 3 p.s.f.; acc. shifted by conv. ו (§ 8.r.7)	בדל
הִבְדִּילֹו	)'(id. 3 pers. sing. masc., suff. 3 pers. s. m.	בדל
הִבְדִּילוּ	id. pret. 3 pers. pl.	בדל
הַבַּדִּים	pref. הַ)(noun masc., pl. of בַּד dec. 8 d.	בדד
הַבְדֵּל	Hiph. inf. absolute	בדל
הִבָּדְלוּ	)'(Niph. imp. pl. masc.	בדל
הַבְדָּלָה	pref. הַ)(noun masc. sing.	בדל
הִבְדַּלְתָּ	)(Hiph. pret. 2 pers. s. m.; acc. shifted by conv. ו (§ 8. rem. 7)	בדל
הִבְדַּלְתִּי	id. pret. 1 pers. sing.	בדל
הִבְדַּלְתָּם	id. pret. 2 p. sing. masc., suff. 3 pers. pl. masc.	בדל
הִבְדַּלְתֶּם	)'(id. pret. 3 pers. pl. masc.	בדל
הַבְּדֶרֶךְ	preff. בְּ, and הַ interr. f. הֲ)(noun com. sing. (suff. דַּרְכִּי) dec. 6 a.	דרך
הָבָה	Kal. imp. sing. masc. with parag. ה.	יהב
הַבְהָבַי	n. m. pl., suff. 1 p. s. fr. [הַבְהָב] (§ 31. r. 5)	יהב
הִבְהִילַנִי	Hiph. pret. 3 pers. sing. m., suff 1 pers. s.	בהל
הַבֶּהֱמָה	)'(pref. הַ)(noun fem. s. d. 12, constr. בֶּהֱמַת (§ 42. rem. 4 & 5, & § 44. rem. 3)	בהם
הַבֶּהָרֹת	pref. id.)(noun f. s. pl. בֶּהָרֹות (§ 44. r. 5)	בהר
הָבוּ / הָבֻוּ	} Kal. imp. pl. masc. (§ 20. rem. 1).	יהב
הָבוֹא	pref. הַ)(Kal inf. absolute	בוא
הֲבוֹאתִים	)'(Kh., transpos. for הֲבֵאֹותִים, Hiph. pret. 1 p. sing., suff. 3 pers. pl. masc.; ו for ו conv.	בוא
הַבּוֹגֵד	pref. הַ)(Kal part. act. sing. masc. dec. 7 b.	בגד
הַבּוֹגְדִים	pref. id.)(id. pl., absolute state	בגד

a Je. 7. 19.	g Mi. 6. 2.	n Is. 41. 22.	t 2 Sa. 23. 20.	z Ge. 33. 11.	f Je. 25. 9.	m Eze. 22. 26.	s 1 Ki. 8. 53.	y Ho. 4. 18.
b Eze. 41. 16.	h 1 Sa. 9. 3.	o Je. 25. 13.	u Ge. 26. 15.	a Eze. 40. 4.	g Eze. 23. 22.	n Is. 56. 3.	t Le. 20. 25.	z Ge. 37. 10.
c Ju. 6. 31.	i De. 7. 19.	p Eze. 39. 2.	v 1 Sa. 27. 12.	b De. 21. 12.	h Ps. 66. 11.	o Nu. 16. 21.	u Eze. 20. 30.	a Ne. 1. 9.
d Mi. 6. 7.	k Pr. 30. 15.	q Je. 35. 2.	w Ex. 5. 21.	c 2 Sa. 14. 10.	i Le. 13. 47, 58.	p Err. 11. 11.	v Ho. 8. 13.	b Is. 21. 2.
e Job 1. 14.	l 1 Sa. 10. 22.	r Is. 30. 5.	x Job 33. 16, 22.	d Is. 37. 26.	k Ex. 26. 33.	q Nu. 8. 14.	w Le. 13. 22, 28.	c Ps. 25. 3.
f Ki. 8. 2.	m Hag. 1. 6.	s Ps. 38. 6.	y Ge. 41. 35.	e Is. 48. 15.	l De. 29. 20.	r Le. 20. 24, 25.	x Job 23. 16.	

Hebrew	Description	Root
הַבּוּז	pref. ה)(noun masc. sing.	בוז
הַבּוּזִי	pref. id.)(gent. noun, from בּוּז	בוז
הִבָּזוֹ	Niph. inf. absolute.	בזז
הַבּוֹטֵחַ	pref. ה)(Kal part. act. sing. m. dec. 7b.	בטח
הַבּוֹנֶה	pref. id.)(Kal part. act. sing. masc. dec. 7b.	בנה
הַבּוֹנִים	pref. id.)(id. pl., absolute state	בנה
הִבָּקַע	Niph. inf. absolute, for הַבָּקַע	בקע
הַבְּאֵר	pref. ה)(noun masc. sing. dec. 1a.	באר
הַבַּז	pref. id.)(with dist. acc. for בַּז n. m. s. d. 6e.	בזז
הַבִּזָּה	pref. id.)(noun fem. sing.	בזז
הַבְּזָק	pref. id.)(noun masc. sing.	בזק
הַבַּחוּרִים	pref. id.)(n. m., pl. of בָּחוּר [for בָּחֻר]	בחר
הַבֹּחֵר	pref. id.)(Kal part. act. masc. sing.	בחר
הַבַּחֲרוּמִי	pref. id.)(gent. noun, from בַּחֻרִים	בחר
הַבֵּט / הַבֶּט-	} Hiph. imp. sing. masc. (§ 11. rem. 5)	נבט
הַבֹּטְחָה	pref. ה)(Kal part. fem. sing. dec.10.	בטח
הַבִּטָּחוֹן	pref. id.)(noun masc. sing.	בטח
הַבְּטֻחִים	pref. id.)(Kal part. act. m., pl. of בָּטֻחַ d. 7b.	בטח
הִבְטַחְתָּ	Hiph. pret. 2 pers. sing. masc.	בטח
הִבְטַחְתָּ	Hiph. pret. 2 pers. sing. m.; acc. shifted by conv. ו (§ 8. rem. 7)	נבט
הִבְטַחְתֶּם	id. pret. 2 pers. pl. masc.	נבט
הַבֶּטֶן / הַבָּטֶן	} pref. ה)(noun fem. s. d. 6a. (suff. בְּטֻנִי, but comp. § 35. rem. 2)	בטן
הָבִי	Kal imp. fem. sing.	יהב
הָבִיא	Hiph. imp. sing. masc. for הָבֵא	בוא
הָבִיא	id. inf. constr.	בוא
הֵבִיא	id. pret. 3 pers. sing. masc.	בוא
הָבִיאָה	id. imp. sing. masc. with parag. ה	בוא
הֵבִיאָה	id. pret. 3 pers. sing. fem.	בוא
הֵבִיאָה	id.id.; acc. shifted by conv. ו (comp. §8.r.7)	בוא
הֱבִיאָהּ	id. pret. 3 pers. sing.masc., suff. 3 pers. sing. fem.; ו bef. conv.	בוא
הָבִיאוּ	id. imp. 2 pers. pl. masc.	בוא
הָבִיאוּ	Kh. הָבִיאוּ (q. v.), K. הָבִיאוּ (q. v.).	בוא
הֵבִיאוּ	Hiph. pret. 3 pers. s. m., suff. 3 pers. s. m.	בוא
הֵבִיאוּ	id. pret. 3 pers. pl.	בוא
הֱבִיאוּהוּ	id. id., suff. 3 pers. sing. masc.	בוא
הֱבִיאוּךְ	id. id., suff. 2 pers. sing. fem.	בוא
הֱבִיאוּם	id. id., suff. 3 pers. pl. m.; ו bef. conv.	בוא
הֲבִיאוֹתִיהוּ	id. pret. 1 pers. sing., suff. 3 pers. sing. masc.; ו bef. conv.	בוא
הֲבִיאוֹתִיךָ	id. id., suff. 2 pers. sing. masc.; ו id.	בוא
הֲבִיאוֹתִים	id. id., suff. 3 pers. pl. masc.; ו id.	בוא
הָבִיאִי	id. imp. sing. fem.	בוא
הֲבִיאֲךָ	id. inf. (הָבִיא), suff. 2 pers. sing. masc. d.3a.	בוא
הֱבִיאֲךָ	id. pret. 3 pers. sing. masc., suff. 2 pers. sing. masc.; ו bef. conv.	בוא
הֲבִיאֲכֶם	id. inf. (הָבִיא) with suff. 2 p. pl. m. d.3a.	בוא
הֱבִיאָם	id. pret. 3 pers. pl., suff. 3 pers. pl. masc.; ו before conv.	בוא
הֱבִיאַנִי	id. pret. 3 pers. sing. masc., suff. 1 pers. sing.	בוא
הֲבִיאֹנוּם	id. pret. 1 pers. pl., suff. 3 pers. pl. masc.	בוא
הֲבֵיאתָ	id. pret. 2 pers. sing. masc. (§ 21. rem. 13)	בוא
הֲבֵאתָ	ו id. id.; acc. shifted by ו conv.	בוא
הֲבֵאתִי	ו id. pret. 1 pers. sing.; acc. id.	בוא
הֲבִיאֹתִיהָ	id. id., suff. 3 p. sing. fem. (comp. parad. קום)	בוא
הֲבִיאֹתִיו	id. id., suff. 3 p. sing. masc.; ו bef. conv.	בוא
הֲבֵאֹתֶם	id. pret. 2 pers. pl. masc.; ו id.	בוא
הֲבֵאֹתֻנוּ	id. pret. 2 pers. sing. masc., suff. 1 pers. pl.	בוא
הֲבֵאֹתַנִי	id. id., suff. 1 pers. sing.	בוא
הַבֵּט	Hiph. imp. sing. masc. for הַבֵּט	נבט
הַבֵּט	ו id. inf. construct	נבט
הַבִּיטָ	Kh. הַבֵּיט q. v., K. הַבִּיטָה (q. v.).	נבט
הִבִּיט	ו Hiph. pret. 3 pers. sing. masc.	נבט
הַבִּיטָה	ו id. imp. sing. masc. with ה paragogic	נבט
הַבִּיטוּ	ו id. imp. pl. masc.	נבט
הִבִּיטוּ	ו id. pret. 3 pers. pl.	נבט
הָבֵן	Hiph. inf. construct.	בין
הֵבִין	id. pret. 3 pers. sing. masc.	בין
הָבִינוּ	id. imp. pl. masc.	בין
הֵבִינוּ	id. pret. 3 pers. pl.	בין
הֲבִינֹתֶם	id. pret. 2 pers. pl. masc.	בין
הֲבִינֵנִי	id. imp. sing. masc., suff. 1 pers. sing.	בין
הַבִּצִּים	pref. ה)(n. fem. with pl. m. term. [fr. בֵּיצָה]	בוץ
הַבִּירָה	pref. id.)(noun fem. sing.	ביר
הֹבִישׁ	Hiph. pret. 3 pers. sing. masc.	יבש
הֹבִישָׁה	id. pret. 3 pers. sing. fem.	יבש
הֹבִישׁוּ	ו id. pret. 3 pers. pl., or imp. pl. masc.	יבש
הֲבִישׁוֹתָ	Hiph. pret. 2 pers. sing. masc. (§ 21. rem. 14)	בוש
הֲבִישֹׁתָה	id. (§ 8. rem. 5)	בוש
הַבַּיִת / הַבָּיְת	} pref. ה)(noun masc. sing. irr. (§ 45)	בית
הַבַּיְתָה / הַבָּיְתָה	} pref. id.)(id. with paragogic ה	בית
הַבַּיִת	pref. id.)(noun masc. sing. dec. 2b.	בית
הַבְּכָא	pref. id.)(noun masc. sing. dec. 4a.	בכא
הַבְּכָאִים	pref. id.)(id. pl., absolute state.	בכא
הַבְּכוֹר	pref. id.)(noun masc. sing. dec. 1a.	בכר
הַבְּכֹרִים	pref. id.)(noun masc., pl. of בְּכוֹר dec. 1b.	בכר
הַבֹּכִים	pref. id.)(pr. name of a place.	בכה

a Is. 24. 3.   g Nu. 31. 32.   o Je. 49. 4.   t 1 Sa. 20. 40.   x Eze. 17. 20.   h Nu. 32. 17.   k 1 Sa. 16. 17.   r Nu. 21. 9.   x Ps. 53. 6.
b Ps. 86. 2.   h 2 Ch. 28. 14.   n Am. 6. 1.   u Ge. 27. 4.   y Eze. 38. 16.   i Is. 43. 23.   l Is. 45. 23.   s La. 1. 11.   y 2 Ch. 34. 8.
c Ps. 32. 10.   i Eze. 1. 14.   o Le. 15. 29.   v 2 Sa. 3. 13.   z Le. 23. 14, 15.   k 2 Ki. 9. 2.   m Nu. 16. 14.   t Is. 40. 21.   z Est. 7. 7, 8.
d Am. 9. 6.   k Am. 8. 13.   p 1 Sa. 2. 32.   w Is. 16. 3.   a Le. 17. 5.   l Nu. 14. 31.   n Ps. 142. 5.   u De. 22. 6.   a Ps. 84. 7.
e Ne. 4. 12.   l Zec. 3. 2.   q Is. 22. 11.   x 2 Ch. 28. 27.   b Eze. 27. 26.   m 2 Ki. 19. 25.   o Hab. 2. 15.   v Zec. 10. 5, 11.   b Nu. 28. 26
f Is. 24. 3.   r Ruth 3. 15.   n Ge. 43. 9.   p Hab. 1. 13.   c Ps. 123. 4.
                          o La. 5. 1.   q La. 1. 11.

הַבְּכִירָה	pref. id. ✗ adj. fem. sing. from [בָּכִיר] m. בכר
הַבְּכֹר	pref. id. ✗ noun masc. sing. dec. 1 a. בכר
וְהַבְּכֹרָה	pref. id. ✗ noun fem. sing. dec. 10. בכר
הַבְּכֹרוֹת	pref. id. ✗ noun fem., pl. of [בַּכֹּרָה] dec. 10. בכר
הַבְּכֹרִי	pref. id. ✗ gent. noun from בָּכָר . בכר
הַבִּכֻּרִים	defect. for הַבִּכּוּרִים (q. v.) . בכר

§ 35. וְ] הֶבֶל masc. dec. 6. (with suff. הַבְלִי, pl. c. הַבְלֵי rem. 4)—I. *breath, vapour, mist*, comp. Ps. 62. 10; Is. 57. 13, הבלא Syr. and Chald. *breath, vapour.* —II. *vanity, something vain, foolish.*—III. *idols.*— IV. adv. *in vain, vainly.*—V. pr. name of the second son of Adam.

הֲבֵל masc. *vanity,* Ec. 1. 2; 12. 8.

הָבַל, fut. יֶהְבַּל, prop. *to become a vapour* (so Sym. on Ps. 62. 11, Μὴ γίνεσθε Ατμἰς) hence *to be* or *become vain, to act vainly, foolishly, sinfully.* Hiph. *to cause to act vainly,* Je. 23. 16.

הָבֶל	id. in pause (§ 35. rem. 2) . הבל
הֶבֶל	noun masc. sing. . . הבל
הֶבְלוֹ	noun masc. sing., suff. 3 pers. sing. masc. from הֶבֶל d. 6. (§ 35. rem. 4) הבל
הַבְלֵי	id. pl., construct state . הבל
הַבְלִי	id. *s*ing. suff. 1 pers. sing. . הבל
הֲבָלִים	וְ] id. pl. absolute state; וַ before (ָ) הבל
הַבְּלִיַּעַל הַבְּלִיָּעַל	pref. הַ ✗ noun masc. sing. compd. of יַעַל & בְּלִי see . . } בלה
הֶבְלְךָ	noun masc. sing., suff. 2 pers. sing. masc. [for הֶבְלְךָ] from הֶבֶל (q. v.) . הבל
הַבַּלְעִי	pref. הַ ✗ gent. noun from בֶּלַע . בלע
הַבָּמָה	pref. id. ✗ noun fem. sing. dec. 10 (pl. c. בָּמֹתֵי); also pr. name . בום
הַבָּמוֹת	וְ] pref. id. ✗ id. pl., absolute state בום
הַבְּמַחֲנִים	preff. בְּ, and הַ interr. for הֲ ✗ noun masc., pl. of מַחֲנֶה dec. 9 a. חנה
הַבָּמָתָה	pref. הַ ✗ noun fem. sing. with paragogic ה from בָּמָה (q. v.) . בום
הָבֵן	וְ] Hiph. imp. sing. masc. R. בון, see בין
הַבֵּן הַבֵּן	וְ] pref. הַ } noun masc. sing. irr. (§ 45) pref. הַ } בנה
הַבַּנְהָרִים	preff. בְּ bef. (ַ), and הַ ✗ noun masc., pl. of נָהָר dec. 4. נהר
הַבָּנוּי	pref. הַ ✗ Kal part. p. sing. masc. dec. 3 a. בנה
הַבְּנוּיָה	pref. id. ✗ fem. of the prec. . בנה
הַבָּנוֹת	pref. id. ✗ noun fem., pl. of בַּת irr. (§ 45) בנה

[הָבְנִי]	masc. pl. הָבְנִים, (Kh. הוֹבְנִים) (ebony, Eze. 27. 15, from הבן perhaps i. q. אבן *to be hard.*
הַבִּנְיָה	וְ] pref. הַ ✗ noun fem. sing. בנה
הַבָּנִים	וְ] pref. id. ✗ noun masc. pl. [as if from בֵּן dec. 2] see [בֵּן] (§ 45) } בנה
הַבָּנֵים	pref. הֲ ✗ noun masc., du. of [בֵּיָן] dec. 6 h. בין
הַבֹּנִים	pref. id. ✗ Kal part. act. masc., pl. of בֹּנֶה dec. 9 a. . בנה
הַבֶּנֶן	וְ] pref. id. ✗ noun masc. sing. גנה
הַבְּסוֹד	preff. בְּ, and הַ interr. for הֲ ✗ n. m. s. dec. 1. סד
הַבֹּסֶר	pref. הַ art. ✗ noun masc. sing. בסר
בַּעֲדִי	pref. הַ interr. for הֲ ✗ prep., with suff. (§ 35. rem. 10) . בעד
הַבַּעַל הַבַּעַל	pref. הַ art. ✗ noun masc. sing. dec. 6 d, also pr. name . } בעל
הַבְּעָלִים	pref. id. ✗ id. pl., absolute state, pr. name . בעל
הִבְעַרְתִּי	וְ] Hiph. pret. 1 pers. sing.; acc. shifted by conv. וְ (§ 8. rem. 7) בער
הַבְּעֵרָה	pref. הַ ✗ noun fem. sing. בער
הַבֵּץ	pref. id. ✗ noun masc. sing. בוץ
הַבָּצוּר	pref. id. ✗ Kh. בָּצוּר part. pass., K. בָּצִיר adj. masc. dec. 3 a. . בצר
הַבְּצָלִים	pref. id. ✗ noun masc., pl. of [בָּצֶל] dec. 6. בצל
הַבָּצַע	pref. id. ✗ noun masc. sing. for בֶּצַע (q. v.) בצע
הַבָּצֵק	pref. id. ✗ noun masc. sing. dec. 5 a. בצק
הַבְּצָרוֹת	pref. id. ✗ noun fem., pl. of בַּצָּרָה dec. 10. בצר
הַבְּצוּרוֹת	וְ] pref. id. ✗ Kal part. p. fem., pl. of בְּצוּרָה d. 10. בצר
הַבַּקְבֻּק	pref. id. ✗ noun masc. sing. בקק
הַבָּקְעָה	Hoph. pret. 3 pers. sing. fem. בקע
הַבִּקְעָה	pref. הַ ✗ noun fem. sing. dec. 12 b. בקע
הַבָּקָר	וְ] pref. id. ✗ noun com. sing. dec. 4 a. בקר
הַבֹּקֶר	וְ] pref. id. ✗ noun masc. sing., d. 6 c. (§ 35. r. 9) בקר

[הָבַר] prop. *to cut, divide,* so in the Arab., whence הֹבְרֵי שָׁמַיִם *they who divide the heavens, astrologers,* Is. 47. 13.

הַבָּר	pref. הַ ✗ noun masc. sing. ברר
הִבָּרַאֲךָ	Niph. inf. [הִבָּרֵא] suff. 2 pers. sing. m. d. 7 b. ברא
הִבָּרַאֲךָ	id. id. & verbal suff. (§ 3. r. 2) 2 p. s. m. pause ברא
הִבָּרְאָם	id. with suff. 3 pers. pl. masc. ברא
הַבְּרָב	preff. בְּ, & הַ interr. ✗ for לְרָב n. m. s. d. 8 c. רבב
הַבָּרָד	וְ] pref. id. ✗ noun masc. sing. ברד
הַבְּרֻדִּים	וְ] pref. id. ✗ adj. masc., pl. of [בָּרֹד] dec. 8 c. (§ 37. Nos. 2 & 3) ברד
הַבֵּרָה	pref. id. ✗ noun masc. sing. with parag. ה from בּוֹר dec. 1 a. באר
[הָבֵרוּ]	Hiph. imp. masc. pl. [for הָבֵרוּ] ברר

a 1 Ch. 5. 2.	f Ec. 5. 6.	l Da. 9. 23.	q Ps. 123. 3.	u Job 15. 3.	c 1 Ch. 4. 21.	r Je. 14. 1.
b Je. 24. 2.	g 2 Sa. 16. 7.	m Eze. 18. 19.	r Isa. 41. 13.	v Je. 31. 39.	d Zec. 11. 2.	s De. 28. 52.
c Le. 23. 26.	h Nu. 13. 19.	n Je. 31. 39.	s Job 22. 12.	w Nu. 11. 5.	e Je. 19. 10.	t Ge. 5. 2.
d Ec. 6. 12.	i Nu. 13. 19.	o Hab. 3. 3.	t 1 Sa. 17. 4, 23.	x Na. 2. 14.	f 1 Sa. 3. 3.	u Je. 39. 2.
e Eze. 7. 15.	k 1 Sa. 9. 12.	p Ju. 6. 25.	Eze. 41. 12.	y Ex. 26. 5.	g Ex. 12. 39,etc.	v Je. 23. 23.

Eze. 28. 15.   r Ex.9.29,33,34.
Eze. 28. 15.   Zec. 6. 6.
Ge. 5. 2.   Ge. 37. 24.
Job 23. 6.   Je. 51. 11.
Da. 8. 26.

12*

הֶחָרוּ   Niph. imp. pl. masc. [for הֶחָבְרוּ] .   ברר

הֶחָבְרוּ   Kh. חָבְרוּ Kal pret., K. חָבְרֵי part. act. pl. constr.   הבר

הַבְרוּרִים   pref. הַ)(Kal part. p. m., pl. of בָּרוּר d. 3 a.   ברר

חַבְרוֹשִׁים   )(pref. id.)(noun masc., pl. of בְּרוֹשׁ dec. 1 a.   ברש

הַבָּרוֹת   pref. id.)(noun masc. with pl. fem. term. from בּוֹר dec. 1 a.   באר

הַבַּרְזֶל   )(pref. id.)(noun masc. sing.   ברזל

הַבַּחֲרָמִי   pref. id.)(gent. noun by transp. for בַּחֲרוּמִי from בַּחוּרִים   בחר

הַבְּרִיאָה   pref. id.)(adj. fem. sing. d. 10, from בָּרִיא m.   ברא

הַבְּרִיאוֹת   )(pref. id.)(id. pl.   ברא

הַבְּרִיָּה   )(pref. id.)(noun fem. sing.   ברה

הַבְּרִיחַ   )(pref. id.)(noun masc. sing. dec. 1 a.   ברח

הִבְרִיחוּ   Hiph. pret. 3 pers. pl. masc.   ברח

הַבְּרִיחִם   pref. הַ)(noun masc., pl. of בְּרִיחַ dec. 1 a.   ברח

הַבֵּרִים   pref. id.)(gent. noun pl. from בְּאֵר or בְּאֵרוֹת   באר

הַבְּרִיעִי   pref. id.)(patronym. of בְּרִיעָה q. v.

הַבְּרִית   )(pref. id.)(noun fem. sing. dec. 1 a.   ברה

הַבְּרָכָה   pref. הַ interr. f. הֲ   ברך

הַבְּרָכָה   pref. הַ art. } noun fem. sing. dec. 11 c.

הַבְּרָכָה   pref. id.)(noun fem. sing. dec. 10.   ברך

הַבְּרָכוֹת   pref. id.)(noun fem., pl. of בְּרָכָה dec. 11 c.   ברך

הַבִּרְכַּיִם   pref. id.)(noun fem. du. of בֶּרֶךְ dec. 6 a.   ברך

הַבַּרְקָנִים   pref. id.)(noun masc. pl. [of בַּרְקָן]   ברק

הַבְּאֵרֹתִי   pref. id.)(gent. noun from בְּאֵרוֹת   באר

הֹבִשׁוּ   Hiph. pret. 3 pers. pl. for הוֹבִישׁוּ   יבש

הַבָּשׂוֹר   pref. הַ)(pr. name of a river .   בשׂר

הִבְשִׁילוּ   Hiph. pret. 3 pers. pl.   בשל

הַבֹּשֶׂם   pref. הַ)(noun masc. sing.   בשׂם

הַבְּשָׂמִים   )(pref. id.)(noun masc., pl. of בֶּשֶׂם dec. 6.   בשׂם

הַבָּשָׁן   )(pref. id.)(pr. name of a region .   בשן

הַבָּשָׂר   )(pref. id.)(noun masc. sing. dec. 4 a.   בשׂר

הַבֹּשֶׁת   )(pref. id.)(noun fem. sing. dec. 13 c.   בוש

הַבָּת   pref. id.)(noun masc. sing. dec. 8 d.   בתת

הַבַּת   pref. id. } noun fem. sing. irr. (§ 45)   בנה

הַבְּתוּלָה   pref. הַ)(noun fem. sing. dec. 10.   בתל

הַבְּתוּלוֹת   pref. id.)(id. pl.   בתל

הַבְּתֹת   pref. id.)(noun fem., pl. of [בַּתָּה] dec. 10.   בתת

הַבָּתִּים   pref. id.)(noun masc. pl. irr. of בַּיִת (§ 45)   בית

הַבָּתִּים   pref. id.)(noun masc., pl. of בַּת dec. 8 d.   בתת

הַבִּתְרוֹן   pref. id.)(pr. name of a place   בתר

הַגֵּא   pr. name masc. Est. 2. 3, called הֵגַי ver. 8, 15.

הַגֵּאָיוֹת   pref. הַ)(noun com. pl. of גַּיְא, גֵּי irr. (§ 45)   גיא

הַגֹּאֵל   pref. id.)(Kal part. act. masc. sing. dec. 7 b.   גאל

הַגְּאֻלָּה   pref. id.)(noun fem. sing. dec. 10.   גאל

הַגָּבֹהַּ   )(pref. id.)(adj. masc. sing. dec. 3 a.   גבה

הַגֹּבַהּ   )(pref. id.)(noun m. sing. d. 6 c. (§ 35. r. 5)   גבה

הַגְבֵּהַּ   Hiph. inf. abs. or imp. sing. masc.   גבה

הַגְּבֹהָה   )(pref. הַ)(adj. fem. sing. d. 10, from גָּבֹהַּ m.   גבה

הַגְּבֹהוֹת   pref. id.)(id. pl.   גבה

הַגְּבֹהִים   )(pref. id.)(adj. masc., pl. of גָּבֹהַּ dec. 3 a.   גבה

הַגְּבֹהֹת   pref. id.)(id. pl. fem.   גבה

הִגְבַּהְתִּי   Hiph. pret. 1 pers. sing.   גבה

הַגְּבוּל   Kh. הַגְּבֻל q. v., K. הַגָּדֹל (q. v.) .   גדל

הַגְּבוּל   )(pref. הַ)(noun masc. sing. dec. 1 a.   גבל

הַגִּבּוֹר   pref. id.)((prim. adj.) noun m. sing. dec. 1 b.   גבר

הַגְּבוּרָה   )(pref. id.)(noun fem. sing. dec. 10.   גבר

הַגְּבוּרֹת   )(pref. id.)(noun masc., pl. of גִּבּוֹר dec. 1 b.   גבר

הַגֵּבִים   pref. id.)(pr. name of a place   גוב

הַגָּבִיעַ   pref. id.)(noun masc. sing. dec. 3 a.   נבע

הִגְבִּיר   )(Hiph. pret. 3 pers. masc. sing.   גבר

הַגְּבִירָה   )(pref. הַ)(noun fem. sing. from גְּבִיר m.   גבר

הַגְבֵּל   Hiph. imp. sing. masc.   גבל

הַגְּבֻל   defect. for הַגְּבוּל (q. v.)   גבל

הַגְּבֻלִי   pref. הַ)(gent. n. from גְּבֻל (comp. § 35. r. 10)   גבל

הַגְּבֻלִים   )(pref. id.)(id. pl.   גבל

הִגְבַּלְתָּ   )(Hiph. pret. 2 pers. sing. masc.; acc. shifted by conv.)((§ 8. rem. 7)   גבל

הַגִּבְעָה   pref. הַ)(n. fem. sing. d. 12 b; also pr. name   נבע

הַגִּבְעֹנִי   pref. id.)(gent. noun from גִּבְעוֹן   נבע

הַגְּבָעוֹת   )(pref. id.)(noun fem., pl. of גִּבְעָה d. 12 b.   נבע

הַגִּבְעֹנִי   pref. id.)(gent. noun from גִּבְעוֹן .   נבע

הַגִּבְעֹנִים   )(pref. id.)(id. pl.   נבע

הַגִּבְעָתָה   pref. id.)(pr. name (גִּבְעָה) with parag. ה   נבע

הַגִּבְעָתִי   pref. id.)(gent. noun from גִּבְעָה   נבע

הַגֶּבֶר   pref. id.)(noun masc. sing. dec. 6.   גבר

הַגִּבֹּר   pref. id.)(noun masc. sing. dec. 1 b.   גבר

הַגְּבָרִים   )(pref. id.)(id. pl., absolute state   גבר

הַגְּבָרִים   pref. id.)(noun masc. pl. of גֶּבֶר dec. 6.   גבר

הָגַג   Root not used; Syr. to imagine, cogn. הָנָה. הָגִין masc. dec. 3 a. — I. musing, meditation, Ps. 5. 2.—II. meditation, prayer, 39. 4.

הַגֹּנֶן   Kh. הַגֹּן q. v., K. הַגֹּנֶה (q. v.) .   גנ

הַגֹּן   pref. הַ)(noun masc. sing. dec. 8 a.   גנ

הַגֹּנָה   pref. id.)(id. with parag. ה   גנ

הַגֹּנוֹת   pref. id.)(id. with pl. fem. term. .   גנ

הַגָּד   pref. id.)(pr. name of a river .   נדד

הַגֵּד   )(pref. id.)(Hiph. inf. or imp. sing. masc.   נגד

a Is. 52. 11.   f Ge. 41. 7, 20.   l Ge. 27. 33.   q 1 Ch. 9. 29.   u Is. 7. 19.   z 2 Ch. 3. 4.   f Eze. 17. 24.   h Da. 9. 27.   o De. 10. 17.
b Is. 47. 13.   g Ge. 41. 4.   m De. 28. 2.   r Je. 3. 24.   v Eze. 45. 14, 14.   a Da. 8. 3.   g Jos. 15. 47.   i Je. 29. 2.   p 1 Ch. 29. 24.
c Na. 2. 4.   h Ex. 26. 28.   n Ju. 8. 7, 16.   s Ruth 4. 6, 8.   x Eze. 48. 17.   k Is. 10. 33.   m Ex. 19. 23.   r 1 Sa. 7. 14.
d Ge. 37. 20.   i 1 Ch. 8. 13.   o Je. 8. 9.   t Eze. 45. 11.   y Eze. 21. 31.   l De. 28. 52.   n 1 Ch. 29. 11.   n Ex. 19. 12.   s Zep. 1. 5.
Jos. 6. 24.   k 2 Ki. 17. 38.   p Ge. 40. 10.   s Ge. 17. 17.

הֻגַּד   ו' id. imp. sing. masc. (§ 11. rem. 5)   נגד

הֻגַּד   b' ו' Hoph. pret. 3 pers. sing. masc.   נגד

הֻגֵּד   id. inf. abs.   נגד

הַגֻּדְגֹּד   pr. name in compos. הֹר הַגִּדְגָּד   נדד

הַגִּדְגָּדָה   pref. ה)(pr. name of a place   נדד

הַגְּדוּ   Hiph. imp. pl. m. for הַגִּידוּ (comp. § 11. r. 5)   נגד

הַגְּדוּד   pref. ה)(noun masc. sing. dec. 1 a.   נדד

הַגָּדוֹל   ו' pref. id.)(adj. masc. sing. dec. 3 a.   גדל

הַגְּדוֹלָה   d' ו' pref. id.)(id. fem., dec. 10.   גדל

הַגְּדוּלָה   pref. id.)(noun fem. sing. dec. 10.   גדל

הַגְּדוֹלִים   pref. id.)(adj. masc., pl. of גָּדוֹל dec. 3 a.; also pr. name masc.   גדל

הַגָּדוֹר   pref. id.)(pr. name of a place   גדר

הַגָּדִי   ו' pref. id.)(patronym. of גָּד   גדד

הַגָּדִי   pref. id.)(noun masc. sing. dec. 6 i.   גדה

הִגְדִּיל   ו' Hiph. pret. 3 pers. sing. masc.   גדל

הִגְדִּילוּ   g' id. pret. 3 pers. pl.   גדל

הַגְדֵל   defect. for הַגָּדוֹל (q. v.)   גדל

הַגְדֵל   g' defect. for הִגְדִּיל (q. v.)   גדל

הַגְּדֹלָה   pref. ה)(adj. fem. sing. dec. 10, from גָּדוֹל m.   גדל

הַגְּדֻלָּה   h' pref. id.)(noun fem. sing. dec. 10.   גדל

הַגְּדֹלוֹת   pref. id.)(adj. fem., pl. of גְּדוֹלָה dec. 10, from גָּדוֹל masc.   גדל

הַגְּדֻלּוֹת   i' pref. id.)(noun fem., pl. of גְּדֻלָּה dec. 10.   גדל

הַגְּדֹלִים   pref. id.)(adj. masc., pl. of גָּדוֹל dec. 3 a.   גדל

הַגְּדֹלֹת   pref. id.)(id. fem. pl. of גְּדוֹלָה dec. 10.   גדל

הִגְדַּלְתָּ   Hiph. pret. 2 pers. sing. masc.   גדל

הִגְדַּלְתִּי   id. pret. 1 pers. sing.   גדל

הַגְּדֵרָה   ו' prf. ה)(pr. name of a place   גדר

הַגְּדֵרוֹת   pref. id.)(pr. name of a place   גדר

הַגְּדֵרִי   pref. id.)(gent. noun from בֵּית־גָּדֵר q. v.   בית

הַגְּדֶרֶת   k' pref. id.)(noun fem. sing.   גדר

הַגְּדֵרָתִי   pref. id.)(gent. noun from גְּדֵרָה   גדר

הִגַּדְתָּ   Hiph. pret. 2 pers. sing. masc.   נגד

הִגַּדְתָּ   ו' id. id.; acc. shifted by conv. ו (§ 8. r. 7)   נגד

הִגַּדְתָּה   l' id. id. written fully (§ 8. rem. 5)   נגד

הִגַּדְתִּי   ו' id. pret. 1 pers. sing.   נגד

הִגַּדְתֶּם   m' ו' id. pret. 2 pers. pl. masc.   נגד

הָגָה [הָגָה]   fut. יֶהְגֶּה—I. to murmur, applied to the cooing of doves, the lamenting or sighing of men, the growling of the lion over his prey.—II. poet. to utter, speak.—III. to meditate. Po. to utter, speak, Is. 59. 13. Hiph. to mutter, spoken of enchanters, Is. 8. 19.

הֶגֶה   masc. I. a muttering of thunder, Job 37. 2.—

II. murmuring, sighing, Eze. 2. 10.—III. meditation, thought, Ps. 90. 9 ; Prof. Lee, murmur.

הָגוּת   fem. (construct state) meditation, thought, Ps. 49. 4.

הִגָּיוֹן   masc. dec. 3 c. (constr. הֶגְיוֹן § 32. rem. 3) —I. murmur or sound of the harp.—II. meditation, thought.

II. הָגָה   to separate, to take away.

הָגֹה   n' Kal inf. abs.   הגה

הֻגָּה   o' ו', ף', noun masc. sing.)(for ו see lett. ו   הגה

הִגָּה   p' Hiph. pret. 3 pers. sing. masc.   ינה

הָגוֹ   Kal inf. abs. [for הָגָה § 24. rem. 2]   הגה

הָגוֹ   ו Poel inf. abs. [for הֹגֹה comp. § 24. r. 2]   הגה

הַגּוֹאֵל   pref. ה)(Kal part. act. masc. dec. 7 b.   גאל

הַגּוֹי   r' ו' pref. ה } noun masc. sing. dec. 1 a.   נוה

הַגּוֹי   pref. ה }

הַגּוֹיִם   v' ו' pref. ה)(id.pl.abs. [for גּוֹיִים comp. § 3. r. 1]   גוה

הַגּוֹלָה   pref. id.)(noun fem. sing.   גלה

הַגּוּנִי   pref. id.)(gent. noun [for גּוּנִי] from גּוּנִי   גון

הַגּוֹרָל   pref. id.)(noun masc. sing. dec. 2 b.   גרל

הַגִּזְבָּר   pref. id.)(noun masc. sing.   גזבר

הֲגִיגָה   ו noun fem. sing.   הגה

הַגִּזָּה   b' pref. ה)(noun fem. sing. dec. 10.   גזז

הַגִּזּוֹנִי   pref. id.)(gent. noun from גִּזֹה   גזה

הַגְּזֵלָה   w' pref. id.)(noun fem. sing. dec. 10.   גזל

הַגֶּזֶם   ו' pref. id.,)(noun masc. sing.   גזם

הַגִּזְרָה   d' ו' pref. id.)(noun fem. sing. (no pl.)   גזר

הַגִּזְרִים   pref. id.)(noun masc., pl. of גֶּזֶר dec. 6.   גזר

הַנַּחֲלָקִים   pref. id.)(n. f., pl. of נַחֲלָה d. 13 a. (suff. נַחֲלֹתָם)   נחל

הֲגַי   הֲגַי } pr. name m. Est. 2. 8, 15, called הֵגֵא v. 3.

הַגַּי   ו }

הַגַּיְא   k' } pref. ה)(noun com. sing. irr. (§ 45)   ניא

הַגַּיְא   ו' }

הַגֵּיאָוֹת   pref. id.)(id. pl. abs. Kh. הַגֵּיאָוֹת, K. הַגֵּאָיוֹת (q. v.)   ניא

הֶגְיֹנִי   noun m. s., suff. 1 p. s. from [הָגָיוֹן] d. 3 a.   הגה

הַגֵּיד   Hiph. inf. absolute   נגד

הִגִּיד   ו' id. pret. 3 pers. sing. masc.   נגד

הַגִּידָה   id. imp. sing. masc. with parag. ה   נגד

הִגִּידָה   s' ו' id. pret. 3 pers. sing. fem.   נגד

הִגִּידָהּ   id. pret. 3 pers. sing. masc., suff. 3 pers. s. f.   נגד

הַגִּידוּ   t' ו' id. imp. pl. masc.   נגד

הִגִּידוּ   ו' id. pret. 3 pers. pl.   נגד

הַגִּידִי   id. imp. sing. fem.   נגד

הֶגְיוֹן   noun masc. sing. dec. 3 c. (§ 32. rem. 3)   הגה

a Jos. 7. 19.   f Ps. 38. 17.   k Ju. 14. 16.   p Job 37. 2.   t Is. 59. 13.   x Exr. 1. 8.   c Eze. 41. 13, 14.   h 1 Ch. 4. 39.   m Je. 36. 16.
b De. 17. 4.   g 1 Sa. 12. 24.   l Is. 27. 8.   q Eze. 2. 10.   u Je. 27. 11.   y Ps. 49. 4.   d Ge. 15. 17.   i 1 Sa. 17. 3.   n 2 Sa. 17. 17.
c Is. 27. 1.   h 1 Ch. 29. 11.   l 1 Ch. 29. 11.   r 2 Sa. 20. 13.   w Ge. 20. 4.   z Ju. 6. 37, 38, 38.   f Pr. 6. 28.   k 2 Ki. 2. 16.   o Is. 45. 21.
c Is. 27. 1.   i 1 Ch. 17. 19.   l Ps. 90. 9.   s Pr. 25. 4, 5.   v Is. 60. 12.   a Joel 2. 25.   g Jos. 8. 11.   l Ps. 5. 2.   p Je. 81. 10.
d Da. 8. 4.   k Ese. 42. 12.   n Ge. 45. 13.   o Le. 5. 23.

הֶגְיוֹן	ן id. constr. state . . .	הגה
הֶגְיוֹנָם	ן id. with suff. 3 pers. pl. masc. .	הגה
הַגִּלֹנִי	pref. הַ)(gent. noun from גִּלֹה	גלה
הֲגִינָה	adj. fem. sing. from [הָגִין] masc. .	הגן
הִגִּיעַ	Hiph. pret. 3 pers. sing. masc. . .	נגע
הִגִּיעוּ	ן id. pret. 3 pers. pl. . . .	נגע
הִגִּיעָנוּ	id. inf. (הַגִּיעַ) with suff. 1 pers. pl. dec. 1 b.	נגע
הַגֵּרִים	pref. הַ)(noun masc., pl. of גֵּיר d. 1 a.	גור
הַגִּישָׁה	Hiph. imp. sing. masc. with parag. ה	נגש
הִגִּישָׁהּ	ן id. pret. 3 pers. sing. m., suff. 3 pers. s. f.	נגש
הַגִּישׁוּ	ון id. imp. pl. masc. . . .	נגש
הִגִּישׁוּ	id. pret. 3 pers. pl. . . .	נגש
הִגִּישׁוֹ	ן id. pret. 3 pers. s. m., suff. 3 pers. s. m.	נגש
הִגַּיְתְּ	ן Kal pret. 2 pers. sing. masc. . .	הגה
הִגַּיְתִּי	ן id. pret. 1 pers. sing. . . .	הגה
הַגַּל הַגָּל	} pref. הַ)(noun masc. sing. dec. 8 d. .	נלל
הַגַּלְבִּים	pref. id.)(n. m. pl. [of גַּלְב d. 1 b. § 30. r. 1]	גלב
הַגִּלְבֹּעַ	pref. id.)(pr. n. of a region, see גִּלְבֹּעַ	
הַגַּלְגַּל	pref. id.)(noun masc. dec. 8 e.	נלל
הַגִּלְגָּל	ן pref. id.)(pr. n. of a place (and in compos. with בַּיִת q. v.)	נלל
הַגֻּלְגֹּלֶת	pref. id.)(id. with parag. ה	נלל
הַגֻּלְגֹּלְתָּ	pref. id.)(noun fem. sing. dec. 13 c.	נלל
הֻגְלָה	Hoph. pret. 3 pers. sing. masc. .	גלה
הַגֻּלָּה	pref. הַ)(noun fem. sing. .	גלה
הַגֻּלָּה	pref. id.)(noun fem. sing. dec. 10. .	נלל
הֶגְלָה וְהִגְלָה	} Kal pret. 3 pers. sing. masc. (§ 11. rem. 1)	גלה
הֶגְלוּ	Hoph. pret. 3 pers. pl. . .	גלה
הִגָּלוּ	Niph. imp. pl. masc. . .	גלה
הֶגְלוּ	Hiph. pret. 3 pers. pl. . .	גלה
הַגֹּלוּ	pref. הַ)(Kal part. p. masc. dec. 3 a.	גלה
הַגִּלּוּלִים	pref. id.)(noun masc., pl. of [גִּלּוּל] dec. 1 b.	נלל
הַגֹּלוֹת	ן pref. id.)(noun fem., pl. of גֹּלָה dec. 10.	נלל
הַגְלוֹת	Hiph. inf. const. dec. 1 b. . .	גלה
הַגְלוֹתָם	id. with suff. 3 pers. pl. masc. .	גלה
הַגְלִי	Ch. Aph. pret. 3 sing. masc. (§ 47. rem. 4)	גלא
הַגָּלִיל	pref. הַ)(pr. name of a region .	גלל
הַגְּלִילָה	pref. id.)(id. with parag. ה	גלל
הַגְּלִלָּה	pref. id.)(noun fem. sing. dec. 10.	גלל
הַגִּלְיֹנִים	pref. id.)(noun masc., pl. of גִּלָּיוֹן dec. 3 c.	גלה
הִגְלֵיתָ	Hiph. pret. 2 pers. sing. m. (§ 24. rem. 14)	גלה

הִגְלֵיתִי	id. pret. 1 pers. sing.	גלה
הִגְלֵיתֶם	id. pret. 2 pers. pl. masc. (§ 24. rem. 14)	גלה
הַגַּלָּל	pref. ה art.)(noun masc. dec. 4 a.	גלל
הַגְּלָלִים	pref. id.)(noun masc., pl. of [גָּלָל] d. 1 b.	גלל
הִגְלָם הִגְלָם	} Hiph. pret. 3 pers. s. m., suff. 3 pers. sing. masc. (§ 11. rem. 1) .	גלה
הַגְלֹנִי	pref. הַ)(gent. noun from גִּלֹה	גלה
הַגִּלְעָד	ן pref. id.)(pr. name of a region, see גִּלְעָד	
הַגִּלְעָדָה	pref. id.)(id. with parag. ה	
הַגִּלְעָדִי	pref. id.)(gent. noun from גִּלְעָד q. v.	
הָגְלָת הָגְלָתָה	} Hoph. pret. 3 pers. fem. s. (§ 24. r. 14)	גלה
הִגְלֵתִי	ן Hiph. pret. 1 pers. sing.; acc. shifted by conv. ו (comp. § 8. rem. 7) . .	גלה
הֲגַם	pref. הֲ interr.)(conj. . . .	גמם
הַגָּמוּל	pref. ה art.)(noun masc. sing. dec. 1 a.	גמל
הַגְּמוּלָה	pref. id.)(noun fem. sing. dec. 10.	גמל
הַגְמִיאִינִי	Hiph. imp. sing. fem., suff. 1 pers. sing.	גמא
הַגָּמָל	pref. הַ)(n. m. s. d. 8 a. (§ 37. Nos. 2 & 3)	גמל
הִגָּמֵל	Niph. inf. constr.	גמל
הַגְּמַלִּים	ן pref. הַ)(n. m., pl. of גָּמָל d. 8 a. (§ 37. Nos. 2 & 3)	גמל
הָגֵן	Root not used; Chald. הָגֵן suitable, convenient. הָגִין m. adj. convenient, commodious, Eze. 42. 12.	
הַגַּן	pref. הַ)(noun com. sing. for גַּן dec. 8 d. .	גנן
הַנֶּגֶב	pref. id.)(noun masc. sing. dec. 1 b.	נגב
הַנְגֵּב	pref. הַ)(Kal inf. absolute	נגב
הַנֹּגֵב	pref. ה)(Kal part. act. sing. masc.	נגב
הַגִּנְבָּה	pref. id.)(noun fem. sing. dec. 10.	נגב
הַגַּנּוֹת	pref. id.)(noun fem., pl. of גַּנָּה dec. 10.	גנן
הִגַּעַתְּ	Hiph. pret. 2 pers. sing. fem.	נגע
הִגַּעְתִּיהוּ	ן id. pret. 1 pers. sing., suff. 3 pers. s. m.	נגע
הִגַּעְתֶּם	ן id. pret. 2 pers. pl. masc.	נגע
הַגֵּן	pref. הַ)(noun com. sing. (suff. גַּפְנִי) d. 6 a.	גפן
הַגְּפָנִים	ן pref. id.)(id. pl., absolute state .	גפן
הָגָר	(flight, coll. with the Arab.) pr. name of the hand-maid of Sarah, the mother of Ishmael. הַגְרִי (fugitive), pl. הַגְרִיאִים, הַגְרִים pr. n. of an Arabian people.	
הַגָּר	pref. id.)(Kal part. sing. masc. dec. 1 a.	גור
הַגֵּר	ן pref. id.,)(noun masc. sing. dec. 1 a.	גור
הַגִּרְגָּשִׁי	ן pref. id.)(pr. name of a people, see גִּרְגָּשִׁי	
הַגְּרָה	pref. id.)(noun fem. sing. [for גֵּרָה] .	גרד

a Ps. 19. 15.   g Le. 2. 8.   m Ps. 77. 13.   s 2 Ki. 24. 14.   a Je. 24. 1.   f Je. 29. 4, 7, 14.   l Je. 13. 19.   q Ge. 24. 17.   v Is. 66. 17.
b La. 3. 62.   h Is. 45. 21.   n Ge. 31. 46.   t Is. 49. 9.   b Am. 1. 6.   g 2 Ki. 17. 27.   m Est. 2. 6.   r Ge. 33. 8.   y Est. 4. 14.
c Eze. 42. 12.   i 2 Sa. 17. 29.   o Eze. 5. 1.   u 2 Ki. 17. 28, etc.   c Eze. 47. 8.   h 1 Ki. 14. 10.   n Am. 5. 27.   s Je. 7. 9.   z Eze. 13. 14.
d Ec. 12. 1.   k Ex. 21. 6.   p Ex. 1. 9. 35.   v 2 Ki. 9. 35.   d Is. 3. 23.   i 1 Ch. 8. 7.   o Joel 4. 4.   t Zec. 5. 3.   a Ex. 12. 29.
e 1 Sa. 14. 9.   l Jos 1. 8.   q Est. 2. 6.   w 2 Ch. 4. 12.   e 1 Ch. 5. 26.   k Je. 20. 4.   p 2 Sa. 19. 37.   u Ex. 22. 3.   b Ca. 1. 13.
f 2 Ch. 2. 16.   m Ps. 143. 5.   r Zec. 4. 3.   x Ge. 21. 8.

הַגִּרְזִי ‎| ‎pref. id.)(pr. n. Kh. R. ‎נרז‎ K. ‎גּוְרִי‎ R.   ‎נזר‎

הַגַּרְזֶן ‎| ‎| ‎pref. id.)(noun masc. sing.   ‎גרז‎

הַגְּרִי ‎pr. name masc.   ‎הגר‎

הַגֵּרִים ‎| ‎| ‎pref. id.)(Kal part. masc., pl. of ‎גֵּר‎ d. 1 a.   ‎נור‎

הַגֵּרִים ‎| ‎| ‎pref. id.)(noun masc., pl. of ‎גֵּר‎ dec. 1 a.   ‎נור‎

הַגֵּרִים ‎| ‎pref. id.)(pr. n. of a people, pl. of ‎הַגְרִי‎ ‎הגר‎

הַגַּרְמִי ‎pref. id.)(pr. name masc.   ‎נרם‎

הַגֹּרָלוֹת ‎| ‎pref. id.)(n. m. with pl. f. term. fr. ‎גּוֹרָל‎ d. 2 b.   ‎נרל‎

הַגְּרֵם ‎| ‎Hiph. imp. 2 p. s. m. [‎הַגְרֵם‎] suff. 3 p. pl. m.   ‎נגר‎

הַגֹּרֶן ‎pref. id.)(noun sing. fem., dec. 6 c.   ‎נרן‎

הַגְּרָנוֹת ‎pref. ‎הַ‎)(pl. absolute (§ 35. rem. 9)   ‎נרן‎

הִגַּרְתִּי ‎| ‎Hiph. pret. 1 p. s. acc. shifted by conv.   ‎נגר‎

הַגֵּרְשֻׁנִּי ‎pref. ‎הַ‎)(patronym. of ‎גֵּרְשׁוֹן‎   ‎נרש‎

הַגִּישָׁה ‎Hiph. imp. sing. masc. with parag. ‎ה‎   ‎נגש‎

הַגִּישׁוּ ‎id. imp. pl. masc.   ‎נגש‎

הֻגְּשׁוּ ‎Hoph. pret. 3 p. pl. (some copies have (‎הֻגְּשׁוּ‎   ‎נגש‎

הַגְשׁוּרִי ‎pref. ‎הַ‎)(pr. name of a people, see ‎גְּשׁוּר‎

הַגֶּשֶׁם ‎| ‎| ‎pref. id.)(noun masc. sing. dec. 6 a. (§ 35. rem. 2, but pl. c. (‎גִּשְׁמֵי‎   ‎נשם‎

הַגֹּשֶׁן ‎pref. id.)(pr. name of a region   ‎נשן‎

הִגַּשְׁתֶּם ‎Hiph. pret. 2 pers. pl. masc.   ‎נגש‎

הַגִּתִּי ‎pref. ‎הַ‎)(gent. noun from ‎נַּת‎   ‎נת‎

הַגִּתִּים ‎pref. id.)(id. pl.   ‎נת‎

הַגִּתִּית ‎pref. id.)(noun fem. sing. from ‎נַּת = גַּתִּי‎   ‎נת‎

הֲדַד ‎noun masc. sing.   ‎הדד‎

הַדָּאָה ‎pref. id.)(noun fem. sing.   ‎דאה‎

הַדֹּב ‎pref. id.)(noun masc. sing. dec. 8 c.   ‎דבב‎

הִדְבִּיקֻהוּ ‎Hiph. pret. 3 pers. pl., suff. 3 pers. sing. masc.   ‎דבק‎

הִדְבִּיקַתְהוּ ‎id. pret. 3 pers. sing. fem., suff. 3 pers. s. m.   ‎דבק‎

הַדְּבִיר ‎pref. ‎הַ‎)(noun masc. sing.   ‎דבר‎

הַדְּבָקִים ‎pref. id.)(noun masc., pl. of ‎דֶּבֶק‎ dec. 6.   ‎דבק‎

הַדְּבֵקִים ‎pref. id.)(adj. masc., pl. of ‎דָּבֵק‎ dec. 5 b.   ‎דבק‎

הִדְבַּקְתִּי ‎Hiph. pret. 1 pers. sing.   ‎דבק‎

הִדְבַּקְתִּי ‎| ‎id. acc. shifted by ‎וְ‎ conv. (comp. § 8. rem. 7)   ‎דבק‎

[‎הַדָּבָר‎] Chald. masc. the title of a certain officer in the court of Babylon, Eng. Ver. *counsellor.* Etymology uncertain.

הַדָּבָר ‎| ‎pref. ‎הַ‎ / ‎הָ‎ } noun masc. sing. dec. 4 a.   ‎דבר‎

הַדָּבָר ‎| ‎| ‎pref. ‎הַ‎)(noun masc. sing. dec. 6 a. (§ 35. rem. 2)   ‎דבר‎

הַדְּבַר ‎| ‎pref. id.)(noun masc. sing.   ‎דבר‎

הַדֹּבֵר ‎pref. id.)(Kal part. act. masc. dec. 7 b.   ‎דבר‎

הַדְּבָרוֹ ‎pref. id.)(noun masc. sing., suff. 3 pers. sing. masc. from ‎דָּבָר‎ dec. 6 f.   ‎דבר‎

הַדִּבְּרוֹת ‎pref. id.)(Kal part. act. fem., pl. from ‎דֹּבֵר‎ m.   ‎דבר‎

הַדְבָרַי ‎Ch. noun m. pl., suff. 1 pers. s. [from ‎הַדָּבָר‎   ‎חדבר‎

הַדְבְרֵי ‎Chald. id. pl., construct state   ‎חדבר‎

הַדָּבְרַיָּא ‎Chald. id. pl., emph. state   ‎חדבר‎

הַדְּבָרִים ‎| ‎pref. ‎הַ‎)(noun masc., pl. of ‎דָּבָר‎ dec. 4 a.   ‎דבר‎

הַדֹּבְרִים ‎| ‎pref. id.)(Kal part. act. m., pl. of ‎דֹּבֵר‎ d. 7 b.   ‎דבר‎

הַדְּבֹרִים ‎pref. id.)(n. fem. with pl. m. term. fr. ‎דְּבֹרָה‎   ‎דבר‎

הַדְּבָרַת ‎pref. id.)(pr. name of a place   ‎דבר‎

הַדְּבַשׁ ‎| ‎pref. id.)(for ‎דְּבַשׁ‎ noun masc., (with suff. (‎דִּבְשִׁי‎ dec. 6 (§ 35. rem. 10)   ‎דבש‎

הַדֹּנֵּג ‎pref. id.)(noun masc. sing. dec. 2 a.   ‎דנה‎

הַדָּנָה ‎| ‎pref. id.)(noun fem. sing. dec. 11 a.   ‎דנה‎

הַדָּנִים ‎pref. id.)(noun masc., pl. of ‎דָּן‎ dec. 2 a.   ‎דנה‎

הַדָּנָן ‎| ‎pref. id.)(noun masc. sing. dec. 4 a.   ‎דנה‎

‎הָדַד‎ Root not used; Arab. *to break; to give forth a heavy sound.*

‎הֶד‎ masc. *a shouting,* Eze. 7. 7.

‎הֵידָד‎ masc. *a shouting,* of those who tread the grapes, or of an attacking army.

‎הֲדַד‎ pr. name—I. of a Syrian idol, see ‎בֶּן־הֲדַד‎. —II. of a son of Ishmael, 1 Ch. 1. 30.—III. of a king of Edom.—IV. of an Idumean, 1 Ki. 11. 14— 25, called ‎אֲדַד‎ in ver. 17.

‎הֲדַדְעֶזֶר‎ (whose *help is Hadad,* see the prec.) pr. name of a king of Syria, also called ‎הֲדַרְעֶזֶר‎, comp. 2 Sa. 8. 3 sq. with chaps. 10, 16, 19.

‎הֲדַדְרִמּוֹן‎ (*Hadad, Rimmon,* two Syrian idols) pr. name of a town near Megiddo, Zec. 12. 11.

‎הֲדַי‎ pr. name masc. 2 Sa. 23. 30, for which ‎חוּרַי‎ in 1 Ch. 11. 32.

הֲדַד ‎| ‎| ‎pr. name masc.   ‎הדד‎

הֲדַדְעֶזֶר ‎| ‎| ‎pr. name masc.   ‎הדד‎

הֲדַדְרִמּוֹן ‎pr. name of a place.   ‎הדד‎

‎הָדָה‎ *to thrust, put forth* the hand, Is. 11. 8; Arab. *to lead, direct.*

‎יֶהְדִּי‎ (for ‎יֶהְדִּיָּה‎ whom *the Lord directs*) pr. name masc. 1 Ch. 2. 47.

הֹדָהּ ‎noun m. s., suff. 3 pers. s. m. from ‎הוֹד‎ dec. 1.   ‎הוד‎

[‎הֹדּוּ‎] (for (‎הִנְדּוּ‎ pr. name *Hindustan, India,* Est. 1. 1; 8. 9.

הֹדוּ ‎| ‎(for (‎הוֹדוּ‎ Hiph. imp. pl. masc.   ‎ידה‎

הַדֹּב ‎pref. ‎הַ‎)(for ‎דֹּב‎ noun masc. sing. dec. 8 c.   ‎דבב‎

a Is. 10. 15.   f Ne. 10. 35.   l 2 Sa. 3. 34.   q 2 Sa. 1. 6.   u Je. 13. 11.   x Eze. 7. 15.   f Da. 4. 33.   b Ps. 109. 20.   g Ne. 5. 11.
b 1 Ki. 6. 7.   g Je. 18. 21.   m Am. 5. 25.   r Ju. 20. 42.   w Eze. 29. 4.   y Je. 5. 13.   g Da. 3. 27.   i De. 1. 44.   p Je. 22. 18.
c 1 Ch. 15. 2.   h Mi. 1. 6.   n Ge. 27. 25.   s 1 Ki. 22. 34; &   1 Sa. 2. 18.   z Mi. 2. 12.   k Da. 6. 8.   m Jon. 2. 1.   q Ps. 107. 1.
d 1 Ch. 24. 4.   i Le. 11. 14.   o Le. 11. 14.   2 Ch. 18. 33.   p Ps. 31. 19.   r 1 Ch. 4. 22.   Ex. 7. 18, 21.   r 1 Sa. 17. 34. 36.
e 2 Ch. 30. 25.   k 1 Sa. 13. 9.   p Am. 5. 19, etc.   t De. 4. 4.   w Je. 21. 7.   u Ju. 14. 9.

הַדּוּד־ ׀ הַ)(noun masc., pl. דּוּדִים and דּוּדִים (§ 35. rem. 12 & 13) . . . דוד

הַדּוּדָאִים pref. id.)(n. m. pl. [of דּוּדַי § 35. r. 15 note] . . . דוד

הַדָּוָה ׀ pref. id.)(adj. fem. from דָּוֶה masc. . . דוה

הַדּוּכִיפַת ׀ pref. id.)(noun fem. sing. . . . דוכ

הַדֹּלְנ pref. id.)(Kal part. act. sing. masc. . . דלנ

הַדֹם noun masc. sing. . . . . . הדם

הַדּוּר Kal part. p. sing. masc. dec. 3 a. . . הדר

הַדּוֹר pref. הַ)(noun masc. sing. dec. 1 a. . דור

הַדּוּרִים ׀ Kal part. p. masc., pl. of הָדוּר ; בֵ bef. (־) הדר

הַדּוֹרָם pr. name of a people . . . . הדר

הַדְּחוּיָה pref. הַ)(Kal part. pass. fem. [fr. דָּחוּי m.] דחה

הִדַּחְתִּי Hiph. pret. 1 pers. sing. . . . . נדח

הִדַּחְתִּי ׀ id. acc. shifted by ׀ conv. (§ 8. rem. 7) נדח

הִדַּחְתִּיו ׀ id. id., suff. 1 pers. sing. . . . נדח

הִדַּחְתִּיךָ id. id., suff. 2 pers. sing. masc. . נדח

הִדַּחְתִּים id. id., suff. 3 pers. pl. masc. . . נדח

הִדַּחְתֶּם id. pret. 2 pers. s. m., suff. 3 pers. pl. masc. נדח

הִדַּחְתֶּם id. pret. 2 pers. pl. masc. . . . נדח

הַדִּי pr. name masc. . . . . . הדד

הַדָּיָנִים pref. הַ)(noun masc., pl. of דַּיָּן dec. 1 a. . דונ

הַדָּיָה ׀ pref. id.)(noun fem. sing. dec. 10. . דיה

הִדִּיחַ ׀ Hiph. pret. 3 pers. sing. masc. . . נדח

הִדִּיחוּ id. pret. 3 pers. pl. . . . נדח

הַדִּיחִי id. inf. (הַדִּיחַ) suff. 1 pers. sing. dec. 1 b. . נדח

הִדִּיחֲךָ id. pret. 3 pers. sing. masc., suff. 2 pers. s. m. נדח

הִדִּיחָם id. pret. 3 pers. sing. m., suff. 3 pers. m. pl. נדח

הַדִּיחֵמוֹ id. imp. sing. masc., suff. 3 pers. pl. masc. נדח

הִדִּיחָנוּ Hiph. pret. 3 pers. sing. masc., suff. נ'נוּ or נ'י or 1 pers. pl. or sing. . . . . דוח

הֹדִיעֵנִי Hiph. imp. sing. masc., suff. 1 pers. sing. ידע

[הָדַךְ] to throw down, tread down ; only in the foll. form.

הֲדֹךְ ׀ Kal. imp. sing. masc. ; ׀ before (־) . הדך

הַדַּלִי ׀ pref. הַ)(noun masc. sing. dec. 8 a. . דלל

הַדַּלִּים pref. id.)(id. pl., absolute state . . דלל

הַדְלֵק Hiph. inf. absolute . . . . דלק

הַדֶּלֶת הַדֶּלֶת ׀ pref. הַ)(noun fem. sing. see דֶּלֶת . . דלה

הַדְּלָתוֹת pref. id.)(id. pl. absolute (§ 44. rem. 5), ת treated as if radical . . . . דלה

הָדֹם Root not used ; Arab. to level with the ground ; Syr. and Chald. (הֲדַם) to cut in pieces.

הֲדָם Chald. piece, Da. 2. 5 ; 3. 29.

הֲדֹם m. footstool, everywhere followed by רַגְלַיִם

הָאָדָם ׀ pref. הַ)(noun masc. sing. dec. 2 a. . אדם

הֶאָדָם pref. הַ interr.)(id., construct state . אדם

הֲדֹם elsewhere הֲדֹם, noun masc. sing. . . הדם

הָאֳדָמִים pref. הַ)(noun masc., pl. of אָדָם dec. 2 a. . אדם

הַדָּמִין Chald. noun masc., pl. of [הֲדָם] dec. 1 a. . הדם

הִדְמָּנוּ Hiph. pret. 3 pers. sing. masc. [הָדַם], suff. 1 pers. pl. . . . . . דמם

הַדָּנִי pref. הַ)(gent. noun from דָּן . . דין

הֲדַס ׀ masc. (pl. הֲדַסִּים) myrtle. Hence הֲדַסָּה (myrtle) pr. name, the former name of Esther, Est. 7. 2. . . . . הדס

הַדַּעַת הַדַּעַת ׀ pref. הַ)(noun fem. sing. dec. 13 a. . ידע

[הָדַף] fut. יֶהְדֹּף (§ 13. rem. 5) to push, thrust, repulse.

הֲדָפוֹ Kal pret. 3 pers. sing. m., suff. 3 pers. s. m. הדף

הֲדַפְתִּיךָ ׀ Hiph. pret. 1 pers. s. & suff. ; ׀ for conv. הדף

הַדְקֵק Hiph. inf., used adverbially . . . דקק

הָדֵק ׀ Hiph. pret. 3 pers. sing. m. (§ 18. r. 10) דקק

הַדִּקּוּ Ch. Aph. pret. 3 pers. pl. m. (§ 47. rem. 1 & 5) דקק

הַדַּקּוֹת pref. הַ)(adj., fem. of דַּק dec. 10, fr. דַק m. דקק

הֲדִקּוֹת ׀ Hiph. pret. 2 pers. sing. fem. ; ׀ bef. (־) דקק

הַדַּקַּת defect for הַדַּקּוֹת (q. v.) . . . דקק

הַדֶּקֶת ׀ Chald. Aph. pret. 3 pers. sing. fem. (§ 47. rem. 4, & § 49. rem. 1) . . דקק

I. [הָדַר] i. q. Chald. הֲדַר to turn, whence part. pass. הֲדוּרִים uneven, crooked places, Is. 45. 2, Rabbin. הַדְרִין id., see Buxtorf.

II. [הָדַר] fut. יֶהְדַּר (§ 13. rem. 5).—I. to adorn, decorate, Is. 63. 1.—II. to honour, reverence, respect. Niph. to be honoured, respected, La. 5. 12. Hithp. to show oneself glorious, Pr. 25. 6.

הֲדַר Chald. Pa. to honour.

הָדָר masc. dec. 4 c.—I. ornament, splendour.— II. honour, Ps. 149. 9.

הֶדֶר masc. ornament, splendour, Da. 11. 20.

הֲדַר Ch. m. dec. 3 a, honour, Da. 4. 27, 33 ; 5. 18.

הֲדַר pr. name masc. see הֲדַד.

הַדְרַת or הֲדָרָה fem. only construct הֲדְרַת ornament, splendour, beauty.

הֲדוֹרָם pr. name of an Arab tribe descended from Joktan, Ge. 10. 27.

הָדָר ׀ noun masc. sing. dec. 4 c. . . הדר

הֲדַר ׀ id. construct state ; ׀ bef. (־) . . הדר

a Je. 24. 2.   Ca. 7. 4   Le. 15. 33.   Le. 11. 19.   De. 14. 18.
f Zep. 1. 9.   Is. 63. 1.   Is. 45. 2.   Ps. 62. 4.   Je. 27. 10.
j Joel 2. 20.   Je. 46. 28.   Da. 9. 7.   2 Ch. 13. 9.   Is. 19. 8.
t De. 14. 13.   2 Sa. 15. 14.   Je. 51. 34.   Je. 27. 15.   De. 30. 1.
u Je. 16. 15.   Ps. 5. 11.   Je. 51. 34.   Job 13. 25.   Job 40. 12.
Ju. 6. 15.   Ex. 30. 15.   Je. 39. 10.   Eze. 24. 10.   Ge. 19. 6.
De. 12. 27.   Ps. 110. 1.   Ex. 8. 14.   Is. 41. 19.   Is. 22. 19.
Ex. 30. 36.   2 Ki. 23. 15.   2 Ch. 34. 4.   Da. 6. 25.   Ge. 41. 7.
Mi. 4. 13.   Ge. 41. 24.   Da. 2. 34, 45.   Pr. 20. 29.

הָדָר׳	noun masc. sing.	הדר
הַדְּרָבֹן׳	pref. הַ)(n. m. fr. [דָּרָב] with the term ־ֹן	דרב
הַדְרָא׳	וְ Chald. noun m. s., emph. of [הֲדָר] d. 3a.	הדר
הֲדָרָהּ׳ de	וַ' n. m. s., suff. 3 pers. s. fem. fr. הָדָר dec. 4c.	הדר
הַדָּרֹום	pref. הַ)(noun masc. sing. [for דָּרֹום]	דרר
הַדְּרֹור׳	pref. id.)(noun masc. sing.	דרר
הַדְּרֹות׳	pref. id.)(noun masc. with pl. fem. term. from דֹּור dec. 1a.	דור
הֲדָרִי	noun m. s., suff. 1 pers. s. fr. הָדָר dec. 4c.	הדר
הַדְרִי	Chald. noun masc. sing., suff. 1 pers. sing. from [הֲדָר] dec. 3a.	הדר
הִדְרִיךְ׳	וְ Hiph. pret. 3 pers. sing. masc.	דרך
הִדְרִיכַהּ׳	id. id. (or inf. §11. rem. 4), suff. 3 pers. s. fem.	דרך
הִדְרִיכֻהוּ׳	id. pret. 3 pers. pl., suff. 3 pers. sing. masc.	דרך
הִדְרִיכֵנִי	id. imp. sing. masc., suff. 1 pers. sing.	דרך
הֲדָרְךָ	וַ noun masc. sing., suff. 2 pers. sing. masc. from הָדָר dec. 4c; וְ bef.	הדר
הֲדָרֵךְ׳	n. m. s., suff. 2 pers. sing. fem. fr. הָדָר dec. 4c.	הדר
הַדֶּרֶךְ	pref. הַ)(noun com. sing., dec. 6a. (§ 35. rem. 2)	דרר
הַדֹּרֵךְ	pref. id.)(Kal part. act. sing. masc. dec. 7b.	דרר
הֲדַרְכִּי	pref. הֲ interr.)(noun com. sing., suff. 1 pers. sing. from דֶּרֶךְ dec. 6a.	דרר
הֲדַרְכֵי׳	pref. הֲ interr. for הַ)(id. pl., suff. 1 pers. s.	דרך
הַדְּרָכִים׳	pref. הַ art.)(id. pl., absolute state	דרך
הִדְרַכְתִּיךָ	Hiph. pret. 1 pers. sing., suff. 2 pers. s. m.	דרך
הֲדַרְם	pr. name of a people	הדר
הֲדַרְעֶזֶר }	pr. name masc., see הֲדַדְעֶזֶר	הדד
הֲדַדְעֶזֶר }		
הַדֹּרֵשׁ׳	pref. הַ)(Kal part. act. sing. masc. dec. 7b.	דרש
הָדַרְתָּ׳	וְ Kal pret. 2 pers. sing. masc.; acc. shifted to ult. by וְ conv. (§ 8. rem. 7)	הדר
הַדַּרְתְּ׳	Chald. Pael pret. 2 pers. s. m. (§ 47. rem. 2)	הדר
הֲדָרַת׳	noun fem. sing. constr. [of הֲדָרָה or הֲדָרָה from הָדָר or הֶדֶר masc. dec. 11 or 12]	הדר
הַדְּרֵת׳	וְ Chald. Pael pret. 1 pers. sing.	הדר
הַדֶּשֶׁן׳ }	pref. הַ)(noun m. s. dec. 6a. (with suff. דִּשְׁנִי, though pause דָּשֶׁן § 35.r.2)	דשן
הַדָּשֵׁן׳ }		דשן
הֻדַּשְׁנָה׳	Hoph. pret. 3 pers. sing. fem.	דשן
הַדָּת׳	וְ pref. הַ)(noun fem. sing. dec. 1a.	דת
הָהּ	interj. expressive of grief, Ah! Eze. 30. 2.	
הַהֶבֶל	pref. הַ)(noun m. s. dec. 6. (§ 35. rem. 4)	הבל
הַהָגָרְאִים	pref. id.)(pl. of the following	הגר
הַהַגְרִי	pref. id.)(pr. name of a people	הגר
הַהַגְרִיאִים	pref. id.)(id. pl.	הגר

הַהֲדַרְקִּים׳	pref. id.)(noun masc., pl. of הֲדַם dec. 8 d.	הדם
הַהוּא	pref. id. (interr. Nu. 23. 19))(pers. pron. 3 pers. sing. masc.	הוא
הַהוּא	pref. id.)((read hee) id. 3 p. s. f. (§ 1. r. 3)	הוא
הַהֹוד׳	וְ pref. id.)(noun masc. sing. dec. 1a.	הוד
הַהֹולֵךְ	pref. id.)(Kal part. act. sing. masc. dec. 7b.	הלך
הַהִיא	pref. id.)(pron. pers. 3 pers. sing. fem. see הוא	הוא
הַהֵיטֵב׳	pref. הֵ interr. for הַ)(Hiph. inf. abs. (used adverbially)	יטב
הַהֵיכָל	וְ pref. הַ art.)(noun com. sing. dec. 2b.	היכל
הַהֵימִיר׳	pref. הַ interr. for הַ)(Hiph. pret. 3 p. s. m.	ימר
הַהִין	pref. הַ art.)(noun masc. sing.	הין
הֲהָיְתָה׳	pref. הֲ interr. bef. הַ, for הַ)(Kal pret. 3 pers. sing. fem.	היה
הַהֵכִין׳	pref. הַ relat. art.)(Hiph. pret. 3 pers. s. m.	כון
הַהֹלֵךְ	pref. id.)(Kal part. act. sing. m. d. 7b.	הלך
הַהֹלְכוּא׳	pref. הַ id., bef. הַ for הַ)(Kal pret. 3 pers. pl., (§ 8. rem. 4)	הלך
הַהֹלְכִים	pref. הַ id.)(Kal part. act. m., pl. of הֹלֵךְ d. 7b.	הלך
הַהֹלֶכֶת	pref. id.)(id. fem. sing. dec. 13a.	הלך
הַהֹלְכֹת׳	pref. id.)(id. pl.	הלך
הַהֻלֶּלָה	pref. id.)(Hoph. pret. 3 pers. sing. fem. [for הֻלְלָה comp. § 8. rem. 7]	הלל
הָהֵם	pref. הָ for הַ)(pron. pers. 3 pers. pl. masc.	הם
הָהֵמָּה	pref. id.)(id. with ה parag.	הם
הַהָמֹון׳	Kh. הָמֹון q. v., K. הֲמֹון (q. v.)	המה
הֶהָמֹון׳	וְ pref. הֶ bef. הָ for הַ)(noun m. s. d. 3a.	המה
הַהֲמֵת׳	pref. id. interr.)(Hiph. inf. absolute	מות
הָהֵנָּה	pref. הָ for הַ)(pers. pron. 3 pers. pl. fem., ה parag.	הן
הַהַסְכֵּן׳	pref. הַ interr. for הַ)(Hiph. inf. abs.	סכן
הַהֲפוּכָה׳	pref. הַ art.)(Kal part. p. s. f. [fr. הָפוּךְ m.]	הפך
הַהֻפַּךְ׳	Hoph. pret. 3 pers. sing. masc.	הפך
הַהֲפֵכָה׳	pref. הַ)(noun fem. sing.	הפך
הַהֹפְכִי׳	pref. id.)(Kal part. act. sing. masc. with parag. י (§ 8. rem. 19)	הפך
הַהֹפְכִים׳	pref. id.)(id. pl. dec. 7b.	הפך
הַהִצִּילוּ׳	pref. הַ interr. for הַ)(Hiph. pret. 3 pers. pl.	נצל
הַהַצֵּל׳	pref. id.)(id. inf. absolute	נצל
הַהִצְלִיחַ׳	pref. id.)(Hiph. pret. 3 pers. sing. masc.	צלח
הַהִקְדִּישׁ׳	pref. id.)(Hiph. pret. 3 pers. sing. masc.	קדש
הָהָר׳	וְ pref. הָ for הַ)(with the art. for הַר noun masc. dec. 8. (§ 37. rem. 7)	הרר
הַהַרְאֵל׳	וְ pref. הַ)(noun masc. sing. see אֲרִיאֵל	ארה
הַהֲרֵגָה׳	pref. הַ)(noun sing. fem.	הרג

a Da. 11. 20.   e Is. 41. 4.   m Eze. 27. 10.   t Le. 19. 32.   x Is. 34. 6.   g Hab. 1. 6.   = Jos. 10. 24.   j Je. 26. 19.   v Am. 5. 7.
b 1 Sa. 13. 21.   f Mi. 2. 9.   n Eze. 18. 25.   u Da. 5. 23.   y Est. 4. 8.   h Jon. 4. 4. 9.   ⊥ 1 Sa. 25. 42.   k Nu. 22. 30.   2 Ki. 18. 33.
c Da. 5. 18.   g Da. 4. 27, 33.   o Eze. 18. 29.   p Pr. 14. 28.   z Est. 3. 15, etc.   i Je. 2. 11.   p Eze. 26. 17.   l Job 30. 15.   ⊚ Ge. 24. 21.
d La. 1. 6.   h Is. 11. 15.   p Eze. 21. 26.   q Da. 4. 31.   a Zec. 1. 8, 10, 11.   q Joel 1. 2.   r 2 Ki. 7. 13.   m Ge. 19. 29.   1 Ch. 26. 28.
Is. 5. 14.   i Je. 51. 33.   q Pr. 4. 11.   r Le. 1. 16.   b 1 Ch. 29. 11.   q 2 Ch. 29. 36.   s 1 Sa. 14. 19.   u Ps. 114. 2.   Eze. 43. 15.
Eze. 46. 17.   d Ps. 45. 4.   s Eze. 14. 10.   s Je. 31. 40.   f La. 4. 6.

הַהֲרַח	pref. הָ for הַ)(noun masc. sing. with parag. ה [for הַרָה] from הַר (§ 37. rem. 7) .	הרר
הַהֲרוּגִים	pref. הַ)(Kal part. p. m., pl. of [הָרוּג] d. 3 a.	הרג
הַהֲרוּסָי	pref. הָ bef. הָ for הַ)(Kal part. pass.	הרם
הַהֲרוֹתָי	pref. id.)(adj. pl. fem., suff. 3 pers. sing. fem., fr. הָרָה [fr. הָרָה masc.; § 42. r. 2]	הרה
הֶהָרִים	)(pref. id.)(noun masc., pl. of הַר dec. 8. (§ 37. rem. 7) .	הרר
מַהֲרִימֹוּ	pref. הַ art. relat.)(Hiph. pret. 3 pers. pl.	רום
הַהַרְמֹונָה	pref. הַ art.)(noun masc. sing. with parag. ה [from הַרְמֹון] .	הרם
הֶחָרֶס	pref. id.)(noun masc. sing. .	הרם
הַהָרָרִי	pref. id.)(pr. name of a people .	הרר
הַהָשֵׁב	pref. הָ interr. bef. הָ f. הָ, הֹ)(Hiph. inf. abs	שׁוּב
הַהֵשִׁיב	pref. הָ art. relat.)(Hiph. pret. 3 pers. s. m.	ישׁב
הַהֵשִׁיבוּ	pref. id.)(id. pret. 3 pers. pl.	ישׁב
הֹוּ	interj.	הוי

הוּא), (masc., הִיא fem., pron. 3 pers. sing. (pl. הֵם, הֵן, see their places).—I. *he, she,* neut. *it.*—II. *this, that, same;* הַהוּא הַהִיא *this, that, the same.*—Chald. id.

הוּא	) id. fem. (§ 1. rem. 3).	
הָוָא	Chald. Peal pret. 3 pers. sing. masc. see .	הוה
הֱוֵא	Kal imp. sing. masc. see .	הוה
הוֹאִיל	Hiph. pret. 3 pers. sing. masc.	יאל
הוֹאִילוּ	id. pret. 3 pers. pl.	יאל
הוֹאֵל / הוֹאֶל	} id. imp. sing. masc. .	יאל
הוֹאַלְנוּ	id. pret. 1 pers. pl.	יאל
הוֹאַלְתָּ	id. pret. 2 pers. sing. masc.	יאל
הוֹאַלְתִּי	id. pret. 1 pers. sing.	יאל
הוּבָא	) Hoph. pret. 3 pers. sing. masc.	בוא
הוּבָאוּ	id. pret. 3 pers. pl.	בוא
הוּבַד	) Ch. Hoph. pret. 3 pers. s. m. (§ 47. r. 9)	אבד
הוֹבִישׁ	Hiph. pret. 3 pers. sing. masc.	יבשׁ
הוֹבִישָׁה	id. pret. 3 pers. sing. fem.	יבשׁ
הוֹבִישׁוּ	id. pret. 3 pers. pl.	בושׁ
הוֹבְנִים	) Kh. הוֹבְנִים K. הָבְנִים noun masc. pl. [of הָבְנִי or הוֹבְנִי]	הבן
הוֹבַשְׁתָּ	Hiph. pret. 2 pers. sing. masc.	יבשׁ
הוֹבַשְׁתִּי	id. pret. 1 pers. sing.	יבשׁ
הוֹבַשְׁתִּי	) id.; acc. shifted by ו conv. (comp. § 8. r. 7)	יבשׁ
הוֹנָה	Hiph. pret. 3 pers. sing. masc.	ינה
הוֹנָהּ	id. with suff. 3 pers. sing. fem. (§ 25. No. 2 e)	ינה

הוֹנַעְנוּ	Hiph. pret. 1 pers. pl. [for הוֹנַעְנוּ § 7. r. 8]	ינע
הוֹנַעְתִּיךָ	id. pret. 1 pers. sing., suff. 2 pers. sing. m.	ינע
הוֹנַעְתֶּם	id. pret. 2 pers. pl. masc.	ינע
הוֹנַעְתָּנִי	id. pret. 2 pers. sing. masc. suff. 1 pers. sing.	ינע

הֹוד),), masc. dec. 1 a.—I. *glory, majesty.*—II. *beauty, brightness.*—III. pr. name masc. 1 Ch. 7. 37. Root not defined, the lexicographers fluctuating between נָהַד, יָהַד, הוד.

הֹודִיָּה (*majesty of the Lord*) pr. name of several Levites.

הֹודַוְיָהוּ, הֹודַוְיָה (for הֹודוּ יָהּ *the Lord is his glory*) pr. name masc. of several persons.

הֹודֹו	id., suff. 3 pers. sing. masc. .	הוד
הֹודוּ	) Hiph. pret. 3 pers. pl., or imp. pl. masc.	ידה
הֹודַוְיָה	) pr. name masc. .	הוד
הֹודֹות	) Hiph. inf. constr.	ידה
הֹודִי	) noun m. s., suff. 1 pers. s. fr. הֹוד d. 1 a.	הוד
הֹודִיָּה	pr. name masc.	הוד
הֹודַוְיָהוּ	Kh. הֹודַוְיָה K., pr. name masc.	הוד
הֹודִינוּ	Hiph. pret. 1 pers. pl.	ידה
הֹודִיעַ	Hiph. pret. 3 p. s. m., or inf. constr. Ge. 41. 39.	ידע
הֹודִיעוּ	id. pret. 3 pers. pl., or imp. pl. masc.	ידע
הֹודִיעֲךָ	id. inf. (הֹודִיעַ), suff. 2 pers. sing. m. d. 1 b.	ידע
הֹודִיעָם	id. imp. sing. masc., suff. 3 pers. pl. masc.	ידע
הֹודִיעֵנוּ	id. id., suff. 1 pers. pl.	ידע
הֹודִיעֻנוּ	id. imp. pl. masc., suff. 1 pers. pl.	ידע
הֹודִיעַנִי	id. pret. 3 pers. sing. masc., suff. 1 pers. s.	ידע
הֹודִיעֵנִי	) id. imp. sing. masc., suff. 1 pers. sing.	ידע
הֹודְךָ / הֹודֶךָ	} noun masc. sing., suff. 2 pers. sing. masc. from הֹוד dec. 1 a.	הוד
הֹודַע	Hiph. imp. sing. masc.; or (Le. 4. 23, 28) Hoph. pret. 3 pers. sing. masc. [for הָוְדַע]	ידע
הֹודַע	) Ch. Aph. pret. 3 pers. s. m. (§ 47. r. 4 & 9)	ידע
תֻּודַע	Niph. inf., suff. 1 pers. sing. fr. [הִוָּדַע § 36. rem. 5] dec. 7 b.	ידע
הֹודְעָךְ	Chald. Aph. pret. 3 pers. sing. masc. suff. 2 pers. sing. masc. (§ 47. rem. 4 & 9) .	ידע
הֹודַעְנָא	) Chald. id. pret. 1 pers. pl.	ידע
הֹודַעֲנִי	Hiph. pret. 3 pers. sing. m., suff. 1 pers. s.	ידע
הֹודַעְתָּ	id. pret. 2 pers. sing. masc. (comp. § 8. rem. 7)	ידע
הֹודַעְתָּ	) id. id.; acc. shifted by conv. ו (comp. id.)	ידע
הֹודַעְתָּהּ	) id. id., suff. 3 pers. sing. fem.	ידע
הֹודַעְתִּי	id. pret. 1 pers. sing.	ידע
הֹודַעְתִּי	) id. id.; acc. shifted by conv. ו (comp. § 8. r. 7)	ידע

a Est. 9. 11. | d Am. 4. 3. | h Am. 5. 16. | n Ge. 18. 27, 31. | s Je. 51. 36. | x Is. 43. 24. | d Ps. 98. 2. | i Je. 11. 18. | n Ezr. 4. 14.
1 Ki. 18. 30. | e Is. 19. 18. | i Job 37. 6. | o Ge. 43. 18. | t La. 1. 5. | y Job 40. 10. | e De. 8. 3. | k Da. 2. 15, 17, 45. | o Ex. 33. 13.
b 2 Ki. 15. 16. | f Ge. 24. 5. | k Job 6. 23. | p Da. 7. 11. | u Mal. 2. 17. | 1 Ch. 25. 3. | f Eze. 20. 4. | l Da. 2. 28. | p Job 26. 3.
c Zec. 6. 1. | g Ezr. 10. 14. | l Jos. 7. 7. | q Eze. 27. 15. | v Is. 43. 23. | a Da. 10. 8. | g Je. 31. 19. | m Da. 2. 29. | q Ex. 18. 20.
Ezr. 8. 25. | Ezr. 10. 17. | m 1 Ch. 17. 27 | r Eze. 17. 24. | w Mal. 2. 17. | b Job 37. 19. | h 1 Sa. 6. 2. | | r Eze. 22. 2.
c Ps. 75. 2.

הוֹדַעְתִּיךָ id. id., suff. 2 pers. sing. masc. . ידע

הוֹדַעְתָּם וְ id. pret. 2 pers. s. m., suff. 3 pers. pl. m. ידע

הוֹדַעְתֶּם וְ id. pret. 2 pers. pl. masc. . ידע

הוֹדַעְתֶּנָא Chald. Aph. pret. 2 pers. sing. masc., suff. 1 pers. pl. (§ 47. rem. 4 & 9) . . ידע

הוֹדַעְתַּנִי Heb. & Ch. Hiph. or Aph. pret. 2 pers. sing. masc., suff. 1 pers. sing. (§ 4. rem. 4 & 9) . ידע

[הָוָה] imp. הָוֵא, הֱוֵא fut. יִהְוֶא (§ 24. rem. 3 e & 20).— I. (Arab. *to breathe*) *to exist, to be.*—II. in the deriv. *to desire*, comp. הַוָּה.—III. *to fall, descend*, Job 37.6.

יְהַוֶה הֲוָא, הֲוָה Chald. *to be.* Fut. יֶהֱוֵא, with the pref. ל, לֶהֱוֵא, לְהֶוֵא, pl. לְהֶוֹן, לֶהֱוֹן, see analyt. order.

הַוָּה fem. dec. 10.—I. *desire, lust.*—II. *fall, calamity, destruction*, for which twice is found הַיָּה in Kheth. Job 6. 2 ; 30. 13.

הֹוָה fem. *fall, calamity.*

יְהֹוָה the most sacred name of God, expressive of His *eternal, Self-existence*, first communicated to the Hebrews, Ex. 3. 14, comp. chap. 6. 3. This name appears to be composed of יְהוֹ (fut. of הָוָה, like יְהִי from הָיָה) and וָה (preterite by aphæresis for הָוָה), the verb *to be* being twice repeated as in Ex. 3. 14. If we supply אֲשֶׁר between these words we obtain nearly the same sense as expressed there in the words אֶהְיֶה אֲשֶׁר אֶהְיֶה. The Jews who (from an early date) believed this name incommunicable, substituted, in the pronunciation, the consonants of אֲדֹנָי, the vowels being alike in both words (with the exception of simple and composite Sheva), and according to these the punctuators suited the vowels of the prefixes when coming to stand before יְהֹוָה, as לַיהֹוָה, בַּיהֹוָה, מֵיהֹוָה according to מֵאֲדֹנָי, לַאֲדֹנָי, בַּאֲדֹנָי. Where, however, יְהֹוָה is already preceded by אֲדֹנָי, to avoid repetition, they furnished it with the vowels of אֱלֹהִים, in order that it be pronounced with its consonants, so that אֲדֹנָי יֱהֹוִה is to be read אֲדֹנָי אֱלֹהִים. The punctuators seem to intimate the originality of the vowels of יְהֹוָה by not pointing Yod with Hhateph-Pattah (יֲהֹוָה) to indicate the reading of אֲדֹנָי just as they point it with Hhateph-Segol to indicate the reading of אֱלֹהִים. We could, moreover, not account for the abbreviated forms יוֹ, יְהוֹ prefixed to so many proper names, unless we consider the vowels of יְהֹוָה original.

יָהּ i. q. יְהֹוָה from which it may be an abbre-

viation, and that probably from the first two letters, Kamets being added to assist the enunciation. When affixed to proper names the Mappik in ה is omitted, as אֵלִיָה ; the form is also sometimes prolonged to יְהוֹ=יָהוּ (comp. יְהֹוָה), as אֵלִיָהוּ.

יְהוֹאָחָז (*the Lord holds* him) pr. name—I. of a king of Israel, son of Jehu, comp. 2 Ki. 13. 1—9. —II. of a king of Judah, son of Josiah, comp. 2 Ki. 23. 31—34, also called יוֹאָחָז comp. 2 Ch. 36. 1 with 2.

יְהוֹאָשׁ (*the Lord has bestowed* him, R. אוּשׁ coll. with the Arab. *to give*) pr. name.—I. of a king of Judah, son of Ahaziah, written also יוֹאָשׁ, comp. 2 Ki. 12. 1 with 20.—II. of a king of Israel, son of Jehoahaz, called also יוֹאָשׁ, comp. 2 Ki. 13. 10 with 9.

יְהוֹזָבָד (*the Lord has bestowed* him) pr. name of several men.

יְהוֹחָנָן (*the Lord has graciously bestowed* him) pr. name of several men, especially a commander under Jehoshaphat, comp. 2 Ch. 17. 15.

יְהוֹיָדָע (whom *the Lord knows*, i. e. cares for) pr. name of several men, especially of a priest of great authority, comp. 2 Ki. 11. 4.

יְהוֹיָכִין (*the Lord will establish* him, R. כּוּן) pr. name of a king of Judah, son of Jehoiakim, comp. 2 Ki. 24. 6, 8, sq.; also written יוֹיָכִין Eze. 1. 2, יְכָנְיָה comp. Est. 2. 6, כָּנְיָהוּ Je. 24. 1, Kh., כָּנְיָהוּ comp. Je. 22. 24.

יְהוֹיָקִים (*the Lord will establish* him, R. קוּם) pr. name of a king of Judah, son of Josiah.

יוֹיָרִיב, יְהוֹיָרִיב (*the Lord will defend* his *cause*) pr. name of a distinguished priest at Jerusalem.

יוֹנָדָב, יְהוֹנָדָב (*the Lord liberally bestowed* him) pr. name of two different men.

יוֹנָתָן, יְהוֹנָתָן (whom *the Lord has given*) pr. name of several men, especially of a son of Saul, the friend of David.

יְהוֹעַדָּה (whom *the Lord adorns*) pr. name masc. 1 Ch. 8. 36, called יַעְרָה chap. 9. 42.

יְהוֹעַדָּן (*the Lord* is her *ornament*) pr. name fem. 2 Ki. 14. 2.

יוֹצָדָק, יְהוֹצָדָק (*the Lord is righteous*) pr. name of the father of Joshua the high-priest.

יוֹרָם, יְהוֹרָם (*the Lord is exalted*) pr. name m. —I. of a king of Judah, son of Jehoshaphat, comp. 2 Ki. 8. 16—24.—II. of a king of Israel, son of Ahab, comp. 2 Ki. chap. 3.

ᵃ Pr. 22. 19.   ᵇ De. 4. 9.   ᶜ Jos. 4. 22.   ᵈ Da. 2. 23.

יְהוֹשֶׁבַע (the Lord is her oath) pr. name of a daughter of king Joram, 2 Ki. 11. 2.

יְהוֹשׁוּעַ, יְהוֹשֻׁעַ (the Lord is his salvation) pr. name of several men, especially—I. of the minister of Moses afterwards his successor, called also הוֹשֵׁעַ, יֵשׁוּעַ.—II. of a high-priest contemporary with Zerubbabel, called also יֵשׁוּעַ.

יְהוֹשָׁפָט (whom the Lord judges) pr. name.—I. of a king of Judah son of Asa, comp. 1 Ki. 22. 41—51.—II. of the recorder of king David, comp. 2 Sa. 8. 16.—III. 1 Ki. 4. 17.—IV. 2 Ki. 9. 2, 14.

יוֹאָב (the Lord is his father) pr. name of several men, especially of the chief military officer of David.

יוֹאָח (the Lord is his friend) pr. name of several men, especially—I. of a recorder of Hezekiah, comp. 2 Ki. 18. 18.—II. of a recorder of king Josiah, 2 Ch. 34. 8.

יוֹאֵל (the Lord is his God) pr. name of several men, especially—I. of a prophet, Joel 1. 1.—II. of a son of Samuel, 1 Sa. 8. 2.—III. of a son of king Uzziah, 1 Ch. 6. 21.

יוֹאָשׁ pr. name of several men, contr. for יְהוֹאָשׁ (q. v.) for which it often stands.

יוֹזָבָד (the Lord has bestowed him) pr. name of several Levites.

יוֹזָכָר (whom the Lord remembers) pr. name of the murderer of king Joash, 2 Ki. 12. 22, written also זָבָד in 2 Ch. 24. 26.

יוֹחָא (perhaps transp. for יוֹאָח q. v.) pr. name masc. of two different persons.

יוֹחָנָן (contr. for יְהוֹחָנָן q. v.) pr. name of several men.

יוֹדָע (contr. for יְהוֹיָדָע q. v.) pr. name masc.

יוֹיָקִים (the Lord will establish him) pr. name masc. Ne. 12. 10.

יוֹיָרִיב (contr. for יְהוֹיָרִיב q. v.) pr. n. m. Ne. 11. 5.

יוֹכֶבֶד (the Lord is her glory) pr. name of the mother of Moses.

יוֹנָתָן (contr. for יְהוֹנָתָן q. v.) pr. name masc. of several persons.

יוֹעֵד (the Lord is his witness) pr. n. m. Ne. 11. 7.

יוֹעֶזֶר (the Lord is his helper) pr. n. m. 1 Ch. 12. 6.

יוֹעָשׁ (whom the Lord succours, see עוּשׁ) pr. n. masc. of two different persons.

יוֹקִים (contr. for יוֹיָקִים) pr. n. m. 1 Ch. 4. 22.

יוֹרָם (contr. for יְהוֹרָם q. v.) pr. name masc. 2 Sa. 8. 10, for which הֲדוֹרָם 1 Ch. 18. 10.

יוֹתָם (the Lord is perfect R. תָּמַם) pr. name.—I. of a son of Gideon, Ju. 9. 5.—II. of a king of Judah, son of Uzziah, comp. 2 Ki. 15. 32—38.

הֲוָה Ch. Peal pret. 3 pers. sing. masc. . . . הוה

הֱוֵה⁴ Kal imp. sing. masc. . . . . . הוה

הֹוָה noun fem. sing. . . . . . הוה

הֹוֶה Kal part. act. sing. masc. . . . . **הוה**

הוֹהָם (perh. for יְהוֹהָם Lord of multitude) pr. name of a king of Hebron, Jos. 10. 3.

הֲווֹ⁵ וַ'; Ch. Peal pret. 3 pers. pl. m.; ו bef. (‐ֹ). הוה

הֱווֹ⁶ Ch. id. imp. pl. masc. . . . . . הוה

הַוּוֹת noun fem., pl. of [הַוָּה] dec. 10. . . הוה

הוּחֲדָה Hoph. pret. 3 pers. sing. fem. . . חדד

הוֹחִילִי⁴ Hiph. imp. sing. fem. . . . . יחל

הוּחָל⁵ Hoph. pret. impers. . . . . . חלל

הוֹחֵלִי⁶ defect. for חִילִי (q. v.). . . . . יחל

הוֹחַלְתִּי } Hiph. pret. 1 pers. sing. (comp. § 8. r. 7) יחל
הוֹחַלְתִּי⁷ }

הוֹחָלְתִּי⁸ ו id. ; acc. shifted by conv. ו (comp. id.) . . יחל

הוּטְלוּ⁵ Hoph. pret. 3 pers. pl. . . . . טול

הוֹי interj.—I. of threatening, ho ! wo ! with acc., עַל, אֶל, ל.—II. of grief, alas !—III. of exhortation, ho !

הוֹ interj. expressive of grief, alas ! Am. 5. 16.

הֱוֵי¹ Kal imp. sing. masc. . . . . הוה

הוֹדֵעַ⁴ transpos. for הַיּוֹדֵעַ, pref. ה art.; Kal part. act. m. ידע

הוֹיָה¹ Kal part. act. sing. fem., [from הָוָה masc.] היה

הֲוַיְתָ⁷ Ch. Peal. pret. 2 pers. sing. masc. . . הוה

הֲוֵית Ch. id. pret. 1 pers. sing. . . . . הוה

[הוּך] Ch. fut. יְהָךְ, inf. מְהָךְ (§ 54. rem. 1) to go.

הֻכְּתָה⁸ Hoph. pret. 3 p. s. m. for הֻכָּה (comp. הוּלֶּדֶת) נכה

הוֹכַח⁹ Hiph. imp. sing. masc. . . . . יכח

הוֹכֵחַ וְ'⁵ id. inf. absolute . . . . יכח

הוֹכִיחַ⁵ ו id. pret. 3 pers. sing. masc. . . יכח

הוּכַח⁶ ו Hoph. pret. 3 pers. sing. masc. . . יכח

הוֹכִיחַ⁷ ו Hiph. pret. 3 pers. sing. masc. . . יכח

הוּכַן⁸ וְ' Hop. pret. 3 pers. sing. masc. . . כון

הוֹלִד defect. for הוֹלִיד (q. v.). . . . . ילד

הֻלֶּדֶת⁵ⁿ Niph. inf., [הִוָּלֵד] suff. 3 pers. s. f. d. 7 b. ילד

הֻלַּדְלוֹ⁵ id., suff. 3 pers. sing. masc. . . ילד

הוֹלִדוּ⁵⁵ defect. for הוֹלִידוּ (q. v.). . . . ילד

הוֹלַדְתָּ⁵ Hiph. pret. 2 pers. sing. masc. . . ילד

הֻלֶּדֶת⁵ Hoph. inf. constr. for הָלֶּדֶת (§ 20. rem. 16. & § 10. rem. 5) . . . . ילד

הוֹלִיד וְ'⁵ Hiph. pret. 3 pers. sing. masc. . ילד

הוֹלֵיד⁶ ו id. inf. absolute . . . . . ילד

---

a Ge. 27. 29.   d Ps. 42. 6.   g Job 32. 16.   k Je. 29. 23.   n Ps. 102. 5.   q Ge. 21. 25.   Nu. 26. 58.   x Ec. 7. 1.   z Eze. 16. 4, 5.
b Da. 2. 35.   e Ge. 4. 26.   h Je. 22. 28.   l Ex. 9. 3.   o Pr. 9. 8.   r Job 33. 19.   u Ho. 2. 5.   y Ge. 48. 6.   aa Is. 59. 4.
c Ezr. 4. 22.   f Job 32. 11.   i Is. 16. 4.   m Da. 2. 31, 34.   p Job 13. 3.   s Is. 30. 33.   uu Eze. 47. 22.

הוֹלִידָהּ id. pret. 3 pers. sing. m., suff. 3 pers. s. f. . . . ילד

הוֹלִידוֹ id. inf., (הֹלִיד) suff. 3 pers. sing. m. d. 1 b. . . . ילד

הוֹלִידֻנִי id. pret. 3 pers. pl. masc. or imp. pl. m. . . . ילד

הוֹלִיךְ Hiph. pret. 3 pers. sing. masc. . . . ילך

הוֹלִיכוֹ id., suff. 3 pers. sing. masc. . . . ילך

הוֹלִיכְךָ id., suff. 2 pers. sing. masc. . . . ילך

הוֹלִיכְכֶם id., suff. 3 pers. pl. masc. . . . ילך

הָלֹךְ Kh. הֹלֹךְ q. v.; K. הָלוֹךְ Kal inf. absolute . . . הלך

הֹלֵךְ Kal part. act. sing. masc. dec. 7 b. . . . הלך

הוֹלֵךְ Hiph. imp. sing. masc. . . . ילך

הֹלְכוֹת Kal part. f., pl. of הֹלְכָה or הֹלֶכֶת d. 10, or 13 a. . . . הלך

הֹלְכִים id. masc., pl. of הֹלֵךְ dec. 7 b. . . . הלך

הוֹלַכְתִּי Hiph. pret. 1 pers. s.; acc. shifted by conv. (comp. § 8. rem. 7) . . . ילד

הֻלְלוּ Pual pret. 3 pers. pl. [for הֻלְלוּ comp. § 8 rem. 7. & § 10. rem. 5] . . . הלל

הוֹלֵלוֹת noun fem., pl. of הוֹלֵלָה dec. 10. . . . הלל

הוֹלֵלוּת noun fem. sing. . . . הלל

הוֹלְלִים Kal part. act. masc., pl. of הוֹלֵל dec. 7 b. . . . הלל

הוֹלֵם noun m. [for הֹלֶם], or rather part. act. and acc. drawn back (§ 8. rem. 19) . . . הלם

[הוּם] to move, confound, perturbate, De. 7. 23. Niph. (fut. תֵּהֹם) to be moved, excited. Hiph. to be tumultuous.

מְהוּמָה f. d. 10, confusion, consternation.

תְּהוֹם m. d. 1, pl. ־וֹת —I. wave, billow.—II. the deep, ocean.

הוֹמֶה fem. of the following . . . המה

הוֹמֶה Kal part. act. sing. masc. . . . המה

הוֹמִיָּה id. fem., (comp. § 24. rem. 4) . . . המה

הוֹמָם pr. name masc. . . . המם

הוּמַת ' Hoph. pret. 3 pers. sing. masc. [for הוּמַת comp. § 8. r. 7] . . . מות

הוּן Kal not used; Arab. to be light, easy. Hiph. to make light of, regard as a light thing, De. 1. 41.

הוֹן m. d. 1 a, prop. ease, commodity; hence, wealth, plenty. Adv. plenty, Pr. 30. 15, 16.

הִין masc. a hin, a liquid measure containing twelve לֹג.

הוֹן & הוֹן ' noun m. s. d. 1 a; for see lett. . . . הון

הוֹנָה Hiph. pret. 3 pers. sing. masc. (§ 25. No. 2 e) . . . ינה

הוֹנוֹ noun masc. sing. from הוֹן dec. 1 a. . . . הון

הוֹנֵנ Hiph. pret. 3 pers. sing. masc. (§ 25. No. 2 e) . . . ינה

הוּנַח Hoph. pret. 3 pers. sing. masc. . . . נוח

הוֹנֵךְ noun m. pl. suff. 2 pers. s. f. from הוֹן d. 1 a. . . . הון

הוֹנֵךְ id. sing., suff. 2 pers. sing. fem. . . . הון

הוּנַף Hoph. pret. 3 pers. sing. masc. . . . נוף

הוּסַד Hoph. pret. 3 pers. sing. masc. . . . יסד

הֻסַּדָהּ Niph. inf. from [הֻסַּד] suff. 3 pers. s. f. d. 7 b. . . . יסד

הוֹסַפְתָּ Hiph. pret. 2 pers. sing. masc. . . . יסף

הוּסְפַת Ch. Hoph. pret. 3 pers. s. f. (§ 47. rem. 9) . . . יסף

הוֹסַפְתִּי Hiph. pret. 1 pers. sing.; acc. shifted by conv. (comp. § 8. rem. 7) . . . יסף

הוּסַר Hoph. pret. 3 pers. sing. masc. . . . סור

הִוָּסְרוּ Niph. imp. pl. masc. . . . יסר

הִוָּסְרִי id. imp. sing. fem. . . . יסר

הוּעַד ' Hoph. pret. impers. . . . עוד

הוֹעִיל Hiph. pret. 3 pers. sing. masc. or inf. constr. . . . יעל

הוֹעֵיל id. inf. absolute . . . יעל

הוֹפִיעַ ' Hiph. pret. 3 pers. m. or imp. sing. masc. . . . יפע

הוֹפִיעָה id. imp. sing. masc. with parag. ה . . . יפע

הוֹפַעְתָּ id. pret. 2 p. s. m. [for הוֹפַעְתָּ comp. § 8. r. 7] . . . יפע

הוֹצֵא Kh. הוֹצֵא q.v., K. הַיֵצֵא i.q. הוֹצֵא (§ 20. No. 1) . . . יצא

הוֹצֵא ' Hiph. imp. sing. masc. . . . יצא

הוֹצִא ' Hiph. pret. 3 pers. sing. masc. (for הוֹצִיא) . . . יצא

הוּצְאָה Hoph. pret. 3 p. s. f. (הוּצְאָה comp. § 8. r. 7) . . . יצא

הוֹצִאִי [defect. for הוֹצִיאִי] Hiph.inf., suff.1 p. s. d. 1 b. . . . יצא

הוֹצֵאֲךָ id. pret. 3 pers. sing. masc., suff. 2 pers. s. m. . . . יצא

הוֹצֵאתָ id. pret. 2 pers. sing. masc. (§ 25. No. 2 d) . . . יצא

הוֹצֵאתָ ' id. id.; acc. shifted by conv. (comp. § 8. r. 7) . . . יצא

הוֹצֵאתְ id. pret. 2 pers. sing. fem. . . . יצא

הוֹצֵאתִיו id. pret. 2 pers. sing. masc., suff. 3 p. s. m. . . . יצא

הוֹצֵאתִי id. pret. 1 pers. sing. . . . יצא

הוֹצֵאתִי id. id., acc. shifted by conv. (comp. § 8. r.7) . . . יצא

הוֹצֵאתִיהָ id. suff. 3 pers. sing. fem. . . . יצא

הוֹצֵאתִיךָ id., suff. 2 pers. sing. masc. . . . יצא

הוֹצֵאתִים ' id., suff. 3 pers. pl. masc. . . . יצא

הוֹצֵאתֶם ' id., suff. 2 pers. pl. masc. . . . יצא

הוֹצֵאתָנוּ id. pret. 2 pers. sing. masc., suff. 1 pers. pl. . . . יצא

הוֹצֵאתַנִי } id. pret. 2 pers. sing. masc., suff. 1 p. s. . . . יצא
הוֹצֵאתַנִי }

הוֹצִיא ' id. pret. 3 pers. sing. m.; or inf. constr.; or (Is. 43. 8) imp. sing. masc. . . . יצא

הוֹצֵא Kh. id., K. הוֹצִיא (q. v.) . . . יצא

הוֹצִיאָה Hiph. imp. sing, masc., suff. 3 pers. sing. fem. . . . יצא

הוֹצִיאָה id. imp. sing. masc. with parag. ה . . . יצא

הוֹצִיאֻהוּ id. pret. 3 pers. pl. masc., suff. 3 pers. s. m. . . . יצא

הוֹצִיאוּ ' id. pret. 3 pers. pl., or imp. pl. masc. . . . יצא

ᵃ Is. 55. 10.   ʰ Jos. 6. 13.   ᵒ Ec. 10. 13.   ᵘ Pr. 19. 14.   ᵉ Eze. 27. 27.   Je. 6. 8.   Ge. 8. 17.   Ne. 9. 7.   De. 9. 28.

ᵇ Le. 25. 45.   ᶦ Pr. 28. 26.   Ps. 5. 6.   Eze. 18. 12, 16.   Ex. 29. 27.   Ex. 3. 10.   Zec. 5. 4.   Job 10. 18.

ᶜ Je. 29. 6.   Nu. 11. 11.   Is. 41. 7.   Pr. 28. 8.   Ex. 9. 18.   Je. 23. 32.   De. 22. 14, etc.   Eze. 20. 14.   Je. 7. 22.

ᵈ 2 Ki. 24. 15.   Ne. 6. 17.   1 Ki. 1. 41.   Eze. 22. 7, 29.   1 Ki. 10. 7.   Job 37. 15.   Eze. 38. 8.   Eze. 34. 13.   Job 142. 8.

Pr. 16. 29.   Ge. 37. 25.   Je. 4. 19.   La. 5. 5.   Da. 4. 33.   Ps. 80. 2.   Je. 34. 13.   Ex. 16. 3.   Eze. 24. 6.

ᵉ De. 8. 2.   Ps. 78. 65.   2 Ki. 11. 2.   Eze. 27. 33.   Ps. 2. 10.   Job 10. 3.   1 Ki. 17. 13.   De. 22. 24.   1 Ki. 21. 10.

ᶠ Is. 48. 21.   Eze. 7. 26.   De. 21. 23.

הוֹצִיאוּהָ	id. imp. pl. masc., suff. 3 pers. sing. fem.	יצא
הוֹצִיאִי	id. inf. with suff. 1 pers. s. d. 1 b, or imp. s. f.	יצא
הוֹצִיאֲךָ	id. pret. 3 pers. sing. m., suff. 2 pers. s. m.	יצא
הוֹצִיאָם	id. id., suff. 3 pers. pl. masc.	יצא
הוֹצִיאֵם	id. imp. sing. masc., suff. 3 pers. pl. masc.	יצא
הוֹצִיאֵנוּ	id. pret. 3 pers. sing. masc., suff. 1 pers. pl.	יצא
הוֹצִיאֵנִי	id. id., suff. 1 pers. sing.	יצא
הוֹצִיאֵנִי	id. imp. sing. masc., suff. 1 pers. sing.	יצא
הוֹצֵאתִיהָ	Kh. הוֹצֵיתִיהָ, K. הַצֵּיתֻהָ 'Hiph. pret. 1 p. sing. or imp. pl. masc., suff. 3 pers. sing. fem. (§ 20. rem. 16)	יצת
הוּצַק	Hoph. pret. 3 pers. sing. masc.	יצק
הוּקַם	Hoph. pret. 3 pers. sing. masc.	קום
הוֹקַע	Hiph. imp. sing. masc.	יקע
הוֹקַעֲנוּם	id. pret. 1 pers. pl., suff. 3 pers. pl. masc.	יקע
הוֹרֵן	Kal part. act. sing. masc. dec. 7 b.	הרנ
הוֹרַנֻנוּ	Pual pret. 1 pers. pl. [for הֻרַנֻנוּ, הֻרַ']	הרנ
הוֹרֵד	Hiph. imp. sing. masc.	ירד
הוּרַד	Hoph. pret. 3 pers. sing. masc.	ירד
הוֹרִד'	Hiph. pret. 3 pers. sing. masc. for הוֹרִיד	ירד
הוֹרְדֵהוּ	Hiph. imp. sing. masc., 3 pers. sing. masc.	ירד
הוֹרִדֻהוּ	id. pret. 3 p. pl. m. or imp. pl. m., suff. id. [for הוֹרִידֻהוּ]	ירד
הוֹרִדוּ	id. id. pret. 3 pers. pl. masc. [for הוֹרִידוּ]	ירד
הוֹרִדְנוּ	id. pret. 1 pers. pl.	ירד
הוֹרַדְתָּ	Hiph. pret. 2 pers. s. m.; acc. shifted by ו conv. (comp. § 8. rem. 7)	ירד
הוּרַדְתָּ	Hoph. pret. 2 p. s. m.; acc. id. (comp. id.)	ירד
הוֹרַדְתִּי	Hiph. pret. 1 pers. s.; acc. id. (comp. id.)	ירד
הוֹרִדְתִּיךָ	id. with suff. 2 pers. sing. fem.	ירד
הוֹרִדְתִּים	id. with suff. 3 pers. sing. masc.	ירד
הוֹרַדְתֶּם	id. pret. 2 pers. pl. masc.	ירד
הוֹרַדְתֻּנוּ	id. pret. 2 pers. sing. fem., suff. 1 pers. pl. [for הוֹרַדְתִּינוּ § 16. rem. 5]	ירד
הוֹרֵהוּ	Hiph. pret. 3 p. s. m., suff. 3 p. s. m. (§ 25. No. 2 e)	ירה
הוֹרֻנִי	id. imp. pl. masc., suff. 1 pers. sing.	ירה
הוֹרִי	Kal part. act. pl. m., suff. 1 p. s. fr. הוֹרַי] 9 a.	הרה
הוֹרִיד	Hiph. pret. 3 pers. sing. masc.	ירד
הוֹרִידוּ	id. pret. 3 p. pl. m., or (Ge. 43. 11) imp. pl. m.	ירד
הוֹרִידִי	id. imp. sing. fem.	ירד
הוֹרִדֵמוֹ	id. imp. sing. masc., suff. 3 pers. pl.	ירד
הוֹרֵשׁ	Hiph. inf. absolute	ירש
הוֹרֵשׁ	id. pret. 3 pers. sing. masc.	ירש
הוֹרִישׁ	id. pret., or inf. with suff. 3 pers. sing. masc.	ירש
הוֹרִישׁוּ	id. pret. 3 pers. pl. masc.	ירש
הוֹרִישֵׁם	id. inf., suff. 3 pers. pl. masc.	ירש

הוֹרֵיתִי	ו Hiph. pret. 1 pers. sing.; acc. shifted to ult. by conv. ו (§ 8. rem. 7)	ירה
הוֹרֵיתִיךָ	ו id., suff. 2 pers. sing. masc.	ירה
הוּרַם	Hoph. pret. 3 pers. sing. masc. [for הוֹרַם]	רום
הוֹרַקְנִי	Hiph. imp. sing. masc., suff. 1 pers. sing.	ירד
הוּרַק	Hoph. pret. 3 pers. sing. masc.	רוק
הוֹרֵשׁ	ו Hiph. inf. abs.	ירש
הוֹרַשְׁתָּ	id. pret. 2 pers. sing. masc.	ירש
הוֹרַשְׁתִּים	ו id. pret. 1 pers. sing., suff. 3 pers. pl. masc.	ירש
הוֹרַשְׁתָּם	ו id. pret. 2 pers. s. m., suff. 3 pers. pl. m.	ירש
הוֹרַשְׁתֶּם	ו id. pret. 2 pers. pl. masc.	ירש
הוֹרַשְׁתֻּנוּ	id. pret. 2 pers. sing. masc., suff. 1 pers. pl.	ירש
הוֹרָתִי	Kal part. act. sing. fem., suff. 1 pers. sing. [from הוֹרָה dec. 10, from הֹרֶה masc.]	הרה
הוֹרָתָם	id., suff. 3 pers. pl. masc.	הרה
הוֹרֵתַנִי	Hiph. pret. 2 pers. sing. masc., suff. 1 pers. sing. (for תַּנִי § 2. rem. 1)	ירה
הוֹשֵׁב	Hiph. imp. sing. masc.	ישב
הוּשַׁב	Hoph. pret. 3 pers. sing. masc.	שוב
הוֹשִׁבוֹתִים	ו Hiph. pret. 1 p. s., suff. 3 p. pl. m. mixed form of פ"ע & פ"י, as הוֹשַׁבְתִּים & הֲשִׁיבוֹתִים	ישב
הוֹשַׁבְתִּי	Hiph. pret. 1 pers. sing.	ישב
הוֹשַׁבְתִּי	ו id. id. acc. shifted by ו conv. (§ 8. rem. 7)	ישב
הוֹשַׁבְתִּיךְ	ו id. id., suff. 2 pers. sing. fem.	ישב
הוֹשַׁבְתִּים	ו id., suff. 3 pers. pl. masc.	ישב
הוּשַׁבְתֶּם	ו Hoph. pret. 3 pers. pl. masc.	ישב
הוֹשִׁיבוּ	ו Hiph. imp. pl. masc.	ישב
הוֹשִׁיבֵנִי	id. pret. 3 pers. sing. masc., suff. 1 pers. sing.	ישב
הוֹשִׁיעַ	ו Hiph. pret. 3 pers. sing. masc.; or inf. constr.	ישע
הוֹשִׁיעָה	ו id. pret. 3 pers. sing. fem.; or imp. sing. masc. with parag. ה	ישע
הוֹשִׁיעוֹ	id. pret. 3 pers. sing. m., suff. 3 pers. sing. m.	ישע
הוֹשִׁיעָם	ו id. id., suff. 3 pers. pl. masc.	ישע
הוֹשִׁיעֵנוּ	ו id. imp. sing. masc., suff. 1 pers. pl.	ישע
הוֹשִׁיעֵנִי	ו id. id., suff. 1 pers. sing.	ישע
הוֹשָׁמָע	(for יְהוֹשָׁמָע) pr. name masc. 1 Ch. 3. 18.	
הוֹשַׁע	Hiph. imp. sing. masc.	
הוֹשֵׁעַ	ו id. pret. 3 pers. sing. masc., for הוֹשִׁיעַ	ישע
הוֹשֵׁעַ	ו id. inf. abs.	ישע
הוֹשֵׁעַ	'pr. name masc.	ישע
הוֹשָׁעָה	defect. for הוֹשִׁיעָה (q.v.)	
הוֹשַׁעְיָה	pr. name masc.	
הוֹשָׁעוּ	ו Niph. imp. pl. masc.	
הוֹשַׁעְנִי	ו Hiph. imp. sing. masc., suff. 1 pers. sing	ישע
הוֹשַׁעְתָּ	id. pret. 2 pers. sing. masc.	ישע
הוֹשַׁעְתָּ	ו id. id. acc. shifted by ו conv. (§ 8. rem. 7)	ישע

a Je. 11. 4. Jos. 2. 3.   c Ps. 45. 3.   e Ge. 39. 1; 44. 21.   f Jos. 2. 18.   h Ps. 59. 12.   k Jos. 14. 12.   m Ge. 47. 6.   o Is. 5. 8.   p Je. 2. 27.
b Ge. 19. 5.   d Nu. 25. 4.   Ge. 43. 22.   g 2 Ki. 12. 3.   Ju. 1. 28.   l Ge. 42. 28.   1 Ki. 21. 10.   q Ps. 71. 2.
Eze. 42. 15.   2 Sa. 21. 6.   1 Ki. 2. 9.   i Job 6. 24.   Ju. 2. 23.   Zec. 10. 6.   1 Sa. 9. 16.   r Zec. 12. 7.
Ps. 25. 17.   Ps. 44. 23.   Eze. 31. 18.   Ge. 49. 26.   Ca. 3. 4.   Le. 23. 43.   Ps. 34. 7.   s Is. 45. 22.
1 Ki. 22. 34.   2 Ki. 16. 17.   Eze. 26. 20.   Am. 3. 11.   Ex. 29. 27.   Ho. 2. 7.   Eze. 26. 20.   t 2 Ki. 16. 7.
2 Sa. 14. 30.   n Eze. 32. 18.   Joel 4. 2.   La. 2. 18.   Je. 48. 11.   Ps. 119. 102.   Ho. 11. 11.   2 Sa. 14. 4
      aa Job 26. 2

הוֹשַׁעְתִּי	} id. pret. 1 pers. sing., acc. id.	ישע
הוֹשַׁעְתִּיךָ	} id. id., suff. 2 pers. sing. masc.	ישע
הוֹשַׁעְתִּים	} id. id., suff. 3 pers. pl. masc.	ישע
הוֹשַׁעְתֶּם	id. pret. 2 pers. pl. masc.	ישע
הוֹשַׁעְתָּנוּ	id. pret. 2 pers. sing. masc., suff. 1 pers. pl.	ישע
הַיֹּשֵׁר	Kh. הוֹשֵׁר, K. הַיָּשָׁר Hiph. imp. sing. masc.	ישר
	(§ 20. No. 1)	
הֲוָת הֲוָת/	} Chald. Peal pret. 3 pers. sing. fem.; } ו bef. (-:)	הוה
הֹוַת	} ו noun sing. fem. constr. of [הַוָּה] dec. 10.	הוה
הֹוּת	id. pl. (for הַוּוֹת)	הוה
הוֹתֵב	} Ch. Aph. pret. 3 pers. sing. m. (§ 47. r. 4)	יתב
הוֹתִיר	pr. name masc.	יתר
הוֹתִיר	Hiph. pret. 3 pers. sing. masc.; or inf. constr.	יתר
הוֹתִירְךָ	} id., suff. 2 pers. sing. masc.	יתר
הוּתַל	Hoph. pret. 3 pers. sing. masc.	תלל
הוֹתֵר	Hiph. imp. sing. masc.	יתר
הוֹתֵר	} id. inf. abs.	יתר
הוֹתִרָה	id. pret. 3 pers. sing. fem. [for הוֹתִירָה]	יתר
הוֹתִרְךָ	} id. with suff. 2 pers. sing. masc.	יתר
הוֹתַרְתִּי	} id. pret. 1 pers. sing.; acc. on ult. by conv.	יתר
	ו (§ 8. rem. 7)	
הַזֹּאת הַזֹּאת/	pref. } pref. } pron. demon. sing. fem. see	זה
הַזֹּאתָה	pref. ה } id.,Kheth. זֹאתָה/ id. with parag. ה, K. זֹאת, see	זה
הַזָּב	} ו pref. id. X Kal part. act. sing. masc.	זוב
הַזְּבוּלֹנִי	pref. id. X gent. n. from זְבוּלֹן	זבל
הַזֶּבַח הַזָּבַח/	} ו pref. id. X n. m. s. dec. 6a. (with suff.) } זִבְחִי but see § 35. rem. 2)	זבח
הַזֹּבֵחַ	pref. id. X Kal part. act. sing. masc. dec. 7b.	זבח
הַזְּבָחִים	pref. id. X noun masc., pl. of זֶבַח dec. 6. comp. הַזָּבַח	זבח
הַזֹּבְחִים	pref. id. X Kal part. act. m., pl. of זֹבֵחַ d. 7b.	זבח
הַזָּדוֹן	pref. id. X noun masc. sing. dec. 3a.	זדה
הַזֵּדִים	pref. id. X adj. masc., pl. of זֵד dec. 1a.	זוד
[הָזָה]	to dream, to talk in one's dream, Is. 56. 10; Prof. Lee, to nod, doze.	
הַזֶּה	Hiph. imp. sing. masc.	נזה
הַזֶּה הַזֶּה/	pref. ה } pref. ה } & : pron. demon. sing. masc.	זה
הִזָּה	} Hiph. pret. 3 pers. sing. masc.	נזה
הַזָּהָב	} prf. ה X noun masc. sing. dec. 4a.	זהב
הִזְהִיר	} Hiph. pret. 3 pers. sing. masc.	זהר
הַזְהֵר	Niph. imp. sing. masc.	זהר

הִזְהִירֹה	} Hiph. pret. 3 pers. sing. masc., suff. 3 pers. sing. masc., K. רו'	זהר
הִזְהַרְתָּ	id. pret. 2 pers. sing. masc.	זהר
הִזְהַרְתָּ הִזְהַרְתָּה/	} id. id.; acc. shifted by conv. ו (§ 8. rem. 7, comp. 5)	זהר
הִזְהַרְתּוֹ	} id. id., suff. 3 pers. sing. masc.	זהר
הִזְהַרְתֶּם	} id pret. 2 pers. pl. masc.	זהר
הַזּוּזִים	pref. ה X pr. name of a people	זוז
הַזּוֹנָה	pref. id. X fem. of the following, dec. 10.	זנה
הַזֹּנֶה	pref. id. X Kal part. act. sing. masc. dec. 9a.	זנה
הַזּוּרָה	} pref. id. X Kal part. pass. [זוּר] with term. ה— [for זוּרָה] comp. לְנָה	זור
הַזֹּחֶלֶת	pref. id. X pr. name, see אֶבֶן	אבן
הֵזִידוּ	Hiph. pret. 3 pers. pl. masc.	זוד
הַזֵּידוֹנִים	pref. ה X noun masc., pl. of זֵידוֹן dec. 1b.	זוד
הַזִּיל	Hiph. pret. 3 pers. sing. masc.	נזל
הִזִּילוּהָ	Hiph.pret. 3 pers. pl. masc. with suff., 3 pers. sing. fem., Chald. inflexion (§ 18. rem. 14)	זלל
הַזִּים	Kal part. act. masc., pl. of [הָזָה] dec. 9a.	הזה
הַזֵּיפִים	pref. ה X gent. noun pl. [of זִיף from זִיף]	זוף
הִזִּיר	} Hiph. pret. 3 pers. sing. masc.	נזר
הִזִּירוֹ	id. inf., suff. 3 pers. sing. m. from הַזִּיר d. 1b.	נזר
הַזַּיִת	pref. ה X noun masc. sing. dec. 6h.	זית
הִזֵּיתָ	} Hiph. pret. 2 pers. sing. masc. (§ 24. rem. 14); acc. shifted by ו conv. (§ 8. rem. 7)	נזה
הַזֵּיתִים	pref. ה X noun masc., pl. of זַיִת dec. 6h	זית
הִזַּכּוּ	Hithp. imp. pl. masc. [for הִתְזַכּוּ]	זכה
הִזְכַּרְתִּי	} Hiph. pret. 1 pers. sing.; ו before (-:)	זכר
הַזְכִּיר	Hiph. inf. construct	זכר
הִזְכִּיר	id. pret. 3 pers. sing. masc.	זכר
הַזְכִּירוּ	id. imp. pl. masc.	זכר
הַזְכִּירֵנִי	id. imp. sing. masc. with 1 pers. sing.	זכר
הַזֶּכֶר	pref. ה X noun masc. sing. dec. 4a.	זכר
הַזִּכָּרוֹן	pref. id. X noun masc. sing. dec. 3 c.	זכר
הַזְּכָרִים	pref. id. X noun masc., pl. of זָכָר dec. 4ѕ.	זכר
הַזְכַּרְכֶם	Hiph. inf. [הַזְכֵּר Chald. form.] 2 pers. pl. m.	זכר
הִזָּכֶרְכֶם	Niph. inf. [הִזָּכֵר] suff. 2 pers. s. m. dec. 7 b	זכר
הַזִּכְרֹנוֹת	pref. ה X noun masc. with pl. fem. term. from זִכָּרוֹן dec. 3 c.	זכר
הִזְכַּרְתָּנִי	} Hiph. pret. 2 pers. sing. masc., suff. 1 pers. s.	זכר
הַזַּלְזַלִּים	pref. ה X noun masc., pl. of [זַלְזַל] dec. 8d.	זלזל
הַזֹּלְלִים	pref. id. X Kal part. act., pl. of [זָל] dec. 1a.	זול
הַזִּמָּה	pref. id. X noun fem. sing. dec. 10.	ימם
הַזְּמוֹרָה	pref. id. X noun fem. sing. dec. 10.	זמר
הַזָּמִיר	pref. id. X noun masc. sing.	זמר
הַזְּמַנְתּוּן	Chald. Kh. הַזְדְּמִנְתּוּן, K. הַזְמִנְתּוּן Aph. or	

a 1 Ch. 19. 12.	d Mi. 7. 3.	n Ruth 2. 18.	t 1 Sa. 2. 15.	z Ec. 12. 12.	h Ne. 9. 10, 16, 29.	o Nu. 6. 6.	u Nu. 5. 18.	a Ge. 40. 14.
b Ho. 1. 7.	e Pr. 10. 3.	k Ezr. 4. 10.	v 2 Ch. 7. 1.	i 2 Ki. 6. 10.	i Ps. 124. 5.	p Ex. 29. 21.	v Eze. 21. 29.	b Is. 18. 5.
c Ju. 12. 2.	f Ezr. 4. 19.	l Je. 26. 6.	w Eze. 7. 10.	k Ex. 18. 20.	k Is. 48. 21.	q Is. 1. 16.	w Is. 43. 21.	c Is. 46. 6.
d Ezr. 4. 24.	g De. 30. 9.	m Le. 15. 33.	x Je. 48. 2.	l Eze.3.18,20,21.	l Is. 49. 1.	r Est. 6. 1.	x Job 9. 30.	d Ca. 2. 12.
e Da. 2. 35.	h Is. 44. 20.	o Le. 7. 17.	y Nu. 8. 7.	m Eze. 6. 9.	m Is. 43. 26.	s Ne. 6. 12.	y 2 Sa. 18. 18.	e Da. 2. 9.
	i Ps. 79. 11.	p Eze. 40. 42.	z Eze. 23. 3.	n Is. 29. 5.	n Nu. 6. 12.	t 2 Sa. 18. 18.	z Je. 44. 7.	f 2 Ch. 19. 10.

Ithpa. [for חִתְחַמְּנְתּוּן, אֵתָ' § 47. rem. 4] pret. 2 pers. pl. masc. . . . זמן

הַזָּנָב pref. ה (noun masc. sing. dec. 4a. . זנב

הַזְּנָבוֹת pref. id. (id. pl. absolute (construct זַנְבוֹת § 33. rem. 1) . . זנב

הַזְנֵה Hiph. inf. absolute . . . זנה

הִזְנוּ '(id. pret. 3 pers. pl. . . . זנה

הַזֹּנוֹת '(Kal part. act. fem., pl. of זוֹנָה dec. 10, from זֹנָה masc. זנה

הִזְנִיחַ Hiph. pret. 3 pers. sing. masc. זנה

הִזְנִיחָם id. with suff. 3 pers. pl. masc. זנה

הַזֹּנִים pref. ה (Kal part. act. m., pl. of זוֹנָה dec. 9a. זנה

הִזְנֵיתָ Hiph. pret. 2 pers. sing. asc. (§ 24. rem. 14) זנה

הַזַּעַם pref. ה (noun masc. sing. dec. 6d. (for זַעַם 35. rem. 2) . . זעם

הַזְעֵק Hiph. imp. sing. m. [for הַזְעֵק § 11. rem. 5] זעק

הַזְּעָקָה pref. ה (noun fem. s. dec. 11c. (§ 42. rem. 1) זעק

הַזּוּפִים pref. id. (gent. noun pl. [of זִיפִי fr. זִיף] . זוף

הַזָּקֵן pref. id. (noun com. sing. dec. 4a. זקן

הַזָּקֵן pref. id. (adj. and subst. masc. sing. dec. 5a. זקן

הַזְּקֵנִים '(pref. id. (id. pl. absolute . . . זקן

הַזָּר '(pref. id. (Kal part. act. sing. m. dec. 1a. זור

הַזְּרוֹעַ pref. id. (noun com. sing. dec. 1a. זקן

הַזַּרְחִי pref. id. (patronym. of זֶרַח . . . זרח

הַזָּרִים pref. id. (Kal part. act. m., pl. of זָר dec. 1a. זור

הַזֶּרַע / הַזָּרַע pref. id. (noun masc. sing. dec. 6a. (§ 35. rem. 2 & 5) . . זרע

הַזָּרֻעַ '(pref. id. (noun com. sing. dec. 1a. . זרע

הַזְּרֻעִים pref. id. (noun masc. pl. [of זְרֻעַ] . זרע

הַזֹּרְעִים pref. id. (Kal part. act. m., pl. of זֹרֵעַ dec. 7b. זרע

הַזֹּרֵק pref. id. (Kal part. act. sing. masc. זרק

הֻזַּרְתֶּם '(Hiph. pret. 2 pers. pl. masc. . נזר

הֶחָבְּאוּ Hoph. pret. 3 pers. pl. (הֶחְבָּאוּ comp. § 8. rem. 7] חבא

הֶחְבִּאַתָּה Hiph. pret. 3 pers. sing. fem. with parag. ה (§ 11. rem. 1) . . . חבא

הֶחְבִּיאָה id. 3 pers. sing. fem. חבא

הֶחְבִּיאַנִי id. pret. 3 pers. sing. masc., suff. 1 pers. sing. (§ 11. rem. 1, & 2. rem. 1) . חבא

הַחֶבֶל pref. ה (noun m. s. dec. 6. (§ 35. rem. 4) חבל

הַחֵבֶל pref. id. (noun masc. sing. dec. 7b. חבל

הַחֹבְלִים pref. id. (Kal part. act. m., pl. of חֹבֵל d. 7b. חבל

הַחֶבְרִי pref. id. (patronym. of חֶבֶר . חבר

הַחֶבְרֹנִי pref. id. (patronym. of חֶבְרוֹן . חבר

הַחֹבֶרֶת pref. id. (noun fem. sing. חבר

הַחֲבִתִּים pref. id. (noun masc., pl. of [חֲבִת] dec. 8b. חבת

הֶחָג ו/ pref. ה bef. חָ for הַ (noun m. s. dec. 8a. חג

הֶחָנָב pref. id. (noun masc. sing. dec. 4c. חנב

הֶחָגוּר/ pref. id. (Kal part. p. sing. masc. dec. 3a. חגר

הֶחַגִּי pref. ה (patronym. [for חַגִּי] from חַגִּי . חגג

הֶחָדֵל ו pref. ה bef. חָ for הַ (adj. masc. s. dec. 5a. חדל

הֶחְדַלְתִּי pref. id. interr. (Kal pret. 1 pers. sing. (The form seems to be an error of the transcribers, and to stand for הֶחָדַלְתִּי, like הֶחֳרָבוֹת for הֶחֳרָבוֹת. Some codices have הֶחָדַלְתִּי, Hiph. without the interr. ה) חדל

הֶחָדֵר pref. ה (noun masc. dec. 6. (§ 35. rem. 4) חדר

הֶחַדְרָה pref. id. } id. with paragogic ה . חדר
הֶחָדְרָה pref. ה bef. חָ for הַ }

הֶחָדֶרֶת pref. ה (Kal part. act. sing. fem. חדר

הֶחָדָשׁ ו/ pref. id. (noun masc. sing. dec. 6c. חרש

הֶחָדָשׁ pref. ה bef. חָ for הַ (adj. masc. sing. dec. 4c. חדש

הֶחֲדָשָׁה pref. ה (fem. of the prec. . חדש

הֶחֲדָשִׁים pref. id. (adj. masc., pl. of חָדָשׁ dec. 4c. חדש

הֶחֳדָשִׁים pref. ה bef. חָ for הַ (n. m., pl. of חֹדֶשׁ d. 6c חדש

הַחוֹחַ pref. ה (noun masc. sing. dec. 1a. חוח

הַחוֹמִים pref. id. (id. pl., also once חֲנָמִים (§ 35. r.13) חוח

הַחוּט ו pref. id. (noun masc. sing. חוט

הַחוֹמֵא ו pref. id. (Kal part. act. sing. masc. for חוֹמֵא § 23. rem. 9. . . חטא

הַחִוִּי ו/ pref. id. (pr. name of a people חוה

הַחֲוִילָה pref. id. (pr. name of a country, see חֲוִילָה

הַחִיל pref. id. (noun masc. sing. . חול

הַחִילָה pref. id. (fem. of the foll., dec. 10. חלה

הַחוֹלָה pref. id. (Kal part. act. masc. sing. חלה

הַחוֹמָה pref. id. (noun fem. sing. dec. 10. חמה

הַחֲנֵינִי Chald. Aph. imp. pl. masc., suff. 1 pers. sing. חוה

הַחֹנִים } pref. ה (Kal part. act. masc., pl. of
הַחֹנָם ו/ חֹנֶה dec. 9a. } חנה

הַחֹסֶה ו pref. id. (Kal part. act. sing. m., dec. 9a. חסה

הַחֹסִים pref. id. (id. pl., absolute state . חסה

הַחוּפָמִי pref. id. (patronym. or חוּפָם, see חֻפִּים חפף

הַחִיץ pref. id. (noun masc. sing. dec. 1a. חוץ

הַחוּצָה pref. id. (id. with paragogic ה חוץ

הַחוֹר pref. id. (noun masc. sing. dec. 1a. חור

הַחֹזֶה pref. id. (noun masc. sing. dec. 9a. חזה

הֶחָזֶה pref. ה bef. חָ for הַ (noun masc. dec. 9b. חזה

הֶחָזוֹן pref. id. (noun masc. sing. dec. 3a. חזה

הֶחָזוֹת pref. id. (n. m. with pl. f. term. from חָזֶה חזה

הַחִזָּיוֹן pref. ה (noun masc. sing., dec. 3c. חזה

הַחֹזִים ו/ pref. id. (Kal part. act. masc. or subst., pl. of חֹזֶה dec. 9a. חזה

a Is. 9.14. | g 2 Ch. 29.19. | m Is. 15.8. | t Le. 7.14. | z 2 Sa. 8.2. | f Ju. 18.17. | s Is. 66.22. | q Pr. 27.3. | x Nu. 2.12.
b Ju. 15.4. | h 2 Ch. 11.14. | n Da. 11.6. | u Le. 15.31. | a Jon. 1.6. | g Eze. 3.27. | n Ne. 10.34. | r Eze. 34.4, 16. | y Is. 57.13.
c Ho. 4.18. | i Le. 20.5. | o Eze. 7.21. | v Is. 42.22. | b Zec. 11.14. | h Ju. 9.9, 11, 13. | o Ca. 2.2. | s Mal. 1.13. | z Le. 9.20, 21.
d Ho. 6.10, 18. | j Ho. 6.17. | p De. 7.19. | w 1 Ch. 9.31. | c Eze. 21.19. | i Ec. 4.12. | p Da. 2.6. | a 2 Sa. 7.17.
e Ke. 34.16. | k Da. 8.19. | q Da. 1.12. | x Jos. 6.25. | d 2 Ch. 7.9. | k Est. 9.22. | j Is. 65.20. | t Na. 3.17. | b Eze. 13.16.
f 1 Ki. 52.38. | l 2 Sa. 20.4. | r Ps. 126.5. | y Is. 49.2. | e Ca. 5.4.

Hebrew	Description	Root
הֶחֱזִיק	וֹ Hiph. pret. 3 pers. sing. masc.	חזק
הֶחֱזִיקָה	id. pret. 3 pers. sing. fem.	חזק
הַחֲזִיקוּ	id. imp. pl. masc.	חזק
הֶחֱזִיקוּ	id. pret. 3 pers. pl. masc.	חזק
הַחֲזִיקִי	id. imp. sing. fem.	חזק
הַחֲזִיקִי	id. inf. הַחֲזִיק (§ 11. rem. 4, comp. § 13. rem. 9) with suff. 1 pers. sing.	חזק
הֶחֱזִיקֵךְ	id. pret. 3 pers. sing. m., suff. 2 pers. s. fem.	חזק
הֶחֱזִיקַתְהוּ	id. pret. 3 pers. sing. fem., suff. 3 pers. s. m.	חזק
הֶחָזִיר	pref. הַ)(noun masc. sing.	חזר
הַחֲזֵק	Hiph. imp. sing. masc.	חזק
הֶחָזָק	pref. הַ bef. חָ for חַ)(adj. masc. sing. dec. 4 a & c (§ 33. rem. 1)	חזק
הַחֲזָקָה	pref. הַ)(fem. of the prec.	חזק
הֶחֱזַקְתָּ	וֹ Hiph. pret. 2 pers. sing. masc.	חזק
הֶחֱזַקְתִּי	id. pret. 1 pers. sing.	חזק
הֶחֱזַקְתִּי	id. id. acc. shifted by conv. וֹ (§ 8. rem. 7, and § 13. rem. 10)	חזק
הֶחֱזַקְתִּיךָ	id. id. suff. 2 pers. sing. masc.	חזק
הֶחֱזַקְתָּנוּ	id. pret. 3 pers. sing. fem., suff. 1 pers. pl.	חזק
הֶחֱזַקְתָּנִי	id. id., suff. 1 pers. sing.	חזק
הַחֲטָאָה	pref. הַ)(noun fem. sing. [from חַטָּא masc.]	חטא
הַחֲטָאִים	pref. id.)(noun masc., pl. of [חַטָּא] dec. 1 b.	חטא
הַחַטָּאת	וֹ pref. id.)(noun fem. sing. (§ 39. No. 4, & § 44. rem. 5)	חטא
הַחַטָּאת	pref. הַ id.)(Kal part. act. fem. s. [for חֹטֵאת § 23. rem. 4]	חטא
הַחֲטָה	וֹ pref. id.)(noun fem. sing. (pl. חִטִּים)	חטה
הַחֲטִי	Hiph. inf. constr. for הַחֲטִיא (§ 23. rem. 7)	חטא
הֶחֱטִיא / הֶחֱטִיא	} id. pret. 3 pers. sing. masc. (§ 23. rem. 7)	חטא
הֶחֱטִיאוּ	id. pret. 3 pers. pl.	חטא
הֶחֱטִיאָם	וֹ id. pret. 3 pers. s. m., suff. 3 pers. pl. m.	חטא
הַחִטִּים	וֹ pref. הַ)(n. f. with pl. m. term. from חִטָּה	חטה
הַחַי	pref. הַ for הֶ)(	חיי
הֶחָי	וֹ pref. הֶ dag. impl.)(adj. masc. sing. dec. 8 d. (§ 37. rem. 6); pref. הֶ bef. חָ for הַ	חיי
הַחַיָּה	pref. id.)(noun fem. sing. dec. 10.	חוד
הַחַיָּה	pref. id.)(adj. (Le. 14. 6, 7, 51) or subst. fem. dec. 10, from חַי masc.	חיי
הֶחֱיָה	Hiph. pret. 3 pers. sing. masc.	חיה
הַחֲיֹה	וֹ id. inf. absolute	חיה
הַחֲיוּ	id. imp. pl. masc.	חיה
הַחַיּוֹת	וֹ pref. הַ)(noun fem. pl. of חַיָּה dec. 10.	חיי
הַחַיִּים	pref. id.)(adj. and subst. masc., pl. of חַי dec. 8 d. (§ 37. rem. 6)	חיי

Hebrew	Description	Root
הַחֲיֵינִי	וֹ Hiph. imp. sing. masc., suff. 1 pers. sing.	חיה
הֶחֱיֵיתִי	id. pret. 1 pers. sing.	חיה
הַחֲיִיתֶם	pref. הַ interr. for הֲ)(Piel. pret. 2 pers. pl. m.	זיה
הֵחֵיל	וֹ pref. הֵ art.	חול
הֶחָיִל	pref. הֶ id. bef. חָ for }noun m. s. dec. 6 h.	חול
הַחֲיָלִים	pref. הַ)(id. pl., abs. state (§ 35. rem. 12)	חול
הַחִיצוֹן	pref. הַ)(adj. masc. sing.	חוץ
הַחִיצֹנָה	} pref. id.)(fem. of the prec.	חוץ
הֶחָזָק	וֹ pref. id.)(noun masc. sing. dec. 1 a.	חזק
הֵחִישׁוּ	Hiph. pret. 3 pers. pl.	חוש
הֶחֱיִתֶם	וֹ Hiph. pret. 2 pers. pl. masc. (§ 13. r. 10)	חיה
הֶחֱיִתָנוּ	id. pret. 2 pers. sing. masc., suff. 1 pers. pl.	חיה
הַחֲכִילָה	pref. הַ)(pr. name of a hill	חכל
הֶחָכָם	pref. הֶ bef. חָ for הַ)(adj. masc. dec. 4 c.	חכם
הַחָכְמָה	וֹ pref. הַ)(noun fem. sing. (no pl. abs.)	חכם
הַחַכְמוֹת	pref. id.)(adj. fem., pl. of חֲכָמָה dec. 11 c. from חָכָם masc.	חכם
הַחֲכָמִים	וֹ pref. id.)(noun m., pl. of חָכָם dec. 4 c.	חכם
הָחֵל	Hiph. inf., or imp. sing. masc.	חלל
הַחֵל	pref. הַ)(noun masc. sing. dec. 1 a.	חול
הַחֵל	pref. הַ)(noun masc. sing.	חלל
הֵחֵל	Hiph. pret. 3 pers. sing. masc.; or (Eze. 20. 9, 14, 22) Niph. inf. for הַחֵל § 18. rem. 14]	חלל
הַחֵלֶב	pref. הַ)(noun masc. sing. dec. 6 d.	חלב
הֶחָלָב	pref. הֶ bef. חָ for הַ)(noun masc. dec. 4 c.	חלב
הַחֲלָבִים	וֹ pref. id.)(noun masc., pl. of חֵלֶב dec. 6. (§ 35. rem. 6)	חלב
הַחֶלֶד	pref. id.)(noun masc. sing.	חלד
הַחַלָּה	pref. id.)(noun fem. sing. dec. 10.	חלל
הֶחֱלָה	Hiph. pret. 3 pers. sing. fem.	חלל
הֶחֱלוּ	id. pret. 3 pers. pl.	חלל
הֶחֱלוּ	Hiph. pret. 3 pers. pl.	חלה
הַחֲלֹם	pref. הַ)(noun masc. sing. dec. 1 a.	חלם
הַחַלּוֹן	pref. id.)(noun com. sing. dec. 1 b.	חלל
הַחַלּוֹנִים	וֹ pref. id.)(id. pl.	חלל
הֶחָלָץ	וֹ pref. הֶ bef. חָ for הַ)(Kal part. p. masc. dec. 3 a.	חלץ
הֶחֱלֹתָ	Hiph. pret. 2 pers. sing. masc. [for הַחֲלֹת by Chaldaism, § 18. rem. 14 note]	חלל
הַחֲלִי	pref. הַ)(for חֳלִי (§ 35. r. 14) n. m. s. dec. 6 k.	חלה
הֶחֱלִיא	Hiph. pret. 3 pers. sing. masc. for הֶחֱלָה (§ 24. rem. 17)	חלה
הַחֲלִיפוּ	וֹ Hiph. imp. pl. masc.	חלף

a Je. 51. 12.   g Is. 27. 1.   m Je. 8. 21.   s 2 Ki. 17. 21.   y Eze. 1. 14.   a Eze. 43. 17.   n Job 28. 12, 20.   r 2 Ch. 35. 14.   y Joel 2. 9.
b Na. 3. 14.   h Le. 25. 35.   n 1 Sa. 17. 35.   t 1 Ch. 21. 23.   z Is. 38. 16.   b Ju. 20. 37.   o Je. 9. 16.   s Le. 11. 29.   z Eze. 41. 16.
c Ge. 21. 18.   i 1 Sa. 17. 35.   o Eze. 18. 4, 20.   u Ge. 6. 19.   a Nu. 22. 33.   c Ju. 8. 19.   p Ec. 9. 1.   t Le. 34. 5.   a 2 Ch. 21. 15.
d Eze. 30. 25.   k Ex. 9. 32.   p Ec. 7. 2.   v Nu. 31. 15.   b Ge. 2. 13.   q Ob. 1. 20.   u Ju. 20. 40.   b Is. 53. 10.
e Ex. 31. 32.   l Is. 41. 9.   q Je. 32. 35.   w Jos. 9. 20.   c Eze. 47. 25.   r Ge. 47. 25.   v Le. 10. 10.
f Mi. 4. 9.   a Je. 6. 24.   r 2 Ki. 13. 6.   x Nu. 31. 18.   d Le. 10. 10.   w Ho. 7. 5.   c Ge. 35. 2.
g Je. 50. 43.

הַחֲלִיפוֹת	pref. הַ)(noun fem., pl. of [חֲלִיפָה] dec. 10.	חלף
הֶחֱלִיק	Hiph. pret. 3 pers. sing. masc.	חלק
הֶחֱלִיקָה	id. pret. 3 pers. sing. fem.	חלק
הֶחֱלִיתִי	Hoph. pret. 1 pers. sing.	חלה
הֶחֱלֵיתִי	Hiph. pret. 1 pers. sing.	חלה
הֶחָלָל	pref. הֶ bef. חָ for הַ)(adj. masc. dec. 4 c.	חלל
הַחֲלָלִים	pref. הַ)(id. pl., absolute state	חלל
הַחִלָּם	Hiph. inf. הַחֵל, for הַהֵל, by Chaldaism § 18. rem. 14], suff. 3 pers. sing. masc.	חלל
הַחֲלֹמוֹת	pref. הַ)(noun masc. with pl. fem. term. from חֲלוֹם dec. 1 a.	חלם
הַחַלָּמִישׁ	pref. id.)(noun m. s. (constr. חַלָּמִישׁ) dec. 3 c.	חלמש
הַחַלֹּנוֹת	¹וְ pref. id., &)(n. com., pl. of חַלּוֹן dec. 1 b.	חלל
הֶחֱלַף	וְ Hiph. pret. 3 pers. sing. masc.	חלף
הֶחָלְצוּ	Niph. imp. pl. masc.	חלץ
הַחֵלֶק	pref. הַ)(noun masc. sing. dec. 6 d.	חלק
הֶחָלֶק	pref. הֶ before חָ for הַ)(adj. masc. sing.	חלק
הַחֲלֻקָּה	pref. הַ)(noun fem. (sing.) dec. 12 b.	חלק
הַחֶלְקִי	pref. id.)(patronym. of חֵלֶק	חלק
הַחֲלָקִים	pref. id.)(noun masc., pl. of חֵלֶק dec. 6. (§ 35. rem. 6)	חלק
הַחַלָּשׁ	pref. id.)(noun masc. sing.	חלש
הַחִלֹּתִי	Hiph. pret. 1 pers. sing.; [for הַהִלֹּתִי, by Chaldaism § 18. rem. 14]	חלל
הַחֶמְדָּה	pref. הַ)(noun fem. sing. (no pl.)	חמד
הַחֲמֻדֹת	pref. id.)(Kal part. p. pl. fem. from [חָמוּד]	חמד
הַחֵמָה	pref. id.)(noun fem. sing. dec. 10.	חמם
הַחֵמָה	וְ pref. id.)(noun fem. s. dec. 11 b for [יֶחֱמָה]	יחם
הַחֵמָה	pref. id.)(noun fem. sing. dec. 10.	חמה
הַחֲמֹל	pref. הֶ bef. חָ for הַ)(gent. noun from חָמוּל	חמל
הַחֲמוֹר	וְ pref. id.)(noun masc. sing. dec. 1 a.	חמר
הַחֲמוֹרִים	pref. id.)(id. pl., absolute state	חמר
הַחֹמֹת	pref. id.)(noun fem., pl. of חוֹמָה dec. 1 a.	חמה
הַחֹמֶט	וְ pref. id.)(noun masc. sing.	חמט
הַחֲמִישִׁי	וְ pref. id.)(adj. ord. masc. from חָמֵשׁ	חמש
הַחֲמִישִׁית	pref. id.)(fem. of the prec.	חמש
הַחֲמָנִים	וְ pref. id.)(noun masc., pl. of [חַמָּן] dec. 1 b.	חמם
הַחֲמֻקִּים	pref. הֶ bef. חָ for הַ)(noun masc., dec. 4 c.	חמק
הַחֵמֶר	pref. הַ)(noun masc. sing. dec. 1 a.	חמר
הַחֹמֶר	וְ pref. id.)(noun masc. sing.	חמר
הַחֹמֶר	pref. id.)(noun masc. sing. dec. 6 c.	חמר
הַחֲמֹרִים	pref. id.)(noun masc., pl. of חֲמוֹר dec. 1 a.	חמר
הַחֹמֶשׁ	pref. id.)(noun masc. sing.	חמש
הַחֲמִשָּׁה	pref. id.)(num. card. masc., from חָמֵשׁ fem.	חמש

הַחֲמִשִּׁי	pref. id.)(adj. ord. masc. from חָמֵשׁ	חמש
הַחֲמִשִּׁים	pref. id.)(num. card., com., pl. of חָמֵשׁ	חמש
הַחֲמֻשִׁים	pref. id.)(Kal part. p. m., pl. of [חָמוּשׁ] d. 3 a.	חמש
הַחֲמִישִׁית	pref. id.)(adj. ord., fem. of חָמֵשׁ	חמש
הַחֲמַת	pref. id.)(noun masc. sing., constr.	חמת
הַחֲמָתִי	pref. id.)(gent. noun from חֲמָת	חמה
הַחֹמֹתִים הַחֹמָתַיִם	} pref. id.)(noun fem., du. of חוֹמָה dec. 10.	חמה
הַחֵן	pref. id.)(noun masc. sing. dec. 8 b.	חנן
הַחֲנֻטִים	pref. id.)(noun masc., pl. of [חָנֻט]	חנט
הַחֲנֻיּוֹת	pref. id.)(noun f., pl. of חָנֻת, comp. מַלְכֻיּוֹת, from [כֻת]	חנה
הַחֹנִים	וְ pref. id.)(Kal part. act. m., fr. חָנָה d. 9 a.	חנה
הַחֲנִית וְ הַחֲנִית	וְ Kh. } pref. id.)(noun fem. sing. dec. 1.	חנה
הַחֲנִיתַיִם	pref. id.)(id. pl., absolute state	חנה
הַחֲנֻכִי	pref. id.)(patronym. of חֲנוֹךְ	חנך
הַחִנָּם	pref. הַ interr. for הֲ)(adv., from חֵן and the term. ־ָם.	חנן
הַחֶסֶד	וְ pref. ה art.)(n. m. s. (suff. חַסְדִּי) d. 6 a.	חסד
הַחֲסָדִים	pref. ה id.)(id. pl., absolute state	חסד
הַחֲסוּת	וְ pref. הֶ bef. חָ for הַ)(noun fem. sing.	חסה
הַחֲסִידָה	וְ pref. הַ)(noun fem. sing.	חסד
הֶחָסִיל	וְ pref. הֶ bef. חָ for הַ)(noun masc. sing.	חסל
הַחֹסִים	pref. הַ)(Kal part. act. m., pl. of חֹסֶה d. 9 a.	חסה
הֶחֱסִיר	Hiph. pret. 3 pers. sing. masc. (§ 13. rem. 9)	חסר
הֶחָסֹן	pref. הֶ bef. חָ for הַ)(adj. masc. sing.	חסן
הֶחֱסַנּוּ	Hiph. pret. 1 pers. pl.	חסן
הֶחְפִּיר	Hiph. pret. 3 pers. sing. masc. (§ 13. rem. 9)	חפר
הַחֵפֶץ	pref. הַ)(noun masc. sing. dec. 6. (§ 35. r. 6)	חפץ
הֶחָפֵץ	pref. הֶ bef. חָ for הַ)(adj. masc. sing. dec. 5 c.	חפץ
הֶחָפֹץ	pref. הֶ id. interr.)(Kal inf. absolute	חפץ
הַחָפְשִׁים	pref. הַ art.)(adj. masc., pl. of חָפְשִׁי dec. 5 c.	חפץ
הַחֹפֶר	pref. id.)(pr. n., see נַחַל חֹפֶר	נת
הַחֶפְרִי	pref. id.)(patronym. of חֵפֶר	חפר
הַחָפְשׁוּת הַחָפְשִׁית	} pref. id.)(noun fem. sing.; Kh. חֻשׁוֹת	חפש
הַחֹצֵב	pref. id.)(Kal part. act. sing. masc. dec. 7 b.	חצב
הַחִיצוֹנָה	pref. id.)(adj. fem. sing. from חִיצוֹן masc.	חוץ
הַחֲצִי וְ הַחֲצִי	וְ } pref. id.)(noun masc. sing. dec. 6 i, (suff. § 35. rem. 14)	חצה
הַחֲצִים	pref. id.)(Kh. הַחֲצִי q.v., K. הַחִצִּים (q.v.)	חצץ
הַחֲצִיוֹן	וְ pref. id.)(n. m. s., suff. 3 p. s. m. fr. חֲצִי	חצה
הַחִצִּים	pref. id.)(noun masc., pl. of חֵץ dec. 8 b.	חצץ
הֶחָצִיר	pref. הֶ bef. חָ for הַ)(noun masc. s. dec. 3 a.	חצר
הַחִיצֹנָה	defect. for הַחִיצוֹנָה q. v.	חוצי

a Ju. 14. 19.	e Eze. 41. 16.	i Ge. 27. 15.	n Ge. 11. 3.	r Ge. 50. 3.	w Ge. 32. 11.	⊞ Ex. 16. 18.	ǁ Ne. 1. 11.	☆ 1 Ki. 16. 21.
b Ps. 36. 3.	f Ge. 31. 7.	k Jer. 25. 15.	o Je. 37. 16.	s Is. 30. 3.	x Is. 1. 31.	⊞ 2 Ch. 26. 21.	‖ 1 Sa. 20. 28.
c Mi. 6. 13.	g Nu. 31. 3.	l 2 Sa. 16. 2.	p Ju. 7. 11.	t 1 Sa. 18. 10.	y Da. 7. 22.	⊠ 2 Ki. 15. 5.	♭ Jos. 8. 33.
d De. 21. 2, ¶ 6.	h Am. 7. 4.	ǁ Ca. 5. 7.	q Ge. 21. 15, 19.	u 1 Sa. 26. 22.	z Is. 33. 9.	♯ Is. 10. 15.	♮ Nu. 11. 5.
Ge. 11. 6.	i Joel 4. 10.	o Le. 11. 30.	r Je. 39. 4.	v Joel 2. 25.	⊡ Eze. 18. 23.	♩ 1 Ki. 3. 25, 25.	♪ Eze. 42. 9.
De. 8. 15.	m Is. 3. 16.	2 Sa. 3. 4.	Pr. 31. 30.	f Job 1. 9.	2 Sa. 22. 31.		

Word	Description	Root
הַחֲצֹצְרוֹת	pref. הַ)(noun fem., pl. of חֲצֹצְרָה dec. 10.	חצר
הֶחָצֵר	pref. הֶ bef. חָ for הַ)(noun com. s. d. 5c.	חצר
הַחֶצְרוֹנִי	pref. הַ)(patronym. of חֶצְרוֹן	חצר
הַחֲצֵרוֹת	pref. id.)(noun com., pl. of חָצֵר dec. 5c.	חצר
הַחֲצֵרִים	pref. id.)(id. with pl. masc. term.	חצר
הַחֶצְרֹנִי	pref. id.)(patronym. of חֶצְרוֹן	חצר
הַחֲצֵרֹת	pref. id.)(noun com., pl. of חָצֵר dec. 5c.	חצר
הַחֻקָּה	pref. id.)(noun fem. sing. d. 10, from חֹק m.	חקק
הַחֻקִּים	pref. id.)(noun masc., pl. of חֹק dec. 8c.	חקק
הַחֹקְקִים	pref. id.)(Kal part. act. m., pl. of [חֹקֵק] d. 7b.	חקק
הַחֵקֶר	pref. הַ interr. for הַ)(n. m., חֵקֶר dec. 6b.	חקר
הֶחָרֵב	Hoph. inf. absolute	חרב
הֶחָרֵב	ו)(pref. הַ)(noun fem. sing. dec. 6a.	חרב
הֶחָרֵב	pref. הֶ bef. חָ for הַ)(adj. masc. sing.	חרב
הֶחָרֵב	pref. id.)(in pause for הַחֶרֶב (q. v. § 35. r. 2)	חרב
הַחָרְבָּה	pref. id.)(noun fem. sing.	חרב
הֶחָרְבָּה	Hoph. pret. 3 pers. sing. fem.	חרב
הֶחֳרָבוֹת	)(pref. הַ bef. חָ for הַ)(n. f., pl. of חָרְבָּה d. 12c.	חרב
הַחֲרֵבוֹת	pref. id.)(adj. fem., pl. of חָרֵב stands for הַחֲרֵבוֹת, comp. הֶחֳדַלְתִּי	חרב
הַחֳרְבַת	Ch. Hoph. pret. 3 pers. sing. fem.	חרב
הֶחֱרַבְתִּי	Hiph. pret. 1 pers. sing.	חרב
הֶחֱרַבְתִּי	ו)(id.; acc. shifted by conv. ו (§ 8. rem. 7, & § 13. rem. 10)	חרב
הַחַרְגֹּל	pref. הַ)(noun masc. sing.	חרגל
הַחֲרָדָה	pref. id.)(noun fem. sing., (constr. חֶרְדַּת) dec. 11c. (§ 42. rem. 1)	חרד
הַחֲרֹדִי	pref. id.)(gent. noun from חֲרוֹד	חרד
הַחֲרֵדִים	)(pref. id.)(adj. masc., pl. of חָרֵד dec. 5c.	חרד
הֶחֱרַדְתִּי	ו)(Hiph. pret. 1 pers. sing.; acc. shifted by conv. ו (§ 8. rem. 7, & § 13. rem. 10)	חרד
הֶחֱרָה	Hiph. pret. 3 pers. sing. masc.	חרה
הַחֲרוּפִי	pref. הַ)(Kh. חֲרוּפִי K. חָרִיף gent. n. see	חרף
הַחֲרִיצִן	pref. הֶ bef. חָ for הַ)(noun masc. sing. dec. 3a.	חרץ
הַחֲרֹרִי	once 1 Ch. 11. 27, for הַחֲרֹדִי (q. v.)	חרד
הַחַרְטֻמִּים / הַחַרְטֻמָּם	pref. הַ)(noun m., pl. of [חַרְטֹם] d. 8c.	חרט
הַחֹרִי	pref. id.)(pr. name of a people	חור
הֶחֱרִיב	Hiph. pret. 3 pers. sing. masc.	חרב
הֶחֱרִיבוּ	id. pret. 3 pers. pl.	חרב
הֶחֱרִיד	Hiph. pret. 3 pers. sing. masc.	חרד
הַחֲרִטִים	ו)(pref. הַ)(noun masc., pl. of [חָרִיט] d. 3a.	חרט
הַחֹרִים	pref. id.)(pr. name of a people, pl. of חֹרִי	חור
הַחֹרִים	pref. id.)(noun masc., pl. of חוֹר dec. 1a.	חור
הַחֹרִים	pref. id.)(noun m., pl. of חֹר dec. 1a.	חרר
הֶחֱרִים	ו)(Hiph. pret. 3 pers. sing. masc.	חרם
הַחֲרִימוּ	id. imp. pl. masc.	חרם
הֶחֱרִימוּ	id. pret. 3 pers. pl.	חרם
הַחֲרִימוּךְ	ו)(id. imp. pl. masc., suff. 3 pers. sing. fem.	חרם
הַחֲרִימָם	id. inf. (הַחֲרִים), suff. 3 pers. pl. m. dec. 1b.	חרם
הֶחֱרִימָם	id. pret. 3 pers. sing. masc., suff. 3 p. pl. m.	חרם
הֶחֱרִישׁ	ו)(Hiph. pret. 3 pers. sing. masc.	חרש
הֶחֱרִישׁוּ	id. imp. pl. masc.	חרש
הֶחֱרִישׁוּ	)(id. pret. 3 pers. pl. masc.	ה.רש
הַחֲרִישִׁי	id. imp. sing. fem.	חרש
הֶחֳרָכִים	pref. הַ)(noun masc., pl. of [חֶרֶךְ] dec. 8a.	חרך
הַחֲרֵם	ו)(Hiph. inf. or (De. 13. 16) imp. sing. m.	חרם
הַחֵרֶם	pref. הַ)(noun masc. s. d. 6. (§ 35. rem. 6)	חרם
הֶחֱרֵם	Hiph. pret. 3 pers sing. masc.	חרם
הַחָרְמָה	pref. הַ)(pr. name of a place	חרם
הֶחֱרַמְנוּ	Hiph. pret. 1 pers. pl.	חרם
הֶחֱרַמְתָּה	)(id. pret. 2 pers. sing. masc.; acc. shifted by conv. ו (§ 8. rem. 7, & § 13. rem. 10)	חרם
הֶחֱרַמְתִּי	id. pret. 1 pers. sing.	חרם
הֶחֱרַמְתִּי	)(id. id.)(acc. shifted by conv. ו (§ 8. rem. 7, & § 13. rem. 10)	חרם
הֶחֱרַמְתִּים	)(id. id. with suff. 3 pers. pl. masc.	חרם
הֶחֱרַמְתֶּם / הֶחֱרַמְתֶּם	)(id. pret. 2 pers. pl. masc. (§ 13. rem. 10)	חרם
הַחֹרָנִי	pref. הַ)(gent. noun of חֹרָנִים	חור
הַחֲרֵם	pref. הֶ bef. חָ for הַ)(n.m.s. (for חָרֵם §35 r.2)	חרם
הַחַרְסָה	pref. הַ)(id. with parag. ה	חרם
הַחַרְסוּת	pref. id.)(pr. n. of a gate, Kh. חַרְסוּת, K. סִית	חרם
הֶחָרֵף	pref. id.)(noun masc. sing. dec. 6c.	חרף
הַחֲרֵשׁ	Hiph. inf. abs., or imp. sing. masc.	חרש
הַחֹרֵשׁ	pref. הַ)(Kal part. act. sing. masc. dec. 7b.	חרש
הֶחָרֵשׁ	pref. id.)(noun masc. sing. dec. 6c.	חרש
הֶחָרָשׁ	)(pref. הֶ bef. חָ)(noun masc. sing. dec. 1b. for [חָדָשׁ § 30. rem. 1]	חרש
הֶחֱרֵשׁ	)(Hiph. pret. 3 pers. sing. masc.	חרש
הֶחָרָשִׁים	pref. הַ)(noun masc., pl. of [חֶרֶשׁ] dec. 6a.	חרש
הַחֲרָשִׁים	pref. id.)(adj. m., pl. of חֵרֵשׁ d. 7b. [for חָדָשׁ]	חרש
הֶחֱרַשְׁתִּי	)(Hiph. pret. 1 pers. sing.	חרש
הַחֹשְׁבִים	pref. הַ)(Kal part. act. m., pl. of חָשַׁב d. 7b.	חשב
הֶחֱשׁוּ	Hiph. pret. 3 pers. pl.	חשה
הֶחֱשִׁיךְ	Hiph. pret. 3 pers. sing. masc. (§ 13. rem. 9)	חשך
הֶחֱשֵׁתִי	Hiph. pret. 1 pers. sing. (§ 24. rem. 14)	חשה
הַחֹשֶׁךְ	)(pref. הַ)(noun masc. sing. dec. 6c.	חשך
הֶחֱשַׁכְתִּי	ו)(Hiph. pret. 1 pers. sing.; acc. on ult. by conv. ו (§ 8. rem. 7, & § 13. rem. 10)	חשך
הַחַשְׁמַל	pref. הַ)(noun masc. sing.	חשמל
הַחַשְׁמַלָה	pref. id.)(id. with parag. ה	חשמל

a Eze. 10. 4.	g Eze. 26. 2.	n Le. 11. 22.	t Joel 4. 14, 14.	b 1 Ki. 21. 11.	h Ca. 2. 9.	o Jos. 2. 10.	t Is. 17. 9.	a Am. 5. 8.
b Ex. 8. 9.	h Eze. 36. 10.	o 2 Ki. 4. 13.	a Ex. 8. 15.	c Is. 11. 15.	i Je. 50. 21.	p 1 Sa. 15. 3.	u Nu. 30. 12, 15.	b Ex. 14. 2?.
c Is. 10. 1.	i Eze. 36. 35, 38.	p Is. 66. 5.	b Eze. 19. 7.	d Je. 51. 3.	k Je. 50. 21.	q 1 Sa. 15. 15.	v Ju. 8. 13.	c Am. 8. 9.
d Job 11. 7.	k Ezr. 4. 15.	q Exr. 10. 3.	c Ju. 8. 12.	e Je. 50. 26.	l 1 Sa. 15. 18.	r Ju. 14. 18.	w Ps. 50. 21.	d Is. 2. 4.
e 2 Ki. 3. 23.	l Zep. 3. 6.	r 2 Sa. 17. 2.	d Is. 3. 22.	f 2 Ki. 18. 36.	m 1 Sa. 15. 20.	s Je. 28. 24.	x 2 Ki. 2. 3, 5.	e Eze. 2. 1.
f Je. 33. 12.	m Je. 51. 26.	s Ne. 3. 20.	e 1 Sa. 14. 11.	g 2 Sa. 13. 20.			Je. 25. 9.	Ex. 13. 10.	Mi. 4. 13.

הַחֹשֶׁן	pref. ה × noun masc. sing. . . .	חשן
הַחֻשָׁתִי	pref. id. × patronym. of חֻשָׁה . .	חוש
הֶחָתוּם	pref. הָ before הָ for הַ × Kal part. p. sing. masc. dec. 3a. . . .	חתם
הַחֲתוּגִמים	pref. ה × id. pl., absolute state	חתם
הַחִתִּי	וֹ pref. id. × gent. noun from חֵת	חתת
הַחִתִּים	pref. id. × id. pl. . . .	חתת
הֶחְתִּים	Hiph. pret. 3 pers. sing. masc. (§ 13. r. 9)	חתם
הַחְתֵּל	וֹ Hoph. inf. absolute (§ 11. rem. 11)	חתל
הַחְתֻּמֶת	pref. ה × noun fem. sing., from חוֹתָם masc.	חתם
הַחְתַתָּ	Hiph. pret. 2 pers. sing. masc. [for by Chaldaism § 18. rem. 14 note]	חתת
הַחְתַּתִּי	וֹ id. pret. 1 pers. sing., contr. [for הַחְתַתִּי regular, for הַחְתֵּתִי irr.] (§ 18. r. 13)	חתת
הַט	Hiph. imp. s. m., ap. for הַטֵּה (§ 25. No. 2b)	נטה
הַטּוֹבָה	pref. ה × adj. & subst. f. d. 10, from טוֹב m.	טוב
הַטֹּבוֹת	pref. id. × id. adj. pl.	טוב
הַטִּבְחָה	pref. id. × noun masc. sing. dec. 1b.	טבח
הַטַּבָּחִים	pref. id. × id. pl., absolute state	טבח
הַטּוֹבִים	pref. id. × adj. masc., pl. of טוֹב dec. 1a.	טוב
הֵטַבְנוּ	וֹ Hiph. pret. 1 pers. sing.	יטב
הֻטְבְּעוּ / הָטְבָּעוּ	} Hoph. pret. 3 pers. sing. (comp. § 8. r. 7)	טבע
הַטַּבָּעוֹת	pref. ה × pl. of the foll. (§ 44. rem. 5)	טבע
הַטַּבַּעַת	pref. id. × n. f. s. (with suff. טַבַּעְתּוֹ) d. 13a.	טבע
הַטַּבָּעֹת	pref. id. × id. pl. absolute state (§ 44. r. 5)	טבע
הַטֹּבָת	pref. id. × adj. f., pl. of טֹבָה d. 10, fr. טוֹב m.	טוב
הֵיטַבְתִּי	וֹ Hiph. pret. 1 pers. sing.; acc. shifted by conv. וֹ (comp. § 8. rem. 7)	טוב
הַטֵּה	Hiph. imp. sing. masc. . .	נטה
הָטָה	id. pret. 3 pers. sing. masc. .	נטה
הִטָּהוּ	id. id., suff. 3 pers. sing. masc.	נטה
הַטָּהוֹר	וֹ pref. ה × adj. masc. sing. dec. 3a.	טהר
הַטְּהוֹרָה	pref. ה × id. fem., dec. 10.	טהר
הַטָּהֹר	defect. for הַטָּהוֹר (q. v.)	טהר
הַטָּהֳרָח	pref. ה × noun f. s. (constr. טָהֳרַת; no pl.)	טהר
הַטָּהֳרָה	defect. for הַטָּהֳרָה (q. v.)	טהר
הִטַּהֲרוּ	Hithpa. pret. 3 pers. pl., or imp. pl. masc. [for הִתְטַהֲרוּ]	טהר
הִטֶּהָרוּ	וֹ id. pret. in pause, (§ 14. rem. 3)	טהר
הִטַּהַרְנוּ	id. pret. 1 pers. sing., dag. impl. (§ 14. r. 1)	טהר
הַטּוּ	וֹ Hiph. imp. pl. masc. (§ 25. No. 2b)	נטה
הִטּוּ	id. pret. 3 pers. pl. .	נטה
הַטּוֹב	וֹ pref. ה × adj. and subst. masc. dec. 1a.	טוב
הֲטוֹב	pref. הַ × Kal pret. impers., or (Ju. 11. 25) inf. absolute (§ 21. rem. 2)	טוב

הַטּוֹבָה	pref. הַ × adj. or subst., fem. of טוֹב masc., dec. 10. }	טוב
הַטֹּבָה	pref. הַ × }	טוב
הַטּוֹבִים	pref. הַ × } id. masc., pl. of טוֹב dec. 1a.	טוב
הַטֹּבִים	pref. הַ × }	טוב
הֵטּוֹחַ	Niph. inf. constr.	טוח
הַטּוּר	וֹ pref. הַ × noun masc. sing. dec. 1a.	טור
הַטֹּחַ	defect. for הַטּוֹחַ (q. v.)	טוח
הַטָּחִים	pref. הַ × Kal part. act. m., pl. of [טָח] d. 1a.	טוח
הַטַּחֲנָה	pref. id. × noun fem. sing.	טחן
הַטֹּחֲנוֹת	pref. id. × Kal part. act. fem. pl. [of טֹחֲנָה or טֹחֶנֶת]	טחן
הֵטִּי	וֹ Hiph. imp. sing. fem. (§ 25. No. 2b)	נטה
הֵיטִיבָה	Hiph. imp. sing. masc. with parag. ה	יטב
הֵיטִיבוּ	id. imp. pl. masc.	יטב
הֵיטִיבוּ	Hiph. imp. pl. masc.	טוב
הֵיטִיבֹתָ	Hiph. pret. 2 pers. sing. masc.	טוב
הֵיטִיבִי	Hiph. imp. sing. fem.	יטב
הֵיטִבְתָּ	Hiph. pret. 2 pers. sing. masc.	טוב
הַטִּיחַ	pref. ה × noun masc. sing.	טוח
הֵטִיל	Hiph. pret. 3 pers. sing. masc.	טול
הֱטִילֻנִי	וֹ id. imp. pl. masc., suff. 1 pers. sing.	טול
הֻטְפוּ	וֹ Hiph. pret. 3 pers. pl.	נטף
הַטִּירוֹת	pref. ה × noun fem., pl. of [טִירָה] dec. 10.	טור
הִטִּיתִי	Hiph. pret. 1 pers. sing. (§ 25. No. 2b)	נטה
הִטִּיתֶם	id. pret. 2 pers. pl. masc.	נטה
הַטֵּל / הַטָּל	} pref. ה × noun masc. sing. dec. 8d.	טלל
הַטְּלֻאִים	וֹ Kal part. p., pl. of טָלוּא dec. 3a.	טלא
הַטְּלֻאֹת	וֹ id. pl. fem.	טלא
הִטַּלְתִּי	וֹ Hiph. pret. 1 p. s. [for הַטְלְתִּי § 21. r. 13]	טול
הַטָּמֵא	pref. ה × adj. masc. s. d. 5a. (constr. טְמֵא)	טמא
הַטְּמֵאָה	pref. id. × id. fem. dec. 10.	טמא
הַטֻּמְאָה	pref. id. × noun fem. sing. dec. 10.	טמא
הַטַּמְּאָה	[for הַתְטַמְּאָה] Hothpa. pret. 3 pers. sing. fem. (§ 6. No. 10 note)	טמא
הַטְּמֵאִים	pref. ה × adj. masc., pl. of טָמֵא dec. 5a.	טמא
הִטָּמֵן	וֹ Niph. imp. sing. masc.	טמן
הַטַּנָּא	pref. ה × noun m. s. (suff. טַנְאֲךָ) dec. 6a.	טנא
הִטְעוּ	Hiph. pret. 3 pers. pl. masc.	טעה
הַטֶּף / הַטָּף	} pref. ה × noun masc. sing. dec. 8d.	טפף
הַטִּפוּ	וֹ Hiph. imp. pl. masc. . .	נטף
הַטְּפָחוֹת	pref. ה × noun masc. with pl. fem. term. from טֶפַח dec. 6. (§ 35. rem. 5) .	טפח
הַטְרֵפֵנִי	Hiph. imp. sing. masc., suff. 1 pers. sing.	טרף
הַטֶּרֶם	pref. הַ × adv. .	טרם

a Ne. 10. 2.   g 1 Sa. 9. 24.   m Is. 44. 20.   s Jos. 22. 17.   y Eze. 13. 15.   e′ Ho. 10. 1.   l′ Jon. 1. 12.   r′ Ge. 30. 35.   w′ Eze. 13. 10.
b Le. 15. 3.   h Joel 4. 5.   n Ne. 12. 45.   t Jos. 24. 23.   z Ge. 24. 14.   f′ 2 Ch. 6. 8.   m′ Am. 9. 13.   s′ Ge. 30. 35.   x′ Ge. 47. 12.
c Ese. 16. 4.   i Nu. 10. 29, 32.   o Ezr. 6. 20.   u Nu. 19. 19.   a′ Ps. 45. 11.   g′ Is. 23. 16.   n′ Eze. 46. 23.   t′ De. 24. 4.   y′ Eze. 21. 2, 7.
d Ge. 38. 25.   j Ge. 38. 22.   p Ge. 35. 2.   v Am. 6. 2.   b′ Ps. 195. 4.   h′ Eze. 13. 12.   o′ Pr. 5. 13.   u′ Is. 2. 10.   z′ 1 Ki. 7. 9.
e Is. 9. 3.   k Ge. 41. 28.   q 2 Ch. 30. 18.   w Le. 14. 43.   c′ De. 5. 28.   i′ Jon. 1. 4.   p′ Le. 2. 10.   v′ De. 25. 4.   a″ Pr. 30. 8.
f Je. 42. 37.   l Eze. 33. 11.   r Nu. 8. 7.   x Le. 14. 48.   d′ Ec. 12. 4.   k′ Ec. 12. 3.   q′ Ex. 10. 7.

Form	Description	Root
הַטֻּרְפָה	pref. הַ)(noun fem. sing.	טרף
[for הַטַּתְהוּ]	Hiph. pret. 3 pers. sing. fem., suff. 3 pers. sing. masc. (§ 25. No. 2 b)	נטה
וָ נ	m. s. by syncope [for נְהִי]; for וָ see lett. ו.	נהה
הִיא וְ &	Kh. הִיא q. v., K. הֻוא (q. v.).	חוא
הִיא וְ &	p. pron. 3 p.s.f. see הֻוא; for ו see lett. ו.	הוא
הָיָאבֶה	pref. הַ)(Kal fut. 3 pers. sing. masc.	אבה
הֵיָאכֵל	pref. id.)(Niph. pret. 3 pers. sing. masc.	אכל
הַיֹּאמַר	pref. id.)(Kal fut. 1 pers. sing. (§ 19. r. 1)	אמר
הַיְאֹר	pref. הַ)(noun masc. sing. dec. 1 a.	יאר
הַיְאֹרָה	pref. id.)(id. with parag. ה.	יאר
הַיְאֹרִי	pref. id.)(patronym. of יָאִיר.	אור
הַיְאֹרִים	pref. id.)(noun masc., pl. of יְאֹר dec. 1 a.	יאר
הָיֵאָתֹן	pref. הַ)(Kh. הַיֵאָתֹן, K. הָאִיתֹן noun m. s.	אתה
הַיְבוּסִי	וָ pref. הַ)(gent. noun from יְבוּם	בוס
הַיֹּבֵל	pref. הַ)(noun masc. sing. dec. 7 b.	יבל
הַיֹּבֵל	וְ Ch. Aph. pret. 3 pers. sing. masc.	יבל
הַיֹּבְלִים	pref. id.)(noun masc., pl. of יֹבֵל dec. 7 b.	יבל
הַיְבוּסִי	pref. id.)(gent. noun from יְבוּם	בוס
הַיַּבֹּק	pref. id.)(pr. name of a stream	בקק
הַיַּבָּשָׁה	pref. id.)(noun fem. sing.	יבש
הַיְבֵשׁוֹת	pref. id.)(adj. f., pl. of יְבֵשָׁה d. 10, fr. יָבֵשׁ m.	יבש
הַיֵּנָאֶה	pref. הַ)(Kal fut. 1 pers. sing.	נאה
הַיַּגִּיד	pref. id.)(Hiph. fut. 3 pers. sing. masc.	נגד
הַיָּד	וְ pref. הַ)(noun com. sing. dec. 2 a.	יד
הַיָּד	pref. הַ)(id. constr. state	די
הֲיָדַד	noun masc. sing.	הדד
הַיָּדֹעַ	pref. הַ)(Kal inf. absolute	ידע
הַיָּדוֹת	pref. הַ)(noun fem., pl. of יָד dec. 3 a.	יד
הַיָּדוֹת	noun fem. pl. [of הַיָּדָה]	ידה
הַיָּדַיִם / הַיָּדַיִם	} pref. הַ)(noun com., du. of יָד dec. 2 a.	יד
הַיָּדֹעַ	pref. הַ)(Kal inf. absolute	ידע
הַיֹּדְעִים	pref. הַ)(Kal part. act. m., pl. of יֹדֵעַ d. 7 b.	ידע
הַיְּדַעְנִי	pref. id.)(noun masc. sing. dec. 1.	ידע
הַיְּדַעֹנִים	pref. id.)(id. pl., absolute state	ידע
הֲיָדַעְתָּ	pref. id.)(Kal pret. 2 pers. sing. masc.	ידע
הֲיָדַעְתֶּם	pref. הַ interr. f.)(id. pret. 2 pers. pl. m.	ידע
הַיָּדֹת	defect. for הַיָּדוֹת (q. v.)	יד

הָיָה וְ, fut. יִהְיֶה תִּהְיֶה § 24. r. 20), apoc. יְהִי (r. 3 e); inf. c. הֱיוֹת (once הָיֹה r. 20), with pref. בִּהְיוֹת לִהְיוֹת § 13. r. 13)—I. *to be, to exist; to be to, belong to; to serve for;* before an inf. *to be about* to do any thing.—II. *to become;* הָיָה לְ *to become to be for;* הָיָה כְּ *to become as.*—III. *to fall out, happen, come to pass* (comp. הָוָה No. III);

וַיְהִי וְ, נַיְהִי כְ *and it came to pass that.* Niph —I. *to become, to be brought to pass,* with לְ.— II. *to fall,* Dan. 2. 1, שְׁנָתוֹ נִהְיְתָה עָלָיו his *sleep had fallen upon him;* Dan. 8. 27, נִהְיֵיתִי וְנֶחֱלֵיתִי *I fell and was sick,* i. e. I fell sick. Gesenius in both passages, *to be done for, be ended,* or *be over.* הַוָּה *calamity,* see הַוָּה

Form	Description	Root
הֱיֵה וְ	הֱיֵה)(Kal imp. sing. m., or inf. abs.; וְ bef. (ְ)	היה
הָיֹה	id. inf. absolute	היה
הָיָה וְ	Kh. הָיָה, K. הָיוֹ Kal pret. 3 p. s. or pl. m.	היה
הַיְהֻדִיָּה	pref. הַ)(fem. of the foll.	ידה
הַיְהוּדִי	pref. id.)(gent. noun from יְהוּדָה	ידה
הַיְהוּדִיִּים / הַיְהוּדִים	וְ } pref. id.)(id. pl., Kh. יְהֻדִיִּים	ידה
הַיְהֹוָה	pref. הַ interr. for הֲ)(the name of God, the *Eternal,* see under the root	הוה
הַיִהְיֶה	pref. הַ)(Kal fut. 3 pers. sing. masc.	היה
הַיֵהָפֵךְ	pref. הַ)(Kal fut. 3 pers. sing. masc.	הפך
הָיוּ וְ	Kh. הָיוּ q. v. K. הָיָה (q. v.)	היה
הָיוֹ	Kal inf. absolute, for הָיֹה (§ 24. rem 2)	היה
הָיוּ וְ	id. pret. 3 pers. pl.	היה
הֱיוּ	id. imp. pl. masc.	היה
הֱיוּ וְ	Kh. הֱיוּ q. v., K. יִהְיוּ q. v.	היה
הֱיוּ וְ	Kal imp. m. pl. (§ 13. r. 13); וְ bef. (ְ) for	היה
הַיּוּבַל	pref. הַ)(noun masc. sing. dec. 7 b.	יבל
הַיּוּבָלִים	pref. id.)(id. pl., absolute state	יבל
הַיּוֹדֶךָ	pref. הַ)(Hiph. fut. 3 p. s. m., suff. 2 p. s. m.	ידה
הַיִּוָּדַע	pref. id.)(Niph. fut. 3 pers. sing. masc.	ידע
הַיּוּחַל	pref. id.)(Hoph. fut. 3 pers. sing. masc.	חול
הַיּוּכַל	pref. id.)(Hoph. fut. 3 pers. sing. masc.	יכל
הַיֻּלַּד	pref. הַ)(Pual pret. 3 pers. sing. masc., (§ 10. rem. 5), or part [for מְיֻלָּד, rem. 6]	ילד
הַיּוֹם	וְ pref. id.)(noun com. s., pl. יָמִים (§ 45)	יום
הַיַּיִן	pref. id.)(n. m. s., constr. יֵין (§ 34. r. 1)	יון
הַיּוֹנָה	pref. id.)(Kal part. act. s. f. from יוֹנֶה m.	ינה
הַיּוֹנָה	pref. id.)(noun fem. sing. dec. 10, see יוֹנָה	ינה
הַיְּוָנִים	pref. id.)(patronym., pl. of יְוָנִי fr. יָוָן q. v.	יון
הַיּוֹנָתָן	pref. הַ)(pr. name masc., see יְהוֹנָתָן	הוה
הַיּוֹצֵא	וְ pref. id.)(Kal part. act. sing. masc. d. 7 b.	יצא
הַיּוֹצְאִים	pref. id.)(id. pl. absolute	יצא
הַיּוֹצֵאת	וְ pref. id.)(id. f. s. [for יוֹצֵאת § 23. r. 4]	יצא
הַיּוֹצֵר	pref. id.)(Kal part. act. sing. masc. dec. 7 b.	יצר
הַיּוֹצְרִים	pref. id.)(id. pl., absolute state	צר
הַיֹּצֵאת	contr. for הַיּוֹצֵאת (q. v.)	יצא
הַיֹּרְדוֹת	pref. הַ)(Kal part. act. f., pl. of יֹרְדָה or יוֹרֶדֶת dec. 10, or 13 a. (§ 8. rem. 19)	ירד
הַיֹּרִים	pref. id.)(Kal part. act. m., pl. of יֹרֶה d. 9 a.	ירד

a Ex. 22. 12. | d Job 39. 9. | g Eze. 40. 15. | k Ps. 30. 10. | o Ge. 27. 22. | r Je. 50. 6. | u Je. 18. 23. | x Ps. 78. 19. | a1 Am. 5. 3.
b Pr. 7. 21. | e Job 6. 6. | h Ezr. 5. 14. | l De. 7. 19. | p Je. 40. 14. | s Je. 8. 19. | v Jos. 6. 4, 8, 1 | y Ju. 13. 8. | b1 1 Ch. 4. 23.
c Eze. 2. 10. | f Is. 45. 9. | i Ne. 12. 8. | m 2 Ki. 9. 35. | q 1 Sa. 27. 8. | t 2 Ki. 7. 2, 19. | w De. 30. 10. | z Je. 21. 9. | c1 De. 28. 57.
d Job 31. 11. | e Ex. 1. 22. | k Eze. 37. 4. | n Je. 13. 23. | Eze. 47. 12. | Is. 66. 8. | Zec. 6. 8. | d1 1 Ch. 10. 3.
1 Ki. 17. 15. | Ex. 8. 1. | Job 8. 11. | Eze. 7. 17. | Ge. 47. 24.
Eze. 23. 42.

Word	Description	Root
הַיּוֹרֵשׁ	pref. ה)(Kal part. act. masc. dec. 7 b.	ירשׁ
הַיּוֹשֵׁב	pref. id.)(Kal part. act. masc. dec. 7 b.	ישׁב
הַיּוֹשְׁבִים	ו)(pref. id.)(id. pl., absolute state	ישׁב
הַיּוֹשֶׁבֶת	pref. id.)(id. fem. s. d. 13 a. (§ 8. rem. 19)	ישׁב
הֱיוֹת	Kal inf. constr., dec. 1 a.	היה
הֱיוֹתָהּ	id., suff. 3 pers. sing. fem.	היה
הֱיוֹתוֹ	id., suff. 3 pers. sing. masc.	היה
הֱיוֹתִי	id., suff. 1 pers. sing.	היה
הֱיוֹתֵךְ	id., suff. 2 pers. sing. fem.	היה
הֱיוֹתְךָ	id., suff. 2 pers. sing. masc.	היה
הֱיוֹתְכֶם	id., suff. 2 pers. pl. masc.	היה
הֱיוֹתָם	id., suff. 3 pers. pl. masc.	היה
הֱיוֹתֵנוּ	id., suff. 1 pers. pl.	היה
הַיּוֹתֵר	pref. ה)(noun masc. sing.	יתר
הַיִּזְבָּחוּ	pref. הַ)(Kal fut. 3 p.s.m. (for יִזְבְּחוּ § 8. r. 15)	זבח
הַיִּזְרָח	pref. id.)(patronym. for אֶזְרָחִי q. v.	זרח
הַיִּזְרְעֵאלִי	pref. id.)(gent. noun from יִזְרְעֶאל (q. v.)	זרע
הַיִּזְרְעֵאלִית / הַיִּזְרְעֵאלִת	} pref. id.)(fem. of the preceding	זרע
הַיְבֹרַךְ	pref. ה interr. for הַ)(Pual fut. 3 pers. sing. masc., suff. 2 p. s. m. [for יְבֹרַךְ § 10. r. 5]	חבר
הַיָּחִיד	pref. ה art.)(adj. masc. sing. dec. 3 a.	יחד
הַיִּחְיֶה	pref. ה)(Kal fut. 3 pers. sing. masc.	חיה
הַיְחַיֵּנִי	pref. ה interr for הַ)(Piel fut. 3 p. m. pl.	חיה
הַיַּחְלְאֵלִי	pref. ה art.)(patronym. of יַחְלְאֵל q. v.	יחל
הַיַּחְצְאֵלִי	pref. id.)(gent. noun from יַחְצְאֵל q. v.	חצה
הַיַּחַשׂ	pref. id.)(noun masc. sing.	יחשׂ
הַיִּתְחַתֵּ	pref. הַ)(Kal fut. 3 pers. sing. masc.	חתה
הֵיטִב	ו Hiph. pret. 3 pers. sing. masc.	יטב
הֵיטֵב	id. inf absolute, used also adverbially	יטב
הֵיטִבְךָ	ו id. pret. 3 pers. sing. masc., suff. 2 p. s. m.	יטב
הֵיטַבְתָּ	id. pret. 2 pers. sing. masc.	יטב
הֵיטַבְתְּ	id. pret. 2 pers. sing. fem.	יטב
הֵיטִיב	id. inf. absolute	יטב
הֵיטִיב	id. pret. 3 pers. sing. masc.	יטב
הֵיטִיבָה	id. imp. sing. masc. with opt. ה	יטב
הֵיטִיבוּ	ו)(id. pret. ▫ pers. pl. masc. or imp. pl. m.	יטב
הַיֵּטְמָא	pref. הַ)(Kal fut. 3 pers. sing. masc.	טמא
הֱיִי	Kal imp. fem. sing.	היה
הַיֵּיטַב	pref. ה interr. for הַ)(Kal fut. 3 pers. s. m.	יטב
הַיַּיִן / הַיָּיִן	} pref. ה)(noun masc. sing. dec. 6 h.	יון
הָיִינוּ	ו Kal pret. 3 pers. pl.	היה
הָיִיתָ	ו id. pret. 2 pers. sing. masc.	היה
הָיִית	ו id. pret. 2 pers. sing. fem.	היה
הָיְתָה	Kh. 'תָה q. v., K. חָיְתָה q. v.	חיה
הָיִיתָ	ו Kal pret. 2 pers. sing. masc. (§ 8. rem. 5)	היה
הָיִיתִי	ו id. pret. 1 pers. sing.	היה
הָיִיתִי	id. pret. 2 pers. sing. fem. Kh. 'תִי, K. הָיִית, (§ 8. rem. 5)	היה
הֱיִיתֶם / ון	} id. pret. 2 pers. pl. masc. (§ 13. rem. 13)	היה
הֵיךְ	ו)(Chald. i. q. אֵיךְ how ?	
הַיָּכוֹל	pref. הַ)(Kal inf. absolute	כל
הַיָּכִינִי	pref. ה)(patronym. of יָכִין	כון

הֵיכָל ו)(masc. dec. 2 b.—I. *a large splendid building, a palace.*—II. *the temple* of the Lord at Jerusalem. הֵיכָל Chald. dec. 2 a.—I. *palace.*—II. *temple,* Da. 5. 2, 3, 5.

Word	Description	Root
הֵיכַל	ו)(id., construct state	היכל
הָיָכֹל	pref. ה)(Kal inf. absolute	יכל
הֵיכַל	Chald. pref. ה interr. for הַ)(Peal pret. 3 pers. sing. masc. (§ 47. rem. 6)	יכל
הֵיכְלָא	Chald. noun m. s., emph. of הֵיכַל dec. 2 a.	היכל
הַיְכַלּוּ	pref. ה interr. for הַ)(Piel pret. 3 pers. pl.	כלה
הֵיכָלוֹ	noun m. s., suff. 3 pers. s. m. fr. הֵיכָל dec. 2 a.	היכל
הֵיכָלוֹת	id. with pl. fem. term., absolute state	היכל
הֵיכְלֵי	id. pl. masc., construct state	היכל
הֵיכָלֶךָ	id. sing., suff. 2 pers. sing. masc. [for הֵיכָלְךָ]	היכל
הַיִּכָּרֵת	pref. הַ)(Kal fut. 3 pers. sing. masc.	כרת
הַיֶּלֶד / הַיָּלֶד	} pref. ה)(noun masc. sing. dec. 6 a. (pl. c. יַלְדֵי & יְלָדֵי § 35. rem. 4)	ילד
הַיַּלְדָּה	ו)(pref. id.)(noun fem. sing. dec. 12 a.	ילד
הַיְלָדָהּ	ו)(id.)(Kal part. act. sing. masc. (יוֹלֵד) suff. 3 p. sing. fem. dec. 7 b.	ילד
הַיַּלְדוּת	pref. id.)(noun fem. sing. dec. 1 b.	ילד
הַיַּלְדוֹת	pref. id.)(Kal part. act. fem., pl. of יֹלֶדֶת dec. 13 a. (§ 8. rem. 19)	ילד
הַיְלָדִים	ו)(pref. id.)(noun masc. pl. from יֶלֶד dec. 6 a. (§ 35. rem. 2 ; pl. c. יַלְדֵי & יְלָדֵי rem. 4)	ילד
הַיְלֻדִים	pref. ה)(noun masc., pl. of יִלּוֹד dec. 1 b.	ילד
הַיֹּלַדְתְּ	pref. id.)(Kal part. act. s. f. d. 13 a. (§ 8. r. 19)	ילד
הַיִּלּוֹד	pref. id.)(Kal part. p. sing. masc. dec. 3 a.	ילד
הַיִּלּוֹד	pref. id.)(noun masc. sing. dec. 1 b.	ילד
הַיִּלּוֹדִים	pref. id.)(Kal part. p. m., pl. of יִלּוֹד dec. 3 a.	ילד
הֵילִיכִי	Hiph. imp. sing. fem.	ילך
הֵילִילוּ	ו)(Hiph. imp. pl. masc.	ילל

a 2 Sa. 14. 7.   d Ju. 18. 19, 19.   g Zec. 12. 10.   l De. 30. 5.   p Ge. 24. 60.   s Eze. 16. 31.   Nu. 22. 38.   Job 40. 28.   Je. 16. 3.

b 2 Ch. 30. 25.   e Je. 44. 8.   Job 14. 14.   m Je. 1. 12.   Le. 19. 19.   t 1 Ch. 13. 12.   Da. 6. 21.   Ge. 34. 4.   Le. 1. 5.

Is. 48. 16.   1 Sa. 25. 16.   Ne. 3. 34.   Ruth 3. 10.   Is. 62. 3.   Da. 10. 17.   Ne. 3. 34.   Joel 4. 3.   1 Ki. 8. 26, 27.

Eze. 34. 12.   1 Sa. 15. 15.   Ne. 7. 5.   Ps. 51. 20.   2 Sa. 14. 7.   2 Ch. 32. 13.   Da. 11. 6.   Ps. 45. 9.   1 Ch. 14. 4.

Jon. 4. 2.   1 Ne. 3. 34.   Pr. 6. 27.   Je. 35. 15.   2 Sa. 5. 2.   Is. 44. 28.   Ec. 11. 10.   Ex. 2. 9.

Is. 60. 15.   Ps. 94. 20.   1 Sa. 25. 31.   Hag. 2. 13.   Ju. 11. 6.   Ezr. 3. 6.

הֵילִילִי •	id. imp. sing. fem.	הַיִסֵר /	pref. הַ)(Kal part. act. sing. masc. יסר
הַיֵלֵךְ •	pref. הַ)(Kal fut. 3 pers. sing. masc. ילך	הַיֵעָצָה •	pref. הַ)(Kal part. p. sing. fem. [fr. יָעוּץ m.] יעץ
הַיֵלְכוּ •	pref. id.)(id. fut. 3 pers. pl. ילך	הַיֵעֲזֹב •	pref. הַ)(Kal fut. 3 pers. sing. masc. עזב
הֵילֵל •	noun masc. sing. הלל	הַיֵעַזְבוּ •	pref. id.)(id. pret. 3 pers. pl. m. עזב
הֵילֵל וְ•	Hiph. imp. sing. masc. ילל	הַיָּעִים	pref. הַ)(noun masc. pl. [of עָץ, no vowel change] יעה
הֵילֵל וְ	id. pret. 3 pers. sing. masc. ילל	הַיֵעֲלֶה •	pref. הַ)(Kal fut. 3 pers. sing. masc. יעל
הַיֶלֶק } הַיָלֶק	pref. הַ)(noun masc. sing. (§ 35. em. 2) ילק	הַיְעֵלִים •	pref. הַ)(noun masc., pl. of יָעֵל dec. 5 a. יעל
הַיָם וְ } הַיָּם	וְ pref. id. } הַ pref. } noun masc. sing. dec. 8 a. ים	הַיַעֲמֹד •	pref. הַ)(Kal fut. 3 pers. sing. masc. עמד
הַיָּמָה	pref. הַ)(id. with paragogic ה ים	הַיַעַמְדוּ	pref. id.)(id. fut. 3 pers. pl. עמד
הַיָמִים וְ•	וְ pref. id.)(noun masc. pl. [as if for יָם, see יוֹם § 45] יום	הַיַעֲנָה	pref. הַ)(noun fem. sing. יען
הַיָּמִים •	pref. הַ)(noun masc., pl. of יָם dec. 8 a. ים	הַיָעֵף •	pref. הַ)(adj. masc. sing. dec. 5 a. עוף
הַיָמִין	pref. id.)(noun masc. with Chald. pl. term. see הַיָּמִים יום	הַיְעֵפִים •	pref. id.)(id. pl., absolute state עוף
הַיָמִין	pref. id.)(noun masc. sing. dec. 3 a. ימן	הַיֹעֲצִים •	וְ pref. id.)(Kal part. act. m., pl. of יֹעֵץ dec. 7 b. יעץ
הַיְמִינִי	pref. id.)(patronym. of יָמִין ימן	הַיַעַר } הַיָעַר }	pref. id.)(noun masc. sing. (§ 35. rem. 2) } dec. 6 d. יער
הַיְמִינִי	pref. id.)(gent. noun fr. בִּנְיָמִין q. v. בנה	הַיַעְרָה	pref. id.)(id. with paragogic ה יער
הַיְמִינִי •	pref. id.)(adj. masc. sing. ימן	הַיְעָרִים	pref. id.)(id. pl., absolute state יעי
הַיְמִינִי •	Kh. הַיְמִינִי q. v., K. הַיְמֵנִי (q. v.) ימן	הַיַעֲרֹךְ •	pref. הַ)(Kal fut. 3 pers. sing. masc. ערך
הַיְמִינִי •	Hiph. imp. sing. fem. ימן	הַיַעֲשֶׂה •	pref. id.)(Kal fut. 3 pers. sing. masc. עשה
הַיִמָּלֵט •	pref. הַ)(Niph. fut. 3 pers. sing. masc. מלט	הַיָפָה	pref. הַ)(adj. fem. sing. dec. 11 a, from יָפֶה m. יפה
הַיָמֵם •	defect for הַיָמִים (q. v.) יום	הַיָפוֹת •	pref. id.)(id. pl., absolute state יפה
הַיָמֵם •	pref. הַ)(noun masc. pl. [of יָם q. v.] יום	הַיְפִי •	pref. id.)(noun masc. sing. dec. 6 k. [for יְפִי § 35. rem. 14] יפה
הֵימָם וְ	וְ pr. name masc. המם		
הֵימָן וְ	וְ pr. name masc. אמן	הַיִפָּלֵא •	pref. הַ)(Niph. fut. 3 pers. sing. masc. פלא
הֵימִן	Chald. Aph. pret. 3 pers. sing. masc. (§ 53) אמן	הַיִפְּלוּ •	pref. id.)(Kal fut. 3 pers. pl. m. נפל
הֵימְנָה	pref. הַ)(pr. name masc. ימן	הַיִפְלְטִי	pref. הַ)(patronym. of יִפְלֵט פלט
הַיְמָנִי •	pref. id.)(adj. masc. sing. (from יָמִין) ימן	הַיֹצֵא וְ•	וְ pref. id.)(Kal part. act. masc. s. dec. 7 b. יצא
הַיְמָנִית	pref. id.)(fem. of the prec. ימן	הַיֹצְאִים	pref. id.)(id. pl., absolute state יצא
הֵימִשֵׁנִי •	Kh. וְהֵימִשֵׁנִי נ Hiph. imp. sing., suff. 1 pers. sing. from מָשַׁ, K. וַהֲמִשֵׁנִי id. from מוש	הַיֹצֵאת וְ•	וְ pref. id.)(id. fem. sing. [for יֹצֵאת § 23. rem. 4 ; § 8. rem. 19] יצא
הֵין	וְ noun masc. sing. הון	הַיִצְהָר וְ•	וְ pref. id.)(noun masc. sing. dec. 2 b. צהר
הַיִנָּהֵק •	pref. הַ)(Kal fut. 3 pers. sing. masc. נהק	הַיִצְהָרִי	pref. id.)(patronym. of יִצְהָר צהר
הַיִנָּטֹר •	pref. הַ)(Kal fut. 3 pers. sing. masc. נטר	הַיָצוּעַ •	pref. id.)(Kh. יְצוּעַ Kal part. pass., K. יָצִיעַ noun masc. dec. 3 a. יצע
הַינִיקָה •	Hiph. pret. 3 pers. sing. fem. ינק	הַיַצְלִחַ • } הַיַצְלֵחַ • }	pref. הַ)(Kal fut. 3 pers. sing. masc. } (§ 8. rem. 15) צלח
הַיֹנֵק •	pref. הַ)(Kal part. act. sing. masc. dec. 7 b. ינק		
הַיֹנַקְהוּ וְ	וְ Hiph. imp. sing. fem., suff. 3 pers. sing. masc. ינק	הַיֹצֵר •	pref. הַ)(Kal part. act. sing. masc. dec. 7 b. יצר
הַנָשׁוּף •	pref. הַ)(noun masc. sing. נשף	הַיֹצְרִי •	pref. id.)(patronym. of יֵצֶר יצר
הַיַסְגִרוּ •	pref. הַ)(Hiph. fut. 3 pers. pl. [def. for יַסְגִּירוּ] סגר	הַיַקֹב • } הַיֶקֶב • }	pref. id.)(noun masc. sing. dec. 6 a. (§ 35. rem. 2 ; but pl. c. יְקָבֵי) יקב
הַיַסְגִרֵנִי •	pref. id.)(id. with suff. 1 pers. sing. סגר		
הַיְסוֹד •	pref. הַ)(noun masc. sing. dec. 1 a. יסד	הַיְקָבִים •	pref. id.)(id. pl., absolute state יקב
הַיִסֵּפֵר	pref. הַ interr. for הַ)(Pual fut. 3 pers. sing. masc. ספר	הַיִקְבַּע •	pref. הַ)(Kal fut. 3 pers. sing. masc. קבע
		הַיִקְדֵשׁ •	pref. id.)(Kal fut. 3 pers. sing. masc. (for יְקְדַשׁ § 8. rem. 15) קדש

a Je. 49. 3.   f Je. 47. 2.   Eze. 4. 6.   l 1 Ki. 7. 21.   b Nu. 11. 12.   Je. 18. 14.   2 Sa. 16. 2.   Am. 8. 13.   Eze. 17. 15.
b Ex. 16. 4.   Joel 1. 4.   Eze. 21. 21.   Ju. 16. 26.   c Ex. 2. 9.   Ne. 3. 34.   Ju. 8. 15.   Pr. 31. 30.   Eze. 15. 4.
Am. 3. 3.   Job 7. 12.   f Eze. 17. 15.   Le. 19. 36.   d 1 Sa. 23. 12.   Am. 3. 5.   Eze. 11. 2.   Ge. 18. 14.   Hag. 2. 16.
Zec. 11. 2.   Ne. 9. 6.   Nu. 6. 5.   Ge. 6. 5.   1 Sa. 23. 11.   1 Sa. 24. 3.   Jos. 17. 15.   Je. 8. 4.   Mal. 3. 8.
Je. 14. 12.   Da. 12. 13.   Ge. 36. 24.   Je. 3. 5.   Ps. 94. 10.   m Eze. 22. 14.   Job 36. 19.   1 Ch. 27. 1.   Hag. 2. 12.
Ese. 21. 17.   Ch. 3. 17.   Da. 6. 24.   Ge. 21. 7.   Is. 14. 26.   Est. 3. 4.   Je. 16. 20.   1 Ki. 6. 6. 10.

הַיְקוּם — pref. הַ)(noun masc. sing. . . . קום
הַיֻּקַּח — pref. הַ)(Hoph. fut. 3 p. s. m. (§ 17. r. 8) לקח
הַיְקָר — pref. הַ)(noun masc. sing. dec. 1 a. יקר
הַיְקָרִים — pref. id.)(adj. masc., pl. of יָקָר dec. 4 a. יקר
הַיִּקְרְךָ — pref. הַ)(Kal fut. 3 p. s. m., suff. 2 p. s. m. קרה
הַיָּרֵא — pref. הַ)(adj. masc. sing. d. 5 a. (§ 34. r. 1) ירא
הַיִּרְבֶּה — pref. הַ)(Hiph. fut. 3 pers. sing. masc. רבה
הַיֵּרֵד — pref. id.)(Kal fut. 3 pers. sing. masc. ירד
הַיֹּרֵד — pref. הַ)(Kal part. act. sing. masc. dec. 7 b. ירד
הַיֹּרְדִים — וְ)(pref. id.)(id. pl., absolute state ירד
הַיַּרְדֵּן — וְ)(pref. id.)(pr. name of a river ירד
הַיַּרְדֵּנָה — pref. id.)(id. with parag. ה ירד
הַיֹּרֶדֶת — pref. id.)(id. fem. sing. dec. 13 a. ירד
הַיֹּרָה — pref. id.)(Kal part. act. sing. masc. dec. 9 a. ירה
הַיָּרֵחַ — וְ)(pref. id.)(noun masc. sing. dec. 5 a. ירח
הַיְרַחְמְאֵל — pref. id.)(patronym. of יְרַחְמְאֵל (q. v.) רחם
הַיֹּרִים — pref. id.)(Kal part. act. m., pl. of יֹרֶה d. 9 a. ירה
הַיְרִיעָה — pref. id.)(noun fem. sing. dec. 10. ירע
הַיְרִיעֹת — pref. id.)(id. pl. ירע
הַיָּרֵךְ — pref. id.)(noun fem. sing. dec. 5 a. ירך
הַיָּרֵעַ — pref. הַ)(Kal fut. 3 pers. sing. masc. רעע
הַיִּרְצֶה — pref. id.)(Kal fut. 3 pers. sing. masc. רצה
הַיִרָצוֹן — pref. הַ interr. for הֲ)(Kal fut. 3 pers. pl., with parag. ן רוץ
הֲיִרְצָךְ — pref. הַ)(Kal fut. 3 pers. sing. masc., (יִרְצָה) suff. 2 pers. sing. masc. רצה
הַיָּרֹק — pref. הַ)(noun masc. sing. dec. 4 a. ירק
הַיַּרְקוֹן — pref. id.)(pr. name, see מֵי הַיַּרְקוֹן מוא
הַיֹּרֵשׁ — pref. id.)(Kal part. act. sing. masc. dec. 7 b. ירש
הַיְרֻשָּׁה — pref. id.)(noun fem. sing. dec. 10. ירש
הֲיֵשׁ — pref. הַ)(adv., with suff. יֶשְׁכֶם, comp. dec. 7 a. ישה
הַיִּשָּׂא — pref. id.)(Kal fut. 3 pers. sing. masc. נשא
הַיִּשְׁאַג — pref. id.)(Kal fut. 3 pers. sing. masc. שאג
הַיֹּשֵׁב — וְ)(pref. הַ)(Kal part. act. sing. m. d. 7 b. ישב
הַיֹּשְׁבָה — pref. id.)(id. fem. dec. 10. ישב
הַיֹּשְׁבִי — pref. id.)(id. m., with parag. י (§ 8. r. 19) ישב
הַיָּשֻׁבִי — pref. id.)(patronym. of יָשׁוּב שוב
הַיֹּשְׁבִים — וְ)(pref. id.)(Kal part. act. m., pl. of יֹשֵׁב d. 7 b. ישב
הַיֹּשֶׁבֶת — pref. id.)(id. sing. fem. dec. 13 a. (§ 8. r. 19) ישב
הַיָּשַׁבְתִּי — pref. id.)(id. id. Kh. יָשַׁבְתִּי with parag. י comp. § 8. rem. 19; K. יָשֶׁבֶת ישב
הֲיָשׁוּב — pref. הַ)(Kal fut. 3 pers. sing. masc. שוב
הַיְשׁוֹנִי — pref. הַ)(pr. name masc. שוה
הַיְשׁוּעָה — pref. id.)(noun fem. sing. dec. 10. ישע
הַיְשִׁימוֹן — pref. id.)(noun masc. sing. ישם

הַיְשִׁימוֹת — pref. id.)(pr. name, see בֵּית הַיְ׳ בית
הַיְשִׁימֹן — pref. id.)(noun masc. sing. ישם
הֲיֶשְׁכֶם — pref. הַ)(adv. (יֵשׁ) with suff. 2 pers. pl. m. ישה
הַיֻּשְׁלָם — pref. הַ)(Pual pret. 3 pers. sing. masc. שלם
הַיִּשְׁמְעֵאלִי — pref. id.)(patronym. of יִשְׁמָעֵאל (q. v.) שמע
הַיִּשְׁמְעֵאלִים — pref. id.)(pl. of the prec. שמע
הֲיִשְׁמְעוּ — pref. הַ)(Kal fut. 3 pers. pl. m. שמע
הַיִּשְׁמְעֵלִי — pref. הַ)(patronym. & contr. of יִשְׁמָעֵאל (q. v.) שמע
הַיְשִׁמֹת — pref. id.)(pr. name, see בֵּית הַיְ׳ בית
הַיְשָׁנָה — pref. id.)(adj. fem. sing., from יָשֵׁן masc. ישן
הַיָּשָׁר — וְ)(pref. id.)(adj. & subs. masc. sing. dec. 4 a. ישר
הַיִּשְׂרְאֵלִי — pref. id.)(gent. noun from יִשְׂרָאֵל (q. v.) שרה
הַיִּשְׂרְאֵלִית — pref. id.)(fem. of the prec. שרה
הַיְשָׁרָה — וְ)(pref. id.)(adj. fem. sing. fr. יָשָׁר masc. ישר
הָיִיתָ — וְ)(Kal pret. 2 pers. sing. masc. היה
הָיִתָ — וְ id. pret. 3 pers. sing. fem. Kh. הָיָת (§ 24. rem. 1) K. הָיְתָה היה
הַיֶּתֶד — וְ)(pref. הַ)(noun fem. sing. dec. 5 a. יתד
הַיְתֵד — pref. id.)(id., constr. state יתד
הַיְתֵדֹת — pref. id.)(id. pl., abs. state fem. term. יתד
הָיְתָה / הַיְתָה — } Kal pret. 3 pers. sing. fem. (§ 8. rem. 7) היה
הָיִתָה — וֹ id. pret. 2 pers. sing. masc. (§ 8. rem. 5) היה
הַיָּתוֹם — וֹ noun masc. sing. dec. 3 a. יתם
הָיָתִי — וֹ Kh.; K. הָיִתִי noun fem. sing., suff. 1 pers. sing. from הָיָה or הַוָּה dec. 10. הוה
הַיְתִי — Ch. Aph. pret. 3 pers. sing. masc. (§ 56. rem. 2, comp. § 47. rem. 4) אתה
הַיְתִיו — וְ)(Ch. id. pret. 3 pers. pl. masc. אתה
הַיְתִינוּ — Ch. Hoph. pret. 3 pers. pl. m. (§ 56. r. 2) אתה
הֵיתֵית — וְ Chald. id. pret. 3 pers. sing. fem. אתה
הֱיִיתֶם / הִיתֶם — } Kal pret. 2 pers. pl. masc., וֹ bef. (:.) for } וֹ וְ (§ 13. rem. 13, & § 24. rem. 7) היה
הֲיִתֵּן — pref. הֲ)(Kal fut. 3 pers. sing. masc. נתן
הַיִּתְפָּאֵר — pref. id.)(Hithpa. fut. 3 pers. sing. masc. פאר
הַיִּתְרִי — pref. הַ)(patronym. of יֶתֶר יתר
הַיִּתְרִים — pref. id.)(noun masc., pl. of יֶתֶר (suff. יִתְרוֹ) dec. 6 a. יתר
הַיִּתֶרֶת — pref. id.)(noun fem. sing. יתר
הַךְ — וְ)(Hiph. imp. sing. masc., apoc. for הַכֵּה (§ 25. No. 2b) וכה
הַכְּאֵב — pref. הַ)(noun masc. sing. dec. 1 a. כאב
הִכְאַבְתִּיו — Hiph. pret. 1 pers. sing., suff. 3 pers. sing. m כאב
הַכְאוֹת — Hiph. inf. construct באה
הַכָּבֵד — pref. הַ)(adj. and subst. masc. sing. dec. 5, constr. כְּבֶד & כָּבֵד (§ 34. rem. 2) כבד

a Zec. 11. 13.   e Ec. 3. 21.   i Am. 6. 12.   m Am. 3. 4.   q Je. 3. 1.   u 2 Sa. 15. 33.   y 2 Sa. 10. 11.   C Da. 3. 13.   G Is. 10. 15.
b La. 4. 2.   f Pr. 26. 18.   k Mal. 1. 9.   n Le. 15. 6.   r De. 13. 4.   v 2 Ki. 9. 37.   z Job 6. 2.   D Da. 6. 18.   H Ju. 16. 9.
c Nu. 11. 23.   g 2 Ch. 35. 23.   l De. 11. 10.   o Na. 3. 8.   s Je. 18. 20.   w Ju. 4. 22.   A Da. 5. 12.   E De. 31. 27.   I Job 2. 13.
d Job 40. 27.   h Ge. 32. 33.   m Mi. 1. 15.   p Ps. 123. 1.   t Ju. 16. 14.   x Ex. 38. 20.   B 1 Sa. 12. 14.   F Eze. 13. 22.
1 Sa. 23. 11.   Je. 15. 12.   Je. 32. 8.   Ca. 8. 13.   Mi. 3. 9.   1 Sa. 12. 23.   Da. 6. 17, 25.   Am. 3. 4.   Eze. 13. 22.
Jos. 3. 16.   Mi. 6. 7.   Mal. 1. 8, 9.   Eze. 27. 3.

הַכָּבֵד	pref. הַ)(noun masc. sing. dec. 3 a.	כבד
הַכְבֵּד	וְ)(Hiph. inf., or imp. sing. masc.	כבד
הַכָּבֵד	Niph. imp. sing. masc.	כבד
הַכְבְּדִי	id. inf. (הַכְבֵּד), suff. 1 pers. sing. dec. 7 b.	כבד
הִכְבַּדְתְּ	Hiph. pret. 2 pers. sing. fem.	כבד
הִכְבַּדְתִּי	id. pret. 1 pers. sing.	כבד
הִכְבַּדְתִּים	id. id., suff. 3 pers. pl. masc.	כבד
הַכָּבוֹד	וְ)(noun masc. sing. dec. 3 a.	כבד
הַכְּבֻדָּה	pref. הַ)([for כְּבֻדָּה] adj. fem. sing. from כָּבֹד (§ 39. No. 3, dec. 8)	כבד
הִכְבִּיד	Hiph. pret. 3 pers. sing. masc.	כבד
הִכְבִּידוּ	id. pret. 3 pers. pl.	כבד
הַכַּבֵּס	Hothpael inf. construct [for הִתְכַּבֵּס § 6. rem. 10, note]	כבס
הַכֶּבֶשׂ	pref. הַ)(noun masc. sing. dec. 6.	כבש
הַכִּבְשָׂה	pref.)(noun fem. sing. dec. 12 b.	כבש
הַכְּבָשִׂים	pref. id.)(noun masc., pl. of כֶּבֶשׂ dec. 6.	כבש
הַכִּבְשָׁן	pref. id.)(noun masc. sing.	כבש
הַכַּדִּים	pref. id.)(noun com. pl. abs. from כַּד dec. 8 d.	כדד
הַכֵּה	Hiph. inf., or imp. sing. masc. (§ 25. No. 2 b)	נכה
הִכָּה	וְ)(id. pret. 3 pers. sing. masc.	נכה
הֻכָּה	וְ)(Hoph. pret. 3 pers. sing. m. (§ 25. No. 2 b)	נכה
הַכּוּהָ	Hiph. imp. pl. masc., (הַכּוּ) suff. 3 pers. sing. masc. (§ 25. No. 2 b)	נכה
הִכָּהוּ	וְ)(id. pret. 3 pers. s. m., suff. 3 pers. s. m.	נכה
הִכּוּהוּ	id. pret. 3 pers. pl., (הִכּוּ) suff. 3 pers. s. m.	נכה
הַכֹּהֵן	וְ)(pref. הַ)(noun masc. sing. dec. 7 b.	כהן
הַכֹּהֲנָה	pref. id.)(noun fem. sing. dec. 10.	כהן
הַכֹּהֲנוֹת	pref. id.)(id. pl.	כהן
הַכֹּהֲנִים	וְ)(pref. id.)(noun masc., pl. of כֹּהֵן dec. 7 b.	כהן
הַכּוּ	וְ)(Hiph. imp. pl. masc. (§ 25. No. 2 b)	נכה
הִכּוּ	וְ)(id. pret. 3 pers. pl.	נכה
הֻכּוּ	Hoph. pret. 3 pers. pl. (§ 25. No. 2 b)	נכה
הַכּוֹכָבִים	וְ)(pref. הַ)(noun masc., pl. of כּוֹכָב dec. 2 b. [for כַּבְכָּב]	כבב
הַכּוּם	Hiph. imp. pl. masc., suff. 3 pers. pl. masc. (§ 25. No. 2 b)	נכה
הִכּוּם	id. pret. 3 pers. pl., suff. 3 pers. pl. masc.	נכה
הִכּוֹן	Niph. imp. sing. masc.	כון
הָכוֹנוּ	וְ Kh. הֵכוֹנוּ Niph., K הָכִינוּ Hiph. imp. pl. m.	כון
הִכּוּנִי	וְ)(Hiph. pret. 3 pers. pl., suff. 1 pers. sing. (§ 25. No. 2 b)	נכה
הַכּוֹס	pref. הַ)(noun fem. sing. dec. 1 a.	כוס
הַכּוּשִׁי	pref. id.)(gent. noun from כּוּשׁ	כוש
הַכּוּשִׁים	pref. id.)(pl. of the preceding	כוש
הַכּוֹת	וְ)(Hiph. inf. const. dec. 1. (§ 25. No. 2 b)	נכה
הַכֻּבֹּתְךָ	id., suff. 2 pers. sing. masc. [for הַכֻּבֹּתְךָ]	נכה
הַכֻּתֶּרֶת	pref. הַ)(n. f. s., pl. כֹּתָרוֹת (§ 44. rem. 5)	כתר
הַכָּזֶה	preff. כְּ (q. v.) & הַ)(pron. demon. m. sing.	זה
הַכְזוֹנָה	preff. הַ interr. for הֲ, & כְּ)(Kal part. act. fem. dec. 10, from זוֹנָה masc.	זנה
הַכַּח	וְ)(pref. הַ)(noun masc., dec. 1 a.	כחח
הֶחְחַדְתִּיו	וְ)(Hiph. pret. 1 pers. sing., suff. 3 pers. s. m.	כחד
הֻכַחְתָּ	Hiph. pret. 2 pers. sing. masc. [for הוֹכַחְתָּ]	יכח
הֹכַחְתִּיו	וְ)(id. pret. 1 pers. sing., suff. 3 pers. sing. m.	יכח
הֲכִי	pref. הַ)(conj.	כי
הֲכַיּוֹצֵר	preff. הַ & כַּ for כְּ הַ)(Kal part. act. s. m. d. 7 b.	יצר
הַכִּיּוֹר	pref. הַ)(noun masc. sing. dec. 1 b.	כור
הֵכִיחַ	Hiph. pret. 3 pers. sing. masc. [for הוֹכִיחַ]	יכח
הָכִיל	Hiph. inf. constr.	כול
הַכִּימֵי	preff. הַ, כַּ, & f. כִּימָה)(כִּי)(n. m. pl., constr of יָמִים, irr. of יוֹם (§ 45)	יום
הָכִין	וְ)(Hiph. inf. constr., used as an absolute	כון
הֵכִין	id. pret. 3 pers. sing. masc.	כון
הֱכִינָהּ	id. id., suff. 3 pers. sing. fem.	כון
הָכִינוּ	וְ)(id. imp. pl. masc.	כון
הֲכִינוֹ	id. inf. (הָכִין), suff. 3 pers. sing. m. dec. 3 a.	כון
הֱכִינוּ	id. pret. 3 pers. sing. masc., suff. 3 pers. s. m.	כון
הֵכִינוּ	וְ)(id. pret. 3 pers. pl.	כון
הֲכִינֹנוּ	id. pret. 1 pers. pl.	כון
הֲכִינוֹתָ	וְ)(id. pret. 2 pers. sing. masc.; וַ bef. (-:)	כון
הֲכִינוֹתִי	וַ)(id. pret. 1 pers. sing.; וַ id.	כון
הַכֵּינִי	Hiph. imp. s. m. suff. 1 p. s. (§ 25. No. 2 b)	נכה
הֱכִינַנִי	Hiph. pret. 3 pers. sing. masc., suff. 1 pers. s.	כון
הֲכִינֹתָה	id. pret. 2 p. s. m. (comp. § 8. r. 5); וַ bef. (-:)	כון
הֲכִינֹתִי	id. pret. 1 pers. sing.; acc. shifted by conv. וַ for וְ (§ 8. rem. 7)	כון
הַכִּיר	pref. הַ)(noun masc. sing. dec. 1 b.	כור
הִכִּיר	Hiph. pret. 3 pers. sing. masc.	נכר
הִכִּירֻהוּ	id. pret. 3 pers. pl. (הִכִּירוּ), suff. 3 p. s. m.	נכר
הִכִּירוּ	id. pret. 3 pers. sing. masc., suff. 3 p. s. m.	נכר
הִכִּירוּ	id. pret. 3 pers. pl.	נכר
הַכִּירוֹת / הַכִּירֹת	pref. הַ)(n. m. with pl. f. term. fr. כִּיּוֹר d. 1 b.	כור
הִכִּתָ / הִכִּיתָ	Hiph. pret. 2 pers. sing. m. (§ 24. r. 14); / acc. shifted by conv. וַ (§ 8. r. 7)	נכה
הִכִּתָה / הִכִּיתָה	id. id. (§ 8. rem. 5)	נכה
הִכִּתָהוּ	id. id., suff. 3 pers. sing. masc.	נכה
הִכֵּיתִי / הִכִּיתִי	id. pret. 1 pers. sing. (§ 24. rem. 14); / acc. shifted by conv. וַ (§ 8. rem. 7)	נכה
הֻכֵּיתִי	Hoph. pret. 1 pers. sing. (§ 25. No. 2 b)	נכה

a Ge. 31. 1.   g Ex. 10. 1.   n Ju. 7. 16, 19, 20.   t 1 Sa. 5. 12.   z 2 Ki. 3. 24.   f Ge. 24. 14.   m Jos. 4. 3.   s 1 Ki. 20. 35, 37.   w Job 2. 12.
b Is. 6. 10.   h Je. 30. 19.   o Ex. 22. 1.   u Ec. 12. 2.   a Mi. 6. 13.   g 2 Sa. 7. 14.   n Job 28. 27.   t 1 Ki. 2. 24.   x Ge. 27. 23.
c Ex. 8. 11.   i 1 Ch. 29. 12.   p 2 Ki. 9. 27.   v 2 Ki. 10. 25.   b Is. 58. 5.   h Je. 18. 6.   o Na. 2. 4.   u 2 Sa. 7. 12.   y Je. 5. 3.
d 2 Ki. 14. 10.   k Ju. 18. 21.   q 1 Sa. 2. 36.   w Am. 4. 12.   c Ge. 34. 31.   i Ge. 24. 44.   p Ex. 16. 5.   v 2 Sa. 7. 12.   z 2 Sa. 18. 11.
e Eze. 39. 13.   l Le. 13. 55. 56.   r 2 Sa. 13. 28.   x 2 Ch. 35. 4.   d Le. 11. 30.   k Je. 6. 11.   q 1 Ch. 29. 16.   v De. 33. 9.   aa Zec. 13. 6.
f Is. 47. 6.   m 2 Sa. 12. 6.   s Eze. 9. 5.   y Ge. 34. 30.   e Ex. 23. 23.   l Job 10. 5.   r 2 Ch. 19. 3.

Hebrew	Description	Root
הֲבִיתִיךְ	id., suff. 2 p. s. f. (§ 24. r. 14, § 25. & No. 2b)	נכה
וַהֲבִיתָם׳	id. pret. 2 pers. sing. m., suff. 3 p. pl. m.	נכה
וַהֲבִיתָם׳	id. pret. 2 pers. pl. masc.	נכה
הֲבִיתָנוּ	id. pret. 2 pers. sing. masc. suff. 1 pers. pl.	נכה
הֲבִיתַנִי	id. id., suff. 1 pers. sing.	נכה
וְהִכְּךָ	id. pret. 3 pers. sing. m., suff. 2 pers. s. m.	נכה
הַבְּכֹר	pref. הַ × noun masc. s. dec. 2b; [for בְּכֹר]	בכר
וְהַבֹּל / הַבֹּל	pref. הַ } noun masc. sing. dec. 8c.	בלל
הַבְּלָא	pref. הַ × noun masc. sing. (suff בְּלֹאוֹ) d. 6a.	בלא
הַכֶּלֶב / הֲכֶלֶב	pref. id. } pref. הַ } noun masc. s. (pl. c. כַּלְבֵי) d. 6a.	כלב
וְהַכְּלָבִים	pref. הַ × id. pl., absolute state	כלב
הַכְּלִי / הַכְּלִי	pref. id. × noun masc. sing. irr. (§ 45; comp. § 35. rem. 14)	כלה
הַכְּלִיא	pref. id. × noun masc. s. Kh. כְּלִיא, K. כְּלוּא	כלא
הַכַּלָּיוֹת	pref. id. × n. f., pl. abs. from [כִּלְיָה] d. 12b.	כלה
הַכֵּלִים	pref. id. × noun masc. pl. [as if from בֶּלֶה, see כְּלִי (§ 45)	כלה
הַכְלִים׳	Hiph. inf. constr.	כלם
וְהַכְלִמֹת׳	pref. הַ × n. f. pl. abs. fr. [כִּלְיָה] d. 12b.	כלה
הַכָּלֵם׳	Niph. inf. constr.	כלם
הִכְלִימֹ	Hiph. pret. 3 pers. s. m., suff. 3 pers. s. m.	כלם
וַהֻכְלְמוּ	Hoph. pret. 3 pers. pl.	כלם
וְהִכָּלְמוּ	Niph. imp. pl. masc.	כלם
הֻכְלַמְנוּ	Hoph. pret. 1 pers. pl.	כלם
הִכְלַמְנוּם	Hiph. pret. 1 p. pl., suff. 3 p. pl. m. (§ 11. r.1)	כלם
וְהִכָּם	Hiph. pret. 3 pers. s. m. (הִכָּה) suff. 3 pers. pl. masc. (§ 25. No. 2b)	נכה
הַכְּמֹת׳	preff. הַ interr. for הֲ, & כְּ × noun masc. sing. constr. of מָוֶת dec. 6g.	מות
הַכְּמַכֶּת	preff. id. × noun f. s. contr. of מַכָּה dec. 10.	נכה
הַכְּמָרִים	pref. הַ × n. m. pl. [of כֹּמֶר § 35. rem. 9]	כמר
הָכֵן	וְ Hiph. imp. sing. masc.; or (Jos. 3. 17) inf. abs. as an adv.	כון
הִכּוֹן	Niph. imp. sing. masc.	כון
הֵכִין׳	Hoph. pret. 3 pers. sing. masc. for הוּכַן	כון
הֲכִנּוּ	Hiph. pret. 1 pers. pl. [for הֲכִנֹנוּ § 25. rem.]	כון
הַכִּנּוֹר׳	pref. הַ × noun masc. sing. dec. 1b.	כנר
וְהִכֵּנִי / וַיַּכֵּנִי	Hiph. pret. 3 pers. sing. masc. (הִכָּה), suff. 1 pers. sing. (§ 25. No. 2b)	נכה
הַכָּנִים׳	pref. הַ × noun masc., pl. of כֵּן dec. 6b.	כנן
הִכְנִיעַ׳	Hiph. pret. 3 pers. sing. masc.	כנע
הַכְנִיעָהוּ	Hiph. imp. sing. masc., suff. 3 pers. sing. m.	כנע

Hebrew	Description	Root
הַכְּנַם	pref. הַ × n. m. collect., fr. כֵּן and the term. ◌ָם	כנן
הִכָּנְעוּ (הִכָּנְעוֹ)	Niph. inf. suff. 3 pers. sing. masc. (§ 36. rem. 5)	כנע
וְהַכְּנַעֲנִי	pref. הַ × gent. noun from כְּנַעַן	כנע
הַכְּנַעֲנִים	pref. id. × id. pl.	כנע
הַכְּנַעֲנִית	pref. id. × id. s. fem.	כנע
וְהִכְנַעְתִּי	Hiph. pret. 1 pers. sing.	כנע
הַכָּנָף	pref. הַ × noun fem. sing. dec. 4c.	כנף
הַכְּנָפַיִם / הַכְּנָפָיִם	pref. id. × id. dual, abs. state; Kh. כְּנָפִים	כנף
הַכְנֹתִי	Hiph. pret. 1 pers. sing.	יון
הַכִּסֵּא׳	pref. הַ × noun masc. sing.	כסא
הַכִּסֵּא	pref. id. × noun masc. sing. dec. 7b.	כסא
הִכָּסוֹת	Niph. inf. constr.	כסה
וְהַכְּסִיל	pref. הַ × noun masc. sing. dec. 1a.	כסל
הַכְּסִילִים	pref. id. × id. pl., absolute state	כסל
וְהַכְּסֻלּוֹת	pref. id. × pr. name of a place	כסל
הַכְּסָלִים	pref. id. × n. m., pl. of כֶּסֶל (suff. כְּסָלוֹ) d. 6a.	כסל
וְהַכֶּסֶמֶת	pref. id. × noun fem. sing., pl. כֻּסְּמִים	כסם
הַכֶּסֶף	pref. id. ×	כסף
וְהַכֶּסֶף	pref. id. × noun m. s. (suff. כַּסְפִּי) d. 6a.	כסף
הִכְעִים	Hiph. pret. 3 pers. sing. masc.	כעס
הִכְעִיסוּ׳	id. id., suff. 3 pers. sing. masc.	כעס
הִכְעִיסוּ	id. pret. 3 pers. pl.	כעס
הַכְעִיסֵנִי	id. inf., suff. 1 pers. sing. dec. 1b.	כעס
הַכַּעַס׳	pref. הַ × noun masc. sing. dec. 6d.	כעס
הַכְעַסְאוּנִי	Kh. הַכְעִסוּנִי q. v.; K. הַכְעִסַנִי Hiph. inf., suff. 1 pers. sing.	כעס
הִכְעִסוּנִי	Hiph. pret. 3 pers. pl., suff. 1 pers. sing.	כעס
הַכְּעָסִים	pref. הַ × noun masc., pl. of כַּעַס dec. 6d.	כעס
הַכְעַסְתַּנִי	defect. for הַכְעִיסַנִי (q. v.)	כעס
הַכְעַסְתָּ׳	Hiph. pret. 2 pers. sing. masc.	כעס
וְהִכְעַסְתִּי	id. pret. 1 p. s.; acc. shifted by conv. וְ (§ 8. r.7)	כעס
הַכַּף׳ / הֲכַף׳	pref. הַ } noun fem. sing. dec. 8d.	כף
הַכַּפּוּפִים	pref. הַ × Kal part. pass. m., pl. of כָּפוּף d.3a.	כפף
וְהַכַּפּוֹת	pref. id. × noun fem., pl. of כַּף dec. 8d.	כף
וְהַכְּפִיר׳	pref. id. × noun masc. sing. dec. 1a.	כפר
הַכְּפִירָה	pref. id. × pr. name of a place	כפר
הַכְּפִירִים	pref. id. × noun masc., pl. of כְּפִיר dec. 1a.	כפר
הִכְפִּישַׁנִי	Hiph. pret. 3 pers. sing. masc., suff. 1 pers. s.	כפש
הַכְּפֹר׳	pref. הַ × noun masc. sing. dec. 6c.	כפר
הַכְּפֻרִים	pref. id. × noun masc., pl. of [כַּפֹּר] d. 1b.	כפר
הַכַּפֹּרֶת	pref. id. × noun fem. sing.	כפר
הַכַּפֻּת׳	defect. for הַכַּפּוֹת (q. v.)	כפף
הַכַּפְתּוֹר׳	pref. הַ × noun masc. sing. dec. 1b.	כתר

a De. 7. 2.   b 1 Sa. 17. 43.   l 1 Sa. 20. 34.   r Is. 27. 7.   f Ex. 8. 14.   n Eze. 17. 3.   s 2 Ki. 23. 26.   z 2 Ki. 22. 17.   h Is. 31. 4.
Je. 37. 10.   i Is. 56. 12.   m Je. 14. 11.   s Eze. 38. 7.   g 2 Ch. 28. 19.   o Ne. 3. 37.   t 1 Ki. 21. 22.   i Ps. 104. 21.
Je. 14. 19.   k 1 Sa. 17. 49.   Eze. 36. 32.   t Na. 2. 6.   Job 40. 12.   p 1 Ki. 21. 22.   u Eze. 32. 9.   k Is. 3. 16.
Nu. 22. 28.   Je. 6. 15.   o 1 Sa. 25. 15.   u 2 Ch. 29. 19.   Pr. 7. 20.   v Nu. 7. 86.   l Ca. 1. 14.
1 Ki. 20. 36.   m Le. 19. 9.   p 1 Sa. 25. 7.   v 1 Sa. 16. 23.   1 Ch. 17. 10.   Eze. 24. 8.   w Ju. 8. 6, 15.   m Nu. 4. 7.
c Ec. 3. 20.   f Je. 3. 3.   q Je. 5. 6.   w 1 Sa. 17. 9.   Nu. 15. 38.   x 2 Ki. 23. 26.   y Ps. 145. 14.   n Am. 9. 1.
d Is. 28. 24.   g Je. 8. 12.   q 2 Sa. 3. 33.   Ge. 32. 12.   x 2 Ch. 3. 11, 12.   y Ex. 9. 32.

הַכְצַעֲקָתָהּ preff. הַ interr. f. הֲ, & כְּ)(noun f. s., suff. 3 pers. s. f. from צְעָקָה d. 11 c. (§ 42. r. 1)   צעק

הָכֵר. Hiph. *to amaze, stun,* so תַּהְכְּרוּ (for תַּהְכִּירוּ § 11. rem. 7) Job 19. 13, which Prof. Lee takes as Kal in the sense of *contemning.*

הַכֵּר Hiph. inf., or imp. s. m. [for הַכֵּר § 11. r. 5]   נכר

הַכֹּר pref. הַ)(noun masc. sing. dec. 1 a.   כרב

הַכְּרֻבִים וְ pref. id.)(noun masc., pl. of כְּרוּב d. 1 a.   כרב

הִכִּרֻהוּ Hiph. pret. 3 pers. pl. (הִכִּירוּ) suff. 3 p. s. m.   נכר

הַכְּרוּב pref. הַ)(noun masc. sing. dec. 1 a.   כרב

הַכְּרוּבִים pref. id.)(id. pl., absolute state   כרב

הַכְרִזוּ וְ Ch. Aph. imp. pl. masc. (§ 47. rem. 4)   כרז

הַכָּרִי pref. הַ)(noun masc., prop. participle [כָּרִי] either with the adj. design. ־ִי, or כָּרֵי is the pl. for כָּרִים   כור

הַכְּרֵי Kh. הַכָּרִי q. v., K. הַכָּרֵתִי (q. v.)   כרת

הַכָּרִים pref. הַ)(n. m., pl. of כַּר dec. 8. (§ 37. r. 7)   כרר

הִכְרִיעַ Hiph. pret. 3 pers. sing. masc.   כרע

הַכְרִיעֵהוּ id. imp. sing. masc. suff. 3 pers. sing. masc.   כרע

הַכְרִית Hiph. inf. constr.   כרת

הִכְרִית id. pret. 3 pers. sing. masc.   כרת

הִכְרִיתָהּ וְ id. pret. 3 pers. sing. fem.   כרת

הִכְרִיתוּ וְ id. pret. 3 pers. pl.   כרת

הַכְרִיתְךָ id. inf. (הַכְרִית), suff. 2 pers. sing. m. d. 1 b.   כרת

הַכָּרֵם / הַכֶּרֶם pref. הַ)(noun masc. sing. (and pr. name) in compos. see בַּיִת d. 6 a. (§ 35. r. 2)   כרם

הַכַּרְמִי pref. id.)(patronym. [for הַכַּרְמִי] from כַּרְמִי   כרם

הַכְּרָמִים pref. id.)(n. m., pl. of כֶּרֶם d. 6 a. (suff. כַּרְמֵי)   כרם

הַכַּרְמֶל וְ pref. id.)(noun masc. sing. (with suff. כַּרְמִלּוֹ) dec. 8. § 37. rem. 3 & 5)   כרם

הַכַּרְמֶלָה pref. id.)(pr. n. of a region (כַּרְמֶל) with parag. ה   כרם

הַכַּרְמְלִי pref. id.)(gent. noun of the prec. (§ 37. r. 5)   כרם

הַכַּרְמְלִית pref. id.)(fem. of the prec.   כרם

הַכְרֵעַ Hiph. inf. absolute   כרע

הַכְּרָעַיִם / הַכְּרָעֵים pref. הַ)(noun f. du. from [פֶּרַע] d. 4 a.   כרע

הִכְרַעְתָּנִי Hiph. pret. 2 p. s. f. [for תִּינִי] suff. 1 p. s.   כרע

הָכְרַת Hoph. pret. 3 pers. sing. masc.   כרת

הַכָּרַת noun fem. s. constr. [of הַכָּרָה § 42. No. 3]   נכר

הַכֹּרֵת pref. הַ)(Kal part. act. sing. masc. dec. 7 b.   כרת

הִכָּרֵתִי Niph. inf. constr.   כרת

הַכָּרֵתִי וְ pref. הַ)(noun masc. sing.   כרת

הִכְרַתִּי Hiph. pret. 1 pers. sing. [for הִכְרַתְתִּי § 25. r.]   כרת

הִכְרַתִּי וְ id.; acc. shifted by conv. וְ (§ 8. rem. 7)   כרת

הִכְרַתִּיו id., suff. 3 pers. sing. masc.   כרת

הִכְרַתִּיךָ וְ id., suff. 2 pers. sing. masc.   כרת

הַכֶּשֶׁב pref. הַ)(noun masc. sing. dec. 6.   כשב

הַכְּשָׂבִים וְ pref. id.)(id. pl., absolute state   כשב

הַכַּשְׂדִּים pref. id.)(pr. name of a people, pl. of כַּשְׂדִּי   כשד

הִכְשִׁיל Hiph. pret. 3 pers. sing. masc.   כשל

הַכְשֵׁיר Hiph. inf. absolute   כשר

הַכֻּשִׁית pref. הַ)(gent. noun, fem. of כּוּשִׁי from כּוּשׁ   כוש

הִכְשַׁלְתֶּם Hiph. pret. 2 pers. pl. masc.   כשל

הַכְּתָב pref. הַ)(noun m. sing. dec. 1 a. (§ 30. No. 3)   כתב

הַכְּתֻבִים pref. id.)(Kal part. p. m., pl. of כָּתוּב d. 3 a.   כתב

הַכֹּתְבִים pref. הַ)(id. part. act. m., pl. of כֹּתֵב d. 7 b.   כתב

הֻכְּתָה Hoph. pret. 3 pers. sing. fem. (§ 25. No. 2 b)   נכה

הַכֹּתוֹ Hiph. inf. (הַכּוֹת), suff. 3 pers. sing. masc. dec. 1 b. (§ 25. No. 2 b)   נכה

הַכֹּתֵב pref. הַ)(Kal part. p. sing. masc. dec. 3 a.   כתב

הַכְּתוּבָה pref. id.)(id. fem. dec. 10.   כתב

הַכְּתֻבוֹת pref. id.)(id. fem. pl.   כתב

הַכְּתוּבִים pref. id.)(id. masc. pl. dec. 3 a.   כתב

הַכֹּתִי Hiph. inf. (הַכּוֹת), suff. 1 pers. sing. dec. 1 a. (§ 25. No. 2 b)   נכה

הִכִּתִיו וְ id. pret. 1 pers. sing., suff. 3 pers. sing. m.   נכה

הִכִּתִיךָ וְ id. pret., suff. 2 pers. sing. masc.   נכה

הַכֶּתֶם pref. הַ)(noun masc. sing.   כתם

הַכָּתְנֹת pref. id.)(n. f. pl. constr. from כְּתֹנֶת d. 13 c.   כתן

הַכֻּתֹּנֶת pref. הַ art. or interr.)(noun fem. sing.   כתן

הַכְּתֹנֶת pref. הַ art.)(noun fem. sing. dec. 13 c.   כתן

הַכָּתֵף pref. הַ)(noun fem. sing. dec. 5 b.   כתף

הַכְּתֵפוֹת pref. id.)(id. pl., absolute state   כתף

הַכֹּתָרוֹת / הַכְּתָרֹת וְ pref. הַ id.)(noun fem., pl. [as if from כְּתָרָה] see the following   כתר

הַכֹּתֶרֶת pref. id.)(noun fem. sing. (§ 44. rem. 5)   כתר

הֲל particle of interrogation, De. 32. 6.

הָלָא Niph. *to be removed, cast away,* Mi. 4. 7.

הָלְאָה only with paragogic ה, הָלְאָה adv.—I. of space, *farther, farther off, beyond;* מִשָּׁם וָהָלְאָה *from thence and farther;* מֵהָלְאָה לְ *farther off than, beyond.*—II. of time *farther, forward, onward.*

הֲלֹא pref. הֲ)(adv. of negation   לא

הֲלֹאה וְ adv. [הֲלֹא with parag. ה]; for וְ see lett. וּ   הלא

הַלְאוֹת Hiph. inf. constr.   לאה

הַלְאֵל preff. הַ interr. for הֲ, & לְ)(noun m. s. d. 1 a.   אול

הֶלְאָנִי Hiph. pret. 3 pers. sing. masc. (§ 11. rem. 1)   לאה

הֶלְאָת id. pret. 3 pers. sing. fem. (§ 24. rem. 14)   לאה

a Ge. 18. 21.   c 2 Sa. 20. 23.   e Le. 26. 22.   g Ju. 11. 35.   j Joel 1. 9.   d Eze. 25. 7.   i Ec. 10. 10.   l 1 Sa. 17. 9, 35, 35.   o 2 Ch. 4. 12, 13.
b Eze. 45. 14.   d 1 Sa. 15. 9.   Ju. 4. 24.   Is. 3. 9.   Le. 4. 35.   k Mal. 2. 8.   1 Sa. 17. 46.   2 Ch. 4. 12.
Eze. 10. 3.   Ps. 78. 31.   Jos. 7. 9.   Is. 14. 8.   Le. 1. 10.   Je. 32. 12.   La. 4. 1.   Is. 7. 13.
Ge. 42. 8.   Ps. 17. 13.   Le. 8. 21.   f Is. 48. 9.   Le. 1. 13.   h Ge. 30. 40.   De. 1. 4.   Ex. 39. 27.   x Job 16. 7.
Da. 5. 29.   Je. 44. 8.   Le. 11. 8.   f Is. 29. 17.   Nu. 15. 31.   2 Ch. 34. 24.   1 Ki. 7. 30.   Eze. 24. 12.
2 Ki. 11. 19.   Ju. 11. 35.   Eze. 14. 8.   La. 1. 14.

Hebrew	Description	Root
הִלְאִיתִיךָ	id. pret. 1 pers. sing., suff. 2 pers. sing. masc.	לאה
הַלֵּבָ֫ב	pref. הַ)(noun masc. sing. dec. 8b.	לבב
הַלֵּבָב	pref. id.)(noun masc. sing. dec. 5b.	לבב
הַלְּבָבוֹת	pref. id.)(noun fem., pl. of [לְבִיבָה] dec. 10.	לבב
הַלְּבוֹנָה	)' pref. id.)(noun fem. sing. dec. 10.	לבן
הַלְּבוּשׁ	pref. id.)(noun masc. sing. dec. 1a.	לבש
הֲלַבְזוֹ	preff. הֲ & לְ (q. v.))(Kal inf. constr.	בזז
הֵלְבִּינוּ	Hiph. pret. 3 pers. pl.	לבן
הִלְבִּישָׁה	id. pret. 3 pers. sing. fem.	לבש
הִלְבִּישׁוּ	id. pret. 3 pers. pl.	לבש
הִלְבִּישַׁנִי	id. pret. 3 pers. sing. masc., suff. 1 pers. sing.	לבש
הַלָּבָן	pref. הַ)(adj. masc. sing. dec. 4a.	לבן
הֲלְבֶן	preff. הַ interr. for הֲ, & לְ)(noun masc., constr. of בֵּן irr., (§ 45)	בנה
הַלְּבָנָה	pref. הַ)(noun fem. sing.	לבן
הַלְּבֵנָה	pref. id.)(n. fem. sing. dec. 11c, (§ 42. No. 1)	לבן
הַלְּבֹנָה	pref. id.)(noun fem. sing. dec. 10.	לבן
הַלְּבָנוֹן	)' pref. id.)(pr. name of a mountain	לבן
הַלְּבָנִי	pref. id.)(pr. name masc.	לבן
הַלְּבָנִים	)' pref. הַ)(adj. masc., pl. of לָבָן dec. 4a.	לבן
הַלְּבֵנִים	pref. id.)(noun fem. with pl. masc. term. from לְבֵנָה dec. 11c. (§ 42. rem. 1)	לבן
הַלָּבֻשׁ	pref. id.)(Kal part. p. s. m. d. 3a. (for לָבוּשׁ)	לבש
הַלְבֵּשׁ	)' Hiph. inf. abs.	לבש
הַלְבִּשׁוּ	)' Ch. Aph. pret. 3 pers. pl. masc.	לבש
הִלְבִּישׁוּ	)' Hiph. pret. 3 pers. pl.	לבש
הַלֹּבְשִׁים	pref. הַ)(Kal part. act. m., pl. of לֹבֵשׁ d. 7b.	לבש
הִלְבַּשְׁתָּ	)' Hiph. pret. 2 pers. sing. masc.; acc. shifted by conv. (§ 8. rem. 7)	לבש
הִלְבַּשְׁתִּיו	)' id. pret. 1 pers. sing., suff. 3 pers. sing. m.	לבש
הִלְבַּשְׁתָּם	)' id. pret. 2 pers. sing. m., suff. 3 pers. pl. m.	לבש
הֲלַדְרֹשׁ	preff. הַ, & לְ bef. (:))(Kal inf. constr.	דרש
הֻלֶּדֶת	Hoph. inf. constr. (§ 20. rem. 16)	ילד
הֲלֹא	pref. הֲ)(adv. of negation, Kh. for לֹא	לא
הַלַּהַב	pref. הַ)(noun masc. sing. dec. 6d.	להב
הֲלַהוֹכֵחַ	preff. הַ interr. for הֲ, & לְ)(Hiph. inf. constr.	יכח
הֲלָהֶן	pref. הַ)(adv. see לָהֵן (§ 5. rem. 3)	להן
הֲלַהֲרֹגֵנִי	preff. הַ interr. for הֲ, & לְ)(Kal inf., suff. 1 p.s.	הרג
הֲלוֹא	)'pref. הֲ)(adv.of negation,more frequently הֲלֹא	לא
הַלּוּבִים	)' pref. הַ)(gent. noun pl.	לוב
הַלּוּחִית	pref. id.)(pr. name of a place	לוח
הַלּוֹחֵשׁ	pref. id.)(pr. name masc.	לחש

Hebrew	Description	Root
הַלוּם	pref. id.)(Kal part. act., or noun masc. sing.	לום
הַלֵּוִי	)' pref. id.)(patronym. [for לֵוִי] from לֵוִי	לוה
הַלְוִיִּם	)' pref. id.)(id. pl. dec. 8f.	לוה
הִלְוִיתָ	)' Hiph. pret. 2 pers. sing. masc.	לוה
הָלוֹךְ	Kal inf. absolute	הלך
הַהֻלָּלִים	noun masc., pl. of [הַלֵּל] dec. 1b.	הלל
הַהֲלֻמֵי	Kal part. p. pl. construct masc. from [הָלוּם] dec. 3a.	הלם
הֲלָז	pron. demon. com. gend. sing., apoc. fr. הַלָּזֶה	זה
הַלָּזֶה	preff. הַ & לְ)(pron. demon. masc. sing.	זה
הַלָּזֶה	pron. demon. masc. sing.	זה
הַלֵּזוּ	pron. demon. fem. sing.	זה
הַלְחֹת	pref. הַ)(noun masc. with pl. fem. term. from לוּחַ dec. 1a.	לוח
הַלֶּחִי / הַלְּחִי	pref. id.)(noun fem. sing. dec. 6i, (§ 35. rem. 14)	לחה
הַלְחָיַיִם	)' pref. id.)(id. dual, absolute state	לחה
הַלֶּחֶם / הַלָּחֶם	pref. הַ)(noun com. s. dec. 6a. (§ 35. rem. 2)	לחם
הִלָּחֵם	)'(Niph. imp. sing. masc.	לחם
הִלָּחֶם	)' id. id.; acc. shifted bef. monos. (§ 9. rem. 3)	לחם
הִלָּחֲמוֹ	id. inf., suff. 3 pers. sing. masc.	לחם
הִלָּחֲמוּ	)' id. imp. pl. masc.	לחם
הַלַּחְמִי	gen. noun, see בֵּית הַלַּחְמִי	בית
הַלַּחַץ	pref. הַ)(noun masc. sing. dec. 6d.	לחץ
הַלֹּחֲצִים	pref. id.)(Kal part. act. masc., pl. of [לֹחֵץ] dec. 7b.	לחץ
הַלְחָשִׁים	)' pref. id.)(noun masc., pl. of לַחַשׁ dec. 6d.	לחש
הַלֻּחֹת	)'(pref. id.)(noun masc., with pl. fem. term. from לוּחַ dec. 1a.	לוח
הַלְטָאָה	)' pref. id.)(noun fem. sing.	לטא
הֹלִיד	defect. for הוֹלִיד (q. v.)	ילד
הַלַיהוָה	pref. הַל interr. particle & יְהוָה (q. v.) others read הַ לַיהוָה, הַלַיהוָה, הַל יְהוָה	הוה
הֲלַיֹּעֵץ	preff. הַ interr. for הֲ, & לְ)(Kal part. act. sing. masc. dec. 7b.	יעץ
הֹלִיכוּ	Hiph. imp. pl. masc. [for הוֹלִיכוּ]	ילד
הֲלִיכוֹת	noun fem., pl. of [הֲלִיכָה] dec. 10.	הלך
הֲלִיכוֹתֶיךָ	id. suff. 2 pers. sing. masc.	הלך
הֲלִיכַי	n. m. pl., suff. 1 pers. s. from [הָלִיךְ] dec. 3a.	הלך
הֲלִיכֹת	defect. for הֲלִיכוֹת (q. v.)	הלך
הַלַּיְלָה / הַלָּיְלָה	pref. הַ)(noun masc. sing. with parag. ה from לַיִל dec. 6h.	ליל

a Mi. 6. 3.   g Ge. 27. 16.   n Eze. 9. 3.   t Is. 22. 21.   ‡ Ruth 1. 13, 13.   ¶ Is. 28. 1.   1 Sa. 18. 17.   Is. 3. 20.   2 Ki. 17. 27.
b Je. 17. 9.   h 2 Ch. 28. 15.   o Zec. 3. 4.   u Ex. 2. 14.   † Is. 58. 5.   Ju. 9. 38.   Ex. 32. 16.   Ps. 68. 25.
c De. 20. 8.   i Ge. 7. 17.   p Eze. 20. 3.   v 2 Sa. 15. 35.   Eze. 36. 35.   Zec. 14. 3.   Le. 11. 30.   Job 29. 6.
d 2 Sa. 13. 8, 10.   k Est. 6. 9.   q Da. 5. 29.   w Is. 25. 7, 7.   De. 18. 3.   Is. 3. 9.   De. 32. 6.   Job 6. 19.
e Eze. 38. 13.   l Le. 6. 8.   r Ge. 40. 20.   x De. 28. 12.   Ex 17. 9.   1 Sa. 10. 18.   2 Ch. 25. 16.   Job 3. 3.
f Joel 1. 7.   m Zec. 6. 6.   s Job 6. 26.   Ge. 30. 37.   Ge. 11. 3.

הֲלִילוּ Hiph. imp. pl. masc. . . . ילל

הֲלִיפוֹת pref. הַ)(noun masc. with pl. fem. term.
from לַיְל dec. 6 h. . . . . ליל

הֲלִילִי Kh. הֲלִילִי q. v., K. הֲלִילִי (q. v.) . ילל

הֲלִילִי Hiph. imp. sing. fem. . . ילל

הֲלִינֹתָם Hiph. pret. 2 pers. pl. masc. . . . לון

הֲלִיצֻנִי [הֲלִיצוּ] Hiph. pret. 3 pers. pl.; suff. 1 pers. s. לוץ

הֲלִירְשֵׁנוּ preff. הַ interr. for הֲ, & לְ)(Piel inf. [יָרַשׁ],
suff. 1 pers. pl. dec. 7 b. . . . ירש

הָלַךְ, [& יָלַךְ] fut. יֵלֵךְ וַיֵּלֶךְ (from יָלַךְ), poet. יַהֲלֹךְ;
imp. לֵךְ לְכוּ (from יָלַךְ), also הֲלֹכוּ; inf. הָלוֹךְ;
constr. לֶכֶת, with suff. לֶכְתִּי (from יָלַךְ).—I. to
go, walk, proceed, const. with אֶל, לְ, עַל, acc.,
rarely בְּ, of the place whither one goes. But
also with the acc. to go through or over; with בְּ
to go with, i. e. lead, bring; with אֵת (אֶת)
to accompany; to have intercourse with; with
אַחֲרֵי to go after, to follow.—II. to go, walk, live.
—III. to go away, depart; especially with the
dative לוֹ הָלַךְ לְךָ.—IV. to flow, run, of
liquids.—V. to go on, continue; הָלַךְ וְגָדֵל going
on and growing, i. e. waxing greater; הוֹלֵךְ וְסֹעֵר
going on raging, i. e. continuing tempestuous;
הָלוֹךְ וָשׁוֹב going on and returning, i. e. continually returning. Niph. נֶהֱלַךְ to pass away, disappear, Ps. 109. 23. Pi. i. q. Kal Nos. I, II, III;
part. מְהַלֵּךְ a wanderer. Hiph. הוֹלִיךְ, once
הֵילִיךְ (from יָלַךְ) part. pi. מַהֲלִכִים (§ 11. rem. 8).—
I. to cause to go, to lead, conduct.—II. to lead away,
to remove, Ps. '25. 5.—III. to cause to flow.
Hithp. הִתְהַלֵּךְ.—I. to go, walk about; part.
מִתְהַלֵּךְ a wanderer, Pr. 24. 34.—II. to walk, live.
—III. to flow, of wine, Pr. 23. 31.

הֲלַךְ Chald. Pa. to go, walk, Da. 4. 26. Aph. id.

הֵלֶךְ masc.—I. a going, travelling, used as a
concrete, traveller, 2 Sa. 12. 4.—II. a flowing,
stream, 1 Sa. 14. 26.

הֲלָךְ Chald. masc. way-tax, toll.

הֲלִךְ masc. a going, step, Job 29. 6.

הֲלִיכָה fem. dec. 10.—I. a going.—II. way.—
III. caravan, Job 6. 19.

מַהֲלָךְ masc. dec. 2 b.—I. a walk.—II. way,
journey.

תַּהֲלוּכָה fem. dec. 10, procession, Ne. 12. 31.

הָלַךְ וַיֵּ Kal pret. 3 pers. sing. masc. (comp.
§ 8. rem. 7) . . . הלך

הֲלַךְ Chald. noun masc. sing.; וְ before הלך

הָלַךְ וְ Kal inf. absolute . . . הלך

הַלְּכִי Piel imp. sing. masc. . . הלך

הֲלָךְ Kal inf. construct . . . . הלך

הֵלֶךְ noun masc. sing. . . . . הלך

הֹלֵךְ Kal part. act. sing. masc. dec. 7 b. . הלך

הָלְכָה, הָלְכָה וַ Kal pret. 3 pers. sing. fem. (§ 8. rem. 7) הלך

הֹלֵכָה id. part. act. sing. fem. dec. 10, from הֹלֵךְ m. הלך

הָלְכוּ id. pret. 3 pers. pl. (§ 8. rem. 7) . הלך

הֲלֹכוּ id. imp. pl. masc. . . . . הלך

הִלְּכוּ Piel pret. 3 pers. pl. . . . הלך

הֹלְכוֹת Kal part. act. fem., pl. of הֹלֶכֶת or הֹלְכָה
dec. 13 a, or 10. . . . . . הלך

הֹלְכֵי construct of the following . . הלך

הֹלְכִים וְ Kal part. act. masc., pl. of הוֹלֵךְ dec. 7 b. הלך

הָלַכְנוּ Kal pret. 1 pers. pl. (§ 8. rem. 7) . הלך

הַלְכָה preff. הַ & לְ (see lett. לְ))(Kal inf. constr. כפה

הָלַכְתָּ וְ Kal pret. 2 pers. sing. masc. (§ 8. rem. 7) הלך

הָלַכְתָּ id. id.; acc. shifted by conv. וְ . . הלך

הָלַכְתְּ, הָלַכְתְּ וְ id. pret. 2 pers. sing. fem. . . . הלך

הֹלְכֹת id. part. act. fem., pl. of הֹלֶכֶת or הֹלְכָה
dec. 13 a, or 10. . . . . . . הלך

הָלַכְתִּי Kh., K. הָלָכְתִּי id. pret. 2 pers. sing. fem.
(§ 8. rem. 5 & 7) . . . . הלך

הָלַכְתִּי וְ id. pret. 1 pers. sing. (§ 8. rem. 7) . הלך

הָלַכְתִּי id. id.; acc. shifted by conv. וְ . . הלך

הִלַּכְתִּי Piel pret. 1 pers. sing. (comp. § 8. rem. 7) הלך

הֹלַכְתִּי K. הֹלֶכֶת Kal part. act. sing. fem., Kh.
id. with parag. ' (comp. § 8. rem. 19) . . הלך

הֹלַכְתִּיהָ Hiph. pret. 1 pers. sing., suff. 3 pers. s. fem. ילך

הֲלַכְתֶּם וַ Kal pret. 2 pers. pl. masc.; וְ for conv. הלך

[הָלַל] I. to shine, Job 29. 3.—II. to boast, glory;
הוֹלְלִים boasters, proud. Pi.—I. to praise, celebrate. const.

---

a Is. 13. 6; 23. 6.   c Nu. 14. 29.   e Ec. 11. 9.   g Je. 3. 6.   r Ju. 5. 6, 10.   u Is. 58. 5.   x Eze. 23. 31.   a Je. 31. 21.   f Ps. 38. 7.
b Is. 21. 3.   d Ps. 119. 51.   f Nu. 22. 14.   h Je. 51. 50.   s 2 Sa. 13. 11.   v 1 Ki. 13. 9.   y Eze. 16. 47.   d Ge. 25. 2.   g 2 Ki. 4. 23.
Je. 45. 20.   g Ju. 14. 15.   i Is. 46. 2.   t 2 Ch. 9. 21.   Ge. 34. 17.   w Ex. 17. 5.   z Ex. 2. 5.   e Ju. 4. 8.   h Hos. 2. 16.
Is. 14. 31.   1 Sa. 6. 8.   Na. 3. 10.   Je. 6. 28.

with an acc., הַלְלוּ־יָהּ *praise ye the Lord*; but also with לְ, בְּ (Ps. 44. 9). Hence II.—*to praise, commend.* Pu. *to be praised*; מְהֻלָּל *praised, worthy to be praised.* Po. *to make foolish, to shame.* Hiph.—I. *to cause to shine.*—II. *to shine*, Job 31. 26. Hithpa.—I. *to be praised*, Pr. 31. 30. —II. *to boast oneself*, with בְּ, עִם (Ps. 106. 5) of that in which one glories. Hithpo. *to be* or *become mad.*

הִלֵּל (apt to praise, i. e. devout, comp. § 26. No. 8) pr. name masc. Ju. 12. 13, 15.

הִלּוּלִים masc. pl. (of הִלּוּל) *praises*, meton. *days of praise, festivals of thanksgiving.*

הֵילֵל masc. *the morning star, Lucifer*, Is. 14. 12. Others take it as the imp. of יָלַל *wail, lament.*

הוֹלֵלָה fem. only pl. הוֹלֵלוֹת, *folly.*

הוֹלֵלוּת fem. id. Ec. 10. 13.

יְהַלַלְאֵל (*he shall praise God*) pr. name of two men, 1 Ch. 4. 16; 2 Ch. 29. 12.

מַהֲלָל masc. dec. 2 b, *praise, commendation*, Pr. 27. 21.

מַהֲלַלְאֵל (*praise of God*) pr. name of two men, Ge. 5. 12; Ne. 11. 4.

תְּהִלָּה fem. dec. 10.—I. *praise.*—II. *an object of praise.*—III. *song of praise, hymn, psalm*; pl. תְּהִלִּים the (book of) *Psalms.*—IV. *praise, glory.*

תְּהִלָּה fem. *folly, sin.*

הַלֵּל) Piel inf. constr. · · ·   הלל

הִלֵּל id. pret. 3 pers. sing. masc. · · הלל

הַלְאוֹת pref. הַ X noun pl. absolute fem. [from לוּלַי § 35. rem. 15 note] · לול

הַלְלוּ Piel imp. pl. masc. [for הַלְלוּ § 10. rem. 7] · הלל

הַלְלוּהוּ id., suff. 3 pers. sing. masc. · · הלל

הִלְלוּ) id. pret. 3 pers. pl. · · הלל

הַלְלוּךָ id. id., suff. 2 pers. sing. masc. [for הַלְלוּךָ § 10. rem. 7] · הלל

הִלְלוֹת noun fem., pl. of הוֹלֵלָה dec. 10. · הלל

הַלְלִי Piel imp. sing. fem. [for הַלְלִי § 10. rem. 7] הלל

הִלַּלְנוּ id. pret. 1 pers. pl. · · הלל

הִלַּלְתִּיךָ id. pret. 1 pers. sing., suff. 2 pers. sing. masc. הלל

הִלַּלְתֶּם) id. pret. 2 pers. pl. masc. · · הלל

[הָלַם] fut. יַהֲלֹם—I. *to strike, beat.*—II. *to beat in pieces*, Is. 16. 8.

הֲלֹם adv. *hither* · עַד־הֲלֹם *thus far.*

הֵלֶם (*blow*) pr. name masc. 1 Ch. 7. 35

הַלְמוּת fem. a *hammer*, Ju. 5. 26.

יַהֲלֹם masc. the name of a gem, which the versions variously render by the *diamond, emerald,* and the *jasper.*

מַהֲלֻמּוֹת fem. pl. (of מַהֲלֻמָּה) *beatings, blows.*

הֲלֹם adv. · · · · הלם

הֲלֹם Kal inf. constr.; וֹ bef. (־ָ)   הלם

הֶלֶם pr. name masc. · · · הלם

הָלְמָה) Kal pret. 3 pers. sing. fem.   הלם

הָלְמוּ id. pret. 3 pers. pl. · · הלם

הֲלָמוּנִי id. id. with suff. 1 pers. sing. הלם

הֲלְמַעַנְךָ pref. הֲ interrog. for הַ X prep. לְמַעַן with suff. 2 pers. sing. masc. [prop. pref. לְ & subst. מַעַן] · · ענה

הַלֵּמֵתִים preff. הֲ, & לְ for לְהַ X Kal part. masc., pl. of מֵת dec. 1 a.   מות

הֲלָנוּ pref. הֲ X prep. לְ with suff. 1 pers. pl. (§ 5. parad.) · · ל

הֲלַנֶּצַח preff. הֲ, & לְ (see lett. ל) X noun masc. sing. (suff. נִצְחִי) dec. 6 a (§ 35. rem. 5)   נצח

הַלְעֵנַג pref. הֲ X noun masc. sing. dec. 6 d. · לענג

הַלְעוֹלָם preff. הֲ interr. for הַ, & לְ X n. m. s. dec. 2 b. עלם

הַלְעִיטֵנִי Hiph. imp. sing. masc., suff. 1 pers. sing. לעט

הַלְעוֹלָמִים preff. הֲ interr. for הַ, & לְ X noun masc., pl. of עוֹלָם dec. 2 b. · · עלם

הַלַּפִּידִים הַלַּפִּידִים } pref. הַ X noun masc. sing. dec. 1 b. · לפד

הִלָּקֵחַ Niph. inf. construct (§ 36. rem. 5) לקח

הִלָּקְחוֹ id., suff. 3 pers. sing. masc.   לקח

הַלֹּקְחִים pref. הַ X Kal part. act. m., pl. of לֹקֵחַ dec. 7. לקח

הַלָּקֵשׁ pref. id. X noun m. s. for לֶקֶשׁ (§ 35. r. 2) לקש

הֲלָרָשָׁע preff. הֲ, & לְ for לְהַ X adj. m. dec. 4 a. רשע

הַלָּשׁוֹן pref. הַ X noun com. sing. dec. 3 a. לשן

הַלִּשְׁכָּה) pref. id. X noun fem. sing. dec. 12 b. לשך

הַלְּשָׁכוֹת) pref. id. X id. pl., absolute state לשך

הַלִּשְׁכוֹת pref. id. X id. pl., construct state לשך

הֲלְשַׁלֵּל preff. הֲ, & לְ for לְהַ X Kal inf. construct · שלל

הַלָּשׁוֹן pref. הַ X noun com. sing. dec. 3 a. לשן

הַלְּשׁוֹנוֹת) pref. id. X id. pl. · · · לשן

הֵם (, וְ,) with parag. ה, הֵמָּה pers. pron. 3 pers. pl. masc. *they*; with the article הָהֵמָּה, הָהֵם *these.* Comp. הוּא (§ 1. rem. 6)

Chala. הֵמוֹ, הֵמוֹן *they.*

Ps. 10.3. | Ps. 44.9. | Ju. 5.26. | Jos. 5.13. | Ge. 25.30. | Ex. 20.18. | Je. 23.31. | Eze. 40.46. | Jos. 15.2.
Is. 62.9. | Ps. 119.164. | Pr. 23.35. | 2 Sa. 2.26. | Ps. 77.8. | 1 Sa. 4.19,21. | Am. 7.1. | Eze. 42.5. | Is. 66.18.
Is. 64.10. | Joel 2.26. | Job 18.4. | Ps. 123.4. | Eze. 1.13. | 1 Sa. 21.7. | Ec. 10.11. | Eze. 33.13. | Nu. 16.16.
Ec. 1.17. | 1 Sa. 14.16. | Ps. 88.11 | 2 Ch. 19.2.

הֵם•	Kh. for הֵם (q. v.)	הם
הֵהֵ׀	Kh. הֵם q. v., K. הֵמָּה (q. v.)	הם
הַמֹּאָבִי	pref. הַ ✗ gent. noun from מוֹאָב q. v.	
הַמֹּאָבִיָּה	pref. id. ✗ id. fem.	
הַמֹּאָבִים׀	pref. id. ✗ id. pl. masc.	
הַמְאָדְּמִים•	pref. id. ✗ Pual part. masc., pl. of מֵאָדָּם (§ 10. rem. 5)	אדם
הַמֵּאָה	pref. id. ✗ noun fem. sing. dec. 11 b. (also proper name)	מאה
הַמָּאוֹר	pref. id. ✗ noun masc. sing. dec. 2 b.	אור
הַמֵּאוֹת	׀ pref. id. ✗ noun fem. pl. of מֵאָה dec. 11 b.	מאה
הַמְאָרְנִי•	pref. id. ✗ Piel part. sing. masc. [מְאָרֵ] suff. 1 pers. sing. dec. 7 b.	אזר
הַמֵּאִיּוֹת	pref. id. ✗ Kh. מֵאִיּוֹת (as if from מֵאָיָה), K. מֵאוֹת׳, noun fem. pl. of מֵאָה dec. 11 b.	מאה
הַמַּאֲכִלְךָ	pref. id. ✗ Hiph. part. sing. masc. (מַאֲכִיל) suff. 2 pers. sing. masc. dec. 1 b.	אכל
הַמַּאֲכֶלֶת	pref. id. ✗ noun fem. sing., pl. מַאֲכָלוֹת׳ (§ 44. rem. 5)	אכל
הַמַּאֲמִית	pref. id. ✗ Hiph. part. sing. masc. dec. 1 b.	אמן
הַמְאֲנִים	pref. id. ✗ adj. masc., pl. of [מָאֵן] dec. 7 b.	מאן
הֲמָאֹס•	pref. הַ ✗ Kal inf. absolute	מאס
הַמְאַסֵּף׀	׀ pref. הַ ✗ Piel part. sing. masc. dec. 7 b.	אסף
הַמַּאֲרֵב׀ הַמַּאֲרֵב׀	׀ pref. id. ✗ noun masc. sing. dec. 2 b.	ארב
הַמְאֵרָה	pref. id. ✗ noun fem. sing. d. 10 [for מְאָרָה]	ארר
הַמְאָרְרִים	pref. id. ✗ Piel part. m., pl. of [מְאָרֵר] dec. 7 b.	ארר
הַמְאֹרָשָׂה•	pref. id. ✗ Pual part. fem. [of מְאֹרָשׂ]	ארש
הַמְּאֹרֹת•	pref. id. ✗ noun masc. with pl. fem. term. from מָאוֹר dec. 3 a.	אור
הַמֵּאתַיִם׀ הַמָּאתַיִם׀	׀ pref. id. ✗ noun fem. dual of מֵאָה, [for מָאתַיִם]	מאה
הַמִּבְדָּלוֹת•	pref. id. ✗ noun fem. pl.	בדל
הַמָּבוֹא•	pref. id. ✗ noun masc. sing. dec. 3 a.	בוא
הַמֵּבוֹא	Kh. הַמֵּבוֹא q. v., K. הַמֵּבִיא Hiph. part. sing. masc. dec. 3 b.	בוא
הַמַּבּוּל	׀ pref. הַ ✗ noun masc. sing.	יבל
הַמְּבוֹנִים•	pref. id. ✗ Kh. הַמְּבוֹנִים noun masc. [pl. of מָבוֹן], K. הַמְּבִינִים (q. v.)	בין
הַמַּבּוּעַ•	pref. id. ✗ noun masc. sing. dec. 1 b.	נבע
הַמְּבִי• הַמֵּבִיא•	׀ Hiph. part. masc. sing. dec. 3 b. (comp. § 25. No. 2 f)	בוא
הַמְּבִיאִים•	pref. הַ ✗ id. pl., absolute state	בוא
הַמַּבִּיט•	pref. הַ ✗ Hiph. part. sing. masc.	נבט
הַמֵּבִין	pref. id. ✗ Hiph. part. sing. masc. dec. 3 b.	בין
הַמְּבִינִים	׀ pref. id. ✗ id. pl., absolute state	בין

הֲמִבִּינָתְךָ	preff. הֲ & מִ ✗ noun fem. s., suff. 2 pers. s. m. from בִּינָה dec. 10.	בין
הֲמִבְּלִי	pref. הֲ ✗ adv.	בלה
הַמַּבְלִיג׳	pref. הַ ✗ Hiph. part. sing. masc.	בלג
הֲמִבַּלְעֲדֵי	preff. הֲ & מִ ✗ adv., compound. from בַּל, and עֲדֵי (pl. constr. of עַד)	בלה
הַמַּבְעֵר•	pref. הַ ✗ Hiph. part. sing. masc. [for מַבְעִיר]	בער
הַמִּבְצָר	pref. id. ✗ noun masc. sing. dec. 2 b.	בצר
הַמְבַקְשִׁים	׀ pref. id. ✗ Piel part. masc., pl. of מְבַקֵּשׁ dec. 7 b. (ק f. ק § 10. rem. 7)	בקש
הַמְבֻשָּׁלִים•	pref. id. ✗ Piel part. m., pl. of [מְבֻשָּׁל] d. 7 b.	בשל
הַמְבַשֵּׂר•	pref. id. ✗ Piel part. act. sing. masc.	בשר
הַמְבַשְּׂרוֹת•	pref. id. ✗ id. f., pl. of מְבַשֶּׂרֶת dec. 13 a.	בשר
הַמַּגְבִּיהִי••	pref. id. ✗ Hiph. part. sing. masc. with parag. י (comp. § 8. rem. 19)	נבה
הַמִּגְבָּעֹת•	pref. id. ✗ noun fem. pl. [of מִגְבָּעָה]	נבע
הַמַּגְדִּילִים•	pref. id. ✗ Hiph. part. m., pl. of [מַגְדִּיל] d. 1 b.	נדל
הַמִּגְדָּל׳	׀ pref. id. ✗ noun masc. sing. dec. 2 b.	נדל
הַמִּגְדָּלוֹת• הַמִּגְדָּלִים	pref. id. ✗ id. pl., absolute state	נדל
הַמָּגוֹג	pref. id. ✗ pr. name of a region	נון
הַמַּגִּיד	pref. id. ✗ Hiph. part. sing. masc. dec. 1 b.	נגד
הַמְּגִלָּה	pref. id. ✗ noun fem. sing. dec. 10.	גלל
הַמֻּגְלִים•	pref. id. ✗ Hoph. part. masc. pl. of [מֻגְלֶה] 9 a. (comp. § 11. rem. 10)	גלה
הַמָּגֵן	pref. id. ✗ noun masc. sing. dec. 8 b.	ננן
הַמָּגִנּוֹת• הַמָּגִנִּים•	׀ pref. id. ✗ id. pl. (§ 37. rem. 4)	ננן
הַמִּגְרַעַת•	pref. id. ✗ noun fem. sing.	נער
הַמַּגֵּפָה	׀ pref. id. ✗ noun fem. sing. dec. 10.	ננף
הַמְדַבֵּר	pref. id. ✗ Piel part. sing. masc. dec. 7 b.	דבר
הַמִּדְבָּר הַמִּדְבָּר׳	pref. id.׀ pref. הַ׀ noun masc. sing. dec. 2 b.	דבר
הַמִּדְבָּרָה	pref. הַ ✗ id. with parag. ה	דבר
הַמְדַבְּרִים	pref. id. ✗ Piel part. m., pl. of מְדַבֵּר d 7 b.	דבר
הַמִּדָּה	pref. id. ✗ noun fem. sing. dec. 10.	מדד
הַמְּדוּרָה•	pref. id. ✗ noun fem. sing. dec. 10.	דור
הַמָּדִי	pref. id. ✗ gent. noun from מָדַי q. v.	
הַמְּדִינָה	pref. id. ✗ noun fem. sing. dec. 10, R. דִּין see	דון
הַמְּדִינוֹת	׀ pref. id. ✗ id. pl.	דון
הַמְּדִינִי•	pref. id. ✗ gent. noun from מִדְיָן R. דִּין see	דון
הַמְּדִינִים	pref. id. ✗ id. pl. masc.	דון
הַמְּדִינִית•	pref. id. ✗ id. sing. fem.	דון
הַמְּדָנִים	׀ pref. id. ✗ id. pl. masc. contr. for מִדְיָנִים	דון
הַמַּדָּע•	׀ pref. id. ✗ noun masc. sing. dec. 2 b.	ידע
הַמַּדְרֵגָה•	pref. id. ✗ noun fem. sing. dec. 10.	דרנ

¹ Ne. 2. 13. ² 2 Sa. 21. 9. ³ Ex. 39. 34. ⁴ De. 8. 16. ⁵ Is. 28. 16.
ᵃ Je. 13. 10. ᵇ Je. 14. 19. ᶜ Jos. 6. 9, 13. ᵈ 2 Ch. 13. 13. ᵉ Ju. 9. 35.
ᶠ Nu. 3. 46. ᵍ Eze. 45. 15. ʰ Jos. 16. 9. ⁱ 1 Ch. 9. 19. ʲ Eze. 42. 9.
ᵏ 2 Ch. 35. 3. ˡ Fc. 12. 6. ᵐ 2 Sa. 5. 2. ⁿ 1 Ch. 11. 2. ᵒ Ne. 10. 32.
ᵖ Ne. 8. 9. Ne. 8. 3. ᵠ Job 39. 26. ʳ Ex. 14. 11 ˢ Am. 5. 9.
ᵗ Ex. 22. 5. ᵘ 1 Sa. 25. 26. ᵛ Eze. 46. 24. ʷ 1 Sa. 4. 17. ˣ Ps. 68. 12.
ʸ Ps. 113. 5. ᶻ Ex. 39. 28. Ps. 35. 26. Ne. 3. 25, 26. 1 Ch. 32. 5.
Je. 40. 1. 2 Ch. 23. 9. Ne. 4. 10. De. 28. 20. Nu. 17. 15.
Je. 2. 32. Eze. 24. 9 Ec. 2. 8. 2 Ch. 1. 12. Ca. 2. 14.

הַמַּדְרֵגות*   pref. ה X id. pl. . . . .   דרג
הַמְּדָתָא   pref. id. X pr. name masc., see מְדָתָא

[הָמָה] fut. יֶהֱמֶה to make a *humming* noise.—I. spoken of the sounds of certain animals, *to growl, to howl, to coo, to mourn*; trop. of men *to sigh*.—II. of the noise of a tumultuous crowd, of water, *to bustle, to be turbulent, to roar, rage*; of the harp *to hum*; applied to the emotion of the soul, such as anguish, sorrow, *to be agitated, disquieted*; to the commotion of the inward parts, Is. 16. 11, *my bowels sound* (moan) *like a harp*.

הֶם or הֲם only pl. Eze. 7. 11, i. q. הָמוֹן *riches*.
הֹם or הָם pr. name of an unknown region, Ge. 14. 5.
הָמוֹן masc. dec. 3 a.—I. *noise, sound*, of singing, rain, a multitude.—II. *multitude, crowd*.—III. *multitude of possession, riches, wealth*.—IV. *emotion of the mind, disquietude*, Is. 63. 15.
הֲמוֹנָה (*multitude*) the mystical name of a city, Eze. 39. 16.
הֶמְיָה f. *sound of the harp*, constr. הֶמְיַת Is. 14. 11.

הֵם   ו' pers. pron. masc. pl. (הֵם) with parag. ה   הם
הֹמֶה   Kal part. act. sing. masc.   המה
הַמַּהֲגִים*   ו' pref. ה X Hiph. part. m. pl. of [מַהֲגֶה] d. 9 a.   הגה
הַמְּהוּמָה   pref. id. X noun fem. sing. dec. 10.   המה
הַמְהַלֵּךְ*   pref. id. X Piel part. sing. masc. dec. 7 b.   הלך
הַמְהַלְּכִים   pref. id. X id. pl., absolute state   הלך
הַמְהַלְּלִים'   ו' pref. id. X Piel part. masc. pl. of [מְהַלֵּל] dec. 7 b. (לְ for לְ § 10. rem. 7)   הלל
הַמַּהְפֶּכֶת* / הַמַּהְפֶּכֶת } pref. id. X noun fem. s. (comp. § 35. r. 2)   הפך
הָמוּ   ו' Kal pret. 3 pers. pl.   המה
הֵמּוּ   Ch. pers. pron. 3 pers. masc. pl.   הם
הַמּוֹאָבִי   pref. ה X gent. noun from מוֹאָב q. v.
הַמּוֹאָבִיָּה   pref. id. X id. fem.
הַמּוֹאָבִים   ו' pref. id. X id. pl. masc.
הַמּוֹאָבִית   pref. id. X id. sing. fem.
הַמּוּבָא   pref. id. X Hoph. part. sing. masc. dec. 1 b.   בוא
הַמּוֹט*   pref. id. X noun masc. sing. dec. 1 a.   מוט
הַמּוֹטָה'   pref. id. X noun fem. sing. dec. 10.   מוט
הַמּוֹכֵר*   ו' Kal part. act. sing. masc. dec. 7 b.   מכר
הַמּוֹל   Niph. inf. absolute   מול
הַמּוֹלִדִים*   pref. ה X Hiph. part. act. m., pl. of מוֹלִיד d. 1 b.   ילד
הֲמוּלָה*   noun fem. sing.   המל
הַמּוֹלִיד*   pref. ה X Hiph. part. sing. masc. dec. 1 b.   ילד

הַמּוֹלִיךְ*   pref. id. X Hiph. part. sing. masc. dec. 1 b.   לך
הַמּוֹלִיכֵךְ'   pref. id. X id., suff. 2 pers. sing. masc.   לך
הַמּוּמָתִים   pref. id. X Hoph. part. masc., pl. of מוּמָת   מות
הָמוֹן   noun masc. sing. dec. 3 a.   המה
הֲמוֹן   ו' id., constr. state; ו bef. (־ֲ)   המה
הֹמוֹן   Ch. pers. pron. masc. pl.   הם
הֲמוֹנָהּ   ו' noun masc. sing., suff. 3 pers. sing. fem. from הָמוֹן dec. 3 a.; ו before (־ֲ)   המה
הֲמוֹנָה   pr. name of a place   המה
הֲמוֹנֹה / הֲמוֹנוֹ' } noun masc. sing., suff. 3 pers. sing. m. from הָמוֹן dec. 3 a.; ו bef. (־ֲ)   המה
הֲמוֹנֶיהָ*   id. pl., suff. 3 pers. sing. fem.   המה
הֲמוֹנֵךְ*   id. sing., suff. 2 pers. sing. m. [for הֲמוֹנֵךְ]   המה
הַמְנוּכָא'   ו Ch. in other copies, Kh. הַמְנוּכָא, (read 'נוּ); K. הַמְנִיכָא, noun masc. sing. emph.
הַמֻּנָּךְ   [of הַמְנֻּךְ or הַמְּנֻּךְ]
הַמּוּסָרִים   pref. ה X Hoph. part. m., pl. of מוּסָר d. 2 b.   סור
הַמּוֹעֵד*   ו' pref. id. X noun masc. sing. dec. 7 b.   יעד
הַמּוֹעָדָה'   pref. id. X noun fem. sing.   יעד
הַמּוֹפֵת   ו' pref. id. X noun masc. sing. dec. 7 b.   יפת
הַמּוֹפְתִים   ו' pref. id. X id. pl., absolute state   יפת
הַמּוֹצָאִים   pref. ה X Hoph. part. masc. pl. [of מוּצָא]   יצא
הַמּוֹצִיא   pref. id. X Hiph. part. sing. masc. dec. 1 b.   יצא
הַמּוֹצִיאֲךָ   pref. id. X id., suff. 2 pers. sing. masc.   יצא
הַמּוּקָעִים*   pref. id. X Hoph. part. masc. pl. [of מוּקָע]   יקע
הַמּוֹר*   pref. id. X noun masc. sing. d. 1 a, for 'מֹר   מרר
הַמּוֹרָא'   pref. id. X noun m. s. (suff. מוֹרַאֲכֶם) d. 2 b.   ירא
הַמּוֹרָאָם*   pref. id. X Kh. מוֹרָאָם for K. מוֹרִים Hiph. part. masc., pl. of מוֹרֶה   ירה
הַמּוֹרְדִים*   pref. id. X Kal part. act. m., pl. of מוֹרֵד d. 7 b.   מרד
הַמּוֹרֶה'   pref. id. X subst.; prop. Hiph. part. masc. dec. 9 a; also pr. name   ירה
הַמּוֹרִיָּה   pref. id. X pr. name of a hill, see מֹרִיָּה
הַמּוֹרִינִים*   for הַמּוֹרְגִּים (q. v.) dag. f. resolved in '   מרג
הַמּוֹרִים   pref. ה X Hiph. part. m., pl. of מוֹרֶה d. 9 a.   ירה
הַמּוֹרַשְׁתִּי   pref. id. X gent. noun from מוֹרֶשֶׁת גַּת q. v.   ירש
הַמּוּשָׁב   pref. id. X Hoph. part. sing. masc.   שוב
הַמּוּשִׁי   pref. id. X patronym. [for מוּשִׁיִּי] from מוּשִׁי   מוש
הַמּוֹשִׁיעַ*   pref. id. X Hiph. part. sing. masc. dec. 1 b.   ישע
הַמּוֹשֵׁל*   pref. id. X Kal part. act. sing. masc. dec. 7 b.   משל
הַמּוֹשְׁלִים*   pref. id. X id. pl., absolute state   משל
הַמָּוֶת   ו' pref. id. X noun masc. sing. dec. 6 g.   מות
הֲמֹתוֹ*   Kal part. act. f., pl. of הֹמֶה הוֹמָה m. d. 10, fr.   המה
הַמִּיתָתָהוּ*   pref. ה X noun masc. s. (מָוֶת) with parag. ה   מות
הַמְּזַבֵּחַ   pref. id. X constr. of the following   זבח
הַמִּזְבֵּחַ   ו' pref. id. X noun masc. sing. dec. 7 c.   זבח

a Eze. 38. 20.   h 2 Ch. 23. 12.   l Eze. 7. 12.   q De. 3. 15.   u Eze. 32. 20.   z Jos. 20. 9.   e Ca. 4. 6.   i Joel 2. 23.   o 2 Ch. 23. 20.
b Pr. 20. 1.   i Je. 20. 5.   m Je. 14. 5.   r 2 Ch. 23. 11.   x Eze. 32. 12.   a De. 12. 5.   f De. 34. 12.   k 1 Ch. 21. 23.   p De. 30. 19.
c Is. 8. 19.   i Nu. 4. 19, 12.   n Ps. 65. 8.   s Da. 5. 7, 16, 29.   y De. 34. 11.   b 2 Sa. 11. 24.   l 1 Sa. 14. 39.   q Eze. 7. 16.
d Ps. 104. 3.   e Je. 23. 10, 12.   o Is. 66. 9.   t 1 Sa. 21. 7.   z Eze. 2. 3.   c Ec. 10. 4.   r Ps. 116. 15.
e Ec. 4. 15.   f Eze. 7. 12.   p Je. 2. 6.   u Ju. 20. 26.

הַמִּזְבֵּחָה	pref. ה) id. with parag. ה	זבח
הַמִּזְבְּחוֹת הַמִּזְבְּחֹת	} pref. id.) id. pl.	זבח
הַמָּזוֹג	pref. id.) noun masc. s. [for מָזֶג § 35. r. 2]	מזג
הַמְּזוּזָה	pref. id.) noun fem. sing. dec. 10.	זוז
הַמְּזוּזוֹת הַמְּזוּזֹת	} pref. id.) id. pl.	זוז
הַמָּזוֹן	pref. id.) noun masc. sing.	זון
הַמַּזְכִּיר	pref. id.) Hiph. part. sing. masc. dec. 1 b.	זכר
הַמַּזְכִּירִים	pref. id.) id. pl., absolute state	זכר
הַמַּזְלֵג	pref. id.) noun masc. sing.	זלג
הַמִּזְלָגוֹת הַמִּזְלָגֹת	} pref. id.) n. f., pl. of [מִזְלָגָה] d. 11 a.	זלג
הַמְזַמְּרוֹת	pref. id.) noun f., pl. of [מְזַמֶּרֶת] d. 13 a.	זמר
הַמְּזִמָּתָה	pref. id.) noun f. s. (מְזִמָּה) with parag. ה	זמם
הַמִּזְרָח	pref. id.) noun masc. sing. dec. 2 b.	זרח
הַמִּזְרָק	pref. id.) noun masc. sing. dec. 2 b.	זרק
הַמִּזְרָקוֹת הַמִּזְרָקֹת	} pref. id.) id. pl., absolute state	זרק
הַמַּחֲבֹאִים	pref. id.) noun masc., pl. of [מַחֲבֹא] d. 1 b.	חבא
הַמַּחֲבַת	pref. id.) noun fem. sing.contr. [for מַחֲבֶתּ]	חבת
הַמְּחֹנִים	pref. id.) gent. noun pl.	חוה
הַמַּחֲזִיק	pref. id.) Hiph. part. sing. masc. dec. 1 b.	חזק
הַמְחַטֵּא	pref. id.) Piel part. sing. masc.	חטא
הַמְחַכֶּה	pref. id.) Piel part. sing. masc. dec. 9 a.	חכה
הַמְחַכִּים	pref. id.) id. pl., absolute state	חכה
הַמַּחֲלָה	pref. id.) noun fem. sing.	חלה
הַמַּחֲלִי	pref. id.) gent. noun [for מַחְלִי] from	חלה מַחְלִי
הַמְּחִלּוֹת	) pref. id.) noun fem., pl. of לָה dec. 10.	חול
הַמְחֹלֵל	pref. id.) Pual part. sing. masc.	חלל
הַמְחֹלְלוֹת	pref. id.) Pilel part. f., pl. of [מְחֹלֶלֶת] d. 13 a.	חול
הַמַּחֲלָצוֹת	pref. id.) noun fem., pl. of [מַחֲלָצָה]	חלץ
הַמַּחְלְקוֹת	pref. id.) pl. of the foll. (§ 44. rem. 5)	חלק
הַמַּחֲלֻקְתּוֹ	pref. id.) noun f. s. (suff. מַחֲלֻקְתּוֹ) d. 13 c.	חלק
הַמְּחֹלָתִי	pref. id.) gent. noun from אָבֵל מְחוֹלָה q. v.	אבל
הַמַּחֲנֶה	pref. id.) noun com. sing. dec. 9 a.	חנה
הַמַּחֲנוֹת	) pref. id.) id. with pl. fem. term	חנה
הַמַּחֲנַיִם	pref. id.) id.du.,or perh.pl.of a s.[מַחֲנֶה](§38.r.2)	חנה
הַמַּחֲנֹת	defect. for הַמַּחֲנוֹת (q. v.)	חנה
הַמַּחְצֶבֶת	pref. id.) Hiph. part. sing. fem.	חצב
הַמַּחֲצָה	pref. id.) noun sing. fem. dec. 10.	חצה
הַמְחֻקֶּה	pref. id.) Pual part. sing. masc.	חקק
הַמַּחֲרֶבֶת	pref. id.) Hiph. part. sing. fem. from מַחֲרִיב masc. (§ 39. No. 4 d).	חרב

הַמַּחֲרֶת	pref. id.) noun fem. sing. (const. רַת)	מחר
הַמַּחֲשֶׁבֶת	pref. id.) n. f., pl. abs. fr. מַחֲשָׁבָה (q. v.)	חשב
הַמַּחְתָּה	pref. id.) noun fem. sing. dec. 10.	חתה
הַמַּחְתּוֹת הַמַּחְתֹּת	} pref. id.) id. pl.	חתה
הַמַּטֶּה הַמַּטֶּה	} pref. id.) noun masc. sing. dec. 9 a.	נטה
	} pref. id.) noun fem. sing. dec. 10.	נטה
הַמְטַהֵר	pref. id.) Piel part. sing. m. (§ 14. rem. 1)	טהר
הַמִּטַּהֵר	pref.id.) Hithp. part. s.m.d.7 b. [for מִתְטַהֵר]	טהר
הַמִּטַּהֲרִים	) pref. id.) id. pl., abs. state (comp. §14.r.1)	טהר
הַמַּטּוֹת	pref. id.) n. m. with pl. f. term. fr. מַטֶּה d.9 a.	נטה
הַמַּטּוֹת	pref. id.) noun fem., pl. of מַטֶּה dec. 10.	נטה
הַמַּטִּים	) pref. id.) Hiph. part. masc., pl. of מַטֶּה dec. 9 a (§ 25. No. 2b)	נטה
הִמְטִיר	Hiph. pret. 3 pers. sing. masc.	מטר
הַמַּטְעַמִּים	pref. ה) noun m., pl. of [מַטְעָם] d. 8 a.	טעם
וַהֲמִטְפָּחוֹת	pref. id.) pl. abs. of the following	טפח
הַמִּטְפַּחַת	pref. id.) noun masc. f., pl. פָּחוֹת (§ 44. r. 5)	טפח
הַמָּטָר	pref. id.) noun masc. sing. dec. 4 a.	מטר
הַמַּטָּרָה	pref. id.) noun fem. sing.	נטר
הִמְטַרְתִּי	) Hiph. pret. 1 pers. sing.; acc. shifted by conv. ו (comp. § 8. rem. 7)	מטר
הַמַּטְרִי	pref. ה) pr. name masc.	מטר
הַמַּטֹּת	pref. id.) n. m. with pl. f. term. fr. מַטֶּה d.9 a.	נטה
הֲמִיָּה	Kal part. act. sing. fem. (§ 24. rem. 4)	המה
הֹמִיּוֹת	id. pl. of the preceding	המה
הַמְיַחֲלִים	pref. ה) Piel part. m., pl. of מְיַחֵל d. 7 b. (§14.r.1)	יחל
הַמְיַלֶּדֶת	pref. id.) Piel part. act. fem. sing. dec. 13 a.	ילד
הַמְיַלְּדֹת	pref. id.) pl. of the preceding	ילד
הַמַּיִם הַמָּיִם	} pref. ה) noun masc. pl. [of מַי § 38. rem. 2; comp. § 45]	מי
הַמַּיְמָה הַמָּיְמָה	} pref. id.) id. pl. with loc. ה	מי
הַכְּמֵימֵיךָ	preff. כ & ה) noun masc. pl. (מַיִם), suff. 2 pers. sing. masc. irr. of יוֹם (§ 45)	יום
הֵמִיר	Hiph. pret. 3 pers. sing. masc.	מור
הֲמִירְאָתְךָ	preff. ה & מ) noun fem. sing., suff. 2 pers. sing. masc. from יִרְאָה (no pl.)	ירא
הַמֵּישָׁר	pref. ה) noun masc. sing.	ישר
הַמְיַשְּׁרִים	pref. id.) Piel part. m., pl. of [מְיַשֵּׁר] d. 7 b.	ישר
הָמִית	Hiph. inf. constr. dec. 3 a.	מות
הֵמִית	) id. pret. 3 pers. sing. masc.	מות
הֲמִיתָה	noun fem. sing., const. of [הֲמִיתָה] dec. 10.	המה
הֲמִיתוֹ	Hiph. inf. (הָמִית), suff. 3 pers. s. m. d. 3 a.	מות
הֲמִיתוּ	) id. imp. pl. masc.	מות

a Nu. 3. 31.	h 2 Ch. 11. 23.	o Je. 52. 18.	u Le. 6. 19.	A Ju. 21. 23.	i 1 Ki. 6. 35.	ii Is. 66. 17.	a Am. 4. 7.	d Je. 2. 11.

14

הֵמִיתוּ	id. pret. 3 pers. pl. . . .	מות
הֲמִתִּיו	[for הֲמַתִּיו, id. for הֲמַתְּיו] Kh. נ Hiph. pret. 1 pers. s., suff. 3 p. s. m. (§ 25. r. 1)	מות
הֲמִיתֶךָ	id. pret. 3 p. s. m., suff. 2 p. s. m.; ן for ו conv.	מות
הֲמִיתָם	id. id. with 3 pers. pl. masc.	מות
הֲמִיתֵנִי	id. imp. sing. masc., suff. 1 pers. sing.	מות
הֲמִיתַתְהוּ	id. pret. 3 pers. sing. fem., suff. 3 p. s. m.	מות
הַחֲכַבֵּד	pref. הַ interr. for הֲ)(Piel part. s. m. d. 7 b	כבד
הַמְכֻבָּר	pref. הַ art.)(noun masc. sing.	כבר
הַמַּכָּה	pref. id.)(noun fem. sing. dec. 10.	נכה
הַמַּכֶּה	pref. id.)(Hiph. part. sing. masc. dec. 9 a. (§ 25. No. 2 b) . . .	נכה
הַמֻּכָּה	pref. id.)(fem. of the following	נכה
הַמֻּכֶּה	pref. id.)(Hoph. part. sing. masc. dec. 9 a. (§ 25. No. 2 b) . .	נכה
הַמֻּכֵּהוּ	pref. id.)(Hiph. part. sing. masc., suff. 3 pers. sing. m. from מֻכֶּה dec. 9 a. (§ 25. No. 2 b)	נכה
הֻמְכוּ	ן Hoph. pret. 3 p. pl. [for הוּמַכּוּ § 18. r. 14]	מכך
הַמְּכוֹנָה	pref. הַ)(noun fem. sing. dec. 10.	כון
הַמְּכוֹנָה	pref. id.)(noun fem. sing. dec. 10.	כון
הַמְּכוֹנוֹת	pref. id.)(pl. of the preceding	כון
הַמַּכּוֹת	pref. id.)(noun fem., pl. of מַכָּה dec. 10.	נכה
הַמַּכִּים	pref. id.)(Hiph. part. masc., pl. of מַכֶּה dec. 9 a (§ 25. No. 2 b, or subs. 2 Ki. 8. 29; 9. 15.	נכה
הַמֵּכִין	pref. id.)(Hiph. part. sing. masc.	כון
הַמַּכִּיר	pref. id.)(patronym. of מָכִיר	מכר
הַמִּכְמְתָת	pref. id.)(pr. name of a place, see מִכְמְתָת	
הַמְּכֹנָה	pref. id.)(noun fem. sing. dec. 10.	כון
הַמְּכֹנוֹת	ן pref. id.)(pl. of the preceding	כון
הַמִּכְסָה	pref. id.)(noun m. sing. (suff. מִכְסָם) dec. 6 a.	כסם
הַמְכַסֶּה	ן pref. הַ art., or interr. for הֲ)(Piel part. sing. masc. dec. 9 a.	כסה
הַמַּכְעִסִים	pref. הַ art.) Hiph. part. m., pl. of מַכְעִים [מַכְעִים] d. 1 b.	כעם
הַמַּכְפֵּלָה	pref. id.)(pr. name of a place	כפל
הַמֻּכְרָב	Niph. Inf. [הֻמְכַּר], suff. 3 pers. s. m. dec. 7 b.	מכר
הַמֹּכֶרֶת	pref. הַ)(Kal part. act. sing. fem., from מכר m.	מכר
הַמְּכֵרָתִי	pref. id.)(gent. noun from מְכֵרָה	כור
הַמַּכְשֵׁלָה	ן pref. id.)(noun fem. sing. dec. 10.	כשל
הַמַּכְשֵׁלוֹת	ן pref. id.)(pl. of the preceding	כשל
הַמַּכְשֵׁלִים	pref. id.)(noun masc., pl. of מַכְשֵׁל dec. 1 b.	כשל
הַמִּכְתָּב	ן pref. id.)(noun masc. sing. dec. 2 b.	כתב
הַמִּכְתָּשׁ	pref. id.)(noun masc. sing. (also pr. name)	כתש
הָמֵל	Root not used; Arab. to rain continually.	
	הַמֻלָּה, הֲמוּלָּה fem. probably noise, bustle, tumult.	

הַמָּלֵא	ן pref. הַ)(adj. masc. sing. dec. 5 a, const. מְלֵא (§ 34. rem. 1) . .	מלא
הַמְּלֵאָה	pref. id.)(id. fem.; or subst. (De. 22. 9) d. 10.	מלא
הַמְּלֵאוֹת	ן pref. id.)(id. pl	מלא
הַמְּלֵאִים	pref. id.)(id. pl masc.	מלא
הַמִּלֻּאִים	pref. id.)(noun masc., pl. of [מִלֻּא] dec. 1 b.	מלא
הַמַּלְאָךְ	ן pref. id.)(noun masc. sing. dec. 2 b.	לאך
הַמְּלָאכָה	ו pref. id.)(noun fem. sing., constr. מְלֶאכֶת, with suff. מְלַאכְתֶּךָ (§ 42. rem. 5)	לאך
הַמַּלְאָכִים	pref. id.)(noun masc., pl. of מַלְאָךְ dec. 2 b.	לאך
הַמַּלְאָכִים	Kh. הַמַּלְאָכִים q. v., K. הַמְּלָכִים (q. v.).	מלך
הַמַּלְבּוּשׁ	pref. הַ)(noun masc. sing. dec. 1 b.	לבש
הַמַּלְבִּשְׁכֶם	pref. id.)(Hiph. part. m. s. from [מַלְבִּשׁ, § 11. rem. 8,] suff. 2 pers. pl. masc., dec. 7 b	לבש
הַמְלָה	noun fem. sing.	המל
הִמָּלוּ	Niph. imp. pl. masc.	מול
הַמְּלוֹא	pref. הַ)(noun masc. sing.	מלא
הַמְּלוּכָה	pref. id.)(noun fem. sing.	מלך
הַמָּלוֹן	pref. id.)(noun masc. sing. dec. 3 a. .	לון
הַמֶּלַח / הַמֶּלַח	} pref. id.)(noun masc. sing. K. מֶלַח	מלח
הָמְלֵחַ	ן Hoph. inf. abs.	מלח
הַמְּלָחִים	pref. הַ)(noun masc., pl. of [מֶלַח] dec. 1 b.	מלח
הַמְּלָחִים	ן pref. id.)(noun masc. pl.	מלח
הַמִּלְחָמוֹת	pref. id.)(id. pl. abs. state.	לחם
הַמִּלְחָמָה	ו pref. id.)(noun fem. sing. dec. 11 b; with suff. מֶחֱמֶת from חֲמַתּוֹ 13 a. (§ 42. rem. 5)	לחם
הֻמְלַחַתְּ	Hoph. pret. 2 pers. sing. fem. (§ 11. rem. 10)	מלח
הִמָּלֵט	Niph. inf. or imp. sing. masc.	מלט
הִמָּלְטִי	id. imp. sing. fem.	מלט
הִמְלִיט	ן Hiph. pret. 3 pers. sing. masc.	מלט
הִמְלִיטָה	ן id. pret. 3 pers. sing. fem.	מלט
הִמְלִיךְ	Hiph. pret. 3 pers. sing. masc.	מלך
הִמְלִיכוּ	id. pret. 3 pers. pl.	מלך
הַמֵּלִיץ	pref. הַ)(Hiph. part. sing. masc. dec. 3 b.	לוץ
הַמְלֵךְ	pref. הַ)(Kal inf. abs.	מלך
הֻמְלַךְ	Hoph. pret. 3 pers. sing. masc.	מלך
הַמֶּלֶךְ / הַמֶּלֶךְ	} pref. הֲ)(noun masc. sing. dec. 6 a.	מלך
הַמֹּלֶךְ	pref. הַ)(pr. name of an idol .	מלך
הַמֹּלֵךְ	pref. הַ)(Kal part. act. sing. masc.	מלך
הַמַּלְכָּה	ו pref. id.)(noun fem. sing. dec. 12 a.	מלך

a 1 Sa. 17. 35.	g Nu. 25, 15, 18.	m Je. 27. 19.	t Le. 9. 19.	a Zep. 1. 3.	f Is. 51. 20.	i 2 Ki. 14. 7.	r Eze. 16. 4.	u Ge. 42. 23.
b Is. 15. 15.	h Nu. 25. 14.	n Zec. 13. 6.	u Is. 65. 3.	b Eze. 21. 20.	g 2 Sa. 11. 1.	m Eze. 16. 4.	s Zec. 2. 11.	w Ge. 37. 8.
c Je. 41. 8.	i Is. 9. 12.	o Ps. 147. 8.	v Le. 25. 50.	c Ex. 32. 16.	h 2 Ki. 10. 22.	n Jon. 1. 5.	t Is. 31. 5.	x Da. 9. 1.
d 1 Sa. 20. 8.	k Job 24. 24.	p 1 Ki. 7. 34, 34, 35.	w Na. 3. 4.	d 2 Ki 4. 4.	i 2 Sa. 1. 24.	o Je. 38. 12.	u Is. 66. 7.	y Mi. 4. 9.
e 2 Ch. 22. 11.	l Le. 13. 24, 28.	q 2 Ki. 25. 16.	x Is. 3. 6.	e Ge. 41. 7.	k Eze. 1. 24.	p 1 Ch. 26. 27.	v Ho. 8. 4.	z Est. 7. 6.
f 2 Ki. 9. 15.	m 1 Ki. 7. 27, 28, &c	r Nu. 31. 37.	y Je. 4. 4.					

הַמְּלוּכָה	pref. הַ)(noun fem. sing. defect. for מְלוּכָה	מלך
הַמַּלְכֻוֹת	pref. id.)(noun fem. sing. d. 1 b. (pl. מַלְכִיּוֹת)	מלך
הַמַּלְכִּיאֵל	pref. id.)(patronym. of מַלְכִּיאֵל (q. v.)	מלך
הַמְּלָכִים	'/ pref. id.)(noun masc., pl. of מֶלֶךְ dec. 6 a.	מלך
הַמֹּלֶכֶת	pref. id.)(pr. name fem.	מלך
הַמְלַכְתָּ וְ	Hiph. pret. 2 pers. sing. masc.; acc. shifted by conv. וְ (comp. § 8. rem. 7)	מלך
הַמְלַכְתִּי	id. pret. 1 pers. sing.	מלך
הִמְלַכְתִּיךָ	id. id., suff. 2 pers. sing. masc.	מלך
הִמְלַכְתַּנִי	'/ id. pret. 2 pers. sing. masc., suff. 1 pers. sing.	מלך
הַמְלַמֵּד	pref. הַ)(Piel part. sing. masc. dec. 7 b.	למד
הַמַּלְצַר	pref. id.)(noun masc. sing.	מלצר
הַמַּלְקוֹחַ	pref. id.)(noun masc. sing. dec. 1 b.	לקח
הַמַּלְקָחַיִם וְ	pref. id.)(noun m. du. of מֶלְקָח dec. 2 b.	לקח
הַמְלַקְקִים	pref. id.)(Piel part. masc., pl. of מְלַקֵּק dec. 7 b. (§ 10. rem. 7)	לקק
הַמַּלְתָּחָה	pref. id.)(noun fem. sing.	לתח

הָמַם I. to put in motion, to drive, Is. 28. 28.—II. to put to the rout, disperse, defeat.—III. to destroy.
הוֹמָם (defeat) pr. name masc. 1 Ch. 1. 39; for which הֵימָם Ge. 36. 22.

הֲמָם וְ	Kal pret. 3 p. s. m. [הָם], suff. 3 p. pl. m.	הום
הַמְמֻתִים	pref. הַ)(Kh. מְמוֹתִים noun masc. pl. [of מָמוֹת dec. 3 a], K. מוּמָתִים, Hoph. part. pl. of מוּמָת	מות
הַמִּמְכָּר	pref. id.)(noun masc. sing. dec. 2 b.	מכר
הַמְמַלְּאִים	'/וְ pref. id.)(Piel part. masc., pl. of מְמַלֵּא dec. 7 b. (§ 10. rem. 7)	מלא
הַמְמַלְּטִים	pref. id.)(Piel part. m., pl. מְמַלֵּט d. 7 b.	מלט
הַמַּמְלִיךְ	pref. id.)(Hiph. part. sing. masc.	מלך
הַמַּמְלָכָה וְ	pref. id.)(noun fem. dec. 11 a. (c. לְכַת, suff. לַכְתּוֹ dec. 13 a. § 42. rem. 5)	מלך
הַמַּמְלָכוֹת	pref. id.)(id. pl., absolute state	מלך
הַמַּמְלָכוֹת	pref. id.)(id. pl., constr. state	מלך
הֲמָמָם	Kal pret. 3 pers. sing. masc., suff. 3 p. pl. m.	המם
הֲמִמֶּנּוּ	pref. הַ)(prep. (מִן), suff. 3 p. s. m. (§ 5 parad.)	מנן
הֲמִמֶּנּוּ	Kal pret. 3 pers. sing. masc., suff. Kh. מְנוּ 1 pers. pl., K. מֵנִי 1 pers. sing.	המם
הֲמִמֶּנִּי	pref. הַ)(prep. (מִן), suff. 1 p. s. (§ 5 parad.)	מנן
הַמַּמְעִיט	'/ וְ pref. הַ)(Hiph. part. sing. masc.	מעט
הַמַּמְשָׁלָה	pref. id.)(noun. fem. sing., constr. שֶׁלֶת, suff. שֶׁלְתּוֹ (§ 42. rem. 5)	משל
הַמַּמְשָׁלִים	pref. id.)(noun masc., pl. of מִמְשָׁל d. 2 b.	משל

[הָמֵן]	i. q. הָמָה to make a noise, to rage, Eze. 5. 7.	
הָמָן	(magnificent, Gesen.) pr. name of a Persian at the court of Ahasuerus, who plotted the entire extirpation of the Jews, Est. 3. 1 seq.	
הָמָן	'/ pref. הַ)(noun masc. sing.	מן
הֲמָן	pref. הַ)(prep., with suff. מִמָּךְ, מִמֶּנִּי, מִנִּי &c. (§ 5 parad.)	מנן
הָמֵן וְ	pr. name masc.	אמן
[הַמְּנֹאָפֹת]	pref. הַ)(Piel part. f., fr. מְנָאֵף m. [for מְנָאֶפֶת]	נאף
הַמְנַגֵּן	pref. id.)(Piel part. sing. masc.	נגן
הַמְנַדִּים	pref. id.)(Piel part. m., pl. of מְנַדֶּה d. 9 a.	נדה
הַמָּנָה	pref. id.)(noun fem. sing. dec. 11 a, pl. with suff. מְנוֹתֶיהָ (§ 42. rem. 2)	מנה
הַמָּנֶה	pref. id.)(noun masc. sing. dec. 9 b.	מנה
הַמֹּנָם	n. m. s., suff. 3 pers. s. m. fr. הָמוֹן dec. 3 a.	המה
הַמַּנְהִיג וְ	pref. הַ)(noun masc. sing. dec. 2 b.	נהג
הַמִּנְהָרוֹת	pref. id.)(noun fem. pl. [of מִנְהָרָה	נהר
הַמְּנוּחָה	pref. id.)(noun fem. sing. dec. 10.	נוח
הַמְנֻכָא	Ch. Kh. הַמְנוּכָא, K. הַמְנִיכָא, noun masc. emph. of הַמְנִיךְ or הַמְנוּךְ Da. 5. 7, 16, 29.	נוך
הַמְּנוֹרָה	pref. הַ)(noun fem. sing. dec. 10.	נור
הַמֻּנָּח	pref. id.)(Hoph. part. masc. sing.	נוח
הַמִּנְחָה	'/ pref. id.)(noun fem. sing. dec. 12 b.	מנח
[הַמְנִיךְ]	Ch. see הַמְנֻכָא	
הַהֲמוֹנִים	noun masc. pl. of הָמוֹן dec. 3 a.	המה
הֲמִנְּכֶם	Kal inf., suff. 2 p. s. m. [fr. הָמֵן § 32. r. 7]	המן
הַמִּנְעָל	pref. הַ)(noun masc. sing. dec. 1 b.	נעל
הַמְנָקִיּוֹת	pref. id.)(n. f. pl. [fr. מְנָקִית comp. § 39. r. 1 note]	נקה
הַמְּנֹרָה	'/ pref. id.)(noun fem. sing. dec.	נור
הַמְּנֹרוֹת	pref. id.)(id. pl.	נור
הַמְנַשֶּׁה	pref. id.)(pr. name of a tribe	נשה
הַמְנַשִּׁי	'/ pref. id.)(patronym. of the preceding	נשה

הָמַס Root not used; whence
הַמָסִים Is. 64. 1, coll. with the Arab., according to Gesenius, after the Jewish commentators and Schultens, brushwood. Prof. Lee, slight noises: As the kindling of fire (excites) slight noises, &c. (?). Others, melting, מָסַס—הָמֵס

הַמֵּס / הָמֵס	pref. הַ)(noun masc. sing. dec. 8 b, contr. from מֶכֶס	כסס
הֲמֵס	Niph. inf. constr., used as an abs.	מסס
הַמַּסְגֵּר	'/ pref. הַ)(noun m. sing. (prop. Hiph. part.)	סגר
הַמַּסְגְּרוֹת	pref. id.)(pl. of the following	סגר
הַמִּסְגֶּרֶת	pref. id.)(noun fem. s. (suff. גַּרְתּוֹ) d. 13 a.	סגר
הַמַּסְדְּרוֹנָה	pref. id.)(n. m. s. [מִסְדְּרוֹן] with loc. ה	סדר
הַמְסֻג	Hiph. pret. 3 pers. pl.	מסס

---

a 1 Sa. 10. 25.	f 2 Ch. 1. 9.	l Is. 28. 28.	q 2 Sa. 19. 6.	v Je. 51. 34.	1 Ch. 26. 6.	1 Sa. 9. 23.	Eze. 5. 7.	2 Sa. 17. 10.
b 1 Ki. 3. 7.	g 2 Ch. 1. 8.	m De. 7. 23.	r Eze. 17. 16.	w Je. 32. 27.	Nu. 11. 7.	Eze. 45. 12.	Ca. 5. 5.	Je. 24. 1.
c 1 Sa. 8. 22.	h Da. 1. 11, 16.	n Eze. 17. 16.	s Je. 11. 32.	x Nu. 11. 7.	2 Ki. 9. 20.	Nu. 4. 7; Je. 52. 19.		Ju. 3. 23.
d 1 Sa. 15. 11.	i 2 Ki. 11. 2.	o Je. 26. 26.	t 2 Ch. 15. 6.	y 2 Ki. 3. 15.	Ju. 6. 2.	Nu. 3. 31.		De. 1. 28.
e 2 Ch. 1. 11.	k 2 Ki. 10. 22.	p Is. 65. 11.	u 1 Ki. 20. 33.	z Am. 6. 3.	Joel 4. 14.			uu Eze. 29. 19.

14*

Hebrew	Description	Root
הַמִּסְוֶה°	pref. הַ)(noun masc. sing.	סוה
הַמַּסּוֹת°	pref. id.)(noun fem., pl. of מַסָּה dec. 10.	נסה
הִמְסִיוּ°	Hiph. pret. 3 pers. pl., [by Chaldaism for הַמְסוּ § 24. rem. 17]	מסה
הַמָּסִים°	noun masc. pl. [of הָמָס] dec. 6.	המס
הַמָּסֵךְ°	וַ)' pref. הַ)(noun masc. sing. (constr. מָסַךְ § 37. rem. 4)	סכך
הַמַּסֵּכָה°	וַ)' prf. id.)(noun fem. sing. dec. 10.	נסך
הַמַּסֵּכוֹת°	וַ)' pref. id.)(pl. of the preceding	נסך
הַמְסֻכָּן°	pref. id.)(Pual part. sing. masc.	סכן
הַמִּסְכֵּן°	pref. id.)(noun masc. sing.	סכן
הַמִּסְכְּנוֹת°	pref. id.)(noun fem. pl. fr. [מִסְכְּנֹת] dec. 3.	סכן
הַמַּסֶּבֶת°	pref. id.)(n. f. s. [for מְסִבֶּת comp. § 35. r. 2]	נסב
הַמְסֻלָּאִים°	pref. id.)(Pual part. masc. pl. [of מְסֻלָּא]	סלא
הַמְסִלָּה°	pref. id.)(noun fem. sing. dec. 10.	סלל
הַמְסִלּוֹת°	pref. id.)(pl. of the preceding	סלל
הַמִּסְפֵּד°	pref. id.)(noun masc. sing. d. 7c. (§ 36. r.1)	ספד
הַמִּסְפְּחוֹת°	pref. id.)(noun fem., pl. of [סִפָּחָה] d. 11a.	ספח
הַמִּסְפַּחַת°	pref. id.)(noun masc. sing.	ספח
הַמִּסְפָּר°	pref. id.)(noun masc. sing. dec. 2b.	ספר
הַמַּסֹּת°	pref. id.)(noun fem., pl. of מַסָּה dec. 10.	נסה
הַמַּסְתִּיר°	pref. id.)(Hiph. part. sing. masc.	סתר
הַמַּעְבָּרוֹת°	וַ)' pref. id.)(n. f. pl. abs. fr. [מַעְבָּרָה] d. 11a.	עבר
הַמַּעְבְּרוֹת°	pref. id.)(n. f. pl. abs. fr. [מַעְבְּרֹת] d. 13.	עבר
הַמַּעֲגָלָה°	pref. id.)(noun fem. sing. dec. 11a.	עגל
הַמְעַד°	Hiph. imp. sing. m. (with gutt. for הַמְעֵד)	מעד
הַמָּעוֹז°	pref. הַ)(for מָעֹז, noun masc. sing. dec. 8c. (suff. מָעֻזִּי § 37. rem. 4)	עזז
הַמְּעוֹנִים°	וַ)' pref. id.)(gent. noun pl., see מָעוֹן	עוי
הַמְעַט°	pref. הַ art. & interr.)(subst., adj. & adv.; pl. מְעַטִּים	מעט
הַמַּעֲטָרָה°	pref. הַ art.)(Hiph. part. sing. fem.	עטר
הַמַּעֲטָפוֹת°	וַ)' pref. id.)(noun fem., pl. of [מְטַפָּה]	עטף
הַמְעַטְּרֵכִי°	pref. id.)(Piel part. sing. masc. suff. 2 pers. sing. fem. (§ 2. rem. 2)	עטר
הִמְעַטְּתִּים°	וַ)' Hiph. pret. 1 pers. s., suff. 3 pers. pl. m.	מעט
הִמְעִיטָה°	וַ)' id. pret. 3 pers. sing. fem.	מעט
הַמָּעִיל°	pref. הַ)(noun masc. sing. dec. 1a.	מעל
הַמַּעְיָנוֹת°	pref. id.)(noun m. pl. abs. fr. מַעְיָן dec. 2b.	עין
הַמְּעִינִים°	pref. id.)(Kh. מְעִי', K. מְעֹ', noun masc. pl. of מַעְיָן or מָעוֹן dec. 3a.	עון
הַמְעַכְתִּי°	וַ)' pref. id.)(gent. noun fr. מַעֲכָה	מעך
הַמַּעַל°	pref. id.)(noun masc. sing. dec. 6d.	מעל
הַמַּעֲלָה°	pref. id.)(noun fem. sing. dec. 10.	עלה
הַמַּעֲלֶה°	pref. id.)(Hiph. part. sing. masc. dec. 9a.	עלה

Hebrew	Description	Root
הַמַּעֲלוֹת°	pref. id.)(noun fem., pl. of מַעֲלָה dec. 10.	עלה
הַמַּעֲלְךָ°	pref. id.)(Hiph. part. sing. masc. (מַעֲלֶה), suff. 2 pers. sing. masc. dec. 9a.	עלה
הַמַּעֲלָם°	pref. id.)(id. with (verbal) suff. 3 pers. pl. m.	עלה
הַמַּעֲמִיקִים°	pref. id.)(Hiph. part. m., pl. (מַעֲמִיק) d. 1b.	עמק
הַמֵּעִמְּךָ°	preff. הַ, & מִ f. מִן prep. (עִם) with suff. 2 pers. sing. masc.	עמם
הַמְעֻנָּנָה°	וַ)' pref. הַ)(Pual part. sing. fem.	ענן
הַמַּעֲרָב°	pref. id.)(noun masc. sing.	ערב
הַמְּעָרָה°	וַ)' pref. id.)(noun fem. sing. dec. 10.	עור
הַמְּעָרוֹת°	pref. id.)(pl. of the preceding	עור
הַמַּעֲרָכָה°	pref. id.)(noun fem. sing. dec. 11a.	ערך
הַמַּעֲרֶכֶת° / הַמַּעֲרָכֶת°	} pref. id.)(noun fem. sing., see מַעֲרָכָה	ערך
הַמְעָרַת°	pref. הַ interr. for הֲ)(noun fem. sing., constr. of מְעָרָה dec. 10.	עור
הַמַּעֲשֶׂה°	pref. הַ art.)(noun masc. sing. dec. 9a.	עשה
הַמַּעֲשִׂים°	pref. id.)(id. pl., absolute state	עשה
הַמְעֻשָּׁקָה°	pref. id.)(Pual part. sing. fem.	עשק
הַמַּעֲשֵׂר°	וַ)' pref. id.)(noun m. s. d. 7c. (§ 36. r. 1)	עשר
הַמְעַשְּׂרִים°	pref. id.)(Piel part. m., pl. of [מְעַשֵּׂר] d. 7b.	עשר
הַמַּעְתִּיק°	pref. id.)(Hiph. part. sing. masc.	עתק
הַמִּפְקָד°	pref. id.)(pr. name of a gate	פקד
הַמִּפְקָדִים°	pref. id.)(Hoph. part. masc., pl. of [מֻפְקָד]	פקד
הַמִּפְשָׂעָה°	pref. id.)(noun fem. sing.	פשע
הַמִּפְתָּח°	pref. id.)(n. m. s. constr. מִפְתַּח (§ 36. r. 1)	פתח
הַמַּפְתְּחִים°	וַ)' pref. id.)(noun masc., pl. of מוֹפֵת d. 7b.	יפת
הַמִּפְתָּן°	pref. id.)(noun masc. sing. dec. 2b.	פתן
הַמֵּץ°	pref. id.)(Kal part. act. sing. m. (§ 21. r. 2)	מוץ
הִמָּצֵא°	Niph. inf. used as an absolute	מצא
הַמֹּצְאוֹת°	pref. הַ)(Kal part. act. fem., pl. of מֹצֵאת [for מֹצֵאת § 23. rem. 4]	מצא
הַמֹּצְאִים°	pref. id. m., pl. of מוֹצֵא (§ 23. rem. 9)	מצא
הֲמָצָאתָנִי°	pref. הַ interr. for הֲ)(Kal pret. 2 pers. sing. masc., suff. 1 pers. sing.	מצא
הַמַּצָּב°	pref. הַ art.)(noun masc. sing. (suff. מַצָּבֶךָ § 31. rem. 5)	נצב
הַמַּצְבָּא°	pref. id.)(Hiph. part. sing. m. [for מַצְבִּיא]	צבא
הַמַּצֵּבָה°	pref. id.)(noun fem. sing.	נצב
הַמַּצֵּבָה°	pref. id.)(noun fem. sing. dec. 11b. (constr. מַצֶּבֶת, suff. מַצַּבְתָּהּ dec. 13a, § 42. rem. 5)	נצב
הַמַּצֵּבוֹת°	pref. id.)(id. pl., absolute state	נצב
הַמִּצְפֶּיָה°	pref. id.)(pr. name of a place, see מִצְפֶּה	
הַמַּצֶּבֶת°	pref. id.)(noun fem., pl. of מַצֵּבָה (q. v.)	נצב
הַמְצָדוֹת°	וַ)' pref. id.)(noun masc. with pl. fem. term. fr. מְצָד dec. 1a.	צוד

---

a Ex. 34. 34, 35. g 2 Ch. 34. 3, 4. m Eze. 13. 18. s 1 Sa. 17. 20. x Le. 26. 22. ᵃ Job 34. 33. ᵍ Is. 23. 12. ᵐ Is. 16. 4. ˢ 1 Sa. 14. 14.
b De. 29. 2. h Is. 40. 20. n Ec. 9. 15, 16. t 1 Ch. 27. 24. y Is. 25. 8. ᵇ 2 Ch. 32. 4. ʰ Da. 8. 5. ⁿ Ex. 22. 3. ᵗ 1 Sa. 14. 14.
c Jos. 14. 8. i Is. 16. 13, 14. o De. 7. 19. u Is. 3. 22. z 1 Ch. 4. 41. ᶜ Jos. 12. 16, 31. ⁱ Ne. 10. 38. ᵒ Jos. 2. 23. ᵘ Ge. 31. 51, 52.
d Is. 64. 1. k Nu. 16. 13, 14. p Is. 8. 17. v De. 7. 19. ᵃ Jos. 2. 23. ᵈ Ju. 6. 2. ᵏ Job 9. 5. ᵖ Nu. 15. 33. ᵛ Ju. 6. 2.
e Nu. 3. 31. l La. 4. 3. q Ps. 103. 4. w Is. 3. 22. ᵇ Is. 63. 11. ᵉ Is. 65. 11. ˡ 1 Ch. 19. 4. ᵠ 1 Ki. 21. 20. ʷ Ge. 31. 51, 52.
f Ju. 18. 17, 18. Ju. 20. 32. r Je. 51. 33. Ese. 29. 15. Is. 29. 15. Je. 7. 11. Je. 48. 41.

הַמֹּצָה וְ pref. הַ)(pr. name of a place . .	יצא
הַמְּצוּדָה pref. id.)(noun fem. sing. dec. 10.	צוד
הַמִּצְוָה וְ' pref. id.)(noun fem. sing. dec. 10.	צוה
הַמָּצוֹר pref. id.)(noun masc. sing. dec. 3a. (with suff. מְצוּרֶךָ § 32. rem. 5)	צור
הַמְּצוּרוֹת' pref. id.)(noun fem., pl. of מְצוּרָה dec. 10.	צור
הַמְצֹרָע' pref. id.)(Pual part. masc. sing.	צרע
הַמַּצּוֹת pref. id.)(noun fem., pl. of מַצָּה dec. 10.	מצץ
הַמִּצְוֹת pref. id.)(noun fem., pl. of מִצְוָה dec. 10.	צוה
הַמְצִיאוּ" Hiph. pret. 3 pers. pl.	מצא
הַמַּצִּיל' pref. הַ)(Hiph. part. sing. masc.	נצל
הַמֵּצִיק" pref. id.)(Hiph. part. sing. masc. dec. 3b.	צוק
הַמְצִיקִים' וְ pref. id.)(id. pl., absolute state .	צוק
הִמְצֵאתִךָ Hiph. pret. 1 pers. sing., suff. 2 pers. sing. masc. [for הִמְצָאתִיךָ § 23. rem. 11] .	מצא
הַמַּצְמִיחַ' pref. הַ)(Hiph. part. sing. masc.	צמח
הַמִּצְנֶפֶת / הַמִּגְבַּעַת } pref. הַ art.)(noun fem. s. (comp. § 35. r. 2)	צנף
הַמַּצָּע" pref. id.)(noun masc. sing. (comp. § 20. r. 16)	יצע
הַמְצַפֶּה' pref. id.)(Piel part. sing. masc. dec. 9a.	צפה
הַמִּצְפֶּה וְ' pref. id.)(pr. name of a place .	צפה
הַמִּצְפָּה' pref. id.)(n. m. s., also pr. name of a place	צפה
הַמְצַפְצְפִים pref. id.)(Pilpel (§ 6. No. 4) part. m., pl. of מְצַפְצֵף dec. 7b. .	צפף
הַמִּצְפָּתָה pref. id.)(pr. name of a place (מִצְפָּה) with parag. ה .	צפה
הַמֵּצַר= pref. id.)(n. m. s. (pl. מְצָרִים, dec. 8. § 37. r. 7)	צרר
הַמְּצֹרוֹת pref. id.)(noun fem., pl. of מְצֹרָה dec. 10.	צור
הַמְּצֵרִים" pref. id.)(noun m. pl. of מֵצַר d. 8. (§ 37. r. 7)	צרר
הַמִּצְרִים pref. id.)(gent. noun, pl. of מִצְרִי, fr. מִצְרַיִם	מצר
הַמִּצְרִית' pref. id.)(id. fem.	מצר
הַמִּצְרִיֹּת' pref. id.)(id. pl. fem. (§ 39. No. 4. r. 1 note)	מצר
הַמְצֹרָע" pref. id.)(Pual part. sing. masc.	צרע
הַמְצֹרָעִים" pref. id.)(id. pl., absolute state .	צרע
הָמֵק Hiph. inf. absolute . .	מקק
הַמְקַבְּרִים' pref. הַ)(Piel part. masc., pl. of מְקַבֵּר d. 7b.	קבר
הַמְּקַבֶּת' pref. id.)(noun fem. sing.	נקב
הַמַּקְדִּישׁ' pref. id.)(Hiph. part. sing. masc. dec. 1b.	קדש
הַמִּקְדָּשׁ' pref. id.)(noun masc. sing. dec. 2b.	קדש
הַמְקֻדָּשׁ" pref. id.)(Pual part. sing. masc. dec. 2b.	קדש
הַמִּקְדָּשִׁים' pref. id.)(id. pl., absolute state .	קדש
הַמָּקוֹם pref. id.)(noun com. sing. dec. 3a.	קום
הַמְּקוֹמֹת, הַמְּקֹמֹת pref. id.)(pl. of the preceding .	קום
הַמַּקְחֹרֹת" pref. id.)(n.f. pl. [of מַקָּחָה, comp § 17.r.8]	לקח
הַמַּקְטִירִים' pref. id.)(Hiph. part. pl. masc.	קטר
הַמְקַטְּרוֹת pref. id.)(Piel part. f., pl. of [מְקַטֶּרֶת] d. 13a.	קטר
הַמְקֻטָּרִים pref. id.)(Piel part. m., pl. of [מְקֻטָּר] d. 7b.	קטר
הַמַּקְלוֹת' pref. id.)(noun masc. with pl. fem. term. from מַקֵּל dec. 7b (§ 36. rem. 1) .	מקל
הַמִּקְלָט pref. id.)(noun masc. sing. dec. 2b.	קלט
הַמְקַלֵּל' pref. id.)(Piel part. sing. masc. dec. 7b.	קלל
הַמְּקֹמוֹת וְ' noun com., pl. of מָקוֹם dec. 3a.	קום
הַמְקַנֵּא' pref. הַ interr. for הֲ)(Piel part. sing. masc.	קנא
הַמַּקְנֶה' pref. הַ art.)(Hiph. part. masc. sing. [for מַקְנִיא § 23. rem. 11]	קנא
הַמִּקְנָה' pref. id.)(noun fem. sing. dec. 10.	קנה
הַמִּקְנֶה' pref. id.)(noun fem. sing. dec. 7b.	קנה
הַמַּקְצֹעַ / הַמְּקֻצְעָע' } pref. id.)(noun masc. sing. dec. 1b.	קצע
הַמַּקְצֹעֹת pref. id.)(pl. of the preceding	קצע
הַמִּקְרֶה' pref. id.)(noun fem. sing.	קרר
הַמְקָרֶה' pref. id.)(Piel part. sing. masc., or (Ec. 10. 18) subst. [for מְקָרֶה] . .	קרה
הַמַּקְרִיב' pref. id.)(Hiph. part. masc. sing. dec. 1b.	קרב
הַמְקֻשָּׁרוֹת' pref. id.)(Pual part. fem. pl. [of שָׁרָה]	קשר

הָמַר   Root not used; Arab. *to flow, stream.*
מַהֲמֹרוֹת pl. fem. *streams, floods,* Ps. 140. 11.

הַמַּר^b pref. הַ)(adj. masc. sing. dec. 8 (§ 37. rem. 7)	מרר
הָמֵר' מוֹר)(Hiph. inf. absolute . .	מור or מרר
הֻמַּר pref. הַ)(noun masc. sing. dec. 1a.	מרר
הֵמַר Hiph. pret. 3 pers. sing. masc. (§ 18. rem. 10)	מרר
הַמַּרְאָה pref. הַ)(noun fem. sing. dec. 10.	ראה
הַמַּרְאֶה pref. id.)(noun masc. sing. dec. 9a.	ראה
הַמַּרְבֶּה pref. id.)(Hiph. part. sing. masc. dec. 9a.	רבה
הַמַּרְגִּיז" pref. id.)(Hiph. part. sing. masc. dec. 1b.	רגז
הַמַּרְגְּלִים' וְ pref. id.)(noun masc. pl. of מוֹרָג' dec. 8e.	מרג
הַמַּרְגְּלִים" pref. id.)(Piel part. m., pl. of [מַרְגֵּל] dec. 7b.	רגל
הַמַּרְגֵּעָה' pref. id.)(noun fem. sing.	רגע
הַמַּרְדּוּת' pref. id.)(noun fem. sing.	מרד
הַמֹּרְדִים' pref. id.)(Kal part. act. masc., pl. of [מוֹרֵד] dec. 7b.	מרד
הַמְרוּ' Hiph. pret. 3 pers. pl.	מרה
הַמָּרוֹם' pref. הַ)(noun masc. sing. dec. 3a.	רום
הַמָּרוּץ" pref. id.)(noun masc. sing.	רוץ
הַמְּרוּצָה" pref. id.)(noun fem. sing. [for מְרֻצָּה] .	רצץ
הַמֶּרְחָק pref. id.)(noun masc. sing., pl. חַקִּים' dec. 8a (and pr. name in compos. see בַּיִת)	רחק
הַמֹּרִי' pref. id.)(noun masc. sing. dec. 6i (for מֹרִי § 35. rem. 14) . .	מרה
הַמּוֹרִיָּה' pref. id.)(pr. name of a hill, see מוֹרִיָּה	מרה
הַמָּרִים' pref. id.)(adj. m., pl. of מַר dec. 8e (§ 37. r. 7)	מרר

---

a Eze. 5. 2.   g 2 Sa. 3. 8.   n La. 1. 3.   t Eze. 48. 11.   z Le. 24. 14, 23.   f Ne. 3. 19, 20.   m Le. 27. 10, 33.   q Is. 28. 12.   v Ec. 9. 11.
b 2 Ch. 11. 21.   h Ps. 147. 8.   o Le. 14. 2.   u Ne. 10. 32.   a 2 Ch. 33. 19.   g Ju. 3. 20, 24.   n Zec. 12. 10.   r 1 Sa. 30. 30.   w Je. 22. 17.
c 2 Ki. 5. 11.   i Is. 21. 6.   p 2 Ki. 7. 8.   v 1 Ki. 13. 2.   b Nu. 11. 29.   h Ps. 104. 3.   o Is. 24. 21.   s Eze. 20. 38.   x Je. 22. 17.
d Is. 8. 34.   k 2 Ch. 20. 24.   q Zec. 14. 12.   w 2 Ch. 30. 14.   c Eze. 8. 3.   i Job 9. 6.   p Le. 9. 13.   t Is. 24. 21.   y Nu. 5. 18, 19, 23, 24.
e Is. 51. 13, 13.   l Is. 8. 19.   r Eze. 39. 15.   x Ge. 30. 37, 38, 39, 41.   d Ge. 30. 41.   k 2 Sa. 24. 22.
f Is. 29. 7.   m Ps. 118. 5.   s Ju. 4. 21.   y Je. 32. 11, 12, 14, 16.   e Hab. 1. 6.   l Jos. 6. 22, 23.   w Is. 28. 20.

Hebrew	Description	Root
הַמֹּרִים	pref. הַ)(Kal part. act. masc., pl. of מָרָה dec. 9a.	מרה
הַמְּרִיקִים	pref. id.)(Hiph. part. masc., pl. of [מֵרִיק] dec. 3b.	רוק
הַמֶּרְכָּב	pref. id.)(noun masc. sing. dec. 2b.	רכב
הַמֶּרְכָּבָה	pref. id.)(noun fem. sing. dec. 11a (constr. כַּבְּתוֹ', suff. 13a (§ 42. rem. 5)	רכב
הַמַּרְכָּבוֹת	pref. id.)(pr. name, in compos. בֵּית הַמַּר'	בית
הַמְּרֹנֹתִי	pref. id.)(gent. noun, see מְרֹנֹתִי	
הַמִּרְעֶה	pref. id.)(noun masc. sing. dec. 9a.	רעה
הַמְרַצֵּחַ	pref. id.)(Piel part. sing. masc. dec. 7b.	רצח
הַמַּרְצֵעַ	pref. id.)(noun masc. sing.	רצע
הַמָּרָק	וְ' pref. id.)(noun masc. sing. dec. 4a.	מרק
הַמִּרְקָחָה	pref. id.)(noun fem. sing.	רקח
הַמֶּרְקָחַת	pref. id.)(noun fem. sing.	רקח
הַמְרָרִי	pref. id.)(patronym. [for מְרָרִי] from מְרָר	מרר
הַמַּרְשַׁעַת	pref. id.)(noun fem. sing.	רשע
הַמֹּרַשְׁתִּי	pref. id.)(gent. noun from מוֹרֶשֶׁת גַּת (q. v.)	ירש
הַמַּשָּׂא	pref. id.)(noun masc. sing. dec. 1b.	נשא
הַמַּשְׂאֵת־	וְ pref. id.)(noun fem. sing. [for שְׂאֵת] constr. מַשְׂאַת, pl. מַשְׂאוֹת	נשא
הַמַּשְׂבִּיעַ	pref. id.)(Hiph. part. sing. masc.	שבע
הַמַּשְׂבִּיר	pref. id.)(Hiph. part. sing. masc.	שבר
הַמִּשְׁבְּצוֹת	pref. id.)(noun fem., pl. of [בָּצֶת] dec. 13a.	שבץ
הַמִּשְׂגָּב	pref. id.)(noun masc. sing., constr. גָּב', suff. גָּבִּי dec. 8a.	שגב
הַמְשֻׁגָּע	pref. id.)(Pual part. sing. masc.	שגע
הַמְשֹׁרֵי	pref. id.)(noun masc. sing.	נשר
הַמְשֹׁרֵר	pref. id.)(Pilel part. sing. masc. dec. 7b.	שיר
הַמְשֹׁרְרִים	וְ pref. id.)(id. pl., absolute state	שיר
הַמָּשׁוּחַ	Niph. inf. constr.	משח
הַמָּשְׁחָה	pref. הַ)(noun fem. sing. (no pl.)	משח
הַמְּשֻׁחִים	pref. id.)(Kal part. p. m., pl. of מָשׁוּחַ dec. 3a.	משח
הַמַּשְׁחִית	pref. הַ)(Hiph. part. sing. masc. dec. 1b.	שחת
הַמַּשְׁחִית	וְ' pref. הַ)(Hiph. part. & subst. m. s. dec. 1b.	שחת
הַמַּשְׁחִיתָם	pref. id.)(id. pl., absolute state	שחת
הַמְשַׂחֲקוֹת	pref. id.)(Piel (§ 14. rem. 1) part. fem., pl. of מְשַׂחֶקֶת dec. 13a.	שחק
הַמְּשִׁיחַ	pref. id.)(noun masc. sing. dec. 3a.	משח
הַמִּשְׁלָם	וְ Hiph. pret. 3 pers. s. m., suff. 3 pers. pl. m.	שלם
הַמִּשְׁכָּב	pref. הַ)(noun masc. sing. dec. 2b.	שכב
הַמַּשְׂכִּיל	pref. id.)(Hiph. part. sing. masc. dec. 1b.	שכל
הַמַּשְׂכִּילִים	וְ' pref. id.)(id. pl., absolute state	שכל
הַמִּשְׁכָּן	pref. id.)(noun masc. sing. dec. 2b.	שכן
הַמָּשָׁל	pref. id.)(noun masc. sing. dec. 4a.	משל
הַמָּשֵׁל	Hiph. inf. absolute	משל
הַמָּשֵׁל	pref. הַ interr. for הֲ)(Kal inf. constr.	משל
הַמּשֵׁל	pref. הַ art.)(Kal part. act. sing. m. dec. 7b.	משל
הַמְשַׁלֵּחַ	וְ' pref. id.)(Piel part. sing. masc. dec. 7b.	שלח
הַמְשַׁלְּחִים	pref. id.)(id. pl., absolute state	שלח
הַמֹּשְׁלִים	pref. id.)(Kal part. act. m., pl. of מֹשֵׁל d. 7b.	משל
הַמְשֻׁלָּשׁ	pref. id.)(Pual part. sing. masc.	שלש
הַמְשַׂמֵּחַ	pref. id.)(Piel part. sing. masc. dec. 7b.	שמח
הַמִּשְׁמָר	pref. id.)(noun masc. sing. dec. 2b.	שמר
הַמִּשְׁנֶה	pref. id.)(noun masc. sing. dec. 9a.	שנה
הַמִּשְׁנִים	וְ' pref. id.)(id. pl., absolute state	שנה
הַמִּשְׁעֶנֶת	pref. id.)(noun fem. sing. dec. 13a.	שען
הַמִּשְׁפָּחָה	וְ' pref. id.)(noun fem. sing. dec. 11a (constr. פַּחַת', suff. פַּחְתוֹ', 13a, § 42. r. 5)	שפח
הַמִּשְׁפָּחוֹת	pref. id.)(id. pl., absolute state	שפח
הַמִּשְׁפָּט	pref. id.)(noun masc. sing. dec. 2b.	שפט
הַמִּשְׁפָּטִים	וְ' pref. id.)(id. pl., absolute state	שפט
הַמַּשְׁפִּילִי	pref. id.)(Hiph. part. sing. masc. with paragogic י (compare § 8. rem. 19)	שפל
הַמִּשְׁפְּתַיִם / הַמִּשְׁפְּתָיִם	pref. id.)(noun masc., du. of [מִשְׁפָּת] dec. 2b.	שפת
הַמַּשְׁקֶה	pref. id.)(Hiph. part. sing. masc. dec. 9a.	שקה
הַמַּשְׁקוֹף	pref. id.)(noun masc. sing.	שקף
הַמַּשְׁקִים	pref. id.)(Hiph. part. m., pl. of קֶה' dec. 9a.	שקה
הַמִּשְׁקָל	pref. id.)(noun masc. sing. dec. 2b.	שקל
הַמִּשְׁרָה	pref. id.)(noun fem. sing.	שרה
הַמְשָׁרְעִי	וְ pref. id.)(gent. noun see מִשְׁרָעִי	
הַמְשֹׁרְרִים	וְ' pref. id.)(Pilel part. m., pl. מְשׁוֹרֵר' dec. 1b.	שיר
הַמְשָׁרֵת	pref. id.)(noun masc. sing.	שרת
הַמְשָׁרְתִים	וְ' pref. id.)(Piel part. masc., pl. of מְשָׁרֵת dec. 7b.	שרת
הַמִּשְׁתֶּה	pref. id.)(noun masc. sing. dec. 9a.	שתה
הַמִּשְׁתַּחֲוִים	pref. id.)(Hithpalel (§ 24. rem. 25) part. masc., pl. of וֶה' dec. 9a.	שחה
הַמִּשְׁתַּבֵּר	וְ pref. הַ)(Hithp. part. sing. masc. [for מִתְשַׁבֵּר § 12. rem. 3]	שבר
הָמֵת	וְ' Hiph. inf. absolute	מות
הַמֵּת	וְ' pref. הַ)(Kal part. s. m. dec. 1a (§ 21. r. 2)	מות
הֵמִת	pref. הַ)(id. pret. 3 pers. sing. masc.	מות
הַמִּתְאַבְּלִים	pref. הַ)(Hithpa. part. m., pl of בֵּל' d. 7b.	אבל
הַמִּתְאַנִּים	pref. id.)(Hithpa. part. m., pl. of נֶה' d. 9a.	אוה
הַמְּתֹאָר	pref. id.)(Pual part. sing. masc.	תאר
הַמִּתְבָּרֵךְ	pref. id.)(Hithpa. part. sing. masc.	ברך
הַמֵּתָה	pref. id.)(Kal part. s. f., from מֵת m. (§ 21. r. 2)	מות
הֲמִתָּה	וְ Hiph. pret. 2 p. s. m. [for הֲמַתָּתָ § 21. r. 13]	מות
הֱמִיתֻהוּ	id. pret. 3 pers. pl. (הֵמִיתוּ) suff. 3 p. s. m.	מות

---

a Nu. 20. 10.   h Ju. 6. 19.   p Ex. 28. 25.   w Nu. 3. 3.   d Am. 5. 13.   l Le. 16. 26.   r 1 Sa. 15. 9.   x Ex. 12. 7, 22, 23.   z 2 Sa. 12. 19.
b Zec. 4. 12.   i Eze. 24. 10.   q Ex. 28. 14.   x Eze. 9. 8.   e 2 Ch. 32. 31.   m Nu. 21. 27.   s Jos. 7. 14.   y Ezr. 8. 34.   Is. 66. 10.
c Le. 15. 9.   k 1 Ch. 9. 30.   r 1 Sa. 14. 15.   y Da. 12. 3, 10.   f Ps. 113. 6.   n Ec. 4. 12.   t Is. 9. 5, 6.   z Is. 9. 15.   Jos. 13. 15.
d Eze. 34. 18.   l 2 Ch. 24. 7.   s 2 Ki. 9. 11.   z Job 25. 2.   g Ge. 49. 14.   o Ju. 9. 13.   u 2 Sa. 13. 9.   a Ge. 23. 6.   Is. 65. 16.
e 2 Ki. 6. 32.   m Ju. 20. 40.   t 1 Sa. 6. 5.   a Ju. 9. 2.   h 2 Sa. 13. 3.   p 1 Ch. 15. 18.   v Ju. 5. 16.   Zec. 11. 9.
f De. 15. 17.   n Ps. 103. 5.   u 1 Sa. 18. 7.   b Ge. 24. 2; Ge. 16. 44.   i 2 Ch. 23. 6.   w Ps. 40. 5.   Je. 26. 19.
g Ju. 6. 20.   o Ge. 42. 6.   v 2 Ch. 23. 13.   c Ps. 104. 10.   k Hag. 1. 6.

הלך   'd. 7 b. pref. הַ χ Hithpa. part. m., pl. of הַלַךְ   הַמִּתְהַלְּכִים׃

הלל   pref. id. χ Hithpa. part. sing. masc. dec. 7 b.   הַמִּתְהַלְּלִי

הלל   pref. id. χ id. pl., absolute state (§ 10. r. 7)   הַמִּתְהַלְלִים׃

הפך   pref. id. χ Hithpa. part. s. f., fr. מִתְהַפֵּךְ m.   הַמִּתְהַפֶּכֶת׃

מות   Hoph. pret. 3 pers. pl. [for הֻמְתוּ] .   הֻמְתוּ

חבא   'd. 7 b. pref. הַ χ Hithpa. part. m., pl. of חַבָּא   הַמִּתְחַבְּאִים

חזק   pref. id. χ Hithpa. part. masc., pl. חַזֵּק dec. 7 b. (§ 10. rem. 7)   הַמִּתְחַזְּקִים

מות   Hiph. pret. 1 p. s. [for הֲמַתִּי § 21. r. 13]; acc. shifted by conv. ו (comp. § 8. rem. 7)   וְהֵמַתִּי׃

המם   Kal pret. 1 pers. sing. acc. shifted (v. id.)   וַהֲמֹתִי׃

מות   Hiph. pret. 1 pers. s., suff. 3 pers. s. fem. [for הֲמִתִּיהָ § 21. rem. 13]; ו for conv.   וַהֲמִתִּיהָ׃

ידש   pref. הַ χ Hithpa. (§ 14. rem. 1) part. masc., pl. of יַחֵשׁ dec. 7 b.   הַמִּתְיַחֲשִׂים׃ הַמִּתְיַחְשִׂים׃

מות   pref. id. χ Kal part. m., pl. of מֵת d. 1 a (§ 21. rem. 2)   וְהַמֵּתִים׃

תכן   pref. id. χ Pual part. sing. masc.   הַמְתֻכָּן׃

מות   Hiph. pret. 2 pers. pl. masc. [for הֲמִתֶּם § 21. rem. 13]; ו for conv.   וַהֲמִתֶּם׃

מות   id. pret. 2 p. pl. f. [for הֲמִתֶּן § 21. r. 13]; ו id.   וַהֲמִתֶּן׃

נבא   pref. הַ χ Hithpa. part. sing. masc. dec. 7 b.   הַמִּתְנַבֵּא

נבא   pref. id. χ id. fem. pl. of [בֵּאת=בָּאת]   הַמִּתְנַבְּאוֹת

נדב   pref. id. χ Hithpa. part. sing. masc. dec. 7 b.   הַמִּתְנַדֵּב

נדב   pref. id. χ id. pl., absolute state   הַמִּתְנַדְּבִים

מתן   pref. id. χ gent. noun   הַמַּתְנִי

מות   Hiph. pret. 3 pers. sing. masc. [הֵמִית], suff. 1 pers. sing. (§ 2. r. 1); ו for conv.   וֶהֱמִיתַנִי

נשא   pref. הַ χ Hithpa. part. sing. masc.   וְהַמִּתְנַשֵּׂא

תעב   pref. id. χ Piel (§ 14. rem. 1) part. masc., pl. of מְתָעֵב dec. 7 b.   הַמְתָעֲבִים

תעה   pref. id. χ Hiph. part. masc., pl. of מַתְעֶה d. 9 a.   הַמַּתְעִים

פרץ   pref. id. χ Hithpa. part. m., pl. of פָּרֵץ d. 7 b.   הַמִּתְפָּרְצִים

קדש   pref. id. χ Hithpa. part. m., pl. of קַדֵּשׁ d. 7 b.   הַמִּתְקַדְּשִׁים

קשר   pref. id. χ Hithpa. part. m., pl. of קַשֵּׁר d. 7 b.   הַמִּתְקַשְּׁרִים

הֵן, הֵן וְ—I. interj. behold! lo!—II. whether, of an indirect inquiry, Je. 2. 10.—III. if.

הֵן Ch.—I. lo! surely, Da. 3. 17.—II. whether, Ezr. 5. 17.—III. if; הֵן—הֵן whether—or, Ezr. 7. 26.

הֵנָּה adv. of place.—I. hither; הֵנָּה וָהֵנָּה hither and thither; מִמְּךָ וָהֵנָּה from thee and hither, i. e. on this side of thee; עַד־הֵנָּה hitherto, also spoken of time.— II. here, in this place, Ge. 21. 29; הֵנָּה וְהֵנָּה here—there, Da. 12. 5; הֵנָּה וָהֵנָּה here and there, 1 Ki. 20. 40.

הֵן, הִנֵּה interj. behold! lo! usually expressive of readiness to hear and to obey; with suff. הִנְנִי, הִנְנִי מֵבִיא, הִנְנִי, behold me! lo, I am here! behold, I bring, am about to, or will bring; (note Is. 28. 16 הִנְנִי יִסַּד, where אֲשֶׁר is to be supplied: behold me, who has laid for have laid, &c.); 2 pers. הִנָּךְ, הִנֶּךָּ &c. see analyt. order.

הֵן   only with the prefixes, מֵהֶן, כָּהֶן, בָּהֶן pers. pron. 3 p. pl. f. they, comp. הוּא (§ 1. r. 6). As a separate pronoun it invariably takes parag. ה, as הֵנָּה, with prefixes, בָּהֵנָּה; מֵהֵנָּה as they are i. e. such; כָּהֵנָּה וְכָהֵנָּה such and such things, 2 Sa. 12. 8.

הן   Kh. הֵן q. v., K. הִנֵּה q. v. interj.   הֵנָּ

אהב   pref. הַ χ Niph. part. masc., pl. of [נֶאֱהָב]   הַנֶּאֱהָבִים

אכל   pref. id. χ Niph. part. s. fem. (fr. נֶאֱכָל m.)   הַנֶּאֱכֶלֶת

אמן   pref. id. χ Niph. part. sing. masc. dec. 2 b.   הַנֶּאֱמָן

אמן   pref. id. χ id. pl., absolute state   הַנֶּאֱמָנִים

אנח   pref. id. χ Niph. part. masc., pl. of נֶאֱנָח   הַנֶּאֱנָחִים

אנק   pref. id. χ Niph. part. masc. pl. [of נֶאֱנָק]   וְהַנֶּאֱנָקִים

נאף   pref. id. χ Kal part. act. sing. masc.   הַנֹּאֵף

נאף   pref. id. χ id. fem. [for נֹאֶפֶת] comp. § 35. r. 2]   וְהַנֹּאָפֶת

נבא   pref. id. χ Niph. pret. 3 pers. sing. masc.   הַנִּבָּא

נבא   pref. id. χ Niph. imp. sing. masc.   וְהִנָּבֵא

נבא   Hithp. imp. pl. masc. [for הִתְנַבְּאוּ § 12. r. 3]   הַנִּבְּאוּ

נבא   pref. הַ χ Niph. part. m., pl. of נִבָּא dec. 1 b.   הַנִּבָּאִים

נבא   pref. id. χ noun masc., pl. of נָבִיא dec. 3 a.   הַנְּבִאִים

נבא   pref. הַ χ Niph. part. masc. pl. [of נִבָּא § 23. rem. 6, comp. rem. 9]   הַנִּבָּאִים

בדל   pref. id. χ Niph. part. sing. masc.   הַנִּבְדָּל

נבא   Hithpa. pret. 1 p. s. [for הִתְנַבֵּאתִי § 12. r. 3]   וְהִנַּבֵּאתִי

נבא   pref. הַ χ noun fem. sing. dec. 10.   וְהַנְּבוּאָה

נבא   pref. id. χ noun masc. sing. dec. 3 a.   וְהַנָּבִיא

נבא   pref. id. χ noun fem. sing.   הַנְּבִיאָה

נבא   pref. id. χ noun masc., pl. of נָבִיא dec. 3 a.   וְהַנְּבִיאִים

נבא   Kh. הַנְּבִאִים K. הַנְּבָאִים (q. v.)   הַנְּבִיאִים

נבל   pref. הַ χ noun masc. sing. (§ 35. rem. 2)   הַנֵּבֶל

נבל   pref. id. χ noun masc. sing. dec. 6 b.   הַנָּבֵל

נבל   pref. id. χ noun fem. sing.   הַנְּבֵלָה

נבל   pref. id. χ noun fem. sing. (constr. נִבְלַת, suff. נְבֵלָתִי once § 42. rem. 4)   הַנְּבֵכָה

נבל   pref. id. χ adj. fem. pl. from נָבֵל masc.   הַנְּבָלוֹת

נבל   pref. id. χ n. m., pl. of נֵבֶל d. 6 b, or נֶבֶל d. 4 a.   הַנְּבָלִים

בנה   pref. id. χ Niph. part. sing. masc.   הַנִּבְנֶה

בשן   pref. id. χ pr. name of a place   וְהַנְּבָשָׁן

a 1 Sa. 25. 27.   d 1 Ch. 11. 10.   h 2 Ki. 12. 12.   l 2 Ch. 17. 16.   b Is. 66. 17.   q De. 7. 9.   m Le. 20. 10.   r Eze. 37. 10.   y Ps. 108. 3.
b Je. 9. 23.   e Ex. 23. 27.   i Nu. 17. 6.   m 2 Sa. 14. 32.   c 2 Ch. 24. 26.   h Is. 55. 3.   n 1 Ch. 25. 2, 3.   s Ne. 6. 12.   z Ps. 57. 9.
c Ps. 97. 7.   f Ho. 2. 5.   k 2 Sa. 13. 28.   n 1 Ch. 29. 11.   d Is. 54. 16.   i Eze. 9. 4.   o 2 Ch. 15. 8.   a Job 2. 10.
d Ge. 3. 24.   g Ezr. 2. 62.   l Ex. 1. 16.   o Mi. 3. 9.   e 2 Sa. 1. 23.   k Je. 23. 13.   u 1 Ch. 25. 1.   b Is. 22. 24; Eze. 13. 2.
2 Sa. 21. 9.   Ne. 7. 64.   Je. 29. 27.   Mi. 3. 5.   f Le. 11. 47.   l Eze. 9. 4.   Am. 6. 5.   c 1 Ch. 22. 19.
1 Sa. 14. 22.   Ec. 9. 5.   Eze. 13. 17.   1 Sa. 25. 10.   Le. 20. 10.   p Ezr. 6. 21.

הַנֶּגֶב	] pref. הַ)(noun masc. dec. 6. (§ 35. r. 3)	נגב
הַנֶּגְבָּה	pref. הַ art.)(id. with parag. ה	נגב
הַנֹּגַהּ	pref. id.)(noun masc. s. d 6 c. (§ 35. r. 5)	נגה
הַנָּגִיד	pref. id.)(noun masc. sing. dec. 3a .	נגד
הַנִּגְלָה	pref. הַ)(Niph. inf. absolute . .	נגלה
הַנִּגְלוּ	pref. id.)(id. pret. 3 pers. pl. .	נגלה
הַנִּגְלוֹת	] ן pref. הַ)(id. part. fem., pl. of לָה d. 10. [from לָה masc.] . .	נגלה
הַנֶּגַע	] pref. id.)(noun masc. sing. dec. 6a.	נגע
הַנָּגַע	ן' (§ 35. rem. 2 & 5; but with suff. נִגְעִי)	
הַנֹּגֵעַ	ן' pref. id.)(Kal part. act. sing. masc. d. 7 b.	נגע
הַנְּגָעִים	pref. id.)(id. pl., absolute state .	נגע
הַנֹּגַעַת	pref. id.)(id. fem. sing. dec. 13 a. .	נגע
הַנֶּגֶף / הַנָּגֶף	} pref. id.)(noun masc. sing. (§ 35. rem. 2)	נגף
הַנִּגְרִים	pref. id.)(Niph. part. masc. pl. [of נִגָּר]	נגר
הַנֹּגֵשׂ	pref. id.)(Kal part. act. sing. masc. d. 7 b.	נגש
הַנִּגָּשִׁים	pref. id.)(Niph. part. masc. pl. [of נִגָּשׁ]	נגש
הַנֹּגְשִׂים	ן' pref. id.)(Kal part. act. m., pl. of נֹגֵשׂ d. 7 b.	נגש
הַנְּדָבָה	pref. id.)(noun fem. sing. dec. 11c	נדב
הַנִּדְבָּרִים	pref. id.)(Niph. part. masc. pl. [of נִדְבָּר] .	דבר
הַנִּדָּה	pref. id.)(noun fem. sing. dec. 10.	נדה
הַנִּדָּחָה	ן' pref. id.)(Niph. part. sing. f. fr. נִדָּח m.	נדח
הַנִּדָּחִים	ן' pref. id.)(id. m., pl. of נִדָּח dec 2 b. (suff. נִדְּחוֹ § 15. rem. 2) .	נדח
הַנִּדַּחַת	pref. id.)(id., sing. fem.	נדח
הַנֹּדֵר	pref. id.)(Kal part. act. sing. masc.	נדר
הֵנָּה	ן' pers. pron. 3 pers. f. pl. (הֵן) with parag. ה	הן
הֵנָּה	ן' adv. (הֵן) with parag. ה; for ן' see lett. ו	הן
הִנֵּה	ן' adv. or demon. interj. (הֵן) with parag. ה	הן
הִנֵּה	id., bef. dag. f. conj. (נָא) .	הן
הִנֵּהוּ	ן' Kh., הִנֵּה with suff. 3 pers. sing. masc. K. הִנֵּה הוּא . .	הן
הֶנָּהְיָה	pref. הַ)(Niph. pret. 3 pers. sing. masc.	היה
הַנֶּהֱלָאָה	ן' pref. הַ)(Niph. part. sing. f. (§ 13. r. 6)	הלא
הַנֶּהֱלָלִים	pref. id.)(noun masc., pl. of [נַהֲלָל] d. 1 b.	נהל
הַנָּהָר	א' pref. id.)(noun masc. sing. dec. 4 a. .	נהר
הַנְּהָרוֹת	pref. id.)(id. pl. abs. (constr. נַהֲרוֹת)	נהר
הַנֶּהֱרָסוֹת	ן' pref. id.)(Niph. part. fem., pl. of [רָסָה]	הרס
הַנֶּהֱרָסֶת	defect. for הַנֶּהֱרָסוֹת (q. v.) . .	והר
הַנֹּה	ן' demon. interj. (הִנֵּה) with suff. 3 p. s. m.	הן
הַנֹּגֵעַ	ן' pref. הַ)(Kal part. sing. masc. dec. 7 b.	נגע
הַנָּוָה	ן' pref. id.)(adj. fem. sing. d. 11a, fr. נָוֶה m.	נוה
הַנָּוֶה	pref. id.)(noun masc. sing. dec. 9b. .	נוה
הַנֹּטָה	ן' pref. id.)(Kal part. act. sing. masc. dec. 9 a.	נטה
הַנֹּטֵעַ	pref. id.)(Kal part. act. sing. masc. dec. 7 b.	נטע
הַנּוֹלָדִי	ן' pref. id.)(Niph. part. sing. masc. d. 2 b.	ילד
הַנּוֹלָדִים	pref. id.)(id. pl., absolute state	ילד
הַנּוֹעָדִים	pref. id.)(Niph. part. masc. pl. [of נוֹעָד]	יעד
הַנּוֹצָה	pref. id.)(noun fem. sing. .	נצה
הַנּוֹרָא	ן' pref. id.)(Niph. part. sing. masc.	ירא
הַנּוֹרָאֹת	pref. id.)(id. fem., pl. abs. fr. נוֹרָאָה d. 11c.	ירא
הַנּוֹשָׁבוֹת	pref. id.)(Niph. part. fem. pl. [of שָׁבָה, in use only שָׁבֶת]	ישב
הַנּוֹשֵׂא	ן' pref. id.)(Kal part. act. sing. masc. d. 7 b.	נשא
הַנּוֹתֵן	pref. id.)(Kal part. act. sing. masc. dec. 7 b.	נתן
הַנּוֹתָר	ן' pref. id.)(Niph. part. sing. masc.	יתר
הַנּוֹתָרֹת	pref. id.f. pl. [of תָּרָה; in use only תֶּרֶת]	יתר
הַנּוֹתָרִים	ן' pref. id.)(id. masc., pl. of נוֹתָר	יתר
הַנּוֹתֶרֶת / הַנּוֹתָרֹת	} pref. id.)(id. f. s. & pl., comp. הַנּוֹתָרוֹת	יתר
הַנָּזִיד	pref. id.)(noun m. sing. dec. 3 a. R. זיד see זוד	זוד
הַנָּזִיר	pref. id.)(noun masc. sing. dec. 3 a.	נזר
הַנֶּזֶר	pref. id.)(noun masc. sing. dec. 6 b.	נזר
הַנָּזֵר	Niph. inf., abs.	נזר
הַנֶּזֶם	pref. הַ)(noun masc. s. (suff. נִזְמָהּ) d. 6 a.	נזם
הַנְּזָמִים	pref. id.)(id. pl., absolute state	נזם
הַנְּזִרִים	pref. id.)(noun masc., pl. of נָזִיר dec. 3 a.	נזר
הַנַּח	ן' Hiph. imp. masc. sing. ap. for הַנִּיחַ (§ 21. rem. 24, comp. rem. 19) .	נוח
הַנַּח	id. pret. 3 p. s. m. for הַנִּיחַ (see the prec.)	נוח
הֲנָחָה	ן noun fem. sing.; ן bef. (־) .	נוח
הַנִּיחוּ	Hiph. imp. pl. masc. (§ 21. rem. 24)	נוח
הַנְחִילוּ	Hiph. inf., suff. 3 pers. sing. masc. dec. 1 b.	נחל
הַנְּחִילוֹת	pref. הַ)(noun f. pl. [of נְחִילָה for נְחִילָה]	חלל
הִנְחִיתָם	Hiph. pret. 2 pers. s. m., suff. 3 pers. s. m.	נחה
הַנַּחַל / הַנָּחַל	} pref. הַ)(noun m. s. d. 6d. (§ 35. r. 2)	נחל
הַנַּחֲלָה	pref. id.)(noun fem. sing. dec. 12d.	נחל
הַנַּחֲלֹת	pref. id.)(Niph. part. f., pl. of נַחֲלָה (§ 13. r. 7)	חלה
הַנְּחָלִים	pref. id.)(noun masc., pl. of נַחַל dec. 6 d.	נחל
הַנַּחְלָמִי	pref. id.)(patronym. .	חלם
הַנַּחֲלַת	pref. id.)(noun fem., pl. of נַחֲלָה dec. 12d.	נחל
הִנְחַלְתִּי	Hoph. pret. 1 pers. sing. . .	נחל
הִנְחַלְתִּי / הִנְחַלְתִּי	} Hiph. pret. 1 pers. sing. acc. shifted by conv. ן' (comp. § 8. rem. 7)	נחל
הִנְחַלְתֶּם	ן' id. pret. 2 pers. pl. masc.	נחל
הִנָּחֵם	ן' Niph. imp. sing. masc. or inf. constr.	נחם
הַנִּחֻמִים	pref. הַ)(Niph. part. pl. [for נְחֻמִים Chaldaism for נְחֻמִים § 18. rem. 14]	חמם

a Eze. 1. 28.   h Nu. 19. 22.   p Ezr. 1. 4.   x Mi. 4. 7.   f Is. 40. 22.   n Le. 15. 10.   u Ge. 24. 30, 47.   z 2 Sa. 16. 11.   g Jos. 19. 51.
b 1 Sa. 2. 27.   i Nu. 17. 11.   q Eze. 33. 30.   y Is. 7. 19.   e Je. 11. 17.   o Je. 34. 7.   v Ge. 35. 4.   a De. 21. 16.   h Job 7. 3.
c Job 38. 17.   k 2 Sa. 14. 14.   r Is. 27. 13.   z Ge. 2. 14.   p Is. 30. 9.   m Am. 2. 12.   Ps. 5. 1.   b Ne. 9. 12.   i 1 Ch. 22. 5.
d De. 29. 28.   l Is. 9. 3.   s Is. 27. 13.   a' Ex. 36. 35, 36.   l Le. 10. 12.   n Ho. 4. 17.   c Ne. 9. 12.   Is. 57. 5.
e Le. 13. 55.   m Ex. 19. 22.   t Eze. 34. 4, 16.   b' Ex. 8. 1.   u Nu. 6. 13, 18, 19 20, 21.   1 Ki. 3. 17.   2 Ki. 12. 9.
f Le. 15. 7.   x Ex. 7. 8.   y Ex. 7. 8.   c' Ge. 19. 2.   Est. 2. 18.   De. 12. 9.
g Je. 12. 14.   o Ex. 5. 13.   v De. 4. 32.   Je. 6. 2.   Ex. 12. 20.   rr De. 10. 21.   ss Zec. 7. 3.   tt Eze. 34. 4, 21.

הַנֶּחֱמָרִים	pref. הַ)(Niph. part. masc., pl. of נֶחֱמָר	חמד
הִנֶּחָמְתִּי וְ	Hithpa. pret. 1 pers. sing. [for הִתְנֶחָמְתִּי, § 14. r. 3, & § 42. No. 3 note; see אָח § 45]	נחם
הִנֶחַנִי	Hiph. pret. 3 pers. sing. m., suff. 1 pers. s.	נחה
הַנֶּחֱרִים	pref. הַ)(Niph. part. m., pl. of [נֶחֱרָה] d. 9a.	חרה
הַנָּחָשׁ וְ	pref. id.)(noun masc. sing. dec. 4a.	נחש
הַנְּחָשִׁים	pref. id.)(id. pl., absolute state	נחש
הַנֶּחֱשָׁלִים	pref. id.)(Niph. part. pl. [of נֶחְשָׁל]	חשל
הַנְּחֹשֶׁת וְ	pref. id.)(noun fem. sing. (with suff. נְחֻשׁ & נָחָשׁ) dec. 13c.	נחש
הַנְחֵת	Hiph. imp. sing. masc. [with gutt. for הַנְחֵת]	נחת
הַנְחַת	Chald. Hoph. pret. 3 pers. sing. masc.	נחת
הִנַּחְתָּ וְ	Hiph. pret. 2 pers. sing. masc. (§ 21. rem. 24); acc. shifted by conv. וְ (§ 8. rem. 7)	נוח
הִנַּחְתּוֹ וְ	id. id., suff. 3 pers. sing. masc.	נוח
הֲנַחְתִּי וָ	id. pret. 1 pers. sing.; acc. shifted by וָ for וְ conv. (§ 8. rem. 7)	נוח
הִנַּחְתִּי וְ	id. id. (§ 21. rem. 24)	נוח
הֲנִחֹתִיו	id. id., suff. 3 pers. sing. masc.	נוח
הִנַּחְתָּם וְ	id. pret. 2 pers. s. m., suff. 3 pers. pl. m.	נוח
הִנַּחְתֶּם וְ	id. pret. 2 pers. pl. masc.	נוח
הַנְּטוּיָה	pref. הַ)(Kal part. p. fem. d. 10, fr. נָטוּי m.	נטה
הַנְּטוֹפָתִי	pref. id.)(gent. noun fr. נְטֹפָה	נטף
הַנְּטֻפוֹת וְ	pref. id.)(noun fem., pl. of [פָה] dec. 10.	נטף
הַנְּטִישׁוֹתי	pref. id.)(noun fem., pl. of [שָׁה] dec. 10.	נטש
הַנֹּטֵעַ	pref. הַ)(Kal part. sing. masc. [for נֹטֵעַ comp. § 15. rem. 1]	נטע
הַנְטִפוֹת	noun fem., pl. of [נְטִיפָה] dec. 10.	נטף
הַנְּטֹפָתִי	pref. הַ)(gent. noun fr. נְטֹפָה	נטף
הָנִיא	Hiph. pret. 3 pers. sing. masc.	נוא
הָנִיחַ	Hiph. inf. constr. dec. 3a.	נוח
הֵנִיחַ (וַ/וְ)	id. pret. 3 pers. sing. masc. (§ 21. rem. 24)	נוח
הֱנִיחָה	id. imp. m. s. with parag. ה (v.i. & § 11. r. 5)	נוח
הֱנִיחָתָ וְ	Hoph. pret. 3 pers. sing. fem. (§ 21. r. 24)	נוח
הָנִיחוּ / הֱנִיחוּ }	Hiph. imp. masc. pl. (§ 21. rem. 24)	נוח
הֱנִיחוֹ	id. pret. 3 pers. sing. masc., suff. 3 pers. s. m.	נוח
הֱנִיחֻהוּ / הֱנִיחֻהוּ וְ }	id. pret. 3 pers. pl. (§ 21. rem. 24)	נוח
הֱנִיחֻךְ וְ	id. id., suff. 2 pers. sing. fem.	נוח
הֲנִיחוֹתִי וְ	id. pret. 1 pers. sing.; וָ for וְ conv.	נוח
הַנִּיחֹחַ	pref. הַ)(noun masc. sing. dec. 1b.	נוח
הֲנִיחִי	Hiph. inf. (הָנִיחַ), suff. 1 pers. sing. dec. 3a.	נוח
הִנִּיחָם	id. pret. 3 p. s. m., suff. 3 p. m. (§ 21. r. 24)	נוח
הֲנִיחֹתִי	id. pret. 1 p. s.; acc. shifted by וָ for וְ conv.	נוח
הַנִּים	pref. הַ)(Kh. נִים adj., K. עַ)נִים Kal part. act. m.	נום
הֵנִים	Hiph. pret. 3 pers. sing. masc.	נום
הֵנִיף וְ	Hiph. pret. 3 pers. sing. masc.	נוף
הָנִיפוּ	id. imp. masc. pl.	נוף
הֲנִיפוֹתִי	id. pret. 1 pers. sing.	נוף
הֲנִיפְכֶם	id. inf. (הָנִיף), suff. 2 pers. pl. masc. dec. 3a.	נוף
הֵנִיעָה	Hiph. pret. 3 pers. sing. fem.	נוע
הֲנִיעֵמוֹ	id. imp. masc. sing., suff. 3 pers. pl.	נוע
הֵנִיקוּ	Hiph. pret. 3 pers. pl.	ינק
הִנָּךְ	interj. demon. (הֶן=הִנֵּה), suff. 2 pers. s. fem.	הן
הִנְּךָ / הִנֶּךָּ }	id., suff. 2 pers. sing. masc. (§ 2. rem. 2)	הן
הַנִּכְבָּד	pref. הַ)(Niph. part. sing. masc. dec. 2b, & 8a (§ 37. rem. 5)	כבד
הִנֵּכָה	full form for הִנֵּךְ q. v. (§ 2. rem. 2)	הן
הַנִּכְחָדוֹת / הַנִּכְחֶדֶת וְ }	pref. הַ)(Niph. part. fem. sing. & pl. (§ 44. rem. 5)	כחד
הַנִּכְלָמוֹת	pref. id.)(Niph. part. fem. pl. [of לְמָה]	כלם
הַנִּכְלָמִים	pref. id.)(id. masc., pl. of נִכְלָם	כלם
הִנְּכֶם וְ	interj. demon. (הִנֵּה), suff. 2 pers. s. m.	הן
הַנֵּכָר	pref. הַ)(noun masc. sing. (§ 33. rem. 3)	נכר
הַנָּכְרִי וְ	pref. id.)(adj. masc. sing. [from נֵכָר with adj. term. יִ-], pl. נָכְרִים	נכר
הַנָּכְרִיּוֹת	pref. id.)(fem., pl. of נָכְרִיָּה	נכר
הַנִּכְשָׁל	pref. id.)(Niph. part. masc.	כשל
הַנִּלְוָה	pref. id.)(Niph. pret. 3 pers. sing. masc., for נִלְוָה (§ 24. rem. 18)	לוה
הַנִּלְוִים	pref. id.)(id. part. m., pl. of [נִלְוָה] dec. 9a.	לוה
הַנִּלְחָם	pref. id.)(Niph. part. sing. masc.	לחם
הַנִּלְחָמִים	pref. id.)(id. pl., absolute state	לחם
הַנֵּלֵךְ	pref. הַ)(Kal fut. 1 pers. pl.	ילך
הַנִּלְכָּד	pref. הַ)(Niph. part. sing. masc.	לכד
הִנָּם וְ	interj. demon. (הֵן=הִנֵּה), suff. 3 pers. pl. m.	הן
הִנֹּם	pr. name masc. see גֵּי	
הַנִּמְהָר וְ	pref. הַ)(Niph. part. sing. masc.	מהר
הַנְּמוּאֵלִי	pref. id.)(patronym. of נְמוּאֵל q. v.	
הַנִּמְכָּרִים	pref. id.)(Niph. part. masc. pl. [of נִמְכָּר]	מכר
הַנִּמְלָט וְ	pref. id.)(Niph. part. sing. masc.	מלט
הַנִּמְלִים	pref. id.)(noun fem. with pl. masc. term. from נְמָלָה	נמל
הַנִּמְצָא	pref. הַ)(Kal fut. 1 pers. pl.	מצא
הַנִּמְצָא וְ	pref. id.)(Niph. part. sing. masc. dec. 1b.	מצא
הַנִּמְצָאָה	pref. id.)(id. fem., dec. 11a.	מצא
הַנִּמְצָאוּ	pref. id.)(id. pret. 3 pers. pl.	מצא
הַנִּמְצָאוֹת	pref. id.)(id. part. fem., pl. of [צָאָה] dec. 11a.	מצא

Ps. 19.11. — 1 Ch. 29.2. — Nu. 17.19. — Nu. 19.9. — Eze. 16.39. — Job 31.21. — 2 Ki. 7.2. — Zec. 12.8. — 1 Ki. 19.17.
Eze. 5.13. — Joel 4.11. — Ju. 8.26. — Zec. 5.11. — 1 Ch. 22.9. — Le. 23.12. — Zec. 11.16. — Is. 56.3. — Pr. 30.25.
Ge. 24.48. — Da. 5.20. — Is. 18.5. — Ge. 8.21. — Eze. 24.13. — Ps. 59.12. — Zec. 11.9. — Jos. 7.15. — Ge. 41.38.
Ge. 3.1. — De. 14.28. — Is. 28.12. — Je. 48.44. — La. 4.3. — Eze. 16.27. — Hab. 1.6. — 1 Ch. 29.17.
Nu. 21.6. — De. 26.10. — Is. 3.19. — De. 26.4. — Ex. 9.20. — Ps. 139.8. — 2 Sa. 19.4. — Ne. 5.8.
De. 25.18. — Je. 27.11. — Is. 14.3. — Zec. 6.8. — Is. 13.2 — De. 28.58. — 2 Sa. 7.11. — Ju. 20.48.

הַנִּמְצָאִים } pref. ה X id. masc., pl. of נִמְצָא [or § 23. rem. 6] . . מצא
הַנִּמְצָאִים }

הַנִּמְצָאֹת pref. id. X id. fem., pl. of נִמְצָאָה dec. 11 a. . מצא

הִנְנִי } interj. demon. (הֵן=הִנֵּה), with suff.
הִנְנוּ } 1 pers. pl. (§ 2 note) . . . הן
וְהִנְנוּ }

הִנְנִי, הִנֵּנִי הַנְנִי id. with suff. 1 pers. sing. . . הן

הַנָּס pref. ה X Kal part. act. sing. masc. dec. 1 a נום

הַנֵּס pref. id. X noun masc. sing. dec. 8 b נסס

הֲנִסָּה pref. הֲ X Piel pret. 3 pers. sing. masc. נסה

הַנְּסוֹגִים pref. ה X Niph. part. masc. pl. of נָסוֹג dec. 3 a. סוג

הַנְּסוּכָה pref. ה X Kal part. p. fem. sing. [fr. נָסוּךְ m.] נסך

הַנֶּסֶךְ pref. id. X noun m. s. for נֶסֶךְ (§ 35. rem. 2) נסך

וְהַנֶּסֶךְ וְ pref. id. X noun masc. sing. dec. 6 b. נסך

הַנִּסְפֶּה pref. id. X Niph. part. sing. masc. ספה

וְהַנִּסְתָּרִים וְ pref. id. X Niph. part. masc., pl. of נִסְתָּר סתר

הַנִּסְתָּרֹת pref. id. X id. fem. pl. [of נִסְתָּרָה] סתר

הֲנַע pr. name of a city in Mesopotamia

הַנּוֹעָדִים pref. ה X Niph. part. masc. pl. [of נוֹעַד] יעד

הַנֹּעָה pref. id. X pr. name of a place נוע

הַנְּעוּרִים pref. id. X noun masc., pl. of [נָעוּר] dec. 1 a. נער

וַהֲנִעוֹתִי נ Hiph. pret. 1 pers. sing.; acc. shifted by וְ for וְ conv. (comp. § 8. rem. 7) . נוע

הַנַּעֲזֻבוֹת pref. ה X Niph. part. fem. pl. [of עָזַב=זָבָה] עזב

וְהַנְּעִמִים וְ pref. id. X adj. m., pl. of נָעִים dec. 3 a. נעם

הַנַּעֲלָה pref. id. X n. f. s. dec. 6 d. for נַעַל (§ 35. r. 2) נעל

הֻנְעַל Chald. Aph. pret. 3 pers. s. m. for אֻעַל=הֻעַל (§ 47. rem. 4] dag. f. resolved in נ, comp. § 52. rem. 2 עלל

הַנַּעֲמִי pref. ה X patronym. [for נַעֲמִנִי] from נַעֲמָן נעם

הַנַּעֲמָתִי pref. id. X gent. noun from נַעֲמָה נעם

הַנַּעֲצוּץ pref. id. X noun masc. sing. dec. 1 b. נעץ

הַנַּעֲצוּצִים pref. id. X id. pl., absolute state נעץ

הַנַּעַר } pref. ה X noun masc. sing. dec. 6 d.
וְהַנַּעַר } (§ 35. rem. י) נער

הַנַּעַר וְ pref. id. X Kh. נַעַר com.gen., K. נַעֲרָה (q.v.) נער

הַנַּעֲרָה וְ pref. id. X noun fem. sing. dec. 12 d. נער

הַנְּעָרוֹת pref. id. X id. pl., absolute state . נער

הַנְּעָרִים pref. id. X noun masc., pl. of נַעַר dec. 6 d. נער

הַנַּעֲרֹת pref. id. X noun fem. sing. נער

הַנַּעֲשֶׂה pref. ה X Kal fut. 1 pers. pl. עשה

הַנַּעֲשׂוֹת pref. id. X Niph. part. f., pl. of [נַעֲשֶׂה=שֶׂה m.] עשה

הַנְּפִילִים pref. id. X noun masc., pl. of [נָפִיל] dec. 3 a. נפל

הַנֵּפֶל pref. id. X noun m. s. for נֶפֶל (§ 35. rem. 2) נפל

הַנֹּפֵל pref. id. X Kal part. act. sing. masc. dec. 7 b. נפל

הַנֹּפְלִים noun masc., pl. of [נֹפֵל] dec. 3 a. . נפל

הַנֹּפְלִים וְ pref. id X Kal part. act. masc., pl. of נֹפֵל dec. 7 b. נפל

הַנֹּפֶלֶת pref. id. X id. fem. sing. (§ 8. rem. 19) נפל

הַנְפֵּק Chald. Aph. pret. 3 pers. sing. masc. (§ 47. rem. 4, & § 51. rem. 1) . . נפק

הַנְפִּקוּ Chald. id. pret. 3 pers. pl. masc. . נפק

הַנֶּפֶשׁ } pref. ה X noun com. sing. (suff. נַפְשִׁי)
הַנֶּפֶשׁ } וְ dec. 6 a (§ 35. rem. 2) נפש

הַנְּפָשׁוֹת pref. ה art. X id. pl., absolute state . נפש

הַנֹּפֶת pref. id. X n. f. s. [for נֹפֶת comp. § 35. r. 2] נוף

הִנַּפְתָּ } Hiph. pret. 2 pers. s. m. (§ 21. r. 13 & 14);
וְהִנַּפְתָּ } acc. shifted by conv. וְ (§ 8. rem. 7) } נוף

הַנֵּץ pref. ה X noun masc. sing. . נצץ

הַנִּצָּב pref. id. X Niph. part. or subst. masc. נצב

הַנִּצָּבָה pref. id. X id. part. fem. sing. נצב

הַנִּצָּבוֹת pref. id. X id. fem., pl. absolute נצב

הַנִּצָּבִים pref. id. X id. masc., pl. of נִצָּב נצב

הַנִּצֶּבֶת pref. id. X id. fem. sing. נצב

הֻנְּצוּ Hiph. pret. 3 pers. pl. (§ 21. rem. 13 & 14) נוץ

הַנָּצוּר וְ pref. ה X Kal part. p. masc. dec. 3 a. נצר

הַנֵּצַח וְ pref. id. X noun masc. sing. dec. 6 e. נצח

הַנְּצִבִים pref. id. X Kh. נִצָּבִים pl. of נָצִיב, K. הַנְצִבִים (q. v.) נצב

הִנָּצֵל וְ Niph. imp. masc. sing. נצל

הַנִּצְמָדִים pref. ה X Niph. part. masc. pl. [of נִצְמָד] צמד

הַנִּצָּנִים pref. id. X noun masc. pl. [of נִצָּן] נצן

הַנְקֵב pref. id. X pr. name of a place נקב

הַנִּקְבָּצִים pref. id. X noun masc., pl. of נִקְבָּץ dec. 2 b. קבץ

הַנְּקֻדּוֹת pref. id. X adj. fem. pl. of [נְקֻדָּה] dec. 10, from נָקֹד masc. (§ 26. No. 21) נקד

הִנָּקֹה Niph. inf. absolute נקה

הַנִּקְהָלִים pref. ה X Niph. part. masc. pl. [of נִקְהָל] קהל

הַנָּקִי pref. id. X adj. masc. sing., pl. נְקִיִּם dec. 8 f, (§ 37. No. 4) . . . נקה

הִנָּקִי Niph. imp. sing. fem. נקה

הַנָּקֵל pref. הַ X Niph. pret. 3 pers. sing. masc. קלל

הֲנִקְלָה pref. ה interr. for X id. part. fem. sing. קלל

הַנִּקְלֶה וְ pref. ה art. X Niph. part. sing. masc. . קלה

הִנָּקֵם וְ Niph. imp. sing. masc.; acc. Milêl before monos. (§ 9. rem. 3) נקם

הִנָּקְמוּ id. imp. pl. masc. נקם

הַנִּקְרָא pref. ה X Niph. part. sing. masc. dec. 1 b קרא

הַנִּקְרָאִים pref. id. X id. pl., absolute state . קרא

הַנִּרְאָה pref. id. X Niph. pret. 3 pers. sing. masc. ראה

הַנִּרְאָה pref. id. X id. part. sing. masc. . ראה

■ Ezr. 8.25.   ‡ Eze. 45.17.   * Eze. 36.4.   ‡ Ge. 24.16.   ⁵ Ju. 8.10.   ⁹ Zec. 11.16.   ᵖ Pr. 6.5.   ᵗ Ge. 30.35.   ᵃ Is. 3.5.
● Ge. 19.15.   ⁴ Is. 18.15.   ° Pr. 23.8.   ᵐ Est. 2.9.   ᶜ Am. 9.11.   ˡ 1 Sa. 4.20.   ᵖ Pr. 6.3.   ᵘ Je. 25.29.   ᵇ Is. 3.5.
● Job 38.35.   ʰ De. 7.20.   ᵖ 2 Sa. 1.23.   ⁿ Ju. 16.9.   ᵈ Da. 5.3.   ᵐ 1 Sa. 1.26.   ● Nu. 25.5.   ˣ Eze. 38.7.   ᵉ Je. 50.15.
ᵈ Nu. 21.9.   ᶜ De. 29.28.   ⁹ Deu. 25.10.   ᵍ 2 Sa. 17.6.   ˢ Jos. 17.11.   ᵗ Ca. 2.12.   ᵈ Je. 6.12.   ʸ Nu. 5.19.   ᵏ Je. 50.15.
● Is. 25.7.   ᵈ Ps. 127.4.   ᵗ Is. 55.13.   ᵖ Eze. 9.4.   ᵗ Ex. 20.25.   ᵘ 1 Ch. 29.11.   ᵉ Je. 40.15.   ᵐ 1 Sa. 18.23.   ᵐ Is. 43.7.
● Nu. 4.7.   ᵉ Am. 9.9.   ᶠ Is. 7.19.   ᵉ Ec. 6.3.   ᵍ Ex. 29.24.26.etc.   ᵖ Ch. 8.10.   ᵛ Zep. 1.8.   ᵐ Nu. 13.33.   ⁿ Is. 48.1.

הַנֵּרוֹת	' וְ] pref. הַ](n. m. with pl. f. term. from נֵר d. 1 a.	נור
הַנִּרְצָחָה	pref. id.](Niph. part. sing. f. [from נִרְצָח m.]	רצח
הַנֵּרָה	'ו defect. for הַנֵּרוֹת (q. v.) .	נור
הַנֹּשֵׂא	'וְ] pref. הַ](Kal part. act. sing. masc. dec. 7 b	נשא
הַנָּשֵׂא	Niph. imp. sing. masc.	נשא
וְהַנָּשְׂאוּ	id. imp. pl. masc. .	נשא
הַנְּשֻׂאוֹת	pref. הַ](id. part. fem. pl. [of נְשֻׂאָה, in use נְשֻׂאת .	נשא
הַנֹּשְׂאִים	'וְ] pref. id.](id. part. m., pl. of נֹשֵׂא dec. 1 b	נשא
הַנֹּשְׂאִים	'וְ] pref. id.](Kal part. act. masc., pl. of נֹשֵׂא dec. 7 b	נשא
הַנְּשֻׂאִים	pref. id.](id. part. p., pl. of נָשׂוּא] dec. 3 a	נשא
הַנְּשִׂאִים	} defect. for הַנְּשִׂיאִים (q. v.) .	נשא
הַנִּשְׁאָר	'וְ] pref. הַ](Niph. part. sing. masc. dec. 2 b	שאר
הַנִּשְׁאָרָה	pref. id.](id. part. sing. fem.	שאר
הַנִּשְׁאָרוֹת	'וְ'] pref. id.](id. pl., absolute state	שאר
הַנִּשְׁאָרִים	'וְ] pref. id.](id. masc., pl. of נִשְׁאָר	שאר
הַנִּשְׁאֶרֶת	} pref. id.](id. fem. sing. (comp. § 35. r. 2)	שאר
הַנִּשְׁבָּע	'וְ] pref. id.](Niph. part. sing. masc.	שבע
הַנִּשְׁבָּעִים	'וְ'] pref. id.](id. pl., absolute state .	שבע
הַנִּשְׁבֶּרֶת	} pref. id.](Niph. part. sing. fem. from masc. (comp. § 35. rem. 2)	שבר
הַנָּשֶׁה	pref. id.](noun masc. sing. .	נשה
הַנֹּשֶׁה	'וְ] pref. id.](Kal part. sing. masc. dec. 9 a .	נשה
הֲנָשׁוּב	pref. הַ](Kal fut. 1 pers. sing.	שוב
הַנָּשׁוּךְ	pref. הַ](Kal part. p. sing. masc.	נשך
הַנִּשְׁחָתוֹת	pref. id.](Niph. part. fem. pl. [of נִשְׁחָתָה]	שחת
הַנָּשִׂיא	'וְ] pref. id.](noun masc. sing. dec. 3 a	נשא
הַנְּשִׂיאִם, הַנְּשִׂיאִם, 'וְ	pref. id.](id. pl., absolute state	נשא
הַנָּשִׁים	'וְ] pref. id.](noun fem. with pl. masc. term. by aphaer. for אֲנָשִׁים see אִשָּׁה (§ 45)	אנש
הַנֹּשֵׁךְ	pref. הַ](Kal part. act. sing. masc. dec. 7 b .	נשך
הַנִּשְׁכוֹת	pref. id.](noun fem. pl. absolute from נִשְׁכָּה dec. 12 b, for לִשְׁכָּה q. v.	לשך
הַנִּשְׁכָּחִים	pref. id.](Niph. part. masc. pl. [of נִשְׁכָּח]	שכח
הַנֹּשְׁכִים	pref. id.](Kal part. act. m., pl. of נֹשֵׁךְ d. 7 b	נשך
הַנְּשָׁמָה	pref. id.](noun fem. sing. dec. 11 c	נשם
הַנִּשְׁמָּה	pref. id.](Niph. part. f.s. d. 10, [from נָשַׁם m.]	שמם
הַנְּשַׁמּוֹת	'וְ] pref. הַ id.](id. pl.	שמם
הַנִּשְׁמַע	pref. הַ](Niph. pret. 3 pers. sing. masc. .	שמע
הַנִּשְׁמַעַת	'וְ] pref. הַ](id. part. sing. fem. from נִשְׁמָע m.	שמע
הַנֶּשֶׁק הַנָּשֶׁק	} pref. הַ](noun masc. sing. (§ 35. rem. 2)	נשק
הַנִּשְׁקָף	pref. id.](Niph. part. sing. masc.	שקף

הַנִּשְׁקָפָה	pref. id.](id. fem.	שקף
הַנֶּשֶׁר הַנָּשֶׁר	} pref. id.](noun masc. sing. dec. 6 a, (§ 35. rem. 2) but pl. c. נְשָׁרֵי	נשר
הַנִּשְׁתְּוָן	pref. id.](noun masc. sing.	נשת
הַנְּתָחִים	pref. id.](noun masc., pl. of נֵתַח dec. 6 a	נתח
הַנְּתוּנִים	pref. id.](Kh. נְתוּנִי, K. נְתִינִ', noun masc., pl. of נָתִין or נָתוּן] dec. 3 a	נתן
הַנְּתִינִים	'וְ] pref. id.](noun masc., pl. of נָתִין] d. 3 a	נתן
הַנִּתָּן	pref. id.](Niph. part. masc. sing.	נתן
הַנֹּתֵן	pref. id.](Kal part. act. masc. sing. dec. 7 b	נתן
הַנָּתֹן	Niph. inf. absolute .	נתן
הַנֹּתְנִים	pref. הַ](Kal part. masc., pl. of נֹתֵן d. 7 b	נתן
הַנְּתוּצִים	pref. id.](Kal part. p. m., pl. of נָתוּץ] d. 3 a	נתץ
הַנֶּתֶק	pref. id.](noun masc. sing.	נתק
הַנְתְּקוּ	Hoph. pret. 3 pers. pl.	נתק
הַנּוֹתָר	וְ] pref. הַ](Niph. part. sing. masc. for נוֹתָר	יתר
הַס הַס	} Kal imp. sing. masc. apoc. [for הֲסֵה]	הסה
הָסֵב	Hiph. imp. sing. masc. .	סבב
הֵסֵב	'וְ] id. pret. 3 pers. sing. masc.	סבב
הַסֹּבֵב	pref. הַ](Kal part. act. sing. masc. dec. 7 b	סבב
הַסֹּבְבִים	pref. id.](id. pl., absolute state .	סבב
הֵסַבּוּ	Hiph. pret. 3 pers. pl. masc.	סבב
הָסֵבִּי	id. imp. sing. fem.	סבב
הַסָּבִיב	pref. הַ](noun masc. sing. dec. 3 a	סבב
הַסְּבִיב	full form for הַסֹּבֵב (q. v.) .	סבב
הַסֵּבֶל	pref. הַ](noun masc. sing. dec. 1 b	סבל
הַסַּבָּלִים	pref. id.](id. pl., absolute state .	סבל
הֲסִבֹּתָ הֲסִבֹּתָ	} Hiph. pret. 2 pers. sing. masc.; acc. shifted by וְ, for וְ, conv. (comp. § 8. r.7)	סבב
הֻסַּג	וְ] Hoph. pret. 3 pers. sing. masc.	נסג
הִסְגִּיר	'וְ] Hiph. pret. 3 pers. sing. masc. .	סגר
הִסְגִּירוֹ	id. inf. (הַסְגִּיר), suff. 3 pers. sing. masc. d. 1 b	סגר
הִסְגִּירוֹ	וְ] id. pret. 3 pers. sing. masc., suff. 3 pers. sing. masc.	סגר
הַסְגִּירֵם	id. inf. (הַסְגִּיר), suff. 3 pers. pl. m., d. 1 b	סגר
הִסְגִּירֵם	id. pret. 3 pers. sing. m., suff. 3 pers. pl. m.	סגר
הַסְּגָנִים	'וְ] pref. הַ](noun masc. pl. [of סָגָן or סֶגֶן]	סגן
הֻפְגַּר	Niph. imp. sing. masc.	סגר
הִסְגַּרְתִּי	וְ] Hiph. pret. 1 pers. sing.; acc. shifted by conv. וְ (comp. § 8. rem. 7)	סגר
הִסְגַּרְתַּנִי	id. pret. 2 pers. sing. masc., suff. 1 pers. sing.	סגר
הַסְּדִינִים	'וְ] pref. הַ](noun masc. pl. of סָדִין] dec. 3 a	סדן

הָסָה Pi. imp. apoc. הַס hist! hush! be silent; adv. silently. Hiph. to silence, still, Nu. 13. 30.

a 2 Ch. 4. 21.	h Is. 2. 13.	p Ex. 10. 5.	y Nu. 21. 8.	f Je. 33. 10.	n Ezr. 4. 7 & 7. 11.	u Ex. 12. 10.	be Ne. 4. 4.	kk Am. 1. 9.
b Ju. 20. 4.	i Ne. 4. 11.	q Is. 65. 16.	z Jos. 22. 32.	g Eze. 36. 35.	o Ezr. 8. 17.	v Ezr. 6. 22.	cc 2 Ch. 34. 13.	ll De. 32. 30.
c 1 Ki. 7. 49.	k Is. 46. 3.	r Zep. 1. 5.	aa Ge. 49. 17.	h Je. 41. 56.	p 2 Ki. 22. 7.	w Ge. 2. 11.	dd 1 Ki. 18. 37.	mm Eze. 3. 24.
d Le. 11. 25.	l Ex. 35. 27.	s Eze. 35. 27.	bb Ne. 12. 44.	i 2 Ki. 10. 2.	q 2 Ch. 11. 16.	x Ezr. 7. 22.	ee Am. 6. 8.	
e Le. 11. 28, 40.	m Zec. 12. 14.	t Ge. 32. 33, 33.	cc Job 28. 4.	k Ne. 3. 19.	r Ca. 6. 5.	y Is. 59. 14.	ff Ps. 31. 9	
f Ps. 24. 7.	n Zec. 11. 9.	u 2 Ki. 4. 1.	dd Mi. 3. 5.	l Le. 13. 31-37.	s 1 Ch. 11. 8.	z 1 Sa. 23. 20.	gg 1 Sa. 3. 23.	
g 2. 14.	o Jos. 13. 2.	x Ezr. 9. 14.	ee Eze. 36. 34, 35, 36.	m De. 28. 49.	t Ju. 20. 31.	aa 2 Ki. 8. 21.	hh Le. 13. 5, 26, 54.	ii Eze. 20. 44.

הַסֹּהַר	pref. הַ ✕ noun masc. sing.	סהר
הַסֹּחֵר	pref. id. ✕ noun masc. sing	סהר
הַסֵּה	Piel imp. pl. masc.	הסה
הַסּוֹבֵב	pref. הַ ✕ Kal part. act. sing. masc. dec. 7b	סבב
הַסּוֹבֵךְ	pref. id. ✕ Kal part. act. sing. masc. dec. 7b	סבך
הַסּוּס	pref. id. ✕ noun masc. sing. dec. 1a	סום
הַסּוּסִים	pref. id. ✕ id. pl., absolute state	סום
הַסּוּף	pref. id. ✕ noun masc. sing.	סוף
הַסּוֹפְדִים	pref. id. ✕ Kal part. act. m., pl. of [סוֹפֵד] d. 7b	ספד
הַסּוֹפֵר	pref. id. ✕ Kal part. act. sing. masc. dec. 7b	ספר
הַסּוּרִים	for הָאֲסוּרִים, pref. הָ ✕ Kal part. p. masc., pl. of אָסוּר dec. 3a	אסר
הַסּוֹרְרִים	pref. הַ ✕ Kal part. act. m., pl. of סוֹרֵר d. 7b	סרר
הַסְּחָבוֹת / הַסְּחָבוֹת	pref. id. ✕ noun fem. pl. [of סְחָבָה or סְחָבוֹת; K. סְחַבָה]	סחב
הַסֹּחֲרִים	pref. id. ✕ Kal part. act. m., pl. of סֹחֵר d. 7b	סחר
הַסֵּךְ	Hiph. inf. absolute (§ 11. rem. 2)	נסך
הַסִּין	pref. הַ ✕ pr. name of a people	סין
הֹסִיף	Hiph. pret. 3 pers. sing. masc. for הוֹסִיף	יסף
הָסִיר	Hiph. inf. constr.	סור
הָסִיר	pref. הַ ✕ noun com. sing. dec. 1a	סיר
הֵסִיר	וְ Hiph. pret. 3 pers. sing. masc.	סור
הֵסִירָה	id. pret. 3 pers. s. f.; acc. shifted (§ 11. r. 9)	סור
הֱסִירָהּ	id. pret. 3 pers. sing. m., suff. 3 pers. sing. f.	סור
הֵסִירוּ	וְ id. imp. pl. masc.	סור
הֵסִירוּ	וְ id. pret. 3 pers. sing. masc.	סור
הֲסִירוֹת	pref. הַ ✕ noun com. with pl. fem. term. d. 1a	סיר
הֲסִירֹתִי	Hiph. pret. 1 pers. sing.	סור
הֲסִירִי	id. imp. sing. fem.	סור
הַסִּירִים	pref. הַ ✕ noun com., pl. of סִיר dec. 1a	סיר
הֲסִירְךָ	Hiph. inf. (הָסִיר), suff. 2 pers. sing. m. d. 3a	סור
הֲסִירְכֶם	id., suff. 2 pers. pl. masc.	סור
הֲסִירֹת	noun com. with pl. f. term. from סִיר dec. 1a	סיר
הֲסִירֹתָ	וַ Hiph. pret. 2 pers. sing. m.; וַ for וְ conv.	סור
הֲסִירֹתִי / הֲסִירוֹתִי	id. pret. 1 pers. sing.; acc. shifted by וַ, וַ for וְ conv. (comp. § 9. rem. 11)	סור
הֲסִיתוּךָ	Hiph. pret. 3 pers. pl., suff. 2 pers. sing. masc. (§ 21. rem. 24)	סות
הֱסִיתְךָ / הֱסִיתְךָ	id. pret. 3 pers. sing. masc., suff. 2 pers. sing. masc. (§ 21. rem. 14)	סות
הַסֵּךְ	וְ Hiph. inf., or imp. sing. masc.	נסך
הַסְּכוּ	וְ id. pret. 3 pers. pl.	נסך
הַסֻּכּוֹת	pref. הַ ✕ noun fem. pl. of סֻכָּה dec. 10.	סכך
הַסֹּכֵךְ	pref. id. ✕ Kal part. act. sing. masc. d. 7b	סכך
הַסֶּכֶל	וְ pref. id. ✕ noun masc. sing. dec. 4a	סכל
הַסִּכְלוּ	pref. id. ✕ noun masc. sing.	סכל

הַשִּׂכְלוּת	וְ pref. id. ✕ noun fem. sing.	סכל
הִסְכַּלְתָּ	Hiph. pret. 2 pers. sing. masc.	סכל
הִסְכַּלְתִּי	id. pret. 1 pers. sing.	סכל
הַסֹּכֵן	pref. הַ ✕ Kal part. act. sing. masc.	סכן
הַסְכֵּן־	Hiph. imp. sing. masc., for כֵּן (§ 11. rem. 5)	סכן
הִסְכַּנְתָּה	id. pret. 2 pers. sing. masc.	סכן
הִסְכַּנְתִּי	id. pret. 1 pers. sing.	סכן
הַסְכֵּת	Hiph. imp. sing. masc.	סכת
הַסֻּכֹּת	pref. הַ ✕ noun fem., pl. of סֻכָּה dec. 10.	סכך
הַסַּל	pref. id. ✕ noun masc. sing. dec. 8d	סלל
הַסֹּלֵחַ	pref. id. ✕ Kal part. act. sing. masc.	סלח
הַסְּלִחוֹת	וְ pref. id. ✕ pl. of the following	סלח
הַסְּלִיחָה	pref. id. ✕ noun fem. sing. dec. 10.	סלח
הַסַּלִּים	pref. id. ✕ noun masc., pl. of סַל dec. 8d	סלל
הַסְלֻלּוֹת	pref. id. ✕ noun fem., pl. of סְלֻלָּה dec. 10.	סלל
הַסֶּלַע	pref. id. ✕ noun masc. sing. dec. 6a (suff. סַלְעוֹ § 35. rem. 5)	סלע
הַסְּלָעִים	pref. id. ✕ id. pl., absolute state	סלע
הַסַּלְעָם	pref. id. ✕ noun masc. sing.	סלעם
הַסֹּלֶת	pref. id. ✕ noun com. sing. dec. 6c	סלת
הַסַּמְדָּר	pref. id. ✕ noun masc. sing.	סמדר
הַסַּמִּים	pref. id. ✕ noun masc., pl. of [סַם] dec. 8d	סמם
הַסֵּמֶל	pref. id. ✕ noun masc. sing.	סמל
הַסְּנָאָה	pref. id. ✕ pr. name of a place	סנא
הַסְּנָאָה	pref. id. ✕ pr. name fem.	סנא
הַסְּנֶה	וְ pref. id. ✕ noun masc. sing.	סנה
הַסְּנוּאָה	pref. id. ✕ pr. name fem.	סנא
הַסְּעַפִּים	pref. id. ✕ n. f. with pl. m. term. [fr. סְעַפָּה]	סעף
הַסַּעַר	pref. id. ✕ noun masc. sing. dec. 6d	סער
הַסְּעָרָה	pref. id. ✕ noun fem. sing. dec. 11c	סער
הַסַּף, הַסֵּף	pref. id. ✕ noun masc. sing. dec. 8e	ספף
הַסִּפּוֹת / הַסִּפִּים	pref. id. ✕ id. with pl. masc. & fem.	ספף
הַסְּפִינָה	pref. id. ✕ noun fem. sing.	ספן
הַסַּפִּיר	pref. id. ✕ noun masc. sing. dec. 1b	ספר
הַסֵּפֶל	pref. id. ✕ noun masc. sing.	ספל
הַסַּפֵּן	pref. id. ✕ noun masc. sing.	ספן
הַסֹּפֵר	pref. id. ✕ noun masc. sing. dec. 6b	ספר
הַסֵּפֶר	pref. id. ✕ noun masc. sing.	ספר
הַסֹּפֵר	pref. id. ✕ Kal part. act. sing. masc.	ספר
הַסְּפָרְוֹנִים	וְ pref. id. ✕ gent. noun pl. fr. סְפַרְוַיִם	ספר
הַסְּפָרִים	pref. id. ✕ noun m., pl. of סֵפֶר dec. 6b	ספר
הַסְּפָרַת	pref. id. ✕ pr. name masc.	ספר
הִסְפַּתִּי	וְ Hiph. fut. 1 pers. sing.	ספף

---

a Ca. 7.3. — b Ge. 39.20-23 & 40.3,5. — c Ne. 8.11. — d Est. 6.9. — 2 Ki. 10.2. — Ex. 2.5.

e Ec. 12.5. — f Ec. 4.14. — g Ps. 66.7. — h Je. 38.11. — Je. 38.12. — 2 Ch. 9.14. — Je. 44.17.

2 Ki. 24.7. — Eze. 21.31. — De. 21.13. — Jos. 24.14. — 2 Ki. 2.31. — 1 Sa. 1.14.

Ec. 7.6. — 2 Sa. 5.16. — Jos. 7.13. — 1 Sa. 26.21. — 2 Ki. 13.27. — Eze. 11.19.

Je. 38.22. — Job 36.16. — Nu. 28.7. — Ex. 38.3. — Je. 32.29. — Na. 2.6. — Ec. 16.14.

Ec. 2.13. — Ec. 7.25. — Ge. 31.28. — 1 Sa. 26.21. — Is. 22.15. — Job 22.21. — Ps. 139.3.

Nu. 22.30. — De. 27.9. — De. 16.13. — Ps. 103.3. — Da. 9.9. — Ps. 130.4. — Ge. 40.18.

Le. 11.22. — Ca. 7.13. — Ex. 3.2,2,3,4. — Ex. 3.2. — 1 Ki. 18.21. — Jon. 1.12. — 1 Sa. 26.19.

1 Ki. 7.50. — Jon. 1.5. — Ex. 24.10. — Ju. 6.38. — 1 Ki. 6.15. — 2 Ch. 2.14. — 2 Ki. 20.6.

הַסְקָנוּ	Ch. Aph. pret. 3 pers. pl. masc. (§ 47. r. 4)	נסק
הֻסַּק	Ch. Hoph. pret. 3 pers. sing. masc.	נסק
הָסֵר	Hiph. inf. abs., or imp. sing. masc.	סור
הָסִרוּ	id. imp. pl. masc. for הָסִירוּ	סור
הַסַּרְדִּי	pref. הַ)(patronym. of סֶרֶד	סרד
הַסִּרָה	pref. id.)(pr. name of a well	סור
הַסִּירוֹת	defect. for הַסִּירוֹת (q. v.)	סיר
הַסִּרְיֹנוֹת	pref. הַ)(noun m. s. pl. of סִרְיֹן see שִׁרְיוֹן	שרה
הַסָּרִים	pref. id.)(noun masc. sing., (§ 32. rem. 2)	סרס
הַסָּרִיקִים	pref. id.)(id. pl., absolute state	סרס
הַסְּרָנִים	pref. id.)(noun masc., pl. of סֶרֶן dec. 6 a (סַרְנֵי)	סרן
הַסָּרִסִים	defect. for הַסָּרִיסִים (q. v.)	סרס
הַסַּרְפַּד	pref. הַ)(noun masc. sing.	סרפד
הֲסִרֹתִי	} Hiph. pret. 1 pers. sing.; acc. shifted by conv. וַ (§ 8. rem. 7) {	סור
הַסָּתָה	id. pret. 3 pers. sing. fem. [for הַסִּיתָה § 21. rem. 13]	סות
הַסָּתֻן	pref. הַ K. סָתֻן noun masc. sing.	סתה
הִסְתּוֹפֵף	Hithpoel inf. [for הִתְסוֹפֵף § 12. rem. 3]	ספף
הִסְתִּיר	Hiph. pret. 3 pers. sing. masc.	סתר
הִסְתִּירוּ	id. pret. 3 pers. pl.	סתר
הִסְתִּירֵנִי	id. pret. 3 p. s. m., suff. 1 pers. s. (§ 2. r. 1)	סתר
הַסְתֵּר	id. inf. abs., or imp. sing. masc.	סתר
הִפָּתֵר	Niph. imp. sing. masc.	סתר
הִסְתַּרְתְּ	Hiph. pret. 2 pers. sing. masc.	סתר
הִסְתַּרְתִּי	} id. pret. 1 pers. sing.; acc. shifted by conv. וָ (comp. § 8. rem. 7) {	סתר
הָעֶבֶד	pref. הָ art. for הַ)(noun m. s. (suff. עַבְדִּי)	עבד
הַעֶבֶד	pref. הַ interr. for הֲ)(dec. 6 a (§ 35. r. 2)	עבד
הָעֹבֵד	pref. הָ for הַ)(Kal part. act. sing. masc. dec. 7 b	עבד
הָעֲבֹדָה	pref. id.)(noun fem. sing. dec. 10.	עבד
הָעֲבָדִים	pref. id.)(n. m., pl. of עֶבֶד d. 6 a (suff. עַבְדֵּי)	עבד
הָעֹבְדִים	pref. id.)(Kal part. act. m., pl. of עֹבֵד d. 7 b.	עבד
הַעֲבַדְתִּיךָ	} Hiph. pret. 1 pers. sing., suff. 2 pers. sing. masc., (§ 13. rem. 10) {	עבד
הֶעֱבַדְתַּנִי	id. pret. 2 pers. sing. masc., suff. 1 pers. s.	עבד
הָעֲבוֹדָה	full form for הָעֲבֹדָה (q. v.)	עבד
הָעָבוֹט	pref. הָ for הַ)(noun masc. sing. d. 1 a.	עבט
הַעֲבֵט	Hiph. inf. abs.	עבט
הַעֲבַטְתָּ	id. pret. 2 pers. sing. masc., [for הֶעֱ § 13. rem. 10] acc. shifted by conv.	עבט
הֶעֱבִיד	Hiph. pret. 3 pers. sing. masc.	עבד
הֶעָבִים	pref. הֶ bef. עָ for הַ)(noun masc., pl. of עָב dec. 1. (except constr. once עָב)	עוב
הֶעָבִים	pref. הֶ for הַ)(noun m., pl. of עָב d. 8 c.	עבב
הַעֲבִיר	Hiph. inf. constr. dec. 1 b.	עבר
הֶעֱבִיר	id. pret. 3 pers. sing. masc.	עבר
הֶעֱבִירוּ	id. pret. 3 pers. pl. masc.	עבר
הַעֲבִרוּנִי	id. imp. pl. masc., suff. 1 pers. sing.	עבר
הֶעֱבִירֵנִי	id. pret. 3 pers. sing. masc., suff. 1 pers. s.	עבר
הַעֲבֵר	} id. imp. sing. masc. (§ 11. rem. 5) {	עבר
הָעֵבֶר	pref. הָ for הַ)(noun masc. sing. dec. 6 b	עבר
הָעֹבֵר	pref. id.)(Kal part. act. sing. masc. dec. 7 b	עבר
הָעֶבְרָה	pref. id.)(noun fem. sing.	עבר
הָעִבְרִי	pref. id.)(gent. noun from עֵבֶר	עבר
הָעִבְרִיָּה	pref. id.)(id. fem.	עבר
הָעִבְרִיּוֹת	pref. id.)(id. pl. fem.	עבר
הָעִבְרִיִּים	pref. id.)(id. pl. masc. comp. dec. 8 f	עבר
הָעֲבָרִים	pref. id.)(pr. name of a place	עבר
הָעִבְרִים	pref. id.)(gent. noun, pl. of עִבְרִי, fr. עֵבֶר	עבר
הָעֹבְרִים	pref. id.)(Kal part. act. m., pl. of עֹבֵר d. 7 b	עבר
הָעִבְרִת	pref. id.)(gent. n. f., pl. of רִיָה, fr. עִבְרִי m.	עבר
הַעֲבִרֵנוּ	Hiph. inf. (הַעֲבִיר), suff. 1 pers. pl. dec. 1 b	עבר
הֶעֱבַרְתָּ	} id. pret. 2 pers. sing. masc. (§ 13. rem. 12 & 10) {	עבר
הֶעֱבַרְתִּי	} id. pret. 1 pers. sing. (§ 13. rem. 10) {	עבר
הֶעֱבַרְתֶּם	id. pret. 2 pers. pl. masc. (comp. id.)	עבר
הָעֲבָתִים	} pref. הָ for הַ)(noun com., pl. of עֲבֹת dec. 1 a {	עבת
הָעֲבֹתֹת		
הָעֵגֶל	pref. id.)(noun masc. sing. d. 6. (§ 35. r. 6)	עגל
הָעֶגְלָה	pref. id.)(noun fem. sing. dec. 12 b	עגל
הָעֲגָלָה	pref. id.)(noun fem. sing. dec. 11 c, with suff. עֶגְלָתוֹ (§ 42. rem. 1)	עגל
הָעֲגָלוֹת	} pref. id.)(id. pl. absolute, constr. עֶגְלוֹת {	עגל
הָעֲגָלֹת		
הָעֵד	pref. id.)(noun masc. sing. dec. 1 a.	עוד
הָעֵד	id.)(Hiph. inf. abs., or imp. sing. masc.	עוד
הֵעִד	id. pret. 3 pers. sing. masc. for הֵעִיד	עוד
הָעֵדָה	pref. הָ for הַ)(noun f. s. dec. 11 b (c. עֲדַת)	יעד
הָעֵדֻת	pref. id.)(noun fem. sing., (pl. suff. עֵדְוֹת once עֵדְוֹתַ)	עוד
הַעְדִּיו	Ch. Aph. pret. 3 pers. pl. masc. (§ 47. r. 4)	עדה
הָעֵדִים	pref. הָ for הַ)(noun masc., pl. of עֵד d. 1 a	עוד
הָעֲדֻלָּמִי	pref. id.)(gent. noun from עֲדֻלָּם	עדל
הָעֹדֵף	pref. id.)(Kal part. act. sing. masc. d. 7 b	עדף
הֶעְדִּיף	Hiph. pret. 3 pers. sing. masc. (§ 13. r. 9)	עדף
הָעֹדְפִים	pref. הָ for הַ)(Kal part. act. masc., pl. of עֹדֵף dec. 7 b	עדף

^a Da. 3. 22.   ^g Je. 46. 4.   ^m Ca. 2. 11.   ^s Je. 2. 14.   2 Ch. 35. 10.   ^x Nu. 8. 7.   De. 15. 12.   Jos. 7. 7.   Ge. 43. 3.

^b Da. 6. 24.   ^h Je. 29. 2.   ⁿ Ps. 84. 11.   ^t Is. 59. 2.   2 Ch. 35. 23.   Eze. 37. 2.   De. 15. 6.   Zec. 3. 4.   Da. 5. 20.

^c Ec. 11. 10.   ⁱ Je. 34. 19.   ^o Is. 55. 13.   ^u Eze. 34. 27.   Eze. 29. 18.   Ex. 1. 16.   Ju. 15. 14.   Ex. 16. 18.

^d Je. 4. 4.   ^k Is. 49. 2.   ^p Je. 36. 19.   ^v Is. 43. 23.   Ps. 119. 37, 39.   Ex. 3. 18.   1 Sa. 6. 14.   Nu. 3. 46,

^e Je. 52. 16.   ^l 2 Sa. 7. 15.   ^q Je. 17. 4.   ^w Is. 43. 24.   Ec. 11. 10.   1 Sa. 26. 13.   De. 19. 18.   48, 49.

^f 1 Ki. 21. 25.   De. 31. 17.   Jos. 7. 7.   1 Sa. 14. 21.   De. 2. 29.   De. 24. 11, 13.

הָעֲרֶפֶת ‖ pref. id. הָ for הַ)(id. fem. sing.	עדף
הָעֶדֶר pref. id.)(noun m. sing. dec. 6. (§ 35. r. 6)	עדר
הָעֲדָרִים pref. id.)(id. pl., absolute state	עדר
הָעֵדֹת pref. id.)(noun f., pl. abs. of עֵדָה d. 11b	יעד
הָעֵדָת defect. for הָעֵדוֹת (q. v.)	עוד
הַעִידֹתָ Hiph. pret. 2 pers. sing. masc., for הַעִידֹתָ (§ 8. rem. 5. & § 21. rem. 14 & 24)	עוד
הַעִידֹתִי id. pret. 1 pers. sing. (§ 14. rem. 24)	עוד
הָעוֹד pref. הָ interr. for הַ)(adv., d. 1 a (§ 1 note)	עוד
הָעֹדָם pref. id.)(id., suff. 3 pers. sing. masc.	עוד
הָעֹדֶנּוּ pref. id.)(id., (verbal) suff. 3 pers. sing. m.	עוד
הָעֵוֹה Hiph. inf. absolute	עוה
הֶעֱוָה id. pret. 3 pers. sing. masc.	עוה
הֶעֱווּ id. pret. 3 pers. pl.	עוה
הָעַוִּים וְ pref. הָ for ·)(gent. noun pl. fr. עַוָּא	עוה
הֶעֱוִינוּ וְ Hiph. pret. 1 pers. pl. (§ 24. rem. 14)	עוה
הֶעֱוֵיתִי id. pret. 1 pers. sing.	עוה
הָעֹלָה pref. הָ for · הַ)(subs., or (1 Ch. 26. 16) Kal part. fem. (of עֹלָה) dec. 10.	עלה
הָעֹלֶה וְ pref. id.)(Kal part. act. sing. masc. dec. 9a	עלה
הָעֹלוֹת pref. id.)(noun fem., pl. of עֹלָה dec. 10.	עלה
הָעֹלִים pref. id.)(Kal part. act. masc., pl. of עֹלֶה dec. 9a	עלה
הָעוֹלָם pref. id.)(noun masc. sing. dec. 2 b	עלם
הֶעָוֹן pref. הָ bef. עָ for הַ)(noun masc. s. d. 3a	עוה
הָעוֹף וְ pref. הָ for ·)(noun masc. sing.	עוף
הָעֹפְרֶת pref. id.)(noun fem. sing.	עפר
הָעוּץ pref. id.)(pr. name of a region	עוץ
הָעוֹר pref. id.)(noun masc. sing. dec. 1 a	עור
הָעִוֵּר pref. id.)(adj. masc. sing. dec. 7 b	עור
הָעִוְרִים וְ pref. id.)(id. pl. absolute state	עור
הָעֹז Hiph. imp. pl. masc.	עזז
הֵעֵז Hiph. pret. 3 pers. sing. masc.	עזז
הָעֹזְבִים pref. הָ)(Kal part. act. m., pl. of עֹזֵב dec. 7b	עזב
הָעֹזֶבֶת pref. id.)(id. fem.	עזב
הֶעֱזָה Hiph. pret. 3 p. s. f. [for הֶעֱוָה § 18. r. 15 note]	עזז
הָעֹזוּ Hiph. imp. pl. masc.	עזז
הָעֲזוּבָה pref. הָ for הַ)(noun fem. sing. dec. 10.	עזב
הָעֲזִיאֵלִי pref. id.)(patronym. from עֲזִיאֵל (q. v.)	עזז
הָעִזִּים pref. id.)(noun fem. pl. of עֵז dec. 8b	עזז
הָעֲזַנְיָה וְ pref. id.)(noun fem. sing.	עזנ
הָעֵזֶר / הָעֶזֶר / הָעָזֶר pref. id.)(pr. name, see אֶבֶן עֶזֶר	אבן
הָעֶזְרָה וְ pref. id.)(noun fem. sing.	עזר
הָעֶזְרִי pref. id.)(patronym., see אֲבִיעֶזֶר	אב

הֶעָנָתִי pref. id.)(gent. noun from עֲנָה	עז
הָעֲטֻפִים pref. id.)(Kal part. p. m., pl. of [עָטוּף] d. 3a	עטף
הֶעֱטִיתָ Hiph. pret. 2 pers. sing. masc. (§ 24. rem. 14)	עטה
הָעֲטַלֵּף וְ pref. הָ for הַ)(noun masc. sing. dec. 1 b	עטלף
הָעֲטֻפִים defect. for הָעֲטוּפִים (q. v.)	עטף
הָעֲטָרָה pref. הָ for הַ)(noun fem. sing., constr. עֲטֶרֶת (§ 42. rem. 5)	עטר
וְהָעֲטָרוֹת pref. id.)(id. pl., abs. state (§ 44. rem. 5)	עטר
הָעַי / הָעָי וְ pref. id.)(pr. name of a place	עוה
הֵעִיד Hiph. pret. 3 pers. sing. masc.	עוד
וְהָעִידוּ id. imp. pl. masc.	עוד
הֵעִידוּ id. pret. 3 pers. pl.	עוד
הַעִידֹתָ Hiph. pret. 2 pers. sing. masc. for הַעִידֹתָ (§ 21. rem. 24)	עוד
הַעִידֹתִי id. pret. 1 pers. sing.	עוד
הָעִיזוּ Hiph. imp. pl. masc.	עוז
הָעִיזוּ id. pret. 3 pers. pl.	עוז
הָעַיִט pref. הָ for · הַ)(noun masc. sing. dec. 6h	עיט
הָעָיִט pref. הָ dag. impl.)(noun masc. sing. dec. 6h	עיט
הָעַיִן / הָעָיִן pref. הָ for הַ)(noun fem. sing. dec. 6h	צין
הָעֵינָה pref. id.)(id. with paragogic ה	עין
הָעֲיָנוֹת pref. id.)(id. pl. abs., constr. עֵינוֹת (§ 35. r. 12)	עין
הָעֵינִי pref. הָ interr. for הַ)(id. du., constr. state	עין
הָעִיר Kh. הָעִיר q. v., K. חָצֵר (q. v.)	חצר
הָעִיר וְ pref. הָ for הַ)(noun fem. sing. irr., pl. עָרִים (§ 45)	עור
הֵעִיר Hiph. pret. 3 pers. sing. masc.	עור
הָעִירָה id. imp. sing. masc. with parag. ה (§ 11. r. 5)	עור
הָעִירָה pref. הָ for הַ)(noun fem. sing. (עִיר) with paragogic ה, irr. (§ 45)	עור
הָעִירוּ Hiph. imp. pl. masc.	עור
הַעִירוֹתִי id. pret. 1 pers. s., for הַעִירוֹתִי (§ 21. r. 24)	עור
וְהָעֲיָרִים pref. הָ for הַ)(noun masc. pl. of עַיִר dec. 6h (§ 35. rem. 12)	עיר
הַעִירֹתִיהוּ Hiph. pret. 1 pers. sing., suff. 3 pers. sing. masc. for הַעִיר (§ 21. rem. 24)	עור
הָעַכְבָּר וְ pref. הָ for הַ)(noun masc. sing. dec. 2 b	עכב
הָעַכָּסִים pref. id.)(noun masc., pl. of עֶכֶס dec. 6a	עכס
הַעַל pref. הָ interr.)(prep., pl. c. עֲלֵי, suff. עָלַי, &c. (§ 31. rem. 5)	עלה
הַעֲלֵה וְ Hiph. imp. s. m., ap. for הַעֲלֵה (§ 24. r. 17)	עלה
הָעֹל pref. הָ for הַ)(noun masc. sing. dec. 8c	עלל
הֻעַל Chald. Hoph. pret. 3 pers. sing. masc. [for comp. § 14. rem. 1]	עלל

ᵃ Je. 13. 20.   ᵍ Ps. 106. 6.   ⁿ 2 Sa. 5. 6, 8.   ᵗ Pr. 2. 17.   ʸ De. 14. 12.   ᵈ Zec. 6. 14.   ⁱ 2 Ch. 32. 3.   ᵒ Is. 30. 24.
ᵇ Ex. 19. 23.   ʰ Is. 42. 18.   ᵒ Is. 42. 18.   ᵘ Pr. 7. 13.   ᶻ La. 2. 19.   ᵉ Ge. 15. 11;   ᵏ 2 Ki. 20. 4.   ᵖ Is. 45. 13.
ᶜ Ex. 4. 18.   ⁱ Eze. 45. 17.   ᵖ Ex. 9. 19.   ᵛ Je. 6. 1.   ᵃ Ps. 89. 46.   Je. 12. 9.   ˡ Ps. 35. 23.   ۹ Is. 13. 18.
ᵈ Je. 9. 4.   ᵏ Zec. 5. 8.   ۹ Pr. 21. 29.   ʷ Ge. 30. 42.   ᵇ Ne. 9. 26.   ᵍ Je. 12. 9.   ᵐ Joel 4. 9.   ʳ Ex. 33. 12.
ᵉ 2 Sa. 19. 20.   ˡ De. 26. 29.   ʳ Pr. 2. 15.   ˣ Eze. 21. 31.   ᶜ Je. 4. 6.   ʰ Ge. 24. 16, 45.   ⁿ Is. 41. 25.   ˢ Da. 5. 13.
ᶠ Je. 5. 21.   ᵐ Ex. 26. 12.   ˢ Le. 11. 13.   ʸ Le. 11. 19. De. 14. 18.

הָעֹלָה	ן pref. הָ for הַ ✕ subst. or part. fem. (from הֹלֶה masc.) dec. 10.	עלה
הַעֲלֵה•	Hiph. inf. absolute	עלה
הָעֹלֶה	י׳ pref. הָ for ·הַ ✕ Kal part. act. m. dec. 7 b	עלה
הָעֹלֶה	י׳ pref. הָ bef. ע for הַ ✕ noun m. s. dec. 9 b	עלה
הֶעֱלָה•	} Hiph. pret. 3 pers. s. m. (§ 13. rem. 12)	עלה
וֶ֯		
הֹעֲלָה	Hoph. pret. 3 pers. sing. masc. [for הֶעֱלָה § 13. rem. 12]	עלה
הַעֲלֵהוּ׳	ן Hiph. imp. sing. masc., suff. 3 pers. s. m.	עלה
הַעֲלוּ	id. imp. pl. masc.	עלה
הֵעָלוּ	Niph. imp. pl. masc.	עלה
הֶעֱלוּ	וֶ Hiph. pret. 3 pers. pl.	עלה
הֹעֲלוּ	Hoph. pret. 3 p. pl. [for הָעֳלוּ comp. § 14. r. 1]	עלל
הֶעֱלוּךָ	י׳ Hiph. pret. 3 pers. pl., suff. 2 pers. s. m.	עלה
הַעֲלוֹת	י׳ id. inf. constr.: in 2 Ch. 24. 14, perhaps subst. (with the art. הָ), pl. of עֲלִי	עלה
הָעֹלוֹת	י׳ pref. הָ for הַ ✕ noun fem., pl. of עֹלָה d. 10.	עלה
הֵעָלוֹת	Niph. inf. constr.	עלה
הַעֲלֹתִי	Hiph. inf.(הַעֲלוֹת), suff. 1 pers. sing. dec. 1b	עלה
הַעֲלִי	וֶ׳ Hiph. imp. sing. fem.	עלה
הָעֶלְיָה	pref. הָ for ·הַ ✕ noun fem. sing. dec. 10.	עלה
הָעֲלִיָּה	ן pref. הַ art. relat. before ע for הַ ✕ prep. (עַל), suff. 3 pers. sing. fem.	עלה
הָעֶלְיוֹן	pref. הָ for ·הַ ✕ adj. masc. sing. dec. 1 b.	עלה
הָעֶלְיוֹנָה	pref. id. ✕ id. fem. dec. 10.	עלה
הָעֶלְיוֹנֹת	pref. id. ✕ id. fem. pl.	עלה
הָעֲלִיּוֹת	ן pref. id. ✕ noun fem., pl. of עֲלִיָּה dec. 10.	עלה
הָעֲלִיזָה	pref. id. ✕ adj. fem. sing. from [עָלִיז] masc.	עלז
הָעֲלִילִיָּה	pref. id. ✕ noun fem. sing.	עלל
הָעֹלִים	pref. id. ✕ Kal part. act. m., pl. of עֹלֶה dec. 9 a.	עלה
הֶעֱלִים	Hiph. pret. 3 pers. sing. masc. [for הֶעֱלִים § 13. rem. 9].	עלם
הֶעֱלִימוּ׳	id. pret. 3 pers. pl.	עלם
הֶעֱלֵיתָ•	} Hiph. pret. 2 pers. sing. masc. (§ 24. rem. 14)	עלה
הֶעֱלִיתָ		
הֶעֱלִיתָ•	} id. id. acc. shifted (§ 13. rem. 10, comp. § 8. rem. 7)	עלה
הֶעֱלֵיתָ		
הֶעֱלִית	id. pret. 2 pers. sing. fem.	עלה
הֶעֱלֵיתִי	} id. pret. 1 pers. sing. (§ 13. rem. 10, comp. § 9. rem. 11).	עלה
הֶעֱלִיתִי		
הַעֲלִיתִהוּ	ן id. id., suff. 3 pers. sing. masc.(§ 13. r. 10)	עלה
הַעֲלִיתִיךָ	ן id. id., suff. 2 pers. sing. masc.	עלה

הֶעֱלִיתִים׳	ן id. id., suff. 3 pers. pl. masc.	עלה
הֶעֱלִיתֶם	ן id. pret. 2 pers. pl. masc.	עלה
הֶעֱלִיתָנוּ	id. pret. 2 pers. sing. masc., suff. 1 pers. pl.	עלה
הֶעֱלִיתֻנוּ	id. pret. 2 pers. pl. masc., suff. 1 pers. pl.	עלה
הֶעֱלְךָ	id. pret. 3 pers. sing. masc., suff. 2 pers. sing. masc. (§ 24. rem. 21)	עלה
הָעֹלָם	pref. הָ for הַ ✕ noun masc. sing. dec. 2b (for עוֹלָם)	עלם
הָעֹלָם"	pref. id. ✕ noun m. s. (for עָלָם י׳ § 35. rem. 2)	עלם
הַעֲלֵם•	Hiph. inf. absolute (§ 13. rem. 10)	עלם
הָעַלְמָה•	pref. הָ for הַ ✕ noun fem. sing dec. 12a	עלם
הֶעֱלָנוּ	Hiph. pret. 3 pers. sing. masc., suff. 1 pers. pl. (§ 24. rem. 21)	עלה
הַעֲלֵנִי׳	Chald. Aph. imp. s. m., suff. 1 pers. s. [for אַעֲלֵנִי; comp. § 47. rem. 4, & § 14. rem. 1]	עלל
הָעֹלֹת•	pref. הָ for ·הַ ✕ Kal part. act. fem., pl. of עֹלָה, from עֹלֶה masc.	עלה
הֶעֶלָתָה•	ן Hiph. pret. 3 pers. sing. fem. [for הֶעֱלָתָה; § 13. rem. 10]	עלה
הָעֳלָתָה׳	Hoph. pret. 3 pers. sing. fem. [for הָעֳלָתָה § 13. rem. 12]	עלה
הַעֲלֹתוֹ•	Niph. inf. (הֵעָלוֹת), suff. 3 pers. s. m. dec. 1b	עלה
הַעֲלֹתִי	Hiph. inf. (הַעֲלוֹת), suff. 1 pers. sing. dec. 1b	עלה
הֶעֱלִיתִיךָ׳	id. pret. 1 pers. sing., suff. 2 pers. sing. masc.	עלה
הֶעֱלַתֶם	ן id. pret. 2 pers. pl. masc. (§ 13. rem. 10)	עלה
הֶעֱלָתַם״	id. pret. 3 pers. sing. fem., suff. 3 pers. pl. masc. (§ 24. rem. 21 c)	עלה
הָעָם	ן pref. הָ for הַ ✕ with the art. for עַם, noun com. dec. 8d (§ 45)	עמם
הָעַמּוּד•	pref. id. ✕ noun masc. s. dec. 1b (for עַמּוּד)	עמד
הָעֹמֵד	pref. id. ✕ Kal part. act. sing. masc. dec. 7b	עמד
הַעֲמֵד•	Hiph. imp sing. masc.	עמד
הָעֱמִדָהּ	ן Hiph. pret. 3 pers. s. m., suff. 3 pers. s. fem.	עמד
עֹמְדֹת	pref. הָ for הַ ✕ Kal part. act. fem., pl. dec. 13a (from עֹמֵד masc. § 8. rem. 19)	עמד
הָעֹמְדִים	pref id. ✕ noun masc. pl. (for עַמּוּדִים) from עַמּוּד dec. 1b	עמד
הָעֹמְדִים	pref. id. ✕ Kal part. act. m., pl. of עֹמֵד dec. 7b	עמד
הֶעֱמַדְנוּ׳	ן Hiph. pret. 1 pers. pl.	עמד
הֶעֱמַדְתָּ	} id. pret. 2 pers. s. m. (§ 13. r. 10, & § 8. r. 5)	עמד
הֶעֱמַדְתָּ		
הֶעֱמַדְתָּה׳		
הֶעֱמַדְתִּי	id. pret. 1 pers. sing.	עמד
הֶעֱמַדְתִּיהוּ׳	ן id. id., suff. 3 pers. sing. masc. (§ 13. r. 10)	עמד
הֶעֱמַדְתִּיךָ׳	id. id., suff. 2 pers. sing. masc.	עמד
הָעַמּוּד	pref. הָ for הַ ✕ noun masc. sing. dec. 1b	עמד

ᵃ Eze. 23. 46.   ᵈ Ge. 22. 2.   ⁱ 2 Ch. 31. 3.   ⁿ 2 Ch. 3. 9.   ˢ Ex. 32. 7.   ˣ Ne. 9. 18.   ᵃ 1 Sa. 2. 19.   ᵐ Jos. 2. 6.   ʳ Ne. 10. 33.

ᵇ Je. 48. 44.   ᵉ Nu. 16. 24.   ᵏ 1 Sa. 28. 11.   ᵒ Ze. 2. 15.   ᵗ Ex. 40. 4.   ʸ 1 Ch. 16. 36.   ᵇ Na. 2. 8.   ⁿ Je. 52. 21.   ˢ Ps. 30. 8.

ᶜ Job 18. 25.   ᶠ Da. 5. 15.   ˡ 1 Sa. 28. 8.   ᵖ Is. 57. 6.   ᵘ Ju. 11. 31.   ᶻ Le. 20. 4.   ᶜ Da. 2. 24.   ᵒ Is. 21. 6.   ᵗ 1 Ch. 17. 14.

ᵈ Ge. 8. 13.   ᵍ Kse. 32. 3.   ᵐ 1 Sa. 9. 24.   ᵍ 2 Ki. 4. 27.   ᵛ Mi. 6. 4.   ᵃ Ge. 41. 27.   ᵖ Nu. 5. 16.   ᵘ Ex. 9. 16.

ᵉ Hab. 1. 15.   ʰ 1 Ch. 23. 31.   ᵐ Eze. 42. 5.   ᵐ Eze. 22. 26.   ᵘ Je. 27. 22.   ᵍ 1 Sa. 17. 56.   ᵖᵖ Ge. 50. 25.

Hebrew	Description	Root
הָעֹמוּדִים	י'] pref. הַ for הָ)(id. pl., absolute state	עמד
הָעַמּוֹנִי	pref. id.)(gent. noun from עַמּוֹן	עמם
הָעַמּוֹנִים	pref. id.)(id. pl. masc.	עמם
הָעַמּוֹנִית	pref. id.)(id. sing. fem.	עמם
הַעֲמֵיד	] Hiph. inf. absolute	עמד
הֶעֱמִיד	ו'] id. pret. 3 pers. sing. masc.	עמד
הֶעֱמִידָהָ	] id. inf. sing. masc., suff. 3 pers. sing. fem.	עמד
הֶעֱמִידוֹ	] id. pret. 3 pers. sing. m., suff. 3 pers. s. m.	עמד
הָעַמִּים	pref. הָ for הַ)(n. com., pl. of עַם d. 8 d (§ 45)	עמם
הֵעֵמִים	} Hiph. pret. 3 pers. sing. masc. (§ 13. r. 9)	עמם
הֶעֱמִיק	Hiph. pret. 3 pers. sing. masc.	עמק
הֶעֱמִיקוּ	id. pret. 3 pers. pl.	עמק
הֶעָמָל	pref. הֶ bef. עָ for הַ)(noun masc. sing. dec. 4 c	עמל
הָעֲמָלֵק	pref. הָ for הַ)(pr. name of a people	עמלק
הָעֲמָלֵקִי	ו'] pref. id.)(gent. noun from the preceding	עמלק
הָעֲמֹנִי	pref. id.)(gent. noun from עַמּוֹן	עמם
הָעֲמֹנִים	ו'] pref. id.)(id. pl. masc.	עמם
הָעֲמֹנִית	pref. id.)(id. sing. fem.	עמם
הָעֲמֻסִים	pref. הַ for הָ)(Kal part. pass. masc., pl. of [עָמוּס] dec. 3 a	עמם
הָעֵמֶק	Hiph. imp. sing. masc.	עמק
הָעֵמֶק	pref. הָ for הַ)(noun masc. sing. dec. 6 b (and pr. name in compos. see בֵּית)	עמק
הָעֲמֻקָּה	pref. id.)(adj. fem. sing. dec. 10, from עָמֹק masc. (comp. § 37. No. 3 c)	עמק
הֶעֱמַקוּ	Hiph. pret. 3 pers. pl. for הֶעֱמִיקוּ	עמק
הָעֲמָקִים	ו'] pref. הָ for הַ)(n. m., pl. of עֵמֶק d. 6 b	עמק
הָעֹמֶר	ו'] pref. id.)(noun masc. sing. dec. 6 c	עמר
הָעֹמְרִים	pref. id.)(id. pl., absolute state	עמר
הָעַמְרָמִי	pref. id.)(patronym. of עַמְרָם	עמם
הָעֲנָבִים	pref. id.)(noun masc., pl. of עֵנָב dec. 4 b	ענב
הֶעָנֵג	] pref. הֶ bef. עָ for הַ)(adj. masc. sing.	ענג
הָעֲנֻגָּה	] pref. הַ for הָ)(id. fem. (comp. § 37. No. 3 c)	ענג
הָעֹנָה	pref. id.)(Kal part. act. sing. masc. dec. 9 a	ענה
הָעֲנוֹק	pref. id.)(pr. name masc.	ענק
הֶעָנִי	pref. הֶ bef. עָ for הַ)(adj. m. d 8 (§ 37. No. 4)	ענה
הָעֲנִיִּים	pref. הָ for הַ)(id. pl., absolute state	ענה
הָעֹנִים	pref. id.)(Kal part. act. m., pl. of עֹנֶה d. 9 a	ענה
הָעֲנָן	pref. id.)(noun masc. sing. dec. 2 b	ענה
הַעֲנִיק	Hiph. inf. absolute	ענק
הֶעָנָן	] pref. הֶ bef. עָ for הַ)(noun masc. sing. d. 4 c	ענן
הָעֲנָק	pref. הָ for הַ)(pr. name masc.	ענק
הָעֲנָקוֹת	pref. id.)(noun masc., with pl. fem. term. from עָנָק	ענק
הָעֲנָקִים	pref. id.)(pr. name of a people, pl. of עָנָק	ענק

Hebrew	Description	Root
הֲעָנַתֹתִי / הֲעָנְתֹתִי	} pref. id.)(pr. name of a place	ענה
הָעֹפֶל	pref. id.)(noun masc. sing. dec. 6 c	עפל
הָעָפְנִי	ו'] pref. id.)(gent. noun	עפן
הֶעָפָר	ו'] pref. הֶ bef. עָ f. הַ)(noun masc. s. d 4 c	עפר
הָעֶפְרָת	pref. הָ for הַ)(noun fem. sing. (for עֶפְרָת, comp. § 35. rem. 2)	עפר
הָעֵץ	pref. id.)(noun m. s. d 7 (§ 36. r. 2 & 4)	עצה
הָעֶצֶב	pref. הָ)(noun masc. sing. dec. 6	עצב
הָעֲצַבִּים	pref. הָ for הַ)(id. pl., absolute state	עצב
הָעֲצַבִּים	pref. id.)(noun masc., pl. of [עָצָב] dec. 8 a	עצב
הָעֵצָה	pref. id.)(noun fem. sing. d 11 b [for יַעֲצָה]	יעץ
הָעֵצָה	pref. הָ bef. עָ for הַ)(noun masc. sing.	עצה
הָעֲצוּמִים	pref. הָ for הַ)(adj. masc., pl. of עָצוּם d. 3 a	עצם
הָעֵצִים	ו'] pref. id.)(n. m., pl. of עֵץ (§ 36. r. 2 & 4)	עצה
הֶעָצֵל	pref. הָ bef. עָ for הַ)(adj. masc. sing.	עצל
הָעֲצָמוֹת	ו'] pref. הָ for הַ)(noun fem., pl. of עֶצֶם (suff. עַצְמִי) dec. 6 a	} עצם
הָעֲצָמִים	pref. id.)(Kh. עַצֵינוּ, K. עַצֵנִי, gent. noun; but see under the R.	עצן
הֶעָקֵב	pref. הָ bef. עָ for הַ)(noun masc. sing.	עקב
הָעֲקֻדִּים	pref. הָ for הַ)(adj. masc., pl. of עָקֹד dec. 8 c (§ 37. Nos. 2 & 3)	עקד
הָעֶקְרוֹנִי	ו'] pref. id.)(gent. noun from עֶקְרוֹן	עקר
הָעֶקְרוֹנִים	pref. id.)(id. pl.	עקר
הָעֶרֶב	in pause for הָעֶרֶב q. v. (§ 35. rem. 2)	ערב
הַעֲרֵב	] Hiph. inf. absolute	ערב
הָעֹרֵב	] pref. הָ for הַ)(noun masc. sing. (du. עֹרְבַיִם) dec. 6 a, also pr. name	ערב
הָעֶרֶב	pref. id.)(noun masc. sing.	ערב
הָעֵרֶב	pref. id.)(noun masc. sing. dec. 7 b	ערב
הָעֶרֶב	pref. הָ bef. עָ for הַ)(noun masc. sing.	ערב
הָעֲרָבָה	] pref. הָ for הַ)(noun fem. sing. dec. 11 c, § 42. r. 1 (and pr. n. in compos. see בֵּית)	ערב
הָעֶרָבוֹן	pref. id.)(noun masc. sing.	ערב
הָעַרְבִי	pref. id.)(gent. n. fr. עֲרָב (comp. § 35. r. 10)	ערב
הָעַרְבִיאִים / הָעַרְבִּיִּים	} pref. id.)(id. pl., Kh. עֲרָבִיִּים (§ 37. No. 4, also rem. 5)	} ערב
הָעֲרָבִים	]	
הָעֲרֻבִּים	pref. id.)(n.m., pl. of עָרֹב d. 6 a (comp. the foll.)	ערב
הָעַרְבַּיִם / הָשַׁרְבַּיִם	} pref. id.)(id. du., absolute state	} ערב
הָעֲרָבִים	ו'] pref. id.)(noun masc., pl. of עֵרֶב dec. 7 b	ערב
הָעֲרָבָתָה	pref. id.)(noun f. a (עֲרָבָה) with parag. הַ	ערב
הָעַרְבָתִי	pref. id.)(gent. n. fr. עֲרָבָה (comp. § 42. r. 1)	ערב
הֶעֱרָה	Hiph. pret. 3 pers. sing. masc.	ערה

ᵃ Je. 52. 21.   ᶠ 1 Ki. 12. 11.   Eze. 23. 32.   ᵏ Ge. 40. 11.   ᵘ Je. 44. 20.   ᶻ Je. 22. 28.   ᵏ Eze. 24. 10.   ᵐ 2 Ch. 31. 3.   ʳ Is. 15. 7.
ᵇ Ne. 7. 3.   ᵍ Is. 30. 33.   ⁱ De. 28. 54.   ᵛ De. 15. 14.   ᵈ Ps. 127. 2.   ˡ Eze. 24. 5.   ⁿ Ge. 8. 7.   ˢ 1 Ki. 17. 4.
ᶜ Eze. 24. 11.   ᵏ Ec. 2. 20.   Mi. 1. 4.   Ex. 16. 36.   Ju. 8. 26.   Is. 40. 4.   Ex. 8. 17, 20,   ᵗ 1 Ki. 17. 4.
ᵈ Le. 27. 8.   ⁱ Is. 46. 5.   Ge. 35. 3.   Ne. 4. 4.   Is. 8. 7.   25, 27.   ᵘ Jos. 18. 18.
ᵉ 2 Ch. 12. 11.   ʰ Is. 7. 11.   ʳ Ruth 2. 15.   Is. 41. 17.   Nu. 31. 22.   Pr. 10. 26.   1 Sa. 17. 16.   ᵍ Ge. 38. 18, 26.

הָעֲרוּפָה   pref. הָ for הַ)(Kal part. p. s. f. [fr. עָרוּף m.]   ערף

הָעֵרִי   pref. id.)(pr. name masc.   עור

הֶעֱרִיךְ   וְ Hiph. pret. 3 pers. sing. masc.   ערך

הֶעֱרִיכוּ   id., suff. 3 pers. sing. masc.   ערך

הֶעָרִים   וְ pref. הָ bef. עַ for הַ)(noun fem., prop. pl. of עָר see עִיר (§ 45)   עיר

הָעֲרֵכוֹת   pref. הָ for הַ)(Kal part. p. fem., pl. of עֲרוּכָה dec. 10 (from עָרוּךְ masc.)   ערך

הָעֹרְכִים   pref. id.)(id. part. act. m., pl. of עֹרֵךְ d. 7 b   ערך

הָעֶרְכְּךָ   pref. id.)(noun masc. sing., suff. 2 pers. sing. masc. from עֵרֶךְ dec. 6 (§ 35. rem. 6)   ערך

הֵעָרֵל   וְ Niph. imp. sing. masc.   ערל

הֶעָרֵל   pref. הָ bef. עַ for הַ)(noun masc. sing. d. 5 c   ערל

הָעֲרָלוֹת   pref הָ for הַ)(n. f., pl. of עָרְלָה d. 12 c (p. n.)   ערל

הָעֲרֵלִים   pref. id.)(noun masc., pl. of עָרֵל dec. 5 c   ערל

הָעֶרְמָה   pref. id.)(noun fem. sing. dec. 10.   ערם

הָעֲרֵמוֹת   pref. id.)(id. pl.   ערם

הָעַרְנִי   pref. id.)(gent. noun from עֵרָן   עור

הָעַרְעָר   pref. id.)(adj. masc. sing.   ערר

הָעֲרֹעֵרִי   pref. id.)(gent. noun from עֲרֹעֵר   ערר

הָעֲרָפֶל   וְ pref. id.)(noun masc. sing.   ערפל

הָעַרְקִי   pref. id.)(gent. noun   ערק

הָעֹרְקִים   pref. id.)(Kal part. act. m., pl. of [עֹרֵק] d. 7 b   ערק

הָעֹשֶׂה   pref. id.)(constr. of the following   עשה

הָעֹשֶׂה   pref. id.)(Kal part. act. sing. masc. dec. 9 a   עשה

הָעֹשֵׂהוּ   pref. id.)(id., suff. 3 pers. sing. masc.   עשה

הָעֹשִׂי הָעֹשַׂי   pref. הָ bef. עַ for הַ)(Kal part. p. masc. sing. (§ 24. rem. 4)   עשה

הָעֲשׂוּיָה   pref. הָ for הַ)(id. fem. dec. 10.   עשה

הָעֲשׂוּיִם   pref. id.)(id. pl. absolute masc. dec. 3 a.   עשה

הֵעָשׂוֹתוֹ   Niph. inf. fr. (הֵעָשׂוֹת) suff. 3 p. s. m. d. 1 b   עשה

הָעֲשִׂיָּה   defect. for הָעֲשׂוּיָה (q. v.)   עשה

הָעֹשִׂים   pref. הָ for הַ)(Kal part. act. masc., pl. of עֹשֶׂה dec. 9 a   עשה

הֶעָשִׁיר   pref. הָ bef. עַ for הַ)(noun masc. sing. d. 3 a   עשר

הָעֲשִׂירִי   pref. הָ for הַ)(adj. ord. masc. from עָשָׂר   עשר

הָעֲשִׂירִית   pref. id.)(id. fem.   עשר

הֶעָשֵׁן   pref. הָ bef. עַ for הַ)(noun masc. sing. d. 4 c   עשן

הָעֲשֵׁנִים   pref. הָ for הַ)(adj. masc., pl. of עָשֵׁן d. 5 c   עשן

הָעֹשֶׁק   pref. id.)(noun masc. sing.   עשק

הָעֲשֻׁקוֹת   pref. id.)(Kal part. act. fem. pl. [of עֲשׁוּקָה or עֲשֻׁקֶת § 8. rem. 19]   עשק

הָעֲשֻׁקִים   pref. id.)(id. part. p., pl. of עָשׁוּק dec. 3 a; or noun masc. pl.   עשק

הֶעָשֹׁר   וְ pref. id.)(noun masc. sing. dec. 6 c   עשר

הֶעָשׂר   pref. הָ bef. עַ for הַ)(num. card. masc. sing.   עשר

הָעֲשָׂרָה   pref. הָ for הַ)(id. masc. sing.   עשר

הָעֲשִׂרִי   pref. id.)(adj. ord. masc. from עָשָׂר   עשר

הָעֲשָׂרִים   pref. id.)(num. com. gen., pl. of עֲשָׂרָה   עשר

הָעֲשִׂירִית   pref. id.)(adj. ord., fem. of עֲשִׂירִי m. fr. עָשָׂר   עשר

הֶעֱשַׁרְתְּ   Hiph. pret. 2 pers. sing. fem.   עשר

הֶעֱשַׁרְתִּי   id. pret. 1 pers. sing.   עשר

הָעֹשֹׂת   pref. הָ for הַ)(Kal part. act. fem., pl. of עֹשָׂה dec. 10, (from עֹשֶׂה masc.)   עשה

הָעַשְׁתָּרוֹת   וְ pref. id.)(pr. name, pl. of עַשְׁתֹּרֶת q. v.   עשה

הָעַשְׁתְּרָתִי   pref. id.)(gent. noun from the preceding   עשה

הָעֵת   וְ pref. art. f. הָ)(noun com. sing. d. 8 b   עדה

הַעֵת   pref. הַ interr. f.)([for עֵדֶת]   עדה

הָעַתֻּדִים   pref. הָ for הַ)(noun masc., pl. [עַתּוּד] dec. 1 b   עתד

הָעַתּוּדִים   dec. 1 b   עתד

הָעֲתִידִים   pref. id.)(adj. masc., pl. of עָתִיד dec. 3 a   עתד

הָעִתִּים   pref. id.)(noun com., pl. of עֵת, see הָעֵת   עדה

הֶעְתִּיקוּ   Hiph. pret. 3 pers. pl. [for הֶעֱתִּיקוּ, § 13. r. 9]   עתק

הַעְתִּירוּ   וְ Hiph. imp. pl. m. [for הַעֲתִּירוּ § 13. r. 9]   עתר

הֵעָתֵר   וְ Niph. imp. sing. masc. (§ 9. rem. 3)   עתר

הַעְתַּרְתִּי   וְ Hiph. pret. 1 pers. sing. (§ 13. r. 9 & 10, comp. § 8. rem. 2)   עתר

הַעְתַּרְתֶּם   וְ id. pret. 2 pers. pl. masc.   עתר

הַפְּאָרִים   pref. הַ)(noun masc., pl. of פְּאָר, pl. c. פַּאֲרֵי (§ 35. rem. 12)   פאר

הַפֵּאָת   pref. id.)(noun fem., pl. of פֵּאָה dec. 11 b   פאה

הַפֻּגוֹת   noun fem., pl. of [הֲפוּגָה] dec. 10.   פוג

הִפְגִּיעַ   Hiph. pret. 3 pers. sing. masc.   פגע

הִפְגִּעוּ   id. pret. 3 pers. pl.   פגע

הִפְגַּעְתִּי   id. pret. 1 pers. sing.   פגע

הַפֶּגֶר   pref. הַ)(noun masc. s. (pl. c. פִּגְרֵי) d. 6 a   פגר

הַפְּגָרִים   pref. id.)(id. pl., absolute state   פגר

הָפְדֵּה   וְ Hoph. inf. absolute   פדה

הִפְדָּהּ   וְ Hiph. pret. 3 pers. sing. masc., suff. 3 pers. sing. fem. (§ 11. rem. 1)   פדה

הַפֹּדְךָ   וְ pref. הַ)(Kal part. act. masc., suff. 2 pers. sing. masc. from [פֹּדֶה] dec. 9 a   פדה

הַפִּדְיוֹם   pref. id.)(noun masc. sing.   פדה

הַפְּדֻיִם   pref. id.)(Kh. פְּדוּיִם defect. for the preced., K. פְּדוּיִם noun pl. [of פָּדוּי]   פדה

הַפֶּדֶר   pref. id.)(noun m. s. [for פֵּדֶר § 35. r. 2]   פדר

הַפֵּאָה   pref. id.)(noun m. s. irr. § 45 [for פֵּאָה]   פאה

הָפֹךְ   Kal inf. absolute   הפך

הָפוּךְ   pr. name, in compos. קֶרֶן הַפּוּךְ   קרן

הַהֲפוּכָה   Kal part. pass., fem. of הָפוּךְ masc.   הפך

הַפֹּנָה   pref. הַ)(Kal part. act. sing. masc. dec. 9 a   פנה

הַפּוּנִי   pref. id.)(patronym. of פּוּן   פן

* De. 21. 6.   ⁱ Le. 27. 23.   ᵐ De. 5. 22.   ᵖ 2 Ki. 23. 4.   ˢ Eze. 29. 1.   ᵛ Zec. 10. 3.   ʸ Eze. 35. 13.   ᶠ Je. 15. 11.   ᵏ Nu. 3. 49.
ᵇ 2 Ki. 23. 35.   ʲ Hab. 2. 16.   Jos. 5. 3.   Nu. 28. 6.   Eze. 27. 33.   Job 3. 8.   Is. 3. 20.   Am. 8. 3.   Nu. 3. 51.
ᶜ Le. 27. 8, 12.   Jos. 5. 3.   Eze. 17. 15.   Je. 32. 1.   Ge. 14. 23.   1 Ch. 29. 30.   La. 3. 49.   Le. 19. 20.   1 Ki. 19. 18.
ᵈ Ex. 27. 14.   Ruth 3. 7.   Job 40. 19.   Is. 7. 4.   Le. 18. 29.   Ezr. 10. 13.   Is. 53. 10.   Ex. 21. 8.   Pr. 12. 7.
ᵉ Jos. 2. 6.   Ps. 102. 18.   Job 41. 25.   Ec. 4. 1.   Ec. 10. 17.   2 Ch. 33. 19.   Je. 36. 25.   De. 13. 6.   Ho. 7. 8.
Is. 65. 11.   Ex. 20. 21.   Ne. 3. 16.   1 Ch. 29. 12.   Ge. 31. 10, 12.   Ex. 8. 25.   Eze. 43. 18.   Am. 4. 1.

15

הַפּוֹצָה	pref. ה)(Kal part. act. sing. masc.	פצה
הַפּוּר	pref. id.)(noun masc. sing. dec. 1a	פור
הַפּוּרִים	pref. id.)(id. pl., absolute state	פור
הַפּשְׁעִים	pref. id.)(Kal part. act. masc., pl. of פּשֵׁע dec. 7b	פשע
הַפּוּתִי	pref. id.)(patronym. from פּוּת	פות
הָפַּח	Hiph. inf. absolute	פחח
הַפַּח	pref. ה)(noun masc. sing., pl. פַּחִים dag. forte impl. (§ 37. rem. 7)	פחח
הַפַּחַד	pref. id.)(noun masc. s. (suff. פַּחְדּוֹ) d. 6d	פחד
הַפַּחָה	pref. id.)(noun masc. sing. irr. (§ 45)	פחה
הַפַּחוֹת	pref. id.)(id. pl. absolute	פחה
הִפְחִיד	Hiph. pret. 3 pers. sing. masc.	פחד
הַפַּחַת	pref. ה)(noun masc. sing. dec. 6d	פחת
הִפְחַתִּי	Hiph. pret. 1 pers. sing. [for הִפְחַתִּי comp. § 8. rem. 7]	נפח
הַפַּחְתִּים	pref. ה art.)(noun masc., pl. of פַּחַת d. 6d	פחת
הַפַּחְתֶּם	Hiph. pret. 2 pers. sing. masc.	נפח
הָפִיחִי	Hiph. imp. sing. fem.	פוח
הִפִּיל	Hiph. pret. 3 pers. sing. masc.	נפל
הַפִּילְנָשִׁים	pref. ה)(for פִּלְ (note to § 18. rem. 12) noun fem., pl. of פִּלֶגֶשׁ d. 6 (§ 35. r. 16)	פלגש
הִפִּילָה	Hiph. pret. 3 pers. sing. fem.	נפל
הַפִּילוּ	id. imp. pl. masc.	נפל
הַפִּילוּ	id. pret. 3 pers. s. m., suff. 3 pers. s. m.	נפל
הִפִּילוּ	id. pret. 3 pers. sing. masc.	נפל
הָפִיץ	Hiph. pret. 3 pers. sing. masc.	פוץ
הֲפִיצוֹתִי	id. pret. 1 pers. sing.; acc. shifted by ן for ן conv. (comp. § 8. r. 7, & § 11. r. 9)	פוץ
הֲפִיצוֹתִיךָ	id. id., suff. 2 pers. sing. masc.	פוץ
הֲפִיצוֹתִים	id. id., suff. 3 pers. pl. masc.	פוץ
הֲפִיצוֹתֶם	id. pret. 2 pers. pl. masc.	פוץ
הֲפִיצְךָ	id. pret. 3 pers. sing. masc., suff. 2 pers. sing. masc.; ן for ן conv.	פוץ
הֱפִיצָם	id. id., suff. 3 pers. pl. masc.	פוץ
הֵפִיר	Hiph. pret. 3 pers. sing. masc.	פור

הָפַךְ fut. יַהֲפֹךְ (1 pers. אֶהֱפֹךְ § 13. rem. 5)—I. to turn, turn over. Intrans. to turn back.—II. to overturn, overthrow, ruin.—III. to convert, change, const. with לְ. Intrans. to change, be changed. —IV. to pervert. Niph. נֶהְפַּךְ (§ 13. rem. 7)— I. to turn oneself, to turn back; with בְּ to turn against, with עַל, לְ to, upon any one.—II. to be over- thrown, ruined.—III. to be changed, with לְ. Hoph. הָהְפֵּךְ (§ 13. rem. 11) to be turned, with עַל upon,

Job 30. 15.   **Hithp.**—I. to turn oneself.—II. to be changed, Job 38. 14.—III. to roll oneself, to tumble, Ju. 7. 13.

הֶפֶךְ, הֵפֶךְ masc. reverse, contrary, Eze. 16. 34.	
הֹפֶךְ masc. perverseness, Is. 29. 16; which, how- ever, may be taken as an infinitive.	
הֲפֵכָה fem. overthrow, Ge. 19. 29.	
הֲפַכְפַּךְ masc. turning, crooked, Pr. 21. 8.	
מַהְפֵּכָה fem. dec. 10, overthrow, destruction.	
מַהְפֶּכֶת f. stocks, imprisonment; בֵּית מַ prison-house.	
תַּהְפּוּכָה fem. dec. 10, perverseness, perversion.	

הֲפֹךְ	Kal imp. sing. masc.	הפך
הֶפֶךְ	noun masc. sing.	הפך
הֹפֵךְ	Kal part. act. sing. masc. dec. 7b	הפך
הָפְכָה	Kal pret. 3 pers. sing. fem.	הפך
הָפְכוּ	id. pret. 3 pers. pl.	הפך
הָפְכִי	id. inf., suff. 1 pers. sing.	הפך
הֶפְכְּכֶם	noun m. s., suff. 2 pers. pl. m. fr. [הֹפֶךְ] d. 6c	הפך
הֲפַכְכֶם	Kal pret. 3 pers. s. m., suff. 2 pers. pl. m.	הפך
הֲפַכְפַּךְ	adj. masc. sing.	הפך
הָפַכְתָּ	Kal pret. 2 pers. sing. masc.	הפך
הָפַכְתִּי הָפַכְתִּי	} id. pret. 1 pers. sing.; acc. shifted by conv. ן (§ 8. rem. 7) }	הפך
וְהֲפַכְתֶּם	id. pret. 2 pers. pl. masc. ן for ן conv.	הפך
הִפִּל	Hiph. pret. 3 pers. sing. masc., for הִפִּיל	נפל
הַפְלֵא	Hiph. inf. absolute	פלא
הַפְלֵא הַפְלֵא	} Hiph. pret. 3 pers. sing. m. (§ 23. r. 9)	פלא
הַפְלָאוֹת	pref. ה)(noun m., pl. of פֶּלֶא (פִּלְאֲךָ suff.) dec. 6a	פלא
הַפַּלָּאִי	pref. id.)(patronym. of פַּלּוּא	פלא
הַפְלֵה	Hiph. imp. sing. masc.	פלה
הַפְלֵהָ	Hiph. imp. sing. masc., suff. 3 pers. sing. f.	נפל
הִפְלָה	Hiph. pret. 3 pers. sing. masc.	פלה
הִפְלִהוּ	Hiph. pret. 3 pers. pl. (הִפִּילוּ) suff. 3 pers. s. m.	נפל
הַפְּלוֹנִי	pref. ה)(patronym. of פָּלוֹן	פלה
הַפְלֵטָה	pref. id.)(noun fem. sing. dec. 10.	פלט
הַפַּלְטִי	pref. id.)(pr. name masc.	פלט
הִפְלִיא	Hiph. pret. 3 pers. sing. masc.	פלא
הַפָּלִיט	pref. ה)((prim. adj.) subst. masc. s. dec. 3a	פלט
הַפְּלֵטָה	pref. id.)(noun fem. sing. dec. 10.	פלט
הִפְלֵיתִי	Hiph. pret. 1 pers. sing.; acc. shifted by conv. ן (comp. § 8. r. 7, & § 11. r. 9)	פלה
הִפַּלְנוּ	Hiph. pret. 1 pers. sing.	נפל

a Ps. 144. 10.   g Est. 3. 12.   m Da. 11. 12.   Eze. 22.15,etc.   s De. 28.64.   v Ge. 19. 21.   a Am. 6. 12.   p De. 28. 59.   u Ps. 4. 4.
b Est. 9. 26.   h Est. 9. 28.   n Pr. 7. 26.   Je. 30. 11.   t Ge. 11. 9.   c Je. 23. 36.   b Is. 28. 29.   q Da. 12. 6.   x 2 Ch. 32. 21.
c Est. 9. 28.   i Job 31. 39.   o 1 Sa. 14. 42.   Je. 9. 15.   u Am. 5. 8.   f Job 9. 5.   c Est. 9. 24.   r Ps. 17. 7.   y 2 Ch. 2. 8.
d Eze. 20. 38.   k 2 Sa. 17. 9.   d De. 25. 2.   Eze. 34. 21.   Le. 13. 10.   Pr. 21. 8.   d Is. 29. 14.   s 2 Ch. 2. 8.   z Ex. 8. 18.
e Is. 42. 22.   l Mal. 1. 13.   Je. 22. 7.   De. 30. 3.   Ps. 78. 9.   Am. 4. 11.   2 Ch. 2. 8.   Jos. 15. 3.   Ne. 10. 38.
f Ps. 124. 7.   m Ca. 4. 16.

הַפְּלֹנִי — pref. הַ)(patronym. of פְּלֹן — פלה

הַפְּלִשְׁתִּי — pref. id.)(gent. noun from פְּלֶשֶׁת — פלש

הַפְּלִשְׁתִּים —)ו(pref. id.)(id. pl. — פלש

הַפְּלֵתִי —)ו(pref. id.)(noun masc. sing. — פלת

הִפְלֵטִי)וָ — Hiph. pret. 1 pers. sing.; acc. shifted by conv.)((comp. § 8. rem. 7) — נפל

הִפְלִיטוֹ —)ו(id., suff. 3 pers. sing. masc. — נפל

הִפְלִיטִים —)ו(id., suff. 3 pers. pl. masc. — נפל

הִפְלַטְתָּם — id. pret. 2 pers. sing. masc., suff. 3 pers. pl. m. — נפל

הַפָּנֶה — pref. הַ)(noun fem. sing. dec. 10. — פנן

הַפֹּנֶה — pref. id.)(Kal part. act. masc. dec. 9a — פנה

הִפְנָה — Hiph. pret. 3 pers. sing. masc. — פנה

הָפְנָה — Hoph. pret. 3 pers. pl. — פנה

הִפְנוּ — Hiph. pret. 1 pers. pl. — פנה

הַפֹּנוֹת — pref. הַ)(Kal part. act. fem. pl. of [פֹּנָה] dec. 10 from פֹּנֶה masc.

הַפִּנּוֹת — pref. id.)(noun fem., pl. of פִּנָּה dec. 10. — פנן

הַפָּנָיו — pref. הַ)(noun masc. pl., suff. 3 pers. sing. masc. from [פָּנֶה] dec. 9b — פנה

הַפָּנִים — pref. הַ)(id. pl., absolute state — פנה

הַפְּנִים — pref. id.)(noun masc., pl. of [פֵּן] dec. 8b — פנן

הַפְּנִימִי — pref. id.)(adj. masc. sing. dec. 1b — פנם

הַפְּנִימִיּוֹת — pref. id.)(id. fem., pl. of מִית (comp. § 39. No. 4, rem. 1 note) — פנם

הַפְּנִימִים — pref. id.)(id. masc. pl. — פנם

הַפְּנִימִית — pref. id.)(id. fem. sing., see הַפְּנִימִיוֹת — פנם

הִפְנְתָה — Hiph. pret. 3 pers. sing. fem. — פנה

הַפִּסְגָּה — pref. הַ)(pr. name of a place — פסג

הַפֶּסַח / הַפָּסַח — pref. id.)(noun masc. sing. dec. 6 (§ 35 rem. 2 & 5) — פסח

הַפִּסֵּחַ — pref. id.)(adj. masc. sing. dec. 7b — פסח

הַפְּסָחִים — pref. id.)(noun masc., pl. of פֶּסַח dec. 6 (§ 35. rem. 5) — פסח

הַפִּסְחִים —)ו(pref. id.)(adj. masc., pl. of פִּסֵּחַ dec. 7b — פסח

הַפְּסִילִים —)ו(pref. id.)(noun m., pl. of [פָּסִיל] dec. 3a — פסל

הַפַּסִּים — pref. id.)(noun masc., pl. of [פַּס] dec. 8d — פסס

הַפֶּסֶל / הַפָּסֶל — pref. id.)(noun masc. sing., dec. 6a (§ 35. rem. 2, but with suff. (פִּסְלִי) — פסל

הַפְּסִלִים —)ו(pref. id.)(noun m., pl. of [פָּסִיל] dec. 3a — פסל

הַפַּעַם / הַפָּעַם —)ו(pref. id.)(noun m. s. dec. 6d (§ 35. r. 2) — פעם

הַפַּעֲמֹנִים — pref. id.)(noun masc., pl. of פַעֲמֹן dec. 1b — פעם

הַפְּעוֹר — pref. id.)(pr. name of a mountain — פער

הָפֵץ — Hiph. imp. sing. masc. — פוץ

הֱפִיצֻהוּ —)ו(id. pret. 3 pers. pl. [הֲפִיצוּ], suff. 3 pers. sing. masc.;)ו(before (‥)

הֲפִצוֹתִים — id. pret. 1 pers. sing., suff. 3 pers. pl. masc. — פוץ

הַפְּצִירָה — pref. הַ)(noun fem. sing. — פצר

הַפְצֵר — Hiph. inf. used as a subst. — פצר

הֲפִצֹתִי)וָ — Hiph. pret. 1 pers. sing.; acc. shifted by)ו(for)ו(conv. (comp. § 8. rem. 7) — פוץ

הֲפִצֹתֶם — id. pret. 2 pers. pl. masc. — פוץ

הָפְקַד — Hoph. pret. 3 pers. sing. masc. — פקד

הַפְקֵד — Hiph. imp. sing. masc. — פקד

הִפָּקֵד — Niph. inf. constr. used as an abs. — פקד

הַפְּקֻדָּה — pref. הַ)(noun fem. sing. dec. 10. — פקד

הִפְקִידוּ — Hiph. pret. 3 pers. pl. [for הִפְקִידוּ] — פקד

הַפִּקָּדוֹן — pref. הַ)(noun masc. sing. — פקד

הַפְּקֻדִים — pref. id.)(Kal part. p. m., pl. of [פָּקוּד] dec. 3a — פקד

הַפְּקֻדֹת — pref. id.)(noun fem., pl. of פְּקֻדָּה dec. 10. — פקד

הִפְקַדְתָּ֫נוּ — Hiph. pret. 2 pers. s. m., suff. 3 pers. s. m. — פקד

הִפְקַדְתִּי)וָ — id. pret. 1 pers. sing.; acc. shifted by)ו(conv.)ו((comp. § 8. rem. 7) — פקד

הִפְקַדְתִּיךָ — id., suff. 2 pers. sing. masc. — פקד

הַפָּקִיד — pref. הַ)(noun masc. sing. dec. 3a — קד

הִפְקִיד —)ו(Hiph. pret. 3 pers. sing. masc. — קד

הַפְקִידוּ —)ו(id. imp. pl. masc. — פקד

הַפְּקָעִים — pref. הַ)(n. m., pl. of [פָּקַע] § 35. r. 5] dec. 6 — פקע

הַפָּר — pref. id.)(with the art. for פָּר, noun masc. dec. 8. (§ 37. rem. 7) — פרר

הָפֵר —)ו(Hiph. inf. abs. or imp. sing. masc. — פרר

הֵפֵר / הָפֵר —)ו(id. pret. 3 pers. sing. m. (§ 18. rem. 10) — פרר

הִפָּרֶד / הִפָּרֵד — Niph. inf. or imp. sing. masc., with Mak. or bef. monos. [for הִפָּרֵד § 9. rem. 3] — פרד

הַפֶּרֶד —)ו(pref. הַ)(noun m. s. (suff. פִּרְדוֹ) dec. 6a — פרד

הַפְרָדָה — pref. id.)(noun fem. sing. dec. 10. — פרד

הַפַּרְדֵּס — pref. id.)(noun masc. sing. dec. 1b — פרדס

הַפָּרָה —)ו(pref. id.)(noun fem. sing. dec. 10 [for פָּרָה] from פַּר masc. (comp. § 37. rem. 7) also pr. name — פרר

הֵפֵרָה — Hiph. pret. sing. masc. with parag. ה — פרר

הֵפֵרוּ — id. pret. 3 pers. — פרר

הַפְּרוֹזִים — pref. הַ)(Kh. פְּרוֹזִים, K. פְּרָזִים, noun masc., pl. of פְּרוֹזִי or פְּרָזִי — פרז

הַפְּרוּצָה — pref. id.)(Kal part. pass. fem. [of פָּרוּץ m.] — פרץ

הַפָּרוֹת — pref. id.)(noun fem., pl. of פָּרָה dec. 10, from פַּר masc. (comp. § 37. rem. 7) — פרר

הַפְּרָזוֹת — pref. id.)(noun fem. pl. [of פְּרָזָה] — פרז

הַפִּרְזִי — pref. id.)(noun masc. sing. — פרז

הַפְּרִזִּי —)ו(pref. id.)(pr. name of a people — פרז

הַפֶּרַח —)ו(pref. id.)(n.m.s. (suff. פִּרְחוֹ) d.6a (§35.r.5) — פרח

הַפִּרְחָה — pref. הַ)(Kal pret. 3 pers. sing. fem. — פרח

a Je. 19.7.   b Ps. 73.18.   c Je. 48.39.   d Je. 49.8.   e Eze. 46.19.   f Job 13.8.

g Zec. 14.10.   h 2 Ch. 4.22.   i 1 Ch. 28.11.   k Je. 49.24.   l Mal. 1.13.   l Eze. 29.12.

m 2 Ch. 30.17.   n 2 Sa. 5.6,8.   o 2 Sa. 34.3,4.   p Ju. 18.20,30.   q 2 Ch. 33.19.   r Jos. 10.18.

s Ex. 39.25.   t Job 40.11.   u Job 18.11.   v Eze. 11.16.   w 1 Sa. 13.21.   x 2 Ch. 32.5.

y 1 Sa. 15.23.   z Je. 23.2.   a 1 Ki. 20.39.   b Ho. 9.7.   c Je. 36.20.   d Est. 9.19.

e Le. 5.23.   f Je. 52.11.   g Je. 29.4.   h Is. 62.6.   i Lev. 26.16.   k Ca. 6.11.

k Je. 1.10.   l Ne. 12.42.   m 2 Ch. 12.10.   n 1 Ki. 7.24.   Ps. 85.5.

q Ge. 13.14.   r Ge. 13.9.   s 2 Sa. 18.9.   t Est. 9.19.   u Ne. 3.8.   w 1 Ch. 4.21.

u Nu. 19.5,6, 9,10.   v 1 Ki. 15.13.

Hebrew	Description	Root
הֲפִתִּיתָ	pref. הַ)(Piel pret. 2 p. s. m.; ן bef. (‏ֵ‏), for ן	פתה
הַצֹּאן	ן)(pref. הַ)(noun com. sing. dec. 1a	צאן
הַצֹּאן	‏ ‏	
הַצֹּאִים	pref. הַ)(adj. masc. sing. from [צֹאֵא]	יצא
הַצֶּאֱצָאִים	pref. id.)(noun masc., pl. of [צֶאֱצָא] d. 1b	יצא
הֹצֵאתִי	ן Hiph. pret. 1 pers. sing., acc. shifted by conv. ן (comp. § 8. rem. 7)	יצא
הַצָּב	ן)(pref. הַ)(noun masc. sing. dec. 8a	צבב
הֻצָּב	ן Hoph. pret. 3 pers. sing. masc.	נצב
הַצָּבָא	pref. הַ)(n.m. s.d 4a, constr. צְבָא (§ 33. r. 2)	צבא
הַצֹּבְאוֹת	pref. id.)(Kal part. act. fem. pl. [of צָבְאָה or [צָבָאת]	צבא
הַצְּבָאוֹת	pref. id.)(n. m. with pl. f. term. fr. צָבָא d.4a	צבא
הַצֹּבְאִים	pref. id.)(Kal part. act.m., pl. of [צָבֵא] d. 7b	צבא
הַצְבָאֹת	defect. for הַצְּבָאוֹת (q. v.)	צבא
הַצְּבֹבָה	pref. הַ)(pr. name fem.	צבב
הַצְּבִי	pref. id.)(noun masc. sing. dec. 6i (§ 35. rem. 14 & 15)	צבה
הַצְּבִי		
הַצְּבָיִים	pref. id.)(id. pl. also pr. name, see הַצְּבֹ בֶּרֶת	צבה
הַצְּבֹיִים		
הַצְּבֹעִים	pref. id.)(pr. name of a valley	צבע
הִצַּבְתָּ	Hiph. pret. 2 pers. sing. masc.	נצב
הַצְּבָתִים	pref. הַ)(noun masc. pl. of [צֶבֶת] dec. 6	צבת
הַצֵּג	Hiph. inf. absolute (§ 20. rem. 16)	יצג
הִצַּגְתִּיהָ	ן id. pret. 1 pers. sing., suff. 3 pers. sing. fem.	יצג
הִצַּגְתִּיו	ן id., suff. 3 pers. sing. masc.	יצג
הַצָּד	pref. הַ)(Kal part. act. sing. masc.	צוד
הֲצָדָא	Ch. pref. הַ interr. for הַ)(noun masc. sing.; or for אַצָּדָא, see under R.	צדה
הַצֶּדָּים	pref. הַ art.)(pr. name of a place	צדד
הַצַּדִּיק	pref. id.)(adj. masc. sing. dec. 1b	צדק
הַצְדִּיקוּ	Hiph. imp. pl. masc.	צדק
הִצְדִּיקוּ	ן id. pret. 3 pers. pl.	צדק
הַצַּדִּיקִם	pref. הַ)(adj. masc., pl. of צַדִּיק dec. 1b	צדק
הַצַּדִּיקִם		
הַצֶּדֶק	pref. id.)(noun masc. sing. (suff. צִדְקִי) d. 6c	צדק
הַצְּדָקָה	pref. id.)(noun fem. sing. dec. 11c	צדק
הִצְדַּקְתִּיו	ן Hiph. pret. 1 pers. sing., suff. 3 pers. s. m.	צדק
הַצָּהֹב	pref. הַ)(adj. masc. sing.	צהב
הַצָּהֳרָים	pref. id.)(noun fem., du. of צֹהַר dec. 6f	צהר
הַצָּהֳרָים		
הִצּוּ	Hiph. pret. 3 pers. pl. (§ 25. No. 2)	נצה
הַצּוֹם	pref. הַ)(Kal inf. absolute	צום
הַצֹּמוֹת	pref. הַ)(n. m., with pl. f. term. fr. צוֹם d.1a	צום
הַצּוּר	pref. id.)(noun masc. sing. dec. 1a	צור
הִצְטַיַּדְנוּ	Hithp.pret.1 p.s. [for הִתְצַיַּדְנוּ §12.r.3]	צוד

Hebrew	Description	Root
הִפְרַחְתִּי	Hiph. pret. 1 pers. sing.	פרח
הַפֹּרְטִים	pref. id.)(Kal part. act. m., pl. of [פֹּרֵט] d.7b	פרט
הַפְּרִיד	Hiph. pret. 3 pers. sing. masc.	פרד
הַפָּרִים	pref. הַ)(noun m. pl. of פַּר, d 8 (§ 37. r. 7)	פרר
הַפָּרִים	pref. id.)(noun masc., pl. of פוּר dec. 1a	פור
הִפְרִיסָה	Hiph. pret. 3 pers. sing. fem.	פרס
הִפְרִיסוּ	id. pret. 3 pers. pl.	פרס
הִפְרִיעַ	Hiph. pret. 3 pers. sing. masc.	פרע
הִפְרִיעִתִי	ן Hiph. pret. 1 pers. sing.; acc. shifted by conv. ן (§ 8. rem. 7)	פרה
הַפָּרֹכֶת	pref. הַ)(noun fem. sing.	פרך
הֲפֵרֵם	Hiph. pret. 3 p. s. m. (הֵפֵר), suff. 3 p. pl. m.	פרר
הִפְרַנִי	Hiph. pret. 3 pers. sing. masc. [הִפְרָה], suff. 1 pers. sing. (§ 24. rem. 21)	פרה
הַפֶּרֶס	ן)(pref. הַ)(noun masc. sing.	פרס
הַפַּרְסָה	pref. id.)(noun fem. sing. dec. 12a	פרס
הַפַּרְסִי	pref. id.)(gent. noun from פָּרָס	פרס
הַפַּרְעָתוֹנִי	pref. id.)(gent. noun from פִּרְעָתוֹן	פרע
הַפִּרְעָתֹנִי		
הַפֹּרִץ	pref. id.)(Kal part. act. sing. masc.	פרץ
הַפַּרְצִי	pref. id.)(patronym. of פֶּרֶץ	פרץ
הַפֹּרְצִים	pref. id.)(Kal part., pl. of [פּוֹרֵץ] dec. 3a	פרץ
הַפֶּרֶק	pref. id.)(noun masc. sing.	פרק
הַפַּרְשְׁדֹנָה	pref. id.)(noun m. s. [פַּרְשְׁדֹן] with loc. ה	פרשד
הַפָּרָשִׁים	ן)(pref. id.)(n.m., pl. of פָּרָשׁ (§ 30. Nos. 2 & 3)	פרש
הִפְרֵתָה	ן Hiph. pret. 2 pers. sing. masc. (§ 8. r. 5) R. either פָּרָה (comp. § 18. rem. 13) or פור	פרה
הִפְרֵתִי	ן Hiph. pret. 1 pers. sing.; acc. shifted by conv. ן (comp. § 8. rem. 7)	פרה
הַפַּרְתְּמִים	pref. id.)(noun masc. pl.	פרתם
הַפְשִׁיטוּ	ן Hiph. imp. pl. masc.	פשט
הִפְשִׁיט	ן id. pret. 3 pers. sing. masc.	פשט
הִפְשִׁיטוּ	ן id. pret. 3 pers. pl.	פשט
הִפְשִׁיטוּךָ	ן id. id., suff. 2 pers. sing. masc.	פשט
הַפֶּשַׁע	ן)(pref. הַ)(noun masc. sing. (suff. פִּשְׁעִי) dec. 6a (§ 35. rem. 5)	פשע
הַפֹּשְׁעִים	pref. id.)(Kal part. act. m., pl. of פֹּשֵׁעַ d. 7b	פשע
הַפִּשְׁעָתָה	ן pref. הַ)(noun fem. sing., (with suff. פִּשְׁתִּי)	פשת
הַפִּשְׁתִּים	ן pref. id.)(id. pl., with masc. term.	פשת
הַפְּתוֹת	ן pref. id.)(noun masc. with pl. fem. term. [from פֹּת] comp. פִּתְחָן	פות
הַפֶּתַח	pref. הַ)(noun masc. sing. dec. 6a (§ 35. rem. 2, 5, but with suff. פִּתְחוֹ)	פתח
הַפָּתֻחַ	ן)(	
הַפֶּתְחָה	pref. id.)(id. with parag. ה (§ 35. rem. 18)	פתח
הַפְּתָחִים	pref. id.)(id. pl., absolute state	פתח
הַפְּתִילִים	ן pref. id.)(noun masc., pl. of [פָּתִיל] d. 3a	פתל

ᵃ Eze. 17. 24.   ᵏ 2 Ch. 28. 19.   ᵘ Ne. 4. 1.   ᵛ Job 19. 9.   ᵍ Ex. 9. 31.   ˡ Ge. 38. 25.   ᶜᶜ Na. 2. 8.   ᵖᵖ Ho. 2. 5.   ᶻᶻ 2 Sa. 15. 4.
ᵇ Am. 6. 5.   ˡ Ge. 17. 20, etc.   ᵒ Ob. 14.   ʷ Le. 1. 6.   ᵗ Le. 13. 59.   ᵃᵃ Pr. 24. 28.   ᵈᵈ 1 Sa. 3. 22.   ᵠ Ge. 43. 9.   ᵃᵃᵃ 2 Sa. 5. 2.
ᶜ Ge. 30. 40.   ᵐ Nu. 30. 13.   ᵖ Ju. 3. 22.   ˣ Mi. 3. 3.   ᵘ 1 Ki. 7. 50.   ᵇᵇ Nu. 11. 22.   ᵉᵉ Ex. 38. 8.   ᵣ Ge. 27. 33.   ᵇᵇᵇ 2 Sa. 4. 5.
ᵈ Nu. 8. 12.   ⁿ Ge. 41. 52.   ᵠ Is. 22. 7.   ʸ Eze. 16. 39.   ᵛ Ge. 19. 11.   ᶜᶜ Zec. 3. 4.   ᶠᶠ 2 Sa. 2. 18.   ˢˢ Da. 3. 14.   ᶜᶜᶜ Nu. 26. 9.
ᵉ Est. 9. 29, 31, 32.   ᵒ Le. 11. 13.   ʳ 2 Sa. 15. 34.   ᶻ Eze. 23. 26.   ʷ Eze. 41. 3.   ᵈᵈ Ge. 19. 6.   ᵍᵍ Ruth 2. 16.   ᵗᵗ Ps. 82. 3.   ᵈᵈᵈ Zec. 7. 5.
ᶠ Le. 11. 6.   ᵖ De. 14. 12.   ˢ Le. 17. 6.   ᵃᵃ Da. 9. 24.   ˣ Je. 51. 44.   ᵉᵉ De. 28. 56.   ʰʰ De. 25. 1.   ᵘᵘᵘ Jos. 9. 12.
ᵍ De. 14. 7.   ᵠ Mi. 2. 13.   ᵗ Nu. 20. 26.   ᵇ Da. 8. 13.   ʸ Le. 11. 29.   ᵐᵐ Da. 8. 9.

Hebrew	Description	Root
הֵצִיב־	Hiph. pret. 3 pers. sing. masc.	נצב
הֵצִיבוּ	id. pret. 3 pers. pl.	נצב
הַצִּיבִי	id. imp. sing. fem.	נצב
הַצִּיגוּ	Hiph. imp. pl. masc. (§ 20. rem. 16)	יצג
הִצִּיגַנוּ	id. pret. 3 pers. sing. masc., Kh. עַנּוּ 1 pers. pl., K. עַנִּי 1 pers. sing.	יצג
הִצִּיגַנִי	id. pret. 3 pers. sing. m., suff. 1 pers. sing.	יצג
הַצִּידֹנִי	pref. הַ)(gent. noun from צִידוֹן	צוד
הַצִּידֹנִים	pref. id.)(id. pl. absolute	צוד
הַצִּוּוֹן	pref. id.)(noun masc. sing. dec. 1 b	צוה
הַצִּיל	Hiph. inf. constr.	נצל
הִצִּיל	id. pret. 3 pers. sing. masc.	נצל
הַצִּילָה	id. imp. sing. masc. with parag. הַ (§ 11. r. 5)	נצל
הַצִּילוּ	id. imp. masc. pl.	נצל
הִצִּילוֹ	id. pret. 3 pers. sing. m., suff. 3 pers. s. m.	נצל
הִצִּילוּ	id. pret. 3 pers. pl.	נצל
הִצִּילָם	id. pret. 3 pers. s. m., suff. 3 pers. pl. m.	נצל
הַצִּילֵנוּ	id. imp. sing. masc., suff. 1 pers. pl.	נצל
הִצִּילָנוּ	id. pret. 3 pers. sing. masc., suff. 1 pers. pl.	נצל
הַצִּילֵנִי	id. imp. sing. masc., suff. 1 pers. sing.	נצל
הִצִּילַנִי	id. pret. 3 pers. s. m., suff. 1 p. s. (§ 2. r. 1)	נצל
הַצִּינֹק	pref. הַ)(noun masc. sing.	צנק
הֵצִיף	Hiph. pret. 3 pers. sing. masc.	צוף
הַצִּיץ	pref. הַ)(pr. name of a place	צוץ
הֵצִיקָה	Hiph. pret. 3 pers. sing. fem.	צוק
הֲצִיקוֹתִי	id. pret. 1 pers. sing.; acc. shifted by וְ for conv. (comp. § 8. rem. 7)	צוק
הֱצִיקַתְהוּ	id. pret. 3 pers. sing. fem., suff. 3 pers. s. m.	צוק
הֱצִיקַתְנִי	id. id., suff. 1 pers. sing.	צוק
הִצִּית	Hiph. pret. 3 pers. sing. m. (§ 20. rem. 16)	יצת
הִצִּיתוּ	id. pret. 3 pers. pl.	יצת
הַצֵּל	pref. הַ)(noun masc. sing. dec. 8 b	צלל
הַצֵּל	Hiph. inf., or imp. sing. masc.	נצל
הַצְלָה	noun fem. sing.	
הַצְלַח	Ch. Aph. pret. 3 pers. sing. masc. (§ 47. r. 4)	צלח
הַצְלַח	Hiph. imp. sing. masc.	צלח
הַצְלַחַת	pref. הַ)(noun fem. sing.	
הִצְלַחְתָּ	Hiph. pret. 2 pers. sing. masc.; acc. shifted by וְ conv. (comp. § 8. rem. 7)	צלח
הַצְלִיחַ	id. pret. 3 pers. sing. masc.	צלח
הַצְלִיחָה	id. imp. sing. m. with parag. הַ (§ 11. r. 5)	צלח
הִצְלִיחָה	id. pret. 3 pers. sing. fem	צלח
הַצְלִיחוּ	id. imp. pl. masc.	צלח
הִצְלִיחוּ	id. pret. 3 pers. sing. m., suff. 3 pers. s. m.	צלח

Hebrew	Description	Root
הַצְּלָלִים	pref. הַ)(noun masc., pl. of [צְלָל] dec. 6 b	צלל
הַצְּלֵלְפּוֹנִי	pref. id.)(pr. name masc., see	צלל
הִצַּלְנוּ	Hiph. pret. 1 pers. pl.	נצל
הִצַּלְנִי	id. pret. 3 pers. sing. masc. (הִצִּיל), suff. 1 p.s.	נצל
הַצֶּלַע	pref. הַ)(noun fem. s. d. 4 c (§ 33. No. 2. & r. 3)	צלע
הַצֹּלְעָה	pref. id.)(Kal part. act., fem. of צֹלֵעַ	צלע
הַצְּלָעֹת / הַצְּלָעֹת־	pref. id.)(noun fem. pl. abs. fr. [צֵלָע] dec. 4 c (§ 33. No. 2)	צלע
הַצְּלָצַל־	pref. הַ)(n. m. s. [for צְלָצַל] see under R.	צלל
הִצְלַתָּ / הִצְלַתְּ	Hiph. pret. 2 pers. sing. masc.; acc. shifted by conv. וְ (comp. § 8. r. 7)	נצל
הִצַּלְתִּי	id. pret. 1 pers. sing.; acc. shifted, see the preceding	נצל
הִצַּלְתִּיךָ	id. id., suff. 2 pers. sing. masc.	נצל
הִצַּלְתִּים	id. id., suff. 3 pers. pl. masc.	נצל
הִצַּלְתֶּם	id. pret. 2 pers. pl. masc.	נצל
הַצָּמֵא	pref. הַ)(adj. masc. sing. dec. 5 a	צמא
הַצְּמֵאָה	pref. id.)(id. fem.	צמא
הַצְּמָדִים	pref. id.)(noun masc., pl. of צֶמֶד dec. 3 a	צמד
הַצֹּמֵחַ	pref. id.)(Kal part. act. sing. masc.	צמח
הַצְּמִדִים	pref. id.)(noun masc., pl. of צָמִיד d. 3 a	צמד
הִצְמִיחָה	Hiph. pret. 3 pers. s. m., suff. 3 p. s. f.	צמח
הַצְמִיתֵם	Hiph. imp. sing. masc., suff. 3 pers. pl. masc.	צמת
הַצֶּמֶר	pref. הַ)(noun masc. s. (suff. צַמְרִי) d. 6 a	צמר
הַצָּמְרִי	pref. id.)(pr. name of a people	צמר
הִצְמַתָּה	Hiph. pret. 2 p. s. m. [for הִצְמַתָּ § 25. rem.]	צמת
הַצֵּן	masc. *armament, force,* Eze. 23. 24.	
הַצִּנָּה	pref. הַ)(noun fem. sing. dec. 10.	צנן
הַצָּנִיף	pref. id.)(noun masc. sing. dec. 3 a	צנף
הַצְּנִיפוֹת	pref. id.)(id. pl. with fem. term.	צנף
הַצְנֵעַ	Hiph. inf. absolute (§ 11. rem. 2)	צנע
הַצְּעָדָה	pref. id.)(noun fem. sing. (no vowel change)	צעד
הַצְּעָדוֹת	pref. id.)(id. pl. absolute	צעד
הַצָּעִיף	pref. הַ)(noun masc. sing. dec. 3 a	צעף
הַצָּעִיר	pref. id.)(adj. masc. sing. dec. 3 a	צער
הַצְּעִירָה	pref. id.)(id. fem. dec. 10.	צער
הַצְּעָקָה	pref. הַ)(noun fem. sing. dec. 11 c, constr. צַעֲקַת (§ 42. rem. 1)	צעק
הַצַּעֲקָתֹה	pref. הַ)(id., suff. 3 pers. sing. masc.	צעק
הַצְּעִירָה	defect. for הַצְּעִירָה (q. v.)	צער
הַצֹּעֲרִים	pref. הַ)(Kal part. act. masc., pl. of [צֹעֵר] dec. 7 b	צער
הַצֹּפֶה	pref. id.)(Kal part. act. sing. masc. d. 9 a	צפה

a 1 Ki. 16. 34.   h Ge. 37. 23.   p De. 11. 4.   u 2 Ki. 20.9,10,11.   z Da. 8. 12.   m 1 Ki. 7. 3.   t Is. 29. 8.   a Ps. 54. 7.   g Ge. 24. 65.
b Je. 5. 26.   i Ps. 82. 4.   q Ju. 16. 9.   x Est. 4. 14.   z 2 Ch. 26. 5.   n 1 Sa. 30. 22.   u De. 28. 42.   b Ps. 73. 27.   h Ge. 19. 38.
c Je. 31. 21.   k Ex. 18. 9.   r Is. 29. 2.   v Da. 3. 30 ; 6. 29.   a 1 Sa. 30. 22.   o Ge. 24. 30.   v Zec. 3. 5.   i 1 Sa. 4. 14.
d Am. 5. 15.   l Nu. 35. 25.   s Ju. 14. 17.   w 2 Ki. 21. 13.   b 1 Sa. 17. 37.   p Ex. 10. 5.   c Is. 3. 23.   k 1 Sa. 9. 21.
e Je. 51. 44.   m Ps. 34. 18.   t Job 32. 18.   x 1 Ch. 22. 11.   c Eze. 41. 8.   q Eze. 34. 27.   d Ge. 24. 47.   l Mi. 6. 8.
f Job 17. 6.   n Is. 19. 20.   u Je. 11. 16.   y Ps. 118. 25.   d Eze. 41. 6.   r Jos. 2. 13.   e Is. 55. 10.   f Is. 3. 20.
g 2 Ki. 23. 17.   o Je. 29. 26.   o Je. 32. 29.   y Ne. 1. 11.   u Ch. 14   e Zec. 13. 7.

Hebrew	Parsing	Root
הַצָּפוֹן	וְ pref. ה)(noun com. sing. dec. 3a	צפן
הַצָּפוֹנָה	pref. id.)(id. with loc. ה	צפן
הַצְּפוֹנִי	pref. id.)(patronym. of צָפוֹן, see צפה	צפה
הַצְּפוֹנִי	pref. id.)(adj. masc. sing.	צפן
הַצַּפּוֹר	pref. id.)(noun com. s., pl. צִפֳּרִים (§ 30. r. 2)	צפה
הַצֹּפִים	pref. id.)(Kal part. act. m., pl. of צֹפֶה d. 9a	צפה
הַצְפִּינוֹ	Hiph. inf., suff. 3 pers. sing. masc. dec. 1b	צפן
וְ הַצָּפִיר	pref. ה)(noun masc. sing. dec. 3a	צפר
הַצְּפִירָה	pref. id.)(noun fem. sing. dec. 10.	צפר
הַצַּפִּית	pref. id.)(noun fem. sing.	צפה
וְ הַצְּפַעֹת	pref. id.)(noun f., pl. of [צִפְעָה] d. 10.	צפע
הַצִּפֹּר	pref. id.)(n. com. s., pl. צִפֳּרִים (§ 20. r. 2)	צפר
הַצְפַרְדֵּעַ	pref. id.)(noun masc. sing. dec. 7b	צפר
הַצְפַרְדְּעִים	pref. id.)(id. pl., absolute state	צפר
הַצִּפְרָה	defect. for הַצִּפֹּרָה (q. v.)	צפר
וְ הַצֶּפֶת	pref. ה)(noun masc. sing.	צפת
הַצַּר / הַצַּר	pref. id.)(noun masc. sing. dec. 8 (§ 37. rem. 7)	צרר
הָצֵר	Hiph. inf. constr.	צרר
הַצֻּר	pref. ה)(for צוּר noun masc. sing. dec. 1a	צור
הֵצַר	Hiph. pret. 3 pers. sing. m. (§ 18. r. 10)	צרר
הַצְרָדָה	pref. ה)(pr. name of a place	צרד
הַצָּרָה	pref. id.)(noun fem. sing. dec. 10, fr. צַר masc., (comp. § 37. rem. 7)	צרר
וְ הַצָּרוּעַ	pref. id.)(Kal part. pass. sing. masc.	צרע
הַצָּרוֹת	pref. id.)(noun fem., pl. of צָרָה dec. 10, fr. צַר masc. (comp. § 37. rem. 7)	צרר
הַצְּרִי	pref. id.)(noun masc. sing.	צרה
הַצָּרִיחַ	pref. id.)(noun masc. sing. dec. 1a	צרה
הַצָּרִים	pref. id.)(Kal part. act. m., pl. of [צָר] d. 1a	צור
וְ הַצֹּרִים	pref. id.)(gent. noun fr. צוֹר	צור
וְ הַצָּרִים	pref. id.)(noun masc., pl. of צַר dec. 1a	צור
הַצַּרְעָה	pref. id.)(noun fem. sing.	צרע
הַצָּרְעִי	pref. id.)(gent. noun fr. צָרְעָה	צרע
הַצָּרַעַת / הַצָּרַעַת	pref. id.)(noun fem. s. (suff. צָרַעְתּוֹ) dec. 13a	צרע
הַצָּרְעָתִי	pref. id.)(gent. noun fr. צָרְעָה	צרע
הַצָּרְפִי	pref. id.)(pr. name masc.	צרף
הַצֹּרְפִים	pref. id.)(Kal part. act. m., pl. of צֹרֵף d. 7b	צרף
הַצֹּרֵר	pref. id.)(Kal part. act. sing. masc. dec. 7b	צרר
הֲצַרֹתִי	וְ Hiph. pret. 1 pers. sing. [for הַצְצַרֹתִי]	צרר
הִצַּתִּי	וְ Hiph. pret. 1 pers. sing. [for הִצְצַתִּי § 20. rem. 16, & § 25. rem.]	יצת
הַקָּאת	וְ pref. ה)(n.f.s. without the art. קָאַת, see R.	קוא
הֲקֵאתוֹ	וְ Hiph. pret. 3 pers. sing. masc., suff. 3 pers. s. m. (§ 21. r. 13); acc. shifted (§ 8. r. 7)	קוא

Hebrew	Parsing	Root
הַקָּבָב	pref. ה)(noun masc. sing.	קבב
וְ הַקָּבָה	pref. id.)(noun fem. sing. for נְקֵבָה	נקב
הַקֻּבָּה	pref. id.)(noun fem. sing.	קבב
הַקְּבוּרָה	pref. id.)(noun fem. sing. dec. 10.	קבר
הַקִּבְצוּ	Niph. imp. pl. masc.	קבץ
הַקֶּבֶר	pref. ה)(noun masc. sing. dec. 6a	קבר
הַקְּבָרִים	pref. id.)(id. pl., absolute state	קבר
הַקָּדוֹשׁ	pref. id.)(adj. masc. sing. dec. 3a	קדש
הַקְּדֹשִׁים	pref. id.)(id. pl., absolute state	קדש
הַקַּדַּחַת	pref. id.)(noun fem. sing.	קדח
הַקָּדִים	pref. id.)(noun masc. sing.	קדם
הַקָּדִימָה	pref. id.)(id. with parag. ה	קדם
הִקְדִּמַנִי	Hiph. pret. 3 pers. sing. masc. suff. 1 pers. s.	קדם
הִקְדִּישׁ	Hiph. pret. 3 pers. sing. masc.	קדש
וְ הִקְדִּישׁוּ	id. pret. 3 pers. pl. masc.	קדש
הַקֵּדֶם	pref. ה)(noun masc. sing. (pl. c. קַדְמֵי) d. 6a	קדם
הַקַּדְמוֹנָה	pref. id.)(adj. fem. sing. [from קַדְמוֹן masc.]	קדם
הַקַּדְמוֹנִי	pref. id.)(adj. masc. sing. dec. 1b	קדם
הַקַּדְמֹנִי	pref. id.)(pr. name masc.	קדם
הַקֹּדְרִים	pref. id.)(Kal part. act. m., pl. of קֹדֵר d. 7b	קדר
וְ הִקְדַּרְתִּי	Hiph. pret. 1 pers. sing.; acc. shifted by conv. וְ (§ 8. rem. 7)	קדר
הַקֹּדֶשׁ	pref. ה)(noun masc. sing. dec. 5a	קדש
הַקְדֵּשׁ	Hiph. inf. absolute (§ 11. rem. 2)	קדש
וְ הַקֹּדֶשׁ	pref. ה)(noun masc. sing. dec. 6c	קדש
הַקְּדֵשָׁה	pref. id.)(noun fem. s. d. 10, from קָדֵשׁ m.	קדש
הַקְּדֵשׁוֹת	pref. id.)(id. pl.	קדש
וְ הַקֳּדָשִׁים	pref. id.)(noun masc., pl. of קֹדֶשׁ dec. 6c	קדש
הַקֳּדָשִׁים	pref. id.)(noun masc., pl. of קֹדֶשׁ dec. 4a	קדש
וְ הִקְדַּשְׁתֶּם	Hiph. imp. sing. masc., suff. 3 pers. pl. m.	קדש
הִקְדַּשְׁנוּ	id. pret. 1 pers. pl. (comp. § 8. rem. 7)	קדש
הִקְדַּשְׁתִּי	id. pret. 1 pers. sing. ; acc. shifted by conv. וְ (comp. § 8. rem. 7)	קדש
הִקְדַּשְׁתִּיךָ	id. id., suff. 2 pers. sing. masc.	קדש
הַקְהִילוּ	Hiph. imp. pl. masc.	קהל
הִקְהִילוּ	id. pret. 3 pers. pl.	קהל
וְ הַקָּהָל	pref. ה)(noun masc. sing. dec. 4a	קהל
הַקְהֵל / הַקְהֶל־	Hiph. imp. sing. masc. (§ 11. rem. 5)	קהל
הִקְהַלְתָּ / וְ הִקְהַלְתָּ	id. pret. 2 pers. sing. masc.; acc. shifted by conv. וְ (comp. § 8. rem. 7)	קהל
הַקְּהָתִי / הַקְּהָתִי	pref. ה)(gent. noun from קְהָת or קָהָת	קהת
הַקְּהָתִים / הַקְּהָתִים	pref. id.)(pl. of the preceding	קהת

a Eze. 40. 19.   b Is. 22. 24.   c 2 Ch. 28. 22.   d Je. 8. 22.   e De. 14. 17.   f 2 Ch. 35. 3.   g Eze. 47. 8.   h Ge. 38. 21.   i De. 31. 28.
j Joel 2. 20.   k Ex. 8. 2.   l 1 Ch. 11. 15.   m Ju. 9. 49, 49.   n Pr. 25. 16.   o Le. 26. 16.   p Job 6. 16.   q Ho. 4. 14.   r Nu. 1. 18.
s 1 Sa. 14. 16.   t Eze. 7. 10.   u De. 28. 52, 52.   v Na. 1. 6.   w 2 Ki. 6. 25.   x Eze. 40. 6.   y Eze. 32. 7.   z 2 Ch. 29. 19.   Nu. 20. 8.
Ex. 2. 3.   2 Ch. 3. 15.   Ge. 42. 21.   De. 18. 3.   Job 41. 3.   1 Ki. 22. 47.   De. 4. 16.
Da. 8. 5, 21.   Est. 7. 4.   Le. 14. 3.   Nu. 25. 8.   Is. 29. 23.   2 Ch. 7. 16.   Eze. 36. 13.
Eze. 7. 7.   Zec. 8. 10.   Le. 13. 45.   2 Ch. 26. 23.   Ge. 10. 30.   Da. 9. 26.   Je. 1. 5.   Nu. 8. 9.
Is. 21. 5.   Nu. 10. 9.   Is. 65. 16.   Le. 11. 18.   2 Ki. 23. 17.

הַקּוֹהֶלֶת	pref. ה)(noun fem. sing. .	קהל
וְ" הַקּוֹל	pref. id.)(noun masc. sing. dec. 1a	קול
הַקּוֹלְךָ	pref. הַ)(id., suff. 2 pers. sing. masc.	קול
הַקּוֹלֹת	pref. id.)(id. pl. . .	קול
הַקּוֹמָה	pref. id.)(noun fem. sing. dec. 10.	קום
הַקָּמִים	pref. id.)(Kal part. act. masc., pl. of [קוֹם, for קָם § 21. rem. 2]	קום
הַקּוֹנֶה	pref. id.)(Kal part. act. sing. masc. dec. 9a	קנה
הַקּוֹסֵם	pref. id.)(Kal part. act. sing. masc. dec. 7b	קסם
וְ הַקּוֹסְמִים	pref. id.)(id. pl., absolute state .	קסם
הַקּוֹץ	pref. id.)(pr. name masc. .	קוץ
הַקּוֹצֵר	pref. id.)(Kal part. act. sing. masc. dec. 7b	קצר
הַקּוֹצְרִים	pref. id.)(id. pl., absolute state	קצר
הַקּוֹרֵא	pref. id.)(Kal part. act. sing. masc. dec. 7b	קרא
הַקּוֹרָה	pref. id.)(noun fem. sing. dec. 10.	קרה
הַקְטֵיר	] Hiph. inf. absolute	קטר
הַקְטִיר	וְ] id. pret. 3 pers. sing. masc.	קטר
הַקְטִירוֹ	] id. id., suff. 3 pers. sing. masc.	קטר
הַקְטִירוּ	וְ] id. pret. 3 pers. pl. .	קטר
הַקְטִירָם	] id. pret. 3 pers. sing. masc., suff. 3 p. pl. m.	קטר
הַקָּטֹן	pref. הַ)(adj. masc. sing. (suff. קְטַנָּם) dec. 8a (§ 37. Nos. 2 & 3), also pr. name	קטן
הַקָּטֹן	וְ] pref. id.)(adj. & subst. masc. sing. d. 3a	קטן
הַקְּטַנָּה	pref. id.)(adj. f. s. d.10, fr. קָטֹן m. (§ 37. No.3)	קטן
הַקְטַנּוֹת	pref. id.)(id. pl. . .	קטן
הַקְּטַנִּים	וְ] pref. id.)(id. pl. masc. from קָטֹן dec. 8a	קטן
הַקֹּטְפִים	pref. id.)(Kal part. act. m., pl. of [קֹטֵף] d.7b	קטף
הַקְטֵר	Hiph. imp. sing. masc.	קטר
הַקְטֹר	pref. ה)(noun sing. masc.	קטר
הַקְטֹרֶת	וְ] pref. id.)(noun fem. sing. dec. 13c .	קטר
הַקְטַרְתָּ	] Hiph. pret. 2 pers. sing. masc.; acc. shifted by conv. וְ (comp. § 8. rem. 7)	קטר
הָקֵים	Hiph. inf. absolute	קום
הָקֵים	נ] Ch. Aph. pret. 3 pers. sing. masc. (§ 47. rem. 4); וְ bef. (-:)	קום
הָקִים	Hiph. inf. constr. .	קום
הֵקִים	וְ] id. pret. 3 pers. sing. masc.	קום
הֲקִימֵהּ	Ch. Aph. pret. 3 pers. sing. masc., suff. 3 pers. sing. masc. (§ 47. rem. 4)	קום
הָקִימוּ	Hiph. imp. pl. masc.	קום
הֲקִימוֹ	id. inf. (הָקִים), suff. 3 pers. sing. masc. d. 3a	קום
הֲקִימוּ	נ] Ch. Aph. pret. 3 pers. pl. masc. (§ 47. rem. 4); וְ bef. (-:)	קום
הֵקִימוּ	וְ] Hiph. pret. 3 pers. pl.	קום
הֲקִימֹתִי	נ] id. pret. 1 p. s.; acc. shifted by וְ for conv.	קום

הֲקִימֵנִי	וְ] id. imp. sing. m., suff. 1 pers. s.; וְ bef. (-:)	קום
הֲקִימֵת	Chald. Aph. pret. 1 pers. sing. (§ 47. rem. 4, & § 54. rem. 4) .	קום
הֲקִימְתָּ	Ch. id. pret. 2 pers. sing. masc. .	קום
הֲקִימַת	Ch. id. pret. 3 pers. sing. fem. .	קום
הֻקִימַת	Ch. Hoph. pret. 3 pers. sing. fem.	קום
הֲקִימֹתִי / וַהֲקִימֹתִי	} Hiph. pret. 1 pers. sing.; acc. shifted by conv. וְ (comp. § 8. rem. 7) . {	קום
הַקֵּן	pref. ה)(pr. name of a place .	קון
הַקִּנָּה	pref. id.)(noun fem. sing. dec. 10. .	קון
הַקִּנּוֹת	pref. id.)(id. pl. . .	קון
הַקֵּינִי	pref. id.)(pr. name of a people .	קון
הַקֵּינִים	pref. id.)(gent. noun, pl. of קֵינִי, see קֵינִי	קון
הַקֵּיף	Hiph. inf. absolute .	נקף
הִקִּיף	id. pret. 3 pers. sing. masc. .	נקף
הִקִּיפָה	id. pret. 3 pers. sing. fem. .	נקף
הִקִּיפוּ	וְ] id. pret. 3 pers. pl. .	נקף
הַקִּיפֻהָ	id. imp. pl. masc., suff. 3 pers. sing. fem.	נקף
הִקִּיפֻנִי	id. pret. 3 pers. pl., suff. 1 pers. sing.	נקף
הַקִּיץ / הַקָּיִץ	} pref. ה)(noun masc. sing. dec. 6h {	קוץ
הֵקִיץ	וְ] Hiph. pret. 3 pers. sing. masc. .	קוץ
הָקִיצָה	וְ] id. imp. s. m. with paragogic ה (§11. r.5)	קוץ
הָקִיצוּ	id. imp. pl. masc. .	קוץ
הַקִּיצֹנָה	pref. ה)(adj. fem. s. [fr. קיצון for קָצֹן m.]	קצן
הֲקִיצוֹתָ	נ] Hiph pret. 2 pers. sing. m.)(וְ for וְ conv.	קוץ
הֲקִיצוֹתִי	id. pret. 1 pers. sing. (§ 21. rem. 14)	קוץ
הַקִּיצֹנָה	defect for הַקִּיצוֹנָה (q. v.) .	קצה
הֲקִיצֹתִי	Hiph. pret. 1 pers. sing. (§ 21. rem. 14) .	קוץ
הַקִּיקָיוֹן	pref. ה)(noun masc. sing. .	קיק
הַקִּיר	וְ] pref. id.)(noun masc. sing. dec. 1a .	קיר
הַקִּירוֹת	pref. id.)(id. pl. . .	קיר
הַקַּל	pref. id.)(adj. masc. sing. dec. 8a .	קלל
הָקֵל	וְ] Hiph. imp. sing. masc. .	קלל
הַקֹּל	וְ] pref. ה)(for קוֹל, noun masc. sing. d. 1a	קול
הֵקֵל	Hiph. pret. 3 pers. sing. masc. (§ 18. r. 10)	קלל
הֵקֵלּוּ	pref. ה)(Kal pret. 3 pers. pl. .	קלל
הֵקֵלּוּ	Hiph. pret. 3 pers. pl. (§ 18. rem. 10)	קלל
הַקֹּלוֹת	pref. ה)(noun masc. with pl. fem. term. from קוֹל dec. 1a .	קול
הַקַּלְיָא	pref. id.)(noun masc. sing. for קָלִי	קלה
הַקִּלְךָ	pref. ה)(noun masc. sing., suff. 2 pers. sing. masc. from קוֹל dec. 1a .	קול
הַקְּלָלָה	וְ] pref. ה)(noun fem. sing. dec. 11c	קלל
הַקְּלָלֹת	pref. id.)(id. pl., absolute state	קלל

ᵃ 1 Sa. 26. 17.   ᵇ 2 Ki. 6. 5.   ᵖ 2 Ch. 36. 18.   ᵃ Da. 3. 2, 3, 5, 7.   ᶠ Da. 3. 14.   ⁿ Jos. 6. 3.   ᶻ Am. 3. 15.   ᵈ Jon. 4. 6, 7, 9, 10.   ᵇ Ge. 8. 8.

ᵇ Ex. 20. 18.   ᶜ 1 Ki. 9. 25.   ᵍ Job 30. 4.   ʳ Da. 6. 2.   ˢ Da. 3. 12. 18.   ᵒ Job 19. 6.   ᶻ 2 Sa. 16. 2.   ᵉ Eze. 43. 8.   ᶜ Eze. 22. 7.

ᶜ Is. 10. 33.   ᵈ Le. 5. 11.   ʰ 2 Ki. 16. 15.   ⁱ Da. 7. 5.   ᵗ Da. 7. 5.   ᵖ Is. 29. 8. 8.   ᵘ Je. 46. 6.   ᶠ Ge. 9. 29, 33.

ᵈ 2 Ki. 16. 7.   ᵉ 2 Ch. 29. 7.   ⁱ Je. 44. 21.   ᵏ Je. 51. 12.   ᵛ 2 Ch. 23. 7.   ᑫ Ps. 85. 23.   ˣ Ex. 18. 22.   ᵍ 1 Sa. 17. 17.

ᵉ Jos. 13. 22.   ᶠ Le. 5. 5.   ᵏ Ex. 30. 37.   ˡ Ezr. 6. 18.   ᵐ 1 Sa. 15. 13.   ʳ Ps. 48. 13.   ʸ Pr. 6. 22.   ʰ Ge. 27. 22; 45.16. = 1 Sa. 24. 17.

ᶠ Zec. 10. 2.   ᵍ Ge. 42. 52.   ˡ Ex.29.13,18,25.   ᵐ Nu. 10. 21.   ⁿ 2 Sa. 1. 17.   ˢ Ps. 22. 17.   ᶻ Ps. 3. 6.   ⁱ Is. 8. 23.

ᵍ Je. 9. 21.   Eze. 16. 61.   ᵒ Je. 44. 25.   ᵖ Ps. 41. 11.   = 2 Ch. 35. 25.   ᵗ Ezr. 3. 13.   ᵏ De. 28. 15, 45.

Hebrew	Description	Root
הַקְלַע֫	pref. ה X for קָלַע n. m. s. d. 6a (§ 35. r. 5)	קלע
הַקְּלָעִים֫	pref. id. X noun masc. pl. [of מַקְלַע]	קלע
הַקִלְקַל	pref. id. X adj. masc. sing.	קלל
הַקֹּלֹת֫ ן	pref. ה X noun masc. with pl. fem. term. from קוֹל dec. 1a	קול
הֲקִלֹּתַ֫נִי	Hiph. pret. 2 pers. sing. masc., suff. 1 pers. s.	קלל
הָקֵם וְ	Hiph. inf. absolute, or imp. sing. masc.	קום
הָקַם֫	Hoph. pret. 3 pers. sing. masc. for הוּקַם (§ 21. rem. 24)	קום
הַקָּמָה֫	pref. ה X noun fem. sing. dec. 10.	קום
הַקֶּ֫מַח	pref. id. X noun masc. sing.	קמח
הַקָּמִים	pref. id. X Kal part. act. m., pl. of קָם dec. 1a	קום
הֲקִמֹ֫נוּ נ	Hiph. pret. 1 pers. pl. (§ 21. rem. 14); ו for ו conv.	קום
הֲקִמֹ֫תָ	id. pret. 2 pers. sing. masc.; acc. shifted by ו for ו conv. (§ 8. rem. 7)	קום
הֲקִמֹתוֹ֫ וְ	id. id., suff. 2 pers. sing. masc. (§ 21. rem. 14); ו for ו conv.	קום
הֲקִמֹ֫תִי / הֲקִמֹתִ֫י	id. pret. 1 pers. sing.; acc. shifted by ו for ו conv. (comp. § 8. rem. 7)	קום
הַקִּנְאָה	pref. ה X noun fem. sing. dec. 12b	קנא
הַקְּנָאֹת	pref. id. X id. pl., absolute state	קנא
הַקָּנֶה	pref. id. X noun masc. sing. dec. 9b	קנה
הַקֹּנֶה֫	pref. id. X Kal part. act. sing. masc. dec. 9a	קנה
הַקֵּנִי֫	pref. id. X pr. name of a people	קנז
הַקֵּינִי֫	pref. id. X pr. name of a people	קון
הַקָּנִים	pref. id. X noun masc., pl. of קָנֶה dec. 9b	קנה
הִקְנַ֫נִי	Hiph. pret. 3 pers. s. m. [הִקְנָה], suff. 1 pers. s.	קנה
הַקֶּ֫סֶם	pref. ה X noun masc. sing. dec. 6.	קסם
הַקֹּסְמִים֫ וְ	pref. id. X Kal part. act. masc., pl. of קֹסֵם dec. 7b	קסם
הַקֶּ֫סֶת	pref. id. X noun fem. sing.	קשה
הַקַּעֲרָה	pref. id. X noun fem. sing., constr. קַעֲרַת dec. 11c (§ 42. rem. 1 & 3)	קער
הַקְּעָרֹת	pref. id. X id. pl., absolute state	קער
הַקֵּף	Hiph. inf. absolute	נקף
הַקֹּצְפִים֫	pref. ה X Kal part. act. m., pl. [קֹצֵא] dec. 7b	קפא
הֲקַצְפְּתֶם֫ וְ	Hiph. pret. 2 pers. pl. masc.	נקף
הַקֵּץ	pref. ה	קץ
הַקֵּ֫ץ	pref. ה noun masc. sing. dec. 8b	קץ
הַקָּצֶה	pref. ה X noun masc. sing. dec. 9b	קצה
הִקְצָה	Hiph. pret. 3 pers. pl.	קצה
הַקְּצוּבוֹת	pref. ה X Kal part. p. pl. fem. [fr. קָצוּב m.]	קצב
הַקָּצֹ֫ר	pref. ה X Kal inf. absolute	קצר
הַקְּצָוֹת	pref. ה X noun fem. pl. absolute from קָצֶה comp. מָנֶה (§ 45)	קצה

Hebrew	Description	Root
הַקְצוֹת	Hiph. inf. construct	קצה
הַקָּצִיר	pref. ה X noun masc. sing. dec. 3a	קצר
הַקֶּ֫צֶף	pref. id. X noun m. s. dec. 6 (suff. קִצְפְּךָ, קֶצֶף)	קצף
הִקְצַ֫פְתָּ	Hiph. pret. 2 pers. sing. masc.	קצף
הִקְצַפְתֶּ֫ם	id pret. 2 pers. pl. masc.	קצף
הַקָּצַר֫	pref. ה X Kal pret. 3 pers. sing. masc.	קצר
הַקֹּצְרִים	pref. ה X Kal part. act. m., pl. of קוֹצֵר d. 7b	קצר
הִקְצַרְתְּ	Hiph. pret. 2 pers. sing. masc.	קצר
הַקֵּר	Hiph. imp. sing. m. [for הוֹקֵר, comp. הַשְׁמַע]	יקר
הַקֹּרֵא֫	pref. ה X noun masc. sing.	קרא
הַקֹּרְאִים	pref. id. X Kal part. p. m., pl. of קָרוּא d. 3a	קרא
הַקָּרֵב	pref. id. X adj. masc. sing. dec. 5a	קרב
הַקָּרֵב֫ ן	pref. id. X adj. masc. sing. dec. 3a	קרב
הַקָּרֵב֫ וְ	pref. id. X noun m. s. (suff. קָרְבִּי) dec. 6a	קרב
הַקְרֵב וְ	Hiph. imp. sing. masc.	קרב
הִקְרִיב	id. pret. 3 pers. sing. masc. for הִקְרִיב	קרב
הַקְּרֵבָה֫	pref. ה X adj. fem. s. dec. 10, from קָרוֹב m.	קרב
הַקְרְבוּהִי	Chald. Aph. pret. 3 pers. pl. masc., suff. 3 pers. sing. masc. (§ 47. rem. 4)	קרב
הַקְּרֹבוֹת וְ	pref. ה X adj. fem., pl. of קְרוֹבָה dec. 10, from קָרוֹב masc.	קרב
הַקְּרֵבִים	pref. id. X adj. masc., pl. of קָרֵב dec. 5a	קרב
הַקְּרֹבִים	pref. id. X adj. masc., pl. of קָרוֹב dec. 3a	קרב
הַקָּרְבָּן	pref. id. X noun masc. sing. see קָרְבָּן	קרב
הִקְרַבְתָּ ן	Hiph. pret. 2 pers. sing. masc.; acc. shifted by conv. ו (§ 8. rem. 7)	קרב
הִקְרַבְתִּיו ן	id. pret. 1 pers. sing., suff. 3 pers. s. m.	קרב
הִקְרַבְתָּם ן	id. pret. 2 pers. s. m., suff. 3 pers. pl. m.	קרב
הִקְרַבְתֶּם ן	id. pret. 2 pers. pl. masc.	קרב
הַקַּרְדֻּמוֹת	pref. ה X noun masc., with pl. fem. term. from [קַרְדֹּם] dec. 8c (§ 37. No. 3)	קרדם
הַקְרֵה	Hiph. imp. sing. masc.	קרה
הַקְרֵה	Hiph. pret. 3 p. s. f. (as if fr. קֵרָה § 21. r. 22)	קור
הַקְרֵה	Hiph. pret. 3 pers. sing. masc.	קרה
הַקֹּרְאִים	pref. ה X Kal part. p. m., pl. of [קָרוּא] d. 3a	קרא
הַקָּרוֹב ן	pref. id. X adj. masc. sing. dec. 3a	קרב
הַקְּרוֹבָה֫	pref. id. X id. fem. dec. 10.	קרב
הַקְּרוֹבִים	pref. id. X id. pl. masc. dec. 3a	קרב
הַקֹּרוֹת	pref. id. X noun fem., pl. of קוֹרָה dec. 10.	קרה
הַקָּרֵחַ / הַקֵּרֵחַ	pref. ה X noun masc. sing. (§ 35. rem. 2)	קרח
הַקָּרְחִי	pref. id. X patronym. of קֹרַח	קרח
הַקָּרְחִים	pref. id. X pl. of the preceding	קרח
הַקְּרִיאָה	pref. id. X noun fem. sing.	קרא
הַקְרִיב	Hiph. inf. constr. dec. 1b	קרב
הִקְרִיב וְ	id. pret. 3 pers. sing. masc.	קרב

a 1 Sa. 25. 29.   h 1 Ki. 17. 14, 16.   p Zec. 13. 5.   w Jos. 6. 11.   d Ex. 38. 5.   k Pr. 25. 17.   q De. 21. 3.   w Eze. 43. 24.   c Le. 21. 3.
b 2 Ki. 3. 25.   i Mi. 5. 4.   q Ezs. 21. 27.   x Zep. 1. 12.   e Le. 14. 43.   l 1 Sa. 26. 20.   r Da. 7. 13.   x Ju. 9. 48.   d 2 Ch. 3. 7.
c Ex. 9. 34.   k Ps. 89. 44.   r Mi. 3. 7.   y 2 Ki. 11. 8.   f De. 9. 7.   m Est. 1. 14.   s Eze. 22. 5.   y Ge. 24. 12.   e Job 38. 22.
d 2 Sa. 19. 44.   l Ge. 19. 2.   s Eze. 13. 9.   z Job 16. 3.   g De. 9. 8.   n Le. 1. 13.   t Je. 48. 24.   z Je. 6. 7.   f Eze. 1. 14.
e Ge. 38. 8.   m Eze. 8. 3, 5.   t Eze. 9. 11.   a Le. 14. 41.   h Mi. 2. 7.   o Le. 9. 2.   u Eze. 40. 43.   a Ge. 27. 20.   g Jon. 3. 2.
f 2 Sa. 23. 1.   n Nu. 5. 25, 29.   u Nu. 7. 85.   b Ca. 4. 2.   i Ps. 89. 46.   p Nu. 7. 19.   v Je. 30. 21.   b Eze. 6. 12.   h Nu. 9. 7.
g Ex. 22. 5.   o Le. 25. 28.   v Nu. 4. 7.   c Is. 50. 2.

הַקְרִיבָהּ	id. id., suff. 3 pers. sing. fem.	קרב
הִקְרִיבָה	id. pret. 3 pers. sing. fem.	קרב
הַקְרִיבֵהוּ	id. imp. sing. masc., suff. 3 pers. sing. masc.	קרב
הַקְרִיבוֹ	id. inf., suff. 3 pers. sing. masc. dec. 1b	קרב
הַקְרִיבוּ	Chald. Aph. pret. 3 pers. pl. m. (§ 47. r. 4)	קרב
הִקְרִיבוּ	Hiph. pret. 3 pers. s. m., suff. 3 pers. s. m.	קרב
הִקְרִיבוּ	id. pret. 3 pers. pl.	קרב
הִקְרִיבָם	id. id., suff. 3 pers. pl. masc. (for ן fem. § 2. rem. 5)	קרב
הַקְרִיָּה	pref. ה × noun fem. sing. dec. 10.	קרה
הַקְּרִיּוֹת	pref. id. × pr. name of a city	קרה
הִקְרִיחוּ	Hiph. pret. 3 pers. pl.	קרה
הִקְרִיתֶם	Hiph. pret. 2 pers. pl. masc.	קרה
הַקֶּרֶן	pref. הַ × noun fem. s. (suff. קַרְנִי) dec. 6a	קרן
הַקְּרָנוֹת	pref. id. × id. pl. absolute state	קרן
הַקְּרָנַיִם	} pref. id. × id. du. [as if from קֶרֶן]	קרן
הַקְּרָסִים	pref. id. × noun m. pl., c. קַרְסֵי fr. קֶרֶס d. 6a	קרס
הַקַּרְקַע	} pref. ה art. × noun masc. sing.	קרקע
הַקַּרְקָעָה	pref. id. × pr. name (קַרְקַע) with parag. ה	קרקע
הַקֶּרֶשׁ	} pref. ה × noun masc. sing. (suff. קַרְשֵׁךְ) dec. 6a (§ 35. rem. 2)	קרש
הַקְּרָשִׁים	pref. id. × id. pl., absolute state	קרש
הַקֹּרֵת	pref. id. × Kal part. act. fem. pl. [of קֹרָה, from קֹרָה masc.]	קרה
הַקֹּשְׁאִים	pref. id. × noun masc., pl. of קֹשְׁא dec. 1b	קשא
הַקְשֵׁב	Hiph. imp. sing. masc.	קשב
הִקְשַׁבְתָּ	id. pret. 2 pers. sing. masc.	קשב
הִקְשַׁבְתִּי	id. pret. 1 pers. sing.	קשב
הַקָּשָׁה	pref. ה × adj., fem. of the following, dec. 11a	קשה
הַקָּשֶׁה	pref. id. × adj. masc. sing. dec. 9b	קשה
הִקְשָׁה	Hiph. pret. 3 pers. sing. masc.	קשה
הִקְשׁוּ	id. pret. 3 pers. pl.	קשה
הַקְּשֻׁוֹת	pref. ה × n. fem., pl. of קְשָׂוָה dec. 12a	קשה
הִקְשִׁיב	pref. id. × Hiph. pret. 3 pers. sing. masc.	קשב
הַקְשִׁיבָה	id. imp. s. m. with parag. ה (§ 11. rem. 5)	קשב
הַקְשִׁיבוּ	id. imp. pl. masc.	קשב
הִקְשִׁיבוּ	id. pret. 3 pers. pl.	קשב
הַקְשִׁיבִי	id. imp. sing. fem.	קשב
הִקְשִׁיחַ	Hiph. pret. 3 pers. sing. masc.	קשח
הִקְשִׁיתָ	Hiph. pret. 2 pers. sing. masc.	קשה
הַקֶּשֶׁר	pref. ה × noun m. sing. (suff. קִשְׁרוֹ) dec. 6c	קשר
הַקְּשֻׁרִים	pref. id. × Kal part. p.m., pl. of קָשׁוּר d. 3a	קשר
הַקֹּשְׁרִים	pref. id. × id. part.act.m., pl. of קֹשֵׁר dec. 7b	קשר
הַקְּשָׁרִים	pref. id. × noun masc., pl. of קֶשֶׁר dec. 1b	קשר

הַקֶּשֶׁת	pref. id. × noun com. sing. (with suff. קַשְׁתִּי comp. dec. 13a)	קוש
וְהַקְּשָׁתוֹת	pref. id. × id. pl. abs., constr. ת treated as if radical	קוש
הַר / וְהַר	noun masc. sing. dec. 8 (§ 37. rem. 7), and pr. name in compos. הַר הָרָם	הרר
הֹר	pr. name of a mountain	הרר
הָרָא / וְ	pr. name of a region	הרר
הָרָאה / וְ	pref. הָ for הַ × noun fem. sing.	ראה
הָרְאָה / וְ	Hoph. pret. 3 pers. sing. masc.	ראה
הָרֹאֶה	pref. הָ f. הַ; pref. הַ } Kal part. act. sing. masc. dec. 9a	ראה
וְהֶרְאָה	Hiph. pret. 3 p. s. m. [for הִרְ § 11. rem. 1]	ראה
הֵרָאֶה	Niph. imp. sing. masc.	ראה
וְהָראוּבֵנִי	pref. הָ for הַ × patronym. רְאוּבֵן	ראה
הָרֹאוֹת	pref. id. × Kal part. act. fem., pl. of רֹאָה dec. 10, from רֹאֶה masc.	ראה
הֵרָאוֹת	Niph. inf. constr. dec. 1b	ראה
הַרְאוֹתְכָה	Hiph. inf. (הַרְאוֹת), suff. 2 pers. sing. masc. (§ 3. rem. 2, comp. § 2. rem. 2)	ראה
הַרְאֹתָם	id. with suff. 3 pers. masc. pl.	ראה
הָרְאִיּוֹת	pref. הָ for הַ × Kal part. p. fem. pl. [of רָאוּי from רָאָה] masc.	ראה
הָרֹאִים	pref. id. × id. part. act. m., pl. of רֹאֶה dec. 9a	ראה
הַרְאִינִי	Hiph. imp. sing. fem., suff. 1 pers. sing.	ראה
הָרִאישׁוֹן	Kh. הָרִאשׁוֹן, pref. הָ for הַ × adj. masc. sing.; K. הָרִאשׁוֹן (q. v.)	ראש
הָרָאִיתָ	pref. הָ × Kal pret. 2 pers. sing. masc.	ראה
הָרְאֵיתָ	Hoph. pret. 2 pers. sing. masc.	ראה
הֶרְאִיתָ	Hiph. pret. 2 pers. sing. masc. (§ 24. rem. 14)	ראה
וְהִרְאֵיתִי	id. pret. 1 pers. sing.; acc. shifted by conv. ו (comp. § 8. rem. 7)	ראה
הֶרְאִיתִיךָ	id. id., suff. 2 p. s. m. (§ 11. r. 1, & § 24. r. 14)	ראה
הִרְאִיתִים	id. id., suff. 3 pers. pl. masc. (§ 24. rem. 14)	ראה
הַרְאִיתֶם	pref. ה interr. for הֲ × Kal pret. 2 pers. pl. masc. (for הַרְאִיתֶם, comp. הַכְּתֹנֶת)	ראה
הִרְאִיתֶם	Hiph. pret. 1 pers. sing., suff. 3 pers. pl. masc. (§ 24. rem. 14) for תִים	ראה
הִרְאִיתָנוּ	id. pret. 2 pers. sing. masc., suff., Kh. תָנוּ 1 pers. pl., K. תָנִי 1 pers. sing.	ראה
הִרְאִיתַנִי	id. pret. 2 p. s. m., suff. 1 p. s. (§ 24. rem. 14)	ראה
הֶרְאָךָ	id. pret. 3 pers. sing. masc., suff. 2 pers. sing. masc. (§ 11. rem. 1, & § 24. rem. 21)	ראה
הֶרְאָם	id. id., suff. 3 pers. pl. masc. (§ 11. rem. 1)	ראה
הִרְאַנוּ	id. id., suff. 1 pers. pl.	ראה
הַרְאֵנוּ	id. imp. sing. masc., suff. 1 pers. pl.	ראה

a Le. 2. 8.   h Eze. 27. 31.   p Ex. 26. 11, 33.   v Is. 48. 18.   c Job 39. 16.   h De. 14. 13.   p Eze. 40. 4.   v Ps. 60. 5.   ♦ 2 Ki. 20. 15.
b Ju. 5. 25.   i Nu. 35. 11.   q 1 Ki. 7. 7.   w Je. 8. 6.   d 2 Ki. 2. 10.   i Le. 13. 49.   q Jos. 5. 6.   w Na. 3. 5.   ♠ Ps. 71. 20.
c Nu. 15. 27.   k Da. 3. 8.   r 1 Ki. 6. 16.   x 2 Sa. 15. 12.   e Ex. 37. 16.   k Eze. 8. 6.   r Est. 2. 9.   x De. 34. 4.   ♥ Je. 11. 18.
d Mal. 1. 8.   l Da. 8. 21.   s Ge. 42. 29.   y 1 Ch. 28. 17.   f Is. 30. 7.   l Ec. 2. 24.   s Ca. 2. 14.   y Is. 39. 4.   ♣ De. 4. 36.
e Tc. 7. 16.   m Da. 8. 20.   t Nu. 11. 5.   z Ge. 30. 42.   g Ps 86. 6.   m 1 Sa. 18. 1.   t Is. 39. 4.   z 1 Sa. 10. 24; 17. 25.
f Ezr. 6. 17.   n Da. 8. 6.   u Job 33. 31.   a Is. 3. 20.   n Job 15. 7.   u 2 Sa. 11. 2.
g Nu. 17. 2.   o Da. 8. 3.   b Ne. 4. 10.   o Ex. 26. 30.

הַרְאֵנִי	id. id., suff. 1 pers. sing.	ראה
הַרְאֵנִי	id. pret. 3 pers. sing. masc. (§ 11. rem. 1)	ראה
הֵרָאַנִי	suff. 1 pers. sing. (§ 2. rem. 1)	ראה
הָרֹאשׁ	pref. הָ f. הַ X noun masc. sing.; irr., pl.	ראשׁ
הָרֹאשׁ	pref. הַ (§ 45) רָאשִׁים	
הָרֹאשׁ	pref. הָ for הַ X Kal part. masc. sing. Kh. (§ 21. rem. 1); K. רֹשׁ id. dec. 1a	רושׁ
הָרָאשִׁים	pref. id. X noun m., pl. of רֹאשׁ irr. (§ 45)	ראשׁ
הָרֹאשָׁה	pref. id. X noun fem. sing.	ראשׁ
הָרִאשׁוֹן	pref. id. X adj. masc. sing. dec. 1b	ראשׁ
הָרִאשׁוֹנָה	pref. id. X id. fem. dec. 10.	ראשׁ
הָרִאשׁוֹנִים	pref. id. X id. pl. masc.	ראשׁ
הָרִאשֹׁן	defect. for הָרִאשׁוֹן (q. v.)	ראשׁ
הָרִאשֹׁנָה	defect. for הָרִאשׁוֹנָה (q. v.)	ראשׁ
הָרִאשֹׁנוֹת	pref. הָ for הַ X adj. fem., pl. of רִאשׁוֹנָה dec. 10 from רִאשׁוֹן masc.	ראשׁ
הָרִאשֹׁנִים	pref. id. X id. masc., pl. of רִאשׁוֹן dec. 1b	ראשׁ
הָרִאשֹׁנִית	pref. id. X adj. fem. sing. [from רִאשֹׁנִי masc.]	ראשׁ
הָרֹאֹת	pref. id. X Kal part. act. fem., pl. of רֹאָה, from רֹאָה masc.	ראה
הִרְאֵתָ	Hoph. pret. 2 pers. sing. masc.	ראה
הֵרָאֹתוֹ	Niph. inf. (הֵרָאוֹת), suff. 3 pers. s. m. dec. 1 b	ראה
הֵרָאֹתְךָ	Hiph. inf. (הַרְאוֹת), suff. 2 pers. s. m. dec. 1 b	ראה
הָרָב הָרָב	pref. הָ for הַ X adj. masc. sing. dec. 8d	רבב
הָרָב	pref. הַ X noun masc. sing. dec. 8 c	רבב
הָרָב	pref. id. X Kal inf. abs. R. רוּב see	ריב
הַרְבֵּ	Hiph. imp. s. m. apoc. from הַרְבָּה (§ 24. r.17)	רבה
הָרְבָּה	pref. הָ for הַ X pr. name of a place	רבב
הַרְבֵּה הַרְבֵּה	Hiph. inf. abs. (§ 24. rem. 15)	רבה
הַרְבֵּה	Kh. הַרְבֵּה q. v., K. הֶרֶב (q. v.)	רבה
הִרְבָּה	Hiph. pret 3 pers. sing. masc.	רבה
הַרְבּוּ	id. imp. pl. masc.	רבה
הִרְבּוּ	id. pret. 3 pers. pl.	רבה
הַרְבּוֹת	id. inf. constr. (§ 24. rem. 15)	רבה
הַרְבִּי	id. imp. sing. fem.	רבה
הָרַבִּים	pref. הָ for הַ X adj. m., pl. of רַב d. 8d	רבב
הִרְבִּינוּ	Hiph. pret. 1 pers. pl. (§ 24. rem. 14)	רבה
הָרְבִיעַ	pref. הָ for הַ X adj. ord. m. s. [fr. אַרְבַּע, רָבַע]	רבע
הָרְבִיעָה הָרְבִיעִת	pref. id. X id. fem.	רבע
הָרַבִּית	pref. id. X pr. name of a place	רבב
הִרְבִּיתָ	Hiph. pret. 2 pers. sing. fem.	רבה
הִרְבִּיתָ	id. pret. 2 pers. sing. masc. (§ 24. r. 14)	רבה
הִרְבֵּיתִי	id. pret. 1 pers. sing.	רבה

הִרְבֵּיתִי	id. id.; acc. shifted by conv. וְ (§ 8. r. 7, & § 11. rem. 9)	רבה
הִרְבִּיתָךְ	id. id., suff. 2 pers. sing. m. (§ 24. rem. 14)	רבה
הִרְבִּיתֶם	id. pret. 2 pers. pl. masc.	רבה
הַרְבְּלָה	pref. הָ for הַ X pr. name of a place	רבל
הִרְבְּךָ	Hiph. pret.3 pers. sing. masc., suff. 2 pers. sing. masc. (§ 24. rem. 20)	רבה
הָרְבִעִי	pref. הָ for הַ for רְבִיעִי, adj. ord. masc. sing. [from אַרְבַּע, רָבַע]	רבע
הָרְבֵעִית	pref. id. X id. fem.	רבע
הָרֹבֵץ	pref. id. X Kal part. act. sing. masc. dec. 7b	רבץ
הִרְבָּתָה	Hiph. pret. 3 pers. sing. fem.	רבה
הִרְבִּתִים	id. pret. 1 pers. sing. with suff. 3 pers. masc. pl. (§ 24. rem. 14)	רבה

הָרֹג וְ to kill, slay, in general, man, beast or plant; by the sword, pestilence, viper, or grief. Constr. with acc., לְ, בְּ. Niph. to be killed, slain. Pu. id. הֶרֶג m. a slaying, slaughter.

הֲרֵגָה f. id.; צֹאן הַהֲרֵגָה sheep for the slaughter.

הָרַג	Kal pret. 3 p. s. m. for הָרַג (comp. § 8. r. 7)	הרג
הָרֹג	id. inf. absolute	הרג
הֲרֹג	id. inf. constr.	הרג
הֶרֶג	וְ noun masc. sing.	הרג
הֹרַג	Pual pret. 3 pers. sing. masc. [for הָרַג]	הרג
הֹרֵג	Kal part. act. sing. masc. dec. 7b	הרג
הֲרֵגָה	noun fem. sing.	הרג
הָרְגוּ הָרְגוּ	Kal pret. 3 pers. pl. (§ 8. rem. 7)	הרג
הֲרָגוּ	id. pret. 3 pers. sing. m., suff. 3 pers. s. m.	הרג
הִרְגוּ הִרְגוּ	id. imp. pl. masc. (§ 8. rem. 12)	הרג
הֲרָגֻם	וְ id. pret. 3 pers. pl., suff. 3 pers. pl. masc.; וְ bef. (–)	הרג
הֲרָגֻנִי	וְ id. id., suff. 1 pers. sing.; וְ id.	הרג
הַרְגִּזוּ	Ch. Aph. pret. 3 pers. pl. masc. (§ 47. r. 4)	רגז
הִרְגַּזְתַּנִי	Hiph. pret. 2 pers. sing. m., suff. 1 pers. s.	רגז
הֲרֻגֵי	Kal part. p. pl. constr. m. from [הָרוּג] d. 3.	הרג
הֲרֻגָיו	id. pl., suff. 3 pers. sing. masc.	הרג
הִרְגִּיז	וְ Hiph. pret. 3 pers. sing. masc.	רגז
הֲרֻגִים	Kal part. pass. masc., pl. of [הָרוּג] dec. 3.	הרג
הֹרְגִים	id. part. act. masc., pl. of הֹרֵג dec. 7b	הרג
הַרְגִּיעַ	Hiph. inf. constr. (§ 11. rem. 4)	רגע
הִרְגִּיעָה	id. pret. 3 pers. sing. fem.	רגע
הָרְגֶךָ	Kal part. act., suff. 2 pers. sing. masc. [for הָרֶגְךָ] from הֹרֵג dec. 7b	הרג

ᵃ Ex. 33. 18.   ᵍ Zec. 4. 7.   ⁿ Nu. 35. 8.   ˢ Ps. 51. 4.   • Ge. 48. 4.   ᵖ Ju. 8. 20.   ᵘ Nu. 31. 17.   ʸ 1 Sa. 28. 15.   ᵃ Is. 14. 19.
ᵇ Ese. 11. 25.   ʰ Ex. 12. 15.   ° Job 11. 2.   ᵗ Is. 23. 16.   ᶠ Ese. 11. 6.   ᑫ Est. 9. 5.   ᵛ Ex. 32. 27.   ² Je. 18. 21.   ᵇ 2 Ki. 11. 2.
ᶜ Is. 13. 15, 18.   ⁱ Je. 25. 1.   ᵖ Ju. 11. 25;   ᵘ Is. 8. 7.   ᵍ De. 30. 5.   ʳ Is. 27. 7.   ʷ Jos. 9. 26.   ᵃ Is. 27. 7.   ° Je. 50. 34.
ᵈ 2 Sa. 3. 8.   ᵏ De. 4. 25.   Job 40. 2.   ᵛ Ezr. 10. 13.   ʰ Je. 29. 3.   ˢ Je. 12. 3.   ˣ 1 Ch. 7. 21.   ᵇ Ju. 9. 26.   ᵈ Is. 34. 14.
ᵉ 2 Sa. 12. 4.   ˡ Le. 13. 7.   ᑫ Ju. 20. 38.   ʳ Nu. 3. 16.   ⁱ 1 Sa. 1. 12.   ᵗ Ge. 12. 12.   ʸ Ge. 20. 11.   ᶜ Je. 50. 34.   ᵉ Eze. 28. 9.
ᶠ Ju. 9. 44.   ᵐ Ex. 9. 16.   ʳ Ge. 22. 17.   ʳ 1 Ch. 4. 10.   ᵏ Je. 30. 19.   ⁿ Ge. 4. 25.   ᵗ Ezr 5. 12.

הָרְגָלִים[a]	pref. הָ for הַ)(noun fem., du. of [רֶגֶל]	רגל
הָרְגָלַיִם[b]	dec. 6 a	
הֲרָגֻנוּ[c]	Kal pret. 3 pers. sing. m., suff. 3 pers. pl. m.	הרג
הֲרַגְנוּהוּ	Kal pret. 1 p. pl., suff. 3 p. s. m.; ן for ו conv.	הרג
הֲרַגְנֻם[d]	id. id., suff. 3 pers. pl. masc.; ן id.	הרג
הֲרַגְנִי	id. pret. 3 pers. sing. masc., suff. 1 pers. sing. (§ 2. rem. 1); ן id.	הרג
הֲרָגֻנִי	id. pret. 3 pers. pl., suff. 1 pers. sing.; ן id.	הרג
הָרְגֵנִי[e]	id. imp. sing. m., suff. 1 pers. s. (§ 8. r. 12)	הרג
הֵרָגְעִי[f]	Niph. imp. sing. fem.	רגע
תַרְגִּשׁוּ[g]	Ch. Aph. pret. 3 pers. pl. masc. (§ 47. r. 4)	רגשׁ
הָרַגְתָּ	Kal pret. 2 pers. sing. masc. (§ 8. rem. 7)	הרג
הָרָגְתָּ		
הָרַגְתָּ[h]	ו id. id.; acc. shifted by conv. ו	הרג
הֲרַגְתְּהוּ	id. pret. 3 pers. sing. fem., suff. 3 pers. sing. masc. [for עֲגָתְהוּ § 16. rem. 3]	הרג
הָרַגְתִּי	id. pret. 1 pers. sing.; acc. shifted by conv. ו (§ 8. rem. 7)	הרג
הָרָגְתִּי[i]		
הֲרַגְתִּיךָ[j]	id. id., suff. 2 pers. sing. masc.	הרג
הֲרַגְתִּיךְ[k]	id. id., suff. 2 pers. sing. fem.	הרג
הֲרַגְתִּים[l]	id. id., suff. 3 pers. pl. masc.	הרג
הֲרַגְתָּם	ו id. pret. 3 pers. sing. fem., suff. 3 pers. pl. masc.; ו for ן conv.	הרג
הֲרַגְתֶּם[m]	id. pret. 2 pers. pl. masc.	הרג
הֲרַגְתָּנִי[n]	id. pret. 2 p. s. m., suff. 1 p. s. [for תָּנִי § 2. r. 1]	הרג
הָרֹדֵד	pref. הָ for הַ)(Kal part. act. sing. masc.	רדד
הָרְדִידִים	ו pref. id.)(noun masc., pl. of [רָדִיד] d. 3 a	רדד
הָרֹדִים	pref. id.)(Kal part. act. m., pl of רָדָה d. 9 a	רדה
הִרְדִּיפֻהוּ	Hiph. pret. 3 pers. pl., suff. 3 pers. sing. m.	רדף
הָרֹדְפִים	pref. הָ for הַ)(Kal part. a. m., pl. of רֹדֵף d. 7 b	רדף
הָרָה	ו fut. תַּהֲרֶה apoc. תַּהַר—I. to conceive, become pregnant, const. with לְ to or by whom.—II. to conceive in mind, devise. Pu. הֹרָה to be conceived, Job 3. 3. Po. to devise, Is. 59. 13.	
	הָרָה adj. only fem. הָרָה, constr. הֲרַת, pl. with suff. הָרוֹתֶיהָ (§ 42. rem. 2) pregnant, with child.	
	הָרִי id. only pl. fem. הָרִיוֹתַי Ho. 14. 1.	
	הֵרָיוֹן masc. conception, pregnancy.	
	הֵרוֹן dec. 1 b (§ 30. 2 note) id. Ge. 3. 16.	
הָרָה	adj. fem. s. comp. § 42. r. 2 [from הָרֶה m.]	הרה
הָרֹה	Kal inf. absolute	הרה
הָרָה[o]	noun masc. (הַר) with loc. ה [dag. f. impl. for הָרָה, § 37. r. 7, comp. § 42. No 3 note]	הרר
הֹרָה[p]	Pual pret. 3 pers. sing. masc. [for הֹרְרָה for הֹרֲרָה]	הרה

הֲרִיבֻנִי	Hiph. pret. 3 pers. pl., suff. 1 pers. sing.	רהב
הָרְהָטִים	pref. הָ for הַ)(noun masc., pl. of [רַהַט] dec. 6 d	רהט
הַרְהֹרִין	ו Ch. noun masc., pl. of [הַרְהֹר] dec. 1.	הרר
הָרֹאָה	pref. הָ)(Kal part. act. sing. masc. dec. 9 a	ראה
הָרֹה	Kal inf. absolute for הָרֹה (§ 24. rem. 2)	הרה
הָרוֹ	Poel inf. absolute (§ 6. No. 1, & § 24. r. 2)	הרה
הָרוֹן	ו Kal inf. absolute	הרג
הֲרוּגֶיהָ	Kal part. p. pl., suff. 3 pers. sing. fem. fr. [הָרוֹג] dec. 3 a	הרג
הֲרוּגִים	id. pl., absolute state	הרג
הָרוֹדֵף[q]	pref. הָ for הַ)(Kal part. act. sing. m. d. 7 b	רדף
הָרְוָה[r]	pref. id.)(adj. fem. sing. fr. רָוֶה masc.	רוה
הִרְוָה[s]	Hiph. pret. 3 pers. sing. masc.	רוה
הָרוּחַ	ו pref. הָ for הַ)(noun com. sing. dec. 1 a	רוח
הָרְוָחָה[t]	pref. id.)(noun fem. sing., (suff. רַוְחָתִי) dec. 11 c. (§ 42. rem. 1)	רוח
הָרְוָחֹת	pref. id.)(noun com. with pl. fem. term. fr. רֶוַח dec. 1 a	רוח
הִרְוֵיתִי	Hiph. pret. 1 pers. sing.	רוה
הִרְוִיתַנִי	id. pret. 2 pers. sing. masc. (§ 24. rem. 14), suff. 1 pers. sing. (§ 2. rem. 1)	רוה
הִרְוַנִי	id. pret. 3 pers. sing. masc. (הִרְוָה), suff. 1 pers. sing. (§ 24. rem. 21)	רוה
הָרֹפֵא[u]	pref. הָ for הַ)(Kal part. act. s. m. d. 7 b	רפא
הָרֹצֵחַ[v]	pref. id.)(Kal part. act. sing. masc.	רצח
הָרוֹת	adj. fem., pl. of הָרָה, dec. 11 a (§ 42. rem. 2) fr. הָרֶה masc.	הרה
הָרֹחַב[w]	ו pref. הָ for הַ)(noun masc. sing. dec. 6 f	רחב
הַרְחֵב[x]	Hiph. imp. sing. masc. (§ 11. rem. 2)	רחב
הִרְחִיב[y]	Hiph. pret. 3 pers. sing. masc. for הִרְחִיב	רחב
הָרְחָבָה	ו pref. הָ for הַ)(adj. fem., constr. רַחֲבַת dec. 11 c (§ 42. rem. 1) from רָחָב masc.	רחב
הָרְחֹבוֹת[z]	pref. id.)(noun fem., pl. of רְחוֹב dec. 1 a	רחב
הַרְחֹבִי	defect. for הַרְחִיבִי (q. v.)	רחב
הִרְחַבְתָּ	Hiph. pret. 2 pers. sing. masc.	רחב
הִרְחַבְתְּ	id. pret. 2 pers. sing. fem.	רחב
הִרְחַבְתִּי	ו id. pret. 1 pers. sing.)(acc. shifted by conv. ו (§ 8. rem. 7)	רחב
הָרְחוֹב	pref. הָ for הַ)(noun fem. sing. dec. 1 a	רחב
הָרָחֹק[a]	pref. id.)(adj. masc. sing. dec. 3 a	רחק
הָרְחֹקִים[b]	ו pref. id.)(id. pl., absolute state	רחק
הָרוּחֹת	noun com., pl. of רוּחַ, (for רוּחוֹת)	רוח
הַרְחִיב	Hiph. inf. constr.	רחב
הִרְחִיב	id. pret. 3 pers. sing. masc.	רחב
הִרְחִיבָה	id. pret. 3 pers. sing. fem.	רחב

a Is. 7. 20.	d Je. 47. 6.	g Ho. 6. 5.	k Ps. 7. 15.	o 2 Sa. 15. 27.	r Is. 55. 10.	u Jos. 20. 6.	x Pr. 26. 13.	a Eze. 6. 12.
b 2 Ki. 9. 35.	e Da. 6. 7, 12, 16.	h Am. 9. 4.	l Job 15. 35	p Is. 59. 4.	s Ex. 8. 11.	v Am. 1. 13.	y Mi. 1. 16.	b Is. 46. 12.
c Ps. 78. 34.	f Le. 26. 18.	i Ju. 8. 18.	m Ge. 14. 10.	q Is. 31. 25.	t Eze. 42. 2.	w Ps. 4. 2.	z Is. 9. 20.	
Ju. 16. 2.	Ju. 9. 54.	1 Sa. 24. 19.	Job 3. 3.	Is. 43. 24.	Ps. 81. 11.	Is. 57. 8.	Je. 49. 36.	
Ne. 4. 5.	Ex. 22. 23.	Ps. 144. 2.	Ca. 6. 5.	La. 3. 15.	Is. 30. 23.	Ex. 34. 24.	Am. 1. 13.	
1 Ki. 12. 27.	1 Sa. 24. 12.	Is. 3. 23.	Ex. 2. 16.	Jos. 8. 20.	Ps. 147. 3.	Eze. 23. 32.	Ne. 8. 1, 3.	Is. 5. 14.
Nu. 11. 15.	Nu. 22. 29.	Ju. 20. 43.	Da. 4. 2.	De. 29. 18.				

הְרַחִיבוּ	id. pret. 3 pers. **pl.**	רחב
הַרְחִיבִי	id. imp. sing. fem.	רחב
הָרְחִים	pref. הַ for הָ)(noun masc. dual	רח
הִרְחִיק	Hiph. pret. 3 pers. sing. masc.	רחק
הַרְחִיקֶהָ	id. imp. sing. masc., suff. 3 pers. sing. masc.	רחק
הִרְחִיקוּ	id. pret. 3 pers. pl.	רחק
הַרְחִיקָם	id. inf., suff. 3 pers. pl. masc. dec. 1 b	רחק
הָרְחֵלִים	pref. הַ for הָ)(noun fem., with pl. masc. term. fr. רָחֵל dec. 5a	רחל
הָרַחַם	pref. id.)(noun masc. sing.	רחם
הָרַחֲמָה	pref. id.)(id. with parag. ה	רחם
הָרַחֲמִים	pref. id.)(noun masc. pl. [for רְחָמִים see § 35. rem. 16] from רַחַם dec. 6d	רחם
הָרַחֲצָה	pref. id.)(noun fem. sing.	רחץ
הַרְחֵק / הַרְחֵק	Hiph. inf. absolute (§11.r.2), or imp. s. m.	רחק
הָרְחֵקוֹת	)(pref. הַ for הָ)(adj. fem., pl. of רְחֹקָה dec. 10, fr. רָחֹק masc.	רחק
הָרְחֹקִים	ן pref. id.)(id. masc., pl. of רָחֹק dec. 3a	רחק
הָרְחֹקֹת	defect. see הָרְחֹקוֹת	רחק
הִרְחַקְתָּ	Hiph. pret. 2 pers. sing. masc.	רחק
הִרְחַקְתִּים	id. pret. 1 pers. sing., suff. 3 pers. pl. masc.	רחק
הָרַי / הָרֵי	noun masc. pl., suff. 1 pers. sing. fr. הַר dec. 8. (§ 37. rem. 7)	הרר
הָרֵי	id. pl., constr. state	הרר
הָרִיב	pref. הַ for הָ)(noun masc. sing. dec. 1a	רוב
הָרָיו	noun masc. pl., suff. 3 pers. sing. masc. fr. הַר dec. 8. (§ 37. rem. 7)	הרר
הֵרָיוֹן	noun masc. sing.	הרה
הֵרָיוֹתָיו	ן adj. fem. pl., suff. 3 pers. sing. masc. fr. [חָרִי] masc.	הרה
הָרִיחוֹ	נ Hiph. inf. (הָרִיחַ), suff. 3 pers. sing. masc. dec. 3a; נ before (־ַ).	רוח
הָרִים	noun masc. pl. [for הַהָרִים] fr. הַר dec. 8. (§ 37. rem. 7)	הרר
הָרִים	)(ן Hiph. inf. constr. used also as an abs.	רום
הֵרִים	)(ן id. pret. 3 pers. sing.	רום
הָרִים	Kh. הָרִים q. v.; K. הוּרַם Hoph. pret. 3 p.s.m.	רום
הָרִימָה	Hiph. imp. s. m. with parag. ה (§ 11. r. 5)	רום
הָרִימוּ	)(ן id. imp. pl. masc.	רום
הֵרִימוּ	id. pret. 3 pers. pl.	רום
הֲרִימוֹת / הֲרִימֹתָ	id. pret. 2 pers. sing. masc. (§ 8. rem. 5)	רום
הֲרִימוֹתִי	id. pret. 1 pers. sing.	רום
הָרִימִי	id. imp. sing. fem.	רום
הֲרִימֹתִי	id. pret. 1 pers. sing.	רום
הֲרִימֹתִיךָ	id. id., suff. 2 pers. sing. masc.	רום
הֲרִינוּ	Kal pret. 1 pers. pl.	הרה
הָרִיעוּ	)(ן Hiph. imp. pl. masc.	רוע
הָרִיעוּ	id. pret. 3 pers. pl.	רוע
הָרִיעִי	id. imp. sing. fem.	רוע
הֲרִיעֹתֶם	ן id. pret. 2 pers. pl. masc.; ן for ו conv.	רוע
הָרִיפוֹת	)(pref. הַ for הָ)(noun fem. pl.	רוף
הָרִיקוּ	ן Hiph. pret. 3 pers. pl.	רוק
הֲרִיקֹתִי	ן id. pret. 1 pers. sing.; acc. shifted by ו for ו conv. (§ 8. rem. 7, & § 11. rem. 5)	רוק
הֹרִישׁ	Hiph. pret. 3 pers. sing. masc. for הוֹרִישׁ	ירשׁ
הָרִית	ן Kal pret. 2 pers. sing. fem.	הרה
הָרִיתִי	id. pret. 1 pers sing.	הרה
הָרַךְ	pref. הַ for הָ)(adj. masc. sing. dec. 8d	רכך
הֵרַךְ	Hiph. pret. 3 pers. sing. masc. (§ 18. rem. 10)	רכך
הָרֶכֶב / הָרָכֶב	pref. הַ for הָ)(noun masc. sing. dec. 6 (§ 35. rem. 2, but with suff. (רִכְבִּי)	רכב
הַרְכֵּב	Hiph. imp. sing. masc.	רכב
הָרֹכְבִים	pref. הַ for הָ)(gent. noun from רֵכָב	רכב
הִרְכַּבְתָּ	Hiph. pret. 2 pers. sing. masc.	רכב
הִרְכַּבְתִּיךָ	ן id. pret. 1 pers. sing., suff. 2 pers. sing. m.	רכב
הִרְכַּבְתֶּם	ן id. pret. 2 pers. pl. masc.	רכב
הָרַכָּה	pref. הַ for הָ)(adj. fem. s. dec. 10, from רַךְ m.	רכך
הִרְכִּבֶהָ	ן Hiph. pret. 3 pers. sing., suff. 3 pers. sing. m.	רכב
הָרֹלְכִים	)(ן pref. הַ for הָ)(Kal part. act. masc., pl. of רֹכֵל dec. 7b	יכל
הָרְכוּשׁ	pref. id.)(noun masc. sing. dec. 1 b	רכש
הָרְכֶם	noun masc. sing., suff. 2 pers. pl. masc. from הַר dec. 8. (§ 37. rem. 7)	הרר
הָרְכָסִים	ן pref. הַ art. for הָ)(n. m. pl. of [רָכָס] d. 6	רכס
הָרְכָשׁ	pref. הַ for הָ)(noun masc. sing.	רכשׁ
הָרְכֻשׁ	ן pref. id.)(noun m. sing. for רְכוּשׁ dec. 1a	רכשׁ

הָרָם   Root not used; *to be high*, cogn. אָרַם, רוּם.

הָרֹם (*height*; or *mountaineer*, from הֹר with the ending ם־) pr. name of a king of Canaan, 1 Ch. 4. 8.

הָרָם (*high*) pr. name masc. 1 Ch. 4. 8.

הַרְמוֹן   masc. *palace*, Am. 4. 3.

הָרֵם	pr. name, see בֵּית הָרָם.	בית
הָרֵם / הָרֵם	Hiph. imp. sing. masc., acc. drawn back before monos. (לְךָ) comp. § 11. rem. 5	רום
הָרָם	pr. name masc.	הרם
הָרָם	pr. name masc.	הרם
הָרָמָה	ן pref. הַ for הָ)(pr. name of a place	רום
הָרָמָה	pref. id.)(Kal part. act. sing., fem. of רָם	רום
הָרְמוּ	ן Niph. imp. pl. masc. [for הֵרֹמּוּ]	רמם

a Ps. 25. 17. | e Le. 11. 18. | i Ps. 88. 9, 19. | o Ps. 75. 7. | s Ps. 89. 20. | w Zec. 9. 9. | A De. 28. 54. | E De. 28. 56. | I Ge. 14. 16.
b Is. 54. 2. | f De. 14. 17. | k Eze. 11. 16. | p Eze. 21. 31. | t Is. 40. 9, 9. | x Jos. 6. 10. | B Job 23. 16. | F Est. 6. 9. | K Ge. 14. 21.
c Ex. 11. 5. | g Job 13. 21. | l Is. 65. 9. | q Da. 8. 11. | u Pr. 27. 22. | C 2 Ki. 13. 16. | G Ne. 3. 31, 32. | L 2 Ki. 6. 7.
d Job 11. 14. | h Eze. 48. 24. | m Ruth 4. 13. | r Ps. 74. 3. | v Ge. 39. 15. | z 2 Ch. 28. 3. | D Ps. 66. 12. | H Ps. 11. 1. | M Eze. 17. 22.
Joel 4. 6. | Eze. 22. 5. | Ho. 14. 1. | Jos. 4. 5. | Is. 26. 18. | Joel 2. 1. | Ju. 13. 3. | 1 Ki. 1. 33. | Est. 8. 10, 14.
Ca. 6. 6. | De. 20. 15. | Is. 11. 3. | Is. 37. 23. | Nu. 11. 12. | Nu. 17. 10.

הַרְמוֹן	וְ/ pref. הַ for ·הַ)(noun masc. sing. dec. 1 b, also pr. name	רמם
הַרְמוֹנִים	וְ/ pref. id.)(id. pl., absolute state	רמן
וְהָרְמָחִים	וְ/ pref. id.)(noun masc., pl. of רֹמַח dec. 6 (§ 35. rem. 9 & 5)	רמח
הָרָמִים	pref. id.)(Kal part. act. masc., pl. of רָם dec. 1 a	רום
הָרְמִּים	pref. id.)(gent. noun, pl. of אֲרַמִּים from אֲרָם	ארם
וְהָרְמָכִים	pref. id.)(noun masc., pl. of [רַמָּךְ] dec. 1 b	רמך
הָרִמֹּנִים	noun masc., pl. of רִמּוֹן dec. 1 b	רמם
הָרְמֶשׁ	pref. הַ for ·הַ)(noun masc. sing.	רמשׁ
הָרֹמֵשׂ	pref. id.)(Kal part. act. sing. masc.	רמשׂ
הָרֹמֶשֶׂת	pref. id.)(id. fem.	רמשׂ
הָרָמָתָה	pref. id.)(pr. name of a place (רָמָה) with parag. ה	רום
הָרָמָתִי	pref. id.)(gent. n. from the preceding	רום
וַהֲרִמֹתָ	וַ/ Hiph. pret. 2 pers. sing. masc.; acc. shifted by וַ for וְ conv.	רום
הֲרִימֹתִי	id. pret. 1 pers. sing.	רום
הֲרִימֹתִיךָ	id. id., suff. 2 pers. sing. masc.	רום
וַהֲרִמֹתֶם	וַ/ id. pret. 2 pers. pl. masc.; וַ for וְ conv.	רום
הָרָמָתַיִם	pref. הַ for ·הַ)(pr. name of a place	רום
הָרָן	/הַ pr. name m. (and in compos. with בֵּית q.v.)	הרר
הָרִנָּה	pref. הַ for ·הַ)(noun fem. sing. dec. 10	רנן
הֹרַנִי	Hiph. pret. 3 pers. sing. masc. [הֹרָה], suff. 1 pers. sing. (§ 24. rem. 21, & § 25. No. 2 e)	ירה
הֹרֵנִי	id. imp. sing. masc., suff. 1 pers. sing.	ירה
הַרְנִינוּ	וְ/ Hiph. imp. pl. masc.	רנן
הָרְנְךָ	/הַ noun m. s., suff. 2 p. s. f. from [הָרֹן] dec. 1 b	הרה

הָרַס fut. יַהֲרֹס ,יֶהֱרֹס (§ 13. rem. 4)—I. *to break, pull down, destroy.*—II. intrans. *to break through,* with לְ Ex. 19. 21, 24. Niph. *to be broken, torn down, destroyed.* Pi. *to break, pull down, destroy.*

הֶרֶס masc. *destruction,* Is. 19. 18.
הֲרִיסָה fem. dec. 10, *a ruin,* Am. 9. 11.
הֲרִיסוּת fem. dec. 1 b, *destruction,* Is. 49. 19.

הָרַס	Kal pret. 3 pers. sing. m. for הָרַס (§ 8. rem. 7)	הרס
הָרֹס	Piel inf. absolute	הרס
הֲרֹס	Kal imp. sing. masc. [for הֲרֹס § 8. rem. 18]	הרס
הֹרֵס	Kal part. act. sing. masc.	הרס
הָרְסָהּ	/הַ id. imp. sing. masc., suff. 3 pers. sing. fem.	הרס
הָרְסוּ הָרָסוּ	/הַ id. pret. 3 pers. pl. (§ 8. rem. 7)	הרס
הָרַסְתָּ	/הַ id. pret. 2 pers. sing. masc.; acc. shifted by conv. וְ (§ 8. rem. 7)	הרס
הָרַסְתִּי	/הַ id. pret. 1 pers. sing.; acc. id.	הרס

הֲרִסֹתָיו	/הַ n. fem. pl., suff. 3 p.s.m. from [הֲרִיסָה] d. 10	הרס
הֲרִסֻתֵךְ	noun fem. sing., suff. 2 pers. sing. fem. from [הֲרִיסוּת] dec. 1 b	הרס
הָרֵעַ הָרֵעַ	וְ/ pref. הַ for ·הַ)(noun masc. sing. dec. 8 (§ 37. rem. 7)	רעע
הָרֵעַ	/וְ Hiph. inf. abs. and constr.	רעע
הָרֵעַ	pref. הַ for ·הַ)(noun masc. sing. dec. 1 a	רעה
הֵרַע	/וְ id. pret. 3 pers. sing. masc. (§ 18. rem. 10)	רעע
הָרָעָב	/וְ pref. הַ for ·הַ)(noun masc. sing. dec. 4 a	רעב
הָרָעֵב	pref. id.)(adj. masc. sing. dec. 5 a	רעב
הָרָעָה	pref. id.)(noun fem. sing. dec. 10 [for רַעָה], from רַע masc. (§ 37. rem. 7)	רעע
הָרֹעָה	pref. id.)(Kal part. act. sing. masc. dec. 9 a	רעה
הָרֹעָה	Kh. הָרֹעָה q. v., K. הָרַע (q. v.)	רעע
הֵרֵעוּ	Hiph. pret. 3 pers. pl.	רעע
הֵרֵעוּ	id., as if from רוע, see	רוע
הָרָעוֹת	/וְ pref. הַ for ·הַ)(noun fem., pl. of רָעָה dec. 10 [for רַעָה], from רַע masc. (§ 37. rem. 7)	רעע
הֲרֵעֹתָ	Hiph. pret. 2 pers. sing. masc. [for הֲרֵעֹתָ]	רעע
הֲרֵעֹתִי	id. pret. 1 pers. sing.	רעע
הָרָעִים	pref. הַ for ·הַ)(adj. masc., pl. [for רַעִים from רַע dec. 8 (§ 37. rem. 7)	רעע
הָרֹעִים	/וְ pref. id.)(Kal part. act. m., pl. of רֹעֶה dec. 9 a	רעה
הַרְעִים	Hiph. pret. 3 pers. sing. masc.	רעם
הַרְעֵם	Hiph. imp. pl. masc.	רעף
הֶרְעִלוּ	Hoph. pret. 3 p. pl. [for הָרְעֲלוּ] comp. § 8. r. 7]	רעל
וְהַרְעָלוֹת	/וְ pref. הַ for ·הַ)(noun masc. with pl. fem. term. from רַעַל dec. 6 d	רעל
הַרְעִמָהּ	Hiph. inf. [הַרְעִים], suff. 3 pers. sing. fem. [for הַרְעִימָהּ]	רעם
הָרָעֵשׁ הָרַעַשׁ	/וְ pref. הַ for ·הַ)(noun masc. sing. (§ 35. rem. 2)	רעשׁ
הִרְעַשְׁתָּה	Hiph. pret. 2 pers. s. m. (comp. § 8. rem. 5)	רעשׁ
הִרְעַשְׁתִּי הִרְעַשְׁתִּי	/וְ id. pret. 1 pers. sing.; acc. shifted by conv. וְ (§ 8. rem. 7)	רעשׁ
הָרֵעֹת	/וְ defect. for הָרֵעוֹת (q. v.)	רעע
הֲרֵעֹתָ הֲרֵעֹתָ	/וְ Hiph. pret. 2 pers. sing. masc. [for הֲרֵעֹתָ for תָה see § 8. rem. 5]	רעע
הֲרֵעֹתִי	id. pret. 1 pers. sing.	רעע
הֲרֵעֹתֶם	id. pret. 2 pers. pl. masc.	רעע
וַהֲרֵעֹתֶם	/וַ Hiph. pret. 2 pers. pl. masc. (§ 21. rem. 14); וַ for וְ conv.	רוע
הָרֵף	Hiph. imp. s. m., apoc. for הַרְפֵּה (§ 24. r. 17)	רפה
הָרָפָא	pref. הַ for ·הַ)(pr. name masc.	רפא
הָרֹפֵא	pref. id.)(Kal part. act. sing. masc. dec. 7 b	רפא
הֵרָפֵא	Niph. inf. construct	רפא

a Hag. 2. 19.   c Ge. 14. 22.   e Ge. 3. 16.   f 2 Sa. 11. 25.   h Ps. 51. 6.   j Je. 18. 10.   m Ps. 29. 3.   o Am. 1. 1.   r Nu. 11. 11.
b 1 Ki. 7. 20.   1 Ki. 14. 7.   1 Ki. 19. 10, 14.   1 Ch. 21. 17.   1 Ki. 17. 20.   Is. 45. 8.   Ex. 5. 22.
Je. 46. 4.   d Nu. 18. 26.   Is. 14. 17.   Ju. 6. 25.   Pr. 17. 17; 19. 6.   k 1 Ki. 17. 20.   Na. 2. 4.   p Nu. 10. 9.
Ne. 4. 10.   Job 30. 19.   Ex. 23. 24.   Am. 9. 11.   Jos. 24. 20.   l 1 Ch. 21. 17.   Is. 3. 19.   q Hag. 2. 7.   Ps. 103. 3.
Est. 8. 10.   Job 34. 32.   Ps. 58. 7.   Is. 49. 19.   Je. 2. 8.   1 Sa. 1. 6.   Ge. 41. 27.   Je. 15. 18.
Nu. 31. 26.   Pa. 22. 11.   Je. 45. 4.   2 Sa. 14. 17.   i Je. 29. 8.

הָרְפָאִים ׀ pref. הָ for הַ)(gent. noun, pl. of   רפא

הָרְפָּאִים pref. id.)(noun masc. pl. [of רָפָא]   רפה

הָרֹפְאִים ׀ pref. id.)(Kal part. act. m., pl. of רֹפֵא dec. 7 b   רפא

הָרָפָה pref. id.)(pr. name masc. · רפה

הָרָפֶה pref. הָ)(adj. masc. sing. dec. 9 b   רפה

הַרְפֵּה Hiph. imp. sing. masc. · רפה

הַרְפּוּ id. imp. pl. masc. · · רפה

הָרְפוֹת defect. for הָרִי (q. v.) · רוף

הָרֵץ ׀ Hiph. imp. sing. masc. · רוץ

הָרָצוּץ pref. הָ for הַ)(Kal part. p. sing. m. dec. 3 a   רצץ

הָרֹצֵחַ pref. id.)(Kal part. act. sing. masc.   רצח

הֲרַצְחְתָּ pref. הֲ)(Kal pret. 2 pers. sing. masc.   רצח

הָרָצִים ׀ pref. הָ for הַ)(Kal part. act. masc., pl.
of רָץ dec. 1 a · · רוץ

הָרְצֵצֶה ׀ pref. id.)(noun com. s. (constr. רְצֶפֶת)   רצף

הָרְצָצוֹת pref. id.)(Kal part. act. fem. pl. [of
רֹצְצָה or רְצֶצֶת] · · רצץ

הָרָצָה ׀ Hiph. pret. 3 pers. s. fem. (§ 24. rem. 14)   רצה

הָרֵק ׀ Hiph. imp. sing. masc.   רוק

הֲרַק pref. הֲ)(adv. · · רקק

הָרַקּוֹן ׀ pref. הָ for הַ)(pr. name of a place   רקק

הָרַקּוֹת pref. id.)(adj. fem., pl. [רַקָּה] d. 10, fr. רַק m.   רקק

הָרֵקוֹת pref. id.)(adj. fem., pl. of רֵקָה dec. 10, from
רֵק [or רִיק] masc. · רוק

הָרֶקַח pref. id.)(noun masc. sing.   רקח

הַרְקַח ׀ Hiph. inf. absolute, or imp.   רקח

הָרַקָּחִים pref. הָ for הַ)(n. m., pl. of [רַקָּח] dec. 1 b   רקח

הָרֵקִים pref. id.)(adj. m., pl. of רֵק [or רִיק] dec. 1 a   רוק

הָרָקִיעַ pref. id.)(noun masc. sing. dec. 3 a   רקע

הָרִקְמָה pref. id.)(noun fem. sing. dec. 12 b   רקם

[הָרָר , הֶרֶר] masc. with suff. הֲרָרִי , הַרְרִי ; pl. c. הַרְרֵי ,
with suff. הֲרָרֶיהָ (comp. dec. 4 & 6) mountain,
mostly poetic.

הָרָרִי , הַרְרִי (mountaineer) gent. noun of the
inhabitants of the hill-country of Ephraim or
Judah, 2 Sa. 23. 11, 33; also written אֲרָרִי in
verse 33.

הַר masc. with the art. הָהָר , with ה local
הָרָה , הֶרָה , pl. הָרִים (§ 37. rem. 7)—I. mountain.
—II. mountainous tract.—III. pr. name הַר חֶרֶס
(mount of the sun) a city of the Samaritans, Ju.
1. 35.

הֹר הוֹר pr. name—I. of a mountain in Edom
where Aaron was buried.—II. of a mountain in
Palestine, Nu. 34. 7, 8.

הָרָא (mountainous) pr. name of a region in
Syria, 1 Ch. 5. 26.

הָרָן (mountaineer) pr. name.—I. of a brother of
Abraham, Ge. 11. 26, 27.—II. 1 Ch. 23. 9 ; see
also בֵּית

הַרְאֵל (mount of God) put for the altar of
burnt-offering, Eze. 43. 15, elsewhere אֲרִיאֵל , see
under אָרָה

הָרַר Root not used; Chald. Palp. to think.

הִרְהֹר Chald. masc. thought, Da. 4. 2.

הָרָרִי pr. name of a people · הרר

הֲרָרִי noun m. s. with suff. 1 pers. s. fr. [הָרָר] d. 4 c   הרר

הַרְרֵי noun masc. pl. constr. fr. [הֶרֶר] dec. 6 a   הרר

הָרְשׁוּמִים pref. הָ for הַ)(Kal part. p. masc. sing.   רשם

הִרְשִׁיעַ Hiph. pret. 3 pers. sing. masc.   רשע

הִרְשִׁיעוּ ׀ id. pret. 3 pers. pl.   רשע

הָרָשָׁע ׀ pref. הָ for הַ)(adj. masc. sing. dec. 4 a   רשע

הָרֶשַׁע ׀ pref. id.)(noun masc. sing. dec. 6 (§ 35.
הָרֶשַׁע rem. 2 & 5, yet with suff. רִשְׁעִי)   רשע

הָרְשָׁעָה pref. id.)(adj. fem. sing. from רָשָׁע masc.   רשע

הָרִשְׁעָה pref. id.)(noun fem. sing. dec. 10.   רשע

הָרְשָׁעִים ׀ pref. id.)(adj. masc. pl. of רָשָׁע dec. 4 a   רשע

הִרְשַׁעְנוּ ׀ Hiph. pret. 1 pers. pl. (comp. § 8. rem. 7)   רשע

הָרֶשֶׁת ׀ pref. הָ for הַ)(noun fem. sing. dec. 13 a   ישת
הָרֶשֶׁת (comp. § 35. r. 2, yet with suff. רִשְׁתִּי)

הָרַת adj. fem. sing. constr. of הָרָה dec. 11 a (but
see § 42. rem. 2) from הָרֶה masc.   הרה

הָרָתָה Kal pret. 3 pers. s. fem. [for הָרְתָה § 8. r. 7]   הרה

הֶרְתּוֹק ׀ pref. הָ for הַ)(noun masc. sing. dec. 1 b   רתק

הֹרֹתֵיהֶם ׀ adj. fem. pl., suff. 3 pers. pl. masc. from
הָרֶה (§ 42. rem. 2) from הָרֶה masc.   הרה

הֹרֵתִיךָ Hiph. pret. 1 pers. sing., suff. 2 pers. s. m.   ירה

הַשָּׂא Hiph. inf. absolute   נשא

הַשֹּׁאֲבֹת ׀ pref. הַ)(Kal part. act. fem. pl. [of שֹׁאֲבָה
or שֹׁאֶבֶת] from שָׁאַב masc.   שאב

הַשָּׁאוּלִי pref. id.)(patronym. of שָׁאוּל   שאל

הַשֹּׁאֲמוֹת ׀ pref. id.)(Kal part. act. fem. & masc. pl.
הַשֹּׁאֲטִים [of שָׁאַט שָׁאֲטָה § 21. rem. 1]   שוט

הִשְׁאִיר ׀ Hiph. pret. 3 pers. sing. masc.   שאר

הִשְׁאִירוּ id. pret. 3 pers. pl.   שאר

הַשְּׁאֵלָה pref. הַ)(noun fem. sing., (suff. שְׁאֵלָתִי &
שְׁאֵ) dec. 10 & 11 (§ 42. rem. 4)   שאל

הַשֹּׁאֲלִים pref. id.)(Kal part. act. m., pl. of שֹׁאֵל d. 7 b   שאל

הַשָּׁאַלְתִּי pref. הַ)(Kal pret. 1 pers. sing.   שאל

ᵃ Job 26.5.   ʰ 1 Sa. 17.17.   ˡ Le. 26.34.   ᵍ Ca. 8.2.   ˢ Je. 17.3.   ᵉ Eze. 3.18, 19.   ᵏ Ex. 27.4, 5   ⁿ Pr. 4.11.   ᵗ Joel 2.14.
ᵇ Ge. 50.2, 2.   ⁱ 1 Ki. 21.19.   ᵐ Ps. 35.3.   ʳ Eze. 24.18.   ʸ Da. 10.21.   Zec. 5.8.   Je. 20.17.   Je. 4.10.   Jos. 11.14.
ᶜ Nu. 13.18.   2 Ki. 11.13.   Nu. 12.2.   Ne. 3.8.   2 Ch. 20.35.   Is. 57.20.   Ge. 24.11.   1 Sa. 2.20.
ᵈ Ps. 46.11.   Eze.40.18.   Ge. 41.20, 27.   Eze. 18.21.   Da. 9.5.   Eze. 7.23.   Eze. 16.37.   1 Sa. 8.10.
ᵉ 2 Sa. 7.19.   Am. 1.   Ge. 41.27.   Eze. 17.3.   Ec. 3.16.   Ps. 1.17.   2 Ki. 8.12.   Eze. 28, 24, 26.   2 Ki. 4.28.

Hebrew	Description	Root
הִשְׁאִלְתִּיהוּ	Hiph. pret. 1 pers. sing., suff. 3 pers. sing. masc. (§ 11. rem. 1)	שאל
הַשַּׁאֲנַנִּים	pref. הַ ‖ adj. masc., pl. of שַׁאֲנָן dec. 8a	שאן
הַשֹּׁאֲפִים	pref. id. ‖ Kal part. act. m. pl. of שׁוֹאֵף d. 7b	שאף
הַשְּׁאֵרִית	pref. id. ‖ noun fem. sing. dec. 1b	שאר
הִשְׁאַרְנוּ	Hiph. pret. 1 pers. pl.	שאר
הִשְׁאַרְתִּי	וְ Hiph. pret. 1 pers. sing.; acc. shifted by conv. (comp. § 8. rem. 7)	שאר
הַשְׂאֵת	pref. הַ ‖ noun fem. sing.	שאה
הִשֵּׁאתָ	Hiph. pret. 2 pers. sing. masc. (§ 25, No. 2a)	נשא
הֻשַׁב	in pause for הֻשַׁב (q. v.)	שוב
הֵשַׁב	pref. הַ ‖ Kal pret. 3 pers. sing. masc.	שוב
הָשֵׁב	וְ Hiph. inf. absolute, or imp. sing. masc.	שוב
הֲשָׁבָה	pref. הַ relat. art. ‖ Kal pret. 3 pers. sing. fem.	שוב
הֲשִׁיבֵהוּ	Hiph. imp. sing. masc., suff. 3 pers. sing. m.	שוב
הֵשִׁבוּ	id. pret. 3 pers. pl., for הֵשִׁיבוּ	שוב
הֲשִׁבוּם	‖ id. id., suff. 3 pers. pl. masc.; וְ bef. (־)	שוב
הָשָׁבוּעַ	pref. הָ ‖ noun masc. sing., irr. constr. שְׁבוּעַ, pl. שְׁבֻעִים (§ 32. rem. 1)	שבע
הַשְּׁבוּעָה	pref. id. ‖ noun fem. sing. dec. 10.	שבע
הַשִׁבוֹתִים	וַ Hiph. pret. 1 pers. sing., suff. 3 pers. pl. masc.; וְ for וַ conv.	שוב
וְהַשִׁבוֹתִים	וְ Hiph. pret. 1 pers. sing., suff. 3 pers. pl. masc., after the analogy of עֹ, for הוֹשַׁבְתִּים	ישב
הַשֵּׁבֶט	pref. הַ ‖ noun com. sing. [for שֵׁבֶט § 35. rem. 2] see under שֵׁבֶט	שבט
הַשֵּׁבֶט	וֹ pref. id. ‖ noun com. sing., dec. 6b	שבט
הַשְּׁבָטִים	pref. id. ‖ id. pl., absolute state	שבט
הַשְּׁבִי / הַשֶּׁבִי	pref. id. ‖ noun masc. sing. dec. 6i (§ 35. rem. 14).	שבה
הַשִּׁבְיָה	pref. id. ‖ noun fem. sing.	שבה
הַשָּׁבִים	pref. id. ‖ Kal part. act. m., pl. of שָׁב d. 1a	שוב
הַשְּׁבִיסִים	וְ pref. id. ‖ noun masc. pl. fr. [שָׁבִים] d. 3a	שבס
הִשְׁבִּיעַ	וְ Hiph. pret. 3 pers. sing. masc.	שבע
הִשְׁבִּיעַ	וְוְ Hiph. pret. 3 pers. sing. masc.	שבע
הִשְׁבִּיעוּ	Hiph. pret. 3 pers. s. m., suff. 3 pers. s. m.	שבע
הַשְּׁבִיעִי	pref. הַ ‖ adj. ord. masc. sing. from שֶׁבַע	שבע
הַשְּׁבִיעִית	pref. id. ‖ fem. of the preceding	שבע
הִשְׁבִּיעֶךָ	Hiph. pret. 3 pers. sing. masc., suff. 2 pers. sing. masc. [for בִּיעֲךָ]	שבע
הִשְׁבִּיעַנִי	id., suff. 1 pers. sing.	שבע
הִשְׁבִּיעַנִי	Hiph. pret. 3 pers. s. masc., suff. 1 pers. s.	שבע
הַשְּׁבִיעַת	defect. for עִית (q. v.)	שבע
הִשְׁבִּית	וְ Hiph. pret. 3 pers. sing. masc.	שבת
הַשְׁבִּיתוּ	id. imp. pl. masc.	שבת
הִשְׁבִּיתוּ	וְ id. pret. 3 pers. pl.	שבת
הַשְׁבָּכָה	pref. הַ ‖ noun fem. sing. (no vowel change)	שבך
הַשְּׂבָכוֹת	וְ pref. id. ‖ id. pl., absolute state	שבך
הַשִּׁבֳּלִים	pref. id. ‖ noun fem. with pl. masc. term. from שִׁבֹּלֶת (§ 44. No. 2)	שבל
הֲשִׁיבֵנִי	וְ Hiph. imp. sing. masc., suff. 1 pers. sing.; וְ bef. (־)	שוב
הֱשִׁיבַנִי	וַ id. pret. 3 pers. sing. masc., suff. 1 pers. sing.; וְ for וַ conv.	שוב
הַשֶּׁבַע	וְ pref. הַ ‖ noun masc. sing.	שבע
הַשְׁבֵּעַ	Hiph. inf. absolute	שבע
הַשֶּׁבַע	pref. הַ ‖ num. card. fem. sing.	שבע
הִשָּׁבֵעַ	וְ Niph. inf. absolute	שבע
הִשָּׁבַע	id. inf. constr.	שבע
הַשְּׁבֻעָה	וְ pref. הַ ‖ noun fem. sing. dec. 10.	שבע
הַשִּׁבְעָה	pref. id. ‖ num. card., masc. of שֶׁבַע fem.	שבע
הִשָּׁבְעָה	Niph. imp. s.m. with parag. הָ (comp. § 8. r. 11)	שבע
הִשָּׁבְעוּ	id. imp. pl. masc.	שבע
הַשָּׁבֻעוֹת	pref. הַ ‖ noun masc., with pl. fem. term. abs., from שָׁבוּעַ, (§ 32. rem. 1)	שבע
הַשְּׁבִעִי	defect. for הַשְּׁבִיעִי q. v.	שבע
הַשְּׁבֻעִים	pref. הַ ‖ n. m., pl. of שָׁבוּעַ, c. שְׁבֻעֵי (§32. r. 1)	שבע
הַשְּׁבֻעִים	‖ pref. id. ‖ num. card. com. gen., pl. of שֶׁבַע f.	שבע
הִשְׁבַּעְתְּ	Hiph. pret. 2 pers. sing. fem.	שבע
הִשְׁבַּעְתִּי	וְ id. pret. 1 pers. sing.; acc. shifted by conv. וְ (comp. § 8. rem. 7)	שבע
הִשְׁבַּעְתִּי	Hiph. pret. 1 pers. sing.	שבע
הִשְׁבַּעְתִּיךָ	id. id., suff. 2 pers. sing. masc.	שבע
הִשְׁבַּעְתָּנוּ	id. pret. 2 pers. sing. masc., suff. 1 pers. pl.	שבע
הַשְׁבֵּץ	pref. הַ ‖ noun masc. sing.	שבץ
הַשֶּׁבֶר / הַשֵּׁבֶר	pref. id. ‖ noun masc. sing., dec. 6a (§ 35. rem. 2, yet with suff. שִׁבְרוֹ)	שבר
הַשְּׁבָרִים	pref. id. ‖ id. pl., absolute state	שבר
הָשְׁבַּרְתִּי	Hoph. pret. 1 pers. sing.	שבר
הַשַּׁבָּת	וְ pref. הַ ‖ noun com. sing. dec. 8a, but pl. שַׁבָּתוֹת, c. שַׁבְּתוֹת	שבת
הִשְׁבַּתָּ	Hiph. pret. 2 p. s. m. [for הִשְׁבַּתְתָּ § 25 rem.]	שבת
הַשֶּׁבֶת	pref. הַ ‖ n. f. s. for שֶׁבֶת (comp. § 35. r. 2)	ישב
הִשְׁבַּתָּ	וַ Hiph. pret. 2 pers. s. m. (§ 21. r. 13 & 14); acc. shifted by וְ for וַ conv. (comp. § 8. r. 7)	שוב
הֲשִׁבֹתוֹ	וַ id., suff. 3 pers. sing. masc.; וְ for וַ conv.	שוב
הַשַּׁבָּתוֹת	pref. ה ‖ noun com., pl. abs. see הַשַּׁבָּת	שבת
הֲשִׁבֹתִי	וַ Hiph. pret. 1 pers. sing.; acc. shifted by וְ for וַ conv. (comp. § 8. rem. 7)	שוב
הִשְׁבַּתִּי	Hiph. pret. 1 p. s. [for הִשְׁבַּתְתִּי §25. r.]; acc. shifted by conv. וְ (comp. § 8. r. 7)	שבת
הִשְׁבַּתִּיךָ	וַ Hiph. pret. 1 pers. sing., suff. 2 pers. s. m.	שוב

a 1 Sa. 1. 28.   f 1 Sa. 6. 21.   m Is. 3. 18.   r La. 3. 15.   v Je. 31. 18.   z Ec. 5. 11.   a Je. 15. 9.   g 1 Ki. 2. 42.   n Jos. 7. 5.
b De. 2. 34.   g Da. 9. 27.   n Ps. 107. 9.   s Ex. 37. 14.   w Ge. 37. 14.   a Je. 7. 9.   b Da. 9. 26.   h 2 Sa. 1. 9.   o Je. 8. 21.
c Je. 4. 10.   h Da. 9. 27.   o Is. 58. 11.   t Ruth 4. 14.   x 2 Sa. 15. 25.   c Ge. 15. 9.   c La. 3. 46.   i La. 3. 47.   p Am. 8. 5.
d Ge. 43. 18.   i Zec. 13. 6.   p 2 Ch. 36. 13.   u Is. 30. 11.   y Ge. 41. 30, 31, 34, 47, 53.   d Nu. 30. 3.   d Eze. 27. 33.   k Ge. 43. 2.   q De. 22. 2.
e 1 Ki. 13. 18.   k Ne. 1. 2.   q Ge. 50. 5.   Ge. 41. 7, 24, 36, 27.   z Jos. 22. 25.   e La. 3. 47.   l Da. 9. 11.   e Eze. 32. 4.   l Is. 51. 19.   r Ne. 13. 34.

Hebrew	Parsing	Root
הִשְׁבַּתִּיךָ	Hiph. pret. 1 pers. sing., suff. 2 pers. sing. fem. [for בַּתִּיךָ § 25. rem.]	שבת
הַשְׁבַּתִּים	Hiph. pret. 1 p. s., suff. 3 p. p. m.; ן for ו conv.	שוב
הִשְׁבַּתִּים	Hiph. pret. 1 pers. sing., suff. 3 pers. pl. masc. [for בַּתִּים § 25. rem.]	שבת
הֲשִׁבֹתִים	Hiph. pret. 1 pers. sing., suff. 3 pers. pl. m.	ישב
הֲשִׁבֹתָם	Hiph. pret. 2 pers. sing. masc., suff. 3 pers. pl. masc. (§ 21. rem. 14); ן for ו conv.	שוב
הֲשִׁבֹתֶם	id. pret. 2 pers. pl. masc.	שוב
הִשְׁבַּתֶּם	Hiph. pret. 2 p.p.m. [for הִשְׁבַּתְּתֶם § 25. r.]	שבת
הֲשִׁבֹתֵנוּ	id. pret. 1 pers. pl.	שבת
הַשְׁגֵּן	Hiph. inf. absolute	שגג
הַשְׁגֶּנֶת	pref. ה X Kal part. act. s. f. (from שָׁנַב m.)	שגב
הִשְׁגִּיוּ	Hiph. pret. 3 pers. pl.	שנה
הִשְׁגִּיחַ	Hiph. pret. 3 pers. sing. masc.	שגח
הַשֹּׁגִים	pref. ה X Kal part. act. m., pl. of שָׁגָה d. 9a	שגה
הַשֶּׁגֶל	pref. id. X noun fem. sing.	שגל
הִשְׂגְּנֻנוּ	Hiph. pret. 3 pers. sing. masc., suff. 1 p. pl.	נשג
הִשַּׂגְתֶּם	id. pret. 2 pers. s. m., suff. 3 pers. pl. m.	נשג
הַשַּׂד	pref. ה X noun masc. sing.	שדד
הַשֹּׁדֵד	pref. id. X Kal part. sing. masc. dec. 7 b	שדד
הַשָּׂדֶה	pref. id. X noun masc. sing. dec. 9b	שדה
הַשְּׂדוּדָה	pref. id. X Kal part. pass. fem. of שָׁדוּד m.	שדד
הַשֵּׂדִים	pref. id. X pr. name of a valley	שדם
הַשְּׁדֵמוֹת	pref. id. X n.f., pl. of שְׁדֵמָה d. 11 (§ 42. r. 4)	שדם
הַשְּׂדֵרוֹת	pref. id. X noun fem., pl. of שְׂדֵרָה d.10, see	סדר
הַשְׂדֶּלֶת	pref.id. X n.m.with pl.f.term.,abs.st.,fr. שָׂדֶלֶת d.9b	שדה
הַשֶּׂה	pref. id. X noun com. sing. irr. (§ 45)	שיה
הִשֵּׁה	Hiph. pret.3 p.s.m., suff.3 p.s.f. (§25.No.2b)	נשה
הַשֹּׁהַם	pref. ה X noun masc. sing.	שהם
הַסַּהֲרֹנִים	pref. id. X noun m., pl. of שַׂהֲרֹן d. 1b, see	סהר
הַשּׁוֹא	pref. id. X noun masc. sing.	שוא
הַשּׁוֹבֵבָה	pref. id. X adj. fem. sing.	שוב
הַשּׁוֹדֵד	ן pref. id. X Kal part. act. masc., dec. 7b	שדד
הַשּׁוֹדְדִים	pref. id. X id. pl., absolute state	שדד
הַשּׁוּחִי	pref. id. X patronym. of שׁוּחַ	שוח
הַשּׁוּחָמִי	pref. id. X patronym. of שׁוּחָם	שוח
הַשּׁוֹטֵם	pref. id. X Kal part. act. sing. masc. dec. 7b	שטם
הַשּׁוֹטֵר	pref. id. X Kal part. act. sing. masc. dec. 7b	שטר
הַשּׁוּלַמִּית	pref. id. X pr. name fem., perhaps gent. noun	שלם
הַשּׁוּמִים	pref. id. X noun masc., pl. of [שׁוּם] dec. 1a	שום
הַשּׁוּנִי	pref. id. X patronym. for שׁוּנִי from שׁוּנִי	שון
הַשּׁוּנַמִּית	pref. id. X gent. noun, f. of שׁוּנַמִּי, fr. שׁוּנֵם	שון
הַשּׁוֹעֵר	pref. id. X noun masc. sing. dec. 7b	שער
הַשּׁוֹעֲרִים	ן pref. id. X id. pl., absolute state	שער
הַשֹּׁפֵט	pref. id. X Kal part. act. sing. masc. d. 7b	שפט

Hebrew	Parsing	Root
הַשּׁוּפָמִי	pref. id. X patronym. fr. שׁוּפָם	שפף
הַשֹּׁפֵר	pref. id. X noun masc. sing. dec. 2b	שפר
הַשֹּׁפָרוֹת	pref. id. X id. pl., absolute state	שפר
הַשּׁוֹקִי	pref. id. X noun fem. sing. dec. 1a	שוק
הַשּׁוֹר	ו pref. id. X noun masc. sing., suff. שׁוֹרוֹ, pl. שְׁוָרִים (§ 35. rem. 13)	שור
הַשַּׁח	Hiph. pret. 3 pers. sing. masc. (§ 18. r. 10)	שחח
הַשַּׁחַד	pref. ה X noun masc. sing.	שחד
הַשֹּׁחֲטָה	pref. id. X Kal part. act. sing. masc.	שחת
הַשְּׁחוּטָה / הַשְּׁחֻטָה	pref. id. X Kal part. pass. fem. sing., fr. שָׁחוּט masc.	שחט
הַשּׁוּחִי	pref. id. X patronym. of שׁוּחַ	שוח
הַשְּׁחִין	pref. id. X noun masc. sing.	שחן
הַשְׁחִית	Hiph. inf. constr.	שחת
הִשְׁחִית	ו id. pret. 3 pers. sing. masc.	שחת
הַשְׁחִיתָה	ן id. imp. sing. masc., suff. 3 pers. sing. f.	שחת
הִשְׁחִיתוּ	ו id. pret. 3 pers. pl. masc.	שחת
הַשְׁחִיתְךָ	id. inf., suff. 2 pers. s. m. d. 1b [for חִיתְךָ]	שחת
הַשְׁחִיתָם	id., suff. 3 pers. pl. masc.	שחת
הַשַּׁחַף	pref. ה X noun masc. s. [for שַׁחַף § 35. r. 2]	שחף
הַשַּׁחֶפֶת	pref. id. X noun fem. sing.	שחף
הַשַּׂחֵק	pref. id. X noun masc. sing.	שחק
הַשַּׁחַר / הַשָּׁחַר	pref. id. X noun masc. sing. dec. 6d (§ 35. rem. 2)	שחר
הַשַּׁחֲרוּת	pref. id. X noun fem. sing.	שחר
הַשְּׁחֹרִים	pref. id. X adj. masc., pl. of שָׁחֹר dec. 3a	שחר
הַשַּׁחַת	pref. id. X n. m. s. for שַׁחַת (comp. § 35. r. 2)	שחת
הַשְׁחֵת	Hiph. inf. absolute (§ 11. rem. 2)	שחת
הִשְׁחַתִּי	ן Hiph. pret. 1 p. s. [for הִשְׁחַתְּתִּי § 25. r.]	שחת
הִשְׁחַתֶּם	ן id. pret. 2 pers. pl. m. [for הִשְׁחַתְּתֶם v. i.]	שחת
הַשִּׁטָּה	pref. ה X pr. name in compos. בֵּית הַשִּׁטָּה	שוט
הַשֹּׁטִים	pref. id. X Kal part. act. m., pl. of שָׁט d. 1a	שוט
הַשִּׁטִּים	pref. id. X pr. name of a place (pl. of שִׁטָּה)	שטה
הַשָּׂטָן	ו pref. id. X noun masc. sing.	שטן
הַשֶּׁטֶף	pref. id. X noun masc. sing.	שטף
הַשֹּׁמְרִים	pref. id. X Kal part. act. m., pl. of שׁוֹמֵר d. 7b	שמר
הִשִּׂיא	Hiph. pret. 3 pers. sing. masc.	נשא
הִשִּׂיאוּ	ן Hiph. pret. 3 pers. pl.	נשא
הִשִּׁיאוּךָ	Hiph. pret. 3 pers. pl., suff. 2 pers. sing. m.	נשא
הִשִּׁיאֶךָ	id. pret. 3 p.s.m., suff. 2 p.s.m. [for הִשִּׁיאֲךָ]	נשא
הִשִּׁיאַנִי	id. id., suff. 1 pers. sing.	נשא
הָשֵׁיב	Hiph. imp. sing. masc.	שוב
הָשִׁיב	id. inf. constr.	שוב
הֵשִׁיב	ו id. pret. 3 pers. sing. masc.	שוב
הָשִׁיבָה	id. imp. masc. s. with parag. ה (§ 11. r. 5)	שוב
הֲשִׁיבֹהוּ	ן id. id., suff. 3 pers. sing. masc.; ן bef. (ד)	שוב

a Eze. 16. 41.   h Nu. 15. 28.   p Is. 51. 19.   w Is. 3. 18.   * Nu. 11. 5.   Le. 14. 51.   2 Ki. 13. 23.   De. 31. 29.   Je. 49. 16.
b Eze. 34. 10.   i Ps. 73. 12.   q Je. 6. 26.   x Je. 31. 21; 49. 4.   2 Ch. 31. 14.   Le. 14. 6.   Le. 26. 16.   Je. 51. 20.   Ob. 7.
c Je. 32. 37.   k Ps. 53. 14.   r Ps. 137. 8.   y Is. 21. 2.   Ju. 2. 18, 19.   Is. 65. 8.   Je. 48. 47.   De. 4. 25.   Ob. 8.
d 1 Ki. 8. 34.   l Ps. 119. 21.   s Je. 31. 40.   z Je. 51. 48.   1 Sa. 9. 24.   Ge. 6. 12.   Ec. 11. 10.   Eze. 27. 26.   Ge. 3. 18.
e Ne. 4. 5.   m Ne. 2. 6.   t Ex. 8. 9.   2 Ch. 32. 4.   Ex. 21. 32.   Ju. 2. 19.   Zec. 6. 14.   Zec. 3. 1.   2 Ki. 8. 6.
f 1 Sa. 30. 8.   Ge. 44. 4.   u Job 39. 17.   2 Ch. 26. 11.   Is. 21. 11.   De. 10. 10.   Ps. 49. 10.   Da. 11. 22.   1 Ki. 22. 26.
    2 Sa. 15. 14.   v Ju. 8. 21, 26.

נ id. imp. pl. masc., suff. 3 pers. sing. masc.; ן id. . . . . שוב הֲשִׁיבֻהג

ן id. imp. pl. masc. . . . שוב הָשִׁיבוּ

id. pret. 3 pers. sing. m., suff. 3 pers. s. m. שוב הֲשִׁיבוֹ

ן id. pret. 3 pers. pl. . . . שוב הֵשִׁיבוּ

י'ן Hiph. pret. 3 pers. pl., or imp. pl. masc. ישב הֵשִׁיבוּ

נ Hiph. pret. 3 pers. pl. (הֵשִׁיבוּ), suff. 3 pers. pl. masc. ן before (ָ) . . שוב הֲשִׁיבֻם

id. pret. 2 pers. sing. masc. (§ 21. rem. 14) שוב הֲשִׁיבוֹתָ

ן id. pret. 1 pers. sing.; ן bef. (ָ) שוב הֲשִׁיבוֹתִי

id. pret. 2 pers. sing. masc., suff. 3 pers. pl. masc. (§ 21. rem. 14); ן id. שוב הֲשִׁיבֹתָם

נ id. pret. 3 pers. sing. m. (הֵשִׁיב), suff. 2 pers. sing. m. ן, ן for ן conv. שוב הֱשִׁיבְךָ הֱשִׁיבְךָ

id. imp. sing. masc., suff. 1 pers. pl. שוב הֲשִׁיבֵנוּ

id. pret. 1 pers. pl. . . . שוב הֲשִׁיבֹנוּ

וַ' id. inf., or imp. s. masc., suff. 1 pers. sing.; ן bef. (ָ) . . שוב הֲשִׁיבֵנִי

id. pret. 3 pers. sing. masc., suff. 1 pers. s. שוב הֱשִׁיבֵנִי

נ id. pret. 1 pers. sing.; acc. shifted by ן, for ן conv. (comp. § 8. rem. 7) . שוב הֲשִׁיבֹתִי

נ id. id., suff. 2 pers. sing. masc.; ן bef. (ָ) שוב הֲשִׁיבֹתִיךָ

ן id. id., suff. 3 pers. pl. masc.; ן id. . שוב הֲשִׁיבֹתִים

ן id. pret. 2 pers. pl. m. (§ 21. r. 14); ן id. שוב הֲשִׁיבֹתֶם

ן Hiph. pret. 3 pers. sing. masc. . נשג הִשִּׂיג

י'ן id pret. 3 pers. sing. fem. . נשג הִשִּׂיגָה

ן id. pret. 3 pers. sing. masc., suff. 3 pers. sing. masc. . . . . נשג הִשִּׂיגוֹ

id. pret. 3 pers. pl. . . . נשג הִשִּׂיגוּ

id. id., suff. 3 pers. sing. fem. . נשג הִשִּׂיגוּהָ

ן id. id., suff. 2 pers. sing. masc. . נשג הִשִּׂיגוּךָ

ן id. id., suff. 1 pers. sing. . . נשג הִשִּׂיגוּנִי

ן' defect. for נגש (q. v.) . . נשג הִשִּׁיגֶךָ

pref. הַ)(noun masc., pl. of שִׂיחַ dec. 1a שיח הַשִּׂיחִם

pref. id.)(pr. name of a river . שחר הַשִּׁיחוֹר

pref. id.)(gent. noun fr. שִׁלֹה שלה הַשִּׁילֹנִי הַשִּׁלֹנִי

Hiph. imp. sing. fem. fr. שׂים or שום הָשִׂימִי

ן' Hiph. pret. 3 pers. pl. . . . שוק הִשִּׁיקוּ

ן Hiph. pret. 3 pers. pl. . . . נשק הִשִּׁיקוּ

ן' pref. הַ)(noun masc. sing. dec. 1a שיר הַשִּׁיר

pref. id.)(noun fem. sing. dec. 10 שיר הַשִּׁירָה

Hiph. pret. 3 pers. pl. . . שור הֵשִׁירוּ

pref. הַ)(noun masc., pl. of שִׁיר dec. 1a שור הַשִּׁירִים

Hiph. inf. absolute (§ 11. rem. 2) שכב הַשְׁכֵּב

ן' pref. הַ)(Kal part. act. masc. dec. 7b שכב הַשֹּׁכֵב

ן Hoph. pret. 3 pers. sing. masc. (§ 11. rem. 10) שכב הֻשְׁכַּב

ן id. imp. sing. masc. with parag. ה שכב הַשְׁכִּבָה

pref. הַ)(Kal part. act. m., pl. of שֹׁכֵב dec. 7b שכב הַשֹּׁכְבִים

ן Hiph. pret. 1 pers. sing., suff. 3 pers. pl. m. שכב הִשְׁכַּבְתִּים

pref. id.)(Kal part. pass. pl. constr. from [שָׁכֹן] dec. 3a שכן הַשְּׁכֻנֵי

pref. הַ)(Kal pret. 3 pers. sing. masc. . שכח הַשָּׁכַח

ן Chald. Aph. pret. 3 pers. pl. masc. (§ 47. rem. 4, & § 49. No. 4) . . . שכח הַשְׁכַּחוּ

pref. הַ)(adj. masc., pl. of [שָׁכֵחַ] dec. 5a שכח הַשְּׁכֵחִים

Ch. Aph. pret. 1 p. pl. (§ 47. r. 4, & § 49. No. 4) שכח הַשְׁכַּחְנָא

Chald. id. pret. 1 pers. sing. . שכח הַשְׁכַּחַת

pref. הַ interr. for הַ)(Kal pret. 2 pers. pl. m. שכב הַשְּׁכַבְתֶּם

Hiph. pret. 3 pers. sing. fem. . שכב הִשְׁכִּיבָה

ן Hiph. inf. abs. . . שׂכל הַשְׂכֵּיל

י'ן id. pret. 3 pers. sing. masc. . שׂכל הִשְׂכֵּיל

id. imp. pl. masc. . . שׂכל הַשְׂכִּילוּ

id. pret. 3 pers. pl. . . שׂכל הִשְׂכִּילוּ

Hiph. inf. abs. used adverbially . שכם הַשְׁכֵּם

ן id. pret. 3 pers. sing. masc. . שכם הִשְׁכִּים

id. pret. 3 pers. pl. . . שכם הִשְׁכִּימוּ

pref. הַ)(noun fem. sing. . שכר הַשִּׁכֹּרָה

Hiph. imp. pl. masc., suff. 3 pers. sing. masc. שכר הַשְׁכִּירֻהָ

ן' Hiph. inf. absolute (§ 11. rem. 2) שׂכל הַשְׂכֵּל

id. pret. 1 pers. sing. . . שׂכל הִשְׂכַּלְתִּי

ן' Hiph. inf. abs. (§ 11. rem. 2), or imp. s. m. שכם הַשְׁכֵּם

id. pret. 2 pers. pl. masc. . שכם הִשְׁכַּמְתֶּם

pref. הַ)(patronym. of שֶׁכֶם שכם הַשִּׁכְמִי

pref. id.)(Kal part. act. sing. masc. dec. 7b שכן הַשֹּׁכֵן

pref. id.)(fem. pl. [of שְׁכֵנָה from שָׁכֵן masc.] comp. שְׁכֶנְתָּה שכן הַשְּׁכֵנוֹת

pref. id.)(Kal part. act. m., pl. of שֹׁכֵן dec. 7b שכן הַשֹּׁכְנִים

ן Hiph. pret. 1 pers. sing.; acc. shifted by ן conv. (comp. § 8. rem. 7) שכן הִשְׁכַּנְתִּי

pref. הַ)(noun masc. sing. . שכר הַשֵּׁכָר

ן Hiph. pret. 1 pers. sing.; acc. shifted by ן conv. (comp. § 8. rem. 7) שכר הִשְׁכַּרְתִּי

ן id., suff. 3 pers. pl. masc. . שכר הִשְׁכַּרְתִּים

נ Hiph. pret. 1 pers. sing.; acc. shifted by ן for conv. (comp. § 8. rem. 7, & § 11. rem. 5) שכב הִשְׁכַּבְתִּי

pref. הַ)(noun masc. sing. . שלה הַשֶּׁלַח

pref. id.)(noun masc., pl. of [שֶׁלֶב] dec. 8d (§ 37. No. 3) . . . שלב הַשְׁלַבִּים

ה pref. id.)(noun masc. sing. (§ 35. rem. 2) שלג הַשָּׁלֶג הַשָּׁלֶנ

² 2 Ch. 18. 25.   ³ Ge. 40. 13.   ⁴ Le. 26. 5.   ⁷ De. 28. 2.   ᶠ Ho. 8. 4.   ᵏ Am. 6. 4.   ⁰ 1 Ki. 3. 20.   ˢ Je. 48. 26.   ᵘ Is. 28. 7.
¹ 1 Ki. 13. 20, 23, 26.   ¹ De. 28. 68.   ᵉ Le. 25. 49.   ᵗ Ge. 21. 15.   ᶜ Ca. 1. 1.   ᵐ Ho. 2. 20.   ᵖ Je. 3. 15.   ᵗ Da. 1. 17.   ᵛ Je. 51. 57.
¹ 1 Ki. 19. 9, 12.   ᵈ De. 28. 28.   ᶠ Le. 25. 26.   ᵘ Ez. 21. 21.   ᵈ 2 Sa. 8. 2.   ⁿ Ju. 8. 11.   ᵍ 1 Ch. 28. 19.   ᵗ Ps. 119. 99.   ʷ Je. 51. 39.
ᵈ 1 Ki. 14. 28.   ᵉ Job 13. 22.   ᵍ De. 19. 6.   ᶻ Joel 4. 13.   ᵉ Ps. 77. 10.   ⁿ Je. 23. 5.   ʳ Je. 26. 5.   ⁿ Nu. 17. 20.
⁵ Am. 1. 8.   ᵗ 2 Ki. 19. 28.   ʰ La. 1. 3.   ᵃ Joel 2. 24.   ᶠ Da. 6. 9.   ᵉ Pa. 2. 10.   ᵗ Ruth 4. 17.   ᵖ 2 Sa. 6. 7.
⁶ Ch. 6. 25.   ᵗ 1 Sa. 8. 7.   ⁱ Ps. 40. 13.   ᵇ 2 Ch. 29. 28.   ᵐ Eze. 32. 32.   ᵉ Da. 2. 25.   ᵗ Zep. 3. 7.   ᵗ Je. 25. 24.   ᵘ 1 Ki. 7. 28, 29.
ᵃᵃ Am. 1. 8.   ᵇᵇ Is. 65. 11.   ⁿ Eze. 32. 19.   ᵗ Je. 44. 9.   ᵗ Is. 7. 20.   ᵉ Eze. 32. 4.   ⁱ Is. 55. 10.

הַשָּׁלֵו	pref. הַ)(K. שְׁלָיו, noun masc. sing., pl. שָׁלָוִים, dec. 6 (§ 35. rem. 16) . .	שלו
הַשָּׁלוֹם	)(pref. id. (prim. adj.) noun masc. sing.	שלם
הַשָּׁלוֹם	pref. הַ } dec. 3a . .	שלם
הַשְּׁלִשָׁה	pref. הַ)(num. card. m. s. from שָׁלִשׁ fem.	שלש
הַשְּׁלוֹשִׁים	pref. id.)(Kh. שְׁלֹשִׁים q. v.; K. שְׁלָשִׁים, noun masc. pl. of שָׁלִישׁ dec. 1b	שלש
הַשְּׁלֹשִׁים	pref. id.)(num. card. com. gen., pl. of שָׁלֹשׁ fem.	שלש
הַשֶּׁלַח	)(pref. id.)(noun masc. sing. dec. 6 (§ 35. rem. 5 & 2, but with suff. שִׁלְחוֹ)	שלח
הַשֶּׁלַח	pref. id.)(pr. name of a pool . .	שלח
הַשִּׁלֹחַ	pref. id.)(pr. name of a pool . .	שלח
הַשֹּׁלֵחַ	pref. id.)(Kal part. act. sing. masc. dec. 7b	שלח
הַשֻּׁלְחָן	)(pref. id.)(noun masc. sing. dec. 2b	שלח
הַשֻּׁלְחָנוֹת	pref. id.)(id. pl. absolute (constr. שֻׁלְחֲנוֹת)	שלח
הִשְׁלַחְתִּי	)(Hiph. pret. 1 pers. sing.; acc. shifted by conv. וֹ)((comp. § 8. rem. 7)	שלח
הַשְׁלְמַהּ	)(Ch. Aph. 3 p. s. m., suff. 3 p. s. m. (§ 47. r. 4)	שלם
הַשְּׁלָמִים	pref. id.)(noun masc., pl. of שֶׁלֶם dec. 6a (pl. c. שַׁלְמֵי) . .	שלם
הַשְׁלְמָךְ	)(Ch. Aph. pret. 3 pers. sing. masc., suff. 2 pers. sing. masc. (§ 47. rem. 4)	שלם
הַשַּׁלִּיט	pref. id.)((prim. adj.) noun m. sing. dec. 1b	שלם
הַשְׁלִיטוֹ	)(Hiph. pret. 3 pers. sing. m., suff. 3 pers. s. m.	שלם
הַשְׁלִיךְ	)(Hiph. pret. 3 pers. sing. masc. .	שלך
הִשְׁלִיכָה	id. pret. 3 pers. sing. fem. . .	שלך
הַשְׁלִיכֵהוּ	id. imp. sing. masc., suff. 3 pers. sing. masc.	שלך
הַשְׁלִיכוּ	id. imp. pl. masc. . .	שלך
הַשְׁלִיכוּ	)(id. pret. 3 pers. pl. . .	שלך
הַשְׁלִיכוֹ	id. inf. with suff. 3 p. s. m. [for הַשְׁלִיכוֹ §11.r.4]	שלך
הַשְׁלִיכִי	)(id. imp. sing. fem. . .	שלך
הִשְׁלִיכָם	id. pret. 3 pers. sing. masc., suff. 3 pers. pl. m.	שלך
הַשְׁלִימָה	Hiph. pret. 3 pers. sing. fem. .	שלם
הַשְׁלִימוּ	id. pret. 3 pers. pl. . .	שלם
הַשְּׁלִישִׁי	pref. הַ)(noun masc. sing. dec. 1b	שלש
הַשְּׁלִישִׁי	pref. id.)(adj. ord. masc. sing. from שָׁלִישׁ	שלש
הַשְּׁלִישִׁיָּה הַשְּׁלִישִׁית	} pref. id.)(id. fem.	שלש
הַשֶּׁלֶךְ	pref. id.)(noun masc. sing. .	שלך
הַשְׁלֵךְ	)(Kal inf. abs. (§ 11. rem. 2), or imp. sing. m.	שלך
הָשְׁלַךְ	)(Hoph. pret. 3 pers. sing. masc. (§ 11. rem. 10)	שלך
הַשְׁלְכָה	id. pret. 3 pers. s. fem. [for הָשְׁלְכָה §11. rem.10, comp. § 8. rem. 7]	שלך

הַשְׁלִיכֵהוּ	Hiph. imp. s. m., suff. 3 p. s. m. [for הַשְׁלִיכֵהוּ]	שלך
הַשְׁלִכוּ	defect. for הַשְׁלִיכוּ (q. v.)	שלך
הָשְׁלְכוּ	)(Hoph. pret. 3 pers. pl. (§ 11. rem. 10)	שלך
הָשְׁלַכְתָּ	id. pret. 2 pers. sing. masc.	שלך
הִשְׁלַכְתָּ	} Hiph. pret. 2 pers. sing. masc.; acc. shifted by conv. וֹ)((comp. § 8. rem. 7)	שלך
הִשְׁלַכְתּוֹ	)(id. id.)(with suff. 3 pers. sing. masc.	שלך
הָשְׁלַכְתִּי	Hoph. pret. 1 pers. sing. . .	שלך
הִשְׁלַכְתִּי	} Hiph. pret. 1 pers. sing.; acc. shifted by conv. וֹ)((comp. § 8. rem. 7)	שלך
הִשְׁלַכְתִּיךָ	id. pret., suff. 2 pers. sing. masc. .	שלך
הִשְׁלַכְתֶּנָה	)(id. pret. 2 pers. pl. fem. (§ 8. rem. 6)	שלך
הַשָּׁלָל	pref. הַ)(noun masc. sing. dec. 4a	שלל
הַשֹּׁלְלִים	pref. id.)(Kal part. act. m., pl. of [שֹׁלֵל] dec. 7b	שלל
הַשְׁלֵם	Chald. Aph. imp. sing. masc. (§ 47. rem. 4)	שלם
הַשֶּׁלֶם	pref. הַ)(noun masc. sing. dec. 1b	שלם
הַשְׁלְמָה	Hoph. pret. 3 pers. sing. fem. .	שלם
הַשְׁלְמָהּ	)(Ch. Aph. 3 p. s. m., suff. 3 p. s. f. (§ 47. rem. 4)	שלם
הַשֶּׁלְמִי	pref. הַ)(patronym. of שֶׁלֶם	שלם
הַשְּׁלָמִים	)(pref. id.)(noun masc. pl. (c. שַׁלְמֵי) from שֶׁלֶם dec. 6a	שלם
הַשֵּׁלָנִי	pref. id.)(patronym. of שֵׁלָה	שאל
הַשִּׁלֹנִי	pref. id.)(gent. noun from שִׁילֹה	שלה
הַשְּׁלִשׁ	pref. id.)(num. card. fem. sing.	שלש
הַשְּׁלִשָׁה	pref. id.)(id. masc.	שלש
הַשְּׁלִישִׁי	)(pref. id.)(adj. ord. masc. sing. (for שְׁלִישִׁי)	שלש
הַשְּׁלִישִׁי	pref. id.)(Kh. הַשְּׁלִשִׁי q. v., K. הַשְּׁלִשָׁה (q. v.)	שלש
הַשְּׁלִשִׁי	pref. id.)(abbreviated for the following	שלש
הַשְּׁלִשִׁים	)(pref. id.)(noun masc., pl. of שָׁלִישׁ dec. 1b	שלש
הַשְּׁלֹשִׁים	pref. id.)(num. card. com. gen., pl. of שָׁלֹשׁ fem.	שלש
הַשְּׁלִישִׁים	pref. id.)(adj. ord. m., pl. of שְׁלִישִׁי from שָׁלִישׁ	שלש
הַשְּׁלִשִׁית	)(pref. id.)(id. fem. sing.	שלש
הָשָׁם	pr. name masc. 1 Ch. 11. 34, for which יָשֵׁם in 2 Sa. 23. 32.	
הַשָּׂם	pref. הַ relat. art.)(Kal part. act. sing. masc. dec. 1a, from שִׂים or	שום
הַשָּׁם	pref. הַ art.)(noun masc. sing. dec. 7a	שם
הַשְּׂמֹאול הַשְּׂמֹאל	} pref. id.)(noun m. sing. dec. 1a (וֹ in otio)	שמאל
הַשְּׂמָאלִי	pref. id.)(adj. masc. sing. .	שמאל
הַשְּׂמָאלִית	pref. id.)(id. fem.	שמאל
הַשְׁמֵד	Hiph. inf. abs. (§ 11. rem. 2), or imp. sing. m.	שמד
הִשָּׁמֵד	Niph. inf. constr. used as an abs.	שמד

a Ne. 4. 1.   c 2 Sa. 11. 21.   f Jos. 10. 1.   k Eze. 19. 12.   o Is. 14. 19.   s Je. 7. 15.   x Ezr. 7. 19.   cc De. 19. 2.   hh 2 Ki. 10. 25.
b Da. 2. 48.   d Eze. 43. 24.   g Je. 52. 3.   l 2 Ki. 7. 3, 17, 19.   p Ki. 9. 25, 26.   t Eze. 28. 17.   y 2 Sa. 3. 8.   dd 1 Ki. 5. 8.
b Da. 2. 38.   e Je. 7. 29   i De. 26. 12.   m 2 Ki. 24. 20.   q Je. 51. 63.   u Am. 4. 3.   z 2 Sa. 23. 18.   ee 1 Ch. 6. 29.
c Ec. 5. 18.   f Da. 3. 11.   n Je. 22. 28.   r Ps. 22. 11.   v Zec. 2. 12.   bb 2 Sa. 23. 8.   ff De. 4. 26.
ww Eze. 10. 14.   Da. 5. 26.

הִשְׁמְדוּ	Kal pret. 3 pers. sing. masc. (הִשְׁמִיד), suff. 3 pers. sing. masc. (comp. § 11. rem. 4)	שמר
הִשָּׁמֶדְךָ	Niph. inf. (הִשָּׁמֵד), suff. 2 p. s. m. pause d. 7 b	שמר
הִשָּׁמֶדְךָ	id. with suff. 2 pers. sing. masc. (comp. § 16. rem. 15, & § 36. rem. 3)	שמר
הַשְׁמִדְךָ	Hiph. inf. with suff. 2 p. s. m. (for הַשְׁ § 11. r. 4)	שמר
הִשָּׁמֶדָם	Niph. inf. (הִשָּׁמֵד), suff. 3 pers. pl. m. dec. 7 b	שמר
הַשְׁמִדָם	Hiph. inf., suff. 3 p. s. m. (for הַשְׁ § 11. rem. 4)	שמר
הִשְׁמַדְתִּי	id. pret. 1 pers. sing.; acc. shifted by conv. ו (comp. § 8. rem. 7)	שמר
הִשְׁמַדְתִּיו	id. id., suff. 3 pers. sing. masc.	שמר
הַשֻּׁמָה	pref. הַ relat. art. ⟩⟨ Kal pret. 3 pers. sing. fem.	שום
הַשֻּׁמָה	Hoph. inf. [הָשֵׁם for הוּשַׁם § 18. r. 14] with suff. 3 p. s. fem. ה— for —ָה (§ 3. rem. 3)	שמם
הֻשַּׁמּוּ	ו id. imp. pl. masc. [הוּשַׁמּוּ=הָשַׁמּוּ, compare the preceding]	שמם
הֵשַׁמּוּ	Hiph. pret. 3 pers. pl. (§ 18. rem. 10)	שמם
הַשְּׁמוּעָה	pref. הַ ⟩⟨ noun fem. sing. dec. 10	שמע
הֲשִׁמּוֹתָ	Hiph. pret. 2 pers. sing. masc.	שמם
הֲשִׁמּוֹתִי	ו id. pret. 1 pers. sing.; acc. shifted by ו, for ו conv. (compare § 8. rem. 7)	שמם
הֲשִׁמּוֹתִיהוּ	ו id. id. with suff. 3 pers. sing. masc.	שמם
הַשִּׂמְחָה	pref. הַ ⟩⟨ noun fem. sing. dec. 12 b	שמח
הַשְּׂמֵחִים	pref. id. ⟩⟨ adj. masc., pl. of שָׂמֵחַ dec. 5 a	שמח
הִשְׂמַחְתָּ	Hiph. pret. 2 pers. sing. masc.	שמח
הַשִּׂמְטָה	pref. הַ ⟩⟨ noun fem. sing.	שמט
הַשְׁמֵד	Hiph. inf. absolute	שמד
הִשְׁמִיד	id. pret. 3 pers. sing. masc.	שמד
הִשְׁמִידוֹ	id. inf., suff. 3 pers. sing. masc. dec. 1 b	שמד
הִשְׁמִידוֹ	id. pret. 3 pers. s. m. suff. id.; or (De. 28. 48) inf. for הַשְׁ (§ 11. rem. 4)	שמד
הִשְׁמִידוּ	id. pret. 3 pers. pl.	שמד
הִשְׁמִידוּם	id. id., suff. 3 pers. pl. masc.	שמד
הִשְׁמִידְךָ	ו id. pret. 3 pers. sing. m., suff. 2 pers. sing. m.	שמד
הַשְׁמִידָם	id. inf., suff. 3 pers. pl. masc. dec. 1 b	שמד
הִשְׁמִידָם	defect. for הִשְׁמִידוֹם (q. v.)	שמד
הַשְׁמִידָע	pref. הַ ⟩⟨ patronym. of שְׁמִידָע q. v.	שם
הַשְׂמְאִילִי	Hiph. imp. sing. fem. [for הַשְׂמְאִילִי]	שמאל
הַשָּׁמַיִם	⟩ pref. הַ ⟩⟨ noun masc., pl. of [שַׁם], pl.	שמה
הַשָּׁמַיִם	⟩ c. שְׁמֵי, with suff. שְׁמֵיךָ (§ 38. r. 2)	שמה
הַשָּׁמָיְמָה	⟩ pref. id. ⟩⟨ id. with paragogic ה	שמה
הַשָּׁמָיְמָה	⟩	שמה
הַשְּׁמִינִי	pref. id. ⟩⟨ adj. ord. masc. sing. for שְׁמֹנָה	שמן
הַשְּׁמִינִית	pref. id. ⟩⟨ id. fem.	שמן
הִשְׁמִיעַ	⟩ ו Hiph. pret. 3 pers. sing. masc.	שמע
הִשְׁמִיעוּ	ו id. imp. pl. masc.	שמע
הִשְׁמִיעוּ	⟩ ו id. pret. 3 pers. pl.	שמע
הַשְׁמִיעוּהָ	ו id. imp. pl. masc., suff. 3 pers. sing. fem.	שמע
הִשְׁמִיעֲךָ	id. pret. 3 pers. sing. m., suff. 2 pers. s. m.	שמע
הַשְׁמִיעֵנוּ	id. imp. pl. masc. (הַשְׁמִיעוּ), suff. 1 pers. pl.	שמע
הִשְׁמִיעָנוּ	id. pret. 3 pers. sing. masc., suff. 1 pers. pl.	שמע
הַשְׁמִיעֵנִי	id. imp. sing. fem., suff. 1 pers. sing.	שמע
הַשְׁמִיעֵנִי	id. imp. sing. masc., (§ 11. r. 5) suff. 1 pers. s.	שמע
הַשִּׂמְלָה	pref. הַ ⟩⟨ noun fem. sing. dec. 12 b	שמל
הַשְׁמֵם	Hiph. inf. abs. (uncontracted form § 18. r. 13)	שמם
הַשָּׁמֵם	pref. הַ ⟩⟨ adj. masc. sing.	שמם
הַשֹּׁמֵמוֹת	pref. id. ⟩⟨ Kal part. act. fem. pl. [of שֹׁמֵמָה dec. 13 a, in use only שׁוֹמֵמָה comp. § 42. r. 5.]	שמם
הַשֶּׁמֶן	⟩ pref. הַ ⟩⟨ noun masc. sing. dec. 6 a	שמן
הַשֶּׁמֶן	⟩ (§ 35. rem. 2)	שמן
הַשְׁמֵן	Hiph. imp. sing. masc.	שמן
הֲשָׁמְנָה	pref. הַ art., or interr. for הֲ ⟩⟨ adj. fem. sing. from שָׁמֵן masc.	שמן
הֲשָׁמַע	pref. הַ ⟩⟨ Kal pret. 3 pers. sing. masc.	שמע
הַשֹּׁמֵעַ	pref. הַ ⟩⟨ Kal part. act. sing. masc. dec. 7 b	שמע
הַשֹּׁמְעָה	pref. id. ⟩⟨ pr. name masc.	שמע
הַשְּׁמֻעָה	⟩ pref. id. ⟩⟨ for שְׁמוּעָה, noun fem. s. dec. 10.	שמע
הַשִּׁמְעִי	pref. id. ⟩⟨ patronym. for שִׁמְעִי from שֶׁמַע	שמע
הַשֹּׁמְעִים	pref. id. ⟩⟨ Kal part. act. m., pl. of שֹׁמֵעַ d. 7 b	שמע
הַשִּׁמְעֹנִי	pref. id. ⟩⟨ patronym. of שִׁמְעוֹן	שמע
הִשְׁמַעְתָּ	Hiph. pret. 2 pers. sing. masc.	שמע
הִשְׁמַעְתִּי	ו id. pret. 1 pers. sing.	שמע
הִשְׁמַעְתִּיךָ	id. id., suff. 2 pers. sing. masc.	שמע
הַשֹּׁמֵר	⟩ pref. הַ	שמר
הַשֹּׁמֵר	⟩ pref. הַ ⟩ Kal part. act. sing. masc. dec. 7 b	שמר
הִשָּׁמֵר	⟩	שמר
הִשָּׁמֵר	⟩ Niph. imp. sing. masc. (§ 9. rem. 3)	שמר
הִשָּׁמְרוּ	⟩	שמר
הִשָּׁמְרוּ	⟩ id. imp. pl. masc. (comp. § 8. rem. 7)	שמר
הִשָּׁמְרִי	id. imp. sing. fem.	שמר
הַשֹּׁמְרִים	⟩ pref. הַ⟩ Kal part. act. masc., pl. of שֹׁמֵר	שמר
הַשֹּׁמְרִים	⟩ pref. הַ⟩ dec. 7 b	שמר
הַשֹּׁמְרֹנִי	pref. הַ ⟩⟨ patronym. of שֹׁמְרוֹן	שמר
הַשֹּׁמְרֹנִים	pref. id. ⟩⟨ gent. noun from שֹׁמְרוֹן	שמר
הַשֶּׁמֶשׁ	⟩ pref. id. ⟩⟨ noun masc. sing. dec. 6 a	שמש
הַשֶּׁמֶשׁ	⟩ (§ 35. rem. 2, but with suff. שִׁמְשְׁךָ)	שמש
הַשִּׁמְשִׁי	pref. id. ⟩⟨ gent. noun, see בֵּית הַשִּׁמְשִׁי	בית
הֲשַׂמְתֶּ	pref. הֲ ⟩⟨ Kal pret. 2 pers. sing. m. fr. שִׂים or שׂום	שום
הִשַּׂמְתִּי	ו Hiph. pret. 1 pers. sing., acc. shifted by ו for ו conv. (comp. § 8. rem. 7)	שמם
הַשֻּׁמָתִי	⟩ pref. הַ ⟩⟨ patronym. of שׁוּמָה q. v.	שום
הַשֵּׁן	pref. id. ⟩⟨ noun com. sing. dec. 8 b	שנן
הַשִּׂנְאָה	pref. id. ⟩⟨ noun fem. sing. (no pl.)	שנא

a 1 Ki. 15. 29.	f Eze. 14. 9.	l Eze. 14. 8.	q 2 Ch. 20. 10.	u Is. 30. 30.
b De. 28. 24,	g Is. 51. 10.	m Ps. 89. 43.	r Jos. 11. 20.	v Ju. 13. 23.
45, 51, 61	h Le. 26. 34, 35.	n Am. 9. 8.	s De. 2. 33.	w Is. 41. 22.
De. 28. 20.	2 Ch. 36. 21.	o Jos. 23. 15.	t Eze. 21. 21.	x Ca. 2. 14; 8. 13.
c De. 7. 24.	Job 21. 5.	p Ps. 106. 34.	l Le. 25. 22.	y Ps. 143. 8.
d Jos. 11. 14	Job 16. 7.	pp Am. 2. 9.		z Je. 5. 20.

שנה	pref. הַ) noun fem. sing. dec. 11 a .	הַשָּׁנָה
שנא	וַ) pref. id.) Kal part. pass. s. f. fr. [שָׂנוּא] m.	הַשְּׂנוּאָה
שנה	Niph. inf. constr.	הִשָּׁנוֹת
שנה	pref. הַ) noun m. s., constr. שְׁנֵי, pl. שָׁנִים	הַשָּׁנֵי
שנה	pref. id.) adj. ord. masc. sing. from שְׁנַיִם	הַשֵּׁנִי
שנה	pref. id.) noun fem. with pl. masc. term. from שָׁנָה dec. 11 a .	הַשָּׁנִים
שנה	pref. id.) num. card. masc. dual, constr. שְׁנֵי & שְׁנַיִם .	הַשְּׁנַיִם
שנן	pref. id.) noun com., dual of שֵׁן dec. 8 b	הַשִּׁנַּיִם
שנה	pref. id.) num. card. m. constr. of שְׁנַיִם du.	הַשְּׁנֵים
שנה	וַ) pref. id.) adj. ord., fem. of שֵׁנִי, used also adverbially	הַשֵּׁנִית
שון	pref. id.) gent. noun, fem. of שׁוּנַמִּי fr. שׁוּנֵם	הַשּׁוּנַמִּית
שסע	וַ) pref. id.) Kal part. pass. s. f. [from שָׁסוּעַ] m.]	הַשְּׁסוּעָה
שעה	Hiph. imp. sing. masc. ap. for הַשְׁעֵה ; it stands for הַשַׁע (like הַעַל from עָלָה § 24. rem. 17) comp. the lengthened vowel in יִכְחָה for יַכֵּה , יִרְבֶּה for יֶרֶב .	הָשַׁע
שעע	Hiph. imp. sing. masc. [for הָשֵׁע comp. imp. הֶחְבֵּר § 15. rem. 1, & § 18. rem. 10] .	הָשַׁע
שער	וַ) pref. הַ) noun masc. sing. dec. 3 a .	הַשָּׂעִיר
שער	pref. id.) id. pl., absolute state	הַשְּׂעִירִם
שער	pref. id.) pr. name of a place [שְׂעִירָה] with paragogic ה	הַשְּׂעִירָתָה
שעלב	pref. id.) gent. noun, see שַׁעַלְבִים	הַשַּׁעַלְבֹנִי
שען	וַ) Hiph. imp. pl. masc.	הִשָּׁעֵנוּ
שער	וַ) pref. הַ) noun com. sing. dec. 6 d (§ 35. rem. 2) .	הַשַּׁעַר / הַשָּׁעַר
שער	pref. id.) noun masc. sing. dec. 7 b .	הַשַּׂעַר
שער	pref. id.) noun com. sing. with paragogic ה from שַׁעַר dec. 6 d	הַשַּׁעְרָה
שער	pref. id.) noun fem. sing. (no pl. abs.)	הַשְּׂעֹרָה
שער	in pause for הַשַּׂעֲרָה (q. v. comp. § 35. r. 5)	הַשָּׂעֲרָה
שער	וַ) pref. הַ) noun fem. sing. dec. 10 .	הַשְּׂעָרָה
שער	pref. id.) noun com., pl. of שַׁעַר dec. 6 d	הַשְּׁעָרִים
שער	pref. id.) noun fem. with pl. masc. term. from שְׂעֹרָה	הַשְּׂעֹרִים
שער	pref. id.) adj. masc. pl. [of שָׂעֵר]	הַשְּׂעִרִים
שער	pref. id.) noun masc., pl. of שַׁעַר dec. 7 b	הַשְּׁעָרִים
שפך	pref. id.) Kal part. pass. sing. masc.	הַשָּׁפוּךְ
שפת	contr. for הָאַשְׁפֹּת (q. v.)	הַשְׁפֹּת
שפח	pref. הַ) noun fem. sing. dec. 12 b	הַשִּׁפְחָה
שפח	pref. id.) id. pl., absolute state	הַשְּׁפָחוֹת
שפט	וַ) pref. id.) Kal part. act. sing. masc.	הַשֹּׁפֵט
שפט	pref. הַ) dec. 7 b	הָשֹׁפֵט

שפט	וַ) pref. הַ) id. pl., absolute state	הַשֹּׁפְטִים
שפל	Hiph. inf. construct	הַשְׁפִּיל
שפל	וַ) id. pret. 3 pers. sing. masc.	הִשְׁפִּיל
שפל	וַ) id. imp. sing. masc., suff. 3 pers. sing. m.	הַשְׁפִּילֵהוּ
שפל	id. imp. pl. masc.	הַשְׁפִּילוּ
שפל	id. pret. 3 pers. pl.	הִשְׁפִּילוּ
שפך	Niph. inf. construct	הִשָּׁפֵךְ
שפך	pref. הַ) Kal part. act. m., pl. of שֹׁפֵךְ d. 7 b	הַשֹּׁפְכִים
שפל	pref. id.) adj. masc. sing with paragogic ה, from שָׁפָל dec. 4 a .	הַשְּׁפֵלָה
שפל	וַ) pref. id.) noun fem. sing. dec. 10 .	הַשְּׁפֵלָה
שפל	Aph. pret. 2 pers. sing. masc. (§ 47. rem. 4)	הַשְׁפֵּלְתְּ
שפל	Hiph. pret. 1 pers. sing.	הִשְׁפַּלְתִּי
שפה	pref. הַ) gent. noun from שָׁפָם .	הַשְּׁפָמִי
שפן	וַ) pref. id.) noun masc. sing., pl. שְׁפַנִּים dec. 8 a (§ 37. Nos. 2 & 3)	הַשָּׁפָן
שפר	pref. id.) noun masc. sing. dec. 2 b	הַשֶּׁפֶר
שפת	וַ) pref. id.) noun masc., du. of [שָׁפָת] dec. 8 a (§ 37. rem. 2 & 3) .	הַשְּׁפַתַּיִם
שקק	pref. id.) noun masc. sing. dec. 8 d .	הַשַּׂק
ישקד	pref. id.) noun masc. sing. dec. 5 a .	הַשָּׁקֵד
שקה	וַ) Hiph. pret. 3 pers. sing. masc.	הִשְׁקָה
שקה	וַ) id. id., suff. 3 pers. s. fem. (§ 24. rem. 21)	הִשְׁקָהָ
שקה	id. imp. sing. masc., suff. 3 pers. sing. masc.	הַשְׁקֵהוּ
שקה	id. imp. pl. masc.	הַשְׁקוּ
שקה	וַ) id. pret. 3 pers. pl.	הִשְׁקוּ
שקץ	pref. הַ) noun masc. sing. dec. 1 b .	הַשִּׁקּוּץ
שקץ	pref. id.) id. pl., absolute state	הַשִּׁקּוּצִים
שקה	וַ) Hiph. inf. constr.	הַשְׁקוֹת
שקט	וַ) Hiph. inf. (§ 11. rem. 2), or imp. sing. m.	הַשְׁקֵט
שקט	pref. הַ) Kal part. act. m., pl. of שֹׁקֵט d. 7 b	הַשֹּׁקְטִים
שוק	pref. id.) noun fem. with du. masc. term. from שׁוֹק dec. 1 a .	הַשֹּׁקַיִם
שקה	וַ) Hiph. pret. 1 pers. sing. (§ 24. rem. 14) .	הִשְׁקִינוּ
שקה	id. imp. sing. fem.	הַשְׁקִינִי
שקף	Hiph. pret. 3 pers. sing. masc.	הִשְׁקִיף
שקף	id. imp. sing. m. with parag. ה (§ 11. r. 5)	הַשְׁקִיפָה
שקה	Hiph. pret. 1 p. s. (§ 24. r. 14, & § 8. r. 5); acc. shifted by וַ conv. (comp. § 8. r. 7)	הִשְׁקֵיתִי / וְהִשְׁקֵיתָה
שקה	וַ) id. pret. 1 pers. sing. .	הִשְׁקֵיתִי
שקה	id. id., suff. 3 pers. pl. masc. (§ 24. r. 14)	הִשְׁקִיתִים
שקה	id. pret. 2 pers. s. m., suff. 1 pers. s. (v. id.)	הִשְׁקִיתָנוּ
שקל	וַ) pref. הַ) noun masc. sing. dec. 6 a (§ 35. rem. 2, but pl. c. שְׁקָלֵי) .	הַשֶּׁקֶל / הַשָּׁקֶל
שקם	וַ) pref. id.) noun fem. with pl. masc. term. [from שִׁקְמָה] .	הַשְּׁקָמִים

De. 21. 16, 17.   f Ps. 39. 14.   m De. 25. 7.   t Mi. 7. 3.   b Job 40. 11.   h Da. 5. 22.   r Ge. 29. 7.   u Eze. 38. 11.   b Eze. 32. 6.
De. 21. 15.   a Is. 6. 10.   n Ju. 20. 16.   u Ge. 18. 25.   l Je. 13. 18.   d Eze. 17. 24.   e Ge. 29. 3.   v De. 28. 35.   i Je. 9. 14.
Ge. 41. 32.   c Le. 16. 10.   o Ex. 9. 31.   v De. 19. 17.   Job 22. 29.   Eze. 40. 43.   a Da. 11. 31.   Ge. 29. 8.   Ps. 60. 5.
1 Sa. 2. 13.   d Le. 16. 7.   Je. 29. 17.   f Eze. 21. 31.   Eze. 36. 36.   e Ec. 12. 5.   2 Ch. 15. 5.   De. 16. 15.   Eze. 45. 12.
2 Sa. 16. 19.   Ge. 18. 4.   Ps. 79. 10.   Is. 25. 12.   La. 4. 13.   Nu. 5. 27.   Est. 1. 7.   Je. 25. 15.   1 Ch. 27. 28.
De. 14. 7.   2 Sa. 15. 28.   Ne. 3. 15.   Is. 25. 11.   Eze. 21. 31.   Pr. 25. 21.   Is. 7. 4.

הִשְׁתַּחֲוִיתֶם — id. pret. 2 pers. pl. masc. — שחה

הִשְׁתִּי — pref. הַ)(noun masc. sing. — שתה

הִשְׁתִיָּה —)(pref. id.)(noun fem. sing. — שתה

הַשֹּׁתִים — pref. id.)(Kal part. act. m., pl. of שָׁתָה d. 9a — שתה

הִשְׁתַּכַּח —)(Ch. Ithp. [for הִתְשְׁ § 12. r. 3, for אתְהַ § 47. rem. 4] pret. 3 p. s. m. (§ 48. r. 4) — שכח

הִשְׁתַּכַּחַת — Ch. id. pret. 3 pers. sing. fem. — שכח

הִשְׁתַּכַּחַתְּ —)(id. pret. 2 pers. sing. masc. — שכח

הִשְׁתַּלְחִי — pref. הַ)(patronym. of שֻׁתֶּלַח (q. v.) —

הִשְׁתַּנִּית —)([for הִתְשְׁ § 12. r. 3] Hithpa. pret. 2 p. s. f. — שנה

הִשְׁתַּעְשְׁעוּ — [for הִתְשְׁ § 12. rem. 3] Hithpalp. imp. pl. masc. (§ 6. No. 4) — שעה

הִשְׁתָּרֵר — [for הִתְשָׁרֵר § 12. rem. 3] Hithpa. inf. abs. — שרר

הַתָּא —)(pref. הַ)(noun masc. sing. dec. 1a — תוה

הִתְאַבֵּל — Hithpa. pret. 3 pers. sing. masc. — אבל

הִתְאַבְּלִי — id. imp. sing. fem. — אבל

הִתַּאֲוָה — pref. הַ)(pr. name, see קִבְרוֹת הַתַּ׳ — קבר

הִתְאַוָּה — Hithpa. pret. 3 pers. sing. masc. — אוה

הִתְאַוּוּ — id. pret. 3 pers. pl. — אוה

הִתְאַוִּיתִי — id. pret. 1 pers. sing. — אוה

הִתְאַוִּיתֶם —)(id. pret. 2 pers. pl. masc. (§ 24. rem. 14) — אוה

הַתָּאוֹת — pref. הַ)(n. m. with pl. f. term. for תָּא d. 1a — תוה

הִתְאָרָּ — Hiph. pret. 3 p. s. m. [for הִתְאָאַר § 12. r. 1] — אזר

הִתְאָרְגוּ — id. imp. pl. masc. — אזר

הִתְאַחֲדִי — Hithpa. imp. sing. fem., (§ 14. rem. 1) — אחד

הַתָּאִים — pref. הַ)(noun masc., pl. of תָּא dec. 1a — תוה

הַתַּאֲמִין — pref. הַ)(Hiph. fut. 2 pers. sing. masc. — אמן

הִתְאַמֵּץ — Hithpa. pret. 3 pers. sing. masc. — אמץ

הַתְּאֵנָה —)(pref. הַ)(noun fem. sing. dec. 10. — תאן

הַתְּאֵנִים — pref. id.)(id. pl., absolute state — תאן

הִתְאַנַּף — Hithpa. pret. 3 pers. sing. masc. — אנף

הִתְאַפְּקוּ — Hithpa. pret. 3 p. pl. m. [for אָפְקַ § 12. r. 1] — אפק

הִתְאַשְׁשׁוּ —)(Hithpal. imp. pl. m. [for אִשְׁשׁוּ § 21. r. 20] — איש

הִתְבָּאֲשׁ — Hithpa. pret. 3 pers. pl. — באש

הַתֵּבָה — pref. הַ)(noun fem. sing. dec. 10. — תבה

הַתָּבוֹא — pref. הַ)(Kal fut. 3 pers. sing. fem. — בוא

הַתְּבוּאָה — pref. הַ)(noun fem. sing. dec. 10. — בוא

הַתְּבוּנָה — pref. id.)(noun fem. sing. d. 10. R בּוּן, see בין

הִתְבּוֹנֵן — Hithpal. pret. 3 pers. sing. masc., [for בּוֹנֵן § 21. rem. 20] R. בוּן or — בין

הִתְבּוֹנָן —)(id. imp. sing. masc. — בין

הִתְבּוֹנֲנוּ — id. pret. 3 pers. pl. [for בּוֹנֲנוּ § 21. rem. 20] — בין

הִתְבּוֹנָנוּ —)(id. imp. pl. masc. — בין

הִתְבּוֹנַנְתָּ —)(id. pret. 2 pers. sing. masc. — בין

הַתִּבְטַח — pref. הַ)(Kal fut. 2 pers. sing. masc. — בטח

הַתֶּבֶן —)(pref. הַ)(noun masc. sing. — תבן

הַשֶּׁקֶן — pref. הַ)(noun masc. sing. — שקן

הַשִּׁקּוּצִים — defect. for הַשִּׁקּוּצִים (q. v.) — שקץ

הַשֶּׁקֶר — pref. הַ)(noun masc. sing. dec. 6a (§ 35. rem. 5, but pl. & suff. שִׁקְרֵיהֶם) — שקר

הַשְׁקָתֹת — pref. id.)(n. f. s., pl. שָׁקָתוֹת (§ 35. r. 9 note) — שקה

הִשְׁקָתָה — Hiph. pret. 3 p.s.f. [for הִשְׁקָתָה comp. § 8. r. 7] — שקה

הַשְׁקִתִים —)(defect. for הַשְׁקִתִים (q. v.) — שקה

הַשֹּׁר —)(pref. הַ)(noun masc. sing. dec. 8 (§ 37. rem. 7) — שור

הַשֶּׁרֶב — pref. id.)(noun masc. sing. — שרב

הַשַּׁרְבִיט — pref. id.)(noun masc. sing. — שבט

הַשָּׁרִנִים — pref. id.)(noun masc. pl. of [שָׁרִין] dec. 1b — שרנ

הַשָּׂרֵד — pref. id.)(noun masc. sing. — שרד

הַשָּׁרוֹן —)(pref. id.)(pr. name of a region — ישר

הַשָּׁרוֹנִי — pref. id.)(gent. noun from the preceding — ישר

הַשִּׁרְיוֹן —)(pref. id.)(noun masc. sing. dec. 1b — שרה

הַשָּׁרוֹת —)(pref. id.)(Kal part. act. fem., pl. [שָׁרָה] dec. 10, from שָׁר masc. — שיר

הַשָּׁרוֹת —)(pref. id.)(noun fem., pl. of [שָׁרָה] dec. 10. — שרר

הַשָּׂרִידִים —)(pref. id.)(noun masc., pl. of שָׂרִיד dec. 3a — שרד

הַשָּׁרִים — pref. id.)(Kal part. act. m., pl. of שָׁר d. 1a — שיר

הַשָּׂרִים —)(pref. id.)(noun m., pl. of שַׂר d.8 (§ 37. r.7) — שרר

הַשָּׁרֵן — pref. id.)(noun masc. sing. — שרה

הַשִּׁרְיֹנִים —)(pref. id.)(noun masc., pl. of שִׁרְיוֹן dec. 1b — שרה

הַשַּׁרְמוֹת — pref. id.)(Kheth.; K. שַׁדְמוֹת noun fem., pl. of שְׁדֵמָה dec. 11 (§ 42. rem. 4) — שדם

הַשֹּׂרֵף —)(pref. id.)(Kal part. act. sing. masc. d. 7b — שרף

הַשְׂרֵפָה — pref. id.)(noun fem. sing. dec. 10. — שרף

הַשְּׂרָפִים — pref. id.)(noun masc., pl. of שָׂרָף dec. 4a — שרף

הַשְּׂרֻפִים — pref. id.)(Kal part. p. m. pl. of [שָׂרוּף] d. 3a — שרף

הַשֶּׁרֶץ — pref. id.)(noun masc. sing. (§ 35. rem. 2) — שרץ

הַשֹּׁרֵץ — '. id.)(noun masc. sing. — שרץ

הַשֹּׁרֵץ — pref. id.)(Kal part. act. sing. masc. — שרץ

הַשֹּׁרֶצֶת — pref. id.)(id. fem. (§ 8. rem. 19) — שרץ

הַשָּׁרֵת — pref. id.)(noun masc. sing. — שרת

הַשָּׁשׁ — pref. id.)(noun masc. sing. — שוש

הַשִּׁשָּׁה — pref. id.)(num. card. masc. sing. from שֵׁשׁ f. — שש

הַשִּׁשִּׁי —)(pref. id.)(adj. ord. masc. from שֵׁשׁ — שש

הַשִּׁשִּׁית — pref. id.)(id. fem. — שש

הַשָּׁתוֹת — pref. id.)(n. m. with pl. f. term. fr. [שָׁת] d. 1a — שות

הִשְׁתַּחֲוָה —)([for הִתְשְׁ § 12. r. 3] Hithpalel pret. 3 pers. s.m., 3rd rad. doubled for חֲוָה (§ 24. r. 22) — שחה

הִשְׁתַּחֲווּ —)(id. pret. 3 pers. pl., or, imp. pl. masc. — שחה

הִשְׁתַּחֲוִי —)(id. imp. sing. fem. — שחה

הִשְׁתַּחֲוִיתָ —)(id. pret. 2 pers. sing. masc. — שחה

הִשְׁתַּחֲוֵיתִי —)(id. pret. 1 pers. sing. — שחה

ᵃ 2 Ki. 23. 24.   ᵇ Ge. 40. 12.   ᵒ Je. 31. 40.   Ps. 11. 3.   Ezr. 6. 2.   1 Sa. 15. 35.   Ps. 93. 1.   1 Ch. 19. 6.   Je. 9. 16.

Je. 7. 4.   1 Sa. 17. 5.   Nu. 17. 4.   Da. 5. 27.   2 Sa. 14. 2.   Is. 8. 9.   2 Sa. 24. 12.   Je. 2. 10.

Ge. 24. 20.   Ge. 35. 25.   Le. 11. 31.   1 Ki. 14. 2.   Pr. 31. 26.   Eze. 21. 21.   Le. 25. 21, 22.   Ps. 37. 10.

Ge. 24. 46.   Is. 3. 19.   Le. 11. 46.   Is. 29. 9.   Nu. 11. 4.   Job 39. 12.   1 Ki. 7. 14.   Job 39. 11.

Is. 35. 7.   Joa. 10. 20.   Nu. 4. 12.   Nu. 16. 13.   Je. 17. 16.   Is. 63. 15.   Is. 1. 3.   Ex. 5. 15.

Est. 5. 2.   Ne. 4. 10.   2 Ch. 35. 25.   Le. 13. 52, 56, 58, 59.   Eze. 40. 13.   Nu. 34. 10.   Is. 46. 8.   Job 37. 14.   1 Ki. 5. 8.

2 Sa. 3. 5.   Est. 1. 8.   Eze. 40. 7, 12.   Is. 66. 15

הַתַּבְנִית֙	pref. הַ)(noun fem. sing. dec. 1 b .	בנה
הִתְבֹּנַנְתָּ֫	Hithpal. pret. 2 pers. sing. masc., R. בון or	בין
הִתְבַּקֵּעוּ	Hithpa. pret. 3 pers. pl. [for בָּקְעוּ § 12. r. 1]	בקע
וְהִתְבָּרֵךְ֙	Hithpa. pret. 3 pers. sing. masc.	ברך
הִתְבָּרְכוּ	} id. pret. 3 pers. pl.	ברך
הִתְבָּרֲכוּ		
הִתְגַּדַּלְתִּי	Hithpa. pret. 1 pers. sing. . .	גדל
הִתְגֹּזָֽרֶת֙	Ch. Ithpe. pret. 3 pers. sing. fem. (§47. rem. 4, & § 49. rem. 1) . . .	גזר
הִתְגַּלְגְּלוּ	Hithpalp. (§ 6. No. 4) pret. 3 pers. pl. [for גַּלְגְּלוּ comp. § 12. rem. 1] . .	גלל
וְהִתְגַּלָּח֙	Hithpa. pret. 3 pers. sing. masc. [for גַּלָּח § 12. rem. 1]	גלח
הִתְגַּלְּחוֹ	id. inf. [fr. הִתְגַּלָּח], suff. 3 pers. sing. m.	גלח
הִתְגַּלֵּֽעַ־	Hithpa. inf. constr.	גלע
וְהִתְגָּעֲשׁוּ	Hithpo. pret. 3 pers. pl.	געשׁ
וְהִתְגָּר֙	Hithpa. imp. sing. masc., ap. [for גָּרָה § 24. rem. 12]	גרה
הִתְגָּרִ֫ית	id. pret. 2 pers. sing. fem. . .	גרה
הֲתֵדַע֙	pref. הֲ)(Kal fut. 2 pers. sing. masc.	ידע
הֲתֹהוּ	pref. הֲ)(noun masc. sing. . .	תהה
וְהִתְהַלֵּךְ֙	Hithpa. pret. 3 pers. sing. m., or imp. m.	הלך
הִתְהַלֵּךְ	id. pret. 3 pers. sing. masc. (§ 12. rem. 4)	הלך
הִתְהַלְּכוּ	id. pret. 3 pers. pl., or imp. pl. masc.	הלך
הִתְהַלַּכְנוּ	id. pret. 1 pers. pl.	הלך
הִתְהַלַּכְתָּ֙	id. pret. 2 pers. sing. masc. [for הַלָּכְתָּ comp. § 8. rem. 7] . .	הלך
הִתְהַלָּ֫כְתִּי	} id. pret. 1 pers. sing. (comp. id.)	הלך
וְהִתְהַלָּ֫כְתִּי		
הִתְהֹלְלוּ	Hithpa. imp. pl. masc. [for הֹלְלוּ § 10. r. 7]	הלל
וְהִתְהֹלָ֫לוּ	Hithpo. pret. 3 pers. pl. [for הֹלְלוּ comp. § 8. rem. 7, & § 12. rem. 1]	הלל
וְהִתְהֹלָ֫לוּ	id. imp. masc., or pret. 3 pers. pl.	הלל
הַתָּוִי֙	pref. הַ)(noun m. s. [for תָּוֶה], with suff.	תוה
הַתּוֹדָה֙	)(pref. id.)(noun fem. sing. dec. 10. .	ידה
וְהִתְוַדָּה֙	Hithpa. pret. 3 pers. s. m. (§ 20. No. 1)	ידה
וְהִתְוַדּוּ	id. pret. 3 pers. pl.	ידה
הַתּוֹדֹת֙	pref. הַ)(noun fem., pl. of תּוֹדָה dec. 10.	ידה
הִתְווּ	Hiph. pret. 3 pers. pl.	תוה
וְהִתְוִ֫יתָ	id. pret. 2 pers. sing. masc. (§ 24. rem. 14)	תוה
הַתָּ֫וֶךְ	pref. הַ)(noun masc. sing. dec. 6g	תוך
הַתּוֹלָעִי	pref. id.)(patronym. of תּוֹלָע	תלע
הַתּוֹלַ֫עַת֙	} pref. id.)(noun fem. sing., (suff. תּוֹלַעְתָּם) dec. 13 a	תלע
הַתּוֹלָ֫עַת֙		

הַתּוֹעֵבָה	pref. id.)(noun fem. sing. dec. 11 b	תעב
הַתּוֹעֵבוֹת	} pref. id.)(id. pl., absolute state	תעב
הַתּוֹעֵבֹת		
הַתּוֹעֲבֹת֙	pref. id.)(id. pl., constr. state	תעב
הַתּוֹקֵ֫עַ֙	וְ pref. הַ)(Kal part. act. sing. masc. d. 7 b	תקע
הַתּוֹרִי֙	pref. id.)(noun masc. sing. dec. 1 a	תור
הַתּוֹרִדֵ֫נִי֙	pref. הֲ)(Hiph. fut. 2 pers. sing. masc., suff. 1 pers. sing.	ירד
הַתּוֹרָה	וְ pref. הַ)(noun fem. sing. dec. 10.	ירה
הַתּוֹרֹת֙	וְ pref. id.)(id. pl.	ירה
הַתּוֹשָׁבִים֙	pref. id.)(noun masc., pl. of תּוֹשָׁב dec. 1 b except constr. תּוֹשַׁב (§ 31. rem. 1) .	ישׁב
הַתֵּז	Hiph. pret. 3 pers. sing. masc. [for הַתֵּז § 8. rem. 10] as if fr. תזז, see .	תיז
הִתְחַבְּאוּ	Hithpa. pret. 3 pers. pl. .	חבא
הִתְחַבְּרוּת֙	(prop. Hithp. inf.) subst. fem. sing.	חבר
וְהִתְחוֹלֵל֙	וְ Hithp. imp. sing. masc.	חול
הִתְחַזֵּק	Hithpa. pret. 3 pers. sing. masc., or imp. masc. (§ 12. rem. 1)	חזק
הִתְחַזְּקוּ	id. imp. pl. masc. . .	חזק
הִתְחַזַּ֫קְתִּי	id. pret. 1 pers. sing. .	חזק
וְהִתְחַזַּקְתֶּם֙	וְ id. pret. 2 pers. pl. masc.	חזק
הֶתְחָיֶ֫ינָה֙	pref. הֲ)(Kal fut. 3 pers. pl. fem.	חיה
וְהִתְחַל־֙	וְ Hithpa. imp. s. m. ap. [for חַלָּה § 24. r. 12]	חלה
הַתְּחִלָּה֙	pref. הַ)(noun fem. sing. dec. 10.	חלל
וְהִתְחַלְּקוּ֙	וְ Hithpa. pret. 3 pers. pl.	חלק
הַתַּחְמָס֙	pref. הַ)(noun masc. sing.	חמס
הַתַּחֲנִי	pref. id.)(patronym. of תַּחַן	חנה
הַתְּחִנָּה֙	וְ pref. id.)(noun fem. sing. dec. 10.	חנן
וְהִתְחַנְּנוּ֙	וְ Hitpa. pret. 3 pers. pl.	חנן
הִתְחַנַּ֫נְתָּה֙	id. pret. 2 pers. sing. masc. (§ 8. rem. 5)	חנן
הִתְחַנָּ֫נְתִּי֙	id. pret. 1 pers. sing.	חנן
הִתְחַפֵּשׂ	Hithpa. pret. 3 pers. sing. masc., or imp. m.	חפשׂ
הִתְחָרֵךְ֙	Ch. Ithpa. pret. 3 pers. sing. m. (§ 47. r. 4)	חרך
הַתַּחַשׁ֙	pref. הַ)(noun masc. sing. dec. 6 d	תחשׁ
הַתְּחָשִׁים֙	pref. id.)(id. pl. absolute state	תחשׁ
הַתַּ֫חַת	pref. הַ)(adv. . .	תות
הַתַּחְתּוֹן֙	pref. הַ)(adj. masc. sing.	תות
הַתַּחְתֹּנָה֙	pref. id.)(id. fem., dec. 10.	תות
הִתְחַתֵּן֙	Hithpa. inf., or imp. sing. masc.	חתן
וְהִתְחַנְּנוּ֙	וְ id. imp. pl. masc.	חתן
וְהִתְחַתַּנְתֶּם֙	וְ id. pret. 2 pers. pl. masc.	חתן
הָתֵיב֙	Ch. Aph. pret. 3 pers. sing. m. (§ 47. r. 4)	תוב
הֲתִיבוּנָא֙	Ch. id. pret. 1 pers. pl.	תוב
הֵתָ֫יוּ	Hiph. imp. masc. pl. [for הֶאֱתָ֫יוּ § 25. No. 2 c, & § 24. rem. 5]	אתה

a 1 Ch. 28. 19.   g Eze. 38. 23.   o De. 2. 24.   u Je. 46. 9.   α Le. 14. 52.   π Le. 26. 46.   ι Nu. 13. 20.   σ 1 Ki. 8. 59.   ∞ Ge. 34. 9.
b Job 38. 18.   h Da. 2. 34.   p Je. 50. 24.   v Eze. 9. 6.   β Le. 14. 6, 51.   ρ Le. 25. 45.   κ Eze. 37. 3.   τ Da. 3. 27.   ♦ Jos. 23. 12.
c Jos. 9. 13.   i Job 30. 14.   q Job 37. 15, 16.   w 1 Sa. 12. 21.   γ Is. 18. 5.   ς 2 Sa. 13. 5.   λ Nu. 4. 25.   υ Nu. 11. 17.   ‖ Da. 2. 14.
d De. 29. 18.   k Le. 13. 33.   r 1 Sa. 14. 11.   x Ne. 12. 38.   δ Ne. 4. 12.   ϑ 1 Sa. 14. 11.   μ Ne. 11. 17.   φ Ex. 39. 34.   ◊ Ezr. 5. 11.
e Ge. 22. 18.   l Nu. 6. 19.   s Jos. 18. 8.   y Ne. 12. 40.   ε Ca. 2. 12.   ω Da. 11. 23.   ν Jos. 18. 5.   χ 1 Ch. 7. 24.   ★ Is. 21. 14;
f Ge. 26. 4;   m Pr. 17. 14.   t Ps. 35. 14.   z Ps. 78. 41.   ζ 1 Sa. 30. 15.   ϕ Ps. 37. 7.   ξ 1 Ki. 8. 54.   ψ 2 Ch. 8. 5.   Je. 12. 9.
Je. 4. 2.   Je. 25. 16.   Je. 25. 16.   Eze. 9. 4.   η Ex. 18. 20.   θ 1 Sa. 4. 9.   ο 1 Ki. 9. 3.   ρ 1 Sa. 18. 22, 23.

Hebrew	Description	Root
הִתְיַחֵשׁ	Hithpa. inf. constr. used as a noun (§ 14. r. 1)	יחש
הִתְיַחְשׂוּ	id. pret. 3 pers. pl.	יחש
הִתְיַחְשָׂם	id. inf., suff. 3 pers. plur. masc. dec. 7b	יחש
הֲתֵיטִבְיָ	pref. הֲ)(Kal fut. 2 pers. s. m. (§ 20. r. 14)	יטב
הִתִּיכוּ	Hiph. pret. 3 pers. pl.	נתך
הַתִּיכוֹן	pref. הַ)(adj. masc. sing.	תוך
הַתִּיכוֹנָה	ו'ן pref. id.)(id. fem. dec. 10.	תוך
הַתִּיכֹן	defect. for כוֹן (q. v.)	תוך
הַתִּיכֹנָה	defect. for הַתִּיכוֹנָה (q. v.)	תוך
הַתֵּימָן	pref. הַ)(noun masc. sing.	ימן
הַתֵּימָנִי	pref. id.)(patronym. of תֵּימָן	ימן
הִתְיַצֵּב	ו' Hithpa. imp. sing. masc.	יצב
הִתְיַצָּבָה	id. id. with parag. ה [for יַצְּבָה comp. § 8. rem. 7, & § 12. rem. 1]	יצב
הִתְיַצְּבוּ	ו' id. pret. 3 pers. pl., or imp. pl. masc.	יצב
הַתֵּיצִי	pref. הַ)(gent. noun fr. תֵּי"ץ q. v.	
הַתִּיקֵנוּ	Hiph. inf., suff. 1 pers. pl. dec. 1b	נתק
הַתִּירוֹשׁ	ו' pref. הַ)(noun masc. sing. dec. 1b	ירש
הַתְּיָשִׁים	pref. id.)(noun masc., pl. of תַּיִשׁ dec. 6h (§ 35. rem. 12)	תיש
הֲתָךְ	pr. name of a eunuch at the court of Ahasuerus, Est. 4. 5.	
הִתְכַּבֵּד	Hithpa. imp. sing. masc.	כבד
הִתְכַּבְּדִי	id. imp. sing. fem.	כבד
הַתְּכֵלֶת	pref. הַ)(noun fem. sing.	תכל
הִתַּכְתִּי	ו' Hiph. pret. 1 pers. sing. m. acc. shifted by ו conv. (comp. § 8. rem. 7)	נתך
הָתֵל	Hiph. inf. constr.	תלל
הָתֵל	id. pret. 3 pers. sing. masc.; for הִתֵּל acc. shifted before monos. (בֵּר).	תלל
הַתְּלָאָה	pref. הַ)(noun fem. sing.	לאה
הֲתַלְבִּישׁ	pref. הֲ)(Hiph. fut. 2 pers. sing. masc.	לבש
הֲתֻלִּים	noun m., pl. of [הָתֻל] d. 8c. (§ 37. Nos. 3&4)	תלל
הֲתֵלֵךְ	pref. הֲ)(Kal fut. 2 pers. sing. masc.	ילך
הֲתֵלְכִי	pref. id.)(id. fut. 2 pers. sing. fem.	ילך
הַתֹּלַעַת	defect. for הַתּוֹלַעַת (q. v. comp. § 35. r. 2)	תלע
הֲתִלְתָּ	Hiph. pret. 2 pers. s. m. (comp. § 18. r. 16)	תלל
הָתֵם	Hiph. imp. sing. masc., or inf.	תמם
הִתְמֹנְגֵעַ	Hithpal. pret. 3 pers. pl. (for מֹנֵגַע comp. § 8. rem. 7, & § 12. rem. 1]	מוג
הִתְמַהּוּ	ו' Hithpa. imp. pl. masc. [for הִתְתַמְּהוּ, comp. § 12. rem. 3]	תמה
הִתְמַהְמְהוּ	ו'" Hithpalp. imp. pl. m. (§ 6. No. 4)	מהה
הִתְמַהְמְהַם	id. inf. (מַהְמֵהַ), suff. 3 pers. pl. m. d. 7b	מהה
הִתְמַהְמָהְנוּ	id. pret. 1 p.pl. [for מַהְמָהְנוּ comp. § 8. r.7]	מהה
הִתְמַהְמָהְתִּי	id. pret. 1 p. s. [for מַהְמַהְתִּי comp. id.]	מהה
הֲתַמּוּ	pref. הֲ)(Kal pret. 3 pers. pl.	תמם
הֲתֵמּוּ	Hiph. pret. 3 pers. pl. (§ 18. rem. 10)	תמם
הַתַּמּוּז	pref. ה)(pr. name of an idol see תַּמּוּז	
הִתְמוֹטְטָה	Hithpal. pret. 3 pers. sing. fem.	מוט
הַתְּמוּרָה	pref. ה)(noun fem. sing. dec. 10.	מור
הֲתִמֹּתִי	ו' Hiph. pret. 1 pers. sing.; acc. shifted by ו, for ו conv. (comp. § 8. rem. 7)	תמם
הַתָּמִיד	pref. ה)(noun masc. sing.	עמד
הַתַּמִּים	pref. id.)(noun masc., pl. of תֹם dec. 8c	תמם
הִתְמַכֵּר	Hithpa. pret. 3 pers. sing. masc.	מכר
הִתְמַכֶּרְךָ	id. inf. [מַכֵּר], suff. 2 pers. sing. masc. dec. 7b (comp. § 16. rem. 15, & § 36. rem. 3)	מכר
הִתְמַכַּרְתֶּם	ו' id. pret. 2 pers. pl. masc.	מכר
הֲתִמָּלֵא	pref. ה interr. for הֲ)(Piel fut. 2 pers. s. m.	מלא
הִתְמְלִי	Ch. Ithpe. pret. 3 pers. sing. m. (§ 47. r. 4)	מלא
הֲתִמְלֹךְ	pref. הֲ)(Kal fut. 2 pers. sing. masc.	מלך
הַתֵּימְנִי	pref. ה)(patronym. of תֵּימָן	ימן
הַתִּמְנִי	pref. id.)(gent. noun from תִּמְנָה	מנה
הַתְּמֹרָה	pref. id.)(noun fem. sing. dec. 10.	תמר
הַתְּמֹרוֹת	pref. id.)(id. pl.	תמר
הַתְּמָרִים	pref. id.)(noun masc., pl. of תָּמָר dec. 4a	תמר
הַתִּמֹרִים	ו' pref. id.)(noun fem. with pl. masc. term. from תִּמֹרָה dec. 10.	תמר
הִתְנַבִּי	ו' Chald. Ithpa. pret. 3 pers. s. m. (§ 47. r. 4)	נבא
הִתְנַבִּיתָ	ו' Hithpa. pret. 2 pers. sing. masc.	נבא
הִתְנַגְּשׁוּ	Hithpa. imp. masc. pl.	נגש
הִתְנַדֵּב	Hithpa. inf. constr. dec. 7b	נדב
הִתְנַדַּבוּ	Chald. Ithpa. pret. 3 pers. pl. m. (§ 47. rem. 4)	נדב
הִתְנַדְּבוּ	Hithpa. pret. 3 pers. pl.	נדב
הִתְנַדָּבוּת	Chald. prop. Ithpa. inf., used as a subst.	נדב
הִתְנַדְּבָם	Hithpa. inf. (נַדֵּב'), suff. 3 pers. pl. m. d. 7b	נדב
הִתְנַדַּבְתִּי	id. pret. 1 pers. sing.	נדב
הִתְנוּ	Hiph. pret. 3 pers. pl.	תנה
הִתְנוֹדְדָה	ו' Hithpal. pret. 3 pers. sing. fem.	נוד
הַתְּנוּפָה	pref. ה)(noun fem. sing. dec. 10.	נוף
הַתַּנּוּרִים	pref. id.)(noun masc., pl. of תַּנּוּר dec. 1b	תנר
הִתְנַחֵל	Hithpa. inf. constr. (§ 14. rem. 1)	נחל
הִתְנַחֲלוּם	ו' id. pret. 3 pers. pl., suff. 3 pers. pl. masc.	נחל
הִתְנַחַלְתֶּם	ו' id. pret. 2 pers. pl. masc.	נחל
הַתַּנִּים	pref. הַ)(noun masc. sing., for תַּנִּין as several MSS. have it	תנן
הַתַּנִּין	pref. id.)(noun masc. sing. dec. 1b, also pr. name	תנן
הַתַּנִּינִם	pref. id.)(id. pl., absolute state	תנן
הִתְנַעֲרִי	Hithpa. imp. sing. fem. (§ 14. rem. 1)	נער

---

a Na. 3. 8.   b 2 Ki. 22. 9.   c Eze. 47. 16.   d Ju. 7. 19.   e 1 Ki. 6. 6.   f Ex. 26. 28; 36,33.   g Zec. 6. 6.

h Job 33. 5.   i Jos. 8. 6.   k Na. 3. 15.   l Na. 3. 15.   m Eze. 22. 20.   n Ex. 8. 25.   o Ge. 31. 7.

p Job 39. 19.   q Job 17. 2.   r Ge. 24. 58.   s De. 28. 39.   t Ju.16.10,13,15.   u Eze. 24. 10.

v Na. 1. 5.   w Hab. 1. 5.   x Is. 29. 9.   y Ju. 19. 8.   z Is. 24. 19.   a Ge. 43. 10.

* Ps. 119. 60.   † 1 Sa. 16. 11.   ‡ 2 Sa. 20. 18.   § Eze. 8. 14.   ‖ Is. 24. 19.   ¶ Eze. 22. 15.

* 1 Ki. 21. 25.   † 1 Ki. 21. 20.   ‡ 1 ... 3. 32.   § De. 28. 68.   ‖ Job 40. 31.   ¶ Da. 3. 19.   # Je. 22. 15.

* Ezr. 1. 6.   † Eze. 7. 16.   ‡ Ezr. 7. 15.   § Ezr. 5. 1.   ‖ 1 Ch. 29. 9.   ¶ 1 Ch. 29. 17.   # Is. 45. 20.   ** Ho. 8. 9.

* Is. 24. 20.   † Is. 14. 2.   ‡ Nu. 32. 18.   § Eze. 29. 2   ‖ Ge. 1. 21   ¶ Is. 52. 2

התְנַפַּלְתִּי	Hithpa. pret. 1 pers. sing. [for נַפַלְתּי comp. § 8. rem. 7]	נפל
הִתְנַשֵּׂא	Hithpa. inf. constr.	נשׂא
הַתִּנְשֶׁמֶת / הַתִּנְשֶׁמֶת	pref. הַ ⅄ noun fem. sing. (comp. § 35. rem. 2)	נשׁם
הִתְעֵבָה	pref. id. ⅄ noun fem. sing. dec. 11b	תעב
הִתְעֵבוֹת	pref. id. ⅄ id. pl. absolute (constr. תּועֵבוֹת)	תעב
הִתְעַבֵּר	Hithpa. pret. 3 pers. sing. m. (§ 12. rem. 1)	עבר
הִתְעַבַּרְתָּ	id. pret. 2 pers. sing. masc.	עבר
הִתְעַבְתְּ	Hiph. pret. 2 pers. sing. fem.	תעב
הִתְעָה	Hiph. pret. 3 pers. sing. masc.	תעה
הִתְעוּ	id. pret. 3 pers. pl.	תעה
הַתְעוּדָה	pref. הַ ⅄ noun fem. sing.	עוד
הִתְעוּם	Hiph. pret. 3 pers. pl., suff. 3 pers. pl. masc.	תעה
הַתָעוֹף	pref. הַ ⅄ Kh. תָעוּף Kal fut. 3 pers. sing. fem.; K. תָעִיף Hiph. fut. 2 pers. sing. m.	עוף
הִתְעוֹרְרִי	Hithpal. imp. sing. fem.	עור
הִתְעַוְּתוּ	Hithpa. pret. 3 pers. pl.	עות
הִתְעִיבוּ	Hiph. pret. 3 pers. pl.	תעב
הַתַעֲלֶה	pref. הַ ⅄ noun fem. sing. dec. 10 (§ 42. r. 2)	עלה
הִתְעַלֵּל	Hithpa. pret. 3 pers. sing. masc.	עלל
הִתְעַלְּלוּ	id. pret. 3 pers. pl.	עלל
הִתְעַלַּלְתְּ	id. pret. 2 pers. sing. fem.	עלל
הִתְעַלַּלְתִּי	id. pret. 1 pers. sing.	עלל
הִתְעַלַּמְתָּ	Hithpa. pret. 2 pers. sing. masc.; acc. shifted by conv. (comp. § 8. rem. 7)	עלם
הִתְעַמֵּר	Hithpa. pret. 3 pers. sing. masc. [for עַמֵּר § 12. rem. 4]	עמר
הִתְעַנֵּג	Hithpa. imp. sing. masc. (§ 12. rem. 1)	ענג
הִתְעַנְּגוּ	id. pret. 3 pers. pl.	ענג
הִתְעַנַּגְתֶּם	id. pret. 2 pers. pl. masc.	ענג
הִתְעַנֶּה	Hithpa. pret. 3 pers. sing. masc.	ענה
הִתְעַנִּי	id. imp. sing. fem.	ענה
הִתְעַנִּיתָ	id. pret. 2 pers. sing. masc.	ענה
הִתְעָרֵב	Hithpa. imp. sing. masc., Milêl bef. monos. [for עָרֵב § 12. rem. 4]	ערב
הִתְעָרְבוּ	id. pret. 3 pers. sing.	ערב
הַתַּעֲרֻבוֹת	pref. הַ ⅄ noun fem., pl. of [תַּעֲרֻבָה] dec. 10.	ערב
הִתְעָרְתִּי	Hithpal. pret. 1 pers. sing.	עור
הִתְעַשְׂקוּ	Hithpa. pret. 3 pers. pl.	עשׂק
הִתְעַתְּדוּ	Hithpa. pret. 3 pers. pl.	עתד
הִתְעַתְּעָם	Keri עִתַּם, Hiph. pret. 2 pers. pl. masc.	תעה
הַתֹּף	pref. הַ ⅄ noun masc. sing. dec. 8c	תפף
הִתְפָּאֵר	Hithpa. imp. sing. masc.	פאר
הִתְפָּאַרְתְּ	ו pref. הַ ⅄ noun fem. sing. dec. 13a	פאר

הַתַּפּוּחַ	pref. id. ⅄ noun masc. sing. dec. 1b	נפח
הִתְפּוֹל	pref. הַ ⅄ Kal fut. 3 pers. sing. fem.	נפל
הִתְפּוֹרְרָה	Hithpo. pret. 3 pers. sing. fem.	פרר
הַתְּפִלָּה	pref. הַ ⅄ noun fem. sing. dec. 10.	פלל
הִתְפַּלֵּל	ו Hithpa. pret. 3 pers. sing. m., or imp. s. m.	פלל
הִתְפַּלֶּל־	id. imp. with Mak. (§ 12. rem. 4)	פלל
הִתְפַּלְלוּ	ו id. imp. pl. m., or pret. comp 1 Ki. 8. 33.	פלל
הִתְפַּלַּלְתָּ	id. pret. 2 pers. sing. masc.	פלל
הִתְפַּלַּלְתִּי	id. pret. 1 pers. s. [פַּלַּתִּי comp. § 8. r. 7]	פלל
הִתְפַּלַּלְתֶּם	ו id. pret. 2 pers. pl. masc.	זלל
הִתְפַּלְּשׁוּ	ו Hithpa. imp. pl. masc.	פלשׁ
הִתְפַּלְּשִׁי	ו id. imp. sing. fem.	פלשׁ
הִתְפַּלָּשְׁתִּי	id., Kh. לָשְׁתִּי, pret. 2 pers. sing. fem., K. לָשִׁי in pause for הִתְפַּלְּשִׁי q. v.	פלשׁ
הִתְפָּקְדוּ	Hothpa. pret. 3 pers. pl. [for פָּקְדוּ § 6. No. 10 note, § 12. rem. 5]	פקד
הִתְפָּקְדוּ	Hithpa. pret. 3 p. pl. [for פָּקְדוּ § 12. r. 5]	פקד
הִתְפָּרְדוּ	ו Hithpa. pret. 3 pers. pl.	פרד
הִתְפָּרְקוּ / הִתְפָּרְקוּ	Hithpa. pret. 3 pers. pl. (comp. § 8. r. 7, & § 12. rem. 1)	פרק
הַתֹּפֶת	pref. הַ ⅄ noun fem. sing.	תוף
הִתְפַּתְּחוּ	Kh. חוּ, Hithpa. imp. pl. masc.; K. חִי, s. f.	פתח
הַתָּצוּדֶ־	pref. הַ ⅄ Kal fut. 2 pers. sing. masc.	צוד
הַתֹּצִיאֶ־	pref. id. ⅄ Hiph. fut. 2 pers. sing. masc.	יצא
הַתִּצְלָחֶ־	pref. id. ⅄ Kal fut. 3 pers. sing. fem. [for תִּצְלַח § 8. rem. 15]	צלח
הַתַּצְלִחַ	pref. id. ⅄ Hiph. fut. 3 pers. sing. fem.	צלח
הִתְקַבְּצוּ	Hithpa. pret. 3 pers. pl., or imp. pl. masc.	קבץ
הִתְקַדְּרוּ	Hithp. pret. 3 pers. pl.	קדר
הִתְקַדֵּשׁ	Hithpa. pret. 3 pers. sing. masc. [for קַדֵּשׁ § 12. rem. 4]	קדשׁ
הִתְקַדְּשׁוּ / הִתְקַדְּשׁוּ	ו id. pret. 3 pers. pl., or imp. pl. masc. (comp. § 8. rem. 7, & § 12. rem. 1)	קדשׁ
הִתְקַדַּשְׁתִּי	ו id. pret. 1 pers. sing.; acc. shifted by conv. (§ 8. rem. 7, & § 12. rem. 2)	קדשׁ
הִתְקַדַּשְׁתֶּם	ו id. pret. 2 pers. pl. masc. (§ 12. rem. 2)	קדשׁ
הַתִּקְוָה	pref. הַ ⅄ noun fem. sing. dec. 10.	קוה
הַתְּקוּעָה	pref. id. ⅄ Kal part. pass. s. f. fr. [תָּקוּעַ] m.	תקע
הַתְּקוֹעִי	pref. id. ⅄ gent. noun from תְּקוֹע	תקע
הַתְּקוֹעִים	pref. id. ⅄ id. pl.	תקע
הַתְּקוֹעִית	pref. id. ⅄ id. sing. fem.	תקע
הִתְקֹשֵׁשׁוּ	Hithpo. imp. pl. masc.	קשׁשׁ
הִתְקַלְקְלוּ	Hithpalp. (§ 6. No. 4) pret. 3. pers. pl. [for קַלְקְלוּ comp. § 8. rem. 7]	קלל

---

a De. 9. 25.   h Ho. 4. 12.   p Ec. 12. 3.   y De. 24. 7.   f Ezr. 9. 2.   n 1 Ch. 29. 11.   u Je. 29. 12.   d Eze. 19. 12.   l Is. 30. 29.
b Eze. 17. 14.   i Ge. 20. 13.   q Ps. 14. 1.   z Ps. 37. 1.   g Job 31. 29.   o Ca. 8. 5.   v Je. 25. 34.   e Is. 52. 2.   m 2 Ch. 35. 6.
c Le. 11. 18.   k Is. 19. 13, 14.   r Ps. 52. 2.   a Ps. 37. 11.   h Ge. 26. 20.   p Am. 3. 5.   w Je. 6. 26.   f Job 38. 39.   n Eze. 38. 23.
d Je. 44. 4.   l Ruth 4. 7.   s 1 Sa. 6. 6.   b Is. 66. 11.   i Job 15. 28.   q Is. 24. 19.   x Ju. 20. 15, 17.   g Job 38. 32.   o Zec. 9. 12.
e Ps. 78. 62.   m Je. 50. 6.   t 1 Ki. 2. 26.   c 1 Ki. 2. 26.   k Je. 42. 20.   r Je. 37. 3.   y Ese. 17. 10.   h Eze. 17. 10.   p Is. 22. 25.
f Ps. 89. 39.   n Pr. 23. 5.   u De. 21. 1, 4.   l Je. 37. 3.   s Je. 29. 7.   z Ps. 22. 15.   i Ju. 18. 5.   q Zep. 2. 1.
g Ese. 16. 52.   o Is. 51. 17.   e Ex. 15. 20.   t 1 Sa. 1. 27.   a Ex. 32. 24.   k 1 Ki. 18. 45.   r Je. 4. 24.
     o Ex. 8. 5.

Headword	Description	Root
הֲתִקֵּם	Hiph. imp. sing. masc., הָתִיק § 11. rem. 5] suff. 3 pers. pl. masc.	נתק
הָתְקָנַת	Ch. Hoph. (by Hebraism) pret. 1 pers. sing. [for הָתְקָנַת]	תקן
הַתִּקְעִי	pref. הַ) gent. noun from תְּקוֹעַ	תקע
הַתְּקֹעִים	pref. id.) id. pl.	תקע
הַתְּקֹעִית	pref. id.) id. sing. fem.	תקע
וַהִתְקַצַּף	) Hithpa. pret. 3 pers. sing. masc. (§ 12. r. 1)	קצף
הַתִּקְשֵׁר	pref. הַ) Kal fut. 2 pers. sing. masc. (for תִּקְשׁר § 8. rem. 18)	קשר
הֲתִקְשֹׁר	pref. הֲ interr. for הַ) Piel fut. 2 pers. s. m.	קשר
הִתְקַשְּׁרוּ	Hithpa. pret. 3 pers. pl.	קשר
הַתֵּר	Hiph. inf. absolute	נתר
הַתְרַגֶּזְךָ	Hithpa. inf. (רָגַז), suff. 2 pers. sing. masc. dec. 7b (comp. § 16. rem. 15, & § 36. r. 3)	רגז
הַתְּרוּמָה	) pref. הַ) noun fem. sing. dec. 10.	רום
הִתְרוֹמַמְתָּ	Ch. Ithpal. pret. 2 pers. sing. masc.	רום
הַתְּרוּעָה	pref. הַ) noun fem. sing. dec. 10.	רוע
הִתְרוֹעָעִי	Hithpal. imp. sing. fem. (for רוֹעֲעִי comp. § 8. rem. 7, & § 21. rem. 20)	רוע
הִתְרַחֲצוּ	Ch. Ithpe. pret. 3 pers. pl. m. (§ 47. r. 1 & 4)	רחץ
הִתְרַחַצְתִּי	Hithpa. pret. 1 pers. sing.	רחץ
הַתָּרִים	pref. הַ) Kal part. act. m., pl. of [תָּר] d. 1a	תור
הֲתָרִים	pref. הֲ) Hiph. fut. 2 pers. sing. masc.	רום
הַתָּרִים	pref. הַ) noun masc., pl. of תּוֹר dec. 1a	תור
הַתַּרְעִישֵׁנּוּ	pref. הַ) Hiph. fut. 2 pers. sing. masc., suff. 3 pers. sing. masc.	רעש
הַתַּרְעֵלָה	pref. הַ) noun fem. sing.	רעל
הִתְרוֹעָעָה	Hithpo. pret. 3 pers. sing. fem.	רעע
הַתְּרָפִים	pref. הַ) noun masc. pl.	תרף
הִתְרַפִּיתָ	Hithpa. pret. 2 pers. sing. masc. (comp. § 24. rem. 14)	רפה
הִתְרַפֵּס	Hithpa. imp. sing. masc.	רפס
תִּרְשָׁתָא	pref. הַ) a title, see תִּרְשָׁתָא	
הַתִּשְׁבִּי	pref. id.) gent. noun from תִּשְׁבָּה	שבה
וְהִתְשׁוֹטַטְנָה	) Hithpal. imp. pl. fem.	שוט
הַתְּשׁוּעָה	pref. id.) noun fem. sing. dec. 10.	ישע
הַתַּשְׁחִית	pref. הַ) Hiph. fut. 2 pers. sing. masc.	שחת
הֲתִשְׂחָק	pref. הֲ interr. for הַ) Piel fut. 2 pers. sing. m. [for תְּשַׂחֵק § 10. r. 14, & § 14. r. 1]	שחק
הֲתָשִׂים	pref. הֲ) Kal fut. 2 p. s. m., from שִׂים see שׂום	שׂום
הַתְּשִׁיעִי	pref. הַ art.) adj. ord. masc. sing. from תֵּשַׁע	תשע
הַתְּשִׁיעִית / הַתְּשִׁיעִת	} pref. id.) id. fem.	תשע
הַתִּשְׁכַּח	pref. הַ) Kal fut. 3 pers. sing. fem.	שכח
הֲתִשְׁלַח	pref. הֲ interr. for הַ) Piel fut. 2 pers. sing. m.	שלח
הַתִּשְׁמֹר	pref. הַ) Kal fut. 2 pers. sing. masc.	שמר
הַתְּשֻׁעָה	defect. for הַתְּשׁוּעָה (q. v.)	ישע
הַתְּשִׁעִי	defect. for תְּשִׁיעִי (q. v.)	תשע
הַתְּשִׁעִית	defect. for תְּשִׁיעִית (q. v.)	תשע
הַתִּשְׁפּוֹט / הַתִּשְׁפֹּט	} pref. הַ) Kal fut. 2 pers. sing. masc. (§ 8. rem. 18)	שפט

הָתַת   cogn. חָתַת q. v., hence Po. to break in upon, תְּהוֹוָתְתוּ Ps. 62. 4; Prof. Lee, to attack unjustly. Others derive it from הוּת in the sense of prating, talking.

הֲתִתֵּן	pref. הֲ) Kal fut. 2 pers. sing. masc.	נתן
הֲתִתְּנֵם	pref. id.) id., suff. 3 pers. pl. masc.	נתן

ו

ו, conjunctive or copulative Vav, *and*; וּ before a consonant with simple Sheva, as וּגְלֹל; or before the labials ב, מ, פ, being homogeneous with it in the pronunciation, as וּפַר, וּמִן, וּבֵין; וֹ sometimes before הָ and חָ, as וְחָיוּ, וְהָיוּ (comp. § 13. rem. 1 & 13); before יְ, Yod becoming quiescent, as יְהִי, with וּ prefixed וִיהִי (for וְיְהִי); וֶ, וֵ, וַ before the composite Shevas, taking the corresponding short vowel, as וַעֲמֹד, (contr. וַאדֹנָי for וַאֲדֹנָי), וַחֲלִי, וַאֲכֹל, and sometimes by contraction, as וָחָיָה for וְחָיָה (comp. § 13. rem. 2 & 5), וֵאלֹהִים for וְאֱלֹהִים; וָ (va) immediately before the tone-syllable, but only at the end of a sentence, especially when short words are connected in pairs, as

וָעֹר חָם נָמֵיג וְחֹרֶף וְיוֹם וָלַיְלָה, but on the contrary זֶרַע וְקָצִיר Ge. 8. 22.

As a connective particle, the manner and nature of its connection is to be collected from the series of the discourse. Its principal uses are as follow— I. simply copulative, *and*, *also*, serving to connect words and phrases.—II. adversative, *but*; *yet*; *otherwise*.—III. *for*, *since*, *because*.—IV. eventual, *that*; וַיְהִי־ *it came to pass that*.—V. final, *that*, *to the end that*.—VI. concessive, *though*.—VII. *then*, comp. Ge. 3. 5.—VIII. exegetical, *even*, where properly the *relative* may be expressed instead, Ge. 49. 25. מֵאֵל אָבִיךָ וְיַעְזְרֶךָ *from the God of thy father, even he*, or *who*, *will help thee*; Ps. 68. 10.

---

a Je. 12. 3.   b Job 38. 31.   c Mal. 3. 8.   d Da. 3. 28.   e Job 39. 20.   f Pr. 24. 10.   g Ge. 18. 28.   h Le. 25. 22.   i 2 Sa. 19. 3.
Da. 4. 31.   2 Ch. 24. 25.   Da. 5. 23.   Ps. 60. 10.   Is. 51. 17, 22.   Pr. 6. 3.   Job 40. 29.   Job 38. 35.   Eze. 22. 2, 2.
Is. 8. 21.   Is. 58.   Ps. 60. 10.   Job 38. 34.   Is. 24. 19.   Je. 49. 3.   Job 40. 26.   De. 8. 2.   Ps. 39. 19.
Job 39. 10.

נַחֲלָתְךָ וְנִלְאָה thine inheritance even when weary, or which is weary; 1 Sa. 28. 3. בְּרָמָה וּבְעִירוֹ in Ramah, even in his own city.—IX. וְ‑וְ both—and; whether—or.

וְ, before guttural וְ, a letter which, prefixed to the forms of the Future, gives to them the sense of the Imperfect; hence called by grammarians Conversive Vav, e. g. יִקְטֹל he will slay, וַיִּקְטֹל he slew. It, nevertheless, frequently includes also the copulative power, comp. Ge. 3. 12, she gave me of the tree, וָאֹכֵל and I did eat.

NOTE.—All forms beginning with Vav (the few following excepted) will be found in the alphabetical order of the analysis according to the letter which next follows Vav in each form.

וְדָן Vedan, pr. name of a place in Arabia, Eze. 27. 19 So according to J. D. Michaelis, who judges the letter ו here to be radical, and collated with the Arab., to signify two rivers; Spicileg. Geogr. Hebr. p. 247.

וָהֵב (gift. Arab. והב to give) Vaheb, pr. name of a place, Nu. 21. 14.

[וָו] masc. dec. 1 a, hook or pin, used for suspending the curtain in the tabernacle.

וָוֵי id. pl., construct state.

וָוֵיהֶם id. pl., suff. 3 pers. pl. masc.

וָוִים id. pl., absolute state, Ex. 38. 28.

וָזַר Root not used; Arab. to be loaded, act. to commit crime; hence the following:

וָזָר masc. laden with guilt, guilty, Pr. 21. 8, see the preceding R.

וַיְזָתָא (pure coll. with the Pers.) pr. name of a son of Haman, Est. 9. 9.

וָלַד Root not used; i. q. יָלַד to bear, to bring forth, whence the two following:

וָלָד masc. a child, offspring, Ge. 11. 30; and וָלָד id. 2 Sa. 6. 23. Keri .

וַנְיָה pr. name masc. Ezr. 10. 36.

וָפְסִי pr. name masc. Nu. 13. 14.

וָשְׁנִי pr. name masc. 1 Ch. 6. 13.

וַשְׁתִּי (beauty, coll. with the Pers.) pr. name of the queen of Ahasuerus.

ז

זְאֵב ′ו masc. dec. 1 a.—I. a wolf.—II. pr. name of a prince of Midian.

זְאֵבֵי id. pl., construct state . . . . זאב

זָאמִין Chald. Kh. זָאמִין, K. זָעֵין, Peal part., pl. of [זָע or זָאע] dec. 2 a . . . זוע

זֹאת ′ו pron. demon. fem. sing., see . . זה

זָב Kal pret. 3 pers. sing. masc. (Le. 15. 2), or part. act. sing. masc. . . . זוב

זָבַב Root not used; Arab. זבב to rove up and down in the air.

זְבוּב masc. dec. 1 a, a fly; זְבוּבֵי מָוֶת deadly (i. e. venomous) flies. See also בַּעַל.

[זָבַד] to give, endow, Ge. 30. 20.

זֶבֶד masc. gift, dowry, Ge. 30. 20.

זָבָד (gift) pr. name of several men; for which once יוֹזָכָר comp. 2 Ch. 24. 26, with 2 Ki. 22. 22.

זָבוּד (given) pr. name masc. 1 Ki. 4. 5.

זַבּוּד (id.) pr. name masc. Ezr. 8. 14. Khethib.

זְבוּדָּה (id. fem.) pr. name fem. 2 Ki. 23. 36 Keri; Kh. זְבִידָה.

זַבְדִּי (giver, for זַבְדִּיָה gift of the Lord, Gesen.) pr. name of several men; for which once זִמְרִי comp. Jos. 7. 1, with 1 Ch. 2. 6.

זַבְדִּיאֵל (gift of God) pr. name masc. Ne. 11. 14.

זְבַדְיָהוּ ,זְבַדְיָה (gift of the Lord) pr. name of several men.

זָבָד ′ו pr. name masc. . . . זבד

זֶבֶד′ noun masc. sing. . . . זבד

זַבְדִּי′ & ′ו זְבַדְיָהוּ ,זְבַדְיָה & ′ו ,זַבְדִּיאֵל pr.n.m. זבד

זְבַדְנִי′ Kal pret. 3 pers. sing. masc., suff. 1 pers. sing. זבד

זָבָה′ Kal part. act. fem. dec. 10, from זָב masc. זוב

זֹבֶה′ defect. for זוֹבֶה (q. v.) . . . זוב

זְבוּב pr. name, see בַּעַל זְבוּב .

זְבוּבֵי′ noun masc. pl. constr. from זְבוּב dec. 1 a זבב

זָבוּד ′ו pr. name masc. . . . זבד

זְבִידָה Kh. זְבוּדָּה K. pr. name fem.   זבד

זְבוּלָא
זְבוּאן } pr. name of a man and a tribe; ־וֹ bef. (ı)   זבל

זָבַח ־ֹ to *slaughter* or *kill* animals, especially for sacrifice. Pi. *to sacrifice.*

זֶבַח masc. with suff. זִבְחִי dec. 6 a (§ 35. rem. 5). —I. prop. *a slaughtering*, meton. *the flesh of slaughtered animals*, i. e. *a repast, banquet.*—II. *sacrifice*; זֶבַח הַיָּמִים *a yearly sacrifice*; זֶבַח מִשְׁפָּחָה *a family sacrifice.*—III. pr. name of a king of Midian.

מִזְבֵּחַ masc. dec. 7 c, pl. מִזְבְּחוֹת, *altar.*

זָבַח ־ֹ in pause for זֶבַח (§ 35. rem. 2) q. v.; for ־ֹ see lett. ו   זבח

זְבַח Kal imp. sing. masc.   זבח

זֶבַח ־ֹ, ־ו noun masc. sing. (suff. זִבְחִי) dec. 6. (§ 35. rem. 5) also pr. name; for ־ו see ו   זבח

זְבֹחַ Kal inf. constr.   זבח

זִבַּח Piel pret. 3 pers. sing. masc.   זבח

זֹבֵחַ ־ו Kal part. act. sing. masc. dec. 7 b   זבח

זָבְחוּ id. pret. 3 pers. pl.   זבח

זִבְּחוּ
זִבֵּחַ } Piel pret. 3 pers. pl. (comp. § 8. rem. 7)   זבח

זִבְחוֹ noun masc. sing., suff. 3 pers. sing. masc. from זֶבַח dec. 6. (§ 35. rem. 5)   זבח

זִבְחוּ Kal imp. pl. masc.   זבח

זִבְחֵי noun m. pl. constr. from זֶבַח d. 6. (§ 35. r. 5)   זבח

זְבָחַי id. sing., suff. 1 pers. sing.   זבח

זֹבְחֵי Kal part. act. m., pl. constr. from זֹבֵחַ dec. 7.   זבח

זִבְחֵיהֶם ־ו noun masc. pl., suff. 3 pers. pl. masc. from זֶבַח dec. 6. (§ 35. rem. 5)   זבח

זְבָחֶיךָ ־ו id., suff. 2 pers. sing. masc.; ־ו bef. (ı)   זבח

זִבְחֵיכֶם ־ו id., suff. 2 pers. pl. masc.   זבח

זְבָחִים ־ו id. pl., absolute state; ־ו before (ı)   זבח

זֹבְחִים Kal part. act. masc., pl. of זֹבֵחַ dec. 7 b .   זבח

זִבְחֵימוֹ noun masc. pl., suff. 3 pers. pl. masc. from זֶבַח dec. 6. (§ 35. rem. 5)   זבח

זִבְחֵכֶם id. sing., suff. 2 pers. pl. masc.   זבח

זָבַחְנוּ ו Kal pret. 1 pers. pl.   זבח

זָבַחְתָּ ו id. pret. 2 pers. sing. masc.; acc. shifted by conv. ו (§ 8. rem. 7)   זבח

זָבַחְתִּי id. pret. 1 pers. sing.   זבח

זְבַחְתֶּם ־ו id. pret. 2 pers. pl. masc.; ־ו for ו conv.   זבח

זַבַּי pr. name masc. Ezr. 10. 28; Ne. 3. 20. Keri; for which זַבַּי Ezr. 2. 9; Ne. 7. 14.

זַבְינָא pr. name masc.   זבן

[זְבֻל] *to dwell*, Ge. 30. 20. יִזְבְּלֵנִי *shall dwell with me.*

זְבֻל masc. dec. 1 a.—I. *habitation.*—II. pr. name masc. Ju. 9. 28.

זְבוּלוּן, זְבוּלֻן, זְבוּלוֹן (*habitation*) pr. name of a son of Jacob and the tribe descended from him. Gen. noun זְבוּלֹנִי.

זְבֻל ־ו noun masc. sing. for זְבוּל dec. 1 a, also pr. name; ־ו before (ı)   זבל

זְבֻלָה" id. with parag. ה   זבל

זְבֻלֻן ־ו defect. for זְבוּלוּן (q. v.)   זבל

[זְבַן] Chald. *to buy, gain*, Da. 2. 8.

זְבִינָא (*bought*) pr. name masc. Ezr. 10. 43.

זָבְנִין Ch. Peal part. act. masc., pl. of [זְבַן] dec. 2 b   זבן

זָבַת Kal part. act. f., constr. of זָבָה d. 10, fr. זָב m.   זוב

זָג" masc. *the skin of the grape*, Nu. 6. 4, so called from its transparency. זֻגּ Chald. זנג Samar. *to be pure*, from either of which roots it may be derived.

זֵד" adj. masc. sing. dec. 1 a   זוד

זָדָה Kal pret. 3 pers. sing. fem.   זיד

זָדוּ id. pret. 3 pers. pl. masc.   זוד

זָדוֹן noun masc. sing. dec. 3 a, as if from זרה, (§ 32. rem. 6) see   זוד

זְדוֹן id. construct state   זוד

זֵדִים adj. masc., pl. of זֵד dec. 1 a   זוד

זְדֹנְךָ" noun m. s., suff. 2 pers. s. m. from זָדוֹן (q. v.)   זוד

זֶה ־ו masc.; fem. זֹאת (for זֹאת from a masc. זֶה=זֹה), rarely זֹה, once זֹאתָה (with demonstr. ה) Je. 26. 6, Kheth.; com. זוּ, & pl. אֵלֶּה, אֵל.—I. pron. demonstr. *this*; when put after the subst. it usually has the article, as הַבַּיִת הַזֶּה *this house*; when put before it without an article, it is usually the predicate of the proposition, זֶה הַדָּבָר *this* (is) *the thing*; זֶה—זֶה *this—that, the one—the other*; זֶה אֶל זֶה *one to the other*, Is. 6. 3.—With emphasis, *this same, very*; Ju. 5. 5. זֶה סִינַי *this very Sinai*, comp. Jos. 9. 12; Ps. 48. 15; 104. 25; also by way of contempt, comp. Ex. 32. 1; 1 Sa. 10. 27;—with the interrogative pronouns, מִי זֶה *who is this?* מַה זֶּה *what is this? how then?* לָמָה זֶּה *why then?*—II. rarely for the relative, e. g. Ps. 104. 8. מָקוֹם זֶה יָסַדְתָּ *the place which thou hast founded.*—III. adv. of place, *here*; מִזֶּה *hence*; מִזֶּה וּמִזֶּה *hence and thence*; of time, *now*; זֶה פַּעֲמַיִם *now twice.*—IV. with prefixes;—בָּזֶה

ᵃ 1 Ki. 8. 63.   ᵈ Ps. 50. 14.   ᵍ 1 Sa. 15. 15.   ʰ Ho. 12. 12.   ᵏ Is. 56. 7.   ᵗ Ex. 8. 23.   ᵖ Da. 2. 8.   ʳ Pr. 21. 24.   ˣ Ex. 18. 11.
ᵇ 1 Ki. 12. 2.   ᵉ Je. 17. 26.   ᶠ 2 Ch. 33. 23.   ⁱ Ps. 106. 38.   ˡ Is. 43. 23.   ᵘ Eze. 39. 19.   ⁿ Nu. 6. 4.   ᵗ Je. 50. 29.   ᶻ 1 Sa. 17. 28.
Je. 7. 22.   ᶜ Ki. 5. 17.   ᵍ 2 Ki. 5. 17.   Mal. 1. 14.   ᵐ Le. 7. 16.   ᵛ Ex. 8. 24.   ᵛᵛ Le. 19. 6.   ʷ Hab. 3. 11.

in this place, *here*, comp. No. III; of time, *then* Est. 2. 13; but בָּזֹאת, בְּזֹאת (Ec. 7. 18), *in, on, by this,* &c., comp. בְּ;—כָּזֹאת, כָּזֶה *like this, such; thus,* and so כָּזֹאת Ge. 45. 23; כָּזֶה וְכָזֶה *thus and thus, so and so;*—לָזֹאת וְכָזֹאת *therefore,* Je. 5. 7; but לָזֹאת *to this, at this,* comp. לְ.

זוּ i. q. זֶה comp. Nos. I, II.

הַלָּזֶה masc. and apocopated הַלָּז com. gen. *this.*

הַלָּזוּ id. Eze. 36. 35.

זֹה pron. demon. fem. sing. see the preceding.

זָהָב masc. dec. 4 a.—I. *gold,* after numerals שֶׁקֶל is to be supplied, עֲשָׂרָה זָהָב *ten* (shekels) *of gold.*—II. metaph. *brightness,* or *fair weather,* Job 37. 22.

זְהַב } id., construct state: ⅃ before (ː) for זהב וּזְהַב

זְהַבְ־ }

זְהָבוֹ id., suff. 3 pers. sing. masc. . זהב

זְהָבִי ⅃ id., suff. 1 pers. sing.; ⅃ before (ː) . זהב

זְהָבְךָ

זְהָבֶ֫ } ⅃ id., suff. 2 pers. sing. masc.; ⅃ id. זהב

זְהָבָם ⅃ id., suff. 3 pers. pl. masc.; ⅃ id. . זהב

זָהָה Root not used; Arab. *to shine, be bright, beautiful.*

זִיו Chald. masc. (for זִהְיוּ) dec. 1 a, *brightness, splendour;* pl. *healthy complexion,* Da. 5. 6, 9, 10.

זִו (*beauty,* especially *of flowers*) name of the second month of the Hebrew year, from the new moon of April to that of May, 1 Ki. 6. 1, 37.

זְהִירִין ⅃ Chald. Peal part. pass. masc., pl. of [זְהִיר] dec. 1 a; ⅃ before (ː) . . . זהר

זָהַם Pi. *to loathe, abhor,* Job 33. 20.

זַהַם (*loathing*) pr. name masc. 2 Ch. 11. 19.

זָהַם pr. name masc. [for זָהָם § 35. rem. 2] . זהם

וְזַהֲמַתּוּ ⅃ Piel pret. 3 pers. sing. fem., suff. 3 pers. sing. masc. [for וְזִהֲמַתְהוּ] . . זהם

זָהַר Hiph.—I. *to enlighten, to teach.*—II. *to admonish, warn,* with the acc. of the pers., and מִן of thing from which, or the pers. on whose part, one warns.—III. *to shine,* Da. 12. 3. Niph. *to be admonished, to receive admonition.*

זְהַר Chald., part. pass., *admonished, cautioned,* Ezr. 4. 22.

זֹהַר masc. *brightness, splendour.*

זֹהַר noun masc. sing. . . . . זהר

זִו name of a month . . . . זוה

זוֹ pron. demon. fem. sing. . . זה

זֶה pron. demon. com. gen. sing. . . זה

[זוּב] I. *to flow.*—II. *to overflow, abound with.*—III. *to waste away, expire,* La. 4. 9.

זוֹב masc. dec. 1 a, *flux, issue of blood,* &c.

זוֹבִי noun masc. sing. dec. 1 a . . . זוב

זוֹבָהּ id., suff. 3 pers. sing. fem. . . . זוב

זוֹבוֹ id., suff. 3 pers. sing. masc. . . . זוב

זוֹבֵחַ Kal part. act. sing. masc. dec. 7 b . זבח

[זוּד, זִיד] I. *to boil, seethe,* Ge. 25. 29.—II. *to act insolently, proudly, wickedly* against any one, const. with עַל אֶל. Niph. part. נָזִיד *something sodden, pottage.*

זוּד Chald. Aph. *to act proudly, wickedly,* Da. 5. 20.

זֵד adj. dec. 1 a, *proud, haughty.*

זֵידוֹן adj. m. *overflowing, overwhelming,* Ps. 124

זָדוֹן masc. dec. 3 a (as if from זָדָה § 32. rem. 6) *insolence, pride, haughtiness.*

זָוָה Root not used; Arab. זוי *to hide, conceal.*

זָוִית fem. pl. זָוִיֹּת (§ 39. No. 4. rem. 1) *corner angle* of a building, &c.

מָזֶו masc. only pl. מְזָוִים (comp. dec. 6) *garners,* Ps. 144. 13.

זִין זוּן Root not used; Chald. זוּן *to move, move about;* hence perhaps *to abound,* comp. שָׂרַץ

זוּזִים pr. name of a people on the borders of Palestine, Ge. 14. 5.

זִיז masc. *abundance, wealth;* זִיז שָׂדַי *wealth of the field,* for *beasts pasturing there.*

זִיזָא (*abundance*) pr. name of two different men 1 Ch. 4. 37; 2 Ch. 11. 20.

זִיזָה (id.) pr. name masc. 1 Ch. 23. 11; for which זִינָא in ver. 10.

זִיזָי (*he moves,* or *motion*) pr. name masc. 1 Ch. 27. 31.

מְזוּזָה fem. dec. 10, *door post,* on which the door moves.

זוֹחֵת pr. name masc. 1 Ch. 4. 20.

[זוּל] *to shake, pour out,* Is. 46. 6.

זוּלָה fem. dec. 10 (prop. *a removing*) constr. זוּלַת as a prep. *besides, except;* with suff. *besides me,* &c. with paragogic Yod, זוּלָתִי

זֹלֵל   Kal part. act. sing. masc. dec. 7b .   זלל

זֹלֵלָה   id. fem. sing. . . . .

זֹלְלִים   id. masc. pl., absolute state .   זלל

זוּלַת   prop. noun fem., constr. of [זוּלָה] dec. 10, only as a prep. . . .   זול

זוּלָתָהּ   id., suff. 3 pers. sing. fem. .   זול

זוּלָתִי   id. with paragogic ', or suff. 1 pers. sing.   זול

זוּלָתְךָ
זוּלָתֶךָ } id., suff. 2 pers. sing. masc. . .   זול

זוּן   Hoph. *to be fed, fattened,* Je. 5. 8.

זוּן   Chald. Ithpe., or Ittaph. (§ 47. rem. 10) *to be nourished, fed,* Da. 4. 9.

מָזוֹן   masc. *food, meat.*

מָזוֹן   Chald. masc. id. Da. 4. 9, 18.

זֹנָה   fem. of the following, dec. 10 .   זנה

זֹנֶה   Kal part. act. sing. masc. dec. 9a   זנה

זוּנָּה   Pual pret. 3 pers. s. m. [for זֻנָּה § 10. r. 5]   זנה

זֹנוֹת   Kal part. act. fem., pl. of זֹנָה (q. v.) .   זנה

זוּע   I. *to move, move oneself,* Est. 5. 9.—II. *to be agitated, to shake,* Ec. 12. 3. Pilp. (§ 6. rem. 4) *to agitate, vex,* Hab. 2. 7.

זוּע   Ch. *to be moved, to tremble.*

זְוָעָה & transp. זַעֲוָה fem.—I. *agitation, disquiet.*—II. *terror,* Is. 28. 19.

זַעֲוָן   (*unquiet*) pr. name of a man.

זִיעַ   (*motion*) pr. name masc. 1 Ch. 5. 13.

זוּעָה   noun fem. sing. . . .   זוע

זוּף   Root not used; prob. i. q. זוב *to flow.*

זֶפֶת   fem. *pitch.*

זִיף   (*flux*) pr. name—I. of a town and desert in the tribe of Judah. Gent. noun זִיפִי.—II. of a man, 1 Ch. 4. 16.

זֹקֵף   Kal part. act. sing. masc. . .   זקף

I. [זוּר]   I. *to press, to press or squeeze out.*—II. intrans. *to be pressed out,* Is. 1. 6, זֹרוּ (§ 21. rem. 2), which others take as Pu. of זָרָה *to be sprinkled upon.*

II. [זוּר]   pret. pl. זָרוּ, and זֹרוּ (Ps. 58. 4. § 21. rem. 2).—I. *to be loathsome* (Arab. زار *to loathe*) Job 19. 17, *my breath is loathsome* (others, *estranged,* see the following) *to my wife.*—II. (cogn. to סור) *to turn aside, depart,* hence *to be strange, a stranger;*

part. זָר *a stranger, barbarian, enemy;* fem. זָרָה *a strange woman, a harlot.* Niph. *to turn, to recede, fall off,* Is. 1. 4. Hoph. *to become estranged,* Ps. 69. 9.

זָרָא   fem. (for זָרָה) *loathsomeness,* Nu. 11. 20.

מָזוֹר   masc. dec. 3a, *compression of a wound by bandages,* meton. for *the wound itself.* In Ob. 7, according to some, *a net,* from the Aram. מְזַר *to spread.*

זֹרֵחַ   Kal part. act. sing. masc. . . .   זרח

זֹרֵעַ   Kal part. act. sing. masc. . . .   זרע

זָחַח   Niph. *to be removed, displaced,* Ex. 28. 28 ; 39. 21.

[זָחַל]   I. *to creep, crawl.*—II. *to fear,* Job 32. 6.

זֹחֶלֶת   only in the pr. name אֶבֶן הַזּ *stone of the serpent,* as would appear from this etymology, but see אֶבֶן

זֹחֲלֵי   Kal part. act. pl. c. masc. from [זָחַל] dec. 7b   זחל

זָחַלְתִּי   id. pret. 1 pers. sing. .   זחל

זִיוֵהּ   Chald. noun masc. sing., suff. 3 pers. sing. masc. from [זִיו] dec. 1   זהה

זִיוֹהִי   Chald. id. pl., suff. 3 pers. sing. masc.   זהה

זִיוָנִי   Chald. id. pl., suff. 1 pers. sing. .   זהה

זִיוִי   Chald. id. sing., suff. 1 pers. sing. .   זהה

זִיוָיִךְ   id. pl., suff. 2 pers. sing. masc. .   זהה

זִיו   noun masc. sing. . . . .   זוו

זִיזָא   pr. name, masc. . . .   זוז

זִיזָה   pr. name, masc. . . .   זוז

זִינָא   pr. name, masc., see זִיזָא .   זוז

זִיעַ   pr. name, masc. . . .   זוע

זִיף   pr. name of a place . . .   זוף

זִיפָה   id. with loc. . . .   זוף

זִיקוֹת   noun fem. pl. [for זְנָקוֹת, זִקוֹת]   זנק

זַיִת
זַיִת } masc. dec. 6 h.—I. *olive-tree;* זֵית שֶׁמֶן *oil-olive;* שֶׁמֶן זַיִת *olive-oil;* הַר הַזֵּיתִים *Mount of Olives,* near Jerusalem.—II. *olive, the fruit;* עֵץ הַזַּיִת *an olive-tree.* The etymology is not defined.

זֵיתָן   (Eng. *Oliver*) pr. name masc. 1 Ch. 7. 10.

זֵתָם   (id.) pr. name masc. 1 Ch. 23. 8 ; 26. 22.

זֵית   id., construct state . . .   זית

זֵיתֵיהֶם   id. pl., suff. 3 pers. pl. masc. .   זית

זֵיתֵיכֶם   id. pl., suff. 2 pers. pl. masc. .   זית

זֵיתִים   id. pl., absolute state . .   זית

זֵיתְךָ
זֵיתֶךָ } id. sing., suff. 2 pers. sing. masc. .   זית

זֵיתָן   pr. name masc. . . .   זית

---

a De. 21. 20.   d Pr. 28. 7.   g Ps. 73. 27.   k Is. 28. 19.   n De. 32. 24.   Da. 5. 6.   Da. 4. 33.   Ju. 15. 5.   De. 24. 20.
b Pr. 23. 21.   e 2 Ki. 24. 14.   h Eze. 16. 34.   l Ps. 145. 14.   Da. 5. 9.   Da. 5. 10.   De. 8. 9, etc.   De. 28. 40.
c La. 1. 11.   f 1 Sa. 21. 10.   i Pr. 29. 3.   m Ec. 1. 5.   Da. 2. 31.   Da. 7. 28.   Is. 50. 11.   Nu. 5. 11.

זַךְ
זָךְ } adj. masc. sing.   .   זכך

[זָכָה] to be pure, in a moral sense. **Pi.** to cleanse, purify. **Hithp.** הִזַּכָּה (§ 12. rem. 3) to cleanse oneself, Is. 1. 16.

זָכוּ Chald. fem. purity, innocence, Da. 6. 23.

זַכָּה adj. sing. fem. of זַךְ .   .   .   זכך

זְכוּ Chald. noun fem. sing. .   .   זכה

זַכּוּ Kal pret. 3 pers. pl.   .   .   זכך

זְכוּכִית noun fem. sing.; ‍ before (:)   זכך

זָכוֹר Kal inf. absolute, used also as an imp. .   זכר

זָכוּר id. part. pass. sing. masc.   .   .   זכר

זַכּוּר ‍) pr. name masc.   .   .   .   זכר

זְכוֹר id. imp. sing. masc.   .   .   .   זכר

זְכוּרָהּ noun masc. sing., suff. 3 pers. sing. fem. from [זָכוּר] dec. 3 a   .   .   זכר

זְכוּרְךָ id., suff. 2 pers. sing. masc.   .   זכר

זַכַּי pr. name masc. for זַכָּי   זכך

זִכִּיתִי Piel. pret. 1 pers. sing.   .   .   זכה

[זָכַךְ] to be clean, clear, pure, physically and morally. **Hiph.** to cleanse, Job 9. 30.

זַךְ masc. זַכָּה fem. adj. clean, pure, physically of things; morally of the heart, innocent, upright.

זְכוּכִית fem. glass or crystal, Job 28. 17.

זַכַּי (innocent) pr. name of a man.

זָכַר to remember, recollect, call to mind. **Niph.**—I. to be remembered, recollected, called to mind, with the acc., rarely לְ, בְּ.—II. (from זָכָר) to be born a male, Ex. 34. 19. **Hiph.**—I. to bring to remembrance.—II. to mention, make mention of.—III. to offer a memorial-offering, Is. 66. 3.—IV. to record, מַזְכִּיר a recorder.

זָכָר masc. dec. 4a, male, spoken of men and of animals.

זֵכֶר, זֶכֶר m. dec. 6c.—I. remembrance, memory. —II. memorial.

זָכוּר m. d. 3a, male, spoken of men and animals.

זַכּוּר (mindful) pr. name of several men.

זְכִרִי (renowned) pr. name of several men.

זְכַרְיָהוּ, זְכַרְיָה (whom the Lord remembers) pr. name—I. of a king of Israel, son of Jeroboam.— II. of the well-known prophet Zechariah son of Berachia, comp. Zec. 1. 1, 7.—III. of a prophet son of Jehoiada, comp. 2 Ch. 24. 20, sq. — IV.

of a cotemporary with Isaiah, Is. 8. 2.—V. of a prophet under Uzziah, 2 Ch. 26. 5;—also of several other men.

אַזְכָּרָה fem. dec. 10, a memorial-offering.

זֵכֶר noun masc. sing. dec. 4a; or (Ps. 9. 13) in pause for זֶכֶר q. v.   .   .   זכר

זָכַר ‍) pr. name masc. for זֶכֶר (§ 35. rem. 2); for ‍ see lett. ‍   .   .   .   זכר

זָכֹר Kal inf. absolute, used also as an imp. .   זכר

זֵכֶר noun masc. sing. dec. 6b   .   .   זכר

זְכֹר Kal imp. sing. masc. (§ 8. rem. 13);
זְכָר־ ‍ bef. (:) }   .   .   זכר

זָכְרָה id. pret. 3 pers. sing. fem.   .   .   זכר

זָכְרָה id. imp. sing. m. with parag. ה (§ 8. r. 11)   זכר

זָכְרוּ ‍) id. pret. 3 pers. pl.   .   .   זכר

זִכְרוּ
זְכֹרוּ } id. imp. pl. masc. (§ 8. rem. 11) .   זכר

זָכְרוֹ noun masc. s., suff. 3 p. s. m. from זֵכֶר d. 6b   זכר

זִכָּרוֹן ‍) noun masc. sing. dec. 3c   .   זכר

זִכְרוֹן id., constr. state   .   .   .   זכר

זִכְרוֹנֵךְ id., suff. 2 pers. sing. fem.   .   זכר

זִכְרִי ‍) pr. name masc.   .   .   .   זכר

זִכְרִי noun masc. sing., suff. 1 p. s. from זֵכֶר d. 6b   יכר

זְכַרְיָה
זְכַרְיָהוּ } pr. name masc.; ‍ bef. (:) .   זכר

זִכְרְךָ ‍) noun masc. sing., suff. 2 pers. sing. masc.
זִכְרֶךָ } from זֵכֶר dec. 6b }   זכר

זִכְרָם ‍) id., suff. 3 pers. pl. masc.   .   זכר

זִכְרֹן defect. for זִכָּרוֹן (q. v.)   .   .   זכר

זָכַרְנוּ Kal pret. 1 pers. pl.   .   .   זכר

זְכָרָנוּ id. pret. 3 pers. sing. masc., suff. 1 pers. pl.   זכר

זָכְרֵנִי id. imp. sing. masc., suff. 1 pers. sing. .   זכר

זִכְרֹנֵיכֶם n. m. pl., suff. 2 p. pl. m. from זִכָּרוֹן d. 3c   זכר

זָכַרְתָּ ‍ Kal pret. 2 pers. sing. masc.; acc. shifted by ‍ conv. (§ 8. rem. 7)   .   .   זכר

זָכַרְתְּ
זְכַרְתְּ }‍) id. pret. 2 pers. sing. fem. (§ 8. rem. 7)   זכר

זָכַרְתִּי
זְכַרְתִּי } id. pret. 1 pers. sing. (§ 8. rem. 7) .   זכר

זָכַרְתִּי ‍ id. id.; acc. shifted by conv. ‍   זכר

זָכַרְתְּ Kh., זָכַרְתִּי K. id. pret. 2 pers. sing. fem., (§ 8. rem. 5)   .   .   .   זכר

זְכַרְתִּיךָ id. id., suff. 2 pers. sing. masc. .   זכר

זְכַרְתָּם id. pret. 2 pers. sing. m., suff. 3 pers. pl. m. זכר

זְכַרְתֶּם ‍ id. pret. 2 pers. pl. masc.; ‍ for ‍ conv.   זכר

זְכַרְתַּנִי ‍) id. pret. 2 pers. sing. masc., suff. 1 pers.
זְכַרְתָּנִי } sing.; ‍ bef. (:) }   זכר

• Ps. 41. 6.   ‍ Ps. 132. 1.   ‍ La. 1. 7, 9.   ‍ Ne. 2. 20.   • Ps. 135. 13.   ‍ Est. 9. 28.   • Ps. 115. 12.   • Ese. 16. 61.   ‍ Ps. 88. 6.
‍ Da. 6. 23.   ‍ De. 20. 13.   ‍ Exe. 6. 9.   ‍ Is. 57. 8.   ‍ Ps. 102. 13.   ‍ Ex. 28. 12.   ‍ Job 13. 12.   ‍ Ese. 16. 22, 42.   ‍ 1 Sa. 1. 11.
‍ Job 28. 17.   ‍ Ec. 12. 1.   ‍ Ne. 4. 8.   ‍ Ex. 3. 15.   ‍ Ps. 6. 6.   ‍ Nu. 11. 5.   ‍ Is. 17. 10.   ‍ Ps. 63. 7.   ‍ Ge. 42. 14.
‍ Ps. 103. 14.

זָלַג Root not used; Arab. دلج to draw out, Aram. סְלַק Aph. to bring up.

מַזְלֵג masc. fork, 1 Sa. 2. 13, 14.

מִזְלָגָה fem. dec. 11 a, id.

זְלָעָה noun fem. sing. . . . זלל

[זָלַל] prop. i. q. זוּל to shake or pour out (Arab. زلزل to shake), whence part. זוֹלֵל—I. squanderer, prodigal.—II. vile, debased. Niph. to be shaken, to quake. Hiph. to debase, La. 1. 8.

זֻלּוּת fem. Ps. 12. 9, vileness, baseness; others, trembling, terror.

זַלְזַלִּים masc. pl. twigs, branches of the vine, Is. 18. 5, comp. תַּלְתַּלִּים R. תָּלַל

זַלְעָפָה fem. dec. 11 a, violent heat, spoken of a poisonous wind called Samoom, of famine, of anger. Comp. זָעַף

זַלְעַפוֹת id. pl., constr. state

זַלְעָפוֹת id., pl. absolute for זַלְ

זִלְפָּה (a dropping זָלַף=דָלַף to drop, trickle down) pr. name of the hand-maid of Leah.

זִמָּה noun fem. sing. dec. 10, also pr. name masc. זמם

זִמְרָה noun fem. sing. dec. 10. . . . זמר

זַמּוֹת Kal pret. 2 pers. sing. masc. . . זמם

זִמּוֹת noun fem., pl. of זִמָּה dec. 10. . . זמם

זִמֹּתִי id. with suff. 1 pers. pl. . . . זמם

זַמְזֻמִּים pr. name of a race of giants, De. 2. 20.

זָמִיר noun masc. sing. dec. 1 a, pl. זְמִרוֹת . זמר

זִמְרָה pr. name masc. . . . . . זמר

זָמַם pret. זַמֹּתִי, זָמַמְתִּי (§ 18. rem. 13); fut. pl. יָזֹמּוּ (rem. 15) to devise, purpose, intend, think, especially to intend evil, with לְ against any one.

זָמָם masc. dec. 4 a, device, project, Ps. 140. 9.

זִמָּה fem. dec. 10.—I. device, plan, purpose, for evil.—II. wickedness, sin, especially with reference to unchastity.—III. pr. name of a man.

מְזִמָּה fem. dec. 10.—I. device, machination, contrivance, in a bad sense.—II. thought, consideration, discretion, in a good sense.

זָמַם Kal pret. 3 pers. sing. m. for זָמַם (§ 8. r. 7) זמם

זֹמֵם id. part. act. sing. masc. . . . זמם

זָמְמָה id. pret. 3 pers. sing. fem. . . זמם

זָמְמוּ id. pret. 3 pers. pl. [for זָמְמוּ § 8. rem. 7] זמם

זְמָמוֹ noun m. s., suff. 3 p. s. m., from [זָמָם] d. 4 a זמם

זַמֹּתִי Kal pret. 1 pers. sing. . . . זמם

זְמַן Pu. to be appointed, fixed, determined.

זַמֵּן Ch. Pa. to appoint, determine, Da. 2. 9 Kheth., which according to Keri is Hithp. הִזְדַּמֵּן to agree together.

זְמָן masc. dec. 8 a, time, especially a stated, appointed time.

זְמָן (Da. 2. 16), elsewhere זְמָן Ch. dec. 3 a.—I. time, appointed time.—II. תְּלָתָה זִמְנִין three times, Da. 6. 11.

זְמָן Heb. & Ch. noun masc. s., (suff. זְמַנָּם) d. 8 a זמן

זְמָן Ch. noun masc. sing. dec. 3 b זמן

זִמְנָא Ch. id., emph. state . . . . זמן

זִמְנַיָּא Ch. id. pl., emph. state . . . . זמן

זִמְנִין Ch. id. pl., absol. te state . . . זמן

[זָמַר] to cut, prune, Le. 25. 3, 4. Niph. to be pruned, Is. 5. 6. Pi. (prop. to divide, with reference to rhythmical numbers, hence) to sing hymns, praises, with לְ or the acc. of the person celebrated, with בְּ of the instrument for accompaniment.

זְמָר Ch. dec. 1 a, song, music, Da. 3. 5, 7, 10, 15.

זַמָּר Ch. dec. 1 a, singer, Ezr. 7. 24.

זָמֵר masc. a species of gazelle, De. 14. 5.

זִמְרָה fem. (no pl.) song, praise, music; Ge. 43. 11 זִמְרַת הָאָרֶץ the song of the land, i. e. the most celebrated produce; others, fruit cut off.

זִמְרִי (pruner, or singer) pr. names of several men, especially—I. of a king of Israel, comp. 1 Ki. 16. 9, seq.—II. of a chief of the tribe of Simeon, Nu. 25. 14.

זִמְרָן (id.) pr. name of a son of Abraham by Keturah, and of a tribe descended from him

זִמְרָת fem. i. q. זִמְרָה song, praise.

זְמוֹרָה fem. dec. 10, branch, bough.

זָמִיר masc. pruning-time, Ca. 2. 12.

זָמִיר masc. song, praise, pl. זְמִירוֹת

זְמִירָה (song) pr. name masc. 1 Ch. 7. 8.

מִזְמוֹר masc. song, hymn, psalm.

מְזַמְּרֹת fem. only pl. מְזַמְּרוֹת (dec. 13) snuffers, others, psalteries.

מַזְמֵרָה fem. dec. 11 b, pruning-instruments.

זָמֹר noun masc. sing. [for זֶמֶר § 35. rem. 2]; for זָ see lett. ו . . . . זמר

זַמָּרָא Ch. noun masc., emph. of [זַמָּר] dec. 1 a זמר

זַמְּרָה Piel inf. with fem. term. (§ 10. rem. 2) . זמר

זִמְרָה noun fem. sing. dec. 10. . . . זמר

a Ps. 12. 9.   d Ps. 11. 6.   g Is. 32. 7.   k La. 1. 17.   o Ps. 31. 14.   q Da. 7. 12.   t Da. 7. 25.   y Da. 3. 5, 7,   z Ps. 147.
Ps. 119. 53.   e Nu. 12. 23.   h Job 17. 11.   l Ps. 37. 12.   Ps. 140. 9.   r Da. 7. 23.   u Da. 6. 11.   13, 15.
La. 5. 16.   f Pr. 39. 32.   i Is. 25. 5.   m Pr. 31. 16.   p Zec. 3. 14, 15.   s Da. 2. 21.   x De. 14. 5.

זַמְּרוּ֫ / זַמֵּ֫רוּ } Piel imp. pl. masc. (comp. § 8. rem. 7)   זמר

זְמֹרוֹת noun masc. with pl. f. term. from זָמִיר d. 1 a   זמר

זִמְרִי pr. name masc.   זמר

זִמְרָיָא Ch. noun masc. pl. emph. from זְמָר d. 1 a   זמר

זְמִירֹתָיהֶם noun fem. with pl. masc. term. & suff. 3 pers. pl. m. fr. זְמוֹרָה d. 10; ‡ bef. ₍₎   זמר

זִמְרָן pr. name masc.   זמר

זִמְרָת noun fem. sing.   זמר

זִמְרַת noun fem. sing., constr. of רָה (no pl.)   זמר

זָמֹרַת n. f. s., constr. of זְמוֹרָה d. 10; ‡ bef. ₍₎   זמר

זְמֹרֹת defect. for זְמוֹרֹת (q. v.)   זמר

זִמַּת noun fem. sing., constr. of זִמָּה dec. 10.   זמם

זַמֹּתִי Kal pret. 1 pers. sing.   זמם

זַמֹּתִי Piel inf. [§ 18. rem. 3] suff. 1 p. sing.   זמם

זִמָּתֵךְ noun f. s., suff. 2 p. s. f. from זִמָּה d. 10.   זמם

זִמַּתְכֶנָה id. with suff. 3 pers. pl. fem. (§ 3. rem. 5)   זמם

זַן for זֶן masc., pl. זְנִים (§ 36. r. 5) sort, kind, manner; מִזַּן אֶל־זַן of all kinds.

זַן Ch. masc. id. only pl. constr. זְנֵי Da. 3. 5, 7, 10, 15.

זָנָב ¹ } masc. dec. 4, pl. זְנָבוֹת, constr. זַנְבוֹת, tail of an animal. Pi. to cut off or smite the rear of an army.

זְנָבוֹ id., suff. 3 pers. sing. masc.   זנב

זַנְבוֹת id. pl., constr. state (§ 33. rem. 1)   זנב

זִנַּבְתָּם } Piel pret. 2 pers. pl. masc.   זנב

זָנָה ¹ } to commit whoredom, play the harlot; frequently also to commit spiritual whoredom or idolatry; const. with acc. בְּ, אֶל, אַחֲרֵי of the person with whom, with מִן, מִתַּחַת, מֵאַחֲרֵי, מֵעַל of the person against whom, it is committed. Part. fem. זוֹנָה harlot. Pu. זוּנָּה pass. Eze. 16. 34. Hiph.—I. to cause to commit whoredom.—II. intrans. to commit whoredom.

זְנוּן masc. dec. 1 a, only pl. זְנוּנִים whoredom; frequently applied to idolatry.

זְנוּת fem. dec. 1 a, whoredom, only trop. of idolatry.

תַּזְנוּת fem. dec. 1 b, the same.

זָנֹה Kal inf. absolute   זנה

זֹנָה fem. of the following, dec. 10.   זנה

זֹנֶה Kal part. act. sing. masc. dec. 9 a   זנה

זָנוּ id. pret. 3 pers. pl.   זנה

זָנוֹחַ ¹ pr. name of a man and a place   זנח

זְנוּגֵי noun masc. pl. constr. from [זְנוּן] dec. 1 a   זנה

זְנוּנֶיהָ id. pl., suff. 3 pers. sing. fem.   זנה

זְנוּנַיִךְ id. pl., suff. 2 pers. sing. fem.   זנה

זְנוּנִים id. pl, absolute state   זנה

זְנוּחַ noun fem. sing. dec. 1 a   זנח

זֹנוֹת defect. for זוֹנוֹת (q. v.)   זנה

זְנוּתָהּ noun f. s., suff. 3 pers. s. f. fr. זְנוּת d. 1 a   זנה

זְנוּתְכֶם id. pl. [זְנוּתִים], suff. 2 pers. pl. masc.   זנה

זְנוּתֵךְ id. sing., suff. 2 pers. sing. fem.   זנה

זְנוּתָם id. sing., suff. 3 pers. pl. masc.   זנה

זָנַח I. prop. to be stinking, illsavoured, hence to be abominable, Ho. 8. 5.—II. meton. to reject as abominable, with מִן to thrust away, cast off. Hiph. —I. to stink, Is. 19. 6.—II. to reject, cast off.

זָנוֹחַ (marshy place) pr. name of a place in the tribe of Judah.

זָנֹחַ pr. name of a place for זָנוֹחַ   זנח

זָנַחְתָּ Kal pret. 2 pers. sing. masc.   זנח

זְנַחְתִּים id. pret. 1 pers. sing., suff. 3 pers. pl. masc.   זנח

זְנַחְתָּנוּ id. pret. 2 pers. sing. masc., suff. 1 pers. pl.   זנח

זְנַחְתָּנִי id. id with suff. 1 pers. sing. (§ 2. rem. 1)   זנח

זְנֵי Ch. noun masc. pl. constr., fr. זַן (q. v.)

זָנִים ‡ noun masc., pl. of זַן q. v.; ‡ bef. ₍₎

זֹנִים Kal part. act. m., pl. of זָנָה dec. 9 a   זנה

זָנִיתָ id. pret 2 pers. sing. masc.   זנה

זָנִית id. pret. 2 pers. sing. fem.   זנה

זָנַק Kal not used; Syr. to cast, dart forth.—Pi. to leap spring forth, De. 23. 22.

זֵק masc. (for זֶנֶק § 37. No. 3 b) only pl. זִקִּים arrows, Pr. 26. 18.

זִיקָה fem. (for זְקָה comp. § 18. rem. 12 note) only pl. זִיקוֹת burning arrows, fiery darts, Is. 50. 11

זָנְתָה ¹ } Kal pret. 3 pers. sing. fem.   זנה

זָעַ Kal pret. 3 pers. sing. masc.   זוע

זְעוּמִים Kal part. pass. masc., constr. of [זָעֻם] d. 3 a   זעם

זְעוּמָה fem. of the preceding   זעם

זַעֲוָן } pr. name masc   זוע

זְעֵיר noun masc. sing.   זער

זְעֵירָה Ch. adj. fem. from זְעֵיר masc.   זער

זָעַךְ i. q. דָּעַךְ, only Niph. to be extinguished, extinct, Job 17. 1; Professor Lee, to be swift.

זָעַם ר } fut. יִזְעַם, & יָעֹם Pr. 24. 24 (§ 8. r. 13).—I. to

a Ps. 98. 4.   c Is. 17. 10.   f Eze. 23. 29.   i Job 40. 17.   r Ho. 1. 2.   u Ho. 2. 4.   z Eze. 43. 9.   g 2 Ch. 18. 14.   k Est. 5. 2.
b Ezr. 7. 24.   d Is. 24. 16.   g Eze. 23. 49.   k Is. 7. 4.   o Ho. 4. 15.   v Eze. 23. 29.   a Zec. 10. 6.   h Ho. 9. 1.   l Pr. 23. 14.
Na. 2. 3.   e Je. 4. 28.   h Ps. 144. 13.   m Jos. 10. 19.   p Ju. 2. 17.   w Je. 3. 9.   o Ps. 42. 2.   i Je. 3. 1.   m Mi. 6. 16.
Am. 5. 23.   f Ps. 17. 3.   g Ju. 15. 4.   n De. 31. 16.   q Ex. 34. 15, 16.   x Nu. 14. 33.   p Da. 3. 5, 7, 10, 15.   f Is. 23. 17.   n Da. 7. 8.

be angry, indignant, with acc., עַל.—II. to be insolent, Ps. 7. 12, וְאֵל זֹעֵם בְּכָל־יוֹם and God (judges) the insolent continually. Niph. to be made angry, sullen, Pr. 25. 23.—III. part. pl. cursed.

זַעַם masc. dec. 6 d, with suff. זַעְמִי, זַעְמֶךָ.—I. anger, indignation.—II. insolence, Ho. 7. 16.

זַעַם }
זַעַם } noun masc. sing. dec. 6 d (§ 35. r. 2);
"(וְ') for וְ see lett. וְ } . . . . . זעם

זֹעֵם Kal part. act. sing. masc. . . . זעם

זַעֲמָה id. imp. sing. m. with parag. ה, [for זְעָמָה § 16. rem. 9] . . . . זעם

זַעְמוֹ noun masc. sing., suff. 3 pers. sing. masc. from זַעַם dec. 6 d [for זַעְמוֹ § 35. rem. 5] זעם

זַעְמִי id., suff. 1 pers. sing. [for זַעְמִי v. id.] . זעם

זַעְמְךָ }
זַעְמֶךָ } id., suff. 2 pers. sing. masc. (v. id.) . זעם

זַעַמְתָּ Kal pret. 2 pers. sing. masc. (§ 8. rem. 5) . זעם

[זָעַף] I. to be angry, enraged.—II. to be sullen, sad, gloomy. Hence the two following—

זָעֵף } masc. adj. angry, indignant,

זַעַף masc. dec. 6 d (with suff. זַעְפּוֹ § 35. rem. 5).
—I. anger, rage.—II. metaph. raging of the sea, Jon. 1. 15.

זֹעֲפִים Kal part. act. masc., pl. of [זָעֵף] dec. 7 b זעף

[זָעַק] fut. יִזְעַק, imp. זְעַק, inf. זְעֹק, to cry, call out, especially from pain, for help, with אֶל, לְ, of the person implored; with לְ, עַל, of the cause of suffering. Niph. to be called together; hence, to come together, to assemble. Hiph.—I. to cry out, Job 35. 9.—II. to proclaim.—III. to call together, to assemble.

זְעִק Ch. (§ 47. rem. 6) to cry out, Da. 6. 21.

זַעַק masc. dec. 6 d, cry, outcry, Is. 30. 19.

זְעָקָה fem. dec. 11 c, constr. זַעֲקַת (comp. § 42. rem. 1) cry, outcry, especially from pain, for help.

זְעַק Kal imp. sing. masc. . . . . . זעק

זְעִק Ch. Peal pret. 3 pers. sing. masc. (§ 47. r. 6) זעק

זָעֲקָה } Kal pret. 3 pers. s. f. [for זָעֲקָה § 8. r. 7] זעק

זְעָקָה noun fem. s. d. 11 c (§ 42. r. 1); וְ bef. (:) זעק

זָעֲקוּ } Kal pret. 3 pers. pl. זעק

זַעֲקוּ } id. imp. pl. masc. זעק

זַעֲקִי id. imp. sing. fem. זעק

זַעֲקִי } Kal imp. sing. fem., or pl. masc., Kh. זַעֲקִי, K. זַעֲקוּ in pause for זַעֲקִי or זַעֲקוּ (comp. § 8. rem. 12) . . . . זעק

זַעֲקֵךְ [for זַעֲקֵךְ] noun masc. sing., suff. 2 pers. sing. masc. fr. [זַעַק] dec. 6 d . . זעק

זַעֲקַת noun f. s., constr. of זְעָקָה d. 11 c (§ 42. r. 1) זעק

זָעַקְתִּי Kal pret. 1 pers. sing. . . . . זעק

וְ) noun fem. sing., suff. 3 pers. pl. masc. fr. זְעָקָה dec. 11 c (§ 42. rem. 1) . . זעק

זַעֲקָתָם } וְ Kal pret. 2 pers. pl. masc. וְ for וְ conv. זעק

זָעַר Root not used; i. q. צָעַר to be little.

זְעֵיר masc. a little.

זְעֵיר Ch. small, little, Da. 7. 8.

מִזְעָר masc. littleness, smallness, of time and number; מְעַט מִזְעָר little of smallness, i. e. very little; אֱנוֹשׁ מִזְעָר very few men. Others take this word as an adverb.

זִפִים gent. noun, pl. of זִיף fr. זִיף . . . זוף

זִפְרֹנָה pr. name of a city in the north of Palestine [זִפְרֹן] with loc. ה, Nu. 34. 9.

זִקִּים noun masc., pl. of [זֵק] for [זָנַק] dec. 8 b (§ 36. No. 3 b) . . . . . . זנק

זְקֵנִינוּ adj. pl. masc., suff. 1 pers. pl. fr. זָקֵן dec. 5 a זקן

זְקִיף וְ Ch. Peal part. pass. sing. masc.; וְ bef. (:) זקף

זָקָן com. dec. 4 a.—I. beard.—II. the chin.

זָקֵן to be or grow old. Hiph. to grow old, be old.

זָקֵן masc. dec. 5 a, adj. old, aged, hence as a subst. an old, aged man; זְקֵנִים elders, chiefs of tribes, families or cities; fem. זְקֵנוֹת old, old women.

זֹקֶן masc. old age, Ge. 48. 10.

זִקְנָה fem. constr. זִקְנַת (no pl.) old age.

זְקֻנִים masc. pl. dec. 1 a, old age; בֶּן־זְקֻנִים son of old age, i. e. born when the father was old.

זָקֵן וְ) Kal pret. 3 pers. sing. masc. or adj. sing. masc. dec. 5 a . . . . . . זקן

זְקַן constr. of זָקֵן (Ps. 133. 2) or זָקֵן (Ge. 24. 2) זקן

זָקְנָה Kal pret. 3 pers. sing. fem. זקן

זִקְנָה noun fem. sing. (no pl.) זקן

זְקָנוֹ noun masc. sing., suff. 3 pers. sing. masc. fr. זָקָן dec. 4 a . . . . זקן

זְקֵנוֹת וְ adj. f., pl. of זְקֵנָה fr. זָקֵן masc.; וְ bef. (:) זקן

זְקֵנַי וְ id. pl. masc., suff. 1 pers. pl. fr. זָקֵן dec. 5 a; וְ id. . . . . זקן

זְקָנִי וְ noun masc. sing., suff. 1 pers. sing. from זָקָן dec. 4 a; וְ id. . . . . . . זקן

זִקְנֵי וְ) adj. pl. constr. masc. fr. זָקֵן dec. 5 a זקן

---

a Ps. 78. 49.　d Ps. 102. 11.　g Da. 6. 21.　k Is. 14. 31.　m Is. 30. 19.　o Est. 9. 31.　r Pr. 26. 13.　u Ezr. 6. 11.　x Zec. 8. 4.
b Ps. 7. 12.　e Zec. 1. 12.　 2 Sa. 13. 19.　l Je. 48. 20.　n Ps. 142. 6.　p 1 Sa. 5. 18.　s Jos. 9. 11.　y La. 1. 19.
c Nu. 23. 7.　f Eze. 21. 17.　 Je. 50. 46.　 Ezr. 9. 3.　　　　　　　　q Pr. 25. 23.

17

זְקֵנֶיהָ id. pl., suff. 3 pers. sing. fem. . . זקן

זְקֵנָיו id. pl., suff. 3 pers. sing. masc.; ‡ bef. (.) זקן

זְקֵנֶיךָ id. pl., suff. 2 pers. sing. masc. . . זקן

זְקֵנֵיכֶם id. pl., suff. 2 pers. pl. masc. . . זקן

זְקֵנִים ‡ id. pl., abs. state; ‡ bef. (:) זקן

זְקֵנִים noun masc., pl. dec. 1 a . . זקן

זְקֵנְךָ noun masc. sing., suff. 2 pers. sing. masc.
    [for זְקֵנְךָ] from זָקֵן dec. 4 a . זקן

זְקֵנְכֶם id., suff. 2 pers. pl. masc. . . זקן

זְקֵנָם id., suff. 3 pers. pl. masc. . . זקן

זָקַנְתָּ Kal pret. 2 pers. sing. masc. . . זקן

זִקְנַת noun fem. sing., constr. of זִקְנָה (no pl.) זקן

זָקַנְתָּה Kal pret. 2 pers. sing. masc. (§ 8. rem. 5) זקן

זִקְנָתָהּ n. fem. s., suff. 3 p. s. fem. from זִקְנָה (no pl.) זקן

זִקְנָתוֹ id., suff. 3 pers. sing. masc. . . זקן

זָקַנְתִּי Kal pret. 1 pers. sing. . . זקן

[זָקַף] *to set upright, erect, raise up.*
    זְקַף Ch. *to lift up, hang up,* a criminal, Ezr. 6. 11.

זֹקֵף Kal part. act. sing. masc. . . זקף

[זָקַק] I. *to pour out,* Job 36. 27.—II. *to fuse, refine,* as gold.
—III. in the deriv. i. q. Chald. זְקַק *to join, bind together.* Pi. זִקֵּק *to refine, purify* gold, Mal. 3. 3.
Pu. *to be refined,* spoken of wine, metals.

זִקִּים masc. only pl. זִקִּים *bonds, fetters, chains.*

אָזִקִּים masc. only pl. אֲזִקִּים id.

זִקֵּק ‡ Piel pret. 3 pers. sing. masc. (§ 10. rem. 1) זקק

זֵר ‡ see the Root . . . וזר

זָר ‡ Kal part. act. sing. masc. dec. 1 a . זור

זֵר noun masc. sing. dec. 1 a . . זרר

זָרַב Kal not used; Syr. *to compress,* hence Pu. *to become straitened, narrow,* Job 6. 17. Others, *to become warm,* צָרַב=זָרַב, שָׂרַף.

זְרֻבָּבֶל (for זְרוּבָבֶל *scattered in Babylon;* or זְרוּעַ בָּבֶל *sown* (i. e. begotten) *in Babylon*)
pr. name of a leader of the first colony of Jews returning from the Babylonish captivity, comp. Ezr. 2. 2.

זֶרֶד } pr. name of a valley and of a stream in
זָרֵד } the land of Moab, Chald. זְרַד *to prune*

[זָרָה] I. *to spread, scatter, disperse.*—II. *to winnow.*
Niph. *to be scattered.* Pi. זֵרָה.—I. *to scatter, disperse.*—II. *to sift, discern.* Pu.—I. *to be spread,*

Pr. 1. 17; others, *to be besprinkled,* and so in Is. 1. 6.—II. *to be scattered,* Job 18. 15; here also according to some, זֹרוּ Ps. 58. 4, comp. זוּר.

זֶרֶת fem. *a span,* a measure.

מִזְרֶה masc. *winnowing fan.*

מְזָרֶה masc. prop. *scatterer,* only pl. מְזָרִים (dec. 9) Job 37. 9, poet. for *the north winds;* so according to Kimchi. Others take it as the name of a constellation, comp. מַזָּרוֹת.

זָרָה Kal pret. 3 pers. sing. fem. . . זור

זָרָה id. part. act. fem. dec. 10, from זָר masc. זור

זְרֵה Kal imp. sing. masc. . . . זרה

זֹרֶה Kal part. act. masc.; Is. 30. 24, according to some Pu. part. [for מְזֹרֶה § 10. rem. 6] זרה

זֹרוּ Kal pret. 3 pers. pl. . . . זור

זֵרוּ Piel pret. 3 pers. pl. . . . זרה

זֹרוּ Kal pret. 3 pers. pl. § 21. rem. 2, (less likely to be taken as Pu. of R. זרה) . . זור

זֵרוּהָ ‡ Piel pret. 3 pers. pl., suff. 3 pers. sing. fem. זרה

זְרֻעַ noun masc. sing. dec. 1 b [for זָרוּעַ] זרע

זֶרַע ‡ noun com. sing. dec. 1 a; ‡ bef. (:) זרע

זְרוּעָה Kal part. pass. fem. from זָרוּעַ masc. זרע

זַרְעוֹ n. com. s., suff. 3 p. s. m., from זֶרַע dec. 1 a זרע

זְרֻעוֹת id. with pl. fem. term. . . זרע

זַרְעִי id. sing., suff. 1 pers. sing. . . זרע

זְרֹעֶיהָ noun m. pl., suff. 3 pers. s. f. from זְרוֹעַ (q. v.) זרע

זְרֹעֲךָ ‡ } noun com. sing., suff. 2 pers. sing. masc.}
זְרֹעֶךָ } from זְרוֹעַ dec. 1 a; ‡ bef. (:) } זרע

זַרְעָם ‡ id., suff. 3 pers. pl. masc.; ‡ before (:) זרע

זְרַעְתִּי id. pl., suff. 1 pers. sing. [for עְתִּי] זרע

זְרֹעֹתֶיהָ id. pl., suff. 3 pers. sing. fem. . זרע

זְרֹעֹתָיו id. pl., suff. 3 pers. sing. masc. . זרע

זְרֹעֹתֵיכֶם id. pl., suff. 2 pers. pl. masc. . זרע

זְרֹעֹתָם id. pl., suff. 3 pers. pl. masc. . זרע

זָרוֹת Kal part. act. fem., pl. of זָרָה d. 10, from זָר m. זור

זַרְזִיף noun masc. sing. . . . זרף

זַרְזִיר noun masc. sing. . . . זור

זָרַח fut. יִזְרַח, inf. זְרֹחַ *to rise,* as the sun, light, glory, leprosy, and in the deriv. also of plants.

זֶרַח masc. with suff. זַרְחֲךָ (§ 35. rem. 5).—I. *a rising,* Is. 60. 3.—II. pr. name of a son of Judah by Tamar, and of others. Patronym. זַרְחִי.

זְרַחְיָה (whom *the Lord brings to light*) pr. name —I. of a man, called also יוֹזַרְיָה, comp. 1 Ch. 5. 32 with 7. 3.—II. Ezr. 8. 4.

אֶזְרָח masc. dec. 2 b.—I. *a native tree,* growing

a Ju. 8. 14.	c 1 Ki. 11. 4.	f Ps. 146. 8.	n Nu. 17. 2.	o Ps. 58. 4;	q Je. 2. 2.	s Ca. 8. 6.	u Pr. 31. 17.	x Ps. 72. 5.
b Is. 24. 23.	f Jos. 13. 1.	g Mal. 3. 3.	m Ru. 3. 2.	Is. 1. 6.	p Ps. 37. 17.	y Ps. 44. 4.	v Ese. 13. 20.	y Pr. 30. 31.
c De. 5. 20.	g Ge. 24. 36.	h Pr. 21. 8.	p Zec. 2. 2. 4.	r Is. 51. 2.	q Is. 61. 11.	s Ps. 18. 35.	w Ho. 7. 15.	z Ps. 112. 4.
d 1 Sa. 9. 5.	h 1 Ki. 15. 23.	k Job 19. 17.	pp Le. 11. 37.					

in its own soil, Ps. 37. 35.—II. *a native*, one born in the country.

אֶזְרָחִי patronym. *Ezrahite*, a descendant of אֶזְרָח.

יָזְרָח 1 Ch. 27. 8, with the art., for אֶזְרָחִי.

יְזַרְחָה (whom *the Lord brings to light*) pr. name m.—I. 1 Ch. 7. 3, see זְרַחְיָה.—II. Ne. 12. 42.

מִזְרָח masc. dec. 2 b, *the east*, prop. *the sunrising*; also adv. *eastward*. With local ה, מִזְרָחָה *towards the east, eastward*.

זָרַח	Kal pret. 3 pers. sing. m. for זָרַח (§ 8. rem. 7)	זרח
זֶרַח	pr. name masc. (§ 35. rem. 2) ; for	זרח
זֶרַח	ן see lett. ו . . .	
זָרְחָה	ן id. pret. 3 pers. sing. fem.	זרח
זְרַחְיָה	ה pr. name masc.; ה before (:)	זרח
זַרְחֶךָ	noun masc. sing., suff. 2 pers. sing. fem. from זֶרַח dec. 6 a (§ 35. rem. 5) . . .	זרח
זֹרַיִךְ	Kal part. masc. pl., suff. 2 pers. sing. fem. [for זֹרַיִךְ] from זָר dec. 1 a	זור
זָרִים	ן id. pl., absolute state	זור
זָרִיתָ	Piel pret. 2 pers. sing. masc.	זרה
זָרִיתִי	ן id. pret. 1 pers. sing.; acc. shifted by conv. ן (comp. § 8. rem. 7)	זרה
זֵרִיתִיךָ	ן id. id., suff. 2 pers. sing. masc.	זרה
זֵרִיתִים	ן id. id., suff. 3 pers. pl. masc.	זרה
זֵרִיתָנוּ	id. pret. 2 pers. sing. masc. with suff. 1 pers. pl.	זרה

[זָרַם] *to flow, pour,* hence with an acc. *to overwhelm,* Ps. 90. 5. Po. *to pour down,* Ps. 77. 18.

זֶרֶם masc. *a violent shower, storm*; זֶרֶם בָּרָד *shower of hail*; זֶרֶם קִיר *a shower* (prostrating) *walls.*

זִרְמַת fem. constr. (no pl.) *effusion, emission,* Eze. 23. 20.

זֶרֶם	noun masc. sing. (§ 35. rem. 2) ; for	זרם
זֶרֶם	ן see lett. ו . . .	
זֵרְמוּ	ן Piel pret. 3 pers. s. m. [זֵרָה], suff. 3 p. pl. m.	זרה
זֹרְמוּ	ן	זרם
זִרְמַת	ן noun fem. sing. constr. [of זִרְמָה ; no pl.]	זרם
זְרַמְתָּם	Kal pret. 2 pers. sing. m., suff. 3 pers. pl. m.	זרם
זִרְמָתָם	noun masc. sing., suff. 3 pers. pl. masc. [from זִרְמָה ; no pl.]	זרם

זָרַע prop. *to spread, to scatter,* and so perhaps Zec. 10. 9, cogn. זָרָה, hence—I. *to sow* ; with an acc. of the seed sown, and the field sown upon ; זָרַע זֶרַע *yielding seed.*—II. *to plant,* Is. 17. 10.—III. metaph. of good, evil, &c. Niph.—I. *to be sown,* of seed, a field.—II. trop. *to be propagated,* as a name,

Na. 1. 14 ; of a woman conceiving, Nu. 5. 28. Pu. *to be sown,* Is. 40. 24. Hiph.—I. *to bear, yield seed,* as a plant, Ge. 1. 11, 12.—II. *to conceive,* of a woman, Le. 12. 2.

זֶרַע masc. dec. 6 a (once constr. זְרַע § 35. r. 5, 7) —I. *seed.*—II. *seedtime.*—III. *issue, progeny.*

זְרַע Ch. *seed,* Da. 2. 43.

זְרוֹעַ com. dec. 1 a, pl. ־ים, ־וֹת.—I. *arm.*—II. *foreleg,* of an animal.—III. *strength, power, might.*

זֵרוּעַ masc. (for זְרוּעַ) dec. 1 b, *a sowing, what is sown,* as garden herbs.

זֵרֹעַ m. only pl. זֵרֹעִים *legumes, vegetables,* Da. 1. 12.

זֵרְעֹן masc. only pl. זֵרְעֹנִים (dec. 3 c) id. Da. 1. 16.

אֶזְרוֹעַ dec. 1 b, i. q. זְרוֹעַ *the arm.*

יִזְרְעֶאל, יִזְרְעֶאל (*God planteth*) pr. name—I. of a city in the tribe of Issachar, comp. Jos. 19. 18 ; afterwards the residence of king Ahab and his successors ; עֵמֶק י' the valley Jezreel near the city. Gent. noun יִזְרְעֵאלִי ; fem. יִזְרְעֵאלִית, יִזְרְעֵאלִת.—II. of a city in the tribe of Judah, Jos. 15. 56, 1 Sa. 29. 1.—III. pr. name of several men.

מִזְרָע masc. dec. 2 b, *things sown, crop,* Is. 19. 7

זָרַע	in pause for זֶרַע (q. v. § 35. rem. 2)	זרע
זָרוּעַ	Kal part. pass. sing. masc. [for זְרוּעַ] .	זרע
זַרְעוֹ	ן, ן n. m. s., suff. זַרְעוֹ, dec. 6 a (§ 35. r. 5)	זרע
זְרַע	Kal imp. sing. masc.	זרע
זְרֹעַ	defect. for זְרוֹעַ (q. v.) . .	זרע
זֹרֵעַ	ן Kal part. act. sing. masc. dec. 7 b	זרע
זַרְעָה	noun masc. sing., suff. 3 pers. sing. fem. from זֶרַע dec. 6 a (§ 35. rem. 5) .	זרע
זָרְעוּ	Kal pret. 3 pers. pl. .	זרע
זַרְעוֹ	ן noun masc. sing., suff. 3 pers. sing. masc. from זֶרַע dec. 6 a (§ 35. rem. 5)	זרע
זְרֹעוֹ	ה defect. for זְרוֹעוֹ (q. v.) ; ה before (:)	זרע
זִרְעוּ	Kal imp. pl. masc.	זרע
זְרֻעֶה	Pual pret. 3 p. pl. [for זֹרְעוּ comp. § 8. r. 7]	זרע
זְרֹעוֹת	ה n. com. with pl. f. term. from זְרוֹעַ d. 1 a	זרע
זְרֹעֹתָיו	id. pl., suff. 3 pers. sing. masc.	זרע
זַרְעִי	noun masc. sing., suff. 1 pers. sing. from זֶרַע dec. 6 a (§ 35. rem. 5) . .	זרע
זְרֹעֵי	noun com. pl. constr., from זְרוֹעַ dec. 1 a	זרע
זְרֹעִי	id. sing., suff. 1 pers. sing. .	זרע
זֹרְעֵי	ן Kal part. act. pl. c. masc., from זֹרֵעַ d. 7 b	זרע
זְרֹעַי	ה noun com. pl., suff. 1 pers. sing. from זְרוֹעַ dec. 1 a ; ה bef. (:) .	זרע
זְרֹעָיו	id., suff. 3 pers. sing. masc. .	זרע

a Is. 60. 1.   d Joel 4. 17.   i Is. 32. 2.   m Ps. 77. 18.   Ju. 6. 5.   r Ge. 1. 29, 29.   b Is. 40. 24.   e Ge. 49. 24.   h Job 4. 8.
a Mal. 3. 20.   e Ps. 139. 3.   f Hab. 3. 10.   n Eze. 22. 20.   Ps. 97. 11.   p Pr. 11. 18.   Eze. 30. 24, 25.   f Is. 63. 5.   k Is. 51. 5.
b Is. 60. 3.   g Eze. 22. 15.   k Is. 30. 30.   o Ps. 90. 5.   Je. 35. 9.   Ge. 3. 15.   Ju. 15. 14.   f Is. 32. 20.   l 2 Ki. 9. 2.
c Is. 29. 5.   h Ps. 44. 12.   l 1 Ki. 14. 15.   Eze. 23. 20.   Ec. 11. 6.   Je. 12. 12.

17*

זְרֵעֲיכֶם noun com. pl., suff. 2 pers. pl. masc. from זֶרַע dec. 6a (§ 35. rem. 5) . . . . . זרע

זְרֵעִים noun com. pl. abs. fr. זֶרַע d.1a ; ‍ bef. (:) . זרע

זַרְעֲךָ (ן) noun masc. sing., suff. 2 pers. sing.⎫
זַרְעֲךָ (ן) masc. from זֶרַע dec. 6a (§ 35. rem. 5)⎬ זרע
זַרְעֵךְ (ן) id., suff. 2 pers sing fem . .⎭

זַרְעֶךָ defect. for זְרוֹעֶךָ (q. v.) . . . . זרע

זַרְעֲכֶם noun masc. sing., suff. 2 pers. pl. masc. from זֶרַע dec. 6a (§ 35. rem. 5) . . . . זרע

זַרְעָם id., suff. 3 pers. pl. masc. . . . זרע

זַרְעָם defect. for זְרֹעָם (q. v.) . . . . ארע

זַרְעֹנִים noun masc., pl. of [זֵרָעוֹן] comp. dec. 3c . זרע

זַרְעֹת for זְרֹעוֹת noun com. with pl. fem. term. from זְרֹעַ dec. 1a . . . . זרע

זָרַעְתִּי Kal pret. 1 pers. sing. ; acc. shifted by conv. (ן) (§ 8. rem. 7) . . . זרע

זַרְעֹת noun com. pl., suff. 1 pers. sing., see זְרֹעַ זרע

זְרַעְתָּהּ (ן) Kal pret. 1 p. s., suff. 3 p. s. f.; ‍ for (ן) conv. זרע

זַרְעֹתָיו (ן) noun com. pl., suff. 3 pers. sing. masc., see זְרֹעַת; ‍ bef. (:) . . . . . זרע

זָרַעְתָּם (ן) Kal pret. 2 pers. pl. masc.; ‍ for (ן) conv. זרע

זָרַף Root not used ; Arab. to flow.
זַרְזִיף masc. a copious rain, Ps. 72. 6.

זָרַק (ן) to scatter, sprinkle, spoken of dust, ashes, water, blood. Intrans. to be sprinkled, Ho. 7. 9. Pu. to be sprinkled, Nu. 19. 13, 20.
מִזְרָק masc. dec. 2 b, pl. ‍‑ים, ‍ות, dish or basin, used for sprinkling.

זֹרַק Pual pret. 3 pers. sing. masc. . . זרק

זְרֹק (ן) Kal imp. sing. masc.; ‍ bef. (:) . זרק

זָרְקָה id. pret. 3 pers. sing. tem . . זרק
זְרָקוּ (ן) id. pret. 3 pers. pl. . . . זרק
זְרָקוֹ (ן) id. pret. 3 pers. sing. masc., suff. 3 pers. sing. masc. ; ‍ for (ן) conv. . . זרק
זֹרְקִים id. part. act. masc., pl. of זֹרֵק dec. 7b . זרק
זְרַקְתָּ (ן) id. pret. 2 pers. sing. masc. ; acc. shifted by conv. (ן) (§ 8. rem. 7) . . . . זרק
זְרַקְתִּי (ן) id. pret. 1 pers. sing.; acc. id. . . זרק

I. זָרַר Po. to sneeze, 2 Ki. 4. 35, comp. Chald. זָרִיר a sneezing.

II. זָרַר Root not used ; Arab. to bind, fasten together.
זֵר masc. dec. 1a, wreath, crown, border. This may also be suitably derived from צרר=זור. זַרְזִיר masc. bound together, girded, once Prov. 30. 31 זַרְזִיר מָתְנַיִם girded about the loins, Prof. Lee, compact of loins ; an epithet, according to some, of the war-horse, which used to be ornamented with girths and buckles round the loins. Simonis understands here the Zebra, from its stripes ; some of the Rabbins, the greyhound.

זֶרֶשׁ (ן) (gold, coll. with Pers., Gesenius ; Simon., the star of Venus) pr. name of the wife of Haman, Est. 6. 13.

זָרִיתָ (ן) noun fem. sing. (§ 35. rem. 2) ; for (ן)⎫
זָרִתָ (ן) see lett. ן . . . . .⎬ זרה
זֵרְתִּים (ן) defect. for זֵרִיתִים (q. v.) . . . זרה

זַתּוּא pr. name masc. comp. Ezr. 2. 8, Ne. 7. 13.

זֵתָם (ן) pr. name masc. . . . . . זית

זֵתַר (star, comp. אֶסְתֵּר) pr. name of a eunuch of Ahasuerus, Est. 1. 10.

ח

חָבָא Kal not used ; i. q. חָבָה to hide, conceal. Niph. to be hid, concealed, to conceal oneself, const. with בְּ, אֶל, of the place; followed by an inf. with לְ, as נַחְבֵּאתָ לִבְרֹחַ thou fleddest secretly. Pu. to be made to hide oneself, Job 24. 4. Hiph. to hide, conceal. Hoph. to be hid, Is. 42. 22. Hithp. to hide oneself, to lie hid.
מַחֲבֵא masc. a hiding-place, Is. 32. 2.
מַחֲבֹא masc. id. only pl. מַחֲבֹאִים 1 Sa. 23. 23.

חֻבְּאוּ Pual pret. 3 pers. pl. . . . חבא

[חָבַב] to love, cherish, De. 33. 3.
חֹב masc. dec. 8c, bosom, lap, Job 31. 33. Also (beloved) pr. name of the father-in-law of Moses . . . . חבב
חֹבֵב Kal part. act. sing. masc. . . . חבב

[חָבָה] to hide oneself, Is. 26. 20. Niph. id. 1 Ki. 22. 25 2 Ki. 7. 12.
חוֹבָה (hiding-place) pr. name of a place northward of Damascus, Ge. 14. 15.

a 1 Sa. 8. 15.   c Is. 54. 3.   f Da. 1. 16.   i 2 Sa. 22. 35.   l Hag. 1. 6.   o Nu. 19. 13, 20.   r Le. 1. 5, 11.   u Ex. 29. 16, 20.   x Je. 49. 32, 36.
b Da. 11. 31.   d 1 Sa. 2. 31.   g De. 33. 27.   k Ho. 2. 25.   m Ex. 24. 6.   p Eze. 10. 2.   s Ex. 9. 8.   v Eze. 36. 25.   y Job 24. 4.
c Ge. 17. 9.   e Is. 33. 2.   h Je. 31. 27.   n Da. 10. 6.   q Le. 17. 6.   t 2 Ch. 20. 16.   w 1 Sa. 17. 4.   z De. 33. 3.
d De. 30. 19.

חֲבַיָּה, חֲבַיָּ֫ה (whom *the Lord protects*) pr. name masc. Ezr. 2. 61 ; Ne. 7. 63.

חֶבְיוֹן masc. *a covering, veil,* Hab. 3. 4.

יַחְבָּה (*hidden, protected*) pr. name masc. 1 Ch. 7. 34 Kheth., וְחָבָה Keri.

נַחְבִּי (*hidden*) pr. name masc. Nu. 13. 14.

חבל   חֲבוּלָא Ch. noun fem. sing.

חבר   חֲבוֹר pr. name of a river

חבר   חֲבוּרֵי Kal part. p. masc., constr. of [חָבוּר] d. 3a

חבר   חַבּוּרָה noun fem. sing. dec. 10.

חבר   חַבּוּרֹתֵי id. pl. with suff. 1 pers. pl. [for תֵי]

חבש   חָבוּשׁ Kal part. pass. sing. masc. dec. 3a

חבש   חֲבֹשׁ id. imp. sing. masc.

חבש   חֲבוּשִׁים id. part. pass. masc., pl. of חָבוּשׁ dec. 3a

[חָבַט] fut. יַחְבֹּט (§ 13. rem. 5).—I. *to beat off,* as fruit from a tree.—II. *to beat out, thresh.* Niph. *to be beaten out,* Is. 28. 27.

חבט   חֹבֵט Kal part. act. sing. masc.

חבה   חֲבִי Kal imp. sing. fem.

חבה   חֲבַיָּה חֲבַיָּ֫ה } pr. name masc.

חבה   חֶבְיוֹן noun masc. sing.

ℒ [חָבַל] fut. יַחְבֹּל (§ 13. rem. 5).—I. *to twist, to bind,* only part. pl. חֹבְלִים *binders, bands;* a mystical name given to a shepherd's staff representing the union of *brotherhood,* Zec. 11. 7, 14.—II. *to bind by a pledge,* with an acc. of the pers., comp. Job 22. 6. Meton. *to take as a pledge,* with an acc. of the thing. Pi. *to writhe, to be in pain, to travail,* as a woman in labour.

§35.   חֵבֶל masc. dec. 6, pl. חֲבָלִים, constr. חֶבְלֵי (§ 35. rem. 6).—I. *writhing, pang, the throes of child-bearing.*—II. *pains* generally, Job 21. 16.

חֶבֶל masc. dec. 6, with suff. חֶבְלִי; pl. חֲבָלִים, constr. חֶבְלֵי חַבְלֵי (§ 35. rem. 4).—I. *cord, rope.* —II. *measuring-line.*—III. *a portion measured out,* whence generally, *a district, tract, region.*—IV. *gin, snare.*—V. *company, band of men,* 1 Sa. 10. 5, 10.

חֲבֹל masc. *a pledge, deposit.*

חֲבֹלָה fem. dec. 10, id. Eze. 18. 7.

חֹבֵל masc. *mast of a ship,* Pr. 23. 34.

חֹבֵל masc. dec. 7b, *ship-man, sailor.*

תַּחְבֻּלָה, תַּחְבֻּלוֹת fem. dec. 10, only in the pl. —I. *guidance, direction, management.*—II. *wise counsel.*—III. *cunning devices,* Pr. 12. 5.

II. [חָבַל] prop. *to corrupt, destroy;* hence, *to act corruptly, perversely, wickedly,* Ne. 1. 7 ; Job 34. 31. Niph. *to be destroyed, to perish,* Pr. 13. 13. Pi. *to corrupt, destroy, lay waste.* Pu. *to be destroyed.* Ch. Pa.—I. *to injure, hurt,* Da. 6. 23.— II. *to corrupt, destroy.* Ithpa. *to be destroyed.*

חֲבַל Ch. masc. *hurt, harm,* Da. 3. 25.

חֲבָל Ch. masc. dec. 1a, *hurt, damage,* Ezr. 4. 22.

חֲבוּלָה fem. *fault, crime,* Da. 6. 23.

חבל   חָבַל Kal pret. 3 pers. sing. m. [for חָבֵל § 8. r. 7]

חבל   חָבֹל id. inf. absolute

חבל   חֲבַל Ch. noun masc. sing. dec. 1a

חבל   חֲבֹל Ch. noun masc. sing. ; וַ bef. (◌ָ)

חבל   חֲבֹל Kal inf. constr., or noun masc.

חבל   חֵבֶל noun masc. sing. dec. 6 (§ 35. rem. 6)

חבל   חֶבֶל n. m. s., pl. c. חֶבְלֵי & חַבְלֵי d. 6 (§ 35. r. 4)

חבל   חִבֵּל n. m. s., or Piel pret. 3 pers. sing. m.

חבל   חֹבֵל Kal part. act. sing. masc. dec. 7b

חבל   חֻבַּל Pual pret. 3 pers. sing. masc.

חבל   חֲבָלָא Ch. noun masc. sing., emph. of חֲבָל dec. 1a

חבל   חֻבְּלָה Pual pret. 3 pers. sing. fem. [for חֻבְּלָה comp. § 8. rem. 7]

חבל   חִבְּלָה Piel pret. 3 pers. sing. fem.

חבל   חֲבֹלֵהוּ Kal imp. sing. masc. [חֲבֹל] with suff. 3 pers. sing. masc. (comp. § 16. rem. 10)

חבל   חֶבְלוֹ noun m. s., suff. 3 p. s. m. from חֵבֶל (q. v.)

חבל   חַבֵּלוּהִי Ch. Pael imp. pl. masc., suff. 3 p. s. m.

חבל   חַבְּלֻנִי Ch. id. pret. 3 pers. pl. m., suff. 1 pers. sing.

חבל   חֶבְלֵי noun masc. pl. constr. from חֵבֶל (q. v.).

חבל   חַבְלֵי noun masc. pl. const. from חֶבֶל, or חֵבֶל (§ 35. rem. 6 & 4)

חבל   חֹבְלֵי noun m. pl. constr. from חֹבֵל dec. 7b

חבל   חַבְלֵיהֶם noun masc. pl., suff. 3 pers. pl. masc. from חֶבֶל dec. 6d (§ 35. rem. 6)

חבל   חֲבָלָיו noun m. pl., suff. 3 p. s. m. from חֵבֶל (q. v.)

חבל   חֲבָלַיִךְ id., suff. 2 pers. sing. fem. [for חֲבָלַיִךְ]

חבל   חֹבְלָיִךְ noun masc. pl., suff. 2 pers. sing. fem. [for וְחֹבְלָיִךְ from חֹבֵל dec. 7b

חבל   חֲבָלִים n. m. pl. of חֵבֶל or חֶבֶל (q. v.); וַ bef. (◌ַ)

חבל   חֲבֻלִים Kal part. p. masc., pl. of חָבוּל dec. 3a

חבל   חֹבְלִים id. part. act. masc., pl. of חֹבֵל dec. 7b

חבל   חָבַלְנוּ id. pret. 1 pers. pl.

חבל   חַבָלָתוֹ noun fem. sing., suff. 3 pers. sing. masc. from [חֲבֹלָה] dec. 10

ᵃ Da. 6. 23.   ᵍ Ps. 38. 6.   ᵐ Is. 26. 20.   ˢ Da. 6. 24.   ˣ Ec. 5. 5.   ᶜ Job 17. 1.   ʰ Da. 6. 23.   ᶠ Is. 33. 20.   ᵘ Am. 2. 8.
ᵇ He. 4. 17.   ʰ Jon. 2. 6.   ⁿ Hab. 3. 4.   ᵗ Da. 3. 25.   ʸ Ca. 8. 5.   ᵖ Jon. 17. 5.   ⁱ Is. 38. 23.   ᵛ Zec. 11. 7.
ᶜ Ez. 21. 25.   ⁱ Ju. 19. 10.   ᵒ Eze. 18. 16.   ᵘ Is. 66. 7.   ᶻ Is. 10. 27.   ᵠ Job 18. 10.   ʲ Eze. 27. 29.   ᵂ Eze. 27. 8, 28.   ⁿ Ne. 1. 7.
Is. 1. 6.   ˡ Ju. 6. 11.   ᵖ Ex. 22. 25.   ᵖ Pr. 23. 34.   ᵂ Ezr. 4. 22.   Da. 4. 20.   Job 19. 3.   ᵏ Eze. 27. 27.   ᵡ Eze. 18. 7.

חֲבַלְתָּ֫ךְ Piel pret. 3 pers. sing. fem., suff. 2 pers. sing. masc. [for חֲבֵּלָתֶךְ § 16. rem. 3]   חבל

חֲבַצֶּ֫לֶת fem. the name of a flower, according to the ancient versions, *a lily*, or *a narcissus*; according to Gesenius, *the meadow saffron*, an autumnal flower resembling saffron, springing from a *bulbous* root; the gutt. ח is prefixed to בְּצֵל (bulb) as in חַשְׁמַנִּים from שֶׁמֶן. Fürst suggests, חֲבַצֵּל from חָמַץ=חָבַץ *to have a pungent fragrance*, or *to be bright*, *splendid*, with the termination, ־ל as in שַׂרְפָל, כַּרְמֶל &c.

חֲבַצַּנְיָה pr. name masc. Je. 35. 3.

[חָבַק] I. *to embrace.*—II. *to fold the hands*, as a slothful person, Ec. 4. 5. Pi. *to embrace.*

חִבֻּק masc. *a folding of the hands*, spoken of the sluggard.

חֲבַקּוּק (*embrace*) pr. name of the prophet, Hab. 1. 1; 3. 1.

חִבֻּק noun masc. sing.   חבק

חֹבֵק Kal part. act. sing. masc.   חבק

חִבְּקוּ Piel pret. 3 pers. pl.   חבק

חֲבַקּוּק pr. name masc.   חבק

חֹבֶ֫קֶת Kal part. act., fem. of חֹבֵק   חבק

[חָבַר] I. *to be bound, joined together, to consociate.*—II. *to charm, bind with a spell.* Pi. *to join, attach.* Pu. *to be joined together.* Hiph. *to join or connect* sentences, with בְּ of the object and עַל of the person, Job 16. 4. Hithp. *to join oneself* to any one.

חָבֵר masc. dec. 5c, *associate, companion.*

חֲבֶ֫רֶת fem. *a female companion*, only חֲבֶרְתֵּךְ (§ 44. rem. 3) Mal. 2. 14.

חֲבַר Chald. masc. dec. 3a, *companion*, Da. 2. 13, 17, 18.

חַבְרָה Chald. fem. dec. 8a (§ 64) *female associate*, hence *fellow, other*, Da. 7. 20.

חָבֵר masc. *associate, companion*, only pl. חֲבֵרִים Job 40. 30.

חָבוֹר (perhaps *strong*, כָּבַר=חָבַר) pr. name of a river in Mesopotamia.

חַבּוּרָה fem. dec. 10, *stripe, bruise, scar.*

חַבֻּרָה fem. dec. 10, id. Is. 53. 5.

חֶ֫בֶר masc. dec. 6.—I. *association, company.*— II. *incantation*, Is. 47. 9, 12.—III. pr. name of several men, written חֵבֶר in Nu. 26. 45.— Patronym. חֶבְרִי.

חֶבְרָה fem. *association, company*, Job 34. 8.

חֶבְרוֹן (*alliance*) pr. name.—I. of a town in the tribe of Judah.—II. of several men.—Patronym. חֶבְרֹנִי

חֶבֶ֫רֶת fem. *a joining, junction.*

חֲבַרְבֻּרָה fem. dec. 10, *stripe, streak* of the leopard, Je. 13. 23.

מַחְבֶּ֫רֶת fem. dec. 13a, with suff. בַּרְתּוֹ, *a joining, seam.*

מַחְבֶּ֫רֶת fem. dec. 13.—I. *beam, brace*, for joining a building, 2 Ch. 34. 11.—II. *iron cramps*, 1 Ch. 22. 3.

חָבָר noun masc. sing. dec. 5c   חבר

חָבָר (וְ) noun m. s. dec. 6 (Ho. 6. 9); also pr. name m. (§ 35. rem. 2); for וְ see   חבר
חָבֵר/

חֶ֫בֶר pr. name masc.   חבר

חִבֵּר Piel pret. 3 pers. sing. masc. (§ 10. rem. 1)   חבר

חֹבֵר וְ Kal part. act. sing. masc.   חבר

חֻבָּר וְ Pual pret. 3 pers. sing. masc. [for חֻבַּר comp. § 8. rem. 7]   חבר

חֲבַרְבֻּרֹתַי noun fem. pl., suff. 3 pers. sing. masc. from [חֲבַרְבֻּרָה] dec. 10.   חבר

חָבְרוּ Kal pret. 3 pers. pl.   חבר

חֲבֵרָו noun masc. pl., suff. 3 pers. sing. masc. (K. רָיו § 4. rem. 1) from חָבֵר dec. 5c   חבר

חֲבֵרוֹ id. sing., suff. 3 pers. sing. masc.   חבר

חַבְרוֹהִי וְ Chald. noun masc. pl., suff. 3 pers. sing. masc. from [חֲבַר] dec. 3a   חבר

חֶבְרוֹן וְ pr. name of a man and a place   חבר

חֶבְרוֹנָה id. of a place with paragogic ה   חבר

חֲבֻרוֹת noun fem., pl. of חַבּוּרָה dec. 10.   חבר

חֹבְרוֹת Kal part. act. fem., pl. of [חֹבֶ֫רֶת] dec. 13a   חבר

חַבְרֵי וְ noun masc. pl. constr. from חָבֵר dec. 5c   חבר

חֲבֵרָיו id. pl., suff. 3 pers. sing. masc.   חבר

חֲבֵרַ֫יִךְ noun masc. pl., suff. 2 pers. sing. fem. from חָבֵר dec. 6   חבר

חֲבֵרֶ֫יךָ noun masc. pl., suff. 2 pers. sing. masc. from חָבֵר dec. 5c   חבר

חֲבָרִים noun masc., pl. of [חֶ֫בֶר] dec. 1b   חבר

חֲבֵרִים noun masc., pl. of חָבֵר dec. 6   חבר

חֲבֵרִים noun masc., pl. of חָבֵר dec. 5c   חבר

חֶבְרֹ֫נָה pr. name of a place (חֶבְרֹן) with parag. ה   חבר

חִבַּרְתָּ֫ וְ Piel pret. 2 pers. sing. masc.; acc. shifted by conv. וְ (comp. § 8. rem. 7)   חבר

חֹבְרֹת defect. for חוֹבְרוֹת (q. v.)   חבר

חַבְרָתַהּ Chald. noun fem. sing., suff. 3 pers. sing. fem. [from חַבְרָה § 65] dec. 8a   חבר

• Ca. 8. 5.   ᵈ Ec. 4. 5.   ᵍ Ex. 36. 10.   ʲ Ex. 28. 7.   ᵐ Eze. 37. 16, 19.   ᵖ Da. 2. 13, 18.   ˢ Is. 1. 23.   ᵛ Ca. 1. 7.   ʸ Ex. 26. 6, 9, 11.
ᵇ Ca. 2. 1.   ᵉ 2 Ki. 4. 16.   ʰ De. 18. 11.   ᵏ Je. 13. 23.   ⁿ Ec. 4. 10.   ᵠ Pr. 20. 30.   ᵗ Is. 44. 11.   ʷ Job 40. 30.   ᶻ Da. 7. 20.
Pr. 6. 10; 24. 33.   ᶠ Ho. 6. 9.   ᶦ Ex. 39. 4.   ˡ Ge. 14. 3.   ᵒ Da. 2. 17.   ʳ Eze. 1. 11.   ᵘ Is. 47. 9.   ˣ Ps. 58. 6.

חֲבַרְתֵּךְ noun fem. sing., suff. 2 pers. sing. masc. from [חֲבֶרֶת] dec. 13 (§ 44. rem. 3) .   חבר

[חָבַשׁ] fut. יַחְבֹּשׁ, (§ 13. rem. 4, 5)—I. *to bind, bind round* or *about*, as with ropes; or as a head-dress; *to bind up*, as a wound, const. with לְ.— II. *to gird* or *saddle* a beast.—III. *to restrain, subdue, govern.* Pi.—I. *to bind up*, with לְ, Ps. 147. 3.—II. *to restrain, stop*, Job 28. 11. Pu. *to be bound up*, as a wound.

חֲבֹשׁ Kal inf. constr.   חבש
חִבֵּשׁ Piel pret. 3 pers. sing. masc.   חבש
חֹבֵשׁ Kal part. act. sing. masc.   חבש
חֻבְּשָׁה Pual pret. 3 pers. sing. fem.   חבש
חִבְשׁוּ Kal imp. pl. masc.   חבש
חֻבְּשׁוּ Pual pret. 3 pers. pl. [for חֻבְּשׁוּ § 8. rem. 7]   חבש
חֲבֻשִׁים Kal part. pass. masc., pl. of חָבוּשׁ dec. 3a   חבש
וְחָבַשְׁתָּ id. pret. 2 pers. sing. masc.; acc. shifted by conv. וְ (§ 8. rem. 7)   חבש
חֲבַשְׁתֶּם id. pret. 2 pers. pl. masc.   חבש

חָבֵת Root not used; i. q. Arab חבז *to bake bread.* חַבִּת masc. only pl. חַבִּתִּים (dec. 8b) 1 Ch. 9. 31, *baked cakes* or *pastry.* Others, *pans*, Arab. חבת *to be low* or *flat.* מַחֲבַת fem. (for מַחֲבֶתֶת) *a baking* or *frying-pan.*

חָנ Kal pret. 3 pers. sing. masc.   חונ
חָנ noun masc. sing. dec. 8a   חנג
חָנ id. constr. state, and, followed by לְ, abs. st.   חנג

חָגָב masc. dec. 4c.—I. *locust.*—II. pr. name masc. Ezr. 2. 46. Hence

חֲגָבָא } (*locust*) pr. name masc. Ne. 7. 48; Ezr.
חֲגָבָה } 2. 45.

[חָגַג] i. q. חונ Syr. and Chald. *to move in a circle*, hence—I. *to dance*, 1 Sa. 30. 16.—II. *to keep* or *celebrate a feast.*—III. *to reel, to be giddy*, Ps. 107. 27.

חָג masc. dec. 8a, חַג constr., and, when followed by לְ, abs. (comp. Ex. 12.14; 13. 6).—I. *festival, feast.*—II. meton. *a festival sacrifice.*

חָגָּא fem. (for חָגָּה, as seven of Dr. Kennicott's codices read) *commotion, tremor, fear*, Is. 19. 17.

חַגַּי (i. q. חַגָּי) pr. name of the prophet, Hag. 1. 1.

חַגִּי (*festive*, or perhaps for חַגִּיָּה q. v.) pr. name of a son of Gad; patronym. חַגִּי for חַגִּיִּי Nu. 26. 15.

חַגִּיָּה (*feast of the Lord*) pr. name masc. 1 Ch. 6. 15.

חַגִּית (*festive*) pr. name of one of the wives of David.

וְחֹגְנִים Kal part. act. masc., pl. of חוֹגֵן dec. 7b.   חנג

חָגָה Root not used; prob. i. q. חָקָה *to cut, hew.*
חֲגָוִים masc. pl., only in constr. חַגְוֵי *chinks, clefts* of rocks. Others, *refuges*, Arab. חנא *to take refuge.*

חַנֵּהוּ noun masc. sing., suff. 3 pers. sing. fem. from חָנ dec. 8a.   חנג

חָגוּר Kal part. pass. sing. masc. dec. 3a.   חגר
חֲגוֹר id. imp. sing. masc., or noun m. s. dec. 1a.   חגר
חֲגוֹרָה noun fem. sing. dec. 10.   חגר
חֲגוֹרֵי adj. masc. pl. constr. from [חָגוֹר] dec. 3a.   חגר
חֲגֻרִים Kal part. pass. masc., pl. of חָגוֹר dec. 3a.   חגר
חַגִּי pr. name masc.   חנג
חַגִּי noun m. s., suff. 1 pers. sing. fr. חָנ dec. 8a.   חנג
וְחַגַּי pr. name masc.   חנג
חַגִּי Kal imp. sing. fem. (§ 18. rem. 4).   חנג
חַגִּיָּה pr. name masc.   חנג
חַגֵּיכֶם noun masc. pl., suff. 2 pers. sing. fem. from חָנ dec. 8a.   חנג
חַגֵּיכֶם id. pl., suff. 2 pers. pl. masc.   חנג
חַגִּים id. pl., absolute state.   חנג
חַגִּית pr. name fem.   חנג
חָגְלָה (*partridge*, Syr. חַגְלָא) pr. name fem.; see also בֵּית חָ׳.
חַגֵּינוּ noun m. s., suff. 1 pers. pl. from חָנ dec. 8a.   חנג

[חָגַר] fut. יַחְגֹּר (§ 13. rem. 5).—I. *to bind about, to gird, gird up, gird on*, with the acc. of the part girded, or acc. of the thing girded on and עַל of the part girded (Ps. 45. 4); with double acc. of the person and the thing; with בְּ of the thing girded on.— II. *to gird oneself.*—III. *to be straitened*, 2 Sa. 22. 46; or perh. *dismayed*, comp. חָרַג

חָגוֹר masc. dec. 3a, adj. *girded.* Eze. 23. 15.
חֲגוֹר masc. dec. 1a, *girdle.*
חֲגוֹרָה fem. dec. 10.—I. *girdle.*—II. *apron*, Ge. 3. 7.
מַחֲגֹרֶת fem. *cincture*, Is. 3. 24.

חֲגֹר Kal imp. sing. masc.   חגר
חֹגֵר id. part. act. sing. masc.   חגר
וַחֲגֹרָה defect. for חֲגוֹרָה q. v.; וַ before (ה־)   חגר
חָגְרָה Kal pret. 3 pers. sing. fem.   חגר

---

a Mal. 2. 4.   c Is. 3. 7.   e Is. 1. 6.   h Job 26. 10.   k Ho. 2. 13.   q Eze. 23. 15.   t Na. 2. 1.   x Is. 29. 1.   z 2 Ki. 3. 21.
b Is. 30. 26.   d Eze. 30. 21.   f Ex. 29. 9.   i 2 Ch. 7. 13.   l Pr. 31. 24.   r Ju. 18. 16.   u Na. 2. L   y Ps. 61. 4.   a Pr. 61 17.
Job 22. 11.   1 Ki. 13. 13, 27.   Eze. 34. 4.   1 Sa. 30. 16.   Is. 3. 24.   Ex. 23. 18.

חָגְרוּ id. pret. 3 pers. pl. . . חגר

חֲגֹרוֹ noun masc. sing., suff. 3 pers. sing. masc. from חֲגוֹר dec. 1 a . חגר

חִגְרוּ Kal imp. pl. masc. . . חגר

חִגְרִי id. imp. sing. fem. . . חגר

חֲגֻרִים id. part. pass. pl. masc. (for חֲגוּרִים) from חָגוּר dec. 3 a . חגר

חֲגֹרְנָה id. imp. pl. fem. . . חגר

חָגַרְתָּ id. pret. 2 pers. sing. masc.; acc. shifted by conv. וְ (§ 8. rem. 7) . חגר

חֲגֹרֶת id. part. pass. fem., const. of [חֲגֹרָה] d. 10, from חָגוּר masc. . חגר

חֲגֹרֹת noun fem., pl. of חֲגוֹרָה dec. 10. . חגר

חֹתַם Kal pret. 2 pers. pl. masc. . חגן

חַד Ch. and once Heb. (Eze. 33. 30) num. masc. . אחד

חֲדָא Ch. fem. of the preceding . אחד

[חָדַד] fut. יֵחַד (§ 18. rem. 6)—I. *to be sharp, sharpened,* Pr. 27. 17.—II. *to be fierce,* Hab. 1. 8. Hiph. *to sharpen,* Pr. 27. 17. Hoph. *to be sharpened,* Eze. 21. 14, 15, 16.

חַד adj. fem. חַדָּה *sharp.*

חֲדַד (*sharpness*) pr. name of a son of Ishmael.

חִדּוּד masc. dec. 1 b, *sharp point,* Job 41. 22.

חָדִיד (*sharp*) pr. name of a town in the tribe of Benjamin.

חֲדַד pr. name masc. . . חדד

[חָדָה] fut. apoc. יַחְדְּ (§ 24. rem. 3) *to rejoice, be glad.* Pi. *to make glad,* Ps. 21. 7. Hiph. *to make glad,* in this sense, according to some, יַחַד (§ 24. r. 16) Pr. 27. 17, but see חָדַד.

חֶדְוָה fem. constr. חֶדְוַת (no pl.) *joy, gladness.* חֶדְוָה Ch. fem. id. Ezr. 6. 16.

יַחְדִּיאֵל (*whom God gladdens*) pr.n.m. 1 Ch. 5. 24.

יַחְדִּיָהוּ (*whom the Lord gladdens*) pr. name masc.—I. 1 Ch. 24. 20.—II. 1 Ch. 27. 30.

חַדָּה adj. fem. from [חַד] masc. . חדד

חֲדָה Ch. i. q. חָדָא (q. v.) . . אחד

חָדוּ Kal pret. 3 pers. pl. tone shifted (§ 18. r. 2) . חדד

חִדּוּדֵי noun masc. pl. constr. fr. [חִדּוּד] dec. 1 b . חדד

חֶדְוָה noun fem. sing. dec. 10. . חדה

חַדְוֺתִי Ch. noun masc. pl., suff. 3 pers. sing. masc [fr. חַדְי q. v.] . חדה

חַדֹּן pr. name, see אָסַר חַדֹּן . אסר

חֶדְוַת noun fem. sing., const. of חֶדְוָה dec. 10. . חדה

[חֲדִי] Ch. masc. i. q. Heb. חָזֶה *the breast,* only Da. 2. 32.

חָדִיד pr. name of a place . . חדד

חָדְלוּ ,יֶחְדַּל pret. pl. חָדְלוּ (from חָדַל), fut. יֶחְדַּל (§ 13. rem. 5)—I. *to cease, leave off, fail.*—II. *to forbear, decline, omit.*—Const. with מִן, rarely with an acc.; followed by a verb in the inf. with לְ rarely without it.

חָדֵל adj. masc. dec. 5 c.—I. *ceasing to be, frail,* Ps. 39. 5.—II. *forbearing* to do anything, Eze. 3. 27.—III. *forsaken,* Is. 53. 3.

חָדֵל masc. *ceasing, frailty,* Is. 38. 11, יֹשְׁבֵי חָדֶל *inhabitants of frailty,* i. e. of this frail, transitory world. Eng. vers. "world," as a transposition for חֶלֶד. *Gesenius, place of rest, hades.* Prof. Lee, *leisure.*

חֶדְלַי (*forsaken*; or *idler*) pr. name masc. 2 Ch. 28. 12.

חָדֵל adj. masc. sing. dec. 5 c . חדל

חֶדֶל noun masc. sing. [for חָדֵל § 35. rem. 2] . חדל

חֲדַל Kal imp. sing. masc. (§ 8. rem. 12) . חדל

חֲדַל adj. masc. sing., constr. of חָדֵל dec 5 c; bef. (־) . חדל

חָדְלוּ } Kal pret. 3 pers. pl. (§ 8. rem. 7) . חדל
חָדְלוּ }

חִדְלוּ Kal imp. pl. masc. (§ 8. rem. 12) . חדל

חֶדְלַי pr. name masc. for חֶדְלַי . חדל

חָדַלְנוּ Kal pret. 1 pers. pl. . חדל

חָדַלְתָּ id. pret. 2 pers. sing. masc. acc. shifted by conv. וְ (§ 8. rem. 7) . חדל

חַדֹּן pr. name masc., see אָסַר חַדֹּן . אסר

חָדַק Root not used; Arab. *to sting, to be sharp.* חֵדֶק ,חָדָק masc. a species of *thorn.*

חֶדֶק noun masc. sing. [for חָדָק § 35. rem. 2] חִדֶּקֶל חִדֶּקֶל pr. name, as is supposed, of the river Tigris, Ge. 2. 14; Da. 10. 4. Jewish interpreters suppose it compounded of חַד *sharp,* and קַל *light, swift;* but nearly the same idea may be obtained by deriving it from חָדַק=חֶדֶק, with the termination לְ (like כַּרְמֶל) with dagesh euphon.

[חָדַר] *to enclose, besiege, beset,* Eze. 21. 19.

חֶדֶר masc. dec. 6, constr. חֲדַר, with suff. חַדְרוֹ pl. c. חַדְרֵי (§ 35. rem. 4 & 7) *chamber, inner*

a 1 Sa. 18. 4.   c Je. 6. 26.   e Ex. 29. 9.   g Ge. 3. 7.   i Job 41. 22.   l Da. 2. 32.   n Ps. 39. 5.   p Is. 53. 3.   r Ex. 22. 1.
b 2 Sa. 3. 31.   d Je. 49. 3.   f Joel 1. 8.   h Hab. 1. 8.   k 1 Ch. 16. 27.   m Ne. 8. 10.   o Is. 38. 11.   q Je. 44. 18.   s Pr. 15. 19.
bb Zec. 11. 12.

apartment; חֶדֶר בְּחָדֶר chamber within a chamber, i. e. the innermost, most secluded chamber. Metaph. חַדְרֵי תֵימָן the remotest parts of the south, Job 9. 9, once simply הַחֶדֶר ch. 37. 9; חַדְרֵי בֶטֶן inner parts of the body; חַדְרֵי מָוֶת tombs.

חֲדַר   pr. name masc.   חדר

חֶדֶר   noun masc. sing., (constr. חֲדַר § 35. rem. 7, comp. rem. 4)   חדר

חַדְרֵי   וְ id. pl., constr. state   חדר

חֲדָרָיו   בְּ id. pl., suff. 3 pers. sing. masc.; וַ bef. (–)   חדר

חֲדָרִים   id. pl., absolute state   חדר

חֶדְרָךְ   pr. name of a region near Damascus, Zec. 9. 1

חָדַשׁ   Pi. to make new, to renew, restore. Hithp. to be renewed, Ps. 103. 5.

     חָדָשׁ masc. dec. 4 c, fem. חֲדָשָׁה, pl. חֲדָשׁוֹת, adj. new, recent, fresh.

     חֹדֶשׁ masc. dec. 6 c.—I. new moon.—II. month; חֹדֶשׁ יָמִים a month of days, i. e. a complete month.—III. pr. name fem. 1 Ch. 8. 9; matronym. חָדְשִׁי, 2 Sa. 24. 6.

חָדָשׁ   adj. masc. sing. dec. 4 c   חדש

חַדֵּשׁ   Piel imp. sing. masc.   חדש

חֹדֶשׁ   noun masc. sing. dec. 6 c, also pr. name fem.   חדש

חֲדָשָׁה   id., suff. 3 pers. sing. fem.   חדש

חֲדָשָׁה   בְּ adj. fem. sing., from חָדָשׁ masc., also pr. name; וַ before (–)   חדש

חִדְּשׁוּ   וְ Piel pret. 3 pers. pl.   חדש

חָדְשׁוֹ   noun masc. sing. with suff. 3 pers. sing. masc. from חֹדֶשׁ dec. 6 c   חדש

חֲדָשׁוֹת   וְ adj. fem., pl. of חֲדָשָׁה, fr. חָדָשׁ masc.   חדש

חָדְשֵׁי   noun masc. pl. constr. from חֹדֶשׁ dec. 6 c   חדש

חֲדָשִׁי   pr. name, see תַּחְתִּים חָדְשִׁי   תוח

חָדָשָׁיו   noun m. pl., suff. 3 p. s. m. from חֹדֶשׁ dec. 6 c   חדש

חָדְשֵׁיכֶם   id. pl., suff. 2 pers. pl. masc.   חדש

חֲדָשִׁים   adj. masc., pl. of חָדָשׁ dec. 4 c   חדש

חֳדָשִׁים   noun masc., pl. of חֹדֶשׁ dec. 6 c   חדש

חָדְשֵׁכֶם   defect. for מָדְשֵׁיכֶם q.v.   חדש

חֲדַת   Ch. adj. masc. new, Ezr. 6. 4.

חֲדַתָּה   pr. name, see חָצוֹר חֲדַתָּה   חצר

חַדֹּתָה   Kal pret. 2 pers. sing. masc. (§ 8. rem. 5)   חוד

חוּב   Pi. חִיֵּב to render guilty, to forfeit, Da. 1. 10. Hence

חוֹב   masc. debt, Eze. 18. 7.   חוב

חוֹבָה   pr. name of a place   חבה

חוֹבְרֵי   Kal part. act. sing. masc.   חבר

חֹבְרוֹת   id. fem., pl. of [חֹבֶרֶת] dec. 13 a   חבר

[חוּג]   to draw a circle, to circumscribe, Job 26. 10.

     חוּג masc. circle, sphere.

     מְחוּגָה fem. compass, compasses, Is. 44. 13.

חוּג   וְ noun masc. sing.   חוג

חוֹגֵג   Kal part. act. sing. masc. dec. 7 b   חגג

חוּד   to propose a riddle, problem.

     חִידָה fem. dec. 10.—I. riddle, enigma.—II. proverb, parable; hence, a sublime, spiritual discourse, comp. Ps. 49. 5 ; 78. 2.

     אֲחִידָא Ch. fem. dec. 8 a, riddle, enigma, Da. 5. 12.

חוּד   Kal imp. sing. masc.   חוד

חוּדָה   id. with parag. ה   חוד

חָוָה   Kal not used; cogn. חָיָה to breathe, to live, (comp. חָנָה) ; to breathe out, hence Pi. to declare, shew חִוָּה Chald. Pa. to declare, shew. Aph. id.

     חַוָּה fem. dec. 10.—I. life, but only as a pr. name of the first woman, Eve, Ge. 3. 20; 4. 1.—II. pl. חַוֹּת villages; from the idea of living, dwelling; others compare it with the Arab. חוי to assemble.

     חִוִּי (villager) pr. name of a people of Canaan, Hivite, collect. Hivites.

     אַחְוָה f. dec. 10, declaration, argument, Job 13. 17.

     אַחֲוָיָה Chald. fem. dec. 8 a, declaration, explanation, Da. 5. 12.

     יְחַוְאֵל (whom God preserves alive) pr. name masc. 2 Ch. 29. 14. Kheth.

     מַחֲוִים pr. name of a people, 1 Ch. 11. 46. אֱלִיאֵל הַמַּ Eliel of the Mahavites.

חַוָּה   pr. name fem.   חוה

חָוַז   Root not used; Arab. חֹאז to collect, conj. VII. to decline, recede.

     מָחוֹז masc. dec. 3 a, haven, Ps. 107. 30.

חוֹזֵה   noun masc., constr. of חֹזֶה dec. 9 a   חזה

חוֹזַי   pr. name masc. for חוֹזַי   חזה

חוֹח   וְ masc. pl. חוֹחִים, חֲוָחִים (§ 35. rem. 13).—I. thorn, thorn-bush.—II. fish-hook, Job 40. 26.—III. a hook or ring used for fastening prisoners, 2 Ch. 33. 11.

     חָח masc. with suff. חַחִי, pl. חַחִים (§ 37. r. 7).—I. a hook or ring put into the nose of animals—II. a nose-ring, worn as an ornament, Ex. 35. 22.

---

a Job 9. 9.   d Pr. 24. 4.   f Is. 61. 4.   h Is. 48. 6.   k 1 Ch. 27. 1.   m Ps. 58. 6.   o Job 22. 14.   r Eze. 17. 2.   t 2 Ch. 35. 15.
b Ca. 1. 4.   c Ho. 2. 13.   g 1 Ki. 5. 7.   i Is. 42. 9.   l Ju. 14. 16.   n Eze. 1. 11.   p Ps. 42. 5.   s Ju. 14. 15.   u Is. 34. 13.
1 Ch. 28. 11.

חוט Ch. Aph. *to fasten, join together*, Ezr. 4. 12. Hence

חוט m. חוט masc.—I. *a thread.*—II. *cord, line*, Jos. 2. 18.

חמא חוֹמֵא, חוֹטֵא'ו Kal part. act. sing. masc. dec. 7 b) (§ 23. rem. 9)

חֲוִילָה pr. name—I. of a son of Joktan, Ge. 10. 29, and of a gold country, *Havilah*, Ge. 2. 11.—II. of a son of Cush, Ge. 10. 7, and of a district in southern Arabia.

חכה חוֹכֵי Kal part. act. pl. c. m. from [חוֹכֶה] dec. 9a

חול [חיל &] חוֹל וַתָּחֶל, וַיָּחֶל fut. יָחִיל, יָחוּל apoc. וַתָּחֶל, וַיָּחֶל imp. חוּלִי, חִילִי. According to Gesenius, coll. with the Arab., prop. *to turn about, twist, whirl*, and intrans. *to be turned, twisted, whirled*, hence—I. *to dance*, Ju. 21. 21.—II. *to be hurled, fall upon*, with עַל, בְּ.—III. *to writhe, to be in pain.*—IV. *to bear, bring forth*, Is. 54. 1.—V. *to tremble.*—VI. *to be strong, firm, durable.*—VII. *to wait, stay, delay*, i. q. יָחַל. Hiph. *to shake*, Ps. 29. 8. Hoph. *to be brought forth*, Is. 66. 8. Pil.—I. *to dance*, Ju. 21. 23.—II. *to bear, bring forth*, Job 39. 1; causat. Ps. 29. 2, metaph. *to create, form.*—III. *to tremble*, Job 26. 5.—IV. *to wait*, Job 35. 14. Pul. *to be born.* Hithpal.—I. *to whirl, precipitate itself*, Je. 23. 19.—II. *to writhe* with pain, Job 15. 20.—III. *to wait*, Ps. 37. 7. Hithpalp. (§ 6. No. 4) *to be pained, grieved*, Est. 4. 4.—Comp. Gesenius' Manuale.

חוֹל masc. *sand* ; חוֹל הַיָּם *sand of the sea*, used as the image of multitude, or of *weight.*

חוּל (*pain*) pr. name of a son of Aram, Ge. 10. 23; 1 Ch. 1. 17.

חַיִל masc. dec. 6h, pl. חֲיָלִים (§ 35. rem. 12).—I. *strength, might, valour*; עָשָׂה חַיִל *to do valiantly.*—II. *forces, army, host*; אַנְשֵׁי חַיִל, בְּנֵי חַיִל *men of the host*, i. e. soldiers; שַׂר הַחַיִל *captain of the host*, i. e. general.—III. *wealth, riches* ; עָשָׂה חַיִל *to acquire riches.*—IV. *virtue, integrity.*

חַיִל Chald. masc. dec. 3 d.—I. *strength*, spoken of the voice, Da. 3. 4.—II. *forces, army.*

חֵל, חֵיל masc. dec. 1a.—I. *host, army.*—II. *fortification*, or perhaps, *the space before it, the out-work.*

חִיל m.—I. *pain.*—II. *trembling, fear*, Ex. 15. 14.

חִילָה fem. *pain*, Job 6. 10.

חֵילָה fem. *fortification*, i. q. חֵיל, Ps. 48. 14, where others read חֵילָה, from חֵיל.

חֵילָם (*strength*; or *strength of the people*, for חֵיל עָם) pr. name of a city near the Euphrates, 2 Sa. 10. 16, for which in ver. 17, it is חֶלְאָם Khethib.

חִילֵן pr. name of a city in the tribe of Judah 1 Ch. 6. 43, supposed to be the same as חֹלוֹן q. v.

חֹלוֹן, חֹלֹן (*sandy*; Simonis, *stay, sojourn*, comp. R. No. VII) pr. name—I. of a city in the tribe of Judah, Jos. 15. 51; 21. 15.—II. of a city in Moab, Je. 48. 21.

חֵלֶן (*strong*) pr. name masc. Nu. 1. 9; 2. 7.

חַלְחָלָה fem—I. *pain.* Is. 21. 3.—II. *trembling terror.*

חַלְחוּל (*trembling, terror*) pr. name of a city in the tribe of Judah, Jos. 15. 58.

מָחוֹל masc. dec. 3a.—I. *dance, dancing.*—II. pr. name masc. 1 Ki. 5. 11.

מְחוֹלָה fem. dec. 10, *dance, dancing.*

חול חֻל'ו Kal inf. absolute; also pr. name masc.

חול חוֹל noun masc. sing.

חלה חוֹלָה fem. of the following, dec. 10.

חלה חוֹלֶה Kal part. act. sing. masc. dec. 9a

חול חוּלִי id. imp. sing. fem.

חול חוֹלֶלֶת Pulal pret. 2 pers. sing. masc. [for חֹלַלְתְּ comp. § 8. rem. 7]

חול חוֹלַלְתִּי id. pret. 1 pers. sing. [for חֹלַלְתִּי v. id.]

חלם חוֹלֵם Kal part. act. sing. masc. dec. 7 b

חלק חוֹלֵק Kal part. act. sing. masc.

חלש חוֹלֵשׁ Kal part. act. sing. masc.

חלה חוֹלַת Kal part. act. fem., constr. of חוֹלָה dec. 10, from חוֹלֶה masc.

חום Root not used ; i. q. Arab. חמם *to be black.* Hence—

חום חוּם'ו adj. m. *black*, Ge. 30. 32, 33, 35, 40.

חמה חוֹמָה'ו noun fem. sing. dec. 10.

חמה חוֹמוֹת id. pl.

חמה חוֹמוֹתַיִךְ id. pl., suff. 2 pers. sing. fem.

חמץ חוֹמֵץ'ו Kal part. act. sing. masc.

חמה חוֹמַת'ו noun fem. sing., constr. of חֹמָה' dec. 10.

חמה חוֹמֹת id. pl.

חמה חוֹמָתָהּ id. sing., suff. 3 pers. sing. fem.

חמה חוֹמֹתֶיהָ id. pl., suff. 3 pers. sing. fem.

חמה חוֹמֹתַיִךְ id. pl., suff. 2 pers. sing. masc.

חנן חוֹנֵן Kal part. act. sing. masc.

[חום] fut. תָּחוּם, יָחֹם, יָחוּם (§ 21. rem. 3) *to pity, spare, grieve for*, const. with עַל of the thing ; frequently spoken of the eye as that from which the pity proceeds, comp. Ge. 45. 20 ; De. 7. 16.

חום חוּסָה'ו Kal imp. sing. masc. with parag. ה

חוֹסֵי Kal part. act. pl. c. masc. from חוֹסָה d. 9a. חסה

חוֹסִים* id. pl., absolute state . . . . חסה

חוֹף noun masc. sing. [for חֹף] . . . חפף

חוּץ Root not used; Syr. Pa. to surround.

חוּץ masc. dec. 1a, pl. חוּצוֹת.—I. an open place round about or without the house, and generally for the street.—II. out-field or lands, without the city.—III. adv. out of doors, without, abroad; חוּצָה, הַחוּצָה abroad, without; בַּחוּץ without, in the street, in the open air; לַחוּץ לַחוּצָה id.; מֵחוּץ from without, out of doors, without, מֵחוּץ לָעִיר without the city, מֵחוּצָה לַשַּׁעַר without the gate, אֶל־מֵחוּץ לַמַּחֲנֶה without the camp; חוּץ מִן except, besides, Ec. 2. 25.

חַיִץ masc. wall, Eze. 13. 10.

חִיצוֹן masc. חִיצוֹנָה fem. adj. outer, exterior; hence, civil, in opposition to sacred, 1 Ch. 26. 29; לַחִיצוֹן without.

חוּץ noun masc. dec. 1a, used also as an adv.

חוּץ [ה'] id. with parag. ה; for וְ see lett. ו.

חוּץ [וֹ'] id. with pl. fem. term.

חוּץ id. pl., suff. 3 pers. sing. fem. חוּצוֹתֶיהָ

חוּץ id. pl., suff. 2 pers. sing. fem. [for תַיִךְ] חוּצוֹתַיִךְ

חוּץ id. pl., suff. 3 pers. pl. masc. חוּצוֹתָם*

חוּק Root not used; i. q. Arab. חאק to surround; prob. derived from חָבַק to embrace, ב being softened into ו.

חֵיק masc. i. q. חֵיק the bosom, Ps. 74. 11 Khethib.

חֵק, חֵיק masc. dec. 1a.—I. the bosom.—II. the feelings, affections.—III. bosom or lap of a garment.—IV. the hollow place or the inside of a chariot, 1 Ki. 22. 35; also of an altar where the fire is kept, Eze. 43. 13, 14, 17.

חֻקְּךָ noun masc. sing., suff. 2 pers. sing. masc., Kh. חוֹקֶךָ, K. חֵיקֶךָ from חֹק or חֵיק. חוק

חֻקֹּק pr. name of a place, see חֲקֹק. חקק

חוֹקְרִי* Kal part. act. sing. masc. חקר

[חָוַר] fut. יֶחֱוָר (§ 13. rem. 5) to become white, pale, Is. 29. 22.

חוּר, חֹר masc. white, linen, Est. 1. 6; 8. 15.

חוּר masc. id. only pl. חֹרַי (poet. for חֹרִים) Is. 19. 9.

חִוָּר Ch. masc. white, Da. 7. 9.

חֹרִי (linen-weaver) pr. name masc. 1 Ch. 5. 14.

חֹרִי masc. white bread, Ge. 40. 16.

חוּרָם (free-born, noble, חוּרָם=חוּר q. v.) pr. name—I. of a king of Tyre, 2 Ch. 2. 2, elsewhere חִירָם.—II. of a Tyrian artificer, 2 Ch. 4. 11; 1 Ki. 7. 13; called חִירוֹם 1 Ki. 7. 40, and חִירָם 2 Ch. 4. 11 Kh. As pr. names of the same person are considered, חוּרָם אָבִיו ,חוּרָם אָבִי (my father or his father is noble) 2 Ch. 2. 12 (where the pref. לְ is to be taken as the accusative) and chap. 4. 16.—III. 1 Ch. 8. 5.

חִירָה (nobility, comp. חֹרָם) pr. name masc. Ge. 38. 1, 12.

חֹר Root not used; prob. i. q. כֹּר to dig, bore.

חוֹר ,חֹר masc. dec. 1a.—I. hole, Is. 11. 8; 42. 22.—II. pr. name of several men, espec. (a) of a king of Midian; (b) of the husband of Miriam the sister of Moses.

חוֹר ,חֹר masc. dec. 1a, cavern, aperture, hole.

חוֹרִי more frequently חֹרִי (dweller of caverns) pr. name—I. Horite, collect. Horites, a Canaanitish people.—II. Hori pr. name masc. (a) Ge. 36. 22; (b) Nu. 13. 5.

חַוְרָן (place of caverns) pr. name of a country beyond Jordan, Eze. 47. 16, 18.

בֵּית חֹרוֹן (cavern) pr. name, see בֵּית חֹרוֹן

חֹרֹנַיִם (two caverns) pr. name of a city of the Moabites.—Gent. noun חֹרֹנִי

חֹר Ch. adj. masc. sing. . . . . חַוָּרִי

חוֹר & [וְ'] noun masc. sing., also pr. name masc.; for וְ see lett. ו. חֻרַי*

חֹרֵב pr. name of a place . . . . חרב

בֵּית pr. name, see בֵּית חֹרוֹן R. . . חוֹרוֹן

חוֹר for [חֹרִי], poet. for חֹרִים noun masc., pl. of חוֹר dec. 1. חֹרִי*

חוֹר pr. name masc. . . . . . חֹרִי

הֹדֹר pr. name masc., see הֹדֹר R. . . חֹרִי

חוֹר pr. name masc. . . . . . חֹרֵי

חֹרִים* noun masc., pl. of [חֹר] dec. 1a . . חרר

חוּר] [pr. name masc. . . . . חֹרָם

חוֹר pr. name of a region . . . . חַוְרָן

בֵּית pr. name in compos. בֵּית חֹרוֹן . . חֹרֹן

חרף Kal part. act. pl. masc., suff. 2 pers. sing. masc. from [חֹרֵף] dec. 7b . . . חֹרְפַיִךְ*

חרש Kal part. act. sing. masc. dec. 7b . חוֹרֵשׁ

[חוּשׁ] I. to hasten, make haste.—II. to be incited, ardent, Job 20. 2.—III. (as in Syr.) to feel, to enjoy, Ec. 2. 25. Hiph.—I. to hasten, accelerate.—II. to hasten, make haste.—III. to be excited, confused, confounded, Is. 28. 16.

חֻשָׁה (haste) whence patronym. חֻשָׁתִי Hushathite.

חוּשַׁי (hastening) pr. name of a friend of David.

חֻשִׁים (hastening) pr. name of several men.

חֻשָׁם (haste) pr. name of a king of Edom, 1 Ch. 1. 45.

חִישׁ adj. masc. hastily, Ps. 90. 10.

Kal part. act. sing. masc. dec. 7 b	חֹשֵׁב
Kal imp. sing. m. with parag. ה (§ 21. rem. 5)	חוּשָׁה
pr. name masc.	חוּשׁ
pr. name masc.	חֻשַׁי / חוּשַׁי
Kal inf., suff. 1 pers. sing. dec. 1 a	חוּשׁ
pr. name masc.	חוּשׁ
Kal part. act. sing. masc.	חֹשֵׁךְ
pr. name masc.	חוּשָׁם
noun fem., pl. of [חַוָּה] dec. 10.	חוה
id. with suff. 3 pers. pl. masc.	חַוֹּתֵיהֶם
n. m. s. (no vowel change), also pr. name m.	חתם
Kal part. act. sing. masc.	חתם
Ch. Peal pret. 3 pers. sing. masc. see	חזה
pr. name masc.; בֵּ bef.	חֲזָאֵל

חָזָה fut. יֶחֱזֶה apoc. תַּחַז (§ 24. rem. 3 d).—I. to see, behold, especially a vision, and applied to a prophecy or revelation received in a vision.—II. to look, gaze upon, with בְּ.—III. to look out, choose, select.—IV. to see, perceive; hence perhaps metaph. to feel, experience, Job 8. 17.

חֲזָא, חֲזָה Ch. (§ 55) to see.

חָזֶה masc. dec. 9 b, pl. חָזוֹת, the breast of animals.

חֹזֶה masc. dec. 9 a.—I. part. act. a seer, prophet.—II. league, agreement, Is. 28. 15, comp. חָזוּת

חוֹזַי (seer) pr. name masc. 2 Ch. 33. 19.

חֲזוֹ (vision) pr. name masc. Ge. 22. 22.

חֱזָו Ch. masc. emph. חֶזְוָא dec. 3 c.—I. vision, sight.—II. look, appearance, Da. 7. 20.

חִזָּיוֹן masc. dec. 3 a.—I. vision, sight.—II. revelation.

חָזוֹת fem. dec. 3 a, vision, revelation, 2 Ch. 9. 29.

חֲזוֹת Ch. dec. 1 a, appearance, view, Da. 4. 8, 17.

חָזוּת fem. dec. 1 b (§ 33. No. 3).—I. appearance, conspicuity, קֶרֶן חָזוּת a conspicuous (Eng. Vers. notable) horn, Da. 8. 5, 8.—II. vision, revelation.—III. league, agreement, Is. 28. 18; חָזֶה

i q. חזז Arab. Conj. III. to consent. IV. to enter into an agreement.

חֶזְיוֹן (vision) pr. name masc. 1 Ki. 15. 18.

חִזָּיוֹן masc., dec. 3 c, constr. חֶזְיוֹן (§ 32. rem. 3) —I. vision, sight.—II. revelation.

חֲזָאֵל (whom God beholds), חֲזָהאֵל (2 Ki. 8. 8, 15) pr. name of a king of Syria.

חֲזִיאֵל (vision of God) pr. name masc. 1 Ch. 23. 9.

חֲזָיָה (whom the Lord beholds, comp. (חֲזָאֵל) pr name masc. Ne. 11. 5.

יַחְזִיאֵל (he shall see God) pr. name masc. of several persons.

יַחְזְיָה (he shall see the Lord) pr. name masc Ezr. 10. 15.

מַחֲזֶה masc. dec. 9 a, vision.

מֶחֱזָה fem. window, 1 Ki. 7. 4, 5

מַחֲזִיאוֹת (visions) pr. name masc. 1 Ch. 25. 4, 30.

Ch. for חֲזָא (q. v.)	חזה
Ch. Peal part. act. sing. masc. dec. 6 a (§ 62)	חזה
Ch. id. part. pass. (§ 55 note)	חזה
Kal imp. sing. masc.; or noun masc constr. of [חָזֶה] dec. 9 b; ל bef.	חזה
noun masc., constr. of the following	חזה
Kal part. act. masc. (Eze. 12. 27); or subst dec. 9 a	חזה
pr. name masc., see חֲזָאֵל	חזה
Kal pret. 3 pers. pl.	חזה
pr. name masc.	חזה
Kal imp. pl. masc.	חזה
Ch. noun masc. sing., suff. 3 pers. sing. fem. from [חֱזָו] dec. 3 c	חזה
Ch. id. pl., constr. state	חזה
noun masc. sing. dec. 3 a	חזה
id., constr. state	חזה
noun fem. sing. dec. 1 b (§ 33. No. 3)	חזה
Ch. noun fem. sing., suff. 3 pers. sing. fem. from [חֲזוֹת=חֲזוּת] dec. 9 b	חזה
noun fem. sing., suff. 2 pers. pl. masc. from חָזוּת dec. 1 b (§ 33. No. 3)	חזה

חָזַז Root not used; Arab. to pierce through.

חָזִיז masc. dec. 1 a, lightning

pr. name masc.; ו bef.	חזה
pr. name masc.	חזה
constr. of the foll.; (§ 32. rem. 3) also pr. n.	חזה
noun masc. sing. dec. 3 c	חזה
noun masc., pl. of חָזְיוֹן dec. 1 a	חזה
Kal part. act., pl. of חֹזֶה dec. 9 a	חזה

חֲזֵין Ch. Peal part. act., pl. of חֲזָה dec. 6a (§ 62) — חזה

חֶזְיֹנוֹת noun masc. with pl. fem. term. from חִזָּיֹן dec. 3c (§ 32. rem. 3) . . . — חזה

חֲזִיר noun masc. sing. . . . — חזר

חֲזִיר pr. name masc. . . . — חזר

חָזִיתָ Kal pret. 2 pers. sing. masc. . . — חזה

חָזִית id. pret. 2 pers. sing. fem. . . — חזה

חֲזַיְתָ Ch. Peal pret. 2 pers. sing. masc. — חזה

חֲזֵית Ch. id. pret. 1 pers. sing. . . — חזה

חֲזַיְתָה Ch. id. pret. 2 pers. sing. masc., (§ 47. r. 2) — חזה

חֲזֵיתוּן Ch. id. pret. 2 pers. sing. pl. masc. — חזה

חָזִיתִי Kal pret. 1 pers. sing. . . — חזה

חֲזִיתִךָ id. id., suff. 2 pers. sing. masc. . — חזה

חֲזִיתֶם id. pret. 2 pers. pl. masc.; וֹ bef. (-:) — חזה

חָזַק fut. יֶחֱזַק (§ 13. rem. 5).—I. *to be* or *become strong, firm, fast*; perhaps trans. *to strengthen,* Eze. 30. 21. Const. with מִן *to be stronger than, to prevail over*; with עַל id.—II. *to be confirmed, established.*—III. *to be hardened, obstinate,* spoken of the heart.—IV. *to be strong* upon any one, i. e. *to be urgent, to press upon,* with עַל; once with acc. Je. 20. 7. Pi.—I. *to make strong, firm, to strengthen;* חִזַּק יָד *to strengthen the hand,* i. e. *to encourage, help, assist.*—II. *to harden,* spoken of one's own heart, the face i. e. *to become obstinate, perverse.*—III. *to heal, restore.* Hiph.—I. *to take hold of, to seize,* with בְּ, עַל, לְ; hence, *to hold, retain; to hold, contain,* 2 Ch. 4. 5.—II. *to hold fast, adhere to,* with עַל of the person.—III. *to make firm, strong, to strengthen,* hence, *to repair;* intrans. *to be strong, powerful.*—IV. *to help, assist* with בְּ. Hithpa.—I. *to be strengthened, confirmed, established.* Also *to strengthen oneself, to gather strength, take courage.*—II. *to show oneself strong, courageous,* with לִפְנֵי *against* any one; with בְּ, עִם for any one, i. e. *to help, assist* him.

חָזָק masc. dec. 4c (pl. c. חִזְקֵי), חֲזָקָה fem. adj. —I. *strong, mighty.*—II. *firm, hard,* of the heart, forehead, i. e. *obstinate, daring.*

חָזֵק masc. adj. *strong, powerful, waxing strong.*

חֵזֶק masc. dec. 6b, *strength,* Ps. 18. 2.

חֹזֶק masc. dec. 6c, *strength, might.*

חֶזְקָה fem. constr. חֶזְקַת (no pl.) strictly an inf. (§ 8. rem. 10).—I. *a being* or *becoming strong,* בְּחֶזְקָתוֹ *when he became strong, gained strength.* —II. *an urging on, impelling,* Is. 8. 11.

חָזְקָה fem.—I. *force, vehemence;* בְּחָזְקָה *with force, vehemently, greatly.*—II. *a strengthening, repairing,* 2 Ki. 12. 13.

חִזְקִי (*strong*) pr. name masc. 1 Ch. 8. 17.

חִזְקִיָּה, חִזְקִיָּהוּ (*strength of the Lord*) pr. name masc. of several persons, especially of Hezekiah king of Judah, who is likewise called יְחִזְקִיָּה, יְחִזְקִיָּהוּ (whom *the Lord shall strengthen,* for יְחַזְּקִיָּהוּ=יְחִזְקִיָּהוּ comp. יְחֶזְקֵאל).

יְחֶזְקֵאל (whom *God shall strengthen,* for יְחַזֵּק אֵל=, comp. אֶבְכָּלֶךָ § 24. rem. 21) pr name masc. Ezekiel the prophet, son of Buzi a priest.

חִזְקִיָּה see יְחִזְקִיָּה

יְחִזְקִיָּהוּ pr. name of a man at the time of Ahaz, 2 Ch. 28. 12.

חָזַק Kal pret. 3 pers. sing. m. for חָזֵק (§ 8. r. 7) — חזק

חָזָק וֹ adj. masc. sing. dec. 4c (pl. c. חִזְקֵי) . — חזק

חֲזַק וְ id. imp. sing. masc. (§ 8. rem. 12); — חזק

חֲזַק וַ וֹ bef. (-:) — חזק

חָזָק וֹ adj. masc. sing. . . — חזק

חַזֵּק Piel inf. const.; or imp. sing. masc. — חזק

חִזַּק id. pret. 3 pers. sing. masc. — חזק

חֹזֶק noun masc. sing. dec. 6c — חזק

חָזְקָה } Kal pret. 3 pers. sing. fem. (§ 8. rem. 7) — חזק
חָזְקָה }

חֲזָקָה adj. fem. sing. from חָזָק masc. — חזק

חַזְּקֵהוּ וְ Piel imp. sing. masc., suff. 3 pers. sing. m. — חזק

חָזְקוּ וְ Kal pret. 3 pers. pl. — חזק

חִזְּקוּ id. pret. 3 pers. sing. masc., suff. 3 p. s. m. — חזק

חַזְּקוּ Piel imp. pl. masc. — חזק

חִזְקוּ Kal imp. pl. masc. — חזק

חִזְּקוּ וְ Piel pret. 3 pers. pl. — חזק

חַזְּקִי } Piel imp. sing. fem., (comp. § 8. rem. 12) — חזק
חִזְקִי }

חִזְקֵי וְ noun masc. pl. c., fr. חֵזֶק d. 4 (§ 33. r. 1) — חזק

חִזְקִי וְ noun masc. sing., suff. 1 pers. sing. fr. [חֵזֶק] dec. 6b; also pr. name masc. . — חזק

חִזְקִיָּה וְ } pr. name masc. — חזק
חִזְקִיָּהוּ }

חֲזָקִים adj. masc., pl. of חָזָק dec. 4c (§ 33. rem. 1) — חזק

חַזְּקֵנִי וְ Piel imp. sing. masc., suff. 1 pers. sing. — חזק

חָזַקְתָּ וֹ Kal pret. 2 pers. sing. masc.; acc. shifted by conv. וֹ (§ 8. rem. 7) — חזק

חִזַּקְתִּי Piel pret. 1 pers. sing. — חזק

חִזַּקְתִּי וֹ id. id.; acc. shifted by conv. וֹ (§ 8. r. 7) — חזק

חֲזַקְתֶּם וֹ Kal pret. 2 pers. pl. masc.; וֹ for וְ conv. — חזק

a Da. 3. 27; 5. 23. — c Da. 2. 8.   2 Ch. 26. 15. — m Hag. 2. 4, 4.   q Ps. 147. 13.   t 2 Sa. 16. 21.   w Is. 54. 2.   z Eze. 2. 4.   c Ki. 2. 2.
b Joel 3. 1.   f Job 15. 17.   i Is. 41. 6.   n Ex. 19. 19;   r Hag. 2. 22.   u 2 Ch. 28. 20.   x Na. 3. 14.   a Ps. 18. 2.   d Ho. 7. 15.
c Is. 57. 8.   g Ps. 63. 3.   k Da. 10. 19.   o 2 Sa. 3. 1.   s Eze. 3. 14.   v Is. 35. 3.   y Eze. 3. 7.   b Ju. 16. 28.   e Jos. 23. 6.
d Da. 2. 41, 41.   h Eze. 13. 6.

חֻזַּקְתֶּם Piel pret. 2 pers. pl. masc. . . חזק

חֲזַקְתָּנִי Kal pret. 2 pers. sing. masc., suff. 1 pers. s. חזק

חִזַּקְתָּנִי Piel pret. 2 pers. sing. masc., suff. 1 pers.

sing. (§ 2. rem. 1) . . . . חזק

חָזֹר Root not used; Arab. *to have small eyes*; but this may merely be a denom. of the following noun. Chald. *to return.*

חֲזִיר masc. *hog, swine.*

חֵזִיר (*swine*) pr. name of a man, 1 Ch. 24. 15; Ne. 10. 21.

יַחֲזֵרָה (*whom God shall bring back*) pr. name masc. 2 Ch. 9. 12.

חָח noun masc. sing., irr. see the following . חוח

חָחִי id. with suff. 1 pers. sing., dag. f. impl.

(§ 37. rem. 7) . . . . חוח

חַחִיִּם id. pl., Kh. [חֲחִי] fr. [חָחִי] K. חָחִים חוח

חָחִים id. pl. absolute state . . . חוח

חָטָא fut. יֶחֱטָא.—I. *to miss* a scope or aim, but only in Hiphil q. v.—II. *to miss one's step*, i. e. *to stumble, fall*, Pr. 19. 2.—III. *to miss*, opp. to מָצָא *to find*, so perhaps Pr. 8. 36; Job 5. 24.—IV. *to sin*; with בְּ, לְ or עַל *by, against.*—V. *to forfeit*, with acc. Pi.—I. *to suffer the loss of anything*, Ge. 31. 39.—II. *to offer as a sin-offering*; hence *to expiate, cleanse, free from sin.* Hiph.—I. *to miss* a scope or aim, Ju. 20. 16.—II. *to cause, induce to sin.*—III. *to declare guilty, to condemn*, Is. 29. 21. Hithp.—I. *to miss oneself* as it were, *to be at his wit's end, be astounded*, Job 41. 17.—II. *to purify oneself.*

חֵטְא masc. with suff. חֶטְאוֹ, pl. c. חֲטָאֵי (§ 35. rem. 6), *failure, sin.*

חַטָּא masc. d. 1 b (§ 30. No. 4, & r. 1) *sinner.*

חַטָּאָה fem.—I. *sin.*—II. *sin-offering*, Ps. 40. 7.

חַטָּאָה fem. of חַטָּא.—I. *sinner*, Am. 9. 8.—II. *sin.*

חֲטָאָה Ch. fem. *sin*, Ezr. 6. 17, Keri.

חַטָּאת (for חַטָּאַת § 39. No. 4) fem. constr. חַטַּאת (for חַטָּאַת from חַטָּאָה comp. § 23. r. 2) with suff. חַטָּאתִי, pl. חַטָּאוֹת (§ 44. rem. 5) constr. חַטֹּאות (for חַטָּאוֹת comp. § 23. rem. 2).— I. *sin.*—II. *sin-offering.*—III. *idols, as the cause of sin.*—IV. *punishment for sin.*

חֲטָי Ch. masc. *sin*, with suff. חֲטָיָךְ.

חַטָּת fem. *sin*, Nu. 15. 24, for חַטָּאת.

חֲטֹא Kal inf. constr. . . . . חטא

חִטֵּא ‖ Piel pret. 3 pers. sing. masc. חטא

חָטָא noun masc. sing. dec. 6 (§ 35. rem 6) . חטא

חֹטֵא ‖ Kal part. act. masc. s. dec. 7 b (§ 23. r. 9) חטא
חֹטֵי ∫

חָטְאָה ‖ id. pret. 3 pers. sing. fem. (§ 8. r. 7) חטא
חָטָאָה ∫

חַטָּאָה רַ ‖ noun fem. sing.; ‖ bef. (ָ). . חטא

חַטָּאָה רַ‖ noun fem. sing. from חַטָּא masc. . חטא

חָטְאוּ ‖ Kal pret. 3 pers. pl. (§ 8. rem. 7) . חטא
חָטָאוּ ∫

חֲטָאוֹ noun masc. pl., suff. 3 pers. sing. masc. [for חֲטָאָיו from חֵטְא dec. 6 (§ 35. rem. 6) חטא

חֶטְאוֹ id. sing., suff. 3 pers. sing. masc. . חטא

חִטְּאוֹ רַ ‖ Piel pret. 3 pers. sing. masc., suff. 3 pers. sing. masc. . . . . . חטא

חָטְאוּ רַ ‖ id. pret. 3 pers. pl. חטא

חַטָּאוֹת רַ‖ noun fem. pl. absolute from חַטָּאת, (§ 39. No. 4 d, & § 44. rem. 5) חטא

חַטֹּאות רַ‖ id. pl., const. state [for חַטָּאוֹת] חטא

חַטֹּאותַי id. pl., suff. 1 pers. sing. [for חַטָּאותַי] חטא

חַטֹּאותֶיךָ id. pl., suff. 2 pers. sing. masc. חטא

חַטֹּאותֵיכֶם רַ‖ id. pl., suff. 2 pers. pl. masc. חטא

חַטֹּאותֵינוּ רַ‖ id. pl., suff. 1 pers. pl. חטא

חַטֹּאותָם id. pl., suff. 3 pers. pl. masc. חטא

חֲטָאַי ‖ noun masc. pl., suff. 1 pers. sing. fr. חֵטְא] חטא
חֲטָאָי ∫ dec. 6 (§ 35. rem. 6)

חֲטָאֵי רַ‖ noun masc. pl. constr. fr. [חֵטְא] dec. 1 b חטא

חֲטָאֵי ‖ רַ‖ noun masc. pl. constr. fr. חֵטְא dec. 6 (§ 35. rem. 6) . . . . חטא

חֹטְאִי רַ‖ Kal part. act. sing. masc. (חֹטֵא) suff. 1 pers. sing. dec. 7 b . חטא

חַטָּאֶיהָ רַ‖ noun masc. pl., suff. 3 pers. sing. fem. from [חַטָּא] dec. 1 b . . חטא

חַטָּאֵיכֶם noun masc. pl., suff. 2 pers. pl. masc. fr. חַטָּא dec. 6 (§ 35. rem. 6) . . חטא

חַטָּאִים id. pl., absolute state . . . חטא

חַטָּאִים ‖ noun masc. pl. of [חַטָּא] dec. 1 b חטא

חֹטְאִים רַ‖ Kal part. act. m., pl. of חֹטֵא dec. 7 b (§ 23. r. 4) חטא

חַטָּאם רַ‖ noun masc. sing., suff. 3 pers. pl. masc. fr. חַטָּא dec. 6 (§ 35. rem. 6) חטא

חָטָאנוּ Kal pret. 1 pers. pl. חטא

חָטָאתָ id. pret. 2 pers. sing. masc. חטא

חָטָאת ‖ id. pret. 3 pers. sing. fem. (§ 23. rem. 1) חטא

חַטָּאת ‖ רַ‖ noun fem. sing. (§ 39. No. 4 d, & § 44. rem. 5, and note the following) חטא

חַטַּאת רַ‖ id., constr. state, [for חַטָּאַת חַטָּאָה fr. [חַטָּאָה] חטא

ᵃ Eze. 34. 4.   ᵉ Eze. 29. 4.   ᵏ Ec. 8. 12.   ᵒ Is. 5. 18.   ʳ Eze. 43. 22.   ᵘ Eze. 21. 29.   ᵇ Am. 9. 10.   ᶠ Is. 13. 9.   ᵏ Le. 20. 20.
ᵇ Je. 20. 7.   ᶠ Eze. 3. 21.   ᵗ La. 1. 8.   ᵖ Ex. 34. 7.   ˢ Job 13. 23.   ᵛ Is. 59. 12.   ² Ki. 10. 29.   ᵍ Is. 1. 18.   ˡ Zx. 5. 16.
ᶜ Da. 10. 19.   ᵍ Le. 14. 52.   ᵐ Le. 5. 15.   ᵠ La. 3. 39.   ᵗ 1 Ki. 16. 13.   ʷ Ge. 41. 9.   ʰ Eze. 23. 49.   ᵐ Ec. 10. 4.   ᵐ Eze. 45. 23.
ᵈ Ex. 35. 22.   ʰ Is. 1. 4.   ⁿ Nu. 19. 19.   ᵠ Ps. 40. 7.   ᵗ Ps. 25. 18.   ˣ Is. 38. 17.   Pr. 8. 36.   ʲ 2 Sa. 14. 32.

חַטָּאת	id. pl. constr., comp. חַטֹּאות . חטא
חָטָאתָ	Piel pret. 2 p.s.m. acc. shifted (comp. § 8. r. 7) חטא
חַטָּאתוֹ	noun fem. sing., suff. 3 pers. sing. masc. fr. חַטָּאת (q. v.) . חטא
חַטֹּאתָו	id. pl., suff. (K. חָטָו' § 4. r. 1) 3 pers. s. m. חטא
חֲטֹאתוֹ	Kal inf. (חֲטֹא § 23. rem. 26), suff. 3 pers. sing. masc. . חטא
חָטָאתִי	Kal pret. 1 pers. sing. . חטא
חַטָּאתִי	n. fem. sing., suff. 1 pers. sing. fr. חַטָּאת (q. v. & חַטֹּאות) . חטא
חַטֹּאתֶיהָ	id. pl., suff. 3 pers. sing. fem. חטא
חַטֹּאתֵיהֶם	id. pl., suff. 3 pers. p... masc. חטא
חַטֹּאתָיו	id. pl., suff. 3 pers. sing. masc. חטא
חַטֹּאתֶךָ / חַטֹּאתֶיךָ	id. pl. with suff. 2 pers. sing. fem. חטא
חַטֹּאתֶיךָ	id. pl., suff. 2 pers. sing. masc. חטא
חַטֹּאתֵיכֶם	id. pl., suff. 2 pers. pl. masc. חטא
חַטֹּאתֵינוּ	id. pl., suff. 1 pers. pl. חטא
חַטָּאתְךָ	id. sing., suff. 2 pers. sing. masc. חטא
חַטַּאתְכֶם	id. sing., suff. 2 pers. pl. masc. חטא
חַטָּאתָם	id. sing., suff. 3 pers. pl. masc. חטא
חַטֹּאתָם	id. pl., suff. 3 pers. pl. masc. חטא
חַטַּאתֶם	Kal pret. 2 pers. pl. masc.; ו for י conv. חטא
חַטָּאתֵנוּ	noun fem. sing., suff. 1 pers. pl. from חַטָּאת (q. v. & חַטֹּאות) . חטא
חַטֹּאתֵנוּ	id. pl., suff. 1 pers. pl. חטא

[חָטַב] I. to cut or hew wood.—II. to stripe, mark with stripes, only part. pass. חֲטֻבוֹת striped, variegated, Pr. 7. 16. Pu. to be hewn out. Ps. 144. 12.

חֲטֻבוֹת	Kal part. pass. pl. fem. from [חָטוּב] masc. חטב
חֹטְבֵי	id. part. act. pl. c. m. from 'חוֹטֵב dec. 7 b חטב

חִטָּה fem. wheat; pl. חִטִּים, חִטִּין, constr. חִטֵּי grains of wheat.

חִנְטָה Chald. fem. only pl. חִנְטִין id., dag. forte resolved in נ

חַטּוּשׁ pr. name masc. of several persons.

חֲטִיטָא (a digging, R. חטט Aram. to dig) pr. name m.

חֶטְאֲךָ Chald. noun masc. sing., suff. 2 pers. sing. m. [from חֲטָא]; K. חֲטָאָךְ id. from חֲטָא חטא

חַטִּיל (waving, Arab. חטל to wave to and fro) pr. name masc.

חִטִּים	noun fem. with pl. m. term. fr. חִטָּה (q. v.) חטה
חִטִּין	id. with the Chald. term. . חטה
חֲטִיפָא	pr. name masc. . חטף

[חָטַם] prop. to muzzle, hence to restrain oneself, with ל towards any one. Is. 48. 9.

חָטַף fut. יַחְטֹף (§ 13. rem. 5) to catch, seize. חֲטִיפָא (a catching) pr. name masc.

חֹטְפְתֶּם Kal pret. 2 pers. pl. masc.; ו for י conv. חטף

חֹטֶר masc. stick, rod, Pr. 14. 3; Is. 11. 1.

חַי / וָ	Kal pret. 3 pers. sing. masc.; or, adj.
חַי / וָ	or subst. m. dec. 8 d (§ 37. rem. 6) חיי
חֵי	id. adj. or subst., construct state . חיי
חַיָּא	Chald. adj. masc. sing., emph. of חַי' dec. 5a חיי
חִיאֵל	pr. name masc. . חיה
חִבַּכְתֶּם	Piel pret. 2 pers. pl. masc. . חוב
חִידָה	noun fem. sing. dec. 10. חוד
חִידוֹת	id. pl. . חוד
חִידָתִי	id. sing., suff. 1 pers. sing. חוד
חִידָתְךָ	id. sing., suff. 2 pers. sing. masc. חוד
חִידֹתָם	id. pl., suff. 3 pers. pl. masc. חוד

חָיָה fut. יִחְיֶה; ap. יְחִי (§ 24. rem. 3 e); inf. c. חֲיוֹת, with pref. לִחְיוֹת, imp. with pref. וָחְיֵה, וֶחְיֵה (§ 13. rem. 1 & 13).—I. to live.—II. to revive.—III. to be or become strong, vigorous, to be restored, with מִן, from sickness. Pi.—I. to make alive, to give life, to quicken.—II. to preserve alive, to let live.—III. to revive, strengthen, comfort, refresh. Hiph. הֶחֱיָה.—I. to preserve alive, to let live.—II. to restore to life.

חָיָה, חֲיָא Chald. to live, only imp. חֱיִי. Aph. to preserve alive, Da. 5. 19.

חָיֶה adj., only pl. fem. חָיוֹת lively, strong, Ex. 1. 19.

חֵיוָא, חֵיוָה Chald. fem. dec. 8a, living creature, animal, beast.

יְחִיאֵל (God liveth) pr. name masc. of several persons. Patronym. יְחִיאֵלִי

חִיאֵל (by aphaer. for יְחִיאֵל) pr. name masc. 1 Ki. 16. 34.

יְחִיָּה (the Lord liveth for יְחִיָּהוּ) pr. name masc. 1 Ch. 15. 24, elsewhere called יְחִיאֵל comp. ver. 18.

מִחְיָה fem. dec. 10.—I. preservation of life.—II. means of living, food.—III. indication, sign, mark, (from חִיָּה i. q. חִוָּה to show), Le. 13. 10, 24. According to others, stroke, mark, spot, fr. מִחְיָה q. v

חָיָה	Kal pret. 3 pers. sing. fem. in pause for חָיְתָה (§ 18. rem. 15 note) . חיי
חָיֹה	Kal inf. absolute חיה

a 2 Ki. 21. 17.   d Ne. 9. 2.   g Is. 43. 25.   k De. 20. 18.   n Pr. 7. 16.   q Da. 4. 24.   t Ju. 21. 21.   r Da. 1. 10.   x Ec. 6. 6.
b Eze. 23. 12.   e 1 Ki. 16. 19.   h Eze. 33. 10.   l Je. 16. 10.   o Jos. 9. 21, 27.   r 2 Sa. 17. 28.   u 2 Sa. 12. 22.   s Ju. 14. 11.   y Ez. L. 14.
c Is. 40. 2.   f Is. 44. 22.   i Is. 6. 7.   m 2 Ch. 28. 13.   p Jos. 9. 23.   s Eze. 4. 9.   v Da. 6. 21, 27.   w Pr. 1. 6.

חִיָּה   noun fem. sing. dec. 10, from חַי masc.   חיי

חִיָּה*   Piel pret. 3 pers. sing. masc.   חיה

חֲיֵה   Kal imp. s. m. [for וֶחְיֵה § 13. rem. 1 & 13]   חיה

חָיֹה   Kal inf. absolute for חָיָה (§ 24. rem. 2)   חיה

חָיוּ*   id. pret. 3 pers. pl.   חיה

חָיוּ   Khethib; K. חָיֵי (q. v. comp. § 4. rem. 1)   חיי

חִיּוּ*   Piel pret. 3 pers. pl.   חיה

חְיוּ   Kal imp. pl. masc.; וְ before (ְ) for וָ (§ 13. rem. 1 & 13)   חיה

חֵיוָא* } Chald. noun fem. sing. dec. 8a (§ 55 note)   חיה
חֵיוָה* }

חֵיוָן   Chald. id pl., absolute state   חיה

חַיּוֹת*   adj. fem. pl. [of חָיָה, from חַיָה masc.]   חיה

חַיּוֹת   adj. (Le. 14. 4) or subst. fem., pl. of חַיָה dec. 10, from חַי masc.   חיי

חַיּוּת*   noun fem. sing.   חיי

חֵיוַת   Chald. noun fem. sing., constr. of חֵיוָא dec. 8a   חיה

חֵיוָתָא   Chald. id pl., emph. state   חיה

חֵיוְתָא   Chald. id. sing., emph. state   חיה

חַיּוֹתָם*   Kal inf., suff. 3 pers. pl. masc. dec. 1a   חיה

[חָיַי]   pret. חַי, to live.

חַי, masc. dec. 8d constr. חֵי, pl. חַיִּים (§ 37. rem. 6); fem. חַיָה.—I. adj.—1. living, alive.—2. lively, vigorous.—3. reviving, כָּעֵת חַיָה when this time or season revives, i. e. the coming spring, or, according to others, at this very time next year. Others who render this, according to the time of life, or (as Prof. Lee) as at the season, period of a vigorous woman, taking עֵת in the constr. state, have overlooked the article in כָּ; for we should then expect כְּעֵת־חַיָה.—4. live, raw, of flesh.—II. subst. life, Le. 25. 36, וְחֵי אָחִיךָ עִמָּךְ that the life of thy brother be with thee, i. e. preserved with thee; חֵי פַרְעֹה by the life of Pharaoh, which others take as an adjective, as Pharaoh liveth.—III. pl. חַיִּים.—1. life.—2. living, substance, Pr. 27. 27.

חַי Chald. masc. dec. 5a.—I. adj. living, alive.—II. subst. pl. חַיִּין life.

חַיָה fem. dec. 10 (comp. חַי).—I. living thing, animal, beast.—II. tribe, people, band, troop.—III. life.

חַיוּת fem. life, 2 Sa. 20. 3.

חַיַי* } noun masc. pl., suff. 1 pers. sing. from
חַיָּי } חַי dec. 8d (§ 37. rem. 6)   חיי
חַיֵּי* } id. pl., construct state

חֲיִי*   Kal imp. sing. fem.   חיה

חֱיִי   Chald. Peal imp. sing. masc.   חיה

חַיַּיָּא   Chald. adj. m. pl. emph. from חַי dec. 5a   חיי

חַיָּיהָ*   noun masc. pl., suff. 3 pers. sing. fem. from חַי dec. 8d (§ 37. rem. 6)   חיי

חַיֵּיהוּ*   Piel imp. sing. masc. [חַיָה], suff. 3 pers. sing. masc. (§ 24. rem. 21b)   חיה

חַיֵּיהֶם   noun masc. pl., suff. 3 pers. pl. masc. from חַי dec. 8d (§ 37. rem. 6)   חיי

חַיָּיו   id., suff. 3 pers. sing. masc.   חיי

חַיֶּיךָ   id., suff. 2 pers. sing. masc.   חיי

חַיָּיִךְ*   id., suff. 2 pers. s. fem. [for חַיַּיִךְ § 4. rem. 3]   חיי

חַיֵּיכֶם*   id., suff. 2 pers. pl. masc.   חיי

חַיִּים   id. pl., absolute state, adj. and subst.   חיי

חַיֵּינוּ*   id. pl., suff. 1 pers. pl.   חיי

חָיִיתָ* } Kal pret. 2 pers. sing. masc.   חיה
חֲיִיתֶם } id. pret. 2 pers. pl. masc.; וַ for conv. (§ 13. rem. 1 & 13)   חיה

חִיִּיתַנִי } Piel pret. 2 pers. sing. masc., suff.
חִיִּיתָנִי* } 1 pers. sing. (§ 2. rem. 1) } חיה

חַיְךָ*   defect. for חַיֶּיךָ (q. v.)   חיי

חַיִל } noun masc. sing. dec. 6h (§ 35. rem.
חֵיל } 12), Chald. dec. 3d } חול

חֵיל } id. constr. st.; or (Na. 3. 8) abs. dec. 1a   חול
חַיִל   noun masc. sing.   חול

חֵילָהּ*   noun masc. sing., suff. 3 pers. sing. fem. from חַיִל dec. 6h   חול

חֵילוֹ   id., suff. 3 pers. sing. masc.   חול

חֵילוּ   Kal imp. pl. masc. R. חִיל, see   חול

חֵילִי   noun m. s., suff. 1 pers. s. from חַיִל dec. 6h   חול

חֵילֵיהֶם*   id. pl., suff. 3 pers. pl. masc.   חול

חֲיָלִים   id. pl., abs. st. (§ 35. rem. 12); וַ bef. (ְ)   חול

חֵילֵךְ   id. sing., suff. 2 pers. sing. masc. [for חֵילְךָ]   חול

חֵילֵךְ*   id. sing., suff. 2 pers. sing. fem.   חול

חֵילְךָ   id. sing., suff. 2 pers. sing. masc.   חול

חֵילָם   id. s., suff. 3 pers. pl. m.; also pr. name   חול

חֵילָן   pr. name of a place   חול

חִין   noun masc. sing.   חנן

חַיֵּנִי   Piel imp. sing. masc. [חָיָה], suff. 1 pers. sing. (§ 24. rem. 21)   חיה

חַיִץ*   noun masc. sing.   חוץ

חִיצוֹנָה*   adj. fem. sing. from חִיצוֹן masc.   חוץ

חֵיק   noun masc. sing. dec. 1a   חוק

חֵיקָהּ*   id., suff. 3 pers. sing. fem.   חוק

חֵיקוֹ   id., suff. 3 pers. sing. masc.   חוק

חֵיקִי   id., suff. 1 pers. sing.   חוק

---

a Ps. 22. 30.   *d* Da. 7. 5, 7.   *i* Da. 7. 12, 7, 17.   *n* Pr. 31. 12.   *r* Is. 38. 20.   *w* 2 Sa. 11. 11.   *a* Ec. 10. 10.   *d* Mi. 4. 13.   *g* Eze. 42. 12.
b Nu. 14. 38.   *e* Da. 7. 3.   *k* Jos. 5. 8.   *o* Hab. 3. 3.   *s* De. 20. 16.   *x* Zec. 9. 4.   *b* Eze. 26. 12.   *e* Job 41. 4.   *h* De. 26. 56.
c Ju. 21. 14.   *f* Ex. 1. 19.   *l* Ps. 88. 4.   *p* Ps. 103 4.   *t* Is. 30. 6.   *y* Eze. 27. 11.   *c* 2 Ch. 23. 14.   *f* Ps. 25. 13.
d Da. 4. 13.   *g* 2 Sa 20. 3.   *m* Eze. 16. 6.   *q* De. 32. 47.   *u* Ps. 30. 4.   *z* Hos. 13. 10.

חֵיקֶךָ	id., suff. 2 pers. sing. masc. [for חֵיקְךָ] .	חוק
חֵיקָם	id., suff. 3 pers. pl. masc. .	חוק
חִירָה	וֹ pr. name masc. . . .	חור
חִירוֹם	pr. name masc., see חוּרָם	חור
חִירָם	pr. name masc. see חוּרָם	חור
חֻרָם	Kh. חִירָם, K. חוּרָם (q. v.) .	חור
חִישׁ	adv., R. חוּשׁ, see	חוש
חוּשָׁה	Kh. חִישָׁה, K. חוּשָׁה, Kal imp. sing. masc. with paragogic ה. R. חִישׁ or חוּשׁ	חוש
חַיַּת	וֹ noun fem. sing., constr. of חַיָּה dec. 10, from חַי masc. . . .	חיי
חָיְתָה	וֹ Kal pret. 3 pers. sing. fem. . .	חיה
חָיִיתָ	וֹ id. pret. 2 pers. sing. masc. (§ 24. rem. 7, & § 8. rem. 5) . . .	חיה
חַיָּתוֹ	וֹ noun fem. sing., suff. 3 pers. sing. masc. from חַיָּה dec. 10. .	חיי
חַיְתוֹ	וֹ id. constr. with paragogic וֹ	חיי
חַיָּתִי	id., suff. 1 pers. sing. .	חיי
חַיָּתְךָ	id., suff. 2 pers. sing. masc. .	חיי
חַיָּתָם	וֹ id., suff. 3 pers. pl. masc. .	חיי
חִיַּתְנִי	Piel pret. 3 pers. sing. fem., suff. 1 pers. sing. [for חִיְּתַנִי] . . .	חיה
חֵךְ	וֹ noun masc. sing. [for חֵנְךְ § 37. No. 3b] dec. 8b . . .	חנך
[חָכָה]	to wait, Is. 30. 18, with לְ. Pi. id. with acc. & לְ.	
חֻכָּה	noun fem. sing. . . .	חנך
חַכֵּה	Piel imp. sing. masc. . .	חכה
חֻכָּהּ	noun masc. sing., suff. 3 pers. sing. fem. from חֵךְ [for חֵנְךְ § 37. No. 3b] dec. 8b .	חנך
חִכָּה	Piel pret. 3 pers. sing. masc. .	חכה
חַכּוּ	id. imp. pl. masc. . . .	חכה
חִכּוֹ	noun masc. sing., suff. 3 pers. sing. masc. from חֵךְ [for חֵנְךְ § 37. No. 3b] dec. 8b .	חנך
חִכּוּ	Piel pret. 3 pers. pl. . .	חכה
חִכִּי	noun masc. sing., suff. 1 pers. sing. from חֵךְ [for חֵנְךְ § 37. No. 3b] dec. 8b .	חנך
חֲכִימֵי	Chald. noun masc. pl. c. from [חַכִּים] dec. 1a	חכם
חֲכִימַיָּא	וֹ id. pl., emph. state	חכם
חֲכִימִין	id. pl., absolute state	חכם
חִכִּינוּ	וֹ Piel pret. 1 pers. pl. . .	חכה
חִכִּיתִי	וֹ id. pret. 1 pers. sing. . .	חכה
חִכְּךָ	noun m. sing., suff. 2 pers. sing. m. from חֵךְ [for חֵנְךְ § 37. No. 3b] dec. 8b	חנך
חִכֵּךְ	וֹ id., suff. 2 pers. sing. fem.	חנך
חָכַל	Root not used; signification uncertain. Hence the four following.	

חֲכִילָה	pr. name of a hill in the wilderness of Ziph, 1 Sa. 23. 19; 26. 1, 3. For the signification compare the three following.	
חֲכַלְיָה	pr. name masc. Ne. 10. 2 .	חכל
חַכְלִילִי	adj. Ge. 49. 12. Eng. Vers. red; and so Schultens. LXX. χαροποιοί cheerful. Some of the other Greek Versions, καθαροί bright; θερμοί glowing; διάπυροι fiery. Prof. Lee, refreshed. Gesenius, dim. Vulg. pulchriores more beautiful (than wine), evidently confounding it with כָּחַל . . .	חכל
חַכְלִלוּת	fem. Pr. 23. 29. Eng. Vers. redness. Gesenius, dimness. Prof. Lee, fierceness, comp. the preceding . . .	חכל
חָכַם	fut. יֶחְכַּם (§ 13. rem. 5) to be or become wise. Pi. to make wise, to teach. Pu. to be made wise, to be taught. Hiph. i. q. Pi. Ps. 19. 8. Hithp.— I. to show oneself wise, Ec. 7. 16.—II. to act wisely, cunningly, Ex. 1. 10.	
	חָכָם masc. dec. 4 c, חֲכָמָה fem. dec. 11 c, constr. חַכְמַת (§ 42. rem. 1) adj.—I. wise, intelligent.— II. knowing, skilful, skilled.	
	חַכִּים Chald. masc. dec. 1, adj. wise, wise man, magician.	
	חָכְמָה fem. constr. חָכְמַת, with suff. חָכְמָתִי (no pl.).—I. wisdom.—II. skill, dexterity.	
	חָכְמָה Chald. fem. dec. 8a, wisdom.	
	חָכְמוֹת fem. (secondary form of חָכְמָה) wisdom. חַכְמוֹת fem. id. Pr. 14. 1.	
	חַכְמוֹנִי (wise) pr. name masc. 1 Ch. 11. 11; 27. 32, for which in the parallel passage, 2 Sa. 23. 8, it is תַּחְכְּמֹנִי.	
חָכָם	וֹ adj. masc. sing. dec. 4 c . .	חכם
חֲכַם	וֹ id. imp. sing. masc.; or, constr. of	חכם
חֲכַם	וֹ חָכָם (q. v.)	חכם
חָכְמָה	Kal pret. 3 pers. sing. fem. . .	חכם
חָכְמָה	וֹ noun. fem. sing. (no pl. abs.); Chald. (Da. 5. 11, 14) dec. 8a . .	חכם
חֲכָמָה	adj. fem. sing., dec. 11 c (§ 42. rem. 1) from חָכָם masc. . . .	חכם
חָכְמוּ	Kal pret. 3 pers. pl. . . .	חכם
חֲכָמוּ	וֹ id. imp. pl. masc. for [חַכְמוּ] from sing. חֲכַם	חכם
חַכְמוֹנִי	pr. name masc. . . .	חכם
חָכְמוֹת	noun fem. sing. [for חָכְמָה] . .	חכם
חַכְמוֹת	noun fem. sing. [for חָכְמָה] . .	חכם
חֲכָמוֹת	adj. fem. pl. c. from חֲכָמָה dec. 11 c (§ 42. rem. 1) from חָכָם masc. .	חכם

- Ps. 90. 10.
Ps. 71. 12.
Je. 38. 17.
   ᵈ Ge. 1. 24.
ᵉ Ps. 143. 2.
ᶠ Ps. 68. 11.
   ᵍ Ps. 119. 50.
ʰ Is. 19. 8.
Hab. 2. 3.
   ᵏ Pr. 5. 3.
ˡ Job 32. 4.
ᵐ Zep. 3. 6.
   ⁿ Ps. 106. 12.
ᵒ Da. 5. 15.
ᵖ Da. 2. 12.
   ᵠ Da. 2. 27.
ʳ 2 Ki. 7. 9.
ˢ Is. 8. 17.
   ᵗ Ho. 8. 1.
ᵘ Ca. 7. 10.
ᵛ Pr. 23. 15.
   ˣ Is. 3. 3.
ʸ Zec. 9. 2.
ᶻ De. 32. 29.
   * Ps. 3. 33.
Pr. 14. 1.
Ju. 5. 29

18

חֲכָמֵי '1 id. pl. c. masc. from חָכָם dec. 4 c — חכם

חַכְמֶיהָ [ ] id. pl., suff. 3 pers. sing. fem.;] bef. (־) — חכם

חֲכָמָיו id. pl., suff. 3 pers. sing. masc. — חכם

חֲכָמַיִךְ id. pl., suff. 2 pers. sing. fem. — חכם

חֲכָמֶיךָ id. pl., suff. 2 pers. sing. masc. — חכם

חֲכָמִים [ ] id. pl., absolute state;] before (־) — חכם

חָכַמְתָּ Kal pret. 2 pers. sing. masc. — חכם

חָכְמַת [ ] noun fem. s. constr. of חָכְמָה (no pl. abs.) — חכם

חֲכַמַת adj. fem. sing., constr. of חֲכָם (§ 42. rem. 1) dec. 11 c from חָכָם masc. — חכם

חָכְמְתָא Ch. noun fem. sing., emph. of חָכְמָה dec. 8 a — חכם

חָכְמָתוֹ [ ] noun fem. sing., suff. 3 pers. sing. masc. from חָכְמָה (no pl. abs.) — חכם

חָכַמְתִּי Kal pret. 1 pers. sing. — חכם

חָכְמָתִי noun fem. sing., suff. 1 pers. sing. from חָכְמָה (no pl. abs.) — חכם

חָכְמָתְךָ / חָכְמָתֶךָ } id., suff. 2 pers. sing. masc. — חכם

חָכְמָתֵךְ id., suff. 2 pers. sing. fem. — חכם

חָכְמַתְכֶם id., suff. 2 pers. pl. masc. — חכם

חָכְמָתָם id., suff. 3 pers. pl. masc. — חכם

חִכְּתָה Piel pret. 3 pers. sing. fem. — חכה

חַל־ Piel imp. s. m. apoc. [for חַלֵּה § 24. rem. 12] — חלה

חֵל defect. for חַיִל, noun masc. sing. dec. 1; for] see lett. י — חיל

חֹל noun masc. sing. — חלל

[חָלָא] to be sick, 2 Ch. 16. 12.

חֶלְאָה fem. dec. 10.—I. rust; others, scum, froth.—II. pr. name fem. 1 Ch. 4. 5, 7.

תַּחֲלוּא masc. only pl. תַּחֲלוּאִים diseases.

חֶלְאָה pr. name fem. — חלא

חֲלָיִם noun masc., pl. of חֲלִי dec. 6. (§ 35. rem. 15) — חלה

חֶלְאָמָה Keri חֶלְמָה pr. name of a place (חֵילָם) with local ה — חול

חֶלְאָתָהּ / חֶלְאָתוֹ } noun fem. sing., suff. 3 pers. sing. fem. from [חֶלְאָה] dec. 10. (§ 3. rem. 3) — חלא

חָלָב Root not used; probably to be fat.

חָלָב masc. dec. 4 c, milk.

חֲלֵב masc. id. only in the constr. חֲלֵב.

חֵלֶב, חֵלֶב masc. dec. 6, with suff. חֶלְבּוֹ (§ 35. rem. 6).—I. fat, fatness, hence the best of any thing.—II. pr. name masc. 2 Sa. 23. 29, compare חֶלְדָּי

חֶלְבָּה (fatness, fertility) pr. name of a city in the tribe of Asher, Ju. 1. 31.

חֶלְבּוֹן (fat, fertile) pr. name of a city in Syria, Eze. 27. 18.

חֶלְבְּנָה fem. galbanum, an odoriferous gum, Ex. 30. 34.

אַחְלָב (fatness, fertility) pr. name of a place in the tribe of Asher, Ju. 1. 31.

חֵלֶב [ ] noun masc. sing. dec. 4 c — חלב

חֲלֵב [ ] noun masc. sing. constr. of [חֵלֶב] dec. 5 c — חלב

חֵלֶב [ ] n. m. s. dec. 6. (§ 35. rem. 6), also pr. n. m. — חלב

חֶלְבָּה pr. name of a place — חלב

חֶלְבָּהּ noun masc. sing., suff. 3 pers. sing. fem., from חֵלֶב dec. 6. (§ 35. rem. 6) — חלב

חֶלְבְּהֶן id., suff. 3 pers. pl. fem. (§ 3. rem. 5) — חלב

חֶלְבּוֹ id., suff. 3 pers. sing. masc. — חלב

חֶלְבּוֹן pr. name of a place — חלב

חֶלְבִּי noun m. s., suff. 1 pers. s. from חֵלֶב dec. 4 c — חלב

חֶלְבֵי n. m. pl. constr. from חֵלֶב dec. 6. (§ 35. rem. 6) — חלב

חֶלְבֵּךְ noun masc. sing., suff. 2 pers. sing. fem. from חֵלֶב dec. 4 c — חלב

חֶלְבָּם / חֶלְבָּמוֹ } noun masc. sing., suff. 3 pers. pl. masc. from חֵלֶב dec. 6. (§ 35. rem. 6) — חלב

חֶלְבְּנָה [ ] noun fem. sing. — חלב

חָלַד Root not used; Rabb. to hide, cover; Syr. to dig; Arab. to endure.

חֶלֶד masc. dec. 6, with suff. חֶלְדִּי (§ 35. rem. 3).—I. time, duration of life, lifetime.—II. world.

חֹלֶד masc. a mole, Le. 11. 29.

חֻלְדָּה (mole) pr. name of a prophetess, 2 Ki. 22. 14; 2 Ch. 34. 22.

חֶלְדָּי pr. name masc.—I. 1 Ch. 27. 15, called חֵלֶד chap. 11. 30, and חֵלֶב 2 Sa. 23. 29.—II. Zec. 6. 10, for which חֵלֶם in ver. 14

חֶלֶד n. m. sing. for חֵלֶד dec. 6. (§ 35. rem. 2 & 3) — חלד

חֵלֶד pr. name masc. — חלד

חֻלְדָּה pr. name fem. — חלד

חֶלְדָּי pr. name masc. — חלד

חֶלְדִּי [ ] noun masc. sing., suff. 1 pers. sing. from חֵלֶד dec. 6. (§ 35. rem. 3) — חלד

I. חָלָה I. to be weak, feeble.—II. to be sick, diseased.—III. to be pained, Pr. 23. 35; hence, to be grieved, 1 Sa. 22. 8, with עַל. Niph. נֶחְלָה, part. fem

a 2 Ch. 2. 13.   e Ex. 35. 25.   h Ec. 2. 15.   l Is. 47. 10.   o 1 Ki. 13. 6.   r Ca. 7. 2.   u De. 32. 14.   x Ca. 5. 1.   a Ps. 17. 10.
b Eze. 27. 8.   f Da. 2. 20, 21, 23.   i Ec. 2. 9.   m Da. 4. 6.   p La. 2. 8.   s Eze. 24. 6.   v Le. 4. 31, 35.   y Ex. 25. 4.   b Ex. 30. 34.
c Pr. 29. 8.   g 1 Ki. 11. 41.   k Eze. 28. 5, 17.   n Ps. 33. 20.   q Is. 26. 1.   t Eze. 24. 6, 11, 12.   w Le. 8. 16, 25.   z Nu. 12. 17.   c Ps. 39. 6.
d Pr. 9. 12.

נֶחְלָה (see analyt. order).—I. *to be exhausted, wearied*, Je. 12. 13.—II. *to become* or *be sick*; part. *sore, very sore,* מַכָּה נַחְלָה *a sore* (hardly curable) *wound.*—III. *to be grieved,* Am. 6. 6, with עַל. Pi. חִלָּה.—I. *to make sick, to afflict* with disease, De. 29. 21, with בְּ; חִלּוֹתִי הִיא *this makes me sick,* Ps. 77. 11.—II. *to weaken, soften down, appease.* Always fully חִלָּה פְּנֵי *to appease the face* (i. e. anger) *of any one;* חִלָּה פְּנֵי יְהֹוָה *to appease the face* (anger) *of the Lord,* i. e. to seek his mercy, hence generally, *to beseech, supplicate.* Pu. *to be made weak,* Is. 14. 10. Hiph.—I. *to make sick,* Mi. 6. 13; intrans. *to become sick,* Ho. 7. 5.—II. *to afflict, grieve,* Pr. 13. 12. Hoph. *to be wounded,* 1 Ki. 22. 34. Hithp.—I. *to fall sick,* 2 Sa. 13. 2.—II. *to feign sickness,* 2 Sa. 13. 5, 6.

חֳלִי masc. dec. 6k—I. *sickness, disease.*—II. *affliction, grief,* Ec. 5. 16.—III. *calamity,* Ec. 6. 2.

מַחֲלֶה masc. dec. 9a, *sickness, disease.*

מַחֲלָה fem. (of the preceding) id.

מַחֲלָה (*disease*) pr. name fem. of two different persons.

מַחְלוֹן (*sick*) pr. name masc. Ru. 1. 2, 4, 9.

מַחֲלַיִים masc. pl. מַחֲלַיִים, *disease,* 2 Ch. 24. 25.

מַחְלִי (*sick*) pr. name masc. of two different persons.

מַחֲלַת fem. the name of a certain musical instrument, Ps. 53. 1; 88. 1.

מַחֲלַת pr. name—I. of a daughter of Ishmael, the wife of Esau, Ge. 28. 9.—II. of the wife of Rehoboam, 2 Ch. 11. 18.

II. חָלָה Root not used; Syr. חלי *to be sweet, pleasant,* Pa. *to adorn.*

חֲלִי masc. dec. 6, pl. חֲלָאִים (§ 35. rem. 15) *ornament, necklace.*

חֶלְיָה fem. id., only חֶלְיָתָהּ Ho. 2. 15.

חָלָה Kal pret. 3 pers. sing. fem.; acc. shifted חול
חָלָה by וְ conv. (comp. § 8. rem. 7)
חֻלָּה noun fem. sing. dec. 10. — חלל
חִלָּה Piel pret. 3 pers. sing. masc. — חלה
חֹלֶה Kal part. act. sing. masc. — חלה
חָלוּ id. pret. 3 pers. pl. [for חָלְלוּ, comp. § 8. rem. 7] — חלה
חָלוּ Kal pret. 3 pers. pl.; acc. shifted by חול
חָלוּ conv. וְ (comp. § 8. rem. 7)
חַלּוּ Piel imp. pl. masc. — חלה

חִלּוּ וְ id. pret. 3 pers. pl. — חלה
חֲלוֹם noun masc. sing. dec. 1a — חלם
חַלּוֹן noun com. sing. dec. 1b — חלל
חֹלוֹן pr. name of a place — חול
חַלּוֹנָי וְ noun masc. pl., suff. 3 pers. sing. masc. (§ 4. rem. 1) dec. 1b — חלל
חַלּוֹנוֹת וְ id. with pl. fem. term. — חלל
חַלּוֹנָי id. pl. masc. poetic for חַלּוֹנִים (comp. חֹרֵי) — חלל
חַלּוֹנֵי id. pl. construct state — חלל
חַלּוֹנִים וְ id. pl. absolute state — חלל
חֲלוֹף noun masc. sing. — חלף
חֲלוּץ Kal part. pass. masc. dec. 3a — חלץ
חֲלוּץ id., construct state — חלץ
חֲלוּצֵי id. pl., construct state — חלץ
חֲלוּצִים id. pl., abs. state — חלץ
חֲלוּשָׁה noun fem. sing. — חלש
חַלּוֹת noun fem., pl. of חַלָּה dec. 10. — חלל
חַלּוֹתִי Piel inf., suff. 1 pers. sing.; acc. Milêl bef. monos. (הִיא) comp. § 3. rem. 1. — חלה
[חֲלַח] pr. name of a province in the kingdom of Assyria whither the ten tribes were transported, 2 Ki. 17. 6; 18. 11; 1 Ch. 5. 26.
חַלְחוּל pr. name of a place — חול
חַלְחָלָה וְ noun fem. sing. — חול

חָקַט Hiph. *to make declare* or *confirm,* 1 Ki. 20. 33
חֵלֶא וְ noun masc. sing. pl. חֲלָאִים dec. 6i (§ 35. rem. 15); also pr. name Jos. 19. 25. — חלה
חֲלִי noun masc. sing. dec. 6k (§ 35. rem. 14); וְ bef. (זָ) for וְ — חלה
חֶלְיוֹ id., suff. 3 pers. sing. masc. — חלה
חָלִיל noun masc. sing. dec. 3a — חלל
חָלִילָה adv.; חָלִיל with parag. ה — חלל
חֲלִילִים noun masc., pl. of חָלִיל dec. 6k [for חֲלִילִים], וְ bef. (זָ) for וְ — חלל
חִלִּינוּ Piel pret. 1 pers. pl. — חלה
חָלְיֵנוּ noun masc. pl., suff. 1 pers. pl. from חֳלִי dec. 6k [for חֳלָיֵנוּ] — חלה
חֲלִיפוֹת noun fem., pl. of חֲלִיפָה dec. 10. — חלף
חֲלִיפָתִי id. sing., suff. 1 pers. sing. — חלף
חֲלִיצוֹתָם noun fem. pl., suff. 3 pers. pl. masc. from חֲלִיצָה dec. 10. — חלץ
חָלִית Kal pret. 2 pers. sing. fem. — חלה
חֻלֵּית Pual pret. 2 pers. sing. fem. — חלה

a Is. 54. 1; 66. 8.   Mi. 1. 12.   Ho. 11. 6.   Na. 15. 20.   b Mal. 1. 8.   c Je. 5. 8.   d Job 11. 19.   e Ge. 8. 6.   f De. 2. 25.   g Mal. 1. 9.   h Job 11. 19.   i Ge. 8. 6.   k 1 Ki. 6. 4.   l Ezr. 40. 22.   m Ex. 40. 16, 29, 33.   n Je. 22. 14.   o Ez. 32. 18.   p Ps. 77. 11.   q Pr. 31. 8.   r Nu. 32. 21, 29.   s Ec. 5. 16.   t Pr. 25. 12.   u Ec. 6. 2.   v Na. 2. 11.   w 1 Sa. 10. 5. Is. 5. 12.   x De. 28. 59.   y Da. 9. 13.   z Pr. 25. 12.   a Is. 53. 4.   b Job 14. 16.   c Ju. 14. 19.   d Is. 57. 10.   e Is. 14. 10.

18*

וְחָלִיָּתָהּ noun fem. s., suff. 3 pers. s. f. [from חֶלְיָה] חלה

וְחָלִיתִי Kal pret. 1 pers. sing. . . . חלה

חִלִּיתִי Piel pret. 1 pers. sing. . . חלה

חָלַךְ Root not used; Arab. *to be black*, trop. *sad, wretched.*

חֵלְכָּאִים (for חֵלְכָא) adj. masc. pl. *wretched, poor.*

חֵלְכָּאִים pl. of the following . . . חלך

חֵלְכָה noun masc. sing., with suff. 2 pers. sing. masc. (§ 3. rem. 2), from חֵל, R. חול, or rather, adj. masc. [for חֵלְכָא=חֵלְכָה] . חלך

חָלַל I. *to be pierced, wounded*, Ps. 109. 22.—II. according to the Arab. *to open, to loose*. Pi.—I. *to wound*, Eze. 28. 9.—II. *to make common, to profane, pollute, defile.*—III. *to violate, break*, a covenant.—IV. *to play the pipe or flute*, from חָלִיל, 1 Ki. 1. 40. Pu. *to be wounded*, Eze. 32. 26; *to be profaned*, 36. 23. Poel *to pierce, wound*. Poal, pass. Is. 53. 5. Niph. נָחַל dag. f. impl., inf. הֵחָל (for הֵחָל § 18. rem. 14) *to be profaned, defiled*. Hiph. הֵחָל.—I. *to loose, set free*, Ho. 8. 10.—II. *to profane, defile, violate.*—III. *to open, begin.*—IV. *to begin to be*, Ge. 9. 20. Hoph. *to be begun*, Ge. 4. 26.

חָלָל masc. dec. 4 c, חֲלָלָה adj.—I. *pierced, wounded, slain.*—II. *profane, common*, Eze. 21. 30; *polluted*, by prostitution, Le. 21. 7, 14.

חָלִיל masc. dec. 3 a.—I. *pipe.*—II. adj. *profane*, only in the form חָלִלָה, חָלִילָה used to express detestation of a thing, *profane! fie! far be it!* followed by לְ of the pers. and inf. with מִן, as חָ׳ לְךָ מֵעֲשׂוֹת *far be it from thee to do*, &c.; אִם and the finite verb is added in a solemn declaration, comp. Ps. 95. 11; חָ׳ לִי מֵיהוָֹה אִם־אֶעֱשֶׂה lit. *profane be it to me from the Lord* (i.e. God forbid) *that I should do.*

חֹל masc. *profane, common.*

חַלָּה fem. dec. 10, *cake*, as being perforated with holes, used chiefly in sacred rites.

חַלּוֹן com. dec. 1 b, pl. ־יִם, ־וֹת, *window*; prop. a hole or opening for admitting the light.

נְחִילָה fem. (for נְחֻלָּה *perforated*) *a pipe, flute*, only pl. נְחִילוֹת Ps. 5. 1, comp. חָלִיל.

מְחִלָּה fem. dec. 10, *cave, cavern*, Is. 2. 19.

תְּחִלָּה fem. dec. 10, *beginning*; בַּתְּחִלָּה *at the first, formerly, before.*

חָלָל adj. masc. sing. dec. 4 c   חלל

חַלְּלִי Piel inf. constr.   חלל

חִלֵּל id. pret. 3 pers. sing. masc. . . חלל

חוֹלֵל Pilel inf. constr. . . . . חול

וַחֲלָלָה adj. fem. sing. from חָלָל masc.; וּ bef. (־) חלל

חֲלִלָה defect. for חָלִילָה (q. v.)   חלל

חוֹלְלָה Pilel pret. 3 pers. sing. fem. . חול

חִלְּלוּהוּ Piel pret. 3 pers. pl., suff. 3 pers. sing. masc. חלל

חִלְּלוֹ id. pret. 3 pers. sing. masc., suff. 3 p. s. m. חלל

חִלְּלוּ id. pret. 3 pers. pl. (comp. § 8. rem. 7) חלל

וַחִלְּלוּהָ id. id., suff. 3 pers. sing. fem.   חלל

וַחִלְּלוּהָ id. id., suff., Kh. לוּהָ 3 pers. sing. fem., K. לוּהוּ 3 pers. sing. masc. . . חלל

חַלְלֵי adj. masc. pl. constr. from חָלָל dec. 4 c חלל

חֲלָלֶיהָ id. pl., suff. 3 pers. sing. fem. .   חלל

חַלְלֵיהֶם id. pl., suff. 3 pers. pl. masc. .   חלל

חֲלָלָיו id. pl., suff. 3 pers. sing. masc.   חלל

חֲלָלַיִךְ id. pl., suff. 2 pers. sing. fem.   חלל

חֲלָלֶיךָ id. pl., suff. 2 pers. sing. masc.   חלל

חַלְלֵיכֶם id., suff. 2 pers. pl. masc.   חלל

חֲלָלִים id., pl. absolute state . .   חלל

חֲלָלֵינוּ id., suff. 1 pers. pl. .   חלל

חַלְלָם Piel inf. (חַלֵּל), suff. 3 pers. pl. masc. d. 7 b חלל

חִלַּלְתְּ id. pret. 2 pers. sing. f. [for חִלַּלְתְּ § 8. r. 7] חלל

חִלַּלְתָּ id. pret. 2 pers. sing. masc.; acc. shifted

וַחִלַּלְתָּ by conv. וְ (comp. § 8. rem. 7)   } חלל

חִלַּלְתִּי id. pret. 1 pers. sing. . . . חלל

חִלַּלְתֶּם id. pret. 2 pers. pl. masc.   חלל

חָלַם fut. יַחֲלַם.—I. *to be fat, stout, strong*, Job 39. 4.—II. *to dream*. Hiph.—I. *to make strong, restore to health*, Is. 38. 16.—II. *to cause to dream*, Je. 29. 8.

חֲלוֹם masc. pl. ־וֹת, *a dream.*

חֵלֶם Ch. masc.—I. *a dream.*—II. pr. name masc. Zec. 6. 14, see חֶלְדָּי.

חַלָּמוּת fem. Job 6. 6, Eng. Vers. "egg;" so the Jewish commentators, who consider חַלָּמוּת i. q. חֶלְבּוֹן=חֶלְמוֹן the yolk of an egg, hence רִיר חַ׳ *slime of a yolk*, i. e. the white of an egg. Others, *purslain*, a herb proverbial among the Arabs for its insipidity. Prof. Lee, *cheese.*

אַחְלָמָה the name of a precious stone; according

a Ho. 2. 15.   d Ps. 109. 22.   g Le. 21. 7, 14.   h De. 20. 6.   a Eze. 7. 21.   f Eze. 35. 8.   f Ju. 16. 24.   m Eze. 22. 3.   n Is. 47. 6.
b Ps. 10. 10.   Am. 2. 7.   h Job 26. 13.   i Je. 31. 5.   c Je. 51. 47.   r Is. 22. 2.   k Je. 16. 18.   l Le. 19. 12.   o Eze. 26. 22, 23.
c Ps. 10. 14.   Job 39. 1.   Eze. 36. 21.   Eze. 7. 22.   f Is. 34. 3.   s Ps. 69. 27.

to the LXX, *the amethyst.* Some suppose it to be the *emerald.* Ex. 28. 19; 39. 12.

נַחֲלָמִי *Nehelamite,* patronym. otherwise unknown, Je. 29. 24, 31, 32.

חַלָּמִישׁ masc., constr. חַלָּמִישׁ dec. 3c, *a hard stone, flint.*

חֲלֹם Ch. noun masc. sing. dec. 3c	חלם
חֹלֵם Kal part. act. sing. masc. dec. 7b	חלם
חֶלְמָא חֶלְמָה } Ch. noun masc. sing., emph. of חֲלֹם dec. 3c	חלם
חֲלֹמִי noun m. s., suff. 3 p. s. m. from חֲלוֹם d.1a	חלם
חֶלְמוּת noun fem. sing.	חלם
חֲלֹמוֹת } noun m. with pl. f. term. from חֲלוֹם d.1a	חלם
חֶלְמִי Ch. n. m. s., suff. 1 pers. s. from חֲלֹם d.3c	חלם
חֶלְמִין Ch. id. pl., abs. state	חלם
חַלְמִישׁ noun masc. sing., constr. חַלָּמִישׁ dec. 3c	חלם
חֶלְמָךְ Ch. noun masc. sing., suff. 2 pers. sing. masc. from חֲלֹם dec. 3c	חלם
חֲלַמְנוּ חֲלַמְנוּ } Kal pret. 1 pers. pl. (§ 8. rem. 7)	חלם
חֲלַמְתָּ id. pret. 2 pers. sing. masc. [for חָלַמְתָּ v. id.]	חלם
חֲלַמְתִּי חֲלַמְתִּי } id. pret. 1 pers. sing. (v. id.)	חלם
חֲלֹמֹתָיו noun masc., with pl. fem. term. & suff. 3 pers. sing. masc. from חֲלוֹם dec. 1a	חלם
חֲלֹמֹתֵיכֶם id., suff. 2 pers. pl. masc.	חלם
חֲלֹמֹתֵינוּ id., suff. 1 pers. pl.	חלם
חֵלֶק pr. name masc., see חָלוֹן	חול
חֶלְקֵי } pr. name of a place	חול
חַלֹּנוּ Kal pret. 1 pers. pl.	חול

חָלַף ו } fut. יַחֲלֹף.—I. *to pass by, pass on, pass away;* to *pass beyond* a law, *to transgress,* Is. 24. 5.—II. *to pass through,* only trans. *to pierce.*—III. *to rush upon, to assail.*—IV. *to revive, to flourish,* of a plant; of the spirit. Pi. *to change,* as a garment. Hiph.—I. *to change.*—II. *to renew, to cause to flourish.* Intrans. *to revive, to flourish again.*

חֲלַף Ch. *to pass,* Da. 4. 13, 20, 29.

חֵלֶף masc.—I. *exchange,* only as a prep. *instead of, for,* Nu. 18. 21, 31.—II. pr. name of a place in the tribe of Naphtali, Jos. 19. 33.

חֲלוֹף masc. *a passing away* or *perishing,* Pr. 31. 8, בְּנֵי חֲלוֹף *those who are about to perish.* Others, *children left behind,* i. e. *orphans.*

חֲלִיפָה fem. dec. 10.—I. *change, alternation;* חֲלִיפוֹת בְּגָדִים *changes* (i. e. *suits*) *of raiment.*—II. *reinforcement,* or *relief of guard,* Job 10. 17; where Gesenius renders חֲלִיפוֹת וְצָבָא (by Hendiadys) *changes and hosts* i. e. hosts continually succeeding each other.—III. חֲלִיפוֹת adv. *by courses, alternately,* 1 Ki. 5. 28.

מַחֲלָף masc. only pl. מַחֲלָפִים Ezr. 1. 9, *slaughtering-knives;* Syr. חלפא *knife.*

מַחְלָפָה fem. dec. 11a, only in the pl. *braided locks,* Ju. 16. 13, 19.

חָלַף ו Kal pret. 3 pers. s. m. (for חֲלַף § 8 r. 7)	חלף
חֵלֶף noun masc. sing.	חלף
חָלְפָה ו Kal pret. 3 pers. sing. fem.	חלף
חָלְפוּ id. pret. 3 pers. pl	חלף
חֲלִפוֹת defect. for חֲלִיפוֹת (q. v.)	חלף
חָלַפְתָּ ו Kal pret. 2 pers. sing. masc.; acc. shifted by ו conv. (§ 8. rem. 7)	חלף
חֲלִפֹת defect. for חֲלִיפוֹת (q. v.)	חלף

חָלַץ ו fut. יַחֲלֵץ.—I. *to draw out,* La. 4. 3.—II. *to draw* or *pull off,* as a shoe; חֲלוּץ נַעַל *barefoot.*—III. *to disengage oneself, to withdraw,* with מִן Ho. 5. 6. —IV. part. חָלוּץ *ready, prepared for war, armed;* חֲלוּץ צָבָא *host ready, prepared for action;* חֲלוּצֵי מוֹאָב *the arrayed* (troops) *of Moab.* Niph.—I. *to be drawn out, delivered.*—II. *to get ready, to arm oneself.* Pi.—I. *to draw out,* Le. 14. 40, 43.— II. *to deliver.*—III. *to strip, spoil,* Ps. 7. 5. Hiph. *to make easy, pliant and flexible,* as the bones in their sockets or joints, Is. 58. 11. Others, *to make strong.* LXX. πιανθήσεται *shall be fat.*

חָלָץ masc. dec. 4c, only dual חֲלָצַיִם *the loins,* prob. as the seat of strength and activity, comp. Hiph. of the verb.

חֶלֶץ, חֵלֶץ (*deliverance*) pr. name masc. of two different persons.

חֲלִיצָה fem. dec. 10, *spoil, booty.*

מַחֲלָצָה fem. dec. 11, *costly dress, mantle.*

חֵלֶץ חֶלֶץ ו } pr. name masc. (§ 35. rem. 2)	חלץ
חָלָץ pr. name masc., see חֶלֶץ	חלץ
חִלֵּץ Piel pret. 3 pers. sing. masc.	חלץ
חָלְצָה ו Kal pret. 3 pers. sing. fem.	חלץ
חַלְּצָה Piel imp. sing. masc. with parag. ה (comp. § 8. rem. 11)	חלץ

a Da. 4. 4, 5.   *d* Da. 4. 6.   *g* Da. 2. 28.   *k* Ge. 37. 10.   *m* Is. 26. 18.   *p* Ps. 90. 6.   *t* Ju. 5. 23.   *s* Ho. 5. 6.   *w* De. 25. 9.
b Da. 4. 15.   *e* Da. 5. 12.   *h* Ge. 41. 11.   *i* Ge. 41. 12.   *n* Is. 8. 8.   *r* Nu. 18. 21, 31.   *u* 1 Sa. 10. 3.   *t* Le. 14. 43.   *x* Ps. 6. 5.
Job 6. 4.   *f* Ps. 114. 8.   *i* Ge. 40. 8.

חָלְצוּ Kal pret. 3 pers. pl. . . . חלץ

חֶלְצוֹ Khethib for חֲלָצָיו (q. v. & § 4. rem. 1) . חלץ

וַחִלְּצוּ וְ Piel pret. 3 pers. pl. masc. . . חלץ

חֲלֻצֵי defect. for חֲלוּצֵי (q. v.) . . . חלץ

חֲלָצָיו noun m. du., suff. 3 p. s. m. fr. [חָלָץ] d. 4 c חלץ

חֲלָצֶיךָ id. id., suff. 2 pers. sing. masc. . . חלץ

חֲלָצַיִם id. du., absolute state [for חֲלָצִים] . חלץ

חַלְּצֵנִי וְ Piel imp. sing. m. [חַלֵּץ] suff. 1 pers. s. חלץ

חִלַּצְתָּ id. pret. 2 pers. sing. masc. . . חלץ

חֲלָצָתוּ noun fem. sing., suff. 3 pers. sing. masc. fr.
[חֲלִיצָה] dec. 10. . . . . חלץ

חָלַק fut. יַחֲלֹק.—I. *to be smooth*; metaph. *flattering.*—
II. *to divide, distribute, apportion*, especially by lot,
with לְ *to*, עִם *with any one*, with בְּ *of the thing*.
—III. *to spoil*, 2 Ch. 28. 21. Niph.—I. *to be
divided, distributed.*—II. *to divide oneself*, Ge. 14.
15. Pi.—I. *to divide, distribute, apportion.*—II. *to
disperse*. Pu. *to be divided, distributed*. Hiph.—
I. *to make smooth, flattering.*—II. *to take a portion*,
Je. 37. 12. Hithp. *to divide among themselves*,
Jos. 18. 5.

חָלָק adj. masc.—I. *smooth, without hair; bare,
bald*, of a mountain.—II. *flattering*, Pr. 26. 28.—
III. *slippery, deceitful, false*, Eze. 12. 24.

חֲלָק Ch. dec. 1 a, *portion, lot*, Da. 4. 12, 20.

חֵלֶק masc. dec. 6, with suff. חֶלְקִי (§ 35. r. 6).
—I. *smoothness, bareness*, spoken of a bare, un-
wooded place, Is. 57. 6.—II. *flattery*, Pr. 7. 21.—
III. *part, portion, lot of land.*—IV. pr. name masc.
Patronym. חֶלְקִי Nu. 26. 30.

חֵלֶק adj. masc. *smooth*, 1 Sa. 17. 40.

חֶלְקָה fem. dec. 12 b.—I. *smoothness*, Ge. 27. 16.
—II. *slippery place*, Ps. 73. 18.—III. metaph.
flattery.—IV. *portion, part.*

חֲלָקָה fem. only pl. חֲלָקוֹת *flatteries*, Da. 11. 32.

חֻלְקָה fem. d. 10, *division, partition*, 2 Ch. 35. 5.

חֶלְקִי (*smooth*) pr. name masc. Ne. 12. 15.

חִלְקִיָּהוּ, חִלְקִיָּה (*portion of the Lord*) pr. name
masc. of several persons, especially—I. of a high
priest in the reign of Josiah, 2 Ki. 22. 8, 12.—II.
of the father of Jeremiah the prophet, Je. 1. 1.—
III. of the father of Eliakim, comp. 2 Ki. 18. 18, 26.

חֲלַקְלַקּוֹת only pl. fem.—I. *slippery
places.*—II. *flatteries, hypocrisy*, Da. 11. 21, 24.

מַחֲלֹקֶת fem. dec. 13 c.—I. *course, division, class*.

—II. pr. n. of a place, 1 Sa. 23. 28, סֶלַע הַמַּחְלְקוֹת,
rock of smoothness, i. e. slipping away, escape.

מַחְלְקָא Ch. fem. dec. 8 a, *course, division*, Ezr.
6. 18.

חֲלָק וְ adj. masc. sing. . . . חלק

חֲלָקָא Ch. noun masc. sing. dec. 1 a . . חלק

חַלֵּק Piel imp. sing. masc. . . . חלק

חֵלֶק וְ noun masc. sing. dec. 6 (§ 35. rem. 6),
also pr. name masc. חלק

חֻלַּק וְ Pual pret. 3 pers. sing. masc. . חלק

חֲלָקֵהּ Ch. noun masc. sing., suff. 3 pers. sing. masc.
from חֲלָק dec. 1 a חלק

חֶלְקָה וְ noun fem. sing. dec. 12 b Am. 4. 7. חלק

חָלְקוּ Kal pret. 3 pers. pl. . . . חלק

חֶלְקוֹ noun masc. sing., suff. 3 pers. sing. masc.
from חֵלֶק dec. 6 (§ 35. rem. 6) . . חלק

חִלְּקוּ Piel pret. 3 pers. pl. [for חִלְקוּ, comp. § 8.
rem. 7] . . . . חלק

חִלְקוּ Kal imp. pl. masc. . . . חלק

חֲלָקוֹת noun fem., pl. abs. from חֶלְקָה dec. 12 b חלק

חַלְקֵי noun masc. pl. constr. from [חֵלֶק] . חלק

חִלְקִי for חִלְקִיָּה pr. name masc. for חִלְקִיָּה q. v.

חֶלְקִי וְ noun masc. sing., suff. 1 pers. sing. from
חֵלֶק dec. 6 (§ 35. rem. 6) . . חלק

חִלְקִיָּה
חִלְקִיָּהוּ } pr. name masc.

חֶלְקֵיהֶם noun masc. pl., suff. 3 pers. pl. masc. from
חֵלֶק dec. 6 (§ 35. rem. 6) חלק

חֲלָקִים id. pl., absolute state . . . חלק

חֶלְקֵךְ id. sing., suff. 2 pers. sing. fem. . חלק

חֶלְקְךָ
חֶלְקֶךָ } id. sing. with suff. 2 pers. sing. masc. . חלק

חֲלַקְלַקּוֹת וְ noun pl. fem. from [חֲלַקְלַק] ; וְ bef. (—) חלק

חֶלְקָם noun masc. sing., suff. 3 pers. pl. masc. fr.
חֵלֶק dec. 6 (§ 35. rem. 6) חלק

חִלְּקָם Piel pret. 3 pers. sing. masc. [חִלֵּק] suff. 3
pers. pl. masc. חלק

חֶלְקַת
חֶלְקָת } pr. name of a place and in compos.
חֵלְקַת הַצֻּרִים, see חֶלְקָה . . חלק

חֶלְקַת noun fem. sing., constr. of חֶלְקָה dec. 12 b חלק

חֻלְקַת וְ noun fem. sing., constr. of [חֻלְקָה] d. 10 חלק

חִלְּקַתָּה Piel pret. 3 pers. sing. fem., suff. 3 pers. s. f. חלק

חֶלְקָתִי noun fem. s., suff. 1 p. s. from חֶלְקָה d. 12 b חלק

חֶלְקָתָם id., suff. 3 pers. pl. masc. . . חלק

a La. 4. 3.   d Is. 32. 11.   g Ps. 116. 8.   k Ezr. 4. 16.   n Zec. 14. 1.   r Joz. 22. 8.   u Ho. 5. 7.   y Ps. 35. 6.   b Is. 34. 17.
b Job 31. 20.   e Ps. 140. 2.   h 2 Sa. 2. 21.   l Jos 13. 7.   o Da. 4. 12, 20.   s 1 Sa. 17. 40.   w Is. 57. 6.   z La. 4. 16.   c Je. 12. 10.
c Le. 14. 40.   f Ps. 119. 153.   i Pr. 5. 3.   m Is. 33. 23.   p Joel 4. 2.   t Ps. 73. 26.   x Ps. 50. 18.   a 2 Ch. 35. 5.   d Job 24. 18.

חֲלַקְתֶּם֙ ן Piel pret. 2 pers. s. m., suff. 3 pers. pl. m.   חלק

חֲלַקְתֶּם֙ ן id. pret. 2 pers. pl. masc.   חלק

[חָלַשׁ] I. fut. יַחֲלֹשׁ to overthrow, discomfit.—II fut. יֶחֱלָשׁ, (§ 8. rem. 13) to be weak, feeble, Job 14. 10.

חַלָּשׁ masc. weak, Joel 4. 10.

חֲלוּשָׁה fem. overthrow, defeat, Ex. 32. 18.

חַלַּת ן noun fem. sing., constr. of חַלָּה dec. 10.   חלל

חַלֹּת ן' pl. of the preceding   חלל

חַלֹּתִי Kal pret. 1 pers. sing.   חול

[חָם] masc. irr. with suff. חָמִיךְ (§ 45) father-in-law.

חָמוֹת fem. with suff. חֲמוֹתֵךְ mother-in-law.

חֲמִיטַל, חֲמוּטַל (father-in-law of dew, comp. אֲבִיטַל) pr. name of the wife of king Josiah.

חָם ן' adj. masc. sing. dec. 8a, also pr. name m.   חמם

חָם ן Kal pret. 3 pers. sing. masc.   חמם

חֹם ן noun masc. sing.   חמם

חֵמְאָ Root not used; Arab. to curdle, coagulate.

חֶמְאָה fem. constr. חֶמְאַת (comp. מַחֲמָאוֹת.—I. curdled milk. Eng. Vers. "butter," which modern interpreters reject as hardly known to the orientalists.—II. cheese, Pr. 30. 33.

חֵמָה Job 29. 5, for חֶמְאָה q. v.

מַחֲמָאוֹת fem. pl. milky (i. e. sweet) words, Ps. 55. 22; but Kimchi and others prefer to read here מֶחֱמָאוֹת than cream or butter, as the pl. of חֶמְאָה (dec. 12b).

חֲמָא ן Ch. noun fem. sing; ן bef. (‒:)   יחם
חֵמָא ן

חֶמְאָה ן' noun fem. sing. (no pl.)   חמא

חֶמְאַת id., constr. state   חמא

חָמַד fut. יַחְמֹד, יֶחְמַד (§ 13. rem. 5) to desire, delight in in a good sense; also in a bad sense, to covet; part. חָמוּד desired, hence something desirable, delightful, pleasant. Niph. part. נֶחְמָד (§ 13. r. 7) desirable, pleasant. Pi. to desire, delight in, Ca. 2. 3.

חֶמֶד masc. desirableness; שְׂדֵי חֶמֶד desirable, pleasant fields; בַּחוּרֵי חֶמֶד pleasant, comely young men.

חֶמְדָּה fem. constr. חֶמְדַּת (no pl.)—I. desire. —II. object of desire; חֶמְדַּת כָּל־הַגּוֹיִם the (object of) desire of all nations, i. e. the Messiah, Hag. 2. 7.—III. desirableness, pleasantness; אֶרֶץ חֶ' pleasant land; כְּלֵי חֶ' desirable, precious vessels.

חֲמֻדוֹת, חֲמוּדוֹת fem. pl. desirable, precious things, applied to vessels and other valuables, לֶחֶם חֲ' desirable, pleasant, delicate food; אִישׁ חֲ' man beloved (of God).

חֶמְדָּן (pleasant) pr. name masc. Ge. 36. 26; for which חַמְרָן 1 Ch. 1. 41.

מַחְמָד masc. constr. מַחְמַד, pl. מַחֲמַדִּים d. 8a (§ 37. No. 3c).—I. desire, also object of desire; hence pl. things desirable, precious, costly.—II. pl. loveliness, Ca. 5. 16.

מַחְמֹד masc. pl. מַחֲמֹדִּים d. 8c (§ 37. No. 3c) precious, costly things, La. 1. 7, 11.

חֶמֶד noun masc. sing.   חמד

חֶמְדָּה noun fem. sing. (no pl.)   חמד

חָמְדָה ן' Kal pret. 3 pers. sing.   חמד

חֲמוּדוֹת noun fem. pl. [fr. חֲמוּדָה]   חמד

חֶמְדָּן pr. name masc.   חמד

חֶמְדַּת noun fem. sing., constr. of דָּה חֶ' (no pl.)   חמד

חֲמַדְתִּי id., suff. 1 pers. sing.   חמד

חִמַּדְתִּי Piel pret. 1 pers. sing.   חמד

חֲמַדְתֵּךְ noun fem. sing., suff. 2 pers. sing. fem. fr. חֶמְדָּה (no pl.)   חמד

חֲמַדְתָּם id., suff. 3 pers. pl. masc.   חמד

חֲמַדְתֶּם Kal pret. 2 pers. pl. masc.   חמד

חָמָה Root not used; Arab. חמא to guard, to surround with a wall.

חוֹמָה fem. dec. 10, a wall; dual חֹמָתַיִם double walls.

חֲמָת (fortress) pr. name Hamath, a large city in Syria near the northern boundary of Palestine. Gent. noun חֲמָתִי Hamathite, Ge. 10. 18.

יַחְמְיָה (for יַחְמְיָה whom the Lord guards, defends) pr. name masc. 1 Ch. 7. 2.

חַמָּה noun fem. sing. dec. 10.   חמם

חֵמָה ן' noun fem. sing. dec. 11 b [for יֶחֱמָה]   יחם

חֹמָה defect. for חוֹמָה (q. v.)   חמה

חַמּוּאֵל pr. name masc.   חמם

חֲמוּדוֹ Kal part. p. masc., suff. 3 pers. sing. masc. from [חָמוּד] dec. 3a   חמד

חֲמוּדוֹת noun fem. pl. [of חֲמוּדָה]   חמד

חֲמוּדֵיהֶם ן Kal part. p. pl. masc., suff. 3 pers. pl. masc. from [חָמוּד] dec. 3a   חמד

חֲמֻדֹת defect. for חֲמוּדוֹת (q. v.)   חמד

חֲמוּטַל pr. name fem.   חם

חָמוּל ן pr. name masc.   חמל

חָמוֹן ן' pr. name of a place   חמם

a Eze. 5. 1.   d Is. 23. 4.   f Ps. 39. 4.   h Da. 3. 19.   k Pr. 1. 22.   m Je. 12. 10.   o Eze. 26. 12.   q Is. 1. 29.   s Ps. 39. 12.
b Eze. 47. 21.   e Jos. 9. 12.   g Da. 3. 13.   i De. 33. 14.   l Mi. 2. 2.   n Ca. 2. 3.   p Da. 11. 8.   r Job 30. 28.   t Is. 44. 9
c Ex. 29. 2.   cc Ge. 8. 22.

חָמוּץ adj. masc. *Ang.* . . . . חמץ

חֲמוּץ Kal part. p. masc., constr. of [חָמוּץ] dec. 3 a חמץ

חֲמוּקֵי noun masc. pl. constr. from [חָמוּק] dec. 1 b חמק

חֲמוֹר נ' noun masc. sing. dec. 1 a, also pr. name; ‌‌ ‌‌ ‌‌ ‌‌ ‌‌ ‌‌ ‌‌ ‌‌ ‌‌ ‌‌ ‌‌ ‌‌ ‌‌ ‌‌ ‌‌ ‌‌ ‌‌ ‌‌ ‌‌ חמר

 נ' before (־ִ)

חֲמוֹרֵיכֶם id. pl., suff. 2 pers. pl. masc. . . . חמר

חֲמוֹרִים נ' id. pl. absolute state; ן before (־ִ) חמר

חֹמוֹת noun fem. pl. abs. from חֵמָה dec. 11 b . יחם

חוֹמֹת noun fem., pl. of חוֹמָה dec. 10. . . חמה

חֲמוֹתָהּ noun fem. sing., suff. 3 pers. sing. fem. from ‌‌‌‌‌ חם

[חָמוֹת] dec. 3 a

חֲמוֹתִי Kal pret. 1 pers. sing. (§ 18. rem. 1) חמם

חֲמוֹתֵךְ noun masc. sing., suff. 2 pers. sing. fem. from ‌‌‌‌‌ ‌‌‌‌‌‌ חם

[חָמוֹת] dec. 3 a . . . .

[חֹמֶט] masc. kind of *lizard*, Le. 11. 30.   Hence

חָמְטָה ן (*place of lizards*) pr. name of a city in ‌‌‌‌‌‌‌‌‌‌‌‌‌‌‌‌‌‌ Judah, Jos. 15. 54 . . . חמט

חֲמִיהָ noun masc. sing., suff. 3 pers. sing. fem. from ‌‌ חם

[חָם irr. § 45] . . . .

חֲמִיטַל Kh. חֲמוּטַל K. q. v. חם

חָמִיךְ n. m. s., suff. 2 pers. s. f. [from חָם irr. §45] חם

חַמִּים adj. masc., pl. of חָם dec. 8 a חמם

חָמִיץ adj. masc. sing. . . . חמץ

חֲמִישִׁי adj. ord. masc. sing. from חָמֵשׁ חמש

חֲמִישִׁית fem. of the preceding dec. 1 b . חמש

חֲמִישִׁיתוֹ ‌‌‌‌‌‌ } id. with suff. 3 pers. sing. masc. חמש
חֲמִישִׁתוֹ נ'

חָמַל fut. יַחְמֹל (§ 13. rem. 5).—I. *to pity, have com- passion,* with עַל of the person.—II. *to spare, save,* with אֶל.—III. *to spare, withhold,* with inf. and לְ, with עַל

חָמוּל (*spared*) pr. name masc.—Patronym. חֲמוּלִי Nu. 26. 21.

חֶמְלָה fem. constr. חֶמְלַת (no pl.) *mercy, clemency.*

מַחְמָל masc. dec. 2 b, *object of tender affection,* Eze. 24. 21.

חָמַל Kal pret. 3 pers. s. m. for חָמַל (comp. § 8. r. 7) חמל

חָמַלְתְּ id. pret. 2 pers. sing. masc. [for חָמַלְתָּ ‌‌‌ חמל

§ 8, rem. 7] . . . .

חָמַלְתִּי ן id. pret. 1 pers. s.; acc. shifted (§ 8. r. 7) חמל

חֲמַלְתֶּם id. pret. 2 pers. pl. masc. חמל

[חָמַם] fut. יֵחֹם, יָחֹם, וַיִּחַם יֵחַם (§ 18. rem. 6) *to be or grow warm;* כְּחֹם הַיּוֹם *in the heat of the day,* at noon;

impers. חַם לוֹ, יֵחַם *it is warm to him, he becomes warm.*   Niph. part. *burning, inflamed,* Is. 57. 5. Pi. *to warm, hatch,* Job 39. 14.   Hithp. *to warm oneself,* Job 31. 20.

חָם masc. dec. 8 a.—I. adj. *warm, hot.*—II. pr. name of a son of Noah.—III. *Ham* poet. for Egypt. comp. Ps. 78. 51 ; 105. 23, 27.

חֹם masc. *warmth, heat.*

חַמָּה fem. dec. 10.—I. *heat, glow,* Ps. 19. 7.— II. *the sun.*

חַמּוּאֵל (*warmth of God*) pr. name m. 1 Ch. 4. 26.

חַמּוֹן (*sunny*) pr. name—I. of a town in the tribe of Asher, Jos. 19. 28.—II. of a town in the tribe of Naphtali, 1 Ch. 6. 61.

חַמָּן masc. dec. 1 b, only pl. (חַמָּנִים) *images dedicated to the sun, sun-images.*

חַמַּת (*hot bath*) pr. name of a city in the tribe of Naphtali, Jos. 19. 35.

חַמֹּת דֹּאר (*hot baths of Dor*) pr. name of a city of refuge in the tribe of Naphtali, Jos. 21. 32.

חַמָּנֵיכֶם noun masc. pl., suff. 2 pers. pl. masc. from ‌‌ חמם

[חַמָּן] dec. 1 b . . . .

חַמָּנִים ן id. pl., absolute state חמם

[חָמַס] fut. יַחְמֹם (§ 13. rem. 5).—I. *to do violence to any one, to injure, wrong, oppress;* חָמַס תּוֹרָה *to vio- late the law.*—II. *to tear away with violence,* La. 2. 6. —III. *to shake off* as the tree its fruit, Job 15. 33.

חָמָס masc. dec. 4 c, *violence, wrong, injury;* meton. *what is obtained by violence* or *wrong, ill- gotten wealth,* Am. 3. 10.

תַּחְמָס masc. a species of unclean bird, Le. 11. 16. De. 14. 15.   According to Bochart, *the male ostrich* Vulg. *noctua, night-hawk.*

חָמָס ן noun masc. sing. dec. 4 c . . . חמם

חֲמַס נ' id. construct state ; ן before (־ַ) חמם

חֹמֵס Kal part. act. sing. masc. חמם

חָמְסוּ id. pret. 3 pers. pl. . . . חמם

חֲמָסוֹ noun masc. sing., suff. 3 pers. sing. masc. ‌‌ חמם

from חָמָס dec. 4 c . . .

חֲמָסִי id., suff. 1 pers. sing. חמם

חֲמָסִים id. pl., absolute state חמם

חָמֵץ fut. יַחְמַץ (§ 13. rem. 4, 5).—I. *to be sour, to be leavened,* of bread.—II. part. חָמוּץ, metaph. *splendid,* of the dazzling scarlet colour, Is. 63. 1.— III. i. q. חָמַס, par חֹמֶץ *a violent man,* Ps. 71. 4

* Is. 1. 17.   ᵈ 1 Sa. 8. 16.   ᶠ Pr. 22. 24.   ⁱ Is. 44. 16.   ˡ Job 37. 17.   ⁿ Nu. 5. 7.   ᵖ 1 Sa. 23. 21.   ʳ Hab. 2. 8, 17.   ᵗ Ps. 7. 17.
ᵇ Is. 63. 1.   ᵉ 1 Ch. 5. 21.   ᵍ Je. 51. 58.   ᵏ Ge. 38. 13.   ᵐ Is. 30. 24.   ᵒ Mal. 3. 17.   ᵠ Is. 27. 9.   ˢ Pr. 8. 36.   ᵘ Ex. 12. 39.
ᶜ Ca 7 2.

Hiph. part. מַחְמֶצֶת *soured, leavened.* Hithp. *to be embittered, provoked to anger,* Ps. 73. 21.

חָמֵץ masc. *what is leavened, fermented.*

חָמוֹץ masc. *violent man, oppressor,* Is. 1. 17, which others take in a passive sense, *oppressed.* Vulg. oppressors.

חָמִיץ masc. adj. *salted, seasoned,* Is. 30. 24. Prof. Lee, "a salt, sour plant of the desert much relished by the camels."

חֹמֶץ masc. *vinegar.*

חָמֵץ noun masc. sing.   . חמץ

חֹמֶץ [ו'] noun masc. sing.   .   .   ° חמץ

חֻמְצָתוֹ Kal inf. [חֻמְצָה § 8. rem. 10] suff. 3 pers. sing. masc.   .   .   ° חמץ

חָמַק *to turn oneself, withdraw, depart,* Ca. 5. 6. Hithp. *to wander about,* Je. 31. 22.

חַמּוּק masc. only pl. (חַמּוּקִים) Ca. 7 2. Eng. Vers., "joints." Others, *circuits.* Prof. Lee, *surroundings, clothings;* and as some think, a kind of *drawers* worn by the women of the east.

חָמַר fut. יַחְמֹר (§ 13. rem. 4, 5).—I. *to rise, ferment,* Ps. 75. 9; others, *to be red.*—II. metaph. *to be agitated,* Ps. 46. 4.—III. fut. יַחְמֹר (§ 13. rem. 5) *to daub, cover with bitumen,* Ex. 2. 3; denom. from חֵמָר. Poalal (§ 6. No. 3).—I. *to become excited, troubled.*—II. *to become red, inflamed,* Job 16. 16.

חֵמָר masc. *bitumen or asphaltus,* a glutinous matter issuing from the earth, which springs in a *turbid effervescence* near Babylon, also near the Dead Sea and at its bottom.

חֶמֶר masc. *wine.*

חֲמַר Chald. masc. dec. 3a, id.

חֹמֶר masc. dec. 6c.—I. *a fermenting, foaming,* of waters, Hab. 3. 15; but comp. the following significations.—II. *clay, cement; mire, mud.*—III. *a heap,* Ex. 8. 10.—IV. *measure of capacity,* containing ten Baths.

חֲמוֹר , חֲמֹר masc.—I. *an ass.*—II. i. q. *a heap,* Ju. 15. 16.—III. pr. name masc. comp. Ge. 33. 19.

חֲמֹרָה fem. dec. 10, *a heap,* Ju. 15. 16.

חֶמְרָן pr. name masc. 1 Ch. 1. 41, called חֲמְדָּן in Ge. 36. 26.

יַחְמוּר masc. *goat* or *gazelle* of a brown or reddish colour.

חֲמֹר in pause for חֲמֹר (q. v. § 35. rem. 2)   . חמר

חֲמַר Chald. noun masc. sing. dec. 3a   . חמר

חֲמוֹר noun masc. sing. dec. 1a   .   . חמור

חֵמָר noun masc. sing.   .   .   .   . חמר

חֶמֶר noun masc. sing.   .   .   .   . חמר

חֹמֶר [ו'] noun masc. sing. dec. 6c   .   . חמר

חַמְרָא Chald. noun masc. s., emph. of חֲמַר dec. 3a   חמר

חֲמֹרוֹ [ו] noun masc. sing. dec. 1a;] before (־)   חמר

חֲמֹרֵיהֶם [ו'] id. pl., suff. 3 pers. pl. masc.   חמר

חֲמֹרִים noun masc., pl. of חֹמֶר dec. 6c   . חמר

חֲמֹרִים [ו] noun masc., pl. of חֲמוֹר dec. 1a;] bef. (־)   חמר

חֲמֹרֵינוּ id. pl., suff. 1 pers. pl.   .   .   . חמר

חֲמֹרְךָ [ו] id. sing., suff. 2 pers. sing. masc.;   } חמר

חֲמֹרֶךָ [ו] }] before (־)   .   .   . }

חֲמֹרָם defect. for חֲמֹרִים (q. v.)   .   .   חמר

חֲמַרְמָרָה Kh. מָרָה Poalal pret. 3 pers. sing. fem.; K. מְרוּ (q. v.)   .   .   .   .   .   . חמר

חֳמַרְמָרוּ } id. pret. 3 pers. pl. (§ 6. rem. 3; § 8. r. 7)   חמר
חֳמַרְמָרוּ }

חֶמְרָן pr. name masc.   .   .   .   .   . חמר

חֲמֹרָתַיִם for [תַיִם חֲמֹרָה] noun fem., dual of [חֲמֹרָה] dec. 10.   חמר

חָמֻשׁ only part. pass. חֲמֻשִׁים *brave, ready for battle.* Arab. *to be fat, stout; strong, courageous.*

חֹמֶשׁ masc. *the belly, abdomen.*

חָמֵשׁ [ו] constr. חֲמֵשׁ fem. חֲמִשָּׁה constr. חֲמֵשֶׁת masc. (§ 39. No. 4. rem. 1) num. card. *five;* חֲמִשִּׁים *fifty,* (with suff. חֲמִשָּׁיךְ), שַׂר חֲ *a captain of fifty,* sc. soldiers.

חִמֵּשׁ Piel (denom. of חָמֵשׁ) *to fifth, exact the fifth part,* Ge. 41. 34.

חֹמֶשׁ masc. *fifth part,* Ge. 47. 26.

חֲמִישִׁי , חֲמִשִׁי masc., —ית fem. adj. ordinal, *fifth;* חֲמִישִׁית *fifth part.*

חֲמֵשׁ [ו] constr. of the preceding   .   . חמש

חִמֵּשׁ [ו] Piel pret. 3 pers. sing. masc.   . חמש

חֲמִשָּׁה [ו] num. card. masc. sing. from חָמֵשׁ fem.;] before (־)   .   .   .   . חמש

חֲמִשֵּׁיהֶם id. pl. com. gen. (חֲמִשִּׁים) suff. 3 pers. pl. m.   חמש

חֲמִשָּׁיו [ו] id. pl., suff. 3 pers. sing. masc.;] bef. (־)   חמש

חֲמִשֶּׁיךָ id. pl., suff. 2 pers. sing. masc.   .   חמש

חֲמִשִּׁים [ו] id. pl., absolute state;] before (־)   חמש

חֲמֻשִׁים [ו'] Kal part. p. masc., pl. of [חָמוּשׁ] dec. 3a   חמש

חֲמִשִׁית adj. ord. fem. s. for חֲמִישִׁית from חֲמִישִׁי m.   חמש

חֲמִשִׁיתוֹ id. with suff. 3 pers. sing. masc.   .   חמש

חֲמֵשֶׁת [ו] num. card. masc., constr. of (חֲמִשָּׁה) (§ 39 rem. 1) from חָמֵשׁ fem.   .   חמש

a Nu. 6. 3.   d De. 32. 14.   g Ho. 3. 2.   k Nu. 11. 32.   = Ex. 23. 12.   o De. 5. 14.   r Job 16. 16.   u La. 2. 11.   u Ge. 41. 34.
b Ho. 7. 4.   e Ge. 14. 10.   h Da. 5. 1, 2, 4, 23.   i Ge. 43. 18.   = De. 28. 3   p Ex. 8. 10.   r La. 1. 29.   t Ju. 15. 16.   Ex. 13. 18.
c Ps. 75. 9.   f Is. 27. 2.   i Ge. 44. 3.   m 2 Ki. 1. 14.

חֲמִשָׁתוֹ adj. ord. fem. (חֲמִישִׁית) suff. 3 pers. masc. from חֲמִישִׁי masc. . . . . חמש

חֲמִשְׁתָּיו id. pl. (חֲמִישִׁיתִים), suff. 3 pers. sing. masc. (§ 4. rem. 3); ן before (–͏ֵ) . . חמש

[הֵמֶת] masc. constr. חֵמַת, *skin-bottle.*

חֲמַת (ו׳) pr. name of a place; ן id. . . חמה
חַמַּת

חֵמַת (e׳ו׳) n. fem. s., constr. of חֵמָה dec. 11 b; ן id. . יחם

חֲמֹת pr. name in compos. חֲמֹת דֹּאר . חמם

חֵמַת (ן׳) noun masc. sing., constr. of חֵמָת . חמת

חֵמֹת noun fem. pl. abs. from חֵמָה dec. 11 b . יחם

חֲמָתָה pr. name of a place (חֲמָת) with paragogic ה חמה

חֲמָתוֹ (ן׳) noun fem. sing., suff. 3 pers. sing. masc. from חֵמָה dec. 11 b; ן before (–͏ֵ) . יחם

חֲמָתִי (ן׳) id., with suff. 1 pers. sing. . יחם

חֹמֹתָיִךְ noun fem. pl., suff. 2 pers. sing. masc. from חוֹמָה dec. 10. . . חמה

חֲמָתֶךָ (ו׳ן׳) noun fem. sing., suff. 2 pers. sing. m. from חֵמָה dec. 11 b; ן bef. (–͏ֵ) . יחם

חֲמָתָם id., suff. 3 pers. pl. masc. . . . יחם

חֵן (ן׳) noun masc. sing. dec. 8 b . . חנן

חֲנָדָד pr. name masc. . . . . חנן

חָנָה fut. יַחֲנֶה, apoc. יִחַן (§ 24. rem. 3).—I. *to decline,* of the day, Ju. 19. 9.—II. *to let oneself down, encamp, pitch one's tent;* const. with עַל *to encamp against;* with לְ *about* any one, sc. for his defence. —III. *to dwell,* Is. 29. 1.

חֲנוּת fem. only pl. חֲנֻיוֹת (comp. מַלְכֻיוֹת from מַלְכוּת) Je. 37. 16, *vaults, cells.* Prof. Lee, *wells.*

חֲנִית fem. dec. 1 a, pl. חֲנִיתוֹת & חֲנִיתִים, *spear, lance.*

מַחֲנֶה com. (fem. Ge. 32. 9) dec. 9 a, pl. מַחֲנִים, מַחֲנוֹת, du. מַחֲנַיִם (comp. § 38. rem. 1).—I. *camp, encampment.*—II. *troop, host, army.*—III. *swarm,* of locusts; *drove,* of cattle.

מַחֲנֵה־דָן (*camp of Dan*) pr. name of a place in the tribe of Judah, Ju. 18. 12.

מַחֲנַיִם (*two troops*) pr. name of a town beyond Jordan.

תַּחַן (*encampment*) pr. name masc. Patronym. תַּחֲנִי Nu. 26. 35.

תַּחֲנֶה fem. dec. 10, *place of encampment,* 2 Ki. 6. 8.

חֲנֵה (ו׳ן׳) Kal imp. sing. masc.; ן before (–͏ֵ) חנה
חַנָּה (ן׳) pr. name fem. . . . חנן
חֻנָּה fem. of the following . . . חנה

חֹנֶה Kal part. act. sing. masc. dec. 9 a . חנה
חָנוּ (ו׳) id. pret. 3 pers. pl. . . חנה
חֲנוּ id. imp. pl. masc. . . . . חנה
חִנּוֹ noun m. s., suff. 3 pers. s. m. from חֵן dec. 8 b חנן
חֲנוֹךְ (ן׳) pr. name of a man and a city . חנך
חָנוֹן (ן׳) Kal inf. abs. (§ 18. rem. 13) . חנן
חָנוּן pr. name masc. . . . . חנן
חַנּוּן (ן׳) adj. masc. sing., also pr. name masc. . חנן
חָנֻּונוּ Kal imp. pl. m., suff. 1 pers. pl. (§ 18. rem. 4) חנן
חָנוֹף Kal inf. abs. . . . . חנף
חֲנוֹת Kal inf. constr. (§ 18. rem. 3); or noun fem., [pl. of חַנָּה] חנן
חֲנוֹת Kal inf. construct dec. 1 a . . חנה
חַנּוֹתִי (ן׳) Kal inf. (§ 18. rem. 3), or noun fem. pl., [of חַנָּה] suff. 1 pers. sing. (§ 4. rem. 2) . חנן

[חָנַט] I. *to embalm,* Ge. 50. 2, 26.—II. *to ripen* fruit, Ca. 2. 13.

חֲנָטִים masc. pl. *an embalming,* Ge. 50. 3; which others take as a part. pass. *embalmed bodies.*

חָנְטָה Kal pret. 3 pers. sing. fem. . . חנט
חִנְטִין Ch. noun fem. pl. [of חִנְטָא for חִטָּא], comp. חטה
חֲנִיאֵל (ן׳) pr. name masc. . . חנן
חֲנִיכָיו noun masc. pl., suff. 3 pers. sing. masc. from [חָנִיךְ] dec. 3 a . חנך
חֹנִים Kal part. act. masc., pl. of חֹנֶה dec. 9 a . חנה
חֲנִנָה noun fem. sing. . . . חנן
חֲנִית (ן׳) noun fem. sing. dec. 1 a; ן before (–͏ֵ) חנה
חֲנִיתוֹ (ן׳) id., suff. 3 pers. sing. masc. . חנה
חֲנִיתוֹתֵיהֶם (ן׳) id. pl., suff. 3 pers. pl. masc. חנה
חַנֹּתִי (ן׳) Kal pret. 1 pers. sing. . חנה
חֲנִיתְךָ noun fem. sing., suff. 2 pers. sing. masc. [for חֲנִיתְךָ from חֲנִית dec. 1 a חנה
חֲנִיתֹתֵיהֶם (ן׳) id. pl., suff. 3 pers. pl. masc.; ן before (–͏ֵ) חנה

[חָנַךְ] fut. יַחְנְכוּ (§ 13. rem. 5).—I. *to instruct, initiate,* Pr. 22. 6.—II. *to consecrate, dedicate,* as a house, temple.

חֲנוֹךְ (*initiated*) pr. name—I. of a son of Cain; also of a city named after him, Ge. 4. 17, 18.—II. of the father of Methuselah, Ge. 5. 18—24.—III. of a son of Reuben. Patronym. חֲנֹכִי.—IV. Ge. 25. 4.

חָנִיךְ masc. dec. 3 a, *trained,* Ge. 14. 14.

חֲנֻכָּה fem. dec. 10, *consecration, dedication.*

חֲנֻכָּא Chald. fem. dec. 8 a, id.

חֵךְ masc. dec. 8 b (for חֵנֶךְ § 37. No. 3, Syr.

a Lc. 27. 27.   d Ge. 21. 14.   g Da. 9. 16.   k 2 Sa. 12. 23.   n Is. 30. 19.   r Ps. 77. 10.   t Ca. 2. 13.   x Je. 16. 13.   b Hab. 3. 11.
b Lc. 5. 24.   e Ps. 76. 11.   h Job 6. 4.   l Nu. 1. 52.   o Ju. 21. 22.   s Ju. 19. 9.   u Ge. 14. 14.   y Is. 2. 4.   c Mi. 4. 3.
c Est. 7. 10.   f Est. 1. 12.   Pr. 2. 22.   m Ge. 39. 21.   p Je. 3. 1.   q Job 19. 17.

חֵ֫נֶךְ (חִנְכָּא).—I. *palate, as the seat of taste.*—II. metaph. Pr. 8. 7, as the *seat of perception.*

חַכָּה fem. *hook, angle.*

חֲנֹךְ‬ ‬חַ֫נֹךְ‬ } Kal imp. sing. masc.; also pr. name; וַ id.

חֹנֵךְ Kal part. act. masc. sing. [חֹנֶה], suff. 2 pers. sing. masc. (§ 2 rem. 2) dec. 9a .

חֲנֻכָּה noun fem. sing. dec. 10.

חֲנָכוֹ‬ Kal pret. 3 pers. sing. m., suff. 3 pers. sing. m.

חֲנֻכַּת noun fem. sing., constr. of חֲנֻכָּה dec. 10; Chald. (Ezr. 6. 16) dec. 8a .

חִנָּם adv.; from חֵן with the term. ◌ָם‬.

חֲנַמְאֵל pr. name masc. Je. 32. 7, 9.

[חֲנָמָל] *host*, Ps. 78. 47. Gesenius conjectures, *ants*; Prof. Lee, *a kind of locust.*

חָנַן fut. יָחֹן, יְחַן (§ 18. rem. 13).—I. *to be gracious, merciful, compassionate* to any one, const. with an acc.—II. *to give graciously, to bestow in mercy and kindness.* Niph. נֵחַן (§ 18. rem. 8 & 14) *to be pitiable,* Je. 22. 23. Pi. *to make gracious, pleasant,* Pr. 26. 25. Po. i. q. Kal No. 1. Hoph. *to be favoured, to find favour.* Hithp. *to implore, supplicate favour, mercy,* const. with לִפְנֵי, אֶל, לְ.

חֲנַן Chald. *to show favour, mercy,* Da. 4. 24. Hithpa. *to implore favour,* Da. 6. 12.

חָנָן (*merciful*) pr. name masc. of several persons, comp. בֵּית חָ׳.

חָנוּן (*favoured*) pr. name—I. of a king of the Ammonites.—II. Ne. 3. 30.—III. Ne. 3. 13.

חַנּוּן adj. masc. *gracious, merciful, compassionate.*

חֲנִינָה fem. *grace, favour,* Je. 16. 13.

חֲנַנְאֵל (which *God has graciously given*) pr. name of a tower in Jerusalem.

חֲנָנִי (*gracious*; or for חֲנַנְיָה q. v.) pr. name masc. of several persons, especially—I. of a prophet, the father of Jehu.—II. of a brother of Nehemiah.

חֲנַנְיָה (whom *the Lord has graciously given*) pr. name—I. of a false prophet, comp. Je. 28. 1.—II. of a companion of Daniel, Da. 1. 6, 7, &c.

חֲנַנְיָהוּ (id.) pr. name masc.—I. 2 Ch. 26. 11.—II. 1 Ch. 25. 23.—III. Je. 36. 12.

חֵן masc. dec. 8b.—I. *grace, favour;* נָשָׂא, מָצָא חֵן בְּעֵינֵי פ׳ *to find, obtain favour in the eyes of* any one i. e. with him; נָתַן אֶת־חֵן בְּ׳ בְּעֵינֵי פ׳ *to procure one the favour of another,* Ex. 3. 21; רוּחַ חֵן *the spirit of grace,* i. e. the spirit of God predis-

posing the heart of man to seek reconciliation with God, Zec. 12. 10.—II. *grace, elegance, beauty.*—III. pr. name masc. Zec. 6. 14.

חִין masc. (for חֵן, like אִישׁ from אֱנָשׁ) *grace, beauty,* Job 41. 4. Others compare it with an Arab. root חִין. Prof. Lee, *destruction;* Schultens, *fitness.*

חֲנָדָד (for חֵן הָדָד *favour of Hadad,* comp. הֲדָד) pr. name of a man.

חֲנִיאֵל (*grace of God*) pr. name masc.—I. Nu. 34. 23.—II. 1 Ch. 7. 39.

חִנָּם adv.—I. *gratis, freely, for nothing.*—II. *in vain.*—III. *for nothing, undeservedly.*

חַנָּה fem. dec. 10.—I. *grace, favour,* Ps. 77. 10.—II. *supplication, prayer for favour,* Job 9. 17.—III. pr. name of the mother of Samuel, comp. 1 Sa. 1. 2, &c.

חַנָּתֹן (*favoured place*) pr. name of a place in Zebulun, Jos. 19. 14.

תְּחִנָּה fem. dec. 10.—I. *favour, mercy.*—II. *supplication, prayer for favour, mercy.*—III. pr. name masc. 1 Ch. 4. 12.

תַּחֲנוּן masc. dec. 1b, pl. ◌ִים, ◌וֹת, *supplication, prayer for mercy.*

חָנָן‬ ‬חָנָן pr. name m. (and in compos. with בֵּית q. v.)

חֹנֵן Kal part. act. sing. masc.

חֲנַנְאֵל pr. name masc.

חָנְנוּ Kal pret. 3 pers. pl. [for חָנְנוּ § 8. rem. 7, & § 18. rem. 13]

חָנֻּנוּ id. imp. s. m. [חֹן], suff. 1 pers. pl. (§ 18. r. 4)

חָנָן pr. name masc.

חַנַּנִי Kal pret. 3 pers. sing. m. [חֵן], suff. 1 pers. sing.

חָנֵּנִי‬ id. imp. s. m. [חֹן], suff. 1 p. s. (§ 18. rem. 4)

חָנֻּנִי id. imp. pl. m., suff. 1 pers. sing. (§ 18. rem. 4)

חֲנַנְיָה‬ ‬חֲנַנְיָהוּ } pr. name masc.; וַ before (◌ַ)

חֲנֵּנִי uncontracted (like קָטְלֵנִי) for חָנֵּנִי q. v.

חָנֵס pr. name of a city in Egypt, Is. 30. 4.

[חָנַף] fut. יֶחֱנַף.—I. *to be* or *become profaned, polluted,* or *defiled.*—II. *to be profane, ungodly,* Je. 23. 11.—III. trans. *to profane, pollute,* Je. 3. 9. Hiph. *to profane, pollute; to seduce to apostacy,* Da. 11. 32.

חָנֵף masc. dec. 5c, *profane, ungodly.*

Note.—The sense of *hypocrite* ascribed to this word (and that of *hypocrisy* in the following), is not recognised by modern lexicographers, though it is so rendered by Aqu. and Symm., and this word is

so used by the Rabbis. Syr. חַנְפָא *heathen, ungodly man,* אֲחַנֵּף *to apostatize from the true religion.*

חֹנֶף masc. *profaneness, wickedness,* Is. 32.6; Eng. Vers. *hypocrisy.*

חֲנֻפָּה fem. id. Je. 23.15.

חָנֵף	noun masc. sing. dec. 5c	חנף
חֲנֵף	noun masc. sing.	חנף
חָנְפָה	Kal pret. 3 pers. sing. fem.	חנף
חַנְפָה	noun fem. sing.	חנף
חָנְפוּ	Kal pret. 3 pers. pl. [for חָנְפוּ § 8. rem. 7]	חנף
וְחַנְפֵי	noun masc. pl. constr. from חָנֵף dec. 5c	חנף
חֲנֵפִים	id. pl., absolute state	חנף

חָנַק Niph. *to strangle oneself,* 2 Sa. 17.23. Pi. *to strangle,* Na. 2.13.

מַחֲנָק masc. dec. 2b, *strangling, suffocation, death,* Job 7.15.

וַחֲנֹתִי	Kal pret. 1 pers. sing.; acc. shifted by conv. וַ (§ 8. rem. 7)	חנה
חֲנֹתֵנוּ	Kal inf. (חֲנוֹת) suff. 1 pers. pl. dec. 1a	חנה

חָסַד Kal not used; in the derivatives it has the signification of *kindness and benignity.* Pi. as in the Aram. *to reproach, disgrace,* Pr. 25.10. Hithp. *to show oneself kind, merciful.*

חָסִיד masc. dec. 3a.—I. *kind, benevolent, gracious, merciful.*—II. *pious, godly, holy.*

חֲסִידָה fem. *stork,* prop. *the pious,* from its affection towards its young.

חֶסֶד masc. with suff. חַסְדִּי dec. 6a.—I. *kindness, mercy;* עַל, לְ, עִם with אֶת *to show kindness to any one;* נָטָה חֶסֶד לְ *to procure kindness, favour for any one.*—II. *grace, beauty,* Is. 40.6.—III. *reproach, disgrace,* comp. Pi.—IV. pr. name masc. 1 Ki. 4.10.

חֲסַדְיָה (whom *the Lord loves*) pr. name masc. 1 Ch. 3.20.

חֶסֶד / חָ֫סֶד	noun masc. sing. (suff. חַסְדִּי) d. 6a; for וְ see lett. ו	חסד
חַסְדּוֹ	id. pl., suff. (K. דָיו § 4. rem. 1) 3 pers. sing. masc.	חסד
חַסְדּוֹ	id. sing., suff. 3 pers. sing. masc.	חסד
חַסְדּוֹ	id. sing., suff., Kh. דוֹ 3 pers.sing. masc., K. דָי' 1 pers. sing.	חסד
חֲסָדַי	id. pl., suff. 1 pers. sing.	חסד
חַסְדֵּי	id. pl., constr. state	חסד
חַסְדִּי	id. sing., suff. 1 pers. sing.	חסד

חֲסַדְיָה	pr. name masc.; וְ bef. (-:)	חסד
חֲסָדָיו	noun masc. pl., suff. 3 pers. sing. masc. from חֶסֶד dec. 6a; וְ bef. (-:)	חסד
חֲסָדֶיךָ / חַסְדֶּךָ	id. pl., suff. 2 pers. sing. masc. (§ 4. rem. 1); וְ id.	חסד
חַסְדְּךָ / חַסְדֶּךָ	id. sing., suff. 2 pers. sing. masc.	חסד
חַסְדֵּךְ	id. sing., suff. 2 pers. sing. fem.	חסד
חַסְדְּכֶם	id. sing., suff. 2 pers. pl. masc.	חסד
חַסְדָּם	id. sing., suff. 3 pers. pl. masc.	חסד

[חָסָה] fut. יֶחֱסֶה, יַחְסֶה (§ 13. rem. 5) prop. *to flee* (cogn. חוּשׁ) *for shelter, refuge;* hence, *to trust, confide in,* const. with בְּ.

חָסוּת fem. *trust, confidence,* Is. 30.3.

חֹסֶה (*confiding, confident*) pr. name of a man.

אַחְסְבִּי (prob. for אֶחֱסֶה בְּיָהּ *I will trust in the Lord*) pr. name masc. 2 Sa. 23.34.

מַחְסֶה, מַחֲסֶה masc. dec. 9a, *shelter, refuge.*

חָסָה	Kal pret. 3 pers. sing. masc.; acc. Milêl before monos.	חסה
חָסָה	Kal pret. 3 pers. sing. fem.	חוס
חֹסָה	pr. name masc.	חסה
חֹסֶה	Kal part. act. masc. dec. 9a	חסה
חָסוּ	id et. 3 pers. pl.	חסה
חֲסוּ	id. imp. pl. masc.	חסה
חָסוֹר	Kal inf. absolute	חסר
חֹסִי	Kal part. act. masc. pl. c. from חֹסֶה dec. 9a; acc. Milêl before monos.	חסה
חָסִיד	adj. masc. sing. dec. 3a	חסד
חֲסִידָה	noun fem. sing., prop. fem. of חָסִיד	חסד
חֲסִידָו	Khethib for חֲסִידָיו (§ 4. rem. 1)	חסד
חֲסִידַי	noun masc. pl., suff. 1 pers. sing. [for דַי'] from חָסִיד dec. 3a	חסד
חֲסִידֶיהָ	id., suff. 3 pers. sing. fem.; וְ bef. (-:)	חסד
חֲסִידָיו	id., suff. 3 pers. sing. masc.	חסד
חֲסִידֶיךָ	id., suff. 2 pers. sing. masc.; וְ before (-:)	חסד
חֲסִידֶיךָ	Kh. id. (דָיךָ), K. דְךָ sing., suff. 2 pers. sing. masc.	חסד
חֲסִידִים	id. pl., absolute state	חסד
חֲסִידְךָ	id. sing., suff. 2 pers. sing. m. [for חֲסִידְךָ]	חסד
חָסְיָה	Kal pret. 3 pers. sing. fem. (§ 24. rem. 5)	חסה
חָסְיוּ	id. pret. 3 pers. pl. (v. id.)	חסה
חָסִיל	noun masc. sing.	חסל
חָסִין	adj. masc. sing.	חסן
חַסִּיר	Ch. adj. masc. sing.	חסר
חָסִיתִי	Kal pret. 1 pers. sing.	חסה

a Is. 32.6.   e Job 36.13.   i Pr. 21.21.   m Is. 63.7.   r Jon. 2.9.   º Ps. 37.40.   ᵇ Na. 1.7.   f Ps. 16.10.   l 1 Ki. 8.37.
b Is. 24.5.   f Is. 33.14.   k Ps. 66.20.   n Ps. 25.6.   s Zep. 3.12.   c Ps. 145.17.   g De. 33.8.   ² Ch. 6.28.
c Je. 23.15.   g Ex. 33.19.   l Ps. 59.11.   o Ps. 119.41.   t Ju. 9.15.   d Ps. 50.5.   h Ps. 57.2.   ᵐ Ps. 89.9.
d Je. 23.1.   h Nu. 10.31.   ᵐ Ne. 13.14.   q Ho. 6.4.   u Pr. 14.32.   Ge. 8.5.   Ps. 132.16.   De. 32.37.   Da. 5.27.

[חָסַל] to crop off, to devour, De. 28. 38.

חָסִיל masc. the name of a species of locust.

[חָסַם] fut. יַחְסֹם (§ 13. rem. 5) to stop, Eze. 39. 11; to stop, bind up, muzzle, De. 25. 4.

מַחְסוֹם masc. a muzzle, Ps. 39. 2.

חסם . . . Kal part. act. fem. sing.   חֹסֶמֶת‸

חָסַן Kal not used; Syr. & Chald. to be strong. Niph. to be laid up, hoarded, Is. 23. 18.

חֲסַן Ch. Aph. or Hiph. (§ 47. rem. 9) to possess, have in possession, Da. 7. 18, 22.

חֲסַן Ch. masc. dec. 3b, might, power.

חַסִּן adj. masc. strong, powerful.

חֹסֶן masc. riches, wealth, abundance.

חֲסִין adj. masc. strong, mighty, Ps. 89. 9.

חסן . . . adj. masc. sing. { חָסֹן‸

חסן . . noun masc. sing. . { חֹסֶן

חסן   Ch. noun masc. sing., emph. of [חֲסַן] d. 3b   חָסְנָא‸

חסן   Ch. id. with suff. 1 pers. sing. . חָסְנִי‸

חָסַף Kal not used; prob. i. q. חָשַׂף to peel, scale; hence quadril. part. pass. מְחֻסְפָּס (§ 6. No. 7) scaled off, having the form of scales, Ex. 16. 14.

חֲסַף Ch. masc. dec. 3a, sherds, earthen ware, Da. 2. 33, 34, 35, 41, 42, 43, 45.

חֶסֶף } Ch. noun masc. sing. dec. 3a . חסף
חֲסַף }

חַסְפָּא‸   id., emph. state . . חסף

[חָסַר] fut. יַחְסַר, יַחְסְרוּ (§ 13. rem. 5, 6).—I. to want, lack, be without any thing.—II. to be in want, suffer need.—III. to fail, be diminished.—IV. to fail, be wanting. Pi. to cause to want, lack, with מִן of the thing. Hiph.—I. to cause to want, cause to fail, Is. 32. 6.—II. intrans. to want, lack, Ex. 16. 18.

חָסֵר adj. masc. dec. 5c.—I. wanting, lacking, destitute, with מִן; חֲסַר־לֵב lacking understanding. —II. subst. want, lack, Pr. 10. 21.

חֶסֶר masc. want, poverty.

חֹסֶר masc. id. חֹסֶר כֹּל want of every thing; חֹסֶר לָחֶם want of bread.

חַסִּיר Ch. wanting, deficient, Da. 5. 27.

חַסְרָה pr. name masc. 2 Ch. 34. 22, for which חַרְחַס in 2 Ki. 22. 14.

חֶסְרוֹן masc. want, poverty, Ec. 1. 15.

מַחְסוֹר, מַחְסֹר masc. dec. 1b, want, need, poverty, אִישׁ מ׳ poor man.

חסר . . adj. masc. sing. dec. 5c .   חָסֵר

חסר   id., constr. state; וֹ bef. (ד)   חֲסַר וְ‸

חסר . . noun masc. sing. .   חֶסְרִי‸

חסר   noun masc. sing. . חֹסְרִי‸ וְ

חסר . . pr. name masc.   חַסְרָה

חסר   Kal pret. 3 pers. pl. [for חָסְרוּ § 8. rem. 7]   חָסֵרוּ‸

חסר   noun masc. sing.   חֶסְרוֹן‸ וְ

חסר . . Kal pret. 1 pers. sing.   חָסַרְנוּ‸

חסר   id. pret. 2 pers. sing. masc.   חָסַרְתָּ‸

חום   Kal pret. 2 pers. sing. masc.   חַסְתָּ‸

חפף . . adj. masc. sing.   חַף‸

חָפָא Kal not used; i. q. חָפָה. Pi. to act secretly, clandestinely, 2 Ki. 17. 9.

[חָפָה] to cover, veil. Pi. to overlay, as with gold, silver. Pu. to be covered, protected, Is. 4. 5, with עַל. Niph. נֶחְפָּה (§ 13. rem. 7) to be overlaid, Ps. 68. 14.

חפה . . Piel pret. 3 pers. sing. masc.   חִפָּה‸

חפה . . noun fem. sing. dec. 10.   חֻפָּה‸

חפה . Kal pret. 3 pers. pl.   חָפוּ וְ‸

חפה   id. part. pass. sing. masc. dec. 3a   חָפוּי‸

חפה   id., constr. state; וֹ bef. (ָ)   חֲפוּי‸ וְ

[חָפַז] fut. יַחְפֹּז (§ 13. rem. 5).—I. to start up (cogn. קָפַץ) especially in haste and alarm.—II. to be alarmed, perplexed. Niph. נֶחְפַּז (§ 13. rem. 7) to take to flight, to flee in alarm.

חִפָּזוֹן masc. haste, hurry.

חָפִים } pr. name masc. . . חפף
חֻפָּם }

[חָפַן] m. only dual חָפְנַיִם (d. 8c) the hollow hands, the fists.

חָפְנִי (fighter, comp. Lat. pugnus & pugnator) pr. name of one of the sons of Eli.

חפן . . pr. name masc.   חָפְנִי

חפן   noun masc. du. constr. from [חֹפֶן] dec. 6c   חָפְנֵי‸

חפן   id. du., suff. 3 pers. sing. masc.   חָפְנָיו‸

חפן   id. du., suff. 2 pers. sing. masc.   חָפְנֶיךָ‸

חפן   id. du., suff. 2 pers. pl. masc.   חָפְנֵיכֶם‸

חפן   id. du., absolute state . חָפְנַיִם‸

[חָפַף] I. i. q. חָפָה to cover, protect, De. 33. 12, with עַל. —II. Arab. to scrape, wipe, wash off, comp. deriv חֹף, חַף.

a Eze. 39. 11.   d Da. 4. 27.   g Da. 2. 35, 43, 45.   k Am. 4. 6.   n Je. 44. 18.   q Job 33. 9.   t Je. 14. 3.   x Eze. 10. 7.   bb Ex. 9. 8.
b Am. 2. 9.   e Da. 2. 33.   h Da. 2. 34.   l Ne. 9. 21.   o De. 2. 7.   r 2 Ch. 3. 5, 9.   u 2 Sa. 15. 30.   y Le. 16. 12.   cc Ec. 4. 6.
c Da. 2. 37.   f Da. 2. 41, 42   i Pr. 28. 22.   m Ec. 1. 15.   p Jon. 4. 10.   s Is. 4. 5.   z Est. 6. 12.   aa Eze. 10. 2.

חַף adj. masc. *clean, pure, faultless*, Job 33. 9.

חוֹף masc. *coast, shore* of the sea.

חֻפָּה fem. dec. 10.—I. *a covering, defence*, Is. 4. 5; but see Pu. of חָפָה.—II. *bridal chamber.*—III. pr. name masc. 1 Ch. 24. 13.

חֻפִּים (*coverings*) pr. name masc.—I. Ge. 46. 21.—II. 1 Ch. 7. 12, 15.

חֹפֵף Kal part. act. sing. masc.   .   חפף

חָפֵץ fut. יַחְפֹּץ, יֶחְפַּץ (§ 13. rem. 4, 5).—I. *to bend, incline*, Job 40. 17.—II. intrans. *to incline, to be favourably disposed towards* any one, or any thing, *to delight in, be pleased with*, const. with בְּ, also acc.; followed by an inf. *to will, to desire, to be pleased* to do anything.

חָפֵץ masc. dec. 5c (pl. c. חֶפְצֵי § 34. rem. 2) adj. *willing, desiring, delighting*; אִם חָפֵץ אַתָּה *if thou art willing*; חָפֵץ רָשַׁע *delighting in wickedness*; נֶפֶשׁ חֲפֵצָה *a willing mind.*

חֵפֶץ masc. dec. 6, with suff. חֶפְצִי (§ 37. r. 6).—I. *delight, pleasure.*—II. *wish, will*, Job 31. 16.—III. *preciousness*; אַבְנֵי חֵפֶץ *precious stones*, and simply חֲפָצִים *precious things.*—IV. *business, concern, affair*

חֶפְצִי־בָהּ (*my delight is in her*) pr. name—I. of the mother of king Manasseh, 2 Ki. 21. 1.—II. a symbolic name of Zion, Is. 62. 4.

חָפֵץ Kal pret. 3 pers. s. m.; or adj. masc. d. 5c   חפץ
חֵפֶץ וְ noun masc. sing. dec. 6 (§ 35. rem. 6)   חפץ
חָפְצָה Kal pret. 3 pers. s. f. [for חָפְצָה § 8. r. 7]   חפץ
חֲפֵצָה adj. fem. sing. from חָפֵץ masc.   .   חפץ
חֶפְצָהּ noun masc. sing., suff. 3 pers. sing. fem. from חֵפֶץ dec. 6 (§ 35. rem. 6)   .   חפץ
חֶפְצוֹ id., suff. 3 pers. sing. masc.   .   חפץ
חֶפְצֵי adj. masc. pl. c. from חָפֵץ d. 5c (§ 34. r. 2).   חפץ
חֶפְצִי noun masc. sing., suff. 1 pers. sing. from חֵפֶץ dec. 6 (§ 35. rem. 6)   .   חפץ
חֶפְצֵיהֶם id. pl., suff. 3 pers. pl. masc.   חפץ
חֲפָצֶיךָ id. pl. suff. 2 pers. sing. masc.   חפץ
חֲפָצִים id. pl., absolute state   .   חפץ
חֲפֵצִים adj. m., pl. of חָפֵץ dec. 5c   חפץ
חֶפְצֵךְ noun masc. pl., suff. 2 pers. sing. masc. [for חֲפָצֶיךְ § 4. r. 1] fr. חֵפֶץ d. 6 (§ 35. r. 6)   חפץ
חֶפְצֵךְ id. sing., suff. 2 pers. sing. fem.   .   חפץ
חֶפְצָם id. sing., suff. 3 pers. pl. masc.   .   חפץ
חָפַצְנוּ Kal pret. 1 pers. s. [for חָפַצְנוּ § 8. rem. 7]   חפץ
חָפַצְתָּ id. pret. 2 pers. sing. masc.   .   חפץ

חָפַצְתִּי חָפָצְתִּי } Kal pret. 1 pers. sing. (§ 8. rem. 7) . חפץ
חֲפַצְתֶּם id. pret. 2 pers. pl. masc. . . חפץ

חָפַר fut. יַחְפֹּר (§ 13. rem. 5).—I. *to dig*, as a pit, well.—II. *to search out, explore, investigate, espy.*

חֵפֶר (*pit, well*) pr. name—I. of a city of Canaan.—II. of several men; (a) Nu. 26. 32; Jos. 17. 2, from which patronym. חֶפְרִי Nu. 26. 32; (b) 1 Ch. 11. 36; (c) 1 Ch. 4. 6.

חֲפָרַיִם (*two wells*) pr. name of a town in the tribe of Issachar, Jos 19. 19.

חֲפֹר פֵּרוֹת (with pref. בְּ, לַחְפֹּר פ', comp. § 13. rem. 1, 2, 5) Is. 2. 20, *a mole* or *rat*; lit. *digger of holes*, חֲפֹר constr. of חָפֹר *digger*, פֵּרוֹת for פֵּארוֹת (comp. בּוֹר for בָּאוֹר) *holes*, from פאר Arab. *to dig.* Modern lexicographers, however, agree in reading it as one word (according to three codices by Dr. Kennicott) חֲפַרְפָּרוֹת pl. *moles*, as a form derived from the conj. Pealal (§ 6. No. 3).

[חָפֵר] fut. יֶחְפָּר (§ 13. rem. 5) *to blush, be ashamed, confounded.* Hiph.—I. *to put to shame, cause disgrace.*—II. intrans. *to be ashamed.*

חֵפֶר pr. name of a man and a place   .   חפר
חֹפֵר Kal part. act. sing. masc.   .   .   חפר
חָפְרָה חָפֵרָה וְ } id. pret. 3 pers. sing. fem. (§ 8. rem. 7) חפר
חָפְרוּ חָפֵרוּ וְ } id. pret. 3 pers. pl. (§ 8. rem.7) חפר
חֲפָרוּהָ id. id., suff. 3 pers. sing. fr. חפר
חָפְרַע pr. name of a king of Egypt, Pharaoh Hophra, Je. 44. 30.
חָפַרְתָּ וְ } id. pret. 2 pers. sing. masc. (§ 8. r. 5) } חפר
חָפַרְתָּה acc. shifted by conv. וְ (§ 8. r. 7) }
חָפַרְתִּי id. pret. 1 pers. sing.   .   .   חפר

[חָפַשׂ] fut. יַחְפֹּשׂ (§ 13. rem. 5) *to search out, explore, investigate.* Niph. נֶחְפַּשׂ (§ 13. rem. 7) *to be sought out*, Ob. 6. Pi. *to search, search out, search through.* Pu. *to be sought, sought out.* Hithp. *to disguise oneself.*

חֵפֶשׂ masc. *device, purpose*, Ps. 64. 7.

חָפַשׁ Kal not used; Arab. *to stretch out, to prostrate*, intrans. *to lie prostrate.* In the Heb. only Pu. *to be set free, to be freed*, Le. 19. 20.

a De. 33. 12.   d 1 Ch. 28. 9.   g Pr. 8. 11.   k Ps. 107. 30.   o Job 39. 29.   r Je. 15. 9.   t Is. 24. 23.   v Nu. 21. 18.   x De. 28. 14.
b Is. 53. 10.   e Ps. 111. 2.   h Mal. 3. 1.   l Job 21. 14.   p Ee. 10. 8.   s Je. 50. 12.   u Ge. 26. 33.   w Job 11. 18.   y Ge. 21. 30.
c Is. 66. 3.   f Pr. 3. 15.   i 1 Ki. 5. 22, etc.   m Je. 42. 3.   n Is. 58. 13.

חֵפֶשׁ masc. *a spreading*, Eze. 27. 20. Here we may refer, with Fürst, Ps. 88. 6, בַּמֵּתִים חָפְשִׁי *my couch, bed, is among the dead*; but see חָפְשִׁי.

חֻפְשָׁה fem. *freedom*, Le. 19. 20.

חָפְשִׁי adj. masc. (pl. חָפְשִׁים) *free*, from servitude, taxes; Ps. 88. 6, *free among the dead*, i. e. from the evils of life; but according to others, *prostrate*, i. e. weak, *among the dead*, comp. also חֵפֶשׁ.

חָפְשׁוּת, חָפְשִׁית fem. *freedom*, from business, בֵּית חָ׳ *house of retirement*; others, *sick-house*, comp. the Root.

חֹפֶשׁ	noun masc. sing.	חפש
חֹפֵשׂ	Kal part. act. sing. masc.	חפש
חֵפֶשׁ	noun masc. sing.	חפש
חֻפָּשָׁה	Pual pret. 3 pers. sing. fem. [for חֻפְּשָׁה comp. § 8. rem. 7]	חפש
חֻפְשָׁה	noun fem. sing.	חפש
חַפְּשׂוּ	Piel imp. pl. masc.	חפש
חָפְשׂוּ	וַ id. pret. 3 pers. pl.	חפש
חָפְשִׁי	adj. masc. sing.; or perh. (Ps. 88. 6) subst. masc. with suff. 1 pers. s. fr. חֹפֶשׁ d. 6c	חפש
חָפְשִׁים	id. pl. absolute state	חפש
חִפַּשְׂתִּי	וַ Piel pret. 1 pers. sing.; acc. shifted by conv. וַ (comp. § 8. rem. 7)	חפש
חֵץ	וַ noun masc. sing. dec. 8b	חצץ

חָצַב fut. יַחְצֹב, inf. חֲצֹב (from חָצַב middle A § 8. rem. 13).—I. *to cut, hew, hew out*, as stone, wood; part. חֹצֵב *a hewer*.—II. trop. *to kill, destroy*, Ho. 6. 5. Niph. *to be engraven*, Job 19. 24. Pu. *to be hewn out*, Is. 51. 1. Hiph. *to cut in pieces*, Is. 51. 9. מַחְצֵב masc. *a hewing* of stone, אַבְנֵי מַ׳ *hewn stones*.

חֹצֵב	id. part. act. sing. masc. dec. 7b	חצב
חָצְבָה	Kal pret. 3 pers. sing. fem.	חצב
חֹצְבִי	id. part. act. sing. masc. with parag. י (§ 8. rem. 19) dec. 7b	חצב
חֹצְבִים	id. pl., absolute state	חצב
חָצַבְתָּ	id. pret. 2 pers. sing. masc.	חצב
חָצַבְתִּי	id. pret. 1 pers. sing.	חצב
חֻצַּבְתֶּם	Pual pret. 2 pers. pl. masc.	חצב

חָצָה fut. יֶחֱצֶה, *to divide*, into two, also **several** parts; לֹא־יֶחֱצוּ יְמֵיהֶם *they shall not halve their days*, i. e. shall not live half their life. Niph. *to be divided*.

חֲצוֹת fem. only constr. חֲצוֹת, *middle, midst*.

חֵצִי masc. dec. 6, with dist. acc. חֵצִי, with suff. חֶצְיוֹ (§ 35. rem. 14).—I. *half, part, portion*.—II. *middle, midst*, Ju. 16. 3.—III. *an arrow*.

חֲצִי הַמְּנֻחוֹת (*midst of resting places*) pr. name masc. 1 Ch. 2. 52; patronym. הַמְּנַחְתִּי ver. 54.

יַחְצְאֵל, יַחְצִיאֵל (whom God *assigns a portion*) pr. name masc. Ge. 46. 24; 1 Ch. 7. 13. Gent. noun יַחְצְאֵלִי Nu. 46. 26.

מֶחֱצָה fem. dec. 10, *a half*, Nu. 31. 36, 43.

מַחֲצִית fem. dec. 1b—I. *a half*.—II. *the middle*, Ne. 8. 3.

חֻצָּה	noun masc. sing. (חוּץ) with parag. ה d. 1a	חוץ
חָצוּ	וָ Kal pret. 3 pers. pl.	חצה
חִצּוֹ	noun masc. pl. suff. (K. חָצָיו § 4. rem. 1) 3 pers. sing. masc. fr. חֵץ dec. 8b	חצץ
חִצּוֹ	id. sing., suff. 3 pers. sing. masc.	חצץ
חֲצוּבִים	Kal part. pass. masc., pl. of (חָצוּב) dec. 3a	חצב
חַצְצֹרֹת	noun fem., pl. of חֲצֹצְרָה dec. 10.	חצר
חָצוֹר	׳ pr. n. of a place, also in compos. חָ׳ חֲדַתָּה	חצה
חֲצוֹת	וַ noun fem. sing., constr. of [חָצוֹת] d. 3a	חצה
חִצּוֹת	׳ וַ noun m. with pl. f. term. fr. חוּץ d. 1a	חוץ
חֲצִי	וַ noun masc. sing., dec. 6i (suff. חֶצְיוֹ § 35. r. 14), & pr. name in compos. חֲצִי הַמְּנֻחוֹת	חצה
חֵצִי	וַ id. with dist. acc. (§ 35. r. 14); וַ I see וַ	חצה
חִצַּי	noun masc. pl., suff. 1 pers. sing. fr. חֵץ d. 8b	חצץ
חִצֵּי	id. pl., constr. state	חצץ
חֶצְיִי	id. sing., suff. 1 pers. sing.	חצה
חֶצְיָהּ	noun masc. sing., suff. 3 pers. sing. fem. fr. חֲצִי dec. 6i (§ 35. rem. 14)	חצה
חֶצְיוֹ	id. with suff. 3 pers. sing. masc.	חצה
חִצָּיו	noun masc. pl., suff. 3 pers. sing. masc. from חֵץ dec. 8b	חצץ
חֲצָיִךְ	id. pl., suff. 2 pers. sing. masc.	חצץ
חֶצְיָם	וַ noun masc. sing., suff. 3 pers. pl. masc. fr. חֲצִי dec. 6i (§ 35. rem. 14)	חצה
חִצִּים	וַ noun masc., pl. of חֵץ dec. 8b	חצץ
חֲצֵינוּ	noun masc. sing., suff. 1 pers. p. יַ. חֲצִי dec. 6i (§ 35. rem. 14)	חצה
חָצִיר	noun masc. sing. dec. 3a	חצר
חֲצִיר	id., constr. state	חצר
חָצִיתָ	וַ Kal pret. 2 pers. sing. masc.	חצה
חֶצְם	noun masc. sing., suff. 3 pers. pl. masc. from חֵץ dec. 8b	חצץ

[חֹצֶן, חֵצֶן] masc. dec. 6b&c, *the bosom, folds of a garment covering the breast*.

a Ps. 64 7.   f Le. 19. 20.   i Is. 5. 2.   n Is. 51. 1.   r Ps. 56. 8.   u Ps. 119. 62.   x De. 32. 23, 42.   c Zec. 14. 4.   f Zec. 14. 8.
b Pr. 20. 27.   g 2 Ki. 10. 23.   k Pr. 9. 1.   o Nu. 31. 42.   s Zec. 9. 14.   v Job 34. 20.   y Job 34. 6.   d Nu. 24. 5.   g 2 Sa. 18. 3.
c Ese. 27. 20.   h 1 Ki. 20. 6.   l Is. 22. 16.   p Is. 53. 7.   t Nu. 10. 2.   w 1 Ki. 20. 34.   z Ne. 3. 38.   e Eze. 39. 3.   h Nu. 31. 27
d Le. 19. 20.   i 1 Sa. 25. 23.   m Ho. 6. 5.   q Ex. 21. 35.

חִצְנֵי 1 noun masc. sing., suff. 3 pers. sing. masc. fr. [חֵצֶן] dec. 6 b . . . . חצן

חִצְנִי noun masc. sing., suff. 1 pers. sing. fr. חֹצֶן dec. 6 c . . . . חצן

חֲצַף Ch. Aph. to urge, hasten.

[חָצַץ] i. q. חָצָה to divide, Pr. 30. 27, the locusts have no king, וַיֵּצֵא חֹצֵץ כֻּלּוֹ yet they all go forth dividing into many parts, sc. the prey for themselves. Others, חֹצֵץ (intrans.) divided, i. e. in divisions; Prof. Lee (coll. with the Arab.), rushing on, i. e. making the attack as an army. Pi. part. מְחַצְצִים Ju. 5. 11, those who divide, sc. the booty, spoil. Others, archers, from חֵץ. Pu. to be cut off in the midst, Job 21. 21.

חָצָץ masc. dec. 4 c.—I. small stones, gravel-stones.—II. arrow, trop. for lightning, Ps. 77. 18.

חֵץ masc. d. 8 b.—I. arrow; בַּעֲלֵי חִצִּים archers. —II. trop. lightning.—III. perhaps the iron point of a spear, 1 Sa. 17. 7, Kheth.

חַצְצֹן תָּמָר, חַצֲצֹן תָּמָר (pruning of the palm) pr. name of a place in the desert of Judah, renowned for its palm-trees, Ge. 14. 7; 2 Ch. 20. 2.

חָצָץ noun masc. sing. dec. 4 c . . . חצץ

חֹצֵץ Kal part. act. sing. masc. . . . חצץ

חֻצָּצוּ Pual pret. 3 pers. pl. [for חֻצְצוּ comp. § 8. r. 7] חצץ

חִצֶּיךָ noun masc. pl., suff. 2 pers. sing. masc. fr. חֵץ dec. 4 c . . . . חצץ

חֲצֵרָה noun fem. sing. dec. 10. . . . חצר

חַצְרוֹת id. pl.; וְ bef. (־) . . . חצר

חָצַר Root not used; Arab. (a) to enclose; (b) to be green; (c) to be present; conj. X. to call together, convoke.

חָצֵר com. dec. 5 c, pl. ־ים, ־וֹת.—I. enclosure, area, court.—II. village, hamlet.—III. in the following pr. names of towns or villages—חֲצַר־אַדָּר (village of Addar) in the tribe of Judah, Nu. 34. 4; called simply אַדָּר Jos. 15. 3.—חֲצַר גַּדָּה (village of fortune) in the tribe of Judah, Jos. 15. 27.— חֲ׳ סוּסִים, חֲ׳ סוּסָה (village of horses) in the tribe of Simeon, Jos. 19. 5; 1 Ch. 4. 31.— חֲ׳ עֵינוֹן, חֲ׳ עֵינָן (village of fountains) in the north of Palestine.—חֲצַר שׁוּעָל (village of foxes) in the tribe of Simeon.—חָצֵר הַתִּיכוֹן (middle village) on the border of Syria, Eze. 47. 16.—חֲצֵרוֹת a station of the Israelites in the desert.

חָצוֹר (village, town) pr. name—I. of a town in Naphtali.—II. of a town in Benjamin, Ne. 11. 33. —III. of a region in Arabia, Je. 49. 28.

חָצוֹר חֲדַתָּה (new-town) pr. name of a town in the tribe of Judah, Jos. 15. 25.

חָצִיר masc.—I. enclosure, court, Is. 34. 13.—II. grass; leeks, Nu. 11. 5.

חֶצְרוֹן (enclosed, protected) pr. name—I. of a son of Reuben.—II. of a son of Perez.—Patronym. חֶצְרֹנִי Nu. 26. 6.

חֶצְרַי (id.) pr. name masc. 2 Sa. 23. 35, Keth., Keri חֶצְרוֹן, and so in 1 Ch. 11. 37.

חֲצֹצְרָה fem. (pl. חֲצֹצְרֹת, חֲצֹצְרוֹת) (חָצַץ) a trumpet. Hence denom.

חַצֵּר (§ 6. No. 11) to blow the trumpet, only in the part. מְחַצְּרִים Kheth.; but the Keri has it everywhere מַחְצְרִים Hiph. (§ 11. rem. 8), except in 2 Ch. 5. 13, where it is מְחַצְּרִים Piel (§ 10. rem. 7).—Pilel id. 2 Ch. 5. 12, מְחַצְצְרִים Kheth. (§ 6. No. 2); but Keri מַחֲצְרִים Hiph.

חֲצַרְמָוֶת (court of death) pr. name of a district in Arabia, Ge. 10. 26.

חָצֵר וְ׳ noun com. sing. dec. 5 c, also pr. name חצר

חֲצַר וְ׳ id., constr. state, and in compos. with pr. name, חֲ׳ אַדָּר &c. וְ before (־) . . חצר

חָצֹר pr. name of a place . . . . חצר

חָצֵרָה pr. name (חָצֹר) with paragogic ה . חצר

חֶצְרוֹן Kh. חֶצְרוֹן q. v., K. חָצְרוֹן q. v. . חצר

חֶצְרוֹ pr. name masc., see חֶצְרַי under . חצר

חֶצְרוֹן וְ׳ pr. name of a man and a place . חצר

חֲצֵרוֹת noun masc. with pl. fem. term., absolute state from חָצֵר dec. 5 c; also pr. name . חצר

חַצְרוֹת id. pl. fem. construct state . . . חצר

חַצְרוֹתַי וְ׳ id. pl. suff. 1 pers. s. [for ־תַי]; וְ bef. (־) חצר

חֲצֵרַי id. pl. masc., suff. 1 pers. sing. [for ־רַי] חצר

חַצְרֵי id. pl. masc. construct state . . . חצר

חַצְרֶיהָ id. pl. masc., suff. 3 pers. s. fem.; וְ bef. (־) חצר

חַצְרֵיהֶם id. pl. masc., suff. 3 pers. pl. masc. חצר

חַצְרֵיהֶן id. pl. masc., suff. 3 pers. pl. fem. חצר

חֲצֵרֶיךָ id. pl. masc., suff. 2 pers. sing. masc. חצר

חֲצֵרִים id. pl. masc. absolute state . . חצר

חֲצַרְמָוֶת pr. name masc. . . . . חצר

חֶצְרוֹ וְ׳ pr. name masc. . . . . חצר

חֲצֵרֹת וְ׳ pr. name of a place; וְ before (־) חצר

חַצְרֹתָיו noun masc. with pl. fem. term. and suff. 3 pers. sing. masc. from חָצֵר dec. 5 c חצר

חֻק defect. for חוּק (q. v.) . . . . חוק

חֹק וְ׳ noun masc. sing. dec. 8 c (§ 37. rem. 2) חקק
חֻק וְ׳

חָקָה Kal not used; i. q. חָקַק. Pu. part.—I. *engraven, carved*, 1 Ki. 6. 35.—II. *portrayed, painted*, Eze. 8. 10; 23. 14. Hithp. *to draw oneself a mark or furrow*, Job 13. 27.

חָקֵה Kal imp. sing. masc., suff. 3 pers. sing. fem. חקק

חֻקָּה noun fem. sing. dec. 10, from חֹק masc. .

חֻקָּו Khethib. for חֻקָּיו (q. v. § 4. rem. 1) . חקק

חֻקּוֹ noun m. s., suff. 3 pers. s. m. fr. חֹק dec. 8c חקק

חֲקוּפָא (*bent*, coll. with the Arab.) pr. name masc. Ezr. 2. 51; Ne. 7. 53.

חַקּוֹתָ } Kal pret. 2 pers. sing. masc.; acc. shifted by conv. ו (comp. § 8. rem. 7) . חקק

חֻקּוֹת noun fem., pl. of חֻקָּה dec. 10. . חקק

חֻקּוֹתַי } id. pl., suff. 1 pers. sing. . . חקק

חֻקַּי } noun masc. pl., suff. 1 pers. sing. from חֹק dec. 8c

חֻקַּי id. pl., construct state . . חקק

חֻקִּי id. sing., suff. 1 pers. sing. . . חקק

חֻקָּיו id. pl., suff. 3 pers. sing. masc. . . חקק

חֻקֶּיךָ id. pl., suff. 2 pers. sing. masc. . חקק

חֻקִּים id. pl. absolute state . . חקק

חֻקְּךָ id. sing., suff. 2 pers. sing. masc. . חקק

חֻקֵּךְ id. sing., suff. 2 pers. sing. fem. . חקק

חֻקְּכֶם id. sing., suff. 2 pers. pl. masc. חקק

חֻקָּם id. sing., suff. 3 pers. pl. masc. . חקק

חָקַק I. *to engrave, inscribe*.—II. *to portray*.—III. part. חֹקֵק *legislator*, Ju. 5. 9. Pu. part. *what is prescribed, a law, statute*, Pr. 31. 5. Hoph. *to be engraven, inscribed*, Job 19. 23. Po. *to decide, decree*; part. (a) *lawgiver*; (b) *judge, ruler*.

חֵקֶק masc. dec. 6b (§ 35. rem. 6).—I. *impression, imagination*, Ju. 5. 15.—II. *decree*, Is. 10. 1. חֹק masc. dec. 8c.—I. *something fixed or appointed*; לֶחֶם חֻקִּי *the bread appointed for me*.—II. *appointed portion of labour, a task*.—III. *appointed time*.—IV. *limit, bound*.—V. *statute, law*.—VI. *custom, privilege*.

חֻקָּה fem. dec. 10.—I. *statute, law*.—II. *custom, right, privilege*.

חֻקֹּק (*trench*) pr. name of a town on the borders of Asher and Naphtali, Jos. 19. 34; written חוקֹק 1 Ch. 6. 60.

חֻקָּתָה pr. name of a place (חֻקֹּק) with paragogic ה חקק

חִקְקֵי noun masc. pl. constr. from [חֵקֶק] dec. 6b חקק

חֹקְקִי Kal part. act. s. m. with parag. ' (§ 8. r. 19) חקק

חֲקֻקִים id. part. pass. masc. pl. of [חָקוּק] dec. 3a חקק

[חָקַר] fut. יַחְקֹר (§ 13. rem. 5) *to search, search out, explore, examine, try*. Niph. נֶחְקַר (§ 13. rem. 7) *to be searched out*. Pi. *to search out*, Ec. 12. 9.

חֵקֶר masc. dec. 6b (§ 35. rem. 6).—I. *searching, investigation examination*; לֹא, אֵין חֵקֶר *unsearchable*.—II. *deliberation*, Ju. 5. 16.—III. *secret, most part*, Job 38. 16.

מֶחְקָר masc. dec. 2b, *inmost part*, Ps. 95. 4.

חֲקֹר Kal inf. construct . . חקר

חֵקֶר } noun masc. sing. dec. 6b . חקר

חִקֵּר } Piel pret. 3 pers. sing. masc. . חקר

חֹקֵר Kal part. act. sing. masc. . חקר

חֲקָרָהּ id. pret. 3 pers. sing. m., suff. 3 pers. s. fem. חקר

חֲקָרוֹ } id. id., suff. 3 pers. sing. m.; ו for ו conv. חקר

חִקְרוּ id. imp. pl. masc. . חקר

חִקְרֵי noun masc. pl. constr. from חֵקֶר dec. 6b חקר

חֲקַרְנֻהָ Kal pret. 1 pers. pl. suff. 3 pers. sing. fem. חקר

חָקְרֵנִי id. imp. sing. masc., suff. 1 pers. sing. חקר

חֲקַרְתָּ } id. pret. 2 pers. sing. masc.; acc. shifted by conv. ו (§ 8. rem. 7) . חקר

חֲקַרְתַּנִי id. id., suff. 1 pers. sing. . חקר

חֻקַּת noun fem., constr. of חֻקָּה dec. 10. חקק

חֻקֹּת id. pl. for חֻקּוֹת . חקק

חֻקֹּתַי } id. pl., suff. 1 pers. sing. . חקק

חֻקֹּתָיו } id. pl., suff. 3 pers. sing. masc. . חקק

חַקֹּתִיךְ Kal pret. 1 pers. sing., suff. 2 pers. sing. fem. חקק

חֹר noun masc. sing. dec. 1a חור

חֹר noun masc. sing. [for חוֹר] dec. 1a . חור

חָרָא Root not used; Arab. *to ease oneself, to ease nature*.

חֶרֶא masc. dec. 4c, *excrement, dung*, Is. 36. 12 Kheth.; 2 Ki. 18. 27 חַרְאֵיהֶם Kheth. for חַרְאֵיהֶם; 2 Ki. 6. 25 חֲרֵי יוֹנִים Kheth. (dove's dung) for חַרְאֵי יוֹנִים

מַחֲרָאָה fem. dec. 10, *a sink, privy*, 2 Ki. 10. 27 Kheth.

חַרְאֵיהֶם K. צוֹאָתָם noun fem. s. with suff. R. יצא; Kh.

חַרְאֵיהֶם noun m. pl. with suff. [fr. חָרָא] חרא

[חָרַב] inf. חָרֹב, fut. יֶחֱרַב.—I. *to be dried up, to be dry*.—II. *to be desolate, waste, ruined*.—III. trans. *to waste, destroy*, Je. 50. 21. Niph. *to be laid waste, to be ruined*. Pu. *to be dried up*, Ju. 16. 7, 8. Hiph.—I. *to dry up*, Is. 50. 2.—II. *to lay waste, to destroy, ruin*. Hoph. *to be laid waste, destroyed, ruined*.

a Is. 30. 8.   e Ps. 50. 16.   h Le. 10. 13, 14.   l Ge. 47. 22.   o Pr. 25. 27.   r Job 28. 27.   u Ju. 5. 16.   x De. 13. 15.   A 1 Ki. 11. 34.
b Job 14. 5   f Ex. 18. 16.   i Eze. 16. 27.   m Is. 22. 16.   p Ec. 12. 9.   s Jcb 5. 27.   y Ps. 139. 1.   B Is. 49. 16.
c Pr. 2. 19.   g Ne. 9. 14.   k Ex. 5. 14.   n Eze. 23. 14.   q Je. 17. 10.   t Ju. 18. 2.   z Ps. 139. 23.   C Je. 31. 35.   Is. 36. 12.
d Eze. 4. 1.
19

חֲרַב Chald. Hoph. *to be laid waste, destroyed,* Ezr. 4. 15.

חָרֵב adj. fem. חֲרֵבָה.—I. *dry.*—II. *desolate, waste.*

חֶרֶב fem. dec. 6a, with suff. חַרְבִּי, pl. חֲרָבוֹת —I. *sword.*—II. for other *cutting instruments.*— III. *dryness, drought,* De. 28. 22.

חֹרֵב, חֹרֶב (*dry, desert*) pr. name of one of the summits of Sinai.

חֹרֶב masc.—I. *dryness, drought, heat.*—II. *desolation.*

חָרָבָה fem. (for חַרְבָּה, after the form יַבָּשָׁה) *the dry land.*

חָרְבָּה fem. dec. 12c, *desolation, desolate places, ruins.*

חֵרָבוֹן m. dec. 3 (pl. c. חַרְבֹנֵי) *drought,* Ps. 32. 4. חַרְבוֹנָה, חַרְבוֹנָא pr. name of a Persian eunuch, Est. 1. 10; 7. 9.

חֲרָב	in pause for חָרֵב (q. v. § 35. rem. 2) .	חרב
חָרֵב	adj. masc. sing. . .	חרב
חָרֹב	Kal inf. absolute . .	חרב
חֲרֹב	id. imp. sing. masc. . .	חרב
חֶרֶב	noun fem. sing. dec. 6a (suff. חַרְבִּי)	חרב
חֹרֵב	pr. name of a place . .	חרב
חֹרֶב	noun masc. sing. . .	חרב
חָרְבָּה	noun fem. sing. . .	חרב
חָרְבָּה	noun fem. sing. dec. 12c	חרב
חֲרֵבָה	adj. fem. sing. from חָרֵב masc.	חרב
חָרָבָה	pr. name of a place (חֹרֵב) with paragogic ה	חרב
חָרְבוּ	Kal pret. 3 pers. pl.	חרב
חָרְבּוֹ	noun fem. sing., suff. 3 pers. sing. masc. from חֶרֶב dec. 6a	חרב
חִרְבוּ	Kal imp. pl. masc.	חרב
חֹרְבוּ	Pual pret. 3 pers. pl. [for חֹרְבִי]	חרב
חֲרֹבוּ	Kal imp. pl. masc. (§ 8. rem. 12)	חרב
חַרְבוֹנָא חַרְבוֹנָה	} pr. name masc. . .	חרב
חָרְבוֹת	noun fem., pl. constr. from חֶרֶב dec. 6a	חרב
חֲרָבוֹת	id. pl., absolute state	חרב
חֳרָבוֹת	noun fem. pl. abs., from חָרְבָּה dec. 12c	חרב
חָרְבוֹת	id. pl., constr. state	חרב
חָרְבוֹתֶיהָ	id. pl. suff. 3 pers. sing. fem.	חרב
חָרְבוֹתָם	noun fem. pl., suff. 3 pers. pl. masc. from חֶרֶב dec. 6a	חרב
חַרְבִּי	id. sing., suff. 1 pers. sing.	חרב
חִרְבִי	Kal imp. sing. fem. for חַרְבִּי (חֲרָבִי) a mixed form from middle A and O, חָרֵב and חֲרַב=חָרֵב (comp. § 8. rem. 11 & 12)	חרב

חַרְבְּךָ חָרְבְּךָ	} noun fem. sing., suff. 2 pers. sing. masc. from חֶרֶב dec. 6a	חרב
חַרְבְּכֶם	id., suff. 2 pers. pl. masc. .	חרב
חַרְבָּם	id., suff. 3 pers. pl. masc. .	חרב
חָרְבֹתֶיהָ	n. fem. pl., suff. 3 p. s. fem. from חָרְבָּה dec. 12c	חרב
חָרְבֹתֵיהֶם	n. fem. pl., suff. 3 pers. pl. m. from חֶרֶב dec. 6a	חרב
חָרְבֹתָיו	n. fem. pl., suff. 3 p. s. m. from חָרְבָּה dec. 12c	חרב
חַרְבֹתֶיךָ	id., suff. 2 pers. sing. fem. .	חרב

[חָרַג] (coll. with the Arab.) *to be straitened, troubled* Ps. 18. 46. Others, *to tremble, fear.*

[חַרְגֹּל] masc. *locust,* Le. 11. 22.

חָרַד fut. יֶחֱרַד.—I. *to tremble, to be timid, fearful,* with עַל, לְ; Ge. 42. 28. וַיֶּחֶרְדוּ אִישׁ אֶל־אָחִיו *and they turned trembling to one another.*—II. with אֶל *to care for, be concerned about* any one, 2 Ki. 4. 13. —III. *to hasten,* with מִן *from* a place, Ho. 11. 10, 11. Hiph. *to make afraid, terrify.*

חָרֵד adj. masc. dec. 5c.—I. *trembling, fearful, timid.*—II. *fearing, reverencing.*

חֲרָדָה fem. dec. 11c (constr. חֶרְדַּת § 42. rem. 1). —I. *trembling, terror, fear.*—II. *care, concern,* 2 Ki. 4. 13.—III. pr. name of a station of the Israelites in the desert, Nu. 33. 24.

חֲרֹד (*trembling*) pr. name of a place in the mountain of Gilboa, Ju. 7. 1. Gent. n. חֲרֹדִי 2 Sa. 23. 25.

חָרֵד	adj. masc. sing. dec. 5c	חרד
חֲרֹד	pr. name of a place .	חרד
חָרְדָה	Kal pret. 3 pers. sing. fem.	חרד
חֶרְדַּת	n. fem. s., constr. חֶרְדַּת, dec. 11c (§ 42. rem. 1)	חרד
חָרְדוּ	Kal pret. 3 pers. pl.	חרד
חִרְדוּ	id. imp. pl. masc.	חרד
חֲרָדוֹת	noun fem., pl. abs. from חֲרָדָה (q. v.)	חרד
חָרַדְתְּ	Kal pret. 2 pers. sing.	חרד
חֶרְדַּת	noun fem. sing. constr. of חֲרָדָה (q. v.)	חרד

חָרָה fut. יֶחֱרֶה, ap. יִחַר (§ 24. rem. 3d) *to burn, be kindled; to become hot, angry, wroth;* חָרָה אַפּוֹ with בְּ, עַל, אֶל, לְ; חָרָה לוֹ *his anger was kindled against;* חָרָה בְּעֵינָיו *he was angry, it grieved him.* Niph. נֶחֱרָה *to be angry, wroth,* with בְּ, Is. 41. 11; 45. 24. Hiph. הֶחֱרָה, fut ap. יַחַר (§ 24. r. 16).—I. *to cause to burn to kindle,* as anger, Job 19. 11.—II. *to become ardent zealous, to do with zeal,* Ne. 3. 20. Tiph. (§ 6. No. 5) *to emulate, rival.* Hithpa. *to fret oneself, be vexed*

a Is. 60. 12.   d Exe. 29. 9.   g Is. 19. 6.   k Je. 2. 12.   n Is. 44. 26.   r Is. 51. 3.   v Is. 19. 16.   x Is. 32. 11.   z 2 Ki. 4. 13.
b Je. 50. 21.   e Le. 7. 19.   h Je. 50. 27.   l Jos. 5. 2, 3.   o Is. 44. 27.   s Ezr. 9. 9.   w 10. 29.   y Eze. 26. 16.   † Pr. 29. 25.
c Eze. 30. 12.   f Ge. 8. 13.   i Ju. 16. 7, 8.   m Is. 5. 17.   p Ps. 37. 15.   t Is. 49. 19.

חָרֹן masc. dec. 3 a.—I. *heat, ardour,* Ps. 58. 10. Prof. Lee, *angry person.*—II. *anger, wrath,* fully חֲרוֹן אַף *heat of anger, burning wrath.*

חֲרִי masc. *heat, glow,* only in the phrase, חֲרִי אַף *heat of anger, burning wrath.*

תַּחְרָא masc. *coat of mail;* Eng. Vers. "habergeon." Comp. Tiph. of the Root.

חָרָה וְ] Kal fut. 3 pers. sing. fem. [for תֶּחֱרֶה]   חרר

חָרֹה Kal inf. abs.   חרר

חַרְהֲיָה / חַרְהֲיָה } pr. name masc.   חרר

חָרוּ Kal pret. 3 pers. pl. [for חָרְגוּ]   חרר

חָרוּל noun m. sing., pl. חֲרֻלִּים dec. 8 (§ 37. No. 3 c)   חרל

חַרְמַף pr. name masc.   חרם

חָרוֹן noun masc. sing. dec. 3 a   חרה

חֲרוֹן וְ] id. construct state; וַ before (־)   חרה

חֹרוֹן pr. name in compos. בֵּית חוֹרֹן, see .   בית

חֹרוֹנִי id., suff. 1 pers. sing.   חרה

חֹרוֹנֶיךָ id. pl., suff. 2 pers. sing. masc.   חרה

חֹרוֹנַיִם pr. name of a place   חור

חָרוּץ וְ] Kal part. pass., adj. or subst. masc. dec. 3 a   חרץ

חָרוּץ n. m. sing. for [חֲרוּגִין] dec. 1 b; also pr. n. m.   חרץ

חֲרוּצִים id. pl., absolute state   חרץ

חֲרוּצִים Kal part. pass. masc., pl. of חָרוּץ dec. 3 a   חרץ

חֲרוּשָׁה Kal part. pass. sing. fem. from [חָרוּשׁ] masc.   חרש

חָרוּת Kal part. pass. sing. masc.   חרת

חָרַז Root not used; Syr. *to put in order, dispose regularly.*

חָרוּז masc. only pl. חֲרוּזִים, Ca. 1. 10, *strings of pearls, coral,* or the like. Sept. ὁρμίσκοι *collars, necklaces.*

חַרְחוּר pr. name masc.   חרר

חַרְחַם pr. name masc. see חַסְרָה .   חסר

חָרַט Root not used; Syr. *to engrave.*

חָרִיט masc. *pocket, purse.*

חֶרֶט masc.—I. *graving tool,* Ex. 32. 4.—II. *writing style,* Is. 8. 1.

חַרְטֹם masc. dec. 8 c, only pl. חַרְטֻמִּים *sacred writers, persons skilled in the hieroglyphics,* mentioned very early among the Egyptians, Ge. 41. 8, 24; and in aftertimes applied to *the wise men* among the Babylonians, Da. 1. 20; 2. 2. LXX. ἐξηγηταί *interpreters* of mysteries; ἐπαοιδοί *enchanters;* φαρμακοί *sorcerers, magicians.*

חַרְטֹם Chald. masc. dec. 5 c, id.

חָרְטֻמִים noun masc., pl. of [חָרִיט] dec. 3 a   חרט

חַרְטֹם Chald. noun masc. sing., dec. 5 c .   חרט

חַרְטֻמֵּי Heb. id. pl., construct state, dec. 8 c .   חרט

חַרְטֻמַיָּא Chald. id. pl., emph. st. dec. 5 c .   חרט

חַרְטֻמִּין Chald. id. pl., absolute state .   חרט

חֲרִי noun masc. sing.   חרה

חֹרֵי noun masc. pl. constr. from חוֹר/ dec. 1 a   חור

חֹרֵי noun masc. pl. constr. from חֹר/ dec. 1 a   חור

חוֹרִי noun masc. sing.; also pr. name   חור

חֹרֶיהָ noun m. pl., suff. 3 p. s. fem. from חֹר/ dec. 1 a   חור

חֹרֵיהֶם K. צֹאָתָם n.f.s.,suff. 3 p.pl.from צֹאָה d.10, R. יֵצָא; Kh. חֲרֵיהֶם for חַרְאֵיהֶם, see חרא תֹרָא/

חֹרָיו n. m. pl., suff. 3 pers. s. m. from חוֹר/ dec. 1 a   חור

חֲרִיוֹנִים K. דְּבִיוֹנִים, see R. דבה; Kh. חֲרֵי יוֹנִים see R. חרא

חָרִיף pr. name masc.   חרף

חֲרִיצֵי noun masc. pl. constr. from [חָרִיץ] dec. 3 a   חרץ

חָרִישׁ noun masc. sing. dec. 3 a   חרש

חֲרִישׁוֹ id., suff. 3 pers. sing. masc.   חרש

חֲרִישִׁית adj. fem. sing. [from חֲרִישִׁי masc.]   חרש

[חָרַךְ] perhaps i. q. כָּרַךְ *to wrap round;* hence, *to enclose* or *catch in a net* or *toil,* Pr. 12. 27, LXX. ἐπιτεύξεται *shall obtain.* Others, *to burn, singe, roast,* as in the Chald.

חֲרַךְ Chald. Ithpa. *to be singed,* Da. 3. 27.

חֲרַךְ masc. dec. 4 c, only Ca. 2. 9. חֲרַכִּים *lattices* of windows, from their *reticulate* form.

חָרַל Root not used; perhaps i. q. חָרַר *to burn.*

חָרוּל masc. pl. חֲרֻלִּים (§ 37. No. 3 c) *nettle, nettles,* Job 30. 7; Zep. 2. 9; Pr. 24. 31.

חֲרֻלִּים noun masc., pl. of חָרוּל (q. v.)   חרל

חָרַם in Kal only part. pass. חָרֻם *flat-nosed, mutilated in the nose.* Arab. *to cut, tear off; to shut up; to prohibit.* Hiph. הֶחֱרִים.—I. *to devote to destruction.*—II. *to devote to God, to consecrate.* Hoph. הׇחֳרַם.—I. *to be devoted to destruction.*—II. *to be consecrated,* Ezr. 10. 8.

חָרֵם (*devoted*) pr. name of a town in the tribe of Naphtali, Jos. 19. 38.

חָרֻם (*flat-nosed*) pr. name of a man.

חֵרֶם, חֶרֶם masc. dec. 6, with suff. חֶרְמִי (§ 35. rem. 6).—I. *a net.*—II. metaph. *allurement,* Ec. 7. 26.—III. *devotion to destruction;* אִישׁ חֶרְמִי *a man devoted by me to destruction.*

חׇרְמָה (*devoted to destruction*) pr. name of a city of the Canaanites.

a Job 30. 30.   d Is. 24. 6.   g Job 14. 5.   i 2 Ki. 5. 23.   m De. 29. 23.   p Is. 34. 12.   r Na. 2. 13.   t Ge. 45. 6.   x Jon. 4. 8.
b Eze. 24. 11.   e Eze. 7. 14.   h Je. 17. 1.   k Da. 2. 10.   n Job 30. 6.   q 2 Ki. 18. 27.   s 1 Sa. 17. 18.   u 1 Sa. 8. 12.   y Pr. 24. 31.
l Is. 20. 7.   f Ps. 68. 17.   i Ex. 32. 16.   o Da. 4. 4, 6.   oo 2 Ki. 6. 25.

9*

חֶרְמוֹן **pr.** name of a ridge or spur of Anti-Libanus, pl. חֶרְמוֹנִים several summits or ridges belonging to the same.

חֲרוּמַף (for חָרוּם אַף *flat-nosed*) **pr.** name masc. Ne. 3. 10.

חָרֵם	**pr.** name masc. . . . . חרם
חָרֵם[c]	Kal part. pass. sing. masc. . . . חרם
חֳרֵם	**pr.** name of a place . . . . . חרם
חֵרֶם }	noun masc. sing. dec. 6 (suff. חֶרְמִי חֶרְמִי[b] } § 35. rem. 6) . . . } חרם
חָרְמָה[c]	**pr.** name of a place . . . . . חרם
חֶרְמוֹ	noun masc. sing., suff. **3 pers. sing. masc.** from חֵרֶם dec. 6 (§ 35. rem. 6) . חרם
חֶרְמוֹן	**pr.** name of a mountain . . . . חרם
חֶרְמוֹנִים	id. pl. . . . . חרם
חֶרְמִי	noun masc. sing., suff. 1 pers. sing. from חֵרֶם dec. 6 (§ 35. rem. 6) . . חרם
חֲרָמִים[d]	id. pl., absolute state; בְ bef. (–֫) . חרם

חֶרְמֵשׁ masc. *sickle*, De. 16. 9 ; 23. 26.

חָרָן	**pr.** name of a man and a place . . חרר
חָרֹן	**pr.** name, see בֵּית חוֹרוֹן . . . בית
חָרָנָה	**pr.** name of a place (חָרָן) with parag. ה חרר
חֹרֹנַיִם	**pr.** name of a place . . . . . חרר
חֲרֹנְךָ[e]	noun m. s., suff. 2 pers. s. m. from חָרוֹן d. 3a חרה
חַרְנֶפֶר	**pr.** name masc. . . . . . . נחר

חָרֵס Root not used ; prob. *to be dry, hot* ; which signification seems to lie in the syllable חַר, comp. חָרַר, חָרָה ; Arab. *to scratch* ; *to be scratched, be rough.*

חֶרֶס masc.—I. *the sun*, Ju. 8. 13 ; 14. 18 ; עִיר הַחֶרֶס mystical name of a city in Egypt, Is. 19. 18 ; where others read הַהֶרֶס.

שַׁעַר הַחַרְסוּת fem. *pottery* (comp. חֶרֶשׂ) ; *pottery-gate*, one of the gates of Jerusalem, Je. 19. 2 Kheth., חַרְסִית Keri.

חֶרֶס **pr.** name, see הַר חֶרֶס under the Root הרר

[חָרֵף] fut. יֶחֱרַף (prim. to pluck, to gather fruit, comp. חֹרֶף autumn ; hence)—I. *to pass the autumn, winter*, Is. 18. 6.—II. *to reproach, scorn.* Pi. *to reproach, scorn* ; חֵרֵף נַפְשׁוֹ *to scorn*, i.e. *expose one's life.* Niph. part. נֶחֱרֶפֶת *abandoned* i.e. exposed, sc. to a man, Le. 19. 20.

חֲרוּפִי or חֲרִיפִי patronym. of an unknown חָרִי 1 Ch. 12. 5.

חָרִיף (*autumnal rain*, coll. with the Arab.) **pr.**

name masc. Ne. 7. 24 ; 10. 20 ; called Ezr. 2. 18 יוֹרָה (*autumnal rain*).

חָרֵף (*plucking of*) **pr.** name masc. 1 Ch. 2. 51.

חֹרֶף masc. dec. 6c, *autumn*, frequently including the winter.

חֶרְפָּה fem. dec. 12b.—I. *reproach, contempt.*—II. *object of reproach.*

חָרֵף	**pr.** name masc. . . . . חרף
חָרֵף	**pr.** name masc. . . . . חרף
חֵרֵף	Piel pret. 3 pers. sing. masc. . . . חרף
וְחֵרֵף	noun masc. sing. dec. 6c ; for וְ see lett. וְ חרף
וְחֶרְפָּה[g]	noun fem. sing. dec. 12b . . . חרף
חֵרְפוּ	Piel pret. 3 pers. pl. . . . . . חרף
חֵרְפוּךָ[f]	id., suff. 2 pers. sing. masc. . . . חרף
חֵרְפוּנִי	id., suff. 1 pers. sing. . . . . . חרף
וְחֶרְפוֹת[g]	noun fem. pl. constr. from חֶרְפָּה d. 12b חרף
חֶרְפִּי[f]	noun masc. sing. suff. 1 pers. sing. from חֹרֶף dec. 6c . . . . חרף
חֹרְפִי	Kal part. act. sing. masc. suff. 1 pers. sing. from [חָרַף] dec. 7b . . . חרף
חֵרַפְתָּ	Piel pret. 2 pers. sing. masc. . . . חרף
וְחֶרְפַּת	noun fem. sing., const. of חֶרְפָּה dec. 12b חרף
וְחֵרְפַתּוֹ[i]	id., suff. 3 pers. sing. masc. . . . חרף
חֵרַפְתִּי[h]	Piel pret. 1 pers. sing. . . . . חרף
חֶרְפָּתִי	noun f. s., suff. 1 pers. s. from חֶרְפָּה d. 12b חרף
חֶרְפָּתֵךְ[k]	id., suff. 2 pers. sing. fem. . . . חרף
חֶרְפָּתְךָ[l]	id., suff. 2 pers. sing. masc. . . . חרף
חֶרְפָּתָם	id., suff. 3 pers. pl. masc. . . . חרף
חֵרַפְתֶּם[m]	Piel pret. 2 pers. pl. masc. . . . חרף
חֶרְפָּתֵנוּ	noun fem. sing., suff. 1 pers. pl. from חֶרְפָּה dec. 12b . . . . . . חרף

חָרַץ fut. יֶחֱרַץ.—I. *to cut in, to wound, lacerate*, only part. pass. חָרוּץ *slightly wounded, lacerated*, Le. 22. 22.—II. *to sharpen, point*, only Ex. 11. 7 not a dog *shall sharpen* or *point his tongue.*—III. *to decide, determine.*—IV. *to be sharp, active, quick*, 2 Sa. 5. 24. Niph. part. נֶחֱרָצֶת, נֶחֱרָצָה *decided determined, decreed.*

חָרוּץ masc. dec. 3a.—I. *ditch, trench*, Da. 9. 25 —II. *sharpened, pointed*, Is. 41. 15 ; as a subst. a *threshing-sledge*, furnished underneath with *teeth of stone or iron* ; pl. חֲרוּצוֹת.—III. *what is decided, decision, judgment*, Joel 4. 14.—IV. *gold.*

חָרוּץ masc. dec. 1b (for חָרִיץ § 32. No. 3).—I. *active, diligent.* Prof. Lee, *sharpened, instructed, prudent.*—II. **pr.** name masc. 2 Ki. 21. 19

חָרִיץ masc. dec. 3a.—I. *a piece cut off, a slice*

1 Sa. 17. 18.—II. *threshing-sleage*, comp. חָרוּץ No. II.

חַרְצָן masc. dec. 8 a, only pl. חַרְצַנִּים (sharp) *sour grapes*, Nu. 6. 4.

[חֲרַץ] Ch. m. d. 3 a, *loin, loins*, Da. 5. 6; comp. Heb. חָלָץ.

חַרְצֹב Root not used; coll. with the Arab. *to bind fast a cord*. Hence

חַרְצֻבּוֹת pl. fem. [fr. חַרְצֹב dec. 8 c].—I. *tight bonds*, Is. 58. 6.—II. *pains, pangs*, Ps. 73. 4.   חרצב

חֲרָצָהּ Ch. noun masc. sing., suff. 3 pers. sing. m. fr. [חֲרַץ] dec. 3 a .   .   .   .   חרץ

חֲרֻצִים defect. for (חָרוּצִים q. v.)   .   .   חרץ

חָרַצְתְּ Kal pret. 2 pers. s. m. [for חָרַצְתָּ § 8. rem. 7]   חרץ

חָרַק fut. יַחֲרֹק, *to grind*, gnash the teeth.

חָרֹק Kal inf. absolute   .   .   .   חרק

וְחֹרֵק id. part. act. sing. masc.   .   .   חרק

[חָרַר] I.—*to burn, glow*.—II. *to be dried up*, Job 30. 30. Niph. נָחַר & נֵחַר (dag. f. impl. § 18. rem. 14), fut. יֵחַר (for יֵחַר) *to be burned, scorched*; *to be dried up*. Pilp. (§ 6. No. 4) *to kindle*, as contention, Pr. 26. 21.

חֲרֵרִים masc. pl. (fr. חָרֵר dec. 4 c) *dry, parched places*, Je. 17. 6.

חֹר masc. dec. 1 a, only pl. (חוֹרִים חֹרִים) *nobles, free-born*.

חָרָן (*parched, scorched*) pr. name—I. of a city of Mesopotamia.—II. of a man, 1 Ch. 2. 46.

חַרְחֻר masc.—I. *inflammation, burning fever*, De. 28. 22.—II. pr. name of a man.

חַרְחֲיָה (*he was burning, hot*) pr. n. m. Ne. 3. 8.

חֲרֵרִים noun masc., pl. of [חָרַר] dec. 5 c   .   חרר

חֶרֶשׂ Root not used; i. q. חָרַם *to scratch, to be rough*.

חֶרֶשׂ masc. dec. 6 a (pl. c. חַרְשֵׂי) *sherd, potsherd*; כְּלִי חָרֶשׂ *earthen vessel*.

חַרְשֶׂת *sherd*, see קִיר חֲרָשֶׂת R.

[חָרַשׁ] fut. יַחֲרֹשׁ.—I. *to plough, till*.—II. *to engrave*, Je. 17. 1.—III. *to form, work, fabricate*. Metaph. *to devise, machinate evil*.—IV. fut. יֶחֱרַשׁ (prop. to be blunted, dull) *to be dumb, silent, deaf*. Niph. *to be ploughed*. Hiph.—I. *to fabricate, devise evil*, 1 Sa. 23. 9.—II. *to keep silent, be silent, quiet*;

with לְ of the thing, to permit it silently, with אֶל to conceal it; with מִן of the person, to hear him silently, also to desist from him, with acc. to permit it silently, also to pass anything in silence, to conceal it. Hithpa. *to keep still*, Ju. 16. 2.

חָרָשׁ masc. dec. 1 b, but constr. חָרַשׁ (§ 30. No. 4, & rem. 1).—I. *engraver*, Ex. 28. 11.—II. *worker, artificer*, in wood, stone, metal, Eze. 21. 36; חָרָשֵׁי מַשְׁחִית *forgers of destruction*.

חֵרֵשׁ masc. (for חִרֵשׁ § 26. No. 9) d. 7 b, *deaf*.

חֶרֶשׁ masc.—I. *artificial, cunning work* (see גֵּי חֲרָשִׁים).—II. adv. *silently*, Jos. 2. 1.—III. pr. name masc. 1 Ch. 9. 15.

חֹרֵשׁ masc. *cutting instrument*, Ge. 4. 22.

חֹרֶשׁ masc. dec. 6 c, *wood, forest* (Chald. חֲרַשׁ *to be entangled*).

חַרְשָׁא (Chald. *enchanter, magician*) pr. name masc.—I. Ezr. 2. 52.—II. Ne. 7. 54.

חֲרֹשֶׁת fem.—I. *sculpture*, Ex. 31. 5; 35. 33.—II. pr. name of a city in the north of Palestine.

חֲרִישׁ masc. dec. 3 a.—I. *a ploughing, tilling the land*; also, *time of ploughing*.

חֲרִישִׁי fem. חֲרִישִׁית adj. *silent, still, gentle*, Jon. 4. 8.

מַחֲרֶשֶׁת, מַחֲרֵשָׁה fem., with suff. מַחֲרַשְׁתּוֹ, pl. מַחֲרֵשׁוֹת, two kinds of *cutting instruments*, perhaps *the ploughshare* and *the coulter*.

חֲרָשׁ noun masc. sing. [for חָרָשׁ] dec. 1 b   .   חרש

חָרַשׁ id. constr. state (§ 30. rem. 1)   .   חרש

חָרַשׁ in pause for חָרֵשׁ (q. v. § 35. rem. 2)   .   חרש

חֵרֵשׁ noun masc. sing. dec. 7 b   .   חרש

חֶרֶשׁ noun m. (used as an adv.) pl. חֲרָשִׁים subst.   חרש

חֹרֶשׁ noun masc. sing. (pl. c. חָרְשֵׁי) dec. 6 a   חרש

חֹרֵשׁ Kal part. act., or (Ge. 4. 22) n. m. s. d. 7 b   חרש

וְחֹרֶשׁ noun masc. sing. dec. 6 c   .   חרש

חַרְשָׁא pr. name masc. (see תֵּל חַרְשָׁא)   .   חרש

חַרְשָׁה noun masc. sing. (חֹרֶשׁ) with parag. ה .   חרש

חָרְשׁוּ Kal pret. 3 pers. pl.   .   חרש

חֹרְשׁוֹת id. part. act. fem. pl. [of חֹרֶשׁ or חֹרְשָׁה]   חרש

וְחָרָשֵׁי noun masc. pl. constr. fr. חָרָשׁ (q. v.)   חרש

חָרְשֵׁי noun masc. pl. constr. fr. חֹרֶשׁ dec. 6 a   חרש

חֹרְשֵׁי Kal part. act. pl. const. masc. fr. חֹרֵשׁ d. 7 b   חרש

חֲרָשֶׁיהָ noun m. pl., suff. 3 pers. s. f. fr. חָרָשׁ d. 6 a   חרש

וְחָרָשִׁים noun masc. pl. absolute fr. חָרָשׁ (q. v.)   חרש

חֲרָשִׁים noun masc. pl. absolute fr. חֶרֶשׁ dec. 6   חרש

וְחֵרְשִׁים noun masc. pl. abs. from חֵרֵשׁ (q. v.)   חרש

חֹרְשִׁים Kal part. act. masc., pl. of חֹרֵשׁ dec. 7 b   .   חרש

a Da. 5. 6.   f Job 16. 9.   g Je. 17. 6.   i Is. 42. 19.   l Exe. 31. 3.   o Ps. 129. 3.   p Is. 45. 9.   r Exe. 23. 34.   t Is. 43. 8.
b Ps. 73. 4.   c Ps. 25. 16.   h 1 Sa. 13. 19.   k Jos. 2. 1.   m 1 Sa. 23. 16.   q Job 1. 14.   q Job 4. 8.   s Is. 35. 5.   u Ps. 129. 3.
c 1 Ki. 20. 42.   e Ps. 37. 12.

חֲרֹשֶׁת
חֲרֹשֶׁת } pr. name in compos.   קִיר חֲרֹשֶׁת   קור

חרש   חָ֑ רֹֽשׁ הַגּוֹיִם   pr. name in compos.

חרש   חֲרַשְׁתֶּם   Kal pret. 2 pers. pl. masc.

[חָרַת]   to cut in, engrave, Ex. 32. 10.

חֶרֶת   (for חֶרֶת § 35. r. 2) pr. name of a wood in the tribe of Judah, 1 Sa. 22. 5.

חוש   חָשׁ וְ' Kal pret. 3 pers. sing. masc.

חָשַׁב וְ'   fut. יַחֲשָׁב־, יַחְשֹׁב (§ 13. rem. 5).—I. to think, purpose, intend to do anything, with לְ before the inf. of the action; usually in a bad sense, to invent, devise, with עַל, אֶל of the person, and acc. of the thing; in a good sense with לְ to care for, part. חֹשֵׁב deviser, artificer, especially a weaver in figures of various colours, a damask-weaver.—II. to think, regard, count as, with acc. and לְ Ge. 38. 15, כְּ Job 19. 11; absolute to esteem, value.—III. to impute, reckon to any one what does not properly belong to him. Niph. נֶחְשַׁב (§ 13. rem. 7).—I. to be computed, reckoned, counted, with עַל, לְ.—II. to be regarded, counted as, with כְּ, לְ, בְּ.—III. to be imputed to any one, with לְ. Pi.—I. to compute, reckon, with אֵת, עִם.—II. to think upon, consider.—III. to think, purpose; to devise, plan; metaph. to be about to do or suffer, Jon. 1. 4. Hithp. to reckon oneself, with בְּ Nu. 23. 9.

חֲשַׁב   Ch. to regard, count, Da. 4. 32.

חָשׁוּב   (considerate) pr. name masc. of two different persons.

חֲשֻׁבָה   (esteemed) pr. name masc. 1 Ch. 3. 20.

חֵשֶׁב   masc. the belt or girdle of the ephod, prob. so called from its being richly embroidered.

חֶשְׁבּוֹן   masc.—I. result of an account or computation, Ec. 7. 27.—II. intelligence, understanding.—III. pr. name of a city formerly the residence of an Amorite king, afterwards assigned to the Levites in the borders of Reuben and Gad.

חִשְּׁבֹנוֹת   masc. only pl.—I. warlike engines, 2 Ch. 26. 15.—II. artifices, devices, Ec. 7. 29.

חֲשַׁבַּדָּנָה   (for בַּדָּנָה חֹשֵׁב thought in judgment) pr. name masc. Ne. 8. 4.

חֲשַׁבְיָהוּ, חֲשַׁבְיָה   (whom the Lord esteems) pr. name of several Levites.

חֲשַׁבְנְיָה, חֲשַׁבְנָה   (?) pr. name masc. of several persons.

מַחֲשֶׁבֶת, מַחֲשָׁבָה   with suff. מַחֲשַׁבְתּוֹ, pl.

מַחֲשָׁבוֹת, constr. מַחְשְׁבוֹת (comp. dec. 12 & 13, & § 42. rem. 5).—I. thought, counsel, design, project.—II. work of art or skill.

חשב   חָשָׁב וְ' noun masc. sing.

חשב   חִשֵּׁב וְ' Piel pret. 3 pers. sing. masc. (§ 10. r. 1)

חשב   חֹשֵׁב וְ' Kal part. act. sing. masc. dec. 7 b

חשב   חֶשְׁבַּדָּנָה וְ' pr. name masc.

חשב   חֲשָׁבַהּ Kal pret. 3 pers. sing. m., suff. 3 pers. s. f.

חשב   חֲשָׁבָה וְ' pr. name masc.

חשב   חִשְּׁבָה Piel pret. 3 pers. sing. fem.

חשב   חָשְׁבוּ
חִשְּׁבוּ } Kal pret. 3 pers. pl. (§ 8. rem. 7)

חשב   חֶשְׁבּוֹן noun masc. sing., also pr. name

חשב   חֹשְׁבֵי וְ' Kal part. act. pl. constr. m. fr. חֹשֵׁב d 7 b

חשב   חֲשַׁבְיָה
חֲשַׁבְיָהוּ } pr. name masc.; וְ bef. (–)

חשב   חֹשְׁבִים Kal part. act. masc., pl. of חֹשֵׁב dec. 7 b

חשב   חֲשַׁבְנָה pr. name masc.

חשב   חֲשָׁבְנֻהוּ Kal pret. 1 pers. pl., suff. 3 pers. sing. masc.

חשב   חִשְּׁבֹנוֹת noun m. with pl. fem. term. fr. [חֶשְׁבּוֹן] dec. 3 c

חשב   חֲשַׁבְנְיָה pr. name masc.

חשב   חֲשַׁבְתָּ
חֲשַׁבְתָּ } Kal pret. 2 pers. sing. masc.; acc. shifted by conv. וְ (§ 8. rem. 7)

חשב   חֲשַׁבְתָּה id., full form for חָשַׁבְתָּ (§ 8. rem. 5)

חשב   חֲשַׁבְתִּי id. pret. 1 pers. sing.

חשב   חִשַּׁבְתִּי Piel pret. 1 pers. sing.

חשב   חֲשַׁבְתֶּם Kal pret. 2 pers. pl. masc.

[חָשָׁה]   fut. יֶחֱשֶׁה to be silent, still, quiet. Hiph.—I. to silence, still, quiet.—II. to be silent, still, quiet.

חשב   חָשׁוּב וְ' pr. name masc.

חשף   חֲשׁוּפָא pr. name masc.

חשף   חֲשׂוּפָה Kal part. pass. fem. [from חָשׂוּף]

חשף   חֲשׂוּפַי וְ' id. sing. masc. pl. const. dec. 3 a ; וְ bef. (–)

חשק   חֲשֻׁקֵיהֶם וְ' noun m. pl., suff. 3 pers. pl. m. [fr. חָשֻׁק]

[חֲשַׁח]   Chald.—I. to be needed, necessary, Ezr. 6. 9.—II to have need, occasion, Da. 3. 16.

חַשְׁחוּ   Chald. fem. dec. 8 c, need, what is needful Ezr. 7. 20.

חשח   חַשְׁחֻת Chald. noun fem. s., constr. of [חַשְׁחוּ] dec. 8 c

חשח   חַשְׁחִין Chald. Peal part. act. pl. masc. [for חָשְׁחִין from חֲשַׁח § 58. rem. 1]

חשח   חַשְׁחָן Chald. id. pl. fem. [for חָשְׁחָן v. id.]

חשב   חֲשִׁיבִין Chald. Peal part. pass. m., pl. of [חֲשִׁיב] d 1 a

חוש   חֻשִׁים pr. name masc.

חוש   חֲשִׁים Kal part. pass. masc., pl. of [חוּשׁ]

---

a De. 32. 35.   b Ge. 50. 20.   c Jon. 1. 4.   d Ps. 10. 2.   e Ec. 7. 27.   f Ex. 35. 35.   g Job 35. 2.   h Eze. 38. 10.   i 2 Sa. 14. 13.   j Je. 18. 8.   k Ge. 50. 20.   l Eze. 4. 7.   m Is. 20. 4.   n Ezr. 7. 20.   o Da. 3. 16.   p Ezr. 6. 9.   q Da. 4. 32.   r Nu. 32. 17.

חָשַׂךְ fut. יַחְשֹׂךְ אֶחְשֹׂךְ, אֶחֱשָׂךְ (§ 13. rem. 5).—I. *to hold back, restrain,* const. with acc., מִן *of the thing from* which.—II. *to save, preserve, deliver,* const. id.—III. *to withhold,* const. id.—IV. *to spare, keep back.* Niph.—I. *to be restrained,* Job 16. 6. —II. *to be reserved,* Job 21. 30.

חָשַׁךְ fut. יֶחְשַׁךְ (§ 13. rem. 5).—*to be* or *become obscure, dark.* Hiph.—I. *to darken, make dark, obscure.* —II. *to cause darkness,* Ps. 139. 12; Je. 13. 16.

חָשֵׁךְ adj. masc., pl. חֲשֵׁכִים (§ 37. No. 3c) *obscure, mean,* Pr. 22. 29.

חֹשֶׁךְ masc. dec. 6c.—I. *darkness.*—II. *calamity, misery.*—III. *ignorance,* Job 37. 19.

חֲשׁוֹךְ Chald. masc. dec. 1a, *darkness,* Da. 2. 22.

חֲשֵׁכָה, חֲשֵׁיכָה fem., constr. חֶשְׁכַת (comp. dec. 11, and § 42. rem. 4), pl. חֲשֵׁכִים, *darkness.*

חֶשְׁכָה fem. *darkness,* Mi. 3. 6.

מַחְשָׁךְ masc. pl. מַחֲשַׁכִּים (dec. 8a, § 37, No. 3c).—I. *darkness.*—II. *dark place.*

חֲשֹׁךְ Kal pret. 3 pers. s. m. for חָשַׁךְ (§ 8. rem. 7) ... חשך

חֲשֹׂךְ Kal imp. sing. masc. ... חשך

חֹשֵׂךְ Kal part. act. sing. masc. ... חשך

חֹשֶׁךְ noun masc. sing. dec. 6c ... חשך

חֲשֵׁכָה noun fem. sing., dec. 11 (§ 42. rem. 4) ... חשך

חָשְׁכָה Kal pret. 3 pers. sing. fem. ... חשך

חָשְׁכוּ
חָשְׁכוּ } Kal pret. 3 pers. pl. (§ 8. rem. 7) ... חשך

חָשְׁכוּ Kal pret. 3 pers. pl. ... חשך

חֶשְׁכִּי noun m. s., suff. 1 pers. s. from חֹשֶׁךְ dec. 6c ... חשך

חֲשֵׁכִים noun fem. with pl. m. term. fr. חֲשֵׁכָה (q. v.) ... חשך

חֲשֵׁכִים adj. m., pl. of חָשֵׁךְ dec. 8c (§ 37. No. 2 & 3) ... חשך

חָשַׁכְתָּ Kal pret. 2 pers. sing. masc. ... חשך

חֶשְׁכַת noun fem. sing. constr. of חֲשֵׁכָה dec. 11. (§ 42. rem. 4) ... חשך

חָשַׁכְתִּי Kal pret. 1 pers. sing. ... חשך

חָשַׁל Niph. part. *debilitated, enfeebled,* De. 25. 18.

חֲשַׁל Chald. *to beat small, pound,* Da. 2. 40.

חָשֵׁל ו Chald. Peal part. act. sing. masc. ... חשל

חָשַׁם Root not used; Arab. *to be fat; to be rich, opulent.*

חָשֻׁם (*rich*) pr. name of a man.

חָשְׁמוֹן (*fat soil*) pr. name of a town in the tribe of Judah, Jos. 15. 27.

חַשְׁמֹנָה (id.) pr. name of a station of the Israelites in the desert, Nu. 33. 29.

חַשְׁמָן masc. only pl. חַשְׁמַנִּים Ps. 68. 32, *rich, opulent, noble.* Michaelis takes it as a pr. name, *Hushmoneans,* the inhabitants of Ashmunein, a city in Egypt.

חֻשָׁם ו pr. name masc. ... חשם

חֻשָׁם pr. name masc., see חוּשָׁם ... חוש

חֻשָׁם pr. name masc., see חוּשָׁם ... חוש

חַשְׁמַל masc. *a kind of polished brass,* comp. Re. 1. 15. According to others, *a mixed metal of gold and silver,* supposing that the LXX. meant the same in rendering it ἤλεκτρον (not *amber*). The Hebrew word is supposed to be compounded of נְחֹשׁ *brass* (dropping the initial נ) and מָל from מָלַל Chald. *to rub, polish,* or מַלְלָא=מָל Chald. *gold.*

חֶשְׁמוֹן ו pr. name masc. ... חשם

הַחַשְׁמַנִּים noun masc., pl. of [חַשְׁמָן] dec. 8a ... חשם

חָשַׁן Root not used; Arab. *to be beautiful; to adorn* Hence

חֹשֶׁן masc. prop. *ornament,* spoken of the *breast-plate* of the high-priest. LXX. once περίστηθιον *a breast-plate,* elsewhere λογιον or λογειον *oracle.* ... חשן

חָשַׂף fut. יַחְשֹׂף.—I. *to strip, make bare, uncover.*—II. *to uncover,* i. e. remove the covering, Is. 47. 2.—III. *to draw, draw off,* as water.

חֲשׂוּפָא (*bare, naked*) pr. name of a man.

חָשִׂיף masc. dec. 3a, *flock, a small separated flock,* 1 Ki. 20. 27.

מַחְשֹׂף masc. *a making bare,* Ge. 30. 37.

חָשֹׂף Kal inf. absolute ... חשף

חֲשׂוּפָא pr. name masc., see חֲשׂוּפָא ... חשף

חֲשָׂפָהּ Kal pret. 3 pers. sing. masc., suff. 3 pers. s. f. ... חשף

חֲשִׂפֵי noun masc. pl. constr. from [חָשִׂיף] dec. 3a ... חשף

חִשְׂפִי Kal imp. sing. fem. (§ 13. rem. 3) ... חשף

חָשַׂפְתִּי id. pret. 1 pers. sing. ... חשף

חָשַׁק I. *to be attached, to cleave to* any one from affection, with בְּ.—II. *to desire, be pleased* to do anything, with לְ before the inf. of the action. Pi. *to connect, join together,* Ex. 38. 28. Pu. pass. of Piel.

חֵשֶׁק masc. dec. 6b, *desire, delight.*

חֲשֻׁקִים masc. pl. (of חָשׁוּק) *the poles*

a Is. 14. 6.   d Ge. 15. 12.   g Je. 14. 10.   k Ec. 12. 3.   n Ps. 18. 12.   Da. 2. 40.   r Ps. 68. 32.   t Joel 1. 7.   x 1 Ki. 20. 27.
b Ps. 19. 14.   e Is. 8. 22.   h Job 30. 10.   Is. 50. 10.   o Job 38. 26.   q Ezc. 1. 27.   s Is. 52. 10.   u Joel 1. 7.   y Is. 47. 2.
c Pr. 11. 24.   f Mi. 3. 6.   i La. 5. 17.   m Pr. 22. 29.

or *rods* which connected the pillars of the court of the tabernacle, and from which the curtains were suspended.

חֲשֻׁקִים masc. pl. (of חָשׁוּק) *spokes of a wheel*, 1 Ki. 7. 33.

חֵשֶׁק noun masc. sing. dec. 6b . . . חשק

חָשַׁק וַ Piel pret. 3 pers. sing. masc. (§ 10. rem. 1) חשק

חָשְׁקָה Kal pret. 3 pers. sing. fem. . חשק

חִשְׁקִי noun m. s., suff. 1 pers. s. from חֵשֶׁק dec. 6b חשק

חֲשַׂכְתֶּם וַ defect. for חָשׂוּ (q. v.) . . חשק

חֲשֻׁקֵיהֶם וַ noun m. pl., suff. 3 pers. pl. m. [fr. חָשׁוּק] חשק

חֲשַׂקְתָּ Kal pret. 2 pers. sing. masc.; acc. shifted
חֲשַׂקְתִּי by conv. וַ (§ 8. rem. 7) . . } חשק

חָשַׂר Root not used; Arab. *to collect*.

חַשְׁרָה fem. dec. 11 (§ 42. rem. 1) *a collection of waters*, 2 Sa. 22. 12.

חִשֻּׁרִים masc. pl. (of חִשּׁוּר) *the nave of a wheel*, 1 Ki. 7. 33.

חִשֻּׁרֵיהֶם וַ noun m. pl., suff. 3 pers. pl.m. [from חִשּׁוּר] חשר

חֶשְׁרַת noun fem. sing. constr. [of חַשְׁרָה or חֶשְׁרָה] חשר

חֲשַׁשׁ וַ masc. *dried grass, hay*, Is. 5. 24; 33. 11.

חַשְׁתִּי Kal pret. 1 pers. sing. . . . חשׁ

חַת [for חַת] noun masc. sing. dec. 8d & e חתת

חַת Kal pret. 3 pers. sing. masc. . . חתת

חֵת pr. name masc. . . . . חתת

חָתָה [חָתָה] fut. יַחְתֶּה (§ 13. rem. 5) *to take, lay hold of, seize*, spoken especially of taking *fire, coals*.

מַחְתָּה fem. dec. 10.—I. *fire-shovel* or *fire-pan*.—II. *censer*.—III. *snuff-dishes*; others, *snuffers*.

מַחַת (*taking, removal*) pr. name of a man.

חָתָה וַ Kal pret. 3 pers. sing. fem. (comp. § 8.
חָתָה rem. 7); for וַ see lett. וַ . } חתת

חֹתָה Kal part. act. sing. masc. . . חתת

חָתוּ וַ Kal pret. 3 pers. pl. (comp. §8. rem. 7);
חַתּוּ for וַ see lett. וַ . } חתת

חַתּוּ וַ id. imp. pl. masc.; וַ id. . חתת

חִתּוּל וַ noun masc. sing. . . . חתל

חָתוֹם וַ Kal inf. absolute . . . חתם

חָתוּם id. part. pass. sing. masc. dec. 3a חתם

חֲתוֹם id. imp. sing. masc. . . . חתם

חַתְחַתִּים וַ adj. masc., pl. of [חַתְחַת] dec. 8d חתת

חִתִּים adj. masc. pl. of [חַת] dec. 8d חתת

חִתִּית gent. noun, fem. of חִתִּי from חֵת חתת

חִתִּית noun fem. sing. dec. 1b . . חתת

חִתִּית gent. noun fem., pl. of חִתִּית from חִתִּי masc., see חֵת . . . . . חתת

חִתִּיתוֹ noun fem. sing., suff. Kh. תּוֹ' 3 pers. sing. masc., K. תִּי' 1 pers. s., from חִתִּית d. 1b חתת

חִתִּיתָם id., suff. 3 pers. pl. masc. . חתת

חָתַךְ Kal not used; Chald. *to cut, divide*. Niph. *to be determined*, Da. 9. 24.

הִתְכֶם וַ noun masc. sing., suff. 2 pers. pl. masc. from [חַת] dec. 8d . . . חתת

חָתַל Pu. & Hoph. *to be bandaged, swaddled*, Eze. 16. 4. חֲתֻלָּה fem. dec. 10, *bandage, swaddling band*, Job 38. 9.

חִתּוּל masc. *bandage* for a wound, Eze. 30. 21.

חִתְלוֹן (*covered place*) pr. name of a town 'n Syria.

חָתֹל pr. name of a place . . . . חתל

חִתַּלְתְּ Pual pret. 2 pers. sing. fem. [חֻתַּלְתְּ, comp. § 8. rem. 7] . . . . חתל

הֲחִתֻּלָתוֹ n. f. s., suff. 3 p. s. m. from [חֲתֻלָּה] d. 10 חתל

[חָתַם] fut. יַחְתֹּם (§ 13. rem. 5).—I. *to seal, seal up*, with the acc.; with בְּ of the seal-ring, also בְּעַד; rarely with בְּ, בְּעַד of the object, comp. Job 9. 7; 33. 16; 37. 7.—II. *to make an end of, finish*, Da. 9. 24.

חֲתַם Ch. *to seal, seal up*, Da. 6. 18.

חוֹתָם m. (no vowel change).—I. *seal, signet*.—II. pr. name masc. of two persons, 1 Ch. 7. 32; 11. 14.

חֹתֶמֶת fem. *seal, signet*, Ge. 38. 25.

חֲתֹם וַ Kal imp. sing. masc.; וַ bef. (-ִ) . חתם

חָתֻם id. part. pass. sing. masc. for חָתוּם . חתם

חֹתֻם defect. for חוֹתָם (q. v.) . . . חתם

חֲתַמַהּ וַ Ch. Peal pret. 3 pers. sing. masc., suff. 3 pers. sing. fem. . . . חתם

חִתְּמוּ Piel pret. 3 pers. pl. . . . חתם

חִתְמוּ וַ Kal imp. pl. masc. . . . חתם

חֲתֻמִים וַ id. part. p. masc., pl. of חָתוּם dec. 3a חתם

חֹתָמְךָ noun masc. sing., suff. 2 pers. sing. masc. from חוֹתָם (no vowel change) . חתם

[חָתַן] *to marry, give in marriage*, only part. חֹתֵן *father-in-law, the wife's father*; fem. חֹתֶנֶת *mother-in-law, the wife's mother*. Hithpa. *mutually to give and take daughters in marriage, to contract affinity by marriage*, with אֵת, בְּ, לְ.

ᵃ Ex. 38. 28.   ᵉ Is. 38. 17.   ⁱ Ps. 119. 60.   ᵐ Pr. 25. 22.   ᵠ Je. 32. 44.   ᵗ Eze. 32. 32.   ˣ Joo 38. 9.   ᵇ Ex. 28. 11.   ᵉ Est. 8. 8.
ᵇ Ge. 34. 8.   ᶠ De. 21. 11.   ᵏ Job 41. 25.   ⁿ Is. 8. 9. 9.   ʳ Is. 8. 16.   ᵘ Ge. 9. 2.   ʸ Da. 12. 4.   ᶜ Da. 6. 18.   ᶠ Da. 12. 9.
ᶜ Is. 21. 4.   ᵍ 1 Ki 7. 33.   ˡ Je. 50. 2.   ᵒ Eze. 30. 21.   ˢ Ec. 12. 5.   ᵛ Eze. 16. 4.   ᶻ Job 14. 17.   ᵈ Job 24. 16.   ᵍ Ge. 38. 18.
ᵈ 1 Ki. 7. 33.   ʰ 2 Sa. 22. 12.   ᵐ Je. 48. 1.   ᵖᵖ Je. 50. 36.   ⁿⁿ Eze. 32. 23, 27.

חָתָן masc. dec. 4 c.—I. *bridegroom, spouse*; Ex. 4. 25 חֲתַן דָּמִים *bridegroom of blood*, i. e. saved and become again her husband through her son's blood of circumcision, which Moses (as the intended mediator between God and Israel) had neglected and, on account of it, almost lost his life.— II. *son-in-law.*—III. *relative by marriage*, 2 Ki. 8. 27.

חֲתֻנָּה fem. dec. 10, *marriage*, Ca. 3. 11.

חֹתֵן noun masc. sing. dec. 4 c . . . . חתן

חֹתֵן ('ח) id. constr. state ; וְ bef. (־ֶ) . . חתן

חֹתֵן Kal part. act. sing. masc. dec. 7 b . . חתן

חֲתָנֵו noun m. s., suff. 3 pers. s. m. from חָתָן d. 4 c חתן

חֹתְנוֹ Kal part. act. sing. masc. (חֹתֵן) suff. 3 pers. sing. masc. dec. 7 b . . . חתן

חֲתָנָיו noun m. pl., suff. 3 p. s. m. from חָתָן d. 4 c חתן

חֹתֶנְךָ Kal part. act. sing. masc. (חֹתֵן) suff. 2 pers. sing. masc. (§ 36. rem. 1) . . . חתן

חֲתֻנָּתוֹ noun fem. sing., suff. 3 pers. sing. masc. from [חֲתֻנָּה] dec. 10 . . . חתן

חֹתַנְתּוֹ Kal part. act. sing. fem. [חֹתֶנֶת], suff. 3 pers. sing. masc. dec. 13 a, from חֹתֵן masc. חתן

[חָתַף] *to catch, seize*, Job 9. 12.

חֶתֶף masc. *prey, rapine*, Pr. 23. 28.

חָתַר fut. יַחְתֹּר (§ 13. rem. 15).—I. *to dig, break through.* —II. *to row*, Jon. 1. 13.

מַחְתֶּרֶת fem. *a digging through, breaking in.*

חֲתֹר Kal imp. sing. masc. [for חֲתָר § 8. rem. 18] חתר

חָתַרְתִּי id. pret. 1 pers. sing. . . . חתר

[חָתַת] fut. יֵחַתּוּ, יֵחַת (§ 18. rem. 6).—I. *to be broken* Is. 7. 8 ; 51. 6.—II. *to be terrified, dismayed, confounded.* Const. with מִפְּנֵי, מִן. Niph. *to be dismayed*, Mal. 2. 5.—Pi.—I. *to be broken in pieces, be shivered*, Je. 51. 56.—II. *to terrify, dismay*, Job 7. 14. Hiph.—I. *to break in pieces*, Is. 9. 3.— II. *to terrify, confound, confuse.*

חֲתַת masc.—I. *terror, dismay*, Job 6. 21.—II. pr name masc. 1 Ch. 4. 13.

חַת masc. dec. 8 e.—I. adj. *broken*, 1 Sa. 2. 4.— II. *terrified, dismayed*, Je. 46. 5.—III. subst. *terror dread.*

חֵת (*terror*) pr. name of the second son of Ca naan, Ge. 10. 15, &c. Gent. noun חִתִּי pl. חִתִּים.

חִתָּה fem. dec. 10, *terror, fear*, Ge. 35. 5.

חִתִּית fem. dec. 1 b, *terror, dread.*

חַתְחַת adj. masc. dec. 8 d, *terrified, dismayed*, Ec. 12. 5.

מְחִתָּה fem. dec. 10.—I. *destruction, ruin.*— II. *terror, fear.*

חֲתַת noun masc. sing., also pr. name masc. . חתת

חִתַּת noun fem. sing., constr. of [חִתָּה] dec. 10 חתת

חִתְּתָה Piel pret. 3 pers. sing. fem. . . . חתת

חִתְּתַנִי וַ id. pret. 2 pers. sing. masc. [for חִתַּתָּ § 25. rem.], suff. 1 pers. sing. . . . חתת

ט

טְאֵב Ch. *to be glad*, Da. 6. 24.

טָאֲמָתִים וַ Pilp. (§ 6. No. 4) pret. 1 pers. sing., suff. 3 pers. sing. fem. . . . טוא

טָב Ch. adj. masc. sing. . . . . טוב

טַבְאֵל, טָבְאַל } pr. name masc. . . . . . טוב

טוֹבוּ Kal pret. 3 pers. sing. (§ 21. rem. 2) . טוב

טָבוּחַ Kal part. pass. sing. masc. . . טבח

טְבוּלִים noun masc., pl. of [טָבוּל] dec. 3 a . . טבל

טָבּוּר noun masc. sing. . . . . טבר

טֻבוֹת וְ defect. for טוֹבוֹת (q. v.) . . . טוב

[טָבַח] *to slaughter*, especially *animals, but also of men, to slay, kill.*

טַבָּח masc. dec. 1 b.—I. *a cook*, 1 Sa. 9. 23, 24.

—II. *executioner, or guard*; for princes anciently employed their own *guards* as *executioners.*

טַבָּח Ch. masc. dec. 1 a, *executioner, or guard,* see Heb. טַבָּח

טַבָּחָה fem. *a cook*, 1 Sa. 8. 13.

טֶבַח masc. dec. 6 a (with suff. טִבְחָה ; but in pause טָבַח § 35. rem. 1 & 5).—I. *slaughter of animals, but also of men.*—II. *animals slaughtered, meat.*—III. pr. name masc. Ge. 22. 24.

טִבְחָה fem. (no pl.) i. q. טֶבַח.

טִבְחַת pr. name of a city in Syria, 1 Ch. 18. 8; but written בֶּטַח in 2 Sa. 8. 8.

מַטְבֵּחַ masc. *slaughter*, Is. 14. 21.

טֶבַח וְ noun masc. sing. dec. 6 a (suff. טִבְחָה § 35. rem. 5) also pr. name . . . טבח

טְבֹחַ[a] ׳ה Kal inf., or imp. sing. masc.; ה bef. (:) טבח

טָבְחָה id. pret. 3 pers. sing. fem.   .   . טבח

טִבְחָה noun fem. sing. (no pl.)   .   . טבח

טִבְחֹה noun masc. sing., suff. 3 pers. sing. fem. from
    dec. 6 a (§ 35. rem. 5) .   .   . טבח

טְבָחוֹ ה Kal pret. 3 pers. sing. masc., suff. 3 pers.
    sing. masc.; ה for ו conv.   .   . טבח

טַבָּחַיָּא Ch. noun masc. pl. emph. from ׳טְבָח dec. 1 a טבח

טַבָּחִים Heb. id. pl. abs. dec. 1 b   .   . טבח

טָבַחְתָּ Kal pret. 2 pers. sing. masc.   .   . טבח

טָבַחְתִּי id. pret. 1 pers. sing.   .   .   . טבח

טִבְחָתִי noun f. s., suff. 1 pers. s. from טִבְחָה (no pl.) טבח

טָבְיָה ו pr. name masc.   .   .   .   . טוב

טֹבִים ׳ו adj. masc., pl. of טוֹב dec. 1 a   . טוב

טְבַלְיָהוּ pr. name masc.   .   .   . טבל

טָבַל ו I. *to dip, immerse.*—II. *to stain,* Ge. 37. 31.
Arab. *to dye with colours.* Niph. pass. Jos. 3. 15.

טְבוּל masc. prop. *something dyed;* hence, *coloured
head-bands, turbans,* Eze. 23. 15. Others compare
this word with the Ethiop. טבל *to wrap, wind*
round.

טְבַלְיָהוּ (*whom the Lord has purified*) pr. name
masc. 1 Ch. 26. 11.

טֹבֵל ו id. part. act. masc. sing.   .   . טבל

טָבַלְתְּ ו id. pret. 2 pers. sing. fem.   .   . טבל

טְבַלְתֶּם ו id. pret. 2 pers. pl. masc.; ה for ו conv. . טבל

[טָבַע] I. *to sink,* as in water, mud.—II. *to sink, enter in,
penetrate,* 1 Sa. 17. 49. Pu. *to sink, be immersed,*
Ex. 15. 4. Hoph. *to be sunk, settled.*

טַבַּעַת fem. with suff. טַבַּעְתּוֹ, pl. טַבָּעוֹת (§ 44.
rem. 5).—I. *seal, seal-ring.*—II. *any ring.*

טַבָּעוֹת (*rings,* or *impressions*) pr. name of a
man, Ezr. 2. 43.

טָבְעוּ Kal pret. 3 pers. pl.   .   .   . טבע

טֻבְּעוּ Pual pret. 3 pers. pl.   .   .   . טבע

טַבְּעוֹת pr. name masc.   .   .   .   . טבע

טַבְּעֹת pl. of the following, see טַבַּעַת   . טבע

טַבַּעַת ׳ן n. f. s. d. 13 a, but pl. טַבָּעֹת (§ 44. r. 5) טבע

טַבָּעֹת id. pl. abs. state   .   .   .   . טבע

טַבְּעֹת id. pl., constr. state   .   .   . טבע

טַבַּעְתּוֹ id. sing., suff. 3 pers. sing. masc.   . טבע

טָבַעְתִּי Kal pret. 1 pers. sing.   .   .   . טבע

טַבְּעֹתֵיהֶם noun fem. pl., suff. 3 pers. pl. masc. (§ 4.
טַבְּעֹתָם rem. 2) from טַבַּעַת dec. 13 a

טָבַר Root not used; hence

טַבּוּר masc. h...h, *eminent place.* Comp. Chald. טור

טַבְרִמֹּן pr. name masc.   .   .   .   . טוב

טִבָּת (*celebrated* i. q. Syr. טָבִיבָא) pr. name of a
town in the tribe of Ephraim, Ju. 7. 22.

טֹבַת adj. fem. s., constr. of טוֹבָה d. 10, fr. טוֹב m. טוב

טֵבֵת *Tebeth,* the tenth month of the Hebrew year,
Est. 2. 16.

טֹבֹת ׳ן adj. or subst. f., pl. of טוֹבָה from טוֹב m. טוב

טֹבֹתָם ו id. subst. sing., suff. 3 pers. pl. masc. טוב

טָהוֹר adj. masc. sing. dec. 3 a   .   . טהר

טְהוֹר id. const. state   .   .   .   . טהר

טְהוֹר Kh. טְהֹר q. v., K. טָהֹר (q. v.) .   . טהר

טְהוֹרָה adj. fem. sing. dec. 10, from טָהוֹר masc. טהר

טְהוֹרִים id. pl. masc. dec. 3 a .   .   . טהר

טָהֵר ן *to be* or *become clean, pure,* in a physical and
moral sense. Pi. טִהַר (§ 14. rem. 1).—I. *to cleanse,
purify.*—II. *to pronounce* or *declare clean.* Pu. *to
be cleansed,* Eze. 22. 24. Hithp. הִטַּהֵר, הִטָּהֵר
(for הִתְטַהֵר § 12. rem. 3; § 14. rem. 1) *to cleanse
or purify oneself.*

טָהוֹר masc. dec. 3 a (טָהֹר § 32. rem. 7), טְהוֹרָה
fem. dec. 10, adj. *clean, pure,* in a physical and
moral sense.

טֹהַר masc. dec. 6 f.—I. *brightness, clearness,
splendour.*—II. *purification,* Le. 12. 4, 6.

טָהֳרָה fem. constr. טָהֳרַת (no pl.).—I. *purity*
of heart, 2 Ch. 30. 19.—II. *cleansing, purification.*

טַהֵר Piel inf. constr. (§ 14. rem. 1)   .   . טהר

טִהַר ו Piel pret. 3 pers. sing. masc. (§ 14. rem. 1) טהר

טְהַר ה Kal imp. sing. masc. [for טְהָר]; ו bef. (:) טהר

טְהָר ה with Mak. for טָהֹר q. v. (§ 32. rem. 7) טהר

טָהֲרָה ן Kal pret. 3 pers. sing. fem. (§ 8. rem.
טָהֳרָה ׳ן 1 a & 7) *Le. 12. 8.   .   .   .

טָהֳרָה noun fem. sing. dec. 10   .   .   . טהר

טָהֳרֹה noun m. s., suff. 3 p. s. fem. from ׳טֹהַר dec. 6 f טהר

טְהֹרָה ׳ן adj. fem. s. dec. 10, from טָהוֹר m.; ו bef. (:) טהר

טִהֲרוֹ ן Piel pret. 3 pers. sing. masc., suff. 3 pers.
    sing. masc. (§ 14. rem. 1)   .   . טהר

טִהֲרוּ ן id. pret. 3 pers. pl.   .   .   . טהר

טְהֹרוֹת adj. fem., pl. of טְהוֹרָה dec. 10, from טָהוֹר m. טהר

טַהֲרִי Piel inf. (§ 14. rem. 1) suff. 1 p. s. dec. 7 b טהר

טְהֹרִים ה adj. masc., pl. of טָהוֹר dec. 3 a; ה bef. (:) טהר

טִהֲרֵנוּ Piel pret. 1 pers. pl. (§ 14. rem. 1) טהר

טַהֲרֵנִי id. imp. sing. masc., suff. 1 pers. sing. טהר

טָהַרְתְּ Kal pret. 2 pers. sing. fem.   .   . טהר

a Esc. 21. 15.   e Pr. 9. 2.   i 1 Sa. 25. 11.   n Ru. 3. 14.   r Ex. 35. 22.   w Ge. 6. 2.   a Eze. 39. 12.   f Le. 12. 7.   h Pr. 15. 26.
b Ge. 43. 16.   f Kr. 21. 37.   k 1 Sa. 25. 11.   o Ex. 12. 22.   s Ps. 69. 3.   x De. 25. 7.   b 2 Ki. 5. 10, 13.   g Le. 12. 4, 5.   l 2 Ch. 29. 18.
c Pr. 9. 2.   g Da. 2. 14.   l 1 Ki. 2. 32.   p Ex. 15. 4.   t Ex. 26. 29.   y Hab. 1. 13.   c Job 17. 9.   h Le. 12. 4, 6.   m Ps. 51. 4.
d Ps. 44. 26.   h La. 2. 21.   m De. 33. 34.   q Nu. 31. 50.   u Ex. 36. 34.   z Pr. 22. 11.   d Le. 15. 28.   i Nu. 5. 28.   n Eze. 24. 13.

טִהַרְתְּ[a] וְ Piel pret. 2 pers. sing. fem. (§ 14. rem. 1);
acc. shifted by conv. וְ (comp. § 8. rem. ?)   טהר

טׇהֳרַת noun fem. sing., constr. of טׇהֳרָה (no pl.)   טהר

טׇהֳרָתוֹ[b] id., suff. 3 pers. sing. masc.   טהר

טִהַרְתִּי } Kal pret. 1 pers. sing. (§ 8. rem. 7)   טהר
טׇהַרְתִּי }

טִהַרְתִּי וְ Piel pret. 1 pers. sing. (§ 14. rem. 1); acc.
shifted by וְ conv. (comp. id.)   .   טהר

טִהַרְתִּיךָ id., suff. 2 pers. sing. fem.   טהר

טִהַרְתִּים וְ id., suff. 3 pers. pl. masc.   טהר

טִהַרְתֶּם וְ Kal pret. 2 pers. pl. masc.; וְ for conv.   טהר

טוֹא Root not used; Syr. *to fast*.
טוׇת Chald. *a fasting*, Da. 6. 19.

טוּא Kal not used; probably *to remove* or *be removed*,
cogn. זוע. Pilp. טִאטֵא (§ 6. No. 4) *to remove*
dirt or *mire, to sweep away*, Is. 14. 23.
מַטְאֲטֵא masc. *besom*, Is. 14. 23.
טִיט masc. *mire, mud*. Talmud. טיאוט *a sweeping out*.

טוֹב וְ pl. טֹבוּ (§ 21. rem. 2).—I. *to be good, well,*
agreeable, pleasant; impers. טוֹב לִי *it is well with*
me; טוֹב בְּעֵינַי *it pleases me*; it is also followed
by עַל, אֶל.—II. *to be cheerful, joyful.* Hiph.
I. *to do well, act rightly.*—II. *to do good*, Eze. 36. 11.
—III. *to make fair, beautiful*, Ho. 10. 1.—IV. *to*
make cheerful, Ec. 11. 9.

טוֹב masc. dec. 1a, טוֹבָה fem. dec. 10, adj.—
I. *good, agreeable, pleasant.*—II. *goodly, fair, beau-*
tiful.—III. *happy, prosperous.*—IV. *cheerful, joyful.*
—V. adv. *well, rightly.* Subst. (masc. and fem.).—
I. *good, what is good.*—II. *goodness*, Ps. 16. 2; 65. 12.
—III. *wealth*, Ec. 5. 10.—IV. *prosperity, happiness*,
Ps. 106. 5. טוֹב pr. name of a region beyond Jordan.
טוֹב אֲדֹנִיָּה pr. name masc. 2 Ch. 17. 8.
טוּב masc. dec. 1a.—I. *goodness.*—II. concr. *the*
good, the best.—III. *wealth.*—IV. *beauty.*—V. *pros-*
perity, happiness.—VI. *cheerfulness.*
טוֹבִיָּהוּ, טוֹבִיָּה (*the Lord is good*) pr. name masc.
of several persons.
טב Chald. *good, pleasing.*
טׇבְאֵל in pause טׇבְאָל (*God is good*) pr. name
masc.—I. Is. 7. 6.—II. Ezr. 4. 7.
טַבְרִמּוֹן (*Rimmon is good*) pr. name of the
father of Benhadad, king of Syria, 1 Ki. 15. 18.

טוֹב נָ, רָ, adj. or subst. masc. sing. dec. 1a, also
pr. name; for ? see lett. ו.   טוב

טוּב noun masc. sing. dec. 1a   טוב

טוֹבָה וְ adj. or subst. fem. dec. 10, from טוב masc.   טוב

טֻבָּהּ[g] נָ n. m. s., suff. 3 p. s. fem. from טוב dec. 1a   טוב

טוּבוֹ id., suff. 3 pers. sing. masc.   טוב

טֹבוֹת adj. or subst. fem., pl. of טוֹבָה (q. v.)   טוב

טוּבִי noun m. s., suff. 1 pers. sing. from טוב dec. 1a   טוב

טוֹבֵי וְ adj. masc. pl. constr. from טוב dec. 1a   טוב

טוֹבִיָּה וְ } pr. name masc.   טוב
טוֹבִיָּהוּ וְ }

טוֹבִים וְ adj. masc., pl. of טוב dec. 1a   טוב

טוּבְךָ noun m. s., suff. 2 p. s. m. from טוב dec. 1a   טוב

טוּבָם noun masc. sing., suff. 3 pers. pl. masc. from
טוב dec. 1a   טוב

טוּבָם[k] noun m. s., suff. 3 p. pl. m. from טוב dec. 1a   טוב

טוֹבַת וְ adj. fem. sing., constr. of טוֹבָה dec. 10,
from טוב masc.   טוב

טוֹבָתִי[m] id. (subst.), suff. 1 pers. sing.   טוב

טוֹבֹתָיו id. (subst.) pl., suff. 3 pers. sing. masc.   טוב

טוֹבָתֶךָ[n] id. (subst.) s., suff. 2 pers. s. m. [for טֹבָתְךָ]   טוב

טוֹבָתָם וְ id. id., suff. 3 pers. pl. masc.   טוב

[טׇוָה] *to spin*, Ex. 35. 25, 26.
מַטְוֶה masc. *yarn*, Ex. 35. 25.

טׇווּ[o] Kal pret. 3 pers. pl.   טוה

[טוּחַ] *to besmear, daub, plaster* or *cover over*, as a wall;
metaph. the eyes, so as not to see. Niph. pass.
Le. 14. 43, 48.
טֻחוֹת fem. pl. (of מֻחָה) *the inward parts, the*
reins, Job 38. 36; Ps. 51. 8.
טִיחַ masc. *a plastering*, Eze. 13. 12.

טֹחֵן[p] Kal part. act. sing. masc.   טחן

טוּל Hiph. *to throw, cast, to cast out* or *forth.* Hoph.
to be cast down, out or *forth.* Pilp. (§ 6. No. 4)
to cast forth with violence, Is. 22. 17.
טַלְטֵלָה fem. *a casting forth*, Is. 22. 17.

טוּף Root not used; Arab. *to surround, bind round.*
טוֹטָפוֹת fem. pl. (for טָפְטָפוֹת, like כּוֹכָב for
כַּבְכָּב) *frontlets, phylacteries.*

טוּר וְ masc. dec. 1a, *series, order, range, row.*
טִירָה fem. dec. 10.—I. *row* or *range of build-*
ings or chambers, Eze. 46. 23.—II. *castle* or *palace.*

יְטוּר (*castle*) pr. name of a son of Ishmael and of a people descended from him.

[טְוֹר] Ch. masc. dec. 1 a, *mountain*, Da. 2. 35, 45. Targ. טוּר, cogn. טַבּוּר q. v.

טוֹרֵד Kal part. act. sing. masc.

טוּרֵי noun masc. pl. constr. from טוּר dec. 1 a

טוּרִים id. pl., absolute state

[טוּשׁ] *to fly swiftly*, Job 9. 26.

טוּחַ Chald. noun fem. sing.

טָח Kal pret. 3 pers. sing. masc.

טָח id. id. as if from R. טחח (§ 21. rem. 2) see טוח

טָחָה Kal not used; Arab. *to expand*; perhaps *to impel, drive, shoot*, cogn. דָּחַק, דָּחַף, דָּחָה. Pilel part. (§ 6. No. 2, & § 24. r. 22) מְטַחֲוֵי קֶשֶׁת *extenders or shooters of the bow*, i. e. *bowmen, archers*, Ge. 21. 16.

טָחֲנוּ Kal pret. 3 pers. pl.

טָחוֹן Kal inf. abs.

טָחוֹן noun masc. sing.

טָחֲיֵ construct of the following:

טָחִים Kal part. masc., pl. of טָח dec. 1 a

[טָחַן] *to bruise; grind with a hand-mill*; Is. 3. 15, *to grind the face of the poor*, i. e. to oppress him.
   טַחֲן masc. *hand-mill*, La. 5. 13.
   טַחֲנָה fem. id. Ec. 12. 4.

טָחֲנוּ Kal pret. 3 pers. pl.

טַחֲנִי id. imp. sing. fem.

טָחַר Root not used; Syr. *to pant, to strain hard in discharging the fæces.*
   טְחֹרִים masc. pl. (of טְחֹר dec. 1 a) *tumors in the anus, hemorrhoids,* in Keri, for Kheth. עֲפָלִים.

טְחֹרֵי Keri, noun masc. pl. constr. from [טְחוֹר] dec. 1. Kh. עֲפֹלֵי (q. v.)

טְחֹרֵיהֶם Keri, id., suff. 3 pers. pl. masc., Kh. עֲפֹלֵיהֶם

טַחְתֶּם Kal pret. 2 pers. pl. masc.

טִיט noun masc. sing.; for ן see lett. ו

[טִין] Ch. masc. *clay, potter's clay*, only in the following form.

טִינָא Ch. noun masc. sing. emph. of [טִין] dec. 1 a.

טִירוֹתֵיהֶם n.fem.pl., suff. 3 p.pl.m. from [טִירָה] dec.10.

טִירֹת id. sing., construct state

טִירָתָם id. sing., suff. 3 pers. pl. masc.

טִירֹתָם id. pl., suff. 3 pers. pl. masc. (§ 4. rem. 2)

טַל / וְטַל noun masc. sing. dec. 8 d

טָלָא only part. pass. טְלוּא *patched*, i. e. *spotted*. Pu. part. *patched, clouted,* Jos. 9. 5.

טְלֻאוֹת Kal part. pass. pl. fem. from טָלָא masc.

טְלָאִים noun m., pl. of [טְלִי] dec. 6 i (§ 35. rem. 15)

טְלֻאִים Kal part.p.m.,pl. of טָלָא dec.3 a; bef.

טָלֵה Root not used; Syr. *to be fresh, young.*
   טָלֶה masc. dec. 9 b, *young lamb.*
   טְלִי masc. only pl. טְלָאִים (§ 35. rem. 15).—I. *lambs*, Is. 40. 11.—II. pr. name of a place in the tribe of Judah, 1 Sa. 15. 4, supposed to be the same which is called טֶלֶם in Jos. 15. 24.

טָלֶה noun masc. sing. dec. 9 b

טְלֵה id., construct state

טָלוּא Kal part. pass. sing. masc. dec. 3 a

טַלְטֵלָה noun fem. sing.

טַלְךָ noun masc. sing., suff. 2 pers. sing. masc. [for טַלְּךָ] from [טַל] dec. 8 d

טָלַל Root not used; Arab.—I. *to moisten.*—II. *to shade, to cover.* Pi. *to cover, to roof*, Ne. 3. 15.
   טְלַל Ch. Aph. *to take shade*, Da. 4. 9.
   טַל masc. dec. 3 c, *dew.* Chald. id.

טֶלֶם Root not used; Arab. *to oppress.*
   טֶלֶם (*oppression*) pr. name of a city in the tribe of Judah, Jos. 15. 24, comp. also טְלִי R. טָלֶה.
   טַלְמוֹן (*oppressed*) pr. name masc. Ezr. 2. 42; Ne. 7. 45, &c.

טַלָּם noun m.s.with suff. 3 p.pl. m.from טַל dec.8 d

טֶלֶם pr. name of a city

טַלְמוֹן / טַלְמֹן pr. name masc.

טָמֵא *to be unclean, defiled*, with בְּ *with* anything.
   טָמֵא masc. dec. 5 a (constr. טְמֵא § 34. rem. 1), טְמֵאָה fem. dec. 10, adj. *unclean, defiled*; טְמֵאַת הַשֵּׁם *infamous.*
   טֻמְאָה Mi. 2. 10, & טָמְאָה fem. dec. 10.—I. *uncleanness, pollution.*—II. concr. *an unclean thing.*

טָמֵא adj. masc. sing. dec. 5 a

טמא	Piel inf. constr. used also as an abs. . . טמא
טָמֵא	adj. m. s., constr. of טָמֵא dec. 5 a (§ 34. rem. 1) טמא
טִמֵּא '1	Piel pret. 3 pers. sing. masc. . . . טמא
טָמְאָה 1	Kal pret. 3 pers. sing. fem. . . . טמא
טֻמְאָה	noun fem. sing. . . . . . טמא
טְמֵאָה	adj. fem. sing. dec. 10, from טָמֵא masc. טמא
טֻמְאָה	noun fem. sing. dec. 10. . . . טמא
טָמְאוּ 1	Kal pret. 3 pers. pl. . . . . טמא
טַמְּאוּ	Piel imp. pl. masc. . . . . . טמא
טִמְּאוֹ 1	id. pret. 3 pers. s. m., suff. 3 pers. s. m. טמא
טִמְּאוּ '1	id. pret. 3 pers. pl. . . . . טמא
טִמְּאוּהָ	id. id., suff. 3 pers. sing. fem. . . טמא
טֻמְאוֹתֵיכֶם	n. f. pl., suff. 2 p. pl. m. fr. טֻמְאָה d. 10. טמא
טְמֵאִים	adj. masc., pl. of טָמֵא d. 5 a; 1 bef. (:) טמא
טָמֵאת	Kal pret. 2 pers. sing. fem. (§ 23. rem. 1) טמא
טְמֵאַת	adj. fem. sing., constr. of טְמֵאָה, fr. טָמֵא m. טמא
טִמֵּאת	Piel pret. 2 pers. sing. fem. . . טמא
טֻמְאָתָהּ	noun fem. sing., suff. 3 pers. sing. fem. fr.
	טֻמְאָה dec. 10. . . . . טמא
טֻמְאָתוֹ '1	id., suff. 3 pers. sing. masc. . . טמא
טֻמְאָתֵךְ	id., suff. 2 pers. sing. fem. . . . טמא
טִמֵּאתֶם '1	Piel pret. 2 pers. pl. masc. . . . טמא
טֻמְאֹתָם '1	noun fem. pl., suff. 3 pers. pl. masc. from
	טֻמְאָה dec. 10. . . . . טמא
טָמָה.	Niph. to be unclean, despised, Job 18.3, but comp.
	§ 23. rem. 11.
טָמוּן	Kal part. pass. sing. masc. dec. 3 a . . טמן
טְמוּנָה	id. fem. sing. . . . . . טמן
טְמוּנֵי	id. pl. constr. masc. . . . . טמן
טָמַן	I. to hide, conceal, especially in the earth.—II. to
	hide, reserve, with לְ for any one. Niph. to hide
	oneself, Is. 2. 10. Hiph. to hide, 2 Ki. 7. 8.
	מַטְמוֹן masc. dec. 1 b, (pl. c. מַטְמֹנֵי § 30. r. 4)
	store, treasure.
טָמְנֵהוּ 1	Kal imp. sing. masc., suff. 3 pers. sing. m. טמן
טָמְנוּ 1	
טָמְנוּ	} Kal pret. 3 pers. pl. (§ 8. rem. 7) . טמן
טְמֻנִים	id. part. pass. masc., pl. of טָמוּן dec. 3 a טמן
טָמְנָם	id. imp. sing. masc., suff. 3 pers. pl. masc. טמן
טָמַנְתִּי	id. pret. 1 pers. sing. [for טָמַנְתְּי § 8. r. 7] טמן
טְמָנְתִּיו	id. id., suff. 3 pers. sing. masc. . טמן
טְמַנְתָּם	id. pret. 2 pers. sing. masc., suff. 3 pers.
	pl. masc.; 1 for 1, conv. . . טמן
[טֶנֶא]	masc. dec. 6 a, basket, De. 26. 2, 4; 28. 5, 17.

טִנְּאֲךָ	id. with suff. 2 pers. sing. masc. . . טנא
טָנַף.	Pi. to soil, pollute, Ca. 5. 3.
טָעָה	Kal not used; i. q. תָּעָה. Hiph. to cause to err, to seduce, Eze. 13. 10.
טָעַם	I. to taste.—II. metaph. to perceive, discriminate.
	טְעֵם Ch. Aph. to cause to taste, i. e. make to eat, to feed.
	טַעַם masc. dec. 6 d.—I. taste.—II. discernment, judgment.—III. decree, edict, Jon. 3. 7.
	טְעֵם Ch. masc. edict, decree.
	טְעֵם Ch. masc. dec. 3 a.—I. taste, Da. 5. 2.—II. discernment, judgment.—III. decree, edict; בְּעֵל טְעֵם master of the decrees, an officer under the Persian government, as Master of the rolls.
	מַטְעָם masc. only pl. מַטְעַמּוֹת, מַטְעַמִּים dainty meat.
טַעַם	} noun masc. sing. dec. 6 d (suff. טַעְמוֹ
טַעַם '1	} § 35. rem. 5) } טעם
טָעֹם	Kal inf. absolute . . . . . טעם
טְעֵם '1	Ch. noun masc. sing. dec. 3 a; 1 bef. (:) טעם
טַעְמָא	} Ch. id., emph. state.
טַעְמָא	}
טָעֲמָה	Kal pret. 3 pers. sing. fem. . . . טעם
טַעֲמוּ	id. imp. pl. masc. . . . . . טעם
טַעְמוֹ '1	noun masc. sing., suff. 3 pers. sing. masc. from טַעַם dec. 6 d (§ 35. rem. 5) . . טעם
טַעְמֵךְ	id., suff. 2 pers. sing. fem. (§ 35. rem. 5) טעם
טָעַמְתִּי	Kal pret. 1 pers. sing. . . . טעם
[טָעַן]	I. to load, as beasts of burden, Ge. 45. 17.—II. Pu. to be thrust through, Is. 14. 19.
טַעֲנוּ	Kal imp. pl. masc. . . . . טען
טַף	n. masc. sing. dec. 8 d; for 1 see lett. 1 טפף
טָפוֹף	Kal inf. absolute . . . . טפף
טָפַח.	Pi.—I. to spread out, to extend, Is. 48. 13.—II. denom. of טֶפַח to stroke with the palm of the hand, to caress or dandle, La. 2. 22. Eng. Vers. " swaddle," from the idea of spreading out, which is perhaps to be preferred; comp. מִטְפַּחַת.
	טֶפַח masc. dec. 6 a (§ 35. r. 5).—I. palm, hand-breadth, a measure.—II. pl. coping stones of a building, 1 Ki. 7. 9.
	טֹפַח masc. hand-breadth, a measure.

a Ml. 2. 10.   c Eze. 43. 8.   k Eze. 22. 5, 10.   g Le. 16. 16.   t Pu. 9. 16.   e Je. 13. 7.   d Job 12. 20.   h Pr. 31. 18.   m 1 Sa. 14. 29, 43.
b Le. 15. 18.   f Eze. 36. 18.   l Eze. 5. 11.   u Jos. 7. 21.   f Je. 43. 9.   c 1 Sa. 14. 43.   i Ps. 34. 9.   n Ge. 45. 17.
Eze. 9. 7.   g Ese. 36. 25, 29   Eze. 22. 15.   v De. 33. 19.   r Job 40. 13.   d Da. 2. 14.   k Ex. 16. 31.   o Je. 40. 7.
Le. 13. 8, 11.   h Le. 11. 35.   Eze. 33. 26.   w Je. 13. 4.   y Je. 43. 10.   e 1 Sa. 14. 24.   g Ex. 5. 5.   l 1 Sa. 25. 53.   p Is. 2. 16.
M. 32.   i Eze. 22. 4.   Is. 30. 22.

טְפֻחִים masc. pl. (of טְפֻח) *a nursing of children,* La. 2. 20, comp. the Root.

מִטְפַּחַת fem. pl. מִטְפָּחוֹת (§ 44. rem. 5) *upper garment, mantle, cloak.*

טֶפַח   noun masc. sing. dec. 6 (§ 35. rem. 5) . . . טפח

טֹפַח   ןֹ noun masc. sing.; for ןֹ see lett. ו . . . טפח

טִפְּחָה   Piel pret. 3 pers. sing. fem. . . . טפח

טִפֻּחוֹת   noun masc. with pl. fem. term. fr. טֶפַח d. 6 (§ 35. rem. 5) . . . טפח

טְפֻחִים   noun masc. pl. [from טֶפַח] . . . טפח

טִפַּחְתִּי   Piel pret. 1 pers. sing. . . . טפח

טַפְּכֶם   ןֹ noun masc. sing., suff 2 pers. pl. masc. from טַף dec. 8 d . . . טפף

[טָפַל]   *to devise, contrive, forge* (Talm. *to join, to sew on*). Prof. Lee, *to cover, conceal.*

טָפְלוּ   Kal pret. 3 pers. pl. . . . טפל

טֹפְלֵי   id. part. act. pl. c. masc. fr. [טֹפֵל] dec. 7 b . . . טפל

טַפָּם   ןֹ noun masc. sing., suff. 3 pers. pl. masc. from טַף dec. 8 d . . . טפף

טַפֵּנוּ   ןֹ id. with suff. 1 pers. pl. . . . טפף

טִפְסַר   masc. *general, chief.*

טַפְסְרַיִך   ןֹ id. pl., suff. 2 pers. sing. fem.

[טָפַף]   *to trip, mince,* Is. 3. 16.

טַף   masc. dec. 8 d, *little ones, little children.*

[טְפַר]   Chald. masc. dec. 3 b.—I. *nail* of a man, Da. 4. 30. —II. *claw* of an animal, Da. 7. 19.

טִפְרַיָּא   ןֹ Ch. noun masc. pl., suff. 3 pers. sing. fem. from [טְפַר] dec. 3 b . . . טפר

טִפְרוֹהִי   ןֹ Ch. id., suff. 3 pers. sing. masc. . . . טפר

טָפַשׁ   *to be fat,* only metaph. *to be stupid,* Ps. 119. 70.

טָפַת   pr. name fem. . . . נטף

טֹרֵד   only part. act. *beating, tempestuous,* of rain, comp. Chald. טְרַד; others, *continual* i.e. *continual dropping.* טְרַד Chald. *to thrust forth, to drive out.* מַטְרֵד (*expeller*) pr. name masc. Ge. 36. 39.

טֹרֵד   Kal part. act. sing. masc. . . . טרד

טָרְדִין   Ch. Peal part. act. masc., pl. of [טְרַד] d. 2 b . . . טרד

טָרָה   Root not used; Arab. *to be fresh, new.*

טְרִי   adj. fem. טְרִיָּה, *fresh, moist*

טָרַח   Hiph. *to load, burden,* Job 37. 11. טֹרַח masc. dec. 6 c (§ 35. rem. 5) *burden, trouble.*

טָרְחֲכֶם   noun masc. sing., suff. 2 pers. pl. masc. from טֹרַח dec. 6 c (§ 35. rem. 5) . . . טרח

טְרִיד   Ch. Peal part. pass. sing. masc. . . . טרד

טְרִיָּה   adj. fem. sing. [from טְרִי masc.] . . . טרה

טְרִים   noun masc. (for טוֹרִים) pl. of טוּר dec. 1 a . . . טור

טֶרֶם   ןֹ adv. *not yet*; conj. בְּטֶרֶם *when not yet, before that*; מִטֶּרֶם, טֶרֶם id. טְרוֹם *not yet,* Ru. 3. 14. Khethib.

טָרַף   ןֹ fut. יִטְרֹף, יִטְרָף *to tear in pieces, to rend.* Niph. pass. Pu. id. Hiph. *to feed, provide for,* Pr. 30. 8. טָרָף adj. masc. *fresh, new,* Ge. 8. 11. Others, *plucked off.* טֶרֶף masc. dec. 6 a (with suff. טַרְפּוֹ).—I. *prey.*—II. *food, provision.*—III. *leaf,* Eze. 17. 9, from th. idea of *freshness,* comp. טָרָף. טְרֵפָה fem. *any thing torn by wild beasts*

טָרָף   ןֹ Kal pret. 3 pers. s. m. for טָרַף (§ 8. r. 7) . . . טרף

טָרָף   adj. masc. sing. . . . טרף

טָרֹף   Kal inf. absolute . . . טרף

טֶרֶף, טָרֶף   ןֹ noun masc. sing. dec. 6 a (§ 35. r. 2) . . . טרף

טֹרַף, טֹרָף   } Pual pret. 3 pers. s. m. (comp. § 8. r. 7) . . . טרף

טֹרֵף   Kal part. act. sing. masc. dec. 7 b . . . טרף

טְרֵפָה   ןֹ noun fem. sing.; ןֹ bef. ⟨:⟩ . . . טרף

טַרְפּוֹ   noun masc. sing., suff. 3 pers. sing. masc. from טֶרֶף dec. 6 a . . . טרף

טַרְפֵּי   id. pl., constr. state . . . טרף

טֹרְפֵים   Kal part. act. pl. c. masc. fr. טֹרֵף dec. 7 b . . . טרף

טַרְפֵּךְ   noun masc. sing., suff. 2 pers. sing. fem. fr. טֶרֶף dec. 6 a . . . טרף

טַרְפְּלָיֵא   Ch. pr. name of a people, Ezr. 4. 9.

a Is. 48. 13.   d La. 2. 22.   g Nu. 16. 27.   k Na. 3. 17.   n Pr. 19. 13.   q 1 Ki. 7. 20.   t Ho. 6. 1.   v Ge. 44. 28.   z Ese. 17. 9.
b Ps. 39. 6.   e Ps. 119. 69.   h Nu. 14. 3.   l Da. 7. 19.   o Da. 4. 22, 29.   r 1 Sa. 3. 7.   u Ge. 8. 11.   w Ge. 37. 33.   a Ese. 22. 27.
c La. 2. 20.   f Job 14. 4.   i Je. 51. 27.   m Da. 4. 30.   p De. 1. 12.   s Job 16. 9.   x Am. 3. 4.   y Is. 31. 4.   d Na. 2. 14.

י

[יָאַב] to desire, long for, with לְ.   Ps. 119. 131

יְאַבֵּד־ / יֹאבֶד־ } Piel fut. 3 pers. sing. masc. (§ 10. rem. 4)   אבד

וַיְאַבֵּד [for וַיֹּאבַד, וַיֹּאבֵד] . id. with conj. וְ   אבד

יֹאבַד / יֹאבֵד } Kal fut. 3 pers. sing. masc. (§ 19. rem. 1)   אבד

יֹאבְדוּ Chald. Peal fut. 3 pers. pl. masc. (§ 53) .   אבד

יֹאבֵדוּ Kh. יֹאבְדוּ q. v., K. וְאָבְדוּ (q. v.)   אבד

יֹאבְדוּ / וַיֹּ' } Kal fut. 3 pers. pl. masc. (§ 19. rem. 1); וְ conv.   אבד

וַיֹּאבְדֵם } Piel fut. 3 pers. pl. masc., suff. 3 pers. pl. masc.; וְ id.   אבד

יְאַבְּדֵם } id. fut. 3 pers. sing. m., suff. 3 pers. pl. m.   אבד

יֹאבֶה Kal fut. 3 pers. sing. masc. (§ 25. No. 2c)   אבה

יֹאבוּ id. fut. 3 pers. pl. masc.   אבה

יַאֲבֵל־ } Hiph. fut. 3 pers. sing. masc. ap. [for יַאֲבֵל § 11. rem. 7]; וְ conv.   אבל

יֵאָבֵק } Niph. fut. 3 pers. sing. masc.; וְ id.   אבק

יַאֲבֵר } Hiph. fut. 3 pers. sing. masc. ap. [for יַאֲבִיר § 11. rem. 7]   אבר

יָאַבְתִּי Kal pret. 3 pers. s. [for יָאַבְתָּ § 8. rem. 7]   יאב

יַאֲדִימוּ Hiph. fut. 3 pers. pl. m. (§ 13. rem. 5 & 9)   אדם

יַאֲדִיר Hiph. fut. 3 pers. s. m. (§ 13. rem. 5 & 9)   אדר

[יָאָה] to be suitable, becoming, with לְ.   Je. 10. 7.

יֶאֱהַב / יֶאֱהָב / וַיֶּ' } Kal fut. 3 pers. sing. masc. (§ 8. rem. 15, & § 13. rem. 5); וְ conv.   אהב

יֶאֱהָבֶהָ } id., suff. 3 pers. sing. fem. (§ 16. rem. 12)   אהב

יֶאֱהָבֵהוּ } id., suff. 3 pers. sing. masc. (v. id.)   אהב

יֶאֱהָבֵן } id., suff. 3 pers. sing. masc., Kh. בֹ', K. בֵהוּ   אהב

יֶאֱהָבֵךְ } id., suff. 2 pers. s. m. for [הָבְךָ] (§ 2. r. 2)   אהב

יֶאֱהָבֵנִי id. with suff. 1 pers. sing. (§ 16. rem. 12)   אהב

יַאֲהִיל Hiph. fut. 3 pers. sing. masc.   אהל

יַאֲהֵל } Kal fut. 3 pers. sing. masc.; וְ conv.   אהל

יְאֹר noun masc. sing. dec. 1a   יאר

יְאֹרֵי id. pl., constr. state   יאר

יֹאשִׁיָּהוּ Kh., יֹאשִׁיָּהוּ K. (q. v.)   אשה

יַאֲזִין Hiph. fut. 3 pers. sing. masc.   אזן

יַאֲזִינוּ id. fut. 3 pers. pl. masc.   אזן

יַאֲזַנְיָה / יַאֲזַנְיָהוּ } pr. name masc.   אזן

יַאֲזְרֵנִי Kal fut. 3 pers. sing. masc. יֵאֹזֹר comp. תֵּאֹזֹר [§ 13. rem. 4], suff. 1 pers. s. (§ 13. rem. 6)   אזר

יֹאחֵז / וַיֹּ' } Kal fut. 3 pers. sing. masc., acc. shifted by conv. וַ (§ 19. rem. 2)   אחז

יֹאחֵז] id., with moveable א (§ 19. rem. 4); וְ id.   אחז

יֵאָחֵז] Niph. fut. 3 pers. sing. masc.; וְ id.   אחז

יֹאחֲזוּ] Kal fut. 3 pers. pl. masc.; וְ id.   אחז

יֹאחֲזֶנָּה] id. id., suff. 3 pers. sing. masc.; וְ id.   אחז

יֹאחֲזֵךְ] id. id., suff. 2 pers. sing. fem.   אחז

יֹאחֲזוּן] id. id. with parag. ן (§ 8. rem. 17)   אחז

יֹאחֲזֵנִי] id. id., suff. 1 pers. sing.   אחז

יֹאחֲזֵמוֹ] id. fut. 3 pers. sing. masc., suff. 3 pers. pl. m.   אחז

יְאַחֵר Piel fut. 3 pers. sing. masc. (§ 14. rem. 1)   אחר

יַאֲטֵם Hiph. fut. 3 pers. sing. masc. ap. [יַאֲטֵם, § 13. rem. 9, fr. יַאֲטִים]   אטם

יָאִיץ] Hiph. fut. 3 pers. sing. masc.; וְ conv.   אוץ

יָאִיר] pr. name masc.   אור

יָאִיר Hiph. fut. 3 pers. sing. masc.   אור

יָאִירוּ id. fut. 3 pers. pl. masc.   אור

יַאֲכִילֵהוּ] Hiph. fut. 3 pers. sing. masc., suff. 3 pers. sing. masc.; וְ conv.   אכל

יֵאָכֵל / וַיֵּ'] Niph. fut. 3 pers. sing. masc.; וְ id.   אכל

יֵאכֻל Chald. Peal fut. 3 pers. sing. masc. (§ 53)   אכל

יֹאכַל / וַ' / יֹאכֵל / וַ' / יֹאכַל / וַ' } Kal fut. 3 pers. sing. masc.; acc. shifted by conv. וַ, but not so with distinctive accent (§ 19. rem. 1)   אכל

יֹאכְלֵהוּ id. fut. 3 pers. pl. masc., suff. 3 pers. s. m.   אכל

יֵאָכְלוּ / יֵאָכֵלוּ } Niph. fut. 3 pers. pl. masc. (comp. § 8. rem. 15)   אכל

וַיֹּאכְלוּ / יֹאכְלוּ } Kal pret. 3 pers. pl. masc. (§ 19. rem. 1); וְ conv.   אכל

יֹאכְלֻהָ] id., suff. 3 pers. sing. fem.   אכל

יַאֲכִלֻם] Hiph. fut. 3 pers. pl. masc. [יַאֲכִיל], suff. 3 pers. pl. masc.; וְ conv.   אכל

יֹאכְלוּם Kal fut. 3 pers. pl. masc., suff. 3 pers. pl. m.   אכל

יֹאכְלוּן / יֹאכֵלוּן } id. fut. 3 pers. pl. masc. with parag. ן (§ 8. rem. 17)   אכל

יַאֲכִלְךָ] Hiph. fut. 3 pers. sing. masc. [יַאֲכִיל], suff. 2 pers. sing. masc.; וְ conv.   אכל

יֹאכְלֵם / וַיֹּ' / יֹאכְלֵמוֹ } Kal fut. 3 pers. sing. masc., suff. 3 pers. pl. masc.; וְ id.   אכל

a Ec. 9. 18.   f La. 2. 8.   k Is. 42. 21.   p Job 25. 5.   u 2 Sa. 6. 6.   Is. 13. 8.   Nu. 8. 2.   2 Ki. 1.41,42,43.   De. 18. 1.

b Pr. 29. 3.   g Ge. 32. 25.   l 1 Sa. 16. 21.   q Ge. 13. 12, 18.   Ge. 47. 27.   Ps. 81. 17.   Le. 6. 9.   De. 4. 28.

c Je. 10. 11.   h Job 39. 26.   m 1 Sa. 18. 1.   r Ps. 135. 17.   Ju. 1. 6;12.6.   Nu. 12. 19.   Pr. 30. 17.   De. 8. 3.

d Je. 6. 21.   i Ps. 119. 131L   n Pr. 9. 5.   s Job 80. 18.   Ju. 16. 21.   Ps. 58. 5.   2 Ch. 28. 15.   Ps. 78. 45.

e Eze. 3. 7.   j Is. 1. 18.   o Ge. 29. 32.   t Job 20. 9.   Je. 12. 21.   Ge. 19. 15.   Le. 11. 13.   Eze. 44. 29.   Ex. 15. 7.

תֹּאכֲלֶנָּה id., suff. 3 pers. sing. fem. (§ 2. rem. 3) . אכל

יֹאכִלֵנוּ Hiph. fut. 3 pers. s. m., [יַאֲכִיל] suff. 1 pers. pl. אכל

יֹאכֲלֶנּוּ Kal fut. 3 pers. sing. masc., suff. 3 pers. sing. masc. (§ 2. rem. 3) . אכל

וַיֹּאכֲלֵנִי Hiph. fut. 3 p. s. m.,[יַאֲכִיל]suff. 1 p.s.; וַ conv. אכל

I. יָאַל . Niph. נוֹאַל to be foolish, to act foolishly.

II. יָאַל . Hiph. הוֹאִיל.—I. to begin, undertake.—II. to be willing, contented.

וַיֹּאֶל Hiph. fut. 3 pers. s. m. ap. [fr. יָאִיל]; acc. drawn back by conv. וַ (§ 20. rem. 9) } יאל

וַיֹּאֶל Hiph. fut. 3 pers. sing. masc. ap. [for יֹאֲלָה § 25. No. 2c, comp. § 19. rem. 8] . אלה

יֶאְלֶף Piel fut. 3 pers. sing. masc. . אלף

יַאֲמִין Hiph. fut. 3 pers. sing. masc. . אמן

וַיַּאֲמִינוּ id. fut. 3 pers. pl. masc. ; וַ conv. אמן

וַיַּאֲמֵן id. fut. 3 pers. sing. masc. ap. fr. יַאֲמִין . אמן

יֵאָמֵן Niph. fut. 3 pers. sing. masc. (§ 9. rem. 3) } אמן

יֵאָמֵן אמן

יֵאָמְנוּ id. fut. 3 pers. pl. masc. אמן

וַיַּאֲמֵץ Hiph. fut. 3 pers. sing. m. ap. [fr. יַאֲמִיץ] אמן

וַיְאַמֵּץ Piel fut. 3 pers. sing. masc. ; (§ 10. rem. 4) ; וַ conv. } אמץ

יַאֲמֵץ Kal fut. 3 pers. sing. masc. [for יֶאֱמַץ, comp. § 8. rem. 15] . אמץ

וַיְאַמְּצֵהוּ the foll. with suff. 3 pers. sing. m. ; וַ conv. אמץ

וַיְאַמְּצוּ Piel fut. 3 pers. pl. masc. ; וַ id. אמץ

וַיַּאַמְצוּ Kal fut. 3 pers. pl. masc. ; וַ id. . אמץ

יֹאמֶר Kh. or וַיֹּאמֶר 2 Sa. 1. 8, & Ne. 7. 3, or וַיֹּאמֶר Ne. 5. 9, & Zec. 4. 2, Kal or Niph. fut. 3 pers. sing. masc. (§ 19. rem. 2, & § 9. rem. 4 & 5) ; Keri וַיֹּאמֶר Kal fut. 1 pers. s. with וַ, for וְ, conv. (§ 19. rem. 2 b) } אמר

וַיֵּאָמֵר יֵאָמֵר Niph. fut. 3 pers. sing. m. (§ 9. rem. 4 & 3) } אמר
יֵאָמֵר

וַיֵּאמַר Chald. Peal fut. 3 pers. sing. masc. (§ 53) אמר

וַיֹּאמֶר יֹאמַר Kal fut. 3 pers. sing. m. (§ 19. rem. 1 & 2) } אמר
יֹאמֶר

וַיֹּאמֶר Kh. for וַיֹּאמְרוּ (q. v.) . אמר

יֹאמְרוּ Kal fut. 3 pers. pl. masc. (§ 19. rem. 1) ; וַ conv. } אמר
וַיֹּאמְרוּ

יֹאמְרוּ Kh. for מְרוּ q. v., K. מְרוּ (q. v.) אמר

תֹּאָנֶה Pual fut. 3 pers. sing. masc. אנה

יֵאָנַח Niph. fut. 3 pers. sing. masc. ; Milêl before monos. (comp. § 9. rem. 4) . אנח

וְיֵאָנְחוּ id. fut. 3 pers. pl. masc. ; וְ conv. . אנח

יֶאֱנֹף Kal fut. 3 pers. sing. masc. . אנף

יֶאֱנֹק Kal fut. 3 pers. sing. masc. (§ 13. rem. 4) . אנק

וַיֵּאָנֵשׁ Niph. fut. 3 pers. sing. masc. ; [for יֵאָנֵשׁ § 9. rem. 4] ; וְ conv. . . אנש

וַיֵּאָסֵף יֵאָסֵף Niph. fut. 3 pers. sing. masc. (§ 9. rem. 3) ; וְ id. . } אסף

וַיֵּאָסֵף for וַיֹּסֵף Hiph. fut. 3 pers. sing. masc., with conv. וַ for יֹסֵף, ap. fr. יֹוסִיף . סף

וַיֶּאֱסֹף Kal fut. 3 p. s. m. (§ 13. rem. 4) ; וְ conv. אסף

וַיַּאַסְפֶהָ id. with suff. 3 pers. sing. fem. (§ 13. rem. 6) אסף

וַיַּאַסְפֵהוּ וַ, id. with suff. 3 pers. sing. masc. (v id.) אסף

וַיַּאַסְפוּ id. fut. 3 pers. pl. masc. (v. id.) ; וְ conv. אסף

יֵאָסְפוּ וַיֵּאָסְפוּ Niph. fut. 3 pers. pl. masc. (comp. § 8. rem. 15) ; וְ id. . } אסף

יֵאָסְפוּן id. with parag. ן (comp. § 8. rem. 17) . אסף

יַאַסְפְךָ Kal fut. 3 pers. sing. masc. [יֶאֱסֹף] suff. 2 pers. sing. masc. (§ 13. rem. 4 & 6) אסף

וַיַּאַסְפֵם id., suff. 3 pers. pl. masc. (v. id.) ; וְ conv. אסף

יַאַסְפֵנִי id. with suff. 1 pers. sing. (v. id.) אסף

יֵאָסֵר Niph. fut. 3 pers. sing. masc. אסר

וַיֶּאֱסֹר יֶאְסֹר Kal fut. 3 pers. sing. masc. (§ 13. rem. 4 & 5) ; וְ conv. . } אסר

וַיַּאַסְרֵהוּ id. id., suff. 3 pers. sing. masc. (§ 13. rem. 6) אסר

וַיַּאַסְרוּהוּ יַאַסְרוּ id. fut. 3 pers. pl. masc., suff. 3 pers. sing. masc. (v. id.) ; וְ conv. } אסר

וַיַּאַסְרוּם id. id., suff. 3 p. pl. m. (ם for fem. § 2. rem. 5) אסר

יַאַסְרֻנִי יַאַסְרוּנִי id. id., suff. 1 pers. sing. (v. id.) . } אסר

וַיֶּאֱפֹד Kal fut. 3 p. s. m. (§ 13. rem. 5) ; וְ conv. אפד

וַיֹּאפוּ Kal fut. 3 p. pl. m. (§ 25. No. 2c) ; וְ id. אפה

וַיֵּאָצֵל Hiph. fut. 3 pers. sing. masc. ap. with conv. וַ [for יַאֲצֵל, יַאֲצִיל § 19. rem. 8] . אצל

יֵאָצֵר Niph. fut. 3 pers. sing. masc. . אצר

יְאֹר , יְאוֹר masc. dec. 1 a, river, especially the Nile; pl. יְאֹרִים streams, especially the artificial canals of the Nile.

יָאֵר יֹואֵר Hiph. fut. 3 p. s. m. ap. (§ 21. rem. 18) for אור } אור

יֹאֵר for יֵאוֹר Niph. fut. 3 pers. s. m. ; וְ conv. אור

וַיֶּאֱרֹב Kal fut. 3 p. s. m. (§ 13. rem. 4) ; וְ id. ארב

יֶאֶרְבוּ יֶאֶרְבוּ id. fut. 3 pers. pl. masc. (§ 8. rem. 15) } ארב

a Le. 6. 11, 19.   q Job 15. 5.   z 2 Ch. 36. 13.   f Jos. 2. 2.   φ Ex. 2. 23.   ‡ 1 Sa. 14. 52.   ω Ps. 27. 10.   ♁ Is. 23. 18.
b Nu. 11. 4, 18.   r Job 15. 31.   i 1 Ch. 17. 24.   g Ge. 25. 23.   χ Is. 44. 14.   ∥ Hab. 1. 15.   π Ge. 42. 19.   ♂ Ju. 16. 7.
c Eze. 3. 2.   s 1 Ki. 8. 26.   k 1 Ch. 24. 13.   h Da. 4. 32.   ψ Je. 51. 52.   ⸿ 1 Ki. 20. 14.   ϱ Is. 8. 7.   ♃ Eze. 29. 9.
d Job 6. 9.   t Ge. 42. 20.   l 2 Ch. 34. 13.   i Ge. 12. 15.   ⸹ Ps. 104. 22.   ⸷ Ge. 12. 39.   σ Eze. 46. 20.   ♄ 2 Sa. 2. 32.
e 1 Sa. 17. 39.   u Am. 2. 14.   m 2 Ch. 11. 17.   j Pr. 12. 21.   ⸺ 1 Sa. 18. 29.   † Is. 58. 8.   τ Ex. 12. 39.   ♅ Ps. 10. 9.
f 1 Sa. 14. 24.   n 2 Ch. 13. 18.   o Pr. 29. 2.   s 2 Sa. 11. 27.   ⸻ 2 Ch. 29. 4.   ⸼ 1 Sa. 6. 10.   υ Nu. 11. 25.   ♆ Ju. 9. 43.

יָאַרְגוּ	Kal fut. 3 pers. pl. masc. [for יַאֲרֹג, from sing. § 8. rem. 15, & § 13. rem. 4] ארג
יְאֹרֵי	noun masc. pl., constr. from יְאֹר dec. 1 a יאר
יְאֹרִי	id. sing., suff. 1 pers. sing. יאר
יְאֹרֵיהֶם	id. pl., suff. 3 pers. pl. masc. יאר
יְאֹרָיו	id. pl., suff. 3 pers. sing. masc. יאר
יַאֲרִיךְ	Hiph. fut. 3 pers. sing. masc. ארך
יְאֹרֶיךָ	noun m. pl., suff. 2 pers. s. m. from יְאֹר dec. 1 a יאר
וַיַּאֲרִיכוּ	Hiph. fut. 3 pers. pl. masc.; וַ conv. ארך
יַאֲרִיכֻן / יַאֲרִיכוּן	} id. with paragogic ן ארך
יְאֹרִים	noun masc. pl. abs. from יְאֹר dec. 1 a יאר
יַאֲרְכוּ	1 Ki. 8. 8, defect. for יַאֲרִיכוּ (q.v.) ארך
יַאַרְכוּ	Kal fut. 3 pers. pl. masc. ארך
יַאַרְכֻן	defect. for יַאֲרִיכוּן (q.v.) ארך
יָאֵשׁ	Kal not used; Arab. to despair, despond. Niph. נוֹאָשׁ id., with מִן to despair of, desist from, 1 Sa. 27. 1; part. desperate; neut. there is no hope, it is in vain. Pi. to render hopeless, Ec. 2. 20.
יֹאָשׁ	pr. name masc. for יְהוֹאָשׁ, יוֹאָשׁ (q. v.) הוה
יֹאשִׁיָּה / יֹאשִׁיָּהוּ	} pr. name masc. אשה
וַיָּאשֶׁם	וַ Kal fut. 3 pers. sing. masc. (§ 13. rem. 5); וַ conv. אשם
יַאֲשְׁמוּ / וַיַּאְשְׁמוּ	} id. fut. 3 pers. pl. masc. (v. id. & § 8. rem. 15); וַ conv. אשם
יְאֻשַּׁר	Kh. Pual fut. 3 pers. sing. masc.; K. וְאָשֵׁר pret. 3 pers. sing. masc. אשר
יְאַשְּׁרֵהוּ	Piel fut. 3 pers. pl. masc., suff. 3 pers. sing. m. אשר
יְאַשְּׁרוּהָ	וַ id., suff. 3 pers. sing. fem.; וַ conv. אשר
יֵאָת	וַ Kal fut. 3 pers. sing. masc. ap. [for יֶאֱתֶה from יָאֲתָה, with conv. וַ, § 24. rem. 16, see § 19. rem. 3, & § 25. No. 2c] אתה
יָאֲתָה	Kal pret. 3 p. s. fem. [for יָאֲתָה § 8. rem. 7] יאה
יֶאֱתֶה	Kal fut. 3 pers. sing. masc. אתה
וַיֵּאָתוּ	וַ Niph., or Kal (comp. יֵבוֹשׁ from בּוֹשׁ) fut. 3 pers. pl.; וַ conv. אות
יֶאֱתָיוּ	Kal fut. 3 pers. pl. masc. (§ 24. rem. 5) אתה
יֶאֱתָיוּן	וַ id. with parag. ן; וַ conv. (v. id. & comp. § 8. rem. 17) אתה
יַאְתִנִי	וַ id. with suff. 1 pers. sing. (§ 5. rem. 24); וַ id. אתה
יַאְתְרַי	pr. name masc. 1 Ch. 6. 6.
יָבֵא	וַ Hiph. fut. 3 pers. s. m. ap. fr. יָבִיא; וַ conv. בוא
יָבֹא	וַ, וַיָּ Kal fut. 3 pers. sing. masc. (§ 21. rem. 3, & § 25. No. 2); וַ conv. בוא
יָבֵא	Hiph. fut. 3 pers. sing. masc. defect. for יָבִיא בוא

יָבֹא	Kh. יָבֹא q. v.; K. וּבָא Kal pret. 3 pers. s. masc.; וַ for וַ conv. בוא
יְבִיאֶהָ	וַ Hiph. fut. 3 pers. sing. masc. (יָבִיא), suff. 3 pers. sing. fem.; וַ conv. בוא
יְבִיאֵהוּ	וַ id. id., suff. 3 pers. sing. masc. בוא
יְבִיאֻהוּ	וַ id. fut. 3 pers. pl. m. (יָבִיאוּ), suff. 3 p. s. m. בוא
יָבִאוּ	וַ id. fut. 3 pers. pl. masc. defect. for יָבִיאוּ בוא
יָבֹאוּ	וַ, וַיָּ Kal fut. 3 pers. pl. masc. (§ 21. rem. 3, & § 25. No. 2f); וַ conv. בוא
יָבֹאוּ	וַ Kh. יָבֹאוּ q. v., K. יָבֹא (q. v.) בוא
יְבֹאוּ	Kh. יְבֹאוּ q. v., K. וּבָאוּ Kal pret. 3 pers. pl.; וַ for וַ conv. בוא
יְבִיאוּם	וַ Hiph. fut. 3 pers. pl. masc. (יָבִיאוּ), suff. 3 pers. pl. masc.; וַ conv. בוא
יָבֹאוּן	Kal fut. 3 pers. pl. masc. with parag. ן (§ 21. rem. 3, & § 25. No. 2f) בוא
יְבֹאוּנִי	id. fut. 3 pers. pl. m. with suff. 1 pers. s. (v. id.) בוא
יַבְאִישׁ	Hiph. fut. 3 pers. sing. masc. באש
יְבִיאֵם	וַ Hiph. fut. 3 pers. sing. masc. (יָבִיא), suff. 3 pers. pl. masc.; וַ conv. בוא
יְבִיאֵנוּ	וַ id. with suff. 1 pers. pl. בוא
יְבִיאֵנִי	וַ id. with suff. 1 pers. sing. בוא
יְבֹאֵנִי	וַ for וַיְבֹאֵנִי, defect. for יְבִיאֵנִי (q.v.) בוא
יְבִיאֶנּוּ	Kal fut. 3 pers. s. m. (יָבוֹא), suff. 3 pers. s. m. (§ 21. rem. 3, & § 25. No. 2f, & § 2. rem. 3) בוא
יִבְאַשׁ	וַ Kal fut. 3 pers. sing. masc.; וַ conv. באש
יַבֵּב	Pi. to call aloud, to cry out, Ju. 5. 28. יוֹבָב (crier; Simonis, for יָאוֹב אָב, desire of the father) pr. name—I. of a descendant of Joktan and a people descended from him.—II. of a king of Edom.—III. of a king of the Canaanites, Jos. 11. 1.—IV. 1 Ch. 8. 9.—V. ibid. ver. 18.
יִבְגֹּד	Kal fut. 3 pers. sing. masc. בגד
וַיִּבְגְּדוּ	וַ id. fut. 3 pers. pl. masc.; וַ conv. בגד
יַבְדִּיל	Hiph. fut. 3 pers. sing. masc. בדל
וַיַּבְדִּלוּ	וַ id. fut. 3 pers. pl. masc.; וַ conv. בדל
יַבְדִּילֵם	וַ id. fut. 3 pers. sing. masc., suff. 3 pers. pl. masc.; וַ id. בדל
יַבְדִּילֵנִי	id. id., suff. 1 pers. sing. for לֵנִי בדל
יַבְדֵּל	וַ id. fut. 3 pers. s. m. ap. fr. יַבְדִּיל; וַ conv. בדל
וַיִּבָּדֵל	וַ Niph. fut. 3 pers. sing. masc.; וַ id. בדל
יִבָּדְלוּ	וַ id. fut. 3 pers. pl. masc.; וַ id. בדל
יַבְהִילוּהוּ	וַ Hiph. fut. 3 pers. pl. masc., suff. 3 pers. sing. masc.; וַ id. בהל
יִבָּהֵל	וַ Niph. fut. 3 pers. sing. masc.; וַ id. בהל
יְבַהֲלֵ	Piel fut. 3 pers. s. m. (§ 14. r. 1); וַ id. בהל

Is. 59. 5.	2 Ch. 5. 9.	Ho. 13. 1.	Je. 10. 7.	Pr. 18. 17.	Ps. 95. 11.	Pr. 28. 22	Ne. 13. 3.	1 Ch. 23. 13.
Eze. 29. 3.	Ex. 20. 12.	Ese. 6. 6.	Ge. 34. 22.	Ex. 22. 12.	Ps. 119. 77.	Mal. 2. 15	2 Ch. 25. 10.	2 Ch. 26. 29
Eze. 29. 3.	De. 5. 16.	Ps. 41. 3.	2 Ki. 12. 9.	Eze. 19. 9	De. 26. 9.	Is. 33. 1.	Is. 56. 3.	Ju. 20. 41.
Eze. 29. 4, 5, 10.	Ese. 12. 23.	Ps. 72. 17.	Is. 41. 5.	Ju. 6. 5.	Ps. 119. 41.	Eze. 39. 14	Ezr. 10. 8.	Est. 2. 9.
De. 25. 15.	D⁴. 6. 2.	Is. 41. 25.	Job 8. 25.	Jos. 7. 23.	1 Ki. 5. 8.	Ps. 119. 77.		

20

יְבַהֲלֻהֽוּ	id. fut. 3 pers. pl. masc., suff. 3 pers. s. m.	בהל
יְבַהֲלֻ֫	Hiph. fut. 3 pers. pl. masc.; וְ conv.	בהל
יִבָּהֲלֽוּ	וְ Niph. fut. 3 pers. pl. masc.	בהל
יְבַהֲלוּךְ	Ch. Pael fut. 3 pers. pl. masc., suff. 2 pers. sing. masc. (comp. § 14. rem. 1)	בהל
יִבָּהֲלוּן	Niph. fut. 3 pers. pl. masc. with parag. ן (comp. § 8. rem. 17)	בהל
יְבַהֲלוּנֵּהּ	Ch. Pael fut. 3 pers. pl. masc., suff. 3 pers. sing. masc. (§ 50)	בהל
יְבַהֲלָךְ	Ch. id. fut. 3 pers. s. m., suff. 2 pers. s. m.	בהל
יְבַהֵל	וְ Piel fut. 3 pers. sing. m. [יְבַהֵל § 14. r. 1], suff. 2 pers. s. m. with conj. וְ [וַיְ׳, וַיְבַהֵל]	בהל
יְבַהֲלֵמוֹ	id., suff. 3 pers. pl. masc.	בהל
יְבַהֲלִנֵּהּ	Ch. Pael fut. 3 pers. sing. masc., suff. 3 pers. sing. masc. (§ 50)	בהל
יְבַהֲלַנִּי	Ch. id., suff. 1 pers. sing.	בהל
יָבוֹא	וְ Kheth., for יָבֹא K. (q. v.)	בוא
יָבֹא	וַיָּ׳ Kal fut. 3 p. s. m. (§ 21. r. 3); וְ conv.	בוא
יָבֹאוּ	וַיָּ׳, וְ׳ id. fut. 3 pers. pl. masc. וְ id.	בוא
יְבוֹאֵנוּ	id. fut. 3 pers. sing. masc., suff. 1 pers. pl.	בוא
יְבוֹאֶנּוּ	id. id., suff. 3 pers. sing. masc.	בוא
יָבוֹז	Kal fut. 3 pers. sing. masc.	בוז
יָבֹזּוּ	id. fut. 3 pers. pl. masc.	בוז
יְבוֹל	וַ Kal fut. 3 pers. sing. masc. Kheth. יָבֹל (§ 18. rem. 2) K. יָבֵל; וְ conv.	בלל
יִבֹּל	Kal fut. 3 pers. sing. masc. (§ 17. rem. 3)	נבל
יְבוּל	noun masc. sing. dec. 1 a	יבל
יְבוּלָהּ	id., suff. 3 pers. sing. fem., with cop. וְ [וַיְ׳, וִיבוּלָהּ]	יבל
יְבוּלָם	id., suff. 3 pers. pl. masc.	יבל
יְבוֹנְנֵהוּ	Pilel fut. 3 pers. sing. m., suff. 3 pers. s. m.	בין
יְבוּם	Kal fut. 3 pers. sing. masc.	בום
יְבוּם	pr. name of a place	בום
יְבוּסִי	gent. noun from the preceding	בום
יָבוֹשׁ	Kal inf. abs.	יבש
יֵבֹשׁ	וְ Kal fut. 3 pers. sing. masc. (§ 21. rem. 6)	בוש
יֵבֹשׁוּ	id. fut. 3 pers. pl. masc.	בוש
יָבֶז	וַ Kal fut. 3 p. s. m. ap. [for יִבְזֶה]; וְ conv.	בזה
יִבְזֶהָ	וַיִּ׳ id. id., suff. 3 pers. sing. masc.; וַ id.	בזה
יִבְזֻהוּ	וַ id. fut. 3 pers. pl. masc., suff. 3 pers. s. m.	בזה
יָבֹזּוּ	וַיָּ׳, וְ׳ Kal fut. 3 pers. pl. masc.; וְ conv.	בזז
יָבֹזּוּ	Kal fut. 3 pers. pl. masc.	בזז
יָבֹזּוּ	וְ Kal fut. 3 pers. pl. masc.; וְ conv.	בזז
יְבֻזּוּם	Kal fut. 3 pers. pl. masc. (יָבֹזּוּ), suff. 3 pers. pl. masc. (§ 18. rem. 5)	בזז

יִבְזֹר	Kal fut. 3 pers. sing. masc. (§ 8. rem. 18)	בזר
יִבָּחֵן	Niph. fut. 3 pers. sing. masc.	בחן
יִבְחַן	Kal fut. 3 pers. sing. m. [fr. יָבְחַן § 8. r. 15]	בחן
יִבָּחֲנוּ	וְ Niph. fut. 3 pers. pl. masc.	בחן
יִבְחֲנוּ	Kal fut. 3 pers. sing. masc.	בחן
יִבְחָר	וְ pr. name masc.	בחר
יִבְחַר יִבְחָר	Kal fut. 3 pers. sing. masc. (§ 8. rem. 15); וַיִּ׳ וְ conv.	בחר
יִבְחָר	Kheth. Pual fut. 3 pers. sing. m. (dag. impl. comp. § 14. r. 1) R. בחר; K. יְחֻבַּר id., R.	חבר
יְבַחֲרוּ	וְ Kal fut. 3 pers. pl. masc.	חבר
יְבַחֶרְךָ	וְ id. fut. 3 pers. sing. masc. (יִבְחַר), suff. 2 pers. sing. masc. (§ 16. r. 12, & § 2. r. 2)	חבר
יַבֵּט	וְ Hiph. fut. 3 pers. sing. masc., ap. fr. יַבִּיט; וְ conv.	נבט
יְבַטֵּא	וַיְ׳ Piel fut. 3 pers. sing. masc.; וְ id.	בטא
יַבְטֵחַ	וַ Hiph. fut. 3 pers. sing. masc. ap. fr. יַבְטִיחַ; וְ id.	בטח
יִבְטָח יִבְטַח	Kal fut. 3 pers. sing. masc. (§ 8. rem. 15); וְ id.	בטח
יִבְטְחוּ	וְ, וַיִּ׳ id. fut. 3 pers. pl. masc.; וְ id.	בטח
יָבִא	וַ for וַיָּבֹא, ap. from יָבִיא (q. v.)	בוא
יָבִיא	וַיָּ׳ Hiph. fut. 3 pers. sing. masc.; וְ conv.	בוא
יְבִיאֶהָ	וְ id. id., suff. 3 pers. sing. fem.	בוא
יְבִיאֵהוּ	וַ id. id., suff. 3 pers. sing. masc.	בוא
יְבִיאֻהוּ	וַ id. fut. 3 pers. pl. masc. (יָבִיאוּ), suff. 3 pers. sing. masc.	בוא
יָבִיאוּ	וַיָּ׳ id. fut. 3 pers. pl. masc.	בוא
יְבִיאוּם	וַ id. id., suff. 3 pers. pl. masc.	בוא
יְבִיאוּן	id. id. with parag. ן	בוא
יְבִיאוּנִי	id. id., suff. 1 pers. sing.	בוא
יְבִיאֲךָ	id. fut. 3 pers. s. m. (יָבִיא), suff. 2 p. s. m.	בוא
יְבִיאֵם	וַ id. id., suff. 3 pers. pl. masc.	בוא
יְבִיאֶנָּה	id. id., suff. 3 pers. sing. fem. (§ 2. rem. 3)	בוא
יְבִיאֶנּוּ	id. id., suff. 3 pers. sing. masc. (v. id.)	בוא
יְבִיאֵנִי	id. id., suff. 1 pers. sing.	בוא
יַבִּיט	Hiph. fut. 3 pers. sing. masc.	נבט
יַבִּיטוּ	id. fut. 3 pers. pl. masc.	נבט
יָבִין	pr. name masc.	בין
יָבֵין	Hiph. or Kal, fut. 3 pers. s. masc. R. בון or	בין
יְבִינֵהוּ	וַ Hiph. fut. 3 pers. sing. masc., suff. 3 pers. sing. masc. R. בון see	בין
יָבִינוּ	וַיָּ׳ Kal fut. 3 pers. pl. masc.; וְ conv.	בין
יַבִּיעַ	Hiph. fut. 3 pers. sing. masc.	נבע
יַבִּיעוּ	id. fut. 3 pers. pl. masc.	נבע
יַבִּיעוּן	id. id. with parag. ן	נבע

a Da. 11. 44.	g Job 22. 10.	n Job 15. 21.	t Zec. 11. 17.	a Ne. 2. 19.	a Ps. 11. 4.	a Ps. 106. 33.	a Ne. 8. 2.	a Nu. 7. 17.
b Est. 6. 14.	h Ps. 2. 5.	o Pr. 23. 9.	u Is. 29. 22.	b Zep. 2. 9.	b Ec. 9. 4.	b Je. 29. 31.	b Ex. 35. 5.	b Le. 4. 12.
c Da. 5. 10.	i Da. 4. 16.	p Ju. 19. 21.	v 1 Sa. 17. 42.	c Da. 11. 24.	c 1 Ki. 18. 23.	c Pr. 28. 1.	c 1 Ch. 9. 28.	c Is. 40. 14.
d Ps. 104. 29.	k 1 Ki. 13. 2.	q De. 32. 22.	w 1 Sa. 10. 27.	d Job 34. 36.	d Is. 49. 7.	d Ps. 52. 9.	d Ex. 18. 26.	d Ne. 8. 8.
e Da. 5. 6.	l Eze. 33. 31.	r Ps. 78. 46.	x Ps. 109. 11.	e Le. 5. 4.	e Le. 5. 4.	e Eze. 40. 3.	e Ps. 43. 3.	e Is. 40. 14.
f Da. 4. 16.	m Is. 28. 15.	s De. 32. 10.	Ca. 8. 1.	f Ge. 42. 16.	f Ps. 11. 5.	f Is. 28. 9.		f Ps. 52. 9.

יָבֵישׁ   pr. name of a place, see יָבֵשׁ . . . יבש

יָבֵישָׁה   id. with parag. ה . . . . . יבש

יָבְךְּ   ] Kal fut. 3 pers. sing. masc. ap. [fr. יִבְכֶּה § 24. rem. 3] ; וְ conv. . . . . בכה

וַיִּבְכּוּ   id. fut. 3 pers. pl. masc. . . . . בכה

יִבְכָּיֻן   id. id. with parag. ן (§ 24. r. 5, & § 8. r. 17) בכה

יְבַכֵּר   Piel fut. 3 pers. sing. masc. . . . בכר

יְבֻכַּר   Pual fut. 3 pers. sing. masc. . . . בכר

יָבַל   Kal not used ; Arab. *to flow, run*. Hiph. הוֹבִיל *to lead, bring, bring forth, carry*. Hoph. pass.

יְבַל   Ch. Aph. *to bring*, Ezr. 5. 14 ; 6. 5.

יָבָל   masc. dec. 4 a.—I. *stream, river*.—II. pr. name of a son of Lamech, Ge. 4. 20.

יָבָל , fem. יַבָּלֶת (§ 39. No. 4) *flowing, running*, as a sore, Le. 22. 22.

יוֹבֵל   masc. dec. 7 b.—I. *protracted sound*, hence קֶרֶן הַיּוֹבֵל *the horn* by which the like *sound* is produced ; in the same sense pl. שׁוֹפְרוֹת יוֹבְלִים , הַיּוֹבְלִים ; ellipt. יוֹבֵל for the instrument, Ex. 19. 13.—II. שְׁנַת הַיּוֹבֵל and ellipt. יוֹבֵל , *the year of jubilee*, celebrated every fiftieth year and so called from *the sounding of trumpets* on the tenth day of the seventh month, by which it was announced to the people, comp. Le. 25. 9.

יוּבַל   masc.—I. *river*, Je. 17. 8.—II. pr. name of a son of Lamech, Ge. 4. 21.

יְבוּל   masc. dec. 1 a.—I. *produce, increase* of the earth.—II. *provision, wealth*, Job 20. 28.

בּוּל   masc. (for יְבוּל).—I. *produce, increase*, Job 40. 20 ; בּוּל עֵץ *trunk of wood*, Is. 44. 19.—II. the name of the eighth Hebrew month, answering to our October, . Ki. 6. 38.

אָבָל אוּבָל   masc. *river, canal*, Da. 8. 2, 3, 6.

מַבּוּל   masc. *inundation, deluge*.

תֵּבֵל   fem. (for תֵּיבֵל).—I. *the world, the earth*, especially the inhabited part of it.—II. *the world, the inhabitants of the world*.

תֻּבַל , תֻּבָל   (*diffusion, propagation*) pr. name of a son of Japheth, used meton. for his descendants, a people of Asia Minor.

תּוּבַל קַיִן   (*propagation of Cain*) pr. name of the third son of Lamech by Zillah, Ge. 4. 22.

יָבָל   pr. name masc. . . . . . יבל

יְבַלָּא   Ch. Pael fut. 3 pers. sing. masc. R. בְּלָא see בלה

יְבַלֶּה   Kal fut. 3 pers. sing. masc. . . . בלה

יְבוּלָהּ   ן noun masc. sing. with suff. from יְבוּל dec. 1 a, with conj. וְ [for וְי , וְיְבוּלָהּ] . . יבל

יְבַלּוּ   Piel fut. 3 pers. pl masc. . . . בלה

יְבַלּוּ   Kal fut. 3 pers. pl. masc. . . . בלה

יַבְלוּ   Kal fut. 3 pers. pl. masc. [§ 17. rem. 3, for יִבְלוּ § 8. rem. 15] . . . נבל

יִבְלוּהָ   Hiph. fut. 3 pers. pl. masc. (יוֹבִיל) suff. 3 pers. sing. masc. . . . . . יבל

יַבְלוּן   Kal fut. 3 pers. pl. masc. with parag. ן (§ 17. rem. 3, & § 8. rem. 17) . . . . בל

יִבְלֵי   noun masc. pl. constr. from יָבָל dec. 4 a יבל

יְבִילֵנִי   Hiph. fut. 3 pers. s. m. (יוֹבִיל) suff. 1 pers. s. יבל

יְבַלַּע   Piel fut. 3 pers. sing. masc. . . . בלע

יִבְלַע } Kal fut. 3 pers. sing. masc. (comp. § . . }

וַיִּבְלַע } rem. 15) ; וְ conv. . . . } בלע

יְבֻלַּע } Pual fut. 3 pers. sing. masc. (comp. § 8. }

יְבֻלָּע } rem. 15) . . . } בלע

יִבְלָעֵהוּ   Kal fut. 3 pers. pl. masc. (יִבְלְעוּ) from sing. (יִבְלַע), suff. 3 pers. sing. m. (§ 16. r. 12) בלע

יְבַלְּעֵם   Piel fut. 3 pers. s. m. (יְבַלַּע), suff. 3 pers. pl. m. בלע

יִבְלְעֵם   וְ pr. name of a place . . . . בלע

יִבְלָעֶהָ   Kal fut. 3 pers. sing. masc. (יִבְלַע), suff. 3 pers. sing. fem. (§ 16. rem. 12) . . בלע

יְבַלְּעֵנוּ   Piel fut. 3 pers. s. m. (יְבַלַּע), suff. 3 pers. s. m. בלע

יַבֶּלֶת   (prop. adj.) subst. fem. sing. [from יָבָל m.] יבל

[יָבָם]   masc. dec. 4 a, *brother-in-law, husband's brother*, who when the husband died without issue, was obliged to marry the widow, to raise up seed to him. Hence

Pi. יִבֵּם *to marry the brother's wife*.

יְבֵמֶת   fem. dec. 13 b, *a sister-in-law*, a brother's wife ; also *the wife of a husband's brother*.

יַבֵּם   ] Piel imp. sing. masc. . . . . יבם

יִבְּמָהּ   ] id. pret. 3 pers. s. m., suff. 3 p. s. f.; וְ conv. יבם

יִבְמָהּ   noun m. s., suff. 3 pers. s. fem. fr. [יָבָם] dec. 4 a יבם

יַבְּמִי   Piel inf. [יַבֵּם], suff. 1 pers. sing. dec. 7 b . יבם

יְבָמִי   noun m. s., suff. 1 pers. s. fr. [יָבָם] dec. 4 a יבם

יְבִמְתּוֹ   noun f. s., suff. 3 pers. s. m. fr. [יְבֵמָת] d. 13 b יבם

יְבִמְתֵּךְ   id., suff. 2 pers. sing. fem. . . . יבם

יַבְנְאֵל   וְ pr. name of a place . . . . בנה

יַבְנֶה   pr. name of a place . . . . בנה

יָבֶן   ] Kal fut. 3 pers. sing. masc., ap. fr. יָבִין } בין

יָבֵן   ] acc. drawn back by וְ conv. }

וַיִּבֶן   וַיִּ , וְ Kal fut. 3 pers. sing. masc., ap. fr. וַיִּ ; יִבְנֶה id. . . . . . בנה

a Job 31. 38.   c Le. 27. 26.   f De. 32. 22.   i Pr. 19. 28.   m Job 37. 20.   p Ps. 21. 10.   s Ge. 38. 8.   u De. 25. 7.   x Ru. 1. 15.

Is. 33. 7.   d Da. 7. 25.   g Ps. 37. 2.   k Job 20. 18.   n 2 Sa. 17. 16.   q Is. 28. 4.   t De. 25. 5.   w De. 25. 7.   y Ezr. 1. 3.

b Eze. 47 12.   e Job 13. 28.   h Ps. 108. 11.   l Ex. 7. 12.   o Ho. 8. 7.   r Le. 22. 22.   De. 25. 5.   De. 25. 7, 9.   bb Is. 23. 7.

20*

יִבָּנֶה	Niph. fut. 3 pers. sing. masc.	בנה
יִבְנֶה	[יִ'] Kal fut. 3 pers. sing. masc.	בנה
יִבְנֵהוּ	[וַיִּ'] id. id., suff. 3 pers. sing. m. (§ 24. r. 21)	בנה
יִבְנוּ	[יִ'] id. fut. 3 pers. pl. masc.	בנה
יִבְנוֹן	Chald. Peal fut. 3 pers. pl. masc.	בנה
יִבְנְיָה יִבְנְיָה	} pr. name masc.	בנה
יִבְנֵם	Kal fut. 3 pers. sing. masc. (יִבְנֶה), suff. 3 pers pl. masc. (§ 24. rem. 21)	בנה
יִבְנֵנוּ	id. with suff. 3 pers. sing. masc. (v. id.)	בנה
יִבְעֵא	Chald. Peal fut. 3 pers. sing. masc.	בעא
יִבְעוֹן	Chald. Pael fut. 3 pers. pl. masc. (dag. forte impl. comp. § 14. rem. 1)	בעא
יִבְעַט	Kal fut. 3 pers. sing. masc.; וַ' conv.	בעט
יִבְעַל	Kal fut. 3 pers. sing. masc.	בעל
יִבְעָלוּךְ	id. fut. 3 pers. pl. [יִבְעָלוּ], suff. 2 pers. sing. fem. (§ 16. rem. 12)	בעל
יַבְעֵר וַיַּבְעֶר	} Hiph. fut. 3 pers. sing. masc. apoc. (§ 11. rem. 7); וַ' conv.	בער
יְבַעֵר	Piel fut. 3 pers. sing. masc. (§ 14. rem. 1)	בער
יִבְעַר וַיִּבְעַר	} Kal fut. 3 pers. sing. masc. (comp. § 8. rem. 15)	בער
יְבַעֲרוּ	Piel fut. 3 pers. pl. masc. (§ 14. rem. 1)	בער
יִבְעֲרוּ	Kal fut. 3 pers. pl. masc.	בער
יְבַעֲתַהוּ	Piel fut. 3 pers. pl. m. (§ 14. rem. 1), suff. 3 pers. sing. masc.	בעת
יְבַעֲתוּנִי יְבַעֲתוּנִי	} id. with suff. 1 pers. sing.	בעת
יְבַצֵּעַ	Piel fut. 3 pers. sing. masc.	בצע
יִבְצַע	Kal fut. 3 pers. sing. masc. [for יִבְצַע, comp. § 8. rem. 15]	בצע
יִבְצְעוּ	id. fut. 3 pers. pl. masc. [for יִבְצְעוּ v. id.]	בצע
יְבַצְעֵנִי יְבַצְעֵנִי	} Piel fut. 3 pers. sing. masc., suff. 1 pers. sing. with cop. וְ [for וַיְ', וַיְבַצְּעֵנִי]	בצע
יִבָּצֵר	Niph. fut. 3 pers. sing. masc.	בצר
יִבְצֹר	Kal fut. 3 pers. sing. masc.	בצר
יִבְצְרוּ	id. fut. 3 pers. pl. masc.; וְ' conv.	בצר
יַבֹּק	pr. name of a torrent	בקק
יִבָּקַע יִבָּקַע	} Niph. fut. 3 pers. sing. masc. (§ 15 rem. 1)	בקע
יְבַקַּע	[וְ'] Piel fut. 3 pers. sing. masc.	בקע
יִבְקַע	[וַ'] Kal fut. 3 pers. sing. masc.; וְ' conv.	בקע
יִבָּקְעוּ	[וַ'] Niph. fut. 3 pers. pl. masc.; וְ' id.	בקע
יְבַקְּעוּ	[וְ'] Piel fut. 3 pers. pl. masc.; וְ' id.	בקע
יִבְקְעוּ	[וְ'] Kal fut. 3 pers. pl. masc.; וְ' id.	בקע
יְבֻקְּעוּ	Pual fut. 3 p. pl. m. [for יְבֻקְּעוּ comp.§ 8. r. 15]	בקע

יִבְקָעוּהָ	[וַ] Kal fut. 3 pers. pl. masc. (יִבְקָעוּ fr. sing. יִבְקַע), suff. 3 pers. sing. fem. (§ 16. r. 12)	בקע
יִבְקְקוּ	[וַ'] Poel fut. 3 p. pl. m.; with cop. וְ [for וַיְ', וַיְ']	בקק
יְבַקַּר	Chald. Pael fut. 3 pers. sing. m. (§ 49. r. 4)	בקר
יְבַקֵּר	Piel fut. 3 pers. sing. masc.	בקר
יְבַקֵּשׁ יְבַקֶּשׁ	} Piel fut. 3 pers. sing. masc. (§ 10. rem. 4); וְ conv.	בקשׁ
יְבֻקַּשׁ	[וְ'] Pual fut. 3 pers. sing. masc.; וְ id.	בקשׁ
יְבַקְשֶׁהוּ	[וְ'] Piel fut. 3 pers. sing. masc. (יְבַקֵּשׁ), suff. 3 pers. sing. masc. (§ 10. rem. 7); וְ id.	בקשׁ
יְבַקְשֻׁהוּ	[וְ'] id. id. fut. 3 pers. pl. masc., suff. 3 pers. s. m.	בקשׁ
יְבַקְשׁוּ יְבַקְּשׁוּ	} id. id. fut. 3 pers. pl. masc. (comp. § 8. rem. 15, & § 10. rem. 7); וְ conv.	בקשׁ
יְבַקְשׁוּ	[וַיְ', וַיְבַקְּשׁוּ] id. id. with cop. וְ [for וַיְ']	בקשׁ
יִבְרָא	[וַיִּ'] Kal fut. 3 pers. sing. masc.; וְ conv.	ברא
יִבְרָאוּן	Niph. fut. 3 pers. pl. masc. with parag. ן (comp. § 8. rem. 17)	ברא
יִבְרַח וַיִּבְרַח	} Kal fut. 3 pers. sing. masc. (comp. § 8. rem. 15); וְ conv.	ברח
יִבְרְחוּ	[וַיִּ'] id. fut. 3 pers. pl. masc.	ברח
יַבְרִיחַ	Hiph. fut. 3 pers. sing. masc.	ברח
יַבְרִיחוּ	[וַ] id. fut. 3 pers. pl. masc.; וְ conv.	ברח
יַבְרִיחֶנּוּ	id. fut. 3 pers. sing. masc., suff. 3 pers. s. m.	ברח
יַבְרֵךְ	[וַיְ'] Hiph. fut. 3 pers. sing. masc. ap. [fr. יַבְרִיךְ]; וְ conv.	ברך
יִבְרַךְ	[וַ'] Kal fut. 3 pers. sing. masc.; וְ id.	ברך
יְבָרֵךְ יְבָרֶךְ יְבָרֶךְ	} Piel fut. 3 pers. sing. masc. with cop. וְ [for וַיְ', וַיְבָרֶךְ]; acc. drawn back by conv. וְ (§ 14. rem. 2)	ברך
יְבֹרַךְ	} Pual fut. 3 pers. sing. masc. (comp. § 8. rem. 15)	ברך
יְבָרֲכֶהוּ יְבָרֲכֶהוּ	} Piel fut. 3 pers. sing. masc., suff. 3 pers. sing. masc.; וְ conv.	ברך
יְבָרֲכוּ יְבָרֲכוּ	} id. fut. 3 pers. pl. masc.; וְ conv.; with cop. וְ [for וַיְ', וַיְבָרֲכוּ,יְבָרֲכוּ]	ברך
יְבָרֲכוּכָה	id. id., suff. 2 pers. sing. masc. (§ 2. rem. 2)	ברך
יְבֶרֶכְיָהוּ	pr. name masc.	ברך
יְבָרֶכְךָ יְבָרֶכְךָ יְבָרֶכְךָ	} Piel fut. 3 pers. sing. masc., suff. 2 pers. sing. masc. (§ 2. rem. 2); with cop. וְ [for וַיְ', וַיְבָרֶכְךָ]	ברך
יְבָרֲכֵם יְבָרֲכֵם	} id. id., suff. 3 pers. pl. masc.; וְ conv.	ברך
יְבָרֲכֶנְהוּ	id. id. with epenth. נ (§ 16. rem. 13) & suff. 3 pers. sing. masc.	ברך

a Ps. 69. 36.   b De. 32. 15.   c Is. 62. 1.   d Is. 10. 12.   e Ju. 9. 27.   1 Sa. 6. 14.   o Est. 2. 23.   q Je. 52. 7.   s Ps. 62. 5.
b Job 20. 19.   c Is. 62. 5.   e La. 2. 3.   f Job 27. 8.   g Is. 58. 8.   h Ho. 14. 1.   v 1 Sa. 23. 14.   r Pr. 19. 26.   t Ne. 9. 5.
c 1 Ki. 6. 38.   d Is. 62. 5.   f Eze. 39. 10.   g Joel 2. 8.   h Job 32. 19.   i 2 Ch. 21. 17.   w Nu. 16. 30.   s 1 Ch. 12. 15.   u Ps. 145. 10.
d Ezr. 6. 7.   e Ex. 22. 4.   g Je. 10. 8.   h Is. 38. 12.   i Ps. 78. 15.   k Je. 51. 2.   x Ge. 1. 21, 27.   t Job 41. 20.   f Job1. 11; 2. 5.
e Ps. 28. 5.   f Ju. 15. 5.   h Job 6. 9.   i Ps. 104. 30.   y Er. 4. 15.   l Ge. 24. 60.   g Ge. 49. 25.
f Ne. 3. 14, 15.   h 1 Ki. 14. 10.   i 2 Sa. 22. 5.   j Ps. 76. 13.   z Je. 50. 20.   m Job 20. 24.   n 2 Ch. 6. 13.   h Ps. 72. 15.
g Da. 6. 8, 13.   nn Da. 4. 33.

יְבָרֲכֵנוּ } id. id. with suff. 1 pers. pl.; with cop. וּ ברך

וַיְבָרֲכֵנוּ } [for וַיְבָרֲכֵנוּ]   .   } ברך

יְבָרֲכֵנִי } id. id. with suff. 1 pers. sing.; ן conv.   ברך

יָבֵשׁ { fut. יִיבַשׁ, to be or become dry, to dry up. Pi. to make dry, to dry up. Hiph.—I. to dry up; (b) intrans. to be dried up.—II. cogn. בּוּשׁ to make ashamed, 2 Sa. 19. 6; (b) intrans. to be ashamed, to be put to shame, be disgraced; (c) to act shamefully, Ho. 2. 7.

יָבֵשׁ masc. dec. 5a, adj. יְבֵשָׁה fem. dec. 10.—I. dry.—II. pr. name of a town in Gilead, written also יָבֵישׁ.—III. pr. name of a man, 2 Ki. 15. 10, 13, 14.

יַבֶּשֶׁת, יַבָּשָׁה fem. dry land.

יַבֶּשֶׁת Chald. fem. id. emph. יַבֶּשְׁתָּא, Da. 2. 10.

יָבֵשׁ adj. masc. dec. 5a, also pr. name   .   יבש

יָבוֹשׁ Kal inf. absolute   .   .   .   יבש

וַיִּיבַשׁ id. fut. 3 pers. s. m. for יִיבַשׁ; וַ conv.   יבש

יָבֵשָׁה pr. name of a place (יָבֵשׁ) with parag. ה יבש

יַבָּשָׁה noun fem. sing.   .   .   .   יבש

יְבֵשָׁה adj. fem. sing. dec. 10, from יָבֵשׁ masc. יבש

יָבְשָׁה Kal pret. 3 pers. sing. fem.   .   יבש

יַבְּשֵׁהוּ } Piel imp. masc. s., with suff. 3 pers. s. m. יבש

יָבְשׁוּ } Kal pret. 3 pers. pl. (§ 8. rem. 7)   .   יבש
יָבֵשׁוּ }

וַיֵּבֹשׁוּ } וַ Kal fut. 3 p. pl. m. (§ 21. r. 6); וַ conv. בוש

וַיֵּבֹשׁוּ { וַ Kal fut. 3 pers. pl. masc. [for יִיבְשׁוּ § 8. rem. 15]; ן conv.   .   יבש

יְבֵשׁוֹת adj. fem., pl. of יְבֵשָׁה dec. 10, fr. יָבֵשׁ masc. יבש

יְבֵשִׁים { id. masc., pl. of יָבֵשׁ d. 5a [for וַיְבַ׳/וַיִּבַ׳] יבש

יַבְשֵׁלוּ } וַ Piel fut. 3 pers. pl. masc.; ן conv. בשל

יִבְשָׂם } pr. name masc.   .   .   .   בשם

יַבְשְׂרוּ Piel fut. 3 p. pl. m. יְבַשְּׂרוּ comp. § 8. r. 15] בשר

יַבֶּשֶׁת } noun fem. sing.   .   .   .   יבש

יַבֶּשֶׁת Kal inf. constr. (§ 20. rem. 3)   .   יבש

יַבֶּשְׁתָּא Ch. noun fem. sing., emph. of יַבֶּשֶׁת יבש

יִבָּתֵר } וַ Piel fut. 3 pers. sing. masc.; ן conv. בתר

יִנָּאֶה } וַ Kal fut. 3 pers. sing. masc.; וַ id. נאה

יִגָּאֵל Niph. fut. 3 pers. sing. masc.   נאל

יִגְאָל } pr. name masc.   .   .   .   נאל

יִגְאַל } Kal fut. 3 pers. sing. masc. (comp. § 8. נאל
יִגְאָל { rem. 15)

יִגְאָלוּהוּ id. fut. 3 p. pl. m., suff. 3 p. s.m. (§ 16. r. 12) נאל

יִגֹּאֲלוּ } וַ Pual fut. 3 pers. pl. masc.; ן conv. נאל

יִגְאָלֶךָ Kal fut. 3 pers. sing. masc. (יִגְאַל), suff. 2 pers. sing. fem. (§ 16. rem. 12)   .   נאל

יִנְאָלֵם } id., suff. 3 pers. pl. masc. (v. id.)   .   נאל

יִנְאָלֶנָּה id., suff. 3 pers. sing. f. (v. id. & § 2. r. 3) נאל

יִנְאָלֶנּוּ id. with suff. 3 pers. sing. masc. (v. id.)   .   נאל

[יָגַב] i. q. גּוּב to plough, till; part. pl. יֹגְבִים plough-men, 2 Ki. 25. 12, Keri, Je. 52. 16.

יֶגֶב masc. dec. 5a, field, Je. 39. 10.

וַיִּגְבַּהּ } וַ Kal fut. 3 pers. sing. masc.; וַ conv. נבה

יִגְבְּהָה } וַ pr. name of a place   .   .   נבה

יִגְבְּהוּ } וַ Kal fut. 3 pers. pl. (§ 8. r. 15); נבה
יִגְבְּהוּ { וַ conv.   .   .   .   }

יִגְבּוֹל Kal fut. 3 pers. sing. masc. (§ 8. rem. 18) נבל

יַגְבִּיהַּ Hiph. fut. 3 pers. sing. masc.   .   נבה

יַגְבִּיהֶהָ id. id., suff. 3 pers. sing. fem.   נבה

יַגְבִּיהוּ id. fut. 3 pers. pl. masc.   .   נבה

יְגָבִים } noun m. pl. of יֶגֶב d. 5c [for וַיְגַ׳/וַיִּגַ׳ נב

יְגַבֵּר } Piel fut. 3 pers. sing. masc.   .   נבר

יִגְבַּר } Kal fut. 3 pers. sing. masc.   .   נבר

יִגְבְּרוּ } וַ id. fut. 3 pers. pl. masc.; ן conv. נבר

יָגֹד } Kal fut. 3 pers. sing. masc. [for יִנְגֹד] . נוד

יַגֵּד } Hiph. fut. 3 pers. sing. masc. ap. נגד
וַיַּגֵּד } וַ , וַ (§ 11. rem. 7); ן conv. נגד

יֻגַּד } וַ Hoph. fut. 3 pers. sing. masc.; ן conv. נגד

יַגִּדָהּ } וַ Hiph. fut. 3 pers. sing. masc. (יַגִּיד), suff. 3 pers. sing. fem.   .   .   נגד

וַיַּגִּדוּ } וַ id. fut. 3 pers. pl. masc.; ן conv. נגד

יַגְדִּיל Hiph. fut. 3 pers. sing. masc.   .   נדל

יַגְדִּילוּ } וַ id. fut. 3 pers. pl. masc.; ן conv. נדל

יַגְדֶּלְךָ } Piel fut. 3 pers. sing. masc., suff. 2 pers. sing. masc. [for יַגְדֶּלְךָ § 16. rem. 16] נגד

יְגַדֵּל } Piel fut. 3 pers. sing. masc.; ן conv., נדל
וִיגַדֵּל } with cop. וִיגַדֵּל for וַיְגַדֵּל נדל

וַיִּגְדַּל } Kal fut. 3 pers. sing. masc. (comp. נדל
וַיִּ׳, ן { § 8. rem. 15); ן conv.   . נדל

יְגַדְּלֶהוּ } Piel fut. 3 pers. sing. masc. (יְגַדֵּל), suff. 3 pers. sing. masc.; ן id.   נדל

יִגְדְּלוּ } id. fut. 3 pers. pl. masc.   .   נדל

יִגְדְּלוּ } Kal fut. 3 pers. pl. masc. (§ 8. rem. 15); נדל
יִגְדְּלוּ { ן conv.   .   .   .   }

יִגְדַּלְיָהוּ pr. name masc.   .   .   .   נדל

וַיְגַדֵּעַ } Piel fut. 3 pers. sing. masc.; ן conv. נדע

יְגַדְּעוּ } id. fut. 3 pers. pl. masc.   .   נדע

יָגָה Niph. נוּגָה (§ 20. rem. 5) to be afflicted, grieved. Pi. to afflict, grieve, La. 3. 33.

a Ps. 67. 7, 8.   e Is. 44. 3.   n Job 12. 15.   t Is. 60. 6.   b Ru. 3. 13.   h Job 36. 7.   Je. 39. 10.   v Zep. 2. 8, 10.   c 2 Ch. 1. 1.
b Ps. 67. 2.   f Nu. 11. 6.   o Is. 40. 24.   u Ps. 95. 5.   c Job 3. 5.   i Eze. 31. 14.   p Ec. 10. 10.   w De. 32. 7.   d Ho. 9. 12.
c Ge. 30. 27.   g Ge. 8. 14.   p Eze. 37. 2.   v Ps. 106. 10.   d Jos. 18. 20.   k 1 Sa. 2, 9.   q Ge. 7. 18, 24.   x 1 Ch. 29. 25.   e 2 Ch. 14. 2.
d Eze. 17. 10.   h Na. 1. 4.   q Nu. 6. 3.   w Da. 2. 10.   e Le. 27. 13.   l Ge. 49. 19.   r 1 Ch. 29. 25.   y 2 Ch. 14. 2.
e Is. 19. 7.   i Joel 1. 12.   r Eze. 46. 20, 24.   x Ge. 15. 10.   f Le. 25. 48, 49.   m 2 Ch. 33. 14.   s Je. 9. 11.   z 2 Ch. 31. 1.
f Ps. 102. 5.   k Job 18. 16.   s 2 Ch. 35. 13.   y Job 10. 16.   g Pr. 18. 12.   n Job 5. 7.   t Je. 9. 11.   u Ge. 48. 19.

Hiph. הוֹגָה.—I. *to afflict grieve.*—II. *to remove,* 2 Sa. 20. 13.

יָגוֹן masc. dec. 3a, *affliction, grief, sorrow.*

תּוּגָה fem. dec. 10, *sorrow, grief, vexation.*

וַ יָּגַהּ	Piel fut. 3 pers. sing. masc. [for וַיִּגַּהּ § 20. rem. 8] ; וַ conv.	ינה
יִגְּהֶהּ	Kal fut. 3 pers. sing. masc.	נגה
יִנְהֶה	Kal fut. 3 pers. sing. masc.	נהה
יִנְהַר	וַ Kal fut. 3 pers. sing. masc. ; וַ conv.	נהר
יָגֹדּוּ	Kal fut. 3 pers. pl. masc. [for יָנֹדּ § 18. rem. 2]	נדד
יְנֻדֶּנּוּ	Kal fut.3 p.s.m., suff.3 p.s.m. or 1 p. pl.(§2.r.3)	נוד
יָגֹל	Kh. יָגֹל , K. יָגִיל Kal fut. 3 pers. sing. masc. R. or נוֹל	ניל
יָגֹן	וַ noun masc. sing. dec. 3a	ינה
יָנוֹעַ	Kal fut. 3 pers. sing. masc. (§ 8. rem. 15) ; וַ conv.	נוע
וַיָּנֹעַ		
יָנֹעוּ	Kal fut. 3 pers. pl. masc. (§ 8. rem. 15)	נוע
וַיָּנֹעוּ		
יְנוֹעוּן	id. with parag. וּ (§ 8. rem. 17)	נוע
יָנוֹד	adj. or part. sing. masc. (§ 26. No. 3, § 8. rem. 1, § 9. rem. 20)	ינר
יָנֹגַר	וַ Kal fut. 3 pers. sing. masc.; also pr. name	נור
יָנֹרוּ	id. fut. 3 pers. pl. masc.	נור
יְנֹרֵם	Kal fut. 3 pers. sing. masc. [יָנֹר], suff. 3 pers. pl. masc. [for יָנֹרֵם=יָנֹרֵם § 18. rem. 5]	נרד
וַיָּגָז	וַ Kal fut. 3 pers. sing. masc. with conv. וַ [for יָגָז § 18. rem. 5]	נזז
וַיָּגָז	וַ Kal fut. 3 pers. sing. masc. with conv. וַ [for יָגָז ap. from יָנֹז]	נוז
וַיִּגְזֹל	וַיַּ Kal fut. 3 pers. sing. masc.; וַ conv.	נזל
וַיִּגְזְלוּ	וַיַּ id. fut. 3 pers. pl. masc. ; וַ id.	נזל
יִגְזֹר	וַ Kal fut. 3 pers. sing. masc. ; וַ id.	נזר
יִגְזְרוּ	וַ id. fut. 3 pers. pl. masc. ; וַ id.	נזר
יָנַּח	Kal fut. 3 pers. sing. m. (comp. § 8. rem. 15)	ננח
יָנַּח		
יַגִּיד	according to some copies	נגד
יַגִּיד	Hiph. fut. 3 pers. sing. masc.	
יַגִּידֶךָ	וַ id. id., suff. 3 pers. sing. fem.	נגד
יַגִּידוּ	וַיַּ וַ id. fut. 3 pers. pl. masc. ; וַ conv.	נגד
יַגִּיהַּ	Hiph. fut. 3 pers. sing. masc.	נגה
יָנִיחַ	Kal fut. 3 pers. sing. masc.	ניח
יָגִיל	Kh. יָגִיל q.v., K. יָגֵל ap. from יָגִיל (§ 22. r. 3)	ניל
וַיָּגֶל	וַ Kal fut. 3 pers. sing. masc.	ניל
יָגִילוּ	id. fut. 3 pers. pl. masc.	ניל
יְגִילוּן	id. id. with parag. וּ	ניל

יִגַּע	וַ Hiph. fut. 3 pers. sing. masc.	נגע
יָגַע	noun masc. sing. dec. 1a	ינע
יְגִיעָהּ	id., suff. 3 pers. sing. fem.	ינע
יָגִיעוּ	וַ Hiph. fut. 3 pers. pl. masc. ; וַ conv.	נגע
יְגִיעוֹ	noun masc. sing., suff. 3 pers. sing. masc. from יָגִיעַ dec. 1a	ינע
יְגִיעַי	id. pl. with suff. 1 pers. sing.	ינע
יְגִיעֵי	adj. masc. pl. constr. from [יָגִיעַ] dec. 3a	ינע
יְגִיעֲךָ	noun masc. sing., suff. 2 pers. sing. masc. from יָגִיעַ dec. 1a	ינע
יְגִיעֶךָ		
יְגִיעֵךְ	id. with suff. 2 pers. sing. fem.	ינע
יְגִיעֲכֶם	id., suff. 2 pers. pl. masc. with cop. וַ [for וְיַ , וְיָ]	ינע
יְגִיעָם	id., suff. 3 pers. pl. masc. comp. preceding	ינע
יַגִּיעֶנָּה	Hiph. fut. 3 pers. s. m., suff. 3 pers. sing. fem.	נגע
יָגִיפוּ	Hiph. fut. 3 pers. pl. masc.	נוף
יַגִּירֻהוּ	Hiph. fut. 3 pers. pl. m. [יַגִּירוּ], suff. 3 p. s. m.	נגר
וַיַּגִּישׁוּ	וַ Hiph. fut. 3 pers. pl. masc. ; וַ conv.	נגש
יָגֵל	Kal fut. 3 pers. sing. masc., ap. from יָגִיל (§ 22. rem. 3)	ניל
יָגֵל		
וַיָּגֶל	וַ Hiph. fut. 3 pers. sing. masc. with conv. וַ [for יָגֵל § 18. rem. 11]	נלל
יְגַל	וַ Piel fut. 3 pers. s. m. ap. for יְגַלֶּה ; וַ conv.	נלה
יֶגֶל	וַ Hiph. fut. 3 pers. sing. masc. ap. [fr. וַיַּגְלֶה]	נלה
וַיִּגֶל	וַיַּ , וַ Kal fut. 3 p. s. m. ap. fr. יִגְלֶה ; וַ conv.	נלה
וַיִּגָּל	וַ Niph. fut. 3 pers. sing. masc.	נלל
יַגְלֶהָ	וַ Hiph. fut. 3 pers. sing. masc., suff. 3 pers. sing. fem. (§ 24. rem. 21)	נלה
יִגָּלֶה	Niph. fut. 3 pers. sing. masc.	נלה
יְגַלֶּה	Piel fut. 3 pers. sing. masc.	נלה
יִגְלֶה	Kal fut. 3 pers. sing. masc.	נלה
וַיִּגָּלוּ	וַ Niph. fut. 3 pers. pl. masc. ; וַ conv.	נלה
יְגַלּוּ	Piel fut. 3 pers. pl. masc.	נלה
יִגְלוּ	Kal fut. 3 pers. pl. masc.	נלה
יַגְלוּם	וַ Hiph. fut. 3 p. pl. m., suff. 3 p. pl. m. ; וַ conv.	נלה
יְנַלַּח	וַ Piel fut. 3 pers. sing. masc. (§ 15. rem. 1) ; וַ conv.	נלח
יְנַלַּח		
יִגְלָחוּ	id. fut. 3 p. pl. m. [for יְגַלְּחוּ comp. § 8.rem. 15]	נלה
יְנַלְּחֶם	id. fut. 3 p. s. m., suff. 3 pers. pl. m.; וַ conv.	נלה
יְנַלְּחֶנּוּ	id. id., suff. 3 pers. sing. masc. (§ 2. rem. 3)	נלה
יִנְלִי	pr. name masc.	נלה
יַגְלֵם	וַ Hiph. fut. 3 pers. sing. masc. [יַגְלֶה], suff. 3 pers. pl. masc. (§ 24. rem. 21)	נלה
יְנַלֵּם	וַ Kal fut. 3 pers. sing. masc. ; וַ conv.	נלם

a La. 3. 33.   h Zec. 13. 8.   p Eze. 18. 7.   x Ec. 10. 20.   f Da. 12. 12.   = Job 39. 11.   o Ps. 63. 11.   * Job 36. 15.   g Job 20. 27.
b Job 18. 5.   i Job 36. 12.   q Job 24. 9, 19.   y Is. 44. 7.   g Ps. 107. 18.   ‡ Eze. 23. 29.   z Is. 41. 22.   † Am. 5. 34.   h Am. 6. 7.
c Ho. 5. 13.   k Ps. 104. 29.   r Ju. 9. 25.   z Job 40. 23.   h Ps. 109. 11.   s Is. 55. 2.   z 2 Ch. 29. 23.   ‡ 2 Ki. 16. 9.   i 1 Ch. 8. 6.
d Ps. 94. 21.   l Je. 22. 25 ; 39. 17.   s Is. 9. 19.   a Pa. 21. 2.   k Ho. 12. 9.   r Ps. 78. 46.   a Ps. 16. 9.   z 1 Sa. 3. 7.   k 1 Ch. 5. 6.
e Pr. 23. 24.   m Pr. 31. 7.   t 2 Ki. 6. 4.   b Zep. 3. 17.   l Job 3. 17.   s Is. 26. 5.   b Ge. 29. 10.   z De. 23. 1.   l Nu. 6. 9.
f Ge. 6. 17.   n Job 1. 20.   u Ex. 21. 31.   c Hab. 1. 15.   m De. 28. 33.   t Ne. 7. 3.   c Job 20. 28.   † 2 Sa. 22. 16.   m 2 Ki. 2. 3.
g Job 34. 15.   o Nu. 11. 1.   w Ex. 21. 28, 31.   d Ps. 89. 17.

יְנַמֵּא Piel fut. 3 pers. s. m. [for יְנַמֵּא § 10. rem. 4]   נמא

יִנָּמֵל } Niph. fut. 3 pers. sing. masc. (§ 9. rem.   נמל
יִנָּמֶל } 3 & 4) ; וَ conv.

יִנְמַל } Kal fut. 3 pers. sing. masc. ; וَ id.   נמל
יִנְמְלֵנִי id. with suff. 1 pers. sing.   נמל

יִנְמֹר } Kal fut. 3 pers. sing. masc. (§ 8. rem. 18)   נמר
יִנָּמֵר }

יִנֹּן Kal fut. 3 pers. sing. masc.   ננן

יִנָּנֵב Niph. fut. 3 pers. sing. masc.   ננב

וַיִּנְנֹב Kal fut. 3 pers. sing. masc. ; וَ conv.   ננב

יְנַנֵּב } Piel fut. 3 pers. sing. masc. ; וَ id.   ננב

יְנֻנַּב Pual fut. 3 pers. sing. masc. [for יְנֻנַּב comp. § 8. rem. 15]   ננב

יִנְנְבוּ Kal fut. 3 pers. pl. masc.   ננב

יִנְנוֹב Kal fut. 3 pers. sing. masc. (§ 8. rem. 18)   ננב

[יָנַע] fut. יִינַע.—I. *to labour, toil.*—II. *to be wearied, fatigued with labour,* with בְּ. Pi. *to weary, fatigue.* Hiph. *to weary, be troublesome.*

יֶנַע masc. *labour,* meton. *earnings,* Job 20. 18.

יָנֵעַ adj. masc. dec. 5a, *weary, fatigued, exhausted.*

יָגֵיעַ adj. masc. dec. 3a, id. Job 3. 17.

יְגִיעַ masc. dec. 1a.—I. *labour, toil.*—II. *fruit of labour, earnings, gain, wealth.*

יְגִיעָה fem. dec. 10, *labour, exertion,* Ec. 12. 12.

יְגַע noun masc. sing.   ינע

יָגֵעַ adj. masc. sing. dec. 5a   ינע

יָגַע } Hiph. fut. 3 pers. s. m. ap. fr. יַגִּיעַ ; וَ conv.   ננע

וַיִּיגַע Kal fut. 3 pers. sing. masc. ; וَ id.   ננע

יָגְעָה Kal pret. 3 pers. sing. fem.   ינע

יִגְעֶה Kal fut. 3 pers. sing. masc.   נעה

יִיגְעוּ } Kal fut. 3 pers. pl. masc. [for יִיגְעוּ, § 20. rem. 2, & § 8. rem. 15]   ינע
יִגְעוּ }

יָגְעוּ Kal fut. 3 pers. pl. masc.   ינע

יְגֵעִים adj. masc., pl. of יָגֵעַ dec. 5a   ינע

יַגְעֵל Hiph. fut. 3 pers. sing. masc. [for יַגְעִיל]   נעל

יָגַעְנוּ Kal pret. 1 pers. pl.   ינע

יִיגַר } Kal fut. 3 pers. sing. masc. ; וَ conv.   נער

יְגֹעֲשׁוּ Pual fut. 3 pers. pl. masc.   נעש

יָגַעְתָּ Kal pret. 2 pers. sing. masc.   ינע

יָגַעַתְּ } Kal pret. 2 pers. sing. fem. (§ 8. rem. 15)   ינע
יָגַעַתְּ }

יְגִעַת noun fem. sing., constr. of [יְגִיעָה] dec. 10.   ינע

יָגַעְתִּי Kal pret. 1 pers. sing.   ינע

וַיִּגֶף Kal fut. 3 pers. sing. masc. (§ 17. r. 3) ; וَ conv.   ננף

יִנְפֵהוּ } id., suff. 3 pers. sing. masc. (§ 2. rem. 3, & § 8. rem. 14)   ננף
יִנְפֵנוּ }

[יָגֹר] 2 pers. יָגֹרְתָּ (§ 8. rem. 1) *to fear, be afraid,* with מִפְּנֵי.

יָגוֹר adj. masc. *fearing, afraid,* Je. 22. 25; 39. 17.

יְגָר Ch. masc. *heap of stones,* Ge. 31. 47.

יַּגֵּר } Hiph. fut. 3 pers. sing. masc. ap. [fr. [וַיַּגֵּר .... conv.   נגר

יָגֹר } Kal fut. 3 pers. sing. masc. [with וَ conv. for יָגֹר, ap. fr. [וַיָּגָר.   נור

יִנָּגֵר Niph. fut. 3 pers. sing. masc. [for יִנָּגֵר]   נרר

יָגְרֶה Piel fut. 3 pers. sing. masc.   נרה

יָגְרֵהוּ Kal fut. 3 pers. sing. masc. [יָגֹר], suff. 3 pers. sing. masc. [for יָגֹרֵהוּ § 18. rem. 5]   נרר

יָגָרְךָ Kal fut. 3 pers. sing. masc. (יָגֹר), suff. 2 pers. sing. masc.   גור

יְגָרֵם Piel fut. 3 pers. sing. masc.   נרם

יְגָרֵס } Hiph. fut. 3 pers. sing. masc. ap. [from [וַיַּגְרִיס ; וَ conv.   נרס

יְגָרַע Piel fut. 3 pers. sing. masc.   נרע

יִגָּרַע } Niph. fut. 3 pers. sing. masc. (§ 15. rem. l, comp. § 8. rem. 15)   נרע
יִגָּרֵעַ }

יִגְרַע } Kal fut. 3 pers. sing. masc. (§ 8. rem. 15)   נרע
יִגְרָע }

יְגָרֵשׁ } Piel fut. 3 pers. sing. masc. (§ 10. rem. 4); וَ conv.   נרש
וَ }

יְגָרְשֵׁהוּ id. id., suff. 3 pers. sing. masc.; וَ conv.   נרש

יְגָרְשׁוּ id. fut. 3 pers. pl. masc.; וَ id.   נרש

יְגֹרְשׁוּ Pual fut. 3 pers. pl. masc. [for יְגֹרְשׁוּ comp. § 8. rem. 15]   נרש

יִגְרְשׁוּ } Kal fut. 3 pers. pl. masc.; וَ conv.   נרש

יְגָרְשׁוּהָ Piel fut. 3 pers. pl. masc., suff. 3 pers. s. f.   נרש

יְגָרְשׁוּם id. id., suff. 3 pers. pl. masc. (for וֵ fem. § 2. rem. 5); וَ conv.   נרש

יְגָרְשֵׁם id. fut. 3 pers. sing. m., suff. 3 pers. pl. m.   נרש

יָגַרְתָּ Kal pret. 2 pers. sing. masc. (§ 8. rem. 1)   ינר

יָגַרְתִּי id. pret. 1 pers. sing. (v. id.)   ינר

יַגֵּשׁ } Hiph. fut. 3 pers. sing. masc. ap. [for
יַגֵּשׁ } יַגִּישׁ § 11. rem. 6 & 7]; וَ conv.   ננש
יַגֵּשׁ }

יִגַּשׁ } Kal fut. 3 pers. sing. masc. (§ 8. rem.
וַיִּגַּשׁ } 15); וَ conv.   ננש

יִגֹּשׁ Kal fut. 3 pers. sing. masc. (§ 17. rem. 3)   ננש

וַיַּגִּשׁוּ Hiph. fut. 3 p. pl. m. (for [וַיַּגִּישׁוּ); וَ conv.   ננש

a Job 39. 24.   h Ex. 21. 37.   o Job 20. 18.   u Is. 40. 30.   z Zec. 3. 2.   f Ps. 75. 9.   p Job 36. 27.   y Ju. 11. 2.   d De. 28. 60.
b Ge. 21. 8.   i Ge. 31. 20.   q 2 Sa. 17. 2.   x Is. 65. 23.   a Job 34. 20.   g Le. 11. 7.   q Nu. 36. 3.   z Job 30. 5.   e Job 40. 19.
c 1 Sa. 1. 22.   k 2 Sa. 15. 6.   r De. 25. 18.   y Je. 47. 15.   b Is. 47. 15.   h Hab. 1. 15.   r Ex. 21. 10.   a Is. 57. 20.   f Ju. 6. 19.
d Nu. 17. 23.   l Job 4. 12.   s 2 Sa. 5. 8.   z Ec. 1. 8.   c Ec. 12. 12.   i Ps. 5. 5.   s Job 36. 7.   b Zep. 2. 4.   g Ge. 27. 25.
e Ps. 138. 8.   m Ob. 5.   t 2 Sa. 23. 10.   a Job 21. 10.   z 2 Ch. 13. 20.   k Nu. 24. 8.   t Ex. 11. 1.   c Ex. 2. 17.   h Ps. 91. 7.
Ps. 7. 10.   n Pr. 6. 30.   i Job 6. 5.   b La. 5. 5.   h 1 Sa. 26. 10.   La. 3. 16.   u Ps. 34. 1.   c Ex. 6. 1.   De. 15. 2.
g Ex. 22. 11.

וַיִּגְּשׁוּ יִגְּשׁוּ Kal fut. 3 pers. pl. masc. (§ 8. rem. 15); וַיִּ— conv. . . .   נגש

יָד com. dec. 2a (with grave suff. יֶדְכֶם § 31. rem. 3).—I. *hand*; followed by prepositions: the hand to be or go forth עִם, אֵת, (rarely) לְ *with* any one, i. e. *to assist, aid him*; followed by אֶל, לְ *upon* or *against* any one, i. e. *to trouble him*, and but seldom in a good sense; by עַל *upon* any one, i. e. *to strengthen and inspire him*; hence, Is.8.11 בְּחֶזְקַת הַיָּד *with the power of the hand*, i. e. *the power of inspiration*; נָתַן יָד *to give the hand*, as a pledge of agreement, also, of submission; פָּתַח יָד *to open the hand*, i. e. *to give liberally*; קָפַץ יָד *to shut the hand*, i. e. *to be illiberal*; Pr. 11. 21 יָד לְיָד *hand in hand*, i. e. *throughout all generations, ever*; this, however, is explained by others, " joining my hand to yours, I promise;" יָד לְפֶה *hand to mouth*, i. e. *be silent.*—II. *power, strength, might*; בְּאֶפֶס יָד, לֹא בְיָד *without human power.*—III. *care, protection*; תַּחַת יַד פ׳ *under the care of any one.*—IV. *part* (prop. *handful*); Da. 1. 20 עֶשֶׂר יָדוֹת עַל *ten parts above*, i. e. *ten times more.* —V. *side*, as of a river; רְחַב יָדַיִם *large on both sides*, i. e. *spacious.*—VI. *space, place*; אִישׁ עַל יָדוֹ *every one in his place.*—VII. *memorial, monument.* —VIII. pl. יָדוֹת *artificial hands* (different from du. יָדַיִם the human hands) as, (a) *tenons of planks*; (b) *axletrees for wheels*, 1 Ki. 7. 32, 33; (c) *the arms of a throne*, 1 Ki. 10. 19.—With prepositions; בְּיַד *with*; *by*; כְּיַד *according to the means of*; מִיַּד *from, out of*; אֶל יַד, בְּעַד יָד, עַל יָד *at, on, by the side of*; עַל יְדֵי, לְיַד *under the care* or *guidance of* any one.

יַד Ch. com. dec. 2a (with grave suff. יְדָהֹם § 58. rem. 3) *the hand; power*.

יַד וְ id. constr.; also Chald. dec. 2a .   יד

יְדִי Kh. יַד id., K. יְדִי (q. v.) . .   יד

וַיַּדְא Kh. וַיַּדְא Hiph. fut. 3 pers. sing. masc., ap. [from יַדְיא R. נדא, K. יַדֵח id. R.   נדח

וַיֵּרָא Kal fut. 3 pers. sing. masc. ap. from יֵרָאֶה (§ 24. rem. 3); וַ— conv. .   דאה

יְדָא Ch. noun com. sing. emph. of יַד dec. 2a   יד

יִדְאַג Kal fut. 3 pers. sing. masc. [for יִדְאַן § 8. rem. 15] . . . .   דאן

יִדְאֶה g׳ Kal fut. 3 pers. sing. masc. .   דאה

וִידָאֲלָה pr. name of a place in Zebulun, Jos. 19. 15.

יַדְבִּיקוּ וְ Hiph. fut. 3 pers. pl. masc.; וַ— conv.   דבק

יִדְּבֶנּוּ Kal fut. 3 pers. sing. masc., suff. 3 p. s. m.   נדב

וַיַּדְבֵּק Hiph. fut. 3 pers. sing. masc. ap. [fr. יַדְבִּיק; וַ— conv. . . .   דבק

וַיִּדְבַּק Kal fut. 3 pers. sing. masc.; וַ— id.   דבק

Pual fut. 3 pers. pl. masc. [for יְדֻבְּקוּ comp. § 8. rem. 15] . . . . .   דבק

יַדְבִּיקוּ וְ Hiph. fut. 3 pers. pl. for יַדְבִּיקוּ (§ 11. r. 7)   דבק

יִדְבְּקוּ m׳ Kal fut. 3 pers. pl. masc. .   דבק

וַיַּדְבֵּר m׳ Hiph. fut. 3 pers. sing. masc. ap. [from יַדְבִּיר; וַ— conv. . . .   דבר

יְדַבֵּר וַיְ Piel fut. 3 pers. sing. masc. (§ 10. rem. 4); וַ— id. . . . . .   דבר
יְדַבֶּר—

יְדַבְּרוּ וַיְ Piel fut. 3 pers. pl. masc.; וַ— id. .   דבר
יְדַבְּרוּ

וַיְ וִידַבְּרוּ id. id. with conj. וְ [for יְדַבְּרוּ] .   דבר

יְדַבְּרֵם וִי id. fut. 3 pers. sing. masc., suff. 3 pers. pl. masc.; וַ— conv. . . . .   דבר

יִדְבָּשׁ וְ pr. name masc. . . . .   דבש

יִדְּגוּ וַיִ Kal fut. 3 pers. pl. masc.; וַיִ— conv.   דגה

I. [יָדָד] *to throw, cast*, Joel 4. 3; Na. 3. 10; Ob. 11.

II. [יָדַד] Root not used; i. q. דוד *to love.*

יָדִיד masc. dec. 3a.—I. *beloved, friend.*—II. adj. *lovely, pleasant*, Ps. 84. 2.—Pl. יְדִידוֹת *love*, שִׁיר יְדִידוֹת *a song of love*, Ps. 45. 1.

יְדִידָה (*beloved*) pr. name of the mother of king Josiah, 2 Ki. 22. 1.

יְדִידוּת fem. *love, object of love*, Je. 12. 7.

יְדִידְיָה (*beloved of the Lord*) a title of Solomon, 2 Sa. 12. 25.

יָדוֹ (for יָדוֹן *loving*) pr. name masc.—I. 1 Ch. 27. 21.—II. Ezr. 10. 43.

יַדַּי (id.) pr. name masc. Ezr. 10. 43 Keri.

מֵידָד (*love*) pr. name masc. Nu. 11. 26, 27.

יֻדַּד וְ Hoph. fut. 3 pers. sing. masc. .   נדד

יִדְּדוּן Kal fut. 3 pers. pl. masc. with parag. וְ .   נדד

יְדִדוּת noun fem. sing. . . . .   ידד

[יָדָה] *to throw, cast*, Je. 50. 14. Pi. id. Hiph. הוֹדָה, fut. יוֹדֶה (§ 25. No. 2e).—I. *to confess openly and freely.*—II. *to give thanks, to praise.* Hithp. הִתְוַדָּה (§ 20. r. 1).—I. *to confess, make confession.* —II. *to praise*, with לְ 2 Ch. 30. 22.

יְדָא Ch. Aph. *to praise, celebrate.*

יְדִדוֹת pl. fem. *songs of praise, hymns*, Ne. 12. 8.

תּוֹדָה fem. dec. 10.—I. *confession.*—II. *praise*

---

a Ge. 45. 4.   d Ps. 18. 11.   g Je. 49. 22.   i De. 28. 21.   l 2 Ki. 18. 6.   o Ps. 47. 4.   p Ps. 73. 8.   Ge. 48. 16.   t Ps. 68. 13.
b 2 Ki. 12. 12.   e Da. 5. 5, 24.   h Ex. 25. 2.   k Ge. 31. 23.   m Nu. 36. 7, 9.   Ps. 18. 48.   q 1 Sa. 8. 21.   s Job 20. 8.   u Je. 12. 7.
c 2 Ki. 17. 21.   f Je. 17. 8.

thanksgiving.—III. *a company of persons singing songs of praise, a choir of singers.*

יְדִיתוּן, יְדֻתוּן, יְדוּתוּן (*praising*) pr. name of a Levite skilled in music, whom David appointed one of the choristers.

יְדָיָה (*who praises the Lord*) pr. name masc.— I. 1 Ch. 4. 37.—II. Ne. 3. 10.

יְהוּדָה (*praised*) pr. name—I. of the fourth son of Jacob, also of the tribe descended from him, and ultimately applied to the kingdom and house of David, including Benjamin, in contra-distinction to the other ten tribes or the kingdom of Israel.—II. pr. name masc. of several persons less known.

יְהוּד Ch. *Judah, the kingdom of Judah.*

יְהוּדִי pl. יְהוּדִים, יְהוּדִיִּים—I. *a Jew, Jews;* fem. יְהוּדִיָּה *Jewess.*—II. pr. name masc. Je. 36. 14, 21.

יְהוּדָאִין Ch. *a Jew*, only pl. יְהוּדָאִין dec. 7.

יָהַד (denom. from יְהוּד) Hithpa. *to become a Jew*, Est. 8. 17.

יְהוּדִית.—I. adv. *Jewish*, in the language of the Jews.—II. pr. name fem. Ge. 26. 34.

יָדָהּ	noun com. sing., suff. 3 pers. sing. fem. from יָד dec. 2a	יד
יְדַהּ	Ch. n. com. s., suff. 3 p. s. m. from יָד d. 2a	יד
יָדוֹ	‹ noun com. du., suff. (K. יָדָיו § 4. rem. 1) 3 pers. sing. masc., from יָד dec. 2a	יד
יָדוֹ	‹ id. sing., suff. 3 pers. sing. masc. .	יד
יַדּוֹ	Kh. יַדּוֹ K. יַדּוֹ pr. name masc. .	ידד
יָדְדוּ	Kal pret. 3 pers. pl.	ידד
יַדּוּ	‹ Piel fut. 3 pers. pl. masc. with ‹ conv. [for וַיִּדּוּ § 20. rem. 8]	ידה
יַדּוּ	Kal imp. pl. masc.	ידד
יַדּוֹ	pr. name masc.	ידד
יָדָיו	‹ Kh. יָדָיו וְיָדָיו q. v.; K. וִידָיו (q. v.)	יד
יִדֹּד	Kal fut. 3 p. s. m. (§ 17. rem. 1, & § 8. r. 18)	נדד
יָדוֹן	‹ Kal fut. 3 p. s. m.; also pr. n. (Ne. 3. 7)	דון
יָדוֹעַ	Kal inf. abs.	ידע
יַדּוּעַ	‹ pr. name masc.	ידע
יֹדֵעַ	‹ [for וְיֹדֵעַ] Kal part. p. masc., constr. of [יֹדֵעַ] dec. 3a ; ‹ conj., for ‹, bef. (:)	ידע
יְדוֹשֶׁנּוּ	Kal fut. 3 pers. sing. masc. [יָדוֹשׁ], suff. 3 pers. sing. masc. (§ 2. rem. 3) .	דושׁ
יָדוֹת	‹ noun com. pl. abs. from יָד dec. 2a	יד
יְדוֹת	‹ id. pl. constr., with conj. ‹ [for וְיָדוֹת]	יד
יְדוּתוּן	‹ pr. name m., with conj. ‹ [for וְיָדֻ]	יד

יְדוֹתָם	noun com. pl. (יָדוֹת), suff. 3 pers. pl. masc. from יָד dec. 2a	יד
וַיַּדַּח	‹ Hiph. fut. 3 pers. sing. masc. with gutt. [for יַדִּיחַ ap. from יָדִּים ; ‹ conv.	נדח
יִדַּח	Kal fut. 3 pers. sing. masc.	נדח
יִדְחֶה	Niph. fut. 3 pers. sing. masc.	דחה
יִדָּחוּ	Niph. fut. 3 pers. pl. masc. [dag. f. implied in ח, for יִדָּחוּ]	דחח
יְרַחֲלַנִּי	‹ Ch. Pael fut. 3 pers. sing. masc., suff. 1 pers. sing. with conj. ‹ [for וִידַ, וִידַ]	דחל
יִדְחָקוּן	Kal fut. 3 p. pl. m. with parag. ‹ (§ 8. r. 17)	דחק
יָדַי	‹ noun com. du., suff. 1 pers. s. fr. יָד	יד
יָדַי	‹ d. 2a (perh. for יָדַיִם in Eze. 13. 18)	יד
יָדִי	‹ id. sing., suff. 1 pers. sing.	יד
יְדַי	Ch. n. com., du., suff. 1 pers. s. fr. יָד dec. 2a	יד
יְדֵי	‹ noun com. du. constr. from יָד dec. 2a,	יד
יְדֵי	‹ with cop. ‹ [for וִידֵי, וִידֵי]	יד
יְדִיד	noun masc. sing., constr. of [יָדִיד] d. 3a	ידד
יְדִידָה	pr. name fem.	ידד
יְדִידוֹת	adj. pl. fem. [from יָדִיד]	ידד
יְדִידְיָה	pr. name masc.	ידד
יְדִידֶיךָ	noun masc. pl., suff. 2 pers. sing. masc. fr. [יָדִיד] dec. 3a	ידד
יְדִידֹת	noun fem. pl. fr. יָדִיד masc.	ידד
יְדָיָה	pr. name masc.	ידה
יָדֶיהָ	‹ noun com. du., suff. 3 pers. sing. fem. fr. יָד dec. 2a	יד
יָדֵיהוּ	id., suff. 3 pers. sing. masc. (§ 4. rem. 5)	יד
יְדֵיהֶם	‹ id., suff. 3 pers. pl. masc. with cop. ‹ [for וִידֵי, וִידֵי]	יד
יְדֵיהֶן	id., suff. 3 pers. pl. fem.	יד
יָדָיו	‹ id., suff. 3 pers. sing. masc.	יד
יָדִיחַ	Hiph. fut. 3 pers. sing. masc.	דוח
יָדִיחוּ	id. fut. 3 pers. pl. masc.	דוח
וַיַּדִּיחוּ	‹ Hiph. fut. 3 pers. sing. masc.; ‹ conv.	נדח
יָדֶיךָ	‹ noun com. dual, suff. 2 pers. sing. fem.	יד
יָדֶיךָ	‹ from יָד dec. 2a	יד
יָדֶיךָ	‹ id., suff. 2 pers. sing. masc.; Kh. יָדֶיךָ K. יָדָךְ (q. v.)	יד
יְדֵיכֶם	id., suff. 2 pers. pl. masc.	יד
יָדַיִם	‹ id. dual, absolute state	יד
יָדַיִן	Kal fut. 3 pers. sing. masc. R. דִּין see	דון
יָדֵינוּ	noun com. du., suff. 1 pers. pl. fr. יָד d. 1a	יד
יָדִיעַ	Ch. Peal part. pass. sing. masc.	ידע
יְדִיעֵאל	& יְדִיעֵאל pr. name masc., with cop. ‹ [for וִידִי, וִידִי]	ידע

a Ezr. 6. 12.   e Eze. 1. 8.   i Is. 53. 3.   m 2 Ch. 21. 11.   q Je. 23. 12.   t Ca. 5. 5.   v De. 33. 12.   b Eze. 10. 12.   De. 13. 14.
b Job 5. 18.   f Na. 3. 7.   k Ge. 6. 3.   n 2 Ch. 9. 18.   r Da. 4. 2.   1 Sa. 24. 13, 14.   w Ps. 84. 2.   c Eze. 23. 42.   Zep. 3. 16.
c La. 3. 53.   g Ge. 6. 3.   l 1 Ki. 32.   o 2 Sa. 14. 14.   s Pr. 14. 32.   Joel 2. 8.   x Hab. 3. 10.   d Is. 4. 4.
d Je. 50. 14.   h Jos. 22. 13.   1 Ki. 7. 33.   p Is. 28. 28.   Da. 3. 15.   u Ps. 45. 1.   f Je. 2. 37.

Form	Definition	Root
יְדִיעוּ	Hiph. fut. 3 pers. pl. masc.	ידע
יְדִיתֻן	Kh. יְדִיתֻן for K. יְדֻעְתֻן (q. v.)	ידה
יָדְךָ	noun com. sing., suff. 2 pers. sing. masc. fr. יָד dec. 2 a	יד
יָדֵךְ	id., suff. 2 pers. sing. fem.	יד
יְדָךְ	Ch. noun com. sing., suff. 2 pers. sing. masc. from יַד dec. 2 a	יד
יְדֻכָּא	Pual fut. 3 pers. sing. masc.	דכא
וְיִדַכֵּא	Piel fut. 3 pers. sing. masc., with conj. [for וַיְ, וְיִדַכֵּא]	דכא
יִדַּכְּאוּ	Hithpa. fut. 3 pers. pl. masc. (§ 12. rem. 3, comp. § 8. rem. 15)	דכא
יְדַכְּאוּ	Piel fut. 3 pers. pl. masc.	דכא
יְדַכְּאוּם	id. id., suff. 3 pers. pl. masc.	דכא
וְיִדַכְּאֵנִי	id. fut. 3 pers. sing. masc., suff. 1 pers. sing. with conj. [for וַיְ, וְיִדַכְּאֵנִי]	דכא
יָדְכָה	noun com. sing., suff. 2 pers. sing. masc. (§ 3. rem. 2) from יָד dec. 2 a	יד
יֶדְכֶם	id., suff. 2 pers. pl. m. [for יַדְכֶם § 31. r. 3]	יד
יְדֵיכֶם	id. dual, suff. 2 pers. pl. masc. for יְדֵיכֶם	יד
וַיִּדַל	Niph. fut. 3 pers. sing. masc.; וַ conv.	דלל
יְדַלֵּג	Piel fut. 3 pers. sing. masc.	דלג
יַדְלִיקֵם	Hiph. fut. 3 pers. sing. m., suff. 3 pers. pl. m.	דלק
יִדְלֶנָּה	Kal fut. 3 pers. sing. masc., suff. 3 pers. sing. fem. (§ 2. rem. 3)	דלה
יִדְלָף	pr. name masc.	דלף
יִדְלְפוּ	Kal fut. 3 pers. sing. masc.	דלף
יִדְלְקוּ	Kal fut. 3 pers. sing. masc.	דלק
יָדָם	noun com. sing., suff. 3 pers. pl. masc. fr. יָד dec. 2 a	יד
וַיִּדֹּם	Kal fut. 3 pers. sing. masc. [for יָדֹּם § 18. rem. 14]	דמם
יְדַמֶּה	Piel fut. 3 pers. sing. masc.	דמה
יִדְמֶה	Kal fut. 3 pers. sing. masc.	דמה
יִדְמוּ	Niph. fut. 3 pers. pl. masc. (comp. § 8. rem. 15)	דמם
יִדְמוּן	Kal fut. 3 pers. pl. masc., Chald. form. (§ 18. rem. 14 & rem. 7 note)	דמם
יָדֵנוּ	noun com. s., suff. 1 pers. pl. fr. יָד d. 2 a	יד

יָדַע fut. יֵדַע, inf. c. דַּעַת (§ 20. r. 3).—I. *to know, perceive, discern, be aware of.*—II. *to know, be acquainted with*; part. יָדוּעַ *acquainted.*—III. *to know, recognize, acknowledge.*—IV. *to know carnally.*—V. *to regard, care for.* Niph. I. *to be or become known.*—II. *to be made to know,* Pr. 10. 9; Je. 31.

19. Pi. *to make to know, to appoint,* Job 38. 12. Pu. part. מְיֻדָּע *known, acquaintance, familiar.* Poel (§ 6. No. I), *to show, appoint,* 1 Sa. 21. 3. Hiph. הוֹדִיעַ, imp. הוֹדַע *to make known, show, inform, teach.* Hoph. *to be made known.* Hithp. הִתְוַדַּע (§ 20. rem. 1) *to make oneself known,* with אֶל.

יְדַע Ch. fut. יִנְדַּע (§ 52. r. 2) *to know, perceive, understand.* Aph. הוֹדַע *to make known, to show.*

יָדָע (*knowing*) pr. name masc. 1 Ch. 2. 28, 32.

יָדוּעַ (*known*) pr. name masc.—I. Ne. 10. 22.—II. Ne. 12. 11, 22.

יְדָעְיָה (*whom the Lord knows*) pr. name masc. 1 Ch. 9. 10; 24. 7.

יְדִיעֲאֵל (*known of God*) pr. name of a son of Benjamin.

יִדְּעֹנִי masc. pl. יִדְּעֹנִים.—I. *wizard, soothsayer.*—II. *spirit of divination,* Le. 20. 27.

דֵּעַ masc. dec. 1 a, *knowledge, opinion.*

דֵּעָה fem. pl. דֵּעוֹת, *knowledge.*

דַּעַת fem. dec. 13 a (with suff. דַּעְתִּי).—I. *knowledge, the act of knowing.* בִּבְלִי דַעַת *without knowing, unawares.*—II. *intelligence, understanding, wisdom.*

מוֹדָע, מֹדָע masc. *acquaintance, friend,* Ru. 2. 1; Pr. 7. 4.

מוֹדַעַת fem. id. Ru. 3. 2.

מַדָּע, מַדַּע masc. with suff. מַדָּעֲךָ.—I. *knowledge.*—II. *thought, mind,* Ec. 10. 20.

מַנְדַּע Ch. dec. 1 a.—I. *knowledge.*—II. *intelligence, intellect,* Da. 4. 31, 33.

מַדּוּעַ (contr. for מָה יָדוּעַ) adv. interrog. *why? wherefore?*

Form	Definition	Root
יָדַע	Ch. Peal part. act. sing. masc. (§ 49. No. 4) dec. 2 a	ידע
יָדָע	pr. name masc.	ידע
יָדַע	Kal pret. 3 pers. sing. m. for יָדַע (§ 8. r. 7)	ידע
יָדֹעַ	id. inf. abs.	ידע
יֵדַע	id. fut. 3 pers. sing. masc. (comp. § 8. rem. 15)	ידע
וַיֵּדַע	id. id.; acc. drawn back by conv. וַ (§ 20. rem. 1 & 3)	ידע
יוֹדַע	Hiph. fut. 3 pers. sing. masc. with gutt., [for יֹדִיעַ] ap. from יוֹדִיעַ (§ 20. r. 9)	ידע
יְדַע	Ch. Peal pret. 3 pers. sing. masc.	ידע
יָדַע	Kal part. act. sing. masc. dec. 7 b	ידע

a Job 32.7.   b 2 Ch. 6. 22.   c Da. 3. 17.   d Job 22. 9.   e Ps. 72. 4.   f Job 34. 25.   g Job 5. 4.   h Ps. 94. 5.   i Job 4. 19.   j Jo. 6. 9.   k Ju. 6. 6.   l Ex. 13. 16.   m Ps. 134. 2.   n Is. 17. 4.   o Ec. 10. 18.   p Ps. 10. 2.   q Is. 11.   r Pr. 20. 5.   s La. 3. 28.   t Is. 10. 7.   u Ps. 30. 13;   Am. 5. 13   v 1 Sa. 2. 9.   w Je. 49. 26; 50. 30.   x Ex. 15. 16;   Ps. 31. 12;   La. 2. 10.   y Ge. 37. 27.   z Je. 9. 23.   a Job 21. 19.   b Nu. 16. 5.   c Ju. 8. 16.

יָדְעָה — Kal pret. 3 pers. sing. fem. — ידע

יְדָעָהּ — id. pret. 3 pers. sing. m., suff. 3 pers. s. f. — ידע

יְדָעוּהוּ — id. pret. 3 pers. pl., suff. 3 pers. sing. masc. — ידע

יָדְעוּ / יְדָעוּ — id. pret. 3 pers. pl. (§ 8. rem. 7) — ידע

יְדָעוֹ — id. pret. 3 pers. sing. m., suff. 3 pers. s. m. — ידע

יֵדְעוּ, וַיֵּ׳ — id. fut. 3 pers. pl. masc.; וַ conv. — ידע

יֹדְעָו — id. part. act. pl. masc., suff. 3 pers. sing. masc. (K. עָיו § 4. rem. 1) — ידע

יְדָעוּךָ — id. pret. 3 pers. pl., suff. 2 pers. sing. masc. — ידע

יְדָעוּם — id. id., suff. 3 pers. pl. masc. — ידע

יֵדְעוּן — id. id. with parag. ן (§ 8. rem. 4) — ידע

יֵדְעוּן — id. fut. 3 pers. pl. m. with parag. ן (§ 8. rem. 17) — ידע

יְדָעוּנִי — id. pret. 3 pers. pl., suff. 1 pers. sing. — ידע

יָדְעֵי — Chald. Peal part. act. pl. constr. masc. from יְדַע dec. 2 a — ידע

יֹדְעַי — Kal part. act. pl. m., suff. 1 p. s. fr. יֹדֵעַ d. 7 b — ידע

יֹדְעֵי — id. pl. construct state — ידע

יְדָעְיָה — pr. name masc. — ידע

יֹדְעָיו — Kal part. act. pl. m., suff. 3 p. m. s. fr. יֹדֵעַ dec. 7 b — ידע

יֹדְעִים — id. pl., absolute state — ידע

יְדֻעִים — Kal part. p. pl. abs. masc. from יָדוּעַ dec. 3 a, with cop. וְ [for וִידֻעִים, וִידֻעִים] — ידע

יָדְעִין — Chald. Peal part. act. pl. abs. masc. from יְדַע (§ 49. No. 4) dec. 2 a — ידע

יֵדַע / יֵדָע — Kal fut. 3 pers. sing. masc. (§ 8. rem. 15) — דע

יְדָעֵם — Kal fut. 3 p. s. m., suff. 3 p. pl. m. (§ 16. r. 12) — ידע

יָדַעְנוּ / וַיֵּ׳ — Kal pret. 1 pers. pl. (§ 8. rem. 7) — ידע

יְדָעַנוּ — id. pret. 3 pers. sing. masc., suff. 1 pers. pl. — ידע

יֵדָעֵנוּ — id. fut. 3 pers. sing. masc., suff. 3 pers. sing. masc. (§ 16. rem. 12, & § 2. rem. 3) — ידע

יֹדְעֵנוּ — id. part. act. s. m., suff. 1 p. pl. from יֹדֵעַ dec. 7 b — ידע

יְדַעֲנוּךָ — id. pret. 1 pers. pl., suff. 2 pers. sing. masc. — ידע

יְדַעֲנוּם — id. id., suff. 3 pers. pl. masc. — ידע

יִדְּעֹנִי — noun masc. sing. dec. 1 b * Le. 20. 27. — ידע

יִדְּעֹנִים — id. pl. absolute state — ידע

יָדַעְתָּ — Kal pret. 2 pers. sing. masc. (§ 8. rem. 7) — ידע

יָדַעְתָּ — id. id.; acc. shifted by conv. וְ (v. id.) — ידע

יָדַעַתְּ / וַ׳ — id. pret. 2 pers. sing. fem. (v. id.) — ידע

יָדַעַתְּ — Kh. עַתְּ q. v., K. עֲתִּי q. v. — ידע

יְדַעְתְּ — Chald. Peal pret. 2 pers. sing. masc., [for יְדַעְתָּ § 47. rem. 2] — ידע

(יִדַּעְתָּ הַשַּׁחַר) — Keri, Piel pret. 2 p. s. m. (read הַשָּׁחַר) — ידע

יִדְעֵת — Chald. Peal pret. 1 pers. sing. — ידע

יֹדַעַת — Kal part. act. sing. fem. from יָדַע masc. (§ 8. rem. 19, & § 39. No. 4) — ידע

יְדַעְתָּה — full form for יָדַעְתָּ q. v. (§ 8. rem. 5) — ידע

יְדַעְתָּ֫ה / יְדַעְתָּ — Kh. יְדַעְתָּה, full form for יָדַעְתָּ (read שָׁחַר comp. § 8. rem. 5) Piel pret. 2 p. s. m. — ידע

יְדַעְתּוֹ — Kal pret. 2 pers. sing. masc., suff. 3 pers. sing. masc. — ידע

יָדַעְתִּי / יָדָ֫עְתִּי — id. pret. 1 pers. sing. (§ 8. rem. 7) — ידע

יָדַעְתִּי — id. id.; acc. shifted by וְ conv. (v. id.) — ידע

יְדַעְתִּיהָ — id. id., suff. 3 pers. sing. fem. — ידע

יְדַעְתִּיו — id. id., suff. 3 pers. sing. masc. — ידע

יְדַעְתִּיךָ — id. id., suff. 2 pers. sing. masc. — ידע

יְדַעְתִּים — id. id., suff. 3 pers. pl. masc. — ידע

יְדַעְתִּין — id. id., suff. 3 pers. pl. fem. — ידע

יְדַעְתָּם — id. pret. 2 pers. sing. masc., suff. 3 pers. pl. m. — ידע

יְדַעְתֶּם / וַיֵּדַעְתֶּם — id. pret. 2 pers. pl. masc. with conv. וְ [for וַיֵּ׳ וִידַעְתֶּם] — ידע

יְדַעְתֶּן־ / וַ׳ יֵדַעְתֶּן־ — id. pret. 2 pers. pl. fem. with conv. וְ [for וַיֵּ׳ וִידַעְתֶּן] — ידע

יְדַעְתָּנִי — id. pret. 2 p. s. m., suff. 1 p. s. [for תַּנִי § 2. r. 1] — ידע

יִדְפְּנֵּהוּ — Kal fut. 3 pers. sing. masc., suff. 3 pers. s. m. — נדף

יָדֵק / וַ׳ — Hiph. fut. 3 pers. sing. masc. with conv. וְ [for יַדֵּק § 18. rem. 11] — דקק

יָדְקֻּנּוּ — Kal fut. 3 pers. sing. masc. [יָדֹק], suff. 3 pers. sing. masc. (§ 18. rem. 5, & § 2. rem. 3) — דקק

יִדָּקֵר — Niph. fut. 3 pers. sing. masc. — דקר

יִדְקֹר / וַ׳ — Kal fut. 3 pers. sing. masc.; וְ conv. — דקר

יִדְקְרֵהוּ / וַ׳ — id., suff. 3 pers. sing. masc.; וַ id. — דקר

יַדֵּר / יִדֹּר / וַ׳ — Kal fut. 3 pers. sing. masc. (§ 8. rem. 13); וַ id. — נדר

יִדְּרוּ / וַ׳ — id. fut. 3 pers. pl. masc.; וַ id. — נדר

יִדְּרוֹן — Ch. Kh. יִדְּרוּן, Peal fut. 3 p. pl. m. (K. רָן) fem. — דור

יִדְרֹשׁ — Kal fut. 3 pers. sing. m., for יִדְרוֹשׁ (§ 8. rem. 18) — דרשׁ

יַדְרֵיכֶם / וַ׳ — Hiph. fut. 3 pers. sing. masc. [יַדְרִיךְ], suff. 3 pers. pl. masc.; וַ conv. — דרך

יַדְרֵךְ — id. fut. 3 pers. sing. masc. ap. [fr. יַדְרִיךְ] — דרך

יִדְרֹךְ — Kal fut. 3 pers. sing. masc. — דרך

יַדְרְכוּ / וַ׳ — Hiph. fut. 3 pers. pl. masc., from the ap. יַדְרֵךְ (§ 11. rem. 7); וַ conv. — דרך

יִדְרְכוּ / וַ׳ — Kal fut. 3 pers. pl. masc.; וַ id. — דרך

יִדְרְכוּן — id. with parag. ן (§ 8. rem. 17) — דרך

יַדְרִכֵנִי — Hiph. fut. 3 pers. s. m. [יַדְרִיךְ], suff. 1 pers. s. — דרך

יִדְרֹשׁ / וַיֵּ׳ — Kal fut. 3 pers. sing. masc.; וַ conv. — דרשׁ

יִדְרְשֵׁהוּ / וַיֵּ׳ — id., suff. 3 pers. sing. masc.; וַ id. — דרשׁ

a Ge. 24. 16; b Je. 2. 8. c Da. 5. 23. d Je. 17. 9. e Da. 5. 22. f Eze. 11. 5. g Job 32. 13. h Da. 4. 9. i Ju. 9. 27.
1 Ki. 1. 4. Ezr. 7. 25. Pr. 20. 20. Is. 48. 8. Ge. 18. 19. Is. 28. 28. Job 39. 8. Ps. 11. 2.
Da. 11. 38. Job 19. 13. Ho. 14. 10. Ho. 8. 2. Da. 4. 6. Pr. 30. 18. Ps. 107. 7. Hab. 3. 19.
De. 34. 10; Job 42. 11. Ge. 29. 5. Is. 59. 12. 2 Sa. 2. 26. Is. 48. 7. Nu. 25. 8. Je. 25. 9. 2 Ch. 24. 22.
Job 28. 7. 2 Ki. 17. 26. 1 Sa. 6. 9. 2 Ki. 21. 6. Job 38. 12. Ge. 31. 6. Ju. 9. 54. Ps. 9. 2. Job 3. 4.
Job 34. 1. Job 34. 2. Is. 63. 16. Je. 50. 24. De. 22. 2. Eze. 13. 21, 23. Jon. 1. 16. 1 Sa. 5. 5. Ch. 1. 5.
De. 8. 3, 16. De. 1. 13, 15.

יִדְרְשׁוּ / וְיִדְרְשׁוּ Kal fut. 3 p. pl. m. (§ 8. rem. 15); וַ conv.   דרשׁ

יִדְרְשׁוּהוּ id. id., suff. 3 pers. sing. masc.   דרשׁ

יִדְרְשׁוּן id. id. with parag. ן (§ 8. rem. 17)   דרשׁ

יִדְרְשֶׁנּוּ id. fut. 3 p. s. m., suff. 3 p. s. m. (§ 2. rem. 3)   דרשׁ

יֻדְשַׁן Pual fut. 3 p.s.m. [for יְדֻשַׁן comp. § 8. rem.15]   דשׁן

יְדַשְּׁנֶה Piel fut. 3 p. s. m. with parag. ה (§ 8. rem. 13)   דשׁן

יְדֹת ' noun com. pl. abs. from יָד dec. 2 a   יד

יְדֹתָו defect. for יְדוֹתָו q. v.   ידה

יְדֹתֶיהָ noun com. pl., suff. 3 pers. sing. fem. from יָד dec. 2 a   יד

יְדֹתָיו id. pl., suff. 3 pers. sing. masc.   יד

יָהּ i. q. יְהֹוָה from which it is abbreviated   הוה

[יָהַב] imp. הַב, with ה parag. הָבָה, fem. הָבִי, pl. הָבוּ —I. *to give.*—II. *to set, place.* הָבָה adv. *come, come on! go to!*

יְהַב Chald.—I. *to give.*—II. *to set, place.* Ithpe. *to be given, delivered over.*

יְהָב masc. *burden, trouble,* Ps. 55. 23; but which some take as a verb and render it, הַשְׁלֵךְ עַל־יְהֹוָה יְהָבְךָ *cast upon the Lord what he has given* or *laid upon thee,* i. e. thy lot, for אֲשֶׁר יָהַב לָךְ. הַבְהָבִים masc. pl. *gifts,* Ho. 8. 13.

יָהֲבִי Chald. Peal part. act. masc. dec. 2 b .   יהב

יְהַב Chald. Peal pret. 3 pers. sing. masc.   יהב

יְהִיב Chald. id. part. pass. sing. masc. (for יְהִיב)   יהב

וִיהִיבוּ ו id. pret. 3 pers. pl. masc. with conj. ו [for וַיְ, וִיהִיבוּ]   יהב

יָהֲבִין Chald. id. part. act. masc., pl. of יָהֵב dec. 2 b   יהב

יְהָבְךָ Kal pret. 3 pers. sing. masc., suff. 2 pers. sing. m.; or rather noun m. [יְהָב] with suff., &c.   יהב

יַהְבִּלוּ ו Kal fut. 3 pers. pl. m. [for יַהְבִּלוּ § 8. rem. 15, & § 13. rem. 4 & 5]; ו conv.   הבל

יְהַבְתְּ Chald. Peal pret. 2 pers. sing. masc.   יהב

יֶהְגֶּה Kal fut. 3 pers. sing. masc. (§ 13. rem. 5)   הגה

יֶהְגּוּ id. fut. 3 pers. pl. masc. (v. id.)   הגה

יָהֻד ן pr. name of a place, for יְהוּד (ן, for ו cop.)   ידה

יֶהְדִּי pr. name masc. for יֶהְדָּי   הדה

יֶהְדֹּף Kal fut. 3 pers. sing. masc. (§ 13. rem. 5)   הדף

יֶהְדְּפֻהוּ id. fut. 3 pers. pl. m., suff. 3 pers. s. m. (v. id.)   הדף

יֶהְדְּפֻם id. fut. 3 pers. sing. masc., suff. 3 pers. pl. masc. (v. id. & § 8. rem. 14) .   הדף

יֶהְדְּפֶנּוּ id. id., suff. 3 pers. s. m. (v. id. & § 2. rem. 3)   הדף

יְהוּא Kal fut. 3 pers. sing. masc. [for יֶהֱוֶה ap. for יֶהֱוֶה § 24. rem. 3] .   הוה

יְהוּא (*he shall exist, live,* contr. for יְהִי=יֶהֱוֶה יֶהֱוֶא)

---

pr. name of several men, especially—I. of a king of Israel, comp. 2 Ki. ch. 9.—II. of a prophet in Samaria, comp. 1 Ki. 16. 1.

יְהוֹאָשׁ יְהוֹאָחָז pr. names masc. .   הוה

יְהוֹבְדוּן Ch. Aph. fut. 3 pers. pl. masc. (§ 53. No. 1)   אבד

יְהוּד pr. name of a country .   ידה

יְהוּדָאִין Chald. gen. noun, pl. of יְהוּדָי [יְהוּדָי] dec. 7   יהד

וִיהוּדָה ויהי pr. name of a man and a tribe, with cop. ן [for וַיְ, וִיהוּדָה]   ידה

יְהוֹדָה Hiph. fut. 3 pers. sing. masc. (§ 20. rem. 10)   ידה

יְהוֹדֻךָ id. fut. 3 pers. pl. m., suff. 2 pers. s. m. (v. id.)   ידה

יְהוּדִי gent. noun from יְהוּדָה; also pr. name masc.   יהד

יְהוּדָיֵא Chald. gen. m. pl. emph. from יְהוּדָי (§ 63)   יהד

יְהוּדִים gent. noun., pl. of יְהוּדָה from יְהוּדִי   יהד

יְהוּדִית id. s. fem., used also as an adv.; or pr. n. f.   יהד

יְהוֹדַע Chald. Aph. fut. 3 pers. s. m. (§ 52 note)   ידע

יְהוֹדְעוּן Chald. id. fut. 3 pers. pl. masc. (v. id.)   ידע

יְהוֹדְעִנַּנִי Chald. id. fut. 3 pers. s. m., suff. 1 p. s. (v. id.)   ידע

יְהוֹדְעֻנַּנִי Chald. id. fut. 3 pers. pl. m., suff. 1 p. s. (v. id.)   ידע

יְהֹוָה, וַיהֹוָה the most sacred name of God, with the vowels of אֲדֹנָי except (־֫), with ו cop. וַיהֹוָה corresponds to the form וַאֲדֹנָי for וְאֲדֹנָי, see lett. ו, but see under   הוה

אֲדֹנָי id. with the vowels of אֱלֹהִים, when precedes   הוה

יְהוֹיָכִין, וַיְהִי, יְהוֹיָדָע & יְהוֹיָע & יְהוֹתָנ, וַיְהִי & יְהוֹבָד וַיְהוֹיָרִיב, יְהוֹיָקִים pr. names masc.   הוה

יְהוֹכַל pr. name masc. .   יכל

יְהוֹלֵל Poel fut. 3 pers. sing. masc.   הלל

יְהוֹעַדָּן, יְהוֹעַדָּה, וַיְהִי & יְהוֹנָתָן, וַיְהִי & יְהוֹשֶׁבַע וְיְהִי & יְהוֹרָם & וַיְהִי & יְהוֹצָדָק & יְהוֹשׁוּעַ, יְהוֹשַׁבְעַת pr. names masc.   הוה

יוֹשִׁיעַ Hiph. fut. 3 pers. sing. masc. (§ 20. r. 10) .   ישׁע

יְהוֹשֻׁעַ וַיְהִי defect. for יְהוֹשׁוּעַ (q. v.) .   הוה

יְהוֹשָׁפָט וַיְהִי pr. name of a man and a place, with cop. ן [for וַיְ, וִיהי] .   הוה

יַחֲחַוֵּה Ch. Aph. fut. 3 pers. s. m. (§47.r.4, &§ 55 note)   חוה

יְהִי (וַיְ) Kal fut. 3 pers. s. m., ap. for יִהְיֶה (§ 24. rem. 3 e, comp. § 35. r. 14); ו conv.   היה

יְהִי ו id. with conj. ו [for וַיְ, וִיהִי] .   היה

יְהִיב Chald. Peal part. pass. sing. masc. .   יהב

יְהִיבוּ ן Chald. id. with the afformative of 3 pers. pl. masc. יְהִיבוּ, see § 47. rem. 11, with conj. ן [for וַיְ, וִיהִיבוּ] .   יהב

יְהִיבַת / וִיהִיבַת Chald. id., with the afformative 3 pers. sing. fem., comp. the preceding .   יהב

יְהִיתָה Kh. יִהֱוָה q. v., K. וִהְיָה Kal pret. 3 pers. s. m.   היה

a Ju. 6. 29.   c Ps. 20. 4.   g Da. 2. 21.   m Pr. 10. 3.   q Ec. 11. 3.   v Da. 2. 25.   a Da. 4. 3.   e Esr. 5. 14.
b Ps. 119. 2.   d Ex. 36. 22.   h Da. 6. 3.   n Job 18. 18.   r Da. 2. 18.   w Da. 2. 30.   b 1 Sa. 17. 47.   f Da. 7. 12, 27.
Is. 58. 2.   e 1 Ki. 10. 19.   i Ps. 55. 23.   o Ne. 11. 17.   s Da. 7. 16.   x Ps. 116. 6.   c Ese. 16. 15.   g Ese 45. 5.
De. 22. 22.   f 1 Ki. 7. 35, 36.   k Jos. 23. 5.   l Da. 2. 23.   p Nu. 35. 20.   t Ps. 45. 18.   u Da. 7. 14. 22.   z Da. 3. 28.   d Da. 7. 4. 6.

יִהְיֶה	Kal fut. 3 pers. sing masc.	היה
יֶהֱיֶה	Kh. יִהְיֶה q. v., K. יֶהֱיֶה (q. v.)	היה
יִהְיוּ	'‚, וַ'‚ Kal fut. 3 pers. pl. masc.; וֹ' conv.	היה
יִהְיוּ	Kh. יֶהֱיוּ q. v., K. וַיְהִיוּ Kal pret. 3 pers. pl.	היה
יְהֵילִילוּ	Hiph. fut. 3 pers. pl. masc. (§ 20. rem. 14)	ילל
יָהִיר	adj. masc. sing.	יהר
יְהָךְ	Chald. Peal fut. 3 pers. sing. masc. (§ 54.	
יְהָךְ	rem. 1), with conj. וֹ [for וְיִהָךְ] .	הוד
יָהֵל	Hiph. fut. 3 pers. sing. masc.	הלל
יַהֵל	Piel fut. 3 pers. s. m. [for יְאַהֵל § 19. r. 10]	אהל
יָהֵלּוּ	Hiph. fut. 3 pers. pl. masc.	הלל
יֵלֵךְ	וַ' Kal fut. 3 pers. sing. masc.	הלך
יְהַלֵּךְ	וֹ' Piel fut. 3 pers. sing. masc.	הלך
יֵלְכוּ	Kal fut. 3 pers. pl. m. [for יֵלְכוּ § 8. r. 15]	הלך
יְהַלְּכוּ	Piel fut. 3 pers. pl. m. [for יְהַלְּכוּ comp. id.]	הלך
יְהַלְּכוּן	id. with parag. ן (§ 8. rem. 17, & § 10. r. 4)	הלך
יְהַלֵּל	Piel fut. 3 pers. s. m. [for יְהַלֵּל § 10. r. 4]	הלל
יְהֻלַּל	Pual fut. 3 pers. sing. masc.	הלל
יְהַלְלְאֵל	pr. name masc.	הלל
יְהַלְלֶהָ	וֹ Piel fut. 3 pers. sing. masc., suff. 3 pers. sing. fem. (§ 10. rem. 7); וֹ conv.	הלל
יְהַלְלוּ	וַ' id. fut. 3 pers. pl. masc. (§ 10. rem. 7b); וֹ' id.	הלל
יְהַלְלוּהָ	וֹ id. id., suff. 3 pers. sing. fem.; וֹ conv.; with conj. וֹ [for וְיִ', וַיִ']	הלל
יְהַלְלוּהוּ	id. id., suff. 3 pers. sing. masc.	הלל
יְהַלְלוּךְ	id. id., suff. 2 pers. sing. masc.	הלל
יְהַלֶּלְךָ	id. fut. 3 pers. sing. masc., suff. 2 pers. sing. masc. (§ 16. rem. 15, & § 2. r. 2)	הלל
יֶהֱלֹם	וֹ noun masc. sing.	הלם
יַהֲלֹמוּן	Kal fut. 3 pers. pl. masc. with parag. ן [for יַהֲלֹמוּן § 8. rem. 17, & § 13. rem. 5]	הלם
יַהֲלֹמֵנִי	id. fut. 3 pers. s. m., suff. 1 pers. s. (§ 13. r. 4)	הלם
יֵהֹם	וֹ Kal fut. 3 p. s. m. with conv. וֹ [for וַיָּהֹם	המם
יֶהֱמֶה	Kal fut. 3 pers. sing. masc.	המה
יֶהֱמוּ	וַ' id. fut. 3 pers. pl. masc.; וֹ' conv.	המה
יֶהֱמָיוּן	id. id. with parag. ן (§ 8. rem. 17, & § 24. r. 5)	המה
יָהֹם	וֹ Kh. יֶהֱמָם q.v.K. וַיָּהֹם in pause for יֶהֱמָם q.v. (§ 21. rem. 8)	המם
יְהֻמֵּם	וֹ Kal fut. 3 pers. sing. masc. (יָהֹם), suff. 3 pers. pl. masc. (§ 18. rem. 5); וֹ conv.	המם
יַהַס	וֹ Hiph. fut. 3 pers. sing. masc. ap. [fr. יָהַס § 24. rem. 16]; וֹ' id.	הסה

יְהַעְדּוֹן	Ch. Aph. fut. 3 pers. pl. masc. (§ 47. r. 4)	עדה
יַהֲפֹךְ	וַ' Kal fut. 3 pers. sing. masc. (§ 8. r. 18);	הפך
יַהֲפָךְ	וֹ' conv.	הפך
יֵהָפֵךְ	וַ' Niph. fut. 3 pers. sing. masc.; וֹ' id.	הפך
יַהַפְכֵהוּ	וֹ Kal fut. 3 pers. sing. masc., suff. 3 pers. sing. masc.; וֹ id.	הפך
יַהַפְכוּ	וֹ', וַ' id. id. fut. 3 pers. pl. masc.; וֹ' id.	הפך
יֵהָפְכוּ	וֹ Niph. fut. 3 pers. pl. masc.; וֹ' id.	הפך
יַהַץ	יַהֲצָה (place trodden down; coll. with the Arab.) pr. name of a city of Moab, afterwards reckoned to the tribe of Reuben.	
יָהֵקִים	Ch. Aph. fut. 3 pers. sing. masc. (§ 47. rem. 4, & § 54. rem. 4)	קום
יָהֵר	Root not used; prob. to be high, cogn. הָרַר, הָרָה. יָהִיר adj. masc. elated, haughty, vain.	יהר
יַהֲרֹג	וַ' Kal fut. 3 pers. sing. masc. (§ 8. rem. 18); וֹ' conv.	הרג
יֵהָרֵג	Niph. fut. 3 pers. sing. masc.	הרג
יַהַרְגֵהוּ	וֹ Kal fut. 3 pers. sing. masc., suff. 3 pers. sing. masc.; וֹ' conv.	הרג
יַהַרְגֵהוּ	וֹ id. fut. 3 pers. pl. masc., suff. 3 pers. sing. masc.; וֹ' id.	הרג
יַהַרְגֵנוּ	id. fut. 3 pers. pl. masc. (§ 8. rem. 15); וֹ' id.	הרג
יַהַרְגֻנִם	וֹ id. id., suff. 3 pers. pl. masc.; וֹ' id.	הרג
יַהַרְגֵם	וֹ id. fut. 3 pers. sing. masc., suff. 3 pers. pl. masc.; וֹ' id.	הרג
יַהַרְגֻן	id. fut. 3 pers. pl. masc. with parag. ן (§ 8. rem. 17)	הרג
יַהַרְגֻנִי	id. fut. 3 pers. sing. masc., suff. 1 pers. sing.	הרג
יַהַרְגֵנִי	id. fut. 3 pers. pl. masc., suff. 1 pers. sing.	הרג
יַהֲרֹס	Kal fut. 3 pers. sing. masc. (§ 8. rem. 18)	הרס
יֵהָרֵס	Niph. fut. 3 pers. sing. masc.	הרס
יַהַרְסָה	וֹ Kal fut. 3 pers. sing. masc. [יַהֲרֹס], suff. 3 pers. sing. fem. (§ 13. rem. 4); וֹ' conv.	הרס
יַהַרְסוּ	id. fut. 3 pers. pl. masc. (v. id. & § 8. rem. 15)	הרס
יֵהָרְסוּן	Niph. fut. 3 pers. pl. masc. with parag. ן (comp. § 8. rem. 17)	הרס
יַהַרְסְךָ	Kal fut. 3 pers. sing. masc. [יַהֲרֹס § 13. rem. 4], suff. 2 pers. sing. m. [for יַהֲרֹסְךָ	הרס
יַהַרְסֵם	id. id., suff. 3 pers. pl. masc.	הרס
יַהַרְסֶנָּה	id. id., suff. 3 pers. sing. fem. (§ 2. rem. 3)	הרס
יְהַשְׁנֵא	Ch. Aph. fut. 3 pers. sing. masc. (§ 47. r. 4)	שנא
יְהַשְׁפֵּל	Ch. Aph. fut. 3 pers. sing. masc. (§ 47. r. 4)	שפל

Jos. 19. 29. · Is. 13. 10. · Pr. 31. 23. · Pr. 27. 2. · Nu. 13. 30. · Job 12. 15. · 2 Ch. 24. 25. · Je. 31. 40. · Is. 22. 19.
Is. 52. 5. · Job 14. 20. · Ge. 12. 15. · Is. 38. 18. · Da. 7. 26. · 1 Sa. 25. 12. · Zec. 11. 5. · 1 Ch. 20. 1. · Ps. 25. 5.
Ezr. 5. 5; 7. 13. · 1 Ki. 21. 27. · Ca. 6. 9. · La. 3. 3. · Ex. 7. 20. · Ge. 4. 14. · 2 Ki. 3. 25. · Pr. 29. 4.
Ezr. 6. 5. · Job 41. 11. · Pr. 31. 31. · Ps. 74. 6. · 1 Sa. 10. 9. · Job 5. 2. · Ge. 26. 7. · Ex. 19. 21, 24. · Ezr. 6. 11.
Job 31. 26. · Pr. 12. 8. · Ps. 84. 5. · Ps. 141. 5. · Ju. 7. 12. · La. 2. 20. · Job 12. 14. · Ps. 11. 3. · Da. 7. 26.
Is. 13. 20. · 2 Sa. 4. 12. · 2 Sa. 22. 15.

יֵהַתְבְּמוּ	Ch. Aph. fut. 3 pers. pl. masc. (§ 47. r. 4)	תוב
יַהְתֵלִּי	וְ Hiph. fut. 3 pers. sing. masc. uncontracted form [for יַתֵל § 20. rem. 10 & 14, by Chaldaism for יָתֵל § 18. rem. 14]; וְ conv.	תלל
יַהְתָלוּ	id. fut. 3 pers. pl. masc. regular and uncontracted [for יָתֵלוּ, in pause for יַתֵלוּ, comp. § 18. rem. 15 note]	תלל
יוֹאָב	וְ & יוֹאֵל, וְ', יוֹאָחָז & יוֹאָח, וְ' (see יְהוֹאָחָז), וְ' pr. names masc.	הוה
יוֹאֵל	וְ Hiph. fut. 3 pers. sing. masc., with conv. וְ [for יוֹאֵל, ap. from יוֹאִיל]	יאל
יוּאָר	Hoph. fut. 3 pers. sing. masc. [for יוּגָאַר]	ארר
יוֹאָשׁ	וְ' pr. name masc.	הוה
יוֹב	pr. name of a son of Issachar, Ge. 46. 13.	
יוּבָא	Hoph. fut. 3 pers. sing. masc.	בוא
יוּבָאוּ	id. fut. 3 pers. pl. masc. [for יוּבָאוּ comp. § 8. rem. 15]	בוא
יוֹבָב	וְ' pr. name masc.	יבב
יוֹבִילוּ	Hiph. fut. 3 pers. pl. masc.	יבל
יוּבַל	pr. name masc.	יבל
יוּבַל	Hoph. fut. 3 pers. sing. masc.; or (Je. 17. 8) noun masc. sing.	יבל
יוֹבֵל	noun masc. sing. dec. 7 b	יבל
יוּבְלוּ	Hoph. fut. 3 pers. pl. masc. [for יוּגְבְּלוּ comp. § 8. rem. 15]	יבל
יוֹבְלוּן	Hiph. fut. 3 pers. pl. masc. with וְ parag.	יבל
יוֹבְלִים	noun masc., pl. of יוֹבֵל dec. 7 b	יבל
יוֹבִילֵנִי	Hiph. fut. 3 pers. sing. masc., suff. 1 pers. sing.	יבל
יוֹדָה	Hiph. fut. 3 pers. sing. masc. (§ 25. No. 2 e)	ידה
יוֹדוּ	וְ' id. fut. 3 pers. pl. masc.	ידה
יוֹדוּךָ	id. id., suff. 2 pers. sing. masc.	ידה
יוֹדִיעַ	Hiph. fut. 3 pers. sing. masc.	ידע
יוֹדִיעֶנּוּ	id., suff. 3 pers. sing. masc. (§ 2. rem. 3)	ידע
יוֹדֶךָ	Hiph. fut. 3 pers. sing. masc. (יוֹדָה § 25. No. 2 e), suff. 2 pers. sing. masc. [for יוֹדְךָ § 24. rem. 21]	ידה
יוֹדוּךָ	וְ id. fut. 3 pers. pl. masc., suff. 2 pers. s. m.	ידה
יִוָּדַע	וַיִּ Niph. fut. 3 pers. sing. masc. (§ 15. rem. 1); וְ conv.	ידע
יוֹדֵעַ	Kal part. act. sing. masc. dec. 7 b	ידע
יוֹדְעוֹ	id., suff. 3 pers. sing. masc.	ידע
יוֹדְעֵי	id. pl., constr. state	ידע
יוֹדְעֶיךָ	id. pl., suff. 2 pers. sing. masc.	ידע
יוֹדְעִים	id. pl., abs. state	ידע
יוֹדִיעֻם	Hiph. fut. 3 pers. pl. (יוֹדִיעוּ), suff. 3 p. pl. m.	ידע
יוֹדַעְתִּי	Poel fut. 1 pers. sing. (§ 6. No. 1)	ידע

יוּדַק	Hoph. fut. 3 pers. sing. masc. [for יוּגְדַק	דקק
יוּדֹּשׁ	Hoph. fut. 3 pers. sing. masc.	דוש
יוֹזָבָד	וְ' & יוֹחָנָן, וְיוֹחָא, וְ' pr. names masc.	הוה
יוּטָּה	וְ' pr. name of a place	נמ־
יוּטַל יוּטָל	Hoph. fut. 3 pers. sing. masc. (comp. § 8. rem. 15)	מול
יוֹיָדָע	וְ' & יוֹיָרִיב, וְ' & יוֹיָקִים, (יְהוֹיָכִין see) יוֹיָכִין, וְ' יוֹזָבָד pr. names masc.	הוה
יוֹכַח יוֹכִיחַ	וַיִּ, וְ' Hiph. fut. 3 pers. sing. masc., apoc. for יוֹכִח because of 3d rad. gutt., comp. § 10 יוֹשַׁע; וְ conv.	יכח
יוֹכִיחוּ	וְ id. fut. 3 pers. pl. masc.	יכח
יוֹכִיחֶךָ	id. fut. 3 pers. s. m., suff. 2 pers. s. m. [for יוֹכִיחֲךָ	יכח
יוֹכִיחֶנּוּ	id. id., suff. 3 pers. sing. masc.	יכח
יוֹכִיחֵנִי	וְ id. id., suff. 1 pers. sing.	יכח
יוּכַל יוּכָל	Hoph. fut. 3 pers. sing. masc. (comp. § 8. rem. 15)	יכל
יוֹכְלוּ	Kh. יוּכְלוּ q. v., K. יָכְלוּ (q. v.)	יכל
יוֹכְלֻא	Hoph. fut. 3 pers. pl. m. [for יָאָכְלֻא § 19. r. 9]	אכל
יוּכְלוּ יוּכָלוּ	Hoph. fut. 3 pers. pl. masc. (comp. § 8. rem. 15)	יכל
יוּכְלוּן	id. with parag. ן	יכל
יִוָּלֵד יִוָּלֶד	וַיִּ Niph. fut. 3 pers. sing. masc. (§ 9. rem. 3); וְ conv.	ילד
יוֹלֵד	K. וַיּוֹלֶד, Kal part. act. sing. masc. dec. 7 b	ילד
יוֹלֵד	וְ Hiph. fut. 3 pers. sing. masc. with conv. וַ for יוֹלֵד (§ 20. r. 9) ap. fr. יוֹלִיד; וַ conv.	ילד
יֻלַּד יֻלָּד	Pual pret. 3 pers. sing. masc. (comp. § 8. rem. 7, for יֻלַד § 10. rem. 5)	ילד
יוֹלֵדָה	Kal part. act. sing. fem., from יֹלֵד masc.	ילד
יִוָּלְדוּ וַיִּ	Niph. fut. 3 pers. pl. masc. (comp. § 8. rem. 15); וְ conv.	ילד
יוֹלֶדֶת	וְ Kal part. act. fem. dec. 13 a, from יוֹלֵד m.	ילד
יוֹלַדְתְּךָ	id. with suff. 2 p. s. m. (§ 8. r. 19, & § 39. No. 4)	ילד
יוֹלַדְתְּכֶם	id., suff. 2 pers. pl. masc.	ילד
יוֹלִיד	Hiph. fut. 3 pers. sing. masc.	ילד
יוֹלִיךְ	Hiph. fut. 3 pers. sing. masc.	ילד
יוֹלִיכֵהוּ	וְ id. fut. 3 pers. pl. m., suff. 3 p. s. m.; וַ conv.	ילד
יוֹלִיכֵם	וַיִּ id. fut. 3 pers. s. m., suff. 3 p. pl. m.; וַ id.	ילד
יוֹלֵךְ	id. fut. 3 pers. sing. masc. ap. and conv. (§ 20. rem. 9) for יוֹלִיךְ	ילד
יוֹלִכֵנִי	וְ id. with suff. 1 pers. sing.; וַ conv.	ילד
יוֹם	וְ', וַ' masc. with suff. יוֹמִי (d. 1 a), pl. יָמִים (as it fr. יָם d. 2 a, § 45).—I. a day.—II. adv. by day, in	

ᵃ Ezr. 6.5.   ᶠ Job 21.30.   ᵏ Ps. 89.6.   ᵖ Pr. 10.9.   ᵘ Is. 28.28.   ᶻ Ge. 31.37.   ᵉ Eze. 42.5.   ʲ Ps. 78.6.   ᵒ Ps. 125.5.
ᵇ 1 Ki. 18.27.   ᵍ Zep. 3.10.   ˡ Ps. 40.13.14.   ᵠ 1 Sa. 10.11.   ᵛ Is. 28.27.   ᵃ Job 22.4.   ᵍ Is. 66.8.   ᵏ De. 23.9.   ᵖ Ps. 106.9.
ᶜ Je. 9.4.   ʰ Jos. 6.6.   ᵐ Is. 38.1b.   ʳ Eze. 28.19.   ʷ Ps. 37.24.   ᵇ Ps. 5.17.   ʰ Pr. 23.24.   ˡ Pr. 25.25.   ᵠ De. 28.36.
ᵈ Nu. 22.6.   ⁱ Ps. 60.11.   ⁿ Ps. 49.19.   ˢ Eze. 44.23.   ˣ Pr. 16.33.   ᶜ Ps. 141.5.   ⁱ Job 5.7.   ᵐ Je. 50.12.   ʳ Ex. 14.21.
ᵉ Je. 27.22.   ⁱ Ps. 6.6.   ᵒ Est. 2.22.   ᵗ 1 Sa. 21.3.   ʸ Ho. 4.4.   ᵈ Jos. 15.63.   ⁱ Ju. 18.29.   ⁿ Je. 31.8.

the day time ; יוֹם בְּיוֹם, יוֹם וָיוֹם, *day by day, every day, daily* ; הַיּוֹם *this day, to day* ; בַּיּוֹם followed by an inf. *on the day that* or *when* ;— בַּיּוֹם *in the day time*, Je. 36. 30 ; *on this day, immediately ; on that day, lately*, Ju. 13. 10 ;— כְּהַיּוֹם *about this day, this time, now ; at that time, then* ; מִיּוֹם *from the time that, since.* Du. יוֹמַיִם *two days.*—Pl. יָמִים, poet. יְמוֹת (constr. of יָמוֹת). —I. *days, some days* or *time* ; יָמִים מִסְפַּר יָמִים *after many days, some time after.*—II. *time, duration* generally ; כָּל הַיָּמִים *at all times, always* ; יָמֶיךָ כָּל *as long as thou livest* ; בָּא בַיָּמִים *advanced in age* ; חֹדֶשׁ יָמִים *a full month* ; שְׁנָתַיִם יָמִים *two full years.*—III. *a definite time*, as *a year* ; זֶבַח הַיָּמִים *yearly sacrifice* ; מִיָּמִים יָמִימָה *from year to year, annually.*

יוֹם Chald. masc. dec. 1 a, pl. יוֹמִין constr. יוֹמָת, by Hebraism יְמֵי, *day, time, period.*

יוֹמָם adv.—I. *by day, in the day time* ; בְּיוֹמָם id.—II. *daily*, Eze. 30. 16.

יוֹמוֹ id., suff. 3 pers. sing. masc. . יום
יוֹמַיָּא Chald. id. pl. emph. state . יום
יוֹמִים } id. du., absolute state . יום
יוֹמִים }
יוֹמִין Chald. id. pl., absolute state . יום
יוֹמְךָ id. sing., suff. 2 pers. sing. masc. יום
יוֹמָם } id. sing., suff. 3 pers. sing. masc. ; or adv. with the term. ם– (comp. חִנָּם) . יום
יוֹמָת Chald. id. pl. constr. fem. . יום
יוּמַת } Hoph. fut. 3 pers. sing. masc. (comp. § 8. rem. 15) . מות
יוּמָת }
יוּמַת Kh. יוּמָת q. v. ; K. יָמוּת, Kal fut. 3 pers. s. m. מות
יוּמְתוּ } Hoph. fut. 3 pers. pl. masc. (comp. § 8. rem. 15) מות
יוּמָתוּ }

יַיִן Root not used ; to which is ascribed the signification of *heat and fermentation*, comp חָמַר, חֹמֶר ,חֶמֶר

יָוֵן m. constr. יְוֵן *mire, mud* ; הַיָּוֵן טִיט *miry clay.*
יַיִן m. dec. 6 h.—I. *wine.*—II. meton. *intoxication.*
יָוָן וְ pr. name of a son of Japheth, Ge. 10. 2, 4, the founder of the Greeks, *Ionians.* Patronym. יְוָנִי ; בְּנֵי הַיְוָנִים *Greeks.*
יוֹנָדָב contr. for יְהוֹנָדָב q. v. . חוה
יוֹנָה fem. dec. 10, pl. יוֹנִים.—I. *dove.*—II. *Jonah*, pr. name of a prophet.
יוֹנֶה Hiph. fut. 3 pers. sing. masc. (§ 25. No. 2 e) ינה

יוֹנוּ id. fut. 3 pers. pl. masc. . ינה
יוֹנִים Keri, Kal part. act. m., pl. of [יוֹנֶה] dec. 9 a ינה
יוֹנִים noun fem. with pl. masc. term. see . יוֹנָה
יוֹנֵק וְ Kal part. act. or subst. masc. dec. 7 b ינק
יוֹנְקֵי וְ id. pl. construct state . . . ינק
יוֹנִקוֹתֶיהָ id. pl. fem., suff. 3 pers. sing. fem. from [יוֹנֶקֶת] dec. 13 a (§ 8. rem. 19, & § 39. No. 4) ינק
יוֹנִקוֹתָי id. id., suff. 3 pers. sing. masc. ינק
יוֹנַקְתּוֹ וְ id. id. sing., suff. 3 pers. sing. masc. ינק
יוֹנֶקֶת noun fem. sing., constr. of . . ינה
יוֹנַקְתִּי id. with suff. 1 pers. sing. . ינה
יוֹנָתָן וְ pr. name masc. . . . הוה
יוּסַב Hoph. fut. 3 pers. sing. masc. [for יֻסַּב, § 18. rem. 14. comp. § 10. rem. 5] סבב
יוֹסִיף וְ Hiph. fut. 3 pers. sing. masc. יסף
יוֹסִפוּ וַ id. fut. 3 pers. pl. masc. ; וְ conv. יסף
יוֹסִפְיָה pr. name masc. יסף
יוֹסֵף Kh. יוֹסֵף q. v., K. יֹסֵף, Kal pret. 3 pers. s. m יסף
יוֹסֵף וְ pr. name masc. יסף
יוֹסֵף } Hiph. fut. 3 pers. sing. masc., ap.
וַיּוֹסֶף and conv. (§ 20. r. 9) fr. יוֹסִיף
יוֹסֵף for יוֹסִיף q. v. ; or perhaps (Is. 29. 14 ; 38. 5) for יוֹסֵף Kal part. act. (§ 9. rem. 7) . יסף
יוֹסִפוּ וַ Hiph. fut. 3 pers. pl. masc. ; וְ conv. יסף
יוֹסִפוּן id. with parag. ן . . . יסף
יוּסַּר Niph. fut. 3 pers. sing. masc., Milêl before penacute [for יִוָּסֵר § 9. rem. 3] . יסר
יוּסַר Hoph. fut. 3 pers. sing. masc. . סור
יוֹעֵאלָה וְ pr. name masc. 1 Ch. 12. 7.
יוֹעֵד pr. name masc. הוה
יוֹעֲדוּ וְ Niph. fut. 3 pers. pl. masc. ; וְ conv. יעד
יוֹעֲדֵנִי Hiph. fut. 3 pers. sing. masc., suff. 1 pers. sing. (§ 2. rem. 3) יעד
יוֹעֵזֶר וְ pr. name masc. הוה
יוֹעֲדֵנִי Hiph. fut. 3 pers. sing. masc., suff. 1 pers. s. יעד
יוֹעִיל Hiph. fut. 3 pers. sing. masc. יעל
יוֹעִלוּ id. fut. 3 pers. pl. masc. יעל
יוֹעִילֻךְ id. id., suff. 2 pers. sing. fem. יעל
יוֹעֲלוּ defect. for יוֹעִילוּ (q. v.) יעל
יוּעַם Hoph. fut. 3 pers. sing. masc. עמם
יוָּעֵץ וַ Niph. fut. 3 pers. sing. masc. ; וְ conv. יעץ
יוֹעֵץ וְ Kal part. act. sing. masc. dec. 7 b יעץ
יִוָּעֲצוּ וַ Niph. fut. 3 pers. pl. masc. ; וְ conv. יעץ
יוֹעֲצָיו וְ Kal part. act. pl. masc., suff. 3 pers. sing. masc. from יָעַץ dec. 7 b עץ
יוֹעֲצִים id. pl., absolute state עץ
יוֹעֲצֵךְ id. sing., suff. 2 pers. sing. fem. עץ

Je. 50. 31.   Eze. 45. 8.   Ho. 14. 7.   Is. 28. 27.   1 Sa. 27. 4.   1 Ki. 19. 2.   Je. 50. 44.   La. 4. 1.   2 Ch. 30. 23
Exr. 4. 15, 19.   Job 14. 7.   Ec. 1. 10.   2 Sa. 24. 3.   Pr. 29. 19.   Job 9. 19.   Is. 2. 3.   Ezr. 7. 28
2 Ki. 14. 6.   Joel 2. 16.   Ps. 56. 1.   Ge. 37. 5, 8.   Le. 4. 35.   Is. 5., 12.   Is. 45. 21.   Mi. 4. 9.
Eze. 18. 7.   Ps. 80. 13.

Hebrew	Description	Root
יוֹעַצְתּי	id. fem. sing. [יוֹעֶצֶת], suff. 3 pers. sing. masc. dec. 13a (§ 8. rem. 19, & § 39. No. 4)	יעץ
יוֹעָשׁ	pr. name masc.	הוה
יוֹצֵא	Kal part. act. sing. masc. dec. 7b	יצא
יוֹצֵא	וַ Hiph. fut. 3 pers. sing. masc. ap. and defect. for יוֹצִיא ; וַ conv.	יצא
יוֹצִאָהּ	וַ id. with suff. 3 pers. sing. fem.; וַ conv.	יצא
יוֹצְאוֹת	Kal part. act. fem., pl. יוֹצֵאת q. v.	יצא
יוֹצְאֵי	id. pl. constr. masc. from יוֹצֵא dec. 7b	יצא
יוֹצְאִים	id. id., absolute state	יצא
יוֹצִאֲךָ	וַ Hiph. fut. 3 pers. sing. masc., (יוֹצִיא), suff. 2 pers. sing. masc.; וַ conv.	יצא
יוֹצֵאת	Kal part. act. sing. fem. [for יוֹצֵאת § 23. rem. 4, see § 8. rem. 19, & § 39. No. 4]	יצא
יוֹצָדָק	pr. name masc., see יְהוֹצָדָק	הוה
יוֹצִיא	Hiph. fut. 3 pers. sing. masc.	יצא
יוֹצִיאֵהוּ	וַ id. fut. 3 p. pl. m., suff. 3 p. s. m.; וַ conv.	יצא
יוֹצִיאוּ	וַ id. fut. 3 pers. pl. masc.; וַ id.	יצא
יוֹצִיאֻם	id. id., suff. 3 pers. pl. masc.	יצא
יוֹצִיאֵם	וַ id. fut. 3 p. s. m., suff. 3 p. pl. m.; וַ conv.	יצא
יוֹצִיאֵנִי	וַ id. id., suff. 1 pers. sing.; וַ id.	יצא
יוּצַק	Hoph. fut. 3 pers. sing. masc.	יצק
יוֹצֵר	Hoph. fut. 3 pers. sing. masc.	יצר
יוֹצֵר	Kal part. act. sing. masc. dec. 7b	יצר
יוֹצְרוֹ	וַ id., suff. 3 pers. sing. masc.	יצר
יוֹצְרִים	id. pl., absolute state	יצר
יוֹקְשִׁים	Kal part. act. masc., pl. of [יוֹקֵשׁ] dec. 7b	יקש
יֻקָשִׁים	Pual part. pl. masc. (§ 10. rem. 6)	יקש
יוֹר	וַ Hiph. fut. 3 pers. sing. masc., ap. from יוֹרֶה (§ 25. No. 2e); וַ conv.	ירה
יוֹרֵא	Hiph. or Hoph. fut. 3 pers. sing. masc. [for יוֹרֶה, or יוּרֶה comp. הוֹדַע § 20. rem. 12]	ירה
יוֹרֵד	Kal part. act. sing. masc. dec. 7b	ירד
יוֹרֵד	וַ Hiph. fut. 3 pers. sing. masc with conv. [for יוֹרֵד § 20. rem. 9, ap. fr. יוֹרִד]	ירד
יוֹרִדוּ	וַ id. fut. 3 pers. pl. masc. (for יוֹרִידוּ); וַ conv.	ירד
יוֹרִדוּךָ	id. id., suff. 2 pers. sing. masc.	ירד
יוֹרְדוֹת	Kal part. act. fem., pl. of רָדַד' dec. 13a (§ 8. rem. 19, & § 30. No. 4)	ירד
יוֹרְדֵי	id. pl. constr. masc. from יוֹרֵד dec. 7b	ירד
יוֹרְדִים	id. id., absolute state	ירד
יוֹרִדֵם	וַ Hiph. fut. 3 pers. sing. masc. [יוֹרִיד], suff. 3 pers. pl. masc.; וַ conv.	ירד
יוֹרָה	pr. name masc.	ירה
יוֹרֶה	וַ Hiph.fut.3 p. s. m.; or, Kal part. or subst. m.	ירה
יוֹרֵהוּ	id. fut. 3 p. s. m., suff. 3 pers. s. m.; וַ conv.	ירה
יוֹרוּ	id. fut. 3 pers. pl. masc.	ירה

Hebrew	Description	Root
יוֹרֶךָ	id. id., suff. 2 pers. sing. masc.	ירה
יוֹרִי	וַ pr. name masc.	ירה
יוֹרִידוּ	וַ Hiph. fut. 3 pers. pl. masc.; וַ conv.	ירד
יוֹרִידֵנִי	id. fut. 3 pers. sing. masc., suff. 1 pers. sing.	ירד
יוֹרִישׁ	Hiph. fut. 3 pers. sing. masc.	ירש
יוֹרִישְׁךָ	id., suff. 2 pers. sing. masc.	ירש
יוּרָם	Hoph. fut. 3 pers. sing. masc. [for יוּרָם]	רום
יוֹרָם	וַ pr. name masc.	הוה
יוֹרֵנוּ	וַ Hiph. fut. 3 pers. sing. masc. (יוֹרֶה § 25. No. 2e, & § 24. rem. 21), suff. 1 pers. pl.	דה
יוֹרֵנוּ	id. fut. 3 pers. sing. masc. (יוֹרֶה § 25. No. 2e, & § 24. rem. 21), suff. 3 p. s. m. (§ 2. rem. 3)	ירה
יוֹרֵשׁ	Niph. fut. 3 pers. sing. masc.	ירש
יוֹרֵשׁ	Kal part. act. sing. masc. dec. 7b	ירש
יוֹרֵשׁ	וַ Hiph. fut. 3 pers. sing. masc. with conv. [for יוֹרִישׁ, § 20. rem. 9] ap. from יוֹרֵשׁ	ירש
יוֹרִשֶׁנָּה	id. fut. 3 p. s. m., suff. 3 p. s. fem. (§ 2. rem. 3)	ירש
יוֹשֵׁב	pr. name in compos. יוֹשֵׁב חֶסֶד	שוב
יוּשַׁב	וַ Hoph. fut. 3 pers. sing. masc.; וַ conv.	שוב
יוֹשֵׁב	וַ Kal part. act. sing. masc. dec. 7b	ישב
יוֹשֵׁב	וַ Hiph. fut. 3 pers. sing. masc. ap. and convers. (§ 20. rem. 9) for יוֹשִׁיב	ישב
יוֹשְׁבֵי	וַ Kal part. act. pl. constr. m. from יוֹשֵׁב dec. 7b	ישב
יוֹשְׁבָה	id. pl., suff. 3 pers. sing. fem.	ישב
יוֹשְׁבָה	pr. name masc.	ישב
יוֹשְׁבָיו	Kal part. act. pl. masc., suff. 3 pers. sing. masc. from יוֹשֵׁב dec. 7b	ישב
יוֹשְׁבִים	וַ id. pl., absolute state	ישב
יוֹשֶׁבֶת	id. sing. fem. dec. 13a (§ 8. rem. 19, & § 39. No. 4)	ישב
יוֹשַׁבְתִּי	id. id. Kh. יָשַׁבְתִּי, K. יוֹשַׁבְתְּ (comp. § 8.r.5)	ישב
יוֹשָׁר	Hoph. fut. 3 pers. sing. masc. [for יוּשַׁר, comp. § 8. rem. 15]	שרד
יוֹשָׁה	pr. names masc. וִישַׁוְיָה, וַ	ושה
יוֹשֵׁם	וַ Hiph. fut. 3 pers. sing. masc. with conv. וַ [for יוֹשִׁים] ap. fr.	ישם
יוֹשִׁיבוּ	וַיַ Hiph. fut. 3 pers. pl. masc.; וַ conv.	ישב
יוֹשִׁיבֵנִי	וַ id. fut. 3 pers. sing. masc., suff. 1 pers. sing. Kh. בִּינִי, K. בֵּנִי (§ 2. rem. 1)	ישב
יוֹשִׁים	Hiph. fut. 3 pers. sing. masc.	ישם
יוֹשִׁיעַ	Hiph. fut. 3 pers. sing. masc.	ישע
יוֹשִׁיעוּ	id. fut. 3 pers. pl. masc.	ישע
יוֹשִׁיעוּךָ	id. id., suff. 2 pers. sing. masc.	ישע
יוֹשִׁיעוּם	וַ, וַיַ id. id., suff. 3 pers. pl. m.; וַ conv.	ישע
יוֹשִׁיעֲךָ	וַ id. fut. 3 pers. sing. m., suff. 2 pers. sing. m.	ישע
יוֹשִׁיעֵךְ	וַ id. fut. 3 pers. pl. m., suff. 2 pers. sing. fem.	ישע
יוֹשִׁיעֵם	וַ, וַיַ id.fut. 3 p.s.m., suff. 3 p.pl.m.; וַ conv.	ישע

a 2 Ch. 22. 3.   f Mi. 7. 9.   l Ec. 9. 12.   r 1 Ki. 18. 40.   ‖ Jos. 3. 10.   * Ex. 10. 8.   ° 2 Ch. 18. 9.   † 1 Ki. 2. 24.   ¤ Ju. 2. 16.
b Ex. 4. 6. 7   g Is. 54. 17.   m 2 Ki. 13. 17.   s Ex. 15. 25.   t Ju. 11. 24.   † Is. 9. 3.   p Ho. 10. 14.   u Est. 4. 11.   § Ho. 13. 16.
c De. 4. 37.   h Is. 45. 11.   n Pr. 11. 25.   t Nu. 1. 51.   w Le. 4. 19.   ‡ Ge. 47. 11.   q Is. 54. 3.   x Je. 2. 2.   v Pr. 17. 13.
d 3 Ki. 12. 13.   i Is. 30. 14.   o Kse. 28. 8.   u Ob. 3.   y Pr. 23. 21.   ‖ 2Ch.34.24,27,28.   z 2 Ch. 23. 20.   z Ne. 9. 27.   v Ps. 107. 35, 33.

יוֹשִׁיעֵנוּ	וְ [id. id., suff. 1 pers. pl.	ישע
יוֹשִׁיעֶנּוּ	id. id., suff. 3 pers. sing. masc. (§ 2. rem. 3)	ישע
יוֹשִׁיעֵנִי	[וְ id. id., suff. 1 pers. sing.	ישע
יִוָּשַׁע	Niph. fut. 3 pers. s. m. [for יִיָּשַׁע § 15. rem. 1]	ישע
יוֹשִׁיעַ יוֹשַׁע	} Hiph. fut. 3 p.s.m. def. for יוֹשִׁיעַ, ap. and conv. וַיּוֹשַׁע (§ 20. rem. 9) for וַיּוֹשִׁיעַ because of 3d rad. gutt., comp. } יוֹכַח	ישע
יוֹשִׁיעֵךְ	id. with suff. 2 pers. sing. fem.	ישע
יוֹשִׁיעֵן	וְ id. with suff. 3 pers. pl. fem.	ישע
יוֹשָׁפָט	וְ contr. for יְהוֹשָׁפָט q. v.	הוה
יוּשַׁר	Hoph. fut. 3 pers. sing. masc.	שיר
יוּשַׁת	Hoph. fut. 3 pers. sing. masc.	שית
יוֹתִיר	Hiph. fut. 3 pers. sing. masc.	יתר
יוֹתָם	וְ pr. name masc.	הות
יִוָּתֵר יִוָּתְרִי	} וַיִּ Niph. fut. 3 pers. sing. masc. (§ 9. rem. 3); וְ conv. }	יתר
יוֹתֵר	וַיֹּ Hiph. fut. 3 pers. sing. masc., ap. fr. יוֹתִיר; וַיֹּ id.	יתר
יוֹתֵר	Kal part., subst. or adv.	יתר
יִוָּתְרוּ	וַיִּ Niph. fut. 3 pers. pl. masc.; וְ conv.	יתר
יוֹתִרוּ	וְ Hiph. fut. 3 pers. pl. masc.; וְ id.	יתר
יַז	וַ Hiph. fut. 3 pers. sing. masc. ap. fr. יַזָּה (§ 25. No. 2b); וְ id.	נזה
יִזּ וַיֵּז	} וְ Kal fut. 3 pers. sing. masc., ap. fr. יַזָּה (§ 25. No. 2b, comp. § 24. rem. 3) }	נזה
יָזֻבוּ	וְ Kal fut. 3 pers. pl. masc.; וְ conv.	זוב
יְזַבַּח	וַ Piel fut. 3 pers. sing. masc.; וְ id. bef.	זבח
יִזְבַּח	וְ Kal fut. 3 pers. sing. masc.; וְ conv.	זבח
יִזְבָּחֵהוּ	וְ id., suff. 3 pers. sing. m. (§ 16. r. 12); וְ id.	זבח
יְזַבְּחוּ	Piel fut. 3 pers. pl. masc. [for יְזַבֵּחוּ, comp. § 8. rem. 15]	זבח
יִזְבְּחוּ	וַ וְ Kal fut. 3 pers. pl. masc.; וְ conv.	זבח
יִזְבְּלֵנִי	Kal fut. 3 pers. sing. masc., suff. 1 pers. sing.	זבל
יָזֵד יָזִיד	} Hiph. fut. 3 pers. sing. masc. def. & ap. fr. יָזִיד, with conv. וְ (§ 21. rem. 17) }	זוד
יַזֶּה	Hiph. fut. 3 pers. sing. masc. (§ 25. No. 2b)	נזה
יִזֶּה	Kal fut. 3 pers. sing. masc. (§ 25. No. 2b)	נזה
יַזְהִרוּ	Hiph. fut. 3 pers. pl. masc.	זהר
יַזוֹאֵל	Kh. וַיִּזוּאֵל, see K. יְזִיאֵל	
יָזוּב	Kal fut. 3 pers. sing. masc.	זוב
יָזוּבוּ	וְ id. fut. 3 pers. pl. masc.; וְ conv.	זוב
יְזוֹרֵר	וְ Poel fut. 3 pers. sing. masc.; וְ id.	זרר
[וַיְזִיאֵל]	(assembly of God; וַה Arab. to assemble) pr. name masc. 1 Ch. 12. 3.	
יֵזַח	וְ Niph. fut. 3 pers. sing. masc.	זחח
יָזִיד	וְ Hiph. fut. 3 pers. sing. masc.	זוד

יִזְדּוּן	וְ id. fut. 3 pers. pl. masc. with parag. וְ	זוד
יִזְיָה	וְ pr. name masc.	נזה
זִיזָא	pr. name masc.	זוז
יַזִּיר	Hiph. fut. 3 pers. sing. masc.	נזר
יְזַכֶּה	Piel fut. 3 pers. sing. masc.	זכה
יִזְכֶּה	Kal fut. 3 pers. sing. masc.	זכה
יִזְכּוֹר	Kal fut. 3 pers. sing. masc. (§ 8. rem. 18)	זכר
יַזְכִּיר	Hiph. fut. 3 pers. sing. masc.	זכר
יַזְכִּירוּ	id. fut. 3 pers. pl. masc.	זכר
יִזָּכֵר	Niph. fut. 3 pers. sing. masc.	זכר
יִזְכֹּר יִזְכָּר	} וַיִּ, וְ Kal fut. 3 pers. sing. masc. (§ 8. rem. 18); וְ conv. }	זכר
יִזְכְּרָהָ	וְ id., suff. 3 pers. sing. fem.; וְ id.	זכר
יִזָּכְרוּ	Niph. fut. 3 pers. pl. masc.	זכר
יִזְכְּרוּ	וַ וְ Kal fut. 3 pers. pl. masc.; וְ conv.	זכר
יִזְכָּרוּךָ	id., suff. 2 pers. sing. masc.	זכר
יִזְכְּרוּנִי	id., suff. 1 pers. sing.	זכר
יִזַּל	Kal fut. 3 pers. sing. masc.	נזל
יִזְּלוּ	id. fut. 3 pers. sing. masc.	נזל
יִזְלִיאָה	וְ pr. name masc. 1 Ch. 8. 18.	
יִזְמוּ	Kal fut. 3 pers. pl. masc. [for יָזֹמּוּ § 18. rem. 15]	זמם
יִזָּמֵר	Niph. fut. 3 pers. sing. masc.	זמר
יְזַמְּרוּ יְזַמְּרוּ	} Piel fut. 3 pers. pl. masc., with conj. [וַיְ, וַיְזַמְּרוּ for וַיְזַמְּרוּ] }	זמר
יְזַמֶּרְךָ	id. fut. 3 pers. sing. masc., suff. 2 pers. sing. masc. (§ 16. rem. 15)	זמר
יָזַן	Kal not used; Arab. to weigh, be heavy. Pu. part. מְזָנִים Je. 5. 8 Keri, heavy, stout.	
יַזְנֵ	וְ Hiph. fut. 3 pers. sing. masc. ap. [from יַזְנֶה; וְ conv.	זנה
יַזְנֵב	וְ Piel fut. 3 pers. sing. masc.; וְ id. bef.	זנב
יִזְנֶה	Kh. יִזְנֶה, K. יִזְנוּ, Kal fut. 3 p. s. or pl. m.	זנה
יִזְנוּ	וְ Kal fut. 3 pers. pl. masc.; וְ conv.	זנה
יִזְנַח	Kal fut. 3 pers. sing. masc.	זנח
יִזַנְיָה יִזַנְיָהוּ	} וַיַ pr. name masc. with cop. וְ [for יַזַנְ, וַיַזַנְ; see יַאֲזַנְיָהוּ under אזן }	אזן
יַנְקַדַךְ	Hiph. fut. 3 pers. sing. masc., suff. 2 pers. sing. masc.	זנה
יְזַעֵק	Piel fut. 3 pers. sing. masc.	זעק
יֶזַע	Root not used; Arab. to flow. יֶזַע masc. sweat, Eze. 44. 18. יֵזָה fem. dec. 10, (for יֵזֶה) id. Ge. 2. 19.	

---

a Is. 46. 7.   g Is. 26. 1.   m Le. 8. 11, 30.   t 1 Ki. 19. 21.   b Le. 15. 25.   f Nu. 6. 3, 5.   m Ec. 11. 8.   r Nu. 24. 7.   w 2 Ch. 21. 11.
b Ps. 55. 17.   h Ex. 21. 30, 30.   n De. 28. 54.   u 2 Ki. 9. 33.   e 2 Ki. 4. 35.   g Fs. 119. 9.   n 1 Sa. 1. 19.   s Ge. 11. 6.   x De. 25. 18.
c Ps. 57. 4.   i De. 28, 54.   o 2 Ki. 9. 33.   v Ex. 21. 14.   d Ex. 28. 28;   h Ho. 9. 9.   o Ps. 75. 35.   t Is. 5. 6.   y Eze. 25. 42.
d Job 22. 29.   k Ex. 16. 19.   p La. 4. 9.   y Ge. 15. 8.   39. 21.   i Is. 19. 17.   p Ps. 68. 4.   s Is. 5. 6.   z 1 Ch. 28. 9.
e 2 Ki. 6. 27.   l Jos. 18. 2.   q Is. 48. 21.   z Le. 4. 20.   e De. 18. 20.   k Is. 48. 1.   q Zec. 10. 2.   u Ps. 30. 12.   1 Ch. 28. 9.
f Ex. 2. 17.   r Hab. 1. 16.   s Da. 12. 1.   f De. 17. 13.

יַזְעִיקוּ[a]	Hiph. fut. 3 pers. pl. masc.	זעק
וְיַעֲמְּדְהוּ[b]	Kal fut. 3 pers. pl. masc. [יַזְעֲמוּ from sing. יַזְעֵם], suff. 3 pers. sing. m. (§ 16. r. 12)	זעם
וַיִּזְעַף[c]	Kal fut. 3 pers. sing. masc.; וַ conv.	זעף
יַזְעֵק[d]	Hiph. fut. 3 pers. sing. masc. ap. [fr. יַזְעִיק]; וַ id.	זעק
יִזָּעֵק[e]	Niph. fut. 3 pers. sing. masc.; וַ id.	זעק
יִזְעַק	} Kal fut. 3 pers. sing. masc. (§ 8. rem. 15); וַ id.	זעק
וַיִּזְעַק		
יִזָּעֲקוּ[f]	Niph. fut. 3 pers. pl. masc.; וַ id.	זעק
וַיִּזְעֲקוּ[g]	} Kal fut. 3 pers. pl. masc. (§ 8. rem. 15); וַ id.	זעק
וַיִּזְעָקוּ[h]		
וַיִּזְעָקוּךָ[i]	} id., suff. 2 pers. sing. masc. (§ 16. rem. 12); וַ id.	זעק
יִזְקְנוּ	Kal fut. 3 pers. pl. masc.	זקן
יַזְקִין	Hiph. fut. 3 pers. sing. masc.	זקן
וַיִּזְקַן[k]	Kal fut. 3 pers. sing. masc.; וַ conv.	זקן
יֵזֹר[l]	Kal fut. 3 pers. sing. masc. ap. (§ 21. r. 9)	זור
וַיָּזַר[m]	Kal fut. 3 pers. sing. masc. ap. [fr. יִזְרֶה]; וַ conv.	זרה
יְזֹרְבוּ[n]	Pual fut. 3 pers. pl. masc.	זרב
יְזֹרֶה[o]	Pual fut. 3 pers. sing. masc.	זרה
וַיִּזֹּרוּ[p]	Niph. fut. 3 pers. pl. masc.; וַ conv.	זרה
יְזָרֶה[q]	Piel fut. 3 pers. pl. masc.	זרה
יִזְרַח	} Kal fut. 3 pers. sing. masc. (§ 8. rem. 15); וַיִּ id. conv.	זרח
וַיִּזְרַח		
יִזְרַחְיָה	pr. name masc.	זרח
יִזָּרֵעַ	} Niph. fut. 3 pers. sing. masc. (§ 15. rem. 1)	זרע
יִזָּרֵעַ		
יִזְרַע	} Kal fut. 3 pers. sing. masc. (§ 8. rem. 15); וַ conv.	זרע
וַיִּזְרַע		
יִזְרְעֶאל	} pr. name of a man and a place	זרע
יִזְרְעֶאלָה		
יִזְרְעֶאלָה	id. with parag. ה	זרע
יִזְרְעֶנָּה	} Kal fut. 3 pers. sing. masc. (יִזְרַע), suff. 3 pers. sing. fem. (§ 16. r. 12); וַ conv.	זרע
יִזְרְעוּ[r]	} id. fut. 3 pers. pl. masc. (§ 8. rem. 15); וַ id.	זרע
יִזְרָעוּ		
וַיִּזְרֹק[s]	Kal fut. 3 pers. sing. masc.; וַ id.	זרק
יִזְרְקֶהוּ[t]	id. id., suff. 3 pers. sing. masc.; וַ id.	זרק
יִזְרְקוּ[u]	id. fut. 3 pers. pl. masc.; וַ id.	זרק
יְזְתָא	see וַיְזָתָא under lett. וּ.	
יֵחָבְאוּ[v]	} וַיֵּ Niph. fut. 3 pers. pl. masc.; וַ conv.	חבא
יַחְבָּה	pr. name masc.	חבה
יַחֲבוֹשׁ[w]	Kal fut. 3 pers. sing. masc. (§ 8. rem. 18)	חבשׁ
יַחְבֹּט[x]	Kal fut. 3 pers. sing. masc. (§ 13. rem. 5)	חבט

יֵחָבֵט[a]	Niph. fut. 3 pers. sing. masc. bef. penacute [for יֵחָבֵט § 9. rem. 3]	חבט
וְיַחְבִּיאֵם[y]	Hiph. fut. 3 pers. sing. masc., suff. 3 pers. pl. masc.; וְ conv.	חבא
יֵחָבֶל–	Niph. fut. 3 pers. sing. masc. bef. monos. [for יֵחָבֵל § 9. rem. 3]	חבל
יַחְבֹּל[z]	Kal fut. 3 pers. sing. masc.	חבל
יְחַבֶּל–	Piel fut. 3 pers. s. m. [for יְחַבֵּל § 10. r. 4]	חבל
יַחְבְּלוּ[a2]	} Kal fut. 3 pers. pl. masc. (§ 8. rem. 15, & § 13. rem. 5)	חבל
יַחְבְּלוּ[b2]		
יְחַבֵּק[c2]	} Piel fut. 3 pers. sing. masc. (§ 9. rem. 3); וַ conv.	חבק
וַיְחַבֵּק[d2]		
יְחַבְּקֵהוּ[e2]	id., suff. 3 pers. sing. masc.; וַ id.	חבק
יְחַבֵּר[f2]	Piel fut. 3 pers. sing. masc.; וַ id.	חבר
יְחַבְּרֵהוּ[g2]	id., suff. 3 pers. sing. masc.; וַ id.	חבר
יַחֲבֹשׁ[h2]	} Kal fut. 3 pers. sing. masc. (§ 8. r. 18)	חבשׁ
יַחֲבֹשׁ–[i2]	} וַ id.	חבשׁ
יַחֲבֹשׁ[k2]	id. id. in pause for [יַחֲבֹשׁ § 8. r. 15, & § 13. rem. 5]	חבשׁ
יַחְבְּשׁוּ[l2]	וַ id. fut. 3 pers. pl. masc. (v. id.); וַ conv.	חבשׁ
יַחְבְּשׁוּ[m2]	וַ id. fut. 3 pers. pl. masc. (v. id.); וַ conv.	חבשׁ
יַחְבְּשֵׁנוּ[n2]	id. fut. 3 pers. sing. masc., suff. 1 pers. pl. (v. id.); וַ id.	חבשׁ
יַחֲנוּ[o2]	וַ Kal fut. 3 pers. pl. masc.	חנה
וַיַּחֲנוּ[p2]	וַ Kal fut. 3 pers. sing. masc. (§ 13. rem. 5); וַ conv.	חנר
יַחְגְּרֶהָ[q2]	id. id., suff. 3 pers. sing. fem. (v. id.)	חנר
וַיַּחְגְּרוּ[r2]	וַ, וַיַּ id. fut. 3 pers. pl. m. (v. id.); וַ conv.	חנר

[יָחַד] fut. יֵחַד, *to be united, be one,* with בְּ, אֵת. Pi to unite, join, Ps. 86. 11.

יָחִיד masc. dec. 3 a, יְחִידָה fem. dec. 10.—I. *only, alone, only begotten.*—II. *solitary, forsaken.* —III. *only, most dear, darling.*

יַחַד masc.—I. *union,* 1 Ch. 12. 17.—II. adv. *together, in one place; wholly, entirely.*

יַחְדָּיו literally *union of them, they together,* (§ 4. rem. 1) hence—I. *together, in the same place.*—II. *together, at one time,* Ps. 4. 9.—III *mutually, with one another.*

יַחְדּוֹ (for יַחְדָּו *united*) pr. name m. 1 Ch. 5. 14

יַחַת (for יַחְדַּת *union*) pr. name masc. of several men.

יָחַד	in pause for יַחַד adv.	יחד
יָחַד[s2]	Kal fut. 3 pers. sing. masc., middle A [for יֵחַד § 18. rem. 6]	חדד

a Job 35. 9.   b Ex. 2. 23.   c Ex. 32. 20.   d Ge. 32. 32.   e Ps. 107. 37.   f Is. 27. 12.   g Job 24. 9.   h 2 Ch. 20. 36.   i Ex. 5. 1.
b Pr. 24. 24.   d Mi. 3. 4.   f Job 6. 17.   h Na. 1. 14.   j Le. 7. 2; Is. 28. 25.   l Is. 28. 27.   n Job 24. 3.   p 1 Ki. 15. 23.   r Le. 16. 4.
c Pr. 19. 3.   e Eze. 27. 30.   g Job 18. 15.   i Ec. 11. 4.   k Ge. 9. 12, 18.   m 1 Ki. 18. 4.   o Ge. 48. 10.   q Job 5. 18.   s Ps. 109. 19.
d 2 Ch. 26. 19.   f Ne. 9. 28.   h Eze. 36. 19.   j Ge. 26. 12.   l Am. 9. 3.   n Ge. 29. 13.   p 1 Ki. 15. 27.   r Eze. 14. 15.
Is. 15. 5.   h 2 Ch. 24. 15.   j Pr. 15. 7.   l Jos. 10. 16.   n De. 24. 6.   p Ge. 53. 4.   r 1 Ki. 15. 27.   t 2 Sa. 22. 46.
f Jos. 9. 16.   h Ju. 6. 38.   j Ju. 9. 45.   l Job 34. 17.   n rs. 7. 15.   p Ex. 36. 10, 13, 16.   r Ho. 6. 1.
g Ho. b. 3.   i Ho. 8. 7.

•יֵחַד	Hiph. fut. 3 pers. sing. masc. ap. R. חָדָה § 24. rem. 16); or it may be regarded as a Chaldaizing form of Hiph. fut. R. חָדַד, with implicit Dagesh in ח (§ 18. rem. 14) and Pattahh in the final syllable on account of this guttural letter [instead of יֵחַד, see § 18. rem. 6.	
וַיִּחַדּ	ᵇ adv. . . .	יחד
•יַחֵד	Piel imp. sing. masc. (§ 14. rem. 1) .	יחד
יַחְדְּ	Kh. יֵחַד q. v.; K. יַחְדָּו (q. v.) .	יחד
וַיִּחַדּ	Kal fut. 3 pers. sing. masc., ap. [fr. יֶחְדֶּה § 24. rem. 4]; ו conv. .	חדה
יַחְדּוּ	adv. . . .	יחד
יַחְדּוּ	pr. name masc. . . .	יחד
יַחְדִּיאֵל	pr. name masc. . . .	חדה
יֶחְדִּיָּהוּ	pr. name masc. . . .	חדה
יַחְדָּיו	adv. . . .	יחד
יֶחְדָּל	Kh. יַחְדָּל q. v.; K. וַיַּחְדָּל Kal imp. sing. masc.; ו bef. (-:) .	חדל
יֶחְדַּל (וֹ) / יֶחְדָּל (נ)	Kal fut. 3 pers. sing. masc. (§ 13. r. 5, & § 8. rem. 15); ו conv. . }	חדל
יַחְדְּלוּ / יַחְדָּלוּ (נ)	id. fut. 3 pers. pl. masc. (§ 13. rem. 6, & § 8. rem. 15); ו id. }	חדל
יֶחְדָּלוּן	id. id., parag. ן (§ 8. rem. 17) .	חדל
יֶחְדַּשׁ	Piel fut. 3 pers. sing. masc.; ו conv. .	חרש
יְחִיאֵל	Kh. יְחוּאֵל, K. יְחִיאֵל (q. v.) .	חיה
יְחוּאֵל	pr. name masc. . . .	חוה
יֶחֱוּוּ	Kal fut. 3 pers. s. m. (for יַחְווּ § 18. r. 2)	חגה
יְחַוֶּה	Piel fut. 3 pers. sing. masc. . . .	חוה
יָחוּל	Kal fut. 3 pers. sing. masc. . . .	חול
יְחוֹלֵל	Pilel fut. 3 pers. sing. masc. . . .	חול
יְחוֹלְלוּ	Pulal fut. 3 pers. pl. masc. [for יְחֹלְלוּ, comp. § 8. rem. 15] . . .	חול
יְחַוְּנַהּ	Ch. Pael fut. 3 pers. sing. masc., suff. 3 pers. sing. fem. .	חוה
יְחַוְּנַּנִי	Ch. id. with suff. 1 pers. sing. . .	חוה
יֵחֹם	Kal fut. 3 pers. sing. masc. . . .	חום
יַחְקְקוּ	Poel fut. 3 pers. pl. masc. . . .	חקק
יַחְרוּ	Kal fut. 3 pers. pl. masc. [for יֶחֱרוּ comp. § 8. rem. 15] . . .	חור
יֵחָשׁ	Kal fut. 3 pers. sing. masc. . . .	חוש
יֶחֱזֶה	Kal fut. 3 pers. sing. masc. . . .	חזה
וַיֶּחֱזוּ	id. fut. 3 pers. pl. masc.; ו conv. .	חזה
יַחֲזִיאֵל	pr. name masc. . . .	חזה
יְחֶזְיָה	pr. name masc. . . .	חזה
יֶחֱזָיוּן	Kal fut. 3 pers. pl. m. with parag. ן (§ 8. r. 17) .	חזה

יַחֲזֵק	Hiph. fut. 3 pers. sing. masc. .	חזק
וַיַּחֲזִיקוּ	id. fut. 3 pers. pl. masc.; ו conv. .	חזק
יַחֲזֶק (וַ)	id. fut. 3 pers. sing. masc., ap. (§ 11. rem. 7) fr. יַחֲזִיק; ו id. . }	חזק
יְחַזֵּק	Piel fut. 3 pers. sing. masc.; ו id. .	חזק
יֶחֱזַק / יֶחֱזַק (נ, ו) / וַיֶּחֱזַק	Kal fut. 3 pers. sing. masc. (§ 13. rem. 5) }	חזק
יַחְזְקָאל	pr. name masc. . . .	חזק
יְחַזְּקֶהוּ	Piel fut. 3 pers. sing. masc., suff. 3 pers. sing. masc.; ו id. bef. (:) .	חזק
וַיְּחַזְּקוּ	Hiph. fut. 3 pers. pl. masc. (for יַחֲזִיקוּ); ו id. .	חזק
יְחַזְּקוּ	Piel fut. 3 pers. pl. masc.; ו id. .	חזק
יֶחֱזְקוּ / יֶחֱזָקוּ	Kal fut. 3 pers. pl. masc. (§ 13. rem. 5) }	חזק
יְחַזְּקוּם	Piel fut. 3 p. pl. m., suff. 3 p. pl. m.; ו conv. .	חזק
יֶחֱזָקֻם	id. fut. 3 pers. s. m., suff. 3 pers. pl. m.; ו id. .	חזק
יַחְזְקֵנִי	id. id., suff. 1 pers. sing. .	חזק
יְחִזְקִיָּה, יְחִזְקִיָּהוּ & וַיֶּחֱזַק	pr. names masc. .	חזק
יַחְזְרָה	pr. name masc. . . .	חזר
וַיַּחֲטֵא	Hiph. fut. 3 p. s. m. [for יַחֲטִיא]; ו conv. .	חטא
יְחַטֵּא	Piel fut. 3 pers. sing. masc.; ו id. .	חטא
יֶחֱטָא	Kal fut. 3 pers. sing. masc. . . .	חטא
יְחַטְּאָהּ	Piel fut. 3 pers. sing. masc., suff. 3 pers. sing. masc.; ו id. .	חטא
יֶחֱטָאוּ	id. fut. 3 pers. pl. masc.; ו id. .	חטא
יֶחֱטְאוּ	Kal fut. 3 pers. pl. masc. . . .	חטא
יַחְטְבוּ	Kal fut. 3 pers. pl. masc. (§ 13. rem. 5) .	חטב
יַחֲטִיאוּ	Hiph. fut. 3 pers. pl. masc. . . .	חטא
יַחְטֹף	Kal fut. 3 pers. sing. masc. (§ 13. rem. 5) .	חטף
יְחִי (וַ, וְ)	Kal fut. 3 pers. s. m., ap. fr. יִחְיֶה (§ 24. rem. 3e); ו conv.; with וַיְחִי [for וַיִּחְיֶה, וַיְחִי] ו conj.; id. וִיחִי [for וְיִחְיֶה] }	חיה
וִיחִיאֵל	(with cop. ו) pr. name masc. .	חיה
יְחִיאֵלִי	patronym. of יְחִיאֵל . . .	חיה
יָחִיד (וְ)	adj. masc. sing. dec. 3a .	יחד
יְחִידָה	id. fem. dec. 10 . . .	יחד
יְחִידִים	id. masc. pl. abs. dec. 3a .	יחד
יְחִידְךָ, יְחִידֶךָ	id. id. sing. with suff. 2 pers. sing. masc. .	יחד
יְחִידָתִי	id. fem. with suff. 1 pers. sing. dec. 10 .	יחד
יְחַיֶּהָ	Piel fut. 3 p. s. m., suff. 3 p. s. fem.; ו conv. .	חיה
יִחְיֶה	Kh. יְחִיֶה q. v., K. וְחָיָה Kal pret. 3 pers. sing. masc.; ו id. .	חיה
יְחַיֶּה	Piel fut. 3 pers. sing. masc. . . .	חיה

ᵃ Pr. 27. 17.   ᵈ Job 10. 20.   ᵐ Ps. 29. 9.   ᵗ Is. 29. 22.   ˡ 1 Ch. 28. 7.   ʳ Is. 28. 22.   ˡ 2 Ki. 21. 11.   ᵘ Ex. 23. 33.   ˣ Ps. 68. 7.
ᵇ Job 31. 38.   ᵉ Eze. 3. 27.   ⁿ Job 26. 5.   ᵏ Da. 2. 11.   ² 2 Ch. 27. 5.   ˢ Is. 41. 7.   ᵐ 2 Ch. 29. 34.   ᵛ Ps. 10. 9.   ʸ Ge. 22. 2, 12.
ᶜ Ps. 86. 11.   ᶠ Job 14. 6.   ᵒ Da. 2. 11.   ˡ Is. 26. 11.   ᵖ Da. 11. 32.   ⁿ Le. 9. 15.   ˢ Is. 38. 21.   ᶻ Ge. 22. 16.
ᵈ Je. 48. 7.   ᵍ Ex. 9. 29.   ᵖ Is. 26. 5.   ʸ Da. 11. 5, 5.   ᵒ Da. 10. 18.   ⁿ 2 Ch. 29. 24.   ᵖ Pr. 4. 3.   ᵃ 2 Sa. 12. 3.
Job 3. 6.   ʰ 2 Ch. 15. 8.   ᵍ Je. 21. 7.   ᶻ Da. 11. 5, 5.   ᵗ 2 Sa. 2. 16.   ᵖ Eze. 39. 10.   ᵗ Ju. 11. 34.   Je. 21. 9; 38. 2.
Ex. 15. 9.   ᵏ Ps. 107. 27.   ʳ Pr. 8. 15.   ᵐ Ps. 19. 3.

יְחִיָּה   ] pr. name masc. [for יְחִיאֵל (וַיְחִיָּה) see   חיה

יִחְיֶה   Kal fut. 3 pers. sing. masc.   חיה

יְחַיֵּהוּ⁴   ] Piel fut. 3 pers. sing. masc., suff. 3 pers.
sing. masc., with conj. וַ [for (וַי), וִיחַיֵּהוּ   חיה

יְחַיּוּ   id. fut. 3 pers. pl. masc.   חיה

יִחְיוּ   וַי' , וַ' , Kal fut. 3 pers. pl. masc.; וַ' conv.   חיה

יַחֲטוּ⁴   Chald. Aph. fut. 3 pers. pl. masc.   חוט

יְחַיֵּינָה⁴   Piel fut. 3 p s m, suff. 1 p pl. (§ 24. rem. 21)   חיה

יָחִיל   Kal, or Hiph. (Ps. 29. 8), fut. 3 pers. sing.
masc. from חִיל or   חול

יָחִיל   ] adj. masc. sing.   יחל

יָחִילוּ⁵   וַי' Kal fut. 3 pers. pl. m.; וַ' conv., R. חִיל, see   חול

יָחִילוּן⁶   id. with parag. ן   חול

יְחַיֵּנוּ   ] Piel fut. 3 pers. pl. masc., suff. 1 pers. pl.
[for יְחַיֻּנוּ]   חיה

יַחֲשׁ   Hiph. fut. 3 pers. sing. masc.   חוש

יַחִישָׁה⁷   id. with parag. ה (§ 8. rem. 13)   חוש

יְחִתַּן⁴   [for יְחִתַּן] Hiph. fut. 3 pers. sing. masc. [יַחֵת],
suff. 3 pers. pl. fem. (§ 18. rem. 12)   חתת

יְחַכֶּה⁸   Piel fut. 3 pers. sing. masc.   חכה

יְחַכֵּם⁹   Piel fut. 3 pers. sing. masc.   חכם

יֶחְכָּם   } Kal fut. 3 pers. sing. masc. (§ 13.
וַי' , וַ' ,   rem. 5, & § 8. rem. 15); וַ' conv.   חכם

יַחְכְּמוּ⁴   id. fut. 3 pers. pl. masc. [for יֶחְכְּמוּ v. id.   חכם

יְחַכְּמֵנוּ⁴   Piel fut. 3 pers. s. m. [יַחֵכֵּם], suff. 1 pers. pl.   חכם

יָחַל   Kal not used; *to wait*, cogn. חוּל. Pi. יִחֵל (§ 14.
rem. 1).—I. *to cause to wait*, expect, hope, with עַל.—
II. *to wait, expect, hope*, with לְ, אֶל. Hiph. *to wait,
expect*, with לְ. Niph. נוֹחַל, fut. יִיחַל (§ 20. r. 6) id.
יָחִיל adj. masc. *waiting, expecting*, La. 3. 26.
יַחְלְאֵל (*hoping in God*) pr. name masc. Ge. 46. 14.
Patronym. יַחְלְאֵלִי Nu. 26. 26.
תּוֹחֶלֶת (with suff. תּוֹחַלְתִּי) fem. dec. 13 a *expectation, hope.*

יָחֵל⁸   ] Kal fut. 3 pers. sing. masc. ap. [for יָחֵל from
יָחֵלָה § 24. rem. 3 d]; וַ' conv.   חלה

יָחֵל⁸   } Hiph. fut. 3 pers. sing. m. (§ 18. rem. 11)   חלל
וַ'

יָחֶל   ] Kal fut. 3 pers. sing. masc. with conv. וַ' [for
יָחֵל, ap. from יָחִיל § 22. r. 3] R. חִיל, see   חול

יַחֵל⁷   Piel imp. sing. masc. (§ 14. rem. 1)   יחל

יְחֵל⁴   dag. forte impl. in ח [for יְחֵל], Chald. form
for יָחֵל q. v. (§ 18. rem. 14)   חלל

יֵחַל⁴   Niph. fut. 3 pers. sing. masc. [for יֵחֵל, with
gutt. for יֵחֵל]   חלל

יָחֵל   ] Piel fut. 3 pers. s. m. ap. [fr. יְחַלֶּה]; וַ' conv.   חלה

יַחְלָא⁴   ] Kal fut. 3 pers. sing. masc. [for יַחֲלָה § 24.
rem. 19]; וַ' conv.   חלה

יַחְלְאֵל   ] pr. name masc.   יחל

יַחֲלוּ⁴   ] Hiph. fut. 3 pers. pl. masc.; וַ' conv.   חלל

יְחִלּוּ⁴   ] Piel pret. 3 pers. pl. (§ 14. rem. 1, &
וַ' ⁴   § 8. rem. 4)   יחל

יַחְלוּ⁴   ] Kal fut. 3 pers. pl. masc. [for יֶחְלוּ]   חול

יַחֵלּוּ⁴   ] Piel fut. 3 pers. pl. masc.   חלה

יַחְלִטוּ⁴   ] Hiph. fut. 3 pers. pl. masc. [for
§ 11. rem. 7]; וַ' conv.   חלם

יַחֲלִיף⁸   Hiph. fut. 3 pers. sing. masc.   חלף

יַחֲלִיפוּ⁸   id. fut. 3 pers. pl. masc.   חלף

יַחֲלִיפֶנּוּ⁴³   id. fut. 3 p s m, suff. 3 p s m. (§ 2. rem. 3)   חלף

יַחֲלִיץ⁸   Hiph. fut. 3 pers. sing. masc.   חלץ

יַחֲלִיקוּן⁸   Hiph. fut. 3 pers. pl. m. with parag. ן.   חלק

יְחַלֵּל⁸   Piel fut. 3 pers. sing. masc.   חלל

יְחַלְּלָהֻ⁴   id. fut. 3 pers. pl. m. (יְחַלְּלוּ), suff. 3 pers. s. m.   חלל

יְחַלֵּלוּ⁴   } id. fut. 3 pers. pl. masc. (comp. § 8.
וַיְחַלְּלוּ⁴   rem. 15); וַ' conv.   חלל

יְחַלְּלַנּוּ⁴   id. fut. 3 p s m, suff. 3 p s m. (§ 2. rem. 3)   חלל

יַחֲלֹם⁴   וַ' Kal fut. 3 pers. sing. masc.; וַ' conv.   חלם

יַחֲלֹמוּ⁴   } id. fut. 3 pers. pl. masc. (§ 13. rem. 5);
יַחֲלֹמוּ⁴   } וַ' id.   חלם

יַחֲלֹמוּן⁴   id. id. with parag. ן [for יַחֲלֹמוּן § 8. rem. 17]   חלם

יְחַלֵּנוּ⁴³   Piel pret. 1 pers. pl. (§ 14. rem. 1)   יחל

יְחַלֵּף⁴   ] Piel fut. 3 pers. sing. masc.; וַ' conv.   חלף

יַחֲלֹף⁴⁴   וַ' Kal fut. 3 pers. sing. masc.   חלף

יַחֲלֹפוּ⁴   ] id. fut. 3 pers. pl. masc. [for יַחֲלְפוּ or
יַחֲלֹפוּ § 13. rem. 5]   חלף

יַחְלְפוּן⁴³   Chald. Peal fut. 3 pers. pl. masc. (§ 49. rem. 2)   חלף

יְחַלֵּץ⁴   Piel fut. 3 pers. sing. masc.   חלץ

יֵחָלְצוּ⁴   Niph. fut. 3 pers. pl. masc. [for יֵחָלְצוּ comp.
§ 8. rem. 7]   ח־ל־ץ

יֵחָלְצוּן⁴   id. with parag. ן   חלץ

יְחַלְּצֵם⁴   ] Piel fut. 3 pers. sing. masc. (יְחַלֵּץ), suff.
3 pers. pl. masc.; וַ' conv.   חלץ

יְחַלְּצֵנִי⁴   id. with suff. 1 pers. sing.   חלץ

יַחֲלֹק⁴   Kal fut. 3 pers. sing. masc.   חלק

יֵחָלֵק⁴ , וַיֵּ'   } Niph. fut. 3 pers. sing. masc. (§ 9. rem.
3); וַ' conv.   חלק

יְחַלֵּק⁴   } וַ' Piel fut. 3 pers. sing. masc. (§ 10. rem.
יְחַלֵּק⁴   } וַ' 4); וַ' id.   חלק

ᵃ Ps. 41. 3.   ᵍ Ju. 3. 25.   ᵏ Is. 30. 18.   ᵖ Job 35. 11.   ᵇ 2 Ch. 16. 12.   ᵗ Le. 27. 10.   ʸ De. 20. 6.   ᶠ Ps. 33. 22.   ˣ Job 36. 15.
ᵇ Eze. 37. 9.   ʰ Is. 13. 8.   ˡ Ps. 105. 22.   ᵍ Ho. 8. 10.   ˢ Is. 29. 8, 8.   ʳ Ps. 105. 27.   ᶜ Pr. 11. 9.
ᶜ Eze. 37. 10.   ⁱ 2 Ki. 7. 4.   ᵐ Pr. 21. 11.   ᵐ Ju.10.18; 13. 5.   ⁿ Ps. 5. 10.   ᵘ Ge. 40. 5.   ᵖ Ps. 84. 8.
ᵈ Ezr. 4. 12.   ᵏ Is. 28. 16.   ⁿ Pr. 9. 9.   ᵖ Ps.130.7; 131.3.   ᵗ 2 Sa. 3. 9.   ᵛ Le.21.12,15,23.   ᵈ Da. 4. 13, 20,   ʸ Job 38. 24.
ᵉ Ho. 6. 2.   ˡ Is. 5. 19.   ᵒ 1 Ki. 5. 11.   ᵗ Nu. 30. 3.   ⁱ 1 Ki. 20. 33.   ᵉ Le. 22. 9.   22, 29.   ᶻ Jos. 18. 10.
ᶠ La. 3. 26.   ᵐ Hab. 2. 17.   ᵒ Job 32. 9.   ⁱ Is. 48. 11.   ᶠ Job 14. 7.   ᵖ Ps. 89. 32.   ˣ Ge. 14. 15.

יַחְלְקוּ } Kal fut. 3 pers. pl. masc. (§ 13. rem. 5,
וַיַּחְלְקוּ } comp. § 8. rem. 15); וְ conv.   חלק

יְחַלְּקוּ ' Piel fut. 3 pers. pl. masc.; וְ id.   חלק

יַחְלְקוּם } Kal fut. 3 pers. pl. masc., suff. 3 pers. pl. masc. (§ 13. rem. 5); וְ id.   חלק

יֵחָלְקֵם° } Niph. fut. 3 pers. sing. masc. (יֵחָלֵק), suff. 3 pers. pl. masc., others read יַחְלְקֵם Piel, (§ 10. rem. 7)   חלק

וַיַּחֲלֹשׁ } Kal fut. 3 pers. sing. masc. (§ 8. rem.
וַיַּחֲלֹשׁ } 13, comp. § 8. rem. 15); וְ conv.   חלש

יִחַלְתִּי } Piel pret. 1 pers. sing. (§ 14. rem. 1, comp. § 8. rem. 7)   יחל

יִחַלְתָּנִי° id. fut. 2 pers. sing. masc., suff. 1 pers. sing. (§ 2. rem. 1)   יחל

[יָחַם] I. to be hot, warm, Eze. 24. 11.—II. to be hot with anger, De. 19. 6.—III. to conceive, Ge. 30. 38, 39. Pi.—I. to be hot (for sexual intercourse).—II. to conceive, Ps. 51. 7.

חֵמָה fem. dec. 11b.—I. heat, anger, fury.—II. poison, venom, De. 32. 33.

חֲמָא, חֱמָא Ch. fem. heat, anger, Da. 3. 13, 19.

יָחֹם° } Kal fut. 3 pers. sing. masc. (§ 18.
וַיִּחַם } rem. 5)   חמם

יַחֵם' Piel inf. constr. (§ 14. rem. 1)   יחם

יֵחַם° } Kal fut. 3 pers. sing. masc. (§ 18. rem.
יֵחָם } 6, comp. § 8. rem. 15)   חמם

יֵחָם= id., with dag. f. imp. in ח [for יֵחַם] a Chald. form (§ 18. rem. 14)   חמם

יַחְמֹד° Kal fut. 3 pers. sing. masc. (§ 13. rem. 5)   חמד

יַחְמוּ° } Kal fut. 3 pers. pl. masc. (§ 18. rem. 6,
וַיֵּחַמּוּ } 14, & § 13. rem. 12); וְ conv.   חמם

יַחְמוֹל Kal fut. 3 pers. sing. masc. (§ 8. rem. 18, & § 13. rem. 5)   חמל

יַחְמוּר } noun masc. sing.   חמר

יַחְמָי } pr. name masc.   חמה

וַיַּחְמֹל } Kal fut. 3 pers. sing. masc. (§ 13. rem. 5); וְ conv.   חמל

יַחְמְלוּ° id. fut. 3 pers. pl. masc. [for יַחְמְלוּ v. id. & § 8. rem. 15]   חמל

וַיַּחֲמֶנָה } Kal fut. 3 pers. pl. fem. (§ 18. rem. 6, & § 8. rem. 16); וְ conv.   חמם

יַחְמֹס° } Kal fut. 3 pers. sing. masc. (§ 13. rem. 5); וְ id.   חמס

יַחְמֹץ= Kal fut. 3 pers. sing. masc. [for יֶחֱמַץ § 13. rem. 5, & § 8. rem. 15]   חמץ

יַחְמְרוּ Kal fut. 3 pers. pl. masc. (§ 13. rem. 5)   חמר

יְחַמַּתְנִי' Piel pret. 3 pers. sing. fem. suff. 1 pers. sing. [for יֶחֱמַתְנִי § 13. rem. 12]   יחם

יָחֹן° } Kal fut. 3 pers. sing. masc. (§ 18.
יָחֹן } rem. 5)   חנן

וַיָּחַן } Kal fut. 3 pers. sing. masc. ap. (§ 24. rem. 3); וְ conv.   חנה

יֻחַן Hoph. fut. 3 pers. sing. masc. [for יֻחְנַן]   חנן

יַחֲנוּ } '>', Kal fut. 3 pers. pl. masc.; parag.;
יַחֲנוּן } וְ conv.   חנה

וַיַּחֲנוּ== } Kal fut. 3 pers. pl. masc.; וְ id.   חנט

יַחֲנִיף Hiph. fut. 3 pers. sing. masc.   חנף

יְחָנְךָ } Kal fut. 3 pers. sing. masc. (יָחֹן), suff.
יָחָנֵךְ } 2 pers. sing. masc. (§ 18. r. 5, & § 2. r. 2); with conj. וְ [for וַיְחָנֶּךָ]   חנן

יַחְכְּנוּ } Kal fut. 3 pers. pl. m. (§ 13. r. 5); וְ conv.   חנן

יַחְנְנֵנּוּ id. fut. 3 pers. sing. masc., suff. 3 pers. sing. masc. (v. id. & § 2. rem. 3)   חנן

יְחַנֵּן° Piel fut. 3 pers. sing. masc.   חנן

יְחֹנֵן° Kal fut. 3 pers. sing. masc. (§ 18. rem. 13)   חנן

יְחָנֵּנוּ° } id. fut. 3 pers. s. m. (יָחֹן), suff. 1 pers. pl.
וַיְחָנֵּנוּ } (§ 18. r. 5), with conj. וְ [for וַיְחָנֵּנוּ]   חנן

יְחֹנֲנוּ Poel fut. 3 pers. pl. masc. [for יְחֹנֲנוּ comp. § 8. rem. 15]   חנן

וַיְחֻנֵּנוּ°= } Kal fut. 3 pers. sing. masc. (יָחֹן), suff. 3 pers. sing. masc. (§ 2. rem. 3); וְ conv.   חנן

יְחָנֵּנִי Kh. Kal fut. 3 pers. sing. masc. (יָחֹן), K. וַיְחָנֵּנִי pret. 3 pers. sing. masc. [חַן, with וְ conv.], suff. 1 pers. sing.   חנן

יֵחָנֵק° } Niph. fut. 3 pers. s. m. (§ 9. r. 4); וְ conv.   חנק

יָחֹס° Kal fut. 3 pers. sing. masc. (§ 21. rem. 7)   חום

יְחַסְּדֵךְ° Piel fut. 3 pers. sing. masc., suff. 2 pers. sing. masc. (§ 16. rem. 15)   חסד

יֶחְסֶה Kal fut. 3 pers. sing. masc.   חסה

יֶחְסוּ° id. fut. 3 pers. pl. masc.   חסה

יֶחְסָיוּן° id. id. with parag. ן (§ 24. rem. 5)   חסה

יַחְסִיר° Hiph. fut. 3 pers. sing. masc. (§ 13. rem. 9)   חסר

יַחְסְלֶנּוּ Kal fut. 3 pers. sing. masc., suff. 3 pers. sing. masc. (§ 13. rem. 5)   חסל

יֵחָסֵן° Niph. fut. 3 pers. sing. masc.   חסן

יַחְסְנוּן° } Chald. Aph. fut. 3 pers. pl. masc. (§ 49. rem. 2)   חסן

יֶחְסַר } Kal fut. 3 pers. sing. masc. (§ 13. rem.
יַחְסֹר } 5, & § 8. rem. 15)   חסר

וַיַּחְסְרוּ° id. fut. 3 pers. pl. masc. (§ 13. rem. 5); וְ conv.   חסר

kk יַחְסְרוּן id. id. with parag. ן   חסר

---

* Jos. 14. 5.   g Ps. 119. 49.   Ex. 34. 24.   La. 2. 6.   Ex. 14. 2.   De. 20. 5.   Ps. 102. 15.   Ps. 72. 15.   Is. 32. 6.
1 Sa. 30. 24.   Is. 44. 16.   Ho. 7. 7.   Ex. 12. 34.   Ju. 11. 18.   Pr. 26. 25.   Job 33. 24.   Pr. 25. 10.   De. 28. 24.
1 Ki. 18. 6.   Ge. 30. 41; 31. 10.   Ge. 30. 39.   Ps. 46. 4.   Ge. 43. 29;   Am. 5. 15.   Ps. 34. 9.   Is. 23. 12.
1 Ch. 23. 6; 24. 3.   Ec. 4. 11.   Is. 9. 18.   Is. 30. 19.   Ps. 67. 2.   Is. 14. 32.   Da. 7. 18.
Ex. 17. 13.   De. 19. 6; 1 Ki. 19. 11.   Ge. 30. 38.   De. 26. 50.   Mal. 1. 9.   Ps. 86. 8.   Ge. 2. 1.
Job 14. 10.   1 Ki. 1. 1.   Job 15. 23.   2 Ki. 17. 23.   ... 4. 20.   Ge. 13. 22.

יָחֵף֫ ‹ [יָחֵף] unshod, barefoot.

יְחַף 1 Piel fut. 3 pers. sing. masc. ap. [from וַיְּחַפֶּה]; 1 conv.   חפה

יְחַפְּאוּ 1 Piel fut. 3 pers. pl. masc.; 1 id.   חפא

יְחַפְּהֵֽנִי 1 Piel fut. 3 pers. sing. masc., suff. 3 pers. sing. masc. (§ 24. rem. 21); 1 id.   חפה

יַחְפֹּז֫ Kal fut. 3 pers. sing. masc. (§ 8. rem. 18, & § 13. rem. 5)   חפז

יֵחָפְזוּן֫ Niph. fut. 3 pers. pl. masc.; 1 parag. [for יֵחָפְזוּן comp. § 8. rem. 17]   חפז

יַחְפִּיר֫ 1 Hiph. fut. 3 pers. sing. masc. (§ 13. r. 9)   חפר

יַחְפֹּץ } Kal fut. 3 pers. sing. masc. (§ 13. rem. 4
יַחְפָּץ } & 5, & § 8. rem. 15) .   חפץ

יַחְפְּצוּ } id. fut. 3 pers. pl. masc. (v. id. & § 13.
יַחְפֵּצוּ } rem. 6) .   חפץ

יַחְפְּצוּן id. id. with parag. 1 [for יַחְפְּצוּן § 8. r. 17]   חפץ

יַחְפֹּר 1 Kal fut. 3 pers. sing. masc. (§ 13. rem. 5); 1 conv.   חפר

יַחְפְּרֵהוּ 1 id. id., suff. 3 pers. sing. masc.; 1 id.   חפר

יַחְפְּרֻהוּ 1 id. fut. 3 p. pl. m., suff. 3 p. s. m.; 1 id.   חפר

יַחְפְּרוּ } 1', וַ' id. fut. 3 pers. pl. masc. (§ 13. rem.
יַחְפֹּרוּ } 1', וַ' 4, 5, 6, & § 8. rem. 15); 1 id.   חפר

יְחַפֵּשׂ 1 Piel fut. 3 pers. sing. masc.; 1 id.   חפשׂ

יְחֻפַּשׂ Pual fut. 3 pers. sing. masc.   חפשׂ

יַחְפְּשׂוּ Kal fut. 3 pers. pl. masc. (§ 13. rem. 5)   חפשׂ

יַחַץ 1 Kal fut. 3 pers. sing. masc. ap. (§ 24. rem. 3d); 1 conv.   חצה

יַחְצְאֵל }
יַחֲצְאֵל } pr. name masc.   חצה

יַחְצֹב 1 Kal fut. 3 pers. sing. masc. (§ 13. rem. 5); 1 conv.   חצב

יֵחָצְבוּן Niph. fut. 3 pers. pl. masc. with parag. 1   חצב

יֶחֱצֶה Kal fut. 3 pers. sing. masc.   חצה

יֵחָצוּ 1 Niph. fut. 3 pers. pl. masc.; 1 conv.   חצה

יֶחֱצוּ id. acc. drawn back before monos.   חצה

יַחְצוּ Kal fut. 3 pers. pl. masc.   חצה

יֶחֱצוּהוּ id. with suff. 3 pers. sing. masc.   חצה

יֶחֱצוּן id. with parag. 1   חצה

יֶחֱצֵם 1 id. fut. 3 pers. sing. masc., suff. 3 pers. pl. masc.; 1 conv.   חצה

יֻחַקּוּ 1 Hoph. fut. 3 pers. pl. masc. [for יֻחַקְקוּ § 18. rem. 15 note]   חקק

יֵחָקֵר Niph. fut. 3 pers. sing. masc.   חקר

יַחְקֹר } Kal fut. 3 pers. sing. masc. (§ 13. rem. 5,
יַחְקְרוּ } & § 8. rem. 18)   חקר

יֵחָקְרוּ 1 Niph. fut. 3 pers. pl. masc.   חקר

יַחְקְרוּ Kal fut. 3 pers. pl. masc. [for יַחְקֹרוּ § 13. rem. 5, & § 8. rem. 15]   חקר

יַחְקְרֶנּוּ id. fut. 3 pers. sing. masc., suff. 3 pers. s. m.   חקר

[יָחַר] to delay, tarry, 2 Sa. 20. 5. Kheth.

יֵחַר 1 Niph. fut. 3 pers. s. m. [for יֵחַר]; 1 conv.   חרר

יַחַר 1 Hiph. fut. 3 pers. sing. masc. ap. [from יַחֲרֶה § 24. rem. 16]; 1 id.   חרה

יִחַר וַ' 1 Kal fut. 3 pers. sing. masc. ap. (§ 24. rem. 3d); 1 id.   חרה

יֶחֱרַב 1 } Kal fut. 3 pers. sing. masc. (§ 8. rem.
יֶחֱרָב וַ' } 15); 1 id.   חרב

יֶחֶרְבוּ
יֶחֱרָבוּ } id. fut. 3 pers. pl. masc. (v. id.)   חרב

יַחְרֹג 1 Kal fut. 3 pers. pl. masc. (§ 13. rem. 5)   חרג

יֶחֱרַד וַ' 1 Kal fut. 3 pers. sing. masc.; 1 conv.   חרד

יֶחֶרְדוּ
וַ', יֶ' } id. fut. 3 pers. pl. masc. (§ 13.
יֶחֶרְדוּ } rem. 5, & § 8. rem. 15); 1 id.   חרד
יֶחֱרָדוּ }

יֶחֱרֶה Kal fut. 3 pers. sing. masc.   חרה

יֵחָרוּ Niph. fut. 3 pers. pl. masc. [for יֵחָרוּ]   חרר

יַחֲרוֹשׁ Kal fut. 3 pers. sing. masc. (§ 8. rem. 18)   חרשׁ

יַחֲרִימָהּ 1 Hiph. fut. 3 pers. sing. masc., suff. 3 pers. sing. fem.; 1 conv.   חרם

יַחֲרִימוּ 1 id. fut. 3 pers. pl. masc.   חרם

יַחֲרִימֵם 1 id. id., suff. 3 pers. pl. masc.   חרם

יַחֲרִישׁ Hiph. fut. 3 pers. sing. masc.   חרשׁ

יַחֲרִישׁוּ וַ' id. fut. 3 pers. pl. masc.   חרשׁ

יַחֲרֹךְ Kal fut. 3 pers. sing. masc.   חרך

יַחֲרֵם 1 Hiph. fut. 3 pers. sing. masc. ap. [from יַחֲרִים]; 1 conv.   חרם

יַחֲרֵם id. fut. 3 pers. sing. masc. def. [for יַחֲרִים]   חרם

יָחֳרָם
יֻחֳרָם } Hoph. fut. 3 pers. sing. masc. (comp.
יָחֳרָם } § 8. rem. 15)   חרם

יְחָרֵף 1 } Piel fut. 3 pers. sing. masc. (§ 10.
יְחָרֶף וַ' } rem. 4); 1 conv.   חרף

יֶחֱרַף Kal fut. 3 pers. sing. masc.   חרף

יְחָרְפוּנִי Piel fut. 3 pers. pl. masc., suff. 1 pers. sing.   חרף

יְחָרְפֵנִי id. fut. 3 pers. sing. masc., suff. 1 pers. sing.   חרף

יַחֲרֹץ Kal fut. 3 pers. sing. masc.   חרץ

יַחֲרֹק Kal fut. 3 pers. sing. masc.   חרק

יַחַרְקוּ 1 id. fut. 3 pers. pl. masc.; 1 conv.   חרק

יַחֲרֹשׁ
יַחֲרֹשׁ } Kal fut. 3 pers. sing. masc. (§ 13. rem. 4)   חרשׁ

יַחֲרֹשׁוּ 1 Hiph. fut. 3 pers. pl. masc. (§ 13. rem. 9); 1 conv.   חרשׁ

a 2 Sa. 15. 30.   b Is. 20. 2, 3, 4.   c 2 Ch. 3. 7.   d 2 Ki. 17. 9.   e 2 Ch. 3. 5, 8.   f Job 40. 23.   g Ps. 104. 7.
  a Pr. 13. 5.   b Ps. 68. 31.   c Is. 58. 2.   d Ge. 26. 18, 22.   e Ps. 7. 16.   f Job 2. 20.   g Job 39. 21.
  a Pr. 28. 12.   b Ps. 64. 7.   c 2 Ch. 26. 10.   d Ex. 21. 35.   e Is. 30. 28.   f Job 19. 24.   g Ez. 37. 22.
  a Ps. 55. 24.   b Job 40. 30.   c Ju. 9. 43.   d Job 19. 23.   e Ez. 46. 23.   f Ps. 44. 22.
  a Job 13. 9.   b Je. 31. 37.   c Ex. 39. 14.   d Pr. 28. 14.   e Eze. 15. 5.   f Job 37. 1.   g Job 19. 11.
  h Ps. 106. 9.   i Ho. 13. 15.   k Eze. 26. 18.   l Eze. 24. 10.   m Jon. 10. 1.   n 1 Ch. 4. 41.   o Ho. 11. 11.
  p Ho. 11. 10.   q Eze. 26. 18.   r Eze. 24. 19.   s Ps. 74. 12.   t Job 27. 6.   u Ne. 6. 13.
  v Pr. 12. 27.   w Le. 27. 28.   x Ex. 22. 19.   y Ps. 55. 13.   z Ex. 11. 7.   a Ps. 112. 12.   b La. 2. 16.   c Ps. 50. 3.   d Je. 38. 27.

[יָחַשׂ] masc. *lineage, family*; סֵפֶר הַיַּחַשׂ *family register*, Ne. 7. 5.—Hithp. הִתְיַחֵשׂ *to enter one's name in the family register, to be enrolled*; inf. *registration*.

יַחְשֹׁב { Kal fut. 3 pers. sing. masc. (§ 8. rem. 18, & § 13. rem. 5) . . } חשב
יַחֲשֹׁב

יֵחָשֵׁב Niph. fut. 3 pers. sing. masc. . . חשב

יְחַשֵּׁב Piel fut. 3 pers. sing. masc. . . חשב

וַיַּחְשְׁבֶהָ Kal fut. 3 pers. sing. masc., suff. 3 pers. sing. fem. (§ 13. rem. 5); וְ conv. . חשב

יַחְשְׁבוּ { id. fut. 3 pers. pl. masc. (§ 8. rem. 15) } חשב
יַחֲשְׁבוּ

יֵחָשְׁבוּ Niph. fut. 3 pers. pl. masc. . . חשב

יְחַשְּׁבוּ Piel fut. 3 pers. pl. masc. . . חשב

יַחְשְׁבוּן Kal fut. 3 pers. pl. masc.; parag. ן [for יַחְשְׁבוּ § 8. rem. 17] . . חשב

וַיַּחְשְׁבֵנִי id. fut. 3 pers. sing. masc., suff. 1 pers. sing. (§ 13. rem. 4 & 5); וְ conv. . חשב

וַיֶּחֱשֶׂה Kal fut. 3 pers. pl. masc.; וְ id. חשה

יַחְשֵׂךְ { Hiph. fut. 3 pers. sing. masc. (§ 13. rem. 9); וַיַּ id. . . } חשך
וַיַּחְשֵׂךְ

יַחְשֹׁךְ Kal fut. 3 pers. sing. masc. (§ 13. rem. 5) חשך

יֵחָשֵׂךְ { Niph. fut. 3 pers. sing. masc. (§ 9. rem. 3) } חשך

יַחְשְׂכוּ Kal fut. 3 pers. pl. masc. (§ 13. rem. 5) . חשך

וַיַּחְשֹׂף Kal fut. 3 pers. sing. masc.; וְ conv. חשף

יַחַת { pr. name masc. . . . } יחד
יַחַת

יֵחַת { Kal fut. 3 pers. sing. masc. (§ 18. rem. 6, comp. § 8. rem. 7) . . } חתת
יֵחַת

וַיֵּחַת Kal fut. 3 pers. sing. masc. [for וַיֵּנַחַת, יֵחַת] נחת

יֵחַתּוּ id. fut. 3 pers. pl. masc. with euph. dag. [for יֵחַתּוּ, comp. וַיִצֹּתּוּ & § 8. rem. 3] נחת

וַיֵּחַתּוּ Kal fut. 3 pers. pl. masc. (§ 18. rem. 6) חתת

יֵחַתּוֹם Kal fut. 3 pers. sing. masc. (§ 13. rem. 5, & § 8. rem. 18) חתם

יֵחַתְּךָ Kal fut. 3 pers. sing. masc. [יֵחַתָּה for § 13. r. 5], suff. 2 pers. s. m. (§ 24. r. 21) חתת

וַיַּחְתֹּם Kal fut. 3 pers. sing. masc. (§ 13. rem. 5); וְ conv. חתם

יְחִתֵּנִי Hiph. fut. 3 pers. s. m. [וַיֵּחַת], suff. 1 pers. s. חתת

יַחְתֹּף Kal fut. 3 pers. sing. masc. (§ 13. rem. 5) חתף

וַיַּחְתְּרוּ Kal fut. 3 pers. pl. masc. (§ 13. rem. 5); וְ conv. חתר

יֵט { Hiph. fut. 3 pers. sing. masc., ap. from יָטֶה (§ 25, 2b); וְ id. . . } נטה

יֵט { וַיֵּט, וְ Kal fut. 3 pers. sing. masc., ap. from יָטֶה (§ 25, 2b, comp. § 24. rem. 3) } נטה
יַּט

יָטַב used only in the fut. תֵּיטְבִי, יֵטַב, יִיטַב—I. *to be good, well*, with מִן tt. *be better*; יֵיטַב לִי *it shall be well with me*; לְפָנַי, בְּעֵינַי and וַיִּיטַב also with לִי, לְפָנַי, *and it pleased me*.—II. *to be cheerful, joyful*, with לֵב. Hiph. הֵיטִיב.—I. *to make good, to do well*, followed by an inf., as הֵיטִיבוּ נַגֵּן *play well*; הֵיטַבְתָּ לִרְאוֹת *thou hast well or rightly seen*; with a subst. הֵיטִיב דְּרָכָיו *to make good one's way*. Inf. abs. as an adv. *well, rightly*.—II. *to do good to any one*, with אֶל, לְ, עִם.—III. *to make cheerful*, Ju. 19. 22.—IV. *to adjust, dress.*—V. *to be pleasing to any one*, with אֶל, 1 Sa. 20. 13.

יְטַב Chald. id. with עַל *to seem good, be pleasing to any one*, Ezr. 7. 18.

יָטְבָה (*goodness*) pr. name of a place, 2 Ki. 21. 19.

יָטְבָתָה (id.) pr. name of a station of the Israelites in the desert.

מֵיטָב masc. dec. 2b, *the best, best part of anything.*

מְהֵיטַבְאֵל (*God does well*) pr. name—I. masc. Ne. 6. 10.—II. fem. Ge. 36. 39.

וַיִּטֶב defect. for יֵיטַב (q. v.) . . יטב

יָטְבָה pr. name of a place . . יטב

וַיִּטְבֹּל Kal fut. 3 pers. sing. masc.; וְ conv. . טבל

יִטְבְּלוּ id. fut. 3 pers. pl. masc.; וְ id. . טבל

יִטְבַּע id. fut. 3 pers. sing. masc.; וְ id. . טבע

יָטְבָתָה pr. name of a place . . טבע

יַטֶּה Hiph. fut. 3 pers. sing. masc. (§ 25, 2b) נטה

יִטֶּה Kal fut. 3 pers. sing. masc. (§ 25, 2b) נטה

יַטֵּהוּ Hiph. fut. 3 pers. sing. masc. (יַטֶּה q. v.), suff. 3 pers. sing. masc.; וְ conv. . נטה

יִטְהָר { וַיִּ Kal fut. 3 pers. sing. masc. (§ 8. rem. 15); וְ id. . . } טהר
יִטְהַר

יְטַהֵר Piel fut. 3 pers. sing. m. (§ 14. r. 1); וְ id. טהר

יִטְהֲרוּ Hithp. fut. 3 pers. pl. masc. [for יִתְטַהֲרוּ § 12. rem. 3]; וְ id. טהר

יְטַהֲרוּ Piel fut. 3 pers. pl. m. (§ 14. rem. 1); וְ id. טהר

וַיַּטּוּ Hiph. fut. 3 pers. pl. m. (§ 25, 2b); וְ id. נטה

יִטּוּ Kal fut. 3 pers. pl. masc. (§ 25, 2b); וְ id. נטה

יִטּוֹל Kal fut. 3 pers. sing. masc. (§ 17. rem. 3) נטל

יִטּוֹר Kal fut. 3 pers. sing. masc. (§ 17. rem. 3) נטר

יִטּוֹר { pr. name masc., with cop. וְ [for וְ, וַיִּטֹּר } נטר
יִטּוֹר

יִטּוֹשׁ Kal fut. 3 pers. sing. masc. . . נטש

יִטֹּשׁ Kal fut. 3 pers. sing. masc. (§ 17. rem. 3) נטש

יִטְחָן Kal fut. 3 pers. sing. masc.; וְ conv. . טחן

a Is. 13. 17. f Is. 62. 6. i Jos 16. 6. o Job 21. 13. u Job 31. 34. a Zep. 2. 13. f Je. 58. 6. l 2 Ch. 34. 5. a Ps. 10b. 9.
b De. 2. 11. g Is. 107. 29. k Job 21. 30. p 1 Sa. 17. 11. v Job 9. 12. b Ge. 26. 25; g Is. 31. 3. Ne. 12. 50. b Job 9. 25.
c Ps. 35. 20. h Ps. 139. 12. l Job ъ. 9. q Job 57. 7. w Jon. 1. 13. c 1 Ch. 15. 1. h Is. 55. 29. 1 Sa. 8. 3. c Ho. 11. 15.
d Job 52. 16. i Je. 13. 16. m Ps. 29. 9. r Ps. 52. 7. x 2 Sa. 19. 15; d 1 Sa. 24. 5. i Is. 46. 15. 2 Ki. 5. 14. d Ez. 33. 54.
c Job 19. 11. k Ps. 105. 23. n Je. 21. 13. s Est. 8. 10. Ezr. 9. 9. c Ge. 37. 31.

יַטִיבְךָ   ‖ Hiph. fut. 3 pers. sing. masc. [יֵטִיב], suff. 2 pers. s. m., with conj. ‖ [for וַיְ׳ וְיָטִיבְךָ   טוב

יַטִּילֻ   ‖ Hiph. fut. 3 pers. pl. masc.; ‖ conv.   .   טול

יַטִּפֻ   Hiph. fut. 3 pers. pl. masc.   .   נטף

יַטִּפֻן   id. with parag. ‖   .   נטף

יַטֶּךָ   Hiph. fut. 3 pers. sing. masc. (יַטֶּה), suff. 2 pers. sing. masc. (§ 25, 26, & § 2. r. 2)   נטה

יָמֵל   ‖ Hiph. fut. 3 pers. sing. masc. ap. [fr. יָמִיל § 21. rem. 18, from   .   מול

יֻמַּל   Hoph. fut. 3 pers. sing. masc. [for יוּמַל § 21. rem. 24, comp. § 8. rem. 15)   .   מול

יַמִּלֻהֻ   ‖ Hiph. fut. 3 pers. pl. masc. [יָמִיל], suff. 3 pers. sing. masc.; ‖ conv.   .   מול

יֻמַלְלֻנֻ   ‖ Piel fut. 3 pers. sing. masc. [יְמַלֵּל], suff. 3 pers. sing. masc. (§ 2. r. 3) with conj. ‖ [for וַיְ׳ , וְיְמַלֵּל]   .   מלל

יַטַּמָּא   Hithpa. fut. 3 pers. sing. masc. [for יִתְטַמָּא § 12. rem. 3]   .   .   טמא

יִטְמָא   Kal fut. 3 pers. sing. masc.   טמא

יְטַמֵּא   ‖ Piel fut. 3 pers. sing. masc.; ‖ conv.   טמא

יְטַמְּאֵהֻ   ‖ id. with suff. 3 pers. sing. masc.; ‖ id.   טמא

יִטַּמָּא   in pause for יִטְמָא (q. v.)   טמא

יְטַמְּאֻ   ‖ Piel fut. 3 pers. pl. masc.   טמא

יִטַּמְּאֻ   Hithpa. fut. 3 pers. pl. masc. [for יִתְטַמְּאֻ § 12. rem. 3]   טמא

יִטְמְאֻ   ‖ Kal fut. 3 pers. pl. masc.; ‖ conv.   .   טמא

יְטַמְּאֶנֻ   Piel fut. 3 pers. sing. masc., suff. 3 pers. s. m.   טמא

יִטְמֹן   ‖ Kal fut. 3 pers. sing. masc.; ‖ conv.   .   טמן

יִטְמְנֵהֻ   ‖ id. with suff. 3 pers. sing. masc.; ‖ id.   טמן

יַטְמִנֻ   ‖ Hiph. fut. 3 pers. pl. masc.; ‖ id.   טמן

יַטֶּנֻ   Hiph. fut. 3 pers. sing. masc. (יַטֶּה), suff. 3 pers. sing. masc. (§ 25, 2 b, & § 2. r. 3)   נטה

יִטַּע   ‖ וַיְ׳ ‖ Kal fut. 3 pers. sing. masc.; ‖ conv.   נטע

יִטָּעֵהֻ   ‖ id. id., suff. 3 pers. sing. m. (§ 16. r. 12)   נטע

יִטְּעֻ   וַיְ׳ id. fut. 3 pers. pl. masc.   .   נטע

יִטְעַם   Kal fut. 3 pers. sing. masc.   .   טעם

יִטְעֲמֻ   id. fut. 3 pers. pl. masc.   .   טעם

יִטְעֲמֻן   Ch. Pa. fut. 3 pers. pl. masc.   .   טעם

יְטַעֲמֻנַּהּ   Ch. id. with suff. 3 pers. sing. masc.   טעם

יִטְפֻ   Kal fut. 3 pers. pl. masc.   .   נטף

יַטְרִיחַ   Hiph. fut. 3 pers. sing. masc.   .   טרח

יִטָּרֵף   Niph. fut. 3 pers. sing. masc.   .   טרף

יִטְרֹף יִטְרָף   ‖ Kal fut. 3 pers. sing. masc. (A & O § 8. r. 13, comp. r. 15); ‖ וַיְ׳ conv.   טרף

יִטֹּשׁ   וַיְ׳ Kal fut. 3 pers. s. m. (§ 17. r. 3); ‖ id.   נטש

יִטְּשֻׁהֻ   ‖ id. fut. 3 p. pl. m., suff. 3 p. s. m.; ‖ id.   נטש

יִטָּשֵׁנֻ   Kal fut. 3 pers. sing. masc., suff. 1 pers. pl.   נטש

יִיבַשׁ   ‖ וַיְ׳ Kal fut. 3 pers. sing. masc. (comp.)

יִיבָשׁ   ‖ § 8. rem. 15); ‖ conv.   }   יבש

יִיגַע   Kal fut. 3 pers. sing. m. [for יִגַע § 8. r. 15)   יגע

יִיגָעֻ   } id. fut. 3 pers. pl. masc. (v. id.)   יגע

יִיגָעֻ   }

יֵידַע   Kal fut. 3 pers. sing. masc. (§ 20. rem. 15)   ידע

יֵיחַל   ‖ Niph. fut. 3 pers. sing. masc. (§ 20. r. 6); acc. drawn back, conv. ‖ (§ 9. rem. 3)   יחל

יְיַחֵל   Piel fut. 3 pers. sing. masc. (§ 14. rem. 1)   יחל

וַיֹּחֶל   Kh. יַחֵל q. v.; K. יֹּחֶל Hiph. fut. 3 pers. sing. masc. ap. with conv. ‖ (§ 20. r. 9)   יחל

יַיַחֲלֻ   Piel (§ 14. rem. 1) fut. 3 pers. pl. masc. [for יְיַחֲלֻ comp. § 8. rem. 15]   .   יחל

יְיַחֲלֻן   id. with parag. ‖ (§ 10. r. 4, comp. § 8. r. 17)   יחל

וַיֹּחֶר   Kh. יִּיחַר Kal, K. יֹּחַר Hiph. fut. comp. יֹּחֶל   יחר

יֵיטַב   Ch. Peal fut. 3 pers. sing. masc.   יטב

יֵיטֵב   ‖ Hiph. fut. 3 pers. sing. masc. ap. with conv. ‖ [for יֵיטֵב from יֵיטִיב]   .   יטב

יֵיטַב   defect. for יֵיטִיב (q. v.)   .   יטב

יִיטַב   ‖ ׳ , וַיְ׳ ‖ Kal fut. 3 pers. sing. masc.; ‖ conv.   יטב

יִיטְבֻ   ‖ id. fut. 3 pers. pl. masc.; ‖ id.   יטב

יֵיטִיב   }

יֵיטִיב   } Hiph. fut. 3 pers. sing. m. (§ 20. r. 15)   יטב

יֵיטִיב   }

יֵיטִיבֻ   id. fut. 3 pers. pl. masc.   .   .   יטב

יֵילִיל   Hiph. fut. 3 p. s. m. [for יֵהֵלִיל § 20. rem. 15]   ילל

יֵילִילֻ   id. fut. 3 pers. pl. masc.   .   .   ילל

יַיִן   ‖ וַיְ׳ ‖ noun masc. sing. dec. 6 h   .   יין

יֵין   ‖ ׳ , וַיְ׳ ‖ id., construct state   .   .   יין

יֵינָהּ   id., suff. 3 pers. sing. fem.   .   יין

יֵינִי   id., suff. 1 pers. sing.   .   .   יין

יֵינֵךְ   id., suff. 2 pers. sing. fem.   .   יין

יֵינְךָ   id., suff. 2 pers. sing. masc. [for יֵינְךָ]   יין

יֵינָם   id., suff. 3 pers. pl. masc.   .   יין

יִינַק   Kal fut. 3 p. s. m. [for יִנַק comp. § 8. rem. 15]   ינק

יִינְקֻ   id. fut. 3 pers. pl. masc. [for יִנְקֻ v. id.]   ינק

יְיַסְּדֶנָּה   Piel fut. 3 pers. sing. masc. [יְיַסֵּד], suff. 3 pers. sing. fem. (§ 2. rem. 3)   יסד

יִיסַךְ   Kal fut. 3 p. s. m. [for יִסַךְ comp. § 8. rem. 15]   יסך

יְיַסֵּר   Piel fut. 3 pers. sing. masc.   .   יסר

יְעַדְּנָה   Kal fut. 3 pers. sing. masc. [וַיְעַר], suff. 3 pers. sing. fem. (§ 16. rem. 12, & § 2. rem. 3)   יער

יִיעַף   Kal fut. 3 pers. sing. masc.   .   יעף

a Ec. 11. 9.   h Ne. 3. 15.   p 2 Ki. 7. 8, 8.   v Da. 4. 22, 29.   ı 1 Ki. 8. 57.   n Ge. 8. 12.   v Ex. 1. 20.   a De. 32. 38.   De. 33. 19.
b Jon. 1. 5.   i 2 Ki. 23. 8.   q Pr. 21. 1.   w Da. 5. 21.   m Jon. 4. 7.   o Mi. 5. 6.   w Ge. 34. 18.   b Pr. 9. 2.   c Jos. 6. 26.
c Mi. 2. 6.   k 2 Ki. 23. 16.   r Da. 11. 45.   x Joel 4. 18.   n 1 Ki. 17. 7.   p 1 Sa. 13. 8.   x Job 24. 21.   c Ca. 5. 1.   f Ex. 30. 32.
d Mi. 2. 6.   l Ps. 106. 30.   s Is. 5. 2.   y Ge. 49. 27.   o Is. 40. 28.   q Is. 42. 4.   y 1 Ki. 1. 47.   d 1 Sa. 1. 14.   g De. 8. 5.
e Job 36. 18.   m Le. 13. 44.   t Is. 65. 22.   z Ps. 7. 3.   p Is. 40. 31.   r Is. 51. 5.   z Ec. 9. 7.   e Ex. 21. 9.
f Job 41. 1.   n Ge. 35. 4.   u Ps. 107. 37.   s Am. 1. 11.   q 2 Sa. 20. 5.   s Ho. 7. 14.   a Job 20. 16.   h Is. 40. 28.
g Jon. 1. 15.   o Ex. 2. 12.   t Eze. 31. 12, 12.   u Ps. 138. 6.   t Ezr. 7. 18.   aa Job 37. 11.

Hebrew	Gloss	Root
יָעֵפוּ	Kal fut. 3 pers. pl. masc. [for יַעְפוּ comp. § 8. rem. 15]	יעף
וַיִּף	Kal fut. 3 pers. sing. masc. ap. [from יִפֶּה § 25, 2e] ; וַ conv.	יפה
וַיְיַפֵּהוּ	Piel fut. 3 pers. s. m. [וַיְיַפֶּה], suff. 3 pers. s. m.	יפה
וַיִּצֶר	Kal fut. 3 pers. sing. masc. with conv. וַ [for וַיִּיצֶר]	יצר
יִיקַץ / וַיִּיקַץ	Kal fut. 3 pers. sing. masc.; וַ conv.	יקץ
יִיקַר / וַיִּיקַר	Kal fut. 3 pers. sing. masc. (§ 20. rem. 2), וַ id.	יקר
וַיִּרָא	Kal fut. 3 pers. sing. m. (§ 25, 2d); וַ id.	ירא
יִירְאוּ, וַיִּ׳	id. fut. 3 pers. pl. masc. (comp. § 8. rem. 15); וַ id.	ירא
יִירָאוּךָ	id. id., suff. 2 pers. sing. masc.	ירא
יִירָאֻנִי	id. fut. 3 pers. sing. masc., suff. 1 pers. sing.	ירא
יִירֶה	Niph. fut. 3 pers. sing. masc. (§ 20. rem. 6)	ירה
יִירַשׁ, וַיִּ׳	Kal fut. 3 pers. sing. masc. (comp. § 8. rem. 15); וַ conv.	ירש
יְיָרֵשׁ	Piel fut. 3 pers. sing. masc.	ירש
יֹרֵשׁ	Kh. יִירַשׁ q. v.; K. יוֹרֵשׁ q. v.	ירש
יִירְשׁוּ, וַיִּ׳	Kal fut. 3 pers. pl. masc. (comp. § 8. rem. 15); וַ conv.	ירש
יִירָשׁוּהָ	id. id., suff. 3 pers. sing. fem. (§ 16. rem. 12)	ירש
יִירָשׁוּם	id. id., suff. 3 pers. pl. masc. (v. id.)	ירש
יִירָשְׁךָ	id fut. 3 pers. sing. masc., suff. 2 pers. sing. masc. (v. id.)	ירש
יִירָשׁוּם	id. id., suff. 3 pers. pl. masc. (v. id.)	ירש
וַיִּירָשֻׁם	id. fut. 3 pers. pl. masc., suff. 3 pers. pl. masc. (v. id.); וַ conv.	ירש
יֵישִׁירוּ	Hiph. fut. 3 pers. pl. masc. (§ 20. No. 1 b)	ישר
וַיִּישַׁם	Kal fut. 3 pers. sing. masc. with conv. וַ [for וַיִּישַׁם]	ישם
יֹשָׁב	Kh. יִישַׁם q. v.; K. יִישַׁם Hoph. fut. 3 pers. sing. masc.; וַ conv.	שום
וַיִּ׳, יִישַׁן	Kal fut. 3 pers. sing. masc. (comp. § 8. rem. 15); וַ id.	ישן
יְיַשֵּׁר	Piel fut. 3 pers. s. m. (comp. § 10. rem. 4)	ישר
וַיִּ׳	Kal fut. 3 pers. sing. masc.; וַ conv.	ישר
וַיְיַשְּׁרֵם	Kh. וַיְיַשְּׁרֵם Piel fut. 3 pers. s. m., suff. 3 pers. pl. m., for K. וַיַּשְׁרֵם id. (§ 20. rem. 8); וַ id.	ישר
יָךְ	וַ in pause for יַךְ (q. v.)	נכה
יָךְ	Kh. most probably an error of the copyists, for יַךְ	נכה
יַ׳, וַ׳	Hiph. fut. 3 pers. sing. masc., ap. from יַכֶּה (§ 25, 2b); וַ conv.	נכה

Hebrew	Gloss	Root
יֶכְאַב / יִכְאַב	Kal fut. 3 pers. sing. masc. (§ 8. rem. 15)	כאב
יַכְאִיב	Hiph. fut. 3 pers. sing. masc.	כאב
יְכַבֵּד	Piel fut. 3 pers. sing. masc.	כבד
וַ׳	Hiph. fut. 3 p. s. m. ap. [from יַכְבִּיד]; וַ conv.	כבד
וַיִּ׳	Kal fut. 3 pers. sing. masc. (comp. § 8. rem. 15); וַ id.	כבד
יְכֻבַּד	Pual fut. 3 pers. s. m. [for יְכֻבַּד § 8. rem. 15]	כבד
וַיְ׳, וַיְכַבְּדוּ	Piel fut. 3 pers. pl. masc., with conj. וַ [for וַיְכַבְּדוּ]	כבד
וַיְכַבְּדוּ	Kal fut. 3 pers. sing. masc.	כבד
יְכַבְּדוּךָ	Piel fut. 3 pers. pl. masc., suff. 2 pers. sing. m.	כבד
יְכַבְּדֻנְנִי	id. fut. 3 pers. sing. masc. with epenth. נ and suff. 1 pers. sing. (§ 16. rem. 13)	כבד
יִכְבֶּה	Kal fut. 3 pers. sing. masc.	כבה
יְכַבּוּ	Piel fut. 3 pers. pl. masc.; וַ conv.	כבה
יִכְבֹּשׁ	Kal fut. 3 pers. sing. masc. (§ 8. rem. 18)	כבש
וַ Kh. יַכְבִּשׁוּם Hiph., K. יִכְבְּשׁוּם Kal fut. 3 pers. pl. masc., suff. 3 pers. pl. masc.		כבש
יְכַבֶּנָּה	Piel fut. 3 p. s. m., suff. 3 p. s. fem. (§ 2. rem. 3)	כבה
יְכַבֵּס	Piel fut. 3 pers. sing. masc.	כבס
יְכַבְּסוּ	id. fut. 3 pers. pl. masc.; וַ conv.	כבס
יַכְבִּר	Hiph. fut. 3 pers. sing. masc. [for יַכְבִּיר]	כבר
יַכֶּהָ	וַ the following with suff. 3 pers. sing. fem. (§ 24. rem. 21); וַ conv.	נכה
יַכֶּה	וַיַּ Hiph. fut. 3 pers. sing. m. (§ 25, 2b); וַ id.	נכה
יִכְהֶה	Kal fut. 3 pers. sing. masc.	כהה
יַכֵּהוּ	וַ Hiph. fut. 3 pers. sing. masc., suff. 3 pers. sing. m. (§ 25. 2b, & § 24. rem. 21); וַ conv.	נכה
וַיַּכֵּהוּ	וַ id. fut. 3 p. pl. m. (יַכּוּ), suff. 3 p. s. m.; וַ id.	נכה
יְכַהֵן	וַ Piel fut. 3 pers. sing. m. (§ 14. rem. 1); וַ id.	כהן
יְכַהֲנוּ	וַ id. fut. 3 pers. pl. masc.; וַ id.	כהן
וַיַּכּוּ	וַ, וַיַּ Hiph. fut. 3 p. pl. m. (§ 25, 2b); וַ id.	נכה
יַכּוּ	וַ id. fut. 3 pers. sing. masc. (יַכָּה), suff. 3 pers. sing. masc. (§ 24. rem. 21); וַ id.	נכה
יֻכּוּ	וַ Hoph. fut. 3 pers. pl. m. (§ 25, 2b); וַ id.	נכה
יַכּוּהָ	וַ Hiph. fut. 3 pers. pl. masc., suff. 3 pers. sing. fem. (§ 25, 2b); וַ id.	נכה
יַכּוּךָ	id., suff. 2 pers. sing. masc.	נכה
יָכוֹל	Kal pret. 3 pers. sing. masc. (§ 8. rem. 1), or (Nu. 13. 30) inf. absolute	יכל
יֻכּוּם	וַ Hiph. fut. 3 pers. pl. masc., suff. 3 pers. pl. masc. (§ 25, 2b); וַ conv.	נכה
יִכּוֹן	וַ Niph. fut. 3 pers. sing. masc.	כון
יְכוֹנְיָה	Kh. יְכוֹנְיָה, for K. יָכְנְיָה q. v.	כון
יְכוֹנֵן	Pilel fut. 3 pers. sing. masc.	כון

a Eze. 31.7.   h Mal. 2.5.   p Ge. 15.4.   y 1 Ki. 19.5.   e 1 Sa. 4.17.   Is. 66.5.   2 Ch. 29.7.   Is. 42.4.   2 Sa. 14.6.
b Je. 10.4.   i Ex. 19.13.   q Ge. 15.4.   z Pr. 3.6.   Ho. 6.1.   Ex. 9.7.   Mi. 7.19.   Is. 61.10.   Ex. 5.14.
c Ge. 2.7.   k Is. 54.3.   r Ho. 9.6.   Pr. 15.21.   Ho. 14.6.   Ju. 9.9.   Je. 34.11.   1 Ch. 24.2.   2 Ch. 25.16.
d Ge. 9.24.   l De. 28.42.   s De. 2. 21, 22.   Nu. 23.27.   Job 14.22.   Ps. 86.9.   Is. 42.3.   Job 35.16.   Pr. 25.5.
e 1 Sa. 18.30.   m Nu 21.32.   Pr. 4.25.   2 Ch. 32.30.   Pr. 14.31.   Is. 25.3.   Job 5.18.   Mi. 4.14.   Is. 62.7.
f Ps. 72.14.   n De. 10.11.   Ge. 50.26.   2 Ki. 15.16.   Job 5.18.   Ps. 50.23.   Jos.10.28,39,32.   Jos. 7.3.
g Ge. 42.35.   o De. 2.12.   Ge. 24.33

יְכוֹנְנֶהָ   } id. suff. 3 pers. sing. fem. ;] conv. .   כון

יְכוֹנְנֵּי   } id., suff. 3 pers. sing. masc. [for יְכוֹנְנֵנּוּ § 21. rem. 21] ;] id.   כון

יִכּוֹנְנֵּי   } Hithpal. fut. 3 pers. pl. masc. [for יִתְכּוֹנְנוּ comp. § 12. rem. 3] .   כון

יְכוֹנְנֵּי   }] Pilel fut. 3 pers. pl. masc. ;] conv. .   כון

יְכוֹנְנֵנִי   }] id. with suff. 1 pers. sing. ;] id.   כון

יְכַזֵּב   } Piel fut. 3 pers. sing. masc., with conj.]
[וַיְ׳, וַיְכַזֵּב] . . . } כזב

יְכַזְּבוּ   } id. fut. 3 pers. pl. masc. .   כזב

יָכָזְבֵנִי   Hiph. fut. 3 pers. sing. masc., suff. 1 pers. sing. כזב

יָכַח   Hiph. הוֹכִיחַ—I. to show, prove.—II. to reprove, reproach, rebuke, convict, correct, with acc. לְ, אֶל of the person, and בְּ, עַל of the thing.—III. to punish, chasten.—IV. to decide, arbitrate, with בֵּין ; to appoint, destine, for any one, with לְ, Ge. 24. 14, 44. —V. to contend, plead, reason, Job 13. 3 ; 16. 21 ; 22. 4, with אֶל, לְ, acc.   Hoph. to be chastened, Job 33. 19.   Niph. נוֹכַח—I. to be convicted, Ge. 20. 16.—II. to contend, dispute.   Hithp. הִתְוַכַּח (§ 20. No. 1) to contend, Mi. 6. 2.

    תּוֹכֵחָה fem. pl. תּוֹכְחוֹת, punishment, chastisement. תּוֹכַחַת fem. with suff. תּוֹכַחְתִּי, pl. תּוֹכָחוֹת (§ 44. r. 5).—I. proof, argument.—II. reproof, admonition, correction.—III. punishment, chastisement.

יְכַחֵד   }] Hiph. fut. 3 pers. sing. masc. ap. [from יַכְחִיד] ;] conv. .   כחד

יִכָּחֵד   Niph. fut. 3 pers. sing. masc. .   כחד

יַכְחִדֶנָּה   Hiph. fut. 3 pers. s. m., suff. 3 pers. s. fem. כחד

יְכַחֵשׁ   Piel fut. 3 pers. sing. masc. (§ 14. rem. 1) before monos. [for יְכַחֵשׁ § 10. rem. 4] כחש

יְכַחֲשׁוּ   }] Niph. fut. 3 pers. pl. masc.   כחש

יְכַחֲשׁוּ   Piel fut. 3 pers. pl. masc. (§ 14. rem. 1) .   כחש

יוֹכִיחֲךָ   Hiph. fut. 3 pers. m. s. יוֹכִיחַ, suff. 2 p. m. s. יכח

יָכִיל   Hiph. fut. 3 pers. sing. masc.   כול

יִכְלְיָה   Kh., for יְכָלְיָה K. (q.v.)   יכל

יְכִילֶנּוּ   Hiph. fut. 3 p. s. m. (יָכִיל), suff. 3 p. s. m. (§ 2. r. 3) כול

יָכִין   ] pr. name of a man and a pillar .   כון

יָכִין   Hiph. fut. 3 pers. sing. masc. .   כון

יָכִין   Kh. id. ; K יָבִין Kal fut. 3 p. s. m. R. בִּין see   בון

יָכִינוּ   ] Hiph. fut. 3 pers. pl. masc. ;] conv. .   כון

יַכִּיר   Hiph. fut. 3 pers. sing. masc. .   נכר

יַכִּירָהּ   ] id. id., suff. 3 pers. sing. fem. ;] conv. .   נכר

יַכִּירוּם   id. fut. 3 pers. pl. masc., suff. 3 pers. pl. m.   נכר

יַכִּירֵנוּ   id. fut. 3 pers. sing. masc., suff. 1 pers. pl.   נכר

יַכִּירֶנּוּ   id. id., suff. 3 pers. sing. masc.   נכר

יַכֶּכָּה   } Hiph. fut. 3 p. s. m. (יַכֶּה § 25. r. 6), suff.
יַכְּכָה   } 2 p. s. m. [6., יַכְּךָ & וַיַּכֶּךָ § 2. r. 2, & § 24. r. 21] } נכה

יָכֹל   (§ 8. rem. 1) fem. יָכְלָה, 1 pers. יָכֹלְתִּי, with suff. יְכָלְתִּיו, inf. abs. יָכוֹל ; Hoph. fut. יוּכַל.— I. to be able to do any thing ; can, could ; or to be permitted to do it, may, might.—II. to be able to bear, to endure.—III. to prevail over, to overcome, with לְ. יְכִל ,יְכֵל Chald. fut. יִכֵּל (§ 52), Hoph. fut. יוּכַל.—I. to be able.—II. to prevail over, to overcome, with לְ, Da. 7. 21.

    יְהוּכַל ,יוּכַל (enabled, strong) pr. name masc. Je. 37. 3 ; 38. 1.

    יְכָלְיָהוּ ,יְכָלְיָה (the Lord has prevailed) pr. name of the mother of King Uzziah, 2 Ki. 15. 2 ; 2 Ch. 26. 3.

יָכֹל   Kal pret. 3 pers. sing. masc. (§ 8. rem. 1) ; or (1 Sa. 26. 25) inf. absolute . .   יכל

יָכֵל   Chald. Peal part. act. sing. m. (§ 47. rem. 1)   יכל

יֻכַל   ] Hoph. fut. 3 pers. sing. masc. [for יוּכַל comp. § 8. rem. 15] ;] conv. .   יכל

יְכַל   ] Piel fut. 3 pers. s. m., ap. from יְכַלֶּה ;] id.   כלה

יִכֶל   Kal fut. 3 pers. sing. masc., ap. from יִכְלֶה   כלה

יִכֻל   Chald. Peal fut. 3 pers. s. m. (§ 52. rem. 2)   יכל

יִכָּלֵא   ] Niph. fut. 3 pers. sing. masc. ;] conv.   כלא

יִכָּלְאוּ   ] id. fut. 3 pers. pl. masc. ;] id. .   כלא

יָכְלָה   Kal pret. 3 pers. sing. fem. .   יכל

יָכְלָה   ] Chald. Peal part. sing., fem. of יָכֵל (q. v.)   יכל

יְכַלֶּה   Piel fut. 3 pers. sing. masc. . .   כלה

יִכְלָא   Kal fut. 3 pers. s. m. [for יִכְלָא § 23 rem. 11]   כלא

יִכְלֶה   Kal fut. 3 pers. sing. masc. . .   כלה

יְכַלֶּהוּ   ] Piel fut. 3 pers. sing. masc., suff. 3 pers. sing. masc. ;] conv. } כלה

יְכַלֻּהוּ   ] id. fut. 3 pers. pl. masc. (יְכַלּוּ), suff. 3 pers. sing. masc. ;] id. } כלה

יִכְלוּ   ] Kal fut. 3 pers. pl. masc. .   יכל

יַכְלוּ   Hiph. fut. 3 pers. pl. masc. [for יַכְלִילוּ]   כול

יָכְלוּ   Kal pret. 3 pers. pl. for יָכְלוּ (§ 8. r. 1 & 7)   יכל

יְכַלּוּ   ] Piel fut. 3 pers. pl. masc. ;] conv. ;
    and with conj. [for וַיְכַלּוּ, וַיְ׳] } כלה

יְכֻלּוּ   ] Pual fut. 3 pers. pl. masc. ;] conv.   כלה

יֻכְלוּ   } Hoph. fut. 3 pers. pl. masc. (comp. § 8.
יֻכַלוּ   } rem. 15) . . . . } יכל

יִכְלוּ   וַיְ׳] Kal fut. 3 pers. pl. masc. ;] conv. .   כלה

---

a Ps. 7. 13.   e Ps. 119. 73.   i 2 Sa. 18. 13.   m Joel 2. 11.   q Is. 63. 16.   u Eze. 31. 15.   y Ge. 23. 6.   d Je. 10. 25.   g Eze. 43. 27.
b Job 31. 15.   f Nu. 23. 19.   k Job 20. 12.   n Is. 10. 18.   r Ho. 12. 5.   v Da. 7. 21.   z Pr. 22. 8.   e Je. 38. 22.   h Ge. 2. 1.
c Ps. 59. 5.   g Job 24. 25.   l Ho. 9. 2.   o Ge. 37. 33.   s Job 33. 21.   w Is. 10. 18.   a 1 Ki. 6. 9, 14.   f Job 36. 1.   i Je. 20. 11.
d Ps. 107. 36.   h 2 Ch. 32. 21   De. 33. 29.   p Is. 61. 9.   t Da. 3. 29.   x Job 22. 4.

יְכָלְיָה   } pr. name masc.   .   .   יכל
יְכָלְיָהוּ

יְכַלְיוּן Kal fut. 3 p. pl. m. with parag. ן (§ 24. r. 5)   כלה

יְכַלִּים Hiph. fut. 3 pers. sing. masc.   .   כלם

יָכְלִין Chald. Peal part. masc., pl. of יָכֵל (q. v.)   יכל

יְכַלְכֵּל וְ Pilpel (§ 6. No. 4) fut. 3 p. s. m.; ן conv.   כול

יְכַלְכְּלֶהוּ id. fut. 3 pers. pl. masc., suff. 3 pers. s. m.   כול

יְכַלְכְּלוּ id. id., suff. 2 pers. sing. masc.   .   כול

יְכַלְכְּלֶךָ id. fut. 3 pers. s. m. (כַּלְכֵּל), suff. 2 pers. s. m. [for יְכַלְכֵּלְךָ comp. § 16. r. 15, & § 2. r. 2]   כול

יְכַלְכְּלֻךָ id. id. fut. 3 pers. sing. masc., suff. 2 pers. sing. masc.   כול

יְכַלְכְּלֻם ן id. fut. 3 p. pl. m., suff. 3 pers. pl. m.; ן conv.   כול

יִכָּלְמוּ וְ Niph. fut. 3 pers. pl. masc.   כלם

יָכֹלְתָּ ן Kal pret. 2 pers. sing. masc., acc. shifted by ן conv. (for יָכֹלְתָּ § 8. rem. 1 & 7)   יכל

יְכֵלְתְּ Chald. Peal pret. 2 pers. s. m. (§ 47. r. 6 & 2)   יכל

יְכֹלֶת Kal inf. constr. (comp. § 8. r. 1, & § 20. r. 3)   יכל

יָכֹלְתִּי id. pret. 1 pers. sing.   יכל

יְכָלְתִּיו id. id. with suff. 3 pers. sing. masc.   .   יכל

וַיְכֵם Hiph. fut. 3 pers. sing. masc. (יַכֶּה § 25, 2 b), suff. 3 p. pl. m. (§ 24. r. 21); ן conv.   נכה

יָכֵן ן Hiph. fut. 3 pers. sing. masc. ap. and conv. from יָכִין   .   .   כון

יְכַנֶּה Piel fut. 3 pers. sing. masc.   .   כנה

יְכַנּוּ Hiph. fut. 3 pers. sing. masc. (יַכֶּה § 25, 2 b), suff. 3 p. s. m. (§ 24. r. 21, & § 2. r. 3)   נכה

יִכּוֹנוּ וְ ן Niph. fut. 3 pers. pl. masc.   כון

יְכָנְיָה } pr. name masc.   .   .   כון
יְכָנְיָהוּ

וַיְכַנְּעֵם Hiph. fut. 3 pers. sing. masc., suff. 3 pers. pl. masc.; ן conv.   כנע

יְכוֹנְנֶךָ ן Pilel fut. 3 pers. sing. masc. (יְכוֹנֵן), suff. 2 pers. s. m. [for יְכֹנְנֶךָ § 16. r. 15]; ן id.   כון

יְכַנֵּס Piel fut. 3 pers. sing. masc.   כנס

יַכְנִיעַ ן Hiph. fut. 3 p. s. m. ap. [from יַכְנִיעַ]; ן conv.   כנע

יִכָּנַע וַ Niph. fut. 3 pers. sing. masc.; ן id.   כנע

יִכָּנְעוּ ן id. fut. 3 pers. pl. masc. (§ 15. rem. 1)   כנע
יִכָּנֵעוּ ן id.   כנע

יִכָּנֵף Niph. fut. 3 pers. sing. masc.   כנף

יְכַס ן Piel fut. 3 pers. sing. masc., ap. and full form; ן conv.   כסה
יְכַסֶּה

יְכֻסֶּה Pual fut. 3 pers. sing. masc.   .   כסה

יְכַסֵּהוּ Piel fut. 3 p. s. m, suff. 3 p. s. m. (§ 24. r. 21)   כסה

יְכַסּוּהוּ ן id. fut. 3 pers. pl. masc., suff. 3 pers. s. m.   כסה

יְכַסּוּ וְ id. fut. 3 pers. pl. masc.; ן conv.   כסה

יְכֻסּוּ ן Pual fut. 3 pers. pl. masc.; ן id.   כסה

יְכַסּוּמוֹ Kh. יְכַסֻּמוֹ Piel fut. 3 pers. pl. m., K. 3 pers. s. m., suff. 3 pers. pl. (§ 24. r. 21b)   כסה

יִכְסוֹף Kal fut. 3 pers. sing. masc. (§ 8. rem. 18)   כסף

יְכַסּוּמוּ Piel fut. 3 pers. pl. masc. (§ 24. rem. 13), suff. 3 pers. pl. (§ 2. rem. 5)   כסה

יְכַסֵּךְ id. fut. 3 pers. sing. masc., suff. 2 pers. s. f.   כסה

יְכַסְּךָ id. id., suff. 2 pers. sing. masc. [for יְכַסְּךָ § 24. rem. 21, & § 2. rem. 2]   כסה

יִכְסְלוּ ן Kal fut. 3 pers. pl. m. [for יִכְסְלוּ § 8. r. 15]   כסל

יִכְסְמוּ id. id. fut. 3 pers. pl. masc.   כסם

יְכַסֶּנָּה Piel fut. 3 pers. sing. masc. (יְכַסֶּה), suff. 3 pers. sing. fem. (§ 24. r. 21, & § 2. r. 3)   כסה

יְכַסֶּנּוּ id. with suff. 3 pers. sing. masc.   .   כסה

יַכְעִיסֵהוּ defect. for יַכְעִיסוּהוּ (q. v.)   כעס

יַכְעִיסוּ ן Hiph. fut. 3 pers. pl. masc.; ן conv.   כעס

יַכְעִיסוּהוּ ן id., suff. 3 pers. sing. masc.; ן id.   כעס

יַכְעֵס ן id. fut. 3 pers. s. m. ap. [from יַכְעִיס]; ן id.   כעס

יַכְעַס ן Kal fut. 3 pers. s. m.; ן id.   .   כעס

יַכְעִיסוּ ן Hiph. fut. 3 pers. pl. m. (for יַכְעִיסוּ); ן id.   כעס

יִכְפֶּה Kal fut. 3 pers. sing. masc.   כפה

יְכַפֵּר ן Piel fut. 3 pers. sing. masc. (§ 10. rem. 4); ן conv.   } כפר
יְכַפֶּר־

יְכֻפַּר Pual fut. 3 pers. sing. masc.   כפר

יְכַפְּרֶנָּה Piel fut. 3 pers. sing. masc. (יְכַפֵּר), suff. 3 pers. sing. fem.   כפר

יַכֵּר ן Hiph. fut. 3 p. s. m., ap. from יַכִּיר; ן conv.   נכר

יִכָּרֶה Niph. fut. 3 pers. sing. masc.   כרה

וַיִּכְרֶה ן Kal fut. 3 pers. sing. masc.; ן conv.   כרה

יַכִּרֵהוּ ן Hiph. fut. 3 pers. sing. masc. (יַכִּיר), suff. 3 pers. sing. masc.; ן id.   נכר

וַיִּכְרוּ ן Kal fut. 3 pers. pl. masc.; ן id.   כרה

יַכְרִית Hiph. fut. 3 pers. sing. masc.   .   כרת

יַכִּרֵם ן Hiph. fut. 3 pers. sing. masc. (יַכִּיר), suff. 3 pers. pl. masc.; ן conv.   נכר

יְכַרְסְמֶנָּה Piel fut. 3 pers. sing. masc. [יְכַרְסֵם], suff. 3 pers. sing. fem. (§ 7)   כרסם

וַיִּכְרַע ן Kal fut. 3 pers. sing. masc.; ן conv.   כרע

וַיִּכְרְעוּ ן id. fut. 3 pers. pl. masc.; ן id.   כרע

יִכְרְעוּן id. id. with parag. ן   .   כרע

וַיַּכְרֵת ן Hiph. fut. 3 pers. sing. masc., ap. from יַכְרִית; ן conv.   .   כרת

יִכָּרֵת Niph. fut. 3 pers. sing. masc.   .   כרת

יִכְרֹת ן Kal fut. 3 pers. sing. masc. (§ 8. rem. 18); ן conv.   } כרת
יִכְרָת־

a Is. 31. 3.   g 1 Ki. 8. 27.   l Is. 49. 10.   r Le. 26. 41.   x Ge. 7. 19, 20.   c Je. 10. 8.   n Ps. 78. 58.   t Ex. 21. 33.   z Ge. 42. 7.
b Pr. 28. 7.   h 2 Sa. 30. 3.   m Is. 44. 5.   s 1 Ch. 20. 4.   d Eze. 44. 20.   o Ju. 2. 12.   u 2 Ki. 6. 23.   a Ps. 80. 14.
c Ge. 47. 13.   i Pr. 69. 7.   n Pr. 16. 3.   t De. 9. 3.   e Ps. 140. 10.   p Pr. 21. 14.   v 1 Ki. 18. 7.   b Ge. 7. 3.
d 2 Ch. 2. 5.   k Ex. 18. 23.   o Is. 30. 20.   u Rx. 15. 5.   f Ps. 17. 12.   q Pr. 16. 14.   w Job 40. 30.   c Job 31. 10.
e 2 Ch. 6. 18.   l Da. 2. 47.   p De. 32. 6.   v 1 Ki. 1. 1.   g Eze. 26. 10.   r Ps. 106. 29.   x Ge. 26. 35.   d Ps. 109. 15.
f Ps. 55. 23.   e Ps. 13. 5.   q Ps. 147. 2.   w Hab. 2. 14.   s Hab. 2. 17.   s Ps. 94. 13.

יִכְרְתֻהוּ ‹ 1 Kal fut. 3 pers. pl. masc. (יִכְרְתוּ), suff. 3 pers. sing. masc.; 1 conv.   .   כרת

יִכָּרְתוּ } Niph. fut. 3 pers. pl. masc. (comp. § 8. rem. 15)   .   .   .   כרת
יִכָּרֵתוּ }

יִכְרְתוּ } Kal fut. 3 pers. pl. masc. (§ 8. rem. 15); 1 conv.   וַיִּ‹   .   כרת
וַיִּכְרְתוּ }

יִכָּרֵתוּן Niph. fut. 3 pers. pl. masc. with parag. [for יִכָּרְתוּן comp. § 8. rem. 17]   .   כרת

יַכְשׁוֹלוּ ‹ Kh. יִכְשׁוֹלוּ Kal (§ 8. rem. 14) K. יַכְשִׁילוּ Hiph. fut. 3 pers. pl. masc.   .   כשל

יַכְשִׁלֵהוּ ‹ 1 Hiph. fut. 3 pers. pl. masc., suff. 3 pers. sing. masc.; 1 conv.   .   כשל

יַכְשִׁילְךָ ‹ id. fut. 3 pers. sing. masc., suff. 2 pers. sing. masc.   .   .   כשל

יִכָּשֵׁל Niph. fut. 3 pers. pl. masc. bef. monos. [for יִכָּשֵׁל § 9. rem. 3]   .   .   כשל

יִכָּשְׁלוּ } id. fut. 3 pers. pl. masc. (comp. § 8. rem. 15)   .   .   כשל
יִכָּשֵׁלוּ }

יִכָּשְׁלוּ ‹ Kh. יִכָּשֵׁלוּ q. v.; K. וְכָשְׁלוּ Kal pret. 3 pers. pl.   .   .   כשל

יַכְשִׁלוּם ‹ 1 Hiph. fut. 3 pers. pl. masc. [יַכְשִׁילוּ] suff. 3 pers. pl. masc.; 1 conv.   .   כשל

יִכְשַׁר Kal fut. 3 pers. sing. masc.   .   כשר

יֻכַּת ‹ Hoph. fut. 3 pers. sing masc. [for יוּכַת § 18. rem. 14]   .   .   כתת

יִכְתֹּב ‹ וַיִּ‹, וַיִּ‹ Niph. fut. 3 pers. sing. masc.; 1 conv.   כתב

יִכְתָּב־ } וַיִּ‹ Kal fut. 3 pers. sing. masc. (§ 8. rem. 18); 1 id.   .   כתב
יִכְתָּב־ }

יִכָּתֵבוּ Niph. fut. 3 pers. pl. masc. [for יִכָּתְבוּ comp. § 8. rem. 15]   .   .   כתב

יִכְתְּבוּ ‹ וַיִּ‹, וַיִּ‹ Kal fut. 3 pers. pl. masc.; 1 conv.   כתב

יִכְתְּבוּהָ ‹ 1 id. with suff. 3 pers. sing. fem.; 1 id. .   כתב

יִכְתְּבוּן ‹ 1 Niph. fut. 3 pers. pl. masc. with parag. 1   כתב

יִכְתְּבֵם ‹ וַיִּ‹ Kal fut. 3 pers. sing. masc. (יִכְתֹּב), suff. 3 pers. pl. masc.; 1 conv.   כתב

יַכְתֻּ ‹ 1 Hiph. fut. 3 pers. pl. masc., Chald. form (§ 18. rem. 14); 1 id.   .   כתת

יֻכַּתּוּ } Hoph. fut. 3 pers. pl. masc. (§ 18. rem. 14)   .   כתת
יֻכַּתּוּ }

יַכְּתוּם ‹ 1 Hiph. fut. 3 pers. pl. masc., suff. 3 pers. pl. masc. (§ 18. rem. 14); 1 conv.   כתת

יַכְתִּירוּ ‹ } 1 id. fut. 3 pers. pl. masc.   .   כתר
יַכְתִּרוּ ‹ }

יִלְאוּ ‹ 1 Kal fut. 3 pers. pl. masc.; 1 conv.   לאה

יַלְאֻךָ " ‹ 1 Hiph. fut. 3 pers. pl. masc., suff. 2 pers. sing. masc.; 1 id.   .   לאה

יִלְבַּב Niph. fut. 3 pers. sing. masc.   .   לבב

יִלָּבֵט Niph. fut. 3 pers. sing. masc.   .   לבט

יַלְבִּינוּ Hiph. fut. 3 pers. pl. masc.   .   .   לבן

יַּלְבֵּשׁ ‹ 1 id. fut. 3 pers. sing. m. ap. [from יַלְבִּישׁ]; 1 conv.   .   .   .   לבש

יַלְבִּשֵׁהוּ ‹ 1 id. fut. 3 pers. pl. masc., suff. 3 pers. sing. masc.; 1 id.   .   .   לבש

יִלְבַּשׁ } Kal (or Peal, Da. 5. 7, § 47. rem. 6) fut. 3 pers. sing. masc.; וַיִּ‹ id.   לבש
וַיִּלְבַּשׁ }

יִלְבְּשׁוּ ‹ } Kh. יִלְבַּשׁוּ q. v.; K. וְלָבְשׁוּ Kal pret. 3 pers. pl.   .   לבש

יִלְבְּשׁוּ } Kal fut. 3 pers. pl. masc. (§ 8. rem. 15); 1 conv.   .   לבש
וַיִּלְבְּשׁוּ }

יַלְבִּשֻׁם ‹ 1 Hiph. fut. 3 pers. pl. masc. [יַלְבִּישׁוּ], suff. 3 pers. pl. masc.; וַיִּ‹ id.   .   לבש

יַלְבִּשֵׁם ‹ 1 id. fut. 3 pers. sing. masc. [יַלְבִּישׁ], suff. 3 pers. pl. masc.; וַיִּ‹ id.   .   לבש

יַלְבִּשֵׁם‹ Kal fut. 3 pers. sing. masc. (יִלְבַּשׁ), suff. 3 pers. pl. masc. (§ 16. rem. 12)   .   לבש

יַלְבִּשֵׁנִי‹ 1 id. with suff. 1 pers. sing.; 1 conv.   .   לבש

יָלַד וְיֵ‹ fut. יֵלֵד, inf. c. לֶדֶת, לָת, לָדָה‹—I. to bear, bring forth.—II. to beget, as a father. Niph. נוֹלַד to be born. Pi. to help to bring forth, to deliver, Ex. 1. 16; part. מְיַלֶּדֶת midwife. Pu. יֻלַּד, יוּלַּד to be born; metaph. Ps. 90. 2. Hiph. הוֹלִיד.—I. to cause to bring forth.—II. to beget; metaph. Job 38. 28. Hoph. to be born, inf. יוֹם הֻלֶּדֶת the birthday of. Hithp. to declare or enrol one's genealogy or pedigree, Nu. 1. 18.

יֶלֶד (יַלְדֵּי‹.—) masc. dec. 6a (pl. c. יְלָדֵי once יַלְדֵּי‹—I. lad, youth, child.—II. the young of animals.

יַלְדָּה fem. dec. 12a, a girl, maiden.

יַלְדוּת fem. dec. 1b.—I. birth, Ps. 110. 3. Others youth, young men.—II. youth, childhood.

יָלוּד masc. dec. 1b.—I. adj. born.—II. subst. offspring, son.

יָלִיד masc. dec. 3a.—I. adj. born; יְלִיד בַּיִת one born in the house.—II. subst. son, child.

מוֹלִיד (genitor) pr. name masc. 1 Ch. 2. 29.

מוֹלָדָה (birth) pr. name of a town in the tribe of Judah, afterwards yielded to Simeon.

מוֹלֶדֶת (מוֹלַדְתִּי‹.—) fem. dec. 13a (with suff. מוֹלַדְתִּי).—I. birth, nativity.—II. birth-place.—III. offspring, progeny.—IV. family, relatives.

תּוֹלָד (family, race) pr. name of a town in the tribe of Simeon, 1 Ch. 4. 29; called אֶלְתּוֹלַד Jos. 15. 30; 19. 4.

a Eze. 31. 12.	e 2 Ch. 25. 8.	i Ec. 11. 6.	m Jos. 8. 32.	r Job 19. 23.	s Job 4. 20.	z Ps. 142. 3.	e Is. 1. 18.	f Ex. 29. 30.
b Zec. 13. 8.	f Eze. 33. 12.	k Is. 24. 12.	n Jos. 18. 4.	s Is. 10. 19.	w Ge. 19. 11.	d Zec. 3. 5.	g Job 29. 14.
c Pr. 4. 16.	g Na. 3. 3.	l Est. 1. 19.	o Ex. 32. 30.	t Job 11. 12.	x Pr. 14. 18.	e Eze. 42. 14.	h Ps. 7. 15.
d Ps. 64. 9.	h Je. 18. 15.		p Jos. 18. 9.	u De. 1. 44.	y Je. 12. 5.	z Jon. 3. 5.	m 2 Ch. 28. 15.

(תּוֹלֶדֶת or תּוֹלָדָה fem. pl. c. (from תּוֹלֵדוֹת.
—I. *birth,* Ex. 28. 10.—II. *generations, families.*
—III. *family history, origin.*

יָלַד Kal pret. 3 pers. s. m. for יָלַד (§ 8. rem. 7)

יָלַד Kh. for יָלַד q. v.; K. [וַיָּלַד for] noun
masc. sing.   וָלַד

יָלֹד ‖ Kal inf. absolute   ילד

יֵלֵד Kal fut. 3 pers. sing. masc., bef. monos. [for
יֵלַד § 20. rem. 4]   ילד

יֶלֶד ‖ n. masc. s. (pl. c. יַלְדֵי, once יְלָדֵי) d. 6a   ילד

יֹלֵד Kal part. act. sing. masc. dec. 7 b   ילד

יֻלַּד according to most copies, & :
יֻלַּד Pual pret. 3 pers. sing. masc.   ילד

יָלְדָה ‖ Kal pret. 3 pers. sing. fem. (§ 8.
וַיֵּלְדָה rem. 7)   ילד

יֻלְּדָה Pual pret. 3 pers. sing. fem.   ילד

יָלְדוּ ‖ Kal pret. 3 pers. pl. (§ 8. rem. 7)   ילד

יֵלְדוּ ‖ Kal fut. 3 pers. pl. masc. (comp. § 8.
rem. 15); וּ conv.   ילד

יְלִדוֹ Kh. for יְלִדָיו (q. v. § 4. rem. 1)   ילד

יְלָדוֹ Kal pret. 3 pers. sing. masc., suff. 3 pers.
sing. masc.   ילד

יֻלְּדוּ ‖ Pual pret. 3 pers. pl. (comp. § 8. rem. 7)   ילד

יֵלְדוּן Kal fut. 3 pers. pl. masc. with parag. ן [for
יֵלְדוּן comp. § 8. rem. 17]   ילד

יְלָדוֹת וְ noun fem., pl. abs. [with cop. וְ, for וְיַלְדוֹת,
וַיְ] from יַלְדָּה dec. 12a   ילד

יְלָדַי noun masc. pl., suff. 1 pers. sing. from יֶלֶד
(pl. c. יַלְדֵי & יְלָדֵי) dec. 6a   ילד

יְלִידֵי noun masc. pl. constr. from יָלִיד dec. 3a   ילד

יַלְדֵי ‖ noun masc. pl. constr. from יֶלֶד dec. 6a   ילד

יְלָדָיו ‖ id. pl., suff. 3 pers. sing. masc., with
וַיְ cop. וְ [for וַיְ וִילָדָיו   ילד

יַלְדֵיהֶם id. pl., suff. 3 pers. pl. masc.   ילד

יַלְדֵיהֶן וְ id. pl., suff. 3 pers. pl. fem.   ילד

יְלָדָיו id. pl., suff. 3 pers. sing. masc.   ילד

יֹלְדָיו Kal part. act. pl., suff. 3 pers. sing. masc.
from יֹלֵד dec. 7 b   ילד

יְלָדִים noun masc. pl. [with cop. וְ for וַיְ וִילָדִים]
from יֶלֶד dec. 6a   ילד

יְלָדְךָ Kal pret. 3 pers. sing. masc., suff. 2 pers.
יְלָדְךָ sing. masc.   ילד

יְלָדָנוּ id. pret. 1 pers. pl.   ילד

יְלָדְתְּ ‖ id. pret. 2 pers. sing. fem. (§ 8. rem. 7)
יְלָדְתְּ ‖   ילד

יֹלֶדֶת ‖ id. part. act. sing. fem. dec. 13a (§ 39.
יֹלֶדֶת ‖ No. 4. rem. 3)   ילד

יְלָדַתּוּ id. pret. 3 pers. sing. fem., suff. 3 pers.
sing. masc.   ילד

יְלִדְתִּי ‖ id. pret. 1 pers. sing. (§ 8. rem. 7)
יָלַדְתִּי ‖   ילד

יָלַדְתִּי Kh. יָלַדְתִּי & K. יָלַדְתְּ Kal pret. 2 pers. sing.
fem. (§ 8. rem. 5)   ילד

יֻלַּדְתִּי Pual pret. 1 pers. sing.   ילד

יְלִדְתִּיהוּ Kal pret. 1 pers. sing. with suff. 3 pers. sing.
masc. [for יְלִדְ § 8. rem. 1b]   ילד

יְלִדְתִּיךָ id. id. with suff. 2 pers. sing. masc. (v. id.)   ילד

יְלָדַתְךָ ‖ id. pret. 3 pers. s. fem., suff. 2 pers. sing. m.
יְלָדַתְךָ ‖   ילד

יַלְדֻתֶךָ noun fem. sing., suff. 2 pers. sing. masc. from
יַלְדוּת dec. 1b   ילד

יֻלַּדְתֶּם Pual pret. 2 pers. pl. masc.   ילד

יְלָדַתְנִי Kal pret. 3 pers. sing. fem., suff. 1 pers. sing.   ילד

יְלִדְתִּנִי id. pret. 2 pers. s. fem. (§ 8. rem. 1b, & § 16.
rem. 5) with suff., Kh. נְיִ, K. נוּ, 1 p.s. or pl.   ילד

יְלִדְתִּנִי id. pret. 2 pers. sing. fem. with suff. 1 pers. s.   ילד

יְלִיד id. part. p. sing. masc., constr. of יָלִיד dec. 3a   ילד

יֵלְוֶה Niph. fut. 3 pers. sing. masc.   לוה

יִלָּווּ ‖ id. fut. 3 pers. pl. masc.   לוה

יַלְוְךָ Hiph. fut. 3 pers. sing. masc. [יַלְוֶה], suff.
2 pers. sing. masc. (§ 24. rem. 21)   לוה

יָלוֹן וְ pr. name masc.   לון

יַלִּינוּ וְ Kh. יְלוֹנוּ Niph. fut. 3 pers. pl. masc.; K.
יָלִינוּ Hiph. &c. (§ 21. rem. 24)   לון

יַלְוֶנּוּ Kal fut. 3 pers. sing. masc. [יִלְוֶה], suff.
3 pers. sing. masc. (§ 24. rem. 21)   לוה

יָלוֹזוּ Kal fut. 3 pers. pl. masc.   לוז

יַלְחֲכוּ ‖ Piel fut. 3 pers. pl. masc. (§ 14. rem. 1,
יְלַחֲכוּ ‖ comp. § 8. rem. 15)   לחך

יִלָּחֵם ‖ Niph. fut. 3 pers. sing. masc. (§ 9.
וַיִּ ‖ rem. 3) ; ' conv.   לחם

יִלָּחֲמוּ ‖ id. fut. 3 pers. pl. masc.; וַיְ id.   לחם

יִלָּחֲמַנִי ‖ id. id., suff. 1 pers. sing.; וַיְ id.   לחם

a Je. 17. 11. | f Ex. 1. 19. | k Ho. 9. 16. | r Zec. 13, 3, 3. | u Ju. 13. 3. | x Je. 20. 14. | aa Ps. 110. 3. | ee Ge. 29. 34. | ff Ec. 8. 15.
b 2 Sa. 6. 23. | g Ge. 20. 17. | l Zec. 8. 5. | s Ezr. 10. 1. | v Ju. 13. 3. | y Nu. 11. 12. | bb Je. 22. 26. | ff Nu. 18. 3. | gg Pr. 3. 21.
c Job 15. 35. | h Is. 65. 23. | m Nu. 13. 28. | t De. 32. 18. | w Is. 7. 14. | z Ps. 2. 7. | cc Je. 20. 14. | hh De. 28. 44. | Ne. 4. 14.
d Pr. 27. 1. | i Job 38. 41. | n Ho. 1. 2. | p Pr. 23. 22. | Ru. 4. 15. | Ca. 8. 5. | dd Ex. 16. 2; | Ps. 109. 3.
Ge. 41. 50. | Job 38. 29. | o Job 21. 11. | q Is. 26. 18. | 1 Ki. 3. 21. | Je. 2. 27. | mm Is. 57. 4.
Ge. 24. 15. | Ps. 90. 2. | Ge. 33. 6. | 1 Sa. 4. 20. | Eze. 16. 20. | Je. 15. 10. | Nu. 14. 36.

יִלְחָצוּ Kal fut. 3 pers. pl. masc.; וְ conv. . . לחץ

יִלְחָצוּם id. id., suff. 3 pers. pl. masc. (§ 16. rem. 12); וְ conv. . . . . . . לחץ

יִלְחָצֵנִי id. fut. 3 pers. sing. masc. [יִלְחַץ], suff. 1 pers. sing. (§ 16. rem. 12) . . . . לחץ

וַיֶּלֶט וְ Hiph. fut. 3 pers. sing. masc. ap. and conv. [from יָלִיט . . . . לוט

יִלְטֹשׁ Kal fut. 3 pers. sing. masc. (§ 8. rem. 18) . לטש

יְלִיד noun m. sing., constr. of [יָלִיד dec.3a; ילד

יְלִיד with cop. וְ [for [וַיְ, וִילִיד ילד

יְלִידֵי id. pl., construct state . . . . . ילד

יַלִּזוּ Hiph. fut. 3 p.pl. m., Chald. form (§ 21. r. 24) לוז

יָלִין Kal fut. 3 pers. sing. masc., R. לִין see . לון

יָלִינוּ וַיְ id. fut. 3 pers. pl. masc.; וְ conv. . לון

יָלוֹנוּ וַיָּ Kh. יַלִּינוּ Hiph. (§ 21. rem. 24), K. לון
Niph. fut. 3 pers. pl. masc. . .

יָלִיץ Hiph. fut. 3 pers. sing. masc. . . לוץ

[יָלַךְ to go, only fut. יֵלֵךְ, inf. constr. לֶכֶת, the rest being supplied from הָלַךְ q. v. Hiph. הוֹלִיךְ, fut. יוֹלִיךְ, see under הָלַךְ.

לֶכָה (journey, for [יְלֵכָה) pr. name of a place in the tribe of Judah, 1 Ch. 4. 21.

יֵלֵךְ וַיֵּ, וְ
יֵלֵךְ
יֵלֶךְ Kal fut.3 pers.sing. m. (§ 20. rem. 4)
וַיֵּ

וַיֹּלֶךְ וְ Hiph. fut. 3 p. s. m., ap. with conv. וְ for
וַיּוֹלֶךְ יוֹלִיךְ (§ 20. rem. 4) from יוֹלִיךְ ילך

וַיִּלָּכֵד Niph. fut. 3 pers. sing. masc. (§ 9.
יִלָּכֵד rem. 3); וְ conv. . לכד

יִלְכֹּד וְ Kal fut. 3 pers. sing. masc. (§ 8. rem.
וַיִּלְכֹּד 18); וְ id. . . . לכד

יִלְכְּדָהּ וְ id. id., suff. 3 pers. sing. fem.; וְ id. . לכד

יִלְכְּדוּהָ וְ id. fut. 3 pers. pl. m., suff. 3 p. s. fem.; וְ id. לכד

יִלְכְּדֻהוּ וְ id. id., suff. 3 pers. sing. masc.; וְ id. . לכד

וְנִלְכְּדוּ Niph. fut. 3 pers. pl. masc. (comp.
וְ § 8. rem. 15); וְ id. . לכד

יִלְכְּדוּ Kal fut. 3 pers. pl. masc. (§ 8. rem.
וַיִּ 15); וְ id. . . . לכד

יִלְכְּדוּהָ וְ id., suff. 3 pers. sing. fem.; וְ id. . לכד

יִלָּכְדוּן Niph. fut. 3 pers. pl. masc. with parag. ן . לכד

יִלְכְּדֶנָּה Kal fut. 3 pers. sing. m., suff. 3 pers. sing. fem. לכד

יִלְכְּדֵנוּ id. id., suff. 3 pers. sing. masc. . . לכד

יִלְכְּדֵנוּ Kal fut. 3 pers. pl. masc. suff. 3 pers.
sing. masc. . . . . . . לכד

יֵלְכוּ וַיֵּ, וְ Kal fut. 3 pers. pl. masc. (comp.
יֵלֵכוּ וְ § 8. rem. 15); וְ conv. . . ילך

וַיֹּלִיכוּ וְ Hiph. fut. 3 p. pl. m. [for [יֹלִיכוּ] וְ id. ילך

יִלְכֹּד Kal fut. 3 pers. sing. masc. (§ 8. rem. 18) לכד

יֵלְכוּן id. fut. 3 pers. pl. masc.; ן parag. [for יֵלְכוּן comp. § 8. rem. 17] . . . . ילך

[יָלַל Hiph. הֵילִיל, fut. יֵילִיל, יְיֵלִיל (§ 20. rem. 15) to wail, howl, lament.

יְלֵל masc. a howling, De. 32. 10.

יְלָלָה fem. dec. 11c, a wailing, lamentation.

תוֹלֵל masc. he who causes to lament, an oppressor, Ps. 137. 3.

יְלֵל noun masc. sing. . . . . . ילל

יְלָלָה ו noun fem. s. [with cop. ו for [וִילָלָה] dec. 11 c ילל

יִלְלַת וְ id., construct state with cop. ו [for
יִלְלַת ו [וִילְלַת, וִילְלַת . . . . ללל

יִלְלָתָהּ id. with suff. 3 pers. sing. fem. . . ללל

יְלַמֵּד ו Piel fut. 3 pers. sing. masc. (§ 10. rem.4)
יְלַמֵּד וַיְ with conj. ו [for [וַיְ, וִילַמֵּד למד

וַיְלַמֵּד וַיְ Kal fut. 3 pers. sing. masc.; וְ conv. למד

יְלַמְּדָהּ ו Piel fut. 3 pers. sing. masc., suff. 3 pers.
sing. fem. with conj. ו [for [וַיְ, וִילַ למד

יְלַמְּדֵהוּ ו id. id., suff. 3 pers. sing. masc.; וְ conv. למד

יְלַמְּדוּ וַיְ Piel fut. 3 pers. pl. masc.; וְ id. . למד

יִלְמְדוּ וַיִּ Kal fut. 3 pers. pl. masc.; וְ id. . למד

יְלַמְּדוּן Piel fut. 3 pers. pl. masc. with parag. ן [for
§ 10. rem. 4, comp. § 8. rem. 17] . למד

יִלְמְדוּן Kal fut. 3 pers. pl. masc. with parag. ן . למד

יָלֶן ו Kal fut. 3 pers. sing. m. ap. from יָלִין R.
לִין, or Hiph. (Ex. 17. 3) R. . לון

יָלִינוּ ו Kal fut. 3 pers. pl. masc.; וְ conv., R. לִין see לון

יִלֹּנוּ ו Niph. fut. 3 pers. pl. masc.; וְ conv. . לון

[יָלַע cogn. לוּעַ to swallow, devour, Pr. 20. 25. Gesenius to speak rashly, to utter at random. Prof. Lee, to retain.

יַלְעֵג ו Hiph. fut. 3 p. s. m. ap. [from [יַלְעִיג; וְ conv. לעג

יִלְעַג Kal fut. 3 pers. sing. masc. (§ 8. rem. 15)
יִלְעַג לעג

יִלְעֲגוּ id. fut. 3 pers. pl. masc. . . . לעג

* Ju. 1. 34.   ᶠ Pr. 4. 21.   ᵏ Ju. 8. 14.   ᵖ 2 Ch. 32. 18.   ᵘ Pr. 5. 22.   ˣ Zec. 11. 3.   ᵇ Job 21. 22.   ᵍ Is. 40. 14, 14.   ᵐ Jos. 2. 1.
ᵇ Ps. 106. 43.   ᵍ Ex. 16. 2.   ˡ 2 Ch. 22. 4.   ᵍ Job 36. 8.   ᵛ 1 Ki. 1. 38.   ʸ Je. 25. 36.   ᶜ De. 17. 19.   ʰ 2 Ch. 17. 9, 9.   ⁿ Nu. 3. 33.
ᶜ Ps. 56. 2.   ᵍ Ex. 8. 9.   ᵐ Je. 3. 9.   ʳ Jos. 7. 14.   ʷ Is. 15. 5, 5.   ᶻ Ps. 25. 9.   ᵈ Eze. 19. 3, 6.   ᵏ Nu. 100. 35.   ᵒ Job 9. 23.
ᵈ 1 Ki. 19. 13.   ʰ Job 27. 21.   ⁿ Ps. 59. 13.   ˢ Jos. 7. 14.   ᵗ Ps. 25. 9.   ᵃ De. 31. 22.   ˡ De. 4. 19.   ᵖ Ps. 80. 7.
ᵉ Le 22. 11.   ⁱ Ec. 7. 26.   ᵒ Je. 5. 26.   ᵗ De. 32. 10.

יַלְעֵגוּ‏   } Hiph. fut. 3 pers. pl. masc. ; וֹ conv.   לעג
וְיַלְעִינוּ‏   }

יֶלֶף‏   Root not used ; Arab. *to stick fast.*   Hence

יַלֶּפֶת‏   fem. *scab, scurf,* Le. 21. 20 ; 22. 22.

וַיִּלָּפֵת‏   וֹ Niph. fut. 3 pers. sing. masc. ; וֹ conv.   לפת

יִלְפֹּת‏   וֹ Kal fut. 3 pers. sing. masc. ; וֹ id.   לפת

יִלָּפְתוּ‏   Niph. fut. 3 pers. pl. masc.   לפת

יֶלֶק‏   וֹ masc. a species of winged *locust.*

יִלֹּק‏   Kal fut. 3 pers. sing. masc.   לקק

וַיִּלֹּק‏   id. fut. 3 pers. pl. masc. ; וֹ conv.   לקק

יְלַקֵּט‏   וֹ Piel fut. 3 pers. sing. masc. ; וֹ id.   לקט

וַיְלַקְּטוּ‏   וֹ Kal fut. 3 pers. pl. masc. ; וֹ id.   לקט

יִלְקְטוּן‏   id. with parag. וֹ [for יִלְקְטוּ‏ § 8. rem. 17]   לקט

יְלַקֵּשׁוּ‏   Piel fut. 3 pers. pl. masc. [for יְלַקְּשׁוּ‏ comp. § 8. rem. 15]   לקש

יָם‏   וֹ masc. constr. יָם‏, יַם‏ dec. 8 a.—I. *a sea* ; also *a great river* ; הַיָּם הָאַחֲרוֹן‏, הַיָּם הַגָּדוֹל‏ (the great, the hinder sea) the Mediterranean. Hence —II. *the west* ; רוּחַ יָם‏ *the west wind* ; פְּאַת יָם‏ *the western quarter* ; יָמָּה‏ *westward.*

יַם‏ Chald. dec. 5 a, *a sea,* Da. 7. 2. 3.

יַם‏ id. construct state (only in יַם־סוּף‏)

[יַם‏] masc. only pl. יֵמִם‏ Ge. 36. 24, probably *hot springs* ; Vulg. aquæ calidæ.

יַמָּא‏ Chald. noun masc. sing., emph. of [יַם‏] d. 5 a   ים

יְמָאֵן‏ וֹ Piel fut. 3 pers. sing. masc. ; וֹ conv.   מאן

וַיְמָאֲנוּ‏ וֹ id. fut. 3 pers. pl. masc. ; וֹ id.   מאן

וַיִּמָּאֵס‏ וֹ Niph. fut. 3 pers. sing. masc. ; וֹ id.   מאס

יִמְאַס‏   } Kal fut. 3 pers. sing. masc. (§ 8. r. 15) ;
וַיִּמְאַס‏   } וֹ id.

יִמָּאֲסוּ‏ Niph. fut. 3 pers. pl. masc.   מסס

יִמְאֲסוּ‏ וֹ Kal fut. 3 pers. pl. masc. ; וֹ conv.   מאס

יִמְאָסוּן‏ id. id. with parag. וֹ [for יִמְאֲסוּ‏ § 8. r. 17]   מאס

יִמְאָסְךָ‏ וֹ id. fut. 3 pers. sing. masc., suff. 2 pers. sing. masc. (§ 16. rem. 12) ; וֹ conv.   מאס

יִמְאָסֵם‏ וֹ id. id., suff. 3 pers. pl. masc. ; וֹ id.   מאס

יְמַנַּר‏ Ch. Pael fut. 3 pers. sing. masc.   מנר

יָמַד‏ וֹ Kal fut. 3 pers. sing. masc., with conv. וֹ [for יָמֹד‏]   מדד

יִמַּד‏ Niph. fut. 3 pers. sing. masc.   מדד

יְמַדֵּד‏ וֹ Piel fut. 3 pers. sing. masc. ; וֹ conv.   מדד

יְמֹדֵד‏ וֹ Pil. (fr. מוד‏) or Poel fut. 3 p. s. m. ; וֹ id.   מדד

יְמָדְדֵם‏ וֹ Piel fut. 3 pers. sing. masc., suff. 3 pers. pl. masc. ; וֹ conv.   מדד

יָמֹדּוּ‏ וֹ Kal fut. 3 pers. pl. masc. ; וֹ id.   מדד

יִמַּדּוּ‏ Niph. fut. 3 pers. pl. masc.   מדד

יָמָּה‏ וֹ, וֹ noun masc. sing. (יָם‏) with loc. ה‏, for וֹ see lett. וֹ   ים

יַמָּה‏ id. with suff. 3 pers. sing. fem. dec. 8 a   ים

יְמַהֵר‏ וֹ Piel fut. 3 p. s. m. (§ 14. r. 1) ; וֹ conv.   מהר

וַיְמַהֲרוּ‏ וֹ id. fut. 3 pers. pl. masc. ; וֹ conv., with conj. וֹ for וַיְמַ'‏, וַיִּמַ'‏   מהר

יְמַהֲרֶנָּה‏ Kal fut. 3 pers. sing. masc. [יָמַהֵר‏], suff. 3 pers. sing. fem. (§ 16. rem. 12)   מהר

יְמוֹ‏ Kh. for יָמָיו‏ (q. v.)   יום

יְמוּאֵל‏ pr. name masc. Ge. 46. 10, and Ex. 6. 15; for which נְמוּאֵל‏ Nu. 26. 12.

יָמוּט‏ Niph. fut. 3 pers. sing. masc.   מוט

יָמוּטוּ‏ id. fut. 3 pers. pl. masc.   מוט

יָמוּךְ‏ Kal fut. 3 pers sing. masc.   מוך

יִמּוֹל‏ Niph. fut. 3 pers. sing. masc.   מול

יְמוֹלֵל‏ Pilel fut. 3 pers. sing. masc.   מול

יָמוּשׁ‏ Kal fut. 3 pers. sing. masc.   מוש

יָמוּשׁוּ‏ id. fut. 3 pers. pl. masc.   מוש

יָמוּת‏ Kal fut. 3 pers. sing. masc.   מות

יְמוֹת‏ n. com. pl. constr. [of יָמוֹת‏] fr. יוֹם‏ irr. (§ 45)   יום

יְמוּת‏ Kh. for יָמוּת‏ q. v. ; K. יוּמַת‏ Hoph. fut. 3 pers. sing. masc.   מות

וַיָּמֻתוּ‏ וֹ Kal fut. 3 pers. pl. masc. ; וֹ conv.   מות

יְמוּתוּן‏ id. with parag. וֹ   מות

יִמַּח‏ Niph. fut. 3 pers. sing. masc. [for יִמָּחֶה‏] ap. from יִמָּחֶה‏ (§ 24. rem. 10)   מחה

יִמַח‏ id., or, according to some copies, without dag. in מ‏, Kal fut. ap. from יִמְחֶה‏ (§ 24. r. 3)   מחה

יִמְחָא‏ Ch. Pael fut. 3 pers. s. m. (comp. § 14. r. 1)   מחא

יִמְחֲאוּ‏ Kal fut. 3 pers. pl. masc.   מחא

יִמָּחֶה‏ Niph. fut. 3 pers. sing. masc.   מחה

יִמְחֶה‏ Kal fut. 3 pers. sing. masc.   מחה

וַיִּמָּחוּ‏ וֹ Niph. fut. 3 pers. pl. masc.   מחה

יִמְחַץ‏   } Kal fut. 3 pers. sing. masc. (§ 8. r. 15)   מחץ
יִמְחָץ‏   }

יִמְטָא‏ Ch. Peal fut. 3 pers. sing. masc.   מטא

וַיַּמְטֵר‏ וֹ Hiph. fut. 3 pers. sing. masc. ap. [from יַמְטִיר‏] ; וֹ conv.   מטר

יְמֵי‏   } noun com. pl. (יָמִים‏), suff. 1 pers. sing. irr. of יוֹם‏ (§ 45)   יום
וּבִימֵי‏   }

וִימֵי‏   } id. pl., constr. state, with cop. וֹ   יום
[וִימֵי‏]   }

a Ne. 2. 19.   f Ps. 105. 34.   k Ps. 104. 28.   p Ps. 58. 8.   t 2 Sa. 3. 2.   x Je. 51. 36.   ‑ Ps. 90. 6.   ‑ Ge. 7. 23.   y Nu. 24. 8.
b Ps. 22. 8.   h Ju. 7. 5.   o Job 24. 6.   q Is. 31. 7.   u Job 3. 6.   l Na. 2. 6.   ‑ De. 32. 7.   ‑ Da. 4. 32.   ‑ Da. 4. 8, 17.
c Ru. 3. 3.   i 1 Ki. 21. 19.   n Da. 7. 3.   r Ex. 22. 16.   v 1 Sa. 15. 23, 26.   m Ex. 22. 15.   q Ki. 14. 6   ‑ 2 Ki. 21. 13.   ‑ Ps. 11. 6.
d Ju. 16. 29.   k 1 Ki. 22. 38.   o Ex. 22. 16.   s Ho. 9. 17.   w Ex. 16. 13.   n Je. 17. 11.   ‑ Is. 51. 6.   ‑ Ps. 69. 29.   ‑ Job 20. 23.
e Job 6. 13.   l Ex. 16. 5.   f Je. 36. 26.   t 1 Sa. 15. 25.   x Je. 31. 37.   o Le. 25. 35, 35, 39.   r Ps. 109. 13.   ‑ Ge. 7. 23.   ‑ Job 9. 25.
‑ Na. 3. 16.   m Ex. 16. 17, 31.   r Job 7. 5.   Ezr. 6. 12.   u Job 8. 20.   u Ps. 82. 5.

יָמֶיהָ	] id. pl., suff. 3 pers. sing fem.	יום
יָמֵיהֶם	id. pl., suff. 3 pers. pl. masc.	יום
יָמָיו	id. pl., suff. 3 pers. sing. masc.	יום
יָמִיטוּ	Hiph. fut. 3 pers. pl. masc.	מוט
יָמִיטוּ	Kh. יָמִיטוּ q. v.; K. יָמוֹטוּ (q. v.)	מוט
יָמַיִךְ	noun com. pl. (יָמִים), suff. 2 pers. sing. fem. irr. of יוֹם (§ 45)	יום
יָמֶיךָ	id. pl., suff. 2 pers. sing. masc.	יום
יְמֵיכֶם	id. pl., suff. 2 pers. pl. masc.	יום
יָמִים	] id. pl., absolute state	יום
יָמִים	noun masc., pl. absolute from יָם dec. 8 a	ים
יוֹמַיִם	noun com. du. (for יוֹמַיִם) fr. יוֹם (§ 45)	יום
יָמִימָה	id. pl. (יָמִים) with parag. ה	יום
יְמִימָה	(dove, coll. with the Arab.) pr. name of one of Job's daughters, Job 42. 14.	
יָמִין	] pr. name masc.	ימן
יָמִין	] noun masc. sing. dec. 3 a	ימן
יְמִין	id., constr. state	ימן
יְמִינָהּ	] id., suff. 3 pers. sing. fem. with cop. ו [for וַיְ, וַיְמִינָה	ימן
יָמִינוּ	noun com. pl. (יָמִים), suff. 1 pers. pl. irr. of יוֹם (§ 45)	יום
יְמִינוֹ	] noun m. s., suff. 3 pers. s. m. fr. יָמִין dec. 3 a; with cop. ו [for וַיְ, וַיְמִינוֹ	ימן
יְמִינִי	gent. noun from בִּנְיָמִין (q. v.)	בנה
יְמִינִי	] noun masc. s., suff. 1 pers. s. fr. יָמִין dec. 3 a, with cop. ו [for וַיְ, וַיְמִינִי	ימן
יְמִינְךָ	] id., suff. 2 pers. sing. mas.; with cop. ו [for וַיְ see preceding	ימן
יְמִינָם	] id., suff. 3 pers. pl. masc.; with cop. ו see preceding	ימן
יָמִיקוּ	Hiph. fut. 3 pers. pl. masc.	מוק
יָמִיר	Hiph. fut. 3 pers. sing. masc.	מור
יָמִירוּ	] id. fut. 3 pers. pl. masc.; ו conv.	מור
יְמִירֶנּוּ	id. fut. 3 pers. sing. masc., suff. 3 pers. sing. masc. (§ 2. rem. 3)	מור
יָמִישׁ	Hiph. fut. 3 pers. sing. masc.	מוש
יְמִישׁוּן	id. fut. 3 pers. pl. masc. with parag. ן	מוש
יָמִית	Hiph. fut. 3 pers. sing. masc.	מות
יְמִיתֵהוּ	] id. id., suff. 3 pers. sing. masc.; ו conv.	מות
יְמִיתֻהוּ	] id. fut. 3 p. pl. m, suff. 3 p. s. m.; ו id.	מות
יְמִיתוּ	] id. fut. 3 pers. pl. masc.; ו id.	מות
יְמִיתֶהָ	] id. id., suff. 3 pers. s. fem.; ו id.	מות
יְמִיתֻם	] id. fut. 3 p. s. m, suff. 3 p. pl. m.; ו id.	מות
יְמִיתֻנוּ	id. fut. 3 pers. pl. masc., suff. 1 pers. pl.	מות
יִמַּךְ	Niph. fut. 3 pers. sing. masc.	מכך
יִמְכּוּ	] Kal fut. 3 pers. pl. masc.; ו conv.	מכך

יִמָּכֵר	Niph. fut. 3 pers. sing. masc.	מכר
יִמְכֹּר	] Kal fut. 3 pers. sing. masc. (§ 8. r. 18) ו conv.	מכר
יִמְכָּרֵ־	{	מכר
יִמָּכְרוּ	Niph. fut. 3 pers. pl. masc.	מכר
יִמְכְּרוּ	] Kal fut. 3 pers. pl. masc.; ו conv.	מכר
יִמְכְּרֶם	] id. fut. 3 p. s. m., suff. 3 p. pl. m.; ו id.	מכר
יִמָּל	] Kal fut. 3 pers. sing. masc. ap. and conv. [from יָמֻל]	מול
יִמַּל	] Kal fut. 3 pers. sing. masc., Chald. form (§ 18. rem. 14); ו conv.	מלל
יִמָּלֵא	], וַ Niph. fut. 3 pers. sing. masc.; ו id.	מלא
יְמַלֵּא	] Piel fut. 3 pers. sing. masc.; ו conv.; with conj. ו [for וַיְ, וַיְמַלֵּא	מלא
יִמְלָא	pr. name masc.	מלא
יִמָּלְאוּ	], ו Niph. fut. 3 pers. pl. masc.	מלא
יְמַלְּאוּ	} Piel fut. 3 pers. pl. masc. (§ 10. rem. 7 comp. § 8. rem. 15); ו conv.	מלא
יִמְלְאוּ	] וַ Kal fut. 3 pers. sing. masc.; ו id.	מלא
יְמַלְאוּם	] Piel fut. 3 pers. pl. masc. (§ 10. rem. 7), suff. 3 pers. pl. masc. (ם for ן fem. § 2. rem. 5); ו id.	מלא
יִמָּלְאוּן	] Niph. fut. 3 pers. pl. masc.; ו parag.	מלא
יְמַלֵּה	Piel fut. 3 pers. sing. m. for יְמַלֵּא (§ 23. r. 10)	מלא
יִמְלָה	pr. name masc., see יִמְלָא	מלא
יִמְלוּ	Kal fut. 3 pers. pl. masc. [for יִמְלְלוּ § 18. rem. 14]	מלל
יִמֹּלוּ	] Niph. fut. 3 pers. pl. masc.; ו conv.	מול
יִמְלוֹךְ	Kal fut. 3 pers. sing. masc. (§ 8. rem. 18)	מלך
יִמָּלֵט	] וַ Niph. fut. 3 pers. sing. masc.; ו conv.	מלט
יְמַלֵּט	} Piel fut. 3 pers. sing. masc.; with conj. ו [for וַיְ, וַיְמַלֵּט	מלט
יְמַלְּטֶהָ	id. id. with suff. 3 pers. sing. masc.	מלט
יִמָּלְטוּ	} Niph. fut. 3 pers. pl. masc. (comp. § 8. rem. 15); ו conv.	מלט
יְמַלְּטוּ	] Piel fut. 3 pers. pl. masc.; ו id.	מלט
יְמַלִּיכֶהָ	] Hiph. fut. 3 pers. sing. masc., suff. 3 pers. sing. fem.; ו id.	מלך
יַמְלִיכֻהוּ	] id. fut. 3 p. pl. m., suff. 3 p. s. m.; ו id.	מלך
יַמְלִיכוּ	] id. fut. 3 pers. pl. masc.; ו id.	מלך
יַמְלֵךְ	] id. future, 3 pers. sing. masc., ap. [from יַמְלִיךְ], also pr. name	מלך
יִמָּלֵךְ	] Niph. fut. 3 pers. sing. masc.; ו conv.	מלך
יִמְלֹךְ	] וַיִ Kal fut. 3 pers. sing. masc. (§ 8. rem. 18); ו id.	מלך
יִמְלָךְ־	}	מלך

a Ge. 25. 24.   f 2 Ch. 15. 3.   k Ps. 18. 36.   t Le. 27. 33.   p Ec. 10. 18.   u Job 14. 2.   aa Ge. 26. 15;   ff Ps. 107. 20.   r Est. 2. 17.
b Is. 13. 22.   g Nu. 9. 22.   l Ps. 74. 11.   m Ps. 115. 7.   q Le. 25. 15.   v Job 18. 16.   1 Sa. 18. 27.   gg Ps. 41. 2.   z 2 Ch. 30. 1.
c Ps. 55. 4.   h Ju. 7. 20.   n Ps. 89. 13.   o 2 Ki. 21. 23.   r Le. 25. 42.   w Ese. 32. 6.   bb Mal. 3. 15.   y Ne. 5. 7.
d Ps. 140. 11.   i Ju. 5. 26.   o Ps. 73. 8.   s 2 Ch. 23. 15.   Eze. 48. 14.   f Fr. 3. 10.   cc Job 8. 21.   p Da. 11. 41.   hh Is. 32. 1.
Eze. 22. 4.   k Is. 48. 13.   Ps. 106. 20.   2 Ki. 7. 4.   t Ge. 37. 28.   ee Eze. 7. 19.   Ge. 34. 24.   q 2 Ki. 23. 12.   ii Ps. 106. 43.

מלך   וַ יַמְלִכֵהוּ Hiph. fut. 3 pers. sing. masc., suff. 3 pers. sing. masc.; וַ conv.

מלך   יַמְלִכוּ defect. for יַמְלִיכוּ (q. v.).

מלך   יַמְלְכוּ Kal fut. 3 pers. pl. masc. (§ 8. rem. 15); וַ conv.

וַיַּמְלִכוּ וַ conv.

מלל   יְמַלֵּל Piel fut. 3 pers. sing. masc.

מלל   יְמַלֵּל Ch. Pael fut. 3 pers. sing. masc. (§ 47. r. 1 c)

ימן. יָמִין Hiph.—I. *to take the right hand, turn to the right hand.*—II. *to use the right hand,* 1 Ch. 12. 2.

יָמִין masc. dec. 3 a.—I. *the right;* יַד יְמִינוֹ *the hand of his right side, i. e. his right hand;* and also יַד omitted, *the right hand* (fem. gen.); יָמִין פ׳, עַל יָמִין, עַל מִימִין *on the right, at the right;* מִימִין פ׳, לִימִין or אֶל־יָמִין פ׳, עַל *on the right hand, right side of any one;* עַל or אֶל־הַיָּמִין and simply הַיָּמִין *towards the right.*—II. *the south;* מִיָּמִין *on the south of.*—III. pr. name masc. of several persons, especially of a son of Simeon, Ge. 46. 10. Patronym. יְמִינִי Nu. 26. 12.

יְמִינִי.—I. adj. *right, dexter,* only in Kheth. 2 Ch. 3. 17; Eze. 4. 6.—II. gent. noun for בֶּן יְמִינִי *Benjamite* from בִּנְיָמִין, see R. בֵּן.

יִמְנָה (*felicity;* coll. with the Arab.) pr. name of several persons, especially of a son of Asher, Ge. 46. 17.

יְמָנִי, fem. יְמָנִית adj. *right, dexter.*

תֵּימָן masc.—I. *the south;* תֵּימָנָה *towards the south.* Ellipt. (for רוּחַ הַתֵּימָן) *the south wind.*—II. pr. name of a grandson of Esau, and of a city and region in Idumea called *Teman* after him. Patronym. תֵּימָנִי.

תֵּימֵנִי pr. name masc. 1 Ch. 4. 6.

מנה   יָמֶן וַ Piel fut. 3 p. s. m., ap. [from וַיְמַנֶּה]; וַ conv.

מנה   יִמָּנֶה Niph. fut. 3 pers. sing. masc.

מנה   יִמְנָה pr. name masc.

מנה   יִמְנוּ וַ Kal fut. 3 pers. pl. masc.; וַ conv.

מנה   יִמָּנוּ Niph. fut. 3 pers. pl. masc.

מנע   יִמָּנַע וַ Niph. fut. 3 pers. sing. masc.

מנע   יִמְנַע וַ pr. name masc.

מנע   יִמְנַע Kal fut. 3 pers. sing. masc.

מנע   יִמָּנְעוּ וַ Niph. fut. 3 pers. pl. masc.; וַ conv.

מנע   יִמְנָעֶנָּ Kal fut. 3 pers. sing. masc. (יִמְנַע), suff. 3 pers. sing. fem. (§ 16. rem. 12)

מנע   יִמְנָעֵנִי id. with suff. 1 pers. sing.

מסס   יָמֵס, וַיִּמַּס Niph. fut. 3 pers. sing. masc. (comp. § 8. rem. 15); וַ conv.

מסס   יִמַּסּוּ id. fut. 3 pers. pl. masc.; וַ conv.

מסה   יָמֵסְם וַ Hiph. fut. 3 pers. sing. masc. [יָמֵסָה], suff. 3 pers. pl. masc. (§ 24. rem. 21)

מסר   יִמָּסְרוּ וַ Niph. fut. 3 pers. pl. masc.; וַ conv.

מעט   יִמְעַט Kal fut. 3 pers. sing. masc. (§ 8. rem. 15)

מעט   יִמְעֲטוּ Kal fut. 3 pers. pl. masc.; וַ conv. (v.), יִמְעָטוּ id.)

מעט   יַמְעִיט Hiph. fut. 3 pers. sing. masc.

מעל   וַיִּמְעַל Kal fut. 3 pers. sing. masc.; וַ conv.

מעל   יִמְעֲלוּ id. fut. 3 pers. pl. masc.; וַ id.

מצה   יֵמַר וַ Kal fut. 3 pers. sing. masc. ap. [from יִמְצֶה]; וַ id.

מצא   וַיִּמָּצֵא Niph. fut. 3 pers. sing. masc.; וַ id.

מצא   וַיִּמְצָא Kal fut. 3 pers. sing. masc.; וַ id.

מצא   יִמְצָאָה id. with suff. 3 pers. sing. fem.; וַ id.

מצא   יִמְצָאֵהוּ Hiph. fut. 3 pers. sing. masc., suff. 3 pers. sing. masc.

מצא   וַיִּמְצָאֵהוּ Kal fut. 3 pers. sing. masc., suff. 3 pers. sing. masc.; וַ conv.

מצא   וַיִּמְצָאֻהוּ id. fut. 3 p. pl. m., suff. 3 p. s. m.; וַ id.

מצא   יִמְצְאוּ וַ Hiph. fut. 3 pers. pl. masc.; וַ id.

מצא   יִמָּצְאוּ וַ Niph. fut. 3 pers. pl. masc.; וַ id.

מצא   יִמְצְאוּ, וַ Kal fut. 3 pers. pl. masc. (§ 8. rem. 15); וַ id.

מצא   יִמְצָאוּן Niph. fut. 3 pers. pl. masc. with parag. ן

מצא   יִמְצָאֻנְךָ Kal fut. 3 pers. pl. masc. with parag. נ & suff. 3 pers. sing. fem. (§ 16. rem. 14)

מצא   יִמְצָאֲךָ id. fut. 3 pers. sing. masc., suff. 2 pers. s. m.

מצא   יִמְצָאֲכָה id., suff. 2 pers. sing. masc. (§ 2. rem. 2)

מצא   יִמְצָאֵם וַ id. fut. 3 pers. sing. masc.; וַ conv.

מצא   יִמְצָאֵנּוּ Hiph. fut. 3 pers. sing. masc., suff. 3 pers. sing. masc. (§ 2. rem. 3)

מצא   יִמְצָאֵנּוּ Kal fut. 3 pers. sing. masc., suff. 3 pers. sing. masc. (§ 2. rem. 3)

מצא   יִמְצָאֻנִּי id. fut. 3 pers. pl. masc. with parag. נ & suff. 1 pers. sing. (§ 16. rem. 14)

מצה   יִמָּצֶה Niph. fut. 3 pers. sing. masc.

מצה   יִמְצֶה id. fut. 3 pers. sing. masc.

מצה   יִמְצוּ Kal fut. 3 pers. pl. masc.

מקק   יִמַּקּוּ, יִמַּקּוּ Niph. fut. 3 pers. pl. masc. (comp. § 8. rem. 15)

ימר. יֵמֶר Hiph. הֵמִיר *to change, exchange,* Je. 2. 11. Hithp. הִתְיַמֵּר *to change places* with any one, *to take his place* in anything, Is. 61. 6. Others, *to exercise dominion.* According to the Vulg., Chald. & Syr. *to boast oneself,* as if for הִתְאַמֵּר.

a 2 Sa. 2. 9.   b Pr. 8. 15.   c 1 Ki. 11. 24.   d Ps 106. 2.   e Da. 7. 25.   f Ge. 13. 16.   g 2 Ki. 12. 11.   h 2 Ch. 5. 6.   i Job 38. 15.   k Ps. 84. 12.   l Je. 3. 3.   m Job 20. 13.   n 2 Sa. 13. 13.   o Ju. 15. 14.   p Ps. 107. 39.   q Nu. 31. 5.   r Pr. 13. 11.   s Ps. 84. 12.   t Pr. 16. 10.   u 2 Ch. 26. 16.   v Ju. 6. 38.   w Job 37. 13.   x De. 32. 10.   y Job 20. 8.   z Le. 9. 12, 18.   a 1 Sa. 25. 8.   b Ge. 18. 29, 32.   c Je. 2. 24.   d Le. 5. 9.   e 1 Ki. 18. 12.   f 1 Ki. 18. 10.   g Job 34. 11.   h Le. 22. 9.   i Ps. 73. 10.   k Ps. 75. 9.   l Le. 26. 39.   m Le. 26. 39.

יָמֵר^a } Hiph. fut. 3 pers. sing. masc., ap. & | מור
יָמִר } defect. for יָמִיר . . . . .

יִמֹר Kal fut. 3 pers. sing. masc. (§ 18. rem 5) . מרר
וַיִּמְרֹד } Kal fut. 3 pers. sing. masc. (§ 8. ren.. | מרד
וַיִּמְרֹד } 18) ; וַ conv. . . . .
יִמְרְדוּ^b id. fut. 3 pers. pl. masc. ; וַ id. . מרד
יַמְרֶה Hiph. fut. 3 pers. sing. masc. . . מרה
יִמְרֶה וַ pr. name masc. . . . . מרה
יַמְרוּ^c וַ Hiph. fut. 3 p. pl. masc. . . מרה
יַמְרוּהָ^d id. id., suff. 3 pers. sing. masc. . . מרה
יִמְרוּךָ^e Kal fut. 3 pers. pl. masc., suff. 2 pers. sing. masc. [for יֹאמְרוּךָ § 19. rem. 5] . . אמר
יִמְרְחוּ^f וַ Kal fut. 3 pers. pl. masc. ; וַ conv. . מרח
יִמָּרֵט^g Niph. fut. 3 pers. sing. masc. . . מרט
יַמְרִיצֵךָ^h Hiph. fut. 3 pers. sing. masc. with suff. 2 pers. sing. masc. . . . . . מרץ
יְמָרְרֻהוּⁱ וַ Piel fut. 3 pers. pl. masc., suff. 3 pers. sing. masc. ; וַ conv. . . . . מרר
יִמְרְרוּ^k וַ id. fut. 3 pers. pl. masc. ; וַ id. . מרר

יָמֵשׁ Kal not used ; i. q. מָשַׁשׁ. Hiph. הֵימִישׁ to let feel, grope, Ju. 16. 26 Kheth.

יָמֵשׁ^l וַ Hiph. fut. 3 pers. sing. masc. . משׁשׁ
יְמֻשֵׁהוּ^m וַ Kal fut. 3 pers. sing. masc. [יָמֻשׁ], suff. 3 pers. sing. masc. ; וַ conv. . משׁשׁ
יְמֻשֵׁנִי defect. for יְמוּשֵׁנִי (q. v.) . . מושׁ
יִמְשֹׁךְⁿ Kal fut. 3 pers. sing. masc. (§ 8. rem. 18) משׁך
יִמְשֹׁל^o Kal fut. 3 pers. sing. masc. (§ 8. rem. 18) משׁל
וַיִּמְשַׁח^p וַיַּ Kal fut. 3 pers. sing. masc. ; וַ conv. משׁח
יִמְשָׁחֵהוּ וַ the foll. with suff. 3 pers. sing. masc. ; וַ id. . . . . משׁח
יִמְשְׁחוּ^q } Kal fut. 3 pers. pl. masc. (§ 8. rem. 15) ; | משׁח
יִמְשְׁחוּ } וַ id.
יִמְשָׁחֲךָ^r וַ id. fut. 3 pers. sing. masc., suff. 2 pers. sing. masc. (§ 16. rem. 12) ; וַ id. . משׁח
יִמְשְׁחֵם^s וַ id. id., suff. 3 pers. pl. masc. ; וַ id. . משׁח
יִמְשְׁכוּ^t וַ Kal fut. 3 pers. sing. masc. ; וַ id. . משׁך
יִמָּשְׁכוּ^u Niph. fut. 3 p. pl. m. [for יִמָּשְׁכוּ comp. § 8. r. 15] משׁך
יִמְשְׁכוּ^x וַ Kal fut. 3 pers. pl. masc. ; וַ conv. משׁך
יִמְשֹׁל } Kal fut. 3 pers. sing. masc. (§ 8. rem. 18) | משׁל
יִמְשָׁל }
יִמְשְׁלוּ^y } id. fut. 3 pers. pl. masc. (§ 8. rem. 15) ; | משׁל
וַיִּ } וַ conv.
יַמְשֵׁנִי Hiph. fut. 3 pers. sing. masc. [יַמְשֶׁה], suff. 1 pers. sing. (§ 24. rem. 21) . . משׁה
יְמֻשֵּׁנִי^z Kal fut. 3 pers. s. m. [יָמֻשׁ], suff. 1 pers. s. משׁשׁ

יְמַשֵּׁשׁ וַיְ Piel fut. 3 pers. sing. masc. ; וַ conv. . משׁשׁ
יְמַשְׁשׁוּ id. fut. 3 pers. pl. masc. . . . משׁשׁ
יָמֵת וַ Hiph. fut. 3 pers. sing. masc. ap. and conv. from יָמִית . . . מות
יָמֹת^a וַיָּ, וַיְ } Kal fut. 3 pers. sing. masc., ap. and | מות
יָמֵת } conv. from יָמוּת (§ 21. rem. 8.)
יְמִתֵהוּ^b וַ Hiph. fut. 3 pers. sing. masc. (יָמִית), suff. 3 pers. sing. masc. ; וַ conv. . . . מות
יְמִתֻהוּ^c וַ id. fut. 3 p. pl. (יָמִיתוּ), suff. 3 p. s. m. ; וַ id. . מות
וַיָּמֻתוּ^d וַיָּ Kal fut. 3 pers. pl. masc. for יָמוּתוּ ; וַ id. . מות
יְמֻתוּן id. with paragogic וַ . . . . מות
יְמִיתֵהֶם^e וַ Kal fut. 3 pers. sing. masc. [יָמֵת], suff. 3 pers. pl. masc. (§ 16. rem. 12) ; וַ conv. . מות
יְמִיתֵם^m וַ Hiph. fut. 3 pers. sing. masc. (יָמִית), suff. 3 pers. pl. masc. ; וַ id . מות
יְמִיתֵנִי^f id. with suff. 3 pers. sing. m. (§ 2. rem. 3) מות
יְמִתְּקוּ^g } Kal fut. 3 pers. pl. masc. (§ 8. rem. 15); | מתק
וַיִ } וַ conv.
יְמֹתְתֻהוּ^h וַ Pilel fut. 3 pers. sing. masc. [יְמֹתֵת], suff. 3 pers. sing. masc. ; וַ id. . . מות
יִנָּאֲמוּⁱ וַ Kal fut. 3 pers. pl. masc. ; וַ id. . נאם
יִנְאַף^k Kal fut. 3 pers. sing. masc. . . נאף
יִנְאַפוּ^l וַ id. fut. 3 pers. sing. masc. [for יִנְאֲפוּ § 8. rem. 15] ; וַ conv. . . נאף
יְנָאֲפוּ^m וַ Piel fut. 3 pers. pl. m. (§ 14. rem. 1) ; וַ id. נאף
יִנְאֵץ וַ Hiph. fut. 3 pers. sing. masc. by Syriasm [for יִנְאֵץ, comp. בָּאֵר for בָּאַר מְלָאכָה, מַלְאָכָה for מְלָאכָה] . . . נאץ
יְנָאֵץ Piel fut. 3 pers. sing. masc. . . נאץ
יִנְאַץⁿ וַ } Kal fut. 3 pers. sing. masc. (§ 8. rem. | נאץ
וַיִּנְאַץ^o } 15) ; וַ conv. . . . . .
יִנְאָצוּן id. fut. 3 pers. pl. masc. with paragogic וַ [for יִנְאָצוּן § 8. rem. 17] . . . נאץ
יְנַאֲצֵנִי^p Piel fut. 3 p. pl. m., suff. 1 p. s. (§ 14. r. 1) נאץ
יִנְאֲקוּ Kal fut. 3 pers. pl. m. [for יִנְאֲקוּ § 8. r. 15] נאק
יִנָּבֵא וַיִּ Niph. fut. 3 pers. sing. masc. ; וַ conv. נבא
יִנָּבְאוּ^q וַ id. fut. 3 pers. pl. masc. ; וַ id. . נבא
יְנַבֵּל^r וַ Piel fut. 3 pers. sing. masc. ; וַ id. . נבל
יְנַבַּח id. fut. 3 pers. sing. masc. . . . נבח
יִנַּע וַ id. fut. 3 pers. sing. masc. ; וַ conv. . נוע
יִנָּעֲעוּ^s וַ Niph. fut. 3 pers. pl. masc. ; וַ id. . נוע
יְנֻעֲעוּ^t Pual fut. 3 pers. pl. m. [for יְנֹעֲעוּ § 8. r. 15] נוע
יִנָּגֵף^u } Niph. fut. 3 pers. sing. masc. (§ 9. | נגף
יִנָּגֵף } rem. 3) ; וַ conv. . . .
יִנָּגְפוּ^x } id. fut. 3 pers. pl. masc. (comp. § 8. | נגף
יִנָּגְפוּ } rem. 15) ; וַ id. . .

a Eze. 48. 14. b Ps. 139. 20. c Ge. 27. 22. d Nu. 7. 1. e Ge. 31. 34. f Nu. 35. 19. g Je. 5. 7. h La. 2. 6. i De. 32. 15.
k Ps. 15. 4. l Is. 38. 21. m Je. 31. 36. n Ju. 20. 37. o De. 33. 6. p Pr. 9. 17. q Je. 29. 23. r Je. 33. 24. s De. 33. 17.
t Is. 24. 9. u Is. 13. 40, 41. x Job 21. 33. y Is. 13. 22. z Ju. 6. 30. 1 Ki. 21. 10. a Ex. 15. 25. b Ec. 12. 5. c Nu. 14. 11. d Jos. 8. 15.
e Ne. 9. 26. f Job 16. 3. g Pr. 22. 7. h De. 15. 6. i Ge. 5. 5. k 1 Sa. 17. 51. l Ps. 74. 10. m Job 24. 12. n Ps. 73. 5.
o Jos. 1. 18. p Ge. 49. 23. q Le. 16. 32. r Nu. 16. 29. s 1 Sa. 31. 6. t Je. 23. 31. u De. 32. 19. x Je. 26. 20. y 2 Ch 6 24.
z Ps. 106. 43. a Ex. 1. 14. b Am. 6. 6. c Ge. 27. 12. d Is. 40. 22. e Le. 20. 10, 10. f Pr. 15. 12. g Je. 28. 8. h 2 Ch. 40. 21.
x Ps. 78. 40. k Ex. 10. 21. l 1 Sa. 15. 17. m Je. 52. 27.

יַנְדְּרֻהוּ‌ — Hiph. fut. 3 p. pl. m. [וַיָּדֻ], suff. 3 p. s. m.   נדד

יִנְדְּרוּ‌ — וַ Kal fut. 3 pers. pl. masc.; וַ conv.   נוד

יִנְדְּעוּן — Chald. Peal fut. 3 pers. pl. masc. [for יִדְעוּן § 52. rem. 2]   ידע

[יָנָה] — fut. יִנֶה (§ 25. No. 2e) to oppress, vex. Hiph. id.; with מִן to dispossess, drive out.

יְנַהֵג‌ — וַ Piel fut. 3 pers. sing. masc. (§ 14. r. 1); וַ conv.   נהג

יִנְהַג‌ / וַיִ — Kal fut. 3 pers. sing. masc. (§ 8. rem. 15); וַ id.   נהג

יְנַהֲגֵהוּ‌ — וַ Piel fut. 3 pers. sing. masc. (§ 14. rem. 1) with suff. 3 pers. sing. masc.; וַ id.   נהג

יִנְהֲגוּ‌ / וַיִ‌, וְ — Kal fut. 3 pers. pl. masc. (§ 8. rem. 15); וַ id.   נהג

יְנַהֶגְךָ‌ — Piel fut. 3 pers. sing. masc. (§ 14. rem. 1), suff. 2 pers. sing. masc.   נהג

יְנַהֲגֵם‌ — וַ id., suff. 3 pers. sing. masc.; וַ conv.   נהג

יְנַהֲגֵנוּ‌ — id., suff. 1 pers. pl.   נהג

יִנָּהֵ‌ — וַ Niph. fut. 3 pers. pl. masc.; וְ conv.   נהה

יְנַהֵל‌ — Piel fut. 3 pers. sing. masc. (§ 14. rem. 1)   נהל

יְנַהֲלֵם‌ — וַ id. fut. 3 pers. pl. masc., suff. 3 pers. pl. masc.; וַ conv.   נהל

יְנַהֲלֵם‌ — וַ id. fut. 3 pers. s. m., suff. 3 p. pl. m.; וַ id.   נהל

יְנַהֲלֵנִי‌ — id. id., suff. 1 pers. sing.   נהל

יְנַהֵם‌ — וַ Kal fut. 3 pers. sing. masc.   נהם

יִנְהֲקוּ‌ — Kal fut. 3 pers. pl. m. [for יִנְהֲקוּ § 8. r. 15]   נהק

יִנְהֲרוּ‌ — Kal fut. 3 pers. pl. masc.   נהר

יָנוּב‌ — Kal fut. 3 pers. sing. masc.   נוב

יְנוֹבֵב‌ — Pilel fut. 3 pers. sing. masc.   נוב

יְנוֹבוּן‌ — Kal fut. 3 pers. pl. masc. with paragogic ן   נוב

יָנוּד‌ — Kal fut. 3 pers. sing. masc.   נוד

יָנוּחַ‌ — Kal fut. 3 pers. sing. masc.   נוח

יָנוֹחַ‌ — pr. name of a place   נוח

יָנוּחַ‌ — Kal fut. 3 pers. sing. masc.   נוח

יָנוֹחָה‌ — pr. name (יָנוֹחַ) with paragogic ה   נוח

יָנוּחוּ‌ — וַ Kal fut. 3 pers. pl. masc.; וַ conv.   נוח

יָנוּם‌ — Kal fut. 3 pers. sing. masc.   נום

יָנוּם‌ — Kal fut. 3 pers. sing. masc.   נום

יָנוּסוּ‌ — וַיִ‌, וְ id. fut. 3 pers. pl. masc.; וַ conv.   נום

יְנוּסוּן — id. id. with paragogic ן   נום

יִנּוֹעַ‌ — Niph. fut. 3 pers. sing. masc.   נוע

יָנוֹעוּ‌ — וַ Kal fut. 3 pers. pl. masc.   נוע

יִנּוֹעוּ‌ — Niph. fut. 3 pers. pl. masc.   נוע

יִנּוֹעוּן‌ — Kh. יְנוֹעוּן Kal, K. יָנִיעוּן Hiph. fut. 3 pers. masc.; ן paragogic   נוע

יֵעָזֵר‌ — וַ Niph. fut. 3 pers. sing. masc.   נזר

יֵעָזְרוּ‌ — וַ‌, וַיִ‌ id. fut. 3 pers. pl. masc.; וַ conv   נזר

יָנַח‌ — וַ Kal or Hiph. fut. 3 pers. sing. masc. ap. from יָנִיחַ‌, יָנוּחַ (§ 21. rem. 9 & 19)   נוח

יַנַּח‌ — וַ Hiph. fut. 3 p. s. m. with 3rd rad. gutt. [for ap. from יַנִּיחַ‌, Chald. form (§ 21. r. 24)   נוח

יַנִּחֵהוּ‌ — וַ id. id., suff. 3 pers. sing. masc.; וַ conv.   נוח

יַנִּחֵהוּ‌ — וַ id. fut. 3 pers. pl. m., suff. 3 pers. s. m.; וַ id.   נוח

יַנִּיחֵם‌ — וַ id. id., suff. 3 pers. pl. masc. (ם for ן fem. § 2. rem. 5); וַ id.   נוח

יַנְחֵנִי‌ — Hiph. fut. 3 pers. pl. masc., suff. 1 pers. sing.   נחה

יַנְחִיל‌ — Hiph. fut. 3 pers. sing. masc.   נחל

יַנְחִלְךָ‌ — id., suff. 2 pers. sing. masc.   נחל

יַנְחֵל‌ — defect. for יַנְחִיל (q. v.)   נחל

יִנְחַל‌ — Kal fut. 3 pers. sing. masc.   נחל

יִנְחֲלוּ‌ / וַיִ — Kal fut. 3 pers. pl. masc. (§ 8. rem. 15); וַ conv.   נחל

יִנְחָלוּהָ‌ — id., suff. 3 pers. sing. fem. (§ 16. rem. 12)   נחל

יִנְחָלוּם‌ — id., suff. 3 pers. pl. masc.   נחל

יַנְחִלֵם‌ — Hiph. fut. 3 pers. s. m., suff. 3 pers. pl. m.   נחל

יַנְחִלֶנָּה‌ — id., suff. 3 pers. sing. fem.   נחל

יְנַחֵם‌ / וַ — Hiph. fut. 3 pers. sing. masc. [יַנְחֶה], suff. 3 pers. pl. masc. (§ 24. rem. 21); וַ conv.   נחה

יִנָּחֵם‌ / וַיִ id. — Niph. fut. 3 pers. sing. masc. (§ 9. rem. 3); וַ id.   נחם

יְנַחֵם‌ — וַ Piel fut. 3 pers. s. m. (§ 14. rem. 1); וַ id.   נחם

יִנָּחֲמוּ‌ — וַ Niph. fut. 3 p. pl. masc.; וַ id.   נחם

יְנַחֲמוּ‌ — וַ Piel fut. 3 pers. pl. masc. (§ 14. rem. 1); וַ id.   נחם

יְנַחֲמוּן‌ — id. fut. 3 pers. pl. masc.; ן paragogic [for יְנַחֲמוּן comp. § 8. rem. 17]   נחם

יְנַחֲמֻנִי‌ — id. fut. 3 pers. sing. masc., suff. 1 pers. pl.   נחם

יְנַחֲמֵנִי‌ — id. fut. 3 pers. pl. masc., suff. 1 pers. sing.   נחם

יַנְחֵנוּ‌ — Hiph. fut. 3 pers. sing. masc. [יַנְחֶה], suff. 3 pers. sing. m. (§ 24. r. 21, & § 2. r. 3)   נחה

יַנְחֵנִי‌ — id. with suff. 1 pers. sing.   נחה

יְנַחֵשׁ‌ — Piel fut. 3 pers. sing. masc. (§ 14. rem. 1)   נחש

יְנַחֲשׁוּ‌ / יְנַחֲשׁוּ — וַ Piel fut. 3 pers. pl. masc. (§ 14. r. 1. comp. § 8. rem. 15); וַ conv.   נחש

יִנָּטֶה‌ — Niph. fut. 3 pers. sing. masc.   נטה

יִנָּטוּ‌ — id. fut. 3 pers. pl. masc.   נטה

יְנַטְּלֵם‌ — וַ Piel fut. 3 pers. sing. masc. [יְנַטֵּל], suff. 3 pers. pl. masc.; וַ conv.   נטל

יִנָּטְשׁוּ‌ — וַ Niph. fut. 3 pers. pl. masc.; וַ id.   נטש

יָנִי‌ / יָנִיא — Hiph. fut. 3 pers. sing. masc. (§ 25, 2 f)   נוא

ᵃ Job 18. 18   ʰ Ex. 14. 25.   ᵖ Ps. 48. 15.   ᵗ Je. 51. 44.   ᶠ Am. 9. 9.   ᵏ Ho. 9. 10.   ᵖ Ps. 69. 37.   Ps. 106. 45.   ᵗ 2 Ki. 17. 17.
ᵇ Job 42. 11.   ⁱ Job 24. 3.   ᵠ 1 Sa. 7. 2.   ᵘ Zec. 9. 17.   ᵍ Ps. 109. 10.   ˡ 1 Ki. 13. 29.   ᵠ Zep. 2. 9.   ⁱ Job 29. 25.   ᵘ 1 Ki. 20. 33.
ᶜ Da. 4. 14.   ᵏ 1 Sa. 30. 22.   ʳ 1 Sa. 92. 15.   ᵛ Ps. 107. 27.   ʰ Ge. 19. 16.   ᵐ 1 Sa. 2. 8.   ʳ Job 42. 11.   ᵛ Zec. 1. 16.
ᵈ De. 4. 27.   ˡ 1 Sa. 30. 2.   ˢ 2 Ch. 28. 15.   ʷ Hab. 2. 5.   ⁱ Jos. 4. 8.   ⁿ De. 1. 38.   ˢ Zec. 10. 2.   ʷ Je. 6. 4.
ᵉ Ps. 78. 26.   ᵐ De. 26. 37.   ᵗ Is. 49. 10.   ˣ Ps. 59. 16.   ᵏ Ps. 78. 53.   ᵒ Ps. 23. 4.   ᵗ Is. 63. 9.
ᶠ 2 Ki. 9. 20   ⁿ Is. 49. 10.   ᵘ Ps. 23. 2.   ʸ Ps. 68. 2.   ˡ 1 Sa. 25. 9.   ᵖ De. 19. 3.   ᵘ Je. 26. 13.   ˣ Ps. 141. 5.
ᵍ Is. 20. 4.   ᵒ Ps. 78. 53.   ᵛ Job 30. 7.   ᶻ Ps. 104. 7.   ᵐ Le. 22 2.   ᵠ Eze. 14. 7.   ᵛ Ge. 24. 67;   ᵠ Ge. 44. 5, 15.   ʸ Nu. 30. 9.
               ᵗ Eze. 46. 18.

יְנִיאוּ‎ Hiph. fut. 3 pers. pl. masc.; וְ conv.   נוא

יָנִיד‎ וְ Hiph. fut. 3 pers. sing. masc.   נוד

יָנִיחַ‎ } Hiph. fut. 3 pers. sing. masc. (§ 21. יַנִּיחַ‎ } rem. 24)   נוח

וַיַּנִיחֵהוּ‎ id. id., suff. 3 pers. sing. masc.; וְ conv.   נוח

וַיַּנִיחֶהָ‎ id. fut. 3 pers. pl. masc., suff. 3 pers. sing. masc.; וְ id.   נוח

וַיַּנִּחוּ‎ id. fut. 3 pers. pl. masc.; וְ id.   נוח

וַיַּנִּיחוּם‎ id. id., suff. 3 pers. pl. masc.; וְ id.   נוח

יְנִיחֶךָ‎ id. fut. 3 pers. sing. masc. (יָנִיחַ‎), suff. 2 pers. sing. masc. in pause, and with conj. וְ [for וִינִיחֶךָ‎, § 2. rem. 2]   נוח

יַנִּיחֵם‎ id. id. fut. 3 pers. sing. masc. (יַנִּיחַ‎ q. v.), suff. 3 pers. pl. masc.; וְ conv.   נוח

יְנִיחֵנִי‎ id. id. fut. 3 pers. sing. masc. (יָנִיחַ‎), suff. 1 pers. sing.; וְ id.   נוח

יָנִים‎ Kh. יָנִים‎, K. יָנוּם‎ pr. name masc.   נום

יָנִין‎ Kh. יָנִין‎ Hiph., K. יָנוֹן‎ Niph. fut. 3 pers. s. m.   נין

יָנִיסוּ‎ Hiph. fut. 3 pers. pl. masc.   נוס

וַיָּנִיסוּ‎ וְ Kh. יְנִיסוּ‎ q. v., K. יָנוּסוּ‎ (q. v.)   נוס

יָנִיעַ‎ Hiph. fut. 3 pers. sing. masc.   נוע

יָנִיעוּ‎ id. fut. 3 pers. pl. masc.   נוע

יְנִיעוּן‎ id. id. with parag. ן‎   נוע

וַיְנִיפֵהוּ‎ וְ Hiph. fut. 3 pers. sing. masc. [יָנִיף‎], suff. 3 pers. sing. masc.; וְ conv.   נוף

יְנִיפֵנִּוּ‎ id. with suff. 3 pers. sing. masc. (§ 2. r. 3)   נוף

יְנִיקוֹתָיו‎ noun fem. pl., suff. 3 pers. sing. masc. fr. [יְנִיקָה‎] dec. 10   ינק

יִנָּכֵר‎ Niph. fut. 3 pers. sing. masc.   נכר

וַיְנַכְּרוּ‎ וְ Piel fut. 3 pers. pl. masc.; וְ conv.   נכר

יָנָם‎ וַ } Kal fut. 3 pers. sing. masc., ap. & conv. } יִנֹם‎ וְ } from יָנוּם‎ (§ 21. rem. 8) }   נום

וַיָּנֻסוּ‎ וְ, וַ id. fut. 3 pers. pl. m. defect. for יָנוּסוּ‎   נוס

וַיְנַסּוּ‎ וְ Piel fut. 3 pers. pl. masc.; וְ conv.   נסה

וַיְנַסֵּךְ‎ וְ Piel fut. 3 pers. sing. masc.; וְ id.   נסך

וַיְנַסֵּם‎ וְ Piel fut. 3 pers. sing. masc. [יְנַסֶּה‎], suff. 3 pers. pl. masc. (§ 24. rem. 21); וְ id.   נסה

וַיָּנַע‎ וְ Kal or Hiph. fut. 3 pers. sing. masc. ap. and conv. (§ 21. rem. 9 & 19)   נוע

יָנִיעוּ‎ וְ Hiph. fut. 3 p. pl. m. (for יְנִיעוּ‎); וְ conv.   נוע

יָנֻעוּ‎ וְ Kal fut: 3 pers. pl. masc.; וְ id.   נוע

וַיַּעֲלוּם‎ וְ Hiph. fut. 3 pers. pl. masc. [וַיַּעֲלוּ‎], suff. 3 pers. pl. masc.; וְ id.   נעל

יָנַעַם‎ Kal fut. 3 pers. s. m. [for יִנְעַם‎ § 8. r. 15]   נעם

יָנִיעֵם‎ וְ Hiph. fut. 3 pers. sing. masc. [יָנִיעַ‎], suff. 3 pers. pl. masc.; וְ conv.   נעם

יְנַעֵר‎ וְ Piel fut. 3 pers. s. m. (§ 14. r. 1); וְ id.   נער

יִנָּעֲרוּ‎ וְ Niph. fut. 3 pers. pl. masc.   נער

יָנֵף‎ וְ Hiph. fut. 3 pers. sing. masc. ap. and conv. [from יָנִיף‎]   נוף

יְנוֹפֵף‎ Pilel fut. 3 pers. sing. masc.   נוף

יְנַפְּצוּ‎ Piel fut. 3 pers. pl. masc. [for יְנַפְּצוּ‎ comp. § 8. rem. 15]   נפץ

יִנָּפֵשׁ‎ } Niph. fut. 3 pers. s. masc (§ 9. וַיִּנָּפַשׁ‎ } rem. 4); וְ conv.   נפש

וַיִּנָּצוּ‎ וַ Niph. fut. 3 pers. pl. masc.; וְ id.   נצה

יִנָּצֵל‎ Niph. fut. 3 pers. s. masc.   נצל

יִנָּצְלוּ‎ } id. fut. 3 pers. pl. masc. (comp. § 8. יִנָּצֵלוּ‎ } rem. 15)   נצל

וַיְנַצְּלוּ‎ וְ Piel fut. 3 pers. pl.; וְ conv.   נצל

יִנְצְרֵהוּ‎ Kal fut. 3 pers. pl. masc., suff. 3 pers. sing. masc. (§ 17. rem. 3)   נצר

יִנְצֹרוּ‎ id. fut. 3 pers. pl. masc. [for יִנְצְרוּ‎ § 8. rem. 15, see § 17. rem. 3]   נצר

[יָנַק‎] fut. יִינַק‎, to suck; יוֹנֵק‎ a sucking child. Hiph. הֵינִיק‎ to give suck, to suckle; part. מֵינֶקֶת‎ (§ 39. No. 4 d, with suff. מֵינִקְתּוֹ‎ dec. 13 a) a nurse; pl מֵינִיקוֹת‎.

יוֹנֵק‎ masc. dec. 7 b, a sucker, sprout, shoot. יוֹנֶקֶת‎ fem. dec. 13 a (with suff. יוֹנַקְתּוֹ‎), id. יְנִיקָה‎ fem. dec. 10, id.

יִנְקָב־‎ Kal fut. 3 pers. sing. masc. [for יִנְקֹב‎ § 8. rem. 18, see § 17. rem. 3]   נקב

יִנָּקֶה‎ Niph. fut. 3 pers. sing. masc.   נקה

יְנַקֶּה‎ Piel fut. 3 pers. sing. masc.   נקה

וַיְנִקֵהוּ‎ וְ Hiph. fut. 3 pers. sing. masc. [וַיֵּינִיק‎], suff. 3 pers. sing. masc.; וְ conv.   ינק

יְנִקוֹתָיו‎ noun fem. pl. with suff. 3 pers. sing. masc. fr. יוֹנֶקֶת‎ dec. 13 a, see יוֹנֵק‎ masc.   ינק

יוֹנְקִים‎ וְ Kal part. act. or subst. masc., pl. of יוֹנֵק‎ dec. 7 b   ינק

יִנָּקֵם‎ Niph. fut. 3 pers. sing. masc.   נקם

יִנָּקְמוּ‎ וְ id. fut. 3 pers. pl. masc.; וְ conv.   נקם

יִנָּקֵפוּ‎ Kal fut. 3 pers. pl. masc. [for יִנְקְפוּ‎ § 8. rem. 15, see § 17. rem. 3]   נקף

וַיְנַקְּרוּ‎ וְ Piel fut. 3 pers. pl. masc.; וְ conv.   נקר

יְנַקֵּשׁ‎ Piel fut. 3 pers. sing. masc.   נקש

יְנַקְּשׁוּ‎ וְ id. fut. 3 pers. pl. masc.; וְ conv.   נקש

וְנִקֵּתָ‎ וְ Kal pret. 2 pers. sing. fem.; וְ id.   ינק

יִנָּקְתָּם‎ וְ id. pret. 2 pers. pl. masc. with conj. וְ [for וְיִ׳, וְנִקַּתֶּם‎   נק

Nu. 32. 9.   Eze. 40. 42.   Zep. 2. 15.   Pr. 26. 24.   2 Ki. 23. 18.   Ex. 14. 27.   Am. 3. 12.   Eze. 17. 22.   Ju. 16. 21.
Je. 18. 16.   Jos. 6. 23.   Ps. 22. 8.   De. 32. 27.   Is. 7. 2.   Job 38. 13.   Eze. 14. 14.   Ps. 8. 3.   Ps. 109. 11.
Ex. 16. 34.   Pr. 29. 17.   Ps. 109. 25.   Je. 19. 4.   La. 2. 15.   Is. 10. 32.   Ps. 61. 8.   Ex. 21. 20.   Ps. 38. 13.
Is. 46. 7.   Ps. 72. 17.   Is. 8. 29.   Nu. 10. 35.   2 Ch. 28. 15.   Ex. 31. 17.   Job 40. 24.   Eze. 25. 15.   Is. 60. 16.
Le. 24. 12.   De. 32. 30.   Le. 23. 11.   1 Ch. 11. 18.   Nu. 32. 13.   Ex. 23. 12.   De. 32. 13.   Is. 29. 1.   Is. 66. 12.
Eze. 42. 13, 14.   Ju. 7. 21.   Eze. 17. 4.   De. 1. 14.   Ne. 5. 13.   2 Sa. 16. 14.   Je. 48. 12.

יִנָּשֵׂא	וַיִּ׳ Niph. fut. 3 pers. sing. masc.; וָ׳ conv.	נשא
יְנַשְּׂאֵהוּ	וַ׳ Piel fut. 3 pers. sing. masc. [יְנַשֵּׂא], suff. 3 pers. sing. masc.; וַ׳ id.	נשא
יִנָּשְׂאוּ }	Niph. fut. 3 pers. pl. m. (comp. § 8. rem. 15)	נשא
יִתְנַשְּׂאוּ	Hithp. fut. 3 p. pl. m. [for יִתְנַשְּׂאוּ § 12. r. 3]	נשא
יְנַשְּׂאוּהוּ	Piel fut. 3 pers. pl. masc., suff. 3 pers. sing. m.	נשא
יְנַשְּׂאֵם	וַ׳ id. fut. 3 pers. sing. masc. [יְנַשֵּׂא], suff. 3 pers. pl. masc.; וָ׳ conv.	נשא
יִנָּשְׂאוּ	Niph. fut. 3 pers. pl. m. [for יִנָּשְׂאוּ § 23. r. 11]	נשא
יְנָשׁוּף	וָ׳ noun masc. sing.	נשף
יְנַשְּׁכוּ	וָ׳ Piel fut. 3 pers. pl. masc.; וַ׳ conv.	נשך
יְנַשֵּׁל	וָ׳ Piel fut. 3 pers. sing. masc.; וַ׳ id.	נשל
יִנְשַׁק / וַיִּ׳	Piel fut. 3 pers. sing. masc. (§ 10. rem. 4); וַ׳ id.	נשק
יְנַתַּח	וָ׳ Piel fut. 3 pers. sing. masc.; וַ׳ id.	נתח
יְנַתְּחָה	id. id., suff. 3 pers. sing. fem.; וַ׳ id.	נתח
יְנַתְּחֵהוּ	id. id., suff. 3 pers. sing. masc.; וַ׳ id.	נתח
יְנַתְּחֵהוּ	id. id. fut. 3 pers. pl. masc., suff. 3 pers. sing. masc. and conj. וַ׳ [for וַיִּ׳, וַיְנַתְּחֵהוּ]	נתח
יִנָּתֵן / וַיִּ׳ }	Niph. fut. 3 pers. sing. masc. (§ 9. rem. 3)	נתן
יִנְתֵּן	Chald. Peal fut. 3 pers. sing. m. (§ 51. rem. 2)	נתן
יֻנְתַּן	Kh. יֻתַּן q.v., K. יֻתַּן Hoph. fut. 3 pers. s.m.	נתן
יִנָּתְנוּ וַיִּ׳, וַ׳	Niph. fut. 3 pers. pl. masc.; וַ׳ conv.	נתן
יִנְתְּנוּן	Chald. Peal fut. 3 pers. pl. m. (§ 51. rem. 2)	נתן
יְנַתֵּץ	וַ׳ Piel fut. 3 pers. sing. masc.; וַ׳ conv.	נתץ
יְנַתְּצוּ	וַ׳ id. fut. 3 pers. pl. masc., וַ׳ id.	נתץ
יִנָּתֵק	Niph. fut. 3 pers. sing. masc.	נתק
יְנַתֵּק	וַ׳ Piel fut. 3 pers. sing. masc.; וַ׳ conv.	נתק
יִנָּתְקוּ / וַ׳ }	Niph. fut. 3 pers. pl. masc. (comp. § 8. rem. 15); וַ׳ id.	נתק
יְנַתְּקֵם	וַ׳ Piel fut. 3 pers. sing. masc., suff. 3 pers. pl. masc.; וַ׳ id.	נתק
יִנָּתֵשׁ	Niph. fut. 3 pers. sing. masc.	נתש
יִנָּתְשׁוּ	id. fut. 3 pers. pl. masc.	נתש
יָסֹב / יָסֹב }	Kal fut. 3 pers. sing. masc. (§ 21. rem. 8)	סבב
יָסֵב	וַ׳ Hiph. fut. 3 pers. sing. masc. Chald. form (§ 18. rem. 14); וַ׳ conv.	סבב
יָסֹב	וַיָּ׳ Kal fut. 3 pers. s. m. (§ 18. rem. 14); וַ׳ id.	סבב
יְסוֹבֵב	Poel fut. 3 pers. sing. masc. with epenth. ו (§ 16. rem. 13) & suff. 3 pers. sing. masc.	סבב
יְסוֹבְבֵנִי	id. fut. 3 pers. sing. m. with suff. 1 pers. sing.	סבב
יְסֻבֵּהוּ	Kal fut. 3 pers. pl. masc. (יָסֹבּוּ), suff. 3 pers. sing. masc. (§ 18. rem. 5)	סבב

יָסֹבּוּ	וַ׳ Hiph. fut. 3 pers. pl. masc. (§ 18. rem. 14); וַ׳ conv.	סבב
יָסֹבּוּ	וַיָּ׳ Kal fut. 3 pers. pl. masc.; וַ׳ id.	סבב
יִסֹּבּוּ	Niph. fut. 3 pers. pl. masc.	סבב
יְסֻבְּכוּ	Pual fut. 3 p. pl. m. [for יְסֻבְּכוּ comp. § 8. r. 15]	סבך
יִסְבֹּל	Kal fut. 3 pers. sing. masc.	סבל
יִסְבְּלֻהוּ	id. fut. 3 pers. pl. masc., suff. 3 pers. sing. m.	סבל
יְסֻבֵּנּוּ	Kal fut. 3 pers. sing. masc. (יָסֹב), suff. 3 pers. sing. masc. (§ 18. rem. 5)	סבב
יְסֻבֵּנִי	id. id., suff. 1 pers. sing.	סבב
יְסֻבֵּנִי	וַ׳ Hiph. fut. 3 pers. sing. masc. [יָסֵב], suff. 1 pers. sing. (§ 18. rem. 11); וַ׳ conv.	סבב
יִסְבַּר	וַ׳ Chald. Peal fut. 3 pers. sing. masc.	סבר
יִסֹּג	Kal fut. 3 pers. sing. masc.	נסג
יִסְגֹּד / וַ׳	id. fut. 3 pers. sing. masc. [for יָסְגֹּד § 8. rem. 18]; וַ׳ conv.	סגד
יִסְגֻּד	וַ׳ Chald. Peal fut. 3 pers. sing. masc.	סגד
יִסְגְּדוּ	Kal fut. 3 pers. pl. masc.	סגד
יִסְגְּדוּן	Chald. Peal fut. 3 pers. pl. masc.	סגד
יִסֹּג	וַיִּ׳, וַ׳ Niph. fut. 3 pers. pl. masc.; וַ׳ conv.	סוג
יִסְגֹּר / יָסְגֹּר	Kh. יִסְגֹּר, K. יָסְגֹּר Kal fut. 3 p.s.m. (§ 8. r. 18)	סגר
יַסְגִּיר	וַ׳ Hiph. fut. 3 pers. sing. masc.	סגר
יַסְגִּירוּ	id. fut. 3 pers. pl. masc.	סגר
יַסְגִּרֵנִי	id. fut. 3 pers. sing. masc., suff. 1 pers. sing.	סגר
יִסָּגֵר	Niph. fut. 3 pers. sing. masc.	סגר
יַסְגֵּר	וַ׳ Hiph. fut. 3 p. s. m., ap. from יַסְגִּיר; וַ׳ conv.	סגר
יִסְגֹּר	וַיִּ׳, וַ׳ Kal fut. 3 pers. sing. masc.; וַ׳ id.	סגר
יַסְגִּרוּ	defect. for יַסְגִּירוּ (q. v.)	סגר
יִסָּגְרוּ / יִסָּגְרוּ }	Niph. fut. 3 pers. pl. masc. (comp. § 8. rem. 15); וַ׳ conv.	סגר
יִסְגְּרוּ	וַ׳ Kal fut. 3 pers. pl. masc.; וַ׳ id.	סגר
יְסַגְּרֵךְ	Piel fut. 3 pers. sing. masc. [יְסַגֵּר], suff. 2 pers. sing. masc. (§ 16. rem. 15)	סגר
יַסְגִּרֵנּוּ	Hiph. fut. 3 pers. sing. masc. (יַסְגִּיר), suff. 3 pers. sing. masc. (§ 2. rem. 3)	סגר

יָסַד I. *to found, lay the foundation of a building.*—II. *to throw up,* as a heap, 2 Ch. 31. 7.—III. *to settle, establish.*—IV. *to ordain, decree.* Niph. נוֹסַד.—I. *to be founded, established.*—II. *to sit together for consultation, to consult together, to plot.* Pi.—I. *to found.*—II. *to ordain, decree.* Pu. *to be founded.* Hoph. *to be founded;* part. מוּסָד *founded, secure.* יְסוֹד masc. dec. 1 a, pl. ים—, ות *foundation, basis.* סוֹד masc. dec. 1 a.—I. *assembly sitting together,* especially *for consultation.*—II. *consultation,* &c

a Is. 40. 4.   h Je. 10. 5.   p 1 Sa. 11. 7.   y 2 Ch. 34. 7.   f De. 32. 10.   n Je. 52. 21.   ᵃ Da. 3. 6, 10, 11.   ᵐ Mal. 1. 10.
b 2 Ch. 32. 23.   i Is. 34. 11.   q 1 Ki. 18. 23.   z Ju. 16. 9.   g Jon. 2. 4. 6.   o Ps. 49. 6.   ᵇ Is. 46. 6.   ⁱ 1 Sa. 23. 12.
c Est. 3. 1.   k Nu. 21. 6.   r Da. 2. 16.   ᵃ Is. 33. 20.   h Eze. 47. 2.   p Da. 3. 28.   ᶜ Ps. 38. 2.   Job 16. 11.   k Ne. 18. 19.
d Pr. 30. 13.   l 2 Ki. 16. 6.   s 2 Sa. 21. 6.   b Jos. 8. 16.   i Da. 7. 25.   q Ps. 129. 5.   Job 16. 11.   Eze. 46. 2.   Ju. 9. 51.
e Da. 11. 14.   m Ge. 29. 13.   t 2 Ch. 18. 14.   c Job 16. 12.   k Mi. 6. 6.   r Ps. 78. 57.   s Ps. 78. 48, 62.   ⁼ 1 Sa. 17. 40.
f Ezr. 1. 4.   n 1 Ki. 18. 33.   u Je. 31. 40.   d Job 8. 17.   l Is. 44. 15.   Ps. 44. 17.   t Job 12. 14.   v Le. 13. 11.
g Is. 63. 9.   o Ju. 19. 29.   v Ezr. 4. 13.   e Ju. 11. 18.   m Is. 46. 7.

liberation.—III. *familiar intercourse. intimacy.*—
IV. *secret.*

סוֹרִי (*confidant, familiar*) pr. name m. Nu.13.10.

בְּסוֹדְיָה (*in the secret of the Lord*) pr. name
masc. Ne. 3.6.

יְסֹד masc. *beginning*, Ezr. 7.9.

מוֹסָד masc. dec. 2b, pl. ‑ִם, ‑וֹת *foundation,
support, prop.*

יְסוּדָה fem. dec. 10, *foundation*, Ps. 87.1.

מוּסָד masc. dec. 2b, *foundation.*

מוּסָדָה fem. dec. 11a.—I. *foundation*, Eze. 41.8.
—II. *appointment, decree*, Is. 30.32.

מְיֻסָּד masc. *foundation*, 1 Ki. 7.9.

יִסַּד **Piel** pret. 3 pers. sing. masc. (§ 10. rem. 1).
In Is. 28.16, it is either Pi. pret. with
אֲשֶׁר implied; or it is Kal fut. according
to § 20. rem. 16 . . . . . יסד

וְיֹסֵד Kal part. act. sing. masc. . . יסד

יֵסֹד noun masc. sing. . . יסד

יֻסַּד / יֻסָּד } Pual pret. 3 pers. sing. masc. (comp.
§ 8. rem. 15) . . . . . } יסד

יָסְדָה Kal pret. 3 pers. sing. fem. . . יסד

יְסָדָהּ id. pret. 3 pers. sing. m., suff. 3 pers. s. fem. . יסד

יִסְּדָהּ Piel pret. 3 pers. sing. masc. (יִסַּד q. v.), suff.
3 pers. sing. fem. . . . . יסד

יְסוֹדוֹ noun m. s., suff. 3 pers. s.m. from יְסוֹד dec. 1a . יסד

וְיִסְּדוּ Piel pret. 3 pers. pl. masc. . יסד

יְסֹדוֹתֶיהָ noun masc. with pl. fem. term. & suff. 3 pers.
sing. fem. from יְסוֹד dec. 1a . . יסד

יְסֹדֶיהָ id. with pl. masc. term. & suff. 3 pers. sing.
fem. with cop. וְ [וְיְ, וְיִסֹדֶיהָ for] . יסד

יִסַּדְתָּ Kal pret. 2 pers. sing. masc. . יסד

יִסַּדְתָּ Piel pret. 2 pers. sing. masc. . יסד

יְסַדְתּוֹ Kal pret. 2 pers. sing. m., suff. 3 pers. sing. m. יסד

יְסַדְתֶּיהָ noun masc. with pl. fem. term. & suff. 3 pers.
sing. fem. from יְסוֹד dec. 1a . . יסד

יִסַּדְתִּיךְ } Kal fut. 1 pers sing., suff. 2 pers. sing. fem.
with conv. וְ [וְיְ, וַיִּסַּד for] . יסד

יְסַדְתָּם id. pret. 2 pers. sing. m., suff. 3 pers. pl. m. יסד

יָסוֹב Kal fut.3 pers. s.m. Chald. form (§ 18. rem.14) סבב

יְסוֹבֵבְתָּ Poel fut. 3 pers. pl. masc. [יְסוֹבְבֻן], suff.
3 pers. sing. fem. . . . . סבב

יְסוֹבְבֻנְג id. fut. 3 p. pl. m. with conv. וְ [וְיְ, וַיִּסֹב for] סבב

יְסוֹבְבֶנּוּ id. fut. 3 p. s. m., suff. 3 p. s. m. (§ 2. rem. 3) סבב

יְסוֹד / יְסוֹד } noun masc. sing. dec. 1a; with cop. }
[וְיְ, וַיְסוֹד for] } יסד

יְסֹרֵם id. with suff. 3 pers. pl. masc. . . יסר

יְסוּדָּתוֹ n. f. s., suff. 3 p. s. m. from [יְסוּדָה] dec. 10 יסר

יָסוּף Kal fut. 3 pers. sing. masc. . . סוף

יָסוּר / וְיְ Kal fut. 3 pers. sing. masc. . . סור

יָסוֹר noun masc. sing. (after the form נָבוֹר). יסר

וַיָּסֻרוּ Kal fut. 3 pers. pl. masc.; וְ conv. . סור

יְסוּרַי Kh. noun masc. pl., suff. 1 pers. sing. from
יָסוֹר (comp. רִיב from רָיב); K. יְסוּרַי וְסוּרַי
Kal part. pass. pl. & suff. 1 pers. sing. סור

יִסְחָבוּם Kal fut. 3 pers. pl. masc. [יִסְחַב], suff. 3 pers.
pl. masc. (§ 16. rem. 12) . . סחב

יִפַּח Kal fut. 3 pers. sing. masc. . . נסח

יִפְחוּ id. fut. 3 pers. pl. masc. . . נסח

יִפָּחֲךָ id. fut. 3 pers. sing. masc., suff. 2 pers. sing.
masc. (§ 16. rem. 12) . . . .

יִסְחָרוּ Kal fut. 3 pers. pl. masc. . . סחר

יָסִיכוּ Hiph. fut. 3 pers. pl. masc.; וְ conv. . נסך

יָסִיף Hiph. fut. 3 pers. sing. masc. (§ 20. rem. 11) יסף

וַיֹּסִיפוּ id. fut. 3 pers. pl. masc.; וְ conv. . יסף

יָסִיר Hiph. fut. 3 pers. sing. masc. . . סור

יְסִירֶהוּ id. id., suff. 3 pers. sing. masc.; וְ conv. סור

וַיָּסִירוּ / וְיְ id. fut. 3 pers. pl. masc.; וְ id. סור

יְסִירֶנָּה id. fut. 3 pers. sing. masc. with suff. 3 pers.
sing. fem. (§ 2. rem. 3) . . סור

יָסִית Hiph. fut. 3 p. s. m., Chald. form (§ 21. r. 24) סות

יְסִיתֵהוּ id. id. [יָסִית], suff. 3 pers. sing. masc. . סות

יְסִיתְךָ id. id., suff. 2 pers. sing. masc. . סות

יְסִיתֵם id. id., suff. 3 pers. pl. masc.; וְ conv. סות

וַיָּסֶךְ / יָסֶךְ Hiph. fut. 3 p. s. m., with conv. וְ [יָסֵךְ for] סכך

יָסֵךְ Hiph. fut. 3 pers. sing. masc. ap. and conv. וְ
[יָסִיךְ from] . . . . . סוך

יָסֵךְ Hiph. fut. 3 p. s. m. ap. [יָסִיךְ for]; וְ conv. נסך

יָסַךְ Hoph. fut. 3 pers. sing. masc. R. נָסַךְ, or as
a Chald. form (§ 18. rem. 14) from R. סכך

יִסְכָּה pr. name of a sister of Lot, Ge. 11.29.

יְסַכֵּהוּ the foll. (יְסֹכּוּ), suff. 3 pers. s. m. (§ 18. rem.5) סכך

יָסֹכּוּ Kal fut. 3 pers. pl. masc. וְ conv. . סכך

יָסְכוּ Kal fut. 3 pers. pl. masc. . . נסך

יְסֻכֻּם Kal fut. 3 pers. pl. masc. [יְסֻכּוּ], suff.
3 pers. pl. masc.; וְ conv. . . סוך

יִסְכּוֹן Kal fut. 3 pers. sing. masc. (§ 8. rem. 18) . סכן

יְסַכֵּל Piel fut. 3 pers. sing. masc. . . סכל

יִסָּכֵן Niph. fut. 3 pers. sing. masc., before monos.
[יִסָּכֵן for § 9. rem. 3] . . . כן

יִסְכֹּן / יִסְכַּךְ } Kal fut. 3 pers. sing. masc. (§ 8. rem. 18) סכן

a Ezr. 7.9.   b Ezr. 3.6.   c Is. 48.13.   d 1 Ki. 16.34.   e Eze. 13.14.   f Zec. 4.9.   g Ezr.3.10.   h Eze. 30.4.   i Mi. 1.6.   k Ps.8.3.   l Ps.55.11.   m Hab. 1.12.   n La. 4.11.   o Is. 54.11.   p Zec. 14.10.   q Est. 9.28.   r Job 15.30.   s Ps. 32.10.   t 2 Ch. 24.27.   u Ps. 87.1.   v Ps. 57.7,15.   w Job 40.2.   x Ju. 18.3,15.   y Je. 17.13.   z Je. 49.20; 50.45.   a Pr. 7.25.   b Pr. 2.22.   c Ps. 52.7.   d Ge. 31.21.   e Eze. 20.28.   f 2 Sa. 7.10.   g 2 Ch. 36.3.   h Job 34.20.   i Le. 3.4,10,15.   k 2 Ch. 18.2.   l 2 Ch. 18.31.   m Ps. 91.4.   n 2 Sa. 12.20.   o Job 40.22.   p 1 Ki. 8.7.   q Ho. 9.4.   r 2 Ch. 28.15.   s Is. 44.25.   t Ec. 10.9.   u Job 22.2.

יְסַכְסֵךְ	Pilp. fut. **3** pers. sing. masc. (§ 6. No. 4)	סכך
יִסָּכֵר	Niph. fut. 3 pers. sing. masc.	סכר
יִסָּכְרוּ	ן id. fut. 3 pers. pl. masc.; ·וְ conv. .	סכר
יָסֹלּוּ	ן Kal fut. 3 pers. pl. masc.; ·וְ id.	סלל
יִסְלַח	Kal fut. 3 pers. sing. masc. . .	סלח
יְסַלֵּף	Piel fut. 3 pers. sing. masc.; ן conv.;	סלף
יְסַלֵּף	with conj. ן [for וַיִּסְלַף, וַיִּ״	
יִסָּמֵךְ	·וַ Nipn. fut. 3 pers. sing. masc.; ·וְ conv.	סמך
יִסְמֹךְ	ן Kal fut. 3 pers. sing. masc.; ·וַ id.	סמך
יִסָּמְכוּ	ן Niph. fut. 3 pers. pl. masc.; ·וְ id.	סמך
יִסְמְכוּ	·וַ Kal fut. 3 pers. pl. masc.; ·וְ id.	סמך
יְסַמְכְיָהוּ	ן pr. name masc.	סמך
יִסְמְכֵנִי	Kal fut. 3 pers. sing. m. (יִסְמֹךְ), suff. 1 pers. s.	סמך
יִסַּע	·וַ Hiph. fut. 3 pers. sing. masc.; ·וְ conv.	נסע
יִסַּע	·וַ Kal fut. 3 pers. sing. masc.; ·וְ id. .	נסע
יִסְעָד	Kal fut. 3 pers. s. m. [for יִסְעַד § 8. rem. 15]	סעד
יִסְעָדֶךָ	id., suff. 2 pers. sing. masc. (§ 16. rem. 12, & § 2. rem. 3)	סעד
יִסְעָדֶנּוּ	id., suff. 3 pers. sing. masc. (v. id.)	סעד
יִסְעָדֵנִי	id., suff. 1 pers. sing. . . .	סעד
יַסְעִיעוּ	ן Hiph. fut. 3 pers. pl. m. [for יַסְעִיעוּ]; ·וְ conv.	נסע
יַסְעוּ, ·וַיִּ״, יִ״ / יִסְעוּ	Kal fut. 3 p. pl. m.; יְסָעוּ for יִסְעוּ on account of Sheva under ס, comp. § 10. rem. 7; ·וְ id.	נסע
יַסְעֵם	ן id. fut. 3 pers. sing. masc., suff. 3 pers. pl. masc. (§ 16. rem. 12); ·וְ id. .	נסע
יִסָּעֵר	ן Niph. fut. 3 pers. sing. masc.; ·וְ id.	סער
יְסֹעֵר	Poel fut. 3 pers. sing. masc. (§ 6. No. 1)	סער
יִסְעֲרוּ	Kal fut. 3 pers. pl. masc.	סער

יָסַף ן Kal and Hiph. (fut. יוֹסִיף ap. יֹסֵף).—I. *to add*, with אֶל, עַל.—II. *to increase, enlarge*, with עַל, לְ, acc.—III. *to add to do, to do again* any thing, const. with an inf. with or without לְ, when it may generally be rendered by *again* or *more*; וְיֹסֵף שַׁלַּח *he shall rise no more*; וַיֹּסֶף שַׁלַּח אֶת־הַיּוֹנָה *and again he sent forth the dove*. Niph. נוֹסַף.—I. *to be added*, Nu. 36. 3, 4, with עַל.—II. *to join oneself*, Ex. 1. 10.—III. *to increase, grow*, Pr. 11. 24. Part. נוֹסָפוֹת, Is. 15. 9, *additions* sc. of calamities.

יְסַף Chald. Hoph. *to be added*, Da. 4. 33.

יוֹסֵף, once יְהוֹסֵף (*He shall add*, sc. the Lord, comp. Ge. 30. 24.) pr. name—I. of a son of Jacob; applied also to the two tribes descended from his sons, Ephraim and Manasseh, and stands poetically

for the kingdom of Israel or the ten tribes, of which the tribe of Ephraim was chief.—II. 1 Ch. 25. 2, 9.—III. Ne. 12. 14.—IV. Ezr. 10. 42.

יוֹסִפְיָה (whom *the Lord will increase*) pr. name masc. Ezr. 8. 10.

יָסַף	Kal pret. 3 pers. sing. m. for יָסַף (§ 8. rem. 7)	יסף
יֹסֵף	ן Hiph. fut. 3 pers. s. m. (§ 20. rem. 10)	יסף
יֹסֵף	ן ap. and conv. from יוֹסִיף .	
יֶסֶף	ן Kal fut. 3 pers. s. m. for וַיֶּאְסֹף (§ 19.rem.4)	אסף
יִסָּפְדוּ	Niph. fut. 3 pers. pl. masc.	ספד
יִסְפְּדוּ	·וַ Kal fut. 3 pers. pl. masc.; · conv.	ספד
יָסְפָה	ן Kal pret. 3 pers. sing. fem.	יסף
יָסְפוּ	ן id. pret. 3 pers. pl. (§ 8. rem. 7)	יסף
יָסֻפוּ	Kal fut. 3 pers. pl. masc.	סוף
יֹסְפוּ	·וַ Hiph. fut. 3 pers. pl. masc. (for יוֹסִפוּ § 20. rem. 11); ·וְ conv.	יסף
יִסְפּוֹק	Kal fut. 3 pers. sing. masc. (§ 8. rem. 18)	ספק
יִסְפּוֹר	Kal fut. 3 pers. sing. masc. (§ 8. rem. 18)	ספר
יְסֻפְּחוּ	Pual fut. 3 pers. pl. masc. [for יְסֻפְּחוּ comp. § 8. rem. 15]	ספח
יֹסְפִים	Kal part. act. pl. masc. from [יֹסֵף] dec. 7 b	יסף
יִסָּפֵן	ן Kal fut. 3 pers. sing. masc.; ·וְ conv.	ספן
יִסְפְּנוּ	Kal pret. 1 pers. pl.	יסף
יִסְפְּק	ן Kal fut. 3 pers. sing. masc.; ·וְ conv.	ספק
יְסַפֵּר, יְסַפֶּר־	ן Piel fut. 3 pers. sing. masc. (§ 10. rem. 4); ·וְ id.	ספר
יְסֻפַּר, יְסֻפָּר	ן Pual fut. 3 pers. sing. masc. (comp. § 8. rem. 15)	ספר
יִסָּפֵר	Niph. fut. 3 pers. sing. masc.	ספר
יִסְפֹּר	·וַ Kal fut. 3 pers. sing. masc.; ·וְ conv.	ספר
יְסַפְּרֶהָ	ן Piel fut. 3 pers. sing. masc. (יְסַפֵּר), suff. 3 pers. sing. fem.; ן id.	ספר
יְסַפְּרוּ, ·וַ	ן id. fut. 3 pers. plur. masc. (comp. § 8. rem. 15); ן id.	ספר
יְסַפְּרוּ	ן id. with cop. [for וַיְ״, וַיְסַפְּרוּ] ן	ספר
יִסָּפְרוּ	·וַ Niph. fut. 3 pers. pl. masc.; ן conv.	ספר
יִסְפְּרוּ	Kal fut. 3 pers. pl. masc. . .	ספר
יְסַפְּרוּם	ן Piel fut. 3 pers. pl. masc., suff. 3 pers. pl. masc.; ן conv.	ספר
יִסְפְּרֵם	ן Kal fut. 3 pers. sing. masc. (יִסְפֹּר), suff. 3 pers. pl. masc.; ·וְ id. .	ספר
יָסַפְתָּ / יָסַפְתְּ	ן Kal pret. 2 pers. sing. masc.; acc. shifted by conv. ן (§ 8. rem. 7) .	יסף
יָסַפְתִּי	ן id. pret. 1 pers. sing. acc. shifted (§ 8. r. 7)	יסף
יִסָּקֵל	Niph. fut. 3 pers. sing. masc. . .	סקל

a Is. 9. 10.   *f* 2 Ch. 32. 8.   *l* Ps. 104. 15.   *r* Ex. 14. 15.   *x* De. 5. 22.   *c* De. 19. 20.   *i* 1 Ki. 6. 9.   *n* Ps. 22. 31.   *r* Eze. 44. 26.

b Ps. 68. 12.   *g* Nu. 8. 12.   *m* Ps. 20. 3.   *s* Ju. 16. 3.   *y* 2 Sa. 6. 1.   *d* Job 34. 37.   *k* 1 Sa. 12. 19.   Ps. 87. 6.   *s* Ezr. 1. 8.

c Job 12. 19.   *h* Ps. 3. 6.   *n* Ps. 41. 4.   *t* 2 Ki. 6. 11.   *z* Ge. 8. 12.   *e* Job 31. 4.   *l* Nu. 24. 10.   *o* Job 28. 27.   *t* De. 19. 9.

d Pr. 22. 12.   *i* Ps. 78. 26.   *o* Ps. 94. 18.   *u* Ho. 13. 3.   *a* Nu. 11. 25.   *f* Job 30. 7.   *m* 1 Ki. 13. 11.   *p* 1 Ch. 23. 3.   *u* Le. 26. 18, 21.

Ju. 16. 29.   *k* Is. 33. 20.   *p* 1 Ki. 5. 31.   *v* Hab. 3. 14.   *b* Is. 66. 17.   *g* De. 5. 25.   *h* Hab. 1. 5.   *g* Ge. 8. 2.

יַסָּקֵל] Piel fut. 3 pers. sing. masc.;] conv.	סקל
יִסָּקְלֻהוּ] id., suff. 3 pers. sing. masc.;] id.	סקל
יִסְקְלֻהוּ] Kal fut. 3 pers. pl. m., suff. 3 p. s. m.;] id.	סקל
יִסְקְלוּ] id. fut. 3 pers. pl. masc.;] id.	סקל
יִסְקְלֻנוּ id. id. with suff. 1 pers. pl.	סקל

[יָסַר] fut. with suff. אֲפָרֵם (§ 20. rem. 16, & § 8. rem. 14); and Pi. יִסַּר.—I. *to chasten, correct, punish.*—II. *to admonish, exhort, instruct;* with מִן *to dehort from* any thing. Hiph. *to chasten,* Ho. 7. 12. Niph. נוֹסַר *to be admonished.* Nithp. נִוַּסָּר (§ 6. No. 10) id. Eze. 23. 48.

יְסוּר masc. (after the form גִּבּוֹר) *a corrector, reprover, censurer,* Job 40. 2. Others regard this word as a future of Kal.

מוּסָר masc. dec. 2b.—I. *chastisement, correction.*—II. *admonition, warning.*—III. *instruction, learning, doctrine.*

מֹסָר masc. *admonition, instruction,* Job 33. 16.

יָסֹר] Kal or Hiph. fut. 3 pers. sing. masc., ap. and conv. (§ 21. rem. 9 & 19)	סור
יָסֵר]׳ Hiph. fut. 3 pers. sing. m., ap. from יָסִיר	סור
יָסֹר ׳ Kal inf. absolute (§ 8. rem. 8)	יסר
יָסֻר Kal fut. 3 p. s. m. defect. for יָסוּר 2 Ki. 4. 8; or id. ap. Pr. 9. 4, 16 (§ 21. rem. 7)	סור
יַסֵּר Piel imp. sing. masc.	יסר
יַסֹּר id. inf. absolute	יסר
יִסַּר id. pret. 3 pers. sing. masc. (§ 10. rem. 1)	יסר
יֹסֵר Kal part. act. sing. masc. (§ 8. rem. 19)	יסר
יְסָרֶהָ] Hiph. fut. 3 pers. sing. masc. (יָסִיר), suff. 3 pers. sing. fem.;] conv.	סור
יְסָרֵהוּ] id. id., suff. 3 pers. sing. masc.;] id.	סור
וַיָּסֻרוּ] Kal fut. 3 p. pl. m. defect. for יָסוּרוּ;]׳ id.	סור
יִסְּרוּ] Piel pret. 3 pers. pl.	יסר
יִסְּרוּ] id. pret. 3 pers. sing. m., suff. 3 pers. s. m.	יסר
יִסְּרוּנִי id. pret. 3 pers. pl., suff. 1 pers. sing.	יסר
יְסָרֵם] Hiph. fut. 3 pers. sing. masc. (יָסִיר), suff. 3 pers. pl. masc.;] conv.	סור
יַסְּרֵנִי Piel imp. sing. masc., suff. 1 pers. sing.	יסר
יִסְּרַנִּי]} id. pret. 3 pers. sing. masc., suff. 1 pers.	
יִסְּרֵנִי } sing. (§ 2. rem. 1)	יסר
יִסַּרְתָּ id. pret. 2 pers. sing. masc.	יסר
יִסְּרַתְהוּ id. pret. 3 pers. sing. fem., suff. 3 pers. s. m.	יסר
יִסַּרְתִּי]} id. pret. 1 pers. sing.; acc. shifted by	
וְיִסַּרְתִּי } conv.] (comp. § 8. rem. 7)	יסר

יִסַּרְתִּיךָ] id. id., suff. 2 pers. sing. masc.	יסר
יְסָרַתְּנִי id. pret. 2 pers. sing. masc., suff. 1 pers. sing.	יסר
יָסֵת] Hiph. fut. 3 pers. sing. masc. ap. and conv. [from יָסִית]	סות
יִסְתַּבֵּל] Hithpa. fut. 3 pers. sing. masc. [for יִתְסַבֵּל § 12. rem. 3]	סבל
יַסְתִּיר Hiph. fut. 3 pers. sing. masc.	סתר
יַסְתִּירֵנִי id. with suff. 1 pers. sing.	סתר
יִסָּתְמוּ } Kal fut. 3 pers. pl. masc. (§ 8. r 15);	סתם
יִסְתְּמוּ }]׳ conv.	
יְסַתְּמֻם] Piel fut. 3 pers. pl. masc., suff. 3 pers. pl. masc.;] id.	סתם
יִסָּתֵר]׳ Niph. fut. 3 pers. sing. masc.;] id.	סתר
יַסְתֵּר]]׳ Hiph. fut. 3 pers. sing. masc. ap. [fr. יַסְתִּיר]]׳ id.	סתר
יִסָּתֵר] Kh. יִסָּתֵר q. v., K. יִסָּתֵר (q. v.)	סתר
יַסְתִּרוּ] Hiph. fut. 3 pers. pl. m.;]׳ conv.	סתר
יִסָּתְרוּ Niph. fut. 3 pers. pl. masc.	סתר
יַסְתִּרֵם] Hiph. fut. 3 pers. sing. masc. (יַסְתִּיר), suff. 3 pers. pl. masc.;] conv.	סתר
יַעֲבֹד] Hiph. fut. 3 pers. sing. masc., ap. [fr. יַעֲבִיד]]׳ id.	עבד
יַעֲבֹד וַ׳ Kal fut. 3 pers. sing. masc.;] id.	עבד
יֵעָבֵד Niph. fut. 3 pers. sing. masc.	עבד
יַעַבְדֻהוּ] defect. for יַעֲבֹדוּהוּ (q. v.)	עבד
יַעַבְדוּ] Hiph. fut. 3 pers. pl. masc.;]׳ conv.	עבד
יַעַבְדוּ וַ׳,]׳ Kal fut. 3 pers. pl. masc. (§ 8.	עבד
יַעַבְדוּ]׳ rem. 15);] id.	
יַעַבְדֻהוּ id. id., suff. 3 pers. sing. masc.	עבד
יַעַבְדֻךָ id. id., suff. 2 pers. sing. masc.	עבד
יַעַבְדֻם] id. id., suff. 3 pers. pl. masc.	עבד
יַעַבְדֻנִי id. id., suff. 1 pers. sing.	עבד
יַעַבְדֶנּוּ id. fut. 3 pers. sing. m., suff. 3 pers. s. m.	עבד
יַעַבְדֵם] id. id., suff. 3 pers. pl. masc.;] conv.	עבד
יַעַבְדֵנִי] id. id., suff. 1 pers. sing.	עבד
יַעַבְדֵנִי]׳ defect. for יַעֲבֻדֵנִי (q. v.)	עבד
יַעֲבֹר Kh. יַעֲבֹר q. v., K. יַעֲבִיר Hiph. fut. 3 pers. sing. masc.	עבר
יַעֲבֹר Kh. יַעֲבֹר q. v., K. יַעֲבָר q. v. (§ 8. r. 18)	עבר
יַעֲבֹר וַ׳ Kal fut. 3 pers. sing. masc. (§ 8. r. 18)	עבר
יְעַבְּטוּן] Piel fut. 3 pers. pl. masc. with parag.]	עבט
יַעֲבִירֻהוּ] Hiph. fut. 3 pers. pl. masc., suff. 3 pers. sing. masc.;] conv.	עבר
יַעֲבִירוּ וַ׳,]׳ id. fut. 3 pers. pl. masc.;]׳ id.	עבר
יַעֲבִירוּ] Kh. וַיַּעֲבִירוּ q. v., K. הֶעֱבִירוּ q. v.	עבר
יַעֲבִירֻנִי Hiph. fut. 3 pers. pl. masc., suff. 1 pers. s.	עבר

a 2 Sa. 16. 6, 13. d 1 Ch. 15. 22. n Is. 28. 26. t Ho. 7. 15. b 2 Ki. 3. 25. g 2 Ki. 11. 2. m 1 Ch. 19. 19. r Ps. 18. 44. y Joel 2. 7.
b Is. 5. 2. e Ps. 118. 18. o Ps. 16. 7. u Le. 26. 28. c Am. 9. 3. n Ex. 1. 13. s 2 Ch. 33. 22. z 2 Ch. 35. 24.
c 1 Ki. 21. 13. f Pr. 9. 7. p Je. 10. 24. v 2 Ch. 32. 4. d Je. 36. 26. o Ex. 10. 7. t Ex. 4. 23. a Ne. 8. 15.
d Jos. 7. 25. g 1 Ki. 15. 13. q Je. 31. 18. w Ge. 26. 18. e Ex. 34. 33. p Ge. 15. 14. u Ex. 48. 14. b 2 Sa. 19. 41
Ex. 8. 22. h 1 Sa. 13. 13. r Ps. 118. 18. x Is. 8. 11. f De. 21. 4. q Job 36. 11. v Is. 26. 20. c Ne. 2. 7
Job 9. 34. m Ex. 25. 15. s Pr. 31. 1. y 1 Sa. 20. 2. f Pr. 22. 3. Ps. 27. 5.

יַעֲבִירֵם*	Hiph. fut. 3 pers. sing. masc., suff. 3 pers. pl. masc.; וַ conv. . . . . עבר
יַעְבֵּץ	pr. name—I. of a man, 1 Ch. 4. 9, 10, which see for the signification.—II. of a place in the tribe of Judah, 1 Ch. 2. 55.
יַעֲבֵר / יַעֲבֶר	Hiph. fut. 3 pers. sing. masc., ap. from יַעֲבִיר (§ 11. rem. 7); וַ conv. עבר
יַעֲבֹר / וַיַּ׳	Kal fut. 3 pers. sing. masc. (§ 8. rem. 18); וַ id. . . . עבר
יֵעָבֵר	Niph. fut. 3 pers. sing. masc. עבר
יְעַבֵּר	Piel fut. 3 pers. sing. masc.; וַ conv. . עבר
יַעֲבְרֵהוּ	Hiph. fut. 3 pers. sing. masc., suff. 3 pers. sing. masc.; וַ id. . . . עבר
יַעַבְרוּ / וַיַּ׳	Kal fut. 3 pers. pl. masc. (§ 8. rem. 15); וַ id. . . . עבר
יַעֲבִרוּ	Hiph. fut. 3 pers. pl. masc. for יַעֲבִירוּ וַ id. . . . . עבר
יַעֲבְרֵם	id. with suff. 3 pers. pl. masc. (for ן fem. § 2. rem. 5); וַ id. . . עבר
יַעֲבְרֵם	Kal fut. 3 pers. plur. masc. (יַעֲבֹר), suff. 3 pers. pl. masc. . . . עבר
יַעַבְרוּן	id. id. with parag. ן [for יַעֲבֹרוּן § 8. r. 17] עבר
יַעַבְרֻם	defect. for יַעֲבִירֵם (q. v.) עבר
יַעַבְרֶנְהוּ	Kal fut. 3 pers. sing. masc. (יַעֲבֹר) with epenth. נ & suff. 3 pers. s. m. (§ 16. r. 13) עבר
יַעַבְרֶנְהוּ	id. fut. 3 pers. pl. masc. with parag. ן & suff. 3 pers. sing. masc. (§ 16. rem. 14) עבר
יַעַבְרֶנּוּ	id. fut. 3 pers. sing. m., suff. 3 pers. s. m. עבר
יַעַבְרֵנִי	Hiph. fut. 3 pers. sing. masc., suff. 1 pers. sing.; וַ conv. . . . עבר
יְעַבְּתוּהָ	Piel fut. 3 pers. pl. m., suff. 3 p. s. f.; וַ id. עבת

[יָעַד] fut. יִיעַד.—I. *to appoint,* as a place, or time.—II. *to betroth,* Ex. 21. 8, 9. Niph. נוֹעַד.—I. *to meet with* any one *at an appointed place, by appointment,* with ל, אֶל.—II. *to meet together at an appointed time and place, by appointment;* also generally *to come together.*—III. *to agree,* Am. 3. 3. Hiph. הוֹעִיד *to appoint for* any one, especially a time for trial, *to arraign.* Hoph. *to be fixed, set, directed.*

יַעְדּוֹ pr. name masc. 2 Ch. 9. 29, Kheth., Keri יֶעְדִּי.

עֵדָה fem. dec. 11 b.—I. *assembly, congregation.*—II. *a private party, a gang, faction.*—III. *family, household.*—IV. *swarm of bees,* Ju. 14. 8.

מוֹעֵד masc. dec. 7 b, מוֹעֲדִים, מוֹעֲדוֹת.—I. *a set time* or *season;* especially *festival days.*—II. *a*

coming together, assembly, congregation; אֹהֶל מוֹעֵד *tabernacle of the congregation;* קְרִיאֵי מוֹעֵד *those called to the assembly.*—III. *place appointed.*—IV. *appointed sign,* a *signal,* Ju. 20. 38.

מוֹעָד masc. dec. 2 b, *assembly, host,* Is. 14. 31.

מוֹעָדָה f. d. 11 a, *festival, solemn feast,* 2 Ch. 8. 13.

מוּעָדָה fem. *appointment;* עָרֵי הַמּוּעָדָה *appointed cities* for refuge, Jos. 20. 9.

מוֹעַדְיָה (*festival of the Lord*) pr. name masc. Ne. 12. 17; called מַעַדְיָה v. 5, see R. עָדָה.

נוֹעַדְיָה (*with* whom *the Lord meets*) pr. name— I. masc. Ezr. 8. 33.—II. fem. Ne. 6. 14.

יָעַד	Hiph. fut. 3 pers. sing. masc., ap. & conv. (§ 21. rem. 19) עוד
יְעָדַהּ	Kal pret. 3 pers. sing. m., suff. 3 pers. s. f. יעד
יַעֲדֵהּ	Ch. Peal fut. 3 pers. s. m. (comp. § 49. r. 2) עדה
וַיָּעִידוּ / [וְיָעִידוּ]	Hiph. fut. 3 p. pl. m., suff. 3 p. s. m.; וַ conv.; ן conj. [for וְיָעִדֻהוּ] עוד
יְעָדוֹ	Kal pret. 3 pers. sing. m., suff. 3 pers. s. m. יעד
יֶעְדִּי / יַעְדּוֹ	Kh. יֶעְדִּי, K. יַעְדּוֹ pr. name masc. יעד
יֵעָדֵר	Niph. fut. 3 pers. sing. masc. עדר
יְעַדְּרוּ	Piel fut. 3 pers. pl. masc. עדר
יֵעָדְרוּן	Niph. fut. 3 pers. pl. masc.; ן parag. [for יֵעָדְרוּן comp. § 8. rem. 17] עדר

יָעָה ן *to carry, sweep away,* Is. 28. 17.

יָע masc. (pl. יָעִים, with suff. יָעָיו) *shovel.*

יְעִיאֵל, יְעוּאֵל (*a carrying away of God*) pr. name masc. of several persons.

יְעוּאֵל / יְעִיאֵל / וִיעִ׳	pr. name masc., Kh. יְעִיאֵל . . יעה
יְעוֹדֵד	Pilel fut. 3 pers. sing. masc. עוד
יָעֹז	Kal fut. 3 pers. sing. masc. for יָעֹז (§ 18. r. 2) עזז
יְעַלֵּז	Piel fut. 3 pers. sing. masc. עלז
יְעֹלְלוּ	Poel fut. 3 pers. pl. masc. . . עלל
יָעוּף	Kal fut. 3 pers. sing. masc. . . עוף
יְעוֹפֵף	Pilel fut. 3 pers. sing. masc. . . עוף
יַעֲיָן	pr. name masc. . . . עין
יָעוֹר / יָעֵר	Kh. יָעוֹר, K. יָעֵר pr. name masc. עור
יְעֹרֵר	Piel fut. 3 pers. sing. masc. עור
יֵעוֹר	Niph. fut. 3 pers. s. m. (comp. conj. 1 gutt.) עור
יֵעוֹרוּ	id. fut. 3 pers. pl. masc. עור
יְעוּשׁ / וִיעוּשׁ	pr. name masc. . . עושׁ
יָעֵת	Piel fut. 3 pers. sing. masc. . עות

יָעֵז Kal not used; prob. i. q. עָזַז *to be strong, firm.* Niph. part. נוֹעַז *firm, obstinate,* Is. 33. 19.

^a Ps. 78. 13.   ^d Job 34. 20.   ^g Is. 8. 13.   ^k Je. 5. 22.   ⁿ Da. 7. 14.   ^r 2 Sa. 20. 5.   ^t Is. 7. 25.   ^w Da. 11. 12.   ^z Je. 6. 9.
^b Eze. 47. 5.   ^e 2 Sa. 19. 42.   ^h Ps. 104. 9.   ^l Je. 5. 22.   ^o 1 Ki. 21. 13.   ^s Is. 5. 6.   ^u Ps. 146. 9   ^y Is. 26. 10.   [*] Joel 4. 12.
1 Ki. 5. 21.   ^f Jos. 4. 3.   Ge. 32. 24.   ^m Mi. 7. 3.   1 Ki. 21. 10.   1 Ki. 5. 7.   ^{vw} Job 8. 3.

יָעֹז	Kal fut. 3 pers. sing. masc. . .	עזז
וַיַּעֲזֹב	} Kal fut. 3 pers. sing. masc. (§ 8. rem.	עזב
וַיַּעֲזָב־	} 18) ; וַ conv. .	עזב
וַיַּעַזְבֻהוּ	} id. fut. 3 p. pl. m., suff. 3 p. s. m ; וַ id.	עזב
יַעַזְבוּ	} id. fut. 3 pers. pl. masc. (§ 8. rem.	עזב
וַיַּעַזְבוּ	} 15) ; וַ id. . .	עזב
יֵעָזְבוּ	Niph. fut. 3 pers. pl. masc. . .	עזב
יַעֲזָבֶךָ	Kal fut. 3 pers. sing. masc., suff. 2 pers. sing. masc. [for יַעַזְבְךָ § 2. rem. 3] . .	עזב
יַעַזְבוּךָ	id. fut. 3 pers. pl. masc., suff. 2 pers. s. m.	עזב
יַעַזְבֶנָּה	id. fut. 3 pers. sing. masc., suff. 3 pers. sing. fem. (§ 2. rem. 3) . .	עזב
יַעַזְבֵנוּ	id. id., suff. 1 pers. pl. . .	עזב
יַעַזְבֶנּוּ	id. id., suff. 3 pers. sing. masc.	עזב
יַעַזְבֵנִי	} id. id., suff. 1 pers. sing. ; וַ conv.	עזב
וַיַּעַזְבֵנִי	} id. fut. 3 pers. pl. masc., suff. 1 pers. s., וַ id.	עזב
יֵעָזוֹב	id. fut. 3 pers. sing. masc. (§ 8. rem. 18)	עזב
יַעֲזִיאֵל וְ יַעֲזִיָּהוּ	pr. names masc. . .	עזה
יַעֲזֵיר	pr. name of a place	עזר
יַעַזְקֵהוּ	} Piel fut. 3 pers. sing. masc. [יְעַזֵּק], suff. 3 pers. sing. masc. ; וַ conv.	עזק
וַיַּעַזְר־	} וַ Kal fut. 3 pers. sing. masc. [for	עזר
	§ 8. rem. 18] ; וַ id. .	עזר
וַיַּעְזֵר	וַ pr. name of a place . .	עזר
יַעַזְרֶהָ	Kal fut. 3 pers. sing. masc. [יַעֲזֹר], suff. 3 pers. sing. fem. (§ 13. rem. 5 & 6)	עזר
וַיַּעַזְרֵהוּ	} וַ id. id., suff. 3 p. s. m. (§ 13. r. 5); וַ conv.	עזר
וַיַּעַזְרֻהוּ	} וַ id. fut. 3 pers. pl. m., suff. 3 p. s. m.; וַ id.	עזר
יַעַזְרוּ	} id. fut. 3 pers. pl. masc. (§ 13. rem. 5,	עזר
וַיַּעַזְרוּ	} & § 8. rem. 15) ; וַ id. . .	עזר
וַיֵּעָזְרוּ	} Niph. fut. 3 pers. pl. masc. ; וַ id.	עזר
וַיַּעַזְרוּנִי	} וַ Kal fut. 3 pers. pl. masc., suff. 1 pers. sing. (§ 13. rem. 5) . .	עזר
וַיַּעַזְרֶךָ	} וַ id. fut. 3 pers. sing. masc., suff. 2 pers. sing. masc. [for יַעַזְרֶךָ v. id. & § 2. rem. 2]	עזר
יַעַזְרֶכֶם	} וַ id. fut. 3 pers. pl. masc., suff. 2 pers. pl. masc. (§ 13. rem. 5) . .	עזר
יַעַזְרֻם	} וַ id. fut. 3 pers. sing. masc., suff. 3 pers. pl. masc. ; וַ conv.	עזר
יַעַזְרֵנִי	id. fut. 3 pers. sing. masc., suff. 1 pers. sing.	עזר
[יָעַט]	to clothe, cover, Is. 61. 10.	
[יְעַט]	Ch. i. q. Hebr. יָעַץ to advise, counsel, Ezr. 7. 14, 15. Ithp. to consult together, Da. 6. 8.
	עֵטָא Ch. fem. counsel, wisdom, Da. 2. 14.

יָעֵט	} Kal fut. 3 pers. sing. masc. ap. & conv.	עיט
	(§ 22. rem 3) . . .	עיט
יַעַט	} ap. for the following (§ 24. rem. 3)	עטה
יַעֲטֶה	Kal fut. 3 pers. sing. masc. (§ 13. rem. 5)	עטה
יַעַטוֹהִי	Ch. defect. for יַעֲטוּהִי (q. v.) .	יעט
וַיַּעֲטוּ	וַ Kal fut. 3 pers. pl. masc. .	עטה
יַעַטוֹהִי	} Ch. Peal part. pl. masc., suff. 3 pers. sing. m. [from s. יָעַט for יְעַט, comp. § 54. r. 1]	יעט
יַעֲטוֹף	Kal fut. 3 pers. sing. masc. (§ 8. rem. 18)	עטף
יַעְטְנִי	Kal pret. 3 p. s. m., suff. 1 p. s. (§ 2. r. 1)	עטף
יַעֲטֹף יַעֲטֹף־ יַעֲטָף־	} Kal fut. 3 pers. sing. masc. (§ 13. rem. 5, & § 8. rem. 18) . . .	עטף
יַעַטְפוּ	id. fut. 3 pers. pl. masc. . .	עטף
יְעִי יְעִיאֵל	pr. name masc. . . .	עיה
יָעִיב	Hiph. fut. 3 pers. sing. masc. .	עוב
וַיָּעִידוּ	וַ Hiph. fut. 3 pers. pl. masc. .	עוד
יְעִידֶנִּי	defect. for יוֹעִידֵנִי (q. v. § 20. rem. 11)	יעד
וַיָּעִיוּ	} וַ noun masc. pl., suff. 3 pers. sing. masc. [from יָע] besides only in the abs. יָעִים	יעה
יַעִילוּ	Hiph. fut. 3 p. pl. m. (for יוֹעִילוּ § 20. r. 11)	יעל
יָעִיר	Hiph. fut. 3 pers. sing. masc. . .	עור
יְעִירֶנּוּ	Kh. יַעִירֶנּוּ Hiph., K. יָעֵר Kal fut. 3 pers. sing. masc., suff. 3 pers. sing. masc.	עור
וַיְעִירֵנִי	} וַ Hiph. fut. 3 pers. sing. masc. (יָעִיר), suff. 1 pers. sing. ; וַ conv. . .	עור
יָעִישׁ	Kh. יָעִישׁ K. יְעוּשׁ pr. name masc. . .	עושׁ
יַעְכָּן	וַ pr. name masc. . .	עכן
יַעַבְּרֶךָ	Kal fut. 3 pers. sing. masc. [יַעֲבֹר], suff. 2 pers. sing. masc. (§ 13. rem. 5) . .	עכר

יָעַל Kal not used; prob. i. q. עָלָה q. v. Hiph. הוֹעִיל —I. to profit, help, with לְ.—II. intrans. to receive profit, to be benefited.

   יָעֵל masc. dec. 5a (pl. c. יַעֲלֵי).—I. the mountain goat, wild goat, ibex.—II. pr. name of a judge in Israel, Ju. 5. 6.—II. pr. name fem. Ju. 4. 17, 18 ; 5. 24.—III. צוּרֵי הַיְּעֵלִים (rocks of the wild goats) pr. name of a rock in the desert of Engedi, 1 Sa. 24. 3.

   יַעֲלָה fem. dec. 10.—I. wild she-goat, female ibex, Pr. 5. 19.—II. pr. name of a man.

יַעַל וַ יַעַל	} וַ Kal or Hiph. fut. 3 pers. s. m., ap. from עָלָה (§24. r.3 & 16)	עלה
יַעֲלֵ וַ	} וַ conv.	עלה
יַעֲל וַ	Kh. יַעַל q. v., K. יַעֲלוּ (q. v.) .	עלה
יָעֵל	pr. name fem. . .	יעל

a Ge. 2. 24.   f Pr. 5. 3.   k Is. 5. 2.   o 2 Ch. 32. 3.   s Is. 44. 2.   v 1 Sa. 25. 14.   z Ezr. 7. 15.   p Ps. 73. 6.   z Zec. 4. 1.
b 1 Ch. 16. 37.   g Job 20. 13.   l Is. 50. 7, 9.   p 1 Ki. 1. 7.   t Ge. 49. 25.   w Is. 59. 17.   a Is. 57. 16.   q La. 2. 1.   y Jos. 17. 25.
c 2 Ch. 29. 6.   h 1 Ki. 8. 57.   m 1 Sa. 30. 13.   q 1 Sa. 21. 17.   u Da. 11. 34.   x De. 32. 38.   b Is. 61. 10.   r Je. 49. 19.   z 2 Ch. 36. 23.
d Jon. 2. 9.   i 1 Sa. 8. 8.   n 2 Ch. 26. 7.   r 2 Ch. 28. 23.   y Ps. 37. 40.   c Ez. 27. 3.   a 1 Sa. 2. 6.
e 1s. 18 6.   r Job 6. 14.   m Ps. 65. 14.   w 2 Ch. 24. 19.   z Ps. 119. 175.   d Ps. 109. 29.   ob 41. 2.   b Ezr. 3. 3.
   s Ps. 71. 13.   c Job 23. 9.

יֵעְלָא	pr. name masc. for יַעְלָה (q. v.) .	.	יעל
יֵעָלֶה	Niph. fut. 3 pers. sing. masc. .	.	עלה
יַעְלָה	pr. name masc. .	.	יעל
וַיַּֽעֲלֵהֶ	Kh. יַעְלֶה q. v., K. יַעֲלֵהוּ (q. v.)	.	עלה
וְיַ׳	Kal or Hiph. fut. 3 pers. sing. masc. (comp. יַעַל); וַ׳ conv. .	.	עלה
וַ יַּעֲלֵהוּ	Hiph. fut. 3 pers. sing. masc., suff. 3 pers. sing. masc.; וַ׳ id. .	.	עלה
וַ יַּעֲלוּהוּ	id. fut. 3 pers. pl. masc., suff. 3 pers. sing. masc.; וַ׳ id. .	.	עלה
וַ יֵּעָלוּ	Niph. fut. 3 pers. pl. masc.; וַ׳ id. .	.	עלה
וְיַ׳	Kal or Hiph. fut. 3 pers. pl. m.; וַ׳ id.	.	עלה
וַ יַּעֲלוּהוּ	Hiph. fut. 3 pers. pl. masc., suff. 3 pers. sing. masc.; וַ׳ id. .	.	עלה
וַ יַּעֲלִי	Kal fut. 3 pers. sing. masc.; וַ׳ id. .	.	עלז
יַעְלֹזוּ / יַעֲלֹזוּן	id. fut. 3 pers. pl. masc. (§ 8. rem. 15, & § 13. rem. 5)	.	עלז
יַעֲלֵי	noun masc. pl. constr. from יָעֵל dec. 5	.	יעל
יַעֲלִימוּ	Hiph. fut. 3 pers. pl. masc. (§ 13. rem. 9)		עלם
יַעְלָם / וַיַּעְלָם	} pr. name masc. .	. .	עלם
וַ יְעַלְּלֻהוּ	Poel fut. 3 pers. pl. masc., suff. 3 pers. sing. masc.; וַ׳ conv.	.	עלל
וַ יַּעַל / יַעְלֵם	} Hiph. fut. 3 p. s. m. [יַעֲלֶה], suff. 3 p. pl. m. (§ 13. r. 9, & § 24. r. 21); וַ׳ id.		עלה
יַעֲלֶֽהָ	Kal fut. 3 pers. sing. masc. (יַעֲלֶה), suff. 3 pers. sing. fem. (§ 24. rem. 21, & § 2. r. 3)		עלה
וַ יַּעֲלֵנִי	Hiph. fut. 3 pers. sing. masc. (יַעֲלֶה), suff. 1 pers. sing. (§ 24. rem. 21); וַ׳ conv.		עלה
יַעֲלֹם	Kal fut. 3 pers. sing. masc.	.	עלם
יַעֲלֹעוּ	Piel fut. 3 pers. pl. masc. (§ 10. rem. 7)		עלע
יַעֲלִיץ	Kal fut. 3 pers. sing. masc.	.	עלץ
יַעַלְצוּ / וְיַעֲלְצוּ	} id. fut. 3 pers. pl. masc. (§ 13. rem. 5) .		עלץ
וַ יַּעֲלַת	noun fem. sing. constr. [of יַעֲלָה]		יעל
וַ יַּֽעֲמֵד	Hiph. fut. 3 pers. sing. masc., ap. from		עמד
וַ יַּעֲמִיד	יַעֲמִיד (§ 11. rem. 7); וַ׳ conv. .	.	עמד
וַ יַּעֲמֹד / יַעֲמֹד	} Kal fut. 3 pers. sing. masc. (§ 8. rem. 18); וַ׳ id. .		עמד
יָעֳמַד	Hoph. fut. 3 pers. sing. masc. .	.	עמד
וַ יַּעֲמִדֵהוּ	Hiph. fut. 3 pers. sing. masc. (יַעֲמִיד), suff. 3 pers. sing. masc.; וַ׳ conv. .		עמד
וַיַּ׳ / יַעֲמֹדוּ	} וַ׳ Kal fut. 3 p. pl. m. (§ 8. r. 15); וַ׳ id.		עמד

יַעַמְדוּ	Kh. יַעֲמֹדוּ q. v., K. עָמְדוּ (q. v.)	.	עמד
יַעֲמֹדְנָה	Kal fut. 3 p. pl. fem. for תַּעֲמֹדְנָה (§ 8. r. 16)		עמד
וַיַּ׳	id. fut. 3 pers. sing. masc. (§ 8. rem. 18); וַ׳ conv. .	.	עמד
וַיַּ׳	Hiph. fut. 3 pers. sing. masc. .	.	עמד
יַעֲמִידֶהָ	id. id., suff. 3 pers. sing. fem.; וַ׳ conv.		עמד
יַעֲמִידוּ	id. fut. 3 pers. pl. masc.; וַ׳ id. .		עמד
וְיַעֲמִידוּ	Kh. יַעֲמִידוּ q. v., K. יַעֲמִיד (q. v.)	.	עמד
וַ יַּעֲמִידֵם	Hiph. fut. 3 pers. sing. masc., suff. 3 pers. pl. masc.; וַ׳ conv.		עמד
וַיַּ׳ / יַעֲמִידֵנִי	id. with suff. 1 pers. sing.; וַ׳ id.		עמד
יַעֲמֹל	Kal fut. 3 pers. sing. masc.	.	עמל
יַעֲמֹם / וַ יַּעֲמָס	} Kal fut. 3 pers. sing. masc. (§ 8. rem. 18); וַ׳ conv. .		עמם

יַעַן   Root not used; Syr. *to be greedy, voracious.*

יָעֵן masc. dec. 5a, *ostrich*, La. 4. 3.

יַעֲנָה fem. always בַּת הַיַּעֲנָה *the female ostrich*; pl. בְּנוֹת הַיַּעֲנָה.

יַעַן	prep. and conj. .	.	ענה
וַ יַּעַן	Kal fut. 3 pers. sing. masc., ap. from יַעֲנֶה (§ 24. rem. 3); וַ׳ conv. .	.	ענה
יַעֲנֶה	noun fem. sing. .	.	יען
וַ יַּעַן	Kal fut. 3 pers. sing. masc.; וַ׳ conv.		ענה
יֵעָנֶה	Niph. fut. 3 pers. sing. masc.		ענה
יְעַנֶּה	Piel fut. 3 pers. sing. masc.		ענה
יַעֲנֶהָ	id., suff. 3 p. s. fem. (§ 24. r. 21); וַ׳ conv.		ענה
וַ יַּעֲנֵהוּ	Kal fut. 3 pers. sing. masc. (יַעֲנֶה), suff. 3 pers. sing. masc. (§ 24. rem. 21); וַ׳ id.		ענה
וַ יַּעֲנוּ	id. fut. 3 pers. pl. masc.; וַ׳ id.		ענה
יְעַנּוּ	Piel fut. 3 pers. pl. masc.		ענה
יַעַנְךָה	Kal fut. 3 p. pl. m., suff. 2 p. s. m. (§ 2. r. 2)		ענה
וַ יַּעֲנוּגוּ	Piel fut. 3 p. pl. m., suff. 1 p. pl.; וַ׳ conv.		ענה
יַעֲנִי	pr. name masc.		ענה
יַעַנְךָ	Kal fut. 3 pers. sing. masc. (יַעֲנֶה), suff. 2 pers. sing. masc. (§ 24. rem. 21)		ענה
יְעַנְּךָ	Piel fut. 3 pers. sing. masc. (יְעַנֶּה), suff. 2 pers. sing. masc. (§ 24. rem. 21); וַ׳ conv.		ענה
וַיַּ׳ / וְ׳ / יַעֲנֵם	Kal fut. 3 pers. sing. masc. (יַעֲנֶה), suff. 3 pers. pl. masc. (§ 24. rem. 21); וַ׳ id.		ענה
יְעַנֵּם	Piel fut. 3 pers. sing. masc. (יְעַנֶּה), suff. 3 pers. pl. masc. (§ 24. rem. 21); וַ׳ id. .		ענה
יַעֲנֶהָ	Kal fut. 3 pers. sing. masc. (יַעֲנֶה), suff. 3 pers. sing. fem. (§ 24. r. 21, & § 2. r. 3)		ענה
יַעֲנֵנוּ	id., suff. 1 pers. pl.		ענה
יַעֲנֵנּוּ	id., suff. 3 pers. sing. masc. .	.	ענה

a Ex. 49. 37.   f Ps. 28. 7.   l De. 28. 61   q 1 Ch. 16. 32.   u 2 Sa. 2. 23.   c Pr. 29. 4.   g Ge. 44. 13.   n Je. 7. 27.   r Ps. 55. 20.
b 1 Sa. 7. 9.   g Ps. 149. 5.   m Is. 35. 9.   r Ps. 5. 12.   w Jos. 3. 13.   d Ne. 3. 14.   h Ps. 68. 20.   o De. 26. 6.   s 2 Ch. 10. 15.
c Je. 39. 5.   h Job 39. 1.   n Job 32. 1.   s Pr. 5. 19.   x Eze. 47. 10.   e Ne. 3. 15.   i 2 Ki. 1. 10.   p De. 8. 3.   t 2 Ki. 17. 20.
d Ju. 15. 13.   i Le. 20. 4.   o Job 20. 18.   t 2 Ch. 11. 15.   y Da. 8. 22.   f Nu. 22. 26.   k Job 37. 23.   q Ps. 99. 6.
e Ps. 96. 12   j Ju. 20. 45.   p Job 39. 30.   t Le. 16. 10.   z Ec. 8. 17.   — Ps. 20. 7.   l Ps. 20. 10.

יַעֲנֶנּוּ Piel fut. 3 pers. sing. masc. (יְעַנֶּה), suff. 3 pers. sing. masc. (§ 24. rem. 21, & § 2. r. 3) . . ענה

וַיַּעֲנֵנִי וגו׳ Kal fut. 3 pers. sing. masc. (יַעֲנֶה), suff. 1 pers. sing. (§ 24. rem. 21); וְ conv. . . ענה

יַעֲנֵנִיּ וְ Piel fut. 3 pers. sing. masc. (יְעַנֶּה), suff. 1 pers. sing. (§ 24. rem. 21); וְ id. . ענה

יֵעָנֵשׁ Niph. fut. 3 pers. sing. masc. . . ענש

וַיֵּעָנֵשׁ וְ Kal fut. 3 pers. sing. masc.; וְ conv. . ענש

יְעַרְעֲרוּ Pilpel (§ 6. No. 4) fut. 3 pers. pl. masc. [for יַעֲרְעֲרוּ, יְעַרְעֲרוּ, ר softened to ו] . . עור

[יָעֵף] fut. יִיעַף to be wearied, fatigued. Arab. وعف to run swiftly. Hoph. part. מֻעָף Da. 9. 21, wearied, faint; others, flying, swift.

    יָעֵף adj. masc. dec. 5a, weary, fatigued.

    יָעֵף masc. flight, swift course, Da. 9. 21.

    תּוֹעָפוֹת fem. pl. (from תּוֹעָפָה dec. 11a).—I. swiftness.—II. wealth, treasure. Perhaps primarily, brightness, splendour, יָפַע=יָעַף to be bright, to shine.

וַיָּעָף Kal fut. 3 p. s. m. ap. & conv. (§ 21. r. 9) עוף

יָעֵף adj. masc. sing. dec. 5 . . . עוף

וַיָּעַף Kal fut. 3 pers. sing. masc. ap. & conv. from יָעוּף (§ 21. rem. 8) . . . עוף

וַיָּעַף Kal fut. 3 pers. sing. masc. for יִיעַף (§ 20. rem. 2, & § 8. rem. 15); וְ conv. . יעף

יָעֲפוּ id. pret. 3 pers. pl. [for יָעֵפוּ § 8. r. 1 & 7] יעף

יָעֻפוּ Kal fut. 3 pers. pl. masc. . . עוף

יָעֻפוּ Kal fut. 3 pers. pl. masc. [for יִיעֲפוּ § 20. rem. 2, comp. § 8. rem. 15] . . . יעף

יַעֲפִילוּ וְ Hiph. fut. 3 pers. pl. masc. [for יַעֲפִילוּ § 13. rem. 9]; וְ conv. . . עפל

יָעַץ fut. יִיעַץ.—I. to counsel, advise, with לְ; part. יוֹעֵץ counsellor.—II. to take counsel, to decree, with עַל, אֶל against any one.—III. to direct, as the eye, Ps. 32. 8, with עַל towards any one, i. e. to care or provide for him.—IV. to instruct, Nu. 24. 14. Niph. נוֹעַץ.—I. to be counselled, advised.—II. to consult, take counsel together, with עִם, אֶל, אֵת. Hithp. to consult together, Ps. 83. 4.

    עֵצָה fem. dec. 11b (for יְעֵצָה).—I. counsel, advice.—II. deliberation, purpose, plan; בְּעֵצָה advisedly.

    מוֹעֵצָה fem. dec. 11b, counsel, device.

יָעַץ Kal pret. 3 pers. sing. m. for יָעֵץ (§ 8. rem. 7) יעץ

יֹעֵץ id. part. act. sing. masc. dec. 7b . יעץ

יֵעָצֵב Niph. fut. 3 pers. sing. masc. . . עצב

יַעַצְבוּ Piel fut. 3 p. pl. m. [for יְעַצְּבוּ comp. § 8. r. 15] עצב

יְעָצָהוּ Kal pret. 3 pers. sing. masc., suff. 3 pers. s. f. יעץ

יְעָצֻהוּ id. pret. 3 pers. pl., suff. 3 pers. sing. masc. יעץ

יְעָצוּ id. pret. 3 pers. pl. . . . יעץ

יוֹעֲצֵי וגו׳ id. part. act. pl. constr. from יוֹעֵץ dec. 7b יעץ

יַעֲצִיבוּהוּ Hiph. fut. 3 pers. pl. m., suff. 3 pers. s. m. עצב

יֹעֲצָיו וְ Kal part. act. pl., suff. 3 pers. sing. masc. from יוֹעֵץ dec. 7b . . . יעץ

יֹעֲצַיִךְ וְ id., suff. 2 pers. sing. fem. . . יעץ

יַעְצֵם וְ Piel fut. 3 pers. sing. masc.; וְ conv. . עצם

יַעְצְמֻהָ וְ Hiph. fut. 3 p. s. m., suff. 3 p. s. m; וְ id. עצם

יַעַצְמוּ וְ Kal fut. 3 pers. pl. masc.; וְ id. . עצם

יְעָצַנִי Kal pret. 3 pers. sing. masc. with suff. 1 pers. sing. (§ 2. rem. 1) . . . יעץ

יַעְצֹר   יַעֲצָר־ Kal fut. 3 pers. sing. masc. (§ 8. rem. 18, & § 13. rem. 5) עצר

יַעַצְרֶהוּ וְ id., suff. 3 pers. sing. masc.; וְ conv. . עצר

יַעַצְרְכָה id., suff. 2 pers. sing. masc. (§ 2. rem. 2) עצר

יָעַצְתָּ Kal pret. 2 pers. sing. masc. . . יעץ

יָעַצְתִּי id. pret. 1 pers. sing. . . . יעץ

יַעֲקֹב וגו׳ pr. name masc. . . . עקב

יַעְקֹב Kal fut. 3 pers. sing. masc. (§ 13. rem. 5) . עקב

יַעֲקֹבָה וְ pr. name masc. . . . עקב

יַעְקְבֵם Piel fut. 3 pers. sing. masc., suff. 3 pers. pl. masc. (§ 10. rem. 7) עקב

יַעְקְבֵנִי וְ Kal fut. 3 pers. sing. masc. (יַעֲקֹב q. v.), suff. 1 pers. sing.; וְ conv. . . . עקב

יַעֲקֹד וְ Kal fut. 3 pers. sing. masc.; וְ id. עקד

יַעֲקוֹב pr. name of a people, see יַעֲקֹב . עקב

יַעֲקָן pr. name masc., see בְּנֵי יַעֲקָן עקן

יַעְקֵר וְ Piel fut. 3 pers. sing. masc.; וְ conv. . עקר

יַעַקְשׁוּ Piel fut. 3 pers. pl. masc. [for יְעַקְּשׁוּ comp. § 8. rem. 15] . . . עקש

יַעְקְשֵׁנִי וְ Kal fut. 3 pers. sing. masc. [יַעֲקֹשׁ], suff. 1 pers. sing. (§ 13. rem. 5); וְ conv. . עקש

יַעַר masc. dec. 6c (with suff. יַעְרִי, § 35. rem. 5; pl יְעָרִים, יְעָרוֹת).—I. honeycomb, Ca. 5. 1.—II thicket, wood, forest.—III. pr. name of a town, Ps. 132. 6, prob. i. q. קִרְיַת יְעָרִים.

    יַעְרָה fem.—I. honeycomb, only constr. יַעְרַת, 1 Sa. 14. 27.—II. pr. name masc. 1 Ch. 9. 42; called יְהוֹעַדָּה in chap. 8. 36.

    יַעוֹר masc. wood, forest, Eze. 34. 25. Kheth.

    יַעֲרֵי אֹרְגִים (woods of the weavers) pr. name masc. 2 Sa. 21. 19; but in the parallel passage, 1 Ch. 20. 5, it is יָעִיר, in Kheth. יָעוּר, or perhaps יָעוֹר, compare the preceding.

a Ps. 89. 23.   c Is. 15. 5.   e Is. 6. 6.   m Is. 40. 30.   r Is. 23. 9.   w Ps. 78. 40.   c Ps. 105. 24.   i 1 Ki. 17. 4.   l Ge. 27. 36.
b Job 30. 11.   d Ju. 4. 21;   f Is. 44. 12.   n Nu. 14. 44.   p Ps. 62. 5.   x Ezr. 8. 25.   d Ex. 1. 7, 20.   k 1 Ki. 18. 44.   m Ge. 22. 9.
c Ex. 21. 22.   1 Sa. 14. 28.   h Hab. 1. 8.   o Na. 1. 11.   s Is. 19. 11.   y Is. 1. 26.   o Ps. 16. 7.   k Je. 9. 3.   l Mi. 3. 9.
d 2 Ch. 36. 3.   g Is. 50. 4.   l Hab. 2. 13.   p Ps. 56. 6.   t Job 3. 14.   z Is. 29. 10.   d 2 Ch. 2. 5.   h Job 37. 4.   m Job 9. 22.
w Je. 51. 58, 64.

Form	Description	Root
יָעַר	in pause for יַעַר (q. v.)	
יָעַר	Hiph. fut. 3 pers. sing. masc., ap. & conv. from עוּר (§ 21. rem. 19)	עור
יֶעְרַב	Kal fut. 3 pers. sing. masc.	ערב
יֶעְרְבוּ	id. fut. 3 pers. pl. masc.	ערב
יַעְרָה	pr. name masc.	יער
יַעְרָה	noun masc. sing., suff. 3 pers. sing. fem. from יַעַר dec. 6d (§ 35. rem. 5)	יער
יֵעָרֶה	Niph. fut. 3 pers. sing. masc.	ערה
יְעָרֶה	Piel fut. 3 pers. sing. masc.	ערה
יַעְרוֹ	noun masc. sing., suff. 3 pers. sing. masc. from יַעַר dec. 6d (§ 35. rem. 5)	יער
יֵעֹרוּ	Niph. fut. 3 pers. pl. masc.	עור
יְעָרוּ	Piel fut. 3 pers. pl. masc. with conj. וְ [for וִיעָרוּ, וַיְעָרוּ]	ערה
יְעָרוֹת	noun masc. with pl. fem. term. abs., from יַעַר dec. 6d	יער
יַעֲרֵי	pr. name in compos. יַעֲרֵי אֹרְגִים	יער
יַעְרִי	noun masc. sing., suff. 1 pers. sing. from יַעַר dec. 6d (§ 35. rem. 5)	יער
יַעֲרֹךְ	Hiph. fut. 3 pers. sing. masc.	ערד
יַעֲרָכֶנּוּ	id. with suff. 3 pers. sing. masc.	ערד
יְעָרִים	pr. name see קִרְיַת יְעָרִים	קרה
יַעֲרִימוּ	Hiph. fut. 3 pers. pl. masc.	ערם
יַעֲרִיצוּ	Hiph. fut. 3 pers. pl. masc.	ערץ
יַעֲרֹךְ	Kal fut. 3 pers. sing. masc.; וְ conv.	ערד
יַעַרְכֶהָ	id. id., suff. 3 pers. sing. fem. (§ 13. r. 5)	ערד
יַעַרְכוּ	id. fut. 3 pers. pl. masc.; וְ conv.	ערד
יַעַרְכוּנִי	id. id. with suff. 1 pers. sing.	ערד
יַעַרְכֶנָּה	id. fut. 3 pers. sing. masc., suff. 3 pers. s. f.	ערד
יַעַרְכֶנּוּ	id. id., suff. 3 pers. sing. masc.	ערד
יַעֲרֵם	Hiph. fut. 3 pers. sing. masc. (§ 13. rem. 5)	ערם
יַעֲרֹף	Kal fut. 3 pers. sing. masc.	ערף
יַעַרְפוּ	id. fut. 3 pers. pl. masc.	ערף
יֶעְשָׂה	(whom the Lord makes fat, i. e. prosperous; עַרשׂ Syr. to fatten) pr. n. m. 1 Ch. 8. 27.	
יַעַשׂ	Kal fut. 3 pers. sing. m., ap. from	עשה
יַעַשׂ	יַעֲשֶׂה (§ 24. rem. 3); וְ conv.	עשה
יַעַשׂ	Kh. q. v., K. יַעַשׂ, Kal fut. 3 pers. sing. masc. [for יַעַט § 21. rem. 24]	עיט
יַעֲשֶׂה	the following with suff. 3 pers. sing. fem.	עשה
יַעֲשֶׂה	Kal fut. 3 pers. sing. masc.; וַיְ conv.	עשה
יַעֲשֶׂה	Kh. יַעֲשֶׂה q. v., K. יַעַשׂ (q. v.)	עשה
יֵעָשֶׂה	Niph. fut. 3 pers. sing. masc.	עשה
יַעֲשֵׂהוּ	וַיְ, וַיְ Kal fut. 3 pers. sing. masc. (יַעֲשֶׂה), suff. 3 pers. s. m. (§ 24. r. 21); וְ conv.	עשה

Form	Description	Root
יַעֲשֹׂן	Kh. יַעֲשֹׂי, K. שִׂי, שִׂי pr. name masc.	עשה
יַעֲשׂוּ	וַיְ, וְ Kal fut. 3 pers. pl. masc. וְ conv.	עשה
יֵעָשׂוּן	Niph. fut. 3 pers. pl. masc.	עשה
יַעֲשׂוּהָ	Kal fut. 3 pers. pl. m. with suff. 3 pers. s. f.	עשה
יַעֲשׂוּן	id. with parag. ן	עשה
יַעֲשׂוּנִי	id. with suff. 1 pers. sing.; וְ conv.	עשה
יַעֲשִׂיאֵל	pr. name masc.	עשה
יַעֲשִׂיר	Hiph. fut. 3 pers. sing. masc.	עשר
יַעֲשִׂרֻן	id. fut. 3 pers. pl. masc.; וְ conv.	עשר
יַעֲשָׂם	וְ Kal fut. 3 pers. sing. masc. (יַעֲשֶׂה), suff. 3 pers. pl. masc. (§ 24. rem. 21)	עשה
יַעֲשֹׁן	Kal fut. 3 pers. sing. masc. (§ 13. rem. 5)	עשן
יַעֲשֶׂנָּה	Kal fut. 3 pers. sing. masc. (יַעֲשֶׂה), suff. 3 pers. sing. fem. (§ 24. rem. 21)	עשה
יַעֲשֵׂנוּ	וְ Kal fut. 3 pers. pl. m. [for יַעֲשֵׂנוּ § 8. r. 15]	עשן
יַעֲשֹׁק	Kal fut. 3 pers. sing. masc.	עשק
יַעַשְׁקֵנִי	id. fut. 3 pers. pl. masc., suff. 1 pers. sing.	עשק
יַעֲשֵׂר	defect. for יַעֲשִׂיר (q. v.)	עשר
יַעֲשֵׂר	Kal fut. 3 pers. sing. masc. (§ 13. rem. 5)	עשר
יַעֲשֵׂר	Kal fut. 3 pers. sing. masc. (§ 13. rem. 5)	עשר
יַעֲשִׂרֶנּוּ	Hiph. fut. 3 pers. sing. m. [ap. יַעֲשֵׂר], suff. 3 pers. sing. m. [for יַעֲשִׂירֶנּוּ § 16. r. 16]	עשר
יַעְתֵּק	וְ Hiph. fut. 3 pers. sing. masc. ap. (§ 13. rem. 9); וְ conv.	עתק
יֶעְתַּק	וְ Kal fut. 3 pers. sing. masc. (§ 13. r. 5)	עתק
יֶעְתָּר	וַיְ Kal fut. 3 pers. sing. masc. (§ 13. rem. 5); וְ conv.	עתר
יֵעָתֵר	וַיְ Niph. fut. 3 pers. sing. masc. (§ 9. rem. 3); וְ id.	עתר
יֵעָתֵר		עתר
יְפָאֵר	Piel fut. 3 pers. sing. masc.	פאר
יָפֻג	וְ Kal fut. 3 p. s. m. ap. & conv. [from יָפוּג]	פוג
יַפְגִּיעַ	Hiph. fut. 3 pers. sing. masc.	פגע
יִפְגַּע	וְ Kal fut. 3 pers. sing. masc.; וְ conv.	פגע
יִפְגְּעוּ	וַיְ id. fut. 3 pers. pl. masc.; וְ id.	פגע
יִפְגְּעוּן	id. id. with parag. ן	פגע
יִפְגְּעֵנוּ	id. fut. 3 pers. sing. masc., suff. 1 pers. pl. (§ 16. rem. 12)	פגע
יִפְגְּשֵׁהוּ	וְ Kal fut. 3 pers. sing. masc., suff. 3 pers. sing. masc.; וְ conv.	פגש
יְפַגְּשׁוּ	Piel fut. 3 pers. pl. masc.	פגש
יִפְגְּשֻׁם	וְ Kal fut. 3 pers. pl. masc., suff. 3 pers. pl. masc.; וְ conv.	פגש
יִפְגָּשְׁךָ	id. fut. 3 pers. sing. masc. [יִפְגֹּשׁ], suff. 2 pers. sing. masc. (§ 16. rem. 12)	פגש
יִפָּדֶה	Niph. fut. 3 pers. sing. masc.	פדה
יִפְדֶּה	Kal fut. 3 pers. sing. masc.	פדה

ᵃ Da. 11. 25.   ᵍ Is. 10. 18, 19.   ⁿ Ps. 83. 4.   ᵗ Job 23. 13.   ˡ Is. 46. 6.   ᵍ Ec. 6. 12.   ᵐ Job 15. 29.   ʳ Ps. 149. 4.   ˣ Ex. 4. 24. 3?.
ᵇ Ps. 104. 34.   ʰ 2 Ch. 24. 11.   ᵒ Is. 29. 23.   ᵏ 2 Sa. 2. 6.   ᵘ Ge. 20. 9.   ʰ Job 40. 23.   ⁿ 1 Sa. 17. 25.   ˢ Ge. 45. 26.   ʸ Job 5. 14.
ᶜ Ho. 9. 4.   ⁱ Ps. 29. 9.   ᵖ Is. 44. 7.   ˡ 1 Sa. 14. 32.   ᵛ Mi. 2. 1.   ⁱ Ps. 119. 122.   ᵒ Job 14. 18.   ᵗ Is. 53. 12.   ᶻ 2 Sa. 2. 13.
ᵈ Je. 46. 23.   ᵏ Ca. 5. 1.   ᵠ Job 6. 4.   ᵐ Ru. 1. 8.   ʷ Job 10. 8.   ᵏ Ps. 49. 17.   ᵖ Job 18. 4.   ᵘ Jos. 17. 10.   ᵃ Ge. 32. 18.
Is. 32. 15.   ˡ Le. 27. 14.   Le. 24. 8.   ˣ Eze. 12. 25, 28.   ʸ Je. 5. 27.   ˡ 1 Sa. 8. 15, 17.   ᵠ Job 33. 26.   ᵛ Ex. 5. 3.   ᵇ Le. 27. 2?.
ᶠs. 3. 17.   ᵐ Le. 27. 8.   ˢ Ue. 33. 28.   ᵈ Is. 44. 13.

יִפְדּוּ	Kal fut. 3 pers. pl. masc.; וַ conv. .	פדה
יִפְדְּיָה	pr. name masc.	פדה
יִפְדְּךָ	Kal fut. 3 pers. sing. masc., suff. 2 pers. sing. masc. (§ 24. rem. 21); וַ conv. .	פדה

[יָפָה] fut. וְיָפָה, ap. יִיף, *to be fair, comely, beautiful.* Pi. *to beautify,* Je. 10. 4. Pu. יֻפְּיָה (§ 6. No. 9) *to be very beautiful.* Hithp. *to beautify oneself,* Je. 4. 30.

יָפֶה masc. dec. 9b, יָפָה fem. dec. 11a, adj.— I. *fair comely, beautiful.*— II. *good, excellent,* Ec. 3. 11; 5. 17.

יָפוֹ, יָפוֹ pr. name *Joppa,* a maritime city in the territory of Dan.

יְפִי, יָפִי, in pause יֹפִי, dec. 6k.— I. *beauty.*— II. *excellence, splendour.*

יְפֵה־פִיָּה adj. fem. *very beautiful,* Je. 46. 20.

יָפָה	fem. of the following, d. 11a (§ 42. rem. 1)	יפה
יָפֶה	adj. masc. sing. dec. 9b . .	יפה
יָפֶה / [וְיָפֶה]	id., constr. state, with cop. וְ [for וְיָפֶה,]	יפה
יְפֵה־פִיָּה	adj. fem. sing. see in its place under	יפה
יָפוֹ	pr. name of a place	יפה
יָפוּ	Kal pret. 3 pers. pl.	יפה
יָפוֹא	pr. name of a place	יפה
יִפּוֹל	Kh. יִפּוֹל, K. יִפֹּל Kal fut. 3 pers. sing. masc. (§ 8. rem. 18)	נפל
יִפּוֹל	Kal fut. 3 pers. s. m. (§ 8. r. 18, & § 17. r. 3)	נפל
יָפוּצוּ	Kal fut. 3 pers. pl. masc. . . .	פוץ
יָפוֹת	adj. fem., pl. abs. of יָפָה dec. 11a (§ 42. rem. 1) from יָפֶה masc.	יפה
יְפוֹת	id. pl., constr. state . . .	יפה
יָפֹזוּ וַ	Kal fut. 3 pers. pl. masc., וַ conv.	פזז
יְפָרֵר	Piel fut. 3 pers. sing. masc. . .	פזר

יָפַח Kal not used; i. q. פוּחַ, נָפַח *to breathe.* Hithp. *to pant, sigh,* Je. 4. 31.

יָפֵחַ adj. masc. dec. 5a, *breathing, puffing out,* Ps. 27. 12.

יָפִיחַ וַ	Kal fut. 3 p. sing. masc. ap. from פוח	יָפִיחַ
יָפַח וַ	Kal fut. 3 pers. sing. masc.; וַ conv. .	נפח
יְפֵחַ	adj. masc. constr. [יָפֵחַ], with cop. וְ, for (וְיָ), וְיָפֵחַ from יָפֵחַ dec. 5a .	יפח
יִפְחַד	Kal fut. 3 pers. s. m. [for יִפְחַד § 8 r. 15]	פחד
יִפְחֲדוּ / יִפְחֲדוּ	id. fut. 3 pers. pl. masc. (§ 8. rem. 15)	פחד

יַפְטִירוּ	Hiph. fut. 3 pers. pl. masc. . .	פטר
יִפְטַר וַ	Kal fut. 3 pers. sing. masc.; וַ conv. .	פטר
יְפִי	noun masc. sing.	יפה
יֳפִי	noun masc. sing. dec. 6k [for יָפְיְ, § 35. r. 14]	יפה
יָפְיָה	id., suff. 3 pers. sing. fem. . .	יפה
יָפְיוֹ	id., suff. 3 pers. sing. masc. . .	יפה
יָפִיחַ וַ	Hiph. fut. 3 pers. sing. masc. . .	פוח
יָפִיחוּ	id. fut. 3 pers. pl. masc. . . .	פוח
יָפְיֵךְ	noun m. s., suff. 2 pers. s. f. fr. [יָפְיְ] d. 6k	יפה
יַפִּיל	Hiph. fut. 3 pers. sing. masc. . .	נפל
יַפִּילוּ וַ	id. fut. 3 pers. pl. masc.; וַ conv. .	נפל
יַפִּילוּן	id. id. with parag. ן	נפל
יַפִּילֵם וַ	id. fut. 3 pers. sing. masc., suff. 3 pers. pl. masc.; וַ conv.	נפל
יָפִיעַ וַ	pr. name of a place	יפע
יָפְיָפִיתָ	Pu. pret. 2 pers. sing. masc. (§ 6. No. 9)	יפה
יָפִיץ	Hiph. fut. 3 pers. sing. masc. . .	פוץ
יְפִיצֵם וַ	id., suff. 3 pers. pl. masc.; וַ conv. .	פוץ
יָפִיק	Hiph. fut. 3 pers. sing. masc. . .	פוק
יָפַלְתְּ	Kal pret. 2 pers. sing. fem. . .	נפל
יַפֵּל וַ	Hiph. fut. 3 pers. sing. masc., ap. fr. יַפִּיל	נפל
יִפֵּל / יִפֵּל	Ch. Peal fut. 3 pers. sing. masc.	נפל
יִפֹּל / יִפֹּל	Kal fut. 3 pers. sing. masc. (comp. § 8. rem. 18); וַ conv.	נפל
יַפְלֵא	Hiph. fut. 3 pers. sing. masc. . .	פלא
יִפָּלֵא וַ	Niph. fut. 3 pers. sing. masc.; וַ conv. .	פלא
יַפְלֶה	Hiph. fut. 3 pers. sing. masc. . .	פלה
יַפְלוּ	defect. for יַפִּילוּ q. v. . . .	נפל
יִפְּלוּ / וַיִּ	Kal fut. 3 pers. pl. masc. (§ 8. r. 15); וַ conv.	נפל
יְפַלַּח וַ	Piel fut. 3 pers. sing. masc.; וַ id.	פלח
יִפְלְחוּן	Ch. Peal fut. 3 pers. pl. masc. . .	פלח
יַפְלֵט	pr. name masc.	פלט
יְפַלְּטֵהוּ וַ	Piel fut. 3 pers. sing. masc. [וַיְפַלֵּט], suff. 3 pers. sing. masc.	פלט
יְפַלְּטֵם וַ	id., suff. 3 pers. pl. masc.; וַ conv. .	פלט
יַפְלִיט וַ	Hiph. fut. 3 pers. sing. masc. . .	פלט
יְפַלֵּל וַ	Piel fut. 3 pers. sing. masc.; וַ conv. .	פלל
יַפְלֵם	defect. for יַפִּילֵם (q. v.) . . .	נפל
יְפַלֵּם	Piel fut. 3 pers. sing. masc. . .	פלם
יִפֶן וַ	Hiph. fut. 3 pers. sing. masc. ap. [from יִפְנֶה]; וַ conv.	פנה
יִפֶן / יִפְנֶה	Kal fut. 3 pers. sing. masc. ap. & full form; וַ id. . . .	פנה

a 1 Sa. 14. 45.   f Ge. 41. 2.   l Ps. 27. 12.   p Ps. 22. 8.   t Pr. 29. 8.   x Job 37. 11.   a 2 Sa. 2. 23.   d 2 Ki. 4. 39.   m Ps. 106. 30.
b Ge. 39. 6.   g Ge. 49. 24.   m Is. 19. 17.   q 1 Sa. 19. 10.   u Ex. 21. 27.   y Ca. 7. 7.   2 Sa. 13. 2.   i Ps. 22. 9.   n Ps. 140. 11.
c Pr. 22. 14.   h Ps. 147. 16.   n Mi. 7. 17.   r Eze. 28. 7.   v Ps. 78. 55.   z Da. 3. 6, 10, 11.   k Ex. 11. 7.   o Ps. 37. 40.   o Ps. 78. 56.
d Ps. 68. 2.   i Hab. 2. 3.   o Is. 44. 11.   s Ps. 45. 3.   c Ezr. 7. 20.   g Jon. 1. 7.   l Is. 5. 29.   u Ju. 15. 4.
e Job 42. 15.   k Ge. 2. 7.   Job 29. 24.

יְפַנֶּה	pr. name masc	פנה
יִפְנוּ	וַיִּ Kal fut. 3 pers. pl. masc.; וְ conv.	פנה
יִפְסַח	וַ Niph. fut. 3 pers. sing. masc.; וְ id.	פסח
יְפַסְּחוּ	וַ Piel fut. 3 pers. pl. masc.; וְ id.	פסח
יִפְסֹל	וַ Kal fut. 3 pers. sing. masc.; וְ id.	פסל
יִפְסְלוּ	וַ id. fut. 3 pers. pl. masc.; וְ id.	פסל

יָפַע. Hiph. הוֹפִיעַ.—I. *to cause to shine*, Job 37. 15.—
II. *to shine forth*.

פֻּעָה (for יְפוּעָה *splendid*) pr. name f. Ex. 1. 15.
יִפְעָה f. (no pl.) *brilliancy, beauty*, Eze. 28. 7, 17.
יָפִיעַ (*splendid*) pr. name—I. of a town in the
tribe of Zebulon, Jos. 19. 12.—II. of a king of
Lachish, Jos. 10. 3.—III. of a son of David,
2 Sa. 5. 15.

מֵפַעַת, מֵיפַעַת (*splendour*) pr. name of a Levitical city in the tribe of Reuben.

יִפְעַל / יְפַעֵל	} Kal fut. 3 pers. sing. masc. (§ 8. rem. 15)	פעל
יִפְעָלֵהוּ	וַ id., suff. 3 pers. sing. masc. (§ 16. r. 12); וְ conv.	פעל
יִפְעָתֵךְ	noun fem. sing., suff. 2 pers. sing. masc. [for יִפְעָתֵךְ, from יִפְעָה]	יפע
יָפֶץ / יָפֵץ	} Hiph. fut. 3 pers. sing. masc., ap. and וְ conv. from יָפִיץ	פוץ
יִפְצֶה	Kal fut. 3 pers. sing. masc.	פצה
יַפְצוּ	וַיִּ, וְיִּ Kal fut. 3 pers. pl. masc.; וְ conv.	פוץ
יִפְצְחוּ	Kal fut. 3 pers. pl. masc.	פצח
יִפְצְחוּ	Kh. יַפְצְחוּ q. v.; K. וּפְצְחוּ Kal imp. pl. m., וּ before labial	פצח
יְפַצֵּל	וַ Piel fut. 3 pers. sing. masc.; וְ conv.	פצל
יְפַצְפְּצֵנִי	וַ Pilpel fut. 3 pers. sing. masc. [יְפַצְפֵּץ, § 6. No. 4], suff. 1 pers. sing.; וְ id.	פוץ
יְפַצֵּץ	Pilel fut. 3 pers. sing. masc.	פוץ
יִפְצַר	וַ Kal fut. 3 pers. sing. masc.; וְ conv.	פצר
יִפְצְרוּ	וַ id. fut. 3 pers. pl. masc.; וְ id.	פצר
יָפֶק	וַ Hiph. fut. 3 pers. sing. masc. ap. and conv. from יָפִיק	פוק
יַפְקֵד	וַ, וַיַּ Hiph. fut. 3 pers. sing. masc. ap. fr. יַפְקִיד; וְ conv.	פקד
יִפָּקֵד / יִפָּקֵד	} וַיִּ Niph. fut. 3 pers. sing. masc. (§ 9. rem. 3); וְ id.	פקד
יִפְקֹד	וַ, וַיִּ Kal fut. 3 pers. sing. masc.; וְ id.	פקד
יַפְקִדֵהוּ	וַ Hiph. fut. 3 pers. sing. masc., suff. 3 pers. sing. masc.; וְ id.	פקד
יַפְקִדוּ	וַ id. fut. 3 pers. pl. masc.; וְ id.	פקד

יִפָּקְדוּ / יִפָּקְדוּ	} Niph. fut. 3 pers. pl. masc. (comp. § 8. rem. 15); וְ conv.	פקד
יִפְקְדוּ / יִפְקְדוּ	} Kal fut. 3 pers. pl. masc. (§ 8. rem. 15); וְ id.	פקד
יִפְקְדֵם	וַיִּ id. fut. 3 p. s. m., suff. 3 p. pl. m.; וְ id.	פקד
יִפְקְדֵנִי	id. id., suff. 1 pers. sing.	פקד
יִפְקוֹד	full form for יִפְקֹד q. v., (§ 8. rem. 18)	פקד
יַפְקִיד	Hiph. fut. 3 pers. sing. masc.	פקד
יִפְקַח	וַ Kal fut. 3 pers. sing. masc.; וְ conv.	פקד
יַפְקִידֵם	וַ Hiph. fut. 3 p. s. m., suff. 3 p. pl. m.; וְ id.	פקד
יֶפֶר / יָפֵר	} Hiph. fut. 3 pers. sing. m. (§ 18. rem. 11.)	פרר
יָפַר	וַ Hiph. fut. 3 pers. sing. masc. ap. [from יִפְרֶה]; וְ conv.	פרה
יִפָּרֵד	Niph. fut. 3 pers. sing. masc.	פרד
יַפְרִדוּ	וַ Hiph. fut. 3 pers. pl. masc.; וְ conv.	פרד
יִפָּרְדוּ / יִפָּרְדוּ	} Niph. fut. 3 pers. pl. masc. (§ 8. rem. 15); וְ id.	פרד
יְפָרְדוּ	Piel fut. 3 p. pl. m. [for יְפָרֵדוּ comp. § 8. r. 15]	פרד
יִפְרֶה	Kal fut. 3 pers. sing. masc.	פרה
יַפְרַח	defect. for יַפְרִיחַ (q. v.)	פרה
יִפְרוּ	וַ Hiph. fut. 3 pers. pl. masc.; וְ conv.	פרה
יִפְרוּ	וַיִּ, וְיִּ Kal fut. 3 pers. pl. masc.; וְ id.	פרה
יִפְרַח / יִפְרָח	} Kal fut. 3 pers. sing. masc. (§ 8. rem. 15)	פרח
יִפְרְחוּ / יִפְרְחוּ	} id. fut. 3 pers. pl. masc. (§ 8. rem. 15)	פרח
יַפְרִיא	Hiph. fut. 3 pers. sing. masc.	פרה
יַפְרִיד	Hiph. fut. 3 pers. sing. masc.	פרד
יַפְרִיחַ	Hiph. fut. 3 pers. pl. masc.	פרח
יַפְרִיחוּ	id. fut. 3 pers. pl. masc.	פרח
יַפְרִיס	Hiph. fut. 3 pers. sing. masc.	פרס
יַפְרֵךְ	וַ Hiph. fut. 3 pers. sing. masc. [יִפְרֶה], suff. 2 pers. sing. masc. (§ 24. rem. 21); וְ conv.	פרה
יִפְרֹם	Kal fut. 3 pers. sing. masc.	פרם
יַפְרְנוּ	Hiph. fut. 3 pers. sing. masc. (יִפְרָ), suff. 3 pers. sing. masc. [for יַפְרֶנּוּ]	פרר
יִפְרְסוּ	Kal fut. 3 pers. pl. masc.	פרס
יִפָּרַע	Niph. fut. 3 pers. sing. masc.	פרע
יִפְרַע	Kal fut. 3 pers. s. m. [for יִפְרָע § 8. rem. 15]	פרע
יְפָרְפְּרֵנִי	וַ Pilp. fut. 3 pers. sing. masc., suff. 1 pers. sing. (§ 6. No. 4); וְ conv.	פרר
יִפְרֹץ / יִפְרָץ	} וַיִּ Kal fut. 3 pers. sing. masc. (§ 8. rem. 18); וְ id.	פרץ
יִפְרְצוּ / יִפְרְצוּ	} id fut. 3 pers. pl. masc. (§ 8. rem. 15); וְ id.	פרץ

a 2 Sa. 4. 4.   e Eze. 28. 7, 17.   i Ge. 30. 37.   n Je. 37. 21.   r 1 Ch. 26. 32.   t Ge. 13. 11.   w Is. 45. 9.   z Pr. 14. 11.   y Je. 16. 7.
b 1 Ki. 18. 26.   f Job 38. 24.   k Job 16. 12.   o Je. 3. 16.   s Ne. 4. 9.   u Ho. 4. 14.   x Ge. 4. 27.   z Ps. 92. 14.   y Pr. 29. 18.
c Ex. 34. 4.   g Job 35. 16.   l Je. 23. 29.   p 1 Sa. 14. 17.   t Ps. 105. 24.   v Is. 11. 1.   x Pr. 11. 28.   e Le. 11. 5.   z Le. 21. 10.
d 1 Ki. 5. 32.   h Nu. 10. 35.   m 1 Sa. 20. 25, 27.   q Zep. 2. 7.   t 2 Ki. 2. 11.   o Job 14. 9.   p Ho. 14. 8.   e Ge. 28. 3.   z Job 16. 12.
e Ps. 7. 14, 16.   i Is. 55. 12.   n Pr. 19. 23.   r 1 Sa. 20. 6.   f Ge. 25. 23.   u Eze. 44. 7.   q Ho. 13. 15.   e Le. 21. 10.   z Ex. 19. 24.
f Is. 44. 12   m Is. 49. 13.   o Ge. 39. 4.   s Is. 10. 28.   ff Nu. 30. 14

יִפְרְצֵנִי	Kal fut. 3 pers. sing. masc., suff. 1 pers. sing.	פרץ
יְפָרֵק	Piel fut. 3 pers. sing. masc.	פרק
יִפְרְקֵנִי	‍וַ Kal fut. 3 pers. sing. masc., suff. 1 pers. sing.; וַ conv.	פרק
יַפְרִשׁ	Hiph. fut. 3 pers. sing. masc.	פרש
יְפָרֵשׁ	Piel fut. 3 pers. sing. masc.	פרש
יִפְרֹשׁ	וַ, וַיִּ Kal fut. 3 pers. sing. masc.; וַ conv.	פרש
יִפְרְשֵׂהוּ	‍וַ id., suff. 3 pers. sing. masc.; יִפְרֹשׂ	פרש
יִפְרְשׂוּ	Niph. fut. 3 pers. pl. masc. [for יִפָּרְשׂוּ, comp. § 8. rem. 15]	פרש
יִפְרְשׂוּ	וַיִּ Kal fut. 3 pers. pl. masc.; וַ conv.	פרש
יִפְשֶׂה	Kal fut. 3 pers. sing. masc.	פשה
יִפְשַׁחֲנִי	Piel fut. 3 pers. s. m., suff. 1 pers. s.; וַ conv.	פשח
יַפְשֵׁט	‍וַ Hiph. fut. 3 pers. sing. masc. ap. [from יַפְשִׁיט]; וַ id.	פשט
יִפְשֹׁט	‍וַ Kal fut. 3 pers. sing. masc.; וַ id.	פשט
יַפְשִׁטוּ	‍וַ Hiph. fut. 3 pers. pl. masc.; וַ id.	פשט
יִפְשְׁטוּ וַיִּ	Kal fut. 3 pers. pl. masc. (§ 8. rem. 15); וַ id.	פשט
יַפְשִׁיטֻהוּ	Hiph. fut. 3 p. pl. m., suff. 3 p. s. m.; וַ id.	פשט
יִפְשְׁטוּ	וַ id. fut. 3 pers. pl. masc.; וַ id.	פשט
יִפְשַׁע	‍וַיִּ Kal fut. 3 pers. sing. masc.; וַ id.	פשע
יִפְשְׁעוּ	וַ id. fut. 3 pers. pl. masc.; וַ id.	פשע

יֵפְתְּ	Root not used; Arab. وفت to be entire, perfect, conj. III, to arrive (Lee).
מוֹפֵת	masc. dec. 7 b.—I. sign, wonder.—II. mark, intimation, portent.
יֶפֶת	pr. name masc. for יַפְתְּ (comp. § 35. rem. 2)	פתה
יַפְתְּ	Hiph. fut. 3 pers. sing. masc. ap. [from § 24. rem. 16] יַפְתֶּה	פתה
יִפְתְּ	‍וַ Kal fut. 3 pers. sing. masc. ap. (from יִפְתֶּה § 24. rem. 3) ; וַ conv.	פתה
יְפַת וְיֹפַת	adj. f. s. constr. [with cop. וַ, for וַיִּ, וַיֹּפַת] from יָפֶה dec. 11 a, from יָפֶה masc.	יפה
יְפַת יְפֹת	id. pl., construct state (comp. preceding)	יפה
יִפְתָּח	‍וַ pr. name masc.; for וַ see lett. וַ	פתה
יְפַתֶּה	Piel fut. 3 pers. sing. masc.	פתה
יִפְתֶּה	Kal fut. 3 pers. sing. masc.	פתה
יְפֻתֶּה	Pual fut. 3 pers. sing. masc.	פתה
יְפַתּוּהוּ	‍וַ Piel fut. 3 p. pl. m., suff. 3 p. s. m.; וַ conv.	פתה
יְפַתּוּךָ	id., suff. 2 pers. sing. masc.	פתה
יִפָּתַח יִפָּתֵחַ	‍וַיִּ Niph. fut. 3 pers. sing. masc. (§ 15. rem. 1); וַ conv.	פתה
יִפְתַּח	‍וַ Piel fut. 3 pers. sing. masc.; וַ id.	פתח
יִפְתָּח	pr. name masc.	פתח

יִפְתַּח	‍וַ, וַיִּ Kal fut. 3 pers. sing. masc.; וַ conv.	פתח
יִפְתָּחֵהוּ	וַ Piel fut. 3 p. s. m., suff. 3 p. s. m.; וַ id.	פתח
יִפָּתְחוּ	Niph. fut. 3 pers. pl. masc.	פתח
יִפְתְּחוּ וַיִּ	Kal fut. 3 pers. pl. masc. (§ 8. rem. 15); וַ conv.	פתח
יִפְתָּחוּם	id., suff. 3 pers. pl. masc. (§ 16. rem. 12)	פתח
יָפָתִי	adj. fem. sing., suff. 1 pers. sing. from יָפֶה (§ 42. rem. 2), from יָפֶה masc.	יפה
יִפְתָּר	וַ Kal fut. 3 pers. sing. masc. [for יִפְתֹּר § 8. rem. 18]; וַ conv.	פתר

יָצָא וַ fut. יֵצֵא, imp. צֵא, inf. c. צֵאת (§ 25. No. 2 d) —I. to go out, go forth; with מִן, also acc. of the place whence, with בְּ (rarely מִן) of the place through or by which one goes out.—II. to come forth, to issue, descend, of children, posterity.—III to escape, as danger, with אֶת Ecc. 7. 18.—IV. to rise, as the sun, stars, &c.—V. to shoot forth, spring up, as plants; to spring forth, of water.—VI. to go forth, be issued, published, as a decree.—VII. to go out, to end, of a period of time. Hiph. הוֹצִיא.— I. to cause to go, come out or forth, to lead, bring forth or out.—II. to cause to spring up, to yield, as the earth plants.—III. to cause to lay out, as money, to exact, with עַל, 2 Ki. 15. 20.—IV. to spread abroad, to publish, with לְ, עַל of the person. —V. to produce, make, Is. 54. 16.—VI. to take out, to separate, Je. 15. 19. Hoph. to be led, brought forth or out.

יָצֵא Chald. Shaph. שֵׁיצֵי, שֵׁיצִי (§ 48) to bring to an end, to finish.

יָצִיא masc. dec. 3 a, issued, proceeded, 2 Ch. 32. 21.

צֵאָה fem. dec. 10 (for יְצֵאָה) excrement, ordure.

צוֹא or צוֹאָ adj. masc. filthy, Zec. 3. 3, 4.

צֵאָה, צוֹאָה fem. dec. 10, excrement, ordure, filth.

צֶאֱצָאִים m. pl. (of צֶאֱצָא dec. 1, § 31. rem. 1).— I. productions of the earth.—II. offspring, children.

מוֹצָא masc. dec. 1 b (§ 31. rem. 1).—I. a going out, an outgoing; a rising, of the sun.—II. the place of going or coming out, applied to a gate, fountain, the east (where the sun rises).—III. that which comes out, i. e. proceeds, is uttered, as words, speech.—IV. origin, race, breed, 1 Ki. 10. 28.—V. pr. name masc. of two different persons.

מוֹצָאָה fem. dec. 10 (comp. § 31. rem. 1).—I. a going out, origin, Mi. 5. 1.—II. draught-house, 2 Ki. 10. 27.

⁴ Job 16. 14.	⁵ Is. 25. 11.	Le. 13. 35.	¹ Sa. 31. 9.	ʳ Ge. 37. 23.	ᵍ Ge. 41. 4.	ᵇ Pr. 1. 10.	ᶠ Job 11. 5.	ᵏ Ge. 44. 11.
⁵ Zec. 11. 16.	⁶ Je. 49. 22.	¹ La. 3. 11.	³ Eze. 26. 16.	ˢ Pr. 28. 21.	ʸ Ge. 41. 18.	ᶜ Eze. 24. 27.	ᵍ Ps. 105. 20.	¹ Ne. 13. 19.
Ps. 136. 24.	ᵍ Eze. 17. 21.	Nu. 20. 28.	⁶ Eze. 44. 19.	ᵗ Ge. 9. 27.	ᵈ De. 11. 16.	ᵈ Eze. 33. 22.	⁷ Ne. 7. 3.	ᶜCa. 2. 10, 12.
Pr. 23. 32.	ᵃ Nu. 4. 7, 11.	¹ Sa. 19. 24.	¹ Ch. 10. 9.	ᵘ Job 31. 27.	ᵃ Ps. 78. 36.	ᵉ Is. 28. 24.	ˡ Ju. 3. 25.	ᵍ Ge. 41. 12.

תּוֹצָאוֹת fem. pl. (of תּוֹצָאָה dec. 11 a).—I. *termination, extremity.*—II. *deliverance, escape,* Ps. 68. 21.—III. *issue, result,* Pr. 4. 23.

יצא   יָצֹא Kal inf. absolute . . . .

יצא   יֵצֵא ',יֵ' id. fut. 3 pers. sing. masc.; וַ conv.

יצא   יֹצֵא Hiph. fut. 3 pers. sing. masc., ap. from יוֹצִיא (§ 20. rem. 11); וַ id. . .

יצא   יֹצֵא[a] Kal part. act. masc. dec. 7 b . .

יצא   יֹצֵא[c] וַ defect. for יוֹצִיא (q. v.) .

יצא   } יָצְאָה / יָצְאָ 'וַ } Kal pret. 3 pers. sing. fem. (§ 8. rem. 7)

יצא   יֹצִאֵהוּ } Hiph. fut. 3 pers. pl. masc. (יוֹצִיאוּ), suff. 3 pers. sing. masc.; וַ conv.

יצא   } יָצְאוּ / יָצְא 'וַ } Kal pret. 3 pers. pl. (§ 8. rem. 7)

יצא   יָצְאוּ Kh. q. v., K. יֵצְא (q. v.) .

יצא   } יֵצְאוּ [g] 'וַ', / יֵ'וַ } Kal fut. 3 pers. pl. masc. (comp. § 8. rem. 15); וַ conv.

יצא   יֵצְאוּ Kh. יֵצְאוּ q. v., K. צֵאוּ (q. v.)

יצא   יֹצִאוּ 'וַ Hiph. fut. 3 pers. pl. for יוֹצִיאוּ; וַ conv.

יצא   יֹצְאוֹת Kal part. act. fem., pl. of יֹצֵאת (§ 23. rem. 4) from יֹצֵא masc. . .

יצא   יֹצְאֵי id. pl. construct masc. dec. 7 b .

יצא   יֹצְאִים id. id., absolute state . .

יצא   יֹצִיאָךְ[h] וַ Hiph. fut. 3 p. s. m. (יוֹצִיא), suff. 2 p. s. m.; וַ conv.

יצא   יֹצִיאֵנוּ[i] וַ id. with suff. 1 pers. pl.; וַ id.

יצא   יָצָאנוּ[c] וַ Kal pret. 1 pers. pl. .

יצא   יָצָאנִי[k] id. pret. 3 pers. pl. with suff. 1 **pers. sing.**

יצא   יָצָאתָ וַ id. pret. 2 pers. sing. masc.

יצא   יָצָאתְ[l] וַ id. pret. 2 pers. sing. fem.

יצא   יֹצְאֹת pl. of the following . .

יצא   יֹצֵאת Kal part. act. fem. [for יֹצֵאת § 23. **rem. 4**] from יֹצֵא masc. . .

יצא   יָצָאתִי 'וַ id. pret. 1 pers. sing. .

יצא   } יְצָאתֶם / וִיצָאתֶם } id. pret. 2 pers. pl. masc., with conj. וַ [for וַ', וִיצָאתֶם] . .

יָצַב Kal not used; i. q. נצב *to set, put, place.* Hithp. הִתְיַצֵּב.—I. *to set* or *place oneself,* const. with לִפְנֵי, עַל.—II. *to stand; to stand before* (לִפְנֵי) any one, i. e. *to minister unto him.*—III. *to stand firm,* as a conqueror, with לִפְנֵי, בִּפְנֵי, עִם.—IV. *to stand up* for any one, *to assist him,* with לְ of the person.

יָצַב Chald. Pa. *to certify,* Da. 7. 19.

יַצִּיב Chald. adj. *firm, fixed, settled,* Da. 6. 13. —II. *certain, true;* מִן יַצִּיב *certainly,* Da. 2. 8.

נצב   } יַצֵּב וַיַּ' / יַצֵּב } Hiph. fut. 3 pers. sing. masc., ap. from יַצִּיב (§ 11. r. 7); וַ conv.

צבא   יִצְבָּא Chald. Peal fut. 3 pers. sing. masc. .

צבא   יִצְבְּאוּ וַ Kal fut. 3 pers. pl. masc.; וַ conv.

נצב   יַצִּבוּ[a] וַ Hiph. fut. 3 pers. pl. masc.; וַ id.

צבט   יִצְבָּט[c] וַ Kal fut. 3 pers. sing. masc. [for יִצְבֹּט § 8 rem. 18]; וַ id. . .

צבר   יִצְבֹּר וַיִּ' Kal fut. 3 pers. sing. masc.; וַ id. .

צבר   יִצְבְּרוּ 'וַ, 'וַיִּ' id. fut. 3 pers. pl. masc.; וַ id. .

יָצַג Kal not used; cogn. יצק, יצב. Hiph. הִצִּיג (§ 20. rem. 16).—I. *to set, put, place.*—II. *to establish,* Am. 5. 15.—III. *to let stay, to leave,* Ge. 33. 15. Hoph. הֻצַּג *to be left,* Ex. 10. 24.

יצג   יַצֵּג וַ Kal fut. 3 p. s. m. ap. [from וַיַּצֵּג]; וַ conv.

יצג   יֻצַּג[b] Hoph. fut. 3 pers. sing. masc. [for יֻצַּג comp. § 8. rem. 15] . . .

יצג   יַצִּיגוּ וַ Hiph. fut. 3 pers. pl. masc.; וַ conv.

יצג   יַצִּיגֵם[c] וַ id. fut. 3 pers. sing. masc., suff. 3 pers. pl. masc.; וַ id. . . .

צדק   יַצְדִּיק Hiph. fut. 3 pers. sing. masc. .

צדק   } יִצְדַּק / יִצְדָּק } Kal fut. 3 pers. sing. masc. (§ 8. rem. 15)

צדק   } יִצְדְּקוּ[l] / יִצְדָּקוּ[a] } id. fut. 3 pers. pl. masc. (§ 8. rem. 15)

צהר   יַצְהִירוּ[f] Hiph. fut. 3 pers. pl. masc. . .

צהל   יִצְהֲלוּ Kal fut. 3 pers. pl. m. [for יִצְהֲלוּ § 8. r. 15]

צהר   יִצְהָר 'וַ noun masc. sing. dec. 2 b, also pr. name m.

צהר   יִצְהָרֶיךָ[a] וַ id. pl., suff. 2 pers. sing. masc.

צהר   [יִצְהָרֶךָ] וַ id. sing., suff. 2 pers. sing. m. [for יִצְהָרְךָ]

צוה   יְצַו'[f] 'וַ Pi. fut. 3 pers. sing. masc. ap. for יְצַוֶּה

צוה   יְצַו[m] וַ Kh. יְצַו q. v., K. יְצַוּ (q. v.)

יצא   יָצוֹא Kal inf. absolute . . .

צוד   יָצוּד[m] Kal fut. 3 pers. sing. masc. .

צוד   יָצוּדוּ[a] id. fut. 3 pers. pl. masc. .

צוד   יְצוּדֶנּוּ id. fut. 3 pers. sing. masc., suff. 3 pers. s. m.

צוה   יְצַוֶּה 'וַ Piel fut. 3 pers. sing. masc.; וַ conv.

צוה   יְצֻוֶּה[f] Pual fut. 3 pers. sing. masc. .

צוה   יְצַוֵּהוּ וַ Piel fut. 3 pers. sing. masc., suff. 3 pers. sing. masc.; וַ conv.

צוה   יְצַוֵּהוּ וַ Kh. יְצַוֵּהָ q. v., K. יְצַוֶּה (q. v.) .

צוה   יְצַוּוּ וַ Piel fut. 3 pers. pl. masc.; וַ conv.

צוה   יְצֻוְּחוּ Kal fut. 3 pers. pl. m. [for יְצֻוְּחוּ § 8. rem. 15]

צוה   } יְצֻוֶּךָ וַיְ', / וַ } Piel fut. 3 pers. s. m. (יְצֻוֶּה), suff. 2 pers. s. m. (§ 24. r. 21); with conj. וַ [for וִיצֻוְּךָ]

צום   יָצוֹם[m] וַ Kal fut. 3 pers. sing. masc. ap. [for יָצֹם § 21. rem. 7 & 8]; וַ conv. . .

a Je. 37. 4.   f Eze. 46. 9.   l 1 Ki. 10. 29. 2 Ki. 10. 26.   q Je. 31. 4.   v Nu. 31. 7.   c 2 Sa. 6. 17.   h Job 24. 11.   m Le. 17. 13.   r 2 Ki. 16. 15.
b Job 28. 11.   g Je. 15. 1.   De. 5. 15.   f Ge. 24. 13.   Je. 5. 8.   Mi. 7. 2.   Is. 42. 11.
Ju. 19. 25.   Ge. 34. 26.   Nu. 11. 20.   1 Sa. 17. 35.   De. 7. 13.   Ps. 140. 12.   1 Ch. 22. 12.
Ju. 28. 29.   Je. 46. 9.   1 Sa. 11. 3.   De. 32. 8.   Is. 53. 11.   Ex. 34. 34.   1 Ki. 21. 27.
Ge. 19. 16.   Je. 50. 8.   Je. 10. 20.   Pr. 15. 25.   Ex. 10. 24.   Is. 45. 25.   Ju. 21. 20.   Nu. 20. 16.

23

יְצַוֵּם וֹ׳	Piel fut. 3 pers. sing. masc. (יְצַוֶּה), suff. 3 pers. pl. masc. (§ 24. rem. 21) ; וֹ conv.	צוה
יְצוּמוּ וַ	Kal fut. 3 pers. pl. masc. ; וַ id.	צום
יְצַוֵּנוּ וַ	Piel fut. 3 pers. sing. masc. (יְצַוֶּה), suff. 1 pers. pl. (§ 24. rem. 21) ; וַ id.	צוה
יָצוּעַ	Kh. יָצוּעַ Kal part. p., K. יָצִיעַ noun m. s. d. 3a	יצע
יְצוּעַי	Kal part. p. pl., suff. 1 p. s. from יָצוּעַ dec. 3a	יצע
יְצוּעֵי	id. pl., construct state	יצע
יְצוּעִי	id. sing. with suff. 1 pers. sing.	יצע
יָצוּק	Kal fut. 3 pers. sing. masc.	צוק
יָצוּק וַ׳	Kal part. pass. sing. masc. dec. 3a	יצק
יְצוּקִים	id. pl., absolute state	יצק
יִצְחָק וְ׳	pr. name masc.	צחק
יִצְחַק־ יִ	Kal fut. 3 pers. sing. masc. (§ 8. rem. 15, comp. § 35. rem. 17) ; וַ conv.	צחק
יְצַחֵק	Piel fut. 3 pers. s. m. (§ 14. rem. 1) ; וַ id.	צחק
יִצְהָר	Kh. יִצְהָר, K. וְצֹהַר pr. name masc.	צהר
יִצְטַבַּע	Chald. Ithpa. fut. 3 pers. sing. masc. [for יִתְצַבַּע, comp. § 12. rem. 3]	צבע
יִצְטַיָּרוּ וַ	Hithpa. fut. 3 pers. pl. masc. [for יִתְצַיָּרוּ, § 12. rem. 3] ; וַ conv.	ציר
יְצִיאֻהוּ וַ	Hiph. fut. 3 pers. pl. masc., suff. 3 pers. sing. masc. [for יוֹצִיאוּהוּ § 20. r. 11] ; וַ id.	יצא
יְצִיאוּ וַ׳	id. fut. 3 pers. pl. masc. (v. id.) ; וַ id.	יצא
יְצִיאֵנוּ	id. fut. 3 pers. s. m., suff. 1 pers. pl. (v. id.)	יצא
יַצִּיב	Hiph. fut. 3 pers. sing. masc.	נצב
יַצִּיב וֹ׳	Chald. adj. masc. dec. 1	יצב
יַצִּיבָא וֹ׳	id., emph. state	יצב
יַצִּיבֵנִי וַ	Hiph. fut. 3 pers. sing. masc., suff. 1 pers. sing. ; וַ conv.	נצב
יַצִּיגוּ וַ	Hiph. fut. 3 pers. pl. masc. ; וַ id.	יצג
יַצִּיל	Hiph. fut. 3 pers. sing. masc.	נצל
יַצִּילֶהָ וַ	id. id., suff. 3 pers. sing. fem. ; וַ conv.	נצל
יַצִּילֵהוּ	id. id., suff. 3 pers. sing. masc.	נצל
יַצִּילוּ	id. fut. 3 pers. pl. masc.	נצל
יַצִּילוּתָ וַ	id. id., suff. 3 pers. sing. fem. ; וַ conv.	נצל
יַצִּילְךָ יַ	id. fut. 3 pers. sing. masc., suff. 2 pers. sing. masc. (§ 2. rem. 2)	נצל
יַצִּילְךָ		
יַצִּילְכֶם	id. fut. 3 pers. pl. masc., suff. 2 pers. s. fem.	נצל
יַצִּילָם	id. fut. 3 pers. sing. masc., suff. 3 pers. pl. m.	נצל
יַצִּילֶנָּה	id. id., suff. 3 pers. sing. fem. (§ 2. rem. 3)	נצל
יַצִּילְנוּ וַ	id. id., suff. 1 pers. pl.	נצל
יַצִּילֶנּוּ	id. id., suff. 3 pers. sing. masc.	נצל
יַצִּילֵנִי	id. id., suff. 1 pers. sing.	נצל

יָצִיעַ	Hph. fut. 3 pers. sing. masc. (§ 20. rem. 16)	יצע
יָצִיק	Hiph fut 3 pers. sing. masc.	צוק
יָצִיקוּ וְ׳	id. fut. 3 pers. pl. masc. ; וַ conv.	צוק
יָצִיק	Hiph. fut. 3 pers. sing. masc.	צוק
יָצִיקוּ	id. fut. 3 pers. pl. masc.	צוק
יַצִּיתוּ וַ	Hiph. fut. 3 p. pl. m. (§ 20. r. 16) ; וַ conv.	יצת
יַצֵּל וַ׳ וַ	Kal fut. 3 pers. sing. masc. ap. from יַצִּיל ; וַ id.	נצל
יִצְלֶה	Kal fut. 3 pers. sing. masc.	צלה
יַצְלִהֵהוּ וַ	Hiph. fut. 3 pers. sing. masc., suff. 3 pers. sing. masc. ; וַ conv.	נצל
יַצְלִחַ וַ	Hiph. fut. 3 p. s. m., ap. from יַצְלִיחַ ; וַ id.	צלח
יִצְלַח יַ	Kal fut. 3 pers. sing. masc. (§ 8. rem. 15)	צלח
יַצְלִיחַ	Hiph. fut. 3 pers. sing. masc.	צלח
יַצְלִיחוּ וַ׳ וַ	id. fut. 3 pers. pl. masc ; וַ conv.	צלח
יַצְּלֵם וַ	Hiph. fut. 3 p. s. m., suff. 3 p. pl. m. ; וַ id.	נצל
יַצְּלֵנִי וַ	id. with suff. 1 pers. sing.	נצל
יָצֹם וַ	Kal fut. 3 pers. s. m., ap. and conv. fr. יָצוּם	צום
יִצְמָא וַ	Kal fut. 3 pers. sing. masc. ; וַ conv.	צמא
יִצְמָאוּ וַ	id. fut. 3 pers. pl. masc. [for יִצְמְאוּ § 8. rem. 15]	צמא
יִצָּמֵד	Niph. fut. 3 p. s. m. (§ 9. rem. 3) ; וַ conv.	צמד
יִצְמְדוּ וַ	id. fut. 3 pers. pl. masc. ; וַ id.	צמד
יָצֻמּוּ וַ	Kal fut. 3 p. pl. m. def. for יָצוּמוּ ; וַ id.	צום
יַצְמַח וַ	Hiph. fut. 3 p. s. m. ap. from יַצְמִיחַ ; וַ id.	צמח
יְצַמֵּח	Piel fut. 3 pers. sing. masc.	צמח
יִצְמַח יִ	Kal fut. 3 pers. sing. masc. (§ 8. rem. 15) ; וַ conv.	צמח
יִצְמָח וַ		
יִצְמְחוּ	id. fut. 3 pers. pl. m. [for יִצְמָחוּ § 8. rem. 15]	צמח
יַצְמִיחַ	Hiph. fut. 3 pers. sing. masc.	צמח
יַצְמִיתֵם	Hiph. fut. 3 pers. sing. m., suff. 3 pers. pl. m.	צמת
יִצְנֹף	Kal fut. 3 pers. sing. masc.	צנף
יִצְנָפְךָ	id., suff. 2 pers. sing. masc.	צנף

[יָצַע] to spread down, to strew ; only part. יָצוּעַ, (a) bed, couch ; (b) floor, story, 1 Ki. 6. 5, 6, 10. Kh. Hiph. הִצִּיעַ (§ 20. rem. 16) to spread down, to strew. Hoph. יֻצַּע pass. of Hiph.

יָצִיעַ masc. floor, story, 1 Ki. 6. 5, 6, 10. Keri. מַצָּע masc. bed, couch, Is. 28. 20.

	Hoph. fut. 3 pers. sing. masc. (§ 20. r. 16)	יצע
יַצְעִד	Kal fut. 3 pers. sing. m. [for יִצְעַד § 8. r. 15]	צעד
יִצְעֲדוּ	id. fut. 3 pers. pl. masc. [for יִצְעֲדוּ v. id.]	צעד
יִצְעַן	Kal fut. 3 pers. sing. masc. [for יִצְעַן v. id.]	צען

a Job 37. 12.   b De. 6. 24.   c 1 Ki. 6. 5.   d 1 Ki 17. 14.   e 1 Ch. 5. 1.   f Job 28. 2: 29. 6.

g Job 41. 16.   h 2 Ch. 4. 3.   i Ge. 17. 17.   k Ge. 21. 6.   l Ju. 16. 25.   m 1 Ki. 21. 13.   n Jos. 9. 4.

o Da. 2. 8.   p Da. 2. 45.   q Da. 7. 16.   r La. 3. 12.   s 2 Sa. 23. 12.   t Ps. 22. 9.   u Ezr. 8. 31.

v 1 Ch. 11. 14.   w Ps. 91. 3.   x Ps. 21. 6.   y Is. 57. 13.   z Ho. 2. 12.   a Je. 19. 9.

b Ps. 34. 20.   c Is. 58. 5.   d Ps. 72. 16.   e Ps. 92. 8.   f De. 28. 53, 55, 57.   g Ex. 18. 8.

h 1 Sa. 7. 3.   i Is. 44. 16.   k Ge. 37. 21.   l Is. 49. 10.   m Is. 5. 28.   n 2 Ch. 14. 6.   o Nu. 25. 3.

p 1 Sa. 26. 24.   q Ex. 18. 4.   r 2 Sa. 12. 16.   s Is. 49. 10.   t Job 24. 11.   u Eze. 17. 6.

v Ps. 106. 28.   w Je. 14. 12.   x Ge. 2. 9.   y Job 5. 6.   z Pr. 7. 8.   a Job 8. 19.

Ps. 94. 23.   b Le. 14. 4.   c Is. 22. 18.   d Pr. 7. 8.   e Je. 10. 5.   f Je. 33. 20.

יַצְעֵק וְ	Hiph. fut. **3** pers. sing. masc. ap. [from	צעק
	וַ [יַצְעִיק; conv. . .	
יִצָּעֵק וְ	Niph. fut. **3** pers. sing. masc.; וְ id. .	צעק
וַיִּצְעַק	Kal fut. **3** pers. sing. masc.; וְ id. .	צעק
יִצָּעֲקוּ וְ	Niph. fut. **3** pers. pl. masc.; •וְ id. .	צעק
וַיִּצְעֲקוּ	Kal fut. **3** pers. pl. masc.; •וְ id. .	צעק
יִצְעֲרוּ }		
וְ }	Kal fut. **3** pers. pl. masc. (§ 8. rem. 15)	צער
יָצִיף וְ	Hiph. fut. **3** pers. sing. masc. ap. & conv.	צוף
	[from יָצִיף]	
יָצֶף	Kal fut. **3** pers. sing. masc. ap. [from יָצְפָּה]	צפה
יְצַף וְ	Piel fut. **3** pers. sing. masc. ap. [from	
	יְצַפֶּה; וְ conv. . . .	צפה
יְצַפֵּהוּ וְ	id. id., suff. **3** pers. sing. masc.; וְ id. .	צפה
יִצָּפוּ וְ	id. fut. **3** pers. pl. masc.; וְ id. .	צפה
Kh. יַצָּפִנוּ	Hiph., K. יִצְפּוֹנוּ, Kal fut. **3** pers.	צפן
	pl. masc. (§ 8. rem. 18)	
יְצַפֵּם וְ	Piel fut. **3** pers. sing. masc. [יְצַפֶּה], suff.	
	3 pers. pl. masc. (§ 24. rem. 21); וְ conv.	צפה
יִצְפֹּן	Kal fut. **3** pers. sing. masc. . .	צפן
יִצְפְּנוּ }		
יִצְפֹּנוּ }	id. fut. **3** pers. pl. masc. (§ 8. rem. 15)	צפן
יִצְפְּנֵנִי	id. fut. **3** pers. sing. masc., suff. 1 pers. sing.	צפן
יִצְפֹּר וְ	Kal fut. **3** pers. sing. masc. . .	צפר
יָצֶץ וְ	Hiph. fut. **3** pers. s. m. ap. & conv. fr. יָצִיץ	צוץ

יָצַק וְ [וְ] fut. יָצֹק (§ 20. rem. 16), וַיָּצָק; imp. צַק, יְצֹק; inf. צֶקֶת; *to pour, pour out*; intrans. *to be poured out*, 1 Ki. 22. 35; Job 38. 38; part. יָצוּק *poured out, cast*, of metal, and hence *hard, firm*. Pi. *to pour out*, 2 Ki. 4. 5 Kheth. Hiph. הִצִּיק *to put down, place, lay out*. Hoph. הוּצַק *to be poured out*; part. מֻצָּק *cast, molten*, 1 Ki. 7. 23; מְצָק *firm*, Job 11. 15.

יְצֻקָה fem. dec. 10, *casting* of metal 1 Ki. 7. 24.

מוּצָק masc. *something cast, a casting*.

מוּצָקָה fem. *a funnel*, pl. מוּצָקוֹת Zec. 4. 2.

מוּצֶקֶת fem. dec. 13 a, *a casting*, 2 Ch. 4. 3.

יִצֹּק וְ }	Kal fut. **3** pers. sing. masc. (§ 20. rem. }	יצק
יָצֹק וַ }	16); וְ conv. . . . }	
יְצֹק	id. imp. sing. masc. (§ 20. rem. 1) .	יצק
יִצְקוּ וְ	Hiph. fut. **3** p. pl. m. (§ 20. r. 16); וְ conv.	יצק
יִצְקוּ וַ	Kal fut. **3** pers. pl. masc.; וְ id. .	יצק
יִצְקוּ	id. imp. pl. masc. (§ 20. rem. 1) .	יצק
יֹצְקֹת	Kal part. p. f. pl. [of יָצְקָה] d. 10, fr. יָצוּק m.	יצק
יְצֻקִים	id. masc., pl. of יָצוּק dec. 3 a .	יצק
יְצֻקֵם	id. pret. **3** pers. sing m., suff. 3 pers. pl. m.	יצק

יַצְקֻם וַ	Hiph. fut. **3** pers. pl. masc. [יַצִּיקֻן], suff.	
	3 pers. pl. masc. (§ 20. rem. 16); וְ conv.	יצק
יָצַקְתָּ וְ	Kal pret. **2** pers. sing. masc.; acc. shifted	
	by conv. וְ (§ 8. rem. 7) . .	יצק
יָצַקְתְּ וְ	id. pret. **2** pers. sing. fem. . .	יצק

יָצַר I. fut. יֵצֶר, *to be straitened, to be distressed, anxious*; וַיֵּצֶר לוֹ *and he was distressed*.—II. fut. יִצֹר (§ 20. rem. 16), וַיִּיצֶר; וַיָּצַר; (*a*) *to form, fashion, make*; part. יוֹצֵר *maker, creator, potter*; (*b*) *to devise, meditate*, with עַל *against* any one. Niph. נוֹצַר *to be formed, created*, Is. 43. 10. Pu. id. Ps. 139. 16. Hoph. הוּצָר id. Is. 54. 17.

יֵצֶר masc. dec. 6 b.—I. *something formed, form, frame*.—II. *imagination, thought*.—III. pr. name masc. Ge. 46. 24. Patronym. יִצְרִי Nu. 26. 49; also the pr. name of a man, 1 Ch. 25. 11.

יְצָרִים masc. pl. (of יֵצֶר dec. 1) *things formed, members*, Job 17. 7.

יָצַר	Kal pret. **3** pers. sing. masc. in pause for יָצַר	יצר
וַיָּצַר	Hiph. fut. **3** pers. sing. masc. with conv. וְ	צרר
	[for יָצֵר § 18. rem. 11] . .	
יָצַר וַ	Kal fut. **3** p. s. m., ap. & conv. (§ 21. r. 9)	צור
יָצֹר	Kal fut. **3** pers. sing. masc. . .	צרר
יֵצֶר }	Kal fut. **3** pers. sing. masc. (§ 20. rem. }	יצר
וַיִּצֶר }	1 & 4); וְ conv. . . . }	
יֵצֶר וְ	noun masc. s. dec. 6 b, also pr. name m.	יצר
יֶצֶר וַ	Kal fut. **3** pers. sing. masc., defect. & with	
	conv. וַ [for וַיִּיצֶר § 20. rem. 2] .	יצר
יִצֹּר	Kal fut. **3** pers. sing. masc. . .	נצר
יֹצֵר וְ	Kal part. act. sing. masc. dec. 7 b .	יצר
יְצָרָהּ	id. pret. **3** pers. sing. masc., suff. 3 pers. s. f.	יצר
יֹצְרָהּ וְ	id. part. act. s. m. (יֹצֵר), suff. 3 p. s. f. d. 7 b	יצר
יִצְרֵהוּ	id. fut. **3** pers. sing. masc. [יָצַר § 20. rem.	יצר
	16], suff. 3 pers. sing. masc. . .	
יְצָרוּ	id. pret. **3** pers. pl. [for יָצְרוּ § 8. rem. 7]	יצר
יָצֹרוּ וְ	Hiph. fut. **3** pers. pl. masc.; וְ conv. .	צרר
יָצוּרוּ	Kal fut. **3** pers. pl. masc.; וְ id. .	צור
יִצְרוּ	Kal fut. **3** pers. pl. masc. . .	יצר
יִצְרוֹ	noun m. s., suff. 3 p. s. m. from יֵצֶר dec. 6 b	יצר
יִצֹּרוּ	Kal fut. **3** pers. sing. masc. . .	נצר
יֹצְרוֹ וְ	Kal part. act. sing. masc. (יֹצֵר), suff. 3 pers.	יצר
	sing. masc. dec. 7 b . . .	
יֻצָּרוּ	Pual pret. **3** p. pl. [for יֻצְּרוּ comp. § 8. r. 7]	נצר
יִצְרוּנִי	Kal fut. **3** pers. pl. masc., suff. 1 pers. sing.	נצר
יֹצְרַי	Kal part. act. pl. c. m. from יֵצֶר dec. 7 b	יצר
יֹצְרִי	id. sing. with suff. 1 pers. sing. . .	יצר

ᵃ 1 Sa. 10. 17.	ᶠ 2 Ch. 3. 10.	ˡ Nu. 17. 23.
ᵇ Je. 30. 19.	ᵍ Ps. 56. 7.	ᵐ Le. 2. 1.
ᶜ Job 14. 21.	ʰ Ex. 36. 36.	ⁿ 1 Ki. 22. 35.
ᵈ 2 Ki. 6. 6.	ⁱ Ps. 27. 5.	ᵒ Eze. 24. 3.
ᵉ Ge. 31. 49.	ᵏ Ju. 7. 3.	ᵖ 2 Sa. 15. 24.

ᵠ 2 Ki. 4. 40.	ˢ 2 Ki. 4. 4.	ᵇ 2 Ch. 28. 20.
ʳ 1 Ki. 18. 34.	ᵗ Is. 44. 10.	ᶜ Is. 11. 13.
ˢ 1 Ki. 7. 30.	ᵘ Ge. 2. 8.	ᵈ Pr. 4. 12.
ᵗ 1 Ki. 7. 24.	ᵛ 1 Ki. 8. 37;	ᵉ Zec. 12. 1.
ᵘ Jos. 7. 23.	2 Ch. 6. 28.	ᶠ Is. 45. 18.
		ᵍ Is. 29. 16.

ᵍ Ge. 2. 19.	ᵐ Is. 44. 12.	ʳ Is. 27. 11.
ʰ Is. 11. 13.	ⁿ Ps. 95. 5.	ˢ Ps. 139. 16.
ⁱ Pr. 3. 1.	ᵒ Ne. 9. 27.	ᵗ Is. 44. 9.
ᵏ Job 20. 22.	ᵖ Job 18. 7.	ᵘ Is. 44. 4.
ˡ Is. 22. 11.	ᵠ Pr. 20. 28.	ᵛ Is. 49. 5.

23*

יְצָרִי   ] noun masc. pl., suff. 1 pers. sing. with cop.] [for וַי׳, וַיְצָרֵי from יֵצֶר dec. 1 a   יצר

יַצְרִיחַ‎ Hiph. fut. 3 pers. sing. masc.   צרח

יֹצְרֶךָ] Kal part. act. sing. masc. (יֹצֵר), suff. 2 pers. sing. masc. dec. 7 b (§ 36. rem. 3)   יצר

יִצְרֶנְהוּ Kal fut. 3 pers. sing. m. (יֵצֶר) with epenth. ן & suff. 3 pers. sing. masc. (§ 16. r. 13)   נצר

יִצְרֵנוּ noun masc. s., suff. 1 pers. pl. from יֵצֶר d. 6 b   יצר

יֹצְרֵנוּ Kal part. act. s. m. (יֹצֵר), suff. 1 p. pl. d. 7 b   יצר

יִצָּרְפוּ] Niph. fut. 3 pers. pl. masc.   צרף

יָצַרְתָּ id. pret. 2 pers. sing. masc.   יצר

יָצַרְתִּי id. pret. 1 pers. sing.   יצר

יְצַרְתִּיהָ] id. id., suff. 3 pers. sing. fem. with conj.] [for וַי׳, וַיְצַרְתִּיהָ]   יצר

יְצַרְתִּיו id. id., suff. 3 pers. sing. masc.   יצר

יְצַרְתִּיךָ id. id., suff. 2 pers. sing. masc.   יצר

יְצַרְתָּם id. pret. 2 pers. sing. m., suff. 3 pers. pl. m.   יצר

יָצַת only fut. יִצַּת (§ 20. rem. 16).—I. to set on fire, to kindle, with בְּ Is. 9. 17.—II. to be burned, consumed. Niph. נִצַּת.—I. to be burned, consumed. —II. to burn with anger, with בְּ against any one. Hiph. הִצִּית, הוֹצִית to set on fire, to kindle.

וַיַּצֶּת־] Hiph. fut. 3 pers. sing. masc. ap. & conv. (§ 11. rem. 7, & § 20. rem. 16)   יצת

יִצְּתוּ‎ Kal fut. 3 pers. pl. masc. with dag. euph. [for יִצַּתוּ, in pause for יִצָּתוּ, comp. יֶחֱתּוּ, also § 8. rem. 3, 4, 7, & § 20. rem. 16]   יצת

יָצַתִי id. Kal pret. 1 pers. sing. for יָצַאתִי (§ 23. r. 1)   יצא

וַיָּקָא] Hiph. fut. 3 pers. sing. masc. ap. [from וַי׳ conv. ;   וַיָּקִיא]   קוא

וַיְקִאֶנּוּ] id., suff. 3 pers. sing. masc. (§ 2. rem. 3)   קוא

יֶקֶב] [וַי׳] masc. dec. 6 a (with suff. יִקְבְךָ).—I. wine-vat. —II. wine-press, i. e. the trough in which grapes are trodden out.

יָקֶב noun masc. seg. [as if from יָקַב § 35. rem. 1 & 2] but see יֶקֶב   יקב

יִקֹּב] Kal fut. 3 pers. sing. masc. ;] conv.   נקב

יִקְבֻהוּ id. fut. 3 pers. pl. masc., suff. 3 pers. s. m.   נקב

יִקְבֵי‎ noun masc. pl. constr. from יֶקֶב dec. 6 a   יקב

יְקָבֶיךָ‎ id. pl., suff. 2 pers. sing. masc.   יקב

יְקָבִים‎ id. pl., absolute state   יקב

וִיקַבְּלוּ] Piel fut. 3 pers. pl. masc. ;] conv.   קבל

וַיְקַבְּלוּן] Ch. Pael fut. 3 pers. pl. masc. with conj.] [for וַי׳, וַיְקַבְּלוּן]   קבל

יְקַבְּלֵם] Piel pret. 3 p. s. m., suff. 3 p. pl. m. ;] conv.   קבל

יִקָּבֶנּוּ Kal fut. 3 pers. sing. masc. ([יִקֹּב]), suff. 3 pers. sing. masc. (§ 8. r. ר 4, & § 2. r. 3)   נקב

יִקְבֹּץ] Kal fut. 3 pers. sing. masc. (§ 8. rem. 18);] conv.   }   קבץ
וְיִקְבֹּץ־] }

יְקַבֵּץ Piel fut. 3 pers. sing. masc.   קבץ

וַיִּקָּבְצוּ] Niph. fut. 3 pers. pl. masc. ;] conv.   קבץ

וַיִּקְבְּצוּ] וַי׳] Kal fut. 3 pers. pl. masc. ;] id.   קבץ

יְקַבֶּצְךָ] Piel fut. 3 pers. sing. masc., suff. 2 pers. sing. masc. (§ 16. rem. 15)   קבץ

יְקַבְּצֵם] Kal fut. 3 p. s. m., suff. 3 p. pl. m. ;] conv.   קבץ

יְקַבְּצֶנּוּ Piel fut. 3 p. s. m., suff. 3 p. s. m. (§ 2. r. 3)   קבץ

יִקְבָּצֶנּוּ Kal fut. 3 p. s. m., suff. 3 p. s. m. (§ 2. r. 3)   קבץ

וַיִּקָּבֵר] Niph. fut. 3 pers. sing. masc. ;] conv.   קבר

יִקְבֹּר] Kal fut. 3 pers. sing. masc. ;] id.   קבר

יִקְבְּרֻהוּ] id. fut. 3 p. pl. m., suff. 3 p. s. m. ;] id.   קבר

יִקְבְּרוּ Niph. fut. 3 pers. pl. masc. [for יִקָּבְרוּ, comp. § 8. rem. 15]   קבר

וַיִּקְבְּרוּ־] Kal fut. 3 pers. pl. masc. ;] conv.   קבר

[יָקַד] fut. יָקַד, יִיקַד to burn, as fire; part. pass. יָקוּד burning mass upon the hearth, Is. 30. 14. Hoph. הוּקַד to be kindled, to burn.

יְקַד Ch. id. Da. 3. 6, 11, 15, 17, 20, 21, 23, 26

יְקֵדָא fem. dec. 8, a burning, Da. 7. 11.

יְקוֹד masc. id. Is. 10. 16.

מוֹקֵד masc. dec. 7 b.—I. burning, Is. 33. 14.— II. firebrand, Ps. 102. 4.

מוֹקְדָה fem. hearth where the burnt-offerings were consumed, Le. 6. 2.

יֵקַד־ Kal fut. 3 pers. sing. masc. (§ 20. rem. 2)   יקד

יְקֹד noun masc. sing.   יקד

יִקֹּד] Kal fut. 3 pers. sing. masc., Chald. form (§ 18. rem. 14);] conv.   קדד

יִקְּדוּ] id. fut. 3 pers. pl. masc. ;] id.   קדד

יַקְדִּישׁ Hiph. fut. 3 pers. sing. masc.   קדש

יַקְדִּישׁוּ id. fut. 3 pers. pl. masc.   קדש

יְקַדְּמוּ Piel fut. 3 pers. pl. masc.   קדם

יְקַדְּמֻנִי id. id., suff. 1 pers. pl.   קדם

יְקַדְּמוּנִי id. id., suff. 1 pers. pl.   קדם

יְקַדְּמֻנָה id. 3 pers. sing. masc., suff. 3 pers. s. fem.   קדם

יְקַדְּמֻנִי id. id., suff. 1 pers. sing.   קדם

יְקַדְּמֻנִי־ defect. for יְקַדְּמוּנִי (q. v.)   קדם

יַקְדֵּעָם‎ pp] (possessed of the people, Syr. קְדָ to possess)   קדע

וַיִּקָּדֵשׁ] Niph. fut. 3 pers. sing. masc. ;] conv.   קדש

יַקְדִּשׁ־ defect. for יַקְדִּישׁ (q. v.)   קדש

ᵃ Job 17. 7.   ᵍ Ps. 104. 26.   ᵐ La. 4. 11.   ˢ Job 20. 15.   ʸ Pr. 3. 10.   ᵉ Is. 62. 2.   ⁱ 2 Ch. 32. 6.   ᵐ Is. 10. 16.   ʳ Ps. 79. 8.
ᵇ Is. 42. 13.   ʰ 2 Ki. 19. 25.;   ⁿ Is. 33. 12.;   ᵗ Is. 5. 2.   ᶻ Job 24. 11.   ᶠ Je. 31. 10.   ᵏ Is. 31. 9.   ⁿ Is. 10. 16.   ˢ Ps. 18. 19.
ᶜ De. 32. 10.   Is. 37. 25.   ᵒ Je. 51. 58.   ᵘ Ho. 9. 2.   ² Ch. 29. 16, 22.   ᵍ Is. 60. 7.   ˡ Pr. 28. 8.   ᵖ Le. 27. 14, 18,   ᵗ Ps. 59. 11.
ᵈ Ps. 103. 14.   ⁱ Is. 43. 21.   ᵖ Job 1. 21.   ᵛ Nu. 18. 30.   ᵃ Da. 7. 18.   ʰ 1 Ch. 13. 2.   22, 26,   ⁿ 2 Sa. 22. 12.
ᵉ Is. 64. 7.   ᵏ Is. 44. 21.   ᵠ Jon. 2. 11.   ᵂ Zec. 14. 10.   ᵇ 1 Ch. 12. 18.   ⁱ De. 30. 4.   ᵐ Je. 19. 11.   ᵠ Ps. 89. 15.   ᵘ Nu. 20. 12.
ᶠ Da. 12. 10.   ˡ Ps. 74. 17.   ᵖᵖ Jos. 15. 56.   ᵘᵘ Le. 27. 14.

יַקְדֵּשׁ ‹ Piel fut. 3 pers. sing. masc.; ‹ conv. . קדש

יַקְדֵּשׁ ‹ Kal fut. 3 pers. sing. masc. (§ 8. rem. 15) קדש

יַקְדִּשֵׁהוּ ‹ Piel fut. 3 pers. sing. masc. with suff. 3 pers. sing. masc.; ‹ conv. . . קדש

יַקְדִּשׁוּ ‹ defect. for יַקְדִּישׁוּ q. v. . . קדש

יַקְדִּשׁוּ Piel fut. 3 pers. pl. masc. (comp. § 8. rem. 15); ‹ conv. . . קדש

יַקְדִּשׁוּ ‹ Kal fut. 3 pers. pl. masc. [for § 8. rem. 15]; ‹ id. . . קדש

יַקְדִּשֵׁם ‹ Piel fut. 3 pers. sing. masc., suff. 3 pers. pl. masc.; ‹ id. . . קדש

יֹקֶדֶת Kal part. act. sing. fem. [from יָקַד masc. § 8. rem. 19] . . יקד

יָקֶדְתָּא Ch. Peal part. act. sing. fem. emph. [of יָקְדָא, from יָקַד masc. § 47. rem. 1] . . יקד

יָקֵה Root not used; Arab. *to venerate*.

יָקֶה (*pious*) pr. name masc. Pr. 30. 1

יְקוּתִיאֵל (*veneration of God*) pr. name masc. 1 Ch. 4. 18.

יָקַה Root not used; Arab. וקה *to obey*.

יְקָהָה fem. dec. 11 c (constr. יְקַהַת with dag. forte euph. comp. § 33. rem. 1) *obedience*, Ge. 49. 10; Pr. 30. 17.

יָקֶה pr. name masc. . . . יקה

יַקְהִיל ‹ Hiph. fut. 3 pers. sing. masc. . קהל

יַקְהֵל ‹ ap. from the preceding; ‹ conv. . קהל

יִקָּהֵל ‹ Niph. fut. 3 pers. sing. masc.; ‹ id. . קהל

יַקְהִלוּ ‹ Hiph. fut. 3 pers. pl. masc.; ‹ id. . קהל

יִקָּהֲלוּ ‹ Niph. fut. 3 pers. pl. masc.; ‹ id. . קהל

יְקַהַת noun fem. sing. constr. of [יְקָהָה] dec. 11 c, dag. forte euph. in ק . . . יקה

יְקַו ‹ Piel fut. 3 pers. sing. masc. ap. and יְקַוֶּה full form; ‹ conv. . . קוה

יִקָּווּ Niph. fut. 3 pers. pl. masc. . . קוה

יְקַווּ Piel fut. 3 pers. pl. masc. . . קוה

יָקוֹט Kal fut. 3 pers. sing. m. [for יָקָט § 18. r. 2] קטט

יָקוּם ‹ Kal fut. 3 pers. sing. masc. . . קום

יְקוּם Chald. Peal fut. 3 pers. sing. masc. . קום

יָקוּם Kal fut. 3 pers. sing. masc. (for יָקָם § 8. rem. 18, & § 17. rem. 3) . . נקם

יָקוּמוּ ‹ Kal fut. 3 pers. pl. masc.; ‹ conv. . קום

יְקוּמוּן id. with parag. ‹; Chald. Da. 7. 10, 17 קום

יְקוֹמֵם Pilel fut. 3 pers. sing. masc. . קום

יְקוֹמְמוּ Pilel fut. 3 pers. pl. masc. [for יְקוֹמְמוּ comp. § 8. rem. 15] . . . קום

יְקוֹנֵן ‹ Pilel fut. 3 pers. sing. masc.; ‹ conv. קין

יְקוֹסֵם Poel fut. 3 pers. sing. masc. . . קסם

יָקוֹשׁ noun masc. sing. . . . יקש

יָקוּשׁ noun masc. sing. dec. 3 a . . . יקש

יְקוּשִׁים id. pl., absolute state . . . יקש

יְקוּתִיאֵל pr. name masc. . . . יקה

יִקַּח Kal fut. 3 pers. sing. masc. (§ 17. rem. 8); ‹ conv. . . . לקח

יֻקַּח Hoph. fut. 3 pers. sing. masc. (§ 17. rem. 8) . . . . לקח

יִקָּח Kh. יָקַח q. v., K. יִקְחוּ (q. v.) . לקח

יִקָּחֶהָ Kal fut. 3 pers. sing. masc. (יִקַּח), suff. 3 pers. sing. fem. (§ 16. rem. 12, & § 17. rem. 8) ; ‹ conv. . . . לקח

יִקָּחֵהוּ id. id., suff. 3 pers. sing. masc.; ‹ id. לקח

יִקָּחֻהוּ id. fut. 3 pers. pl. m. with suff. 3 pers. s. m. לקח

יִקְּחוּ id. fut. 3 pers. pl. masc. (§ 8. rem. 15); ‹ conv. . . . לקח

יִקָּחוּם id. id., suff. (יִקַּח), 3 p. pl. m. (§ 16. rem. 12) לקח

יִקָּחֲךָ id. fut. 3 pers. sing. masc., suff. 2 pers. sing. masc. (v. id.) . . . לקח

יִקָּחֵם id. id., suff. 3 pers. pl. masc. (v. id.); ‹ conv. לקח

יִקָּחֶנָּה id. id., suff. 3 pers. s. fem. (v. id. & § 2. rem. 3) לקח

יִקָּחֵנּוּ id. id., suff. 3 pers. sing. masc. (v. id.) . לקח

יִקָּחֵנִי id. id., suff. 1 pers. sing. (v. id.); ‹ conv. לקח

יַקְטִיר Hiph. fut. 3 pers. sing. masc. . . קטר

יַקְטִרוּ Kh. יַקְטִירוּ Hiph. fut. 3 pers. pl.; K. יַקְטִרוּ (q. v.) . . . קטר

יַקְטִירֶנָּה Hiph. fut. 3 pers. sing. masc., suff. 3 pers. sing. fem. (§ 2. rem. 3) . . . קטר

יִקְטֹל Kal fut. 3 pers. s. m. [for יִקְטֹל § 8. rem. 18] קטל

יִקְטְלֵנִי id. with suff. 1 pers. sing. . . קטל

יָקְטָן pr. name masc. . . . קטן

יִקָּטֵף Niph. fut. 3 pers. sing. masc. . . קטף

יַקְטֵר ‹ Kal fut. 3 pers. s. m. ap. from יַקְטִיר; ‹ conv. קטר

יְקַטֵּר ‹ Piel fut. 3 p. s. m.; ‹ conv.; with ‹ conj. קטר

יַקְטֵר ‹ [וַיְ, וַיִּקְטַר [for וַיִּקְטֵר קטר

יְקַטְּרוּ id. fut. 3 pers. pl. masc. (comp. § 8. rem. 15); ‹ conv. . . . קטר

יַקְטִרוּן Hiph. fut. 3 pers. pl. masc. with parag. ‹ קטר

יְקַטְּרוּן Piel fut. 3 pers. pl. masc.; ‹ paragogic [for יְקַטְּרוּן comp. § 8. rem. 17] . . קטר

יָקִדְתָּא Chald. full form for יָקֶדְתָּא (q. v.) . יקד

יָקִים Hiph. fut. 3 pers. sing. masc. . . קום

יָקִים pr. name masc. . . . קום

---

a 1 Sa. 21. 6.   f Nu. 17. 3.   i Job 11. 10.   t Is. 5. 2, 7.   *Mi. 2. 8.   c Je. 5. 26.   h De. 30. 4.   *2 Ch. 34. 25.   ‡ 2 Ch. 25. 14.
b Jos. 20. 7.   g Job 1. 5.   k 1 Ki. 8. 1.   u Ge. 1. 9.   y Is. 61. 4.   d Ge. 42. 16.   i Ge. 32. 24.   q Ex. 30. 7, 8.   † Hab. 1. 16.
c Eze. 44. 24.   h Is. 65. 5.   l Nu. 20. 10.   v Job 8. 14.   z 2 Ch. 35. 25.   e Ge. 18. 4.   k De. 20. 7.   r Job 24. 24.   g Ho. 11. 2.
d Eze. 44. 19.   i Da. 3. 26, 23, 26.   m Ge. 49. 10.   w Ec. 12. 4.   * Eze. 17. 9.   f 2 Ki. 20. 18.   l Job 40. 24.   s Job 15. 15.   Da. 3. 6, 11,
e Ch. 29. 17.   k Ch. 5. 2.   n Job 3. 9.   x De. 32. 43.   † Ho. 9. 8.   g Job 15. 12.   = Eze. 8. 3; Am. 7. 15.   t Job 8. 12   15, 17, 21.
        == 1 Sa. 2. 15, 16.

יָקִים	Chald. Aph. fut. 3 pers. sing. masc.	קום
יְקִימֶהָ	וַ Hiph. fut. 3 pers. sing. masc. (יָקִים), suff. 3 pers. sing. fem.; וַ conv.	קום
וַיָּקִימוּ	id. fut. 3 pers. pl. masc.; וַ id.	קום
יָקִימוּן	id. id. with parag.	קום
יְקִימְךָ	id. fut. 3 pers. s. m. (יָקִים), suff. 2 pers. s. m.	קום
יְקִימֶנָּה	id. id., suff. 3 pers. sing. fem. (§ 2. rem. 3)	קום
יְקִימֶנּוּ	id. id., suff. 3 pers. sing. masc. (v. id.)	קום
וַיְקִימֵנִי	וַ id. id., suff. 1 pers. sing.; וַ conv.	קום
וַיְקִיעֵם	וַ Hiph. fut. 3 pers. pl. m., suff. 3 pers. pl. m. defect. [for יוֹקִיעֵם § 20. r. 2]; וַ id.	יקע
יָקִיפוּ	Hiph. fut. 3 pers. pl. masc.	נקף
יָקִיצוּ	Hiph. fut. 3 pers. pl. masc.	קוץ
יָקִיר	adj. masc. sing.	יקר
וְיַקִּירָא	וַ Chald. adj. masc. sing., emph. of יַקִּיר dec. 1	יקר
יַקִּירָה	Chald. id. fem., absolute state	יקר
יָקֵל	Hiph. fut. 3 pers. sing. masc.	קלל
וַיָּקְלָהוּ	Kh. יָקְלָהוּ וַ Niph. fut. 3 pers. pl. masc., transposed for K. יִקָּהֲלוּ (q. v.)	קהל
יֵקַלּוּ	Kal fut. 3 pers. pl. m. [for יֵקַלּוּ § 18. rem. 6]	קלל
יֵקַלּוּ	Niph. fut. 3 pers. pl. masc.	קלל
יְקַלֵּל	וַ/ Piel fut. 3 pers. sing. masc.; וַ conv.; with וַ conj. [וַיְקַלֵּל for וַיְקַלֵּל]	קלל
יְקֻלַּל	Pual fut. 3 pers. sing. masc. [for יְקֻלַּל comp. § 8. rem. 15]	קלל
וַיְקַלְלוּ	וַ/ Piel fut. 3 pers. pl. m. (§ 10. r. 7); וַ conv.	קלל
יְקַלֶּלְךָ	id. fut. 3 pers. sing. masc. [יְקַלֵּל], suff. 2 pers. sing. masc. (§ 16. rem. 15)	קלל
וַיְקַלְלֵם	וַ id. id., suff. 3 p. pl. m. (§ 10. rem. 7); וַ conv.	קלל
וַיִּקְלַע	וַ Piel fut. 3 pers. sing. masc.; וַ id.	קלע
יִקְלַעֶנָּה	id., suff. 3 pers. sing. fem.	קלע
יָקֶם / יֵקֶם	Hiph. fut. 3 pers. sing. masc., ap. and conv. from יָקִים	קום
יָקָם / וַיָּקָם	וַ/וַ Kal fut. 3 pers. sing. masc., ap. and conv. from יָקוּם (§ 21. r. 7 & 8)	קום
יָקֹם	Kal fut. 3 pers. sing. masc. (§ 17. rem. 3)	נקם
יוּקַם	Hoph. fut. 3 pers. sing. masc. (comp. § 8. rem. 15)	נקם
וַיָּקֻמוּ	וַ/ וַ defect. for יָקוּמוּ (q. v.)	קום
יָקוּמֻן	Chald. defect. for יָקוּמוּן (q. v.)	קום
יָקָמְיָה	וַ/ וְיָקַמְיָה וַיָּקַם pr. name m., with cop. וַ [for יָקֻמֶנִּי	קמה
יְקַמְנוּ	defect. for יְקִימֻנוּ (q. v.)	קום
יְקַמְעָם	וַיָּקַם & יָקַמְעָם וַ pr. names masc.	קמה
יָקֶן	וַ Kal fut. 3 pers. s. m. ap. from יִקְנֶה; וַ conv.	קנה
וַיְקַנֵּא	וַ/ Piel fut. 3 pers. sing. masc.; וַ id.	קנא

יְקַנְאֵהוּ	defect. for יְקַנְאֻיֹאֻהוּ (q. v.)	קנא
יְקַנְאֵהוּ	וַ the following with suff. 3 pers. sing. masc.	קנא
וַיְקַנְאוּ	וַ Piel fut. 3 pers. pl. m. (§ 10. rem. 7); וַ conv.	קנא
יִקְנֶה	Kal fut. 3 pers. sing. masc.	קנה
וַיִּקְנֵהוּ	וַ id., suff. 3 pers. s. m. (§ 24. rem. 21); וַ conv.	קנה
יִקָּנֶה	Niph. fut. 3 pers. sing. masc.	קנה
יִקְנוּ	Kal fut. 3 pers. pl. masc.	קנה
יַקְנִיאֻהוּ	Hiph. fut. 3 pers. pl. m., suff. 3 pers. sing. m.	קנא
יָקֹנֵן	וַ Pilel fut. 3 pers. sing. masc.; וַ conv.	קון
יְקַנְּנוּ	Piel fut. 3 pers. pl. masc. [for יְקַנְּנוּ comp. § 8. rem. 15]	קנן
יִקְנָעַם	pr. name of a place	קנה
יִקְסֹמוּ / וַיִּקְסְמוּ	} Kal fut. 3 pers. pl. masc. (§ 8. rem. 15); וַ conv.	קסם
יָקַע	only fut. יֵקַע.—I. to be dislocated, Ge. 32. 26.—II. to be alienated from any one, with מֵעַל, מִן. Hiph. הוֹקִיעַ to suspend, hang. Hoph. to be hanged, 2 Sa. 21. 13.	
וַיָּקֶף	וַ Hiph. fut. 3 pers. sing. masc. ap. [from וַיַּקִּיף]; וַ conv.	נקף
יִקְפְּאוּן	Kh. יִקְפָּאֻן Kal fut. 3 pers. pl. masc., וַ parag. (§ 8. rem. 17); K. וְקָפָאֻן n. masc. sing.	קפא
יַקִּפוּ	וַ Hiph. fut. 3 pers. pl. masc.; וַ conv.	נקף
יִקְפְּצוּ	Kal fut. 3 pers. pl. masc.	קפץ
וְיִקָּפְצוּן	Niph. fut. 3 pers. pl. masc.; וַ parag.	קפץ
יָקַץ	only fut. יָקַץ, יִיקַץ, וַיִּיקַץ (§ 20. rem. 16), to awake.	
וַיָּקַץ	וַ Kal fut. 3 p. s. m. ap. and conv. [fr. וַיָּקוּץ]	קוץ
יִקַץ / וַיִּקַץ / יִיקַץ	} וַ Kal fut. 3 pers. sing. masc., for יִיקַץ (§ 8. rem. 15, and § 20. rem. 2); וַ conv.	יקץ
יִקָּבֶ־	וַ Kal fut. 3 pers. sing. masc. [for יִקֹּב § 8 rem. 18]; וַ id.	קבב
יִקְצוּ	וַ Kal fut. 3 pers. pl. masc.; וַ id.	קוץ
יִקְצוּ	וַ Kal fut. 3 p. pl. m. [for יִיקְצוּ § 20. rem. 2]	קץ
יִקְצֹר / יִקְצוֹר	Kh. יִקְצוֹר q. v., K. יִקְצָר with Mak. for Kal fut. 3 pers. sing. masc. (§ 8. rem. 18)	קצר
וַיַּקְצִפוּ	וַ Hiph. fut. 3 pers. pl. masc.; וַ conv.	קצף
יַקְצִרוּ	Kh. יַקְצִרוּ Hiph. fut. 3 pers. pl. masc., K. יִקְצְרוּ (q. v.)	קצר
יַקְצִעַ	Hiph. fut. 3 pers. sing. masc.	קצע
וַיִּקְצֹף	וַ/ Kal fut. 3 pers. sing. masc.; וַ conv.	קצף
יִקְצְפוּ	וַ id. fut. 3 pers. pl. masc.; וַ id.	קצף
יְקַצֵּץ	וַ Piel fut. 3 pers. sing. masc.; וַ id.	קצץ

a Jos. 24. 26.   f 2 Sa. 21. 9.   u 2 Sa. 20. 14.   r Pr. 30. 10.   b Jos. 10. 13   c De. 32. 16.   o Ps. 104. 17.   u Is. 52. 15.   cc Hab. 2. 7.
b Nu. 1. 51.   g Ps. 17. 9.   n 1 Sa. 2. 30.   s 2 Ki. 2. 24.   c Ge. 4. 15.   d Eze. 31. 9.   p Mi. 3. 11.   v 1 Ki. 18. 27.   dd Pr. 22. 8.
c Job 4. 4.   h Je. 31. 20.   o Is. 30. 16.   t 1 Sa. 17. 49.   d Jos. 18. 4.   e Ge. 39. 1.   q 2 Ki. 17. 17.   w 1 Ki. 3. 15.   ee Ps. 106. 32.
De. 28. 9.   i Esr. 4. 19.   p 2 Sa. 16. 11.   u 1 Sa. 25. 29.   e Da. 7. 24.   f La. 3. 5.   r Zec. 14. 6.   x 1 Ki. 6. 6.   ff Job 24. 6.
d Nu. 23. 19.   j Da. 2. 11.   q Is. 65. 20.   v Job 22. 28.   f Ho. 6. 2.   g Je. 32. 44.   s Ps. 78. 58.   y 2 Ki. 6. 14.   b Ex. 1. 12.   gg Ju. 16. 20.
f Job 16. 12.   k 1 Sa. 6. 5.   r Ju. 9. 27.   w Ge. 27. 31.   g Joel 2. 18   t Ps. 78. 58.

יְקַצְצוּ	Piel fut. 3 pers. pl. masc. ; ‍ conv.	קצץ
יְקַצְּרֻהוּ	Kal fut. 3 pers. pl. m., suff. 3 pers. sing. m.	קצר
יִקְצְרוּ	id. fut. 3 pers. pl. m. [for יִקְצְרוּן § 8. rem. 15]	קצר
יִקְצְרוּן	id. with parag. ‍ (§ 8. rem. 17) .	קצר

[יָקַר] fut. יָקַר, יִיקַר, יֵיקָר; (Arab. وقر *to be heavy*).—I. *to be dear, precious, esteemed.*—II. *to be estimated, prized,* Zec. 11. 13.—III. *to be honoured, respected,* 1 Sa. 18. 30. Hiph. הוֹקִיר *to make rare.*

יָקָר masc. dec. 4 a, יְקָרָה fem. dec. 11 c, adj.—I. *precious, dear.*—II. *splendid, beautiful.*—III. *honoured, respected,* Ec. 10. 1.—IV. *rare,* 1 Sa. 3. 1.—V. *quiet,* Pr. 17. 27.

בְּלִי יְקָר יְקָר masc. dec. 1 a.—I. *preciousness, precious vessel;* also *what is precious, precious thing.*—II. *splendour, glory, honour.*—III. *value, price,* Zec. 11. 13.

יְקָר Chald. dec. 1 b.—I. *costly things.*—II. *honour, glory.*

יַקִּיר adj. masc. *dear, beloved,* Je. 31. 20.

יַקִּיר Chald. adj. masc. dec. 1 a.—I. *hard, difficult,* Da. 2. 11.—II. *honourable, noble,* Ezr. 4. 10.

יָקָר	adj. masc. sing. dec. 4 b .	יקר
יִקֶר	‍ Kal fut. 3 pers. s. m., ap. fr. יִקְרָה ; וַ conv.	קרה
יֵקֶר	‍ Niph. fut. 3 p. s. m., ap. from יִקָּרָה ; וַ id.	קרה
יַקֵר	‍ Kal fut. 3 pers. sing. masc. (§ 20. rem. 2)	יקר
יְקָר	‍ noun masc. sing. dec. 1 a; with cop. ‍	יקר
יְקָר	‍ [for וַיְקָר]	
יִקְרָא	‍, וַ Niph. fut. 3 pers. sing. masc. ; וַ conv.	קרא
יִקְרָא	וַ Kal fut. 3 pers. sing. masc. ; וַ id.	קרא
יְקָרָא	‍ noun masc. sing. emph. [with cop. ‍, for וַיְקָרָא] from יְקָר dec. 1 b .	יקר
יִקְרָאֶהָ	‍ Kal fut. 3 p. s. m., suff. 3 p. s. f.; וַ conv.	קרא
יִקְרָאֶהָ	וַ id. id., suff. 3 pers. sing. masc. .	קרא
יִקְרָאֵהוּ	id. fut. 3 pers. sing. masc. (יִקְרָאוּ), suff. 3 pers. sing. masc. (§ 16. rem. 13) .	קרא
יִקְרְאוּ	‍ וַ Niph. fut. 3 pers. pl. masc. ; וַ conv.	קרא
יִקְרָאוּ	Kal fut. 3 pers. sing. masc. (יִקְרָא), suff. 3 pers. sing. masc. [for יִקְרָאוּ comp. § 16. r. 12]	קרא
יִקְרְאוּ	וַ id. fut. 3 pers. pl. masc. (§ 8. rem. 15) ; וַ conv.	קרא
יִקְרְאוּ	וַ, וַ id.	
יִקְרָאֻם	‍ id. fut. 3 pers. sing. m., suff. 3 pers. pl. m.	קרא
יִקְרָאֻנּוּ	id. id., suff. 3 pers. sing. masc.	קרא
יִקְרָאֻנִי	id. id., suff. 1 pers. sing.	קרא
יִקְרָאֻנְנִי	id. fut. 3 pers. pl. masc. with parag. ‍ and suff. 1 pers. sing. (§ 16. rem. 12 & 13) .	קרא
יַקְרֵב	defect. for יַקְרִיב (q. v.) . .	קרב

יַקְרֵב	‍ Hiph. fut 3 p.s.m. ap. from יַקְרִיב ; וַ conv.	קרב
יִקְרַב	Kal fut. 3 pers. sing. masc. (§ 8. rem.)	קרב
יִקְרַב	וַ (§ 8. rem. 15) ; וַ id.	קרב
יַקְרִבוּ	‍ defect. for יַקְרִיבוּ (q. v.) .	קרב
יִקְרְבוּ	Kal fut. 3 pers. pl. masc. (§ 8. rem.)	קרב
יִקְרְבוּ	וַ (§ 8. rem. 15) ; וַ conv.	קרב
יָקְרָה	Kal pret. 3 pers. sing. fem. .	יקר
יְקָרָה	adj. fem. sing. dec. 11 c, from יָקָר masc.	יקר
יְקָרָהּ	noun masc. sing., suff. 3 pers. sing. fem. from יְקָר dec. 1 a .	יקר
יְקָרֵה	‍ Chald. for וַיִּקְרָא (q. v.) .	יקר
יִקָּרֵה	Niph. fut. 3 pers. sing. masc.	קרה
יִקְרֶה	Kal fut. 3 pers. s. m., for יִקְרָה (§ 24. r. 19 a)	קרה
יִקְרֵה	Chald. Peal fut. 3 pers. sing. masc. [for יִקְרָא § 55 note]	קרא
יִקְרֶה	Kal fut. 3 pers. sing. masc. .	קרה
יָקְרוּ	Kal pret. 3 pers. pl. .	יקר
יִקְּרוּהָ	Kal fut. 3 pers. pl. masc., suff. 3 pers. s. fem.	נקר
יִקְרוֹן	Chald. Peal fut. 3 pers. pl. masc. .	קרא
יְקָרוֹת	adj. fem., pl. of יְקָרָה dec. 11 c, from יָקָר m.	יקר
יִקָּרֶחָ	Niph. fut. 3 pers. sing. masc. .	קרה
יִקְרְחוּ	Keri יִקְרְחוּ, Kal fut. 3 pers. pl. masc. .	קרח
יַקְרִיב	Hiph. fut. 3 pers. sing. masc. .	קרב
יַקְרִיבוּ	וַ id. fut. 3 pers. pl. masc.	קרב
יַקְרִיבֶנּוּ	id. fut. 3 pers. sing. masc., suff. 3 pers. s. m.	קרב
יִקְרֵךְ	Kal fut. 3 pers. sing. masc. (יִקְרָה), suff. 2 pers. sing. fem. (§ 24. rem. 21) .	קרה
יִקְרְמֵם	‍ Kal fut. 3 pers. sing. masc. ; וַ conv. .	קרם
יִקְרֵנִי	Kal fut. 3 pers. sing. masc. (יִקְרָה), suff. 1 pers. sing. (§ 24. rem. 21) .	קרה
יִקָּרֵעַ	Niph. fut. 3 pers. sing. masc. (§ 15.)	קרע
יִקָּרֵעַ	וַ rem. 1) ; וַ conv.	קרע
יִקְרַע	‍ Kal fut. 3 pers. sing. masc. ; וַ id. .	קרע
יִקְרָעֶהָ	וַ id. id., suff. 3 pers. sing. f. (§ 16. r. 12)	קרע
יִקְרְעוּ	‍ id. fut. 3 pers. pl. masc. .	קרע
יִקְרָעֵם	‍ id. fut. 3 pers. sing. masc., suff. 3 pers. pl. masc. (§ 16. rem. 12)	קרע
יִקְרְצוּ	Kal fut. 3 pers. pl. masc. . .	קרץ
יָקַרְתְּ	Kal pret. 2 pers. sing. fem. .	יקר
יְקָרֹת	adj. pl. absolute fem. from sing. יְקָרָה dec. 11 c, from יָקָר masc.	קר
יָקְרַת	id. sing., constr. state . .	יקר
יָקַרְתִּי	Kal pret. 1 pers. sing. .	יקר

[יָקַשׁ] *to lay snares;* יֹקֵשׁ *fowler,* Ps. 124. 7. Niph נוֹקַשׁ *to be ensnared.* Pu. id. Ec. 9. 12.

יָקוּשׁ, יָקֹשׁ masc. dec. 3 a, *fowler.*

* Job 4. 8.   * Ps. 49. 9.   ‡ Jon. 3. 8.   ‖ Eze. 46. 4.   ᵃ Da. 5. 20.   ᶠ Ps. 139. 17.   ʰ Le. 21. 5.   ᵏ 1 Sa. 15. 27.   ᵗ Is. 43. 4.
ᵇ Ru. 2. 9.   ᵈ Is. 41. 3.   ᵍ 2 Ki. 19. 14.   Nu. 18. 3.   Da. 23. 3.   ᵍ Pr. 30. 17.   1 Sa. 28. 10.   ᵏ Je. 36. 23.   1 Ki. 7. 9.
ᶜ Ru. 2. 3.   ᵉ Je. 23. 6.   ‖ Ge. 42. 4.   1 Sa. 26. 21.   Da. 10. 14.   Da. 5. 15.   Eze. 37. 8.   1 Ki. 11. 30.   Zec. 11. 13.
ᵈ Nu. 23. 4. 16.   2 Ki. 19. 30.   ᵐ Pr. 1. 28.   Je. 20. 5.   Da. 5. 7.   Je. 16. 6.   Ec. 2. 15.   Ps. 35. 19.   Is. 28. 16.

יָקְשָׁן (fowler) pr. name of a son of Abraham by Keturah, Ge. 25. 2, 3.

מוֹקֵשׁ masc. dec. 7 b (pl. ־וֹת, ־ים), snare, gin.

וַיָּקֶשׁ] Hiph. fut. 3 pers. sing. masc., ap. [from
קשה [וַ׳ conv. ; יַקְשֶׁה

וַיִּקֶשׁ] Kal fut. 3 pers. s. m. ap. fr. יִקְשֶׁה; וַ׳ id.   קשה

וַיַּקְשֵׁב] Hiph. fut. 3 pers. s. m. ap. fr. יַקְשִׁיב; וַ׳ id.   קשב

יִקְשֶׁה Kal fut. 3 pers. sing. masc.   קשה

יִקְשׁוּ Kal pret. 3 pers. pl.   יקש

יִקְשׁוּן Kal fut. 3 p. pl. m. (קוֹשׁ § 21. r. 3) with parag. ן   קוש

וַיַּקְשׁוּ] Hiph. fut. 3 pers. pl. masc.; וַ׳ conv.   קשה

יַקְשִׁיב Hiph. fut. 3 pers. sing. masc.   קשב

יָקְשָׁן pr. name masc.   יקש

יִקְשֹׁר] Kal fut. 3 pers. sing. masc. (§ 8. rem.
וַ׳] 18); וַ׳ conv.   קשר

וַיִּקְשְׁרוּ] id. fut. 3 pers. pl. masc.; וַ׳ id.   קשר

וָאֶקְשְׁתִּי Kal pret. 1 pers. sing. (§ 8. rem. 1)   יקש

יְקוּתִיאֵל] (subdued of God; Arab. קתא to serve) pr.
name—I. of a town in the tribe of Judah,
Jos. 15. 38.—II. of a city in Arabia,
2 Ki. 14. 7.

יָרֵא וְ׳] pret. יָרֵאתָ, יְרֵאתֶם (from יָרֵא § 23. rem. 1);
fut. יִירָא, יִרָא; inf. c. יָרֹא, יִרְאָה (§ 8. rem. 10).
—I. to fear, be afraid; with acc., מִן of the
person or thing feared; with לְ to fear, be anxious
for any person or thing; with an inf. and לְ or
מִן to be afraid to do anything; with פֶּן, lest any
thing happen.—II. to reverence, honour, with אֵת,
מִלִּפְנֵי. Niph. נוֹרָא to be feared, Ps. 130. 4.
Part. נוֹרָא, (a) fearful, dreadful, terrible; (b) awful,
holy; (c) marvellous, wonderful; נוֹרָאוֹת marvellous
deeds. Pi. to make afraid, to alarm.

יָרֵא masc. dec. 5 a (constr. יְרֵא § 34. rem. 1);
יְרֵאָה fem. dec. 11 c (constr. יִרְאַת Pr. 31. 30) adj.
—I. fearing, reverencing; יָרֵא אָנֹכִי אֹתוֹ I fear
him; יְרֵא אֱלֹהִים fearing God.—II. fearful, timid,
De. 20. 8.

יִרְאָה fem. (no pl.).—I. inf. of the verb יָרֵא, to
fear; hence לְיִרְאָה אֶת־שְׁמֶךָ to fear thy name.—
II. subst. fear, terror.—III. reverence, awe.

יִרְאוֹן (fearful) pr. name of a city in the tribe
of Naphtali, Jos. 19. 38.

מוֹרָא masc. dec. 2 b.—I. fear, Ge. 9. 2.—II.
reverence, awe.—III. object of fear or reverence.—
IV. fearful, stupendous act.

תִּירְיָא (fear) pr. name masc. 1 Ch. 4. 16.

יָרֵא adj. masc. sing. dec. 5 (§ 34. rem. 1)   ירא

וַיִּרָא] Kal fut. 3 pers. sing. masc., ap. and conv.
from יִרְאָה (§ 24. rem. 3); or (2 Ki. 11. 4)
Hiph., ap. from יַרְאָה (§ 24. rem. 16)   ראה

וַיֵּרָא יֵ׳ וַ׳] Niph. fut. 3 pers. sing masc. ap. from
יֵרָאֶה; וַ׳ conv.   ראה

וַיַּרְא] Kal fut. 3 p. s. m. ap. fr. יִרְאָה (§ 24. r. 3 c) ראה

יִרָא] id. fut. 3 pers. sing. masc. for יִירָא (§ 20.
rem. 2); וַ׳ conv.   ירא

יֵרָא Kh. יֵרָא q. v., K. יִרְאָה (q. v.)   ראה

וַיֵּרָא Kh. וַיֵּרָא q. v., K. וַיִּרְאָה (q. v.)   ראה

יְרָא Kal imp. sing. masc.   ירא

יְרֵא וּ׳] adj. masc. sing., constr. of יָרֵא dec. 5;
with cop. וּ׳ [for וַיְ׳, וַיְרָא]   ירא

יִרְאָ Kal inf. constr.   ירא

יָרְאָה דָּֽרְאָה יִרְאָה] Kal pret. 3 pers. sing. fem. (§ 8. rem.
1 a & 7)   ירא

יַרְאֶה Hiph. fut. 3 pers. sing. masc.   ראה

יֵרָאֶה Niph. fut. 3 pers. sing. masc.   ראה

וַיִּרְאָהָ] Kal fut. 3 pers. sing. masc. (יִרְאֶה), suff.
3 pers. sing. fem. (§ 24. rem. 21); וַ׳ conv.   ראה

יִרְאָה וְ׳] noun fem. sing. (no vowel change)   ירא

וַיִּרְאֵהוּ וַיֵּ׳ וַ׳] Kal fut. 3 pers. sing. masc.; וַ׳ conv. ראה

וַיִּרְאֵהוּ] Hiph. fut. 3 pers. sing. masc. (יִרְאֶה), suff.
3 pers. sing. masc. (§ 24. rem. 21); וַ׳ id.   ראה

וַיַּרְאֵהוּ] Kal fut. 3 pers. sing. masc. (יִרְאֶה), suff.
3 pers. sing. masc. (§ 24. rem. 21); וַ׳ id.   ראה

יִרְאֵהוּ] id. fut. 3 pers. pl. m., suff. 3 p. s. m.; וַ׳ id. ראה

וַיִּרְאוּ] Kal pret. 3 pers. pl.   ירא

וַיֵּרָאוּ וַיֵּ׳] Niph. fut. 3 pers. pl. masc.; וַ׳ conv.   ראה

יִרְאוּ (read, yĕroo) Kal. imp. pl. masc. [for יְראוּ
§ 23. rem. 3]   ירא

יִירְאוּ וַיִּ׳] Kal fut. 3 pers. pl. masc. for יִירְאוּ
(§ 20. r. 2, & § 8. r. 15); וַ׳ conv.   ירא

וַיִּרְאוּ] Kal fut. 3 pers. pl. masc.; וַ׳ id.   ראה

יִרְאוּ Kh. (§ 24. rem. 19, & § 23. rem. 3), K. יִרְאוּ
Hiph. fut. 3 pers. pl. masc. (§ 25. 2 e)   ירה

יִרְאוּהָ Kal fut. 3 pers. pl. masc., suff. 3 pers. s. fem. ראה

יְרֵאוּהָ Kal pret. 3 pers. pl. (יָרְאוּ, from יָרֵא sing.),
suff. 3 pers. sing. masc. (§ 16. rem. 1)   ירא

יִירְאוּךָ id. fut. 3 pers. pl. m. (יִירְאוּ, from יִירָא), suff.
2 p. s. m. (§ 16. rem. 12, & § 20. rem. 2)   ירא

יְרֵאוּךָ id. pret. 3 p. pl. (יָרְאוּ), suff. 2 p. s. m. (§ 16. r. 1) ירא

יִרְאוּם] Hiph. fut. 3 p. pl. m., suff. 3 p. pl. m.; וַ׳ conv. ראה

יִרְאוּן] Kal fut. 3 pers. pl. masc. with parag. ן [for
יִירְאוּן § 20. rem. 2, & § 8. rem. 17]   ירא

יִרְאוּן Kal fut. 3 pers. pl. masc. with parag. ן   ראה

a 2 Ch. 36. 13.   c Is. 29. 21.   e Ne. 7. 2.   g Job 42. 16.   i Ge. 38. 15.   l Ju. 19. 3.   o 2 Ki. 17. 28.   r Job 37. 24.   v Nu. 13. 26
b 2 Sa. 19. 44.   d Is. 42. 23.   f Ex. 34. 3.   h Jos. 22. 25.   k Ese. 1. 18.   m 2 Sa. 2. 15.   p 2 Sa. 11. 24.   s 1 Ki. 8. 40.   t De. 13. 12.
c Mal. 3. 16.   d 2 Ki. 15. 30.   f Le. 9. 6.   h Ge. 18. 15.   k 2 Ki. 6. 17.   m Da. 1. 13.   p Nu. 14. 22.   u 119. 63.   w De. 4. 28.
z Ps. 141. 9.   d Je. 50. 34.   f Jo. 17. 3.   h Is. 30. 30.

יִרְאוֹן	‍ pr. name of a place . . .	ירא
יְרָאוּנִי	Kal pret. 3 p. pl. (יָרְאוּ, fr. יָרֵא sing.), suff. 1 pers. sing. (§ 16. rem. 1) . .	ירא
יִרְאוּנוּ	Kal fut. 3 pers. pl. masc., suff. 1 pers. sing.	ראה
יִרְאֵי	adj. masc. pl. constr. from יָרֵא dec. 5	ירא
יִרְאָיו	id. pl. with suff. 3 pers. sing. masc.	ירא
יִרְאִיָּה	pr. name masc.	ראה
יִרְאֶיךָ	adj. masc. pl., suff. 2 p. s. m. from יָרֵא dec. 5a	ירא
יִרְאִים	id. pl., absolute state . .	ירא
יִרְאֲךָ	Kal fut. 3 pers. sing. masc. (יִירָא), suff. 2 pers. sing. masc. (§ 20. rem. 2) . .	ירא
וַיִּרְאֵם	Hiph. fut. 3 pers. sing. masc. (יַרְאֶה), suff. 3 pers. pl. masc. (§ 24. rem. 21) ; וَ conv.	ראה
וַיִּרְאֵם	Kal fut. 3 pers. sing. masc. (יִרְאֶה), suff. 3 pers. pl. masc. (§ 20. rem. 21) ; וَ id.	ראה
יִרְאֶנָּה	id., suff. 3 pers. sing. fem. .	ראה
יָרֵאנוּ	Kal pret. 1 pers. pl. (§ 23. rem. 1)	ירא
יַרְאֵנוּ	Hiph. fut. 3 pers. sing. masc. (יַרְאֶה), suff. 1 pers. pl. (§ 24. rem. 21) . .	ראה
וַיִּרְאֵנִי	id. with suff. 1 pers. sing. ; וَ conv. .	ראה
יַרְאֵנִי	Kal fut. 3 pers. sing. masc. (יִרְאֶה), suff. 1 pers. sing. (§ 24. rem. 21) ; וَ id.	ראה
יְרָאֻנִי	Piel pret. 3 pers. pl., suff. 1 pers. sing. .	ירא
יִרְאֵנִי	Kal fut. 3 pers.sing.masc. (יִרְאֶה), suff. 1 pers. sing. (§ 24. rem. 21) . . .	ראה
וְיָרֵאתָ	Kal pret. 2 pers. sing. masc. (§ 23. rem. 1)	ירא
יִרְאַת	noun f. s., constr. of יִרְאָה, or (Pr. 31. 30) adj. f. constr. of יָרֵא dec. 11 c, from יָרֵא m.	ירא
יִרְאָתוֹ	id. with suff. 3 pers. sing. masc. .	ירא
יָרֵאתִי	Kal pret. 1 pers. sing. (§ 23. rem. 1) .	ירא
יִרְאָתִי	noun fem. s., suff. 1 p. s. from יִרְאָה (no pl.)	ירא
יִרְאָתְךָ	id. with suff. 2 pers. sing. masc.	ירא
יְרֵאתֶם	Kal pret.2 p.pl.m.as if from יָרֵא, comp.	ירא
יִרְאָתָם	noun fem. sing. with suff. 3 pers. pl. masc. from יִרְאָה (q. v.)	ירא
יְרֵאתֶם	Kal pret. 2 pers. pl. masc. (§ 23. rem. 1)	ירא
יָרֶב וַיָּ יֶרֶב	Kal fut. 3 pers. sing. masc. ap. and conv. from יָרִיב	ריב
וַיִּרֶב	Kal fut. 3 pers. sing. masc., ap. from יִרְבֶּה ; וَ conv. . . .	רבה
יֶרֶב וַיֶּ יַרְבֶּה	Hiph. fut. 3 pers. sing. masc. ap. and full form ; וَ id. . .	רבה
יִרְבֶּה	Kal fut. 3 pers. sing. masc. . .	רבה
וַיִּרְבּוּ	id. fut. 3 pers. pl. masc ; וَ conv. .	רבה
יִרְבּוּן יִרְבְּיֻן	id. id. with parag. ן (§ 24. rem. 5)	רבר
יַרְבִּיעֶנִּי	Hiph. fut. 3 pers. sing. masc.,suff. 1 pers. sing.	רבץ

וְיַרְבֶּךָ	[for יַרְבְּךָ] Hiph. fut. 3 pers. sing. masc. (יַרְבֶּה), suff. 2 pers. s. m. (§ 24. rem. 21)	רבה
יְרֻבַּעַל יְרֻבֶּעַל	pr. name masc. R. רוב see . .	רוב
וְיָרָבְעָם	pr. name masc. R. רוב, see . .	ריב
יִרְבַּץ	Kal fut. 3 pers. sing. m. [for יִרְבַּץ § 8. rem. 15]	רבץ
יַרְבִּצוּ	Hiph. fut. 3 pers. pl. masc.	רבץ
יִרְבְּצוּ יִרְבָּצוּ	Kal fut. 3 pers. pl. masc. (§ 8. rem. 15)	רבץ
יִרְבָּצוּן	id. with parag. ן [for יִרְבְּצוּן § 8. rem. 17]	רבץ
יְרֻבֶּשֶׁת	pr. name masc. R. רוב, see . .	ריב
יִרְגַּז וַיִּ יִרְגָּז	Kal fut. 3 pers. sing. masc. (§ 8. rem. 15) ; וَ conv. . .	רגז
יִרְגְּזוּ וַיִּרְגְּזוּ	id. fut. 3 pers. pl. masc. ; וَ id. .	רגז
יִרְגָּזוּן יִרְגְּזוּן	id. with parag. ן (§ 8. rem. 17) . .	רגז
וַיְרַגֵּל	Piel fut. 3 pers. sing. masc. ; וَ conv.	רגל
וַיִּרְגְּלוּ	id. fut. 3 pers. pl. masc. ; וَ id. .	רגל
וַיִּרְגְּמֻהוּ	Kal fut. 3 pers. pl. m., suff. 3 pers. sing. m.	רגם
וַיִּרְגְּמוּ	id. fut. 3 pers. pl. masc. ; וَ conv. .	רגם
יִרְגְּנוּ	Niph. fut. 3 pers. pl. masc. ; וَ id. .	רגן

יָרַד ‍ fut. יֵרֵד ; imp. רֵד, רְדָה, inf. c. רֶדֶת, –רָדַת, parag. ה, also acc. of the place *whither*.—II. *to go down, decline*, Ju. 19. 11, יַרְד הַיּוֹם *the day was declining*.—III. *to flow, run down*, as the eye with tears ; Is. 15. 3, יֵרֵד בְּבֶכִי *melting in tears*.—IV. *to be cast down, to fall.* Hiph. הוֹרִיד.—I. *to cause to go down* or *descend* ; *to send, bring, carry down*.—II. *to cast down.* Hoph. *to be brought down.*

יֶרֶד (*descent*) pr. name masc.—I. Ge. 5. 15.— II. 1 Ch. 4. 18.

יַרְדֵּן (*flowing, river*) pr. name, the river *Jordan* in Palestine flowing into the Dead Sea.

מוֹרָד masc. dec. 2b.—I. *descent, declivity.*—II. 1 Ki. 7. 29, מַעֲשֵׂה מוֹרָד *hanging work, festoons.* Others, *inlaid* or *inrun work*, the gold being *run down* into the engraved figures. Prof. Lee, *sloping*, i. e. in the manner of a declivity.

יָרַד	Kal pret. 3 pers. sing. m. for יָרַד (§ 8. rem. 7)	ירד
וַיֵּרְדְּ	Hiph. fut. 3 pers. sing. masc. conv. [for יֹרֶד]	רדד
יֶרֶד	pr. name masc. for יֶרֶד (§ 35. rem. 2)	ירד
יָרֹד	Kal inf. absolute . . .	ידד
יַרְדֶּה	Hiph. fut. 3 pers. sing. masc. ap. [from יָרָה § 24. rem. 16] . . .	ידה

• Mal. 3. 5.   ₁ 2 Sa. 1. 7.   ⌐ Je. 32. 40.   ₚ Is. 29. 13.   ₜ Job 34. 37.   ▸ Ps. 23. 2.   ◂ Is. 28. 21.   ▴ 2 Sa. 19. 26.   ⌐ 2 Sa. 11. 12.
⌐ Je. 10. 7.   ₓ 2 Sa. 14. 15.   ⌐ Job 4. 16.   ∗ Ho. 4. 4.   ⌐ Pr. 4. 16.   ⌐ Ge. 28. 8.   ₓ 2 Sa. 19. 1.   ⌐ Le. 20. 2.   ⌐ 1 Ki. 6. 32.
⌐ 2 Ki. 2. 24.   ⌐ Ex. 33. 20.   ⌐ De. 2. 25.   ⌐ 1 Sa. 24. 16.   ⌐ Ps. 139. 18.   ⌐ Is. 13. 20.   ⌐ Ex. 15. 14.   ⌐ 2 Ch. 24. 21.   ⌐ Ge. 43. 20.
⌐ Ho. 10. 1.   ⌐ 2 Sa. 1. 14.   ⌐ Jos. 4. 24.   ⌐ Ge. 1. 22 ; Ex. 1. 20.   ⌐ De. 8. 14.   Is. 11. 7 ; 14. 30.   ⌐ Hab. 3. 7.   ⌐ Ps. 104. 25.   ₚ Is. 41. 2.
⌐ Ps. 4. 7.   ⌐ Ex. 20. 20.   ⌐ Is. 5. 25.

וַיֵּרֶד[1]	Kal fut. 3 pers. sing. masc.	ירד
יֵרֶד וַיֵּרְד	} id. with conv. וַ (§ 20. rem. 4)	ירד
יֵרְדְּ	Kal fut. 3 pers. sing. masc., ap. [for יִרְדֶּה § 24. rem. 3]; וַ conv.	רדה
יֶרֶד	pr. name masc.	ירד
יֹרֵד	Kal part. act. sing. masc. dec. 7b	ירד
וַיֹּרֶד	} Hiph. fut. 3 pers. sing. masc. ap. & conv. [for יוֹרִד § 20. rem. 11]	ירד
יְרֵד	Kal imp. s. m. (others, Piel fut. ap. from רדה)	ירד
יָרְדָה יָרְדָה	} id. pret. 3 pers. sing. fem. (§ 8. rem. 7)	ירד
יֹרֶדֶת	id. part. act. sing., fem. of יֹרֵד	ירד
יִרְדֶּהוּ	} Kal fut. 3 pers. sing. masc. [יִרְדֶּה], suff. 3 pers. sing. masc. (§ 24. rem. 21); וַ conv.	רדה
יֹרִדֵהוּ	} Hiph. fut. 3 pers. sing. masc. [יוֹרִיד], suff. 3 pers. sing. masc. (§ 20. rem. 11); וַ id.	ירד
יֹרִדוּהוּ	} id. fut. 3 pers. pl. m., suff. 3 pers. s.m.; וַ id.	ירד
יָרְדוּ	} Kal pret. 3 pers. pl.	ירד
וַיֵּרְדוּ	} id. fut. 3 pers. pl. masc.; וַ conv.	ירד
יִרְדּוּ, וַיִּרְדּוּ	} Kal fut. 3 pers. pl. masc.	רדה
יֹרִדוּ	Hiph. fut. 3 p. pl. m. [for יוֹרִידוּ § 20. rem. 11]	ירד
יֹרְדוֹת	Kal part. act. fem., pl. of יֹרֶדֶת dec. 13a from יֹרֵד masc. (§ 8. rem. 19)	ירד
יֹרְדֵי	id. pl. constr. masc. from יֹרֵד dec. 7b	ירד
יֹרְדִים	} id. pl., absolute state	ירד
וַיֵּרָדֶם	} Niph. fut. 3 pers. sing. masc. [for יֵרָדֵם § 9. rem. 4]; וַ conv.	רדם
יִרְדֶּנָּה	} Kal fut. 3 pers. sing. masc. [יִרְדֶּה], suff. 3 pers. s. f. (§ 24. r. 21, & § 2. r. 3); וַ id.	רדה
יַרְדֵּן	pr. name of a river	ירד
יֹרִדֵנוּ, וַ	} Kal pret. 3 pers. pl.	ירד
יִרְדֶּנּוּ	Kal fut. 3 pers. sing. masc. [יִרְדֶּה], suff. 3 pers. sing. masc. (§ 24. rem. 21)	רדה
יִרְדְּף	Piel fut. 3 pers. s. m. [for יְרַדֵּף § 10. r. 4]	רדף
יִרְדֹּף	mixed form of Kal & Piel fut., יִרְדֹּף & יְרַדֵּף	רדף
יִרְדֹּף וַיִּרְדֹּף	} Kal fut. 3 pers. sing. masc. (§ 8. rem. 18); וַ conv.	רדף
יִרְדְּפֵהוּ	} id. id., suff. 3 pers. sing. masc.; וַ id.	רדף
יִרְדְּפוּ	id. id., suff. 3 pers. sing. masc.	רדף
יִרְדְּפוּ וַיִּרְדְּפוּ	} id. fut. 3 pers. pl. masc. (§ 8. rem. 15); וַ conv.	רדף
יִרְדְּפוּם	} id. id., suff. 3 pers. pl. masc.; וַ id.	רדף
יִרְדְּפוּנִי	id. id., suff. 1 pers. sing.	רדף
יִרְדָּפְךָ	id. fut. 3 pers. sing. masc., suff. 2 pers. sing. masc. for יִרְדָּפְךָ (§ 8. rem. 15), יִרְדָּפְךָ	רדף
וַיִּרְדְּפֵם	} id. id., suff. 3 pers. pl. masc.; וַ conv.	רדף

יָרָה fut. יִירֶה; inr. c. יָרֹה, יָרֹת; imp. יְרֵה (§ 25. No. 2e, & § 24. rem. 2).—I. *to throw*, *cast*; *to shoot*, as an arrow; part. יוֹרִים *archers.*—II. *to cast, lay a foundation.*—III. *to sprinkle*, *to water*, Ho. 6. 3. Niph. *to be shot*, Ex. 19. 13. Hiph. הוֹרָה.—I. *to throw*, *cast*; *to shoot*, as arrows.—II. *to put forth*, as the finger, *to point out, show.*—III. *to teach, instruct*; with the acc. of the thing, also with a double acc.; with בְּ, אֶל, כְּמוֹ *to instruct in* any thing.

יוֹרֶה masc. *the former* or *early rain*, falling in Judea about the beginning of November.

יוֹרָה (*former rain*) pr. name masc. Ezr. 2. 18.

יוֹרִי (for יוֹרִיָה *whom the Lord teaches*) pr. name masc. 1 Ch. 5. 13.

מוֹרֶה masc. dec. 9a, prop. Hiph. part.—I. *archer* —II. *teacher.*—III. *former rain*; comp. יוֹרֶה.

תּוֹרָה fem. dec. 10.—I. *instruction, direction, precept.*—II. *law.*—III. *mode, manner*, 2 Sa. 7. 19.

תֹּר masc. i. q. תּוֹרָה *mode, manner*, 1 Ch. 17. 17. תֹּר, however, may stand for תֹּאַר, תֹּאר *form, figure*, and hence perhaps *type*, comp. בָּאַר & מוּם, מְאוּם, בּוֹר.

יְרוּאֵל (*founded of God*) pr. name of a desert 2 Ch. 20. 16.

יְרוּשָׁלַיִם, יְרוּשָׁלֵם (*foundation of peace*) pr. name, *Jerusalem*, the royal city of Palestine on the confines of Judah and Benjamin; called שָׁלֵם Ge. 14. 18; Ps. 76. 3; in the Chald. יְרוּשְׁלֵם, יְרוּשָׁלֵם.

יְרִיאֵל (*established of God*) pr. name masc. 1 Ch. 7. 2.

יְרִיָּהוּ, יְרִיָּה (*established of the Lord*) pr. name masc. 1 Ch. 23. 19; 24. 23; 26. 31.

יָרֵא only fut. תִּירְהוּ (for תִּירְאוּ) *to fear, be afraid*, Is. 44. 8.

יָרֹה	Kal inf. absolute	ירה
יְרֵה	id. imp. sing. masc.	ירה

Pr. 21. 22.   Ju. 14. 9.   Ge. 1. 26.   La. 1. 13.   Na. 1. 8.   Ju. 9. 40.   2 Sa. 2. 28.   Is. 41. 5.   Ru. 3. 3.
Ju. 5. 13.   1 Ki. 1. 53.   1 Ki. 5. 23.   La. 1. 13.   Ps. 7. 6.   Ho. 8. 3.   Ps. 23. 6.   1 Sa. 17. 28.   Ex. 19. 14.
Is. 38. 8.   Je. 5. 31.   Pr. 5. 5.   Le. 25. 53.   Jos. 23. 10.   Le. 26. 8, etc.   Kze. 35. 6.   1 Sa. 25. 29.   Ki. 12. 17.
La. 1. 16.   1 Sa. 17. 8.   Ge. 28. 12.   Jon. 1. 5.

יְרַהֲבֻ	Kal fut. 3 pers. pl. masc. . . .	רהב
יְרָהֻ	the following with suff. 3 pers. sing. masc.	ירה
יֹרֻ	Hiph. fut. 3 pers. pl. masc. for יוֹרֻ, (§ 20. rem. 11, & § 25. No. 2a); וֹ conv.	ירה
יְרוּאֵל	pr. name of a place . . .	ירה
יְרֹחַ	pr. name masc. . . .	ירח
וַיָּנַח	Kal fut. 3 pers. sing. masc.	רוח
יְרִיעֻן	Kal fut. 3 p. pl. m. with parag. ן (§ 24. r. 5)	רוח
יְרֻגֶּךָ	Piel fut. 3 pers. pl. m. [יְרַגְּ], suff. 2 p. s. m.	רוח
יָרֻם	Kal fut. 3 pers. sing. masc.	רום
יָרֹם	Kh. יָרֹם q. v., K. וְרָם (q. v.) .	רום
יָרֹמֻ	Kal fut. 3 pers. pl. masc.	רום
וַיֵּרֹמֻ	וַיְּ Niph. fut. 3 pers. pl. masc.; וֹ conv.	רמם
יְרֹמֵם	Pilel fut. 3 pers. sing. masc.	רום
וִירֹמְמֻהֻ	וֹ id. fut. 3 pers. pl. masc., suff. 3 pers. sing. masc. with cop. וֹ [for וַיְּ, וְיִרֹ] . .	רום
יְרֹמִמְךָ	וֹ id. fut. 3 p. s. m., suff. 2 p. s. m., see preced.	רום
יְרֹמְמֵנִי	id. id., suff. 1 pers. sing. . .	רום
יְרַנֵּן	Kal fut. 3 pers. sing. m. [for יְרַן § 18. r. 12]	רנן
יֵרֹעַ	Niph. fut. 3 pers. sing. masc.	רוע
יְרֻפְּפֻ	Pulal fut. 3 pers. pl. masc. [for יְרֹפְפֻ comp. § 8. rem. 15]	רוף
יָרֻץ	Kal fut. 3 pers. sing. m. [for יָרֹץ § 18. r. 12]	רצץ
יָרֻץ	Kal fut. 3 pers. sing. masc.	רוץ
וַיְּ	וַיְּ id. fut. 3 pers. pl. masc.; וֹ conv.	רוץ
יְרֻצֻן	id. with parag. ן . . .	רוץ
יְרֹצְצֻ	Pilel fut. 3 pers. pl. masc. [for יְרֹצְצֻ comp. § 8. rem. 15]	רוץ
יָרֹק	noun masc. sing. . . .	ירק
יְרֻשָׁא יְרֻשָׁה	} pr. name fem. . . .	ירש
יְרֻשָׁלְַמָה	the following with loc. ה . .	ירה
יְרֻשָׁלַם	וִירֻ pr. name of a place; with cop. וּ	
יְרֻשָׁלַם	וַיְרֻ [for וַיְּ, וְיִרֻ]	ירה
יְרֻשָׁלֵם יְרֻשָׁלֵם	} Chald. pr. name of a place .	ירה
יְרֻשָׁלְַמָה	pr. name m. (יְרֻשָׁלַיִם) with loc. ה, K. לֵמָה	ירה
יֵרָזֶה	Niph. fut. 3 pers. sing. masc.	רזה
יְרֻזְמֻן	Kal fut. 3 pers. pl. masc. with parag. ן	רזם
יֶרַח	וֹ masc. dec. 5a, the moon.	
	יֶרַח masc. dec. 6a (pl. c. יַרְחֵי; § 35. rem. 5).—	
	I. month, lunar month.—II. pr. name of a descendant of Joktan, Ge. 10. 26.	
	יְרַח Chald. dec. 3a, month.	
	יָרֹחַ (moon) pr. name masc. 1 Ch. 5. 14.	
יֶרַח	pr. name of a people and region, for יָרֵחַ (§ 35. rem. 2) . . .	ירח
יָרַח וַיָּרַח	} Hiph. fut. 3 pers. sing. masc. ap. & conv. from יָרֵחַ (§ 21. rem. 19)	רוח
יֵרַח	noun masc. sing. dec. 6a (§ 35. rem. 5) .	ירח
יְרֵחוֹ	pr. name of a place, see יְרִיחוֹ	רוח
יַרְחֵי	n. m., pl. constr. from יֶרַח d. 6 (§ 35. r. 5)	ירח
יָרִיב	Hiph. fut. 3 pers. sing. masc. .	רחב
וַיָּרִיבֻ	וֹ id. fut. 3 pers. pl. masc.; וֹ conv.	רחב
יְרָחִים	noun masc. pl. (constr. יַרְחֵי) from יֶרַח d. 6 (§ 35. rem. 5) . . .	ירח
	Chald. noun masc., pl. of יְרַח dec. 3a	ירח
יַרְחִיקֶנָּה	Hiph. fut. 3 p. s. m., suff. 3 p. s. f. (§ 2. r. 3)	רחק
יְרֵחֲךָ	וֹ noun m. s., suff. 2 pers. s. m. with cop. וֹ [for וַיְּ, וְיִרֵחֲךָ § 35. r. 5] from יֶרַח d. 5	ירח
יְרַחֵם	Piel fut. 3 pers. sing. masc. (§ 14. rem. 1)	רחם
יְרֹחָם	pr. name masc.	רחם
יְרֻחַם יְרֻחָם	} Pual fut. 3 pers. sing. masc. (§ 14. rem. 1, comp. § 8. rem. 15) . . .	} רחם
יְרַחְמְאֵל	pr. name masc.	רחם
יְרַחֲמֶהֻ	וֹ Piel fut. 3 pers. sing. masc. (יְרַחֵם q. v.), suff. 3 p. s. m. with cop. וֹ [for וַיְּ, וְיִרַחֲמֶהֻ	רחם
יְרַחֲמֻ	id. fut. 3 pers. pl. masc. [for יְרַחֲמֻ, comp. § 8. rem. 15]	רחם
יְרַחֲמֵם	וֹ id. fut. 3 p. s. m., suff. 3 p. pl. m.; וֹ conv.	רחם
יְרַחֲמֻהֻ	id. id., suff. 3 pers. sing. masc.	רחם
יְרַחֲמֵנֻ	id. id., suff. 1 pers. pl.	רחם
יַרְחַע	pr. name of an Egyptian slave, 1 Ch. 2. 34, 35.	
יְרַחֵף	Piel fut. 3 pers. sing. masc. (§ 14. rem. 1)	רחף
יִרְחַץ יִרְחָץ	} Kal fut. 3 pers. sing. masc. (§ 8. rem. 15); וֹ conv.	} רחץ
יִרְחֲצֻ וַיִּ	} Kal fut. 3 p. pl. m. (§ 8. r. 15); וֹ id.	} רחץ
יֵרָחֵק	Kh., יֵרָתֵק K., Niph. fut. 3 pers. sing. masc. from רחק or . . .	רתק
יִרְחַק	Kal fut. 3 pers. sing. masc.	רחק
יְרַחֲקֻ	Piel fut. 3 pers. pl. masc. (§ 14. rem. 1)	רחק
יִרְחֲקֻ	Kal fut. 3 pers. pl. masc.	רחק
יָרַט	I. to cast down, precipitate, Job 16. 11.—II. to be perverse, destructive, Nu. 22. 32.	
יִרְטְבֻ	Kal fut. 3 p. pl. m. [for יִרְטְבֻ § 8. r. 15]	רטב
יִרְטֵנִי	or יַרְטֵנִי Kal fut. 3 pers. sing. masc., suff. 1 pers. sing. from רטה or . . .	ידט
יְרֻטְּשֻׁ יְרֻטְּשֻׁ	} Pual fut. 3 pers. pl. masc. (comp. § 8. rem. 15)	} רטש
יְרִיאֵל	pr. name masc.	רה

a Is. 3. 5.	f Ps. 18. 47.	k Ps. 107. 32.	p Job 26. 11.	u Joh 39. 8.	z Ps. 35. 21.	e Ho. 14. 4.	m De. 32. 11.	s Job 5. 4.
b Ps. 64. 5.	g Da. 11. 12.	l Ps. 87. 34.	q Is. 44. 26.	v Is. 17. 4.	a Da. 4. 26.	f Is. 45. 7.	l Le. 17. 16.	t Nu. 22. 32.
c Job 32. 20.	h Eze. 10. 17.	m Ps. 27. 5.	r Jos. 8. 19.	w Job 15. 12.	b Pr. 22. 15.	g 2 Ki. 13. 23.	o Ex. 40. 32.	u Job 34. 8.
d Pr. 5. 19.	i Eze. 10. 19.	n Pr. 29. 6.	s Joel 2. 4, 7.	x Is. 60. 20.	c Is. 27. 11	h Is. 27. 11	p Ec. 12. 6.	x Job 16. 11.
e Ho. 11. 7.		o Pr.11.15;13.20	t Na. 2. 5.	y Job 7. 3.	d Pr. 28. 13.	i Mi. 7. 19.	q Eze. 43. 9.	y Ho. 14. 1.
f 2 Sa. 11. 20. 2 Ch. 35. 25.		pp Is. 55. 5.						

יָרִיב	′ן pr. name masc.	ריב
יָרִיב	Kal fut. 3 pers. sing. masc.	ריב
יָרִיבוּ	ן id. fut. 3 pers. pl. masc.; וְ conv.	ריב
יְרִיבוּן	ן id. id. with parag. ן ; ן id.	ריב
יְרִיבַי	noun masc. pl., suff. 1 pers. sing. from [יָרִיב] dec. 3a	ריב
יָרִיבַי	′ן pr. name masc. (יָרִיבַי) with cop. ן [for וַ′, וְיָרִיבַי]	ריב
יְרִיבְךָ	noun masc. sing., suff. 2 pers. sing. masc. from [יָרִיב] dec. 3a	ריב
יְרִיבֻן	defect. for יְרִיבוּן (q. v.)	ריב
יְרִיָּה / יְרִיָּהוּ	ן pr. name masc.	ירה
יְרִידוּ	ן Hiph. fut. 3 pers. pl. masc. for יוֹרִידוּ (§ 20. rem. 2); וְ conv.	ירד
יְרִידוּם	ן id., suff. 3 pers. pl. masc.; וְ id.	ירד
יָרִיחַ	Hiph. fut. 3 pers. sing. masc.	רוח
יְרִיחָה / יְרִיחוֹ	pr. name of a place [with cop. ן for וַ′, וִירִיחוֹ (וִירִיחוֹ)]	רוח
יְרִיחוֹן / יְרִיחֹן	Hiph. fut. 3 pers. pl. masc. with parag. ן	רוח
יָרִים	Hiph. fut. 3 pers. sing. masc.	רום
יְרִימֶהָ	ן id. id., suff. 3 pers. sing. fem.; וְ conv.	רום
יָרִימוּ	id. fut. 3 pers. pl. masc.	רום
יָרִימוּ	Kh. יָרִימוּ q. v., K. יָרֻמוּ (q. v.)	רום
יְרִימוֹת / יְרִמוֹת	′וְ pr. name masc. [with cop. ן, for וַ′, וְיְרֵ′, וַ′]	ירם
יָרִיעַ	Hiph. fut. 3 pers. sing. masc.	רוע
יָרִיעוּ	וַ id. fut. 3 pers. pl. masc.; וְ conv.	רוע
יְרִיעוֹת	noun fem., pl. of יְרִיעָה dec. 10, also pr. n. m. [with cop. ן for וַ′, וִירִיעוֹת]	ירע
יְרִיעֹתַי	id., suff. 1 pers. sing. [for תַי]	ירע
יְרִיעוֹתֵיהֶם	id., suff. 3 pers. pl. masc.	ירע
יְרִיעֹת	defect. for יְרִיעוֹת (q. v.)	ירע
יְרִיצוּ	ן Hiph. fut. 3 pers. pl. masc.; וְ conv.	רוץ
יָרִיק	Hiph. fut. 3 pers. sing. masc.	רוק
יָרִיקוּ	id. fut. 3 pers. pl. masc.	רוק
יָרִיתִי	′וְ Kal pret. 1 pers. sing	ירה

יָרֵךְ fem. dec. 5b.—I. thigh; יֹצְאֵי יָרֵךְ the comers out of the thigh, i. e. the descendants of; שֹׁק עַל־יָרֵךְ hip upon thigh, i. e. wholly; סָפַק עַל־יָרֵךְ to smite upon the thigh, in token of distress.—II. of inanimate things, the shank of the candlestick in the tabernacle; side of a tent. Du. יְרֵכַיִם both thighs. יַרְכָה fem., with suff. יַרְכָתוֹ dec. 11c (§ 39. No. 3. r. 3), a side, as of a country, Ge. 49. 13. Du.

יַרְכָתַיִם, constr. יַרְכְּתֵי (strictly from יָרֵךְ=יַרְכָּה).—1. hinder part, hinder side, of a building.—II. hindmost, innermost parts, recesses.—III. remotest parts, as of the earth, the north.

יַרְכָא	Chald. fem. dec. 8, the thigh, Da. 2. 32.	
יֵרֶךְ	Kal fut. 3 pers. sing. masc. (§ 18. rem. 6)	ובך
יֶרֶךְ	noun fem. sing., constr. of יָרֵךְ dec. 5 b	ירך
יַרְכֵּב	ן Hiph. fut. 3 pers. sing. masc. ap. [from יַרְכִּיב]; ן conv.	רכב
וַיַּרְכֵּב	וַ Kal fut. 3 pers. sing. masc.; ן id.	רכב
יַרְכִּבֵהוּ	ן Hiph. fut. 3 pers. pl. masc. (יַרְכִּיבוּ), suff. 3 pers. sing. masc.; ן id.	רכב
יַרְכִּבֵהוּ	id. fut. 3 pers. s. m. [יַרְכִּיב], suff. 3 pers. s. m.	רכב
יַרְכִּבוּ	ן id. fut. 3 pers. pl. m. for יַרְכִּיבוּ; וְ conv.	רכב
יִרְכְּבוּ / יִרְכְּבוּן	Kal fut. 3 pers. pl. masc. (§ 8. rem. 15); וְ id.	רכב
יַרְכִּבֵם	ן Hiph. fut. 3 pers. sing. masc., [יַרְכִּיב] suff. 3 pers. pl. masc.; וְ id.	רכב
יְרֵכָהּ	noun fem. s., suff. 3 p. s. fem. from יָרֵךְ dec. 5 b	ירך
יְרֵכוֹ	id., suff. 3 pers. sing. masc.	ירך
יְרֵכִי	id., suff. 1 pers. sing.	ירך
יַרְכִּיבֵהוּ	ן Hiph. fut. 3 p. s. m., suff. 3 p. s. m.; ן conv.	רכב
יַרְכִּיבֶהָ	ן id. fut. 3 pers. pl. m., suff. 3 p. s. m.; ן id.	רכב
יַרְכִּיבוּ	ן id. fut. 3 pers. pl. masc.; ן id.	רכב
יְרֵכָיִךְ	n. f. du., with suff. 2 p. s. m. from יָרֵךְ d. 5 b	ירך
יְרֵכַיִם	id. du., absolute state	ירך
יְרֵכֵךְ	id. sing., suff. 2 pers. sing. fem. Nu. 5. 21.	ירך
יִרְכְּסוּ	ן, וַ′ וַ Kal fut. 3 pers. pl. masc.; ן conv.	רכס
יַרְכָתֵהּ	ן Chald. noun fem. sing. with suff. 3 pers. sing. m. [from יַרְכָּה] dec. 8a	ירך
יַרְכָתוֹ	ן noun fem. sing., suff. 3 pers. sing. m. [from יַרְכָּה comp. dec. 11c § 39. No. 3. rem. 3]	ירך
יַרְכְּתֵי	id. dual constr. [from יַרְכָּה]	ירך

יָרַם Root not used; Arab. ורם to be high, (§ 20. No. 1).

יַרְמוּת (height) pr. name—I. of a city in the tribe of Judah.—II. of a city assigned to the Levites in the tribe of Issachar, Jos. 21. 29; called רָמָת ch. 19. 21.

יְרִימוֹת, יְרֵמוֹת, יְרֵימוֹת (heights) pr. name masc. of several persons.

יַרְמִי (highlander) pr. name masc. Exr. 10. 33.

יָרֵם / יָרֶם	ן וַ Hiph. fut. 3 pers. sing. masc., ap. and conv. from יָרִים	רום
יָרֹם / יָרֻם / וַיָּרָם	ן וַ ן Kal fut. 3 pers. sing. masc., ap. and conv. from יָרוּם (§ 21. rem. 6 & 7).	רום

a Ge. 26. 20, 21.   d Is. 49. 25.   g Job 39. 25.   k Ps. 66. 7.   r Hab. 1. 17.   u 2 Ki. 23. 30.   z Est. 6. 11.   f Ex. 28. 42.   i Ge. 49. 13.
b Ju. 8. 1.   e Ex. 21. 18.   f Ex. 21. 18.   l Ps. 115. 6.   s Is. 54. 2.   v De. 32. 13.   c 2 Ch. 35. 24.   g Ex. 28. 28.   t Nu. 24. 7.
c Je. 18. 19.   f 2 Ki. 11. 19.   h De. 4. 28.   q Je. 49. 29.   t Jos. 15. 6.   w 2 Sa. 13. 29.   d 1 Ch. 13. 7.   h Ex. 39. 21.   m 2 Sa. 22. 47.
d Ps. 35. 1.   f Jos. 10. 27.   m Ge. 31. 45.   p 2 Ch. 35. 13.   t Le. 15. 9.   x Ex. 4. 20.   t Ca. 7. 2.   i Da. 2. 32.   n Ex. 16. 20.

וַ יְ׳, יֶרֶם Hiph. fut. 3 pers. sing. masc. (יוֹרֶה), suff. 3 pers. pl. m. (§ 25. No. 2e); וַ conv. . . ירה

יֵרָמּוּ Niph. fut. 3 pers. pl. masc.; וַ id. . . רמם

יֵרְגְּמֻן Kal fut. 3 pers. pl. masc. (יִרְגְּמוּ) with parag. . רגם

יְרָמוּת pr. name of a place . . . . ירם

וַיְ׳, יְרֵימוֹת pr. name masc., see יְרֵימוֹת . . ירם

יִרְמְיָ pr. name masc. . . . . ירם

(יִ׳) יִרְמְיָה
(יִ׳) יִרְמְיָהוּ } pr. name masc. . . . . רמה

יִרְמֹס (יְ׳) } Kal fut. 3 pers. sing. masc. (§ 8. rem. 18) מם

יִרְמְסֶהֻ id. fut. 3 p.s.m., suff. 3 p.s.m.; וַ conv. . רמם

יִרְמְסֶהָ id. fut. 3 pers. pl. m., suff. 3 pers. s. m.; וַ id. . רמם

יִרְמְסוּ id. fut. 3 pers. pl. masc.; וַ id. . . רמם

יִרְמְסֶנָּה id. fut. 3 pers. sing. masc., suff. 3 pers. sing. fem. (§ 2. rem. 3); וַ id. . . . רמם

וַיָּרֹנּוּ Kal fut. 3 pers. pl. masc.; וַ id. . . רנן

יַרְנִי Hiph. fut. 3 pers. sing. masc. (יוֹרֶה), suff. 1 pers. sing. (§ 25. No. 2e); וַ id. . . ירה

יְרֻנַּן Pual fut. 3 pers. sing. masc. (for יְרֻנַּן) comp. § 8. rem. 15, & § 18. rem. 13] . רנן

יְרַנְּנוּ
יְרַנְּנוּ } Piel fut. 3 pers. pl. masc. (comp. § 8. rem. 15) . . . . רנן

יְרַנְּנוּ id. with cop. וַ [for וַיְ׳, וַיְרַנְּנוּ] . רנן

[יָרֵע] to be fearful, distressed, Is. 15. 4; perhaps primarily, to tremble.

יְרִיעָה fem. dec. 10, a curtain, a hanging, so called from its tremulous motion; so Gesenius, but compare Prof. Lee under יָרַע.

יְרִיעוֹת (curtains) pr. name fem. 1 Ch. 2. 18.

יָרַע וַ Hiph. fut. 3 pers. sing. masc. ap. and conv. from יָרַע (§ 21. rem. 19) . . רוע

יֵרַע וַ
יֵרַע } Hiph. fut. 3 pers. sing. masc. (§ 18. rem. 11, comp. § 15. rem. 1) . רעע

יֵרַע
יֵרַע } Kal fut. 3 pers. sing. masc. (§ 18. rem. 6) רעע

וַיֵּ׳, יֵ׳ id. bef. penacute or by conv. וַ (v. id. comp. also rem. 5) . . . .

יִרַע Kal fut. 3 pers. sing. masc. ap. from יִרְעֶה (§ 24. rem. 3) . . . . רעה

יִרְעַב
יִרְעָב } Kal fut. 3 pers. sing. masc. (§ 8. rem. 15) רעב

יִרְעֲבוּ id. fut. 3 pers. pl. masc. [for יִרְעָבוּ v. id.] רעב

יַרְעִבֶךָ וַ Hiph. fut. 3 pers. sing. masc., suff. 2 pers. sing. masc. [for וַיַּרְעִבֶךָ]; וַ conv. רעב

יָרְעָה Kal pret. 3 pers. sing. fem. . . . ירע

יֵרָעֶה Kal fut. 3 pers. sing. masc. . . ירע

יֵרֵעוּ, וַיֵּ׳ Hiph. fut. 3 pers. pl. masc.; וַ conv. . רעע

יֵרֵעוּ defect. for יָרֵעוּ (q. v) . . . . רוע

יֵרֵעוּ Kal fut. 3 pers. pl. masc. (as if from ירע comp. § 18. rem. 6) . . . . . רעע

יִרְעוּ, וַיִּ׳ Kal fut. 3 pers. pl. masc.; וַ conv. . רעה

יִרְעוּךָ id. fut. 3 pers. sing. m., suff. 2 pers. sing. fem. רעה

יִרְעוּן id. id. with parag. וַ . . . . . . רעה

יַרְעִיב Hiph. fut. 3 pers. sing. masc. . . . רעב

וַ יַּ׳ Hiph. fut. 3 p.s.m., ap. [fr. יַרְעִים]; וַ conv. . רעם

יַרְעֵם וַ Hiph. fut. 3 pers. sing. masc. [יַרְעֶה], suff. 3 pers. pl. masc. (§ 24. rem. 21); וַ id. רעה

יִרְעַם Kal fut. 3 pers. sing. masc. . . . . רעם

יִרְעֵם Kal fut. 3 pers. sing. masc. (יִרְעֶה), suff. 3 pers. pl. masc. (§ 24. rem. 21) . . . רעה

יִרְעֶנָּה id. with suff. 3 pers. sing. fem. (§ 2. rem. 3) רעה

יְרֹעַע Pulal fut. 3 p.s.m. [for יְרֹעַע comp. § 8. rem. 15] רוע

יִרְעֲפוּ Kal fut. 3 pers. pl. masc. . . . . רעף

יִרְעֲפוּן id. with parag. וַ . . . . רעף

יִרְעֲצוּ וַ Kal fut. 3 pers. pl. masc.; וַ conv. . רעץ

יִרְעַשׁ Kal fut. 3 pers. sing. masc. . . . . רעש

וַיִּ׳, יִ׳ id. fut. 3 pers. pl. masc.; וַ conv. . רעש

יִרְפֶּה וַ Kal fut. 3 pers. sing. m. ap. from יִרְפֶּה; וַ id. רפה

וַיְ׳ Piel fut. 3 pers. sing. masc.; וַ id. . רפא

וַיִּ׳ Kal fut. 3 pers. sing. masc.; וַ id. . רפא

יִרְפְּאֵל pr. name of a place . . . . רפא

וַיֵּ׳ Niph. fut. 3 pers. pl. masc. . . . רפא

יְרַפְּאוּ Piel fut. 3 pers. pl. masc.; וַ conv. . רפא

יִרְפָּאֵם Kal fut. 3 pers. sing. m., suff. 3 pers. pl. m. רפא

יִרְפָּאֵנוּ id. with suff. 1 pers. pl. . . . . רפא

יִרְפֹּד Kal fut. 3 pers. sing. masc. . . . רפד

יִרְפֶּה Kal fut. 3 pers. sing. masc. . . . רפה

יֵרָפוּ וַ Niph. fut. 3 pers. pl. masc. [for יֵרָפְאוּ § 23. rem. 11]; וַ conv. . . . . . רפא

יְרַפּוּ וַ Piel fut. 3 pers. pl. masc. for יְרַפְּאוּ (§ 23. rem. 11); וַ id. . . . . . רפא

וַיִּ׳ Kal fut. 3 pers. pl. masc.; וַ id. . רפה

יַרְפְּךָ Hiph. fut. 3 pers. sing. masc. [יַרְפֶּה], suff. 2 pers. sing. masc. (§ 24. rem. 21) . . רפה

יָרָץ
וַיָּ׳
יָ׳ } Kal fut. 3 pers. sing. masc., ap. and conv. from יָרוּץ (§ 21. rem. 7 & 8) } רוץ

יֵרָצֶה Niph. fut. 3 pers. sing. masc. . . . רצה

יִרְצֶה Kal fut. 3 pers. sing. masc. . . . רצה

יִרְצֵהֻ וַ id. with suff. 3 pers. sing. masc.; וַ conv. . רצה

ª 2 Ki. 17. 27.   ᵇ Is. 41. 25.   ᵐ Is. 16. 10.   ᵗ 2 Sa. 20. 6.   ª De. 8. 3.   ᶠ Ps. 78. 72.   Am. 9. 1.   Je. 6. 14.   ᵇ Je. 8. 11.
ᵇ Ps. 64. 8.   De. 8. 7.   Is. 15. 4.   Ne. 2. 10.   Is. 14. 4.   Ps. 80. 14.   Is. 24. 18.   Ps. 107. 20.   2 Sa. 4. 1.
ᶜ Eze. 10. 15.   2 Ki. 7. 17.   Jos. 6. 20.   Ne. 2. 5.   Is. 16. 10.   Ez. 4. 26.   Ho. 6. 1.   Job 16. 14.
ᵈ Is. 49. 11.   2 Ki. 7. 17.   1 Ki. 16. 25.   Pr. 6. 30.   Je. 2. 16.   1 Ki. 18. 30.   Job 41. 22.   Job 16. 14.
ᵉ Eze. 26. 11.   2 Ki. 9. 33.   Zep. 1. 12.   Is. 8. 21.   Zep. 2. 7.   Ju. 10. 8.   Eze. 47. 11.   Is. 5. 24.   Job 32. 22.
ᵍ Ps. 7. 6.   Pr. 4. 4.   Job 34. 24.   Is. 49. 12.   Pr. 10. 3.   Ps. 78. 16.   Eze. 47. 9.   2 Ki. 2. 22.   Le. 9. 24.

יְרַצֵּהוּ¹] Hiph. fut. 3 pers. pl. masc. [יְרִצוּ], suff. 3 pers. sing. masc.;] conv.   רוץ

יְרֻצּוּ² וַ Kal fut. 3 pers. pl. masc. for יְרוּצוּ;] id.   רוץ

יֵרָצוּ³ Niph. fut. 3 pers. pl. masc. .   רצה

יְרַצּוּ⁴ Piel fut. 3 pers. pl. masc. .   רצה

יִרְצוּ Kal fut. 3 pers. pl. masc. .   רצה

יְרֻצוּן Kal fut. 3 pers. pl. m. with parag.] for ירוצון   רוץ

יִרְצַח Kal fut. 3 pers. sing. masc. .   רצח

יְרַצְּחֵהוּ / יְרַצְּחֻהוּ } Piel fut. 3 pers. pl. masc. (comp. § 8. rem. 15)   רצח

יִרְצֶךָ⁵ Kal fut. 3 pers. sing. masc. [יִרְצֶה], suff. 2 pers. sing. masc. (§ 24. rem. 21) for יִרְצְךָ   רצה

יְרַצֵּץ⁶] Piel fut. 3 pers. sing. masc.;] conv.   רצץ

יְרֹצְצוּ⁷] Poel fut. 3 pers. pl. masc.;] id.   רצץ

יָרָק masc. dec. 4a, *greenness, verdure,* 2 Ki. 19. 26; Is. 37. 27; more frequently, *green herb, vegetable.*

יֶרֶק masc. *greenness, verdure, foliage;* יֶרֶק עֵשֶׂב *greenness of herb,* i. e. *green herb.*

יָרוֹק masc. *green herb,* Job 39. 8.

יֵרָקוֹן masc. *a yellowish livid paleness,* spoken—I. of a disease in corn, Eng. Vers. *mildew.*—II. of the human countenance when suddenly affrighted, Je. 30. 6.

יְרַקְרַק, pl. fem. יְרַקְרַקֹּת.—I. adj. *greenish, yellowish,* Le. 13. 19; 14. 37.—II. *gold colour,* Ps. 68. 14.

יָרַק *to spit,* const. with בִּפְנֵי *in the presence of.*

יָרֶק] Hiph. fut. 3 p. s. m. ap. and conv. from יָרִיק   רוק

יָרֹס Kal inf. absolute . .   ירד

יָרַק Kal fut. 3 pers. sing. masc.   רקק

יֶרֶק noun masc. sing. .   ירק

יֶרֶק] adj. masc. constr. [with cop.] for וִירַק, וַי], from יָרָק dec. 4a   ירק

יִרְקַב / יֵרָקֵב } Kal fut. 3 pers. sing. masc. (§ 8. rem. 15)   רקב

יִרְקָה] Kal pret. 3 pers. sing. fem.   ירק

יְרַקְּדוּ Piel fut. 3 pers. pl. masc.   רקד

יְרַקְּדוּן id. with parag.] [for יְרַקְּדוּ § 8. rem. 17]   רקד

יִרָקוֹן] noun masc. sing. .   ירק

יִרְקַח Kal fut. 3 pers. sing. masc.   רקח

יַרְקִיעַם] Hiph. fut. 3 pers. sing. masc., suff. 3 pers. pl. masc.;] conv.   רקד

יָרְקְעָם pr. name of a place .   רקע

יְרַקְּעוּ] Piel fut. 3 pers. pl. masc.;] conv.   רקע

יְרַקְּעוּם id. id., suff. 3 pers. pl. masc. (ם for fem. § 2. rem. 5)   רקע

יְרַקְעֶנּוּ Piel fut. 3 p. s. m., suff. 3 p. s. m. (§ 2. r. 3)   רקע

יְרַקְרַק adj. masc. sing. .   ירק

יְרַקְרַקֹּת id. pl. fem. from [יְרַקְרַקָּה] dec. 10 .   ירק

יָרַשׁ] pret. pl. with suff. יְרֵשׁוּךָ, יְרֵשׁוּהָ (from § 16. r. 1); fut. יָרַשׁ, יִירַשׁ; imp. יְרַשׁ, רַשׁ; inf. c. רֶשֶׁת.—I. *to take, seize upon; to take possession of.*—II. *to dispossess, to drive out.*—III. *to possess, hold in possession.*—IV. *to inherit;* part. יֹרֵשׁ *heir.* Niph. *to become poor.* Pi. יָרֵשׁ—I. *to take possession of,* De. 28. 42.—II. *to dispossess, impoverish,* Ju. 14. 15. Hiph. הוֹרִישׁ—I. *to cause or make to possess, give for a possession,* with double acc.—II. *to take possession of.*—III. *to dispossess, to drive out.*—IV. *to make poor,* 1 Sa. 2. 7.—V. *to destroy,* Nu. 14. 12.

יְרֵשָׁה fem. *possession,* Nu. 24. 18.

יְרֻשָּׁה fem. dec. 10.—I. *possession.*—II. *heritage,* Je. 32. 8.

יְרוּשָׁה, יְרוּשָׁא (*possessed*) pr. name of the mother of King Jotham, 2 Ki. 15. 33; 2 Ch. 27. 1.

רֶשֶׁת fem. dec. 13a (with suff. רִשְׁתִּי), *net;* מַעֲשֵׂה רֶשֶׁת *net-work,* Ex. 27. 4.

מוֹרָשׁ masc. dec. 1b (but constr. מוֹרַשׁ, § 31. rem. 1), מוֹרָשָׁה fem. *possession.*

מוֹרֶשֶׁת גַּת (*possession of Gath*) pr. name of a town near Gath. Gent. noun מוֹרַשְׁתִּי.

תִּירוֹשׁ, תִּירֹשׁ masc. dec. 1b, *new wine, must.*

יָרֶשׁ] Hiph. fut. 3 pers. sing. masc. ap. and conv. from יוֹרִישׁ (comp. § 20. rem. 11) .   ירש

יִירַשׁ] Kal fut. 3 p. s. m. for יִירַשׁ (§ 20. rem. 2)   ירש

יְרָשָׁה id. imp. s. m. [וַיְרַשׁ] with parag. ה (§ 8. r. 12)   ירש

יְרֵשָׁה noun fem. sing.   ירש

יְרֻשָּׁה noun fem. sing. dec. 10   ירש

יָרְשׁוּ] Kal pret. 3 pers. pl.   ירש

יִירְשׁוּ וַיִּ Kal fut. 3 pers. pl. masc. for יִירְשׁוּ (§ 20. rem. 2);] conv.   ירש

יְרָשׁוּהָ] id. fut. 3 pers. pl. masc. (יִירְשׁוּ from), suff. 3 pers. sing. masc. (§ 16. rem. 12)   ירש

יְרֵשׁוּהָ] id. pret. 3 pers. pl. (יָרַשׁ, fr. s. § 16. r. 1), suff. 3 pers. s. m. with conj.] [for וַיְ, וַיִּרָשׁוּ]   ירש

יְרֵשׁוּךָ] id. id., suff. 2 p. s. m. with cop.], see prec.   ירש

יֹרְשָׁיו id. part. act. pl., suff. 3 p. s. m. fr. יוֹרֵשׁ d. 7b   ירש

יֹרְשִׁים id. pl., absolute state   ירש

יַרְשִׁיעַ Hiph. fut. 3 pers. sing. masc. .   רשע

וַיַּרְשִׁיעוּ id. fut. 3 pers. pl. masc. .   רשע

יַרְשִׁיעֶךָ id. fut. 3 pers. sing. masc., suff. 2 pers. s. m.   רשע

ᵃ Ge. 41. 14.   ᶠ Ho. 6. 9.   ᵏ Nu. 12. 14.   ᵒ Pr. 10. 7.   ᵗ 1 Ki. 8. 37.   ˣ Ex. 39. 3.   Le. 14. 37.   Ob. 1. 20.   De. 12. 2.
ᵇ Is. 40. 31; 59. 7.   ᵍ 2 Sa. 24. 23.   ˡ Ge. 14. 14.   ᵖ Is. 40. 20.   2 Ch. 6. 28.   ʸ Nu. 17. 4.   Je. 49. 1.   Jos. 21. 43.   Ps. 94. 21.
ᶜ Le. 22. 25.   ⁱ 2 Ch. 15. 10.   ᵐ Nu. 12. 14.   ᵍ Ge. 25. 9.   Ex. 30. 33.   ᶻ Is. 40. 19.   Ge. 22. 17.   Eze. 36. 12.   Job 33. 2.
Job 20. 12.   Ju. 10. 8.   Le. 15. 3.   Le. 13. 21.   Ps. 29. 6.   Le. 13. 49.   De. 33. 23.   Je. 49. 2.   Job 14. 6.
Ps. 94. 5.

יַרְשִׁיעֻן	Hiph. fut. 3 pers. pl. masc. with parag.	רשע
יַרְשִׁיעֶנּוּ	id. fut. 3 pers. sing. masc., suff. 3 pers. s. m.	רשע
יַרְשִׁיעֵנִי	id. id., suff. 1 pers. sing.	רשע
יַרְשֵׁם	וַ Hiph. fut. 3 pers. sing. masc. (יוֹרִישׁ), suff. 3 pers. pl. masc. (§ 20. rem. 11); וַ conv.	ירש
יִרַשְׁנוּ	וְ Kal pret. 1 pers. pl.	ירש
יִרָשֶׁנּוּ	Hiph. fut. 3 pers. sing. masc. (יוֹרִישׁ), suff. 3 pers. sing. masc. (§ 20. rem. 11)	ירש
יְרַשְׁנוּהָ	וְ Kal pret. 1 pers. pl. (יְרַשְׁנוּ), suff. 3 pers. sing. fem. with conv. וְ for וַ, וַיִּרָשְׁנוּ	ירש
יַרְשִׁעַ	defect. for יַרְשִׁיעַ (q. v.)	רשע
יַרְשֵׁשׁ	Pilel fut. 3 pers. sing. masc.	רוש
יָרַשְׁתָּ יָרַשְׁתְּ	Kal pret. 2 pers. sing. masc., acc. shifted by conv. וְ (§ 8. rem. 7)	ירש
יְרֵשַׁת	noun fem. sing., constr. of יְרֵשָׁה dec. 10	ירש
יֹרַשְׁתְּ	Kal part. act., fem. of יוֹרֵשׁ (§ 8. rem. 19)	ירש
יְרִשְׁתָּהּ	וְ id. pret. 2 p. s. m. (יָרַשְׁתָּ), suff. 3 p. s. fem. (§ 8. r. 1 b); with conv. וְ for וַ, וַיִּרָשְׁתָּהּ	ירש
יְרֻשָּׁתוֹ	noun fem. sing., suff. 3 pers. sing. fem. from יְרֵשָׁה dec. 10	ירש
יְרֻשַּׁתְכֶם	id., suff. 3 pers. pl. masc.	ירש
יִרִשְׁתֶּם	וַ Kal pret. 2 pers. sing. masc. (יָרַשְׁתָּ), suff. 3 pers. pl. masc. (§ 8. rem. 1 b); with conv. וַ, וַיִּרַשְׁתֶּם for	ירש
יְרִשְׁתֶּם	וַ id. pret. 2 p. pl. m. with conv. וַ, see prec.	ירש
יַרְתִּיחַ	Hiph. fut. 3 pers. sing. masc.	רתח
יֵשׁ יֶשׁ	prop. subst., used as an adv., with suff. יֶשְׁךָ, יֶשְׁכֶם, (d. 7. § 36. r. 3)	ישה
יִשָּׂא	defect. for יִשָּׂיא (q. v.)	נשא
יִשָּׂא	וַ Kal fut. 3 p. s. m. (§ 25. No. 2a); וַ conv.	נשא
יִשְׁאֲבוּ	וְ Kal fut. 3 pers. pl. masc.; וַ id.	שאב
יִשְׁאֲבוּן	id. with paragogic וּן	שאב
יִשְׁאַן יִשְׁאַן	Kal fut. 3 pers. sing. masc. (§ 8. rem. 15)	שאן
יִשְׁאֲנוּ	id. fut. 3 pers. pl. masc. (v. id.)	שאן
יִשָּׂאֶהָ	Kal fut. 3 pers. sing. m., suff. 3 pers. sing. fem. (§ 16. rem. 12, & § 25. No. 2a); וַ conv.	נשא
יִשָּׂאֵהוּ	וַ id. id., suff. 3 pers. s. m. (v. id.); וַ id.	נשא
יִשָּׂאֻהוּ	וְ, וַ id. fut. 3 pers. pl. masc., suff. 3 pers. sing. fem. (v. id.); וַ id.	נשא
יִשְׂאוּ יִשְׂאוּ	id. fut. 3 pers. pl. masc. (v. id. & § 8. rem. 15); וַ id.	נשא
יִשָּׂאוּם	וַ id. id., suff. 3 pers. pl. masc. (§ 16. rem. 12, & § 25. No. 2a); וַ id.	נשא
יִשָּׂאוּן	Niph. fut. 3 pers. pl. masc. with paragogic וּן	שאה

יִשָּׂאוּנְךָ	Kal fut. 3 pers. pl. m. parag. וּ and suff. 2 pers. sing. m. (§ 16. rem. 12 & 14, & § 25. No. 2a)	נשא
יַשְׁאִיר	Hiph. fut. 3 pers. sing. masc.	שאר
יַשְׁאִירוּ	id. fut. 3 pers. pl. masc.	שאר
יִשָּׁאֲךָ	Hiph. fut. 3 pers. sing. m., suff. 2 pers. s. m.	נשא
יִשָּׂאֲךָ	Kal fut. 3 pers. sing. masc., suff. 2 pers. sing. masc. (§ 16. rem. 12, & § 25. No. 2a)	נשא
יִשְׁאָל	Kh. יִשְׁאַל q. v. K. וְשָׁאַל Kal pret. 3 p. s. m.	שאל
יִשְׁאַל וַיִּשְׁאַל	Kal fut. 3 pers. sing. masc. (§ 8. rem. 15); וַ conv.	שאל
יִשְׁאָלֵהוּ	וַ id., suff. 3 pers. s. m. (§ 16. r. 12); וַ id.	שאל
יְשַׁאֲלוּ	Piel fut. 3 pers. pl. masc.	שאל
יִשְׁאֲלוּ וַיִּ, וְ	Kal fut. 3 pers. pl. masc. (§ 8. rem. 15); וַ conv.	שאל
יַשְׁאִלוּם	וְ Hiph. fut. 3 pers. pl. masc. [יַשְׁאִיל], suff. 3 pers. pl. masc.; וַ id.	שאל
יִשְׁאָלוּן	Kal fut. 3 pers. pl. masc. with parag. וּן (§ 8. rem. 17, comp. § 16. rem. 12)	שאל
יִשְׁאָלוּנִי	id. id. with suff. 1 pers. sing. (v. id.)	שאל
יִשְׁאָלְךָ	id. fut. 3 pers. sing. masc., suff. 2 pers. s. m.	שאל
יִשְׁאֲלֻנְכוֹן	Chald. Peal fut. 3 pers. s. m., suff. 2 p. pl. m.	שאל
יִשָּׂאֵם	וַ Kal fut. 3 pers. sing. masc., suff. 3 pers. pl. m. (§ 16. rem. 12, & § 25. No. 2a); וַ conv.	נשא
יִשָּׂאֵם	וַ id. fut. 3 pers. pl. masc., suff. 3 pers. pl. masc. (v. id.) וַ id.	נשא
יִשָּׂאֶנָּה	id. fut. 3 pers. sing. masc., suff. 3 pers. sing. fem. (v. id. & § 2. rem. 3)	נשא
יִשָּׂאֻנוּ	id. fut. 3 pers. pl. m., suff. 1 pers. pl. (v. id.)	נשא
יִשָּׂאֻנִי	id. fut. 3 pers. s. m., suff. 1 pers. s. (v. id.)	נשא
יִשָּׂף	Kal fut. 3 pers. sing. masc.	שאף
יִשָּׁאֵר וַ	Niph. fut. 3 pers. sing. masc. (§ 9. rem. 3); וַ conv.	שאר
יִשָּׁאֲרוּ וַיִּ	וַיִּ id. fut. 3 pers. pl. masc.; וַ id.	שאר

יָשַׁב וְ fut. יֵשֵׁב; inf. c. שֶׁבֶת; imp. שֵׁב, שְׁבָה; וַ — I. to sit, sit down; with בְּ, עַל of the place; וַתֵּשֶׁב לָהּ and she sat down by herself.—II. to remain, stay, abide.—III. to dwell, dwell in, inhabit; with בְּ, עַל of the place; part. יוֹשֵׁב inhabitant.—IV. to be inhabited, as a place, country. Niph. נוֹשַׁב, to be inhabited. Pi. to set, place, Eze. 25. 4. Hiph. הוֹשִׁיב—I. to cause to sit, to sit.—II. to cause to dwell; to let dwell.—III. to cause to be inhabited. Hoph.—I. to be made to dwell, Is. 5. 8.—II. to be inhabited, Is. 44. 26.

a Ex. 22. 8.   b Ps. 37. 33.   c Jos. 13. 12.   d De. 3. 12.   e Nu. 17. 30.   f Job 24. 15.   g Eze. 35. 10.   h Job 34. 29.   i Je. 5. 17.   k 1 Ki. 21. 19.   l Nu. 36. 8.   m De. 2. 12.   n Jos. 1. 15.   o Job 41. 23.   p 2 Ki. 10. 15.   q Ge. 47. 6.   r Is. 36. 14.   s Ru. 2. 9.   t Je. 51. 35.   u Je. 2. 15.   v Ju. 9. 45.   x 2 Ki. 4. 20.   y Is. 46. 7.   z 2 Ch. 24. 11.   a 1 Ch. 23. 22.   b Ps. 91. 12.   c De. 28. 51.   d 1 Ki. 18. 12.   e Pr. 20. 4.   f Ho. 4. 12.   g 2 Sa. 20. 18.   h Je. 50. 5.   i Ex. 11. 2.   k Ez. 12. 36.   l Jos. 4. 6. 21.   m Ezr. 7. 21.   n 2 Sa. 5. 21.   o Le. 10. 5.   p Ex. 18. 14.   q Is. 64. 5.   r Job 32. 22.   s Job 7. 2.   t Is. 11. 14.   u Ge. 7. 23.   v Eze. 36. 36.   x Nu. 11. 20.

יֹשֵׁב בַּשֶּׁבֶת (*dwelling in quiet*) pr. name of one of David's chief officers, 2 Sa. 23. 8.

יֶשְׁבְּאָב (*father's dwelling*) pr. name masc. 1 Ch. 24. 13.

יִשְׁבּוֹ בְנֹב (*his seat is in Nob*) pr. name m. 2 Sa. 21. 16. Kheth., K. יִשְׁבִּי בְנֹב (*my seat is in Nob*).

יָשָׁב בְּקָשָׁה (for יֹשֵׁב בְּקָשָׁה *seat in a hard place*) pr. name masc. 1 Ch. 25. 4, 24.

שִׁיבָה fem. dec. 10, *abode, stay*, 2 Sa. 19. 33.

שֶׁבֶת fem. *a sitting, seat*, 2 Sa. 23. 7; 1 Ki. 10. 19.

יְשַׁבְיָה (*whom the Lord settles*) pr. name masc. 1 Ch. 4. 35.

מוֹשָׁב masc. dec. 2b (pl. c. מוֹשְׁבֵי, מוֹשְׁבוֹת).—I. *seat.*—II. *seat, dwelling, residence.*—III. *time of residing*, Ex. 12. 40.—IV. *inhabitants*, 2 Sa. 9. 12.—V. *site, situation*, 2 Ki. 2. 19.

תּוֹשָׁב masc. dec. 2 b (but comp. § 31. rem. 1) *settler, sojourner.*

יָשַׁב Kal pret. 3 pers. sing. m. for יָשֵׁב (§ 8. r. 7)

יָשֹׂב Kh. יָשֵׂב q.v.; K. יָשֵׂם ap. from יָשִׂים (q.v.)

יֹשֵׁב Hiph. fut. 3 pers. sing. masc., ap. and conv. for יָשִׁיב

יֹשֵׁב Kal inf. absolute

וַיֵּשֶׁב Kal fut. 3 pers. sing. masc. ap. & conv. (§ 21. rem. 7 & 8)

וַיֹּשֶׁב Hiph. fut. 3 pers. s. m. ap. [from יָשִׁיב] נשב

וַיֵּשֶׁב Kal fut. 3 pers. sing. masc., with conv. וַ in pause (§ 20. rem. 4)

וַיֵּשֶׁב id. with Mak., bef. monos., or with conv. וַ

יֵשֵׁב Kal fut. 3 pers. sing. masc. ap. [from יִשְׁבֶּה § 24. rem. 3b]; וַ conv. שבה

וְיֹשֵׁב Kal part. act. masc. dec. 7b (also pr. name in compos. יֹשֵׁב בַּשֶּׁבֶת) ישב

וְיֹשֵׁב Hiph. fut. 3 pers. sing. masc. ap. & conv. [from יָשִׁיב, comp. § 20. rem. 11]

יֹשֵׁב Kh. יָשֵׁב q.v., K. יֹשְׁבִי (q. v.)

יֶשְׁבְּאָב pr. name masc.

וְיֹשְׁבָה Kal pret. 3 pers. sing. masc. שבה

וְיֹשִׁבָהּ Hiph. fut. 3 pers. sing. masc. (יָשִׁיב), suff. 3 pers. sing. fem.; וַ conv. שוב

וְיֹשִׁבֻהוּ id. fut. 3 pers. pl. masc. (יָשִׁיבוּ) suff. 3 pers. sing. masc.; וַ id. שוב

יָשְׁבוּ Kal pret. 3 pers. pl. (§ 8. rem. 7)

וַיָּשִׁבוּ Hiph. fut. 3 pers. pl. masc. (for יָשִׁיבוּ); וַ conv. שוב

וַיֵּשְׁבוּ Kal fut. 3 p. pl. m. (for יֵשְׁבוּ); וַ conv. שוב

יֵשְׁבוּ Kal fut. 3 pers. pl. masc. (comp. § 8. rem. 15, & § 20. rem. 4); וַ id. ישב

וַיְשַׁבוּ Piel pret. 3 pers. pl. שבה

יִשְׁבּוּ Kal fut. 3 pers. pl. masc; וַ conv. שבה

יֹשְׁבֵי Kh. יֹשְׁבֵי q. v., K. יֹשְׁבֵי (q. v.) שב

וְיִשְׁבֹּם Hiph. fut. 3 pers. pl. masc. (יָשִׁיבוּ), suff. 3 p. pl. m. with conj. וַ [for וַיְשִׁבֹם שוב

יֹשְׁבוּ Kh. יֹשְׁבוּ, K. יֹשְׁבִי pr. name masc. in compos. with בְּנֹב. ישב

יֵשׁוּבוּן Kal fut. 3 p. pl. m. with parag. ן [for יֵשְׁבוּן שוב

יִשְׁבֹּר Kal fut. 3 pers. sing. masc. (§ 8. rem. 18) שבר

יִשְׁבֹּת Kal fut. 3 pers. sing. masc. (§ 8. rem. 18) שבת

יֹשְׁבוֹת Kal part. act. fem., pl. of יֹשֶׁבֶת dec. 13a, from יֹשֵׁב masc. (§ 8. rem. 19) ישב

יְשַׁבֵּחַ Piel fut. 3 pers. sing. masc. שבח

יִשְׁבָּח pr. name masc. שבח

יְשַׁבְּחוּנֶךָ Piel fut. 3 pers. pl. masc. with parag. נ & suff. 2 pers. sing. masc. (§ 16. rem. 14) שבח

יְשַׁבְּחֶנָּה id. fut. 3 p. s. m., suff. 3 p. s. f. (§ 2. r. 3) שבח

יֹשְׁבִי Kal part. act. pl. c. from יֹשֵׁב dec. 7b. ישב

יֹשְׁבִי Kh. יֹשְׁבִי, K. וְיֹשְׁבִי Kal imp. sing. fem. (reg. or irreg. § 20. rem. 2); וַ bef. (ַ) for ן ישב

יֹשְׁבֵי pr. name in compos. יֹשְׁבֵי לֶחֶם שוב

יֹשְׁבֶיהָ וַ Kal part. act. pl. masc., suff. 3 pers. sing fem. from יֹשֵׁב dec. 7b. ישב

יֹשְׁבֵיהֶם וַ id., suff. 3 pers. pl. masc. ישב

יֹשְׁבֵיהֶן וַ id., suff. 3 pers. pl. fem. ישב

יֹשְׁבָיו id., suff. 3 pers. sing. masc. ישב

וְיֹשְׁבֵים id. pl., absolute state ישב

יַשְׁבִּיעֶךָ Hiph. fut. 3 pers. sing. masc., suff. 2 p. s. f. שבע

יַשְׁבִּיעֵם id., suff. 3 pers. pl. masc. שבע

יַשְׁבִּית Hiph. fut. 3 pers. sing. masc. שבת

וַיֹּשִׁבֵם Kal fut. 3 p. m. s. [יֹשְׁבֵה], suff. 3 p. pl. m. שבה

יִשְׁבְּנוּ Kal pret. 1 pers. pl. ישב

וַיֹּשִׁבֵנִי Hiph. fut. 3 p. s. m. (יָשִׁיב), suff. 1 p. s.; וַ conv. שוב

וַיַּשְׁבַּע Hiph. fut. 3 pers. sing. masc. ap. [from יַשְׁבִּיעַ]; וַ id. שבע

וַיִּשָּׁבַע Niph. fut. 3 pers. sing. masc.; וַ id. שבע

יִשְׁבַּע Kal fut. 3 pers. sing. masc. (§ 8. rem. 15); וַ id. שבע

יִשָּׁבְעוּ Niph. fut. 3 pers. pl. masc. (comp. § 8. rem. 15); וַ id. שבע

יְשַׁבְּעוּ Piel fut. 3 pers. pl. masc. [for יְשַׂבְּעוּ comp. § 8. rem. 15] שבע

יִשְׂבְּעוּ וַ, וַיִּ Kal fut. 3 pers. pl. masc. (§ 8. rem. 15); וַ conv. שבע

---

a Da. 11. 18.	f Ru. 4. 1.	k 2 Ki. 14. 22.	l 1 Ch. 2. 55.	r Ps. 145. 4.	z Is. 42. 10.	e Ps. 105. 40.	g Eze. 47. 1, 6.	l Exr. 10. 5.
b Da. 11. 18, 19.	g Ps. 55. 20.	l Eze. 36. 35.	m Je. 23. 22.	s Ps. 63. 4.	a 2 Ki. 22. 16, 19.	d Pr. 18. 18, etc.	h Is. 44. 16.	m Eze. 7. 19.
c 1 Sa. 20. 5.	h 2 Ki. 17. 6, 24.	m Ru. 4. 1.	n Is. 42. 3.	t Pr. 29. 11.	c Ge. 34. 16.	f 2 Ch. 24. 15.	n Ps. 22. 27.
d Ps. 147. 18.	i Ju. 1. 27.	n Eze. 25. 4.	o Ho. 7. 4.	u Ps. 147. 14.	f 2 Sa. 15. 8.	h Je. 5. 2.	o Ho. 13. 6.
e Ge. 15. 11.	k La. 1. 1, 3.	o De. 1. 22.	p Je. 41. 10.			

יִשְׁבְּעוּן*	Kal fut. 3 pers. pl. masc. with parag.	שבע
יִשְׁבָּעֲךָ[b]	id. fut. 3 pers. sing. masc. (יִשְׁבַּע), suff. 2 pers. sing. masc. (§ 16. rem. 12)	שבע
יָשְׁבְעָם	' pr. name masc.	שוב
יַשְׁבְּעֵנִי	Hiph. fut. 3 pers. sing. masc., suff. 1 pers. s.	שבע
יַשְׁבִּעֵנִי	וַ Hiph. fut. 3 p. s. m., suff. 1 p. s.; וַ conv.	שבע
יִשְׁבָּק	' pr. name masc.	שבק
יָשְׁבְקָשָׁה	pr. name masc.	יוב
יִשָּׁבֵר	וַ Niph. fut. 3 pers. sing. masc.; וַ conv.	שבר
יְשַׁבֵּר	וַ Piel fut. 3 pers. sing. masc.; וַ id.	שבר
יִשְׁבֹּר	' וַ Kal fut. 3 pers. sing. masc.; וַ id.	שבר
יִשְׁבְּרֵהוּ	וַ id. fut. 3 p. s. m., suff. 3 p. s. m.; וַ id.	שבר
יִשָּׁבְרוּ	וַ Niph. fut. 3 pers. pl. masc. (comp. § 8. rem. 15); וַ id.	שבר
יִשְׁבָּרוּ	וַ Kal fut. 3 pers. pl. masc.; וַ id.	שבר
יְשַׁבְּרוּ	וַ Piel fut. 3 pers. pl. masc. (comp. § 8. rem. 15)	שבר
יְשַׁבְּרוּ	וַ Piel fut. 3 pers. pl. masc.; וַ conv.	שבר
יִשְׁבְּרוּהוּ	Kal fut. 3 pers. pl. m., suff. 3 pers. s. m.	שבר
יְשַׁבְּרוּן	Piel fut. 3 pers. pl. masc. parag. [for יְשַׁבְּרוּן § 10. rem. 4] .	שבר
יָשַׁבְתָּ		
יָשַׁבְתָּ	} Kal pret. 2 pers. sing. masc. (§ 8. r. 7)	ישב
יָשַׁבְתָּ		
יָשַׁבְתְּ	' וַ id. pret. 2 pers. sing. fem.	ישב
יַשְׁבֵּת	וַ Hiph. fut. 3 p. s. m. ap. from יַשְׁבִּית; וַ conv.	שבת
יִשְׁבֹּת	' וַ, Kal fut. 3 pers. sing. masc.; וַ id.	שבת
יֹשֶׁבֶת	} Kal part. act. fem. dec. 13 a, from יָשַׁב masc. (§ 8. rem. 19)	ישב
יֹשְׁבֹת	pl. of the preceding. 1 Ki. 3. 17.	ישב
יֹשַׁבְתָּה	וַ in full for יָשַׁבְתְּ q. v. (§ 8. rem. 5)	ישב
יָשַׁבְתּוּ	} Kal fut. 3 pers. pl. masc. (§ 8. rem. 15); וַ conv.	שבות
וַיֵּ֫שְׁבוּ		
יָשַׁבְתִּי	' וַ Kal pret. 1 pers. sing.	ישב
יֹשַׁבְתִּי	Kh. יֹשַׁבְתִּי, K. יֹשֶׁבֶת Kal part. act. fem. (§ 39. rem. 3, comp. § 8. rem. 5)	ישב
יְשַׁבְתֶּם	} Kal pret. 2 pers. pl. masc., with conv. וַ [for וַ, וִישַׁבְתֶּם]	ישב
יְשַׁבְתֶּם		
יַשֵּׁג	וַ, וַיַ Hiph. fut. 3 pers. sing. masc., ap. for יַשִּׂיג; וַ conv.	נשג
יִשְׁגֵּא	Ch. Peal fut. 3 pers. sing. masc.	שגא
יְשַׂגֵּב	וַ Piel fut. 3 pers. sing. masc.; וַ conv.	שגב
יְשֻׁגָּב	Pual fut. 3 pers. sing. masc. [for יְשֻׁגַּב comp. § 8. rem. 15]	שגב-
יְשַׂגֶּבְךָ	Piel fut. 3 p. s. m., suff. 2 p. s. m. (§ 16. r. 15)	שגב
יִשְׁגֶּה	Kal fut. 3 pers. sing. masc.	שנה
יִשְׁגֶּה	Kal fut. 3 pers. sing. masc.	שנה

יַשְׁגִּנוּ	וַ Hiph. fut. 3 pers. pl. m. for יַשִּׂיגֻנוּ; וַ conv.	נשג
יִשְׁגֻּנוּ	Kal fut. 3 pers. pl. masc.	שנה
יַשְׁגִּיב*	Hiph. fut. 3 pers. sing. masc.	שגב
יַשְׁגִּיחוּ	Hiph. fut. 3 pers. pl. masc.	שגח
יִשְׁלָגֶהָ	Kh. Kal fut. 3 pers. sing. masc. [יִשְׁלַג], suff. 3 pers. sing. fem. (§ 16. r. 12, & § 2. r. 3)	שגל
וַיַשְׂגֵּם	וַ Hiph. fut. 3 pers. sing. masc., suff. 3 pers. pl. masc. for יַשִּׂיגֵם; וַ conv.	נשג
יְשַׁדֵּד	} Piel fut. 3 pers. sing. masc., with conj.	
יְשַׁדֵּד*	} וַ [וַיְ, וִישַׁדֵּד for]	שדד
יְשָׁד*	id. with Makkaph (§ 10. rem. 4)	שדד
יְשׁוֹדֵד	Poel fut. 3 pers. sing. masc.	שדד
יְשָׁדֵּם	Kal fut. 3 pers. sing. masc. [יִשֹׁד], suff. 3 pers. pl. masc. [for the contracted form § 18. rem. 13, comp. rem. 5]	שדד

יֵשׁ Root not used; to be, exist, subsist; to be firm. Comp. Prof. Lee under יֵשׁ; Arab. وشی to help.

יֵשׁ, יֵשׁ.—I. substance, wealth, Pr. 8. 2.—II adv. there is, there are; with suff. יֶשְׁךָ thou art; he is, יֶשְׁכֶם ye are; יֵשׁ וָיֵשׁ it is truly so, I have; יֶשׁ־לִי there are those who.

יִשַׁי, אִישַׁי (wealthy) pr. name Jesse, the father of David.

יוֹשָׁה (wealth) pr. name masc. 1 Ch. 4. 34.

יוֹשַׁוְיָה (whom the Lord establishes) pr. name masc. 1 Ch. 11. 46.

מֵישָׁא (wealth) pr. name masc. 1 Ch. 8. 9.

תּוּשִׁיָּה fem.—I. help, deliverance, Job 6. 13; Pr. 2. 7; Mi. 6. 9. Others render these passages either by wealth, wisdom or security.—II. purpose, enterprise, Job 5. 12; Prof. Lee wealth, abundance.—III. counsel, wisdom.

יַשֶּׁה	Hiph. fut. 3 pers. sing. masc.	נשה
וַיֵּשׁוֹב	Kh. וַיֵּשׁוֹב וַיָּשָׁב for וַיָּשָׁב q. v., K. וַיָּשָׁב (q. v.)	שוב
יֵשׁוּב	Kh. יֵשׁוּב q. v., K. יָשׁוּב (q. v.)	שוב
יָשׁוּב	pr. name masc.	שוב
יָשׁוּב	Kal fut. 3 pers. sing. masc.	שוב
יְשׁוֹבֵב	Pilel fut. 3 pers. sing. masc.	שוב
וַיָּשֻׁבוּ	וַ Kal fut. 3 pers. pl. masc.; וַ conv.	שוב
יְשׁוּבוּן	id. with parag. וַ	שוב
יְשׁוֹדֵד*	Kal fut. 3 pers. sing. masc.	שוד
יְשַׁוֶּה*	Piel fut. 3 pers. sing. masc.	שוה
יְשׁוָה	וַ pr. name masc.	שוה
יְשׁוּ*	Kal fut. 3 pers. pl. masc.	שוה
יְשׁוֹחַח*	Pilel fut. 3 pers. sing. masc.	שיח
יְשׁוֹחָיָה	וַ pr. name masc. [for וַיְ, וַיָּשֻׁ]	שיח

a Ps. 104. 28.　e Je. 19. 11.　i Ps. 145. 15.　l De. 8. 12.　p De. 17. 11.　t Ps. 7. 6.　x Job 36. 22.　a Is. 28. 24.　f Eze.18. 28
b Pr. 25. 17.　f Ge. 41. 56.　k Is. 38. 18.　m Je. 3. 2.　y Ge. 8. 22.　u Ge. 31. 25.　c Is. 14. 16.　b Ho. 10. 11.　g Ps. 23. 3.
c Jo 9. 18.　g Da. 11. 22.　i 2 Ch. 31. 1.　n Eze. 23. 41.　z Je. 31. 36.　v Pr. 29. 25.　d Is. 28. 24.　c Ho. 10. 2.　h Ps. 91. 6.
d Ge. 24. 37.　h Ju. 7. 20.　k 2 Ch. 20. 37.　o Da. 11. 26.　q Pr. 22. 10.　w Ps. 20. 2.　e Ge. 44. 6.　d Je. 5. 6.　i Ho. 10. 1.
e Je. 50. 23.　　　l Ps. 104. 27.　r 2 Ki. 4. 12.　s Je. 22. 23.　g Pr. 5. 23.　e Job 39. 10.　f Job 11. 6.　j Is. 53. 8.

יְשׁוֹטְמֽוּ	Pilel fut. 3 pers. pl. masc. . . שׁוט
יְשׁוִֽי	} pr. name masc. . . . שׁוה
יָשׂוּם	Kal fut. 3 pers. sing. masc. . . שׂום
יֵשׁוּעַ	} (*he shall be a deliverance, i. e. deliverer,* for יִהְיֶה יֵשׁוּעַ comp. (יְהוּא) pr. name of several persons, and stands often for יְהוֹשֻׁעַ
יְשׁוּעָה / יְשׁוּעָה	} noun fem. sing. dec. 10, with cop. [for וְיִשׁוּעָה], וַיֽ] . . } ישׁע
יְשׁוּעֽוּ / יְשׁוּעוּ	} Piel fut. 3 pers. pl. masc. (comp. § 8. rem. 15, & § 15. rem. 2) . . } שׁוע
יְשׁוּעוֹת	noun fem., pl. of יְשׁוּעָה dec. 10 . ישׁע
יְשׁוּעַת	id. sing., constr. state . . . ישׁע
יְשֻׁעֹת	id pl. defect. for יְשׁוּעוֹת . . ישׁע
יְשׁוּעָתָה	id. sing. with parag. ה . . . ישׁע
יְשׁוּעָתֹֽה	} id. sing., suff. 3 pers. sing. fem. [for וִישׁוּעָתָה, וַיֽ] . } ישׁע
יְשׁוּעָתוֹ	id. sing., suff. 3 pers. sing. masc. . ישׁע
יְשׁוּעָתִֽי / יְשׁוּעָתִי	} id. sing., suff. 1 pers. sing. with cop. [for וִישׁוּעָתִי, וַיֽ] . } ישׁע
יְשׁוּעָתֶֽךָ / יְשׁוּעָתֶךָ	} id. sing., suff. 2 pers. sing. masc. . ישׁע
יְשׁוּעָתֵנוּ	id. sing., suff. 1 pers. pl. . . ישׁע
יְשׁוּפְךָ	Kal fut. 3 pers. sing. masc. [יָשׁוּף], suff. 2 pers. sing. masc. . . שׁוף
יְשׁוּפֵֽנִי	id. with suff. 1 pers. sing. . . שׁוף
יְשׁוּרֽ	Kal fut. 3 pers. sing. masc. . . שׁור
יְשׁוּרֶֽנָּה	id., suff. 3 pers. sing. fem. (§ 2. rem. 3) . שׁור
יְשׁוּרֶֽנּוּ	id., suff. 3 pers. sing. masc. (§ 2. rem. 3) . שׁור
יְשׁוֹרֵר	Pilel fut. 3 pers. sing. masc. . . שׁיר
יְשֵׁיזִֽב	Chald. Peil fut. 3 pers. sing. masc. (§ 48) שׁזב

[יֵשַׁח]	masc. *emptiness of stomach, hunger,* Mi. 6. 14. So Gesenius, coll. with Arab. وحش *to be empty.* Others, *lowness, faintness,* שָׁחַח=יֵשַׁח q. v.
יֵשַׁח	Kal fut. 3 pers. sing. masc . . שׁחח
יִשַּׁח	} Niph. fut. 3 pers. sing. masc.; וַֽ conv. . שׁחח
יִשְׁחֽוּ	} וַיֽ Kal fut. 3 pers. pl. masc.; וַֽ id. שׁחח
יֵשַֽׁחוּ	} Niph. (dag. impl. in ח) fut. 3 pers. pl. m. שׁחח
יִשְׁחֲטוּ	Niph. fut. 3 pers. sing. masc. . . שׁחט
יִשְׁחָֽט	} (וַיֽ) Kal fut. 3 pers. sing. masc. (§ 8. rem. 15); וַֽ conv. . } שׁחט
יִשְׁחֲמֵ֫הוּ	} id. id., suff. 3 p. s. m. (§ 16. r. 12); וַֽ id. שׁחט
יִשְׁחֲטוּ	} (וַיֽ) id. fut. 3 pers. pl. masc. (§ 8. rem. 15); וַֽ id. . } שׁחט
יִשְׁחָטֽוּהָ	} וַֽ id. id., suff. 3 p. s. m. (§ 16. r. 12); וַֽ id. שׁחט
יִשְׁחָטֽוּם	} id. id., suff. 3 pers. pl. masc.; וַֽ id. שׁחט

יִשְׁחָתֵם	} וַֽ Kal fut. 3 pers. sing. masc., suff. 3 pers. pl. masc. (§ 16. rem. 12); וַֽ conv. . שׁחת
יַשְׁחִית	Hiph. fut. 3 pers. sing. masc. . . שׁחת
יַשְׁחִיתוּ	} וַיֽ id. fut. 3 pers. pl. masc.; וַֽ conv. שׁחת
יַשְׁחִיתֶֽךָ	id. fut. 3 p. s. m., suff. 2 p. s. m. [for רָחִיתְךָ] . שׁחת
יַשְׁחֶֽנָּה	} Hiph. fut. 3 pers. sing. masc. [יַשְׁחֶה], suff. 3 pers. sing. fem. (§ 24. r. 21, & § 2. r. 3) . שׁחה
יִשְׁחֲךָ	} noun masc. sing., suff. 2 pers. sing. masc. from [יֵשַׁח] dec. 6 (§ 35. rem. 3 & 5) . ישׁח
יִשְׂחָק / יִצְחָק	} Kal fut. 3 pers. sing. masc. (§ 8. r. 15) שׂחק
יְשַׂחֶק	} Piel fut. 3 pers. sing. masc. [for יִשַׂחֵק § 14. r. 1 & 2] with conj. וַֽ [for וַיֽ], וַיְשַׂחֵק . } שׂחק
יְשַׂחֲקוּ	} id. fut. 3 pers. pl. masc., with conj. וַֽ [for וַיְשַׂחֲקוּ], וַיֽ . } שׂחק
יִשְׂחֲקוּ	Kal fut. 3 pers. pl. m. [for יִשְׂחֲקוּ § 8. r. 15] שׂחק
יְשָׂחֲרֻֽנְנִי	Piel (§ 14. rem. 1) fut. 3 pers. pl. masc., with parag. נ & suff. 1 p. s. (§ 16. r. 14) שׁחר
יַשְׁחֵת	} (וַֽ) Hiph. fut. 3 pers. sing. masc. apoc. & defect. for יַשְׁחִית; וַֽ conv. . } שׁחת
יַשְׁחִֽתוּ	} id. fut. 3 p. pl. m., defect. for יַשְׁחִיתוּ; וַֽ id. שׁחת

יָשֵׁט	Hiph. הוֹשִׁיט *to stretch out, extend,* Est. 4. 11; 5. 2; 8. 4.
יֵשְׁטֽ	Kal fut. 3 p. s. m. apoc. [fr. יִשְׁטֶה § 24. r. 3] שׁטה
יָשׁוֹטוּ	} וַֽ Kal fut. 3 p. pl. m. [for יְשׁוּטוּ]; וַֽ conv. שׁוט
יִשְׁטֹף	Kal fut. 3 pers. sing. masc. (§ 8. rem. 18) שׁטף
יִשְׁטְחֽוּ	} וַֽ Kal fut. 3 pers. pl. masc.; וַֽ conv. שׁטח
יְשׁוֹטְטֽוּ	Pilel fut. 3 pers. pl. masc. . . שׁוט
יָשִֽׂימוּ	} וַֽ Kal fut. 3 pers. sing. masc.; וַֽ conv. שׂום
יְשִׂימֵ֫הוּ	} id. fut. 3 p. pl. m., suff. 3 p. s. m.; וַֽ id. שׂום
יְשִׂימֻ֫נִי	} id. id., suff. 1 pers. sing. . . שׂום
יְשִׂימֵֽנִי	id. fut. 3 pers. sing. masc., suff. 1 pers. s. שׂום
יְשִׂימֵ֫נִי	} וַֽ id. id., suff. 1 pers. sing.; וַֽ conv . שׂום
יְשִׂימֻ֫נִי	Kal fut. 3 pers. pl. masc., suff. 1 pers. sing. שׂום
יִשָּׁטֵף	Niph. fut. 3 pers. sing. masc. . . שׁטף
יִשָּׁטֵֽף	} וַֽ Kal fut. 3 pers. sing. masc.; וַֽ conv. שׁטף
יִשָּׁטְפֽוּ	Niph. fut. 3 pers. pl. masc. . . שׁטף
יִשְׁטְפֽוּ / יִשְׁטְפֻֽהוּ	} Kal fut. 3 pers. pl. masc. (§ 8. rem. 15) שׁטף
יִשְׁטְפֽוּהָ	id., suff. 3 pers. sing. fem. . . שׁטף
יִשְׁטְפֽוּךָ	id., suff. 2 pers. sing. masc. . . שׁטף
יִשַׁי / יִשָׁי	} pr. name masc. . . . ישׁה
יַשִּׂיא	Hiph. fut. 3 pers. sing. masc. . . נשׁא
יַשִּׂיאוּ	id. fut. 3 pers. pl. masc. . . נשׁא

---

a Am. 8. 12.	g Ge. 3. 15.	m Job 38. 40.	r Le. 8. 15, 19, 23.	y Mi. 6. 14.	e Ps. 52. 8.	i Nu. 11. 32.	o Ge. 50. 15.	f Je. 47. 2.
b Ex. 4. 11.	h Je. 5. 26.	n Ps. 107. 39.	s Le. 9. 15.	z Job 41. 21.	a 1 Ch. 20. 1.	k Da. 12. 4.	p Job 16. 9.	u Ca. 8. 7.
c Ps. 118. 15.	i Zep. 2. 14.	o Ec. 19. 4.	t Eze. 40. 41.	a Ju. 16. 25.	b Pr. 7. 25.	l Ge. 27. 41.	q Le. 15. 12.	v Is. 43. 2.
Job 38. 41.	k Da. 3. 17.	p Nu. 11. 32.	u Ju. 12. 6.	b Job 40. 20.	c 2 Sa. 24. 8.	m Ge. 49. 23.	r 1 Ki. 22. 38.	w Ps. 89. 23, etc.
Is. 62. 1.	l Ps. 10. 10.	q Le. 17. 3.	v Pr. 12. 25.	c 2 Sa. 2. 14.	d Da. 11. 26.	n Ps. 55. 4.	s Da. 11. 22.	x Je. 29. 8.
Ps. 69. 30.	u Job 34. 29.							

יָשִׁיב	Kh. יָשׁוּב, K. יָשׁוּב pr. name masc.	שוב
יָשִׁיב	Kh. יָשׁוּב q. v., K. יָשׁוּב (q. v.)	שוב
יָשִׁיב	Hiph. fut. 3 pers. sing. masc.	שוב
יְשִׁיבֶהָ	id. id., suff. 3 pers. sing. fem.; ו conv.	שוב
יְשִׁיבֶהוּ	id. id., suff. 3 pers. sing. masc.; ו id.	שוב
יְשִׁיבָהוּ	id. fut. 3 pers. pl. masc., suff. 3 pers. sing. masc. with conj. ו [for וַיְשִׁיבֻהוּ]	שוב
יָשִׁיבוּ	ו, וַיָּ id. fut. 3 pers. pl. masc.; וַ conv.	שוב
וַיְשִׁיבֻם	Hiph. fut. 3 pers. pl. masc. [יֹשִׁיבֻן § 20. rem. 11], suff. 3 pers. pl. masc.; וַ id.	ישב
יְשִׁיבֻנִי	Hiph. fut. 3 pers. pl. m. (וַיְשִׁיבֻ), suff. 1 p. s.	שוב
יְשִׁיבֵם	Hiph. fut. 3 pers. sing. masc. [יֹשִׁיב § 20. rem. 11], suff. 3 pers. pl. masc.; ו conv.	ישב
יְשִׁיבֵם	id. fut. 3 pers. pl. m., suff. 3 pers. pl. m.	ישב
יְשִׁיבֵם	Hiph. fut. 3 pers. sing. masc. (יָשִׁיב), suff. 3 pers. pl. masc.; ו conv.	שוב
יְשִׁיבֶנָּה	id., suff. 3 pers. sing. fem. (§ 2. rem. 3)	שוב
יְשִׁיבֶנּוּ	id., suff. 3 pers. sing. masc. (§ 2. rem. 3)	שוב
יַשִּׁיגוּ	Hiph. fut. 3 pers. sing. masc.	נשג
יַשִּׂיגוּ	וַיָּ id. fut. 3 pers. pl. masc.; ו conv.	נשג
יַשִּׂיגוּן	id. id. with parag. ן	נשג
יַשִּׂיגֵם	id. fut. 3 pers. sing. masc., suff. 3 p. pl. m.	נשג
יְשַׁיָּה	ו pr. name masc.	נשה
יְשַׁיָּהוּ	ו	נשה
יְשֵׁיזְבִנָּךְ	Chald. Peil fut. 3 pers. sing. masc. (יְשֵׁיזִיב), suff. 2 pers. sing. masc. (§ 48)	שוב
יְשֵׁיזְבִנְכוֹן	Chald. id. with suff. 2 pers. pl. masc.	שוב
יָשִׂיחַ	Kal fut. 3 pers. sing. masc.	שיח
יָשִׂיחוּ	id. fut. 3 pers. pl. masc.	שיח
יָשִׂים	Kal fut. 3 pers. sing. masc., R. שׂים see	שׂום
יַשִּׂים	Hiph. fut. 3 pers. sing. masc. for יָשֵׂם (§ 18. rem. 12 & 14)	שׂמם
יְשִׂימֶהָ	Kal fut. 3 pers. sing. masc. (יָשִׂים, R. שׂים) with suff. 3 pers. sing. fem.; ו conv., see	שׂום
יְשִׂימֵהוּ	id. id. with suff. 3 pers. sing. masc.; ו conv.	שׂום
יְשִׂימֻהוּ	id. fut. 3 p. pl. m. with suff. 3 p. s. m.; ו id.	שׂום
יָשִׂימוּ	ו, וַיָּ id. fut. 3 pers. pl. masc.; ו id.	שׂום
יִשְׂמָעֵאל	pr. name masc.	שׂום
יְשִׂימוֹת	Kh. יְשִׂמוֹת noun pl. R. ישם; K. מָנַת יְשֵׁי; see (מָנַת) יְשִׁי for יְשָׁיא (q. v. & § 23. r. 7)	נשׂא
יְשִׂימְךָ	Kal fut. 3 pers. sing. masc., (יָשִׂים, R. שׂים), suff. 2 pers. sing. masc.; ו conv., see	שׂום
יְשִׂימֵם	id. with suff. 3 pers. pl. masc.	שׂום
יְשִׂימֵנִי	id. with suff. 1 pers. sing.; ו conv.	שׂום
יַשִּׁיעֵנִי	Hiph. fut. 3 pers. sing. masc. (יוֹשִׁיעַ § 20. rem. 11), suff. 1 pers. pl.	ישע

יַשִּׁיק	Hiph. fut. 3 pers. sing. masc.	נשק
יָשִׁיר	Kal fut. 3 pers. sing. masc.	שיר
יָשִׁירוּ	ו/ id. fut. 3 pers. pl. masc.	שיר
יְשִׁישׁ	noun masc. sing. dec. 3a	ישׁישׁ
יָשִׁישׂ	ו/ Kal fut. 3 pers. sing. masc. R. שׂושׂ, see	שׂושׂ
יָשִׂישׂוּ	ו/ id. fut. 3 pers. sing. masc.	שׂושׂ
יִשְׁוִישַׁי	pr. name masc.	ישׁישׁ
יְשִׁישִׁים	noun masc. pl. [with cop. ו, for וִישִׁישִׁים], from יָשִׁישׁ dec. 3a	ישׁישׁ
יָשִׁית	Kal fut. 3 pers. sing. masc.	שית
יָשִׁת	Kh. יָשִׁית q. v.; K. וְשִׁת Kal imp. sing. masc.	שית
וַיְשִׁיתֵהוּ	Hiph. fut. 3 pers. sing. m. (יָשִׁית) and suff. 3 p. s. m. with conj. ו [for וַיְשִׁיתֵהוּ]	שית
יְשִׁיתֻהוּ	ו/ id. fut. 3 pers. pl. masc.; ו conv.	שית
יְשִׁיתֻגָהוּ	id. id., suff. 3 pers. sing. masc.	שית
יֶשְׁךָ	adv. יֵשׁ with suff. 2 pers. sing. masc. comp. dec. 7a (§ 36. rem. 3)	ישה
יֵשֵׁךְ	Kal fut. 3 pers. s. m. [for יֵשֵׁךְ § 8. rem. 15]	נשך
יִשֹּׁךְ	id. middle O (§ 17. rem. 3)	נשך
יִשְׁכַּב	וַיָּ Kal fut. 3 pers. sing. masc. (§ 8. rem. 15); ו conv.	שכב
יִשְׁכָּב	וַיָּ	שכב
וַיַּשְׁכִּבֵהוּ	ו Hiph. fut. 3 pers. sing. masc. (וַיַּשְׁכִּיב), suff. 3 pers. sing. masc.; ו id.	שכב
יִשְׁכְּבוּ	Kal fut. 3 pers. pl. masc. (§ 8. rem. 15); ו id.	שכב
יִשְׁכָּבוּ	וַיָּ	שכב
יִשְׁכָּבוּן	id. with parag. ן (§ 8. rem. 17)	שכב
יִשְׁכְּנוּ	ו Kal fut. 3 pers. pl. masc.; ו conv.	שכן
יִשְׁכֹּן	וַיָּ Kal fut. 3 p. s. m. (§ 8. rem. 18); ו id.	שכן
יִשְׁכֹּנוּ	id. fut. 3 pers. pl. masc.	שכן
יִשְׁכַּח	Niph. fut. 3 pers. sing. masc.	שכח
יִשְׁכַּח	ו, וַיָּ Kal fut. 3 pers. sing. masc.; ו conv.	שכח
יִשְׁכָּחֵהוּ	וַיָּ id. id., suff. 3 p. s. m. (§ 16. rem. 12); ו id.	שכח
יִשְׁכָּחוּ	וַיָּ id. fut. 3 pers. pl. masc.; ו id.	שכח
יַשְׁכִּיב	Hiph. fut. 3 pers. sing. masc.	שכב
וַיַּשְׁכִּבֵהוּ	ו id. fut. 3 p. pl. m., suff. 3 p. s. m.; ו conv.	שכב
יַשְׁכִּיל	Hiph. fut. 3 pers. sing. masc.	שׂכל
יַשְׂכִּילוּ	ו/ id. fut. 3 pers. pl. masc.	שׂכל
יַשְׁכִּימוּ	ו Hiph. fut. 3 pers. pl. masc.; ו conv.	שכם
יַשְׁכִּינֵנִי	ו Hiph. fut. 3 pers. sing. masc.; ו id.	שכן
יַשְׁכֵּם	ו Hiph. fut. 3 p. s. m. ap. [from יַשְׁכִּים]; ו id.	שכם
יֶשְׁכֶם	adv. יֵשׁ with suff. 2 pers. pl. masc. (comp. הַיֶשְׁכֶם & § 36. rem. 3)	ישה
יִשְׁכְּמוּ	ו defect. for יַשְׁכִּימוּ (q. v.)	שכם
וַיַּשְׁכֵּן	וַ Hiph. fut. 3 pers. sing. masc. apoc. [from יַשְׁכִּין]; ו conv.	שכן

a 2 Ch. 26. 2.   e 2 Ch. 19. 4.   i Ps. 119. 23.   l 1 Ki. 10. 9.   o Job 39. 21.   s Ps. 17. 11.   w Ge. 8. 1.   z Ho. 8. 14.   δ De. 32. 29.
b 2 Ch. 24. 11.   f Le. 26. 5.   " Ps. 69. 13.   m De. 7. 15.   p Ps. 68. 4.   t Je. 2. 15.   x Job 15. 28.   a Job 24. 20.   ε Is. 41. 20.
2 Sa. 12. 8.   g Is. 51. 11.   k Je. 49. 20; 50. 45.   n 1 Sa. 4. 3.   q Ps. 84. 7.   u Ps. 102. 29.   y Ge. 40. 23.   β Jos. 18. 1.   ζ Ge. 24. 49.
d Job 20. 2.   h Ps. 69. 25.   Is. 44. 15.   r Ec. 10. 11.   Ps. 9. 19.   Is. 18. 11.
Job 36. 7.   Da. 6. 17.   2 Ki. 10. 27.   Ps. 138. 5.   1 Ki. 17. 19   y Job 38. 37.   2 Ch. 16. 14.   Ps. 7. 6.
1 Sa. 30. 21.   Da. 3. 15.   Ps. 55. 16.   Job 15. 10.   1 Sa. 2. 22.   De. 4. 31.

יִשְׁכֹּן ׀ וַיִּ׳, וְיִ׳, Kal fut. 3 pers. sing. masc. (§ 8. rem. 18) ; וַ׳ conv.   שׁכן

יִשְׁכָּנּוּ Kal fut. 3 pers. sing. masc. (comp. יִשֹּׁךְ & יִשֹּׁךְ) suff. 3 pers. sing. masc.   נשׁך

יִשְׁכְּנוּ ׀ וַיִּ׳, וְיִ׳, Kal fut. 3 pers. pl. masc. (§ 8. rem. 15) ; וַ׳ conv.   שׁכן

יִשְׁכְּנָן Chald. Peal fut. 3 pers. pl. fem.   שׁכן

יִשְׁכַּר וַ׳ Kal fut. 3 pers. sing. masc. [for יִשְׁכַּר § 8. rem. 15]; וַ׳ conv.   שׁכר

יִשְׁכַּר וַ׳ Kal fut. 3 pers. sing. masc. ; וַ׳ id.   שׁכר

יִשְׁכְּרֵהוּ Piel fut. 3 pers. s. m., suff. 3 pers. s. m.; וַ׳ id.   שׁכר

יִשְׁכְּרוּ וַיִּ׳ Kal fut. 3 pers. pl. masc. ; וַ׳ id.   שׁכר

יִשְׁכְּרוּן וַ׳ Kal fut. 3 pers. pl. masc. ; וַ׳ id.   שׁכר

id. with parag. ן [for יִשְׁכְּרוּן § 8. rem. 17]   שׁכר

יִשְׁכְּרֵנִי וַ׳ Kal fut. 3 pers. s. m., suff. 1 pers. s.; וַ׳ conv.   שׁכר

יִשָּׁל Kal fut. 3 pers. sing. masc.   נשׁל

יִשָּׁל Kal fut. 3 p. s. m. ap. [for יִשְׁלֶה § 24. rem. 3]   שׁלה

יִשָּׁלוּךָ Kal fut. 3 pers. pl. masc. [יִשְׁלוּ], suff. 2 pers. sing. masc. (§ 18. rem. 5)   שׁלל

יִשְׁלַח וַיִּ׳ Piel fut. 3 pers. sing. masc.; וַ׳ conv.; with conj. וַ׳ [for וַיִּשְׁלַח, וְיִ׳   שׁלה

יִשְׁלָח id. in pause (§ 15. rem. 1)   שׁלה

יֻשְׁלַח Pual fut. 3 pers. sing. masc.   שׁלה

יִשְׁלַח וַיִּ׳, וַ׳ Kal or (Chald.) Peal fut. 3 p. s. m.; וַ׳ conv.   שׁלה

יִשְׁלָחֶהָ וַ׳ Piel fut. 3 pers. s. m., suff. 3 pers. s. fem.; וַ׳ id.   שׁלה

יִשְׁלָחֵהוּ וַ׳ id., suff. 3 pers. sing. masc. ; וַ׳ id.   שׁלה

יִשְׁלָחֵהוּ וַ׳ Kal fut. 3 pers. sing. masc. (יִשְׁלַח), suff. 3 pers. sing. masc. (§ 16. rem. 12); וַ׳ id.   שׁלה

יִשְׁלְחוּ וַ׳ Piel fut. 3 pers. pl. masc. (comp. § 8. rem. 15) ; וַ׳ id.   שׁלה

יִשְׁלְחוּ וַ׳ id. with conj. ו [for וַיִּשְׁלְחוּ, וְיִ׳   שׁלה

יִשְׁלְחוּ וַיִּ׳ Kal fut. 3 pers. pl. masc.; וַ׳ conv.   שׁלה

יִשְׁלָחוּהָ וַ׳ Piel fut. 3 p. pl. m., suff. 3 p. s. fem.; וַ׳ id.   שׁלה

יִשְׁלָחוּם וַ׳ id., suff. 3 pers. pl. masc. ; וַ׳ id.   שׁלה

יִשְׁלָחֲךָ וַיִּ׳ Kal fut. 3 pers. sing. masc. (יִשְׁלַח), suff. 2 pers. sing. masc. (§ 16. rem. 12); וַ׳ id.   שׁלה

יִשְׁלָחֵם וַ׳ Piel fut. 3 p. s. m., suff. 3 p. pl. m.; וַ׳ conv.; with conj. ו [for וַיִּשְׁלְחֵם, וְיִ׳   שׁלה

יִשְׁלָחֵם וַ׳ Kal fut. 3 pers. sing. masc. (יִשְׁלַח), suff. 3 pers. pl. masc. (§ 16. rem. 12); וַ׳ conv.   שׁלה

יִשְׁלָחֵנוּ וַ׳ Piel fut. 3 pers. sing. m., suff. 1 pers. pl.; וַ׳ id.   שׁלה

יִשְׁלָחֵנוּ id., suff. 3 pers. sing. masc.   שׁלה

יִשְׁלָחֵנּוּ Kal fut. 3 pers. sing. masc. (יִשְׁלַח), suff. 3 pers. sing. masc. (§ 16. rem. 12)   שׁלה

יִשְׁלָחֵנִי וַ׳ Kal fut. 3 pers. sing. masc., with suff. 1 pers. sing. (§ 16. rem. 10) ; וַ׳ conv.   שׁלה

יִשְׁלְטוּ Chald. Peal fut. 3 pers. sing. m. (§ 47. rem. 6 b)   שׁלט

יִשְׁלֹט וַ׳ Kal fut. 3 pers. sing. masc.   שׁלט

יִשְׁלְטוּ id. fut. 3 pers. pl. masc.   שׁלט

יִשְׁלִיו Kal fut. 3 pers. pl. masc. (§ 24. rem. 5)   שׁלה

יַשְׁלִיטֶנּוּ Hiph. fut. 3 pers. sing. m., suff. 3 pers. sing. m.   שׁלט

יַשְׁלִיךְ Hiph. fut. 3 pers. sing. masc.   שׁלך

יַשְׁלִיכֵהוּ וַ׳ id. id., suff. 3 pers. sing. masc.; וַ׳ conv.   שׁלך

יַשְׁלִיכוּ וַיִּ׳ id. fut. 3 pers. pl. masc.; וַ׳ id.   שׁלך

יַשְׁלִיכֻם id. id., suff. 3 pers. pl. masc.; וַ׳ id.   שׁלך
יַשְׁלִיכֵם וַ׳

יַשְׁלִים Hiph. fut. 3 pers. sing. masc.   שׁלם

יַשְׁלִימוּ וַ׳ id. fut. 3 pers. pl. masc. ; וַ׳ conv.   שׁלם

יַשְׁלֵךְ וַיַּ׳, וַ׳ Hiph. fut. 3 pers. sing. masc., apoc. יַשְׁלֵךְ [from יַשְׁלִיךְ]; וַ׳ conv.   שׁלך

יַשְׁלִכֵהוּ id. fut. 3 pers. pl. m., suff. 3 pers. s. m.; וַ׳ id.   שׁלך

יַשְׁלִכוּ defect. for יַשְׁלִיכוּ (q. v.)   שׁלך

יֻשְׁלְכוּ Hoph. fut. 3 p. pl. m. [for יֻשְׁלְכוּ comp. § 8. r. 15]   שׁלך

יַשְׁלִכֶם וַ׳ Hiph. fut. 3 p. s. m., suff. 3 p. pl. m.; וַ׳ conv.   שׁלך

יַשְׁלֵם וַ׳ Hiph. fut. 3 pers. sing. masc., apoc. and defect. for יַשְׁלִים ; וַ׳ id.   שׁלם

יִשְׁלַם וַ׳ Kal fut. 3 p. s. m. [for יִשְׁלַם § 8. r. 15]; וַ׳ id.   שׁלם

יְשַׁלֵּם Piel fut. 3 pers. sing. masc. (§ 10. rem. 4)   שׁלם
יְשַׁלֶּם־

יְשֻׁלַּם Pual fut. 3 pers. sing. masc. (comp. § 8. rem. 15)   שׁלם
יְשֻׁלָּם־

יְשַׁלְּמוּ וַ׳ Hiph. fut. 3 pers. pl. masc.; וַ׳ conv.   שׁלם

יְשַׁלְּמֻנִי Piel fut. 3 pers. pl. masc., suff. 1 pers. sing.   שׁלם

יְשַׁלֶּמְךָ id. fut. 3 p. s. m., suff. 2 p. s. m. (§ 16. rem. 15)   שׁלם

יְשַׁלְּמֶנָּה id. id., suff. 3 pers. sing. fem. (§ 2. rem. 3)   שׁלם

יִשְׁלֹף וַ׳ Kal fut. 3 pers. sing. masc. ; וַ׳ conv.   שׁלף

יִשְׁלְפָהּ וַ׳ id., suff. 3 pers. sing. fem. ; וַ׳ id.   שׁלף

יְשַׁלְּשׁוּ וַ׳ Piel fut. 3 pers. pl. masc. [for יְשַׁלֵּשׁוּ comp. § 8. rem. 15]; וַ׳ id.   שׁלשׁ

יָשֶׂם only fut. וַיָּשֶׂם.—I. to put, place, Ju. 12. 3. Kheth
—II. to be put, placed, Ge. 50. 26 ; 24. 33. Kheth

יָשֵׁם only fut. תֵּשַׁם, תִּישַׁמְנָה, to be desolate, laid waste. יְשִׁמָא (for יְשִׁמָה desolation) pr. name m. 1 Ch. 4. 3

יְשִׁימָה fem. only pl. יְשִׁימוֹת desolations, Ps. 55. 16. Kheth. Compare בֵּית־הַיְשִׁימוֹת.

a Ge. 9. 27.   g Ge. 9. 21.   m De. 28. 40.   t Eze. 44. 20.   z 1 Sa. 6. 6.   g Ge. 19. 13.   — Ec. 6. 2.   — Is. 34. 3.   y Ps. 35. 12.
b Ec. 10. 8.   h 2 Sa. 11. 13.   n Job 27. 8.   u Je. 34. 10.   a Je. 42. 5.   l Is. 18. 5.   i Is. 2. 20.   o De. 29. 27.   z 1 Sa. 24. 20.
c Je. 49. 31.   i Is. 46. 6.   o Hab. 2. 8.   v Job 21. 11.   b 1 Sa. 15. 18.   k Da. 5. 7.   l Da. 8. 7.   p 1 Ki. 22. 45.   a Ru. 4. 8.
d Ps. 37. 29.   k Ex. 6. 11.   p Nu. 5. 2.   w Ex. 6. 11.   c Ch. 25. 12.   l Ec. 2. 19.   m 2 Ch. 25. 12.   q Job 9. 4.   b Is. 17. 51.
e Ge. 25. 18.   i Is. 49. 26.   q Pr. 17. 11.   x Ps. 125. 3.   d Job 12. 15.   i Est. 9. 1.   n Jos. 10. 27.   r Ps. 68. 2.   c 1 Ki. 18. 34.
f Lu. 4. 18.   ~ Ju. 18. 4.   s Ge. 37. 14.   y Ju. 19. 25.   e 1 Ch. 19. 19.   # 2 Ki. 2. 21.   tt 2 Sa. 10. 19.

יְשִׁימוֹן masc. *waste, desert.*

יְשִׁימוֹן (for יְשִׁימוֹן *desert*) pr. name m. 1 Ch. 4. 20.

יִשְׁמָה (for יִשְׁמָה *desolation*; Gesenius, *garlic*) pr. name whence patronym. יִשְׁמָתִי 1 Ch. 2. 53.

יָשֵׂם } Kal fut. 3 pers. sing. masc., apoc. and

יָשֵׂם } conv. from יָשִׂים, R. שׂים see . } שׂום

[a] defect. for יָשִׂים (q. v.) . . שׂום

יָשֵׂם Kal fut. 3 p. s. m., Chald. form (§ 18. rem. 14) שׂמם

יִשְׁמָא } pr. name masc . . . . ישׁם

יַשְׁמֵד } Hiph. fut. 3 pers. sing. m., ap. from יַשְׁמִיד שׁמד

יִשָּׁמֵד } Niph. fut. 3 pers. sing. masc. . . שׁמד

יְשִׂמֶהָ } Kal fut. 3 pers. sing. masc. (יָשִׂים R. שׂים), suff. 3 pers. sing. fem.; } conv., see . שׂום

יְשִׂמֵהוּ } id., suff. 3 pers. sing. masc.; } id. . . שׂום

יְשִׂמוּ } id. fut. 3 pers. pl. m. defect. for יָשִׂימוּ; } id. . שׂום

יָשֵׂמוּ Kal fut. 3 pers. pl. masc. . . . שׂמם

יִשְׂמַח [c] } Piel fut. 3 pers. sing. masc.; } conv . שׂמח

יִשְׂמַח } Kal fut. 3 pers. sing. masc. (§ 8.

יִשְׂמַח } [d] וַ, } rem. 15); } id. . . . } שׂמח

יִשְׂמְחוּ } Piel fut. 3 pers. pl. masc. . . . שׂמח

יִשְׂמְחוּ } וַ, } Kal fut. 3 pers. pl. masc. (§ 8.

יִשְׂמְחוּ } וַ, } rem. 15); · conv. . . } שׂמח

יְשַׂמְּחֶנָּה Piel fut. 3 pers. sing. masc., suff. 3 pers sing. fem. (§ 2. rem. 3) . . . . שׂמח

יְשַׂמְּטוּהָ } Kal fut. 3 pers. pl. masc., suff. 3 pers. sing. fem.; } conv. . . . . שׁמט

יַשְׁמִיד } Hiph. fut. 3 pers. sing. masc. . . שׁמד

יַשְׁמִידוּ [f] } id. fut. 3 pers. pl. masc. . . . שׁמד

יַשְׁמִידֵם } } id. id., suff. 3 pers. pl. masc.; } conv. . שׁמד

יַשְׁמִידֵם [k] } וַ, } id. id. fut. 3 pers. sing. masc., suff. 3 pers. pl. masc.; } id. . . . . שׁמד

יַשְׁמִינוּ } Hiph. fut. 3 pers. pl. masc.; } id. . שׁמן

יַשְׁמִיעַ } Hiph. fut. 3 pers. sing. masc. . . שׁמע

יַשְׁמִיעוּ [m] } וַ, וַ, } id. id. fut. 3 pers. pl. masc.; } conv. . שׁמע

יַשְׁמִיעֵנוּ } id. id. with suff. 1 pers. pl. . . שׁמע

יְשִׂמְךָ } Kal fut. 3 pers. sing. masc. (יָשִׂים R. שׂים), suff. 2 pers. sing. masc. (for יְשִׂימְךָ), see שׂום

יְשִׂמֵם [g] } id. with suff. 3 pers. pl. masc.; } conv. . שׂום

יַשְׂמֵם } Hiph. fut. 3 pers. sing. masc. [יָשֵׂם], suff. 3 pers. pl. masc.; } id. . . . שׂמם

יַשְׁמֵן } Kal fut. 3 pers. sing. masc.; } id. . שׁמן

יְשִׁימוֹן } noun masc. sing. defect. for יְשִׁימוֹן . ישׁם

יְשִׂמֵנִי [n] } Kal fut. 3 pers. sing. masc. (יָשִׂים R. שׂים), suff. 1 pers. sing. (for יְשִׂימֵנִי), see . שׂום

יְשַׂמַּע } Piel fut. 3 pers. sing. masc. } conv. . שׁמע

יִשָּׁמַע } Niph. fut. 3 pers. sing. masc. (§ 15.

יִשָּׁמַע } rem. 1); } id. . . . . } שׁמע

יִשְׁמַע } Kal fut. 3 pers. sing. masc. (§ 8.

יִשְׁמַע } וַ, } rem. 15); } conv. . . } שׁמע

יִשְׁמַע Ch. Peal fut. 3 pers. sing. m. (§ 49. No. 4) שׁמע

יִשְׁמָעֵאל } pr. name masc. . . . . שׁמע

יִשְׁמְעֵאלִים } gent. noun pl. from the preceding . שׁמע

יִשָּׁמְעוּ [a] } Niph. fut. 3 pers. pl. masc.; } conv. . שׁמע

יִשְׁמְעוּ [b] } Kal fut. 3 pers. pl. masc. (§ 8.

יִשְׁמְעוּ } וַ, } rem. 15); } id. . . . } שׁמע

יִשְׁמְעוּן } id. id. with parag. } . . . . שׁמע

יִשְׁמַעְיָה } } pr. name masc. . . . . שׁמע

יִשְׁמַעְיָהוּ } }

יִשְׁמָעֲךָ } Kal fut. 3 pers. sing. masc. (יִשְׁמַע), suff. 2 pers. sing. m. (§ 16. r. 12, & § 2. r. 2) שׁמע

יַשְׁמִעֵנוּ } Hiph. fut. 3 pers. sing. masc. (יַשְׁמִיעַ), suff. 3 pers. pl. . . . . שׁמע

יִשְׁמָעֵנִי } Kal fut. 3 pers. sing. masc. (יִשְׁמַע), suff. 1 pers. sing. (§ 16. rem. 12) . . . שׁמע

יִשְׁמֹר } וַ, } Kal fut. 3 pers. sing. masc. (§ 8. rem.

יִשְׁמָר } וַ, } 18); } conv. . . . } שׁמר

יִשְׁמְרֵהוּ [d] } id. id., suff. 3 pers. sing. masc. . . שׁמר

יִשְׁמְרוּ } } id. fut. 3 pers. pl. masc. (§ 8.

יִשְׁמְרוּ } וַ, } rem. 15); } conv. . . } שׁמר

יִשְׁמְרִי } pr. name masc. . . . . שׁמר

יִשְׁמָרְךָ [h] } Kal fut. 3 pers. sing. masc., suff. 2

יִשְׁמָרְךָ } וַ, } pers. sing. masc. . . . } שׁמר

יִשְׁמְרֵנוּ [k] } id. id., suff. 1 pers. pl.; } conv. . שׁמר

יִשְׁמְרֶנּוּ } id. id., suff. 3 pers. sing. masc. (§ 2. r. 3) שׁמר

יִשְׁמְרֵנִי [m] } id. id., suff. 1 pers. sing. . . שׁמר

יְשַׁמְּשׁוּנֵּהּ Chald. Pael fut. 3 pers. pl. masc., suff. 3 pers. sing. masc. . . . . שׁמשׁ

[יָשֵׁן, יָשַׁן] fut. יִישַׁן.—I. *to fall asleep, to sleep.* Niph.—I. *to be dry*, Le. 26. 10.—II. *to grow old*, Le. 13. 11, De. 4. 25. Pi. *to make to sleep*, Ju. 16. 19.

יָשֵׁן masc. dec. 4 a, יְשֵׁנָה fem. adj. *old.*

יָשֵׁן masc. dec. 5 a (pl. c. יְשֵׁנֵי § 4. rem. 2), יְשֵׁנָה fem. adj.—I. *sleeping, asleep.*—II. pr. name masc. 2 Sa. 23. 32.

יָשֵׁן (*old*) pr. name of a city in the tribe of Judah, 2 Ch. 13. 19.

שֵׁנָה fem. dec. 11 b (once שֵׁנָא).—I. *sleep.*—II *dream*, Ps. 90. 5.

שְׁנָא Chald. fem. dec. 9 a, *sleep*, Da. 6. 19.

שְׁנָת fem. *sleep*, Ps. 132. 4.

יָשֵׁן [o] } adj. masc. sing. dec. 4 a . . . ישׁן

יָשֵׁן adj. masc. sing. dec. 5 a, also pr. name m. ישׁן

יִשָּׁנֵא [p] Niph. fut. 3 pers. sing. masc. . . שׁנא

יִשְׂנָא Kal fut. 3 pers. sing. masc. . . . שנא

יִשְׁנֵא Ch. Peal fut. 3 pers. sing. masc., see under שנא

יִשְׁנֶא Kal fut. 2 pers. s. m. [for יִשְׁנֶה § 24. r. 19 b] שנה

יִשָּׁנֵא Pual fut. 3 pers. s. m. [for יִשָּׁנֶה § 24. r. 19 b] שנה

יִשְׂנָאֶהָ ‍] Kal fut. 3 pers. sing. masc., suff. 3 pers. sing. fem.; ‍] conv. . . שנא

יִשְׂנָאוּ וַיִּ‍] id. fut. 3 pers. pl. masc.; ‍] id. . שנא

יִשְׂנָאֶךָ id. fut. 3 pers. sing. masc., suff. 2 pers. sing. masc. (§ 2. rem. 3) . . . שנא

יִשְׁנֶה pr. name of a place . . . ישן

יִשְׁנֶהָ ‍] the foll. with suff. 3 pers. s. fem.; ‍] conv. שנה

יְשַׁנֶּה ‍] Piel fut. 3 pers. sing. masc., with conj. ‍] [for וַיִּ‍], וַיְשַׁנֶּה] . . . שנה

יְשֵׁנָה adj. fem. sing. from יָשֵׁן masc. . ישן

יְשַׁנּוּ ‍] Piel fut. 3 pers. sing. masc. (יְשַׁנֶּה), suff. 3 pers. sing. masc. (§ 24. r. 21); ‍] conv. שנה

יֶשְׁנוֹ adv. יֵשׁ with epenth. נ and suff. 3 pers. sing. masc. (§ 36. rem. 3) . . . ישה

יִשְׁנוּ ‍] Kal pret. 3 pers. pl. . . ישן

יִישְׁנוּ id. fut. 3 pers. pl. m. [for יִישְׁנוּ § 20. r. 2] ישן

יִשְׁנוּ וַיִּ‍] Kal fut. 3 pers. pl. masc.; ‍] conv. שנה

יִשְׁנוּן Chald. Peal fut. 3 pers. pl. masc., see under שנה

יְשֵׁנִים adj. masc., pl. of יָשֵׁן dec. 4 a ישן

יְשֵׁנִים adj. masc., pl. of יָשֵׁן dec. 5 a ישן

יְשַׁנֵּם ‍] Piel fut. 3 pers. sing. masc.; ‍] conv. שנם

יְשַׁנְתִּי Kal pret. 3 pers. sing. ישן

יְשַׂשֶּׂה Kal fut. 3 pers. sing. masc. שסה

יָשֹׁסּוּ ‍] Kal fut. 3 pers. pl. m.; ‍] conv. שסס

יִשַּׁסּוּ Niph. fut. 3 pers. pl. masc. . שסס

יְשַׁסַּע ‍] Piel fut. 3 pers. sing. masc.; ‍] conv. שסע

יְשַׁסְּעֵהוּ ‍] id., suff. 3 pers. sing. masc.; ‍] id. שסע

יְשַׁסֵּף ‍] Piel fut. 3 pers. sing. masc.; ‍] id. שסף

יָשַׁע Hiph. הוֹשִׁיעַ fut. יוֹשִׁיעַ, apoc. יֹשַׁע, יֹשַׁע.—I. *to deliver, save, set free,* with מִן, מִיָּד *from any thing.*—II. *to help, succour,* with acc., לְ. Niph. נוֹשַׁע.—I. *to be delivered, saved.*—II. *to be helped, succoured.* Part. נוֹשָׁע *aided, supported.*

יֶשַׁע, יֵשַׁע masc. dec. 6 e (see § 35. rem. 6), *deliverance, freedom, safety, salvation.*

יְשׁוּעָה f. d. 10, *deliverance, help, safety, salvation.*

יִשְׁעִי (*salutary*) pr. name masc.—I. 1 Ch. 2. 31. —II. 1 Ch. 5. 24.—III. 1 Ch. 4. 20, 42.

יְשַׁעְיָהוּ (*salvation of the Lord*) pr. name masc. —I. *Isaiah,* the prophet under the reign of Uzziah, Jotham, Ahaz and Hezekiah.—II. 1 Ch. 25. 3, 15. —III. 1 Ch. 26. 25.

יְשַׁעְיָה (id.) pr. name masc.—I. 1 Ch. 3. 21.— II. Ezr. 8. 7.—III. Ezr. 8. 19.—IV. Ne. 11. 7.

הוֹשֵׁעַ (*deliverance*) pr. name—I. of the minister of Moses before he was called יְהוֹשֻׁעַ, *Joshua,* Nu. 13. 8, 16.—II. of a king of Israel.—III. of a prophet, Ho. 1. 1, 2.

הוֹשַׁעְיָה (whom *the Lord delivers*) pr. name masc. of several persons.

מוֹשָׁעוֹת fem. pl. (of מוֹשָׁעָה) *deliverances* Ps 68. 21.

מֵישַׁע (*deliverance*) pr. name of a king of Moab, 2 Ki. 3. 4.

מֵישָׁע (id.) pr. name masc. 1 Ch. 2. 42.

יֶשַׁע noun masc. sing. dec. 6 e . . . ישע

יֵשַׁע noun masc. sing. dec. 6 e (§ 35. r. 5) . ישע

יְשַׁע ‍] Kal fut. 3 pers. s. m. ap. fr. יְשָׁעָה; ‍] conv. שעה

יֵשַׁע וַיִּ‍], וַיִּ‍] Hiph. fut. 3 pers. sing. masc., apoc. and conv. from יוֹשִׁיעַ (§ 20. rem. 11) ישע

יִשְׁעֶה Kal fut. 3 pers. sing. masc. . . שעה

יִשְׁעוֹ noun masc. sing., suff. 3 pers. sing. masc. from יֶשַׁע dec. 6 e . . . ישע

יִשְׁעוּ Kal fut. 3 pers. pl. masc. . . שעה

יְשׁוּעוֹת noun fem., pl. of יְשׁוּעָה dec. 10 ישע

יִשְׁעִי ‍] pr. name masc. . . . ישע

יִשְׁעִי noun m. s., suff. 1 pers. s. from יֶשַׁע d. 6 e ישע

יְשַׁעְיָה וַיִּשַׁע‍], וַיִּשַׁע‍] pr. name masc. ישע
יְשַׁעְיָהוּ

יִשְׁעֲךָ ‍] noun masc. sing., suff. 2 pers. sing. masc. from יֶשַׁע dec. 6 (§ 35. rem. 6) ישע

יִשְׁעֵךְ id., suff. 2 pers. sing. fem. . . ישע

יִשְׁעֶךָ id., suff. 2 pers. sing. masc. [for יִשְׁעֲךָ] ישע

יֹשִׁיעֲכֶם ‍] Hiph. fut. 3 pers. sing. masc. (יֹשִׁיעַ § 20. rem. 11), suff. 2 pers. pl. m. [for יֹשִׁיעֲכֶם § 16. rem. 16 note] . . ישע

יִוָּשַׁע וְ‍] Niph. fut. 3 pers. sing. masc. שע

יִוָּשְׁעוּ Niph. fut. 3 pers. pl. masc. [for יִוָּשַׁעוּ comp. § 8. rem. 15] . . . . שע

יִשְׁעֵנוּ noun masc. s., suff. 1 pers. pl. fr. יֵשַׁע d. 6 e ישע

יוֹשִׁיעֵנוּ Hiph. fut. 3 pers. sing. masc. with suff. 1 pers. pl. [for יוֹשִׁיעֵנוּ] . . . ישע

יִשְׂעָרֵהוּ ‍] Piel fut. 3 pers. sing. masc. [for יְשָׂעֵר § 14. rem. 1], suff. 3 pers. sing. masc. with cop. ‍] [for וַיִּ‍], וַיְשָׂעֲרֵהוּ] . שער

יִשְׂעֲרוּ Kal fut. 3 pers. pl. masc. . . שער

יִשְׂעָרֶנּוּ id. fut. 3 pers. sing. masc. (יְשָׂעֵר), suff. 3 pers. sing. masc. (§ 16. rem. 12) שער

יְשַׁעְשְׁעוּ Pilpel fut. 3 pers. pl. masc. (§ 6. No. 4) שעע

a Da. 7. 24.   e Pr. 9. 8.   i Pr. 4. 16.   m Ca. 7. 14.   r Is. 13. 16.   v Ps. 20. 7.   b Ps. 53. 7.   f Job 8. 15.   j Eze. 32. 10.
b La. 4. 1.   d Est. 2. 9.   k Job 29. 22.   n 1 Ki. 18. 46.   s 1 Sa. 24. 8.   w Ge. 4. 4.   c Ps. 27. 1.   g 1 Sa. 10. 27.   k Ps. 58. 10.
c Ec. 8. 1.   g Pr. 31. 5.   l 1 Ki. 18. 34.   p Job 3. 13.   t Ju. 14. 6.   x Pr. 20. 22.   d Ps. 85. 8.   h Is. 17. 7, 8.   l Ps. 94. 19.
d Ge. 37. 4.   h 1 Sa. 21. 14.   Da. 4. 12.   q Ho. 13. 15.   u 1 Sa. 15. 33.   z Is. 17. 7, 8.   i Is. 35. 4.

יִשְׁעָתוֹ‎ noun f. s., suff. 3 pers. s. m. fr. יֵשׁוּעָה d. 10   ישע

יִשְׁעָתִי‎ id. with suff. 1 pers. sing. . . .   ישע

יִשְׁעֲתֶךָ‎ id., suff. 2 pers. sing. masc. . .   ישע

יָשְׁפֵה‎ } masc. jasper, a variegated gem, Ex. 28. 20 ;
39. 13 ; Eze. 28. 13.

יָשְׁפֵה‎ } pr. name masc. . . . .   שפה

יִשְׁפּוֹט‎ Kal fut. 3 pers. sing. masc. (§ 8. rem. 18)   שפט

יִשְׁפּוֹטוּ‎ id. fut. 3 pers. pl. masc. (§ 8. rem. 14) .   שפט

יִשְׁפֹּט‎ } וַיִ‎, id. fut. 3 pers. sing. masc. (§ 8.
יִשְׁפָּט־‎ } rem. 18) ; וַ‎ conv. . }   שפט

יִשָּׁפְטוּ‎ Niph. fut. 3 pers. pl. masc. . .   שפט

יִשְׁפְּטוּ‎ }
יִשְׁפֹּטוּ‎ } Kal fut. 3 pers. pl. masc. (§ 8. rem. 15)   שפט

יִשְׁפְּטֵנִי‎ } id. fut. 3 pers. sing. masc., suff. 1 pers. s.   שפט

יַשְׁפִּיל‎ Hiph. fut. 3 pers. sing. masc. . .   שפל

יַשְׁפִּילֶהָ‎ }
יַשְׁפִּילֶנָּה‎ } id., suff. 3 pers. sing. fem. (§ 2. rem. 3)   שפל

יַשְׁפִּיקוּ‎ Hiph. fut. 3 pers. pl. masc. . .   שפק

יִשָּׁפֵךְ‎ וַיִ‎, Niph. fut. 3 pers. sing. masc.; וַ‎ conv.   שפך

יִשְׁפֹּךְ‎ וַיִ‎, רֵ‎, Kal fut. 3 pers. sing. masc.; וַ‎ id.   שפך

יִשְׁפְּכוּ‎ וַ‎ id. fut. 3 pers. pl. masc. ; וַ‎ id. .   שפך

יִשְׁפְּכֵם‎ וַ‎ id. fut. 3 pers. sing. masc., suff. 3 pers. pl.
masc. ; וַ‎ id. . . . .   שפך

יִשְׁפַּל‎ וַ‎ Kal fut. 3 pers. sing. masc. ; וַ‎ id. .   שפל

יִשְׁפְּלוּ‎ id. fut. 3 pers. pl. m. [for יִשְׁפְּלוּ‎ § 8. r. 15]   שפל

יִשְׁפָּן‎ } pr. name masc. . . .   שפה

יִשְׁפֹּק‎ Kal fut. 3 pers. sing. masc. . .   שפק

יִשְׁפַּר‎ Chald. Peal fut. 3 pers. sing. m. (§ 47. r. 6 b)   שפר

יַשְׁקְ‎ } Hiph. fut. 3 pers. sing. masc., apoc. and
conv. from יַשְׁקֶה‎ (§ 24. rem. 16) .   שקה

יִשֹּׁק‎ }
יַשֵּׁק‎ } Kal fut. 3 pers. sing. masc. (comp. § 8.
וַיִ‎ } rem. 15) ; וַ‎ conv. . . . }   נשק

יִשְׁקֹד‎ וַ‎ Kal fut. 3 pers. sing. masc.; וַ‎ id. .   שקד

יַשְׁקֶה‎ Hiph. fut. 3 pers. sing. masc. . .   שקה

יֻשְׁקֶה‎ Pual fut. 3 pers. sing. masc. . .   שקה

יַשְׁקֻהָנ‎ וַ‎ Hiph. fut. 3 pers. pl. masc., suff. 3 pers.
sing. masc. ; וַ‎ conv. . . .   שקה

יַשְׁקֵהוּ‎ וַ‎ Kal fut. 3 pers. sing. masc. (יַשְׁקְ‎), suff.
3 pers. sing. masc. (§ 16. rem. 12) ; וַ‎ id.   נשק

יַשְׁקוּ‎ Kal fut. 3 pers. pl. masc. . .   שקק

יַשְׁקוּ‎ Hiph. fut. 3 pers. pl. masc. . .   שקה

יִשָּׁקוּ‎ Kal fut. 3 pers. pl. masc. [for יִשְׁקוּ‎ comp.
§ 10. rem. 7] ; וַ‎ conv. . .   נשק

יִשְׁקוֹד‎ Kal fut. 3 pers. sing. masc. (§ 8. rem. 18)   שקד

יַשְׁקֵם‎ וַ‎ Hiph. fut. 3 pers. pl. masc., suff. 3 pers.
pl. masc. ; וַ‎ conv. . . .   שקה

יִשְׁקוֹן‎ Kal fut. 3 pers. pl. masc. with parag. ן [for
§ 8. rem. 17] . . . .   נשק

יַשְׁקֵנִי‎ Hiph. fut. 3 pers. pl. masc., suff. 1 pers sing.   שקה

יִשְׁקֹט‎ defect. for יִשְׁקוֹט‎ (q. v.) . .   שקט

יִשְׁקֹט‎ Kal fut. 3 pers. sing. masc. . .   שקט

יַשְׁקִיט‎ Hiph. fut. 3 pers. sing. masc. . .   שקט

יַשְׁקִיף‎ Hiph. fut. 3 pers. sing. masc. . .   שקף

יַשְׁקִיפוּ‎ וַ‎ id. fut. 3 pers. pl. masc. ; וַ‎ conv. .   שקף

יִשָּׁקֵל‎ Niph. fut. 3 pers. sing. masc. . .   שקל

יִשְׁקֹל‎ וַיִ‎ Kal fut. 3 pers. sing. masc. ; וַ‎ conv. .   שקל

יִשְׁקְלוּ‎ }
יִשְׁקֹלוּ‎ } Kal fut. 3 pers. pl. masc. (§ 8. rem.
וַ‎ } 15) ; וַ‎ id. . }   שקל

יִשְׁקְלֵנִי‎ id. fut. 3 pers. sing. masc., suff. 1 pers. sing.   שקל

יַשְׁקֵנוּ‎ } Hiph. fut. 3 pers. sing. masc. (יַשְׁקֶה‎), suff.
1 pers. pl. (§ 24. rem. 21) ; וַ‎ conv. .   שקה

יַשְׁקֵנִי‎ id., suff. 1 pers. sing. . . .   שקה

יִשָּׁקֵנִי‎ Kal fut. 3 pers. sing. masc. (יִשַּׁק‎), suff. 1 pers.
sing. (§ 16. rem. 12) . . .   נשק

יַשְׁקֵף‎ } Hiph. fut. 3 pers. sing. masc., apoc. from
וַ‎ } יַשְׁקִיף‎ ; וַ‎ conv. . . .   שקף

יַשְׁקִפוּ‎ } id. fut. 3 pers. pl. masc. ; וַ‎ id. .   שקף

יְשַׁקֵּר‎ Piel fut. 3 pers. sing. masc. . .   שקר

יְשַׁקְּרוּ‎ id. fut. 3 p. pl. m. [for יְשַׁקְּרוּ‎ comp. § 8. r. 15]   שקר

יָשַׁר‎ fut. יָשֹׁר‎, יִישַׁר‎ (§ 20. rem. 16) to be straight, even,
right ; metaph. יָשַׁר בְּעֵינַי‎ it is right in my eyes,
i. e. is pleasing to me. Pi.—I. to make straight,
even, the way ; metaph. to make one's way even,
i. e. to make successful, prosperous.—II. to direct,
lead, an aqueduct.—III. to esteem right, approve,
Ps. 119. 128. Pu. part. smoothed, spread, 1 Ki.
6. 35. Hiph. הַיְשִׁיר‎ or הֹושִׁיר‎ (Kheth.) to make
even, the way ; of the eyes, to look straight forwards, Pr. 4. 25.

יָשָׁר‎ masc. dec. 4, יְשָׁרָה‎ fem. adj. straight, even,
opp. to עָקֵשׁ‎ ; metaph. right, upright, righteous,
true, especially with דֶּרֶךְ‎, יִשְׁרֵי לֵב‎, לִפְנֵי‎, בְּעֵינֵי‎,
upright in heart, walk ; neut. יָשָׁר‎ what is right ;
סֵפֶר הַיָּשָׁר‎ Eng. Ver. "book of Jasher." LXX.
according to the Complutension edition, τοῦ βιβλίου
τοῦ εὐθοῦς, the right or correct book, i. e. probably
the authentic record ; and as Josephus (Ant. lib. v.
cap. 1. § 17) explains it by, the writings laid up in
the temple.

יֶשֶׁר‎ (uprightness, concr. upright) pr. name masc.
1 Ch. 2. 18.

ᵃ De. 32. 15.   ᶠ 1 Ki. 7. 7.   ⁱ Is. 26. 5.   ᵖ Pr. 24. 26.   ˢ 1 Sa. 30. 11.   ᵛ Ho. 13. 2.   ᵃ La. 3. 50.   ᵐ Is. 46. 6.   ᵗ Ca. 1. 2.
ᵇ Job 30. 15.   ᵍ Ps. 9. 20.   ᵏ Is. 2. 6.   ᵠ Ge. 41. 40.   ⁴ Joel 2. 9.   ᵈ Ps. 69. 22.   ᵇ 2 Ki. 9. 32.   ⁿ Zec. 11. 12.   ʳ Ge. 18. 16.
ᶜ Ps. 35. 3.   ʰ 1 Sa. 24. 16.   ˡ 1 Ki. 13. 5.   ᵗ Da. 9. 14.   ᵍ 1 Sa. 20. 41.   ᵉ Job 34. 28.   ⁱ Ex. 22. 16.   ᵒ Job 31. 6.   ᵘ 1 Sa. 15. 29
ᵈ Ex. 12. 26.   Ps. 75. 8.   ᵐ Da. 11. 15.   ᵘ Nu. 5. 26.   ʰ Job 21. 32.   ᶠ Ru. 3. 18.   ᵏ Je. 8. 14.   ᵖ Je. 35. 3.   ᵛ Is. 63. 8.
ᵉ Ex. 5. 21.   ᶦ Is. 95. 5.   ⁿ Da. 4. 24.   ᵒ Job 21. 24.   ² 2 Ch. 28. 15.   ᵍ Pr. 15. 18.

יֹ֫שֶׁר masc. dec. 7c, *uprightness, rectitude, integrity*; Pr. 11. 24 מִישָׁר *more than is right, meet.*

יִשְׂרְאֵלָה (*upright towards* or *with God*) pr. name masc. i Cn. 25. 14.

יִשְׁרָה or יָשְׁרָה f. *uprightness, integrity*, 1 Ki. 3. 6.

יְשֻׁרוּן masc. a periphrastic name of Israel, *the right, righteous; or the little righteous people;* if וֹן be really a termination of diminutives.

שָׁרוֹן (for יִשְׁרוֹן *plain, level*) pr. name invariably הַשָּׁרוֹן, *Sharon*, the plain between Joppa and Cesarea.

מִישׁוֹר masc.—I. *a plain, a level country.*—II. *righteousness, equity*, Ps. 45. 7; adv. *righteously, justly*, Ps. 67. 5.

מֵישָׁר masc. only pl. מֵישָׁרִים—I. *straightness*, of a way, Is. 26. 7; with pref. בְּ, לְ, *straight, right.*—II. *righteousness, justice, truth*, adv. *righteously*; Ca. 1. 4, *truly, sincerely*, which others take as a concr. *righteous men.*—III. *agreement, concord*, Da. 11. 6.

יָשֹׁר וֹ] adj. and subst. masc. sing. dec. 4a . . שׁר

יָשֹׁר וֹ] Kal fut. 3 pers. sing. masc. apoc. & conv. (§ 21. rem. 9) . . . . שׁור

יָשֹׁר[a] Kal fut. 3 pers. sing. masc. R. שָׁרַר, or id. apoc. from יָשׁוּר R. . . . שׁור

יָשֹׁר[a] וַ] Kal fut. 3 pers. sing. masc. for יִישָׁר (§ 20. rem. 2); וַ conv. . . . . יָשַׁר

יְשַׁר[a] adj. masc. sing., constr. of יָשָׁר dec. 4a . יָשַׁר

יֶשֶׁר pr. name masc. . . . . . . יָשַׁר

יָשָׁר[d]וֹ] noun masc. sing. dec. 6c; for וֹ see lett. ו יָשַׁר

יִשְׂרָאֵל[e]וֹ] pr. name of a man and a people . שׂרה

יִשְׂרְאֵלָה pr. name masc. יָשַׁר

יִשְׂרְאֵלִ֫ית gent. noun, fem. of יִשְׂרְאֵלִי from יִשְׂרָאֵל . שׂרה

יִשְׂרְגוּ[f]וֹ Pual fut. 3 pers. pl. masc. [for יְשֹׂרְגוּ comp. § 8. rem. 15] . . . . שׂרנ

יָשְׁרָה Kal pret. 3 pers. sing. fem. . . . יָשַׁר

יְשָׁרָה adj. fem. sing. dec. 11c, from יָשָׁר masc. יָשַׁר

יִשְּׁרֻ֫הוּ[g] Piel pret. 3 pers. sing. masc., suff. 3 pers. sing. masc. [for יִשְּׁרֻהוּ § 10. rem. 7] . יָשַׁר

יָשְׁרוּ[g] Kal fut. 3 pers. pl. masc. . . . . שׂרר

יָשְׁרוּ[h] Kal pret. 3 pers. pl. . . . . שׂרר

יַשְּׂרוּ Piel imp. pl. masc. . . . . שׂרר

יָשְׁרוֹ[i] noun masc. sing., suff. 3 pers. sing. masc. from יָשָׁר dec. 6c . . . . יָשַׁר

יְשֻׁרוּן
יְשֹׁרוּן } noun masc. s., with cop. וַ [for [וַ], וַיְשֻׁרוּן יָשַׁר

יְשָׁרוֹת- adj. fem., pl. of יְשָׁרָה dec. 11c, from יָשָׁר m. יָשַׁר

יִשָּׁרְטוּ[j] Niph. fut. 3 pers. pl. masc. [for יִשָּׂרְטוּ comp. § 8. rem. 15] . . . . שׂרט

יִשְׂרְטוּ[j] Kal fut. 3 pers. pl. masc. . . . שׂרט

יֻשְׁרִי constr. of the following: . . . . יָשַׁר

יְשָׁרִים } adj. masc. pl. absolute [with cop. וַ, for
יְשָׁרִים } [וַ] from יָשָׁר dec. 4a } יָשַׁר
יִשְׁרָ֫נָה וַ] [for תִּשְׁרָנָה § 8. rem. 16] Kal fut. 3 pers. pl. fem. (§ 20. rem. 16); וַ conv. . שׂרר

יִשָּׂרֵף Niph. fut. 3 pers. sing. masc. . . . שׂרף

יִשְׂרֹף[k] וַ] Kal fut. 3 pers. sing. masc.; וַ conv. . שׂרף

יִשְׂרְפֶ֫הָ[l] וַ] id. with suff. 3 pers. sing. fem.; וַ id. שׂרף

יִשָּׂרְפוּ[m]וַ] Niph. fut. 3 pers. pl. masc.; וַ id. . שׂרף

יִשְׂרְפוּ } Kal fut. 3 pers. pl. masc. (§ 8. rem.
יִשְׂרְפוּ[n] וַ] } 15); וַ id. } שׂרף

יִשְׂרְפֻ֫הָ[o] וַ] id. id., suff. 3 pers. sing. fem.; וַ id. שׂרף

יִשְׂרְפֵם וַ] id. fut. 3 pers. sing. masc., suff. 3 pers. pl. masc.; וַ id. . . . . . שׂרף

יִשְׁרֹץ[p] Kal fut. 3 pers. sing. masc. . . . שׂרצ

יִשְׁרְצוּ[q] וַ] id. fut. 3 pers. pl. masc.; וַ conv. . שׂרצ

יִשְׁרֹק[r] וַ] Kal fut. 3 pers. sing. masc. . . . שׂרק

יַשְׁרִשׁ Hiph. fut. 3 pers. sing. masc., ap. from יַשְׁרִישׁ שׁרשׁ

יְשֹׁרְשׁוּ[s] Pual fut. 3 pers. pl. masc. [for יְשֹׁרְשׁוּ comp. § 8. rem. 15] . . . . שׁרשׁ

יְשָׁרֵת וַ] Piel fut. 3 pers. sing. masc.; acc. drawn back by conv. וַ . . . . . שׁרת

יְשָׁרְתֶ֫הוּ[t] וַ] id. id., suff. 3 pers. sing. masc.; וַ conv. שׁרת

יְשָׁרְתֻ֫הוּ[u] id. fut. 3 pers. pl. masc., suff. 3 pers. s. m. שׁרת

יְשָׁרְתוּ id. fut. 3 pers. pl. masc. . . . שׁרת

יְשָׁרְתֻ֫נְךָ[v] } id. id., suff. 2 pers. sing. masc. and conj. וַ
[for [וַ], וַיְשָׁרְתוּךָ } שׁרת

יְשָׁרְתֻ֫נְכָה[w] id. id. with parag. נ (§ 16. rem. 14) and suff. 2 pers. sing. fem. (§ 2. rem. 2) . . שׁרת

יֵשַׁרְתִּי Piel pret. 1 p. s. [for יֵשָׁרַתִּי comp. § 8. r. 7] יָשַׁר

יְשָׁרְתֵ֫נִי Piel fut. 3 pers. s. m. (יְשָׁרֵת), suff. 1 p. s. שׁרת

יָשֵׁשׁ וֹ] masc. *old, aged man*, 2 Ch. 36. 17.

יָשִׁישׁ masc. dec. 3a, id.

יְשִׁישַׁי (*of aged*, sc. *parents*) pr. name masc. 1 Ch. 5. 14.

יְשִׁישׂוּם[x] Kal fut. 3 p. pl. m. [וְישִׁישׂוּ], suff. 3 p. pl. m. שׂושׂ

יִשָּׂשכָר וֹ] pr. name masc. . . . . . שׂכר

יָשֵׁת וֹ] } Kal fut. 3 pers. sing. masc., apoc. and
יָשֶׁת[y]וַ] } conv. from שִׁית יָשִׁית R. see . } שׁות

יֵשְׁתְּ[z]וַ] וַ] Kal fut. 3 pers. sing. masc. apoc. from יִשְׁתֶּה, (§ 24. rem. 3); וַ conv. . . . שׁתה

יִשָּׁתֶה- Niph. fut. 3 pers. sing. masc. . . . שׁתה

יֵ֫שְׁתְּ[aa]וַ] Kal fut. 3 pers. sing. masc.; וַ conv. שׁתה

---

a Job 33. 27.   b Job 40. 17.   c Is. 40. 3.   d Zec. 12. 3.   e Eze. 23. 47.   f Ge. 1. 20.   g 1 Ki. 19. 21.   h Ps. 119. 128.   i Ps. 18. 12.
j 1 Sa. 18. 20, 26.   k Job 37. 3.   l Job 33. 23.   m Le. 21. 5.   n 2 Ki. 10. 26.   o Ex. 1. 7.   p Nu. 1. 50.   q Ps. 101. 6.   r 1 Ki. 13. 18.
s Pr. 29. 27.   t Is. 32. 1.   u 1 Sa. 44. 2.   v 1 Sa. 6. 12.   w 2 Ki. 23. 4.   x Is. 27. 6.   y Is. 60. 7, 10.   z Job 9. 33.   aa 1 Ki. 19. 2.
bb Ps. 25. 21.   cc 1 Ki. 9. 12.   dd Eze. 1. 22.   ee 1 Ki. 9. 16.   ff Eze. 47. 9.   gg Job 31. 8.   hh Is. 35. 1.   ii Le. 11. 34.
jj 1 Ch. 14. 12.

יָתֵד I com. dec. 5ᵃ.—I. *pin, peg, nail*; especially *a tent-pin* or *stake*.—II. *a vointed stake* or *paddle*, De. 23. 14.

יְתֵת (for יָתֵדַת *pin, nail*) pr. n. m. Ge. 36. 40.

יתד   יְתֵדᵇ id., constr. state . . .

יתד   יִתְדֹת id. pl., constr. state . . .

יתד   וִיתֵדֹתֶיהָ id. pl. with suff. 3 pers. sing. fem. with cop. וְ [for וַיְ,וִיתֵדֹתֶיהָ]

יתד   יְתֵדֹתָיו id. pl., suff. 3 pers. sing. masc. . .

יתד   וִיתֵדֹתֶיךָ id. pl. with suff. 2 pers. sing. fem. with cop. וְ [for וַיְ,וִיתֵדֹתַיִךְ]

יתד   יְתֵדֹתָם id. pl., suff. 3 pers. pl. masc. with cop. וְ comp. preceding

הלל   יִתְהוֹלֲלוּ Hithpo. fut. 3 pers. pl. masc. . .

ית   יָתְהוֹן Chald. sign of the accusative (יָת) with suff. 3 pers. pl. masc. . . . .

הלך   יִתְהַלֵּךְ / וַיְ / יִתְהַלֶּךְ Hithpa. fut. 3 pers. sing. masc. (§ 12. rem. 1 & 4) ; וְ conv. . .

הלך   יִתְהַלְּכוּ / וַיְ ,וְיִ id. fut. 3 pers. pl. masc. (§ 12. rem. 1) ;

הלך   יִתְהַלָּכוּן id. with parag. ן [for הַלְּכוּן § 8. rem. 17, & § 12. rem. 4]

הלל   יִתְהַלָּל / יִתְהַלֵּל Hithpa. fut. 3 pers. sing. masc. (§ 12. rem. 1) . .

הלל   וַיִּתְהַלֵּל Hithpo. fut. 3 pers. sing. masc. ; וְ conv.

הלל   יִתְהַלְּלוּ / וְ יִ Hithpa. fut. 3 pers. pl. masc. (§ 12. rem. 1)

הלל   יִתְהוֹלָלוּ / וְ יִ Hithpo. fut. 3 pers. pl. masc. (comp. § 21. rem. 20) .

תוה   וַיְתָו Piel fut. 3 pers. sing. masc. ap. [from יְתַוֶּה § 24. rem. 12] ; וְ conv. . .

תוב   יְתוּב Chald. Peal fut. 3 pers. sing. masc.

ידה   וַיְתוֹדוּ Hithpa. fut. 3 p. pl. m. (§ 20.No.1); וְ conv.

יכח   יִתְוַכַּח Hithpa. fut. 3 pers. sing. masc. (§ 12. rem. 1)

יתם   יָתוֹם noun masc. sing. dec. 3a . . .

יתם   יְתוֹמִים / יְתוֹמִים / וַיְ ,וִיתוֹמִים id. pl. abs., with cop. וְ [for

תור   יְתוּרֵי noun masc. sing.

זון   יִתְּזִין Chald. Ithpe. or Ittaphal fut. 3 pers. sing. masc. (§ 47. rem. 10) . . .

יָתַח Root not used ; Arab. *to beat with a club*. תּוֹתָח masc. *club*, Job 41. 21.

חבא   וַיְּ id. Hithpa. fut. 3 pers. sing. masc. conv.

חבא   יִתְחַבָּא / יִתְחַבְּאוּ / יִתְחַבָּאוּ id. fut. 3 pers. pl. masc. (§ 12. rem. 1) ; וְ id.

חבר   יִתְחַבְּרוּ Hithpa. fut. 3 pers. pl. masc. (§ 12. rem. 1)

חזק   וַיִּתְחַזַּק / וְיִתְחַזֵּק id Hithpa. fut. 3 pers. sing. masc. (§ 12. rem. 1) ; וְ conv.

חזק   יִתְחַזְּקוּ id. fut. 3 pers. pl. masc. (v. id.) . .

חטא   יִתְחַטָּא Hithpa. fut. 3 pers. sing. masc. .

חטא   יִתְחַטָּאוּ / יִתְחַטָּאוּ id. fut. 3 pers. pl. masc. (comp. § 8. rem. 15) ; וְ conv.

חלה   יִתְחַל Kal fut. 3 pers. sing. masc. ap. [from יִתְחַלֶּה § 24. rem. 12] ; וְ id.

חמם   יִתְחַמָּם Hithpa. fut. 3 pers. sing. masc. (§ 12. rem. 1)

חמץ   יִתְחַמֵּץ Hithpa. fut. 3 pers. sing. masc. . .

חנן   וַיִּתְחַנֵּן / וַיִּתְחַנֶּן Hithpa. fut. 3 pers. sing. masc. (§ 12. rem. 4) ; וְ conv.

חפש   וַיְּ id. Hithpa. fut. 3 pers. sing. masc. ; וַיְ id.

חרש   יִתְחָרְשׁוּ / וְ Hithpa. fut. 3 pers. pl. masc. ; וַיְ id.

חשב   יִתְחַשָּׁב Hithpa. fut. 3 pers. sing. masc. (§ 12. rem. 1)

חתן   יִתְחַתַּן / וְ Hithpa. fut. 3 pers. sing. masc. ; וְ conv.

תוב   יְתִיבוּן Chald. Aph. fut. 3 pers. pl. masc. . .

יהב   יִתְיְהֵב Chald. Ithpe. fut. 3 pers. s. m. (§ 47. rem. 1 b)

יהב   יִתְיַהֲבוּן Chald. id. fut. 3 pers. pl. masc.

נתך   יַתִּיכוּ / וְ Hiph. fut. 3 pers. pl. masc. ; וְ conv.

ילד   יִתְיַלְּדוּ / וְ Hithpa. fut. 3 pers. pl. masc. ; וְ id.

יעץ   יִתְיָעֲצוּ / וְ Hithpa. fut. 3 pers. pl. masc.

יצב   יִתְיַצָּב / וַיִּ יִתְיַצֵּב Hithpa. fut. 3 pers. sing. masc. (§ 12. rem. 1) ; וְ conv.

יצב   יִתְיַצְּבוּ / וְ ,וַיְ id. fut. 3 pers. pl. masc. ; וְ id.

יתר   יַתִּיר pr. name masc. . . .

יתר   יַתִּיר Chald. adj. masc. sing. dec. 1a

יתר   יַתִּירָא / יַתִּירָה Chald. id., emph. st.

נתר   יַתִּירֶנּוּ Hiph. fut. 3 p. s. m., suff. 3 p. s. m.; וְ conv.

תור   יָתוּרוּ / וְ Hiph. fut. 3 pers. pl. masc. ; וְ id.

נתך   יִתְּכוּ Kal fut. 3 pers. pl. masc. ; וְ id.

כון   יִתְכּוֹנָן Hithpal. fut. 3 pers. sing. masc. (§ 21. rem. 20)

כחש   יִתְכַּחֲשׁוּ Hithpa. fut. 3 pers. pl. masc. (§ 14. rem. 1)

תכן   יִתָּכֵן Niph. fut. 3 pers. sing. masc. . .

תכן   יִתְכְּנוּ / יִתָּכְנוּ id. fut. 3 pers. pl. masc. (comp. § 8. rem. 15)

כסה   וַיִּתְכַּס Hithpa. fut. 3 p.s.m.ap. [fr. יִתְכַּסֶּה]; וְ conv.

כסה   יִתְכַּסּוּ / וְ id. fut. 3 pers. pl. masc.

כפר   יִתְכַּפֵּר Hithpa. fut. 3 pers. sing. masc. . .

לבן   יִתְלַבְּנוּ Hithpa. fut. 3 pers. pl. masc.

תלה   יִתְלָה pr. name of a place . . .

ᵃ De. 23. 14.   ᵇ Ps. 39. 7.   ᵖ Da. 4. 31,33,33.   ʲ 1 Sa. 23. 23.   ᵈ Job 41. 17.   ᵏ Ho. 12. 5.   ᵘ Da. 7. 25.   ᵍ Da. 5. 12.   Exe.18.25.
ᵇ Ju. 4. 21.   ᵈ Jos. 18. 4.   𝑞 Ne. 9. 2.   ᵍ Ge. 3. 8.   ᵉ Nu. 8. 21.   ˡ Job 30. 18.   ᵛ 2 Ch. 34. 17.   ᵖ Ps. 105. 20.   ᶠ Exe. 18. 29.
ᶜ Ex. 39. 40.   ᵉ Pa. 12. 9.   ʳ Mi. 6. 2.   ʰ Job 38. 30.   ᶠ 2 Sa. 13. 6.   ᵐ Ju. 16. 2.   ʷ Nu. 1. 18.   𝑞 Ju. 1. 23.   ᵍ Is. 59. 6.
ᵈ Is. 54. 2.   ᶠ Pr. 20. 14.   ˢ Ps. 94. 6.   ᶦ 1 Sa. 13. 6.   ᵍ Job 31. 20.   ⁿ Nu. 23. 9.   ˣ Ps. 83. 4.   ʳ Pr. 24. 3.   ʰ Jon. 3. 8.
ᵉ Na. 2. 5.   ᵍ 1 Sa. 21. 14.   ᵗ Job 39. 8.   ᵏ Da. 11. 6.   ʰ Ps. 73. 21.   ᵒ Ezr. 5. 5.   ʸ Job 38. 10.   ᵍ 2 Sa. 22. 45.   ᶦ 1 Sa. 3. 14.
ᶠ Da. 3. 12.   ʰ Je. 50. 38.   ᵘ Da. 4. 9.   ˡ Eze. 7. 13.   ᶦ 2 Ki. 1. 13.   ᵖ Da. 2. 31.   ᶻ Da. 2. 31.   ᵏ Da. 12. 10.
ᵍ Pr. 23. 31.   ᶦ 1 Sa. 21. 14.

יִתָּלֶה [a] וְ Niph. fut. 3 pers. pl. masc.; ·וְ conv.   תלה

יִתְלוּ [c] וַ, וְ Kal fut. 3 pers. pl. masc.; וְ id.   תלה

יִתְלוֹנֵן Hithpal. fut. 3 pers. sing. m. (§ 21. rem. 20)   לון

יִתְלַחֲשׁוּ [d] Hithpa. fut. 3 pers. pl. masc. (§ 14. rem. 1)   לחש

יִתְלַכְּדוּ
יִתְלַכָּדוּ } Hithpa. fut. 3 pers. pl. masc. (§ 12. rem. 1)   לכד

יִתְלֵם [h] וְ Kal fut. 3 pers. sing. masc. (יִתְלֶה), suff. 3 pers. pl. masc. (§ 24. rem. 21); ·וְ conv.   תלה

יִתְלֹנֵן וְ defect. for יִתְלוֹנֵן (q ..)   לון

יִתְלַקְטוּ [i] וְ Hithpa. fut. 3 pers. pl. masc.; ·וְ conv.   לקט

יָתַם Root not used; to be lonely, bereaved.
    יָתוֹם masc. dec. 3 a, an orphan.
    יִתְמָה (orphanage) pr. name masc. 1 Ch. 11. 46.
    אֹתֶם (solitary) pr. name of a place in the boundary of the Arabian desert.

יַתֵּם וְ Hiph. fut. 3 p. s. m. Chald. form (§ 18. r. 14)   תמם

יַתֵּם [m] וַיְ Kal fut. 3 p. s. m. (§ 18. r. 14); ·וְ conv.   תמם

יִתְמוֹדֵד וְ Hithpo. fut. 3 pers. sing. masc.; ·וְ id.   מדד

יִתְמָה וְ pr. name masc.   יתם

יִתְמְהוּ
יִתְמָהוּ } וַיְ, וְ Kal fut. 3 pers. pl. masc. (§ 8. rem. 15); ·וְ conv.   תמה

יִתְמַהְמָהּ וַיְ Hithpalp. fut. 3 pers. sing. m. (§ 6. No. 4)   מהה

יִתַּמּוּ Niph. fut. 3 pers. pl. masc.   תמם

יִתַּמּוּ
יִתַּמּוּ } Kal fut. 3 pers. pl. masc., Chald. form (§ 18. rem. 14); ·וְ conv.   תמם

יִתְמְחָא Chald. Ithpe. fut. 3 pers. sing. masc.   מחא

יְתֹמָיו noun m. pl., suff. 3 p. s. m. from יָתוֹם dec. 3a   יתם

יְתֹמֶיךָ id. pl., suff. 2 pers. sing. masc.   יתם

יְתֹמִים id. pl., absolute state   יתם

יִתָּמֵךְ Niph. fut. 3 pers. sing. masc.   תמך

יִתְמֹךְ
יִתְמָךְ } [e] וַיְ Kal fut. 3 pers. sing. masc. (§ 8. rem. 18); ·וְ conv.   תמך

יִתְמְכוּ
יִתְמְכוּ } id. fut. 3 pers. pl. masc. (§ 8. rem. 15)   תמך

יִתְמַכְּרוּ וְ Hithp. fut. 3 pers. pl. masc.; ·וְ conv.   מכר

יִתְמַלָּאוּן Hithpa. fut. 3 pers. pl. masc.; וְ parag. (comp. § 8. rem. 17)   מלא

יִתְמַלְּטוּ Hithpa. fut. 3 pers. pl. masc. (§ 12. rem. 1)   מלט

יִתְמוֹלְלוּ Hithpal. fut. 3 pers. pl. masc. (§ 21. rem. 20)   מול

יִתְמַרְמַר [k] וַיְ, וְ Hithpalp. fut. 3 pers. sing. masc. (§ 6. No. 4); ·וְ conv.   מרר

יָתַן Root not used; Arab. to be perennial, to flow constantly; hence, to be constant, stable, firm, Gesenius.

אֵיתָן masc. (no vowel change).—I. adj. perennial, constant; subst. perennity, constancy, of streams.—II. firm, strong, mighty; subst. firmness. יֶרַח הָאֵיתָנִים the month Ethanim, the seventh month of the Hebrew year, otherwise called Tishri.—III. pr. name masc. 1 Ki. 5 ; Ps. 89. 1.

יִתֵּן יִתֵּן
יִתֶּן יִתֶּן } וַיְ, וְ Kal fut. 3 pers. sing. masc. (§ 17. rem. 3); ·וְ conv.   נתן

יֻתַּן וַיְ Hoph. fut. 3 pers. sing. masc.; ·וְ id.   נתן

יִתְנַבֵּא וַיְ Hithpa. fut. 3 pers. sing. masc.; ·וְ id.   נבא

יִתְנַבְּאוּ וְ id. fut. 3 pers. pl. masc.; ·וְ id.   נבא

יִתְנַגַּח Hithpa. fut. 3 pers. sing. masc.   נגח

יִתְנַגְּפוּ Hithpa. fut. 3 pers. pl. masc.   נגף

יִתְנַדְּבוּ וְ Hithpa. fut. 3 pers. pl. masc.; ·וְ conv.   נדב

יִתְּנֶהָ וְ Kal fut. 3 pers. sing. masc. (יִתֵּן), suff. 3 pers. sing. fem.; ·וְ id.   נתן

יִתְּנֶה [g] וְ Kh. יִתְּנֶה Kal fut. 3 pers. pl. masc., suff. 3 pers. sing. fem.; K. יִתְּנֶהָ (q. v.)   נתן

יִתְּנֵהוּ וְ Kal fut. 3 pers. s. m., suff. 3 p. s. m.; ·וְ conv.   נתן

יִתְּנֵהוּ [g] וַיְ id. fut. 3 pers. pl. m., suff. 3 p. s. m.; ·וְ id.   נתן

יְתַנּוּ [g] Piel fut. 3 pers. pl. masc.   תנה

יִתְּנוּ
יִתְּנוּ } וַיְ, וְ Kal fut. 3 pers. pl. masc. (§ 17. rem. 3, & § 8. rem. 15); ·וְ conv.   נתן

יִתְנוּ Kal fut. 3 pers. pl. masc.   תנה

יִתְנַדְּדוּ [a] Hithpo. fut. 3 pers. pl. masc.   נדד

יִתְּנוּהוּ [e] וְ Kal fut. 3 pers. pl. m., suff. 3 p.s.m.; ·וְ conv.   נתן

יִתְּנוּם [g] וְ id., suff. 3 pers. pl. masc.; ·וְ id.   נתן

יִתְנַחֵם [f] וְ Hithpa. fut. 3 pers. s. m. (§ 14. rem. 1 & 3)   נחם

יְתַנְאֵל pr. name masc.   תנה

יִתֶּנְךָ וַיְ Kal fut. 3 pers. sing. masc. (יִתֵּן), suff. 2 pers. sing. masc. (§ 17. rem. 3); ·וְ conv.   נתן

יִתְנַכְּלוּ וְ Hithpa. fut. 3 pers. pl. masc., ·וְ id.   נכל

יִתְנַכֵּר
יִתְנַכֵּר } וְ Hithpa. fut. 3 pers. sing. masc. (§ 12. rem. 4); ·וְ id.   נכר

יִתְּנֵם וַיְ Kal fut. 3 pers. sing. masc. (יִתֵּן), suff. 3 pers. pl. masc. (§ 17. rem. 3); ·וְ id.   נתן

יִתְּנֵם/ וְ id. fut. 3 p. pl. m., suff. 3 p. pl. m.; וְ id.   נתן

יִתְּנָן וְ pr. name of a city   תנה

יִתְּנֶנָּה [g] Kal fut. 3 pers. sing. masc. (יִתֵּן), suff. 3 pers. sing. fem. (§ 17. rem. 3)   נתן

יִתְנַנֵּהּ
יִתְנַנֵּהּ } Chald. Peal fut. 3 pers. sing. masc. [וַיִתֵּן] with suff. 3 pers. sing. fem.   נתן

יִתְּנֵנִי וְ Kal fut. 3 pers. sing. masc. (יִתֵּן), suff. 1 pers. pl. (§ 17. rem. 3); ·וְ conv.   נתן

יִתְּנֻנּוּ id., suff. 3 pers. sing. masc.   נתן

יִתְּנֵנִי id., suff. 1 pers. sing.   נתן

a Est. 2. 23.   b Jos. 10. 26.   c Job 26. 11.   d Ezr. 6. 11.   e Pr. 4. 4.   f Da. 8. 7.   g 2 Ki. 12. 15.   h 3 Ch. 35. 25.   i Mi. 5. 2.
a Est. 9. 13.   f Job 39. 28.   h Ge. 43. 33.   c Is. 9. 16.   d 2 Ki. 17. 17.   e Ju. 5. 11.   f Nu. 23. 19.   g Ex. 39. 18, 20.
a Est. 5. 14.   h Ju. 11. 3.   i Hab. 2. 3.   k Je. 49. 11.   l Job 16. 10.   f Je. 38. 20.   m 2 Ch. 9. 8.   n Ge. 23. 9.
a Ps. 91. 1.   b 2 Ki. 22. 4.   i Ge. 19. 16.   j Pr. 5. 22.   k Job 41. 11.   l Je. 13. 16.   m Ho. 8. 10.   n Da. 4. 22, 29.
a Ps. 41. 8.   m Eze. 47. 12.   o Ps. 102. 28.   p Pr. 29. 23.   q Ps. 58. 8.   r 1 Ch. 29. 6.   s Ps. 64. 9.   t Ge. 42. 7.   u Da. 4. 14.
a Job 38. 30.   n Ge. 47. 15.   o De. 34. 8.   p Ge. 48. 17.   q Da. 11. 11.   r 2 Ki. 22. 5.   s 2 Ch. 34. 17.   t Pr. 20. 11.   u Ju. 6. 13.
a Job 41. 9.   o 1 Ki. 17. 21.

יִתְנַסַּח Chald. Ithpe. fut. 3 pers. s. m. (§ 49. r. 4)   נסה

וְיִתְנַצְּלוּ Hithpa. fut. 3 pers. pl. masc.; וְ conv.   נצל

יִתְנַשָּׂא Hithpa. fut. 3 pers. sing. masc. (§ 12. rem. 1)   נשא

וַיַּתְעֶ וְ Hiph. fut. 3 pers. sing. masc. ap. [from יַתְעֶה comp. § 24. rem. 3] ; וְ conv. .   תעה

וַיַּתְעֵב וְ Hiph. fut. 3 pers. sing. masc. ap. [from וַיַּתְעִיב ; וְ id. . . .   תעב

יַתְעֵב Piel fut. 3 pers. sing. masc.; וְ   תעב

יִתְעָבוּ id. fut. 3 pers. pl. masc. [for יִתְעָבוּ comp. § 8. rem. 15] . . .   תעב

יִתְעַבֵּד Chald. Ithpe. fut. 3 pers. sing. m. (§ 49. r. 2)   עבד

וַיִּתְעַבֵּר Hithpa. fut. 3 pers. sing. masc. (§ 12.

וַיִּתְעַבַּר rem. 1) ; וְ conv. . .   עבר

וַיִּתְעַדְּנוּ וְ Hithpa. fut. 3 pers. pl. masc.; וְ id. .   עדן

וַיַּתְעוּ וְ Hiph. fut. 3 pers. pl. masc.; וְ id. .   תעה

יִתְעוּ Kal fut. 3 pers. pl. masc. . . .   תעה

וַיַּתְעוּם וְ Hiph. fut. 3 pers. pl. masc., suff. 3 pers. pl. masc. ; וְ conv. . .   תעה

יִתְעוֹפֵף Hithpal. fut. 3 pers. sing. masc.   עוף

יִתְעַל Hithpa. fut. 3 pers. s. m. ap. [from יִתְעַלֶּה]   עלה

וְיִתְעַלְּלוּ וְ Hithpa. fut. 3 pers. pl. masc.; וְ conv.   עלל

יִתְעַלָּם Hithpa. fut. 3 pers. sing. masc. (§ 12. rem. 4)   עלם

וְיִתְעַלֶּה וְ Hithpa. fut. 3 p. s. m. (§ 12. r. 1) ; וְ conv.   עלה

וַיַּתְעֵם וְ Hiph. fut. 3 pers. sing. masc. [יַתְעֶה], suff. 3 pers. pl. masc. (§ 24. rem. 21); וְ id.   תעה

יִתְעַנֵּנִי Hithpa. fut. 3 pers. sing. masc. (§ 12. rem. 1)   ענן

יִתְעַנּוּ Hithpa. fut. 3 pers. pl. masc.   ענה

וְיִתְעַצֵּב וְ Hithpa. fut. 3 pers. sing. masc.; וְ conv.   עצב

וַיִּתְעַצְּבוּ וְ id. fut. 3 pers. pl. masc.; וְ id. .   עצב

יִתְעָרֵב Hithpa. fut. 3 pers. sing. masc., acc. Milêl before monos. (comp. § 12. rem. 4)   ערב

וַיִּתְעָרְבוּ וְ id. fut. 3 pers. pl. masc.; וְ conv. .   ערב

יִתְעוֹרֵר Hithpal. fut. 3 pers. s. m. (comp. § 21. r. 20)   עור

יִתְעַשֵּׁת Hithpa. fut. 3 pers. sing. masc. . .   עשת

יִתְפָּאֵר Hithpa. fut. 3 pers. sing. masc. (§ 12. rem. 1) . . . .   פאר

וְיִתְפַּלֵּל וְ, וְנִ Hithpa. fut. 3 pers. sing. masc. (§ 12. rem. 4); וְ conv.   פלל

יִתְפַּלְּלוּ id. fut. 3 pers. pl. masc. (§ 12. rem. 1, comp. § 10. rem. 7)   פלל

יִתְפַּלָּצוּן Hithpa. fut. 3 pers. pl. masc.; ן parag. [for פַּלְּצוּן comp. § 8. rem. 17, & § 12. rem. 1]   פלץ

יִתְפַּלָּשׁוּ Hithpa. fut. 3 pers. pl. masc. (§ 12. rem. 1)   פלש

וַיִּתְפָּצְצוּ וְ Hithpal. fut. 3 pers. pl. masc.; וְ conv.   פוץ

וַיִּתְפָּקֵד וְ Hithpa. fut. 3 pers. s. m. (§ 12. r. 5) ; וְ id.   פקד

יִתְפָּקְדוּ וְ Hithpa. fut. 3 pers. pl. masc. (§ 12. rem. 5)   פקד

יִתְפָּרְדוּ Hithpa. fut. 3 pers. pl. masc. (§ 12.

וְיִתְפָּרְדוּ rem. 1)   פרד

יִתְפֹּרוּ וְ Kal fut. 3 pers. pl. masc.; וְ conv. .   תפר

יִתְפָּרְקוּ וְ Hithpa. fut. 3 pers. pl. masc.; וְ id. .   פרק

וַיִּתְפֹּשׂ וְ Kal fut. 3 pers. sing. masc.; וְ id. .   תפשׂ

יִתְפְּשֶׂהָ וְ id. id., suff. 3 pers. sing. masc.; וְ id. .   תפשׂ

יִתָּפְשׂוּ Niph. fut. 3 pers. pl. masc.   תפשׂ

יִתְפְּשׂוּ וְ Kal fut. 3 pers. pl. masc.; וְ conv. .   פשׂה

יִתְפְּשׂוּם וְ id. id., suff. 3 pers. pl. masc.; וְ id. .   פשׂה

וַיִּתְפַּשֵּׁט וְ Hithpa. fut. 3 pers. sing. masc.; וְ id. .   פשׁט

יִתְפְּשֵׂם וְ Kal fut. 3 pers. sing. masc. (יִתְפֹּשׂ), suff. 3 pers. pl. masc.; וְ id. .   פשׂה

וַיִּתֵּץ וְ Kal fut. 3 pers. s. m. (§ 17. r. 3) ; וְ id. .   נתץ

יֻתַּץ Hoph. fut. 3 pers. sing. masc. [for יֻתַּץ comp. § 2 rem. 15] . . . . .   נתץ

the following with suff. 3 pers. sing. masc.   נתץ

יִתְּצֻהוּ Kal fut. 3 pers. pl. masc. (§ 8. rem. 15);

וְיִתְּצוּ וְ conv. . . . .   נתץ

יִתְּצֶךָ id. fut. 3 pers. s. m. (יִתֹּץ), suff. 2 pers. s. m.   נתץ

יִתְּצֵנִי id. id. with suff. 1 pers. sing.   נתץ

וַיִּתְקַבְּצוּ וְ Hithpa. fut. 3 pers. pl. masc.; וְ conv. .   קבץ

יִתְקַדְּשׁוּ Hithpa. fut. 3 pers. pl. masc. (§ 12.

וַיִּתְקַדְּשׁוּ rem. 1) ; וְ id. . . .   קדש

יִתְקַלֶּס Hithpa. fut. 3 pers. sing. masc. (§ 12. r. 1)   קלס

וַיִּתְקַלְּסוּ וְ id. fut. 3 pers. pl. masc.; וְ conv. .   קלס

יִתָּקַע Niph. fut. 3 pers. sing. masc. (§ 15.

יִתְקַע rem. 1)   תקע

יִתְקַע Kal fut. 3 pers. sing. masc. (§ 8. rem.

וְיִתְקַע 15); וְ conv. . . . .   תקע

יִתְקָעֶהָ id. id., suff. 3 pers. sing. fem. (§ 16. rem. 12) ; וְ id. . . . .   תקע

יִתְקָעֵהוּ id. id., suff. 3 pers. sing. masc.; וְ id. .   תקע

יִתְקְעוּ id. fut. 3 pers. pl. masc. (§ 8. rem.

וַיִּתְקְעוּ 15); וְ id. . . . .   תקע

יִתְקָעֵם id. fut. 3 pers. sing. masc., suff. 3 pers. pl. masc. (§ 16. rem. 12); וְ id. .   תקע

יִתְקְפוֹ Kal fut. 3 pers. sing. m., suff. 3 pers. s. m.   תקף

יִתְקְרִי Ch. Ithpe. fut. 3 pers. sing. masc.   קרא

יִתְקַשָּׁר וְ Hithpa. fut. 3 pers. sing. masc.; וְ conv.   קשר

[יָתַר] to remain, be left, only part. יוֹתֵר the rest, 1 Sa. 15. 15. Hiph. הוֹתִיר.—I. to cause to abound, with acc. of the pers. and בְּ of the thing.—II. to let remain, leave.—III. to abound, excel, Ge. 49. 4 Niph. נוֹתַר to be left, remain; part. that which is left

a Ezr. 6. 11.	*k* Am. 5. 10.	*r* Je. 51. 3.	*y* Ge. 34. 7.	*f* 1 Sa. 2. 25.	*m* Ju. 20. 15.	*t* 1 Sa. 18. 4.	*d* Is. 44. 11.	*l* Ju. 3. 21.

Full footnote key:

a Ezr. 6. 11.   *k* Am. 5. 10.   *r* Je. 51. 3.   *y* Ge. 34. 7.   *f* 1 Sa. 2. 25.   *m* Ju. 20. 15.   *t* 1 Sa. 18. 4.   *d* Is. 44. 11.   *l* Ju. 3. 21.
b Ex. 33. 6.   *l* Ps. 78. 21, 59.   *s* Ju. 19. 25.   *z* Pr. 14. 10.   *g* Is. 45. 14.   *n* Ps. 92. 10.   *u* Eze. 26. 9.   *e* Ex. 19. 22.   *m* Ex. 10. 19.
c Nu. 23. 24.   *m* De. 3. 26.   *t* Job 6. 16.   *a* Ps. 106. 35.   *h* 2 Ch. 7. 14.   *o* Ge. 3. 7.   *v* Le. 11. 35   *f* Hab. 1. 10.   *n* Nu. 10. 4.
2 Ch. 33. 9.   *n* Ne. 9. 25.   *u* Jon. 4. 8.   *b* Job 17. 8.   *i* Ex. 32. 3.   *p* Is. 3. 6.   *w* Eze. 26. 19   *g* Ese. 23. 5.   *o* 2 Sa. 18. 14.
1 Ki. 21. 26.   *o* Je. 23. 13, 32.   *w* Job 27. 10.   *c* Jon. 1. 6.   *k* 2 Ki. 10. 27.   *q* 2 Ki. 2. 23.   *h* Job 17. 3.   *p* Ec. 4. 12.
d Ps. 5. 7.   *p* Am. 2. 4.   *x* Ps. 107. 17.   *d* Is. 44. 23.   *l* Ki. 16. 9.   *r* Ps. 52. 7.   *i* Job 19. 10.   *q* Zec. 9. 14.   *r* Da. 5. 12.
Ps. 106. 40.   *q* Ho. 9. 11.   *q* Ge. 6. 6.   *e* Ju. 7. 2.   *m* Ju. 21. 9.   *s* Ps. 10. 2.   *k* Job 19. 10.   *s* 2 Ki. 9. 14.

יֹתֵר, יֶתֶר masc.—I. *abundance, profit*, Ec. 6. 8.
—II. adv. (a) *more, further*; (b) *too much, over much*, Ec. 7. 16; (c) *besides*; יוֹתֵר שֶׁ conj. *besides that*.

יֹתֶרֶת fem. *the great lobe of the liver*, followed by מִן הַ׳, עַל־הַ׳, הַכָּבֵד.

יֶתֶר masc. dec. 6a (with suff. יִתְרוֹ).—I. *abundance*; adv. *abundantly*.—II. *remainder, residue, rest*.—III. *excellence, pre-eminence*.—IV. *cord, string*.—V. pr. name masc. of several persons, especially of the father-in-law of Moses, elsewhere called יִתְרוֹ, Ex. 4. 18. Patronym. יִתְרִי.

יִתְרָא (*residue*) pr. name masc. 2 Sa. 17. 25, for יֶתֶר 1 Ki. 2. 5.

יִתְרָה fem. *remainder, residue, rest*, Is. 15. 7, constr. יִתְרַת Je. 48. 36.

יִתְרְעָם (*abundance of the people*) pr. name masc. 2 Sa. 3. 5; 1 Ch. 3. 3.

יַתִּיר (*excellent*) pr. name of a town in the tribe of Judah.

יַתִּיר Chald. masc. dec. 1a, adj. *very great, excellent*; fem. יַתִּירָה *very, exceedingly*.

יִתְרוֹ (*pre-eminence*) pr. name of the father-in-law of Moses, called also יֶתֶר & חֹבָב.

יִתְרוֹן masc.—I. *gain, profit*.—II. *excellence, pre-eminence*, Ec. 2. 13.

יִתְרָן (id.) pr. name, 1 Ch. 7. 37, for יֶתֶר ver. 38.

מוֹתָר masc. dec. 2b.—I. *abundance*.—II. *excellence*, Ec. 3. 19.

מֵיתָר masc. dec. 2b, *string, cord*.

יָתֵר Hiph. fut. 3 pers. sing. m. ap. [from יָתִיר תור
יָתַר in pause for יֶתֶר [as if from יָתַר § 35. rem. 5] but with suff. יִתְרוֹ . . . . . . יתר

וַיַּתַר Hiph. fut. 3 pers. sing. masc. ap. from
יָתִיר; וְ conv. . . . . . . נתר

יַתִּר by Chaldaism for יֶתֶר q. v. (§ 21. rem.
24); וְ id. . . . . תור

וְיֶתֶר Kal fut. 3 pers. sing. masc. . . . . נתר

יַתָּר pr. name of a place for יַתִּיר . . . . יתר

וְ׳ יֶתֶר noun masc. sing. (suff. יִתְרוֹ) dec. 6a, also
pr. name masc. . . . . . . יתר

יֹתֵר וְ׳ adv. comp. יוֹתֵר . . . . . . יתר

יִתְרָא pr. name masc. . . . . . . יתר

וְ יִתְרָאוּ Hithpa. fut. 3 pers. pl. masc.; וַ conv. . ראה

יִתְרָה/וְ׳ noun fem. sing. (no pl.) . . . . . יתר

יִתְרוֹ pr. name masc. . . . . . . יתר

וַ׳ וְ׳ יִתְרוּ Kal fut. 3 pers. pl. masc.; וְ conv. . תור

וְ יִתְרוֹ} noun masc. sing., suff. 3 pers. sing. masc.
יִתְרִי} (K. יִתְרִי suff. 1 pers. s.) fr. יֶתֶר d. 6a} יתר

וְ יִתְרוֹמֵם Hithpal. fut. 3 pers. sing. masc. . . רום

וְ יִתְרוֹן noun masc. sing. . . . . . . יתר

יִתְרוֹעֲעוּ Hithpal. fut. 3 pers. pl. masc. . . . רוע

יְתָרִים n. m., pl. of יֶתֶר d. 6a (comp. the following) יתר

וְ׳ יִתְרָם id. sing., suff. 3 pers. pl. masc. . . יתר

יִתְרְמָא Ithpe. fut. 3 pers. sing. masc. R. רמא , see רמה

וְ יִתְרָן pr. name, see יֶתֶר . . . . . . יתר

יִתְרְעָם pr. name masc. . . . . . . יתר

יִתְרַצֶּה Hithpa. fut. 3 pers. sing. masc. . . רצה

וְ יִתְרַצְּצוּ Hithpo. fut. 3 pers. pl. masc.; וַ conv. . רצץ

יִתְרַת noun fem. sing. constr. from יִתְרָה (no pl.) יתר

וְ׳ יֹתֶרֶת noun fem. sing. . . . . . . יתר

יִתְּשֵׁם Ch. Ithpe. fut. 3 pers. sing. masc. . . שום

וַ יִתְּשֵׁם Kal fut. 3 pers. sing. masc. [יִישֵׁשׁ], suff.
3 pers. pl. masc.; וְ conv. . . . . נתש

יִתְּשְׁמוּן Ch. Ithpe. fut. 3 p. pl. m. (comp. § 12. r. 3) שום

יָתֵת pr. name masc. . . . . . . יתד

כ

כ everywhere with Sheva except in the following
cases:—כְּ before a word beginning with Sheva, as
כִּבְשֵׂר for כְּבְשֵׂר; before יֹ, Yod becoming quiescent, as יְדֵי with כ pref. כִּידֵי for כְּיְדֵי;—כָ, כַּ,
כָּ) before the composites (ָ), ֳ), ֱ), as כָּאֲרִי
(and contr. כָּאסֻף for כַּאֲדֹנָי), (כַּאֲדֹנָי and
contr. כֵּאלֹהִים for כְּאֱלֹהִים), but there is no example extant for Kamets-khatuph;—כַ, כָ, כָ,
when displacing the article ה (q. v.), as כַּדָּם for
כְּהַדָּם;—כְּהָחָצִיר for כֶּחָצִיר, כָּהאוֹר for כָּאוֹר

כְּ rarely before the tone-syllable, as כָּזֶה, כָּזֶה.
כָּאֵלֶּה, כָּהֵם, כָּזֹאת. For כ with suffixes see § 5.
—I. adv. (a) *as*, of quality: —כְּ, —וּכְ, כֹּ—, כ—;
כֵּן *as—so; so—as*, e. g. Is. 24. 2, כָּעָם כַּכֹּהֵן *as the
people so the priest*; Ge. 44. 18, כָּמוֹךָ כְּפַרְעֹה *so
thou* (art) *as Pharaoh* (is);—(b) relat. *how, in
what way*, Ec. 11. 5;—(c) indef. *about, nearly,
almost*, before words of measure, number or time;
כְּאֵיפָה *about an ephah*; כְּכָעֶשֶׂר שָׁנִים *about ten
years*; כָּעֵת מָחָר *about this time to-morrow*; hence,

---

a Pr. 19. 26.   d Job 37. 1.   g Nu. 13. 2, 21.   i Job 30. 11.   l Ps. 65. 14.   o Ex. 23. 11.   p 1 Sa. 29. 4.   s Je. 48. 36.   t Ezr. 4. 21
b Pr. 17. 7.   e Ec. 2. 15.   k Is. 44. 19.   h Da. 11. 36.   m Ju. 16. 7, 8.   q Da. 3. 6, etc.   r Ge. 25. 22.   v Le. 9. 19.   x Dc. 29. 27
c 2 Sa. 22. 23   f Is. 15. 7.   hh Job 6. 9.   kk Da. 2. 5.

כַּיּוֹם *about this day*, i. e. *to-day*, but not limited to any particular time of the day; כְּרֶגַע *in a moment*; especially with the inf. *when*, as; e. g. כְּדַבְּרָהּ *about* (the time of) *her speaking*, i. e. *when, as soon as she spoke*; Is. 10. 15, *as if*.—II. prep. (*a*) *as, like, as if*, of resemblance; כָּאֵלֶּה, כָּזֹאת, כָּזֶה, *like this, these, or such*; כָּזֹאת וְכָזֹאת *thus and thus, so and so*;—(*b*) *according to, after*;—(*c*) noting intensity (so Gesenius; others, כְּ veritatis); Ne. 7. 2, כְּאִישׁ אֱמֶת *as a man of truth*, sc. can possibly be; 1 Sa. 10. 27, וַיְהִי כְּמַחֲרִישׁ *he was as quiet*, sc. as possible; Is. 1. 7, כְּמַהְפֵּכַת זָרִים *as an overthrow of strangers*, sc. can possibly make it; כִּמְעַט *very little*.—III. conj. i. q. כַּאֲשֶׁר *as, like as*, Is. 8. 23.

[כָּאַב] fut. יִכְאַב *to be pained, be in pain*; trop. *to be grieved*, with עַל Job 14. 22. Hiph.—I. *to cause pain, sadness*.—II. *to mar, destroy*, 2 Ki. 3. 19.

כְּאֵב masc. dec. 1a, *pain*; trop. *grief, sorrow*.

מַכְאוֹב masc. dec. 1b, pl. ‑ִים, ‑וֹת id.

כְּאָבִי pref. כְּ)(noun m. s., irr. (§ 45); ן bef. (‑ָ)

כְּאָב׳ ן noun masc. sing. dec. 1a; ן id.

כְּאָבוֹת pref. כְּ)(noun masc. with pl. fem. term. fr. אוֹב dec. 1a

כַּאֲבוֹתֵיכֶם pref. כְּ bef. (‑ָ))(noun masc. pl., suff. 2 pers. pl. masc. fr. אָב irr. (§ 45)

כַּאֲבוֹתָם pref. id.)(id., suff. 3 pers. pl. m. (§ 4. r. 2)

כְּאָבִי׳ ן noun masc. sing., suff. 1 pers. sing. from כְּאָב dec. 1a; ן bef. (‑ָ)

כְּאָבָיו pref. כְּ)(noun masc. sing., suff. 3 pers. sing. masc. from אָב irr. (§ 45)

כָּאִים Kal part. act. masc., pl. of כּוֹאֵא dec. 7b

כְּאַבִּירִי Kh. כְּאַבִּיר׳ pref. כְּ, see אַבִּיר; K. כַּבִּיר adv.

כַּאֲבָל־ pref. כְּ bef. (‑ָ))(adj. masc. sing., bef. Mak. [for כְּאָבֵל], constr. of אָבֵל (§ 34. No. 2, & rem. 1)

כְּאֵבֶל׳ pref. כְּ)(noun masc. sing. d. 6 (§ 35. r. 6)

כְּאֶבֶן‑ / כַּאֶבֶן׳ / כָּאֶבֶן׳ pref. כְּ f. כְּה, כְּ)(noun fem. sing. (suff. אַבְנוֹ) dec. 6a (§ 35. rem. 2). pref. כְּ q. v.

כְּאַבְנֵי׳ pref. id.)(id. pl., constr. state

כָּאֲבָנִים pref. כְּ for כְּה; כְּה)(id. pl., absolute state

כְּאָבָק׳ / כָּאָבָק׳ pref. id. / pref. כְּ)(noun masc. sing. dec. 4c

כָּאַבִּרִים pref. כְּ for כְּה; כְּה)(adj. or subst. masc., pl. of אַבִּיר dec. 1b

כְּאַבְשָׁלוֹם pref. כְּ)(pr. name masc.; ן before (‑ָ)

כַּאֲבֹתֵיכֶם׳ defect. for כַּאֲבוֹתֵיכֶם (q. v.)

כְּאָמָן׳ pref. כְּ)(noun masc. sing.

כְּאָדָם pref. id.)(noun masc. sing.

כְּאַדְמָה pref. id.)(pr. name of a place

כַּאדֹנָיו׳ pref. כַּ, contr. for כַּאֲדֹנָיו)(noun masc. pl., suff. 3 pers. sing. m. fr. אָדוֹן d. 3a

כְּאַדַּרְתּ׳ pref. כְּ)(noun fem. s., (suff. אַדַּרְתּוֹ) d. 13a

כָּאָה. Hiph. *to cause to despond*, as the heart, Eze. 13. 22. Niph. *to be dejected, faint-hearted*.

כָּאֶה masc. dec. 9b, *desponding, dejected*, P 10. 10, Keri.

כְּאַהֲבָם׳ pref. id.)(noun masc. sing., suff. 3 pers. pl. masc. from [אָהַב] dec. 6f

כְּאַהֲבַת׳ pref. id.)(noun f. s., constr. of אַהֲבָה (no pl.)

כְּאֹהֶל׳ / כָּאֹהֶל׳ pref. כְּ f. כְּה, כְּ)(noun masc. sing. d. 6 (§ 35. rem. 9) pref. כְּ q. v.

כְּאָהֳלֵי׳ pref. id.)(id. pl., constr. state

כָּאֹהָלִים׳ pref. כַּ bef. (‑ָ))(noun masc. only in the pl.

כְּאוֹב׳ pref. כְּ)(noun masc. sing. dec. 1a

כְּאוּד׳ pref. id.)(noun masc. sing. dec. 1a

כְּאוֹיֵב pref. id.)(Kal part. act. sing. masc. dec. 7b

כְּאוּלָם׳ pref. כְּ for כְּה; כְּה)(noun masc. sing. (pl. c. אֻלַמֵּי) dec. 8a

כְּאִוַּלְתּוֹ׳ pref. כְּ)(noun fem. sing., suff. 3 pers. sing. masc. from אִוֶּלֶת dec. 13a

כְּאוֹר׳ / כָּאוֹר׳ pref. כְּ f. כְּה)(noun m. sing. dec. 1a; ן pref. כְּ q. v. ן bef. (‑ָ)

כְּאוֹרָה׳ pref. כְּ for כְּה; כְּה)(noun fem. sing.

כְּאֵזוֹר׳ pref. id.)(noun masc. sing.

כְּאֶזְרַח׳ / כָּאֶזְרַח pref. id. / pref. כְּ)(noun masc. sing. dec. 2b

כָּאֶזְרָח׳ pref. id.)(id., constr. state

כְּאָח pref. id.)(noun masc. sing. irr. (§ 45)

כְּאָחָאב pref. id.)(pr. name masc.

כְּאָחָב ן pref. id.)(pr. name masc., ן bef. (‑ָ)

כְּאַחַד׳ / כָּאֶחָד pref. id.)(num. card. masc. constr. and abs., irr. (§ 45); ן id.

כְּאָחִיו pref. id.)(noun masc. sing., suff. 3 pers. sing. masc. from אָח (§ 45)

כְּאֶחָיו׳ pref. id.)(id. pl., suff. 3 pers. sing. masc.

וּכְאֲחֵיכֶם׳ ן pref. כַּ bef. (‑ָ))(id. pl., suff. 2 pers. pl. m.

כָּאַחֲרוֹנָה ן pref. כְּ for כְּה; כְּה)(adj. fem. sing. from אַחֲרוֹן masc.

כְּאַחַת pref. כְּ)(num. card. [for אֶחָת] fem. of אֶחָד irr. (§ 45)

• Job 31. 18.   ✶ Ps. 39. 3.   ! Am. 8. 10.   ⁂ Is. 5. 24.   ⁑ Is. 24. 2.   ⁜ Is. 38. 12.   ‡ Am. 4. 11.   ² 2 Sa. 23, 4.   ᵖ Ps. 82. 7.
• Pr. 3. 12.   ᵍ Ki. 3. 2.   ᵐ Ex. 15. 16.   Is. 29. 5.   ᵏ Ge. 25. 25.   ᵈ Ca. 1. 5.   ᵉ La. 2. 4, 5.   ᵗ Ps. 139. 12.   ᵛ Ge. 38. 11.
Is. 17. 11.   ᶜ Ge. 34. 25.   ⁿ Job 38. 30.   Ho. 9. 10.   Nu. 24. 6.   1 Ki. 7. 8.   Je. 13. 10.   ² 2 Ch. 30. 7.
Job 33. 19.   ᵈ Is. 10. 13.   ᵖ Esc. 10. 1.   Ho. 3. 1.   Is. 29. 4.   Pr. 26. 4, 5.   Ex. 12. 46.   Da. 11. 29.
Ps. 78. 8, 57.   ᵏ Ps. 35. 14.   ᶠ Is. 27. 9.   Is. 58. 5.   Is. 40. 29.

Hebrew	Description	Root
כְּאִיּוֹב	pref. כְּ)(pr. name masc.	איב
כָּאֵיל	וֹ' pref. כָּ f. כְּהָ, כְּה(noun m. sing. dec. 1 b	אול
כְּאֵילָה	pref. כְּ q. v. § 30. No. 3)	
כְּאֵילוֹת	pref. כְּ for כְּהָ, כְּה)(noun fem., pl. of אֵלָה (§ 42. rem. 5)	אול
כְּאֵילִים	pref. כְּ)(n. m., pl. of אַיִל dec. 1 b (§ 30. No.3)	אול
כְּאֵילִים	pref. id.)(noun masc., pl. of אַיִל dec. 6 h	אול
כְּאָן	pref. id.)(noun masc. sing. dec. 6 h	און
כְּאָן	וּ pref. id.)(id. constr. st. as an adv.; וּ bef.	און
כְּאֵיפָה	pref. id.)(noun fem. sing. dec. 10	איף
כָּאִישׁ	pref. כָּ f. כְּהָ, כְּה(noun masc. sing. dec. 1 a	אישׁ
כְּאִישׁ	pref. כְּ q. v. (but comp. § 45)	אישׁ
כְּאִישׁוֹן	pref. id.)(noun masc. sing.	אישׁ
כֶּאֱכֹל	pref. כֶּ bef.)(Kal inf. constr.	אכל
כְּאָכְלָם	pref. כְּ Kal inf. with suff. 3 pers. pl. masc.	אכל
כְּאֵל	pref. כְּ for כְּהָ, כְּה)(noun m. sing. dec. 1 a	אול
כְּאֵלָה	pref. id.)(noun fem. sing.	אול
כָּאֵלֶּה	וּ' pref. כָּ, see lett. כ)(pron. demon. com. pl.	אל
כְּאֵלָה	pref. כְּ)(noun fem. sing.	אול
כָּאֵלֶּה	pref. id.)(pron. demon. com. pl.	אל
כֵּאלֹהֵי	pref. כֵּ, contr. for כֵּאלֹהֵי, noun masc. pl. constr. from אֱלֹהַּ dec. 1 a	אלה
כֵּאלֹהִים	pref. כֵּ id.)(id. pl., abs. st.	אלה
כֵּאלֹהֵינוּ	pref. כֵּ id.)(id., suff. 1 pers. pl.	אלה
כָּאֵלוֹן	וּ pref. כָּ for כְּהָ, כְּה)(noun m. sing. dec. 2 b	אלל
כָּאֵלוֹנִים	pref. כָּ id.)(id. pl., abs. st.	אלל
כְּאִלֵּם	וּ pref. כְּ)(adj. masc. sing. dec. 7 b; וּ bef.	אלם
כְּאָמְנָה	pref. id.)(noun fem. sing. dec. 11 a	אלם
כְּאָמְנוֹת	pref. id.)(id. pl., abs. st.	אלם
כְּאַלְּפֵי	pref. id.)(for אַלּוּף, noun masc. sing. dec. 1 b	אלף
כְּאַלְפֵי	pref. id.)(noun m. s. dec. 6 a (comp. the foll.)	אלף
כְּאַלְפַּיִם	pref. id.)(id. du., abs. st.	אלף
כְּאִמָּהּ	pref. id.)(noun fem. sing., suff. 3 pers. sing. masc. (§ 3. rem. 3) from אֵם dec. 8 b	אם
כְּאִמּוֹ	וּ pref. id.)(id., suff. 3 pers. s. m.; וּ bef.	אם
כֶּאֱמֹר	pref. כֶּ bef.)(Kal inf. constr.	אמר
כְּאִמְרָתֶךָ	pref. כְּ)(noun fem. sing., suff. 2 pers. sing. masc. from [אִמְרָה] dec. 12 b	אמר
כְּאַמָּתַיִם	וּ pref. id.)(n. fem. du. of אַמָּה d. 10; וּ bef.	אם
כֶּאֲנִיּוֹת	pref. כֶּ bef.)(noun fem., pl. of אֳנִיָּה dec. 10	אנה
כֶּאֱנָשׁ	Chald. pref. כֶּ bef.)(noun m. sing. dec. 1	אנשׁ
כַּאֲנָשֵׁי	pref. כַּ)(noun masc. pl. constr. [as if from אֱנָשׁ] see אֱנָשׁ, & אִישׁ (§ 45)	אנשׁ
כַּאֲנָשִׁים	pref. כַּ bef.)(id. pl., abs. st.	אנשׁ

Hebrew	Description	Root
כֶּאֱסֹף	וֹ' pref. כֶּ bef.)(Kal inf. constr.	אסף
כְּאַסְפִּי	pref. כְּ)(noun m. pl. constr. from אֹסֶף dec. 6 c	אסף
כְּאַפִּי	pref. id.)(noun masc. sing., suff. 1 pers. sing. from אַף dec. 8 d (§ 37. No. 3 b)	אנף
כַּאֲפִיק	pref. כַּ bef.)(n.m.s., constr. of [אָפִיק] d. 3 a	אפק
כַּאֲפִיקִים	pref. כַּ id.)(id. pl., abs. st.	אפק
כְּאַפְּךָ	pref. כְּ)(noun masc. sing., suff. 2 pers. sing. masc. from אַף dec. 8 d (§ 37. No. 3 b)	אנף
כְּאָפְלָה	pref. כְּ for כְּהָ, כְּה)(noun fem. sing. dec. 10	אפל
כְּאֶפֶס	וּ pref. כְּ)(n.m.s. (du. אֲפָסַיִם) dec. 6 a; וּ bef.	אפס
כְּאֹפֶר	pref. כְּ for כְּהָ, כְּה)(noun masc. sing.	אפר
כְּאֶפְרַיִם	pref. כְּ)(pr. name masc.	אפר
כְּיֹאר	contr. for כַּיְאוֹר (q. v.)	יאר
כְּאַרְבֶּה	pref. כְּ for כְּהָ, כְּה)(noun masc. sing.	רבה
כְּאַרְבַּע	pref. כְּ)(num. card. fem. (§ 31. rem. 5)	רבע
כְּאַרְבָּעִים	pref. id.)(id. pl. com. gen.	רבע
כְּאַרְבַּעַת	pref. id.)(id.s.m., constr. of אַרְבָּעָה (§ 42.r.5)	רבע
כְּאֹרֵג	pref. כְּ for כְּהָ, כְּה)(Kal part. a. m. dec. 7 b	ארג
כְּאַרְגָּמָן	pref. כְּ id.)(noun masc. sing.	ארג
כְּאֶרֶז	pref. כְּ)(noun masc. sing. (pl. c. אֲרָזֵי) dec. 6 a	ארז
כַּאֲרָזִים	pref. כַּ f. כְּהָ, כְּה(id. pl., abs. st.	ארז
כַּאֲרָזִים	pref. כַּ bef.)(	ארז
כְּאֹרַח	pref. כְּ)(noun com. sing. dec. 6 (§ 35. rem. 5 & 9); וּ bef.	ארח
כְּאֹרֵחַ	וּ pref. id.)(Kal part. act. masc. dec. 7 b; וּ id.	ארח
כַּאֲרִי	pref. כַּ for כְּהָ, כְּה(n. m. s. d. 6 i (§ 35. r. 14)	ארה
כַּאֲרִי	Kal part. act. pl. masc. [for כְּאֵרִים § 21. r. 1]	בור
כְּאֲרִי	וּ' pref. כְּ bef.)(n. m. s. d. 6 i (§ 35. r. 14)	ארה
כַּאֲרִיאֵל	pref.id.)(n.m., compound of אֲרִי & אֵל see R.	ארה
כְּאַרְיֵה	pref. כְּ)(noun masc. sing., אֲרִי, with parag. ה (§ 35. rem. 14)	ארה
כְּאַרְכֻּבֹּן	pref. id.)(noun masc. sing., suff. 3 pers. pl. fem. from אֶרֶךְ dec. 6 c	ארך
כְּאַרְפַּד	pref. id.)(pr. name of a place	רפד
כָּאָרֶץ	pref. כָּ f. כְּהָ, כְּה(noun fem. sing. dec. 6 a	ארץ
כְּאֶרֶץ	pref. כְּ q. v. (§ 35. rem. 1 d)	ארץ
כְּאַרְצְכֶם	pref. id.)(id., suff. 2 pers. pl. masc.	ארץ
כָּאִשׁ	pref. כָּ f. כְּהָ, כְּה(noun com. sing. dec. 8 b	אשׁ
כְּאִשׁ	pref. כְּ q. v.	אשׁ
כְּאִשָּׁה	pref. id.)(noun fem. sing. dec. 10 (comp. § 45)	אנשׁ
כְּאֶשְׁכְּלוֹת	pref. כְּ)(noun masc. with pl. fem. term. from אֶשְׁכֹּל (§ 36. rem. 6, & § 44. rem. 5)	שׁכל
כָּאִישֵׁם	וֹ' pref. כָּ for כְּהָ, כְּה)(noun m. s. dec. 4 c	אשׁם
כְּאִשֵׁם	pref. כְּ)(adj. masc. sing. dec. 5 c	אשׁם
כַּאֲשֶׁר	וּ' pref. כַּ bef.)(pref. כ forming an adv. with אֲשֶׁר (q. v.)	אשׁר

a Is. 35. 6.   d 2 Ki. 4. 40.   g Ps. 38. 14.   k Jos. 6. 8.   Joel 2. 7.   q Job 6. 15.   Am. 8. 8.   Ca. 5. 14.   Eze. 42. 11.
b Ps. 42. 2.   Is. 6. 13.   La. 1. 1.   Ps. 119. 41, 58.   Ju. 9. 36.   Ps. 126. 4.   Jos. 4. 13.   Nu. 24. 6.   Is. 36. 17.
La. 1. 6.   Is. 1. 30.   La. 2. 5.   Ps. 119. 76.   Is. 17. 5.   Eze. 35. 11.   1 Sa. 4. 2.   Job 34. 11.   Ca. 7. 9.
Is. 59. 10.   2 Ch. 32. 17.   Zec. 9. 7.   115, 170.   Is. 10. 14.   Pr. 4. 19.   Is. 38. 12.   Is. 38. 13.   Le. 7. 7.
Ru. 2. 17.   1 Sa. 2. 2.   Ju. 9. 49.   Nu. 11. 31.   Mi. 7. 1.   Is. 41. 12.   Ca. 7. 6.   Ps. 22. 17.   Le. 6. 10.
Ju. 8. 21.   Is. 6. 13.   Eze. 16. 44.   Pr. 31. 14.   Eze. 25. 14.   Ps. 147. 16.   Ps. 92. 13.   Nu. 23. 24.   2 Sa. 14. 13.
Is. 5. 24.   Am. 3. 9.   2 Ki. 3. 2.   Da. 7. 4.   Jer. 14. 8.

כְּאֶתְמוֹל pref. בְּ)(adv.   מול

כְּבֹא [a] pref. בְּ)(Kal inf. defect. for בּוֹא (§ 21. rem. 3) dec. 1 a ; ‹ bef. (ִ)   בוא

כְּבֹאֹה [b] pref. בְּ)(id., suff. 3 pers. sing. masc.   בוא

כְּבֹאִי pref. id.)(id., suff. 1 pers. sing.   בוא

כְּבֹאֲךָ pref. id.)(id., suff. 2 pers. sing. masc.   בוא

כְּבֹאֲכֶם pref. id.)(id., suff. 2 pers. pl. masc.   בוא

כְּבֹאָם pref. id.)(id., suff. 3 pers. pl. masc.   בוא

כְּבֹאֲנָה pref. id.)(id., suff. 3 pers. pl. fem. (§ 3. rem. 5) בוא

כָּבַב Root not used ; Arab. and Ethiop. *to roll up*.

כַּבּוֹן (*cake*, Syr. כבונא) pr. name of a place in the tribe of Judah, Jos. 15. 40.

כּוֹכָב masc. dec. 2 b (for כַּבְכָּב) *star*.

כַּבֶּגֶד pref. כַּ for כְּהַ)(noun masc. sing. (suff.

כְּבִגְדִי [c] ‹ pref. בְּ q. v. ((בְּגָדִי) dec. 6 a .   בגד

כָּבֵד , וְ כָבֵד [d] (Ge. chaps. 12. 13. 43. 47 ; Ex. 7. 18 ; Nu. 11 ; 2 Sa. 14 ; all of these, however, may be taken as adjectives) fut. יִכְבַּד.—I. *to be heavy*.—II. *to be weighty, honoured, respected, mighty*.—III. *to be or become vehement, violent, great*.—IV. *to be grievous, burdensome*, with עַל *upon* or *to any one*.—V. *to be dull*, of the senses, also of the mind. Niph.—I. *to be, become*, or *show oneself honoured, renowned, glorious* ; part. נִכְבָּד *glorious* ; נִכְבָּדוֹת *glorious things*.—II. *to be abounding*, Pr. 8. 24. Pi.—I. *to honour*.—II. *to make obdurate, to harden*, the heart, 1 Sa. 6. 6. Pu. *to be honoured*. Hiph.—I. *to make heavy, grievous*.—II. *to honour, make honourable* ; intrans. *to acquire honour*, 2 Ch. 25. 19. Hithp.—I. *to show oneself honourable, boast oneself*, Pr. 12. 9.—II. *to multiply oneself, become numerous*, Na. 3. 15.

כָּבֵד masc. dec. 5 a & b (§ 34. rem. 2).—I. adj. *heavy* ; Is 1. 4, כֶּבֶד עָוֹן *laden with iniquity*.—II. *abounding, numerous*.—III. *heavy, grievous, sore*.—IV. *difficult, arduous*.—V. *slow of utterance*, Ex. 4. 10.—VI. subst. *the liver*.

כָּבוֹד masc. dec. 3 a.—I. *honour, glory* ; adv. *unto glory*, Ps. 73. 24.—II. *splendour, majesty*.—III. *abundance, wealth*.—IV. *heart, mind, soul*.

כְּבֻדָּה adj. only fem. כְּבוּדָּה (for כְּבֻדָּה) *glorious, magnificent* ; subst. *precious things*, Ju. 18. 21.

כֹּבֶד masc.—I. *weight*, Pr. 27. 3.—II. *vehemence, violence*, Is. 21. 15 ; 30. 27.—III. *abundance, multitude*, Na. 3. 3.

כְּבֵדֻת fem. *heaviness, difficulty*, Ex. 14. 25.

כָּבֵד וְ [f] adj. masc. sing. dec. 5 a & b (§ 34. rem. 2)   כבד

כָּבֵד [h] defect. for כָּבוֹד (q. v.) .   כבד

כַּבֵּד Piel inf., or imp. sing. masc.   כבד

כְּבַד [i] ‹ adj. m. sing. constr. of כָּבֵד dec. 5 a & b
כְּבַד [k] { (§ 34. rem. 2) ; ‹ bef. (ִ) . }   כבד

כֹּבֶד וְ noun masc. sing. .   כבד

כְּבֹד [l] ‹ n. m. s., constr. of כָּבוֹד dec. 3 a ; ‹ bef. (ִ) כבד

כָּבְדָה [m] } Kal pret. 3 pers. sing. fem. (§ 8. rem. 1 a)
כָּבְדָה {   כבד

כָּבְדוּ [n] id. pret. 3 pers. pl. .   כבד

כַּבְּדוּ [o] Piel imp. pl. masc. .   כבד

כְּבֵדוֹ noun masc. sing., suff. 3 pers. sing. masc. from כָּבֵד dec. 5 (§ 34. rem. 2) .   כבד

כְּבֹדוֹ n. m. s., suff. 3 pers s. m. from כָּבוֹד d. 3 a כבד

כִּבְּדוּ Piel pret. 3 pers. pl. .   כבד

כִּבְּדוּהוּ [p] id. imp. pl. masc., suff. 3 pers. sing. masc. כבד

כִּבְּדוּנִי id. pret. 3 pers. pl., suff. 1 pers. sing. כבד

כְּבֵדִי n. m. s., suff. 1 pers. s. fr. כָּבֵד d. 5 (§ 34. r. 2) כבד

כְּבֹדִי noun m. s., suff. 1 pers. s. from כָּבוֹד d. 3 a כבד

כְּבֹדֵי וְ constr. of the foll.   כבד

כְּבֵדִים adj. masc., pl. of כָּבֵד dec. 5 (§ 34. rem. 2) כבד

כַּבֶּדְךָ Piel inf. (כַּבֵּד), suff. 2 pers. sing. masc. for [כַּבֶּדְךָ] dec. 7 b (§ 16. r. 16, & § 36. r. 3) כבד

כְּבֹדֶךָ noun masc. sing., suff. 2 pers. sing. masc. [for כְּבוֹדְךָ] from כָּבוֹד dec. 3 a .   כבד

כְּבֹדָם id., suff. 3 pers. pl. masc. .   כבד

כִּבַּדְנוּךָ וְ Piel pret. 1 pers. pl., suff. 2 pers. sing. m. כבד

כַּבְּדֵנִי id. imp. sing. masc. (כַּבֵּד), suff. 1 pers. s. כבד

כִּבַּדְתּוֹ וְ id. pret. 2 p. s. m. [כִּבַּדְתָּ], suff. 3 p. s. m. כבד

כִּבַּדְתַּנִי id. id., suff. 1 pers. sing. .   כבד

[כָּבָה] *to be extinguished*. Pi. *to extinguish, to quench*.

כַּבֶּהֱמָה pref. כַּ for כְּהַ)(noun f. s. d. 11 (§ 42. r. 5) בהם

כַּבְּהֵמוֹת pref. id.)(id. pl., abs. st. .   בהם

כָּבוּ [q] Kal pret. 3 pers. pl.   כבה

כִּבּוּ [s] ‹ Piel pret. 3 pers. pl. .   כבה

כְּבוֹא ‹ pref. בְּ)(Kal inf. c. (§ 21. rem. 3) dec. 1 a ; ‹ bef. (ִ) .   בוא

כָּבוֹד וְ noun masc. sing. dec. 3 a   כבד

כְּבוֹד ‹ id. constr. state ; ‹ bef. (ִ) .   כבד

כְּבוֹדָהּ [h] id. with suff. 3 pers. sing. fem.   כבד

כְּבוּדָּה adj. f. [for כְּבֻדָּה, fr. כָּבֵד m. § 39. No. 3. d. 8] כבד

כְּבוֹדוֹ ‹ noun masc. sing., suff. 3 pers. sing. masc. from כָּבוֹד dec. 3 a ; ‹ bef. (ִ) .   כבד

כְּבוֹדִי ‹ id., suff. 1 pers. sing. ; ‹ id. .   כבד

כְּבוֹדְךָ [‹] id., suff. 2 pers. s. m. [for כְּבוֹדְךָ] ; ‹ id. כבד

כְּבוֹדֵךְ [‹] id., suff. 2 pers. sing. fem.   כבד

a De. 23. 12.   e Is. 64. 5.   h Na. 2. 10.   n Ju. 20. 34.   q 1 Sa. 6. 6.   u Eze. 3. 5, 6.   x Ju. 13. 17.   * Ps. 49. 13, 21.   ‖ Is. 65. 11.
b 1 Ki. 14. 5.   f Is. 24. 20.   k Ex. 4. 10   o Ge. 48. 10.   r Ps. 22. 24.   v Ex. 17. 12.   y 1 Sa. 15. 30.   ‖ Is. 43. 17.   ‖ Ps. 63. 3.
  Ge. 44. 30.   g Ge. 50. 10 ;   l Is. 1. 4.   p Is. 24. 15.   s Is. 29. 13.   z Nu. 22. 37.   * Is. 58. 13.   a 2 Sa. 14. 7.   A Is. 66. 2.
  Ru. 1. 19.   1 Sa. 4. 18.   Pr. 25. 2, 2.   t La. 2. 11.   Pr. 25. 27.   c Is. 43. 23.

כְּבוֹדְכֶם id., suff. 2 pers. pl. masc. . . . . . כבד

כְּבוֹדָם id., suff. 3 pers. pl. masc. . . . . . . כבד

כָּבוּל pr. name of a place . . . . כבל

כַּבּוֹן וְ pr. name of a place . . . . כבב

כְּבוֹצֵר pref. כְּ)(Kal part. act. sing. masc. dec. 7 b בצר

כִּבְחֹן pref. כְּ bef. (:))(Kal inf. constr. . . . בחן

כִּבְחֲצִי preff. כְּ, & בַּ bef. (-:))(noun masc. sing.
    (with suff. חֲצִיו) dec. 6i (§ 35. rem. 14) . חצה

כַּבִּיר adj. masc. sing. dec. 1 b . . . . כבר

כְּבִיר וְ noun masc. sing.; וְ bef. (:) . . . . כבר

כַּבִּירִים adj. masc., pl. of כַּבִּיר dec. 1 b . . . . כבר

כְּבֵית וְ pref. כְּ)(noun masc. sing. constr. of בַּיִת
    irr. (§ 45) ; וְ bef. (:) . . . . בית

כִּבְכוּרָהּ pref. כְּ)(noun masc. sing., suff. 3 pers. sing.
    fem. from [בִּכּוּר] dec. 1 b . . . . כבר

כְּבִכּוּרָהּ pref. id.)(noun fem. sing. . . . . . כבר

כְּבִכְרָתוֹ pref. כְּ bef. (:))(noun fem. sing., suff. 3 pers.
    sing. masc. from בִּכְרָה dec. 10 . . . . כבר

כָּבֵל Root not used ; prob. i. q. נָבֵל, חָבַל to twist, in
    the kindred dialects, to bind together.

    כֶּבֶל masc. dec. 6a (pl. c. כַּבְלֵי) fetter, Ps. 105.
    18 ; 149. 8.

    כָּבוּל (district) pr. name—I. of a district in
    Galilee, 1 Ki. 9. 13.—II. of a town in the tribe of
    Asher, Jos. 19. 27.

כְּבַלַע pref. כְּ)(Piel inf. constr. . . . . . בלע

כִּבְנוֹת pref. כְּ bef. (..))(noun fem. pl., constr. of
    בָּנוֹת, irr. of sing. בַּת (§ 45) . . . . . בנה

כִּבְנֵי pref. id.)(noun masc. pl., constr. of בָּנִים
    irr. of sing. בֵּן, (§ 45) . . . . בנה

כִּבְנֵיהֶם pref. id.)(id. pl. with suff. 3 pers. pl. masc. בנה

[כָּבַס] to wash ; only part. כּוֹבֵס washer, fuller. Pi.
    כָּבֵּס, כִּבֵּס (§ 9. rem. 4) to wash, as clothes ; me-
    taph. to cleanse, purify. Pu. to be washed, Le. 13.
    58 ; 15. 17. Hothp. הֻכַּבֵּס (§ 6. No. 10 note)
    id. Le. 13. 55, 56.

כִּבֵּס } Piel pret. 3 pers. sing. masc (§ 10.
כִּבֵּס וְ } rem. 1) . . . . כבס

כֻּבַּס וְ Pual pret. 3 pers. sing. masc. . . . . כבס

כִּבְּסוּ וְ Piel pret. 3 pers. pl. . . . . כבס

כַּבְּסִי id. imp. sing. fem. . . . . כבס

כַּבְּסֵנִי id. imp. sing. masc., suff. 1 pers. sing. . כבס

כִּבַּסְתֶּם וְ id. pret. 2 pers. pl. masc. . . . . . כבס

כָּבַע Root not used ; i. q. גָּבַע to be high.

כּוֹבַע masc. (constr. כּוֹבַע, pl. כּוֹבָעִים (§ 31.
    rem. 5) a helmet.

כַּבֹּקֶר pref. כַּ for כְּהַ)(noun com. sing. dec. 4a . בקר

כַּבָּקָר pref. id.)(noun masc. sing. dec. 6 c . . בקר

כְּבָקָרַת pref. כְּ)(noun f. s., constr. of [בַּקָּרָה] d. 10 בקר

כָּבַר Kal not used ; i. q. cogn. נָבֵל, חָבַל to twist ; Arab.
    to be great, powerful. Hiph. to multiply, Job
    35. 16 ; part. abundance, Job 36. 31, לְמַכְבִּיר
    abundantly.

    כְּבָר.—I. adv. already, formerly.—II. pr. name
    of a river in Mesopotamia, called also חָבוֹר.

    כְּבִיר masc. quilt, mattrass, 1 Sa. 19. 13, 16.

    כַּבִּיר adj. masc. dec. 1 b.—I. great, mighty ;
    כַּבִּיר יָמִים very old.—II. copious, numerous, many.

    כְּבָרָה fem. a sieve, Am. 9. 9.

    כִּבְרָה fem. only constr. כִּבְרַת, an unknown
    measure of length.

    מִכְבָּר masc. dec. 2b, lattice-work of brass.

    מַכְבֵּר masc. cloth of a coarse texture, 2 Ki. 8. 15.

כַּבָּר pref. כַּ for כְּהַ)(noun masc. sing. dec. 1 a . ברר

כְּבָר adv. ; also pr. name of a river . . . . כבר

כְּבַר Ch. pref. כְּ)(noun masc. sing. dec. 2 a . ברא

כְּבַר pref. id.)(noun masc. sing. dec. 1 a . . ברר

כְּבָרֹאשֹׁנָה preff. כְּ, & בָּ for בְּהָ, בָּה)(adj.,f. of רֹאשׁ רֵאשֹׁן

כִּבְרֹשׁ pref. כְּ bef. (:))(noun masc. sing. dec. 1 a ברש

כַּבַּרְזֶל pref. כַּ for כְּהַ)(noun masc. sing. . . ברזל

כְּבָרִי pref. כְּ)(n. m. s., suff. 1 p. s. from בַּר d. 1 a ברר

כִּבְרִיחַ pref. כְּ bef. (:))(noun masc. sing. dec. 1 a ברח

כִּבְרִית וְ pref. כְּ)(noun fem. sing.; וְ bef. (:) ברר

כַּבְּרִית pref. כְּ f. כְּהַ)(noun fem. sing. dec. 1 a ברת
כִּבְרִית pref. כְּ bef. (:))(}

כְּבִרְכַּת pref. כְּ)(noun fem., constr. of בְּרָכָה d. 11 c ברך

כְּבִרְכַּת pref. כְּ bef. (:))(n. f., constr. of בְּרָכָה d. 10 ברך

כְּבִרְכָתוֹ pref. כְּ)(n. f. s., suff. 3 p. s. m. fr. בְּרָכָה d. 11 c ברך

כַּבָּרָק pref. כַּ for כְּהַ)(noun masc. sing. dec. 4 a ברק

כַּבְּרָקִים pref. id.)(id. pl., abs. st. . . . . . ברק

כִּבְרַת noun fem. constr. [of כִּבְרָה]. . . . . כבר

כֶּבֶשׂ וָ)', (' masc. dec. 6a, lamb ; by transp. כֶּשֶׂב
    which, though of less frequent occurrence, may
    yet be the primary form, כָּסַף=כָּשַׂב to be white.
    כַּבְשָׂה, כִּבְשָׂה fem. dec. 12 b, ewe-lamb

[כָּבַשׁ] I. to trample, tread under foot ; metaph. to dis-
    regard, Mi. 7. 19.—II. to subdue, subject.—III. to
    humble, force, ravish, Est. 7. 8. Niph. pass. of

a Is. 10. 3.   c 1 Sa. 19. 13, 16.   h Nu. 4. 20.   = Ps. 51. 4.   p Ese. 34. 12.   t Le. 26. 19.   x Mal. 3. 2.   a Na. 2. 9.   d Na. 2. 5.
b Je. 6. 9.   f Is. 28. 4.   k Ne. 5. 5.   o Nu. 31. 32.   q Is. 1. 25.   u 2 Sa. 22. 25.   y Je. 31. 32.   b Ge. 49. 28.   e Ese. 46. 12.
c Zec. 13. 9.   g Ho. 9. 10.   l Je. 4. 14.   o Job 11. 17.   r Ho. 14. 9.   w Pr. 18. 19.   z 2 Ch. 34. 32.   c Zec. 9. 14.   f Le. 9. 3.
d 1 Sa. 14. 14.   h Ge. 43. 33.

25

Kal, Nos. II. & III. (Ne. 5. 5). Pi. *to subdue*, 2 Sa. 8. 11. Hiph. id. Je. 34. 11, Kheth.

כֶּבֶשׁ masc. *footstool*, 2 Ch. 9. 18.

כִּבְשָׁן masc. *smelting furnace.*

וְכֶבֶשׁ	noun masc. sing.	כבש
כִּבֵּשׁ	Piel pret. 3 pers. sing. masc.	כבש
וְכִבְשָׂה	noun fem. sing. from כֶּבֶשׂ masc.	כבש
כִּבְשָׂה	noun fem. sing. dec. 12 b, from כֶּבֶשׂ masc.	כבש
כִּבְשֻׁהָ	Kal imp. pl. masc., suff. 3 pers. sing. fem.	כבש
וְכִבְשׁוּ	id. pret. 3 pers. pl.	כבש
כְּבָשַׂי	noun m. pl., suff. 1 pers. s. from כֶּבֶשׂ d 6	כבש
כְּבָשִׂים	id. pl., abs. st. ; ↓ bef. (:)	כבש
כֹּבְשִׁים	Kal part. act. masc., pl. of [כֹּבֵשׁ] dec. 7 b	כבש
כְּבַשֵּׁל	pref. כְּ)(Piel inf. constr.	בשל
כַּבֹּשֶׂם	pref. כַּ for כְּהַ)(noun masc. sing.	בשם
כִּבְשָׂן	noun masc. sing.	כבש
וּכְבַשַׂר	↓ pref.)(noun masc. sing. d. 4 a; ↓ bef. (:)	בשר
כִּבְשַׂר	pref. כְּ bef. (:))(id., constr. st.	בשר
כִּבְשָׂרוֹ	pref. id.)(id., suff. 3 pers. sing. masc.	בשר
כְּבָשֹׂת	noun fem. pl. abs., from כִּבְשָׂה dec. 12 b	כבש
כְּבֹשֶׁת	pref. כְּ)(noun fem. sing. dec. 13 c	בוש
כִּבְשַׂת	noun fem. sing., constr. of כִּבְשָׂה dec. 12 b	כבש
כִּבְשֹׂת	id. pl., constr. state	כבש
כְּבַת	pref. כְּ)(noun fem. s. [for בֶּנֶת, בַּת [§ 45]	בנה
כִּבְתוּלָה	pref. כְּ before (:))(noun fem. sing. dec. 10	בתל
כִּבְתְחִלָּה	preff. כְּ, & בְּ for בְּהַ)(noun f. sing. d. 10	חלל
כִּגְאוֹן	pref. כְּ bef. (:))(noun masc. sing., constr. of גָּאוֹן dec. 3 a	נאה
כְּגֻבַּהּ	pref. כְּ)(noun masc. sing. d. 6 c (§ 35. r. 5)	גבה
כִּגְבֹהַּ	pref. כְּ bef. (:))(Kal inf. constr.	גבה
כַּגִּבּוֹר	pref. כַּ f. כְּהַ)(adj. or subst. masc. sing.}	נבר
כִּגְבּוֹר	pref. כְּ q. v. } dec. 1 b	נבר
כִּגְבֹּרִים	pref. id.)(id. pl., abs. st.	נבר
כִּגְבוּרֹתֶיךָ	↓ pref. כְּ bef. (:))(noun fem. pl., suff. 2 pers. sing. masc. from גְּבוּרָה dec. 10	גבר
כַּגִּבְנָה	↓ pref. כַּ for כְּהַ)(noun fem. sing.	גבן
כִּגְבַּר	↓ pref. כְּ)(noun masc. sing. d. 6; ↓ bef. (:)	גבר
כִּגְבֹּרִים	defect. for כִּגְבּוֹרִים (q. v.)	נבר
כִּגְבֻרְתָּהּ	pref. כַּ for כְּהַ)(noun fem. sing., suff. 3 pers. sing. fem. from גְּבֻרָת dec. 13 a	גבר
כַּגָּדוֹל } כַּגָּדֹל }	pref. id.)(adj. masc. sing. dec. 3 a	גדל
כִּגְדֹל	pref. כְּ)(noun masc. sing. dec. 6 c	גדל
כִּגְנֹבַי	pref. id.)(noun m. sing., pl. or collect.	נוב
כִּגְנֹי	pref. id.)(noun masc. sing. dec. 1 a	נוה
כַּגּוֹיִם	pref. כַּ for כְּהַ)(id. pl., abs. st., for גּוֹיִם (comp. § 3. rem. 1)	נוה
כִּגְנוֹרָי	pref. כְּ)(noun m. pl. constr. fr. [גּוֹר] d. 1 a	נור
כִּגְנַחֲלֵי	pref. id.)(noun fem. with pl. masc. term., constr. of נְחָלִים, fr. נַחֲלָת (q. v.)	נחל
כְּגִילְכֶם	pref. כְּ)(n. m. pl., suff. 2 p. pl. m. from נִּיל d. 1 a	ניל
כַּגַּלְגַּל	pref. כַּ for כְּהַ)(noun masc. sing. d. 8 e;	נלל
כְּגַלְגַּל	↓ pref. כְּ q. v. ↓ before (:)	נלל
כִּגְלֵי	pref. כְּ)(noun m. pl. constr. from נַל d 8 d	נלל
כְּגַלִּים	pref. id.)(id. pl., abs. st.	נלל
כְּגַלְלוֹ	pref. id.)(noun masc. sing., suff. 3 pers. sing. masc. from נָלָל dec. 6 (§ 35. rem. 3)	נלל
כַּגְלָלִים	pref. כַּ for כְּהַ)(id. pl., abs. st.	נלל
כִּגְמוּל	pref. כְּ bef. .)(noun masc. sing. dec. 1 a	נמל
כַּגָּמֻל	pref. כַּ f. כְּהַ)(Kal part. pass. sing. masc.}	נמל
כִּגְמֻלִי	pref. כְּ q. v. } (for נָּמוּל) dec. 3 a	נמל
כַּגַּן	pref. כַּ f. כְּהַ } noun com. sing. dec. 8 d	נגן
כְּגַן	pref. כְּ q. v. }	נגן
כַּגַּנָּב	pref. כַּ for כְּהַ)(noun m. s. d. 1 b (§ 30. r. 1)	ננב
כְּגַנָּה	↓ pref. כְּ)(noun fem. sing. d. 10 ; ↓ bef. (:)	ננן
כְּגַנֹּת	pref. id.)(id. pl.	ננן
כְּגַנַּעַת	pref. id.)(Kal inf. constr.	ננע
כַּגֶּפֶן	{pref. כַּ f. כְּהַ } noun com. sing. (suff. נַפְנִי)	נפן
כְּגֶפֶן	} dec. 6 a (§ 35. rem. 2) }	נפן
כִּגְפֶן	pref. כְּ q. v. }	נפן
כַּגֵּר	pref. כַּ for כְּהַ)(n. m. s. dec. 1 a (נֵּר Je. 14.8)	נור
כִּגְרֹן	pref. כְּ)(noun fem. sing. dec. 6 c	נרן
כַּגְּשָׁמִים	pref. כַּ for כְּהַ)(n. m. s. (pl. c. נִשְׁמֵי) d. 6 c	נשם
כַּד	noun com. sing. dec. 8 d	כדד

כְּדַב Chald. not used as a verb (in the Bible); i. q. Heb. כָּזַב *to lie, deceive.*

כְּדַב Chald. adj. m. d. 3 b, *lying, false*, Da. 2. 9

כִּדְּב	pref. כְּ)(noun masc. sing. dec. 8 c	דבב
כִּדְבָה	Chald. adj. fem. sing. [from כְּדַב masc.]	כדב
כַּדֻּבִּים	pref. כַּ for כְּהַ)(noun m., pl. of דֹּב d. 8 c	דבב
כִּדְבַר	pref. id.)(noun masc. sing. dec. 4 a	דבר
כְּדַבֵּר	pref. כְּ)(Piel inf. constr. dec. 7 b	דבר
כִּדְבַר	pref. כְּ bef. (:))(n. m., constr. of דָּבָר d. 4 a	דבר
כְּדַבְּרָהּ	pref. כְּ)(Piel inf. (דַּבֵּר), suff. 3 pers. sing. fem. dec. 7 b	דבר
כִּדְבְרֵי	pref. id.)(noun m. pl. constr. fr. דָּבָר d. 4 a	דבר
כִּדְבָרֶיךָ	pref. כְּ bef. (:))(id. pl. (Kh. כִּדְבָרֶיךָ), suff. 2 pers. sing. masc., K. כִּדְבָרְךָ id. sing.	דבר
כְּדִבְרֵיכֶם	pref. id.)(id. pl., suff. 2 pers. pl. masc.	דבר

a 2 Ch. 9.18.   g Ne. 5.5.   n Je. 2.26.   t Na. 2.3.   z Je. 23.9.   f Je. 51.38.   m Ho. 12.12.   s Nu. 24.6.   y Da. 2.9.
b 2 Sa. 8.11.   h 1 Sa. 2.13.   o 2 Sa. 12.4.   u Ps. 103.11.   a Zec. 10.5.   g Eze. 1.13.   n Job 20.7.   t Ho. 14.8.   z Is. 59.11.
c 2 Sa. 12.3.   i Ex. 9.8.   p Ge. 21.28.   v Is. 42.13.   b Is. 24.2.   h Da. 1.10.   o Zep. 1.17.   u Ps. 128.3.   a Ge. 39.10.
d Je. 1.28.   k Mi. 3.3.   q 2 Sa. 12.3.   w Joel 2.7.   c De. 1.17.   i Ps. 83.14.   p Ps. 131.1.   v Je. 51.33.   b Is. 29.11.
e Eze. 9.15.   l Ex. 4.7.   r Joel 1.8.   x De. 3.24.   d Na. 3.17.   k Ps. 131.2.   q Ho. 6.3.   w Ezr. 10.12.
f Job 31.20.   m Ge. 21.29, 30.   s Is. 1.28.   y Job 10.10.   e Is. 58.2.   l La. 2.6.   r Ho. 13.8.   x Eze. 17.10.

כַּדְּבָרִים pref. כְּ for כְּהַ)(id. pl., abs. st. . . דבר

כִּדְבֹרִים pref. כְּ bef. (:))(noun fem. with pl. masc. term. from דְּבֹרָה dec. 10 . . דבר

כִּדְבָרְךָ in pause for כִּדְבָרְךָ (q. v.) . . דבר

כִּדְבָרְךָ pref. כְּ bef. (:))(noun masc. sing., suff. 2 pers. sing. fem. from דָּבָר dec. 4 a . . דבר

כִּדְבָרֶךָ pref. id.)(id., suff. 2 pers. sing. masc. . דבר

כְּדַבֶּרְכֶם pref. כְּ)(Piel Inf. (דַּבֵּר) suff. 2 pers. pl. masc. dec. 7 b (§ 16. rem. 15, & § 36. rem. 3) . דבר

כְּדִבְרָם pref. id.)(noun masc. sing., suff. 3 pers. pl. masc. from [דִּבֵּר] dec. 6 c . . דבר

כְּדִבְשִׁי pref. כְּ bef. (:))(noun masc. sing. (suff. דִּבְשִׁי) dec. 6 (§ 35. rem. 10) . . דבש

כְּדָגְנִי pref. id.)(noun m. pl. constr. from דָּן dec. 2 a דנה

כַּדָּגִים pref. כַּ for כְּהַ)(id. pl., abs. st. . . דנה

כַּדָּגָן pref. id.)(noun masc. sing. dec. 4 a . דנה

כְּדָנַת pref. כְּ bef. (:))(n. fem., constr. of דָּנָה dec. 11 a . דנה

כָּדַד Root not used; i. q. כָּתַת to beat, strike; Arab. to hammer, to toil; to draw out of a well.

כַּד com. dec. 8 d, earthen jar, espec. for drawing water, a pitcher; but also for keeping meal, 1 Ki. 17. 12, 14, 16.

כִּידוֹד masc. dec. 1 b, Job 41. 11, a spark; Arab. כיד to strike fire.

כַּדְכֹּד masc. a sparkling or flashing gem, supposed to be a ruby.

כַּדָּהּ n. com. s., suff. 3 p. s. f. from כַּד dec. 8 d

כַּדֹּב pref. כְּ)(for דֹּב, noun masc. sing. dec. 8 c דבב

כְּדֹד pref. id.)(pr. name masc. . דוד

כְּדוּד pref. id.)(noun masc. sing., pl. דּוּדִים and דּוּדָים (§ 35. rem. 13) . . דוד

כְּדֻדָי pref. כְּ bef. (:))(noun masc. pl. constr. from דֻּדַי (comp. § 38. rem. 2) . דוד

כְּדָוִיד pref. כְּ)(pr. name masc., see דָּוִד דוד

כִּדְעֹנֶן / כַּדּוֹעֵן pref. כְּ for כְּהַ)(noun masc. sing. דנן

כַּדּוּר pref. id.)(noun masc. sing. . . דור

כְּדִי pref. כְּ)(noun masc. sing. dec. 8 d (§ 37. rem. 6); ו bef. (:)

כְּדֵי pref. כְּ)(id., constr. st. . . די

כְּדִי Chald. pref. כְּ)((prim. pron. relat.) conj., see דִּי; ו bef. (:) . . די

כַּדִּים noun com., pl. of כַּד dec. 8 d . כדד

כַּדֵּךְ id. sing., suff. 2 pers. sing. fem. . כדד

כַּדְכֹּד noun masc. sing. . . . כדד

כַּדֹּם pref. כַּ for כְּהַ)(noun masc. sing. dec. 2 a אדם

כִּדְמָה pref. כְּ)(noun fem. sing. [from דֹּם masc.] דמם

כִּדְמוּת pref. כְּ bef. (:))(noun fem. sing. dec. 1 a דמה

כִּדְמוּתֵנוּ pref. id.)(id., suff. 1 pers. pl. . דמה

כְּדָמִי ו pref. id.)(n. m. pl. constr. from דָּם d. 2 a אדם

כְּדָמָן pref. id.)(noun masc. sing. . דמן

כְּדַמֶּשֶׂק pref. id.)(pr. name of a place . דמשק

כְּדֵנָה Chald. pref. כְּ bef. (:))(emph. or fem. of דֵּן pron. demonst. . . דן

כְּדָנִיֵּאל pref. כְּ)(pr. name masc. . . דן

כְּדַעְתְּכֶם pref. id.)(noun fem. sing., suff. 2 pers. pl. masc. from דַּעַת dec. 13 a (§ 44. No. 1) ידע

כַּדַּק pref. כַּ for כְּהַ)(adj. or subst. masc. sing. דקק

כְּדֹק pref. id.)(noun masc. sing. . . דקק

כָּדַר Root not used; Arab. to be agitated, troubled.

כִּידוֹר masc. Job 15. 24, tumult, warlike tumult. Prof. Lee, attack, onset.

כַּדַּרְבֹּנוֹת pref. id.)(noun pl. fem. . . דרב

כַּדְּרוֹר pref. id.)(noun masc. sing. . דרר

כְּדַרְכִּי pref. כְּ)(noun com. sing. (suff. דַּרְכִּי) dec. 6 a; ו bef. (:) . . דרך

כְּדֹרֵךְ pref. id.)(Kal part. act. masc. dec. 7 b . דרך

כִּדְרָכָו / כִּדְרָכָיו pref. כְּ bef. (:))(noun com. pl., suff. 3 pers. sing. masc. from דֶּרֶךְ dec. 6 a דרך

כִּדְרָכֶךָ / כִּדְרָכַיִךְ pref. id.)(id. pl., suff. 2 pers. sing. fem. דרך

כְּדַרְכֵיכֶם pref. id.)(id. pl., suff. 2 pers. pl. masc. דרך

כְּדֹרְכִים pref. id.)(Kal part. act. m., pl. of דֹּרֵךְ d. 7 b דרך

כִּדְרָכֵינוּ pref. כְּ bef. (:))(n. com. pl., suff. 1 p. fr. דֶּרֶךְ d. 6 a דרך

כְּדַרְכָּם pref. כְּ)(id. sing., suff. 3 pers. pl. masc. דרך

כְּדָרְלָעֹמֶר / כְּדָרְלָעֹמֶר (handful of sheaves; coll. with the Arab. by Simonis) pr. n. of a king of Elam, Ge. 14. 1, 9.

כַּדֶּשֶׁא pref. כַּ for כְּהַ)(noun masc. sing. . רשא

כַּדָּת pref. id.)(noun f. s. dec. 1 a; but comp. כְּדָת דת

כְּדָת Chald. and Heb. pref. כְּ)(noun fem. sing. dec. 1 a (but comp. דָּתְכוֹ) . . . רת

כִּדְת pref. id.)(id. constr. (but this reading is doubtful) . . . . ית

כֹּה ו / כֹּה adv.—I. so, thus; כָּכֹה—כֹּה in this manner—in that manner, 1 Ki. 22. 20.—II. of place, here hither; עַד־כֹּה yonder, Ge. 22. 5; כֹּה—כֹּה here—there, on this side—on the other side, Nu. 11. 31; כֹּה וָכֹה hither and thither, Ex. 2. 12.—III. of time, now; עַד־כֹּה until now, hitherto, Ex. 7. 16; Jos 17. 14; עַד־כֹּה וְעַד־כֹּה till now and then, i. e. meanwhile, 1 Ki. 18. 45.

---

* Ps. 118. 12.   f Hab. 1. 14.   * Ge. 24. 16, 18, 20, 46.   * Job 6. 7.   f Ju. 7. 16.   * Eze. 27. 32.   * Is. 40. 15.   † Is. 63. 2.   † Je. 25. 30.
† 1 Ki. 17. 13.   g Ec. 9. 12.   h Ge. 24. 14.   p Ps. 22. 15.   g Ge. 24. 14.   † Ge. 1. 26.   f Is. 40. 22.   ‡ Je. 17. 10.   ‡ Zec. 1. 16.
‡ Ex. 12. 31.   h Nu. 18. 27.   i Ge. 24. 15, 45.   a Is. 1. 18.   r Is. 54. 12.   ‡ Eze. 16. 36.   g Ec. 12. 11.   * Eze. 7. 3, 8.   ‡ Eze. 36. 19.
§ Is. 5. 17.   i Eze. 47. 10.   k 2 Sa. 17. 8.   b Da. 12. 20.   s Eze. 27. 16.   ‖ Eze. 7. 27.   h Pr. 26. 2.   ‡ Eze. 24. 14.   ‡ Is. 66. 14.
‖ Esz. 2. 13.   * Job 41. 11.   c 1 Ki. 18. 34.   t 2 Ki. 3. 22.   * Job 13. 2.   * Nu. 11. 31.   ‡ Eze. 20. 44.   ‖ Est. 2. 12.

5*

כָּה Chald. i. q. כה, only Da. 7. 28, עַד־כָּה *hitherto, thus far.*

כְּהִנָּלוֹת pref. כְּ)(Niph. inf. constr. . . נלה
כְּהִדּוּשׁ• pref. id.)(Niph. inf. constr. (§ 21. rem. 12) דוש

[כָּהָה] fut. יִכְהֶה, apoc. וַתֵּכַהּ (§ 24. rem. 3) *to become weak, languid, faint,* Is. 42. 4; of the eyes, *to become dull, dim.* Pi. כֵּהָה.—I. intrans. *to become faint, timid,* Eze. 21. 12.—II. *to make timid, to admonish,* 1 Sa. 3. 13.

כֵּהָה adj. only fem. כֵּהָה dec. 10.—I. *weak, faint,* of the mind, Is. 61. 3; *dull, dim,* of the eyes; פִּשְׁתָּה כֵהָה *dim wick* of a lamp about to go out, Is. 42. 3.—II. *faint, pale,* of spots of leprosy.

כֵּהָה fem. *weakening, relaxation, mitigation,* Na. 3. 19.

כָּהֹה• Kal inf. abs. . . . כהה
כֵּהָה• subst. or adj. fem. s. dec. 10 [from כֵּהֶה m.] כהה
כִּהָה• Piel pret. 3 pers. sing. masc. (comp. קָהָה, נֶחְלָּת) according to Gesenius, in an intrans. sense, *to become pale* . . כהה
כְּהֶה• id. with dag. forte impl. (§ 14. rem. 1) . כהה
כְּהֹלֵךְ' pref. פַּ for כְּהַ)(Kal part. act. masc. dec. 7b הלך
כְּהוֹצִיאָם pref. כְּ)(Hiph. inf. (הוֹצִיא), suff. 3 pers. pl. masc. dec. 1b יצא
כֵּהוֹת adj. fem., pl. of כֵּהָה dec. 10 [from כֵּהֶה m.] כהה
כְּהַזְכִּירוֹ• pref. כְּ)(Hiph. inf. (הַזְכִּיר), suff. 3 pers. sing. masc. dec. 1b זכר
כְּהַזְנוֹת aa pref. id.)(Hiph. inf. constr. dec. 1b זנה
כְּהֶחָכָם• preff. כְּ, & הַ bef. חָ for הַ)(adj. m. dec. 4c חכם
כְּהַחַלֹּנוֹת preff. כְּ, & הַ for הַ)(noun com., pl. of חַלּוֹן dec. 1b חלל
כְּהַיָּמִים preff. כְּ, & הַ)(noun masc. dec. 1, pl. יָמִים irr. (§ 45) . . . יום
כְּהַכּוֹתָם• pref. כְּ)(Hiph. inf. (הַכּוֹת § 25. No. 2), suff. 3 pers. pl. masc. dec. 1b . נכה
כְּהָקִין• pref. id.)(Hiph. inf. constr. dec. 3a . כון
כְּהִכָּנַע■ pref. id.)(Niph. inf. constr. dec. 7 (§ 36. r. 5) כנע

[כְּהַל] *to be able, can;* הַאִיתָיךָ כָּהֵל לְ *canst thou?* &c.
כָּהֵל Chald. Peal part. act. dec. 2b כהל
כָּהֲלִין• Chald. id. pl., abs. st. . כהל
כָּהֶם•)(pref. כָּ q. v.)(pron. pers. masc. pl. . הם
כָּהֵם prep. (כְּ) with suff. 3 pers. pl. m. (§ 5. parad.) כ
כָּהֵמָּה• pref. כָּ q.v.)(pron. 3.m.pl.(הֵם) with parag. ה הם

כַּהֲמוֹת pref. כַּ bef. (־))(Kal inf. constr. . . המה
כְּהִמָּס• pref. כְּ)(Niph. inf. constr. (§ 18. rem. 7) . מסס
כְּהָמֵר pref. id.)(Hiph. inf. constr. . . מרר

כָּהַן Kal not used; prob. i. q. כּוּן *to stand,* whence Pi. כִּהֵן (§ 14. rem. 1).—I. *to prepare, make ready, adjust* or *adorn* (comp. הֵכִין) Is. 61. 10.—II. *to minister, act* or *officiate as a priest.*

כֹּהֵן masc. dec. 7b (pl. כֹּהֲנִים).—I. *priest;* כֹּהֵן הַגָּדוֹל כּ׳ הָרֹאשׁ *the high priest,* also called, כּ׳ הַמָּשִׁיחַ *the anointed priest.*—II. *minister of civil affairs,* 2 Sa. 8. 18, comp. 1 Ch. 18. 17; some refer here, 2 Sa. 20. 26; 1 Ki. 4. 5; Job 12. 19.

כָּהֵן, כַּהֵן (Ezr. 7. 13) Chald. masc. dec. 2b, *priest.*
כְּהֻנָּה fem. dec. 10, *priesthood, office of the priest.*

כָּהֵן• pref. כָּ)(pron. 3 p. fem. pl. (comp. הוּא) הן
כִּהֵן')(Piel pret. 3 pers. sing. masc. (§ 14. rem. 1) כהן
כֹהֵן)(noun masc. sing. dec. 7b . . . כהן
כַּהֲנָא• Ch. n. m. s. emph. [of כַּהֵן for כָּהֵן] d. 2b כהן
כְּהִנָּבֵא• pref. כְּ)(Niph. inf. (הִנָּבֵא), suff. 1 p s. d. 7b נבא
כְּהִנָּדֹף• pref. id.)(Kal inf. constr. (§ 9. rem. 2) נדף
כְּהֵנָּה')(pref. כְּ q. v.)(pron. 3 p. fem. pl. (הֵן) with parag. ה (comp. § 5. parad.) הן
כְּהֻנָּה noun fem. sing. dec. 10 כהן
כִּהֲנוּ)(Piel pret. 3 pers. pl. (§ 14. rem. 1) כהן
כַּהֲנוֹהִי)(Ch. n. m. pl., suff. 3 pers. s. m. fr. כָּהֵן d. 2b כהן
כֹּהֲנַי• noun m. pl., suff. 1 pers. s. from כֹּהֵן dec. 7b כהן
כֹּהֲנֵי• id. pl., constr. st. . . . . כהן
כָּהֲנַיָּא•)(Ch. noun m. pl. emph. from [כָּהֵן] d. 2b כהן
כֹּהֲנֶיהָ)(noun m. pl., suff. 3 p. s. f. from כֹּהֵן d. 7b כהן
כֹּהֲנֵיהֶם•)(id. pl., suff. 3 pers. pl. masc. . כהן
כֹּהֲנָיו)(id. pl., suff. 3 pers. sing. masc. . כהן
כֹּהֲנֶיךָ id. pl., suff. 2 pers. sing. masc. . כהן
כֹּהֲנִים s')(id. pl., abs. st. . . . . כהן
כֹּהֲנֵינוּ id. pl., suff. 1 pers. pl. . . . כהן
כְּהָנִיף• pref. כְּ)(Hiph. inf. constr. dec. 3a נוף
כְּהֻנַּת noun fem. sing., constr. of כְּהֻנָּה dec. 10 כהן
כְּהֻנַּתְכֶם• id., suff. 2 pers. pl. masc. . . כהן
כְּהֻנָּתָם• id., suff. 3 pers. pl. masc. . . כהן
כְּהַעֲלוֹת• pref. כְּ)(Hiph. inf. constr. dec. 1b עלה
כְּהָפְנֹתוֹ w pref. id.)(Hiph. inf., suff. 3 p. s. m. d. 1b פנה
כְּהָצֵר• 1 pref. כְּ)(Hiph. inf. constr.; 1 bef. (:) צרר
כְּהַקִּיר• pref. כְּ)(Hiph. inf. constr. . . קור
כְּהַר pref. id.)(noun masc. sing. d. 8 (§ 37. r. 7) הרר
כְּהָרֹן• pref. id.)(noun masc. sing. . . הרן
כְּהָרִים y•)(pref. כְּ)(Hiph. inf. constr. dec. 3a רום

---

a 2 Sa. 6. 20. | b Is. 30. 29. | c 2 Ch. 12. 1. | d Je. 36. 32. | e 1 Ch. 5. 36. | f Ezr. 7. 13. | g Je. 2. 26. | h Nu. 3. 10. | i Je. 6. 7.
Is. 25. 10. | 1 Sa. 4. 18. | 2 Ch. 33. 23. | Is. 17. 12. | La. 1. 19. | 2 Ch. 13. 10. | Is. 27. 7.
Zec. 11. 17. | Ec. 8. 1. | Da. 5. 8, 15. | Ps. 68. 3. | Ezr. 7. 12, 21. | Eze. 26. 3. | Is. 27. 7.
Le. 13. 6, 56. | Eze. 40. 35. | 2 Sa. 24. 3. | Ps. 68. 3. | Ps. 68. 3. | 1 Sa. 40. 9. | Is. 10. 15.
1 Sa. 3. 13. | Eze. 9. 8. | 2 Ki. 17. 15. | Eze. 18. 14. | 2 Ch. 21. 13. | Je. 32. 32. | Ch. 5. 13.

כְּהָרִימִי pref. בְּ bef. ־)(id. with suff. 1 pers. sing. . רום

כְּהָרְרֵי pref. בְּ)(n. m. pl. constr. from הָרָר d. 4c הרר

כְּהַשְׁחִית pref. בְּ)(Hiph. inf. constr. d. 2 b ; ו bef. (ְ) שחת

כֵּהָתָה Kal pret. 3 pers. sing. fem. . . . כהה

כֵּהֲתָה ן Piel pret. 3 pers. sing. fem. (§ 14. rem. 1) כהה

כְּהִתְוַדֹּתֹו ן pref. בְּ)(Hithpa. inf., suff. 3 pers. sing. masc. (§ 20. No. 1) ; ו bef. (ְ) . ידה

כְּהִתֹּודֵד pref. בְּ)(noun masc. sing. . . . נתך

כְּהַתִּימְךָ ן pref. בַּ bef. ־)(Hiph. inf., suff. 2 pers. sing. masc. [for הַתִּמָּ § 18. rem. 12] . תמם

כְּהִתְכַּנֵּס pref. בְּ)(Hithpa. inf. constr. . . כנס

כַּהֲתֵל pref. id.)(Hiph. inf. constr. . . תלל

כְּהָתֵם pref. id.)(Hiph. inf. constr. . . תמם

כְּהִתְעֹות pref. id.)(Niph. inf. constr. . . תעה

כְהִתְפַּלֵּל ן pref. id.)(Hithpa. inf. constr. d. 7 b ; ו bef. (ְ) פלל

כֹואֵב ן Kal part. act. sing. masc. dec. 7 b . . כאב

כּוּב ן (thorn, paliurus, Syr.) pr. name of an unknown country, Eze. 30. 5.

כֹובֵס Kal part. act. sing. masc. . . . כבס

כֹובַע ן

כֹּובַע ן noun masc. sing. (§ 31. rem. 5) . . כבע

כֹּובַע ן

כֹובַע ן id. constr. st. . . . . . כבע

כֹובָעִים ן id. pl., abs. st. . . . . כבע

כָּוָה Niph. to be burned, scorched.

    כִּי masc. (for כְּוִי § 27. No. VI, 4) brand, mark burnt in, Is. 3. 24.

    כְּוִיָּה fem. a burning, branding, Ex. 21. 25.

    מִכְוָה fem. dec. 10, inflamed part in the body, Le. 13. 24, 25, 28.

כַּו Root not used ; prob. i. q. נָקַב, קָבַב, to hollow out.

    כַּו Chald. masc. dec. 5a, window, Da. 6. 11.

כֹּוחַ in full for כֹּחַ (q. v.) . . . כחח

כֹּוּיָה noun fem. sing. . . . . . כוה

כַּוִּין ן Chald. noun masc., pl. of כַּו dec. 5a כוו

כֹּוכַב noun masc. sing. dec. 2 b [for כַּבְכָּב] כבב

כֹּוכַב id., constr. st. . . . . . . כבב

כֹּוכְבֵי id. pl., constr. st. . . . . כבב

כֹּוכָבִים ן id. pl., abs. st. . . . . . כבב

[כּוּל] to measure, Is. 40. 12. Pilp. כִּלְכֵּל (§ 6. No. 4). —I. to contain.—II. to sustain, hold out, endure.— III. to sustain, maintain, nourish.—IV. to maintain one's cause, Ps. 55. 23. Polp. כָּלְכַּל to be sustained, provided for, 1 Ki. 20. 27. Hiph. הֵכִיל. I. to contain.—II. to sustain, hold out, endure.

כַּלְכֹּל (sustenance) pr. name of a wise man, 1 Ki. 5. 11 ; 1 Ch. 2. 6.

כֻּלָּם (for כָּלָּם) n. m. s., suff. 3 p. pl. m. fr. כֹּל d. 8c כלל

כּוּם Root not used ; Arab. to heap up.

    כִּימָה fem. the constellation of the pleiades.

כָּמָז ן noun masc. sing. . . . . כמז

[כּוּן] Kal not used ; to stand, Arab. to exist, hence Pil. כֹּונֵן.—I. to set up, fix, confirm, establish.— II. to prepare, fashion, form.—III. to adjust, direct, aim, with acc. and עַל against ; abs. to prepare, dispose, apply oneself, Job 8. 8 ; Is. 51. 13. Pul.— I. to be established, Ps. 37. 33.—II. to be prepared, Eze. 28. 13. Hiph. הֵכִין.—I. to set up, establish, strengthen.—II. to constitute, appoint, with עַל over.—III. to adjust, direct, aim, with לְ against —IV. to prepare, make ready ; הֵכִין לֵב לְ to prepare, set his heart, purpose to do anything, or towards any one ; so also abs. (without לֵב comp. 1 Ch. 28. 2. Hoph.—I. to be set up, established, Is. 16. 5.—II. to be prepared, ready. Niph.—I. to be set up, confirmed, fixed, established ; שַׂחַר נָכֹון the fixed day, i. e. full noon ; נְכֹון הַיֹּום the fixed, steady dawn, as opposed to the premature twilight in the East ; metaph. to be upright, right, sincere, true ; אֶל־נָכֹון truly, certainly.—II. to be suitable, becoming.—III. to be prepared, ready. Hithpal. הִכֹּונֵן, הִתְכֹּונֵן.—I. to be established.—II. to prepare oneself, Ps. 59. 5.

    כּוּן (stability) pr. name of a town in Syria, 1 Ch. 18. 8.

    כֵּן.—I. adj. masc. dec. 1a, upright, right, true, honest.—II. adv. (a) right, rightly, well ; (b) so, thus ; כַּאֲשֶׁר—כֵּן, כְּ־כֵּן as—so ; כֵּן—כַּאֲשֶׁר so — as ; (c) with prepositions, אַחֲרֵיכֶן, אַחַר כֵּן afterwards ; בְּכֵן then, so ; לָכֵן אֲשֶׁר therefore, because ; עַל־כֵּן therefore, because ; עַד־כֵּן till now, hitherto, Ne. 2. 16.

    כֵּן Chald. so, thus.

    כֵּן masc. only pl. כַּוָּנִים small cakes ; Chald. כַּן to prepare.

    כִּיּוּן Am. 5. 26, according to Kimchi, cake (i. q. כַּוָּן). Others take it as a pr. name of an idol, called Ῥεμφὰν, Acts 7. 43, the planet Saturn. Vulg. imaginem.

    אָכֵן adv.—I. surely, certainly, truly.—II. but, yet

a Ge. 32. 13. | d De. 24. 7. | g Eze. 22. 24. | j Job 13. 9. | m Ezr. 10. 1. | p Eze. 27. 10. | s 2 Ch. 26. 14. | v Da. 6. 11. | y Am. 5. 26.
b Ps. 86. 7. | e Eze. 21. 12. | h Is. 33. 1. | k Da. 8. 23. | n Ps. 69. 30. | q 1 Sa. 17. 5 ; | t Da. 11. 6. | w Nu. 24. 17. | z Je. 31. 34.
c 1 Ch. 21. 15. | f Ezr. 10. 1. | i Le. 28. 20. | l Is. 19. 14. | o Eze. 38. 5. | Is. 59. 17. | u Ex. 21. 25.

יָכִין (*He shall establish*) pr. name—I. of a son of Simeon, Ge. 46. 10 (for which יָרִיב 1 Ch. 4. 24); Patronym. יָכִינִי Nu. 26. 12.—II. of one of the columns of the temple of Solomon, 1 Ki. 7. 21.

כְּנָיָה, יְכָנְיָהוּ, יְכָנְיָה (whom *the Lord establishes*) pr. name of a king, see יְהוֹיָכִין.

מָכוֹן masc. dec. 3 a.—I. *place, habitation.*— II. *foundation, basis.*

מְכֹנָה, מְכוֹנָה fem. with suff. מְכֹנָתָהּ (comp. § 30. rem. 4 ; § 32. rem. 5 ; § 39. No. 3. rem. 1), pl. מְכֹנוֹת—I. *place*, Ezr. 3. 3.—II. *base, stand.* —III. pr. name of a town in the tribe of Judah, Ne. 11. 28.

נָכוֹן (*established*) pr. name of a threshing-floor, 2 Sa. 6. 6.

תְּכוּנָה fem. dec. 10.—I.—*place, seat*, Job 23. 3. —II. *arrangement*, Eze. 43. 11.—III. *furniture, store*, Na. 2. 10.

כַּנִּים n. m. pl. of [כֵּן] d. 1 b (§ 30. No. III. & r. 1) כון

כּוֹנֵן Pilel pret. 3 pers. sing. masc., or (Job 8. 8) imp. sing. masc. . . . . כון

כּוֹנֲנָה id. imp. sing. masc. with parag. ה . . כון

כּוֹנֲנֶהָ id. pret. 3 pers. sing. masc., suff. 3 pers. s. f. כון

כּוֹנֲנֵהוּ id. imp. sing. masc., suff. 3 pers. sing. masc. כון

כּוֹנָנוּ [for כּוֹנָנוּ from כּוֹנֵן] Pulal pret. 3 pers. pl. כון

כּוֹנֲנוּ Pilel pret. 3 pers. pl. . . . . . כון

כְּנַנְיָהוּ Kh. כּוֹנַנְיָהוּ K. (q. v.) . . . . כון

כּוֹנַנְתָּ Pilel pret. 2 pers. sing. masc. (comp. § 8. rem. 5, and rem. 7) . . . . . . כון

כּוֹנַנְתָּהּ id. id., suff. 3 pers. sing. fem. . . . כון

כּוֹס fem. dec. 1 a.—I. *cup.*—II. *pelican.* The Root is doubtful ; according to Gesenius, it stands for כְּנָס, from כָּנַס *to collect.* Others derive it from כָּסָה *to cover.* But the signification of the obsol. כּוּס may be i. q. כָּסָה *to cover*; whence *to hide, preserve.* Hence perhaps also

כִּיס masc. dec. 1 a, *bag, purse.*

כּוֹסֹה id. with suff. 3 pers. sing. masc. . . כוס

כּוֹסִי id. with suff. 1 pers. sing. . . כוס

כּוֹסָם id. with suff. 3 pers. pl. masc. . . כוס

[כּוּר] *to dig, pierce*, only Ps. 22. 17 (comp. § 21. rem. 1).

כָּרִי masc. (prop. *piercer, stabber*, hence) *an executioner, sheriff*, attached to a kind of body-guard.

כּוּר masc. *a furnace* for smelting metals.

כּוּר עָשָׁן (*smoking furnace*) pr. name of a city

in the tribe of Simeon, 1 Sa. 30. 30, elsewhere called עָשָׁן.

כִּיר masc. only du. כִּירַיִם Le. 11. 35, *pot or jar*, prob. consisting of *two* compartments.

כִּיּוֹר masc. dec. 1 b, pl. ־ִים, ־וֹת.—I. a *firepan* or *basin*, Zec. 12. 6.—II. *basin, wash-basin, laver* —III. *chafingdish*, 1 Sa. 2. 14.—IV. *pulpit*, 2 Ch. 6. 13.

מְכֵרָה fem. dec. 10, *sword*, Ge. 49. 5.

מְכֵרָתִי gentile noun from מְכֵרָה, a place otherwise unknown, 1 Ch. 11. 36.

מְכוּרָה, מְכֹרָה fem. dec. 10, *place of origin or nativity.*

כּוּר noun masc. sing. . . . . כור

כּוּרִין Chald. noun masc., pl. of כֹּר dec. 1 a . כרד

כֹּרֶשׁ pr. name masc., see כֹּרֶשׁ.

כּוּשׁ (*terror*; coll. with the Arab.) pr. name—I. of a son of Ham, Ge. 10. 6, and a country, *Ethiopia*, so called after him, and applied also to its inhabitants, *Ethiopians.*—II. of a Benjamite, Ps. 7. 1.

כּוּשִׁי masc.—I. gent. noun from כּוּשׁ No. 1, a *Cushite, Ethiopian*; pl. כּוּשִׁיִּים, כּוּשִׁים. Fem. כּוּשִׁית an *Ethiopian woman*, Nu. 12. 1.—II. pr. name, *Cushi*, father of the prophet Zephaniah, Zep. 1. 1.

כּוּשָׁן fem. i. q. כּוּשׁ *Ethiopia*, Hab. 3. 7.

כּוּשַׁן רִשְׁעָתַיִם (*Ethiopian of great wickedness*) pr. name of a king of Mesopotamia, Ju. 3. 8, 10.

כּוּשִׁי gent. noun masc. from the preced. . כוש

כּוּשִׁים id. pl. . . . . כוש

כֹּשֵׁל Kal part. act. sing. masc. . . . . כשל

כּוּשָׁן pr. name of a country . . . . כוש

כּוּשַׁן pr. name in compos. כּו' רִשְׁעָתַיִם . . כוש

כּוּת pr. n. of a region where the ten tribes were colonised after the depopulation of their kingdom, 2 Ki. 17. 30, called כּוּתָה in ver. 24.

כְּזֹאֵב pref. כְּ bef. (ּ) ✗ pr. name masc. . . . זאב

כִּזְאֵבִים pref. id. ✗ noun masc., pl. of זְאֵב dec. 1 a זאב

כָּזֹאת pref. כְּ or ✗ q. v. ✗ pron. demon. fem. ✗ זה

כְּזֹאת sing., see . . . . . .

[כָּזַב] *to lie, speak falsehood*, Ps. 116. 11. Pi.—I. *to lie, deceive.*—II. metaph. *to deceive, fail* of water, Is. 58. 11. Hiph. *to convict of falsehood*, Job 24. 25. Niph. *to be proved false, fallacious.*

כָּזָב masc. dec. 4 a, *lie, falsehood.*

כֹּזְבָא (*lying, false*) pr. name of a place, 1 Ch. 4. 22.

כָּזְבִּי (id.) pr. name of a Midianitish princess, Nu. 25. 15, 18.

a Ps. 90. 17.   c Ps. 90. 17.   e Ps. 68. 10.   g Eze. 23. 31.   h Ge. 23. 5.   i Ps. 16. 5.   k Ps. 11. 6.   Ezr. 7. 22.   Ge. 45. 23.

b Is. 45. 13.   d Ps. 8. 4.   f Ge. 40. 11.   ff Eze. 22. 27.

כְּזִיב   pr. name of a town in the tribe of Judah, Ge. 38. 5.

אַכְזָב   adj. masc. false, deceitful, failing.

אַכְזִיב   (false, deceitful) pr. name—I. of a town in the tribe of Asher.—II. of a town in the tribe of Judah.

כָּזָב	noun masc. sing. dec. 4 a . . .	כזב
כִּזֵּב	Piel pret. 3 pers. sing. masc. . .	כזב
כֹּזֵב	Kal part. act. sing. masc. . . .	כזב
כֹּזְבָא	pr. name of a place . . .	כזב
כֹזְבָה	(pref. כְּ)(pr. name masc.; 1 bef. (וֹ)	זבה
כָּזְבִּי	pr. name fem.	כזב
כְּזָבֵיהֶם	noun masc. pl., suff. 3 pers. pl. masc. from כָּזָב dec. 4 a . .	כזב
כְּזָבִים	id. pl., abs. st. . . .	כזב
כָּזֶה / כָּזֶה	(וְ) pref. כְּ (see lett. כ))(pron. demon. masc. and fem. sing.	זה
כַּזָּהָב	pref. כַּ for כְּהַ)(noun masc. sing dec. 4 a .	זהב
כְּזֹהַר	pref. כְּ)(noun masc. sing. . .	זהר
כְּזֵיתֵי	pref. id.)(noun fem. pl. [of זַיִת comp. § 39, 4. rem. 1]	זוה
כַּזּוֹנָה	pref. כַּ for כְּהַ)(Kal part. act. fem. dec. 10, from זוֹנָה masc.	זנה
כְּזֹחֲלֵי	pref. כְּ)(Kal part. act. pl. c. masc. from [זֹחֵל] dec. 7 b . . .	זחל
כַּזַּיִת / כִּזַיִת	pref. כַּ f. כְּהַ / pref. כְּ q. v.)(noun masc. sing. dec. 6 h	זית
כְּזִכְרִי	pref. כְּ bef. (וֹ))(Kal inf. constr. .	זכר
וּכְזִמַנָּם	(וְ) pref. id.)(noun masc. sing., suff. 3 pers. pl. masc. from זְמָן dec. 8 a . .	זמן
כְּזִמָּתְכֶנָה	pref. כְּ)(noun fem. sing., suff. 2 pers. pl. fem. (§ 3. rem. 5) from זִמָּה dec. 10	זמם

כָּזַר   Root not used; Syr. to be valiant, daring.

אַכְזָר   adj. masc.—I. bold, daring, Job 41. 2.—II. cruel, fierce.—III. deadly of poison, De. 32. 33. Vulg. insanabile, incurable.

אַכְזָרִי   adj. masc. fierce, cruel.

אַכְזְרִיּוּת   fem. cruelty, fierceness, Pr. 27. 4.

כְּזֹרֵחַ	pref. כְּ bef. (וֹ))(Kal inf. constr. .	זרח
כְּזֶרֶם	pref. כְּ)(noun masc. sing. . .	זרם
כְּזַרְעֵי	pref. id.)(noun masc. sing. (suff. זַרְעוֹ) dec. 6 a (§ 35. rem. 5)	זרע
כְּזֹרֵעַ	pref. כְּ bef. (וֹ))(id. constr. st. (§ 35. rem. 7)	זרע
כֹּחַ	(וְ) noun masc. sing. dec. 1 a . .	כחח
כַּחֲבַצֶּלֶת	pref. כַּ bef. (וַ))(noun fem. sing. [for חֲבַצֶּלֶת, comp. § 35. rem. 2] . . .	חבצל

כְּחֻנֵּי	pref. כְּ for כְּהַ)(bef. כְּהָ for כְּהַ)(n. m. s. d. 8 a	חנן
כַּחֲנָבִים	pref. כַּ bef. (וַ))(noun m., pl. of חָנָב d. 4 c	חנב

כָּחַד   Pi. כִּחֵד (§ 14. rem. 1) to keep back, conceal, with acc. of the thing and לְ or מִן of the person. Hiph.—I. to hide, Job 20. 12.—II. to destroy, bring to nought. Niph.—I. to be concealed.—II. to be destroyed.

כִּחֵד	Piel pret. 3 pers. sing. masc. (§ 14. rem. 1)	כחד
כַּחֲדָה	Chald. pref. כַּ bef. (וַ))(num. adj. fem. of חַד, with pref. כַּ adv. . . .	אחד
כְּחַדְגוּ / כְחַדֻּנוּ	} Piel pref. 3 p. pl. (§ 14. r. 1, comp. § 8. r. 7)	כחד
כַּחֲדֹק	pref. כְּ)(noun masc. sing.	חדק
כִּחַדְתִּי	Piel pret. 1 pers. sing. (§ 14. rem. 1) .	כחד
כֹּחָהּ	noun masc. s., suff. 3 pers. s. f. fr. כֹּחַ d. 1 a	כחח
כֹּחוֹ	id. with suff. 3 pers. sing. masc.	כחח
כֹּחִי	Kh. כֹּחוֹ q. v., K. כֹּחִי (q. v.)	כחח
כַּחוּט	pref. כַּ f. כְּהַ / pref. כְּ q. v. } noun masc. sing.	חוט
כְּחוּט		
כַּחוֹמָא	pref. כַּ for כְּהַ)(Kal part. act. masc. dec. 7 b	חטא
וְכָחוֹל / וּכְחוֹל	(וְ) pref. id. / (וּ) pref. כְּ } noun masc. sing.; 1 bef. (וֹ)	חול
כַּחוֹלָה	pref. id.)(Kal part. act. fem. d. 10, from חָלָה m.	חלה
כַּחוֹמָה	(וֹ) pref. id.)(noun fem. sing. d. 10; 1 bef. (וֹ)	חמה
וְכַחוּץ	(וְ) pref. כְּ for כְּהַ)(noun masc. sing. dec. 1 a	חוץ
כַּחוֹתָם	pref. id.)(noun masc. sing. (no vowel change)	חתם
כַּחֲזֵה	pref. id.)(noun m. sing., constr. of חָזֶה d. 9 b	חזה
כְּחֶזְיוֹן	pref. כְּ)(noun masc. sing., constr. of חִזָּיוֹן dec. 3 c (§ 32. rem. 3) . .	חזה
וּכְחֶזְקָתוֹ	(וּ) pref. id.)(noun fem. sing. constr. [of חֶזְקָה, no pi.]; 1 bef. (וֹ)	חזק

כָּחַח   Root not used; i. q. Syr. כחי to pant, then, to exert oneself (Gesenius).

כֹּחַ, once כּוֹחַ (Da. 11. 6) masc. dec. 1 a.—I. strength, vigour, power, ability.—II. substance, wealth, riches.—III. a species of lizard, Le. 11. 30

כַּחֲטָאֵינוּ	pref. כַּ bef. (וַ))(noun masc. pl., suff. 1 pers. pl. from חֵטְא dec. 6 (§ 35. rem. 6)	חטא
כַּחַטָּאת	pref. כַּ for כְּהַ)(n.f.s. (§ 39. No.4, & § 44.r.5)	חטא
כְּחַטֹּאתֵיכֶם	pref. כְּ)(id. pl. (חַטֹּאת for חַטָּאֹת), suff. 2 pers. pl. masc.	חטא
כְּחֹטְבֵי	pref. id.)(Kal part. act. pl. c. from חֹטֵב d. 7 b	חטב
כֹּחִי	noun m. sing., suff. 1 pers. sing from כֹּחַ d. 1 a	כחח
כַּחַיִל	pref. כַּ for כְּהַ)(noun masc. sing. dec. 6 h	חול
כְּחַיִל	pref. כְּ)(id. constr. st. . .	חול

a Mi. 2. 11.   e Eze. 16. 31.   i Est. 9. 27.   m Is. 35. 1.   r Job 15. 18.   u Ju. 16. 12.   z Je. 4. 31.   f Job 20. 8.   k Je. 46. 22.
b Ps. 116. 11.   f Mi. 7. 17.   j Ps. 52. 10.   n 1 Ki. 11. 32.   s Is. 3. 9.   v Ca. 4. 3.   a Pr. 18. 11.   g Ps. 103. 10.   l 1 Ki. 20. 25.
c Am. 2. 4.   g Ps. 52. 10.   k Ex. 16. 31.   o 1 Sa. 3. 18.   t Mi. 7. 4.   w Ee. 9. 2.   b Is. 51. 23.   h Le. 26. 21.   m Job 20. 18.
d Da. 12.   h Je. 17. 2.   l Nu. 11. 7.   q Da. 2. 35.   q Ps. 102. 24.   x Ps. 78. 27.   c Nu. 18. 18.

כְּחָךְ
כְּחָֽךְ֒
כְּחָה֒
} noun masc. sing., suff. 2 pers. sing. masc. from כֹּחַ dec. 1a (§ 3. rem. 2) { כחח

כְּחַבִּ֒ י pref. כְּ) Piel inf. constr. by Chaldaism [for § 24. rem. 20] חכה

כְּחַכֶם֒ noun m. s., suff. 2 pers. pl. m. from כֹּחַ d. 1a כחח

כְּחָכְמַת pref. כְּ) noun fem. sing., constr. of חָכְמָה Chald. dec. 8a (no pl.) . . . חכם

כְּחָכְמָתָֽךְ֒ pref. id.) id. with suff. 2 p. s. m. for חָכְמָתְךָ חכם

[כָּחַל] to blacken or paint the eyes with stibium, a kind of powder, see פּוּךְ, Eze. 23. 40.

כַּחֵלֶב֒ pref. כַּ for כְּהַ) noun masc. sing. dec. 6 חלב
כְּחֵלֶב֒ pref. כְּ q. v. ((§ 35. rem. 6) }

כְּחֵלֶב֒ pref. כְּ for כְּהַ, bef. הָ for כְּהָ) n. m. dec. 4c חלב
כַּחֲלוֹם֒ pref. כַּ bef. (-:)) noun masc. sing. dec. 1a חלם
כֶּחָלָל֒ pref. כְּ for כְּהַ, bef. הָ for כְּהָ) adj. m. s. d. 4c חלל
כְּחֹלְלִים֒ pref. כְּ) Kal part. act. pl. of [חֹלֵל] dec. 7b חלל
כַּחֲלִילִים֒ pref. כַּ bef. (-:)) noun m., pl. of חָלִיל dec. 3a חלל
כַּחֲלֹמוֹ֒ pref. id.) noun masc. sing., suff. 3 pers. sing. masc. from חֲלוֹם dec. 1a חלם
כְּחֹלְמִים֒ pref. כְּ) Kal part. act. m., pl. of חֹלֵם dec. 7b חלם
כַּחֲלָמִישׁ֒ pref. כַּ for כְּהַ) noun masc. sing. (constr. חַלָּמִישׁ) dec. 3c . . . חלמש
כְּחֵלֶק֒ pref. כְּ) noun masc. sing. d. 6 (§ 35. r. 6) חלק
כַּחֲלַקְלַקּוֹת֒ pref. כַּ bef. (-:)) noun pl. fem. [from חֲלַקְלַק] חלק
כְּחַלְתְּ֒ Kal pret. 2 pers. sing. fem. כחל
כֹּחַם֒ pref. כְּ) noun masc. sing. dec. 8c . חמם
כֹּחָם֒ noun m. s., suff. 3 pers. pl. m. from כֹּחַ d. 1a כחח
כַּחֲמָה֒ pref. כַּ for כְּהַ) noun fem. sing. dec. 10 חמם
כַּחֲמִין֒ pref. id.) noun masc. sing. חמץ
כַחֹמֶר֒ } pref. id. } noun masc. sing. dec. 6c חמר
כְּחֹמֶר֒ } pref. כְּ }
כַּחֲמֵשֶׁת֒ pref. כַּ bef. (-:)) num. card. masc. constr. of חֲמִשָּׁה (§ 39. No. 4. rem. 1) from חָמֵשׁ fem. חמש
כַּחֲמָתִי֒ pref. id.) noun fem. sing., suff. 1 pers. sing. from חֵמָה dec. 11b . . . יחם
כַּחֶסֶד֒ pref. כַּ for כְּהַ) noun masc. sing. dec. 6a חסד
כְּחַסְדְּךָ֒
כְּחַסְדֶּךָ֒ } pref. כְּ) id., suff. 2 pers. sing. masc. . חסד
כַּחֲצֵי֒ pref. כַּ bef. (-:)) noun masc. sing. dec. 6i (suff. חָצְיוֹ § 35. rem. 14) . . חצה
כַּחֲצָאִים֒ pref. כְּ) noun masc., pl. of חֵץ dec. 8b . חצץ
כֶּחָצִיר֒ pref. כַּ bef. (-:)) constr. of the foll. . חצר
כְּחָצִיר֒ pref. כְּ for כְּהַ, bef. הָ for כְּהָ) noun m. d. 3a חצר

כַּחֲצֹת pref. כַּ bef. (-:)) n. m. s., consti. of [חֲצוֹת] d. 3a חצה
כְּחֻקָּת֒ pref. כְּ) noun fem. sing., constr. of חֻקָּה d. 10 חקק
כְּחֻקָּתָם֒ pref. id.) id. pl., suff. 3 pers. pl. masc. חקק
כַּחֶרֶב֒ pref. כַּ f. כְּהַ) noun fem. sing. (suff. חַרְבִּי)
כְּחֶרֶב֒ pref. כְּ q. v. } dec. 6a } חרב
כְּחֶרֶב֒ pref. id.) id. noun masc. sing. } חרב
כַּחֲרָשֵׁי֒ pref. כַּ for כְּהַ) n. m. s. (pl. c. חֲרָשֵׁי) d. 6a חרש
כֶּחָרָשׁ֒ pref. כְּ) adj. s. m. d. 7b [for חָרֵשׁ § 36. No. 1] חרש

כָּחַשׁ to fail, waste away, Ps. 109. 24. Pi. כִּחֵשׁ (§ 14. rem. 1).—I. to deny; with בְּ of the person and thing, to disavow.—II. to lie, to speak falsehood, with לְ.—III. to fail, deceive, flatter. Niph. to feign, flatter, De. 33. 29. Hithp. id. 2 Sa. 22. 45.

כַּחַשׁ masc. dec. 6d.—I. leanness, Job 16. 8.—II. lie, falsehood, deceit.

כָּחָשׁ m. a lying, false, only pl. כָּחָשִׁים Is. 30. 9.

כָּחַשׁ } noun masc. sing. dec. 6d . . כחש
כַּחֵשׁ }
כַּחֵשׁ }) Piel inf. abs. or constr. (§ 14. rem. 1) . כחש
כִּחֵשׁ }
וַיְכַחֵשׁ }) id. pret. 3 pers. sing. masc. (§ 10. rem. 1) . כחש
כִּחֵשׁ }
כִּחֲשׁוּ id. pret. 3 pers. pl. . . . כחש
כַּחֲשִׁי or כַּחַשׁ, n. m. s., suff. 1 p. s. from כַּחַשׁ d. 6d כחש
כְּחֶשְׁכָּה pref. כַּ bef. (-:)) noun fem. sing. dec. 10 . חשך
כֶּחָשִׁים noun m. pl. [of כַּחַשׁ for כַּחַשׁ, dec. 1b (§ 30. rem. 3, comp. also § 42. No. 3, note) כחש
כִּחַשְׁתִּי) Piel pret. 1 pers. sing. (§ 14. rem. 1) . כחש
כֶּחָתָן֒ pref. כַּ for כְּהַ, bef. הָ for כְּהַ) and
כְּחָתָן֒ pref. כְּ q. v.) noun masc. sing. dec. 4c } חתן
כְּחָתֵף֒ pref. id.) noun masc. sing. . . . חתף
כְּטָהֳרַת pref. id.) n. fem. s., constr. of טָהֳרָה (no pl.) טהר
כַּטּוֹב֒ pref. כַּ for כְּהַ) adj. or subst. and
כְּטוֹב֒ pref. כְּ q. v.) inf. or adj. m. sing. dec. 1a } טוב
כְּטִיט֒ pref. id.) noun masc. sing. [for טָאִיט] טוא
כַּטַּל֒) pref. כַּ for כְּהַ) noun masc. sing. dec. 8a;
כְּטַל֒) pref. כְּ q. v.) bef. (-:) } טלל
כְּטָמֵא֒ pref. כַּ for כְּהַ) adj. masc. sing. dec. 4a (constr. טָמֵא § 34. rem. 1) . . טמא
כְּטֻמְאַת pref. כְּ) noun f. s., constr. of טֻמְאָה d. 10 טמא
כְּטֻמְאָתָם֒ pref. id.) id., suff. 3 pers. pl. masc. . טמא
כְּטַעֲמוֹ֒ pref. id.) n. m. s. d. 6d (suff. טַעְמוֹ § 35. r. 5) טעם

כִּי) particle.—I. supposed (by Gesenius and Fürst, but disputed by Prof. Lee) to be primarily a relative pron. i. q. אֲשֶׁר which, espec. in the passages

* Ju. 16. 6, 15.   ʰ Ps. 119. 70.   ⁿ Ps. 126. 1.   ʳ Pr. 10. 26.   ᵇ Ps. 129. 6.   ᵉ Ps. 22. 16.   ˡ Le. 5. 21.   ᶠ Job 31. 28.   ⁿ 2 Ch. 30. 19.
ᵇ Pr. 5. 10.   ⁱ Le. 4. 26.   ° 1 Sa. 30. 24.   ˢ Job 27. 16.   ᶜ Ex. 11. 4.   ᶠ Ps. 38. 14.   ᵐ Le. 5. 22;   ᵍ Pr. 30. 9.   ° Pr. 19. 12.
ᶜ Pr. 24. 10.   ᵏ Job 10. 10.   ᵖ Je. 23. 12.   ᵗ Eze. 25. 14.   ᵈ Nu. 9. 14.   ᵍ Ps. 109. 24.   Job 8. 18.   ʰ Is. 61. 10.   ᵖ Is. 64. 5.
ᵈ Ho. 6. 9.   ˡ Ps. 87. 7.   ᵠ Eze. 23. 40.   ᵘ Ge. 21. 23.   ᵉ 2 Ki. 17. 34.   ʰ Ho. 10. 13.   ʰ Job 16. 8.   ⁱ Ps. 76. 6.   ᵠ Eze. 39. 24.
ᵉ Le. 26. 20.   ᵐ Je. 48. 36.   ʳ Pr. 20. 29.   ˣ Eze. 16. 51.   ᶠ Ps. 64. 4.   ⁱ Ps. 139. 12.   ⁱ Pr. 23. 28.   Nu. 11. 1.
ᶠ 1 Ki. 2. 6.   ⁿ Ge. 41. 12.   Ps. 127. 1.   Ca. 6. 10.   ᵃ Is. 25. 5.   Zec. 13. 4.   ʲ Is. 30. 9.

Ge. 3. 19 (כִּי מִמֶּנָּה); Ge. 4. 25 (כִּי הֲרָגוֹ); Is. 54. 6 (כִּי תְמָאֵס); Is. 57. 20.—II. relat. conj. (a) *that*, especially after the verbs of seeing, knowing, hearing, believing, saying, &c. as מִי הִגִּיד לְךָ כִּי *who told thee that*, &c.; also after an adv. e. g. Job 12. 2, *no doubt that* (כִּי) *ye are the people*; הֲכִי *is it that? is it not that?* עַל כִּי יַעַן כִּי *on account of, that, because*; עַד כִּי *until that*; אֶפֶס כִּי *except that*; תַּחַת כִּי עֵקֶב כִּי *because that*; (b) *for, because*; וְכִי־כִּי *because—and because*; (c) *but*, preceded by a negation, comp. Ge. 24. 4; also, *nay but, nay for*, espec. after an interrogation including a negation though not expressed, comp. Job 31. 14; without a negation, *but yet, nevertheless*; (d) of time, *if; when; so, then*, comp. Nu. 22. 33.—III. כִּי אִם (a) *that if*, the אִם referring to a parenthetic clause, e. g. 1 Sa. 20. 9; *that since; for if; but if*; (b) *unless, except, if not; but; yet, nevertheless; that*.

כִּי noun masc. sing. [for כִּוִי]   כוה

כִּי Kh. כִּי q. v. K. כֹּה (q. v.)   כה

כִּיאֹר / כִּיאֹר } pref. כַּ for כָּה) noun masc. sing.} dec. 1 a   יאר

כִּיאֹר pref. כְּ) n.m. יְאֹר with pref. כְּ [for כִּיאֹר, כִּיאֹר   יאר

כִּיבוּסִי pref. id.) gent. n. יְבוּסִי (see preced.) fr. יְבוּס   בום

כִּיבִין pref. כְּ) pr. name masc.   בין

[כִּיד] masc. dec. 1 a, *ruin, destruction*, Job 21. 20.

כִּידוֹן masc.—I. *spear, or javelin*.—II. גֹּרֶן כִּי (*threshing-floor of spears*) pr. name of a place near Jerusalem, 1 Ch. 13. 9; for which גֹּרֶן נָכוֹן 2 Sa. 6. 6.

כְּיַד pref. כְּ) noun com. s., constr. of יָד d. 2 a   יד

כִּידוֹ noun m. s., suff. 3 pers. s. m. fr. כִּיד d. 1 a   כיד

כִּידוֹדֵי noun masc. pl. constr. from [כִּידוֹד] dec. 1 b   כדד

כִּידוֹן וְ) noun masc. sing.   כיד

כִּידֵי pref. כְּ [for כְּיָדֵי, כִּי) (noun com. pl. constr. from יָד dec. 2 a   יד

כִּידוֹן וְ) noun masc. sing., also pr. name masc. the most sacred name of God with the vowels of אֲדֹנָי; pref. כַּ bef. (-:)   הוה

כַּיֹּלֵדָה pref. כַּ for כָּה) Kal part. act. s. f. of יֹלֵד   ילד

כַּיּוֹם pref. id.) noun masc. sing. irr. (§ 45);   יום
כְּיוֹם כְ׳ pref. כְּ) bef. (:)

כִּיּוּן noun masc. sing.   כון

כַּיּוֹנָה pref. כַ for כָּה) noun fem. sing. dec 10;
כְּיוֹנָה כְ׳ pref. כְּ q. v. } bef. (:)   יונה

כִּיּוּנֵי pref. כְּ) noun fem. pl., constr. st.   זנה

כַּיּוֹנִים וְ) pref. כַּ f. כָּה } id. pl., abs. st.   יונה
כְּיוֹנִים כְ׳ pref. כְּ q. v. }

כַּיֹּנֵק pref. כַּ for כָּה) noun masc. sing. dec. 7 b   ענ

כִּיּוֹר noun masc. sing. dec. 1 b   כור

כְּיֹרְדֵי pref. כְּ) Kal part. act. pl. c. m. fr. יֹרֵד d. 7 b   ירד

כִּיּוֹרִים noun masc., pl. of כִּיּוֹר dec. 1 b   כור

כִּיטוֹב Kh. q. v., K. (כְּטוֹב כִּי טוֹב (q. v.)   טוב

כַּיַּיִן pref. כַּ) noun masc. sing. dec. 6 h   יון

כְּיֵין pref. כְּ) id., constr. st.   יון

כַּיֹּלֵדָה pref. כַּ for כָּה) Kal part. act. s., f. of יֹלֵד   ילד

כִּילַפּוֹת וְ) noun pl. fem.   כלף

כַּיֶּלֶק / כַּיָּלֶק } pref. כַּ f. כָּה } noun masc. s. (§ 35. r. 2)   ילק
כְּיֶלֶק pref. כְּ q. v. }

כַּיָּם pref. כַּ for כָּה) noun masc. sing. dec 8 a   ים

כִּימָה וְ׳ noun fem. sing.   כום

כִּימוֹת pref. כְּ [for כְּיָמוֹת, כִּי) (n.m. with pl. f. term., constr. of יָמוֹת [as if fr. יָם] see יוֹם (§ 45)   יום

כִּימֵי וְ׳ pref. כְּ [for כְּיָמֵי, כִּי) (id. pl. masc., constr. of יָמִים   יום

כְּיָמֶיךָ וּ) pref. כְּ) id. pl. with suff. 2 p. s. m.; וּ bef. (:)   יום

כַּיָּמִים pref. כַּ f. כָּה } id. pl. abs. masc.   יום
כְּיָמִים כְ׳ pref. כְּ q. v. }

כִּים noun masc. sing. dec. 1 a   כום

כִּיעֲנִים Kh. (pl. of עֹנָה כִּי עֹנָה q. v.); K.   כִּיעֲנִים
pref. כַּ for כָּה) noun m., pl. of יַעַן d. 5 a   יען

כִּיקוֹד pref. כְּ [for כְּיָקוֹד, כִּי) (noun masc. sing.   יקד

כִּיקָר pref. כְּ [for כְּיָקָר, כִּי) (adj. masc. sing., constr. of יָקָר dec. 4 a   יקר

כְּיִרְאָתְךָ וּ) pref. כְּ) noun fem. sing., suff. 2 pers. sing. masc. fr. יִרְאָה (no pl.); וּ bef. (:)   ירא

כִּירוּשָׁלַ͏ִם pref. כְּ [for כְּיָרוּ, כִּי) (pr. name of a place   ירה

כִּירוֹת noun masc. with pl. f. term. fr. כִּיּוֹר dec. 1 b   כור

כְּיֶרַח pref. כְּ) noun masc. sing. dec. 4 a   ירח

כִּירְחֵי pref. id.) (n. m. pl. c. fr. יֶרַח d. 6 a (§ 35. r. 5)   ירח

כִּיּרִים וְ) noun masc., du. of [כִּיר] dec. 1 a   כור

כַּיְרִיעָה pref. כַּ for כָּה) noun fem. sing. dec. 10   ירע

כִּירִיעוֹת pref. כְּ [for כִּיר, כִּי) (id. pl.   ירע

כִּירָק כְ׳ pref. כְּ) noun masc. sing.; וּ bef. (:)   ירק

כִּישָׁן pref. id.) adj. masc. sing. dec. 5 a   ישן

כַּיָּשָׁר וְ) pref. כַּ for כָּה) adj. m. s. d. 4 a; וּ bef. (:)   ישר

כִּישְׂרָאֵל pref. id.) (pr. name of a people   שרה

כִּיתְרוֹן transp. and contr. [for כִּיתְרוֹן], noun masc. sing., יִתְרוֹן, with pref. כְּ   יתר

כַּכָּבוֹד pref. כַּ for כָּה) noun masc. sing. dec. 3 a   נבד

a Is. 3. 24. f Job 41. 21. i Ho. 11. 11. † Ju. 16. 25. ‡ Je. 51. 27. ° Ge. 29. 20. ♭ Ps. 90. 11. ‖ Le. 11. 35. ♯ Ps. 37. 2.
b 2 Sa. 12. 10. g Ge. 27. 23. k Eze. 7. 16. * Job 32. 19. ♪ Job 9. 9. " La. 4. 3. ‖ 1 Ki. 7. 38. ‖ Ca. 1. 15. † Ps. 78. 65.
Je. 46. 8. h Je. 50. 42. ⁎ Ca. 5. 12. ° Je. 22. 23. ♩ Ps. 90. 15. ° Is. 10. 16. ⁕ Ps. 89. 38. ‖ Ca. 1. 5. ‖ Ec. 2. 13.
d Job 21. 20. i Ho. 2. 17. ‖ Is. 53. 2. d Ps. 74. 6. ⁑ Job 7. 1. ♦ Ps. 37. 20. ‖ Job 29. 2. ‖ Ge. 9. 5. ‖ Eze. 3. 21.
Job 41. 11. k Am. 5. 26. ♭ 2 Ch. 4. 6. ✝ Na. 3. 15. ♦ De. 33. 25. ♫ Pr. 1. 12.

כבד	pref. בְּ bef.)(id., constr. st.	בִּכְבוֹד־
כבב	the foll. with suff. 3 pers. pl. masc.	בִּכְבֵיהֶם׳
כבב	ו noun masc. pl. abs. from כּוֹכָב dec. 2 b	וְכֹכָבִים
כבש	pref. כְּ)(noun masc. sing. dec. 6 a	בְּכֶבֶשׂ
	כָּכָה adv. thus; contr. from כָּה כָּה i. q. כֹּה כֹּה so and so. Others take it as the pref. כ with suff., hoc tibi.	וְ׳
כהן	pref. בַּ for בְּהַ)(noun masc. sing. dec. 7 b	בַּכֹּהֵן
כבב	pref. כְּ)(noun m. pl. constr. from כּוֹכָב d. 2 b	כְּכוֹכְבֵי
כבב	pref. בַּ for בְּהַ)(id. pl., abs. st.	בַּכּוֹכָבִים
כום	pref. בְּ)(noun fem. sing. dec. 1 a	בְּכוֹם׳
כחח	ו pref. id.)(noun m. sing. dec. 1 a; ו bef.	בְּכֹחִי
סחח	pref. id.)(id., suff. 3 pers. pl. masc.	בְּכֹחָם׳
כור	pref. בְּ)(noun masc. sing. dec. 1 b	בְּכוּר׳
כבב	defect. for בְּכוֹכְבֵי (q. v.)	בְּכֹכְבֵי
כלל	pref. בַּ f. בְּהַ)(noun masc. sing. dec. 8 c (§ 37. rem. 2); ו bef.	בַּכֹּל֫ בְּכֹל֫ וּכְכֹל־
כלב	pref. בַּ f. בְּהַ)(noun masc. sing. (pl. c. בַּכְּלָבִ׳) dec. 6 a	בַּכֶּ֫לֶב בַּכְּלָבִ׳
כלל	ו pref. בַּ for בְּהַ, &)(noun fem. sing. d. 10	בַּכַּלָּה־
כלב	pref. בְּ bef.)(noun masc. sing.	בְּכֶלְיוֹב־
כלה	ו pref. כְּ)(Piel inf. constr. d. 1 b; ו bef.	בְּכַלּוֹת
כלה	pref. בְּ bef.)(Kal inf. constr.	בְּכַלּוֹת׳
כלה	pref. בְּ)(Piel inf. (כַּלּוֹת), suff. 2 pers. s. m.	בְּכַלּוֹתְךָ־
כלה	ו pref. id.)(id., suff. 3 pers. pl. masc.; ו bef.	בְּכַלּוֹתָם
כלה	pref. בְּ bef.)(pl. constr. of the foll.	בִּכְלֵי
כלה	pref. id.)(noun masc. sing. irr. (§ 45)	בִּכְלִי
כלה	pref. בְּ)(for כַלּוֹת Piel inf. c. dec. 1 b	בְּכַלּוֹת
כלה	pref. id.)(id., suff. 3 pers. sing. masc.	בְּכַלֹּתוֹ
כלה	pref. id.)(id., suff. 2 pers. sing. masc.	בְּכַלֹּתְךָ
כ	pref. prep. כ with suff. 3 p. pl. m. (§ 5 parad.)	כָּכֶם
כנר	pref. בַּ for בְּהַ)(noun masc. sing. dec. 1 b	בַּכִּנּוֹר־
כנף	pref. בְּ)(n. fem. pl. c. from כָּנָף d. 4 a (§ 33. r. 1)	בְּכַנְפֵי׳
כסף	ו pref. בַּ for בְּהַ)(noun masc. sing. dec. 6 a (for כֶּסֶף § 35. rem. 2)	בַּכַּ֫סֶף׳
כפף	pref. בְּ)(noun fem. sing. dec. 8 d	בְּכַף
	ו pref. בַּ for בְּהַ)(noun masc. sing. dec. 1 a	בַּכְּפִיר־ בִּכְפִיר
כפר	pref. בַּ for בְּהַ)(id. pl., abs. st.	בַּכְּפִירִים׳
כפר	pref. id.)(noun masc. sing. dec. 1 a	בַּכְּפֹר־
כפר	defect. for בַּכְּפִירִים (q. v.)	בַּכְּפֵרִים׳
כרר	noun fem. sing. dec. 2 b [for כְּרְכָּר]	בִּכָּר
כרר	ו id., constr. st.	בִּכַּר
כרר	id. pl. fem. constr. [of בִּכָּרוֹת]	בִּכְּרוֹת

כרר	noun pl. masc. constr. (of בִּכָּרִים)	בִּכְּרֵי
כרר	pref. בְּ)(n. m., pl. of כַּר dec. 8 (§ 37. rem. 7)	בְּכָּרִים׳
כרר	noun fem. with du. masc. term. from כִּכָּר dec. 2 b [for בִּכְרָר]	בִּכְרַיִם׳
כרר	id. pl., abs. st.	בִּכָּרִים
כרר	id. du. (see כִּכָּר under the Root)	בִּכָּרַיִם׳
כרר	Chald. id. pl. abs. st.	בְּכִרִין
כרר	pref. בְּ)(pr. name of a place	בְּכַרְכְּמִישׁ
כרם	ו pref. בַּ for בְּהַ)(pr. name of a place; ו bef.	בַּכַּרְמֶל׳
כתב	Ch. pref. בְּ bef.)(n. m., constr. of כְּתָב d. 1 b	בִּכְתָב׳
כתב	pref. בְּ)(noun masc. sing., suff. 3 pers. sing. fem. from כְּתָב dec. 1 (§ 30. rem. 1)	בְּכָתְבָהּ
כתב	pref. id.)(id. with suff. 3 pers. pl. masc.	בְּכָתְבָם
כתב	pref. בַּ for בְּהַ)(Kal part. pass. s. m. d. 3 a	בַּכָּתוּב
כול	ו Kal pret. 3 pers. sing. masc.	כָּל׳
כלל	ו noun masc. sing. dec. 8 c, comp. § 37. rem. 2 (Chald. dec. 5)	כֹּל כָּל־ וְכָל־

[כָּלָא] I. to shut up, confine; intrans. to be shut up, Hag. **1.** 10.—II. to restrain, withhold, with מִן of the person or thing. Niph. to be restrained.

כֶּלֶא masc. dec. 6 a (with suff. כִּלְאוֹ).—I. prison, and so when preceded by בַּיִת.—II. separation, hence du. כִּלְאַיִם separate or distinct species of animals, seeds or materials for clothing, Le. 19. 19; De. 22. 9.

כְּלוּא masc. prison, Je. 37. 4; 52. 31, Keri, Kheth. כְּלִיא.

מִכְלָה masc. (for מִכְלָא) pl. c. מִכְלְאוֹת fold or pen for flocks, sheepfold.

כלא	defect. for כְּלוּא (q. v.)	כְּלָא־
כלא	noun masc. sing. (suff. כִּלְאוֹ) dec. 6 a	כֶּלֶא
כלל	Ch. by Syriasm [for כְּלָא], emph. of כֹּל (q. v.)	כֹּלָּא
כלל	for כֻּלֹּה q. v. (§ 3. rem. 3)	כֻּלָּא־
	pr. name of a son of David, 2 Sa. 3. 3. Etymon uncertain.	כִּלְאָב
כלא	Kal pret. 3 pers. sing. fem.	כָּלְאָה־
לאה	ו pref. כְּ)(pr. name fem.; ו bef.	כְלֵאָה
כלא	Kal pret. 3 pers. pl.	כָּלְאוּ׳
כלא	id. pret. 3 pers. sing. masc., suff. 3 pers. s. m.	כְּלָאוֹ׳
כלא	noun m. s., suff. 3 p. s. m. from כֶּלֶא d. 6 a	כִּלְאוֹ׳
כלא	id. pl., abs. st.	כְּלָאִים׳
כלא	id. dual, abs. st.	כִּלְאַ֫יִם כִּלְאָ֫יִם׳

a Is. 17. 3.   f Ezr. 2. 69.   k Pr. 26. 11.   o 2 Sa. 11. 19.   s Zec. 5. 9.   w Is. 5. 29.   a 2 Ki. 5. 23.   l Is. 40. 12.   p Hag. 1. 10.
b Ese. 32. 7.   g Zec. 12. 6.   m Is. 49. 18.   p Eze. 12. 4, 7.   t 2 Ki. 5. 23.   x Ex. 16. 14.   b 2 Ki. 5. 23.   m Ps. 88. 9.   q Je. 32. 3.
c Joel 4. 15.   h Job 24. 24.   n Is. 61. 10.   q De. 20. 9.   u Mal. 3. 3.   y Je. 51. 38.   c Ezr. 7. 22.   n Eze. 36. 5.   r Is. 49. 20.
d Da. 12. 3.   i Nu. 9. 3.   Je. 5. 27.   r Je. 51. 63.   v Ho. 5. 14.   z Je. 51. 40.   d Ezr. 6. 18.   o Hag. 1. 10.   s De 19. 19.
e Jos 14. 11.   j Ps. 50. 7, 15.   Ps. 71. 9.   Is. 15. 11.   Ps. 17. 12.   Ps. 102. 7.

כלא   כְּלָאֵם[a] Kal imp. sing. masc., suff. 3 pers. pl. masc.

כלא   כְּלָאתִי[b] id. pret. 1 pers. sing. (§ 23. rem. 9)

כָּלֶב Root not used; supposed to be onomatopoetic, as imitating the sound of striking, Eng. *clap*, hence *to bark*; Arab. *to plait, braid*.

כָּלֵב (*barker*) pr. name—I. of a contemporary of Joshua, patronym. כָּלִבִּי 1 Sa. 25. 3.—II. 1 Ch. 2. 18, 19, כְּלוּבָי in ver. 9.—III. 1 Ch. 2. 50.—IV. כָּלֵב אֶפְרָתָה of an unknown place, 1 Ch. 2. 24.

כֶּלֶב masc. dec. 6a (pl. c. כַּלְבֵי) *dog*.

כְּלוּב masc.—I. *fruit-basket*, Am. 8. 1, 2.—II. *bird-cage*, Je. 5. 27.—III. pr. name masc. of two different persons, 1 Ch. 4. 11 ; 27. 26.

כלב   כָּלֵב וְ pr. name masc.

כלב   כֶּלֶב } noun masc. sing. dec. 6a (§ 35. rem. 2) כְּלָבּ־ כְּלֶב־

לבב   כְּלֵב pref. כְּ)(noun masc. sing. dec. 6b

לבב   כִּלְבַב pref. בְּ bef. (.))(n. m., constr. of לֵבָב d. 4b

לבב   כִּלְבָבוֹ pref. id.)(id., suff. 3 pers. sing. masc.

לבב   כִּלְבָבֶךָ pref. id.)(id., suff. 2 pers. s. m. (for לְבָבְךָ)

כלב   כְּלִבּוֹ Kh. appellative (*as his own heart*); K. patronym. of כָּלִבִּי

לבש   כַּלְבֻשׁ pref. כַּ for כְּהַ)(noun masc. sing. dec. 1a

כלב   כַּלְבֵי־ noun masc. pl. constr. from כֶּלֶב dec. 6a

לבב   כְּלִבִּי pref. כְּ)(n. m. s., suff. 1 p. s. from לֵב d. 8b

לבא   כַּלְבִיא pref. כַּ f.)(כְּלָבִיא וְ pref. בְּ q. v. } noun masc. sing. , וְ bef. (.)

כְּלָבֶיךָ noun masc. pl., suff. 2 pers. sing. masc. from כֶּלֶב dec. 6a

לבב   כִּלְבָךְ וּ pref. בְּ)(noun masc. sing., suff. 2 pers. sing. masc. from לֵב dec. 8b; וּ bef. (.)

כלב   כְּלָבִים noun m. pl. abs. (c. כַּלְבֵי) from כֶּלֶב d. 6a

לבן   כַּלְבָנֶה pref. בַּ for כְּהַ)(noun fem. sing.

לבן   כַּלְבָנוֹן pref. id.)(pr. name of a mountain

כָּלָה   כָּלָה וְ fut. וַתֵּכֶל ,יִכְל תִּכְלֶה apoc. (§ 24. rem. 3).—I. *to be completed, finished, ended*; hence *to be accomplished, fulfilled.*—II. *to be spent, wasted, destroyed; to waste away, pine.* Pi. כִּלָּה—I. *to complete, finish, end.*—II. *to waste, ruin, destroy; also to cause to languish; to cause to vanish.* Pu. כֻּלָּה (§ 10. rem. 5) *to be completed, finished.*

כָּלֶה כָּלָה f. adj. *languishing, pining*, De. 28. 32.

כָּלָה fem.—I. *completion*, only as an adv. *entirely, wholly.*—II. *destruction.*

כְּלִי masc. dec. 6 i, but pl. כֵּלִים (see § 45) constr. כְּלֵי.—I. *vessel, utensil.*—II. *boat, skiff.*—III. *implement, tool.*—IV. *weapons, arms.*—V. *equipment, clothing, dress.*

כִּלְיוֹת fem. dec. 12b, only pl. (כְּלָיוֹת) *the reins, kidneys;* meton. *the inward, secret parts,* denoting *the secret workings and affections of the soul.*

כִּלָּיוֹן masc. dec. 3c.—I. *consumption, destruction,* Is. 10. 22.—II. *a pining, wasting of the eyes,* De. 28. 65.

כִּלְיוֹן (*a pining*) pr. name, Ru. 1. 2 ; 4. 9.

מִכְלָה f. only pl. מִכְלוֹת *perfection,* 2 Ch. 4. 21.

תִּכְלָה fem. *perfection,* Ps. 119. 96.

תַּכְלִית f.—I. *completeness, perfection.*—II. *end, extremity, boundary.*

כלה   כָּלָה וְ Kal pret. 3 pers. sing. masc., or noun f. s.

כלה   כַּלָּה וֹ noun fem. sing. dec. 10

כלה   כַּלֵּה וְ[m] Piel inf., or imp. sing. masc.

לא   כְּלָא Chald. pref. כְּ for לָא adv.

כלה   כִּלָּה וְ Piel pret. 3 pers. sing. masc.

כלל   כֻּלֹּה noun m. s., suff. 3 pers. s. m. from כֹּל d. 8c

כלל   כֻּלֹּה id. with suff. 3 pers. sing. masc.

להב   כְּלַהֲבָה[n] וּ pref. כְּ)(noun fem. sing., pl. לֶהָבוֹת, constr. dec. 11a (§ 42. No. 3 note); וּ bef. (.)

כלל   כְּלַהֲוֹן Chald. for כֻּלְּהֵן (§ 37. rem. 2) ; noun masc. sing. with suff. (Kh. הוֹן 3 pers. pl. (K. הֵן) 3 pers. pl. fem. from כֹּל (q. v.)

כלל   כֻּלְּהֶם[o] n. m. s., suff. 3 p. pl. m. (§ 3. r. 5) fr. כֹּל d. 8c

כלא   כָּלוּ Kal pret. 3 pers. pl. for כָּלְאוּ (§ 23. rem. 11)

כלה   כָּלוּ Kal pret. 3 pers. pl.

כלה   כַּלּוּ Piel imp. pl. masc.

כלה   כַּלּוּ id. pret. 3 pers. pl.

כלה   כֻּלּוּ Pual pret. 3 pers. pl. [for כֻּלְּאוּ § 10. rem. 5]

כלל   כֻּלּוֹ וְ noun m. s., suff. 3 p. s. m. from כֹּל d. 8c

כלא   כָּלוּא Kal part. pass. sing. masc.

ל   כְּלוֹא pref. כְּ)(לוֹא for לֹא adv. (q. v.)

כלב   כְּלוּב וֹ noun m. s., also pr. name m. ; וֹ bef. (.)

כלב   כְּלוּבָי pr. name masc., see כָּלֵב

לוה   כַּלֹּוֶה pref. כַּ for כְּהַ)(Kal part. act. sing. masc

כְּלוּהַי Kh. K. כְּלוּהָי K. כְּלֻהַי pr. name masc. Ezr. 10. 35. Etymon uncertain.

כלל   כְּלוּלֹתַיִךְ [for תַיִךְ כְּלוּלֹת] n. f. pl., suff. 2 p. s. f.

a Nu. 11. 28.   b Ps. 119. 101.   c Pr. 26. 17.   d 1 Sa. 25. 3.   e Job 30. 1.   Je. 3. 15.   g Is. 5. 29.   h Ps. 68. 24.   i Ca. 6. 10.   k Joel 2. 16.   l Da. 4. 32.   Ps. 83. 15.   m Da. 7. 19.   n 1 Sa. 3. 12.   p 1 Sa. 6. 10.   q Ex. 5. 13.   r Ps. 72. 20.   s Je. 32. 2.   t Ob. 1. 16.   u Am. 8. 1, 2.   x Is. 24. 2.   y Je. 2. 2.

כלה   Piel pret. 3 pers. pl., suff. 3 pers. pl. masc.   כִּלּוּם

כלה   id. with suff. 1 pers. pl.   כִּלּוּנִי

כלה   adj. f. pl. of [כָּלֶה m.] d. 11a, [from   כָלוֹת

כלה   Piel inf. constr. dec. 1 b   כַּלּוֹת

כלה   Kal inf. constr. dec. 1 a   כְּלוֹת

כלה   Piel inf. (כַּלּוֹת), suff. 1 pers. sing. dec. 1 b   כַּלּוֹתִי

כלל   n. f. pl., suff. 2 pers. pl. m. fr. כַּלָּה d. 10   כַלּוֹתֵיכֶם

כלה   Piel inf. (כַּלּוֹת), suff. 2 pers. sing. m. d. 1 b   כַּלּוֹתְךָ

כלה   id., suff. 3 pers. pl. masc.   כַּלּוֹתָם

כלה   Kal inf. (כְּלוֹת), suff. 3 pers. pl. m. dec. 1 a   כְּלוֹתָם

[כֶּלַח] masc.—I. old age, full age, Job 5. 26; 30. 2.—
II. pr. name of a city, Ge. 10. 11, 12.

כלח   noun masc. sing. for כֶּלַח, (§ 35. rem. 2)   כָּלַח

לחך   pref. כְּ bef. (:) X Kal inf. constr.   כִּלְחֹךְ

לחם   pref. כַּ f. (כְּהַ) noun com. sing. (suff. לַחְמִי)   כַּלֶּחֶם

     pref. כְּ q. v. dec. 6 a   כִּלְחֶם

נכל   adj. or subst. masc. sing. [for נִכְלֵי]   כִּלַי

כלה   noun m. pl., suff. 1 p. pl., irr. of כְּלִי (§ 45)   כֵּלַי

כלה   id. pl. constr. st.; bef. (:)   כְּלֵי

כלה   id. sing. abs. st. (§ 35. rem. 14); id.   כְּלִי

כלה   id. pl., suff. 3 pers. sing. masc. (§ 45)   כֵּלָיו

כלה   id. id., suff. 3 pers. pl. masc.   כְּלֵיהֶם

כלה   id. id., suff. 3 pers. sing. masc.   כֵּלָיו

כלה   noun masc. sing. dec. 3 c   כִּלָּיוֹן

כלה   id., constr. st.; also pr. name masc.   כִּלְיוֹן

כלה   noun fem. pl. abs. from [כִּלְיָה] dec. 12 b;   כְּלָיוֹת

כלה   bef. (:)

כלה   id. pl., constr. st.   כִּלְיוֹת

כלה   id. pl. with suff. 1 pers. sing.   כִּלְיֹתַי

כלה   noun m. pl., suff. 2 p. s. m. irr. of כְּלִי (§ 45)   כֵּלֶיךָ

כלה   id. sing., suff. 2 pers. sing. masc.   כֶּלְיְךָ

כלה   id. pl., suff. 2 pers. pl. masc.   כְּלֵיכֶם

כלל   adj. masc. sing. dec. 3 a   כָּלִיל

לול   pref. כַּ for כְּהַ X noun masc. sing. dec. 6 h   כַּלַּיִל

לול   pref. כְּ X id., constr. st.   כְּלֵיל

כלל   adj. m. s. constr. of כָּלִיל dec. 3 a; bef. (:)   כְּלִיל

לול   pref. כַּ for כְּהַ X noun masc. sing. לַיִל q. v.) with parag. ה   כַּלַּיְלָה

כלל   adj. fem., constr. of [כְּלִילָה] d. 10, fr. כָּלִיל m.   כְּלִילַת

בלה   noun masc. pl. irr. of כְּלִי (§ 45)   כֵּלִים

בלה   Kal pret. 1 pers. pl.   כָּלִינוּ

כלה   Piel pret. 1 pers. pl.   כִּלִּינוּ

כלה   Piel pret. 2 pers. sing. masc. X acc. shifted by conv. (comp. § 8. rem. 7)   כִּלִּיתָ

כלה   Kal pret. 1 pers. sing.   כָּלִיתִי

כלה   Piel pret. 1 pers. sing.   כִּלִּיתִי

כלה   noun fem. pl., suff. 1 pers. sing. from [כִּלְיָה] dec. 12 b   כִּלְיֹתַי

כלה   Piel pret. 1 pers. sing. acc. shifted by conv. (§ 11. r. 24; comp. § 8. r. 7)   כִּלִּיתִי

כלה   id. id., suff. 2 pers. sing. masc.   כִּלִּיתִיךָ

כלה   id. id., suff. 3 pers. pl. masc.   כִּלִּיתִים

כלה   id. pret. 2 pers. sing. m., suff. 3 pers. pl. m.   כִּלִּיתָם

כלה   Kal pret. 2 pers. pl. masc.; for conv.   כְּלִיתֶם

כלה   Piel pret. 2 pers. pl. masc.   כִּלִּיתֶם

כלל   noun masc. sing., suff. 2 pers. sing. fem. from כֹּל dec. 8 c (§ 3. rem. 2)   כֻּלֵּךְ

בול   Pilpel inf. constr. (§ 6. No. 4)   כַּלְכֵּל

בול   pr. name masc.   כַּלְכֹּל

בול   Pilpel pret. 3 pers. sing. masc. (§ 6. No. 4)   כִּלְכֵּל

בול   Pulpal pret. 3 pers. pl. (§ 6. No. 4)   כָּלְכְּלוּ

בול   Pilpel pret. 3 pers. pl. (§ 6. No. 4)   כִּלְכְּלוּ

בול   id. pret. 3 pers. s. m., suff. 3 pers. pl. m.   כִּלְכְּלָם

בול   id. pret. 1 pers. sing., acc. shifted by conv. (comp. § 8. rem. 7)   כִּלְכַּלְתִּי

בול   id. pret. 2 pers. sing. m., suff. 3 pers. pl. m.   כִּלְכַּלְתָּם

כלל   noun m. s., suff. 2 p. pl. m. fr. כֹּל d. 8 c   כֻּלְּכֶם

[כָּלַל] to complete, Eze. 27. 4, 11.

כְּלַל Chald. Shaph. שַׁכְלֵל (§ 48) to complete finish. Ishtaph. to be finished, Ezr. 4. 13, 16.

כְּלָל (perfection) pr. name masc. Ezr. 10. 30.

כֹּל, כָּל־ (בוֹל only Je. 33. 8), dec. 8 c.—I. the whole, expressive of totality; הַכֹּל the whole; before a noun sing with the art.; also without it, when the noun is in the constr. st. or it has suff., or being a pr. name, as כָּל־הָאָרֶץ the whole earth; כָּל־יִשְׂרָאֵל the whole congregation of Israel; the whole (people) of Israel; בְּכָל־לְבָבְךָ with thy whole heart; כֻּלֹּה the whole of it.—II. all, before noun pl., as כָּל־הַגּוֹיִם all nations; abs. כֹּל. all, they all; כֻּלָּנוּ all of us; כֻּלְּכֶם all of you, &c.; before a noun sing. collective, כָּל־הַחַיָּה all

a 2 Ch. 8. 8.   f Eze. 4. 8.   i Ho. 9. 4.   p Ps. 73. 21.   r Eze. 28. 12.   v Ps. 39. 11.   A Ex. 33. 5.   m Ex. 5. 14.   r 1 Ki. 20. 27.
Ps. 119. 87.   g Je. 44. 27.   k Is. 32. 7.   q Job 5. 14.   s De. 23. 25.   w Nu. 25. 11.   B Eze. 22. 31.   n Is. 14. 29, 31.   1 Ki. 18. 4.
De. 28. 32.   h Job 30. 2.   l Is. 10. 22.   t Ge. 45. 20.   u Ps. 139. 13.   C Je. 5. 3.   o Je. 20. 9.   t Ne. 9. 31.
d Nu. 7. 1.   i Nu. 22. 4.   De. 28. 65.   u Is. 16. 3.   x Job 19. 27.   D Mal. 3. 6.   t 2 Sa. 19. 33.   x Is. 65. 12.
e Ho. 4. 13, 14.   Ps. 102. 10.   Ps. 7. 10.   Is. 30. 29.   Eze. 4. 6.   Is. 49. 4.   Eze. 13. 14.

living things.—III. every, before a noun without
the art., כָּל־אִישׁ every man.—IV. any one, any
thing; כָּל־דָּבָר any thing, whatever; with לֹא, אֵין
not any, no.—V. of all kinds, sorts.—VI. adv.
altogether, Ps. 39. 6; כָּל־עֹד as long as, Job 27. 3;
כָּל־עֻמַּת שֶׁ wholly as, just as, Ec. 5. 15.

כָּל, כֹּל Chald. emph. כֹּלָּא, with suff. כָּלְּהוֹן
(§ 61) i. q. Heb. כֹּל Nos. I, II, IV, VI.

כָּלִיל masc. dec. 3a.—I. adj. complete, perfect;
fem. כְּלִילַת, adverb, wholly, entirely.—II. subst.
(a) the whole; (b) whole burnt-offering.

כְּלוּלֹת (of כְּלוּלָה) fem. pl. bridal state, Je. 2. 2;
Eng. Ver. "espousals."

כַּלָּה fem. d. 10.—I. bride, spouse.—II. daughter-
in-law.

מִכְלוֹל masc. perfection, Eze. 23. 12; 38. 4.
מִכְלָל masc. dec. 2b, id. Ps. 50. 2.
מַכְלֻלִים masc. pl. (of מַכְלוּל) splendid things, of
costly garments, Eze. 27. 24.

כָּלָל	‍ pr. name masc.; ‍ bef. (:)	כלל
כָּלְלוּ	Kal pret. 3 pers. pl.	כלל

כָּלַם Hiph. הַכְלִים, הִכְלִים (§ 11. rem. 1).—I. to put to
shame, make ashamed.—II. to injure, hurt. Hoph.
pass. 1 Sa. 25. 15; Je. 14. 3. Niph. to be put to
shame; also to feel ashamed, with מִן, בְּ on account
of anything.

כְּלִמָּה fem. dec. 10, shame, ignominy.
כְּלִמּוּת fem. id. Je. 23. 40.

כִּלְּמָם	Piel pret. 3 pers. sing. masc. (כִּלָּה), suff. 3 pers. pl. masc. (§ 24. rem. 21)	כלה
וְכִלָּם	‍ noun m. s., suff. 3 p. pl. m. from כֹּל d. 8c	כלל
כִּלְמַד	pr. name of a region or city, Eze. 27. 23.	
כְּלִמָּה	‍ noun fem. sing. dec. 10; ‍ bef. (:)	כלם
כַּלִּמּוּדִים	pref. כַּ for כְּהַ)(adj. or subst. masc. pl. of [לִמּוּד] dec. 1b	למד
כְּלִמּוֹת	‍ noun fem., pl. of כְּלִמָּה dec. 10	כלם
כְּלִמּוּת	‍ noun fem. sing.; ‍ bef. (:)	כלם
כְּלִמַּת	noun fem. sing., constr. of כְּלִמָּה dec. 10	כלם
כְּלִמָּתִי	‍ id., suff. 1 pers. sing.; ‍ bef. (:)	כלם
כְּלִמָּתֶךָ	id., suff. 2 pers. sing. fem.	כלם
כְּלִמָּתָם	id., suff. 3 pers. pl. masc.	כלם
כְּלִמָּתֵנוּ	id., suff. 1 pers. pl.	כלם

כַּלְנֶה, כַּלְנֵה, כַּלְנוֹ pr. name of a city on the river
Tigris, Ge. 10. 10; Is. 10. 9; Am. 6. 2.

כָּלְנָהּ	noun masc. sing., suff. 3 pers. sing. fem. (§ 3. rem. 5) from כֹּל dec. 8c	כלל
כַּלְנוֹ	pr. name of a place, see כַּלְנֶה.	
כִּלָּנוּ	Piel pret. 3 pers. sing. masc. (כִּלָּה), suff. 1 pers. pl. (§ 24. rem. 21)	כלה
וְכֻלָּנוּ	‍ noun m. sing., suff. 1 pers. pl. from כֹּל d. 8c	כלל
כַּעֲנֵה	pref. כַּ for כְּהַ)(noun fem. sing.	לען

כָּלַף Root not used; prob. to strike, comp. כָּלָב.
כֵּילַפּוֹת fem. pl. hammers or axes, Ps. 74. 6.

כַּלַּפִּיד	‍ pref. כְּ)(noun masc. sing. d. 1b; ‍ bef. (:)	לפד
כְּלַפִּידֵי	pref. כְּ)(id. pl., constr. st.	לפד
כַּלַּפִּידִים	pref. כַּ for כְּהַ)(id. pl., abs. st.	לפד
כִּלְשׁוֹן	‍ pref. כְּ bef. (:))(noun com. sing., constr. of לָשׁוֹן dec. 3a	לשן
כִּלְשׁוֹנוֹ	pref. id.)(id., suff. 3 pers. sing. masc.	לשן
וְכִלְשׁוֹנָם	‍ pref. id.)(id., suff. 3 pers. pl. masc.	לשן
כִּלְשֹׁנוֹ	defect. for כִּלְשׁוֹנוֹ (q. v.)	לשן
כַּלָּתָה	in pause for כַּלָּתָה (q. v. § 8. rem. 7)	כלה
כַּלָּתָהּ	n. fem. s., suff. 3 pers. s. fem. from כַּלָּה d. 10	כלל
כָּלָתָה	Kal pret. 3 pers. sing. fem.	כלה
וְכִלְּתָה	‍ Piel pret. 3 pers. sing. fem.	כלה
כַּלָּתוֹ	n. fem. s., suff. 3 pers. s. m. from כַּלָּה d. 10	כלל
כַּלֹּתוֹ	Piel inf. (כַּלּוֹת), suff. 3 pers. sing. masc. d. 1b	כלה
וְכִלַּתּוּ	‍ Piel pret. 3 pers. sing. fem., suff. 3 pers. sing. masc. (§ 24. rem. 21)	כלה
כְּלֹתוֹ	Kal inf. (כְּלוֹת), suff. 3 pers. sing. masc. d. 1a	כלה
וְכַלֹּתֶיהָ	‍ n. fem. pl., suff. 3 p. s. fem. from כַּלָּה d. 10	כלל
כַּלָּתְךָ	)(id. sing., suff. 2 pers. sing. masc.	כלל
כַּלָּתֵךְ	)(id. id., suff. 2 pers. sing. fem.	כלל
כַּלֹּתָם	defect. for כַּלּוֹתָם (q. v.)	כלה
כְּלִתְנִי	Kal pret. 2 pers. sing. fem. with suff. 1 pers. sing. (§ 23. rem. 11)	כלא
כְּמַאֲכֶלֶת	pref. כְּ)(noun fem. sing.	אכל
כְּמֵאמַר	Chald. pref. כְּ)(noun masc. sing.	אמר
כְּמָבוֹא	pref. כְּ bef. (:))(n. m. s., constr. of מָבוֹא d. 3a	בוא
כִּמְבוֹאֵי	pref. id.)(id. pl., constr. st.	בוא
כִּמֵבִיא	pref. id.)(Hiph. part. sing. masc. dec. 3b	בוא
כְּמַבְכִּרָה	pref. id.)(Hiph. part. sing. fem.	בכר
כְּמִבְנֵה	pref. id.)(noun m. sing., constr. of [בָּנֶה] d. 9a	בנה
כִּמְבַשֵּׂר	pref. כְּ bef. (:))(Piel part. sing. masc.	בשר
כְּמִגְדַּל	pref. כְּ)(noun m. sing., constr. of מִגְדָּל d. 2b	גדל
כַּמִּגְדָּלוֹת	pref. כַּ for כְּהַ)(id. with pl. fem. term., abs. st.	גדל

---

a Eze. 27, 4, 11.   e Ps. 69. 20.   i 2 Sa. 19. 7.   o Da. 10. 6.   s Est. 8. 9.   w Zec. 5. 4.   a' Ge. 38. 24.   e' Ezr. 6. 9.   i' Je. 4. 31.
b La. 2. 22.   f Je. 3. 25.   k Pr. 5. 4.   p Na. 2. 5.   t Est. 3. 12.   x 2 Ch. 8. 16.   b' Ru. 4. 15.   f' Eze. 33. 31.   m' Eze. 40. 2.
c Is. 50. 4.   g Ge. 42. 36.   l Is. 62. 1.   q Est. 1. 22.   u 1 Ki. 17. 16   y Ru. 1. 6, 7, 8.   c' 1 Sa. 25. 33.   k' Eze. 26. 10.   n' 2 Sa. 4. 10.
Mi. 2. 6.   Pr. 31. 29.   m Zec. 12. 6.   r Ne. 13. 24.   v Ho. 11. 6.   z Le. 18. 5.   d' Is. 9. 18.   l' Ps. 74. 5.   o' Ca. 8. 10.
Je. 23. 40.   2 Sa. 21. 5.   1 Sa. 4. 19.

כַּמַּגֵּפָה pref. id.)(noun fem. sing. dec. 10 . נגף

כַּמִּדְבָּר pref. כַּ for כְּהַ)(noun masc. sing. dec. 2 b דבר

כְּמִדִּי pref. כְּ)(noun masc. sing., suff. 3 pers. sing. masc. from מַד dec. 8 d & e . מדד

כַּמִּדּוֹת pref. כַּ f.)(כְּהַ
כְּמִדּוֹת pref. כְּ q. v. }noun fem., pl. of מִדָּה dec. 10 מדד

כְּמִדְיָן pref. id.)(pr. name of a people . דין

כְּמַדְקְרוֹת pref. id.)(noun fem. pl. c. [from מַדְקָרָה or קָרָה] dec. 11 . . . דקר

כְּמִדַּת pref. id.)(noun fem. s., constr. of מִדָּה d. 10 מדד

כָּמַהּ to long for, desire ardently, Ps. 63. 2.

כִּמְהָם (longing) pr. name masc. ; written also כְּמוֹהָם (Kh.), and כִּמְהָן.

כַּמָּה)וּ'/ pref. כַּ for כְּהַ)(pron. interrog. with
כַּמֶּה} the pref. adverbially }מה

כְּמָה Chald. pref. כְּ)(pron. interrog. . מה

כְמוֹהֻ ו'/ defect. for כָּמוֹהוּ (q. v.) . . מו

כַּמְהַלֵּךְ pref. כְּ bef. (:))(Piel part. sing. masc. d. 7 b הלך

כִּמְהָם
כִּמְהָן וּ'/} pr. name masc. . . . כמה

כְּמַהְפֵּכַת pref. כְּ)(n. fem. s., constr. of [מַהְפֵּכָה] d. 10 הפך

כְּמַהֵר pref. id.)(Piel inf. constr. (§ 14. rem. 1) מהר

כְּמֹהַר pref. id.)(noun masc. sing. . . מהר

כְּמוֹ ו'/ adv., prep. or conj. ; וּ bef. (:) מו

כָּמוֹהָ id., suff. 3 pers. sing. fem. (§ 5, parad.) . מו

כָּמוֹהוּ id., suff. 3 pers. sing. masc. . . מו

כְּמוֹהֶם id., suff. 3 pers. pl. masc. . . מו

כְּמוֹהָם Kh. כְמוֹהָם, K. כְּמֵהָם pr. name masc. . כמה

כָּמוֹךָ adv. or prep. (כְּמוֹ), suff. 2 p. s. m. (§ 5, parad.) מו

כְּמוֹכֶם id., suff. 2 pers. pl. masc. . . מו

כַּמּוֹכֵר pref. כַּ for כְּהַ)(Kal part. act. sing. m. d. 7 b מכר

כָּמוֹנוּ adv. (כְּמוֹ) with suff. 1 pers. pl. . מו

כָּמוֹנִי id. (& prep.) with suff. 1 pers. sing. . מו

כְּמוֹפֵת pref. כַּ f.)(כְּהַ
כְּמוֹפֵת pref. כְּ q. v. }noun masc. sing. dec. 7 b יפת

כְּמוֹץ pref. כְּ)(noun masc. sing. . . מוץ

כְּמוֹצָא וּ pref. כְּ)(n. m. s. d. 1 b (§ 31. r. 1) ; וּ bef.(:) יצא

כְּמוֹצָא pref. id.)(Kal part. act. sing. masc. dec. 7 b מצא

כְּמוֹצָאֵי pref. id.)(n. m. pl. c.fr. מוֹצָא d. 1 b (§ 31. r. 1) יצא

כְּמוֹצֵאת pref. id.)(Kal part. act. fem. [for צֵאת § 23. rem. 4], from מוֹצָא masc. מצא

כְּמוֹקֵר pref. id.)(noun masc. sing. dec. 7 b יקד

כְּמוֹשׁ (perhaps subduer (כָּבַשׁ=כָּמַשׁ) pr. name of an idol of the Moabites and Ammonites; עַם כְּ the Moabites, Nu. 21. 29.

כַּמָּוֶת pref. כַּ for כְּהַ)(noun masc. sing. dec. 6g מות

כְּמוֹת pref. כְּ)(id., constr. st. . . . מות

כְּמוֹתוֹ וּ pref. id.)(id. with suff. 3 pers. s. m.; וּ bef. (:) מות

כָּמַז Root not used; Arab. to gather or compress into a roundish form.

כּוּמָז masc. bracelet, prob. of gold beads, Ex. 35. 22; Nu. 31. 50.

כַּמִּזְרָק pref. כַּ for כְּהַ)(noun masc. sing. dec. 2 b זרק

כַּמִּזְרָקִים pref. id.)(id., pl. absolute . זרק

כְּמַחֲבֵא pref. כְּ)(noun masc. sing. . . חבא

כְּמַחְלְקֹתָם pref. id.)(noun fem. pl., suff. 3 pers. pl. masc. from מַחֲלֶקֶת dec. 13 c חלק

כְּמַחְלַת pref. כְּ bef. (:))(noun fem. sing., constr. of [מַחֲלָה] dec. 10 חול

כְּמַחֲנֵה)(noun m. s., constr. of מַחֲנֶה d. 9a חנה

כְּמַחֲרִישׁ pref. id.)(Hiph. part. sing. masc. d. 1 b חרש

כִּמְטַחֲוֵי pref. כְּ bef. (:))(Pilel (§ 6. No. 2) part. pl. c. [from מְטַחֲוֶה 3rd rad. ה doubled and changed to ו [for מְטַחֲחֶה § 24. r. 25] מחה

כְּמַטִּיל pref. id.)(noun masc. sing. . . מטל

כְּמַטְמֹנִים וּ pref. כְּ)(noun masc., pl. of מַטְמֹן dec. 1 b (§ 30. rem. 4) . . טמן

כַּמָּטָר וּ'/ pref. כַּ f.)(כְּהַ
כְּמָטָר pref. כְּ q. v. }noun masc. sing. dec. 4 a מטר

כַּמַּטָּרָא pref. כַּ for כְּהַ)(for מַטָּרָה noun fem. sing. נטר

כַּמַּיִם pref. id.
כְּמַיִם וּ'/ pref. id. }noun masc. pl. [of מַי irr.
כְּמַיִם pref. כְּ } § 45, comp. § 38. rem. 2] }מי

כְּמִישׁ Kh. כְּמִישׁ, K. כָּמֹשׁ q. v.

כִּמְכְאֹבַי pref. id.)(n. m. s., suff. 1 p. s. fr. מַכְאֹב d. 1 b נאב

כָּמְכָה prep. (כְּמוֹ) with suff. 2 pers. sing. masc. (§ 5, parad. & § 3. rem. 2) מו

כְּמַכַּת pref. כְּ)(noun fem. s. constr. of מַכָּה d. 10 נכה

כַּמִּכְתָּב pref. כַּ for כְּהַ)(noun masc. sing. dec. 2 b כתב

כַּמְלֵאָה וּ pref. id.)(noun fem. sing. dec. 10 מלא

כִּמְלֹאות with וּ in otio, see כִּמְלֹאת מלא

כְּמַלְאַךְ pref. כְּ)(noun m. s., constr. of מַלְאָךְ d. 2 b לאך

כְּמַלְאָכִי pref. id.)(id. with suff. 1 pers. sing. לאך

כִּמְלֹאת pref. כְּ bef. (:))(Kal inf. constr. (§ 23. r. 2) מלא

כַּמִּלֹנָה pref. כַּ for כְּהַ)(noun masc. sing. . לוה

כַּמְּלוּנָה pref. כַּ for כְּהַ
כִּמְלוּנָה pref. כְּ bef. (:) }noun fem. sing. לון

כַּמִּלְחָמָה pref. כַּ for כְּהַ)(noun fem.sing. (suff. מִלְחַמְתוֹ § 42. rem. 5) . . . לחם

⸗ Zec. 14.15.   ƒ Zec. 2. 6.   ᵏ Job 12. 3.   ⁿ Is. 58. 11.   ʳ 2 Ch. 24. 22.   ᵘ 1 Ch. 12. 22.   ˣ Pr. 26. 1.   ᵃ Ex. 15. 11.   ᵉ Is. 42. 19.
ᵇ Ps. 109. 18.   ᵍ Da. 3. 33.   ˡ Is. 24. 2.   ᵒ Ps. 119. 162.   ˢ Zec. 9. 15.   ᵛ 1 Sa. 10. 27.   ʸ Ps. 72. 6.   ᵇ Is. 10. 26.   ᶠ Is. 24. 2.
ᶜ Eze. 40. 28,   ʰ Pr. 6. 11.   ᵐ Is. 14. 10.   ᵖ Eze. 12. 4.   ᵗ Zec. 14. 20.   ʷ Ge. 21. 16.   ᶻ La. 3. 12.   ᶜ De. 10. 4.   ᵍ Is. 24. 20.
29, 35.   ⁱ Pr. 7. 23.   ⁿ 1 Ki. 13. 5.   ᵠ Ca. 8. 10.   ⁱ Is. 32. 2.   ˣ Job 40. 18.   ᵈ Nu. 11. 27.   ʰ Is. 1. 25.
ᵈ Pr. 12. 18.   ʲ Ex. 22. 16.   ᵒ Ps. 71. 7.   ᵠ Ps. 102. 4.   Ca. 7. 1.   ʸ Pr. 2. 4.   ᵉ La. 1. 12.   ⁱ Je. 25. 12.
ᵉ Eze. 40. 21, 22.   ᵏ Ese. 5. 9.   ᶠ 1 Ki. 7. 9, 11.   ᵗᵗ Zeph. 2. 2.   Je. 29. 22.

כְּמֶלֶךְ   pref. כְּ)(noun masc. sing. (suff. מַלְכִּי), d. 6a   מלך

כְּמָלְכוֹ   pref. id.)(Kal inf. with suff. 3 pers. sing. m.   מלך

כְּמַלְכֵי   pref. id.)(noun masc. pl. c. from מֶלֶךְ d. 6a   מלך

כְּמַלְקוֹשׁ   pref. id.)(noun masc. sing. . . . לקש

כְּמַלְקֵט   pref. כְּ bef. (:))(Piel part. sing. masc. d. 7b   לקט

כָּמַן   Root not used ; Syr. & Arab. *to lay up.*

מִכְמָן masc. *treasure,* only pl. c. מִכְמַנֵּי (dec. 8a) Da. 11. 43

וְ כַּמֹּן] masc. *cummin,* a herb, Is. 28. 25, 27.

כְּמִנְהַג   pref.)(noun m. s., constr. of מִנְהָג d. 2b   נהג

כָּמֹנוּ   prep. (כְּמוֹ) with suff. 1 pers. pl. (§ 5, parad.)   מו

כִּמְנוֹר   pref. כְּ bef. (:))(noun masc. sing. constr. of מָנוֹר dec. 3a, R. נור see . . . ניר

כַּמִּנְחָה   וְ)(pref. כַּ for כְּהַ)(noun fem. sing. dec. 12b   מנח

כְּמִנְחַת   pref. כְּ)(id. constr. st. . . . . מנח

כָּמֹנִי   defect. for כָּמוֹנִי (q. v.) . . . מו

כִּמְנַשֶּׁה   וְ)(pref. כְּ bef. (:))(pr. name masc. . נשה

כָּמַס]   *to lay up, treasure up,* De. 32. 34.

מִכְמָס (*treasure*), also מִכְמָשׂ, מִכְמָשׁ pr. name of a city in the tribe of Benjamin, 1 Sa. 13. 2, 5 ; Ezr. 2. 27 ; Ne. 11. 31.

כָּמֻס   Kal part. pass. sing. masc. [for כָּמוּס]   כמס

כִּמְסֹם   pref. כְּ bef. (:) Kal inf. constr.   מסם

כְּמַסִּיגֵי   pref.)(Hiph. part. pl. c. m. fr. מַסִּיג d. 1b   נסג

כְּמִסְפַּד   pref. id.)(constr. of the following . . ספד

כְּמִסְפֵּד   pref. id.)(noun masc. sing. dec. 7c   ספד

כַּמִּסְפָּר   pref. כַּ for כְּהַ)(noun masc. sing. dec. 2b   ספר

כְּמִסְפַּר   pref. כְּ)(id. constr. st. . . ספר

כְּמִסְפָּרָם   pref. id.)(id., suff. 3 pers. pl. masc. . ספר

כְּמַסְתִּיר   וְ pref. id.)(Hiph. part. for מַסְתִּיר (§ 11. rem. 8) ; וְ bef. (:) . . . . . סתר

כִּמְעוֹתָיו   pref. כְּ bef. (:))(noun masc. with pl. fem. term. and suff. from [מֵעָ] dec. 7a . מע

כִּמְעַט   pref. id.)(adj. masc. sing. (pl. מְעַטִּים) dec. 8 d
כְּמַעַט   מעט

כַּמְעִיל   pref. כַּ f. כְּהַ)(noun masc. sing. dec. 1a . מעל
כִּמְעִיל   pref. כְּ bef. (:))(

כְּמַעַלְלָיו   pref.)(noun masc. pl., suff. 3 pers. sing. masc. from [מַעֲלָל] dec. 2b   עלל

כְּמַעַלְלֵינוּ   וְ)(pref. id.)(id. pl., suff. 1 p. pl. ; וְ bef. (:)   עלל

כְּמַעַר   וְ)(pref.)(noun masc. sing. (with suff. מַעֲרֵךְ)   ערה

כַּמַּעֲשֵׂה   pref. כַּ for כְּהַ)(noun masc. sing. dec. 9a   עשה

כְּמַעֲשֵׂה   וְ)(pref. כְּ)(id. constr. st. ; וְ bef. (:)   עשה

כְּמַעֲשֵׂהוּ   pref. id.)(id., suff. 3 pers. sing. masc. . עשה

כְּמַעֲשֵׂיהֶם   pref. id.)(id. pl., suff. 3 pers. pl. masc   עשה

כְּמַעֲשָׂיו   pref. id.)(id. pl., suff. 3 pers. sing. masc   עשה

כְּמַעֲשֶׂיךָ   pref. id.)(id. pl., suff. 2 pers. sing. masc.   עשה

כְּמִפְּנֵי   pref. id.)(noun masc. pl., constr. of פָּנִים, from [פָּנָה] dec. 9b . . . פנה

כִּמְפַתֵּחַ   pref. כְּ bef. (:))(Piel part. sing. masc. . פתח

כַּמֹּץ   pref. כַּ f. כְּהַ)(
כְּמֹץ   וְ pref. כְּ q. v.)(noun masc. sing.; וְ bef. (:)   מוץ

כְּמִצְבַּיַּהּ   וְ Chald. pref. id.)(Peal inf. [מִצְבָּא], suff. 3 pers. sing. masc. dec. 6a ; וְ id. . . צבא

כְּמִצְוָה   וְ pref. כַּ for כְּהַ)(noun fem. sing. dec. 10   צוה

כְּמִצְוַת   וְ pref. כְּ)(id. constr. st. ; וְ bef. (:) . . צוה

כִּמְצַחֵק   pref. כְּ bef. (:))(Piel inf. constr. (§ 14. r. 1)   צחק

כַּמָּקֵק   pref. כַּ for כְּהַ)(noun masc. sing.   מקק

כִּמְקוֹם   pref. כְּ bef. (:))(noun com. sing., constr. of מָקוֹם dec. 3a . . . . . קום

כְּמִקְרְבֵהּ   וְ Chald. pref. כְּ)(Peal inf. [מִקְרַב], suff. 3 pers. sing. fem. dec. 2a ; וְ bef. (:)   קרב

כְּמִקְרֶהָ   pref. כְּ)(noun m. s., constr. of מִקְרֶה dec. 9a   קרה

כָּמַר   Niph.—I. *to be burned, be black with burning,* La. 5. 10.—II. trop. *to be warmed, kindled,* of love, or compassion.—III. according to the derivatives, i. q. כָּבַר *to plait, braid.*

כֹּמֶר masc. only pl. (כְּמָרִים § 35. rem. 9) *idolatrous priests.*

כַּמְרִיר masc. dec. 1b, *blackness or heat,* trop. *or calamity,* Job 3. 5.

מַכְמֹר, מִכְמָר masc. dec. 2b, *a net, snare,* Ps. 141. 10 ; Is. 51. 20.

מִכְמֶרֶת f. d. 13a (with suff. מַרְתִּי) *fishing-net.*

כְּמַר   pref. כְּ)(noun masc. sing. dec. 8 (§ 37. r. 7)   מרר

כַּמַּרְאֶה   pref. כַּ for כְּהַ)(noun masc. sing. dec. 9a   ראה

כְּמַרְאֵה   וְ pref. כְּ)(id. constr. st. ; וְ bef. (:) . . ראה

כִּמְרַגְּלִים   pref. כְּ bef. (:))(Piel part. masc., pl. of [מְרַגֵּל] dec. 7b . . . רגל

כִּמְרִיבָה   pref. id.)(pr. name of a place   ריב

כִּמְרִיבֵי   pref. id.)(Kal part. pl. c. m. from [מְרִיב] d. 3b   ריב

כִּמְרִימֵי   pref. id.)(Hiph. part. pl. c. m. from מֵרִים d. 3b   רום

כִּמְרִירוֹ   וְ noun masc. pl. (כְּמָרִים), suff. 3 pers. sing. m.   כמר

כִּמְרִירֵי   noun masc. pl. constr. from [כַּמְרִיר] dec. 1b   כמר

כְּמַרְעִיתָם   pref. כְּ)(noun fem. sing., suff. 3 pers. pl. masc. from מַרְעִית dec. 1b   רעה

כִּמְרֻצַת   pref. כְּ bef. (:))(n. fem. s., constr. of מְרוּצָה d. 10   רוץ

כַּמִּרְקָחָה   pref. כַּ for כְּהַ)(noun fem. sing. . . רקח

a 1 Ki. 15. 29.   f Le. 5. 13.   k Zec. 12. 11.   p Is. 53. 8.   u 1 Ki. 7. 36.   z 1 Ki. 20. 11.   e Is. 5. 24.   k Eze. 43. 3.   q Job 3. 5.

b 2 Ki. 17. 2.   g Eze. 45. 25.   l Zec. 12. 10.   q Is. 48. 19.   v 1 Ki. 7. 8.   a Da. 4. 32.   f Je. 19. 13.   l Ge. 42. 30.   r Ho. 13. 8.

c Ho. 6. 3.   h De. 32. 34.   m Nu. 15. 12.   r Job 29. 14.   w Ex. 23. 24.   b 2 Ki. 17. 34.   g Da. 6. 21.   m Ho. 4. 4.   s 2 Sa. 18. 27.

d Is. 17. 5.   i Is. 10. 18.   n 1 Ki. 18. 31.   s Ho. 12. 3.   x Ne. 6. 14.   c 2 Ch. 30. 6.   h Ec. 2. 15.   n Ho. 11. 4.   t Job 41. 23.

e 2 Ki. 9. 20.   j Ho. 5. 10.   o Nu. 15. 12.   t Zec. 1. 6.   y Le. 26. 37.   d Ge. 19. 14.   i Is. 40. 15.   o Ho. 10. 5.

כְּמַשָּׂא׳   pref. כְּ)(noun masc. sing. dec. 1b   נשא

כְּמשֶׁה   pref. id.)(pr. name masc.   משה

כְּמֵשִׁיב׳   pref. id.)(Hiph. part. sing. masc. dec. 3b   שוב

כְּמִשְׁכָּב׳   pref. id.)(noun m. s., constr. of מִשְׁכָּב d.2b   שכב

כְּמִשְׁכַּ֫חַת   pref. כְּ bef. (:))(noun fem. sing. constr. of [מְשׂוּכָה] dec. 10 . . .   שׂור

כְּמָשְׁלֹו   pref. כְּ)(Kal inf., suff. 3 pers. sing. masc.   משל

כְּמֻשְׁלָם   pref. כְּ bef. (:))(Pual part. sing. masc.   שלם

כְּמִשְׁלֹשׁ   pref. כְּ)(noun masc. sing.   שלש

כְּמִשְׁפָּחָה   pref. id.)(noun fem. pl., constr. from מִשְׁפָּחָה dec. 11a (but comp. § 42. rem. 5)   שפח

וּכְמִשְׁמָרֹות׳   pref. id.)(for מִשְׁמָרֹות noun masc. with pl. fem. term. from [מִשְׁמָר] dec.7b; וּ bef. (:)   שמר

כַּמִּשְׁפָּט   pref. כַּ f. [כְּהַ } noun masc. sing. dec. 2b .   שפט
כְּמִשְׁפָּט   pref. כְּ q. v. }

כְּמִשְׁפָּט   pref. id.)(id. constr. st.   שפט

כְּמִשְׁפָּטֹו׳   pref. id.)(id., suff. 3 pers. s. m.; וּ bef. (:)   שפט

כְּמִשְׁפְּטֵי   וּ pref. id.)(id. pl., constr. st.; וּ id.   שפט

כְּמִשְׁפְּטֵיהֶן   וּ pref. id.)(id. pl., suff. 3 pers. pl. m.; וּ id.   שפט

כְּמִשְׁפָּטֶיךָ־   pref. כְּ)(id. pl., suff. 2 pers. sing. masc.   שפט

כַּמִּשְׁפָּטִים   pref. כַּ for כְּהַ)(id. pl., abs. st.   שפט

כְּמִשְׁפָּטֶ֫ךָ   pref. כְּ)(id.pl., suff. 2 p.s.m.for [טֶיךָ] (§4.r.1)   שפט

כְּמִשְׁפָּטָם   pref. כְּ)(id.s.,suff.3 pers. pl. m.; וּ bef. (:)   שפט

כְּמַשַּׁק׳   pref. כְּ)(noun masc. sing. constr. [of מַשָּׁק]   שקק

כְּמִשְׁתֵּה׳   pref. id.)(noun m. s., constr. of מִשְׁתֶּה d.9a   שתה

כַּמֵּת׳   pref. כַּ f. [כְּהַ] Kal part. sing. masc. dec. 1a   מות
כְּמֵת׳   pref. כְּ q. v.   (§ 21. r. 2, & § 30. No. 3) }

כְּמִתְאֹנְנִים׳   pref.id.)(Hithpo.part.pl.m.fr.[מִתְאֹנֵן] d.7b   אנן

כְּמֵתֵי   pref. כְּ)(Kal part. pl. masc. constr. from מֵת dec. 1a (§ 21. rem. 2, & § 30. No. 3)   מות

כַּמֵּתִים׳   pref. כַּ for כְּהַ)(id. pl., abs. st. .   מות

כְּמִתְלַהְלֵהַּ   pref. כְּ)(Hithpalp. part. sing. masc. (§ 6. r. 4)   להה

כְּמִתְלַהֲמִים   pref. id.)(Hithpa. (§ 14. rem. 1) part. masc., pl. of [מִתְלַהֵם] dec. 7b   להם

כְּמַתְּנַת׳   pref. id.)(n. fem. s., constr. of מַתָּנָה d. 11a   נתן

כְּמִתְעַתֵּעַ   pref. כְּ bef. (:))(Pilp. part. sing. m. (§ 6. r. 4)   תעע

כֵּן   noun m.s. (suff. כַּנֹּו, pl. כֵּנִים d. 8b, § 37.r.1)   כנן
כֵּן }
כֵּן } adj. masc. sing. dec. 1a; or adv. .   כון
כֵּ֫ן }

כְּנֹאד׳   pref. כְּ)(noun masc. sing. dec. 1a   נאד

כְּנָבָל   pref. id.)(pr. name masc.   נבל

כִּנְבֹל   pref. כְּ bef. (:))(Kal inf. constr.   נבל

כְּנֹבֶ֫לֶת   וּ pref. כְּ)(Kal part. act. sing. fem. (§ 8. rem. 19) ; וּ bef. (:)   נבל

כְּנֶגְדֹּו   pref. id.)(prep. נֶגֶד with suff. 3 pers. sing. masc. dec. 6 (§ 35. rem. 3)   נגד

כְּנָנָה׳   pref. כַּ for כְּהַ)(noun masc. sing. (suff. נֶגְהֹו), dec. 6c (§ 35. rem. 5) . . .   נגה

כְּנַגֵּן   pref. כְּ)(Piel inf. constr.   נגן

כְּנֶ֫גַע׳   pref. id.)(n. m. s. (suff. נִגְעִי), d.6a (§ 35.r.5)   נגע

כַּנֵּדֵר׳   pref. כַּ for כְּהַ)(noun masc. sing.   נדר

כַּנִּדְגָּלֹות׳   pref. id.)(Niph. part. fem. pl. [of נִדְגָּלָה from נִדְגָּל masc.] . . . .   דגל

כְּנִדָּתָהּ׳   pref. כְּ)(n. fem. s., suff. 3 p. s. from נִדָּה d. 10   נדה

כָּנָה.   Pi.—I. *to call by name.*—II. *to call by flattering names* or *titles,* i. e. *to flatter,* Job 32. 21, 22.

כְּנָת   fem. *companion, associate,* only pl. כְּנָוָת (§ 45) Ezr. 4. 7.

כְּנָת   Chald. fem. id. pl. with suff. כְּנָוָתֵהּ, comp. the preceding.

כְּנֵמָא   Chald. adv. (for כְּנָאמָא) *namely; hence, thus, in this manner.* Others take כְּ as a prefix and נֵמָא for נָאמָא (from נָאם) *according to the saying;* or נֵמָא for נֵימָא, נֵימַר, נֵאמַר (from אמר) *as is said,* or *as we say.*

וְכַנֵּן׳   noun fem. sing.   כנן

כְּנֶחֱמַת׳   pref. כְּ)(noun fem. sing., constr. of [נֶחָמָה] dec. 11c (§ 42. rem. 1) . .   נחם

כַּנָּהָר   pref. כַּ f. [כְּהַ } noun masc. sing. dec. 4a
כְּנָהָר׳   pref. כְּ q. v. }   נהר

וְכַנְּהָרֹות׳   pref. כַּ for כְּהַ)(id. pl., abs. st. .   נהר

וְכַנֶּה   pr. name of a place, see כַּלְנֵה.

וְכַנֹּו׳   noun m. s., suff. 3 p. s. m. from כֵּן d.8d & e   כנן

כִּנֹוֹחַ׳   pref. כְּ)(Kal inf.constr. (§21.r.3); וּ bef. (:)   נוח

כְּנֹוּס׳   pref. id.)(Kal inf.constr. (§21.r.3), orimp.s.m.   כנס

כְּנֹוּעַ׳   pref. id.)(Kal inf. constr. (§ 21. rem. 3)   נוע

וְכִנֹּור׳   noun masc. sing. dec. 1b   כנר

כִּנֹּרֹותֵ֫ינוּ׳   id. pl. fem., suff. 1 pers. pl.   כנר

כִּנֹּרֶ֫יךָ׳   id. pl. masc., suff. 2 pers. sing. fem. .   כנר

כְּנָוָתֵהּ׳   וּ Chald. noun. fem. sing., suff. 3 pers. sing. m. [from כְּנָת irr. § 45] ; וּ bef. (:)   כנה

כְּנָוָתְהֹון׳   וּ Chald. id. with suff. 3 pers. pl. masc.   כנה

כְּנָוָתֹו׳   Heb. id. pl., suff. 3 pers. sing. masc.   כנה

כַּנַּ֫חַל׳   pref. כַּ for כְּהַ)(noun masc. sing. dec. 6d;
כְּנַ֫חַל   b pref. כְּ q.v. } וּ bef. (:)   נחל

כַּנְּחָלִים׳   pref. כְּ bef. (:))(id. pl., abs. st. .   נחל

כַּנָּחָשׁ   pref. כַּ f. [כְּהַ } noun masc. sing. dec. 4a
כְּנָחָשׁ׳   pref. כְּ q. v. }   נחש

כַּנְּחֻשָׁה׳   pref. כַּ for כְּהַ)(adj. fem. sing. from נָחוּשׁ m.   נחש

כִּנְטֹות׳   pref. כְּ bef. (:))(Kal inf. c. dec. 1b   נטה

כִּנְטֹותֹו׳   pref. id.)(id., suff. 3 pers. sing. masc.   נטה

כְּנִטְעִים pref. id. ✕ noun masc., pl. of [נָטִיעַ] dec. 3 a   נטע

כַּנִּי noun m. s., suff. 1 pers. s. from כֵּן d. 8 d & e   כנן

כְּנַנְיָהוּ pr. name masc., see יְהוֹיָכִין   הוה

כֵּנִים adj. masc., pl. of כֵּן dec. 1 a   כון

כֵּנִים noun masc., pl. of כֵּן dec. 8 b (§ 37. rem. 1)   כון

כַּנֶּךָ id. sing., suff. 2 pers. sing. masc. [for כַּנְּךָ]   כון

כַּנְלֹתְךָ pref. כַּ ✕ contr. [for כְּהַכְלֹתְךָ] Hiph. inf., suff. 2 pers. sing. masc.   כלה

כְּנֵמָא Chald. adv. ; וּ bef. (ְ)   כנה

כְּנָמֵר pref. כְּ ✕ noun masc. sing. dec. 5 a   נמר

כִּנְמַר Chald. pref. כְּ bef. (ְ) ✕ noun masc. sing.   נמר

כְּנִמְרֹד pref. כְּ ✕ pr. name masc.   מרד

כָּנַן Root not used ; prob. i. q. כּוּן q. v. In the Arab. *to protect.*

כֵּן masc. dec. 8 (with suff. כַּנִּי § 37. rem. 1).— I. *place, station.*—II. *base, pedestal,* of the base or foot of the laver.

כֵּן masc. (in the sing. perhaps, Is. 51. 6) pl. כִּנִּים *lice* ; Sept. σκνῖφες, Vulg. *sciniphes,* a species of small *gnats.*

כַּנָּה fem. *plant ;* or *stock, root,* Ps. 80. 16.

כִּנָּם i. q. the preceding כִּנִּים *lice* or *gnats,* Ex. 8. 13, 14.

כְּנַנִי (*protector*) pr. name masc. Ne. 9. 4.

כְּנַנְיָהוּ (whom *the Lord protects*) pr. name masc. כְּנַנְיָהוּ (id.) pr. name masc. called also כְּנַנְיָה comp. 1 Ch. 15. 22, with ver. 27.

כְּנָנִי pr. name masc.   כנן

כְּנַנְיָה
כְּנַנְיָהוּ } pr. name masc. ; וּ bef. (ְ)   כנן

כֹּנַנְתִּי Pilel pret. 1 pers. sing. ; acc. shifted by conv. וְ (comp. § 8. rem. 7)   כון

[כָּנַס] *to collect, gather together, assemble.* Pi. id. Hithp. *to collect oneself,* i. e. *to wrap oneself up,* Is. 28. 20.

מִכְנָס m. d. 2 b, only in pl. or du. constr. *trowsers* or *drawers,* for the priests, comp. Hithp.

כְּנֵס pref. כַּ for כְּהַ ✕ noun masc. sing. dec. 8 b   נסס

כֹּנֵס Kal part. act. sing. masc.   כנס

כְּנִסְכָּה pref. כְּ ✕ noun masc. sing., suff. 3 pers. sing. fem. from נֶסֶךְ dec. 6 a ; וּ bef. (ְ)   נסך

כְּנִסְכּוֹ pref. id. ✕ id., suff. 3 pers. sing. masc. ; וּ id.   נסך

כָּנַסְתִּי Kal pret. 1 pers. sing.   כנס

כִּנַּסְתִּי Piel pret. 1 pers. sing. ; acc. shifted by conv. וְ (comp. § 8. rem. 7)   כנס

כְּנַסְתִּים id. with suff. 3 pers. pl. masc.   כנס

כָּנַע Hiph. *to bow down, bring low, humble, subdue.* Niph.—I. *to be humbled, subdued.*—II. *to humble oneself, to submit,* with מִלְפְנֵי, מִפְּנֵי, לִפְנֵי.

כְּנֵעָה fem. dec. 11 c, *bundle, package, bale,* from the idea of *folding together,* Je. 10. 17.

כְּנַעַן (*low*) pr. name—I. of a son of Ham.—II. of the land inhabited by his posterity.—III. *merchant* (comp. כְּנַעֲנִי No. II.); pl. with suff. כְּנַעֲנֶיהָ (§ 35. r. 5).

כְּנַעֲנִי, fem. כְּנַעֲנִית, pl. masc. כְּנַעֲנִים gent. noun —I. *Canaanite,* inhabitant of Canaan, collect. *Canaanites.*—II. *merchant,* like כַּשְׂדִּי *Chaldean,* for *astrologer.*

כִּנְעוּרֶיהָ pref. כְּ bef. (ְ) ✕ n. m. pl. (נְעוּרִים) suff. 3 p. s. m.   נער

כְּנַעַן
כְּנַעַן } וּ pr. name of a man and a people ; וּ bef. (ְ)   כנע

כְּנַעַן noun masc. sing. (§ 35. rem. 5)   כנע

כְּנַעֲנָה וּ pr. name masc. ; וּ bef. (ְ)   כנע

כְּנַעֲנִי gent. noun from כְּנַעַן, also as an appellative   כנע

כְּנַעֲנֶיהָ noun masc. pl., suff. 3 pers. sing. fem. from כְּנַעַן dec. 6 (§ 35. rem. 5)   כנע

כְּנַעֲנִים gent. noun, pl. of כְּנַעֲנִי from כְּנַעַן   כנע

כְּנַעֲנִים noun masc., pl. of כְּנַעֲנִי (comp. § 35. rem. 5)   כנע

כַּנַּעַר pref. כַּ for כְּהַ ✕ noun masc. sing. dec. 6 d   נער

כִּנְעָתֵךְ noun fem. sing., suff. 2 pers. sing. fem. [from כְּנָעָה or כִּנְעָה]   כנע

כָּנָף fem. dec. 4 a (du. c. כַּנְפֵי, pl. c. כַּנְפוֹת § 33. rem. 1).—I. *wing* of a bird ; עוֹף כָּנָף *bird of wing,* i. e. *winged bird ;* בַּעַל כָּנָף *possessor of wings,* i. e. *bird.* Metaph. for *swiftness,* כַּנְפֵי רוּחַ שַׁחַר 'כַּ *wings of the wind, morning ;* as the means of protection, צֵל כְּנָפַיִם *shadow of wings.*—II. *wing* of an army, Is. 8. 8.—III. *extremity, extreme part, corner,* as of the earth.—IV. *skirt* of the loose flowing upper garment.—V. perhaps *pinnacle,* Da. 9. 28, *upon the pinnacle of abomination,* i. e. the temple filled with abominations.

כָּנַף Niph. *to be removed to a distant part,* Is. 30. 20. Others, *to be hid,* or *hide oneself,* coll. with the Arabic.

כְּנַף וּ id. constr. st. ; וּ bef. (ְ)   כנף

כְּנָפָיו id. pl., suff. 3 pers. sing. masc. (§ 4. rem. 1)   כנף

כִּנְפֹל pref. כְּ bef. (ְ) ✕ Kal inf. constr.   נפל

כַּנְפוֹת noun fem. pl. constr. [of כְּנָפוֹת] from כָּנָף dec. 4 a (§ 33. rem. 1)   כנף

כַּנְפֵי id. dual masc. constr. of כְּנָפַיִם   כנף

כְּנָפִי id. sing., suff. 1 pers. sing.   כנף

a Ps. 144. 12.   d Ge. 40. 13.   g Ho. 13. 7.   k Ps. 33. 7.   o Ec. 2. 8.   r Le. 22. 13.   u Is. 23. 8.   x Je. 10. 17.   a 2 Ch. 3. 11.
Ge. 41. 13.   e Is. 33. 1.   h Da. 7. 6.   l Ex. 29. 41.   p Eze. 22. 21.   s Ho. 12. 8 ;   v Job 40. 30.   y Job 39. 26.   b Eze. 18. 8.
Ge. 42. 11. 19.   f Ezr. 5. 11.   i Is. 30. 17.   m Nu. 28. 8.   q Eze. 39. 28.   Zep. 1. 11.   w 2 Sa. 18. 32.   z 2 Sa. 3. 34.

26

כנפיהם–כסף

כַּנְפֵיהֶם	וּ] id. dual, suff. **3** pers. pl. **masc.**	כנף
כַּנְפֵיהֶן	id. dual, suff. **3** pers. pl. fem.	כנף
כְּנָפָיו	id. dual, suff. **3** pers. sing. masc.	כנף
כְּנָפֶיךָ	id. dual, suff. **2** pers. sing. masc.	כנף
כְּנָפַיִם	} id. dual abs. st.	כנף
כְּנָפָיִם		
כְּנָפֶךָ	id. sing., suff. 2 pers. sing. masc. [for כְּנָפְךָ]	כנף
כְּנָפֵל	pref. כְּ)(noun masc. sing.	נפל
כִּנְפֹל	pref. כְּ bef. (:))(Kal inf. constr.	נפל
כְּנֶפֶשׁ	וּ] pref. כְּ)(noun com. sing. d. 6 a; וּ] bef. (:)	נפש
כְּנַפְשׁוֹ	pref. id.)(id., suff. 3 pers. sing. masc.	נפש
כְּנַפְשְׁךָ	pref. id.)(id., suff. 2 pers. sing. masc.	נפש
כְּנֶצֶר	pref. id.)(noun masc. sing.	נצר
כְּנֹקֵף	pref. id.)(noun masc. sing.	נקף

כָּנַר Root not used; prob. imitating a *tremulous and stridulous sound.*

    כִּנּוֹר masc. dec. 1 b (pl. ‑יִם, ‑וֹת) *harp or lyre.*

    כִּנֶּרֶת, כִּנְּרוֹת, כִּנָּרוֹת pr. name of a city in the tribe of Naphtali, near the sea of Galilee, called יָם כִּנֶּרֶת Nu. 34. 11.

כִּנְּרוֹת	} pr. name of a place, כִּנֶּרֶת	כנר
כִּנָּרוֹת		
כִּנֹּרוֹת	וּ] noun m. with pl. fem. term. fr. כִּנּוֹר d. 1 b	כנר
כִּנֹּרִי	id. sing., suff. 1 pers. sing.	כנר
כִּנְּרָה	} pr. name of a place	כנר
כִּנְּרֹר		

[כְּנַשׁ] Chald. *to collect, assemble,* Da. 3. 2. Ithpa. pass. Ge. 3. 3, 27.

כִּנְשֹׂא	pref. כְּ bef. (:))(Kal inf. constr.	נשא
כַּנֹּשֶׁה	} pref. כַּ f. [כְּהַ)(Kal part. act. sing. masc.	נשה
כִּנְשֶׁה	} pref. כְּ q. v. dec. 9 a	
כַּנָּשִׁים	pref. כַּ for כְּהַ)(noun fem. with pl. masc. term. see אֱנוֹשׁ and אִישׁ (§ 45)	אנש
כַּנֶּשֶׁף	pref. id.)(noun masc. sing. (suff. נִשְׁפּוֹ) d. 6 a	נשף
כַּנֶּשֶׁר	} pref. id. noun masc. sing. (pl. c. נִשְׁרֵי)	נשר
כְּנֶשֶׁר	} pref. כְּ dec. 6 c	
כַּנְּשָׁרִים	pref. כַּ for כְּהַ)(id. pl., abs. st.	נשר
כְּנִשְׁרִין	Chald. pref. כְּ)(noun masc., pl. of נְשַׁר d. 3 b	נשר
	noun masc. sing.	כסא

כָּסָא Root not used; 1. q. כָּסָה *to cover.*

    כֶּסֶה, כֶּסָא masc. *the new moon,* Pr. 7. 20; Ps. 81. 4; Arab. كسا *to cover with brightness* (Prof. Lee).

    כִּסֵּא masc. dec. 7 b (with suff. כִּסְאֲךָ § 36.

rem. 3) pl. כִּסְאוֹת for כִּסְאוֹת.—I. *seat,* of the high-priest, of a judge.—II. *throne, royal throne.*

    כִּסֵּה masc. *throne,* 1 Kl. 10. 19; Job 26. 9.

    כֵּס masc. id. Ex. 17. 16.

כִּסֵּא	וּ] noun masc. sing. dec. 7 b	כסא
כִּסְאוֹ	וּ] id., suff. 3 pers. sing. masc.	כסא
כִּסְאוֹת	id. pl.	כסא
כִּסְאוֹתָם	id. pl., suff. 3 pers. pl. masc.	כסא
כִּסְאִי	id. sing., suff. 1 pers. sing.	כסא
כִּסְאֲךָ	} id. sing., suff. 2 pers. sing. masc. (§ 36. r. 3)	נסא
כִּסְאֶךָ		
כְּסָבְאָם	וּ] pref. כְּ)(noun masc. sing. with suff. 3 pers. pl. masc. from סֹבֶא dec. 6 c; וּ] bef. (:)	סבא
כַּסְדָּיָא	Chald. Kh. דָּיָא, K. דָּאֵי gent. n., emph. of כַּשְׂדִּי	כשד
	dec. 7, see כַּשְׂדִּי	
כְּסֶלֶם	pref. כְּ bef. (:))(pr. name of a place	סלם

[כָּסָה].—I. *to cover, conceal.* Niph. *to be covered.* Pi. כִּסָּה—I. *to cover,* with acc.; with עַל, לְ, *to cover over;* with acc. or עַל of the person covered, and acc. or בְּ of the covering. כְּסוּי חֲטָאָה *covered* (as to) *sin,* i. e. *whose sin is covered, pardoned.*—II. *to put on, to cover oneself.*—III. *to cover, hide, conceal.* Intrans. Ps. 143. 9, *to thee I hide myself,* i. e. to thee I hasten or flee to hide myself. Pu. כֻּסָּה, כָּסָּה (§ 10. rem. 5) *to be covered,* with בְּ, also without it. Hithp. *to cover oneself,* with בְּ, also without it.

    כְּסָי masc. dec. 3 a, *a covering,* Nu. 4. 6, 14.

    כְּסוּת fem. dec. 10.—I. *a covering.*—II. *garment,* De. 22. 12.

    סוּת fem. *clothing, garment,* Ge. 49. 11; but see Root סָוָה.

    כֶּסֶת fem. only pl. כְּסָתוֹת, constr. כְּסָתוֹת (ת treated as if radical, comp. דֶּלֶת) *cushions,* Eze. 13. 18, 20.

    מְכַסֶּה masc. dec. 9 a, *a covering.*

    מְכַסֶּה masc. dec. 9 a (§ 38. rem. 1).—I. *covering.*—II. *the caul* which covers the intestines, Le. 9. 19.

כִּסָּה	וּ] Piel pret. 3 pers. sing. masc.	כסה
כִּסֶּה	noun masc. sing. for כֶּסָא (q. v.)	כסא
כֹּסֶה	וּ] Kal part. act. sing. masc.	כסה
כִּסָּהוּ	וּ] Piel pret. 3 pers. sing. m., suff. 3 pers. s. m.	כסה
כִּסּוּ	וּ] Piel pret. 3 pers. pl.	כסה
כֻּסּוּ	Pual pret. 3 pers. pl. [for כָּסּוּ § 10. rem. 5]	כסה
כַּסּוּחָה	pref. כַּ for כְּהַ)(noun fem. sing.	סוח
כְּסוּחָה	Kal part. pass. sing. fem. [of כָּסוּחַ]	כסח

a Eze. 1. 24, 25.   d 2 Sa. 17. 9.   g Is. 14. 19.   k Is. 24. 2.   n Is. 40. 31.   p Ps. 122. 5.   t Job 26. 9.   w Nu. 17. 7.   z Is. 5. 25.
b Eu. 3. 9.   e Eze. 18. 4.   h Job 30. 31.   l Ex. 22. 24.   o Da. 4. 30.   r Exe. 26. 16.   u Pr. 12. 16, 23.   y Le. 17. 12.   z Ps. 80. 17.
c Job 3. 16.   f 1 Sa. 18. 1, 3.   i Is. 18. 3.   m Is. 59. 10.   x Ex. 17. 16.   s Na. 1. 10.

כְּסוּחִים	Kal part. pass. pl. masc. [of כָּסוּחַ] dec. 3a	כסה
כְּסוּי	Kal part. p. or subst. m., constr. of [כָּסוּי] d. 3a	כסה
וְכִסּוּךָ	Piel pret. 3 pers. pl., suff. 2 pers. sing. fem.	כסה
כָּסוֹם	Kal inf. abs.	כסם
כַּסּוּנְגּ	Piel imp. pl. masc., suff. 1 pers. pl.	
כְּכַה	pref. כַּ f. } noun masc. sing. dec. 1a	סום
כְּסוּסִים	pref. כַּ q. v. }	
כִּסוּסִי	pref. id. ✕ id. pl., suff. 1 pers. sing	סום
כְּסוּסֶיךָ	pref. id. ✕ id. pl., suff. 2 pers. sing. masc.	סום
כַּסּוּפָהּ	pref. כַּ for כְּה ✕ noun fem. sing. dec. 10	סוף
כְּסוּפוֹת	pref. כַּ ✕ id. pl.	סוף
כַּסּוֹת	Piel inf. constr.	כסה
כְּסוּת	noun fem. sing. dec. 1a	כסה
וּכְסוֹת	noun fem., pl. of כוֹם dec. 1a	כום
כְּסוּתֹה	noun f. s., suff. 3 pers. s. f. fr. כְּסוּת d. 1a	כסה
כְּסוּתֹה	id., suff. 3 pers. sing. masc.	כסה
כְּסוּתְךָ	id., suff. 2 pers. sing. masc.	כסה
כְּסוּתָם	id., suff. 3 pers. pl. masc.	כסה

[כָּסַח] to cut off, Is. 33. 12; Ps. 80. 17.

כְּסִיל	noun m. s. d. 1a, also pr. name; וּ bef.	כסל
כְּסִילוּת	noun fem. sing.	כסל
כְּסִילֵיהֶם	noun masc. pl., suff. 3 pers. pl. masc. fr. כְּסִיל dec. 1a; וּ bef.	כסל
כְּסִילִים	id. pl., abs. st.; וּ id.	כסל
כִּסִּינוּ	Piel pret. 1 pers. pl.	כסה
כְּסִירָא	pref. כְּ ✕ pr. name masc., see סִיסְרָא.	
כַּסִּיר	pref. כַּ for כְּה ✕ noun com. sing. dec. 1a	סיר
כִּסִּיתִי	Piel pret. 2 pers. sing. masc.	כסה
כִּסִּיתוֹ	id. id., suff. 3 pers. sing. masc.	כסה
כִּסִּיתִי	id. pret. 1 pers. sing. (§ 24. rem. 11)	כסה
כִּסִּיתִיךָ	id. id., suff. 2 pers. sing. masc.	כסה
כְּסִכָּה	noun fem. sing. dec. 1b; וּ bef.	סכך

כָּסַל to be foolish, only fut. יִכְסָל Je. 10. 8. In the derivatives (according to Gesenius) to be fat, strong; hence to be firm, confident.

כֶּסֶל masc. dec. 6a (with suff. כִּסְלִי).—I. loin; loins.—II. inward parts, viscera, Ps. 38. 8.—III. confidence, hope.—IV. folly, Ec. 7. 25.

כִּסְלָה fem. (no vowel change).—I. confidence, hope, Job 4. 6.—II. folly, Ps. 85. 9.

כִּסְלֵו Chislev, the ninth month of the Hebrew year, beginning with the new moon of our December.

כְּסִיל masc. dec. 1a.—I. fool.—II. the constel-

lation Orion.—III. pr. name of a city in Judah, Jos. 15. 30.

כְּסִילוּת fem. folly, Pr. 9. 13.

כִּסְלוֹן (hope) pr. name of a town in the borders of Judah, Jos. 15. 10.

כִּסְלוֹן (id.) pr. name masc. Nu. 34. 21.

כְּסֻלּוֹת (hopes) pr. name of a town in Issachar, Jos. 19. 18.

כִּסְלֹת תָּבֹר (confidence of Tabor) pr. name of a town at the foot of mount Tabor, Jos. 19. 12.

כְּסָל	in pause, Seg. [as if from כָּסָל § 35. rem. 5] }	כסל
כֶּסֶל	noun masc. sing. (suff. כִּסְלוֹ), dec. 6a }	כסל
כִּסְלֵו	name of a month	כסל
כִּסְלוֹ	noun m. s., suff. 3 pers. s. m. from כֶּסֶל d. 6a	כסל
כִּסְלוֹן	pr. name of a place	כסל
כִּסְלוֹן	pr. name masc.	כסל

כַּסְלֻחִים pr. name of a people, Ge. 10. 14; 1 Ch. 1. 12.

כְּסָלַי	noun m. pl., suff. 1 pers. sing. from כֶּסֶל d. 6a	כסל
כִּסְלִי	id. sing., suff. 1 pers. sing.	כסל
כִּסְלָם	id. sing., suff. 3 pers. pl. masc.	כסל
כִּסְלֹת	pr. name in compos. כִּסְלֹת־תָּבֹר	כסל
כִּסְלָתְךָ	noun masc. sing., suff. 2 pers. sing. masc. [for כְּסָלָתְךָ from כִּסְלָה (no pl.)	כסל

[כָּסַם] to shave, poll the head, Eze. 44. 20. Prof. Lee, to adorn.

כֻּסֶּמֶת fem. pl. כֻּסְּמִים, a kind of corn, spelt.

כִּסְמוֹ	Piel pret. 3 pers. s. m. (כִּסָּה), suff. 3 p. pl. m.	כסה
וּכְסֻמִּים	pl. abs. of the foll.	כסם
וּכֻסֶּמֶת	noun fem. sing. dec. 13	כסם

[כָּסַס] to number, reckon, Ex. 12. 4.

מֶכֶס masc. (with suff. מִכְסָם) tribute.

מִכְסָה fem. only constr. מִכְסַת.—I. number, Ex. 12. 4.—II. price, Le. 27. 23.

מַס masc. (contr. from מֶסֶס?) pl. מִסִּים, tribute, tax; מַס עֹבֵד tribute-service; הָיָה לָמַס to become tributary; נָתַן לָמַס שׂוּם to impose tribute, make tributary; שָׂרֵי מִסִּים tribute masters.

מִסָּה fem. dec. 10, tribute, offering, De. 16. 10.

[כָּסַף] prop. as in the Chald. to be pale, wan; hence, to desire greatly, to long after, const. with לְ of the person. Niph.—I. to be ashamed, Zep. 2. 1.—II. to long after.

כֶּסֶף masc. dec. 6a (with suff. כַּסְפִּי).—I. silver;

a Is. 33. 12.   d Eze. 44. 20.   h Mal. 2. 13.   m De. 22. 12.   q Ge. 37. 26.   u Ps. 104. 6.   z Is. 1. 8.   e Job 8. 14.   i Job 4. 6.
b Ps. 32. 1;   e Ho. 10. 8.   i Is. 35. 5.   n Is. 50. 3.   r Is. 58. 7.   a Job 27. 18.   f Ps. 38. 8.   j Ex. 15. 10.
Nu. 4. 6, 14.   f Is.5.28; Pr.1.27.   k Ex. 21. 10.   o Pr. 9. 13.   s Eze. 32. 7.   c Job 15. 27.   g Job 31. 24.   k Eze. 4. 9.
Eze. 26. 19.   g Is. 21. 1.   l Ex. 22. 26.   Iz. 13. 10.   De. 23. 14.   t Is. 51. 16.   d Ne. 1. 1.   h Ps. 73. 7.   l Is. 29. 26.

20*

שֶׁקֶל כָּסֶף *a shekel of silver*; with the numeral שֶׁקֶל is omitted, as עֶשְׂרִים כָּסֶף *twenty shekels of silver*.—II. *money*.

כְּסַף Chald. masc. dec. 3a, *silver*.

כָּסְפְיָא pr. name of a country, according to others, of a town, Ezr. 8. 17.

כָּסֶף ן' in pause for כֶּסֶף (q. v. § 35. rem. 5)   כסף

כַּסְף' } Chald. noun masc. sing. dec. 3a   כסף
כְּסַף }

כָּסֶף ן', ן' noun masc. sing. (suff. כַּסְפִּי), dec. 6a; for ן see lett. ו.   כסף

כַּסְפָּא ן' Chald. noun m. sing., emph. of כְּסַף dec. 3a   כסף

כַּסְפּוֹ noun m. s., suff. 3 pers. s. m. from כֶּסֶף d. 6a   כסף

כַּסְפִּי id. with suff. 1 pers. sing.   כסף

כַּסְפֵּיהֶם ' id. pl., suff. 3 pers. pl. masc.   כסף

כַּסְפֵּךָ } id. id., suff. 2 pers. sing. masc.   כסף
כַּסְפְּךָ }

כַּסְפֵּךְ id. id., suff. 2 pers. sing. fem.   כסף

כַּסְפְּכֶם' id. id., suff. 2 pers. pl. masc.   כסף

כַּסְפָּם id. id., suff. 3 pers. pl. masc.   כסף

כַּסְפֵּנוּ id. id., suff. 1 pers. sing.   כסף

כַּסְפַּר' pref. בַּ for כְּהַ (noun masc. sing. dec. 6b   ספר

כִּסְּתָה ן' Piel pret. 3 pers. sing. fem.   כסה

כְּסָתוֹת' noun fem. pl. abs. from [כֶּסֶת] dec. 13a   כסה

כִּסְּתוֹתֵיכֶנָה id. pl., suff. 2 pers. pl. fem. ת retained as if radical, (comp. דֶּלֶת קֶשֶׁת)   כסה

כִּסֵּתִי' defect. for כִּסֵּיתִי (q. v.)   כסה

כִּסִּתְנִי' Piel pret. 3 pers. sing. f. (כִּסְּתָה), suff. 1 p. s.   כסה

כָּעַב pref. בְּ f. כְּהַ (כְּהַ noun com. s. d. 1a (once
כְּעַב ו' pref. בְּ q. v. constr. of עָב); בֶּ bef. (.:)   עוב

כָּעֶבֶד' } pref. בְּ f. כְּהַ } noun masc. sing. dec. 6a   עבד
כְּעֶבֶד } pref. בְּ q. v. }

כְּעַבְדִּי pref. id. (id. with suff. 1 pers. sing.   עבד

כַּעֲבָדִים' pref. בַּ bef. (.:) (id. pl., abs. st.   עבד

כַּעֲבוֹדַת' pref. id. (noun fem. s., constr. of 'דָה d. 10   עבד

כַּעֲבוֹר' pref. id. (Kal inf. constr.   עבר

כַּעֲבוֹת ו' suff. id.; noun m. s., constr. of עָבֹת d. 3a   עבת

כַּעֲבֹר' pref. id. (Kal inf. constr.   עבר

כְּעָבְרָם' pref. בְּ (id., suff. 3 pers. pl. masc.   עבר

כָּעֵגֶל' pref. id. (noun masc. sing. d. 6 (§ 35. r. 6)   עגל

כְּעֶגְלָה' pref. id. (noun fem. sing. dec. 10   עגל

כְּעֶגְלֵי' pref. id. (noun masc. pl. constr. of עֵגֶל dec. 6 (§ 35. rem. 6)   עגל

כָּעֲדִי' pref. בַּ bef. (.:) (noun masc. sing. (suff. עֶדְיוֹ) dec. 6i (§ 35. rem. 14)   עדה

כְּעֶדֶן pref. בְּ (pr. name of a place   עדן

כָּעֵדֶר' } pref. בְּ f. כְּהַ, (כְּהַ noun masc. sing. dec. 6   עדר
כְּעֵדֶר } pref. בְּ q. v. (§ 35. rem. 6) }

כַּעֲדָתוֹ ן' pref. בַּ bef. (.:) (noun fem. sing., suff. 3 pers. sing. masc. from עֵדָה dec. 11b   יעד

כְּעֹל' pref. בְּ (noun masc. sing.   עול

כַּעֲוֹן' pref. בַּ bef. (.:) (n. m. s. constr. of עָוֹן d. 3a   עוה

כַּעֲוֹנֹתֵנוּ' pref. id. (id. pl., suff. 1 pers. pl.   עוה

כָּעוֹף' } pref. בְּ f. כְּהַ, (כְּהַ noun masc. sing.   עוף
כְּעוֹף } pref. בְּ q. v. }

כְּעוֹפֶרֶת' pref. בְּ for כְּהַ, (כְּהַ noun fem. sing.   עפר

כְּעוּר' Chald. pref. בְּ (noun masc. sing.   עור

כָּעוֹרֵב' pref. בְּ for כְּהַ, (כְּהַ noun masc. sing. d. 7b   ערב

כָּעוֹרִים' pref. בַּ for כְּהַ (adj. masc., pl. of עִוֵּר d. 7b   עור

כַּעֲזוּבַת' pref. בַּ bef. (.:) (n. f. s., constr. of עֲזוּבָה d. 10   עזב

כְּעֹטְיָה' pref. id. (Kal part. act., fem. (§ 24. rem. 5)   עטה

כְּעֵין' pref. id. (noun fem. s. constr. of עַיִן d. 6h   עין

כְּעֵינֵי' Chald. pref. id. (id. pl. constr. dec. 3d   עין

כְּעֵינֵי' pref. id. (id. pl. constr. st.   עין

כָּעִיר' pref. id. (noun fem. sing. irr. (§ 45)   עור

כֶּעָכֶם' ו pref. בְּ (noun masc. sing. d. 6; ו bef. (.:)   עכס

כְּעַל' pref. בְּ (prep. עַל (prop. constr. of עָלה)   עלה

כַּעֲלֶה' ו' pref. בְּ for כְּהַ כְּהַ bef. עֲ for כְּהַ (n. m. d. 9b   עלה

כַּעֲלֻקָה' pref. בַּ for כְּהַ, (כְּהַ noun fem. sing. d. 10   עלה

כַּעֲלוֹת' pref. בַּ bef. (.:) (Kal inf. constr. dec. 1b   עלה

כַּעֲלִילוֹתַיִךְ' ן' pref. id. (noun fem. pl., suff. 2 pers. sing. fem. from עֲלִילָה dec. 10   עלל

כְּעֲלִילוֹתֵיכֶם' ן' pref. id. (id., suff. 2 pers. pl. masc.   עלל

כַּעֲלִילוֹתָם' ן' pref. id. (id., suff. 3 pers. pl. m. (§ 4. r. 2)   עלל

כָּעֹלְלִים' pref. id. (noun masc., pl. of עוֹלֵל dec. 7b   עלל

כְּעֹלֵלֹת' pref. id. (constr. of the foll.   עלל

כְּעֹלֵלֹת' pref. id. (noun fem. pl. dec. 11b   עלל

כָּעָם } pref. בְּ f. כְּהַ, (כְּהַ noun masc. sing. dec. 8   עמם
כְּעָם } pref. בְּ q. v. (but comp. § 45) }

כְּעָמְדוֹ' ו pref. בְּ (Kal inf., suff. 3 p. s. m.; ו bef.   עמד

כְּעַמּוּדֵי' pref. id. (noun m. pl. constr. fr. עַמּוּד d. 1b   עמד

כְּעַמֵּי' pref. id. (n. m. pl. c. fr. עַם d. 8a (comp. §45)   עמם

כְּעַמִּי' pref. id. (id. sing., suff. 1 pers. sing.   עמם

כָּעַמִּים' pref. בְּ for כְּהַ, (כְּהַ id. pl., abs. st.   עמם

כֶּעָמִיר' } pref. בְּ f. כְּהַ bef. עֲ f. כְּהַ dag. forte impl. (&
כָּעָמִיר' } ו pref. בְּ q. v. (noun masc. s.; ו bef. (.:)   עמר

כַּעֲמָךְ' ו' } pref. id. (noun masc. sing., suff. 2 p.
כַּעֲמֶךָ } sing. m. from עַם d. 8a (comp. § 45)   עמם

כָּעֵמֶק' pref. id. (noun masc. sing. dec. 6b   עמק

כְּעֵמֶר' Chald. בְּ bef. (.:) (noun masc. sing.   עמר

a Da. 2. 32.   g Eze. 13. 20.   m 1 Ch. 28. 15.   s Je. 50. 11.   b Ps. 103. 10.   h Ca. 1. 7.   Eze. 45. 25.   n Is. 24. 13.   t Mi. 4. 12.
b Ge. 42. 25, 35.   h Eze. 31. 15.   n Pr. 10. 25.   t Is. 49. 18.   c Ho. 9. 11.   i Da. 7. 8.   m Eze. 24. 11.   o Joel 2. 5.   u Je. 9. 21.
c Is. 1. 22.   i Ps. 44. 16.   o Is. 5. 18.   u Ps. 78. 52.   d Ps. 123. 2.   k Ex. 15. 10.   o Eze. 20. 44.   p Da. 11. 4.   v 2 Ch. 18. 3.
d Ge. 43. 23.   k Job 30. 15.   p 1 Ki. 18. 29.   v Nu. 17. 5.   e Pr. 7. 22.   l Eze. 36. 19.   p Eze. 42. 6.   g Eze. 28. 21.   w Is. 28. 21.
e Is. 34. 4.   l Is. 24. 2.   q Job 27. 7.   w Ca. 5. 11.   f Is. 64. 5.   m Job 3. 16.   r 2 Ch. 13. 9.   r Da. 7. 2.
f Ex. 13. 13.   f Ec. 10. 7.   r Je. 31. 18.   x Eze. 14. 10.   g Is. 17. 9.   m Pr. 11. 28.   g Mi. 7. 1.   s Ho. 9. 1.

בַּעֲמָרָה   pret. id.)(pr. name of a place   עמר

כְּעַן   Chald. adv. *now;* עַד כְּעַן *until now.* Hence a fem. form כְּעֶנֶת, contr. כְּעֶת adv. *so on, so forth.* Etymon doubtful.

כַּעֲנָבִים   pref. כַּ bef. (־ַ))(noun m., pl. of עֵנָב d. 4 b   ענב

כַּעֲנַן   pref. id.)(constr. of the foll.   ענן

כֶּעָנָן   )(וְ pref. כַּ f. כְּהֶ bef. עָ f. כְּהָ)(n. m. s. d. 4 c   ענן

כַּעֲנָנִים   pref. כַּ bef. (־ַ))(id. pl., abs. st.   ענן

כַּעֲנָקִים   pref. id.)(noun m. pl. abs. from עֲנָק d. 4 c   ענק

כְּעֶנֶת   Chald. adv. see כְּעַן; וּ bef. (־ְ).

כָּעַס)(fut. יִכְעַם *to be vexed, irritated, provoked, angry.* Pi. כִּעֵם *to irritate, provoke.* Hiph. הִכְעִים *to vex, grieve; to irritate, provoke to anger.*

כַּעַם masc. dec. 6 d (with suff. כַּעֲסוֹ, כַּעֲסוֹ § 35. r. 5).—I. *vexation, grief, sadness.*—II. *anger;* pl. כְּעָסִים *excitements to anger,* 2 Ki. 23. 26.

כַּעַשׁ masc. dec. 6 d, id. only Job 5. 2; 6. 2; 10. 17; 17. 7.

כָּעַם)(וְ Kal pret. 3 pers. s. m. for כַּעַם (§ 8. r. 7)   כעם

כָּעַם   )(־וְ noun masc. sing. dec. 6 d; for ־וְ see

כַּעַם   )(וְ, lett. ו.   כעם

כַּעֲסוֹ   id., suff. 3 pers. s. m. [for כַּעֲסוֹ § 35. r. 5]   כעם

כִּעֲסוּנִי   Piel pret. 3 pers. pl. (§ 14. r. 1), suff. 1 p. s.   כעם

בַעֲסִי   )(noun masc. sing., suff. 1 pers. sing. from כַּעַם dec. 6 d [for כַּעֲסִי § 35. rem. 5]   כעם

כֶּעָסִים   )(וְ pref. כַּ for כְּהֶ bef. עָ for כְּהָ; n. m. s. d. 3 a   כעם

כַּעַסְךָ   noun m. s., suff. 2 pers. s. m. from כַּעַם d. 6 d   כעם

כִעֲסָתָה   )(וְ Piel pret. 3 p. s. f. (§ 14. r. 1), suff. 3 p. s. f.   כעם

כְּמִפְעַל   pref. כְּ)(n. m. pl. constr. fr. [פַּעַל] d. 8 d   עוף

כַּעֲפָר   pref. כַּ bef. (־ַ))(constr. of the foll.   עפר

כֶּעָפָר   )(pref. כַּ for כְּהֶ bef. עָ for כְּהָ &   עפר

כְּעָפָר   pref. כְּ)(noun masc. sing. dec. 4 c   עפר

כָּעֵץ   pref. כַּ f. כְּהֶ, כְּהָ)(noun m. s. d. 7 a (but   עצה

כְּעֵץ   pref. כְּ q. v.   comp. § 36. r. 2 & 4)   עצה

כַּעֲצָם   )(וְ pref. כַּ)(n. f. s. (suff. עַצְמִי) d. 6 a; וּ bef. (־ְ)   עצם

כְּעַצְמוֹ   )(וְ pref. id.)(Kal inf., suff. 3 p. s. m.; וּ id.   עצם

כַּעֲצָמִים   )(pref. כַּ bef. (־ַ))(noun fem. pl. of עֶצֶם (suff. עַצְמִי) dec. 6 a   עצם

כְּעֶצֶת   pref. id.)(noun f. s., constr. of עֵצָה d. 11 b   יעץ

כְּעֹרֵב   pref. כְּ)(pr. name masc.   ערב

כַּעֲרָבָה   pref. כַּ for כְּהֶ, כְּהָ)(noun fem. sing. d. 11 c   ערב

כַּעֲרָבִי   pref. כַּ bef. (־ַ))(gent. noun from עֲרָב   ערב

כָּעֲרָבִים   pref. id.)(n. m. pl. (c. עַרְבֵי) from עֶרֶב d. 6 a   ערב

כַּעֲרוּגַת   pref. id.)(n. f. s. constr. of [עֲרוּגָה] d. 10   ערג

כָּעֲרוֹעֵר   pref. id.)(adj. masc. sing.   ערד

כְּעָרִים   pref. כַּ for כְּהֶ bef. עָ for כְּהֶ)(noun fem., pl. of עִיר see (§ 45)   עיר

כְּעֶרְכּוֹ   pref. כְּ)(noun masc. sing., suff. 3 pers. sing. masc. from עֶרֶךְ dec. 6 (§ 35. rem. 6)   ערך

כְּעֶרְכִּי   pref. id.)(id. with suff. 1 pers. sing.   ערך

כְּעֶרְכְּךָ   pref. id.)(id., suff. 2 pers. sing. masc.   ערך

כְּעַרְעָר   pref. id.)(adj. masc. sing.   ערר

כְּעֹרֶף   pref. id.)(noun masc. sing. dec. 6 c   ערף

כָּעָשׂ   pref. כַּ for כְּהֶ, כְּהָ)(noun masc. sing.   עשׁשׁ

כָּעָשׂ   for [כָּעַשׂ] noun masc. sing. dec. 6 d   כעם

כָּעָשָׁב   pref. כַּ f. כְּהֶ, כְּהָ)(noun masc. sing. dec. 6   עשׁב

כְּעֵשֶׂב   pref. כְּ q. v.   (§ 35. rem. 6)   עשׁב

כַּעֲשִׂי   noun masc. sing., suff. 1 pers. sing. [for כַּעֲשִׂי § 35. rem. 5] from [כַּעַשׂ] dec. 6 d   כעם

כַּעַשְׂךָ   id. with suff. 2 pers. sing. masc.   כעם

כֶּעָשָׁן   )(וְ pref. כַּ for כְּהֶ bef. עָ for כְּהָ &   עשׁן

כְּעָשָׁן   וּ pref. כְּ)(noun masc. s. d. 4 c; וּ bef. (־ְ)   עשׁן

כַּעֲשַׁן   וּ pref. כְּ)(id. constr. st. (§ 33. r. 3); וּ id.   עשׁן

כַּעֲשֶׂר   pref. id.)(num. card. fem.   עשׁר

כַּעֲשָׂרִים   pref. id.)(id. pl. com. gen. (§ 35. rem. 16)   עשׁר

כַּעֲשֶׂרֶת   pref. כַּ bef. (־ַ))(id. sing. masc., constr. of עֲשָׂרָה (§ 42. rem. 5)   עשׁר

כָּעֵת   )(וְ pref. כַּ f. כְּהֶ, כְּהָ)(noun com. sing. dec. 8 b; וּ bef. (־ְ)   עדה

כְּעֵת   וּ pref. כְּ q. v.   dec. 8 b; וּ bef. (־ְ)

כְּעֶת   וּ Chald. adv. see כְּעַן; וּ id.

כְּעִתּוּדִים   pref. כְּ)(noun masc., pl. of [עַתּוּד] dec. 1 b   עתד

כֵּף

masc. *a rock,* only pl. כֵּפִים, Je. 4. 29; Job 30. 6.

כַּף
כָּף   וְ)(noun fem. sing. dec. 8 a.   כפף

כִּפְנֵי   pref. כְּ)(noun masc. s. (pl. c. פְּנֵי) d. 6 a   פנר

כִּפְנֹשׁ   pref. כְּ bef. (־ְ))(Kal inf. constr.   פנשׁ

[כָּפָה] *to cover, extinguish,* cogn. חָפָה, חָבָא, כָּבָא, only metaph. of anger, *to appease,* Pr. 21. 14. Others, *to bend, to avert,* cogn. כָּפַף.

כַּפָּה   noun f. s., suff. 3 pers. s. fem. fr. כַּף d. 8 d   כפף

כֻּפָּה   noun fem. sing. dec. 10   כפף

כַּפּוֹ   Kh. for כַּפָּיו (q. v. § 4. rem. 1)   כפף

כַּפּוֹ   noun fem. s., suff. 3 pers. s. m. fr. כַּף d. 8 d   כפף

כָּפוּל   Kal part. pass. sing. masc.   כפל

כְּפוּפִים   Kal part. pass. masc., pl. of [כָּפוּף] dec. 3 a   כפף

כְּפוֹר   וְ noun masc. sing. dec. 1 a; וּ bef. (־ְ)   כפר

כְּפוֹרֵי   id. pl., constr. st.; וּ id.   כפר

כַּפּוֹת   וְ noun fem., pl. of כַּף dec. 8 d   כפף

כַּפְטִישׁ   וְ pref. כְּ)(noun masc. sing.; וּ bef. (־ְ)   פטשׁ

a Ho. 9. 10.   f Ps. 112. 10.   l De. 32. 21.   r Ps. 18. 43.   x Ca. 5. 13.   e Je. 17. 6.   h Ho. 13. 5.   k Je. 50. 8.   l Ch. 28. 17.
b Eze. 38. 9, 16.   g Ec. 1. 18.   m Sa. 1. 16.   s Ex. 24. 10.   y Je. 48. 6.   d Job 6. 2.   i Ex. 19. 18.   l Is. 14. 19.   m Ezr. 1. 10.
c Je. 4. 13.   h Pr. 21. 19.   n Is. 49. 26.   t Da. 8. 8.   z 2 Ki. 23. 35.   e Job 10. 17.   k Ru. 1. 4.   m Je. 41. 6.   n Ezr. 6. 27.
d Ec. 5. 16.   i Pr. 27. 3.   o Ps. 85. 5.   u Ec. 11. 5.   a Is. 51. 6.   f Is. 44. 4.   l Ju. 13. 23.   o Ps. 146. 8.   o Je. 23. 29.
e 2 Ki. 17. 14.   k Pr. 12. 16.   p 1 Sa. 1. 6.   v Is. 44. 4.   b Le. 27. 12, 17.   g Pr. 10. 26.   m Ezr. 4. 17.   p Ps. 147. 16.   p Job. 41. 10.
   q Ki. 17. 14.   kk Job 5. 2.   pp Da. 9. 2L.

כפף   כַּפַּי   noun fem. dual, suff. 1 pers. sing. from

כַּפַּי   dec. 8 d . . . . .

כפף   id. dual, constr. st.

כפף   id. sing. with suff. 1 pers. sing.

פאה   כַּפִּי   pref. כְּ)(noun masc. sing., constr. of פֶּה, or (Je. 15. 19), with suff. 1 pers. s. irr. (§ 45)

כפף   וְכַפֶּיהָ[b]   noun f. du., suff. 3 pers. s. f. fr. כַּף d. 8 d

כפף   כַּפֵּיהֶם[dd]   id. dual, suff. 3 pers. pl. masc.

כפף   וְכַפָּיו[c]   id. dual, suff. 3 pers. sing. masc.

כפף   כַּפֶּיךָ   id. dual, suff. 2 pers. sing. masc.

כפף   כַּפַּיִךְ[b]   id. dual, suff. 2 pers. sing. fem.

פאה   כְּפִיךָ   pref. כְּ)(noun masc. sing., suff. 2 pers. sing. masc. from פֶּה irr. (§ 45)

כפף   כַּפֵּיכֶם   noun f. du., suff. 2 pers. pl. m. fr. כַּף d. 8 d

כַּפַּיִם   id. dual, abs. st.

כַּפָּיִם

כפף   וְכִפִּי[c]   noun masc. pl. [of כַּף q. v.]

כפף   כַּפֵּימוֹ[e]   noun fem. du., suff. 3 pers. pl. fr. כַּף d. 8 d

כפף   כַּפֵּינוּ   id. dual, suff. 1 pers. pl.

כפם   וְכָפִים[f]   noun masc. sing.

כפר   כְּפִיר[g]   noun masc. sing. dec. 1 a; וְ bef. (:)

כפר   כְּפִירָה   pr. name of a place

כפר   כְּפִרֶיהָ[h]   noun m. pl., suff. 3 pers. s. f. fr. כְּפִיר d. 1 a

כפר   כְּפִרַיִךְ[i]   id. pl., suff. 2 pers. sing. fem.; וְ bef. (:)

כפר   כְּפִרִים   id. pl., abs. st.

כפף   כַּפֵּךְ[k]   noun fem. sing., suff. 2 pers. sing. masc.

כַּפֵּךְ[l]   from כַּף dec. 8 d

כפף   כַּפָּכָה[m]   id. with parag. ה (§ 3. rem. 2)

[כָּפַל]   to double; part. כָּפוּל doubled. Niph. to be doubled, Eze. 21. 19.

כֶּפֶל masc. dec. 6 a, a doubling, Job 41. 5, see רֶסֶן; dual כִּפְלַיִם double, twice as much, Is. 40. 2; double, manifold, Job 11. 6.

מַכְפֵּלָה (a doubling) pr. name of a place, perhaps a plain near Hebron.

פלג   כְּפַלְגֵּי[o]   pref. כְּ)(noun m. pl. constr. fr. פֶּלֶג d. 6 a

פלח   כְּפֶלַח   pref. id.)(noun masc. sing.

כפל   כִּפְלַיִם   noun masc., dual of כֶּפֶל dec. 6 a

כפל   וְכָפַלְתָּ   Kal pret. 2 pers. sing. masc; acc. shifted by conv. וְ (§ 8. rem. 7)

פלש   כַּפְּלִשְׁתִּים   pref. כְּ for כְּהַ)(gent. noun, pl. of פְּלִשְׁתִּי from פְּלֶשֶׁת

[כָּפַן]   to languish, be languid, Eze 17. 7.

כָּפָן masc. hunger, Job 5. 22; 30. 3.

כפן   כָּפְנָה[p]   Kal pret. 3 pers. sing. fem.

כָּפַם   Root not used ; Syr. to connect, join.

כָּפִים masc. cross beam, rafter, Hab. 2. 11.

סבח   כַּבֶּסַח   pref. כְּ for כְּהַ)(noun m. s. d. 6 (§ 35. r. 5)

פעל   כְּפָעֳלֹהּ[q]   pref. כְּ)(noun masc. sing., suff. 3 pers. sing. fem. from פֹּעַל dec. 6 f .

פעל   כְּפָעֳלוֹ   pref. id.)(id., suff. 3 pers. sing. masc.

פעל   כְּפָעֳלָם   pref. id.)(id., suff. 3 pers. pl. masc.

פעם   כְּפַעַם   pref. id.)(noun fem. sing. dec. 6 d .

כָּפַף to bend, bow down. Intrans. to be bowed down, Ps. 57. 7. Niph. to bow, humble oneself, Mi. 6. 6.

כַּף fem. dec. 8 d.—I. the hollow, palm of the hand, often also for the hand itself; dual כַּפַּיִם, pl. כַּפּוֹת; in animals the paw; כַּף רֶגֶל, the sole of the foot.—II. pan, spoon, dish; כַּף הַקֶּלַע the hollow, cavity of a sling; כַּף הַיָּרֵךְ the hollow of the thigh, i. e. the socket of the hip-bone.—III. handle of a bolt, Ca. 5. 5.—IV. כַּפּוֹת תְּמָרִים palm-branches, Le. 23. 40.

כִּפָּה fem. dec. 10, palm-branch , also branch in general, Job 15. 32.

כָּפַר to cover, overlay, with pitch, to pitch, Ge. 6. 14. Pi. כִּפֶּר (§ 10. rem. 1).—I. to cover over sin, i. e. to forgive, pardon sin, const. with בְּעַד, לְ, עַל.—II. to expiate an offence, with עַל, בְּעַד ; מִן; to make atonement for an offender, to purify, with עַל, בְּ, בְּעַד.—III. to appease, pacify, with acc. of the person ; of calamity, to avert, with בְּ of the sacrifice. Pu.—I. pass. of Pi. No. II.—II. to be abolished, Is. 28. 18. Hithp. and Nithpa. (§ 6. No. 10) to be expiated.

כָּפָר masc. dec. 4 a, village, hamlet.

כְּפַר הָעַמֹּנִי (village of the Ammonites) pr. name of a place in the tribe of Benjamin, Jos. 18. 24.

כְּפוֹר m. dec. 1 a.—I. cup, bowl.—II. hoar frost.

כְּפִיר masc. dec. 1 a.—I. young lion.—II. village, Ne. 6. 2.

כֹּפֶר masc. dec. 6 c.—I. village, 1 Sa. 6. 18.—II. pitch, Ge. 6. 14.—III. cyprus-flower, Alhenna of the Arabs, a shrub or low tree with fragrant whitish flowers growing in clusters like grapes (Gesenius), which when dried and reduced to powder is used by the women for colouring their eyebrows or nails.—IV. ransom.

כִּפֻּרִים masc. pl. (of כִּפּוּר) atonement, expiation ; יוֹם הַכִּפֻּרִים day of atonement.

a La. 2. 19.   c Job 30. 6.   e Ps. 44. 21.   g Is. 11. 6.   i Na. 2. 14.   l Job 40. 32.   n Is. 32. 2.   p Eze. 17. 7.   r Pr. 24. 12, 29.

b Job 33. 6.   d Job 27. 23.   f Hab. 2. 11.   h Eze. 38. 13.   k Job 13. 21.   m Ps. 139. 5.   o Ex. 26. 9.   q Je. 50. 29.   s Ps. 57. 7.

bb Pr. 31. 19.   dd Le. 8. 28.

כַּפֹּרֶת fem. *covering of the ark, the mercy-seat;* בֵּית הַכַּפֹּרֶת *the holy of holies,* where the ark of the covenant was placed, 1 Ch. **28. 11.**

כַּפֵּר׳	וֹ Piel imp. sing. masc.	כפר
כִּפֶּר	וֹ id. pret. 3 pers. sing. masc. (§ 9. rem. 1)	כפר
כֹּפֶר	noun masc. sing. dec. 6 c .	כפר
כֻּפַּר׳	וֹ Pual pret. 3 pers. sing. masc. .	כפר
כְּפֹר	וֹ defect. for כָּפוֹר (q. v.) .	כפר
כְּ הָעֲמֹנִי	pr. name in compos. .	כפר
כְּפָרֹאתֶיךָ	pref. כְּ transp. for פָּארֹתֶיךָ (q. v.) .	פאר
כִּפְרֹד	pref. id.)(noun masc. sing. (suff. פִּרְדּוֹ) d. 6 a	פרד
כַּפְּרֹה׳	Piel inf. (כַּפֵּר), suff. 3 pers. sing. fem. dec. 7 b	כפר
כַּפָּרָה	pref. כְּ)(noun f. s. d. 10 [for פָּרָה] fr. פַּר m.	פרה
וְכָפְרוּ׳ Kh. K. יְכַפְּרוּ	Piel pret. or fut. 3 p. pl.	כפר
כָּפְרוֹ	noun m. s., suff. 3 pers. s. m. from כֹּפֶר d. 6 c	כפר
כְּפַרְזְלָא	וֹ Chald. pref. כְּ)(noun masc. sing. emph. of פַּרְזֶל dec. 2 a (§ 58. rem. 2); וֹ bef. (:)	פרזל
כְּפֹרֵחַת׳	pref. כְּ)(Kal part. act. s. f. d. 13 a, fr. פֹּרַח m.	פרח
וְכִפְרֵי	pref. כְּ bef. (:))(noun masc. sing. dec. 6 i	כפרה
כְּפִרִים	noun masc., pl. of כֹּפֶר dec. 6 c (§ 35. rem. 9)	כפר
כְּפִרִים	defect. for כְּפִירִים (q. v.) .	כפר
כְּפֹרִים	noun masc., pl. of [כָּפוֹר] dec. 1 b	כפר
כָּפְרְךָ	noun m. s., suff. 2 p. s. m. from כֹּפֶר d. 6 c	כפר
כְּפַרְעֹה	pref. כְּ)(pr. name masc., see פַּרְעֹה	פרעה
כְּפַרְץ	pref. id.)(n. m. s. (pl. with suff. פִּרְצֵיהֶם) d. 6 c	פרץ
וְכִפְרֹץ׳	וֹ pref. כְּ bef. (:))(Kal inf. constr. .	פרץ
כְּפָרָשִׁים	וֹ pref. כְּ)(noun masc., pl. of פָּרָשׁ dec. 1 b (§ 30. No. 3); וֹ bef. (:)	פרש
וְכָפַרְתָּ׳	וֹ Kal pret. 2 pers. sing. masc.; acc. shifted by conv. וֹ (§ 8. rem. 7)	כפר
כַּפֹּרֶת	noun fem. sing. .	כפר
וְכִפַּרְתָּהֻג׳	וֹ Piel pret. 2 pers. s. m., suff. 3 pers. s. m.	כפר
וְכִפַּרְתֶּם׳	וֹ id. pret. 2 pers. pl. masc.	כפר

כָּפַשׁ Hiph. *to cover over,* La. **3. 16.**

כְּפֶשַׁע׳	pref. כְּ)(noun masc. sing. .	פשע
וֹ כְּפִשְׁעֵיהֶם׳	pref. id.)(noun m. pl., suff. 3 pers. pl. m. from פֶּשַׁע dec. 6 a (§ 35. r. 5); וֹ bef. (:)	פשע
כַּפִּשְׁתָּה	pref. כַּ for כְּהַ)(noun fem. sing.	פשת
כַּפִּשְׁתִּים	pref. id.)(id. with pl. masc. term.	פשת

[כְּפַת] Chald. *to bind, fetter.* Pret. Peil, Da. **3. 21.** Pa. id. Da. **3. 20, 23, 24.**

כַּפֹּת׳	noun fem., pl. of כַּף dec. 8 d .	כפף
כַפֹּתוֹ׳	וֹ noun f. s., suff. 3 p. s. m. from כַּפָּה d. 10	כפף
כְּפִתוּ׳	Chald. Peil pret. 3 pers. s. m. masc. (§ 47. r. 6)	כפת

וֹ כְּפִתְחוֹ׳	pref. כְּ)(Kal inf. [פְּתֹחַ], suff. 3 pers. sing. masc. (§ 16. rem. 10); וֹ bef. (:) .	פתח
וֹ כְּפִתְחֵי׳	pref. id.)(noun masc. pl. c. from פֶּתַח dec. 6 a (§ 35. rem. 5); וֹ id.	פתח
וֹ כְּפִתְחֵיהֶן׳	pref. id.)(id. pl., suff. 3 p. pl. fem.; וֹ id.	פתח
וְכַפֹּתָיו׳	noun f. pl., suff. 3 p. s. m. from כַּף d. 8 d	כפף
כִּפְתָּמִים׳	pref. כְּ)(noun fem., pl. of פַּת dec. 8 d	פתת
כַּפְתּוֹר	pr. name of a place .	כפתר

וְ כַפְתֹּר masc. dec. 1 b.—I. *a round* or *spherical knob,* an ornament on the golden candlestick; LXX. σφαιρωτήρ, and Vulg. sphærula; then the *knob* or *capital of a pillar,* Am. **9. 1;** Zep. **2. 14.** Etymon uncertain.—II. pr. name of a country; pl. כַּפְתֹּרִים of its inhabitants.

כִּפְתְרוֹן	pref. כְּ)(noun masc. sing. dec. 1 b .	פתר
כַּפְתֹּרֶיהָ	noun m. pl., suff. 3 p. s. m. from כַּפְתֹּר d. 1׳	כפתר
כַּפְתֹּרֵיהֶם	id. pl. with suff. 3 pers. pl. masc.	כפתר
כַּפְתֹּרִים	gent. noun, pl. of כַּפְתֹּרִי from כַּפְתֹּר	כפתר
כַּצֹּאן	pref. כַּ for כְּהַ)(noun com. sing. dec. 1 b ;}	צאן
כְּצֹאן וֹ׳	וֹ pref. כְּ q. v. } וֹ bef. (:) .	צאן
כְּצֵאת׳	pref. כְּ)(Kal inf. constr. dec. 1 a [for צֵאָת § 25, n. 2 d, comp. § 23. rem. 2 & 4]	יצא
כְּצֵאתִי׳	pref. id.)(id. with suff. 1 pers. sing. .	יצא
וֹ כִּצְבָאָם׳	וֹ pref. כְּ bef. (:))(n. m., pl. of צְבִי (§ 35. r. 15)	צבה
כִּצְבֹאָם׳	pref. id.)(pr. name of a place .	צבה
כַּצְּבִי׳	pref. כַּ f. כְּהַ } noun masc. sing. dec. 6 i	צבה
כִּצְבִי׳	pref. כְּ bef. (:) } (§ 35. rem. 14 & 15) }	צבה
כַּצַּדִּיק׳	pref. כַּ for כְּהַ)(noun masc. sing. dec. 1 b	צדק
כַּצַּדֹנִים׳	pref. id.)(gent. noun, pl. of צִידֹנִי fr. צִידוֹן	צוד
כְּצִדְקוֹ׳	pref. כְּ)(noun masc. sing. from צֶדֶק dec. 6 a	צדק
כְּצִדְקִי׳	pref. id.)(id. with suff. 1 pers. sing. .	צדק
כִּצְדְקִיָּהוּ	pref. id.)(pr. name masc. .	צדק
כְּצִדְקָךָ׳	pref. id.)(noun masc. sing., suff. 2 pers. sing. masc. from צֶדֶק dec. 6 a .	צדק
כְּצִדְקָתוֹ	pref. id.)(noun fem. sing., suff. 3 pers. sing. masc. from צְדָקָה dec. 11 c .	צדק
כְּצִדְקָתִי׳	pref. id.)(id. with suff. 1 pers. sing. .	צדק
כַּצָּהֳרַיִם	pref. כַּ for כְּהַ)(noun m., dual of צֹהַר d. 6 f	צהר
כְּצוּר	pref. כְּ)(pr. name of a place .	צור
כְּצוּרֵנוּ׳	pref. id.)(noun masc. sing., suff. 1 pers. pl. from צוּר dec. 1 a .	צור
כַּצִּיץ׳	pref. id.)(noun masc. sing., pl. צִצִּים	צוץ
כְּצִירֵי׳	pref. id.)(noun m. pl. constr. from צִיר d. 1 a	ציר
כַּצֵּל	pref. כַּ f. כְּהַ } noun masc. sing. dec. 6 b .	צלל
כְּצֵל	pref. כְּ q. v. }	צלל

 a De. 21. 8.   f Is. 47. 11.   i Ge. 40. 10.   p 2 Ch. 31. 5.   s 1 Sa. 20. 3.   c Job 15. 32.   m Ex. 37. 16.   m Ex. 9. 29.   r Ps. 35. 24.
b Ex. 29. 33.   g Ho. 4. 16.   k Je. 32. 19.   q Joel 2. 4.   Exe. 39. 24.   d Da. 3. 21.   n Ex. 35. 29.   o 1 Ch. 12. 8.   s 2 Sa. 22. 21, 25.
c Is. 28. 18.   h Exe. 43. 26.   l Ca. 4. 13.   Ge. 6. 14.   Is. 43. 17.   e Ne. 8. 5.   o Ps. 147. 17.   p Ge. 18. 25.   t De. 32. 31.
d Job 38. 29.   i Ps. 49. 8.   m Le. 23. 28.   Ju. 15. 14.   f Exe. 42. 12.   q Is. 13. 14.   p Ps. 7. 18.   u Is. 21. 3.
e Exe. 31. 3.   k Da. 3. 24.   o Is. 43. 3.   Exe. 45. 20.   Is. 23. 40.   Exe. 42. 11.

בְּצַלְמָנֶע⁴	pref. id.) pr. name m., see [צֶלֶם],) bef.	
כְּצֶמַח•	pref. id.) noun masc. sing. (suff. צִמְחָה) dec. 6 (§ 35. rem. 5)	צמח
כַּצֶּמֶר }	pref. כַּ for כְּהַ) noun masc. sing. (suff.	צמר
כְּצַמְרִי}	צְמְרִי) dec. 6a (§ 35. rem. 2)	
כַּצִנָּה	pref. id.) noun fem. sing. dec. 10	צנן
כְּצִנַּת	pref. כְּ) id. constr. st.	צנן
כְּצַעֲרָתוֹ	pref. כְּ bef. (:)) noun fem. sing., suff. 3 pers. sing. masc. from [צְעָרָה] dec. 10	צער
כַּצִּפּוֹר	pref. כַּ for כְּהַ } noun com. sing., pl. צִפֳּרִים	צפר
כְּצִפּוֹר⁴}	pref. כְּ q. v. } (§ 30. r. 1);) bef. (:)	
כְּצִפִּיחִת	pref. id.) noun fem. sing.	צפח
כְּצִפְעֹנִי⁴	pref. id.) noun masc. sing. d. 1 b;) bef. (:)	צפע
כַּצִּפֳּרִים וְ }	pref. כַּ f. כְּהַ } noun com., pl. of צִפּוֹר	צפר
כְּצִפֳּרִים }	pref. כְּ q. v. } (§ 30. rem. 1)	
כְּצִפֳּרֵין⁴	Ch. pref. id.) n. com. pl. [f.] צִפְּרִין fr. [צְפַר] d. 2 a	צפר
כַּצַּר• }	pref. כַּ f. כְּהַ } noun masc. sing. dec. 8 (§ 37.	צרר
כְּצַר• }	pref. כְּ q. v. } rem. 7)	
כִּצְרוֹר⁴	pref. כְּ bef. (:)) n. masc. sing. dec. 1 a	צרר
כְּצָרָיו	pref. כְּ) noun masc. pl., suff. 3 pers. pl. masc. from צַר dec. 8c (§ 37. rem. 7)	צרר
כִּצְרֹף• }	pref. כְּ bef. (:)) Kal inf. constr. (§ 8.	צרף
כִּצְרָף־• }	rem. 18)	
כְּקִבְרָ•	pref. כְּ) noun masc. sing. (suff. קִבְרִי) d. 6 a	קבר
כִּקְדֹחַ	pref. כְּ bef. (:)) Kal inf. constr.	קדח
כְּקֶדֶם	pref. כְּ) noun masc. s. (pl. c. קַדְמֵי) d. 6a	קדם
כְּקַדְמוּתְכֶם▪	pref. id.) noun masc. pl., suff. 2 pers. pl. masc. [from קַדְמָה no pl. abs.]	קדם
כְּקוֹל	pref. id.) noun masc. sing. dec. 1a	קול
כַּקּוֹמָה•	pref. כַּ for כְּהַ) Kal part. act. sing. m. d. 9a	קנה
כְּקוֹץ•	pref. כְּ) noun masc. sing. dec. 1a	קוץ
כַּקָּטֹן	pref. כַּ for כְּהַ) adj. masc. sing. (pl. קְטַנִּים) dec. 8a (§ 37. No. 3)	קטן
כַּקָּטֹן	pref. id.) adj. masc. sing. dec. 3a	קטן
כְּקִיטֹר	pref. כְּ) noun masc. sing.	קטר
כְּקִיר•⁴	pref. id.) noun masc. sing. dec. 1a	קיר
כַּקֵּן•	pref. כַּ for כְּהַ) noun masc. sing. dec. 8b	קנן
כְּקִנְאָתְךָ▪ }	pref. כְּ) noun fem. sing., suff. 2 pers. sing. masc. from קִנְאָה dec. 12 b;) bef. (:)	קנא
כְּקֹסֵם	pref. כְּ bef. (:)) Kh. קֹסֵם, K. קֶסֶם, Kal inf. constr. (§ 8. rem. 18)	קסם
כִּקְצָף▪	pref. כְּ) n. m. s. d. 6 (suff. קַצְפּוֹ & קַצְפִּי)	קצף
כִּקְרֹא	pref. כְּ bef. (:)) Kal inf. constr.	קרא
כְּקָרְבְכֶם	pref. כְּ) Kal inf., suff. 2 p. pl. m. (§ 16. r. 8)	קרב
כְּקֹרַח	pref. id.) pr. name masc.	קרח
כַּקַּשׁ }	pref. כַּ f. כְּהַ } noun masc. sing.	קשש
כְּקַשׁ }	pref. כְּ q. v. }	

כַּקֶּשֶׁת	pref. id.) noun com. sing., suff. קַשְׁתִּי, pl. קְשָׁתוֹת, c. קַשְׁתוֹת ת treated as if radical, comp. dec. 6a	קוש
כַּר	noun masc. sing. dec. 8, § 37. rem. 7 (and pr. name in compos. with בַּיִת q. v.)	כרר
כָּר•⁴	noun masc. sing. (pl. כָּרִים) dec. 1a	כרר

כְּרָא Chald. Ithpe. *to be pained, grieved,* Da. 7. 15.

כִּרְאוּבֵן	pref. כְּ bef. (:)) pr. name masc.	ראה
כִּרְאוֹת וְ	pref. id.) Kal inf. constr.	ראה
כִּרְאוֹתָהּ⁴	pref. id.) id., suff. 3 pers. sing. fem.	ראה
כִּרְאוֹתוֹ	pref. id.) id., suff. 3 pers. sing. masc.	ראה
כִּרְאוֹתָם וְ⁴	pref. id.) id., suff. 3 pers. pl. masc.	ראה
כְּרָאִי	pref. כְּ) noun masc. s. [for רְאִי § 35. r. 14]	ראה
כִּרְאִי•⁴	pref. כְּ bef. (:)) noun masc. sing.	ראה
כִּרְאֵם⁼	pref. id.) noun masc. sing. dec. 1a	ראם
כְּרֹאשׁ⁴	pref. כְּ f. כְּהַ, כְּ } noun masc. sing. irr.	ראש
כְּרֹאשׁ•⁴	pref. כְּ q. v. } (§ 45);) bef. (:)	
כָּרִאשׁוֹן	pref. כַּ for כְּהַ, כְּהָ) adj. masc. sing. d. 1b	ראש
כָּרִאשֹׁנָה	pref. id.) id. fem. dec. 10	ראש
כָּרִאשֹׁנִים	pref. id.) id. pl. masc.	ראש
כִּרְאֹת	pref. כְּ bef. (:)) Kal inf. constr. d. 1 b (for כִּרְאוֹת)	ראה
כִּרְאֹתוֹ	pref. id.) id., suff. 3 pers. sing. masc.	ראה
כִּרְאֹתְכֶם *	pref. id.) id., suff. 2 pers. pl. m. *Jos. 3. 3	ראה

כָּרַב Root not used; whence

כְּרוּב masc. dec. 1 a.—I. *cherub,* a certain symbolical figure described Eze. 1. 6 sq.; etymon uncertain.—II. pr. name masc. Ezr. 2. 59; Ne. 7. 61.

כְּרוּב⁴▪	pref. כְּ) noun masc. s. d. 8c;) bef. (:)	רבב
כְּרוּבִים וְ⁴	pref. כְּ bef. (:)) noun masc. pl.	רבב
כְּרֻבִים	defect. for כְּרוּבִים (q. v.)	כרב

כַּרְבֵּל only part. pass. מְכָרְבָּל *girded, clothed,* 1 Ch. 15. 27.

כַּרְבְּלָא Ch. fem. dec. 1 a, *a mantle, cloak,* Da. 3. 21.

וְכַרְבְּלָתְהוֹן⁴	Chald. noun fem. pl., suff. 3 pers. pl. masc. from [כַּרְבְּלָא] dec. 9a	כרבל
כְּרֻבָּם▪	pref. כְּ) noun masc. sing., suff. 3 pers. pl. masc. from רֹב dec. 8c	רבב
כְּרָגַע	pref. id.) noun m. s. d. 6, for רֶגַע (§ 35. r. 5)	רגע

כָּרָה I. *to dig;* trop. of plots and devices against any one; Ps. 40. 7 אָזְנַיִם כָּרִיתָ לִּי *mine ears hast thou digged,* i. e. *opened,* given me a listening ear. Niph. *to be dug,* Ps. 94. 13.—II. Kal *to buy, purchase.*—III. *to give a feast,* 2 Ki. 6. 23.

a Eze. 16. 7.   g Ps. 25. 13.   m Ec. 9. 12.   r Pr. 26. 8.   x Is. 64. 1.   Ge. 19. 28.   Ho. 10. 7.   Na. 3. 6.   Is. 63. 7.
b Ps. 147. 16.   h Ge. 43. 33.   n Is. 31. 5.   s Job 19. 11.   y Eze. 36. 11.   Ps. 62. 4.   De. 20. 2.   Job 37. 18.   De. 32. 2.
c Is. 1. 18.   i Pr. 6. 5.   o Da. 4. 30.   t Zec. 13. 9.   z Is. 24. 2.   Is. 10. 14.   1 Ki. 5. 2, 25.   Ho. 10. 4.   Da. 3. 21.
d Is. 51. 8.   k Ex. 16. 31.   p Is. 5. 28.   u Ps. 66. 10.   Ge. 35. 11.   Ge. 39. 13.   Job 24. 24.   Ho. 4. 7.
e Ps. 5. 12.   l Pr. 23. 32.   q La. 2. 4.   w Je. 5. 16.   2 Sa. 23. 6.   Eze. 21. 28.   2 Ch. 24. 11.   c. 9. 15.   Ps. 92. 11.
2 Ch. 31. 15.

כֵּרָה fem. dec. 11 b.—I well, cistern, Zep. 2. 6.
—II. feast, banquet, 2 Ki 6. 23.

מִכְרָה masc. dec. 9 a, pit, Zep. 2. 9.

כרה noun fem. sing. . . . . .

כרה Kal part. act. sing. masc. . . .

כרה id. pret. 3 pers. pl. . . .

כרב n. m. s. d. 1 a, also pr. name m. ; ו bef. (:)

כרב id. pl., abs. st. ; ו id.

כרה Kal pret. 3 pers. pl., suff. 3 pers. sing. fem.

כרז Chald. noun m. s., emph., of [כָּרוֹז] d. 1 a

רוח { pref. כ f. כְּה, כָּה ; } noun com. sing. dec. 1 a
pref. כ q. v.

כרת Kal inf. abs. . .

כרת id. part. pass. sing. masc. dec. 3 a.

כרת id. constr. st. ; ו bef. (:)

כְּרַז Chald. Aph. to cry out, proclaim, Da. 5. 29.
כָּרוֹז Chald. masc. dec. 1 a, herald, Da. 3. 4.

רחל pref. כְּ ✗ noun fem. sing. d. 5 a ; ו bef. (:)

רחל pref. id. ✗ pr. name fem.

רחם pref. id. ✗ Piel (§ 14. r. 1) inf. constr. d. 7 b

רחם pref. id. ✗ noun masc. pl., suff. 3 pers. sing.
masc. [for רַחֲמִים from רַחַם (§ 35. r. 16)

רחם pref. id. ✗ id., suff. 2 p. s. m. ; ו bef. (:)

רחם pref. כְּ bef. (:) ✗ Kal inf. constr. .

רוח pref. כְּ ✗ noun masc. sing. dec. 1 a

כרר noun masc., pl. of כַּר dec. 8 (§ 37. rem. 7)

כרר noun masc., pl. of כֹּר dec. 1 a

כרה Kal pret. 2 pers. sing. masc. .

כרת pr. name of a brook .

כרת noun fem. sing. dec. 1 b .

כרה Kal pret. 1 pers. sing.

כרת for תוּת', noun fem. sing. dec. 1 b

כרת id. pl., suff. 3 pers. sing. masc.

כָּרַך Root not used ; Syr. and Chald. to surround ; to wrap round.

תַּכְרִיךְ masc. robe, Est. 8. 15.

כַּרְכְּמִישׁ (fortress of Camosh, compounded of כְּמוֹשׁ & כָּרַך i. q. כְּמוֹשׁ the name of an idol) pr. name of a city on the Euphrates.

כַּרְכֹּב masc. dec. 8 c, margin, border, or ledge going round the inside of the altar. Vulg. arula, hearth. Ex. 27. 5 ; 38. 4.

רכב pref. כְּ for כְּה, כָּה ✗ n. m. s. (suff. רִכְבִּי) d. 6 c

כרכב noun m. s., suff. 3 pers. s. m. from כַּרְכֹּב d. 8 c

כַּרְכֹּם masc. saffron, Ca. 4. 14.

כַּרְכְּמִישׁ pr. name of a place

כַּרְכַּס pr. name of a eunuch of Ahasuerus, Est. 1. 10, coll. with the Persic Eagle (Gesenius).

כֶּרֶם masc. (fem. Is. 27. 2, 3) dec. 6 a, with suff. כַּרְמִי, vineyard : with זַיִת an olive-yard, Ju. 15. 5.

כֹּרֵם masc. dec. 7 b, vine-dresser.

כַּרְמִי (vine-dresser) pr. name masc.—I. Ge. 46. 9 ; Ex. 6. 14 ; also patronym. (for כַּרְמִי) Nu. 26. 6.— II. Jos. 7. 1.

כַּרְמֶל masc. with suff. כַּרְמִלּוֹ (§ 37. No. 3) with loc. ה כַּרְמֶלָה.—I. well-cultivated plain, garden, orchard, field ; גֶּרֶשׂ כַּ' grits of the garden or of the best cultivated grounds, Le. 2. 14.—II. pr. name Carmel ; (a) a fruitful hill south of Asher on the Mediterranean ; (b) a mountain and city westward from the Dead sea, Jos. 15. 55 ; 1 Sa. 15. 12 ; 25. 5 ; Gent. n. כַּרְמְלִי for ־יִת.

כרם id. in pause (§ 35. rem. 2)

רום pref. כְּ ✗ Kal inf. constr. (for רום)

כרם noun m. s., suff. 3 pers. s. m. from כֶּרֶם d. 6 a

כרם id. pl., constr. st.

כרם pr. name masc.

כרם noun m. sing., suff. 1 pers. sing. from כֶּרֶם d. 6 a

כרם id. pl., suff. 3 pers. sing. masc.

כרם id. pl., suff. 3 pers. pl. masc.

כרם id. pl., suff. 2 pers. pl. masc.

כרם n. m. pl., suff. 2 pers. pl. m. from [כֶּרֶם] d. 7 b

כרם masc. crimson, 2 Ch. 2. 6, 13 ; 3. 14.

כרם noun masc., pl. of כֶּרֶם (q. v.) dec. 6 a

כרם noun masc., pl. of [כֹּרֶם] dec. 7 b

כרם noun masc. pl., suff. 1 pers. pl. from כֶּרֶם (q v.) dec. 6 a ; ו bef. (:)

כרם } id. sing., suff. 2 pers. sing. masc.

כרם noun m. sing., d. 8 (§ 37. r. 3) also pr. name

כרם id. with loc. ה (pr. name)

כרם id., suff. 3 pers. sing. masc.

רמש pref. כְּ ✗ noun masc. sing.

כרן (harp, Arab. כראן) pr. name m. Ge. 36. 26.

כָּרֵם Root not used ; prob. i. q. כָּרַשׂ to be curved ; hence

כרם Chald. noun fem. seat, throne

כרם Chald. id. pl. as if from כָּרְסֵי (comp. dec. 9)

כרם Chald. id. s., suff. 3 p. s. m. [as if from כָּרְסִי

² 2 Ki. 6. 23.   ᵈ Je. 18. 17.   ᵍ Is. 53. 7.   ᵏ Ne. 9. 27.   ʳ Ge. 50. 5.   ᵘ Ex. 38. 4.   ᵇ Ho. 2. 17.   ᶠ 2 Ch. 26. 10.   ᵏ Da. 5. 20.
¹ 1 Ki. 7. 29.   ᵉ Ne. 9. 8.   ʰ Ps. 103. 13.   ˡ Ps. 103. 12.   ˢ De. 24. 1, 3.   ˣ Nu. 16. 14.   ᶜ 1 Sa. 8. 15.   ᵍ Le. 25. 3.   ˡ Da. 7. 9.
ᵇ Nu. 21. 18.   ᶠ Le. 22. 24.   ¹ Is. 63. 7.   ᵐ Ps. 40. 7.   ᵗ Je. 3. 8.   ʸ Ps. 12. 9.   ᵈ Is. 61. 5.   ʰ Is. 10. 18.   ᵐ Da. 7. 9.
ᵈ Da. 3. 4.   ᵉ De. 23. 2.   ᵏ Ne. 9. 28.   ⁿ Is. 50. 1.   ¹ 1 Ki. 20. 25.   ᶻ Ex. 22. 4.   ᵉ Joel 1. 11.   Hab. 1. 14.

[כִּרְסֵם] (§ 7) *to devour*, Ps. 80. 14.

כָּרַע fut. יִכְרַע, *to bend, bow, sink down*, of the knees, Is. 45. 23; of a person כָּרַע עַל־בִּרְכַּיִם *to bow down upon the knees*, i. e. *to kneel*; of an animal *bowing the legs in order to lie down*; of persons in token of reverence or worship, with לְ, לִפְנֵי before any one; as an indication of weakness, בִּרְכַּיִם כֹּרְעוֹת *sinking*, i. e. *feeble knees*, Job 4. 4, comp. Ju. 5. 27; hence of females in labour. Hiph. *to cause to bow down, to prostrate.* Meton. *to depress, afflict.*

כֶּרַע fem. dec. 4 a, only dual כְּרָעַיִם *the legs* or *leg bones*; also of the springing legs of the locust, Le. 11. 21.

כֹּרֵעַ pref. כְּ)(noun masc. sing. dec. 1 a   .   רעה

כֹּרֵעַ Kal part. act. sing. masc. dec. 7 b   כרע

וּכְרֵעַ ‍ pref. כְּ)(noun masc. sing.; וּ bef. (:)   רעע

כֹּרְעָה pref. id.)(Kal part. act. sing. masc. dec. 9 a   רעה

כָּרְעוּ Kal pret. 3 pers pl.   .   .   .   כרע

כִּרְעוֹת Chald. כְּ bef. (:))(noun fem. sing. constr. of [רְעוּ] dec. 9 b   .   .   .   רעה

כֹּרְעוֹת Kal part. act. f., pl. of [כֹּרַעַת] d. 13 a fr. כֹּרֵעַ m.   כרע

כְּרָעָיו ‍ noun fem. du., suff. 3 pers. s. m., see the foll.   כרע

כְּרָעַיִם id. du. abs. from [כֶּרַע] dec. 4 a   .   כרע

כֹּרְעִים Kal part. act. m., pl. of כֹּרֵעַ dec. 7 b   כרע

כְּרָעָתוֹ pref. כְּ)(noun fem. sing., suff. 3 pers. sing. m. from רָעָה dec. 10 [for רָעָה] from רַע m.   רעע

כְּרָפְאִי pref. id.)(Kal inf., suff. 1 pers. sing.   .   רפא

כַּרְפַּס masc. *a fine white cotton cloth* or *linen*, Est. 1. 6.

כִּרְצוֹן pref. כְּ bef. (:))(n. m. s., constr. of רָצוֹן d. 3 a   רצה

כִּרְצוֹנוֹ ‍ pref. id.)(id., suff. 3 pers. sing. masc.   רצה

כִּרְצוֹנָם pref. id.)(id., suff. 3 pers. pl. masc.   .   רצה

כִּרְצֹנוֹ defect. for כִּרְצוֹנוֹ (q. v.)   .   .   רצה

וּכְרָקָב ‍ pref. כְּ f., [כְּה, כָּה,] noun m. sing. d. 4 a; } רקב
וּכְרָקָב ‍ pref. כְּ q. v.   } וּ bef. (:)   .   }

כָּרַר Pilp. כִּרְכֵּר (§ 6. No. 4) *to leap, dance,* 2 Sa. 6. 14, 16.

כַּר masc. pl. כָּרִים (§ 37. rem. 7).—I. *fatted lamb*, so called from its *leaping.*—II. meton. *pasture* where lambs feed, Ps. 65. 14; Is. 30. 23.—III. *battering-ram*, Eze. 4. 2; 21. 27.—IV. כַּר הַגָּמָל Ge. 31. 34, *camel's saddle*, "the *haudaj*, or *portable chamber*, in which the Eastern women ride on the backs of camels," (Prof. Lee).

כֹּר masc. dec. 1 a, *a cor*, a measure of capacity, containing ten baths.

כּוֹר Chald. masc. id. Ezr. 7. 22.

כִּרְכָּרָה fem. only pl. כִּרְכָּרוֹת Is. 66. 20, *dromedaries*, from their agility and swiftness.

כִּכָּר fem. d. 2 b (du. כִּכָּרַיִם, כִּכָּרִים pl. כִּכָּרוֹת).—I. *a circuit, circumjacent tract* of country.—II. *a cake* or *round loaf* of bread.—III. *a talent*, a weight of gold, silver or lead.

כִּכָּר Chald. masc. id. pl. כַּכָּרִין Ezr. 7. 22.

כָּרֵשׂ Root not used; *to be curved*, cogn. כָּרַס, כָּרָם.

כָּרֵשׂ masc. dec. 1 a, *the belly*, Je. 51. 34.

כּוֹרֶשׂ (*sun*) pr. name, *Cyrus*, king of Persia.

כִּרְשׂוֹ noun m. s., suff. 3 pers. s. m. from [כֶּרֶשׂ] d. 1 a   כרש

כִּרְשׂוֹן pref. כְּ)(noun masc. sing.   .   רשה

כַּרְשְׁנָא pr. name of a prince in the court of Ahasuerus, Est. 1. 14.

כְּרָשָׁע ‍ pref. כְּ f. [כָּה, כְּה,] } adj. masc. sing. dec. 4 a   רשע
כִּרְשָׁע ‍ pref. כְּ q. v.   }

כָּרַת וֹ pret. 1 & 2 pers. כָּרַתָּ, כָּרַתִּי (for כָּרַתִּי, &c. § 25. rem.) fut. יִכְרֹת.—I. *to cut, cut off, cut down*; כֹּרֵת עֵצִים *wood-cutter*; De. 23. 2, *cut off* as to his privy members, i. e. *eunuch*, and simply כָּרוּת Le. 22. 24.—II. *to cut off, destroy.*—III. כָּרַת בְּרִית (and sometimes ellipt. without בְּרִית) *to make a covenant, agreement*, from the ancient custom of *cutting up* victims on such occasions; const. with אֵת, אֶת, עִם, לְ. Niph.—I. *to be cut off* or *down.*—II. *to be divided, separated.*—III. *to be destroyed.*—IV. *to perish, fail.* Pu. כֹּרַת (§ 10. rem. 5) *to be cut off* or *down.* Hiph. *to cut off, destroy;* trop. *to cut off,* i. e. *to withdraw,* with acc. and מִן, 1 Sa. 20. 15. Hoph. *to be cut off, to perish,* Joel 1. 9.

כְּרֻתוֹת fem. pl. *hewn beams.*

כְּרִית (*a cutting*) pr. name of a brook which falls into Jordan below Beth-shan, 1 Ki. 17. 3, 5.

כְּרִיתוּת fem. dec. 1 b, *separation, divorce;* with סֵפֶר, *bill of divorce.*

כְּרֵתִים pl. כְּרֵתִים.—I. pr. name of a portion of the Philistines residing on the south-west shore of Judea.—II. the title of a certain class of soldiers in the army of David, supposed to have been of Philistine origin. According to Gesenius, *executioners*, attached to David's body-guard; hence הַכְּרֵתִי וְהַפְּלֵתִי *executioners and couriers.*

וְכָרַתָּ וֹ Kal pret. 2 pers. s. m. [for כָּרַתָּ § 25. r.]   כרת

---

a Ps. 35. 14.   d Ezr. 7. 18.   f Est. 3. 2.   h Ho. 7. 1.   l Da. 11. 3, 16.   n Ho. 5. 12.   o Pr. 12. 4.   r Ezr. 3. 7.   t Job 27. 7.
b Est. 3. 5.   c Job 4. 4.   g 2 Sa. 3. 39.   i Est. 1. 8.   m Da. 8. 4.   k Job 13. 28.   p Je. 51. 34.   s Ge. 18. 25.   u De. 20. 20.
Ps. 28. 4.

כָּרֹת	Kal inf. abs.	כרת
כֹּרַת	Pual pret. 3 pers. sing. masc. (§ 10. rem. 5)	כרת
כְּרֹת	noun fem. pl. constr. from [כָּרָה or כֵּרָה] d.11	כרה
כְּרֹת	Kal inf. constr.	כרת
כְּרֹת	id. imp. masc. sing. (for כְּרֹת § 8. rem. 18)	כרת
כֹּרֵת	id. part. act. sing. masc. d. 7 b	כרת
כָּרְתָה	id. imp. sing. masc. with parag. ה (§ 8. r. 11)	כרת
כָּרְתָה	Pual pret 3 p. s. f. [for כֻּרְתָה comp. § 8. r. 7]	כרת
וְכָרְתוּ	Kal pret. 3 pers. pl.	כרת
כְּרָתוֹ	id. pret. 3 pers. sing. m., suff. 3 pers. s. m.	כרת
כִּרְתוּ	id. imp. pl. masc.	כרת
כְּרֻתוֹת	noun fem. pl.; or, Kal part. pass. fem., pl. [of כְּרוּתָה] from כָּרוּת masc.	כרת
כָּרַתִּי	Kal pret. 1 pers. sing. [for כָּרַתִּי § 25. rem.], acc. shifted by conv. וְ (§ 8. r.7)	כרת
כֹּרְתֵי	id. part. act. pl. c. masc. fr. כֹּרֵת dec. 7 b	כרת
כְּרֵתִים	gent. noun, pl. of כְּרֵתִי	כרת
כֹּרְתִים	Kal part. act. masc., pl. of כֹּרֵת dec. 7 b	כרת
כְּרַתְנוּ	id. pret. 1 pers. pl.	כרת
כָּרַתְּ	defect. for כְּרֵתוֹת (q. v.)	כרת
כִּשְׁאָלָה	pref. כְּ)(Kh. שְׁאָלָה noun f. comp. נַאֲוָה, (K. שׁוֹאָה q. v.)	שאה
כִּשְׁאוֹל	pref. כְּ bef. (:))(noun com. sing. dec. 1 a	שאל
כִּשְׁאוֹן	pref. id.)(noun m. s., constr. of שָׁאוֹן d. 3 a	שאה

כֶּשֶׂב

וְ masc. dec. 6 a, *lamb*, comp כֶּבֶשׂ.

כִּשְׂבָּה fem. *ewe-lamb*, Le. 5. 6; comp. כִּבְשָׂה.

כִּשְׂבָּא	preff. כְּ & שֶׁ)(Kal pret. 3 pers. sing. masc.	בוא
כִּשְׂבָּה	noun fem. sing. from כֶּשֶׂב masc.	כשב
כִּשְׂבֻוֹת	pref. כְּ bef. (:))(Kal part. act. fem. pl. [of שְׁבֻיָה from שָׁבוּי masc.]	שבה
כִּשְׂבִים	noun masc., pl. of כֶּשֶׂב dec. 6	כשב
כְּשֶׁבֶר	pref. כְּ)(noun masc. sing. dec. 6 b	שבר
כְּשִׁבְתּ	pref. id.)(Kal inf. constr. (suff. שִׁבְתִּי) d. 13 a	ישב
כְּשִׁבְתּוֹ	pref. id.)(id. with suff. 3 pers. sing. masc.	ישב
כִּשְׁנַנָּה	pref. כְּ bef. (:))(noun fem. sing. dec. 11 c	שנן

כֶּשֶׂד

pr. name of a son of Nahor; the progenitor of the Chaldeans, Ge. 22. 22.

כַּשְׂדִּי, only pl. כַּשְׂדִּים (once כַּשְׂדִּים Eze. 23. 14, Kh.).—I. Gent. noun *the Chaldeans*, the inhabitants of Babylon; אֶרֶץ כַּשְׂדִּים *Chaldea*; with ה loc. כַּשְׂדִּימָה *to Chaldea*.—II. meton. *Chaldeans for astrologers*, Da. 2. 2, 4.

כַּשְׂדָּי Ch. dec. 7, i. q. Heb. כַּשְׂדִּי Nos I, II.

כְּשֶׂדֶר	pref. כְּ)(noun masc. sing.; וּ bef. (:)	שדר
כַּשְׂדָּאִין	Chald. gent. noun, pl. of כַּשְׂדָּי dec. 7	כשד
כִּשְׂדֵּה	pref. כְּ bef. (:))(noun masc. sing., constr. of שָׂדֶה dec. 9 b	שדה
וְכַשְׂדִּי	Chald. for כַּשְׂדָּי, gent. noun sing. dec. 7	כשד
כַּשְׂדָּיָא	Ch. Kh. כַּשְׂדָּאָה, K. כַּשְׂדָּאָה, id., emph. st. (§ 63)	כשד
כַּשְׂדָּיֵא	Ch. Kh. כַּשְׂדָּיֵא, K. כַּשְׂדָּאֵי, id. pl. emph.	כשד
כַּשְׂדִּיים	gent. noun, pl. of כַּשְׂדִּי, Kh. כַּשְׂדִּים dec. 8 f (§ 37. rem. 5)	כשד
כַּשְׂדִּימָה	id. with parag. ה	כשד

[כָּשָׂה] *to be covered with fat*, De. 32. 15.

כָּשֶׂה	pref. בְּכֹה f. — noun com. sing. irr. (§ 45)	שה
כָּשֶׂה	pref. בְּ q. v.	שה
כְּשָׂהָיָה	preff. כְּ & שֶׁ)(Kal pret. 3 pers. sing. masc.	היה
כְּשָׂהַסָּכָל	Kh. כִּשֶׁהַסָּכָל, preff. כְּ, שֶׁ & הַ)(n. m. s. d. 4 a	סכל
כְּשׂוֹאָה	pref. בְּ for בְּכֹה)(noun fem. sing. dec. 10	שוא
כְּשׂוּב	וּ pref. כְּ)(Kal inf. c. dec. 1 a; וּ bef. (:)	שוב
כְּשׂוֹל	Kal inf. abs.	כשל
כְּשׂוֹפֵר	pref. בְּ for בְּכֹה)(noun masc. sing. dec. 2 b	שפר
כְּשׂוֹק	וּ pref. כְּ)(noun fem. sing. d. 1 a; וּ bef. (:)	שוק
כְּשׂוֹר	pref. כְּ)(noun masc. sing (§ 35. rem. 13)	שור
כְּשׂוֹשַׁנָּה	pref. בְּ f. — noun fem. sing. dec. 10	שוש
כְּשׂוֹשַׁנָּה	pref. בְּ q. v.	שוש
כְּשׂחוֹק	pref. בְּ bef. (:))(noun masc. sing.	שחק
כְּשׂחַל	pref. בְּ for בְּכֹה)(noun masc. sing.	שחל
כְּשׂחַק	וּ pref. כְּ)(noun masc. s. d. 6 d; וּ bef. (:)	שחק
כַּשָּׂחַר	pref. בְּ f. — noun masc. sing. dec. 6 d	שחר
כַּשָּׂחַר	pref. בְּ q. v.	שחר
כַּשְׂיִים	gent. noun, pl. of כּוּשִׂי (comp. dec. 8 f, § 37. rem. 5) from כּוּשׂ	כוש
וְכַשְׂיִם		
כְּשִׂיר	pref. id.)(noun masc. sing. dec. 1 a	שיר
כְּשִׂרַת	pref. id.)(noun f. s., constr. of שִׁירָה d. 10	שיר
כָּשִׂיתָ	Kal pret. 2 pers. sing. masc.	כשה
כּוּשִׂית	gent. noun, fem. of כּוּשִׂי from כּוּשׂ	כוש
כְּשֹׂךְ	pref. כְּ)(Kal inf. constr. (§ 18. rem. 3)	שכך
כְּשֵׂכֶב	pref. id.)(Kal part. act. s. m. d. 7 b; וּ bef. (:)	שכב
כְּשׂכָב	וּ pref. כְּ bef. (:))(id. inf. constr.	שכב
כִּשְׂכּוֹר	pref. בְּ for בְּכֹה)(noun masc. sing. dec. 1 b.	שכר
כְּשִׂכִיר	וּ pref. כְּ)(noun masc. sing. d. 3 a; וּ bef. (:)	שכר
כְּשִׂכִיר	pref. בְּ bef. (:))(id. constr. st.	שכר

כָּשַׁל וְ fut. יִכְשׁוֹל (Pr. 4. 16).—I. *to totter, stagger*; part. כּוֹשֵׁל *feeble, weary*.—II. *to stumble*, with בְּ *against any thing*. Niph. *to totter, stumble from weakness*. Pi. *to cause to fall*, Eze. 36. 14. Kheth. Hiph.—I. to

---

a Ho. 10. 4.   f Ju. 6. 28.   n Ne. 10. 1.   t Le. 5. 6.   b Joel 1. 15.   g Ec. 10. 3.   o Is. 58. 1.   r Is. 40. 15.   y Je. 5. 26.
b Eze. 16. 4.   h Je. 22. 7.   o Is. 28. 15.   u Ge. 31. 26.   c Le. 27. 21.   h Is. 38. 9.   p Nu. 18. 18.   s Is. 58. 8.   z Est. 2. 1.
c Zep. 2. 6.   i Je. 10. 3.   p Pr. 1. 27.   v De. 14. 4.   c Is. 53. 7.   i 2 Sa. 17. 3.   q Pr. 7. 22.   t Eze. 33. 32.   a Pr. 23. 34.
d Je. 34. 8.   k 1 Sa. 5. 4.   q Je. 17. 12, 13.   w Is. 30. 14.   d Ps. 119. 176.   k Is. 17. 57.   q Ho. 14. 6.   u Is. 23. 15.   c Job 7. 2.
1 Sa. 11. 1.   l 1 Ki. 7. 2.   r Le. 7. 23.   x Est. 1. 2.   e Ec. 12. 7.   l Is. 40. 30.   r Pr. 10. 23.   x De. 32. 15.   c Le. 25. 53.
e 2 Sa. 3. 12.   m Ps. 59. 6.   s Ec. 5. 14.   y Ec. 10. 5.   f Ca. 2. 2.   m 1 Ki. 1. 21

cause to totter to make feeble, La. 1. 14.—II. *to cause to stumble and fal.*; metaph. *to seduce*, Mal. 2. 8. Hoph. *to be made to stumble*, Je. 18. 23.

כַּשִּׁיל masc. *an axe*, Ps. 74. 6.

כִּשָּׁלוֹן masc. *fall, ruin*, Pr. 16. 18.

מִכְשׁוֹל m. d. 1 b.—I. *a cause of stumbling, a stumbling-block.*—II. in a moral sense, *cause of offence.*

מַכְשֵׁלָה fem. dec. 10.—I. *ruin*, Is. 3. 6.—II. *cause of offence*, Zep. 1. 3.

כְּשַׁלֵן / כַּשַּׁלֵן } pref. כַּ for כְּה)(noun masc. sing. (§ 35. rem. 2) . . . . שלג

כָּשְׁלָה Kal pret. 3 pers. sing. fem. . . כשל

כְּשִׁלֹה pref. כְּ)(pr. name of a place . . שלה

כָּשְׁלוּ / וְ } Kal pret. 3 pers. pl. (§ 8. rem. 7) . . כשל

בְּשִׁלֹה pref. כְּ)(pr. name of a place, see שִׁלֹה . שלה
noun masc. sing. . . . . כשל

כִּשְׁלוֹן noun masc. sing.

כֹּשְׁלוֹת Kal part. act. pl. fem. from כֹּשֵׁל masc. . כשל

כְּשַׁלְּחוֹ pref. כְּ)(Piel inf. (שַׁלֵּחַ for שַׁלַּח), suff. 3 pers. sing. masc. dec. 7 b (§ 36. rem. 5) . שלה

כְּשַׁלְמָה pref. כַּ for כְּה)(noun fem. sing. dec. 12 a שלם

כָּשַׁלְנוּ Kal pret. 1 pers. pl. . . . . כשל

כַּשְּׁלָשִׁים / כִּשְׁלֹשִׁים } pref. כְּ bef. (:))(num. card. com. gen., pl. of שָׁלִשׁ fem. . שלש

כִּשְׁלֹשֶׁת pref. כְּ bef. (:))(num. card. masc. constr. of שְׁלֹשָׁה (§ 42. rem. 5) from שָׁלֹשׁ fem. . שלש

כְּשַׁלְתָּ / וְ } Kal pret. 2 pers. sing. masc., acc. shifted by conv. וְ (§ 8. rem. 7) . . . כשל

כְּשֵׁם pref. כְּ)(noun masc. sing. dec. 7 a . שם

כְּשֻׁם Chald. pref. כְּ)(n. masc. sing. irr. (§ 68) שם

כִּשְׁמוֹ pref. כְּ bef. (:))(noun masc. sing., suff. 3 pers. sing. masc. from שֵׁם 7 a . . . שם

כְּשֻׂמֹחַ pref. id.)(Kal inf. constr. . . שמח

כְּשִׂמְחַת pref. כְּ)(noun fem. s., constr. of שִׂמְחָה d. 12 b שמח

כְּשִׂמְחָתְךָ pref. id.)(id. with suff. 2 pers. sing. masc. שמח

כְּשָׁמִיר pref. id.)(noun masc. sing. dec. 3 a שמר

כִּשְׁמֶךָ pref. כְּ)(n. m. s., suff. 2 pers. s. m. fr. שֵׁם d. 7 a שם

כַּשֶּׁמֶן / וְ } pref. כַּ for כְּה)(noun masc. sing. dec. 6 a (§ 35. rem. 5) . . . שמן

כְּשֵׁמַע pref. כְּ)(noun masc. sing. dec. 6 e שמע

כִּשְׁמֹעַ / וְ pref. כְּ bef. (:))(Kal inf. constr. . שמע

כְּשָׁמְעוֹ)(pref. id.)(id., suff. 3 pers. sing. masc.; וְ bef. (:) שמע

כְּשָׁמְעִי / וְ pref. id.)(id., suff. 1 pers. sing.; וְ id. שמע

כְּשָׁמְעֲךָ pref. id.)(id., suff. 2 pers. sing. masc. שמע

כְּשָׁמְעֲכֶם pref. כְּ)(id., suff. 2 pers. pl. masc. שמע

כְּשָׁמְעָם pref. כְּ)(id. suff. 3 pers. pl. masc. . שמע

כְּשָׁמְעָתוֹ pref. id.)(id. with fem. term. [שִׁמְעָה], and suff. 3 pers. sing. masc. (§ 8. rem. 10) . שמע

כְּשֹׁמְרֵי pref. כְּ)(Kal part. act. pl. c. fr. שֹׁמֵר d. 7 b שמר

כַּשֶּׁמֶשׁ pref. כַּ f. כְּה)(n. com. s. (suff. שִׁמְשֵׁךְ) d. 6 c שמש

כַּשֵּׁמֹת pref. id.)(n. m. with pl. f. term. abs. fr. שֵׁם d. 7 a שם

כְּשָׁנָה pref. כְּ)(noun fem. sing. dec. 11 a שנה

כִּשְׁנֵי pref. כְּ)(id. pl. c.; or num. card. constr. of שְׁנַיִם (q. v.) . . שנה

כַּשָּׁנִים pref. כַּ for כְּה)(id. pl. abs. st.; or (Is. 1. 18) id. . שנה
כִּשְׁנַיִם / וְ pref. כְּ q. v.;)(pl. of שָׁנִי ; וְ bef. (:)

כְּשַׁסַּע pref. כְּ)(Piel inf. constr. . . . שסע

כְּשַׁעֲתָא pref. id.)(noun fem. sing. [emph. שַׁעְתָּא] . שעה

כִּשְׂעִירִים pref. כְּ bef. (:))(noun masc. pl. under שער

כְּשֻׁעָלִים pref. כְּ)(n. m., pl. of שׁוּעָל (no vowel change) שעל

כִּשֵּׁף Piel, *to practise magic, use witchcraft*; part. מְכַשֵּׁף *magician, wizard*; f. מְכַשֵּׁפָה *sorceress, witch.*

כֶּשֶׁף m. d. 6, only pl. כְּשָׁפִים *incantations, sorceries.*

כַּשָּׁף masc. dec. 1 b, *magician*, Je. 27. 9.

אַכְשָׁף (*incantation*) pr. name of a city in Asher, Jos. 12. 20; 19. 25.

כִּשֵּׁף / וְ Piel pret. 3 pers. sing. masc. . . כשף

כַּשִּׁפְחָה pref. כַּ for כְּה)(noun fem. sing. dec. 12 b שפח

כְּשָׁפַיִךְ)(noun masc. pl., suff. 3 pers. sing. masc. fr. [כֶּשֶׁף] dec. 6; וְ bef. (:) כשף

כְּשָׁפַיִךְ id. pl. with suff. 2 pers. sing. fem. . כשף

כְּשָׁפֵיכֶם n. m. pl., suff. 2 pers. pl. m. fr. [כֶּשֶׁף] d. 1 b כשף

כְּשָׁפִים noun masc., pl. of [כֶּשֶׁף] d. 6 . כשף

כִּשְׁפָקִים pref. כַּ for כְּה)(noun fem. with pl. masc. term. [fr. שִׁקְמָה § 35. rem. 16] . שקם

כָּשֵׁר fut. יִכְשַׁר *to be right, proper, acceptable.* Hiph. *to give success*, Ec. 10. 10.

כּוּשָׁרָה f. d. 10, *prosperity, success*, Ps. 68. 7.

כִּישׁוֹר masc. *distaff*, Pr. 31. 19.

כִּשְׁרוֹן masc. *prosperity, success.*

כִּשְׁרוֹן noun masc. sing. . . . . כשר

כַּשֶּׁרֶץ pref. כַּ for כְּה)(noun masc. sing. . שרה

כִּשְׂרֵפַת pref. כְּ bef. (:))(noun sing. fem., constr. of שְׂרֵפָה dec. 10 שרף

כַּשֹּׁרֶשׁ / וְ pref. כַּ for כְּה)(noun masc. sing. dec. 6 c שרש

כְּשֵׁשׁ pref. כְּ)(num. card. fem. . . שש

כִּשְׁתֵּל pref. כְּ bef. (:))(noun masc. pl. constr. [from שָׁתִיל or שְׁתִל] . שתל

כְּשֶׁתְּפוּלִי preff. כְּ & שֶׁ)(Kal fut. 3 pers. sing. fem. נפל

כְּתַאֲנִי pref. כְּ bef. (:))(constr. of the foll. . תאן

ᵃ Pr. 16. 18. ᵈ 1 Sa. 9. 22. ⁱ Eze. 35. 14. ᵐ Eze. 45. 25. ᵖ Is. 30. 19. ˢ Mal. 3. 4. ᵛ 2 Ch. 33. 6. ᵞ Je. 27. 9. ˣ Is. 53. 2.
ᵇ Is. 35. 3. ᵉ Ho. 14. 2. ᵏ Is. 9. 2. ⁿ Ps. 109. 18. ᵍ Is. 4. 17. ᵗ Ju. 14. 6. ʷ Est. 8. 5. ᶻ Ps. 128. 3.
ᶜ Ex. 11. 1. ᶠ Ho. 4. 5. ˡ Eze. 35. 15. ᵒ 2 Ch. 15. 3. ʳ Ps. 89. 37. ᵘ De. 32. 2. ᵏ 2 Ki. 9. 22. ˣ Is. 59. 17. ᶜ Ec. 9. 12.
Ps. 104. 2. Da. 4. 5. Eze. 3. 9. Ge. 24. 39. Ge. 26. 13 Eze. 13. 4. Is. 47. 9, 12. 2 Ch. 21. 19. Je. 24. 2.
Is. 59. 10. 1 Sa. 25. 25. Ps. 48. 11. Ne. 1. 4. 2 Ki. 17. 4. Da. 4. 16.

כְּתָאֵנִים *a* ןֵ'׀ pref. בְּ for כְּהַ)(noun fem. with pl. masc. term. from תְּאֵנָה dec. 10 . . . תאן	כְּתָבֹת ﬞ noun masc. sing.; ﬞ bef. (ִ:) . . . . בתב
כְּתֹאֲרִי pref. כְּ)(noun masc. sing. dec. 6 f . . . תאר	כָּתַבְתִּי Kal pret. 1 pers. sing., acc. shifted by conv. ﬞ (§ 8. rem. 7) . . . } בתב
כָּתַב ﬞ'׀ fut. יִכְתֹּב.—I. *to write, engrave,* with אֶל, לְ, עַל, בְּ, or acc. of the thing written upon; also with acc. of the thing written; כָּתַב סֵפֶר אֶל *to write a letter to any one.*—II. *to describe, write down.*—III. *to write, ordain, decree,* Is. 65. 6; Job 13. 26. Niph. *to be written down.* Piel *to write, decree,* Is. 10. 1.	כְּתַבְתִּם ﬞ id. pret. 2 pers. sing. masc., suff. 3 pers. pl. masc.; ﬞ for ﬞ conv. . . בתב
	כַּתֻּהוּ pref. כַּ for כְּהַ)(Seg. noun for [תֹּהוּ] תהה
	כְּתַהֹמֹת pref. כְּ bef. (ִ:))(noun com., pl. of תְּהוֹם d. 1 a הום
	כִּתְבוּ Kal imp. pl. masc. . . . כתת
	כִּתְבֹוא pref. כְּ)(n. m. s. by transp. & contr. for תָּבֹא תאה
כְּתָב Chald. *to write.*	כָּתוֹב ﬞ Kal inf. abs. . . . . בתב
כְּתָב m. d. 1 a (§ 30. No. 3).—I. *a writing.*—II. *epistle, letter,* 2 Ch. 2. 10.—III. *register, record.* —IV. *scripture,* Da. 10. 21.	כָּתוּב ﬞ id. part. pass. sing. masc. dec. 3 a . בתב
	כְּתוֹב־ *b* Kh. כְּתוֹב, K. כְּתָב, Kal imp. sing. masc. (§ 8. rem. 18) . . . . בתב
כְּתָב Chald. masc. dec. 1 b.—I. *a writing.*—II. *precept, prescription,* Ezr. 6. 18; 7. 22.	כְּתוּבָה Kal part. p. sing. fem. dec. 10, fr. כָּתוּב m. בתב
כְּתֹבֶת f. *a writing, mark,* Le. 19. 28.	כְּתוּבִים id. masc., pl. of כָּתוּב dec. 3 a בתב
מִכְתָּב masc. dec. 2 b.—I. *writing.*—II. *thing written, a writing, letter;* hence, *composition, ode,* Is. 33. 9.	כְּתוֹלְדֹתָם *c* pref. כְּ)(noun fem. pl. (תּוֹלְדוֹת), suff. 3 pers. pl. masc. . . . ילד
כְּתָב *'''* ﬞ noun m. s. dec. 1 a, Ch. dec. 1 b; ﬞ bef. (ִ:) כתב	כַּתֹּלַע *d* pref. כַּ f. כְּהַ)(n. m. s. (no vowel change) תלע
כְּתַב ﬞ'׀ Chald. Peal pret. 3 pers. sing. masc. . כתב	כְּתוֹעֲבוֹת pref. כְּ)(n. f. pl. constr. fr. תּוֹעֵבָה dec. 11 b תעב
כְּתֹב ﬞ'׀ Kal imp. sing. masc. (§ 8. rem. 18); ﬞ bef. (ִ:) } כתב	כְּתוֹעֲבוֹתֵיהֶן ﬞ pref. id.)(id., suff. 3 pers. pl. fem.; ﬞ bef. (ִ:) תעב
כְּתָבָא *e* Ch. noun m. s., emph. of כְּתָב dec. 1 b כתב	כְּתֹעֶבֹת defect. for כְּתוֹעֲבוֹת (q. v.) . . תעב
כָּתְבָא Ch. Peal part. act. fem. dec. 10 [from כְּתַב] כתב	כְּתוֹעֲפֹת pref. כְּ)(noun fem. pl. c. fr. [תּוֹעָפָה] d. 11 a יעף
כָּתְבָהּ Kal imp. sing., suff. 3 pers. sing. fem. . כתב	כְּתֹרָה pref. id.)(noun masc. sing. dec. 1 a . ירה
כְּתָבָה Ch. n. m. s. (for כְּתָבָא), emph. of כְּתָב d. 1 b כתב	כַּתּוֹרָה ﬞ pref. כַּ f. כְּהַ)(noun fem. sing. dec. 10 ירה
כָּתְבוּ Kal pret. 3 pers. pl. . . . . כתב	כְּתֹרִין Ch. pref. כְּ)(noun masc., pl. of [תֹּר] d. 1 a תור
כְּתַבוּ Chald. Peal pret. 3 pers. pl. masc. . . כתב	כְּתוֹרַת *g* pref. id.)(n. f. sing., constr. of תּוֹרָה d. 10 ירה
כִּתְבוּ ﬞ'׀ Kal imp. pl. masc. . . . . כתב	כְּתוֹרָתֶךָ pref. id.)(id., suff. 2 pers. s. m. (for רָתֶךָ) ירה
כִּתְבֵי Piel pret. 3 pers. pl. [for כִּתְּבוּ comp. § 8. r. 7] כתב	כְּתוֹשָׁב pref. id.)(noun masc. sing. dec. 1 b (except constr. תּוֹשַׁב § 31. rem. 1) . . שׁב
כִּתְבוּאַת־ ﬞ'׀ pref. כְּ bef. (ִ:))(n. f. s., constr. of תְּבוּאָה d. 10 בוא	כָּתֹת Kal inf. abs. . . . . . כתת
כְּתַבֹּר pref. כְּ)(pr. name of a place . . תבר	כָּתוּת *k* ﬞ id. part. pass. sing. masc. . . כתת
כֹּתְבִים ﬞ Kal part. act. m., pl. of כֹּתֵב d. 7 b . כתב	כַּתּוֹתִי ﬞ id. pret. 1 pers. sing. . . . כתת
כְּתֻבִים defect. for כְּתוּבִים (q. v.) . . . כתב	כְּתִיב Ch. Peal part. pass. sing. masc. . . כתב
כָּתְבֵם Kal imp. sing. masc., suff. 3 pers. pl. masc. [ם for ﬞ fem. in Pr. 7. 3, § 2. rem. 5] כתב	כִּתִּיִּים gent. noun, pl. of כִּתִּי, K. כִּתִּים (§ 37. rem. 5) } כתב
כְּתָבָם n. m. s., suff. 3 pers. pl. m. fr. כְּתָב dec. 1 a כתב	כִּתִּיִּם id., Kh. כִּתִּים, K. כִּתִּיִּם (§ 37. rem. 5) כתב
כָּתְבָן ﬞ Chald. Peal part. act. fem., pl. of כְּתָבָא dec. 10 [from כְּתַב masc.] . . כתב	כְּתִימָרוֹת *m* pref. כְּ)(n. f. pl. constr. fr. [תִּימָרָה] dec. 11 a תמר
כְּתֶבֶן ﬞ pref. כְּ)(noun masc. sing. . . תבן	כָּתִית noun masc. sing. . . . . כתת
כְּתַבְנִית pref. id.)(noun fem. sing. dec. 1 b . בנה	כֹּתֶל masc. dec. 6 c, *wall,* Ca. 2. 9.
כְּתַבְתְּ ﬞ'׀ Kal pret. 2 pers. sing. masc. (§ 8. rem. 7) } כתב	כֹּתֶל Ch. id. Da. 5. 5; pl. כֹּתְלַיָּא (from כֻּתַל) Ezr. 5. 8.
כָּתַבְתָּ ﬞ'׀ id.; acc. shifted by conv. ﬞ (§ 8. rem. 7) כתב	כְּתַלִּישׁ (prob. for כֹּתֶל אִישׁ *wall of man*) pr. name of a town in Judah, Jos. 15. 40.
	כְּתַל Chald. noun masc. sing. . . כתל
	כְּתַלְג Chald. pref. כְּ bef. (ִ:))(noun masc. sing. תלג

---

a Je. 24. 8.	*f* Is. 30. 8.	*k* Jos. 18. 8.	*o* Da. 5. 5.	*t* Le. 19. 28.	*y* Joel 4. 10.	*c* Ex. 28. 10.	*e* 2 Ch. 30. 16.	*i* Ps. 89. 24.
b Ju. 8. 18.	*g* Da. 5. 7, 15.	*l* Is. 10. 1.	*p* Job 21. 18.	*u* Ex. 34. 1.	*z* Is. 51. 20.	*d* Is. 1. 18.	*f* Ps. 119. 85.	*m* Ca. 3. 6.
Je. 36. 18.	*h* Ezr. 4. 6.	*m* Nu. 18. 30.	*q* Is. 44. 13.	*v* Is. 40. 23.	*a* Je. 32. 44.	*e* Eze. 16. 47.	*g* Is. 30. 14.	*n* Da. 5. 5.
Da. 5. 24.	*i* Ezr. 4. 8.	*n* Ne. 19. 1.	*r* Ex. 32. 32.	*w* Ps. 78. 15.	*b* Eze. 24. 2.	*f* 1 Ch. 17. 17.	*h* Le. 22. 24.	Da. 7. 9.
Da. 5. 5.	*u* Ezr. 4. 7.	*s* Le. 25. 40.						

כְּתָלִישׁ] וְ pr name of a place . . . כתל

כְּתָלֵּנוּ [n. ɪɛ. sing., suff. 1 pers. pl. fr. [כֹּתֶל] d. 6 c כתל

כָּתַם Kal not used; *to shut up, hide*; cogn. חָסַם, חָתַם,
    חָטַם, hence Niph. Je. 2. 22, *to be shut, laid up.*
    Others, according to the Syr. *spotted, stained*; hence
    Eng. vers. " marked."

    כֶּתֶם masc. *fine gold*; used only poetically for זָהָב.
    מִכְתָּם m. in the superscription of several Psalms,
    prob. *a golden poem.*

כְּתָם^b
כְּתֵם^c } noun masc. sing. . . . . כתם

כְּתֻמִּם^d pref. כְּ ✗ noun masc. sing. dec. 8 c . תמם

כְּתָם־^e pref. id. ✗ Kal inf. constr. for תֹּם dec. 8 c
    (§ 18. rem. 3) . . . . . תמם

כְּתְמוֹל pref. כְּ bef. (:) ✗ adv. . . . מול

כְּתֻמִּי^f וּ pref. כְּ ✗ noun masc. sing., suff. 1 pers.
    sing. fr. תֹּם dec. 8 c ; וּ bef. (:) . תמם

כְּתְמוֹל defect. for כְּתְמוֹל (q. v.) . . . מול

כְּתֻמָּם^g pref. כְּ ✗ noun masc. sing., suff. 3 pers. pl.
    masc. fr. תֹּם dec. 8 c . . . תמם

כַּתָּמָר^h pref. כַּ ✗ for כְּהַ ✗ noun masc. sing. dec. 4 a תמר

כְּתָמָרⁱ pref. כְּ ✗ noun masc. sing. . . תמר

כָּתַן Root not used; *to cover, hide*, cogn. כָּתַם.

    כֻּתֹּנֶת, כְּתֹנֶת fem. dec. 13 c (with suff. כֻּתָּנְתִּי,
    pl. כֻּתֳּנוֹת, constr. כָּתְנוֹת § 44. rem. 6) *an under
    garment, shirt.*

כַּתַּנּוּר pref. כַּ f. ✗ כְּהַ ✗ } noun masc. sing. dec. 1 b
כְּתַנּוּר pref. כְּ q. v. { see . . . תנר

כְּתֻנּוֹת^k וּ see כָּתֹנֶת defect. . . . כתן

כַּתַּנִּים pref. כַּ for כְּהַ ✗ n. m. pl. [of תַּן or תַּן] d. 8 תנן

כַּתַּנִּין pref. id. ✗ noun masc. sing. dec. 1 b תנן

כְּתֹנֶת^l וּ noun fem. sing. ; וּ bef. (:) . . כתן

כֻּתֳּנֹת^m וּ noun fem. pl. constr. fr. כֻּתֹּנֶת dec. 13 c . כתן

כֻּתֳּנֹת id. pl., abs. st. . . . . . כתן

כֻּתָּנְתּוֹ id. sing., suff. 3 pers. sing. masc. . . כתן

כֻּתָּנְתִּי id. sing., suff. 1 pers. sing. . . . כתן

כֻּתָּנְתֶּךָⁿ ✗. sing., suff. 2 pers. sing. masc. . כתן

כְּתֹעֵבוֹת pref. כְּ ✗ n. f. pl. constr. fr. תּוֹעֵבָה d. 11 b תעב

כְּתֹעֲבֹתֵיהֶם pref. id. ✗ id. pl., suff. 3 pers. pl. masc. . תעב

כְּתַעַר^o pref. כְּ ✗ noun masc. sing. dec. 6 d . תער

כָּתֵף] וְ fem. dec. 5 b (pl כְּתֵפוֹת, constr. כִּתְפוֹת, with
    suff. כְּתֵפָי).—I. *snoulder.*—II. trop. *side of an
    edifice, of the sea, of a city or region.*—III. pl. (a)
    shoulder-pieces of a garment; (b) *sides, jambs* of

doors *or gates*, Eze. 41. 2, 26 ; (c) *shoulders* of an
axle, 1 Ki. 7. 30, 34.

כָּתֵף id. constr. st. . . . . . כתף

כְּתִפְאֶרֶת pref. כְּ ✗ noun fem. sing. constr. d. 13 a, abs.
    תִּפְאָרָה (§ 42. rem. 5) . . . פאר

כַּתַּפּוּחַ pref. id. ✗ noun masc. sing. dec. 1 b נפח

כַּתַּפּוּחִים pref. כַּ for כְּהַ id. pl., abs. st. . . נפח

כְּתֵפוֹת^u noun fem. pl. abs. fr. כָּתֵף dec. 5 b . . כתף

כְּתֵפוֹת] וְ id. pl., constr. st. . . . כתף

כְּתֵפִי^v id. sing., suff. 1 pers. sing. . . . כתף

כְּתֵפֶיהָ id. pl., suff. 3 pers. sing. fem. . . כתף

כְּתֵפָיו id. id., suff. 3 pers. sing. masc. . . כתף

כְּתָפְשְׂכֶם^w pref. כְּ ✗ Kal inf., suff. 2 pers. pl. masc. . תפש

כְּתֻפֹת defect. for כְּתֵפוֹת (q. v.) . . . כתף

כְּתָפַת pref. כְּ ✗ pr. name of a place . . . תפת

כְּתֻפֹת defect. for כְּתֵפוֹת (q. v.) . . . כתף

כִּתְקֹעַ^x וְ pref. כְּ bef. (:) ✗ Kal inf. constr. . . תקע

כָּתַר Piel.—I. *to surround, encompass* in a hostile
    manner.—II. *to wait*, as in Syr. & Chald. Job
    36. 2. Hiph.—I. *to surround*, with בְּ.—II. in-
    trans. *to be crowned with*, Pr. 14. 18. Prof. Lee,
    trans. *to comprehend.*

    כֶּתֶר masc. *diadem, crown*, Est. 1. 11 ; 2. 17 ;
    6. 8.

    כֹּתָרוֹת fem. pl. (§ 44. rem. 5) *capital,
    chapiter* of a column.

כַּתֵּר־^y Piel imp. sing. masc. (comp. § 10. rem. 3) כתר

כֶּתֶר noun masc. sing. . . . . . כתר

כִּתְּרוּ^z Piel pret. 3 pers. pl. . . . כתר

כִּתְרוּמַת^a pref. כְּ bef. (:) ✗ n. f. s., constr. of תְּרוּמָה d. 10

כִּתְּרוּנִי^b Piel pret. 3 pers. pl., suff. 1 pers. sing. . כתר

כֹּתָרוֹת^c noun fem. pl. abs. [as if from כֹּתָרָה dec. 11 a],
    see כֹּתֶרֶת (§ 44. rem. 5) . . . כתר

כַּתִּרֹזָן^d pref. כַּ for כְּהַ ✗ noun masc. sing. dec. 6 c תרן

כְּתִרְצָה^e pref. כְּ ✗ pr. name of a place . . רצה

כְּתַרְשִׁישׁ^f pref. id. ✗ noun masc. sing. . . רשש

כֹּתְרֹת
כֹּתְרֹת } noun fem. pl. & sing. (§ 44. rem. 5) . כתר

[כָּתַשׁ] *to bruise, pound*, Pr. 27. 22.

    מַכְתֵּשׁ masc.—I. *mortar*, Pr. 27. 22.—II. prob.
    a hole in the shape of a mortar, Ju. 15. 19.—
    III. pr. name of a valley near Jerusalem, Zep. 1. 11

[כָּתַת] fut. יִכֹּת.—I. *to beat, hammer, forge*, Joel 4. 10.
    —II. *to beat, break in pieces*; Le. 22. 24   כָּתוּת^g

^a Ca. 2. 9.   ^e Is. 18. 5.   ⁱ Je. 10. 5.   ^m Is. 22. 21.   ^q Is. 44. 13.   ^u Eze. 41. 2.   ^y Jos. 8. 8.   ^c Ju. 20. 43.   ^g 1 Ki. 7. 16.
^b Pr. 25. 12.   ^f Ps. 7. 9.   ^k Ne. 7. 72.   ⁿ Ezr. 9. 1.   ^r Ps. 52. 4.   ^v Job 31. 22.   ^z Ca. 2. 3.   ^d Nu. 15. 20.   ^h Is. 30. 17.
^c Ca. 5. 11.   ^g Is. 47. 2.   ^l Je. 51. 34.   ^o Ps. 52. 4.   ^s Ca. 7. 9.   ^w 1 Ki. 7. 44.   ^a Job 36. 2.   ^e Ps. 22. 13.   ⁱ Da. 10. 6.
^d Ps. 78. 79.   ^h Ps. 92. 13.   ^m Ezr. 2. 69.   ^p Eze. 24. 4.   ^t 1 Ki. 7. 34.

one crushed, i. e. as to his testicles.—III. *to beat down, rout,* as enemies, Ps. 89. 24. Pi. כִּתֵּת i. q. Kal. Pu. *to be broken.*

כָּתִית masc. *beaten oil,* from olives beaten in a mortar.

כִּתִּי, only pl. כִּתִּים כִּתִּיִּם gent. noun, *the Chittim,* according to Gesenius the inhabitants of Cyprus ; and, in a wider sense, also those of the islands and coasts of the Mediterranean sea, especially the northern parts.

מְכִתָּה fem. dec. 10, *a breaking in pieces,* Is. 30. 14

כתת   .   .   כִּתֵּת וְ[a] Piel pret. 3 pers. sing. masc. (§ 10. r. 1)

כתת   .   .   כִּתְּתוּ וְ id. pret. 3 pers. pl.

כתת   .   .   כֻּתְּתוּ[b] וְ Pual pret. 3 pers. pl.

ל

ל everywhere with Sheva except in the following cases ;—ל before a word which has Sheva under the first letter, as לִפְרִי for לְפְרִי ;—before יְ, so that Yod becomes quiescent, as לִיהוּדָה, with ל pref. לִיהוּדָה (for לְיְהוּדָה ; לָ, לֶ, לָ before the composites לָאדֹנִי, לָעֲזֹר, as לַ עֲמֹד (and contr. לָ עֲמֹד) for לֶאֱהֹב, (לָאֲדֹנִי, לָעֲזֹר and contr. לֶ אֱכֹל ל for לֶאֱמֹר, לֶאֱהֹב for לֶאֱמֹר), לֶ חֳלִי, לְ חֳדָשָׁיו ל ;— לָ, לָ, לֶ when displacing the art. ה (q. v.), as לֶהָרִים for לְהֶהָרִים, לְהָאוֹר for לְהַהָאוֹר, לַדּוֹר for לְהַדּוֹר, לֶהָרִים ;—frequently before the tone-syllable, as before several forms of the pronouns, and the infinitives of verbs, as לָזֶה, לָאֵלֶּה, לָקוּם, לָלֶכֶת ; moreover before substantives, usually at the end of a sentence, and especially when short words are connected in pairs (comp. lett. וּ), comp. לַמָּיִם Ge. 1. 6, לַנֶּגַע De. 17. 8. For ל with suffixes see § 5.

Prep.—I. noting motion or direction *towards* any object, *to, unto, towards,* hence with verbs of motion, longing, and the like affections ; but also of rest, delay, and condition, *at, on, in,* as לַפֶּתַח אָהֳלֹ *at the door of his tent,* לְעֵינֵי פ׳ *in the sight of any one* ; of the time in which any thing is done, as לַבֹּקֶר וְלָעֶרֶב *in the morning and in the evening,* לִשְׁלֹשֶׁת הַיָּמִים *within three days* ; with the plural, distribut., as לַבְּקָרִים *every morning.*—II. *into,* of the transition into another state, as נֶהְפַּךְ לְאֵבֶל is *turned into mourning* ; הָיָה–לְ *to be, become, be made into* anything.—III. sign of the dative, after verbs of giving, assigning, &c. ; also as dative *commodi* and *incommodi,* מִי יֵלֶךְ–לָנוּ *who shall go for us* ; הָיָה לִי, יֵשׁ לִי *there is to me,* i. e. *I have* ; frequently pleonastic with the verb, דְּמֵה לְךָ *be thou like,* Ca. 2. 17 ; 8. 14.—IV. noting possession, *to, belonging to,* equivalent to the genitive, as מִזְמוֹר לְדָוִד *a psalm belonging to,* or *of David* ; בֶּן לְיִשַׁי *a son of Jesse* ; לַיהוָה הַיְשׁוּעָה *to the Lord belongs salvation.*—V. adverbs with ל put before nouns take the force of prepositions: סָבִיב לְ *round about,* מִתַּחַת לְ *beneath, under,* &c. ; with nouns it frequently serves for a periphrasis of the adv., as לְבֶטַח *securely,* לְבַד *separately.*—VI. by later writers ל is also used for the accusative, comp. Je. 40. 2 ; 5. 2.—VII. *at,* noting occasion, e. g. לְשֵׁמַע *at the fame,* Ps. 18. 45.—VIII. *as to, in respect to.*—IX. *on account of, because* ; לְהֵן, לָכֵן *therefore.*—X. *about, concerning.*—XI. *according to, after,* as לְמִינוֹ *after its kind* ; also *as if, as though, like.*—XII. prefixed to the infinitive, it may be variously rendered, *to* ; *till that ; so that ; because ; when ; as though.*

ל Chald.—I. *to, unto, towards* ; also before the infin.—II. as sign of the dative, accusative, and genitive.—III. conj. *that,* prefixed to the future.

לֹא וְ[a] לֹו rarely לוֹא, also לֹו (15 times) adv. of negation.—I. *not,* noting an absolute negation of the verb, whether in the preterite or future ; though also found with the future, indicating prohibition or dissuasion, i. q. אַל comp. Le. 19. 4 ; Pr. 22. 24 where both are used indiscriminately. In combination with substantives and adjectives it conveys a negative signification, e. g. לֹא עֵץ *not wood,* i. e. that which is not wood, a man, Is. 10. 15 ; לֹא חָסִיד *impious,* Ps. 43. 1.—II. *no, nay,* in answer to a question.—III. *without,* comp. 1 Ch. 2. 30 ; לֹא כֹל *no one, none* ; לֹא דָבָר *nothing.*—IV. *not yet,* 2 Ki. 20. 4 ; Ps. 139. 16.—V. with prefixes ; בְּלֹא (a) of time, *when not, before* ; (b) *without* ; (c) often ellipt. for בַּאֲשֶׁר לֹא *for that which not.*—הֲלֹא *is not ? lo ! surely !*—לְלֹא (a) *without,* 2 Ch. 15. 3 ; (b) ellipt. for לַאֲשֶׁר לֹא comp. Is. 65. 1.

לָה , לָא (Da. 4. 32) Chald.—I. *not*.—II. *nothing*, Da. 4. 32.

לֹא דְבָר (*no pasture*) pr. name of a town in Gilead, 2 Sa. 17. 27 ; but לוֹ דְבָר in 2 Sa. 9. 4, 5, comp. לֹא.

לֹא עַמִּי (*not my people*) symbolical name given to the prophet Hosea, Ho. 1. 9.

לֹא רֻחָמָה (*not pitied*) symbolical name given to a daughter of Hosea.

לָא ; וְ Chald. adv. . . . . לא

לֵא Kh. ; K. לוֹ pref. prep. לְ with suff. 3 p. s. m. . ל

לֻא ; וְ Kh. לֹא q. v., K. לוֹ (q. v.) . . . לו

לָאַב Root not used ; Arab. *to thirst*.

תַּלְאוּבָה fem. dec. 10, *thirst, drought*, Ho. 13. 5.

לְאָב pref. לְ)(noun masc. sing irr. (§ 45) . . אב

לְאָב pref. id.)(id. constr. st. . . . . אב

לְאַבֵּד ו' pref. לְ)(Piel inf. constr. d. 7 b , ו bef. (:) . אבד

לַאֲבֹדוֹן pref. לְ for לְהַ ,לְהֶ)(noun masc. sing. . אבד

לְאַבְּדָם ו'' pref. לְ)(Piel inf. (אַבֵּד), suff. 3 pers. pl. masc. dec. 7 b ; ו bef. (:) . . . . אבד

לְאַבְּדֵנִי' pref. id.)(id. with suff. 1 pers. sing. . . אבד

לְאָבוֹת pref. id.)(noun masc. with pl. fem. term. abs. from אָב irr. (§ 45) . . . . אב

לְאַב תֵּיהֶם ו'' ו' pref. לְ bef. (:))(id. pl., suff. 3 p. pl. m. אב

לַאֲבוֹתֵיכֶם pref. id.)(id. pl., suff. 2 pers. pl. masc. אר

לַאֲבֹתָם pref. id.)(id. pl., suff. 3 p. pl. m. (§ 4. r. 2) אב

לַאֲבִי' pref. id.)(id. sing., constr. st. . . . אב

לְאָבִי pref. לְ)(id. sing., suff. 1 pers. sing. . . אב

לַאֲבִיגַיִל' וְ, לַאֲבִינָ'ל Kh., לַאֲבִיָּה pref. לְ bef. (:))(pr. names . . . . אב

לְאָבִיהָ pref. id.)(noun masc. sing., suff. 3 pers. sing. fem. from אָב irr. (§ 45) . . . . אב

לַאֲבִיהֶם' pref. לְ bef. (:))(id., suff. 3 pers. pl. masc. אב

לְאָבִיו ו' pref. לְ)(id., suff. 3 pers. s. m. ו bef. (:) אב

לְאֶבְיוֹן pref. לְ for לְהַ ,לְהֶ)(adj. masc. sing. d. 1 b אבה

לְאֶבְיוֹנִים pref. id.)(id. pl., absolute state . . אבה

לְאֲבִיטַל pref. לְ bef. (:))(pr. name fem. . . אב

לְאָבִיךְ pref. לְ)(noun masc. sing., suff. 2 pers. sing. masc. from אָב irr. (§ 45) . . . . אב

לַאֲבִימֶלֶךְ pref. לְ bef. (:))(pr. name masc. . . אב

לְאָבִינוּ pref. לְ)(noun masc. sing., suff. 1 pers. pl. from אָב irr. (§ 45) . . . . . אב

לְאֶבְיֹנִים pref. לְ for לְהַ ,לְהֶ)(adj. m., pl. of אֶבְיוֹן d. 1 b אבה

לְאָבִינֶךָ' ו pref. לְ)(id. s., suff. 2 pers. s. m. ; וְ bef. (:) אבה

לָאַבִּיר' pref. לְ bef. (ֵ))(noun masc. sing. constr. of [אָבִיר] dec. 3 a . . . . אבר

לַאֲבִירָם וְ pref. id.)(pr. name masc. . . . אב

לְאֶבְיָתָר ו' pref. לְ)(pr. name masc. ; ו bef. (:) אב

לְאֵבֶל pref. id.)(noun masc. sing. d. 6 (§ 35. r. 6) אבל

לַאֲבֵלֵי' pref. לְ bef. (ֵ))(adj. masc. pl. constr. from אָבֵל dec. 5 (§ 34. rem. 2) . . . . אבל

לַאֲבֵלָיו ו' pref. id.)(id. pl., suff. 3 pers. sing. masc. אבל

לָאֶבֶן ו' ו pref. לְ f. לְהָ ,לְהֶ)(noun fem. sing. dec. 6 a (§ 35. rem. 2)

לָאָבֶן וְ pref. לְ q. v.

לְאֶבֶן ו bef. (:)

לַאֲבָנֵי' ו') pref. id.)(id. pl., constr. st. ; ו id. אבן

לַאֲבָנִים pref. לְ for לְהַ ,לְהֶ)(id. pl., abs. st. . אבן

לְאַבְנֵר pref. לְ)(pr. name masc. . . . אב

לְאָבָק' pref. id.)(noun masc. sing. dec. 4 c . אבק

לְאַבְרָהָם ו' , לְאַבְשָׁלוֹם ו' , לְאַבְשָׁם ו' pref. לְ)(pr. names masc. ; ו bef. (:) . . אב

לַאֲבֹתֵיהֶם ו' pref. לְ bef. (:))(noun masc. pl., suff. 3 pers. pl. masc. from אָב irr. . . . אב

לַאֲבֹתָיו pref. id.)(id., suff. 3 pers. sing. masc. אב

לַאֲבֹתֶיךָ ו' pref. id.)(id., suff. 2 pers. sing. masc. אב

לַאֲבֹתֵיכֶם ו' pref. id.)(id., suff. 2 pers. pl. masc. אב

לַאֲבֹתֵינוּ ו' pref. id.)(id., suff. 1 pers. pl. אב

לַאֲבֹתָם pref. id.)(id., suff. 3 pers. pl. m. (§ 4. r. 2) אב

לָאֲגֻדָּה' pref. id.)(noun fem. sing. dec. 10 . אגד

לַאֲגוֹרַת' pref. id.)(noun f. s. constr. of [אֲגוֹרָה] d. 10 נרר

לָאֲגַם pref. לְ bef. (ֵ))(noun masc. sing., pl. constr. אֲגַמֵּי (§ 35. rem. 10)

לַאֲגַם pref. לְ q. v.

לְאֵדוֹ' pref. לְ)(noun masc. sing., suff. 3 pers. sing. masc. from אֵד dec. 1 a . . . . אוד

לֶאֱדוֹם pref. לְ bef. (ֱ))(pr. name of a people . אדם

לָאֲדוֹן' pref. לְ bef. (ֲ))(constr. of the foll. דון

לְאָדוֹן ו' pref. לְ)(noun masc. s. dec. 3 a ; ו bef. (:) דון

לְאַדִּיר' ו pref. לְ contr. [for לְהַאֲדִיב] Hiph. inf. constr. (§ 11. rem. 3) אדב

לָאַדִּירִים' pref. לְ)(adj. or subst. m., pl. of אַדִּיר d. 1 b אדר

לָאָדָם pref. לְ f. לְהָ ,לְהֶ)(noun masc. sing. also pr.

לְאָדָם ו' pref. לְ q. v.

name ; ו bef. (:)

לָאֲדָמָה' pref. לְ for לְהַ ,לְהֶ)(noun fem. sing. d. 11 c אדם

לְאַדְמַת pref. id.)(id. constr. st. (§ 42. rem. 1) אדם

לְאַדְמָתוֹ' pref. id.)(id., suff. 3 pers. sing. masc. . אדם

ᵃ 2 Sa. 19. 7.   ᵈ Est. 9. 24.   ˡ De. 22. 19, 29.   ° Ps. 132. 2, 5.   ʳ Hab. 2. 19.   ᵘ Ex. 9. 9.   ᵇ 1 Sa. 2. 36.   ᵉ Mi. 4. 13.   ʰ Ju. 5. 13.
ᵇ 2 Sa. 18. 12.   ᵉ Ps. 119. 95.   ᵐ 1 Ki. 13. 11.   ᵖ Is. 61. 3.   ˢ Is. 54. 12.   ᵛ 2 Ch. 6. 25.   ᶜ Is. 35. 7.   ᶠ Ge. 45. 8, 9.   ⁱ Ps. 83. 11.
ᶜ Ge. 17. 4.   ᶠ 1 Ki. 14. 15.   ⁿ Est. 9. 22.   ᵠ Is. 57. 18.   ᵗ 2 Ch. 26. 14.   ʷ Ex. 13. 11.   ᵈ Job 36. 27.   ᵍ 1 Sa. 2. 33.   ᵏ Ps. 146. 4.
ᵈ Job 26. 6.   ᵍ Je. 24. 10.   = De. V. 11.   ᵠ Je. 2. 27.   ᵘ Je. 43. 10.   ᵡ 2 Sa. 2. 25.

לָאָדֹן pref. ל q. v.)(noun masc. sing. dec. 6a [for אָדֶן § 35. rem. 2] . . . . ארן

לַאדֹנָי pref. ל, contr. [for לַאֲדֹנָי])(the name of God   דון

לַאֲדֹנִי pref. ל bef. (-:))(noun m. pl. c. fr. אָדֹן d. 3a   דון

לַאדֹנָי pref. ל contr. [for לַאֲ])(id. s., suff. 1 p. s.   דון

לַאֲדֹנֶיהָ pref. ל id.)(id. pl., suff. 3 pers. sing. fem.   דון

לַאֲדֹנֵיהוּ pref. ל bef. (-:))(pr. name masc.   דון

לַאֲדֹנֵיהֶם pref. id.)(noun masc. pl., suff. 3 pers. pl. m. from אָדֹן dec. 3a   דון

לַאֲדֹנָיו pref. ל, contr. [for לַאֲ])(id. pl., suff. 3 p. s. m.   דון

לַאֲדֹנֶיךָ pref. ל id.)(id. pl., suff. 2 pers. sing. masc.   דון

לַאֲדֹנֵינוּ pref. ל bef. (-:))(id. pl., suff. 1 pers. pl.   דון

לַאֲדַרְכֹּנִים pref. id.)(noun masc. pl. [of אֲדַרְכֹּן]   אדרכ'

לְאַדְרַמֶּלֶךְ pref. ל)(pr. name of an idol   אדר

[לָאָה] fut. תִּלְאָה, ap. וַתֵּלֶא (§ 24. rem. 3).—I. *to labour*, especially *in vain*, Ge. 19. 11.—II. *to be weary, faint*. Niph.—I. *to labour, exert oneself*, Je. 9. 4; espec. *to labour in vain*.—II. *to be weary, faint*.—III. *to be grieved, vexed*.—IV. *to dislike, loathe*, Ex. 7. 18. Hiph. הֶלְאָה (§ 11. rem. 1) *to make weary, to vex*.

לֵאָה (*wearied*) pr. name of Laban's elder daughter, wife of Jacob.

תְּלָאָה fem. *weariness, trouble, vexation.*

לֵאָה)(pr. name fem. . . . . . לאה

לְאַהֵב pref. ל bef. (v:))(Kal inf. constr. (§ 8. r. 10) אהב

לְאַהֲבָה pref. ל q. v. }

לְאֹהֲבַי } pref. ל)(id. part. act. pl. masc., suff.

לְאֹהֲבָיו } 1 pers. sing. from אָהֵב dec. 7b } אהב

לְאֹהֲבֵי pref. id.)(id. id. constr. st. . . . אהב

לְאֹהֲבָיו pref. id.)(id. id. with suff. 3 pers. pl. masc. אהב

לָאֹהֶל pref. ל f. לָה, לָהּ)(noun masc. sing. dec. 6c } אהל

לָאֹהֶל pref. ל q. v. (§ 35. rem. 9) }

לְאָהֳלוֹ pref. id.)(id. sing., suff. 3 pers. sing. masc. אהל

לְאָהֳלָו pref. id.)(id. pl., suff. 3 pers. sing. masc. (א by Syr. § 35. rem. 9) אהל

לְאֹהָלַי pref. id.)(id. pl., suff. 1 pers. sing. אהל

לְאָהֳלֵיהֶם pref. id.)(id. pl., suff. 3 pers. pl. masc. אהל

לְאֹהָלָיו pref. id.)(id. pl., suff. 3 p. s. m. (א by Syr. § 35. r. 9) אהל

לְאֹהָלֶיךָ pref. id.)(id. pl., suff. 2 pers. s. m. (א id.) אהל

לְאָהֳלֵיכֶם pref. id.)(id. pl., suff. 2 pers. pl. masc. . אהל

לְאָהֳלֶךָ pref. id. [for אָהְלֶךָ])(id. sing., suff. 2 pers. sing. masc. (א by Syr. § 39. rem. 9) . אהל

לְאַהֲרֹן pref. ל)(pr. name masc.; ꝩ bef. (:) אהר

לְאֹבֵד pref. id.)(Kal part. act. sing. masc. . . אבד

לְאֹיֵב pref. id.)(Kal part. act. sing. masc. dec. 7b איב

לְאֹיְבִים pref. id.)(id. pl., abs. st. . . . איב

לְאֱוִיל pref. ל bef. (v:))(noun masc. sing. dec. 1a . אול

לְאוּלָם pref. ל f. לָה, לִי)(noun masc. sing. (pl. c.) } אול

לְאוּלָם pref. ל q. v. (אֻלָמֵי) dec. 8a }

לְאֻוַּלְתִּי pref. id.)(noun fem. sing., suff. 1 pers. sing. from אִוֶּלֶת dec. 13a . . . אול

לְאֹם for לְאֹם, noun masc. sing. dec. 8c . לאם

לְאֻמִּי id., suff. 1 pers. sing. (§ 37. r. 2); ꝩ bef. (:) לאם

לְאֻמִּים id. pl., abs. st. . . . . לאם

לְאָוֶן pref. ל)(noun masc. sing. dec. 6g און

לְאֹנֵן pref. id.)(pr. name masc. און

לְאוֹפַנִּים pref. ל for לָה)(noun m., pl. of אוֹפָן d. 8d אפן

לְאוֹצָר pref. id.)(noun masc. sing. dec 2b אצר

לְאוֹצַר pref. ל)(id., constr. st. אצר

לְאוֹצָרוֹת pref. ל for לָה)(id. pl., abs. st. אצר

לְאוֹר pref. id.)(noun masc. sing. dec. 1a אור

לְאוֹר pref. ל, contr. [for לְהָאוֹר], Niph. inf. constr. (comp. § 9 rem. 6) . . . . אור

לְאוֹר pref. ל)(noun masc. sing. dec. 1a . אור

לְאוֹרוֹ pref. id.)(id., suff. 3 pers. sing. masc. אור

לַאֲוֵרוֹת pref. ל bef. (-:))(noun fem. pl. [by transp. for אֲרָוֹת i. q. אֲרֻוֹת see אֻרָה אֲרָיָה] ארה

לְאוּרִיָּה לְאוּרִיאֵל pref. ל)(pr. names masc. אור

לְאוּרִים pref. id.)(noun masc., pl. of [אוּר] dec. 1a אור

לְאוֹרֵךְ pref. id.)(noun masc. sing., suff. 2 pers. sing. fem. from אוֹר dec. 1a אור

לְאוֹת pref. id.)(noun com. sing. dec. 1a [for אָות] אות

לְאַזְכָּרָה pref. id.)(noun fem. sing. dec. 10 . זכר

לְאָזְנִי pref. id.)(pr. name masc. . . . אזן

לְאֶזְרָח pref. ל for לָה)(noun masc. sing. d. 2b זרח

לְאֶזְרַח pref. ל)(id. constr. st.; ꝩ bef. (:) זרח

לְאָח pref. id.)(noun masc. sing. irr. (§ 45) אח

לְאַחְאָב pref. id.)(pr. name masc.; ꝩ bef. (:) אח

לְאֶחָד pref. ל f. לָה, לִי)(num. card. sing. masc. } אחד

לְאֶחָד pref. ל q. v. irr. (§ 45); ꝩ bef. (:) }

לְאַחַד pref. ל)(id. constr. st.; ꝩ id. אחד

לַאֲחָדִים pref. ל bef. (-:))(id. pl. abs. אחד

לֶאֱחֹז pref. ל bef. (v:))(Kal inf. constr. אחז

לְאָחוֹר pref. ל)(noun masc. sing. dec. 3a אחר

לַאֲחוֹת pref. id.)(noun fem. s. irr. (§ 45); ꝩ bef. (:) אח

a Ex. 38. 27.	c Ne. 8. 10.	e Ex. 20. 6.	g Ju. 19. 9.	i 2 Ch. 29. 17.	k Is. 55. 4.	m Job 36. 30.	o Le. 24. 7.	r Zec. 11. 7.
b Ps. 136. 3.	d Ezr. 8. 27.	f Ps.119.132,165.	h Pr. 31. 6.	l Ps. 69. 6.	n Am. 5. 5.	p Job 29. 3.	q Nu. 9. 14.	s Eze. 37. 17.
c Ex. 21. 4.	d Ec. 3. 8.	e 2 Ki. 14. 12.	f Ps 139. 22.	m Pr. 11. 26.	n Eze. 10. 13.	o 2 Ch. 32. 28.	p Eze. 44. 25.	q Job 38. 13.
1Ki 18.3,11,14.	De. 5. 10.	Job 19. 12.	1 Ki. 7. 8.	Is. 51. 4.	Ne. 7. 70.	Ge. 60. 3.	Ec. 4. 11.	Eze. 44. 25.

27

וְלַאֲחוֹתֵיכֶם — pref. לְ bef. (-:))(id. pl., suff. 2 pers. pl. m — אח

לַאֲחוֹתֵךְ — pref. id.)(id. sing., suff. 2 pers. sing. fem. — אח

לַאֲחוֹתֵנוּ — pref. id.)(id. sing., suff. 1 pers. pl. — אח

לֶאֱחֹז — וְ pref. לְ bef. (v:))(Kal inf. constr. — אחז

לֶאֱחֹז — pref. לְ)(pr. name masc. — אחז

לַאֲחֻזָּה — pref. לְ bef. (-:))(noun fem. sing. dec. 10 — אחז

לַאֲחַזְיָהוּ — pref. id.)(pr. name masc. — אחז

וְלַאֲחֻזַּת — pref. id.)(noun fem. s., constr. of אֲחֻזָּה d. 10 — אחז

לַאֲחֻזָּתוֹ — pref. id.)(id. with suff. 3 pers. sing. masc. — אחז

לְאֶחָיו — pref. id.)(noun m.pl.constr. from אָח irr. (§ 45) — אח

לְאָחִי — pref. לְ)(id. sing., suff. 1 pers. sing. — אח

לְאַחַי — pref. id.)(id. pl., suff. 1 pers. sing. [for אַחַי] dag. forte impl. in ח (§ 45) — אח

לַאֲחִיָּה — pref. לְ bef. (-:))(pr. name masc. — אח

לַאֲחִיָּה — pref. לְ)(noun masc. sing., suff. 3 pers. sing. fem. from אָח irr. (§ 45) — אח

לַאֲחִיהֶם — וְ pref. לְ bef. (-:))(id. pl., suff. 3 pers. pl. m. — אח

לְאָחִיו — וְ pref. לְ)(id. s., suff. 3 pers. s. m.; וּ bef. (:) — אח

לְאֶחָיו — וְ pref. id.)(id. pl., suff. 3 pers. sing. masc. (dag. forte impl. in ח § 45); וּ id. — אח

לְאָחִיךָ — וּ pref. id.)(id. sing., suff. 2 pers. s. m.; וּ bef. (:) — אח

לְאָחִיךְ — pref. id.)(id. sing., suff. 2 pers. sing. fem. — אח

לְאַחֶיךָ — pref. id.)(id. pl., suff. 2 pers. sing. masc. (dag. forte impl. in ח § 45) — אח

לַאֲחִיכֶם — pref. id. bef. (-:))(id. pl., suff. 2 pers. pl. masc. — אח

לַאֲחִימֶלֶךְ — pref. id.)(pr. name masc. — אח

לַאֲחִינוּ — pref. לְ)(noun masc. sing., suff. 1 pers. pl. from אָח irr. (§ 45) — אח

לַאֲחִינֹעַם m., לַאֲחִירָם fem.; pref. לְ bef. (-:))(pr. names — אח

לְאַחֵר — pref. לְ)(adj. masc. sing., dag. forte impl. in ח, irr. (§ 45) — אחר

לַאֲחֵרִים — וְ pref. לְ bef. (-:))(id. pl.abs. [as if from אָחֵר] — אחר

לְאַחֲרִיתָהּ — pref. לְ)(noun fem. sing., suff. 3 pers. sing. fem. from אַחֲרִית dec. 1 b — אחר

לְאַחֲרִיתוֹ — pref. id.)(id., suff. 3 pers. sing. masc. — אחר

לְאַחֲרִיתֵךְ — pref. id.)(id., suff. 2 pers. sing. fem. — אחר

לְאַחֲרִיתָם — pref. id.)(id., suff. 3 pers. pl. masc. — אחר

לַאֲחֳרָן — Chald., pref. id.)(adj. masc. sing. — אחר

לָאַחֲרֹנָה — pref. לְ for לְהָ, לְהַ)(adj. fem. from אַחֲרוֹן m. — אחר

לָאַחֲרֹנִים — pref. id.)(id. pl. masc. dec. 1 b — אחר

לְאַחֶרֶת — pref. id.)(adj. fem. from אַחֵר masc. (dag. forte impl. in ח § 45) — אחר

לַאֲחַשְׁדַּרְפְּנֵי — pref. לְ bef. (-:))(constr. of the foll. — אחשר

לַאֲחַשְׁדַּרְפְּנַיָּא — Chald., pref. id.)(noun masc. pl., emph. from [אֲחַשְׁדַּרְפַּן] dec. 2a — אחשר

לְאַחַת / לְאַחַת — pref. לְ)(num. card. [for אֶחָת], fem. of אֶחָד (§ 45) — אחד

וְלַאֲחֹתוֹ — וְ pref. לְ bef. (-:))(noun fem. s., suff. 3 pers. sing. masc. from אָחוֹת irr. (§ 45) — אח

לַאֲחֹתוֹ — וּ pref. לְ)(id. with dag. forte impl. in ח; וּ bef. (:) — אח

לָאט — to vail, cover the face, 2 Sa. 19. 5.

לָאט / לָאט — pref. לְ or לָ q. v.)(subst. masc., with the prefix used adverbially — אטם / לט

לְאִטִּי — pref. לְ)(id. with suff. 1 pers. sing. dec. 8 e — אטם

לְאֹיֵב — pref. id.)(Kal part. act. sing. masc. dec. 7 b — איב

לְאֹיְבֵי — pref. id.)(id. pl., constr. st. — איב

לְאֹיְבָיו — pref. id.)(id. pl., suff. 3 pers. sing. masc. — איב

לְאֹיְבֵךְ — pref. id.)(id. pl., suff. 2 pers. sing. fem. — איב

לְאֹיְבֶיךָ — pref. id.)(id. pl., suff. 2 pers. sing. masc. — איב

לְאֹיְבִים — pref. id.)(id. pl., abs. st. — איב

לְאֵיד — pref. id.)(noun masc. sing. dec. 1 a — אוד

לְאִיּוֹב — pref. id.)(pr. name masc. — איב

לְאִיזֶבֶל — pref. id.)(pr. name fem., see אִיזָבֶל.

לְאִיִּים — pref. לְ f. לְהָ)(noun masc., pl. of אִי — אוה

לָאִיִּים — pref. id.)(q. v. dec. 8 (§ 37. No. 4) —

לָאַיִל / לְאַיִל — pref. לְ for לְהָ, לְהַ)(noun m. sing. d. 6 h — אול

לְאֵילִים / לְאֵלִים — pref. id.)(id. pl., abs. st. — אול

לְאֵילָמוֹ — וּ pref. לְ)(noun masc. pl., suff. 3 pers. sing. masc. from [אֵילָם] dec. 8 a; וּ bef. (:) — אול

לָאַיִן — pref. id.)(for אַיִן, noun masc. sing. dec. 6 h — אין

לְאֵין — pref.id.)(id., constr.st. (adverbially); וּ bef.(:) — אין

לְאֵיפָה — pref. id.)(for לְהָ)(noun fem. sing. dec. 10 — אוף

לְאִישׁ — וְ pref. id.)(noun masc. sing. dec. 1 a (but comp. § 45); וּ pref. לְ — איש

לְאִשָּׁהּ — וְ pref. id.)(id., suff. 3 pers. sing. fem. — איש

לְאִישִׁי — pref. id.)(id., suff. 1 pers. sing. — איש

לְאִישֵׁךְ — pref. id.)(id., suff. 2 pers. sing. fem. — איש

לְאִיתִיאֵל — pref. id.)(pr. name masc. — אית

לְאִיתָמָר — וּ pref. id.)(pr. name masc.; וּ bef. (:) — אוה

לְאֵיתָן — pref. id.)(pr. name masc. — יתן

לְאֵיתָנוֹ — pref. id.)(noun masc. sing., suff. 3 pers. sing. masc. from אֵיתָן (no vowel change) — יתן

---

a Ho. 2. 3.   e Ec. 2. 3.   i De. 23. 21.   n Je. 5. 31.   Ec. 1. 11.   r Nu. 6. 7.   u 1 Sa. 25. 22.   y Da. 11. 18.   Ju. 19. 24.
Eze. 16. 52.   f Nu. 27. 10.   k Ge. 20. 16.   o Da. 11. 4.   Eze. 24. 24.   v Job 15. 11.   De. 28. 31, 63.   z Nu. 29. 8.   1 Sa. 25. 19.
Ca. 8. 8.   g 1 Ki. 2. 15.   l Ru. 4. 3.   p Je. 31. 17.   Ear. 8. 36.   w Ge. 23. 14.   La. 1. 2.   Eze. 40. 25.   Ki. 4. 28.
1 Ch. 13. 9.   Ge. 24. 53.   Da. 11. 4.   Da. 5. 17.   Le. 21. 3.   Je. 6. 25.   Pr. 17. 5.   Is. 40. 29.   Ex. 14. 27.

לָאַךְ Root not used; Ethiop. *to send; to minister.*

מַלְאָךְ masc. dec. 2 b.—I. *messenger.*—II. *angel.*—III. perh. *priest*, Ec. 5. 5, comp. Mal. 2. 7.

מַלְאָךְ Chald. dec. 2 a, *angel*, Da. 3. 28; 6. 23.

מְלָאכָה fem. (for מְלָאכָה), constr. מְלֶאכֶת, with suff. מְלַאכְתּוֹ; pl. c. מַלְאֲכוֹת (§ 42. rem. 5).—I. *work, business, labour.*—II. *acquisition, wealth, property*, Ex. 22. 7, 10; hence, *cattle*, comp. Ge. 33. 14.

מַלְאָכוּת fem. dec. 3 a, *message*, Hag. 1. 13.

מַלְאָכִי (*messenger*) pr. name, *Malachi*, the prophet, Mal. 1. 1.

לֶאֱכוֹל pref. לְ bef. (ֱ) (Kal inf. constr. (§ 8. r. 18) אכל

לֶאֱכָל־ Kh. לֶאֱכוֹל (q. v.), K. לֶאֱכָל־ (q. v. & § 8. r. 18) אכל

לְאַכְזָב pref. לְ (adj. masc. sing. כזב

לְאַכְזָר pref. id. (adj. masc. sing. כזר

לְאַכְזָרִי pref. id. (adj. masc. sing. כזר

לֶאֱכֹל pref. לְ for לֶה, לֶה (Kal part. act. s. m. d. 7 b אכל

וְלֶאֱכֹל pref. לְ bef. (ֱ) (id. inf. constr. (§ 8. rem. 18) אכל

לְאָכְלָה pref. לְ (noun fem. sing. אכל

לְאָכְלוֹ pref. id. (Kal inf., suff. 3 pers. sing. masc. אכל

לְאָכְלוֹ pref. id. (noun masc. sing., suff. 3 pers. sing. masc. from אֹכֶל dec. 6 c אכל

לְאָכְלְכֶם pref. id. (id. with suff. 2 p. pl. m. ; bef. (:) אכל

לָאֵל pr. name masc. אול

לָאֵל pref. לְ for לֶה, לֶה (noun masc. sing. d. 1 a אול

לָאֵל pref. לְ (noun masc. sing. (אֵל elsewhere adv.) אלל

לָאֵל pref. id. (noun masc. sing. dec. 1 a אול

לְאֵלֶּה pref. לְ for לֶה, לֶה (pron. demon. com. pl. אל

לֵאלָה pref. לְ (noun fem. sing. dec. 10 (§ 42. r. 2) אלה

לֶאֱלָהּ Chald., pref. לְ bef. (ֱ) (noun masc. s. d. 1 a אלה

לֵאלֹהַּ pref. id. (noun masc. sing. dec. 1 a אלה

וְלָאֵלֶּה pref. לְ (pron. demon. com. pl.; bef. (:) אל

לֵאלָהָא Chald., pref. לְ, contr. [for לְאֵל] (noun masc. sing., emph. of אֱלָהּ dec. 1 a אלה

לֵאלָהֲהוֹ Ch. pref. id. (id. with suff. 3 pers. pl. masc. אלה

לֵאלָהוֹ Ch. pref. id. (noun masc. sing., suff. 3 pers. sing. masc. from אֱלוֹהַּ dec. 1 a אלה

לֵאלָהִי Ch., pref. id. (noun masc. sing., suff. 1 pers. sing. from אֱלָהּ dec. 1 a אלה

לֵאלֹהַי pref. id. (noun masc. pl., suff. 1 pers. pl. from אֱלוֹהַּ dec. 1 i אלה

לֵאלָהַי Ch., pref. id. (noun m. pl. c. from אֱלָהּ d. 1 a אלה

לֵאלֹהֵי pref. id. (noun masc. pl. c. from אֱלוֹהַּ dec. 1 a אלה

לֵאלֹהֵיהֶם pref. id. (id. pl., suff. 3 pers. pl. masc. אלה

לֵאלֹהֵיהֶן pref. id. (id. pl., suff. 3 pers. pl. fem. אלה

לֵאלֹהָיו pref. id. (id. pl., suff. 3 pers. sing. masc. אלה

לֵאלָהָךְ Ch., pref. id. (noun masc. pl. (K. הָךְ sing.), suff. 2 pers. sing. masc. from אֱלָהּ dec. 1 a אלה

לֵאלֹהֵיכֶם pref. id. (noun masc. pl., suff. 2 pers. pl. masc. from אֱלוֹהַּ dec. 1 a אלה

לֵאלֹהִים pref. לְ f. לֶה, לֶה (id. pl. abs. st. אלה
לֵאלֹהִים pref. לְ, contr. [for וְלָאֵל] (אלה

לֵאלֹהֵינוּ pref. id. (id. pl., suff. 1 pers. pl. אלה

לֶאֱלוֹהַּ וְ pref. לְ bef. (ֱ) (id. sing. abs. אלה

לְאֵלוּל pref. id. (name of a month אלל

לְאֵלוֹן pref. id. (pr. name masc. אול

לַאֲלִיָה pref. לְ bef. (ֱ) (noun masc. pl., suff. 3 pers. sing. fem. from [אֱלִיל] dec. 1 a אלל

לֶאֱלִימֶלֶךְ, לֶאֱלִיעֶזֶר pref. לְ bef. (ֱ) (pr. n. m. אלה

לֶאֱלִישִׁיב, לֶאֱלִיקִים pref. לְ (pr. names masc. אלה

לֶאֱלִתָה, לֶאֱלִישׁע pref. לְ bef. (ֱ) (pr. names masc. אלה

לְאֵלֶם pref. לְ (adj. masc. sing. dec. 7 b אלם

לָאֵלֶם pref. id. (noun masc. sing. (pl. c. אֵלְמֵי) dec. 8 a; bef. (:) אול

לְאֵלֻמּוֹ pref. id. (noun masc. pl., suff. 3 pers. sing. masc. from [אֵלֶם] dec. 8 a; bef. (:) אול

לְאַלְמוֹת pref. לְ for לֶה, לֶה (id. with pl. fem. term. אול

לָאַלְמָנָה pref. id. (noun fem. sing. dec. 11 a אלם

לְאַלְמָתִי pref. לְ bef. (:) (noun fem. sing., suff. 1 pers. sing. from [אֲלֻמָּה] dec. 10 אלם

לְאֶלְנָתָן, pref. לְ (pr. n. m. ; bef. (:) אלה

לָאֵלֶּה pref. לְ f. לֶה, לֶה (אלה
לָאֵלֶה pref. לְ q. v. noun masc. sing. dec. 6 a (§ 35. rem. 2) אלף
לָאֲלֵי

לְאַלְפֵי pref. id. (id. pl., constr. st. אלף

לְאַלְפֵיהֶם pref. id. (noun masc. pl., suff. 3 pers. pl. masc. from אַלּוּף dec. 1 b אלף

לְאַלְפֵיכֶם pref. id. (noun masc. pl., suff. 2 pers. pl. masc. from אֶלֶף dec. 6 a; bef. (:) אלף

לַאֲלָפִים pref. לְ f. לֶה, לֶה (id. pl., abs. st. אלף
וְלַאֲלָפִים pref. לְ bef. (ֱ) (אלף

לְאֹם masc. dec. 8 c (with suff. לְאֻמִּי or לְאוּמִי Is. 51. 4).—I. *people, nation.*—II. לְאֻמִּים pr. name of a people, Ge. 25. 3.

Eze 44. 3.   Ge. 47. 24.   Job 24. 25.   Da. 3. 28.   Da. 5. 4, 23.   Da. 11. 38.   1 Ki. 7. 12.   1 Ch. 12. 14.   Ex. 34. 7.
Mi. 1. 14.   Eze. 33. 27.   Da. 11. 38.   Hab. 1. 11.   Ex. 23. 32.   Ne. 6. 15.   Eze. 40. 29, 32.   Ge. 36. 30.   Pr. 14. 28.
Pr. 5. 9.   Job 20. 21.   1 Ch. 26. 12.   Da. 3. 14.   Da. 3. 18, 12.   Is. 10. 11.   Eze. 40. 16.   1 Sa. 10. 19.   Ge. 25. 23.
Is. 55. 10.   Ge. 47. 24.   Da. 5. 23.   Ps. 69. 5.   Ex. 22. 19.   Pr. 31. 8.   Ge. 87. 7.

לְאֹם   bef. (:) ; pref. לְ)(noun fem. sing. d. 8 b   אם

לְאִמָּה   pref. id.)(noun fem. sing. irr. (§ 45)   אמה

לְאִמָּהּ   pref. id.)(noun fem. sing., suff. 3 pers. sing. fem. from אֵם dec. 8 b ; bef. (:)   אם

לְאִמּוֹ   pref. id.)(id., suff. 3 pers. sing. m. ; id.   אם

לְאֲמוֹנָה   pref. לְ bef. (v:))(noun fem. sing. dec. 10   אמן

לְאֵמוֹר   in full for לֵאמֹר (q. v. & § 8. rem. 18)   אמר

לְאִמּוֹת   pref. לְ)(noun fem., pl. of אָמָה dec. 10   אם

לְאִמִּי   pref. id.)(noun fem. sing., suff. 1 pers. sing. from אֵם dec. 8 b ; bef. (:)   אם

לְאֻמִּים   pref. id.)(noun masc., pl. of לְאֹם dec. 8 c, also pr. name ; id.   לאם

לְאָמְנוֹן   pref. id.)(pr. name masc., id.   אמן

לְאֹמְנַת   pref. id.)(Kal part. act. f. d. 13 a, fr. אָמַן m.   אמן

לְאֲמַצְיָהוּ   pref. לְ bef. (־:))(pr. name masc.   אמץ

לֵאמֹר   pref. לְ, contr. [for לְאָמֹר])(Kal inf. constr.   אמר

לְאֵמֶר   pref. לְ)(pr. name masc.   אמר

לְאֱמֹרִי   pref. לְ for לְהָ ,לְהַ)(pr. name of a people   אמר

לְאֲמָרַי   pref. לְ bef. (־:))(noun masc. pl., suff. 1 pers. sing. from [אֵמֶר] dec. 6 b   אמר

לְאִמְרֵי   pref. לְ)(id. pl., constr. st.   אמר

לְאֲמַרְיָה   pref. לְ bef. (־:))(pr. name masc.   אמר

לְאִמְרַת   pref. לְ)(noun fem. sing., constr. of [אִמְרָה] dec. 12 b ; bef. (:)   אמר

לְאִמְרָתְךָ / לְאִמְרָתֶךָ   pref. id.)(id. with suff. 2 pers. sing. masc.   אמר

לֶאֱמֶת   pref. לְ bef. (v:))(noun fem. sing. dec. 8 [for § 37. No. 3 b]   אמן

לַאֲמָתְךָ / וְלַאֲמָתֶךָ   pref. לְ bef. (־:))(noun fem. sing., suff. 2 p. s. m. fr. אָמָה d. 11 a, pl. irr. (§ 45)   אמה

לְאִמֹּתָם   pref. לְ)(noun fem. pl., suff. 3 pers. pl. masc. from אֵם dec. 8 b   אם

לְאִמֹּתָם   pref. id.)(noun fem. pl., suff. 3 pers. pl. masc. from אָמָה dec. 10   אמם

לֶאֱנֹשׁ   pref. לְ bef. (v:))(n. m. s. irr. (see אִישׁ § 45)   אנש

לְאַנְשֵׁי   pref. לְ)(id. pl. constr. [prop. from אֱנָשׁ]   אנש

לְאַנְשֵׁיהֶם   pref. id.)(id. pl., suff. 3 p. pl. m. ; bef. (:)   אנש

לְאַנְשָׁיו   pref. id. bef. (־:))(id. pl., suff. 3 pers. sing. m.   אנש

לְאֲנָשֶׁיךָ   pref. id.)(id., suff. 2 pers. sing. masc.   אנש

לֶאֱנָשִׁים   pref. לְ f. לְהָ ,לְהַ)(id. pl., abs. st.   אנש

לֶאֱנָשִׁים   pref. id. bef. (־:))(אנש

לְאָסָא   pref. לְ)(pr. name masc.   אסה

לֶאֱסוֹר   in full for לֶאֱסֹר (q. v. & § 8. rem. 18)   אסר

לַאֲסוּרִים   pref. לְ bef. (־:))(Kal p. p. pl. m. fr. אָסוּר d. 3 a   אסר

לַאֲסוּרִין   Chald., pref. לְ bef. (v:))(noun masc., pl. of אֱסוּר dec. 1 a   אסר

לְאָסָף   pref. לְ)(pr. name masc.   אסף

לֶאֱסֹף   pref. לְ bef. (v:))(Kal inf. constr. dec. 6 c   אסף

לַאֲסֻפִּים   pref. לְ for לְהָ ,לְהַ)(noun masc., pl. of [אָסֻף] dec. 8 c (§ 37. No. 3 c)   אסף

לְאֵסֶר   pref. לְ)(noun masc. sing., constr. of אֵסָר dec. 2 b ; bef. (:)   אסר

לֶאֱסֹר / לֶאֱסוֹר   pref. לְ bef. (v:))(Kal inf. constr. (§ 13. rem. 2)   אסר

לְאָסְרְךָ   pref. id.)(id. with suff. 2 pers. sing. masc.   אסר

לְאֶסְתֵּר   pref. לְ)(pr. name fem., see אֶסְתֵּר.   אסר

לְאֵפֹד   pref. לְ for לְהָ ,לְהַ)(noun masc. sing.   אפד

לְאַפּוֹ   pref. לְ)(noun masc. sing., suff. 3 pers. sing. masc. from אַף dec. 8 d (§ 37. No. 3 b)   אנף

לְאֵפוֹד / לְאֵפוֹד   pref. לְ f. לְהָ ,לְהַ)(noun masc. sing.   אפד

לְאֵפוֹד   pref. לְ q. v.   אפד

לְאֹפוֹת   pref. id.)(Kal part. act., pl. of [אֹפֶה] dec. 10, from אָפָה masc. ; bef. (:)   אפה

לְאַפֵּי   pref. id.)(noun masc. du. constr., from אַף dec. 8 d (§ 37. No. 3 b)   אנף

לְאַפִּי   pref. id.)(id. sing., suff. 1 pers. sing.   אנף

לְאַפָּיו   pref. id.)(id. du., suff. 3 pers. sing. masc.   אנף

לַאֲפִיקִים   pref. לְ f. לְהָ ,לְהַ)(noun masc., pl. of [אָפִיק] dec. 3 a   אפק

לַאֲפִיקִים   pref. לְ bef. (־:))(אפק

לְאַפְּסֵי   pref. לְ)(noun m. du. constr. fr. אֶפֶס d. 6 a   אפס

לְאֵפֶר   pref. id.)(noun masc. sing.   אפר

לְאֶפְרַיִם / לְאֶפְרַיִם   pref. id.)(pr. name of a man and a tribe   אפר

לְאָצֵל   pref. id.)(pr. name masc. ; bef. (:)   אצל

לְאֹצָרוֹת   pref. לְ, for לְהָ ,לְהַ)(noun masc. with pl. fem. term. abs. from אוֹצָר dec. 2 b   אצר

לְאֹצְרוֹת   pref. לְ)(id. pl. constr. st. ; bef. (:)   אצר

לְאַרְצֹתָיו   pref. id.)(id. pl., suff. 3 pers. sing. masc.   אצר

לְאַרְאֵלִי   pref. id.)(pr. name masc., see אַרְאֵל   ארה

לְאֹרֵב   pref. id.)(Kal part. act. sing. masc. dec. 7 b   ארב

לְאַרְבֶּה   pref. לְ for לְהָ ,לְהַ)(noun masc. sing.   רבה

לְאַרְבַּע   pref. לְ)(num. card. fem. (§ 31. rem. 5)   רבע

לְאַרְבָּעָה   pref. id.)(id. masc. (comp. § 42. rem. 5)   רבע

לְאַרְבַּעַת   pref. id.)(id. id. constr.   רבע

לְאַרְבַּעְתָּם   pref. id.)(id. id. with suff. 3 pers. pl. masc.   רבע

לְאַרְבַּעְתָּן   pref. id.)(id. id. with suff. 3 pers. pl. fem.   רבע

a 1 Ki. 2. 19.   f Ru. 4. 16.   l Is. 42. 3.   q Ge. 19. 8.   u Is. 61. 1.   w Nu. 30. 3.   z Ex. 35. 9, 27.   Is. 13. 3.   g 1 Sa. 22. 8, 13.

b Exe. 44. 25.   g Pr. 4. 20.   m 1 Ki. 1. 17.   r Ezr. 7. 26.   Ju. 15. 12.   f Ju. 8. 27.   Eze. 36. 6.   Eze. 1. 15.

c Ca. 6. 9.   h Ps. 119. 123.   n La. 2. 12.   Ju. 15. 10.   1 Ch. 26. 17.   Ex. 25. 7.   1 Sa. 8. 13.   Eze. 22. 18.   Eze. 1. 10.

d Ge. 24. 53.   Ps. 119. 154.   Ge. 25. 16.   Is. 49. 9.   Nu. 30. 13.   Ps. 78. 50.   1 Sa. 25. 22.   2 Ch. 8. 15.   13.

e 2 Ch. 2. 11.   Ps. 119. 82.   Ju. 8. 15.   Ex. 21. 7.   Ps. 59. 14.   Is. 2. 7.

לָאֲרוֹד   pref. לְ bef. (־ַ))(pr. name masc. . .   ארד

לָאָרוֹן   pref. לְ for לְהַ, לְהָ)(noun masc. sing. d. 3 a   ארה

לָאֲרוֹן   pref. לְ bef. (־ַ))(id. constr. st. .   ארה

לָאֲרָזִי   pref. לְ)(noun masc. sing. (pl. c. אֲרָזֵי) d. 6 a   ארז

לָאֹרַח   pref. לְ for לְהַ, לְהָ)(noun com. sing. dec. 6   ארה
     (§ 35. rem. 5 & 9)

לָאֹרֵחַ   pref. id.)(Kal part. act. sing. masc.   ארה

לָאֲרִיאֵל   pref. לְ bef. (־ַ))(compound noun masc. from   ארה
     אֵל & אֲרִי, see

לָאַרְיֵה   pref. לְ for לְהָ)(n. m. s., אֲרִי, with parag. ה   ארה

לָאֲרִיוֹד   pref. לְ)(pr. name masc. .   ארה

לָאֲרָיוֹת   pref. לְ bef. (־ַ))(noun masc. with pl. fem.   ארה
     term. from אֲרִי dec. 6 i (§ 35. rem. 14)

לָאֶרֶךְ   pref. לְ)(noun masc. sing. .   ארך

לָאָרֹךְ   pref. id.)(noun masc. sing. dec. 6 c   ארך

לָאָרְכָּהּ   pref. id.)(id., suff. 3 pers. sing. fem.   ארך

לָאֲרָם   pref. לְ bef. (־ַ))(pr. name of a people   ארם

לָאַרְנוֹן   pref. לְ)(pr. name of a river   רנן

לָאָרְנָן   pref. לְ)(pr. name masc. .   ארן

לָאַרְעִיתָ   Chald., pref. id.)(noun fem. sing., constr. of   ארע
     [אַרְעָי] dec. 8 b

לָאָרֶץ   וְ pref. לְ f. לְהָ, לְהָ)(noun fem. sing. d. 6 a   ארץ

לָאָרֶץ   pref. q. v.   (§ 35. rem. 2)   ארץ

לָאַרְצָהּ   pref. id., suff. 3 pers. sing. masc.   ארץ

לָאַרְצוֹ   pref. id., suff. 3 pers. sing. masc.   ארץ

לָאַרְצִי   ‌ pref. id)(id., suff. 1 pers. sing.; ‌ bef. (־ַ)   ארץ

לָאַרְצֶךָ } pref. id)(id., suff. 2 pers. sing. masc.   ארץ
לָאַרְצֵךְ }

לָאַרְצֵךְ   ‌ pref. id., suff. 2 pers. s. fem.; ‌ bef. (־ַ)   ארץ

לָאַרְצָם   ‌ pref. id)(id., suff. 3 pers. pl. masc.; ‌ id.   ארץ

לָאַרְתַּחְשַׁסְתָּא } pref. id)(pr. name masc., see   ארתח
לָאַרְתַּחְשַׁשְׁתָּא }

לָאֵשׁ } pref. לְ f. לְהָ)(} noun com. sing. dec. 8 b   אש
לָאֵשׁ } pref. לְ q. v. }

לָאֶשְׁבָּל   pref. id.)(pr. name masc. see אֶשְׁבָּל .   אשב

לָאַשְׁדּוֹד   pref. id.)(pr. name of a place .   שדד

לָאִשָּׁה } וְ pref. לְ f. לְהָ)(noun fem. sing. irr.   אנש
לָאִשָּׁה } ‌ pref. לְ q. v. } (§ 45); ‌ bef. (־ַ)

לָאַשּׁוּר   ‌ pref. id.)(pr. name of a country; ‌ id.   אשר

לָאֲשְׁחוּר   ‌ pref. id.)(pr. name masc.; ‌ id. .   שחר

לָאֲשֵׁי   pref. id.)(noun masc. pl., suff. ֿ pers. sing.   אש
     from אֵשׁ dec. 9 a

לָאֲשִׁישֵׁי   pref. לְ bef. (־ַ))(noun masc. pl. constr. from   אשש
     [אֲשִׁישׁ] dec. 3 a .

לָאֶשְׁכְּלוֹתָ   pref. לְ)(noun masc. with pl. fem. term., abs.   שכל
     from אֶשְׁכֹּל (q. v.) . .

לָאָשָׁם } וְ pref. לְ f. לְהָ)(} noun masc. sing. d. 1 c   אשם
לָאָשָׁם } pref. לְ q. v. }

לָאַשְׁמָה   pref. id.)(noun fem. sing. dec. 12 a .   אשם

לָאַשְׁמַת   pref. id.)(id., constr. st. .   אשם

לָאִשְׁפַיָּא   Chald., pref. id.)(noun masc. pl. emph. [as if   אשף
     from אַשָּׁף dec. 2 b] see אַשָּׁף

לָאַשְׁפִּים   ‌ וְ pref. לְ for לְהָ, לְהָ)(n. m., pl. of אַשָּׁף d. 1 b   אשף

לָאַשְׁפְּנַז   pref. לְ)(pr. name masc., see אַשְׁפְּנַז.

לָאַשְׁקְלוֹן   pref. id.)(pr. name of a place .   שקל

לָאֲשֶׁר   ‌ וְ pref. לְ bef. (־ַ))(pron. relat. com. s. & pl.   אשר

לָאָשֵׁר   ‌ pref. לְ)(pr. name of a tribe; ‌ bef. (־ַ)   אשר

לָאֲשֵׁרָה   ‌ וְ pref. לְ f. לְהָ, לְהָ)(} noun fem. sing. dec. 10   אשר
לָאֲשֵׁרָה   ‌ pref. לְ bef. (־ַ) }

לָאֲשֵׁרוֹ   pref. id.)(noun masc. sing., suff. 3 pers. sing.   אשר
     masc. from [אָשׁוּר] dec. 3 a .

לָאֵשֶׁת   pref. לְ)(noun fem. sing. d. 13 b (comp. § 45)   איש

לָאִשְׁתּוֹ   ‌ pref. id.)(id., suff. 3 pers. s. m.; ‌ bef. (־ַ)   איש

לָאִשְׁתִּי   pref. id.)(id., suff. 1 pers. sing. .   איש

לָאת   defect. for לְאוֹת (q. v.) . .   אוה

לָאָתוֹן   pref. לְ for לְ, לְהָ)(noun fem. sing. dec. 3 a   אתן

לָאַתּוּן   Ch., pref. לְ)(noun m. s. dec. 1 a [for אַתְנוּן]   תנן

לָאַתּוּנָא   Ch., pref. id.)(id., emph. st. . .   תנן

לָאתוֹת   pref. id.)(n. com., pl. of אוֹת d. 1 a [for אֹנֻת   אוה

לָאֲתִים   ‌ וְ pref. לְ for לְהָ, לְהָ)(noun masc. pl. [of   אֵת
לָאִתִּים   ‌ pref. לְ q. v. } אֵת § 37. rem. 5]

לָאֲתֹנוֹת   ‌ וְ pref. לְ bef. (־ַ))(noun f., pl. of אָתוֹן d. 3 a   אתן

לָאֶתְנַנָּה   pref. לְ)(noun masc. sing., suff. 3 pers. sing.   תנה
     (§ 3. rem. 3) fem. from אֶתְנַן dec. 8 a

לָאַתְרֵהּ   Ch., pref. id.)(noun masc. sing., suff. 3 pers.   אתר
     sing. masc. from אֲתַר dec. 3 a .

לָאָתֹת   pref. id.)(defect. for לָאוֹתֹת see אוֹתֹת   אוה

לֵב } ‌ וְ pref.)(noun masc. sing. dec. 8 b (comp. §   לבב
לֵב־ } ‌ וְ pref.)(} 36. rem. 3); for וְ see lett. ו

לָבָא   or לָבָה Root not used; most prob. onomatopoetic,
imitating the sound of *lowing*, *roaring* (Gesenius).

לְבִי—I. pl. masc. לְבָאִים (§ 35. rem. 15) *lions*,
Ps. 57. 5.—II. pl. fem. לְבָאוֹת, (a) *lionesses*, constr

a Eze. 17. 23.   d 1 Ki. 7. 29.   h Nu. 35. 33.   l De. 31. 4.   p Is. 16. 7.   s Da. 2. 2.   w Ge. 3. 21.   y Da. 3. 20.   k 1 Sa. 9. 20.
b Job 31. 32.   e Je. 15. 15.   2 Sa. 7. 23.   m 1 Sa. 28. 24.   Ca. 7. 5.   x 2 Ki. 23. 4, 7.   Job 19. 17.   z Da. 3. 19.   l 1 Sa. 23. 17.
c 2 Sa. 12. 4.   f Ge. 13. 17.   Ge. 32. 10.   n Is. 45. 10.   q Le. 7. 37.   t Pr. 14. 15.   u Ex. 12. 13.   a Is. 8. 18.   m Esr. 6. 5.
1 Ki. 13. 26.   g Da. 6. 25.   Is. 62. 4.   o Nu. 28. 2.   r Da. 5. 7.   u Ju. 14. 15.   v Nu. 22. 29.   1 Sa. 13. 21.   n Ge. 1. 14.
i Is. 29. 2.   AA Ge. 30. 25.

לְבָאוֹת Na. 2. 13; (b) בֵּית לְ (house of lionesses) pr. name of a town in the tribe of Simeon, Jos. 19. 6.

לָבִיא lion; according to others, lioness.

לְבִיָּא fem. (for לְבִיָּה) lioness, Eze. 19. 2.

לְבֹא   לְבוֹא   } defect. for לְבוֹא, לָבוֹא (q. v.)   בוא

לְבָאוֹת ½ pr. n. of a place (see also בֵּית לְבָ); ⅓ bef. (ะ)   לבה

לָבָא ְ pref. לְ f. לָה } Kal part. sing. masc. dec. 1 a   בוא

לְבָאִים◌ pref. id. } id. pl., abs. st.   בוא

לָבָאֹם◌ noun m., pl. of לָבִי (לְבִי) dec. 6 i (§ 35. rem. 15)   לבה

לַבְּאֵר◌ pref. לְ f. לָה; לָה } n. f. s. d. 1 a (but pl. c.) } באר
לִבְאֵר◌ pref. לְ bef. (ะ) } בְּאֵרֹת § 35. rem. 10)}

לֵב, לֵבָב masc. dec. 4 d & 8 b (pl. לְבֹבוֹת, לְבָבִים)—I. the heart, in the physical sense; frequently for life, the vital principle. To the heart is ascribed, thought, reasoning, understanding, will, judgment, design, affection, love, hatred, courage, fear, joy, sorrow; חֲכַם לֵב wise in heart; חֲסַר לֵב wanting in understanding, foolish; אַנְשֵׁי לֵב men of understanding; also men of courage; בְּלֵב וָלֵב with a double heart, i. e. deceitfully.—II. middle, midst, inner part.

לֵב, לְבַב Chald. masc. dec. 3 b & 5 b, id.

לֵבָב denom. Niph. to become wise, acquire understanding, Job 11. 12. Piel, Ca. 4. 9, to encourage, embolden; others, to ravish the heart.

לִבָּה fem. dec. 10, the heart.

לְבִיבָה f. d. 10, cake, pancake, 2 Sa. 13. 6, 8, 10.

לֵבֵב denom. Pi. to make such cakes, 2 Sa. 13. 6, 8.

לְבַב ⅓ Heb. & Chald., noun masc. sing., constr. of לֵבָב dec. 4 d (Ch. d. 3 b); ⅓ bef. (ะ)   לבב

לְבָבָהּ id., suff. 3 pers. sing. fem.   לבב

לִבְבֵהּ ⅓ Chald., noun masc. sing., suff. 3 pers. sing. masc. from לֵבַב dec. 3 b .   לבב

לְבָבְהֶן noun masc. pl., suff. 3 pers. pl. [for לְבִבְיהֶן] from לֵבָב dec. 4 b   לבב

לְבָבוֹ ⅓ id. sing., suff. 3 pers. sing. masc.; ⅓ bef. (ะ)   לבב

לְבָבוֹת◌ id. pl. abs. with fem. term.   לבב

לְבָבוֹת◌ noun fem., pl. of לְבִיבָה dec. 10   לבב

לְבָבִי ⅓ נ n. m. sing., suff. 1 pers. sing. fr. לֵבָב d. 4 b   לבב

לְבָבֶךָ
לְבָבְךָ } id., suff. 2 pers. sing. masc.; ⅓ bef. (ะ)   לבב

לְבָבֵךְ id., suff. 2 pers. sing. fem.   לבב

לְבָבֵךְ Chald., noun masc. sing., suff ꝰ pers. sing. masc. from לֵבַב dec. 3 b   לבב

לִבַבְכֶם n. m. s., suff. 2 pers. pl. masc. from לֵבָב d. 4 b   לבב

[לִבְבֵל] pref. לְ } pr. n. of a country [for בָּבֶל]   בלל

לְבַבְכֶם noun masc. sing., suff. 3 pers. pl. masc. from לֵב dec. 4 b .   לבב

לְבָבֵנוּ id. with suff. 1 pers. pl.   לבב

לִבַּבְתִּנִי Piel pret. 2 pers. sing. fem., suff. 1 pers. sing.   לבב

לִבֵּן◌ pref. לְ } see בֵּן; K. לְבֵן (q. v.)   בנן

לְבֶגֶד◌ pref. id. } noun masc. s. (suff. בִּגְדִּי), d. 6 a   בגד

לִבְגֹּד◌ pref. לְ bef. (ะ) } Kal inf. constr. .   בגד

לְבִגְדֵי◌ ⅓ pref. לְ } noun masc. pl. constr. from בֶּגֶד dec. 6 a; ⅓ bef. (ะ)   בגד

לְבַד
לַבָּד } pref. id. } noun masc. sing., with the pref. used adverbially; ⅓ id. } בדד

לְבַדֵּד pref. id. } n. m. s. with the pref. used adverbially   בדד

לְבַדָּהּ pref. id. } adv. לְבַד (q. v.), with suff. 3 p. s. f.   בדד

לְבַדְּהֶן pref. id. } id., suff. 3 pers. pl. fem.   בדד

לְבַדּוֹ pref. id. } id., suff. 3 pers. sing. masc.   בדד

לִבְדּוֹק◌ pref. לְ bef. (ะ) } Kal inf. constr. (§ 8. r. 8)   בדק

לְבַדִּי pref. לְ } adv. לְבַד (q. v.), with suff. 1 pers. s.   בדד

לַבַּדִּים pref. לְ f. לָה }   בדד
לְבַדִּים pref. לְ q. v. } noun masc., pl. of בַּד dec. 8 d   בדד

לְבַדֶּךָ
לְבַדְּךָ } pref. id. } id. sing., suff. 2 pers. sing. masc., adverbially   בדד

לְבַדְּכֶם pref. id. } id. sing., suff. 2 pers. pl. masc.   בדד

לְבַדָּם pref. id. } id. sing., suff. 3 pers. pl. masc.   בדד

לְבַדָּנָה pref. id. } id. s., suff. 3 pers. pl. f. (§ 3. r. 5)   בדד

לְבִדְקֵי pref. id. } noun masc. s. (suff. בִּדְקֵךְ) d. 6 a   בדק

לִבָּהּ noun masc. sing., suff. 3 pers. sing. fem. from לֵב dec. 8 b .   לבב

לַבֶּהָלָה pref. לְ for לְהַ } noun fem. sing. dec. 10   בהל

לְבַהֲלָם◌ ⅓ pref. לְ } Piel inf. [בַּהֵל § 14. r. 1], suff. 3 pers. pl. dec. 7 b; ⅓ bef. (ะ)   בהל

לְבַהֲלֵנִי pref. id. } id. with suff. 1 pers. sing.   בהל

לִבְהֵמָה ⅓ pref. לְ f. לָה } noun fem. sing. (§ 42. r. 5,
לַבְּהֵמָה◌ pref. לְ bef. (ะ) } & § 44. rem. 3) }

לְבֶהֱמַת ⅓ pref. לְ } id. constr. st. (comp. § 42. r. 4);
⅓ bef. (ะ)   בהם

לְבֶהֶמְתְּךָ
לִבְהֶמְתֶּךָ } pref. לְ bef. (ะ) } id., suff. 2 p. s. f. [prop. from בְּהֵמַת § 42. r. 5, & § 44. r 8] } בהם

לִבְהֶמְתָּם◌ pref. id. } id., suff. 3 pers. pl. masc.   בהם

לִבְהֶמְתֵּנוּ pref. id. } id., suff. 1 pers. pl   בהם

לַבֶּהָרֶת ⅓ pref. לְ for לְהַ } noun fem. sing., in pause for בַּהֶרֶת q.v. (§ 44. rem. 5)   בהר

a Pr. 23. 30.   Da. 5. 21.   ꞔ 2 Sa. 13. 8.   Ca. 4. 9.   Ex. 35. 21.   1 Ch. 34. 10.   ꝑ Is. 65. 23.   Ps. 147. 9.   Nu. 20. 5.
b Ps. 75. 5.   Ps. 2. 8.   Ps. 73. 26.   Ex. 25. 7.   Ju. 8. 36.   Ge. 21. 29.   2 Ch. 32. 18.   De. 11. 12.   Jos. 21. 2.
c Ge. 16. 14.   1 Ch. 28. 9.   Is. 7. 4.   Is. 59. 6.   Ge. 21. 28.   2 Ki. 12. 8.   2 Ch. 35. 21.   Le. 13. 7.   Le. 14. 56.
d Ps. 55. 21.   ee Is. 33. 1.

לִבּוֹ וֹ	noun masc. sing., suff. 3 pers. sing. masc.
	from לֵב dec. 8 b לבב
לָבוֹא וֹ	pref. לְ or לָ q. v.) Kal inf. constr.
לָבוֹא	(§ 21. rem. 2, & § 25. No. 2) dec. 1 a בוא
לְבוֹאָם	pref. לְ) id., suff. 3 pers. pl. masc. בוא
לְבוֹ	in full for לְבוֹא (q. v.) בוז
לְבוֹז	pref. לְ, see lett. ל) noun masc. sing. בוז
לְבוּל	pref. לְ) noun masc. sing. for יְבוּל יבל
לִבוֹנָה וֹ	pref. id.) noun fem. s. d. 10 ; וּ bef. (:) לבן
לָבוּר וְ	pref. לָ, see lett. ל) Kal inf. constr. בור
לָבוֹשׁ	Kal inf. abs. לבש
לָבוּשׁ	id. part. pass. sing. masc. dec 3 a. לבש
לְבוּשׁ	id. id. constr.; or noun masc. sing. dec. 1a לבש
לְבוּשָׁהּ	noun masc. sing., suff. 3 p. s. f. fr. לְבוּשׁ d. 1 a לבש
לְבוּשֵׁהּ	Chald. id., suff. 3 pers. sing. masc. לבש
לְבוּשׁוֹ	id., suff. 3 pers. sing. masc. לבש
לְבוּשִׁי	id., suff. 1 pers. sing. לבש
לְבוּשֵׁיהוֹן וּ	Ch. id. pl., suff. 3 pers. pl. m.; וּ bef. (:) לבש
לְבוּשְׁכֶן	id. sing., suff. 2 pers. pl. fem. לבש
לְבוּשָׁם	id. sing., suff. 3 pers. pl. masc. לבש
לִבּוֹת	noun fem., pl. of לִבָּה dec. 10 לבב
לָבַז	pref. לָ (see lett. ל)) noun m. s. d. 8 e בזז
לָבֹז וְ	pref. id.) Kal inf. constr. בזז
לְבַז	pref. לְ) noun masc. sing. dec. 8 e בזז
לְבִזָּה	pref. id.) noun fem. sing. בזז
לְבִזֹה	pref. לְ bef. (:)) adj. m., constr. of בָּזֹה d. 3 a בזה
לְבֹזְזִים	pref. לְ) Kal part. act. m., pl. of בֹּזֵז d. 7 b בזז
לְבֹזְזֵינוּ	pref. id.) id. with suff. 1 pers. pl. בזז
לִבְחִירָי	pref. לְ bef. (:)) adj. pl. masc., suff. 1 pers.
	pl. from בָּחִיר dec. 3 a בחר
לִבְחִירִי	pref. id.) id. sing., suff. 1 pers. sing. בחר
לָבַט	Niph. to *stumble, fall*, Pr. 10. 8, 10 ; He. 4. 14.
לְבַטֵּא	pref. לְ) Piel inf. constr. בטא
לְבֶטַח	pref. לְ, see lett. ל) noun masc. with the pref.
	as an adv. בטח
לְבַטָּלָא	Chald., pref. id.) Pael inf. בטל
לִבִּי וְ	noun m. s., suff. 1 pers. s. from לֵב d. 8 b לבב
לָבִיא	pref. לָ, contr. for לְהָבִיא, Hiph. inf. (comp.
	§ 11. rem. 3) בוא
לָבִיא	noun masc. sing. לבא
לְבִיָּה	[for לְבִיָּה] noun fem. sing. לבה
לְבִים וְ	pr. name of a people, see לוּבִים לוב

לְבֵין וֹ	pref. לְ) prep. [prop. constr. of בֵּין] dec. 6 h בין
לְבִינָה	pref. לְ for לְהָ) noun fem. sing. dec. 10 בין
לַבַּיִת וְ	pref. לְ for לְהָ) noun masc. sing. dec. בית
לַבָּתִּים וְ	6 m, pl. irr. בָּתִּים (§ 45) . בית
לְבֵית וֹ	pref. לְ) id. constr. st. Heb. & Ch., also
	pr. name in compos., as לְבֵית־אֵל &c. בית
לְבֵיתָהּ	pref. id.) id., suff. 3 pers. sing. fem. בית
לְבַיְתֵהּ	Ch., pref. id.) id., suff. 3 pers. sing. m. (§ 68) בית
לְבֵיתוֹ וֹ	pref. id.) id. with suff. 3 p. s. m.; וּ bef. (:) בית
לְבֵיתִי	pref. id.) id., suff. 1 pers. sing. בית
לְבֵיתֶךָ וֹ	pref. id.) id., suff. 2 pers. sing. masc.;
לְבֵיתְךָ	וּ bef. (:) בית
לְבֵיתֵךְ	pref. id.) id., suff. 2 pers. sing. fem. בית
לְבָךְ	noun masc. sing., suff. 2 pers. sing. masc. לבב
לִבָּךְ וְ	from לֵב dec. 8 b
לִבֵּךְ	id., suff. 2 pers. sing. fem. לבב
לַבִּכּוּרִים וְ	pref. לְ for לְהָ) n. m., pl. of בִּכּוּר d. 1 b בכר
לִבְכּוֹת	pref. לְ bef. (:)) Kal inf. constr. dec. 1 b בכה
לִבְכִּי	pref. לְ, or לִ bef. (:)) noun masc. sing.
לְבֶכִי	dec. 6 i (§ 35. rem. 14) בכה
לְבַבְכֶם	noun m. s., suff. 2 pers. pl. m. from לֵב d. 8 b לבב
לְבַכֵּר	pref. לְ) Piel inf. constr. בכר
לְבֶכֶר	pref. id.) pr. name masc. בכר
לְבִכְרָה	pref. לְ for לְהָ) noun fem. sing. dec. 10 בכר
לִבְכֹּתָהּ וְ	pref. לְ bef. (:)) Kal inf. בְּכוֹת, suff.
	3 pers. sing. fem. dec. 1 b בכה
לְבֵלְאשַׁצַּר	pref. לְ) pr. name masc., see בֵּלְשַׁאצַּר.
לְבִלְגָּה	pref. id.) pr. name masc. בלג
לְבָלָה	pref. לְ for לְהָ) adj. f. s. d. 11 a, from בָּלֶה m. בלה
לִבְלוֹם	pref. לְ bef. (:)) Kal inf. constr. (§ 8. r. 18) בלם
לְבַלּוֹת	pref. לְ) Piel inf. constr. בלה
לְבִלְי	pref. לְ bef. (:)) adv. with & without the pref. בלה
לְבֶלַע	pref. לְ) pr. name masc. (§ 35. rem. 2) בלע
לְבֶלַע	pref. לְ bef. (:)) Kal inf. constr. בלע
לְבַלֵּעַ	pref. לְ) Piel inf. (בִּלַּע), suff. 3 pers. sing.
	masc. dec. 7 b (§ 36. rem. 5) בלע
לְבִלְעָם	pref. id.) pr. name masc. בלע
לְבָלָק	pref. id.) pr. name masc. בלק
לְבַלֹּתוֹ	pref. id.) Piel inf. (בַּלּוֹת), suff. 3 p. s. m. d. 1 b בלה
לְבִלְתִּי וֹ	pref. id.) adv. (בָּלַת), with parag. י; וּ bef. (:) בלת
לְבָבָם וְ	noun m. s., suff. 3 p. pl. m. from לֵב d. 8 b לבב

a Ec. 9. 1.   c 2 Sa. 1. 24.   e Is. 49. 7.   h Ps. 89. 4.   l Pr. 31. 15, 21.   o Ne. 13. 31.   s De. 21. 16.   u Ese. 23. 43.   f Jon. 2. 1.
b Hag. 1. 6.   d Je. 10. 9.   f Is. 42. 24.   i Le. 5. 4.   m De. 26. 11.   p Is. 15. 2.   t 1 Ch. 5. 1.   w Job 33.
c Da. 7. 9.   f Ese. 23. 46.   g Is. 17. 14.   k Ese. 19. 2.   n Is. 22. 12.   q Ps. 49. 15.   y 1 Ch. 17. 2.
d Da. 3. 21.   f 2 Ch. 20. 25.   n Is. 65. 15.   l Is. 59. 2.   Ps. 93. 5.   w Ne. 3. 36.

לַבָּמָה pref. לְ for לָהּ)(noun f. s. d. 10 (pl. c. בָּמָתֵי) בום

לַבָּמוֹת pref. id.

לַבָּמוֹת pref. לְ } id. pl., abs. st. . . בום

[לָבַן] Kal not used.—I. *to be white.*—II. from לְבֵנָה, *to make bricks.* Hiph.—I. *to make white, clean,* Da. 11. 35.—II. intrans. *to become white.* Hithp. *to cleanse oneself,* Da. 12. 10.

לָבָן masc. dec. 4 a.—I. adj. *white;* fem. לְבָנָה, pl. לְבָנוֹת.—II. pr. name of the father-in-law of Jacob.—III. pr. name of a place in the desert, De. 1. 1.

לָבֵן adj. masc. *white,* only constr. לְבֶן־ Ge. 49. 12 (§ 34. No. 2).

לְבָנָה fem.—I. *the moon,* from her whiteness. —II. pr. name masc. Ezr. 2. 45; called לְבָנָא Ne. 7. 48.

לְבֵנָה fem. dec. 10 (pl. לְבֵנִים) *brick or tile.*

לִבְנֶה masc. *the white poplar,* Ge. 30. 37; Ho. 4. 13.

לִבְנָה fem.—I. *whiteness, clearness;* only constr. לִבְנַת Ex. 24. 10.—II. pr. name of a city in the tribe of Judah.—III. pr. name of a station of the Israelites in the desert, Nu. 33. 20.

לְבֹנָה, לְבוֹנָה fem. dec. 10.—I. *frankincense.*— II. pr. name of a city near Shiloh, Ju. 21. 19.

לְבָנוֹן (*white*) pr. name, *Mount Lebanon,* on the confines of Syria and Palestine.

לִבְנִי (id.) pr. name of a son of Gershon; also patronym. for לִבְנִי.

מַלְבֵּן masc. *brickkiln.*

לָבֵן adj. masc. sing. d. 4 a, also pr. name masc. לבן

לַבֵּן pref. לְ f. לָהּ }
לָבֵן pref. לְ q. v. } noun masc. sing. irr. (§ 45) בנה

לְבֶן־ pref. id.)(id. constr. before Mak. (also pr. name in composition) . . . בנה

לְבַד־ adj. masc. [for לָבָד], constr. of לָבָד dec. 5 a (§ 34. No. 2); בef. . . לבן

לָבֵן noun m. s., suff. 3 p. pl. fem., from לֵב d. 8 b לבב

לָבָן pr. name masc., see לְבָנָה לבן

לְבֵנָא Chald., pref. לְ (for לְמִבְנָא), Peal inf. בנה

לְבָנָה pr. name masc. . . . לבן

לְבָנָה adj. fem., pl. לְבָנוֹת, from לָבָן masc. לבן

לְבֵנָה noun masc. sing. dec. 11 (§ 42. rem. 4) לבן

לַלְבָנָה noun fem. sing. dec. 10; בef. . לבן

לִבְנָה pr. name of a place . . . לבן

לִבְנֶה noun masc. sing. . . . לבן

לִבֵּנוּ noun m. sing., suff. 1 pers. pl. from לֵב d. 8 b לבב

לִבְנוֹ pref. לְ bef.)(noun masc. sing., suff. 3 pers. sing. masc. from בֵּן irr. (§ 45) בנה

לְבָנוֹן pr. name of a mountain; bef. לבן

לְבוֹנָה id. with parag. ה לבן

לִבְנוֹת pref. לְ)(n. f. pl., as if of בָּנָה, see ירת irr. (§ 45) בנה

לְבָנוֹת adj. pl., fem. of לְבָנָה, from לָבָן masc. לבן

לִבְנוֹת pref. לְ bef.)(Kal inf. constr. dec. 1 a בנה

לִבְנוֹת pref. id.)(noun fem. pl., constr. of בָּנוֹת, irr. of בַּת (§ 45) . . . בנה

לִבְנוֹתֶיהָ pref. id.)(id. pl., suff. 3 pers. sing. fem. בנה

לִבְנוֹתָיו pref. id.)(id. pl., suff. 3 pers. sing. masc. בנה

לְבָנַי pref. לְ)(noun masc. pl. (בָּנִים), suff. 1 pers. sing., irr. of בֵּן (§ 45); bef. בנה

לִבְנֵי pref. לְ bef.)(id. pl., constr. st. בנה

לִבְנִי pr. name masc. . . . לבן

לִבְנִי pref. לְ bef.)(noun masc. sing., suff. 1 pers. sing., from בֵּן irr. (§ 45) . בנה

לִבְנָיָהוּ pref. id.)(pr. name masc., see בְּנָיָהוּ בנה

לִבְנֵיהֶם pref. id.)(noun masc. pl. (בָּנִים), suff. 3 pers. pl. masc. irr. of בֵּן (§ 45) . בנה

לִבְנֵיהֶן pref. id.)(id. pl., suff. 3 pers. pl. fem. בנה

לְבָנָיו pref. לְ)(id. pl., suff. 3 pers. s. m.; bef. בנה

לְבָנֶיךָ pref. id.)(id. pl., suff. 2 pers. sing. m.; id. בנה

לִבְנֵיכֶם pref. לְ bef.)(id., suff. 2 pers. pl. masc. בנה

לַבֹּנִים pref. לְ for לָהּ)(Kal part. act. masc., pl. of בּוֹנֶה dec. 9 a בנה

לְבָנִים adj. m., pl. of לָבָן d. 4 a; bef. לבן

לְבָנִים pref. לְ)(noun masc. pl. irr. of בֵּן (§ 45) בנה

לְבֵנִים noun fem. with pl. masc. term. from לְבֵנָה dec. 11 (§ 42. rem. 4); bef. לבן

לְבִנְיָמִין pref. לְ)(pr. name of a tribe . בנה

לַבֵּנְיְמִינִי pref. לְ for לָהּ)(בֶּן־יְמִינִי K. Kh., gent. noun of the preceding . . . בנה

לְבִנְיָמִן pref. לְ)(pr. n. of a man and a tribe; bef. בנה

לִבְנֵינוּ pref. id.)(noun masc. pl., suff. 1 pers. pl. irr. of בֵּן (§ 45); id. . . . בנה

לְבִנְךָ pref. לְ or לְ bef.)(id. sing., suff. }
לִבְנֶךָ 2 pers. sing. masc.; id. } בנה

לִבְנֵךְ pref. לְ bef.)(id. s., suff. 2 pers. s. fem. בנה

לִבְנֹת defect. for לִבְנוֹת (q. v.) . . . לבן

לִבְנַת pr. name, see שִׁיחוֹר לִבְנַת under . . . שחר

ᵃ 2 Ch. 1. 3, 13.   ᵈ Eze. 44. 25.   ᵍ Ex. 35. 26.   ᵏ Ge. 30. 37.   ⁿ Ge. 30. 37.   ᵖ Ge. 31. 28.   ᵗ Ge. 31. 43.   ᶻ Ex. 5. 16.   ᶜ¹ 1 Ki. 17. 13.
ᵇ 2 Ch. 11. 15.   ᵉ Job 35. 8.   ᶠ Esr. 5. 3, 13.   ⁱ Ho. 4. 13.   ᵐ Ese. 16. 61.   ᵒ 1 Ki. 20. 7.   ᵘ Zec. 1. 8.   ᵃ¹ 1 Sa. 25. 8.   ᵈ¹ Le. 13. 38, 39.
ᶜ Ps. 9. 1.   ᶜ Ge. 49. 12.   ʰ Ese. 4. 1.   ᵐ Ese. 16. 61.   ᵖ Ge. 32. 1.   ᵠ 1 Ki. 17. 12.   ᵛ Is. 38. 19.

לְבִנַת־	noun fem. sing. constr. [of לְבֵנָה] .	לבן
לִבְנֹתֽ־	pref. לְ bef. (.:) χ Kal inf. constr.	בנה
לִבְנָתֶהֽ	noun fem.s. with suff. 3 p.s.fem.fr. לְבוֹנָה d.10	לבן
לִבְנֹתֵּי־	וְ pref. לְ bef. χ noun fem. pl. (בָּנוֹת), suff.	בנה
וְ לִבְנֹתֵי־	1 pers. pl. irr. of בַּת (§ 45)	
לִבְנֹתָיו	pref. id. χ id., suff. 3 pers. sing. masc.	בנה
וְ לִבְנֹתֶךָ	pref. id. χ id., suff. 2 pers. sing. masc.	בנה
לְבַעֲבוּר	preff. לְ, & בַּ bef. (.:) χ in this form only as a conj. comp. בַּעֲבוּר	עבר
לְבְעֹז	pref. לְ χ pr. name masc.	בעז
לְבַעַל	}	
לְבַעַל	} pref. לְ for לְהַ { noun masc. sing. dec.	בעל
לְבַעַל	} pref. לְ q. v. 6d (also pr. name) }	
לִבְעָלֶיהָ	pref. לְ bef. (.:) χ id. pl., suff. 3 pers. s. fem.	בעל
לִבְעָלֵיהֶן	pref. לְ χ id. pl., suff. 3 pers. pl. fem.	בעל
לִבְעָלָיו	pref. לְ bef. (.:) χ id. pl., suff. 3 pers. sing. masc.	בעל
לִבְעָלִים	pref. לְ for לְהַ χ id. pl., abs. st.	בעל
לְבַעֵר	pref. לְ χ Piel inf. constr.	בער
לְבַעֲרָםֽ	pref. id. χ id. [בַּעֵר § 14. rem. 1] with suff. 3 pers. pl. masc. dec. 7b	בער
לְבַעֲשָׁא	pref. id. χ pr. name masc.	בעש
לְבִצְעוֹֽ	pref. id. χ noun masc. sing., suff. 3 pers. sing. masc. from בֶּצַע dec. 6 (§ 35. rem. 5)	בצע
לְבַצֵּר־	pref. id. χ Piel inf. constr.	בצר
לְבִצְרוֹןֽ	pref. id. χ noun masc. sing.	בצר
לְבִקְעָהֽ	pref. id. χ noun fem. sing. dec. 12b	בקע
לְבִקְעָםֽ	pref. id. χ Kal inf. [בְּקַע], suff. 3 pers. pl. masc. (§ 16. rem. 10)	בקע
לַבָּקֶר	וּ noun com. sing. dec. 4a	בקר
לַבָּקָר	וְ pref. לְ for לְהַ χ noun m. s., d.6c (§ 35. r. 9)	בקר
לְבַקֵּר	וּ pref. לְ χ Piel inf. constr.; וּ bef. (:)	בקר
לְבַקָּרָהֽ	Chald., pref. id. χ Pael inf. (§ 47. rem. 5)	בקר
לִבְקָרוֹ־	pref. לְ bef. (.:) χ noun com. sing., suff. 3 pers. sing. masc. from בָּקָר dec. 4a	בקר
לַבְּקָרִים	pref. לְ for לְהַ } noun masc., pl. of בֹּקֶר	בקר
לִבְקָרִים	pref. לְ bef. } dec. 6c (§ 35. rem. 9)	בקר
לְבַקֵּשׁ	וּ pref. לְ χ Piel inf. c. dec. 7b; וּ bef. (:)	בקש
לְבַקְשׁוֹ־	pref. id. χ id., suff. 3 p. s. m. (ק for קְ §10. r.7)	בקש
לְבַקֶּשְׁךָֽ	pref. id. χ id., suff. 2 pers. sing. masc.	בקש
לְבַקְשֵׁנִיֽ	pref. id. χ id., suff. 1 pers. sing.	בקש
לִבְרִי	Chald., pref. id. χ noun masc. sing. dec. 2a	ברא
לְבָרָדֽ	pref. לְ for לְהַ χ noun masc. sing.	ברד

לְבָרוֹתֽ	pref. לְ χ Piel inf. constr., or subst. fem. sing.	ברה
לַבַּרְזֶלֽ	וְ pref. לְ for לְהַ χ noun masc. sing.	ברזל
לְבַרְזֵלֽ	pref. לְ χ pr. name masc.	ברזל
לִבְרֹחַ	pref. לְ bef. (.:) χ Kal inf. constr.	ברח
לִבְרֵי־	pref. לְ χ adj. pl. constr. masc. fr. בַּר dec. 8 (§ 37. rem. 7)	ברר
לַבְּרִיחִם	pref. לְ for לְהַ χ noun m., pl. of בְּרִיחַ d.1a	ברח
לִבְרִיעָה	pref. לְ bef. (.:) χ pr. name masc.	ברע
לַבְּרִית־	pref. לְ for לְהַ } noun fem. sing. dec. 1a	ברה
לִבְרִית	pref. לְ bef. (.:) }	ברה
לְבָרֵךְ	וּ pref. לְ χ Piel inf. constr.; וּ bef. (.:)	ברך
לִבְרָכָה	pref. לְ bef. (.:) χ noun fem. sing. dec. 11c	ברך
לְבָרְכוֹֽ	pref. לְ χ Kal inf. with suff. 3 pers. sing. m.	ברך
לְבָרְכוֹ־	וּ pref. id. χ Piel inf. (בָּרֵךְ), suff. 3 pers. sing. masc. dec. 7b; וּ bef. (:)	ברך
לְבָרְכָםֽ	pref. id. χ Kal inf. [בָּר § 18. rem. 3], suff. 3 pers. pl. masc. dec. 8 (§ 37. rem. 7)	ברך
לְבָרָק	pref. id. χ noun m. s. dec.4a; also pr. name m.	ברק
לְבָרֵרֽ	וּ pref. id. χ Piel inf. constr.; וּ bef. (:)	ברר

לָבַשׁ & וְ, לְבֹשׁ (Ps. 93. 1) fut. יִלְבַּשׁ.—I. to put on a garment, to be clothed.—II. metaph. to be clothed or covered, with flocks, worms, glory, justice, &c. Part. pass. לָבוּשׁ clothed. Pu. part. clothed. Hiph. to clothe, invest.

לְבַשׁ Chald. fut. יִלְבַּשׁ id. Da. 5. 7, 16. Aph. to clothe, Da. 5. 29.

לְבוּשׁ masc dec. 1a, garment, vestment. Chald. id. Da. 3. 21, 7. 9.

מַלְבּוּשׁ masc. dec. 1b, id.

תִּלְבֹּשֶׁת fem. id. Is. 59. 17.

לָבֵשֽׁ	defect. for לָבוּשׁ (q. v.)	לבש
לְבַשׁ	Kal imp. sing. masc.	לבש
לָבֵשׁ־	participle or subst. defect. for לָבוּשׁ (q. v.)	לבש
לָבְשָׁה	Kal pret. 3 pers. sing. fem.	לבש
וְ לָבְשׁוּֽ	וְ id. pret. 3 pers. pl.	לבש
לְבֻשׁוֹ	defect. for לְבוּשׁוֹ (q. v.)	לבש
לִבְשׁוּֽ	Kal imp. pl. masc.	לבש
לְבֻשֵׁיֽ	id. part. pass. pl. constr. from לָבוּשׁ d. 3a	לבש
לְבֹשׁ	וְ id. imp. sing. masc.	לבש
לְבֵשָׁםֽ	וּ id. pret. 3 pers. sing. masc. (לָבֵשׁ § 16. r. 1), suff. 3 pers. pl. masc.; וּ bef. (:)	לבש

a Ex. 24. 10.   f Nu. 38. 2.   l Is. 56. 11.   q Ps. 27. 4.   u 1 Ki. 18. 10.   z 1 Ch. 29. 2.   d 2 Sa. 8. 10;   m Eze. 10. 7;   r Je. 46. 4.
b Ge. 11. 8.   g Nu. 18. 11, 19.   m Is. 22. 10.   r Ezr. 7. 14.   u 1 Sa. 27. 1.   a 1 Ch. 22. 14, 16.   1 Ch. 18. 10   Is. 14. 19.   s Eze. 23. 6, 12.
c Le. 2, 2. 16.   h Nu. 18. 5. 10.   n Zec. 9. 12.   s 1 Sa. 11. 7.   b Da. 3. 25.   e Ec. 3. 18.   o Ps. 65. 14.   t 2 Sa. 14. 2.
d Ge. 31. 28.   i Est. 1. 20.   o Is. 40. 4.   t Job 7. 18.   c Da. 11. 35.   o Eze. 44. 19.   u Le. 16. 4.
e Ge. 31. 43.   k 2 Ch. 4. 20.   p 2 Ch. 32. 1.   v 1 Sa. 13 10.   d Pr. 31. 21.   ** 2 Ch. 35. 12.   w 1 Ki. 7. 29.
   s La. 4. 16.   z Ps. 74. 20.   z Ps. 78. 48.

לַבְשָׂמִים	pref. ל for [לְהַ] noun masc., pl. of בֶּשֶׂם dec. 6	בשם
לִבְשָׂמִים׳	pref. ל bef.	
לַבָּשָׂר	pref. ל)(noun masc. sing. dec. 4a	בשר
לְבַשֵּׂר	pref. id.)(Piel inf. constr.	בשר
לִבְשָׂרִי	pref. ל bef.)(noun masc. sing., suff. 1 pers. sing. from בָּשָׂר dec. 4a	בשר
לָבַשְׁתָּ	Kal pret. 2 pers. sing. m. [for לָבַשְׁתָּ § 8. r. 7]	לבש
לַבֹּשֶׁת	pref. ל for [לְהַ] noun fem. sing. dec. 13c;	בוש
לְבֹשֶׁת	pref. ל q. v. bef.	
לָבַשְׁתִּי	Kal pret. 1 pers. sing.	לבש
לְבָשְׁתֵּךְ	pref. ל)(noun fem. sing., suff. 2 pers. sing. masc. from בֹּשֶׁת dec. 13c	בוש
לְבַת	pref. id.)(noun fem. sing. irr. (§ 45); also pr. name in compos.; bef.	בנה
לְבִתּוֹ	pref. id.)(noun fem. sing., suff. 3 pers. sing. masc. from בַּת irr. (§ 45); id.	בנה
לִבְתוּאֵל	pref. ל bef.)(pr. name masc., see בְּתוּאֵל	
לִבְתוּלַת	pref. id.)(noun f. s., constr. of בְּתוּלָה d. 10	בתל
לַבָּתִּים	pref. ל f. [לְהַ] noun masc. pl. irr. of בַּיִת	בית
לַבָּתִּים	pref. ל q. v. (§ 45)	
לְבִתְּךָ	pref. id.)(noun fem. sing., suff. 2 pers. sing. masc. from בַּת irr. (§ 45)	בנה
לְבָתֵךְ	noun fem. s., suff. 2 p. s. f. from [לִבָּה] d. 10	לבב
לְבָתָם׳	id. pl., suff. 3 pers. pl. masc.	לבב
לֹג	masc. a Log, a measure for liquids, containing the twelfth part of a Hin, Le. 14. 10, 12, 15, 21, 24.	
לִנְאֹל	pref. ל bef.)(Kal inf. constr., Kh. לִנְאֹל	נאל
לִגְאֹל	q. v., K. לִנְאָל id. with Mak. (§ 8. r. 18)	
לְנָאוֹן	pref. ל)(noun masc. sing. dec. 3a	נאה
לִנְאוֹן	pref. ל bef.)(id. constr. st.	נאה
לְנֵאיוֹנִים	pref. ל)(Kh. לִנְאיוֹנִים noun masc. pl. [of גֵּאי יוֹנִים; K. [גֵּאיוֹן] pref. ל bef. adj. pl. c. masc. from גֵּאֶה dec. 9 (§ 38. No. 1 & 2) and יוֹנִים (q. v.)	נאה
לַגֵּאָיוֹת	pref. ל for [לְהַ])(noun com. pl. transp. [for גֵּאָיוֹת from גַּיְא irr. (§ 45)	ניא
לַגְּאָל	pref. id.)(Kal part. act. sing. masc. dec. 7b	נאל
לְגַאֲלָהּ	pref. ל)(id. inf. with suff. 2 p. s. f. (§ 16. r. 8)	נאל
לְנַב	Ch., pref. id.)(noun m. s. d. 5c; bef.	נבב
לְנַבָּא	Chald., pref. id.)(id. emph. st.	נבב
לְנַבֵּה	pref. id.)(Kal inf. constr. (§ 8. rem. 11)	נבה
לִגְבוּל	pref. ל bef.)(noun masc. sing. dec. 1a	נבל

לִגְבוּלָם	pref. id.)(id., suff. 3 pers. pl. masc.	נבל
לִגְבוּלֹתֶיהָ	pref.id.)(n.f.s. suff. 3 p.s.f. from [נְבוּלָה] d. 10	נבל
לִגְבוּרָה	pref. id.)(noun fem. sing. dec. 10	נבר
לִגְבוּרִי	pref. ל)(noun m. pl. constr. from נִבּוֹר d. 1b	נבר
לַגִּבּוֹרִים	pref. ל for [לְהַ] id. pl., abs. state	נבר
לִגְבִי	pref. ל)(noun m. pl. constr. from נָב d. 8d	נבר
לַגִּבִּים	pref. id.)(Kh. לִגְבִים pl. of נוּב R. נוב K. לַגְּבִים q.v.	נבר
לִגְבִירָה	pref. ל for [לְהַ])(noun fem. sing.	נבר
לִגְבֻלֹתֶיהָ	defect. for לִגְבוּלֹתֶיהָ (q. v.)	נבל
לַגֶּבַע	pref. ל)(pr. name of a place	נבע
לְגִבְעָה	pref. ל for [לְהַ])(pr. name of a place	נבע
לַגִּבְעֹנִים	pref. id.)(gent. noun, pl. of נִבְעֹנִי fr. נִבְעוֹן	נבע
לַגְּבָעוֹת	pref. id.)(noun f. pl. abs. fr. נִבְעָה d. 12b	נבע
לַגֶּבֶר	pref. id.	
לְגֶבֶר	pref. ל)(noun masc. sing. dec. 6	נבר
לְגֻבְרַיָּא	Chald., pref. id.)(noun masc. pl. emph. [as if from נֶּבֶר] dec. 2b	נבר
לַגְּבָרִים	pref. ל f. [לְהַ])(noun masc., pl. of נֶּבֶר	
לִגְבָרִים	pref. ל bef.)(dec. 6a	נבר
לְגֻבְרִין	Ch., pref. ל)(noun m. pl. [as if from נֶּבֶר] dec. 2b; bef.	נבר
לְנַגּוֹ	pref. ל)(noun masc. sing., suff. 3 pers. sing. masc. from נַב dec. 8d	נג
לַגַּגּוֹת	pref. ל for [לְהַ])(id. pl. fem.	נג
לְנַגְּךָ	pref. ל)(id. s., suff ? pers. s. m. [for נַגְּךָ]	נג
לַגֵּד	pref. ל for [לְהַ])(noun masc. sing.	נדד
לְגָד	pref. ל)(pr. name of a tribe; bef.	נדד
לִגְדוּד	pref. ל bef.)(noun masc. sing. dec. 1a	נדד
לִגְדוּדָיו	pref. id.)(id. pl., suff. 3 pers. sing. masc.	נדד
לַגְּדֻפִים	pref. ל)(noun masc., pl. of נִדּוּף dec. 1b	נדף
לְגָדִי	pref. ל for [לְהַ])(pr. name of a tribe	נדד
לְגַדֵּל	pref. ל)(Piel inf. constr. dec. 7b	נדל
לְגַדְּלָם	pref. id.)(id., suff. 3 pers. pl. m.; bef.	נדל
לִגְדֻלָּתוֹ	pref. ל bef.)(noun fem. sing., suff. 3 pers. sing. fem. from נְדֻלָּה dec. 10	נדל
לְגִדַּלְתִּי	pref. ל)(pr. name masc.	נדל
לְגִדְעוֹן	pref. id.)(pr. name masc.; bef.	נדע
לַגֹּדְרִים	pref. ל for [לְהַ])(Kal part. act. masc., pl. of נֹדֵר dec. 7b	נדר
לְגַנּוּ	pref. ל)(noun masc. sing. dec. 1a	נוה
לְגֹא	Ch., pref. id.)(n. m. s., constr. of נַו irr. (§ 68)	נוא
לְנוֹב	Chald. in full for לֻנּב (q. v.)	נבב

---

1 Ch. 9. 30.   Job 29. 14.   Eze. 16. 30.   Eze. 36. 4, 6.   Je. 31. 17.   Je. 13. 18.   1 Ch. 23. 3.   Is. 65. 11.   Ps. 145. 3.
2 Ch. 32. 27.   1 Sa. 20. 30.   Is. 44. 18.   Ru. 4. 3.   Is. 28. 6.   Nu. 34. 2, 12.   Da. 3. 20.   Job 25. 3.   2 Ki. 12. 13.
Ps. 102. 6.   Ese. 44. 25.   Ru. 4. 4, 6.   Ru. 4. 6.   Ch. 26. 12.   La. 3. 27.   Eze. 40. 13.   Is. 43. 28.   Da. 3. 6, 11.
Ps. 104. 1.   Le. 21. 3.   Da. 3. 13.   Is. 60. 15.   Da. 6. 21.   Da.3.27; Ezr.6.8.   1 Ch. 29. 12.   Is. 22. 1.   15, 21, 24.
Is. 30. 3, 5.   La. 1. 15.   Is. 60. 15.   Da.6.17,20,21.   Job 13. 12.   Jos.7.14,17,18.   De. 22. 6.   Da. 1. 5.   Da. 6. 6.
1 Sa. 20. 30.   De. 22. 17.   Ps. 123. 4.   Zep. 3. 11.   2 Ki. 25. 12.

לְגֹוג	pref. לְ ✗ pr. name masc. . . . נוג
לַגֹּוִי	pref. לְ for [לְהַ ✗ noun masc. sing. dec. 1a
לִגְוִי	pref. לְ q. v. (§ 3. rem. 1) .
לַגְוִיָהֿ	pref. לְ for [לְהַ ✗ noun fem. sing. dec. 10
לִגְוִיָהֶם	pref. לְ ✗ noun masc. pl., suff. 3 pers. pl. masc. from גֹּוי dec. 1a (§ 3. rem. 1) .
לַגֹּויִם / לִגֹּויִם	pref. לְ f. [לְהַ } id. pl., abs. st. / pref. לְ q. v. }
לִגְוֻנִי	pref. id. ✗ pr. name masc. . . . גוי
לָגֹוּעַ	pref. לְ bef. (..) ✗ Kal inf. constr. . נוע
לָגֹור	pref. לְ (see lett. לְ) ✗ Kal inf. constr. . גור
לָגַז	pref. id. } Kal inf. constr. (§ 18. rem. 13)
לִגְזֹז	pref. לְ bef. (..) } גזז
לְגֹזְזַי	pref. id. ✗ id. part. act. pl., suff. 1 pers. sing. from גָּזַז dec. 7b . . . גזז
לִגְזֹל	ו pref. לְ bef. (..) ✗ Kal inf. constr. גזל
לְגֹזֵר	pref. לְ ✗ Kal part. act. sing. masc. גזר
לִגְזָרִים	pref. לְ bef. (..) ✗ noun m. pl. of [גֶּזֶר] d. 6b גזר
לַנְּחָלִים	pref. לְ ✗ noun fem. pl. [as if from נַחֲלָה] see נַחֲלַת (§ 44. rem. 5, & § 42. No. 3 note) נחל
לַגֹּוי	pref. לְ for [לְהַ ✗ noun com. sing. irr. (§ 45) ניא
לַגֵּיאֹות	ו pref. id. ✗ id. pl., Kh. גֵּיאֹות, K. by transp. גֵּאֹות . ניא
לַגִּיד	Kh. לַגִּיד contr. for K. [לְהַגִּיד (q. v. & § 11. r.3) ננד
לְנִיחֹון	pref. לְ ✗ pr. name of a river . . ניה
לְנִיחֳזִי	pref. id. ✗ pr. name masc. . . ניא
לַגָּל	pref. לְ for [לְהַ ✗ for גַּל noun masc. s. d. 8d נלל
לַגַּלְגַּל	pref. id. ✗ noun masc. sing. dec. 8e . נלל
לְגִלְגָּל	pref. id. ✗ pr. name of a place . נלל
לַגֻּלְגֹּלֶת	pref. לְ for [לְהַ ✗ noun fem. sing. dec. 13c נלל
לַגֻּלְגְּלֹתָם	pref. id. ✗ id. pl., suff. 3 pers. pl. masc. נלל
לְגֻלָּה	pref. לְ for [לְהַ ✗ noun fem. sing. . נלה
לְגֻלֻּלֵיהֶם	pref. ✗ n. m. pl., suff. 3 p. pl. m. fr.] d. 1b נלל
לִגְלֹות	pref. id. ✗ noun fem. s. d. 1b (§ 32. No. 3) נלה
לִגְלֹות	pref. id. ✗ Piel inf. constr. . נלה
לְגָלֻתֵינוּ / לְגָלֻתֵּנוּ	pref. id. ✗ noun fem. sing., suff. 1 pers. pl. fr. גָּלֻת d. 1b (§ 32. No. 3; & § 4. r. 1) } נלה
לְגַלָּיו	pref. id. ✗ n. m. pl., suff. 3 p. s. m. fr. גַּל d. 8d נלל
לַגַּלִּים	pref. id. ✗ id. pl., abs. st. . נלל
לַגִּלְעָד	pref. לְ f. [לְהַ pr. name of a man and a place, / pref. לְ q. v. } see גִּלְעָד. }
לְגָמוּל	pref. id. ✗ pr. name masc. . . . נמל

לִנְמַלֵיהֶם	ו pref. לְ bef. (..) ✗ noun masc. pl., suff. 3 pers. pl. masc. from נָמָל dec. 8a (§ 37. No. 2) נמל
לִנְמַלֶיךָֿ	pref. id. ✗ id., suff. 2 pers. sing. masc. . נמל
לִנְמַלִּים	pref. לְ for [לְהַ ✗ id. pl., abs. st. . נמל
לַנֵּן	pref. לְ ✗ noun com. sing. dec. 8d . . ננן
לַנֶּגֶב	pref. לְ for [לְהַ ✗ noun masc. sing. dec. 1b ננב
לְנַגְּנֹו	pref. לְ ✗ n. com. s., suff. 3 p. s. m. fr. נֵן d.8d ננן
לְנַגְּנִי	pref. id. ✗ id. with suff. 1 pers. sing. ננן
לִנְגַּתֹון	pref. id. ✗ pr. name masc. . . . ננן
לָנַעַת	pref. לְ (see lett. לְ) ✗ Kal inf. constr. . ננע
לַגֶּפֶן / לַגֶּפֶן / לִגְפֶן	pref. לְ f. [לְהַ noun com. sing. dec. 6a (§ 35. rem. 2) / pref. לְ q. v. } גפן
לְגָפְרִית	pref. id. ✗ noun fem. sing. from גָּפֶר masc. נפר
לְגֵר / וְ	pref. לְ for [לְהַ ✗ noun masc. sing. dec. 1a נור
לְנַרְגְּרֹתֶיךָ	pref. לְ ✗ n. f. pl., suff. 2 p.s.m. fr. [גַּרְגֶּרֶת] d. 13 נרר
לִנְרֹעַ	pref. לְ bef. (..) ✗ Kal inf. constr. נרע
לְגֹרָלְךָ	pref. לְ ✗ n. m. s., suff. 2 p. s. m. fr. גֹּורָל d. 2b נרל
לִנְרֹר	pref. לְ bef. (..) ✗ pr. name of a place . נרר
לְגָרֵשׁ	pref. לְ ✗ Piel inf. constr. . . נרש
לְגֵרְשֹׁון	pref. id. ✗ pr. name masc. . . נרש
לְגָרְשֵׁנוּ	pref. id.)✗ Piel inf. (גָּרֵשׁ), suff. 1 p. pl. d. 7b נרש
לַגֵּרְשֻׁנִּי	pref. לְ for [לְהַ ✗ patronym. of גֵּרְשֹׁון . נרש
לְגֶשֶׁם	ו pref. לְ ✗ pr. name masc.; ו bef. (..) נשם
לָגֶשֶׁת	ו pref. לְ (see lett. לְ) ✗ Kal inf. constr. (suff. גִּשְׁתֹּו) dec. 13a . . ננש
לְגַת	pref. לְ ✗ pr. name of a place . . נת
וָלָד & לָד	see under lett. ו.
לֹד	pr. name of a town in the tribe of Benjamin.
לְדָא	Chald., pref. לְ ✗ pron. demon. sing. fem. דא
לְדָאֲבָה	pref. id. ✗ noun fem. sing. . . ראב
לִדְבַֿ	Chald., pref. id. ✗ noun m. sing., comp. Heb. דָּב דבב
לַדְּבֹורָה	ו pref. לְ for [לְהַ ✗ noun fem. s. (pl. דְּבֹורִים) d. 10 דבר
לַדְּבִיר	ו pref. id. ✗ noun masc. sing. דבר
לַדֶּבֶק	pref. id. ✗ noun masc. sing. dec. 6a דבק
לִדְבְקָה	ו pref. לְ ✗ Kal inf. constr. (§ 8 r.10); ו bef. (..) דבק
לַדָּבָר	pref. לְ for [לְהַ ✗ noun masc. sing. dec. 4a דבר
לְדָבָר / לְדָבָר	pref. לְ f. [לְהַ noun masc. sing. dec. 6 (§ 35. rem. 2); ו bef. (..) } דבר
לִדְבַר	pref. לְ ✗ noun masc. sing. dec. 4a . דבר
לְדַבֵּר / לְדַבֵּר	pref. id. ✗ Piel inf. constr. (§ 10. rem. 4); ו bef. (..) } דבר

לִדְבַר	pref. לְ bef. (:) X n. m. s., constr. of דְּבַר d. 4a	דבר
לִדְבִּר	pref. id. X for 'דְּבִיר, noun masc. sing., also pr. name of a place	דבר
לִדְבִּרָה	pref. id. X pr. name (דְּבִיר with loc. ה)	דבר
וְלִדְבָרוֹ	'וְ pref. id. X n.m.s., suff. 3 p.s.m.fr. דְּבָר d. 4a	דבר
לְדִבְרֵי	pref. X id. pl. constr. st.	דבר
לִדְבָרַי	pref. X bef. (:) X id. pl., suff. 1 pers. sing.	דבר
לִדִבְרֵיהֶם	pref. X id. pl., suff. 3 pers. pl. masc.	דבר
לִדְבָרֶיךָ	pref. לְ bef. (:) X id. pl. (Kh. רֶיךָ), K. דֶּרֶךְ sing., suff. 2 pers. sing. masc.	דבר
לְדִבְרֵיכֶם	pref. X id. pl., suff. 2 pers. pl. masc.	דבר
לִדְבָרִים	pref. X for לָה X id. pl., abs. st.	דבר
לִדְבָרֶךָ	pref. X bef. (:) X id. sing., suff. 2 pers. s. m.	דבר
לַדְּגֵ	pref. X for לָה X noun masc. sing. dec. 2a	דגה
לְדָגוֹן	pref. לְ X pr. name of an idol	דגה
לְדִגְלֵיהֶם	pref. id. X n.m.pl., suff. 3 p. pl. m. fr. דֶּגֶל d. 6a	דגל
לֶדֶת	Kal inf. constr. (§ 20. rem. 3)	ילד
לַדַּגַּיִם	pref. לְ X Kh. noun masc. pl. [from דַּיָּן], K. 'דָיָנִים [from דִּין] dec. 1b	דון
לְדָוִד	pref. id. X pr. name masc.	דוד
לְדוֹדִי	pref. id. X noun m. s., suff. 1 p. s. fr. דּוֹד d. 1a	דוד
לְדֹאֵג	pref. id. X pr. name masc., K. דּוֹאֵג	דאג
לְדָוִיד	pref. id. X pr. name masc., see דָּוִד	דוד
לְדוֹר	pref. לְ (see לֹ)	דור
לְדוֹר	pref. לְ for לָה X noun masc. sing. dec. 1a	דור
לְדוֹר	pref. לְ (q. v.)	דור
לָדוּשׁ	pref. לְ (see lett. לֹ) X Kal inf. constr.	דושׁ
לִדְחוֹת	pref. לְ bef. (:) X Kal inf. constr.	דחה
לָדִין	pref. לְ (see lett. לֹ) X Kal inf. constr. R. see דִּין	דון
לְדַיָּן	pref. לְ X noun masc. sing. dec. 2b, R. דִּין see	דון
לְדִין	pref. id. X noun masc. sing. dec. 1a, R. דִּין see	דון
לַדַּךְ	pref. לְ for לָה X for דַּךְ, adj. masc. sing. d. 8d	דכך
לְדַכֵּא	pref. לְ X Piel inf. constr.	דכא
לַדָּל / לְדַל	pref. לְ for לָה X adj. masc. sing. dec. 8d	דלל
לִדְלָיָהוּ	pref. לְ bef. (:) X pr. name masc.	דלה
לְדֹלְקִים	pref. לְ X Kal part. act. m., pl. of דָּלַק d. 7b	דלק
לְדַלָּת	pref. לְ X noun fem. sing., comp. דֶּלֶת	דלה
לְדַלְתוֹת	pref. לְ for לָה X id. pl. abs. (§ 44. rem. 5), ת treated as if radical	דלה
לְדַלְתוֹת	pref. לְ X id. pl., constr. st. (§ 44. rem. 1)	דלה
לְדָלְתֵי	pref. לְ X noun fem., constr. of דְּלָתַיִם from [דֶּלֶת] dec. 11a (§ 44. rem. 1)	דלה
לָדָם	pref. לְ for לָה X {noun masc. sing. dec. 2a	אדם
לְדָם	pref. לְ q. v.	אדם
לְדַם	pref. id. X id. constr. st.	אדם
לְדָמִים	pref. id. X id. pl., abs. st.	אדם
לְדָמָם	pref. id. X id. sing., suff. 3 pers. pl. masc	אדם
לְדָמָה	pref. לְ bef. (:) X noun fem. sing.	דמם
לְדָמֶן	pref. לְ X noun masc. sing.	דמן
לְדַמֶּשֶׂק / לְדַמֶּשֶׂק	} pref. id. X pr. name of a place	דמשׂק
לְדָן	'לְ pref. id. X pr. name of a tribe; וְ bef. (:)	דון
לְדָנִיֵּאל	'לְ pref. id. X pr. name masc.; וְ id.	דון
לָדַעַת	pref. id. X Kal inf. constr. (§ 20. rem. 3)	ידע
לְדַעַת	pref. לְ (see lett. לֹ) X for דַּעַת n.fem.s.d.13a	ידע
וְלָדַעַת	וְ pref. id. X Kal inf. constr. d. 13a (§ 20. r. 3)	ידע
לְדַעְתָּהּ	pref. לְ X id., suff. 3 pers. sing. fem.	ידע
לְדַעְתּוֹ	pref. לְ X id., suff. 3 pers. sing. masc.	ידע
לְדַעְתִּי	pref. id. X n. fem. s., suff. 1 p. s. fr. דַּעַת d. 13a	ידע
לְדֹר	defect. for לְדוֹר (q. v.)	דור
לִדְרְאוֹן	pref. לְ X noun masc. sing. constr. [of דְּרָאוֹן § 32. Nos. 1 & 2]	דרא
לַדָּרוֹם	pref. לְ for לָה X noun masc. sing. [for דָּרוֹם	דרר
לִדְרֹשׁ	in full for לִדְרֹשׁ (q. v.)	דרשׁ
לְדַרְיָוֶשׁ	pref. לְ X pr. name masc., see דָּרְיָוֶשׁ	דרשׁ
לִדְרְיֹושׁ	pref. id. X Piel inf. [for דַּרֹשׁ § 8. rem. 10]	דרשׁ
לְדַרְכְּ / לְדַרְכֶּךָ / לְדַרְכֶּךָ	} pref. לְ f. לָה X noun com. sing. dec. 6a (§ 35. rem. 2) / pref. לְ q. v.	דרך
לְדַרְכָּהּ	pref. id. X id., suff. 3 pers. sing. fem.	דרך
לְדַרְכּוֹ	pref. id. X id., suff. 3 pers. sing. masc.	דרך
לְדַרְכְּךָ	pref. id. X id., suff. 2 pers. sing. masc.	דרך
לְדַרְכְּכֶם	pref. id. X id., suff. 2 pers. pl. masc.	דרך
לְדַרְכָּם	pref. id. X id., suff. 3 pers. pl. masc	דרך
לִדְרֹשׁ / לִדְרָשׁ	} pref. לְ bef. (:) X Kal inf. constr. (§ 8. rem. 18)	דרשׁ
לְדָרְשֵׁנִי	pref. לְ X id. with suff. 1 pers. sing.	דרשׁ
לְדֹרֹת	pref. לְ X noun masc., pl. of דּוֹר dec. 1a	דור
לְדֹרֹתָיו	pref. id. X id., suff. 3 pers. sing. masc.	דור
לְדֹרֹתֵיכֶם	pref. id. X id., suff. 2 pers. pl. masc.	דור
לְדֹרֹתָם	pref. id. X id., suff. 3 pers. pl. m. (§ 4. r. 2)	דור

a 1 Ki. 6. 16. f Ps. 119. 147. k Je. 13. 21. p Ps. 140. 5. u Job 5. 16. z Nu. 35. 33. e Ex. 2. 4. j Da. 12. 2. o 1 Ki. 19. 15.
b Ps. 106. 24. g Job 32. 11. l Je. 16. 16. q Ps. 7. 14. x 1 Sa. 14. 16. a Le. 16. 15. f Is. 32. 4. k Eze. 41. 11. p Eze. 14. 7.
c Ps. 130. 5. h 1 Ki. 10. 7. m Is. 34. 10. r De. 17. 3. y Esc. 41. 24. b Mi. 7. 9. g Ge. 38. 26. l Ezr. 10. 16. q Je. 87. 7.
d Job 16. 3. i Ps. 119. 81, 114. n Ps. 22. 31. s Ps. 9. 10. z Eze. 41. 24. c Pr. 1. 18. h Is. 7. 15. m Jos. 9. 11. r Ge. 9. 13.
e Pr. 4. 20. j Jon. 2. 11. o Ho. 10. 11. t La. 3. 34. d 1 Ki. 7. 50. i Ps. 107. 29. n Pr. 12. 17. 1 Sa. 1. 18. s Le. 25. 30.
f 2 Cb. 9. 6. m Nu. 2. 17, 31, 34.

לָדֹש   defect. for לָדוֹשׁ (q. v.) . . . דוש

לְדַשְּׁנוֹ   pref. לְ ✗ Piel inf. [דִּשֵּׁן], suff. 3 pers. sing. masc. dec. 7 b . . . דשן

לָדֶת   Kal inf. const. dec. 13 a . . . ילד

לְדִתָּהּ   id. with suff. 3 pers. sing. fem. . . ילד

לְדָתָן   pref. לְ ✗ pr. name masc. . . . דת

לְדִתְּנָה   Kal inf. (לֶדֶת), suff. 3 pers. pl. fem. dec. 13 a (§ 3. rem. 5) . . . ילד

לָהּ   וְ Heb. & Ch., pref. prep. לְ with suff. 3 pers. sing. fem. (§ 5, parad.) . . . ל

לֵהּ   וְ Ch., pref. prep. לְ with suff. 3 pers. s. m. . . ל

לֵהּ   Kh. לָה q. v.; K. לִי (q. v.) . . ל

לְהַאֲבִיד   ו pref. ✗ Hiph. inf. constr. d. 1 h; ו bef. (ַ) . . אבד

לְהַאֲבִידוֹ   pref. id. ✗ id., suff. 3 pers. sing. masc. . אבד

לְהַאֲבִידֵנוּ   pref. id. ✗ id., suff. 1 pers. pl. . . אבד

לְהָאִיר   pref. id. ✗ Hiph. inf. constr. . . אור

לְהַאֲלֹתוֹ   pref. id. ✗ Hiph. inf. [הַאֲלוֹת], suff. 3 pers. sing. masc. dec. 1 b . . אלה

לַהַב   Root not used; Arab. *to burn, flame.*

לַהַב   masc. dec. 6 d.—I. *flame.*—II. *glitter of a sword or spear,* i. e. *the blade* or *iron-head.*

לֶהָבָה   fem. dec. 11 a (pl לְהָבוֹת, constr. לַהֲבוֹת § 42. No. 3 note), and לַהֶבֶת.—I. *flame.* —II. *iron-head of a spear,* 1 Sa. 17. 7.

לַבָּה   fem. for לֶהָבָה *flame,* Ex. 3. 2.

לְהָבִים   pr. name of a people, Ge. 10. 13; prob. *Libyans,* comp. לוּבִים.

שַׁלְהֶבֶת   fem. *flame,* Job 15. 30; Ca. 8. 6, שַׁלְהֶבֶתְיָה *flame of the Lord,* i. e. intense flame.

לַהַב   וְ noun masc. sing. dec. 6 d . . להב

לְהַבְאִישֵׁנִי   pref. לְ ✗ Hiph. inf. [הַבְאִישׁ], suff. 1 pers. sing. dec. 1 b . . . באש

לְהַבְדִּיל   ו pref. id. ✗ Hiph. inf. constr.; ו bef. (ַ) בדל

לֶהָבָה   וְ noun fem. sing. d. 11 a (§ 42. No. 3 note) . להב

לַהֲבוֹת   id. pl., constr. st. . . . להב

לְהָבוֹת   id. pl., abs. st. . . . להב

לְהַבְזוֹת   pref. לְ ✗ Hiph. inf. constr. . . בזה

לְהָבִיא   ו pref. id. ✗ Hiph. inf. constr. d. 3 a; ו bef. (ַ) בוא

לַהֲבִיאֲךָ   ו pref. לְ bef. (ַ) ✗ id., suff. 2 pers. sing. m. בוא

לַהֲבִיאָם   pref. id. ✗ id., suff. 3 pers. pl. masc. . בוא

לְהַבִּיט   pref. לְ ✗ Hiph. inf. constr. dec. 1 b . נבט

לַהֲבִיטָם   pref. id. ✗ id., suff. 3 pers. pl. masc. . נבט

לֵהָב   pr. name of a people . . . להב

לְהָבִים   noun masc., pl. of לַהַב dec. 6 d . . להב

לְהָבִין   pref. לְ ✗ Hiph. inf. constr. dec. 3 a . בין

לַהֲבִינֶךָ   pref. לְ bef. (ַ) id., suff. 2 pers. sing. masc. בין

לַהֲבֵל   pref. לְ for לְהֶ ✗ noun m. s. d. 6 a (§ 35. r. 4) הבל

לְהִבָּנוֹת   pref. לְ ✗ Niph. inf. constr. . . בנה

לְהַבְקִיעַ   pref. id. ✗ Hiph. inf. constr. . . בקע

לְהִבָּקֵעַ   pref. id. ✗ Niph. inf. constr. [for הִבָּקַע § 15. rem. 1] . . . בקע

לְהָבַר   pref. id. ✗ Hiph. inf. constr. (§ 18. rem. 10) ברר

לְהַבְרוֹת   pref. id. ✗ Hiph. inf. constr. . . ברה

לְהַבְרִיאֲכֶם   pref. id. ✗ Hiph. inf. [הַבְרִיא], suff. 2 pers. pl. masc. dec. 1 b . . . ברא

לַהֲבָת   וְ noun fem. sing., pl. לֶהָבוֹת from לַהֲבָה (§ 42. No. 3 note, comp. rem. 5) . . להב

לַהַג   וְ masc. *study,* Ec. 12. 12.

לְהַגְדּוּד   preff. לְ & הַ ✗ noun masc. sing. dec. 1 a . נדד

לְהַגְדִּיל   ו pref. לְ ✗ Hiph. inf. constr.; ו bef. (ַ) נדל

לְהַגִּיד   ו pref. id. ✗ Hiph. inf. constr.; ו id. . נגד

לְהִגָּלוֹת   pref. id. ✗ Niph. inf. constr. . . . גלה

לְהַגְלוֹת   ו pref. id. ✗ Hiph. inf. constr. d. 1 b; ו bef. (ַ) גלה

לְהַגְלוֹתֵךְ   pref. id. ✗ id. with suff. 2 pers. sing. fem. . גלה

לַהַגֵּרִים   ו preff. לְ & הַ ✗ n. m., pl. of גֵּר d. 1 a; ו bef. (ַ) גור

לֶהַד   [for לָהַד] pr. name masc. 1 Ch. 4. 2.

לְהַדְבְּרוֹהִי   Chald., pref. לְ ✗ noun masc. pl., suff. 3 pers. sing. masc. [from הַדָּבָר] . . . דבר

לַהֲדַדְעֶזֶר   pref. לְ bef. (ַ) ✗ pr. name masc. . . הדד

לְהֹדוֹת   ו defect. for לְהוֹדוֹת (q. v.) . . . ידה

לְהַדִּיחַ   pref. לְ ✗ Hiph. inf. constr. dec. 1 b . נדח

לְהַדִּיחֲךָ   pref. id. ✗ id., suff. 2 pers. sing. masc. . נדח

לְהֹדִיעַ   defect. for לְהוֹדִיעַ (q. v.) . . . ידע

לַהֲדֹם   ו pref. לְ bef. (ַ) ✗ noun masc. sing. . הדם

לַהֲדֹף   pref. id. ✗ Kal inf. constr. . . הדף

לְהָדְפָהּ   pref. לְ ✗ id., suff. 3 pers. sing. fem. . הדף

לְהַדֵּק   pref. id. ✗ Hiph inf. constr. (§ 18. rem. 10) דקק

לַהֲדַרְעֶזֶר   pref. לְ bef. (ַ) ✗ pr. n. m., see הֲדַדְעֶזֶר under הדד

לְהַדְרַת   pref. לְ ✗ n. f. s. constr. [of הֲדָרָה or הַדְרָה] הדר

[לָהָה]   fut. apoc. וַתֵּלַהּ (§ 24. rem. 3) *to be weary, faint,* Ge. 47. 13. Hithpalp. (§ 6. No. 3) part. מִתְלַהְלֵהַּ *insane, mad person,* Pr. 26. 18.

a 2 Ki. 13. 7.	f Ju. 16. 18.	l Ps. 105. 32.	r La. 4. 16.	x Eze. 30. 16.	d 1 Sa. 17. 7.
b Ex. 27. 3.	g De. 28. 63.	m Est. 1. 17.	s Is. 13. 8.	y Je. 4. 11.	e 1 Ch. 22. 5.
c Ge. 38. 27.	h Jos. 7. 7.	n De. 4. 38.	t Da. 10. 14.	z 2 Sa. 3. 35.	f Am. 8. 5.
Job 39. 2.	i Ge. 34. 30.	o Ex. 23. 20.	u Ps. 144. 4.	a 1 Sa. 2. 29.	g Is. 56. 1.
Da. 7. 14.	k Ps. 29. 7.	p Jon. 2. 5.	w 2 Ki. 3. 26.	b Eze. 21. 3.	h Est. 4. 8.

e Je. 43. 3.   l Ps. 62. 5.   r De. 19. 9.
i La. 4. 22.   m De. 13. 6, 11.   q 2 Ki. 4. 27.
k Eze. 47. 22.   n 1 Ch. 17. 19.   s 2 Ch. 34. 7.
o 1 Ch. 28. 2.   t 2 Ch. 20. 21.
p Da. 3. 24.

Headword	Description	Root
לֶהֱוֵא	Ch., pref. לְ bef. (יִ))(contr. [for לְיֶהֱוֵא] preform. ' omitted, Peal fut. 3 pers. sing. m.	הוה
לְהוֹבָרָא	Chald., pref. לְ)(Aph. inf. constr. (§ 53.	אבד
לְהוֹבָדַהּ	rem. 1, & § 47. rem. 5); ו bef. (:)	
לְהוֹדְוָה	pref. id.)(K. הוֹדְיָה (q. v.)	הוד
לְהוֹדוֹת	pref. id.)(Hiph. inf. constr.; ו bef. (:)	ידה
לְהוֹדִיעַ	pref. id.)(Hiph. inf. constr. dec. 1 b	ידע
לְהוֹדִיעֲךָ	pref. id.)(id., suff. 2 pers. sing. masc.	ידע
לְהוֹדִיעָם	pref. id.)(id., suff. 3 pers. pl. masc.	ידע
לְהוֹדִיעֵנִי	pref. id.)(id., suff. 1 pers. sing.	ידע
לְהוֹדָעָה	Chald., pref. id.)(Aph. inf. constr. (§47. r.5)	ידע
לְהוֹדָעוּתַנִי	Ch., pref. id.)(id., suff. 2 p.s. m. [fr. הוֹדָעוּת]	ידע
לְהוֹדָעוּתַנִי / לְהוֹדָעֻתַנִי	Chald., pref. id.)(id., suff. 1 pers. sing.	ידע
לֶהֱוֵה	Chald., pref. לְ bef. (יִ))(Peal fut. 3 pers. sing. masc., comp. לֶהֱוֵא	הוה
לֶהֶוְיָן	Chald., pref. id.)(id. fut. 3 pers. pl. fem.	הוה
לְהוֹכִיחַ	pref. לְ)(Hiph. inf. constr.	יכח
לַהוֹלְלִים	pref. לְ for לְהַ)(Kal part. act., pl. of הוֹלֵל d. 7 b	הלל
לָהֶם	Chald., pref. prep. לְ with suff. 3 pers. pl. m.	ל
לַהוֹן	pref. לְ for לְהַ)(noun masc. sing. dec. 1a	הון
לְהוֹן	Chald., pref. לְ bef. (יִ))(Peal fut. 3 pers. pl. masc. comp. לֶהֱוֵא	הוה
לְהֹן	Chald., pref. prep. לְ with suff. 3 pers. pl. m.	ל
לְהוֹתָם	pref. לְ)(Hiph. inf. [הוֹנוֹת], suff. 3 pers. pl. masc. (§ 25. No. 2 e)	ינה
לְהוֹסִיף	pref. id.)(Hiph. inf. constr.	יסף
לְהוֹעִיל	pref. id.)(Hiph. inf. constr.	יעל
לְהוֹצִיאֵהוּ	pref. id.)(the foll. with suff. 3 pers. s. m.	יצא
לְהוֹצִיא	pref. id.)(Hiph. inf. constr. dec. 1 b	יצא
לְהוֹצִיאָם	pref. id.)(id., suff. 3 pers. pl. masc.	יצא
לְהוֹצִיאֵנוּ	pref. id.)(id., suff. 1 pers. pl.	יצא
לַהוֹרְגִים	pref. id.)(Kal part. act. m., pl. of הֹרֵג d. 7 b	הרג
לְהוֹרִיד	pref. id.)(Hiph. inf. constr.	ירד
לְהוֹרִישׁ	pref. id.)(Hiph. inf. constr. dec. 1 b	ירש
לְהוֹרִישָׁם	pref. id.)(id., suff. 3 pers. pl. masc.	ירש
לְהוֹרֹת	pref. id.)(Hiph. inf. constr. (§ 25. No. 2e)	ירה
לְהוֹרֹתָם	pref. id.)(id., suff. 3 pers. pl. masc.	ירה
לְהוֹשִׁיב	pref. id.)(Hiph. inf. constr. dec. 1 b	ישב
לְהוֹשִׁיבִי	pref. id.)(id. with parag. '	ישב
לְהוֹשֵׁעַ	pref. id.)(Hiph. inf. constr. d. 1 b; ו bef. (:)	ישע
לְהוֹשִׁיעָה	pref. id.)(id., suff. 3 pers. sing. fem.	ישע

Headword	Description	Root
לְהוֹשִׁיעֲךָ / לְהוֹשִׁיעֶךָ	} pref. לְ)(id., suff. 2 pers. sing. masc.	ישע
לְהוֹשִׁיעֵנִי	pref. id.)(id., suff. 1 pers. sing.	ישע
לְהוֹשֵׁעַ	pref. id.)(pr. name masc.	ישע
לְהוֹתִיר	pref. id.)(pr. name masc.	יתר
לְהַזְדָּה	Ch., pref. לְ bef. (-))(Aph. inf. (§ 21. r. 15, & § 47. rem. 4)	זוד
לְהַזְהִיר	pref. לְ)(Hiph. inf. constr.	זהר
לְהִזָּהֵר	pref. id.)(Niph. inf. constr.	זהר
לְהַזִּיר	pref. id.)(Hiph. inf. constr. dec. 1 b	נזר
לְהַזְכִּיר	pref. id.)(Hiph. inf. constr.; ו bef. (:)	זכר
לְהַזְנוֹתָהּ	pref. id.)(Hiph. inf. (הַזְנוֹת), suff. 3 pers. sing. fem. dec. 1 b	זנה
לְהַזְעִיק	pref. id.)(Hiph. inf. constr.	זעק
לְהֵחָבֵא	pref. id.)(Niph. inf. constr.	חבא
לְהַחְבָּה	pref. id.)(Niph. inf. constr.	חבה
לְהַחֲוָיָה	Ch., pref. id.)(Aph. inf. constr. (§ 47. r. 4, & § 35. rem. 3)	חוה
לְהַחְוֹמָה	preff. לְ & הַ)(noun fem. sing. dec. 10	חמה
לְהַחֲזִיק	pref. לְ)(Hiph. inf. constr.	חזק
לְהַחֲטִיא	pref. id.)(Hiph. inf. constr.	חטא
לְהַחֲיוֹת / לְהַחֲיֹת	} pref. id.)(Hiph. inf. constr. dec. 1 b; ו bef. (:)	חיה
לְהַחֲיֹתוֹ	pref. id.)(id. with suff. 3 pers. sing. masc.	חיה
לְהֵחָלוֹ	pref. id.)(Niph. inf. [הֵחָל], suff. 3 pers. sing. masc. (§ 18. rem. 7)	חלל
לְהַחֲרִיד	pref. id.)(Hiph. inf. constr.	חרד
לְהַחֲרִים	pref. id.)(Hiph. inf. constr. d. 1 b; ו bef. (:)	חרם
לְהַחֲרִימָם	pref. id.)(id. with suff. 3 pers. pl. masc.	חרם

[לָהַט] to burn, flame, only part. לֹהֵט flaming. **Pi.** לַהֵט (§ 14. rem. 1) to kindle, inflame.

לַהַט masc. flame, glittering, Ge. 3. 24.

לְהָטִים masc. pl. (of לַהַט) flames; hence dazzlings, delusions, Ex. 7. 11. Others, take it to stand for לָטִים enchantments from לוּט; or suppose the signification of the Root לָהַט to be the same as לוּט.

Headword	Description	Root
לַהַט	noun masc. sing.	להט
לִהַט	Piel pret. 3 pers. sing. masc. (§ 14. r. 1)	להט
לֹהֵט	Kal part. act. sing. masc.	להט
לִהֲטָה	Piel pret. 3 pers. sing. fem. (§ 14. rem. 1)	להט
לִהְטוֹת	pref. לְ)(Hiph. inf. constr. (§ 25. No. 2 b)	נטה

* Da. 2. 24.   ƒ 1 Sa. 28. 15.   ʰ Hab. 1. 12.   ᵏ Je. 39. 14.   ⁿ Ps. 113. 8.   ᵖ Ec. 4. 13.   ˢ 2 Ch. 18. 24.   ᵘ Eze. 13. 22.   ˣ Ge. 3. 24.
ᵇ Da. 2. 12.   ᵍ Da. 5. 8.   Ps. 75. 5.   1 Sa. 25. 31.   Nu. 6. 2.   Ne. 12. 38.   Le. 21. 4.   ʸ Mal. 3. 19.
ᶜ Da. 7. 26.   Ezr. 5. 10.   Ex. 14. 11.   Je. 4. 31.   Je. 15. 20.   1 Ch. 16. 4.   1 Ki. 16. 19.   2 Ch. 20. 23.   ᶻ Ps. 104. 4.
ᵈ 1 Ch. 16. 4.   Da. 4. 22.   Pr. 28. 22.   Ge. 37. 25.   Le. 19. 29.   Ge. 50. 20.   Da. 11. 44.   1 Jo. 1. 19.
Pr. 22. 21.   Da. 5. 17.   Eze. 46. 18.   Ex. 24. 12.   Da. 5. 20.   2 Sa. 20. 5.   1 Sa. 2. 8.

לְהֵיטִיב	defect. for לְהֵיטִיב (q. v.) . . .	יטב
לַהֲטִים	Kal part. act. masc., pl. of לַהַט dec. 7 b	להט
לְהַטּוֹת	pref. לְ)(for הַטּוֹת, Hiph. inf. constr. (§ 25. No. 2 b)	נטה
לְהַטֹּתָהּ	pref. id.)(id. with suff. 3 pers. sing. fem.	נטה
לְהֵיבָלָה	Ch., pref. id.)(Aph. inf. (§ 47. r. 4); ו bef. (:)	יבל
לִהְיוֹת	ו/ pref. לְ bef. (:))(Kal inf. constr. dec. 1 a (§ 13. rem. 13) . . .	היה
לִהְיוֹתְכֶם	pref. id.)(id. with suff. 2 pers. pl. masc.	היה
לְהֵיטִבְךָ	pref. לְ)(the foll. with suff. 2 pers. sing. m.	יטב
לְהֵיטִיב	ו/ pref. id.)(Hiph. inf. constr. d. 1 b; ו bef. (:)	יטב
לְהֵיטִיבִי	pref. id.)(id. with suff. 1 pers. sing. .	יטב
לְהֵיכַל	pref. לְ for הֵיכָל)(noun com. sing. dec. 2 b	היכל
לְהֵיכְלָא	Chald., pref. לְ)(id., emph. of הֵיכַל dec. 2 a	היכל
לְהֵיכְלָהּ	Chald., pref. id.)(id., suff. 3 pers. sing. m.	היכל
לְהֵיכְלֵיכֶם	pref. id.)(id. pl., suff. 2 pers. pl. masc. .	היכל
לְהֵימָן	pref. id.)(pr. name masc. . .	אמן
לְהֵינִיק	pref. id.)(Hiph. inf. constr. . .	ינק
לִהְיֹת	defect. for לִהְיוֹת (q. v.) . . .	היה
לַהֲוָתִי	pref. לְ)(noun f. s., suff. 1 pers. s., see הַוָּה	הוה
לְהֶיְתָיָה	Ch., pref. id.)(Aph. inf. (§ 56. r.2, & §55. r. 3)	אתה
לִהְיוֹתְךָ	ו pref. לְ bef. (:))(Kal inf. (הֱיוֹת), suff. 2 pers. sing. masc. (§ 13. rem. 13) . . .	היה
לְהַכְבִּיד	pref. לְ)(Hiph. inf. constr.	כבד
לְהַכּוֹת	ו/ pref. id.)(Hiph. inf. constr. (§25. No. 2 b)	נכה
לְהַכְחִיד	ו pref. id.)(Hiph. inf. constr.; ו bef. (:)	כחד
לְהַכִּילִי	pref. id.)(Hiph. inf. constr. (§ 19. rem. 8) [contr. for הַאֲכִיל] . . .	אכל
לְהָכִיל	pref. id.)(Hiph. inf. constr.	כול
לְהָכִין	ו/ pref. id.)(Hiph. inf. constr. d. 3 a; ו bef. (:)	כון
לַהֲכִינָהּ	pref. לְ bef. (_:))(id. with suff. 3 pers. s. f.	כון
לְהַכִּירֵנִי	pref. לְ)(Hiph. inf. [הַכִּיר], suff. 1 p. s. f. d. 1 b	נכר
לְהַכְעִיס	pref. id.)(Hiph. inf. constr. dec. 1 b	כעס
לְהַכְעִיסוֹ	pref. id.)(id., suff. 3 pers. sing. masc.	כעס
לְהַכְעִסֵנִי / לְהַכְעִסֵנִי	} pref. id.)(id., suff. 1 pers. sing.	כעס
לְהַכְרִית	ו/ pref. id.)(Hiph. inf. constr. d. 1 b; ו bef. (:)	כרת
לְהַכְרִיתוֹ	pref. id.)(id., suff. 3 pers. sing. masc. .	כרת
לְהַכְשִׁיל	ו pref. id.)(Hiph. inf. constr. d. 1 b; ו bef. (:)	כשל
לְהַכְשִׁילוֹ	pref. id.)(id., suff. 3 pers. sing. masc. .	כשל
לְהַכֹּתָהּ	pref. id.)(Hiph. inf. הַכּוֹת, suff. 3 pers. sing. fem. dec. 1 b (§ 25. No. 2 b)	נכה

לְהַכֹּתוֹ	pref. לְ)(id., suff. 3 pers. sing. masc.	נכה
לְהַכֹּתְךָ	pref. id.)(id., suff. 2 pers. sing. masc.	נכה
לְהַכֹּתָם	pref. id.)(id., suff. 3 pers. pl. masc. .	נכה
לְהַלְבִּישׁ	pref. id.)(Hiph. inf. constr. .	לבש
לְהַלָּז	pref. id.)(pron. demon. com. gen. sing., ap. for הַלָּזֶה (q. v.) . . .	זה
לְהַלֶּחֶם	ו/ Kh.)(וְהַלֶּחֶם preff. הַ art., לְ, & ו bef. (:) K. וְהַלֶּחֶם, pref. הַ)(noun com. sing. d. 6 a	לחם
לְהִלָּחֵם / לְהִלָּחֵם	{ (ו) pref. לְ)(Niph. inf. constr. (§ 9. rem. 3); ו bef. (:) }	לחם
לְהֹלִיכוֹ	pref. id.)(Hiph. inf. [הוֹלִיךְ], suff. 3 p.s.m. d. 1 b	ילך
לַהֲלֹךְ	pref. לְ bef. (_:))(Kal inf. constr.	הלך
לַהֹלֵךְ	pref. לְ for הַ)(Kal part. act. m. dec. 7 b	הלך
לַהֹלְכֵי	pref. לְ)(id. pl., constr. st. .	הלך
לַהֹלְכִים	pref. לְ for הַ)(id. pl., abs. st. .	הלך
לְהַלֵּל	ו/ pref. לְ)(Piel inf. constr.; ו bef. (:)	הלל
לְהַלְמוּת	pref. id.)(noun fem. sing. .	הלם
לָהַם	Root not used; Arab. *to swallow greedily.* Hithpa. part. מִתְלַהֲמִים *dainties,* which are greedily swallowed, Pr. 18. 8 ; 26. 22.
לָהֶם	ו/ pref. prep. לְ with suff. 3 p.pl.m. (§ 5, parad.)	ל
לְהוֹן	Ch., pref. prep. לְ with suff. 3 p.pl. m. for לְהוֹן	ל
לָהֵמָּה	pref. לְ (see lett. לְ))(pron. pers. masc. pl. (הֵם) with parag. ה . . .	הם
לְהִמּוֹל	pref. לְ)(Niph. inf. constr.	מול
לַהֲמוֹן	pref. לְ bef. (_:))(n. m. s., constr. of הָמוֹן d. 3 a	המה
לַמִּזְבֵּחַ	preff. לְ & הַ)(noun masc. sing. dec. 7 c	זבח
לְהַמְטִיר	pref. לְ)(Hiph. inf. constr. .	מטר
לְהֵימִן	pref. id.)(Hiph. inf. constr. .	ימן
לְהָמִית	ו/ pref. id.)(Hiph. inf. constr. d. 3 a; ו bef. (:)	מות
לַהֲמִיתוֹ	ו/ pref. לְ bef. (_:))(id., suff. 3 pers. sing. m.	מות
לַהֲמִיתֶךָ	pref. id.)(id., suff. 2 pers. s. m. [for הֲמִיתֶךָ]	מות
לַהֲמִיתָם	pref. id.)(id., suff. 3 pers. pl. masc.	מות
לַהֲמִיתֵנוּ	pref. id.)(id., suff. 1 pers. pl.	מות
לַהֲמִיתֵנִי	pref. id.)(id., suff. 1 pers. sing.	מות
לְהִמֹּל	defect. for לְהִמּוֹל (q. v.) . .	מול
לְהִמָּלֵט	pref. לְ)(Niph. inf. constr.	מלט
לְהַמְלִיךְ	pref. id.)(Hiph. inf. constr. dec. 1 b	מלך
לְהַמְלִיכוֹ	pref. id.)(id., suff. 3 pers. sing. masc.	מלך
לַהֲמָם	pref. id.)(Kal inf. [הֹם], suff. 3 p. pl. m. d. 8 c	המם
לְהָמָן	pref. id.)(pr. name masc. . .	המן

---

a Je. 32. 41.   f Est.8.13; 2 Ch. 29.11.   l Da. 6. 19.   r 2 Ch. 25. 19.   v Je. 33. 2.   z Nu. 22. 25.   d 2 Ch. 36. 6.   h Job 39. 7.   l 1 Sa. 19. 11.
b Ps. 57. 5.   g Eze. 36. 3.   m Joel 4. 5.   o Is. 58. 4.   s Ru. 2. 10.   x Je. 40. 14.   a 2 Ch. 29. 27.   i 1 Sa. 19. 2.
c Ex. 23. 2.   h De. 8. 16.   n 1 Ki. 3. 21.   p 1 Ki. 13. 34.   t Je. 51. 62.   y Da. 8. 16.   b Pr. 2. 7.   p Job 38. 26.   j 1 Sa. 2. 25.
d Nu. 22. 23.   i Je. 4. 22.   o Job 30. 13.   q Eze. 21. 33.   u 3 Ch. 25. 8.   z 3 Sa. 16. 2.   c Ju. 5. 26.   r Ge. 34. 15.
Exr. 7. 15.   k Je. 32. 40.   p De. 26. 19.   2 Ch. 2. 8.   2 Ch. 28. 23.   2 Ch. 32. 3.   Je. 14. 16.   1 Ki. 17. 18.   Est. 4. 4

לְהִמָּנֹות	pref. לְ)(Niph. inf. constr. . . .	מנה
לַהֲמִתָם	defect. for לַהֲמִיתָם (q. v.) . . .	מות
לָהֵן	Chald., i.q. Heb. לָכֵן.—I. *therefore*.—II. *nevertheless*, *but*, *except*.	
לְ	pref. prep. לְ with suff. 3 pers. pl. fem.	
לְהִנָּבֵא	pref. לְ)(Niph. inf. constr. dec. 7 b	נבא
לְהֵנָּה	)ו' pref. לְ (see lett. לְ) pron. pers. fem. pl.	הן
לְהַנְזָקַת	Chald., pref. לְ)(Aph. inf. constr. [of הַנְזָקָה § 47. rem. 4] . . .	נזק
לְהַנְחִיל	pref. id.)(Hiph. inf. constr. . . .	נחל
לְהִנָּחֵם	pref. id.)(Niph. inf. constr. . . .	נחם
לְהַנִּחֹתָם	pref. id.)(Hiph. inf. [הַנִּחֹת], suff. 3 pers. pl. masc. dec. 1 b . . .	נחה
לְהָנִיד	pref. id.)(Hiph. inf. constr. . . .	נוד
לְהָנִיחַ	pref. id.)(Hiph. inf. constr. . . .	נוח
לַהֲנִיחֹו	pref. id.)(Hiph. inf. [הַנִּיחַ], suff. 3 pers. sing. masc. (§ 21. rem. 24) . . .	נוח
לַהֲנִיחָם	pref. id.)(id., suff. 3 pers. pl. masc. dec. 1 b	נוח
לְהָנִיס	pref. id.)(Hiph. inf. constr. . . .	נוס
לְהָנִיף	pref. id.)(Hiph. inf. constr. dec. 3 a	נוף
לְהַנְסָקָה	Chald., pref. id.)(Aph. inf. constr. (§47. r.4)	נסק
לְהַנְעָלָה	Chald., pref. id.)(Aph. inf. [for הַעֲלָה] dag. forte resolved in נ	עלל
לַהֲנָפָה	pref. לְ bef. (..))(Hiph. inf. (§ 21. rem. 15)	נוף
לְהִנָּצֵל	pref. לְ)(Niph. inf. constr. . . .	נצל
לְהִנָּקֵם	pref. id.)(Niph. inf. constr. . . .	נקם
לְהַנְתִּיךְ	pref. id.)(Hiph. inf. constr. . . .	נתך
לְהִנָּתֵן	pref. id.)(Niph. inf. constr. . . .	נתן
לְהָסֵב	pref. id.)(Hiph. inf. constr. . . .	סבב
לְהַסְגִּיד	pref. id.)(Hiph. inf. constr. . . .	סגר
לְהֹסִיף	pref. id.)(Hiph. inf. constr. (for הֹוסִיף § 20. rem. 11) . . .	יסף
לְהָסִיר	pref. id.)(Hiph. inf. constr. d.3a; bef. (:)	סור
לַהֲסִירָהּ	pref. לְ bef. (..))(id. with suff. 3 pers. sing. fem.	סור
לְהָסֵךְ	pref. לְ)(Hiph. inf. constr. . . .	סכך
לְהָסֵךְ	pref. id.)(Hiph. inf. constr. [for הָסִיךְ §11.r.2]	נסך
לְהִסָּתֵם	pref. id.)(Niph. inf. constr. . . .	סתם
לְהִסָּתֵר	pref. id.)(Niph. inf. constr. (§ 9. rem. 3)	סתר
לְהַעֲבִיד	pref. id.)(Hiph. inf. constr. . . .	עבד
לְהַעֲבִיר	pref. id.)(Hiph. inf. constr. dec. 1b	עבר
לְהַעֲבִרֹו	pref. id.)(id., suff. 3 pers. sing. masc.	עבר
לְהֵעָזֵר	pref. id.)(Niph. inf. constr. . . .	עזר

לְהַעֲלָה	Chald., pref. לְ)(Aph. inf. constr. [dag. impl. for הַעֲלָה, comp. § 42. No. 3 note, & § 47. rem. 4 & 5]	עלל
לְהַעֲלֹות	pref. id.)(Hiph. inf. constr. dec. 1b .	עלה
לְהַעֲלֹותָם	pref. id.)(id., suff. 3 pers. pl. masc.	עלה
לְהַעֲלֹת	pref. id.)(defect. for לְהַעֲלֹות (q. v.) .	עלה
לְהַעֲלֹתֹו	ו pref. id.)(id. with suff. 3 pers. s. m.; ו bef. (:)	עלה
לָהֶם	pref. id.)(noun com. s. d. 8 a (but comp. § 45)	עמם
לְהַעֲמִיד	ו pref. id.)(Hiph. inf. constr. d. 1 b; ו bef. (:)	עמד
לְהַעֲמִידֹו	pref. id.)(id. with suff. 3 pers. sing. masc.	עמד
לְהַעֲצֵבָה	pref. id)(Hiph. inf. [הַעֲצֵיב], suff. 3 p.s.f. d.1 b	עצב
לְהֵעָשֹׂות	pref. id.)(Niph. inf. constr. . . .	עשה
לְהַעֲשִׁיר	pref. id.)(Hiph. inf. constr. . . .	עשר
לְהַפִּיל	ו pref. id.)(Hiph. inf. constr.; ו bef. (:)	נפל
לְהָפִיץ	pref. id.)(Hiph. inf. constr. dec. 3a	פוץ
לַהֲפִיצֵנִי	pref. לְ bef. (..))(id. with suff. 1 pers. sing.	פוץ
לְהָפֵיר	pref. לְ)(Hiph. inf. constr. for הָפֵר	פרר
לַהֲפֹךְ	pref. לְ bef. (..))(Kal inf. constr. .	הפך
לְהֶפֶךְ	pref. לְ)(noun masc. sing. . . .	הפך
לְהָפְכָהּ	ו pref. id.)(Kal inf., suff. 3 p. s. f.; ו bef. (:)	הפך
לְהַפְלִיא	pref. id.)(Hiph. inf. constr. . . .	פלא
לְהַפְצֵץ	preff. לְ & הַ)(pr. name masc. .	פצץ
לְהִפָּקֵד	pref. לְ)(Niph. inf. constr. . . .	פקד
לְהָפֵר	pref. id.)(Hiph. inf. constr. . . .	פרר
לְהַפְרְכֶם	pref. id.)(id. with suff. 2 pers. pl. masc. [for הַפְרְכֶם comp. § 36. rem. 3]	פרר
לְהַפְשִׁיטֹו	pref. id.)(Hiph. inf. constr. . . .	פשט
לְהִפָּתֵחַ	pref. id.)(Niph. inf. constr. . . .	פתח
לְהַצְדִּיק	ו pref. id.)(Hiph. inf. constr.; ו bef. (:)	צדק
לְהַצְהִיל	pref. id.)(Hiph. inf. constr. . . .	צהל
לְהַצִּיב	ו/ו pref. id.)(Hiph. inf. constr.; ו bef. (:)	נצב
לְהַצִּיל	ו/ו pref. id.)(Hiph. inf. constr. dec. 1 b; ו id.	נצל
לְהַצִּילֹו	pref. id.)(id., suff. 3 pers. sing. masc.	נצל
לְהַצִּילְךָ	pref. id.)(id., suff. 2 pers. sing. masc.; ו bef. (:)	נצל
לְהַצִּילָם	pref. id.)(id., suff. 3 pers. pl. masc.	נצל
לְהַצִּילֵנִי	pref. id.)(id., suff. 1 pers. sing.	נצל
לְהַצָּלָה	Ch., pref. id.)(Aph. inf. constr. (§47. r.4 & 5)	נצל
לְהַצָּלֹותֵהּ	Ch., pref. id.)(id. inf. [הַצָּלֹות], suff. 3 pers. sing. masc.	נצל
לְהַצִּלֵךְ	defect. for לְהַצִּילֵךְ (q. v.)	נצל
לְהַצְמִיחַ	ו pref. לְ)(Hiph. inf. constr.; ו bef. (:)	צמח

a Ec. 1. 15.   g Eze. 44. 20.   l Is. 30. 28.   t 1 Sa. 24. 4.   o 2 Ch. 26. 15.   u Est. 9. 1, 14.   x Eze. 16. 34.   m Ps. 104. 15.   s Je. 15. 20.
b De. 9. 28.   h Nu. 32. 15.   m Eze. 22. 20.   k Je. 44. 19, 25.   p Da. 5. 7.   v Ps. 106. 27.   y 2 Sa. 10. 3.   n 1 Ch. 18. 3.   t Da. 3. 29.
c Zec. 5. 9.   i Est. 3. 8.   n Am. 1. 6.   l Ne. 4. 1.   q Ju. 20. 38.   w Eze. 20. 23.   z Ju. 21. 3.   o 1 Sa. 13. 21.   u Da. 6. 15.
d Ezr. 1. 22.   k Ju. 6. 11.   o 2 Ch. 28. 13.   m Job 34. 22.   r Ex. 3. 8.   x Hab. 3. 14.   a Le. 26. 15.   p Je. 42. 11.   v Je. 1. 8.
e Ne. 9. 19.   l Da. 6. 24.   Est. 4. 4.   n 2 Ch. 2. 17.   s 2 Ch. 10. 7.   y Zec. 11. 10.   b 2 Ch. 29. 34.   q Ex. 3. 8.   g Job 38. 27.
f 2 Ki. 21. 2.   m Da. 4. 3.   Je. 32. 31.   s 1 Sa. 20. 36.   t Je. 44. 19.   z 1 Ch. 19. 3.   c a. 51. 14.   r Je. 1. 19.

Headword	Description	Root
לְהַקְבֵּץ	pref. לְ)(Niph. inf. constr.	קבץ
לְהַקְדִּישׁ	pref. id.)(Hiph. inf. constr. dec. 1 b	קדשׁ
לְהַקְדִּישׁוֹ	pref. id.)(id., suff. 3 pers. sing. masc.	קדשׁ
לְהַקְדִּישֵׁנִי	pref. id.)(id., suff. 1 pers. sing.	קדשׁ
לְהַקְהֵל	pref. id.)(Niph. inf. constr.	קהל
לְהַקּוֹץ	preff. לְ & הַ)(pr. name masc.	קוץ
לְהַקְטִין	pref. id.)(Hiph. inf. constr.	קטן
לְהַקְטִיר	pref. id.)(Hiph. inf. constr.	קטר
לְהָקִים	' pref. id.)(Hiph. inf. constr. d.3a; וּ bef. (:)	קום
לַהֲקִימוֹ	pref. לְ bef. (ֲ))(id., suff. 3 pers. sing. masc.	קום
לְהָקֵל	pref. לְ)(Hiph. inf. constr.	קלל
לַהֲקָמֻתַהּ	Chald., pref. לְ bef. (ֲ))(Aph. inf. [הֲקָמוּת], suff. 3 pers. sing. fem. (§ 47. rem. 4)	קום
וּ לְהַקַּרְדֻּמִּים	וּ preff. לְ & הַ)(noun masc., pl. of [קַרְדֹּם] dec. 8c; וּ bef. (:)	קרדם
לְהַקְרִיב	pref. לְ)(Hiph. inf. constr.	קרב
לְהַקְשִׁיב	pref. id.)(Hiph. inf. constr.	קשב
לַהֲקָת	noun fem. sing. constr. [of לְהָקָה by transp. for קְהָלָה] assembly, company	קהל
לָהָר	pref. id.)(noun masc. sing. dec. 8 (§ 37. r. 7)	הרר
לְהֵרָאֹה	pref. id.)(Niph. inf. abs. (used as a constr.)	ראה
לְהֵרָאוֹת	pref. id.)(Hiph. inf. constr. dec. 1 b	ראה
לְהֵרָאוֹת	pref. id.)(Niph. inf. constr.	ראה
לְהַרְבֵּה	pref. id.)(Hiph. inf. used adverbially (§ 24. r. 15)	רבה
לְהַרְבּוֹת	וּ pref. id.)(id. inf. constr.; וּ bef. (:)	רבה
לָהֶרֶג	pref. לְ for לָהּ)(noun masc. sing.	הרג
לַהֲרֹג	pref. לְ bef. (ֲ))(Kal inf. constr.	הרג
לְהָרְגוֹ	pref. לְ)(id. with suff. 3 pers. sing. masc.	הרג
לְהַרְגִּיעוֹ	pref. id.)(Hiph. inf. [הִרְגִּיעַ], suff.3 p.s.m.d.1 b	רגע
לַהֲרָגֶךָ / לְהָרְגֶךָ	pref. id.)(Kal inf., suff. 2 pers. sing. masc. (§ 16. rem. 7)	הרג
לְהָרְגֵנוּ	pref. לְ)(id. with suff. 1 pers. pl.	הרג
לַהֲרֹן	in full for לַהֲרֹן (q. v. § 8. rem. 18)	הרג
וּ לָהֲרֹם	וּ in full for לָהֲרֹם (q. v. § 8. rem. 18)	הרם
לְהָרִיחַ	pref. לְ)(Hiph. inf. constr.	רוח
לֶהָרִים	pref. לְ for לָה, bef. הָ for לָה)(noun masc. pl. of הַר dec. 8d (§ 37. rem. 7)	הרר
לְהָרִים	pref. לְ)(Hiph. inf. constr.	רום
לְהָרִיעַ	pref. id.)(Hiph. inf. constr.	רוע
לְהָרִיק	pref. id.)(Hiph. inf. constr.	רוק
וּ לָהֲרֹס	וּ pref. לְ bef. (ֲ))(Kal inf. constr.	הרם

Headword	Description	Root
לְהָרַע / לְהָרֵעַ	pref. לְ)(Hiph. inf. constr. (comp.) § 15. rem. 1); וּ bef. (:)	רעע
לְהַרְפָּא	preff. לְ & הָ for הַ)(pr. name masc.	רפא
לְהֵרָפֵא	pref. לְ)(Niph. inf. constr.	רפא
לְהַרְפֵּה	preff. לְ & הָ for הַ)(pr. name masc.	רפה
לְהֵרָפֵה	pref. id.)(Niph. inf. constr. for הֵרָפֵא (§ 23. r. 10)	רפא
לַהֲרָרִי	pref. id.)(n. m. s., suff. 1 p. s. fr. [הֲרָר] d.6a	הרר
לְהַרְשִׁיעַ	pref. id.)(Hiph. inf. constr.	רשע
לְהַשְׁאוֹת	pref. id.)(Hiph. inf. constr.	שאה
לְהַשְׁאִיר	pref. id.)(Hiph. inf. constr.	שאר
לְהַשְׁבִּיעַ	pref. id.)(Hiph. inf. constr.	שבע
לְהַשְׁבִּיעַ	pref. id.)(Hiph. inf. constr.	שבע
לְהַשְׁבִּית	pref. id.)(Hiph. inf. constr.	שבת
לְהִשָּׁבֵעַ	pref. id.)(Niph. inf. constr. (§ 15. rem. 1)	שבע
לְהִשָּׁבֵר	pref. id.)(Niph. inf. constr.	שבר
לְהַשּׁוֹת	contr. and defect. for לְהַשְׁאוֹת (q. v.)	שאה
לְהַשְׁחִית	וּ pref. לְ)(Hiph. inf. constr. d.1b; וּ bef. (:)	שחת
לְהַשְׁחִיתָהּ	pref. id.)(id., suff. 3 pers. sing. fem.	שחת
לְהַשְׁחִיתֶךָ	pref. id.)(id., suff. 2 p. s. m. [for הַשְׁחִיתְךָ]	שחת
לְהַשְׁחִיתוֹ	pref. id.)(id., suff. 3 pers. sing. masc.	שחת
לְהָשִׁיב	' pref. id.)(Hiph. inf. constr. d.3a; וּ bef. (:)	שוב
לְהָשִׁיב	defect. for לְהָשִׁיב (q. v.)	ישב
לַהֲשִׁיבָה	pref. לְ bef. (ֲ))(Hiph. inf. (הָשִׁיב), suff. 3 pers. sing. fem. dec. 3a	שוב
לַהֲשִׁיבוֹ	pref. id.)(id., suff. Kh. בוֹ 3 p. s. m., K. בָהּ	שוב
לַהֲשִׁיבוֹ	pref. id.)(id., suff. 3 pers. sing. masc.	שוב
לַהֲשִׁיבָם	pref. id.)(id., suff. 3 pers. pl. masc.	שוב
לְהַשְׁכָּחָה	Chald., pref. לְ)(Aph. inf. constr. (§ 47. r. 4)	שכח
לְהַשְׁכִּיחִי	pref. id.)(Hiph. inf. constr.	שכח
לְהַשְׂכִּיל	וּ pref. id.)(Hiph. inf. constr. d. 1b; וּ bef. (:)	שכל
לְהַשְׂכִּילְךָ	pref. id.)(id., suff. 2 pers. sing. masc.	שכל
לְהַשְׂכִּילָם	pref. id.)(id., suff. 3 pers. pl. masc.	שכל
לְהַשְׁלִיחַ	pref. id.)(Hiph. inf. constr.	שלח
לְהַשְׁלִיךְ	pref. id.)(Hiph. inf. constr.	שלך
לְהַשְׁמָדָה	Chald, pref. id.)(Aph. inf. constr. (§ 47. r. 4)	שמד
לְהַשָּׁמְדָם	pref. id.)(Niph. inf. (הִשָּׁמֵד), suff. 3 pers. pl. masc. dec. 7 b	שמד
לְהַשְׁמִיד	וּ pref. id.)(Hiph. inf. constr. d. 1 b; וּ bef. (:)	שמד
לְהַשְׁמִידוֹ	pref. id.)(id., suff. 3 pers. sing. masc.	שמד
לְהַשְׁמִידָם	pref. id.)(id., suff. 3 pers. pl. masc.	שמד
לְהַשְׁמִידֵנוּ	pref. id.)(id., suff. 1 pers. pl.	שמד

---

a Ezr. 10. 7.   h Da. 6. 4.   o Je. 31. 2.   u 2 Ch. 11. 12.   Ps. 30. 8.   Ps. 8. 3.   2 Ch. 25. 16.   Da. 6. 5.   y Ec. 3. 5, 6.
b 1 Ch. 23. 13.   i 1 Sa. 13. 21.   p 1 Sa. 24. 11.   Is. 32. 6.   Is. 37. 26.   Je. 12. 16.   2 Ki. 18. 25.   Da. 6. 27.   Da. 7. 26.
c Est. 8. 11.   k 1 Sa. 19. 20.   q Ex. 5. 21.   Je. 31. 28.   Ezr. 9. 8.   Jon. 1. 4.   Ge. 42. 25.   Da. 9. 21.   Ps. 92. 8.
d Am. 8. 5.   l De. 28. 63.   r Ec. 3. 3.   Je. 31. 28.   1 Sa. 20. 17.   2 Ki. 19. 25.   Ne. 13. 27.   Ne. 9. 20.   De. 9. 26.
e 2 Sa. 3. 10.   Pr. 24. 11.   s Je. 1. 10.   De. 28. 27, 35.   Job 38. 27.   Je. 15. 3.   Ju. 19. 3.   2 Ki. 15. 37.   De. 1. 27.
f Jon. 1. 5.; Is. 23. 9.   Ex. 21. 14.   Ex. 30. 38.   e. 19. 11.

לְהַשְׂמִיל ° pref. לְ)(Hiph. inf. constr.; ו bef. (׃)   שמאל

לְהַשְׁמִיעַ pref. id.)(Hiph. inf. constr.   שמע

לְהַשְׁמָעוּתִי pref. id.)(noun fem. sing. (formed from Hiph.)   שמע

לְהַשְׁנָיָא } Chald., pref. id.)(Aph. inf. constr. (§ 47.
לְהַשְׁנָיָה } rem. 4 & 5)   שנה

לְהִשָּׁעֵן pref. id.)(Niph. inf. constr.   שען

לְהַשְׁפָּלָה Ch., pref. id.)(Aph. inf. constr. (§47. r.4 & 5)   שפל

לְהַשְׁקוֹת pref. id.)(Hiph. inf. constr.   שקה

לְהַשְׁקִיט pref. id.)(Hiph. inf. constr.   שקט

לְהַשְׁקֹתְוֹ pref. id.)(Hiph. inf. (הַשְׁקוֹת), suff. 3 pers. sing. masc. dec. 1 b   שקה

לְהִשְׁתַּבֵּחַ pref. id.)(Hithpa. inf. constr. [for הִתְשַׁבֵּחַ § 12. rem. 3]   שבח

לְהִשְׁתַּגֵּעַ pref. id.)(Hithpa. inf. constr. [for הִתְשַׁגֵּעַ § 12. rem. 3]   שגע

לְהִשְׁתַּחֲוֺת ° pref. id.)(Hithpalel inf. c. [for הִתְשַׁחֲוֹת comp. § 12. r. 3, § 6. No. 2, & § 24. r. 25]   שחה

לְהִתְאַפֵּק pref. id.)(Hithpa. inf. constr.   אפק

לַהֲתָבוּתְהֵ Ch., pref. לְ bef. (ָ))(Aph. inf. [הֲתָבוּת], suff. 2 pers. sing. masc. (§ 47. rem. 4)   תוב

לְהִתְגֹּלֵל pref. לְ)(Hithpoel inf. constr.   גלל

לְהִתְגָּרֵד pref. id.)(Hithpa. inf. constr.   גרד

לְהִתְהַלֵּךְ pref. id.)(Hithpa. inf. constr.   הלך

לְהִתְהַלֵּל pref. id.)(Hithpa. inf. constr.   הלל

לְהִתְחַזֵּק pref. id.)(Hithpa. inf. constr.   חזק

לְהִתְחַלּוֹת pref. id.)(Hithpa. inf. constr.   חלה

לְהִתְחַנֶּן pref. id.)(Hithpa. inf. constr. (for חַנֵּן § 12. rem. 4)   חנן

לְהִתְחַתֵּן ° pref. id.)(Hithpa. inf. constr.; ו bef. (׃)   חתן

לְהִתְיַחֵשׂ ° pref. id.)(Hithpa. inf. constr. (§ 14. rem. 1); ו id.   יחש

לְהִתְיַצֵּב pref. id.)(Hithpa. inf. constr.   יצב

לְהִתְחַתֵּד pref. לְ bef. (ָ))(pr. name masc.   התד

לְהִתְמַהְמֵהַּ° pref. id.)(Hithpalp. inf. constr. (§ 6. r. 4)   מהה

לְהִתְנַדֵּב } pref. id.)(Hithpa. inf. constr. (§ 12.
לְהִתְנַדָּב } rem. 4)   נדב

לְהִתְנוֹסֵס° pref. id.)(Hithpal. inf. fr. נום, or Hithpoel fr.   נסס

לְהִתְנַחֵם° pref. id.)(Hithpa. inf. constr. (§ 14. rem. 1)   נחם

לְהִתְנַכֵּל pref. id.)(Hithpa. inf. constr.   נכל

לְהִתְנַפֵּל° ° pref. id.)(Hithpa. inf. constr.; ו bef. (׃)   נפל

לְהִתְעוֹלֵל pref. id.)(Hithpoel inf. constr.   עלל

לְהִתְעַלֵּם° pref. id.)(Hithpa. inf. constr.   עלם

לְהִתְעַנּוֹת° pref. לְ)(Hithpa. inf. constr.; ו bef.   ענה

לְהִתְפָּאֵר pref. id.)(Hithpa. inf. constr.   פאר

לְהִתְפַּלֵּל pref. id.)(Hithpa. inf. constr.   לל

לְהִתְפֵּשׂ° pref. id.)(Niph. inf. constr.   תפש

לְהִתְקַדֵּשׁ° pref. id.)(Hithpa. inf. constr.   קדש

לְהִתְקַטְלָה° Ch., pref. id.)(Ithpeel inf. constr. (§47. r.4)   קטל

לְהִתְרוֹעֵעַ pref. id.)(Hithpoel inf. constr.   רעע

לְהִתְרַפֵּא pref. id.)(Hithpa. inf. constr.   רפא

לֹא , לוֹא , & וְ לוּ I. conj. if.—II. interj. O if.
O that! would that!

לוּלֵי , לוּלֵא (from לוּ if and לֹא , לְ , i. q. לֹא not)
if not, unless.

לְ ° pref. prep. לְ with suff. 3 p.s.m. (§ 5, parad.)   ל

לוֹא ° more usually לֹא adv.   לא

לוּ ° interj. & conj.   לו

לוּבִים ° gent. n. Libyans, inhabitants of the desert, west of Egypt; written לֻבִּים Da. 11. 43, and לְהָבִים Ge. 10. 13   לוב

לוּד ° pr. name—I. of a people descended from Shem, Ge. 10. 22, according to Josephus the Lydian in Asia Minor.—II. of a people in Africa; pl. לוּדִים.   לוד

לוּדִיים } gent. n., pl. of לוּד; Kh. לוּדִים, pl.
לוּדִי } of לוּדִים   לוד

[לָוָה] fut. יִלְוֶה.—I. to be joined to, adhere to, Ec. 8. 15.— II. to borrow; part. לֹוֶה borrowing; borrower. Niph. to join oneself to any one, const. with אֶל , עִם , עַל. Hiph. to lend, with acc. of the person, with double acc. of the person and thing; part. מַלְוֶה lender.

לֵוִי (adhesion, comp. Ge. 29. 34).—I. pr. name Levi, son of Jacob by Leah.—II. patronym. (for לֵוִיִּ), Levite, pl. לְוִיִּם (& בְּנֵי לֵוִי) Levites.

לֵוָי Ch.m. dec. 7, Levite.

לִוְיָה fem. garland, crown, only constr. Pr. 1. 9; 4. 9.

לֹיָה fem. (from masc. לוֹי after the form גּוֹי) only pl. לֹיוֹת wreaths, festoons, in architecture, 1 Ki. 7. 29, 30, 36.

לִוְיָתָן masc.—I. sea-monster, generally.—II. large serpent.—III. crocodile, Job 40. 25, sq.

לְוָת Ch., prep. by, with, Ezr. 4. 12.

לֹוֶה Kal part. act. sing. masc.   לוה

ᵃ 2 Sa. 14. 19.   ᵉ Da. 4. 34.   ⁱ Ge. 45. 1.   ᵐ Ps. 106. 5.   ᵖ 2 Ch. 31. 18.   ʳ Ps. 60. 6.   ᵘ Ge. 43. 18.   ᵃ Ezr. 8. 21.   ᵍ 2 Ch. 29. 34.
ᵇ Eze. 24. 26.   ᶠ Ps. 94. 13.   ᵏ Da. 3. 16.   ⁿ 2 Sa. 13. 2.   Ex. 12. 39.   ʸ Ge. 37. 35.   ᵇ Ps. 141. 4.   ᵉ Da. 10. 12.   ᵏ Da. 2. 13.
ᶜ Ezr. 6. 12.   ᵍ Ge. 24. 19.   ˡ Ge. 43. 18.   Est. 4. 8.   ¹ 1 Ch. 29. 14.   ᵗ Ps. 105. 25.   ᶜ De. 22. 3.   ˣ Esc. 21. 28.   Pr. 18. 24.
ᵈ Is. 10. 20.   ʰ 1 Sa. 21. 16.   Job 2. 3.   Ezr. 5. 14.   1 Ch. 29. 17.

[לוז] to turn aside, to decline, depart, Pr. 3. 21. Niph. part. נָלוֹז perverse; also neut. what is perverse, Is. 30. 12. Hiph. i. q. Kal, Pr. 4. 21. Hence

לוז ׳ masc.—I. almond-tree, Ge. 30. 37.—II. pr. name of a city, afterwards called בֵּית־אֵל, in the tribe of Benjamin.—III. pr. name of another city, Ju. 1. 26 . . . . לוז

לוּזָה pr. name (לוּז) with parag. ה . . לוז

לוּחַ masc. dec. 1 a (pl. לֻחֹת, לוּחֹת).—I. tablet of stone or wood; trop. tablet of the heart, Pr. 3. 3; Je. 17. 1.—II. leaf or valve of a folding-door, Ca. 8. 9.—III. du. לֻחֹתַיִם Eze. 27. 5, the boarding or deck of a ship.

לֻחִית (tabulata, i. e. built of boards) pr. name of a city in Moab.

לוּחֹת noun m. with pl. fem. term. for לוּחַ dec. 1 a

[לוט] to wrap up, to cover, conceal; part. בְּלָאט, בַּלָּט (§ 21. rem. 1) secretly; pl. לָטִים secret arts. Hiph. to wrap up, cover, 1 Ki. 19. 13.

לוֹט, לֹט masc.—I. veil, covering, Is. 25. 7.—II. Ge. 37. 25; 43. 11, ladanum, a fragrant resinous gum. Vulg. stacte, the purest kind of myrrh, distilling from the trees of its own accord. Syr. pistacia.—III. pr. name Lot, nephew of Abraham.

לוֹטָן (covering) pr. name masc. Ge. 36. 20, 29.

לוֹט ׳ pr. name masc. . . . . . לוט
לוֹטָה Kal part. pass. sing. fem. [from לוט masc.] לוט
לוֹטָן pr. name masc. . . . . . לוט
לֵוִי ׳ pr. name masc., also patronym. [for לְוִי] לוה
לֵוָיֵא Chald., gent. n. pl. emph. from לֵוִי d. 7 (§ 63) לוה
לָוִינִי Kal pret. 1 pers. sing. . . . . לוה
לְוִיֵּנוּ gent. n. (לֵוִי) with suff. 1 pers. pl. dec. 8 f לוה
לִוְיַת noun fem. sing. [constr. of לִוְיָה] . לוה
לִוְיָתָן noun masc. sing. . . . . . לוה

לוּל Root not used; prob. to wind, turn, move round, cogn. גָּלַל.

לוּל masc. pl. לוּלִים winding-stairs, 1 Ki. 6. 8.

לֻלָי, only pl. לֻלָאֹת, constr. לֻלְאֹת (§ 35. rem. 15 note) loops or eyes for hooks.

לוּא conj. compounded of לוּ & לֹא . . . לו
לוּלֵי conj. compounded of לוּ & לֵי . . . לו

I. **[לוּן]** & [לִין] inf. (gerund.) לָלִין, לָלוּן; imp. לִין; fut. יָלִין, ap. וַיָּלֶן.—I. to lodge, remain, or pass the night.—II. to abide, remain. Hiph. to let remain Je. 4. 14. Hithpal. to lodge, remain.

II. **לוּן** Niph. fut. יִלּוֹן (§ 21. rem. 24) to complain, murmur, const. with עַל against any one. Hiph. הַלִּין, הֵלִין id.

יָלוֹן (abiding) pr. name masc. 1 Ch. 4. 17.

מָלוֹן masc. dec. 3 a, lodging-place, an inn.

מְלוּנָה fem. lodge, hovel, hut, Is. 1. 8; 24. 20

תְּלוּנָה fem. dec. 10, a murmuring, complaining.

[לוּע] to swallow, Ob. ver. 16.

לֹעַ masc. dec. 1 a, throat, Pr. 23. 2.

[לוּץ] I. Arab. to turn, twist; also, to speak in obscure sentences, comp. Hiph.—II. Heb. to mock, deride, scorn; part. לֵץ (§ 21. rem. 2) scorner, scoffer. Hiph.—I. to interpret; only part. מֵלִיץ interpreter; also, intercessor.—II. to mock, deride. Pil. part. scorners, scoffers, Ho. 7. 5. Hithpal. to show oneself a mocker, Is. 28. 22.

לָצוֹן masc. derision, scorn.

מְלִיצָה fem.—I. obscure saying, enigma, Pr. 1. 6. —II. satire, Hab. 2. 6.

[לוּשׁ] to knead. Arab. to be strong; hence

לַיִשׁ masc.—I. lion.—II. pr. name of a man, 1 Sa. 25. 44; Kh. לוּשׁ 2 Sa. 3. 15.—III. pr. name of a place in the north of Palestine.

לָיִשׁ Kh. לוּשׁ, K. לַיִשׁ (q. v.) pr. name masc. לושׁ
לוּשִׁי Kal imp. sing. fem. . . . . . לושׁ
לְוָתָךְ Chald., prep. [לְוָת] with suff. 2 pers. sing. m. לוה
לָזֹאת pref. לָ or לְ q. v. { pron. demon. fem. }
לָזֹאת { sing., see . } זה
לַזְּבוּב pref. לְ for לְהַ)(noun masc. sing. dec. 1 a זבב
לִזְבֹּחַ pref. לְ bef. (:))(Kal inf. constr. (§ 8. r. 18) זבח
לִזְבוּלֻן ׳ pref. id.)(pr. name of a tribe זבל
לַזֹּבֵחַ ׳ pref. לְ for לְהַ)(Kal part. act. sing. m. d. 7 b זבח
לָזֶבַח pref. id.) in pause, Seg. n. as if fr. זָבַח (§ 35.)
לַזֶּבַח ׳ pref. לְ r. 2) but see זֶבַח;) bef. (:) זבח
לִזְבֹּחַ pref. id.)(Piel inf. constr. (§ 15. rem. 1) . זבח
לְזֶבַח ׳ pref. id.)(n. m. s. (suff. זִבְחִי) d. 6 a;) bef. (:) זבח
לִזְבֹּחַ ׳ pref. id.)(Kal inf. constr. זבח

ᵃ 1 Sa. 21. 10.   ᶜ Ge. 18. 6.   ᵈ Ezr. 4. 12.   ᵉ Is. 7. 15.   ᶠ 2 Ch. 11. 16.   ᵍ Ec. 9. 2.   ʰ Jos. 22. 26, 29.   ¹ 1 Ki. 12. 32.   ᵏ 1 Sa. 1. 3.
Ne. 5. 4.

28*

לְזִבְחֵי‎   pref. לְ‎)(noun masc. pl. constr. from זֶבַח‎ dec. 6a (§ 35. rem. 5) . . . . זבח

לָזֶה‎   Root not used; prob. i. q לוּז‎ q. v.
לָזוּת‎ fem. *perverseness,* Pr. 4. 24.

לָזֶה‎   pref. לְ‎ (see lett. לְ‎))(pron. demon. masc. s. זה

לַזָּהָב‎   pref. לְ‎ f. לַהְ‎)(noun masc. sing. dec. 4a; ‎ זהב

לְזָהָב‎   ‎ pref. לְ‎ q. v. ‎ bef. (:)   } זהב

לִזְהָבִי‎   ‎ pref. לְ‎ bef. (:))(id. with suff. 1 pers. sing. זהב

לְזוֹנָה‎   pref. לְ‎)(Kal part. act. s. f. d. 10, fr. זוֹנָה‎ m. זנה

לִזְוָעָה‎   pref. id.)(Kh. זְוָעָה‎, K. by transp. זַעֲוָה‎ n. f. s. זוע

לָזוּל‎   ‎ noun fem. sing.; ‎ bef. (:) . . לזה

לַזַּיִת‎   pref. לְ‎ for לַהְ‎)(noun masc. sing. dec. 6h זית

לְזֵיתֶךָ‎   pref. לְ‎)(id., suff. 2 pers. sing. m. [for זֵיתְךָ‎] זית

לַזֵּכֶר‎   pref. לְ‎ for לַהְ‎)(noun masc. sing. dec. 4a זכר

לְזֵכֶר‎   pref. לְ‎)(noun masc. sing. dec. 6b זכר

לִזְכֹּר‎   pref. לְ‎ bef. (:))(Kal inf. constr. . זכר

לְזִכָּרוֹן‎   ‎ pref. לְ‎)(noun masc. s. d. 3c; ‎ bef. (:) זכר

לְזֹכְרֵי‎   ‎ pref. id.)(Kal part. act. pl. c. masc. from [זֹכֵר‎] dec. 7b; ‎ id.   זכר

לִזְכַרְיָה‎   ‎ pref. לְ‎ bef. (:))(pr. name masc. זכר

לִזְכָרִים‎   pref. id.)(noun masc., pl. of זָכָר‎ dec. 4a זכר

לְזִכְרֹן‎   defect. for לְזִכָּרוֹן‎ (q. v.) . . זכר

לְזִכְרְךָ‎   ‎ pref. לְ‎)(noun masc. sing., suff. 2 pers. sing. masc. from זֵכֶר‎ dec. 6b; ‎ bef. (:) . זכר

לְזַמֵּר‎   ‎ pref. id.)(Piel inf. constr.; ‎ id. . זמר

לְזָנָב‎   pref. id.)(noun masc. sing. d. 4a (§ 33. r. 1) זנב

לִזְנוּנִים‎   pref. לְ‎ bef. (:))(noun m. pl. [of זְנוּן‎] d. 1a זנה

לִזְנוֹת‎   ‎ } pref. id.)(Kal inf. constr. . זנה
לִזְנֹת‎   ‎ }

לְזַעֲוָה‎   pref. לְ‎)(noun fem. sing., by transp. for זְוָעָה‎ זוע

לִזְעֹק‎   ‎ pref. לְ‎ bef. (:))(Kal inf. constr. . זעק

לְזַעֲקָתִי‎   pref. לְ‎)(noun fem. sing., suff. 1 pers. sing. from זְעָקָה‎ dec. 11c (§ 42. rem. 1) . זעק

לְזֶפֶת‎   pref. id.)(noun fem. sing. . . זוף

לַזָּקֵן‎   pref. id.)(adj. or subst. masc. sing. dec. 5a זקן

לְזִקְנֵי‎   ‎ pref. id.)(id. pl. constr.; ‎ bef. (:) . זקן

לְזִקְנֵיהֶם‎   pref. לְ‎ bef. (:))(id. pl., suff. 3 pers. sing. m. זקן

לִזְקֵנָיו‎   pref. id.)(n. m. pl., suff. 3 p. s. m. fr. [זָקֵן‎] d. 1a זקן

לַזְּקֵנִים‎   pref. לְ‎ f. לַהְ‎)(adj. or subst. m., pl. of זָקֵן‎ d. 5a זקן

לַזָּר‎   ‎ } pref. id. ‎ }
לְזָר‎   ‎ pref. לְ‎   } Kal part. act. sing. masc. dec. 1a זור

לְזָרָא‎   pref. לְ‎)(noun fem. sing. [for זָרָה‎] זור

לְזָרוֹ‎   pref. id.)(n. m. s., suff. 3 p. s. m. fr. זָר‎ d. 1a זור

לִזְרוֹת‎   pref. לְ‎ bef. (:))(Kal inf. constr. . זרה

לְזָרוֹת‎   ‎ pref. לְ‎)(Piel inf. constr. dec. 1; ‎ bef. (:) . זרה

לְזָרוֹתָהּ‎   pref. id.)(id., suff. 3 pers. sing. fem. . זרה

לְזָרוֹתָם‎   ‎ pref. id.)(id., suff. 3 p. pl. m.; ‎ bef. (:) זרה

לְזֶרַח‎   pref. id.)(pr. name masc. . . זרח

לַזַּרְחִי‎   pref. לְ‎ for לַהְ‎)(patronym. of the preced. . זרח

לַזָּרִים‎   ‎ pref. id.) Kal part. act. masc., pl. of זָר‎ } זור
לְזָרִים‎   ‎ pref. לְ‎   dec. 1a . . . }

לַזֶּרַע‎   pref. לְ‎ for לַהְ‎)(Kal part. act. sing. m. d. 7b דע

לְזֶרַע‎   ‎ pref. לְ‎)(noun masc. sing. dec. 6a (§ 35. } רע
לָזָרַע‎   ‎ rem. 5 & 7) . . . . . }

לִזְרֹעַ‎   pref. לְ‎ bef. (:))(Kal inf. constr. . זרע

לְזַרְעוֹ‎   ‎ pref. לְ‎)(noun masc. sing., suff. 3 pers. s. m. from זֶרַע‎ d. 6 (§ 35. r. 5); ‎ bef. (:) זרע

לִזְרֹעוֹ‎   ‎ pref. לְ‎ bef. (:))(noun com. sing., suff. 3 pers. sing. masc. from זְרֹעַ‎ dec. 1a . זרע

לְזַרְעֲךָ‎   ‎ pref. לְ‎)(noun m. s., suff. 2 pers. s. m. } רע
לְזַרְעֶךָ‎   ‎ from זֶרַע‎ dec. 6 (§ 35. r. 5); ‎ bef. (:) }

לְזַרְעֲכֶם‎   pref. id.)(id., suff. 2 pers. pl. masc. . זרע

לְזַרְעָם‎   ‎ pref. id.)(id., suff. 3 p. pl. m.; ‎ bef. (:) זרע

לִזְרֹק‎   ‎ pref. לְ‎ bef. (:))(Kal inf. constr. . זרק

לְזָרֶשׁ‎   pref. לְ‎)(pr. name fem. . . זרש

לְחַ‎   ‎ } adj. masc. sing., pl. לַחִים‎ (§ 37. rem. 7] לחח
לָח‎   ‎ }

לְחָבָב‎   pref. לְ‎)(pr. name masc. . . חבב

לַחֲבֹק‎   pref. לְ‎ bef. (ֲ))(Kal inf. constr. (§ 8. r. 18) חבק

לְחַבֵּל‎   pref. לְ‎)(Piel inf. constr. . . חבל

לְחַבָּלָה‎   Chald., pref. id.)(Pael inf. constr. (§ 47. r. 5) חבל

לַחֲבָלִים‎   pref. לְ‎ bef. (ֲ))(n. m., pl. of חֶבֶל‎ d. 6 (§ 35. r. 4) חבל

לַחֲבַקּוּק‎   pref. id.)(pr. name masc. . . חבק

לְחַבֵּר‎   pref. לְ‎)(Piel inf. constr. . . חבר

לְחֶבֶר‎   pref. id.)(pr. name masc. . . חבר

לְחֶבְרָה‎   pref. id.)(noun fem. sing. . . חבר

לְחֶבְרוֹן‎   pref. id.)(pr. name of a place . חבר

לַחֶבְרֹנִי‎   pref. לְ‎ for לָהְ‎)(gent. noun from the preced. חבר

לַחֲבֻרָתִי‎   pref. לְ‎)(n. f. s., suff. 1 p. s. fr. חַבּוּרָה‎ d. 10 חבר

לַחֲבֹשׁ‎   pref. לְ‎ bef. (ֲ))(Kal inf. constr. . חבש

לְחָבְשָׁהּ‎   pref. לְ‎)(id., suff. 3 pers. sing. fem. חבש

לַחֲנֹג‎   ‎ pref. לְ‎ (see lett. לֲ‎))(Kal inf. constr. חנג

a Nu. 25. 2.   h Ps. 103. 18.   o Le. 20. 6.   u Le. 9. 1.   a Job 19. 15.   g Ps. 106. 27.   k Eze. 22. 6.   q Ec. 3. 5.   w Ge. 4. 23.
b 1 Ki. 20. 7.   i Ex. 28. 12, 29.   p 2 Sa. 19. 29.   v Jos. 23. 2.   b Je. 3. 13.   h Ge. 28. 13.   l Ezr. 6. 12.   r Is. 61. 1.
c Pr. 4. 24.   k Is. 26. 8.   q Job 16. 18.   w Ge. 21. 2.   c Je. 4. 11.   i Is. 55. 10.   m Ex. 32. 13.   s Je. 38. 12.   x Eze. 30. 31.
d Ju. 9. 8.   l Ps. 92. 2.   r Is. 34. 9.   w Ru. 4. 9.   d Eze. 20. 23.   l Le. 18. 20.   n Eze. 43. 18.   t Ex. 36. 18.   y Zec. 14. 14.
e Ex. 23. 11.   m De. 28. 13, 44.   s De. 28. 50.   x Pr. 6. 1.   e Zec. 2. 4.   i Is. 28. 24.   o Eze. 17. 24.   u Job 34. 3.   18. 19.
f Ex. 13. 9.   n Ge. 38. 24.

לַחֲנָא   pref. ל‎) noun fem. sing. [for חָנָּה‎]   חנא
לַחֲנִי   pref. id.) pr. name masc.   חנן
לַחְגֹּר‎ וְ‎ pref. ל‎ bef. (ֲ)) Kal inf. constr.   חגר
לַחֲדָשׁ   pref. ל‎ for לָה‎) noun masc. sing. dec. 6c   חדשׁ
לְחַדֵּשׁ   pref. ל‎) Piel inf. constr.   חדשׁ
לַחֹדֶשׁ   pref. id.) noun masc. sing. dec. 6c   חדשׁ
לְחָדְשֵׁי   pref. id.) id. pl. constr. st.   חדשׁ
לְחָדָשָׁיו‎ pref. ל‎ bef. (ֲ)) id. pl., suff. 3 p. s. masc.   חדשׁ
לֶחֳדָשִׁים‎ וְ‎ pref. ל‎ f. לָה‎ bef. חֲ‎ f. לָה‎) id. pl. abs. st.   חדשׁ

לְחָה   Root not used ; hence
לְחִי‎ fem. dec. 6i (§ 35 rem. 14 & 15).—I. cheek.—II. jaw-bone.—III. pr. name of a place on the borders of Philistia.

לֵחֹה‎ n. m. s., suff. 3 pers. sing. masc. fr. [לֵחַ‎] d. 1 a   לחח
לַחוֹטֵא‎ וְ‎ pref. ל‎ for לָה‎) Kal part. act. sing. m. d. 7b   חטא
לָחוּל   pref. ל‎ (see lett. ל‎)) Kal inf. constr.   חול
לְחוֹמָה   pref. ל‎ f. לָה‎) noun fem. sing. dec. 10   חמה
לְחוֹמַת‎ וְ‎ pref. ל‎) id. constr. st. ; וְ‎ bef. (ֲ)   חמה
לְחוֹנֵן   pref. id.) Kal part. act. sing. masc.   חנן
לַחוֹסִים   pref. ל‎ f. לָה‎) Kal part. a., pl. of חוֹסֶה‎ d. 9a   חסה
לָחוֹף   pref. ל‎) noun masc. sing.   חפף
לְחוּפָם   pref. id.) pr. name masc., see חֻפִּים‎   חפף
לַחוּצִי‎ וְ‎ pref. ל‎ for לָה‎) noun masc. sing. dec. 1 a   חוץ
לַחוּצָה‎ וְ‎ pref. id.) id. with loc. ה‎   חוץ
לְחוֹקְקֵי   pref. ל‎) Kal part. act. pl. c. m. fr. [חֹקֵק‎] d.7b   חקק
לַחוֹרֵם   pref. id.) pr. name masc.   חור
לְחוּשִׁי   pref. id.) pr. name masc.   חושׁ
לָחוֹת   defect. [for לָחוֹת‎], see לוּחוֹת‎   לוח
לַחֲזָאֵל   pref. ל‎ bef. (ֲ)) pr. name masc.   חזה
לַחֲזוֹת   pref. id.) Kal inf. constr.   חזה
לֶחָזֶה   pref. id.) noun masc. sing. dec. 1a   חזה
לַחֲזִים‎ וְ‎ pref. ל‎ for לָה‎) noun m., pl. of חֹזֶה‎ d. 9a   חזה
לַחֲזִיר   pref. ל‎) pr. name masc.   חזר
לְחַזֵּק‎ וְ‎ pref. id.) Piel inf. constr. ; וְ‎ bef. (ֲ)   חזק
לַחֲזָקָה   pref. id.) noun fem. sing.   חזק
לְחָזְקָה   pref. id.) Kal inf., suff. 3 pers. sing. fem.   חזק
לְחִזְקִיָּה
לְחִזְקִיָּהוּ‎ } pref. id.) pr. name masc.   חזק

לָחַח   Root not used ; Chald. & Ethiop. לחֵח‎ to moisten.

לָח‎ m. pl. לַחִים‎ (§ 37. rem. 7) adj. moist, fresh
לֵחַ‎ masc. dec. 1, freshness, vigour, De. 34. 7.
לַחְטֹא‎ pref. ל‎ bef. (ֲ)) Kal inf. constr.   חטא
לַחֲטֵא‎ pref. ל‎) Piel inf. constr.   חטא
לַחֲטָאָה‎ pref. ל‎ bef. (ֲ)) noun fem. sing.   חטא
לַחַטָּאוֹת‎ וְ‎ pref. ל‎ for לָה‎) noun fem., pl. abs. from חַטָּאת‎ (q. v.)   חטא
לְחַטֹּאותֵיכֶם‎ pref. ל‎) id. pl., suff. 2 p. s. m. ; וְ‎ bef. (ֲ)   חטא
לַחַטֹּאת‎ וְ‎ pref. ל‎ f. לָה‎) id. s. abs. [for חַטָּאת‎ § 39. No. 4 d] pl. חַטָּאוֹת‎ (comp. prec. & §44.r.5)   חטא
לְחַטֹּאת‎ pref. ל‎) pref. id.) id. constr. st. [for חַטָּאת‎, comp. § 23. rem. 2 & 4] prop. from חֲטָאָה‎   חטא
לְחַטָּאתִי‎ pref. id.) id. s., suff. 1 pers. s. ; וְ‎ bef. (ֲ)   חטא
לְחַטָּאתָם‎ pref. id.) id., suff. 3 pers. pl. masc. ; וְ‎ id.   חטא
לְחַטָּאתֵנוּ‎ pref. id.) id., suff. 1 pers. pl. ; וְ‎ id.   חטא
לִכְתֹּב‎ pref. ל‎) Kal inf. constr. [for לַחְטֹב‎ comp. § 13. rem. 1 & 2].   חטב
לַחֹטְבִים‎ pref. ל‎ for לָה‎) Kal part. act. masc., pl. of חֹטֵב‎ dec. 7 b   חטב
לַחֲטוֹף‎ pref. ל‎) Kal inf. constr. [for לַחֲטֹף‎ comp. § 13. rem. 1 & 2, & § 8. rem. 18]   חטף
לַחֲטִיא‎ pref. ל‎ contr. [for לְהַחֲטִיא‎]) Hiph. inf. constr. (§ 11. rem. 3)   חטא
לְחַטְּיָא‎ Chald., pref. ל‎) Kh. for חַטָּאָה‎ Keri n. f. s.   חטא
לַחַטָּת‎ defect. for לְחַטָּאת‎ (q. v.)   חטא
לְחַי רֹאִי‎ pr. name, see בְּאֵר‎ under   באר
לֶחָי‎ pref. ל‎ for לָה‎, bef. חַ‎ for לָה‎) adj. masc. sing. dec. 8a (for חַי‎ § 37. rem. 6)   חיי
לְחַי‎ Chald., pref. ל‎) adj. m. s. d. 5a ; וְ‎ bef. (ֲ)   חיי
לְחִי‎
לֶחִי‎ } noun fem. sing. dec. 6i (suff. לֶחְיוֹ‎ § 35. rem. 14), also pr. name   לחה
לַחַיָּה‎ וְ‎ pref. ל‎ for לָה‎) n. f. s. d. 10, from חַי‎ m.   חיי
לְחַיָּתָהּ‎ noun f. s., suff. 3 pers. s. f. from לְחִי‎ (q. v.)   לחה
לְחָיֵהֶם‎ id. du. [for לְחָיִם‎ § 35. rem. 15], suff. 3 p. pl. m.   לחה
לְחָיָו‎ id. du. [לְחָיַיִם‎], suff. 3 p. s. m. (§ 4. r. 1 & 2)   לחה
לֶחְיוֹ‎ id. sing., suff. 3 pers. sing. masc. (§ 35. r. 14)   לחה
לְחַיּוֹת‎ pref. ל‎) Piel inf. constr. ; וְ‎ bef. (ֲ)   חיה
לַחֲיוֹת‎ pref. ל‎ bef. (ֲ)) Kal inf. constr. (§ 13. r. 13)   חיה
לְחֵיוָתָא‎ Chald., pref. ל‎) n. f. s., emph. of חֵיוָא‎ d. 8a   חוה
לְחַיּוֹתָם‎ וְ‎ pref. id.) Piel inf. (חַיּוֹת‎), suff. 3 pers. pl. masc. dec. 1b ; וְ‎ bef. (ֲ)   חיה

לֶחָיַי֜ noun fem. du., suff. 1 pers. sing. from לחה dec. 61; ו bef. (:) — לחה

לְחָיֵי id. pl., constr. st. — לחה

לְחָיֵי pref. לְ)(noun masc. pl. c. from חַי dec. 8 d (§ 37. rem. 6), Chald. (Ezr. 6. 10) dec. 5 a — חיי

לְחָיֶיךָ noun fem. du., suff. 2 p. s. f. from חִי d. 61 — לחה

לַחַיִּים pref. לְ f. [לְהַ)(noun masc., pl. of חַי dec. 8 d (§ 37. rem. 6) — חיי

לַחַיִם pref. לְ q. v.

לְחַיִל pref. id.)(noun masc. sing. dec. 6 h — חול

לְחַיִל pref. id.)(id. constr. st. — חול

לְחַיְלָה pref. id.)(id., suff. 3 pers. sing. fem.; the general reading is חֵילָה noun fem. — חול

לְחַיְלוֹ pref. id.)(id., suff. 3 pers. s. m.; ו bef. (:) — חול

לָחִים adj. masc., pl. of לַח (§ 37. rem. 7) — לחח

לַחִיצוֹן pref. לְ for לְהַ)(adj. masc. sing. — חוץ

לְחֵירָם pref. לְ)(pr. name masc., see חירם — חור

לְחַיַּת pref. id.)(noun fem. sing., constr. of חַיָּה dec. 10, from חַי masc. — חיי

לְחַיְתוֹ pref. id.)(id. constr. with parag. ו (for dag. omitted in יְ comp. § 10. rem. 7) — חיה

לְחַיֹּתוֹ pref. id.)(Piel inf. (חַיּוֹת), suff. 3 pers. sing. masc. dec. 1 a — חיה

לְחַיֹּתֵנוּ pref. id.)(id. with suff. 1 pers. pl. — חיה

[לָחַךְ] i. q. לָקַק only Nu. 22. 4, and Pi. לִחֵךְ (§ 14. r. 1) to lick, lick up, as an ox in feeding; to lap up, as a dog in drinking.

לִחֲכָה Piel pret. 3 pers. sing. fem. [for לִחֲכָה, comp. § 7. rem. 8, & § 14. rem. 1] — לחך

לְחִ. כִּי pref. לְ)(noun masc. sing., suff. 1 pers. sing. from חֵךְ [for חִנְךְּ] dec. 8 b — חנך

לְחַכִּימֵי Ch., pref. id.)(noun m. pl. c. fr. [חַכִּים] d. 1 a — חכם

לְחַכִּימִין h., pref. id.)(id. pl., abs. state — חכם

לַחֲכַם pref. לְ bef. (-:))(constr. of the foll. — חכם

לְחָכָם pref. לְ f. לְהָ)(adj. masc. sing. dec. 4 c — חכם

לֶחָכָם pref. לְ q. v.

לַחְכַּם pref. id.)(noun masc. sing., suff. 3 pers. pl. masc. from חֵךְ [for חִנְךְּ] dec. 8 b — חנך

לְחָכְמָה pref. לְ for לְהַ)(noun fem. sing. (no pl.) — חכם

לַחָכְמָה pref. לְ q. v.

לַחֲכָמִים pref. לְ bef. (-:))(adj. m., pl. of חָכָם d. 4 c — חכם

לְחָכְמָתִי pref. לְ)(noun fem. sing., suff. 1 pers. sing. from חָכְמָה (no pl.) — חכם

לְחֹל pref. לְ)(noun masc. sing. — חלל

לַחֲלֹף pref. לְ bef. (-:))(Kal inf. constr. (§ 8. r. 18) — חלף

לְחַלּוֹת ו pref. לְ)(Piel inf. constr.; ו bef. (:) — חלה

לְחֵלַח pref. לְ for לְהַ)(pr. name of a province — חלח

לַחֲלִי pref. לְ bef. (-:))(noun masc. sing. dec. 6 k — חלה

לְחֶלְכָּה pref. לְ)(adj. masc. sing. [for חֵלְכָא] — חלך

לְחַלֵּל ו pref. id.)(Piel inf. constr. d. 7 b; ו bef. (:) — חלל

לְחַלְּלוֹ pref. id.)(id. with suff. 3 pers. sing. masc. — חלל

לְחֵלֶם pref. id.)(pr. name masc. — חלם

לְהַחֲלִיק pref. לְ, contr. & defect. [for לְהַחֲלִיק] Hiph. inf. constr. (§ 11. rem. 3) — חלק

לַחֲלֹק pref. לְ bef. (-:))(Kal inf. constr. — חלק

לְחֵלֶק pref. לְ)(noun masc. sing. dec. 6 b (§ 35. rem. 6), also pr. name masc. — חלק

לְחִלְקִיָּה pref. id.)(pr. name masc. — חלק

[לָחַם] fut. יִלְחַם—I. to eat, consume, with acc., בְּ of the food; metaph. לְחֻמֵי רֶשֶׁף consumed of fever, Da. 32. 24.—II. to war, fight, with אֶת, לְ of the person. Niph. נִלְחַם to make or wage war, to fight, with בְּ, עִם, אֶל, עַל against, and לְ, עַל for whom.

לָחֻם or לְחוּם masc.—I. eating, feasting, with suff. לְחֻמוֹ Job 20. 23.—II. flesh, body, Zep. 1. 17, where the MSS. and editions differ between לְחֻמָם & לְחֻמָם.

לֶחֶם com. dec. 6 a (with suff. לַחְמִי).—I. food, meat; applied also to fruit, Je. 11. 19; meton. meal, feast.—II. bread, as the principal part of the food of men; לֶחֶם הַפַּעֲרֶכֶת, לֶחֶם הַפָּנִים shew-bread, the bread arranged or piled up in the tabernacle in the presence of the Lord; שְׁתֵּי לֶחֶם two loaves; meton. bread-corn, Is. 28. 28; אַנְשֵׁי לֶחֶם food necessary for men; אַנְשֵׁי לַחְמְךָ men who eat thy food.

לְחֵם Chald. meal, feast, Da. 5. 1.

לָחֶם masc. (for לָחֶם לָחֶם) war, only constr. לֶחֶם Ju. 5. 8.

לַחְמִי pr. name masc. 1 Ch. 20. 5; see also under בֵּית.

מִלְחָמֶת and מִלְחָמָה fem. dec. 11 a, & 13 a (with suff. מַחֲמֹתִי, pl. חָמוֹת § 42. rem. 5).—I. a warring, fighting, Is. 7. 1; hence, fight, battle —II. war, עָשָׂה מִלְחָמָה (with אֶת, עִם) to make

war with any one; אִישׁ מִ׳ warrior, soldier;
כְּלֵי מִ׳ weapons of war, arms.—III. event of war,
victory, Ec. 9. 11.

לֶחֶם   in pause for לֶחֶם (q. v. & § 35. rem. 2)   .   לחם

לֶחֶם   noun masc. sing. constr. [of לֶחֶם; some
MSS. read לֶחֶם, others לֶחֶם .   .   .   לחם

לְחַם   Kal imp. sing. masc.   .   .   .   לחם

לָחֶם   וְ׳, וַ׳ noun com. s. d. 6 a (and pr. name in
compos. with בֵּית q. v.); for וְ see lett. ו   לחם

לְחֵם   Chald. noun masc. sing.   .   .   לחם

לָחֶם   pref. לְ וְ noun masc. sing. dec. 8 c   חמם

לֹחֵם   Kal part. act. sing. masc. dec. 7 b   .   לחם

לַחְמָהּ   noun com. s., suff. 3 pers. s. f. fr. לֶחֶם d. 6a   לחם

לָחֲמוּ   Kal pret. 3 pers. pl.   .   .   .   לחם

לָחֲמוּ   id. imp. pl. masc.   .   .   .   לחם

לַחְמוֹ   noun com. s., suff. 3 p. s. m. from לֶחֶם d. 6a   לחם

לְחָמוּל   pref. לְ וְ pr. name masc.   .   .   חמל

לַחֲמוֹרִי   pref. לְ bef. (־) וְ noun masc. sing. dec. 1a   חמר

לַחֲמוֹרֵיהֶם   pref. id. וְ id., suff. 3 pers. pl. masc.   .   חמר

לַחֲמוֹרִים   pref. id. וְ id. pl., abs. st.   .   .   חמר

לַחֲמוֹרֵינוּ   pref. id. וְ id. pl., suff. 1 pers. pl.   .   חמר

לַחֹמוֹת   וְ׳ pref. לְ וְ n. f., pl. of חוֹמָה d. 10; וְ bef. (׃)   חמה

לַחֲמוֹתָהּ   pref. לְ bef. (־) וְ noun fem. sing., suff. 3
pers. sing. fem. from [חָמוֹת] dec. 3a   .   חם

לַחְמִי   pr. name masc.   .   .   .   לחם

לַחְמִי   וְ׳ noun com. s., suff. 1 p. s. from לֶחֶם d. 6a   לחם

לֹחֲמַי   Kal part. act. pl. m., suff. 1 p. s. fr. לֶחֶם d. 7 b   לחם

לְחֻמֵי   וְ id. part. pass. pl. constr. masc. from [לָחוּם]
d. 3 a; Milêl bef. penacute (רֶשֶׁף); וְ bef. (׃)   לחם

לֹחֲמִים   id. part. act. masc., pl. of לֶחֶם dec. 7 b   לחם

לַחְמְךָ   וְ׳ noun com. sing., suff. 2 pers. sing.
לַחְמֶךָ   masc. from לֶחֶם dec. 6a   לחם

לַחְמְכֶם   id., suff. 2 pers. pl. masc.   .   .   לחם

לַחְמְלָה   pref. לְ וְ Kal inf. constr. with fem. term.
(§ 8. rem. 10)   .   .   .   חמל

לַחְמָם   noun com. s., suff. 3 p. pl. m. from לֶחֶם d. 6a   לחם

לַחְמָם   pref. לְ, contr. [for לַחֲמָם], Kal inf. constr.
(after the form קְטַל comp. § 13. rem. 2
& 13, & § 18. rem. 13)   .   .   חמם

לַחְמָם   וְ for לַחֲמָם (as other copies read) n. m., suff.
3 p. pl. m. [fr. לָחֻם or לֶחֶם] וְ bef. (׃)   לחם

לַחְמֵנוּ   noun m., suff. 1 pers. pl. from לֶחֶם dec. 6a   לחם

לַחְמָס   וְ pr. n. of a place in the tribe of Judah, Jos. 15. 40.

לַחְמָס   pref. לְ וְ noun masc. sing. dec. 4c   .   חמם

לַחְמָר   pref. לְ for לְהָ וְ noun masc. sing. dec. 6 c   חמר

לַחֲמֹרוֹ   pref. לְ bef. (־) וְ noun masc. sing., suff. 3
pers. sing. masc. from חֲמוֹר dec. 1a   .   חמר

לַחֲמֹרֵיהֶם   pref. id. וְ id., suff. 3 pers. pl. masc.   חמר

לַחֲמֵשׁ   pref. לְ for לְהָ וְ noun masc. sing.   .   חמש

לַחֲמִשָּׁה   pref. לְ bef. (־) וְ num. card. m. from חֲמֵשׁ f. חמש

לַחֲמִשִּׁים   pref. id. וְ id. com. gen., pl. of חָמֵשׁ   .   חמש

לַחֲמֵשֶׁת   pref. id. וְ id. masc. sing., constr. of חֲמִשָּׁה
(§ 39. No. 4. rem. 1)   .   .   חמש

לְחֵן   Chald. Root not used; Arab. to be rancid, corrupt;
metaph. to be obscene.

לְחֵנָא   Chald. fem. d. 8a, concubine, Da. 5. 2, 3, 23.

לְחָן   וְ pref. לְ וְ pr. name masc.; וְ bef. (׃)   חנן

לְחַנָּה   וְ pref. id. וְ pr. name fem.; וְ id.   .   חנן

לַחֲנוֹךְ   pref. לְ bef. (־) וְ pr. name masc.   .   חנך

לְחָנֻן   pref. לְ וְ pr. name masc.   .   .   חנן

לַחֲנֹט   pref. לְ bef. (־) וְ Kal inf. constr.   .   חנט

לַחֲנֻכַּת   Heb. & Chald., pref. id. וְ noun fem. sing.,
constr. of חֲנֻכָּה dec. 10, Chald. dec. 8a   חנך

לְחַנְּנָהּ   pref. לְ וְ Piel or Kal inf., suff. 3 pers. sing.
fem. [for חַנְּנָהּ, comp. § 10. rem. 7; or
for חַנְנָהּ, from חָנַן, § 16. rem. 10]   חנן

לַחֲנַנְיָהוּ, לַחֲנַנְיָהוּ   וְ pref. לְ bef. (־) וְ pr. names masc.   חנן

לַחֲנֶּכֶם   pref. id. וְ Kal inf. [חָנַן], suff. 2 pers. pl.
masc. (§ 16. rem. 10)   .   .   חנן

לְחֶנָתָהּ   וְ Chald. noun fem. sing., suff. 3 pers. sing.
fem. from [לְחֵנָא] dec. 8a; וְ bef. (׃)   לחן

לְחֶנָתָךְ   וְ Chald. id. with suff. 2 pers. sing. masc.; וְ id.   לחן

לַחֲנֹתְכֶם   pref. לְ bef. (־) וְ Kal inf. (חֲנוֹת), suff. 2
pers. pl. masc. dec. 1a   .   חנה

לְחֶסֶד   pref. לְ וְ noun masc. sing. d. 6a (see the foll.)   חסד

לְחַסְדּוֹ   וְ pref. id. וְ id., suff. 3 pers. s. m.; וְ bef. (׃)   חסד

לְחַסְדֵי   pref. id. וְ id. pl., constr. st.   .   חסד

לְחָסָה   וְ pref. id. וְ pr. name masc.; וְ bef. (׃)   חסה

לַחֲסוֹת   וְ׳ pref. לְ bef. (־) וְ Kal inf. constr.   חסה

לַחֲסִידָיו   pref. id. וְ adj. pl. m., suff. 3 p. s. m. fr. חָסִיד d. 3a   חסד

לַחֲסִידֶךָ   pref. id. וְ id., suff. 2 pers. sing. fem. for חֲסִידֶךָ   חסד

לֶחָסִיל   pref. לְ for לְהָ, bef. הַ for לְהָ וְ noun m. sing.   חסל

לַחֲסִים   pref. לְ for לְהָ וְ Kal part. m., pl. of חֹסֶה d. 9a   חסה

לַחֲסַר   pref. לְ bef. (־) וְ adj. m. s., constr. of חָסֵר d. 5c   חסר

לַחֲפִים   pref. לְ וְ pr. names masc.   .   חפף

---

a Ju. 5. 8.	f Ps. 56. 2.	l Ju. 19. 21.	p Ps. 35. 1.	u Le. 26. 5, 26.	z Hab. 1. 9.	e Ne. 6. 15.	Da. 5. 2, 3.	n Ps. 89. 20.
b Ps. 35. 1.	g Pr. 4. 17.	m Ju. 19. 19.	q De. 32. 24.	v Eze. 16. 5.	aa Ge. 6. 18.	f 1 Sa. 6. 18.	Da. 1. 33.	o Ps. 78. 46.
c Ge. 45. 23.	h Pr. 9. 5.	n Ne. 4. 1.	r Ps. 56. 3.	y Is. 47. 14.	bb Ge. 47. 26.	g Ge. 50. 2.	i 2 Ch. 6. 42.	p Pr. 30. 5.
d Da. 5. 1.	i Pr. 26. 3.	o Je. 1. 18.	s Je. 5. 17.	Zep. 1. 17.	cc 1 Ch. 25. 22.	h Ps. 102. 14	m Is. 30. 2.	q Pr. 15. 21.
Hag. 1. 6.	k Jos. 9. 4.	p Eze. 16. 19.	t Je. 30. 18.	aa Da. 5. 23.	dd Ps. 116. 15.			

לַחְפֹּר־ pref. ל contr. for [לַחְפֹּר], Kal inf. constr. (comp. § 13. rem. 2 & 9) . . . חפר

לַחְפֹּר׳ see חֲפֹר פֵּרוֹת under . . . חפר

לַחֲפְשִׁי pref. ל for לֶה χ adj. masc. sing. dec. 1 b . חפש

לַחַץ fut. יִלְחַץ.—I. to press, squeeze.—II. to oppress, afflict. Niph. to press oneself, with אֶל against, Nu. 22. 25. Hence

לַחַץ masc. dec. 6 d (§ 35. rem. 2) oppression, affliction . לחץ

לָחַץ

לַחַץ׳ pref. ל f. לֶה χ noun masc. sing. dec. 8 b . חצץ

לַחֵץ׳ pref. ל q. v.

לַחֲצֹב׳ pref. ל χ Kal inf. constr. [for לַחֲצֹב, comp. § 13. rem. 2 & 9] . חצב

לַחֹצְבֵי׳ pref. ל χ Kal part. act. pl. c. masc. from חֹצֵב dec. 7 b ; ו bef. (:) . חצב

לַחֹצְבִים׳ pref. ל for לֶה χ id. pl., abs. st. . חצב

לַחֲצוּ ׳ו Kal pret. 3 pers. pl. . . . לחץ

לַחֲצֹב in full for לַחְצֹב (q. v. & § 8. rem. 18) חצב

לַחֲצִי׳ pref. ל bef. (–:) noun m. s. (suff. חָצִיו) dec. 6 (§ 35. rem. 14)

לַחֲצִי׳ pref. ל for לֶה χ

לַחֲצֵיהֶם Kal part. act. pl. masc., suff. 3 pers. pl. masc. from [לֹחֵץ] dec. 7 b . . חלץ

לַחֲצָיו id. pl. with suff. 3 pers. sing. masc. . . חלץ

לַחֲצָיו ו pref. ל χ noun m. sing., suff. 3 pers. sing. m. from חֲצִי dec. 6 (§ 35. r. 14); ו bef. (:) חצה

לַחֲצִיכֶם the foll. with suff. 2 pers. pl. masc. . . חלץ

לַחֲצִים Kal part. act. masc., pl. of [לֹחֵץ] dec. 7 b . חלץ

לַחֲצֵנוּ ׳ו noun masc. sing., suff. 1 pers. pl. from לַחַץ dec. 6 d . . . . . לחץ

לַחֲצֵר ׳ו pref. ל bef. (–:) constr. of the foll. . חצר

לַחֲצֵר ׳ו pref. ל for לֶה, bef. חָ for לֹה χ noun com. sing. dec. 5 c . . . . הצר

לַחֲצֵרוֹת pref. ל χ id. pl., constr. st. . . חצר

לַחַצְרוֹתֶיהָ pref. id. χ id. pl., suff. 3 pers. sing. masc. חצר

לַחֲצֹרוֹ pref. id. χ pr. name masc. . . חצר

לַחֲצַתֶּם ו Kal pret. 2 pers. pl. masc.; ו for ו conv. לחץ

לַחֹק pref. ל χ noun masc. sing. dec. 8 c (§ 37. rem. 2)

לַחֲקֹר in full for לַחְקֹר (q. v. & § 8. rem. 18) חקר

לַחֻקִּים pref. ל χ noun masc., pl. of חֹק dec. 8 c חקק

לַחֲקֹר׳ pref. id. χ noun masc. sing. dec. 6 b . חקר

לַחְקֹר׳ pref. ל χ Kal inf. constr. [for לַחֲקֹר comp. § 13. rem. 2 & 3] חקר

לַחְקְרָהּ pref. ל χ Kal inf., suff. 3 p. s. fem.; ו bef. (:) חקר

לַחֻקַּת pref. id. χ noun fem. s., constr. of חֻקָּה d. 10 חקק

לַחָרְבִּי pref. ל for לֶה χ noun fem. s. (suff. חָרְבִּי) d. 6 a חרב

לַחֲרֹב pref. id. χ noun masc. sing. . . חרב

לַחֶרֶב pref. ל for לֶה, bef. חָ for לֹה χ in pause for חֶרֶב (q. v. & § 35. rem. 2) חרב

לַחֶרְבָּ׳ pref. ל χ noun masc. sing. . . חרב

לַחָרְבָּה pref. ל for לֶה, bef. חָ for לֹה χ noun fem. sing. חרב

לַחָרְבָּה pref. ל χ noun fem. sing. dec. 12 c . חרב

לַחֳרָבוֹת pref. ל bef. (–:) χ n. fem. pl. abs. fr. חֶרֶב d. 6 a חרב

לַחֳרָבוֹת ו pref. ל for לֶה, לֹה χ noun fem. pl. abs. from חׇרְבָּה dec. 12 c חרב

לַחָרְבוֹת ׳ו pref. ל χ id. constr. st.; ו bef. (:) חרב

לַחֲרָדָה pref. ל bef. (–:) χ noun fem. sing. dec. 11 c חרד

לַחֲרַדַּת pref. ל χ id. constr. st. (§ 42. rem. 1) . חרד

לַחֲרוֹת pref. ל bef. (–:) χ Kal inf. constr. חרה

לַחַרְחַר pref. ל χ Pilpel inf. constr. (§ 6. rem. 4) חרר

לַחַרְטֻמִּים pref. ל for לֶה χ noun m., pl. of [חַרְטֹם] d. 6 c חרטם

לַחֹרִים ו pref. id. χ noun masc., pl. of חֹר dec. 1 a חרר

לַחָרִם pref. ל χ pr. name masc. . . חרם

לַחֵרֶם pref. ל f. לֶה χ noun masc. sing. dec. 6 b חרם

לַחֵרֶם pref. ל q. v. (§ 35. rem. 6) חרם

לַחֶרְמוֹ pref. id. χ id., suff. 3 pers. sing. masc. חרם

לַחֶרְמוֹן pref. id. χ pr. name of a ridge . חרם

לַחֲרָמִים pref. ל bef. (–:) χ noun masc., pl. of חֵרֶם dec. 6 b (§ 35. rem. 6) חרם

לַחֵרֶם pref. ל for לֶה χ noun masc. sing. . חרם

לַחֲרֹף pref. ל χ Piel inf. constr. . . חרף

לַחֶרְפָּה pref. id. χ noun fem. sing. d. 12 b; ו bef. (:) חרף

לַחֲרָפוֹת pref. ל bef. (–:) χ id. pl., abs. st. . חרף

לַחֲרֹשׁ ׳ו pref. id. χ Kal inf. constr. . חרש

לַחָרָשֵׁי pref. ל χ noun masc. pl. constr. from חָרָשׁ (q. v.) dec. 1 b . . . . חרש

לַחָרָשִׁים ו pref. ל for לֶה, לֹה χ id. pl., abs. st. חרש

לַחַשׁ Pi. לַחֵשׁ (§ 14. rem. 1) to whisper, mutter, only part. pl. מְלַחֲשִׁים whisperers, charmers, Ps. 58. 6. Hithp. to whisper among themselves, 2 Sa. 12. 19 ; Ps. 41. 8.

לֹחֵשׁ (charmer) pr. name m. Ne. 3. 12 ; 10. 25

---

a Jos. 2. 2, 3.	e Je. 2. 13.	i 1 Ch. 22. 2.	n Ju. 6. 9.	r 1 Ch. 28. 12.	v Job 8. 8.	z Ex. 14. 21.	d 1 Sa. 14. 15.	h Is. 43. 28.
b Is. 2. 20.	Is. 2. 20.	2 Ki. 12. 13.	1 Ki. 16. 21.	De. 26. 7.	Ps. 96. 8.	1 Ch. 19. 3.	Joel 4. 10.	2 Sa. 24. 1.	Hab. 1. 16.
Is. 30. 20.	Ezr. 3. 7.	Ju. 2. 18.	Ps. 44. 25.	2 Ki. 6. 32.	Ju. 18. 2.	Eze. 36. 4.	Pr. 26. 21.	Eze. 47. 10.
La. 3. 12.	Ju. 10. 12.	Je. 30. 20.	1 Ki. 7. 12.	Pr. 23. 30.	Je. 25. 9.	Da. 2. 2.	Job 9. 7.
Is. 49. 2.	Am. 6. 14.	Jos. 22. 7.	Ex. 38. 29.	2 Ch. 19. 10.	Je. 49. 13.	Is. 21. 4.	Ne. 3. 16.	1 Sa. 8. 12.
								Ezr. 3. 7.

לַחַשׁ masc. dec. 6 d.—I. *a whispering*, of prayer, Is. 26. 16.—II. *incantation, charm.*—III. *amulet*, Is. 3. 20.

לַחַשׁ } noun masc. sing. dec. 6 d (§ 35. rem. 2)   לחש
לַחֲשׁ־ }

וָּ לַחְשֹׁב pref. לְ)(Kal inf. constr. [for לַחְשֹׁב comp. § 13. rem. 2 & 13] .   חשב

לַחֲשֹׁב pref. לְ)(noun masc. sing.   חשב

וּ לַחשְׁבֵי pref. id.)(Kal part. act. pl. c. masc. from חשֵׁב dec. 7 b ; וּ bef. (:)   חשב

לַחֲשַׁבְיָה pref. לַ bef. (-:))(pr. name masc.   חשב

וָּ לַחֲשׁוֹף in full for לַחְשֹׁף (q. v. & § 8. rem. 18)   חשף

לַחֲשׂוֹת pref. לַ bef. (-:))(Kal inf. constr.   חשה

וְּ לַחְשֵׁךְ pref. לַ f. לְה)(noun masc. sing. dec. 6 c   חשך
לַחֲשֵׁךְ pref. לְ q. v. }

וְּ לַחֲשֵׁן pref. לַ for לְה)(noun masc. sing.   חשן

ﭏ לַחֲשֹׁף pref. לְ)(Kal inf. constr. [for לַחְשֹׁף comp. § 13. rem. 2 & 13] .   חשף

לָחֹת for לֻחֹת, n. m. with pl. f. term. fr. לוּחַ dec. 1 a   לוח

לַחְתֹּת pref. לְ)(Kal inf. constr. [for לַחְתֹּת comp. § 13. rem. 2 & 13] .   חתה

לֻחֹתַיִם noun masc. du. from לוּחַ dec. 1 a   לוח

וָּ לַחְתֹּם pref. לְ)(Kal inf. constr. [for לַחְתֹּם § 13. rem. 2 & 13]   חתם

וּ לַחֲתֹם Kh. וְלַחְתֹּם q. v.; K. וְלַחֲתָם pref. לְ)(Hiph. inf. constr.; וּ bef. (:)   חתם

לַחְתְּנוֹ pref. לַ)(Kal part. act. masc., suff. 3 pers. sing. masc. from חתֵן dec. 7 b   חתן

לָט וְּ noun masc. sing.; for וְּ see lett. ו .   לוט

לָמָא Root not used; Arab. *to adhere to the ground*.

לְטָאָה fem. a species of *poisonous lizard*, Le. 11. 30. Vulg. stellio, *a newt*.

לְטֹבָה defect. for לְטוֹבָה (q. v.)   טוב

לִטְבֹּחַ pref. לְ bef. (:))(Kal inf. constr. (§ 8. r. 18)   טבח

לַטָּבַח in pause for לַטֶּבַח (q. v.)   טבח

לַטַּבָּח pref. לְ for לְה)(noun masc. sing. dec. 1 b   טבח

לַטֶּבַח pref. id. } noun masc. sing. dec. 6 a (with
לְטֶבַח pref. לְ } suff. טִבְחָה, but comp. § 35.
לַטֶּבַח pref. id. } rem. 2)

לְטִבְחָה pref. id.)(noun fem. sing. (no pl.)   טבח

לַטַּבָּחוֹת וּ pref. id.)(n. f., pl. of [טַבָּחָה] d. 10; וּ bef. (:)   טבח

לְטָהוֹר pref. לְ q. v.

לַטָּהוֹר }
וּ לְטָהֹר } pref. לְ f. לְה)(adj. masc. sing. dec. ż a   טהר
לַטָּהֹר }

לְטָהֹר pref. לְ (see lett. לְ))(noun masc. sing. d. 6 f   טהר

לְטַהֵר pref. לְ)(Piel inf. constr. (§ 14. r. 1) dec. 7 b   טהר

לְטַהֲרָה־ pref. id.)(id., suff. 3 pers. sing. fem.   טהר

לְטַהֲרוֹ pref. id.)(id., suff. 3 pers. sing. masc.   טהר

לְטַהֲרָם pref. id.)(id., suff. 3 pers. pl. masc.   טהר

לְטַהֲרָתוֹ pref. id.)(n. f. s., suff. 3 p. s. m. fr. [טָהֳרָה] d. 10   טהר

וְּ לַטֹּב pref. לַ f. לְה)((prim. adj.) subst. masc. }
לַטּוֹב pref. לַ q. v. } sing. dec. 1 a . } טוב

לַטּוֹבָה pref. לַ f. לְה)((prim. adj.) subst. fem. sing. }
לְטוֹבָה pref. לַ q. v. dec. 10 } טוב

וּ לְטוֹבִיָּה pref. id.)(pr. name masc.; וּ bef. (:)   טוב

לַטּוֹבִים־ pref. לַ for לְה)(adj. masc., pl. of טוֹב d. 1 a   טוב

לָטוּחַ pref. לְ (see lett. לְ))(Kal inf. constr.   טוח

וּ לְטוֹטָפֹת pref. לְ)(n. f. pl. [for טַפְטָפֹת]; וּ bef. (:)   טוף

לְטוּר־ Chald., pref. id.)(noun masc. sing. dec. 1 a   טור

לְטוּשִׁם וּ pr. name of a people; וּ bef. (:)   לטש

לְטֹפֶת defect. for לְטוֹטָפֹת (q. v.).   טוף

לְטִירוֹתָם pref. לְ)(n.f. pl., suff. 3 p. pl. m. fr. [טִירָה] d. 10   טור

וּ לַטָּמֵא וְּ pref. לַ for לְה)(adj. masc. sing. dec. 5 a   טמא

לְטַמֵּא pref. לְ)(Piel inf. constr. dec. 7 b   טמא

לַטְּמֵאָה־ pref. לְ for לְה)(adj. fem. sing. dec. 10   טמא

לְטָמְאָה pref. לְ)(Kal inf. constr. (§ 8. rem. 10)   טמא

לְטַמְּאוֹ pref. id.)(Piel inf. (טִמֵּא), suff. 3 p. s. m. d. 7 b   טמא

לְטַמְמוֹן pref. לְ bef. (:))(Kal inf. constr.   טמן

לְטָמְנוֹ־ pref. לְ)(id. with suff. 3 pers. sing. masc.   טמן

לִטַּעַת־ pref. לְ (see lett. לְ))(Kal inf. constr. (§ 20. r.1)   נטע

לְטַפְּכֶם pref. לְ)(n. m. s., suff. 2 p. pl. m. fr. טַף d. 8 d   טפף

לְטַפֵּנוּ וְּ pref. id.)(id. with suff. 1 p. pl.; וּ bef. (:)   טפף

לָטֹרַח pref. לְ (see lett. לְ))(n. m. s. d. 6 c (§ 35. r.5)   טרח

לַטָּרֶף pref. לְ for לְה)(noun masc. sing. dec. 6 a (for § 35. rem. 2)   טרף

לִטְרֹף־ }
לַטְרֹף־ } pref. לְ bef. (:))(Kal inf. constr. (§ 8. r. 18)   טרף

[לָטַשׁ] *to sharpen*; metaph. *to sharpen the eye*, i. e. to cast a *sharp, penetrating* look, Job 16. 9. Pu. part. *sharpened*, Ps. 52. 4.

לְטוּשִׁם (*sharpened, sharp*) pr. name of ar Arabian people, Ge. 25. 3.

ᵃ Is. 26. 16.	ᶠ Ge. 1. 5.	ᵏ Da. 9. 24.	ᵖ Je. 12. 3.	ᵘ Eze. 39. 14.	ᵃ 1 Ch. 29. 4.	ᵍ De. 6. 8.	ᶫ Le. 20. 25.	ᵖ Nu. 32. 16.
ᵇ Mal. 3. 16.	ᵍ Hag. 2. 16.	ˡ Ex. 18. 8, 15.	ᵠ 1 Sa. 8. 13.	ᵛ Le. 13. 59.	ᵇ De. 11. 18.	ʰ 1 Ch. 6. 39.	ᵐ Le. 20. 25.	ᵠ Ezr. 8. 21.
ᶜ Is. 30. 14.	ʰ Is. 30. 14.	ᵐ 1 Sa. 9. 23.	ʳ Ke. 9. 2.	ʷ Is. 5. 20.	ᶜ Ex. 13. 16.	ⁱ Nu. 19. 17.	ⁿ Je. 13. 6.	ʳ Ps. 17. 12.
ᵈ Ec. 3. 7.	ⁱ Ese. 27. 5.	ⁿ Ese. 21. 20.	ˢ Le. 20. 25.	ˣ Ne. 2. 18.	ᵈ Da. 2. 35.	ᵏ Ec. 9. 2.	ᵒ Ec. 3. 2.	ˢ Ec. 3. 2.
ᵉ Job 28. 3.	ᵉ Da. 9. 24.	ᵒ Ese. 21. 33.	ᵗ Ex. 24. 10.	ʸ Ps. 125. 4.				ᵗ Eze. 19. 3.

לִטֵּשׁ — Kal part. act. sing. masc.   לטש

לִי — ו' pref. prep. ל with suff. 1 p. s. (§ 5, parad.)   ל

לָנוּ — Kh. לִי q. v.; K. לָנוּ id. with suff. 1 pers. pl.   ל

לְיָאֵשׁ — pref. ל X Piel inf. constr.   יאש

לְיָאשִׁיָּהוּ — pref. id. X pr. name masc.   אשה

לַיַּבָּשָׁה — pref. ל f. לְהַ ⎫ noun fem sing.   יבש

לַיַּבָּשָׁה — pref. ל q. v. ⎭   יבש

לִנְגָבִים — ו' pref. id. X Kal part. act. masc., pl. of נֶגֶב dec. 7 b; ו bef. (:)   ינב

לְיָד — pref. id. X noun com. sing. dec. 2a   יד

לְיַד — pref. id. X id. constr. (used with the suff. as a prep.)   יד

לְיָדוֹ — pref. id. X id. with suff. 3 pers. sing. masc.   יד

לְיַדּוֹת — pref. id. X Piel inf. constr.   ידה

לִידוּתוּן — pref. ל [for לְיִדּ] X pr. name masc.   ידה

לְיָדִי — pref. ל X noun com. sing., suff. 1 pers. sing. from יָד dec. 2 a   יד

לִידִידוֹ — pref. ל [for לְי , לִידִידוֹ] X noun masc. sing., suff. 3 pers. sing. masc. fr. [יָדִיד] d. 3 a   ידד

לִידִידַי — pref. id. X id. with suff. 1 pers. sing.   ידד

לִידִיתוּן — Kh. לִידִיתוּן, K. לִידוּתוּן (q. v.)   ידה

לְיֹדְעַי — pref. id. X Kal part. act. pl. masc., suff. 1 pers. sing. from יָדַע dec. 7 b   ידע

לְיָדְעֵי — Ch., pref. id. X Peal part. act. pl. c. masc. from יְדַע dec. 2 a   ידע

לִידַעְיָה — ו' pref. ל [for לְיָדַע] X pr. name masc.   ידע

לְיָדְעֶךָ — pref. ל X the following with suff. 2 pers. s. m.   ידע

לְיֹדְעָיו — pref. ל for לְהַ X Kal part. act. masc., pl. of יָדַע dec. 7 b   ידע

לִידְתָן — defect. for לִידוּתָן (q. v.)   ידה

לְיֵהוּא — pref. ל X pr. name masc., see יֵהוּא.   הוה

לִיהוֹאָחָז — pref. ל [for לְיָהוֹ] X pr. name masc.   הוה

לִיהוּד — Ch., pref. id. X pr. name of a country   ידה

לִיהוּדָה — ו' pref. id. X pr. name of a man and a tribe   ידה

לִיהוּדִים — ו' pref. ל for לְהַ X gent. masc., pl. of יְהוּדִי from יְהוּדָה   ידה

לַיהֹוָה — ו' the most sacred name of God (יהוה), with the vowels of אֲדֹנָי, whence pref. ל bef. (-:)   הוה

לֵיהֹוָה — ו' id. with the vowels of אֱלֹהִים hence with pref. לֵאלֹהִים (q. v.)   הוה

לִיהוֹשֻׁעַ, לִיהוֹרָם, ו' לִיהוֹנָתָן, לִיהוֹיָרִיב, לִיהוֹיָקִים, לִיהוֹיָדָע — pref. ל [for לְיָהוֹ] X pr. names m.   הוה

ו' לִיהוֹשָׁפָט, pref. ל [for לְיָהוֹ] X pr. names m.; ו bef. (:)   הוה

ו' לְיוֹאָשׁ, pref. ל X pr. names m.; ו bef. (:)   הוה

ו' לְיָרִיב, pref. ל X (pr. name m. (see יְהוֹיָרִיב); ו bef. (:)   הוה

לְיוֹלַדְתָּהּ — pref. id. X Kal part. act. sing. fem., suff. 3 pers. sing. fem. from יָלֶדֶת dec. 1? a   ילד

לְיוֹלַדְתּוֹ — pref. id. X id. with suff. 3 pers. sing. masc   ילד

לְיוֹם — pref. ל for לְהַ X noun m. s. d. 1, but pl. irr.

ו' לְיוֹם — pref. ל q. v. ⎭ יָמִים (§ 45); ו bef. (:)   יום

לְיוֹנָדָב — pref. id. X pr. name masc. (see יְהוֹנָדָב)   הוה

לְיוֹנָה — pref. id. X pr. name masc., see יוֹנָה.   הוה

לְיוֹנָתָן — ו' pref. id. X pr. name masc.; ו bef. (:)   הוה

לְיוֹסֵף — ו' pref. id. X pr. name masc.; ו id.   יסף

לְיוֹעֲצֵי — ו' pref. id. X Kal part. act. pl. c. masc. from יוֹעֵץ dec. 7 b; ו id.   יעץ

לְיוֹצֵא — ו' pref. ל for לְהַ X Kal part. act. s. m. d. 7 b.   יצא

לְיוֹרָם — pref. ל X pr. name masc.   הוה

לְיוֹרְשִׁים — pref. id. X Kal part. act. m., pl. of יוֹרֵשׁ d. 7 b   ירש

לְיוֹשֵׁב — pref. ל for לְהַ ⎫ Kal part. act. s. m. d. 7 b

לְיוֹשֵׁב — pref. ל q. v. ⎭   ישב

לְיוֹשְׁבֵי — pref. id. X id. pl. constr. st.   ישב

לְיוֹשְׁבֵינוּ — ו' pref. id. X id., suff. 3 pers. s. m.; ו bef. (:)   ישב

לְיוֹת — ו' noun fem. pl. of [לֹיָה] dec. 10   לוה

לְיוֹתָם — pref. ל X pr. name masc.   הוה

לְיִזְרְעֶאל — pref. id. X pr. name of a place   זרע

לְיַחַד — pref. id. X for יַחַד, adv. with and without pref.   יחד

לְיִחֶזְקִיָּהוּ, לְיִחֶזְקִיָּה — pref. ל [for לְיִחֵז], לְיִחֶזְקֵאל, pr. names masc.   חזק

לְיַחְלְאֵל — pref. ל X pr. name masc.   יחל

לְיַחְמֶנָּה — pref. id. X Piel inf. (§ 14. rem. 1), suff. 3 pers. sing. fem.   יחם

לְיַחְצְאֵל — pref. id. X pr. name masc.   חצה

לְיַיִן — pref. ל for לְהַ X noun masc. sing. dec. 6 h   יון

לְיָכִין — pref. ל X pr. name masc.   בון

לֵיל — masc. dec. 6 h, most frequently with ה parag. (לַיְלָה) (pl. לֵילוֹת) *night*; trop. for *calamity, adversity*; adv. לֵילוֹת, בַּלֵּילוֹת, בַּלַּיְלָה, לַיְלָה *by night*; הַלַּיְלָה *this night, to-night.*

לֵילֵי — Ch. m. *night*, only in the emph. st. לֵילְיָא. לִילִית fem. *screech-owl*, Is. 34. 14.

לֵיל — noun masc. sing., constr. of לַיִל dec. 6 h   ליל

לַיְלָדֶר — pref. ל for לְהַ X noun masc. sing. dec. 6 a, for יֶלֶד (§ 35. rem. 2)   ילד

וָ', וְ', לַיְלָה — noun masc. sing. (לַיִל) with parag. ה, dec. 6 h; for וָ see lett. ו   ליל

a Ge. 4. 22.   e Ps. 66. 6.   i Job 17. 3.   m Da. 2. 21.   p Ca. 6. 9.   r Pr. 12. 20.   s Je. 8. 10.   x 1 Ki.7. 29,30,36.   ᵈ Mi. 2. 11.
b 2 Sa. 21. 4.   f Je. 52. 16.   k Ps. 127. 2.   n Ex. 21. 13.   q Pr. 17. 25.   2 Ch. 15. 5.   t Ia. 28. 6.   y 1 Ch. 13. 17.   z Ex. 12. 42.
c Ec. 2. 20.   g Ex. 21. 13.   l Ps 35. 4.   o Ec. 9. 11.   Ho. 9. 5.   Zec. 8. 10.   u Je. 19. 13.   v Ge. 30. 41.   2 Ki. 4. 26.
d Ge. 1. 10.   h Zec. 3. 4.

Hebrew	Description	Root
וְּ	id. with pl. fem. term.	ליל
לֵילְיָא	Ch. noun masc. sing. emph. [of לֵילִי]	ליל
לֵילִית	noun fem. sing.	ליל
לַיָּם	pref. לְ for לְהַ‎ ⟩ noun masc. sing. dec. 8a	ים
לְיָם	pref. לְ ⟩ id. constr. st.	ים
לְיַמָּא	Ch., pref. id. ⟩ id. emph. st. dec. 5a	ים
לְיָמָּה	pref. לְ for לְהַ ⟩ id. with loc. ה	ים
לִימֵי	pref. לְ [for לְיְמֵי] ⟩ constr. of the foll.	יום
לַיָּמִים	pref. לְ for לְהַ ⟩ n. m. pl. [as if fr. יָם d. 2a]	יום
לְיָמִים	pref. q. v. see יוֹם (§ 45); וּ bef. (.:)	יום
לַיָּמִין	pref. לְ for לְהַ ⟩ noun masc. sing. dec. 3a	ימן
לְיָמִין	pref. לְ ⟩ pr. name masc.	ימן
לִימִין	pref. לְ [for לְיְ לִימִין] ⟩ noun masc. sing., constr. of יָמִין dec. 3a	ימן
לִימִינוֹ	pref. id. ⟩ id., suff. 3 pers. sing. masc.	ימן
לִימִינִי	pref. id. ⟩ id., suff. 1 pers. sing.	ימן
לִימִינְךָ	pref. id. ⟩ id., suff. 2 pers. sing. masc.	ימן
לְיָמְנָה	pref. id. ⟩ pr. name masc.	ימן
לִין	וְּ ⟩ Kal imp. sing. masc. R. לִין, see	לון
לִינוּ	וְּ ⟩ id. imp. pl. masc.	לון
לִינִי	id. imp. sing. fem.	לון
לְיַסֵּד	pref. לְ ⟩ Piel inf. constr.	יסד
לִיסוֹד / לְיַסֵּר	pref. לְ [for לִיסוֹד] ⟩ Kal inf. constr. (§ 8. rem. 18)	יסד
לְיַסְּרָה	pref. לְ ⟩ Piel inf. [יַסֵּר] with fem. term.	יסר
לְיַסְּרֵךְ	pref. id. ⟩ id. with suff. 2 p. s. m. (§ 2. r. 2)	יסר
לַעֲזַנְיָהוּ	pref. id. ⟩ pr. name masc.	עזה
לַיְעֵלִים	pref. לְ for לְהַ ⟩ noun masc., pl. of יָעֵל d. 5	יעל
לָיָּעֵף	pref. id. ⟩ adj. masc. sing. dec. 5a	יעף
לְיַעֲקֹב	pref. לְ ⟩ pr. name masc.; וּ bef. (:)	עקב
לַיַּעַר / לְיַעַר	pref. לְ f. לְהַ ⟩ / pref. q. v. ⟩ noun masc. sing. dec. 6d	יער
לְיַפֵּת	pref. id. ⟩ pr. name masc.	פתה
לִיפְתָּח	pref. id. ⟩ pr. name masc.	פתה
לְיַצְבָּא	Chald., pref. id. ⟩ Pael inf. constr.	יצב
לְיִצְהָרִי	pref. לְ for לְהַ ⟩ patronym. of יִצְהָר	צהר
לְיִצְחָק	pref. id. ⟩ pr. name masc.; וּ bef. (:)	צחק
לְיֵצֶר	pref. id. ⟩ noun masc. sing. dec. 6b	יצר
לְיֵצֶר	pref. id. ⟩ pr. name masc.	יצר
לְיֹצְרוֹ	pref. id. ⟩ Kal part. act. masc., suff. 3 pers. sing. masc. from יוֹצֵר dec. 7b	יצר
לַיִּצְרִי	pref. לְ for לְהַ ⟩ patronym. of יֵצֶר	יצר

Hebrew	Description	Root
לִיקֵדַת	Chald., pref. לְ [for לְיְ, לִיקֵדַת] ⟩ noun fem. sing., constr. of [יְקֵדָא] dec. 8a	יקד
לִיקֵהַת	pref. id. ⟩ n. f. s. constr. [of יְקָהָה or יַקָּהָה]	יקה
לְיָקִים	pref. לְ ⟩ pr. name masc.	קום
לְיָקְמְעָם	pref. id. ⟩ pr. name of a place	קמה
לִיקָר	וְּ Chald., pref. לְ [for לִיקָר] ⟩ noun masc. sing., constr. of יְקָר dec. 1b	יקר
לִירְאָה	pref. לְ ⟩ Kal inf. constr. (§ 8. r. 10); וּ bef. (.:)	ירא
לִירְאֵי	pref. id. ⟩ adj. pl. constr. masc. from יָרֵא d. 5a	ירא
לִירֵאָיו	pref. לְ [for לְיְ] ⟩ id. pl., suff. 3 pers. s. m.	ירא
לִירֵאֶיךָ	pref. id. ⟩ id. pl., suff. 2 pers. sing. masc.	ירא
לְיָרְאָם	pref. לְ ⟩ Piel inf. [יָרֵא], suff. 3 p. pl. m. d. 7b	ירא
לְיִרְאֵנִי	pref. id. ⟩ id. with suff. 1 pers. sing.	ירא
לְיִרְאָתֶךָ	pref. id. ⟩ noun fem. sing., suff. 2 pers. sing. masc. from יִרְאָה (no pl.)	ירא
לְיָרָבְעָם	pref. id. ⟩ pr. name masc.	ריב
לַיַּרְדֵּן / לְיַרְדֵּן	pref. לְ f. לְהַ ⟩ / pref. לְ q. v. ⟩ pr. name of a river	ירד
לִירוֹא	pref. לְ [for לִירוֹא] ⟩ Kal inf. constr. [for § 24. rem. 18]	ירה
לִירוּשָׁלַיִם / לִירוּשָׁלַיְמָה / לִירוּשְׁלֶם	וְּ / וְּ / Ch. pref. לְ [for לִירוּ] ⟩ pr. name of a city	ירה
לִירוֹת	pref. לְ [for לִירֹת] ⟩ Kal inf. constr.	ירה
לַיָּרֵחַ	וְּ pref. לְ for לְהַ ⟩ noun masc. sing. dec. 5a	ירח
לְיָרֵחַ	Chald., pref. לְ [for לְיְ, לִירַח] ⟩ n. m. s. d. 3a	ירח
לִירַחְמְאֵל	pref. id. ⟩ pr. name masc.	רחם
לְיָרֵחַע	pref. לְ ⟩ pr. name masc., see יָרָחַע	רוח
לִירִיחוֹ	pref. לְ [for לְיְ] ⟩ pr. name of a place	
לְיַרְכְּתֵי	pref. לְ ⟩ noun fem. du., constr. [from יָרֵךְ=יַרְכָּה m. § 39. No. 3. r. 3]; וּ bef. (:)	ירך
לַיַּרְכָתַיִם	pref. לְ f. לְהַ ⟩ id. du. abs. [fr. יָרֵךְ=יַרְכָה m.]	ירך
לִירֵמוֹת	pref. לְ [for לְיְ] ⟩ pr. name masc.	ירם
לְיִרְמְיָה / לְיִרְמְיָהוּ	pref. לְ ⟩ pr. name masc.	רמה
לְיֵרָקוֹן	pref. id. ⟩ noun masc. sing.	ירק
לִירֻשָּׁתוֹ	pref. לְ [for לִירֻשׁ] ⟩ noun fem. sing., suff. 3 pers. sing. fem. from יְרֻשָׁה dec. 10	ירש
לַיִשׁ	וְּ n. m. s., also pr. name; for וּ see lett. וּ	לוש
לְיִשְׁבָּאב	pref. לְ ⟩ pr. name masc.	ישב
לְיֹשְׁבֵי	וְּ pref. id. ⟩ constr. of the foll.; וּ bef. (:)	ישב
לַיּשְׁבִים	pref. לְ for לְהַ ⟩ Kal part. act. masc., pl. of יוֹשֵׁב dec. 7b	ישב

לִישָׁבְקָשָׁה	pref. לְ)(pr. name masc.	ישב
לִישָׁה	} pr. name of a place (לַיִשׁ) with loc. ה	לוש
לִישָׁה	}	
לִישׁוּב	pref. לְ)(pr. name masc.	שוב
לִישְׁוִי	pref. id.)(pr. name masc.	שוה
לִישׁוֹן	pref. לְ [for לְיִ, לִישׁוֹן])(Kal inf. constr.	ישן
לִישׁוּעַ	pref. לְ)(pr. name masc., see יְשׁוּעַ.	
לִישׁוּעָה	pref. לְ [for לְיִשׁוּ])(noun fem. sing. dec. 10	ישע
לִישׁוּעָתְךָ	} pref. id.)(id., suff. 2 pers. sing. masc.	ישע
לִישׁוּעָתֶ(י	}	
לִישְׂחָק	pref. לְ)(pr. name masc., see יִצְחָק under	צחק
לִישִׁי	pref. id.)(pr. name masc.	ישה
לִישְׁמָעֵאל	pref. id.)(pr. name masc.; בֶ bef. (:)	שמע
לַיִּשְׁמְעֵאלִים	pref. לְ for לְהָ)(patronym. pl. from the prec.	שמע
לְיֵשַׁע	pref.)(noun masc. sing. dec. 6 (§ 35. r. 6)	ישע
לִישׁוּעָתָה	pref. לְ [for לִישׁוּ, לְיִ])(noun fem. sing. (יְשׁוּעָה) with parag. ה	ישע
לְיִשְׂרָאֵל	בֶ pref. לְ)(pr. name of a man and a people; בֶ bef. (:)	שרה
לִישָׁרַי	בֶ pref. id.)(constr. of the foll.; בֶ id.	ישר
לִישָׁרִים	pref. לְ for לְהָ)(adj. pl. masc. from יָשָׁר dec. 4 a.	ישר
לַיְשָׁרִים	וֶ pref. לְ [f. לְיִשׁ])(	
לְיִשָּׂשכָר	pref. לְ)(pr. name masc.	שכר
לַיָתֵד	pref. לְ for לְהָ)(noun fem. sing. dec. 5 a	יתד
לַיָתוֹם	pref. id.)(noun masc. sing. dec. 3 a	יתם
לִיתוֹמָיו	pref. לְ [for לְיִ, לִיתָ])(id. pl., suff. 3 p. s. m.	יתם
לַיֶתֶר	בֶ pref. לְ)(noun masc. sing. (suff. יִתְרוֹ) dec. 6 a; בֶ bef. (:)	יתר
לַיֶתֶר	pref. id.)(pr. name masc.	יתר
לָךְ	בֶ pref. prep. לְ with suff. 2 p. s. f. (§ 5, parad.)	ל
לָךְ	בֶ id. with suff. 2 pers. sing. m.; בֶ bef. (:) בֶ	ל
לָךְ	בֶ בֶ in pause	
לֵךְ	בֶ בֶ } Kal imp. sing. masc. (§ 20. rem. 3); for בֶ see lett. בֶ }	ילך
לֵךְ	}	
לֵךְ		
לִכְבוֹד	בֶ pref. לְ)(noun masc. sing. d. 3 a; בֶ bef. (:)	כבד
לִכְבוֹדִי	בֶ pref. לְ bef. (:))(id. with suff. 1 pers. sing.	כבד
לִכְבשׁ	in full for לִכְבֹּשׁ (q. v. & § 8. rem. 18)	כבש
לְכַבּוֹת	pref. לְ)(Piel inf. constr.	כבה
לַכֶּבֶשׂ	pref. לְ for לְהָ)(noun masc. sing. dec. 6 a	כבש
לִכְבֹּשׁ	pref. לְ bef. (:))(Kal inf. constr.	כבש
לִכְבָשִׂים	בֶ pref. לְ for לְהָ)(noun m., pl. of כֶּבֶשׂ d. 6 a	כבש

וְלָכַד	m] I. to take, catch.—II. to intercept, Ju. 7. 24.—III. to take, choose, by lot, Jos. 7. 17. Niph. to be taken, caught. Hithp. to take or catch hold on each other, to hang together, Job 38. 30; 41. 9.	
לֶכֶד	masc. capture, Pr. 3. 26.	
מַלְכֹּדֶת	fem. dec. 13 c, snare, trap, Job 18. 10.	
לָכַד	Kal pret. 3 pers. sing. masc. for לָכַד (§ 8. r. 7)	לכד
לֹכֵד	id. part. act. sing. masc.	לכד
לָכְדָהּ	בֶ id. imp. sing. masc., suff. 3 pers. sing. fem.	לכד
לְכָדָהּ	בֶ id. pret. 3 pers. sing. masc., suff. 3 pers. sing. fem.; בֶ for בֶ conv.	לכד
לְכָדָהּ	בֶ id. pret. 3 p. pl. [לָכְדוּ], suff. 3 p. s. f.; בֶ id.	לכד
לָכְדוּ	בֶ id. imp. pl. masc.	לכד
לְכָדוּהָ	id. pret. 3 pers. pl., suff. 3 pers. sing. fem.; בֶ for בֶ conv.	לכד
לְכָדְנוּ	id. pret. 1 pers. pl. [for לָכַדְנוּ § 8. rem. 7]	לכד
לָכַדְתִּי	id. pret. 1 pers. sing.	לכד
לָכָה	pr. name of a place	לך
לְכָה	בֶ } Kal imp. sing. masc. with parag. ה (§ 20. rem. 3); בֶ bef. (:)	ילך
לְכָה	בֶ }	
לְכָה	בֶ pref. prep. לְ with suff. 2 pers. sing. masc. (§ 5. rem. 3); בֶ id.	ל
לַכֹּהֵן	pref. לְ for לְהָ)(noun masc. sing. dec. 7 b	כהן
לְכַהֵן	pref. לְ)(Piel inf. constr. (§ 14. rem. 1)	כהן
לְכֹהֵן	בֶ pref. id.)(noun masc. sing. d. 7 b; בֶ bef. (:)	כהן
לְכַהֲנוֹ	pref. id.)(Piel inf. [כַּהֵן § 14. rem. 1], suff. 3 pers. masc. dec. 7 b	כהן
לְכַהֲנֶיהָ	pref. id.)(the foll. with suff. 3 pers. sing. fem.	כהן
לַכֹּהֲנִים	בֶ pref. לְ for לְהָ)(noun masc., pl. of כֹּהֵן d. 7 b	כהן
לִכְהֻנֵּינוּ	בֶ pref. לְ)(id. with suff. 1 pers. pl.; בֶ bef. (:)	כהן
לִכְהֻנַּת	pref. לְ bef. (:))(n. f. s., constr. of כְּהֻנָּה d. 10	כהן
לְכוּ	בֶ } Kal imp. pl. masc.; בֶ bef. (:), בֶ bef. pause	ילך
לְכוּ	בֶ }	
לָכוֹד	בֶ } Kal inf. abs.	לכד
לִכְוֹכְבֵי	pref. לְ)(constr. of the foll.	כבב
לְכוֹכָבִים	pref. לְ for לְהָ)(noun masc., pl. of כּוֹכָב dec. 2 b [for כַּבְכָּב]	כבב
לְכֹל	pref. לְ)(Kh. לְכֹל, K. לְכָל; noun masc. sing. [כֹּל] dec. 8 c (§ 37. rem. 2)	כלל
לְכוֹן	Chald., pref. prep. לְ with suff. 2 pers. pl. m.	ל
לְכוֹרֵשׁ	pref. לְ)(pr. name masc.	כרש
לַכּוּשִׁי	pref. לְ for לְהָ)(gent. noun from כּוּשׁ	כוש
לְכַח	pref. לְ)(noun masc. sing. dec. 1 a	כוח

a Ec. 5. 11.   b Ps. 97. 11.   c Est. 7. 8.   d Am. 3. 4.   e Ju. 7. 24.   f 1 Sa. 23. 27.   g Ex. 28. 1, 3, 4.   h Ex. 40. 15.   i Je. 33. 8.
d Ps. 119. 123.   f Ju. 5. 26.   g Ca. 8. 7.   h Job 5. 13.   Is. 3. 6.   Je. 1. 18.   Am. 3. 5.   Je. 37. 8.
Hab. 3. 13.   Ps. 109. 12.   2 Ch. 28. 10.   2 Sa. 12. 28.   De. 2. 35.   Ge. 27. 37;   Ne. 9. 22.   Is. 14. 12.   Job 9. 12.
Ps. 80. 3.   Is. 43. 7.   Je. 37. 8.   2 Sa. 12. 27.   2 Sa. 18. 22.   Ps. 125. 4.   Ps. 147. 1.

לְכִי	Kh. לְכִי q. v., K. לַךְ (q. v.) . . .	ל
לְכִי		
לְכִי }	Kal imp. sing. fem.; ᵈ bef. (:) .	ילך
לְכִידֹד•	pref. ל for לְהַ)(noun masc. sing. .	כדר
לַכִּילְיָ¹	ᵈ pref. ל)(noun m. sing. [for וְנָכִילְי] ᵈ bef. (:)	נכל
לַכִּיר•	pref. ל for לְהַ)(noun masc. sing. dec. 1 b	כור
לָכִישׁ	pr. name of a fortified city in the tribe of Judah.	
לָכִישָׁה	id. with parag. ה.	
לִכְבָּרִים	pref. ל)(n. f., pl. of כְּבָר d. 2 b [for כְּרְכָּר	כבר
לְכָל	pref. ל for לְהַ)(	
לְכָל	} noun masc. sing. dec. 8 c	
לְכָל ᵈ }	pref. ל q. v. (§ 37. rem. 2); ᵈ bef. (:)	כלל
לְכַלֵּא	pref.id.)(Piel inf.constr. for לְכַלֵּה (§ 24. r. 19)	כלה
לְכַלָּא	Chald., pref. id.)(noun masc. emph. by Syriasm [for כַּלָּא] from כֹּל dec. 5c .	כלל
לְכָלֵב	pref. ל for לְהַ)(n. m. s. (pl. c. כָּלְבֵי) d. 6 a	כלב
לְכָלֵב	ᵈ pref. ל)(pr. name masc.; ᵈ bef. (:)	כלב
לִכְלָבֵי	pref. id.)(noun masc. s. (pl. c. כָּלְבֵי) d. 6 a	כלב
לְכַלָּה	pref. id.)(noun fem. sing. .	כלה
לְכַלֵּה	pref. id.)(Piel inf. constr.	כלה
לְכַלּוֹתָנָה³	pref. id.)(noun masc. sing., suff. 3 pers. pl. fem. (§ 3. rem. 5) from כֹּל dec. 8 c	כלל
לִכְלוֹא⁴	pref. ל bef. (:))(Kal inf. constr. (§ 8. r. 18)	כלא
לִכְלוֹת	pref. ל)(Piel inf. constr.	כלה
לִכְלוֹת⁵	pref. ל bef. (:))(Kal inf. constr. .	כלה
לְכִלְיוֹן	pref. ל)(pr. name masc.	כלה
לְכִלְכֵּל⁶	pref. id.)(Pilp. (§ 6. No. 4) inf. constr. dec. 7 b; ᵈ bef. (:) . . .	כול
לְכַלְכְּלֶךָ, לְכַלְכְּלֶךָ }	pref. id.)(id. with suff. 2 pers. sing. masc.	כול
לְכַלְכֶם	pref. id.)(n. m. s., suff. 2 p. pl. m. fr. כֹּל d. 8 c	כלל
לְכַלָּם	pref. id.)(id., suff. 3 pers. pl. masc.	כלל
לְכַלִּמָּה	pref. ל bef. (:))(noun fem. sing. dec. 10	כלם
לְכַלָּנוּ	pref. ל n. m. s., suff. 1 p. pl. from כֹּל d. 8 c	כלל
לְכַלָּתָהּ⁷	pref. id.)(n. f. s., suff. 3 p. s. f. fr. כַּלָּה d. 10	כלה
לְכַלּוֹתָם⁸	pref. id.)(Piel inf. (כַּלּוֹת), suff. 3 pers. pl. masc. dec. 1 b	כלה
לְכֶם	ᵈ pref. prep. ל with suff. 2 p. pl. m. (§ 5, parad.)	ל
לְכֹם⁹	ᵈ Chald. id. with suff. 2 pers. pl. masc.	ל
לִכְמוֹשׁ¹⁰	ᵈ pref. ל bef.(:))(pr. name of an idol, see כְּמוֹשׁ	
לְכֵן¹¹	ᵈ pref. ל (see lett. ל))(adv. .	כון
לֵכְנָה	Kal imp. pl. f., for לֵכְנָה (comp. § 8. r. 16)	ילך
לָכֶנָה	pref. prep. ל with suff. 2 pers. pl. fem. (§ 5, parad. & rem ᵍ)	ל
לֵכְנָה	Kal imp. pl. fem.	ילך
לִכְנוֹם¹²	וְ pref. ל bef. (:))(Kal inf. constr. (§ 8. r. 18)	כנם
לְכֶם	pref. ל)(noun masc., pl. of כֵּן dec. 8 b .	כן
לַכְּנַעֲנִי	pref. ל for לְהַ)(gent. noun from כְּנַעַן	כנע
לַכְּנַעֲנִי¹³	pref. id.)(noun masc. sing., pl. כְּנַעֲנִים .	כנע
לְכָנָף¹⁴	pref. ל bef. (:))(noun f. s. d. 4 a (§ 33. r. 1)	כנף
לַכִּסֵּא	pref. ל f. לְהַ)(	
לַכִּסֵּא	} noun masc. sing. dec. 7 b .	כסא
לְכִסְאוֹ¹⁵	ᵈ pref. id.)(id., suff. 3 pers. s. m.; ᵈ bef. (:)	כסא
לַכִּסֶּה¹⁶	for לַכִּסֵּא (q. v.)	כסא
לְכַסּוֹת	pref. ל)(Piel inf. constr. dec. 1 b	כסה
לַכְּסִיל	pref. ל bef. (:))(noun masc. sing. dec. 1 a	כסל
לְכִסְלָה	pref. ל)(noun fem. sing. (no pl.)	כסל
לַכֶּסֶף	וְ pref. ל f. לְהַ)(	
לְכֶסֶף	} noun masc. sing. dec. 6 a	כסף
לְכַסְפִּי¹⁷	ᵈ pref. id.)(id., suff. 1 pers. sing.; ᵈ bef.	כסף
לְכַסְפָּם¹⁸	pref. id.)(id., suff. 3 pers. pl. masc.	כסף
לְכַסּוֹת¹⁹	pref. id.)(Piel inf. constr. dec. 1 b	כסה
לְכַסֹּתוֹ	pref. id.)(id., suff. 3 pers. sing. masc.	כסה
לִכְעֹם²⁰	pref. ל bef. (:))(Kal inf. constr. (§ 8. r. 18)	כעם
לַכַּף	pref. ל)(noun fem. sing. dec. 8 d	כפף
לִכְפוֹר²¹	pref. ל bef. (:))(noun masc. sing. dec. 1 a	כפר
לִכְפוֹרֵי²²	וְ pref. id.)(id. pl., constr. st.	כפר
לְכָפֶן	ᵈ pref. ל)(noun masc. sing.; ᵈ bef. (:)	כפן
לְכַפֵּר²³	pref. id.)(Piel inf. constr. dec. 7 b; ᵈ id.	כפר
לַכְּפִירִים²⁴	pref. ל for לְהַ)(noun m., pl. of כְּפִיר dec. 1 a	כפר
לְכַפָּתָה²⁵	Chald., pref. ל)(Pael inf. constr. (§ 47. r. 5)	כפת
לַכְּרֻבִּים²⁶	defect. for לַכְּרוּבִים (q. v.) .	כרב
לְכָרוּב	pref. ל f. לְהַ)(	
לִכְרוּב	} noun masc. sing. dec. 1 a	כרב
לַכְּרוּבִים²⁷	pref. ל for לְהַ)(id. pl., abs. st. .	כרב
לִכְרוֹת	in full for לִכְרֹת (q. v. & § 8. rem. 18)	כרת
לְכָרִי	pref. ל for לְהַ)(noun masc. either sing. or pl. comp. הַכָּרִי	כור
לְכַרְמוֹ²⁸	pref. id.)(noun masc. sing., suff. 3 pers. sing. masc. from כֶּרֶם dec. 6 a	כרם
לְכַרְמִי	pref. id.)(pr. name masc. .	כרם
לְכַרְמִי²⁹	pref. id.)(noun masc. sing., suff. 1 pers. sing. from כֶּרֶם dec. 6 a	כרם
לִכְרָמִים	pref. id.)(noun masc., pl. of [כֶּרֶם] dec. 7 b	כרם

---

a Job 15. 24.   f Ex. 22. 30.   l 1 Ki. 4. 7.   q Ru. 2. 20.   u Eze. 13. 18.   z 2 Ch. 3. 11, 12.   e Ho. 9. 6.   i 1 Ch. 28. 17.   o Eze. 41. 18.
b Is. 32. 5.   g Ec. 9. 4.   m Ru. 4. 15.   r Ex. 32. 12.   v 1 Ki. 2. 33.   Nu. 4. 15.   Eze. 10. 7.
c 1 Ki. 7. 30.   h 1 Ki. 1. 37.   n 1 Ki. 17. 9.   s Ezr. 5. 3, 9;   w Ec. 2. 26.   Na. 2. 12.   1 Ki. 11. 4.
d Da. 9. 24.   i Ec. 8. 8.   1 Ki. 17. 4.   7. 24.   x Ec. 7. 9.   Da. 3. 20.   Is. 5. 1.
e Da. 4. 9, 18.   k 2 Ch. 36. 22, etc.   1 Sa. 22. 7.   Ru. 1. 12.   r. 31. 24.   1 Ki. 20. 7.   1 Ch. 28. 17.   Eze. 10. 7, 8.   Is. 5. 4, 1.

לִכְרָמִים	pref. לְ for לָה)(noun m., pl. of כֶּרֶם d. 6a	כרם
לְכַרְמְךָ	pref. לְ)(id. sing., suff. 2 pers. sing. masc.	כרם
לַכַּרְמֶל	pref. לְ for לָה)(pr. name of a place	כרם
לִכְרֹת	pref. לְ bef. ⟨:⟩)(Kal inf. constr. (§ 8. rem. 18)	כרת
לְכֹרְתֵי	pref. לְ)(Kal part. act. pl. c. fr. כֹּרֵת d. 7 b	כרת
לַכַּשְׂדִּים	pref. לְ for לָה)(gent. noun, pl. of כַּשְׂדִּי	כשׂד
לְכַשְׂדָּיֵא	Ch., pref. id.)(Kh. כַּשְׂדָּיֵא, K. כַּשְׂדָּאֵי gent. noun pl. emph. fr. כַּשְׂדַּי dec. 7 (§ 63)	כשׂד
לֶכֶת לֶכֶת	Kal inf. constr. (suff. לֶכְתּוֹ) dec. 13a (§ 44. rem. 3)	ילך
לִכְתֹּב	pref. לְ bef. ⟨:⟩)(Kal inf. constr.	כתב
לְכָתּוֹ	Kal inf. (לֶכֶת), suff. 3 pers. sing. m. d. 13 (§ 44. rem. 3)	ילך
לֶכְתִּי	id., suff. 1 pers. sing.	ילך
לֶכְתְּךָ	id., suff. 2 pers. sing. masc.	ילך
לֶכְתֵּךְ	id., suff. 2 pers. sing. fem.	ילך
לֶכְתָּם	id., suff. 3 pers. pl. masc.	ילך
לַכֶּתֶם	pref. לְ for לָה)(noun masc. sing.	כתם
לַכָּתֵף	pref. id.)(noun fem. sing. dec. 5 b	כתף
לְכֶתֶף	pref. לְ)(id. constr. st.	כתף
לַכְּתָרֹת לַכְּתָרֹת	pref. לְ for לָה)(noun fem. pl. & sing. (§ 44. rem. 5)	כתר
לֹא	pref. לְ)(adv. (in 2 Ch. 15. 3, it forms a prep. with the pref.); ו bef. ⟨:⟩	לא
לְלֵאָה	pref. id.)(pr. name fem.; ו id.	לאה
לְלָאֹת	noun pl. abs. fem. [fr. לוּלָי § 35. r. 15 note]	לול
לֻלָאֹת	id. pl., constr. st.	לול
לִלְבֹאתָיו	pref. לְ)(noun pl. fem. [לְבָאוֹת], suff. 3 pers. sing. masc. [fr. לְבִי § 35. rem. 15]	לבא
לַלְּבָב	pref. לְ for לָה)(noun masc. sing. dec. 4 b	לבב
לִלְבָבָם	pref. לְ bef. ⟨:⟩)(id., suff. 3 pers. pl. masc.	לבב
לְלִבְנָה	pref. id.)(pr. name of a city	לבן
לִלְבוּשֶׁךָ	pref. id.)(noun masc. sing., suff. 2 pers. sing. masc. [for לִלְבוּשְׁךָ fr. לְבוּשׁ dec. 1a	לבשׁ
לִלְבִיא	pref. לְ)(noun masc. sing.	לבא
לְלָבָן	pref. id.)(pr. name masc.; ו bef. ⟨:⟩	לבן
לְלָבָן	pref. id.)(adj. masc. sing. dec. 4 a	לבן
וְלַלְבֵּן	ו pref. לְ, contr. [for לְהַלְבֵּן] Hiph. inf. constr. (§ 11. rem. 2 & 3)	לבן
לִלְבֹּן	pref. לְ bef. ⟨:⟩)(Kal inf. constr.	לבן
לְלִבְנָה	pref. לְ)(pr. name of a place	לבן

לִלְבֹּשׁ	pref. לְ bef. ⟨:⟩)(Kal inf. constr.	לבשׁ
לְלֵדָה	pref. לְ)(Kal inf. with fem. term. (§ 20. r. 3)	ילד
לָלֶדֶת	pref. לְ (see lett. לְ))(id. inf. constr. d. 13a	ילד
לְלִדְתִּי	pref. לְ)(id. with suff. 1 pers. sing.	ילד
לְלֶהָבָה	pref. id.)(noun fem. sing. dec. 11 a	להב
לְלוֹא	in full for לְלֹא (q. v.)	לא
לְלוֹט	pref. לְ)(pr. name masc.	לוט
לַלֵּוִי	pref. לְ for לָה)(pr. name masc., or gent.	לוה
לְלֵוִי	ו pref. לְ q. v.)(noun [for לֵוִי]	לוה
וְלַלְוִיִּם	ו pref. לְ for לָה)(pl. of the preceding	לוה
לָלוּן	pref. לְ (see lett. לְ))(Kal inf. constr.	לון
לִלְחוּם	pref. לְ bef. ⟨:⟩)(Kal inf. constr.	לחם
לַלֶּחֶם וְלַלֶּחֶם לַלָּחֶם וְלַלָּחֶם	}pref. לְ f. לָה){ }pref. לְ q. v){ noun com. s. d. 6a (§ 35. rem. 1); ו bef. ⟨:⟩	לחם
לְלַחְמְךָ	pref. id.)(io. with suff. 2 pers. sing. masc.	לחם
לִלְטֹשׁ	pref. לְ bef. ⟨:⟩)(Kal inf. constr. (§ 8. r. 18)	לטשׁ
לְלַיְלָה	pref. לְ)(noun masc. sing. (לַיִל) with parag. ה dec. 6 h	ליל
לָלִין	pref. לָ (see lett. לְ))(Kal inf. constr. R. לִין, see	לון
לְלָכְדָהּ	pref. לְ)(Kal inf., suff. 3 pers. sing. fem.	לכד
לְלָכְדֵנִי	pref. id.)(id. with suff. 1 pers. sing.	לכד
לְלָכִישׁ	pref. id.)(pr. name of a place, see לָכִישׁ	
לָלֶכֶת וְלָלֶכֶת	}pref. לָ (see lett. לְ))(Kal inf. constr. dec. 13 (§ 44. rem. 3)	ילך
לְלַמֵּד	pref. לְ)(Piel inf. constr. d. 7 b; ו bef. ⟨:⟩	למד
לְלַמְּדָם	pref. id.)(id., suff. 3 pers. pl. masc.; ו id.	למד
לְלַעַג	pref. id.)(noun masc. sing. dec. 6 d; ו id.	לעג
לְלַעְדָּן	pref. id.)(pr. name masc.	לעד
לְלַעֲנָה	pref. id.)(noun fem. sing.	לען
לַלֵּצִים	pref. לְ for לָה)(Kal part. act. masc., pl. of לִיץ (§ 21. rem. 2) dec. 1a	לוץ
לְלַקֵּט	pref. לְ)(Piel inf. constr.	לקט
לִלְקֹט	ו pref. לְ bef. ⟨:⟩)(Kal inf. constr.	לקט
לְלִשְׁכַּת	pref. לְ)(noun f. s., constr. of לִשְׁכָּה d. 12 b	לשׁך
לְלֶשֶׁם	pref. id.)(pr. name of a place	לשׁם
לִלְשׁוֹנוֹ	pref. לְ bef. ⟨:⟩)(noun com. sing., suff. 3 pers. sing. masc. from לָשׁוֹן dec. 3 a	לשׁן
לִלְשׁוֹנֵנוּ	pref. id.)(id., suff. 1 pers. pl.	לשׁן
לִלְשֹׁנֹתָם	pref. id.)(id. pl., suff. 3 pers. pl. masc.	לשׁן

ᵃ Ca. 7. 13.	ᶠ De. 2. 7.	ᵏ Eze. 40. 41.	ᵖ Na. 2. 13.	ᵘ Da. 11. 35.
ᵇ Ex. 23. 11.	ᵍ Je. 2. 2.	ˡ 1 Ki. 7. 17.	ᑫ 1 Sa. 16. 7.	ᵛ Ex. 5. 7, 14.
ᶜ 2 Ch. 2. 9.	ʰ 2 Sa. 17. 21.	ᵐ 1 Ki. 7. 17.	ʳ Ho. 7. 2.	ʷ 1 Ki. 3. 18
ᵈ 1 Ki. 16. 31.	ⁱ Job 31. 24.	18, 31.	ˢ Job 38. 39.	ˣ Is. 10. 17.
ᵉ 1 Ki. 2. 8.	ʲ Ex. 27. 14.	ⁿ 2 Ch. 15. 3.	ᵗ Le. 13. 16.	ʸ Is. 65. 1.

ᶻ Pr. 23. 1.	ᵍ Pr. 27. 27.	ᵐ Je. 18. 22.	ʳ Ca. 6. 2.
ᵃ Ge. 41. 55.	ʰ 1 Sa. 13. 20.	ⁿ Ec. 1. 7.	ˢ Je. 35. 4.
ᵇ Je. 42. 14.	ⁱ Ps. 19. 3.	ᵒ Ezr. 7. 10.	ᵗ Ge. 10. 15.
ᶜ Eze. 4. 9.	ʲ Ge. 24. 23.	ᵖ Ju. 3. 2.	ᵘ Ps. 12. 5.
ᵈ 1 Ch. 23. 29.	ˡ Je. 32. 24.	ᑫ Da. 1. 4.	ᵛ Ge. 10. 20, 11.

לְלֶת[a]	pref. לְ (see lett. ל))(Kal inf. constr., contr. from לֶדֶת (§ 25. rem.) . . .	ילד
לְמָא	Chald., pron. i. q. Heb. מָה . . .	מה
לְמֵאֹד[b]	pref. לְ bef. (ְ))(noun masc. sing. dec. 1 a	אוד
לְמֵאָדָם	preff. לְ, & מֶ for מִ)(noun masc. sing. .	אדם
לַמֵּאָה[c]	pref. לְ f. לָה)){ noun fem. sing. dec. 11 b .	מאה
לְמֵאָה	pref. לְ q. v.) }	
לְמְאַהֲבַי[d]	pref. לְ for לָה)(Piel (§ 14. rem. 1) part. pl., suff. 1 pers. sing. from [מָאַהַב] dec. 7 b	אהב
לְמֵאוּמָה	pref. לְ bef. (ְ))(see מְאוּמָה under	מה
לַמֵּאוֹר[e]	pref. לְ f. לָה)){ noun masc. sing. dec. 3 a	אור
לְמֵאוֹר	pref. לְ q. v.) }	
לְמְאוֹר[f]	pref. לְ bef. (ְ))(id., constr. st. .	אור
לִמְאוֹרֹת[g]	pref. id.)(id., pl. with fem. term. .	אור
לִמְאוֹת	pref. לְ)(noun f. pl. abs. from מֵאָה d. 11 b	מאה
לִמְאֹת[h]	Kh. לִמֵאוֹת q. v., K. לְמַאת (q. v.) .	מאה
לַמְאַחֲרִים[i]	pref. לְ for לָה)(Piel (§ 14. rem. 1) part. pl. masc. from [מְאַחֵר] dec. 7 b .	אחר
לְמֵאִישׁ[k]	preff. לְ, & מֵ f. מִ)(n. m. s. d. 1 a (comp. §45)	איש
לְמַאֲכָל	pref. לְ)(noun masc. sing. dec. 2 b	אכל
לְמֵאמַר[l]	Chald., pref. id.)(Peal inf. constr. (§ 53) .	אמר
לְמֵאנַי[m]	Chald., pref. id.)(n. m. pl. constr. fr. [מָאן] d. 1 a	מאן
לְמֵאנָיָא[n]	Chald., pref. id.)(id. pl., emph. st.; וּ bef. (ְ)	מאן
לַמְאֹר[o]	defect. for לַמָּאוֹר (q. v.) . . .	אור
לִמְאַת[p]	pref. לְ bef. (ְ))(n. f., constr. of מֵאָה d. 11 b	מאה
לִמְבוֹא	pref. id.)(noun m. s., constr. of מָבוֹא d. 3 a	בוא
לַמַּבּוּל[q]	pref. לְ f. לָה) }{ noun masc. sing. dec. 1 b	יבל
לְמַבּוּל[r]	pref. לְ q. v.) }	
לְמַבּוּעֵי[s]	pref. id.)(noun m. pl. constr. fr. [מַבּוּעַ] d. 1 b	נבע
לְמִבְטָח	pref. id.)(noun m. s. d. 2 & 8 (§ 37. r. 5)	בטח
לַמֵּבִין[t]	pref. לְ for לָה)(Hiph. part. sing. m. d. 3 b	בין
לְמִבֵּית[u]	preff. לְ & מִ)(noun masc. sing., constr. of בַּיִת d. 6 h, pl. irr. בָּתִּים (§ 45); וּ bef. (ְ)	בות
לְמִבֶּן	preff. id.)(n. m. s., constr. of בֶּן irr. (§ 45)	בנה
לְמִבְנָא	Chald., pref. לְ)(Peal inf. . .	בנה
לְמִבְנְיָה	Chald., pref. id.)(id. emph. st. dec. 6 a	בנה
לְמִבְעֵא[v]	Chald., pref. id.)(Peal inf. . .	בעה
לְמִבְצָרַי	pref. id.)(noun m. pl. constr. fr. מִבְצָר d. 2 b	בצר
לְמִבְּרֵאשֹׁנָה[w]	pref. id.)(compounded of מָה (q. v.) & בָּרִאשֹׁנָה (q. v.) .	ראש
לְמִגְדּוֹל[x]	preff. לְ & מִ)(adj. masc. sing. dec. 3 a	נדל
לְמִגְדַּל	pref. לְ)(noun m. s., constr. of מִגְדָּל d. 2 b	נדל

לְמִנְדָּנוֹת[y]	pref. לְ)(n. f. pl. abs. [fr. [מִגְדָּנָה]; וּ bef. (ְ)	מנד
לִמְנוֹר[z]	pref. id.)(noun masc. s. d. 3 a (§ 32. r. 5)	נור
לְמַגִּידִי[a]	pref. id.)(Hiph. part. pl. constr. m. fr. מַגִּיד d. 1 b	נגד
לְמִנְלָא	Chald., pref. id.)(Peal inf. . .	גלה
לְמָגִנִּים[b]	pref. id.)(noun masc., pl. of מָגֵן dec. 8 b (§ 37. No. 3); וּ bef. (ְ) .	מנן
לְמַגֵּפָה[c]	pref. id.)(noun fem. sing. dec. 10 .	נגף
לְמִגְרָשׁ[d]	pref. id.)(noun masc. s. d. 2 b; וּ bef. (ְ)	נרש

לָמַד—fut. יִלְמַד.—I. *to accustom oneself*, with אֶל Je. 10. 2.—II. *to learn*, with לְ and an inf.; with acc. Pi.—I. *to accustom*, Je.9.4.—II. *to teach*, with acc. of the pers.; with double acc.; with acc. of the thing and לְ of the pers.; with בְּ of the pers.; and with מִן Ps. 94. 12. Pu. *to be accustomed, trained, taught.*

לָמֵד, לִמּוּד adj. masc. dec. 1 b.—I. *accustomed*, Je. 2. 24.—II. *trained, taught*; hence, *a disciple.*

מַלְמָד masc. dec. 2 b, *ox-goad*, Ju. 3. 31.

תַּלְמִיד masc. *learner, disciple*, 1 Ch. 25. 8.

לָמֹד[e]	Kal inf. abs.	למד
לָמֹד[f]	pref. לְ (see lett. ל))(Kal inf. constr. .	מדד
לַמֵּד	! Piel inf. constr. dec. 7 b	למד
לִמַּד[g]	id. pret. 3 pers. sing. masc. (§ 10. rem. 1) .	למד
לֻמַּד[h]	Pual pret. 3 p. s. m. [for לָמַּד] comp. § 8. r.7]	למד
לִמֻּד[i]	[defect. for לִמּוּד] adj. masc. sing. dec. 1 b	למד
לַמְּדַבֵּר[k]	pref. לְ f. לָה) }{ noun masc. sing. dec. 2 b .	דבר
לְמְדַבֵּר[l]	pref. לְ q. v.) }	
לְמִדְבַּר	pref. id.)(id. constr. st. . .	דבר
לַמְּדֵהוּ[m]	! Piel imp. sing. m. [לַמֵּד], suff. 3 pers. s. f.	למד
לָמְדוּ[n]	י')(Kal pret. 3 pers. pl. .	למד
לִמְדוּ[o]	id. imp. pl. masc. . .	למד
לִמְּדוּ	Piel pret. 3 pers. pl. . .	למד
לִמְּדוּם[p]	id. with suff. 3 pers. pl. masc.	למד
לַמַּדְחֵפֹת[q]	pref. לְ)(noun fem. pl. [of מַדְחֵפָה]	דחף
לְמָדַי[r]	pref. id.)(pr. name of a country, see מָדַי.	
לְמַדַּי[s]	pref. id.)(for מַה־דַּי, comp. דַּי & מָה.	
לְמֻדַי[t]	defect. for לִמּוּדַי (q. v.) . .	למד
לְמֻדָּיו[u]	pref. id.)(noun masc. pl., suff. 3 pers. sing. masc. from מַד dec. 8 d & c, &c.	מדד
לַמְּדִינוֹת[v]	pref. לְ for לָה)(n. f., pl. of מְדִינָה d. 10. R. דִּין see ו ן	
לְמָדָן	preff. לְ & מָ)(pr. name of a tribe .	דון

לַמְרֵנָה וְ	Piel imp. pl. fem. . . .	למד
לַמְרֵב וְ	id. imp. sing. masc. [לְמַד], suff. 1 pers. s.	למד
לְמִדָּה	pref. לְ ✗ noun fem. s., constr. of מָדָה d. 10	מרד
לָמַדְתִּי	Kal pret. 1 pers. sing. . .	למד
לִמַּדְתִּי	Piel pret. 1 pers. sing. .	למד
	id.pret.2 p.s.f.Kh. לְמַדְתְּ, K. לְמַדְתָּ (§ 8. r.5)	למד
לִמַּדְתֶּם וְ	id. pret. 2 pers. pl. masc.	למד
לְמַדְתֶּם וְ	Kal pret. 2 pers. pl. m. ; וְ bef. (:) for וְ conv.	למד
לִמַּדְתַּנִי	id. pret. 2 pers. sing. masc., suff. 1 pers. sing.	למד
לָמָה	&, (כַּמָּה, בַּמָּה comp. לְהָמָּה, לָמָּה, לָמָה (for וְ & לָמָה וְ (chiefly bef. א, ה, ע, and the name יְהֹוָה) & לָמָה וְ (three times) adv. interr., from the pref. לְ & מָה or מֶה q. v.	מה
לָמֶה	Chald., adv. interr., from the pref. לְ & מָה q. v.	מה
לְמֹהֻמָן	pref. לְ bef. (:) ✗ pr. name masc.	אמן
לְמֶהֱוֵא	Chald., pref. id. ✗ Peal inf. .	הוך
לְמַהֲלֻמּוֹת	pref. לְ ✗ noun fem., pl. of [מַהֲלֻמָּה] dec. 10	הלם
לְמַהֵר	pref. id. ✗ Piel inf. constr. (§ 14. rem. 1)	מהר
לָמוֹ	pref. prep. לְ with suff. 3 pers. pl. or sing. masc. (§ 5. rem. 2)	ל
לְמוֹ	pref. לְ ✗ parag. syl. forming one word with the pref. prepp. בְּ, כְּ, לְ without affecting the signification, see	מו
	pref. id. ✗ pr. name of a country, see מוֹאָב ; וְ bef. (:)	
לְמוֹאֵל	pref. id. ✗ prep., K. מוֹל (q. v.) לְמוֹאֵל, לְמוֹאֵל (to God, sc. dedicated ; for לְאֵל, comp. לְמוֹ) title of king Solomon, Pr. 31. 1, 4.	מול
לְמָגֵן	pref. לְ, (see lett. לְ) ✗ Kal inf. constr.	מגן
לִמּוּדֵי	adj. pl. constr. masc. from [לִמּוּד] dec. 2b	למד
לִמֻּדֵי	Kal part. pass. pl. constr. masc. from [לָמֻד] dec. 3a ; וְ bef. (:)	למד
לִמּוּדִים	adj. pl. masc. from [לִמּוּד] dec. 2b	למד
לָמוּט	pref. לְ for לְהָ ✗ noun masc. sing. dec. 1a	מוט
לְמוֹכִיחַ וְ	pref. id. ✗ Hiph. part. sing. masc. dec. 1b	יכח
לְמוֹכִיחִים וְ	pref. id. ✗ id. pl. abs.	יכח
לְמוֹלַדְתֶּךָ וְ	pref. לְ ✗ noun fem. sing., suff. 2 pers. s. m. from מוֹלֶדֶת d. 13a; וְ bef. (:)	ילד
לְמוֹלַדְתֵּנוּ וְ	id., suff. 1 pers. pl. ; וְ id.	ילד
לְמוֹלִיךְ	pref. id. ✗ Hiph. part. sing. masc. dec. 1b	ילך
לְמוּלֹת	pref. לְ for לְהָ ✗ noun f., pl. of [מוּלָה] d. 10	מול
לְמוֹסָדוֹת	pref. לְ ✗ noun masc. with pl. fem. term., abs. from [מוֹסָד] dec. 2b	יסד
לְמוּסָר	pref. לְ for לְהָ ✗ noun masc. sing. dec. 2b	יסר
לְמֹסְרַי	pref. לְ ✗ n.m.pl., suff. 1 p.s. [fr. מוֹסָר for מַאְסָר]	אסר
לְמוֹעֵד	pref. לְ f. לְהָ ✗ } noun masc. sing dec. 7b	יעד
לְמוֹעֵד	pref. לְ q. v. ✗ }	יעד
לְמוֹעֲדָהּ	pref. id. ✗ id. pl. constr. st.	יעד
לְמוֹעֲדוֹת וְ	pref. לְ for לְהָ ✗ id. pl. abs. fem.	יעד
לְמוֹעֲדַי וְ	pref. לְ ✗ id. pl. c. m. R. יעד, or Kal part. R.	מער
לְמוֹעֵדְיָה	pref. id. ✗ pr. name masc.	יעד
לְמוֹעֲדִים וְ	pref. לְ f. לְהָ ✗ noun masc., pl. of מוֹעֵד	יעד
לְמוֹעֲדִים וְ	pref. לְ q. v. ✗ dec. 7b ; וְ bef. (:)	
לְמוֹפֵת וְ	pref. id. ✗ noun masc. sing. d. 7b; וְ id.	יפת
לְמוֹפְתִים וְ	pref. id. ✗ id. pl., abs. st.; וְ id. .	יפת
לְמוֹצָאַי	pref. id. ✗ n.m.pl. constr. fr. מוֹצָא d.1b(§31.r.1)	יצא
לְמוֹצָאֵיהֶם	pref. id. ✗ id. pl., suff. 3 pers. pl. masc.	יצא
לְמוּצַק	pref. לְ for לְהָ ✗ noun masc. sing.	יצק
לְמוֹקֵשׁ וְ	pref. לְ ✗ noun masc. sing. d. 7b; וְ bef. (:)	יקש
לְמוֹרָא	pref. לְ f. לְהָ ✗ n. m. s. d. 2b (§ 31. r. 1 & 3)	ירא
לְמוֹרֶנּוּ	pref. לְ ✗ noun masc. s. (pl. מוֹרִים) d. 8e	מרה
לְמוֹרָשׁ	pref. id. ✗ noun masc. sing. [constr. of מוֹרָשׁ, but see § 31. rem. 1]	ירש
לְמוֹרָשָׁה	pref. id. ✗ noun fem. sing.	ירש
לְמוֹשָׁב	pref. id. ✗ noun masc. sing. dec. 2b	ישב
לְמוֹשִׁיעַ	pref. id. ✗ Hiph. part. sing. masc. dec. 1b	ישע
לְמוֹשָׁעוֹת	pref. id. ✗ noun fem. pl. [of מוֹשָׁעָה]	ישע
לָמוּת	pref. לְ (see lett. לְ) ✗ Kal inf. constr. dec. 1a	מות
לָמָוֶת	pref. לְ f. לְהָ ✗ } noun masc. sing. dec. 6g	מות
לָמָוֶת	pref. לְ q. v. ✗ }	מות
לְמוֹת	Chald., pref. id. ✗ noun masc. sing.	מות
לְמוֹתוֹ	pref. id. ✗ n. m. s., suff. 3 p. s. m. fr. מָוֶת d.6g	מות
לְמוֹתָם	pref. id. ✗ id., suff. 3 pers. pl. masc.	מות
לְמוֹתַר	pref. id. ✗ noun masc. sing. dec. 2b	יתר
לְמוֹתֵת	pref. id. ✗ Pilel inf. constr.	מות
לְמֵזֵא	Chald., pref. id. ✗ Peal inf. (§ 53 & 56, 2)	אזא
לַמִּזְבֵּחַ וְ	pref. לְ for לְהָ ✗ noun masc. sing. dec. 7c	זבח
לַמִּזְבֵּחַ וְ	pref. לְ ✗ id., constr. st.; וְ bef. (:)	זבח
לְמִזְבְּחוֹת	pref. לְ for לְהָ ✗ id. pl. fem.	זבח
לְמִזְרֶה	pref. לְ ✗ noun masc. sing. dec. 3a	זור
לְמֵזַח וְ	pref. id. ✗ noun masc. sing.; וְ bef. (:)	מזח

---

a e. 9.19.   h Ps. 71.17.   p Ne. 12.38.   w Ge. 31.3.   c Ps. 116.16.   i Ge. 1.14.   q Job 38.38.   x Ps. 118.18.   d Ps. 109.16.
b Ne. 5.4.   i Ezr.4.22; 7.23.   q Eze. 21.20.   x Ge. 32.10.   d Ge. 32.10.   k Eze. 24, 27.   r Ps. 76.12.   y 2 Sa. 15.21.   e Je. 30.13.
c Pr. 30.3.   k Ezr. 7.13.   r Is. 54.13.   y Ge. 43.7.   e 2 Ch. 8.13.   l De. 28.46.   s Is. 41.15.   z Ezr. 7.26.   f 2 Ch. 26.19.
d De. 4.5.   l Pr.18.5.   s 1 Ch. 5.18.   z Ps. 136.16.   f 2 Ch. 2.3.   m Is. 8.18.   t Is. 14.23.   a Pr. 11.19.   g Ho. 11.1.
e Je.2.33; 13 21.   m Ge.9.26,27;   t Is. 50.4.   aa Ex. 4.26.   g Ne. 10.34.   n Is. 41.18.   u Is. 63.8.   b Pa. 73.4.   h Je. 30.13.
f De.11.19.   n Is.44.45;53.5;   u Is. 29.21.   bb Je. 51.26.   h Job 12.5.   o Nu. 33.2.   v Ps. 68.21.   c Ir. 91.5.   i Ps. 109.19.
g De.5.1.   o Ps. 28.8.   v Pr. 24.25.   2 Ch. 31.3.

לְמֶזְיֵהּ°	Chald., pref. לְ)(Peal inf. (מְזָא §53 & 56, 2), suff. 3 pers. sing. masc. dec. 6a	אזא
לַמַּוְּלוֹת¹	וּ pref. לְ for לְהָ)(noun pl. fem. [from מַוָּל]	מזל
לִמְזִמָּה	pref. לְ bef. (:))(noun fem. sing. dec. 10	זמם
לִמְזַמְּרוֹת	pref. לְ)(noun f. pl. abs. fr. [מַזְמֵרָה] d. 11b	זמר
לַמִּזְרָח	" pref. לְ for לְהָ)(noun masc. sing. dec. 2b	זרח
לְמִזְרָח	pref. לְ)(id., constr. st.	זרח
לְמִזְרָחָה²	pref. לְ for לְהָ)(id. with loc. ה	זרח
לַמַּחְבְּרוֹת³	וְ/ pref. id.)(noun f., pl. of [מַחְבֶּרֶת] d. 13a	חבר
לַמַּחְבַּת⁴	וּ pref. id.)(noun fem. sing. [for מַחֲבַרְתּ comp. §25. rem.]	חבת
לִמְחוֹל⁵	pref. id.)(noun masc. sing. dec. 3a	חול
לִמְחוֹת	pref. id.)([for לְהָמְחוֹת], Hiph. inf. constr. (§11. rem. 3); but see מָחָה	מחה
לִמְחוֹת	pref. לְ bef. (:))(Kal inf. constr.	מחה
לְמֶחֱזֵא⁶	Chald., pref. לְ)(Peal inf. (§49. No. 2)	חזא
לְמַחֲזִיאוֹת	pref. id.)(pr. name masc.	חזא
לְמַחֲזִיר⁷	pref. id.)(Hiph. part. sing. masc. dec. 2b	חזק
לַמַּחֲזִיקִים⁸	pref. לְ for לְהָ)(id. pl., abs. st.	חזק
לְמֶחֱזָיָה⁹	pref. לְ)(noun masc. sing. dec. 10	חיה
לִמְחַכֵּה°	pref. לְ bef. (:))(Piel part. sing. masc., constr. of מְחַכֶּה dec. 9a	חכה
לְמַחְלִי	pref. לְ)(pr. name masc.	חלה
לְמַחְלְקוֹת	וּ/ pref. id.)(n.f., pl. of מַחֲלֹקֶת d. 13c; וּ bef. (:)	חלק
לַמַּחֲנֶה / לְמַחֲנֶה	pref. לְ f. לְהָ } noun com. sing. dec. 9a / pref. לְ q. v.	חנה
לְמַחֲנֵה	pref. id.)(id., constr. st.	חנה
לְמַחֲנוֹת	pref. id.)(id. pl. fem.	חנה
לְמַחֲסֶה	וּ pref. id.)(noun masc. s. d. 9a; וּ bef. (:)	חסה
לְמַחְסוֹר	pref. id.)(noun masc. sing. dec. 1b	חסר
לַמְחַצְצְרִים°	pref. לְ for לְהָ)(Kh. מְחַצְצְרִים Peopel (§6. No. 7) K. מְחַצְרִים or מַחֲצְרִים Piel or Hiph. part. pl. masc.	חצר
לְמָחָר	pref. לְ)(noun masc. or adv.	מהר
לְמַרְאוֹת	pref. id.)(Kh. מַחֲרָאוֹת noun fem. pl. [of מוֹצָאֹת R. יצא; (K. [מַחֲרָאָה]	חרא
לְמַחֲרֵשׁוֹת	pref. לְ for לְהָ)(noun fem. pl. [of מַחֲרֵשָׁה]	חרש
לַמָּחֳרָת	pref. id.)(noun fem. sing.	מחר
לְמָחֳרָת	pref. לְ)(id., constr. st.	מחר
לְמָחֳרָתָם°	pref. id.)(adv (comp. רֵיקָם, אָמְנָם).	מחר
לִמְחִתָּה	וְ pref. לְ bef. (:))(noun fem. sing. dec. 10	חתת
לַמַּטֶּה	pref. לְ for לְהָ)(noun masc. sing. dec. 9a	נטה
לְמַטָּה¹	pref. לְ)(prop. subst. [מַט] with loc. ה, } /	נטה
לְמַטָּה¹'	as an adv.; וּ bef. (:)	נטה
לְמַטֶּה¹	pref. id.)(noun masc. s. d. 9a; וּ id.	נטה
לְמַטֵּה¹	pref. id.)(id., constr. st.; וּ id.	נטה
לְמִטַּהֵר'	pref. לְ for לְהָ)(Hithpa. part. sing. masc. [for מִתְטַהֵר §12. r. 3, & §14. r. 1] d. 7b	טהר
לְמַטּוֹת	pref. id.)(noun masc. with pl. fem. term. fr. מַטֶּה dec. 9a	נטה
לְמַטָּעֵי⁴	pref. id.)(noun m. pl. constr. fr. מַטָּע d. 1b	נטע
לְמַטַּעֲמוֹתָיו / לְמַטְעַמֹּתָיו	pref. id.)(noun pl. fem., suff. 3 pers. sing. masc. from [מַטְעָם] dec. 8a	טעם
לַמָּטָר	pref. לְ for לְהָ)(noun masc. sing. dec. 4a	מטר
לִמְטַר'	pref. לְ bef. (:))(id., constr. st.	מטר
לְמַטְרָה	pref. לְ)(noun fem. sing.	מטר
לְמֵי'	pref. id.)(noun masc. pl., constr. of מַיִם [fr. sing. irr. §38. r. 2, & §45]	מים
לְמִי'	' pref. id.)(pron. pers. interrog.; וּ bef. (:)	מה
לִמְיֻדָּעָי'	pref. לְ bef. (:))(for עָ'; Pual part. pl. masc., suff. 1 pers. sing. [fr. מְיֻדָּע]	ידע
לְמִיּוֹם	preff. לְ & מִ)(noun masc. sing. dec. 1a, pl. irr. יָמִים (§45)	יום
לַמְיַחֲלִים°	pref. לְ for לְהָ)(Piel (§14. rem. 1) part. masc., pl. of מְיַחֵל dec. 7b	יחל
לְמִיכָה / לְמִיכָיְהוּ / לְמִיכָיָהוּ	וּ pref. לְ)(pr. name masc., see מִיכָה; וּ bef. (:)	
לְמִיכַל	וּ pref. id.)(pr. name f.; וּ bef. (:), see מִיכַל.	
לַמְיַלְּדֹת°	pref. לְ for לְהָ)(Piel part. fem., pl. of מְיַלֶּדֶת dec. 13a	ילד
לְמַיִם° / לַמַּיִם° / לָמַיִם / לְמָיִם°	pref. לְ (see לְ) / pref. לְ f. לְהָ / pref. לְ q. v. } noun masc. pl. [of מֵי irr. §38. r. 2, & §45] id. in pause for the preced.	מים
לְמֵימֵי	pref. id.)(id. pl. constr. st.	מים
לְמִימֵי	[for לִימֵי] preff. לְ & מִ)(constr. of the foll.	יום
לְמִימִים''	וּ preff. id.)(n.m.pl.irr. of יוֹם (§45); וּ bef. (:)	יום
לְמִימִן	pref. לְ)(pr. name masc., see מִימִן.	יום
לְמִינָהּ	pref. id.)(noun masc. sing., suff. 3 pers. sing. fem. from [מִין] dec. 1a	מן
לְמִינֵהוּ	pref. id.)(id., suff. 3 pers. sing. masc.	מן
לְמִינֵיהֶם°	pref. id.)(id. pl., suff. 3 p. pl. m. [for מִינֵיהֶם]	מן
לְמִינוֹ	pref. id.)(id. sing., suff. 3 pers. sing. masc.	מן
לְמִישָׁאֵל	וּ pref. id.)(pr. name m., see מִישָׁ'; וּ bef. (:)	

° Da. 3. 19. ' 1 Ch. 22. 3. ' Ezr. 4. 14. ' 1 Ch. 28. 13. ² 2 Ki. 10. 27. ° Je. 17. 17. ° Mi. 1. 6. ° Ps. 31. 12. ° Je. 14. 2.
² 2 Ki. 23. 5. ² 1 Ch. 23. 29 = Da. 21. 1. ' 1 Ch. 12. 22. ' 1 Sa. 13. 21. ' Je. 48. 39. ' Pr. 23. 3. ' Ps. 33. 18. ' Jos. 7. 5.
³ Je. 139. 20. ⁴ Ps. 30. 12. ' Pr. 3. 18. ' Jon. 9. 18. ' Jon. 1. 4. ' 1 Ch. 27. 23. ' Pr. 23. 6. ' Ex. 1. 15,18,20. ' Da. 12. 6,7.
⁴ 2 Ch. 31. 14. ' Pr. 31. 3. ' Ge. 45. 5. ' Is. 4. 6. ' 1 Ch. 29. 21 ' Le. 14. 4. ' Ge. 1. 6. ' Ge. 1. 21.
⁴ 2 Ch. 34. 11. ' 2 Ki. 14. 27. ' Is. 64. 3. ' 9 Ch. 5. 13. ' 1 Sa. 30. 17.

לְמִישׁוֹר pref. לְ)(noun masc. sing. . .	ישר
לְמֵישָׁרִים pref. id.)(noun masc., pl. of [מֵישָׁר], with the prefix as an *adv.* . .	ישר
לֶמֶךְ }(§ 35. rem. 2) pr. name masc. *Lamech.* וְ'}	
לְמַכְאוֹבָי pref. לְ)(noun masc. sing., suff. 3 pers. sing. fem. from מַכְאוֹב dec. 1 b . .	כאב
לְמַכְבִּירֵי pref. id.)(Hiph. part. as a *subst.* .	כבר
לְמִכְבָּר pref. id.)(noun m. s., constr. of מִכְבָּר d. 2 b	כבר
לְמַכֵּה pref. id.)(Hiph. part. sing. masc., constr. of מַכֶּה dec. 9 a . . .	נכה
לְמַכֵּהוּ pref. id.)(id. with suff. 3 pers. sing. masc.	נכה
לִמְכוֹנָה pref. לְ for לָהּ)(noun fem. sing. dec. 10	כון
לְמִיָּמִים וּ preff. מְ & לְ)( )(noun masc. pl. abs. (as if from יָם dec. 2 a) see יוֹם (§ 45); וּ bef.	יום
לִמְכוּרֹי pref. לְ bef.)(Kal inf. constr. (§ 8. r. 18)	מכר
לְמַכִּים pref. לְ)(Hiph. part. masc., pl. of מַכֶּה d. 9 a	נכה
לְמָכִיר וּ pref. id.)(pr. name masc.; וּ bef.	מכר
לְמִכְמַרְתּוֹ pref. id.)(noun fem. sing., suff. 3 pers. sing. masc. from [מִכְמֶרֶת] dec. 13 a .	כמר
לְמִכְמָשׁ pref. id.)(pr. name of a place, see מִכְמָס	כמס
לְמִכְנַשׁ Ch., pref. id.)(Peal inf. . .	כנש
לְמָכְרָהּ pref. id.)(Kal inf., suff. 3 pers. sing. fem.	מכר
לְמִכְסֶה וּ pref. לְ bef.)(noun masc. sing. d. 9 a	כסה
לְמִכְשׁוֹל וּ pref. לְ)(noun masc. sing. dec. 1 b	כשל
לִמְכַשְּׁפִים וּ pref. לְ for לָהּ)(Piel part. masc., pl. of מְכַשֵּׁף dec. 7 b	כשף
לְמַלֵּא dd'וּ pref. לְ)(Piel inf. constr. d. 7 b; וּ bef.	מלא
לִמְלֹאות with וּ in otio for לִמְלֹאת (q. v.) .	מלא
לַמַּלְאָךְ pref. לְ for לָהּ)(noun masc. sing. dec. 2 b	לאך
לַמְּלָאכָה pref. לְ id. } noun fem. sing., constr.	לאך
לַמְּלָאכָה pref. לְ bef.)(מְלֶאכֶת (§ 42. rem. 5) }	לאך
לְמַלְאֲכֵי pref. לְ)(constr. of the following	לאך
לְמַלְאָכִים pref. לְ for לָהּ)(noun m., pl. of מַלְאָךְ d. 2 b	לאך
לִמְלֶאכֶת pref. לְ bef.)(noun fem. sing. constr. of מְלָאכָה (§ 42. rem. 5)	לאך
לִמְלַאכְתּוֹ pref. id.)(id., suff. 3 pers. sing. m. d. 13 a	לאך
לְמַלְּאָם וּ pref. לְ)(Piel inf. (מַלֵּא), suff. 3 pers. pl. masc. dec. 7 b; וּ bef.	מלא
לְמַלֹּאת pref. id.)(Piel inf. with f. term. [for מַלֵּאת § 23. rem. 2 & 4]	מלא
לְמִלָּה pref. id.)(noun fem. sing. d. 10 (pl. מִלִּים)	מלל
לְמִלּוּאִים וּ pref. לְ for לָהּ)(noun m., pl. of [מִלּוּא] d.1 b	מלא

לִמְלוּכָה pref. לְ bef.)(noun fem. sing. .	מלך
לְמָלְכִי pref. לְ)(Kh. (לְ)מַלֻּכִי, K. (לְ)מְלִיכוּ, see מַלֻּךְ	מלך
לְמַלּוֹתִי pref. לְ)(pr. name masc.	מלל
לְמֶלַח pref. id.)(noun masc. sing. . .	מלה
לַמְּלֵחָה pref. לְ bef.)(noun fem. sing. .	מלה
לַמִּלְחָמָה וּ pref. לְ f. לָהּ)(n.f.s.d.11 a, with suff.	לחם
לַמִּלְחָמָה pref. לְ q. v. } fr. חֵמָה d. 13 a (§ 42. r.5) }	
לַמִּלִּין pref. id.)(noun fem. with pl. masc. term. from מִלָּה dec. 10 .	מלל
לַמֶּלֶךְ וּ pref. לְ for לָהּ)(noun masc. sing. dec. 6 a	מלך
לַמֹּלֶךְ pref. id. } pr. name of an idol; וּ bef.	מלך
לַמּוֹלֶךְ וּ pref. }	מלך
לְמֶלֶךְ pref. id.)(noun masc. s. d. 6 a; Chald. d. 3 a	מלך
לִמְלֹךְ pref. לְ bef.)(Kal inf. constr. .	מלך
לְמַלְכָּא Chald., pref. לְ)(noun masc. sing., emph. of מֶלֶךְ (§ 59) dec. 3 a . .	מלך
לְמַלְכָּהּ וּ pref. id.)(noun masc. sing., suff. 3 pers. sing. fem. from מֶלֶךְ dec. 6 a; וּ bef.	מלך
לְמַלְכּוֹ pref. id.)(id. with suff. 3 pers. sing. masc.	מלך
לִמְלֹכוֹ pref. id.)(Kal inf., suff. 3 pers. sing. masc.	מלך
לְמַלְכוּת pref. לְ f. לָהּ)(noun fem. sing. dec. 10 ; Ch.	מלך
לְמַלְכוּת pref. לְ q. v. } constr. of מַלְכוּ dec. 8 c }	
לְמַלְכוּתוֹ pref. id.)(id. with suff. 3 pers. sing. masc.	מלך
לְמַלְכֵי וּ pref. id.)(noun masc. pl. constr. from מֶלֶךְ dec. 6 a ; וּ bef.	מלך
לְמַלְכִּיָּה, לְמַלְכִּיאֵל pref. id.)(pr. name masc.	מלך
לִמְלָכִים pref. לְ for לָהּ)(noun m. pl. of מֶלֶךְ d. 6 a	מלך
לְמַלְכֵנוּ pref. לְ bef.)(id. pl., suff. 1 pers. pl.	מלך
לְמַלְכָּם וּ pref. לְ)(pr. name of an idol; וּ bef.	מלך
לְמַלְכֵּנוּ pref. id.)(noun masc. sing., suff. 1 pers. pl. from מֶלֶךְ dec. 6 a .	מלך
לְמַלְכַּת pref. id.)(n. fem. s., constr. of מַלְכָּה d. 12 a	מלך
לְמַלְכֶּת pref. לְ bef.)(noun fem. sing. .	מלך
לְמַלְּמְדַי וּ pref. id.)(Piel part. pl. masc., suff. 1 pers. sing. from מְלַמֵּד dec. 7 b	למד
לְמַלְקוֹשׁ pref. לְ)(noun masc. sing. .	לקש
לְמַמְלָכָה pref. id.)(noun fem. sing., constr. לָבֵת with suff. לְבֵתוֹ (§ 42. rem. 5)	מלך
לְמַמְלְכֹת וּ pref. id.)(id. pl. constr. st.	מלך
לְמֵמַר Chald., pref. id.)(for מֵאמַר Peal inf. (§ 53)	אמר
לְמִמְשְׁלוֹת pref. id.)(pl. of the foll.	משל
לְמֶמְשֶׁלֶת pref. id.)(noun fem. sing. dec. 13a (used as the constr. of מֶמְשָׁלָה § 42. rem. 5) .	משל

a Ca. 7. 10.   *b* Ps. 136. 10.   *c* Ne. 10. 32.   *d* Ex. 21. 8.   *e* 1 Sa. 11. 9.   *f* Eze. 16. 13.   *g* Jos. 10. 30.   *h* Ps. 47. 7.   *i* Is. 10. 10.

j Je. 51. 8.   *k* La. 3. 30.   *l* Is. 50. 6.   *m* Is. 23. 18.   *n* Je. 33. 5.   *o* Eze. 47. 11.   *p* 1 Sa. 2. 10.   *q* Pr. 5. 13.   *r* Je. 49. 28.

s Job 36. 31.   *t* 1 Ki. 7. 30.   *u* Hab. 1. 16.   *v* 1 Sa. 25. 31.   *w* Job 30. 9.   *x* Ps. 107. 34.   *y* Est. 4. 14.   *z* Job 29. 23.   *aa* Ezr. 5. 11.

bb Ex. 38. 5.   *cc* 1 Ch. 17. 10.   Da. 3. 2.   1 Ki. 20. 9.   Le. 7. 37.   Job 18. 2.   1 Ki. 15. 29.   2 Ch. 22. 9.   Ps. 136. 9.

dd Ex. 29. 29.

לַמְמֵתִים־ pref. לְ for לָה X Hiph. part. masc., pl. of מֵמִית dec. 3 b . . . מות

לְמָן Chald., pref. לְ X pron. interrog.; ז bef. (:) מן

לְמִן ז pref. id. X prep. (§ 5, parad.) . . מנן

לִמְנַאֲצֵי־ pref. לְ bef. (:) Piel (§ 14. rem. 1), part. pl., suff. 1 pers. sing. from [מְנָאֵץ] dec. 7 b נאץ

לְמָנָה pref. לְ X noun f. s., d. 10 & 11 a (§ 42. r. 2) מנה

לִמְנוּחָיְכִי־ pref. לְ bef. (:) X noun masc. pl. with suff. 2 p. s. f. fr. מָנוֹחַ d. 3 a (§ 30. r. 5 & § 4. r. 4) נוח

לִמְנוּחָתֵךְ־ pref. id. X noun fem. sing., suff. 2 pers. sing. masc. from מְנוּחָה dec. 10 . . נוח

לִמְנוֹרָה׳ pref. id. X noun fem. sing. dec. 10 . נור

לִמְנוֹת pref. id. X Kal inf. constr. . . . מנה

לַמֻּנָּח־ pref. לְ for לָה X Hoph. part. sing. masc. [Chald. form for מוּנָח § 21. rem. 24] . נוח

לַמִּנְחָה / לַמִּנְחָה pref. id. / pref. לְ q. v. } noun fem. sing. dec. 12 b . מנה

לְמִנְחָה־ pref. id. bef. (:) for מִנְחָה׳, noun f. s. d. 10 נוח

לַמְנַחֲמִים־ ז pref. לְ for לָה X Piel (§ 14. rem. 1) pl. masc. from מְנַחֵם dec. 7 b . נחם

לְמִנְחַת־ pref. לְ X noun f. s., constr. of מִנְחָה d. 12 b מנה

לְמִנְחֹתֵיכֶם־ ז pref. id. X id. pl., suff. 2 p. pl. m.; ז bef. (:) מנה

לַמְּנִי־ pref. לְ for לָה X pr. name of an idol . מנה

לְמִנִּי־ ז pref. לְ X prep. מִן with parag. ׳ see מִן (§ 5, parad.) . . . מנן

לְמִנְיָמִין pref. id. X pr. name masc., see מִיָּמִין.

לְמִנְיָן׳ Chald., pref. id. X noun masc. sing. . מנה

לַמְנַצֵּחַ pref. לְ for לָה X Piel part. sing. masc. d. 7 b נצח

לַמְּנֹרוֹת־ ז pref. לְ bef. (:) X noun f., pl. of מְנוֹרָה d. 10 נור

לִמְנַשֶּׁה ז pref. id. X pr. name of a tribe . נשה

לִמְנַשִּׁי pref. לְ for לָה X gent. noun from the prec. נשה

לְמִנְתֻן־ Chald., pref. לְ X Peal inf. . נתן

לָמָס pref. לְ (see lett. לְ) X noun masc. sing. dec. 8 e, contr. from מֶכֶס . . . כסס

לְמַס־ pref. לְ for לָה X noun masc. sing. . מסס

לְמַס־ pref. לְ X noun m. s. d. 8 e, contr. from מֶכֶס כסס

לַמִּסְגְּרוֹת pref. לְ for לָה X noun f., pl. of מִסְגֶּרֶת d. 13 a סגר

לְמִסְגַּרְתּוֹ pref. id. X id. sing., suff. 3 pers. sing. masc. סגר

לַמֵּסֶךְ־ / לַמֶּסֶךְ־ pref. לְ f. לָה / pref. לְ q. v. } noun masc. sing. (constr.) מָסָךְ § 37. rem. 4) סכך

לְמִסָּךְ־ pref. לְ bef. (:) X Kal inf. constr. . מסך

לְמַסֵּכָה pref. לְ X noun fem. sing. dec. 10 . נסך

לַמְסִלָּה / לַמְסִלָּה־ pref. לְ for לָה / pref. לְ bef. (:) } noun fem. sing. dec. 10 . סלל

לִמְסַמְּרוֹת־ pref. לְ X noun pl. fem and masc. [from מַסְמֵר] dec. 7 b } סמר
לַמַּסְמְרִים־ pref. לְ f. לָה

לְמַסַּע־ ז pref. לְ X noun masc. sing. dec. 2 (§ 31. rem. 5); ז bef. (:) . . נסע

לְמַסְעֵיהֶם pref. id. X id. pl., suff. 3 pers. pl. masc. . נסע

לְמַסָּעָיו־ pref. id. X id. pl., suff. 3 pers. sing. masc. נסע

לְמִסְפֵּר־ ז pref. id. X noun masc. s. dec. 7 c; ז bef. (:) ספר

לְמִסְפַּר־ pref. id. X noun m. s., constr. of מִסְפָּר dec. 2 b ספר

לְמִסְפָּרָם pref. id. X id. with suff. 3 pers. pl. masc. ספר

לִמְסֹר־ pref. לְ bef. (:) X Kal inf. constr. [for מָסֹר § 8. rem. 18] מסר

לְמַסַּת pref. לְ X noun fem. s., constr. of מַסָּה d. 10 נסה

לְמִסְתּוֹר־ ז pref. id. X noun masc. sing.; ז bef. (:) סתר

לְמֶעְבַּד Chald., pref. id. X Peal inf. (§ 49. No. 2) עבד

לַמּוֹעֲדִים־ ז pref. לְ f. לָה X noun masc., pl. of מוֹעֵד dec. } ידע
לַמֹּעֲדִים־ ז pref. לְ q. v. 7 b; ז bef. (:)

לְמַעֲדַנִּים־ pref. id. X noun masc., pl. of [מַעֲדָן] dec. 8 a עדן

לְמָעוֹז־ ז pref. id. X noun masc. sing. (suff. מָעֻזִּי § 37. rem. 4) dec. 8 c עזז

לְמָעוּזֵּי־ pref. id. X id. pl., constr. st. (§ 37. rem. 2) עזז

לַמַּעְגָּל־ pref. לְ bef. (:) X Kh. לְמַעְגּוֹל, K. לְמַעְגַּל, and } עגל
לַמַּעְגּוֹל־ pref. id. X Kal inf. constr. (§ 8. rem. 18) }

לִמְעוֹן pref. id. X noun m. s., constr. of מָעוֹן dec. 3 a עון

לְמַעֲזַיָהוּ pref. לְ X pr. name masc. . . עזה

לְמַעַט־ / לְמַעַט־ ז pref. לְ f. לָה / pref. לְ bef. (:) } subst. and adj. masc. (pl. מְעַטִּים) dec. 8 d } מעט

לְמַעֲיְנוֹ־ pref. לְ X noun masc. sing. (מַעְיָן) with parag. ו (חֲיָתוֹ comp.) . . . עין

לִמְעַל־ / לַמְעַל־ pref. לְ bef. (:) X Kal inf. constr. (§ 8. rem. 18) } מעל

לַמַּעֲלָה / לַמַּעֲלָה ז pref. לְ X subst. m. (מַעַל) with parag. ה, as an adv.; ז bef. (:) } עלה

לְמַעֲלָה pref. id. X noun m. s., constr. of עלה d. 9 a עלה

לְמַעֲלוֹת־ pref. לְ for לָה X noun f., pl. of מַעֲלָה d. 10 עלה

לְמַעַן ז prep.; prop. subst. masc. (מַעַן) with pref. לְ; ז bef. (:) } ענה

לְמַעֲנֵהוּ־ pref. לְ for לָה X noun masc. sing., suff. 3 pers. sing. masc. from מַעֲנֶה dec. 9 a . ענה

לְמַעֲנוֹתָם־ pref. לְ X Kh. מַעֲנִיתָם, K. מַעֲנִיתָם, noun f. s., suff. 3 pers. pl. m. [fr. מַעֲנִית or נִית] ענה

ª Job 33. 22.   ᵈ 1 Ch. 28. 15.   ʰ Nu. 29. 39.   ᵍ Ezr. 7. 20.   ᵏ Is. 5. 22.   ᵒ Ge. 13. 3.   ˢ Zec. 8. 19.   ᵛ Da. 11. 19.   ᶻ Eze. 14. 15.
² 2 Sa. 7. 11.   ᵉ Eze. 41. 11.   ⁱ Is. 65. 11.   ᵖ Job 6. 14.   ˡ 2 Ch. 3. 9.   ᵖ Is. 22. 12.   ᵗ La. 4. 5   ᵂ 2 Ch. 36. 14.   ᵃ Ps. 121. 1.
³ Je. 22. 17.   ᶠ 2 Sa. 14. 17   Mi. 7. 12.   ᵖ 1 Ki. 7. 32.   ᵐ 1 Ch. 22. 3.   Nu. 31. 16.   Na. 1. 7.   2 Ch. 28. 22.   Pr. 16. 4.
⁴ Ps. 116. 7.   ᵍ Ps. 69. 21.   Ezr. 6. 17.   Ex. 26. 37.   De. 10. 11.   Job 9. 23.   Da. 11. 1.   Ps. 114. 8.   Ps. 129. 3.
⁵ Ps. 132. 8.   Ezr. 9. 4.   1 Ch. 28. 15, 15.   Ps. 105. 39.   Nu. 10. 2.   Is. 4. 6.   Ju. 21. 19.   1 Ch. 23. 31

29*

לְמַעֲנִי — prep. לְמַעַן [prop. subst. masc., מַעַן, with pref. לְ], suff. 1 pers. sing. — ענה

לְמַעֲנֶךָ — id. with suff. 2 pers. sing. masc. — ענה

לְמַעֲנְכֶם — id. with suff. 2 pers. pl. masc. — ענה

לְמַעֲצֵבָה — pref. לְ ✕ noun fem. sing. — עצב

וְלְמַעֲרָב — pref. לְ for לְהָ ✕ noun masc. sing. dec. 2b — ערב

לְמַעֲשֵׂה — pref. לְ ✕ noun m. s., constr. of מַעֲשֶׂה d. 9a — עשה

לְמַעֲשֵׂהוּ — pref. id. ✕ id., suff. 3 pers. sing. masc. — עשה

לְמַעֲשֵׂי — pref. id. ✕ id. pl., constr. st. — עשה

וְלְמַעְשְׂרוֹת — pref. לְ for לְהָ ✕ noun masc. with pl. fem. term. from מַעֲשֵׂר dec. 7c — עשר

לְמִפְגָּע — pref. לְ ✕ noun masc. sing. — פגע

וְלְמִפִיבֹשֶׁת — pref. לְ bef. (:) ✕ pr. name masc. — פאה

לְמִפְלַגּוֹת — pref. לְ ✕ noun fem., pl. of [מִפְלַגָּה] dec. 10 — פלג

לְמַפָּלָה — pref. id. ✕ noun fem. sing. — נפל

לְמִפְשַׁר — Chald., pref. id. ✕ Peal inf. — פשר

לִמְצֹא — pref. לְ bef. (:) ✕ Kal inf. constr. — מצא

לְמוֹצָאֵי — pref. לְ ✕ noun masc. pl. constr. from מוֹצָא dec. 1b (§ 31. rem. 1) — יצא

לְמוֹצָאֵי — pref. id. ✕ Kal part. act. pl. constr. masc. from מוֹצָא dec. 7b — מצא

לְמוֹצָאֵיהֶם — pref. id. ✕ id. pl. with suff. 3 pers. pl. masc. — מצא

לַמַּצֶּבֶת — pref. לְ for לְהָ ✕ noun fem. sing. (suff. מַצַּבְתּוֹ) dec. 13a — נצב

לַמָּצֹד — pref. id. ✕ noun masc. sing. dec. 1 — צוד

לַמָּצֹד — pref. id. ✕ id. constr. (by exception comp. § 30. No. 1) — צוד

לִמְצֹדָה — pref. לְ bef. (:) ✕ for מְצוּדָה noun f. s. d. 10 — צוד

לְמִצְוֹא — pref. id. ✕ Kal inf. constr. — מצא

לְמִצְוָה — pref. id. ✕ noun fem. sing. dec. 10 — צוה

לִמְצוֹר — pref. id. ✕ noun fem. sing. dec. 3a — צור

לְמִצְוֹתַי — pref. id. ✕ noun fem. pl., suff. 1 pers. sing. from מִצְוָה dec. 10 — צוה

לְמִצְוֹתָיו — pref. id. ✕ id., suff. 3 pers. sing. masc. — צוה

לְמִצְוֹתֶיךָ — pref. id. ✕ id., suff. 2 pers. sing. masc. — צוה

לְמִצְעָר — pref. לְ for לְהָ ✕ noun masc. sing. dec. 2b — צער

לְמִצְפֶּה — pref. לְ ✕ pr. name of a place — צפה

לְמִצְרַיִם / לְמִצְרַיִם — pref. id. ✕ pr. name of a country; וּ bef. (:) — מצר

לְמִקְדַּשׁ — pref. לְ f. לְהָ ✕ noun masc. sing. dec. 2b — קדש

לְמִקְדָּשׁ — pref. לְ q. v. ✕

לְמִקְדָּשׁוֹ — pref. id. ✕ id., suff. 3 pers. sing. masc. — קדש

לְמִקְדָּשַׁי — pref. לְ bef. (:) ✕ Pu. part. pl. masc., suff. 1 pers. sing. from מְקֻדָּשׁ — קדש

וְלְמִקְוֵה — pref. לְ ✕ noun masc. sing., constr. of מִקְוֶה dec. 9a; וּ bef. (:) — קנה

וְלַמָּקוֹם — pref. לְ for לְהָ ✕ noun com. sing. dec. 3a — קום

לִמְקוֹמוֹ — pref. לְ bef. (:) ✕ id., suff. 3 pers. sing. masc. — קום

לִמְקוֹמֶךָ — pref. id. ✕ id., suff. 2 pers. s. m. (for מְקוֹמְךָ) — קום

לִמְקוֹמָם — pref. id. ✕ id., suff. 3 pers. pl. masc. — קום

לְמִקָּטֹן — preff. id. ✕ & מִ ✕ adj. masc. sing. dec. 3a — קטן

לְמִקְּטַנָּם — preff. id. ✕ adj. masc. sing., suff. 3 pers. pl. masc. from קָטָן dec. 8a (§ 37. No. 3c) — קטן

לְמִקְלָט — pref. לְ ✕ noun masc. sing. dec. 2b — קלט

לִמְקֹמָהּ — pref. לְ bef. (:) ✕ noun com. sing., suff. 3 pers. sing. fem. from מָקוֹם dec. 3a — קום

לִמְקֹמוֹ — pref. id. ✕ id., suff. 3 pers. sing. masc. — קום

לִמְקֹמֹתָם — pref. id. ✕ id. pl., suff. 3 pers. pl. masc. — קום

לְמִקְנֶה — pref. לְ ✕ noun fem. sing. dec. 10 — קנה

לְמִקְנֵהוּ — pref. id. ✕ noun masc. sing., suff. 3 pers. sing. masc. from מִקְנֶה dec. 9a; וּ bef. (:) — קנה

לְמִקְנֵיהֶם — pref. id. ✕ id. pl., suff. 3 pers. pl. masc. — קנה

לְמִקְנֵנוּ — pref. id. ✕ id. sing., suff. 1 pers. pl. — קנה

לִמְקֹנְנוֹת — pref. לְ for לְהָ ✕ Pil. part. pl. fem. [from מְקוֹנֵן dec. 13, from מְקוֹנֶנֶת masc.] — קון

לְמִקְצֶה — [for לְמִקְצֵה] preff. לְ & מִ ✕ noun masc. sing., constr. of קָצֶה dec. 9b; וּ bef. (:) — קצה

לְמִקְצְעֹת — pref. לְ bef. (:) ✕ Pu. part. pl. constr. fem. from [מְקֻצְעָה] dec. 11a — קצע

לְמִקְצָת — preff. id. ✕ & מִ ✕ noun fem. sing., pl. קְצָוֹת, comp. מְנָת (§ 45); וּ bef. (:) — קצה

לְמִקְרָא — pref. לְ ✕ noun masc. sing. dec. 1b (pl. c. מִקְרָאֵי § 31. rem. 1) — קרא

לְמִקְרָא — Chald., pref. id. ✕ Peal inf. — קרא

לְמָר — pref. id. ✕ for מַר adj. masc., pl. מָרִים, dec. 8 (§ 37. rem. 7) — מרר

לְמַרְאֶה — pref. id. ✕ noun masc. sing. dec. 9a — ראה

לְמַרְאֵה — pref. id. ✕ id., constr. state — דאה

לְמַרְכְּבָה — pref. id. ✕ for מַרְכָּבָה, noun masc. sing., constr. of מֶרְכָּבָה dec. 9a — רכב

וְלַמֶּרְכֶּבֶת — pref. לְ for לְהָ ✕ Hoph. part. sing. fem. [from מֻרְכָּב masc.] — רכב

לְמַרְבֵּץ — pref. id. ✕ noun masc. sing., constr. of מַרְבֵּץ dec. 7 (§ 36. rem. 1) — רבץ

לְמַרְגִּיזֵי — pref. id. ✕ Hiph. part. pl. c. m. fr. מַרְגִּיז d. 1b — רגז

a Da. 9. 19.   b Job 7. 20.   c Pr. 4. 22.   d Ec. 8. 17.   e Is. 63. 18.   f 2 Sa. 15. 19.   g Jos. 14. 4.   h Da. 1. 18.   i Is. 9. 6.
Is. 50. 11.   2 Ch. 35. 12.   2 Sa. 18. 18.   2 Ch. 19. 10.   2 Ch. 30. 8.   Je. 31. 34.   Nu. 32. 16.   Nu. 10. 2.   1 Ch. 23. 29.
1 Ch. 26. 16, 18.   Da. 1. 16.   1 Ch. 12. 16.   1 Ch. 11. 5.   Is. 13. 3.   Je. 9. 16.   De. 4. 32.   Is. 5. 20.   Eze. 25. 5.
Is. 54. 16.   Ps. 107. 35.   1 Ch. 12. 8.   Is. 48. 18.   Ge. 1. 10.   Ge. 36. 40.   Ex. 26. 23; 36. 28.   Ne. 12. 44.   Job 12. 6.
Je. 1. 16.   Pr. 8. 9.   Eze. 13. 21.   Ex. 15. 26.   Je. 7. 14.   Ge. 23. 18.   Ne. 12. 44.   Ge. 33. 17.

לִמְרֹד˙	pref. לְ bef. (ִ) ✕ Kal inf. constr. . . מרד
לְמָרְדְּכַי	} pref. לְ ✕ pr. name m., see מָרְדְּכַי; וּ bef. (ִ)
לְמָרְדְּכָי	}
לִמְרָדְכֶם˙	pref. לְ bef. (ִ) ✕ Kal inf., suff. 2 pers. pl. m. מרד
לִמְרוֹד˙	in full for לִמְרֹד (q. v. & § 8. rem. 18) מרד
לַמָּרוֹם˙	pref. לְ f. [לְהַ] } noun masc. sing. dec. 3a רום
לַמָּרוֹם	pref. לְ q. v. }
לַמָּרוֹת	pref.לְ✕[f.לְהַמָרוֹת] Hiph.inf.constr. (§11.r.3) מרה
לַמַּרְחֵב˙	pref. לְ for לְהַ ✕ noun masc. sing. dec. 2b רחב
לְמֶרְחֲבֵי˙	pref. לְ ✕ id. pl., constr. st. . רחב
לְמֵרָחוֹק˙	preff. לְ, & מִ for מִן ✕ (prim. adj.) subst. masc. sing. dec. 3a . . . רחק
לְמָרְטָה˙	pref. לְ ✕ Kal inf. constr. (§ 8. rem. 10) . מרט
לְמֹרְטִים˙	pref. id. ✕ id. part. masc., pl. of [מֹרֵט] d. 7b מרט
לְמָרִי	pref. id. ✕ adj. pl. constr. masc. [for מָרֵי] from מַר dec. 8 (§ 37. rem. 7) . מרר
לְמָרְיוֹת˙	pref. לְ bef. (ִ) ✕ pr. name masc. . מרה
לִמְרִים˙	pref. לְ ✕ noun masc. pl. abs. [for מָרִים] from מַר dec. 8 (§ 37. rem. 7) מרר
לְמִרְיָם˙	pref. id. ✕ pr. name fem. . . מרה
לְמֶרְכָּבוֹ˙	pref. id. ✕ noun masc. sing., suff. 3 pers. sing. masc. from מֶרְכָּב dec. 2b רכב
לְמַרְכְּבֹתָיו˙	pref. id. ✕ noun fem. pl., suff. 3 pers. sing. m. fr. מֶרְכָּבָה, constr. מַרְכֶּבֶת (§42. r.5) רכב
לְמִרְמָא˙	Chald., pref. id. ✕ Peal inf. . רמה
לְמִרְמָה˙	pref. id. ✕ noun fem. sing. dec. 10 . רמה
לְמִרְמָס˙	pref. id. ✕ noun masc. sing. dec. 2b . רמס
לְמִרְמָכ˙	"וּ pref. id. ✕ id. constr. st.; וּ bef. (ִ) רמס
לְמֵרֵע˙	preff. לְ, & מִ for מִן ✕ with dist. acc. for רֵעַ, adj. masc. sing. dec. 8 (§ 37. rem. 7) . רעע
לְמֵרֵעֵהוּ˙	pref. לְ ✕ n. m. s., suff. 3 p. s. m. fr. [רֵעַ] d.1b רעה
לְמֵרֵעֶךָ˙	pref. לְ ✕ id. with suff. 2 p. s. m. [for עַךָ] רעה
לְמֶרְרִי˙	pref. לְ bef. (ִ) ✕ pr. name masc. . מרר
לְמֶרֵשָׁה˙	pref. לְ ✕ pr. name of a place, see מָאֵרֵשָׁה ראש
לְמַשָּׂא˙	וּ pref. id. ✕ noun masc. s. d. 1b; וּ bef. (ִ) נשא
לְמַשָּׂאוֹת˙	pref. id. ✕ Kal inf. with preformative מ in the manner of the Chald. and the ending וֹת after the verb לה (§23. r.3 & 9, & §8. r.10) נשא
לְמַשְׂאוֹת˙	defect. for לְמַשּׂוּאוֹת (q. v.) . . שוא
לְמִשְׁבַּק˙	Chald., pref. לְ ✕ Peal inf. . שבק
לְמוֹשְׁבֹתָם˙	pref. id. ✕ noun masc., pl. fem., suff. 3 pers. pl. masc. from מוֹשָׁב dec. 2b ישב

לְמִשְׂגָּב˙	pref. לְ ✕ noun masc. sing., dec. 8a (suff. § 37. No. 3c) . . שגב מִשְׂגַּבּוֹ
לְמַשְׁנֵת˙	pref. id. ✕ Hiph. part. sing. fem. . נשל
לְמֹשֶׁה˙	pref. id. ✕ pr. name masc. . משה
לְמַשּׂוּאוֹת˙	pref. id. ✕ noun fem., pl. of [מַשּׂוּאָה] d. 10 שוא
לְמִשּׁוּבָתַי˙	pref. id. bef. (ִ) ✕ noun fem. sing., suff. 1 pers. sing. from מְשׁוּבָה dec. 10 . . שוב
לִמְשׁוֹךְ˙	pref. id. ✕ Kal inf. constr. (§ 8. rem. 18) משך
לִמְשׁוֹל˙	pref. id. ✕ Kal inf. constr. (§ 8. rem. 18) משל
לִמְשׁוּסָה˙	pref. id. ✕ Kh. מְשׁוּסָה, K. מְשַׁסָּה noun fem. sing. dec. 10 . . . שסס
לִמְשֹׁחַ˙	וּ pref. id. ✕ Kal inf. constr. . משח
לְמָשְׁחָה˙	pref. לְ ✕ id. with fem. term. (§ 8. rem. 10); noun fem. Nu. 18. 8 . . משח
לְמַשְׁחִית˙	pref. id. ✕ noun masc. sing. . שחת
לְמָשְׁחֲךָ˙	pref.לְbef. (ִ) ✕ Kal inf. [מְשֹׁחַ], suff. 2 pers. sing. masc. (§ 16. rem. 10 & 11; but others read מְשׁחֲךָ from מָשַׁח) . משח
לְמֵשִׁיב˙	pref. לְ ✕ Hiph. part. sing. masc. dec. 3b שוב
לְמָשִׁיחַ˙	pref. לְ bef. (ִ) ✕ n. m. s., constr. of מָשִׁיחַ d.3a משח
לִמְשִׁיחוֹ˙	pref. id. ✕ id., suff. 3 pers. sing. masc. משח
לִמְשִׁיחִי˙	pref. id. ✕ id., suff. 1 pers. sing. משח
לְמִשְׁכָּבִי˙	pref. לְ ✕ noun masc. sing. dec. 2 b שכב
לְמִשְׁכָּב˙	pref. id. ✕ id., constr. st. . שכב
לְמַשְׂכִּיל˙	pref. id. ✕ Hiph. part. sing. masc. dec. 1b שכל
לַמִּשְׁכָּן˙	pref. לְ for לְהַ ✕ noun masc. sing. dec. 2b שכן
לְמִשְׁכַּן˙	pref. לְ ✕ id. constr. st. . . שכן
לְמִשְׁכְּנוֹתָיו˙	pref. id. ✕ id. pl. fem., suff. 3 pers. sing. m. שכן
לְמָשָׁל˙	וּ pref. id. ✕ noun masc. s. d. 4a; וּ bef. (ִ) משל
לִמְשֹׁל˙	וּ pref. לְ bef. (ִ) ✕ Kal inf. constr., or לִמְשָׁל-	(Job 17. 6) subst. masc. (§ 8. r. 18) משל
לְמִשְׁלֹחַ˙	pref. לְ ✕ noun m. s., constr. of [מִשְׁלֹחַ] d. 2b שלח
לְמִשְׁלִים˙	וּ pref. לְ bef. (ִ) ✕ noun m., pl. of מָשָׁל d. 4a משל
לִמְשֻׁלָּם˙	וּ pref. id. ✕ pr. name masc. . . שלם
לִמְשֶׁלֶמְיָהוּ˙	וּ pref. id. ✕ pr. name masc. . שלם
לְמִשְׂמוֹת˙	pref. id. ✕ noun fem., pl. of מַשְׂמָה dec. 10 שמם
לְמַשְׁמִיעִים˙	pref. לְ ✕ Hiph. part. m., pl. of מַשְׁמִיעַ d.1b שמע
לְמַשְׁמַע˙	pref. id. ✕ n. m. s., constr. of [מִשְׁמַע] d.2b שמע
לְמִשְׁמָר˙	pref. id. ✕ noun masc. sing. dec. 2b שמר
לְמִשְׁמָרוֹת˙	pref. id. ✕ pl. of the foll. (§ 44. rem. 5) . שמר
לְמִשְׁמַרְתִּי˙	} pref. id. ✕ noun fem. sing. (suff. מַרְתּוֹ) dec. 13a שמר

a Jos. 22. 29.   f Eze. 21. 16.   l Ps. 24. 4.   q Eze. 17. 9.   v Ho. 11. 7.   c Da. 9. 24.   h Ps. 132. 17.   m Job 17. 6.   r Je. 48. 34.
b Jos. 22. 15.   g Is. 50. 6.   m Mi. 7. 10.   r Ps. 74. 3.   w Ec. 2. 3.   d Ex. 29. 29.   i Ge. 1. 1.   n 1 Ch. 16. 42.
c Ne. 6. 6.   h Nu. 5. 24, 27.   n Is. 7. 25.   s Da. 4. 23.   x Eze. 19. 14.   e 1 Sa. 15. 1.   k Joel 2. 17.   o Is. 11. 3.
d Job 5. 11.   i 1 Ki. 5. 6.   o Ju. 15. 2.   t 1 Ch. 21. 12.   y Is. 42. 24.   f Ru. 4. 15.   l Je. 24. 9.   p Eze. 14. 8.   s Ex. 16. 34.
e Hab. 1. 6.   k Is. 2. 7.   p Nu. 4. 24.   u Ps. 73. 18.   z Ju. 9. 8.   g Ge. 36. 43.   pp Is. 7. 25.   a Eze. 38. 7.

לְמְשַׂנְאַי וְ pref. לְ bef. (:) X Piel (§ 10. rem. 7) part. pl. m., suff. 1 pers. s. from [מְשַׂנֵּא] d. 7 b   שׂנא

לְמִשְׁנֶה pref. לְ X noun masc. sing. dec. 9 a   שׁנה

לְמִשְׁסָּה וְ pref. לְ bef. (:) X noun fem. sing. & pl. dec. 10   שׁסס
לְמִשִׁסּוֹת

לְמִשְׁעִי pref. לְ X noun masc. sing.   משׁע

לְמִשְׁעֵנוּ pref. id. X noun masc. sing. dec. 2 b   שׁען

לְמִשְׁעָר preff. לְ & מְ X noun com. sing. dec. 6 d   שׁער

לְמִשְׁפָּחַת וּ pref. לְ X noun fem. sing. dec. 11 a (c. פַּחַת', suff. פַּחְתּוֹ' dec. 13 a, § 42. r. 5); וּ bef. (:)   שׁפח

לְמִשְׁפְּחוֹת pref. לְ f. [לָהּ] id. pl., abs. st.   שׁפח
לְמִשְׁפָּחוֹת pref. לְ q. v.

לְמִשְׁפְּחֹת וּ' pref. id. X id. pl., constr. st.; וּ bef. (:)   שׁפח

לְמִשְׁפְּחוֹתֵיהֶם pref. id. X id. pl., suff. 3 pers. pl. masc. (§ 4. rem. 2)   שׁפח
לְמִשְׁפְּחוֹתָם

לְמִשְׁפַּחַת pref. id. X id. sing., constr. st.   שׁפח

לְמִשְׁפַּחֹת pref. id. X id. pl., constr. st.   שׁפח

לְמִשְׁפְּחֹתָו pref. id. X id. pl., suff. 3 p. s. m. (§ 4. r. 1)   שׁפח

לְמִשְׁפְּחֹתֵיהֶם pref. id. X id. pl., suff. 3 pers. pl. masc.   שׁפח

לְמִשְׁפַּחְתּוֹ וּ pref. id. X id. sing., suff. 3 p. s. m.; וּ bef. (:)   שׁפח

לְמִשְׁפְּחֹתָיו pref. id. X id. pl., suff. 3 pers. sing. masc.   שׁפח

לְמִשְׁפְּחֹתֵיכֶם pref. id. X id. pl., suff. 2 pers. pl. masc.   שׁפח

לְמִשְׁפְּחֹתָם pref. id. X id. pl., suff. 3 pers. pl. m. (§ 4. r. 2)   שׁפח

לְמִשְׁפָּט pref. לְ for [לָהּ] noun masc. sing. dec. 2 b;   שׁפט
לְמִשְׁפָּט וּ' pref. לְ q. v. וּ bef. (:)

לְמִשְׁפַּט pref. id. X id., constr. st.   שׁפט

לְמִשְׁפָּטִי pref. id. X id. with suff. 1 pers. sing.   שׁפט

לְמִשְׁפְּטִי pref. לְ bef. (:) X Poel (§ 6. No. 1) part., suff. 1 pers. sing. from [מְשֹׁפֵט] dec. 7 b   שׁפט

לְמִשְׁפָּטֶיךָ pref. id. X noun masc. pl., suff. 2 pers. sing. masc. from מִשְׁפָּט dec. 2 b   שׁפט

לְמִשְׁפָּטִים וּ pref. id. X id. pl., abs. st.; וּ bef. (:)   שׁפט

לְמִשְׁפָּטֶךָ pref. id. X id. sing., suff. 2 p. s. m. [for מִשְׁפָּטְךָ]   שׁפט

לְמִשְׁקְלַת pref. id. X n. f. s. [for מִשְׁקֶלֶת] comp. § 35. r. 2]   שׁקל

לְמִשְׁרֵא Chald., pref. id. X Peal inf.   שׁרא

לְמְשֹׁרְרִים וְ pref. לְ for [לָהּ] X Pilel part. masc., pl. of מְשׁוֹרֵר dec. 7 b   שׁיר

לְמָתֵי pref. לְ & q. v. X Kal part. act. sing. masc. dec. 1 a (§ 21. rem. 2, & § 30. No. 3)   מות
לְמֵת

לִמְמְתֵא Chald., pref. לְ X Peal inf. [for מֵאתָא § 53. No. 1, & § 56. No. 2]   אתא

לְמָתוֹק pref. לְ X adj. m. s. (pl. § 32. r. 5) מְתוּקִים   מתק

לְמִתַּחַת preff. לְ & מְ X (prop. noun masc.) as a prep., with suff. תַּחְתִּי see תַּחַת   תוח

לְמָתַי pref. לְ X adv. interrog.   מתה

לִמְתָעֵב pref. לְ bef. (:) X Piel part. sing. masc.   תעב

לְמִתְפָּרוֹת pref. id. X Piel part. f. pl., of [מְתָפֵּרֶת] d. 13 a   תפר

לָן וְ' Kal pret. 3 pers. sing. masc.   לון

לָנָא Chald., pref. prep. לְ with suff. 1 pers. pl.   ל

לְנֶאֱמָנִים pref. לְ X Niph. part. m., pl. of נֶאֱמָן dec. 2 b   אמן

לַנְּבָאִים pref. לְ for [לָהּ] noun masc., pl of נָבִיא   נבא
לִנְבָאִים pref. לְ bef. (:) dec. 3 a

לִנְבוּכַדְנֶצַּר pref. id. X pr. name masc.   נבא
לִנְבוּכַדְרֶאצַּר

לְנָבוֹן pref. לְ X Niph. part. sing. masc. dec. 3 a   בין

לִנְבוֹת pref. id. X pr. name masc.   נוב

לְנֹבַח pref. id. X pr. name of a place   נבח

לִנְבֹּחַ pref. לְ bef. (:) X Kal inf. constr.   נבח

לַנָּבִיא pref. לְ f. [לָהּ]   נבא
לִנְבִיא pref. לְ q. v. noun masc. sing. dec. 3 a

לִנְבִיאַי וְ pref. לְ bef. (:) X id. pl., suff. 1 pers. sing.   נבא

לִנְבִיאֵי pref. id. X id. pl., constr. state   נבא

לִנְבִיאֵינוּ וְ pref. id. X id. pl., suff. 1 pers. pl.   נבא

לְנֵבֶל pref. לְ X noun masc. s. d. 4 a, also pr. name   נבל

לְנִבְלֵי pref. id. X noun m. pl. constr. fr. נֵבֶל d. 6 b   נבל

לַנְּבֹנִים pref. לְ for [לָהּ] X Niph. part. m., pl. of נָבוֹן d. 3 a   בין

לַנֶּגְבָּה pref. id. X n. m. s. (נֶגֶב) with loc. ה (§ 35. r. 3)   נגב

לְנֶגֶד pref. לְ X (prop. subst. masc.) as a prep., dec. 6 (§ 35. rem. 3)   נגד

לְנֶגְדּוֹ pref. id. X id., suff. 3 pers. sing. masc.   נגד

לְנֶגְדִּי pref. id. X id., suff. 1 pers. sing.   נגד

לְנֶגְדֶּךָ pref. id. X id., suff. 2 pers. s. m. (for נֶגְדְּךָ)   נגד

לְנֶגְדְּכֶם pref. id. X id., suff. 2 pers. pl. masc.   נגד

לְנֶגְדָּם pref. id. X id., suff. 3 pers. pl. masc.   נגד

לְנֹגַהּ וּ' pref. id. X noun m. s. d. 6 c (§ 35. r. 5)   נגה

לִנְגֹהוֹת pref. לְ bef. (:) X noun f., pl. of [נְגֹהָה] d. 10   נגה

לִנְגֹּעַ in full for לִנְגֹּעַ (q. v. & § 8. rem. 18)   נגע

לְנָגִיד וּ' pref. לְ X noun m. s. dec. 3 a; וּ bef. (:)   נגד

לִנְגִיד וּ' pref. id. X id., constr. st.   נגד

לְנַגֵּן pref. id. X Piel inf. constr.   נגן

לְנֶגַע pref. לְ or q. v. X noun masc. sing.   נגע
לִנְגַע (suff. נִגְעוֹ) dec. 6 a (§ 35. rem. 5)

a 2 Ki. 21. 14.   f Jos. 7. 14.   l Ge. 8. 19.   r Ps. 119. 91.   x De. 14. 1.   d Ge. 32. 22.   Is. 56. 10.   u Jos. 5. 13.   1 Ch. 5. 2.
b Hab. 2. 7.   g Ne. 4. 7.   m Ju. 21. 24.   s 2 Ch. 19. 10.   b Da. 3. 2.   e 2 Sa. 12. 16.   Ps. 105. 15.   v Is. 1. 7.   c Eze. 28. 2.
c Eze. 16. 4.   h Jos. 21. 20, 34.   n Ju. 30. 25.   t Ps. 119. 43.   c 1 Ki. 7. 32.   f Ezr. 4. 14.   Ne. 9. 32.   w Is. 59. 9.   d 1 Sa. 18. 13.
d Ps. 18. 19.   i Nu. 3. 30.   o 2 Ch. 19. 8.   u Is. 28. 17.   d Ex. 8. 5.   g Job 12. 20.   La. 4. 2.   x Is. 59. 9.   e De. 17. 8.
e Zec. 14. 10.   j Job 18. 2.   p 2 Ch. 19. 8.   w Is. 49. 7.   e Is. 25. 9.   h Ec. 9. 11.   Job 6. 7.   y Le. 13. 2.
f Ju. 18. 19.   k 1 Sa. 10. 21.   q Ps. 35. 23.   z Job 9. 15.   c 2 Ch. 5. 13   Eze. 13. 18.   Am. 2. 11.   1 Ch. 26. 17.   De. 32. 41.

לִנְגֹּעַ	pref. לְ bef. (:))(Kal inf. constr.	נגע
לִנְגֹּף	pref. id.)(Kal inf. constr.	נגף
לִנְדָבָה	pref. id.)(noun fem. sing. dec. 1 c	נדב
לַנֶּדֶר	pref. לְ for לְהַ)(Kal part. act. s. m. d. 7 b	נדד
לְנִדָּה	pref. לְ)(noun fem. sing. d. 10; ו bef. (:)	נדד
לִנְדֹּחַ	pref. לְ bef. (:))(Kal inf. constr.	נדח
לְנָדִיב	pref. לְ)((prim. adj.) noun masc. sing. d. 3a	נדב
לִנְדֹּר	pref. לְ bef. (:))(Kal inf. constr.	נדר
לְנֶגֶר	ו pref. לְ)(noun masc. sing. d. 6 b; ו bef. (:)	נדר
לִנְדָרָי	pref. לְ bef. (:))(id. pl., suff. 1 p. s. (for נְדָרַי)	נדר
לִנְדָרֶיהָ	pref. id.)(id. pl., suff. 3 pers. sing. fem.	נדר
לָנָה	ו Kal pret. 3 pers. sing. fem. [for לָנָה, comp. הַזֻּרָה for הַזֻּרָה]	לון
לַנַּהַר	pref. לְ for לְהַ)(noun masc. sing. dec. 4 a	נהר
לַנְּהָרֵי	pref. לְ)(id. pl., constr. st.	נהר
לָנוּ	־נֶ ,־ו)(pref. prep. לְ with suff. 1 pers. pl. (§ 5, parad.); ו see lett. ו	ל
לַגֻּ	ו Kal pret. 1 pers. pl. [for לַנְנוּ § 25. rem.]	לון
לָנוּד	pref. לְ (see lett. לְ))(Kal inf. constr.	נוד
לִנְוֵה	pref. לְ bef. (:))(noun m., constr. of נָוֶה d. 9 b	נוה
לָנוּחַ	pref. לְ (see lett. לְ))(Kal inf. constr.	נוח
לְנִיחֶךָ	pref. לְ)(noun masc. sing., suff. 2 pers. sing. masc. from נוֹחַ (comp. § 30. rem. 4)	נוח
לָנוּם	pref. לְ (see lett. לְ))(Kal inf. constr.	נום
לָנֻם	pref. id.)(Kal inf. constr.	נום
לָנוּעַ	pref. id.)(Kal inf. constr.	נוע
לְנֹועַדְיָה	pref. לְ)(pr. name fem.	יער
לַנּוֹתָרִים	pref. לְ for לְהַ)(Niph. part. m., pl. of נוֹתָר	יתר
לַנְּזָרִים	pref. לְ bef. (:))(noun m., pl. of נָזִיר d. 3 a	נזר
לְנֹחַ	pref. לְ)(pr. name masc.	נוח
לְנָחוֹר	pref. id.)(pr. name masc.	נחר
לַנַּחֲלִ	pref. לְ f. לְהַ)(noun masc. sing. dec. 6 d	נחל
לַנַּחַל	pref. לְ q. v.	
לְנַחֵל	pref. id.)(Piel inf. constr. (§ 14. rem. 1)	נחל
לִנְחֹל	pref. לְ bef. (:))(Kal inf. constr.	נחל
לְנַחֲלָה	pref. לְ)(noun fem. sing. dec. 12 d	נחל
לְנַחֲלַת	pref. id.)(id., constr. st.	נחל
לְנַחֲלָתוֹ	pref. id.)(id., suff. 3 pers. sing. masc.	נחל
לְנַחֵם	pref. id.)(Piel (§ 14. r. 1) inf. constr. d. 7 b	נחם
לְנַחֲמוֹ	־ ו pref. id.)(id., suff. 3 pers. s. m.; ו bef. (:)	נחם

לְנַחֲמֵנִי	pref. לְ)(id., suff. 1 pers. sing.	יחם
לָנַחַשׁ	pref. id.)(noun masc. sing. dec. 4 a	נחש
לַנְּחֹשֶׁת	ו' לְ pref. לְ f. לְהַ)(	נחש
לִנְחֹשֶׁת	pref. לְ bef. (:))(noun com. sing., dec. 13c	נחש
לַנְּחֻשְׁתַּיִם	pref. id.)(id. dual, abs. st. (§ 44. rem. 4)	נחש
לִנְחֻשְׁתָּם	pref. id.)(id. sing., suff. 3 pers. pl. masc.	נחש
לַנְחֹתָם	pref. לְ contr. for לְהַנְחֹתָם, Hiph. inf. with suff. 3 pers. pl. masc. (§ 11. rem. 3)	נחה
לִנְטֹועַ	ו in full for לִנְטֹעַ (q. v. & § 8. rem. 18)	נטע
לִנְטוֹת	pref. לְ bef. (:))(Kal inf. constr.	נטה
לִנְטֹעַ	pref. id.)(Kal inf. constr.	נטע
לַנֹּטְרִים	pref. לְ f. לְהַ)(Kal part. act. masc., pl. of נוֹטֵר dec. 7 b	נטר
לְנֹטְרִים	pref. לְ q. v.	
לִנְטֹת	defect. for לִנְטוֹת (q. v.)	נטה
לְנִדֹּה	pref. לְ)(noun fem. sing. R. נוד; or for נִדָּה, dag. forte resolved in Yod	נדד
לָנִים	Kal part. act. masc. pl. [of לָן § 21. rem. 2, & § 30. No. 3] dec. 1a	לון
לְנִינִי	ו pref. לְ)(noun masc. sing., suff. 1 pers. sing. from נִין dec. 1a; ו bef. (:)	נון
לְנִיצוֹץ	pref. id.)(noun masc. sing.	נצץ
לִנְכָּדִי	ו pref. id.)(noun masc. sing., suff. 1 pers. sing. fr. נֶכֶד dec. 6 (§ 35. r. 3); ו bef. (:)	נכד
לְנֹכַח	pref. id.)((prop. subst. m.) as a *prep. & adv.*	נכה
לַנֵּכְרִי	pref. לְ f. לְהַ)(	נכר
לְנָכְרִי	pref. לְ q. v.)(adj. masc. sing.	נכר
לַנֵּכָרִים	pref. id.)(id. pl., abs. st.	נכר
לַנִּמְהָרֵי	pref. id.)(Niph. part. pl. constr. masc. from נִמְהָר dec. 2b	מהר
לִנְמוּאֵל	pref. לְ bef. (:))(pr. name masc., see נְמוּאֵל	
לָנֻם	defect. for לָנוּם (q. v.)	נום
לַנֵּס	pref. לְ)(noun masc. sing. dec. 8b	נסס
לְנַסּוֹת	pref. id.)(Piel inf. constr. dec. 1b	נסה
לְנַסּוֹתוֹ	pref. id., suff. 3 pers. sing. masc.	נסה
לַנֶּסֶךְ	pref. לְ for לְהַ)(noun m. s. (suff. נִסְכִּי) d.6a	נסך
לִנְסֹךְ	ו pref. לְ bef. (:))(Kal inf. constr.	נסך
לְנַסָּכָה	Chald., pref. לְ)(Pael inf. constr. (§ 47. r. 5)	נסך
לְנִסְכֵּיכֶם	ו pref. id.)(noun masc. pl., suff. 2 pers. pl. masc. from נֶסֶךְ dec. 6a; ו bef. (:)	נסך
לַנְסֹתוֹ	pref. id.)(Piel inf. (נַסּוֹת), suff. 3p. s. m. d.1b	נסה
לִנְסֹתְךָ	pref. id.)(id., suff. 2 pers. sing. masc.	נסה

ᵃ Ex. 12. 22.   ᵍ Ps. 61. 6.   ᵐ 2 Sa. 21. 10.   ᵗ Jos. 17. 9, 9.   ᵃ 1 Ch. 29. 2.   ᶠ Ex. 13. 21.   ˡ La. 1. 8.   ⁿ De. 23. 21.   ˢ Is. 30. 1.
ᵇ Je. 49. 5.   ʰ Nu. 30. 13.   ⁿ 2 Ch. 6. 41.   ᵘ Nu. 34. 29.   ᵇ 1 Ch. 22. 14, 16.   ᵍ 1 Ki. 25. 16.   ᵐ Ne. 13. 21.   ᵒ De. 14. 21.   ᵗ Da. 2. 46.
ᶜ Zec. 13. 1.   ⁱ Zec. 5. 4.   ᵒ Is. 56. 10.   ᵛ Eze. 35. 15.   ᶜ 2 Ki. 25. 16.   ʰ Ca. 8. 11.   ⁿ Ge. 21. 23.   ᵖ La. 5. 2.   ᵘ Nu. 29. 39.
ᵈ De. 20. 19.   ᵏ 1 Ki. 14. 15.   ᵖ Ju. 21. 7, 16.   ʷ Is. 61. 2.   ᵈ 2 Sa. 3. 34.   ⁱ Is. 35. 4.   ᵒ Is. 1. 31.   ᵠ 2 Ch. 32. 31.   ᵛ 1 Ki. 10. 1.
ᵉ Pr. 17. 7.   ˡ Esr. 4. 3.   ᵠ Am. 2. 11.   ˣ Job 2. 11.   ᵉ Je. 52. 20.   ᵏ Ex. 23. 2.   ʳ Ge. 21. 23.   ʳ De. 8. 2.
ᶠ Le. 22. 23.   ᵐ Ju. 19. 13.   ʳ Jos. 15. 7.

לְנָעֳמִי	ᵃ pref. ל ✗ pr. name fem ; ו bef. (:)	נעם
לְנַעֲמָן	pref. id. ✗ pr. name masc.	נעם
לַנַּעַר / לַנָּעַר	{ pref. ל f. [לָה] } noun masc. sing. dec. 6 d	נער
לַנַּעַר	pref. ל q. v.	נער
לַנַּעֲרָ	ᵇ pref. ל for [לָה] Kh. נַעַר com. gen. (q.v.); K. נַעֲרָה noun fem. sing. dec. 12 d	נער
לְנַעֲרוֹ	ᶜ pref. ל ✗ noun masc. sing., suff. 3 pers. sing. masc. from נַעַר dec. 6 a	נער
לְנַעֲרוֹתֶיךָ	pref. id. ✗ noun fem. pl., suff. 2 pers. sing. masc. from נַעֲרָה dec. 12 d	נער
לְנַעֲרֶיהָ	pref. ל bef. (:) ✗ noun masc. pl., suff. 3 pers. sing. fem. from נַעַר dec. 6 d	נער
לַנְּעָרִים	pref. ל for [לָה] ✗ id. pl., abs. st.	נער
לְנַעֲרַת	pref. ל bef. (:) ✗ noun fem. sing.	נער
לְנַעֲרֹתֶיהָ	pref. ל ✗ noun fem. pl., suff. 3 pers. sing. fem. from נַעֲרָה dec. 12 d	נער
לַנְפֵּל	ᵈ ו pref. ל contr. [לְהַנְפִּיל Hiph. inf. constr. (§ 11. rem. 3, & § 17. rem. 6)	נפל
לִנְפֹּל	pref. ל bef. (:) ✗ Kal inf. constr. (§ 17. r. 1)	נפל
לְנִפְלְאֹתֶיהָ	pref. ל ✗ Niph. part. pl., suff. 3 pers. sing. masc. from נִפְלָא dec. 11 a, from נִפְלָאָה m.	פלא
לְנֶפֶשׁ / לַנֶּפֶשׁ / לַנָּפֶשׁ / לְנָפֶשׁ	{ pref. ל (see ל) } { pref. ל for [לָה] noun com. sing. dec. 6 a (§ 35. rem. 2) } { pref. ל q. v. }	נפש
לְנַפְשָׁהּ	pref. id. ✗ id., suff. 3 pers. sing. fem.	נפש
לְנַפְשׁוֹ	pref. id. ✗ id., suff. 3 pers. sing. masc.	נפש
לְנַפְשִׁי	pref. id. ✗ id., suff. 1 pers. sing.	נפש
לְנַפְשֶׁךָ / לְנַפְשֶׁךָ	pref. id. ✗ id., suff. 2 pers. sing. masc.	נפש
לְנַפְשֵׁךְ	pref. id. ✗ id., suff. 2 pers. sing. fem.	נפש
לְנַפְשְׁכֶם	pref. id. ✗ id., suff. 2 pers. pl. masc.	נפש
לְנַפְשָׁם	pref. id. ✗ id., suff. 3 pers. pl. masc.	נפש
לְנַפְשֹׁתֵיכֶם	pref. id. ✗ id. pl., suff. 2 pers. pl. masc.	נפש
לְנַפְשֹׁתֵינוּ	pref. id. ✗ id. pl., suff. 1 pers. pl.	נפש
לְנַפְשֹׁתָם	pref. id. ✗ id. pl., suff. 3 pers. pl. m. (§ 4. r. 2)	נפש
לְנָפַת	pref. id. ✗ noun fem. sing. constr. of [נֹפָה] dec. 10, also pr. name	נוף
לְנַפְתָּלִי	ᵉ pref. id. ✗ pr. name of a tribe ; ו bef.	פתל
לְנֵצַח	pref ל (see lett. ל) ✗ noun masc. sing. (suff. נִצְחִי) dec. 6 a (§ 35. rem. 5)	נצח
לְנַצֵּחַ	pref. ל ✗ Piel inf. constr.	נצח
לְנֵצַח	pref. id. ✗ noun masc. sing. dec. 6 e	נצח
לִנְצֹר	pref. ל bef. (:) ✗ Kal inf. constr.	נצר
לְנֹצְרֵי	pref. ל ✗ id. part. pl. constr. m. from נֹצֵר d. 7 b	נצר
לַנְּקֵבָה	ו pref. ל for [לָה] ✗ noun fem. sing.	נקב
לִנְקַבְצָיו	pref. ל ✗ Niph. part. pl. masc., suff. 3 pers. sing. masc. [from נִקְבָּץ]	קבץ
לַנְּקִי	ᵇ pref. id. ✗ adj. masc. (constr. נְקִי, pl. נְקִיִּם) dec. 8 (§ 37. No. 4)	נקה
לִנְקֹם	pref. ל bef. (:) ✗ Kal inf. constr.	נקם
לַנֵּרוֹת	pref. ל for [לָה] ✗ noun masc. with pl. fem. term. from נֵר dec. 1 a	נור
לְנֹשֵׂא	pref. ל ✗ Kal part. act. sing. masc. dec. 7 b	נשא
לְנִשְׁבָּרֵי	pref. id. ✗ Niph. part. pl. constr. masc. from נִשְׁבָּר dec. 2 b	שבר
לַנִּשְׁבֶּרֶת	ו pref. ל for [לָה] ✗ id. sing. fem.	שבר
לְנָשַׁי	ᵍ pref. ל ✗ noun fem. with pl. masc. term. (נָשִׁים), suff. 1 pers. s. see אִשָּׁה irr. (§ 45)	אנש
לַנָּשִׂיא / לְנָשִׂיא	{ ו pref. ל f. [לָה] } { pref. ל q. v. } noun masc. sing. dec. 3 a	נשא
לְנָשָׁיו	pref. id. ✗ noun fem. pl. (נָשִׁים), suff. 3 pers. sing. masc. see אִשָּׁה irr. (§ 45)	אנש
לִנְשֵׁיכֶם	ᶜ ו pref. ל bef. (:) ✗ id. with suff. 2 pers. pl. m.	אנש
לַנָּשִׁים / לְנָשִׁים	{ pref. ל for [לָה] id. pl., abs. st. } { pref. ל q. v. }	אנש
לְנַשֵּׁק	ᵐ pref. id. ✗ Piel inf. constr.	נשק
לִנְשֹׁק	ⁿ pref. ל bef. (:) ✗ Kal inf. constr. [for נָשֹׁק § 8. rem. 18, & § 17. rem. 1]	נשק
לִנְתִיבוֹת	pref. id. ✗ noun fem. pl. of נְתִיבָה dec. 10	נתב
לְנָתָן	ᵒ pref. ל ✗ pr. name masc. ; ו bef. (:)	נתן
לִנְתַנְאֵל	ᵖ ו pref. ל bef. (:) ✗ pr. name masc.	נתן
לִנְתוֹץ	ᵠ ו pref. id. ✗ Kal inf. constr. (§ 8. r. 18, & § 17. r. 1)	נתץ
לִנְתֹּשׁ	pref. id. ✗ Kal inf. constr. (§ 8. r. 18, & § 17. r. 1)	נתש
לִנְתָחֶיהָ	pref. id. ✗ noun masc. pl., suff. 3 pers. sing fem. from נֶתַח dec. 6 e	נתח
לִנְתָחָיו	pref. id. ✗ id. pl., suff. 3 pers. sing. masc.	נתח
לִנְתִיבָתִי	pref. id. ✗ noun fem. sing., suff. 1 pers. sing. from נְתִיבָה dec. 10	נתב
לַנָּתֵק	ᵠ ו pref. ל for [לָה] ✗ n. m. s. (for נֶתֶק § 35. r. 2)	נתק
לְנַתֵּר	pref. ל ✗ Piel inf. constr.	נתר
לִסְבֹּב	ʳ pref. ל bef. (:) ✗ Kal inf. constr. (§ 18. r. 13)	סבב
לִסְבִיבוֹתֵינוּ	pref. id. ✗ noun masc. with pl. fem. term. and suff. 1 pers. pl. from סָבִיב dec. 3 a	סבב

ᵃ Ju. 19. 19.   ᶠ Pr. 31. 15.   Nu. 9. 10.   ⁱ Is. 51. 23.   ᵘ Is. 34. 10.   Pr. 1. 11.   ᶻ 1 Ki. 20. 7.   ᶠ Ge. 45. 19.   ᵖ Ps. 119. 105.
ᵇ Pr. 1. 4.   ᵍ Nu. 5. 22.   ˡ Pr. 16. 24.   Je. 6. 6.   Pr. 9 8   ᶜ Eze. 24. 8.   Eze. 45. 7.   Ge. 31. 28.   ᵗ Le. 14. 54.
De. 22. 26.   Ps. 111. 4.   ᵐ Pr. 13. 19.   Jos. 9. 24.   Ps 25. 10.   Zec. 4. 2.   Nu. 17. 21.   2 Sa. 20. 9.   Le. 11. 21.
ᵈ 1 Sa. 25. 19.   Nu. 5. 2.   De. 21. 14.   Pr. 1. 18.   12 7.   1 Sa. 31 4.   Ge. 4. 23.   Je. 6. 16.   Nu. 21. 4.
Is. 1. 31,   Le. 19. 28 ;   Pr. 2. 10.   Jos. 12. 23.   Is. 56. 8.   Eze. 34. 4, 16.

לִסְבֹּל־	pref. לְ bef. (ְ))(Kal inf. constr.	סבל
לְסִבְלֹתֵיכֶם‎	pref. לְ)(noun fem. pl., suff. 2 pers. pl. masc. [from סְבָלָה or סֻבְלָה]	סבל
לִסְגּוֹר	pref. לְ bef. (ְ))(Kal inf. constr. (§ 8. r. 18)	סגר
לִסְגִים	pref. לְ)(noun m. pl. abs. for סִינִים fr. סִין	סוג
לְסֻגָלָתוֹ	pref. לְ bef. (ְ))(noun fem. sing., suff. 3 pers. sing. masc. from סְגֻלָה dec. 10	סגל
לַסְּגָנִים‎	וְ pref. לְ for לְהַ)(noun masc. pl. [of סָגָן or סֶגֶן § 35. rem. 12]	סגן
לְסוֹנֵי‎	pref. לְ)(Kh. סוֹג; K. סִין, noun masc. sing. dec. 1a, comp. לְסָנִים	סוג
לָסוּס	pref. לְ for לְהַ)(noun masc. sing. dec. 1a	סוס
לְסוּסָיו‎	pref. לְ)(id. pl., suff. 3 pers. sing. masc.	סוס
לַסּוּסִים‎	pref. לְ for לְהַ)(id. pl., abs. st.	סוס
לְסוֹף‎	Chald., pref. לְ)(noun masc. sing. dec. 1a	סוף
לְסוּר‎	pref. לְ (see lett. לְ))(Kal inf. constr.	סור
לִסְחֹב‎	pref. לְ bef. (ְ))(Kal inf. constr.	סחב
לִסְחֹר‎	pref. לְ for לְהַ)(Kal part. act. sing. m. d. 7b	סחר
לְסִיחוֹן לְסִיחֹן	} pref. לְ)(pr. name masc.	סוח
לְסִיסְרָא‎	pref. id.)(pr. name masc., see סִיסְרָא	
לְסִיר־‎	pref. id.)(noun com. sing. dec. 1a	סיר
לִסְלֹחַ‎ לִסְלֹחַ‎	} pref. לְ bef. (ְ))(Kal inf. constr. (§ 8. rem. 18)	סלח
לְסַלֵּי‎	pref. לְ)(pr. name masc.	סלל
לְסַנְבַּלַּט‎	pref. id.)(pr. name masc., see סַנְבַּלַּט	
לִסְסָתִי‎	pref. id.)(noun fem. sing., suff. 1 pers. sing. from [סוּסָה] dec. 10	סוס
לִסְפֹּד‎ לִסְפּוֹד‎	} pref. לְ bef. (ְ))(Kal inf. constr. (§ 8. r. 18)	ספד
לְסֹלֶת‎	pref. לְ)(noun com. sing. dec. 6c; וּ bef. (ְ)	סלת
לְסַעֲדָהּ‎	pref. id.)(Kal inf. [סָעַד], suff. 3 pers. sing. fem. (§ 16. rem. 10); וּ id.	סעד
לִסְפּוֹת‎	pref. לְ bef. (ְ))(Kal inf. constr.	ספה
לִסְפּוֹתָהּ‎	pref. id.)(id. with suff. 3 pers. sing. fem.	ספה
לַסַּפַּחַת‎	וְ pref. לְ for לְהַ)(noun fem. sing.	ספח
לְסַפֵּר‎	וְ pref. לְ)(Piel inf. constr.; וּ bef. (ְ)	ספר
לִסְפֹּר‎	pref. לְ bef. (ְ))(Kal inf. constr.	ספר
לְסָקְלוֹ‎	pref. לְ)(Kal inf., suff. 3 pers. sing. masc.	סקל
לְסֶרֶד‎	pref. id.)(pr. name masc.	סרד
לְסָרִיסָיו‎	pref. id.)(noun masc. pl., suff. 3 pers. sing. masc. from סָרִים d. 1b (but see § 32. r. 2)	סרס
לַסָּרִיסִים‎	pref. לְ for לְהַ)(id. pl., abs. st.	סרס
לְסָרְנֵי‎	pref. לְ)(noun m. pl. constr. from [סֶרֶן] d. 6a	סרן
לְסַרְגֵיכֶם‎	וּ pref. id.)(id. pl., suff. 2 p. pl. m.; וּ bef. (ְ)	סרן
לִסְתּוֹם‎	pref. לְ bef. (ְ))(Kal inf. constr. (§ 8. rem. 18)	סתם
לְסַתֵּר‎	pref. לְ)(contr. and defect. [for לְהַסְתִּיר] Hiph. inf. constr. (§ 11. rem. 3)	סתר
לָעֵב‎	Hiph. to mock at, to deride, 2 Ch. 36. 16.	
לְעַב‎	pref. לְ (see lett. לְ))(noun com. sing. dec. 1a (except constr. once עַב)	עוב
לַעֲבֹד‎	וְ pref. לְ bef. (ֲ))(Kal inf constr.	עבד
לְעֶבֶד‎	pref. לְ)(noun masc. sing. (suff. עַבְדִּי) dec. 6a, also pr. name in compos. עֶבֶד מֶלֶךְ	עבד
לְעֹבֵד‎	וּ pref. id.)(pr. name in compos. עֹבֵד אֱדֹם	עבד
לַעֲבֹדָה‎	pref. לְ bef. (ֲ))(noun fem. sing. dec. 10	עבד
לְעָבְדָהּ‎	pref. לְ)(Kal inf., suff. 3 pers. sing. fem.	עבד
לְעָבְדוֹ‎	וּ pref. id.)(id., suff. 3 pers. s. m.; וּ bef. (ְ)	יבד
לְעָבְדוֹהִי‎	Chald., pref. id.)(noun masc. pl., suff. 3 pers. sing. masc. from עֲבַד dec. 3a	עבד
לְעַבְדִּי‎	pref. id.)(noun masc. sing., suff. 1 pers. sing. from עֶבֶד dec. 6a	עבד
לְעֹבְדֵי‎	pref. id.)(Kal part. act. pl. constr. masc. from עָבַד dec. 7b	עבד
לְעֹבַדְיָה‎	וּ pref. id.)(pr. name masc.; וּ bef. (ְ)	עבד
לְעֹבְדֵיהֶם‎	pref. id.)(Kal part. act. pl., suff. 3 pers. pl. masc. from עָבַד dec. 7b	עבד
לְעַבְדֵיהֶם‎	pref. id.)(noun masc. pl., suff. 3 pers. pl. masc. from עֶבֶד dec. 6a	עבד
לַעֲבָדָיו‎	וְ pref. לְ bef. (ֲ))(id. pl., suff. 3 pers. s. m.	עבד
לְעַבְדָּךְ‎	Chald., pref. לְ)(noun masc. pl., suff. (K. דָּךְ) 2 pers. sing. masc. from עֲבַד dec. 3a	עבד
לַעֲבָדֶיךָ‎	וְ pref. לְ bef. (ֲ))(noun masc. pl., suff. 2 pers. pl. masc. from עֶבֶד dec. 6a	עבד
לַעֲבָדִים‎	pref. id.)(id. pl., abs. st.	עבד
לְעׇבְדֶךָ‎ לְעׇבְדֶךָ‎	} pref. לְ)(id. sing., suff. 2 pers. sing. masc.; וּ bef. (ְ)	עבד
לְעׇבְדָם‎	pref. id.)(Kal inf., suff. 3 pers. pl. masc.	עבד
לַעֲבֹדַת‎	וְ pref. לְ bef. (ֲ))(noun fem. sing., constr. of עֲבוֹדָה dec. 10	עבד
לְעׇבְדָתוֹ‎	וְ pref. id.)(id., suff. 3 pers. sing. masc.	עבד
לְעׇבְדָתָם‎	pref. id.)(id., suff. 3 pers. pl. masc.	עבד
לַעֲבֹדָתָם‎	pref. לְ)(noun fem. sing., suff. 3 pers. pl. masc. from [עֲבֹדוּת] dec. 10	עבד

a Ge. 49. 15.   f Eze. 22. 18.   i Ge. 23. 16.   p Ca. 1. 9.   Nu. 32. 14.   u 1 Sa. 30. 6.   d 1 Sa. 6. 4.   h Zec. 2. 13.   m 1 Ch. 26. 30.
b Ex. 5. 4.   g De. 11. 4.   k Eze. 11. 11.   q Je. 16. 5.   r Ps. 40. 15.   v 1 Sa. 8. 15.   e 2 Ch. 32. 3.   l Zec. 2. 13.   n 1 Ch. 23. 26.
c Jos. 2. 5.   h 1 Ki. 5. 8.   l Is. 55. 7.   r Je. 15. 29.   s Le. 14. 56.   w Is. 56. 4.   f Is. 29. 15.   k Da. 2. 4.   o Ps. 104. 26.
d Ps. 135. 4.   i Da. 4. 8, 19.   m 2 Ki. 24. 4.   t Is. 9. 6.   t Ps. 26. 7.   x Ju. 16. 18.   g Ge. 2. 15.   l Le. 25. 6.   p Ne. 9. 17.
e Ne. 2. 16.   Je. 15. 3.

לַעֲבוֹד	in full for לַעֲבֹד (q. v. & § 8. r. 18) .	עבד
לַעֲבוֹדָה	pref. לְ bef. (־ֲ) ⟩(noun fem. sing. dec. 10	עבד
לַעֲבוֹדַת	pref. id. ⟩(id., constr. st. .	עבד
לַעֲבוֹדָתָם	pref. id. ⟩(id., suff. 3 pers. pl. masc.	עבד
לַעֲבוּר	pref. id. ⟩(Kh. לַעֲבוֹר q. v., K. לַעֲבֻר q. v. (§ 8. rem. 18)	עבד
לַעֲבֹר	in full for לַעֲבֹר (q. v. & § 8. rem. 18)	עבר
לַעֲבֹט	pref. לְ bef. (־ֲ) ⟩(Kal inf. constr. .	עבט
לַעֲבִידַת	Chald., pref. id. ⟩(noun fem. sing., constr. of [עֲבִידָא] dec. 8a .	עבד
לַעֲבִיר	contr. for לְהַעֲבִיר (q. v. & § 11. rem. 3) .	עבר
לַעֲבֹר	pref. לְ bef. (־ֲ) ⟩(Kal inf. constr. (§ 8. rem. 18) .	עבר
לַעֲבֵר	pref. לְ bef. (־ֲ) ⟩(noun masc. sing. dec. 6 (§ 35. rem. 6), also pr. name masc.; וּ bef. (־ֲ)	עבר
לַעֲבָדוֹ	pref. id. ⟩(id., suff. 3 pers. sing. masc.	עבר
לְעֹבְרֵי	pref. id. ⟩(Kal part. act. pl. c. masc. from עֹבֵר dec. 7b	עבר
לָעִבְרִים	pref. לְ f. לְהָ, לְהַ ⟩(gent. n., pl. of עִבְרִי fr. עֵבֶר .	עבר
לָעִבְרִים	pref. לְ for לְהָ ⟩(id. pl., abs. st.	עבר
לְעָבְדְךָ	pref. לְ ⟩(Kal inf., suff. 2 pers. sing. masc.	עבר

[לָעֵג]	fut. יִלְעַג, to mock, deride, scorn. Niph. to stammer, Is. 33. 19. Hiph. to mock, deride, with בְּ, עַל, לְ.
(לָעֵג)	adj. masc. dec. 5 (only pl. c. לַעֲגֵי).—I. stammering, stammerer, Is. 28. 11; Gesenius, speaking in a foreign or barbarous tongue.—II. mocker, jester, Is. 28. 11 לַעֲגֵי מָעוֹג cake jesters, i. e. parasites, who act the part of jesters at the table.
לַעַג	masc. dec. 6 d, scorn, derision, scoffing; meton. cause of derision, Ho. 7. 16.

לַעַג	noun masc. sing. dec. 6 d .	לען
לֹעֵג	Kal part. act. sing. masc.	לען
לָעֲגָה	id. pret. 3 pers. sing. fem.	לען
לַעֲגֵי	adj. pl. constr. masc. from [לָעֵג] dec. 5c	לען
לַעֲדָה	pref. לְ ⟩(pr. name fem. .	ענל
לַעֲדָלוֹן	pref. id. ⟩(pr. name of a man and a place .	ענל
לַעֲדָלוֹת	pref. id. ⟩(noun f., pl. c. fr. עֲדָלָה (no pl. abs.)	ענל
לַעֲדָלִים	וְ pref. לְ bef. (־ֲ) ⟩(noun masc., pl. of עֲדָל dec. 6 (§ 37. rem. 6)	ענל
לַעֲדָם	noun masc. sing., suff. 3 pers. pl. masc. from לַעַד dec. 6 d	לען

לָעַד	Root not used; Arab. to put in order.	
לַעֲדָה	(order) pr. name masc. 1 Ch. 4. 21.	
לַעֲדָּן	(put in order) pr. name masc. of two different persons.	
לָעַד, לַעֲדִי	pref. לְ & לָ לְ q. v. ⟩(prep. עַד, constr. with suff. עֲדֵי (§ 21. rem. 5)	עדה
לָעַד	pref. id. ⟩(noun masc. s. d. 1a; וּ bef. (־ָ)	עוד
לָעֵדָה	pref. לְ for לְהָ, לְהַ ⟩(noun fem. sing. d. 11b	יעד
לַעְדָּה	pr. name masc. .	לעד
לָעֵדָה	pref. לְ ⟩(noun fem. sing. dec. 10	עוד
לְעֵדְוֹתָיךָ	וּ pref. id. ⟩((read ēhdĕvō-) noun fem. pl., suff. 2 p. s. m. from עֵדוּת (q. v.); וּ bef. (־ְ)	עוד
לַעֲדִיא	pref. id. ⟩(Kh. עֲדִיא, K. עֲדּוֹא (q. v.)	עדד
לַעְדָּן	pr. name masc. .	לעד
לַעֲדְרִיאֵל	pref. לְ ⟩(pr. name masc. .	עדר
לַעֲדֹר	וּ pref. לְ bef. (־ֲ) ⟩(Kal inf. constr.	עדר
לָעֲדָרִים	pref. id. ⟩(n. m., pl. of עֵדֶר d. 6 (§ 37. r. 6)	עדר
לַעֲדַת	pref. id. ⟩(noun f. s., constr. of עֵדָה d. 11b	יעד
לַעֲדָת	pref. לְ for לְהָ, לְהַ ⟩(noun fem. sing. (pl. with suff. עֵדֹתֶיךָ) .	עוד
לַעֲדָתָם	pref. לְ bef. (־ֲ) ⟩(noun fem. sing., suff. 3 pers. pl. masc. from עֵדָה dec. 11b .	יעד

[לָעָה]	to be rash, in speaking, Job 6. 3.

לָעוּ	[for לָעֲוּ] Kal pret. 3 pers. pl.	לעה
לָעוּ	וְ Kal pret. 3 pers. pl. .	לוע
לְעוֹג	וּ pref. לְ ⟩(pr. name masc.; וּ bef. (־ְ)	עוג
לָעוּז	pref. לְ (see lett. לְ) ⟩(Kal inf. c. R. עוז, or for עֹז (§ 18. rem. 2) R.	עזז
לְעֻגֵּל	pref. לְ ⟩(noun masc. sing. .	עול
לְעוֹלָה	pref. לְ for לְהָ, לְהַ ⟩(noun fem. sing. d. 10	עלה
לְעוֹלָה	pref. id. ⟩(Kal part. act. sing. masc. dec. 9a	עלה
לְעוֹלָה	וּ pref. לְ ⟩(noun fem. sing. dec. 10; וּ bef. (־ְ)	עלה
לְעוֹלְלֵיהֶם	pref. id. ⟩(noun masc. pl., suff. 3 pers. pl. masc. from עוֹלֵל dec. 7b	עלל
לְעוֹלָם	וּ pref. id. ⟩(noun masc. s. d. 2b; וּ bef. (־ְ)	עלם
לְעוֹלַת	וּ pref. id. ⟩(n. f. s., constr. of עוֹלָה d.10; וּ id.	עלה
לַעֲוֹן	pref. לְ bef. (־ֲ) ⟩(n. m. s., constr. of עָוֹן d. 3a	עוה
לַעֲוֹנוֹתֶיךָ	pref. id. ⟩(id. pl., suff. 2 pers. sing. masc.	עוה
לַעֲוֹנִי	pref. id. ⟩(id. sing., suff. 1 pers. sing.	עוה
לַעֲוֹנָם	pref. id. ⟩(id. sing., suff. 3 pers. pl. masc.	עוה
לַעֲוֹנֵנוּ	pref. id. ⟩(id. sing., suff. 1 pers. pl.	עוה

ᵃ 2 Ch. 33. 16.   ᶠ Ezr. 6. 7.   ᵏ Is. 51. 23.   ᵖ 1 Ki. 12. 32.   ᵗ Is. 19. 20.   ˣ Ex. 31. 7.   ᵈ Is. 30. 2.   ʰ Jos. 22. 26, 28.   ᵐ Ne. 10. 34.
ᵇ 2 Ch. 34. 13.   ᵍ 2 Sa. 19. 19.   ˡ De. 29. 11.   ᵠ 2 Ch. 11. 15.   ᵘ Ne. 9. 34.   ʸ Ho. 7. 12.   ᵉ Job 31. 3.   ⁱ Eze. 45. 15.   ⁿ Nu. 14. 19.
ᶜ 2 Ch. 31. 16.   ʰ 1 Ki. 18. 6.   ᵐ Ps. 35. 16.   ʳ Ho. 7. 16.   ᵛ 1 Ch. 12. 33.   ᶻ Job 6. 3.   ᶠ Eze. 40. 42.   ᵏ Ps. 17. 14.   ᵒ Job 22. 5.
ᵈ Na. 2. 1.   ⁱ Is. 47. 15.   ⁿ Ho. 10. 5.   ˢ Zep. 3. 8.   ʷ Nu. 19. 9.   ᵃ Ob. 1. 16.   ᵍ Eze. 40. 40.   ˡ Ps. 119. 160.   ᵖ Eze. 54. 9.
ᵉ De. 24. 10.   ʲ Pr. 9. 15.

לְעוּף*	pref. ל for ,לָה לְהַ) X noun masc. sing. .	עוף
לְעוּף*	pref. ל (see lett. ל) X Kal inf. constr. .	עוף
לָעוּף	וְ pref. ל X noun masc. sing.; וְ bef. (־:)	עוף
לָעוּר*	pref. ל for ,לָה לְהַ) X adj. masc. sing. d. 7 b	עור
לָעוּת*	pref. ל (see lett. ל) X Kal inf. constr. .	עות
לְעַוֵּת*	וְ pref. ל X Piel inf. constr.; וְ bef. (־:)	עות

[לָעַז] to speak in a barbarous or foreign tongue, Ps. 114. 1. Syr. id.

לֹעֵז	Kal part. act. sing. masc.	לעז
לַעֲזָאזֵל*	pref. ל bef. (־:) X see under עֲזָאזֵל.	
לַעֲזֹב	pref. id. X Kal inf. constr. .	עזב
לְעֹזֵב*	pref. ל X id. part. act. sing. masc. dec. 7 b	עזב
לְעָזְבֵךְ*	pref. id. X id. inf., suff. 2 pers. sing. fem.	עזב
לְעַזָּה	pref. id. X pr. name of a place	עזה
לַעֲזֹור־	in full for לַעֲזֹר & § 8. r. 18)	עזר
לְעַזָּרֵל*	pref. ל for ,לָה לְהַ) X patronym. of עֲזִיאֵל q. v.	עזז
לַעֲזָיָה	pref. ל X pr. name masc. . .	עזז
לַעֲזָיָהוּ		
לַעֲזִיר־	Kh. לְעָזִיר pref. ל, for לְהַעֲזִיר Hiph. inf. c. (§ 11. rem. 3); K. לָעֲזִר (q. v.) .	עזר
לַעֲזֹר	pref. ל bef. (־:) X Kal inf. constr. (comp. § 13. rem. 2 & 1)	עזר
לְעֵזֶר*	pref. ל X noun masc. sing. dec. 6 (§ 35. r. 6)	עזר
לְעֶזְרָא*	pref. id. X pr. name masc. .	עזר
לְעֶזְרָה	pref. ל bef. (־:) X noun fem. sing.	עזר
לְעֶזְרָה	pref. ל X noun fem. sing. dec. 12 b	עזר
לְעָזְרוֹ	pref. id. X Kal inf., suff. 3 pers. sing. masc.	עזר
לַעֲזַרְיָה	וְ pref. ל bef. (־:) X pr. name masc. .	עזר
לַעֲזַרְיָהוּ		
לְעֹזְרֶיךָ*	pref. ל X Kal part. act. pl., suff. 2 pers. sing. masc. [for עֹזְרֶיךָ § 4. r. 1] from עֹזֵר d. 7 b	עזר
לְעֶזְרֵנוּ	pref. id. X id. inf., suff. 1 pers. pl.	עזר
לְעֶזְרֵנִי	pref. id. X id. id., suff. 1 pers. sing. .	עזר
לְעֶזְרָת*	pref. id. X noun f. s., constr. of עֶזְרָה d. 12 b	עזר
לְעֶזְרָתִי	pref. id. X id. with suff. 1 pers. sing.	עזר
לַעֲנָתִים*	pref. ל f. לָה ,לְהַ) X gent. n., pl. of עֲנָה fr.	עזז

לָעַט Hiph. to give to eat, Ge. 25. 30.

לַעֲטַלֵּפִים*	וְ pref. ל for ,לָה לְהַ) X noun masc., pl. of עֲטַלֵּף dec. 1 b (§ 36. No. 1)	עטלף

לַעֲטֶרֶת*	pref. ל bef. (־:) X n. f. s., pl. עֲטָרוֹת (§ 44. r. 5)	עטר
לְעַי	pref. ל for ,לָה לְהַ) X pr. name of a place	עוה
לְעָי		
לָעִי*	pref. ל X n. s. m., pl. עָיִים d. 8 (§ 37. No. 4)	עוה
לְעִיט*	pref. id. X noun m. s., constr. of עַיִט d. 6 h	עוט
לָעֵיִּים*	pref. id. X noun m., pl. of עִי dec. 8 (§ 37. No. 4)	עוה
לַעֲיֵלוֹם*	pref. id. X noun masc. sing.	עלם
לָעָוֹן*	pref. ל for ,לָה לְהַ) X noun fem. sing. d. 6 k	עין
לָעָוֹן*		
לְעֵינַי	pref. ל X id. du., suff. 1 pers. sing.	עין
לְעֵינֵי		
לְעֵינֵי*	וְ pref. id. X id. du. constr. st.; וְ bef. (־:)	עין
לְעֵינֵיהֶם	pref. id. X id. du., suff. 3 pers. pl. masc.	עין
לְעֵינָיו	pref. id. X id. du., suff. 3 pers. sing. masc. .	עין
לְעֵינֶיךָ	pref. id. X id. du., suff. 2 pers. sing. masc.	עין
לְעֵינֵיכֶם	pref. id. X id. du., suff. 2 pers. pl. masc.	עין
לָעֵינָיִם*	pref. ל for ,לָה לְהַ)	עין
לָעֵינַיִם*		
לָעֵינַיִם*	pref. ל f. לָה) (dag. f. impl.)	
לָעֵינָיִם*	pref. ל q. v.	
לְעֵינֵינוּ	pref. id. X id. du., suff. 1 pers. pl.	עין
לְעָיֵף*	pref. ל for ,לָה לְהַ) X adj. masc. sing. dec. 5 c	עיף
לַעֲיֵפָה*	pref. ל bef. (־:) X id. fem.	עיף
לָעִיר	pref. ל f. לָה) X noun fem. sing. irr. (§ 45)	עור
לָעִיר	pref. ל q. v.	
לְעִירוֹ*	pref. id. X id. with suff. 3 pers. sing. masc.	עור
לַעֲלֶה	pref. ל f. ,לָה לְהַ) X noun fem. sing. dec. 10	עלה
לַעֲלֶה	pref. ל q. v.	
לַעֲלוֹת*	pref. ל bef. (־:) X Kal inf. constr. (§ 8. rem. 18)	עלה
לַעֲלֻקָה	Ch., pref. id. X noun fem. pl. abs. fr. [עֲלוּ] d. 8 c	עלה
לַעֲלוּקָה*	pref. id. X noun fem. sing.	עלק
לַעֲלוֹת	pref. id. X Kal inf. constr. dec. 1 b	עלה
לַעֲלוֹת	pref. ל f. ,לָה לְהַ) X nour fem., pl. of עוֹלָה	עלה
לַעֲלוֹת*	pref. ל q. v. dec. 10	עלה
לְעַלִּי	pref. id. X pr. name masc.	עלה
לְעַלָּא*	וְ Chald., pref. id. X adj. masc. sing. emph. [of עֲלִי]; K. עֲלָאָה, dec. 7; וְ bef. (־:)	עלה
לְעֶלְיוֹן	pref. id. X adj. masc. sing. dec. 1 b	עלה
לָעֶלֶם*	pref. ל for ,לָה לְהַ) X noun masc. sing. .	עלם
לָעֹלָם	pref. ל X noun masc. sing. dec. 2 b	עלם
לְעָלְמַיָא*	Chald., pref. id. X noun masc. pl. emph. from עָלַם dec. 2 a	עלם

- Le. 7. 26.
- Pr. 26. 2.
- Job 29. 15.
- Is. 50. 4.
- Is. 2. 20.

- La. 3. 36.
- Am. 8. 5.
- Ps. 114. 1.
- Le. 16. 8, 10, 26.

- Ge. 44. 22.
- Pr. 15. 10.
- Ru. 1. 16.
- 2 Ch. 25. 8.

- 2 Sa. 18. 3.
- Ju. 5. 23.
- 2 Ch. 4. 9.
- 1 Ch. 12. 22.

- 1 Ch. 12. 18.
- Is. 28. 5.
- Mi. 1. 6.

- Ps. 79. 1.
- 2 Ch. 33. 7.
- Eze. 12. 12.

- Pr. 10. 26.
- Ge. 3. 6.
- Nu. 34. 11.
- Is. 28. 12.

- Is. 46. 1.
- Is. 23. 12.
- Ezr. 6. 9.
- Pr. 30. 15.

- 2 Ch. 31. 2.
- Da. 4. 31.
- 1 Sa. 20. 22.
- Da. 2. 44.

לְעֹלָמִיםּ	pref. לְ)(noun masc., pl. of עוֹלָם dec. 2 b	עלם
לְעָלְמִין	Ch., pref. id.)(noun m. pl. abs. from עָלַם d. 2 a	עלם
לַעֲלֹת	pref. לְ bef. (=))(Kal inf. constr.	עלה
לַעֲלַתּ	pref. לְ)(noun fem. sing., constr. of עֹלָה d. 10	עלה
לְעֹלֹתֵיכֶם	pref. id.)(id. pl., suff. 2 pers. pl. masc.	עלה
לְעָם	ן' pref. לְ f. לָה, לְ	
לְעַם	} pref. לְ q. v. { noun com. s. d. 8 a (§ 45); וּ bef. (:)	עמם
לֶעָם	וּ'	
לַעֲמֹד	ן' pref. לְ bef. (=))(Kal inf. constr.	עמד
לַעֲמְדָהּ	pref. לְ)(id. with suff. 3 pers. sing. fem.	עמד
לָעֲמֻדִים'	pref. לְ for לָה, לְ)(noun masc. pl. (for עַמּוּדִים from עַמּוּד) dec. 1 b	עמד
לְעַמּוֹ	pref. לְ)(noun com. sing., suff. 3 pers. sing. masc. from עַם dec. 8 d (§ 45)	עמם
לַעֲמוֹד	in full for לַעֲמֹד (q. v. & § 8. rem. 18)	עמד
לָעַמּוּד	pref. לְ f. לָה, לְ } noun masc. sing. dec.	עמד
לְעַמּוּדֵּ	וּ pref. לְ q. v. } 1 b ; וּ bef. (:)	
לָעַמּוּדִים'	pref. לְ for לָה, לְ)(id. pl., abs. st.	עמד
לַעֲמוֹק	pref. לְ)(pr. name masc.	עמק
לַעֲמוֹתּ	pref. id.)((prop., noun fem. pl. of עֻמָּה dec. 10) as a prep.	עמם
לְעַמִּיּ	pref. id.)(n. com. pl. constr. fr. עַם d. 8 a (§45)	עמם
לְעַמִּי	pref. id.)(id. sing., suff. 1 pers. sing.	עמם
לַעֲמִיתֶךָּ	pref. לְ bef. (=))(noun fem. sing., suff. 2 pers. sing. masc. from עֲמִית dec. 3 a	עמה
לְעַמִּים'	pref. לְ)(noun com., pl. of עַם dec. 8 a (§ 45)	עמם
לְעַמֶּךָ	} pref. id.)(id. sing., suff. 2 pers. sing.	
לְעַמֶּךָ	וּ' } masc.; וּ bef. (:)	עמם
לְעַמֵּךְ	pref. id.)(id. sing., suff. 2 pers. sing. fem.	עמם
לְעָמֵל	pref. id.)(noun masc. sing. dec. 4 c	עמל
לֶעָמֵל	pref. id.)(adj. masc. sing. dec. 5 c	עמל
לַעֲמָלֵק	pref. לְ bef. (=))(pr. name of a people	עמלק
לָעֵמֶק	pref. לְ for לָה, לְ)(noun masc. sing. dec. 6 b	עמק
לְעֵמֶק	pref. לְ)(noun masc. sing.	עמק
לָעֵמֶק	pref. לְ)(noun masc. sing. dec. 6 b	עמק
לַעֲמֹרָה	pref. לְ bef. (=))(pr. name of a place	עמר
לַעֲמְרָם	pref. לְ)(pr. name masc., see עַמְרָם	עמם
לַעֲמְרָמִי	pref. לְ for לָה, לְ)(patronym. of the prec.	עמם
לַעֲמָשָׂא	ן' pref. לְ bef. (=))(pr. name masc.	עמש
לְעֻמַּת	pref. id.)((prop. noun fem. sing., constr. of עֻמָּה dec. 10) prep.	עמת
לְעֻמָּתוֹ	pref. id.)(id., suff. 3 pers. sing. masc.	עמת

לְעֻמָּתָם	pref. לְ)(id., suff. 3 pers. pl. masc.	עמת
לָעַן	Root not used; Arab. *to reject, detest;* also *to curse.* Hence	
לַעֲנָה	ן' fem. *wormwood;* metaph. of *distress*	לען
לַעֲנָוֵיּ	pref. לְ)(adj. pl. constr. masc. fr. עָנָו d. 4 c	ענה
לַעֲנוֹת	pref. לְ bef. (=))(Kal inf. constr.	ענה
לְעַנּוֹתּ	pref. לְ)(Piel inf. constr. dec. 1 b	ענה
לְעַנּוֹתוֹּ	pref. id.)(id., suff. 3 pers. sing. masc.	ענה
לְעַנּוֹתֶךָּ	pref. id.)(id., suff. 2 pers. s. m. [for עַנּוֹתְךָ]	ענה
לֶעָנִי	pref. לְ for לָה, bef. עָ for לָה; &	ענה
לֶעָנִי'	pref. לְ)(adj. masc. s. d. 8 (§ 37. No. 4) }	ענה
לַעֲנִיִּם'	ו' pref. לְ bef. (=))(id. pl. abs. (Kh. עֲנִיִּים'); K. עֲנָוִים (q. v.)	ענה
לְעָנְיֶךָּ	pref. id.)(id. sing., suff. 2 pers. sing. masc.	ענה
לַעֲנֵשׁ'	Chald., pref. id.)(noun masc. sing.	ענש
לַעֲנֹתּ	pref. לְ, contr. [for לְהַעֲנֹת], Niph. inf. constr. (§ 9. rem. 6)	ענה
לְעַנֹּתּ'	pref לְ)(Piel inf. constr.	ענה
לְעֹפֶל	pref. לְ for לָה, לְ)(pr. name of a tower	עפל
לְעַפְעַפָּיּ	pref. id.)(noun masc. du., suff. 1 pers. sing. from [עַפְעַף] dec. 8 d	עוף
לְעַפְעַפֶּיךָּ	pref. id.)(id., suff. 2 pers. sing. masc.	עוף
לֶעָפָר	pref. לְ for לָה, bef. עָ for לָה; & }	עפר
לְעָפָר	pref. לְ)(noun masc. sing. dec. 4 c }	עפר
לְעָפָר'	ו pref. לְ bef. (=))(id., constr. st.	עפר
לְעֹפֶר	pref. לְ)(noun masc. sing. dec. 6 c	עפר
לְעָפְרָה	pref. id.)(pr. name of a place	עפר
לְעֶפְרֹן	pref. id.)(pr. name masc.	עפר
לָעֵץ	pref. לְ f. לָה, לְ }noun masc. sing. dec. 7 a	עצה
לְעֵץ	pref. לְ q. v. } (§ 36. rem. 2 & 4) }	עצה
לְעַצְבוֹתָםּ	pref. id.)(noun fem. pl., suff. 3 pers. pl. masc. from עַצֶּבֶת q. v.	עצב
לְעַצְבֵּיּ	pref. לְ bef. (=))(noun masc. pl. constr. fr. [עֶצֶב] dec. 8 a	עצב
לְעַצְבֶּיהָּ	ו pref. id.)(id. with suff. 3 pers. sing. fem.	עצב
לַעֲצַבִּים'	pref. לְ for לָה, לְ)(id. pl., abs. st.	עצב
לְעֵצָה'	pref. לְ)(noun fem. sing. dec. 11 b	יעץ
לַעֲצִיוֹן	pref. id.)(pr. name in compos. עֶצְיוֹן גֶּבֶר	עצה
לָעֵצִים	pref. לְ for לָה, לְ)(noun masc., pl. of עֵץ dec. 7 a (§ 36. rem. 2 & 4)	עצה
לְעֶצֶם'	pref. id.)(noun fem. sing. dec. 6 a (for עֶצֶם) § 35. rem. 2)	עצם

a Ec. 1. 10.	f Ex. 38. 17.	l Le. 25. 14.	q Job 5. 7.	u De. 29. 17.	y Ju. 16. 6.
b Nu. 28. 23.	g Je. 1. 18.	m Is. 2. 4.	r Job 3. 20.	v Ps. 102. 1.	z Ex. 10. 3.
c Nu. 29. 39.	h Ex. 38. 28.	n Ex. 32. 12.	s Ju. 1. 34.	w Ps. 88. 1.	a Nu. 30. 14.
d Je. 1. 18.	i Eze. 45. 7.	o Ex. 8. 5.	t Ru. 1. 10.	x Ju. 16. 5, 19.	b Ps. 132. 4.
e Esc. 17. 14.	k Ne. 10. 31.	p Ru. 1. 10.		y De. 15. 11.	

לְעַצְמוֹת	pref. לְ for לָהּ, לָהּ X id. pl. abs. fem.	עצם
לְעַצְמוֹתָי	pref. לְ X id. pl. fem., suff. 2 pers. sing. m.	עצם
לַעֲצָמָיהָ	pref. לְ bef. (-:) X id. pl. m., suff. 3 pers. s. f.	עצם
לַעְצֹר	pref. id. X Kal inf. constr.	עצר
לַעֲצָתוֹ	pref. id. X noun fem. sing., suff. 3 pers. sing. masc. from עֵצָה dec. 11 b	יעץ
לַעֲצָתִי	pref. id. X id. with suff. 1 pers. sing.	יעץ
לַעֲקוֹר	pref. id. X Kal inf. constr. (§ 8. rem. 18)	עקר
לְעֵקֶר	pref. לְ X noun masc. sing.	עקר
לְעֶקְרוֹן	pref. id. X pr. name of a place	עקר
לְעֵר	pref. id. X pr. name masc.	עור
לְעֶרֶב / לָעֶרֶב	pref. לְ for לָהּ, לָהּ X noun com. sing. dec. 6c (§ 35. rem. 2)	ערב
לְעָרְבֵי	pref. לְ X noun masc. sing. dec. 7 b	ערב
לַעֲרֹב	pref. לְ bef. (-:) X Kal inf. constr.	ערב
לְעֹרוֹ	pref. לְ X noun masc. sing., suff. 3 pers. sing. masc. from עוֹר dec. 1a	עור
לַעֲרוֹב	in full for לַעֲרֹב (q. v. & § 8. rem. 18)	ערב
לַעֲרוּגוֹת	pref. לְ bef. (-:) X n. f., pl. of [עֲרוּגָה] dec. 10	ערג
לְעָרַי	pref. לְ X noun fem. pl. constr. (prop. from עָר see עִיר § 45) ; ן bef. (:)	עור
לְעָרֵי	pref. id. X pr. name masc.	עור
לְעָרֶיהָ	pref. id. X noun fem. pl., suff. 3 pers. sing. fem. (prop. from עָר see עִיר § 45)	עור
לְעָרֵיהֶם	pref. id. X id. with suff. 3 pers. pl. masc.	עור
לְעָרָיִךְ	Chald., pref. id. X noun masc. pl., suff. 2 pers. sing. masc. from עָר dec. 1a	עיר
לְעָרִים / וְ	pref. לְ for לָהּ, bef. for לָהּ X noun fem. pl. of עָר see עִיר (§ 45)	עור
לַעֲרִיץ	pref. id. X noun masc. sing., pl. עֲרִיצִים d. 1 b	ערץ
לַעֲרֹךְ	pref. לְ bef. (-:) X Kal inf. constr.	ערך
לְעֶרֶן	pref. לְ X pr. name masc.	עור
לַעֲרָפֶל	pref. לְ bef. (-:) X noun masc. sing.	ערף
לַעֲרֹץ	pref. id. X Kal inf. constr.	ערץ
לְעֹשֶׂה	pref. לְ for לָהּ X Kal part. act. sing. masc. dec. 9a	עשה
לַעֲשֵׂה	pref. לְ X id., constr. st.	עשה
לַעֲשֵׂהוּ	pref. id. X id. with suff. 3 pers. sing. masc.	עשה
לְעַשּׂוּ	pref. id. X pr. name masc.	עשה
לַעֲשׂוּקִים	pref. לְ bef. (-:) X Kal part. pass. masc., pl. of עָשׁוּק dec. 3a	עשק
לַעֲשׂוֹת / וְ	pref. id. X Kal inf. constr. dec. 1 b	עשה

לַעֲשׂוֹתָם	pref. לְ bef. (-:) X id., suff. 3 pers. pl. masc.	עשה
לְעֹשֵׂי	pref. לְ X Kal part. act. pl. constr. masc. from עֹשֶׂה dec. 9a	עשה
לֶעָשִׁיר / לַעֲשִׁיר	pref. לְ f. לָהּ, לָהּ / pref. לְ q. v. } noun masc. sing. dec. 3a	עשר
לַעֲשֹׁק	pref. לְ bef. (-:) X Kal inf. constr.	עשק
לְעֹשְׁקַי	pref. לְ X id. part. act. pl. masc., suff. 1 pers. sing. from עֹשֵׁק dec. 7b	עשק
לְעָשְׁקָם	pref. id. X id. inf., suff. 3 pers. pl. masc.	עשק
לַעְשֵׂר	pref. לְ, contr. [for לְהַעְשֵׂר], Hiph. inf. constr. (§ 11. rem. 2 & 3)	עשר
לַעֲשֵׂר	pref. לְ X num. card. fem.	עשר
לְעֹשֶׁר	pref. id. X noun masc. sing. dec. 6c	עשר
לַעֲשָׂרִים	pref. id. X card. num. com., pl. of עֶשֶׂר (§ 35. rem. 16)	עשר
לַעֲשֹׂת	pref. לְ bef. (-:) X Kal inf. constr.	עשה
לַעֲשֹׂתָה	pref. id. X id., suff. 3 pers. sing. fem.	עשה
לַעֲשֹׂתוֹ	pref. id. X id., suff. 3 pers. sing. masc.	עשה
לַעֲשָׁתוֹת	pref. לְ X noun fem., pl. of עֶשֶׁת dec. 6a	עשת
לַעֲשְׁתֹּת	pref. id. X n.f.s. (a different reading of the prec.)	עשת
לְעַשְׁתֵּי עָשָׂר / לְעַשְׁתֵּי עֶשְׂרֵה	pref. id. { id. pl. constr. of עֶשֶׁת only in combination with the num. ten, making together eleven }	עשת
לַעֲשׂתְכֶם	pref. לְ bef. (-:) X Kal inf. (עֲשׂוֹת), suff. 2 pers. pl. masc. dec. 1b	עשה
לַעֲשׂתָם	pref. id. X id., suff. 3 pers. pl. masc.	עשה
לָעַשְׁתָּרוֹת / וְ	pref. לְ for לָהּ, לָהּ X pl. of the foll. (§ 44. rem. 5).	עשת
	pref. לְ X pr. name of an idol, see עַשְׁתֹּרֶת	
לָעֵת / וְ / לְעֶת-	pref. id. X noun com. sing. dec. 8b (§ 36. rem. 3) ; ן bef. (:)	עדה
לָעַתּוּדִים / וְ	pref. לְ for לָהּ, לָהּ X n. m., pl. of [עַתּוּד] d. 1b	עתד
לְעִתּוֹת	pref. לְ X noun com. with pl. fem. term. from עֵת dec. 8b	עדה
לָעִתִּים	pref. לְ f. לָהּ, לָהּ X id. with pl. masc. term. ;	עדה
לְעִתִּים / וְ	pref. לְ q. v. } ן bef. (:)	עדה
לִעְתְנִיאֵל	pref. id. X pr. name masc., see עָתְנִיאֵל	
לִפְאָה	pref. לְ f. לָהּ } noun fem. sing. dec. 11b	פאה
לִפְאַה	pref. לְ q. v. }	פאה
לְפָאֵר	pref. id. X Piel inf. constr.	פאר
לִפְאַת / וְ	pref. לְ bef. (-:) X n. f., constr. of פֵּאָה d. 11b	פאה
לִפְגֹּעַ	pref. id. X Kal inf. constr.	פגע

a Eze. 37. 5.   e Ec. 3. 2.   i Ex. 22. 26.   q 2 Ch. 31. 1.   u Nu. 15. 29.   c Ho. 12. 8.   h Job 12. 5.   m Eze. 34. 17.   r Ne. 9. 22.
b Pr. 3. 8.   f Le. 25. 47.   k Ju. 19. 9.   r Da. 4. 16.   v Is. 29. 16.   d Ps. 119. 121.   i Job 12. 5.   n 1 Ch. 12. 32.   s Ex. 38. 11,
c Ju. 19. 29.   g 1 Ch. 23. 30.   l Ca. 6. 2.   s Eze. 36. 4.   w Ps. 146. 7.   e De. 26. 12.   k De. 4. 14.   o Eze. 12. 27.   12, 13.
d 2 Ch. 22. 9.   p Job 38. 41.   m Is. 44. 26.   t Job 15. 20.   x Ps. 103. 18.   f 1 Ki. 7. 38.   l Je. 14. 19.   p Ex. 27. 9.   t 1 Sa. 22. 17.
e Ps. 105. 13.   h Eze. 27. 9.   n Nu. 32. 33.   o Je. 13. 16.   g Ec. 5. 11.   l 1 Ch. 25. 27.

לָפַד Root not used; prob. *to shine*, whence Gr. λάμπω (μ inserted after the first radical) and subst. λαμπάς, Chald. לַמְפַּד, Syr. לְמְפִּידָא *lamp*.

לַפִּיד masc. dec. 1 b.—I. *lamp, torch.*—II. *flame.*

לַפִּידוֹת (*lamps*) pr. name of the husband of the prophetess Deborah, Ju. 4. 4.

לִפְדּוֹת pref. לְ bef. (.ְ) χ Kal inf. constr. . . . פרה

לַפִּדִים‸ ₁ defect. for לַפִּידִים (q. v.) . . . . לפד

לְפֶּה ‍₂ pref. לְ (see לְ)‌} noun masc. sing. irr. (§ 45) פאה

לְפֶה pref. לְ q. v. }

לְפֻּאָה pref. id. χ pr. name masc., see פֻּאָה

לִפוֹטִיפַר pref. id. χ pr. name masc., see פוֹטִי

לְפוּל pref. id. χ pr. name masc. . . . . פול

לִפוּקָה‸ pref. id. χ noun fem. sing. . . . . פוק

לְפַח‸ pref. id. χ noun masc. sing., pl. (פַּחִים) } פחת
לְפָח (§ 37. rem. 7) . . . . }

לְפַחַד‸ pref. id. χ noun masc. sing. dec. 6 d . . פחד

לַפְחֹת‸ pref. לְ (see lett. לְ) χ Kal inf. constr. . נפח

לִפְחֶתֶךָ‸ pref. לְ χ noun masc. sing. with fem. term. and suff. 2 pers. s. m. from פֶּחָה irr. (§ 45) פחה

לְפִי‸ ₁ pref. id. χ noun masc. constr., or with suff. 1 p. s. from פֶּה irr. (§ 45); ₁ bef. (.ְ) . פאה

לַפִּיד‸ ₁ noun masc. sing. dec. 1 b . . . . לפד

לַפִּידוֹת pr. name fem. . . . . . . לפד

לַפִּידִים noun masc., pl. of לַפִּיד dec. 1 b . . לפד

לְפִיהוּ‸ pref. לְ χ noun masc. sing., suff. 3 pers. sing. masc. from פֶּה irr. (§ 45) . . . פאה

לְפִיהֶם‸ pref. id. χ id., suff. 3 pers. pl. masc. . . פאה

לְפִיהֶן‸ pref. id. χ id., suff. 3 pers. pl. fem. . . פאה

לְפִיו‸ pref. id. χ id., suff. 3 pers. sing. masc. . . פאה

לְפִלֹא‸ pref. id. χ Piel inf. constr. . . . . פלא

לִפְלַגּוֹת‸ pref. לְ bef. (.ְ) χ noun f., pl. of [פְּלַגָּה] d. 10 פלג

לִפְלַגּוֹת‸ pref. id. χ noun fem., pl. of [פְּלַגָּה] dec. 10 פלג

לְפַלּוּא‸ pref. לְ χ pr. name masc. . . . . פלא

לִפְלְחָן Chald., pref. id. χ noun masc. sing., constr. of [פֶּלְחָן] dec. 1 b . . . . פלח

לְפַלְטִי‸ pref. id. χ pr. name masc. . . . . פלט

לִפְלֵיטָה‸ pref. לְ bef. (.ְ) χ noun fem. sing. dec. 10 פלט

לִפְלֵיטַת‸ pref. id. χ id. constr. st. . . . . פלט

לְפִלְכּוּ‸ pref. לְ χ noun masc. sing., suff. 3 pers. sing. masc. from פֶּלֶךְ dec. 6 a . . . פלך

לַפְּלֹמֹנִי‸ pref. לְ for לְהַ χ by contr. for פְּלֹנִי אַלְמֹנִי see פלה

לַפְּלִשְׁתִּים pref. לְ for לְהַ χ gent. noun, pl. of פְּלִשְׁתִּי‸ פלש

לִפְנֵי‸ pref. לְ χ noun fem. sing. dec. 10 . . פנה

לִפְנוֹת pref. לְ bef. (.ְ) χ Kal inf. constr. dec. 1 a . פנה

לְפָנַי pref. לְ χ noun masc. pl. (פָּנִים), suff. 1 } פנה
לְפָנַי pers. sing. from [פָּנֶה] dec. 9 b . }

לִפְנֵי [for [לִפְנֵי adj. m. fr. the pl. constr. (q. v.) . פנה

לִפְנֵי‸ ₁ pref. לְ bef. (.ְ) χ noun masc. pl. constr. [from פָּנֶה], as a *prep* פנה

לְפָנֶיהָ pref. לְ χ id., suff. 3 pers. sing. fem. פנה

לִפְנֵיהֶם‸ ₁ pref. לְ bef. (.ְ) χ id., suff. 3 pers. pl. masc. פנה

לְפָנָיו‸ ₁ pref. id. χ id., suff. 3 pers. s. m.; ₁ bef. (.ְ) פנה

לְפָנֶיךָ‸ ₁ pref. id. χ id., suff. 2 pers. sing. masc.; ₁ id. פנה

לִפְנֵיכֶם‸ pref. לְ bef. (.ְ) χ id., suff. 2 pers. pl. masc. . פנה

לַפָּנִים‸ dd pref. לְ χ id. pl. abs. . . . . פנה

לְפָנִים‸ pref. לְ χ id. pl. abs. *adverbially* . . פנה

לִפְנִימָה pref. לְ bef. (.ְ) χ n. m. s. (פָּנִים) with loc. ה פנה

לְפָנֵינוּ pref. לְ χ noun masc. pl. (פָּנִים), suff. 1 pers. pl. from [פָּנֶה] dec. 9 b . . . . פנה

לִפְנֻנָּה pref. לְ bef. (.ְ) χ pr. name fem. . . פנן

לְפֶסַח‸ pref. לְ for לְהַ χ adj. masc. sing. dec. 7 b פסח

לִפְסָחִים‸ pref. id. χ noun masc., pl. of פֶּסַח dec. 6 a פסח

לִפְסִילִים‸ x pref. id. χ noun masc., pl. of [פָּסִיל] d. 3 a פסל

לְפִסְלוֹ‸ pref. לְ χ n. m. s., suff. 3 p. s. m. fr. פֶּסֶל d. 6 a פסל

לִפְסִלִים‸ ₁ defect. for לַפְּסִילִים (q. v.) . . פסל

לְפָעֳלוֹ‸ pref. לְ χ n. m. s., suff. 3 p. s. m. fr. פֹּעַל d. 6 f פעל

לִפְעֻלּוֹת‸ pref. לְ bef. (.ְ) χ noun f., pl. of [פְּעֻלָּה] d. 10 פעל

לְפֹעֲלִי‸ ₁ pref. לְ χ Kal part. act., suff. 1 pers. sing. from פֹּעַל dec. 7 b ; ₁ bef. (.ְ) פעל

לְפָעֳלֵי pref. id. χ id. pl., constr. st. . . . פעל

לְפָעֳלָם‸ pref. id. χ n. m. s., suff. 3 p. pl. m. fr. פֹּעַל d. 6 f פעל

לִפְעֻלָּתֵךְ‸ pref. לְ bef. (.ְ) χ noun fem. sing., suff. 2 pers. sing. fem. from [פְּעֻלָּה] dec. 10 . פעל

לִפְעֻלַּתְכֶם pref. id. χ id., suff. 2 pers. pl. masc. . פעל

לְפָעֳמוֹ‸ g pref. לְ χ Kal inf. [פָּעַם], suff. 3 pers. sing. masc. (§ 16. rem. 10) . . . . פעם

לִפְעָמַי‸ pref. לְ bef. (.ְ) χ n.f. pl., suff. 1 p. s. fr. פַּעַם d. 6 d פעם

לִפְצָעִי‸ pref. לְ χ noun masc. sing., suff. 1 pers. sing. from פֶּצַע dec. 6 a (§ 35. rem. 5) . . פצע

לִפְקֹד‸ k ₁ pref. לְ bef. (.ְ) χ Kal inf. constr. . פקד

לִפְקֻדָּה‸ pref. id. χ noun fem. sing. dec. 10 . . פקד

לִפְקִדוֹן‸ m pref. לְ χ noun masc. sing. . . . פקד

לִפְקֻדֵיהֶם defect. for לִפְקוּדֵיהֶם (q. v.) . . פקד

‸ Ju. 15. 4.   * Job 39. 22.   ‡ Ec. 6. 7.   ₙ 2 Ch. 35. 5.   ₒ Je. 51. 26.   ₚ Is. 42. 8.   ₐ Ps. 17. 4.   f 2 Ch. 15. 7.   ‖ Ho. 12. 3.

b Ju. 7. 16.   f Mal. 1. 8.   k Job 29. 9.   ₒ Ezr. 7. 19.   q 1 Ki. 6. 17.   r Is. 44. 17.   s Job 36. 3.   g Ju. 13. 25.   l 1 Ch. 23. 11.

c 1 Sa. 25. 31.   g Ge. 15. 17.   l Le. 25. 51.   ₙ Ne. 3. 17.   o Ho. 11. 2.   s Job 37. 12.   h Ge. 41. 36.

d Ps. 69. 23.   h Job 41. 11.   m Ju. 5. 16.   n Da. 3. 13.   p 2 Ch. 35. 7, 8, 9.   q Ps. 104. 23.   e Je. 31. 16.   ₚ Ps. 57. 7.   i Ge. 4. 23.   ₓ Eze. 22. 20.

לִפְקֻדָּתָם֯ pref. לְ bef. (.))(noun fem. sing., suff. 3 pers. pl. masc. from פְּקֻדָּה dec. 10 . פקד

לִפְקוּדֵיהֶםי pref. id.)(Kal part. pass. pl. masc., suff. 3 pers. pl. masc. from [פָּקוּד] dec. 3a פקד

לִפְקוּדֶיךָ pref. לְ)(noun masc. pl., suff. 2 pers. sing. masc. from [פָּקוּד] dec. 1b פקד

לְפֶקַח pref. id.)(pr. name masc. . . . פקח

לִפְקֹחַּ pref. לְ bef. (.))(Kal inf. constr. . . פקח

לַפָּר pref. לְ for לְהַ פָּר, with the art. ; &

לְפַרי pref. לְ)(noun masc. sing. d. 8 (§ 37. r. 7) פרר

לְפַרְבָּרי pref. לְ for לְהַ)(noun masc. sing. פרבר

לִפְרֹץי pref. לְ bef. (.))(Kal inf. constr. (§ 8. r. 18) פרץ

לְפִרְחוֹתʰ pref. לְ)(Kal part. act. fem., pl. of פֹּרַחַת dec. 13, from פֶּרַח masc. . . פרח

לְפִרְיוֹ pref. id.)(n. m. s., suff. 3 p. s. m. fr. פְּרִי d. 6i פרה

לַפָּרִים pref. לְ for לְהַ)(noun masc. pl. [for פָּרִים from פָּר dec. 8 (§ 37. rem. 7) פרר

לַפָּרֹכֶת pref. id. }
לִפְרֹכֶתי pref. לְ } noun fem. sing. . . . פרך

לְפָרָס pref. id.)(pr. name of a country . . פרס

לְפַרְעֹה pref. id.)(pr. name masc., see פַּרְעֹה. פרעה

לְפֶרֶץ pref. id.)(pr. name masc. . . . פרץ

לִפְרֹשׂי pref. לְ bef. (.))(Kal inf. constr. פרש

לִפְרָשִׁים pref. לְ)(noun masc., pl. of פָּרָשׁ dec. 1b (§ 30. rem. 1); ו bef. (.) . פרש

לְפֹרְשִׂיםי pref. id.)(Kal part. act. m., pl. of פּוֹרֵשׂ d. 7b . פרש

לְפַשֵּׂט pref. id.)(Piel inf. constr. . . פשט

לְפִשְׁעִי pref. id.)(n. m. s. (suff. פִּשְׁעִי) d. 6a (§ 35. r. 5) פשע

לִפְשֹׁעַ pref. לְ bef. (.))(Kal inf. constr. . . פשע

לַפֹּשְׁעִיםי ו pref. לְ f. לְהַ)(id. part. a. m., pl. of פֹּשֵׁעַ d. 7b פשע

לְפִשְׁעֲכֶם pref. לְ)(noun masc. sing., suff. 2 pers. pl. masc. from פֶּשַׁע dec. 6a (§ 35. rem. 5) . פשע

לַפִּשְׁתִּיםי pref. לְ for לְהַ)(noun fem. with pl. masc. term. from פִּשְׁתָּה dec. 10 . . פשת

[לָפַת] fut. יִלְפָּת, to embrace, Ju. 16. 29. LXX περιέλαβε; Vulg. apprehendens. Targ. prehendit; Prof. Lee, intrans. to turn towards; const. with אֶת. Niph. —I. to turn aside, Job 6. 18.—II. to turn oneself, turn round, Ru. 3. 8.

לִפְתָאִים pref. לְ bef. (.))(noun masc., pl. of [פְּתִי] dec. 6i (§ 35. rem. 15) פתה

לְפֹתֵהַּᵘ ו pref. לְ)(Kal part. act. sing. m. ; ו bef. (.) פתה

לַפֶּתַחᵖ pref. לְ for לְהַ)(noun masc. sing. (suff. פִּתְחוֹ) dec. 6a (§ 35. rem. 5) . פתח

לְפַתֵּחַי ו pref. לְ)(Piel inf. constr.; ו bef. (.) פתח

לְפִתְחָ pref. id.)(n. m. s. (suff. פִּתְחִי) d. 6a (§ 35. r. 5) פתח

לִפְתֹּחַ pref. לְ bef. (.))(Kal inf. constr. . פתח

לִפְתַחְיָה pref. id.)(pr. name masc., see פְּתַחְיָה . פתח

לְפֶתַע pref. לְ (noun masc.) only adverbially פתע

לִפְתֹּרי pref. לְ bef. (.))(Kal inf. constr. . פתר

לְפַתֹּתְךָֽי pref. לְ)(Piel inf. [פַּתֹּת], suff. 2 p. s. m. d. 1b פתה

לָץֵ ו Kal part. act. sing. masc. dec. 1a (§ 21. rem. 2, & § 36. rem. 2) . . . לוץ

לַצֹּאןֵ pref. לְ for לְהַ)(noun com. sing. dec. 1a צאן

לְצֹאנִיֵ pref. לְ)(id., suff. 1 pers. sing. צאן

לְצֹאנְךֵָ pref. id.)(id., suff. 2 pers. s. m. (for צֹאנֶךָ) צאן

לְצֹאנָםֵ pref. id.)(id., suff. 3 pers. pl. masc. . צאן

לְצֵאתֵ ו pref. לְ, when not followed by a genit., &

לְצֵאתֵ pref. לְ when followed by a genit.)(Kal inf. constr. dec. 1a (comp. § 23. rem. 4) יצא

לְצֵאתָם pref. id.)(id. with suff. 3 pers. pl. masc. יצא

לַצָּבָא pref. לְ for לְהַ)(noun m. s. d. 4a (§ 33. r. 2) צבא

לְצָבָא pref. לְ)(pr. name masc. for צִיבָא נצב

לִצְבָאי pref. לְ bef. (.))(noun masc. sing., constr. of צָבָא dec. 4a (§ 33. rem. 2) . צבא

לִצְבָּא pref. id.)(Kal inf. constr. . . . צבא

לִצְבָאֲךָי pref. id.)(n. m. s., suff. 2 p. s. m. fr. צָבָא d. 4a צבא

לְצִבְאֹתָם pref. לְ)(id. with pl. f. & suff. 3 pers. pl. m. צבא

לַצְבּוֹתᵈ pref. לְ [for לְהַצְבּוֹת], Hiph. inf. constr. צבה

לִצְבִּי pref. לְ bef. (.))(noun masc. sing. dec. 6i צבה

לְצִבְעוֹן pref. לְ)(pr. name masc. צבע

לְצַדד Chald., pref. id.)(noun masc. sing. צדד

לְצָדוֹק ו pref. id.)(pr. name masc. ; ו bef. (.) צדק

לַצְדִּיםֵ pref. id.)(noun masc., pl., of צַד dec. 8e צדד

לַצַּדִּיק pref. לְ f. לְהַ)(adj. masc. sing. dec. 1b צדק
לְצַדִּיקᵍ pref. לְ q. v.

לַצִּידֹנִים pref. לְ for לְהַ)(gent. n., pl. of צִידֹנִי fr. צִידוֹן fr. צוד צדק

לְצִדְקֹᵏ pref. לְ)(noun masc. sing. (suff. צִדְקִי) d. 6a צדק

לִצְדָקָה pref. לְ bef. (.))(noun fem. sing. dec. 11c צדק

לְצִדְקִיָּהוּ pref. לְ)(pr. name masc. . . . צדק

לְצֻוָּהי pref. לְ (see lett. לְ)(for צַו, noun masc. sing. צוה

לְצַוְּארֵיᵈᵈ pref. לְ)(noun m. pl. constr. from צַוָּאר d. 2b צור

לָצוּדᵈᵈ pref. לְ (see lett. לְ))(Kal inf. constr. צוד

לְצוֹדֵדי pref. לְ)(Pilel inf. constr. צוד

ᵃ 1 Ch. 24. 3. ᵇ Le. 4. 20. ᶜ Le. 24. 3. ᵈ Le. 13. 48. ᵉ Ge. 41. 15. ᶠ Eze. 34. 22. ᵍ Zep. 1. 5. ʰ Ju. 2. 3. ⁱ Is. 28. 10, 13.
ᵏ 1 Ch. 23. 24. ˡ 1 Ch. 26. 18. ᵐ Le. 24. 12. ⁿ Pr. 1. 4. ᵒ 2 Sa. 3. 25. ᵖ Ex. 22. 29. ᵠ Ju. 8. 6. ʳ Pr. 9. 9. ˢ Ju. 5. 30.
ᵗ Ps. 119. 40. ᵘ Ec. 3. 3. ᵛ 1 Ch. 28. 18. ʷ Ge. 4. 7. ˣ Pr. 13. 1. ʸ 1 Ch. 4. 39, 41. ᶻ Nu. 5. 22. ᵃᵃ Is. 52. 1. ᵇᵇ Eze. 13. 18.
ᶜᶜ Is. 42. 7. ᵈᵈ Ho. 10. 1. Is. 53. 12. 2 Ch. 2. 13. Ge. 47. 4. Jos. 14. 11. Da. 7. 25. Eze. 13. 20. ᵉᵉ Pr. 20. 19
ᵈᵈ Gen. 27. 5.

לְצַוֺּת   ? pref. ל X Piel inf. constr.; ? bef. (:)   צוה

לְצוּלָתִי   pref. ל for לה X noun fem. sing.   צול

לָצוּץ   noun masc. sing.   לוץ

לָצוּר   pref. ל (see lett. ל) X Kal inf. constr.   צור

לְצוֹר   pref. ל X pr. name of a place   צור

לְצוּר   ? pref. id. X noun m. sing. dec. 1a; ? bef. (:)   צור

לַצּוֹרֵף   pref. ל for לה X Kal part. act. masc. dec. 7 b   צרף

לְצַוֺת   defect. for לְצַוֺּת (q. v.)   צוה

לְצִחִיחַ   pref. ל bef. (:) X noun m. s. Eze. 26. 4, 14.   צחח

לִצְחֹק   } pref. ל X Piel inf. constr. (§ 10. rem. 4,
לַצְחֹק   } & § 14. rem. 1)   צחק

לִצְחֹק   pref. ל bef. (:) X noun masc. sing.   צחק

לְצִיבָא   ? pref. ל X pr. name masc.; ? bef. (:)   נצב

לְצִידֹן   ? pref. id. X pr. name of a place   צוד

לְצִידֹנִים   pref. ל for לה X gent. n. pl. from the preced.   צוד

לְצִיּוֹן   ? pref. ל X pr. name of a place; ? bef. (:)   ציה

לְצִיִּים   pref. id. X noun masc. pl. [of צִי]   ציה

לְצִים   וּ? Kal part. act. masc., pl. of לוץ dec. 1a (§ 21. rem. 2, & § 36. rem. 2)   לוץ

לְצִיצִת   pref. ל X noun fem. sing. [for צִיצִית]   צוץ

לְצִיקְלָג   pref. id. X pr. name of a place, see צִיקְלַג.

לַצֵּל   pref. ל f. [לה X
לְצֵל   pref. ל q. v. } noun masc. sing. dec. 8 b   צלל

לִצְלוֹת   pref. ל bef. (:) X Kal inf. constr.   צלה

לְצַלְם   ? Ch., pref. ל X noun m. sing. d.3a; ? bef. (:)   צלם

לְצַלְמָא   Chald., pref. id. X id. emph. st.   צלם

לְצַלְמָוֶת   pref. id. X noun f. s. compd. of צֵל & מָוֶת, see   צלל

לְצַלְעָה   pref. ל for לה X noun fem. sing. dec. 4c (§ 33. No. 2, & rem. 3)   צלע

לְצַלְעֹ   pref. ל X noun m.s. (suff. צַלְעִי) d.6a (§35.r.5)   צלע

לְצֵלָע   ? pref. id. X noun fem. sing., constr. of צֵלָע (§ 33. rem. 3); ? bef. (:)   צלע

לְצַלְעוֹ   pref. id. X id., suff. 3 pers. sing. m. (§33.No.2)   צלע

לְצַלְעוֹת   pref. ל for לה X id. pl., abs. st.   צלע

לְצָלָפְחָד   ? pref. ל bef. (:) X pr. name masc. see צְלָפְחָד

לְצָמָאוֹן   pref. ל X noun masc. sing.   צמא

לְצִמְאִי   ? pref. ל bef. (:) X noun masc. sing., suff. 1 pers. sing. from צָמָא d. 4a (§ 33. rem. 2)   צמא

לִצְמָאָם   pref. id. X id., suff. 3 pers. pl. masc.   צמא

לְצַמֵּחַ   pref. ל X Piel inf. constr.   צמח

לִצְמִיתֻת   pref. ל for לה X noun fem. sing.   צמת

לְצֶמֶר   ו? pref. ל f. [לה X for צֶמֶר, n.m.s.d 6a (§35.r.2)   צמר

לְצִמֻּתֶךָ   pref. ל X noun f.s., suff. 2 p.s.f.fr. [צָמָה] d. 10   צמם

לִצְמִתֻת   pref. ל bef. (:) X noun fem. s., comp.   צמת

לְצַאנְכֶם   pref. ל X noun com. s., suff. 2 pers. pl. m. dec. 7 b, R. צנא, or by transp. for צֹאנְכֶם q.v.   צאן

לְצִנִּינִים   ו? pref. ל bef. (:) X noun masc. pl. [from
לִצְנִנִים   וּ? צְ' or צְנִין }   צנן

לְצַעֲקָ   pref. id. X Kal inf. constr.   צעק

לְצֹפֶה   pref. ל X Kal part. act. sing. masc. dec. 9a   צפה

לַצָּפוֹן   pref. ל for לה X noun masc. sing. dec. 3a   צפן

לְצִפוֹן   pref. ל bef. (:) X pr. name masc., see צְפִיוֹן   צפה

לְצָפוֹנָה   pref. ל for לה X n. m. s. (צָפוֹן) with parag. ה   צפן

לִצְפוּנָיו   pref. ל bef. (:) X Kal part. pass. pl. masc., suff. 3 pers. sing. masc. from צָפוֹן dec. 3 a   צפן

לְצִפּוֹר   pref. ל X noun com. s., pl. צִפֳּרִים (§ 30. r. 1)   צפר

לְצִפִּירַת   ו? pref. ל bef. (:) X noun fem., constr. of צְפִירָה dec. 10   צפר

לְצִיצִים   Pil. part. p. pl. m. [for מְלוֹצְצִים comp. §10.r.6]   לוץ

לָצֶקֶת   pref. ל (see lett. ל) X Kal inf. constr.   יצק

לְצֹר   pref. ל X pr. name of a place, for צוֹר   צור

לְצָרָה   pref. id. X noun fem. sing. dec. 10 [for צָרָה] from צַר masc.   צרר

לִצְרוֹף   pref. ל bef. (:) X Kal inf. constr. (§ 8. r. 18)   צרף

לְצָרַי   } pref. ל X noun masc. pl., suff. 1 pers.
לְצָרָי   } sing. from צַר dec. 8 (§ 37. rem. 7)   צרר

לְצָרָיו   pref. id. X id. pl., suff. 3 pers. sing. masc.   צרר

לְצָרֶיךָ   pref. id. X id. pl., suff. 2 pers. sing. masc.   צרר

לַצָּרִים   וּ? pref. ל for לה X gent. n. pl. of צָרִי from צוֹר   צרר

לְצָרֵינוּ   pref. ל X noun masc. pl., suff. 1 pers. pl. from צַר dec. 8 (§ 37. rem. 7)   צרר

לְצָרַעַת   ? pref. id. X noun fem.sing.dec.13a; ? bef. (:)   צרע

לַצֹּרֵף   pref. ל for לה X Kal part. act. sing. masc. d.7b   צרף

לִצְרֹר   pref. ל bef. (:) X Kal inf. constr.   צרר

לַצְתָּ   וּ? Kal pret. 2 pers. sing. masc.   לוץ

לִקְאַת   ? pref. ל bef. (:) X n. f. s., constr. of קָאַת (q.v.)   קוא

לָקַב   pref. ל (see lett. ל) X Kal inf. constr.   קבב

לִקְבוֹר   in full for לִקְבֹּר (q. v. & § 8. rem. 18)   קבר

לְקַבֵּל   וּ? Chald., pref. ל bef. (::) X and contr.
לְקַבֵּל   } לָק' X prep.   קבל
לָקֳבֵל   }

לְקָבְלָךְ   ? Chald., pref. ל X id. with suff. 2 pers. sing. m.   קבל

לְקַבֵּץ   pref. id. X Piel inf. constr. dec. 7b   קבץ

a Est. 4. 8.   a Ps. 1. 1.   a Da. 3. 5, 7, 10, 12, 14, 18.   a Job 18. 12.   a Le. 25. 30.   a 2 Ki. 8. 3.   a Ho. 7. 5.   a Is. 64. 1.   a Ps. 102. 7.

b Is. 44. 27.   b Pr. 1. 22.   b Je. 13. 16.   b Eze. 41. 6, 7.   b Le. 13. 48.   b Eze. 33. 2.   b Ex. 38. 27.   b Jos. 5. 13.   b Je. 19. 11.

c 1 Sa. 23. 8.   c Nu. 15. 39.   c Eze. 41. 9.   c Ps. 107. 33.   c Le. 25. 23.   c 1 Ch. 26. 17.   c Da. 11. 35.   c Le. 14. 55.   c Ja. 5. 1.

d Is. 8. 14.   d 2 Ki. 20. 10.   d Ps. 38. 18.   d Nu. 32. 24.   d Nu. 33. 55.   d Job 20. 26.   d De. 32. 41.   d Pr. 25. 4.   d Da. 2. 31.

e Ex. 32. 6.   e Is. 4. 6.   e Ne. 9. 15, 20.   e Eze. 39. 17.   e 1 Ch. 12. 17   e Le. 18. 18.   e Is. 66. 13.

f Eze. 23. 32.   f 1 Sa. 2. 15.   f Ex.26.20;36.25.   f Ju. 16. 22.   f Jos. 23. 13.   f Is. 28. 5.   f Pr. 9. 12.   f Ju. 17. 4.

Hebrew	Description	Root
לְקַבְצִי	pref. לְ)(Kal inf., suff. 1 pers. sing.	קבץ
לְקִבְרִי	pref. לְ for לְהָ)(noun m. s. (suff. קִבְרִי) d.6a	קבר
לְקַבֵּר	pref. לְ)(Piel inf. constr.	קבר
לִקְבֹּר	pref. לְ bef. (:))(Kal inf. constr.	קבר
לְקָבְרָהּ	pref. לְ)(id., suff. 3 pers. sing. fem.	קבר
לְקָבְרוֹ	וְ pref. id.)(id., suff. 3 pers. s. m.; וְ bef. (:)	קבר
לְקִבְרוֹת	pref. לְ bef. (:))(noun masc. with pl. fem. term. abs. from קֶבֶר dec.6a	קבר
לְקִבְרֵי	pref. לְ)(id. pl. constr. masc.	קבר
לִקְדֹשׁ	וְ pref. לְ bef. (:))(adj. masc. sing., constr. of קָדֹשׁ dec.3a	קדש
לִקְדֹשִׁים	pref. id.)(id. pl., abs. st.	קדש
לַקָּדִים	וְ pref. לְ for לְהָ)(noun masc. sing. with ה parag., קָדִימָה	קדם
לְקַדִּישֵׁי	וְ Chald., pref. לְ)(adj. pl. constr. masc. from קַדִּישׁ dec.1a; וְ bef. (:)	קדש
לְקַדְמִיאֵל	pref. id.)(pr. name masc.	קדם
לְקַדְמַתְכֶוּ	pref. id.)(noun fem. sing., suff. 2 pers. pl. fem. from קַדְמָה (no pl. abs.)	קדם
לְקַדְמָתָן	pref. id.)(id. with suff. 3 pers. pl. fem.	קדם
לְקַדְקֹד	וְ pref. id.)(noun masc. sing. (suff. קָדְקֳדוֹ & קָדְקֹד § 36. rem. 6)	קדד
לְקֶדָר	pref. id.)(pr. name of a tribe	קדר
לִקְדֹשׁ	וְ pref. לְ for לְהָ)(noun masc. sing. dec.6c	קדש
לְקֶדֶשׁ	pref. לְ)(pr. name in compos. קֶדֶשׁ בַּרְנֵעַ	קדש
לְקַדֵּשׁ	וְ pref. id.)(Piel inf. constr.; וְ bef. (:)	קדש
לְקֹדֶשׁ	pref. id.)(noun masc. sing. dec.6c	קדש
לְקָדְשׁוֹ	pref. id.)(id., suff. 3 pers. sing. masc.	קדש
לְקַדְּשׁוֹ	pref. id.)(Piel inf. (קַדֵּשׁ), suff. 3 p. s. m. d.7b	קדש
לַקֳּדָשִׁים	וְ pref. לְ for לְהָ)(noun m., pl. of קֹדֶשׁ d.6c	קדש
לְקַדְּשָׁם	pref. לְ)(Piel inf. (קַדֵּשׁ) suff. 3 p. pl. m. d.7b	קדש
לְקָהֵל	pref. לְ f. לְהָ)(noun masc. sing. dec.4a	קהל
לִקְהַל	pref. לְ q. v.	קהל
לַקָּהָל	pref. לְ bef. (:))(id., constr. st.	קהל
לִקְהָת	וְ pref. id.)(pr. name masc.	קהת
לְקָו	pref. לְ (see לְ))(noun masc. sing. (suff.	קוה
לְקָו	pref. לְ q. v. (קָו) d.8a (§ 37. r.4)	קוה
לְקוֹיָו	pref. id.)([for קֹוָיו] Kal part. act. pl., suff. 3 pers. sing. masc. from קָוָה dec.9a	קוה
לָקוֹחַ	Kal inf. abs.	לקח
לְקוֹל	pref. לְ)(noun masc. sing. dec.1a	קול
לְקוֹלִי	pref. id.)(id., suff. 1 pers. sing.	קול
לְקוֹלֶךָ	pref. id.)(id., suff. 2 pers. sing. fem.	קול

לָקּוּם (*fortress;* Arab. لقم *to stop the way*) pr. name of a town in the tribe of Naphtali, Jos. 19. 33.

Hebrew	Description	Root
לָקוּם	pref. לְ (see lett. לְ))(Kal inf. constr. d.1a	קים
לַקֹּצְרִים	pref. לְ for לְהָ)(Kal part. act. masc., pl. of קוֹצֵר dec.7b	צר

לָקַח וְ fut. יִקַּח (see more under § 17. rem. 8).—I. *to take, to take hold of,* with acc. of the pers., and בְּ *by;* לְ אִשָּׁה *to take a wife.*—II. *to take away.*—III. *to take possession of, seize, capture.*—IV. *to take, receive.* Niph. נִלְקַח *to be taken.* Pu. and Hoph. id. Hithpa. part. אֵשׁ מִתְלַקַּחַת *continuous fire,* prop. *taking hold of itself.*

לֶקַח masc. dec. 6 (with suff. לִקְחִי § 35. r. 5) —I. *captivating, persuasive speech,* Pr. 7. 21.—II *doctrine, instruction.*

Hebrew	Description	Root
לִקְחִי	(*captivating*) pr. name masc. 2 Ch. 19. 7	
מַלְקוֹחַ	masc. dec. 1 b.—I. *spoil, booty.*—II. du.	
מַלְקוֹחַיִם	the jaws, Ps. 22. 16.	
מַלְקָח, מֶלְקָח	masc. dec. 2 b, only du. קָחַיִם.—I. *tongs,* for the fire, Is. 6. 6.—II. *snuffers.*	
מִקָּח	masc. *receiving, accepting,* 1 Ch. 19. 7.	
מַקָּחוֹת	f. pl. (fr. מַקָּחָה) *merchandise,* Ne. 10. 31.	
לָקַח	Kal pret. 3 pers. sing. m. for לָקַח (§ 8. r. 7)	לקח
לָקֹחַ	id. inf. abs.	לקח
לֶקַח	noun m. s. (suff. לִקְחִי) d. 6 a (§ 35. r. 5)	לקח
לְקַח	וְ Kal imp. sing. masc.; וְ bef. (:)	לקח
לֹקֵחַ	וְ id. part. act. sing. masc. dec. 7 b	לקח
לֻקַּח	וְ Pual pret. 3 pers. s. m. (comp. § 8. r. 7)	לקח
לָקְחָה	וְ Kal pret. 3 pers. sing. fem.	לקח
לְקָחָהּ	וְ id. pret. 3 pers. sing. masc., suff. 3 pers. sing. fem.; וְ bef. (:)	לקח
לִקְחָהּ	noun masc. sing., suff. 3 pers. sing. fem. fr. לֶקַח dec. 6 a (§ 35. rem. 5)	לקח
לֻקָּחָה	Pual pret. 3 pers. s. f. [for לֻקְּחָה § 10. r. 7]	לקח
לָקְחוּ	וְ Kal pret. 3 pers. pl. (§ 8. rem. 7)	לקח
לֻקְּחוּ	Pual pret. 3 pers. pl.	לקח
לְקָחוּם	וְ Kal pret. 3 pers. pl., suff. 3 pers. pl. masc.; וְ for וְ conv.	לקח
לִקְחִי	וְ pr. name masc.	לקח
לִקְחִי	Kal imp. fem. (1 Ki. 17. 11), or noun masc. with suff. 1 pers. s. fr. לֶקַח d. 6 a (§ 35. r. 5)	לקח

לְקֻחֵי	Kal part. act. pl. constr. m. fr. לָקַח dec. 7 b	לקח
לְקֻחִים	id. part pass pl. abs. from [לָקוּחַ] dec. 3 a	לקח
לְקָחָם	id. pret. 3 pers sing. masc., suff. 3 pers. pl. m.	לקח
וַיִּקָּחֵנוּ	id. pret. 1 pers. pl.	לקח
לְקָחָנִי	id. pret. 3 pers. sing. masc., suff. 1 pers. sing.	לקח
וְלָקַחַת	pref. לְ (see lett. ל) X id., inf. constr. (קַחַת § 17. rem. 8) dec. 13 a	לקח
לְקַחְתָּ לְקַחְתָּ	id. pret. 2 pers. sing. masc.; acc. shifted by conv. וָ (§ 8. rem. 7)	לקח
וְלָקַחַתְּ	id. pret. 2 pers. sing. fem.	לקח
לֻקָּחְתָּ	Pual pret. 2 p. s. m. [for לֻקַּחְתָּ comp. § 8. r. 7]	לקח
לְקַחְתָּה	pref. לְ X Kal inf. (קַחַת) dec. 13 a, § 17. rem. 8, with suff. 3 pers. fem. sing.	לקח
לְקַחְתּוֹ	pref. id. X id., suff. 3 pers. sing. masc.	לקח
לְקַחְתִּי לְקַחְתִּי לְקַחְתִּי	id. pret. 1 pers. sing.; acc. shifted by conv. וָ (§ 8. rem. 7)	לקח
לְקַחְתִּיו	id. id., suff. 3 pers. sing. masc.	לקח
לְקַחְתִּיךָ	id. id., suff. 2 pers. sing. m.; וָ for וְ conv.	לקח
לְקַחְתִּים	id. id., suff. 3 pers. pl. masc.; וָ id.	לקח
לְקַחְתֵּךְ	pref. לְ X id. inf. constr. (קַחַת § 17. rem. 8), suff. 2 pers. sing. fem. dec. 13 a	לקח
לְקַחְתֶּם	id. pret. 2 pers. pl. masc.; וָ for וְ conv.	לקח
לְקַחְתָּנוּ	id. pret. 2 pers. sing. masc., suff. 1 pers. pl.	לקח
[לָקֵט]	to collect, gather, glean. Pi. id. Pu. to be gathered together. Hithp. id.	
לֶקֶט	masc. a gleaning, Le. 19. 9; 23. 22.	
יַלְקוּט	masc. bag, scrip, 1 Sa. 17. 40.	
לֶקֶט	noun masc. sing.	לקט
לָקְטָה וַ	Piel pret. 3 pers. sing. fem. (comp. § 8. rem. 7)	לקט
לָקְטוּ וַ	Kal pret. 3 pers. pl. (§ 8. rem. 7)	לקט
לִקְטוּ	id. imp. pl. masc.	לקט
לְקַטְלָה	Chald., pref. לְ X Peal inf. constr. (§ 47. r. 5)	קטל
לְקַטֵּר	pref. id. X Piel inf. constr.	קטר
וְלִקְטֹרֶת	pref. לְ bef. (:) X noun fem. sing. dec. 13 c	קטר
לִקַּטְתְּ	Piel pret. 2 pers. sing. fem.	לקט
לְקַיֵּם	pref. לְ X Piel inf. constr.	קום
לְקַיָּמָה	Chald., pref. id. X Pael inf. constr. (§ 47. r. 5)	קום
לְקַיִן	pref. id. X pr. name masc.	קין

לְקִינָה	pref. לְ X noun fem. sing. dec. 10	קון
לְקִיר	pref. id. X noun masc. sing. dec. 1 a	קיר
לַקִּירוֹת	pref. לְ for לָה X id. pl.	קיר
לְקִישׁ	pref. לְ X pr. name masc.	קושׁ
לְקֹל	pref. id. X noun masc. sing. dec. 1 a, for קוֹל	קול
לְקֹלִי	pref. id. X id., suff. 1 pers. sing.; וָ bef. (:)	קול
לַקַּלִּים	pref. לְ for לָה X adj. pl. masc. from קַל 1. 8 d	קלל
לְקֹלְךָ	pref. לְ X for לְקֹלְךָ, noun masc. sing., suff. 2 pers. sing. masc. from קוֹל dec. 1 a	קול
לְקַלֵּל	pref. id. X Piel inf. constr. dec. 7 b	קלל
וְלִקְלָלָה	וַ pref. לְ bef. (:) X noun fem. sing. dec. 11 c	קלל
לְקַלְלוֹ	pref. לְ X Piel inf. (קַלֵּל), suff. 3 pers. sing. masc. dec. 7 b (§ 10. rem. 7)	קלל
לְקַלֶּלְךָ	pref. id. X id., suff. 2 pers. sing. masc. [for § 2. rem. 2, & § 10. rem. 7]	קלל
לְקֹלָם	pref. id. X noun masc. sing., suff. 3 pers. pl. masc. from קוֹל dec. 1 a	קול
לְקַלֵּם	pref. id. X Piel inf. constr.	קלם
לְקָלֵס	וַ pref. id. X noun masc. sing.; וָ bef. (:)	קלס
לִקְמָצִים	pref. לְ bef. (:) X noun masc., pl. קֹמֶץ dec. 6 c (§ 35. rem. 9)	קמן
לְקָנֶה	pref. לְ X noun masc. sing. dec. 9 b	קנה
לַקֹּנֶה	pref. לְ for לָה X Kal part. act. sing. m. d. 9 a	קנה
וְלִקְנוֹת	וַ pref. לְ bef. (:) X id. inf. constr. dec. 1 b	קנה
לְקִנְיָנָם	וַ pref. לְ X noun masc. sing., suff. 3 pers. pl. masc. from קִנְיָן dec. 2 b; וָ bef. (:)	קנה
לִקְסָם־	pref. לְ bef. (:) X [for קְסֹם § 8. rem. 18] Kal inf. constr.	קסם
לַקֹּסְמִים	וַ pref. לְ for לָה X id. part. act. masc., pl. of קֹסֵם dec. 7 b	קסם
לַקֵּץ לְקֵץ	pref. לְ for לָה X noun masc. sing. dec. 8 b; וָ pref. לְ q. v.; וָ bef. (:)	קצץ
לְקִצְבֵי	pref. id. X noun m. pl. constr. fr. קֶצֶב d. 6 a	קצב
לְקַצּוֹת	pref. id. X Piel inf. constr.	קצץ
לִקְצוֹת	pref. לְ bef. (:) X noun fem. pl. constr. from קָצָה dec. 11 a	קצה
לְקָצִין	וַ pref. לְ X noun masc. s. d. 3 a; וָ bef. (.:)	קצה
לַקָּצִיר	pref. לְ for לָה X noun masc. sing. dec. 3 a	קצר
לְקִצְפָה	pref. לְ bef. (:) X noun fem. sing.	קצף
לִקְצֹר־	וַ pref. id. X Kal inf. constr.	קצר
וְלִקְצָת	וַ Chald., pref. id. X noun fem. sing., constr. of קְצָת dec. 1 b	קצה

a Pr. 24. 11.	f Ge. 3. 19.	l Am. 9. 3.	q Ex. 16. 18.	u Da. 6. 8.	a Ne. 13. 2.	h Is. 35. 7.	m 1 Sa. 6. 2.	s Am. 4. 7.
b Je. 27. 20.	g De. 24. 19.	m 1 Sa. 25. 40.	r Ex. 16. 22.	v Eze. 41. 25	b Eze. 16. 31.	k 2 Ki. 12. 13.	n Jon. 2. 7.	t Joel 1. 7.
c Ge. 24. 7.	h Nu. 23. 20.	n Ex. 14. 11.	s Da. 2. 14.	w Ex. 4. 8.	c Je. 20. 8.	l 2 Ki. 10. 32.	o Le. 19. 9.	
d Eze. 22. 12.	i Ju. 17. 2.	o Ru. 2. 17, 18.	t Ex. 40. 5.	x 2 Ki. 10. 6.	d Joa. 14. 4.	l Job 28. 24.	p 1 Sa. 8. 12.	
e 1 Ki. 14. 3.	k Ge. 27. 45.	p Ru. 2. 16.		y Ru. 2. 19.	e Ge. 41. 47.	= Eze. 21. 26.	r Ju. 11. 6, 11.	y Da. 4. 26, 31.

[לָקַק] pret. לָקְקוּ, fut. יָלֹק *to lick, lap.* Pi. id. Ju. 7. 6, 7. | לקק

לָקְקוּ Kal pret. 3 pers. pl. | לקק

לִקְרֹא pref. לְ bef. (:) ⟩ Kal inf. constr. | קרא

וְ"לִקְרַאת pref. id. ⟩ prep. [prop. noun fem. contr. for לִקְרַאת, constr. of [קְרָאָה] | קרא

לִקְרָאתָהּ pref. id. ⟩ id., suff. 3 pers. sing. fem. | קרא

לִקְרָאתוֹ pref. id. ⟩ id., suff. 3 pers. sing. masc. | קרא

לִקְרָאתִי pref. id. ⟩ id., suff. 1 pers. sing. | קרא

לִקְרָאתֶךָ
לִקְרָאתֶךָ' } pref. id. ⟩ id., suff. 2 pers. sing. masc. | קרא

לִקְרַאתְכֶם pref. id. ⟩ id., suff. 2 pers. pl. masc. | קרא

לִקְרָאתָם pref. id ⟩ id., suff. 3 pers. pl. masc. | קרא

לִקְרָאתֵנוּ pref. id. ⟩ id., suff. 1 pers. pl. | קרא

לְקֶרֶב pref. לְ for לְהַ ⟩ n. m. s. d. 1 a (§ 30. No. 30) | קרב

לְקָרְבָה pref. לְ ⟩ Kal inf. constr. (§ 8. rem. 10) | קרב

לְקָרְבַּן pref. id. ⟩ noun m s., constr. of קָרְבַּן d. 2 b | קרב

וּ לְקָרְבַּן' ⟩ pref. id. ⟩ noun masc., constr. of [קָרְבַּן] dec. 2 b ; וּ bef. (:) | קרב

לִקְרֹועַ pref. לְ bef. (:) ⟩ Kal inf. constr. (§ 8. r. 18) | קרע

וְ לְקָרוֹב' ⟩ pref. לְ for לְהַ ⟩ adj masc. sing. dec. 3 a | קרב

לִקְרוֹת' ⟩ pref. לְ ⟩ Piel inf. constr.; וּ bef. (:) | קרה

וְ לְקֹרַח' ⟩ pref. לְ for לְהַ ⟩ noun masc. sing. | קרח

לְקֹרַח pref. לְ ⟩ pr. name masc. | קרח

וּ לְקָרְחָה ⟩ pref. id. ⟩ noun fem. s. (no pl.) ; וּ bef. (:) | קרח

לַקָּרְחִים pref. לְ for לְהַ ⟩ patronym. pl. of קָרְחִי fr. קֹרַח | קרח

וּ לִקְרָנוֹת ⟩ pref. לְ ⟩ noun fem. pl. constr. (abs. קְרָנוֹת) from קֶרֶן dec. 6 a ; וּ bef. (:) | קרן

לְקָדֵשׁ pref. לְ for לְהַ ⟩ noun masc. sing. dec. 6 a | קדש

לְקָדֵשִׁי pref. לְ ⟩ id. pl., constr. st. | קדש

לָקַשׁ Kal not used ; Syr. *to be late.* Pi. *to glean, to gather the last fruits,* Job 24. 6.

לֶקֶשׁ masc. *latter grass, aftermath,* Am. 7. 1.

אֶלְקֹשִׁי gent. noun, *Elkoshite,* of the prophet Nahum from a place אֶלְקֹשׁ (more prob. from the Root קֹשׁ, אֶל being the art.) Na. 1. 1.

מַלְקוֹשׁ masc. *the latter rain,* which falls in Palestine in the months of March and April.

לְקֹשֵׁשׁ pref. לְ ⟩ noun masc. sing. | קשש

לֹקֵשׁ noun masc. sing. | לקש

לִקְשֵׁה' pref. לְ bef. (:) ⟩ adj. m. s., constr. of קָשֶׁה d. 9 b | קשה

לְקֹשֵׁשׁ' pref. לְ ⟩ Poel inf. constr. | קשש

לִירֹא' pref. לְ [contr. for לְיִרֹא, לִירֹא], Kal inf. constr. | ירא

לִרְאוּבֵן pref. לְ bef. (:) ⟩ pr. name of a tribe | ראה

לִרְאוּבֵנִי' וְ' pref. לְ for לְהַ, לֶהָ ⟩ gent. n. fr. the preced. | ראה

לִרְאַוָּה' pref. לְ ⟩ Kal inf. constr. (§ 24. rem. 2) | ראה

לִרְאוֹת contr. for לְהִרְאוֹת (q. v. & § 9. rem. 6) | ראה

לִרְאוֹת וְ' pref. לְ bef. (:) ⟩ Kal inf. constr. dec. 1 a | ראה

לִרְאוֹתוֹ pref. id. ⟩ id., suff. 3 pers. sing. masc. | ראה

[לִרְאוֹתֶךָ]• pref. id. ⟩ id., suff. 2 p. s. m. [for רְאוֹתְךָ] | ראה

לְרֹאִי' pref. לְ ⟩ Kal part. a. pl. constr. m. fr. רֹאֶה d. 9 a | ראה

לַרְאִים• pref. לְ for לְהַ, לֶהָ ⟩ id. pl., abs. st. | ראה

לְרֹאשׁ
לְרֹאשׁ } pref. id.
pref. לְ } noun masc. sing. irr. (§ 45) | ראש

לְרֹאשׁוֹ• pref. id. ⟩ id., suff. 3 pers. sing. masc. | ראש

לְרֹאשֵׁי pref. id. ⟩ id. pl., constr. st. | ראש

לְרֹאשִׁי pref. id. ⟩ id. sing., suff. 1 pers. sing. | ראש

וּ לְרָאשָׁיו ⟩ pref. id. ⟩ id. pl., suff. 3 p. s. m. ; וּ bef. (:) | ראש

לְרֵאשִׁית• pref. לְ for לְהַ, לֶהָ ⟩ noun fem. sing. d. 1 a | ראש

לְרֹאשֶׁךָ
לְרֹאשְׁךָ• } pref. לְ ⟩ noun masc. sing., suff. 2 pers. sing. masc., from רֹאשׁ (§ 45) } | ראש

לָרִאשֹׁנָה pref. לְ for לְהַ, לֶהָ ⟩ adj,. fem. of רִאשׁוֹן, used *adverbially* | ראש

לְרֹאשֵׁנוּ' pref. לְ ⟩ n. m. s., suff. 1 p. pl. fr. רֹאשׁ (§ 45) | ראש

לָרִאשֹׁנִים' pref. לְ for לְהַ, לֶהָ ⟩ adj. m., pl. of רִאשׁוֹן (q. v.) | ראש

לִרְאֹת pref. לְ bef. (:) ⟩ Kal inf. constr. dec. 1 a | ראה

לִרְאֹתָהּ• pref. id. ⟩ id., suff. 3 pers. sing. fem. | ראה

לְרַאֹתְכֶם• pref. לְ (contr. for לְהַרְאֹתְכֶם § 11. rem. 3), Hiph. inf., suff. 2 pers. pl. masc. dec. 1 b | ראה

לִרְאֹתָם' pref. לְ bef. (:) ⟩ Kal inf. (רְאֹות), suff. 3 pers. pl. masc. dec. 1 a | ראה

לָרֹב pref. לְ for לְהַ, לֶהָ• ⟩ adj. masc. sing. d. 8 d | רבב

לָרֹב defect. for לָרִיב (q. v.) | ריב

לָרֹב pref. לְ (see lett. לְ) ⟩ noun masc. dec. 8, used *adverbially* ; or (Ge. 6. 1) Kal inf. constr. | רבב

לִרְבָבָה' pref. לְ for לְהַ, לֶהָ• ⟩ noun fem. sing. d. 11 c | רבב

לָרַבִּים
לָרַבִּים } pref. id.
pref. לְ } adj. masc., pl. of רַב dec. 8 d | רבב

לִרְבְּעָה• pref. id. ⟩ Kal inf. constr. (§ 8. rem. 10) | יבע

לְרִבְעָהּ• pref. id. ⟩ Kal inf. [רָבַע], suff. 3 pers. sing. fem. (§ 16. rem. 10) | רבע

לְרִבֵץ• pref. id. ⟩ noun masc. sing. dec. 6 b | רבץ

לְרִבְקָה וּ' pref. id. ⟩ pr. name fem. ; וּ bef. (:) | רבק

ᵃ 1 Ki. 21. 19.	ᶠ Ne. 13. 31.	ˡ 2 Ch. 34. 11.	ᵖ Am. 7. 1.	ᵘ Eze. 28. 17.	ʸ Is. 30. 10.	ᶜ Pr. 1. 9.	ᵍ De. 28. 68.	Ju. 20. 10.
ᵇ Ge. 32. 7.	ᵍ Ec. 3. 7.	ᵐ Je. 36. 30.	ᵠ Job 30. 25.	ˣ 2 Sa. 13. 6.	ᶻ 2 Ch. 11. 22.	ᵈ Pr. 4. 8.	ʰ De. 1. 33.	ˡ Le. 20. 16.
ᶜ Ps. 144. 1.	ʰ Is. 57. 19.	ⁿ Is. 22. 12.	ʳ Ex. 5. 12.	ʷ 2 Sa. 13. 5.	ᵃ Ps. 21. 4.	ᵉ Ps. 66. 12.	ᶦ Ex. 14. 13.	ᵐ Is. 65. 16.
ᵈ Ex. 36. 2.	ᶦ Je. 2. 8.	ᵒ Je. 17. 1.	1 Sa. 18. 29.	ˢ Ec. 7. 11.	ᵇ Ne. 12. 44.	ᶠ Ec. 1. 11.	ᵏ Pr. 25. 8.	
ᵉ Le. 22. 27.	ᵏ 1 Sa. 30. 21.							

30*

לְדַבְרְבָנוֹהִי — Ch., pref. ל) noun masc. pl., suff. 3 pers. sing. masc. from רַבְרְבָן dec. 1 . **רבב**

לִרְגּוֹם — pref. ל bef. (:)) Kal inf. constr. (§ 8. r. 18) **רגם**

לְרַגֵּל — ו pref. ל) Piel inf. constr. d. 7b; ו bef. (:) **רגל**

לְרַגְלוֹ — ו pref. id.) noun com. sing. dec. 6a; ו id. **רגל**

לְרַגְלָהּ — pref. id.) id., suff. 3 pers. sing. fem. . **רגל**

לְרַגְּלָהּ — ו pref. id.) Piel inf. (רַגֵּל), suff. 3 pers. sing. fem. dec. 7b; ו bef. (:) **רגל**

לְרַגְלִי — pref. id.) n. com. s., suff. 3 p.s.m. fr. רֶגֶל d. 6a **רגל**

לְרַגְלַי / לְרַגְלָי — } pref. id.) id. du., suff. 1 pers. sing. . **רגל**

לְרַגְלִי — pref. id.) id. sing., suff. 1 pers. sing. . **רגל**

לְרַגְלָיו — pref. id.) id. du., suff. 3 pers. sing. masc. **רגל**

לְרַגְלֶיךָ — pref. id.) id. du., suff. 2 pers. sing. masc. **רגל**

לְרַגְלֶךָ — pref. id.) id. s., suff. 2 pers. s. m. (for לְךָ) **רגל**

לִרְגָעִים — pref. ל bef. (:)) n.m., pl. of רֶגַע d. 6 (§ 35. r. 5) **רגע**

לִרְדָּד — pref. ל) Kal inf. constr. (§ 18. rem. 3) . **רדד**

לִרְדֹּף — pref. ל bef. (:)) Kal inf. constr. **רדף**

לְרָדְפְּךָ — pref. id.) id., suff. 2 pers. sing. masc. . **רדף**

לָרֶדֶת — pref. ל (see lett. ל)) Kal inf. constr. (suff. רִדְתִּי) dec. 13a . **ירד**

לִרְבוֹב — pref. id.) Kh. רוֹב Kal inf.R. רוב; K. רִיב id.R. **ריב**

לִרְבּוֹב — pref. ל) Kal inf. constr. (§ 18. rem. 2) **רבב**

לָרֹב — pref. ל) for רֹב, noun masc. sing. dec. 8d **רבב**

לְרוֹזְנִים — ו pref. id.) Kal part. act. masc., pl. of [רוֹזֵן] dec. 7b; ו bef. (:) **רזן**

לָרוּחַ — pref. ל for לְהָ, לְהַ, noun com. sing. dec. } **רוח**

לָרוּחַ — ו pref. ל q. v. } 1a; ו id.

לְרוּחוֹ — pref. id.) id. with suff. 3 pers. sing. masc. **רוח**

לְרוּחָתִי — pref. id.) noun fem. sing., suff. 1 pers. sing. from רְוָחָה dec. 11c (§ 42. rem. 1) **רוח**

לָרְוָיָה — pref. ל for לְהָ, לְהַ) noun fem. sing. . **רוה**

לָרוּם — pref. ל (see lett. ל)) Kal inf. constr. or (Pr. 25. 3) subst. . . **רום**

לְרוֹמֵם — pref. ל) Pilel inf. constr. **רום**

לְרוֹמַמְתִּי — pref. id.) pr. name in compos. רִי עֶזֶר **רום**

לָרוּץ — pref. ל (see lett. ל)) Kal inf. constr. **רוץ**

לִרְקֹעַ — pref. ל) Kal part. act., constr. of [רֹקֵעַ] d.7c **רקע**

לְרַחְבָּהּ — ו pref. id.) noun masc. sing., suff. 3 pers. sing. fem. from רֹחַב dec. 6c; ו bef. (:) **רחב**

לִרְחַבְיָהוּ — pref. ל bef. (:)) pr. name masc. . **רחב**

לִרְחַבְעָם — pref. id.) pr. name masc. . **רחב**

לִרְחוֹב — pref. ל bef. (:)) noun fem. sing. dec. 1a **רחב**

לְרָחֹק — pref. ל for לְהָ, לְהַ) adj. masc. sing. d. 3a **רחק**

לְרָחֵל — pref. ל) pr. name fem. . **רחל**

לְרַחֲמִים — ו pref. id.) noun masc. pl. [for רְחָמִים § 35. rem. 16] from רַחַם . **רחם**

לְרַחֶמְכֶם — pref. id.) Piel inf. (רַחֵם § 14. rem. 1), suff. 2 pers. pl. masc. dec. 7b . **רחם**

לִרְחֹץ — pref. ל bef. (:)) Kal inf. constr. . **רחץ**

לְרָחְצָה — pref. ל) id. with fem. term. (§ 8. rem. 10) **רחץ**

לִרְחֹק — pref. ל bef. (:)) Kal inf. constr. . **רחק**

לְרָחְקָה — pref. ל) id. with fem. term. (§ 8. rem. 10) **רחק**

לָרִיב — pref. ל (see lett. ל)) Kal inf. constr. . **ריב**

לָרִיב — ו pref. ל f. לְהָ } noun masc. sing. dec. 1a **ריב**

לָרִיב — pref. ל q. v. }

לְרִיבִי — pref. id.) id., suff. 1 pers. sing. **ריב**

לְרֵיחַ — pref. id.) noun masc. sing. dec. 1a . **רוח**

לָרִיק / לָרִק — } pref. ל or לַ (see lett. ל)) prim. adj. masc. as an adv. . **רוק**

לְרֶכֶב — pref. ל for לְהָ, לְהַ) noun masc. sing. d. 1b **רכב**

לְרֹכֵב — pref. id.) Kal part. act. sing. masc. dec. 7b **רכב**

לִרְכֹּב — pref. ל) noun masc. sing. (suff. רִכְבִּי) d. 6a **רכב**

לִרְכֹּב — pref. ל bef. (:)) Kal inf. constr. **רכב**

לְרִכְבָּהּ — pref. ל) noun fem. sing. **רכב**

לְרִכְבּוֹ — pref. id.) noun masc. sing., suff. 3 pers. sing. masc. from רַכָּב dec. 1b . **רכב**

לְרִכְבּוֹ — ו pref. id.) noun masc. sing., suff. 3 pers. sing. masc. from רֶכֶב dec. 6a; ו bef. (:) **רכב**

לְרֹכְבוֹ — ו pref. id.) Kal part. act. sing. masc. (רֹכֵב), suff. 3 pers. sing. masc. dec. 7b; ו id. **רכב**

לְרֶכֶשׁ / לָרֶכֶשׁ — } ו pref. ל for לְהָ, לְהַ) noun masc. sing. (§ 35. rem. 2) **רכש**

לְרִכְשָׁם — ו pref. ל bef. (:)) noun masc. sing., suff. 3 pers. pl. masc. from רְכוּשׁ dec. 1a **רכש**

לְרָמָה — pref. ל for לְהָ, לְהַ) noun fem. sing. **רמם**

לִרְמוֹן — pref. ל) pr. name masc. **רמם**

לְרַמּוֹתַנִי — pref. id.) Piel inf. [רַמּוֹת], suff. 1 pers. s. d.1b **רמה**

לִרְמָחִים — pref. ל bef. (:)) noun masc., pl. of רֹמַח dec. 6b (§ 35. rem. 5 & 9) **רמח**

לְרִנָּתִי — pref. ל) noun fem. s., suff. 1 p.s. fr. רִנָּה d. 10 **רנן**

לָרֶסֶן — pref. ל (see lett. ל)) Kal inf. constr. . **רסן**

לָרַע / לָרֵעַ — } pref. ל for לְהָ, לְהַ) subst. masc. sing. dec. 8 (§ 37. rem. 7) } **רעע**

---

a Da. 5.1.   b Is. 41. 2.   c 1 Sa. 25. 29.   d Pr. 25. 28.   e Ge. 13. 17.   f Ec. 3. 5.   g 2 Ch. 18. 33.   h De. 11. 4.   i Job 17. 14.

k Nu. 14. 10.   l Je. 18. 22.   m Ju. 21. 22.   n La. 3. 56.   o 2 Ch. 29. 4.   p Eze. 8. 6.   q Ps. 68. 5, 34.   r Job 39. 18.   s Ch. 12. 17

Ch. 19. 3.   La. 1. 3.   1 Ch. 4. 38.   Ps. 66. 12.   2 Ch. 19. 8.   Eze. 27. 20.   1 Ki. 5. 8.   Mi. 1. 13.   Joel 4. 10.

Ge. 35. 14, 14.   Ps. 110. 1.   Est. 10. 3.   Eze. 10. 16.   Is. 57. 19.   Da. 1. 9.   Ps. 35. 23.   Nu. 35. 3.   Ps. 88. 3.

1 Sa. 25. 42.   De. 33. 3.   Pr. 31. 4.   Ezr. 9. 9.   Job 39. 16.   Je. 47. 3.   Eze. 46. 14.

2 Sa. 10. 3.   Is. 45. 1.   Ps. 136. 6.

לְרֵעַ — pref. ל (see lett. ל) X noun masc. sing. . רעע

לְרָע / pref. ל X noun masc. sing. dec. 8. (§ 37.
לְרַע } rem. 7) . . . . . רעע

לְרָעָב — pref. ל for לְהִ, לְהַ· X noun masc. sing. d. 4a בּ רעב

לְרָעָב — pref. id.} adj. masc. sing. dec. 5a רעב
לְרָעָב — pref. ל }

לְרַעֲבִים — pref. ל for לְהַ, לְהִ· X id. pl., abs. st. רעב

לְרַעֲבָם — pref. ל bef. (:) X noun masc. sing., suff. 3 pers. pl. masc. from רָעָב dec. 4a . רעב

לְרָעָה — pref. ל f. לְהָ, לְהַ· } n.fem.s.d 10 [for רָעָה] רעע
לְרָעָה — ּו pref. ל q.v. from רַע m.; ּו bef. (:)

לְרֹעֶה — pref. ל X Kal part. act. sing. masc. dec. 9a רעה

לְרֹעֵהוּ — pref. id. X noun masc. sing., or (1 Sa. 30. 26) pl. for רֵעֵיהוּ, suff. 3 pers. sing. masc. (§ 4. rem. 5) from רֵעַ dec. 1a (§ 36. rem. 4) רעה

לִרְעוֹת — pref. ל bef. (:) X Kal inf. constr. dec. 1b רעה

לִרְעוּתָהּ — pref. id. X noun fem. sing., suff. 3 pers. sing. fem. from רְעוּת dec. 1a . רעה

לְרֵעִי — pref. ל X noun masc. sing., suff. 1 pers. sing. from רֵעַ dec. 1a (§ 36. rem. 4) רעה

לְרֵעֶיךָ — pref. id. X id. pl., or sing. (2 Sa. 12. 11, Pr. 3. 28, Kh. § 38. r. 1), suff. 2 p. s. m. from רֵעַ d. 9a רעה

לְרֹעִים — pref. ל for לְהָ, לְהִ· X Kal part. act. masc. pl. of רֹעֶה dec. 9a . רעה

לְרֵעֶךָ / pref. ל X noun masc. sing., suff. 2 pers.
לְרֵעֶךָ } sing. masc. from רֵעַ d. 1a (§ 36. r. 4) רעה

לְרַעַשׁ — pref. id. X noun masc. sing. רעש

לְרָעוֹת — pref. id. X noun fem., pl. of רָעָה d. 10, fr. רַע m. רעע

לְרָעָתוֹ — pref. id. X id. sing., suff. 3 pers. sing. masc. רעע

לִרְפֹּא / pref. ל bef. (:) X Kal inf. constr. (§ 8.
לִרְפּוֹא } rem. 18) . . . . . רפא

לְרָצוֹן — pref. ל X noun masc. sing. dec. 3a . רצה

לִרְצוֹת — pref. ל bef. (:) X Kal inf. constr. dec. 1a רצה

לָרָצִים / וי pref. ל for לְהָ, לְהִ· X Kal part. act. masc. pl. of רָץ dec. 1a . רוץ

לִרְצֹנוֹ — pref. ל bef. (:) X noun masc. sing., suff. 3 pers. sing. masc. from רָצוֹן 3a . רצה

לִרְצֹנְכֶם — pref. id. X id., suff. 2 pers. pl. masc. רצה

לְרֻקָּחוֹת — pref. ל X noun fem., pl. of רַקָּחָה dec. 10 . רקח

לָרָקִיעַ — pref. ל for לְהָ, לְהִ· X noun masc. sing. dec. 3a רקע

לִרְקִיעִי / ּו pref. ל bef. (:) X noun masc. pl. constr. from רָקִיק dec. 3a רקס

לְרִקְמוֹת — pref. ל bef. (:) X n. f. pl. abs. from רִקְמָה d. 12 b רקם

לָרוֹשׁ / ּו pref. ל for לְהָ, לְהִ· X Kal part. act. m. d. 1a רוש

לְרָשָׁע / ּו pref. id.} adj. masc. sing. dec. 4 a . רשע
לְרָשָׁע — pref. ל }

לְרִשְׁעָה — pref. id. X noun fem. sing. (no pl.) רשע

לְרָשֵׁעי — ּו pref. id. X noun masc. pl. constr. from רָשָׁע dec. 4a ; ּו bef. (:) רשע

לָרְשָׁעִים / ּו pref. ל for לְהָ, לְהִ· X id. abs. st. רשע

לָרְשָׁפִים — pref. id. X noun masc. pl. (constr. (רִשְׁפֵי) from רֶשֶׁף dec. 6a . . . רשׁף

לָרֶשֶׁת / pref. ל (see lett. ל) X Kal inf. constr.
לָרֶשֶׁת } (suff. רִשְׁתּוֹ) dec. 13 b ירשׁ

לְרִשְׁתָּהּ — pref. ל X id., suff. 3 pers. sing. fem. ירשׁ

לְרִשְׁתּוֹ — pref. id. X id., suff. 3 pers. sing. masc. ירשׁ

לְרִשְׁתְּךָ — pref. id. X id., suff. 2 pers. sing. masc. ירשׁ

לִשְׁאֹב — pref. ל bef. (:) X Kal inf. constr. . שאב

לִשְׁאוּל — ּו pref. ל X pr. name masc. ; ּו bef. (:) שאל

לִשְׁאוֹל- — Kh. לִשְׁאוֹל q.v., K. לִשְׁאָל q.v. (§ 8. rem. 18) שאל

לִשְׁאוֹל — pref. ל bef. (:) X n. m. s.; or Kal inf. see לִשְׁאֹל שאל

לִשְׁאוֹלָה — pref. id. X id. with loc. ה שאל

לִשְׁאֹל /
לִשְׁאָל- } pref. id. X Kal inf. constr. (§ 8. rem. 18) שאל

לִשְׁאָר — pref. id. X noun masc. sing. שאר

לִשְׁאָרוֹ — pref. id. X noun masc. sing., suff. 3 pers. sing. masc. from שְׁאָר dec. 1a שאר

לִשְׁאֵרִית / וי pref. id. X noun fem. sing. dec. 1 b שאר

לָשֵׂאת / וי pref. לָ (see lett. ל) X Kal inf. constr. (§ 25. No. 2a) . נשׂא

לָשֵׂאת / pref. ל for לְהַ X n. f. s. (suff. שְׂאֵתוֹ) d. 1a נשׂא

לְשַׁבָּאִים — pref. ל bef. (:) X gent. noun pl. from שְׁבָא שׁבא

לִשְׁבוּיִם — pref. id. X Kal part. p. m., pl. of (שָׁבוּי) d. 3a שׁבה

לִשְׁבוּעָה — pref. id. X noun fem. sing. dec. 10 שׁבע

לִשְׁבוּרֵי — pref. id. X Kal part. p. pl. constr. fr. שָׁבוּר d. 3a שׁבר

לְשֵׁבֶט — pref. ל f. לְהַ·X [n. m. s. שֵׁבֶט § 35. r. 2] see שׁבט

לְשֵׁבֶט — p ּו pref. ל X noun com. sing. d. 6b; ּו bef. (:) שׁבט

לְשִׁבְטוֹ — pref. id. X id., suff. 3 pers. sing. masc. . שׁבט

לְשִׁבְטֵי — pref. id. X id. pl., constr. st. שׁבט

לְשִׁבְטֵיהֶם — pref. id. X id. pl., suff. 3 pers. pl. masc. . שׁבט

לְשִׁבְטֵי — pref. ל bef. (:) X id. pl., suff. 3 pers. sing. m. שׁבט

לְשִׁבְטֶךָ — pref. id. X id., suff. 2 pers. sing. masc. שׁבט

לְשִׁבְטֵיכֶם — pref. ל X id. pl., suff. 2 pers. pl. masc. שׁבט

a Ge. 41. 19.   f Pr. 6. 18.   l Job 41. 21.   q Ps. 77. 8.   v 1 Ch. 23. 29.   z Eze. 7. 21.   f 1 Ki. 21. 16, 18.   s Is. 15. 9.   x Ps. 147. 3.
b Is. 58. 7, 10.   g Je. 28. 8.   m Ex. 23. 2.   r 2 Ki. 11. 4.   w Ps. 45. 15.   a Ps. 75. 5.   g Ge. 28. 4.   t Le. 14. 56.   y Jos. 13. 33.
c Eze. 18. 7, 16.   h Eze. 34. 23.   n Ec. 5. 12.   s Le. 1. 3.   x 2 Sa. 12. 3.   b Ps. 78. 48.   h 1 Ch. 18. 10.   u Is. 61. 1.   z Ju. 21. 24.
d Ps. 146. 7.   i Ps. 139. 2.   o Ho. 5. 13.   t 1 Sa. 8. 13.   y Eze. 5. 6.   c Ne. 9. 23.   i Ps. 9. 18.   v Is. 65. 15.   a De. 16. 18.
e Ne. 9. 15.   k Eze. 34. 2.   p Ec. 8. 3.   u Ge. 1. 7, 8, etc.   aa Ex. 1. 19.

לָשֶּׁבִי } pref. לְ for לְהַ)(noun masc. sing. dec. 6 i   שׁבה
לִשְׁבִי } (§ 35. rem. 14)

לְשָׁבֵי וּ pref. לְ)(Kal part. act. pl. const. masc. from שָׁב dec. 1 a (§ 30. No. 3), וּ bef.   שׁוב

לְשָׁבֵי וּ Chald., pref. id.)(Peal part. act. pl. constr. masc. from [שָׁב] d. 1 a (§ 30. No. 3); וּ id.   שׁיב

לְשָׁבַיָּא Chald., pref. id.)(id. pl., emph. st.   שׁיב

לְשֹׁבֵיהֶם pref. id.)(Kal part. act. pl. masc., suff. 3 pers. pl. masc. from [שָׁבָה] dec. 9a   שׁבה

לַשְׁבִּית וְ pref. לְ contr. (for לְהַשְׁבִּית), Hiph.inf.constr.   שׁבת

לְשִׁבְכָה pref. לְ for לְהַ)(n. f. s., pl. שְׂבָכוֹת (no pl. c.)   שׂבך

לִשְׁבַנְיָה pref. לְ bef.)(pr. name masc.   שׁבן

לְשֶׁבַע pref. לְ (see lett. לְ))(n. m. s. d. 6 c (§ 35. r. 5)   שׁבע

לְשֶׁבַע pref. לְ)(num. card. fem.   שׁבע

לְשֶׁבַע pref. id.)(noun masc. sing. dec. 6 c (§35. r. 5)   שׁבע

לִשְׁבֹּעַ pref. לְ bef.)(Kal inf. constr.   שׁבע

לִשְׁבֻעָה pref. לְ)(noun fem. sing. (no pl.)   שׁבע

לִשְׁבֻעָה וּ defect. for לִשְׁבוּעָה (q.v.)   שׁבע

לְשִׁבְעָה pref. id.)(num. card. masc. from שֶׁבַע fem.   שׁבע

לְשִׁבְעַת pref. id.)(id. constr. state   שׁבע

לִשְׁבֹּר } pref. לְ bef.)(Kal inf. constr. (§ 8. rem. 18)
לִשְׁבֹּר }

לְשִׁבְרֶךָ pref. לְ)(noun masc. sing., suff. (for דְךָ) 2 pers. sing. masc. fr. שֶׁבֶר dec. 6 b   שׁבר

לְשִׁבְרֵךְ pref. id.)(id., suff. 2 pers. sing. fem.   שׁבר

לָשֶׁבֶת } pref. לְ, when not followed by a Genitive, otherwise לְשֶׁבֶת (q. v.)
לָשֶׁבֶת }

לְשַׁבַּת pref. לְ for לְהַ)(noun com. sing. (suff. שַׁבַּתּוֹ, pl. שַׁבָּתוֹת)   שׁבת

לָשֶׁבֶת pref. לְ)(Kal inf. constr. dec. 13 a   ישׁב

לְשִׁבְתּוֹ pref. id.)(id., suff. 3 pers. sing. masc.   ישׁב

לְשַׁבְּתוֹת pref. לְ for לְהַ)(noun com. pl. abs. (constr. שַׁבְּתוֹת) from שַׁבָּת (q. v.)   שׁבת

לְשִׁבְתִּי pref. לְ)(Kal inf. constr. (שֶׁבֶת), suff. 1 pers. sing. dec. 13 a   ישׁב

לְשִׁבְתְּךָ pref. id.)(id., suff. 2 pers. sing. masc.   ישׁב

לְשִׁבְתֵּנוּ pref. id.)(id., suff. 1 pers. pl.   ישׁב

לְשִׁגְנָה pref. לְ bef.)(noun fem. sing. dec. 11 c   שׁגג

לְשִׁגּוֹת pref. id.)(Kal inf. constr.   שׁגה

לָשַׁד masc. dec. 8 d.—I. moisture, vital power, Ps. 32. 4 (Arab. לשׁד to suck).—II. הַשָּׁמֶן לְ oil cake, Nu. 11. 8.

לִשְׁדֵי pref. לְ)(noun masc. sing.   שׁדד

לִשְׁדְדִים pref. id.)(Kal part. act. m., pl. of שׁוֹדֵד d. 7 b   שׁדד

לְשָׂדֶה pref. id.)(noun masc. sing. dec. 9 b   שׂדה

לְשָׂדֵהוּ pref. id.)(id., suff. 3 pers. sing. masc   שׂדה

לְשַׁדֵּר pref. לְ bef.)(Kal inf. constr.   שׁדד

לְשַׁדַּי pref. לְ)(noun m. [שַׁד] with the pl. term. ־ַי   שׁדד

לְשַׁדַּי noun m. s., suff. 1 pers. sing. fr. שַׁד dec. 8 d   שׁד

לִשְׂדֵי pref. לְ bef.)(noun masc. pl. constr. fr. שָׂדֶה dec. 9 b   שׂדה

לַשֵּׁדִים pref. לְ for לְהַ)(noun m., pl. of [שֵׁד] d. 1 a   שׁוד

לַשַּׁדְרַךְ pref. לְ)(pr. name masc.   שׁדר

לַשְּׁדֵרֹת pref. לְ for לְהַ)(noun fem., pl. of [שְׂדֵרָה] dec. 10, see   סדר

לְשֵׁר pref. לְ (see lett. לְ))(noun masc. sing. irr.   שׁיה
לְשִׁי pref. לְ for לְהַ)((§ 45)

לַשּׁוְא pref. id.)(noun masc. sing.   שׁוא

לְשׁוֹאָה pref. לְ)(noun fem. s. d. 10; וּ bef.   שׁוא

לְשׁוּב וְ pref. לְ (see lett. לְ))(Kal inf. constr.   שׁוב

לְשׁוֹבֵב pref. לְ)(Pilel inf. constr.   שׁוב

לְשׁוֹבָל pref. id.)(pr. name masc.   שׁבל

לָשׁוּחַ pref. לְ (see lett. לְ))(Kal inf. constr.   שׁוח

לְשׁוּחָם pref. id.)(pr. name masc.   שׁוח

לָשׁוּם וְ pref. לְ (see lett. לְ))(Kal inf. constr.   שׂום

לָשׁוֹן וְ noun com. sing. dec. 3 a   לשׁן

לְשׁוֹן וּ id. constr. st. ; וּ bef.   לשׁן

לְשׁוֹנָה וּ id., suff. 3 pers. sing. fem.   לשׁן

לְשׁוֹנוֹ וּ id., suff. 3 pers. sing. masc. ; וּ bef.   לשׁן

לְשׁוֹנִי וּ id., suff. 1 pers. sing. ; וּ id.   לשׁן

לְשׁוֹנִי pref. לְ)(pr. name masc., for שָׁאוֹנִי   שׁאן

לְשׁוֹנְךָ } noun com. sing., suff. 2 pers. sing. masc. from לָשׁוֹן dec. 3 a; וּ bef.
לְשׁוֹנֶךָ }

לְשׁוֹנֵךְ id., suff. 2 pers. sing. fem.   לשׁן

לְשׁוֹנְכֶם id., suff. 2 pers. pl. masc.   לשׁן

לְשׁוֹנָם וּ id., suff. 3 pers. pl. masc. ; וּ bef.   לשׁן

לְשׁוּנַמִּית pref. לְ for לְהַ)(gent. noun, fem. of שׁוּנַמִּי from שׁוּנֵם   שׁון

לְשׁוֹנֵנוּ וּ noun com. sing., suff. 1 pers. pl. from לָשׁוֹן dec. 3 a; וּ bef.   לשׁן

לְשׁוּעָתִי pref. לְ)(noun fem. sing., suff. 1 pers. sing. from שׁוּעָה (no pl.)   שׁוע

לָשׁוּר pref. לְ (see lett. לְ))(Kh. שׁוּר Kal inf. R. שׁיר K. שִׁיר id. R.   שׁיר

לָשׁוֹרּ	pref. לְ for לְהַ)(noun masc. s. (§ 35. r. 13)	שׁוֹר
לָשׁוּשׁיּ	pref. לְ (see lett. לְ))(Kal inf. constr.	שׁוּשׁ
לוֹשׁ	Kal part. act. fem. pl. [of לָשָׁה dec. 10, from לוּשׁ masc.]	
לְשׁוּתֶלַח	pref. לְ)(pr. name masc., see שׁוּתֶלַ	
לִשְׁחוֹט	in full for לִשְׁחֹט (q. v. & § 8. rem. 18)	שׁחט
לִשְׁחוֹק	pref. לְ bef. (:))(Kal inf. constr. (§ 8. rem. 18); or noun masc. sing.	שׁחק
לִשְׁחוֹת	pref. id.)(Kal inf. constr.	שׁחה
לִשְׁחֹט	pref. id.)(Kal inf. constr.	שׁחט
לִשְׁחֹן	pref. id.)(noun masc. sing.	שׁחן
לְשַׁחֵק	pref. לְ)(Piel (§ 14. rem 1) inf. constr. [for § 10. rem. 4]	שׁחק
לִשְׁחֹקִי	pref. לְ bef. (:))(noun masc. sing.	שׁחק
לִשְׂחָקִים	pref. id.)(noun masc., pl. of שַׂחַק dec. 6d	שׁחק
לְשַׁחֵר	pref. לְ)(Piel inf. constr. (§ 14. rem. 1)	שׁחר
לָשַׁחַת	pref. לְ for לְהַ)(noun fem. sing. dec. 13a	שׁוח
לְשַׁחַת	pref. לְ)(noun masc. sing.	שׁחת
לְשַׁחֵת	pref. לְ)(Piel (§ 14. rem 1) inf. constr. d. 7b	שׁחת
לְשַׁחֲתָהּ	pref. id.)(id., suff. 3 pers. sing. fem.	שׁחת
לְשַׁחֶתְכֶם	pref. id.)(id., suff. 2 pers. pl. masc.	שׁחת
לְשׁוֹטֵט	וּ pref. id.)(Pilel inf. constr.; וּ bef. (:)	שׁוט
לְשָׂטָן	pref. id.)(noun masc. sing.	שׁטן
לְשִׂטְנוֹ	pref. id.)(Kal inf. [שְׂטֹן], suff. 3 pers. sing. masc. (§ 16. rem. 10)	שׁטן
לְשֶׁטֶף	pref. לְ for לְהַ)(noun masc. sing.	שׁטף
לְשֶׁטֶף	pref. לְ)(noun masc. sing.	שׁטף
לְשֹׁטְרֵי	וּ Chald., pref. לְ bef. (:))(noun masc. sing.	שׁטר
לְשֹׁטְרָיו	וּ pref. לְ)(the foll. with suff. 3 pers. sing. masc.; וּ bef. (:)	שׁטר
לְשֹׁטְרִים	pref. id.)(Kal part. act. m., pl. of שֹׁטֵר d. 7b	שׁטר
לְשִׂיבָה	pref. id.)(noun fem. sing. dec. 10	שׁיב
לָשִׂיד	pref. לְ for לְהַ)(noun masc. sing.	שׁוד
לְשֵׁיזָבוּתֵּהּ	Chald., pref. לְ)(Peel inf. [שֵׁיזָבוּת], suff. 3 pers. sing. fem. (§ 48)	שׁזב
לְשֵׁיזָבוּתָךְ	Chald., pref. id.)(id., suff. 2 pers. sing. m.	שׁזב
לְשֵׁיזָבוּתַנָא	Chald., pref. id.)(id., suff. 1 pers. pl.	שׁזב
לָשִׂיחַ	pref. לְ (see lett. לְ))(Kal inf. constr.	שׁיח
לְשֻׂמוֹ	וּ pref. לְ)(Kh. לְשִׂימוֹ, K. לְשׂוּמוֹ, Kal inf. with suff. R. שׂים or שׂום	
לָשִׁית	pref. לְ (see lett. לְ))(Kal inf. constr. d. 1a	שׁית
לְשִׁית	וּ pref. לְ for לְהַ)(noun masc. sing. dec. 6m	שׁית

לָשַׁךְ	Root not used; prob. i. q. Arab. לשק, לצק to be joined, to adhere to (Lee).	
לִשְׁכָּה	fem. dec. 12b, chamber, espec. those attached to the sides of the temple, written also נִשְׁכָּה by interchange of the liquids.	
לִשְׁכַּב	pref. לְ bef. (:))(Kal inf. constr.	שׁכב
לִשְׁכָּה	וּ noun fem. sing. dec. 12b	לשך
לִשְׁכֹּה	pref. לְ for לְהַ)(noun masc. sing.	שׁכה
לִשְׁכּוֹן	in full for לִשְׁכֹּן (q. v. & § 8. rem. 18)	שׁכן
לְשָׁכוֹת	noun fem. pl. abs. from לִשְׁכָּה dec. 12b	לשך
לִשְׁכוֹת	id., constr. st.	לשך
לִשְׁכִּים	pref. לְ)(noun masc., pl. of [שֵׁךְ] dec. 8b	שׁכך
לִשְׂכִירֶךָ	וּ pref. לְ bef. (:))(noun masc. sing., suff. 2 pers. sing. masc. from שָׂכִיר dec. 3a	שׂכר
לְשֵׂכֶל	pref. לְ)(noun masc. sing. dec. 6b	שׂכל
לְשַׁכְלָלָה	Chald., pref. id.)(Shaph. inf. constr. (§ 48)	כלל
לְשַׁכְּלָם	pref. id.)(Piel inf. [שַׁכֵּל], suff. 3 pers. pl. masc. dec. 7b	שׁכל
לְשַׁכֵּן	pref. id.)(Piel inf. constr.	שׁכן
לִשְׁכֹּן	pref. לְ bef. (:))(Kal inf. constr.	שׁכן
לְשָׁכְנוֹ	pref. לְ)(noun masc. sing. with suff. 3 pers. sing. masc. from [שָׁכֵן] dec. 6a	שׁכן
לְשָׁכְנִי	pref. id.)(Kal inf., suff. 1 pers. sing.	שׁכן
לִשְׁכַנְיָה לִשְׁכַנְיָהוּ	pref. לְ bef. (:))(pr. name masc., see שְׁכַנְיָה	שׁכן
לִשְׁכֵנִי	וּ pref. id.)(noun masc. pl., suff. 1 pers. sing. from שָׁכֵן dec. 5a	שׁכן
לִשְׁכֵנָיו	pref. id.)(id., suff. 3 pers. sing. masc.	שׁכן
לִשְׁכֵנֵינוּ	pref. id.)(id., suff. 1 pers. pl.	שׁכן
לְשֶׂכֶר	וּ pref. לְ for לְהַ)(noun masc. sing.	שׂכר
לִשְׂכֹּר	pref. לְ bef. (:))(Kal inf. constr.	שׂכר
לְשִׁכְרָה	pref. לְ)(Kal inf. constr. (§ 8. rem. 10)	שׁכר
לְשִׁכְרָה	pref. id.)(noun fem. sing. from שִׁכּוֹר masc.	שׁכר
לְשִׁכָּרוֹן	pref. id.)(noun masc. sing.	שׁכר
לְשָׁכֹת	noun fem., pl. of לִשְׁכָּה dec. 12b	לשך
לְשָׁכַּת	id. sing., constr. st.	לשך
לְשָׁכָּתָה	id. sing. with parag. ה	לשך
לְשָׁלָא	pref. לְ for לְהַ)(noun masc. sing.	שׁלג
לִשְׁלָה	pref. id.)(pr. name masc.	שׁאל
לְשִׁלֹה	pref. id.)(pr. name of a place	שׁלה
לִשְׁלוֹט	pref. לְ bef. (:))(Kal inf. constr. (§ 8. r. 18)	שׁלט

a Nu. 15. 11.   f Ex. 9. 9.   k Eze. 5. 16.   l 1 Ch. 26. 29.   b Ps. 119. 148.   h Eze. 40. 38.   o Ezr. 5. 3, 9.   r Ps. 89. 42.   u Eze. 39. 19.
b De. 30. 9.   e Ps. 104. 26.   l Jos. 23. 13.   n Job 41. 23.   i Is. 10. 6.   p Eze. 36. 12.   s Mi. 2. 11.   v Eze. 45. 5.
c Je. 7. 18.   g Je. 48. 39.   m Zec. 3. 1.   o Am. 2. 1.   k Job 30. 1.   q De. 12. 5.   t 1 Ch. 19. 6.   w 1 Sa. 9. 22.
d Eze. 40. 39.   h Job 37. 18.   n Job 38. 25.   p Da. 6. 15.   l Nu. 33. 55.   r Ex. 29. 46.   s Hag. 1. 6.   x Job 37. 6.
e Is. 25. 11.   i Pr. 7. 15.   o Ps. 32. 6.   q Da. 6.   m Le. 25. 6.   s 2 Sa. 11. 11.   t 1 Sa. 1. 15.   y Est. 9. 1.
f Ge. 22. 10.   e Job 17. 14.   p Da. 7. 5.   r Da. 3.   n Ne. 13. 5.   o Pr. 23. 9.

לִשְׁלוֹם	'י pref. לְ)((prim. adj.) subst. m. s. d. 3 a; ' bef. (:)	שלם
לִשְׁלוֹם	'י' pref. לְ bef. (:))(id. constr. st.	שלם
לִשְׁלוֹמִים	' pref. id.)(id. (adj.) pl., abs. st.	שלם
לִשְׁלוֹשׁ	pref. לְ)(num. card. fem. comp. שְׁלֹשׁ	שלש
לִשְׁלָוְתֵהּ	Chald., pref. לְ bef. (:))(noun fem. sing., suff. 2 pers. sing. masc. from [שְׁלָוָה] d. 8 a	שלה
לִשְׁלַח לִשְׁלֹחַ	'י' } pref. לְ)(Piel inf. constr. dec. 7 (§ 15. rem. 1) ; ' bef. (:)	שלה
לִשְׁלֹחַ	pref. לְ bef. (:))(Kal inf. constr.	שלה
לִשְׁלָחֲהּ	pref. לְ)(Piel inf. (שְׁלַּח), suff. 3 p. s. f. d. 7 b	שלה
לִשְׁלָחוֹ	pref. id.)(id. with suff. 3 pers. sing. masc.	שלה
לִשְׁלְחָיו	pref. id.)(Kal part. act. pl. masc., suff. 3 pers. sing. masc. from שׁוֹלֵחַ dec. 7 b	שלה
לִשְׁלָחֲךָ	pref. id.)(id. with suff. 2 pers. sing. masc.	שלה
לִשְׁלָחָם	pref. id.)(Piel inf. (שְׁלַּח), suff. 3 p. pl. m. d. 7 b	שלה
לִשְׁלָחָן	pref. id.)(noun masc. sing. dec. 2 b	שלה
לְשַׁלְּחֵנוּ	pref. id.)(Piel inf. (שְׁלַּח), suff. 1 p. pl. d. 7 b	שלה
לְשֻׁלְחָנוֹת	pref. id.)(noun masc. with pl. fem. term., constr. of חֻנוֹת from שֻׁלְחָן dec. 2 b	שלה
לְשַׁלְּחֵנִי	pref. id.)(Piel inf. (שְׁלַּח), suff. 1 p. s. d. 7 b	שלה
לִשְׁלָחֶךָ	pref. id.)(n. m. s., suff. 2 p. s. m. fr. שֶׁלַח d. 2 b	שלה
לִשְׁלָל	pref. לְ for לָהּ } noun masc. sing. dec. 4 a	שלל
לִשְׁלֹל	pref. לְ q. v. }	שלל
לִשְׁלֹל	pref. לְ bef. (:))(Kal inf. constr.	שלל
לִשְׁלֻם	defect. for לִשְׁלוֹם (q. v.)	שלם
לְשַׁלֵּם	pref. לְ)(Piel inf. constr.	שלם
לְשַׁלֵּם	לִשְׁלֵּם, pref. id.)(pr. names masc.	שלם
לִשְׁלֹמֹה	'י' pref. לְ bef. (:))(pr. name masc.	שלם
לְשַׁלְּמוּ	pref. לְ)(Piel inf. (שְׁלַּם), suff. 3 p. s. m. d. 7 b	שלם
לְשַׁלְּמִי	pref. id.)(id. with suff. 1 pers. sing.	שלם
לְשֶׁלֶמְיָהוּ	pref. id.)(pr. name masc.	שלם
לְשַׁלֵּמְכֶם	'י pref. id.)(the foll. with suff. 2 p. pl. m.; ' bef. (:)	שלם
לִשְׁלָמִים	'י pref. לְ bef. (:))(n. m., pl. of שֶׁלֶם d. 6 a	שלם
לְשָׁלֹשׁ	pref. לְ)(num. card. fem.	שלש
לִשְׁלֹשׁ	'י' pref. לְ bef. (:))(id., constr. st.	שלש
לִשְׁלֹשָׁה	pref. לְ)(id. masc. from שָׁלֹשׁ fem.	שלש
לִשְׁלֹשִׁים	' pref. לְ for לָהּ)(n. m., pl. of שָׁלֹשׁ d. 1 b	שלש
לִשְׁלֹשֶׁת	pref. לְ bef. (:))(num. card. masc., constr. of שְׁלֹשָׁה (§ 42. rem. 5)	שלש
לְשִׁלְשָׁתָם	pref. id.)(id. with suff. 3 pers. pl. m. d. 13 c	שלש
לְשֶׁם	masc. — I. ligure, a precious stone, Ex. 28. 19:	

39. 12.—II. pr. name of a city, Jos. 19. 47, else where called דָּן & לַיִשׁ.

לְשֵׁם	'י pref. לְ)(n. m. s. d. 7 a; also pr. n. m.; ' bef. (:)	שם
לִשְׂמֹאלוֹ	pref. לְ bef. (:))(noun masc. sing., suff. 3 pers. sing. masc. from שְׂמֹאל dec. 1 a	שמאל
לְשַׁמֵּד	contr. & defect. for לְהַשְׁמִיד (q. v. & § 11. r. 3)	שמד
לְשַׁמָּה	'י pref. לְ)(noun fem. sing. d. 10 ; ' bef. (:)	שמם
לִשְׁמוֹ	pref. לְ bef. (:))(noun masc. sing., suff. 3 pers. sing. masc. from שֵׁם dec. 7 a	שם
לִשְׁמוּאֵל	pref. id.)(pr. name masc.	שמע
לְשַׂמֹּחַ	'י in full for לְשַׂמֵּחַ (q. v. § 8. rem. 18)	שמח
לִשְׁמוֹנָה	pref. לְ bef. (:))(num. card. m., from נֶה f.	שמן
לִשְׁמוֹעַ	in full for לִשְׁמֹעַ (q. v. & § 8. rem. 18)	שמע
לִשְׁמוּעָה	pref. לְ bef. (:))(noun fem. sing. dec. 10	שמע
לִשְׁמוֹר	'י in full for לִשְׁמֹר (q. v. & § 8. rem. 18)	שמר
לִשְׁמוֹת	pref. לְ bef. (:))(noun masc. with pl. fem. term. constr. from שֵׁם dec. 7 a	שם
לִשְׂמֹחַ	'י' pref. id.)(Kal inf. constr.	שמח
לְשִׂמְחָה	'י pref. לְ)(noun fem. sing. d. 12 b ; ' bef. (:)	שמח
לְשִׂמְחַת	' pref. id.)(id. constr. st. ; ' id.	שמח
לִשְׁמִי	pref. לְ bef. (:))(noun masc. sing., suff. 1 pers sing. from שֵׁם dec. 7 a	שם
לִשְׁמַיָּא	Ch., pref. id.)(n. m. pl. emph. [from שְׁמֵה]	שמה
לַשָּׁמַיִם	pref. לְ for לָהּ)(noun masc. pl. constr. שָׁמַיִם, suff. שְׁמֵיךָ, [from שָׁמֵי § 38. r. 2]	שמה
לְשָׁמִיר	pref. id.)(noun masc. sing. dec. 3 a	שמר
לִשְׁמֶךָ	pref. לְ bef. (:))(noun m. s., suff. 2 pers. s.	שם
לִשְׁמָךְ	'י pref. לְ q. v. } m. fr. שֵׁם d. 7 a; ' bef. (:)	שם
לְשִׂמְלָתוֹ	pref. id.)(noun fem. sing., suff. 3 pers. sing. masc. from שִׂמְלָה dec. 12 b	שמל
לִשְׁמָמָה	'י pref. id.)(noun fem. sing.	שמם
לְשַׁמָּה	pref. לְ bef. (:))(noun fem. sing. dec. 11 c	שמם
לְשַׁמּוֹת	pref. לְ)(id. pl., constr. st.	שמם
לִשְׁמָן	'י pref. id.)(n. m. s. (suff. שְׁמָנִי) d. 6 a; ' bef. (:)	שמן
לְשַׁמֵּעַ	contr. & defect. for לְהַשְׁמִיעַ (q. v. & § 11. r. 3)	שמע
לְשֵׁמַע	pref. לְ)(noun masc. sing. dec. 6 e	שמע
לִשְׁמֹעַ	'י' pref. לְ bef. (:))(Kal inf. constr.	שמע
לְשִׁמְעוֹן	pref. לְ)(pr. name of a tribe	שמע
לְשִׁמְעוֹנִי	pref. לְ for לָהּ)(gent. noun from the preced.	שמע
לִשְׁמְעִי	'י pref. לְ)(pr. name masc ; ' bef. (:)	שמע
לִשְׁמַעְיָה	'י' pref. לְ bef. (:))(pr. name masc.	שמעיה
לְשִׁמְעֹנִי	pref. לְ for לָהּ)(gent. noun from שִׁמְעוֹן	שמע

* 2 Sa. 11. 7.   ᵉ Ne. 8. 12.   ⁱ Ex. 13. 15.   ᵐ 2 Ki. 3. 23.   ¹ 1 Ki. 10. 22.   ᵖ Is. 23. 11.   ᵘ Nu. 26. 55.   ⁱ Da. 4. 8, 17, 19, 31.   ᵉ Je. 25. 12.
ᵇ Ps. 69. 23.   ᶠ De. 22. 19.   ᵏ 1 Ch. 28. 16.   ⁿ Pr. 22. 27.   ᵒ Le. 25. 21.   ᵠ Ps. 135. 3.   ᵛ Ps. 106. 5.   ʸ Is. 7. 23.   ᵈ Ex. 35. 8, 26.
ᶜ Ch. 9. 21.   ᵍ Pr. 22. 21.   ⁱ 2 Sa. 13. 16.   ᵒ Ps. 61. 9.   ᵖ 1 Sa. 13. 21.   ʳ Ec. 3. 12 ; 8. 15.   ʷ Ec. 5. 18.   ᵉ De. 22. 3.   ᵉ Ps. 26. 7.
ᵈ Da. 4. 24.   ʰ 1 Ch. 28. 16.   ᵐ Ps. 128. 3.   ᵗ Nu. 29 so.   ° Ki. 10. 24.   ᵗ Eze. 16. 56.   ˣ Je. 15. 16.   ᵈ Eze. 35. 7.   ᵗ De. 26. 17.

לְשָׁמְעָתֵנוּ	pref. לְ bef. (:))(noun fem. sing., suff. 1 pers. pl. from שְׁמוּעָה dec. 10 . . . שמע
לְשִׁמְצָה⁰	pref. לְ)(noun fem. sing. . . שמץ
לִשְׁמֹר	וְ pref. לְ bef. (:))(Kal inf. constr. . שמר
לְשָׁמְרָה⁰	pref. לְ)(id., suff. 3 pers. sing. fem.; וֹ bef. (:) שמר
לְשָׁמְרוֹ⁰	pref. id.)(id., suff. 3 pers. sing. masc. שמר
לְשֹׁמְרוֹן	pref. id.)(pr. name of a place . שמר
לְשֹׁמְרֵי	וֹ pref. id.)(Kal part. act. pl. constr. masc. from שׁוֹמֵר dec. 7 b; וֹ bef. (:) שמר
לְשָׁמְרֶךָ	pref. לְ bef. (:))(id. inf., suff. 2 pers. sing. m. שמר
לְשָׁמְרָם⁰	pref. לְ)(id. id., suff. 3 pers. pl. masc. שמר
לְשִׁמְרֹן	pref. id.)(pr. name masc. . . שמר
לְשִׁמְשׁ⁰	pref. לְ for לַה)(noun com. sing. (suff. שמש
לְשִׁמְשֶׁךָ⁰	וֹ)(שִׁמְשֶׁךָ) dec. 6a (§ 35. rem. 2) שמש
לְשִׁמְשׁוֹן	pref. id.)(pr. name masc. . . שמש
לָשֹׁן	Root not used; in Po. and Hiph. (only as denom. of לָשׁוֹן) to slander, Ps. 12. 8; Pr. 30. 10.
	לָשׁוֹן com. dec. 3a (pl. לְשׁוֹנוֹת).—I. tongue; לִ תַּהְפּוּכוֹת slanderer; אִישׁ לָ stammerer; לָ perverse, deceitful tongue.—II. speech, Job 15 5.— III. tongue, dialect.—IV. applied to inanimate things; זָהָב לְ bar of gold; אֵשׁ לְ flame of fire.
	לִשָּׁן Chald., d.1a, tongue, dialect, Da.3.4,29, &c.
לִשָּׁן⁴	וֹ Chald., noun com. sing. dec. 1 . לשן
לִשְׁנֹא⁰	וֹ pref. לְ bef. (:))(Kal inf. constr. . שנא
לְשֹׂנְאוֹ⁴	pref. לְ)(Kal part. act. sing. masc., suff. 3 pers. sing. masc. from שׂוֹנֵא dec. 7 b שנא
לְשֹׂנְאַי	pref. id.)(id. pl., suff. 1 pers. sing. . שנא
לְשֹׂנְאֵי	וֹ pref. id.)(id. pl., constr. st.; וֹ bef. (:) שנא
לְשֹׂנְאָיו⁻	pref. id.)(id. pl., suff. 3 pers. sing. masc. שנא
לְשַׂנְאָךְ⁴	Chald., pref. id.)(Peal part. act. pl. masc., suff. 2 pers. sing. masc. from [שְׂנָא] d. 2 b שנא
לְשָׁנָה	pref. לְ for לַה)(noun fem. sing. dec. 11a שנה
לְשֹׁנוֹ	defect. for לְשׁוֹנוֹ (q. v.) . . לשן
לְשַׁנּוֹת	pref. לְ)(Piel inf. constr. . שנה
לְשֹׁנוֹת	noun com., pl. of לָשׁוֹן dec. 3 a . לשן
לִשְׁנֵי⁰	pref. לְ bef. (:))(num. card. m., constr. of שְׁנַיִם שנה
לִשָּׁנַיָּא⁴	וֹ Chald., noun com. pl. emph. from לִשָּׁן d. 1 לשן
לְשָׁנְיָאה⁴	pref. לְ for לַה)(adj. sing. fem. [of שַׁנְיָא] שנא
לִשְׁנֵיהֶם⁴	pref. לְ)(n. com. du., suff. 3 p. pl. m. שֵׁן d. 8b שנן
לִשְׁנֵיהֶם	pref. לְ bef. (.))(num. card. masc. (שְׁנַיִם, c. שׁנֵי), suff. 3 pers. pl. masc. שנה
לִשְׁנַיִם⁰	pref. לְ for לָה)(noun com., du. of שֵׁן d. 8b שנן
לְשָׁנִים	pref. לְ)(noun fem. with pl. masc. term. from שָׁנָה dec. 11a . . . שנה
שְׁנַיִם וְי׳	} num. card. masc. . . . שנה
לִשְׁנֵים	pref. לְ bef. (:))(id. constr. (only with עָשָׂר to express twelve) שנה
לִשְׁנִינָה⁰	וֹ pref. id.)(noun fem. sing. . . שנן
לִשְׁנַת⁰	pref. id.)(noun fem. sing., constr. of שָׁנָה d. 11a שנה
לְשָׁנָתַיִם⁻	pref. id.)(id. du., abs. st. . שנה
לָשַׁע	[for לֶשַׁע] pr. name of a place, Ge. 10. 19.
לִשְׂעִירִים⁰	וֹ pref. לְ for לָה)(noun masc., pl. of שָׂעִיר dec. 3a שער
לִשְׂעָרִם⁴	pref. לְ bef. (:))(noun m., pl. of [שֵׂעָל] d. 6d שעל
לְשַׁעַר⁰	pref. לְ)((see lett. ל.) שער
לַשַּׁעַר⁻	} pref. לְ for לָה)(noun com. sing. dec. 6d שער
לְשַׁעֲרֵ	pref. id.)(noun masc. sing. dec. 4b . שער
לַשַּׁעַר⁴	וֹי׳ pref. לְ)(noun com. sing. d. 6d; וֹ bef. (:) שער
לִשְׁעָרַי	pref. id.)(id. pl., constr. st. שער
לִשְׁעָרֵי⁴	pref. id.)(noun m.pl.constr. from שֹׁעֵר d. 7b שער
לַשְּׁעָרִים⁰	pref. לְ for לָה)(noun com., pl. of שַׁעַר d. 6d שער
לַשֹּׁעֲרִים	pref. לְ)(noun masc., pl. of שׁוֹעֵר dec. 7b שער
לְשֹׁעֲרִים	pref. לְ bef. (:))(pr. name masc. . שער
לִשְׁפֹּט⁰	in full for לִשְׁפֹּט (q. v. & § 8. rem. 18) שפט
לִשְׁפֹּךְ⁴	in full for לִשְׁפֹּךְ (q. v. & § 8. rem. 18) שפך
לְשִׁפְעָם	pref. לְ)(pr. name masc. . . שפע
לְשִׁפְחָה	pref. לְ)(noun fem. sing. dec. 12b שפח
לִשְׁפָחוֹת	וֹ pref. id.)(id. pl., abs. st. שפח
לְשִׁפְחָתְךָ⁰	וֹי׳ pref. לְ)(id. sing., suff. 2 p. s. m.; וֹ bef. (:) שפח
לְ שִׁפֹּט⁰	Kh. לִשְׁפֹּט q. v. K. (לְמִשְׁפָּט (q. v.) שפט
לִשְׁפֹּט⁴	pref. לְ bef. (:))(Kal inf. constr. . שפט
לְשָׁפְטֵי	וֹ pref. לְ)(the foll. with suff. 3 pers. sing. m. שפט
לְשֹׁפְטִים⁰	וֹ pref. לְ f. לָה)(Kal part. act. masc., pl. of שפט
לְשֹׁפְטֵים	וֹ pref. לְ)(שׁוֹפֵט d. 7b; וֹ bef. (:) שפט
לְשָׁפְטֵנוּ	pref. id.)(id. inf., suff. 1 pers. pl. שפט
לְשָׁפִים	וֹ pref. id.)(pr. name masc.; וֹ bef. (:) שפף
לִשְׁפֹּךְ⁰	pref. לְ bef. (:))(שפך
לִשְׁפֹּךְ⁻	וֹי׳ pref. id.)(Kal inf. constr. (§ 8.rem.18) שפך
לַשְׁפַנִּים⁰	pref. לְ for לָה)(noun masc., pl. of שָׁפָן שפן
	dec. 8a (§ 37. No. 3c) . . .
לִשְׂפַת⁰	pref. לְ bef. (:))(n. f. s., constr. of שָׂפָה d. 11a שפה

ᵃ Is. 53. 1.   ʲ Eze. 8. 16.   ᵍ 2 Ch. 19. 2.   ʳ Ps. 124. 6.   ˣ Je. 24. 9.   ᵇ 1 Ki. 20. 10.   ᵏ Ex. 27. 16.   ᵐ Je. 22. 17.   ᵗ 1 Ch. 26. 29.
ᵇ Ex. 32. 25.   ᶠ De. 17. 3.   ᵐ De. 7. 10.   ʳ Pr. 10. 26.   ʸ 2 Ch. 15. 10.   ᶜ Ex. 32. 27.   ᵏ Je. 22. 19.   ⁿ 2 Ki. 4. 2.   ᵘ 1 Sa. 8. 5, 6.
ᶜ Ge. 2. 15.   ᵍ De. 3. 29.   ᵏ Da. 4. 16.   ˢ 2 Ch. 11. 17.   ᶻ 2 Sa. 13. 23.   ᵈ 1 Ch. 16. 42.   ˡ 2 Ch. 23. 4.   ᵒ 2 Sa. 14. 6.   ᵛ 1 Sa. 25. 31.
ᵈ 1 Sa. 19. 11.   ʰ 2 Sa. 19. 7.   ⁱ Je. 2. 36.   ᵗ 1 Ki. 3. 25.   ᵃ 2 Ch. 11. 15.   ᵉ Eze. 40. 16, 44.   ᵐ Ju. 5. 11.   ᵖ Eze. 44. 24.   ʷ Ps. 104. 18.
ᵉ Jos. 10. 18.   ⁱ De. 7. 10.   ᵖ De. 21. 15.   ᵘ Jos. 6. 22.   ᵇ Le. 17. 7.   ᶠ Le. 13. 36.   ⁿ 1 Ch. 16. 33.   ᵠ 2 Ch. 1. 2.   ˣ Da. 12. 5.

pref. לְ)(id., suff. 1 pers. sing.	שרת לְשָׁרְתֵנִי
pref. id.)(num. card. f., pl. שִׁשִּׁים (com. gen.)	שש לְשֵׁשׁ
pref. id.)(pr. name masc., see לְשֵׁשְׁבַּצַּר	לְשֵׁשְׁבַּצַּר
pref. id.)(num. card. masc. (constr. שֵׁשֶׁת) from שֵׁשׁ fem.	שש לְשִׁשָּׁה
pref. id.)(noun masc. sing. dec. 3 a	שוש לְשָׂשׂוֹן
pref. id.)(pr. name masc.; וּ bef. (:)	שוש וּלְשֵׁשָׁן
pref. id.)(num. card. masc., constr. of שִׁשָּׁה (§ 39. No. 4. rem. 1) from שֵׁשׁ fem.	שש לְשֵׁשֶׁת
pref. id.)(pr. name masc.; וּ bef. (:)	שית וּלְשֵׁת
pref. לְ bef. (:))(Kal inf. constr. dec. 1 a	שתה וְלִשְׁתּוֹת
pref. id.)(id., suff. 3 pers. sing. fem.	שתה לִשְׁתּוֹתָהּ
pref. id.)(id., suff. 3 pers. pl. masc.	שתה לִשְׁתּוֹתָם
pref. id.)(num. card. du., constr. of שְׁתַּיִם, fem. of שְׁנַיִם	שנה לִשְׁתֵּי
pref. id.)(id. with suff. 3 pers. pl. masc.	שנה לִשְׁתֵּיהֶן
pref. לְ)(Kal part. act. pl. masc., suff. 3 pers. sing. masc. from שָׁתָה dec. 9 a	שתה לִשְׁתָיו
defect. for לִשְׁתּוֹת (q. v.).	שתה לִשְׁתֹּת
pref. לְ)(noun fem. sing.	תאב לְתַאֲבָה
pref. id.)(noun fem. sing. dec. 10	אוה לְתַאֲוָה
pref. לְ for לְהַ)(noun fem. sing. dec. 10	תאן לַתְּאֵנָה
pref. id.)(noun fem. sing. dec. 10	תבה לַתֵּבָה
pref. לְ bef. (:))(noun fem. sing., constr. of תְּבוּאָה dec. 10	בוא לִתְבוּאַת
pref. לְ for לְהַ)(noun f. s. d. 10. R. see בון	בין לַתְּבוּנָה
pref. לְ bef. (:))(id., suff. 3 pers. sing. masc.	בין לִתְבוּנָתוֹ
pref. id.)(id., suff. 1 pers. sing.	בין לִתְבוּנָתִי
pref. לְ f. לְהַ } noun masc. sing.	תבן לַתֶּבֶן
pref. לְ q. v. }	לַתֶּבֶן
pref. id.)(noun fem. sing. d. 1 b; וּ bef. (:)	בנה לִתַבְנִית
pref. id.)(Seg. noun [for תֹּהוּ]	תהה לְתֹהוּ
pref. לְ bef. (:))(noun fem. sing. dec. 10	הלל וְלִתְהִלָּה
pref. לְ)(noun fem. sing. dec. 10	ינה לְתוֹגָה
pref. id.)(noun fem. sing. dec. 10	ידה לְתוֹדָה
pref. id.)(noun fem. sing., suff. 1 pers. sing. from כָחַת dec. 13 a, pl. תוֹכָחוֹת (§ 44. r. 5)	יכח לְתוֹכַחְתִּי
pref. id.)(noun fem. pl. תוֹלֵדוֹת q. v.), suff. 3 pers. pl. masc.	ילד לְתוֹלְדֹתָם
pref. id.)(pr. name masc.	תלע לְתוֹלָע
pref. id.)(noun fem. sing. dec. 11 b	תעב לְתוֹעֵבָה
וְ pref. לְ (see lett. לְ))(Kal inf. constr.	תור וְלָתוּר

pref. לְ bef. (:))(id. with suff. 3 pers. s. m.	שפה לִשְׂפָתוֹ
pref. id.)(Kal inf. constr.	שקד לִשְׁקֹד
pref. id.)(Kal inf. constr. (§ 8. rem. 18)	שקל לִשְׁקוֹל
pref. id.)(noun masc. pl. (c. שִׁקְלֵי) from שֶׁקֶל dec. 6 a	שקל לִשְׁקָלִים
pref. לְ for לְהַ)(noun masc. sing. (pl.) suff. (שִׁקְרֵיהֶם) d. 6 a (comp. § 35. r. 2) }	שקר לַשֶּׁקֶר / לַשָּׁקֶר
וּ pref. לְ)(noun masc. sing. dec. 8 (§ 37. rem. 7); וּ bef. (:) }	שרר לְשָׂר / לָשָׂר
pref. id.)(pr. name masc., see שֵׁרֵבְיָ׳	לְשֵׁרֵבְיָה
וּ pref. id.)(pr. name fem., וּ bef. (:)	שרר וּלְשָׂרָה
pref. לְ for לְהַ)(pr. name of a region	ישר לַשָּׁרוֹן
וּ pref. id.)(noun masc. pl. constr. fr. שַׂר dec. 8 (§ 37. rem. 7); וּ bef. (:)	שרר וּלְשָׂרֵי
pref. id.)(id. pl. with suff. 3 pers. sing. fem.	שרר לְשָׂרֶיהָ
pref. לְ bef. (:))(pr. name masc., see שְׂרָיָה	שרה לִשְׂרָיָה
pref. לְ)(noun masc. pl., suff. 3 pers. sing. masc. from שַׂר dec. 8 (§ 37. rem. 7)	שרר לְשָׂרָיו
pref. לְ for לְהַ)(Kal part. act. masc., pl. of שָׁר dec. 1 a (§ 30. No. 1)	שיר לַשָּׁרִים
וּ pref. id. } noun masc., pl. of שַׂר d. 8 e	שרר לַשָּׂרִים / לַשָּׂרִים
וִּ pref. לְ q. v. } (§ 37. r. 7); וּ bef. (:)	
pref. id.)(id. pl. with suff. 1 pers. pl.	שרר לְשָׂרֵינוּ
pref. id.)(noun masc. sing., suff. 2 pers. sing. masc. from [שֹׁר] dec. 8 c	שרר לְשָׁרֵךְ
pref. id.)(noun masc. sing., suff. 2 pers. sing. masc. from שׁוֹר (§ 35. rem. 13)	שור לְשׁוֹרְךָ
pref. לְ bef. (:))(Kal inf. constr.	שרף לִשְׂרֹף
pref. id.)(noun fem. sing. dec. 10	שרף לִשְׂרֵפָה
pref. לְ)(Kal inf., suff. 3 pers. sing. masc.	שרף לְשָׂרְפוֹ
pref. לְ bef. (:))(noun fem. sing., constr. of שְׂרֵפָה dec. 10	שרף לִשְׂרֵפַת
וּ pref. לְ for לְהַ)(noun fem. sing.	שרק לַשְּׁרֵקָה
וְ pref. לְ bef. (:))(noun fem. sing.	שרק וְלִשְׁרֵקָה
pref. לְ)(Kal part. act. pl., suff. 1 pers. sing. fr. [שׁוֹרֵר] dec. 7 b	שרר לְשׁוֹרְרָי
Ch., pref. לְ bef. (:))(Kh. שֶׁרְשִׁי, K. שָׁרְשִׁי, noun fem. sing.	שר־שׁ לְשָׁרֹשִׁי
וִּ pref. לְ)(Piel inf. constr. dec. 7 b (comp. § 10. rem. 3); וּ bef. (:) }	שרת לְשָׁרֵת / לְשָׁרֶת
וִּ pref. id.)(id., suff. 3 pers. s. m.; וּ id.	שרת לְשָׁרְתוֹ
pref. id.)(id., suff. 3 pers. pl. masc.	שרת לְשָׁרְתָם

ᵃ 1 Ki. 7. 24.   ᶠ Je. 1. 15.   ⁱ Is. 32. 1.   ᵍ Ge. 49. 11.   ᵐ De. 17. 12.   ᵖ Is. 51. 22.   ᵗ Pr. 18. 1.   Pr. 2. 2, 3.   ᵇ Is. 49. 4.
Pr. 8. 34.   ᵍ 2 Ch. 17. 7.   ᵐ Pr. 3. 8.   ʳ Ps. 54. 7.   ⁿ 1 Ch. 15. 2.   ᵍ Eze. 23. 13.   ᶠ Ju. 9. 10.   ᵏ Pr. 5. 1.   ᵖ Pr. 17. 21.
Est. 4. 7.   ᵏ Ge. 9. 11.   ᵏ Ex. 22. 29.   Ezr. 7. 26.   ᶻ Ex. 38. 26.   ᵏ Is. 24. 9.   ᵍ Job 41. 19.   ᶜ Ps. 100. 1.
2 Ch. 3. 9.   ᵉ Nu. 22. 40.   ᵏ Ju. 9. 52.   2 Ch. 8. 14.   ᶜ 1 Ch. 25. 23.   ᵈ Ps. 119. 20.   ᵍ 2 Ch. 32. 28.   ᵈ 1 Ch. 28. 18.   ʳ Pr. 1. 23.
1 Ch. 11. 6.   ᵈ Ps. 45. 17.   ⁱ Is. 64. 10.

לְתּוֹרָה   pref. לְ f. {לָהּ} noun fem. sing. dec. 10 .   ירה

לְתוֹרָה   pref. לְ q. v.}

לְתוֹרֹתִיו   pref. id.)(id., suff. 3 pers. s. m. ; וּ bef. (:)   ירה

לְתֹשָׁב   pref. לְ for לָהּ)(noun m. s. d. 1 b (§ 31. r. 1)   ישב

לְתוֹשָׁבֶךָ   וּ pref. לְ)(id., suff. 2 pers. s. m. ; וּ bef. (:)   ישב

לִתְוּשִׁיָה   pref. id.)(noun fem. sing. . . .   ישה

לְתַח   Root not used; perh. *to spread out,* i. q. מָתַח, Sam. נתח (Gesenius).

מֶלְתָּחָה fem. *wardrobe, vestry,* 2 Ki. 10. 22.

לְתַחַן   pref. לְ)(pr. name masc. . .   חנה

לַתֵּיכוֹנָה   pref. לְ for לָהּ)(adj. f. s. d. 10, fr. תֵּיכוֹן ’m.   תוך

לְתֵימָן   וּ' pref. לְ)(noun masc. sing. (with parag. ה, תֵּימָנָה ; וּ bef. (:) .   ימן

לֶתֶךְ } masc. *measure,* of capacity, Ho. 3. 2.

לִתְכוּנָה   pref. לְ for לָהּ)(noun fem. sing. dec. 10 .   כון

לְתָלִי   pref. לְ)(noun masc. sing. dec. 8b . .   תלל

לְתֹלְדוֹתָם   pref. id.)(n. m. pl. (תּוֹלְדוֹת), suff. 3 pers. pl. m.   ילד

לְתֹלְדֹתָיו   pref. id.)(id. with suff. 3 pers. sing. masc.   ילד

לְתֹלְדֹתָם   defect. for לְתוֹלְדוֹתָם (q. v.)   ילד

לִתְלוֹת   pref. לְ bef. (:))(Kal inf. constr. .   תלה

לְתַלְפִּיוֹת   pref. לְ)(noun fem. pl. . .   תלה

לְתֻמָּם   pref. לְ for לָהּ)(noun masc. sing. dec. 8c   תמם

לְתֻמּוֹ   pref. לְ)(id., suff. 3 pers. sing. masc.   תמם

לְתַמִּים   וּ pref. id.)(id. pl., abs. st.; וּ bef. (:)   תמם

לְתֻמָּם   pref. id.)(id. sing., suff. 3 pers. pl. masc.   תמם

לְתָמָר   pref. id.)(pr. name fem. . .   תמר

לְתָמָר   pref. id.)(noun masc. sing. dec. 4a   תמר

לִתְנוּפָה   pref. לְ bef. (:))(noun fem. sing. dec. 10 .   נוף

לְתַנּוֹת   pref. לְ)(Piel inf. constr. . .   תנה

לְתַנּוֹת   pref. id.)(noun fem., pl. of [תַּנָּה] dec. 10 .   תנה

לְתַנִּים   pref. id.)(noun masc., pl. of [תַּן] dec. 8d   תנן

לְתַנִּין   pref. id.)(noun masc. sing. dec. 1b   תנן

לְתַנִּינָם   pref. id.)(id. pl., abs. st.   תנן

לְתַע   Root not used; Arab. *to bite.*

מַלְתָּעָה fem. dec. 11a, pl. *teeth,* Ps. 58. 7; by transp. מְתַלְּעוֹת Pr. 30. 14; Job 29. 17; Joe. 1. 6.

לְתֶעוּדָה   וּ pref. לְ bef. (:))(noun fem. sing. .   עוד

לְתִפְאָרֶת   וּ' pref. .)(noun fem. sing. dec. 13a (comp. § 35. rem. 2); וּ bef. (:)}   פאר

לְתִפְאַרְתֵּךְ   pref. id.)(id. with suff. 2 pers. sing. fem. .   פאר

לִתְפֹּר   pref. לְ bef. (:))(Kal inf. constr. (§ 8. r. 2   חפר

לַתְּפִלָּה   pref. לְ for לָהּ)(noun fem. sing. dec. 10 .   פלל

לִתְפִלַּת   pref. לְ bef. (:))(id., constr. st. .   פלל

לִתְפֹּשׂ   pref. id.)(Kal inf. constr.   תפש

לְתָפְשָׂהּ   pref. לְ)(id., suff. 3 pers. sing. fem.   תפש

לְתָפְשָׂם   pref. לְ)(id., suff. 3 pers. pl. masc.   תפש

לִתְקוֹעַ   pref. לְ bef. (:))(Kal inf. constr. (§ 8. r. 18)   תקע

לִתְקוּפַת   pref. id.)(noun f. s., constr. of [תְּקוּפָה] d. 10   קוף

לְתַקֵּן   pref. לְ)(Piel inf. constr.   תקן

לִתְקֹן   pref. לְ bef. (:))(Kal inf. constr.   תקן

לִתְקָפָה   וּ Chald., pref. לְ)(Pael inf. constr. (§ 47. rem. 5); וּ bef. (:)   תקף

לִתְקוּפוֹת   pref. לְ bef. (:))(noun f., pl. of תְּקוּפָה d. 10   קוף

לִתְרוּמוֹת   pref. לְ for לָהּ)(noun f., pl. of תְּרוּמָה d. 10   רום

לִתְרוּמַת   pref. לְ bef. (:))(id. sing., constr. st   רום

לִתְרוּפָה   pref. id.)(noun fem. sing. .   רוף

לִתְרַע   pref. id.)(noun masc. sing. . .   תרע

לִתְשׁוּבַת   וּ pref. id.)(n. f. s., constr. of [תְּשׁוּבָה] d. 10   שוב

לִתְשׁוּעָה   pref. id.)(noun fem. sing. dec. 10 .   שוע

לִתְשׁוּעַת   pref. id.)(id., constr. st. . .   שוע

לִתְשׁוּעָתְךָ   pref. id.)(id. with suff. 2 pers. sing. masc.   שוע

לַתְּשִׁיעִי   pref. לְ for לָהּ)(num. ord. masc., from תֵּשַׁע   תשע

לְתִשְׁעָה   pref. לְ)(num. card. masc. from תֵּשַׁע fem. .   תשע

לִתְשַׁעַת   pref. id.)(id., constr. st. . .   תשע

לָתֵת   וּ' pref. לָ (see lett. לְ))(Kal inf. constr.) / וְ לָתֶת- [for תֵּנֵת § 17. rem. 8]}   נתן

לְתִתָּהּ   pref. id.)(id. with suff. 3 pers. sing. f. d. 8b   נתן

לְתִתִּי   pref. id.)(id., suff. 1 pers. sing. .   נתן

לְתִתְּךָ   וּ' pref. id.)(id., suff. 2 pers. s. m.; וּ bef. (:)   נתן

לְתִתָּם   pref. id.)(id., suff. 3 pers. pl. masc.   נתן

לְתִתֵּן   pref. id.)(Kal fut. 2 pers. sing. masc. (*that thou mayest put*), but some MSS. read לְתִתּוֹ inf. with suff. . .   נתן

לְתִתֵּנוּ   וּ pref. id.)(Kal inf. (תֵּת § 17. rem. 1), suff. 1 pers. pl. 8b; וּ bef. (:) . . .   נתן

---

a Ne. 8. 7.   f Eze. 41. 7.   m Ca. 4. 4.   r Le. 14. 21.   w Is. 8. 20.   a De. 20. 19.   g Ec. 1. 15.   n Da. 3. 26.   Ezr. 9. 8, 9.
b Is. 8. 20.   g Job 39. 26.   n Pr. 10. 29.   s Ju. 11. 40.   x 2 Ch. 3. 6.   b 1 Sa. 23. 26.   h 2 Ch. 36. 10.   o De. 26. 19.
c Is. 42. 4.   h Is. 43. 6.   o Ezr. 2. 63.   t Mal. 1. 3.   y Is. 60. 19.   c Da. 6. 8.   i 1 Sa. 1. 20.   p 2 Ch. 35. 12.
Nu. 35. 15.   i Na. 2. 10.   p 2 Sa. 15. 11.   u Job 30. 29.   z Ec. 3. 7.   d 2 Ch. 24. 23.   k La. 3. 26.   q 1 Ki. 6. 19.
Le. 25. 6.   k Je. 49. 2.   q Ca. 7. 8.   v Ex. 7. 12.   Ne. 11. 17.   e Ne. 12. 44.   l Ps. 119. 81.   r Esr. 9. 8.
Job 11. 6.   l 1 Ch. 26. 31.   Ec. 7. 13.   f Eze. 47. 12.   m 1 Ch. 25. 24.

ב

מ, מ (before guttural) pref. prep. i. q. מן q. v. Root מנן.

מְאַבְּדִים — Piel part. masc., pl. of [מְאַבֵּד] dec. 7 b — אבד

מֵאֲבֹתָם — pref. מ for מן X noun masc., with pl. fem. term. & suff. 3 pers. pl. m. fr. אָב irr. (§ 45) — אב

מַאֲבִידִי — Hiph. part. sing. masc. — אבד

מֵאָבִיהָן — pref. מ for מן X noun masc. sing., suff. 3 pers. pl. fem. from אָב irr. (§ 45) — אב

מוֹאֲבִיּוֹת — gent. noun fem., pl. of מוֹאֲבִיָּה, masc. מוֹאָבִי, from מוֹאָב q. v.

מֵאָבִיךְ — pref. מ for מן X noun masc. sing., suff. 2 pers. sing. masc. from אָב irr. (§ 45) — אב

מֵאָבִיךְ — pref. id. X id., suff. 2 pers. sing. fem. — אב

מֵאֲבִימֶלֶךְ — pref. id. X pr. name masc. — אב

מֵאָבִינוּ — pref. id. X noun masc. sing., suff. 1 pers. pl. from אָב irr. (§ 45) — אב

מֵאֵבֶל — pref. id. X noun masc. sing. dec. 6 (§ 35. rem. 6); bef. lab. — אבל

מֵאָבֵל — pref. id. X pr. name in compos. אָבֵל מְחוֹלָה — אבל

מֵאֶבֶן — pref. id. X noun fem. sing. dec. 6a (also pr. name in compos. אֶבֶן הָעֵזֶר) — אבן

מֵאַבְנֵי — pref. id. X id. pl. constr. — אבן

מֵאֲבֻסֶיהָ — noun masc. pl., suff. 3 pers. sing. fem. from [מֵאֲבוּס] dec. 1 b — אבס

מֵאַבְרָהָם — pref. מ for מן X pr. name masc. — אב

מֵאָבֵת — pref. id. X pr. name of a place — אוב

מֵאֲבֹתַי — pref. id. X noun masc. with pl. fem. term. and suff. 1 pers. sing. from אָב irr. (§ 45) — אב

מֵאֲבֹתֶיךָ — pref. id. X id., suff. 2 pers. sing. masc. — אב

מֵאֲבֹתֵיכֶם — pref. id. X id., suff. 2 pers. pl. masc. — אב

מֵאֲנָג — pref. id. X pr. name masc. — אנג

מְאֹד — noun masc. sing. dec. 1a, generally as an adv. — אוד

מְאֹדוֹ — id. with suff. 3 pers. sing. masc. — אוד

מֵאֱדוֹם — pref. מ for מן X pr. name of a country — אדם

מֵאַדִּירֵי — pref. id. X adj. pl. constr. m. from אַדִּיר d. 1 b — אדר

מֵאָדְךָ — [for מְאֹדְךָ] noun masc. sing., suff. 2 pers. sing. masc. from מְאֹד dec. 1a — אוד

מֵאָדָם — pref. מ for מן X noun masc. sing. — אדם

מְאָדָּם — Pual part. sing. masc. [for מְאֻדָּם § 10. r. 5] — אדם

מֵאֲדָמָה — pref. מ for מן X noun fem. sing. dec. 11 c (§ 42. rem. 1); bef. lab. — אדם

מְאָדָּמִים — Pual part. masc., pl. of מְאָדָּם (q. v.) — אדם

מֵאֲדֹנִי — pref. מ for מן X noun masc. sing., suff. 1 pers. sing. from אָדוֹן dec. 3a — דון

מֵאֲדֹנֵינוּ — pref. מ for מן X id. pl., suff. 3 pers. sing. m. — דון

מֵאָה — 'i fem. constr. מְאַת dec. 11 b.—I. *a hundred*; qualifying other words either in apposition, as מֵאָה שָׁנָה, or in the state of construction, as מְאַת שָׁנָה *a hundred years*; more rarely this numeral follows, comp. 2 Ch. 3. 16; 4. 8; Ezr. 2. 69; du. מָאתַיִם (for מְאָתַיִם) *two hundred*; pl. מֵאוֹת (and in Kh. מֵאִיוֹת) *hundreds*.—II. adv. *hundred times*, Pr. 17. 10; Ec. 8. 12.—III. *the hundredth*, sc. part, of money, &c., Ne. 5. 11.—IV. pr. name of a tower in Jerusalem, Ne. 3. 1; 12. 39

מְאָה — Chald. *hundred*; dual מָאתַיִן, Ezr. 6. 17.

מֵאַהֲבָה — pref. מ for מן X noun fem. sing. (no pl.) — אהב

מְאַהֲבַי } Piel (§ 14. rem. 1) part. pl. masc., suff. 1 pers. sing. from [מְאַהֵב] dec. 7 b } — אהב

מְאַהֲבֶיהָ — id. pl., suff. 3 pers. sing. fem. — אהב

מְאַהֲבַיִךְ }
מְאַהֲבֵיךְ } id. pl., suff. 2 pers. sing fem.; bef. lab. — אהב

מֵאַהֲבַת — pref. מ for מן X noun fem. sing., constr. of אַהֲבָה (no pl.) — אהב

מֵאֹהֶל — pref. id. X noun masc. sing. d. 6 c (§ 35. r. 9) — אהל

מֵאָהֳלוֹ — pref. id. X id., suff. 3 pers. sing. masc. — אהל

מֵאָהֳלֵי — pref. id. X id. pl., constr. st. — אהל

מֵאָהֳלֵיהֶם — pref. id. X id. pl., suff. 3 pers. pl. masc. — אהל

מֵאֹהָלֶיךָ — pref. id. X id. pl., suff. 2 pers. sing. masc. — אהל

מְאֻצָּל — Pual part. sing. masc. [for מְאֻצָּל § 10. r. 5] — אצל

מֵאוֹיֵב — pref. מ for מן X Kal part. act. s. m. d. 7 b — איב

מֵאוֹיְבַי — pref. id. X id., suff. 1 pers. sing. — איב

מֵאוֹיְבֵיהֶם — pref. id. X id. pl., suff. 3 pers. pl. masc. — איב

מַאֲוַיֵּי — noun masc. pl. constr. from [מַאֲוַי] dec. 8 d (§ 37. No. 4) — אוה

מְאוּם — Kh., see the foll.; K. מוּם (q. v.) — מום

מְאוּם — noun masc. sing. elsewhere contr. מוּם — מאם

מְאוּמָה — 'i compounded fr. מָה וּמָה; bef. lab. — מה

מֵאוֹן — pref. מ for מן X noun masc. sing. dec. 6 g — און

מָאוֹס — 'i Kal inf. abs.; bef. lab. — מאס

מֵאוּפָז — pref. מ for מן X pr. name of a place, see אוּפָז

מֵאוֹפִיר — pref. id. X pr. name of a country — אפר

מֵאוֹצָר — pref. id. X noun masc. sing. dec. 2 b — אצר

מֵאוֹצְרוֹתָיו — pref. id. X id. pl. fem., suff. 3 pers. s. m. — אצר

מָאוֹר — noun masc. sing. dec. 3 a — אור

מֵאוֹר — pref. מ for מן X noun masc. sing. dec. 1a — אור

מְאוֹר — noun masc. sing., constr. of מָאוֹר dec. 3 a — אור

---

a Je. 23. 1.   f Est. 9. 22.   l 1 Ki. 19. 4.   q Je. 25. 35.   v Ge. 47. 18.   Job 18. 14.   2 Ch. 20. 27.   Job 36. 10.   Ps. 135. 7.
De. 8. 20.   g Is. 62. 10.   m De. 30. 5.   r Job 3. 19.   Job 3. 19.   Mal. 2. 12.   Ps. 140. 9.   Is. 7. 15.   Ps. 74. 16.
c Ge. 19. 36.   h Ge. 28. 11.   n Je. 16. 12.   s De. 6. 5.   Ho. 2. 7.   Da. 1. 4.   Job 22. 23.   Is. 3. 45.   Job 18. 18.
d Je. 15. 10.   i Je. 50. 26.   2 Ki. 23. 25.   t Na. 2. 4.   Job 22. 23.   La. 3. 45.   Job 31. 7.   Pr. 15. 16.   Pr. 15. 30.
e 2 Sa. 6. 21.   k Jos. 3. 14.   Eze. 27. 19.   u Job 5. 6.   Je. 22. 22.   Is. 1. 24.   Pr. 15. 16.

מָאֹגֵר	pref. מְ for מִ)(pr. name of a place .	אור
מְאוֹרֵי	noun masc. pl. constr. from מָאוֹר dec. 3 a	אור
מְאוּרַת	noun fem. sing., constr. of [מְאוּרָה] dec. 10	אור
מֵאוֹת	noun fem., pl. of מֵאָה dec. 11 b .	מאה
מֵאוֹתוֹ	pref. מְ for מִי)(as if אוֹת with suff. 3 pers.	
	sing. masc., see אֵת (§ 5, parag.) .	את
מֵאוֹתִי	pref. id.)(id., suff. 1 pers. sing. .	את
מֵאוֹתָךְ	pref. id.)(id., suff. 2 pers. sing. fem.	את
מֵאוֹתְךָ	pref. id.)(id., suff. 2 pers. sing. masc.	את
מֵאוֹתֵיכֶם	pref. id.)(noun com. pl., suff. 2 pers. sing.	
	masc. from אוֹת dec. 1 a .	אוה
מֵאָז	פ pref. id.)(adv.; ו bef. lab.	אז
מֹאזְנֵי	ו constr. of the foll.; ו id.	אזן
מֹאזְנַיִם	noun masc. du. [for מֹאזֵן] dec. 7 b .	אזן
מְאזְּרִי	Piel part. pl. constr. masc. fr. [מְאַזֵּר] d. 7 b	אזר
מֵאָח	pref. מְ for מִי)(noun masc. sing. irr. (§ 45)	אחד
מֵאַחַד	pref. id.)(num. m., constr. of אֶחָד irr. (§ 45)	אחד
מֵאָחוֹר	פ pref. id.)(noun masc. s. d. 3 a; ו bef. lab.	אחר
מְאָחֲזִים	Piel part. sing. masc. (§ 14. rem. 1)	אחז
מְאֻחָזִים	Hoph. part. masc. pl. [of מְאֻחָז] .	אחז
מֵאֲחֻזַּת	פ pref. מְ for מִי)(noun fem. sing., constr.	
	of אֲחֻזָּה dec. 10; ו bef. lab.	אחז
מֵאֲחֻזָּתוֹ	pref. id.)(id., suff. 3 pers. sing. masc. .	אחז
מֵאֲחֻזָּתָם	pref. id.)(id., suff. 3 pers. pl. masc.	אחז
מֵאַחַי	pref. id.)(n.m. pl., suff. 1 p. s. fr. אָח irr. (§ 45)	אח
מֵאַחֵי	pref. id.)(id. pl., constr. st.	אח
מֵאֲחֵיהֶם	pref. id.)(id. pl., suff. 3 pers. pl. masc.	אח
מֵאֶחָיו	pref. id.)(id. sing., suff. 3 pers. sing. masc.	אח
מֵאֶחָיו	pref. id.)(id. sing., suff. 3 pers. sing. masc.	אח
מֵאָחִיךְ	pref. id.)(id. sing., suff. 2 pers. sing. fem.	אח
מֵאָחִיךָ	pref. id.)(id. sing., suff. 2 pers. sing. masc.	אח
מֵאֲחִיכֶם	pref. id.)(id. sing., suff. 2 pers. pl. masc.	אח
מֵאַחַר	pref. id.)((prim. subst. masc.) as a prep.	אחר
מֵאַחֲרֵי	} pref. id.)(id. pl., suff. 1 pers. sing.;	אחר
מֵאַחֲרַי	} ו bef. lab. .	
מֵאַחֲרֵי	pref. id.)(id. pl., constr. st. . .	אחר
מְאַחֲרֵי	Piel (§ 14. rem. 1) part. pl. constr. masc.	
	from [מְאַחֵר] dec. 7 b .	אחר
מֵאַחֲרֶיהָ	pref. מְ for מִי)(prep. (אַחַר) with pl. suff.	
	3 pers. sing. fem. . .	אחר
מֵאַחֲרֵיהֶם	pref. id.)(id. with suff. 3 pers. pl. masc.	אחר
מֵאַחֲרָיו	pref. id.)(id. with suff. 3 pers. sing. masc.	אחר
מֵאַחֲרַיִךְ	pref. id.)(id., suff. 2 pers. sing. fem.	אחר
מֵאַחֲרֶיךָ	pref. id.)(id., suff. 2 pers. sing. masc.	אחר
מֵאַחֲרֵיכֶם	pref. id.)(id., suff. 2 pers. pl. masc.	אחר
מֵאַחֶרֶת	pref. id.)(adj. f., pl. אֲחֵרוֹת fr. אַחֵר m. irr. (§ 45)	אחר

מֵאַחַת	pref. מְ for מִי)(num. adj. [for אַחֶרֶת], fem. of	
	אֶחָד (§ 45)	אחד
מְאַיְבֵי	} pref. id.)(Kal part. act sing. masc.	איב
מְאֹיְבַי	} dec. 7 b; ו bef. lab. .	
מְאֹיְבִי	pref. id.)(id. s.ng., suff. 1 pers. sing. .	איב
מְאֹיְבֵיהֶם	pref. id.)(id. pl., suff. 3 pers. sing. masc.	איב
מְאֹיְבֶיךָ	pref. id.)(id. pl., suff. 2 pers. sing. masc.	איב
מְאֹיְבֵיכֶם	pref. id.)(id. pl., suff. 2 pers. pl. masc. .	איב
מְאֹיְבִים	pref. id.)(id. pl., abs. st. .	איב
מֵאַיֵּי	פ pref. id.)(n.m. pl. constr. fr. אִי d. 8 (§ 37. No. 4)	אוה
מְאֵיל	pref. id.)(noun masc. s. d. 1 b (§ 30. No. 3)	אול
מְאֵיל	pref. id.)(noun m. s., constr. of אַיִל d. 6 h	אול
מְאֵילוֹת	pref. id.)(pr. name of a place	אול
מֵאֵילִים	pref. id.)(noun masc., pl. of אַיִל dec. 1 a	אול
מֵאֵילָם	pref. id.)(pr. name of a place	אול
מֵאֵילַת	pref. id.)(pr. name of a place	אול
מֵאַיִן	פ pref. id.)(adv. of inter.; ו bef. lab. .	אי
מֵאַיִן	פ pref. id.)(noun masc. sing. dec. 6 h .	אין
מֵאֵין	פ pref. id.)(id. constr. as an adv.; ו bef. lab.	אין
מֵאִיר	Hiph. part. sing. masc.	אור
מְאִירוֹת	id. fem., pl. of [מְאִירָה] dec. 10	אור
מְאִירַת	id. id sing., constr. st.	אור
מֵאִישׁ	pref. מְ for מִי)(n. m. s. d. 1 a (comp. § 45)	איש
מֵאִשָּׁהּ	פ pref. id.)(id. suff. 3 p. s. f.; ו bef. lab.	איש
מֵאֵיתָן	pref. id.)(pr. name of a place .	יתן
מַאֲכִיל	Hiph. part. sing. masc. dec. 1 b	אכל
מַאֲכִילָם	id., suff. 3 pers. pl. masc.	אכל
מַאֲכָל	פ noun masc. sing. dec. 2 b; ו bef. lab.	אכל
מַאֲכַל	פ id., constr. st.; ו id.	אכל
מֶאֱכֹל	pref. מֶ for מִי)(Kal inf. constr.	אכל
מַאֲכָלָהּ	noun m. s., suff. 3 pers. s. f. fr. מַאֲכָל d. 2 b	אכל
מַאֲכָלוֹ	ו id., suff. 3 pers. sing. masc.; ו bef. lab.	אכל
מַאֲכַלְכֶם	id., suff. 2 pers. pl. masc.	אכל
מַאֲכָלוֹת	ו noun fem. pl. abs. [as if from מַאֲכָלָה] see	
	מַאֲכֶלֶת (§ 44. rem. 5); ו bef. lab.	אכל
מַאֲכָלְךָ	ו n. m. s., suff. 2 p. s. m. fr. מַאֲכָל d. 2 b; ו id.	אכל
מַאֲכֶלֶת	noun fem. sing. . .	אכל
מֵאֵל	pref. מֶ f. מִי)(n. m. s. d. 1 a, or constr. of אַיִל d. 6 h	אול
מֵאֵלָה	ו pref. id.)(n. f. s. d. 10 (§ 42. r. 2); ו bef. lab.	אלה
מֵאֵלֶּה	ו pref. id.)(pron. demon. pl. com. gen.; ו id.	אל
מֵאֱלֹהַי	} pref. id.)(noun masc. pl., suff. 1 pers.	אלה
מֵאֱלֹהֵי	} sing. from אֱלוֹהַּ dec. 1 a; ו id.	
מֵאֱלֹהֵי	pref. id.)(id. pl., constr. st.	אלה
מֵאֱלֹהָיו	pref. id.)(id. pl., suff. 3 pers. sing. masc. .	אלה

ᵃ Eze. 32. 8.   ᶠ Ps. 65. 9.   ᵏ Job 26. 9.   ᵖ Ne. 4. 13.   ᵘ De. 29. 21.   ˣ Eze. 27. 6, 7.   ᵇ Pr. 29. 13.   ᵉ Je. 9. 14.   ⁱ Eze. 4. 10.
ᵇ Is. 11. 8.   ᵍ Ex. 5. 23.   ˡ 2 Ch. 9. 18.   ᵍ De. 15. 7.   ᵛ 2 Sa. 13. 16.   ʸ Is. 11. 11.   ᶜ Is. 27. 11.   ᶠ Ezr. 3. 7.   ᵏ Is. 9. 4.
ᶜ 1 Ki. 22. 7;   ʰ Is. 40. 15.   ᵐ Nu. 35. 8.   ʳ 2 Sa. 2. 22.   ʷ 2 Sa. 22. 4.   ᶻ 1 Ki. 5. 3.   ᵈ Ps. 19. 9.   ᵍ Ps. 102. 5.   ˡ Ps. 59. 13.
2 Ki.3.11; S.8.   ⁱ Is. 50. 11.   ⁿ Eze. 48. 22.   ˢ Je. 3. 19.   Ju. 11. 36.   ᵃ Is. 1. 29.   ᵉ Le. 21. 7.   ʰ Pr. 6. 8.   ᵐ 1 Ch. 11. 19.
ᵈ Is. 54. 15.   ⱼ Is. 9. 11.   ᵒ Eze. 46. 18.   ᵗ Jos. 8. 2.   ⁱ Nu. 10. 9.   Is. 41. 24:   ᶠ Ru. 1. 5.   ⁱ Hab. 1. 16.   ⁿ Is. 40. 27.
ⱼ Ki. 20. 25.   ᵏ 2 Sa. 10. 9.   ᵖ Ne. 1. 2.   ᵗ Ru. 1. 16.   ᵖ Ps. 68. 24.   Je. 30. 7.   ᵍ Je. 23. 15.   ᵏ Da. 1. 10.   ᵒ Je. 51. 8.
ᵉ Sa. 24. 24.   ᵐᵐ Pr. 30. 14.

מַאֲלֹהֶיךָ	pref. מֵ for מִ) וּ id. pl., suff. 2 pers. sing. m.	אלה
מֵאֱלֹהִים	וּ pref. id.)(id. pl., abs. st.; וּ bef. lab.	אלה
מֵאֱלֹהֵינוּ	pref. id.)(id. pl., suff. 1 pers. pl.	אלה
מֵאֱלוֹהַּ	pref. id.)(id. sing., abs.	אלה
מֵאֵלוֹן	pref. id.)(noun masc. sing. dec. 1 b	אלל
מֵאֶלְתֹּלַשׁ	pref. id.)(pr. name of a place	אלש
מֵאֱלִיָּהוּ	pref. id.)(pr. name masc.	אול
מַאֲלִיפוֹת	Hiph. part. f. pl. [of מַאֲלִיפָה fr. מֵאֲלִיף m.]	אלף
מְאַלְּמִים	Piel part. masc., pl. of [מְאַלֵּם] dec. 7 b	אלם

מֵאָלֶף / מֵאֶלֶף — pref. מֵ for מִ)(noun masc. sing. dec. 6 a (§ 35. rem. 2)   אלף

מֵאַלְפֵי	pref. id.)(id. pl., constr. st.	אלף
מֵאָלָתִי	pref. id.)(noun fem. sing., suff. 1 pers. sing. from אָלָה dec. 10 (§ 42. rem. 2)	אלה

מָאַם

Root not used; hence
מאוּם m. (for מְאוּם) Da. 1. 4; Job 31. 7, and
מוּם (contr.) masc. dec. 1 a, *spot, blemish,* in a
physical and moral sense.

מַאֲמִינִם	Hiph. part. masc., pl. of מַאֲמִין dec. 1 b	אמן
מְאַמֵּץ	Piel part. sing. masc. [for מְאַמֵּץ]	אמץ
מַאַמַצֵּי	noun masc. pl. constr. from [מַאֲמָץ] d. 8 a	אמץ
מַאֲמַר	וּ n. m. s., constr. of [מַאֲמָר] d. 2 b; וּ bef. lab.	אמר
מֵאמַר	וּ Chald. noun masc. sing. (§ 53. r. 1); וּ id.	אמר
מֵאִמְרֵי	pref. מֵ for מִ; n. m. pl. constr. fr. [אֵמֶר] d. 6 b	אמר

מָאֵן. Pi. מֵאֵן *to refuse, to be unwilling.*
מָאֵן adj. masc. *refusing, unwilling.*
מֵאֵן masc. (for מְאֵן) d. 7 b, *refusing,* Je. 13. 10.

[מָאן]	Chald. masc. dec. 1 a, *vessel.* Da. 5. 2, 3, 23; Ezr. 5. 14; 7. 19.	
מָאֵן	adj. masc. s.; or (Ex. 22. 16) Piel inf. abs.	מאן
מֵאִי	pref. מֵ for מִ)(Kh. מֵאֵין see אַי, K. מֵאַיִן (q. v.)	אי
מֵאֵן	Piel pret. 3 pers. sing. masc.	מאן
מֵאֲנָה	id. pret. 3 pers. sing. fem.	מאן
מֵאֲנוּ	id. pret. 3 pers. pl.	מאן
מֵאֱנוֹשׁ	pref. מֵ for מִ)(n. m. s. irr. (see אִישׁ § 45)	אנש
מָאנַיָּא	Chald. noun masc. pl. constr. fr. [מָאן] d. 1 a	מאן
מָאנַיָּא	וּ Chald. id. pl. emph.; וּ bef. lab.	מאן
מֵאַנְיוֹתֵיהֶם	pref. מֵ for מִ)(noun fem. pl., suff. 3 pers. pl. masc. from אֳנִיָּה dec. 10	אנה
מֵאֲנָקַת	pref. id.)(noun fem. sing., constr. of אֲנָקָה' dec. 11 c (§ 42. rem. 1)	אנק

מֵאַנְשֵׁי	וּ pref. מֵ for מִ)(noun masc. pl. constr. [as if from אֱנָשׁ], see אֱנוֹשׁ. וּ bef. lab.	אנש
מֵאַנְתָּ	Piel pret. 2 pers. masc. sing.	מאן
מֵאַנְתְּ	id. pret. 2 pers. sing. fem.	מאן
מֵאַנְתֶּם	id. pret. 2 pers. pl. masc.	מאן

I. מָאַס fut. יִמְאַס.—I. *to reject.*—II. *to despise, lightly esteem,* with בְּ; inf. מָאוֹס La. 3. 45, *aversion, contempt.* Niph. *to be contemned, despised.*

II. מָאַס Kal not used; i. q. מָסַס, Niph. *to melt, dissolve, waste away,* Ps. 58. 8; Job 7. 5.

מָאֹס	Kal inf. abs.	מאס
מֹאֵס	id. part. act. sing. masc.	מאס
מָאֲסוּ / מָאָסוּ	id. pret. 3 pers. pl. (§ 8. rem. 7)	מאס
מָאָסְכֶם	id. inf., suff. 2 pers. pl. (§ 16. rem. 8)	מאס
מָאֲסָם	id. id., suff. 3 pers. pl. masc.	מאס
מְאָסָם	id. pret. 3 pers. sing. m., suff. 3 pers. pl. m.	מאס
מְאַסֵּף	Piel part. sing. masc. dec. 7 b	אסף
מְאֻסָּף	Pual part. sing. masc.	אסף
מְאַסְפָיו	Piel part. pl. masc., suff. 3 pers. sing. masc. from מְאַסֵּף dec. 7 b	אסף
מֵאַסְפְּכֶם	וּ id., suff. 2 pers. pl. masc.; וּ bef. lab.	אסף
מָאַסְתָּ	Kal pret. 2 pers. sing. masc.	מאס
מֹאֶסֶת	id. part. act. sing., fem. of מוֹאֵס	מאס
מְאַסְתָּה	id. pret. 2 pers. sing. masc. (§ 8. rem. 5)	מאס
מָאַסְתִּי / מְאַסְתִּי	id. pret. 1 pers. sing., acc. shifted by וּ for וָ conv. (§ 8. rem. 7)	מאס
מְאַסְתִּיהוּ	id. id., suff. 3 pers. sing. masc.	מאס
מְאַסְתִּינוּ	id. id., suff. 3 pers. sing. masc.	מאס
מְאַסְתִּיךָ	id. id., suff. 2 pers. sing. masc.	מאס
מְאַסְתִּים	id. id., suff. 3 pers. pl. masc.	מאס
מְאַסְתֶּם	id. pret. 2 pers. pl. masc.	מאס
מְאַסְתָּנוּ	id. pret. 2 pers. sing. masc., suff. 1 pers. pl.	מאס
מֵאֶסְתֵּר	pref. מֵ for מִ)(pr. name fem., see אֶסְתֵּר	
מֵאַף	pref. id.)(noun m. sing. d. 8 d [for אַנְף, אָנֶף]	אנף
מַאֲפֵה	noun masc. sing., constr. of [מַאֲפָה] dec. 9 a	אפה
מֵאֹפֶה	pref. מֵ for מִ)(Kal part. sing. masc. dec. 9 a	אפה
מֵאַפְּכֶם	pref. id.)(noun masc. sing., suff. 2 pers. pl. masc. from אַף dec. 8 d [for אָנֶף, אַנְף]	אנף
מַאְפֵּל	noun masc. sing.	אפל
מַאְפֵּל	וּ pref. מֵ for מִ)(noun masc. s.; וּ bef. lab.	אפל
מַאְפֵּלְיָה	n. m. (for מַאְפֵּל q. v.) with the term. יָה for יָּה (q. v.)	אפל
מֵאֹפֶס	pref. מֵ for מִ)(noun masc. sing. dec. 6 a	אפס
מֵאַפְסֵי	pref. id.)(id. du., constr. st.	אפס

a 2 Ch. 22. 7.   e Ec. 7. 28.   h Est. 9. 32.   l Eze. 27. 29.   p Ex. 16. 28.   t Ps. 53. 6.   x 2 Ki. 23. 27.   b La. 5. 22.   f Jos. 24. 7.
b Ezr. 8. 23.   d Ge. 24. 41.   i De. 1. 32.   m Da. 4. 14.   q Is. La. 2.   u Is. 33. 15.   y 1 Sa. 16. 7.   c Ps. 37.   y Je. 2. 31.
c Job 4. 17.   d De. 1. 32.   k 2 Ki. 5. 25.   n Ps. 59. 3.   r Is. 62. 9.   v 1 Sa. 16. 1.   c Le. 2. 4.   z Je. 40. 17.
d Ps. 144. 13.   e Pr. 24. 5.   l Da. 5. 3; Ezr. 6. 5.   o Ex. 10. 3.   s Is. 52. 12.   w Ho. 7. 4.   c Nu. 11. 20.   z Je. 16. 19.
e Ge. 37. 7.   g Job 36. 19.   j Ezr. 5. 14; 7. 19.   k Je. 3. 3.   s Am. 2. 4.   w Eze. 21. 15, 18.   c Le. 26. 44.
f Ps. 84. 11.

מָאְפָע   pref. מְ for מִ)([for אָפָע] noun masc. sing.   אפע

מָאְפָרִים   pref. id.)(pr. name of a tribe   אפר

מֵאֲצִילֶיהָ   pref. id.)(noun masc. pl., suff. 3 pers. sing. fem. from [אָצִיל] dec. 3 a; bef. lab.   אצל

מֵאֵצֶל   pref. id.)((prop. subst. masc. dec. 6. § 35. rem. 6) as a prep.   אצל

מֵאֶצְלוֹ   pref. id.)(id., suff. 3 pers. sing. masc.   אצל

מֵאֶצְלִי   pref. id.)(id., suff. 1 pers. sing.   אצל

מֵאֶצְלָם   pref. id.)(id., suff. 3 pers. pl. masc.   אצל

מֵאֹצְרוֹת   pref. id.)(noun masc. with pl. fem. term., constr. of צְרוֹת from אוֹצָר dec. 2 b   אצר

מֵאוֹצְרוֹתָיו   pref. id.)(id., suff. 3 pers. sing. masc.   אצר

מֵאֹצְרֹתָיו   pref. id.)(id., suff. 3 pers. sing. masc.   אצר

מָאַר   Hiph. הֵמְאִיר to irritate, pain; part. painful.

מֵאַרְבֶּה   pref. מְ for מִ)(noun masc. sing.   רבה

מֵאָרְבֹּה   pref. id.)(noun fem. sing. dec. 10   ארב

מְאָרְבִים   Piel part. masc., pl. of [מְאָרֵב] dec. 7 b   ארב

מֵאַרְבַּע   pref. מְ for מִ)(num. card. fem. (§ 31. rem. 5)   רבע

מְאֵרוֹת   noun fem., pl. of מְאֵרָה dec. 10 [for מְאָרָה]   ארר

מֵאֲרִי   pref. מְ for מִ)(noun m. sing. d. 6 i (§ 35. r. 14)   ארה

מֵאֲרָיוֹת   pref. id.)(id. pl. abs. fem.   ארה

מֵאֲרִיךְ   Hiph. part. sing. masc.; bef. lab.   ארך

מֵאֲרָם   pref. מְ for מִ)(pr. name of a country   ארם

מֵאַרְנוֹן   } pref. id.)(pr. name of a river   רנן
מֵאַרְנֹן

מֵאַרְעָא   Chald., pref. id.)(noun fem. sing., emph. of [אֲרַע] dec. 3 a   ארע

מֵאֶרֶץ   } pref. id.)(noun fem. sing. dec. 6 a (§ 35. rem. 2); bef. lab.   ארץ
מֵאָרֶץ

מֵאַרְצוֹ   pref. id.)(id., suff. 3 pers. sing. masc.; id.   ארץ

מֵאֲרָצוֹת   pref. id.)(id. pl., abs. st.; id.   ארץ

מֵאַרְצוֹת   pref. id.)(id. pl., constr. st.   ארץ

מֵאַרְצְךָ   pref. id.)(id. sing., suff. 2 pers. sing. masc.   ארץ

מֵאַרְצָם   pref. id.)(id. sing., suff. 3 pers. pl. masc.   ארץ

מְאֵרָשָׂה   Pual part. sing. fem. [of מְאֹרָשׂ]   ארש

מְאֵרַת   noun f. s., constr. of מְאֵרָה d. 10 [for מְאָרָה]   ארר

מְאֹרֹת   noun m. with pl. fem. term. from מָאוֹר d. 3 a   אור

מֵאֵשׁ   pref. מְ for מִ)(noun com. sing. dec. 8 b   אש

מֵאַשְׁדּוֹד   pref. id.)(pr. name of a place   שדד

מֵאִשָּׁה   pref. id.)(noun fem. sing. dec. 10 [for אַנְשָׁה]   אנש

מֵאַשּׁוּר   pref. id.)(pr. name of a country; bef. lab.   אשר

מֵאֲשֵׁי   pref. id.)(noun masc. pl., suff. 1 pers. sing. from אִשֶּׁה dec. 9 a   אש

מֵאִשֵּׁי   pref. id.)(id. pl., constr. st.   אש

מֵאַשְׁפֹּת   pref. id.)(noun masc. sing.   שפת

מֵאַשְׁקְלוֹן   pref. מְ for מִ)(pr. name of a place   שקל

מֵאָשֵׁר   pref. id.)(pr. name of a man and a tribe; bef. lab.   אשר

מֵאֲשֶׁר   pref. id.)(pron. relat. of all genders and numbers; id.   אשר

מְאֻשָּׁר   Pual part. sing. masc.   אשר

מְאַשְּׁרֵי   Piel part. pl. constr. masc. fr. מְאַשֵּׁר d. 7 b   אשר

מְאֻשָּׁרָיו   Pual part. pl., suff. 3 p.s.m. fr. מְאֻשָּׁר; bef. lab.   אשר

מְאַשְּׁרֶיךָ   the foll. with suff. 2 pers. sing. masc.   אשר

מְאַשְּׁרִים   Piel part. masc., pl. of [מְאַשֵּׁר] dec. 7 b   אשר

מֵאִשֵּׁת   pref. מְ for מִ)(noun fem. sing. dec. 13 b   איש

מֵאֶשְׁתָּם   Kh. מֵאֶשְׁתָּם pref. מְ for מִ)(noun fem. sing., suff. 3 pers. pl. masc. from [אֶשֶׁת] from אֵשׁ K. מֵאֵשׁ (q. v.) & תָּם 3 pers. sing.   תמם

מְאַת   noun f. s., constr. of מֵאָה d. 11 b; bef. lab.   מאה

מֵאֹת   id. pl. abs. st.   מאה

מֵאֵת   pref. מְ for מִ)(prep. (אֵת), comp. dec. 8 b; bef. lab.   את

מֵאִתּוֹ   pref. id.)(id., suff. 3 pers. sing. masc.   את

מֵאֹתוֹ   pref. id.)(as if אוֹת with suff. 3 pers. sing. masc. see אֵת (§ 5, parad.)   את

מֵאֹתוֹת   pref. id.)(noun com., pl. of אוֹת dec. 1 a [for אֹתוֹת]; bef. lab.   אוה

מֵאִתִּי   pref. id.)(prep. אֵת with suff. 1 p. s. (comp. d. 8 b)   את

מָאתַיִם   } noun fem., by Syriasm [for מְאָתַיִם,] du. of מֵאָה dec. 11 b; bef. lab.   מאה
מָאתַיִם

מָאתַיִן   Chald. [for מְאָתַיִן], noun fem., dual of מְאָה   מאה

מֵאִתְּךָ   pref. מְ for מִ)(prep. אֵת with suff. in pause for מֵאִתְּךָ (q. v.), or (1 Ki. 2. 16, 20) 2 p.s.f.   את

מֵאִתָּךְ   pref. id.)(id. with suff. 2 pers. sing. fem.   את

מֵאִתְּךָ   pref. id.)(id. with suff. 2 pers. sing. masc.   את

מֵאִתְּכֶם   pref. id.)(id. with suff. 2 pers. pl. masc.   את

מֵאֵיתָם   pref. id.)(pr. name of a place   יתם

מֵאִתָּם   pref. id.)(prep. אֵת with suff. 3 pers. pl. masc. (comp. dec. 8 b)   את

מֵאֶתְמוּל   } pref. id.)(adv.   מול
מֵאִתְמוֹל

מֵאֶתְנַן   pref. id.)(noun m. sing., constr. of אֶתְנָן d. 2 b   תנה

מְבֹא   defect. for מָבוֹא (q. v.)   בוא

מְבֹאוֹ   defect. for מְבוֹאוֹ (q. v.)   בוא

מְבִאֵי   Hiph. part. pl. constr. masc. from מֵבִיא dec. 3 b; bef. lab.   בוא

מְבִאִים   id. pl. abs. (comp. מְבִיאִים)   בוא

מִבְּאֵר   pref. מְ)(pr. name in compos. בְּאֵר שֶׁבַע   באר

מִבְּאֵר   pref. id.)(Kh. בְּאֵר q. v., K. בֹּר (see מִבּוֹר)   באר

מִבְּאֵרֹת   pref. id.)(pr. name in compos. בְּאֵרֹת בְּנֵי יַעֲקָן   באר

a Is. 41. 24.   d Je. 10. 13.   Ju. 14. 18.   i Ps. 107. 3.   m Pr. 3. 33.   q Is. 9. 15.   t Je. 6. 29.   x Is. 30. 33.   * Ps. 50. 1.
b Is. 41. 9.   e Je. 51. 16.   h 2 Sa. 1. 23.   k Eze. 39. 27.   n Ge. 1. 14.   r Is. 9. 15.   u Je. 10. 2.   y 1 Sa. 16. 11.   † Je. 17. 26; 33. 11.
c 1 Ki. 3. 20.   f Je. 46. 23.   * Ec. 7. 15; 8. 12.   l De. 2. 5.   o Is. 3. 12.   s Mal. 3. 15.   v Exr. 6. 17.   z Mi. 1. 7.   ‡ Je. 17. 26; 33. 11.
Eze. 10. 16.   g Ho. 13. 3.   Je. 10. 11.   De. 22. 23.   p Le. 6. 10.   Is. 54. 10.   w 2 Ki. 23. 11.   2 Sa. 23. 15, 16.
2 Ch. 16. 2.   Pr. 28. 27.   Eze. 36. 20.   Pr. 3. 18.

מִבָּבֶל   pref. מ׳)(pr. name of a place   .   בלל

מִבָּבֶלָה   pref. id.)(id. with parag. ה   .   בלל

מִבֹּגְדָה   pref. id.)(Kal part. act., fem. of בֹּגֵד (§ 39. No. 3. rem. 4)   בגד

מִבְּנָדֶיךָ   pref. id.)(noun masc. pl., suff. 2 pers. sing. fem. from בֶּגֶד dec. 6a   בגד

מַבְדִּיל   Hiph. part. sing. masc. dec. 1 b   בדל

מַבְדִּלִים   id. pl., abs. st.   .   בדל

מְבֹהָלִים   Pual part. masc. pl. [of מְבֹהָל]   בהל

מִבֶּהֱמוֹת   pref. מִ׳)(noun fem. pl., constr. of בְּהֵמוֹת, from בְּהֵמָה (§ 42. rem. 1 & 5)   בהם

מָבוֹא   noun masc. sing. dec. 3a   .   בוא

מְבוֹא   id., constr. st.   .   בוא

מִבּוֹא   pref. מ׳)(Kal inf. constr. (§ 25. No. 2f)   בוא

מְבוֹאוֹ   noun m. s., suff. 3 pers. s. m. fr. מָבוֹא d. 3a   בוא

מְבוֹאֶךָ   Kh. מְבוֹאָךְ id. with suff. [for מְבוֹאֶךָ] 2 pers. sing. masc.; K. מוֹבָאֶךָ from מוֹבָא d. 2 b   בוא

מְבוֹאֹת   noun masc. with pl. fem. term. fr. מָבוֹא d. 3a   בוא

מְבוּכָה   ו noun fem. sing. dec. 10 ; ו bef. lab.   בוך

מְבוּכָתָם   id., suff. 3 pers. pl. masc.   .   בוך

מַבּוּל   noun masc. sing.   .   יבל

מְבוּסָה   ו noun fem. sing. ; ו bef. lab.   בוס

מַבּוּעֵי   noun masc. pl. constr. from מַבּוּעַ׳ dec. 1 b   נבע

מְבוּקָה   ו noun fem. sing. ; ו bef. lab.   בוק

מִבּוֹר   pref. מ׳)(n. m. s. d. 1a, contr. for בְּאֵר=בֹּאר   באר

מִבּוֹרֶךָ   pref. id.)(id., suff. 2 pers. s. m. [for בּוֹרְךָ]   בור

מִבְחוֹר   noun masc. sing.   .   בחר

מִבַּחוּרֵיכֶם   ו pref. id.)(noun masc. pl. בַּחוּרִים, dag. forte impl. in ח), suff. 2 pers. pl. masc. from בָּחוּר [for בַּחוּר] ; ו bef. lab.   בחר

מִבְחוֹרִים   pref. מ׳)(pr. name of a place   בחר

מְבֻחֶלֶת   Kh. Pual part. s. f. R. בחל, K. מְבֻחֶלֶת R. בהל

מִבְחָר   pr. name masc.   .   בחר

מִבְחַר   ו noun masc. sing., constr. of [מִבְחָר] dec. 2 b ; ו bef. lab.   בחר

מִבְחָרָיו   id. pl., suff. 3 pers. sing. masc.   בחר

מִבְחֻרָיו   pref. מ׳)(n. m. pl. [בַּחֻרִים], suff. 3 p. s. m.   בחר

מִבְחָרִים   pref. מ׳)(pr. name of a place   בחר

מִבְטָא   noun masc. sing. constr. (§ 31. rem. 1)   בטא

מִבְטָה   noun masc. sing., suff. 3 pers. sing. fem. [for מַבְטָהּ from מַבָּט comp. אָח § 45] dec. 1 b   נבט

מִבְטָח   ו pref. מ׳)(pr. name of a place ; ו bef. lab.   בטח

מִבְטַח   noun masc. sing., constr. of מִבְטָח׳, dec. 2 b   בטח

מִבְטַח   pref. מ׳)(Kal inf. constr.   .   בטח

מִבְטָחָהּ   noun masc. sing., suff. 3 pers. s. f. (§ 3. r. 3) from מִבְטָח d. 8 (§ 37. r. 7, comp. אָח § 45)   בטח

מִבְטָחוֹ   } id., suff. 3 pers. sing. masc.   .   בטח

מִבְטַחִי   } id., suff. 1 pers. sing.   .   בטח

מִבְטַחִים   id. pl., abs. st.   .   בטח

מִבְטַחֲךָ   id. sing., suff. 2 pers. sing. m. [for מִבְטָחֲךָ]   בטח

מִבְטַחָם   id. sing., suff. 3 pers. pl. m. (comp. אָח § 45)   בטח

מַבְטִיחִי   Hiph. part. sing. masc., suff. 1 pers. sing. from [מַבְטִיחַ] dec. 1 b   בטח

מַבָּטָם   noun masc. sing., suff. 3 pers. pl. masc. from [מַבָּט] dec. 1 b   נבט

מִבֶּטֶן   } pref. מ׳)(noun fem. sing. dec. 6 a (§ 35.) r. 2, but with suff. (בִּטְנִי) ; ו bef. lab.   בטן

מַבִּטְנֵנוּ   noun m. s., suff. 1 pers. pl. fr. [מַבָּט] d. 1 b   נבט

מִבִּטְנֵנוּ   noun fem. sing., suff. 3 pers. s. m. fr. בֶּטֶן d. 6 a   בטן

מֵבִי   Kh. for מֵבִיא Keri (q. v. & § 23. rem. 7)   בוא

מֵבִיא   Hiph. part. sing. masc. dec. 3 b   בוא

מְבִיאֶיהָ   ו id. pl., suff. 3 pers. sing. fem. ; ו bef. lab.   בוא

מְבִיאִים   ו id. pl. abs. st. ; ו id.   בוא

מְבִיאֲךָ   id. sing., suff. 2 pers. sing. masc.   בוא

מֵבִין   ו ״ Hiph. part. sing. masc. ; ו bef. lab.   בין

מִבִּין   ו pref. מ׳)([prim. noun masc. sing., constr. of בַּיִן dec. 6 a] prep. ; ו id.   בין

מְבִינוֹת   pref. id.)(id. with pl. fem. term.   בין

מְבִינֵי   ו constr. of the foll. ; ו bef. lab.   בין

מְבִינִים   Hiph. part. masc., pl. of מֵבִין dec. 3 b   בין

מִבִּינָתִי   pref. מ׳)(noun fem. sing., suff. 1 pers. sing. from בִּינָה dec. 10   בין

מִבִּינָתְךָ   pref. id.)(id., suff. 2 pers. sing. masc.   בין

מִבֵּיצֵיהֶם   noun fem. with pl. masc. term. (בֵּיצִים) and suff. 3 pers. pl. masc. [from בֵּיצָה sing.]   בייץ

מֵבִישׁ   Hiph. part. sing. masc.   בוש

מְבִישָׁה   id. part. sing. fem.   בוש

מִבַּיִת   } pref. מ׳)(noun masc. sing. irr. (§ 45) .   בית

מִבֵּית   ו pref. id.)(id. constr. st. (also pr. name in composition, as בֵּית אֵל &c.) ; ו bef. lab.   בית

מִבֵּיתָה   pref. id.)(id. with loc. ה   .   בית

מִבֵּיתוֹ   pref. id.)(id., suff. 3 pers. sing. masc.   בית

מִבֵּיתִי   pref. id.)(id., suff. 1 pers. sing.   בית

מִבֵּיתְךָ   } pref. id.)(id., suff. 2 pers. sing. masc.   בית

מְבַכָּה   Piel part. sing. fem. dec. 10 [from מְבַכֶּה m.]   בכה

מִבְּכוֹר   pref. מ׳)(noun masc. sing. dec. 1a   בכר

מְבַכּוֹת   Piel part. fem., pl. of מְבַכָּה dec. 10 [from מְבַכֶּה masc.]   בכה

---

a Je. 3. 11.   g 2 Sa. 3. 25.   l Is. 49. 10.   r Da. 11. 15.   y Pr. 21. 22.   d Pr. 22. 19.   i Da. 11. 6.   o Job 20. 3.   u Ho. 9. 15.

b Eze. 16. 16.   h Eze. 27. 3.   m Na. 2. 11.   s Nu. 11. 28.   z Job 18. 14.   e Ne. 13. 15.   k Is. 48. 13.   p Pr. 23. 4.   v 2 Sa. 12. 10. 11.

c Ge. 1. 6.   i Is. 22. 5.   n Pr. 5. 15.   t Nu. 30. 7, 9.   a Ps. 71. 5.   f Ps. 22. 10.   l Is. 59. 5.   q Is. 31. 15.

d Is. 59. 2.   k Mi. 7. 4.   o Am. 2. 11.   u Zec. 9. 5.   b Job 31. 24.   g De. 8. 23.   m Is. 20. 6.   r Pr. 12. 4.   w Is. 50. 9.

e Est. 8. 14.   t Ge. 9. 11.   p Pr. 20. 21.   x Ps. 118. 8, 9.   c Is. 32. 18.   h Is. 20. 5.   n Da. 1. 4.   s 1 Ki. 6. 15.   x Ese. 8. 14.

f Job 31. 11.   u Je. 38. 14.

מְבַכִּי	} pref. מְ)(noun masc. sing. dec. 6 i	בכה
מִבְכִּי	} (§ 35. rem. 14)	
מִבְכֹּר	pref. id.)(noun masc. sing. dec. 1 a	בכר
מִבְכֹרוֹת	pref. id.)(noun fem., pl. of בְּכֹרָה dec. 10	בכר
מְבַלֵּהֵים	ק Kh. מְבַלְהִים Piel part. pl. masc. R. בלה;	
	K. מְבַהֲלִים Piel (dag. forte impl.) part.	
	pl. masc. R.	בהל
מִבְּלִי	ף pref. מְ)((prim. subst. comp. Is. 38. 17)	
	adv.; ף bef. lab.	בלה
מַבְלִינִיתִי	noun fem. s., suff. 1 p. s. fr. [מַבְלִינִית] d. 1 b	בלה
מְבַלֵּעַ	pref. מְ)(Piel inf. constr. for בַּלֵּעַ (§ 15. r. 1)	בלע
מִבַּלְעָדַי	ף pref. id.)(the foll. with suff. 1 p. s.; ף bef. lab.	בלה
מִבַּלְעֲדֵי	pref. id.)(adv. compd. of בַּל,& עֲדֵי pl. constr. of עַד	בלה
מְבַלַּעֲךָ	Piel part. pl., suff. 2 pers. sing. fem. [from	
	מְבַלֵּעַ, מְבַלֵּעַ § 15. rem. 1] dec. 7 b	בלע
מְבֻלָּעִים	Pual part. masc. pl. [of מְבֻלָּע]	בלע
מִבַלֵּק	pref. מְ)(pr. name masc.	בלק
מִבֻלָּקָה	ף Pual part. sing. fem. [of מְבֻלָּק]; ף bef. lab.	בלה
מִבַּלֲקִי	pref. מְ)(adv. [בְּלַת] with parag. י)	בלה
מִבָּמוֹת	ף pref. id.)(pr. name of a place; ף bef. lab.	בום
מִבֵּן	ף pref. id.)(n. m. s., constr. of בֵּן irr. (§ 45); ף id.	בנה
מִבֵּן יָמִין	pref. id.)(pr. n. of a tribe, for בִּנְיָמִן (q. v.)	בנה
מִבָּנוֹת	ף pref. id.)(noun fem. pl. abs. irr. of בַּת	בנה
	(§ 45); ף bef. lab.	
מִבְּנוֹת	pref. id.)(id., constr. st., or Kal inf. constr.	בנה
מִבְּנוֹתֵינוּ	pref. id.)(id., suff. 1 pers. pl.	בנה
מִבְנַי	pr. name masc., see סְבַכַי under	סבך
מִבְּנֵי	ף pref. מְ)(noun masc. pl., constr. of בָּנִים	
	[as if from בֵּן] see בֵּן irr. (§ 45) also pr.	
	name in compos.; ף bef. lab.	בנה
מִבְּנֵיהֶם	pref. id.)(id., suff. 3 pers. pl. masc.	בנה
מִבָּנָיו	pref. id.)(id., suff. 3 pers. sing. masc.	בנה
מִבָּנֶיךָ	ף pref. id.)(id., suff. 2 p. s. m.; ף bef. lab.	בנה
מִבְּנֵיכֶם	pref. id.)(id., suff. 2 pers. masc.	בנה
מִבָּנִים	pref. id.)(id. pl., abs. st.	בנה
מִבָּנִים	pref. id.)(Kal part. act. masc. pl. [of בֵּן]	בין
מִבִּנְיָמִן	ף pref. id.)(pr. name of a tribe; ף bef. lab.	בנה
מִבְּנֹתֵיהֶם	pref. id.)(noun fem. pl. (בָּנוֹת), suff. 3 pers.	
	pl. masc. irr. of בַּת (§ 45)	בנה
מִבְּנֹתֵיו	pref. id.)(id., suff. 3 pers. sing. masc.	בנה
מִבְּנֹתֵינוּ	pref. id.)(id., suff. 1 pers. pl.	בנה
מִבַּעַד	pref. id.)((prop. subst. masc. dec. 6 d) prep.	בעד
מַבְעִירֹ	Hiph. part. sing. masc.	בער
מִבַּעַל	pref. מְ)(pr. name in compos., as בַּעַל גָּד &c.	בעל
מִבַּעֲלָה	pref. id.)(pr. name of a place	בעל
מִבַּעֲלֵי	ף pref. מְ)(n. m. pl., constr. fr. בַּעַל d. 6 d	בעל
מִבַּעֲלָיו	pref. id.)(id., suff. 3 pers. sing. masc.	בעל
מִבַּעֲרִים	Piel (§ 14. r. 1) part. m., pl. of [מְבָעֵר] d. 7 b	בער
מִבֹעֶרֶת	Pual part. sing. fem. [for מְבֹעֶרֶת]	בער
מִבְעֶתְּךָ	[contr. for תְּךָ, מִבְעַתְתְּךָ] Piel part. sing.	
	fem. [מְבַעֶתֶת], suff. 2 pers. sing. masc.	
	comp. dec. 13 (§ 25 rem.)	בעת
מִבְצַר	pref. מְ)(noun m. s., constr. of בְּצִיר d. 3 a	בצר
מִבְצַק	pref. id.)(pr. name of a place	בצק
מִבְצָר	noun m. s. d. 2 b; also pr. name of a place	בצר
מִבְצַר	ף id. constr. st.; ף bef. lab.	בצר
מִבָצְרָה	pref. מְ)(pr. name of a place	בצר
מִבְצָרוֹת	n. m. with pl. f. term., abs. fr. מִבְצָר d. 2 b	בצר
מִבְצָרֵי	id. pl. constr. masc.	בצר
מִבְצְרֵיהֶם	id. id., suff. 3 pers. pl. masc.	בצר
מִבְצָרָיו	id. id., suff. 3 pers. sing. masc.	בצר
מִבְצָרֵיִךְ	} id. id., suff. 2 pers. sing. fem.	בצר
מִבְצָרַיִךְ	}	בצר
מִבְצָרֶיךָ	id. id., suff. 2 pers. sing. masc.	בצר
מִבְצָרִים	id. pl., abs. st.	בצר
מִבְקָעָה	Pual part. sing. fem. [of מְבֻקָּע]	בקע
מִבֻקָּעִים	ף id. part. masc. pl. [of מְבֻקָּע]; ף bef. lab.	בקע
מִבִּקְעַת	pref. מְ)(noun f. s., constr. of בִּקְעָה d. 12 b	בקע
מִבְּקָר	pref. id.)(n. m. s. (pl. בְּקָרִים) d. 6 c (§ 35. r. 9)	בקר
מִבְּקָרוֹ	ף pref. id.)(noun com. sing., suff. 3 pers. sing.	
	masc. from בָּקָר dec. 4 a; ף bef. lab.	בקר
מִבְּקָרְךָ	pref. id.)(id., suff. 2 pers. sing. masc.	בקר
מְבַקֵּשׁ	} ף Piel part. sing. masc. dec. 7 b; ף bef.	
מְבַקֵּשׁ	} lab.	בקש
מְבַקְשֵׁי	ף id. pl. constr. [for מְבַקְשֵׁי] § 10. rem. 7]	בקש
מְבַקְשֶׁיהָ	id. pl., suff. 3 pers. sing. fem.	בקש
מְבַקְשָׁיו	id. pl., suff. 3 pers. sing. masc.	בקש
מְבַקְשֶׁךָ	id. pl., suff. 2 pers. sing. masc.	בקש
מְבַקְשִׁים	id. pl., abs. st.	בקש
מַבְרִיחַ	Hiph. part. sing. masc. [for מַבְרִיחַ]	ברח
מִבְרִחְנוֹ	noun masc. pl., suff. 3 pers. sing. masc. (K.	
	חָיו) from [מִבְרָח] dec. 2 b	ברח
מִבְרִיתְךָ	pref. מְ)(n. f. s., suff. 2 p. s. f. fr. בְּרִית d. 1 a	ברה
מְבֹרָךְ	Piel (Peal Da. 2. 20) part. sing. masc. d. 7 b	ברך
מְבֹרָךְ	ף Pual part. sing. masc.; ף bef. lab.	ברך
מְבֹרְכָיו	id. pl., suff. 3 pers. sing. masc.	ברך
מְבָרֲכֶיךָ	Piel part. pl. masc., suff. 2 pers. sing.	
	m. (for יךָ) from מְבָרֵךְ d. 7 b; ף bef. lab.	ברך
מְבֹרֶכֶת	Pual part. sing., fem. of מְבֹרָךְ	ברך
מִבִּרְכָתְךָ	ף pref. מְ)(noun fem. sing., suff. 2 pers. sing.	
	masc. from בְּרָכָה dec. 11 c; ף bef. lab.	ברך

ᵃ Je. 31. 16.	ᵍ Is. 44. 6.	ᵐ Ps. 78. 4.	ᵗ Ne. 5. 5.	ᵃ Je. 36. 22.	ᵍ La. 2. 2.	ᵐ Jos. 9. 4.	ᵖ Je. 2. 24.	ᵘ 1 Ch. 17. 27.
ᵇ Ge. 4. 4.	ʰ Is. 49. 19.	ⁿ 1 Ch. 17. 11.	ᵘ 1 Ki. 16. 3.	ᵇ 1 Sa. 15. 15.	ʰ 2 Ki. 8. 12.	ⁿ Am. 1. 5.	ᵠ Ezr. 8. 22.	ᵛ Ps. 37. 22.
ᶜ Ezr. 4. 4.	ⁱ Is. 9. 15.	ᵒ Am. 2. 11.	ᵛ Ju. 9.20; 2 Sa.6.2.	ᶜ Ju. 8. 2.	ⁱ Na. 3. 12.	ᵒ Job 4. 20.	ʳ Ex. 26 28.	ʷ Ge. 27. 29.
Job 24. 7.	ᵏ Na. 2. 11.	ᵖ Je. 49. 7.		ᵈ Pr. 3. 27.	ᵏ Da. 11. 14.	ᵖ 2 Sa. 12. 4.	ˢ Eze. 17. 21.	ˣ De. 33. 13.
ᵈ Je. 8. 18.	ˡ Is. 56. 5.	ᵠ Ex. 34. 16.		ᵉ Is. 25. 12.	ˡ Eze. 26. 10.	ᵠ De. 12. 21.	ᵗ Eze. 16. 61.	ʸ 2 Sa. 7. 29.
ᶠ La. 2. 8.	ᵐ Ju. 21. 7, 18.			ᶠ Je. 7. 18				

31

מְבֻשָּׁל   Pual part. sing. masc.   .   .   .   בשל

מְבַשְּׁלוֹת   noun f., pl. of [מְבַשֶּׁלֶת] d. 13; ꜳ bef. lab.   בשל

מִבְשָׂם   pr. name of a place; ꜳ id.   .   .   בשם

מִבְשָׂן   pref. מִ (pr. name of a region   .   בשן

מְבַשֵּׂר   Piel part. sing. masc.   .   .   .   בשר

מִבְשַׂר   pref. מִ (noun m. s., constr. of בָּשָׂר d. 4 a   בשר

מִבְשָׂרוֹ   pref. id. (id., suff. 3 pers. sing. masc.   .   בשר

מִבְּשָׂרִי   ꜳ pref. id. (id., suff. 1 pers. s.; ꜳ bef. lab.   בשר

מִבְּשָׂרְךָ   } pref. id. (id., suff. 2 pers. sing. masc.;   בשר

מִבְּשָׂרֶךָ   } ꜳ id.   .   .   .   .   .   בשר

מִבְּשַׂרְכֶם   pref. id. (id., suff. 2 pers. pl. masc.   .   בשר

מִבְּשָׂרָם   pref. id. (id., suff. 3 pers. pl. masc.   .   בשר

מְבַשֶּׂרֶת   Piel part. sing. fem. dec. 13, from מְבַשֵּׂר m.   בשר

מִבַּת   pref. מִ (noun f. s. irr. [for בַּת=בַּנְת § 45]   בנה

מְבַת־שׁוּעַ   pref. id. (pr. name fem.   .   .   בנה

מִבָּתֵּיהֶם   pref. id. (noun masc. pl. (בָּתִּים), suff. 3   pers. pl. masc. irr. of בַּיִת (§ 45)   .   בית

מִבָּתֶּיךָ   ꜳ pref. id. (id., suff. 2 pers. s. m.; ꜳ bef. lab.   בית

מִבָּתֵּיכֶם   pref. id. (id., suff. 2 pers. pl. masc.   בית

מִבָּתֵּינוּ   pref. id. (id., suff. 1 pers. pl.   .   בית

מַג   masc. magian, a Persian or Median priest, only Je. 39. 3, רַב־מָג chief of the magi.

מִגְּאוֹן   pref. מִ (noun m. s., constr. of גָּאוֹן d. 3 a   נאה

מְגֹאָל   Pual part. sing. masc.   .   .   .   נאל

מְגָאֵל   pref. מִ (Kal part. sing. masc. dec. 7 b   נאל

מְגָאֲלֵנוּ   pref. id. (id. (some read לֵינוּ pl.), suff. 1 p. pl.   נאל

מִגְבָּא   pref. id. (noun masc. sing. dec. 6   .   נבא

מִגְבֹּהַּ   pref. id. (adj. masc. sing. dec. 3 a   .   נבה

מִגְּבֹהַּ   pref. id. (adj. m. s., constr. of [גָּבֹהַּ] d. 4 a   נבה

מִגְּבוּל   pref. id. (noun masc. sing. dec. 1 a   .   נבל

מִגִּבּוֹר   pref. id. ((prim. adj.) subst. masc. s. d. 1 b   נבר

מִגְּבוּרָה   pref. id. (noun fem. sing. dec. 10   .   נבר

מִגְּבוּרֹתָם   pref. id. (id., suff. 3 pers. pl. masc.   נבר

מַגְבִּיהַּ   Hiph. part. sing. masc.   .   .   נבה

מִגְּבִירָה   pref. מִ (noun fem. sing.   .   .   נבר

מַגְבִּישׁ   pr. name of a place   .   .   .   נבש

מִגְבֹּל   pref. מִ (noun masc. sing. dec. 1 a, defect. for מִגְּבוּל (q. v.)   .   .   נבל

מִגְּבֻלְכֶם   pref. id. (id., suff. 2 pers. pl. masc.   נבל

מִגְבָּלֹת   noun fem. pl. abs. [from מִגְבָּלָה]   נבל

מִגְבָּע   } pref. מִ (pr. name of a place (§ 35. rem. 2)   } נבע

מִגְבַּע

מִגְבְּעוֹן   pref. id. (pr. name of a place   .   נבע

מִגְּבָעוֹת   ꜳ pref. id. (noun fem., pl. abs from גִּבְעָה dec. 12 b; ꜳ bef. lab.   .   .   נבע

מִגְּבָעוֹת   ꜳ noun f. pl. abs. [fr. מִגְבָּעָה]; ꜳ bef. lab.   נבע

מִגִּבְעַת   pref. מִ (noun fem. sing., constr. of גִּבְעָה dec. 12 b, also pr. name   נבע

מִגֶּבֶר   pref. id. (noun masc. sing. dec. 6   נבר

מִגִּבֹּרֵי   pref. id. ((prim. adj.) subst. masc. pl. constr. from גִּבּוֹר dec. 1 b   .   .   נבר

מִגִּבְּתוֹן   pref. id. (pr. name of a place   נבב

מִגַּן   pref. id. (noun masc. s., constr. of גַּן d. 8 a   גן

מָגַד   Root not used; Arab. to be honoured, to be noble, excellent.

מֶגֶד   masc. dec. 6 a, what is most precious, excellent, pleasant.

מַגְדִּיאֵל   (noble of God) pr. name of a prince of Edom.

מִגְדָּנוֹת   fem. pl. (of מִגְדָּנָה) choice, precious things.

מִגְדּוֹל   ꜳ pr. name of a place; ꜳ bef. (:)   נדל

מִגְּדוֹל   pref. מִ (adj. masc. sing. dec. 3 a   .   נדל

מִגְּדוֹלָם   pref. id. (id., suff. 3 pers. pl. masc.   נדל

מִגְדּוֹן   pr. name of a place   .   .   נדל

מַגְדִּיאֵל   pr. name masc.   .   .   .   מנד

מִגְדָּיו   noun m. pl., suff. 3 pers. sing. m. fr. מֶגֶד d. 6   מנד

מַגְדִּיל   Kh. מַגְדִּיל Hiph. part. s.m.; K. מִגְדּוֹל n.m.s.   נדל

מְגָדִים   noun masc. pl. of מֶגֶד dec. 6   מנד

מִגְדִּישׁ   pref. מִ (noun masc. sing.   נדש

מִגְדֹּל   defect. for מַגְדִּיל (q. v.)   נדל

מִגְדָּל   ꜳ noun m. sing. dec. 2 b   נדל

מִגְדַּל   ꜳ id. constr. st., and pr. name in compos. as מִגְדַּל־אֵל &c.; ꜳ bef. lab.   .   נדל

מִגְדֹּל   pr. name of a place   .   .   נדל

מִגְדְּלוֹת   noun m. with f. pl. term., constr. fr. מִגְדָּל d. 2 b   נדל

מִגְדְּלֶיהָ   id. with pl. m. term. and suff. 3 pers. sing. fem.   נדל

מְגַדְּלִים   Piel part. masc. pl. of [מְגַדֵּל] dec. 7 b   נדל

מְגֻדָּלִים   Pual part. masc. pl. of [מְגֻדָּל]   נדל

מִגְדָּלִים   ꜳ noun masc. pl. of מִגְדָּל d. 2 b; ꜳ bef. lab.   נדל

מִגְדְּלֹתַיִךְ   ꜳ id. with fem. term. and suff. 2 p. s. fem.; ꜳ id.   נדל

מִגְדָּנוֹת   ꜳ noun fem. pl. abs. from [מִגְדָּנָה]; ꜳ id.   מנד

מִגְדָּנֹת   ꜳ   מנד

מְגַדֵּף   ꜳ Piel part. sing. masc.; ꜳ id.   נדף

מִגְדֻּפֹתָם   ꜳ pref. מִ (noun m. with pl. fem. term. and suff. 3 pers. pl. m. from [גִּדּוּף] d. 1 b; ꜳ id.   נדף

מַגֶּדֶת   Hiph. part. sing., f. of מַגִּיד (§ 39. No. 4 d)   נגד

מָגוֹג   ꜳ pr. name masc.; ꜳ bef. lab.   גוג

מִגֹּוַהּ   pref. מִ (noun sing. fem.   נוה

a Eze. 46. 23.   f Is. 40. 9.   l Mal. 1. 7, 12.   r Ec. 9. 16.   x Ex. 28. 14.   c 2 Ch. 34. 30.   h Ps. 18. 51.   n Eze. 26. 9.   s Ps. 44. 17.
b Ge. 2. 23.   g 1 Ch. 2. 3.   m Ru. 2. 20.   s Eze. 32. 30.   y Ex. 28. 40.   d Jon. 3. 5.   i Ge. 11. 4.   o 2 Ch. 32. 23.   t Is. 51. 7.
c Ec. 11. 10.   h Je. 18. 22.   n Is. 30. 14.   t Pr. 17. 19.   z Job 33. 17.   c Ca. 4. 16.   k 2 Sa. 22. 51.   p Ge. 24. 53.   u Est. 2. 20.
d Is. 58. 7.   i Ex. 8. 5, 7.   o Ec. 12. 5.   u Nu. 21. 13.   a Ca. 3. 7.   f 2 Ki. 10. 6.   q Nu. 15. 30.   v Job 20. 3.
e Eze. 36. 26.   k Jos. 9. 12.   p Ec. 7. 8.   w Am. 6. 2.   b Eze. 40. 13.   g Ju. 15. 5.   m Ps. 144. 12.   r Nu. 23. 9.

מָגוֹי	pref. ·מְ)(noun masc. sing. dec. 1a (§ 3. r. 1) נוה
מָגוֹיִם	pref. id.)(id. pl. abs. (for גּוֹיִים' comp. § 3. r. 1) נוה
מְגוִיַּת	pref. id.)(noun fem. s., constr. of גְּוִיָּה d. 10 נוה
[מְגוֹלָלָה]	Poal part. sing. fem. [of . . . נלל
מָגוֹר	noun masc. sing., see § 32. rem. 5 (also pr. name in compos.) נור
מְגוּרוֹתַי	noun fem. pl., suff. 1 pers. s. from מְגוֹרָה' d. 10 נור
מְגוּרַי	noun m. pl., suff. 1 pers. s. from [מָגוֹר] d. 3a נור
מְגוּרַי	noun m. pl., suff. 1 pers. s. fr. מָגוֹר (§ 32. r. 5) נור
מְגוּרֵי	Kal part. pass. pl. c. m. from [מָגוֹר] dec. 3a מגר
מְגוּרֵי	noun masc. pl. constr. from [מָגוֹר] dec. 3a נור
מְגוּרֵיהֶם	id. pl., suff. 3 pers. pl. masc. . . נור
מְגוֹרַת	noun fem. sing., constr. of [מְגוֹרָה] dec. 10 נור
מְגוֹרָתָם	noun fem. pl., suff. 3 pers. pl. masc. (§ 4. rem. 2) from מְגוֹרָה dec. 10; bef. lab. נור
מָגֵּז	pref. מְ)(noun masc. sing. dec. 8b ; id. נזז
מְגַזְלוֹ	pref. id.)(Kal part. act. sing. masc., suff. 3 pers. sing. masc. from גּוֹזֵל dec. 7b נזל
מְגֻזָּע	pref. id.)(noun masc. sing. (suff. גְּזָעוֹ) d. 6a נזע
מֵגִיד	Hiph. part. sing. masc. dec. 1b ; bef. lab. נגד
מֵגִיחַ	Hiph. part. sing. masc. R. נוח or . . ניח
מְגִיחָן	Chald. Aph. part. pl. fem. [from מֵגִיחַ masc.] נוח
מַגִּיעַ	Hiph. part. sing. masc. . . . נגע
מַגִּיעֵי	id. pl., constr. st. . . . נגע
מַגִּישׁ	Hiph. part. sing. masc. ; bef. lab. נגשׁ
מַגִּישֵׁי	id. pl., constr. st. . . . נגשׁ
מַגִּישִׁים	id. pl., abs. st. . . . נגשׁ
מָגָל	noun masc. sing. . . . נגל
מְגַלֶּה	Piel part. sing. masc. . . . נלה
מְגִלָּה	noun fem. sing. dec. 10 נלל
מְגֻלָּה	Pual part. sing. fem. [from מְגֻלֶּה masc.] נלה
מְגַלָּה	pref. מְ)(pr. name of a place . . נלה
מְגַלְחֵי	Pual part. pl. constr. masc. from [מְגֻלָּח] d. 2b נלה
מְגַלִּים	pref. מְ)(pr. name of a place . . נלל
מִגְלְעָד	pref. id.)(pr. name of a region, see גִּלְעָד.
מְגִלַּת	noun fem. sing., constr. of מְגִלָּה dec. 10 נלל
מַמְגֵּל	pref. מְ)(noun masc. sing. d. 8a (§ 37. No. 3c) נמל
מַגְמַלֵּי	pref. id.)(id. pl., constr. st. נמל
מְגַמַּת	noun fem. sing., constr. of [מְגַמָּה] dec. 10 נמם
מָגֵן	Pi. מִגֵּן—I. to give over, deliver, Ge. 14. 20; with double acc. Pr. 4. 9.—II. to make one to or as any thing, Ho. 11. 8, comp. נָתַן to give, to make. Others take it as denom. of מָגֵן shield (R. נָּגֵן) (a) to protect, surround, Pr. 4. 9; Ho. 11. 8; (b) privat.

to deprive one of his shield, to disarm, Ge. 14. 20, מִ' צָרֶיךָ בְּיָדֶךָ disarmed thine enemies by thy hand.	
מָגֵן	noun masc. sing. (suff. מָגִנּי) dec. 8b (§ 37. rem. 4) ; bef. lab. ננן
מִגֵּן	pref. מִ)(noun com. sing. dec. 8d ננן
מִגֵּן	Piel pret. 3 pers. sing. masc. מגן
מְגַנְּבֵי	Piel part. pl. constr. masc. from [מְגַנֵּב] d. 7b ננב
מָגִנֵּי	noun masc. pl. constr. from מָגֵן d. 8a (§ 37. r. 4) ננן
מָגִנִּי	id. sing., suff. 1 pers. sing. ; bef. lab. ננן
מָגִנֶּיהָ	id. pl., suff. 3 pers. sing. fem. ננן
מָגִנָּיו	id. pl., suff. 3 pers. sing. masc. ננן
מָגִנִּים	id. pl., abs. st. ; bef. lab. ננן
מָגִנָּם	id. sing., suff. 3 pers. pl masc. ; id. ננן
מָגִנֵּנוּ	id. sing., suff. 1 pers. pl. ; id. ננן
מִגְנַת	noun fem. sing., constr. of [מִגְנָה] dec. 10 ננן
מִגְנַת	pref. מְ)(noun fem. sing., constr. of נִּגְנָה d. 10 ננן
מִגְעָר	pref. id.)(Kal inf. constr. [for גְּעָר § 8. rem. 18] ; bef. lab. נער
מִגְעֶרֶת	pref. id.)(n. f., constr. of גְּעָרָה d. 11c (§ 42. r. 1) נער
מִגְעַרְתוֹ	pref. id.)(id., suff. 3 pers. sing. masc. נער
מִגְעַרְתָךְ	pref. id.)(id., suff. 2 pers. sing. masc. נער
מַגַּעַת	Hiph. part. sing., fem. of מַגִּיעַ (§ 39. No. 4d) נגע
מַגֵּפָה	noun fem. sing. (constr. מַגֵּפַת) dec. 10 נגף
מַגְפִּיעָשׁ	pr. name masc. Ne. 10. 21.
מִגְפָּן	pref. מְ)(noun com. sing. (suff. גַּפְנוֹ) d. 6a נפן
מַגֵּפַת	noun fem. sing., constr. of מַגֵּפָה dec. 10 נגף
מַגֵּפֹתַי	id. pl. with suff. 1 pers. sing. נגף

מָגַר	only part. pl. c. מְגֻרֵי fallen, delivered up, Eze 21. 17. Pi. to cast down, to overthrow, Ps. 89. 45. מָגַר Ch. Pa. to cast down, to overthrow, Ezr. 6. 12. מִגְרוֹן (precipice) pr. name of a town in Benjamin, 1 Sa. 14. 2 ; Is. 10. 28.

מְגֻרֶיהָ	pref. מְ)(noun m. pl., suff. from גּוּר d. 1a. נור
מְגֻרֵיהֶם	noun m. pl., suff. 3 p. pl. m. from מָגוֹר d. 3a נור
מְגֻרֶיךָ	id. pl., suff. 2 pers. sing. masc. נור
מֻגָּרִים	Hoph. part. masc. pl. [of מֻגָּר] נגר
מִגָּרְךָ	pref. מְ)(noun masc. sing., suff. 2 pers. sing. masc. from גֵּר dec. 1a (§ 30. No. 3) נור
מִגּוֹרָלִי	pref. id.)(noun masc. sing. constr. of גּוֹרָל dec. 2b ; bef. lab. נרל
מִגְרֹן	pref. id.)(noun masc. sing. dec. 6c נרן
מִגְרַנְךָ	pref. id.)(id. with suff. 2 p. s. m.; bef. lab. נרן
מִגְרָעוֹת	noun fem. pl. abs. [from מִגְרָעָה] נרע
מִגְרָפֹתֵיהֶם	noun fem. pl., suff. 3 pers. sing. masc. from [מִגְרָפָה] dec. 11a . . נרף

a Eze. 38. 2.   f Pr. 10. 24.   k Da. 7. 2.   r Je. 41. 5.   y Ge. 14. 20.   c Ps. 115. 9,10,11.   h Ps. 80. 17.   t Eze. 19. 3, 5.   x Hos. 13. 3.
b Ju. 14. 9.   g Job 31. 20.   l Is. 5. 8.   s Mal. 2. 12.   z Je. 23. 30.   d Ps. 33. 20.   i La. 3. 65.   u Ex. 6. 4.   v De. 16. 13.
c Is. 9. 4.   h Ps. 35. 10.   m Mal. 3. 3.   t Ho. 4. 18.   a Est. 7. 8.   e 2 Ch. 3. 11.   i Mi. 1. 4.   v De. 15. 14.
d Ps. 34. 5.   i Is. 11. 1.   n Hab. 1. 9.   u Job 15. 26.   s Is. 54. 9.   f Zec. 14. 15.   p Ex. 9. 14.   y 1 Ki. 6. 6.
La. 2. 22.   j Ju. 20. 33.   o Pr. 27. 5.   x 2 Ch. 32. 5.   d De. 24. 14.   z Joel 1. 17.
f Eze. 21. 17.   a Ge. 3. 23.   u Nu. 26. 3.

31 *

מְגֻרָר	pref. ·מְ·) pl. name of a place . .	נרר
מְגֻרָרוֹת	Pual part. f. pl. abs. [fr. מְגֹרָרָה, fr. מְגֹרָר m.]	נרר
מַגְרֵשׁ	b'וּ noun masc. sing. dec. 2 b; וּ bef. lab.	נרשׁ
מִגְרַשׁ	id., constr. st.	נרשׁ
מִגְרָשָׁהּ	Kal inf. [מִגְרָשׁ § 8. rem. 10], suff. 3 p. s. f.	נרשׁ
מִגְרָשֶׁהָ	defect. for מִגְרָשֶׁיהָ (q. v.) . . .	נרשׁ
מִגְרָשֵׁהּ	pref. מְ·) noun masc. sing., suff. 3 pers. sing. fem. from גֵּרֶשׁ dec. 6 a	נרס
מִגְרָשׁוֹת	n. pl. f. abs. st. (prop. fr. מִגְרֶשֶׁת) see מִגְרָשׁ	נרשׁ
מִגְרְשֵׁי	g' וּ noun masc. pl. constr. from מִגְרָשׁ dec. 2 b; וּ bef. lab.	נרשׁ
מִגְרָשֶׁיהָ	g' id., suff. 3 pers. sing. fem.; וּ id.	נרשׁ
מִגְרְשֵׁיהֶם	g' id., suff. 3 pers. pl. masc.; וּ id.	נרשׁ
מִגְרְשֵׁיהֶן	g' id., suff. 3 pers. pl. fem.; וּ id.	נרשׁ
מִגְרָת	וּ pref. ·מְ·) Kal part. act. f., constr. of [נֵרָה] dec. 10, fr. נֵר m. (comp. § 30. No. 3); וּ id.	נור
מִגֵּרְתָּה	Piel pret. 2 pers. sing. masc. (comp. § 8. r. 5)	מגר
מֻגָּשׁ	Hoph. part. sing. masc.	נגשׁ
מַגְשׁוּר	pref. ·מְ·) pr. name of a place, see גְּשׁוּר	נגשׁ
מַגְשִׂים	defect. for מַגְשִׂים (q. v.) . . .	נגשׁ
מַגְשִׁימִים	Hiph. part. masc., pl. of [מַגְשִׁם] dec. 1 b	נגשׁם
מַגֶּשֶׁת	pref. ·מְ·) Kal inf. constr. (suff. נִגְשְׁתּוֹ) d. 13 b	נגשׁ
מַגְּת מַגֵּת	} pref. id.) pr. name of a place . .	נת
מִדְאָנָה	pref. id.) noun fem. sing.	דאן
מַדְבְּחָה	Chald. noun masc. sing. [for מַדְבְּחָא] emph. of [מַדְבַּח] dec. 2 a . .	דבח
מֻדְבָּק	Hoph. part. sing. masc. (§ 11. rem. 10) .	דבק
מְדַבֵּר	g''וּ Piel part. sing. masc. dec. 7 b; וּ bef. lab.	דבר
מְדֻבָּר	Pual part. sing. masc.	דבר
מִדְבָּר	pref. ·מְ·) noun masc. sing. dec. 4 a .	דבר
מִדְבָּר	וּ pref. id.) noun masc. sing. dec. 6 (for דְּבָר § 35. rem. 2) ; וּ bef. lab.	דבר
מְדַבֵּר	pref. id.) Piel inf. constr. . .	דבר
מִדַּבֵּר	g''וּ Hithpa. part. s. m. [for מִתְדַּבֵּר § 12. r. 3.]	דבר
מְדַבֵּר	pref. ·מְ·) noun masc. s.; constr. of דָּבָר d. 4 a	דבר
מִדְבָּר	noun masc. sing. dec. 2 b	דבר
מִדְבַּר	id., constr. st. . . .	דבר
מְדֻבָּר	pref. ·מְ·) noun masc. sing. dec. 6	דבר
מִדְבָּרָה	noun masc. s. with parag. ה (מִדְבָּר) dec. 2 b	דבר
מִדְבָּרָהּ	id. with suff. 3 pers. sing. masc.	דבר
מִדְבָּרָה	id. constr. with parag. ה, comp. מִדְבָּר	דבר
מְדַבְּרוֹת	Piel part. f. pl. of מְדַבֵּר d. 13, fr. מְדַבֵּר m.	דבר
מְדִבְרֵי	pref. ·מְ·) noun m. pl. constr. fr. דָּבָר d. 4 a	דבר
מִדִּבְרֵיהֶם	וּ pref. id.) id., suff. 3 pers. pl. m.; וּ bef. lab.	דבר
מִדִּבְרֶיךָ	וּ pref. id.) id. pl. (Kh. רָיךָ), or sing. (K. בְרְךָ) with suff. 2 pers. sing. m.; וּ id.	דבר

מְדַבְּרִים	Piel part. masc., pl. of מְדַבֵּר dec. 7 b	דבר
מְדַבֶּרְךָ	וּ noun masc. sing., suff. 2 pers. sing. fem. from מִדְבָּר dec. 2 b ; וּ bef. lab.	רבר
מְדַבֶּרֶת	Piel part. sing. fem. from מְדַבֵּר masc.	דבר
מְדַבְּרֹתַיִךְ	pref. מְ·) noun f. pl., suff. 2 pers. s. m. fr [דַּבְּרָה] d. 10; or Hithpa. part. pl. with suff. [fr. מִתְדַּבְּרֶת=מְדַבְּרֶת § 12. r. 3]	רבר
מְדֻבָּשׁ	pref. id.) noun masc. sing. d. 6 (§ 35. r. 10)	רבשׁ

מָדַד

מָדַד 'pret. מָדַדְתִּי, מָדֹדוּ.—Arab. to extend, hence—'. ta measure.—II. metaph. to apportion, Is. 65. 7. Niph. to be measured. Pi. to measure. Po. מוֹדֵד id. Hab. 3. 6, but see מוּד. Hithpo. to extend, stretch oneself, 1 Ki. 17. 21.

מַד masc. dec. 8 (with suff. מַדּוֹ, מִדּוֹ, pl. מַדִּים, מִדִּין).—I. vestment, garment.—II. covering or carpet, Ju. 5. 10.—III. measure.

מִדָּה fem. dec. 10.—I. extension; מ' אִישׁ a man of extension, a tall man; בֵּית מִדּוֹת spacious house. —II. measure.—III. vestment, garment, Ps. 133. 2. —IV. tribute, Ne. 5. 4.

מִנְדָּה, מִדָּה (dag. forte. resolved in נ) Chald. fem. dec. 8 a, tribute.

מִדִּין (measures) pr. name of a town in the tribe of Judah, Jos. 15. 61.

מֵמַד masc. dec. 8 d, measure, Job 38. 5.

מָדַד	g Kal pret. 3 pers. sing. m. for מָדַד (§ 8. r. 7)	מדד
מַד	h noun masc. sing. constr. [of מַד for [מֶמַד] ; וּ bef. lab. . .	נדד
מָדְדוּ	וּ Kal pret. 3 pers. pl.; וּ id.	מדד
מְדָדוֹ	וּ id. pret. 3 pers. s. m., suff. 3 p. s. m.; וּ id.	מדד

מָדָה

מָדָה Root not used ; i. q. מָדַד to extend.

מַדְוֶה masc. dec. 9 a, vestment, garment, 2 Sa. 10. 4; 1 Ch. 19. 4.

מָדוֹן masc. extension, 2 Sa. 21. 20, אִישׁ מ' tall man, comp. מַד under preced. root.

מִדָּה	וּ noun fem. sing. dec. 10; וּ bef. lab.	מדד
מִדָּה	k וּ Chald. noun fem. sing. dec. 8 a; וּ id.	מדד
מִדָּהּ	m noun m. s., suff. 3 p. s. f. fr. [מַד] d. 8 d & e	מדד
מַרְהֵבָה	noun fem. s. (some prefer מַרְהֵבָה R. רהב)	דהב
מַדְהֵרוֹת	pref. מְ·) n. f. pl. constr. [fr. דַּהֲרָה or דַּהֲרָה]	דהר
מַדּוֹ	noun m. s., suff. 3 p. s. m. from [מַד] d. 8 e	מדד
מָדוֹד	pref. ·מְ·) noun masc. sing. dec. 1 a	דוד
מִדּוּד	pref. id.) noun masc. sing. pl. דּוּדִים & דּוּדִים (§ 35. rem. 13) . .	דוד
מְדוּדָאֵי	noun m. pl. constr. [fr. דּוּדַי § 35. r. 15, note]	דוד

a 1 Ki. 7.9.   e Nu. 35. 4.   i 1 Ki. 5. 1.   n Ps. 22. 16.   r 2 Sa. 14. 13.   u Is. 19. 18.   z Ca. 4. 3.   f Eze. 42. 15, 20.   p Ju. 5. 22.
b Nu. 35. 2.   f Jos. 21. 40.   k Je. 14. 22.   o Ps. 87. 3.   s Ps. 91. 3, 6.   v 1 Sa. 23. 20.   a De. 33. 3.   k Ezr. 4. 20.   p Ca. 5. 9.
c Eze. 36. 5.   g Ex. 3. 22.   l Ex. 34. 30.   p Jos. 22. 24.   t Is. 51. 3.   w Eze. 42. 18.   b Job 11. 9.   q Ps. 81. 7.
d Le. 2. 16.   h Ps. 89. 45.   m Jos. 22. 24.   q Eze. 12. 16.   u 1 Ki. 19. 15.   x Ps. 119. 161.   c Job 7. 4.   l Is. 14. 4.   r Ge. 30. 14.
  Eze. 27. 28.   b Mal. 1. 11.   Ezr. 7. 17.

מִדְוָה	noun masc. sing., constr. of [מַדְוֶה] dec. 9a	דוה
מַדּוּחִים	¹ noun m., pl. of [מַדּוּחַ] d. 1b; ⁴ bef. lab.	נדח
מִדְוֵי	noun masc. pl. constr. from [מַדְוֶה] dec. 9a	דוה
מַדְוֵיהֶם	noun m. pl., suff. 3 p. pl. m. fr. [מַדְוֶה] d. 6a	מדה
מָדוֹן	⁴ noun masc. sing., also pr. name	דון
מְדָנִים	⁵ id. pl. abs. Kh. מְדוֹנִים, or מִדְיָנִים comp. § 32. rem. 8, & § 35. rem. 13 (Keri. מִדְיָנִים q. v.); ⁴ id.	דון
מַדּוּעַ	⁶ adv. of interrog., compnd. of מַה (q. v.) & יָדוּעַ part. pass. see	מה
מָדוֹר	pref. מְ)(noun masc. sing. dec. 1a	דור
מָדוּר	pref. id.)(Kal inf. constr.	דור
מְדוֹרֵהּ	Chald. n. m. s., suff. 3 p. s. m. fr. [מְדוֹר] d. 1a	דור
מִדּוֹת	noun fem., pl. of מִדָּה dec. 10	מדד
מִדּוֹתֶיהָ	id., suff. 3 pers. sing. fem.	מדד
מִדּוֹתָיו	id., suff. 3 pers. sing. masc.	מדד
מֻדָּח	Hoph. part. sing. masc.	נדח
מִדְחֶה	noun masc. sing.	דחה
מַדְחִי	pref. מְ)(noun m. s. (for דְּחִי [§ 35. r. 14]	דחה
מָדַי	} Media; meton. the Medes. Gent. noun מָדַי a Mede, Da. 11. 1.—Chald. Gent. noun, מָדַי Mede. Da. 6. 1.	
מַדַּי	⁷ pref. מְ)(noun masc. sing. constr. of דַּי dec. 8 (§ 37. rem. 6); ⁴ bef. lab.	די
מָדַיָא	Chald. Kh. מָדַיָא; K. מָדָאָה gent. noun, emph. of מָדַי dec. 7	מרי
מְדִיבְן	pref. מְ)(pr. name masc.	דוב
מְדִיבוֹתַי	⁴ Hiph. part. fem. pl. [of מְדִיבָה from מָדִיב masc.]; ⁴ bef. lab.	דוב
מַדָּיו	⁷ noun masc. pl., suff. 3 pers. sing. masc. from [מַד] dec. 8d; ⁴ id.	מדד
מַדַּיִךְ	id. pl., suff. 2 pers. sing. fem. dec. 8e	מדד
מָדִין	Kh. מָדִין R. מדד (q. v.); K. מָדוֹן (q. v.)	דון
מִדְיָן	⁴ pr. name of a people and country; ⁴ bef. lab.	דון
מִדְיָן	pr. name of a place	מדד
מַדִּין	noun m. pl. abs. [for מַדִּים from מַד] d. 8b	מדד
מְדִינֵי	pref. מְ)(noun masc. s. d. 1a. R. דִּין see	דון
מְדִינָה	⁴ noun fem. s. d. 10 R. דִּין; ⁴ bef. lab., see	דון
מְדִינוֹת	pl. of the preced.	דון
מְדִינֵי	noun m. pl. constr. fr. מָדִין d. 2b. R. דִּין see	דון
מְדִינִים	id. pl., abs. st.; also gent. noun, pl. of מָדִין	דון
מְדִינָן	⁴ Chald. noun fem. pl. abs. from [מְדִינָא] dec. 8a. R. דִּין; ⁴ bef. lab., see	דון
מְדִינַת	Chald. id. sing., constr. st. R. דִּין see	דון
מְדִינָתָא	Chald. id. pl., emph. st.	דון
מְדִינְתָּא	Chald. id. sing., emph. st.	דון
מְדֻכָּא	Pual part. sing. masc.	דכא
מְדֻכָּאִים	id. pl., abs. st.	דכא
מְדַלֵּג	¹ Piel part. sing. masc.	דלג
מִדְלָה	¹ pref. מְ)(noun fem. sing. dec. 10	דלל
מִדְלוֹת	⁴ pref. id.)(id. pl.; ⁴ bef. lab.	דלל
מִדְלִי	pref. id.)(noun masc. sing.	דלה
מִדָּלְיָו	pref. id.)(noun masc. pl., suff. 3 pers. sing. masc. [from דְּלִי]. The form דְּלָיו (dol-yav) stands for דְּלָיָו=דְּלָיָיו (comp. קָדְשָׁיו, & קָדְשָׁיו 2 Ch. 15. 18), and having taken the shorter form by dropping ָ under ל according to § 35. rem. 16, it has irregularly retained the Metheg.	דלה
מִדְלָק	⁵ pref. id.)(Kal inf. constr.	דלק
מִדַּלַת	⁴ pref. id.)(noun fem., constr. of דַּלָּה dec. 10; ⁴ bef. lab.	דלל
מִדַּלְתֵי	pref. id.)(noun fem. du., constr. of דְּלָתַיִם from [דְּלָה] dec. 11a (§ 44. rem. 1)	דלה
מָדָם	pref. id.)(noun masc. sing. dec. 2a	אדם
מִדַּם	⁴ pref. id.)(id. constr. st.; ⁴ bef. lab.	אדם
מִדָּמָהּ	pref. id.)(id., suff. 3 pers. sing. fem.	אדם
מִדָּמוֹ	pref. id.)(id., suff. 3 pers. sing. masc.	אדם
מִדְּמֵי	pref. id.)(id. pl., constr. st.	אדם
מִדָּמִים	pref. id.)(id. pl., abs. st.	אדם
מִדָּמְךָ	pref. id.)(id. sing., suff. 2 pers. sing. masc.	אדם
מִדָּמָם	pref. id.)(id. sing., suff. 3 pers. pl. masc.	אדם
מַדְמֵן	pr. name of a place	דמן
מַדְמַנָּה	⁴ pr. name of a place; ⁴ bef. lab.	דמן
מַדְמֵנָה	noun fem. sing., also pr. name of a place	דמן
מִדְמְעָה	pref. מְ)(noun fem. sing. dec. 12b	דמע
מִדַּמֶּשֶׂק	} pref. id.)(pr. name of a place, see דַּמֶּשֶׂק	
מַדָּן	⁴ pr. name masc.; ⁴ bef. lab.	דון
מְדָן	pref.)(pr. name of a tribe	דון
מִדְנָאֵל	pref. id.)(pr. name masc.	דון
מְדָנִים	noun masc., pl. of [מָדוֹן] dec. 1a	דון
מְדָנַיִם	Kh. מְדָנִים q.v.; K. מְדוֹנִים pl. of מָדוֹן (q.v.)	דון
מַדָּע	⁴ noun masc. sing. dec. 1b; ⁴ bef. lab.	ידע
מַדַּע	⁴ noun masc. sing.; ⁴ id.	ידע
מַדֻּעַ	defect. for מַדּוּעַ (q. v.)	מה
מֹדַע	⁴ for [מוֹדָע] noun masc. sing.; ⁴ bef. lab.	ידע
מַדַּעַת	pref. מְ)(noun fem. sing. dec. 13a	ידע
מַדַּעְתִּי	pref. id.)(id. with suff. 1 pers. sing.	ידע
מוֹדַעְתָּנוּ	noun fem. sing., suff. 1 pers. pl. (§ 3. rem. 4) from [מוֹדַעַת] dec. 13a	ידע
מִדְפְּקָה	pref. מְ)(pr. name of a place	דפק
מַדְקָה	⁴ Ch. Aph. part. s. fem. [of מְדַק]; ⁴ bef. lab.	רקק

ᵃ De. 28. 60. ᵈ Is. 34. 10. ⁱ Is. 13. 14. ᵖ 2 Sa. 21. 20. ᵘ Ezr. 4. 15. ᶜ Is. 38. 12. ᵉ Le. 16. 18. ᵏ Pr. 6. 14. ᵖ Pr. 7. 4.
ᵇ La. 2. 14. ᵉ Ps. 84. 11. ᵏ Is. 66. 23. ʳ Ju. 5. 10. ᵛ Da. 3. 2, 3. ᵈ Je. 52. 15, 16. ᶠ Ps. 51. 16. ˡ 2 Ch. 1. 11. ᵍ Is. 48. 4.
ᶜ De. 7. 15. ᶠ Da. 5. 21. ˡ Le. 26. 16. ˢ Is. 19. 13. ʷ Is. 53. 5. ᵉ Eze. 32. 6. ᵍ Is. 25. 10. ᵐ 2 Ch. 1. 10. ʰ Ru. 3. 2.
ʰ Hab. 1. 3. ᵍ Eze. 48. 16. ᵐ 1 Sa. 17. 38. ᵗ Pr. 19. 13. ˣ Is. 19. 10. ᶠ Nu. 24. 7. ʰ Je. 31. 18. ⁿ Eze. 18. 19. ⁱ Da. 7. 7. 19.
ⁱ Pr. 18. 19. ʰ Ps. 133. 2. ⁿ Je. 13. 25. ᵗ Pr. 18. 18. ʸ Ca. 2. 8. ᵍ 1 Sa. 17. 53.

מְדֻקָּרִים   ᵃʰ Pual part. masc., pl. of [מְדֻקָּר]; ʰ bef. lab.   דקר

מְדֹר   defect. for מָדוֹר (q. v.)   דור

מִדָּרְהוֹן   Ch. n. m. s., suff. 3 pers. pl. m. from [מְדָר] d. 1 a   דור

מִדָּרוֹם   pref. מִ ‌⟩‌ noun masc. sing. [for דָּרוֹם]   דרר

מַדְרִיכֶךָ   Hiph. part. s. [מַדְרִיךְ], suff. 2 pers. s. m. d. 2 b   דרך

מְדֹרְךָ   Chald. noun masc. sing., suff. 2 pers. sing. masc. from [מְדוֹר] dec. 1 a   דור

מִדָּרֶךְ   ᵍ in pause for מִדֶּרֶךְ (q. v. § 35. rem. 2)   דרך

מִדְרָךְ   ⁱ noun masc. sing., constr. of [מִדְרָךְ] dec. 2 b   דרך

מִדֶּרֶךְ   pref. מִ ‌⟩‌ noun com. sing. dec. 6 a   דרך

מִדַּרְכּוֹ   ʰ pref. id. ‌⟩‌ id., suff. 3 pers. sing. m.; ʰ bef. lab.   דרך

מִדַּרְכֵיהֶם   pref. id. ‌⟩‌ id. pl., suff. 3 pers. pl. masc.   דרך

מִדַּרְכָיו   pref. id. ‌⟩‌ id. pl., suff. 3 pers. sing. masc.   דרך

מִדַּרְכֵיךָ   pref. id. ‌⟩‌ id. pl., suff. 2 pers. sing. masc.   דרך

מִדַּרְכֵיכֶם   pref. id. ‌⟩‌ id. pl., suff. 2 pers. pl. masc.   דרך

מִדַּרְכֵּךְ   ᵏ pref. id. ‌⟩‌ id. sing., suff. 2 pers. sing. fem.   דרך

מִדַּרְכְּכֶם   ʰ pref. id. ‌⟩‌ id. s., suff. 3 p. pl. m.; ʰ bef. lab.   דרך

מִדְרַשׁ   noun masc. sing., constr. of [מִדְרָשׁ] dec. 2 b   דרש

מְדוּרָתָהּ   noun fem. s., suff. 3 pers. s. f. from מְדוּרָה d. 10   דור

מִדָּשֶׁן   pref. מִ ‌⟩‌ noun masc. sing. (suff.) [דֶּשֶׁן] d. 6 a   דשן

מְדֻשָׁתִי   noun fem. s., suff. 1 pers. s. from [מְדוּשָׁה] d. 10   דוש

מִדַּת   ʳʰ noun fem. sing., constr. of מִדָּה dec. 10, Chald. 8 a, ʰ bef. lab.   מדד

מַדֹּתִי   ⁱ Kal pret. 1 pers. sing.; acc. shifted by ⁱ, for וְ, conv. (§ 8. rem. 7)   מדד

מַדֹּתֶם   ⁱ id. pret. 2 pers. pl. masc.; ⁱ bef. lab.   מדד

מָה   ⁱ every where in pause, except before א and ר, as מָה רְאִיתֶם; rarely before הָ, הֶ, ה, עֶ, עָ, מַה־; מַה־ (followed by Dag. forte) before non-guttural letters, as מַה־שְּׁמוֹ (& contr. מַזֶּה, מַלְּכֶם, for מַה־זֶּה, מַה־לָּכֶם; (מַה־לֶּכֶם (Dag. forte impl.) before the harsher gutturals, as מַה־הוּא; — מֶה before הָ, חָ, עֶ (once עַ 1 Sa. 20. 1), as מֶה עָשִׂיתָ, מֶה חָדַל. This latter form stands also frequently before non-gutturals, chiefly at the beginning of a sentence. It is still more frequently found with prefixes, as לָמָה, כַּמָּה, בַּמָּה.

Part.—I. pron. interrog. what? (of things) in a direct and indirect question, espec. with the verbs אָמַר, שָׁאַל; frequently also in the genit. after constr. חָכְמַת מָה wisdom, of what (thing)?—מַה־לִּי וָלָךְ what wilt thou? מַה־לָּךְ what have I to do with thee?—II. pron. indefinite, whatever, anything, something; מָה שֶׁ that which.—III. pron. relat. what.—IV. adv. of interrog.; (a) why? wherefore? (b) how? in what manner? (c) how!

how much!—V. with prepositions; בַּמֶּה, בַּמָּה in what? whereby? on what account?—בַּמָּה, כַּמָּה how great? how long? how many? how often?—לָמָּה, לָמָה (the latter usually before א, ה, ע, and the name יְהֹוָה) wherefore? why? לָמָה זֶּה why then? שֶׁלָּמָה that not, lest; 1 Ch. 15. 13, לְמַבָּרִאשֹׁנָה (for לְמַה־בָּ) because that from the beginning; 2 Ch. 30. 3, לְמַדַּי (for לְמַה־דַּי to what is enough) sufficiently;—עַד־מָה till when? how long?—עַל־מָה, עַל־מֶה wherefore? why?

מָה, מָא Chald.—I. what?—II. what, whatever; מָה דִּי whatever (it is) which; כְּמָה how! how very! מָה, לָמָה wherefore? or lest, that not. מְאוּמָה (for מָה וּמָה i. e. whatever) anything whatever, something; with לֹא, אַל, אֵין nothing.

מַדּוּעַ adv. (for מַה־יָדוּעַ) why? wherefore? on what account? also in indirect question.

מֵהָאֹרֵב   preff. מֵ for מִ, & הָ for הַ ‌⟩‌ Kal part. act. sing. masc. dec. 7 b   ארב

מֵהָאֹכֵל   preff. id. ‌⟩‌ Kal part. act. sing. masc. dec. 7 b   אכל

מֵהָאֱלֹהִים   preff. id. ‌⟩‌ noun masc., pl. of אֱלוֹהַּ dec. 1 a   אלה

מֵהָאֲנָשִׁים   preff. id. ‌⟩‌ n. m. pl. (as if fr. אֱנוֹשׁ d. 6) see אֱנוֹשׁ   אנש

מֵהָאֲרִאֵל   ⁱ preff. id. ‌⟩‌ for אֲרִיאֵל (q. v.); ⁱ bef. lab.   ארה

מֵהָאָרֶץ   preff. id. ‌⟩‌ with the art. (הָ) for אֶרֶץ noun fem. sing. dec. 6 a (§ 35. rem. 2)   ארץ

מֵהָאֵשׁ   preff. id. ‌⟩‌ noun com. sing. dec. 8 b   אש

מֵהַבְּאֵר   preff. מֵ for מִ, & הַ ‌⟩‌ noun fem. sing. dec. 1 a (except pl. c. בְּאֵרֹת)   באר

מֵהָבִיא   pref. מֵ for מִ ‌⟩‌ Hiph. inf. constr.   בוא

מֵהַבִּיט   pref. id. ‌⟩‌ Hiph. inf. constr.   נבט

מֵהַבַּיִת }   preff. מֵ for מִ, & הַ ‌⟩‌ noun masc. sing.
מֵהַבָּיְתָ }   irr. (§ 45)   בית

מֵהֶבֶל   pref. מֵ for מִ ‌⟩‌ noun m. sing. d. 6 (§ 35. r. 4)   הבל

מַהֲבִלִים   ᵍ Hiph. part. masc. pl. [of מַהֲבִיל § 13. r. 9]   הבל

מֵהַבָּמָה   preff. מֵ for מִ, & הַ ‌⟩‌ n. f. s. d. 10 (§ 36. r. 6)   בום

מֵהַבֹּקֶר   preff. id. ‌⟩‌ noun masc. sing. d. 6 c (§ 35. r. 9)   בקר

מֵהַגְּבָעוֹת   preff. id. ‌⟩‌ noun fem. pl. abs. from גִּבְעָה d. 12 b   נבע

מֵהַגְּדוּד   preff. id. ‌⟩‌ noun masc. sing. dec. 1 a   גדד

מֵהַגּוֹלָה   preff. id. ‌⟩‌ noun fem. sing.   נלה

מֵהַגִּיד   pref. מֵ for מִ ‌⟩‌ Hiph. inf. constr.   נגד

מֵהַנַּגֹּות   ⁱⁱ preff. מֵ for מִ, & הַ ‌⟩‌ n. f., pl. of נַגָּה dec. 10   נגן

מֵהַגֵּר   ⁱ preff. id. ‌⟩‌ noun masc. s. d. 1; ⁱ bef. lab.   נור

מֵהַגּשָׁמַיִם   ⁱ preff. id. ‌⟩‌ n. m. pl. (c. גִּשְׁמֵי) fr. גֶּשֶׁם d. 6 a; ⁱ id.   נשם

מַהֵדוּ   pref. מֵ for מִ ‌⟩‌ pr. name of a country, see הֹדוּ   הדו

מְהַדֵּק   Ch. Aph. part. act. s. m. [for מַדֵּק § 47. r. 4]   דקק

מֵהֲדַר   ⁱ pref. מֵ for מִ ‌⟩‌ noun masc. sing., constr. of הָדָר dec. 4 c; ⁱ bef. lab.   הדר

ᵃ Je. 51. 4.   ᵈ Da. 4. 22, 29.   ⁱ Eze. 16. 27.   ᵏ Ps. 36. 9.   ˢ Is. 65. 7.   ᵛ 1 Sa. 30. 22.   ᵉ Ex. 36. 6.   ᵍ Je. 23. 16.   ⁱ 1 Sa. 3. 15.
ᵇ Ex. 17. 16.   ᵉ Job 24. 4.   ᶠ Ju. 2. 19.   ˡ Is. 21. 10.   ᵗ Nu. 35. 5.   ʷ Eze. 43. 15.   ᵈ Ex. 3. 6.   ʰ Zep. 1. 10.   ᵐ Eze. 14. 7.
ᶜ Da. 2. 11.   ᵉ De 2. 5.   ᵍ 2 Ch. 24. 27.   ᵐ Ps. 39. 5.   ᵘ Jos. 8. 7.   ˣ Eze. 15. 7.   ᵉ 2 Sa. 3. 22.   ⁱ Ezr. 10. 9.   ⁿ Eze. 14. 7.
ᵈ Job 37. 16.   ⁱ Is. 63. 17.   ʰ Is. 30. 33.   ⁿ Ju. 14. 14.   ʸ 2 Sa. 17. 21.   ᵃ Eze. 40. 7, 8.   ᶠ Ezr. 6. 21.   ᵏ Da. 2. 40.
Is. 48. 17.   ⁱ Is. 1. 29.

מְהַדַּר׳ ‡ Chald. Pael part. sing. masc.; ‡ bef. lab. — הדר

מָהַהּ Hithpalp. הִתְמַהְמֵהַּ (§ 6. No. 4) *to delay, tarry, wait.*

מֵהָהָר׳ preff. מְ for מִ, & הָ for הַ) noun masc. sing., with the art. for הַר, dec. 8 (§ 37. rem. 7) — הרר

מְהוֹדְרָא׳ Ch. Aph. part. s. m., for מוֹדָא (§ 47. r. 4) — ידה

מְהוֹדְךָ׳ pref. מְ for מִ) noun masc. sing., suff. 2 pers. sing. masc. from הוֹד dec. 1 a — הוד

מְהוֹדְעִין Ch. Aph. part. masc., pl. of [מְהוֹדַע § 47. rem. 4] dec. 2 a — ידע

מֻהְגָּל Kal part. pass. sing. masc. — מהל

מְהוֹלָל Poal part. sing. masc. — הלל

מְהוֹלָלַי id. pl. with suff. 1 pers. sing. — הלל

מְהוּמָה ‡ noun fem. sing. dec. 10 ; ‡ bef. lab. — הום

מְהוּמוֹת id. pl. comp. מְהוּמֹת — הום

מְהוּמַת id. sing., constr. st. — הום

מְהֻמֹת id. pl. defect. (for מְהוּמוֹת) — הום

מְהוֹנְךָ׳ pref. מְ for מִ) noun masc. sing., suff. 2 pers. sing. masc. from הוֹן dec. 1 a — הון

מְהוֹשִׁיעַ׳ pref. id.) Hiph. inf. constr. — ישע

מֵהַחוּץ׳ preff. מְ for מִ, & הַ) noun masc. dec. 1 a — חוץ

מְהָחֵל׳ pref. מְ for מִ) Hiph. inf. constr. — חלל

מְהַחְצָפָה׳ Ch. Aph. part. s. f. [for מַחְצְפָה § 47. r. 4] — חצף

מֵהֶחָצֵר׳ preff. מְ f. מִ, & הֶ bef. חָ f. הַ) n. m. d. 5 c — חצר

מְהַחְתִּין׳ Ch. Aph. (comp. § 14. rem. 1) part. masc., pl. of [מְהַחַת § 47. rem. 4] dec. 2 b — נחת

מֵהַיּוֹם׳ preff. מְ for מִ, & הַ) noun com. s. irr. (§45) — יום

מְהִיוֹת׳ pref. מְ) Kal inf. constr. dec. 1 a — היה

מִהְיוֹתְךָ׳ pref. id.) id., suff. 2 pers. sing. masc. — היה

מִהְיוֹתָם׳ pref. id.) id., suff. 3 pers. pl. masc. — היה

מְהֵיטַבְאֵל pr. name masc. — יטב

מְהֵיכַל׳ pref. מְ for מִ) noun com. sing. dec. 2 b — היכל

מֵהֵיכַל׳ pref. id.) id., constr. st. — היכל

מְהֵיכָלוֹ׳ pref. id.) id., suff. 3 pers. sing. masc. — היכל

מֵהֵיכָלְךָ׳ pref. id.) id., suff. 2 pers. sing. masc. — היכל

מֵהַיָּם׳ preff. מְ for מִ, & הַ) noun masc. s. d. 8 a — ים

מְהֵימְן׳ ‡ Ch. Aph. part. sing. masc. (§ 53 & 47. rem. 4); ‡ bef. lab. — אמן

מָהִיר adj. masc. sing. dec. 3 a — מהר

מְהִית defect. for מְהִיוֹת (q. v.) — היה

מֵהַכֹּהֲנִים preff. מְ for מִ, & הַ) noun masc., pl. of כֹּהֵן dec. 7 b — כהן

מְהַכְּבוֹת pref. מְ f. מִ) Hiph. inf. constr. (§ 25. No. 2b) — נכה

מְהַכְּבוֹתוֹ pref. id.) id., suff. 3 pers. sing. masc. — נכה

מְהָכִיל׳ pref. מְ for מִ) Hiph. inf. constr. — בול

מָהָל only part. pass. מָהוּל *adulterated*, of wine, Is. 1. 22.

מֵהַלְאָה pref. מְ for מִ) adv. — הלא

מֵהַלְּבָנוֹן preff. מְ for מִ, & הַ) pr. n. of a mountain — לבן

מֵהַלְוִים ‡ preff. id.) patronym., pl. of לֵוִי d. 8 f; ‡ bef. lab. — לו־

מֵהֲלָךְ׳ pref. מְ for מִ) Kal inf. constr. for הֲלָךְ (§ 8. rem. 18) — הלך

מַהֲלַךְ noun masc. sing., constr. of [מַהֲלָךְ] dec. 2b — הלך

מְהַלֵּךְ׳ Chald. Pael part. sing. masc. — הלך

מֵהֲלֹךְ׳ pref. מְ for מִ) Kal inf. constr. — הלך

מַהְלְכִים׳ Hiph. part. masc. pl. [of מַהֲלֵךְ ap. for § 11. rem. 8] dec. 7 b — הלך

מַהְלְכִין Chald. Aph. part. masc., pl. of [מַהְלֵךְ] d. 2 b — הלך

מַהֲלָכֶךְ׳ noun masc. sing., suff. 2 sing. masc. from [מַהֲלָךְ] dec. 2b — הלך

מְהֻלָּל ‡ Pual part. sing. masc.; ‡ bef. lab. — הלל

מַהֲלַלְאֵל pr. name masc. — הלל

מַהֲלָלוֹ׳ noun m. s., suff. 3 pers. s. m. fr. [מַהֲלָל] d. 2 b — הלל

מְהֻלָּלִים ‡ Piel part. m., pl. of [מְהֻלָּל] d. 7 b; ‡ bef. lab. — הלל

מַהֲלֻמּוֹת ‡ noun fem., pl. of [מַהֲלֻמָה] dec. 10 ; ‡ id. — הלם

מֵהֶם׳ Kh. contr. from מָה הֵם (q. v.) — מה & הם

מֵהֶם ‡ pref. prep. מְ, bef. gutt. for מִ, with suff. 3 pers. pl. masc., see מִן (§ 5); ‡ bef. lab. — מן

מֵהַמְדַבֵּר׳ preff. מְ for מִ, & הַ) noun masc. sing. d. 2 b — דבר

מֵהֵמָּה׳ pref. מְ for מִ) pron. pers. masc. pl. (הֵם) with parag. ה — הם

מֵהֲמֵהֶם ‡ pref. id.) noun masc. pl., suff. 3 pers. pl. masc. [for הֲמֵיהֶם from הָם] — המה

מֵהֲמוֹן׳ pref. id.) noun m. s., constr. of הָמוֹן d. 3 a — המה

מֵהֲמוֹנָם׳ ‡ pref. id.) id., suff. 3 pers. pl. m.; ‡ bef. lab. — המה

מֵהַמּוֹרִים׳ preff. מְ for מִ, & הַ) Hiph. part. masc., pl. of מוֹרֶה dec. 9 a — ירה

מְהַמְטִיר׳ pref. מְ for מִ) Hiph. inf. constr. — מטר

מֵהַמֶּלֶךְ׳ preff. מְ for מִ, & הַ) n. m. s. (suff. מַלְכִּי) d. 6 a — מלך

מְהֵמָן׳ pr. name masc. — המן

מֵהַמְּעָרָה׳ preff. מְ for מִ, & הַ) noun fem. sing., constr. מְעָרָה, dec. 10 — עור

מֵהַמַּעֲרָכָה׳ preff. id.) noun fem. sing. dec. 11 a — ערך

מֵהֵן׳ pref. מְ for מִ) pron. pers. fem. pl. — הן

מֵהַנְּבִיאִים׳ preff. מְ for מִ, & הַ) n. m., pl. of נָבִיא d. 3 a — נבא

מֵהֵנָּה׳ pref. מְ for מִ) pron. pers. fem. pl. (הֵן) with parag. ה — הן

מֵהַנָּזִיד׳ preff. מְ for מִ, & הַ) n. m. s. d. 3a, R. זיד see — זוד

Da. 4. 34.	Ps. 102. 9.	Eze. 41. 25.	Hag. 2. 16.	2 Sa. 8. 13.	Zec. 3. 7.	Eze. 8. 6.	Eze. 7. 11.	1 Sa. 24. 8.
Jos. 2. 23.	Pr. 15. 16.	Is. 66. 6.	1 Ki. 8. 64.		Ne. 2. 6.	Je. 10. 2;	Is. 31. 4.	1 Sa. 4. 12.
Da. 2. 23.	2 Ch. 15. 5.	Eze. 42. 9.	Ps. 68. 30.	Ec. 6. 9.		Pr. 27. 21.	Ec. 12. 12.	1 Sa. 31. 3.
Nu. 27. 20.	Am. 3. 9.	Ezr. 6. 1.	Is. 19. 5.	Da. 4. 26.	1 Ch. 23. 5.	Eze. 7. 11.	Is. 5. 6.	Eze. 16. 47, 52
Is. 1. 22.	Pr. 3. 9.	Is. 49. 6.	Da. 2. 45; 6. 5.	Nu. 22. 16.	Pr. 19. 29.	Ps. 37. 16.	2 Sa. 3. 37.	1 Ki. 20. 41.
Ec. 3. 2.	Is. 58. 1.							2 Ki. 4. 40.

מְהַנְזְקַת^a ᵃ Chald. Aph. part. sing. constr. [of
מְהַנְזְקָא d. 8 a, fr. נְזֵק m. § 47. r. 4]; ᵇ bef. lab.   נזק

מְהַנַּחֲלִי^b preff. for מִ, & הַ)(noun masc. sing. d. 6 d   נחל

מְהַנְּעָרִים preff. id.)(noun masc., pl. of נַעַר dec. 6 d   נער

מְהַנְּשֶׁף^c preff. id.)(noun masc. sing. (suff. נִשְׁפּוֹ) d. 6 a   נשף

מְהַסַּלְעֲ^d preff. id.)(noun masc. sing. (suff. כַּלְעִי)
dec. 6 a (§ 35. rem. 5)   סלע

מְהִסְתַּפֵּחַ pref. מְ for מִ)(Hithpa. inf. constr. [for
הִתְסַפֵּחַ § 12. rem. 3]   ספח

מְהָעֶבֶר^e preff. מְ for מִ, & הָ for הַ)(noun masc.
sing. dec. 6 (§ 35. rem. 6)   עבר

מְהַעֲדָה^f Chald. Aph. part. sing. masc. (§ 47. rem. 4)   עדה

מְהָעֵדֶר^g preff. מְ for מִ, & הָ for הַ)(noun masc.
sing. dec. 6 (§ 35. rem. 6)   עדר

מְהָעוֹלָם^h preff. id.)(noun masc. sing. dec. 2 b   עלם

מְהָעוֹףⁱ preff. id.)(noun masc. sing.   עוף

מְהָעֶזְרָה^k ᵏ preff. id.)(noun fem. sing.; ᵏ bef. lab.   עזר

מְהָעִיר preff. id.)(noun fem. sing. irr. (§ 45)   עור

מְהַעֲלוֹת^l pref. מְ for מִ)(Hiph. inf. constr.   עלה

מְהָעָם pref. מְ for מִ, and הָ for הַ)(noun com.
sing. dec. 8 a, also irr. עֲמָמִים (§ 45)   עמם

מְהָעֲמוֹנִים preff. id.)(gent. noun, pl. of עַמּוֹנִי fr. עַמּוֹן   עמם

מְהֶעָרִים preff. מְ id., & הֶ bef. עָ for הַ)(noun fem.
pl. irr. of עִיר (§ 45)   עור

מְהַקְּדֵמִים^m preff. מְ id., & הַ)(noun masc. sing.   קדם

מְהַקֹּדֶשׁⁿ preff. id.)(noun masc. sing. dec. 6 c   קדש

מְהָקִּים^o ᵒ Aph. part. sing. m. (§ 47. r. 4); ᵒ bef. lab.   קום

מְהָקֵין^p pref. מְ for מִ)(Hiph. inf. constr.   קין

מְהַקְצֻעוֹ^q Hoph. part. fem. pl. [of מְהַקְצֻעָה from
מְהֻקְצָע masc.]   קצע

מְהַקָּרְבִין Chald. Aph. (§ 47. rem. 4) part. masc., pl.
of מְהַקְרֵב dec. 2 b   קרב

מְהַקַּרְקַע^r preff. מְ for מִ, & הַ)(noun masc. sing.   קרקע

I. [מָהַר] to haste, hasten, Ps. 16. 4. Pi. מִהַר (§ 14. rem. 1)
to hasten, make haste, be quick; מִהֲרוּ שָׁכְחוּ they
hasted, they forgot, i. e. they quickly forgot;
מִהַר לִמְצֹא he found quickly. Niph. to be hasty,
rash, Job 5. 13. Part. נִמְהָר (a) hasty, rash, in-
considerate, Is. 32. 4; (b) impetuous, Hab. 1. 6;
(c) timid, with לֵב, Is. 35. 4.

מָהִיר adj. masc. dec. 3 a, quick, ready, skilful.
מַהֵר masc.—I. adj. hasty, speedy, Zep. 1. 14.—
II. adv. quickly, speedily.

מְהֵרָה fem. haste, speed; as an adv. quickly,
speedily.

מַהֲרַי (ready, skilful) pr. name of one of David's
captains.

II. [מָהַר] cogn. מוּר q. v. to purchase a wife, by a dowry
or present to the father, Ex. 22. 15.

מֹהַר masc. price or dowry, tendered by the
bridegroom to the parents of the bride.

מָהֹר Kal inf. abs.   מהר

מַהֵר^s ˢ Piel (§ 14. rem. 1) imp. sing. masc.; or
adv.; or (Zep. 1. 14) adj.; ᵗ bef. lab.   מהר

מֵהַר pref. מְ for מִ)(noun m. sing. d. 8 (§ 37. r. 7)   הרר

מֵהַר pref. id.)(pr. name of a mountain   הרר

מִהַר Piel pret. 3 pers. sing. masc. (§ 14. rem. 1)   מהר

מֹהַר^t noun masc. sing.   מהר

מְהִיר^u ᵘ adj. m. sing., constr. of מָהִיר d. 3 a; ᵘ bef. lab.   מהר

מֵהָרֹאשׁ preff. מְ for מִ, and הָ for הַ)(noun masc.
sing. irr. (§ 45)   ראשׁ

מַהַרְבֵּה^x pref. מְ for מִ)(Hiph. inf. abs. as an adv.
(§ 24. rem. 15)   רבה

מֵהַרְבִּית^y pref. id.)(id. inf. constr., Kh. בִּית', K. בַּת',   רבה

מַהֲרָה Piel imp. s. m. (מַהֵר § 14. r. 1) with parag. ה   מהר

מִהֲרָה id. pret. 3 pers. sing. fem.   מהר

מְהֵרָה noun fem. s. (Ps. 147. 15); used also adverbially   מהר

מָהֲרוּ^z ᶻ Kal pret. 3 pers. pl. [for מָהֲרוּ § 8. rem. 7]   מהר

מַהֲרוּ Piel imp. pl. masc. (§ 14. rem. 1)   מהר

מִהֲרוּ id. pret. 3 pers. pl.   מהר

מַהֲרַי pr. name masc.   מהר

מַהֲרִי^a Piel imp. sing. fem.   מהר

מֵהָרֵי^b pref. מְ for מִ)(noun masc. pl. constr. fr. הַר
dec. 8 (§ 37. rem. 7)   הרר

מְהֵרָיוֹן^c ᶜ pref. id.)(noun masc. sing.; ᶜ bef. lab.   הרה

מְהָרְסַיִךְ^d Piel part. pl. masc., suff. 2 pers. sing. fem.
from [מְהָרֵם] dec. 7 b   הרס

מֵהָרֵעַ^e pref. מְ for מִ)(Hiph. inf. constr. (§ 18. r. 10)   רעע

מֵהָרְרֵי^f pref. id.)(noun m. pl. constr. from [הָרָר] d. 4 c   הרר

מֵהֲרָרַיִךְ^g ᵍ pref. id.)(id., suff. 3 pers. s.; ᵍ bef. lab.   הרר

מִהַרְתְּ^h Piel pret. 2 pers. sing. masc. (§ 14. rem. 1)   מהר

מִהַרְתְּⁱ id. pret. 2 pers. sing. fem.   מהר

מִהַרְתֶּם^k ᵏ id. pret. 2 pers. pl. m.; ᵏ bef. lab. for וְ, conv.   מהר

מִהַרְתֶּן id. pret. 2 pers. pl. fem.   מהר

מְהַשֵּׁבִי preff. מְ for מִ, & הַ)(noun masc. sing. d. 6 i   שׁבה

מַהַשְׁחִית^l pref. מְ for מִ)(Hiph. inf. constr. dec. 1 b   שׁחת

מְהַשְׁחִיתָם^m pref. id.)(id., suff. 3 pers. pl. masc.   שׁחת

מְהַשִּׁטִּים preff. מְ for מִ, & הַ)(pr. name of a place,
see שִׁטָּה

מְהַשְׂכִּילⁿ pref. מְ for מִ)(Hiph. inf. constr.   שׂכל

ᵃ Ezr. 4. 15.   ᶠ 1 Sa. 14. 4.   ˡ Eze. 43. 14.   ᵠ Eze. 46. 22.   ˣ Zep. 1. 14.   ᵇ Je. 42. 2.   ᵍ Ge. 18. 6.   ˡ 1 Sa. 25. 34.   ˣ Ge. 45. 13.
ᵇ 1 Ki. 17. 4.   ᵍ Da. 2. 21.   ᵐ Eze. 42. 9.   ʳ Ezr. 6. 10.   ʸ 1 Ki. 7. 7.   ᶜ 2 Sa. 14. 11.   ʰ Nu. 33. 48.   ᵐ De. 8. 9.   ʸ Ps. 106. 23.
ᶜ 1 Sa. 30. 17.   ʰ 1 Sa. 17. 34.   ⁿ Eze. 42. 14.   ˢ Da. 2. 21.   ᶻ Is. 16. 5.   ᵈ Je. 48. 16.   ⁱ Ho. 9. 11.   ⁿ 1 Sa. 25. 34.   ᶻ Je. 13. 14.
ᵈ Ju. 1. 36.   ⁱ Ge. 6. 20.   ᵒ Ps. 41. 14.   ᵗ Eze. 22. 15.   ᵃ Is. 44. 14.   ᵉ 2 Sa. 16. 1.   ᵏ Ps. 16. 4.   ᵐ Is. 49. 17.
ᵉ 1 Sa. 26. 19.   ᵏ Ge. 6. 20.   ᵖ Ps. 73. 20.

מֵהַשָּׁלֵל preff. מְ for מִ, & הַ ⟩(noun masc. s. d. 4 a שלל

מֵהַשְּׁלִשִׁים preff. id. ⟩(num. card. com., pl. of שָׁלִשׁ fem. שלש

מֵהַשְּׂמֹאול preff. ia. ⟩(noun masc. sing. dec. 1 a שמאל

מֵהַשָּׁמַיִם preff. id. ⟩(noun masc. pl. [of שָׁמֶה], constr. שָׁמֵי, suff. שָׁמֶיךָ (§ 38. rem. 2) שם

מֵהַשְׁנֵא Chald. Aph. part. sing. masc. (§ 47. rem. 4) שנה

מֵהַשְׁפִּילְךָ pref. מֵ for מִ ⟩(Hiph. inf. (הַשְׁפִּיל), suff. 2 pers. sing. masc. dec. 1 b שפל

מֵהִשְׁתָּרֵעַ pref. id. ⟩(Hithpa. inf. constr. [for הִתְשָׁרֵע § 12. rem. 3] שרע

מֵהִתְהַלֶּךְ pref. id. ⟩(Hithpa. inf. constr.; bef. lab. הלך

מֵהַהִתְחַתְּנוֹת preff. מְ for מִ, & הַ ⟩(adj. pl. fem. from נָה dec. 10, from תַּחְתּוֹן masc. תחת

מֵהַתִּיכוֹנוֹת preff. id. ⟩(adj. fem., pl. of נָה, dec.
מֵהַתִּיכֹנוֹת 10, from תִּיכוֹן masc.; bef. lab. תוך

מֵהִתְיַצֵּב pref. מֵ for מִ ⟩(Hithpa. inf. constr. יצב

מֵהַתְּלֹאות noun fem., pl. of [מַהֲתַלָּה] dec 10 תלל

מֵהִתְנַבּוֹת pref. מֵ for מִ ⟩(Hithpa. inf. c. as if from נבא (§ 23. rem. 11)

מֵהִתְעַנֵּג pref. id. ⟩(Hithpa. inf. constr. ענג

מֵהַתֹּפֶת preff. מְ for מִ, & הַ ⟩(pr. name of a place תוף

מוֹ (prob. i. q. מָה what) does not occur as a separate word, but is merely annexed to the prefixes בְּ, כְּ, לְ to make them independent words, the signification not being affected thereby. Hence

בְּמוֹ i. q. בְּ.—I. in, noting rest; into, to, noting motion, Job 37. 8.—II. with, Job 16. 4, 5.

כְּמוֹ, כְמוֹ (the latter form only before light suffixes, comp. § 5) i. q. כְּ.—I. adv. thus, Ps. 73. 15.—II. prep. as, like; repeated, as—so.—III. conj. i. q. כַּאֲשֶׁר when.

לְמוֹ i. q. לְ so, at; for; upon. Only Job 27. 14; 29. 21; 38. 40; 40. 4.

מוֹאָב (water, i. e. progeny, of the father; מוֹ i. q. מֵי) pr. name—I. Moab, a descendant of Lot.—II. of the people descended from him, and the region between the Dead Sea and the river Arnon. Gent. noun מוֹאָבִי, fem. מוֹאָבִית, see also the foll.

מוֹאָבִיָּה sing.⎫ gent. noun, fem. of מוֹאָבִי from מוֹאָב
מוֹאָבִיּוֹת pl.⎭ q. v.

מוֹאָס Kal part. act. sing. masc. מאס

מוּבָאוֹת Hoph. part. f., pl. [of מוּבָאָה fr. מוּבָא m.] בוא

מוּבָאָיו noun masc. pl., suff. 3 pers. sing. masc. from [מוּבָא] d. 1 b (§ 31. r. 1); bef. lab. בוא

מוּבָאִים Hoph. part. m., pl. of מוּבָא d. 1 b (§ 31. r. 1) בוא

מוּבָס Hoph. part. sing. masc. בוס

[מוּג] to melt, flow down, dissolve, metaph. from fear; trans. to cause to melt, despond, Is. 64. 6. Niph. to be dissolved, undone, 1 Sa. 14. 16; metaph. to melt away, from fear. Pil. to dissolve, soften, Ps. 65. 11; metaph. to cause to waste away, Job 30. 22. Hithpal. to flow down, to melt, Am. 9. 13; metaph. to despond, from fear.

מוֹנַיִךְ Hiph. part. pl. masc., suff. 2 pers. sing. fem. from [מוֹנָה] dec. 9 a ינה

מוּד Kal not used; Arab. to be moved, cogn. מוט. Hence perhaps Pil. to move, shake, Hab. 3. 6, but see מָדַד.

תָּמִיד masc.—I. continuance, perpetuity; עֹלַת הַתָּמִיד continual, i. e. daily burnt-offering; for which simply הַתָּמִיד id.; לֶחֶם הַתָּמִיד the continual bread, i. e. the shew-bread.—II. adv. constantly, continually, always.

מוֹרֵא Ch. Aph. part. s. m. (§ 56. No. 3); bf. lab. ידה

מוֹרֶה Hiph. part. s. m. (§ 25. No. 2 e) d. 9 a; id. ידה

מוֹרִים id. pl., abs. st. ידה

מוֹדִיעִים Hiph. part. masc., pl. of [מוֹדִיעַ] dec. 1 b; bef. lab. ידע

מוֹדִיעֲךָ id. sing., suff. 2 pers. sing. masc. ידע

מוֹדִיעָם id. sing., suff. 3 pers. pl. masc. ידע

מְיֻנָּנִים K. מְיֻנָּנִים Pu. part. pl. m. R. זון; Kh. מוּזָנִים Hoph. part. masc. pl. [of מוּזָן masc.] זון

מוּזָר Hoph. part. sing. masc. זור

מוֹט fut. יָמוּט to totter, shake; of the foot, to slip, slide; of the hand, to be weak, to fail, trop. of prosperity, Le. 25. 35. Niph. to be moved, shaken. Hiph. to cause to fall or come down, Ps. 55. 4; 140. 11. Kheth. Hithpa. i. q. Kal, Is. 24. 19.
מוֹט masc. dec. 1 a.—I. a tottering, shaking.—II. pole, staff.—III. yoke, Na. 1. 13.
מוֹטָה fem. dec. 10.—I. pole, staff.—II. yoke.

מוֹט noun masc. sing. dec. 1 a מוט

מוֹטָה noun fem. sing. dec. 10 מוט

מוֹטוֹת pl. of the preced. מוט

[מוּךְ] to become reduced, to wax poor.

מִיכִי (reduced, thin) pr. name masc. Nu. 13. 15.

מוֹכִיחַ Hiph. part. sing. masc. dec. 1 b; bef. lab. יכח

מוּכָן Hoph. part. sing. masc. כון

---

a 2 Sa. 23. 13.   d Is. 28. 20.   g Eze. 42. 6.   m Pr. 15. 32.   q Is. 51. 23.   t Is. 47. 13.   w Je. 16. 21.   z Is. 24. 19.   f Je. 28. 13.
b 2 Ch. 7. 1.   e Job 1. 7; 2. 2.   h Is. 30. 10.   n Ps. 45. 15.   r Da. 6. 11.   u 2 Ch. 23. 13.   x Je. 5. 8.   a Ps. 55. 23.   g Pr. 9. 7.
c Da. 2. 21.   f Eze. 42. 5. 6.   i 1 Sa. 30. 13.   o Eze. 43. 11.   s Pr. 28. 13.   v Da. 8. 19.   y Ps. 69. 9.   b Is. 58. 6, 6, 9.   h Pr. 31. 31.
d Pr. 25. 7.   Eze. 42. 5.   De. 28. 56.   Is. 14. 19.   1 Ch. 29. 13.

מוּכָנִים• id. pi., abs. st. . . . . כון
מוֹכְרִים•ᶥ Kal part. act. masc., pl. of מוֹכֵר' dec. 7b;
ᶥ bef. lab. . . . . . מכר

[מוּל] to circumcise. Niph. to be circumcised, to circumcise oneself. Pil. to cut off, Ps. 90. 6. Hiph. to cut off, destroy, Ps. 118. 10, 11, 12. Hithpal. to be cut off, destroyed, Ps. 58. 8; where others refer the verb to חָצִיר, and render it, to be blunted.
מוּלָה fem. dec. 10, circumcision, Ex. 4. 26.

מוּל ᵍᵈ'ᵘ, once מוֹל (De. 1. 1), contr. from מוֹאָל (Ne. 12. 38), for מוֹאָל (compounded of מוֹ i. q. מָה what, that which is, & אֶל towards, before; hence, that which is in front, opposite) prep.—I. over against, opposite.—II. before, Ex. 18. 19.—III. with prepositions: אֶל־מוּל over against, towards;—מִמּוּל, (a) from before; (b) before, opposite, noting rest.
(אֶת־מוּל for) אֶתְמוֹל, אֶתְמוּל adv.—I. before, formerly.—II. yesterday.
תְּמוֹל (for אֶתְמוֹל) adv. yesterday; frequently coupled with שִׁלְשׁוֹם the day before yesterday.

מוּלᵈ ᶥ adv.; ᶥ bef. lab. . . . מול
מוּל• Kal part. pass. sing. masc. dec. 1a מול
מוֹלָדָה ᶥ pr. name of a place; ᶥ bef. lab. . ילד
מוֹלְדוֹתַיִךְ ᶥ pl. of the foll. with suff. 2 pers. s. f.; ᶥ id. ילד
מוֹלֶדֶת•ᵍ noun fem. sing. dec. 13a ילד
מוֹלַדְתָּהּ id., suff. 3 pers. sing. fem. . ילד
מוֹלַדְתּוֹ id., suff. 3 pers. sing. masc. . ילד
מוֹלַדְתִּי id., suff. 1 pers. sing. . . ילד
מוֹלַדְתְּךָ
מוֹלַדְתֶּךָʰ } id., suff. 2 pers. sing. masc.; ᶥ bef. lab. ילד
מוֹלַדְתֵּךְ id., suff. 2 pers. sing. fem. . . ילד
מוֹלַדְתָּם• id., suff. 3 pers. pl. masc. . . ילד
מוֹלַדְתֵּנוּ id., suff. 1 pers. sing. . . ילד
מוֹלִיד pr. name masc. . . . . ילד
מוֹלִיךְ Hiph. part. sing. masc. dec. 1b . ילד
מוֹלִיכְכֶם• id., suff. 3 pers. pl. masc. . . ילד
מוֹלִיכוֹת• id. pl. fem. [from מוֹלִיכָה•] dec. 10 ילד
מוֹלִכֵךְᵍ id. sing. masc., suff. 2 pers. sing. fem. ילד
מוֹלֵל• Kal part. act. sing. masc. . . מלל
מוּם•ᶥʰ noun m. s. d. 1a (for מְאוּם); ᶥ bef. lab. מאם
מוּמוֹ id., suff. 3 pers. sing. masc. . . מאם
מוֹמְכָן Kh. מוּמְכָן, K. מְמוּכָן q. v.

מוּמָם•ᵃ noun masc. sing., suff. 3 pers. pl. masc. from מוּם (for מְאוּם•) dec. 1a . . . מאם
מוּמָת•ᵇ Hoph. part. sing. masc. . . . מות

מִן & מֵין Root not used; signification uncertain, perhaps i. q. מָנָה to appoint, define; Fürst, to devise, form, fashion, cogn. Arab. مان mentiri ementiri.
מִין masc. dec. 1a, species, sort, kind.
תְּמוּנָה fem. dec. 10.—I. image, likeness.—II. form, appearance.

מוֹנֶה Kal part. sing. masc. . . . מנה
מוֹנַיִךְᵇ Hiph. part. pl., suff. 2 pers. sing. fem. from [מוֹנֶה] dec. 9a . . . ינה
מוּסָב•ᶜ noun masc. sing. . . . סבב
מוּסַבּוֹת•ᵈ } Hoph. part. fem. pl. [of מוּסַבָּה dec. 10,
מוּסַבַּת } from מוּסָב masc.] . . סבב
מוּסָד•ᵇ Hoph. part. sing. masc. (§ 20. rem. 16) יסד
מוּסָד•ᵈ noun masc. sing. dec. 2b . . יסד
מוּסַד•ᵈ id. constr. st. . . . יסד
מוּסָדָה noun fem. sing. dec. 11a . . יסד
מוֹסְדוֹת noun masc. with pl. fem. term., constr. of מוֹסְדוֹת, from [מוֹסָד] dec. 2b . יסד
מוֹסְדֵיᶠᶥ id. pl. constr. masc.; ᶥ bef. lab. . יסד
מוֹסִיפִים•ᵍ Hiph. part. masc., pl. of [מוֹסִיף•] dec. 1b . יסף
מוּסָר•ʰ Hoph. part. sing. masc. . . סור
מוּסָרᶥ noun masc. sing. dec. 2b; ᶥ bef. lab. . יסר
מוּסַר•ᶥ id. constr. st.; ᶥ id. . . . יסר
מוֹסֵרָה pr. name of a place (מוֹסֵר) with loc. ה אסר
מוֹסֵרוֹת noun masc. with pl. fem. term. abs. [from מוֹסֵר for מַאְסֵר] dec. 7b . . אסר
מוֹסְרוֹתֵיהֶם•ᶥ id. pl., suff. 3 pers. pl. masc.; ᶥ bef. lab. אסר
מוֹסְרוֹתֵיךָᵈᶥ id. pl., suff. 2 pers. sing. masc.; ᶥ id. אסר
מוֹסְרוֹתַיִךְ id. pl., suff. 2 pers. sing. fem. . אסר
מוֹסְרוֹתֵימוֹᵐ id. pl., suff. 3 pers. pl. masc. . אסר
מוֹסְרֵיᵒ id. pl., constr. masc. . . . אסר
מוֹסֵרִי•ᵖ noun m. s., suff. 1 pers. s. from מוּסָר d. 2b יסר
מוֹסְרֵיכֶם• noun masc. pl., suff. 2 pers. pl. masc. [from מוֹסֵר for מַאְסֵר] dec. 7b . . אסר
מוֹסָרְךָ•ᵠ noun m. s., suff. 2 p. s. m. from מוּסָר d. 2b סר
מוֹסְרֹתֶיךָᵗ ᶥ defect. for מוֹסְרוֹתֶיךָ• (q. v.) אסר
מוֹעָד noun masc. sing. dec. 7b . . . יעד
מוֹעֲדָהᵘ id., suff. 3 pers. sing. masc. . . עד
מוֹעֲדַיᵛ
מוֹעֲדַיᵛ } id. pl., suff. 1 pers. sing. . . עד
מוֹעֲדֵי id. pl., constr. st. . . . יעד
מוֹעֲדֶיהָ id. pl., suff. 3 pers. sing. fem. . יעד

• Eze. 40. 43. ᶜ Eze. 16. 4. ᶠ Ru. 2. 11. ᵍ Je. 2. 17. ᵏ 1 Sa. 19. 11. ᵇ Is. 28. 16. ᵏ Is. 17. 1. ᵐ Is. 52. 2. ᵖ Ho. 2. 13.
ᵇ Ne. 13. 16. ᵈ Le. 18. 9, 11. ᵏ Eze. 23. 15. ʰ Pr. 6. 13. ᵗ Is. 49. 26. ᵢ 2 Ch. 8. 16. ᵏ Ps. 107. 14. ᵒ Pr. 8. 10. ᵠ Le. 23. 2.
ᶜ 1 Ki. 7. 5. ᵉ Est. 2. 10. 20. ᵏ Je. 46. 16. ᵢ Ca. 4. 7. ᵘ Eze. 41. 7. ᵏ Is. 30. 32. ᵏ Je. 30. 8. ᵖ Is. 26. 16. ᵏ Ge. 44. 24.
ᵈ 1 Ki. 7. 5. ᶠ Ge. 31. 13. ᵏ Is. 63. 13. ᵏ Pr. 9. 7. ᵛ Ps. 18. 8. ᵏ Je. 2. 20. ᵏ Is. 26. 16. ᵏ Je. 8. 7.
Je. 9. 24. ᵍ Ge. 48. 6. ᵏ Zec. 5. 10. ᵏ De. 32. 5. ᵏ Is. 28. 16. ᵏ Ne. 13. 18. ᵏ Ps. 2. 3. ᵏ Na. 1. 13.

מֹעֲדֵיכֶם	id. pl., suff. 2 pers. pl. masc.; וּ bef. lab.	יעד
מֹעֲדִים	id. pl., abs. st.	יעד
מֹעָדִים	Hoph. part. masc. pl. [of מוּעָד]	יעד
מֹעָדֶךָ	noun masc. pl., suff. 2 pers. sing. masc. [for דֶּיךָ § 4. rem. 1] from מוֹעֵד dec. 7 b	יעד
מֹעֲדֵנוּ	id. sing., suff. 1 pers. pl.	יעד
מֹעֶדֶת	Kal part. fem. [for מֹעֲדֶת]; or Pual part. fem. [for מְמֹעֲדֶת § 10. rem. 6]	מעד
מֹעִיל	Hiph. part. sing. masc.	יעל
מֹעָף	noun masc. sing.	עוף
מוּעָקָה	noun fem. sing.	עוק
מוּפָז	Hoph. part. sing. masc.	פזז
מוֹפַעַת	Kh. מֹ׳, K. מֵי׳, pr. name of a place	יפע
מוֹפֵת	וּ noun masc. sing. dec. 7 b; וּ bef. lab.	יפת
מוֹפְתִי	id. pl., suff. 1 pers. sing.	יפת
מוֹפְתָיו	id. pl., suff. 3 pers. sing. masc.; וּ bef. lab.	יפת
מוֹפְתִים	וּ id. pl. abs.	יפת
מוֹפְתֵכֶם	id. sing., suff. 2 pers. pl. masc.	יפת

מוּץ to press, only part. מֵץ (§ 21. r. 2) oppressor, Is. 16. 4.
מֹץ מוֹץ masc. chaff.
מֵץ masc. pressing, of cream to make butter, churning, Pr. 30. 33.

מוֹצָא	וּ noun m. s. d. 1 b, also pr. name; וּ bef. lab.	יצא
מוֹצִא	Hiph. part. sing. masc. apoc. from מוֹצִיא	יצא
מֹצֵא	וּ Kal part. act. s. m. (§ 23. r. 9); וּ bef. lab.	מצא
מוֹצָאוֹ	noun masc. sing., suff. 3 pers. sing. masc. from מוֹצָא dec. 1 b (§ 31. rem. 1)	יצא
מוֹצָאוֹת	Hoph. part. pl. f. [from מוּצָאָה from מוּצָא] m.	יצא
מוֹצָאֵי	n. m. pl. constr. for מוֹצָא d. 1 b (§ 31. r. 1)	יצא
מוֹצִאֵי	Hiph. part. pl. constr. from מוֹצִיא dec. 1 b	יצא
מוֹצָאֵיהֶם	noun masc. pl., suff. 3 pers. pl. masc. from מוֹצָא dec. 1 b (§ 31. rem. 1)	יצא
מוֹצָאֵיהֶן	id. pl., suff. 3 pers. pl. fem.	יצא
מוֹצָאָיו	וּ id. pl., suff. 3 pers. sing. masc.; וּ bef. lab.	יצא
מוֹצָאִים	defect. for מוֹצִיאִים (q. v.)	יצא
מוֹצָאֲךָ	n. m. s., suff. 2 p. s. m. fr. מוֹצָא d. 1 b (§ 31. r. 1)	יצא
מוּצֵאת	Hoph. part. sing. fem. [for מוּצָאת], pl. מוּצָאוֹת (§ 44. rem. 5)	יצא
מוֹצָאֹתַי	וּ noun fem. pl., suff. 3 pers. sing. masc. [from מוֹצָאָה § 31. r. 1] d. 10; וּ bef. lab.	יצא
מוֹצִיא	וּ Hiph. part. sing. masc. dec. 1 b; וּ id.	יצא
מוֹצִיאוֹ	id., suff. 3 pers. sing. masc.	יצא
מוֹצִיאִי	וּ id., suff. 1 pers. sing.; וּ bef. lab.	יצא
מוֹצִיאִים	וּ id. pl., abs. st.; וּ id.	יצא
מוֹצִיאָם	id. sing., suff. 3 pers. pl. masc.	יצא

מוּצָק	Hoph. part. s. m., or (1 Ki. 7. 37) n. m. s.	יצק
מוּצָק	noun masc. sing.	צוק
מוּצָק	noun masc. sing.	צוק
מוּצָקוֹת	noun fem. pl. abs. [from מוּצָקָה]	יצק

מוּק Hiph. to mock, deride, Ps. 73. 8.

מוֹקְדָה	noun fem. sing.	יקד
מוֹקְדֵי	noun masc. pl. constr. from מוֹקֵד dec. 7 b	יקד
מוֹקֵשׁ	וּ noun masc. sing. dec. 7 b; וּ bef. lab.	יקש
מוֹקְשֵׁי	id. pl., constr. st.	יקש
מוֹקְשִׁים	id. pl., abs. st.	יקש

מוֹר Niph. to be changed, altered, Je. 48. 11. Hiph.—
I. to exchange, with בְּ of the thing for which.—
II. to change, undergo change, Ps. 15. 4; 46. 3.
תְּמוּרָה fem. dec. 10.—I. exchange, transfer.—
II. restitution, Job 20. 18.—III. equivalent, recompense.

מוֹרִי	noun m. s. (with suff. מוֹרִי) for מֹר (q. v.)	מרר
מוֹרָא	noun masc. sing. dec. 2 b	ירא
מוֹרָאָה	Kal part. act. fem. [of מוֹרָא R. מרא]; or it stands for מוֹרֶה, fem. of מוֹרֶה R.	מרה
מוֹרָאוֹ	n. m. s., suff. 3 p. s. m. fr. מוֹרָא d. 2 b (§ 31. r. 3)	ירא
מוֹרָאִי	id., suff. 1 pers. sing.	ירא
מוֹרַאֲכֶם	וּ id., suff. 2 pers. pl. masc.; וּ bef. lab.	ירא
מוֹרָד	noun masc. sing. dec. 2 b	ירד
מוֹרָה	וּ noun masc. s. with fem. term.; וּ bef. lab.	מרה
מוֹרָה	for מוֹרָא (q. v.) noun masc. sing.	ירא
מוֹרֶה	וּ participial n.m.s.d. 9a, also pr. n.; וּ bef. lab.	ירה
מוֹרֶה	וּ Kal part. sing. masc. dec. 9 a; וּ id.	מרה
מוֹרָט	וּ Pual part. sing. m. for מְמֹרָט (§ 10. r. 6)	מרט
מוֹרַי	participial n. m. pl., suff. 1 p. s. fr. מוֹרֶה d. 9a	ירה
מוֹרִי	n. m. s., suff. 1 p. s. for מֹרִי fr. מֹר d. 1 a	מרר
מוֹרִיד	Hiph. part. sing. masc.	ירד
מוֹרֶיךָ	participial noun masc. pl., suff. 2 pers. sing. masc. from מוֹרֶה dec. 9 a	ירה
מוֹרִישׁ	Hiph. part. sing. masc. dec. 1 b	ירשׁ
מוֹרִישָׁם	id. with suff. 3 pers. pl. masc.	ירשׁ
מוֹרָשָׁה	noun fem. sing.	ירשׁ
מוֹרָשֵׁי	noun masc. pl. constr. from מוֹרָשׁ dec. 1 b (exc. sing. constr. מוֹרַשׁ § 31. rem. 1)	ירשׁ
מוֹרָשֵׁיהֶם	id. pl. with suff. 3 pers. pl. masc.	ירשׁ
מוֹרֶשֶׁת	pr. name in compos. מוֹרֶשֶׁת גַּת	ירשׁ

I. [מוּשׁ] I. to move, withdraw, depart.—II. to remove, put away, Zec. 3. 9. Hiph.—I. to let remove, go on

a Is. 1. 14.   f Is. 8. 23.   p Ec. 7. 26.   y Je. 38. 23.   Nu. 24. 8.   j Job 36. 16.   Ps. 64. 6.   Is. 8. 13.   Ca. 5. 1.
b Da. 12. 7.   g Ps. 66. 11.   q Ps. 19. 7.   z 2 Sa. 3. 25.   Zec. 4. 2.   Ca. 5. 5, 5, 13.   1 Ki. 7. 29.   1 Sa. 2. 6.
c Je. 24. 1.   h 1 Ki. 10. 18.   r Je. 38. 22.   a Ne. 6. 19.   Mi. 5. 1.   Le. 6. 2.   Mal. 2. 5.   Ju. 16. 17.   Is. 30. 20, 20.
d Ps. 74. 4.   i Ps. 78. 43.   s Nu. 14. 37.   b Ge. 38. 25.   2 Ch. 9. 28.   Is. 33. 14.   Zep. 3. 1.   Ps. 9. 21.   De. 9. 4, 5.
e Is. 33. 20.   k Joel 3. 3.   t Nu. 33. 2.   c Eze. 12. 11.   Nu. 26. 22.   Am. 3. 5.   Is. 8. 12.   Is. 18. 2, 7.   Job 17. 11.
Pr. 25. 19.   l Pr. 25. 19.   u Eze. 42. 11.   d Is. 54. 16; Pr. 10. 18.   Is. 8. 13.   Is. 18. 6.   Mal. 1. 6.   Pr. 5. 13.   Ob. 1. 17.
Je. 16. 19.   m Ps. 135. 7.   w Eze. 43. 11.

escape, hence to *withdraw*, Na. 3. 1; Mi. 2. 3.—
II. *to withdraw, depart.*

II. [מוּשׁ] i. q. מָשַׁשׁ *to feel, touch,* Ge. 27. 21. Hiph. id.
Ps. 115. 7; Ju. 16. 26, Keri.

מוּשִׁי, מֹשִׁי (*tried*) pr. name masc.—Patronym.
מוּשִׁי for מוּשִׁיִּי.

מוֹשָׁב	noun masc. sing. dec. 2 b .	ישב
מוֹשַׁב	’i id., constr. st.; i bef. lab. .	ישב
מוֹשָׁבוֹ	id., suff. 3 pers. sing. masc. .	ישב
מוֹשְׁבוֹתֵיהֶם	id. pl. fem., suff. 3 pers. pl. masc.	ישב
מוֹשְׁבוֹתֵיכֶם	id. id., suff. 2 pers. pl. masc. .	ישב
מוֹשְׁבֹתָם	id. id., suff. 3 pers. pl. masc. (§ 4. rem. 2)	ישב
מוֹשָׁבִי	id. sing., suff. 1 pers. sing. .	ישב
מוֹשְׁבֵי	id. pl. constr. st. .	ישב
מוּשָׁבִים	Hoph. part. masc., pl. of מוּשָׁב’ .	שוב
מוֹשָׁבֶךָ	noun masc. sing., suff. 2 pers. sing. masc.	
	(for שִׁבְךָ’) from מוֹשָׁב dec. 2 b	ישב
מוֹשְׁבָם	id., suff. 3 pers. pl. masc. .	ישב
מוֹשְׁבֹתֵיהֶם	id. pl. fem., suff. 3 pers. pl. masc.	ישב
מוֹשְׁבֹתֵיכֶם	id. id., suff. 2 pers. pl. masc. .	ישב
מוֹשְׁבֹתָם	id. sing., suff. 3 pers. pl. masc. (§ 4. rem. 2)	ישב
מוֹשִׁי	’i pr. name masc.; i bef. lab. .	מוש
מוֹשִׁיב	Hiph. part. sing. masc. .	ישב
מוֹשִׁיבִי	id. constr. with parag. ’i .	ישב
מוֹשִׁיעַ	’i Hiph. part. sing. masc. dec. 1 b; i bef. lab.	ישע
מוֹשִׁיעוֹ	id., suff. 3 pers. sing. masc. .	ישע
מוֹשִׁיעִים	id. pl., abs. st. .	ישע
מוֹשִׁיעֶךָ	} id. sing., suff. 2 pers. sing. masc. .	ישע
מוֹשִׁיעֵךְ	id. sing., suff. 2 pers. sing. fem. .	ישע
מוֹשִׁיעָם	id. sing., suff. 3 pers. pl. masc. .	ישע
מוֹשְׁכוֹת	noun fem., pl. of מוֹשֶׁכֶת’ dec. 13 .	משך
מוֹשֵׁל	’i Kal part. act. sing. masc. dec. 7 b; i bef. lab.	משל
מוֹשַׁעֲךָ	defect. for מוֹשִׁיעֲךָ (q. v.) *Je. 46. 27	ישע

[מוּת] pret. מֵת, 1 pers. מַתִּי (§ 21. rem. 2, & 25. rem.)
—I. *to die,* both naturally and by violence; with
בְּ, מִפְּנֵי of the cause; part. מֵת *a dead person.*—
II. *to perish, be destroyed,* of a state. Pil. מוֹתֵת *to
kill, slay.* Hiph. הֵמִית, 1 pers. הֵמַתִּי (§ 25. rem.),
to put to death, kill, slay. Hoph. הוּמַת *to be put
to death.*

מָוֶת masc. dec. 6 g.—I. *death;* כְּלֵי מָוֶת *weapons
of death;* אִישׁ מָוֶת, בֶּן־מָוֶת *guilty of death;*
מִשְׁפַּט מָוֶת *sentence of death.*—II. *the grave.*
חַדְרֵי מָוֶת, שַׁעֲרֵי מָוֶת *gates, chambers of hell.*—
III. *pestilence.*—IV. *destruction, ruin.*

מוֹת Chald., masc. *death,* Ezr. 7. 26.

מוּת masc. id. Ps. 48. 15; מוּת לַבֵּן in the title
of Ps. 9, signification not known; Gesenius (without sufficient ground) proposes the reading of
עַלְמוּת *female voices* (see עַלְמָה) for the first
passage, and עֹלְמוּת *eternity,* for the second.

מָמוֹת masc. dec. 3 a, only pl. מְמוֹתִים—I. *deaths,*
Je. 16. 4; Eze. 28. 8.—II. as a concrete, *the dead,
slain,* 2 Ki. 11. 2, Kheth.

תְּמוּתָה fem. *death;* only בֶּן־תִּ’ *condemned to
death,* Ps. 79. 11; 102. 21.

מוֹת	’i noun masc. sing. dec. 6 g; for i see lett. i	מות
מוֹת	id. constr. st.; or Kal inf. abs. .	מות
מוֹתי	noun masc. sing. or inf., but see under the Root	מות
מוֹתָהּ	noun m. s., suff. 3 pers. s. fem. from מָוֶת d. 6 g	מות
מוֹתָהּ	Kal inf. (מֹת’), suff. 3 pers. sing. fem. dec. 1 a	מות
מוֹתוֹ	noun m. s., suff. 3 pers. s. m. from מָוֶת d. 6 g	מות
מוֹתֵי	id. pl., constr. st. .	מות
מוֹתִי	id. sing., suff. 1 pers. sing. .	מות
מוֹתִי	Kal inf. (מֹת’), suff. 1 pers. sing. dec. 1 a	מות
מוֹתֵנוּ	id. with suff. 1 pers. pl. .	מות
מוֹתַר	noun masc. sing. dec. 2 b .	יתר
מוֹתַר	i id. constr. st.; i bef. lab. .	יתר
מוֹתְתַנִי	Pilel pret. 3 pers. s. m. [מוֹתֵת], suff. 1 pers. s.	מות
מֹתְתֵנִי	i id. imp. sing. masc. [מוֹתֵת], suff. 1 pers.	
	sing.; i bef. lab. .	מות
מֵאֲבֵי	pref. מ’ X noun m. pl. constr. from זְאֵב d. 1 a	זאב
מִזֹּאת	pref. id. X pron. demon. fem. sing., see	זה
מִזְּבוּל	pref. id. X noun masc. sing. dec. 1 a .	זבל
מִזְּבוּלֻן	i pref. id. X pr. name of a tribe; i bef. lab.	זבל
מְזַבֵּחַ	Piel part. sing. masc. .	זבח
מִזְבֵּחַ	pref. מ’ X Seg. noun in pause for זֶבַח [as if	
	from זָבַח § 35. r. 2] but with suff. זִבְחִי’	זבח
מִזְבַּח	i noun masc. sing., constr. of מִזְבֵּחַ dec. 7 c	זבח
מִזְבְּחָה	pref. מ’ X n. m. s. (suff. זִבְחִי’) d. 6 a (§ 35. r. 5)	זבח
מִזְבֵּחַ	noun masc. sing. dec. 7 c .	זבח
מִזְבְּחוֹ	id. with suff. 3 pers. sing. masc. .	זבח
מִזְבְּחוֹ	pref. מ’ X noun masc. sing., suff. 3 pers. sing.	
	masc. from זֶבַח dec. 6 a (§ 35. rem. 5)	זבח
מְזַבְּחוֹת	i Piel part. fem. pl. [of מְזַבַּחַת or מְזַבְּחָה]	
	i bef. lab. .	זבח
מִזְבְּחוֹת	noun masc. with pl. fem. term. fr. מִזְבֵּחַ d. 7 c	זבח
מִזְבְּחוֹתֵיהֶם	id., suff. 3 pers. pl. masc. .	זבח
מִזְבְּחוֹתֶיךָ	id., suff. 2 pers. s. masc. .	זבח
מִזְבְּחוֹתֵיכֶם	id., suff. 2 pers. pl. masc. .	זבח
מִזְבְּחוֹתָם	id., suff. 3 p. pl. m. K. חֹתָם’; Kh. חֹתִים’	זבח
	with a double pl. comp. בָּמוֹתַי מְרֵאשֹׁתַי	זבח

a Eze. 6. 14.	e Eze. 34. 13.	i 1 Ch. 4. 33.	n Is. 43. 3.	r 2 Sa. 6. 23.	x 2 Sa. 19. 1.	b Je. 20. 17.	f Is. 63. 15.	1 Ki. 11. 8.
b Eze. 6. 6.	f Je. 27. 16.	k Ps. 68. 7.	o Ps. 106. 21.	s 1 Sa. 4. 20.	y Ex. 16. 3.	c Ju. 9. 54.	g 1 Ki. 3. 3.	Ps. 84. 4.
c 1 Ch. 6. 39.	g Ge. 10. 30.	l Ps. 113. 9.	p Job 38. 31.	t Ge. 27. 10, etc.	z Pr. 14. 23.	d Hab. 1. 8.	h Pr. 21. 3.	2 Ch. 34. 5.
d Job 29. 7.	h Eze. 37. 23.	m Je. 14. 8.	q Ps. 9. 1; 48. 15.	u Eze. 28. 10.	a Ec. 3. 19.	e 2 Sa. 6. 22.	i Ex. 34. 15.	Jer. 30. 10.

מִזְבְּחוֹתָם	id., suff. 3 pers. pl. masc. (§ 4. rem. 2) .	זבח
מִזְבְּחִי	id. sing., suff. 1 pers. sing.	זבח
מִזְבְּחֵי	pref. מ) noun masc. pl. constr. from זֶבַח dec. 6a (§ 35. rem. 5)	זבח
מִזְבְּחִי	pref. id.) id. sing. with suff. 1 pers. sing.	זבח
מְזַבְּחִים	Piel part. masc., pl. of זָבַח dec. 7b	זבח
מִזְבַּחֲךָ / מִזְבְּחֶךָ	} noun masc. sing., suff. 2 pers. sing. masc. from מִזְבֵּחַ dec. 7c {	זבח
מִזְבְּחֹת	id. pl. fem. comp.	זבח
מִזְבְּחֹתָו	id. id., suff. 3 pers. sing. m. (K. תָּיו § 4. r. 1)	זבח
מִזְבְּחֹתֵיהֶם	id. id., suff. 3 pers. pl. masc.	זבח
מִזְבְּחֹתָיו	id. id., suff. 3 pers. sing. masc.	זבח
מִזְבְּחֹתֶיךָ	id. id., suff. 2 pers. sing. masc.	זבח
מִזְבְּחֹתָם	id. id., suff. 3 pers. pl. masc. (§ 4. rem. 2)	זבח
מִזְבְּחֹתָם	noun masc. with pl. fem. term. & suff. 3 pers. pl. m. (§ 4. r. 2) fr. זֶבַח d. 6a (§ 35. r. 5)	זבח
מִזְבֻּל	defect. for זְבֻל (q. v.)	זבל
מִזְבֻּלֻן	pref. מ) pr. name of a tribe, see זְבוּלֻן	זבל
מֶזֶג	Root not used; i. q. מָסַךְ to mix.	
מֶזֶג	masc. mixed wine, Ca. 7. 3.	
מְזָרִים	pref. מ) adj. masc., pl. of זָר dec. 1a (§ 21. rem. 2, & § 30. No. 3)	זוד
מָזָה	Root not used; i. q. מָצָה, מָצַץ to suck, suck out.	
מָזֶה	adj. masc. dec. 9b, sucking, only De. 32. 24, מְזֵי רָעָב sucking famine, i. e. exhausted with famine.	
מַזֶּה	4 Hiph. part. sing. masc., constr. of [מַזֶּה] dec. 9a (§ 25. No. 2a); 4 bef. lab.	נזה
מַזֶּה	contr. for מַה־זֶּה see	מה
מֵזָה	4 (fear; Root מזה i. q. מָסַס q. v.) pr. name masc. Ge. 36. 13, 17.	
מִזֶּה	4 pref. מ) pron. demon. masc. sing., as an adv.; 4 bef. lab.	זה
מִזָּהָב	4 pref. id.) noun masc. sing. d. 4a; 4 id.	זהב
מִזְהַב	pref. id.) id. constr. st.	זהב
מִזְהָבִי	pref. id.) id. with suff. 1 pers. sing.	זהב
מִזּוֹב	pref. id.) noun masc. sing. dec. 1a	זוב
מִזּוֹבָהּ	pref. id.) id., suff. 3 pers. sing. fem.	זוב
מִזּוֹבוֹ	pref. id.) id., suff. 3 pers. sing. masc.	זוב
מְזוּזוֹת	noun fem., pl. of מְזוּזָה dec. 10	זוז
מְזוּזַת	id. sing., constr. st.	זוז
מְזֻזֹת	id. pl., defect. for מְזוּזוֹת	זוז
מְזוּזָתִי	id. sing., suff. 1 pers. sing.	זוז
מְזוּזֹתָם	4 id. sing., suff. 3 pers. pl. masc.; 4 bef. lab.	זוז
מְזוֹנֵינוּ	noun masc. pl., suff. 1 pers. pl. fr. [מָזוֹן] d. 6	זוה

מְזֹלֵל	pref. מ) Kal part. act. sing. masc. dec. 7b	זלל
מָזוֹן	4 Ch. & Heb. noun masc. sing.; 4 bef. lab.	זון
מְזוֹנָה	pref. מ) Kal part. act. s. f. d. 10, fr. זֹנָה m.	זנה
מָזוֹר	noun masc. sing. dec. 3a	זור
מְזֹרָה	[for מְזֹרָה] Pual part. sing. f. [of מְזֹרָה m.]	זרה
מְזֻזוֹת	defect. for מְזוּזוֹת (q. v.)	זוז
מֵזַח, מָזִיחַ	masc. a girdle, Ps. 109. 19; Is. 23. 10.	
מִזֵּי	adj. pl. constr. masc. from [מָזֶה] dec. 9a	מזה
מָזִין	pref. מ) noun masc. sing.	זון
מָזִיחַ	4 noun masc. sing.; 4 bef. lab.	מזח
מַזִּין	Hiph. part. sing. masc. [for מַאֲזִין § 19. r. 8]	אזן
מַזְכִּיר	Hiph. part. sing. masc. dec. 1b	זכר
מַזְכֵּר	pref. מ) noun masc. sing. dec. 4a	זכר
מַזְכֶּרֶת	Hiph. part. s., fem. of מַזְכִּיר (§ 39. No. 4d)	זכר
מִזְלַנֹתָיו	4 noun fem. pl., suff. 3 pers. sing. masc. from [מִזְלָנָה] dec. 11a; 4 bef. lab.	זלג
מְזִמָּה	4 noun fem. sing. dec. 10; 4 id.	זמם
מִזְמוֹר	noun masc. sing.	זמר
מְזִמּוֹת	4 noun fem., pl. of מְזִמָּה d. 10, 4 bef. lab.	זמם
מְזִמּוֹתָיו	id. with suff. 3 pers. sing. masc.	זמם
מְזֻמָּנוֹת	Pual part. f. pl. [of מְזֻמָּנָה from מְזֻמָּן m.]	זמן
מְזֻמָּנִים	id. masc., pl. of [מְזֻמָּן] dec. 2b	זמן
מַזְמֵרוֹת	noun fem., pl. of [מַזְמֵרָה] dec. 13	זמר
מַזְמְרוֹתֵיכֶם	4 noun fem. pl., suff. 2 pers. pl. masc. from [מַזְמֵרָה] dec. 11b; 4 bef. lab.	זמר
מִזְמֶרֶת	pref. מ) noun f. s., constr. of זִמְרָה (no pl.)	זמר
מִזְמָתוֹ	noun f. s., suff. 3 p. s. m. from מְזִמָּה d. 10	זמם
מִזָּן	pref. מ) noun masc. s., pl. זָנִים (§ 36. r. 5)	זן
מִזָּנִי	pref. id.) noun m. pl. constr. fr. [זָנִין] d. 1a	זנה
מְזַעְזְעֶיךָ	Pilp. (§ 6. No. 4) part. pl. masc., suff. 2 pers. sing. masc. [from מְזַעֲזֵעַ § 36. rem. 5]	זוע
מִזַּעַם	pref. מ) noun masc. sing. dec. 6d	זעם
מִזַּעְפּוֹ	pref. id.) noun masc. sing., suff. 3 pers. sing. masc. from זַעַף dec. 6d (§ 35. rem. 5)	זעף
מִזְעֹק	pref. id.) Kal inf. constr.	זעק
מִזַּעֲקַת	pref. id.) noun fem. sing., constr. of זְעָקָה dec. 11c (§ 42. rem. 1)	זעק
מִזְעָר	noun masc. sing.	זער
מִזָּקֵן	pref. מ) Heb. noun masc. sing.	זקן
מִזִּקְנֵי	4 pref. id.) adj. or subst. masc. pl. constr. from זָקֵן dec. 5a; 4 bef. lab.	זקן
מִזְּקֵנִים	pref. מ) id. pl., abs. st.	זקן
מְזֻקָּק	Pual part. sing. masc. dec. 2b	זקק
מְזֻקָּקִים	id. pl., abs. st.	זקק
מִזָּרָה	constr. of the foll.	זרה

a Eze. 39. 19.   b Ho. 4. 19.   c Eze. 16. 17.   d Eze. 43. 8.   e Pr. 1. 17.   f Pr. 17. 4.   g Ps. 10. 4.   h Je. 51. 11.   i Jon. 1. 15.
k De. 33. 10.   l Ps. 49. 15.   m Eze. 16. 17.   n Le. 15. 30.   o De. 6. 9.   p Nu. 5. 3.   q Nu. 13. 31.   r Ps. 144. 13.   s Ge. 48. 10.
t Nu. 23. 1, 14, 29.   u Ps. 19. 14.   v Le. 15. 28.   w Je. 15. 19.   x Nu. 5. 15.   y 2 Ki. 12. 14.   z Eze. 23. 11.   a Je. 19. 1.
b Ex. 11. 18.   c Nu. 19. 21.   d Le. 13. 13, 15.   e Ps. 45. 23.   f Ex. 27. 3.   g Joel 4. 10.   h Hab. 1. 2.   i Is. 25. 6.
k De. 7. 5.   l Ex. 4. 2.   m Pr. 8. 34.   n Da. 4. 9, 18.   o Job 12. 21.   p Job 21. 27.   q Ge. 43. 11.   r Ho. 7. 16.   s Je. 31. 12.
t 1 Ki. 19. 10, 14.   u Pr. 22. 1.   v Eze. 43. 8.   w Eze. 16. 41.   x 1 Sa. 7. 8.

מְזָרֶה Piel part. sing. masc. dec. 9 a .   זרה

מְזוֹרוֹ noun m. s., suff. 3 pers. s. m. from מָזוֹר d. 3 a   זור

מִזְרוֹעַ pref. מְ)(noun com. sing. dec. 1 a .   זרע

מְזָרוֹת noun pl. fem. .   מזר

מִזְרָח noun masc. sing. dec. 2 b .   זרח

מִזְרַח id., constr. st. .   זרח

מִזְרָחָה id. abs. & constr. with loc. ה ; bef.
מִזְרָחָה } lab. .   זרח

מַזְרִיעַ Hiph. part. sing. masc. .   זרע

מִזְרָם pref. מִ)(noun masc. sing. .   זרם

מִזְרָע pref. id.)(noun masc. sing. (suff. זַרְעוֹ)
dec. 6 a (§ 35. rem. 5) ; bef. lab.   זרע

מִזְרַע noun masc. sing., constr. of [מִזְרָע] dec. 2 b   זרע

מִזְרָעוֹ pref. מִ)(noun masc., suff. 3 pers. sing.
masc. from זֶרַע d. 6 a (§ 35 r.5); bef. lab.   זרע

מִזְרָעֶךָ pref. id.)(id., suff. 2 pers. sing. m. ; id.   זרע

מִזְרָעָם pref. id.)(id., suff. 3 pers. pl. masc. .   זרע

מִזְרָק noun masc. sing. dec. 2 b   זרק

מִזְרָקוֹת id. with pl. fem. term. abs.   זרק

מִזְרְקֵי id. pl. constr. masc. .   זרק

מִזְרְקֹתָיו id. with pl. f. term.& suff. 3 p. s. m.; bef. lab.   זרק

מֹחַ noun masc. sing. ; id. .   מחח

[מָחָא] to strike, clap the hands, exultingly. Pi. id. Eze.
25. 6.

מְחָא Ch. to strike, smite. Pa. id. with בִּיַד to
strike upon the hand, i. e. to hinder, restrain, Da.
4. 32. Ithpe. to be fastened or nailed to, with
עַל, Ezr. 6. 11.

מָחָא or מַחְיָא Ch. by Syriasm [for מַחְיָא] Aph.
part. sing. masc.   חיה

מַחֲאֲךָ Piel inf. [מָחָא § 14. rem. 1], suff. 2 pers.
sing. masc. dec. 7 b (§ 36. rem. 3) .   מחא

מְחַבֵּל pref. מְ for מִ)(noun m. s. d. 6 (§ 35. r. 6)   חבל

מְחַבֵּל pref. id.)(noun masc. sing. dec. 6 a (pl. c.
חֶבְלֵי & חַבְלֵי § 35. rem. 4)   חבל

מְחַבְּלִים Piel part. masc., pl. of [מְחַבֵּל] dec. 7 b   חבל

מְחַבֵּק pref. מְ for מִ)(Piel inf. constr. .   חבק

מַחְבְּרוֹן pref. id.)(pr. name of a place   חבר

מַחְבְּרֶיךָ pref. id.)(n. m. pl.,suff. 2 p. s. m. fr. חָבֵר d. 5 c   חבר

מַחְבַּרְתּוֹ noun f. s., suff. 3 p. s. m. from מַחְבֶּרֶת d. 13 a   חבר

מְחַבֵּשׁ Piel part. sing. masc. ; bef. lab.   חבש

מַחֲבַת noun fem. sing. [for מַחֲבַתְ] .   חבת

מַחֲגֹרֶת noun fem. sing. .   חגר

מְחַדֵּל pref. מְ for מִ)(Kal inf. constr. .   חדל

מְחַדְּרוֹ pref. id.)(noun masc. sing., suff. 3 pers. sing.
masc. from חֶדֶר, dec. 6 a (§ 35. rem. 4)   חדר

מְחָדָרִים pref. מְ for מִ)(id., pl., abs. st. ; bef. lab.   חדר

מְחֻדָּשׁ pref. id.)(noun masc. sing. dec. 6 c ; id.   חדש

מָחָה I. to strike, wipe out or away.—II. to blot out,
destroy.—III. with עַל to strike upon, reach unto,
Nu. 34. 11. Niph (fut. ap. יִמַּח § 24. rem. 10)
to be blotted out, destroyed. Pi. not used; i. q.
Arab. مخح to take out the marrow; hence Pu.
part. מְמֻחָי (§ 38. rem. 1) taken from the marrow,
Is. 25. 6. Hiph. (fut. ap. תֶּמַח § 24. rem. 16)
to blot out, destroy.

מָחָה fem. מָחָה (dec. 11 a) destroying, cor-
rupting, Pr. 31. 3, לַמְחוֹת מְלָכִין to (women)
destroying kings. לַמְחוֹת for לִמְחוֹת, not for
לְהַמְחוֹת, לַמְחוֹת, unless this is supposed to be
one of the exceptions where the article stands
with the noun in the constr. st.

מְחִי masc. a striking, of battering-rams, Eze.
26. 9.

מְחוּיָאֵל, מְחִיָּיאֵל (smitten of God) pr. name
masc. Ge. 4. 18.

מָחֹה Kal inf. abs. .   מחה

מְחֵה id. imp. sing. masc. .   מחה

מֹחֶה id. part. act. sing. masc. .   מחה

מְחוֹז noun masc. sing., constr. of [מָחוֹז] dec. 3 a   חוז

מָחוּט pref. מִ)(noun masc. sing. .   חוט

מְחוּיָאֵל pr. name masc. .   מחה

מַחֲוִילָה pref. מֵ for מִ)(pr. name of a region, see חֲוִילָה

מָחוֹלָה noun masc. sing. dec. 3 a, also pr. name;
bef. lab.   חול

מְחוֹל pref. מֵ for מִ)(noun masc. sing.   חול

מְחוֹלָה see אָבֵל מְחוֹלָה under אבל

מְחֹלֵל Poal part. sing. masc. .   חלל

מְחוֹלֵל Pilel part. sing. masc. .   חול

מְחוֹלֶלֶת Poel part. sing. fem. [of מְחוֹלֵל masc.]   חלל

מְחוֹלְלֵנוּ noun masc. sing., suff. 1 pers. pl. from
מְחוֹל dec. 3 a   חול

מְחוֹמַת pref. מֵ for מִ)(noun fem. sing., constr. of
חוֹמָה dec. 10 .   חמה

מְחוֹנֵן Poel part. sing. masc. ; bef. lab.   חנן

מְחוּץ pref. מִ)(noun fem. sing. dec. 1 a ; id.   חוץ

מְחוּצָה pref. id.)(id. with loc. ה ; id.   חוץ

מְחוּצוֹת pref. מֵ for מִ)(id. pl. ; id.   חוץ

מַחֲוֹת pref. id.)(Piel inf. constr.   חוה

מַחֲזֵה noun masc. sing., constr. of [מַחֲזֶה] dec. 9 a   חזה

מַחֲזֶה noun fem. sing.; bef. lab. .   חזה

a Pr. 20. 8, 26.   e Ge. 1. 11, 12.   i Est. 9. 28.   n Eze. 25. 6.   r Ps. 45. 8.   v De. 32. 25.   z Is. 43. 25.   f Pr. 25. 10.   * Eze. 40. 40, 44.
b Ho. 5. 13.   f Da. 1. 3.   k Is. 19. 7.   o Nu.7.13,19,&c.   s Ps. 147. 3.   w Est. 3. 7.   g Ps. 107. 30.   k Is. 51. 9.   y Je. 7. 34.
c Job 35. 9.   g Is. 19. 7.   l Ex. 27. 3.   p Jos. 19. 29.   t Is. 3. 24.   x Ge. 14. 23.   h Ps. 150. 4.   m Job 32. 6.
d Job 38. 32.   h 2 Sa. 4. 8.   m Job 21. 24.   q Jos. 19. 9.   u 1 Sa. 12. 26.   y Joel 2. 16.   i 1 Sa. 31. 12   n 1 Ki. 7. 4, 4, 5.
De. 3. 27.   d Le. 18. 21.   Da. 5. 19.   Eze. 2. 5.   Ps. 51. 3, 11.   Is. 52. 5.   Pr. 14. 21.

מֶחֱזוֹן	pref. מ for מ)(noun masc. sing. dec. 3 a	חזה
מַחֲזִיאֹת	pr. name masc.	חזה
מֶחֱזְיוֹנוֹת	pref. id)(noun masc. with pl. fem. term. from חִזָּיוֹן dec. 3 c; ִ bef. lab.	חזה
מַחֲזִינוּ	pref. id.)(id. sing., suff. 3 pers. sing. masc.	חזה
מַחֲזִיק	ִ Hiph. part. sing. masc. d. 1 b; ִ bef. lab.	חזק
מַחֲזִיקֵי	id. pl. constr. st.	חזק
מַחֲזִיקִים	ִ id. pl., abs. st.; ִ bef. lab.	חזק
מַחֲזָק	pref. מ for מ)(adj. masc. sing. dec. 4 c (but pl. c. (חֲזָקִ	חזק
מְחַזֵּק	Piel part. sing. masc. dec. 7 b	חזק
מַחֲזִיקָהִ	ִ Hiph. part. sing. masc. (מַחֲזִיק), suff. 3 pers. sing. fem. dec. 1 a	חזק
מְחַזְּקִים	Piel part. masc., pl. of מְחַזֵּק dec. 7 b	חזק
מַחֲזֶקֶת	Hiph. part. sing., f. of מַחֲזִיק (§ 39. No. 4d)	חזק

מָחַח   Root not used; to be marrowy.

    מֵחַ adj. masc. dec. 1 a.—I. fat, Ps. 66. 15.—II. rich, Is. 5. 17.

    מֹחַ masc. marrow, Job 21. 24.

מֵחֲטֹא	pref. מ for מ)(Piel inf. constr.	חטא
מֵחֲטֹא	pref. id.)(Kal inf. constr.	חטא
מֵחַטֹּאות	pref. id.)(noun fem. pl. constr. from חַטָּאת see מֵחַטֹּאת	חטא
מֵחַטֹּאַי	pref. id.)(noun masc. pl., suff. 1 pers. sing. from חַטָּא dec. 6 (§ 35. rem. 6)	חטא
מֵחַטֹּאת	pref. id.)(noun fem. s. [for חַטָּאת] constr. of חַטָּאה see חַטָּא (§ 39. No.4d, & §44. r.5)	חטא
מֵחַטֹּאת	pref. id.)(id. pl. [for חַטָּאות] constr. of חַטָּאות	חטא
מֵחַטֹּאתוֹ	pref. id.)(id. sing., suff. 3 pers. sing. masc.	חטא
מֵחַטֹּאתִי	ִ pref. id.)(id. sing., suff. 1 p. s.; ִ bef. lab.	חטא
מֵחַטֹּאתָם	ִ pref. id.)(id., suff. 3 pers. pl. m.; ִ id.	חטא
מֵחֹטֵב	pref. id.)(Kal part act. sing. masc.	חטב
מַחְשְׁבוֹת	Pual part. pl. f. [of מַחְשָׁבָה from מַחְשָׁב m.]	חטב
מֵחֲטוֹ מֵחֲטוֹא	} pref. מ for מ)(Kal inf. constr. (§ 23. r. 2)	חטא
מַחֲטִיאֵי	Hiph. part. pl. constr. m. from מַחֲטִיא d. 1 b	חטא
מְחִידָא	pr. name masc.	חוד
מֵחִי	ִ noun masc. sing.; ִ bef. lab.	מחה
מְחַיֶּה	ִ Piel part. sing. masc.; ִ id.	חיה
מְחִיָּה	noun masc. sing. dec. 10	חיה
מְחִיַּי	pref. מ for מ)(noun masc. pl., suff. 1 pers. sing. from חַי dec. 8 d (§ 37. rem. 6)	חיי
מְחִיָּיאֵל	ִ pr. name masc., see מְחוּיָאֵל; ִ bef. lab.	
מֵחַיִּים	pref. מ for מ)(n. m., pl. of חַי d. 8 d (§37. r.6)	חיי
מְחִיל	pref. id.)(noun masc. sing. dec. 6h	חול

מֵחִים	adj. masc. pl. [of מֵחַ]	מחח
מֵחֻקִּים	ִ pref. מ for מ)(noun m. s. d. 1 a; ִ bef. lab.	חוק
מֵחֻקָּהּ	pref. id.)(id., suff. 3 pers. sing. fem.	חוק
מֵחֻקּוֹ	pref. id.)(id., suff. 3 pers. sing. masc.	חוק
מָחִיר	ִ n. m. s. d. 1 a, also pr. name m.; ִ bef. lab	מחר
מְחִירָהּ	id., suff. 3 pers. sing. fem.	
מָחִיתָ	Kal pret. 2 pers. sing. masc.	מחה
מִחְיַת	ִ pref. מ for מ)(noun fem. sing., constr. of חַיָּה dec. 10, from חַי masc.; ִ bef. lab.	חיי
מִחְיַת	ִ noun fem. s., constr. of מִחְיָה d. 10; ִ id.	חיה
מָחִיתִי	ִ Kal pret. 1 pers. sing.; ִ id.	מחה
מְחִיתְךָ	ִ n. f. s., suff. 2 p. s. m. fr. מִחְיָה d.10; ִ id.	חיה
מַחְכִּימַת	Hiph. part. constr. f. [of מַחְכִּימָה fr. מַחְכִּים m.]	חכם
מֶחְכַּם	ִ pref. מ for מ)(adj. masc. sing. dec. 4 c	חכם
מֻחְכָּם	Hoph. part. sing. masc.	חכם
מַחְכְּמָה	pref. מ for מ)(noun fem. sing. (no pl.)	חכם
מֻחְכָּמִים	Hoph. part. masc., pl. of מֻחְכָּם	חכם
מַחְכְּמַת	ִ pref. מ for מ)(n.f.s.constr. of חָכְמָה (no pl.)	חכם
מַחְלִיל	Hiph. part. sing. masc.	חלל
מֵחָלָב	pref. מ for מ)(noun masc. sing. dec. 4 c	חלב
מֵחָלָב מֵחֵלֶב	} pref. id.)(noun masc. sing. dec. 6 (§ 35. rem. 6)	חלב
מֵחֶלְבְּהֶן	ִ pref. id.)(id. pl., suff. 3 pers. pl. fem [for בֵּיהֶן § 4. rem. 1]; ִ bef. lab.	חלב
מַחְלֵד	pref. id.)(noun masc. sing. d. 6 (§ 35. r. 4)	חלד
מַחְלְדִי	pref. id.)(pr. name masc.	חלד
מַחְלָה	noun fem. sing.; or (Pr. 13. 12) Hiph part. fem. [of מַחֲלֶה masc.]	חלה
מַחְלָה	pr. name fem.	חלה
מַחֲלֵהוּ	noun m. s., suff. 3 p. s. m. from מַחֲלֶה d. 9a	חלה
מַחְלוֹן	ִ pr. name masc.; ִ bef. lab.	חלה
מַחְלִי	pr. name masc.	חלה
מַחְלִי	pref. מ for מ)(noun masc. sing. dec. 6k	חלה
מַחְלִיוֹ	pref. id.)(id., suff. 3 pers. sing. masc.	חלה
מַחֲלִיק	Hiph. part. sing. masc.	חלק
מְחַלֵּל	Piel part. sing. masc. dec. 7 b	חלל
מֵחַלְּלוֹ	pref. מ for מ)(Piel inf. (חַלֵּל), suff. 3 pers. sing. masc. dec. 7 b	חלל
מְחֹלְלִי	pref. id.)(adj. pl. constr. masc. fr. חָלָל d. 3 c	חלל
מְחֹלָלִי	Pual part. pl. constr. masc. from [מְחֹלָל] dec. 2 b (§ 10. rem. 7)	חלל
מְחֹלְלֶיהָ	the foll. with suff. 3 pers. sing. f. (§ 10. r. 7)	חלל
מְחֹלְלִים	ִ Piel part. m., pl. of מְחֹלֵל d. 7 b; ִ bef. lab.	חלל
מְחֹלֶלְךָ	id. s., suff. 2 pers. s. m. [for מְחֹלֶלְךָ § 10. r. 7]	חלל

ᵃ Mi. 3. 6.	ᵈ Ex. 14. 17.	ʰ Ps. 51. 11.	ᵖ Ps. 144. 12.	ᶠ Jon. 4. 3,8.	ˢ Ps. 9. 6.	ᶜ Je. 18. 18.	ᵇ Ge. 4. 4.	ⁱ Is. 56. 2, 6.
ᵇ Job 4.13; 7.14.	ᵉ Da. 11. 6.	ⁱ La. 4. 6.	ᑫ Ge. 20. 6.	ᵍ Ps. 84. 8.	ᵗ Job 5. 22.	ᵈ Ps. 58. 6.	ᵏ Ps. 17. 14.	ᵐ La. 4. 9.
Zec. 13. 4.	2 Ki. 12. 8.	2 Ki. 13. 6.	Ps. 39. 2.	Is. 5. 17.	Le. 13. 10, 24.	Pr. 30. 24.	Pr. 18. 31.	Eze. 32. 26.
2 Sa. 3. 29.	Ne. 4. 11.	Ps. 51. 4.	Is. 29. 21.	Is. 44. 22.	1 Ki. 5. 10.	Is. 38. 9.	Ex. 31. 14.
Is. 27. 9, 27.	1 Sa. 12. 23.	2 Ch. 6. 26.	Eze. 26. 9.	Ju. 17. 10.	Is. 25. 29.	Is. 41. 7.	Ne. 13. 17.
Is. 56. 4, 6.	1 Sa. 12. 23.	1 Ki. 8. 35.	Ne. 9. 6.	Ex. 4. 7.	Is. 34. 6, 6.	Eze. 24. 21.
Ps. 35. 10.	2 Ki 15. 9, 24.	De. 29. 10.	1 Sa. 2. 6.	Job 28. 15.

מְחֹלְלֶךָ	Pilel part. sing. masc., suff. 2 pers. sing. masc. [for מְחֹלֶלְךָ] from מְחוֹלֵל dec. 7 b . . חול
מְחֹלֶלֶת	Piel part. sing., fem. of מְחֹלֵל . . חלל
מַחֲלִמִים	Hiph. part. masc. pl. [of מַחֲלִם apoc. for § 11. rem. 8] מַחֲלִים . . חלם
מֵחַלָּמִישׁ	pref. מֵ for מִן n.m.s., constr. of חַלָּמִישׁ d. 3 c . . חלמש
מֵחֵלֶף	pref. id. ⟩(pr. name of a place . . חלף
מַחְלְפוֹת	noun fem. pl. constr. from [מַחְלָפָה] d. 11 a . . חלף
מַחֲלָפִים	noun masc. pl. [of מַחֲלָף] . . חלף
מַחֲלָצוֹת	noun fem., pl. of [מַחֲלָצָה] dec. 11 a . . חלץ
מֵחֲלָצֶיךָ	pref. מֵ for מִן ⟩(noun masc. du. (חֲלָצַיִם), suff. 2 pers. sing. masc. from [חָלָץ] d. 4 c . . חלץ
מֵחֵלֶק	pref. id. ⟩(Piel inf. constr. . . חלק
מַחְלְקוֹת	noun fem., pl. of מַחֲלֹקֶת dec. 13 c . . חלק
מַחְלְקוֹתָם	id., suff. 3 pers. pl. masc. . . חלק
מַחֲלֹקֶת	id. sing., abs. st. . . חלק
מֵחֶלְקַת	pref. מֵ for מִן ⟩(n. f., constr. of חֶלְקָה d. 12 b . . חלק
מֵחֶלְקָתוֹ	noun fem. sing., suff. 3 pers. sing. masc. from מַחֲלֹקֶת dec. 13 c ; bef. lab. . . חלק
מַחְלְקֹתָם	id. pl., suff. 3 pers. pl. masc. . . חלק
מַחֲלַת	noun fem. sing., also pr. name fem. . . חלה
מְחֹלֹת	noun fem., pl. of מְחֹלָה [for מְחוֹלָה] dec. 10 ; bef. lab. . . חול
מַחֲמָאֹת	noun fem., pl. of [מַחֲמָאָה] dec. 11 a . . חמא
מַחְמַד	noun masc. sing., constr. of [מַחְמָד] dec. 8 a . . חמד
מַחֲמַדֵּי	id. pl., constr. st. (§ 37. No. 3 c) . . חמד
מַחֲמַדַּי	id. pl., suff. 1 pers. sing. ; bef. lab. . . חמד
מַחֲמַדֶּיהָ	id. pl., suff. 3 pers. sing. fem. . . חמד
מַחֲמֻדֶּיהָ	noun masc. pl., suff. 3 pers. sing. fem. from [מַחְמֹד] dec. 8 c (§ 37. No. 3 c) . . חמד
מַחֲמֻדִּים	noun m., pl. of [מַחְמֹד] d. 8 a (§ 37. No. 3 c) . . חמד
מַחֲמַדֵּינוּ	id. pl. with suff. 1 pers. pl. . . חמד
מַחֲמוֹדֵּיהֶם	K. מַדֵּיהֶם id. pl. with suff., Kh. [for מַחְמֹד from מְדֵּיהֶם] dec. 8 c . . חמד
מַחְמַל	noun masc. sing., constr. of [מַחְמָל] dec. 2 b ; bef. lab. . . חמל
מֵחַמָּס	pref. מֵ for מִן ⟩(noun m. s. d. 4 c ; id. . . חמס
מֵחֲמַס	pref. id. ⟩(id., constr. st. . . חמס
מֵחֵמֶץ	pref. id. ⟩(noun masc. sing. . . חמץ
מַחֲמֶצֶת	noun fem. sing., formed from Hiph. part. . . חמץ
מֵחֹמֶר	pref. מֵ for מִן ⟩(noun masc. sing. dec. 6 c . . חמר
מֵחֲמֵשׁ	pref. id. ⟩(num. card. fem., constr. of חָמֵשׁ . . חמש
מֵחַמַּת	pref. id. ⟩(pr. name of a place . . חמם
מֵחֲמַת	pref. id. ⟩(pr. name of a place ; bef. lab. . . חמה

מֵחֲמַת	pref. מֵ for מִן ⟩(noun f. s., constr. of חֵמָה dec. 11 b ; bef. lab. . . יחם
מֵחֲמָתוֹ	pref. id. ⟩(noun fem. sing., suff. 3 pers. sing. masc. from חֵמָה dec. 10 . . חמם
מַחֲנֵה	constr. of the foll., and pr. name in compos. מַחֲנֵה דָן ; bef. lab. . . חנה
מַחֲנֶה	noun com. sing. dec. 9 a . . חנה
מַחֲנֵהוּ	id. with suff. 3 pers. sing. masc. . . חנה
מַחֲנוֹת	id. pl. with fem. term. . . חנה
מַחֲנִי	Kal imp. s. (מְחֵה), suff. 1 p. s. (§ 24. r. 21) . . מחה
מַחֲנֵיהֶם	noun com. sing., suff. 3 pers. pl. masc. from מַחֲנֶה dec. 9 a ; bef. lab. . . חנה
מַחֲנֶיךָ	id. pl., suff. 2 pers. sing. masc. . . חנה
מַחֲנֵיכֶם	id. pl., suff. 2 pers. pl. masc. . . חנה
מַחֲנַיִם / מַחֲנָיִם	} pr. name of a place . . חנה
מַחֲנָיְמָה	id. with parag. ה . . חנה
מַחֲנֶךָ	defect. for מַחֲנֶיךָ (q. v.) . . חנה
מַחֲנַק	noun masc. sing., constr. of [מַחֲנָק] dec. 2 b . . חנק
מֵחַנֵּק	Piel inf. constr. ; bef. lab. . . חנק
מַחְסֶה / מַחֲסֶה	} noun masc. sing. dec. 9 a . . חסה
מַחְסֵה	id., constr. st. . . חסה
מַחְסֵהוּ	id., suff. 3 pers. sing. masc. . . חסה
מַחְסוֹם	noun masc. sing. . . חסם
מַחְסוֹר	noun masc. sing. dec. 1 b . . חסר
מַחְסוֹרְךָ	id., suff. 2 pers. sing. masc. . . חסר
מַחֲסִי / מַחֲסִי	} noun masc. sing., suff. 1 pers. sing. from מַחֲסֶה dec. 9 a (comp. § 35. rem. 5) . . חסה
מַחֲסֵיָה	pr. name masc. . . חסה
מַחֲסֵנוּ	noun m. s., suff. 1 pers. pl. fr. מַחֲסֶה d. 9 a . . חסה
מְחֻסְפָּס	Pu. (§ 6. No. 7) part. sing. masc. . . חסף
מְחַסֵּר	Piel part. sing. masc. ; bef. lab. . . חסר
מַחְסֹרוֹ	noun masc. sing., suff. 3 pers. sing. masc. from מַחְסוֹר dec. 1 b . . חסר
מַחְסֹרֶיךָ	id. pl., suff. 2 pers. sing. masc. ; bef. lab. . . חסר
מַחְסֹרְךָ	id. sing., suff. 2 pers. sing. masc. ; id. . . חסר
מַחְפִּיר	Hiph. part. sing. masc. ; id. . . חפר
מֵחֵפֶץ	pref. מֵ for מִן ⟩(noun masc. sing. dec. 6 (§ 35. rem. 6) . . חפץ
מְחֻפָּשׂ	Pual part. sing. masc. . . חפש
מֵחֻפָּתָהּ	pref. מֵ for מִן ⟩(noun fem. sing., suff. 3 pers. sing. fem. from חֻפָּה dec. 10 . . חפף
מֵחֻפָּתוֹ	pref. id. ⟩(id., suff. 3 pers. sing. masc. . . חפף

מָחַץ I. *to dash, plunge*, as the foot in blood, Ps.

a De. 32. 18.   g Zec. 3. 4.   m Ex. 32. 19.   s La. 1. 11.   y Nu. 31. 28.   e De. 23. 15.   k Ps. 14. 5.   q Ec. 4. 8.   x Job 31. 16.
b Le. 21. 9.   h 1 Ch. 27. 4.   n Ps. 55. 21.   t Eze. 24. 21.   z Job 21. 20.   f Job 7. 15.   l Ps. 39. 2.   r De. 15. 8.   y Ps. 64. 7.
c Je. 29. 8.   i Pr. 6. 24.   o Joel 4. 5.   u 2 Sa. 23. 3.   a Na. 2. 13.   g Ju. 19. 20.   m Pr. 24. 34.   z Joel 1. 4.
d De. 32. 13.   k 1 Ch. 27. 2,   p Joel 4. 5.   v Ps. 72. 14.   b Ex. 32. 32.   h Is. 25. 4.   n Pr. 6. 11.   a Pr. 19. 6.
e Ju. 16. 13, 19.   4, 7, &c.   q La. 1. 7.   w Ca. 5. 16.   c Is. 28. 15.   i Is. 28. 17.   o Pr. 19. 23.   b Nu. 24. 17.
f Ear. 1. 9.   l Eze. 48. 29.   r Is. 64. 10.   x Ez. 12. 19, 20.   d Am. 4. 5.   f Am. 4. 10.   p Ex. 16. 14.

68. 24.—II. *to dash, break in pieces*; metaph. *to crush*, of wisdom, Job 26. 12.

מַחַץ masc. *contusion, bruise*, Is. 30. 26.

מְחַץ	Kal imp. sing. masc. . . . . מחץ
מַחַץ	﹜ noun masc. sing. ; ﹜ bef. lab. . מחץ
מִמַּחַץ	pref. מִ for מִן) (noun masc. sing. dec. 8 b חצץ
מַחְצֵב	noun masc. sing. . . . . חצב
מָחֲצָה	﹜ Kal pret. 3 pers. sing. fem. ; ﹜ bef. lab. מחץ
מִמַּחֲצָה	﹜ pref. מִ for מִן) (noun masc. sing. dec. 6 i (§ 35. rem. 14) ; ﹜ id. . . מחץ
מֶחֱצִיוֹ	pref. id.) (id. with suff. 3 pers. sing. masc. . חצה
מַחֲצִית	noun fem. sing. dec. 1 b חצה
מַחֲצִיתָהּ	﹜ id., suff. 3 pers. sing. fem. ; ﹜ bef. lab. חצה
מַחֲצִיתוֹ	id., suff. 3 pers. sing. masc. . חצה
מַחְצְפָה	Chald. Aph. part. sing. masc. (§ 47. rem. 5) חצף
מְחַצְצִים	Piel part. m., pl. of [מְחַצֵּץ] d. 7 b (§ 10. r. 7) חצץ
מַחְצְצִים	Kh. מַחֲצֵרִים part. pl. masc. (from חָצַר § 6. No. 11) ; K. מַחֲצְרִים Hiph. part. pl. [of מַחְצֵר for מַחְצִיר § 11. rem. 8] חצר
מֵחֲצַר	pref. מִ for מִן) (noun com. s., constr. of חָצֵר d. 5 c, also pr. name in compos. חצר
מַחֲצֵרוֹת	pref. id.) (pr. name of a place, see חָצֵר . חצר
מַחְצְרִים	Kh. מְחַצְרִים Pilel part. pl. masc. [from מְחַצְרֵר § 6. No. 2]; for Keri see מַחְצְצִים חצר
מַחֲצְרֹת	pref. מִ for מִן) (pr. name of a place, see חָצֵר חצר
מָחַצְתָּ	Kal pret. 2 pers. sing. masc. . . מחץ
מֶחֱצָת	noun f. s., constr. of מֶחֱצָה dec. 10 חצה
מָחַצְתִּי	Kal pret. 1 pers. sing. . . . מחץ

[מָחַק] *to strike, smite*, Ju. 5. 26.

מָחֹק	defect. for מָחוֹק (q. v.) . . . . חוק
מָחֲקָה	Kal pret. 3 pers. sing. fem. . . מחק
מְחֻקֶּה	Pual part. sing. masc. . . . חקה
מִמְּחֻקּוֹת	pref. מִ for מִן) (noun fem., pl. of חֻקָּה dec. 10 חקק
מֵחֻקַּי	pref. id.) (noun masc. pl., suff. 1 pers. sing. from חֹק dec. 8 c חקק
מְחֻקִּי	pref. id.) (id. sing., suff. 1 pers. sing. . חקק
מְחֻקֵּיךָ	pref. id.) (id. pl., suff. 2 pers. sing. masc. . חקק
מְחֹקֵק	﹜ Poel part. sing. masc., dec. 7 b ; ﹜ bef. lab. חקק
מְחֻקָּק	Pual part. sing. masc. . . . חקק
מְחֹקְקִי	Poel part. s. m. (מְחֹקֵק), suff. 1 pers. s. d. 7 b חקק
מְחֹקְקִים	id. pl., abs. st. . . . . חקק
מְחֹקְקֵנוּ	id. sing., suff. 1 pers. pl. . חקק
מֶחְקְרֵי	noun masc. pl. constr. from [מֶחְקָר] dec. 1 b חקר

מָחַר Root not used ; prob. i. q. מָכַר *to sell*.

מְחִיר	masc. dec. 1 a.—I. *price*.—II. *hire, wages.*—III. pr. name masc. 1 Ch. 4. 11.

מָחָר & מָחָר I. *to-morrow* ; כְּעֵת מָחָר , יוֹם מָחָר , לְמָחָר id. , כָּעֵת מָחָר *about this time to-morrow* כָּעֵת מָחָר הַשְּׁלִשִׁית *this time the day after to-morrow.*—II. *in time to come, in future time.*

לְמׇחֳרָת , constr. מׇחֳרַת fem. *the morrow* ; מׇחֳרָת *the next day* ; עַד־מׇחֳרָת *until the next day* ; מִמׇּחֳרַת הַשַּׁבָּת *the day after the sabbath.* מׇחֳרָתָם adv. *the day after*, 1 Sa. 30. 17.

מֵחַר	pref. מִ for מִן) (pr. name in compos. נדד
'הֹר הַגִּדְגָּד , see under . . נדד
מִמַּחֲרֵב	pref. id.) (noun fem. sing. (suff. חׇרְבִּי) d. 6 a חרב
מֵחָרֵב	pref. id.) (pr. name of a mountain . חרב
מֵחֹרֶב	pref. id.) (noun masc. sing. . . חרב
מׇחֳרָבוֹת	Hoph. part. pl. fem. [from מׇחֳרָבָה=מׇחֳרָב m.] חרב
מֵחׇרְבוֹתֵיהֶם	pref. מִ for מִן) (noun fem. pl., suff. 3 pers. pl. masc. from חׇרְבָּה dec. 12 c חרב
מֵחׇרְדָּה	pref. id.) (pr. name of a place . חרד
מֵחֲרוֹן	pref. id.) (noun m. sing., constr. of חָרוֹן d. 3 a חרה
מֵחׇרֹנִים	pref. id.) (pr. name of a place . חור
מֵחׇרוֹץ	﹜ pref. id.) (noun m. sing. d. 3 a ; ﹜ bef. lab. חרץ
מַחֲרִיב	Hiph. part. sing. masc. dec. 1 b חרב
מַחֲרִיכֵךְ	﹜ id. pl., suff. 2 pers. sing. fem. ; ﹜ bef. lab. חרב
מַחֲרִיד	Hiph. part. sing. masc. . . חרד
מַחֲרִישׁ	Hiph. part. sing. masc. dec. 1 b חרש
מֵחׇרָן	pref. מִ for מִן) (pr. name of a place . חרר
מֵחׇרֹנִים	pref. id.) (pr. name of a place חור
מְחָרֵף	Piel part. sing. masc. . . . חרף
מֵחֵרֶף	pref. מִ for מִן) (noun masc. sing. dec. 6 c חרף
מֵחֶרְפַּת	pref. id.) (noun fem. sing., constr. of חֶרְפָּה dec. 12 b (comp. § 35. rem. 6) . חרף
מֵחׇרְצַנִּים	pref. id.) (n. m., pl. of [חַרְצָן] d. 6 a (§ 37. No. 3) חרץ
מַחֲרִשִׁים	Hiph. part. masc., pl. of מַחֲרִישׁ dec. 1 b חרש
מֵחֲרֹשֶׁת	pref. מִ for מִן) (pr. n. in compos. חֲרֹשֶׁת הַגּוֹיִם חרש
מַחֲרַשְׁתּוֹ	noun fem. sing., suff. 3 pers. sing. masc. from [מַחֲרֶשֶׁת] dec. 13 a חרש
מַחֲרַשְׁתּוֹ	noun m. s., suff. 3 pers. s. m. [from מַחֲרֵשָׁה חרש
מְחַשֵּׁב	Piel part. sing. masc. . . . חשב
מַחֲשָׁבָה	noun fem. s. d. 11 a, constr. מַחֲשֶׁבֶת (§ 42. r. 5) חשב
מֵחֶשְׁבּוֹן	﹜ pref. מִ for מִן) (pr. name of a place ; ﹜ bef. lab. חשב
מַחֲשָׁבוֹת	noun masc., pl. of מַחֲשָׁבָה dec. 11 a חשב
מַחְשְׁבוֹת	id. pl., constr. st. . . . חשב
מַחְשְׁבוֹתַי	﹜ id. pl., suff. 1 pers. sing. ; ﹜ bef. lab. חשב
מַחְשְׁבֹתָיו	﹜ id. pl., suff. 3 pers. sing. masc. ; ﹜ id. . חשב
מַחְשְׁבוֹתֵיכֶם	id. pl., suff. 2 pers. pl. masc. חשב

---

a De. 33. 11.   *f* Zec. 14. 4.   Je. 39. 14.   *p* Pr. 17. 23.   *s* Ps. 119. 118.   *u* Is. 33. 22.   *b* Ju. 16. 24.   *e* Ne. 5. 9.   *l* Sa. 13. 20.
b Is. 30. 26.   *g* Le. 6. 13, 13.   *m* 2 Ch. 5. 12.   *q* Ju. 5. 26.   De. 33. 21.   *d* Ps. 95. 4.   *k* Is. 49. 17.   *v* Nu. 6. 4.   *r* Pr. 24. 8.
c Ps. 91. 5.   *h* Ex. 30. 23.   *n* Hab. 3. 13.   *r* Le. 18. 30.   Ge. 49. 10.   Eze. 29. 12.   Ps. 44. 17.   *w* 2 Sa. 19. 11.   Is. 55. 8.
d Ju. 5. 26.   Da. 3. 22.   Nu. 31. 43.   Mal. 3. 7.   Pr. 31. 5.   Ps. 109. 10.   Pr. 20. 4.   1 Sa. 13. 20.   Is. 55. 9.
Jos. 21. 27.   *e* Ju. 5. 11.   *o* De. 32. 39.   Job 23. 12.   *t* Ju. 5. 14.   Pr. 3. 14.

32

מַחְשְׁבוֹתֵינוּ	id. pl., suff. 1 pers. pl.	חשׁב
מַחֲשָׁבֶת	in pause for מַחֲשֶׁבֶת (q. v. & comp. § 35. r. 2)	חשׁב
מַחֲשָׁבֹת	pl. abs. of מַחֲשָׁבָה, see the following	חשׁב
מַחֲשֶׁבֶת	noun fem. sing. dec. 13 a, used for the constr. of מַחֲשָׁבָה (§ 42. rem. 5)	חשׁב
מַחְשְׁבֹת	id. pl., constr. st.	חשׁב
מַחֲשַׁבְתּוֹ	id. sing., suff. 3 pers. sing. masc.	חשׁב
מַחְשְׁבֹתֵיהֶם	id. pl., suff. 3 pers. pl. masc.; ‹ bef. lab.	חשׁב
מַחְשְׁבֹתָיו	id. pl., suff. 3 pers. pl. masc.	חשׁב
מַחְשְׁבֹתֶיךָ	id. pl., suff. 2 pers. sing. masc.; ‹ bef. lab.	חשׁב
מַחְשְׁבֹתָם	id. pl., suff. 3 pers. pl. masc. (§ 4. rem. 2)	חשׁב
מַחֲשֶׂה	Hiph. part. sing. masc. dec. 9 a	חשׂה
מַחֲשִׂיךְ	Hiph. part. sing. masc.	חשׂך
מַחֲשִׂים	Hiph. part. masc., pl. of מַחְשִׂים dec. 9 a	חשׂה
מֶחֱשִׁים	‹ pref. מ for מִי) pr. name masc.; ‹ bef. lab.	חושׁ
מַחְשָׁךְ	noun masc. sing. dec. 8 a, comp. מַחֲשֻׁכֵּי	חשׁך
מַחְשַׁךְּ	‹ pref. מ for מִי) n. m. s. d. 6 c; ‹ bef. lab.	חשׁך
מַחֲשֻׁכֵּי	noun masc. pl. constr. from מַחְשָׁךְ dec. 8 a (§ 37. No. 3)	חשׁך
מַחְשְׁמַנָּה	pref. מ for מִי) pr. name of a place	חשׁם
מַחְשֹׂף	noun masc. sing.	חשׂף
מַחְשַׁקִּים	Pual part. pl. masc. [from מְחֻשָּׁק]	חשׁק
מַחַת	‹ pr. name masc.; ‹ bef. lab.	חתה
מָחַת	‹ Chald. Peal pret. 3 pers. sing. fem.; ‹ id.	מחא
מָחֲתָה	‹ Kal pret. 3 pers. sing. fem.; ‹ id.	מחה
מַחְתָּה	‹ noun fem. sing. dec. 10; ‹ id.	חתת
מַחְתּוֹת	} noun fem., pl. of מַחְתָּה dec. 10	חתת
מַחְתֹּת	noun fem. sing., constr. of מַחְתָּה dec. 10	חתת
מַחְתָּתוֹ	noun fem. s., suff. 3 p. s. m., fr. מַחְתָּה d. 10	חתת
מַחְתֹּתֶיהָ	‹ id. pl., suff. 3 pers. sing. fem.; ‹ bef. lab.	חתת
מַחְתֹּתָיו	‹ id. pl., suff. 3 pers. sing. fem.; ‹ id.	חתה
מָט	Kal part. sing. masc. dec. 1 a (§ 30. No. 3)	מוט

מְטָה, מְטָא Chald. I. *to come on* or *to, to arrive at*; with עַל *to come upon* any one, *to happen* to him.— II. *to reach to*, Da. 4. 8, 17, 19.

מֵיטִב	‹ defect. for מֵיטִיב (q. v.)	יטב
מִטְבָּח	noun masc. sing.	טבח
מִטְבָּחַת	‹ pref. מ) pr. name of a place; ‹ bef. lab.	טבח
מֵיטְבֵי	defect. for מֵיטִיבֵי (q. v.)	יטב
מִטַּבְּעֹתוֹ	pref. מ) noun fem. pl., suff. 3 pers. sing. masc. fr. טַבַּעַת (§ 44. rem. 5)	טבע
מָטָה	‹ Kal pret. 3 pers. sing. fem.; ‹ bef. lab.	מוט
מַטָּה מַטָּה	} prop. subst. (מַט) with loc. ה, as an *adv.*	נטה

מַטֵּ	‹ constr. of the following	נטה
מַטֶּה	‹ Hiph. part. or noun masc. sing. dec. 9 a; ‹ bef. lab.	נטה
מְטָה	Ch. Peal pret. 3 pers. sing. masc.	מטא
מִטָּה	noun fem. sing. dec. 10	נטה
מַטֶּה	noun masc. sing.	נטה
מַטֵּהוּ	‹ noun masc. sing., suff. 3 pers. sing. m.	נטה
מַטֶּה	*א.* dec. 9 a, ‹ bef. lab.	נטה
מוֹטֵהוּ	noun masc. sing., suff. 3 pers. sing. masc. fr. מוֹט dec. 1 a	מוט
מְטַהֵר	‹ Piel part. sing. m. (§ 14. r. 1); ‹ bef. lab.	טהר
מְטֹהָרָה	Pual part. sing. fem. [fr. מְטֹהָר masc.]	טהר
מְטַהֲרוֹ	pref. מ) noun masc. sing. with suff. 3 pers. sing. masc. [for טָהֳרוֹ] fr. טֹהַר dec. 1 a	טהר
מִטַּהֲרִים	Hithpa. part. masc. pl. of מִטַּהֵר [for מִתְטַהֵר § 12. rem. 3] dec. 7 b	טהר
מָטוּ	Kal pret. 3 pers. pl.	מוט
מְטוֹ	Ch. Peal pret. 3 pers. pl. masc.	מטא
מִטּוֹב	pref. מ) noun masc. sing. dec. 1 a	טוב
מִטּוּב	pref. id.) noun masc. sing. dec. 1 a	טוב
מִטּוֹבָה	pref. id.) noun fem. sing. d. 10, fr. טוֹב m.	טוב
מַטֹּוֶה	noun masc. sing.	טוה
מְטוּרָא	Ch. pref. מ) noun masc. sing., emph. of טוּר dec. 1 a	טור
מַטּוֹת	noun masc. with pl. f. term. fr. מַטֶּה d. 9 a	נטה
מִטּוֹת	noun fem., pl. of מִטָּה dec. 10	נטה
מֹטוֹת	‹ defect. for מוֹטוֹת (q. v.)	מוט
מַטּוֹת	noun fem., pl. of [מַטֶּה] dec. 10	נטה
מַטּוֹתָם	noun masc. with pl. fem. term. and suff. 3 pers. pl. masc. fr. מַטֶּה dec. 9 a	נטה
מַטֵּי	‹ Hiph. part. pl. constr. masc. fr. מַטֶּה (§ 25. No. 2 b) dec. 9; ‹ bef. lab.	נטה
מֵיטִב	‹ defect. for מֵיטִיב (q. v.)	יטב
מְטִיט	pref. מ) noun masc. sing.	טוא
מָטִים	‹ Kal part. act. masc., pl. of מָט dec. 1 a (§ 30. No. 3); ‹ bef. lab.	מוט
מַטִּיף	Hiph. part. sing. masc.	נטף
מַטֵּךְ	‹ noun masc. sing., suff. 2 pers. sing. fem. fr. מַטֶּה dec. 9 a; ‹ bef. lab.	נטה

מְטַל Root not used; Arab. *to forge iron.*

מְטִיל	masc. dec. 3 a, *bar of iron*, Job 40. 18.	
מְטַל	} pref. מ) noun masc. sing. dec. 8 d	טלל
מִטְלֵי	} ‹ bef. lab.	טלל
מְטֻלָּא=מְטַלְּאוֹת	‹ Pual part. pl. fem. [fr. מְטֻלָּא masc.]; ‹ id.	טלא

a Je. 18. 12.   g Is. 29. 18.   m Nu. 16. 17.   r Da. 7. 13, 22.   w Le. 25. 35.   d Is. 10. 24, 26.   i Ne. 13. 22.   o Da. 2. 45.   t Ps. 119. 66.
b Is. 66. 18.   h Ps. 74. 20.   n Nu. 4. 9.   s Eze. 33. 32.   x De. 28. 43.   e Na. 1. 13.   k Ps. 46. 7.   p Je. 27. 2.   u Pr. 24. 11.
c Ps. 40. 6.   i Ge. 30. 37.   o Ex. 27. 3.   t Is. 14. 21.   y Is. 10. 5.   f Mal. 3. 3.   l Da. 6. 25.   q Is. 8. 8.   v Mi. 2. 11.
d Is. 57. 11.   k Da. 2. 34, 35.   p Pr. 25. 26.   u Pr. 30. 29.   z Ex. 28. 28; 39.21.   g Eze. 22. 24.   m Ec. 4. 8.   r Nu. 17. 21.   w Ge. 27. 28.
e Job 38. 2.   l Pr. 30. 20.   q Da. 4. 25.   v Eze. 9. 9.   a Ps. 89. 45.   h Ex. 35. 25.   n Mal. 3. 5.   x Jos. 9. 5.
f Ps. 107. 14.

מְטַלְטְלְךָ Pilp. part. sing. masc. [מְטַלְטֵל] suff. 2 pers. sing. masc. dec. 7 b . . . . טול

מִטַּמֵּא pref. מ) adj. masc. sing. dec. 5 a (constr. טְמֵא § 34. rem. 1) . . . . טמא

מְטֻמְּאָה Pual part. sing. fem. [of מְטֻמָּא masc.] טמא

מִטֻּמְאַת pref. מ) noun f. s., constr. of טֻמְאָה d. 10 טמא

מִטֻּמְאֹת pref. id.) id. pl. constr. . . . טמא

מִטֻּמְאָתָהּ pref. id.) id. sing., suff. 3 pers. sing. fem. טמא

מִטֻּמְאָתוֹ pref. id.) id. sing., suff. 3 pers. sing. masc. טמא

מִטֻּמְאָתֵךְ pref. id.) id. sing., suff. 2 pers. sing. fem. טמא

מִטֻּמְאָתָם pref. id.) id. sing., suff. 3 pers. pl. masc. טמא

מַטְמוֹן noun masc. sing. dec. 1 a . . . טמן

מַטְמֹנֵי id. pl. constr. (§ 30. rem. 4) ; bef. lab. טמן

מַטְמֹנִים id. pl., abs. st. . . . . טמן

מַטָּע noun masc. sing. d. 2 b (except pl. c. מַטְּעֵי) נטע

מַטַּע id., constr. st. . . . . נטע

מַטָּעָהּ id., suff. 3 pers. sing. fem. . . נטע

מַטָּעוֹ id. pl. with suff. Kh. עֵי 3 pers. sing. masc., K. עֵי 1 pers. sing. . . . נטע

מִטְעַם pref. מ) noun masc. sing. dec. 6 d טעם

מִטְעַם Ch., pref. id.) noun m. s. d. 3 a ; bef. lab. טעם

מַטְעַמִּים noun m., pl. of [מַטְעָם] d. 8 a (§ 37. No. 2) טעם

מִטְעֲנֵי Pual part. pl. constr. masc. fr. [מְטֹעָן] d. 2 b טען

מִטְפַּ pref. מ) noun masc. sing. (for טַף) d. 8 d טפף

מָטָר Hiph. הִמְטִיר to rain, cause or give rain; applied to the sending of hail, lightning, fire and brimstone, manna; const. with acc. בְּ of the thing rained down, and עַל upon anything. Niph. to be rained upon, Am. 4. 7.

מָטָר masc. dec. 4 a (pl. c. מְטָרוֹת) rain.

מַטְרִי (rain of the Lord, for מַטְרִיָּה) pr. name masc. 1 Sa. 10. 21.

מָטָר noun masc. sing. dec. 4 a ; bef. lab. מטר

מְטַר id., constr. st. ; id. . . מטר

מַטְרֵד pr. name masc. . . . . טרד

מַטְרוֹת noun masc. with pl. fem. term. constr. [of מַטְרוֹת from מָטָר] dec. 4 a מטר

מִטֶּרֶם pref. מ) adv. . . . . טרם

מְטֹרָף pref. id.) noun masc. sing. (suff. טַרְפּוֹ) d. 6 a טרף

מְטָת Chald. Peal pret. 3 pers. s. f. ; bef. lab. מטא

מַטַּת noun fem. sing., constr. of מִטָּה dec. 10 נטה

מִטֹּת defect. for מוֹטֹת (q. v.) . . מוט

מִטָּתוֹ noun fem. s., suff. 3 pers. s. m. fr. מִטָּה d. 10 נטה

מִטָּתִי id., suff. 1 pers. sing. . . נטה

מִטָּתְךָ id., suff. 2 pers. sing. masc. [for מִטָּתֶךָ] . נטה

מִטֹּתָם defect. for מַטֹּתָם (q. v.) . . נטה

מֵי an obsol. sing. water (a trace of which is found in the pr. name אֲחִימִי brother of water) ; pl. מַיִם, constr. מֵי and reduplicated מֵימֵי, with suff. מֵימָיו (§ 38. rem. 2, & § 45).—I. waters, water ;. joined with the adj. and verb in the pl., with the latter sometimes also in the sing. מֵי רֹאשׁ juice of poppies ; מֵי רַגְלַיִם water of the feet, by euphemism for urine. Emblemat. of abundance, overwhelming danger, terror, arrogance.—II. in pr. names. מֵי זָהָב (water, i. e. lustre of gold) of a man, Ge. 36. 39.—מֵי הַיַּרְקוֹן (water of a greenish yellow) of a town in the tribe of Dan, Jos. 19. 46.—מֵי־נֶפְתּוֹחַ (waters of opening) of a fountain in the tribe of Judah, Jos. 15. 9; 18. 15.

מֵידְבָא (water of rest, see Root דָּבָא) pr. name of a city in the tribe of Reuben.

מִי, מ׳, וָ׳ pron. pers.—I. interrog. who? usually of persons, rarely of things, as מִי־שְׁמֶךָ what is thy name? put in the genitive, בַּת־מִי whose daughter? With prep. לְמִי to whom? מִמִּי from whom, more than who? אֶת־מִי whom? בְּמִי by whom?—II. without interrogation, whoever, any one; מִי אֲשֶׁר whosoever.

מֵי noun masc. pl., constr. of מַיִם, [from מֵי § 45] ; also pr. n. in compos. as מֵי זָהָב, &c. מי

מֵיאֹתִי Kh. מִי אֹתִי, K. מֵאֹתִי, see מִי, מֵי, את

מֵיבַשׁ pref. מ) pr. name of a place . . יבש

מֵינֹון pref. id.) noun masc. sing. dec. 3 a . ינה

מֵינֹונָם pref. מ) [for מֵינֹו]) id., suff. 3 pers. pl. m. ינה

מֵינִיעוֹ pref. id.) n. m. s. (יְגִיעַ), suff. 3 p. m. s. d. 1 a ינע

מֵיָד pref. מ) noun com. sing. dec. 2 a . יד

מִיַּד pref. id.) id. constr. st. ; bef. lab. . יד

מֵידְבָא pr. name of a place . . . . מי

מֵידָד pr. name masc. ; bef. lab. . . ידד

מִיָּדָהּ pref. מ) n. com. s., suff. 3 p. s. f. fr. יָד d. 2 a יד

מִיָּדַיְו pref. id.) id. du. (יָדַיִם), suff. 3 pers. s. m. יד

מִיָּדוֹ pref. id.) id. sing., suff. 3 pers. sing. masc. יד

מִיָּדִי pref. id.) id. sing., suff. 1 pers. sing. יד

מִידֵי pref. מ) [for מִיָּדֵי]) id. du., constr. of יָדַיִם יד

מִיָּדְךָ pref. id.) id. sing., suff. 2 pers. sing. masc. יד

מִיָּדֵךְ pref. id.) id. sing., suff. 2 pers. sing. fem. יד

מִיָּדְךָ pref. id.) id. sing., suff. 2 p. s. m.; bef. lab. יד

מִיֶּדְכֶם pref. id.) id. sing., suff. 2 pers. pl. masc. [for § 31. rem. 2] יד

מִיֶּדְכֶן pref. id.) id. sing., suff. 2 pers. pl. fem. יד

מִיָּדָם pref. id) id. sing., suff. 3 pers. pl. masc. יד

a Is. 22. 17.   b Job 14. 4.   c Ezr. 6. 21.   d Le. 16. 16, 19.   e 2 Sa. 11. 4.   f Le. 14. 19.   g Eze. 24. 13.   h Le. 15. 31.   i Ge. 43. 23.   k Is. 45. 3.   l Je. 41. 8.   m Eze. 34. 22.   n Le. 6. 3.   o Is. 60. 21.   p Jon. 3. 7.   q Is. 6. 14.   r Ge.27.4,7,9,etc.   s Is. 14. 19.   t Ex. 19. 37.   u Zec. 10. 1.   v Job 27. 6.   a Hag. 2. 15.   b Ge. 49. 9.   c Ja. 2. 13.   d Le. 26. 13.   e Ps. 6. 7.   f Ex. 7. 28.   g Ex. 7. 12.   h Ex. 10. 8.   i Is. 44. 24.   k Est. 9. 22.   l Je. 31. 13.   m Ne. 5. 13.   n Ex. 32. 19.   o 1 Ch. 29. 14.   p Eze. 13. 21, 23.

32*

מִידָּנוּ	pref. מ) (id. sing., suff. 1 pers. pl. יד
מֹידַע	Kh. מִידָע Pual part. s. m.; K. מוֹדָע subst. ידע
מִידְּעֵי	id. pl. with suff. 1 pers. sing.; ו bef. lab. ידע
מִידָּעִי	id. sing., suff. 1 pers. sing.; ו id. ידע
מִידָּעָיו	id. pl., suff. 3 pers. sing. masc.; ו id. ידע
מֹידַעַת	Kh. מִידַּעַת, K. מוּדַעַת Pu. or Hoph. part., fem. of מִידָע or מוּדָע ידע
מֵיהוּדָה	ו pref. מ [for מִיהוּדָה], pr. name of a man and a tribe; ו bef. lab. ידה
מֵיהוָה	ו the most sacred name of God (יהוה) with the vowels of אֲדֹנָי, whence pref. מֵ bef. gutt. for מִ הוה
מִיּוֹם	ו pref. מ) (noun masc. sing. dec. 1 a, but pl. irr. (§ 45); ו bef. lab. יוֹם
מִיּוֹרְדֵי	pref. id.) (Kh. יוֹרְדֵי Kal part. pl. c. masc.; K. יָרְדֵי inf. with suff. 1 pers. sing. ירד
מִיּוֹשֵׁב	pref. id.) (Kal part. act. sing. masc. dec. 7 b ישב
מִיּוֹשְׁבֵי	pref. id.) (id. pl., constr. st. ישב
מִיּזְרְעֵאל	pref. id.) (pr. name of a place זרע
מִיחִים	according to some copies, see מֵחִים מחח
מְיַחֵל	Piel (§ 14. rem. 1) part. sing. masc. dec. 7 b יחל
מְיַחֵף	pref. מ) (adj. masc. sing. יחף
מֵיטָב	ו noun masc. sing., constr. of [מֵיטָב] d. 2 b יטב
מִיטַבְתָּה	pref. מ) (pr. name of a place יטב
מֵיטִיב	Hiph. part. sing. masc. dec. 1 b יטב
מֵיטִיבֵי	id. pl., constr. st. יטב
מֵיטִיבִים	id. pl., abs. st. יטב
מִיַּיִן / מִיַּיִן	) pref. מ) (noun masc. sing. dec. 6 h יון
מִיֵּין	ו pref. id.) (id. constr. st.; ו bef. lab. יון
מִיֵּינָהּ	pref. id.) (id. with suff. 3 pers. sing. fem. יון
מִיֵּינוֹ	pref. id.) (id., suff. 3 pers. sing. masc. יון
מִיכָא	pr. name masc., see מִיכָה.
מִיכָאֵל	(who is like unto God?) pr. name—I. Michael the archangel.—II. of several men.
מִיכָה	(for מִיכָיְהוּ q. v.) pr. name masc.—I. Micah, the prophet.—II. 2 Ch. 34. 20, called מִיכָה in 2 Ki. 22. 12.—III. stands for מִיכָיְהוּ & מִיכָיְהוּ q. v.
מִיכָיָה	(who is like unto the Lord?) pr. name masc. —I. Ne. 12. 35, for which מִיכָא Ne. 11. 17, 22.—II. Ne. 12. 41. See also מִיכָה.
מִיכָיָה / מִיכָיְהוּ	pr. name m. Kh. מִיכָיָה, K. מִיכָה, Je. 26. 18.
מִיכָיְהוּ	(i. q. מִיכָיָה q. v.) pr. name—I. masc. 2 Ch. 17. 7.—II. fem., wife of Rehoboam, 2 Ch. 13. 2.
מִיכָיְהוּ	(id.) pr. name masc.—I. Ju. 17. 1, 4, called

מִיכָה	vers. 5, 8, 9, 10.—II. of a prophet, 1 Ki. 28. 8 ; 2 Ch. 18. 7, called מִיכָיְהוּ ver. 24, מִיכָהוּ ver. 8, Kh.
מִיכָל	noun masc. [constr. of מִיכָל dec. 2 b] a brook, 2 Sa. 17. 20. Root uncertain.
מִיכָל / מִיכָל	} pr. name of the daughter of Saul, the wife of David.
מִילְדֵי	pref. מ) (noun masc. pl. constr. fr. יֶלֶד d. 6 a לד
מִילְּדֵי	pref. מ [for מִילְדֵי], noun masc. pl. constr. from [יָלִיד] dec. 3 a לד
מַיִם / מֵם	} noun m. pl. [of מֵי irr. § 38. r. 2, & §45]; ו bef. lab., for ן see lett. ן ם
מִיָּם	ו pref. מ) (noun masc. s. d. 8 a; ו bef. lab. ם
מִיָּם	pref. id.) (id. constr. st. (only before סוֹף) ם
מִיָּמַי	pref. id.) (noun masc. pl. (יָמִים), with suff. 1 pers. sing. irr. of יוֹם (§ 45) יום
מִיָּמַי	ו the foll. with suff. 1 pers. s.; ו bef. lab. מי
מֵימֵי	noun masc. pl. constr., a reduplicated form from מַיִם (§ 45) מי
מֵימֵי	pref. מ [for מִימֵי], noun m., pl. c. of יָמִים, irr. of יוֹם (§ 45) יום
מֵימֶיהָ	noun m. pl., suff. 3 p. s. f. irr. of מַיִם (§ 45) מי
מֵימֵיהֶם	id., suff. 3 pers. pl. masc.; ו bef. lab. מי
מֵימָיו	id., suff. 3 pers. sing. masc. מי
מִימָיו	pref. מ) (noun masc. pl. (יָמִים), suff. 3 pers. sing. masc. irr. of יוֹם (§ 45) יום
מֵימֶיךָ	ו noun masc. pl. [מֵימִים], suff. 2 pers. sing. masc. irr. of מַיִם (§ 45); ו bef. lab. מי
מִימֶיךָ	pref. מ) (the foll. with suff. 2 pers. sing. m. יום
מִיָּמִים	pref. id.) (noun masc. pl., irr. of יוֹם (§ 45) יום
מִיָּמִים	pref. id.) (noun masc., pl. of יָם dec. 8 a ם
מִיָּמִים	pref. id.) (n. m., du. of יוֹם d. 1 a (comp. § 45) יום
מִימִין	(at the right hand) pr. name masc.—I. 1 Ch. 24. 9.—II. of another person, called also מִנְיָמִין, comp. Ne. 12. 5 with vers. 17, 41.
מִיָּמִין	pref. מ) (noun masc. sing. dec. 3 a מן
מִיָּמִין	pref. מ [for מִיָּמִין], id., constr. st. ימן
מֵימִינוּ	noun masc. pl. [יָמִים], suff. 1 pers. pl. irr of מַיִם (§ 45) מי
מִימִינוֹ	pref. מ [for מִיְמִינוֹ], noun masc. sing., suff. 3 pers. sing. masc. from יָמִין dec. 3 a ימן
מִימִינִי	pref. id.) (id. with suff. 1 pers. sing. ימן
מַיְמִינִים	Hiph. part. m. pl. [of מַיְמִין § 20. r. 14] d. 1 b ימן
מִימִינֶךָ	pref. מ [for מִיְמִי], noun masc. sing., suff. 2 pers. sing. masc. from יָמִין dec. 3 a ימן
מִימִינֶךְ	pref. id.) (id., suff. 2 pers. sing. fem. ימן
מִימִינָם	pref. id.) (id., suff. 3 pers. pl. masc. ימן

a Ju. 13. 23.   b 2 Ki. 10. 11.   c Ju. 21. 9, 12.   d Ex. 22. 4.   e Da. 1. 5.   f 1 Ch. 20. 4.   g Ho. 2. 7.   h 1 Sa. 25. 25.   i 1 Ch. 12. 2.
a Ru. 2. 1.   Is. 12. 5.   Ps. 66. 15.   1 Sa. 16. 17.   Je. 51. 7.   2 Ki. 6. 22.   Ho. 6. 2.   Ps. 91. 7.
Ps. 88. 9, 19.   Le. 22. 27.   Ps. 69. 4.   Pr. 30. 29.   Ge. 9. 24.   Job 27. 6.   1 Ki. 1. 6.   La. 5. 4.   Eze. 16. 46.
Job 19. 14.   Ps. 30. 4.   Je. 2. 35.   Ju. 19. 22.   Ex. 3. 6.   1 Sa. 25. 11.   Ese. 12. 19.   Ps. 16. 8.   Ex. 14. 22, 29.
Ps. 55. 14.   Is. 49. 19.

מִימָן — pr. name masc., see מֵימִין; ‡ bef. lab.

מִינוֹחָה — pref. מִ)(pr. name of a place (יָנוֹחַ) with parag. ה — נוח

מֵינִיקוֹת — Hiph. part. fem., pl. of מֵינִיקָה dec. 10 — ינק

מֵינִיקוֹתָיִךְ — id. pl. with suff. 2 pers. sing. fem. — ינק

מֵינֶקֶת — id. sing. dec. 13a — ינק

מֵינַקְתּוֹ — id. sing., suff. 3 pers. sing. masc. — ינק

מְיֻסָּד — ‡ Pual part. sing. masc.; ‡ bef. lab. — יסד

מִיסָדוֹת — Kh. מֵיסָדוֹת, K. מוֹסָדוֹת, noun fem. pl. constr. from מוֹסָדָה, or מֵיסָדָה dec. 11a — יסד

מְיֻסָּדִים — Pual part. masc., pl. of מְיֻסָּד dec. 2b — יסד

מֵיסָךְ — Kh. מֵיסַךְ [for מְסַךְ], K. מוּסָךְ, noun masc. sing., constr. [of סָךְ] — סכך

מְיֻסָּרְךָ — [for מְיֻסָּרְ § 2. rem. 2]; Piel part. [מְיֻסָּרְ], suff. 2 pers. sing. masc. dec. 7b — יסר

מִיַעֲקֹב — pref. מִ)(pr. name of a man and a people — עקב

מִיָּעַר — pref. id.)(noun masc. sing. dec. 6d — יער

מִיָּפַעַת — pref. id.)(pr. name of a place — יפע

מִיץ — ‡ noun masc. sing.; ‡ bef. lab. — מוץ

מִיצָאֵי — pref. מ [for מְיֹצֵ], K. אֵי adj. pl. constr. masc., Kh. אֵי, with suff. 3 pers. sing. masc. from [יֹצֵא] dec. 3a; ‡ id. — יצא

מִיצֶקֶת — Kh. מֵיצֶקֶת, K. מוֹצֶקֶת, Hiph. part. s. fem. — יצק

מִיקְבִים — pref. מִ)(noun masc. pl. of יֶקֶב dec. 6a — יקב

מִיקְבְּךָ — pref. id.)(id. sing., suff. 2 pers. sing. masc. for בְּךָ; ‡ bef. lab. — יקב

מִיקוֹד — pref. id.)(Kal part. pass. sing. masc. — יקד

מְיָרְאִים — Piel part. masc., pl. of מְיָרֵא dec. 7b — ירא

מִירְאָתוֹ — pref. מִ)(Kal inf. from (יָרְאָה), suff. 3 pers. sing. masc. (§ 8. rem. 10) — ירא

מִירְאָתְךָ — pref. id.)(id. (subst.) with suff. 2 pers. sing. m. — ירא

מִיַּרְדֵּן — pref. id.)(pr. name of a river — ירד

מִירוּשָׁלַם / מִירוּשָׁלָיִם — pref. מ [for מְיְרוּ], pr. name of a place — ירה

מִירִיחוֹ — pref. id.)(pr. name of a place — רוח

מִירְכְּבוֹתַי — pref. מִ)(Kh. יַרְכּוֹתִי, K. יַרְכְּתַי see the foll. — ירך

מִירְכְּתַי — pref. id.)(noun fem., du., constr. of יַרְכָתַיִם [from יְרֵכָה § 39. No. 3. rem. 3] — ירך

מִירֻשָּׁתְךָ — pref. id.)(noun fem. sing., suff. 2 pers. sing. masc. from יְרֻשָּׁה dec. 10 — ירש

מֵישָׁא — pr. name masc. — ישה

מִישָׁאֵל — (who is what God is? comp. מִי, שֶׁ, שֵׁ or שֶׁ) pr. name m. of several persons, especially one of the companions of Daniel, Da. 1.6; 2.17.

מִישְׁבִּי — defect. for מוֹשָׁבִי (q. v.) — ישב

מִישׁוּעָתִי — pref. מ [for מְיְשׁוּ], noun fem. sing., suff. 1 pers. sing. from יְשׁוּעָה dec. 10 — ישע

מִישׁוֹר — noun masc. sing. — ישר

מֵישַׁךְ — Chald. pr. name masc. Da. 2.49; 3.12. —

מִישְׁנֵי — pref. מִ)(adj. pl. constr. masc. from יָשֵׁן dec. 5a (§ 34. rem. 2) — ישן

מִישָׁע — ‡ pr. name masc.; ‡ bef. lab. — ישע

מִישַׁע — pref. מִ)(noun masc. sing. (suff. יִשְׁעִי) dec. 6a (§ 35. rem. 5) — ישע

מְיֻשָּׁר — Pual part. sing. masc. — ישר

מִישָּׁר — pref. מִ)(noun masc. sing. d. 6c *Pr.11.24. — ישר

מִישָׁר — defect. for מִישׁוֹר (q. v.) — ישר

מִישְׂרָאֵל — ‡ pref. מִ)(pr. name of a people; ‡ bef. lab. — שרה

מֵישָׁרִים — ‡ noun m.pl. [of מֵישָׁר], also adverbially; ‡ id. — ישר

מִיֶּתֶר — ‡ noun masc. sing. (suff. יִתְרוֹ) dec. 6a; ‡ id. — יתר

מִיתְרֵי — noun masc. pl., suff. 1 pers. s. fr. [מֵיתָר] d. 2b — יתר

מֵיתְרֵיהֶם — ‡ id., suff. 3 pers. pl. masc.; ‡ bef. lab. — יתר

מֵיתָרָיו — id., suff. 3 pers. pl. masc. — יתר

מֵיתָרַיִךְ — id., suff. 2 pers. sing. fem. — יתר

מָךְ — ‡ Kal pret. 3 pers. sing. masc., or (Le. 27.8) part. sing. masc.; ‡ bef. lab. — מוך

מַכְאָב — Hiph. part. sing. masc. — כאב

מַכְאֵב — pref. מִ)(noun masc. sing. dec. 1a — כאב

מַכְאֹבוֹ — ‡ noun masc. sing., suff. 3 pers. sing. masc. from מַכְאוֹב dec. 1b; ‡ bef. lab. — כאב

מַכְאֹבוֹת — id. with pl. fem. term. — כאב

מַכְאֹבִי — id. sing., suff. 1 pers. sing. — כאב

מַכְאֹבָיו — id. pl. masc., suff. 3 pers. sing. masc. — כאב

מַכְאֹבִים — id. pl., abs. st. — כאב

מַכְאֹבֵינוּ — ‡ id. pl., suff. 1 pers. pl.; ‡ bef. lab. — כאב

מַכְאֹבְךָ — id. sing., suff. 2 pers. sing. fem. — כאב

מַכְאוֹב — id. sing. abs. st. dec. 1b — כאב

מַכְאֹבִי — ‡ id. sing., suff. 1 pers. sing.; ‡ bef. lab. — כאב

מַכְאֹבִים — id. pl., abs. st. — כאב

מְכֻבָּד — Pual part. sing. masc. — כבד

מְכַבְּדוֹ — ‡ Piel part. sing. masc. (מְכַבֵּד), suff. 3 pers. sing. masc. dec. 7b; ‡ bef. lab. — כבד

מִכְּבוֹדוֹ — pref. מִ)(noun masc. sing., suff. 3 pers. sing. masc. from כָּבוֹד dec. 3a — כבד

מְכַבְּדַי — Piel part. pl. masc., suff. 1 p. s. fr. מְכַבֵּד d. 7b — כבד

מַכְבִּיד — ‡ Hiph. part. sing. masc.; ‡ bef. lab. — כבד

מְכַבְּדֶיהָ — Piel part. pl. masc., suff. 3 pers. sing. fem. from מְכַבֵּד dec. 7b — כבד

מְכַבֶּה — Piel part. sing. masc. — כבה

מִכָּבוֹד — pref. מִ)(noun masc. sing. dec. 3a — כבד

a Ge. 32.16.   f Ca. 5.15.   l 2 Ch. 32.21.   q 2 Sa.3.11.   v Ps. 22.2.   a Je. 10.20.   f Is. 65.14.   k Is. 53.4.   p Pr. 14.31.
b Is. 49.23.   g 2 Ki. 16.18.   m 2 Ki. 4.5.   r Da. 12.2.   w Nu. 3.37;4.32.   b 2 Ch.6.29.   g Je. 30.15.   l Eze. 43.12.
c Ch. 22.11.   h De. 8.5.   n Je. 48.33.   s 1 Ki. 6.16.   x Job 5.4.   c Is. 54.2.   h Ps. 38.18.   m 1 Sa.2.30
d 1 Ki. 7.10.   i Ps. 80.14.   o Is. 30.14.   t 2 Ch. 20.11.   y 1 Ki 6.35.   d Le. 25.47.   i Ex. 3.7.   n Ps. 32.10.   q Hab. 2.6.
e Eze. 41.8.   k Pr. 30.33.   p Ne. 6.9.14.   u Ju. 20.15.   z Le. .4.17.   e Eze. 28.24.   k Ec. 2.23.   o Is. 58.13.   r La. 1.8.

מַכְבֵּנָא	(*circuit*, or *band*, Syr. כבן *to bind round*) pr. name of a town in Judah. 1 Ch. 2. 49.	
מַכְבַּנַּי	(*binder*) pr. name masc. 1 Ch. 12. 13.	
מְכַבְּסִים	Piel part. masc., pl. of [מְכַבֵּס] dec. 7 b	כבס
מִכְבָּר	noun masc. sing. dec. 2 b	כבר
מִכְבַּר	id., constr. st.	כבר
מִכְבָּדֵךְ	pref. מִ ⟩〈 noun com. sing., suff. 2 pers. sing. fem. from כַּד dec. 8 d	כדד
מַכָּה	⟩ noun fem. sing. dec. 10; ⟩ bef. lab.	נכה
מַכַּת	⟩ constr. of the foll.; ⟩ id.	נכה
מַכֶּה	Hiph. part. sing. masc. (§ 25. No. 2b) d. 9a	נכה
מֻכֶּה׳	Hoph. part. sing. masc., constr. of מֻכֶּה׳ d. 9a	נכה
מַכֵּהוּ	Hiph. part. sing. masc. מַכֶּה § 25. No. 2b), suff. 3 pers. sing. masc. dec. 9a	נכה
מִכַּהֵן	pref. מִ ⟩〈 Piel inf. constr. (§ 14. rem. 1)	כהן
מִכֹּהֵן	pref. id. ⟩〈 noun masc. sing. dec. 7 b	כהן
מִכּוֹכְבֵי׳	pref. id. ⟩〈 noun m. pl. constr. fr. כּוֹכָב d. 2 b	כבב
מָכוֹן	⟩ noun masc. sing. dec. 3 a; ⟩ bef. lab.	כון
מְכוֹן	id., constr. st.	כון
מִכּוֹן	⟩ pref. מִ ⟩〈 pr. name masc.; ⟩ bef. lab.	כון
מְכוֹנוֹ	noun m. s., suff. 3 pers. s. m. fr. מָכוֹן d. 3 a	כון
מְכוֹנֶיהָ	id. pl., suff. 3 pers. sing. fem.	כון
מְכוֹנֹתֶיהָ	noun f. pl., suff. 3 pers. s. m. fr. מְכוֹנָה d. 10	כון
מָכוֹר	pref. מִ ⟩〈 noun masc. sing.	כור
מְכֻרֹתָם	noun f. s., suff. 3 p. pl. m. fr. [מְכוּרָה] d. 10	מכר
מַכּוּשׁ	⟩ pref. מִ ⟩〈 pr. name of a country; ⟩ bef. lab.	כושׁ
מַכּוּשִׁים	pref. id. gent. noun, pl. of כּוּשִׁי	כושׁ
מַכּוֹת	⟩ noun fem., pl. of מַכָּה d. 10; ⟩ bef. lab.	נכה
מְכוֹנַת׳	noun fem. sing., constr. of מְכוֹנָה dec. 10	כוה
מְכוּתָה	⟩ pref. מִ ⟩〈 pr. name of a region; ⟩ bef. lab.	כות
מַכּוֹתָהּ מַכּוֹתֶיהָ	noun fem. pl., suff. 3 pers. sing. fem. from מַכָּה dec. 10	נכה
מַכּוֹתָם	id. with suff. 3 pers. pl. masc. (§ 4. rem. 2)	נכה
מִכְבֵּחַ	pref. מִ ⟩〈 noun masc. sing. dec. 1 a	כחח
מִכְבַּחֲכֶם	pref. id. ⟩〈 id. with suff. 2 p. m. pl.; ⟩ bef. lab.	כחח
מִכְחַשׁ	⟩ pref. id. ⟩〈 noun masc. s. d. 6 d; ⟩ bef. lab.	כחשׁ
מִיכָי	pr. name masc.	מוך
מֻכֵּי	Hoph. part. pl. constr. masc. from מֻכֶּה (§ 25. No. 2b) dec. 9a	נכה
מִיכָיְהוּ	defect. for מִיכָיְהוּ q. v.	
מֻכִּים׳	Hoph. part. m., pl. of מֻכֶּה׳ (§ 25. No. 2b) d. 9a	נכה
מַכִּין׳	Hiph. part. sing. masc.	כון
מִכִּיס׳	pref. מִ ⟩〈 noun masc. sing. dec. 1 a	כוס
מָכִיר	pr. name masc.	מכר
מַכִּיר	Hiph. part. sing. masc. dec. 1 b	נכר
מַכִּירִים	id. pl., abs. st.	נכר
מַכִּירֵךְ׳	id. sing., suff. 2 pers. sing. fem.	נכר

[מכךְ]	*to waste, pine away*, Ps. 106. 43. Niph. *to decay*, or *sink*, Ec. 10. 18. Hoph. *to decay, perish*, Job 24. 24.	
מַכֵּךְ׳	Hiph. part. sing. masc. מַכֶּה § 25. No. 2b), suff. 2 pers. sing. fem. dec. 9a	נכה
מִכְּל	⟩ pref. מִ ⟩〈 noun masc. sing. dec. 8 c;	כלל
מִכָּל־	⟩ bef. lab.	כלל
מְכַלֶּה	Piel part. sing. masc.	בלה
מִכְלוֹל	noun masc. sing.	כלל
מְכַלּוֹת	Piel part. f. pl. [of מְכַלָּה d. 10] fr. מְכַלֶּה m.	בלה
מִכְלוֹת	noun fem., pl. of [מִכְלָה] dec. 10	כלה
מִכְלִי׳	⟩ pl. constr. of the foll.; ⟩ bef. lab.	כלה
מִכְּלִי׳	pref. מִ ⟩〈 noun m. s. d. 6 i, pl. irr. כֵּלִים (§ 45)	כלה
מְכַלִּים׳	Hiph. part. sing. masc.	כלם
מִכְלָיִם׳	pref. מִ ⟩〈 noun m. pl. [prop. from כְּלֶה=כְּל see כְּלִי (§ 45)	כלה
מִכְלֵינוּ׳	pref. id. ⟩〈 id. pl. with suff. 1 pers. pl.	כלה
מִכְלְיֹתֵיהֶם׳	pref. id. ⟩〈 noun masc. pl., suff. 3 pers. pl. masc. from [כִּלְיָה] dec. 12b	כלה
מְכַלְכֵּל	Pilp. part. sing. masc. (§ 6. No. 4)	כול
מִכְלַל	noun masc. sing., constr. of [מִכְלָל] dec. 2 b	כלל
מַכְלִם׳	defect. for מַכְלִים (q. v.)	כלם
מִכְלָם׳	⟩ pref. מִ ⟩〈 noun masc. sing., suff. 3 pers. sing. masc. from כֹּל dec. 8 c; ⟩ bef. lab.	כלל
מִכְּלִמּוֹת׳	pref. id. ⟩〈 noun fem., pl. of כְּלִמָּה dec. 10	כלם
מִכֻּלָּנוּ׳	pref. id. ⟩〈 n. m. s., suff. 1 p. pl. fr. כֹּל d. 8c	כלל
מַכֹּלֶת׳	noun fem. sing. contr. from מַאֲכֹלֶת	אכל
מִכֶּם	pref. prep. מִן with suff. 2 p. pl. m. see מִן (§ 5)	מנן
מִכְמֹשׁ	pref. מִ ⟩〈 pr. name of an idol, see כְּמוֹשׁ.	
מַכְמָם	pr. name of a place	כמם
מַכְמָר׳	noun masc. sing.	כמר
מִכְמֹרֶת׳	noun fem. sing.	כמר
מִכְמָשׁ מִכְמָשׂ	pr. name of a place, see מִכְמָס	כמס
מִכְמְתָת	pr. name of a town on the borders of Ephraim and Manasseh, Jos. 16. 6; 17. 7.	
מַכְנַדְבַּי	pr. name masc. Ezr. 10. 40.	
מִכְנְסֵי׳	⟩ noun fem. du. constr. [of מִכְנָסַיִם, from מִכְנָם] dec. 2 b; ⟩ bef. lab.	כנס
מִכְּנַף׳	pref. מִ ⟩〈 noun fem. s., constr. of כָּנָף d. 4 a	כנף
מִכְנֶרֶת	pref. id. ⟩〈 pr. name of a place	כנר
מִמְּכֻנָתָהּ	n. f. s., suff. 3 p.s. f. fr. מְכֻנָה see under the R.	כון
מִכְסָם׳	noun masc. sing. (with suff. מִכְסָם) dec. 6 a	כסס
מִכְסָא׳	pref. מִ ⟩〈 noun masc. sing. d. 7 b (§ 36. r. 3)	כסא
מִכְסָאוֹ׳	pref. id. ⟩〈 id., suff. 3 pers. sing. masc.	כסא

a Mal. 3. 2.	f Ezr. 2. 68.	l Le. 13. 24.	q Je. 18. 21.	u Is. 14. 29.	y Ju. 18. 7.	a Ps. 50. 2.	x 2 Ki. 9. 5.	k Zec. 5. 11.
b Ge. 24. 17, 43.	g Ps. 104. 5.	m Je. 49. 17.	r Ex. 5. 16.	v Le. 26. 16.	z Est. 1. 7.	b Job 11. 3.	y 1 Ki. 5. 25.	l Nu. 31. 28, 41.
c Is. 53. 4.	h Ezr. 4. 2.	n Ps. 64. 8.	s 2 Ch. 4. 21.	w 1 Sa. 9. 7.	a Da. 11. 5.	c Is. 51. 20.	z 1 Ki. 1. 37.
d Na. 3. 16.	i Eze. 29. 14.	o Je. 48. 45.	t Ps. 142. 5.	x 2 Ch. 36. 7.	b Je. 12. 2.	d Is. 19. 8.	a Jon. 3. 6.
e 2 Ch. 6. 2.	k Pr. 20. 30.	p Ps. 59. 13.	t Ru. 2. 19.	e Je. 48. 11.	c Mal. 3. 2.	f Is. 24. 14.	e Job 6. 22.

מַכְסָאוֹתָם   pref. ·מַ)(id. pl. f., suff. 3 p. pl. m. (§ 4. r. 2)   כסא

מִכָּסְאָךָ   pref. id.)(id. sing., suff. 2 p. s. m. (for כְּסָאֲךָ)   כסא

מְכַסֶּה   Piel part. sing. masc.   .   .   כסה

מְכַסֵּה   constr. of the foll. ; וּ bef. lab.   .   כסה

מִכְסֶה   noun masc. sing. dec. 9a   .   .   כסה

מִכְסֵהוּ   id., suff. 3 pers. sing. masc.   .   כסה

מִכְסֵהוּ   pref. מְ)(noun fem. sing., suff. 3 pers. sing. masc. from כּוֹס dec. 1a ; וּ bef. lab.   כוס

מְכַסּוֹת   Piel part. f. pl. [of מְכַסֶּה d. 10], fr. מְכַסֶּה m.   כסה

מְכֻסּוֹת   Pual part. fem. pl. [of מְכֻסֶּה dec. 10, from מְכֻסֶּה masc.]   כסה

מְכַסֶּיךָ   noun masc. pl. (or sing. § 38. rem. 1), suff. 2 pers. sing. m. fr. מְכַסֶּה d. 9a ; וּ bef. lab.   כסה

מְכַסִּים   Piel part. masc. pl. of מְכַסֶּה dec. 9a   כסה

מְכֻסִּים   Pual part. masc. pl. of [מְכֻסֶּה] dec. 9a   כסה

מְכַסֵּךְ   noun masc. sing., suff. 2 pers. sing. fem. from מְכַסֶּה dec. 9a   כסה

מִכְסָם   noun masc. sing., suff. 3 pers. pl. masc. from מֶכֶס ; וּ bef. lab.   .   כסס

מַכְסֵף / מִכְסֵף   pref. מַ)(noun masc. sing. dec. 6a (§ 35. rem. 2)   כסף

מִכַסְפִּי   pref. id.)(id., suff. 1 pers. sing. ; וּ bef. lab.   כסף

מִכַסְפָּם   pref. id.)(id., suff. 3 pers. pl. masc.   כסף

מִכְסַת   noun fem. sing., constr. of מִכְסָה dec. 10   כסס

מַכְעִיסִים   Hiph. part. masc., pl. of [מַכְעִים] dec. 1b   כעס

מַכְעַס   pref. מַ)(noun masc. sing. dec. 6d   כעס

מַכְעִיסִים   defect. for מַכְעִיסִים (q. v.)   כעס

מַכְעֵשׁ   pref. מַ)(noun masc. sing. dec. 6d   כעש

מִכַּף   pref. id.)(noun fem. s. d. 8d ; וּ bef. lab.   כפף

מִכְּפִירִים   pref. id.)(noun masc., pl. of כְּפִיר dec. 1a   כפר

מִכַּפֵּר   pref. id.)(Piel inf. constr.   כפר

מִכַּפְתּוֹר   pref. id.)(pr. name of a region   כפתר

מְכַבְּתִין   Chald. Pael part. m., pl. of [מְכַבַּת] dec. 2b   כפת

מִכַּפְתּוֹר   pref. ·מְ)(pr. name of a region   .   כפתר

מָכַר   fut. יִמְכֹּר. I. to sell.—II. to give in marriage, for a price, Ge. 31. 15 ; Ex. 21. 7.—III. to deliver, give up into the power of another.   Niph. I. to be sold.—II. to be delivered up.   Hithp. I. to be sold, De. 28. 68.—II. to sell oneself, give oneself up, sc. to do evil.

מָכִיר   (sold) pr. name—I. of a son of Manasseh ; patronym. מָכִירִי Nu. 26. 29.—II. 2 Sa. 9. 4, 5 ; 17. 27.

מֶכֶר   masc. dec. 6a (with suff. מִכְרֹה)—I. ware, merchandise, Ne. 13. 16.—II. price, value.

מְכְרִי   (price of the Lord, for מִכְרִיָּה) pr. name masc. 1 Ch. 9. 8.

מִמְכָּר   masc. dec. 2b.—I. sale.—II. thing sold.—III. ware, merchandise.

מִמְכֶּרֶת   fem. sale, Le. 25. 42.

מָכֹר   Kal inf. abs. ; וּ bef. lab.   .   מכר

מֶכֶר   noun masc. sing. (suff. מִכְרֹה) dec. 6a   מכר

מֹכֵר   Kal part. sing. masc. dec. 7b   .   מכר

מְכֻרְבָּל   Pual part. sing. masc. (§ 7)   .   כרבל

מָכְרָה   Kal pret. 3 pers. sing. fem.   .   מכר

מָכְרָה   id. imp. s. m. [מְכֹר] with parag. ה (§ 8. r. 11)   מכר

מִכְרֹה   noun masc. s., suff. 3 pers. s. f. fr. מֶכֶר d. 6a   מכר

מְכֵרָה   noun masc. sing., constr. of [מְכֵרָה] dec. 9a ; וּ bef. lab.   כרה

מַכֵּרוֹ   noun masc. s., suff. 3 p. s. m. fr. [מַכָּר] d. 1b   נכר

מָכְרוּ   Kal pret. 3 pers. pl. ; וּ bef. lab.   .   מכר

מְכָרוֹ   id. pret. 3 pers. sing. masc., suff. 3 pers. sing. masc. ; וּ id.   .   מכר

מְכֵרוֹתַיִךְ   noun fem. pl., suff. 2 pers. sing. masc. from [מְכוּרָה] dec. 10   .   כור

מְכָרוּם   Kal pret. 3 pers. pl., suff. 3 pers. pl. masc. ; וּ bef. lab.   .   מכר

מִכְרִי   pr. name masc.   .   .   מכר

מִכְרִי   Kal imp. sing. fem.   .   .   מכר

מַכִּרֵי   id. part. pl. constr. masc. from מֹכֵר dec. 7b ; וּ bef. lab.   .   מכר

מַכִּירֵהֶן   id., suff. 3 pers. pl. fem. ; וּ id.   מכר

מַכִּרֵיכֶם   noun m. pl., suff. 2 p. pl. m. tr. [מַכָּר] d. 1b   נכר

מְכַרְכֵּר   Pilp. part. sing. m. (§ 6. No. 4) ; וּ bef. lab.   כור

מְכָרָם   Kal pret. 3 pers. sing. m., suff. 3 pers. pl. m.   מכר

מִכְרָם   id. inf. [מְכֹר § 16. rem. 10] with suff. ; or (Nu. 20. 19) subst. masc. with suff. 3 pers. pl. masc. from מֶכֶר dec. 6a   מכר

מַכַרְמֵל   pref. ·מַ)(pr. name of a place   כרם

מְכָרָנוּ   Kal pret. 3 pers. s. m., with suff. 1 pers. pl.   מכר

מִכְרֵעַ   pref. ·מַ)(Kal inf. constr.   .   כרע

מְכַרְתִּי / מָכַרְתִּי   Kal pret. 1 pers. sing. ; acc. shifted by conv. וּ, bef. lab. for וּ (§ 8. rem. 7)   מכר

מְכֵרֹתֵיהֶם   noun fem. pl., suff. 3 pers. pl. masc. from [מְכֵרָה] dec. 10   כור

מְכוּרֹתַיִךְ   noun fem. pl., suff. 2 pers. sing. fem. from [מְכוּרָה] dec. 10   כור

מְכַרְתֶּם   Kal pret. 2 pers. pl. masc.   .   מכר

מִכַּשְׂדִּים   pref. ·מִ)(gent. noun, pl. of כַּשְׂדִּי   כשד

מִכְשׁוֹל / מִכְשֹׁל   noun masc. sing. dec. 1b ; וּ bef. lab.   כשל

מַכְשִׁלִים   Hoph. part. masc. pl. [of מֻכְשָׁל § 11. r. 10]   כשל

ᵃ Is. 14. 9.   ᶠ Is. 11. 9.   ˡ Hos. 13. 2.   ᵖ Da. 3. 23, 24.   ᵘ Le. 25. 16.   ᶻ Zep. 2. 9.   ᵍ Joel 4. 8.   ² Sa. 6. 14, 16.   Ge. 42. 5.
ᵇ 1 Ki. 1. 47.   ᵍ 1 Ch. 21. 16.   ᵐ Le. 27. 23.   ᵠ Le. 25. 25.   ᵛ Ch. 15. 27.   ᵃ 2 Ki. 12. 6.   ʰ 2 Ki. 4. 7.   ᵇ De. 32. 30.   Ge. 49. 5.
ᶜ 2 Sa. 12. 3.   ʰ Eze. 27. 7.   ⁿ Job 17. 7.   ʳ De. 14. 21.   ᵂ Ru. 4. 3.   ᵇ Ex. 21. 35.   ᵢ Ne. 13. 20.   ᶜ Ge. 31. 15.   Le. 19. 14.
ᵈ Eze. 41. 16.   ⁱ Nu. 31. 38, 39, 40.   ᵒ Ps. 35. 17.   ˢ De. 21. 14.   ˣ Ge. 25. 31.   ᶜ Ex. 21. 37.   ᵏ Zec. 11. 5.   ⁱ 1 Ki. 8. 54.   Ja. 18. 23.
ᵉ Is. 14. 11.   ᵏ Eze. 16. 17.   ᵖ Le. 16. 20.   ᵗ Ne. 13. 16.   ᵧ Pr. 31. 10.   ᵈ Eze. 21. 35.   ˡ 2 Ki. 12. 8.   ᵏ La. 50. 1.

מְבֻשָּׁלִים noun masc., pl. of מְבֻשָּׁל dec. 1 b .   בשל

מְבַשֵּׁף
מְבַשְּׁפָה‎[a] } Piel part. sing. masc. & fem. dec. 7 b)
(§ 39. No. 3. r. 4.); ‎ו bef. lab. } בשף

מַכַּת noun fem. sing., constr. of מַכָּה dec. 10 .   נכה

מִכְתָּב noun masc. sing. dec. 2 b .   כתב

מִכְתַּב id., constr. st. .   כתב

מְכַתְּבִים‎ו Piel part. masc. pl. [of מְכַתֵּב] dec. 7 b ;
‎ו bef. lab. .   כתב

מַכֹּתֶהָ noun fem. pl., suff. 3 pers. sing. fem. from
מַכָּה dec. 10, defect. for מַכּוֹתֶיהָ   נכה

מַכֹּתוֹ id. sing., suff. 3 pers. sing. masc. .   נכה

מַכֹּתַי‎[b]‎ו id. sing., suff. 1 pers. sing.; ‎ו bef. lab. .   נכה

מַכְתִּיר Hiph. part. sing. masc. .   כתר

מַכָּתְךָ‎[c] noun fem. s., suff. 2 pers. s. m. fr. מַכָּה d. 10   נכה

מַכָּתֵךְ id., suff. 2 pers. sing. fem. .   נכה

מַכֹּתֶךָ id. pl., suff. 2 p. s. m. [for מַכּוֹתֶיךָ § 4. r. 2]   נכה

מִכְתָּם noun masc. sing. .   כתם

מִכֶּתֶם‎[d] pref. מִ)(noun masc. sing. .   כתם

מִכֶּתֶף pref. id.)(noun fem. s., constr. of כָּתֵף d. 5 b .   כתף

מָל‎[e]‎ו Kal pret. 3 pers. sing. masc.; ‎ו, bef. lab.
for ‎ו, conv. .   מול

מָל‎ו Kal imp. sing. masc. .   מלל

מָלֵא (and middle Kametz מָלֹאוּ Est. 7. 5) fut. יִמְלָא.—
I. to be full, filled, with the acc. of that with
which anything is filled.—II. to be fulfilled, com-
pleted, of time.—III. trans. to fill, make full, with
double acc. of the space filled and the thing filling
it; Ex. 32. 29, מִלְאוּ יֶדְכֶם לַיהוָֹה fill your hands,
i. e. to act fully, for the Lord, Est. 7. 5, אֲשֶׁר
מְלָאוֹ לִבּוֹ whose heart has filled him, i. e. was
filled with courage, was bold enough. Niph. I.
to be filled, with acc., also לְ, מִן.—II. to be ful-
filled, completed, of time, Ex. 7. 25; Job 15. 32.
Pi. מִלֵּא (once מִלָּא).—I. to fill, with acc., double
acc., less frequently עַל, בְּ, מִן to
fill his hand, i. e. give over to him, the priesthood;
מִ׳ יָדוֹ לַיהוָֹה to fill one's (own) hand, i. e. be
liberal, towards the Lord; מִ׳ יָדוֹ בַּקֶּשֶׁת to fill his
hand with the bow, i. e. to seize the bow.—II. to
fulfil, complete, of time, promise, desire.—III. to
fill up, complete, as a number, words.—IV. ellipt.
and adverbially מִ׳ [לָלֶכֶת] אַחֲרֵי יְהוָֹה to follow
the Lord fully; מִ׳ הַקֶּשֶׁת to [bend] the bow fully,
sc. with full strength; Je. 4. 5, קִרְאוּ מַלְאוּ cry
fully, i. e. aloud.—V. to fill in, insert, set, as
precious stones. Pu. part. filled in, inserted, set,

of gems, Ca. 5. 14. Hithp. to set themselves
against, with עַל, Job 16. 19.

מְלָא Ch. to fill, Da. 2. 35. Ithpe. pass. Da. 3. 19.

מָלֵא masc. dec. 5 a (constr. מְלֵא § 34. rem. 1),
מְלֵאָה fem. dec. 10; adj.—I. filling.—II. filled,
full; מְלֵא יָמִים full of days, i. e. advanced in
age; neut. fulness, מֵי מָלֵא abundant water.—
III. adv. in full, fully.

מְלֹא, מְלוֹא, מְלֹא masc. dec. 1 a.—I. fulness
מְלֹא כַף the fulness of the hand, i. e. handful.—
II. multitude.

מְלֵאָה f. d. 10, fulness, plenty, of grain and wine.

מִלּוֹא masc.—I. a certain part of the citadel of
Jerusalem, called also בֵּית מִלּוֹא 2 Ki. 12. 21.—
II. a castle of the Shechemites, Ju. 9. 6, 20.

מִלֻּאָה, מְלֻאָה f. d. 10, insertion, setting of gems
מִלֻּאִים masc. pl. (of מִלֻּא dec. 1 b).—
I. consecration to the priestly office; meton. the
sacrifice of consecration.—II. insertion, setting of
gems.

מִלֻּאַת fem. setting, bezel of a ring; applied to
the socket of the eye, Ca. 5. 12.

מַלֵּא, יִמְלָא (He (God) will fill him) pr. name
masc. 1 Ki. 22. 8, 9.

מָלֵא‎[f]‎ו adj. masc. dec. 5 a (§ 34. r. 1); ‎ו bef. lab.

מַלֵּא‎[g]‎ו Piel imp. sing. masc.; ‎ו id.

מְלֵא adj. m. s., constr. of מָלֵא dec. 5 a (§ 34. r. 1)

מְלֹא‎ו noun masc. sing. dec. 1 a; ‎ו bef. lab. .

מִלֵּא Piel pret. 3 pers. sing. masc. .

מִלֵּא‎[h]‎ו id. pret. 3 pers. sing. masc.; ‎ו for ‎ו conv.

מִלֹּא‎[gg] noun masc. sing.

מִלֹּא pref. מִ)(pr. name in compos., לֹא דְבָר   לא

מָלְאָה‎[i]‎ו Kal pret. 3 pers. sing. fem.; ‎ו for ‎ו conv.

מְלֵאָה adj. fem. sing. dec. 10, from מָלֵא masc. .

מִלְאָה pref. מִ)(pr. name fem.   לאה

מְלֵאָה‎ו defect. for מְלוֹאָה (q. v.)

מָלְאוּ‎[k]‎ו } Kal pret. 3 pers. pl. (§ 8. rem. 1 & 7);
וּ‎ו } ‎ו for ‎ו conv. }

מַלְּאוּ‎[l]‎ו Piel imp. pl. masc. (§ 10. r. 7); ‎ו bef. lab.

מְלָאוֹ Kal pret. 3 pers. sing. m., suff. 3 pers. sing. m.

מִלְאוּ‎ו id. imp. pl. masc.; or [for מִלְּאוּ] Piel pret.
3 pers. sing. masc. (§ 10. rem. 7); ‎ו bef. lab.

מִלֹּאוֹ‎ו noun masc. sing., suff. 1 pers. sing. from
מִלֹּא dec. 1 a; ‎ו id.

‎a Je. 6. 21.   ‎c Je. 19. 8.   ‎h Je. 15. 18.   ‎o Je. 30. 12.   ‎t Jos. 5. 4, 7.   ‎x De. 33. 23.   ‎bb Je. 51. 34.   ‎ii Nu. 7. 14, 20,   ‎gg Je. 4. 5.
‎b De. 15. 10.   ‎f Is. 30. 26.   ‎i Hab. 1. 4.   ‎m De. 28. 59.   ‎p De. 30. 6.   ‎z Eze. 10. 2.   ‎cc Le. 21. 10.   26, &c.   ‎hh Ene. 9. 7.
‎c Ex. 22. 17.   ‎g Je. 10. 19.   ‎k Na. 3. 19.   ‎n Is. 13. 12.   ‎s Jos. 5. 2.   ‎aa Je. 6. 11.   ‎dd Le. 19. 29.   ‎l Is. 1. 15.   ‎d Est. 7. 5.
Is. 10. 1.   ‎gg 2 Ki. 12. 22.

מְלָאוּהָ׳	Piel pret. 3 pers. pl., suff. 3 pers. sing. fem. (§ 10. rem. 7); ו bef. lab.	מלא
מְלָאוּךְ	id. with suff. 2 pers. sing. fem.	מלא
מְלֵאוֹת	adj. fem., pl. constr. of מָלֵא d. 10, fr. מָלֵא m.	מלא
מִלֻּאֵיכֶם	noun m. pl., suff. 2 pers. pl. m. fr. [מִלֻּא] d. 1 b	מלא
מְלֵאִים	adj. masc., pl. of מָלֵא dec. 5a (§ 34. rem. 1)	מלא
מְלֹאִים	noun masc., pl. of [מְלֹא] dec. 1 b	מלא
מַלְאָךְ	noun masc. sing. dec. 2b; ו bef. lab.	לאך
מַלְאַךְ	id., constr. st.; ו id.	לאך
מַלְאֲכָהּ	Chald. id., suff. 3 pers. sing. fem. dec. 2a	לאך
מְלָאכָה	noun fem. sing. dec. 11c (comp. מְלָאכוֹת), constr. מְלֶאכֶת (§ 42. rem. 5); ו bef. lab.	לאך
מַלְאָכוֹ	noun masc. sing., suff. 3 pers. sing. masc. from מַלְאָךְ dec. 2b	לאך
מַלְאֲכוֹת	noun fem. pl. constr. [of מְלָאכוֹת] from מְלָאכָה (q. v.) dec. 11c	לאך
מַלְאֲכוֹתֵיךְ	id. pl. with suff. 2 pers. pl. masc.	לאך
מַלְאֲכֵי	noun masc. pl. constr. trom מַלְאָךְ dec. 2b	לאך
מַלְאָכִי	pr. name masc.	לאך
מַלְאָכִי	noun masc. s., suff. 1 pers. sing. fr. מַלְאָךְ d. 2a	לאך
מַלְאָכָיו	id. pl., suff. 3 pers. sing. masc.; ו bef. lab.	לאך
מַלְאָכֶיךָ	id. pl., suff. 2 pers. sing. masc.	לאך
מַלְאָכִים	id. pl., abs. st.; ו bef. lab.	לאך
מַלְאָכֵכָה	id. pl., suff. 2 pers. sing. fem. (§ 4. rem. 4)	לאך
מְלֶאכֶת	noun fem. sing. (used as the constr. of מְלָאכָה § 42. rem. 5) dec. 13a	לאך
מְלַאכְתּוֹ	id., suff. 3 pers. sing. fem.	לאך
מְלַאכְתְּךָ / מְלַאכְתֶּךָ	id., suff. 2 pers. sing. masc.	לאך
מִלְאֹם	pref. מְ noun masc. sing. (suff. לְאֻמִּי) d. 8c	לאם
מִלֵּאנוּ	Piel pret. 1 pers. pl.	מלא
מְלֵאת	Kal pret. 2 pers. sing. masc.	מלא
מְלָאת	Chald. Peal pret. 3 pers. sing. fem.; ו bef. lab.	מלא
מְלֵאת	defect. for מְלֵאוֹת (q. v.)	מלא
מְלֹאת	Kal inf. constr. (§ 23. rem. 2)	מלא
מִלֵּאתָ / מִלֵּאת	Piel pret. 2 pers. sing. masc.; acc. shifted by conv. ו, bef. lab. for וְ (§ 8. r. 7)	מלא
מְלֵאת	noun fem. sing. [for מְלֵאָת]	מלא
מְלֹאת	noun fem. sing., constr. of [מְלֹאָה] dec. 10	מלא
מִלֵּאתִי	Kal pret. 1 pers. sing.	מלא
מְלֵאֲתִי	adj. fem. constr. [מְלֵאַת], with parag. י from מְלֵאָה dec. 10, from מָלֵא masc.	מלא

מִלֵּאתִי / מִלֵּאתִי	Piel pret. 1 pers. sing.; acc. shifted by conv. ו, bef. lab. for וְ (§ 8. rem. 7)	מלא
מִלֵּאתִיו	id., suff. 3 pers. sing. masc.	מלא
מִלֵּאתִיךְ	id., suff. 2 pers. sing. fem.	מלא
מִלֵּאתִים	Kh. מִלֵּאתִים, id., suff. 3 pers. pl. masc.; K. מִלֵּאתָם (q. v.); ו bef. lab.	מלא
מְלֵאתֵךְ	noun fem. sing., suff. 2 pers. sing. masc. from מְלֵאָה dec. 10 (§ 42. rem. 4)	מלא
מִלֵּאתֶם	Piel pret. 2 pers. pl. masc.	מלא
מִלֵּאתַנִי	id. pret. 2 pers. s. m., suff. 1 pers. s. (§ 2. r. 1)	מלא
מִלֵּב	pref. מְ noun masc. sing. dec. 8b	לבב
מִלְּבְּךָ	pref. id. noun masc. sing., suff. 2 pers. sing. masc. from לֵב dec. 4b	לבב
מִלְּבַד	preff. מְ & לְ subst. masc., with the preff. לְ & מְ as an adv.; ו bef. lab.	בדד
מִלְּבַדּוֹ	Kh. מִלְּבַד q. v.; K. מִלְּבוֹ (q. v.)	לבב
מִלְבַדּוֹ	adv. מִלְבַד (q. v.) with suff. 3 pers. sing. m.	בדד
מִלִּבְּהֶן	pref. מְ noun masc. sing., suff. 3 pers. pl. fem. (§ 3. rem. 5) from לֵב dec. 8b	לבב
מִלִּבּוֹ	pref. id. id., suff. 3 pers. sing. masc.	לבב
מִלְּבוֹא	preff. מְ & לְ Kal inf. constr. (§ 25. No. 2f)	בוא
מַלְבּוּשׁ	noun masc. sing. dec. 1b	לבש
מַלְבּוּשַׁי	id. pl., suff. 1 pers. sing.	לבש
מַלְבּוּשֵׁיהֶם	id. pl., suff. 3 pers. pl. masc.; ו bef. lab.	לבש
מַלְבּוּשֵׁךְ	id. sing., suff. 2 pers. sing. fem.; ו id.	לבש
מִלִּבִּי	pref. מְ noun masc. sing., suff. 1 pers. sing. from לֵב dec. 8b	לבב
מִלִּבֶּךָ / מִלִּבֶּךָ	pref. id. id., suff. 2 pers. sing. masc.	לבב
מִלִּבְּכֶם	pref. id. id., suff. 3 p. pl. m.; ו bef. lab.	לבב
מַלְבֵּן	noun masc. sing.	לבן
מַלְבְּנָה	pref. מְ pr. name of a place	לבן
מַלְבְּנוֹן	pref. id. pr. name of a mountain	לבן
מִלִּבְנֵיכֶם	pref. id. noun fem. with pl. m. term. & suff. 2 pers. pl. masc. fr. לְבֵנָה d. 11 (§ 42. r. 4)	לבן
מַלְבֻּשֵׁיהֶם	defect. for מַלְבּוּשֵׁיהֶם (q. v.)	לבש
מַלְבִּשִׁים	Pual part. masc. pl. [of מְלֻבָּשׁ]	לבש
מִלֵּן	pref. מְ noun masc. sing.	לן
מִלֵּדָה	pref. id. Kal inf., or subst. fem. (§ 20. r. 3)	ילד
מִלֶּדֶת	pref. id. id. inf. constr. dec. 13a	ילד
מִלְּדֹתַיִךְ	defect. for מוֹלְדֹתַיִךְ (q. v.)	ילד
מִלָּה	noun fem. sing. dec. 10, Chald. dec. 8a	מלל
מָלְאוּ	Kal pret. 3 pers. pl. for מָלְאוּ (§ 23. rem. 11)	מלא

a Ezr. 9. 11.   f 2 Ch. 17. 13.   l Na. 2. 14.   q Da. 2. 35.   u Je. 51. 14.   z Le. 23. 38.   f Na. 3. 14.   l Ho. 9. 12.
b Ki. 3. 25.   g Ge. 24. 7, 40.   m Jon. 1. 8.   r Ca. 5. 12.   v Eze. 11. 6.   a Eze. 16. 13.   g Ec. 11. 10.   m Eze. 16. 3.
c Is. 23. 2.   h 1 Ch. 28. 19.   n Ge. 25. 23.   s Is. 1. 21.   w Ex. 22. 28.   b 1Ki. 12. 33.   h Ne. 6. 8.   n Ex. 5. 19.
d Eze. 36. 38.   i Ps. 72. 28.   o Ex. 28. 17.   t Ex. 28. 3.   x Je. 15. 17.   c De. 4. 35.   i 1 Ki. 22. 10.   o Ps. 189. 4.
e Le. 8. 33.   k Jos. 9. 13.   p Job 36. 17.   y Is. 63. 3.   d Eze. 13. 17.   k Le. 14. 15.   p Da. 2. 9.
  e Job 8. 10.   q Ese. 26. 16.

מָלְאוּ	Kal pret. 3 pers. pl. . . .	מול
מְלֹא⁴	defect. for מְלוֹא (q. v.) . .	מלא
מְלוֹ	pr. name in compos. see לֹא דְ׳ לוֹ דָבָר under לֹא	לא
מִלּוֹא	noun masc. sing. . . .	מלא
מִלֹּא	noun masc. sing. dec. 1 a	מלא
מְלֹאָה⁶	ᴵ id., suff. 3 pers. sing. fem.; ᴵ bef. lab.	מלא
מְלֹאוֹ	ᴵ id., suff. 3 pers. sing. masc.; ᴵ id.	מלא
מִלֻּאִים	ᴵ noun masc., pl. of [מִלֻּא] dec. 1 b; ᴵ id.	מלא
מְלוֹהַ⁶	constr. of the foll. . . .	לוה
מַלְוֶה⁶	ᴵ᷍ Hiph. part. sing. masc. d. 9 a; ᴵ bef. lab.	לוה
מַלֵּחַ⁶	noun masc. sing. . . .	מלח
מַלּוּךְ	pr. name masc. . . .	מלך
מְלוֹכָה⁴	Kh. מְלוֹכָה, K. מָלְכָה Kal imp. sing. masc. with parag. ה (§ 8. rem. 12)	מלך
מְלוּכָה	noun fem. sing.	מלך
מְלוֹכִי⁶	Kh. מְלוֹכִי, K. מָלְכִי Kal imp. sing. fem. (§ 8. rem. 12)	מלך
מָלוֹן⁶	noun masc. sing. dec. 3 a . .	לון
מְלוֹן	id., constr. st. . . .	לון
מַלּוֹשׁ⁶	pref. מִ ✗ Kal inf. constr. .	לוש
מְלוֹשְׁנִי⁶⁶	Kh. מְלוֹשְׁנִי Poel part. (§ 6. No. 1), K. מַלְשְׁנִי for מְלַשְׁנִי Piel part. (§ 10. r. 7 b), suff. 1 pers. sing.	לשן
מַלּוֹתִי	pr. name masc. . . .	מלל

מָלַח. Niph. *to pass away, vanish,* Is. 51. 6. מְלָחִים masc. pl. (from מָלַח) *decay, rottenness,* Je. 38 12, בְּלוֹיֵ מְ׳ *rotten rags.*

מֶלַח וְ׳ masc. *salt;* יָם הַמֶּלַח *the salt sea,* i. e. the Dead Sea; בְּרִית מֶלַח *covenant of salt,* i. e. lasting covenant; salt as the emblem of perpetuity.

מְלַח Chald. masc. *salt.*

מָלַח *to salt,* Le. 2. 13. Pu. pass. Ex. 30. 35. Hoph. *to be salted, washed with salt water,* Eze. 16. 4.

מְלַח Chald. *to eat salt,* Ezr. 4. 14.

מַלָּח masc. dec. 1 a, *seaman, mariner.*

מַלּוּחַ masc. ἅλιμος, *sea-purslain,* a marine plant, the leaves of which are eaten by the poor, Job 30. 4.

מְלֵחָה fem. *salt, barren land.*

מְלַח ⁿ᷍ᵃ Chald. noun masc. sing.; ᴵ bef. lab. | מלח |
מְלֵחָה noun fem. sing. | מלח |

מַלְחֵיהֶם⁶	ᴵ noun masc. pl., suff. 3 pers. pl. masc. fr. [מֶלַח] dec. 1 b; ᴵ bef. iab. .	מלח
מַלְחַיִךְ⁶	id. pl., suff. 2 pers. sing. fem. . .	מלח
מַלָּחִים⁶	id. pl., abs. st. . . .	מלח
מְלָחִים	noun masc. pl. of [מֶלַח] dec. 6 .	מלח
מִלָּחֶם	pref. מִ ✗ noun com. sing. (suff. לַחְמִי) d. 6 a	לחם
מִלְחָמָה	ᴵ᷍ noun f. s. d. 11 a (§ 42. r. 5); ᴵ bef. lab.	לחם
מִלַּחְמוֹ	pref. מִ ✗ noun com. sing., suff. 3 pers. sing. masc. fr. לֶחֶם dec. 6 a	לחם
מִלְחָמוֹת	ᴵ᷍᷍ noun fem. pl. abs. fr. מִלְחָמָה dec. 11 a (§ 42. rem. 5); ᴵ bef. lab. . .	לחם
מִלְחֲמוֹת מִלְחֲמֹת	} id. pl. constr.; ᴵ id.	לחם
מִלְחֶמֶת	noun fem. sing. dec. 13 a, see מִלְחָמָה	לחם
מִלְחַמְתָּהּ	id., suff. 3 pers. sing. fem. . .	לחם
מִלְחַמְתּוֹ	id., suff. 3 pers. sing. masc. . .	לחם
מִלְחַמְתִּי	id., suff. 1 pers. sing. . .	לחם
מִלְחֲמֹתָיו	id. pl., suff. 3 pers. sing. masc. .	לחם
מִלְחֲמֹתֵינוּ	id. pl., suff. 1 pers. pl. . .	לחם
מִלְחַמְתֶּךָ	id. sing., suff. for מִלְחַמְתְּךָ (q. v.)	לחם
מִלְחַמְתֵּךְ	id. sing., suff. 2 pers. sing. fem. .	לחם
מִלְחַמְתְּךָ	id. sing., suff. 2 pers. sing. masc. .	לחם
מִלְחַמְתָּם	id. sing., suff. 3 pers. pl. masc. .	לחם
מִלְחַמְתֵּנוּ	defect. for מִלְחֲמֹתֵינוּ (q. v.) .	לחם
מְלַחְנָא	Chald. Peal pret. 1 pers. pl. .	מלח
מְלַחֲשִׁים	Piel (§ 14. r. 1) part. m., pl. of [מְלַחֵשׁ] d. 7 b	לחש

מָלַט Pi. מִלֵּט, מִלַּט (§ 10. rem. 1).—I. *to let escape* or *slip, to deliver.*—II. *to lay eggs,* Is. 34. 15. Hiph. I. *to deliver,* Is. 31. 5.—II. *to bring forth,* Is. 66. 7. Niph. *to be delivered; to deliver oneself, escape.* Hithp. *to escape,* Job 19. 20; 41. 11.

מֶלֶט masc. *mortar, cement,* Je. 43. 9.

מְלַטְיָה (whom *the Lord delivers*) pr. name masc. Ne. 3. 7.

מַלֵּט	Piel inf. abs. & constr. . .	מלט
מִלַּט⁶ᵏ מִלֵּט	} ᴵ᷍ id. pret. 3 pers. sing. masc. (§ 10.rem.1); } ᴵ bef. lab. . . .	מלט
מַלְּטָה⁶	id. imp. sing. masc. with parag. ה	מלט
מַלְּטוּ⁶	ᴵ᷍ id. imp. pl. masc.; ᴵ bef. lab. .	מלט
מַלְּטוּנִי⁶	ᴵ id. id. with suff. 1 pers. sing.; ᴵ id.	מלט
מַלְּטִי⁶	ᴵ᷍ id. imp. sing. fem.; ᴵ id. .	מלט
מַלְטִיָּה⁶	pr. name masc. . . .	מלט

ᵃ Jos. 5. 5, 7.   ᶠ Ps. 112. 5.   ᵏ Ho. 7. 4.   ᵖ Eze. 27. 27.   ᵗ 1 Ch. 22. 8.   ˣ Je. 50. 30.   ᵈ Is. 41. 12.   ʰ Ezr. 4. 14.   ᵐ Je. 48. 6.
ᵇ Eze. 41. 8.   ᵍ Job 30. 4.   ᵐ De. 29. 22.   ᵠ Eze. 27. 29.   ᵘ 2 Ch. 12. 15.   ʸ 2 Ch. 35. 21.   ᵉ Eze. 27. 10, 27.   ᶦ Ps. 58. 6.   ⁿ Je. 51. 6, 45.
ᶜ 1 Ch. 29. 2.   ʰ Ju. 9. 8.   ⁿ Ju. 9. 12.   ʳ Ezr. 7. 22.   ᵛ Nu. 21. 14.   ᶻ 2 Ch. 27. 7.   ᶠ 2 Sa. 11. 25.   ᵏ Ec. 9. 15.   ᵒ Job 6. 23.
Pr. 19. 17.   ᶦ Ju. 9. 12.   ˢ Eze. 27. 9.   ˢ Pr. 22. 9.   ᵂ 1 Sa. 13. 22.   ᵃ 2 Ch. 32. 8.   ᵍ 1 Sa. 8. 20.   ˡ Ps. 116. 4.   ᵖ 1 Ki. 1. 12.
Pr. 22. 7.   ᵏ Is. 10. 39.   ᵒ 1 Ch. 16. 32.   ᵗ Ps. 101. 5.   ʸʸ Eze. 33. 5.

מִלַּטְנוּ Piel pret. 3 pers. s. m. (מִלַּט), suff. 1 pers. pl. מלט

מְלֻטָּשׁ Pual part. sing. masc. . . . . לטש

מִלַּי [for מִלָּי] noun fem. with pl. masc. term. & suff. 1 pers. sing. from מִלָּה dec. 10 . מלל

מִלַּי Chald. noun fem. with pl. masc. term., constr. st. from מִלָּה [for מִלָּא] dec. 8 a . מלל

מִלַּיָּא Chald. id. pl., emph. st. . מלל

מִלֵּיהֶם noun fem. with pl. masc. term. & suff. 3 pers. pl. masc. from מִלָּה dec. 10 . מלל

מִלֶּיךָ id. pl. with suff. 2 pers. sing. masc. . מלל

מֵלֵיל pref. מֵ)(noun m. sing., constr. of לַיִל d. 6 h   ליל

מֵלֵילָה pref. id.)(id. abs. with parag. ה . ליל

מִלֵּילֹת noun fem., pl. of [מִלֵילָה] dec. 10 . מלל

מִלִּים noun fem. with pl. masc. term. from מִלָּה dec. 10 ; וּ bef. lab. . מלל

מְלִלִים Kal part. pass. masc., pl. of מוּל dec. 1 a מול

מִלִּין Heb. & Chald. noun fem. with pl. masc. term. fr. מִלָּה d. 10, Chald. d. 8 a ; וּ bef. lab. מלל

מְלִיצִים Hiph. part. masc. pl. [of מֵלִין], Chald. form (§ 21. rem. 24) . . } לוץ
מְלִינָם

מֵלִיץ Hiph. part. sing. masc. dec. 3 b . לוץ

מְלִיצָה noun fem. sing. ; וּ bef. lab. . לוץ

מְלִיצַי Hiph. part. pl. m., suff. 1 p. s. fr. מֵלִיץ d. 3 b לוץ

מְלִיצֶיךָ id. pl. with suff. 2 pers. sing. m.; וּ bef. lab. לוץ

מָלַךְ fut. יִמְלֹךְ.—I. to reign, to be king, with בְּ, עַל over.—II. to be made king. Hiph. to make king, with acc., also לְ. Hoph. to be made king, Da. 9. 1. Niph. to consult, take counsel, Ne. 5. 7; comp. מֶלֶךְ.

מֶלֶךְ masc. dec. 6 a (with suff. מַלְכִּי).—I. king; applied to God, and also false gods.—II. pr. name masc., also with the art. הַמֶּלֶךְ.

מֶלֶךְ Chald. masc. dec. 3 a, king.

מְלַךְ Chald. m. d. 3 b, advice, counsel, Da. 4. 24.

מֹלֶךְ with the art. הַמֹּלֶךְ (the king) Moloch, pr. name of an idol of the Ammonites.

מַלְכָּה fem. dec. 12 a, queen.

מַלְכָּא Chald. fem. dec. 8 a, queen.

מִלְכָּה (counsel) pr. name of a daughter of Haran, Ge. 11. 29 ; 22. 20.

מַלּוּךְ (counsellor) pr. name masc. of several persons ; for which also מַלּוּכִי Kh., but מְלִיכִי Keri, comp. Ne. 12. 2, with ver. 14.

מַלְכוּ Chald. fem. dec. 8 c.—I. dominion, reign, rule.—II. kingdom, realm.

מְלוּכָה fem., kingship or royalty.

מַלְכוּת fem. dec. 1 b (pl. מַלְכָיוֹת).—I. kingdom, dominion, reign, rule.—II. royalty, royal dignity, בֵּית מַ royal palace; לְבוּשׁ מַ royal garments also לְבוּשׁ omitted, Est. 5. 1.—III. kingdom, realm.

מַלְכִּיאֵל (king of, i. e. appointed by, God) pr name masc. Ge. 46. 17.

מַלְכִּיָּהוּ, מַלְכִּיָּה (king of the Lord; see preced.) pr. name masc. of several persons.

מַלְכִּירָם (the king is exalted; part. of רוּם) pr. name masc. 1 Ch. 3. 18.

מַלְכִּישׁוּעַ, מַלְכִּי־שׁוּעַ (king of help or wealth) pr. name of a son of Saul.

מַלְכָּם pr. name.—I. i. q. מַלְכֹּם, an idol of the Moabites and Ammonites.—II. of a man, 1 Ch. 8. 9.

מִלְכֹּם pr. n., i. q. מֹלֶךְ, an idol of the Ammonites.

מְלֶכֶת fem. queen, only in the phrase מְלֶכֶת הַשָּׁמַיִם the queen of heaven, the Astoreth, Astarte of the Phenicians, i. e. the Diana or Venus.

מַלְכֶת (queen) pr. name fem. 1 Ch. 7. 18.

יַמְלֵךְ (whom he, sc. God, shall cause to reign) pr. name masc. 1 Ch. 4. 34.

מַמְלַכְתִּי fem. constr. מַמְלֶכֶת, with suff. מַמְלַכְתִּי, pl. מַמְלָכוֹת (§ 42. rem. 5) i. q. מַלְכוּת q. v.

מַמְלָכָה fem. dec. 3 c, kingdom, realm.

מָלַךְ Kal pret. 3 pers. sing. masc. for מָלַךְ (§ 8. r. 7) מלך

מָלֹךְ id. inf. abs. . . . מלך

מֶלֶךְ 'וּ, רְ noun masc. sing. dec. 6 a, Chald. 3 a, also pr. name ; וּ bef. lab., for וֶ see lett. ו מלך

מְלֹךְ Kal inf. constr. . . מלך

מְלָךְ id. with Mak., or (Ju. 9. 14) imp. sing. masc. (§ 8. rem. 18) . . . מלך

מֹלֵךְ id. part. act. sing. masc. . מלך

מַלְכָּא 'וּ Chald. noun m. sing., emph. of מֶלֶךְ d. 3 a מלך

מִלְכֹּד pref. מִ)(noun masc. sing. [for לָכֹד] לכד

מִלֹּכֵד pref. id.)(Kal part. act. sing. masc. . לכד

מַלְכֹּדְתּוֹ 'וּ noun fem. sing., suff. 3 pers. sing. masc. from [מַלְכֹּדֶת] dec. 13 c ; וּ bef. lab. לכד

מַלְכָּה Chald. in some copies for מַלְכָּא (q. v.) . מלך

מַלְכָּהּ noun masc. s., suff. 3 pers. s. m. fr. מֶלֶךְ d. 6 a מלך

מַלְכָּה 'וּ pr. name fem. ; וּ bef. lab. . מלך

מָלְכוֹ Kal inf., suff. 3 pers. sing. masc. . מלך

מָלְכוּ id. pret. 3 pers. pl. . . מלך

a 2 Sa. 19. 19.   d Da. 7. 11, 16.   g Is. 21. 11.   k Da. 7. 25.   m Job 33. 23.   o Is. 43. 27.   q Je. 33. 21.   s Pr. 16. 32.   u Da. 4. 16.
Ps. 52. 4.   e Ps. 19. 5.   h De. 23. 26.   l Nu. 14. 27.   Job 16. 20.   p 1 Sa. 24. 21.   r Pr. 3. 26.   t Job 18. 10.   x 2 Ki. 25. 27.
b Da. 5. 10.   f Is. 21. 11.   i Jos. 5. 5.   n Job 15. 3.

מַלְכּוֹ — noun masc. sing., suff. 3 pers. sing. masc. from מֶלֶךְ dec. 6a . . . מלך

מַלְכוּ — 'ª Chald. noun fem. sing. dec. 8c ; ו bef. lab. . . מלך

מַלְכְוָת׳ — Chald. id. pl., constr. st. . . מלך

(מַלְכֻיּוֹת) — Ch. id. s. constr.; or Heb. n. f. (pl.) מלך

מַלְכֻיּוֹת — noun fem. pl. abs. from מַלְכָּה dec. 12a מלך

מַלְכוּתָא — 'ª Ch. noun fem. sing., emph. of מַלְכוּ d. 8c מלך

מַלְכְוָתָא — Chald. id. pl., emph. st. . . מלך

מַלְכוּתָה — 'ª Chald. id. sing., emph. for מַלְכוּתָא (q. v.) מלך

מַלְכוּתָהּ — ª id. sing., suff. 3 pers. sing. fem.; ו bef. lab. מלך

מַלְכוּתֵהּ — ª Chald. noun fem. sing., suff. 3 pers. sing. masc. from מַלְכוּ dec. 8c ; ו bef. lab. מלך

מַלְכוּתוֹ — 'ª noun fem. sing., suff. 3 pers. sing. masc. from מַלְכוּת (pl. מַלְכֻיּוֹת); ו id. מלך

מַלְכוּתִי — Ch. noun fem. s., suff. 1 pers. s. fr. מַלְכוּ d. 8. מלך

מַלְכוּתָךְ — Chald. id., suff. 2 pers. sing. masc. מלך

מַלְכוּתְךָ — ª'ª noun fem. sing., suff. 2 pers. sing. masc.
מַלְכוּתֶךָ — fr. מַלְכוּת, (pl. מַלְכֻיּוֹת); ו bef. lab. מלך

מַלְכוּתָם — id., suff. 3 pers. pl. masc. מלך

מַלְכִּי — Kal imp. sing. fem. (§ 8. rem. 12) . מלך

מַלְכֵי — ª noun m. pl. constr. fr. מֶלֶךְ d. 6a; ו bef. lab. מלך

מַלְכִּי — id. sing., suff. 1 pers. sing. מלך

מַלְכִּי — ª pr. name in compos. as מַלְכִּי צֶדֶק, &c.; ו bef. lab. מלך

מַלְכִּי — Ch. noun m. s., suff. 1 pers. s. fr. [מֶלֶךְ] d. 3b מלך

מַלְכַיָּא — Chald. noun masc. pl. emph. from מֶלֶךְ dec. 3a מלך

מַלְכִּיאֵל — ª pr. names masc.; ו bef. lab. מלך

מַלְכֵיהָ — noun m. pl., suff. 3 pers. s. fem. fr. מֶלֶךְ d. 6a מלך

מַלְכִּיָּהוּ — pr. name masc., see מַלְכִּיָּה מלך

מַלְכֵיהֶם — ª noun masc. pl., suff. 3 pers. pl. masc. from מֶלֶךְ dec. 6a; ו bef. lab. מלך

מַלְכֻיּוֹת — noun fem., pl. of מַלְכוּת . . מלך

מַלְכְּכֶם — noun masc. pl., suff. 2 pers. pl. m. fr. מֶלֶךְ d. 6a מלך

מַלְכִים — Ch. n. m. pl. with Heb. term. for מַלְכִין (q. v.) מלך

מְלָכִים — ª noun masc., pl. of מֶלֶךְ dec. 6a; ו bef. lab. מלך

מַלְכִין — ª' Ch. noun masc., pl. of מֶלֶךְ [or מְלַךְ] d. 3a מלך

מְלָכֵינוּ — noun masc. pl. with Chald. term. fr. מֶלֶךְ d. 6a מלך

מְלָכֵינוּ — id. pl. with suff. 1 pers. pl. מלך

מַלְכִּירָם — ª pr. name masc.; ו bef. lab. מלך

מַלְכִּישׁ — pref. מִ ℵ pr. name of a place לבש

מַלְכִּישׁוּעַ — ª pr. name masc.; ו bef. lab. מלך

מַלְכְּךָ — noun m. s., suff. 2 pers. s. m. fr. מֶלֶךְ d. 6a מלך

מַלְכֵּךְ — id., suff. 2 pers. sing. fem. מלך

מַלְכְּכֶם — id., suff. 2 pers. pl. masc. מלך

מַלְּכֶם׳ — Kh. for K. מַה־לָכֶם, see לָכֶם, & מה

מַלְכָּם — pr. name masc. מלך

מַלְכָּם — noun m. s., suff. 3 pers. pl. m. fr. מֶלֶךְ d. 6a מלך

מִלְכֹּם — pr. name masc. מלך

מַלְכֵּנוּ — noun masc. s., suff. 1 pers. pl. fr. מֶלֶךְ d. 6a מלך

מָלַכְתִּ׳ — Kal pret. 2 pers. sing. masc.; acc. shifted
מָלַכְתָּ — ו by conv. ו, bef. lab. for וְ (§ 8. r. 7) מלך

מַלְכַּת — ª noun fem. sing., constr. of מַלְכָּה dec. 12a מלך

מָלֶכֶת — pref. מִ ℵ Kal inf. constr. . . ילך

מֹלֶכֶת — Kal part. act. sing. fem., from מֹלֵךְ masc. . מלך

מַלְכְּתָא — Ch. noun fem. sing., emph. of [מַלְכָּא] d. 8a מלך

מַלְכֻתוֹ — defect. for מַלְכוּתוֹ (q. v.) מלך

I. [מָלַל] — to speak, Pr. 6. 23. Pi. to speak, declare, announce.

    מְלַל Ch. Pa. to speak, with עִם with any one, Da. 6. 22 ; to declare, with acc.

    מַלְלַי (eloquent) pr. name masc. Ne. 12. 36.

    מִלָּה fem. dec. 10 (pl. מִלִּים, מִלִּין).—I. word, saying, discourse ; meton. object of discourse, Job 30. 9.—II. thing, Job 32. 11.

    מִלָּה Ch. fem. dec. 8a (§ 64) pl. מִלִּין.—I. word, espec. order, mandate.—II. thing.

    מַלּוֹתִי (I spoke, comp. גְּדַלְתִּי, רוֹמַמְתִּי) pr. name masc. 1 Ch. 25. 4, 26.

II. [מָלַל] — I. to circumcise, Jos. 5. 2.—II. intrans. fut. יָמַל (§ 18. rem. 14) to be cut off, as grass, &c. Niph. to be circumcised, Ge. 17. 11 ; comp. also נָמַל. For Po. and Hithpo. which might properly be referred here, see מוּל.

    מְלִילָה fem. dec. 10, an ear of corn, De. 23. 26.

מַלִּל — Ch. Peal pret. 3 pers. sing. masc. (§ 47. r. 1) מלל

מִלֵּל — Piel pret. 3 pers. sing. masc. . . מלל

מִלְּלוּ — id. pret. 3 pers. pl. [for מִלְּלוּ comp. § 8. r. 7] מלל

מַלְלַי — pr. name masc. מלל

מְלַמֵּד — Piel part. sing. masc. dec. 7b מלד

מְלֻמָּדָה — Pual part. sing. fem. [of מְלֻמָּד] מלד

מְלַמְּדַי — Piel part. pl., suff. 1 pers. s. fr. מְלַמֵּד d. 7b מלד

מְלֻמְּדֵי — Pual part. pl. constr. from [מְלֻמָּד] dec. 2b מלד

מְלַמֶּדְךָ — Piel part. s. מְלַמֵּד, suff. 2 pers. s. m. d. 7b מלד

מִלְמַטָּה — preff. מִ & לְ ℵ prop. subst. מַט with loc.
    ה as an adv. יטה

ᵃ Da. 7. 27.   ᵈ Da. 7. 24.   ᶠ Ps. 103. 19.   ʲ Ju. 9. 10.   ᵐ Je. 44. 21.   ᵖ Pr. 31. 3.   ˢ 2 Sa. 16. 8.   ᵛ Ge. 21. 7.   ᵞ Is. 48. 17.
ᵇ Ca. 6. 8, 9.   ª Da. 2. 44.   ᵍ 1 Sa. 20. 31.   ᵏ Da. 4. 24.   ⁿ Ezr. 4. 13.   ᵠ Zec. 9. 9.   ᵗ Da. 5. 10, 10.   ʷ Job 33. 3.   ᶻ Ex. 27. 5.
ᶜ Da. 7. 22, 27.   ᶠ Est. 1. 19.   ʰ Ps. 145. 11, 13.   ˡ Da. 8. 22.   ° Je. 4. 20.   ʳ Is. 3. 15.   ᵘ Da. 6. 22.   ˣ Ps. 119. 99.

מִלְמַעְלָה preff. מִ & לְ)(prop. subst. מַעַל 'with loc. עלה
מִלְמַעְלָה *kk* ה as an *adv.*; ‹ bef. lab. }
מִלְמַעְלָה preff. id.)(n. m. s., constr. of מַעֲלָה d. 9a עלה
מַלְעִיבִים Hiph. part. masc. pl. [of מַלְעִיב] dec. 1b לעב
מַלְעִינִים Hiph. part. m. pl. [of מַלְעִין] d. 1b; ‹ bef. lab. לען
מִלְּעֻמַּת preff. מִ & לְ)(prop. subst., constr. of עֻמָּה
   dec. 10, as a *prep.* עמת
מֵאַלְּפֵנוּ [for מְאַלְּפֵנוּ § 19. rem. 10] Piel part. sing.
   [מְאַלֵּף], suff. 1 pers. pl. dec. 7b אלף
מִלִּפְנֵי preff. מִ & לְ)(the foll. with suff. 1 pers. פנה
מִלְּפָנֵי sing. }
מִלִּפְנֵי *oo* preff. מִ, & לְ bef. (:))(noun masc. pl.
   constr. fr. פָּנֶה d. 9b, as a *prep.* or *adv.* פנה
מִלְּפָנָיו preff. מִ & לְ)(id., suff. 3 pers. sing. masc. פנה
מִלְּפָנֶיךָ preff. id.)(id., suff. 2 pers. sing. masc. פנה
מִלִּפְנֵיכֶם preff. מִ, & לְ bef. (:))(id., suff. 2 p. pl. m. פנה
מִלְּפָנִים ‹ preff. מִ & לְ)(id.pl.abs. adverbially; ‹ bef. lab. פנה
מִלִּפְנִים preff. מִ, & לְ bef. (:))(noun masc. sing. פנם
מִלְּפָנֵינוּ ‹ preff. מִ & לְ)(noun masc. pl., suff. 1 pers.
   pl. as an *adv.* comp. מִלִּפְנֵי פנה

מָלַץ Niph. *to be smooth, agreeable,* Ps. 119. 103.
מֶלְצַר only with the art. הַמֶּלְצַר, a certain officer
   in the Babylonian court; coll. with the
   Persic, according to some, *master of the*
   wine, chief butler; according to others,
   treasurer, Da. 1. 11. 16.

מָלַק ‹ *to wring* or *pinch off,* Le. 1. 15; 5. 8.
מַלְקוֹחַ ‹ noun masc. sing. dec. 1b; ‹ bef. lab. לקח
מַלְקוֹחָי id. du. [מַלְקוֹחַיִם], with suff. 1 pers. sing. לקח
מַלְקוֹשׁ ‹ noun masc. sing.; ‹ bef. lab. לקש
מַלְקָחֶיהָ ‹ noun masc. du. [מַלְקָחַיִם], suff. 3 pers.
   sing. fem. from [מַלְקָח] dec. 2b; ‹ id. לקח
מְלַקְּטִים Piel part. masc., pl. of מְלַקֵּט dec. 7b לקט
מַלְשֵׁון pref. מִ)(noun com. sing. dec. 3a לשן
מַלְשֻׁן pref. id.)(id., constr. st.*Jos. 15. 5. לשן
מִלְשַׁת pref. id.)(noun fem., constr. of לִשְׁכָּה d. 12b לשך
מִלַּת ‹ ‹ Ch. noun fem. sing. constr. of מִלָּה [for
   מְלָא dec. 8a; ‹ bef. lab. מלל
מִלְּתָא ‹ Ch. id., emph. st.; ‹ id. מלל
מַלֹּתָה ‹ Kal pret. 2 pers. sing. masc. (§ 8. rem. 5);
   acc. shifted by ‹ for וַ, conv. (§ 8. rem. 7) מול
מִלְּתֵהּ Ch. for מִלְּתָא (q. v.) מלל

מִלָּתוֹ ‹ noun fem. sing., suff. 3 pers. sing. masc
   from מִלָּה dec. 10; ‹ bef. lab. מלל
מָלִתִי Kal pret. 1 pers. sing. for מָלָאתִי (§ 23. r. 11) מלא
מִלָּתִי noun fem. sing., suff. 1 pers. s. fr. מִלָּה d. 10 מלל
מְלָתֶם ‹ Kal pret. 2 pers. pl. masc.; ‹ for וַ, conv. מול
מַלְתָּעוֹת noun fem. pl. constr. of [מַלְתָּעָה] dec. 11a לתע
מַמְאִיר Hiph. part. sing. masc. מאר
מַמְאֶרֶת id. fem. (§ 39. No. 4d) מאר
מִמֶּגֶד ‹ pref. מִ)(noun masc. sing. dec. 6 מגד
מִמִּגְדּוֹ pref. id.)(pr. name of a place מגד
מִמִּגְדַּל pref. id.)(n. m. s., constr. of [מִגְדָּל] d. 2b מגד
מִמִּגְדָּל pref. id.)(pr. name of a place מגד
מִמָּגוֹר *a* pref. id.)(noun masc. sing. (§ 30. rem. 4) נור
מִמְּגֻרוֹת *b* noun fem., pl. of [מְגֻרָה] dec. 10 נור
מִמִּדְבָּר ‹ pref. מִ)(noun masc. s. d. 2b; ‹ bef. lab. דבר
מִמִּדְבַּר pref. id.)(id., constr. st. דבר
מִמַּדֵּיהֶם *c* noun m. pl., suff. 3 p. s. f. fr. [מַד] d. 8d מדד
מִמְּדִין pref. מִ)(pr. name of a country, R. דִּין see דון
מִמְּדִינוֹת *d* pref. id.)(n. f., pl. of מְדִינָה d. 10, R. דִּין see דון
מִמְּמַהֵר ‹ *f* Piel part. sing. m. (§ 14. r. 1); ‹ bef. lab. מהר
מִמַּהֲרוֹת *g* id. fem., pl. of [מְמַהֶרֶת] dec. 13 מהר
מִמּוֹאָב ‹ pr. name of a people, see מוֹאָב; ‹ bef. lab.
מְמוּכָן pr. name of a prince at the court of Ahasuerus, Est. 1. 14, 16, 21.
מִמּוּל pref. מִ)(*prep.* (suff. מִמֻּלִי) dec. 1a מול
מִמּוֹלַדְתְּךָ ‹ pref. id.)(noun fem. sing., suff. 2 pers.
   sing. masc from מוֹלֶדֶת d. 13a; ‹ bef. lab. לד
מִמְּמוּם pref. id.)(noun m. s. d. 1a, for מְאוּם מאם
מִמּוֹעֵד *h* pref. id.)(noun masc. sing. dec. 7b יעד
מִמּוֹעֲצוֹתֵיהֶם *ii* pref. id.)(noun fem. pl., suff. 3 pers.
   pl. masc. from מוֹעֵצָה dec. 11b; ‹ bef. lab. יעץ
מִמּוֹצָא *k* pref. id.)(noun masc. sing. d. 1b (§ 31. r. 1) יצא
מִמּוֹקְשֵׁי pref. id.)(noun m. pl. constr. fr. מוֹקֵשׁ d. 7b יקש
מִמּוֹשְׁבֹתֵיכֶם pref. id.)(noun masc. with pl. fem. term.
   & suff. 2 pers. pl. masc. from מוֹשָׁב d. 2b ישב
מִמְּמֻנָת pref. id.)(noun masc. sing. dec. 6g מות
מִמּוֹתֵי noun masc. pl. constr. from [מֹמוֹת] dec. 3a מות
מְמוֹתֵת *l* Pilel part. sing. masc. מות
מַמְזֵר masc. *bastard;* according to the Mishna (Je-
   bamoth) the offspring of adultery or incest;
   De. 23. 3; Zec. 9. 6. Etymo. uncertain.
מִמִּזְרָח pref. מִ)(noun masc. sing. dec. 2b זרח
מִמִּזְרַח *m* pref. id.)(id. constr. st.; ‹ bef. lab. זרח
מִמִּזְרָחִים ‹ pref. id.)(noun m., pl. of [מִזְרָח] dec. 9a זרח
מְמֻחִים Pual (§ 14. rem. 1) part. masc. pl. [of מְמֻחֶה
   § 38. rem. 1] מחה

* Ju. 8. 13.   *f* Is. 41. 26.   *l* Nu. 4. 9.   *r* Ex. 12. 44.   *a* Ps. 58.7.   *h* Joel 1. 17.   *g* Pr. 6. 18.   *f* Pr. 1. 31.   *p* 1 Sa. 14. 13
2 Ch. 36. 16.   *g* 1 Ki. 6. 29.   *m* Ps. 120. 2.   *s* Da. 2. 5.   *b* Eze. 23. 24.   *i* Ge. 12. 1.   *h* Ps. 75. 7.   *m* Is. 59. 19.
2 Ch. 30. 10.   *h* Ec. 1. 10.   *n* Je. 36. 21.   *t* 2 Sa. 23. 2.   *c* De. 33. 13, 14,   *k* Job 11. 15.   *i* Pr. 14. 27.   *n* Job 37. 9.
1 Ki. 7. 20.   *i* Is. 49. 25.   *o* Da. 2. 10, 23.   *u* Job 32. 18.   15, 16.   *l* Mal. 3. 5.   *k* Zep. 3. 18.   *o* Is. 25. 6.
Job 25. 11.   *k* Ps. 22. 16.   *p* Ps. 3. 28.   *a* Is. 31. 9.   *d* Is. 31. 9.   *m* Ge. 41. 32.   *l* 1 Ki. 7. 11.   *oo* 2 Ch. 32. 7   *q* Ho. 11. 8.
e De. 10. 16.

מְמַחֲלִיק pref. מִ ✕ Hiph. part. sing. masc. — חלק

מִמַּחֲנֵה pref. id. ✕ noun m. s., constr. of מַחֲנֶה d. 9a — חנה

מִמַּחֲנוֹתᵇ pref. id. ✕ id. with pl. fem. term. — חנה

מִמַּחֲנַיִםᵍ pref. id. ✕ pr. name of a place; ו bef. lab. — חנה

מִמַּחֲצִיתᵍ pref. id. ✕ noun fem. sing. dec. 1 b; ו id. — חצה

מִמַּחֲצִיתָםᶜ pref. id. ✕ id., suff. 3 pers. pl. masc. — חצה

מִמַּחֲצַתᵈ defect. for מִמַּחֲצִית (q. v.) — חצה

מִמָּחֳרָתᵉ pref. מִ ✕ noun fem. sing.; ו bef. lab. — מחר

מִמָּחֳרָת pref. id. ✕ id., constr. st. — מחר

מִמַּחְשְׁבֹתֵיכֶם pref. id. ✕ noun fem. pl., suff. 2 pers. pl. masc. from מַחֲשָׁבָה or מַחֲשֶׁבֶת — חשב

מִמְּחִתָּהᶠ pref. id. ✕ noun fem. sing. d. 10; ו bef. lab. — חתת

מִמַּטֵּהᵍ pref. id. ✕ constr. of the foll.; ו id. — נטה

מִמַּטֶּה pref. id. ✕ noun masc. sing. dec. 9a — נטה

מִמַּטּוֹתᵍ pref. id. ✕ id. with pl. fem. term. — נטה

מֵמִטִיר Hiph. part. sing. masc. — מטר

מִמַּטְמוֹנִיםᵍ pref. מִ ✕ noun masc. pl. of מַטְמוֹן dec. 1a — טמן

מִמָּטָרᵍ pref. id. ✕ noun masc. s. d. 4a; ו bef. lab. — מטר

מִמֵּיᵍ pref. id. ✕ noun masc. pl. constr. [from מַי § 38. rem. 2, & § 45] — מי

מִמֵּי pref. id. ✕ pron. pers. interr. — מי

מִמֵּימֵי pref. id. ✕ n. m. pl. [of מַי § 38. r. 2, & § 45] — מי

מִמֵּימֵי pref. id. ✕ id. constr. st. (§ 45) — מי

מֵמִיתᵏ Hiph. part. sing. masc. dec. 3b — מות

מְמִיתִיםᵐ id. pl., abs. st. — מות

מִמְּךָ / מִמֶּךָּ } prep. מִן with suff. 2 pers. sing. m. (§ 5) — מנן

מִמֵּךְ id. with suff. 2 pers. sing. fem. — מנן

מִמְּכוֹן pref. מִ ✕ noun m. s., constr. of מָכוֹן d. 3a — כון

מִמַּבֹּלוֹתֶיךָ pref. id. ✕ noun fem. pl., suff. 2 pers. sing. fem. from מַבָּה dec. 10; ו bef. lab. — נכה

מִמִּכְלְאֹת pref. id. ✕ n. f. pl. constr. fr. [מִכְלָאָה] d. 11a — כלא

מִמִּכְלְאֹתֶיךָ pref. id. ✕ id., suff. 2 pers. sing. masc. — כלא

מִמִּכְלָה pref. id. ✕ id. sing. abs. [for מִכְלָאָה] — כלא

מִמִּכְמָשׁ pref. id. ✕ pr. name of a place, see מִכְמָשׂ — כמס

מִמְכָּר noun masc. sing. dec. 2b — מכר

מִמְכָּר id. constr. st. — מכר

מִמְכָּרוֹ id. with suff. 3 pers. sing. masc. — מכר

מִמְכָּרָיו id. pl., suff. 3 pers. sing. masc. — מכר

מִמְכֶּרֶת noun sing. fem. — מכר

מְמַלֵּא Piel part. sing. masc. dec. 7b — מלא

מִמַּלֵּא pref. מִ ✕ noun masc. sing. dec. 1a — מלא

מִמַּלֵּאָה pref. id. ✕ id., suff. 3 pers. sing. fem. — מלא

מְמֻלָּאִים Pual part. masc. pl. [of מִלֵּא] — מלא

מִמְּלָאכְתּוֹ pref. מִ ✕ noun fem. sing., suff. 3 pers. sing.

masc. from מְלֶאכֶת (dec. 13a), constr. of מְלָאכָה (§ 42. rem. 5) — לאך

מִמֶּלַחᵈ Pual part. sing. masc. — מלח

מִמִּלְחָמָה pref. מִ ✕ noun fem. sing. dec. 11 a, (suff. חֲמָתוֹ, from חֵמָה dec. 13a, § 42. rem. 5) — לחם

מְמַלֵּט Piel part. sing. masc. dec. 7 b — מלט

מִמֻּלִיᵍ pref. מִ ✕ prep. (מוּל) with suff. 1 p. s. d. 1a — מול

מִמֶּלֶךְ pref. id. ✕ noun masc. sing. dec. 6a — מלך

מִמְּלֹךְ pref. id. ✕ Kal inf. constr. — מלך

מַמְלָכָהᵍ noun fem. sing. dec. 11 a, but constr. מַמְלֶכֶת (§ 42. rem. 5); ו bef. lab. — מלך

מַמְלָכוֹתᵍ id. pl., abs. st.; ו id. — מלך

מַמְלְכוֹת id. pl., constr. st. — מלך

מַמְלָכוּת noun fem. sing. — מלך

מַמְלֶכֶת noun fem. sing., constr. of מַמְלָכָה (§ 42. r. 5) — מלך

מַמְלַכְתּוֹ id., suff. 3 pers. sing. masc. (comp. dec. 13) — מלך

מַמְלַכְתִּיᶠ id., suff. 1 pers. sing.; ו bef. lab. for ו — מלך

מַמְלַכְתְּךָᵍ id., suff. 2 pers. sing. masc.; ו id. — מלך

מְמַלֵּלᵏ Ch. Pael part. sing. masc. — מלל

מְמַלִּלᵐ Ch. id. part. sing. masc — מלל

מְמַלְּלָאᵐ Ch. id. part. sing. fem. — מלל

מִמַּמְלָכָהᵖ pref. מִ ✕ noun fem. sing., comp. מַמְלָכָה — מלך

מִמֶּנָּהᵍ prep. (מִן) with suff. 3 p.s.f. (§5); ו bef. lab. — מנן

מִמֶּנּוּᵍ id. with suff. 3 pers. s. masc. or 1 pers. pl. — מנן

מִמְּנוֹחַᵃ pref. מִ ✕ noun m. s., constr. of מָנוֹחַ d. 3a — נוח

מִמֶּנִּי prep. (מִן) with suff. 1 pers. sing. (§ 5) — מנן

מְמֻנִּיםᵇ Pual part. masc., pl. of [מְמֻנֶּה] dec. 9a — מנה

מִמְנַשֶּׁהᵍ pref. מִ ✕ pr. name of a tribe; ו bef. lab. — נשה

מִמַּסְגֵּר pref. id. ✕ (prop. Hiph. part.) subst. masc. s. — סגר

מִמַּסְגְּרֹתֵיהֶם / מִמַּסְגְּרוֹתָם / מִמַּסְגְּרֹתֵיהֶם } pref. מִ ✕ noun fem. pl., suff. 3 pers. pl. masc. (§ 4. rem. 2) fr. מִסְגֶּרֶת dec. 13 a — סגר

מִמַּסְפֵּד pref. id. ✕ noun masc. sing.; ו bef. lab. — יסד

מִמְּסֻכָהᵃ pref. id. ✕ noun fem. sing. [for מְשׂוּכָה] — שׂוך

מִמְסָךְ noun masc. sing. — מסך

מִמְּסִלּוֹתָםᵍ pref. מִ ✕ noun fem. pl., suff. 3 pers. pl. masc. from מְסִלָּה dec. 10 — סלל

מִמִּסְרוֹת pref. id. ✕ pr. name of a place, see מוֹסֵר — אסר

מִמָּעוֹן pref. id. ✕ noun masc sing., constr. of מָעוֹן dec. 3a (§ 32. rem. 5) — עון

מִמְּעֵיᵍ pref. id. ✕ n. m. pl., suff. 1 p. s. fr. [מֵעַ] d. 7 a — מע

מִמְּעֵי pref. id. ✕ id. pl., constr. st. — מע

מִמֵּעַיִךְᵈ pref. id. ✕ id. pl., suff. 2 pers. sing. fem. — מע

מִמֵּעֶיךָ pref. id. ✕ id. pl., suff. 2 pers. sing. masc. — מע

ᵃ Pr. 28. 23.   ᵍ Nu. 36. 8.   ⁿ 2 Ki. 17. 26.   ᵗ Le. 25. 27, 28, 29, 50.   ˣ Ex. 36. 4.   ² 2 Sa. 3. 28.   ᶜ Ps. 105. 13.   ʰ Ps. 142. 8.   ᵐ Mi. 7. 4.
ᵇ 1 Sa. 17. 4.   ʰ Job 3. 21.   ᵒ 1 Ch. 16. 20.   ᵘ De. 18. 8.   ʸ Ex. 30. 35.   ᵃ 1 Ch. 16. 20.   ᵈ Ps. 18. 46.   ⁱ Ju. 5. 20.
ᶜ Nu. 31. 29.   ⁱ 2 Sa. 23. 4.   ᵖ Ps. 78. 70.   ᵛ 1 Sa. 19. 11.   ᶻ Da. 7. 8.   ᵇ Je. 30. 7.   ᵉ 2 Sa. 22. 46.   ᵏ Je. 25. 30.
ᵈ Nu.31.30,42,47.   ᵏ Is. 4. 6.   ᵠ Ps. 50. 9.   ʷ Nu. 22. 5.   ᵃ Da. 7. 20.   ᶜ Da. 7. 11.   ᶠ Mi. 7. 17.   ˡ 2 Sa. 16. 4.
ᵉ Is. 55. 9.   ˡ Is. 48. 1.   ʳ Hab. 3. 17.   ˣ Le. 25. 42.   ᵇ 1 Ch. 6. 16.   ᵈ 1 Ch. 9. 29.   ᵍ 1 Ki 7. 9.   ᵇ Ge. 25. 23.
ᶠ Is. 54. 14.   ᵐ 1 Sa. 2. 6.   ˢ Le. 25. 25, 33.   ʸ Ca. 5. 14.   Ge. 20. 9.

מִמַּעְיָנֵי — pref. מִ (noun m. pl. constr. fr. מַעְיָן d. 2 b — עין

מִמַּעַל / מִמָּעַל — } pref. id. ((prop. subst.) as an adv.; / ו bef. lab. — עלה

מִמַּעֲלָה — pref. id. (noun m. s., constr. of מַעֲלָה d. 9 a — עלה

מִמַּעֲלֵי — pref. id. (Hiph. part. pl. constr. fr. מַעֲלָה d. 9 a — עלה

מִמַּעַלְלֵיהֶם — pref. id. (noun masc. pl., suff. 3 pers. pl. masc. fr. [מַעֲלָל] dec. 2 b — עלל

מִמַּעֲמַדְּךָ — ו pref. id. (noun masc. sing., suff. 2 pers. sing. masc., from [מַעֲמָד] d. 2 b; ו bef. lab. — עמד

מִמַּעֲמַקֵּי — ו pref. id. (constr. of the foll.; ו id. — עמק

מִמַּעֲמַקִּים — pref. id. (noun masc., pl. of [מַעֲמָק] d. 8 a — עמק

מִמַּעֲנוֹת — pref. id. (noun fem., pl. of מַעֲנָה [or מְעוֹנָה] dec. 10 — עון

מִמַּעֲנָתוֹ — pref. id. (id. sing., suff. 3 pers. sing. masc. — עון

מִמַּעֲצוּצוֹתֵיהֶם — defect. for מִמַּעֲצוּצוֹתֵיהֶם (q. v.) — יעץ

מִמַּעֲרָב — ו pref. מִ (noun masc. s. d. 2 b; ו bef. lab. — ערב

מִמַּעֲרָבָה — ו pref. id. (noun fem. sing. fr. מַעֲרָב; ו id. — ערב

מִמַּעֲרָה — pref. id. (noun m. s., constr. of [מַעֲרָה] d. 9 a — ערה

מִמַּעֲרוֹת — pref. id. (Kh. מַעֲרוֹת [pl. c. of [מַעֲרָה] R. מַעֲרָה; K. מַעֲרְכוֹת (q. v.) — ערך

מִמַּעֲשָׂיו — prf. id.(n. m. pl., suff. 3 p. m. s. fr. מַעֲשֶׂה d. 9 a — עשה

מִמַּעֲשֵׂנוּ — pref. id. (id. sing., suff. 1 pers. pl. — עשה

מִמַּעְשְׂרוֹ — pref. id. (noun masc. sing., suff. 3 pers. sing. masc. from מַעֲשֵׂר dec. 7 b — עשר

מִמַּפְרִיסֵי — } ו pref. id. (Hiph. part. pl. constr. fr. מַפְרִיס dec. 1 b; ו bef. lab. — פרס

מִמַּצָּב — ו pref. id. (noun m. s., constr. of [מַצָּב] d. 2 b — נצב

מִמַּצָּבֶךָ — ו pref. id. (id., suff. 2 pers. s. m. [for מַצָּבְךָ] — נצב

מִמְּצֹא — pref. id. (Kal inf. constr. — מצא

מִמְּצוּקוֹתַי — pref. id. (noun fem. pl., suff. 1 pers. sing. from מְצוּקָה dec. 10 — צוק

מִמְּצוּקוֹתֵיהֶם — pref. id. (id., suff. 3 pers. pl. masc. — צוק

מִמִּצְוֺת — pref. id. (noun fem., pl. of מִצְוָה dec. 10 — צוה

מִמִּצְוֺתֶיךָ — pref. id. (id., suff. 2 pers. sing. masc. — צוה

מַמְצִיא — Hiph. part. sing. masc. — מצא

מִמְּצֻלוֹת — pref. מִ (noun fem., pl. of מְצוּלָה dec. 10 — צול

מִמִּצְפֶּה — ו pref. id. (pr. name of a place; ו bef. lab. — צפה

מִמְּצֻקוֹתֵיהֶם — ו defect. for מִמְּצוּקוֹ (q. v.) — צוק

מִמִּצְרַיִם / מִמִּצְרָיְנוּ — } pref. מִ (pr. name of a country; ו bef. lab. — מצר

מִמַּקֵּדָה — pref. id. (pr. name of a place — נקד

מִמִּקְדְּשִׁי — ו pref. id. (noun masc. sing., suff. 1 pers. sing. from מִקְדָּשׁ dec. 2 b; ו bef. lab. — קדש

מִמִּקְדָּשֵׁיךָ — pref. id. (id. pl., suff. 2 pers. sing. masc. — קדש

מִמַּקְהֵלוֹת — pref. id. (pr. name of a place — קהל

מִמָּקוֹם — pref. מִ (noun com. sing. dec. 3 a — קום

מִמְּקוֹם — ו pref. id. (id. constr. st.; ו bef. lab. — קום

מִמְּקוֹמָהּ — pref. id. (id., suff. 3 pers. sing. fem. — קום

מִמְּקוֹמוֹ — pref. id. (id., suff. 3 pers. sing. masc. — קום

מִמְּקוֹמְךָ — pref. id. (id., suff. 2 pers. sing. masc. — קום

מִמְּקוֹמְכֶם — pref. id. (id., suff. 2 pers. pl. masc. — קום

מִמְּקוֹמָם — pref. id. (id., suff. 3 pers. pl. masc. — קום

מִמָּקוֹר — pref. id. (noun m. sing., constr. of מָקוֹר d. 3 a — קור

מִמְּקֹמוֹ — defect. for מִמְּקוֹמוֹ (q. v.) — קום

מִמִּקְנֶה — ו pref. מִ (noun masc. sing., constr. of מִקְנֶה dec. 9 a; ו bef. lab. — קנה

מִמָּקֹר — defect. for מִמָּקוֹר (q. v.) — קור

מִמּוֹקְשֵׁי — defect. for מִמּוֹקְשֵׁי (q. v.) — יקש

מִמָּרֵא — ו pr. name of a man and a place; ו bef. lab. — מרא

מִמֵּר — ו noun masc. sing.; ו id. — מרר

מִמַּרְאֵה — ו pref. מִ (noun masc. sing., constr. of מַרְאֶה dec. 9 a; ו id. — ראה

מִמָּרָה — pref. id. (pr. name of a place — מר

מִמָּרוֹם — pref. id. (noun masc. sing. dec. 3 a — רום

מִמְּרוֹם — pref. id. (id. constr. st. — רום

מִמְּרוֹמִים — pref. id. (id. pl., abs. st. — רום

מַמְּרוֹרִים — noun masc. pl. [of מַמְּרוֹר] — מרר

מִמֶּרְחָק — noun masc. sing. (pl. מֶרְחַקִּים & מַרְ׳) d. 8 a — רחק

מִמָּרֵט — Pual part. sing. masc. — מרט

מַמְרִים — Hiph. part. masc., pl. of [מַמְרֶה] dec. 9 a — מרה

מִמָּרְדָתוֹ — pref. מִ (noun fem. sing., suff. 3 pers. sing. fem. from [מָרְדָה] dec. 10 — מר

מִמְּרֵשָׁה — pref. id. (pr. name of a place — ראש

מִמַּשָּׂא — pref. id. (noun masc. sing. dec. 1 b — נשא

מִמַּשָּׂא — pref. id. (pr. name of a place, see מַשָּׂא — נשא

מִמַּשְׂאוֹת — pref. id. (noun f., pl. of מַשְׂאֵת [for מַשְׂאָת] — נשא

מִמִּשְׁבְּצוֹת — pref. id. (noun fem., pl. [מִשְׁבֶּצֶת] dec. 13 — שבץ

מִמְשָׁח — noun masc. sing. — משח

מִמְשָׁךְ — Pual part. sing. masc. — משך

מִמִּשְׁכָּה — id. part. sing. fem. — משך

מִמִּשְׁכָּן — ו pref. מִ (noun masc. sing. dec. 2 b; ו bef. lab. — שכן

מִמִּשְׁכַּן — pref. id. (id. constr. st. — שכן

מִמַּשֵּׁל — Piel part. 2 pers. sing. masc. — משל

מִמָּשָׁל — noun masc. sing., pl. מְשָׁלִים — משל

מַמְשְׁלוֹתָיו — the foll. with suff. 3 pers. sing. masc. — משל

מֶמְשַׁלְתְּ — noun fem. sing. dec. 13 a, used as the constr. of מֶמְשָׁלָה (§ 42. rem. 5) — משל

מֶמְשַׁלְתּוֹ — id., suff. 3 pers. sing. masc. — משל

מֶמְשַׁלְתְּךָ — ו id., suff. 2 pers. sing. masc.; ו bef. lab. — משל

---

a Is. 12.3. | b Am. 3.4. | c Ge. 5.29. | d Is. 58.13. | e Ps. 107.28. | f Job.9.6; Is.13.13. | g Pr. 17.25. | h Ho. 8.10. | i 1 Ch. 17.5.
Ju. 1.36. | Ps. 5.11. | Le. 27.31. | Je. 9.6. | Jos. 3.3. | Ps. 102.20. | Ge. 43.34. | 2 Ch. 29.6.
Is. 22.19. | Is. 45.6. | De. 14.7. | Ps.107.6,13,19. | Job 6.17. | Job 31.2. | Ps. 45.14. | Eze. 21.5.
Ps. 69.15. | Ju. 20.33. | Le. 11.4. | Est. 4.14. | Ps. 68.36. | Job 9.18. | Eze. 28.14. | Da. 11.3,5.
Ps. 130.1. | 1 Sa. 17.23. | Jos. 4.3. | Zec. 11.6. | 2 Ch. 6.21. | Ex. 9.6,7 | 1 Ki. 7.45. | Is. 18.2,7. | Ps. 114.2.
Ca. 4.8. | Ex. 5.4. | Is. 22.19. | Ps. 68.23. | Ec. 8.10. | Le. 12.7. | Job 20.25. | Pr. 13.12. | Je. 34.1.

מִמִּשְׁפָּחָה pref. מִ)(noun fem. sing. dec. 11a, suff. פַּחְתִּי dec. 13a, from פַּחַת (§ 42. rem. 5) — שפח

וּמִמִּשְׁפָּחוֹת ו pref. id.)(id. pl., constr. of מִשְׁפָּחוֹת — שפח

מִמִּשְׁפַּחַת pref. id.)(id. sing., dec. 13a — שפח

מִמִּשְׁפְּחֹת pref. id.)(id. pl. constr. st. — שפח

מִמִּשְׁפַּחְתּוֹ pref. id.)(id. sing., suff. 3 pers. sing. masc. — שפח

מִמִּשְׁפַּחְתִּי pref. id.)(id. sing., suff. 1 pers. sing. — שפח

וּמִמִּשְׁפַּחְתָּם ו pref. id.)(id. sing., suff. 3 pers. pl. masc.; ו bef. lab. — שפח

מִמִּשְׁפָּט ו pref. id.)(noun masc. sing. dec. 2b; ו id. — שפט

מִמִּשְׁפָּטֶיךָ ו pref. id.)(id. pl., suff. 2 pers. sing. m.; ו id. — שפט

מִמְשַׁק noun masc. sing., constr. of מִשָׁק dec. 2b — משק

מִמַּשְׁקֵה pref. מִ)(noun m. s., constr. of מַשְׁקֶה d. 9a — שקה

מִמַּשְׂרֵקָה pref. id.)(pr. name of a place — שרק

מְמַשֵּׁשׁ Piel part. sing. masc. — משש

מִמִּשְׁתֵּה pref. מִ)(noun m. s., constr. of מִשְׁתֶּה d. 9a — שתה

מְמִתִים defect. for מְמִיתִים (q. v.) — מות

מִמְּתִים pref. מִ)(noun m. pl. of מַת d. 7 (§ 36. r. 5) — מתה

מִמִּתְכַּבֵּד pref. מִ)(Hithpa. part. sing. masc. — כבד

מִמַּתָּנָה pref. id.)(pr. name of a place; ו bef. lab. — נתן

מִמְתֵנוּ pref. id.)(Kal inf. (מוּת), suff. 1 pers. pl. d. 1a — מות

מִמָּתְנֵי pref. id.)(noun m. du., constr. of מָתְן d. 6c — מתן

וּמִמָּתְנָיו ו pref. id.)(id. du., suff. 3 p. s. m.; ו bef. lab. — מתן

מִמָּתְנַיִם pref. id.)(id. du., abs. st. — מתן

מִמְּתָקָה pref. id.)(pr. name of a place — מתק

מִמְּתִקוֹלְמֵי pref. id.)(the foll. with suff. 1 pers. sing. — קום

מִמִּתְקוֹמְמִים pref. id.)(Hithpal. part. masc. pl. [of מִתְקוֹמֵם] dec. 7b — קום

מַמְתַּקִּים noun masc., pl. of מַמְתָּק dec. 8a — מתק

מָן masc. once with suff. מַנּוֹ Ne.9.20, (according to some MSS. מַנֵּךְ) *manna,* the *miraculous* food with which God fed the Israelites in the wilderness, described Ex. 16. 31; Nu. 11. 7. Etymo. uncertain. According to Ex. 16.15, its name is derived from the words מָן הוּא *what is this?* (comp. Chald. מָן) or, *it is a portion;* from the Root מָנָן q. v.

מַן Chald. [with Mak. for מָן] pron.—I. interrog. *who? what?*—II. relat. מַן־דִּי *whoever, whosoever.*

מֵן Piel imp. sing. masc. ap. [from מַנֵּה] — מנה

מִן ו Heb. & Chald. prep. (§ 5) — מנן

מִן בָּהּ Kh. מִן בָּהּ: K. מֵהַבְּהֵמָה pref. מֵ for מִ see הַבְּהֵמָה.

מְנָא Chald. Peal part. pass. sing. masc. — מנא

מְנָא pref. מִ)(pr. name of a place — נא

מְנָאוֹת noun fem., pl. of מְנָת irr. (§ 45) — מנה

מְנָאֵף Piel part. sing. masc. dec. 7b — נאף

מְנָאֲפִים id. pl., abs. st. — נאף

מְנַאֲפִים id. id. dag. forte impl. (§ 14. rem. 1) — נאף

וּמְנָאֶפֶת ו id. sing. fem. [for מְנָאֶפֶת]; ו bef. lab. — נאף

מִתְנָאֵץ [for מִתְנָאֵץ] Hithpoal (§ 6. No. 1) part. s. m. — נאץ

מְנַאֲצַי Piel part. pl., suff. 1 pers. s. fr. [מְנָאֵץ] d. 7b — נאץ

מְנַאֲצֶיךָ id. pl., suff. 2 p. s. f., dag. f. impl. (§ 14. r. 1) — נאץ

מִנַּאֲקָתָם pref. מִ)(noun fem. sing., suff. 3 pers. pl. masc. from [נְאָקָה] dec. 11c (§ 42. r. 1) — נאק

וּמִנָּבִיא ו pref. id.)(noun masc. s. d. 3a; ו bef. lab. — נבא

מִנְּבִיאֵי pref. id.)(id. pl., constr. st. — נבא

מְנוּבָל pref. id.)(pr. name masc. — נבל

מְנַבֵּל Piel part. sing. masc. — נבל

מִנִּבְלָתָהּ pref. מִ)(noun fem. sing., suff. 3 pers. sing. fem. from נְבֵלָה dec. 11c (§ 42. rem. 4) — נבל

מִנִּבְלָתָם pref. id.)(id. with suff. 3 pers. pl. masc. — נבל

מִנֶּגֶב ו pref. id.)(noun masc. sing. (§ 35. rem. 3); ו bef. lab. — נגב

מִנֶּגֶד pref. id.)((prop. noun masc. sing., dec. 6) as a *prep.* (§ 35. rem. 3) — נגד

מִנֶּגְדּוֹ pref. id.)(id., suff. 3 pers. sing. masc. — נגד

מִנֶּגְדִּי pref. id.)(id., suff. 1 pers. sing. — נגד

מִנֹּגַהּ pref. id.)(n. m. s. (suff. נָגְהָם) d.6c (§ 35. r. 5) — נגה

מְנַגֵּחַ Piel part. sing. masc. — נגח

מַנְגִּינָתָם noun f. s., suff. 3 p. pl. m. fr. [מַנְגִּינָה] d. 10 — נגן

מִנְגִּינָתָם pref. מִ)(noun fem. sing., suff. 3 pers. pl. masc. from נְגִינָה dec. 10 — נגן

מְנַגֵּן Piel part. sing. masc. — נגן

מֻנְגָּד Hoph. part. sing. m. [for מֻנְגָּד § 21. r. 24] — נגד

מִנְדָּה Ch. dag. forte resolved in נ for מִדָּה (q. v.) — מדד

מְנֻדָּח Pual part. sing. masc. — נדח

מְנַדֵּיכֶם Piel part. pl. masc., suff. 2 pers. pl. masc. from [מְנַדֶּה] dec. 9a — נדה

מַנְדַּע ו Ch. noun masc. sing., dag. forte resolved in נ for מַדַּע dec. 2a; ו bef. lab. — ידע

מַנְדְּעָא ו Ch. id., emph. st.; ו id. — ידע

מַנְדְּעִי ו Ch. id., suff. 1 pers. sing.; ו id. — ידע

מִנְּדָרֵיכֶם pref. מִ)(n. m. pl., suff. 2 p. pl. m. fr. נֶדֶר d.6a — נדר

מָנָה I. *to separate, appoint.*—II. *to number.* Niph. *to be numbered.* Pi. *to appoint, constitute, destine;* with לְ *to appoint, assign.*

מְנָא, מְנָה Ch. *to number.* Pa. *to appoint, constitute.*

מָנֶה masc. dec. 9b, *Maneh,* a Hebrew weight,

a Je. 3. 14.   e Is. 53. 8.   l Je. 26. 15.   r Ps. 59. 2.   x Is. 57. 3.   e Is. 60. 14.   m La. 3. 63.   q Da. 5. 12.
b Jos. 21. 40.   f Ps.119.102,120.   m Ps. 17. 14.   s Ps. 17. 7.   y Ho. 7. 4.   f Ju. 2. 18.   37, 38.   n La. 5. 14.   r Da. 4. 31, 32.
c 1 Ch. 6. 51.   g Zep. 2. 9.   n Pr. 12. 9.   t Ps. 61. 8.   z Pr. 30. 20.   g Is. 6. 13.   h Ju. 21. 19.   o 2 Sa. 23. 6.   s Nu. 29. 39.
d Ge. 24. 40.   h Eze. 45. 15.   o Ex. 14. 12.   u Ho. 3. 1.   a 1 Ki. 18. 13.   i Nu. 10. 5.   k Is. 8. 22.   p Is. 22. 21.   t Nu. 23. 10.
Ju. 18. 2.   i De. 28. 29.   p Eze. 8. 2.   v Da. 5. 25, 26.   b Mi. 7. 6.   Le 11. 25, 35,   l Le. 11. 40.
Le. 25. 45.   k Est. 7. 7.   q Ex. 28. 42.   w Ne. 12. 44.   c Ca. 6. 5.   d Da. 8. 4.

consisting of **100 shekels**; for smaller kinds, see Eze. 45. 12.

מָנֶה fem. constr. מְנַת, but pl. with suff. מְנוֹתֶהָ (§ 42. rem. 2) *part, portion*.

מֹנֶה masc. only pl. מֹנִים *times*, Ge. 31. 7, 41, *ten times*.

מְנִי, the name of an idol, prob. the god of *destiny, fortune*, Is. 65. 11.

מְנָת fem. pl. מָנִיוֹת, מְנָאוֹת (§ 45) *part, portion*. מִנְיָן Ch. dec. 1 b, *number*, Ezr. 6. 17.

תִּמְנָה (*portion, possession*) pr. name—I. אַ a city in the tribe of Judah.—II. תִּמְנָתָה, prob. another city in the tribe of Dan. Gent. noun תִּמְנִי Ju. 15. 6.

תִּמְנַת־סֶרַח (*portion of abundance*) pr. name of a city in the tribe of Ephraim, Jos. 19. 50; 24. 30; called also (by transp.) תִּמְנַת הֶרֶס Ju. 2. 9.

מָנֶה noun fem. sing. dec. 11 a (§ 42. rem. 2) . מנה

מְנָה Ch. Peal pret. 3 pers. sing. masc. (§ 55. r. 1) מנה

מְנֵה Kal imp. sing. masc. . מנה

מִנָּהּ Piel pret. 3 pers. sing. masc. . מנה

מִנַּהּ Ch. prep. מִן with suff. 3 p. s. f.; וּ bef. lab. מנן

מִנֵּהּ Ch. id. with suff. 3 pers. sing. m.; וּ id. מנן

מְנַהֲגוֹת Piel (§ 14. rem. 1) part. fem. pl. [of מְנַהֶגֶת dec. 13, from מְנַהֵג masc.] . . נהג

מֶנְהֻגִי } prep. מִן with suff. 3 pers. sing. masc. (§ 5) מנן
מֶנְהֻגִּי }

מִנְהֵווֹן } Chald. prep. מִן with suff. 3 pers. pl. מנן
מִנְהוֹן } masc., K. הֵן fem.; וּ bef. lab. }

מְנַהֵל Piel part. sing. masc. (§ 14. rem. 1) . נהל

מֵהֶם prep. מִן with suff. 3 pers. pl. masc. (§ 5) מנן

מַהֲמַת pref. מִי)(noun fem. sing., constr. of [נְהָמָה] dec. 11 c (§ 42. rem. 1) . . נהם

מִנְהָר וּ pref. id.)(noun masc. s. d. 4 a; וּ bef. lab. נהר

מִנְהַר pref. id.)(id., constr. st. . נהר

מַנּוּ Piel pret. 3 pers. pl. . מנה

מָנוֹד noun masc., constr. of [מָנוֹד] dec. 3 a נוד

מָנוֹס וּ noun m. s., dec. 3 a, also pr. n.; וּ bef. lab. נוס

מְנוּחָה וּ noun fem. sing. dec. 10; וּ id. נוח

מְנֻחֹת id. pl. . . נוח

מְנֻחָתִי id. sing., suff. 1 pers. sing. . . נוח

מְנִיוֹת pref. מִי)(Kh. נָוִית, K. נָיוֹת, pr. n. of a place נוה

מָנוֹן noun masc. sing. . . נון

מָנוֹס וּ noun masc. sing. dec. 3 a; וּ bef. lab. . נוס

מְנוּסִי וּ id. with suff. 1 pers. sing. (§ 32. r. 5); וּ id. נוס

מְנוֹרָה וּ noun fem. sing. dec. 10; וּ id. נור

מְנֹרֹת וּ/וּ id., constr. st; וּ id. נור

מְנֻשָּׁי pref. מִי)(Kal part. pl. masc., suff. 1 pers. sing. from נֹשֶׁה dec. 9 a . . נשה

מָנוֹת noun fem. pl. abs. from מָנֶה dec. 11 a . מנה

מְנוֹתֶהָ id. pl., suff. 3 pers. sing. fem. (§ 42. rem. 2) מנה

מִנְּזָרַיִךְ noun m. pl., suff. 2 p. s. f. fr. [מִנְזָר] d. 2 b נזר

מָנַה **Root not used**; Arab. *to give*.

מִנְחָה fem. dec. 12 b.—I. *gift, present*.—II. *tribute*.—III. *an offering to God, a sacrifice*, Ge. 4. 3 4, 5; especially a bloodless offering.

מִנְחָה Ch. fem. dec. 8 a, id. Da. 2. 46; Ezr. 7. 17

מֻנָּח Hoph. part. sing. m. [for מוּנָח § 21. r. 24] נוח

מְנֻחָה defect. for מְנוּחָה (q. v.) . . נוח

מִנְחָה וּ noun fem. sing. dec. 12 b; וּ bef. lab. . מנח

מַנְחִיל Hiph. part. sing. masc. . . נחל

מִנְחִירָיו pref. מִי)(n. m. du. [נְחִירַיִם], suff. 3 p. pl. m. נחר

מִנַּחַל pref. id.)(noun masc. sing. dec. 6 d . נחל

מִנַּחְלָה pref. id.)(noun fem. sing., dec. 12 d . נחל

מִנַּחֲלֵי pref. id.)(noun m. pl. constr. fr. נַחַל d. 6 d נחל

מִנַּחֲלִיאֵל וּ pref. id.)(pr. name masc.; וּ bef. lab. נחל

מִנַּחֲלַת וּ pref. id.)(noun fem. sing., constr. of נַחֲלָה dec. 12 d; וּ id. . . נחל

מִנַּחֲלָתוֹ pref. id.)(id., suff. 3 pers. sing. masc. נחל

מִנַּחֲלָתְךָ pref. id.)(id., suff. 2 pers. sing. masc. נחל

מִנַּחֲלָתָם pref. id.)(id., suff. 3 pers. pl. masc. . נחל

מְנַחֵם Piel (§ 14. r. 1) part. s. m. d. 7 b, also pr. n. נחם

מְנַחֲמֵי id. pl., constr. st. . . נחם

מְנַחֲמִים id. pl., abs. st. . . נחם

מְנַחֶמְכֶם id. sing., suff. 2 pers. pl. masc. . . נחם

מְנַחֵשׁ וּ Piel part. sing. masc. (§ 14. r. 1); וּ bef. lab. נחש

מָנַחַת וּ pr. name of a place; וּ id. . . נוח

מִנְחַת וּ noun fem. sing., constr. of מִנְחָה dec. 12 b (Chald. 8 a); וּ id. . . מנח

מִנְחָתָהּ וּ id., suff. 3 pers. sing. fem.; וּ id. . מנח

מִנְחָתְהוֹן וּ Chald. noun fem. pl., suff. 3 pers. pl. masc. from מִנְחָה dec. 8 a; וּ id. . . מנח

מְנֻחָתוֹ noun fem. sing., suff. 3 pers. sing. masc. from מְנוּחָה dec. 10 . . נוח

מִנְחָתוֹ וּ noun fem. sing., suff. 3 pers. sing. masc. from מִנְחָה dec. 12 b; וּ bef. lab. מנח

מִנְחָתִי id., suff. 1 pers. sing. . . מנח

מִנְחֹתֶיךָ id. pl., suff. 2 pers. sing. masc. . מנח

מִנְחֹתֵיכֶם וּ id. pl., suff. 2 pers. pl. masc.; וּ bef. lab. . מנח

מִנְחָתְךָ } id. sing., suff. 2 pers. sing. masc. . מנח
מִנְחָתֶךָ }

מִנְחָתָם וּ id. sing., suff. 3 pers. pl. masc.; וּ bef. lab. מנח

1 Sa. 1. 5.	ƒ Da. 4. 9.	ⁱ Da. 6. 3.	ⁿ Ps. 44. 15.	ᵗ 2 Ch. 13. 11.	ᵍ Ge. 49. 15.	ᶻ 2 Sa. 23. 30;
Da. 5. 26.	ᵍ Na. 2. 8.	ᵏ Is. 51. 18.	° Je. 45. 3.	Je. 50. 1.	ᵈ De. 12. 10.	1 Ch. 11. 32.
2 Sa. 24. 1.	ʰ Job 4. 12.	ˡ Job 11. 20.	ᵖ Ps. 23. 2.	ˣ Est. 2. 9.	ᵉ Job 41. 12.	ᵐ Job 16. 2.
Da. 1. 10, 11.	ⁱ Pr. 28. 24.	ᵐ Ps. 38. 9.	ᑫ Pr. 29. 21.	ᵛ Na. 3. 17.	ⁱ Eze. 46. 17.	ⁿ Is. 51. 12.
Da. 7. 24.	ᵉ Da. 2. 33, 41, 42.	ⁿ Job 7. 3.	ʳ 1 Ch. 28. 15.	Eze. 41. 9.	ⱼ Je. 17. 4.	° De. 18. 10.
						ᵖ Ezr. 7. 17.
						ᵗ Ps. 20. 4.
						ᵃ Am. 5. 25.
						ᵇ Le. 2. 13.
						ᶜ Le. 2. 13.

מַנִּי*	י' Chald. Pael pret. 3 pers. sing. masc. ; י' id.	מנה
מַנִּי*	Chald. id. imp. sing. masc.	מנה
מֶנִּי	prep. מִן with suff. 1 pers. sing. (§ 5)	מן
מִנִּי*	(as if pl. constr. of מִן) used poetically for the prep. מִן	מן
מִנִּי*	pr. name of a province	מן
מִנִּים*	perh. for מִנִּים pl. of [מֵן] dec. 8 b	מן
מִנִּי*	י' prep. מִן with suff. 1 pers. sing., or parag. ' ; י' bef. lab.	מן
מָנָיוֹת	noun fem., pl. of מָנָת irr. (§ 45)	מנה
מֵנִיחַ*	} Hiph. part. sing. masc. (§ 21. rem. 24)	נוח
מֵנִיחַ*		
מָנִים	noun masc., pl. of מָנֶה dec. 9 a	מנה
מֹנִים*	noun masc., pl. of [מֹנֶה] dec. 9 a	מנה
מִנְיָמִין	י' pr. name masc. see מִיָמִין ; י' bef. lab.	
מֵנִיף	Hiph. part. sing. masc. dec. 3 b	נוף
מְנִיפוֹ	id. with suff. 3 pers. sing. masc.	נוף
מַנִּית*	Chald. Pael pret. 2 pers. sing. m. (§ 47. r. 2)	מנה
מִנִּית	pr. name of a place	מן
מָנִיתִי*	י' Kal pret. 1 pers. sing. ; י' for וְ conv.	
מִנֶּךָ*	י' noun masc. sing., suff. 2 pers. sing. masc. from מִן q. v. ; י' bef. lab.	
מִנָּךְ	Chald., prep. מִן with suff. 2 pers. sing. masc.	מן
מִנִּכְסֵי*	י' Chald. noun masc. pl. constr. from [נְכַס] dec. 3 b ; י' bef. lab.	נכס
מִנָּכְרִיָּה	pref. מִ)(adj. fem. s. dec. 10, from נָכְרִי m.	נכר
מִנְלָם*	noun masc. sing., suff. 3 pers. pl. masc. from [מִנְלָה] dec. 9 a	נלה
מְנַמֵּרִים*	noun masc., pl. of נָמֵר dec. 4 a	נמר

מָנַן

Root not used ; Arab. *to divide, apportion.*

מֵן masc.—I. *part, portion* ; not used as a subst. in this sense, yet it is a primary form, of which the prep. מִן is the constr. st.—II. pl. מִנִּים Ps. 150. 4, for which מִנִּי Ps. 45. 9, *strings of an in-strument.*

מִן, as a prefix מִ with dag. forte, sometimes also without it, when the next letter has sheva, especially when this letter is Yod, which then becomes quiescent (e. g. מִידֵי for מִיְדֵי) ; before guttural מֵ, rarely מִ with dag. forte impl. (as מֵחוּץ, מִחְיוֹת) poet. מִנִּי, מִנֵּי, with suff. מִמֶּנִּי (see § 5) prep.—I. *of,* noting a part taken *from* or *out of* a whole, both with reference to number and quantity ; מִן הָעָם *some of the people ;* מִן הַדָּם *some of the blood ;* with a negation *nothing of,* comp. De. 16. 4 ; hence מֵאֵין, מֵאֶפֶס *nothing at all.*—II. *from,* noting motion, departing, fleeing,

trembling, fearing, derivation, distance, &c. Hence as marking cause and means ; (*a*) *before, in the presence of* ; (*b*) *by, through* ; (*c*) *because, on account of* ; (*d*) *according to* ; (*e*) *about, concern-ing* ; (*f*) *far from, away from* ; (*g*) *without* ; (*h*) *besides* ; (*i*) מִן–אֶל, מִן–עַד *from—to ;* both—and.—III. *out of, from,* after verbs of going or bringing out, delivering.—IV. *out of, of,* indicating the material of which anything is made.—V *more than,* noting comparison.—VI. *at, in, on, by* in specification of space and time ; (*b*) *from, since, after,* of time ; מִנְּעֻרַי *from my youth ;* מִיָּמִים *after some time.*—VII. before an inf. (*a*) *because* ; (*b*) *after that, since* ; (*c*) *so that not, lest* ; (*d* *more than.*—VIII. with a finite verb, *so that not lest,* De. 33. 11. Before other particles, see תַּחַת, פָּנִים, עִם, עַל, בַּעַד, בֵּין, אֶת, אַחַר.

מִן Ch. with suff. מִנְּהוֹן, מִנַּהּ, מִנָּה, מִנָּךְ, מִנִּי. —I. *part of,* comp. Da. 2. 33.—II. *from,* i. q. Heb. No. II ; hence of time, Da. 3. 22.—III. *out of, from,* of the author and cause ; hence, (*a*) *on account of, because of,* Da. 5. 19 ; (*b*) *according to,* Ezr. 6. 14 ; (*c*) מִן יַצִּיב, מִן קְשֹׁט *of a truth, truly, certainly.*—IV. *more than,* of comparison, Da. 2. 30.

מִנִּי (perh. *allotted*) pr. name of a region, Je. 51. 27.

מִנִּית (id.) pr. name of a place in Ammon, Ju. 11. 33 ; Eze. 27. 17.

מִנָּס*	pref. מִ)(noun masc. sing. dec. 8 b	נסס
מְנַסֶּה*	Piel part. sing. masc.	נסה
מְנֻסַּת*	noun fem. sing., constr. of מְנוּסָה dec. 10	נוס
מִסְתַּתְּרוֹת	Niph. part. pl. abs. [fr. נְסְתָּר, fr. נִסְתַּר m.]	סתר

מָנַע

I. *to restrain, hold back,* with מִן *from any thing.*—II. *to restrain, keep back, withhold, refuse,* with acc. of the thing, and מִן, rarely with לְ of the person. Niph. I. *to be restrained, hindered.*—II. *to be withheld* or *withdrawn,* Job 38. 15.

יִמְנָע (whom *He withholds*) pr. name masc. 1 Ch. 7. 35.

תִּמְנָע (*restraint*) pr. name—I. of the concubine of Eliphaz, the son of Esau.—II. of one of the tribes of Edom.

מְנַע*	Kal imp. sing. masc.	מנע
מֹנֵעַ	id. part. sing. masc.	מנע
מָנְעוּ*	id. pret. 3 pers. pl.	מנע
מַנְעוּלָיו*	noun masc. pl., suff. 3 pers. sing. masc. from [מַנְעוּל] dec. 1 b	נעל

a Da. 2. 24, 49.   d Ps. 45. 9.   g Ge. 31. 7, 41.   k Is. 65. 12.   o Job 15. 29.   r Is. 31. 9.   r Le. 26. 36.   t Ge. 30. 2.   x Je. 5. 25.
b Ezr. 7. 25.   e Ec. 5. 11.   h Is. 10. 15.   l Ne. 9. 20.   p Hab. 1. 8.   s De. 13. 4.   u Ps. 19. 13.   w Pr. 1. 15.   y Ne. 3. 6.
c Is. 30. 11.   f Jos. 1. 13.   i Da. 3. 12.   m Ezr. 6. 8.

מְנְעוּרַי	pref. ·מ)(noun masc. pl., suff. 1 pers. sing. from [נָעוּר] dec. 1 a	נער
מִנְּעוּרָיו	pref. id.)(id., suff. 3 pers. sing. masc.	נער
מִנְּעוּרַיִךְ	pref. id.)(id., suff. 2 pers. sing. fem.	נער
מִנְּעוּרֵינוּ	pref. id.)(id., suff. 1 pers. pl.	נער
מְנַע	Kal imp. sing. fem.	מנע
מְנָעֶךָ	id. pret. 3 pers. sing. masc., suff. 2 pers. sing. masc.	מנע
מִנְּעָלָיו	ו defect. for מַנְעוּלָיו (q. v.) ; ו bef. lab.	נעל
מִנְעָלְךָ	[for מִנְעָלֶךָ] noun masc. sing., suff. 2 pers. sing. masc. from [מִנְעָל] dec. 2 b	נעל
מְנָעַנִי	Kal pret. 3 pers. sing. masc., suff. 1 pers. s.	מנע
מִנַּעַר	pref. ·מ)(noun masc. sing. dec. 6 d	נער
מִנַּעַר	pref. id.)(noun masc. sing.	נער
מִנְּעָרַי	ו pref. id.)(the following with suff. 1 pers. sing. ; ו bef. lab.	נער
מִנַּעֲרֵי	pref. id.)(noun m. pl. constr. fr. נַעַר d. 6 d	נער
מִנְּעָרַי	pref. id.)(noun masc. pl., suff. 1 pers. sing. from [נָעוּר] dec. 1 a	נער
מִנְּעָרָיו	pref. id.)(id., suff. 3 pers. sing. masc.	נער
מִנְּעָרֵיךְ	pref. id.)(id., suff. 2 pers. pl. masc.	נער
מִנַּעֲרוֹתֵיהֶם	pref. id.)(noun fem. pl. [נְעָרוֹת], suff. 3 pers. pl. masc.	נער
מָנַעְתָּ	Kal pret. 2 pers. sing. masc.	מנע
מָנַעְתִּי	id. pret. 1 pers. sing.	מנע
מִנֹּף	pref. ·מ)(pr. name of a place, see נֹף.	
מְנֻפָצוֹת	Pual part. f. pl. [of מְנֻפָּצָה from נָפַץ m.]	נפץ
מִנֶּפֶשׁ	pref. ·מ)(noun com. sing. (suff. נַפְשִׁי) d. 6 a	נפש
מִנַּפְתָּלִי	ו pref. id.)(pr. name of a tribe ; ו bef. lab.	פתל
מְנַצְּחִים	ו Piel part. masc., pl. of [מְנַצֵּחַ] d. 7 b ; ו id.	נצח
מִנֵּצֶר	pref. ·מ)(noun masc. sing.	נצר
מִנְּקִיקֵי	ו pref. id.)(noun m. pl. constr. fr. [נָקִיק] or [נְקִיק] ; ו bef. lab.	נקק
מְנִקֹתָיו	ו noun fem. pl., suff. 3 pers. sing. masc. [from מֵנֶקֶת § 39. rem. 1, note]	נקה
מֵנִקְתָּהּ	Hiph. part. sing. fem. מֵינֶקֶת, suff. 3 pers. sing. f. d. 13 a [fr. מֵינִיק m. § 39. No. 4 d]	ינק
מֵנִקְתּוֹ	id., suff. 3 pers. sing. masc.	ינק
מְנֹרָה	noun fem. sing. dec. 10	נור
מְנֹרוֹת	id. pl.	נור
מְנֹרַת	id. sing., constr. st.	נור
מִנְּשׂוֹא	pref. ·מ)(Kal inf. constr.	נשא
מְנַשְּׂאִים	Piel part. masc., pl. of [מְנַשֵּׂא] dec. 7 b	נשא
מְנַשֶּׁה	ו pr. name of a man and a tribe ; ו bef. lab.	נשה
מִנְשֵׁי	pref. ·מ)(constr. of the following	אנש

מִנָּשִׁים	pref. ·מ)(noun fem. with pl. masc. term., for אֶשָּׁה אִשָּׁה see (§ 45)	אנש
מִנְּשִׁיקוֹת	pref. id.)(noun fem., pl. of [נְשִׁיקָה] dec. 10	נשק
מִנִּשְׁמַת	pref. id.)(noun f. s., constr. of נְשָׁמָה d. 11 c	נשם
מִנֶּשֶׁק	pref. id.)(noun masc. sing.	נשק
מִנִּשְׁרֵי	pref. id.)(constr. of the following	נשר
מִנְּשָׁרִים	pref. id.)(noun masc., pl. of נֶשֶׁר dec. 6 a	נשר
מְנָת	י noun fem. sing. irr. (§ 45) ; ו bef. lab.	מנה
מְנָת	noun f. s., constr. of מָנָה d. 11 a (§ 42. r. 2)	מנה
מִנְּתִיבָתָם	pref. ·מ)(n. f. s., suff. 3 p. m. fr. נְתִיבָה d. 10	נתב
מַס	noun m. s. (pl. מִסִּים) d. 8 b, contr. fr. מֶכֶס	מסס
מֵסַב	prop. noun masc. sing. (with suff. מְסִבּוֹ) dec. 8 d, as an adv.	סבב
מֵסֵב	Hiph. part. sing. masc.	סבב
מְסִבּוֹת	noun fem., pl. [of מְסִבָּה dec. 10]	סבב
מְסִבַּי	noun m. pl., suff. 1 pers. s. fr. מֵסַב d. 8 d	סבב
מְסִבֵּי	ו id. pl., constr. st. ; ו bef. lab.	סבב
מִסָּבִיב	pref. ·מ)((prop. noun masc. sing. dec. 3 a) as an adv. or prep	סבב
מִסְּבִיבוֹת	ו pref. id.)(id. with pl. fem. term., as a prep.; ו bef. lab.	סבב
מִסְּבִיבֹתָם	pref. id.)(id. (subst.) with pl. fem. term. and suff. 3 pers. pl. masc. (§ 4. rem. 1)	סבב
מִסְּבְּכוֹ	pref. id.)(noun masc. sing., suff. 3 pers. sing. masc., dag. euph. [fr. סֹבֶךְ § 35. rem. 17]	סבך
מְסֻבָּל	pref. id.)(noun masc. sing.	סבל
מְסֻבָּלִים	Pual part. masc., pl. of מְסֻבָּל	סבל
מִסִּבְלֹתָם	pref. ·מ)(noun fem. pl., suff. 3 pers. pl. masc. [fr. סָבְלָה or סִבְלָה]	סבל
מַסַּבֹּת	defect. for מוּסַבּוֹת (q. v.)	סבב
מִסְגֵּר	noun masc. sing.	סגר
מִסְגְּרוֹת	pl. of the foll. ; ו bef. lab.	סגר
מִסְגְּרֹת	ו defect. for מִסְגָּרוֹת q. v. ; ו bef. lab. f.	סגר
מִסְגֶּרֶת	ו Pual part. sing. fem. [of מְסֻגָּר] ; ו bef. lab.	סגר
מִסְגֶּרֶת	noun fem. sing. (suff. מִסְגַּרְתּוֹ) dec. 13 a	סגר
מִסְגְּרֹתֶיהָ	ו noun fem. pl., suff. 3 pers. sing. fem. fr. מִסְגֶּרֶת dec. 13 a ; ו bef. lab.	סגר
מִסְגְּרֹתֵיהֶם	id., suff. 3 pers. pl. masc. ; ו id.	סגר
מִסְדֹרוֹת	defect. for מוּסָדוֹת (q. v.)	יסד

מָסָה 1. q. מָסַס, only Hiph. *to cause to flow down*, dis solve, melt.

מַסָּה	noun fem. sing. dec. 10	נסה
מְסוֹבְלִין	Ch. Poal (§ 48) part. m., pl. of [מְסוֹבַל] d. 2 a	סבל
מִסוֹד	pref. ·מ)(noun masc. sing. d. 1 a [for יְסוֹד]	יסד
מַסְוֶה	noun masc. sing.	סוה

^a Je. 48. 11.   ^f Ne. 13. 19.   ^m Is. 27. 9.   ^s 2 Ki. 11. 2.   ^a 2 Ch. 31. 3.   ^f Job 37. 12.   ^z Je. 4. 7.   ^f 1 Ki. 7. 28.   ^a 2 Sa. 22. 16.
^b Is. 47. 12.   ^g Is. 10. 18.   ⁿ Is. 10. 18.   ^t 2 Ch. 4. 7.   ^b Je. 13. 25.   ^g Ps. 140. 10.   ^m Ps. 81. 7.   ^u 1 Ki. 7. 29.   ^b Ps. 95. 8.
Ne. 3. 6, 13,   ^h 1 Ki. 18. 12.   ^o 2 Ch. 2. 17.   ^u Ge. 4. 13.   ^c Pr. 1. 15.   ^h 2 Ki. 23. 5.   ⁿ Ps. 144. 14.   ^v Jos. 6. 1.   ^c Ezr. 6. 3.
14, 15.   ⁱ Sa. 12. 2.   ^p Je. 16. 16.   ^v Ca. 1. 2.   ^d Je. 16. 29.   ⁱ Ex. 5. 5.   ^o 1 Ki. 7. 35, 36.   ^d Ps. 64. 3.
^c De. 33. 25.   ^k 2 Sa. 19. 8.   ^r Ex. 25. 29; 37. 16.   ^w Job 20. 24.   ^e Je. 21. 4.   ^k Is. 24. 22.   ^p 1 Is. 5. 5.   ^e Ex. 34. 33.
1 Sa. 25. 34.   ^l Je. 32. 30.   ^s Ge. 24. 59.   ^x La. 4. 19.

33*

מַסָּח־ noun masc. sing. . נסח

מִסְתָּר־ pref. ·מִ)(noun m. s., constr. of [סָתָר] d. 4 a   סתר

י n. m. s., constr. of [מִסְתָּר] d. 2 b; וֹ bef. lab.   סתר

מַסִּיג־ Hiph. part. sing. masc. dec. 1 b . נסג

מֵסִיךְ־ Hiph. part. sing. masc. [for מֵסֵךְ § 18. r. 12]   סכך

מְסִים־ noun masc., pl. of מַס d. 8 b, contr. from מְסִכֶם   כסס

מְסִינִי pref. ·מִ)(pr. name of a mountain . סין

מֵסִיעַ־ Hiph. part. sing. masc. . נסע

מֵסִיר־ Hiph. part. sing. masc. . סור

מֵסִית־ Hiph. part. sing. masc. [for מְסִית § 21. r. 24]   סות

מָסַךְ־ *to mix, mingle.*

    מֶסֶךְ m. *mixture,* i. e. mixed or spiced wine, Ps. 75. 9.

    מִמְסָךְ masc. id. Pr. 23. 30; Is. 65. 11.

מָסָךְ noun masc. sing. (§ 37. rem. 4)   סכך

מָסַךְ וֹ id. constr. st.; וֹ bef. lab.   סכך

מֵסֶךְי noun masc. sing. . מסך

מָסְכָה־ Kal pret. 3 pers. sing. fem.   מסך

מַסֵּכָה וֹ noun fem. sing. dec. 10; וֹ bef. lab.   נסך

מַסֵּכוֹת־ id. pl.; וֹ id. . נסך

מַסְכְּנוֹת־ pref. ·מִ)(pr. name of a place   סכך

מִסְכְּנֻת noun masc. sing. . סכן

מִסְכְּנוֹת־ וֹ noun fem., pl. of [מִסְכֶּנֶת] d. 13; וֹ bef. lab.   סכן

מַסֶּכֶת־ noun fem. sing., constr. of מַסֵּכָה dec. 10   נסך

מַסֶּכֶת pref. ·מִ)(pr. name of a place   סכך

מַסְכְתִּי Kal pret. 1 pers. sing. [for מָסַכְתִּי § 8. r. 7]   מסך

מְסֻכָּתְךָ־ [for כֻּתְּךָ] noun fem. sing., suff. 2 pers. sing. masc. from [מְסֻכָה] dec. 10   סכך

מַסֵּכְתָּם־ noun fem. sing., suff. 3 pers. pl. masc. from מַסֵּכָה dec. 10 . נסך

מְסִלּ־ יֹ pref. ·מִ)(noun m. sing. d. 8 a, וֹ bef. lab.   סלל

מְסִלָּה־ noun fem. sing. dec. 10   סלל

מַסְלוּל־ noun masc. sing.   סלל

מְסִלּוֹת־ noun fem., pl. of מְסִלָּה dec. 10   סלל

מִסְלָע־ pref. ·מִ)(noun masc. sing. (suff. סַלְעִי dec. 6 a, § 35. rem. 5)   סלע

מְסַלֵּף־ Piel part. sing. masc.   סלף

מְסִלַּת־ noun fem. sing., constr. of מְסִלָּה dec. 10   סלל

מְסִלַּת־ pref. ·מִ)(noun com. sing. dec. 6 c   סלת

מְסֻלָּתָהּ־ pref. id.)(id., suff. 3 pers. sing. fem.   סלת

מְסִלֹּתַי־ וֹ noun fem. pl., suff. 1 pers. sing. from מְסִלָּה dec. 10; וֹ bef. lab.   סלל

[מָסַם] i. q. מָסָה *to flow down,* melt; only trop. *to faint,* Is. 10. 18. Niph. נָמֵס, in pause נָמַס & נָמֵס

(§ 18. rem. 7).—I. *to melt, flow down.*—II. *to become weak, faint,* as the heart, of fear, grief, sorrow. Hiph. *to cause to faint, make faint-hearted,* De. 1. 28.

    מֵס masc. *faint, unhappy,* Job 6. 14.

    תֶּמֶס masc. *a melting, wasting away,* Ps. 58. 9.

מַסָּע־ noun masc. sing. . נסע

מִסְעָד־ noun masc. sing. . סעד

מִסְעָדִין־ Chald. Pael part. masc., pl. of [מְסַעֵד dag. forte impl. comp. § 14. rem. 1] dec. 2 a   סעד

מַסְעֵי noun m. pl. constr. [for מַסְּעֵי] from מַסָּע d. 2 b   נסע

מַסְעֵיהֶם־ id. pl., suff. 3 pers. pl. masc. [for מַסְּעֵיהֶם]   נסע

מְסָעֵף־ Piel part. sing. masc.   סעף

מִסְעַר־ pref. ·מִ)(for סַעַר, noun masc. sing. dec. 6 d   סער

מִסְפַּד־ constr. of the foll.   ספד

מִסְפֵּד וֹ noun m. sing. d. 7 c (§ 36. r. 1); וֹ bef. lab.   ספד

מִסְפְּדִי־ id. with suff. 1 pers. sing.   ספד

מִסְפּוֹא וֹ noun masc. sing.; וֹ bef. lab.   ספא

מְסַפֵּחַ־ Piel part. sing. masc.   ספח

מִסְפַּחַת noun fem. sing.   ספח

מִסְפְּחֹתֵיכֶם־ noun fem. pl., suff. 2 pers. pl. masc. from [מִסְפָּחָה] dec. 11 a   ספח

מְסַפֵּר־ Piel part. sing. masc. dec. 7 b   ספר

מְסַפֵּר־ pref. ·מִ)(Piel inf. constr.   ספר

מִסְפָּר־ וֹ noun m. s. d. 2 b, also pr. name; וֹ bef. lab.   ספר

מִסְפַּר־ וֹ id., constr. st.; וֹ id.   ספר

מִסְפָּר־ pref. ·מִ)(noun masc. sing. dec. 6 b   ספר

מִסְפְּרֵי־ noun masc. pl. constr. from מִסְפָּר dec. 2 b   ספר

מִסְפָּרִי־ pref. ·מִ)(noun masc. sing., suff. 1 pers. sing. from סָפָר dec. 6 b   ספר

מְסַפְּרִים Piel part. masc., pl. of מְסַפֵּר dec. 7 b   ספר

מִסְפָּרְךְ־ pref. ·מִ)(noun masc. sing., suff. 2 pers. sing. masc. from סָפָר dec. 6 b   ספר

מִסְפַּרְכֶם־ noun m. s., suff. 2 pers. pl. m. fr. מִסְפָּר d. 2 b   ספר

מִסְפָּרָם id. with suff. 3 pers. pl. masc.   ספר

מִסְפֶּרֶת pr. name masc. . ספר

[מָסַר] as in the Chald. *to deliver, offer;* hence *to teach,* Nu. 31. 16. Prof. Lee, *to stir up.* Niph. *to be delivered, given up,* Nu. 31. 5.

מָסֹרוֹת־ וֹ noun masc. with pl. fem. term., constr. st. [from מוֹסֵר for מַאְסֵר] dec. 7 b; וֹ bef. lab.   אסר

מְסַרְסִי noun masc. pl. constr. from סָרִים (§ 32. r. 2)   סרם

מְסָרְפוֹ־ וֹ Piel part. sing. masc. [מְסָרֵף], suff. 3 pers. sing. masc. dec. 7 b; וֹ bef. lab.   סרף

מִסַּת־ n. f., constr. of [מִסָּה] contr. fr. מִכְסָה=מָכַס   כסס

a 2 Ki. 11. 6.   f Ec. 10. 9.   k 2 Ch. 32. 28.   p Le. 8. 26.   u Le. 2. 2.   d Ezr. 5. 2.   i Ge. 24. 32.   n Nu. 23. 10.   s Nu. 14. 29.

b Pr. 3. 14.   g Is. 19. 14.   l Ps. 75. 9.   q Eze. 28. 13.   v Is. 49. 11.   e Ex. 40. 36, 38.   k Hab. 3. 15.   o Ps. 69. 29.   t Job 39. 5.

c 1 Ki. 10. 15.   h Is. 35. 8.   m Ps. 78. 16.   r 1 Ki. 6. 7;   w Is. 10. 33.   l Le. 13. 6.   1 Ch. 12. 23.   p Est. 4. 5.

d De. 27. 17.   i Pr. 9. 2.   n Nu. 33. 52.   Job 41. 18.   x Ps. 55. 9.   m Eze. 13. 21.   r Ex. 32. 33.   y Am. 6. 10.

e Ju. 3. 24.   j 2 Ch. 28. 2.   o Ex. 29. 23.   t Le. 6. 8.   1 Ki. 10. 12.   x Ps. 30. 12.   s Ps. 40. 6.   z Ex. 32. 32.   z De. 16. 10.

f 1. 11.   =1 Ki. 14. 9.

מִסְתּוֹלֵל Hithpoel part. s. m. [for מִתְסוֹלֵל § 12. r. 3.] סלל

the foll. with suff. 3 pers. sing. masc. סתר

מִסְתָּרִים noun masc., pl. of מִסְתָּר dec. 2 b סתר

מְסֻתֶּרֶת [for תֶּרֶת Pual part. s. fem. [of מְסֻתָּר m.] סתר

מְסַתְּרָתָא Chald. Pael part. pass. fem., emph. st. from מִסְתַּרָא d. 8 a, fr. [מְסַתַּר m.; ו bef. lab. סתר

מִסְתַּתֵּר Hithpa. part. sing. m. [for מִתְסַתֵּר § 12. r. 3] סתר

מֵעַ masc. sing. not used; pl. מֵעִים, constr. מְעֵי (d.7a), with suff. מֵעַי מֵעֶיהָם (§ 36. rem.4).—I. *intestines, bowels.*—II. meton. *belly.*—III. *womb.*—IV. *viscera,* trop. for *heart, mind.*—V. pl. מֵעוֹת Is. 48. 19, *the bowels,* trop. of the sea.

מְעָא Ch. masc. d. 2b, only pl. מְעִין *belly,* Da. 2. 32.

מָעַי (*compassionate*) pr. name masc. Ne. 12. 36.

מֵעֲבַדָה ו pref. מ for מִ X noun fem. s. d. 10; ו bef. lab. עבד

מַעֲבָדוֹהִי Chald. noun masc. pl., suff. 3 pers. sing. masc. from [מַעֲבָד] dec. 1 a עבד

מַעֲבָדֵי pref. מ for מִ X noun masc. pl. c. fr. עֶבֶד d. 6 a עבד

מַעֲבָדֵיהֶם noun m. pl., suff. 3 pers. pl. m. fr. [מַעֲבָּד] d. 1 b עבד

מַעֲבָדָיו pref. מ for מִ X noun masc., suff. 3 pers. sing. masc. from עֶבֶד dec. 6 a עבד

מַעֲבָדֶיךָ ו pref. id. X id., suff. 2 pers. s. m.; ו bef. lab. עבד

מַעֲבִדִים Hiph. part. masc., pl. of [מַעֲבִיד] dec. 1 b עבד

מַעֲבָדְךָ pref. מ for מִ X noun masc. sing., suff. (for דְךָ) 2 pers. sing. masc. from עֶבֶד dec. 6 a עבד

מַעֲבִדֵנוּ pref. id. X Kal inf., suff. 1 pers. pl. עבד

מַעֲבֹדַת pref. id. X noun f. s., constr. of עֲבוֹדָה d. 10 עבד

מַעֲבֹדַתְכֶם pref. id. X id., suff. 2 pers. pl. masc. עבד

מַעֲבֹדָתָם pref. id. X id., suff. 3 pers. pl. m. (§ 4. r. 2) עבד

מַעֲבוֹד pref. id. X Kal inf. constr. (§ 8. rem. 18) עבד

מַעֲבוֹדַת pref. id. X noun f. s., constr. of עֲבוֹדָה d. 10 עבד

מַעֲבוֹר pref. id. X Kal inf. constr. (§ 8. rem. 18) עבר

מַעֲבוּר pref. id. X noun m. s., constr. of [עֲבוּר] d. 3 a עבר

מַעֲבִיר Hiph. part. sing. masc. dec. 1 b עבר

מַעֲבַר noun masc. sing., constr. of [מַעֲבָר] dec. 2 b עבר

מַעֲבֹר pref. מ for מִ X Kal inf. constr. עבר

מַעֲבָר ו pref. id. X noun masc. sing. dec. 6 (§ 35. rem. 6); ו bef. lab. עבר

מַעֲבֵר pref. id. X Kal part. act. sing. masc. dec. 7 b עבר

מַעֲבָרָה noun fem. sing. dec. 11 a עבר

מַעְבְּרוֹת id. pl., abs. st. עבר

מַעְבְּרוֹת id. pl., constr. st. עבר

מַעֲבִרִים Hiph. part. masc., pl. of מַעֲבִיר dec. 1 b עבר

מַעֲבָרִם pref. מ for מִ X pr. name of a place עבר

מַעֲבְרִים pref. id. X Kal part. act. m., pl. of עֹבֵר d. 7 b עבר

מַעְבְּרֹנָה pref. מ for מִ X pr. name of a place עבר

מַעְגָּל noun masc. sing. dec. 2 b עגל

מַעְגַּל id., constr. st. עגל

מַעְגִּלוֹנָה pref. מ for מִ X pr. name of a place (עֶגְלוֹן) with parag. ה עגל

מַעְגָּלֶיךָ ו noun masc. pl., suff. 2 pers. sing. masc. from מַעְגָּל dec. 2 b; ו bef. lab. עגל

מַעְגְּלֹתֶיהָ noun fem. pl., suff. 3 p. s. f. fr. מַעְגָּלָה d. 11 a עגל

מַעְגְּלֹתָיו id. with suff. 3 pers. sing. masc. עגל

[מָעַד] *to vacillate, totter.* Hiph. *to make to vacillate, totter,* Ps. 69. 24. Pu. *to be made to vacillate,* Pr. 25. 19, מְעָד, מְמֹעֶדֶת, for מוֹּעֶדֶת, מְמוּעֶדֶת (§ 10. r. 6). Gesenius takes this as a participle of Kal, for מֹעֶדֶת *vacillating.*

מַעֲדָה Hiph. part. sing. masc. עדה

מָעֲדוּ Kal pret. 3 pers. pl. מעד

מָעֲדוֹ noun masc. s., suff. 3 p. s. m. fr. מוֹעֵד d. 7 b יעד

מֻעָדוֹת Hoph. part. fem. pl. [of מוּעָדָה fr. מוּעָד m.] יעד

מַעְדֹּתֶיךָ pref. מ for מִ X noun fem. pl., suff. 2 pers. sing. masc. from עֵדוּת (comp. Chald. d. 8 c) עוד

מַעֲדִי pr. name masc. עדה

מֹעֲדִי defect. for מוֹעֲדִי (q. v.) יעד

מַעֲדְיָה pr. name masc. עדה

מַעֲדָן pref. מ for מִ X pr. name of a place עדן

מַעֲדַנּוֹת noun fem. pl. by transp. [for מַעֲדָנוֹת] ענד

מַעֲדַנֵּי noun masc. pl. constr. from [מַעֲדָן] dec. 8 a עדן

מַעֲדַנַּי pref. מ for מִ X noun masc. pl., suff. 1 pers. sing. from עֶדֶן dec. 6 (§ 35. rem. 6) עדן

מַעֲדַנִּים } noun masc., pl. of [מַעֲדָן] dec. 8 a עדן

מַעֲדַנּוֹת }

מַעֲדַת pref. מ for מִ X noun fem. sing., constr. of עֵדָה dec. 11 b יעד

מַעֲדֹתֶיךָ pref. id. X noun fem. pl., suff. 2 pers. sing. masc. from עֵדָה dec. 10 עוד

מֵעַוָּא ו pref. id. X pr. name of a place; ו bef. lab. עוה

מָעוֹן noun masc. sing. עון

מְעוֹדֵד Pilel part. sing. masc. עוד

מְעוֹדִי pref. מ for מִ X adv. עוֹד with suff. 1 p. s. d. 1 a עוד

מְעוֹדְךָ pref. id. X id. with suff. 2 pers. sing. masc. עוד

מְעוֹהִי Chald. noun masc. pl., suff. 3 pers. sing. masc. from [מְעַ] dec. 2 b מע

מָעוֹז ו noun masc. sing., for מָעֹז (suff. מָעֻזִּי) dec. 8 c (§ 37. rem. 2 & 4); ו bef. lab. עזז

מָעֻזּוֹ id., suff. 3 pers. s. m. [for מָעֻזּוֹ § 37. r. 2] עזז

מָעֻזִּי id., suff. 1 pers. sing. (v. id.) עזז

מָעֻזָּם id., suff. 3 pers. pl. masc. (v. id.) עזז

a Ex. 9. 17.   f Ex. 6. 9.   k Ps. 69. 18.   p Je. 40. 9.   u Is. 10. 29.   Ps. 65. 12.   Pr. 119. 157.   Pr. 22. 17   Nu. 22. 80.
b Je. 49. 10.   g Da. 4. 34.   l Ex. 14. 5.   q 2 Ch. 10. 4.   Is. 16. 2.   Le. 23. 44.   1 Sa. 15. 32.   Da. 2. 32.
c Pr. 27. 5.   h Job 34. 25.   m 1 Ki. 12. 4.   La. 3. 44.   1 Sa. 2. 24.   Pr. 25. 20.   Job 38. 31.   Ps. 119. 152.   2 Sa. 22. 33.
d Da. 2 22.   i Ex. 8. 7.   Ex. 5. 11.   Jos. 5. 11, 12.   Mi. 2. 8.   Ge. 49. 20.   Ps. 147. 6.   Ps. 37. 39.
e   j Ex. 6.   Ex. 6. 6.   Zec. 7. 14; 9. 8.   Ps. 140. 6.   Eze. 21. 21.   Je. 51. 34.   Ge. 48. 15.

מָעוֹךְ   pr. name masc.   .   .   .   מעך

מָעוּךְ   ו Kal part. pass. sing. masc.; ו bef. lab.   מעך

מְעוּכָה   fem. of the preced.   .   .   מעך

מָעוֹל   ו Kal inf. abs. (§ 8. rem. 8); ו bef. lab.   מעל

מְעֹל   pref. מְ for מִ)(noun masc. s. (§ 35. r. 11)   עול

מְעוֹלֵל   Piel part. sing. masc.   .   עול

מְעוֹלֵל   pref. מְ for מִ)(noun masc. sing. dec. 7 b   עלל

מְעוֹלֵל   Poel part. or subst. masc.   .   עלל

מֵעוֹלָם   ו pref. מְ for מִ)(noun m. s. d. 2 b ; ו bef. lab.   עלם

מָעוֹן   ו noun masc. sing. d. 3 a, also pr. name ; ו id.   עון

מְעוֹן   pref. מְ for מִ)(noun masc. sing. dec. 3 a   עוה

מְעוֹן   noun masc. sing., constr. of מָעוֹן dec. 3 a   עון

    (also pr. name in compos. see בֵּית)   .

מְעוֹנָה   id., suff. 3 pers. sing. fem.   .   עון

מְעוֹנוֹ   id., suff. 3 pers. sing. masc.   .   עון

מְעוֹנֹתַי   ו pr. name masc. ; ו bef. lab.   .   עון

מְעוֹנֹתֵיהֶם   pref. מְ for מִ)(noun masc. with pl. fem. and suff. 3 pers. pl. masc. from עוֹן dec. 3 a

מְעוֹנוֹתֵינוּ   pref. id.)(id. pl., suff. 1 pers. pl.   עוה

מְעוֹנִי   ו)(pref. id.)(id. s., suff. 1 p. s. ; ו bef. lab.   עוה

מְעוֹנִי   in full for מְעֹנִי (q. v.)   .   ענה

מְעוּנִים   pr. name of a people, see מָעוֹן   עון

מְעוֹנֵינוּ   pref. מְ for מִ)(noun masc. pl. [עֲוֹנִים], suff. 1 pers. pl. from עָוֹן dec. 3 a

מְעוֹנְךָ   pref. id.)(id. sing., suff. 2 pers. sing. masc.   (for עֲוֹנְךָ)

מְעוֹנְךָ   [for מְעֹנְךָ] noun masc. sing., suff. 2 pers. sing. masc. from מָעוֹן dec. 3 a   עון

מְעוֹנֵן   Poel (§ 6. No. 1) part. sing. masc. dec. 7 b   ענן

מְעוֹנְנוּ   pref. מְ for מִ)(noun masc. sing., suff. 1 pers. pl. from עָוֹן dec. 3 a   עוה

מְעוֹנְנִים   ו Poel (§ 6. No. 1) part. masc., pl. of מְעוֹנֵן dec. 7 b ; ו bef. lab.   ענן

מְעוֹנָתוֹ   ו noun fem. sing., suff. 3 pers. sing. masc. from מְעוֹנָה dec. 10 ; ו id.   עון

מְעוֹנֹתָיו   ו id. pl., suff. 3 pers. sing. masc. ; ו id.   עון

מְעוֹנֹתֵיהֶם   ו defect. for מְעוֹנוֹתֵיהֶם (q. v.)   עוה

מְעוֹנֹתָם   noun fem. pl., suff. 3 pers. pl. masc. (§ 4. rem. 1) from מְעוֹנָה dec. 10   עון

מָעוֹף   ו pref. מְ for מִ)(noun masc. s. ; ו bef. lab.   עוף

מְעוֹף   noun masc. sing., constr. of [מָעוֹף] dec. 3 a   עוף

מְעוֹפֵף   Pilel part. sing. masc.   .   עוף

מְעוֹר   pref. מְ for מִ)(noun masc. sing. dec. 1 a   עור

מְעוֹרֵיהֶם   noun m. pl., suff. 3 p. pl. m. fr. [מָעוֹר] d. 3 a   עור

מְעוֹרָת   Pual part. sing. masc.   .   עות

מָעֹז   ו pref. מְ for מִ)(adj. m. s. d. 8 d ; ו bef. lab.   עזז

מָעוֹז   noun masc. sing. (suff. מָעֻזִּי) d. 8 c (§ 37. r. 4)   עזז

מְעֹזֵב   pref. מְ for מִ)(Kal inf. constr.   עזב

מָעֻזֹּה   n. m. s., suff. 3 p. s. m. fr. מָעוֹז d. 8 c (§ 37. r. 4)   עזז

מְעֻזָּה   pref. מְ for מִ)(pr. name of a place   עזז

מָעֻזִּי   ו)(n. m. s., suff. 1 p. s. fr. מָעוֹז d. 8 c (§ 37. r. 4)   עזז

מַעֲזְיָה   pr. name masc.   .   עזה

מָעֻזִּים   noun masc., pl. of מָעוֹז dec. 8 c (§ 37. rem. 4)   עזז

מָעֻזֵּךְ   id. sing., suff. 2 pers. sing. fem.   עזז

מָעֻזְּכֶם   id. sing., suff. 2 pers. pl. masc.   עזז

מָעֻזְּכֶן   id. sing., suff. 2 pers. pl. fem.   עזז

מָעֻזָּם   id. sing., suff. 3 pers. pl. masc.   עזז

מָעֻזְנֶיהָ   id. pl., epenth. נ & suff. 3 p. s. f. (§ 4. r. 5)   עזז

מַעְזִרִים   Hiph. part. masc. pl. [of מַעֲזֵר § 11. rem. 8]   עזר

[מָעַט]   to be or become little, few. Pi. id. Ec. 12. 3. Hiph. I. to make small, few, to diminish.—II. to make or do little.—III. to give little.

מָעַט, מְעַט, masc. pl. מְעַטִּים dec. 8.—I. smallness, fewness; hence, a little, few; מְעַט מַיִם a little water; מְתֵי מְעַט men of fewness, i. e. a few men.—II. adj. small, few; בֵּין רַב לִמְעַט between many and few; יִהְיוּ יָמָיו מְעַטִּים let his days be few.—III. adv. a little; of time, for a little, a little while; מְעַט מְעַט by little and little.—IV. כִּמְעַט lit. as a little; (a) nearly, almost; (b) shortly, soon; כִּמְעַט שֶׁ little that, i. e. scarcely; (c) intens. very little; of number, very few; לִמְעַט i. q. מְעַט Hag. 1. 9; 2 Ch. 29. 34.

מָעֹט, fem. מְעֹטָה adj. Eze. 21. 20, naked, drawn, of a sword (Arab. מעט smooth, bare). Gesenius, polished, sharp.

מְעַט   ו)(noun masc. sing., also adv. (pl. מְעַטִּים) dec. 8 d ; ו bef. lab.   מעט

מְעַט   Kal inf. constr.   .   מעט

מַעֲטֵה   noun masc. sing., constr. of מַעֲטֶה dec. 9 a   עטה

מְעֻטָּה   adj. fem. [from מָעֹט masc. dec. 8] R. מעט ; or Pual part. fem. [of מְעֻטֶּה masc.]   עטה

מִעֲטוּ   Piel (§ 14. rem. 1) pret. 3 pers. sing. [for מֵעֲטוּ, comp. § 8. rem. 7]   מעט

מְעַטִּים   adj. masc., pl. of מְעַט dec. 8 d   מעט

מֵעַי   pr. name masc.   .   מע

מֵעַי   ו)(noun masc. pl. [מֵעִים], suff. 1 pers. sing. [fr. מֵע § 36. r. 4]; ו bef. lab.   מע

מֵעִי   noun masc. sing. [for מְעִי]   עוה

מֵעִיד   Hiph. part. sing. masc.   .   עוד

מֵעִיהֶם   ו noun masc. pl. [מֵעִים], suff. 3 pers. pl. masc. [from מֵע § 36. rem. 4]; ו bef. lab.   מע

---

a Le. 22. 24.   f Zep. 3. 7.   l Ps. 107. 41.   q Ezr. 9. 13.   ᵖ Ps. 104. 22.   c Ju. 14. 14.   h Ne. 8. 10.   m Le. 25. 16.   r Ca. 5. 4.
b 1 Sa. 26. 7.   g 2 Ch. 36. 15.   m Da. 9. 13.   r Mi. 5. 11.   y Is. 8. 22.   d Pr. 10. 29.   i Is. 23. 14.   n Is. 61. 3.   s Is. 17. 1.
c 2 Ch. 28. 19.   h Eze. 43. 10.   n Job 11. 6.   s Ps. 76. 3.   z Da. 11. 10.   e Je. 16. 19.   k Eze. 24. 25.   o Eze. 21. 20.   t De. 32. 46.
d Ps. 71. 4.   i Is. 53. 5.   o Ps. 91. 9.   t Na. 2. 13.   a Hab. 2. 15.   f Is. 23. 11.   l Ec. 12. 3.   p Eze. 7. 19.
e Is. 3. 12.   k Job 10. 14.   p De. 18. 10.   u Ps. 107. 17.   b Ec. 1. 15.   g Is. 17. 10.   2 Ch. 28. 22.

מֵעָיו id. with suff. 3 pers. sing. masc.	מע
מֵעַיִים pref. מֵ for מִ) pr. name of a place	עוה
מֵעֶיךָ) noun masc. pl., suff. 2 pers. sing. masc. [from מַע § 36. rem. 4]; bef. lab.	מע
מְעִיל) noun masc. sing. dec. 1 a; id.	מעל
מְעִילוֹ id., suff. 3 pers. sing. masc.	מעל
מְעִילִי) id., suff. 1 pers. sing.; bef. lab.	מעל
מְעִילֵיהֶם id. pl., suff. 3 pers. pl. masc.	מעל
מְעִילִים id. pl., abs. st.	מעל
מְעִילְךָ id. sing., suff. 2 pers. sing. masc.	מעל
מְעִילָם) pref. מֵ for מִ) pr. name of a province ; bef. lab.	עלם
מַעְיָן) noun masc. sing. dec. 2 b, id.	עין
מַעְיַן id., constr. st.	עין
מַעְיַן pref. מֵ for מִ) pr. name in compos. עֵין גַּדִּי	עין
מַעְיָנוֹ noun m., suff. 3 pers. sing. m. fr. מַעְיָן d. 2 b	עין
מַעְיָנוֹת id. pl. abs. fem.	עין
מַעְיְנוֹת id. pl. constr. fem.	עין
מַעְיְנֵי id. pl. masc. (מַעְיָנִים), suff. 1 pers. sing.	עין
מַעְיְנֵי id. pl., constr. st.	עין
מֵעֵינַי pref. מֵ for מִ) noun fem. du. (עֵינַיִם), suff. 1 pers. sing. from עַיִן dec. 6 h	עין
מֵעֵינֵי pref. id.) id. du., constr. st.	עין
מֵעֵינָיו pref. id.) id. du., suff. 3 pers. sing. masc.	עין
מֵעֵינַיִךְ pref. id.) id. du., suff. 2 pers. sing. fem.	עין
מֵעֵינֶיךָ pref. id.) id. du., suff. 2 pers. sing. masc.	עין
מַעְיָנִים noun masc., pl. of מַעְיָן dec. 2 b	עין
מַעְיְנֹת id. pl. constr. fem.	עין
מַעְיְנֹתֶיךָ id. pl. fem., suff. 2 pers. sing. masc.	עין
מֵעִיק Hiph. part. sing. masc.	עוק
מֵעִיר Hiph. part. sing. masc. dec. 3 b	עור
מֵעִיר pref. מֵ for מִ) Kal inf. constr. Ho. 7. 4; and perhaps (Job 24. 12) noun m. s. see עִיר	עור
מֵעִיר pref. id.) noun fem. sing. irr., pl. עָרִים more usually עָרִים (§ 45)	עור
מֵעִירוֹ pref. id.) id., suff. 3 pers. sing. masc.	עור
מֵעִירְךָ pref. id.) id., suff. 2 pers. sing. masc.	עור
מֵעָרֵם Hiph. part. masc., pl. of מֵעִיר dec. 3 b	עור

[מָעַךְ] *to press*, 1 Sa. 26. 7 ; part. Le. 22. 24, מָעוּךְ *bruised, castrated.* Pu. *to be pressed*, Eze. 23. 3.

מָעוֹךְ (*oppression*) pr. name masc. 1 Sa. 27. 2 ; otherwise called מַעֲכָה, comp. 1 Ki. 2. 39.

מַעֲכַת, מַעֲכָה (id.) pr. name—I. of a region and city near Mount Hermon. Gent. מַעֲכָתִי.—II. of several persons, male and female.

מַעֲכָה) pr. name of a man and a region (and in compos see בֵּית); bef. lab.	מעך
מֹעֲכוּ Pual pret. 3 pers. pl.	מעך
מַעֲכַת) pr. name of a region, see מַעֲכָה) bef. lab.	מעך

מָעַל *to act perversely, treacherously, to be faithless*, with בְּ of the thing or person.

מַעַל masc. dec. 6 d, *perverseness, treachery, sin*, against God.

מְעִיל masc. dec. 1 a, *long and full upper garment*, worn by persons of dignity (men and women), *robe, mantle.*

מַעַל } noun masc. sing. dec. 6 d (§ 35. rem. 2) מַעַל }	מעל
מַעַל pref. מֵ for מִ) adv.	עלה
מַעַל) pref. id.) prep. see עַל; bef. lab.	עלה
מֵעַל pref. id.) Kh. מֵעַל q. v., K. מֵעֲלֵי see עֲלֵי	עלה
מָעֲלָה) Kal pret. 3 pers. sing. fem.; , for וְ conv.	מעל
מַעֲלֵה constr. of the foll.	עלה
מַעֲלֶה) Hiph. part. or subst. m. d. 9 a; bef. lab.	עלה
מַעֲלָה id. part., fem. of the preced., dec. 10	עלה
מַעֲלָה } adv. [מַעַל] with loc. ה, for וְ see lett. ו מָעְלָה }	עלה
מָעֲלוּ Kal pret. 3 pers. pl.	מעל
מַעֲלָיו noun masc. pl., suff. 3 pers. sing. masc. (§ 4. rem. 1) fr. מַעֲלָה dec. 9 a	עלה
מַעֲלוֹ) noun masc. sing., suff. 3 pers. sing. masc. fr. מַעַל dec. 6 d; bef. lab.	מעל
מַעֲלוֹ) pref. מֵ for מִ) noun masc. sing., suff. 3 pers. sing. masc. fr. עַל dec. 8 c; id.	עלל
מְעֻלּוֹ defect. for מְעִילוֹ (q. v.)	מעל
מַעֲלוֹת) noun fem., pl. of מַעֲלָה d. 10; bef. lab.	עלה
מַעֲלוֹת pref. מֵ for מִ) Kal inf. constr.	עלה
מֵעֲלוֹת pref. id.) noun f., pl. of עֹלָה or עוֹלָה d. 10	עלה
מַעֲלוֹתָו noun fem. pl., suff. 3 pers. sing. masc. (§ 4. rem. 1) fr. מַעֲלָה dec. 10	עלה
מֵעֲלַי } pref. מֵ for מִ) prep. (עַל), pl. with suff. מֵעָלַי } 1 pers. sing. (§ 31. rem. 5) }	עלה
מֵעֲלֵי (or מֵעַל) Ch. noun masc. pl. constr. [fr. מֵעַל or מֵעַל] dec. 1 a	עלל
מֵעָלֶיהָ pref. מֵ for מִ) prep. (עַל) pl. with suff. 3 pers. sing. fem. (§ 31. rem. 5)	עלה
מֵעֲלֵיהֶם pref. id.) id., suff. 3 pers. pl. masc.	עלה
מֵעָלָיו) pref. id.) id., suff. 3 p. s. m.; bef. lab.	עלה

a Eze. 3. 3.   b 2 Sa. 13. 18.   i Ps. 87. 7.   n Ge. 8. 2.   r Joel 4. 7.   x Je. 50.   c Eze. 40. 31,   e 2 Ch. 33. 19.   f Am. 9. 6.
c 1 Sa. 15. 27.   f Joel 4. 18.   k Ju. 6. 21.   o Pr. 5. 16.   s Eze. 23. 3.   y Le. 11. 26.   34, 37.   g Job 1. 20; 2. 12.   g Da. 6. 15.
d Esr. 9. 3, 5.   h Ho. 13. 15.   l Ca. 4. 9.   p Am. 2. 13.   t 21. 34; Nu.   z De. 28. 43.   Eze. 17. 20.   Ho. 6. 6.   Pr. 14. 14.
e Eze. 26. 16.   h Ge. 7. 11.   m Ps. 104. 10.   q Da. 9. 16.   u 1 Ki. 20. 41.

מַעֲלִיּוֹתָיו	pref. מְ for מִי ‖ noun fem. pl., suff. 3 pers. sing. masc. fr. עָלִיָּה dec. 10 . . עלה
מַעֲלֵךְ	pref. id. ‖ prep. (עַל) pl. with suff. 2 pers. sing. fem. (§ 31. rem. 5) . . עלה
מַעֲלֶיךָ	pref. id. ‖ id., suff. 2 pers. sing. masc. עלה
מַעֲלֵיכֶם	pref. id. ‖ id., suff. 2 pers. pl. masc. עלה
מַעֲלֵילֵיכֶם׳ Kh.	noun masc. pl., suff. 2 pers. pl. masc. from [מַעֲלִיל] dec. 1 b; K. מַעֲלְלֵיכֶם (q. v.); ‖ bef. lab. עלל
מַעֲלִים	Hiph. part. masc., pl. of מַעֲלֶה dec. 9 a עלה
מַעֲלִים׳	Hiph. part. sing. masc.; ‖ bef. lab. עלם
מַעֲלֵינוּ	pref. מְ for מִי ‖ prep. (עַל) pl. with suff. 1 pers. pl. (§ 31. rem. 5) . . עלה
מַעֲלְלֵי	noun masc. pl. constr. fr. [מַעֲלָל] dec. 2 b עלל
מַעֲלְלֵיהֶם׳	id. pl., suff. 3 pers. pl. masc.; ‖ bef. lab. עלל
מַעֲלְלֵיהֶם׳	id. pl., suff. 3 p. pl. m.; K. כֶם 2 p. pl. m. עלל
מַעֲלְלָיו׳	id. pl., suff. 3 pers. sing. m.; ‖ bef. lab. עלל
מַעֲלְלֵךְ	id. pl., suff. 2 pers. sing. masc. עלל
מַעֲלְלָיִךְ׳	id. pl., suff. 2 pers. sing. fem.; ‖ bef. lab. עלל
מַעֲלְלֵיכֶם׳	id. pl., suff. 2 pers. pl. masc.; ‖ id. עלל
מַעֲלָלִים׳	id. pl., abs. st. עלל
מַעֲלָם׳	noun masc. sing., suff. 3 pers. pl. masc. fr. מַעַל dec. 6 d מעל
מַעֲלָם׳	pref. מְ for מִי ‖ pr. name of a place עלם
מָעַלְנוּ׳	Kal pret. 1 pers. pl. מעל
מְעֻלָּפֶת	Pual part. sing. fem. [of מְעֻלָּף] עלף
מַעֲלַת	Hiph. part. sing. fem., constr. of מַעֲלָה dec. 10, from מַעֲלֶה masc. עלה
מָעַלְתָּ׳	Kal pret. 2 pers. sing. masc. מעל
מַעֲלָתְהֶג׳	‖ noun fem. pl., suff. 3 pers. sing. masc. fr. מַעֲלָה dec. 10 (§ 4. rem. 1 & 2); ‖ bef. lab. עלה
מָעַלְתֶּם	Kal pret. 2 pers. pl. masc. . . מעל
מֵעִם	‖ pref. מְ for מִי ‖ noun com. s. (pl. עַמִּים) מעם
מֵעִם׳	d. 8 d, & irr. עֲמָמִים (§ 45); ‖ bef. lab.
מֵעִם׳	‖ pref. id. ‖ prep. (§ 5); ‖ id. מעם
מַעֲמָד	‖ noun m. sing., constr. of [מַעֲמָד] d. 1 b; ‖ id. עמד
מָעֳמָד׳	Hoph. part. or subst. masc. sing. עמד
מֵעָמְדִי׳	pref. מְ for מִי ‖ prep. [עָמַד] with suff. 1 p. s. עמד
מַעֲמָדִים	noun m. s., suff. 3 pers. pl. m. fr. [מַעֲמָד] d. 3 a עמד
מֵעַמּוֹ׳	‖ pref. מְ for מִי ‖ noun com. sing., suff. 3 pers. sing. masc. from עַם dec. 8 d (§ 45) . עמם
מֵעַמּוֹ׳	pref. id. ‖ prep. (עַם) with suff. 3 p. s. m. (§ 5) עמם
מֵעַמֵּי׳	pref. id. ‖ n. com. pl. constr. fr. עַם d. 8 d (§ 45) עמם
מֵעַמִּי׳	‖ pref. id. ‖ id. sing. suff. 1 pers. s.; ‖ bef. lab. עמם

מֵעִמִּי	pref. מְ for מִי ‖ prep. עִם with suff. 1 p s. (§ 5) עמם
מַעֲמִיד׳	Hiph. part. sing. masc. עמד
מֵעַמֶּיהָ	pref. מְ for מִי ‖ noun com. pl., suff. 3 pers. sing. fem. from עַם dec. 8 d (§ 45) . עמם
מֵעַמָּיו	pref. id. ‖ id. pl., suff. 3 pers. sing. masc. עמם
מֵעַמִּים׳	‖ pref. id. ‖ id. pl., abs. st. : ‖ bef. lab. עמם
מֵעִמָּךְ׳	‖ pref. id. ‖ id. sing., suff. 2 pers. sing. masc.; ‖ id. עמם
מֵעִמָּךְ	pref. id. ‖ prep. (עִם) with suff. 2 pers. sing. fem., or 2 pers. masc. in pause for the foll. עמם
מֵעִמָּךְ	pref. id. ‖ id., suff. 2 pers. sing. masc. עמם
מֵעִמָּכֶם׳	pref. id. ‖ id., suff. 2 pers. pl. masc. . עמם
מֵעֲמַל	pref. id. ‖ noun m. sing., constr. of עָמָל d. 4 c עמל
מֵעֲמָלֵקִי׳	‖ pref. id. ‖ gent. n. fr. עֲמָלֵק (q. v.); ‖ bef. lab. עמל
מֵעִמָּנוּ	pref. id. ‖ prep. (מִן) with suff. 1 pers. pl. (§ 5) עמם
מַעֲמָסָה׳	noun fem. sing. עמס
מַעֲמָק	pref. מְ for מִי ‖ noun masc. sing. dec. 6 b עמק
מַעֲמַקֵּי׳	noun masc. pl. constr. from [מַעֲמָק] dec. 8 a עמק
מְעַמֵּר	Piel part. sing. masc. עמר
מַעֲנֶה	noun fem. sing. dec. 10 ענה
מַעֲנֶה	noun masc. sing. constr. & abs. dec. 9 a ענה
מַעֲנֶה	
מְעֹנָה׳	noun fem. sing. dec. 10 עון
מְעֻנֶּה׳	‖ Pual part. sing. masc.; ‖ bef. lab. ענה
מַעֲנוֹת	pref. מְ for מִי ‖ Kal inf. constr. ענה
מַעֲנִי׳	pref. id. ‖ adj. masc., pl. עֲנִיִּים d. 8 (§ 37. r. 4) ענה
מֵעֳנִי	pref. id. ‖ noun masc. sing. dec. 6 k ענה
מֵעֳנִי׳	(§ 35. rem. 14) . . .
מְעַנֵּךְ	Piel part. pl. masc. [מְעַנִּים], suff. 2 pers. sing. fem. from [מְעַנֶּה] dec. 9 a ענה
מְעֹנְנִים׳	defect. for מְעוֹנְנִים (q. v.) ענן
מַעֲשִׂים׳	pref. מְ for מִי ‖ n. m. s., constr. of עָשִׂים d. 3 a עשם
מָעָף׳	Hoph. part. sing. masc. [for מוּעָף] יעף
מֵעָפָר׳	‖ pref. מְ for מִי ‖ noun m. s. d. 4 c; ‖ bef. lab. עפר
מֵעֲפַר׳	pref. id. ‖ id., constr. st. עפר
מַעַץ	(anger, Gesenius) pr. name masc. 1 Ch. 2. 27.
מַעֵץ׳	‖ pref. מְ for מִי ‖ noun masc. sing. dec. 7 b עצה
מַעֵץ׳	(§ 36. rem. 2 & 4); ‖ bef. lab.
מֵעִצְּבוֹן׳	‖ pref. id. ‖ noun m. sing. constr. of עִצָּבוֹן dec. 3 c; ‖ id. עצב
מֵעָצְבֵּךְ	pref. id. ‖ noun m. s., suff. 2 p. s. m. fr. עֹצֶב d. 6 c עצב
מַעֲצָד	noun masc. sing. עצד
מַעְצוֹר׳	noun masc. sing. עצר
מֵעֲצֵי׳	pref. מְ for מִי ‖ noun m. pl. constr. fr. עֵץ d. 7 b עצה
מֵעֵצְיוֹן׳	‖ pref. id. ‖ pr. name in compos., see עֶצְיוֹן עצה
	גֶּבֶר; ‖ bef. lab.

* Ps. 104. 13.   f Je. 21. 12.   Eze. 39. 26.   l 1 Sa. 18. 12.   " 2 Ch. 18. 34.   k Is. 53. 11.   f De. 33. 27.   " De. 18. 14.   ' Ge. 5. 29.
b Zec. 1. 4.   g Ho. 4. 9.   Ezr. 10. 2.   1 Ki. 22. 35;   Eze. 38. 8.   Zec. 12. 3.   Is. 53. 4.   " Ca. 8. 2.   Is. 14. 3.
c Job 42. 3.   De. 28. 20.   Ca. 5. 14.   Ps. 69. 3.   l Is. 63. 3.   Is. 51. 10.   Job 32. 1.   Da. 9. 21.   Is. 44. 12.
d Pr. 28. 27.   i Je. 4. 18.   2 Ch. 26. 18.   Ex. 8. 4.   Ex. 8. 7.   Ps. 129. 7.   Eze. 18. 17.   Nu. 19. 17.   1 Sa. 14. 6.
e Is. 3. 8.   1 Sa. 25. 3.   Eze. 43. 17.   Ge. 31. 31.   2 Sa. 15. 28.   1 Sa. 14. 14.   Ex. 3. 17.   Ge. 2. 17.   Ca. 3. 9.
f Is. 18. 7.

מֵעֲרֹעֵר	pref. מ for מִ)(pr. name of a place .	ערר
מֵעָרָה	וֹ pr. name of a place ; וֹ bef. lab. .	ערה
מְעָרַת	noun fem. sing., constr. of מְעָרָה dec. 10 (comp. § 39. No. 3) .	עור
מַעֲשֶׂה / מַעֲשֵׂה	וֹ } noun masc. sing. constr. & abs. dec. 9a; וֹ bef. lab. .	עשׂה
מַעֲשֵׂהוּ	וֹ id., suff. 3 pers. sing. masc. ; וֹ bef. lab. .	עשׂה
מַעֲשֵׂהוּ	pref. מ for מִ)(Kal part. act., suff. 3 pers. sing. masc. from עֹשֶׂה dec. 9a .	עשׂה
מֵעֲשׂוֹת	pref. id.)(Kal inf. constr. dec. 1a .	עשׂה
מַעֲשַׂי	וֹ } **noun m. pl. with suff. 1 pers. s. fr.** מַעֲשֶׂה dec. 9a (also pr. name); וֹ bef. lab. }	עשׂה
מַעֲשֵׂי	id. pl. constr. st. .	עשׂה
מַעֲשֵׂיָה	וֹ pr. name masc. ; וֹ bef. lab. .	עשׂה
מַעֲשֶׂיהָ	noun masc. pl., suff. 3 pers. sing. fem. from מַעֲשֶׂה dec. 9a .	עשׂה
מַעֲשֵׂיָהוּ	וֹ pr. name masc., see מַעֲשֵׂיָה ; וֹ bef. lab. .	עשׂה
מַעֲשֵׂיהֶם	וֹ noun masc. pl., suff. 3 pers. pl. masc. from מַעֲשֶׂה dec. 9a ; וֹ id.	עשׂה
מַעֲשָׂיו	id. pl., suff. 3 pers. sing. masc. .	עשׂה
מַעֲשֶׂיךָ	id. pl., suff. 2 pers. sing. masc. .	עשׂה
מַעֲשַׂיִךְ	} id. pl., suff. 2 pers. sing. fem. .	עשׂה
מַעֲשֵׂיכֶם	id. pl., suff. 2 pers. pl. masc. .	עשׂה
מַעֲשִׂים	id. pl., abs. st. .	עשׂה
מַעֲשֵׂינוּ	id. pl., suff. 1 pers. pl. .	עשׂה
מַעֲשִׂיר	וֹ Hiph. part. sing. masc. ; וֹ bef. lab. .	עשׂר
מַעֲשֵׂק	accord. to some copies for מַעֲשֵׂי (q. v. & §4. r. 1)	עשׂה
מַעֲשָׁק	pref. מ for מִ)(noun masc. sing. .	עשׁק
מַעֲשַׁקּוֹת	noun fem., pl. of [מַעֲשַׁקָּה] dec. 10 .	עשׁק
מַעֲשֵׂר / מַעֲשַׂר	} noun masc. sing. constr. & abs., suff. מַעֲשְׂרוֹ , dec. 7c .	עשׂר
מַעְשַׂר	וֹ id., constr. st. ; וֹ bef. lab. .	עשׂר
מֵעֶשֶׂר	pref. מ for מִ)(noun masc. sing. dec. 6c .	עשׂר
מַעֲשָׂרָה	pref. id.)(num. card. masc. constr. עֲשֶׂרֶת , see עֶשֶׂר fem. .	עשׂר
מַעְשְׂרֹתֵיכֶם	noun masc. with pl. fem. term. and suff. 2 pers. pl. masc. from מַעֲשֵׂר (q. v.)	עשׂר
מֵעֲשׂת	pref. מ for מִ)(Kal inf. constr. 1a, see מֵעֲשׂוֹת	עשׂה
מֵעֲשׂתִי	pref. id.)(id. with suff. 1 pers. sing. .	עשׂה
מֵעֵת	וֹ pref. id.)(noun com. sing. dec. 8b [for עֵדֶת] ; וֹ bef. lab. .	עדה
מֵעַתָּה / מֵעָתָּה	} pref. id.)(adv. .	עדה
מֹף	pr. name, *Memphis*, a city of Egypt, Ho. 9. 6, otherwise called נֹף Is. 19. 13 ; Je. 2. 16.	
מִפְּארָן	pref. מ)(pr. name of a place .	פאר

מֵעֲצְמוֹן	pref. מ for מִ)(pr. name of a place	עצם
מֵעַצְמוֹתָי	pref. id.)(noun fem. pl., (עֲצָמוֹת), suff. 1 pers. sing. from עֶצֶם dec. 6a	עצם
מֵעֲצָמַי	pref. id.)(id. pl. m. (עֲצָמִים), suff. 1 pers. s.	עצם
מַעֲצָר	noun masc. sing. .	עצר
מֵעֹצֶר	pref. מ for מִ)(noun masc. sing. .	עצר
מַעֲצַת	perh. constr. of עֵצָה R. .	עצה
מֵעֲצַת	pref. מ for מִ)(n. f. s., constr. of עֵצָה d. 11b	יעץ
מֵעֲצָתוֹ	pref. id.)(id. with suff. 3 pers. sing. masc.	יעץ
מַעֲקֶה	noun masc. sing. .	עקה
מְעֻקָּל	Pual part. sing. masc. .	עקל
מֵעֶקְרוֹן	pref. מ for מִ)(pr. name of a place .	עקר
מְעֻקָּשׁ	pref. id.)(adj. masc. sing. dec. 7b .	עקשׁ
מְעַקֵּשׁ	וֹ Piel part. sing. masc. ; וֹ bef. lab. .	עקשׁ
מַעֲקַשִּׁים	וֹ noun masc., pl. of [מַעֲקָשׁ] dec. 8a ; וֹ id.	עקשׁ
מְעָרֵב	Chald. Pael part. sing. masc. (§ 49. rem. 3)	ערב
מֵעֶרֶב	pref. מ for מִ)(n. com. s. (du. עַרְבַּיִם) d. 6a	ערב
מַעֲרָבָה	noun masc. sing. [מַעֲרָב] with parag. ה, d. 2b	ערב
מַעֲרָבַיִךְ	וֹ id. pl., suff. 2 pers. sing. fem. ; וֹ bef. lab.	ערב
מַעֲרָבֵךְ	id. sing., suff. 2 pers. sing. fem. .	ערב
מֵעַרְבֹת	pref. מ for מִ)(noun fem. pl. constr. from עֲרָבָה dec. 11c (§ 42. rem. 1)	ערב
מֵעֲרֻגוֹת	pref. id.)(noun fem., pl. of [עֲרוּגָה] dec. 10	ערג
מְעָרָה	וֹ noun fem. s. (constr. מְעָרַת) d. 10; וֹ bef. lab.	עור
מֵעָרֹעֵר	pref. מ for מִ)(pr. name of a place .	ערר
מֵעָרוֹת	noun fem. plural, abs. of מְעָרָה dec. 10 (comp. § 39. No. 3) .	עור
מֵעָרֵי	pref. מ for מִ)(noun fem. pl. constr. prop. from עָר see עִיר (§ 45)	עור
מֵעָרֵיהֶם	pref. id.)(id. pl., suff. 3 pers. pl. masc. .	עור
מֵעָרָיו	pref. id.)(id. pl., suff. 3 pers. sing. masc. .	עור
מַעֲרִיצְכֶם	Hiph. part. or subst. masc. (מַעֲרִיץ), suff. 2 pers. pl. masc. dec. 1b	ערץ
מַעֲרֵךְ	noun masc. sing., suff. 2 pers. sing. fem. from מַעַר [contr. from מַעֲרֶה] .	ערה
מַעֲרָכָה	noun fem. sing. dec. 11a .	ערך
מַעֲרָכוֹת	id. pl., abs. st. .	ערך
מַעַרְכוֹת	id. pl., constr. st. .	ערך
מַעַרְכֵי	noun masc. pl. constr. from [מַעֲרָךְ] dec. 2b .	ערך
מַעֲרָכְּךָ	pref. מ for מִ)(noun masc. sing., suff. 2 pers. sing. masc. from עֵרֶךְ dec. 6 (§ 35. rem. 6) .	ערך
מַעֲרֶכֶת	וֹ noun fem. sing. ; וֹ bef. lab. .	ערך
מַעֲרֶכֶת	noun fem. pl. constr. of מַעֲרָכָה .	ערך
מֵעֲרֵלִים	pref. מ for מִ)(adj. masc., pl. of עָרֵל d. 5b .	ערל
מֵעֲרֵמוֹת	pref. id.)(noun fem., pl. of עֲרֵמָה constr. עֲרֵמַת dec. 10 .	ערם
מֵעֲרֵמֵיהֶם	noun m. pl., suff. 3 p. pl. m. fr. [מַעֲרָם] d. 8c	ערם

a Job 7. 15. | e Ho. 10. 6. | i Da. 2. 41, 43. | p Eze. 17. 7. | s Na. 3. 5. | z Eze. 32. 27. | f Ec. 2. 4. | k Ge. 20. 9. | p Pr. 22. 1.
b Ge. 2. 23. | f De. 22. 8. | k Eze. 27. 33. | t 1 Sa. 24. 4. | t Le. 24. 6. | k Ne. 3. 34. | g Pr. 31. 31. | l Is. 26. 12. | p Ge. 18. 25.
c Pr. 25. 28. | g Hab. 1. 4. | l Eze. 27. 13, 17. | r Jos. 13. 4. | u Pr. 4. 17. | l 2 Ch. 28. 15. | h Is. 1. 16, 16. | m 1 Sa. 2. 7. | r 2 Sa. 23. 17.
d Pr. 27. 9. | h Pr. 10. 9. | 25, 27, 34. | s Is. 32. 14. | v Le. 27. 8, 18. | m Job 4. 17. | i Eze. 1. 16, 16. | n De. 15. 10. | s Ho. 2. 9.
  2 Sa. 17. 14. | Is. 42. 16. | De. 34. 1. | Is. 8. 13. | | 2 Ch. 2. 3 ; 13. 11.

מִפְּאַת	ᵃ pref. מִ)(noun fem., constr. of פֵּאָה dec. 11 b; ᴉ bef. lab. . . .	פאה
מַפְנִיעַ	Hiph. part. sing. masc. . .	פנע
מִפְדּוֹתᵇ	pref. מִ)(noun fem. sing . .	פדה
מִפְדָּן	pref. id.)(pr. name of a place .	פדן
מִפְדַּן אֲרָם	pref. id.)(pr. name of a place, פַּדַּן אֲ׳	פדן
מִפֶּה	pref. id.)(noun masc. sing. irr. (§ 45)	פאה
מִפֹּה מִפּוֹ	} pref. id.)(adv. ; ᴉ bef. lab. . .	פה
מִפּוּנֹן	pref. id.)(pr. name of a place .	פון
מִפָּזᶜ	ᴉ pref. id.)(noun masc. sing. ; ᴉ id. .	פזז
מְפַזֵּז	Piel part. sing. masc. . .	פזז
מְפַזֵּר	Piel part. sing. masc. . .	פזר
מְפֹזָרᵈ	Pual part. sing. masc. . .	פזר
מִפָּחʰ	noun masc. sing., bef. penacute for מַפָּח .	נפח
מַפֵּחַ	noun masc. sing. . .	נפח
מִפָּח	pref. מִ)(noun m. s., pl. פַּחִים (§ 37. r. 7)	פחח
מְפַחֵדᵏ	Piel part. sing. masc. (§ 14. rem. 1) .	פחד
מִפַּחַד מְפַּחֵד	} pref. מִ)(noun masc. sing. dec. 6 d (§ 35. rem. 2) .	פחד
מִפַּחְדְּךָᵍ	pref. id.)(id., suff. 2 pers. s. m. (§ 35. r. 5)	פחד
מִפִּי	ᵐᴉ pref. id.)(noun masc. sing. constr., or with suff. 1 p. s. fr. פֶּה irr. (§ 45); ᴉ bef. lab.	פאה
מְפִיבֹשֶׁת	ᴉ noun masc. ; ᴉ id. . . .	פאה
מִפִּיָהⁿ	pref. מִ)(noun masc. sing., suff. 3 pers. sing. fem. from פֶּה irr. (§ 45) . .	פאה
מִפִּיהוּᵒ	pref. id.)(id., suff. 3 pers. sing. masc.	פאה
מִפִּיהֶם	pref. id.)(id., suff. 3 pers. pl. masc. .	פאה
מִפִּיו	pref. id.)(id., suff. 3 pers. sing. masc.	פאה
מִפִּיךָ	pref. id.)(id., suff. 2 pers. sing. masc.	פאה
מִפִּיכֶם	pref. id.)(id., suff. 2 pers. pl. masc.	פאה
מַפִּיל	ᵖᴉ Hiph. part. sing. masc. d. 1 b ; ᴉ bef. lab.	נפל
מַפִּילִיםᵠ	id. pl., abs. st. . .	נפל
מֻפִּים	pr. name masc. Ge. 46. 21 ; called שְׁפוּפָם in Nu. 26. 39.	
מִפִּינוּᵣ	pref. מִ)(noun masc. sing., suff. 1 pers. pl. from פֶּה irr. (§ 45) . .	פאה
מֵפִיץ	Hiph. part. s. m. dec. 3 b, subs. in Pr. 25. 18.	פוץ
מְפִיקִיםˢ	Hiph. part. masc., pl. of מֵפִיק dec. 3 b	פוק
מְפַכִּיםᵗ	Piel part. masc., pl. of מִפְכֶּה dec. 9 a .	פכה
מִפְלᵘ	ᴉ noun m. s., constr. of מַפָּל d. 2 b; ᴉ bef. lab.	נפל
מַפְלִיאᵛ	ᴉ Hiph. part. sing. masc. [for מַפְלִיא]; ᴉ id.	פלא
מִפְלָאוֹתʷ	noun fem. pl. constr. from [מִפְלָאָה] dec. 11 a	פלא
מַפְלָהˣ	noun fem. sing. . . .	נפל
מִפְלָטᵇ	noun masc. sing. . . .	פלט

מִפַלְטִיᵃ	ᴉ Piel part. sing. masc. [מְפַלֵּט], suff. 1 pers. sing. dec. 7 b ; ᴉ bef. lab.	פלט
מַפְלִיᵇ	noun masc. pl. constr. from [מַפָל] dec. 2 b	נפל
מְפַלֵּסᶜ	Piel part. sing. masc. . .	פלס
מִפְלֶצֶת מִפְלַצְתˢ	} noun fem. sing. dec. 13 a (comp. § 35. rem. 2)	פלץ
מִפְלַצְתָּהּ	id. with suff. 3 pers. sing. fem.	פלץ
מִפְלְשֵׁיᵏ	noun masc. pl. constr. from [מִפְלָשׁ] dec. 2 b	פלש
מִפְלִשְׁתִּים	ᴉ pref. מִ)(gent. n., pl. of פְּלִשְׁתִּי; ᴉ bef. lab.	פלש
מַפֶּלֶתˡ	noun fem. sing. dec. 13 a	נפל
מַפַּלְתּוֹᵐ	id., suff. 3 pers. sing. masc.	נפל
מַפַּלְתֵּךְ	id., suff. 2 pers. sing. fem.	נפל
מַפַּלְתֶּךָⁿ	id., suff. 2 pers. sing. masc. for תְּךָ׳	נפל
מֻפְנֶהᵐ	Hoph. part. sing. masc.	פנה
מַפְנֶהⁿ	Hiph. part. sing. masc.	פנה
מִפָּנַי מִפָּנָי	} pref. מִ)(the foll. with suff. 1 pers. sing. ; ᴉ bef. lab.	פנה
מִפְּנֵי	ᴉ pref. id.)(noun masc. pl., constr. of פָּנִים [from פָּנֶה] dec. 9 b ; ᴉ id.	פנר
מִפָּנֶיהָ	pref. id.)(id., suff. 3 pers. sing. fem. .	פנה
מִפְּנֵיהֶםᵖ	ᴉ pref. id.)(id., suff. 3 pers. pl. m. ; ᴉ bef. lab.	פנה
מִפָּנָיו	pref. id.)(id., suff. 3 pers. sing. masc.	פנה
מִפְּנִים	pref. id.)(Kh., פָּנִים Keri (q. v.) .	פנן
מִפָּנֶיךָ	ᵣᴉ pref. id.)(noun masc. pl. (פָּנִים), suff. 2 pers. sing. masc. [from פָּנֶה] dec. 9 b	פנה
מִפְּנֵיכֶם	pref. id.)(id. pl., suff. 2 pers. pl. masc.	פנה
מִפְּנִים	pref. id.)(id. pl., abs. st. .	פנה
מִפָּנִימָה	pref. id.)(noun masc. sing. פָּנִים׳ with loc. ה	פנם
מִפָּנֵינוּ	pref. id.)(noun masc. pl. (פָּנִים), suff. 1 pers. pl. [from פָּנֶה] dec. 9 b	פנה
מִפְּנִינִים	pref. id.)(noun masc. pl. abs.	פנן
מְפַנֵּקᵗ	Piel part. sing. masc. . .	פנק
מִפְתֵּחַⁿ	pref. מִ)(adj. masc. sing. dec. 7 b	פסח
מִפֶּסֶל	pref. id.)(Seg. noun m. sing. dec. 6 a, in pause for פָּסֶל (§ 35. rem. 2), but with suff. פִּסְלִי	פסל
מִפְעָלוֹת	noun fem. pl. constr. from [מִפְעָלָה] dec. 11 a	פעל
מִפְעֲלֵיᵛ	pref. מִ)(Kal part. act. pl. c. from פֹּעַל d. 7 b	פעל
מִפְעָלָיוᵘ	noun masc. pl., suff. 3 pers. sing. masc. from [מִפְעָל] dec. 2 b . .	פעל
מִפַּעַת	ᴉ pr. name for מֵיפַעַת (q. v.) ; ᴉ bef. lab.	יפע
מַפָּץ	noun masc. sing. . .	נפץ
מַפָּצוֹᵇ	noun m. s., suff. 3 pers. s. m. fr. [מַפָּץ] d. 2 b	נפץ
מְפִיצִיםᵃ	ᴉ Hiph. part. m., pl. of מֵפִיץ d. 3 b; ᴉ bef. lab.	פוץ
מְפַקֵּדᶜ	Piel part. sing. masc. . .	פקד

ᵃ Is. 59. 16.	ᵍ Est. 3. 8.	ᵏ Ho. 2. 19.	ᵗ Ps. 144. 13.	ᵖ Ps. 55. 9.	1 Ki. 15. 13.	ᵐ Eze. 9. 2.	ᵣ Ge. 4. 14.	ʸ Pr. 8. 22.
Is. 50. 2.	ʰ Job 11. 20.	ˡ Mal. 2. 7.	ᵘ Eze. 47. 2.	ᵠ Ps. 18. 49.	ʲ Job 37. 16.	ⁿ Na. 2. 9.	ˢ 2 Sa. 10. 9.	Je. 51. 20.
Ezr. 9. 11.	ᵢ Je. 6. 29.	ᵐ Da. 9. 20.	Am. 8. 6.	ᶜ Job 41. 15.	Ju. 14. 8.	Ho. 2. 4.	ᵗ Pr. 29. 21.	ᶻ Je. 23. 1.
Is. 13. 12.	ᵢ Pr. 28. 14.	ⁿ Da. 9. 18.	ᵛ Ju. 13. 19.	ᵣ Ps. 5. 21.	Eze. 31. 13, 16.	Eze. 2. 6.	ᵘ Pr. 26. 7.	Eze. 23. 1.
2 Sa. 6. 16.	ᵏ Job 21. 9.	ᵒ Je. 44. 17.	Job 37. 16.	ᵣ 2 Ch. 15. 16.	Eze. 32. 10.	Pr. 3. 15.	ᵛ Ps. 59. 5.	Is. 13. 4.
Pr. 11. 24.	ᵐ Is. 48. 3.	ᵖ Na. 2. 2.	Is. 17. 1.	ᵧ Ps. 119. 120.				

מִפְקָד   noun masc. sing., constr. of מִפְקָד׳ dec. 2 b   פקד

מִפְקָדִים   Hoph. part. m., pl. of [מִפְקָד] § 11. r. 10] d.2 b   פקד

מְפֻקֻּדֵי׳   pref. מְ)(Kal part. pass. pl. constr. from [פָּקוּד] dec. 3 a   פקד

מִפְקוּדֶיךָ׳   ו pref. id.)(noun masc. pl., suff. 2 pers. sing. masc. from [פָּקוּד] d. 1 b; ו bef. lab.   פקד

מַפְרֵד   Hiph. part. sing. masc.   פרד

מְפֹרָד   ו Pual part. sing. masc.; ו bef. lab.   פרד

מִפְרִי׳   ו׳ו pref. מְ)(noun masc. sing. dec. 6i; ו id.   פרה

מַפְרִיד   Hiph. part. sing. masc.   פרד

מִפְרְיוֹ׳   pref. מְ)(noun masc. sing., suff. 3 pers. sing. masc. from פְּרִי dec. 6i   פרה

מַפְרִיס   Hiph. part. sing. masc. dec. 1 b   פרס

מַפְרֵךְ   Hiph. part. s. m. [מַפְרֶה], suff. 2 p. s. m. d.9 a   פרה

מַפְרֶסֶת   Hiph. part. s., fem. of מַפְרִיס (§ 39. No. 4 d)   פרס

מִפְרְעֹה   pref. מְ)(pr. name masc., see פַּרְעֹה.   פרה

מִפְרְצָיו׳   noun m. pl., suff. 3 pers. s. m. fr. [מִפְרָץ] d.2 b   פרץ

מְפֹרֶצֶת׳   Pual part. sing. fem. [of מִפְרָץ]   פרץ

מְפָרֵק׳   Piel part. sing. masc.   פרק

מַפְרַקְתּוֹ׳   noun fem. sing., suff. 3 pers. sing. masc. from [מַפְרֶקֶת] dec. 13 a   פרק

מְפָרַשׁ   Chald. Pael part. pass. sing. masc. (§ 19. r. 3)   פרש

מְפֹרָשׁ   Pual part. sing. masc.   פרש

מִפְרָשֵׂי׳   noun masc. pl. constr. from [מִפְרָשׂ] dec. 2 b   פרש

מִפְרָשֵׂךְ׳   id. sing., suff. 2 pers. sing. fem.   פרש

מַפְשִׁיטִים   Hiph. part. masc., pl. of [מַפְשִׁיט] dec. 1 b   פשט

מִפֶּשַׁע   pref. מְ)(noun masc. sing. dec. 6 a (§ 35. r. 5)   פשע

מִפִּשְׁעֵיהֶם   ו pref. id.)(id. pl., suff. 3 p. pl. m.; ו bef. lab.   פשע

מִפְּשָׁעֵינוּ   pref. id.)(id. pl., suff. 1 pers. pl.   פשע

מְפַשֵּׁר׳   Chald. Pael part. act. sing. masc.   פשר

מִפֶּתֶ׳   Keri pref. מְ)(noun fem. sing. dec. 8 e   פתת

מִפֶּתְבַּג׳   pref. מְ)(noun m. s., constr. of [פַּתְבַּג] d.2 b   פתבג

מִפִּתּוֹ׳   pref. id.)(noun fem. sing., suff. 3 pers. sing. masc. from פַּת dec. 8 e   פתת

מִפְתּוֹר   pref. id.)(pr. name of a place   פתר

מַפְתֵּחַ׳   noun masc. sing. dec. 7 b   פתח

מְפַתֵּחַ׳   Piel part. sing. masc.   פתח

מִפְתָּח׳   ו pref. מְ)(noun masc. sing. (suff. פִּתְחוֹ) dec. 6 a (§ 35. rem. 5); ו bef. lab.   פתח

מִפְתַּח׳   ו noun masc. sing., constr. of מִפְתָּח (§ 36. rem. 1); ו id.   פתח

מְפֻתָּחֹת   Pual part. fem. pl. [of מְפֻתָּחָה fr. מְפֻתָּח m.]   פתח

מִפְתָּיו׳   ו pref. מְ)(noun masc. sing. dec. 6i [for פְּתִי § 35. rem. 15]; ו bef. lab.   פתה

מְפַתֶּיהָ   Piel part. pl. masc., suff. 3 pers. sing. fem. from [מְפַתֶּה] dec. 9 a   פתה

מִפְּתָיו   the foll. with suff. 3 pers. sing. masc.   יפת

מִפְתִים   ו noun masc., pl. of מוֹפֵת d. 7 b; ו bef. lab.   יפת

מִפְתַּן   noun masc. sing., constr. of מִפְתָּן dec. 2 b   פתן

מִפַּתְרוֹם   ו pref. מְ)(pr. name of a country, see פַּתְרוֹם.   פתרום

מָצָא   ו׳ו fut. יִמְצָא.—I. to come to, reach to, arrive at, with עַד, Job 11. 7.—II. to obtain, acquire.—III. to find, discover.—IV. to come upon any one, to befall, happen, with acc., לְ of pers.—V. to be sufficient, enough, for anything, with לְ. Niph. נִמְצָא.—I. to be obtained, acquired by any one, with לְ.—II. to be found.—III. to be present, at hand; נִמְצָא מְאֹד very present, or is readily found. Hiph. הִמְצִיא.—I. to cause to come to, i. e. to deliver, give up.—II. to cause to obtain.—III. to offer, present, with אֶל Le. 9. 12, 13, 18.

מְצָא   ו׳ו Kal imp. sing. masc.; ו bef. lab.   מצא

מְצֹא   ו id. inf. constr.   מצא

מֹצִא׳   defect. for מוֹצִא (q. v.)   יצא

מָצְאָה   ו׳ו Kal pret. 3 pers. sing. fem.; ו bef. lab.   מצא

מְצָאָה   ו׳ו id. pret. 3 pers. sing. masc., suff. 3 pers. sing. fem.; ו id.   מצא

מְצָאָהוּ׳   ו id. pret. 3 pers. pl., suff. 3 p. s. m.; ו id.   מצא

מָצְאוּ׳   } id. pret. 3 pers. pl. (§ 8. rem. 7); }   מצא
מָצָאוּ   ו׳ו } ו id.   }

מְצָאוֹ׳   id. pret. 3 pers. sing. masc., suff. 3 pers. sing. masc.; bef. monos. for מְצָאוֹ   מצא

מֹצְאוֹ׳   defect. for מוֹצָאוֹ (q. v.)   יצא

מֹצְאוֹ׳   Kal part. sing. masc. fr מוֹצֵא, suff. 3 pers. sing. masc. dec. 7 b   מצא

מִצְאוּ׳   ו id. imp. pl. masc.; ו bef. lab.   מצא

מְצָאוּךְ   ו id. pret. 3 pers. pl. with suff. 2 pers. sing. masc.; ו id. conv.   מצא

מְצָאוּנִי   id. id. with suff. 1 pers. sing.   מצא

מֹצְאַי׳   ו defect. for מוֹצְאַי (q. v.)   יצא

מֹצְאִי   Kal part. act. sing. masc., suff. 1 pers. sing. fr. מוֹצֵא dec. 7 b   מצא

מֹצְאֵיהֶם׳   id. pl., suff. 3 pers. pl. masc.   מצא

מִצֹּאן׳   pref. מְ)(noun com. sing. dec. 1 a   צאן

מְצֶאןָ׳   ו Kal imp. pl. f. (comp. § 8.r.16); ו bef. lab.   מצא

מְצָאַנְהוּ׳   the following with suff. 3 pers. sing. masc.   מצא

מְצָאנוּ   Kal pret. 1 pers. pl.   מצא

מְצָאַנוּ   ו id. pret. 3 pers. sing. masc., suff. 1 pers. pl.; ו for וַ, conv.   מצא

מִצֹּאנוּ   pref. מְ)(noun com. sing., suff. 3 pers. sing. masc. fr. צֹאן dec. 1 a   צאן

a 2 Ch. 34. 12.   g Ge. 48. 4.   * Ne. 8. 8.   i Da. 5. 12.   o Zec. 3. 9.   t 1 Sa. 20. 21, 36.   l De. 22. 23.   r Ho. 6. 3.   x Am. 6. 4.
b Nu. 26. 64.   h Ju. 5. 17.   * Job 36. 29.   k Da. 1. 5.   p Pr. 8. 6.   u 2 Ki. 2. 17.   m Ki. 2. 17.   s Ge. 4. 15.   y Ru. 1. 9.
c Ps.119.104,110.   i Ne. 1. 3.   p Eze. 27. 7.   l Da. 1. 5.   q Ex. 39. 6.   v De. 31. 17.   n Je. 6. 16.   z Job 37. 23.
d Est. 3. 8.   k 1 Ki. 19. 11.   p Da. 1. 5.   p Ch. 35. 11.   r Eze. 45. 20.   w Da. 9. 25, etc.   o 2 Ch. 32. 4.   p Ps. 107. 33.   a 2 Ki. 7. 9.
e Ge. 3. 3.   l 1 Sa. 4. 18.   p Le. 16. 16.   y Is. 22. 22.   s Ho. 2. 16.   x Ex.22.5;Is.34.14.   p Job 31. 29.   q Je. 50. 7.   b 2 Sa. 12. 4.
f Ge. 3. 6.   m Ezr. 4. 18.   n Is. 53. 5.

מְצָאֲנוּךְ Kal pret. 1 pers. pl., suff. 3 pers. sing. fem. מצא

מְצָאֲנִי defect. for מְצָאוּנִי (q. v.) . . מצא

מְצָאֲךָ ׀ pref. מְ) noun com. sing., suff. 2 pers. sing. masc. from צֵא dec. 1 a; ׀ bef. lab. צאן

מָצָאתָ Kal pret. 2 pers. sing. masc. . מצא

מָצָאתָ ׀ id. id.; acc. shifted by conv. ׀, for וְ, but וּמָצָאתָ De. 4. 29, in pause (§ 8. r. 7) מצא

מָצָאת id. pret. 2 pers. sing. fem. . מצא

מֹצֵאת id. part. sing. fem. (§ 23. r. 4) fr. מוֹצֵא m. מצא

מְצָאַתְךָ ׀ ׀ id. pret. 2 p. s. m., suff. 3 p. s. f.; ׀ for וְ conv. מצא

מְצָאתוֹ ׀ pref. מְ) noun fem. sing., suff. 3 pers. sing. masc. fr. צוֹאָה dec. 10; ׀ bef. lab. יצא

מָצָאתִי Kal pret. 1 pers. sing. . . מצא

מְצָאתִיהָ id., suff. 3 pers. sing. fem. . מצא

מְצָאתִיהוּ ׀
מְצָאתִיו ׀ } id., suff. 3 pers. sing. masc. מצא

מְצָאתִים id. pret. 1 pers., or 2 pers. f., suff. 3 p. pl. m. מצא

מְצָאתְךָ pref. מְ) Kal inf. constr. צֵאת (§ 25, 2 d), suff. 2 pers. sing. fem. dec. 1 a. יצא

מְצָאתַם Kal pret. 3 pers. f. sing., suff. 3 pers. pl. m. מצא

מְצָאתֶם ׀ id. pret. 2 pers. pl. masc.; ׀ for וְ, conv. מצא

מְצָאתָנוּ ׀
מְצָאתָנוּ ׀ } id. pret. 3 pers. sing. fem., suff. 1 pers. pl. מצא

מַצָּב ׀ ׀ noun m. s., constr. of מַעֲצָב d. 2 b; ׀ bef. lab. נצב

מֻצָּב Hoph. part. sing. masc. נצב

מִצְבָּא pref. מִ) n. m. s., constr. of צָבָא d. 4 a (§ 33. r. 2) צבא

מַצָּבָה noun fem. sing. . נצב

מַצֶּבֶת ׀ n. f. s. (constr. מַצֶּבֶת) d. 11 b; נצב

מַצֵּבָה pref. מַ) pr. name of a country . . נצב

מַצֵּבוֹת ׀ ׀ noun f. pl. abs. fr. מַצֵּבָה d. 11 b; ׀ bef. lab. נצב

מַצְּבוֹת ׀ ׀ id. pl., constr. st.; ׀ id. נצב

מַצֵּבֹתֶיךָ ׀ id. pl., suff. 2 p. s. m. (comp. § 42. r. 4); ׀ id. נצב

מַצֵּבֹתָם id. pl., suff. 3 pers. pl. masc. (v. id.) נצב

[מִצְבָּיָה] pr. name of a place otherwise unknown, 1 Ch. 11. 47, where it stands with the article as a gentile noun.

מְצֹבְּעִין Ch. Pael part. act. m., pl. of [מְצַבַּע] d. 2 a צבע

מַצֶּבֶת noun fem. sing., constr. of מַצֵּבָה dec. 11 a נצב

מַצֶּבֶת noun fem. sing. dec. 13 a . נצב

מַצַּבְתָּה id., suff. 3 pers. sing. fem. . נצב

מַצְּבֹתֵיהֶם ׀
מַצַּבְתָּם ׀ } noun fem. pl. (retaining (..) under צ, comp. § 42. r. 4), suff. 3 p. pl. m. d. 10 (§ 4. r. 2) נצב

מֵצַד pref. מֵ) noun masc. sing. dec. 8 e צדד

מְצֹדְרוֹת Pilel part. f. pl. [of מְצֹדֶרֶת d. 13, fr. מְצוֹדֵר m.] צוד

מְצָדָּה pref. מְ) n. m. s., suff. 3 p. s. f. fr. צַד d. 8 e צדד

מְצָדוֹ pref. id.) id., suff. 3 pers. sing. masc. . צדד

מְצָדוֹת noun masc. with pl. fem. term., abs. st., from מֵצַד dec. 1 a (comp. § 30. No. 3) . צוד

מִצָּדֶיהָ pref. מִ) n. m. pl., suff. 3 p. s. f. fr. צַד d. 8 b צדד

מַצְדִּיק Hiph. part. sing. masc. dec. 1 b . צדק

מַצְדִּיק pref. מַ) adj. masc. sing. dec. 1 b . צדק

מַצְדִּיקֵי ׀ Hiph. part. pl. constr. masc. from מַצְדִּיק dec. 1 b; ׀ bef. lab. . צדק

מַצְדִּיקִי id. sing. with suff. 1 pers. sing. . צדק

מִצָּדְךָ pref. מִ) n. m. s., suff. 2 p. s. m. fr. צַד d. 8 e צדד

מִצְדָקָה pref. id.) noun fem. sing. dec. 11 c . צדק

מִצִּדְקוֹ pref. id.) n. m. s., suff. 3 p. s. m. fr. צֶדֶק d. 6 a צדד

מִצִּדְקָתוֹ pref. id.) n. f. s., suff. 3 p. s. m. fr. צְדָקָה d. 11 c צדד

מְצֻדַת noun fem. sing., constr. of מְצוּדָה dec. 10 צוד

מְצֻדָתָהּ ׀ noun fem. sing., suff. 3 pers. sing. fem., from מְצוּדָה dec. 10; ׀ bef. lab. . צוד

מְצֻדָתִי ׀ noun f. s., suff. 1 p. s. fr. מְצוּדָה d. 10; ׀ id. צוד

[מָצָה] to suck, drain, wring out. Niph. pass.

מֹצָה noun fem. sing. dec. 10 . . מצץ

מֹצָה ׀ noun fem. sing.; ׀ bef. lab. . נצה

מֻצְהָב Hoph. part. sing. masc. (§ 11. rem. 10) . צהב

מַצְהֲלוֹת noun fem. pl., constr. from [מִצְהָלָה] dec. 11 a צהל

מִצְהֲלוֹתַיִךְ ׀ id. pl., suff. 2 pers. sing. fem.; ׀ bef. lab. צהל

מִצְהֲרַיִם ׀ pref. מִ) noun f., du. of צֹהַר d. 6 f; ׀ id. צהר

מִצֹּבָה ׀ pref. id.) pr. name of a country; ׀ id. נצב

מְצוֹד noun masc. sing., constr. of [מָצוֹד] dec. 3 a צוד

מְצוֹדָה ׀ noun fem. sing. dec. 10; ׀ bef. lab. צוד

מְצוֹדוֹ ׀ noun masc. sing., suff. 3 pers. sing. masc. from [מָצוֹד] § 32. rem. 5]; ׀ id. . צוד

מְצוֹדוֹת noun fem., pl. of מְצוּדָה dec. 10 . צוד

מְצוֹדִים noun masc., pl. of [מָצוֹד] dec. 3 a . צוד

מְצוֹדָתִי ׀ noun fem. sing., suff. 1 pers. sing. from מְצוּדָה dec. 10; ׀ bef. lab. . צוד

מְצַוֶּה Piel part. sing., fem. of מְצַוֶּה . צוה

מְצַוֶּה ׀ ׀ id. part. sing. masc. dec. 9 a; ׀ bef. lab. צוה

מִצְוָה ׀
מִצְוֹת ׀ } noun fem. sing. & pl. dec. 10; ׀ id. צוה

מְצַוֶּךָ ׀
מְצַוְּךָ ׀
מְצַוְּךָ ׀ } Piel part. sing. masc., suff. 2 pers. sing. masc. (§ 2. rem. 2) from מְצַוֶּה dec. 9 a צוה

מְצוּלָה ׀
מְצוּלֹת ׀ } noun fem. sing. & pl. dec. 10 . צול

מָצוֹם pref. מָ) noun masc. sing. dec. 1 a צום

מָצוֹעָר pref. id.) pr. name of a place צער

מָצוֹק ׀ ׀ noun masc. sing.; ׀ bef. lab. צוק

a Ps. 132. 6.   b Ca. 5. 7.   c De. 12. 21; 15. 14.   d Is. 57. 10.   e 2 Sa. 18. 22.   f Ge. 38. 23.   g De. 22. 3.   h Pr. 30. 12.   i Ge. 38. 22.   k Ca. 5. 6.   l Ca. 3. 1, 2.   m Je. 2. 34.   n Ez. 18. 8.   o Nu. 20. 14.   p 2 Sa. 23. 14.   q Is. 29. 3.   r Zec. 9. 8.   s 1 Ki. 14. 23.   t Eze. 26. 13.   u Mi. 5. 12.   v Ho. 10. 2.   w Da. 4. 22.   x Is. 6. 13.   y Job 36. 7.   z Ex. 23. 24.   aa De. 7. 5.   bb Eze. 26. 11.   cc 1 Sa. 6. 8.   dd Is. 33. 16.   ee Pr. 17. 15.   ff Job 11. 17.   gg Is. 29. 7.   hh 2 Sa. 22. 2.   ii Is. 50. 8.   kk Ps. 91. 7.   ll Is. 46. 12.   mm Eze. 3. 20.   nn Job 11. 17.   oo Pr. 13. 12.   pp Is. 58. 4.   qq Ezr. 8. 27.   rr Je. 8. 16.   ss Je. 13. 27.   tt Job 27. 8.   uu Ge. 27. 8.   vv Is. 55. 4.   ww Job 39. 28.   xx Job 19. 6.   yy Ps. 31. 3.   zz Ec. 7. 26.   Ge. 27. 8.   Ne. 9. 14.   De. 6. 2.   Zec. 10. 11.   Ps. 109. 24.   1 Sa. 22. 2.   Ps. 119. 143.

מָצוֹק	noun masc. sing. dec. 3a . . .	צוק
מְצוּקָה	ᵃ noun fem. sing. dec. 10 ; ᵇ bef. lab.	צוק
מָצוֹר	pr. name of a country . . .	מצר
מָצוֹר	noun masc. sing. dec. 3a (§ 32. rem. 5) .	צור
מְצוֹר	id., constr. st.	צור
מִצּוּר	ᶜ pref. ·מִ)(noun masc. s. d. 1a ; ᵈ bef. lab.	צור
מְצוּרָה מְצֻרוֹת	} noun fem. sing. and pl. dec. 10 . .	צור
מְצוּרֶךָᵉ	noun masc. sing., suff. 2 pers. sing. masc. [for	
	[מְצוּרְךָ from מָצוֹר dec. 3a (§ 32. rem. 5)	צור
מִצַּוְּרֹנֶיךָ	pref. ·מִ)(.n.m.pl., suff.2 p. s. f. fr. [צַוָּרֹן] d.3c	צור
מְצֹרָעᶠ	in full for מְצֹרָע (q. v.) . . .	צרע
מִצְוֹת	ᵍ noun fem., pl. of מַצָּה dec. 10 ; ᵇ bef. lab.	מצץ
מִצְוַת	noun fem. sing., constr. of מִצְוָה dec. 10	צוה
מִצְוֹת	ᵉᵍ id. pl. ; ᵇ bef. lab.	צוה
מִצְוָתוֹᵍ	id. sing., suff. 3 pers. sing. masc. .	צוה
מִצְוֹתָיו	id. pl., suff. 3 pers. s. m. (for ·וֹתָיו § 4. r. 1)	צוה
מִצְוֹתַי מִצְוֹתָי	} id. pl., suff. 1 pers. sing.; ᵇ bef. lab.	צוה
מִצְוֹתָיו	ᵍ id. pl., suff. 3 pers. sing. masc.; ᵇ id.	צוה
מִצְוֹתֶיךָ	ᵍⁱ id. pl., suff. 2 pers. sing. masc.; ᵇ id.	צוה
מִצְוָתְךָ	id. sing., suff. 2 pers. sing. masc. .	צוה
מִצְוֹתֶךָᵈ	defect. for מִצְוֹתֶיךָ (q. v. & § 4. rem. 1)	צוה

מֵצַח ᶦᵍ masc. dec. 6e (pl. c. מִצְחוֹת), *forehead, brow, front.*

מִצְחָה fem. *greaves, armour of the legs,* only constr. מִצְחַת 1 Sa. 17. 6.

מִצְחוֹ	id., suff. 3 pers. sing. masc. . .	מצח
מִצְחוֹתᵏ	id. with pl. fem. term., constr. st.	מצח
מִצְחֲךָ מִצְחֶךָ	} id. sing., suff. 2 pers. sing. m.; ᵇ bef. lab.	מצח
מִצְחָםᵍ	id. sing., suff. 3 pers. pl. masc.	מצח
מְצַחֵק	Piel part. sing. masc. (§ 14. rem. 1)	צחק
מִצְחַתᵐ	ᵍ noun fem.sing.constr. [of מִצְחָה]; ᵇ bef. lab.	מצח
מַצִּיבᵇ	Hiph. part. sing. masc. . .	נצב
מַצִּיגᵛ	Hiph. part. sing. masc. (§ 20. rem. 16)	יצג
מְצִידᵖ	pref. ·מִ)(noun m. sing., constr. of צֵיד d. 6h	צוד
מְצִידוֹᵍ	pref. id.)(id. with suff. 3 pers. sing. masc.	צוד
מְצִידוֹן	pref. id.)(pr. name of a place . .	צוד
מְצִידִיʸ	pref. id.)(noun masc. sing., suff. 1 pers. sing.	
	from צֵיד dec. 6h . . .	צוד
מְצִידָםˢ	pref. id.)(id. with suff. 3 pers. pl. masc.	צוד
מְצִידֹן	pref. id.)(pr. name of a place .	צוד
מְצִידֹנִים	pref. id.)(gent. n. pl. from the preced.	צוד
מְצִיֹּון	ᵍ pref. id.)(pr. name of a place; ᵇ bef. lab.	ציה

מַצִּיל	Hiph. part. sing. masc. . . .	נצל
מֵצִיץᵃ	Hiph. part. sing. masc. . . .	צוץ
מָצִיתᵇ	ᶜᵍ Kal pret. 2 pers. sing. fem.; ᵇ for ן, conv.	מצה
מַצִּיתᵈ	Hiph. part. sing. masc. (§ 20. rem. 16)	יצת
מַצִּלᵉ	ᶠ defect. for מַצִּיל (q. v.) . . .	נצל
מַצֵּל	Hiph. part. sing. masc. (§ 18. rem. 10)	צלל
מֻצָּל	Hoph. part. sing. masc. . . .	נצל
מְצַלֵּאᵃ	ᵍ Chald. Pael part. sing. masc. d. 6a ; ᵇ bef. lab.	צלא
מַצְלוֹᵃ	pref. ·מַ)(noun masc. sing., suff. 3 pers. sing.	
	masc. from צֵל dec. 8b . . .	צלל
מְצֻלּוֹת	noun fem., pl. of [מְצֻלָּה] dec. 10	צלל
מַצְלַחᵃ	ᵍ Ch. Aph. part. sing. masc. d. 2b ; ᵇ bef. lab.	צלח
מַצְלְחִיןᵇ	ᵍ id. pl. abs.; ᵇ id.	צלח
מַצְלִיחַ	Hiph. part. sing. masc.	צלח
מַצְלְחִיןᵐ	ᵍ Ch. Aph. part. m., pl. of מַצְלַא d. 6a; ᵇ bef. lab.	צלא
מַצְלֵמֹנָה	pref. ·מַ)(pr. name of a place .	צלם
מַצְלְעֹתָיוⁿ	pref. id.)(noun fem. pl., suff. 3 pers. sing.	
	masc. from צֵלָע dec. 4b (§ 33. 2c & r. 3)	צלע
מְצִלְתַּיִם	ᵃ } noun fem. du. from [מְצֵלֶת] dec. 13b;	צלל
מְצִלְתָּיִם	ᵇᵍ } ᵇ bef. lab. . . . . }	
מַצְמֵאָהᵃ	pref. ·מַ)(noun fem. sing. . .	צמא
מַצְמֶדֶתᵃ	Pual part. sing. fem. [of מֻצְמָד] . .	צמד
מַצְמִיחַ ᵃᵃ	Hiph. part. sing. masc. . .	צמח
מַצְמִיתַי	Hiph. part. pl. masc., suff. 1 pers. sing. from	
	[מַצְמִית] dec. 1b . . .	צמת
מַצְמֶרֶתᵃ	pref. ·מַ)(noun fem. s. (suff. צַמַּרְתּוֹ) d. 13a	צמר
מַצָּנִיםᵃ	pref. id.)(noun masc., pl. of [צֵן] dec. 8b	צנן
מִצְנֶפֶת	noun fem. sing. . . .	צנף
מַצְעָדֵי	noun masc. pl. constr. from [מִצְעָד] dec. 2b	צעד
מַצְעִירָהᵃ	noun fem. sing. compnd. of מִן & צְעִירָה	צער
מְצַעֵקᵃ	Piel part. sing. masc. (§ 14. rem. 1)	צעק
מִצְעָר	noun masc. sing. . . .	צער
מִצְעָר	pref. ·מִ)(pr. name of a place .	צער
מְצַפֶּה	Piel part. sing. masc. dec. 9 a	צפה
מְצֻפֶּהᵃ	Pual part. sing. masc. dec. 9 a	צפה
מִצְפֶּהʸᵍ	} pr. name of a place	צפה
מִצְפֶּה		
מִצְפֶּהᵇ	noun masc. sing. dec. 9 a	צפה
מַצְפֹּוןᵍ	ᵍ pref. ·מַ)(noun masc. sing. d. 3a; ᵇ bef. lab.	צפן
מַצְפּוֹן	pref. ·מַ)(id. constr. st.	צפן
מִצְפֹּונָהᶜ	pref. id.)(id. abs. with parag. ה	צפן
מִצְפּוֹנָהᵇ	pref. id.)(id. constr. with parag. ה	צפן
מְצַפֶּיךָᵈ	Piel part. pl. masc., suff. 2 pers. sing. masc.	
	from מְצַפֶּה dec. 9a	צפה
מְצַפִּיםˢ	Pual part. pl. masc. from מְצֻפֶּה dec. 9a	יפה

ᵃ 1 Sa. 14. 5.   ᵍ Ne. 9. 13.   ᵐ Eze. 3. 8.   ᵗ Ju. 6. 37.   ᵇ Is. 51. 17.   ᵏ Eze. 31. 12.   ⁱ 1 Ch. 15. 16.   ᵘ Eze. 17. 22.   ᵃ Is. 21. 3.

ᵇ Eze. 4. 7.   ʰ Nu. 15. 31.   ⁿ Is. 48. 4.   ᵖ Ge. 27. 25, 31.   ᶜ Eze. 23. 34.   ᵗ Zec. 14. 20.   ᵛ Ne. 12. 27.   ᵛ Job 5. 5.   ᵇ Ju. 21. 19.

ᶜ Ps. 81. 17.   ⁱ Ps. 119. 166.   ᵒ Ps. 48. 9.   ᵠ Ge. 27. 30.   ᵈ Eze. 21. 3.   ᵘ Ezr. 5. 8.   ʷ 1 Ch. 16. 42.   ᵃ Da. 8. 9.   ᶜ Mi. 7. 4.

ᵈ Eze. 4. 8.   ʲ Ps. 119. 98.   ᵖ Eze. 3. 8.   ʳ Ge. 27. 19.   ᵉ Da. 6. 28.   ᵛ Ezr. 14.   ˣ 2 Sa. 25.   ᵇ 2 Ki. 2. 12.   ᵈ Ex. 26. 32.

ᵉ Ca. 4. 9.   ᵏ Je. 3. 3.   ᵠ 1 Sa. 17. 6.   ˢ Jos. 9. 14.   ᶠ Eze. 31. 3.   ʷ Ezr. 6. 10.   ʸ 2 Sa. 20. 8.   ᶜ Pr. 26. 23.   ᵉ Ex. 26. 32.

ᶠ 2 Ch. 26. 23.   ˡ Eze. 9. 4.   ʳ 1 Sa. 15. 12.   ᵗ Ca. 2. 9.   ᵍ Da. 6. 11.   ˣ Ge. 2. 21.   ᵃ Pa. 69. 5.   ᵈ Ps. 104. 14.   ᶠ 1 Sa. 4. 13.

מַצְפֻּנָיו[a]	n. m. p., suff. 3 pers. s. m. [fr. מַצְפֻּן § 3. r. 4]	צפן
וּמְצַפְצֵף[b]	ו Pilp. (§ 6. No. 4) part. s. m. d. 7 b; וּ bef. lab.	צפף

מָצַץ *to suck*, Is. 66. 11.

מַצָּה fem. dec. 10, *unleavened bread*, or *cake* (either from the idea of *pressing, extending by pressure,* or *sweetness* supposed to be contained in the root); חַג הַמַּצּוֹת חַלּוֹת מַצּוֹת *unleavened cakes;* *the feast of unleavened bread, the passover.*

מֻצָּק[c]	Hoph. part. sing. masc. dec. 2 b (§ 20. r. 16)	יצק
מֻצָּק[d]	id. constr. st.	יצק
מְצֻקֵי[e]	noun masc. pl. constr. from מָצוּק dec. 3 a	צוק

מָצָר Root not used; prob *to shut;* Arab. *to limit, border.*

מָצוֹר (*fortified,* or *border*) pr. name, *Egypt;* יְאֹרֵי מָ the streams or canals of the Nile.

מִצְרַיִם pr. name—I. of one of the sons of Ham.— II. *Egypt;* frequently for *Egyptians.* Gent. n. מִצְרִי (fem. מִצְרִית, pl. מִצְרִים, fem. מִצְרִיּוֹת) *Egyptian.*

מֵצַר מֵצַר	pref. מְ ⟩(noun masc. sing. dec. 8 (§ 37. rem. 7)	צרר
מֵצַר	pref. id. ⟩(noun masc. sing. (Eze. 3. 9) also pr. name for צוֹר	צור
מְצָרָה	pref. id. ⟩(noun fem. sing. dec. 10 [for צָרָה] from צַר masc.	צרר
מְצָרָה[g]	Hiph. part. sing. fem. [for מַצְרָה fr. מֵצַר 'm.]	צרר
מְצָרוֹת[h]	pref. מְ ⟩(noun fem., pl. of צָרָה dec. 10 [for צָוָה] from צַר masc.	צרר
מְצָרַי	pref. id. ⟩(noun masc. pl., suff. 1 pers. sing. from צַר dec. 8 (§ 37. rem. 7)	צרר
מְצָרֵי[i]	ו noun masc. pl. constr. from מֵצַר dec. 8 e (§ 37. rem. 7); וּ bef. lab.	צרר
מִצְרִי	gent. noun masc. from מִצְרַיִם	מצר
מִצְרָיו	pref. מְ ⟩(noun masc. pl., suff. 3 pers. sing. masc. from צַר dec. 8 (§ 37. rem. 7)	צרר
מִצְרַיִם מִצְרַיִם	pr. name of a country; וּ bef. lab.	מצר
מִצְרָיְמָה מִצְרָיְמָה	id. with parag. ה	מצר
מְצָרֵינוּ	pref. מְ ⟩(noun masc. sing., suff. 1 pers. pl. from צַר dec. 8 (§ 37. rem. 7)	צרר
מִצְרִית	gent. noun, fem. of מִצְרִי from מִצְרַיִם	מצר
מְצֹרָע	וֹ Pual part. sing. masc.; וּ bef. lab.	צרע
מְצֹרָעָה	pref. מְ ⟩(pr. name of a place	צרע
מְצֹרָעִים[n]	Pual part. masc., pl. of מְצֹרָע	צרע

מְצֹרַעַת[o] מְצֹרַעַת	} id. sing. fem.	צרע
מְצֹרַעְתּוֹ[p]	pref. מְ ⟩(noun fem. sing., suff. 3 pers. sing. masc. from צָרַעַת [for צָרַעַת] dec. 13 a	צרע
מַצְרֵף	noun masc. sing.	צרף
מְצָרֵף	Piel part. sing. masc.	צרף
מְצָרְרִים	ו Pual part. masc., pl. of מְצֹרָר; וּ bef. lab.	צרר
מְצֻרֹת[r]	defect. for מְצוּרוֹת (q. v.)	צור
מְצָרָתוֹ	pref. מְ ⟩(noun fem. sing., suff. 3 pers. sing. masc. from צָרָה dec. 10, from צַר masc.	צרר
מְצָרָתֵינוּ	pref. id. ⟩(id. sing. (written in full) or pl. with suff. 1 pers. pl. (§ 4. rem. 3)	צרר
מִצֹּת	defect. for מִצּוֹת (q. v.)	מצץ
מָצָתִי[s]	Kal pret. 1 pers. s. for מָצָאתִי (§ 23. r. 1)	מצא
מַצֻּתֵךְ[t]	noun f. s., suff. 2 p. s. m. fr. [מַצּוּת] d. 1 b	נצה
מַק	noun masc. sing.	מקק
מַקָּבוֹת[u]	ו noun fem., pl. of מַקָּבָה; וּ bef. lab.	נקב
מַקְבִּילֹת	Hiph. part. fem. pl. [of מַקְבִּילָה fr. מַקְבִּיל 'm.]	קבל
מְקַבֵּץ	Piel part. sing. masc. dec. 7 b	קבץ
מִקַּבְצְאֵל	pref. מְ ⟩(pr. name of a place, see יַקַבְצְאֵל	קבץ
מְקַבְּצָיו	ו Piel part. pl. masc., suff. 3 pers. sing. masc. from מְקַבֵּץ dec. 7 b; וּ bef. lab.	קבץ
מְקַבְּצָם	id. sing., suff. 3 pers. pl. masc.	קבץ
מְקֻבֶּצֶת	Pual part. sing. fem. [of מְקֻבָּץ § 39. No. 4]	קבץ
מְקַבֵּר	Piel part. sing. masc. dec. 7 b	קבר
מְקַבֵּר[v]	pref. מְ ⟩(Kal inf. constr.	קבר
מִקְבְּרוֹת	pref. id. ⟩(pr. n. in compos. קִבְרוֹת הַתַּאֲוָה	קבר
מִקִּבְרֹתֵיכֶם	pref. id. ⟩(noun masc. with pl. fem. term. and suff. 2 pers. pl. masc. fr. קֶבֶר d. 6 a	קבר
מְקַבְּרֵיהֶם[x]	pref. id. ⟩(id. pl. masc., suff. 3 pers. pl. masc.	קבר
מְקַבְּרִים	Piel part. masc., pl. of מְקַבֵּר dec. 7 b	קבר
מִקִּבְרְךָ[y]	pref. מְ ⟩(n. m. s., suff. 2 p. s. m. fr. קֶבֶר d. 6 a	קבר
מִקְבֶּרֶת	pref. id. ⟩(pr. name in compos. קִבְרוֹת הַתַּאֲוָה	קבר
מַקֶּבֶת[z]	noun fem. sing.	נקב
מַקֵּדָה	וֹ pr. name of a place; וּ bef. lab.	נקר
מִקְדָּשׁ[k]	pref. מְ ⟩(adj. masc. s., constr. of קָדוֹשׁ d. 3 a	קדשׁ
מִקֶּדֶם[l]	וֹ pref. id. ⟩(noun masc. s. d. 6 a; וּ bef. lab.	קדם
מִקַּדְמֵי[m]	pref. מְ ⟩(id. pl., constr. st.	קדם
מִקַּדְמַת[n]	Chald. noun f. s., constr. of [קַדְמָא] dec. 8 a	קדם
מְקַדֵּשׁ[u]	Piel part. sing. masc. dec. 7 b	קדשׁ
מִקְדָּשׁ	pref. מְ ⟩(pr. name of a place	קדשׁ
מִקְדָּשׁ[o]	וֹ noun masc. sing. dec. 2 b ; וּ bef. lab.	קדשׁ
מִקְדַּשׁ[p]	וֹ id., constr. st. ; וּ id.	קדשׁ
מְקַדֵּשׁ	pref. מְ ⟩(pr. name of a place	קדשׁ
מִקְדָּשׁ	pref. id. ⟩(noun masc. sing. dec. 6 c	קדשׁ
מִקְדָּשָׁה[q]	noun masc. sing., suff. 3 pers. sing. fem. from מִקְדָּשׁ dec. 2 b	קדשׁ

a Ob. 6.	f Ps. 32. 7.	l 2 Sa. 3. 29.	q Jos. 9. 4.	■ Nu. 11. 11.	s Is. 62. 9.	c Ge. 23. 6.	Is. 51. 1.	v Ezr. 5. 11.
b Is. 10. 14.	g Je. 48. 41; 49. 22.	m 2 Ki. 7. 3.	r Is. 29. 3.	n Is. 41. 12.	t Je. 32. 37.	f Eze. 37. 12, 13.	e Is. 51. 5.	Eze. 45. 4.
c Job 11. 15.	h Pr. 21. 23.	n Nu. 12. 10.	s Is. 46. 7.	s Is. 3. 24.	u Eze. 38. 8.	g Je. 8. 1.	l Is. 46. 10.	Eze. 48. 21.
d 1 Ki. 7. 16.	i Is. 1. 24.	o 2 Ki. 5. 3, 6, 7.	t 2 Ch. 20. 9.	p 1 Ki. 6. 7.	x Je. 14. 16.	h Is. 14. 19.	n Pr. 8. 23.	v La. 1. 10.
1 Sa. 2. 8.	k Ps. 116. 3.	p Mal. 3. 2. 3.	u Eze. 37. 28.				

מְקַדְּשׁוֹ Piel part. sing. masc., suff. 3 pers. sing. masc. from מְקַדֵּשׁ dec. 7 b . . קדש

מְקַדְּשׁוֹ } noun m. s., suff. 3 p. s. m. fr. מִקְדָּשׁ d. 2 b)
מְקַדָּשִׁי } [the latter form as if from מִקְדָּשׁ d. 7 b]   קדש

מְקַדְּשֵׁי pref. מִ) (noun m. pl. constr. fr. קֹדֶשׁ d. 6 c   קדש

מְקַדְּשֵׁי noun masc. pl., suff. 1 p. s. fr. מִקְדָּשׁ d. 2 b   קדש

מְקַדְּשֵׁי id. sing., suff. 1 pers. sing.; ו bef. lab. . קדש

מְקַדְּשֵׁי id. pl., constr. st.; ו id. . . קדש

מְקַדְּשֵׁיהֶם Piel part. pl. masc., suff. 3 pers. pl. masc. from מְקַדֵּשׁ dec. 7 b . . קדש

מְקַדְּשֶׁיךָ noun masc. pl., suff. 2 pers. sing. masc. from מִקְדָּשׁ dec. 2 b . . קדש

מְקַדְּשֵׁיכֶם id. with suff. 2 pers. pl. masc. . קדש

מַקְדִּשִׁים Hiph. part. masc., pl. of מַקְדִּישׁ dec. 1 b   קדש

מִקְדָּשִׁים noun masc., pl. of מִקְדָּשׁ dec. 2 b . קדש

מְקֻדָּשִׁים pref. מִ) (adj. masc., pl. of קָדֹשׁ dec. 3 a . קדש

מִקְדָּשְׁךָ } noun masc. sing., suff. 2 pers. sing. masc.)
מִקְדָּשֶׁךָ } from מִקְדָּשׁ dec. 2 b . } קדש

מְקַדִּשְׁכֶם Piel part. sing. masc., suff. 2 pers. pl. masc. from מְקַדֵּשׁ dec. 7 b . . קדש

מְקַדְּשָׁם id. with suff. 3 pers. pl. masc. . קדש

מְקַדְּשָׁם noun masc. s., suff. 3 p. pl. m. fr. מִקְדָּשׁ d. 2 b   קדש

מְקַדְּשֵׁנוּ id. with suff. 1 pers. pl. . קדש

מַקְהֵל pref. מִ) (noun m. s., constr. of קָהָל d. 4 a   קהל

מַקְהֵלֹתָה pref. id.) (pr. name of a place, (קְהֵלָה), ה parag.   קהל

מִקְוֵא for מִקְוֶה (q. v.); ו bef. lab. . קוה

מִקְוֶה noun fem. sing. from מִקְוֶה masc.; ו id. . קוה

מִקְוֵה } noun masc. sing. constr. & abs. dec.)
מִקְוֶה } 9 a; ו id. . } קוה

מְקוֹל pref. מִ) (noun masc. sing. dec. 1 a   קול

מְקוֹלָם pref. id.) (id., suff. 3 pers. pl. masc.   קול

מָקוֹם noun com. sing. dec. 3 a; ו bef. lab.   קום

מְקוֹם id., constr. st.; ו id. . קום

מְקוֹמָה id., suff. 3 pers. sing. fem. . קום

מְקוֹמוֹ id., suff. 3 pers. sing. masc. . קום

מְקוֹמִי id., suff. 1 pers. sing. . קום

מְקוֹמְךָ } id. with suff. 2 pers. sing. masc.)
מְקוֹמֶךָ } קום

מְקוֹמָם id., suff. 3 pers. pl. masc. . קום

מְקוֹמֹתֵיכֶם id. pl., suff. 2 pers. pl. masc.   קום

מִקוֹמֹתָם id. pl., suff. 3 pers. pl. masc. (§ 4. rem. 2)   קום

מָקוֹר noun masc. sing. dec. 3 a; ו bef. lab. . קור

מְקוֹר id., constr. st. . קור

מְקוֹרָה id., suff. 3 pers. sing. fem. . קור

מְקוֹרוֹ id., suff. 3 pers. sing. masc. . קור

מְקוֹרְךָ id., suff. 2 pers. sing. masc. . קור

מִקָּח noun masc. sing., constr. of [מִקָּח] dec. 2 b; ו bef. lab. . לקח

מְקַחַת pref. מִ) (Kal inf. constr. (§ 17. rem. 8)   לקח

מַקְטֵב pref. id.) (noun masc. sing.   קטב

מַקְטִיר Hiph. part. sing. masc. d. 1 b; ו bef. lab. . קטר

מַקְטִירוֹת id. pl. fem. [from מַקְטִירָה] dec. 10   קטר

מַקְטִירִים id. pl. masc. dec. 1 b   קטר

מִקְטָל pref. מִ) (noun masc. s. [for קֶטֶל § 35. r. 2]   קטל

מִקְטָן pref. id.) (adj. masc. sing. dec. 3 a   קטן

מִקְטַנֵּי pref. id.) (adj. pl. masc. constr. from קָטָן dec. 8 a (§ 37. No. 2)   קטן

מִקְטַנָּם pref. id.) (id. sing., suff. 3 pers. pl. masc.   קטן

מִקְטָר noun masc. sing., constr. of [מִקְטָר] dec. 2 b   קטר

מָקְטָר Hoph. part. sing. masc. (§ 11. rem. 10)   קטר

מְקֻטָּרוֹת Piel part. f., pl. of מְקֻטֶּרֶת d. 13 [fr. מְקֻטָּר m.]   קטר

מַקְטְרִים defect. for מַקְטִירִים q. v.; ו bef. lab. . קטר

מְקַטְּרִים Piel part. masc., pl. of [מְקַטֵּר] d. 7 b; ו id.   קטר

מְקֻטֶּרֶת Pual part. sing. fem. [of מְקֻטָּר § 39. No. 4]   קטר

מִקְטֶרֶת noun fem. sing. dec. 13 a   קטר

מִקְטַרְתּוֹ id., suff. 3 pers. sing. masc.   קטר

מֵקִים Hiph. part. sing. masc. dec. 3 b; ו bef. lab.   קום

מְקִימָהּ id., suff. 3 pers. sing. fem.   קום

מְקִימִי id. with parag. י (comp. § 8. rem. 19)   קום

מִקְיָן pref. מִ) (pr. name masc.   קון

מַקִּיפִים Hiph. part. masc., pl. of [מַקִּיף] dec. 1 b   נקף

מַקְיץ Hiph. part. sing. masc.   קוץ

מְקִיר pref. מִ) (noun m. s. d. 1 a (also pr. name)   קיר

מַקֵּל masc. dec. 7 b (constr. מַקַּל, מַקֵּל, with suff. מַקְלִי, מַקֶּלְכֶם § 36. rem. 1 & 3).—I. shoot, twig, Ge. 30. 37—39, 41; Je. 1. 11.—II. staff, stick; מַקֵּל יָד a javelin.—III. mace, badge of authority, Je. 48. 17. Root coll. with the Ethiop. to shoot, sprout.

מִקְלוֹת (shoots) pr. name masc. of two different persons.

מַקֵּל id. constr. st. . מקל

מִקְלָל pref. מִ) (for קָל, adj. masc. sing. dec. 8 d   קלל

מְקַל defect. for מְקֻל (q. v.)   קלל

מַקְלֶה Hiph. part. sing. masc. dec. 9 a   קלה

מַקְלוֹ noun masc. sing., suff. 3 pers. sing. masc. [for מַקְלוֹ] from מַקֵּל dec. 7 b; ו bef. lab.   מקל

מַקְלוֹת id. with pl. fem. term. [for מַקְלוֹת]   מקל

מִקְלוֹת pref. מִ) (noun masc. with pl. fem. term. from קוֹל dec. 1 a   קול

מִקְלוֹת pr. name masc.; ו bef. lab. . מקל

מִקְלָט noun masc. sing. dec. 2 b   קלט

a Le. 21. 15.   f Eze. 21. 7.   — Ezr. 10. 8.   ▲ Am. 4. 6.   ♭ Pr. 5. 18.   ‖ 1 Sa. 9. 21.   ● 2 Ch. 26. 19.   ‡ 2 Ch. 4. 3.   ● De. 27. 16.
b Nu. 18. 29.   g Job 5. 1.   n 2 Ch. 1. 16, 16.   ▼ Ne. 12. 27.   i Zec. 13. 1.   a 1 Sa. 26. 12.   ● Eze. 8. 11.   a 1 Sa. 26. 12.   ● 1 Sa. 17. 40.
c Am. 7. 9.   h Is. 63. 18; Ps. 74. 7.   o Is. 22. 11.   w Ps. 91. 6.   j Ex. 30. 1.   m Je. 10. 20.   ● Ge. 30. 37.   k Ho. 4. 12.
d Eze. 7. 24.   i Da. 9. 17.   p Is. 31. 4.   x Pr. 25. 26.   k Mal. 1. 11.   n Am. 5. 2.   a Am. 2. 14.   Zec. 11. 7.
e Le. 26. 31.   k 2 Ch. 36. 17.   q Nu. 24. 11.   y Je. 51. 36.   l 1 Ch. 6. 34.   s Je. 44. 15.   o Ps. 113. 7.   s Je. 3. 9.   Ps. 93. 4.
f Ne. 12. 47.   — Je. 17. 12.   r Ee. 10. 4.   z Ho. 13. 15.   p Ob. 1, 9.   t Ca. 3. 6.   ss Eze. 18. 18.

מְקַלֵּט   id., constr. st.   קלט

מְקַלְטוֹ   id. with suff. 3 pers. sing. masc.   קלט

מַקְלִי   noun masc. sing., suff. 1 pers. sing. [for מַקְלִי] from מַקֵּל dec. 7 b   מקל

מַקֶּלְכֶם   ᵃ id., suff. 2 p. pl. m. (§ 36. r. 3); ᵇ bef. lab.   מקל

מְקַלֵּל   ᵇ Piel part. sing. masc. dec. 7 b; ᵃ id.   קלל

מְקַלְלוֹנִי or מְקַלְלֵנִי   id. with suff. 1 pers. sing., an anomalous form, perh. for מְקַלְלוּנִי a participle with the afformative of the plural. Ewald proposes מְקַלְלֵנִי, with epenth. נ. Gesenius takes it as a mixed form made up from two readings קִלְּלוּנִי & מְקַלְלֵנִי part. and pret.   קלל

מְקַלְלָיו   ᵃ Pual part. pl. masc. with suff. 3 pers. sing. fem. from [מְקֻלָּל] dec. 2 b; ᵇ bef. lab.   קלל

מְקַלְלִים   ᵉ Piel part. masc., pl. of מְקַלֵּל dec. 7 b   קלל

מְקַלֶּלְךָ   } id. sing., suff. 2 pers. sing. masc. (§ 10. rem. 7); ᵇ bef. lab.   קלל

מְקַלְעוֹת   } noun fem. pl. abs. and constr. [as if from מְקַלְעָה] see the foll.   קלע

מְקַלַּעַת   ᵐ id. sing. (§ 44. rem. 5)   קלע

מְקוֹמָהּ   ⁿ noun com. sing., suff. 3 pers. sing. fem. from מָקוֹם dec. 3 a   קום

מְקוֹמוֹ   id., suff. 3 pers. sing. masc.   קום

מְקוֹמוֹת   id. pl. fem.   קום

מְקִימַי   ᵖ pref. מְ ✕ Kal part. pl. masc., suff. 1 pers. sing. fr. קָם d. 1 a (§ 30. No. 3); ᵇ bef. lab.   קום

מִקְנֶהָ   pref. id. ✕ noun masc. sing., suff. 3 pers. sing. fem. from קָנֶה dec. 9 b   קנה

מִקְנֶה   ᵗ } noun masc. sing. constr. and abs. dec. 9 a; ᵇ bef. lab.   קנה

מִקְנֵהוּ   ʳ id., suff. 3 pers. sing. masc.; ᵇ id.   קנה

מִקְנֵהֶם   id. pl., suff. 3 pers. pl. masc. for מִקְנֵיהֶם   קנה

מִקְנַי   ᵗ id. pl., suff. 1 pers. sing.; ᵇ bef. lab.   קנה

מִקְנֵיָהוּ   ᵘ pr. name masc.; ᵇ id.   קנה

מִקְנֵיהֶם   ᵛ noun masc. pl., suff. 3 pers. pl. masc. from מִקְנֶה dec. 9 a; ᵇ id.   קנה

מִקְנֶךָ   id. sing. (§ 38. rem. 1), suff. 2 pers. pl. masc.   קנה

מִקְנֵיכֶם   ˣ id. pl., suff. 2 pers. pl. masc.; ᵇ bef. lab.   קנה

מִקְנְךָ   id. sing., suff. 2 pers. sing. masc.   קנה

מִקְנֵכֶם   ʸ id. pl., suff. 3 pers. pl. masc. for מִקְנֵיכֶם; ᵇ bef. lab.   קנה

מִקְנֵנוּ   id. sing., suff. 1 pers. pl.   קנה

מִקְנַנְתִּי   Kh. קָנִתִי, K. קָנַת Pual part. s. f. [for the Seg. מְקֻנֶּנֶת § 39. No. 4. r. 3, comp. § 8. r. 19]   קנן

מִקְנַת   ᵃ noun f. s., constr. of מִקְנָה d. 10; ᵇ bef. lab.   קנה

מִקְנָתוֹ   id. with suff. 3 pers. sing. masc.   קנה

מִקְסָם   ᵇ n. m. s., constr. of [מִקְסָם] d. 2 b; ᵇ bef. lab.   קסם

מִקְסֹם   ᵈ pref. מְ ✕ Kal inf. constr.   קסם

מִקְעֵילָה   pref. id. ✕ pr. name of a place, see קְעִילָה.

מַקְפִים   ᵉ defect. for מַקִּיפִים (q. v.)   נקף

מְקַפֵּץ   ᶜ Piel part. sing. masc.   קפץ

מִקֵּץ   pref. מְ ✕ noun masc. sing. dec. 8 b   קץ

מִקְצָה   pref. id. ✕ noun fem. sing. dec. 11 a   קצה

מִקַצֶּה   ᵈ Piel part. sing. masc.   קצה

מִקְצֶה   pref. מְ ✕ noun masc. sing. dec. 9 b   קצה

מִקְצֵה   ᵉ } pref. id. ✕ id., constr. st.; ᵇ bef. lab.   קצה

מִקְצֵהוּ   pref. id. ✕ id. with suff. 3 pers. sing. masc.   קצה

מִקְצוֹעֵי   noun masc. pl. constr. from מִקְצוֹעַ dec. 1 b   קצע

מִקְצֹעוֹת   pref. מְ ✕ noun fem. pl. constr. fr. קָצָה d. 11 a   קצה

מִקְצֹעוֹתָם   pref. id. ✕ id. with suff. 3 pers. pl. masc.   קצה

מִקְצֵיהֶם   ᵍ pref. id. ✕ n. m. pl., suff. 3 p. m. fr. קָצֶה d. 9 a   קצה

מִקְצָעֹת   noun masc. with pl. f. term. fr. מִקְצוֹעַ d. 1 b   קצע

מִקְצֹעוֹתָיו   ⁱ id. with suff. 3 pers. sing. masc.; ᵇ bef. lab.   קצע

מִקְצֶף   ᵏ pref. מְ ✕ noun masc. sing. (suff. קִצְפִּי) d. 6 a   הצף

מִקְצֹף   ˡ pref. id. ✕ Kal inf. constr.   קצף

מִקִּצְפּוֹ   ᵐ pref. id. ✕ n. m. s., suff. 3 p. s. m. fr. קֶצֶף d. 6 a   קצף

מַקְצִפִים   ⁿ Hiph. part. masc. pl. [of מַקְצִיף] dec. 1 b   קצף

מְקֻצָּצִים   ᵒ Pual part. masc. pl. [of מְקֻצָּץ]   קצץ

מִקְצָר   ᵖ pref. מְ ✕ noun masc. sing.   קצר

מִקְצָת   ᵠ pref. מְ [for מִקְצָת] ✕ noun fem. sing., pl. קְצָוֹת comp. מְנָת (§ 45); ᵇ bef. lab.   קצה

מִקְצָתָם   ʳ pref. id. ✕ id., suff. 3 pers. pl. masc.; ᵇ id.   קצה

מָקַק   Niph. נָמַק.—I. to be melted, to melt, flow, run.—II. to waste, consume away. Hiph. הֵמֵק to cause to waste away, Zec. 14. 12.

     מָק masc. rottenness, Is. 3. 24.

מִקְרָא   noun masc. sing. dec. 1 b   קרא

מִקְרָאֶהָ   noun m. pl., suff. 3 pers. s. f. [for מִקְרָאֶיהָ]   קרא

מִקְרָאֵי   id. pl., constr. st.   קרא

מְקֹרָאֵי   Pual part. s., suff. 1 p. s. fr. [מְקֹרָא] d. 1 b   קרא

מִקְרֹב   defect. for מִקָּרוֹב (q. v.)   קרב

מִקְרַב   ᵃ pref. מְ ✕ noun masc. sing. dec. 1 a   קרב

מִקֶּרֶב   pref. id. ✕ (prop. subs. m. s. d. 6 a) as a prep.   קרב

מִקִּרְבָּהּ   pref. id. ✕ id., suff. 3 pers. sing. fem.   קרב

מִקִּרְבּוֹ   pref. id. ✕ id., suff. 3 pers. sing. masc.   קרב

מִקִּרְבֵּךְ   } pref. id. ✕ id., suff. 2 pers. sing. masc.   קרב

מִקִּרְבֵּךְ   pref. id. ✕ id., suff. 2 pers. sing. fem.   קרב

מִקִּרְבְּכֶם   ᵛ pref. id. ✕ id., suff. 2 pers. pl. masc.   קרב

ᵃ Jos. 21. 13, 21, 27, 32, 36.   ᶠ Ps. 37. 22.   ⁱ 1 Ki. 6. 29, 32.   ᵠ Job 31. 22.   ᵘ Ge. 47. 16.   ᶜ Ca. 2. 8.   ᵏ Eze. 46. 22.   ⁿ De. 9. 22.   ˢ Is. 48. 12.
Zec. 11. 10, 14.   ᵍ 1 Sa. 3. 13.   ʳ 1 Ki. 6. 18.   ʳ Job 1. 10.   ʸ De. 3. 19.   ᵈ Pr. 26. 6.   ˡ Eze. 41. 22.   ᵗ Jud. 1. 7.   ᵗ Ps. 55. 19.
Ex. 12. 11.   ᵇ Ge. 12. 3.   ᵗ Ge. 38. 21.   ˢ Ex. 17. 3.   ᶻ Je. 22. 23.   ᵉ Ge. 47. 2.   ᵐ Je. 50. 13.   ᵖ Ex. 6. 9.   ᵘ De. 18. 15.
Pr. 20. 20.   ᵈ Ps. 103. 22.   ˣ 1 Ki. 7. 31.   ᵗ Nu. 20. 19.   ᵃ Mi. 3. 6.   ᶠ Eze. 46. 21.   ⁱ Is. 54. 9.   ᵠ Da. 1. 5.   ᵛ Zep. 3. 11.
Je. 5. 10.   ᵉ 1 Ki. 7. 24.   ᵖ 2 Sa. 22. 49.   ⁱ Is. 30. 28.   ᵍ Eze. 38. 2.   ᵉ Je. 10. 10.   ⁱ Is. 4. 5.   ʸ Jos. 7. 12, 13.

מְקֹרְבָּם	pref. מ׳)(id., suff. 3 pers. pl. masc.	קרב
מְקֹרָה	defect. for מְקוֹרָה (q. v.) . . .	קור
מִקְרֶהָ	noun masc. sing., suff. 3 pers. sing. fem. fr. מִקְרָה dec. 9 a	קרה
מִקְרֵה	pref. מ׳)(noun m. s., constr. of [קרה] d. 9 b	קרה
מִקְרֶה	noun masc. sing. dec. 9 a ; ו bef. lab.	קרה
מִקְרוֹב	pref. מ׳)((prim. adj. masc. dec. 3 a) with the pref. as an adv. . . .	קרב
מָקְרָח	Hoph. part. sing. masc. (§ 11. rem. 10)	קרח
מַקְרִיב	Hiph. part. sing. masc. dec. 1 b	קרב
מַקְרִיבֵי	id. pl., constr. st. . . .	קרב
מַקְרִיבִם	id. pl., abs. st. . . .	קרב
מִקְרִיּה	pref. מ׳)(noun fem. sing. (no pl.) .	קרה
מִקְרִית	pref. id.)(id., constr. st., also pr. name in compos. ק׳ יְעָרִים . . .	קרה
מַקְרִן	Hiph. part. sing. masc. defect. [for מַקְרִין]	קרן
מַקְרַנֵּי	ו pref. מ׳)(noun fem. du., constr. of קַרְנַיִם from קֶרֶן dec. 6 a; ו bef. lab.	קרן
מִקַּרְקַע	pref. id.)(noun masc. sing.	קרקע
מְקַרְקַר	Pilpel (§ 6. rem. 4) part. sing. masc.	קור
מַקְשֶׁה	ו Hiph. part. sing. masc.; ו bef. lab.	קשה
מִקְשָׁה	noun fem. sing. . . .	קשה
מִקְשֶׁה	noun masc. sing. . . .	קשה
מִקְשׁוֹת	ו noun masc. with pl. fem. term. fr. מוֹקֵשׁ dec. 7 b; ו bef. lab.	יקש
מִקְשֵׁי	id. pl. constr. masc. . .	יקש
מַקְשִׁיב	Hiph. part. sing. masc. dec. 1 b	קשב
מַקְשִׁיבִים	id. pl., abs. st. . .	קשב
מִקְשִׁים	defect. for מוֹקְשִׁים (q. v.) . .	יקש
מְקַשֵּׁשׁ מְקֹשֶׁשֶׁת	} Poel part. sing. masc. and fem.	קשׁשׁ
מְקֻשָּׁת	pref. מ׳)(noun com.s.,suff. קַשְׁתוֹ pl. קְשָׁתוֹת, ת treated as if radical, comp. d. 6 a	קושׁ
מַר מֵר מָר מָרִי	} Kal pret. 3 pers. s. m.; or adj. m. d.8 e (§ 37. rem. 7); for ו see lett. ו } noun masc. sing. (§ 37. rem. 2) .	מרר

I. מָרָא *to be rebellious*, cogn. מָרָה, only part. fem. מוֹרְאָה Zep. 3. 1. Hiph. *to fly*, Job 39. 18 (Talm. מְרָא *to fly*; the primary idea may be that of *rising*).

II. מָרָא Root not used; Arab. *to be well fed, be fat*.
מְרִיא adj. masc.d. 1 a—I. *fattened, fat*, Eze. 39. 18.
—II. *a fatling*, espec. *a fatted calf*.
מֻרְאָה fem. dec. 10, *crop*, of birds, Le. 1. 16.
מַמְרֵא (*fattening*; or *causing rebellion*) pr. name

—I. of an Amorite, a confederate of Abraham, Ge. 14. 13, 24.—II. אֵלוֹנֵי מ׳ (*oaks of Mamre*) and simply מַמְרֵא, a place near Hebron.

מָרֵא ו׳	Ch. masc. (with suff. מָרִאי Kh. מָרִי K.), *lord*.	
מָרֵא	adj. fem. for מָרָה (q. v.) . . .	מרר
מְרֹאדַךְ	pr. name in compos. מְרֹאדַךְ בַּלְאֲדָן see	
מַרְאָהּ ו׳	noun masc. sing., suff. 3 pers. sing. fem. from מַרְאָה dec. 9 a; ו bef. lab.	ראה
מַרְאֵה ו׳	id., constr. st.; ו id. . . .	ראה
מַרְאֶה ו׳	Hiph. part. sing m. (Ex. 25. 9; Eze. 40. 4) or subst. dec. 9 a; ו id.	ראה
מָרְאֶה	Hoph. part. sing. masc.	ראה
מַרְאֵהוּ ו	noun masc. sing., suff. 3 pers. sing. masc. from מַרְאָה dec. 9 a; ו bef. lab.	ראה
מְרֹאוֹן	pr. name in compos. שֹׁמְרוֹן מְרֹאוֹן see	שמר
מַרְאוֹת ו׳	noun masc. with pl. fem. term. from מַרְאָה dec. 9 a; ו bef. lab. . .	ראה
מֵרְאוֹת	pref. מ׳ for מ׳)(Kal inf. constr. dec. 1 a	ראה
מָרְאִי	Chald. Kh. מָרִא noun masc. sing. with suff. from מָרֵא dec. 2 b, K. מָרִי [from מָר] d. 1	מרא
מֵרְאִי	pref. מ׳ for מ׳)(Kal part. pl. masc., suff. 1 pers. sing. from רָאָה dec. 9 a	ראה
מֵרְאִי	pref. id.)(noun m. sing. (for רְאִי § 35. r. 14)	אה
מַרְאֵיהֶם	ו noun masc. pl., or sing. (§ 38. rem. 1), suff. 3 pers. pl.masc.from מַרְאָה d. 9 a; ו bef.lab.	ראה
מַרְאֵיהֶן	ו id., suff. 3 pers. pl. fem.; ו id.	ראה
מַרְאָיו	id., suff. 3 pers. sing. masc.	ראה
מַרְאַיִךְ	id., suff. 2 pers. sing. fem.	ראה
מַרְאַיִךְ	ו id., suff. 2 pers. sing. fem., Kh. מַרְאַיִךְ q. v., K. מַרְאֵךְ; ו bef. lab.	ראה
מַרְאֵינוּ	id., suff. 1 pers. pl.	ראה
מַרְאֵשׁ	ו׳ pref. מ׳ for מ׳)(n.m.s.irr. (§ 45); ו bef. lab.	ראשׁ
מַרְאֵשָׁה	ו pr. name of a place; ו id. . . .	ראשׁ
מַרְאֵשׁוֹ	pref. מ׳ for מ׳)(noun masc. sing., suff. 3 pers. sing. masc. from רֹאשׁ irr. (§ 45)	ראשׁ
מֵרִאשׁוֹן	pref. id.)(adj. masc. sing. dec. 1 b	ראשׁ
מֵרָאשֵׁי	ו pref. id.)(noun masc. pl. constr. from רֹאשׁ irr. (§ 45); ו bef. lab. . . .	ראשׁ
מֵרֵאשִׁית	ו׳ pref. id.)(noun fem. sing. dec. 1 b; ו id.	ראשׁ
מֵרֵאשִׁיתוֹ	pref. id.)(id. with suff. 3 pers. sing. masc.	ראשׁ
מְרַאֲשֹׁתַי	Kh., מְרַאֲשֹׁתַי K. (q. v.) . . .	ראשׁ
מְרַאֲשֹׁתוֹ	defect. for מְרַאֲשׁוֹתוֹ . . .	ראשׁ
מְרַאֲשֹׁת	pref. מ׳ for מ׳)(noun fem. with pl. m. term., constr. st. [from רָאֲשֹׁתִים, see ראשׁ [רָאֲשׁוֹת]	
	n. f. pl. [מְרַאֲשֹׁתָו], suff. 3 p s. m., *adverbially*	ראשׁ

a Ju. 10. 16.   *f* Nu. 16. 35.   *k* Is. 22. 5.   *o* 2 Sa. 22. 6.   *s* Is. 22. 3.   *w* Ru. 1. 20.   *A* Da. 4. 16, 21.   *P* Da. 1. 13.   *u* Ec. 7. 8.
b Le. 20. 18.   *g* Le. 21. 6.   *l* Mi. 4. 10.   *p* Pr. 29. 1.   *t* Je. 2. 19.   *x* Nu. 12. 8.   *B* Job 41. 1.   *Q* De. 33. 15.   *v* 1 Sa. 26. 7,
c Ru. 2. 3.   *h* Pu. 4. 10.   *m* Pr. 28. 14.   *q* Pr. 28. 14.   *u* Ex. 30. 23.   *y*   *C* Ca. 2. 14.   *R* Le. 13. 12.   11, 16.
d Ec. 23. 11.   *i* Ps. 69. 32.   *n* Is. 3. 24.   *r* Nu. 15. 32, 33.   *v* Da. 5. 23.   *z* Ex. 25. 40.   *D* Ca. 2. 14.   *S* Je. 17. 12.
e Ec. 3. 19.   *j* Ps. 22. 22.   *s* 1 Ki. 17. 10, 12.   *w* Da. 2. 47.   *G* Eze. 1. 1; 43. 3.   *E* Ca. 2. 14.   *T* Pr. 3. 9.   *t* Job 42. 12.
f Eze. 29. 18.   *n* 1 Ki. 6. 15.   *w* Ps. 141. 9.   *u* 1 Sa. 26. 12

34

מְרַאֲשֹׁתֵיכֶם֙ pref. מֵ for מִ X noun fem. pl., suff. 2 pers. pl. [from רֵאשָׁה] . ראש

מַרְאֲשֹׁתֵיכֶם֙ noun fem. pl. [מַרְאָשׁוֹת], suff. 2 pers. pl. m. ראש

מַרְאֹת defect. for מַרְאוֹת (q. v.) . . . ראה

מַרְאֵתוֹ֙ noun fem. sing., suff. 3 pers. sing. masc. [from מַרְאֶה, no pl.] . . . . . מרה

מֶרַב pr. name fem. . . . . . . רבב

מִרְבַּד֙ pref. מֵ for מִ X [noun m. s. d. 8c; ו bef. lab. רבב

מַרְבְּבָה֙ pref. id. X noun fem. sing. dec. 11 c רבב

מַרְבְּבוֹת֙ pref. id. X id. pl., constr. of רְבָבוֹת . רבב

מְרֻבָּבוֹת֙ Pual part. fem. pl. [of מְרֻבָּבָה fr. מְרֻבָּב m.] רבב

מַרְבְבֹת֙ defect. for מַרְבְבוֹת (q. v.) . . רבב

מַרְבַּדִּים noun masc., pl. of [מַרְבָד] dec. 8a רבד

מַרְבֶּה֙ Hiph. part., fem. of the foll. . . רבה

מַרְבֵּה֙ id. masc., constr. of the foll. . . רבה

מַרְבֶּה Hiph. part., or (Is. 33. 23) subst. m. sing. d. 9a רבה

מִרְבֶּה֙ noun masc. sing. . . . רבה

מַרְבִּים (ו) Hiph. part. m., pl. of מַרְבֶּה d. 9a; ו bef. lab. רבה

מַרְבִּים֙ pref. מֵ for מִ X adj. masc., pl. of רַב d. 8d רבב

מַרְבִּיץ֙ Hiph. part. sing. masc. dec. 1 b רבץ

מִרְבִּית֙ noun fem. sing. dec. 1 b . . רבה

מַרְבִּיתָם֙ id. with suff. 3 pers. pl. masc. . רבה

מֵרַבְּכֶם֙ pref. מֵ for מִ X noun masc. sing., suff. 2 pers. pl. masc. from רַב dec. 8c . . רבב

מֻרְבֶּכֶת֙ Hoph. part. sing. fem. [of מָרְבָּךְ § 39. No. 4] רבך

מְרֻבָּע֙ Pual part. sing. masc. . . רבע

מְרֻבָּעוֹתי֙ [as if fr. מְרֻבָּעָה] as the pl. of the foll. (§44.r.5) רבע

מְרֻבָּעַת֙ [for מְרֻבַּעַת] Pual part. sing. fem. of מְרֻבָּע רבע

מַרְבֵּץ֙ noun m. sing. d. 7 b (constr. מִרְבַּץ׳ § 36. r. 1) רבץ

מַרְבִּצִים֙ Hiph. part. masc. pl. of מַרְבִּיץ dec. i b רבץ

מִרְבָּק֙ noun masc. sing. . . . רבק

מְרַבַּת֙ pref. מֵ for מִ X pr. name of a place . רבת

מָרַג Root not used ; whence

מוֹרַג masc. (pl. מוֹרִגִּים, מוֹרִגִּים, dag. resolved in Yod) threshing-sledge, a kind of dray, in which are inserted wooden rollers, and in these are fixed teeth of iron, stone, &c.

מַרְגּוֹעַ֙ noun masc. sing. . . . . רגע

מֵרָגְזֶךָ֙ ו pref. מֵ for מִ X noun masc. sing., suff. 2 pers. sing. masc. from רֹגֶז dec. 6c ; ו bef. lab. רגז

מַרְגִּיז֙ Hiph. part. sing. masc. . ' רגז

מַרְגְּלוֹתָיו֙ Kh. for מַרְגְּלֹתָיו (q. v.) . . רגל

מַרְגְּלִים֙ Hiph. part. masc. pl. of [מְרַגֵּל] dec. 7 b רגל

מַרְגְּלִים֙ pref. מֵ for מִ X pr. name of a place . רגל

מַרְגְּלֹתָיו֙ n. f.pl. [מַרְגְּלוֹת], suff. 3 p. s. m.; ו bef. lab. רגל

מַרְנֶשֶׁת֙ pref. מֵ for מִ X noun f. s. constr. [of רַנֶשֶׁת] רנש

מָרַד fut. יִמְרֹד to rebel, revolt, cause sedition, with בְּ, עַל of the pers. against whom ; מֹרְדֵי אוֹר who rebel against the light, are enemies of the light.

מְרַד Chald. rebellion, Ezr. 4. 19.

מֶרֶד masc.—I. rebellion, defection, Jos. 22. 22 —II. pr. name masc. 1 Ch. 4. 17, 18.

מָרָד Chald. adj. rebellious, only fem. מָרָדָא dec. 8a, Ezr. 4. 12, 15.

מַרְדּוּת fem rebellion, contumacy, 1 Sa. 20. 30.

נִמְרֹד (rebel, or, let us rebel) pr. name, Nimrod, the founder of Babylon, Ge. 10. 8, 9. נ׳ אֶרֶץ Babylonia, Mi. 5. 5.

מָרַד֙ Kal pret. 3 pers. sing. m. [for מָרַד § 8. r. 7] רד

מֶרֶד֙ } pr. name masc. (§ 35. r. 2); ו bef. lab. . מרד
מֶרֶד֙ }

מְרַד֙ ו Ch. Peal pret. 3 pers. sing. masc. ; ו id. מרד

מָרְדָא֙ Ch. adj. fem. dec. 11 [fr. מָרַד masc.] . מרד

מֵרֶדֶת֙ pref. מֵ for מִ X Kal inf. constr. (§ 20. r. 3) ירד

מָרְדוּ֙ } Kal pret. 3 pers. pl. (§ 8. rem. 7) . מרד
מָרְדוּ֙ }

מֹרְדִים֙ id. part. masc., pl. of [מוֹרֵד] dec. 7 b . מרד

מְרֹדָךְ pr. name, Merodach, an idol of the Babylonians, prob. the planet Mars. Je. 50. 2.

מְרֹאדַךְ בַּלְאֲדָן (Merodach is his lord) pr. name of a king of Babylon, Is. 39. 1.

מָרְדֳּכַי֙ } pr. name, Mordecai, a Jew of the tribe of
מָרְדֳּכַי֙ } Benjamin, living in Persia, who was the foster-father of Esther, and afterwards prime minister in the court of Ahasuerus, Est. 2. 5 seq.

מָרַדְנוּ֙ } ו Kal pret. 1 pers. pl. (§ 8. rem. 7) ; ו bef. } מרד
מָרַדְנוּ֙ } lab. . . . . . . }

מְרַדֵּף֙ ו Piel part. sing. masc.; ו id. . . רדף

מֵרְדֹף֙ pref. מֵ X Kal inf. constr. . . רדף

מִרְדָּף֙ noun masc. sing. . . . . רדף

מֹרְדְפַי֙ (ו) ו } pref. מֵ for מִ X Kal part. act. pl., suff. } רדף
מֹרְדְפַי֙ } 1 pers. sing. from רֹדֵף dec. 7 b }

מָרַדְתָּ֙ Kal pret. 2 pers. sing. masc. . . מרד

מֵרִדְתִּי֙ pref. מֵ f. X Kal inf.constr. (suff. רִדְתִּי) d. 13a ירד

מָרָדְתָּא֙ Ch. adj. f., emph. of מָרָדָא d. 11 [fr. מָרָד m.] מרד

מָרָה I. to rebel, be disobedient, const. with בְּ, acc.— II. i. q. מָרַר to be bitter, 2 Ki. 14. 26. Hiph. הִמְרָה—I. to resist, contend with, const. with עַם

---

* Eze. 36. 11.   ⨍ Ps. 3. 7.   ˡ Eze. 23. 32.   ⁱ De. 7. 7.   ᵒ Je. 33. 12.   ᶜ Ru. 3. 4, 7, 8.   ᵍ Ge. 46. 3.   * Pr. 19. 7.   ʳ Je. 15. 15.
ᵇ Je. 13. 18.   ᵍ Ps. 144. 13.   ᵐ 1 Ch. 8. 40.   ʲ Eze. 45. 2.   ᵖ Je. 6. 16.   ᵈ Da. 10. 6.   ʰ Ge. 14. 1.   ⁱ Is. 14. 6.   ˢ Job 33. 24.
ᶜ Ge. 27. 1.   ʰ De. 33. 2.   ⁿ Ne. 7. 2.   ᵏ 1 Ki. 7. 31.   ⁱ Is. 14. 3.   ᵉ Ps. 64. 3.   ⁱ Eze. 2. 3.   ᵖ Ps. 142. 7.   ᵗ Ezr. 4. 12.
ᵈ Le. 1. 16.   ⁱ Ne. 9. 37.   ᵒ Is. 54. 11.   ˡ Eze. 40. 47.   ᵐ Is. 14. 16.   ⨍ 2 Ch. 36. 13.   ⱼ Da. 9. 5.   ᵍ Ps. 31. 16.   ᵘ 1 Ki. 13. 26.
ᵉ Ca. 5. 10.   ᵏ Le. 11. 42.   ᵖ 1 Ch. 12. 29.   ⁿ Zep. 2. 15.   ⁿ Ru. 3. 14.   ᵍ Ezr. 4. 19.   ᵐ Da. 9. 9.   ᵏ Ezr. 4. 15.   ᵛ Ne. 2. 19.

—II. *to be rebellious, disobedient*, with acc., בְּ.—
III. *to embitter, grieve*, with the acc.

מוֹרָה masc. *a razor.* Its connection with the
Root is not obvious.

מְרִי masc. dec. 6 i.—I. *rebellion, contumacy.*—
II. *bitterness*, Job 23. 2.

מְרִי בַעַל (i. q. מְרִיב בַּעַל *contender against Baal,*
see R. רִיב) pr. name masc. 1 Ch. 9. 40.

מֶרָיָה (*rebellion*) pr. name masc. Ne. 12. 12.

מֵרָיוֹת (*rebellions*) pr. name masc. of several
persons.

מִרְיָם (*rebellion*) pr. name fem. *Miriam.*—I. sister
of Moses, a prophetess.—II. 1 Ch. 4. 17.

מְרָתַיִם (*double rebellion*) symbolical name for
Babylon, Je. 50. 21.

יִמְרָה (*refractory*) pr. name masc. 1 Ch. 7. 36.

מָרָה [for מָרֶה] *a* adj. or subst. fem. sing. dec. 10
from מַר masc.; also pr. name; ו bef. lab.

מָרָה Kal pret. 3 pers. sing. fem. [for מָרְרָה]   מרר

מֹרָה pr. name of a place · · · ירה

מֹרֶה defect. for מוֹרֶה (q. v.) · · ירה

מֹרֶה *a* Kal part. act. sing. masc. d. 7 b; ו bef. lab.   מרה

מָרֹה *c* Kal inf. abs. [for מָרָה § 24. rem. 2] · מרה

מָרוּ id. pret. 3 pers. pl. · · · מרה

מְרִיב in full for מְרָב (q. v. & § 18. rem. 2) · רבב

מְרוּדִי *d* noun masc. sing., suff. 1 pers. sing. from
[מָרוּד] dec. 3 a; ו bef. lab.

מְרוּדֶיהָ *d* id. pl., suff. 3 pers. sing. fem.; ו id.   רוד

מְרוּדִים id. pl., abs. st. · · · רוד

מְרוֶּה *e* Hiph. part. sing. masc.; ו bef. lab.   רוה

מְרוֹז pr. name of a place · · · ארז

מְרוֹחַ *h* adj. masc. sing., constr. of [מָרוֹחַ] dec. 3 a   מרח

מֵרוּחַ *k* ו pref. מֵ for מִן n. com. s. d. 1 a; ו bef. lab.   רוח

מְרוּחִים Pual part. masc. pl. [of מְרוּחַ] · רוח

מֵרוּחֲךָ pref. מֵ for מִן X noun com. sing., suff. 2 pers.
sing. masc. [for רוּחֲךָ] from רוּחַ dec. 1 a

מְרוּטָה Kal part. pass. sing. fem. [from מָרוּט masc.]   מרט

מָרוֹם noun masc. sing. dec. 3 a · · רום

מֵרוֹם pr. name of a place · · · רום

מְרוֹם noun masc. sing., constr. of מָרוֹם dec. 3 a   רום

מְרוֹמֵי id. pl., constr. st. · · · רום

מְרוֹמִים id. pl., abs. st. · · · רום

מְרוֹמָם *p* ו Pulal part. sing. masc.; ו bef. lab.   רום

מְרוֹמְמוּ *r* ו Heb. & Ch. Pilel part. s. m. d. 7 b; ו id.   רום

מְרוֹמְמִי id. with suff. 1 pers. sing. · · רום

מְרוּצַת *s* noun fem. sing., constr. of מְרוּצָה dec. 10   רוץ

מְרוּצָתָם *u* noun fem. sing., suff. 3 pers. pl. masc. · רוץ

מָרוּק Kal part. pass. sing. masc. · · מרק

מְרוּקֵיהֶן *y* noun m. pl., suff. 3 p. pl. f. fr. [מָרוּק] d. 1 a   מרק

מְרוֹרַת noun fem. sing., constr. of מְרוֹרָה dec. 10   מרר

מָרוֹת pr. name of a place · · · מרר

מָרְזַח *a* noun masc. sing. dec. 7 b · · רזח

מִרְזַח *b* id., constr. st. (§ 36. rem. 1) · רזח

[מָרַח] *to rub, bruise, crush*, Is. 38. 21, *and crush them over
the ulcer*, i. e. apply them crushed, softened.

מָרוֹחַ masc. dec. 3 a, *bruised, crushed*, Le. 21. 20
מְרוֹחַ אָשֶׁךְ *crushed at the testicles.*

מֶרְחָב *c* pref. מֶ for מִן X noun fem. sing. dec. 1 a   רחב

מֶרְחָבָה *d* pref. id. X id. sing., suff. 3 pers. sing. fem.   רחב

מֶרְחֲבוֹת *e* pref. id. X id. pl. fem.; also pr. name · רחב

מֵרָחוֹק *gg* pref. id. X adj. masc. sing. d. 3 a, as an *adv.*   רחק

מַרְחִיב Hiph. part. sing. masc. · · רחב

מְרַחֵם in pause for מְרַחֵם (q. v. & § 35. rem. 2)   רחם

מְרַחֵם *g* pref. מְ for מִן X Piel inf. constr. (§ 14. r. 1)   רחם

מֵרַחַם *h* pref. id. X noun masc. s. (suff. רַחְמָה) d. 6 a   רחם

מְרַחֵם *h* Piel part. sing. masc. (§ 14. rem. 1) dec. 7 b   רחם

מְרַחֲמֵךְ id., suff. 2 pers. sing. fem. · · רחם

מְרַחֲמָם *k* id., suff. 3 pers. pl. masc. · רחם

מְרַחֶפֶת Piel (§ 14. r. 1) part. sing. f. [of מְרַחֵף m.]   רחף

מְרַחֹק defect. for מֵרָחוֹק (q. v.) · רחק

מֶרְחָק noun masc. sing. dec. 8 a (see the foll.)   רחק

מֶרְחַקֵּי id. pl., constr. st. · · רחק

מֶרְחַקִּים id. pl., abs. st. · · רחק

מֶרְחֶשֶׁת *n* noun fem. sing. · · רחש

[מָרַט] *to make smooth.*—I. of a sword, *to polish, sharpen.*
—II. of the head, *to pluck out the hair, make it bald.*
Niph. *to become bald*, Le. 13. 40, 41. Pu. I. *to
be polished*, of metal, 1 Ki. 7. 45.—II. *to be sharpened, sharp*, of a sword.—III. Is. 18. 2, 7, part.
מוֹרָט (for מְמֹרָט) *made bald, peeled*; but Gesenius
(who thinks that that prophecy refers to the *Ethiopians*) takes it as a noun, *destruction*, and renders
גּוֹי מוֹרָט *a destructive* nation.

מְרַט Chald. pret. pass. *to be plucked*, Da. 7. 4.

מֹרָטָה [for מְמֹרָטָה & dag. forte euph.] Pual part.
sing., fem. of מְמֹרָט (§ 10. rem. 6) · מרט

מָרֵי *o* adj. pl. constr. masc. from מַר dec. 8 e
(§ 37. rem. 7); ו bef. lab. · · מרר

מְרִי noun masc. s. d. 6 i (§ 35. r. 14), also pr.
מְרִי name in compos. } ג *a* id. } מרה

---

a Pr. 6. 13.   *f* Is. 58. 7.   *l* Je. 22. 14.   *p* Ne. 9. 5.   *t* 2 Sa. 18. 27.   *x* Job 20. 14.   *d* Ps. 55. 12.   *h* Ps. 116. 5.   *m* Is. 8. 9.
b 2 Ki. 14. 26.   *g* Pr. 11. 25.   *m* Ps. 139. 7.   *q* 1 Sa. 2. 7.   *u* Je. 23. 10.   *y* Je. 16. 5.   *e* Je. 9. 20.   *i* Is. 54. 10.   *n* Le. 2. 7.
c La. 1. 20.   *h* Le. 21. 20.   *n* Ju. 5. 18.   *r* Da. 4. 34.   *2* Ch. 4. 16.   *z* Am. 6. 7.   *f* De. 33. 20.   *k* Is. 49. 10.   *o* Ju. 18. 25.
d La. 3. 19.   *i* Ps. 55. 9.   *o* Is. 33. 16.   *s* Ps. 9. 14.   *v* Est. 2. 12.   *2* Sa. 21. 12.   *g* Is. 49. 15.   *l* Ge. 1. 2.   *p* 2 Sa. 17. 8.
e La. 1. 7.   *k* Job 4. 9.   *gg* Job 39. 25
34.*

מָרִיא	adj. masc. sing. dec. 1 a; ‹ bef. lab.	מרא
מְרִיאֵי	id. pl., constr. ‹‹	מרא
מְרִיאֵיכֶם	id. pl., suff. 2 pers. pl. masc.	מרא
מְרִיאִים	id. pl., abs. st.	מרא
מֵרִיב	pref. מֵ for מִ)(noun masc. sing. dec. 1 a	ריב
מְרִיב	pr. name in compos. = מְרִיב בַּעַל; ‹ bef. lab.	ריב
מְרִיבָה	noun fem. sing. d. 10, also pr. name; ‹ id.	ריב
מְרִיבֹת	Hiph. part. pl. masc., suff. 3 pers. sing. masc. (§ 4. rem. 1) fr. [מֵרִיב] dec. 3 b	ריב
מְרִיבוֹת	noun fem., pl. of מְרִיבָה dec. 10	ריב
מְרִיבֵי	pref. מֵ for מִ)(noun m. pl. c. fr. רִיב d. 1 a	ריב
מְרִיבַת	noun fem. sing., constr. of מְרִיבָה dec. 10	ריב
מֹרִיד	defect. for מוֹרִיד (q. v.); ‹ bef. lab.	ירד
מְרָיָה	pr. name masc.	מרה
מֹרִיָּה	(for מָרְאֶה יָהּ=מָרְאִיָּה shown of the Lord; or, chosen of the Lord, comp. Ge. 22. 14), pr. name, Moriah, a hill near Jerusalem where Isaac was to have been offered, and where afterwards the temple was built by Solomon.	
מְרָיוֹת	pr. name masc.	מרה
מֵרִיחַ	pref. מֵ for מִ)(noun masc. sing. dec. 1 a	רוח
מְרִיטוּ	Ch. part. p., or Peil, 3 pers. pl. m. (§ 47. r. 11)	מרט
מֶרְיְךָ	noun masc. pl., suff. 2 pers. sing. masc. fr. מְרִי dec. 6 i (§ 35. rem. 14)	מרה
מָרִים	Chald. Aph. part. sing. masc. (§ 54. rem. 5)	רום
מָרִים	adj. masc., pl. of מַר dec. 8 (§ 37. rem. 7)	מרר
מָרִים	Hiph. part. sing. masc. d. 3 b; ‹ bef. lab.	רום
מִרְיָם	pr. name fem.; ‹ id.	מרה
מְרִימֶנּוּ	Hiph. part. pl. m., suff. 3 p. pl. m. fr. מֵרִים d. 3 b	רום
מָרִינוּ	Kal pret. 1 pers. pl.; ‹ bef. lab.	מרה
מְרִיעִים	Hiph. part. masc. pl. [of מֵרִיעַ] dec. 3 b	רוע
מְרִיקִים	Hiph. part. masc. pl. [of מֵרִיק] dec. 3 b	רוק
מְרִירִי	adj. masc. sing.	מרר
מָרִיתָ	Kal pret. 2 pers. sing. masc.	מרה
מָרִיתִי	id. pret. 1 pers. sing.	מרה
מְרִיתֶם	id. pret. 2 pers. pl. masc.; ‹ for ן, conv.	מרה
מֶרֶךְ	pref. מֵ for מִ)(noun masc. sing.; ‹ bef. lab.	רכך
מֹרֶךְ	noun masc. sing.	רכך
מֶרְכָּבָה	noun fem. sing. dec. 11 a, constr. מֶרְכֶּבֶת, suff. מֶרְכַּבְתּוֹ (§ 42. rem. 5); ‹ bef. lab.	רכב
מֶרְכָּבוֹ	noun masc. sing., suff. 3 pers. sing. masc. from מֶרְכָּב dec. 2 b	רכב
מַרְכְּבוֹת	noun fem. pl. abs. from מֶרְכָּבָה dec. 11 (comp. § 42. rem. 5); ‹ bef. lab.	רכב
מַרְכְּבוֹת	id. pl., constr. st.	רכב
מֶרְכְּבוֹתַי	id. pl., suff. 3 pers. sing. masc.	רכב
מֶרְכֶּבֶת	id. pl., constr. st. for מֶרְכָּבוֹת (q. v.)	רכב

מֶרְכַּבְתּוֹ	id. sing., suff. 3 pers. sing. masc. (from constr. מֶרְכֶּבֶת dec. 13 a)	רכב
מַרְכְּבֹתֵיהֶם	id. pl., suff. 3 pers. pl. masc.	רכב
מַרְכְּבֹתָיו	id. pl., suff. 3 pers. sing. masc.	רכב
מַרְכְּבֹתֶיךָ	id. pl., suff. 2 pers. sing. masc.	רכב
מֶרְכֻּגּשׁ	pref. מֵ for מִ)(noun masc. sing. dec. 1 a	רכש
מֶרְכֻּסֵי	pref. id.)(noun masc. pl. constr. from [רֶכֶם] dec. 6 c (§ 35. rem. 9)	רכם
מִרְמָה	noun f. s. d. 10, also pr. name; ‹ bef. lab.	רמה
מֵרֵמוֹת	pr. name of a place	רום
מִרְמוֹת	noun fem., pl. of מִרְמָה dec. 10; ‹ bef. lab.	רמה
מְרֹמֵי	pref. id.)(noun masc. pl. constr. from מְרוֹמֵי, &c. (q.v.) defect. for	רום
מְרֹמְמַתְךָ	pref. מֵ for מִ)(noun fem. sing., suff. 2 pers. sing. masc. from [רוֹמְמוּת] dec. 3 b	רום
מַרְמֹן	pref. id.)(pr. name in compos. see רִמּוֹן פֶּרֶץ	רמם
מִרְמָס	noun masc. sing. dec. 2 b	רמם
מִרְמַס	id. constr., also abs. Is. 10. 6	מס
מְרֵמֹת	pr. name masc.	יום
מֶרֹנֹתִי	gent. noun, 1 Ch. 27. 30; Ne. 3. 7.	
מֶרֶס	pr. name of a Persian prince, Est. 1. 14	
מַרְסָה	pref. מֵ for מִ)(pr. name of a place	רסם
מַרְסְנָא	pr. name of a Persian prince, Est. 1. 14.	
מֵרַע	Hiph. part. in pause for מֵרַע (q.v.); ‹ bef. lab.	רעע
מֵרַע	pref. מֵ for מִ)(noun masc. sing. dec. 8 (§ 37. rem. 7)	רעע
מֵרֵעַ		
מֵרַע	Hiph. part. sing. masc. [with gutt. for מֵרַע § 18. rem. 10]	רעע
מֵרֵעַ	pref. מֵ for מִ)(noun masc. s.; ‹ bef. lab.	רעע
מַרְעֵב	pref. id.)(noun masc. sing. dec. 4 a	רעב
מֵרְעֵב	pref. id.)(adj. masc. sing.; ‹ bef. lab.	רעב
מֵרָעָה	pref. id.)(adj. or subst. fem. sing. dec. 10 [for רָעָה from רַע masc.	רעע
מֵרָעָה	pref. id.)(noun masc. sing., suff. 3 pers. sing. fem. from רֵעַ (§ 36. rem. 4)	רעה
מִרְעֶה	noun masc. sing., constr. and abs., dec. 9 a; ‹ bef. lab.	רעה
מִרְעֵה	pref. מֵ for מִ)(Kal part. act. sing. m. d. 9 a	רעה
מֵרֵעֵהוּ	pref. id.)(noun masc. sing., suff. 3 pers. sing. masc. from רֵעַ (§ 36. rem. 4)	רעה
מֵרֵעֵהוּ	noun m. s., suff. 3 p. s. m. fr. [מֵרֵעַ] d. 1 b	רעה
מִרְעֵהוּ	noun masc. sing., suff. 3 pers. sing. masc. from מִרְעֶה dec. 9 a	רעה
מִרְעֹת	pref. מֵ for מִ)(Kal inf. constr.	רעה
מַרְעִיד	Hiph. part. sing. masc.	רעד
מַרְעִידִים	id. pl., abs. st.	רעד
מִרְעֵיכֶם	noun masc. pl., suff. 2 pers. pl. masc. from מִרְעֶה dec. 9 a	רעה

* 2 Sa. 6. 13, etc. / 1 Sa. 2. 10. ' Da. 5. 19. ₴ Ezr. 3. 13. ■ Le. 26. 36. Ps. 31. 21. ‖ Is. 9. 16. ■ Je. 3. 20. ♦ Job 39. 8.
Eze. 39. 18. ² Eze. 47. 19. ⁿ Ex. 15. 23. ' Ge. 42. 35. ♪ Na. 3. 2. ♭ Ps. 35. 20. ‖ Job 28. 28. ‖ Is. 32. 14. Eze. 34. 10.
Am. 5. 22. ' 2 Sa. 22. 48. ' Ps. 3. 4. ' De. 32. 24. ♦ Ca. 2. 10. Pr. 8. 2; 9. 3, 14. ₤ Pr. 17. 4. ₣ Ge. 26. 26. Is. 33. 3.
Is. 1. 11. ' Da. 7. 4. ' Is. 10. 15. ' 1 Ki. 13. 21. ' Is. 33. 3. • Da. 8. 13. Job 22. 7. 2 Sa. 3. 8; Pr. 19. 7. Ezr. 10. 9.
Ex. 17. 7. ' De. 31. 27. ' La. 3. 42. ♪ De. 28. 56. ᵇ 2 Ch. 35. 7. Job 14. 9. Eze. 34. 12.

מְרֵעִים־	noun masc. pl. of [מֵרֵעַ] dec. 1 b	רעה
מְרֵעִים	Hiph. part. pl. m. [for מְרֵעִים] fr. מֵרַע (q. v.)	רעע
מַרְעִישׁ	Hiph. part. sing. masc.	רעש
מַרְעִיתוֹ	noun f. s., suff. 3 p. s. m. fr. [מַרְעִית] d. 1 b	רעה
מַרְעִיתִי	id., suff. 1 pers. sing.	רעה
מַרְעִיתֶךָ	id., suff. 2 pers. sing. masc. [for מַרְעִיתְךָ]	רעה
מַרְעִיתָם	id., suff. 3 pers. pl. masc.	רעה
מַרְעֲלָה	וּ pr. name of a place ; וּ bef. lab.	רעל
מַרְעֹמֶס	pref. מֵ for מִ) (pr. n. of a place, see רַעְמְסֵס.	
מַרְעֵעַ	Chald. Pael part. sing. m. (§ 49. Nos 3 & 4)	רעע
מַרְעֵשׁ	pref. מֵ for מִ) (noun masc. sing.	רעש
מַרְעֶה	pref. id.) (noun fem. sing., constr. of רָעֶה dec. 10 [for רַעֶה] from רָעָ masc.	רעע
מַרְעָתוֹ	pref. id.) (id., suff. 3 pers. sing. masc.	רעע
מַרְעָתָם	pref. id.) (id., suff. 3 pers. pl. masc.	רעע
מַרְפֵּא	וּ noun masc. sing. ; וּ bef. lab.	רפא
מַרְפֵּא	Piel part. sing. m. [for מְרַפֵּא § 24. r. 19c]	רפה
מַרְפֵּה	noun masc. sing. for מַרְפֵּא (§ 23. rem. 10)	רפא
מְרַפִּידִים / מַרְפִּידִים	} pref. מֵ for מִ) (pr. name of a place	רפד
מַרְפֵּיוֹן	pref. id.) (noun masc. sing.	רפה
מַרְפִּים	Piel part. masc. pl. [of מְרַפֶּה] dec. 9 a	רפה
מַרְפֵּשׁ	וּ noun masc. sing., constr. of [מִרְפָּשׂ] dec. 2 b ; וּ bef. lab.	רפש

מָרַץ Kal not used ; Arab. *to be diseased, weak*, in body or mind. Niph. *to be weak*, ironically, Job 6. 25 ; part. *diseased, pernicious, foul*, Mi. 2. 10 ; 1 Ki. 2. 8. Hiph. *to make weak, foolish*, Job 16. 3.—Note. Kimchi, on the contrary, ascribes to this verb the signification of *being strong, forcible, vehement*, which Gesenius supports by making it cogn. with פָּרַץ q. v. comp. also Eng. vers.

מְרַצְּחִים	Piel part. masc. pl. of מְרַצֵּחַ dec. 7 b	רצח
מַרְצֶפֶת	noun fem. sing.	רצף

[מָרַק] *to make clean, bright by rubbing, to polish, furbish.* Pu. *to be cleansed,* Le. 6. 21.

מָרָק masc. dec. 4 a, *broth.*

מְרוּקִים m. pl. (of מָרוּק) *purification,* Est. 2. 12.

תַּמְרוּק masc. dec. 1 b, *purification,* Est. 2. 12. Meton. *precious ointments, perfumes,* Est. 2. 3, 9.

תַּמְרוּק masc. *cleansing, remedy,* Pr. 20. 30 Kh., תַּמְרוּק K.

מֹרַק	וּ Pual part. sing. masc. ; וּ for וְ conv.	מרק
מְרֻקָּד	Piel part. sing. masc.	רקד
מְרֻקָּדָה	id. part. sing. fem.	רקד
מֹרְקוּ	Kal imp. pl. masc.	מרק
מִרְקָחִים	noun masc. pl. [of מִרְקָח]	רקח
מְרֻקָּחִים	Pual part. masc. pl. [of מְרֻקָּח]	רקח
מִרְקַחַת	noun fem. sing.	רקח
מֻרְקָע	Pual part. sing. masc.	רקע

מָרַר fut. יֵמַר (§ 18. rem. 6).—I. *to be bitter* ; impers. מַר לִי *it is bitter to me, it grieves me.*—II. *to be embittered, exasperated,* 1 Sa. 30. 6.—III. Arab. *to flow, drop,* whence derivv. מֹר q. v. Pi. I. *to make bitter, to embitter* ; מָרֵר בַּבְּכִי *to weep bitterly.*—II. *to irritate, provoke,* Ge. 49. 23. Hiph. הֵמַר (§ 18. rem. 10).—I. *to embitter,* with נֶפֶשׁ Job 27. 2 ; ellipt. הֵ׳ לִי *has embittered me,* sc. life, Ruth 1. 20.—II. *to weep bitterly,* Zec. 12. 10.

מַר masc.—I. *a drop,* Is. 40. 15.—II. adj. (pl. מָרִים, c. מָרֵי § 37. rem. 7) fem. מָרָה dec. 10 ; *bitter* ; neut. as subst. *bitterness.* Metaph. for (a) *sad, sorrowful* ; subst. *sadness, grief* ; (b) *bitter, lamentable,* of a cry, grief ; (c) *violent, cruel* ; (d) *deadly, pernicious* ; (e) adv. *bitterly,* of lamentation.

מֹר, מוֹר masc. (with suff. מוֹרִי) *myrrh.*

מָרָא (*bitter, sad*) pr. name fem. Ruth 1. 20.

מָרָה (*bitterness*) pr. name of a fountain in the desert of Sinai.

מָרָה fem. dec. 10, *bitterness,* Pr. 14. 10.

מֹרָה fem. dec. 10, *bitterness, grief.* Ge. 26. 35

מָרוֹת (prob. *bitter fountains*) pr. name of a place in the tribe of Judah, Mi. 1. 12.

מְרֵרָה fem. dec. 10, *gall,* Job 16. 13.

מְרֹרָה fem. dec. 10.—I. *bitterness,* De. 32. 32 ; metaph. pl. *bitter, severe things,* Job 13. 26.—II. *gall,* Job 20. 25.—III. *poison,* Job 20. 14.

מְרֹרִים masc. pl. (of מָרֹר dec. 3 a) *bitter herbs.*

מְרָרִי (*bitter, sad*) pr. name of a son of Levi, also patronym. Nu. 26. 57.

מְרִירִי adj. masc. *bitter, poisonous,* De. 32. 24.

מְרִירוּת f. *bitterness, sorrow, trouble,* Eze. 21. 11

מָמֵר masc. *grief, sorrow,* Pr. 17. 25.

מַמְּרֹרִים m. pl. (of מַמְרֹר) *bitter things,* Job 9. 18.

תַּמְרוּרִים masc. pl. (of תַּמְרוּר) *bitterness* ; adv. *bitterly,* Ho. 12. 15.

מְרֹרוֹת	noun fem. pl. of [מְרוֹרָה] dec. 10	מרר
מְרָרִי	וּ pr. name masc. ; וּ bef. lab.	מרר
מְרֹרִים	וּ noun masc. pl. of [מָרֹר] dec. 3 a ; וּ id.	מרר
מְרֹרֹת	defect. for מְרֹרוֹת (q. v.)	מרר
מְרָרָתִי	noun fem. s., suff. 1 pers. s. fr. [מְרֹרָה] d. 10.	מרר
מָרֵשָׁה	pr. name of a place, see מַרְאֵשָׁה	ראש

• Ju. 14. 11.   d Je. 44. 5.   g Je. 47. 3.   k Is. 1. 21.   n 1 Ch. 15. 29.   q Ca. 5. 13.   t Je. 10. 9.   w Ex. 12. 8.   z De. 32. 32.
b Da. 2. 40.   e Je. 38. 4.   Ezr. 4. 4.   i 2 Ki. 16. 17.   o Na. 3. 2.   r 2 Ch. 16. 14.   u Job 13. 26.   x Nu. 9. 11.   a Job 16. 13.
c Je. 47. 2.   Je. 8. 15.   Eze. 34. 19.   m Le. 6. 21.   p Je. 46. 4.   Ex. 30. 25.   Job 13. 26.

מַרְשִׁיעַ	ו Hiph. part. sing. masc. dec. 1 b ; ו bef. lab.	רשע
מַרְשִׁיעִי	ו id. pl., constr. st. ; ו id.	רשע
מֵרְשִׁית	defect. for מֵרֵאשִׁית (q. v.) . . .	ראש
מֵרָשָׁע	pref. מ for מִ)(adj. masc. sing. dec. 4 a	רשע
מֵרֶשַׁע	pref. id.)(noun masc. sing. d. 6 a (§ 35. r. 5)	רשע
מֵרִשְׁעוֹ	pref. id.)(id. with suff. 3 pers. sing. masc.	רשע
מֵרְשָׁעִים	pref. id.)(adj. masc. pl. of רָשָׁע dec. 4a	רשע
מֵרִשְׁעָתוֹ	pref. id.)(noun fem. sing., suff. 3 pers. sing. masc. from רִשְׁעָה (no pl.) .	רשע
מֵרֶשֶׁת	pref. id.)(noun fem. s. (suff. רִשְׁתִּי) d. 13 b	ירש
מָרַת	adj. fem. sing., constr. of מָרָה dec. 10 [for מָרָה] from מַר masc. . .	מרר
מָרַת	noun fem. sing. constr. [of מָרָה fr. מֹר m.]	מרר
מֹרַת	noun fem. sing. constr. [of מָרָה fr. מֹר m.]	מרר
מָרֵתָה	pr. name of a place (מָרָה) with loc. ה	מרר
מָרָתָה מָרָתָה	} Kal pret. 3 pers. sing. fem. (§ 8. rem. 7)	מרה
מָרָתַיִם	noun fem. du. from [מָרָה] dec. 11a	מרה
מֵרְתְמָה	pref. מֵ for מִ)(pr. name of a place	רתם
מָשׁ	ו Kal pret. 3 pers. sing. m. ; ו for ו, conv.	מוש
וָמָשׁ	pr. name of a son of Aram, Ge. 10. 23.	
מַשָּׂא	ו noun m. s. d. 1 b, also pr. name ; ו bef. lab.	נשא
מַשָּׂא	ו noun masc. sing. ; ו id.	נשא
[מֵשָׁא]	pr. name, Mesha, one of the boundaries of the district inhabited by the descendants of Joktan, Ge. 10. 30.	
מַשָּׂא	ו noun masc. sing. ; ו bef. lab.	נשא
מַשָּׂאבִים	noun masc. pl. of [מַשְׁאָב] dec. 8a	שאב
מַשָּׂאָה	noun fem. sing.	נשא
מַשֻּׂאָה	ו defect. for מְשׂוּאָה (q. v.) ; ו bef. lab. .	שוא
מַשָּׂאוֹ	noun masc. sing., suff. 3 pers. sing. masc. from מַשָּׂא dec. 1 b	נשא
מְשׁוּאֵל	pref. מִ)(pr. name masc.	שאל
מְשׁוּאֵל	pref. id.)(noun com. sing. dec. 1 a	שאל
מַשֻּׂאוֹת	noun fem. pl. abs. from מַשֻּׂאָה dec. 11a	נשא
מַשְׂאוֹת	noun fem. pl. of מַשְׂאֵת (q. v.) . .	נשא
מַשְׂאוֹתֵיכֶם	id. with suff. 2 pers. pl. masc.	נשא
מְשׂאֵיהֶם	pref. מִ)(noun masc. pl., suff. 3 pers. pl. masc. from [שׂוֹא] dec. 1a	שוא
מַשַּׂאֲכֶם	ו noun masc. sing., suff. 2 pers. pl. masc. from מַשָּׂא dec. 1 b (§ 21. rem. 1) ; ו bef. lab.	נשא
מְשׁאֵל	ו pr. name masc. ; ו id.	שאל
מִשְׁאֲלוֹת	noun fem. pl. constr. from [מִשְׁאָלָה] d. 11a	שאל
מִשְׁאֲלוֹתֶיךָ	id. with suff. 2 pers. sing. masc.	שאל
מַשָּׂאָם	noun m. s., suff. 3 pers. pl. m. fr. מַשָּׂא d. 1 b	נשא
מַשְׂאֵר	pref. מִ)(noun masc. sing. dec. 1 a	שאר

מִשְׁאַרְתֶּךָ	ו noun fem. sing., suff. 2 pers. sing. masc. from [מִשְׁאֶרֶת] dec. 13a ; ו bef. lab.	שאר
מִשְׁאֲרוֹתָם	id. pl. with suff. 3 pers. pl. masc. .	שאר
מַשְּׂאֵת	[for מַשְׂאֵת] n. m. s. constr. of [מַשְׂאָה] d. 11a	נשא
מַשְׂאֵת	[for מַשְׂאֵת] noun fem. constr. as if from מַשְׂאָה, see מַשָּׂא ; ו bef. lab. . .	נשא
מַשְׂאֵת	n. f. s. [for מַשְׂאֵת § 39. No. 4. r. 2] ; ו id.	נשא
מַשְׂאֵת	ו pref. מִ)(n. f. s., constr. of שׂוֹאָה d. 10 ; ו id.	שוא
מַשְׂאֵתוֹ	ו pref. id.)(noun fem. sing., suff. 3 pers. sing. m. from שְׂאֵת (§ 39. No. 4. r. 2) ; ו id.	נשא
מֵשֵׁב	ו pref. id.)(Kal part. sing. masc. dec. 1 a (§ 30. No. 3) , ו id. . .	שוב
מְשֵׁבָא	pref. id.)(pr. name of a region .	שבא
מְשׁוּבָה	noun fem. sing. [for מְשׁוּבָה] dec. 10	שוב
מְשׁוּבוֹתֵיהֶם	id. pl., suff. 3 pers. pl. masc.	שוב
מְשׁוּבֹתֶיךָ	ו id. pl., suff. 2 pers. sing. masc. ; ו bef. lab.	שוב
מִשְׁבֻּתָם	ו defect. for מְשׁוּבֹתָם q. v. ; ו id. .	ישב
מְשַׁבַּח	ו Ch. Pael part. sing. m. (§ 49. No. 4) ; ו id.	שבח
מַשְׁבֵּט	pref. מִ)(Seg. n. as if for שֶׁבֶט=שֵׁבֶט see שֵׁבֶט	שבט
מִשְׁבְּטֵי	pref. id.)(n. com. pl. constr. fr. שֵׁבֶט d. 6b	שבט
מִשְׁבִּי	pref. id.)(noun masc. sing. d. 6i (§ 35. r. 14)	שבה
מַשְׁבִּיחַ	Hiph. part. sing. masc.	שבח
מַשְׁבִּיעַ	ו Hiph. part. sing. masc. ; ו bef. lab.	שבע
מַשְׁבִּיעֶךָ	Hiph. part. sing. masc., suff. 2 pers. sing. masc. [for מַשְׁבִּיעֲךָ, from מַשְׁבִּיעַ] dec. 1 b	שבע
מַשְׁבִּיר	Hiph. part. sing. masc. .	שבר
מַשְׁבִּית	Hiph. part. sing. masc. .	שבת
מִשְׁבְּלַת	pref. מִ)(noun fem. sing., pl. שִׁבֳּלִים d. 13c	שבל
מִשְׁבְעָה	pref. id.)(num. card. m., constr. שִׁבְעַת fr. שֶׁבַע f.	שבע
מִשְׁבֻעָה	pref. id.)(noun masc. sing., suff. 3 pers. s. f.	שבע
מִשְׁבֻעָתִי	pref. id.)(n. f. s., suff. 1 p. s. fr. שְׁבוּעָה d. 10	שבע
מִשְׁבֻעָתֵךְ	pref. id.)(id., suff. 2 pers. sing. fem. .	שבע
מִשְׁבְּצוֹת	noun fem. pl. of [מִשְׁבֶּצֶת] dec. 13	שבץ
מְשֻׁבָּצִים	Pual part. masc. pl. [of מְשֻׁבָּץ] .	שבץ
מִשְׁבְּצֹת	defect. for מִשְׁבְּצוֹת (q. v.) . .	שבץ
מַשְׁבֵּר	noun masc. sing., constr. מִשְׁבָּר (§ 36. r. 1)	שבר
מְשַׁבֵּר	ו Piel part. sing. masc. ; ו bef. lab.	שבר
מִשִּׁבְרוֹ	ו pref. מִ)(n. m. s. (suff. שִׁבְרוֹ) d. 6a; ו id.	שבר
מִשִּׁבְרֵי	noun masc. pl. constr. from [מִשְׁבָּר] dec. 2b	שבר
מִשִּׁבְרִי	pref. מִ)(n. m. s., suff. 1 p. s. fr. [שֶׁבֶר] d. 6b	שבר
מִשִּׁבְרַיִךְ	noun m. pl., suff. 2 p. s. m. fr. [מִשְׁבָּר] d. 2b	שבר
מִשְׁבָּרִים	pref. מִ)(noun masc. pl. of שֶׁבֶר dec. 6b	שבר
מִשַּׁבַּת	pref. id.)(n. com. s. (suff. שַׁבַּתּוֹ, pl. שַׁבָּתוֹת)	שבת
מִשַּׁבֵּת	pref. id.)(Kal inf. constr. (suff. שִׁבְתִּי) d. 13a	ישב
מִשַּׁבַּתָּהּ	[for תָּהּ § 4. rem. 1] noun masc. pl., suff. 3 pers. sing. fem. from [מִשְׁבָּת] dec. 8a	שבת

a Pr. 17. 15.   a Ge. 26. 35.   e Ne. 5. 7, 10; 32.   a Pr. 22. 26.   c Nu. 4. 27, 31, 32.   i Je. 40. 5.   p 1 Ch. 7. 28.   u Is. 27. 12.   a 1 Ki. 19. 11.
Da. 11. 32.   b Je. 4. 17.   f 2 Ch. 19. 7.   u Eze. 20. 40.   d Le. 25. 49.   k Pr. 3. 25.   q Da. 2. 23 ; 4. 34.   v Ru. 2. 18.   b Is. 65. 14.
De. 11. 12.   c Ho. 14. 1.   g Ju. 5. 11.   v Is. 30. 27.   e De. 28. 5, 17.   l Ps. 62. 5.   r Jos. 4. 2, 4.   v Ge. 24. 8.   c Ps. 119. 118.
Ps. 17. 13.   d Je. 50. 21.   h Ju. 5. 11.   w Dc. 1. 12.   f Ex. 12. 34.   m Nu. 31. 23.   s Ps. 65. 8.   x Jos. 2. 17, 20.   d Job 41. 17.
Job 34. 10.   e Zec. 14. 4.   i Job 30. 3.   x Ps. 37. 4.   g De. 24. 10.   n Je. 5. 6.   t Ps. 145. 16.   y Ex. 28. 11.   e Is. 58. 13.
1 Sa. 1. 10.   n Je. 23. 36.   k Nu. 4. 19, 49.   y Ps. 20. 6.   h Am. 5. 11.   o Je. 2. 19.   u Pr. 11. 26.   z Ex. 28. 20.   f La. 1. 7.
g Pr. 14. 10.

מִשַׁבַּתּוֹתַי	1 pref. מ (noun com. pl., suff. 1 pers. sing. from שַׁבָּת, comp. מִשְׁבַּת ; 1 bef. lab.	שבת
מִשְׁבְּתֵיכֶם	defect. for מוֹשְׁבֹתֵיכֶם (q. v.)	ישב
מִשְׂגָּב	noun masc. sing. dec. 8a	שׂגב
מִשְׂגַּב	id., constr. st.	שׂגב
מִשְׂגַּבּוֹ	id., suff. 3 pers. sing. masc.	שׂגב
מִשְׂגַּבִּי	id., suff. 1 pers. sing.	שׂגב
מַשְׂגֶּה	1 Hiph. part. sing. masc.; 1 bef. lab.	שׂנה
מִשְׂגֶּה	noun masc. sing.	שׂנה
מַשְׂגִּיא	Hiph. part. sing. masc.	שׂנה
מַשְׂגִּיחַ	Hiph. part. sing. masc.	שׂנח
מְשֻׁגָּע	Pual part. sing. masc. dec. 2b	שׁגע
מְשֻׁגָּעִים	id. pl., abs. st.	שׁגע
מַשֶּׂגֶת	Hiph. part. sing. f. [of מַשִּׂיג § 39. No. 4 d]	נשׂג
מִשְׂדֵ	pref. מ (noun masc. sing.	שׂדה
מִשְׂדַּ	pref. id. (noun masc. sing.	שׂדד
מְשַׂדֵּד	Piel part. s. m. [for מְשַׂדֵּד comp. § 10. r. 4]	שׂדד
מִשְׂדֶּה	m 1 n. m. s., constr. of שָׂדֶה d. 9 b ; 1 bef. lab.	שׂדה
מִשְׂדְרוֹת	1 pref. id. (id. with pl. fem. term., constr. of שָׂדְרוֹת ; 1 id.	
מְשַׁדַּי	pref. מ (name of God, the Almighty, שַׁדָּי with the pl. term. ־ֵ	שׂדד
מִשְׂדֵי	pref. id. (noun masc. pl. constr. fr. שָׂדֶה d. 9 b	שׂדה
מִשְׂדַיִם	pref. id. (for שָׂדַיִם, noun masc. du., constr. שְׂדֵי from שַׁד (§ 31. rem. 5)	שׂדד
מִשְׂדְמוֹת	1 pref. id. (noun fem. pl. constr. from שְׂדֵמָה dec. 11 c (§ 42. rem. 4); 1 bef. lab.	שׂדם

[מָשָׁה] to draw out, Ex. 2. 10. Hiph. id. 2 Sa. 22. 17; Ps. 18. 17.

    מֹשֶׁה (drawing out, deliverer ; or, in a passive sense, drawn out) pr. name, Moses, the great leader, lawgiver and prophet of the Israelites, the son of Amram, of the tribe of Levi.

    מֶשִׁי masc. silk, Eze. 16. 10, 13.

    נְמֻשִׁי (drawn out) pr. name masc. 1 Ki. 19. 16; 2 Ki. 9. 2.

מַשֶּׁה	noun masc. sing., constr. of [מַשֶּׁה] dec. 9 a	נשׂה
מֹשֶׁה	pref. מ (noun masc. sing. irr. (§ 45)	שׂיה
מֹשֶׁה	1 pr. name masc. ; 1 bef. lab.	משה
מָשׁוּ	Kal pret. 3 pers. pl.	מוש
מַשׁאָה	1 noun fem. sing ; 1 bef. lab.	שׁוא
מָשׁוּב	pref. מ (Kal inf. constr. dec. 1 a	שׁוב
מְשׁוֹבֵב	1 pr. name masc. ; 1 bef. (:)	שׁוב
מְשׁוֹבֵב	Pilel part. sing. masc.	שׁוב
מְשׁוֹבֶבֶת	Pulal part. sing. fem. [of מְשׁוֹבָב § 39. No. 4]	שׁוב
מְשׁוּבַת	noun fem. sing. constr. of [מְשׁוּבָה] dec. 10	שׁוב
מְשׁוּבֹתֵיכֶם	id. pl., suff. 2 pers. pl. masc.	שׁוב

מְשׁוּבֹתֵינוּ	id. pl., suff. pers. pl.	שׁוב
מְשׁוּבָתָם	id. sing., suff. 3 pers. pl. masc.	שׁוב
מְשׁוּגָתִי	noun fem. s., suff. 1 pers. s. fr. [מְשׁוּגָה] d. 10	שׁוג
מָשׁוֹד	in full for מָשֹׁד (q. v.)	שׁדד
מַשְׁוָה	Hiph. part. sing. masc.	שׁוה
מָשׁוֹחַ	1 Kal inf. abs.; 1 bef. lab.	משח
מָשׁוּחַ	1 id. part. pass. sing. masc. ; 1 id.	משח
מָשׁוֹט	noun masc. sing.	שׁוט
מְשׁוֹט	qq pref. מ (Kal inf. constr.	שׁוט
מְשׁוֹטְטִים	Pilel part. masc. pl. [of מְשׁוֹטֵט] dec. 7 b	שׁוט
מְשׁוֹטַיִךְ	noun masc. pl., suff. 2 pers. sing. fem. from [מָשׁוֹט] dec. 1 b	שׁוט
מִשֻׁכַּבְתּוֹ	noun fem. sing., suff. 3 pers. sing. masc. [from מָשְׁכָּבָה for מִשְׁכָּבָה]	שׁכב
מְשׁוֹלִי	Kal inf. abs.	משׁל
מְשׂוּמִי	pref. מ (Kal inf., suff. 1 pers. s. d. 1 a	שׂום
מְשׁוֹמֵם	Poel part. sing. masc.	שׁמם
מְשַׁוֵּעַ	Piel part. sing. masc. [for מְשַׁוֵּעַ § 15. rem. 1]	שׁוע
מָשׁוֹר	pref. מ (noun masc. sing.	שׁור
מְשׂוֹרָה	noun fem. sing.	משׂר
מְשׁוֹרֵר	Pilel part. sing. masc. dec. 7 b	שׁיר
מָשׂוֹשׂ	noun masc. sing. dec. 3 a	שׂושׂ
מְשׂוֹשׂ	1 id., constr. st.; 1 bef. lab.	שׂושׂ
מְשׂוֹשָׂהּ	id., suff. 3 pers. sing. fem.	שׂושׂ
מְשׂוֹשִׂי	id., suff. 1 pers. sing.	שׂושׂ
מָשׁוּזָר	Hoph. part. sing. masc.	שׁזר

[מָשַׁח] ו' fut יִמְשַׁח, inf. מְשֹׁחַ, מָשְׁחָה, prop. as in Arab. to draw the hand over anything ; hence Syr. to measure.—I. to smear or rub over ; with oil, to anoint ; with paint, to paint, Je. 22. 14.—II. to anoint, to consecrate by unction.—III. to consecrate, appoint, constitute.—IV. to anoint oneself, with בְּ Am. 6. 6. Niph. to be anointed.

    מְשַׁח Chald. masc. oil, Ezr. 6. 9 ; 7. 22.

    מָשִׁיחַ masc. dec. 3 a.—I. adj. anointed.—II. subst. the anointed, applied to priests, kings ; hence the Messiah, Christ.

    מָשְׁחָה fem. constr. מִשְׁחַת (no vowel change) —I. an anointing, unction.—II. portion, Le. 7. 35.

    מִשְׁחָה fem. part, portion, Nu. 18. 8, and perh. so in Ex. 40. 15.

    מִמְשַׁח masc. extension, spreading out, Eze. 28. 14

מְשַׁח	1 Chald. noun masc. sing.; 1 id.	משח
מְשָׁחֵהוּ	Kal imp. masc. sing. [מְשַׁח], suff. 3 pers. sing. masc. (§ 16. rem. 11)	משח
מָשְׁחוֹ	id. inf., suff. 3 pers. sing. masc.	משח

a Eze. 22. 26.   f Job 12. 23.   l Pr. 19. 26.   q De. 15. 2.   v Eze. 38. 8.   Job 19. 4.   Zec. 4. 10.   1 Ch. 23. 29.   1 Ki. 1. 34.
b Is. 25. 12.   g Ca. 2. 9.   m Le. 27. 28.   r Ex. 12. 4.   y Pr. 1. 32.   Job 5. 21.   Eze. 27. 6.   2 Ch. 29. 28.   Ezr. 6. 9; 7. 22.
Is. 33. 16.   h 1 Sa. 21. 16.   n Ne. 12. 29.   s Nu. 14. 44.   z Je. 3. 32.   Is. 5. 5.   Ho. 2. 13.   1 Sa. 16. 12.
Job 12. 16.   i Le. 14. 21.   o Is. 28. 9.   t 2 Ch. 36. 13.   Je. 14. 7.   Ge. 37. 8.   Je. 49. 25.   Le. 7. 36.
Ge. 43. 12.   k Job 24.9; Is.66.11.   p De. 32. 32.   u Is. 58. 12.   Ho. 14. 5.   Eze. 27. 29.   Is. 44. 7.   qq Job 1. 7.

מָשְׁחוּ	id. pret. 3 pers. pl. . . .	משח
מְשָׁחוֹ	id. pret. 3 pers. sing. m., suff. 3 pers. sing. m.	משח
מִשְׁחוּ	id. imp. pl. masc. . . .	משח
מִשְׂחוֹק	pref. מִ)(noun masc. sing. . .	שחק
מִשְׁחוֹר	pref. id.)(noun masc. sing. . .	שחר
מְשֻׁחִים	Kal part. pass. masc. pl. of מָשׁוּחַ dec. 3 a	משח
מֹשְׁחִים	id. part. act. masc. pl. [of מֹשֵׁחַ] dec. 7 b	משח
מְשִׁיחִים	Hiph. part. masc. pl. [of מָשִׁיחַ] dec. 1 b	שחק
מַשְׁחִית	Hiph. part. or subst. m. d. 1 b ; ּו bef. lab.	שחת
מִשְׁחִיתוֹתָם	pref. מִ)(noun fem. pl., suff. 3 pers. pl. masc. from [שְׁחִית] dec. 1 a .	שחה
מַשְׁחִיתִים	Hiph. part. masc. pl. of מַשְׁחִית dec. 1 b	שחת
מַשְׁחִיתָם	id. sing., suff. 3 pers. pl. masc. .	שחת
מַשְׁחִתָם	defect. for מַשְׁחִיתָם (q. v.) .	שחת
מְשָׁחֲךָ	Kal pret. 3 pers. sing. m., suff. 2 pers. sing. m.	משח
מְשַׁחְנוּ	id. pret. 1 pers. pl. .	משח
מְשַׁחֵק	ְו Piel (§ 14. r. 1) part. s. m. d. 7 b ; ּו bef.lab.	שחק
מִשְׂחָק	noun masc. sing. .	שחק
מְשַׂחֲקִים	Piel (§ 14. r. 1) part. masc. pl. of מְשַׂחֵק d. 7 b	שחק
מְשַׂחֶקֶת	id. part. sing. fem. dec. 13	שחק
מִשְׁחָר	noun masc. sing. .	שחר
מַשְׁחֲרֵי	ּו the foll. with suff. 1 pers. sing.; ּו bef. lab.	שחר
מְשַׁחֲרֵי	Piel part. pl. constr. [fr. מְשַׁחֵר §14. r. 1] d. 7 b	שחר
מָשַׁחְתָּ	Kal pret. 2 pers. sing. masc.; acc. shifted	משח
מָשַׁחְתָ	by conv. ּו, bef. lab. for ְו (§ 8. r. 7)	משח
מִשְׁחַת	pref. מִ)(noun fem. sing. dec. 13 a	שחת
מִשְׁחָת	ּו noun fem. sing., constr. of מִשְׁחָה (no pl.); ּו bef. lab.	משח
מִשְׁחַת	noun masc. sing.,constr. of [מִשְׁחָת] dec. 2 b	שחת
מָשְׁחָת	Hoph. part. sing. masc. dec. 2 b	שחת
מָשְׁחַת	id., constr. st. .	שחת
מָשְׁחָתוֹ	noun masc. sing., suff. 3 pers. sing. masc. [from מָשְׁחָת]	שחת
מְשַׁחְתוֹ	ְו Kal pret. 2 pers. sing. masc., suff. 3 pers. sing. masc.; ּו for ְו, conv.	משח
מְשַׁחְתִּיו	id. pret. 1 pers. sing., suff. 3 pers. sing. masc.	משח
מְשַׁחְתִּיךָ	id. id., suff. 2 pers. sing. masc.	משח
מַשְׁחִתִים	defect. for מַשְׁחִיתִים (q. v.)	שחת
מַשְׁחִתָם	noun m. sing., suff. 3 pers. pl. m. [fr. מַשְׁחָת]	שחת
מָשְׁחָתָם	Kal inf. [מָשְׁחָה § 8. r. 10], suff. 3 p. pl. m.	משח
מַשְׁחִתָם	pref. מִ)(Piel inf. (שַׁחֵת § 14. rem. 1), suff. 3 pers. pl. masc. dec. 7 b	שחת
מִשְׁטֵי	pref. id.)(Kal inf. constr. defect. for שׁוּט	שוט
מִשְׂטוֹחַ	noun masc. sing. .	שטח
מִשְׁטַח	noun masc. sing., constr. of [מִשְׁטָח] d. 2 b	שטח
מְשֹׁטְטוֹת	Pilel part. fem. pl. [of מְשׁוֹטֵט dec. 13, from שׁוֹט masc.]	שוט

מַשְׂטֵמָה	noun fem. sing. . . .	שטם
מִשְׁטָרוֹ	noun m. s., suff. 3 pers. s. m. [fr. מִשְׁטָר]	שטר
מֵשִׁי	ּן n. m. s. [for מְשִׁי § 35. r. 14]; for ן see lett. ּו	משה
מֵשִׁי	ּו pr. name masc., see מוּשִׁי; ּו bef. lab.	מוש
מֵשִׁיב	Hiph. part. sing. masc. dec. 3 b .	שוב
מְשִׁיבוֹ	pref. מִ)(noun masc. sing., suff. 3 pers. sing. masc. [fr. שֵׁיב or שָׁיב]	שיב
מְשִׁיבֵי	constr. of the foll. . .	שוב
מְשִׁיבִים	Hiph. part. masc. pl. of מֵשִׁיב dec. 3 b	שוב
מְשִׁיבַת	id. part. sing. fem. constr. [of מְשִׁיבָה] dec. 10	שוב
מַשִּׂיג	Hiph. part. sing. masc. dec. 1 b	נשג
מַשִּׂיגֵהוּ	id. with suff. 3 pers. sing. masc.	נשג
מְשֵׁיזָב	Ch. Peil part. sing. masc. (§ 48) .	שוב
מְשֵׁיזַבְאֵל	pr. name masc.	שוב
מָשִׁיחַ	noun masc. sing. dec. 3 a . .	משח
מְשִׁיחַ	id., constr. st. . . .	משח
מְשִׁיחוֹ	id., suff. 3 pers. sing. masc.	משח
מְשִׁיחִי	id., suff. 1 pers. sing.	משח
מְשִׁיחֶךָ	id., suff. 2 pers. sing. masc. [for מְשִׁיחֲךָ]	משח
מְשִׂים	Hiph. part. sing. masc.	שום
מַשִּׁיקוֹת	Hiph. part. fem. pl. [of מַשִּׁיקָה dec. 10, from מַשִּׁיק masc.]	נשק
מְשִׁיר	pref. מִ)(noun masc. sing. dec. 1 a	שיר
מְשִׁירִי	ּו pref. מִ)(id., suff. 1 pers. sing.; ּו bef. lab.	שיר
מְשִׁיתִהוּ	Kal pret. 1 p. s. [מָשִׁיתִי] with suff. 3 p. s. m.	משה

מָשַׁךְ ְו fut. יִמְשֹׁךְ.—I. to draw; to draw any one to a place, with בְּ , אֶל of the place; with מִן to draw out; espec. מָ הַקֶּשֶׁת to draw the bow; מָ הַיּוֹבֵל to draw, i. e. to sound the trumpet, perh. in protracted sounds.—II. to draw out, stretch, hold out the hand, in token of fellowship, Ho. 7. 5.—III. to draw out, prolong, continue a kindness to any one.—IV. to make durable, strengthen, Ec. 2. 3.—V. to scatter, as seed, Am. 9. 13; intrans. to spread out.—VI. to seize, take, Ex. 12. 21; to hold, with בְּ Ju. 5. 14.—VII. to draw, take away, remove. Niph. to be protracted, delayed. Pu. I. protracted, deferred, Pr. 13. 12.—II. Is. 18. 2, 7, Eng. vers. " scattered;" Lee, spoiled; Gesenius (who refers this prophecy to the Ethiopians) stout, strong.

מֶשֶׁךְ masc.—I. acquisition, Job 28. 18.—II. a scattering, Ps. 126. 6.—III. pr. name of a son of Japhet, and a people descended from him.

מֹשְׁכוֹת (מֹשְׁכָה) fem. pl. (of מֹשְׁבָה or מֹשֶׁכֶת) cords, bands, Job 38. 31, Lee, attractions, influences.

מֶשֶׁךְ ְן pr. name of a people; for ן see lett. ּו | משך

מֶשֶׁךְ • ⁿ ׳⁰ noun masc. sing.; ⁱ bef. lab. .   משך

מְשֹׁךְ • Kal imp. sing. masc. . .   משך

מֹשֵׁךְ • id. part. sing. masc. dec. 7 b .   משך

מִשְׁכָּב • noun masc. sing. dec. 2 b .   שכב

מִשְׁכַּב • id., constr. st. . . .   שכב

מֻשְׁכָּב • Hoph. part. sing. masc. (§ 11. rem. 10)   שכב

מִשְׁכְּבֵהּ • Chald. noun masc. sing., suff. 3 pers. sing.

    masc. from [מִשְׁכָּב] dec. 2 a .   שכב

מִשְׁכָּבוֹ • noun m. s., suff. 3 p. s. m. fr. מִשְׁכָּב d. 2 b   שכב

מִשְׁכְּבוֹתָם • id. pl. fem., suff. 3 pers. pl. masc. .   שכב

מִשְׁכָּבִי • id. sing., suff. 1 pers. sing. . .   שכב

מִשְׁכְּבֵי • id. pl., constr. st. . . .   שכב

מִשְׁכְּבִי • Ch. noun m. s., suff. 1 p. s. fr. [מִשְׁכַּב] d. 2 a   שכב

מִשְׁכָּבְךָ • noun m. s., suff. 2 pers. s. f. fr. מִשְׁכָּב d. 2 b   שכב

מִשְׁכָּבְךָ

מִשְׁכָּבֶךָ } id., suff. 2 pers. sing. masc. .   שכב

מִשְׁכְּבָךְ • Chald. noun masc. sing., suff. 2 pers. sing.

    masc. from [מִשְׁכַּב] dec. 2 a .   שכב

מִשְׁכַּבְכֶם • noun m. s., suff. 2 p. pl. m. fr. מִשְׁכָּב d. 2 b   שכב

מִשְׁכַּבְכֶם • id. with suff. 3 pers. pl. masc. .   שכב

מֹשַׁכְתְּ • pref. מִ) (Kal part. act. fem. from שֵׁכָב masc.   שכב

מָשְׁכָה • Kal pret. 3 pers. sing. fem. .   משך

מִשְׁכוּ

מִשְׁכוּ } id. imp. pl. masc. (§ 8. rem. 12) .   משך

מֹשְׁכֵי • id. part. act. pl. constr. masc. fr. מֹשֵׁךְ d. 7 b   משך

מַשְׂכִּיּוֹת • noun fem. pl. of מַשְׂכִּית (q. v.) .   שכה

מַשְׂכִּיל • Hiph. part. sing. masc. . .   שכל

מַשְׂכִּיל • Hiph. part. sing. masc. dec. 1 b .   שכל

מַשְׂכִּילֵי • ⁱ id. pl. constr.; ⁱ bef. lab. .   שכל

מַשְׂכִּים • Hiph. part. sing. masc. dec. 1 b .   שכם

מַשְׂכִּים • id. id. adverbially ; or perhaps Hiph. part.

    pl. [of מַשְׂכָּה] dec. 9 a . .   שכה

מֹשְׂכִים • Kal part. act. masc. pl. of מֹשֵׁךְ dec. 7 b   משך

מַשְׂכִּימֵי • Hiph. part. pl. constr. masc. fr. מַשְׂכִּים d. 1 b   שכם

מַשְׂכִּית • n. f. s., pl. מַשְׂכִּיּוֹת (§ 39. No. 4. r. 1 note)   שכה

מַשְׂכִּיתוֹ • id., suff. 3 pers. sing. masc. .   שכה

מַשְׂכִּיתָם • id. pl., suff. 3 pers. pl. masc. .   שכה

מַשְׂכֵּל • pref. מִ) (for שֵׂכֶל noun m. s. see under שֵׂכֶל   שכל

מְשַׂכֶּלֶת • Piel part. sing. f. [of מְשַׂכֵּל] comp. מְשַׂכֶּלֶת   שכל

מַשְׂכִּלִים • ⁱ Hiph. part. masc. pl. of מַשְׂכִּיל dec. 1 b ;

    ⁱ bef. lab. . . . .   שכל

מַשְׂכֶּלֶת • [for מַשְׂכֶּלֶת] Hiph. part. sing. fem. of מַשְׂכִּיל

    (§ 39. No. 4 d) . . .   שכל

מְשַׂכֶּלֶת

מְשַׂכֵּלָה } ⁱ Piel part. sing. fem. [of מְשַׂכֵּל] comp.

    מְשַׂכֵּלָה; ⁱ bef. lab. . .   שכל

מְשַׂכְּבֵם • pref. מ) (pr. name of a place .   שכם

מִשְׁכָּמָה • pref. מִ) (noun masc. sing., suff. 3 pers.

    sing. fem. (§ 3. r. 3) fr. שֶׁכֶם (§ 35. r. 10)   שכם

מִשְׁכְּמוֹ • pref. id.) (id. with suff. 3 pers. sing. masc.   שכם

מִשְׁכָּן • noun masc. sing. dec. 2 b . .   שכן

מִשְׁכַּן • ⁱ ⁱ id., constr. st.; ⁱ bef. lab. . .   שכן

מִשְׁכְּנֵהּ • Chald. noun masc. sing., suff. 3 pers. sing.

    masc. from [מִשְׁכַּן] dec. 2 a .   שכן

מִשְׁכָּנוֹ • noun m. s., suff. 3 p. s. m. from מִשְׁכָּן d. 2 b   שכן

מִשְׁכְּנוֹת • id. pl. abs. fem. comp. מִשְׁכְּנֵי   שכן

מִשְׁכְּנוֹת • id. pl. constr. fem. . .   שכן

מִשְׁכְּנוֹתָיו • ⁱ id. pl., suff. 3 pers. sing. masc.; ⁱ bef. lab.   שכן

מִשְׁכְּנוֹתַיִךְ • id. pl., suff. 2 pers. sing. fem. .   שכן

מִשְׁכְּנוֹתֶיךָ • id. pl., suff. 2 pers. sing. masc. .   שכן

מִשְׁכְּנוֹתֵינוּ • id. pl., suff. 1 pers. pl. .   שכן

מָשְׁכֵנִי • Kal imp. sing. masc., suff. 1 pers. sing. .   משך

מִשְׁכָּנִי • noun masc. sing., suff. 1 p. s. fr. מִשְׁכָּן d. 2 b   שכן

מִשְׁכְּנֵי • ⁱ id. pl. constr. [of מִשְׁכָּנִים] comp. מִשְׁכְּנוֹת   שכן

מִשְׁכְּנֵיהֶם • id. pl., suff. 3 pers. pl. masc. .   שכן

מִשְׁכַּנְתָּהּ • pref. מִ) ((prop. adj.) subst. fem. sing., suff.

    3 pers. s. f. [fr. שֶׁכֶנֶת d. 13 b] fr. שָׁכֵן m.   שכן

מִשְׁכְּנֹתֶיהָ • noun masc. with pl. fem. term. and suff. 3

    pers. sing. fem. from מִשְׁכָּן dec. 2 b   שכן

מִשְׁכְּנוֹתֶיךָ • id., suff. 2 pers. sing. masc. see מִשְׁכְּנוֹתֶיךָ   שכן

מִשְׁכְּנֹתָם • id., suff. 3 pers. pl. masc. (§ 4. rem. 2) .   שכן

מְשָׁרֶבֶת • Piel part. sing. fem. [of מְשַׁבֵּר]   שבר

מַשְׁבַּרְתִּי • noun f. s., suff. 1 pers. s. fr. [מַשְׁבֶּרֶת] d. 13 c

    (comp. § 35. rem. 8) . .   שבר

מַשְׁבַּרְתֶּךָ • id., suff. 2 pers. sing. masc. (for תְּךָ) .   שבר

מַשְׁבַּרְתֵּךְ • id., suff. 2 pers. sing. fem. .   שבר

מָשַׁכְתָּ • ⁱ Kal pret. 2 pers. sing. masc.; acc. shifted

    bef. ⁱ, for ⁱ, conv. (§ 8. rem. 7) .   משך

מָשַׁכְתִּי • ⁱ id. pret. 1 pers. sing.; acc. id. .   משך

מְשַׁכְתִּיךָ • id. id. with suff. 1 pers. sing. .   משך

מָשַׁל ⁱ ׳⁰ fut. יִמְשָׁל . —I. *to rule, have dominion*; with בְּ,

עַל of that *over* which one rules.—II. *to have power*

to do anything, Ex. 21. 8. Part. מֹשֵׁל *ruler,*

prince. Hiph. *to cause to rule, give dominion to,*

appoint ruler. Inf. הַמְשֵׁל *dominion,* Job 25. 2.

מֶשֶׁל masc. dec. 7 c, *dominion,* Zec. 9. 10.

מִמְשָׁל masc. (no vowel change) *dominion,* Da.

11. 3, 5; pl. concr. *rulers,* 1 Ch. 26. 6.

מֶמְשָׁלָה fem. constr. מֶמְשֶׁלֶת, with suff. מֶמְשַׁלְתּוֹ

(§ 42. rem. 5).—I. *dominion, rule.*—II. *dominion,*

kingdom, 2 Ki. 20. 13.—III. meton. *rulers, lords,*

2 Ch. 32. 9.

ᵃ Ps. 126. 6.   ᵉ Da. 4. 2, 7, 10.   ⁱ Mi. 7. 5.   ⁱ Da. 11. 33.   ⁱ Job 17. 4.   ᵏ Job 31. 22.   ⁱ Je. 9. 18.   ᵗ Je. 51. 30.   ᵘ Ge. 29. 15.

ᵇ Job 28. 18.   ᶠ Is. 57. 7, 8.   ʲ De. 21. 3.   ⁿ Je. 5. 8.   ᵖ Ex. 23. 26.   ˡ Is. 22. 16.   ᵖ Ca. 1. 4.   ˢ Nu. 24. 5.   ᵛ Ru. 2. 12.

ᶜ Ps. 36. 11.   ᵍ 2 Ki. 6. 12.   ᵏ Ex. 12. 21.   ᵒ Ju. 5. 14.   ᵍ Da. 1. 4.   ᵐ 1 Ch. 21. 29.   ᵠ Ps. 46. 5.   ᵏ Ps. 49. 12.   ʷ Ju. 4. 6.

ᵈ Ps. 109. 12.   ʰ Da. 2. 38, 29.   ⁱ Eze. 32. 20.   ᵖ Pr. 19. 14.   ʳ Je. 7. 15.   ⁿ Eze. 25. 4.   ʸ Je. 51. 7.   ˣ Ju. 4. 7.

ⁱ 2 Ki. 4. 32.   ⁱ Ps. 4. 5.   ᵏ Is. 5. 18; 66. 19.   ⁱ Eze. 8. 12.   ˢ 2 Ki. 2. 19, 21.   ⁿ Jos. 22. 29.   ˢ Ex. 3. 22.   ᵏ Ge. 31. 7 41.   Je. 31. 3.

ⁱ Da. 7. 1.   ᵏ Is. 57. 8.   ⁱ Ps. 73. 7.   ⁿ Nu. 33. 52.   Eze. 36. 13.   ⁱ Is. 54. 2.

מָשָׁל

מָשָׁל ‹‹ר'›› masc. dec. 4 a.—I. *similitude, parable.*—II. *sentiment, sententious saying, maxim.*—III. *proverb.* —IV. *by-word; subject of a taunting proverb.*

מָשַׁל.—I. *to utter a comparison* or *similitude,* with בְּ, עַל, אֶל *concerning* any one in derision, Joel 2. 17.—II. *to use a proverb.* Part. מֹשְׁלִים *using similitudes, poets,* Nu. 21. 27. Niph. *to be* or *become like, similar,* with בְּ, עִם, אֶל. Pi. *to use a parable,* Eze. 21. 5. Hiph. *to compare,* Is. 46. 5. Hithp. *to become like, similar,* Job 30. 19.

מָשָׁל masc. *something like, similar,* Job 41. 25.

מָשָׁל masc. *taunt, by-word,* Job 17. 6.

מָשַׁל ‹ר'› Kal pret. 3 pers. sing. masc. for מָשַׁל (§ 8. rem. 7); ו bef. lab.   .   .   .   .   משל

מֹשֶׁל noun masc. sing., constr. of מָשָׁל dec. 4 a   משל

מְשֹׁל ‹ר'› Kal inf. constr. or imp. sing. masc. (§ 8. rem. 18); ו bef. lab.   .   .   .   משל

מָשְׁלֶבֶת Pual part. fem. pl. [of מְשֻׁלָּבָה fr. מָשְׁלָב m.]   שלב

מִשְׁלֵנַי / מִשְׁלָנַי ‹ר'› pref. מִ ✗ noun masc. sing. (§ 35. rem. 2); ו bef. lab.   .   .   שלנ

מָשְׁלָה ‹ר'› Kal pret. 3 pers. s. f. [for מָשֲׁלָה § 8. r. 7]   .   משל

מִשְׁלֹה pref. מִ ✗ pr. name of a place, see שִׁילֹה   שלה

מֹשְׁלָה Kal part. sing., fem. of מוֹשֵׁל   משל

מָשְׁלוּ id. pret. 3 pers. pl.   משל

מֹשְׁלוֹ ‹ר'› id. part. act. sing. masc., suff. 3 pers. sing. masc. from מוֹשֵׁל dec. 7 b; ו bef. lab.   משל

מְשָׁלוֹ ‹‹r'›› n.m.s., suff. 3 p.s.m. fr. [מָשָׁל] d. 6 c; ו id.   משל

מֹשְׁלָיו Kal part.pl., suff. 3 p.s.m. (§ 4. r. 1) fr. מוֹשֵׁל d. 7 b   משל

מָשְׁלוֹ noun m. s., suff. 3 pers. s. m. fr. מֹשֶׁל d. 4 a   משל

מִשְׁלוֹ pref. מִ ✗ pr. name of a place, see שִׁילֹה   שלה

מִשְׁלוֹחַ ‹ר'› noun masc. sing.; ו bef. lab.   שלח

מִשְׁלוֹם ‹ר'› pref. מִ ✗ noun masc. sing. dec. 3 a   שלם

מְשַׁלֵּחַ ‹ר'› Piel part. sing. masc. dec 7 b; ו bef. lab.   שלח

מְשֻׁלָּח Pual part. sing. masc.   שלח

מִשְׁלַח noun masc. sing., constr. of [מִשְׁלָח] dec. 2 b   שלח

מְשַׁלֵּחַ pref. מִ ✗ Kal inf. constr.   שלח

מִשְׁלֹחַ ‹ר'› defect. for מִשְׁלוֹחַ (q. v.)   שלח

מְשַׁלְּחֵי / מְשַׁלְּחִים Piel part. pl. masc. constr. and abs. from מְשַׁלֵּחַ dec. 7 b   שלח

מְשַׁלֶּחְךָ id. sing., suff. 2 pers. sing. masc. (§ 16. r. 15)   שלח

מִשְׁלַחַת noun fem. sing.   שלח

מִשְׁלֵי noun masc. pl. constr. from מָשָׁל dec. 4 a   משל

מֹשְׁלֵי Kal part. pl. constr. masc from מוֹשֵׁל d. 7 b   משל

מַשְׁלִיחַ ‹‹ר'›› Hiph. part. sing. masc.   שלה

מַשְׁלִיךְ Hiph. part. sing. masc. dec. 1 b   שלך

מַשְׁלִיכֵי id. pl., constr st.   שלך

מְשָׁלִים noun masc. pl. of מָשָׁל dec. 4 a   משל

מֹשְׁלִים Kal part. act. masc. pl. of מוֹשֵׁל dec. 7 b   משל

מֻשְׁלָךְ Hoph. part. sing. masc. (§ 11. rem. 10)   שלך

מֻשְׁלָכִים ‹d› id. pl., abs. st.   שלך

מֻשְׁלֶכֶת id. part. sing. fem.   שלך

מִשְׁלָל ‹ר'› pref. מִ ✗ noun masc. s. d. 4 a; ו bef. lab.   שלל

מִשְׁלַל ‹ר'› pref. id. ✗ id., constr. st.; ו id.   שלל

מְשַׁלֵּם ‹ר'› Piel part. sing. masc. dec. 7 b; ו id.   שלם

מְשֻׁלָּם ‹ר'› pr. name masc.; ו id.   שלם

מְשֻׁלָּמָה pref. מִ ✗ pr. name masc.   שלם

מְשֻׁלֵּמוֹת pr. name masc.   שלם

מְשַׁלְּמֵי ‹ר'› Piel part. pl., constr. masc. from מְשַׁלֵּם dec. 7 b; ו bef. lab.   שלם

מְשֶׁלֶמְיָה / מְשֶׁלֶמְיָהוּ pr. name masc.   שלם

מְשֻׁלָּמִים ‹c› Piel part. masc., pl. of מְשֻׁלָּם dec. 7 b   שלם

מְשֻׁלֶּמֶת pr. name masc.   שלם

מְשֻׁלֶּמֶת pr. name fem.   שלם

מִשֶּׁלָּנוּ preff. מִ & שֶׁ (for מִן אֲשֶׁר) ✗ pref. prep. ל with suff. 1 pers. pl. (§ 5)   ל

מְשֻׁלָּשׁ Pual part. sing. masc.   שלש

מְשֻׁלָּשׁוֹת ‹‹ר'›› id. part. pl. fem. [prop. from מְשֻׁלָּשָׁה] see מְשֻׁלֶּשֶׁת (§ 44. rem. 5)   שלש

מִשְׁלָשֹׁם ‹‹m›› pref. מִ ✗ adv.   שלש

מְשֻׁלֶּשֶׁת ‹‹n›› Pual part. s., fem. of מְשֻׁלָּשׁ, comp. מְשֻׁלָּשׁוֹת   שלש

מָשַׁלְתָּ / מָשָׁלְתָּ Kal pret. 2 pers. sing. masc.; acc. shifted ‹ו› by ו, for וְ conv. (§ 8. rem. 7)   משל

מִשָּׁם ‹ר'› pref. מִ ✗ adv.; ו bef. lab.   שם

מִשְׂמֹאול ‹c› / מִשְׂמֹאל pref. id. ✗ noun masc. sing. dec. 1 a   שמאל

מִשְּׂמֹאלוֹ ‹ר'› pref. id. ✗ id., suff. 3 p. s. m.; ו bef. lab.   שמאל

מַשְׂמְאִילִים ‹ר'› Hiph. part. pl. m. [for מַשְׂמִאלִים]; ו id.   שמאל

מִשְּׂמֹאלָם ‹ר'› pref. מִ ✗ noun masc. sing., suff. 3 pers. pl. masc. from שְׂמֹאל dec. 1 a; ו id.   שמאל

מִשְׁמָה ‹ר'› noun fem. sing. dec. 10; ו id.   שמם

מִשָּׂמוֹ ‹ר'› pref. מִ ✗ Kal inf. constr. (שׂוּם), suff. 3 pers. sing. masc. dec. 1 a   שום

מִשְׁמֹעַ in full for מִשְּׁמֹעַ (q. v.)   שמע

מִשְּׁמוּעָה ‹ר'› pref. מִ ✗ noun fem. sing. dec. 10   שמע

---

* Pr. 26. 7, 9.   ƒ La. 4. 7.   ɪ Job 41. 25.   ᵏ La. 3. 17.   ᵖ 1 Sa. 6. 3.   ᵘ 2 Sa. 20. 21.   ᵃ Joel 4. 4.   ᵉ Ge. 15. 9.   ⁱ 1 Ch. 12 2.

ᵇ Da. 11. 4, 5.   ᵍ Ps. 51. 9.   = Zec. 9. 10.   ˡ Pr. 6. 19.   ᵠ Je. 28. 16.   ᵛ Je. 14. 16.   ᵇ 2 Ki. 6. 11.   ᶠ Is. 63. 19.   ᵏ Ex. 14. 22, 29.

ᶜ 1 Sa. 24. 14.   ʰ Ps. 105. 19.   ᵐ Is. 52. 5.   ⁿ 1 Sa. 26. 11.   ʳ Is. 28. 14.   ˣ 1 Sa. 30. 19.   ᶜ Ge. 15. 9.   ᵍ De. 15. 6.   ˡ Nu. 24. 23.

ᵈ Ju. 8. 22.   ⁱ Is. 40. 10.   ⁿ Is. 11. 14.   ᵒ Est. 9. 19.   ˢ Ex. 8. 17.   ʸ 2 Sa. 8. 12.   ᵈ Eze. 42. 6.   ʰ 2 Ch. 4. 6, 7, 8.   Ps. 112. 7.

ᵉ Pr. 31. 21.   ʲ Je. 30. 21.   ᵉ Est. 9. 23.   ᵖ Is. 32. 20.   ᵗ Je. 19. 8.   ᶻ Ps. 38. 21.   = Ex. 4. 10.   ⁱ 1 Ki. 7. 39.

מִשְׂמוֹת٠	noun fem. pl. of מִשְׂמָה dec. 10 .	שמם
מְשַׂמְּחֵי٠	Piel part. pl. constr. masc. from שָׂמַח d. 7 b	שמח
מִשְּׁמֵי٠	pref. מִ)(noun masc. pl., constr. of שָׁמַיִם [from שָׁמַי § 38. rem. 2]	שמה
מַשְׁמִים	Hiph. part. sing. masc. .	שמה
מִשָּׁמַיִם	} pref. מִ)(noun masc. pl. [of שָׁמַי § 38. rem. 2] . .	שמה
מִשָּׁמַיִם	}	שמה
מַשְׁמִיעַ٠	Hiph. part. sing. masc. dec. 1 b ; ו bef. lab.	שמע
מַשְׁמִיעִים	id. pl., abs. st. . . .	שמע
מִשָּׁמְךָ٠	} pref. מִ)(noun masc. sing., suff. 2 pers.	שם
מִשִּׁמְךָ٠	} sing. masc. from שֵׁם dec. 7 a .	שם
מִשָּׁמָם	defect. for מִשּׁוֹמֵם (q. v.) . .	שמם
מִשָּׁמָן	} pref. מִ)(noun masc. sing. dec. 6 a	שמן
מִשָּׁמָן	} (§ 35. rem. 2) ; ו bef. lab.	שמן
מִשְׁמַן٠	noun masc. sing., constr. of [מִשְׁמָן] dec. 8 a (pl. c. [מַשְׁמַנֵּי]) ; ו id.	שמן
מִשַּׁמְנָהּ	} pref. מִ)(noun masc. sing., suff. 3 pers. sing. fem. from שֶׁמֶן dec. 6 a ; ו id.	שמן
מִשְׁמַנָּה	pr. name masc. . . .	שמן
מִשְׁמַנֵּי٠	} pref. מִ [for מִשְׁמַנֵּי])(noun m. pl. constr. fr. [שֶׁמֶן] dec. 8 a (§ 37. No. 3 c) ; ו bef. lab.	שמן
מִשְׁמַנִּים٠	noun masc. pl. of [מִשְׁמָן] dec. 8 a	שמן
מִשְׁמָע٠	pr. name masc. ; ו bef. lab.	שמע
מִשְׁמָע	pref. מִ)(Kal inf. constr. .	שמע
מִשְׁמָעוֹן٠	pref. id.)(pr. name of a tribe ; ו bef. lab.	שמע
מַשְׁמִעִים	defect. for מַשְׁמִיעִים (q. v.) .	שמע
מִשְׁמַעְתּוֹ	noun f. s., suff. 3 p. s. m. fr. [מִשְׁמַעַת] d. 13 a	שמע
מִשְׁמַעְתֶּךָ٠	id., suff. 2 pers. sing. masc. [for תְּךָ]	שמע
מִשְׁמַעֲתָם٠	id., suff. 3 pers. pl. masc.	שמע
מִשְׁמָר	noun masc. sing. dec. 2 b .	שמר
מִשְׁמָרוֹ٠	} pref. מִ)(Kal inf., suff. 3 p. s. m. ; ו bef. lab.	שמר
מִשְׁמְרוֹן٠	pref. id.)(pr. name of a country ; ו id.	שמר
מִשְׁמָרוֹת	noun fem., pl. abs. from מִשְׁמֶרֶת (§ 44. r. 5)	שמר
מִשְׁמָרוֹת٠	id. pl., constr. st. . .	שמר
מִשְׁמְרוֹתָם	id. pl., suff. 3 pers. pl. masc. (§ 4. rem. 2) .	שמר
מִשֹּׁמְרִי	pref. מִ)(Kal part. act. pl. constr. masc. from שֹׁמֵר dec. 7 b	שמר
מְשַׁמְּרִים٠	Piel part. masc. pl. of [מְשַׁמֵּר] dec. 7 b	שמר
מִשֹּׁמְרִים٠	pref. מִ)(noun masc. pl. of שׁוֹמֵר dec. 7 b	שמר
מִשְׁמַרְכֶם٠	noun masc. sing., suff. 2 pers. pl. masc.	שמר
מִשְׁמֶרֶת٠	} noun f. s. d. 13 a, comp. מִשְׁמָרוֹת ; ו bef. lab.	שמר
מִשְׁמַרְתּוֹ٠	id., suff. 3 pers. sing. masc.	שמר
מִשְׁמַרְתִּי٠	id., suff. 1 pers. sing.	שמר
מִשְׁמַרְתְּךָ٠	id., suff. 2 pers. sing. masc.	שמר
מִשְׁמַרְתָּם٠	id., suff. 3 pers. pl. masc. ; ו bef. lab.	שמר
מִשְּׁמֹתָם	pref. מִ)(noun masc. with pl. fem. term. and suff. 3 pers. pl. m. (§ 4. r. 2) from שֵׁם d. 7 a	שם

מְשַׂנְּאַי٠	Piel part. pl. masc., suff. 1 pers. sing. [fr. מְשַׂנֵּא § 10. rem. 7] dec. 7 b ; ו bef. lab.	שׂנא
מְשַׂנְּאַי٠	id. pl., constr. st.	שׂנא
מְשַׂנְּאִי	id. sing. with suff. 1 pers. sing. .	שׂנא
מְשֹׂנְאַי٠	} pref. מִ)(Kal part. act. pl., suff. 1 pers.	שׂנא
מְשֹׂנְאַי٠	} sing. from שׂוֹנֵא dec. 7 b ; ו bef. lab.	שׂנא
מְשַׂנְאָיו٠	Piel part. pl. masc., suff. 3 pers. sing. masc. [from מְשַׂנֵּא § 10. rem. 7] dec. 7 b ; ו id.	שׂנא
מְשַׂנְאֶיךָ٠	id. pl., suff. 2 pers. pl. masc. ; ו id.	שׂנא
מְשַׂנְאֵינוּ٠	id. pl., suff. 1 pers. pl. ; ו id.	שׂנא
מִשִּׂנְאָתוֹ٠	pref. מִ)(noun fem. sing., suff. 3 pers. sing. masc. from שִׂנְאָה (no pl.) ; ו id.	שׂנא
מִשֹּׂנְאָתֶיךָ٠	id. sing. (§ 4. r. 3), suff. 2 pers. sing. masc.	שׂנא
מְשַׁנֶּה٠	Piel part. sing. masc.	שנה
מִשְׁנֶה٠	noun masc. sing. dec. 9 a ; ו bef. lab. .	שנה
מִשְׁנֵה٠	id., constr. st.	שנה
מִשְׁנֵהוּ٠	id. with suff. 3 pers. sing. masc., ו bef. lab.	שנה
מִשְׁנֵי٠	pref. מִ)(num. card. masc., constr. of שְׁנַיִם	שנה
מְשַׁנְיָה٠	Chald. Pael part. sing. fem. [of מְשַׁנֵּא]	שנה
מִשְּׁנֵיהֶם٠	pref. מִ)(num. card. masc. (שְׁנַיִם) with suff. 3 pers. pl. masc.	שנה
מִשְּׁנָיו٠	pref. id.)(noun com. du., suff. 3 pers. sing. masc. from שֵׁן dec. 2 b ; ו bef. lab.	שנן
מִשְׁנִים٠	noun masc., pl. of מִשְׁנֶה dec. 9 a .	שנה
מִשְּׂנִיר٠	pref. מִ)(pr. name of a mount, see שְׂנִיר .	
מִשִּׁנְעָר٠	pref. id.)(pr. name of a country, see שִׁנְעָר ; ו bef. lab.	
מִשְׁנַת٠	pref. מִ)(noun fem. sing., constr. of שָׁנָה d. 11 a	שנה
מִשְׁנָתוֹ٠	pref. id.)(noun fem. s., constr. of שָׁנָה d. 11 b	ישן
מִשְּׁנָתְךָ٠	pref. id.)(id., suff. 2 pers. sing. m. [for שְׁנָתְךָ]	ישן
מִשְּׁנָתָם٠	pref. id.)(id., suff. 3 pers. pl. masc. .	ישן
מִשְׁסָה٠	noun fem. sing. dec. 10 . .	שסם

מָשַׁע   Root not used ; Arab. *to cleanse*.

    מֶשַׁע٠ masc. *a cleansing*, with pref. לְ adv. *clean*, Eze. 16. 4.

    מֵישָׁע (*cleansing*) pr. name masc. 1 Ch. 8. 12.

מַשְׁעִי٠	Hiph. part. sing. masc., suff. 1 pers. sing. [for מוֹשִׁיעִי] from מֹשִׁיעַ dec. 1 b	ישע
מִשָּׂעִיר٠	pref. מִ)(pr. name of a country	שׂער
מִשָּׁעָם٠	pr. name masc. ; ו bef. lab.	שעם
מִשְׁעָן٠	noun masc. sing.	שען
מִשְׁעָן٠	noun masc. sing. dec. 2 a	שען
מִשְׁעַן٠	id., constr. st.	שען
מִשְׁעֵנָה٠	} noun fem. sing. ; ו bef. lab.	שען
מִשְׁעֶנֶת٠	noun fem. sing. dec. 13 a	שען
מִשְׁעַנְתּוֹ٠	id., suff. 3 pers. sing. masc.	שען

a Is. 15. 6.   f 1 Ch. 15. 16.   i Ge. 27. 28, 39.   l De. 7. 8.   m Nu. 18. 3.   p Ps. 18. 18.   k Eze. 35. 11.   n Ezr. 1. 10.   r Is. 3. 1.
b Ps. 19. 9.   g 1Ki. 1. 47.   k Ne. 8. 10.   Ne. 7. 3.   Ex. 28. 10.   Ps. 68. 2.   Job 14. 20.   Pr. 6. 9.   2 Sa. 22. 19.
c Ps. 20. 7.   h Na. 1. 14.   1 Ch. 15. 28.   Jon. 2. 9.   Ps. 83. 3.   1 Sa. 8. 2.   Da. 7. 7.   Is. 42. 22.   Is. 3. 1.
d Eze. 3. 15.   Ex. 29. 21.   1 Sa. 22. 14.   Ps. 130. 6.   Ps. 44. 8, 11.   Is. 42. 22.   Is. 3. 1.
e Je. 4. 15.   Is. 17. 4.   Is. 11. 14.   Ge. 42. 19.   Ps. 9. 14.   De. 9. 28.   Job 29. 17.   2 Sa. 22. 3.

מִשְׁעַנְתִּי	id., suff. 1 pers. sing.	שׁען
מִשְׁעַנְתֶּךָ	id., suff. 2 pers. sing. m. [for תְּךָ]; וּ bef. lab.	שׁען
מִשְׁעָר	pref. מִ ‖ noun fem. sing. dec. 6 d; וּ id.	שׁער
מִשְׁעַר	pref. id. ‖ noun m. sing. constr. of שַׁעַר d. 4 d	שׁער
מִשְׁעֲרוֹת	pref. id. ‖ noun fem. pl. constr. from שַׁעֲרָה (no pl. abs.)	שׁער
מִשְׁעֲרִי	pref. id. ‖ noun fem. pl. constr. of שֵׂעָר d. 6 d	שׁער
מִשְׁעֶרֶת	pref. id. ‖ n. f. s., constr. of שַׂעֲרָה (no pl. abs.)	שׁער
מִשְׁעַרְתּוֹ	pref. id. ‖ id., suff. 3 pers. sing. masc.	שׁער
מִשְׁפָּה	noun masc. sing.	שׁפה
מִשְׁפָּחָה	noun fem. sing., constr. מִשְׁפַּחַת dec. 11 & 13 (§ 42. rem. 5); וּ bef. lab.	שׁפה
מִשְׁפָּחוֹת	id. pl., abs. st.; וּ id.	שׁפה
מִשְׁפְּחוֹת	id. pl., constr. st.; וּ id.	שׁפה
מִשְׁפְּחוֹתֶיהָ	id. pl., suff. 3 pers. sing. fem.	שׁפה
מִשְׁפַּחַת	id. pl., abs. st.	שׁפה
מִשְׁפַּחַת	id. sing., constr. st.; וּ bef. lab.	שׁפה
מִשְׁפַּחַת	id. pl., constr. st.; וּ id.	שׁפה
מִשְׁפַּחְתּוֹ	id. sing., suff. 3 pers. sing. masc.	שׁפה
מִשְׁפַּחְתִּי	id. sing., suff. 1 pers. sing.; וּ bef. lab.	שׁפה
מִשְׁפַּחְתָּם	id. sing., suff. 3 pers. pl. masc.	שׁפה
מִשְׁפְּחֹתָם	id. pl., suff. 3 pers. pl. masc. (§ 4. rem. 2)	שׁפה
מִשְׁפָּט	noun masc. sing. dec. 2 b; וּ bef. lab.	שׁפט
מִשְׁפַּט	id., constr. st. וּ id.	שׁפט
מִשְׁפָּטָהּ	id., suff. 3 pers. sing. fem.	שׁפט
מִשְׁפָּטוֹ	id. pl., suff. 3 pers. sing. masc. (§ 4. rem. 1)	שׁפט
מִשְׁפָּטוֹ	id. sing., suff. 3 pers. sing. masc.	שׁפט
מִשְׁפָּטַי	id. pl., suff. 1 pers. sing.; וּ bef. lab.	שׁפט
מִשְׁפָּטִי	id. sing., suff. 1 pers. sing.; וּ id.	שׁפט
מִשְׁפְּטִי	pref. מִ ‖ Kal part. act. sing. masc. (שׁוֹפֵט), suff. 1 pers. sing. dec. 7 b	שׁפט
מִשְׁפְּטֵי	n. m. pl. constr. fr. מִשְׁפָּט d. 2 b; וּ bef. lab.	שׁפט
מִשְׁפְּטֵי	pref. מִ ‖ Kal part. act. pl. constr. masc. from שׁוֹפֵט dec. 7 b	שׁפט
מִשְׁפְּטֵיהֶם	noun masc. pl., suff. 3 pers. pl. masc. from מִשְׁפָּט dec. 2 b	שׁפט
מִשְׁפָּטָיו	id. pl., suff. 3 pers. sing. masc.; וּ bef. lab.	שׁפט
מִשְׁפָּטֶיךָ	id. pl., suff. 2 pers. sing. masc.; וּ id.	שׁפט
מִשְׁפָּטַיִךְ	id. pl., suff. 2 pers. sing. fem.	שׁפט
מִשְׁפָּטִים	id. pl., abs. st.; וּ bef. lab.	שׁפט
מִשְׁפָּטֶךָ	id. s., suff. 2 p. s. mas. [for מִשְׁפָּטְךָ]; וּ id.	שׁפט
מִשְׁפָּטָם	id. sing., suff. 3 pers. pl. masc.	שׁפט
מִשְׁפָּטָן	id. sing., suff. 3 pers. pl. fem.	שׁפט
מַשְׁפִּיל	Heb. & Chald. def. Da. 5. 19. Hiph. part. s. m.	שׁפל
מִשְׁפָּם	pref. מִ ‖ pr. name of a place	שׁפה
מִשְׁפְּעַת	pref. id. ‖ n. f. s. constr. [of שִׁפְעָה, no pl.]	שׁפע
מִשְׁפַּת	pref. מִ ‖ noun f. s., constr. of שָׂפָה d. 11 a	שׁפה
מִשְׁפָּתוֹ	pref. id. ‖ id., suff. 3 pers. sing. masc.	שׁפה
מֶשֶׁק	masc. i. q. מֶשֶׁק possession, Ge. 15. 2, בֶּן־מֶ׳ son of possession, possessor. R. מָשַׁק i. q. מָשַׁק	
מִמְשָׁק	masc. dec. 2 b, possession, Zep. 2. 9. Lee, overspreading.	
מַשְׁקְרִים	Pual part. masc. pl. [of מְשֻׁקָּד]	שׁקד
מַשְׁקֶה	Hiph. part. or subst. m. d. 9 a; וּ bef. lab.	שׁקה
מַשְׁקֵה	id., constr. st.	שׁקה
מַשְׁקֵהוּ	id., suff. 3 pers. sing. masc.	שׁקה
מַשְׁקָיו	id. (subst.) pl., suff. 3 p. s. m.; וּ bef. lab.	שׁקה
מִשְׁקָל	noun masc. sing. dec. 2 b; וּ id.	שׁקל
מִשְׁקַל	id., constr. st.; וּ id.	שׁקל
מִשְׁקָלָהּ	id., suff. 3 pers. sing. fem.; וּ id.	שׁקל
מִשְׁקָלוֹ	id., suff. 3 pers. sing. masc.	שׁקל
מִשְׁקָלָם	id., suff. 3 pers. pl. masc.	שׁקל
מִשְׁקֹלֶת	noun fem. sing.	שׁקל
מִשְׁקָע	noun masc. sing., constr. of [מִשְׁקָע] dec. 2 b; וּ bef. lab.	שׁקע
מִשְׁקְרוֹת	Piel part. fem. pl. [of מְשַׁקֶּרֶת dec. 13, from מִשְׁקָר masc.]; וּ id.	שׁקר
מָשַׁר	Root not used, Arab. to divide. מְשׂוּרָה fem. measure for liquids. Others, derive it from שׂוּר to divide, saw.	
מִשְׂרָה	pref. מִ ‖ noun masc. sing. d. 8 (§ 37. r. 7)	שׂרר
מְשָׁרֵא	Ch. Pa. part. sing. masc.; וּ bef. lab.	שׁרא
מַשְׁרוֹקִיתָא	Ch. noun f. s., emph. of [מַשְׁרוֹקִי] d. 8 b	שׁרק
מִשְׂרֵי	pref. מִ ‖ noun masc. pl. constr. [for שָׂרֵי] from שַׂר dec. 8 e (§ 37. rem. 7)	שׂרר
מִשְׂרָד	pref. id. ‖ pr. name of a place	שׂרד
מֵישָׁרִים	defect. for מֵישָׁרִים (q. v.)	ישׁר
מְשָׁרֵשׁ	Hiph. part. sing. masc.	שׁרשׁ
מְשָׁרֶכֶת	Piel part. sing. [from מְשָׁרֵךְ masc.]	שׁרך
[מִשְׁרָעִי]	gent. noun from an unknown town מִשְׁרָע 1 Ch. 2. 53.	
מִשְׂרֵפָה	pref. מִ ‖ noun fem. sing. dec. 10	שׂרף
מִשְׂרְפוֹת	noun fem. pl. constr. fr. [מִשְׂרֵפָה] dec. 11 a, also pr. name in compos. מֵי מַיִם	שׂרף
מְשָׁרְרוֹת	Pilel part. fem. pl. [of מְשׁוֹרֶרֶת dec 10, fr. מְשׁוֹרֵר masc.]; וּ bef. lab.	שׁיר
מְשֹׁרְרִים	id. part. masc. pl. of מְשׁוֹרֵר dec. 7 b	שׁיר
מְשָׁרֵשׁ	pref. מִ ‖ noun masc. sing. dec. 6 c	שׁרשׁ
מְשָׁרְשֹׁהָ	pref. id. ‖ id. pl., suff. 3 pers. s. f. (§ 35. r. 9)	שׁרשׁ
מְשָׁרְשָׁיו	pref. id. ‖ id. pl., suff. 3 pers. sing. masc.	שׁרשׁ

---

2 Ki. 4. 29.   Is. 5. 7.   Zec. 12. 12, 14.   1 Ch. 4. 27.   Ps. 109. 31.   Nu. 27. 5.   Nu. 7. 13, 19, &c.   Is. 3. 16.   Job 5. 3.

Ps. 23. 4.   Est. 9. 23.   Nu. 3. 21, 27, 33.   Nu. 1. 18.   Eze. 20. 18.   Eze. 26. 10.   2 Sa. 12. 30.   Da. 1. 8.   Je. 2. 23.

Ru. 4. 10.   Na. 3. 4.   1 Ch. 4. 8, 21.   Je. 51. 9.   Ps. 119. 108, etc.   Ps. 120. 2.   Ge. 24. 22.   Da. 5. 12.   Am. 4. 11.

Ezr. 9. 3.   1 Ch. 2. 53, 55.   Ge. 24. 38, 41.   Is. 51. 4.   Zep. 3. 15.   Is. 32. 6.   2 Ki. 21. 13.   Da. 3. 5, 7, 10, 15.   Eze. 17. 9.

Ps. 9. 14.   Jos. 6. 23.   Job 23. 7.   1 Ki. 20. 40.   Ge. 40. 13, 21.   Eze. 34. 18.   Pr. 1. 3.   Is. 11. 1.

1 Ki. 1. 52.

[מַשְׂרֵת]   m. *frying-pan,* 2 Sa. 13. 3. Etymology doubtful.

מְשָׁרֵת   Piel part. sing. masc. dec. 7 b   .   שרת

[מְשָׁרֶתֶת]   id. fem. [for   .   שרת

מְשָׁרֵת   noun fem. sing., constr. of [מְשָׁרֶת] dec. 10   שרת

מְשָׁרְתוֹ   Piel part. sing. masc. (מְשָׁרֵת), suff. 3   שרת
pers. sing. masc. dec. 7 b ; bef. lab.

מְשָׁרְתַי   id. pl., suff. 1 pers. sing. for תֵי'   שרת

מְשָׁרְתֵי   id. pl., abs. st.   .   .   שרת

מְשָׁרְתָיו   id. pl., suff. 3 pers. sing. masc.   שרת

מְשָׁרְתִים   id. pl., abs. st. ; bef. lab.   שרת

[מָשַׁשׁ]   *to touch, feel,* Ge. 27. 12, 22.   Pi. I. *to feel, examine by feeling.*—II. *to feel one's way, grope.*   Hiph. *to grope,* with acc. Ex. 10. 21.

מְשַׁשְׁתָּ   Piel pret. 2 pers. sing. masc.   .   משש

מִשְׁתָּאֵה   Hithpa. part. s. m. [for מִתְשָׁאֵה § 12. r. 3]   שאה

מִשְׁתַּבְּשִׁין   Chald. Ithpa. part. masc. pl. [of מִשְׁתַּבֵּשׁ for   שבש
מִתְשַׁבֵּשׁ § 12. rem. 3] dec. 2 b

מִשְׁתַּגֵּעַ   Hithpa. part. sing. masc. [for מִתְשַׁגֵּעַ v. id.]   שגע

מִשְׁתַּדּוֹר   preff. מִ & שֶׁ Kal fut. 2 pers. sing. masc.   נדר

מִשְׁתַּדַּר   Ch. Ithpa. part. s. m. [for מִתְשַׁדַּר § 12. r. 3]   שדר

מִשְׁתֶּה   noun masc. sing. dec. 9 a ; bef. lab.   שתה

מִשְׁתֵּה   id., constr. st.   .   .   שתה

מִשְׁאֵתוֹ   pref. מִ for שְׂאֵתוֹ noun fem. sing., suff. 3   נשא
pers. sing. m. fr. שְׂאֵת (§ 35. No. 4. r. 2)

מִשְׁתּוֹלֵל   Hithpoel part. s. m. [for מִתְשׁוֹלֵל § 12. r. 3]   שלל

מִשְׁתַּחֲוֶה   [for מִתְשַׁ § 12. r. 3] Hithpal. (3rd rad. ה   שחה
doubled, for חֲוָה) part. s. m. d. 9 a ; bef. lab.

מִשְׁתַּחֲוִים   id. pl., abs. st. ; id.   שחה

מִשְׁתַּחֲוִיתֶם   prob. an error for מִשְׁתַּחֲוִים, as some   שחה
MSS. read   .   .   .

מַשֹׁתִי   Kal pret. 1 pers. sing. ; acc. shifted by ,   מוש
for , conv. (comp. § 8. rem. 7)

מִשְׁתֵּי   pref. מִ num. card. fem., constr. of שְׁתַּיִם,   שנה
from שְׁנַיִם masc.

מִשְׁתְּיָא   Chald. noun masc. s., emph. of [מִשְׁתֵּי] d. 6 b   שתה

מִשְׁתֵּיהֶם   pref. מ noun masc. pl. or sing. (§ 38.   שתה
rem. 1), suff. 3 pers. s. m. fr. מִשְׁתֶּה d. 9 a

מִשְׁתָּיו   pref. id. id., suff. 3 pers. sing. masc.   שתה

מִשְׁתֵּיכֶם   pref. id. id., suff. 2 pers. pl. masc.   שתה

מִשְׁתַּיִם   pref. id. num. card. fem., constr. of שְׁתַּיִם   שנה

מִשְׁתִּין   Hiph. part. sing. masc.   .   .   שתן

מִשְׁתַּכֵּל   Ch. Ithpa. part. s. m. [for מִתְשַׁכֵּל § 12. r. 3]   שכל

מִשְׁתַּבֵּר   Hithpa. part. sing. masc. [for מִתְשַׁבֵּר v. id.]   שבר

מִשְׁתָּרַיִן   Chald. Ithpa. part. masc. pl. [of מִשְׁתָּרֵא for   שרא
מִתְשָׁרֵא § 12. rem. 3] dec. 6 a

מֵת   Kal pret. 3 pers. sing. masc. ; or part.   מות
(§ 21. rem. 2) ; bef. lab., for see lett.

מֻת   id. imp. s. m. (§ 21. r. 5) ; preff. id.   מות

מִתְאָב   Piel part. sing. masc.   .   .   תאב

מִתְאַבֵּל   Hithpa. part. sing. masc. dec. 7 b   אבל

מִתְאַבְּלִים   id. pl., abs. st.   .   אבל

מִתְאַבֶּלֶת   id. part. sing. fem.   .   אבל

[מִתְאַוָּה]   Hithpa. part. sing. fem. [of   אוה

מִתְאַוָּתָם   pref. מִ noun fem. sing., suff. 3 pers. pl.   אוה
masc. from תַּאֲוָה dec. 10

מַתְאִימוֹת   Hiph. part. f. pl. [of מַתְאִימָה, fr. m.]   תאם

מִתְאַמֶּצֶת   Hithpa. part. sing. fem. [of מִתְאַמֵּץ]   אמץ

מִתְאַנֶּה   Hithpa. part. sing. masc.   .   אנה

מִתְאַנֶּה   pref. מִ noun fem. sing. dec. 10   תאן

מִתְבָּהַל   Ithpa. part. sing. masc. (§ 49. rem. 3)   בהל

מִתְבוּאַת   pref. מִ noun f. s., constr. of תְּבוּאָה d. 10   בוא

מִתְבוּאֹתֵיכֶם   pref. id. id. pl., suff. 2 pers. pl. masc.   בוא

מִתְבּוֹסֶסֶת   Hithpal. part. sing. masc.   .   בוס

מִתְבֵּל   pref. מִ noun fem. sing. ; bef. lab.   יבל

מִתְבֵּן   noun masc. sing.   .   .   תבן

מִתְבְּנֵא   Chald. Ithpe. part. sing. masc. R. בְּנָא see   בנה

מֶתֶג   masc. dec. 6 a (with suff. מִתְגִּי) *a bridle.*

מִתְגּוֹדְדִים   Hithpoel part. masc. pl. [of מִתְגּוֹדֵד] dec.   נדד
7 b ; bef. lab.

מִתְגּוֹרֵר   Hithpalel part. sing. masc.   .   גור

מִתְגּוֹרֵר   Hithpoel part. sing. masc.   .   גרר

מִתְגִּי   noun masc. sing., suff. 1 pers. sing. from   מתג
מֶתֶג dec. 6 a ; bef. lab.

מִתְגַּלָּל   Hithpoel part. sing. masc.   .   גלל

מִתְגֶּרֶת   pref. מִ noun f. s., constr. of וַתִּגְרָה d. 10   גרה

מִתְדַּפְּקִים   Hithpa. part. masc. pl. [of מִתְדַּפֵּק] dec. 7 b   דפק

מָתָה   Root not used ; Arab. مَتَى مَتَا, *to extend* ; cogn. מָתַח.

מֵת   masc. *man* (prop. *adult*) ; only pl. מְתִים,
constr. מְתֵי (§ 36. rem. 5) *men* ; מְתֵי מִסְפָּר *men of number,* i. e. that can be numbered, *a few* ;
מְתֵי אֹהֶל *men of tent,* i. e. *domestics* ; others, *tent-companions.*

מְתוּשָׁאֵל (*man of God* ; מְתוּ־שֶׁ־אֵל) pr. name of one of the descendants of Cain.

מְתוּשֶׁלַח (*man of dart*) pr. name of the son of Enoch.

מָתַי   adv. *when?* Also without interrog. Pr. 23.

ᵃ 1 Ki. 1. 15.   ᵍ Ge. 24. 21.   ᵐ Is. 59. 15.   ˢ Hag. 1. 6.   ʸ 2 Ch. 35. 24.   ᵍ 2 Ki. 7. 7.   ᶠ Eze. 16. 6, 22.   ᵏ 1 Ki. 17. 20.
ᵇ Nu. 6. 3.   ʰ Da. 5. 9.   ⁿ Est. 3. 5.   ᵗ Da. 5. 6.   ᶻ 2 Sa. 14. 2.   ᵍ Is. 34. 4.   ᵍ Job 18. 18.   ˡ Je. 30. 23.
ᶜ Ex. 38. 11.   ⁱ 1 Sa. 21. 15.   ᵒ Eze. 8. 16.   ᵘ De. 32. 50.   ᵃ Pr. 13. 4.   ᵉ Is. 25. 10.   ᵍ Jos. 5. 12.   ᵐ 2 Sa. 20. 13.
ᵈ Je. 33. 21.   ᵏ Ec. 5. 4.   ᵖ Zec. 3. 9.   ᵛ Jon. 4. 11.   ᵇ Ps. 78. 30.   ᵗ Ezr. 5. 8, 16.   ᵍ Ps. 39. 11.
ᵉ Eze. 14. 11.   ˡ Da. 6. 15.   ᵍ Ju. 16. 28.   ᵂ Da. 7. 8.   ᶜ Am. 6. 8.   ᵈ Ru. 1. 18.   ᵉ Je. 12. 13.   ᵉ Je. 41. 5.   ʰ Ju. 19. 22.
ᵍᵉ 31. 37.   ᵐ Job 41 17.

אַחֲרֵי־מָתַי , לְמָתַי , עַד מָתַי *how long?* after 35; *how long?*

מָתֹם perh. adv. *all, every one,* Ju. 20. 48; comp. the forms שִׁלְשׁם פִּתְאֹם.

מַתָּה וָ Kal pret. 2 pers. sing. masc. [for מַתְתָּה , § 25. r.]; וָ bef. dist. acc. for וָ conv. — מות

מֵתָה e'וָ Kal pret. 3 pers. s. f. (§ 21. r. 2); וָ id. — מות

מֵתָה id. part. sing. fem. of מֵת masc. — מות

מְתַהוֹם וָ pref. מ')(noun com. sing. d. 1 a; וָ bef. lab. — הום

מִתְּהוֹמוֹ וָ pref. id.)(id. pl. fem.; וָ id. — הום

מִתְהַלֵּךְ Hithpa. part. sing. masc. dec. 7 b — הלך

מִתְהַלֶּכֶת id. part. sing. fem. — הלך

מִתְהַלֵּל Hithpa. part. sing. masc. dec. 7 b — הלל

מִתְהַפֵּךְ Hithpa. part. sing. masc. — הפך

מְתוֹ Kal part. sing. masc. (מֵת § 21. rem. 2), suff. 3 pers. sing. masc. dec. 1 a (§ 30. No. 3) — מות

מֵתוּ וָ , וָ id. pret. 3 pers. pl.; וָ bef. lab., & וָ bef. pause & dist. acc., for וָ , conv. — מות

מֹתוֹ defect. for מוֹתוֹ (q. v.) — מות

מִתְוַנֶּה pref. מ')(noun fem. sing. dec. 10 — ינה

מִתְוַדֶּה וָ Hithpa. (§ 20. No. 1) part. sing. masc. dec. 9 a; וָ bef. lab. — ידה

מִתְוַדִּים וָ , וָ id. pl., abs. st.; וָ id. — ידה

מִתּוֹךְ pref. מ')(noun masc. sing. for תָּוֶךְ — תכך

מִתּוֹךְ pref. id.)(noun masc. sing., constr. of תָּוֶךְ dec. 6 g (as a prep.) — תוך

מִתּוֹכָהּ וָ pref. id.)(id., suff. 3 p. s. f.; וָ bef. lab. — תוך

מִתּוֹכְךָ pref. id.)(id., suff. 2 pers. sing. masc. — תוך

מִתּוֹכְכֶם pref. id.)(id., suff. 2 pers. pl. masc. — תוך

מִתּוֹכָם pref. id.)(id., suff. 3 pers. pl. masc. — תוך

מָתוֹק וָ adj. masc. sing.; וָ bef. lab. — מתק

מְתוּקָה id. fem. (§ 39. No. 3. rem. 1) — מתק

מְתוּקִים וָ id. pl. masc. (§ 32. rem. 5); וָ bef. lab. — מתק

מִתּוּר pref. מ')(Kal inf. constr. — תור

מִתּוֹרָתֶךָ } pref. id.)(noun fem. sing., suff. 2 pers.
מִתּוֹרָתֶךָ וָ'וֹ } sing. m. fr. תּוֹרָה d. 10; וָ bef. lab. — ורה

מְתוּשֶׁלַח & מְתוּשָׁאֵל וָ'וָ pr. names masc. — מתה

מִתַּזְנוּתֵךְ וָ'וָ pref. מ')(Kh. תֵּךְ , K. תַּיִךְ , noun fem. sing. or pl., suff. 2 p. s. sing. f. fr. תַּזְנוּת d. 1 b. — זנה

[מָתַח] *to stretch out,* Is. 40. 22.

אַמְתַּחַת fem., with suff. תַּחְתִּי' (dec. 13 a) *a sack* or *bag.*

מִתְחַבֵּא Hithpa. part. sing. masc. dec. 7 b — חבא

מִתְחַבְּאִים id. pl., abs. st. — חבא

מִתְחוֹלֵל Hithpal. part. sing. masc. — חול

מִתְחַזֵּק Hithpa. part. sing. masc. dec. 7 b — חזק

מִתְּחִלַּת pref. מ')(noun f. sing., constr. of תְּחִלָּה d. 10 — חלל

מִתְחַנֵּן וָ Ch. Ithpa. part. s. m.; וָ bef. lab. — חנן

מִתְּחִנָּתִי וָ'וָ pref. מ')(noun f. sing., constr. of תְּחִנָּה d. 10 — חנן

מִתְחָרֶה Tiphal part. sing. masc. (§ 6. No. 5) — חרה

מִתַּחַת' } pref. id.)(adv. (see the foll.), also pr.
מִתַּחַת וָ'וֹ } name; וָ bef. lab. } — תחת

מִתַּחְתָּהּ וָ pref. id.)(id. with suff. 3 pers. sing. fem. Kh. מִתַּחְתֶּהָ ; וָ id. — תחת

מִתַּחְתָּיו וָ'וֹ pref. id.)(id. pl. with suff. 3 p. s. m.; וָ id. — תחת

מִתַּחְתִּיּוֹת' pref. id.)(adj. fem. pl. of תַּחְתִּית [from תַּחְתִּי § 39. No. 4. rem. 1 note] masc. — תחת

מִתַּחְתֶּיךָ' pref. id.)(adv. (תַּחַת) with pl. suff. 2 p. s. m. — תחת

מָתַי } adv. interr.; וָ bef. lab. — מתה
מָתַי מ'וָ }

מַתִּי' וָ Kal pret. 1 pers. sing. [for מַתְתִּי § 25. rem.]; וָ bef. pause for וָ , conv. — מות

מֵתֵי' id. part. pl. constr. masc. from מֵת (§ 21. rem. 2, & § 30. No. 3) dec. 1 a — מות

מֵתִי id. sing. with suff. 1 pers. sing. — מות

מְתֵי n. m. pl., constr. of מְתִים [fr. מַת § 36. r. 5] — מתה

מִתְיַהֵב Chald. Ithpe. part. sing. masc. dec. 2 b — יהב

מִתְיַהֲבָא' Chald. id. part. sing. fem. — יהב

מִתְיַהֲבִין' Chald. id. part. pl. masc. dec. 2 b — יהב

מִתְיַהֲדִים' Hithpa. (§ 14. rem. 1) part. masc. pl. [of מִתְיַהֵד] dec. 7 b — ידה

מְתָיו noun masc. pl. (מְתִים), suff. 3 pers. sing. masc. [from מַת § 36. rem. 5] — מתה

מְתַיִךְ' id. pl. with suff. 2 pers. sing. fem. — מתה

מֵתַיִךְ' the foll. with suff. 2 pers. sing. masc. — מות

מֵתִים Kal part. masc. pl. of מֵת (§ 21. rem. 2, & § 30. No. 3) dec. 1 a — מות

מְתִים noun masc. pl. [of מַת § 36. rem. 5] — מתה

מֵיתִימָן וָ'וֹ noun masc. s., also pr. name; וָ bef. lab. — ימן

מֵיתִיר' Hiph. part. sing. masc. — נתר

מֵתְךָ } Kal part. sing. masc., suff. 2 pers. s. m.
מֵתֶךָ 'וָ } from מֵת (§ 21. r. 2, & § 30. No. 3) d. 1 a } — מות

מִתְכַּנְּשִׁין וָ Chald. Ithpa. part. m. pl. [of מִתְכַּנֵּשׁ] d. 2 b — כנש

מַתְכֹּנֶת noun fem. sing. dec. 13 c — תכן

מַתְכֻּנְתּוֹ id., suff. 3 pers. sing. masc. (§ 14. rem. 4) — תכן

מִתְכַּסֶּה Hithpa. part. sing. masc. dec. 9 a — כסה

מִתְכַּסִּים id. pl., abs. st. — כסה

מִתְלָל pref. מ')(pr. name in compos. תֵּל מֶלַח — תלל

מַתְלָאָה' תְּלָאָה ; מַה ; (מַה comp.), see תְּלָאָה מַה־תְּלָאָה) for noun fem. sing. — לאה

• Eze. 28. 8.   f Ps. 71. 20.   m Ne. 9. 3.   r Ps. 19. 11.   u 1 Ch. 21. 20.   g Eze. 42. 9.   ʼ Ge. 19. 19.   t De. 33. 6.   ᵃ Ge. 23. 6, 11.
ᵇ Ge. 35. 18; 48. 7;   ᵍ Eze. 1. 13.   ⁿ 2 Ch. 30. 22.   ˢ Nu. 13. 25.   ᵛ 2 Sa. 21. 10.   ʰ Ex. 1ſ. 23.   ⁱ Is. 22. 2.   ᵘ Is. 3. 25.   ᵇ Ge. 23. 15.
Ex. 7. 21;   ʰ Pr. 25. 14.   ᵒ Ps. 72. 14.   ᵗ Ps. 119. 18.   ᵂ Da. 6. 12.   ⁱ Zec. 6. 12.   ᵖ Ge. 23. 4, 8, 13.   ᵛ Is. 26. 19.   ᶜ Da. 3. 3, 27.
ᶜ De. 22. 21.   ⁱ Ge. 23. 3.   ᵖ Le. 1. 4, 5.   ᵘ Ps. 119. 51, 150.   ˣ Ne. 4. 7.   ᵏ Ezr. 6. 8.   ᵍ Jos. 12. 3.   ᵈ Ex. 5. 8.
ᵈ Ge. 30. 1.   ᵏ 2 Ki. 15. 5.   ᵠ 1 Sa. 7. 3.   ᵛ Ps. 94. 12.   ʸ Je. 22. 15.   ᶦ Pr. 22. 27.   ᵖ Ezr. 7. 19.   ʸ Ps. 146. 7.   ᵉ 1 Ki. 11. 29.
ᵉ De. 33. 13.   ˡ Ps. 119. 28.   ᵠ Ec. 5. 11.   ᶻ Eze. 16. 20.   ᶠ Ex. 20. 4, etc.   ᵐ Ne. 2. 6.   ᵠ Est. 8. 17.   ᵃᵃ Mal. 1. 13.

מִתְלַחֲשִׁים Hithpa. part. pl. **masc.** [from מִתְלַחֵשׁ § 14. rem. 1] dec. 7 b — לחשׁ

מַתְלְעוֹת (o.v.) n. f. pl. constr., by transp. for מַלְתָּעוֹת — תלע

מְתַלְּעִים Pual part. masc. pl. [of מְתֻלָּע] — תלע

מְתַלְּעֹתָיו noun fem. pl., suff. 3 pers. s. m., see מַלְתָּעוֹת — תלע

מִתְלַקַּחַת Hithpa. part. sing. fem. [of מִתְלַקֵּחַ masc.] — לקח

מְתִם defect. for מְתִים (q. v.) — מתה

מְתֹם noun masc. sing. — מתם

מִתְמַהְמֵהַּ Hithpalp. part. sing. masc. (§ 6. rem. 4) — מהה

מִתְמוֹל pref. מְ)(adv. — מול

מִתְמֹךְ pref. id.)(Kal inf. constr. — תמך

מִתְמֹל defect. for מִתְמוֹל (q. v.) — מול

מִתְמָר pref. מְ)(pr. name of a place — תמר

מָתַן Root not used; Arab. *to be firm.*
מֹתֶן only du. מָתְנַיִם (dec. 6c) *loins.*
מִתְנִי gent. noun elsewhere unknown, 1 Ch. 11.43.
אֲמִתְנִי Chald. fem. *strong*, Da. 7. 7.

מַתָּן noun m. s. d. 2 b, also pr. n. ◗ bef. lab. — נתן
מֻתָן [for מוּתָן] Kal inf. constr. (מות), suff. 3 pers. pl. fem. dec. 1 a — מות

מִתְנַבֵּא Hithpa. part. sing. m. d. 7 b; bef. lab. — נבא
מִתְנַבְּאִים id. pl., abs. st. — נבא
מִתְנַדַּב Chald. Ithpa. part. sing. masc. dec. 2 a — נדב
מִתְנַדֵּב Hithpa. part. sing. masc. dec. 7 b — נדב
מִתְנַדְּבִין Chald. Ithpa. part. masc., pl. of מִתְנַדַּב d. 2 a — נדב
מַתָּנָה noun fem. sing. dec. 11 a; also pr. name — נתן
מָתְנוּ Kal pret. 1 pers. pl.; conv. see lett. ו — מות
מְתֻנוּבֹת pref. מְ)(noun fem. pl. of תְּנוּבָה dec. 10 — נוב
מִתְנוֹדֵד Hithpal. part. sing. masc. — נוד
מִתְנוֹסְסוֹת Hithpoel part. fem.pl. [from מִתְנוֹסֶסֶת, from מִתְנוֹסֵס masc.] — נסס
מַתָּנֹת noun fem. pl. abs from מַתָּנָה dec. 11a — נתן
מַתְּנֹתֵיכֶם id. pl. with suff. 2 pers. pl. masc. — נתן
מִתְנַחֵם Hithpa. part. sing. masc. (§ 14. rem. 1) — נחם
מָתְנַי } noun masc. du. (מָתְנַיִם), suff. 1 pers. sing. } from [מֹתֶן] dec. 6c — מתן
מָתְנֵי id. du., constr. st.; bef. lab. — מתן
מַתַּנְיָה pr. names masc.; id. — נתן
מָתְנָיו noun m. du., suff. 3 p. s. f. fr. [מֹתֶן] d. 6c — מתן
מַתִּתְיָהוּ pr. name masc., see מַתַּנְיָה — נתן
מָתְנֵיהֶם noun masc. du., suff. 3 pers. pl. masc. from [מֹתֶן] dec. 6c; bef. lab. — מתן
מָתְנָיו id. du., suff. 3 pers. sing. masc.; id. — מתן

מְתָנֶיךָ id. du., suff. 2 pers. sing. masc. — מתן
מָתְנֵיכֶם id. du., suff. 2 pers. pl. masc. — מתן
מָתְנַיִם / מָתְנָיִם } id. du., abs. st. — מתן
מִתְנַכְּרָה Hithpa. part. s. f. [of מִתְנַכֵּר § 39. No. 3. r. 4.] — נכר
מַתָּנָם noun masc. sing., suff. 3 pers. pl. masc. fr. מַתָּן — נתן
מַתְּנָן Chald. noun fem. pl. of [מַתְּנָא] dec. 8a; bef. lab. — נתן
מִתְנַפֵּל Hithpa. part. sing. masc.; id. — נפל
מִתְנַצַּח Chald. Ithpa. part. sing. masc. — נצח
מִתְנַקֵּם Hithpa. part. sing. masc.; bef. lab. — נקם
מִתְנַקֵּשׁ Hithpa. part. sing. masc. — נקשׁ
מִתְנַשֵּׂא Hithpa. part. sing. masc. — נשׂא
מִתְנַשְּׂאָה Chald. Ithpa. part. sing. fem. of מִתְנַשֵּׂא — נשׂא
מַתְּנֹת noun fem. pl. of מַתָּנָה dec. 11a — נתן
מַתְּנֹת id. pl., constr. st. — נתן
מַתְּנֹתֵיכֶם id. pl., suff. 2 pers. pl. masc. — נתן
מַתְּנָתָךְ Chald. noun fem. pl., suff. 2 pers. sing. masc. from [מַתְּנָא] dec. 8a — נתן
מִתְעַבֵּד / מִתְעֲבֵד } Chald. Ithpe. part. sing. masc. — עבד
מִתְעַבְדָא Chald. id. part. sing. fem. — עבד
מִתְעַבֵּר Hithpa. part. sing. masc. — עבר
מִתְעַבְּרוֹ id. with suff. 3 pers. sing. masc. — עבר
מַתְעֶה Hiph. part. sing. masc. dec. 9a — תעה
מִתְעוֹרֵר Hithpal. part. sing. masc. — עור
מַתְעִים Hiph. part. masc. pl. of מַתְעֶה dec. 9a — תעה
מִתְעַנִּיתִי pref. מְ)(noun fem. sing., suff. 1 pers. sing. from [תַּעֲנִית] dec. 1b — ענה
מִתְעָרֵב Chald. Ithpa. part. sing. masc. dec. 2a — ערב
מִתְעָרְבִין Chald. id. pl., abs. st. — ערב
מִתְעָרֶה pref. מְ)(noun masc. sing., suff. 3 pers. sing. fem. from תַּעַר [for תַּעֲרָה] — ערה
מִתְעָרָה Hithpa. part. sing. masc.; bef. lab. — ערה
מִתְעַשֵּׁר Hithpa. part. sing. masc. — עשׁר
מִתַּעְתְּעִים Hithpal. part. pl. masc. [from מִתַּעְתֵּעַ for מִתְעַתְּעַ] dec. .. ; bef. lab. — תעע
מַתַּפּוּחַ pref. מְ)(pr. name of a place — נפח
מִתְפַּלֵּל Hithpa. part. sing. masc. dec. 7b; bef. lab. — פלל
מִתְפַּלְלִים id. pl., abs. st., id. — פלל
מִתְפַּסֵּחַ pref. מְ)(pr. name of a place — פסח
מִתְחַפְּפוֹת Hithpoel part. pl. fem. [from מְתַחַפֶּפֶת d. 13, from מִתְחַפֵּף masc.] — תפף

[מָתַק] fut. יִמְתַּק—I. *to be* or *become sweet.*—II. i. q Syr. *to suck, to feed upon with relish,* Job 24. 20

---

a 2 Sa. 12. 19.   g Is. 33. 15.   n Nu. 14. 2.   s Le. 23. 38.   y Pr. 31. 17.   a Nu. 18. 11.   o Ex. 28. 38.   u Pr. 20. 2.   z Ps. 37. 35.
b Job 29. 17.   h Ge. 34. 12.   o 2 Ki. 7. 4.   t Eze. 44. 18.   z Eze. 44. 18.   b Da. 2. 6, 48.   p Da. 5. 17.   v Is. 64. 6.   Pr. 13. 7.
c Joel 1. 6.   i 2 Sa. 20. 3.   p La. 4. 9.   u Je. 13. 2.   a Ps. 69. 24.   c Da. 5. 17.   q Ezr. 7. 26.   w Ezr. 9. 5.   2 Ch. 36. 16.
d Na. 2. 4.   k Je. 29. 26.   q Je. 31. 18.   v Is. 21. 3.   b Da. 10. 5.   d Ezr. 10. 1.   r Ezr. 4. 19.   x Da. 2. 43.   Is. 45. 20.
e Pr. 30. 14.   l Ezr. 7. 13.   r Zec. 9. 16.   w Je. 13. 11.   c Da. 6. 4.   l 1 Sa. 28. 9.   s Ezr. 5. 8.   y Da. 1. 41.   Na. 2. 8.
f 2 Sa. 15. 28.   m Ezr. 7. 16.   x Est. 9. 22.   d Ex. 12. 11.   n Ezr. 4. 19.   e 1 Ki. 14. 5, 6.   m 1 Ki. 1. 5.

Hiph. I. *to make sweet*, Ps. 55. 15. הַמְתִּיק סוֹד *to take sweet counsel.*—II. *to be sweet*, Job 20. 12.

מָתוֹק masc. pl. מְתוּקִים, fem. מְתוּקָה (§ 32. r.5) adj. *sweet*; neut. *sweet, sweetness; pleasantness.*

מֶתֶק masc. *sweetness*, Pr. 16. 21; 27. 9.

מֹתֶק masc. dec. 6e, id. Ju. 9. 11.

מִתְקָה (*sweetness*) pr. name of a station of the Israelites in the desert, Nu. 33. 28.

מַמְתַּקִּים masc. pl. (of מַמְתָּק dec. 8a) *sweet things.*

מֶתֶק ‹ noun masc. sing.; ‹ bef. lab. . . מתק

מִתְקַדֶּשֶׁת‹ Hithpa. part. sing. fem. [of מִתְקַדֵּשׁ m.] קדש

מָתְקוּ‹ Kal pret. 3 pers. pl. . . . מתק

מִתְקוֹ‹ id. pret. 3 pers. sing. m., suff. 3 pers. sing. m. מתק

מִתְקוֹמְמָה‹ Hithpal. part. sing. fem. [of מִתְקוֹמֵם comp. § 12. rem. 1] . . קום

מִתְקוֹמְמַי‹ id. masc. with suff. 1 pers. sing. [from קוֹמֵם dec. 7b; ‹ bef. lab. . . . קום

מִתְקוֹעַ pref. מִ)(pr. name of a place . תקע

מִתְקַטְּלִין‹ Chald. Ithpa. part. pass. masc. pl. [of מִתְקַטַּל] dec. 2a . . . קטל

מִתְקִי‹ noun m. sing., suff. 1 pers. s. fr. [מֹתֶק] d. 6c מתק

מְתֻרְגָּם‹ Pual part. sing. masc. (§ 7); ‹ bef. lab. תרגם

מִתְרְדָת (Mithra-dat (-datus), *given or dedicated to Mithra, the genius of the sun*) pr. name—

I. of a treasurer of Cyrus, Ezr. 1. 8.—II. of an officer of Artaxerxes, Ezr. 4. 7.

מִתְרוּגֶמֶת‹ pref. מְ)(noun fem. s., constr. of תְּרוּמָה d. 10 רום

מִתְרוֹנֵן‹ Hithpal. part. sing. masc. . רון

מִתְרוֹשֵׁשׁ‹ Hithpal. part. sing. masc. . . רוש

מִתֶּרַח pref. מִ)(pr. name masc. for תֶּרַח (§ 35. r. 2) תרח

מִתְרַפֶּה‹ Hithpa. part. sing. masc. dec. 9a . רפה

מִתְרַפִּים‹ id. pl., constr. st. . . . רפה

מִתְרַפֵּס‹ Hithpa. part. sing. masc. . . רפס

מִתְרַפֶּקֶת‹ Hithpa. part. sing. fem. [of מִתְרַפֵּק masc.] רפק

מִתְרָצָה‹ pref. מִ)(pr. name of a place . רצה

מִתַּרְשִׁישׁ pref. id.)(pr. name of a place, see תַּרְשִׁישׁ.

מִתּוֹשָׁבֵי‹ pref. id.)(noun masc. pl. constr. from תּוֹשָׁב dec. 1b (§ 31. rem. 1) ישׁב

מִתְּשֵׂם‹ Chald. Ithpe. part. sing. masc. שׂום

מַתָּתִי‹ } noun fem. sing. [contr. for מַתָּנָת] נתן
מַתַּת

מִתֵּת‹ pref. מְ)(Kal inf. constr. [for תְּנַת § 17. r. 9] נתן

מַתַּתָה pr. name masc. . . . . נתן

מִתִּתִּי‹ pref. id.)(Kal inf. (תֵּת for תְּנַת), suff. 1 pers. sing. (§ 17. rem. 9) . . . . נתן

מֹתַתִּי‹ Pilel pret. 1 p.s. [for מוֹתַתְתִּי § 25.r.] מות

מַתִּתְיָה‹ } pr. name masc.; ‹ bef. lab. . נתן
מַתִּתְיָהוּ‹

מֹתְתֵנִי‹ Pilel imp. s. m., suff. 1 pers. sing.; ‹ id. מות

נ

נָא interj. noting respectful entreaty or exhortation, *I pray!* used—I. with the imp. optat. and fut. with and without negation, as אִמְרִי נָא *say, I pray thee!* יֻקַּח נָא *let there be taken, I pray thee!* אֵלְכָה־נָּא *let me go, I pray thee!* אַל־נָא תַעֲבֹר *pass not away, I pray thee!*—II. with conj. and interj. אַל־נָא *nay, or not so, I pray thee!* הִנֵּה־נָא *behold, I pray thee!* In many instances the word *now* may be substituted, as אִם־נָא *if now*, or *if indeed*; אוֹי־נָא *woe now! alas!* comp. also Ex. 3. 3. אָסֻרָה־נָּא *let me go now*, comp. No. I.

נָא‹ adj. masc. sing. . . . . ניא

נֹא‹ ‹ fully נָא אָמוֹן נֹא pr. name of an Egyptian city, supposed to be *Thebes.*

נֹאבַד Kal fut. 1 pers. pl. . . . אבד

נֹאבְדָה‹ id. with parag. ה (§ 8. rem. 13) אבד

נֹאד‹ וְ masc. dec. 1a (pl. נֹאדוֹת), *bottle, skin-bottle.* Arab. נאד *to yield water.*

נֹאדוֹת‹ id. pl. with fem. term. . . נאד

נֶאְדָּר‹ Niph. part. sing. masc. (§ 13. rem. 7) אדר

נֶאְדָּרִי‹ id. with parag. ‹ (comp. § 8. rem. 19) . אדר

נָאָה Kal not used; i. q. נָוָה *to sit, dwell*, comp. deriv. נָאָה Pil. נָאוָה (§ 24. rem. 25)—I. *to be suitable, becoming*, with לְ Ps. 93. 5; prop. *to sit well* (Gesenius).—II. *to be comely, beautiful*, cogn. יָאָה. נָאָה fem. dec. 11a, only pl. c.—I. *seats, dwellings, habitations.*—II. *flocks and herds, pastures;* נְאוֹת דֶּשֶׁא *green pastures.*

נָאוָה (for נָאֲוָה) adj. fem.—I. *suitable, becoming.*—II. *comely, beautiful.*

נָאוֹר‹ with ‹ in otio for נֹאד (q. v.) . . . נאד

a 2 Sa. 11. 4.   d Job 20. 27.   f Ju. 9. 11.   k Ps. 78. 65.   m Jos. 18. 3.   o 1 Ki. 17. 1.   q 2 Sa. 1. 16.   s Jon. 1. 14.   u Ex. 15. 11.
b Job 21. 33.   e Job 27. 7.   g Ezr. 4. 7.   i Pr. 13. 7.   n Ps. 68. 31.   Ezr. 5. 8.   1 Sa. 1. 9.   t 1 Sa. 16. 20.   v Ex. 15. 6.
c Job 24 30.   f Da. 2. 13.   Eze. 48. 12.   l Pr. 18. 9.   p Ca. 8. 5.   1 Ki. 15. 7.   r Ex. 12. 9.   Jos. 9. 4, 13.   w Ju. 4. 19.

נָאוָה	*ʻ* fem. of the foll. . . .	נאה
נָאוֶה	adj. masc. sing. [for נָאוֶה], comp. the foll.	נאה
נָאוָה	Pilel pret. 3 p. s. m. (§ 6. No. 2, & § 24. r. 22)	נאה
נָאווּ	id. pret. 3 pers. pl. [for נָאווּ] . .	נאה
נָאוֹף	Kal inf. abs.	נאף
נָאוֹר	Niph. part. sing. masc. . . .	אור
נָאוֹת	Niph. [for נָאוֹת], or Kal (comp. יֵבוֹשׁ from	
	בּוֹשׁ) fut. 1 pers. pl. . . .	אות
נְאוֹת	noun fem. pl. constr. from [נָאָה] dec. 11 a	נאה
נֵאוֹתָה	Niph. or Kal fut. 1 pers. pl. with parag. ה	
	comp. נָאוֹת	יאת
נֶאֱזָר	Niph. part. sing. masc. (§ 13. rem. 7) .	אזר
נֶאֱחָז	Niph. part. sing. masc. . . .	אחז
נֶאֶחֲזוּ	*ʻ* id. pret. 3 pers. pl. (§ 19. rem. 7) .	אחז
נֶאֱכָל	Niph. pret. 3 pers. sing. masc. . .	אכל
נֹאכַל	} Kal fut. 1 pers. pl. (§ 19. rem. 1) .	אכל
נֹאכְלָה	} id. with parag. (ה § 8. rem. 13)	אכל
נֹאכְלֶהוּ	} id. with suff. 3 pers. sing. masc.; וַ com.	אכל
נֹאכְלֶנּוּ		
נֹאֵל	*ʻ* in pause and defect. for נוֹאֵל (q. v.) .	יאל
נֶאֱלַח	Niph. part. sing. masc. . . .	אלח
נֶאֱלָחוּ	id. pret. 3 pers. pl. [for נֶאֶלְחוּ comp. § 8. r. 7]	אלח
נֶאֶלְמָה	Niph. pret. 3 pers. sing. fem. [for נֶאֶלְמָה	
	§ 13. rem. 7, comp. § 8. rem. 7] .	אלם
נֶאֱלַמְתָּ	} id. pret. 2 pers. sing. masc. . .	אלם
נֶאֱלַמְתִּי	} id. pret. 1 p. s. [for נֶאֱלַמְתִּי comp. § 8. r.7]	אלם

[נָאַם] to utter, *speak, declare*, Je. 23. 31, elsewhere in the part. pass. constr. נְאֻם prop. *declared of, by*, as a subst. *declaration, dictum of*; נְאֻם יְהוָה *a declaration of the Lord*, Eng. vers. *saith the Lord*.

נְאֻם	*h* Kal part. pass. sing. masc. constr. [of	
	נָאוּם] dec. 3 a; וַ bef. (:) . .	נאם
נֶאֱמָן	*ʻ* Niph. part. sing. masc. dec. 2 b .	אמן
נֶאֱמָן	*ʻ* id. id., constr. st. or pret. 3 pers. sing. m.	אמן
נֶאֱמָנָה	id. part. sing. fem.	אמן
נֶאֶמְנָה	id. pret. 3 pers. sing. fem. . .	אמן
נֶאֶמְנוּ	} id. pret. 3 pers. pl. (comp. § 8. rem. 7)	אמן
נֶאֶמְנוּ		
נֶאֱמָנוֹת	} id. part. fem. pl. of נֶאֱמָנָה . .	אמן
נֶאֱמָנִים	*b* id. part. masc. pl. of נֶאֱמָן dec. 2 b	אמן
נֶאֶמְנַת	id. part. sing. fem., comp. נֶאֱמָנָה .	אמן
נֶאֱמַר	Niph. pret. 3 pers. sing. masc.	אמר

נֵאמַר	*ʻ* Chald. Peal fut. 1 pers. pl. (§ 53) .	אמר
נֹאמַר	*l* Kal fut. 1 pers. pl. (§ 19. rem. 1)	אמר
נֹאמַר	} id.; acc. drawn back by conv. וַ	אמר
נֶאֱנָח	*k* Niph. part. sing. masc. (§ 13. rem. 7)	אנח
נֶאֶנְחָה	*h* id. part. sing. fem.	אנח
נֶאֶנְחָה	id. pret. 3 pers. sing. fem. . .	אנח
נֶאֶנְחוּ	id. pret. 3 pers. pl. . . .	אנח
נֶאֱנָחִים	id. part. masc., pl. of נֶאֱנָח . .	אנח
נֶאֱסָף	*l* Niph. part. sing. masc. . . .	אסף
נֶאֱסָף	*m* } id. pret. *ʻ* pers. sing. masc.	אסף
נֶאֱסֹף	*n* Kal fut. 1 pers. pl. . . .	סף
נֶאֶסְפָה	} Niph. pret. 3 pers. sing. fem. . .	אסף
נֶאֶסְפוּ	} id. pret. 3 pers. pl.	אסף
נֶאֱסָפִים	id. part. masc. pl. of נֶאֱסָף . .	אסף
נֶאֱסַפְתָּ	} id. pret. 2 pers. sing. masc., acc. shifted.	אסף
	by conv. וַ (§ 8. rem. 7) . .	
נֶאֱסַפְתֶּם	} id. pret. 2 pers. pl. masc. . .	אסף
נֶאֶסׇרְךָ	} Kal fut. 1 pers. pl., suff. 2 pers. sing. masc.	אסר

[נָאַף] fut. יִנְאַף *to commit adultery;* const. with an acc. נָאַף אִשָּׁה *he that committeth adultery with a woman*, Pr. 6. 32. Trop. applied to apostacy from the true God to idolatry. Pi. נִאֵף (§ 14. r. 1) idem. נֹאַף m. d. 1 b, *adultery*, Je. 13. 27; Eze. 23. 43. נַאֲפוּף masc. dec. 1 b, id. Ho. 2. 4.

נָאֹף	} Kal inf. abs.	נאף
נֹאֵף	id. part. act. sing. masc. . .	נאף
נָאֲפָה	*n* Piel pret. 3 pers. sing. fem. (§ 14. rem 1)	נאף
נָאֲפוּ	id. pret. 3 pers. pl. [for נָאֲפוּ comp. § 8 r. 7]	נאף
נַאֲפוּפֶיהָ	*y* n. m. pl., suff. 3 p. s. f. fr. (נַאֲפוּף) d. 1 b	נאף
נֹאֲפוֹת	Kal part. act. fem., pl. of נֹאֶפֶת dec. 13	נאף
נֹאֲפָיִךְ	the foll. with suff. 2 pers. sing. fem.	נאף
נֹאֲפִים	noun masc. pl. [of נֹאֵף, נָאוּף] . .	נאף

נָאַץ *fut.* יִנְאַץ *to deride, despise, contemn, reject.* Pi. נִאֵץ (§ 14. rem. 1).—I to *despise, contemn.*—II. *to give occasion for blasphemy*, 2 Sa. 12. 14. Hiph *intrans.* to be *despised* Ec. 12. 5. Hithpo. *to be despised, contemned*, Is. 52. 5. נֶאָצָה fem. *reproach, insult.* נָאֲצֹתָי fem. id. pl. נָאָצוֹת Ne. 9. 18, 26. Eze. 35. 12.

נִאֵץ	Piel (§ 14. rem. 1) pret. 3 pers. sing. masc.;	
	or, 2 Sa. 1*ʻ*. 14, inf. (§ 10. rem. 2)	נאץ
נֶאָצָה	*ʻ* noun fem. sing.; *ʻ* bef (:) . .	נאץ

---

a Ca. 1. 5.	*g* Ps. 65. 7.	*m* 2 Ki. 6. 29.	*t* Da. 10. 15.	*a* De. 28. 59.	*g* Eze. 21. 12.	*m* Is. 16. 10.	*s* Le. 26. 25.	*y* Ho. 2. 4.
b Ps. 93. 5.	*h* Ge. 22. 13.	*n* 2 Ki. 6. 28, 29.	*u* Je. 42. 5.	*b* De. 28. 59.	*h* La. 1. 21.	*n* Le. 25. 20.	*t* Ju. 15. 13.	*z* Je. 13. 27.
c Je. 23. 14.	*i* Jos. 22. 9.	*o* Je. 50. 36.	*p* 2 Sa. 7. 16;	*c* Ps. 89. 29.	*i* Is. 24. 7.	*o* Je. 48. 33.	*u* Je. 7. 9; Ho. 4. 2.	*a* Eze. 23. 43.
d Ps. 76. 5.	*k* Nu. 32. 30.	*p* Job 15. 16.	Pr. 11. 13.	*d* Da. 8. 26.	*k* La. 1. 4.	*p* De. 3. 8.	*v* Je. 3. 9.	*b* Eze. 23. 43.
e Ge. 34. 15.	*l* Ex. 22. 5.	*q* Is. 53. 7.	*r* Ps. 78. 8.	*e* Da. 2. 36.	*l* Ge. 49. 29.	*q* Ps. 35. 15.	*w* Eze. 23. 37.	*c* Ps. 10. 3, 13.
f Ge. 34. 23.	*m* Nu. 11. 12.	*s* Eze. 3. 26.	*s* Je. 15. 18.	*f* Is. 41. 22.				

35

נָאֲצוּ
נָאֵצוּ } Kal pret. 3 pers. pl. (§ 8. rem. 7) . נאץ

נִאֵצוּ } Piel pret. 3 pers. pl. (§ 14. rem. 1) . נאץ

וַיְנַאֲצוּנִי id. with suff. 1 pers. sing. . נאץ

נָאֲצוֹת noun f. pl. of [נְאָצָה] d. 10 (§ 42. No. 3 note) נאץ

נִאַצְתָּ֫יךָ id. with suff. 2 pers. sing. masc. (vowel under נ lengthened instead of (ֵ) and dag. forte impl. in א) . . . . . נאץ

נֶאֱצַל Niph. pret. 3 pers. sing. masc. . אצל

נֵאַצְתָּ Piel (§ 14. rem. 1) pret. 2 pers. sing. masc. נאץ

נָאַק } fut. יִנְאַק, to groan, lament.
נְאָקָה fem. dec. 11 c (constr. נַאֲקַת § 42. r. 1) a groaning, lamentation.

נַאֲקוֹת n. f. pl. constr. fr. [נְאָקָה] d. 11c (§ 42. r. 1) נאק
נַאֲקַת id. sing., constr. st. . . . נאק
נַאֲקָתָם id. sing., suff. 3 pers. pl. masc. . נאק

נָאַר Pi. (§ 14. rem. 1) to abhor, reject.
נְאָרְכָה Kal fut. 1 p. pl. (נִנְאַר) with opt. ה (§ 8. r. 13) ארב
נֶאֱרִים Niph. part. m. pl. [of נֵאָר, for נֵאָר § 18. r. 14] ארר
נֵאַרְתָּה Piel pret. 2 pers. sing. masc. (comp. § 8. r. 5) נאר
נִשְׁאַר anom. form prob. made up from two readings, נִשְׁאַר Niph. part. & אֲשֶׁאַל Kal fut. שאר
נֶאְשַׁם Kal fut. 1 pers. pl. [for נֶאְשַׁם § 13. rem. 5] אשם
נֶאְשְׁמוּ Niph. pret. 3 pers. pl. [for נֶאְשְׁמוּ § 13. rem. 7, comp. § 8. rem. 7] . אשם

נֹב pr. name of a place . . . נבה

נָבָא Niph. נִבָּא to announce, to prophesy, i. e. to foretell future events, and also generally to teach the Divine will; const. with אֶל, עַל, לְ concerning whom, with בְּ in whose name one prophesies. Hithp. idem.
נְבָא Chald. Ithpa id. Ezr. 5. 1.
נָבִיא masc. dec. 3a, prophet, one inspired and commissioned of God to instruct the people and foretell future events; בְּנֵי הַנְּבִיאִים the sons of the prophets, i. e. the disciples of the prophets.
נְבִיא Chald. masc. idem. See § 68.
נְבִיאָה fem.—I. prophetess.—II. a prophet's wife, Is. 8. 3.
נְבוּאָה fem. dec. 10.—I. prophecy, prediction.— II. prophetical book, 2 Ch. 9. 29.
נְבוּאָה Chald. fem. id. Ezr. 6. 14.

נְבוֹ (for נְבוֹא) pr. name of an idol worshipped by the Chaldeans, supposed to have been Mercury, as the interpreter of the gods, Is. 46. 1, see also נְבוֹ under נָבָה. Hence also the following compounds with נְבוֹ as נְבוּזַרְאֲדָן ,נְבוּכַדְנֶאצַר, נְבוּשַׁזְבָּן which see in their order.

וַיָּבֹא Kal fut. 1 pers. pl. (§ 25. No. 2 f); וְ conv בוא
נָבֹא Niph. pret. 3 pers. sing. masc.; or part. נבא
נָבֹאָה Kal fut. 1 p. pl. with parag. ה (§ 25. No. 2 f) בוא
נָבֹאוּ } id. pret. 3 pers. pl. בוא
וַיָּבֹאוּ }
נְבִיאֵי constr. of נְבִיאִים (q. v.) . . בא
נְבִאִים defect. for נְבִיאִים (q. v.) . . בא
נִבָּאִים Niph. part. masc. pl. [of נָבָא § 23. rem. 9] comp. הַנִּבְּאִים . . . נבא
נִבְאַשׁ Niph. pret. 3 pers. sing. masc. . באש
נִבְאֲשׁוּ id. pret. 3 pers. pl. . . באש
נִבְאַשְׁתָּ id. pret. 2 pers. sing. masc. . באש
נִבֵּאתָ } Niph. pret. 2 pers. sing. masc.; acc.
וַתִּנָּבֵא } shifted by conv. וְ (comp. § 8. r. 7) נבא
וְנִבֵּאתִי } id. pret. 1 pers. sing. . נבא

נָבַב to bore through, to make hollow; only part. נָבוּב hollow; Metaph. empty, stupid, foolish, Job 11. 12.
נִבְגֹּד Kal fut. 1 pers. pl. . . . בגד
נִבְדְּלוּ Niph. pret. 3 pers. pl. . . בדל

נָבָה Root not used; i. q. Arab. נבא to be high.
נְבוֹ (height) pr. name—I. of a mountain and a city in the land of Moab.—II. of a town in the tribe of Judah.
נֹב (for נָבֹה height) pr. name of a city of the Levites near Jerusalem; with ה parag. נֹבָה.
נְבָיוֹת (heights) pr. name of a people descended from Ishmael.
נֹבָה pr. name (נֹב) with ה parag. . . נבה
נִבְהָל Niph. part. sing. masc. . . בהל
נִבְהַל id. pret. 3 pers. sing. masc. . בהל
נִבְהָלָה id. part. sing. fem. of נִבְהָל . בהל
נִבְהֲלָה id. pret. 3 pers. sing. fem. . בהל
נִבְהֲלוּ } Niph. pret. 3 pers. pl. (comp. § 8.
וְנִבְהֲלוּ } rem. 7) . . . . בהל
נִבְהַלְנוּ id. pret. 1 pers. pl. [for נִבְהַלְנוּ v. id.] בהל
נִבְהַלְתִּי } id. pret. 1 pers. sing. (v. id.) . בה

a Ps. 107. 11. b Pr. 1. 30. c Is. 5. 24. d De. 31. 20. e Ne. 9 18, 26. f Eze. 35. 12. g Eze. 42. 6. h 2 Sa. 12. 14. i Ese. 30. 24. k Je. 23. 26, 32. l Eze. 30. 24. m Ex. 6. 5. n Ex. 2. 7. o Pr. 1. 11. p Ma. 3. 9. q Ps. 89. 40. r Eze. 9. 8. s Je. 50. 7. t Joel 1. 18. u 1 Sa. 13. 4. v Je. 23. 21. w Je. 37. 19, etc. x Joel 3. 1. y 2 Sa. 10. 6. z 2 Sa. 16. 21. a Eze. 4. 7. b Mal. 2. 10. c Ps. 30. 8; Pr. 28. 22. d 1 Sa. 28. 21. e Zep. 1. 18. f Ps. 6. 4. g Is. 13. 8. h Eze. 26. 13. i Ps. 90. 7. k Job 21. 6. l Is. 21. 3.

נְבוֹ   pr. name of an idol   נבא

נְבוֹ 'ı pr. name of a place; ı bef. (:)   נבה

סַמְגַּר נְבוֹ.   pr. name, see נְבוֹ

נָבוֹא 'ı, וַ'ı Kal fut. 1 p. pl. (§ 25. No. 2f); ·ı conv.   בוא

נְבוֹאָהʰ 'ı id. with parag. ה (§ 8. rem. 13)   בוא

נְבוּאַתʰ   noun fem. sing., constr. of נְבוּאָה dec. 10   נבא

נָבוּב   Kal part. p. s. m. (or Niph. part. of בוב) d. 3 a   נבב

נְבוּב   id., const. st.   נבב

נְבוּזַרְאֲךָ   (of Nebo prince and lord; compnd. of נְבוֹ q. v. Root נבא, זַר i. q. שָׂר, & אָדָן i. q. אָדוֹן) pr. name of one of Nebuchadnezzar's generals.

נְבוּכַדְנֶאצַּר 'ı   pr. name, Nebuchadnezzar, king of
נְבוּכַדְנֶצּוֹר   Babylon. It is variously inter-
נְבוּכַדְנֶצַּר 'ı   preted. According to Geseniu⸱:
נְבוּכַדְרֶאצּוֹר   of Nebo the god, prince, i. e. prince
נְבוּכַדְרֶאצַּר   of the god Nebo, comp. the preced.;
  chodna or chodan is in the Pers. god;
  Zar, prince. Or נבוך אֶדֶר אַצַּר
  Nebo, god of splendour.

נָבוֹכָה 'ı Niph. pret. 3 pers. sing. fem.   בון

נָבוֹן 'ı Niph. part. sing. masc. dec. 3 a   בין

נְבוֹן 'ı id., constr. st.; ı bef. (:)   בין

נְבוֹנִים   id. pl., abs. st.   בין

נָבוּסׂ   Kal fut. 1 pers. pl.   בוס

נְבוּשַׁזְבָּן 'ı (adorer of Mercury; Gesenius. Comp. נְבוֹ R. נָבָא) pr. name of a prince of Assyria, Je. 39. 13.

נְבוֹת   pr. name of a man   נוב

נִבְזְבָּה 'ı Chald. fem. gift, Da. 2. 6; pl. נִבְזְבָּין (from נִבְזְבָּיָה dec. 9 b), Da. 5. 17. This word is supposed to be of Pers. origin.

נִבְזְבָּיָתָךְ 'ı Chald. noun fem. pl., suff. 2 pers. sing. masc., see the preced.; ı bef. (:)

נָבְזָהˣ 'ı Kal fut. 1 pers. plur. com. [נָבֹז] with parag. ה (§ 8. rem. 13)   בזז

נִבְזֶה 'ı, וַ'ı Niph. part. sing. masc. dec. 9 a   בזה

נִבְזוּ ı Niph. pret. 3 pers. pl.   בזז

נִבְזִיםˢ   Niph. part. masc. pl. of נִבְזֶה dec. 9 a   בזה

[נָבַח]   to bark, Is. 56. 10. Hence

נֹבַח 'ı (o. barking) pr. name—I. of a man, Nu. 32. 42.—II. of a city, Ju. 8. 11   נבח

נִבְחַז   pr. name of an idol of the Avites, 2 Ki. 17. 31.

נִבְחָר   Niph. part. sing. masc.   בחר

נִבְחַר ı id. pret. 3 pers. sing masc.   בחר

נִבְחֲרָהˣ   Kal fut. 1 pers. plur. [נִבְחַר] with parag. ה (§ 8. rem. 13)   בחר

נָבַט וְ ı. Pi. only Is. 5. 30, and Hiph. הִבִּיט.—I. to look, abs.—II. to behold, look at or towards, with אֶל, ל, עַל of the place.—III. with בְּ, to look upon with pleasure, Ps. 92. 12.—IV. to regard, have respect to, with acc., אֶל, ל.—V. to look towards with expectation, with אֶל.

נְבָט   (aspect) pr. name of the father of Jeroboam

מַבָּט   masc. dec. 1 b (with suff. also מֶבָּטֶה), expectation, hope, Zec. 9. 5; meton. object of expectation.

נְבָט   pr. name masc.   נבט

נָבִיא ı'ı Hiph. fut. 1 pers. pl.   בוא

נָבִיא ı'ı noun masc. sing. dec. 3 a   נבא

נְבִיאָה   Chald. noun m. s. emph. [of נְבִיא irr. § 68]   נבא

נְבִיאָהˢ   noun fem. sing. from נָבִיא masc.   נבא

נְבִיאוʸ   Kh. נְבִיאָו for נְבִיאָיו q. v.; K. נְבִיאָי (q. v.)   נבא

נְבִיאֵי 'ı noun m. pl. constr. fr. נָבִיא d. 3 a; ı bef. (:)   נבא

נְבִיאַיָּא 'ı Chald. noun masc. pl. emph. [from נְבִיא
נְבִיאַיָּה   irr. § 68]
נְבִיאֶהָ 'ı noun masc. pl., suff. 3 pers. sing. fem. from נָבִיא dec. 3 a; ı bef. (:)   נבא

נְבִיאֵיהֶם ı id. pl., suff. 3 pers. pl. masc.; ı id.   נבא

נְבִיאָיו   id. pl., suff. 3 pers. sing. masc.   נבא

נְבִיאַיִךְ   id. pl., suff. 2 pers. sing. fem.   נבא

נְבִיאֶיךָ   id. pl., suff. 2 pers. sing. masc.   נבא

נְבִיאֵיכֶם   id. pl., suff. 2 pers. pl. masc.   נבא

נְבִיאִים   id. pl., abs. st.   נבא

נְבִיאֶךָˣ   id. sing., suff. 2 pers. sing. masc. (for נְבִיאֲךָ)   נבא

נְבִיאֲכֶםˢ   id. sing., suff. 2 pers. pl. masc.   נבא

נְבִיאֵם 'ı Hiph. fut. 1 pers. plur. (נָבִיא), suff. 3 pers. pl. masc.; ı for ı, conv.   בוא

נְבָיוֹת   pr. name of a man and a people   נבה
נְבָיֹת

נְבֵּאתָˢ   Niph. pret. 2 p. s. m for נָבֵּאתָ (§ 23. r. 11)   נבא

נָבַךְ   Root not used; prob. i. q. Chald. נְבַע to spring, gush forth.

נֵבֶךְ   m. d. 6 b, fountain, Job 38. 16, so the Sept.

נְבַכַדְנֶאצַּר   pr. name masc. defect., see 'ı נבוכד
נְבַכַדְנֶאצַּר
נְבַכַדְנֶצַּר

נָבְכוּˢ   Niph. pret. 3 pers. pl.   בוך

נִבְכֵי   noun masc. pl. constr. of [נֵבֶךְ] dec. 6 b   נבך

נְבֹכִיםˢ   Niph. part. masc. pl. [of נָבוֹךְ § 32. rem. 5]   בוך

ᵃ 1 Sa. 10. 14.   ᵈ 2 Ch. 9. 29.   ᶠ Da. 5. 17.   ⁱ Am. 3. 11.   ⁿ Job 34. 4.   ʳ 2 Ki. 17. 13.   ᵗ La. 2. 14.   ʸ 2 Ch. 2. 15.   ᵇ Job 38. 16.
ᵇ Ps. 132. 7.   ᵉ Est. 3. 15.   ᵍ 1 Sa. 14. 36.   ᵏ Mal. 2. 9.   ᵖ Ps. 90. 12.   ˢ Ezr. 5. 1.   ᵘ Ex. 7. 1.   ᶻ Je. 26. 9.   ᵉ Ex. 14. 3.
ᶜ Je. 4. 5.   ᶠ Ps. 44. 6.   ʰ Ps. 119. 141.   ᵐ Je. 8. 3.   ᵠ Ju 4. 4.   Ezr. 5. 2.   ˣ Nu. 12. 6.   Joel 1. 18.
35*

נָבֵל fu. יָבֵל.—I. *to wither, fade, fall off*, of leaves and flowers.—II. trop. *to wear, waste, fall away.*—III. *to be weak, to act foolishly*, Pr. 30. 32. Hiph. *to wither, fade*, Is. 64. 5. Pi. נִבֵּל, *to lightly esteem, despise, contemn.*

נָבָל, fem. נְבָלָה (Job 2. 10) adj.—I. *foolish.*—II. *wicked, impious, ungodly.*

נֵבֶל, נֶבֶל masc. dec. 6b or a.—I. *bottle, skin-bottle*, as being shrivelled, flaccid.—II. *any kind of vessel or jar*, made of earthenware.—III. *a musical instrument*, perhaps so called from its shape; generally considered to have been a kind of *lute.*

נְבָלָה fem.—I. *folly.*—II. *impiety, wickedness.*—III. *disgraceful action, crime.*—V. meton. *punishment*, for such an action, Job 42. 8.

נְבֵלָה fem. dec. 11c (with suff. נִבְלָתוֹ, once נִבְלָתִי § 42. rem. 4), *corpse, carcase*, of men and animals; trop. of idols, Je. 16. 18.

נַבְלוּת fem. dec. 1b, *shame, nakedness*, Ho. 2. 12.

נָבֵל (ו') adj. masc. sing. dec. 4a; also pr. name . נבל
נָבֶל Seg. noun in pause for נֵבֶל (§ 35. rem. 2) . נבל
נַּבֵּילָה [for נַבְבִּיל] Hiph. fut. 1 p. pl. ap. [fr. נָבַל], acc. drawn back by conv. וַ [for נַבֵּל] . נבל
נָבֹל Kal inf. abs. . נבל
נָבֵל (וְ') noun masc. sing. dec. 6b or a; for וְ} . נבל
נֵבֶל (וַ') see lett. וַ . }
נֹבֵל Kal part. sing. masc. . נבל
נָבְלָה id. pret. 3 pers. sing. fem. . נבל
נִבְלָה וְ Kal fut. 1 pers. pl. with parag. ה [for § 18. rem. 15, & § 8. rem. 13] . בלל
נְבָלָה 'n. f. s. (no pl. or sing. constr.); וְ bef. . נבל
נְבָלָה וֹ' noun fem. s. d. 11c (§ 42. rem. 4); וֹ id. . נבל
נְבַלָּט pr. name of a town in the tribe of Benjamin, Ne. 11. 34.
נִבְלֵי (וְ') noun masc. pl. constr. from נֵבֶל dec. 6b . נבל
נִבְלֵיהֶם id. pl., suff. 3 pers. pl. masc. . נבל
נְבָלֶיךָ id. pl., suff. 2 pers. sing. masc. . נבל
נְבָלִים וְ' id. pl., abs. st.; וְ bef. . נבל
נִבְלַע Niph. pret. 3 pers. sing. masc. . בלע
נִבְלְעוּ id. pret. 3 pers. pl. . בלע
נִבְלָעֵם Kal fut. 1 pers. pl. [נִבְלַע], suff. 3 pers. pl. masc. (§ 16. rem. 12) . בלע
נֹבֶלֶת Kal part. act. sing. fem. of נָבֵל . נבל
נִבְלְתָּ id. pret. 2 pers. sing. masc.

נִבְלַת noun f. s. constr. of נְבֵלָה d. 11c (§ 42. r. 4) . נבל
נִבְלָתָהּ noun f. s., suff. 3 pers. s. f. fr. [נַבְלוּת] d. 1b . יבל
נִבְלָתָהּ noun fem. sing., suff. 3 pers. sing. fem. from יְבֵלָה dec. 11c (§ 42. rem. 4) . . נבל
נִבְלָתוֹ (וְ') id., suff. 3 pers. sing. masc. . . נבל
נִבְלָתִי id., suff. 1 pers. sing. (‥), immut. § 42. r. 4) . נבל
נִבְלָתֵיךְ וְ Piel pret. 1 pers. sing., suff. 2 pers. sing. f. . יבל
נִבְלָתְךָ noun fem. sing., suff. 2 pers. sing. masc. from נְבֵלָה dec. 11c (§ 42. rem. 4) . . נבל
נִבְלָתָם id., suff. 3 pers. pl. masc. . . נבל
נִבְנָה Niph. pret. 3 pers. sing. masc. . בנה
נִבְנֶה וְ', וַ' Kal fut. 1 pers. pl.; וַ conv. . בנה
נִבְנוּ וְ Niph. pret. 3 pers. pl. . בנה
נִבְנוֹתִי Niph. pret. 1 pers. sing. . בין
נִבְנָיו id. part. pl., suff. 3 pers. s. m. fr. נָבוֹן d. 3a . בין
נְבֹנִים וֹ id. id., abs. st.; וֹ bef. (:) . בין
נִבְנֵית וְ Niph. pret. 2 pers. sing. fem. . בנה
נִבְנְתָה וְ' id. pret. 3 pers. sing. fem. . בנה

[נָבַע] *to gush out, bubble out* or *up*, Pr. 18. 4. Hiph. הִבִּיעַ.—I. *to pour forth, to utter, declare.*—II. *to cause to bubble up*, as fermenting matter, *to render putrid*, Ec. 10. 1.

מַבּוּעַ masc. dec. 1b, *spring* or *fountain.*

נֹבֵעַ Kal part. sing. masc. . נבע
נִבְעָה Niph. part. sing. masc. . בעה
נִבְעוּ id. pret. 3 pers. pl. . בעה
נִבְעָר Niph. pret. 3 pers. sing. masc. . בער
נִבְעָרָה id. part. sing. fem. . בער
נִבְעָרָה וֹ Piel (§ 14. rem. 1) fut. 1 pers. pl. with parag. ה; וֹ bef. (:) . בער
נִבְעֲרוּ Niph. pret. 3 pers. pl. . בער
נִבְעַת Niph. pret. 3 pers. sing. masc. . בעת
נִבְעַתִּי id. pret. 1 pers. s. [for נִבְעַתְתִּי § 25. rem.] . בעת
נִבְקָה וְ Niph. pret. 3 p. s. f. [for נִבְקְקָה § 18. r. 15] . בקק
נַבְקִיעֶנָּה וְ Hiph. fut. 1 pers. pl., suff. 3 pers. sing. f. . בקע
נִבְקַע וְ' Niph. pret. 3 pers. sing. masc. . בקע
נִבְקְעוּ id. pret. 3 pers. pl. (comp. § 8. rem. 7) . בקע
נִבְקָעוּ }
נְבַקֵּשׁ Piel fut. 1 pers. pl. . בקש
נְבַקְשָׁה וְ id. with parag. ה (§ 8. rem. 13); וְ conv. . בקש
נְבַקְשֶׁנּוּ וֹ id. with suff. 3 pers. sing. masc.; וֹ bef. (:) . בקש
נָבָר Niph. part. sing. masc. . ברר
נִבְרָא Niph. part. sing. masc. . ברא
נִבְרְאוּ וַ' id. pret. 3 pers. pl. (comp. § 8. rem. 7) . ברא
נִבְרָאוּ }

• Pr. 30. 22.   ‖ Is. 28. 1. 4.   ‖ Je. 48. 12.   ¶ Pr. 30. 32.   ⁂ Na. 3. 6.   • De. 1. 13.   ‖ Je. 10. 14.   ‖ Is. 19. 3.   ⁂ Exr. 8. 23.
♭ Is. 64. 5.   ᵍ Ge. 11. 7.   ᵐ Ho. 8. 8.   ʳ Ho. 2. 12.   ᵛ Ne. 3. 38.   ᵇ Je. 31. 4.   ᶦ Is. 19. 11.   ᵐ Is. 7. 6.   Ca. 6. 1.
ᶜ Ex. 18. 18.   ᵉ Eze. 41. 4.   ⁿ Is. 28. 7.   ˢ Le. 11. 40.   ʷ Mal. 3. 15.   ᶜ Pr. 18. 4.   ᵏ Ju. 20. 13.   ⁿ Job 26. 8.   ʸ Ps. 102. 19.
ᵈ Ps. 71. 22.   ᵏ 1 Sa. 15. 13.   ° Pr. 1. 12.   ᵗ Je. 36. 30.   ˣ Is. 10. 13.   ᵈ Is. 30. 13.   ᶦ Je. 10. 21.   ° Zec. 14. 4.   ᶻ Ps. 148. 5.
Is. 5. 12.   ‖ Job 32. 37.   ᵖ Is. 1. 30.   ᵘ Is. 26. 19.   ʸ 7.. 29. 14.   ᵇ Ob. L 6.   ᵐ Da. 8. 17.   Ne. 5. 12.   ᵧᵧ Is. 24. 4.

נִבְרֵאת	id. pret. 2 pers. sing. fem.	ברא
נִבְרְחָה[a] ן	Kal fut. 1 pers. pl. with parag. ה (§ 8. r.13)	ברח
נִבְרֵךְ	Piel fut. 1 pers. pl.	ברך
נִבְרְכָה[c]	Kal fut. 1 pers. pl. with parag. ה (§ 8. r.13)	ברך
נִבְרְכוּ ן	Niph. pret. 3 pers. pl.	ברך
נֶבְרַשְׁתָּא	Ch. f., emph. [of נֶבְרְשָׁא d. 9a] *lamp,* Da. 5. 5.	
וּנְבַשֵּׁל[d] ן	Piel fut. 1 pers. pl. ; ן conv.	בשל
[נִנְאַל] וְ נִנְאַל	Niph. pret. 3 pers. sing. masc. [for נִנְאַל]	נאל
נִנְאֲלָה[b] ן	id. part. sing. fem.	נאל
נִנְאַלוּ	pret. 1 pers. sing. (§ 6. No. 10 note)	נאל

נֶגֶב Root not used; Syr. & Chald. *to be dry.* Hence

נֶגֶב masc.—I. *the desert tract of land to the south* of Judea.—II. *the south*; with ה parag. נֶגְבָּה (§ 35. rem. 3) *towards the south, southward*; לְנֶגְבָּה, בַּנֶּגֶב *in the region lying towards the south*; מִנֶּגַב *from the south*; simply נֶגֶב *south, on the south,* comp. Zec. 14. 10   ננב

נֶגְבָּה[a] ן, וְ	id. with loc. ה; for ן see lett. ן	ננב
נַגְבִּיר[e]	Hiph. fut. 1 pers. pl.	נבר

נֶגֶד Kal not used; Arab. *to be clear and manifest.* Hiph. הִגִּיד—I. *to declare, show, tell, announce,* with ל of the pers. to whom.—II. *to publish, proclaim with commendation, to praise.*—III. *to betray,* Job 17. 5. Hoph. הֻגַּד *to be shown, told.*

נְגַד Chald. *to flow,* Da. 7. 10.

נֶגֶד with suff. נֶגְדִּי (§ 35. rem. 3) prep.—I. *before, in the presence* or *sight of.*—II. *over against, in front of, opposite to.*—III. *in comparison with,* Is. 40. 17.—IV. *straight, forwards,* comp. Jos. 6. 5, 20.—V. with prepositions. כְּנֶגֶד Ge. 2. 18, 20. כְּנֶגְדּוֹ *as over against him,* i.e. *corresponding to him, his counterpart;* or, *one like him* (Lee); לְנֶגֶד *before, in the presence of; over against; against, in opposition to; for, appointed to; before,* proceeding on a journey;—מִנֶּגֶד *from before, away from, aloof from; before, in the presence of, over against, opposite,* const. with ל; *against, in opposition to,* with ל.

נֶגֶד Chald. prep. *towards,* Da. 6. 11.

נָגִיד masc. dec. 3a.—I. *leader, chief, prefect, overseer.*—II. *prince.*—III. pl. *nobles;* neut. *noble, excellent thing,* Pr. 8. 6.

נָגִד[i]	Chald. Peal part. sing. masc.	ננד

וַנַּגֵּד ן	Hiph. fut. 1 pers. pl., ap. & conv. from	נגיד
נֶגֶד וְן	(prop. subst. m. d. 6) as a *prep* (§ 35. r. 3)	ננד
נֶגֶד	defect. for נָגִיד (q. v.)	ננד
נֶגְדָּהּ[l]	prep. (נֶגֶד) with suff. 3 p. s. f. (§ 35. r. 3)	ננד
נֶגְדָּה[m]	id. with loc. ה	ננד
נֶגְדּוֹ	id., suff. 3 pers. sing. masc.	ננד
נֶגְדִּי	id., suff. 1 pers. sing.	ננד
נֶגְדְּךָ נֶגְדֶּךָ	} id., suff. 2 pers. sing. masc.	ננד
נֶגְדָּם[n] וְ	id., suff. 3 pers. pl. masc.	ננד
נֶגְדַּע[o] נִגְדַּע[p]	} Niph. pret. 3 p. s. m. (the reading נֶגְדַּע in Je. 50. 23 is only confined to *some* copies) }	נרע
נֶגְדְּעָה[q] ן	id. pret. 3 pers. sing. fem.	נרע
נִגְדְּעוּ ן	id. pret. 3 pers. pl.	נדע
נִגְדַּעְתָּ[r]	id. pret. 2 pers. sing. masc.	ירע

נָגַהּ fut. יִגַּהּ *to shine, give light.* Hiph. הִגִּיהַּ—I. *to cause to shine,* Is. 13. 10.—II. *to make light, enlighten.*

נֹגַהּ masc. dec. 6c (§ 35. rem. 5).—I. *shining, brightness, splendour.*—II. pr. name of a son of David.

נֹגַהּ Chald. masc. dec. 3e, *light,* Da. 6. 20.

נְגֹהָה fem. dec. 10, *shining brightness,* Is. 59. 9.

נֹגַהּ וְ	noun m. s. d. 6c (§ 35. r. 5), also pr. name	ננה
נָגְהָם	id., suff. 3 pers. pl. masc.	ננה
נְגוֹ נְגוֹא	} pr. name in compos. עֲבֵד נְגוֹ see	עבד
נָגוֹגוּ	Niph. pret. 3 pers. pl. [for נָגֹגוּ comp. § 18.r.2]	ננ
נָגוּעַ	Kal part. pass. sing. masc.	ננע
נָגוֹף	Niph. inf. abs. (§ 9. rem. 2, & § 17. rem. 4)	ננף
נִגְזְלָה ן	Niph. pret. 3 pers. sing. fem.	נזל
נִגְזַר	Niph. pret. 3 pers. sing. masc.	נזר
נִגְזְרוּ	id. pret. 3 pers. pl. [for נִגְזְרוּ comp. § 8. r. 7]	נזר
נִגְזַרְנוּ	id. pret. 1 pers. pl.	נזר
נִגְזַרְתִּי	id. pret. 1 pers. s. [for נִגְזַרְתִּי comp. § 8. r. 7]	נזר

[נָגַח] fut. יִגַּח *to push, butt* with the horns, Ex. 21.28, 31, 32. Pi. id. trop. *of a conqueror prostrating nations.* Hithp. with עִם *to engage in conflict with* any one, Da. 11. 40.

נַגָּח masc. *addicted to push* or *butt* with the horns, Ex. 21. 29. 36.

נֹגַהּ	noun masc. sing.	ננה
נָגִיד וְ	noun masc. sing. dec. 3a	ננד
נַגִּיד	Hiph. fut. 1 pers. pl.	ננד

נָגִיד	noun masc. sing., constr. of נָגִיד dec. 3 a	נגד
וְנַגִּידָהֵ	Hiph. fut. 1 p. pl. with parag. ה (comp. §8. r. 13)	נגד
נְגִידִיֵ	} noun masc. pl. constr. & abs. from נָגִיד	נגד
נְגִידִים	} dec. 3 a . . .	
וַנַגִּידֶנּוּᵍ	Hiph fut. 1 pers. pl., suff. 3 pers. sing. m.	נגד
נַגִּילָה	Kal fut. 1 p. pl. with parag. ה (comp. § 8. r. 13)	גול
נְגִינוֹתᶜ	noun fem. pl. of [נְגִינָה] dec. 10; ᵈ bef.	נגן
נְגִינוֹתַיᵉ	id. pl., suff. 1 pers. sing.; ᶠ id.	נגן
נְגִינָתְ	id. sing., constr. st. . .	נגן
נְגִינָתִיᵍ	id. sing., suff. 1 pers. sing.	נגן
נְגִינָתָם	id. sing., suff. 3 pers. pl. .	נגן

נָגַל Root not used; Arab. *to cut, wound.*

מַגָּל masc. *sickle,* Je. 50. 16; Joel 4. 13.

וְנִגְלָה	Niph. pret. 3 pers. sing. masc., or part. fem. dec. 10 [from נִגְלֶה masc.] .	נלה
וְנָגֹלּוּᴴ	Niph. pret. 3 pers. pl. .	נלל
נָגֹלּוּ	Niph. pret. 3 pers. pl. .	נלה
נִגְלוֹתᵢ	id. inf. constr. . .	נלה
וְנִגְלֵינוּᵏ	id. pret. 1 pers. pl. (§ 24. rem. 8)	נלה
נִגְלֵיתִיˡ	id. pret. 1 pers. sing. .	נלה
נִגְלָתָהᵐ	id. pret. 3 p. s. fem. [for נִגְלְתָה comp. §8.r.7]	נלה

[נָגַן] Ps. 68. 26, and Pi. נִגֵּן *to play on a stringed instrument.*

נְגִינָה fem. dec. 10.—I. *music.*—II. *a song;* meton. *subject of a song.*

מַנְגִּינָה fem. d. 10, *song of derision, satire,* La. 3. 62.

נַגֵּן	Piel inf. constr. . .	נגן
נִגֵּןⁿ	id. pret. 3 pers. sing. masc. .	נגן
נִגְנֹבᵏᵇ	Kal fut. 1 pers. pl. . .	נגב
נֹגְנִיםᵖ	Kal part. act. masc. pl. [of נֹגֵן] dec. 7 b	נגן

נָגַע ן ᵍ fut. יִגַּע, inf. c. נְגֹעַ נַּגַּעַת. ᵍ—I. *to touch, meddle with;* const. with בְּ, אֶל; עַל; metaph. *to touch, affect the heart.*—II. *to touch, to reach, come to, arrive at,* with בְּ, עַד, אֶל; עַל; abs. of time, *to arrive.*—III. *to touch with force and violence, to strike, smite.* Niph. *to be smitten, beaten in battle,* Jos. 8. 15. Pi. *to smite, as God does, with disease and calamities.* Pu. pass. Ps. 73. 5. Hiph. הִגִּיעַ.—I. *to cause to touch;* בַּיִת בְּבַיִת ה' *to cause house to touch house,* i. e. to join house to house; הׁ' לָאָרֶץ *to cause to touch* (i. e. cast down to) *the ground.*—II. *to touch,* with אֶל, עַל; עַל.—III. *to reach to,* with עַד, אֶל; אֶל;—IV. *to come to,* with עַד;

hence, *to come upon, happen to;* with לְ *to attain to,* Est. 4. 14; abs. *to come, arrive.*

נֶגַע masc. dec. 6 a (§ 35. rem. 5; w th suff. נִגְעִי).—I. *stroke, blow,* comp. De. 17. 8.—II. *infliction of evil, calamity, plague,* espec. as a divine judgment.—III. *spot, mark,* as of leprosy.

נֶגַע תָּם (for נֶגַע תָּם *calamity is ended*) pr. name masc. Ge. 36. 11, 16.

נֶגַע	} noun masc. sing. (suff. נִגְעִי) dec. 6 a	נגע
וָנֶגַע	} (§ 35. rem. 2 & 5) . .	נגע
נֹגֵעַ	} Kal part. act. sing. masc. dec. 7 b	נגע
נְגֹעַᵗ	ᵗ id. inf. constr.; ᵘ bef.	נע
נָגְעָהᵛ	ᵛ id. pret. 3 pers. sing. fem. .	נע
נָגְעוּ	id. pret. 3 pers. pl. [for נָגְעוּ § 8. rem. 7]	נגע
נִגְּעוֹᵂ	Piel pret. 3 pers. s. m. [נִגַּע], suff. 3 pers. s. m.	נגע
נִגְעוֹ	noun masc. sing., suff. 3 pers. sing. masc. from נֶגַע dec. 6 a (§ 35. rem. 5)	נגע
נִגְעִיˣ	id. with suff. 1 pers. sing. .	נגע
נְגָעִיםᶻ	id. pl., abs. st. . .	נגע
נָגְעֵךְᵃ	Kal inf., suff. 2 pers sing. fem. .	נגע
נִגְעֶךָᵇ	noun masc. sing., suff. 2 pers. sing. masc. [for נִגְעֲךָ] from נֶגַע dec. 6 a (§ 35. rem. 5)	נגע
נִגְעַלᶜ	Niph. pret. 3 pers. sing. masc. .	נעל
נְגַעֲנוּךָᵈ	Kal pret. 1 pers. pl., suff. 2 pers. sing. masc.	נגע
נֹגַעַת	} id. part. sing. and pl. fem. dec. 13 from	נגע
נֹגְעֹתᵉ	} נֹגֵעַ masc. (§ 39. No. 4 b) .	

נָגַף ᶠ ו יִגֹּף.—I. *to strike, smite,* with the hand, a sword, &c.—II. *to smite,* as God does, with disease and calamities, *to plague.*—III. *to thrust, push.*—IV. *to strike, stumble against.* Niph. *to be smitten, defeated.* Hithp. *to strike oneself, stumble against,* Je. 13. 16.

נֶגֶף masc.—I. *infliction of disease, plague,* as a divine judgment.—II. *a stumbling,* Is. 8. 14.

מַגֵּפָה fem. dec. 10.—I. *a plague or pestilence* —II. *a beating, defeat in battle.*

נָגֹףᴴ	Kal inf. abs. . .	נגף
נֶגֶף	noun masc. sing. . .	נגף
נִגָּף	Niph. part. sing. masc. .	נגף
נָגַףᵢ	id. pret. 3 pers. sing. masc. .	נגף
נֹגֵף	id. part. act. sing. masc. .	נגף
וְנָגְפוּᵏ	ן id. pret. 3 pers. pl. .	נגף
נְגָפוֹˡ	id. pret. 3 pers. sing. m., suff. 3 pers. sing. m.	נגף
נִגְּפוּᵐ	} Niph. pret. 3 pers. pl. (comp. § 8. rem. 7)	נגף
נִגְּפוּ		
נֹגְפִים	id. part., pl. of נֹגֵף . .	נגף

ᵃ 2 Ki. 7. 9.   ᵉ Is. 38. 20.   ᵢ 2 Sa. 6. 20.   ᵐ 1 Sa. 16.16,23.   ᵖ Ps. 91. 10.   ʳ 2 Ch. 26. 20.   ᵛ Ps. 39. 11.   ᶠ 2 Ch. 13. 15.   ᵏ Ex. 21. 22.
ᵇ 2 Ch. 35. 8.   ᶠ Ps. 61. ..   ʲ 1 Sa. 14. 8.   Ge. 44. 8.   Le. 11. 36.   ᵞ Ps. 38. 12.   ᶜ 2 Sa. 1. 21.   ᵍ Is. 19. 22.   ˡ 2 Ch. 21. 18.
ᶜ Je. 20. 10.   ᵍ Ps. 77. 7.   ᵏ 1 Sa. 2. 27.   ᵘ Ex. 19. 12.   ᵈ Ge. 12. 17.   ᵉ 3e. 26. 29.   ʰ Is. 19. 22.   ᵐ Ju. 20. 36.
ᵈ Ps. 69. 13.   ʰ Is. 34. 4.   Is. 53. 1.   ᵗ Hag. 2. 12.   Je. 4. 10.   Ru. 2. 9.   ᵢ 1 Ki. 6. 27.   ʲ 2 Sa. 10. 18.

נְגָפָֽנוּ[a]   Kal pret. 3 pers. sing. masc., suff. 1 pers. pl.   נגף

וְ נְגַפְתֶּם[b]   Niph. pret. 2 pers. pl. masc.   נגף

נִגַּר   Niph. נִגַּר.—I. *to be poured out, to flow out.*—II. *to flow, run,* as a wound, Ps. 77. 3. נִגְּרָה יָדִי *my hand* (i. e. the hand upon me), *my wound runs ; others, my hand is put forth, stretched out.* Hiph. הִגִּיר.—I. *'o pour out,* Ps. 75. 9.—II. *to pour, thrust down,* Mi. 1. 6.—III. trop. *to deliver up, give over.* Hoph. *to be poured down,* Mi. 1. 4.

נִגְּרָה   Niph. pret. 3 pers. sing. fem.   נגר

נִגָּרוֹת   Niph. part. fem. pl. [of נִגְּרָה from נָגַר masc. § 18. rem. 14]   נגר

נִגְרַזְתִּי[c]   Niph. pret. 1 pers. sing   נגרז

נִגָּרֵעַ   Niph. fut. 1 pers. pl.   נגרע

נִגְרָע[d]   id. part. sing. masc.   נגרע

וְ נִגְרַע[e]   id. pret. 3 pers. sing. masc.   נגרע

וְ נִגְרְעָה[f]   id. pret. 3 pers. sing. fem.   נגרע

נִגְרָשׁ[g]   Niph. part. sing. masc.   נגרש

וְ נִגְרְשָׁה[h]   id. pret. 3 pers. sing. masc.   נגרש

נִגְרַשְׁתִּי   id. pret. 1 pers. sing.   נגרש

נָגַשׂ   fut. יִגֹּשׂ.—I. *to impel, drive,* Job 39. 7.—II. *to urge any one, to exact,* a task, debt or tax from him ; part. נֹגֵשׂ *an exactor, task-master.*—III. *to oppress ;* part. נֹגֵשׂ *oppressor.* Niph. I. *to be oppressed.*—II. *to be wearied, distressed,* 1 Sa. 14. 24.

[נָגַשׁ]   fut. יִגַּשׁ, imp. גַּשׁ, גְּשָׁה, inf. c. גֶּשֶׁת ; and Niph. נִגַּשׁ *to draw* or *come near, to approach,* constr. with אֶל, בְּ, לְ, עַד, עַל *to any person or thing.* Hiph. הִגִּישׁ.—I. *to bring near.*—II. *to offer, present,* espec. a sacrifice.—III. *to approach,* Am. 9. 10. Hoph. הֻגַּשׁ.—I. *to be brought, placed, put,* 2 Sa. 3. 34. —II. *to be offered,* Mal. 1. 11. Hithp. *to approach,* Is. 45. 20.

וְ נִגַּשׁ[i]   Niph. pret. 3 pers. sing. masc.   נגש

וְ נִגַּשׁ[k]   Niph. pret. 3 pers. sing. masc.   נגש

נֹגֵשׂ   Kal part. act. masc. dec. 7 b   נגש

וְ נִגְּשָׁה[l]   Niph. pret. 3 pers. sing. fem.   נגש

נִגְּשׁוּ[m]   id. pret. 3 pers. pl.   נגש

נֹגְשֵׂי[n]   Kal part. pl. constr. masc. from נֹגֵשׂ dec. 7 b   נגש

נֹגְשָׂיו   id. pl., suff. 3 pers. sing. masc.   נגש

נֹגְשַׂיִךְ   id. pl., suff. 2 pers. sing. fem.   נגש

נְגַשְּׁשָׁה / נְגַשְּׁשָׁה   Piel fut. 1 pers. pl. with parag. ה (comp. § 8. rem. 13 & 15)   נשש

נְגַשְׁתֶּם   Niph. pret. 2 pers. pl. masc.   נגש

וְ נָד[o]   Kal part. act. sing. masc. ; for וָ comp. lett. ו   נוד

נֵד   noun masc. sing. ; or (Is. 17. 11) Kal pret. 3 pers. sing. masc. (§ 21. rem. 2)   נדד

[נָדָא]   i. q. נָדָה Hiph. *to remove, separate,* 2 Ki. 17. 21. Kh.

נָדַב   *to impel, make willing.* Hithp. I. *to show oneself willing, to act voluntarily.*—II. *to give, offer willingly.*

נְדַב   Chald. Ithpa. i. q. Heb. Hithp. inf. הִתְנַדָּבוּת as subst. *free-will offering,* Ezr. 7. 16.

נָדָב   (*liberal*) pr. name masc. of several persons, espec. (a) son of Jeroboam ; (b) son of Aaron.

נְדָבָה   fem. dec. 11 c.—I. *willingness, free will* Ps. 110. 3, עַמְּךָ נְדָבֹת *thy people will be willing-ness,* i. e. *willing.*—II. *voluntary offering.*—III. *liberality, abundance,* Ps. 68. 10.

נָדִיב   masc. dec. 3 a, fem. נְדִיבָה adj.—I. *willing, ready.*—II. *liberal.*—III. *noble, noble-minded.*—IV. *noble,* as a subst. *a noble, a prince.*—V. prob. *libertine,* Job 21. 8 (Lee).

נְדִיבָה   fem. d. 10, *nobility, excellency,* Job 30. 15.

נוֹדָב   (*noble*) pr. name masc. 1 Ch. 5. 19.

נְדַבְיָה   (*noble of the Lord*) pr. name masc. 1 Ch. 3. 18.

וְ נָדָב   pr. name masc.   נדב

נָדְבָה[p]   Kal pret. 3 pers. sing. fem.   נדב

נְדָבָה   noun fem. sing. dec. 11 a   נדב

נְדָבוֹת   id. pl., abs. st.   נדב

נִדְבוֹת   id. pl., constr. st.   נדב

נִדְבֹתָם   id. pl., suff. 3 pers. pl. masc.   נדב

נְדַבְיָה[q]   pr. name masc. ; וּ bef. (:)   נדב

וְ נִדְבָּךְ   Chald. noun masc. sing. dec. 1 a   דבך

נִדְבָּכִין   Chald. id. pl., abs. st.   דבך

נְדַבֵּר   Piel fut. 1 pers. pl.   דבר

נִדְבְּרוּ[r] / נִדְבָּרוּ[s]   Niph. pret. 3 pers. pl. (comp. § 8. rem. 7)   דבר

נִדְבַּרְנוּ[t]   id. pret. 1 pers. pl.   דבר

נְדָבֹת   noun fem. pl. abs. from נְדָבָה d. 11 c, see נדב   נדב

נִדְבַת[u]   id. sing., constr. st.   נדב

נְדִבָתִי[dd]   adj. fem. sing., suff. 1 pers. sing from נְדִיבָה dec. 10, from נָדִיב masc.   נדב

וְ נְדָבֹתֶיךָ   noun fem. pl., suff. 2 p. s. m. fr. נְדָבָה d 11 c   נדב

וְ נִדְבֹתֵיכֶם[x]   id. pl., suff. 2 pers. pl. masc.   נדב

נִדְגֹּל[y]   Kal fut. 1 pers. pl.   דגל

[נָדַד]   fem. נָדְדָה, fut. יִדֹּד.—I. *to move,* as the wing, Is. 10. 14.—II. *to move, wander about.*—III.

a 1 Sa. 4. 3.   c Nu. 9. 7.   i Is. 57. 20.   m Is. 3. 5.   r Is. 59. 10.   x Ex. 35. 29.   cc Ezr. 6. 4.   c Mal. 3. 13.   h De. 12. 17.
b Le. 26. 17.   f Ex. 5. 11.   k Am. 8. 8.   n Is. 59. 10.   s 2 Sa. 11. 20, 21.   y Ps. 119. 23.   f Ps. 110. 3.   t Le. 23. 38.
c Job 20. 28.   g Le. 27. 18.   l Jon. 2. 5.   p Ex. 5. 10, 14.   t Le. 22. 18.   z Mal. 3. 16.   g De. 16. 10.   x Ps. 20. 6.
d Ps. 31. 23.   h Nu. 36. 3.   —2 Ki. 23. 35.   q Is. 60. 17.   u Ge. 4. 12, 14.   cc Ezr. 6. 4.   dd Job. 30. 15.

to flee; of a bird, to fly away. Po. to flee away, Na. 3. 17. Hiph. הֵנַר to chase away, Job 18. 18. Hoph. הֻנַּר (§ 18. rem. 14) fut. יֻדַּר to be made to wander, be driven to and fro. Hithpo. to flee, or be agitated, Ps. 64. 9.

נְדַד Chald. to flee, Da. 6. 19.

נְדֻדִים masc. pl. agitation, restlessness, Job 7. 4.

נֵד masc. heap, mound ; Is. 17. 11 נֵד קָצִיר the heap of the harvest ; but see R. נוד.

נִדָּה fem. dec. 10.—I. uncleanness, impurity, of the female menses.—II. unclean, filthy thing, of idols, of incest.

נִידָה fem. (for נִדָּה dag. forte resolved in Yod) uncleanness, La. 1. 8 ; but comp. R. נוד.

נְדֹד Kal inf. constr. · נדד
נֹדֵד id. part. sing. masc. dec. 7 b   נדד
נָדְדָה id. pret. 3 pers. sing. fem.   נדד
נָדְדוּ / נָדְדוּ } Kal pret. 3 pers. pl. (§ 8. rem. 7)   נדד
נְדֻדִים noun masc. pl. abs.   נדד
נֹדְדִים Kal part. act. masc. pl. of נוֹדֵד dec. 7 b   נדד

נִדָּה Pi. נִדָּה to remove, put away or thrust out.

II. נָדָה Root not used ; to give.
נֵדֶה masc. gift, Eze. 16. 33.
נָדָן masc. dec. 4 a, id. Eze. 16. 33.

נֵדֶה noun masc. sing.   נדה
נֵדָה noun fem. sing. dec. 10   נדד
נִדְהָם Niph. part. sing. masc.   דהם
נָדוּ Kal pret. 3 pers. pl.   נוד
נֹדוּ id. imp. pl. masc.   נוד
נָדוֹן Niph. part. sing. masc.   דון
נָדוֹשׁ Niph. pret. 3 pers. sing. masc.   דוש

[נָדַח] fut. יִדַּח.—I. to impel, force, thrust, De. 20 19.—II. to expel, thrust out, 2 Sa. 14. 14. Niph. נִדַּח.—I. to be impelled, as the hand in striking with an axe, De. 19. 5.—II. to be expelled, driven or cast out.—III. to be impelled, incited, induced to an action. Pu. to be thrust, driven forth, Is. 8. 22. Hiph. הִדִּיחַ.—I. to thrust, cast down, with מִן Ps. 62. 5.—II. to draw or bring down, with עַל 2 Sa. 15. 14.—III. to thrust, drive out, expel.—IV. to urge, seduce, with מִן away from. Hoph. to be driven, chased, Is. 13. 14.

מַדּוּחַ masc. dec. 1 b, seduction, La. 2. 14.

נִדָּח Niph. part. sing. masc. dec. 2 b   נדח
נִדָּחָה id. part. sing. fem.   נדח
נִדְּחָה id. pret. 3 pers. sing. fem.   נדח
נִדְּחוֹ id. part. sing. masc., suff. 3 pers. sing. masc. [as if from נָדַח dec. 7 b, § 15. rem. 2]   נדח
נִדְּחוּ id. pret. 3 pers. pl.   נדח
נִדָּחַי id. part. pl., suff. 1 pers. sing. fr. נָדָח d. 2 b   נדח
נִדְחֵי / נִדְחֵי } id. id. pl., constr. st.   נדח
נִדָּחִים id. id. pl., abs. st.   נדח
נִדַּחֲךָ id. id. sing., suff. 2 pers. sing. masc. [as if from נָדַח dec. 7 b, § 15. rem. 2]   נדח
נִדַּחֲכֶם id. id. sing., suff. 2 pers. pl. masc. (v. id.)   נדח
נִדְחַף Niph. pret. 3 pers. sing. masc.   דחף
נִדְחַתָּ וְ Niph. pret. 2 pers. sing. masc.; acc. shifted by conv. וְ (comp. § 8. rem. 7)   נדח
נִדַחְתֶּם וְ id. pret. 2 pers. pl. masc.   נדח
נְדִי noun masc. sing., suff. 1 pers. sing. from [נוֹד] dec. 1 a   נוד
נָדִיב וְ adj. or subst. masc. sing. dec. 3 a   נדב
נְדִיב id. constr. st.   נדב
נְדִיבָה id. sing. fem. dec. 10   נדב
נְדִיבוֹת id. pl. fem.   נדב
נְדִיבֵי id. pl. constr. masc. dec. 3 a   נדב
נְדִיבִים id. pl. abs. masc.; וּ bef. (:)   נדב
נְדִיבֵמוֹ id. pl. masc. with suff. 3 pers. pl. masc.   נדב
נִדְכָּאִים Niph. part. masc. pl. [of נִדְכָּא]   דכא
נִדְכֶּה וְ Niph. part. sing. masc.   דכה
נִדְכֵּיתִי וְ id. pret. 1 pers. sing.   דכה
נִדְמָה Niph. part. 3 pers. sing. masc.   דמה
נִדְמֶה וְ Kal fut. 1 pers. pl. with opt. ה [for נָדְמֶּה § 18. rem. 14 & 15, comp. § 8. rem. 13]   דמם
נִדְמֶה וְ Kal fut. 1 pers. pl. or Niph. part. sing. m.   דמה
נִדְמֹה Niph. inf. abs.   דמה
נִדְמוּ וְ Niph. pret. 3 pers. pl.   דמם
נִדְמוּ Niph. pret. 3 pers. pl.   דמה
נִדְמֵיתָ / נִדְמֵיתָה } id. pret. 2 pers. sing. masc. (comp. § 8. rem. 5)   דמה
נִדְמֵיתִי id. pret. 1 pers. sing.   דמה
נִדְמְתָה id. pret. 3 pers. sing. fem.   דמה

[נָדָן] masc. dec. 4 a, sheath of a sword, 1 Ch. 21. 27.
נִדְנֶה Ch. masc. sheath, trop. of the body, Da. 7. 15.

נַדְנָהּ noun masc. sing., suff. 3 pers. sing. fem. from [נֵדֶן] dec. 4 a   נדן
נִדְנֶה Ch. noun masc. sing.   דן

a Ps. 55. 8.   f 2 Sa. 19. 10.   k Job 6. 13.   q Je. 49. 36.   v Ps. 56. 9.   y Pr. 8. 16.   e Ps. 38. 9.   f Ho. 10. 15.   k Is. 6. 5.
b Job 7. 4.   g Is. 25. 10.   l De. 19. 5.   r De. 30. 4.   w Is. 32. 8.   z Ps. 83. 12.   d Je. 8. 14.   g Je. 25. 37.   l Je. 47. 5.
c Eze. 16. 33.   h 2 Sa. 14. 14.   m 2 Sa. 14. 14.   s Ne. 1. 9.   x Ps. 51. 14.   a Is. 57. 15.   h Ho. 10. 15 ;   k Eze. 32. 2.   m 1 Ch. 21. 27.
d Je. 14. 9.   i Je. 30. 17.   n Is. 16. 4.   t Je. 49. 5.   b Is. 32. 8.   c Ps. 51. 19.   i Is. 46. 5.   l Ob. 5.   n Da. 7. 15.
e Je. 50. 3.   u Hos. 9. 17.

נְדָנֶיךָ[a] noun masc. pl., suff. 2 pers. sing. fem. fr. נדה [נֵדָן] dec. 4 a

נֵדַע } Kal fut. 1 pers. pl. (§ 20. rem. 1) . ידע
נֵדַע }

נֵדְעָה } id. with opt. ה (§ 8. rem. 13) . ידע
וְנֵדְעָה[b] }

נֶדְעָכוּ Niph. pret. 3 pers. pl. . דעך

וְנֶדְּעֵם[c] } Kal fut. 1 pers. sing. (נֵדַע), with suff. 3 pers. pl. masc. (§ 16. rem. 12) . ידע

וְנֶדְעֶנּוּ[d] } id. with suff. 3 pers. sing. masc. . ידע

נָדַף fut. יִנְדֹּף (§ 17. rem. 3).—I. to drive about, scatter.—II. to put to flight, to rout, an enemy, Job 32. 13. Niph. נִדַּף, inf. c. הִנָּדֵף to be driven about, away.

נִדָּף Niph. part. sing. masc. . נדף
נִדַּף[f] id. pret. 3 pers. sing. masc. . נדף

I. נָדַר fut. יִדֹּר (§ 17. rem. 3) to vow; נָדַר נֶדֶר to make a vow.
נֶדֶר, נֵדֶר masc. dec. 6 b.—I. a vow.—II. thing vowed.

II. נָדַר Root not used; Arab. to cut off.
אִדָּר Ch. masc. dec. 2 b, threshing-floor, Da. 2. 35. But this word is more likely to be derived from אָדַר (q. v.) from the large space the threshing-floor occupies.

נָדַר[g] Kal pret. 3 pers. sing. m. for נָדַר (§ 8. r. 7) נדר
נֶדֶר } noun masc. sing. dec. 6 b or a נדר
[וְ][h] }
נֹדֵר[i] } Kal part. act. sing. masc. נדר
נָדְרָה[k] id. pret. 3 pers. sing. f. [for נָדְרָה § 8. r. 7] נדר
נִדְרָהּ[l] noun masc. sing., suff. 3 pers. sing. fem. from נֶדֶר dec. 6 b . נדר
נָדְרוּ[m] } Kal pret. 3 pers. pl. נדר
נִדְרוֹ[l] noun masc. sing., suff. 3 pers. sing. masc. from נֶדֶר dec. 6 b . נדר
נִדְרוּ[n] Kal imp. pl. masc. . נדר
נִדְרֹשׁ[o] Kal fut. 1 pers. pl. (§ 8. rem. 18) . דרש
נְדָרַי } noun masc. pl., suff. 1 pers. sing. from נֶדֶר dec. 6 b
נִדְרִי } id. sing., suff. 1 pers. sing.
נְדָרֶיהָ[p] id. pl., suff. 3 pers. sing. fem.; וּ bef. (�…)
נִדְרֵיהֶם id. pl., suff. 3 pers. pl. masc.
נְדָרֶיךְ[q] id. pl., suff. 2 pers. sing. fem. [for נְדָרַיִךְ]
נְדָרֶיךָ[r] id. pl., suff. 2 pers. sing. masc.; וּ bef. (⁚)

נִדְרֵיכֶם[s] id. pl., suff. 2 pers. pl. masc. . נדר
נְדָרִים id. pl., abs. st. . נדר
נְדָרֵינוּ[t] id. pl., suff. 1 pers. pl. . נדר
נָדַרְנוּ[u] Kal pret. 1 pers. pl. . נדר
נִדְרָשׁ[v] Niph. pret. 3 pers. sing. masc. [for נִדְרַשׁ comp. § 8. rem. 7] . דרש
וְנִדְרְשָׁה Kal fut. 1 pers. pl. with parag. ה (§ 8. r. 13) דרש
נִדְרְשׁוּ[w] Niph. pret. 3 p. pl. [for נִדְרְשׁוּ comp. § 8. r. 7] דרש
נִדְרַשְׁתִּי id. pret. 1 pers. sing. . דרש
נָדַרְתָּ Kal pret. 2 pers. sing. masc. . נדר
נָדַרְתִּי id. pret. 1 pers. sing. . נדר
נַדַּת[x] Chald. Pael pret. 3 pers. sing. fem. . נדר
נִדַּת[y] noun fem. sing., constr. of נִדָּה dec. 10 . נדר
נִדָּתָהּ[z] id., suff. 3 pers. sing. fem. . נדר
נֹּה masc. Eze. 7. 11, according to some, lamentation, from נָהָה; others (with the Sept.) ornament, beauty, from נוּהּ, i. q. נָאָה, Arab. to be high, magnificent.

I. נָהַג fut. יִנְהַג.—I. to drive, as beasts, a vehicle.—II. to lead, conduct.—III. to lead, carry away, as a spoil.—IV. with בְּ to guide into, accustom to, Ec. 2. 3. Pi. נִהַג (§ 14. rem. 1).—I. to cause to drive, Ex. 14. 25.—II. to lead, bring.—III. to take away, Ge. 31. 26.
מִנְהָג masc. dec. 2 b, a driving of a chariot, 2 Ki. 9. 20.

II. נָהַג Pi. to sigh, Na. 2. 8.
נְהַג[a'] Kal imp. sing. masc. . נהג
נִהַג[b'] Piel pret. 3 pers. sing. masc. (§ 14. rem. 1) . נהג
נֹהֵג Kal part. sing. masc. dec. 7 b . נהג
נֶהְגֶּה[c'] Kal fut. 1 pers. pl. (§ 13. rem. 5) . הגה
נָהֲגוּ[d'] Kal pret. 3 pers. pl. . נהג
נֹהֲגִים id. part. act. masc. pl. of נֹהֵג dec. 7 b . נהג
נִהַגְתָּ Piel 2 pers. sing. masc. (§ 14. rem. 1) . נהג
נֶהְדְּרוּ Niph. pret. 3 pers. pl. [for נֶהְדְּרוּ § 13. rem. 7] הדר

נָהָה[e'] } to wail, lament. Niph. to lament, 1 Sa. 7. 2.
נְהִי masc. lamentation.
נִהְיָה fem. id. Mi. 2. 4.
נְ masc. (for נְהִי) id. Eze. 27. 32
הִי masc. (for נְהִי) id. Eze. 2. 10.

נְהֵה[m'] Kal imp. sing. masc. . נהה
נְהָגִים[n'] Kal part. pass. masc. pl. of (נָהוּג) dec. 3 a . נהג
נְהֹרָא[o'] Ch. n. m. s., emph. of (נְהוֹר) d. 1 a; וּ bef. (⁚) נהר
נְהַחֲוֵה Chald. Pael fut. 1 pers. pl. . חוה

a Eze. 16. 33. f Is. 19. 7. l Nu. 30. 5, 9. r Nu. 30. 5, 6, 7, f De. 12. 6. z Is. 65. 1. e La. 3. 2. l 1 Sa. 30. 20. m Eze. 32. 18.
b Job 34. 4. g Ju. 11. 39. m Is. 19. 21. 8, 12, 15. u Je. 44. 25. a Da. 6. 19. f 2 Ki. 4. 24. k Is. 63. 14. n Is. 60. 11.
c Job 6. 17. h Mal. 1. 14. n Ps. 76. 12. s Ezr. 4. 2. v Le. 22. 18. b Le. 12. 2. g Ex. 10. 13. l La. 5. 12. o Da. 2. 22.
d Ps. 78. 3. i Le. 27. 2. o Na. 2. 1. t 1 Ch. 26. 31. w Le.15.24,25,26. c Is. 59. 11. i Mi. 2. 4. p Da. 2. 7.
e Ju. 19. 22. k Nu. 30. 11. p 2 Sa. 15. 7. u Gen. 42. 22.

נֶהִי (נְ') noun masc. sing. (§ 35. rem. 14); for 1 see lett. ו } נהה

נִהְיֶה Kal fut. 1 pers. pl., ap. for נְהְיֶה (§ 24. rem. 3 c); וַ conv. . . . . היה

נִהְיָה Niph. pret. 3 pers. sing. masc., or (Pr. 13. 19) part. fem. [of נְהְיָה] . . . היה

נִהְיָה noun fem. sing. . . . . . נהה

נִהְיֶה (וַ') וַ Kal fut. 1 pers. pl.; וַ conv. . . היה

נִהְיֵיתָ Niph. pret. 2 pers. sing. masc. . . היה

נִהְיֵיתִי id. pret. 1 pers. sing. . . . היה

נְהִירָא ו Ch., נְהִירָא Cheth., n. m. s. emph. [of נְהִיר], K. נְהוֹרָא (q.v.) . . . . נהר

נַהִירוּ וַ Chald. noun fem. sing. . . . נהר

נִהְיָתָה Niph. pret. 3 pers. sing. fem. (comp. § 8. rem. 7) } היה

נָהַל Pi. נֵהַל (§ 14. rem. 1).—I. to lead, conduct.— II. to sustain, provide. Hithp. to proceed, Ge. 33. 14. נַהֲלֹל m. d. 1 b.—I. pasture, Is. 7. 19.—II. pr.n. of a city in Zebulun, Ju. 1. 30, called נַהֲלָל in Jos. 19. 15.

נְנַהֵל Piel fut. 1 pers. pl. . . . . הלך

נֶהֱלַכְתִּי Niph. pret. 1 pers. sing. [for נֶהֱלַכְתִּי § 13. r. 7] הלך

נַהֲלָל וַ pr. name of a place . . . נהל

נַהֲלֹל pr. name of a place . . . . נהל

נִהַלְתָּ Piel pret. 2 pers. sing. masc. . . נהל

[נָהַם] fut. יִנְהַם.—I. to grumble or growl, as a lion.— II. to murmur, as the sea, Is. 5. 30.—III. to groan, moan, as one in distress. נַהַם m. a growling, as of a lion, Pr. 19. 12; 20. 2. נְהָמָה fem. dec. 11 c (constr. נַהֲמַת § 42. r. 1).— I. a murmuring, roaring of the sea, Is. 5. 30.—II. groaning, moaning of one in affliction, Ps. 38. 9.

נַהַם noun masc. sing. . . . . . נהם

נֹהֵם Kal part. act. sing. masc. . . . נהם

נֶהֱמֶה Kal fut. 1 pers. pl. . . . . המה

נָהַמְתָּ וַ Kal pret. 2 pers. sing. masc.; acc. shifted by conv. וַ (§ 8. rem. 7) . . . נהם

נֶהֱמַתֶּם וַ id. pret. 2 pers. pl. masc.; וַ for וַ, conv. נהם

נֶהֱפוֹךְ וַ Niph. inf. abs. (§ 9. rem. 1) . . הפך

נֶהְפַּךְ נֶהֱפָךְ } Niph. pret. 3 pers. sing. masc. (§ 13. r. 7) הפך

נֶהֶפְכָה id. pret. 3 pers. sing. fem. . . הפך

נֶהֶפְכוּ נֶהֶפְכוּ וַ } id. pret. 3 pers. pl. (§ 13. rem. 7, comp. rem. 4, 5, 6) } הפך

נֶהֶפֶּכֶת id. part. fem. sing. [for פֶּכֶת from הָפַך m.] הפך

נֶהְפַּכְתָּ וַ id. pret. 2 pers. sing. masc.; acc. shifted by conv. וַ (comp. id. & § 8. rem. 7) . הפך

נֶהְפַּכְתִּ id. pret. 2 pers. sing. fem. . . . הפך

[נָהַק] fut. יִנְהַק to bray, as the ass, Job 6. 5; 30. 7.

[נָהַר] I. to flow, run.—II. to shine, be bright. נָהָר masc. dec. 4 a (pl. נְהָרִים, נְהָרוֹת, constr. נַהֲרֵי).—I. current, stream.—II. stream, river. Du. נַהֲרַיִם (from a sing. נָהָר) the two rivers, i. e. Tigris and Euphrates, whence נַ אֲרַם Mesopotamia. נַהֲרָה Ch. m. emph. נַהֲרָא (d. 3 a) a river נְהוֹר Chald. masc. dec. 1 a, light, Da. 2. 22, Keri; נְהִיר Kh. נַהִירוּ or נְהִירוֹ Ch. fem. light, wisdom, Da. 5. 11, 14. נְהָרָה fem. light, daylight, Job 3. 4. מִנְהָרָה fem. only pl. מִנְהָרוֹת Ju. 6. 2, clefts in the mountains, serving as canals to the mountain torrents (Lee).

נָהָר נ' noun masc. sing. dec. 4 a . . . נהר

נְהַר וַ id. constr. st.; & (Da. 7. 10) Chald. noun masc. dec. 3 a . . . . . נהר

נַהֲרָא Chald. id. emph. st., see the preced. . נהר

נַהֲרֹן Kal fut. 1 pers. pl. . . . . הרן

נַהֲרָגֵנוּ וַ id., suff. 3 pers. sing. masc. . . הרן

נַהֲרָה Chald. for נַהֲרָא (q. v.) . . . נהר

נְהָרָה noun fem. sing. . . . . . נהר

נָהַרְנוּ וַ נָהַרוּ } Kal pret. 3 pers. pl. (§ 8. rem. 7) . נהר

נְהָרוֹת נְהָרוֹת וַ } n.m. with pl. f.term.constr. & abs. st.fr. נָהָר d.4 a (comp. § 42.r.1); וַ bef. (:) } נהר

נַהֲרוֹתֶיהָ id. pl. fem., suff. 3 p. s. fem. (comp. § 42. r. 1)

נַהֲרוֹתָם וַ id. pl. fem., suff. 3 pers. pl. masc. (§ 4. r. 2)

נַהֲרֵי id. pl. masc., constr. of נְהָרִים . . נהר

נְהָרַיִם נְהָרַיִם } id. du., pr. name in compos. אֲרַם נַ ארם

נְהָרִים id. pl., abs. st. . . . . . נהר

נֶהֶרְסָה Niph. pret. 3 pers. sing. fem. [for נֶהֶרְסָה comp. § 8. rem. 7] . . . הרם

נֶהֶרְסוּ וַ id. pret. 3 pers. pl. . . . . הרם

נֶהֱרַתְּ וַ Kal pret. 2 pers. sing. fem. . . נהר

נַהֲרַתֶיהָ noun m., pl. f. term., suff. 3 pers. sing. fem. from נָהָר dec. 4 a (comp. § 42. rem. 1) . נהר

נַהֲרַתֶיךָ וַ id., suff. 2 pers. sing. fem. . . נהר

נַהֲרַתָם id., suff. 3 pers. pl. masc. (§ 4. rem. 2) . נהר

נְהַשְׁכַּח Chald. Aph. fut. 1 pers. pl. (§ 47. rem. 4) שכח

---

a Je. 9. 9.   e Da. 8. 27.   i Ex. 15. 13.   n Eze. 24. 23.   r Jon. 3. 4.   x Ezr. 4. 16.   b Ps. 34. 6.   f Job 20. 17.   z Eze. 31. 4.
b Mi. 2. 4.   d Da. 5. 11, 14.   k Pr. 28. 15.   o Est. 9. 1.   s 1 Sa. 10. 6.   y Ge. 31. 21.   c Ca. 8. 7.   g Pr. 24. 31.   i Is. 44. 27.
c Ge. 47. 19.   g Is. 59. 9; Ps. 55. 15.   l Is. 59. 11.   p Job 20. 14.   t Je. 2. 21.   z Ge. 37. 20.   d Eze. 31. 15.   h Is. 60. 5.
d De. 27. 9.   h Ps. 109. 23.   m Pr. 5. 11.   q La. 5. 2.   u 1 Ch. 5. 26.   a Job 3. 4.   e Eze. 32. 14.   ii Da. 2. 22.

נוא Kal not used (except Nu. 32. 7, Kh.) Hiph. הֵנִיא.—I. *to refuse, decline*, Ps. 141. 5.—II. *to hinder, restrain, prohibit*, Nu. 30. 6, 9, 12.—III. *to dissuade, discourage*, with מִן Nu. 32. 7, 9.—IV. *to frustrate*, Ps. 33. 10.

תְּנוּאָה fem. dec. 10, *hinderance, opposition, hostility*, Nu. 14. 34; Job 33. 10.

נוֹאֲלוּ Niph. pret. 3 pers. pl. . . . יאל

נוֹאַלְנוּ id. pret. 1 pers. pl. . . . יאל

נוֹאָשׁ Niph. part. sing. masc. (adverbially) יאש

נוֹאַשׁ id. pret. 3 pers. sing. masc. . יאש

[נוֹב] fut. יָנוּב.—I. *to put forth shoots*, Ps. 92. 15.—II. *to increase*, Ps. 62. 11.—III. *to produce, utter*, Pr. 10. 31.

נוֹב masc. Is. 57. 19. Kh. and

נִיב m. d. 1 a, *produce, fruit*, Is. 57. 19; Mal. 1. 12.

נֵיבַי (*prosperous*) pr. name masc. Ne. 10. 20.

נְבוֹת (*produce, fruit*) pr. name m. 1 Ki. 21. 1, sq.

תְּנוּבָה fem. dec. 10, *produce, increase, fruit*.

נוֹבִי Kh. נוֹב, K. נִיב noun masc. sing. dec. 1 a נוב

נֵיבַי Kh. נוֹבַי, K. נֵיבַי pr. name masc. נוב

נוֹגוֹת Niph. part. fem. pl. [of נוּגָה from נָגָה masc. § 20. rem. 5] . . . ינה

נוּגֵי id. part. pl. constr. masc. [from נוּגָה d. 9 a ינה

נוֹגֵעַ Kal part. act. sing. masc. dec. 7 b . ננע

נוֹגֵשׂ Kal part. act. sing. masc. dec. 7 b ננשׂ

[נוֹד] fut. יָנוּד, ap. תָּנֹד.—I. *to move, be agitated, shaken.*—II. *to be driven about, to wander as a fugitive*; part. נָד *a fugitive.*—III. *to remove, depart, flee*; Is. 17. 11 נֵד קָצִיר *the harvest fleeth*, according to some; but see נֵד.—IV. *to shake* the head, as an expression of pity, *to console, comfort*, with לְ of the person; hence—V. *to deplore, bemoan*, Je. 22. 10. Hiph. הֵנִיד.—I. *to move, shake* the head, with בְּ, Je. 18. 16.—II. *to cause to move, wander*, 2 Ki. 21. 8.—III. *to move, disturb*, Ps. 36. 12. Hithpal.—I. *to shake oneself*, i. e. shake one's head in derision, Je. 48. 27.—II. *to be shaken to and fro, to reel*, Is. 24. 20.—III. *to bemoan oneself*, Je. 31. 18.

נוּד Chald. *to depart, flee*, Da. 4. 11.

נוֹד masc. dec. 1 a.—I. *wandering*, Ps. 56. 9.—II. pr. name of the region whither Cain fled, Ge. 4. 16.

נִיד masc. *a moving* of the lips, Job 16. 5.

נִידָה fem. *a wandering*, La. 1. 8; but see R. נָדַד.

מָנוֹד masc. dec. 3 a, *a shaking* of the head, i. e. the object of it, Ps. 44. 15.

נוֹד pr. name of a region . . . נוד

נוֹדָב } pr. name masc. . . . נדב

נוֹדַד } Poal pret. 3 pers. sing. masc. נדד

נוֹדֵד Kal part. act. sing. masc. dec. 7 b . נדד

נוֹדֶדֶת id. part. sing. fem. . . . נדד

נוֹדֶה Hiph. fut. 1 pers. pl. (§ 25. No. 2e) ידה

נוֹדְרוּ Kh. נוֹדְרִי, K. נוֹדְרֵי sing. fem. נוד Kal imp. pl. masc.,

נוֹדִיעָה } Hiph. fut. 1 pers. pl. with parag. ה (comp. § 8. rem. 13) . . . . ידע

נוֹדָע '' Niph. part. sing. masc. . . ידע

נוֹדַע '' id. pret. 3 pers. sing. masc. . . ידע

נוֹדְעָה id. pret. 3 pers. sing. fem. . ידע

נוֹדְעוּ id. pret. 3 pers. pl. [for נוֹדְעוּ comp. § 8. r. 7] ידע

נוֹדַעְתִּי } id. pret. 1 pers. sing.; acc. shifted by conv. וְ (comp. § 8. r. 7) . } ידע

נוֹדַעְתִּי } id. id.; with conv. וְ, acc. retained bef. monos. (בָּם), comp. the preced. . ידע

[נָוָה] *to sit, dwell quietly*, Hab. 2. 5. Hiph. *to prepare a dwelling*, Ex. 15. 2. Others, *to adorn*, נָוָה i. q נָאָה q. v.

נָוֶה masc. dec. 9 b, fem. נָוָה dec. 11 a.—I. adj. (*a*) *inhabiting*, Ps. 68. 13; (*b*) *comely*, Je. 6. 2; comp נָאָה.—II. subst. (*a*) *dwelling, habitation*; (*b*) *fold* for cattle; others, *pasture*.

נָוָה fem. dec. 11 a, i. q. נָוֶה No. II. Job 8. 6; Zep. 2. 6.

נָוֺית (*habitations*) pr. name of a dwelling-place of the prophets near Ramah, 1 Sa. 19. 18, 19, 22, 23; 20. 1, Kh., in Keri נָיוֹת.

נֹוַהּ noun masc. sing. dec. 9 a . . . נוה

נֹוֵהּ id., constr. st.; וְ bef. (ְ) . . נוה

נָוֵהוּ id., suff. 3 pers. sing. masc. . נוה

נְוֵהֶם id., suff. 3 pers. pl. masc. . נוה

נוֹוַלֵיהֶם וְ the foll. with suff. 3 pers. pl. masc. . נזל

נוֹוְלִים וְ Kal part. act. masc. pl. [of נוֹזֵל dec. 7 b נזל

[נוֹחַ, נוּחַ] fut. יָנוּחַ, ap. וַיָּנַח (§ 21. rem. 9).—I. *to rest, settle down, alight*, with בְּ, עַל.—II. *to rest, be at rest, have repose*. Hence—III. *to abide, continue.*—IV. *to rest, to cease, leave off* speaking, 1 Sa. 25. 9. Hiph. 1. הֵנִיחַ, fut. יָנִיחַ, ap. יָנַח (§ 21. rem. 19).—I. *to set, put, lay or let down; to let fall.*—II. *to cause to rest; to give rest, repose* 2. הִנִּיחַ, fut. יַנִּיחַ, ap. יַנַּח (§ 21. rem. 24).—I. *to set, put or lay down, to place, deposit.*—II. *to let rest, remain.*—III. *to permit, suffer, let alone.*—IV. *to leave behind.* Hoph. I. הוּנַח *rest* is given, La. 5. 5.—II. הֻנַּח *to be set, placed;* part. מֻנָּח *something left,* Eze. 41. 9, 11.

נוֹחַ masc.—I. *rest, quiet,* Est. 9. 16, 17, 18; with suff. נוֹחֲךָ (§ 30. rem. 4), 2 Ch. 6. 41.—II. נֹחַ pr. name, *Noah.*

נוֹחָה (*rest*) pr. name masc. 1 Ch. 8. 2.

נַחַת fem.—I. *a setting, letting down,* Job 36. 16; Is. 30. 30, which may consistently be derived from נָחַת.—II. *rest, quiet.*—III. pr. name m. 1 Ch. 6. 11, called תּוֹחַ in ver. 19.

נִיחוֹחַ masc. dec. 1 b (prop. *acquiescence*) *satisfaction, delight;* רֵיחַ נ׳ *savour of delight,* i. e. *pleasant, sweet savour.*

נִיחוֹחַ Chald. masc. dec. 1 a, *sweet odour, incense.*

הֲנָחָה fem. *rest, release,* Est. 2. 18.

נוֹחַ (*rest*) pr. name of a town on the confines of Ephraim and Manasseh.

מָנוֹחַ masc. dec. 3 a (with suff. מְנוּחֶיךָ § 30. r. 4). —I. *rest, quiet.*—II. *resting-place.*—III. pr. name of the father of Samson.

מְנוּחָה f. d. 10.—I. *rest, quiet.*—II. *resting-place.*

מָנַחַת (*rest*) pr. name.—I. of a man, Ge. 36. 23. —II. of a place, 1 Ch. 8. 6.

נֹחַ ן noun masc. sing., suff. נוּחֶךָ (§ 30. rem. 4) — נוח
נוֹחָה pr. name masc. — נוח
נוֹחֲלָה Niph. pret. 3 pers. sing. fem. — יחל

[נוט] *to move, be shaken,* Ps. 99. 1.

נוֹטֶה Kal part. sing. masc. dec. 9 — נטה
נוֹטֵיהֶם ן id. sing., suff. 3 pers. pl. masc. from נוֹטֶה dec. 9 a (§ 38. r. 1, comp. also § 24. r. 21 b) — נטה
נוֹטֵל Kal part. act. sing. masc. — נטל
נְוֵיהֶן noun masc. pl. (but comp. נוֹטֵיהֶם), suff. 3 pers. pl. fem. from נָוֶה dec. 9 b — נוה
נָוֹת Kh. נָוִית, K. נָיוֹת pr. name of a place — נוה
נָוֶךָ noun masc. sing., suff. 2 p. s. m. fr. נָוֶה d. 9 b — נוה
נוֹטֵר ן Kal part. act. sing. masc. dec. 7 b — נטר
נוֹכָח Niph. part. sing. masc. — יכח
נִוָּכְחָה ן id. fut. 1 pers. pl. [נִוָּכַח] with parag. ה (comp. § 8. rem. 13) — יכח
נוֹכֵל Kal part. act. sing. masc. — נכל
נוּכַל Hoph. fut. 1 pers. pl. — יכל
נוּכְלָה ן id. with parag. ה (comp. § 8. rem. 13) — יכל

נָוֵל Root not used; Chald. Pa. *to dirty, soil.* נְוָלִי, נְוָלוּ Chald. fem. *dunghill,* Da. 2. 5; 3. 29; Ezr. 6. 11.

נוֹלָד Niph. part. sing. masc. dec. 2 b — ילד
נוֹלַד id. pret. 3 pers. sing. masc. — ילד
נוֹלְדוּ id. pret. 3 pers. pl. with euph. dag. [for § 20. rem. 5] — ילד
נְבָלִי Chald. noun fem. sing. — נול
נְבָלֵי Chald. noun fem. sing. — נול

[נום] fut. יָנוּם, *to slumber.*

נוּמָה fem. *slumber,* Pr. 23. 21.

יָנוּם (*slumber*) pr. name of a place in the tribe of Judah, Jos. 15. 53, Kh., יָנוֹם Keri.

תְּנוּמָה fem. dec. 10, *slumber.*

נוּמָה noun fem. sing. — נום

נוּן Niph. in Keri, or Hiph. in Kheth. Ps. 72. 17, *to sprout, flourish;* others, *to propagate.* Comp. derivv. Lee, *drawn out, perpetuated.* The versions seem to have read here יִכּוֹן.

נוּן (*fish;* so Syr. and Chald.) pr. name of the father of Joshua; once נֹן 1 Ch. 7. 27.

נִין masc. dec. 1 a, *offspring, posterity.*

מָנוֹן masc. Pr. 29. 21, *child, son,* comp. Eng. vers. Yarchi, *young master* or *lord.* Others, from מָאַן, *ingratitude;* Lee, *despiser.*

נוּן pr. name masc. — נון
נֹן pr. name masc. — נון

[נוס] fut. יָנוּס.—I. *to flee, flee away, escape* from a person, place or thing, with לִפְנֵי, מִפְּנֵי, מִן.—II. *to proceed, ride swiftly,* Is. 30. 16. Pil. נוֹסֵס *to impel, drive,* Is. 59. 19. Hiph. הֵנִיס.—I. *to cause to flee* for refuge or shelter.—II. *to put to flight,* De. 32. 30.

נִיס masc. *fleeing,* Je. 48. 44, Kh.; Keri נָס part.

מָנוֹס masc. (with suff. מְנוּסִי § 30. rem. 4).—I. *flight,* Je. 46. 5.—II. *place of flight, refuge.*

מְנוּסָה fem. d. 10, *flight,* Le. 26. 36; Is. 52. 12.

נוֹס Kal inf. abs. — נום
נוֹסְדוּ Niph. pret. 3 pers. pl. — יסד
נוֹסָף ן Niph. part. sing. masc. — יסף
נוֹסַף ן id. pret. 3 pers. sing. masc. — יסף
נוֹסְפָה ן id. pret. 3 pers. sing. fem. — יסף
נוֹסָפוֹת ן id. part. fem. pl. [of נוֹסָפָה] as a subst. — יסף
נִתְוַסְּרוּ ן [for נִתְוַסְּרוּ] Hithpa. pret. 3 pers. pl. (§ 20. No. 1, & § 7. No. 10) — יסר

[נוע, נוֹעַ Is. 7. 2.] fut. יָנוּעַ, ap. יָנַע (§ 21. rem. 9).—I. *to move to and fro, be agitated, shaken.*—II. *to*

a Est. 9. 16, 17, 18.   c 2 Sa. 24. 12.   e Na. 1. 2.   h Mal. 1. 14.   m Ezr. 6. 11.   p Pr. 23. 21.   r Ps. 2. 2.   t Je. 36. 32.   x Is. 15. 9.
b Eze. 19. 5.   d Je. 23. 3.   f Job 23. 7.   i Je. 20. 10.   n Da. 2. 5; 3. 29.   q 2 Sa. 18. 3.   s Pr. 11. 24.   u Nu. 36. 4.   y Eze. 23. 48.
g Is. 42. 5.   f Job 5. 24.   l Is. 1. 18.   1 Ch. 3. 5; 20. 8.

stagger, as a drunken man.—III. *to move, be moved*, of the lips.—IV. *to be changeable, variable*, Pr. 5. 6.—V. *to wander, wander about*. Niph. *to be shaken*. Hiph. הֵנִיעַ.—I. *to shake*, as the head or hand.—II. *to agitate, shake, disturb.*—III. *to cause to reel, tremble*, Da. 10. 10.—IV. *to cause to wander about.*

נֵעָה (*a shaking*) pr. name of a place in Zebulun, Jos. 19. 13.

נֹעָה (*moving, motion*) pr. name fem. Nu. 26. 33.

מְנַעַנְעִים masc. pl. (of נַע , מְנַעֲנַע § 36. rem. 5) 2 Sa. 6. 5, the name of a musical instrument. Vulg. sistra, *sistrums*, a kind of *timbrel*, played upon by *shaking* it in cadence.

נֹעַ[b]	וְ[a] Kal inf. abs.	נוע
נִוָּעֵד[d]	Niph. fut. 1 pers. pl.	יעד
נִוָּעֲדָה[f]	וְ[e] id. id. with parag. ה (comp. § 8. rem. 13)	יעד
נוֹעֲדוּ[g]	Niph. pret. 3 pers. pl. (comp. § 8.	יעד
נוֹעָדוּ[i]	וְ[h] rem. 7)	יעד
נוֹעַדְיָה	וְ pr. name masc.	יעד
נוֹעַדְתִּי	וְ id. pret. 1 pers. s.; acc. shifted by conv. וְ	יעד
נוֹעַץ	Niph. pret. 3 pers. sing. masc.	יעץ
נוֹעִיל[l]	Hiph. fut. 1 pers. pl.	יעל
נוֹעַץ	Niph. pret. 3 pers. sing. masc.	יעץ
נִוָּעֲצָה	וְ id. fut. 1 pers. pl. with parag. ה (comp. § 8. rem. 13)	יעץ
נוֹעֲצוּ[q]	id. pret. 3 pers. pl.	יעץ
נוֹעֲצִים	id. part. masc., pl. of נוֹעֵץ	יעץ

[נוף] *to sprinkle*, which is done by *waving, shaking* the hand, Pr. 7. 17, comp. Hiph. הֵנִיף.—I. *to lift up*, as the hand an instrument, with אֶל , עַל *against, over.*—II. *to move to and fro, to wave, shake*, as the hand a sieve; espec. with reference to the priests' *waving* in the presentation of offerings.—III. *to sprinkle, scatter*, Ps. 68. 10. Hoph. *to be waved*, Ex. 29. 27. Pil. נוֹפֵף *to wave, shake* the hand, Is. 10. 32.

נוֹף masc. *elevation*, Ps. 48. 3.

נָפָה fem. dec. 10.—I. *a height*; only in the pr. name נָפַת דּוֹר , נָפוֹת דּוֹר *heights of Dor*, a place near Mount Carmel.—II. *sieve, fan*, Is. 30. 28.

נֶפֶת fem. *high place, height*, Jos. 17. 11.

נֹפֶת fem. *a dropping, distilling*; נֹפֶת צוּפִים *honey as dropped from the honeycomb.*

תְּנוּפָה fem. dec. 10.—I. *a lifting, waving* or *shaking* of the hand.—II. *a waving* of the priest

in the presentation of offerings; meton. *wave-offering.*—III. *agitation, tumult*, Is. 30. 32.

נוֹף[m]	noun masc. sing.	נוף
נוֹפֵל[o]	Kal part. act. sing. masc. dec. 7 b	נפל
נִץ	Hiph. הֵנֵץ (comp. § 21. rem. 14) *to flourish, blossom*, Ca. 6. 11 ; 7. 13.	
נוֹצָה[p]	noun fem. sing.	נצה
נוֹצִיא[q]	Hiph. fut. 1 pers. pl.	יצא
נוֹצַר[r]	Niph. pret. 3 pers. sing. masc.	יצר
נוֹצֵר[s]	Kal part. sing. masc. dec. 7 b	נצר
נוֹצְרִים	id. pl., abs. st.	נצר

נוּק i. q. יָנַק , only Hiph. *to give suck, to suckle*, Ex. 2. 9.

נוֹקֵשׁ[s]	Kal part. sing. masc.	נקש
נוֹקְשׁוּ	וְ Niph. pret. 3 pers. pl.	יקש
נוֹקַשְׁתָּ	id. pret. 2 pers. sing. masc.	יקש

נוּר Root not used ; i. q. נָהַר , Arab. נאר *to shine.*

נוּר Chald. masc. dec. 1 a, *fire.*

נֵר (נֵר) (once) masc. dec. 1 a.—I. *light, lamp*; trop. *prosperity, happiness.*—II. pr. name of the grandfather of Saul.

נֵיר , נֵר masc. *light, lamp*, only metaph.

נֵרִיָּה (*light of the Lord*) pr. name—I. of the father of Baruch, companion of Jeremiah.—II. Je. 51. 59.

מְנוֹרָה fem. dec. 10, *candlestick* or *chandelier.*

נוּר	Chald. noun masc. sing. dec. 1 a	נור
נוֹרָא	וְ[t] Niph. part. sing. masc. (§ 25. No. 2 d)	ירא
נוּרָא	Chald. noun masc. sing., emph. of נוּר dec. 1 a	נור
נוֹרָאָה[u]	Niph. part. sing. fem. dec. 11 a, fr. נוֹרָא m.	ירא
נוֹרָאוֹת	וְ[v] id. pl., abs. st.	ירא
נוֹרְאוֹתֶיךָ	id. pl. with suff. 2 pers. sing. masc.	ירא

[נוש] i. q. אָנַשׁ *to be sick*, Ps. 69. 21.

נוֹשְׂאֵי	Kal part. act. pl. constr. masc. from נָשָׂא (q. v.) dec. 7 b	נשא
נוֹשָׁבָה[a]	Niph. pret. 3 pers. sing. fem. [for נוֹשְׁבָה comp. § 8. rem. 7]	ישב
נוֹשָׁבָה[b]	Kh. נוֹשָׁבָה q. v., K. נוֹשְׁבוּ (q. v.)	ישב
נוֹשְׁבוּ[c]	Niph. pret. 3 pers. pl. (comp. § 8.	ישב
נוֹשָׁבוּ[d]	וְ rem. 7)	ישב
נוֹשָׁבוֹת[e]	Niph. part. fem. pl. of the foll.	ישב
נוֹשֶׁבֶת[f]	id. part. sing. fem., pl. נוֹשָׁבוֹת (§ 44. rem. 5)	ישב
נוֹשֶׁה[h]	Kal part. act. sing. masc. dec. 9 a	נשה

[a] Is. 24. 20.   [b] Am. 3. 3.   [c] Is. 33. 19.   [d] Ps. 48. 3.   [e] Is. 43. 10.   [f] Pr. 6. 2.   [g] Ps. 145. 6.   [h] Eze. 26. 19.   [i] Ex. 16. 35.
[k] Ps. 109. 10.   [l] Ps. 48. 5.   [m] Job 21. 15.   [n] Job 14. 18.   [o] Pr. 28. 7.   [p] Is. 21. 1.   [q] Je. 6. 8.   [r] Eze. 36. 10.   [s] Eze. 26. 17.
[t] Ne. 6. 10.   [u] Nu. 10. 4.   [v] Is. 40. 14.   Eze. 17. 7.   Ps. 9. 17.   1 Ch. 17. 21.   Je. 22. 6.   Eze. 38. 12.   Ps. 109. 11.
Ne. 6. 2.   Ex. 25. 21.   Ne. 6. 7.   Nu. 20. 10.

נוֹשָׁן‎ Niph. part. sing. masc.   ישן

נוֹשֶׁנֶת‎ id. part. sing. fem.   ישן

וְנוֹשַׁנְתֶּם‎ id. pret. 2 pers. pl. masc.   ישן

וְנוֹשַׁע‎ Niph. part. sing. masc.   ישע

נוֹשַׁע‎ id. pret. 3 pers. sing. masc.   ישע

נִוָּשֵׁעַ‎ id. fut. 1 pers. pl. [for נִוָּשַׁע § 15. rem. 1]   ישע

וְנִוָּשֵׁעָה‎ id. id. with opt. ה [for נִוָּשְׁעָה v. i. and § 8. rem. 13]   ישע

נוֹשַׁעְנוּ‎ id. pret. 1 pers. pl.   ישע

וְנוֹשַׁעְתֶּם‎ id. pret. 2 pers. pl. masc.   ישע

נֹשְׁקֵי‎ Kal part. act. pl. constr. m. [fr. נֹשֵׁק d. 7 b]   נשק

נְוַת‎ adj. or subst. fem., constr. of נָוָה dec. 11a, from נָוֶה masc. ו bef. (:)   נוה

נְוֹת‎ noun fem. pl. constr. of נָוָה, see the preced.   נוה

וְנֹתֵן‎ Kal part. act. sing. masc. dec. 7 b   נתן

נוֹתַר‎ Niph. pret. 3 pers. sing. masc. (comp. § 8. rem. 7)   יתר

נוֹתָר‎

וְנוֹתְרָה‎ id. pret. 3 pers. sing. fem.   יתר

נוֹתְרוּ‎ id. pret. 3 pers. pl.   יתר

נוֹתַרְתִּי‎ id. pret. 1 pers. sing.   יתר

נוֹתַרְתֶּם‎ id. pret. 2 pers. pl. masc.   יתר

נִזְבַּח‎ Kal fut. 1 pers. pl.   זבח

וְנִזְבְּחָה‎ id. with parag. ה (§ 8. rem. 13)   זבח

נָזָה‎ only fut. יִזֶּה, ap. וַיֵּז‎, וַיִּז‎ (§ 25. No. 2 e) to spatter, be sprinkled, with עַל‎, אֶל‎ upon anything. Hiph. הִזָּה, fut. יַזֶּה, ap. וַיַּז.—I. to sprinkle, with acc. of the liquid or מִן‎ some of it, and עַל‎ upon whom. —II. to sprinkle, besprinkle, expiate, with acc. of the person, Is. 52. 15. But this passage seems rather to indicate the Messiah's exaltation in judgment (comp. Ps. 2), and this word may be rendered, to scatter; comp. נוּף‎ Kal and Hiph. According to Schultens, to cause to leap or exult, coll. with the Arab.

יִזְיָה‎ (exults in the Lord; comp. Hiph.) pr. name masc. Ezr. 10. 25.

נִזְהָר‎ Niph. part. sing. masc.   זהר

נָזִיד‎ noun masc. sing. dec. 3a   זוד

נְזִיד‎ ו id., constr. st.; ו bef. (:)   זוד

נָזִיר‎ noun masc. sing. dec. 3a   נזר

נְזִיר‎ id., constr. st.   נזר

נְזִירֶיהָ‎ id. pl., suff. 3 pers. sing. fem.   נזר

נְזִירֶךָ‎ id. pl., suff. 3 pers. s. m. [for רֶיךָ § 4. r. 1]   נזר

נַזְכִּיר‎

נַזְכִּירָה‎ } Hiph. fut. 1 pers. pl. (§ 8. rem. 13)   זכר

נִזְכָּרִים‎ Niph. part. masc. pl. [of נִזְכָּר]   זכר

וְנִזְבַּרְתֶּם‎ id. pret. 2 pers. pl. masc.   יכר

[נָזַל]‎ fut. יִזַּל.—I. to sink down, Ju. 5. 5.—II. to drop down, distil, flow. Hiph. הִזִּיל to cause to flow, Is. 48. 21.

מַזָּל‎ masc. wandering star, planet; like Gr. πλανήτης from πλανάω; only pl. מַזָּלוֹת‎ 2 Ki. 23. 5.

נָזְלוּ‎ Kal pret. 3 pers. pl. R. נָזַל; or Niph. for נָזֹלּוּ (§ 18. rem. 15) R.   זלל

נָזֹלּוּ‎ Niph. pret. 3 pers. pl.   זלל

וְנֹזְלִים‎ defect. for נוֹזְלִים (q. v.)   נזל

וְנֶזֶם‎ masc. dec. 6a (with suff. נִזְמָה).—I. nosering. —II. earring.

נִזְמָהּ‎ id. with suff. 3 pers. sing. fem.   נזם

וְנִזְמֵי‎ id. pl., constr. st.   נזם

נְזַמְּרָה‎ ו Piel fut. 1 pers. pl. with parag. ה (comp. § 8. rem. 13)   זמר

נֶעֶזְבוּ‎ Niph. pret. 3 p. pl. [for נֶעֶזְבוּ comp. § 8. r. 7]   זער

נֶעֱזָמִים‎ Niph. part. masc. pl. [of נֶעֱזָם]   זעם

וְנִזְעַק‎ Kal fut. 1 pers. pl.   זעק

נִזְעֲקוּ‎ Niph. pret. 3 pers. pl.   זעק

נִזְעַקְתָּ‎ id. pret. 2 p. s. m. [for נִזְעַקְתָּ comp. § 8. r. 7]   זעק

[נְזַק]‎ Chald. to suffer loss, injury, Da. 6. 3. Aph. to cause loss, endamage, Ezr. 4. 13, 15, 22.

נֵזֶק‎ masc. injury, damage, Est. 7. 4.

נָזִק‎ Chald. Peal part. act. sing. m. (§ 47. r. 1a)   נזק

נָזַר‎ Niph. I. to separate, withdraw oneself, with מֵאַחֲרֵי Eze. 14. 7.—II. to restrict oneself, Zec. 7. 3.—III. to abstain from, with מִן‎, Le. 22. 2.—IV. to devote, consecrate oneself, with ל to anything, Ho. 9. 10. Hiph. הִזִּיר.—I. to set apart, with ל Nu. 6. 12.— II. to cause to avoid, restrict from, with מִן‎.—III. intrans. to abstain from, with מִן‎ Nu. 6. 3.—IV. to devote, consecrate oneself, with ל, Nu. 6. 2, 5, 6

נָזִיר‎ masc. dec. 3a.—I. a Nazarite, one separated and consecrated to God, comp. Nu. 6.—II. the unpruned vine, by application from the unshorn head of the Nazarite, Le. 25. 5, 11.—III. prince, comp. נֶזֶר.

נֶזֶר‎ masc. dec. 6 b.—I. separation, consecration. —II. sign or mark of separation, consecration or distinction; (a) the long hair of the Nazarite; (b) crown, diadem, whether priestly or regal.

מְנֻזָּרִים‎ masc. pl. (of מְנֻזָּר) princes, Na. 3. 17.

a Le. 26. 10.   h Is. 64. 4.   k Job 8. 6.   o Ps. 106. 11.   s Ex. 5. 8, 17.   y Ca. 1. 4.   c Ex. 15. 8.   g Is. 3. 21.   l 2 Ch. 20. 9.
b Le. 13. 11.   e Ps. 80. 4, 8, 20.   l Ps. 68. 13.   p Is. 1. 8.   t Ge. 25. 34.   z Est. 9. 28.   d Ca. 4. 15.   h Ps. 21. 14.   m Ju. 18. 22.
c De. 4. 25.   f Je. 8. 20.   m Zep. 2. 6.   q Is. 30. 17.   u La. 4. 7.   a Nu. 10. 9.   e Ex. 35. 22.   i Job 17. 1.   n Ju. 18. 23.
d Ps. 33. 16.   g Nu. 10. 9.   n Ps. 37. 21.   r Ex. 8. 22.   x Le. 25. 5.   b Ju. 5. 5.   f Ho. 2. 15.   k Pr. 25. 21.   o Da 6. 3.
Zec. 9. 9.   k Ps. 78. 9   nn Nu. 6. 2.

נֵזֶר נֶזֶר	} noun masc. sing. dec. 6 b & a .	נזר
נֵזְרוּ	Niph. pret. 3 pers. pl. .	זור
נִזְרוֹ	noun masc. sing., suff. 3 pers. sing. masc. from נֶזֶר dec. 6 b .	נזר
נְזֶרֶיהָ	defect. for נְזִירֶיהָ (q. v.) .	נזר
נִזְרֶךָ	noun masc. sing., suff. 2 p. s. f. fr. נֶזֶר d. 6 b	נזר
נִזְרַע	Kal fut. 1 pers. pl. [for נִזְרַע comp. § 8. r. 15]	זרע
נִזְרְעָה	Niph. pret. 3 pers. sing. fem. .	זרע
נִזְרַעְתֶּם	id. pret. 2 pers. pl. masc. .	זרע
נָח	pr. name masc. . . .	נוח
נֶחְבָּא	Niph. pret. 3 p. s.; or part. m. (§ 13. r. 7)	חבא
נֶחְבְּאוּ נֶחְבָּאוּ	} id. pret. 3 pers. pl. (v. i. & § 8. rem. 7)	חבא
נֶחְבָּאִים	id. part. masc. pl. [of נֶחְבָּא or בָּא § 23. rem. 6 & 9] . .	חבא
נֶחְבֵּאתָ	id. pret. 2 pers. sing. m. (§ 13. r. 7, note)	חבא
נֵחָבֵה	Niph. inf. (v. i. & § 24. rem. 9) .	חבה
נֶחְבְּתֶם	id. pret. 2 pers. pl. masc. [for נֶחְבָּאתֶם § 23. rem. 5, & § 13. rem. 7]	חבא
נַחְבִּי	pr. name masc. . .	חבה
נַחְדַּל	Kal fut. 1 pers. pl. (§ 13. rem. 7)	חדל
נְחַדֵּשׁ	Piel fut. 1 pers. pl.; וּ bef. (:)	חדש

[נָחָה] to lead, conduct. Hiph. I. to lead, conduct, guide.
—II. to lead back, Job 12. 23.

נָחָה נָחָה	} Kal pret. 3 pers. sing. fem.; acc. shifted by conv. וְ (comp. § 8. rem. 7) }	נוח
נְחֵה	Kal imp. sing. masc. .	נחה
נָחוּ נָחוּ	} Kal pret. 3 pers. pl.; acc. shifted by conv. וְ (comp. § 8. rem. 7) }	נוח
נְחֵוֵא	Chald. Pael fut. 1 pers. pl.	חוה
נַחוּם	pr. names masc. .	נחם
נְחוּמָי	noun masc. pl., suff. 1 p. s. fr. [נחום] d. 1 b	נחם
נָחוּץ	Kal part. pass. sing. masc. .	חוץ
נָחוֹר	pr. name masc. .	נחר
נָחוּשׁ	adj. masc. sing. .	נחש
נְחוּשָׁה	id. sing. fem. .	נחש
נֶחֱזֶה	Kal fut. 1 pers. pl. .	חזה
נֶחֱזַק	Kal fut. 1 pers. pl. .	חזק
נֶחֱטָא	Kal fut. 1 pers. pl.; וְ conv. .	חטא
נִחְיֶה	Kal fut. 1 pers. pl. .	חיה
נְחַיֶּה	Piel fut. 1 pers. pl.; וּ bef. (:)	חיה
נָחִיתָ	Kal pret. 2 pers. sing. masc.	נחה
נֶחָךְ	id. pret. 3 pers. sing. masc. [נָחָה], suff. 2 pers. sing. masc. (§ 24. rem. 21)	נחה

נָחַל וְ fut. יִנְחַל.—I. to obtain, acquire a possession, to possess.—II. to obtain by inheritance, to inherit.—III. to divide for a possession, to apportion, with acc. and also לְ of the thing, acc. of the person. Pi. נִחֵל (§ 14. rem. 1) to give, distribute for a possession, with double acc., also לְ of the person. Hiph. הִנְחִיל.—I. to cause to possess, give as a possession, with double acc.—II. to cause to inherit, give or leave as an inheritance, with double acc., also לְ of the person. Hoph. to be made to possess, Job 7. 3. Hithp. I. to receive as one's own possession, to possess for oneself, with acc.—II. to leave as an inheritance, with acc. of the thing, and לְ of the person.

נַחֲלָה fem. dec. 12 d.—I. the act of taking possession, perh. so Is. 17. 11.—II. possession, property, estate.—III. inheritance.—IV. portion, lot, Job 20. 29; 27. 13; 31. 2.

נַחֲלָת fem. portion, lot, Ps. 16. 6.

נַחַל וְ masc. dec. 6 d (with ה parag. נַחֲלָה).—I. stream, river or brook.—II. torrent.—III. valley through which streams run.—IV. shaft of a mine, so, according to some, in Job 28. 4.

נַחֲלִיאֵל (valley of God) pr. name of a station of the Israelites in the desert, Nu. 21. 19.

נַחַל נַחַל	} noun masc. sing. dec. 6 d (§ 35. rem. 2) . .	נחל
נֶחֱלָל	Niph. pret. 3 p. s. m. [for נֶחְלַל, נָחַל § 18. r. 14]	חלל
נִחֵל	Piel pret. 3 pers. sing. masc. (§ 14. rem. 1)	נחל
נַחֲלָה	noun fem. sing. dec. 12 d	נחל
נַחֲלָה	noun masc. sing. (נַחַל) with parag. ה .	נחל
נַחֲלָה	Niph. part. sing. fem. [from נַחֲלָה § 13. rem. 7, & § 24. rem. 18] .	חלה
נָחֲלוּ	Kal pret. 3 pers. pl.	נחל
נֶחְלוּ	Niph. pret. 3 pers. pl. (§ 13. rem. 7)	חלה
נִחֲלוּ	Piel pret. 3 pers. pl. (§ 14. rem. 1)	נחל
נֶחֱלוּ	Niph. pret. 3 pers. pl. (§ 18. rem. 8 & 14)	חלל
נַחֲלוֹת	noun fem. pl. abs. fr. נַחֲלָה dec. 12 d	נחל
נַחֲלֵי	noun masc. pl. constr. from נַחַל dec. 6 d	נחל
נַחֲלִיאֵל	pr. name masc. .	נחל
נַחֲלָתָהּ	noun m. pl., suff. 3 pers. s. m. fr. נַחַל d. 6 d	נחל
נְחָלִים	id. du., abs. st.	נחל
נְחָלִים	id. pl., abs. st.; וּ bef. (:)	נחל

Ex 39.30.   e Le. 25. 20.   k Jos. 10. 17.   l 1 Ki. 22. 15.   m Is. 7. 19.   o Ca. 7. 1.   r Zec. 2. 16.   x Eze. 25. 3.   c Is. 49. 6.
a Is. 1. 4;   f Nu. 5. 28.   g Ge. 31. 27.   n 1 Sa. 11. 14.   i Is. 11. 2.   p Da. 2. 4.   s 1 Ki. 20. 23.   y Ps. 36. 9.   l Jos. 13. 32.   p Ps. 18. 5.
Eze. 14. 5.   g Eze. 36. 9.   h 1 Sa. 19. 2.   o Is. 11. 8.   q Is. 64. 4.   t Ps. 74. 15.   m Eze. 42. 13.   q Is. 34. 9.
c Le. 25. 11.   h Job 29. 8. 10.   i Je. 49. 10.   p Ex. 32. 34.   r 1 Sa. 21. 9.   u Is. 58. 11.   n Ps. 36. 9.   w Eze. 7. 24.   r Eze. 47. 9.
d Je. 7. 29.   i Jos. 10. 27.   j Jos. 2. 16.   Est. 9. 22.   o Job 6. 12.

נַחֲלִיף Hiph. fut. 1 pers. pl. . . . חלף

וְנֶחֱלֵיתִי Niph. pret. 1 pers. sing. . . חלה

וְנַחְלְמָה Kal fut. 1 pers. pl. [נַחֲלֹם] with parag. ה (§ 8. rem. 13); וְ conv. . חלם

נֵחָלֵץ Niph. fut. 1 pers. pl. . . . חלץ

נֶחֱלָץ id. part. sing. masc. . . . חלץ

נָחַלְתָּ Kal pret. 2 pers. sing. masc.; acc. shifted by conv. וְ (§ 8. rem. 7) . . נחל

נַחֲלַת noun fem. sing. . . . . נחל

וְנַחֲלַת noun fem. sing., constr. of נַחֲלָה d. 12 d נחל

וְנַחֲלָת Niph. pret. 2 pers. sing. fem. [dag. forte impl. for נֶחֱלֹת נֶחֱלָלְתְּ § 18. rem. 14] חלל

וַיְנַחֲלְתוֹ noun fem. sing., suff. 3 pers. sing. masc. from נַחֲלָה dec. 12 d . . נחל

נָחַלְתִּי Kal pret. 1 pers. sing. . . נחל

וְנַחֲלָתִי noun f. s., suff. 1 pers. s. fr. נַחֲלָה d. 12d נחל

נַחֲלָתְךָ id., suff. 2 pers. sing. masc.
נַחֲלָתֶךָ } . נחל

נַחֲלַתְכֶם id., suff. 2 pers. pl. masc. . . נחל

וְנַחֲלָתָם id., suff. 3 pers. pl. masc. . . נחל

נְחַלְתֶּם Kal pret. 2 pers. pl. masc.; וּ for וְ conv. נחל

נְחַלְתֶּנוּ id. pret. 2 pers. s. m., suff. 1 pers. pl.; וּ id. נחל

נַחֲלָתָן noun masc. sing., suff. 3 pers. pl. fem. fr. נַחֲלָה dec. 12 d . . . נחל

נַחֲלָתֵנוּ id., suff. 1 pers. pl. . . נחל

נָחַם Kal not used; as in the Arab. to sigh, cogn. נָהָם; hence Niph. נִחַם (comp. § 14. rem. 1).—I. to mourn, grieve over, with עַל, אֶל, לְ, Ju. 21. 6, 15; Eze. 32. 31.—II. to grieve, feel compassion for, pity, with עַל, אֶל, לְ, מִן.—II. to feel regret, to repent (with עַל, אֶל) so as to produce either a change of conduct or of purpose, which latter case is inapplicable to God, comp. 1 Sa. 15. 29; Ps. 110. 4.—III. to ease, free oneself of any displeasing object, with מִן.—IV. to be comforted, to console oneself, with עַל, אַחֲרֵי. Pi. נִחַם (§ 14. rem. 1) to sympathize with, to console, comfort, with acc. of the pers., with עַל, מִן concerning which. Pu. נֻחַם to be consoled, comforted. Hithp. הִנַּחֵם, הִתְנַחֵם (contr.) i. q. Niph. Nos. II, III, IV, const. with עַל, לְ.

נַחַם (consolation) pr. name masc. 1 Ch. 4. 19.

נֹחַם masc. repentance, Ho. 13. 14.

נֶחָמָה fem. dec. 10, consolation, Job 6. 10; Ps. 119. 50.

נַחוּם (compassionate) pr. name, Nahum, the prophet, Na. 1. 1.

נֹחַם masc. dec. 1 b, only pl.—1. compassion, Ho. 11. 8.—II. consolations.

נְחֶמְיָה (consolation of the Lord) pr. name of a governor of Judea under Artaxerxes, and other persons.

נַחֲמָנִי (compassionate) pr. name masc. Ne. 7. 7.

מְנַחֵם (consoler) pr. name of a king of Israel, Menahem.

תַּנְחֻמִים m. d. 1 b, only pl. consolations, comforts

תַּנְחוּמָה fem. dec. 10, only pl. id. Job 21. 2.

תַּנְחֶמֶת (consolation) pr. name of a man.

נָחַם Kal pret. 3 pers. sing. masc. [נָחַה], suff. 3 pers. pl. masc. (§ 24. rem. 21) . נחה

נַחַם pr. name masc. נחם

וְנָחָם Niph. part. masc.; or נָחַם pret., in pause for the foll. נחם

וְנִחַם id.; or Piel pret. 3 p.s.m. (dag. f. impl. in ח) נחם

נֹחַם noun masc. sing. . . . . נחם

וְנֶחְמָד Niph. part. sing. masc. (§ 13. rem. 7) חמד

נַחְמְדֵהוּ Kal fut. 1 p. pl., suff. 3 p s.m. (§ 13. r.5) חמד

נֶחְמְדָה Pual pret. 3 pers. sing. fem. (§ 14. rem. 1) חמד

נַחֲמוּ Piel imp. pl. masc. (§ 14. rem. 1) נחם

וְנִחֲמוּ id. pret. 3 pers. pl. . . נחם

נְחֶמְיָה pr. name masc. . . . נחם

נְחֻמִים noun masc. pl. [of נֹחַם] dec. 1b . נחם

נַחְמָנִי pr. name masc. . נחם

נֶחְמְסוּ Niph. pret. 3 pers. pl. (§ 13. rem. 7) חמס

נֶחָמָתִי noun fem. sing., suff. 1 p. s. fr. [נֶחָמָה] d. 10 נחם

נִחַמְתִּי Niph. pret. 1 pers. sing. (§ 14. rem. 1,
נִחָמְתִּי } comp. § 8. rem. 7) } נחם

נִחַמְתִּי id. id.; acc. shifted by conv. (comp. § 8. r. 7) נחם

נִחַמְתִּים Piel (§ 14. r. 1) pret. 1 p. s., suff. 3 p.pl. m. נחם

נִחַמְתֶּם Niph. (comp. § 14. r. 1) pret. 2 p. pl. m. נחם

נִחַמְתַּנִי Piel (§ 14. r. 1) pret. 2 p. s. m., suff. 1 p. s. נחם

נַחְנָה Kal fut. 1 pers.; וְ conv. . . חנה

נַחְנוּ pers. pron. 1 pers. pl., by aphaer. for
נַחְנוּ } אֲנַחְנוּ q. v.

נְחָנִי Kal pret. 3 pers. sing. masc. [נָחָה], suff. 1 pers. sing. (§ 24. rem. 21) . . נחה

נְחֵנִי id. imp. s. m. (נְחֵה), suff. 1 p. s.; וּ bef. (:) נחה

נְחֶנְתִּי Kh. נֶחֱנְתִּי, K. נֶחֶנְתְּ Niph. pret. 2 pers. sing. fem. [for נֶחֱנוֹת נִחַנְתְּ § 18. rem. 14] חנן

נֶחְפָּה Niph. part. sing. fem. [of נֶחְפֶּה § 13. r. 7] חפה

נֶחְפָּז Niph. part. sing. masc. (§ 13. rem. 7) . חפז

נֶחְפְּזוּ id. pret. 3 pers. pl. [for נֶחְפָּזוּ v. i. & § 8. r. 7] חפז

* Is. 9. 9.   * Pr. 11. 8.   * Ps. 119. 111.   * Ex. 34. 9.   * Ge. 3. 6.   * Eze. 14. 23.   * Je. 31. 13.   * Ge. 42. 11.   * Ps. 68. 14.
* Da. 8. 27.   * Ex. 23. 30.   * De. 9. 29.   * Nu. 36. 3, 4, 12.   * Is. 53. 2.   * Je. 13. 22.   * Eze. 14. 22.   * Ps. 5. 9.   * 1 Sa. 23. 22.
* Ge. 41. 11.   * Ps. 16. 6.   * Ps. 37. 18.   * Ex. 13. 17.   * Is. 54. 11.   * Zec. 8. 14.   * Ezr. 8. 15.   * Je. 22. 23.   * Ps. 45. 6.
* Nu. 32. 17.   * Eze. 22. 16.   * Eze. 47. 14.   * Ho. 13. 14.   * Is. 40. 1.   * Ru. 2. 13.   * Ps. 86. 17.

נַחְפְּשָׂה‎ Kal fut. 1 pers. pl. [נֶחְפֵּשׂ] with parag. ה (§ 13. rem. 5, & § 8. rem. 13) . חפשׂ

נֶחְפְּשׂוּ‎ Niph. pret. 3 pers. pl. (§ 13. rem. 7) . חפשׂ

נָחֵץ‎ only part. pass. *urgent*, 1 Sa. 21. 9.

נֶחְקַר‎ Niph. pret. 3 pers. sing. masc. (§ 13. rem. 7) . חקר

וְנַחְקְרָה‎ Kal fut. 1 pers. pl. [נֶחְקֹר] parag. ה (§ 13. rem. 5, & § 8. rem. 13) . . . חקר

נָחַר‎ Root not used; Arab. *to snort*.

    נַחַר‎ masc. dec. 6 d, *a snorting*, Job 39. 20.

    נַחֲרָה‎ fem. id. only נַחֲרַת Je. 8. 16.

    נַחֲרַי, נַחֲרִי‎ (*snorer*) pr. name masc. 2 Sa. 23. 37; 1 Ch. 11. 39.

    נָחוֹר‎ (*snoring*) pr. name masc.—I. Ge. 11. 22.— II. of a brother of Abraham, Ge. 11. 26, 27, &c.

    נְחִירַיִם‎ masc. du. *nostrils*, Job 41. 12.

    חַרְנֶפֶר‎ (*snorer*, for נָחַר, & נפר‎ Syr. *to breathe hard*) pr. name masc. 1 Ch. 7. 36.

נֶחֱרַ‎ } Niph. pret. 3 pers. sing. masc. (comp. נֶחֱרָ‎ } § 8. rem. 7) . . . } חרר
נִחַר‎ id., dag. forte impl. [for נֶחַר § 18. rem. 14] . . חרר

נֶחְרְבוּ‎ Niph. pret. 3 pers. pl. . . חרב

נֶחֱרָבוֹת‎ } id. part. pl. & sing. [from נֶחֱרָב masc.‎ נֶחֱרָבָה‎ } § 44. rem. 5, & § 13. rem. 7] . } חרב

נַחְרוֹ‎ noun fem. sing., suff. 3 pers. sing. masc. from נַחַר dec. 6 d [for נַחֲרוֹ § 35. rem. 5] . . נחר

נֶחֶרְגוּ‎ } Niph. pret. 3 pers. pl. [dag. f. impl. for נֶחֱרְגוּ‎ } נֶחֱרְגוּ § 18. rem. 14, comp. § 8. rem. 7] } חרר
נַחֲרַי‎ pr. name masc. . . . . נחר

בַּחֲרֵם‎ Hiph. fut. 1 pers. pl. ap. [fr. נַחֲרִים]; וַ‎ conv. חרם

נֶחֱרֶפֶת‎ Niph. part. sing. fem. [of נֶחֱרָף] . חרף

נֶחֶרְצָה‎ } Niph. part. sing. fem. [of נֶחֱרָץ] . חרץ
נֶחֱרֶצֶת‎ }

נַחֲרֶת‎ noun fem. sing. constr. [of נַחֲרָה, no pl.] נחר

נָחָשׁ‎ וַ‎ masc. dec. 4 a.—I. *serpent*.—II. pr. name; (*a*) of a place, 1 Ch. 4. 12; (*b*) of a king of the Ammonites; (*c*) 2 Sa. 17. 27; (*d*) 2 Sa. 17. 25.

    נִחֵשׁ‎ Pi. (§ 14. rem. 1) denom. of נָחָשׁ ὀφιομαντεία divination by serpents.—I. *to use enchantment, divination.*—II. *to perceive, observe.*

    נַחַשׁ‎ masc. d. 6 d, *enchantment*, Nu. 23. 23; 24. 1.

    נַחְשׁוֹן‎ (*enchanter*) pr. name of a man.

נְחָשׁ‎ וַ‎ Chald. masc. dec. 1 a, *copper, brass*.

    נְחֹשֶׁת‎ fem dec. 13 c (with suff. נְחָשְׁתָּה, נְחָשְׁתִּי).

—I. *brass.*—II. *fetter, chain*, La. 3. 7; du. שְׁתַּיִם‎ *fetters.*—III. *money*, Eze. 16. 36.

    נְחֻשְׁתָּא‎ (*brass*) pr. name fem. 2 Ki. 24. 8.

    נְחֻשְׁתָּן‎ masc. adj. *brazen serpent*, 2 Ki. 18. 4.

    נָחוּשׁ‎ masc. adj. *brazen*, Job 6. 12.

    נְחוּשָׁה‎ fem. *brass.*

נָחָשׁ‎ noun masc. sing. dec. 6 d . . . נחשׁ

נַחֵשׁ‎ Piel inf. constr. for abs. (§ 14. rem. 1) נחשׁ

וַיְנַחֵשׁ‎ id. pret. 3 pers. sing. masc. . . נחשׁ

נְחַשׁ‎ noun masc. sing., constr. of נָחָשׁ dec. 4 a . נחשׁ

נְחָשָׁא‎ Chald. noun masc. sing., emph. of נְחָשׁ d. 1 a נחשׁ

נֶחְשָׁב‎ Niph. part. sing. masc. (§ 13. rem. 7) . חשׁב

נֶחְשַׁב‎ } id. pret. 3 pers. sing. masc. (comp. § 8. r. 7) חשׁב
נֶחְשָׁב‎ }

וְנַחְשְׁבָה‎ Kal fut. 1 pers. pl. with parag. ה (§ 13. rem. 5, comp. § 8. rem. 13) . . חשׁב

נֶחְשְׁבוּ‎ } Niph. pret. 3 pers. pl. (§ 13. rem. 7, נֶחְשָׁבוּ‎ } comp. § 8. rem. 7) . . . } חשׁב

נֶחְשַׁבְנוּ‎ id. pret. 1 pers. pl. . . . חשׁב

נֶחְשַׁבְתִּי‎ id. pret. 1 pers. sing. . . . חשׁב

נַחְשׁוֹן‎ וְ‎ pr. name masc. . . . . נחשׁ

נְחָשִׁים‎ noun masc. pl. of נָחָשׁ dec. 4, or נַחַשׁ dec. 6 a נחשׁ

נְחֹשֶׁת‎ וַ‎ noun fem. sing. dec. 13 c ; וַ‎ bef. (:) נחשׁ

נְחֻשְׁתָּא‎ pr. name fem. . . . . נחשׁ

נְחֻשְׁתָּהּ‎ noun fem. sing., suff. 3 pers. sing. fem. from נְחֹשֶׁת dec. 13 c (§ 44. rem. 4) . נחשׁ

נְחֻשְׁתִּי‎ id. with suff. 1 pers. sing. (v. id.) . נחשׁ

נִחַשְׁתִּי‎ Piel pret. 1 pers. sing. (§ 14. rem. 1) . נחשׁ

נְחֻשְׁתֵּךְ‎ noun fem. sing., suff. 2 pers. sing. fem. from נְחֹשֶׁת dec. 13 a (§ 44. rem. 4) . . נחשׁ

נְחֻשְׁתָּם‎ id. with suff. 3 pers. pl. masc. . . נחשׁ

נְחֻשְׁתָּן‎ noun masc. sing. from נְחֹשֶׁת with the term. ‎ָן . . . . . נחשׁ

נָחַת‎ only fut. יֵחַת, יִנְחַת, *to come down, descend*, with עַל *upon* any one; with בּ *into* any, *to penetrate* him. Niph. נֵחַת (comp. § 14. rem. 1) id. with בּ *to penetrate*, Ps. 38. 3. Pi. נִחַת (§ 14. rem. 1).— I. *to press, bend down*, as a bow.—II. *to level*, as furrows, Ps. 65. 11. Hiph. *to cause to come down, to prostrate*, Joel 4. 11.

    נְחַת‎ Chald. *to come down, descend*, Da. 4. 10, 20. Aph. (§ 51. rem. 1).—I. *to bring* or *carry down*, Ezr. 5. 15.—II. *to lay down, deposit, place*, Ezr. 6. 1, 5. Hoph. הֻנְחַת *to be deposed*, Da. 5. 20.

    נָחֵת‎ adj. *coming down*, only pl. נְחִתִים (with dag. euph. for נְחִתִים) 2 Ki. 6. 9.

a La. 3. 40.   e Je. 6. 29.   i Eze. 26. 19.   m Le. 19. 20.   q Is. 65. 25.   u 2 Ch. 9. 20;   x Je. 18. 18.   d Eze. 24. 11.   g Eze. 16. 36.
b Ob. 6.   f Ps. 69. 4.   k Job 39. 20.   n Da. 11. 36.   r Da. 4. 12, 20.   Is. 2. 22.   y Ps. 88. 5.   e La. 3. 7.   h 2 Ki. 18. 4.
c La. 3. 40.   g 2 Ki. 3. 23.   l Ps. 102. 4.   o Da. 9. 26.   s Nu. 23. 23.   w 1 Ki. 10. 21.   z Nu. 24. 1;   f Ge. 30. 27.
d Eze. 15. 4.   h Eze. 30. 7.   m Ca. 1. 6.   p Je. 8. 16.   t Ge. 44. 5, 15.   Nu. 18. 27, 30. Je. 8. 17.

נָחַת }
וַ֯ } pr. name masc. . . . . נוח
נָחַת
נַ֯חַת } noun fem. sing.; for וַ֯ see lett. וַ֯ . נוח
נָחֵת Chald. Peal part. act. sing. masc. (§ 47. r. 1 a) . נחת
נַחֵת Piel imp. sing. masc. (§ 14. rem. 1) . . נחת
נִחַת Niph. pret. 3 pers. sing. masc. [dag. forte impl. for נָחַת, § 18. rem. 14] . . חתת
וַ֯נַחֲתָה Piel pret. 3 pers. sing. masc. (§ 14. rem. 1) נחת
נִחֲתָה id. pret. 3 pers. sing. fem. . . נחת
נֶחְתּוּ Niph. pret. 3 pers. pl. for [נַחְתוּ, נָחֲתוּ dag. forte impl.] . . . . נחת
וַ֯נַחְתּוֹם Niph. inf. abs. (§ 9. rem. 1) . . חתם
נַחְתִּי for נֻחְתִּי (as some read) Niph. pret. 1 pers. s. נוח
נְחִתִּים adj. masc. pl. [for נְחָתִים from נָחַת] נחת
נֵחַת Niph. pret. 3 pers. sing. masc. (§ 13. rem. 7) חתת
וַ֯נֵחָם Niph. part. sing. masc. (§ 13. rem. 7) חתם
נִטְבְּלוּ Niph. pret. 3 pers. pl. . . . טבל

נָטָה וַ֯ fut. יִטֶּה, ap. יֵט (§ 25. No. 2 b).—I. to stretch out, extend, as the hand, a measure, &c.—II. to stretch, spread out, expand, as a tent.—III. to incline, bow.—IV. to turn, lead to; and intrans. to turn away, decline; with אַחֲרֵי, אֶל to, after, מֵעַם, מִן from any one.—V. to go away, depart, 1 Sa. 14. 7. Niph. נִטָּה to be stretched out, extended. Hiph. הִטָּה, fut. יַטֶּה, ap. יֵט.—I. to stretch out, extend.—II. to spread out, expand.—III. to decline, bow down, lower, with לְ to any one.—IV. to turn, lead away; and intrans. to decline, depart; with אַחֲרֵי, לְ, אֶל.—V. to wrest, pervert.

יָטָּה, יֻטָּה (spread out) pr. name of a city in the tribe of Judah, Jos. 15. 55; 21. 16.

מַטֶּה masc. dec. 9 a (pl. מַטּוֹת, once מַטִּים Hab. 3. 14).—I. branch, bough, Eze. 19. 11, sq.—II. rod, staff; מַ׳ לֶחֶם staff of bread, i. e. bread which supports and strengthens.—III. sceptre.—IV. tribe.

מַט only with ה loc. מַטָּה adv. downwards, De. 28. 43; (a) beneath, Pr. 15. 24; לְמַטָּה downwards; (b) below, beneath; (c) below, under, e. g. twenty years וּלְמַטָּה and under; מִלְמַטָּה from below, underneath.

מִטָּה fem. dec. 10.—I. couch, bed.—II. a bier, for dead bodies, 2 Sa. 3. 31.

מֻטֶּה masc. a wresting of right and judgment, Eze. 9. 9.

מֻטָּה fem. d. 10, a spreading out, expansion, Is. 8. 8.

נְטֵה וַ֯ Kal imp. s. masc.; וַ֯ bef. (:) . נטה
נִטֶּה id. fut. 1 pers. pl. (§ 25. No. 2 b) נטה
נֹטֶה id. part. act. sing. masc. dec. 9 a . נטה
נָטוּ id. pret. 3 pers. pl. . . . נטה
נְטוּוֹת Kh. Niph. part. fem. pl. [or נְטוּיָה from נָטוּ § 24. rem. 4] K. נְטֻיוֹת of נְטוּיָה (q. v.). נטה
נְטוּי Kh. נָטוּי, constr. of נָטוּי q. v.; K. נָטוּי Kal pret. 3 pers. pl. (§ 24. rem. 5) נטה
נָטוּי Kal part. pass. sing. masc. dec. 3 a . נטה
נְטוּיָה id. part. sing. fem. dec. 10 . . נטה
נָטוּעַ Kal part. pass. sing. masc. dec. 3 a . נטע
נְטוּעִים id. pl., abs. st. . . . נטע
נְטוֹפָתִי וַ֯ gent. noun from נְטֹפָה (q v.); וַ֯ bef. (:) נטף
נְטֹשׁ Kal imp. sing. masc. . . נטש
נְטוּשָׁה id. part. pass. sing. fem. [of נָטוּשׁ] נטש
נְטוֹשׁ id. inf. constr. . . . נטש
נִטָּיוּ Niph. pret. 3 pers. pl. (§ 24. r. 8, & § 25. No. 2) נטה
נְטִילֵי noun masc. pl. constr. [from נָטִיל or נְטִיל נטל
נְטִילַת וַ֯ Peal part. pass. 3 pers. sing. fem. (§ 47. rem. 11); וַ֯ bef. (:) נטל
נְטִישׁוֹתֶיהָ noun fem. pl., suff. 3 pers. sing. fem. from [נְטִישָׁה] dec. 10 . . נטש
נְטִישֹׁתַיִךְ id., suff. 2 pers. sing. fem. . . נטש
נָטִיתָ Kal pret. 2 pers. sing. masc. . . נטה
וַ֯נָּטִיתִי id. pret. 1 pers. sing. . . נטה

נָטַל fut. יִטּוֹל.—I. to lift, take up, Is. 40. 15.—II. to lay, impose upon, with עַל. Pi. to take up, Is. 63. 9.
נְטַל Chald. to lift up, Da. 4. 31; pret. pass. Da. 7. 4.
נֵטֶל masc. burden, Pr. 27. 3.
נָטִיל adj. masc. dec. 3 a, laden, Zep. 1. 11.
נֵטֶל וַ֯ noun masc. sing. . . . נטל
נִטְלֵת Chald. Peal pret. 1 pers. sing. . נטל
נִטְמָא Niph. pret. 3 pers. sing. masc. . טמא
נִטְמָאָה }
נִטַּמָּאָה } id. pret. 3 pers. sing. fem. (comp. § 8. r. 7) טמא
נִטְמְאוּ id. pret. 3 pers. pl. . . . טמא
נִטְמְאִים id. part. m., pl. of נִטְמָא or מָ׳ (§ 23. r. 6 & 9) טמא
נִטְמֵאת id. pret. 3 pers. sing. fem. . . טמא
נִטְמֵאתִי id. pret. 1 pers. sing. . . טמא
נִטְמֵאתֶם id. pret. 2 pers. pl. masc. . . טמא
נִטְמֵינוּ Niph. pret. 1 pers. pl. (§ 23. rem. 11) טמא
וַ֯נִטְמָתֶם defect. for נִטְמָאתֶם q. v. (§ 23. rem. 5) טמא

נָטַע fut. יִטַּע, inf. נְטֹעַ נַטַעַת.—I. to plant, as trees, gardens, &c.—II. trop. to plant or settle a people

a Ec. 6. 5.   c Mal. 2. 5.   e Est. 8. 8.   g Est. 3. 12.   i Ec. 3. 2.   k Ju. 19. 3.   b Je. 48. 32.   f Da. 4. 31.   k Je. 2. 23.
Is. 30. 15.   d 2 Sa. 22. 35.   f Job 3. 26.   h Jos. 3. 15.   l Ex. 12. 11.   u Nu. 24. 6.   c Nu. 5. 29.   l Eze. 20. 43.
Da. 4. 10. 20.   e Ps. 18. 35.   g 2 Ki. 6. 9.   l Is. 3. 16.   m Pr. 17. 14.   d Da. 7. 4.   l Le. 18. 24.   m Job 18. 3.
b Ps. 65. 11.   h Ps. 38. 2.   = Da. 9. 24.   f Ps. 73. 2.   = Is. 21. 15.   c Je. 5. 10.   d La. 3. 28.   n Le. 11. 43.
= Zep. 1. 11.   aa Nu. 5. 27. 28.   t Eze. 20. 30. 31.   n Pr. 27. 3.

in a particular country.—III. *to plant, pitch a tent,*
Da. 11. 45.—IV. *to fix, fasten* a nail, Ec. 12. 11.—
V. *to fix, set up* an image, De. 16. 21. Niph. *to be
planted, established,* Is. 40. 24.

נֶטַע masc. dec. 6 (constr. נְטַע, with suff. נִטְעָהּ
§ 35. rem. 5 & 7).—I. *a planting,* Is. 17. 11.—II.
a plant, Job 14 9.—III. *place planted, plantation.*

נָטִיעַ m. *something planted, a plant,* Ps. 144. 12.

מַטָּע masc. dec. 2 b (pl. c. מַטָּעֵי § 31. rem. 1)
ᵃ *planting, plantation.*

• נָטַע Kal pret. 3 pers. sing. masc. for נָטַע (§ 8. r. 7) נטע
ᵇ נֶטַע Seg. noun as if for נֵטַע=נְטַע but pl. c. נִטְעֵי נטע
   (§ 35. rem. 2)

נֶטַע Kh. נֶטַע q. v.—K. נְטָעַי (o. v.) נטע

נְטַע noun masc. sing., constr [of נֶטַע comp. נטע
   נָטַע § 35. rem. 6]

נָטְעָה Kal pret. 3 pers. sing. fem. . . . נטע
ᵍ נָטְעוּ ᴵ id. pret. 3 pers. pl. . . . נטע
ᵉ נִטְּעוּ Niph. pret. 3 pers. pl. [for נִטְעוּ comp. § 8. r. 7] נטע
נִטְעוּ ן Kal imp. pl. masc. . . . נטע
ᵈ נְטָעִים ן noun masc. pl. constr. & abs. from [נֶטַע] נטע
   נֹטְעִים ן dec. 6 a (§ 35. rem. 5)
נֹטְעִים Kal part. masc. pl. of נוֹטֵעַ dec. 7 b . נטע
נְטָעֶךָ noun masc. sing., suff. 2 pers. sing. fem. נטע
   from [נֶטַע] dec. 6 a (§ 35. rem. 5)
ᵈᵈ נְטַעְתָּ Kal pret. 2 pers. s. m. [for נָטַעְתָּ § 8. r. 7] נטע
נָטַעְתִּי ן id. pret. 1 pers. sing.; acc. shifted by נטע
   וָנֶטַעְתִּי ן conv. וָ (§ 8. rem. 7) . .
נְטַעְתִּיהוּ ᵏ id. id., suff. 3 pers. sing. masc.; וָ for וְ, נטע
   וּנְטַעְתִּיו ן conv. . . .
נְטַעְתִּיךְ id. id., suff. 2 pers. sing. fem. נטע
נְטַעְתִּים וָ id. id., suff. 3 pers. pl. masc.; וָ for וְ, conv. נטע
נְטַעְתֶּם id. pret. 2 pers. sing. masc., suff. 3 p. pl. m. נטע
נְטַעְתֶּם וָ ᵍᴵ id. pret. 2 pers. pl. masc.; וָ for וְ, conv. נטע

[נָטַף] fut. יִטֹּף.—I. *to drop, distil;* metaph. of discourse.
—II. *to drop with, let fall in drops.* Hiph. הִטִּיף
to let drop, distil, Am. 9. 13; elsewhere metaph.
of *dropping* sentiments, prophetic declarations, for
to prophesy.

נָטָף masc. dec. 4 a.—I. *a drop,* Job 36. 27.—
II. Sept. στακτή, *myrrh,* Ex. 30. 34.

נְטֹפָה (*a dropping, distilling*) pr. name of a
town near Bethlehem in Judea. Gent. n. נְטֹפָתִי

נְטִיפָה fem. dec. 10, only pl. *drops, pendants* or
earrings.

טָפַת (*drop*; for נִטְפַת) pr. name of a daughter
of Solomon, 1 Ki. 4. 11.

נָטִף noun masc. sing. dec. 4 a . . . נטף
נְטֹפָה ᴵ pr. name of a place; וָ bef. (:) . נטף
נָטְפוּ ן נטף
נָטָפוּ ן Kal pret. 3 pers. pl. (§ 8. rem. 7) . נטף
נֹטְפוֹת id. part. act. fem. pl. [נֹטֵף from נוֹטֵף m.] נטף
נִטְפֵי noun masc. pl., constr. of נָטָף dec. 4 a נטף
נְטֹפָתִי gent. noun, from נְטֹפָה . נטף

[נָטַר] fut. יִנְטֹר, יִטֹּר.—I. *to watch, guard.*—II. *to keep,
retain,* sc. anger, אַף being implied, with לְ, אֶת of
the person.

נְטַר Chald. *to keep, preserve,* Da. 7. 28.

מַטָּרָא, מַטָּרָה fem.—I. *place of custody,* ᵃ
prison.—II. *mark* or *butt,* aimed and shot at.

נֹטְרָה Kal part. act. s., f. of נֹטֵר (§ 39. No. 3. r. 4) נטר
נִטְרֵת Chald. Peal pret. 1 pers. sing. . נטר
נָטַרְתִּי Kal pret. 1 pers. sing. [for נָטַרְתִּי § 8. r. 7] נטר

נָטַשׁ fut. יִטֹּשׁ, יִטּוֹשׁ.—I. *to leave, forsake, abandon.*—
II. *to leave* in charge of any one, with עַל.—III.
to let alone without using, as a field.—IV. *to let
be, to remit* a debt, Ne. 10. 32.—V. *to let be, to
allow, permit,* Ge. 31. 28.—VI. *to let out, draw
out* a sword, Is. 21. 15.—VII. *to spread, scatter*
intrans. *to spread itself,* 1 Sa. 4. 2. Niph. I. *to be
left, forsaken,* Am. 5. 2.—II. *to be loosened,* Is.
33. 23.—III. *to spread itself.* Pu. *to be forsaken,*
Is. 32. 14.

נְטִישׁוֹת fem. pl. (of נְטִישָׁה dec. 10).—I. *shoots*
of a vine.—II. Je. 5. 10, perhaps, *bulwarks;* Prof.
Lee, " *smaller towns,* considered as shoots of the
capital."

נֻטַּשׁ Pual pret. 3 pers. sing. masc. [for נֻטָּשׁ comp. נטש
   § 8. rem. 7] . . . . .
נִטֹּשׁ ן Kal fut. 1 pers. pl. . . נטש
נִטְּשָׁה Niph. pret. 3 pers. sing. masc. נטש
נִטְּשׁוּ id. pret. 3 pers. pl. . . נטש
נְטֻשִׁים Kal part. pass. masc., pl. of נָטוּשׁ dec. 3 a נטש
נְטָשַׁנִי id. pret. 3 pers. sing. masc., suff. 1 pers. pl. נטש
נְטַשְׁתָּ id. pret. 2 pers. sing. masc. נטש
נְטַשְׁתְּ id. pret. 2 pers. sing. fem. נטש
נְטַשְׁתָּה id. pret. 2 pers. sing. masc. (§ 8. rem. 5) נטש
נְטַשְׁתָּהּ וָ id. id., suff. 3 pers. sing. fem.; וָ for וְ conv. נטש
נְטַשְׁתִּי ן id. pret. 1 pers. sing.; acc. shifted by יטש
   וָנֶטַשְׁתִּי ן conv. וָ (§ 8. rem. 7) .

ᵃ Ps. 104. 16.   ᶜ Ps. 80. 16.   ⁱ 1 Ch. 4. 23.   ᵐ 2 Sa. 7. 10.   ʳ Ex. 30. 34.   ᵃ Da. 7. 28.   ᵇ Ne. 10. 32.   ᶜ Ju. 6. 13.   ⁱ Is. 2. 6.
ᵇ Job 14. 9.   ᶠ Je. 31. 5.   ᵏ Je. 31. 5.   ⁿ Je. 2. 21.   ˢ Ca. 5. 13.   ᵇ Ca. 1. 6.   ᶠ Am. 5. 2.   ᶠ 1 Sa. 17. 28.   ᵏ Ex. 23. 11.
ᶜ Pr. 31. 16.   ᵍ Is. 40. 24.   ᴵ Is. 17. 11.   ᵒ Je. 12. 2.   ᵗ Job 36. 27.   ᶜ 1 Sa. 10. 2.   ᵍ Is. 30. 16.   ˡ Je. 15. 5.   ᵏ Je. 12. 7.
ᵈ Is. 5. 7.   ʰ Is. 17. 10.   ⁼1 Ch. 17. 9.   ᵖ Le. 19. 23.   ᵘ Ca. 1. 6.   ᵈ Is. 32. 14.   ᵈᵈ De. 6. 11.

36*

נטש   נְטַשְׁתִּיךָ id. id., suff. 2 pers. sing. masc., ו for ן conv.

נטש   נְטַשְׁתַּנִי id. pret. 2 pers. sing. masc., suff. 1 pers. sing.

נטה   נָטָתָה Kal pret. 3 pers. sing. fem.

נִיא Root not used; Arab. *to be raw.*

נָא adj. masc. *raw, half-boiled,* Ex. 12. 9.

נוב   נִיבוֹ noun m. s., suff. 1 pers. s. fr. [נִיב] d. 1 a

נוד   נִיד noun masc. sing.

נָיָה see וַנָּיָה under lett. ו.

נוח   נִיחוֹחַ noun masc. sing. dec. 1 b

נוח   נִיחֹחֵיהֶם id. pl., suff. 3 pers. pl. masc.

נוח   נִיחוֹחִין Chald. id. pl., abs. st. dec. 1 a

נוח   נִיחֹחַ noun masc. sing. dec. 1 b for נִיחוֹחַ

נוח   נִיחֹחִי id., suff. 1 pers. sing.

נוח   נִיחֹחֲכֶם id., suff. 2 pers. pl. masc.

נון   נִין noun masc. sing. dec. 1 a

נִינְוֵה pr. name, *Nineveh,* the ancient capital of Assyria.

ינה   נִינֵם Kal fut. 1 pers. pl. [נִינֶה], suff. 3 pers. pl. masc. (§ 25. No. 2e)

נִיסָן m. *Nisan,* the first month of the Hebrew year, called also אָבִיב. Etymology not defined.

[נִיר, נוּר] I. *to break up the ground, to till,* Je. 4. 3. —II. *to cultivate,* Ho. 10. 12.

נִיר masc. *fallow-ground, land first broken up.*

מָנוֹר masc. dec. 3, *beam* (prop. *yoke;* comp. Lat. jugum, *a yoke, a beam*) only in the phrase מְנוֹר אֹרְגִים *a weaver's beam.*

נור   נִיר noun masc. sing. R. נִיר or

ירא   נִירָא וַנּ Kal fut. 1 pers. pl.; ו conv.

ניר   נִירוּ Kal imp. pl. masc.

נור   נִירִי noun masc. s., suff. 3 p. s. m. fr. [נִיר] d. 1 a

ירה   נִירָם וַ Kal fut. 1 pers. pl. [נִירָה], suff. 3 pers. pl. masc. (§ 25. No. 2e); ו conv.

ירש   נִירָשׁ Kal fut. 1 pers. pl. [for נִירַשׁ § 8. rem. 15]

ירש   נִירְשָׁה id. with parag. ה (§ 8. rem. 13)

נכה   נַּךְ וַ Hiph. fut. 1 pers. pl., ap. from נָכָה (§ 25. No. 2a); ו conv.

נָכָא Kal not used; i. q. נָכָה *to smite.* Niph. *to be beaten,* Job 30. 8 נִכְאוּ, which some render, *they were frightened,* supposing it to stand for נִכְאוּ from כָּאָה.

נָכָא adj. masc. dec. 4a, *smitten, afflicted,* Is. 16. 7.

נָכֵא adj. masc. dec. 5a, id. רוּחַ נְכֵאָה *an afflicted mind, broken spirit.*

נכא   נְכֹאת fem. with suff. נְכֹאתֹה (prop. *something crushed, bruised*) *spicery, spices;* בֵּית נְכֹתֹה *house of his spices, his perfume house.*

נכא   נְכָאָה adj. fem. sing. [for נָכֵא masc.]

נכא   נִכְאָה וְ Niph. pret. 3 pers. sing. masc.

נכא   נִכְאֶה וְ id. part. sing. m. constr. [of נִכְאָה] d. 9 a

נכא   נִכְאוּ Niph. pret. 3 pers. pl.

נכא   נְכָאִים adj. masc. pl. of [נָכֵא] dec. 4a

נכא   נְכֹאת noun fem. sing. (with suff. נְכֹתֹה)

כבד   נִכְבָּד וְ Niph. part. sing. masc. (§ 37. rem. 5)

כבד   נִכְבַּד id. pret. 3 p. s. m., or (2 Sa. 13. 25) Kal fut. 1 p. pl.

כבד   נִכְבָּדוֹת id. part. fem. pl. [of נִכְבָּדָה fr. נִכְבָּד masc.]

כבד   נִכְבְּדֵי id. part. constr. masc. from נִכְבָּד dec. 8a (§ 37. rem. 5)

כבד   נִכְבַּדֶּיהָ id. id., suff. 3 pers. sing. fem.

כבד   נִכְבַּדֶּהֶם וְ id. id., suff. 3 pers. pl. masc. dec. 2b

כבד   נִכְבָּדִים וְ id. id. pl. abs. dec. 2b

כבד   נִכְבַּדְתָּ id. pret. 2 pers. sing. masc. (comp. § 8. rem. 7)

כבד   נִכְבַּדְתִּי וְ id. pret. 1 pers. sing.; acc. shifted by conv. ו (§ 8. rem. 7)

כבש   נִכְבְּשָׁה וְ Niph. pret. 3 pers. sing. fem.

כבש   נִכְבָּשׁוֹת id. part. fem. pl. [of נִכְבָּשָׁה fr. נִכְבָּשׁ masc.]

נכר   נֶכֶד ,וְ masc. with suff. נֶכְדִּי (§ 35. rem. 3) *progeny,* always with נִין.

נכה   נָכָה Niph. נִכָּה (§ 25. No. 2b) *to be smitten,* 2 Sa. 11. 15 Pu. נֻכָּה *to be beaten down,* Ex. 9. 31, 32. Hiph. הִכָּה; imp. הַךְ, הַכֵּה; fut. יַכֶּה, ap. וַיַּךְ.—I. *to smite, strike,* e. g. with the fist, a stick, sling, arrow, &c.; also with the horn, *to push;* moreover of the rays of the sun, of the cold. Espec. (a) הִכָּה כַף *to clap the hands,* in derision, but also in exultation; (b) trop. of the heart, i. e. the conscience reproving one; (c) with the tongue, *to taunt;* (d) frequently of God's judgments, as disease, pestilence; (e) of enemies, *to vanquish.* —II. *to strike, smite down, beat in pieces,* as hail; *to kill, slay;* הִכָּה נֶפֶשׁ *to strike* (as to) *life, to kill;* הִכָּה לְפִי חֶרֶב *to smite with the edge of the sword.*—III. *to strike root,* Ho. 14. 6. Hoph. הֻכָּה, הֻכָּה *to be smitten,* &c. pass. of Hiph.

נכה   נָכֶה adj. masc. dec. 9b, *smitten.*—I. נְכֵה רַגְלַיִם *injured as to the feet,* i. e. *lame.*—II. נְכֵה רוּחַ *afflicted, contrite in spirit.*

נכה   נָכִים masc. pl. (of נָכֶה) *smiters,* sc. with the

a Ge. 31. 28.	e Eze. 20. 28.	i Le. 26. 31.	n Jos. 9. 24.	r Ps. 83. 13.	z Job 30. 8.	b Ps. 87. 3.	f Is. 26. 15.	k Ne. 5. 5.
b Nu. 22. 33.	f Ezr. 6. 10.	k Job 18. 19.	o 2 Sa. 22. 29.	s De. 2. 33.	a Na. 3. 10.	c Nu. 149. 8.	g Is. 43. 4.	l Job 18. 19.
c Mal. 1. 12.	g Job 2. 46.	l Is. 14. 22.	p Nu. 21. 30.	t Da. 11. 30.	b Ps. 149. 8.	d Nu. 22. 15.	k Eze. 28. 22.	= Is. 14. 22.
d Job 16. 5.	h Nu. 28. 2.	m Ps. 74. 8.	q Ju. 11. 24.	u Ps. 109. 16.	c 2 Sa. 6. 20.		l Jos. 18. 1.	

tongue, *slanderers*, Ps. 35. 15.   Others take it as the pl. of גֵּהּ *a jester*, from נוּהּ i. q. Arab. نأى *to jest.*

מַכָּה fem. dec. 10 (pl. מַכּוֹת, מַכִּים).—I. *a smiting, beating.*—II. *stroke, blow, wound.*—III. *slaughter.*—IV. *calamity from God.*

וְנַכֶּה‎ Hiph. fut. 1 pers. pl. (§ 25. No. 2 b)   נכה

וְנִכָּה‎ Niph. pret. 3 pers. sing. masc.   נכה

נְכוֹ, נְכֹה Pharaoh Necho, pr. name of a king of Egypt.

נָכֶה‎ adj. masc. sing., constr. of [נָכֶה] dec. 9 b; וּ bef. (:)   נכה

וַ נַּכֵּהוּ‎ Hiph. fut. 1 pers. pl. (נַכָּה), suff. 3 pers. sing. masc. (§ 25. No. 2 b); וְ conv.   נכה

נְכוֹ‎ pr. name masc. see נְכֹה.

נֻכּוּ‎ Hoph. pret. 3 pers. pl. (§ 25. No. 2 b)   נכה

נָכוֹן‎ Niph. part. s. m. d. 3 a (also pr. name m.)   כון

נְכוֹן‎ id., constr. st.   כון

נָכוֹנָה‎ id. pret. 3 pers. sing. fem.   כון

נְכוֹנָה‎ id. part. fem of נָכוֹן .   כון

נָכוֹנוּ‎ id. pret. 3 pers. pl.   כון

נִכְזָבָה‎ Niph. pret. 3 pers. sing. fem. [for נִכְזָבָה comp. § 8. rem. 7]   כזב

וְ נִכְזַבְתָּ‎ id. pret. 2 p. s. m. [for נִכְזַבְתָּ comp. §8.r.7]   כזב

נֹכַח‎ prep.—I. *opposite, over against.*—II. *before, in sight of.*—III. with other prep. אֶל נֹכַח *towards,* Nu. 19. 4. לְנֹכַח (a) adv. *straight forward,* Pr. 4. 25; (b) *before,* Ge. 30. 38; (c) *in behalf of,* Ge. 25. 21, עַד נֹכַח *as far as, in front of.*

נָכֹחַ‎ masc. dec. 3 a.— 1. adj. *straight, right, upright,* Pr. 8. 9; Is. 57. , הֹלֵךְ נְכֹחוֹ *he that walketh in what is right with him,* sc. God.—II. fem. נְכֹחָה *right, righteousness.*

נֵכַח‎ i. q. נֹכַח, with suff. נִכְחוֹ (dec. 6 b) *over against.*

נְכַחֵד‎ Piel fut. 1 pers. pl. (§ 14. rem. 1)   כחד

נִכְחַד‎ Niph. pret. 3 pers. sing. masc.   כחד

נִכְחֲדוּ‎ id. pret. 3 p. pl. [for נִכְחֲדוּ comp. § 8. r. 7]   כחד

נִכְחָדוֹת‎ id. part. fem. pl., sing. נִכְחֶדֶת (§ 44. r. 5)   כחד

נְכֹחָה‎ adj. fem. s. d. 10 (fr. נָכֹחַ m.); וּ bef. (:)   נכה

נְכֹחוֹ‎ id. masc., suff. 3 pers. s. m. fr. נָכֹחַ d. 3 a   נכה

נִכְחוֹ‎ prep. [נֵכַח] with suff. 3 pers. sing. m. d. 6 e   נכה

נְכֹחוֹת‎ adj. fem., pl. of נְכֹחָה d. 10 [fr. נָכֹחַ masc.]   נכה

וְ נַכְחִידֵם‎ Hiph. fut. 1 pers. pl., suff. 3 pers. pl. m.   כחד

נְכֹחִים‎ adj. masc. pl. of [נָכֹחַ] d. 3 a; וּ bef. (:)   נכה

וְ נֹכַחַת‎ Niph. part. sing. fem. [of נוֹכַח]   יכח

נָכִים‎ adj. masc. pl. of [נָכֶה] dec. 9   נכה

[נָכַל]‎ *fraudulently to withhold,* Mal. 1. 14. Pi. *to act deceitfully,* Nu. 25. 18. Hithp. *to plot together against,* with אֵת, בְּ .

נֵכֶל‎ masc. dec. 6 b, *craft, deceit,* Nu. 25. 18.

כֵּלַי, כִּילַי‎ m. *churl, miser, niggard,* Is. 32. 5, 7.

נִכְּלוּ‎ Piel pret. 3 pers. pl.   נכל

נִכְלָם‎ Niph. part. sing. masc.   כלם

נִכְלְמוּ‎ id. pret. 3 pers. pl.   כלם

נִכְלָמִים‎ id. part. masc. pl. of כלם   כלם

וְ נִכְלַמְתְּ‎ id. pret. 2 pers. sing. fem.   כלם

נִכְלַמְתִּי }‎
וְ נִכְלָמְתִּי }‎ id. pret. 1 pers. sing. (comp. § 8. r. 7)   כלם

נַכֵּם }‎ Hiph. fut. 1 pers. pl. (נָכָה), suff. 3 pers. pl. masc. (§ 25. No. 2 b); וְ conv.   נכה

נִכְמְרוּ }‎
רֶם. 7) }‎ Niph. pret. 3 pers. pl. (comp. § 8. rem. 7)   כמר

נָכֹנוּ‎ defect. for נָכוֹנוּ (q. v.)   כון

נַכֵּנוּ‎ Hiph. fut. 1 pers. pl. (נָכָה), suff. 3 pers. sing. masc. (§ 25. No. 2 b)   נכה

נְכֹנִים‎ Niph. part. masc., pl. of נָכוֹן dec. 3 a   כון

נִכְנַע‎ Niph. pret. 3 pers. sing. masc.   כנע

נִכְנְעוּ }‎
רֶם. 7) }‎ id. pret. 3 pers. pl. (comp. § 8. rem. 7)   כנע

[נֶכֶס]‎ masc. dec. 6 a, only pl. *riches, treasures.* נְכַס Chald. masc. dec. 3 b, pl. id.

נְכָסִים‎ noun masc. pl. of [נֶכֶס] dec. 6; וּ bef. (:)   נכס

נִכְסִין‎ Chald. noun masc. pl. of [נְכַס] dec. 3 b   נכס

נִכְסָף‎ Niph. part. sing. masc.   כסף

נִכְסֹף‎ id. inf. abs.   כסף

נִכְסְפָה‎ id. pret. 3 pers. sing. fem.   כסף

נִכְסַפְתָּה‎ id. pret. 2 pers. sing. masc. (§ 8. rem. 5)   כסף

נִכְסְתָה‎ Niph. pret. 3 p. s. f. [for סְתָה comp. §8. r.7]   כסה

וְ נִכַּפֵּר‎ Nithpa. pret. 3 pers. sing. masc. [for נִתְכַּפֵּר § 7. No. 10]   כפר

נָכַר‎ Pi. נִכֵּר.—I. *to estrange, alienate,* Je. 9. 4.—II. *to seem strange,* hence (a) *to gaze at, admire,* Job 34. 19; (b) *to mistake,* De. 32. 27; Job 21. 29, (c) *to reject,* 1 Sa. 23. 7. Hiph. הִכִּיר.—I. *to gaze at, regard, have respect to,* with פָּנִים.—II. *to be concerned, care for any one.*—III. *to recognise; to acknowledge; to know, be acquainted*

▪ Nu. 22. 6.   *f* De. 3. 3.   *l* Job 41. 1.   *p* Is. 59. 14.   *t* Ge. 20. 16.   ▪ Is. 50. 7.   *d* La. 5. 10.   *h* 2 Ch. 1. 11.   ▪ Ps. 84. 3.
b Jos. 10. 4.   *g* Ex. 9. 32.   *m* Pr. 30. 6.   *q* Is. 57. 2.   *u* Je. 31. 19.   *a* Eze. 16. 7.   *e* Ezr. 7. 26.   *i* Ge. 31. 30.
c 2 Sa. 11. 15.   *h* Pr. 4. 18.   *n* Job 15. 28.   *r* Ps. 83. 5.   *v* Nu. 25. 18.   *b* Ge. 37. 21.   *f* Zep. 2. 1.   *k* Je. 51. 42.
d Is. 66. 2.   *i* 1 Ki. 2. 46.   *o* Am. 3. 10.   *s* 2 Sa. 15. 3.   *w* Ps. 74. 21.   *c* De. 29. 6.   *g* 2 Ch. 12. 7.   *l* Ge. 31. 39.
Je. 18. 18.   *k* Pr. 19. 29.   *De. 21. 8.

with. — IV. *to know, discriminate* Ezr. 3. 13.
Niph. נִכַּר.—I. *to feign oneself a stranger,* Pr. 26.
24.—II. *to be recognised, known,* La. 4. 8. Hithp.
I. *to feign, dissemble.*—II. *to be recognised, known,*
Pr. 20. 11.

נֵכָר masc. constr. נֵכַר (§ 33. rem. 3) *what is
strange, foreign,* comp. Ne. 13. 30; *strange, foreign part* (comp. Germ. die Fremde). בֶּן־נֵכָר *son
of a foreign land, a stranger, foreigner.*

נֶכֶר masc. *alienation,* Job 31. 3.

נֶכֶר masc. dec. 6c, id. Ob. 12.

נָכְרִי masc. pl. נָכְרִים; fem. נָכְרִיָּה, pl. נָכְרִיּוֹת.
—I. adj. *strange, foreign.*—II. *strange, new, singular,* Is. 28. 21.—III. *stranger, foreigner.*

הַכָּרָה fem. (verbal of Hiph.) *respect, regard,*
Is. 3. 9, הַכָּרַת פְּנֵיהֶם *the respect of persons,* sc. in
judgment. Others, *acknowledgment of their face,*
i. e. the indication in their looks.

מַכָּר masc. dec. 1b, *acquaintance, friend,* 2 Ki.
12. 6, 8.

נֵכֶר	noun masc. sing. dec. 2b	נכר
נֵכֶר	id., constr. st. (§ 33. rem. 3)	נכר
נִכֵּר	Piel pret. 3 pers. sing. masc. (§ 10. rem. 1)	נכר
וְנֵכֶר	noun masc. sing.	נכר
נִכְרוֹ	noun m. s., suff. 3 p. s. m. fr. [נֵכֶר] d. 6c	נכר
נִכְּרוּ	Niph. pret. 3 pers. pl.	נכר
נָכְרִי	adj. masc. sing., pl. נָכְרִים	נכר
נָכְרִיָּה	id. fem. sing. dec. 10	נכר
נָכְרִיּוֹת	id. fem. pl.	נכר
נָכְרִים	id. masc. pl. of נָכְרִי	נכר
נָכְרִים	Kh. q. v.; K. נָכְרִיָּה (q. v.)	נכר
נַכְרִית	Hiph. fut. 1 pers. pl.	כרת
נַכְרִיתֶנָּה	id., suff. 3 pers. sing. fem.	כרת
נִכְרְעָה	Kal fut. 1 pers. pl. with opt. ה [for נִכְרְעָה § 8. rem. 13 & 15]	כרע
נִכְרַתָּ	Niph. pret. 2 pers. sing. masc. [for נִכְרַתָּ § 25. rem.]	כרת
נִכְרַת / וְנִכְרָת	Niph. pret. 3 pers. sing. masc. (comp. § 8. rem. 7)	כרת
נִכְרַת / נִכְרָת	Kal fut. 1 pers. pl. (§ 8. rem. 18)	כרת
נִכְרְתָה	Niph. pret. 3 p. s. f. [for נִכְרְתָה comp. § 8. r. 7]	כרת
נִכְרְתָה	Kal fut. 1 pers. pl. ה parag. (§ 8. rem. 13), or Niph. pret. 3 pers. sing. fem.	כרת
נִכְרְתוּ / נִכְרְתוּ	Niph. pret. 3 pers. pl. (comp. § 8. rem. 7)	כרת

וְנִכְרָתְנּוּ	Kal fut. 1 pers. pl. (נִכְרֹת), suff. 3 p. s. m.	כרת
וְנִכְשַׁל	Niph. pret. 3 pers. sing. masc.	כשל
וְנִכְשְׁלוּ	Niph. pret. 3 pers. pl. (comp. § 8. rem. 7)	כשל
וְנִכְשְׁלוּ	id. part. masc. pl. [of נִכְשָׁל]	כשל
וְנִכְתָּב	Niph. part. sing. masc.	כתב
נִכְתֵּב	Ch. Peal fut. 1 pers. pl.	כתב
נִכְתָּה / נִכְתָּה	noun fem. sing., suff. 3 pers. sing. masc. from נְכֹאת	נכא
נִכְּתָה	Pual pret. 3 p. s. f. [for נִכְּתָה comp. § 8. r. 7]	נכה
נִכְתָּם	Niph. part. sing. masc.	כתם
וְנִלְאָה	Niph. pret. 3 pers. sing. fem.	לאה
וְנִלְאוּ	id. pret. 3 pers. pl.	לאה
נִלְאֵית	id. pret. 2 pers. sing. fem.	לאה
וְנִלְאֵיתִי	id. pret. 1 pers. sing.	לאה
נִלְבְּנָה	Kal fut. 1 pers. pl. with parag. ה (§ 8. r. 13)	לבן
נִלְבַּשׁ	Kal fut. 1 pers. pl. [for נִלְבַּשׁ § 8. rem. 15]	לבש

נָלָה Kal not used; prob. i. q. Arab. نال *to complete,*
hence Hiph. *to complete, accomplish,* Is. 33. 1.
מִנְלֶה masc. dec. 9a, *possession, wealth,* Job 15. 29.

וְנִלְוָה	Niph. pret. 3 pers. sing. masc.	לוה
נִלְווּ	id. pret. 3 pers. pl.	לוה
וְנִלְוֶה	Niph. part. sing. masc. dec. 3a	לוה
נִלְוֶה	id., constr. st.; ו bef. (:)	לוה
נִלְוִים	id. pl., abs. st.	לוה
נִלָּחֵם	Niph. fut. 1 pers. pl.	לחם
נִלְחָם	id. part. sing. masc., or in pause for the foll.	לחם
וְנִלְחַם	id. pret. 3 pers. sing. masc.	לחם
נִלְחֹם	id. inf. abs.	לחם
וְנִלָּחֲמָה	id. fut. 1 pers. pl. (נִלָּחֵם) with parag. ה (comp. § 8. rem. 13)	לחם
נִלְחֲמוּ / נִלְחֲמוּ	id. pret. 3 pers. pl. (comp. § 8. rem. 7)	לחם
נִלְחָמִים	id. part. masc., pl. of נִלְחָם	לחם
נִלְחַמְנוּ	id. pret. 1 pers. pl.	לחם
נִלְחַמְתָּ	id. pret. 2 pers. sing. masc.; acc. shifted by conv. ו (§ 8. rem. 7)	לחם
נִלְחַמְתִּי / נִלְחַמְתִּי	id. pret. 1 pers. sing.; acc. shifted by conv. ו (§ 8. rem. 7)	לחם
נִלְחַמְתֶּם	id. pret. 2 pers. pl. masc.	לחם
וְנָלִין / נָלִינָה	Kal fut. 1 pers. pl. (comp. § 8. rem. 13); R. לין see	לון

---

a De. 31. 16. — b 1 Sa. 23. 7; Job 34. 19. Job 31. 3. — c Ob. 12. — d La. 4. 8.
f Is. 2. 6. — g Ob. 11. — h Pr. 20. 16. — i 1 Ki. 18. 5. — k Je. 48. 2. — l Ps. 95. 6.
m 2 Ch. 2. 15. — n Ezr. 10. 3. — o Ps. 37. 38. — p Jos. 3. 6. — q Je. 11. 19. — r Da. 11. 19.
s Da. 11. 14. — t Da. 11. 33. — u 1 Sa. 2. 4. — v Est. 9. 32. — w Ezr. 5. 10. — x 2 Ki. 20. 13.
y Is. 39. 2. — z Ex. 9. 31. — a Je. 2. 22. — b Ps. 68. 10. — c Je. 9. 4. — d Ps. 69. 9.
e Is. 47. 13. — f Ex. 7. 18. — g Je. 20. 9. — h Ge. 11. 3. — i Is. 30. 12. — k Pr. 14. 2.
l Ps. 83. 9. — m Is. 14. 1. — n Pr. 3. 32. — o Ju. 5. 19, 20. — p Ob. 1. 10.
q Pr. 2. 15. — r 1 Ki. 20. 23. — s Ju. 11. 25. — t De. 1. 41. — u Ge. 31. 44.
v 2 Sa. 12. 27. — w 1 Sa. 4. 9. — x Ge. 10. 2. — y Ju. 19. 11. — z Ca. 7. 12.

נֵלֵךְ ,רְ, וַגֵּ' Kal fut. 1 pers. pl. (§ 20. rem. 4; וְ conv.) — ילד
נֵלֵךְ

נִלְכַּד Niph. pret. 3 pers. sing. masc. — לכד

נִלְכֹּד וְ Kal fut. 1 pers. pl.; וְ conv. — לכד

נִלְכְּדָה וְ Niph. pret. 3 pers. sing. fem. — לכד

נִלְכְּדוּ וְ id. pret. 3 pers. pl. (comp. § 8. rem. 7) — לכד

נִלְכַּדְתָּ id. pret. 2 pers. sing. masc. — לכד

נִלְכַּדְתְּ id. pret. 2 pers. sing. fem. — לכד

נֵלְכָה וְ Kal fut. 1 pers. pl. (נֵלֵךְ) with parag. ה — ילד
נֵלְכָה וְ (comp. § 8. rem. 13 & 15)

נִלְעָג Niph. part. sing. m. constr. [of נִלְעָג] d. 2 b — לעג

נִלְקַח Niph. pret. 3 pers. sing. masc. (comp. § 8. rem. 7) — לקח
נִלְקְחָה

נִלְקְחָה id. pret. 3 pers. sing. fem. [for נִלְקָחָה v. id.] — לקח

נִמְאָס Niph. part. sing. masc. — מאס

נִמְבְזֶה Niph. part. formed from the subst. מִבְזֶה — בזה

נָמֹגוּ Niph. pret. 3 pers. pl. — מוג

נְמֹגִים id. part. masc. pl. [of נָמוֹג] dec. 3 a — מוג

נִמְהָרָה Niph. pret. sing. [for נִמְהֲרָה comp. § 8. r. 7] — מהר

נִמְהָרִים id. part. pl. masc. from נִמְהָר dec. 2 b — מהר

נָמוּ Kal pret. 3 pers. pl. — נום

נְמוּאֵל pr. name masc. Nu. 26. 9; see also יְמוּאֵל. Patronym. נְמוּאֵלִי ver. 12.

נָמוֹג Niph. pret. 3 pers. sing. masc. — מוג

נָמוֹטוּ Niph. pret. 3 pers. pl. — מוט

נָמוֹל Niph. pret. 3 pers. sing. masc., Chald. form for נָמוֹל (§ 21. rem. 24) — מול

נָמוּת Kal fut. 1 pers. pl. — מות

נִמְחוּ וְ Niph. pret. 3 pers. pl. — מחה

נָמִיתֶךָ Niph. fut. 1 pers. pl. [נָמִית], suff. 2 pers. s. m. — מות

נְמִיתֵם id., suff. 3 pers. pl. masc.; וְ for וְ conv. — מות

נִמְכַּר וְ Niph. pret. 3 pers. sing. masc. — מכר

נִמְכְּרוּ וְ id. pret. 3 pers. pl. — מכר

נִמְכַּרְנוּ id. pret. 1 pers. pl. — מכר

נִמְכֹּר וְ Kal fu 1 pers. pl. [נִמְכֹּר], suff. 3 p. s. m. — מכר

נִמְכַּרְתֶּם Niph. pret. 2 pers. pl. masc. — מכר

[נָמַל] to circumcise, Ge. 17. 11; so according to some, but see מָלַל.

נְמָלָה fem. the ant, Pr. 6. 6; from the idea of cutting, consuming. Pl. נְמָלִים Pr. 30. 25.

נְמַלֵּא Piel fut. 1 pers. pl. — מלא

נִמְלָא Niph. part. sing. masc. — מלא

נֶמֶל noun fem. sing. (pl. נְמָלִים) — נמל

נִמְלְאוּ Niph. pret. 3 p. pl. Ch. form [for נִמְלֹאוּ § 21. r. 24] — מול

נִמְלְחוּ Niph. pret. 3 p. pl. [for נִמְלָחוּ comp. § 8. r. 7] — מלח

נִמָּלֵט Niph. fut. 1 pers. pl. — מלט

נִמְלַט וְ Niph. pret. 3 pers. sing. masc. (§ 8. rem. 15) — מלט
נִמְלָט וְ

נִמְלָטָה id. part. sing. masc. with parag. ה — מלט

נִמְלְטָה id. pret. 3 pers. sing. fem. — מלט

נִמְלְטוּ id. pret. 3 pers. pl. (comp. § 8. rem. 7) — מלט
נִמְלָטוּ

נִמְלַטְנוּ id. pret. 1 pers. pl. [for נִמְלָטְנוּ v. id.] — מלט

נִמְלַטְתִּי id. pret. 1 pers. sing.; acc. shifted by וְ conv. (comp. § 8. rem. 7) — מלט
וְ

נַמְלִיךְ וְ Hiph. fut. 1 pers. pl. — מלך

נְמֹלִים Niph. part. pl. m., from נָמוֹל (§ 21. rem. 24) — מול

נִמְלָךְ defect. for נִמְלִיךְ (q. v.) — מלך

נִמְלְצוּ Niph. pret. 3 pers. — מלץ

נִמְלַתֶּם וְ Niph. pret. 2 pers. pl. masc. for נִמְלַתֶּם (§ 18 rem. 15); וְ for וְ conv. — מלל

נִמְנָה Niph. pret. 3 pers. sing. masc. — מנה

נִמְנַע Niph. pret. 3 pers. sing. masc. — מנע

נָמֵס וְ Niph. pret. 3 pers. sing. masc. [for נָמֵס] — מסס

נָמָס וְ id. id. (§ 18. rem. 7) and in pause נָמָס — מסס

נָמַסּוּ וְ id. pret. 3 pers. pl. — מסס

נִמְצָא וְ Niph. pret. 3 pers. s. m.; or Kal fut. 1 pers. pl. — מצא

נִמְצָאָה Kh. נִמְצָאָה Niph. pret. 3 pers. sing. fem.; K. נִמְצָא (q. v.) — מצא

נִמְצְאוּ Niph. pret. 3 pers. pl. (comp. § 8. rem. 7) — מצא
נִמְצָאוּ

נִמְצָאֶיךָ id. part. pl. masc., suff. 2 pers. s. f. fr. נִמְצָא — מצא

נִמְצֵאת id. pret. 2 pers. sing. fem. — מצא

נִמְצֵאתִי id. pret. 1 pers. sing. — מצא

נִמְצָה וְ Niph. pret. 3 pers. sing. masc. — מצה

נִמְקוּ וְ Niph. pret. 3 pers. pl. — מקק

נְמַקִּים id. part. pl. masc. [fr. נָמַק d. 8. § 37. No. 2] — מקק

נִמְקֹתֶם וְ id. pret. 2 pers. pl. masc.; וְ for וְ, conv. — מקק

נָמֵר וְ masc. dec. 5 a, panther, leopard. In the Arab. to be spotted; also to be limpid, comp. בֵּית נִמְרָה. נְמַר Chald. masc. id. Da. 7. 6.

נָמַר Niph. pret. 3 pers. sing. masc. [for נָמַר] — מור

נִמְרֹד pr. name masc. — מרד

נִמְרָה וְ pr. name in compos. בֵּית נִמְרָה see — בית

נִמְרוֹד pr. name masc., see נִמְרֹד — מרד

---

a Je. 51. 9.   h 1 Sa. 9. 10.   s Is. 32. 4.   g Ge. 37. 27.   f Pr. 11. 21.   — Ps. 22. 6.   = 2 Ki. 10. 5.   b Je. 48. 27.   f Le. 1. 15.
b De. 1. 19.   i Is. 33. 19.   t Ps. 76. 6.   h Pr. 1. 13.   s Eze. 17. 15   n Ps. 124. 7.   f Ps. 119. 103.   c De. 22. 28.   g Ps. 38. 6.
c La. 4. 20.   k 1 Sa. 4. 14.   u Is. 22. 2.   i Job 22. 30.   t Ca. 5. 2.   o 2 Sa. 1. 3.   g Eze. 17. 11.   d Is. 22. 3.   h Eze. 33. 10.
d Zec. 14. 2.   l 1 Sa. 4. 17.   x Ge. 17. 26.   k Pr. 5. 6.   u Je. 48. 19.   p 1 Sa. 27. 1.   h Is. 53. 12.   e Je. 50. 24.   i Eze. 24. 23.
e Je. 51. 56.   m 1 Sa. 15. 9.   y Eze. 6. 6.   l Ge. 17. 27.   v Ps. 124. 7.   q Is. 7. 6.   i Joel 1. 13.   f Is. 65. 1.   k Je. 48. 7.
f Pr. 6. 2.   n Ps. 75. 4.   z Ne. 5. 8.   m Is. 51. 6.   w 2 Sa. 4. 6.   r Ge. 34. 22.   k Ps. 97. 5.   g Je. 29. 14.   l Je. 48. 4.
g Je. 50. 24.   o Job 5. 13.   b Est. 7. 4.   n Is. 20. 6.   x Je. 42. 3.   m 1 Sa. 5. 9.

נְמֵרִים — noun masc. pl. of נָמֵר dec. 5 a . נמר

נִמְרִים — pr. name of a place, see בֵּית נִמְרָה . בית

נִמְרָץ — Niph. part. sing. masc. . מרץ

נִמְרְצוּ — id. pret. 3 pers. pl. . מרץ

נִמְרֶצֶת — id. part. sing. fem. . מרץ

נִמְשַׁח — Niph. pret. 3 pers. sing. masc. . משח

נִמְשִׁי — pr. name masc. . משה

נִמְשַׁל — Niph. pret. 3 pers. sing. masc. . משל

נִמְשַׁלְתָּ — id. pret. 2 pers. sing. masc. [for נִמְשַׁלְתָּ comp. § 8. rem. 7] . משל

נִמְשַׁלְתִּי — id. pret. 1 pers. sing. . משל

נְמִיתֶהוּ — Hiph. fut. 1 pers. pl. [נָמִית], suff. 3 pers. sing. masc.; וּ for וְ conv. . מות

נַמְתִּיק — Hiph. fut. 1 pers. pl. . מתק

נְנַגֵּחַ — Piel fut. 1 pers. pl. (§ 15. rem. 1) . נגח

נְנַגֵּן — Piel fut. 1 pers. pl. . נגן

נָנוּס — Kal fut. 1 pers. pl. . נוס

נָנוּסָה — id. with parag. ה (comp. § 8. rem. 13) . נוס

נִנְחַל — Kal fut. 1 pers. pl. . נחל

נִנְעַרְתִּי — Niph. pret. 1 pers. sing. . נער

נְנַתְּקָה — Piel fut. 1 pers. pl. with parag. ה (comp. § 8. r. 13) . נתק

נָס — Kal pret 3 p. s. m.; or part. masc. d. 1 a . נוס

נַס — Piel imp. sing. masc. ap. [fr. נָסָה § 24. r. 11] . נסה

נֵס — noun masc. sing. dec. 8 b . נסס

נָסַב — Niph. pret. 3 pers. sing. masc. . סבב

נָסֵב — Hiph. fut. 1 pers. pl. . סבב

נָסֹב } Kal fut. 1 pers. pl. (§ 18. rem. 5) . סבב

נָסֵבָּה — Kal fut. 1 p. pl. with parag. ה (§ 8. r. 13) . סבא

נָסַבָּה — Niph. pret. 3 pers. sing. fem. (§ 18. rem. 7) . סבב

נָסֵבָּה — Hiph. fut. 1 pers. pl. (נָסֵב) with parag. ה . סבב

נָסֵבָּה — Niph. pret. 3 p. s. f. [for נָסַבָּה § 18. r. 15] . סבב

נִסְבָּה — noun fem. sing. *2 Ch. 10. 15 . סבב

נָסַבּוּ — Niph. pret. 3 pers. pl. . סבב

[נָסַג] — fut. יִסַּג, to recede, depart, Is. 59. 13; Mi. 2. 6. Hiph. הִסִּיג.—I. to remove a boundary.—II. to take away, Mi. 6. 14. Hoph. הֻסַּג, to be turned back, be perverted, Is. 59. 14.

נִסְגַּר — Chald. Peal fut. 1 pers. pl. . סגר

נָסוֹגוּ — Niph. pret. 3 pers. pl. . סוג

נִסְגַּר — Niph. pret. 3 pers. sing. masc. . סגר

נִסְגְּרָה — Kal fut. 1 pers. pl. with parag. ה (§ 8. r. 13) . סגר

נָסָה — Pi. נִסָּה.—I. to try, prove, tempt.—II. to try, attempt, essay.

מַסָּה — fem. d. 10.—I. trial, temptation.—II. trial, calamity, Job 9. 23.

נָסָה — Kal pret. 3 pers. sing. fem. . נוס

נְסָה — Kal imp. s. m., for נְשָׂא, or better inf. (c. מֵרְדָה) . נשא

נִסָּה — Piel pret. 3 pers. sing. masc. . נסה

נִסָּהוּ — id., suff. 3 pers. sing. masc. . נסה

נָסוּ } Kal pret. 3 pers. pl.; acc. shifted by conv.} . נוס

וָנָסוּ { (comp. § 8. rem. 7) .

נֻסוּ — id. imp. pl. masc. . נוס

נָסוֹג — Niph. pret. 3 pers. sing. masc.; or (Ps. 80. 19) Kal fut. 1 pers. pl. . סוג

נָסֹג } Kal inf. abs. . סוג

נְסוֹגִים — Niph. part. pl. masc. [from נָסוֹג] dec. 3 a . סוג

נְסוּגֹּתִי — id. pret. 1 pers. sing. . סוג

נִסּוּנִי — Piel pret. 3 pers. pl., suff. 1 pers. sing. . נסה

נָסוֹעַ } Kal inf. abs. . נסע

נָסוּר — Kal fut. 1 pers. pl. . סור

נָסוּרָה } id. with parag. ה (comp. § 8. rem. 13) . סור

נַסּוֹת — Piel inf. constr. dec. 1 b . נסה

נָסַח — only fut. יִסַּח, to pluck, tear away, spoken of a house, Pr. 15. 25, of a person, Ps. 52. 7; Pr. 2. 22. Niph. to be plucked up, De. 28. 63.

נְסַח — Chald. Ithpe. id. pass. Ezr. 6. 11.

מַסָּח — masc. removing, i. e. a changing or relieving of guards, adverbially 2 Ki. 11. 6. Others, a keeping off.

נִסְחַף — Niph. pret. 3 pers. sing. masc. . סחף

נִסַּחְתֶּם } Niph. pret. 2 pers. pl. masc. . נסח

נִסִּי — noun masc. sing., suff. 1 pers. s. fr. נֵס d. 8 b . נסס

נְסִיכֵי — noun masc. pl. constr. from [נָסִיךְ] dec. 3 a . נסך

נְסִיכֵם — id. sing., suff. 3 pers. pl. masc. . נסך

נְסִיכֵמוֹ — id. pl., suff. 3 pers. pl. masc. [for נְסִיכֵימוֹ] . נסך

נָסִים — Kal part. act. masc., pl. of נָס dec. 1 a . נוס

נִסִּיתוֹ — Piel pret. 2 p. s. m. [נִסִּיתָ], suff. 3 p. s. m. . נסה

נִסִּיתִי — id. pret. 1 pers. sing. . נסה

נִסִּיתֶם — id. pret. 2 pers. pl. masc. . נסה

נָסַךְ I. — 1. to pour, pour out, Is. 29. 10.—II. to pour out, make a libation.—III. to melt, cast, found.—IV. to anoint a king, Ps. 2. 6. Niph. to be appointed, Pr. 8. 23. Pi. 1 Ch. 11. 18, and Hiph. הִסִּיךְ to pour out a libation. Hoph. pass. Ex. 25. 29; 37. 16; these passages, however, may fairly be referred to סָכַךְ to cover.

נְסַךְ Ch. Pa. to pour out, make a libation, Da. 2. 46.

a Ca. 4. 8. — e Ps. 49. 13, 21. — k Is. 38. 20. — p Da. 1. 12. — u Eze. 26. 2. — z Ne. 6. 10. — e Is. 59. 13. — k Ge. 12. 9. — p De. 32. 38.
b Mi. 2. 10. — f Is. 14. 10. — l Ju. 20. 32. — q 2 Ch. 14. 6. — v 1 Ch. 13. 3. — a Is. 10. 29. — f Je. 46. 5. — l Ju. 19. 11. — q Ps. 83. 12.
c Job 6. 25. — g 2 Sa. 14. 7. — m Nu. 32. 19. — r 1 Ch. 13. 3. — w Ps. 4. 7. — b Ps. 4. 7. — g Is. 50. 5. — m Je. 46. 15. — r De. 33. 8.
d 1 Ki. 2. 8. — h Ps. 55. 15. — n 1 Sa. 16. 11. — s Eze. 41. 7. — x Ex. 15. 25. — c Da. 3. 18. — h Je. 46. 15. — n De. 33. 8. — s De. 6. 14.
Ch. 14. 8. — i Ps. 44. 6. — o De. 2. 1. — t Ps. 2. 3. — y Is. 56. 12. — d 1 Sa. 23. 7. — i De. 28. 63. — o

נֶסֶךְ‎, נֵסֶךְ‎ masc. dec. 6 b.—I. *libation, drink-offering.*—II. *molten image.*

נְסַךְ‎ Chald. masc. dec. 3 b, *libation, drink-offer-ing,* Ezr. 7. 17.

נָסִיךְ‎ m. d. 3 a.—I. *drink-offering,* De. 32. 38.—II. *molten image,* Da. 11. 8.—III. *one appointed, a prince.*

מַסֵּכָה‎ fem. dec. 10.—I. *a fusing;* אֱלֹהֵי מ׳‎ *molten gods, images.*—II. *libation,* meton. for *truce, league,* Is. 30. 1.

II. נָסַךְ‎ to cover, only part. pass. Is. 25. 7. Arab. *to weave.*

מַסֵּכָה‎ fem. *a covering,* Is. 25. 7 ; 28. 20.

מַסֶּכֶת‎ fem. *a web,* Ju. 16. 13, 14.

נָסַךְ‎ᵃ	Kal pret. 3 pers. sing. masc. for נָסַךְ‎ (§ 8. r. 7)	נסך
נֶסֶךְ‎ᵇ	ן noun masc. sing. (suff. נִסְכּוֹ‎) dec. 6a	נסך
נֵסֶךְ‎	ן׳ (comp. § 35. rem. 2) ; for ן see lett. ו	
נֶסֶךְ‎	ן noun masc. sing. dec. 6 b	נסך
נְסָכְךָ‎	Kal inf. (נוּס‎), suff. 2 pers. sing. masc. d. 1 a	נוס
נִסְכֹּה‎	ן noun masc. s., suff. 3 p. s. f. fr. נֶסֶךְ‎ d. 6b	נסך
נִסְכֹּה‎ᵈ	ן id., suff. 3 pers. sing. masc., Keri נִסְכּוֹ‎	נסך
נִסְכֵּיהֶם‎	ן id. pl., suff. 3 pers. pl. masc. for נְסִיכֵיהֶם‎	נסך
נִסְכּוֹ‎	ן׳ id. sing., suff. 3 pers. sing. masc.	נסך
נִסְכִּי‎	ן id. sing., suff. 1 pers. sing.	נסך
נִסְכֶּיהָ‎ᵍ	ן id. pl., suff. 3 pers. sing. fem. ; ו bef. (:)	נסך
נִסְכֵּיהוֹן‎	ן Ch. id. pl., suff. 3 p. pl. m. fr. נְסַךְ‎ d. 3 b	נסך
נִסְכֵּיהֶם‎	noun m. pl., suff. 3 p. pl. m. fr. נָסִיךְ‎ d. 3 a	נסך
נִסְכֵּיהֶם‎	ן׳ the foll. with suff. 3 pers. pl. masc.	נסך
נְסָכִים‎ᵏ	ן noun masc., pl. of נֶסֶךְ‎ dec. 6 b ; ו bef. (:)	נסך
נִסְכַּלְתָּ‎ᵗ	ן Niph. pret. 2 pers. sing. masc. (comp.	סכל
נִסְכַּלְתָּ‎ᵐ	} § 8. rem. 7)	
נִסְכַּלְתִּי‎	id. pret. 1 pers. sing.	סכל
נָסַכְתִּי‎	Kal pret. 1 pers. sing.	נסך
נִסַּכְתִּי‎	Piel pret. 1 pers. sing.	נסך
נִסְלְחָה‎	ן Niph. pret. 3 pers. sing. masc.	סלח
נִסְמְכוּ‎ⁿ	Niph. pret. 3 p. pl. [for נִסְמְכוּ‎ comp. § 8. r. 7]	סמך
נִסְמַכְתִּי‎	id. pret. 1 pers. sing.	סמך
נִסְמָן‎	Niph. part. sing. masc.	סמן
נַסְנוּ‎	ן׳ Kal pret. 1 pers. pl.	נוס
נַסֵּנִי‎	ן Piel imp. sing. masc. [נַסֵּה‎], suff. 1 pers.	נסה
	sing. (§ 24. rem. 21, & § 25)	נסה

I. נָסַם‎ to pine, waste away, only part. נֹסֵם‎ Is. 10. 18 ; cogn. נָמַם‎.

II. נָסַם‎. Hithpo. I. *to lift, raise oneself up,* Zec. 9. 16. Others, *to glitter, shine,* i. q. נָצַץ‎ q. v. where the

two ideas seem to be combined.—II. denom. of נֵס‎, to rally round a standard, Ps. 60. 6.

נֵס‎ masc. dec. 8 b.—I. *a standard, banner.*—II. *sail,* Is. 33. 23 ; Eze. 27. 7 ; others, *flag of a ship.*—III. *pole,* Nu. 21. 8, 9.—IV. *sign, token,* Nu. 26. 10.

נֹסֵם‎	Kal part. act. sing. masc.	נסם
נָסְסָה‎	Piel pret. 3 pers. sing. fem.	נום

נָסַע‎, ן‎ fut. יִסַּע‎, imp. סְעוּ‎, inf. נְסֹעַ‎.—I. *to pull, pluck up or out,* as tent pins, &c.—II. *to break up a camp, castra movere.*—III. generally, *to remove, depart.*—IV. *to travel, journey.* Niph. *to be torn away.* Hiph. הִסִּיעַ‎.—I. *to tear up ;* also *to quarry stones.*—II. *to cause to depart,* Ex. 15. 22.—III. *to lead, guide.*—IV. *to put away, remove,* 2 Ki. 4. 4.

מַסַּע‎, מַסָּע‎ masc. dec. 2 b (§ 31. rem. 5).—I. *a removing,* 1 Ki. 6. 7, אֶבֶן מַסָּע‎ *stone* (ready) *for removing ;* Gesenius, *stone of the quarry.*—II. *journey, march.*

מַסָּע‎ masc. *missile, weapon,* Job 41. 18.

נִסַּע‎	Piel pret. 3 pers. sing. masc.	נסע
נִסַּע‎	ן Kal fut. 1 pers. pl. ; וַ‎ conv.	נסע
נֹסֵעַ‎	id. part. act. sing. masc. dec. 7 b	נסע
נִסְעָה‎ᵃ	וַ‎ id. fut. 1 pers. pl. with parag. ה‎ ; וַ‎ conv.	נסע
נָסְעוּ‎ᵇ	} id. pret. 3 pers. pl. (§ 8. rem. 7)	נסע
נָסְעוּ‎	ן׳ }	
נֹסְעִים‎ᶜ	id. part. act. masc., pl. of נֹסֵעַ‎ dec. 7 b	נסע
נִסְפָּה‎ᵈ	ן Niph. pret. 3 pers. sing. masc.	ספה
נִסְפֶּה‎	id. part. sing. masc.	ספה
נִסְפְּחוּ‎	ן Niph. pret. 3 pers. pl.	ספח
נְסַפֵּר‎ᵍ	וַ‎ Piel fut. 1 pers. pl. ; וַ‎ conv.	ספר
נְסַפְּרָה‎ʰ	ה id. with parag. ה‎ ; ו bef. (:)	ספר

נָסַק‎ only fut. יִסַּק‎, *to go up, ascend,* Ps. 139. 8.

נְסַק‎ Chald. Aph. *to cause to ascend, to take* or *bring up.* Hoph. pass. Da. 6. 24.

נִסְרְחָה‎	Niph. pret. 3 pers. sing. fem.	סרח
נִסְרֹךְ‎	pr. name, *Nisroch,* an idol of the Ninevites.	
נִסִּיתָה‎ᵏ	ן Kal pret. 2 pers. sing. masc. (§ 8. rem. 5)	נום
נִסְּתָה‎ˡ	Piel pret. 3 pers. sing. fem.	נסה
נִסִּיתִי‎ᵐ	Kal pret. 1 pers. sing.	נום
נַסֹּתְךָ‎ⁿ	Piel inf. (נַסּוֹת‎), suff. 2 pers. sing. m. d. 1 b	נסה
נִסְּתָם‎ᵒ	id., suff. 3 pers. pl. masc.	נסה
נִסֵּתֶם‎ᵖ	ן׳ Kal pret. 2 pers. pl. masc.	נום
נִסָּתֵר‎ᵠ	ן Niph. fut. 1 pers. pl.	סתר
נִסְתָּר‎	id. part sing. masc.	סתר

ᵃ Is. 44. 10.   ᶠ Is. 48. 5.   ᵏ 1 Sa. 13. 13.   ᵖ Ps. 71. 6.   ᵘ Ps. 26. 2.   ᶜ Ezr. 8. 31.   ᵏ Is. 14. 1.   ˡ Je. 49. 7.   ᵐ De. 8. 16.

ᵇ Joel 1. 13.   ᵍ Nu. 29. 31.   ˡ 2 Ch. 16. 9.   ᵠ Is. 28. 25.   ᵛ Is. 10. 18.   ᵈ Nu. 9. 21.   ˡ Ps. 79. 13.   ᵐ 2 Ki. 9. 3.   Ex. 17. 7.

ᶜ 2 Sa. 24. 13.   ʰ Ezr. 7. 17.   ᵐ Ps. 2. 6.   ʳ Pr. 8. 23.   ʷ Is. 19. 19.   ᵉ Nu. 10. 29.   ᵍ Ge. 41. 12.   De. 28. 56.   Zec. 14. 5.

ᵈ Le. 23. 13.   ⁱ Da. 11. 8.   ⁿ Jos. 8. 5, 6.   Ge. 33. 12.   ᶠ 1 Sa. 26. 10.   Je. 51. 10.   ᵐ 1 Sa. 4. 16.   ᵒ Ge. 31. 49.

ᵉ Nu. 29. 33.   ᵉ Le. 23. 37.   Is. 48. 2.

נִסְתָּרָה	Niph. pret. 3 pers. sing. fem. (comp. § 8. rem. 7)	סתר
וַתִּסְתָּרֵה		סתר
נִסְתָּרוּ	id. pret. 3 pers. pl.	סתר
נִסְתַּרְנוּ	id. pret. 1 p. pl. [for נִסְתָּרֵנוּ comp. § 8. r. 7]	סתר
נִסְתַּרְתָּ	id. pret. 2 pers. sing. masc.; acc. shifted by conv. וְ (comp. § 8. rem. 7)	סתר
נִסְתַּרְתִּי	id. pret. 1 pers. sing.; acc. id.	סתר
נָע	Kal part. act. sing. masc.	נוע
וַנַּעֲבֹד	Kal fut. 1 pers. pl.; וַ conv.	עבד
נֶעֱבַד	Niph. pret. 3 p. s. m. [for נֶעֱבַד § 13. r. 7]	עבד
נַעַבְדָה	Kal fut. 1 pers. pl. (נַעֲבֹד) with parag. ה (comp. § 8. rem. 13)	עבד
וְנַעַבְדֶךָ	id., suff. 2 pers. sing. masc.	עבד
נַעַבְדֵם	Hoph. fut. 1 pers. pl., suff. 3 pers. pl. masc.	עבד
נַעַבְדֶנּוּ	Kal fut. 1 pers. pl. (נַעֲבֹד), suff. 3 pers. s. m.	עבד
נֶעֱבַדְתֶּם	Niph. pret. 2 pers. pl. masc.	עבד
וַנַּעֲבֹר	Kal fut. 1 pers. pl.; וַ conv.	עבר
וְנַעַבְרָה	id. with parag. ה (§ 8. rem. 13, & § 13. rem. 7)	עבר
וַנַּעַבְרָה		עבר
נֶעְדָּר	Niph. pret. 3 pers. sing. masc. (comp. § 8. rem. 7, & § 13. rem. 7)	עדר
נֶעְדָּרִי		עדר
נֶעֶדְרָה	id. pret. 3 pers. sing. fem. [for נֶעְדְּרָה comp. § 8. rem. 7]	עדר
נֶעֶדֶרֶת	id. part. sing. fem. [from נֶעְדָּר masc.]	עדר
נֹעַדְתִּי	defect. for נוֹעַדְתִּי (q. v.)	יעד
נֹעָה	pr. name fem.	נוע
נָעוּ	Kal pret. 3 pers. pl.; acc. shifted by conv. וְ (comp. § 8. rem. 7)	נוע
נָעֻו		נוע
נַעֲוֵה	Niph. part. sing. m., constr. [of נַעֲוֶה d. 9a	עוה
נַעֲוֵיתִי	id. pret. 1 pers. sing. (§ 13. rem. 7, note)	עוה
נָעוּל	Kal part. pass. sing. masc.	נעל
נָעוּר	Kal part. pass. sing. masc.	נער
נֵעוֹר	Niph. pret. 3 pers. sing. masc. (§ 21. rem. 11)	עור
נְעוּרַי	noun masc. pl., suff. 1 pers. sing. from [נָעוּר] dec. 1a	נער
נְעוּרֶיהָ	id., suff. 3 pers. sing. fem.	נער
נְעוּרָיִךְ	id. with suff. 2 pers. sing. fem.	נער
נְעוּרֶיךָ	id., suff. 2 pers. sing. masc.	נער
נְעוּרָיְכִי	id., suff. 2 pers. sing. fem. (§ 4. rem. 4)	נער
נְעוּרִים	id. pl., abs. st.	נער
נָעוֹת	Kal part. act. fem. pl. [of נָעָה dec. 10] from נָע masc.	נוע
נַעֲוַת	Niph. part. sing. fem. constr. [of נַעֲוָה dec. 10, from נַעֲוֶה masc.]	עוה
נַעֲזֹב	Kal fut. 1 pers. pl.	עזב

וְנֶעֱזָב	Niph. part. sing. masc.	עזב
נֶעֱזָב	id. pret. 3 pers. sing. masc.	עזב
נַעַזְבָה	Kal fut. 1 pers. pl. (נַעֲזֹב) with parag. ה (comp. § 8. rem. 13)	עזב
נֶעֶזְבָה	Niph. pret. 3 pers. sing. fem. [for נֶעֶזְבָה comp. § 8. rem. 7]	עזב
וְנֶעֱזַרְתִּי	Niph. pret. 1 pers. sing.	עזר
נְעִיאֵל	pr. name of a place in the tribe of Asher, Jos. 19. 27.	
נָעִים	adj. masc. sing. dec. 3a	נעם
נְעִים	id., constr. st.; וּ bef. (:)	נעם
נֶעְכָּר	Niph. part. sing. masc. (§ 13. rem. 7)	עכר
נֶעְכֶּרֶת	id. part. sing. fem. [for נֶעְכֶּרֶת comp. § 35. r. 2]	עכר
נָעַל	fut. יִנְעַל.—I. to fasten with a bolt or bar, to bolt. —II. to tie or latch the sandals for any one, with acc. of the person, Eze. 16. 10. נַעַל fem. dec. 6d (pl. נְעָלִים, נְעָלוֹת) sandal, shoe; שְׂרוֹךְ נַ׳ shoe-latchet; du. נַעֲלַיִם a pair of shoes. מַנְעוּל masc. dec. 1b, bolt, bar. מִנְעָל masc. dec. 2b, id. De. 33. 25.	
וְנָעַל	Kal pret. 3 pers. sing. masc. for נָעַל (§ 8. r. 7)	נעל
נַעֲלָה	noun fem. sing. dec. 6d	נעל
וַנַּעַל	Kal fut. 1 pers. pl., ap. from נַעֲלֶה; וַ conv.	עלה
וּנְעַל	Kal imp. sing. masc.; וּ bef. (:)	נעל
נַעֲלֶה	Niph. pret. 3 pers. sing. m. (§ 13. r. 7, note)	עלה
וְנַעֲלֶה	Kal fut. 1 pers. pl. (v. id.)	עלה
נַעֲלוֹ	noun fem. sing., suff. 3 pers. sing. masc. from נַעַל dec. 6d	נעל
נְעֻלוֹת	Kal part. fem. pl. [of נְעוּלָה d. 10] fr. נָעוּל m.	נעל
נְעָלוֹת	noun fem. pl. abs. from נַעַל d. 6d; וּ bef. (:)	נעל
נַעֲלִי	id. sing., suff. 1 pers. sing.	נעל
נְעָלָיו	id. pl. (נְעָלִים), suff. 3 pers. sing. masc.	נעל
נְעָלֶיךָ	id. pl., suff. 2 pers. sing. masc.; וּ bef. (:)	נעל
נַעֲלֵיכֶם	id. pl., suff. 2 pers. pl. masc.	נעל
נַעֲלַיִם	id. du., abs. st. [for נַעֲלָיִם]	נעל
נַעֲלֵינוּ	id. pl. (נְעָלִים), suff. 1 pers. pl.; וּ bef. (:)	נעל
נַעֲלֵיתָ	Niph. pret. 2 pers. sing. masc. (§ 13. r. 7 note)	עלה
וְנַעַלְךָ	noun fem. sing., suff. 2 pers. sing. masc. from נַעַל dec. 6d	נעל
נֶעְלָם	Niph. part. sing. masc., pl. נֶעְלָמִים (§ 13. r. 7)	עלם
וְנֶעְלַם	id. pret. 3 pers. sing. masc.	עלם
נֶעְלָמָה	id. part. sing. fem.	עלם

a Is. 40. 27.	g Ec. 5. 8.	m Is. 59. 15.	r Ps. 25. 7.	v Ps. 37. 25.	b Pr. 24. 4.	g Ge. 14. 23.	m Is. 5. 27.	r Jos. 9. 13.
b Nu. 5. 13.	h De. 13. 3.	n Ex. 29. 43.	s Ps. 103. 5.	w Is. 27. 10.	c 2 Sa. 3. 1.	h De. 3. 1.	n Ex. 3. 5.	s Ps. 97. 9.
c Is. 28. 15.	i Eze. 36. 9.	o Pr. 12. 8.	t Is. 54. 6.	x Ps. 39. 3.	d 2 Sa. 13. 17.	i Nu. 9. 21.	o Eze. 24. 17.	t Jos. 5. 15.
d 1 Sa. 20. 19.	j Is. 51. 23.	p Ca. 4. 12.	u 1 Sa. 1. 5.	y Ps. 15. 6.	e Ex. 12. 11.		p 2 Ch. 9. 2.
e 1 Ki. 17. 3.	k 1 Sa. 30. 19.	q Ne. 5. 13.	v 1 Sa. 20. 30.	z Is. 62. 12.	f Ju. 3. 24.	l Eze. 24. 23.	q Na. 3. 11.
f 1 Sa. 20. 5.	l Is. 34. 16.		Zec. 2. 17.	Ne. 10. 40.	Ps. 28.	Ju. 3. 23.	Jos. 9. 5.

וְנֶעְלָמָה [a]	Niph. pret. 3 pers. sing. masc.	עלם
נֶעְלָמִים	id. part. masc., pl. of נֶעְלָם (q. v.)	עלם
נֶעֶלְסָה [b]	Niph. pret. 3 pers. sing. fem. [for נֶעְלְסָה comp. § 8. rem. 7]	עלם

[נָעֵם] fut. יִנְעַם to be pleasant, agreeable, lovely.

נָעִים masc. dec. 3 a, adj.—I. pleasant, agreeable, sweet.—II. lovely, amiable. Pl. נָעִימִים pleasant places, Ps. 16. 6; נְעִימוֹת, נְעִימִים delights, pleasures.

נַעַם (pleasantness) pr. name masc. 1 Ch. 4. 15.

נֹעַם masc.—I. pleasantness.—II. beauty, glory, Ps. 27. 4.—III. kindness, grace, Ps. 90. 17.

נַעֲמָה (pleasant) pr. name—I. of a daughter of Lamech, Ge. 4. 22.—II. of the mother of Rehoboam.—III. of a place in the tribe of Judah, Jos. 15. 41.—IV. of another unknown place, whence the gent. n. נַעֲמָתִי, comp. Job 2. 11.

נַעֲמִי patronym. of pr. name (נַעֲמָן (q. v.) Nu. 26. 40.

נָעֳמִי (my pleasantness; or perh. for נַעֲמִיָּה (pleasantness of the Lord; or for נַעֲמִית pleasant) pr. name of the mother-in-law of Ruth.

נַעֲמָן masc.—I. pl. נַעֲמָנִים pleasantness, Is. 17. 10.—II. pr. name masc. of several persons.

מַנְעַמִּים masc. pl. of (מַנְעָם dec. 8 a) delicacies, Ps. 141. 4.

וְנֹעַם	pr. name masc. [for נֹעַם § 35. rem. 2]; see lett. י	
נֹעַם	noun masc. sing.	נעם
נַעֲמֹד [c]	Kal fut. 1 pers. pl.	עמד
נַעַמְדָה	id. with parag. ה (§ 8. rem. 13)	עמד
נַעֲמָה	י pr. name of a woman and a place	נעם
נָעֵמָה [d]	Kal pret. 3 pers. s. fem. [for נָעֲמָה § 8. r. 1 a]	נעם
נָעֵמוּ [e]	id. pret. 3 pers. pl. [for נָעֲמוּ v. i.]	נעם
נְעֵמוֹת [f]	adj. fem. pl. [of נָעִמָה dec. 10] from נָעִים m.	נעם
נָעֳמִי	pr. name fem.	נעם
וְנַעֲמִיד [g]	Hiph. fut. 1 pers. pl.; וַ conv.	עמד
נַעֲמָן	י pr. name masc.	נעם
נַעֲמָנִים	noun masc., pl. of [נַעֲמָן] dec. 2 b	נעם
נָעַמְתְּ [h] נָעַמְתָּ [h]	} Kal pret. 2 pers. sing. masc. (§ 8. rem. 7)	נעם
נָעַמְתְּ [h]	id. pret. 2 pers. sing. fem.	נעם
נַעֲנָה [i] נֵעָנֶה	} Niph. part. sing. fem. & masc.	ענה
נַעֲנֵיתִי	id. pret. 1 pers. sing. (§ 13. rem. 7, note)	ענה
וְנַעֲנְשׁוּ [k]	Niph. pret. 3 pers. pl. [for נֶעֶנְשׁוּ comp. § 8. rem. 7]	ענש

וַנָּעֻפָה [l]	Kal fut. 1 pers. pl. with parag. ה (comp. § 8. rem. 13); וַ conv.	עוף

נָעַץ Root not used; Chald. to prick.

נַעֲצוּץ masc. d. 1 b, thorn-bush, Is. 7. 19; 55. 13.

נֶעֱצַב	Niph. pret. 3 pers. sing. masc.	עצב
נַעֲצֹר [m]	Kal fut. 1 pers. pl. (§ 13. rem. 5)	עצר
נֶעֱצָר [m]	Niph. part. sing. masc. (§ 13. rem. 7)	עצר
נַעְצְרָה [m]	Kal fut. 1 pers. pl. with parag. ה (§ 8. rem. 13, & § 13. rem. 5)	עצר
[נֶעֶצְרָה]	Niph. pret. 3 pers. sing. fem. [for נֶעֶצְרָה]	עצר
וְנֶעְקַשׁ [n]	Niph. part. sing. masc., constr. of [נֶעְקָשׁ § 13. rem. 7] dec. 2 b	עקש

I. [נָעַר] to roar, as a young lion, Je. 51. 38.

II. [נָעַר] cogn. עוּר, עָרָה.—I. to shake, shake out.—II. to shake off, i. e. cast off foliage, Is. 33. 9. Niph. I. to be shaken, cast out.—II. to shake or rouse oneself, Ju. 16. 20. Pi. נִעֵר (§ 14. rem. 1) to shake, throw out. Hithp. to shake oneself, Is. 52. 2.

נַעַר m. that which is cast or driven out, Zec. 11. 16.

נְעֹרֶת fem. tow, Ju. 16. 9; Is. 1. 31.

וְנַעַר masc. dec. 6 d.—I. a male infant, comp. Ex. 2. 6—II. boy, lad.—III. a youth.—IV. servant.

נֹעַר masc. childhood, youth.

נַעֲרָה fem. dec. 12 a.—I. a girl, maiden.—II. a young woman.—III. handmaid.—IV. pr. name of a woman, 1 Ch. 4. 5.—V. pr. name of a town on the borders of Ephraim, Jos. 16. 7, called נַעֲרָן in 1 Ch. 7. 28.

נְעוּרִים masc. pl. (of נָעוּר dec. 1 a).—I. childhood, Ge. 46. 34.—II. youth, early life.

נְעוּרוֹת fem. pl. (of נְעוּרָה dec. 10) id. Je. 32. 30.

נַעַרְיָה (servant of the Lord) pr. name masc.—I. 1 Ch. 3. 22.—II. 1 Ch. 4. 42.

נַעַר [o]	Kh. נַעַר (q. v.) com. gen.; K. נַעֲרָה (q. v.)	נער
נָעַר [p]	י in pause for נַעַר (§ 35. r. 2); for י see lett. ו	נער
נִעֵר [q]	Piel pret. 3 pers. sing. masc. (§ 14. rem. 1)	נער
נֹעֵר [r]	Kal part. sing. masc.	נער
נַעֲרָה [s]	י noun fem. sing. d. 12 d (also pr. name fem.)	נער
נַעֲרָהּ [t]	noun masc. sing., suff. 3 pers. sing. fem. from נַעַר dec. 6 d	נער
נָעֲרוּ [u]	י Kal pret. 3 pers. pl.	נער
נַעֲרוֹ [v]	י n. m. s., suff. 3 pers. sing. masc. fr. נַעַר d. 6 d	נער
נַעֲרוֹת [w]	constr. of the foll.	נער

a Job 28. 21.   e Ge. 49. 15.   i Ne. 4. 3.   m 2 Sa. 1. 26.   q Pr. 23. 3; 27. 12.   t 1 Sa. 21. 8.   u Pr. 28. 18.   z Ps. 136. 15.   c 2 Ki. 4. 24.
Ps. 26. 4.   f Ps. 141. 6.   k Is. 17. 10.   n Ca. 7. 7.   r Ps. 90. 10.   u Ju. 13. 15.   w De. 22. 23, 28.   s Is. 33. 9, 15.   d Je. 51. 38.
Job 39. 13.   g Ps. 16. 11.   l Ex. 32. 19.   o Is. 58. 10.   s 1 Ch. 29. 14.   v Nu. 17. 15.   x Je. 51. 22.   t Est. 2. 12.   e Est. 4. 4
d 2 Ki. 10. 4.

נְעָרוֹת	noun fem. pl. abs. from נַעֲרָה dec. 12 d	נער
נַעֲרוֹתֶיהָ	id. pl., suff. 3 pers. sing. fem.	נער
נַעֲרוֹתָיו	id. pl., suff. 3 pers. sing. masc.	נער
נַעֲרִי	pr. name masc.	נער
נַעֲרֵי	noun masc. pl. constr. from נַעַר dec. 6 d	נער
נְעָרַי } נְעָרָי	id. pl., suff. 1 pers. sing. ; וֹ bef. (:)	נער
נְעֻרַי	defect. for נְעוּרַי (q. v.)	נער
נַעֲרָיָה	pr. name masc. ; וֹ bef. (:)	נער
נַעֲרֵיהֶם	noun masc. pl., suff. 3 p. pl. m. fr נַעַר d. 6 d	נער
נְעָרָיו	id. pl., suff. 3 pers. sing. masc.	נער
נְעָרֶיךָ	id. pl., suff. 2 pers. sing. masc.	נער
נְעָרִים	id. pl., abs. st. ; וֹ bef. (:)	נער
נַעֲרֹךְ	Kal fut. 1 pers. pl.	ערך
נֶעְרָךְ	noun masc. s., suff. 2 pers. s. m. fr. נַעַר d. 6 g	נער
נֶעֶרְמוּ	Niph. pret. 3 pers. pl.	ערם
נַעֲרָן	pr. name of a place, see נַעֲרָה	נער
נַעֲרָץ	Niph. part. sing. masc.	ערץ
נַעֲרָתָה	pr. name of a place נַעֲרָה with parag. ה	נער
נָעַרְתִּי	Kal pret. 1 pers. sing.	נער
נַעֲרֹתַי וֵנ	noun fem. pl., suff. 1 pers. sing. from נַעֲרָה dec. 12 d	נער
נַעֲרֹתֶיהָ וֵנ	id., suff. 3 pers. sing. fem.	נער
וַנַּעַשׂ	Kal fut. 1 pers. pl., ap. fr. נַעֲשֶׂה ; וֵ conv.	עשה
נַעֲשָׂה וֵנ	Niph. pret. 3 pers. sing. m. (§ 13. r. 7, note)	עשה
נַעֲשֶׂה וַנ	Kal fut. 1 pers. pl. ; or (Ne. 5. 18) Niph. part. dec. 9 a	עשה
נַעֲשׂוּ	Niph. pret. 3 pers. pl. (§ 13. rem. 7, note)	עשה
נַעֲשִׂים וֵנ	id. part. masc., pl. of נַעֲשֶׂה dec. 9 a	עשה
נַעֲשֶׂנָּה	Kal fut. 1 pers. pl. (נַעֲשֶׂה), suff. 3 p. s. f.	עשה
נֶעֶשְׂתָה } נֶעֶשְׂתָה	Niph. pret. 3 pers. sing. fem. (comp. § 8. rem. 7)	עשה
נֶעְתּוֹר	Niph. inf. abs. (§ 9. rem. 1, & § 13. rem. 7)	עתר
נֶעְתָּם	Niph. pret. 3 pers. sing. masc. (§ 13. rem. 7)	עתם
נֶעְתָּר וֵנ	Niph. pret. 3 pers. sing. masc. (§ 13. r. 7)	עתר
נֶעְתָּרוֹת וֵנ	id. part. pl. fem. (§ 13. rem. 7)	עתר
נֹף	pr. name, *Memphis*, see נֹף.	
נֶפֶג	(*sprout*) pr. name masc. of two different persons.	
נִפְגַּע	Kal fut. 1 pers. pl.	פגע
נִפְגְּשׁוּ	Niph. pret. 3 p. pl. [for נִפְגְּשׁוּ comp. § 8. r. 7]	פגש
נִפְדְּתָה	Niph. pret. 3 pers. sing. fem. [for נִפְדְּתָה comp. § 8. rem. 7]	פדה
נִפְדֹּנְתִּי	Niph. pret. 1 pers. sing.	פון
נָפוּחַ	Kal part. pass. sing. masc.	נפח
נָפוֹל	Kal inf. abs.	נפל
נָפוֹץ וֵנ	Kal inf. abs.	נפץ

נָפוּץ	id. part. pass. sing. masc.	נפץ
נָפוּץ	Kal fut. 1 pers. pl.	פוץ
נָפוֹצָה	Niph. pret. 3 pers. sing. fem.	פוץ
נְפוֹצוֹתֶם	id. pret. 2 pers. pl. masc. (§ 21. rem. 12)	פוץ
נְפוֹצִים	id. part. masc. pl. [of נָפוֹץ] dec. 3 a	פוץ
נְפוֹסִים K., נְפִישִׁים Kh. see נְפוּשְׁסִים		
נִפְזָרוּ	Niph. pret. 3 pers. pl.	פזר

[נָפַח] fut. יִפַּח.—I. *to blow, breathe* a breath, or abs. *to blow* ; with בְּ *into* or *upon*.—II. *to blow* a fire, with acc., בְּ ; and עַל *upon* a thing or person ; דּוּד נָפוּחַ *a seething pot.*—III. with נֶפֶשׁ *to expire* Je. 15. 9. Pu. *to be blown*, of a fire, Job 20. 26. Hiph. I. *to cause to breathe out, cause to pant*, Job 31. 39.—II. *to puff at, despise*, Mal. 1. 13.

נֹפַח (*a blowing*) pr. name of a town in Moab, Nu. 21. 30.

מַפֵּחַ masc. dec. 2 b, *an expiring*, with נֶפֶשׁ Job 11. 20.

מַפֻּחַ masc. *bellows*, Je. 6. 29.

תַּפּוּחַ masc.—I. *apple.*—II. *apple-tree.*—III. pr. name (*a*) of a town in Judah ; (*b*) of another between Ephraim and Manasseh, Jos. 16. 8 ; (*c*) of a man, 1 Ch. 2. 43.

נֹפַח	pr. name of a place	נפח
נֹפֵחַ	Kal part. act. sing. masc.	נפח
נֻפַּח	Pual pret. 3 p. s. m. [for נֻפַּח comp. § 8. r. 7]	נפח
נָפְחָה	Kal pret. 3 pers. sing. fem.	נפח
נָפַחְתִּי וֵ	id. pret. 1 pers. sing. ; acc. shifted by conv. (§ 8. rem. 7)	נפח
נַפִּילָה וֵ	Hiph. fut. 1 p. pl. with parag. ה (comp. § 8. r. 13)	נפל
נְפוּסִים Kh. נְפִיסִים K., נְפוּסִים	pr. name masc. Ezr. 2. 50, for which in Ne. 7. 52 נְפוּשְׁסִים Kh. נְפִישִׁים K.	
נָפִישׁ וֵ	pr. name masc.	נפש

נֹפֶךְ masc. name of a precious stone ; kind uncertain LXX. ἄνθρακα, *carbuncle* ; Eng. vers. *emerald* marg. *chrysoprase*, Eze. 28. 13.

נָפַל וֵ fut. יִפֹּל, inf. נְפֹל.—I. *to fall*, of persons and things.—II. *to fall* in battle, by the sword, *to be killed.*—III. *to fall down, to alight, dismount.*—IV. *to be fallen, to lie*, 1 Sa. 19. 24 ; and so frequently in the part. נֹפֵל *fallen, lying.*—V. *to fall, hang down*, as the arms from weakness ; as the countenance in sorrow or anger.—VI. trop. *to fall to*

a Job 29. 5.   d Job 37. 19.   f Ne. 5. 13.   n Je. 35. 10.   q Da. 11. 36.   p Pr. 27. 6.   b Est. 6. 13.   f Je. 10. 21.   i Is. 54. 16.
b Je. 3. 4.   e Ju. 7. 10.   g Ru. 2. 8.   o Eze. 15. 5.   r 1 Ch. 5. 20.   q Job 21. 15.   v Ju. 7. 19.   g Eze. 20. 34.   f Job 20. 26.
Ne. 5. 15.   h Ex. 15. 8.   h Est. 4. 16.   p Is. 9. 18.   s Le. 19. 20.   f Je. 22. 28.   u 2 Ch. 18. 16.   h Is. 15. 9.
l Sa. 25. 8.   h Ps. 89. 8.   m Pr. 9. 3.   q De. 30. 12, 13.   B.C. 4. 1.   Ge. 11. 4.   aa Es 4. 28.   k Ps. 141. 7.   j Jon. 1. 7.

the ground, come to nothing, comp. 2 Ki. 10. 10.
—VII. *to fall out, terminate*, Ru. 3. 18.—VIII.
with עַל (*a*) *to fall upon*, as sleep, terror, divine
revelation, (*b*) upon the sword; (*c*) upon the
neck of any one, to embrace him; (*d*) upon the
face, *to prostrate oneself* before any one; (*e*) upon
any one, *to attack* him; (*f*) נָ׳ גּוֹרָל עַל *the lot fell
upon*.—IX. with מִן *to fall away from* one party to
another, with אֶל . עַל.—X. with לְ (*a*) *to fall to*,
of an inheritance; (*b*) לְמִשְׁכָּב נָ׳ *to fall upon* a
sick-bed, to fall sick.—XI. with מִן *to fall, sink
down*; trop. from counsels, Ps. 5. 11. Hiph.
הִפִּיל.—I. *to cause, make to fall*; hence, *to cast,
throw down*; ה׳ גּוֹרָל *to cast lots*; with לְ *to assign
to* any one.—II. פְּנֵי פ׳ ה׳ *to cause* the countenance of any one *to fall*, i.e. to make sad;
ב פָּנָיו ה׳ *to drop* one's countenance at any one,
to be angry with him; לִפְנֵי תְּחִנָּה ה׳ *to lay down*
one's prayer, petition before any one; עַיִן ה׳ *to
knock out* an eye.—III. הִפִּיל מִן *to desist from*;
אַרְצָה ה׳ *to let fall* to the ground, not to fulfil.—
IV. *to cast, bear, bring forth*. Hithp. I. *to prostrate oneself*.—II. with עַל , *to throw oneself upon*,
to attack, Ge. 43. 18. Pil. נִפֵּל i. q. Kal, Eze. 28. 23.

נְפַל Ch. fut. יִפַּל.—I. *to fall*.—II. *to fall down,
prostrate oneself*.—III. *to be cast down*, Da. 3. 23.
—IV. *to fall out, happen*, Ezr. 7. 20.

נֵפֶל masc. *an untimely birth*.

נָפִיל masc. only pl. נְפִילִים *giants*.

מַפָּל masc. dec. 2 b.—I. *refuse* of corn, Am. 8. 6.
—II. *pendulous, flaccid* parts of the flesh, Job
41. 15.

מַפֵּלָה, מַפֵּלָה fem. *ruins*.

מַפֶּלֶת (מַפַּלְתּוֹ .suff with) fem. dec. 13 a.—I.
fall, ruin, spoken of a man, a kingdom, a fallen
trunk.—II. *a carcase*, Ju. 14. 8.

נָפַל	Kal pret. 3 pers. sing. m. for נָפַל (§ 8. r. 7)	נפל
נְפַל	Chald. Peal pret. 3 pers. sing. masc. .	נפל
נֶפֶל ͣ	noun masc. sing. . .	נפל
נֹפֵל ͣ	'ן Kal part. sing. masc. .	נפל
נִפְלְאוּ ͣ	Niph. pret. 3 pers. pl. .	פלא
נִפְלָאוֹת ͥ	'ן id. part. pl. abs. fem. [from נִפְלָאָה] dec. 11 a, in use נִפְלָאֹת q. v. .	פלא
נִפְלְאוֹת ͩͩ	id. pl., constr. st. .	פלא
נִפְלְאֹתָיו	'ן id. pl., suff. 3 pers. sing. masc. .	פלא
נִפְלְאֹתֶיךָ	id. pl., suff. 2 pers. sing. masc. .	פלא

נִפְלָאִים	id. part. pl. masc. [from נִפְלָא]	פלא
נִפְלָאת ͤ	id. pret. 3 pers. sing. fem. (§ 23. rem. 5)	פלא
נִפְלָאֹת	id. part. pl. abs. fem. see נִפְלָאוֹת	פלא
נִפְלֵאת ͤ	id. part. sing. fem. [for נִפְלָאֶת § 23. rem. 5]	פלא
נִפְלָאתָה ͤ	id. pret. 3 pers. sing. fem. with parag. ה	פלא
נִפְלְאֹתַי	id. part. pl. fem., suff. 1 pers. sing. [from נִפְלָאָה dec. 11 b] .	פלא
נִפְלְאֹתָיו	'ן id. pl., suff. 3 pers. sing. masc.	פלא
נִפְלְאֹתֶיךָ	id. pl., suff. 2 pers. sing. masc. .	פלא
נִפְלְגָה	Niph. pret. 3 pers. sing. fem. .	פלג
נָפְלָה ͫ נָפְלָה	} Kal pret. 3 pers. sing. fem. (§ 8. rem. 7)	נפל
נִפְּלָה ͤ 'ן	id. fut. 1 p.pl. with parag. ה (comp. § 8. r. 13)	נפל
נָפְלוּ ͤ 'ן נָפְלוּ	} id. pret. 3 pers. pl. (§ 8. rem. 7)	נפל
נְפַלוּ ͤ	Chald. Peal pret. 3 pers. pl. masc. .	נפל
נָפְלוֹ ͤ	Kal inf. [נְפֹל], suff. 3 p. s. m. (§ 16. r. 10)	נפל
נָפְלִי ͤ	id. inf. (נְפֹל), suff. 3 p. s. m. (§ 16. r. 7)	נפל
נִפְלוּ ͤ 'ן	id. imp. pl. masc.	נפל
נְפַלַת ͤ	ͥ Ch. Peal pret. 3 p.pl., Kh. נְפַלֻ m., K. נְפַלָה f.	נפל
נֹפְלִים	Kal part. act. masc. pl. of נֹפֵל dec. 7 b	נפל
נָפְלִין ͤ	Ch. Peal part. act. masc. pl. [of נָפֵל] d. 2 b	נפל
נִפְלֵנוּ ͤ	ͥ Niph. pret. 1 pers. pl. (§ 24. rem. 8)	פלה
נִפְלֵתִי ͤ	id. pret. 1 pers. sing. .	פלה
נִפְלַל ͤ	ͥ Pilel pret. 3 pers. sing. masc. (§ 6. No. 2)	פלל
נָפְלָם ͤ	Kal inf. [נְפֹל], suff. 3 p. pl. m. (§ 16. r. 10)	נפל
נָפַלְתָּ ͤ נָפָלְתָּ ͤ 'ן	} id. pret. 2 pers. sing. masc. (§ 8. r. 7)	נפל
נֹפֶלֶת	id. part. sing., fem. of נֹפֵל	נפל
נָפַלְתָּה ͤ 'ן	id. pret. 2 pers. sing. masc. (§ 8. rem. 5)	ופל
נָפַלְתִּי ͤ נָפָלְתִּי ͤ 'ן	} id. pret. 1 pers. sing.; acc. shifted by conv. וְ (§ 8. rem. 7)	נפל
נְפַלְתֶּם ͤ	ͥ id. pret. 2 pers. pl. masc.; וֹ for וְ , conv.	נפל
נִפֶּן	ן Kal fut. 1 pers. pl., ap. [fr. נִפְנֶה] (§ 24. rem. 3); וַ conv. .	פנה
נִפְעַמְתִּי ͤ	Niph. pret. 1 pers. sing. .	פעם

נָפַץ I. *to break, dash in pieces*.—II. *to disperse, scatter*,
Is. 11. 12.—III. of a people, *to disperse themselves,
be scattered abroad*. Pi. i. q. Kal No. I & II.
Pu. *to be dashed* or *broken down*, Is. 27. 9.

נֶפֶץ masc. *a violent shower, flood*, Is. 30. 30.

ᵃ Ps. 58. 9.   ᶜ Ps. 96. 3.   ⁱ De. 30. 11.   ᵐ 2 Sa. 24. 14.   ʳ 1 Sa. 29. 3.   ˣ Da. 3. 7.   ᵉ Je. 49. 21.   ᶜ 2 Ch. 25. 19.   ʰ Ju. 15. 18.
ᵇ 2 Sa. 3. 29.   ᶠ Ps. 139. 14.   ᵏ 2 Sa. 1. 26.   ⁿ Ho. 10. 8.   ˢ Ex. 33. 16.   ʸ Ps. 139. 14.   ᵈ 2 Ki. 14. 10.   ⁱ Ps. 77. 5.
ᶜ Pr. 30. 18.   ᵍ Ps. 118. 23.   ˡ Ex. 3. 20.   ᵖ Da. 3. 23.   ᵗ Je. 25. 27.   ᶻ Mi. 7. 8.   ᵍ Mi. 7. 8.
ᵈ Da. 8. 24, etc.   ʰ Ex. 34. 10.   = Je. 51. 64.   ᵍ 2 Sa. 1. 10.   ᵘ Da. 7. 20.   ᵇ Eze. 28. 23.   ᵈᵈ Job. 37. 14.   1 Sa. 13. 11.

מַפָּץ masc. *a bruising,* only מַפָּצוֹ Eze. 9. 2.

מַפֵּץ m. *hammer,* Je. 51. 20. Eng. vers. "battleaxe."

a נַפֵּץ	Piel inf. constr.	נפץ
b נֶפֶץ	noun masc. sing.	נפץ
c נִפֵּץ וְ	Piel pret. 3 pers. sing. masc.	נפץ
d נָפְצָה	Kal pret. 3 pers. sing. fem.	נפץ
e נָפֹצוּ	id. pret. 3 pers. pl.	נפץ
נָפֹצוּ וְ	Niph. pret. 3 pers. pl.	פוץ
g נְפֹצוֹת	Kh. נְפֹצוֹת q. v.; K. נְפֹצֶת Niph. part. fem.	פוץ
h נְפֻצוֹת	Kal part. pass. fem. pl. [of נָפוּצָה] from	פוץ
	נָפוּץ; וְ bef. (:)	
i נְפוֹצוֹתֶם	defect for נְפוֹצוֹתֶם (q. v.)	פוץ
k נְפֹצִים	defect. for נְפוֹצִים (q. v.)	פוץ
נִפַּצְתִּי וְ	Piel pret. 1 pers. sing.; acc. shifted by conv.	נפץ
	וְ (comp. § 8. rem. 7)	
נִפַּצְתִּים וּ	id., suff. 3 pers. pl. masc.; וּ for וְ, conv.	נפץ
m נְפֹצֹתֶם	defect. for נְפוֹצוֹתֶם (q. v.)	פוץ

נְפַק Chald. *to go forth.* Aph. *to bring forth* or *out.*

נִפְקָא Chald. fem. dec. 8 a, *expense,* Ezr. 6. 4, 8.

n נָפֵק	Ch. Peal part. act. sing. masc. dec. 2 b	נפק
נִפְקַד	Niph. pret. 3 pers. sing. masc.	פקד
p נִפְקַדְתָּ	id. pret. 2 pers. sing. masc.; acc. shifted by conv. וְ (comp. § 8. rem. 7)	פקד
q נְפַקוּ	Ch. Peal pret. 3 p. pl., Kh. נְפַקוּ m., K. נְפָקָה f.	נפק
r נִפְקְחוּ וְ	Niph. pret. 3 pers. pl.	פקח
s נָפְקִין	Ch. Peal part. act. masc., pl. of נָפֵק dec. 2 b	נפק
נֶפְקַת	Ch. id. pret. 3 pers. sing. fem. [for נְפָקַת]	נפק
u נִפְקְתָא וְ	Ch. noun fem. s., emph. of [נִפְקָא] d. 8 a	נפק
נִפְרַד	Niph. part. sing. masc. dec. 2 b	פרד
נִפְרְדוּ	id. pret. 3 pers. pl. (comp. § 8. rem. 7)	פרד
נִפְרְדוּ וְ		
z נִפְרָדִים	id. part. masc., pl. of נִפְרָד	פרד
נִפְרָץ	Niph. part. sing. masc.	פרץ
b נִפְרְצָה	Kal fut. 1 pers. pl. with parag. ה (§ 8. r. 13)	פרץ
c נִפְרֹשׂ וְ	Kal fut. 1 pers. pl.; וְ conv.	פרשׂ
d נִפְרָשׂוֹת	Niph. part. f. pl. [of נִפְרָשָׂה, fr. נִפְרָשׂ m.]	פרשׂ

נָפַשׁ *to respire, take breath, refresh oneself.*

נֶפֶשׁ com. dec. 6 a (with suff. נַפְשִׁי, pl. נְפָשׁוֹת once נְפָשִׁים).—I. *breath;* also *odour, perfume,* Is. 3. 20, בָּתֵּי נֶפֶשׁ *perfume boxes;* and so perhaps in Pr. 27. 9, see עֵצָה R. עֵצָה.—II. meton. any thing that breathes, *an animal.*—III. *person;* שִׁבְעִים נֶ׳ *seventy persons;* נֶ׳ מֵת *one dead, a dead body;* טָמֵא לָנֶפֶשׁ *polluted by a dead body.*—IV.

soul, as the principle of life.—V. *life.*—VI. *self,* as נַפְשִׁי *myself,* נַפְשְׁךָ *thyself.*—VI. *feelings, spirit,* e. g. Ex. 23. 9, נֶפֶשׁ הַגֵּר *the feelings of a stranger;* also used for the *feelings* of an animal, Pr. 12. 10.—VII. *desire, inclination.*

נָפִישׁ (*refreshed, recreated*) pr. name of a man.

נֶפֶשׁ וְ	noun com. sing. dec. 6 a (§ 35. rem. 2)	נפש
נֶפֶשׁ		
נַפְשָׁהּ	id., suff. 3 pers. sing. fem.	נפש
נִפְשׁוּ	Niph. pret. 3 pers. pl.	פוש
נַפְשׁוֹ	Kh. נַפְשׁוֹ q. v.; K. נַפְשׁוֹ (q. v.).	נפש
נַפְשׁוֹ וְ	noun com. s., suff. 3 pers. s. m. fr. נֶפֶשׁ d. 6 a	נפש
g נַפְשׁוֹת וְ	id. pl. constr. fem.	נפש
h נְפָשׁוֹת וּ	id. pl. abs. fem.; וּ bef. (:)	נפש
i נַפְשׁוֹתֵינוּ	id. pl. fem., suff. 1 pers. pl.	
נַפְשִׁי וְ	id. sing., suff. 1 pers. sing.	נפש
k נְפָשִׁים	id. pl. abs. masc.	נפש
נַפְשְׁךָ	id. sing., suff. 2 pers. sing. masc.	נפש
נַפְשֶׁךָ		
נַפְשֵׁךְ	id. sing., suff. 2 pers. sing. fem.	נפש
l נַפְשְׁכֶם וְ	id. sing., suff. 2 pers. pl. masc.	נפש
m נַפְשָׁם וְ	id. sing., suff. 3 pers. pl. masc.	נפש
n נַפְשֵׁנוּ וְ	id. sing., suff. 1 pers. pl.	נפש
o נִפְשַׁע	Niph. part. sing. masc.	פשע
p נַפְשֹׁת	noun com. pl. constr. fr. נֶפֶשׁ dec. 6 a	נפש
נַפְשֹׁת	id. pl., abs. st.	נפש
נַפְשֹׁתֵיכֶם	id. pl., suff. 2 pers. pl. masc., def. Je. 44. 7.	נפש
נַפְשֹׁתֵינוּ	id. pl., suff. 1 pers. pl.	נפש
q נֹפֶת	noun fem. sing., constr. of [נֹפָה] dec. 10	נוף
נֹפֶת וְ	noun fem. sing.	נוף
r נִפְתָּה	Niph. pret. 3 pers. sing. masc.	פתה
נְפָתוֹחַ	pr. name of a place.	פתח
נַפְתּוּלֵי	noun masc. pl. constr. of [נַפְתּוּל] dec. 1 b.	פתל
t נִפְתָּח	Niph. part. sing. masc.	פתח
u נִפְתַּח	id. pret. 3 pers. sing. masc.	פתח
נִפְתְּחָה וְ, *y* וַ	Kal fut. 1 pers. pl. with parag. ה (comp. § 8. rem. 13); וְ conv.	פתה
נִפְתְּחוּ	Niph. pret. 3 pers. pl. (comp. § 8. rem. 7)	פתח
נִפְתְּחוּ		
נַפְתֻּחִים	pr. name of an Egyptian people.	
נַפְתִּי	Kal pret. 1 pers. sing.	נוף
a נִפְתָּל	Niph. part. sing. masc.	פתל
נַפְתָּלִי וְ	pr. name of a man and a tribe	פתל
נִפְתָּלִים	Niph. part. masc., pl. of נִפְתָּל	פתל
נִפְתַּלְתִּי	id. pret. 1 pers. sing	פתל
d נִצִּין	noun masc. sing. dec. 8 b	נצץ

---

a Da. 12. 7.   *g* 2 Sa. 18. 8.   *m* Eze. 20. 41.   *t* Da. 3. 26.   *a* 1 Sa. 3. 1.   *k* Ps. 72. 13.   *n* Nu. 21. 5.   *t* Ge. 30. 8.   *x* Pr. 7. 17.
b Is. 30. 30.   *h* Is. 11. 12.   *n* Da. 2. 14.   *u* Da. 2. 13.   *b* 1 Ch. 13. 2.   *l* Eze. 13. 18.   *o* Pr. 18. 19.   *u* Zec. 13. 1.   *y* Ps. 8. 5.
c Ps. 137. 9.   *i* Eze. 11. 17.   *o* Da. 7. 10.   *z* Ezr. 6. 4. 8.   *c* Ps. 44. 21.   *m* Je. 26. 19.   *p* Le. 21. 11.   *v* Is. 5. 27.   *z* Job 5. 5.
d Ge. 9. 19.   *k* 1 Ki. 22. 17.   *p* 1 Sa. 20. 18.   *b* 2 Sa. 1. 21.   *d* Eze. 34. 12.   *o* Eze. 13. 20.   *q* 1 Ki. 4. 11.   *w* Am. 8. 5.   *a* Ge. 30. 8.
e Is. 33. 3.   *l* Je. 51. 20, 21,   *r* Ge. 10. 5, 32.   *c* Na. 3. 18.   *r* 1 Ch. 22. 19.   *v* Job 31. 9.   *b* Ge. 30. 8.
f Je. 40 15.   22, 23.   *s* Ge. 3. 5.   *s* Ne. 4. 13.   *f* Ps. 24. 4.   *m* Is. 46. 2.   *y* Ge. 43. 21.   *c* Job 39. 26.

נָצָא inf. abs. Je. 48. 9, *to fly away.*

נֵצֵא {וּ} Kal fut. 1 pers. pl. . . . . יצא

נָצַב Kal not used; i. q. יָצַב q. v. Niph. נִצָּב.—I. *to be set, placed* or *appointed,* with עַל *over* any one; part. נִצָּב *one set over, an officer.*—II. *to place, station oneself; to stand.* Hiph. הִצָּב.—I. *to set, place.*—II. *to set up, erect.*—III. *to fix, appoint.* Hoph. הֻצָּב.—I. *to be set, placed, fixed.*—II. *to be set, planted,* Ju. 9. 6.

נְצָב masc. *handle, haft,* Ju. 3. 22.

נִצְבָּא Ch. f. d. 8a, *firmness, strength,* Da. 2. 41.

נְצִיב masc. dec. 1a.—I. *a statue, pillar,* Ge. 19. 26. —II. *garrison.*—III. *officer, overseer,* 1 Ki. 4. 7, 19. —IV. pr. name of a place in the tribe of Judah, Jos. 15. 45.

צוֹבָה, צֹבָא, צֹבָה (for נְצוֹבָה *station*) pr. name of a region in Syria, whence the two cities אֲרָם חֲמַת צוֹבָה & צוֹבָה.

צִיבָא (for נְצִיבָא *statue*) pr. name of a servant of Saul.

מַצָּב masc. d. 2 b.—I. *standing-place,* Jos. 4. 3, 9. —II. *station, office,* Is. 22. 19.—III. *military station, garrison.*

מַצָּב masc. *station, garrison,* Is. 29. 3.

מַצֵּבָה, מַצָּבָה fem. id. 1 Sa. 14. 12 ; Zec. 9. 8.

מַצֵּבָה fem. dec. 11b (but pl. with suff. invariably retaining *Tseri,* comp. § 42. rem. 4).—I. *pillar, monument.*—II. *statue, image of an idol.*

מַצֶּבֶת fem. dec. 13a.—I. *pillar, monument.*— II. *stem, root,* Is. 22. 19.

נִצָּב Niph. part. sing. masc. . . . נצב

נִצְּבָה / נִצְּבָה* } id. pret. 3 pers. sing. fem. (comp. § 8. rem. 7) . . . נצב

נִצְּבוּ / {וּ} id. pret. 3 pers. pl. . . . נצב

נִצָּבִים* noun masc. pl., constr. of נְצִיב dec. 1a נצב

נִצָּבִים id. pl. abs. (comp. נְצִיבִים) . . . נצב

נִצָּבִים Niph. part. masc. pl. of נִצָּב . . . נצב

נִצַּבְתָּ / id. pret. 2 pers. sing. masc. ; acc. shifted by conv. וְ (comp. § 8. rem. 7) . . נצב

נְצִבְתָּא Ch. noun fem. sing., constr. of [נְצִבָּא] d. 8a נצב

נִצְדוּ / Niph. pret. 3 pers. pl. . . . צדה

נִצְדַּק / {וּ} Niph. pret. 3 pers. sing. masc. . צדק

[נָצָה] I. *to fly,* La. 4. 15.—II. *to be desolate, laid waste,* Je. 4. 7. Hiph. הִצָּה *to strive, contend.* Niph.

נִצָּה.—I. *to contend with one another, to quarrel.*— II. *to be desolated.*

נֹצָה, נוֹצָה fem. *feather, pinion.*

מַצָּה fem. *contention, quarrel.*

מַצּוּת fem. dec. 1 b, id. Is. 41. 12.

נִצָּה noun fem. sing. dec. 10 . . . נצץ

נִצּוֹ noun masc. sing., suff. 3 pers. sing. fem. fr. נֵץ dec. 8b . . . . נצץ

נֹצָה defect. for נוֹצָה (q. v.) . . . יצה

נָצוּ Kal pret. 3 pers. pl. R. נצה or . . נוץ

נָצוּמָה / Kal fut. 1 pers. pl. with parag. ה (comp. § 8 rem. 13) ; וַ conv. . . צום

נָצוֹר Kal inf. abs. . . . . נצר

נֶצֹּר Kal fut. 1 pers. sing. . . . . צור

נְצוּרָה Kal part. pass. sing. fem. dec. 10, fr. נָצוּר m. נצר

נָצַח Kal not used; Arab. *to be pure, innocent, faithful;* Syr. *to conquer;* hence Pi. I. *to excel;* especially *to be* or *preside over, to superintend;* part. מְנַצֵּחַ *overseer.*—II. *to lead in music,* 1 Ch. 15. 21; part. מְנַצֵּחַ *leader of music, precentor, chorister.* Niph. *to be entire, perfect, complete,* Je. 8. 5.

נְצַח Chald. Ithpa. *to conquer, surpass,* Da. 6. 4.

נֶצַח, נֵצַח masc. dec. 6e.—I. *truth, uprightness, faithfulness;* 1 Sa. 15. 29, for concr. *the truthful, faithful,* sc. God. — II. *permanency, perpetuity, eternity;* לָנֶצַח, עַד נֵצַח, and נֶצַח adv. *for ever;* לְנֵצַח נְצָחִים *for ever and ever.*—III. *confidence, trust.*—IV. *excellency, glory,* 1 Ch. 29. 11.—V. *completeness, entireness,* לָנֶצַח, and נֶצַח adv. *wholly, entirely.*—VI. *juice,* Is. 63. 3, 6; Arab. נצח *to spatter.*

נְצִיחַ (*excellent;* Syr. נציחא) pr. name of a man.

נֶצַח / נֵצַח } noun masc. sing. dec. 6e (§ 35. rem. 5) נצח

נִצְחִי id. with suff. 1 pers. sing. . . . נצח

נְצָחִים id. pl., abs. st. . . . נצח

נִצְחָם id. sing., suff. 3 pers. pl. masc. . נצח

נִצְּחַת Niph. part. sing. fem. [of נָצַח] . נצח

נִצְטַדָּק Hithpa. fut. 1 pers. pl. [for נִתְצַדָּק § 12. r. 3] צדק

נְצִיב noun m. sing. d. 1a, also pr. n.; וּ bef. (ː) נצב

נְצִיבִים id. pl., abs. st. . . . נצב

נָצִיחַ pr. name masc. . . . נצח

נֹצִים Niph part. masc. pl. [of נָצָה] dec. 9a נצה

נְצִירֵי / Kh. נְצִירֵי adj. pl. constr. masc. [fr. נָצִיר]; K. נְצוּרֵי Kal part. pass. pl. constr. masc., from נָצוּר dec. 3a ; וּ bef. (ː) . . . נצר

a Ps. 45. 10.   d 1 Sa. 10. 5.   g Da. 8. 14.   k Job 39. 13.   m Ezr. 8. 23.   o Ca. 8. 9.   q La. 3. 18.   s Is. 63. 3, 6. Je. 2. 5.   u Ge. 44. 15
b Ex. 15. 8.   e Da. 2. 41.   h Is. 18. 5.   l La. 4. 15.   n Na. 2. 2.   p Is. 1. 8.   r Is. 34. 10.   t Is. 49. 6.
c Ex. 33. 8.   f Zep. 3. 6.   i Ge. 40. 10.

נָצַל **Pi.** נִצֵּל.—I. *to strip off, take away,* 2 Ch. 20. 25.—II. *to snatch away, deliver,* Eze. 14. 14.—III. *to spoil, plunder* any one. **Hiph.** הִצִּיל.—I. *to take away;* with בֵּין *to part, separate,* 2 Sa. 14. 6.—II. *to deliver, rescue,* with מִכַּף, מִיַּד, מִן. **Hoph.** הֻצַּל *to be delivered, rescued.* **Niph.** נִצַּל.—I. *to be delivered, rescued.*—II. *to deliver oneself, to escape.* **Hithp.** *to strip oneself of any thing,* with acc. Ex. 33. 6.

נְצַל **Ch. Aph.** *to deliver, rescue.*

הַצָּלָה fem. *deliverance,* Est. 4. 14.

נִצַּלְנוּ **Niph.** pret. 1 pers. pl. — — נצל

נִצַּלְתֶּם וְ Pl. pret. 2 pers. pl. masc. — נצל

נִצְמָתוּ **Niph.** pret. 3 p. pl. [for נִצְמְתוּ comp. § 8. r. 7] צמת

נִצְמַתִּי id. pret. 1 pers. sing. [for נִצְמַתְתִּי § 25. r.] צמת

נִּצְעַק וְ Kal fut. 1 pers. pl.; וְ conv. צעק

נִצְפַּן **Niph.** pret. 3 pers. sing. masc. — צפן

נִצְפְּנָה Kal fut. 1 pers. pl. [נִצְפֹּן] with parag. ה (§ 8. rem. 13) צפן

נִצְפְּנוּ **Niph.** pret. 3 pers. pl. — — צפן

[נָצַץ] *to glitter, shine,* Eze. 1. 7. In the derivv. also *to flourish, to fly.*

נֵץ masc. dec. 8 b.—I. *flower, blossom,* Ge. 40. 10.—II. *a hawk.*

נִצָּה fem. dec. 10, *flower, blossom.*

נִצָּן masc. id. Ca. 2. 12.

נִיצוֹץ masc. *a spark,* Is. 1. 31.

נֹצְצִים וְ Kal part. act. masc. pl. [of נוֹצֵץ] dec. 7 b נצץ

[נָצַר] fut. יִנְצֹר, יִצֹּר.—I. *to watch, guard, keep, preserve,* Is. 49. 6, נְצוּרֵי יִשְׂרָאֵל *the preserved of Israel,* Kh.; K. נְצִירֵי from a pass. form נָצִיר *preserved.*—II. *to keep, observe,* as a law; *to observe* mercy, truth; *to observe, scrutinize,* Job 7. 20.—III. *to shut up, conceal, hide.*—IV. *to besiege.*

נֵצֶר וְ masc. *shoot, branch;* Arab. نصر *to shine; to be green.*

נְצֹר Kal imp. sing. masc. — — נצר

נֹצֵר וְ id. part. act. sing. masc. dec. 7 b נצר

נִצְרְבוּ וְ **Niph.** pret. 3 pers. pl. — צרב

נִצְרָה Kal imp. sing. masc. with parag. ה (§ 8. r. 13) נצר

נִצְרֶהָ id. id. with suff. 3 pers. sing. fem. נצר

נֹצְרֶהָ id. part. act. sing. masc., suff. 3 pers. sing. fem. from נֹצֵר dec. 7 b נצר

נְצָרוּ id. pret. 3 pers. pl. — — נצר

נְצֻרוֹת וְ id. part. pass. fem. pl. of נְצוּרָה dec. 10, from נָצוּר masc.; וְ bef. (:ְ) נצר

נֹצְרֵי id. part. act. pl. constr. masc. fr. נֹצֵר dec. 7 b נצר

נֹצְרִים id. id. pl., abs. st. — נצר

נְצֻרַת וְ id. part. pass. sing. fem., constr. of נְצוּרָה dec. 10, from נָצוּר masc.; וְ bef. (:ְ) נצר

נָצַרְתִּי id. pret. 1 pers. sing. [for נְצַרְתִּי § 7. r.] נצר

נְצָרַתַם id. pret. 3 pers. sing. fem., suff. 3 pers. pl. m. נצר

נִצְּתָה וְ **Niph.** pret. 3 pers. sing. fem. (§ 20. rem. 16) יצת

נִצְּתָה Kh. נָצְתָה q. v.—K. נִצְּתָה q. v. יצת

נִצָּתוֹ noun fem. sing., suff. 3 pers. sing. masc. fr. נִצָּה dec. 10 נצץ

נִצְּתוּ **Niph.** pret. 3 pers. pl. (§ 20. rem. 16) יצת

נְקֵא **Ch. Peal** part. pass. sing. masc. R. נְקָא see נקה

[נָקַב] fut. יִקֹּב, יִנְקֹב.—I. *to bore, bore through, pierce.*—II. *to mark out, to determine, specify, name.*—III. i. q. קָבַב *to execrate, curse, blaspheme.* **Niph.** *to be specified, by name.*

נֶקֶב masc. dec. 6 a.—I. *a bezel,* the cavity in which a gem is set, Eze. 28. 13, Eng. vers. *pipes.*—II. pr. name of a place in the tribe of Naphtali, Jos. 19. 33.

נְקֵבָה fem. *female,* both of man and beast.

קֵבָה fem. (for נְקֵבָה) *the stomach* or *maw* of a beast, De. 18. 3.

קֻבָּה fem. (for נְקֻבָּה) *the womb,* Nu. 25. 8. Others make it, i. q. קֻבָּה *a tent.*

מַקָּבוֹת fem. *hammer,* only in the pl. מַקָּבוֹת.

מַקֶּבֶת fem.—I. *hammer,* Ju. 4. 21.—II. *hollow* or *shaft* of a rock, Is. 51. 1.

נֹקֵב וְ Kal part. act. sing. masc. — נקב

נְקָבָה וְ id. pret. 3 pers. sing. masc., suff. 3 pers. sing. fem.; וְ for וְ, conv. נקב

נְקֵבָה וְ noun fem. sing.; וְ bef. (:ְ) נקב

נָקְבָה Kal imp. sing. masc. with parag. ה (§ 8 r. 11) נקב

נִקְבוּ **Niph.** pret. 3 pers. pl. נקב

נְקֻבֵי Kal part. pass. pl. constr. masc. from נָקוּב dec. 3 a נקב

נְקָבֶיךָ וְ noun masc. pl., suff. 2 pers. sing. masc. fr. נֶקֶב dec. 6; וְ bef. (:ְ) נקב

נְקַבֵּל Piel fut. 1 pers. pl. קבל

נִקְבְּצוּ וְ Niph. pret. 3 pers. pl. (comp. § 8. rem. 7) קבץ
נִקְבְּצוּ וְ

נְקַבְתָּ Kal pret. 2 pers. sing. masc. נקב

a Je. 7. 10.   e Pr. 1. 11.   i Pr. 24. 12.   m Is. 27. 3.   p Pr. 7. 10.   r Ps. 119. 129.   v Da. 7. 9.   a Am. 6. 1.   e Joel 4. 11.
b Ex. 3. 22.   f Eze. 1. 7.   k Eze. 21. 3.   n Ps. 141. 3.   q Ps. 119. 22, 56, 100.   s Je. 2. 15.   w Le. 24. 14.   b Eze. 28. 13.   f Ho. 2. 2.
c Job 6. 17.   g Is. 60. 21.   l Is. 48. 6.   o Pr. 4. 13.   t Ps. 119. 2.   u Job 23. 17.   x Ps. 15. 33.   z Ge. 35. 26.   d Job 2. 10.   g Hab. 3. 14.
Je. 16. 17.   h Is. 11. 1.   Pr. 22. 12.

נָקֹד ('ו) pl. נְקֻדִּים (§ 37. No. 3) fem. נְקֻדּוֹת adj. *spotted, speckled,* spoken of sheep and goats.

נָקוֹדָא (*marked*) pr. name of a man.

נֹקֵד m. d. 7 b, *shepherd, herdsman* (Arab. نقّاد).

נְקֻדָּה fem. dec. 10, *point, stud,* Ca. 1. 11.

נִקֻּדִים masc. pl. (of נָקֹד).—I. *spots, specks* of mould, Jos. 9. 5, 12. Others, *crumbs.*—II. a kind of *cake,* 1 Ki. 14. 3.

מַקֵּדָה (*place of herdsmen?*) pr. name of a town in the tribe of Judah.

נֹקֶד ('ו) noun masc. sing. dec. 7 b   .   נקד

נְקֻדּוֹת noun fem. pl. of [נְקֻדָּה] dec.10 .   נקד

נְקֻדִּים adj. masc. pl. of נָקֹד dec. 8 c (§ 37. No. 3)   נקד

נִקֻּדִים ('ו) noun masc. pl. of [נִקּוּד] dec. 1 b   נקד

נַקְדְּמָה Kal fut. 1 pers. pl. with parag. ה (comp. § 8. rem. 13)   קדם

נִקְדָּשׁ ('ו) Niph. pret. 3 pers. sing. masc. .   קדשׁ

נִקְדַּשְׁתִּי ('ו) id. pret. 1 pers. sing.; acc. shifted by conv. ('ו) (except bef. monos. comp. § 8. rem. 7)   קדשׁ

[נָקָה] *to be pure, innocent,* Je. 49. 12. Niph. נִקָּה.—I. *to be pure, innocent, blameless,* with מִן from a crime, or regarding a person.—II. *to be clear, free* from punishment, an obligation.—III. *to be cleared, empty, desolate,* of a city, Is. 3. 26: of persons, *to be destroyed,* Zec. 5. 3. Pi. I. *to cleanse,* Joel 4. 21.—II. *to pronounce innocent, to acquit.*—III. *to let go unpunished, to pardon.*

נְקָא Ch. *to be pure, white,* Da. 7. 9.

נָקִי, constr. נְקִי, pl. נְקִיִּם (§ 37. No. 4) adj.—I. *pure, innocent, free from guilt.*—II. *clear, free* from an obligation.

נָקִיא id. Joel 4. 19; Jon. 1. 14. Kh.

נִקָּיוֹן masc. dec. 3c.—I. *cleanness,* Am. 4. 6.—II. *innocency.*

מְנַקִּיּוֹת fem. only pl. (§ 39. No. 4. rem. 1) *bowls* used in making libations. (Syr. מניקיתא id.)

נָקֹה Kal inf. abs. .   .   .   נקה

נַקֵּה ('ו) Piel inf. abs. .   .   .   נקה

נִקָּה ('ו) Niph. pret. 3 pers. sing. masc. .   נקה

נִקְהֲלוּ Niph. pret. 3 pers. pl. .   .   קהל

נָקוּב Kal part. pass. sing. masc. dec. 3 a   נקב

נְקוֹדָא pr. name masc. .   .   .   נקד

נְקַוֶּה ('ו) Piel fut. 1 pers. pl.; ('ו) bef. (:)   קוה

נִקְווּ ('ו) Niph. pret. 3 pers. pl. .   .   קוה

נָקוּם Kal fut. 1 pers. pl. .   .   קום

נָקוּמָה ('ו) id. with parag. ה (comp. § 8. rem. 13)   קום

נָקַח 'ו Kal fut. 1 pers. pl. (§ 17. rem. 8); ('ו) conv.   לקח

נִקְחָה ('ו) id. with parag. ה (comp. § 8. rem. 13)   לקח

נָקַט *to be weary of, to loathe,* only in the following form.

נָקְטָה Kal pret. 3 pers. sing. fem. .   .   נקט

נָקֹטּוּ ('ו) Niph. pret. 3 pers. pl. .   .   קוט

נְקֹטֹתֶם 'ו Niph. pret. 2 pers. pl. masc. (§ 21. rem. 12); 'ו for ('ו) conv. .   .   קוט

נָקִי ('ו) adj. masc. sing. d. 8 (pl. נְקִיִּם § 37. rem. 4)   נקה

נְקִי id., constr. st. .   .   .   נקה

נָקִיא adj. masc. sing., א added to נָקִי .   נקה

נִקָּיוֹן noun masc. sing., constr. of נִקָּיוֹן dec. 3c   נקה

נְקִיִּם ('ו) adj. masc. pl. of נָקִי dec. 8 (§ 37 rem. 4)   נקה

נְקִיֹּן noun masc. sing. dec. 3c.   נקה

נַקִּיצָה 'ו Hiph. fut. 1 pers. pl. [נָקִיץ], suff. 3 pers. sing. fem.; 'ו bef. (:)   קוץ

נְקִיתָ ('ו) Niph. pret. 2 pers. sing. masc. (§ 24. r. 8)   נקה

נִקֵּיתִי ('ו) id. pret., or Piel pret. 1 pers. s. (§ 24. r. 11)   נקה

נָקַל 'ו Niph. pret. 3 pers. sing. m. (§ 18. r. 7)   קלל

נָקְלָה id. pret. 3 pers. sing. fem. .   קלל

נִקְלָה ('ו) Niph. pret. 3 pers. sing. masc. .   קלה

נִקְלֶה ('ו) id. part. sing. masc. .   .   קלה

נָקֹלּתִי 'ו Niph. pret. 1 pers. sing.; 'ו bef. (:)   קלל

[נָקַם] fut. יִקֹּם, inf. נְקֹם.—I. *to avenge, take vengeance for,* with acc.—II. *to take revenge on,* with acc., also לְ.—III. *to revenge* a person, with the acc.; with מִיַּד, מֵאֵת, מִן, עַל on whom. Niph. *to be avenged, to avenge oneself,* with בְּ, מִן on whom. Pi. i. q. Kal No. 1. Hoph. *to be avenged.* Hithp. *to avenge oneself;* part. מִתְנַקֵּם *avenger.*

נָקָם masc. dec. 4a, and נְקָמָה fem. dec. 11c.—I. *vengeance;* הֵשִׁיב נָקָם לְ *to render vengeance to* i. e. to repay an injury; לָקַח, עָשָׂה נָ' *to take vengeance;* נָתַן נְקָמוֹת *to avenge* any one, *to give* him *satisfaction.*—II. *desire of revenge, vindictiveness.*

נֶקֶם ('ו) noun masc. sing. dec. 4a .   .   נקם

נְקֹם Kal inf. abs. .   .   .   נקם

נְקַם noun masc., constr. of נָקָם dec. 4a .   נקם

נְקֹם Kal imp. sing. masc. .   .   נקם

נֹקֵם ('ו) id. part. sing. masc. .   .   נקם

נְקָמָה noun fem. sing. dec. 11c   .   נקם

נִקְמוּ ('ו) Niph. pret. 3 pers. pl. .   .   נקם

a Ge. 30. 32, 33.   d 1 Ki. 14. 3.   i Je. 49. 12.   n Je. 3. 17.   s Eze. 6. 9.   x Am. 4. 6.   a Ge. 24. 8.   2 Sa. 6. 22.   h Nu. 31. 2.
b 2 Ki. 3. 4.   e Ps. 95. 2.   k Zec. 5. 3.   o Ne. 2. 18, 20.   t Eze. 20. 43;   y Je. 2. 34.   b Pr. 14. 6.   d De. 32. 43.   Na. 1. 2.
c Ca. 1. 11.   f Is. 5. 16.   l Hag. 2. 6.   p 1 Sa. 4. 3.   36. 31.   z Ho. 8. 5.   c 2 Ki. 3. 13.   e Ex. 21. 20.   k Eze. 25. 12.
d Jos. 9. 5, 12.   g Ex. 29. 43.   m 'e. 14. 22.   q Job 10. 1.   u Ps. 24. 4.   a Is. 7. 6.   d 1 Sa. 18. 23.

37

נְקָמוֹת noun fem. pl., abs. from נְקָמָה dec. 11 c   נקם

נְקָמַנִי Kal pret. 3 p. s. m., suff. 1 p. s.; וֹ bef. (:)   נקם

נְקָמֹת noun fem. pl. abs., from נְקָמָה dec. 11 c   נקם

נִקְמַת id. sing., constr. st.   נקם

נֹקֶמֶת Kal part. sing. fem. from נָקַם masc.   נקם

נִקַּמְתִּי Niph. pret. 1 pers. sing.   נקם

נִקַּמְתִּי וְ Piel, or (1 Sa. 14. 24) Niph. pret. 1 pers. sing.; acc. shifted by conv. וְ (comp. § 8. r. 7)   נקם

נִקְמָתִי noun fem. s., suff. 1 pers. s. fr. נְקָמָה d. 11 c   נקם

נִקְמָתֵךְ id., suff. 2 pers. sing. fem.   נקם

נִקְמָתְךָ id., suff. 2 pers. sing. masc.   נקם

נִקְמָתָם id., suff. 3 pers. pl. masc.   נקם

נִקְמָתֵנוּ id., suff. 1 pers. pl.   נקם

נִקְנָה וְ Niph. pret. 3 pers. sing. masc.   קנה

נַקֵּנִי Piel imp. s. m. (נַקֵּה), suff. 1 p. s. (§ 24. r. 21)   נקה

נָקַע to be removed, alienated (comp. יָקַע), only in the following form.

נָקְעָה Kal pret. 3 pers. sing. fem.   נקע

נָקַף Kal, only Is. 29. 1, חַגִּים יִנְקֹפוּ let the feasts go or come round ; so Vulg. solennitates evolutæ sunt, the solemn feasts are rolled by, comp. Hiph.; others, " let them kill the sacrifices ;" as in the Chald. and Arab. to smite, hew. Pi. I. to cut down, Is. 10. 34.—II. to destroy, Job 19. 26. Hiph. הִקִּיף.—I. to surround, compass, with acc., עַל.—II. to go or come round, of time.

נֶקֶף masc. a beating or shaking of an olive-tree. נִקְפָּה fem. Is. 3. 24, Eng. vers. " rent." Others, after the Sept. and Vulg. a rope, cord. According to the Rabbis, a bruising, wounding.

נִקַּף וְ Piel pret. 3 pers. sing. masc.   נקף

נִקְפָּה noun sing. fem.   נקף

נִקְּפוּ Piel pret. 3 pers. pl.   נקף

נָקַק Root not used ; whence נָקִיק or נְקִיק masc. cleft of a rock.

[נָקַר] I. to bore, dig or put out an eye, 1 Sa. 11. 2.—II. to pick out, as a bird, Pr. 30. 17. Pi. I. to pierce, Job 30. 17.—II. to put out an eye. Pu. to be dug out, Is. 51. 1.

נִקְרָה fem. dec. 11 c, cleft of a rock.

נִקַּר Piel pret. 3 pers. sing. masc.   נקר

נִקְרָא וְ Kal fut. 1 pers. pl. ; or Niph. 3 pers. s. m.   קרא

נִקְרָא Niph. inf. abs.   קרא

נִקְרָאָה וְ id. pret. 3 pers. sing. fem.   קרא

נִקְרְאוּ id. pret. 3 p. pl. [for נִקְרָאוּ comp. § 8. r. 7]   קרא

נִקְרָאִים id. part. masc. pl. of נִקְרָא   קרא

נִקְרֵאתִי id. pret. 1 pers. sing.   קרא

נַקְרֵב וְ Hiph. fut. 1 p. pl. ap. [fr. נַקְרִיב]; וְ conv.   קרב

נִקְרַב וְ Kal fut. 1 p. pl. ; or Niph. pret. 3 p. s. m.   קרב

נִקְרְבָה id. fut. 1 pers. pl. (נִקְרַב) with parag. ה (§ 8. rem. 13 & 15)   קרב

נִקְרַבְתֶּם וְ Niph. pret. 2 pers. pl. masc.   קרב

נִקְרָה Niph. pret. 3 pers. sing. masc.   קרה

נִקְרֵיתִי id. pret. 1 pers. sing.   קרה

נִקְרָע Niph. part. sing. masc.   קרע

נִקַּרְתֶּם Pual pret. 2 pers. pl. masc.   נקר

[נָקַשׁ] to lay snares, to ensnare, Ps. 9. 17. Niph. to be ensnared, enticed, De. 12. 30. Pi. to lay snares, with לְ for any one. Hithp. id. with בְּ 1 Sa. 28. 9. נְקַשׁ Chald. to smite, strike, Da. 5. 6.

נִקְשֶׁה Niph. part. sing. masc.   קשה

נַקְשִׁיב Hiph. fut. 1 pers. sing.   קשב

נַקְשִׁיבָה id. with parag. ה (§ 8. rem. 13)   קשב

נָקְשָׁן Chald. Peal part. act. fem. pl. [of נָקַשׁ dec. 8 a, נָקֵשׁ masc.]   נקשׁ

נִקְשְׁרָה Niph. pret. 3 pers. sing. fem.   קשר

נִקְתָה וְ Niph. pret. 3 pers. sing. fem. (comp. § 8. rem. 7)   נקה

נֵר noun masc. sing. dec. 1 a, also pr. name   נור

נֵר defect. for נִיר (q. v.)   ניר

נִרָא וְ Kh. נִרָא, ap. form from K. נִרְאֶה (q. v.)   ראה

נִרְאָה וְ Niph. pret. 3 pers. sing. masc.   ראה

נִרְאֶה וַ, וְ Kal fut. 1 pers. pl. ; וְ conv.   ראה

נִרְאֵהוּ id. with suff. 3 pers. sing. masc.   ראה

נִרְאוּ Niph. pret. 3 pers. pl.   ראה

נִרְאוֹת וְ defect. for נוֹרָאוֹת (q. v.)   ירא

נִרְאֲתָה וְ Niph. pret. 3 pers. sing. fem.   ראה

נֵרְגַל וְ pr. name of an idol, 2 Ki. 17. 30.

שַׁרְאֶצֶר נֵרְגַל pr. name masc. Je. 39. 3, 13.

נָרַג Root not used ; Arab. נירג calumniator, whisperer : hence

נִרְגָּן וְ masc. whisperer, slanderer, talebearer   נרג

נֵרְדְּ masc. dec. 6 b (§ 35. rem. 6) spikenard.

נֵרֵד נֵרֵד וַ Kal fut. 1 pers. pl. (§ 20. rem. 4)   ירד

a 1 Sa. 24. 13. | f Je. 51. 36. | m Is. 10. 34. | s Est. 4. 11. | r 1 Sa. 14. 36. | q 1 Ki. 13. 3, 5. | v Is. 41. 23. | aa Ge. 9. 14.
b 2 Sa. 22. 48. | g La. 3. 60. | n Is. 3. 24. | t Nu. 31. 50. | u Ju. 19. 13. | s 1 Sa. 18. 1. | w 1 Sa. 10. 14. | bb Pr. 16. 28.
c Le. 26. 25. | h Je. 20. 10. | o Jos. 8. 5. | p Jos. 7. 14. | z Is. 8. 21. | y Is. 53. 2. | cc Ca. 4. 14.
d Ju. 15. 7. | i Je. 32. 43. | p Job 30. 17. | q Ex. 22. 7. | x Nu. 5. 28. | z 2 Sa. 7. 3. | dd Ge. 43. 5.
e 2 Ki. 9. 7; | k Ps. 19. 13. | q 2 Sa. 1. 6. | y Is. 41. 1. | ee Je. 18. 18. | aa Ju. 19. 30. | s 2 Ki. 10. 11.
Je. 51. 36. | l Eze. 23. 18. 22. 23. | t Is. 48. 2. | w Est. 6. 1.

נֵרְדָּה	id. with parag. ה (comp. § 8. rem. 13)	ירד
נִרְדִּי	n. m. s., suff. 1 p. s. from נֵרְדְּ d. 6 (§ 35. r. 6)	נרד
נְרָדִים	id. pl. abs. state	נרד
נִרְדָּם	Niph. part. sing. masc. . .	רדם
נִרְדָּם	id. pret. 3 pers. sing. masc. .	רדם
נִרְדַּמְתִּי	id. pret. 1 pers. sing. . .	רדם
נִרְדָּף	Niph. part. sing. masc. . .	רדף
נִרְדָּף	Kal fut. 1 pers. pl. [for נִרְדֹּף § 8. rem. 18]	רדף
נִרְדְּפָה	id. with parag. ה (§ 8. rem. 13)	רדף
נִרְדְּפָנּוּ	Niph. pret. 1 pers. pl. [for נִרְדְּפָנוּ § 8. r. 7]	רדף
נֵרֹה	noun masc. sing., suff. 3 p. s. f. fr. נֵר d. 1a	נור
וְנֵרוֹ	h'' id., suff. 3 pers. sing. masc. .	נור
נִרְוֶה	Kal fut. 1 pers. pl. . . .	רוה
נְרוֹמְמָה	Pil. fut. 1 pers. pl. [נְרוֹמֵם] with parag. ה (comp. § 8. rem. 13) ; bef.	רום
נָרוּצָה	Kal fut. 1 pers. pl. [נָרוּץ] with parag. ה (comp. § 8. rem. 13) . .	רוץ
נִרְחָב	Niph. part. sing. masc. . .	רחב
נֵרִי	noun masc. sing., suff. 1 pers. s. fr. נֵר d. 1a	נור
נֵרִיָּה נֵרִיָּהוּ	} pr. name masc. . . .	נור
נָרִיעַ	Hiph. fut. 1 pers. pl. . .	רוע
נָרִיעָה	id. with parag. ה (comp. § 8. rem. 13) .	רוע
נִרְכַּב	Kal fut. 1 pers. pl. [for נִרְכַּב § 8. rem. 15]	רכב
נְרַנְּנָה	Piel fut. 1 pers. pl. [נְרַנֵּן] with parag. ה (comp. § 8. rem. 13); bef.	רנן
נָרַע	Hiph. fut. 1 pers. pl., with gutt. [for נָרֵע]	רעע
נִרְעַב	Kal fut. 1 pers. s. [for נִרְעַב § 8. rem. 15]	רעב
נִרְעָשָׁה	Niph. pret. 3 pers. sing. fem. . .	רעש
נִרְפָּא	Niph. pret. 3 pers. sing. masc. .	רפא
נִרְפְּאוּ	id. pret. 3 pers. pl. (§ 23. rem. 3) .	רפא
נִרְפִּים	Niph. part. masc. pl. [of נִרְפֶּה] dec. 9a .	רפה
נִרְפַּשׁ	Niph. part. sing. masc. R. רפש see	רפס
נִרְפָּתָה	Niph. pret. 3 pers. sing. fem. [for נִרְפְּתָה § 23. rem. 11] as if from R. רפה	רפא
וְנִרְצִין	Niph. pret. 3 pers. sing. masc. (§ 18. r. 7)	רצץ
וְנִרְצָה	Niph. pret. 3 pers. sing. m.	רצה
נֵרֹתַי	noun masc. with pl. fem. term. from נֵר d. 1a	נור
נֵרֹתֶיהָ	id., suff. 3 pers. sing. fem. .	נור
וְנֵרֹתֵיהֶם	id., suff. 3 pers. pl. masc. .	נור

נָשָׂא וְ (§ 25. No. 2a) fut. יִשָּׂא, inf. c. שְׂאוֹ, שְׂאֵת, שְׂאֵת, נָשֹׂא.—I. to lift or raise up; נָ׳ יָד to lift up the hand, as in a solemn promise or prayer, with לְ for any one; with בְּ against any one, to do him violence; נָ׳ רֹאשׁוֹ to lift up one's head, to become cheerful, happy, &c.; to lift up the head

of another, to give him his liberty; with מֵעַל, to behead him, נָ׳ פָּנָיו to lift up one's countenance, of one conscious of innocence; נָ׳ עֵינָיו לְ, אֶל to lift up, cast one's eyes upon, espec. with longing desire; נָ׳ נֶפֶשׁ אֶל to set one's affection upon any thing; נָ׳ לִבּוֹ to be willing; נָ׳ רַגְלָיו to lift up one's feet, i. e. to set out upon a journey; נָ׳ קוֹל to lift up the voice, of weeping, rejoicing, calling aloud; hence to utter, as a parable, prayer.—II. to bear, carry, as an infant in the arms, garments to wear, a tree its fruit; also to bear, take away; hence to bear, endure, suffer; נָ׳ עָוֹן פֶּ׳ to bear the guilt of any one; but also to forgive, pardon sin; נְשָׂא עָוֹן whose sins are forgiven.—III. to lead, bring.—IV. to take up, to take; נָ׳ אִשָּׁה to take a wife; נָ׳ פָּנִים to take, accept the person of any one, i. e. to act with partiality; נָ׳ רֹאשׁ to take the sum of anything. Niph. I. to be lifted up, raised; part. נִשָּׂא lifted up, lofty.—II. to raise oneself.—III. to be borne, carried, carried away. Pi. נִשָּׂא, נִשֵּׂא.—I. to lift up, exalt; נָ׳ נֶפֶשׁ לְ to set one's heart upon.—II. to aid, assist.—III. to present a gift, with לְ 2 Sa. 19. 43.—IV. to carry away, Am. 4. 2. Hiph. הִשִּׂיא.—I. to cause to bear sin, Le. 22. 16.—II. to bring, 2 Sa. 17. 13. Hithp. I. to be elevated, exalted, with עַל above any thing.—II. to lift up, exalt oneself in strength or pride, to rise.

נְשָׂא Chald.—I. to bear or carry away, Da. 2. 35. —II. to take, Ezr. 5. 15. Ithpa. to rise up, with עַל against, Ezr. 4. 19.

נִשְׂאֵת fem. a gift, 2 Sa. 19. 43.

נְשׂוּאָה fem. dec. 10, burden, Is. 46. 1.

נָשִׂיא masc. dec. 3a.—I. chief.—II. prince.—III. pl. vapours; hence clouds.

שִׂיא masc. dec. 1a (for נְשִׂיא) elevation, dignity, Job 20. 6.

שִׂיאֹן (elevated) pr. name of one of the peaks of Hermon, De. 4. 48

שְׂאֵת fem. dec. 1a.—I. a lifting up of the countenance, Ge. 4. 7; according to the Eng. vers. acceptance.—II. a swelling in the skin.—III. exaltation, dignity.—IV. judgment, sentence, Hab. 1. 7.

שֵׂת fem. dec. 1a (for שְׂאֵת) a lifting up, rising, Job 41. 17.

מַשָּׂא masc. dec. 1b.—I. a lifting up, carrying, Eze. 24. 25, מַ׳ נֶפֶשׁ that on which the heart is set.

a Ca. 1. 12.   d Ec. 3. 15.   h Pr. 31. 18.   k Ps. 34. 4.   n Ps. 95. 2.   q Ge. 19. 9.   t Le. 13. 18.   x Pr. 25. 26.   b Is. 40. 2.
b Ca. 4. 13.   e Ho. 6. 3.   i Job 18. 6.   l Is. 30. 23.   o Ps. 95. 1.   r Je. 42. 14.   u Eze. 47. 8.   y Je. 51. 9.   c Le. 1. 4.
c Da. 8. 18.   f La. 5. 5.   g Pr. 7. 18.   m Ps. 18. 29.   p Ps. 90. 11.   s Je. 50. 46.   v Ex. 5. 8, 17.   z Ec. 12. 6.   d Ez. 39. 37
Ju. 2. 21.   g Job 19. 28.

—II. *burden, load*; anything burdensome.—III. *a lifting up of the voice in singing, a singing*, 1 Ch. 15. 27; שַׂר הַמַּשָּׂא *master of song*; but according to Hengstenberg (Christ. vol. ii. p. 78) *master of burden.*—IV. something uttered, *a saying; a solemn declaration; a prophecy*; but according to Hengstenberg (in l. c.) *burden, burdensome prophecy*, in general, and also *a weighty, important sentence.*—V. *tribute*, 2 Ch. 17. 11.—VI. pr. name of a son of Ishmael.

מַשָּׂא masc. 2 Ch. 19. 7 כְּ׳ פָּנִים *preference, respect of persons.*

מַשָּׂאָה fem. *a rising of a flame, a burning, conflagration*, Is. 30. 27. Others, *burden.*

מַשְׂאֵת (for מַשְׂאֶת) fem. constr. מַשְׂאֵת (as if from מַשָּׂאָה), pl. מַשְׂאוֹת.—I. *a lifting up*, Ps. 141. 2; *a rising, ascending* of smoke, Ju. 20. 38, 40.—II. *signal*, Je. 6. 1.—III. *burden*, Zep. 3. 18.—IV. *a prophecy*, La. 2. 14; but comp. מַשָּׂא Nos. II & III.—V. *gift, present.*—VI. *tribute*, 2 Ch. 24. 6, 9.

I. [נָשָׁא] *to err, go astray*, Je. 23. 39. Hiph. הִשִּׁיא.—I. *to lead astray, deceive*, const. with acc., לְ.—II. *to come suddenly upon*, with עַל Ps. 55. 16.—III. *to seduce, corrupt*. Niph. *to be deceived*, Is. 19. 13.

מַשָּׁאוֹן masc. *deceit*, Pr. 26. 26.

II. [נָשָׁא] *to lend* on usury, with בְּ, Ne. 5. 9; part. נֹשֶׁא (§ 23. rem. 9) *a creditor*. Hiph. *to exact*, with בְּ, Ps. 89. 23.

מַשָּׁא masc.—I. *usury*, Ne. 5. 7, 10.—II. *debt*, Ne. 10. 32.

מַשָּׁאָה fem. constr. מַשַּׁאת (for מַשָּׁאֶת), pl. מַשָּׁאוֹת, *debt.*

נָשֹׁא	Kal inf. abs.	.	.	נשא
נָשֹׂא	Kal inf. abs. [for נָשֹׂה § 24. rem. 18]			נשה
נְשָׂא	id. imp. s. m.; or Ch. Peal pret. 3 p. s. m.			נשא
נְשֹׂא	id. inf. constr.	.	.	נשא
נְשֹׂא	defect. for נְשׂוֹא (q. v.)	.	.	נשא
נִשָּׂא	Kal fut. 1 pers. pl. (La. 3. 41); Niph. pret. 3 pers. sing. or part. masc.; Piel pret. 3 pers. sing. masc. (1 Ki. 9. 11; Am. 4. 2)			נשא
נִשֵּׂא	Piel pret. 3 pers. sing. masc.			נשא
נֹשֵׂא	Kal part. sing. masc. dec. 7b			נשא
נֹשֵׂא	Kal part. sing. masc. (§ 23. rem. 9)			נשא
נָשְׂאָה	Kal pret. 3 pers. sing. fem.			נשא
נִשְּׂאָה	Niph. part. sing. fem.			נשא

נָשְׂאוּ				
נָשְׂאוּ	} Kal pret. 3 pers. pl. (§ 8. rem. 7)	.		נשא
נְשָׂאוֹ	id. pret. 3 pers. s. m., suff. 3 p. s. m.; ו bef. (ָ)		נשא
נִשְּׂאוֹ	Piel pret. 3 pers. s. m. (נִשֵּׂא), suff. 3 pers. s. m.		נשא
נִשְּׂאוּ	Niph. pret. 3 pers. pl.		נשא
נִשָּׂא	ו Niph. pret. 3 pers. sing. masc.	.	נשא
נִשָּׂאֵם	ו Kal fut. 1 pers. pl., suff. 3 p. pl. m.; ו bef. (ָ)	נשא
נְשָׂאוֹת	id. part. act. f., pl. of נֹשֵׂאת [for נֹשְׂאֹת § 23. r. 4]	נשא
נְשֻׂאִי	Kh. נְשֻׂאַי q. v.; K. נָשׂוּא (q. v.)		נשא
נֹשְׂאֵי	Kal part. act. pl. constr. masc. fr. נֹשֵׂא d. 7b	נשא
נְשֻׂאֵי	Kh. נְשֻׂאַי q. v.; K. נָשׂוּא (q. v.)		נשא
נְשֻׂאִים	defect. for נְשׂוּאִים (q. v.)	.	נשא
נֹשְׂאִים	ו Kal part. act. masc. pl. of נֹשֵׂא dec. 7b	נשא
נְשֻׂאִים	Kh. נְשֻׂאִים, pl. of נָשׂוּא q. v.; K. נשׂים (q. v.)	נשה
נְשָׂאֲךָ	ו Kal pret. 3 p. s. m., suff. 2 p. s. m.; ו bef. (ָ)	נשא
נִשְׁאַל	Niph. pret. 3 pers. sing. masc.	.	שאל
נִשְׁאֹל	id. inf. abs.	.	.	שאל
נִשְׁאֲלָה	ו Kal fut. 1 pers. pl., with parag. ה (§ 8. r. 7)	שאל
נִשְׁאַלְתִּי	Niph. pret. 1 pers. sing.	.	שאל
נְשַׁאֲמֵם	ו Piel imp. sing. m. [נַשֵּׁא], suff. 3 pers. pl. m.	נשא
נַשְׁאֵר	Hiph. fut. 1 pers. pl. ap. [from נַשְׁאִיר]	שאר
נִשְׁאַר	} Niph. pret. 3 pers. sing. masc. (comp. § 8. rem. 7)	שאר
נִשְׁאָר	}			
נִשְׁאֲרָה	} id. pret. 3 pers. sing. fem. (v. id.)	.	שאר
נִשְׁאָרָה	}			
נִשְׁאֲרוּ	} id. pret. 3 pers. pl. (v. id.)	.	שאר
נִשְׁאָרוּ	}			
נִשְׁאַרְנוּ	id. pret. 1 pers. pl.	.	שאר
נִשְׁאַרְתִּי	id. pret. 1 pers. sing.	.	שאר
נִשְׁאַרְתֶּם	ו id. pret. 2 pers. masc.	.	שאר
נָשָׂאת	ו Kal pret. 3 pers. sing. masc.	.	נשא
נֹשֵׂאת	id. part. act. s. f. [for נֹשְׂאֵת § 23. r. 4] fr. נֹשֵׂא m.	נשא
נְשֻׂאֹת	id. pl., comp. dec. 13	.	נשא
נְשֵׂאת	id. sing. [for נְשֵׂאֶת] .	.	נשא
נִשֵּׂאת	Niph. part. sing. fem. [for נִשֵּׂאֶת comp. § 23. rem. 4]; subst. 2 Sa. 19. 43	.	נשא
נָשָׂאתָ	Kal pret. 2 pers. sing. masc. (§ 8. rem. 5)	.	נשא
נָשָׂאתִי	ו id. pret. 1 pers. sing.	.	נשא
נְשִׂאֹתֵיכֶם	noun f. pl., suff. 2 p. pl. m. [fr. נְשׂוּאָה d. 10	נשא
נְשָׂאתִים	Kal pret. 2 pers. sing. fem., suff. 3 pers. pl. m.	נשא
נְשָׂאתָם	ו id. pret. 2 pers. pl. masc.; ו for ָ, conv.	נשא
נְשָׂאַתְנִי	id. pret. 3 pers. sing. fem., suff. 1 pers. sing.	נשא
נְשָׂאתַנִי	ו id. pret. 2 p. s. m., suff. 1 p. s.; ו for ָ, conv.	נשא

[נָשַׁב] *to blow*, with בְּ, Is. 40. 7. Hiph. I. *to cause to blow*, Ps. 147. 18.—II. Ge. 15. 11, *to drive away,*

a Je. 23. 39.   f 2 Ki. 5. 1.   l Est. 5. 11.   q Ezr. 10. 44.   v 1 Sa. 20. 6, 28.   a 1 Sa. 14. 36.   g 1 Ki. 10. 22.   1 Ch. 14. 2.   s Exe. 16. 58.
b Ps. 10. 12.   g 2 Sa. 5. 12.   m Is. 19. 13.   r 2 Sa. 23. 37.   w 1 Sa. 20. 6, 28.   b Ge. 42. 38.   h Ge. 45. 23.   i Nu. 14. 19.   p Exe. 36. 6.
c Da. 2. 35.   h Est. 5. 2.   n Is. 30. 25.   s Ezr. 8. 36.   x Mal. 2. 9.   c Ge. 14. 7.   k Est. 2. 15.   m Ge. 18. 26.   t Ps. 102. 11.
d Is. 1. 14.   i Mi. 2. 2.   o 2 Ch. 12. 11.   t Ne. 5. 7.   y Ne. 13. 6.   d Je. 37. 10.   l Zec. 5. 7;   n Is. 46. 1.   u Ge. 47. 30.
e Is. 33. 24.   k 2 Ch. 9. 21.   p De. 1. 31.   u Ps. 28. 9.

or *frighten away*, as birds, with a kind of *puffing* noise.

וַנָּשֶׁב‎ }	Hiph. fut. 1 p. pl., ap. & conv. (§ 21. r. 18)	שׁוב
נָשֶׁב‎ נָּשֶׁב‎ }	Kal fut. 1 pers. pl. (§ 20. rem. 4) ; וְ‎ conv.	ישׁב
וַנָּשֶׁב‎ }	Hiph. fut. 1 pers. pl. ap. & conv. [from § 20. rem. 9] נשׁיב‎	ישׁב
נָשְׁבָה‎	Kal pret. 3 pers. sing. fem.	נשׁב
נָשְׁבָה‎	defect. for נָשׁוּבָה‎ (q. v.)	שׁוב
נִשְׁבָּה‎	Niph. pret. 3 pers. sing. masc.	שׁבה
נִשְׁבּוּ‎	id. pret. 3 pers. pl.	שׁבה
נַשְׁבִּיר‎	Hiph. fut. 1 pers. pl.	שׁבר
וְנַשְׁבִּירָה‎	id. with parag. ה‎ (§ 8. rem. 13)	שׁבר
נִשָּׁבֵעַ‎ וַנִּשָּׁבֵעַ‎ }	Kal fut. 1 pers. pl. (§ 8. rem. 15); וְ‎ conv.	שׁבע
וְנִשְׁבַּע‎	Niph. pret. 3 pers. sing. masc.	שׁבע
נִשְׁבְּעָה‎	Kal fut. 1 pers. pl. with parag. ה‎ (§ 8.rem.13)	שׁבע
נִשְׁבְּעוּ‎ נִשְׁבְּעוּ‎ }	Niph. pret. 3 pers. pl. (comp. § 8. rem. 7)	שׁבע
נִשְׁבָּעוֹת‎	id. part. fem. pl. [of נִשְׁבָּעָה‎] fr. נִשְׁבָּע‎ m.	שׁבע
נִשְׁבַּעְנוּ‎	id. pret. 1 pers. pl.	שׁבע
וְנִשְׁבַּעְתָּ‎	id. pret. 2 pers. sing. masc.	שׁבע
נִשְׁבַּעְתִּי‎	id. pret. 1 pers. sing.	שׁבע
נִשְׁבַּעְתֶּם‎	id. pret. 2 pers. pl. masc.	שׁבע
נִשְׁבָּר‎	Niph. part. sing. m. d. 2 b; or in pause for foll.	שׁבר
וְנִשְׁבַּר‎	id. pret. 3 pers. sing. masc.	שׁבר
נִשְׁבְּרָה‎	id. part. sing. fem. of נִשְׁבָּר‎	שׁבר
נִשְׁבְּרָה‎ וְנִשְׁבְּרָה‎ }	id. pret. 3 pers. sing. fem.; or (Ge. 43. 4)} Kal fut. 1 pers. pl. (§ 8. rem. 7 & 15) }	שׁבר
נִשְׁבְּרֵי‎	Kh. נִשְׁבְּרָה‎ q. v.; K. נִשְׁבְּרוּ‎ (q. v.)	שׁבר
נִשְׁבְּרוּ‎ וְנִשְׁבְּרוּ‎ }	Niph. pret. 3 pers. pl. (comp. § 8. rem. 7)	שׁבר
נִשְׁבָּרִים‎	id. part. masc. pl. of נִשְׁבָּר‎ dec. 2 b	שׁבר
נִשְׁבֶּרֶת‎	id. part. sing. fem.	שׁבר
נִשְׁבַּרְתִּי‎	id. part. 1 pers. sing.	שׁבר
וְנִשְׁבַּת‎	Niph. pret. 3 pers. sing. masc.	שׁבת
וְנִשְׁבְּתוּ‎	id. pret. 3 pers. pl.	שׁבת

נָשַׁג‎ Kal not used; cogn. נָסַג‎, סוּג‎. Hiph. הִשִּׂיג‎.—I. *to reach*, as the hand to the mouth, 1 Sa. 14. 26.—II. *to reach, attain to, overtake.*—III. *to come upon, befall.*—IV. *to acquire, obtain.*—V. *to over-pass, go beyond,* Job 24. 2. Others, *to remove*, i. q. סוּג‎.

נִשְׂגָּב‎ וְנִשְׂגָּב‎ }	Niph. part. sing. masc., or (Pr. 18. 10) pret. 3 pers. masc. sing. in pause	שׂגב
וְנִשְׂגָּב‎	id. pret. 3 person. sing. masc.	שׂגב

נִשְׁנָּבָה‎	id. part. sing. fem. of נִשְׁנָּב‎	שׁגב
נִשְׁנָּבָה‎	id. pret. 3 pers. sing. fem.	שׁגב
נִשְׁדַּדְנוּ‎	Niph. pret. 1 pers. pl. [for נָשַׁדּוֹנוּ‎ § 18. r. 16]	שׁדד

I. [נָשָׁה‎] I. *to forget*, La. 3. 17.—II. *to neglect,* Je. 23. 39 Niph. id. Is. 44. 21. Pi. *to cause to forget* Ge. 41. 51. Hiph. הִשָּׁה‎ id. Job 11. 6; 39. 17.

נָשְׁיָה‎ fem. *forgetfulness,* Ps. 88. 13.

מְנַשֶּׁה‎ (*causing to forget*) pr. name, Manasseh.—I. a son of Joseph.—II. a king of Judah.—III. Ju. 18. 30. Kh.—IV. Ezr. 10. 30.—V. Ezr. 10. 33.

II. [נָשָׁה‎] I. *to lend* on usury, with בְּ‎ of *the person;* נֹשֶׁה‎ *a lender, creditor.*—II. *to borrow* on usury, const. abs. Je. 15. 10 ; Is. 24. 2 ; נֹשֶׁה‎ *a usurer.*—III. *to take as usury,* Ne. 5. 11 Hiph. *to lend on usury,* with בְּ‎ of the person.

נְשִׁי‎ masc. dec. 6i, *debt,* 2 Ki. 4. 7.

יְשִׁיָּה‎ (whom *the Lord lendeth*) pr. name masc. of several individuals.

יִשִּׁיָּהוּ‎ (id.) pr. name masc. 1 Ch. 12. 6.

מַשֶּׁה‎ masc. dec. 9 a, *debt,* De. 15. 2.

נָשֶׁה‎ masc. *the ischiatic nerve,* extending through the thigh and leg to the ankles, Ge. 32. 33. Etymology not known.

נֹשֶׁה‎	Kal part. act. sing. masc. dec. 9 a	נשׁה
נָשׁוּ‎	id. pret. 3 p. pl.; acc. drawn back bef. monos.	נשׁה
נָשׂוּ‎	Kal pret. 3 pers. pl. for נָשְׂאוּ‎ (§ 23. r. 11)	נשׂא
נָשׂוֹא‎	Kal inf. abs.	נשׂא
נָשׂוּא‎	id. pret. 3 pers. pl. (§ 23. r. 11, & § 8. r. 4)	נשׂא
נָשׂוּא‎	id. part. pass. sing. masc. constr. [of נָשׂוֹא‎] dec. 3 a ; וְ‎ bef.	נשׂא
נָשׁוּב‎ וַנָּשׁוּב‎ }	Kh. נָשׁוּב‎ וַנָּשָׁב‎ K. וַנָּשָׁב‎ ap. from נָשׁוּב‎ (q. v.)	שׁוב
נָשׁוּבָה‎ וְנָשׁוּבָה‎ }	Kh. נָשׁוּב‎ q. v.; K. נָשׁוּבָה‎ (q. v.)	שׁוב
וְנָשׁוּב‎	Kal fut. 1 pers. pl.	שׁוב
וְנָשׁוּבָה‎	Kal fut. 1 pers. pl. (נָשׁוּב‎) with parag. ה‎ (comp. § 8. rem. 13)	שׁוב
נָשׁוֹן‎	Niph. pret. 3 pers. sing. masc.	שׁוג
נָשׂוּי‎	Kal part. pass. sing. masc., constr. of נָשׂוּי‎ (§ 23. rem. 11) see	נשׂא
וְנַשְׁחִיתָה‎	Hiph. fut. 1 pers. pl. with parag. ה‎ (comp. § 8. rem. 13)	שׁחת
וְנִשְׁחַת‎	Niph. pret. 3 pers. sing. masc.	שׁחת
נִשְׁחֲתָה‎	id. pret. 3 pers. sing. fem. [for נִשְׁחֲתָה‎ comp. § 8. rem. 7]	שׁחת
נָשֵׁי‎	the foll. with suff. 1 pers. sing.	אנש

a Ge. 43. 21.   f Am. 8. 6.   l Ps. 65. 5.   q Ex. 22. 13.   v Eze. 27. 34.   a Ps. 139. 6.   f Eze. 39. 26.   l La. 5. 21.   q Je. 6. 5.
b Je. 42. 13, 14.   g Am. 8. 5.   m Is. 19. 18.   r Ps. 51. 19.   w Eze. 6. 9.   b Mi. 2. 4.   g Je. 10. 5.   m 2 Sa. 1. 22.   r Je. 13. 7.
c Ezr. 10. 2.   h Job 31. 31.   n Je. 4. 2.   s 1 Ki. 22. 49.   x Eze. 24. 11.   c De. 24. 11.   h Ps. 139. 20.   n Ps. 32. 1.   s Je. 18. 4.
d Is. 40. 7.   i Je. 44. 17.   o Jos. 6. 22.   t Je. 2. 13.   y Is. 2. 11, 17.   d Je. 15. 10.   i Ne. 4. 9.   o Je. 11. 19.   t Ge. 30. 26.
e Je. 46. 16   k Le. 5. 22.   p Ps.51.19; 124.7.   u Mal. 1. 4   z Ge. 6. 12.

נְשֵׁי n. fem. with pl. masc. term., constr. of נָשִׁים, irr. of אִשָּׁה (§ 45) ; ‍ו bef. (:)   אנשׁ

נָשִׂיא noun masc. sing. dec. 3 a   נשׂא

נְשִׂיא id., constr. st.; ‍ו bef. (:)   נשׂא

נְשִׂיאֵהֶם id. pl., suff. 3 pers. pl. masc.   נשׂא

נְשִׂיאַי id. pl., suff. 1 pers. sing.   נשׂא

נְשִׂיאֵי id. pl., constr. st.; ‍ו bef. (:)   נשׂא

נְשִׂיאֶיהָ id. pl., suff. 3 pers. sing. fem.   נשׂא

נְשִׂיאֵיהֶם id. pl., suff. 3 pers. pl. masc.   נשׂא

נְשִׂיאִים
נְשִׂיאִם } id. pl., abs. st.   נשׂא

נָשִׁיב Hiph. fut. 1 pers. pl.   שׁוב

נְשִׁיָּה noun fem. sing.*Ps. 88. 13.   נשׁה

נְשַׁיֵּהוֹן Chald. noun fem. with pl. m. term. [נָשִׁין], suff. 3 pers. pl. masc., see the foll.   אנשׁ

נְשֵׁיהֶם noun f. with pl. m. term. (נָשִׁים), suff. 3 pers. pl. m., irr. of אִשָּׁה (§ 45); ‍ו bef. (:)   אנשׁ

נָשָׁיו id. pl., suff. 3 pers. sing. masc.   אנשׁ

נָשֶׁיךָ id. pl., suff. 2 pers. sing. masc.   אנשׁ

נְשִׁיכִי noun masc. sing., suff. 2 pers. sing. fem., Kh. נְשִׁיכִי, K. נִשְׁיֵךְ [fr. נָשִׁי] dec. 6 i   נשׁה

נְשֵׁיכֶם the foll. with suff. 2 p. pl. m.; ‍ו bef. (:)   אנשׁ

נָשִׁים noun fem. with pl. masc. term. irr. of אִשָּׁה. (§ 45)   אנשׁ

נָשִׂים Kal fut. 1 pers. pl. R. שִׂים, see   שׂום

נַשִּׁים Hiph. fut. 1 pers. pl., for נָשִׁם (§ 18. rem. 12, & § 21. rem. 24) ; ‍ו conv.   שׁמם

נֹשִׁים Kal part. masc. pl. of נֹשֶׁה dec. 9 a   נשׁה

נָשִׂימָה Kal fut. 1 pers. pl. with parag. ה (comp. § 8. rem. 13) R. שִׂים, see   שׂום

נָשֵׁינוּ noun fem. with pl. masc. term. (נָשִׁים), suff. 1 pers. pl., irr. of אִשָּׁה (§ 45)   אנשׁ

נְשִׁיקוֹת noun fem. pl. of [נְשִׁיקָה] dec. 10   נשׁק

נָשִׁיר Kal fut. 1 pers. pl.   שׁיר

נָשִׁירָה id. with parag. ה (comp. § 8. rem. 13)   שׁיר

נָשִׁישׁ Kal fut. 1 pers. pl. R. שִׂישׁ, see   שׂישׂ

נָשִׁיתִי Kal pret. 1 pers. sing.   נשׁה

נָשַׁךְ fut. יִשַּׁךְ, יִשֹּׁךְ.—I. to bite.—II. to vex, oppress, Hab. 2. 7.—III. to lend on usury, De. 23. 20. Pu. to bite. Hiph. to take usury, exact interest, De. 23. 20, 21. Hence

נֶשֶׁךְ masc. usury, interest   נשׁך

נִשְׁכְּבָה Kal fut. 1 pers. pl. with parag. ה (§ 8. rem. 13)   שׁכב

נִשְׁכָּה fem. dec. 12 d, for לִשְׁכָּה a chamber (q. v.)   לשׁך

נִשְׁכְּבוּ Piel pret. 3 pers. pl.   נשׁך

נְשָׁכוֹ Kal pret. 3 pers. sing. masc., suff. 3 pers. sing. masc.; ‍ו bef. (:)   נשׁך

נִשְׁכָּח
וְ' } Niph. pret. 3 pers. s. m. (comp. § 8. r. 7)   שׁכח

נִשְׁכַּחַה id. part. sing. fem.   שׁכח

נִשְׁכְּחוּ id. pret. 3 pers. pl.   שׁכח

נִשְׁכַּחַת id. part. sing. fem.   שׁכח

נִשְׁכַּחְתִּי id. pret. 1 pers. sing.   שׁכח

נֹשְׁכֶיךָ Kal part. act. pl. masc., suff. 2 pers. sing. masc. from נֹשֵׁךְ dec. 7 b   נשׁך

נַשְׁכִּימָה Hiph. fut. 1 p. pl. with parag. ה (§ 8. 1 13)   שׁכם

נְשָׁכַם Kal pret. 3 pers. sing. masc., suff. 3 pers. pl. masc. ; ‍ו for ‍ו conv.   נשׁך

נִשְׁכְּרוּ Niph. pret. 3 pers. pl. [for נִשְׁבְּרוּ comp. § 8. rem. 7]   שׁבר

נִשְׁכָּתוֹ noun fem. sing., suff. 3 pers. sing. masc. fr. נִשְׁכָּה dec. 12 d, for לִשְׁכָּה q. v.   לשׁך

נָשַׁל fut. יִשַּׁל.—I. to fall or drop off, De. 28. 40.—II. trans. to draw or put off, as a shoe.—III. to cast or drive out a nation, De. 7. 1, 22. Pi. to cast, drive out, 2 Ki. 16. 6.

נִשְׁלוֹחַ Niph. inf. abs.   שׁלח

נִשְׁלְחָה
וְ' } Kal fut. 1 p. pl. with parag. ה (§ 8. r. 13)   שׁלח

נְשַׁלֵּחֲךָ Piel fut. 1 pers. pl., 2 pers. sing. masc. (§ 16. rem. 15) ; ‍ו conv.   שׁלח

נְשַׁלְּחֶנּוּ id. with suff. 3 pers. sing. masc.   שׁלח

נַשְׁלִיכָה
וְ' } Hiph. fut. 1 p. pl. with parag. ה (§ 8. r. 13)   שׁלך

נַשְׁלִכֵהוּ id. with suff. 3 pers. sing. masc.   שׁלך

נְשַׁלְּמָה Piel fut. 1 pers. pl. with parag. ה (§ 8. rem. 13) ; ‍ו bef. (:) for   שׁלם

[נָשַׁם] to breathe, pant, perhaps so אֶשֹּׁם Is. 42. 14; but which may be from שָׁמַם.

נְשָׁמָה fem. d. 11 c.—I. breath.—II. life; meton. a living thing.—III. mind, spirit.—IV. anger.

נִשְׁמָא Ch. fem. dec. 8 a, breath, life, Da. 5. 23.

תִּנְשֶׁמֶת f. a species of animal, enumerated among the lizards, Le. 11. 30, according to Bochart, the chameleon. In Le. 11. 18; De. 14. 16, it occurs among the waterfowls, according to some, the swan; others, seagull; Sept. πορφυρίον, the crested purple heron.

נִשְׁמַר
וְ' } Niph. pret. 3 pers. sing. masc.   שׁמר

a Nu. 17. 17.   f 2 Ch. 21. 17.   k Nu. 21. 30.   p Pr. 27. 6.   u Nu. 21. 9.   Am. 5. 19.   i Is. 65. 16.   n Am. 9. 3.   s 1 Sa. 6. 2.
b Eze. 32. 29.   g 1 Ki. 20. 3, 5.   l Ne. 5. 10, 11.   Ps. 137. 4.   Je. 3. 25.   Ec. 2. 16.   Is. 23. 15.   1 Sa. 2. 5.   Ps. 2. 3.
c Nu. 17. 21.   h 2 Ki. 4. 7.   1 Ki. 20. 31.   q Ps. 21. 14.   Ge. 19. 32.   Ec. 9. 5.   Ps. 31. 13.   Ne. 3. 30.   Ge. 37. 20.
d Ge. 25. 16.   i Je. 44. 25.   Is. 41. 22.   r Eze. 21. 15.   Ne. 13. 7.   Ge. 41. 30.   Hab. 2. 7.   Est. 3. 13.   Ho. 14. 3.
e Da. 6. 25.   2 Ki. 4. 10.   o 2 Ch. 29. 9.   Je. 23. 39.   Je. 8. 17.   Is. 23. 16.   Ca. 7. 13.   Ge. 26. 29.

נִשְׁמְדָה	id. pret. 3 pers. sing. fem.	שמד
נִשְׁמְדוּ	id. pret. 3 pers. pl.	שמד
נִשְׁמַדְנוּ	id. pret. 1 pers. pl.	שמד
נִשְׁמַדְתִּי	id. pret. 1 pers. sing.; acc. shifted by conv. (comp. § 8. rem. 7)	שמד
נְשָׁמָה	Niph. pret. 3 pers. sing. fem.	שמם
נְשָׁמָה	noun fem. sing. dec. 11 c; bef.	נשם
נְשַׁמָּה	Niph. part. sing. fem. [fr. נָשַׁם m.]; id.	שמם
נָשַׁמּוּ	id. pret. 3 pers. pl.	שמם
נִשְׁמוֹת	noun f. pl. abs. fr. נְשָׁמָה d. 11 c; bef.	נשם
נִשַׁמּוֹת	Niph. part. fem. pl. of נְשַׁמָּה (q. v.)	שמם
נִשְׁמְחָה	Kal fut. 1 pers. pl. with parag. ה (§ 8. r. 13)	שמח
נִשְׁמְטוּ	Niph. pret. 3 pers. pl.	שמט
נַשְׁמִידָה	Hiph. fut. 1 p. pl. with parag. ה (§ 8. r. 13)	שמד
נִשְׁמַע	Kal fut. 1 pers. pl.; conv.; or Niph. pret. 3 pers. s. m. (§ 8. r. 7 & 15)	שמע
נִשְׁמְעָה	id. fut. 1 pers. pl. with parag. ה (§ 8. rem. 13 & 15)	שמע
נִשְׁמְעוּ	Niph. pret. 3 pers. pl.	שמע
נִשְׁמָעִים	id. part. masc. pl. [of נִשְׁמָע]	שמע
נִשְׁמָעֶנָּה	Kal fut. 1 pers. pl., suff. 3 pers. sing. fem.	שמע
נִשְׁמָר	Niph. pret. 3 pers. sing. masc. (comp. § 8. rem. 7)	שמר
נִשְׁמֹר	Kal fut. 1 pers. pl.	שמר
נִשְׁמְרוּ	Niph. pret. 3 pers. pl. (comp. § 8. rem. 7)	שמר
נִשְׁמַרְתָּ	id. pret. 2 pers. sing. masc.; acc. shifted by conv. (comp. § 8. rem. 7)	שמר
נִשְׁמַרְתֶּם	id. pret. 2 pers. pl. masc.	שמר
נִשְׁמַת	noun fem. sing., constr. of נְשָׁמָה d. 11 c	נשם
נִשְׁמָתוֹ	id., suff. 3 pers. sing. masc.	נשם
נִשְׁמָתִי	id., suff. 1 pers. sing.	נשם
נִשְׁמָתָךְ	Ch. n. f. s., suff. 2 pers. s. f., fr. נִשְׁמָא d. 8a	נשם
נִשַּׁנִי	Piel pret. 3 p.s.m., suff. 1 p.s. [for נִשְּׁנִי §10.r.1]	נשה
נִשַּׁפּוּ	Niph. pret. 3 pers. pl.	שסס
נִשְׁעָן	Niph. part. sing. masc.	שען
נִשְׁעָן	id. pret. 3 pers. sing. masc.	שען
נִשְׁעַנּוּ	id. pret. 1 pers. pl. [for נִשְׁעַנּוּ § 25. rem.]	שען
נִשְׁעֲנוּ	id pret. 3 pers. pl.	שען
נִשְׁעַנְתָּ	id. pret. 2 pers. sing. masc.	שען
נִשְׁעֲרָה	Niph. pret. 3 pers. sing. fem.	שער

נָשַׁף to breathe, blow.

נֶשֶׁף masc. dec. 6 a (with suff. נִשְׁפּוֹ) twilight, supposed to be so called from the refreshing breezes of that time.—I. dawn, morning twilight.

—II. dusk, evening twilight.—III. darkness, night.

יַנְשׁוּף, יַנְשׁוֹף masc. the name of an unclean bird, Sept. & Vulg. ibis, the Egyptian heron. Ch. & Syr. the owl.

נֶשֶׁף	in pause, as if for נָשֶׁף (comp. § 35. r. 2)	נשף
נֵשֶׁף	noun masc. sing. (suff. נִשְׁפּוֹ) dec. 6 a	נשף
נִשְׁפָּה	Niph. part. sing. masc.	שפה
נִשְׁפּוֹ	noun m. s., suff. 3 pers. s. m. fr. נֶשֶׁף d. 6a	נשף
נִשְׁפָּט	Niph. part. sing. masc.	שפט
נִשְׁפְּטָה	id. fut. 1 pers. pl. [נִשְׁפָּט] with parag. ה (comp. § 8. rem. 15)	שפט
נִשְׁפַּטְתִּי	id. pret. 1 pers. sing.; acc. shifted by conv. (§ 8. rem. 7)	שפט
נִשְׁפַּךְ	Niph. pret. 3 pers. sing. masc.	שפך
נִשְׁפַּכְתִּי	id. pret. 1 pers. sing.	שפך
נִשְׁפַּתְּ	Kal pret. 2 pers. sing. masc.	נשף

נָשַׁק Hiph. to kindle, set on fire. Niph. pass. Ps. 78. 21.

נָשַׁק fut. יִשַּׁק, in the Arab. to join, to arrange; hence Heb.—I. intrans. to be arranged, to regulate oneself, Ge. 41. 40.—II. to arm oneself.—III. to kiss (i. e. join mouth to mouth), const. with ל of the person. Pi. to kiss. Hiph. to join, touch, with אֶל, Eze. 3. 13.

נֶשֶׁק נֵשֶׁק masc.—I. battle array, Job 39. 21—II. battle, Ps. 140. 8.—III. arms, armour.—IV. armoury, arsenal.

נְשִׁיקָה fem. dec. 10, a kiss.

נָשַׁק	Kal pret. 3 p. s. m. before monos. for נָשַׁק	נשק
נֵשֶׁק	noun masc. sing. (§ 35. rem. 2)	נשק
נֶשֶׁק	noun masc. sing.	נשק
נִשְׁקַד	Niph. pret. 3 pers. sing. masc.	שקד
נִשְׁקְתָה	Kal pret. 3 pers. sing. fem.	נשק
נַשְׁקֶה	Hiph. fut. 1 pers. pl.	שקה
נִשְׁקְתָה	Niph. pret. 3 pers. sing. fem.	שקה
נִשְׁקְתָה	Kh. נָשְׁקָה, K. נָשְׁקְעָה Niph. pret. 3 pers. sing. fem. R. שקה or שקע
נָשְׁקוּ	Kal pret. 3 pers. pl. [for נָשַׁקוּ § 8. rem. 7]	נשק
נַשְּׁקוּ	Piel imp. pl. masc.	נשק
נֹשְׁקֵי	Kal part. act. pl. constr. m. [fr. נֹשֵׁק] d. 7b	נשק
נִשְׁקַל	Niph. pret. 3 pers. sing. masc.	שקל
נַשְׁקֶנּוּ	Hiph. fut. 1 pers. pl. (נַשְׁקֶה), suff. 3 pers. sing. masc. (§ 24. rem. 21)	שקה
נִשְׁקַף	Niph. pret. 3 p. s. m. [for נִשְׁקַף comp. § 8. r. 7]	שקף

---

a Ju. 21. 16.   h Is. 57. 16.   p Da. 10. 12.   r Ps. 37. 28.   z Zec. 14. 2.   n Ps. 50. 3.   u La. 2. 11.   b 2 Ch. 9. 24.   f Ps. 78. 21.
b Ho. 10. 8.   i Ps. 66. 6.   q Ec. 9. 16, 17.   s 1 Sa. 21. 5.   g Nu. 21. 15;   o Is. 40. 24.   v 1 Ki. 13. 3.   c Is. 22. 8.   g Am. 8. 8.
c 3 Sa. 21. 5.   k Ps. 141. 6.   r Ju. 14. 13.   t De. 23. 10.   Is. 10. 20.   p Is. 13. 2.   w Is. 22. 8.   d 1 Ki. 10. 25.   h Ps. 2. 12.
d Ge. 38. 30.   l 2 Sa. 14. 7.   s Ho. 12. 14.   u Is. 10. 20.   h Is. 13. 2.   q Ps. 22. 15.   x 1 Ki. 10. 25.   e La. 1. 14.   i Ezr. 8. 33.
e Da. 10. 17.   m Ex. 24. 7.   t Job 34. 14.   b 2 Ch. 14. 10.   i Job 3. 9.   r Ex. 15. 10.   y La. 1. 14.   f Pr. 7. 13.   k Ge. 19. 34.
f Ps. 69. 26.   n Ex. 20. 19.   u Job 27. 3.   c 2 Sa. 20. 10.   k Is. 43. 26.   s 1 Ki. 19. 18.   z Pr. 7. 13.   g Ge. 19. 32.
g Eze. 32. 15.   o 2 Sa. 17. 5.   v 2 Ki. 6. 10.   d Da. 5. 23.   l 2 Ch. 16. 7   t 2 Sa. 15. 5.   a Ge. 19. 32.
    w De. 6. 25.   e Ge. 41. 51.   m Ps. 85. 11.

נִשְׁקְפָה׳ } id. pret. 3 pers. sing. fem. (v. id.) . שׁקף

נִשְׁקְפָה

נִשְׁקַפְתִּי׳ id. pret. 1 pers. sing. [for נִשְׁקַפְתִּי v. id.] שׁקף

נָשַׂר Root not used; i. q. Chald. נְסַר to saw.
מַשּׂוֹר masc. a saw, Is. 10. 15.

נֶשֶׁר masc. dec. 6a (pl. c. נִשְׁרֵי) an eagle.

נְשַׁר Chald. masc. dec. 3b, id.

נָשֶׁר noun masc. s., in pause for נֶשֶׁר (§ 35. r. 2) נשׁר

נְשָׁרִים׳ id. pl., abs. st. . . . . . נשׁר

נִשְׂרֹף Kal fut. 1 pers. pl. . . . . . שׂרף

נִשְׂרְפָה } id. with parag. ה (§ 8. rem. 13) . שׂרף

[נָשַׁת] I. to dry up, of the tongue from thirst, to be parched, Is. 41. 17.—II. to fail, waste away, of strength, Je. 51. 30. Niph. to dry up, Is. 19. 5.

נָשְׁתָה׳ } Kal pret. 3 pers. sing. fem. (§ 8. rem. 3) נשׁת

נָשְׁתָה

נִשְׁתֶּה׳ } Kal fut. 1 pers. pl. . . . . . שׁתה

נִשְׁתּוּ׳ } Niph. pret. 3 pers. pl. . . . . נשׁת

נִשְׁתַּוֶּה׳ Nithpa. pret. 3 pers. sing. masc. [for נִתְשַׁוֶּה ׳7. No. 10, & § 12. rem. 3] . . . שׁוה

[נִשְׁתְּוָן] masc. epistle, letter. Chald. id.

נִשְׁתְּוָנָא Chald. id. emph. state.

נִשְׁתַּחֲוֶה׳ [for נִתְשַׁ ׳ § 12. rem. 3] Hithpalel (3rd rad. doubled for תַּחֲוֶה׳) fut. 1 pers. pl. (§ 24. rem. 22, & § 6. rem. No. 2) . . שׁחה

נִשְׁתַּעֶה׳ [for נִתְשַׁ ׳ § 12. rem. 3] Hithpa. fut. 1 pers. pl. (נִשְׁתַּעֲוָה) with parag. ה [for נִשְׁתַּעֲוָה] שׁעה

נָתַב Root not used; Arab. to be high, raised; meaning uncertain as regards its connection with the derivatives. Gesenius and Fürst ascribe to it the signification of treading.

נָתִיב masc. dec. 3a, fem. נְתִיבָה dec. 10.—I. adj. trodden, Pr. 12. 28, דֶּרֶךְ נְתִיבָה a trodden way, beaten path (Gesenius), comp. the Root.—II. path, by-way, metaph. course of life.

נָתֹן׳ } Kal inf. abs. . . . . . נתן

נָתוּן׳ id. part. pass. sing. masc. dec. 3a . נתן

נְתוּנִים׳ } id. pl. abs. st. . . . . . נתן

נְתוּנֵם׳

נְתֹן׳ Kal imp. sing. masc. . . . . נתץ

נָתוּק׳ } Kal part. pass. sing. masc. . . . נתק

נָתוֹשׁ׳ Kal inf. abs. . . . . . . נתשׁ

נַתַּח Pi. נִתַּח, to divide, cut in pieces. Hence

נֵתַח׳ masc. dec. 6e, a piece . . . . נתח

נִתַּח׳ ׳] Piel pret. 3 pers. sing. masc. . . נתח

נִתְחַזֵּק׳ } Hithpa. fut. 1 pers. pl. (§ 12. rem. 1) חזק

נִתְחַזְּקָה׳ } id. with parag. ה (comp. § 8. rem. 13) חזק

נְתָחֶיהָ׳ noun masc. pl., suff. 3 pers. sing. fem. from נֵתַח dec. 6e . . . . . . נתח

נְתָחָיו׳ id. pl., suff. 3 pers. sing. masc. . . נתח

נְתָחִים׳ id. pl., abs. st. . . . . . נתח

נִתְחַכְּמָה׳ Hithpa. fut. 1 pers. pl. [נִתְחַכֵּם] with parag. ה (comp. § 8. rem. 13) . . . חכם

נָתִיב noun masc. sing. dec. 3a . . . נתב

נְתִיבָה noun fem. sing. dec. 10; or (Pr. 12. 28) adj., fem. of נָתִיב . . . . . . נתב

נְתִיבוֹת id., pl. of the preced. . . . נתב

נְתִיבוֹתַי id. pl., suff. 1 pers. sing. . . נתב

נְתִיבוֹתֶיהָ׳ } id. pl. with suff. 3 pers. sing. fem.; ׳ bef. (:·) נתב

נְתִיבוֹתֵיהֶם׳ id. pl., suff. 3 pers. pl. masc. . נתב

נְתִיבָתִי׳ id. sing., suff. 1 pers. sing. . . נתב

נְתִיבָתֶיהָ׳ id. pl., suff. 3 pers. sing. fem. . נתב

נְתִינַיָּא׳ Chald. noun masc. pl. emph. fr. [נָתִין] d. 1a נתן

נְתִינִים׳ noun masc. pl. of [נָתִין] dec. 3a . נתן

[נָתַךְ] fut. יִתַּךְ to be poured out, to flow, as water, Jol 3. 24; elsewhere metaph. of anger, curses. Niph. I. i. q. Kal No. 1.—II. to flow down, be melted. Hiph. I. to pour out.—II. to melt, Eze. 22. 20. Hoph. to be melted, Eze. 22. 22.
הִתּוּךְ masc. a melting, Ezr. 22. 22.

נִתַּךְ Niph. pret. 3 pers. sing. masc. . . נתך

נִתְּכָה׳ ׳] id. pret. 3 pers. sing. fem. . . נתך

נִתְּכְנוּ Niph. pret. 3 pers. pl. . . . . תכן

נִתֶּכֶת׳ Niph. part. sing. fem. [of נָתַךְ] . נתך

נִתַּכְתֶּם׳ } id. pret. 2 pers. pl. masc. . . נתך

נִתְּלוּ׳ Niph. pret. 3 pers. pl. . . . . תלה

נָתַן ׳] fut. יִתֵּן, imp. תֵּן, inf. נָתֹן more frequently תֵּת (§ 17. rem. 9).—I. to give, with the acc. of the thing and לְ of the person; מִי יִתֵּן who will give? a formula of wishing, for O that !—II. to grant, permit, suffer.—III. to give forth, an odour, to emit; fruit, to yield, bear; the voice, to speak aloud; the hand, to put forth, Ps. 81. 3, נָ׳ תֹּף to strike the timbrel.—IV. to render, ascribe.—V. to place, set, lay, put, with עַל, לְ, בְּ, אֶל; hence to impose any thing upon; נָ׳ פָּנָיו בְּ to set his face against any one; נָ׳ לִבּוֹ לְ to apply his heart, mind

ᵃ Nu. 21. 20.   ᵉ Ge. 11. 3.   ⁱ Pr. 27. 15.   ᵐ Nu. 3. 9.   ᵠ Eze. 24. 4.   ᵘ Eze. 24. 4.   ʸ Is. 43. 16.   ᵈ Ezr. 7. 24.   ᵏ Je. 7. 29.
ᵇ Pr. 7. 6.   ᶠ Is. 41. 17.   ᵏ Ge. 22. 5.   ⁿ Ps. 58. 7.   ʳ Le. 1. 6, 12; 8, 20.   ᵛ Ex. 29. 17.   ᶻ Ho. 2. 8.   ᵈ Ezr. 8. 20.   ˡ Eze. 22. 21.
ᶜ Da. 7. 4.   ᵍ Je. 51. 30.   ⁱ Is. 41. 23.   ᵒ Le. 22. 24.   ˢ 2 Sa. 10. 12.   ʷ Ju. 19. 29.   ᵃ Is. 59. 8.   ᵉ Eze. 24. 11.   ⁿ La. 5. 12.
ᵈ Ex. 19. 4.   ʰ Is. 19. 5.   ˡ 1 Ch. 6. 33.   ᵖ Je. 12. 17.   ᵗ 1 Ch. 19. 13.   ˣ Ex. 1. 10.   ᵇ Pr. 3. 17.   ⁱ 1 Sa. 2. 3.

to any thing.—VI. *to appoint,* with עַל over any one.—VII. *to make, to do; to make, constitute;* with בְּ *to make like* something else; also *to hold, regard* or *treat* as such. Niph. I. *to be given, delivered.*—II. *to be made.* Hoph. *to be given.*

נְתַן Chald. fut. יִנְתֵּן, יִנְתֵּן *to give.*

נָתָן (*giver*) pr. name masc. of several persons, espec.—I. of a prophet in the time of David.—II. of a son of David, 2 Sa. 5. 14.

נְתַן־מֶלֶךְ (*king's gift*) pr. name m. 2 Ki. 23. 11.

נְתִינִים masc. pl. (of נָתִין dec. 3a) *Nethinim,* servants *devoted* to the service of the temple in waiting upon the Levites; once נְתוּנִים Kh. Ezr. 8. 17.

נְתִינִין Chald. id. Ezr. 7. 24.

נְתַנְאֵל (*gift of God*) pr. name masc. of several persons.

נְתַנְיָה, נְתַנְיָהוּ (*gift of the Lord*) pr. name masc. of several persons.

מַתָּן masc. dec. 1b.—I. *gift;* אִישׁ מַתָּן *liberal man.*—II. pr. name masc. (*a*) of a priest of Baal; (*b*) Je. 38. 1.

מַתָּנָה fem. dec. 11a.—I. *gift, present.*—II. pr. name of a place on the borders of Moab.

מַתְּנָא Chald. fem. dec. 8a, *gift, present.*

מַתַּנְיָהוּ, מַתַּנְיָה (*gift of the Lord*) pr. name masc. of several persons.

מַתְּנַי (id.) pr. name of several men.

מַתַּת fem. (contr. from מַתְּנַת) *gift, present.*

מַתִּתָה (contr. fr. מַתִּתְיָה) pr. n. m. Ezr. 10. 33.

מַתִּתְיָה, מַתִּתְיָהוּ (*gift of the Lord*) pr. name masc. of several persons.

וַיִּתֵּן	pr. name masc.		נתן
נָתַן	Kal pret. 3 pers. sing. m. for נָתַן (§ 8. r. 7)		נתן
נָתֹן	id. inf. abs., comp. נָתוֹן		נתן
נְתַן	pr. name in compos. נְתַן מֶלֶךְ		נתן
תִּתֵּן / תִּתְּ־	} Kal inf. constr. (§ 8. rem. 18)		נתן
נִתָּן	Niph. part. sing. masc.		נתן
וַיִּתֶּן	id. pret. 3 pers. sing. masc.; or (Ju. 16. 5) with Mak. for the foll.		נתן
נִתֵּן	Kal fut. 1 pers. pl.		נתן
נֹתֵן	id. part. act. sing. masc. dec. 7b		נתן
נְתַנְאֵל	pr. name masc.; וּ bef.		נתן
נָתְנָה / נָתְנָה	} Kal pret. 3 pers. sing. fem. (§ 8. rem. 7)		נתן
נְתָנָהּ	id. pret. 3 pers. sing. masc., suff. 3 pers. sing. fem.; וּ bef.		נתן

נָתְנָה / נָתְנָה	} Niph. pret. 3 p.s.fem., or Kal fut. 1 p.pl., ה parag. (comp. § 8. rem. 7, 13 & 15) }		נתן
נִתְּנֶהָ	Kal fut. 1 pers. pl., suff. 3 p.s.f.; וּ conv.		נתן
נִתַּנּוּ	id. pret. 1 pers. pl. [for נְתַנֲנוּ § 17. rem. 9] *Eze. 27. 19		נתן
נָתְנוּ	id. pret. 3 pers. pl.		נתן
נְתָנֻהוּ	id. pret. 3 p. s. m., suff. 3 p. s. m.; וּ bef.		נתן
נִתְּנוּ	Niph. pret. 3 pers. pl. for נִנְתְּנוּ (comp. § 8. r. 7)		נתן
נְתַנּוּ	id. pret. 1 pers. pl. [for נָתַנֲנוּ § 17. rem. 9]		נתן
נְתָנֻנוּ	id. pret. 3 pers. pl.		נתן
נְתָנוּהוּ	Kal part. act. sing. masc. (נֹתֵן), suff. 3 pers. sing. masc. dec. 7b		נתן
נְתַנּוּךָ	id. pret. 1 pers. pl. (נָתַנּוּ q. v.), suff. 2 pers. sing. masc.; וּ bef.		נתן
נְתֻנוֹת	id. part. pass. fem. pl. [of נְתוּנָה] fr. נָתוּן m.		נתן
נֹתְנֵי	id. part. act. pl. constr. masc., from נוֹתֵן d. 7b		נתן
נְתַנְיָה / נְתַנְיָהוּ	} pr. name masc.		נתן
נְתֻנִים	defect. for נְתוּנִים (q. v.)		נתן
נֹתְנִים	Kal part. act. masc. pl. of נוֹתֵן dec. 7b		נתן
נְתָנְךָ	id. pret. 3 pers. sing. masc., suff. 2 pers. sing. masc.; וּ bef.		נתן
נֹתְנֵךְ	id. part. act. sing. masc. (נֹתֵן), suff. 2 pers. sing. fem. (for ךָ § 3. rem. 2) dec. 7b		נתן
נְתָנְךָ	id. id., suff. 2 pers. sing. masc.		נתן
נְתָנָם	id. pret. 3 pers. sing. masc., suff. 3 pers. pl. masc.; וּ bef.		נתן
נְתַנֲנִי	id. id., suff. 1 pers. pl.		נתן
נְתָנַנִי / נְתָנֵנִי	} id. id., suff. 1 pers. sing. (§ 2. rem. 1)		נתן

[נָתַם] *to tear up, destroy,* only in the foll. form.

נָתְסוּ	Kal pret. 3 pers. pl.		נתס

נָתַע Niph. *to be broken out,* Job 4. 10, cogn. נָתַץ.

נִתְעָב	Niph. part. sing. masc.		תעב
נִתְעָב	id. pret. 3 pers. sing. masc.		תעב
נִתְעָה	Niph. pret. 3 pers. sing. masc.		תעה
נִתְעוּ	Niph. pret. 3 p. pl. [for נִתְעֲוּ comp. § 8. r. 7]		נתע
וַתִּתְעוֹרֵר	Hithpa. fut. 1 p.pl. (comp. § 12. r. 1); וַ conv.		עור
נִתְעַלְּסָה	Hithpa. fut. 1 pers. pl. with parag. ה (comp. § 8. rem. 13)		עלס
וַתִּתְפַּלֵּל	Hithpa. fut. 1 pers. pl.; וַ conv.		פלל
נִתְפַּשׂ / וַיִּתְפַּשׂ	} Niph. pret. 3 pers. sing. masc. (comp. § 8. rem. 7)		חפש
נִתְפְּשָׂה / נִתְפָּשֶׂה	} id. pret. 3 pers. sing. fem. (v. id.)		חפש

a Nu. 20. 21.   *d* Ju. 5. 25.   *g* De. 21. 10.   *i* Ezr. 9. 7.   *m* Ju. 15. 13.   *p* Je. 20. 4.   *s* Job 30. 13.   *x* Ps. 20. 9.   *a* Eze. 19. 8.

b Ge. 38. 9.   *e* De. 29. 7.   *h* 1 Ki. 20. 13.   *k* Ezr. 9. 7.   *n* De. 28. 31.   *q* Ps. 124. 6.   *t* 1 Ch. 21. 6.   *y* Pr. 7. 18.   *b* Eze. 19. 4.

c Da. 1. 16.   *f* Ge. 34. 16.   Eze. 47. 11.   *l* 2 Ch. 25. 16.   *o* Ho. 2. 7.   *r* Ps. 118. 18.   *u* Job 15. 31.   *z* Ne. 4. 5.   *c* Je. 29. 4.

m Job 4. 10.

נִתְפָּשׂוּ — id. pret. 3 pers. pl. [for נִתְפְּשׂוּ v. id.] . תפש

וְנִתְפָּשֵׂמוֹ — וְ Kal fut. 1 pers. pl. [נִתְפּשׂ], suff. 3 pers. pl masc. . . . . תפש

נִתְפַּשְׂתְּ — Niph. pret. 2 pers. sing. fem. . . תפש

נָתַץ — וְ fut. יִתֹּץ, inf. נְתֹץ.—I. *to tear* or *break down, destroy,* as houses, &c.; trop. of persons.—II. *to break out* the teeth, Ps. 58. 7. Pi. *to break down, destroy.* Niph. Pu. and Hoph. *to be broken, thrown down.*

נָתַץ — Kal pret. 3 pers. sing. masc. for נְתַץ (§ 8. r. 7) נתץ

נִתֵּץ — Piel pret. 3 pers. sing. masc. (§ 10. rem. 1) נתץ

נֻתַּץ — Pual pret. 3 pers. sing. masc. . . נתץ

נָתְצוּ / נָתְצוּ — } Kal pret. 3 pers. pl. (§ 8. rem. 7) נתץ

נִתְּצוּ — וְ Niph. pret. 3 pers. pl. נתץ

נִתַּצְתֶּם — וְ Piel pret. 2 pers. pl. masc. . . נתץ

נָתַק — I. *to pluck, draw off* or *away.*—II. part. נָתוּק *castrated,* Le. 22. 24. Niph. נִתַּק.—I. *to be torn, broken,* as a string; metaph. Job 17. 11.—II. *to be plucked* or *drawn away, withdrawn.* Pi. נִתֵּק.—I. *to pull up, uproot,* Eze. 17. 9.—II. *to tear* or *break,* as cords, the breasts, a yoke. Hiph. *to draw away* or *out.* Hoph. pass. Ju. 20. 31. Hence

נֶתֶק — masc. *a kind of leprosy, a scall* (prop. *a plucking off of hair*) . . . . נתק

נִתַּק — Niph. pret. 3 pers. sing. masc. . . נתק

נָתְקוּ / נִתְּקוּ — } id. pret. or (Je. 5. 5) Piel 3 pers. pl. (comp. § 8. rem. 7) . . נתק

נְתַקְנוּהוּ — וְ Kal pret. 1 pers. pl., with dag. euph. & suff. 3 pers. sing. masc.; וְ for וַ, conv. . נתק

נִתַּקְתִּי — Piel pret. 1 pers. sing. . . . נתק

נָתַר — in Kal only fut. יִתַּר *to tremble,* of the heart, *to palpitate,* Job 37. 1.—Pi. *to spring, leap,* of the locust, Le. 11. 21. Hiph. הִתִּיר.—I. *to cause to tremble.*—II. *to let loose, loosen.*

נְתַר — Chald. Aph. *to shake off,* Da. 4. 11.

[נֶתֶר] — masc.—I. *nitre,* Pr. 25. 20.—II. *soap* made of *nitre* and oil, Je. 2. 22.

נָתָר — noun masc. sing. for נֶתֶר (§ 35. rem. 2) נתר

נִתְרָאֶה — Hithpa. fut. 1 pers. pl. . . . ראה

נָתַשׁ — וְ fut. יִתֹּשׁ, inf. נְתֹשׁ.—I. *to tear, pluck up,* only metaph. of a people *to be expelled* from a land, comp. Je. 24. 6.—II. *to tear down, destroy.* Niph. I. i. q. Kal No. 1.—II. *to fail,* spoken of water, Je. 18. 14. Hoph. *to be torn, plucked up,* Eze. 19. 12.

נֹתֵשׁ — Kal part. act. sing. masc. dec. 7b . נתש

נָתְשִׁי — id. inf. with suff. 1 pers. sing. . . נתש

נֹתְשָׁם — id. part. act. sing. masc. (נֹתֵשׁ), suff. 3 pers. pl. masc. dec. 7 b . . . נתש

נָתַשְׁתָּ — id. pret. 2 pers. sing. masc. . . נתש

וְנָתַשְׁתִּי — וְ id. pret. 1 pers. sing.; acc. shifted by conv. וְ (§ 8. rem. 7) . . . נתש

נְתַשְׁתִּים — וְ id. id., suff. 3 pers. pl. masc.; וְ for וַ, conv. נתש

נָתַתָּ — וְ Kal pret. 2 pers. s. m. [for נָתַנְתָּ § 17. r. 9] נתן

נָתַתְּ — id. pret. 2 pers. sing. fem. . . נתן

נָתַתָּה — וְ id. pret. 2 pers. sing. masc. (§ 8. rem. 5) נתן

נָתַתִּי / נָתַתִּי — } id. pret. 1 pers. sing. (§ 17. rem. 9, & § 8. rem. 7) } נתן

נָתַתִּי — id. pret. 2 pers. sing. fem., Kh. נָתַתִּי, K. נָתַתְּ (§ 8. rem. 5) . . . נתן

נְתַתִּיהָ — וְ id. pret. 1 pers. sing., suff. 3 pers. sing. fem.; וְ for וַ, conv. . . . נתן

נְתַתִּיהוּ / נְתַתִּיו — } וְ id. id., or (Eze. 16. 19) pret. 2 pers. fem. sing. suff. 3 pers. sing. masc.; וְ id. } נתן

נְתַתִּיךָ — וְ id. id., suff. 2 pers. sing. masc.; וְ id. נתן

נְתַתִּיךְ — וְ id. id., suff. 2 pers. sing. fem.; וְ id. . נתן

נְתַתִּים — וְ id. id., suff. 3 pers. pl. masc.; וְ id. . נתן

נִתַּתֶּם — וְ Niph. pret. 2 p. pl. m. [for נִתַּנְתֶּם § 17. r. 9] נתן

נְתַתֶּם — וְ Kal pret. 2 pers. sing. masc., suff. 3 pers. pl. m. [for נְתַנְתֶּם § 17. r. 9]; וְ for וַ, conv. נתן

נְתַתֶּם — וְ id. pret. 2 pers. pl. masc.; וְ id. נתן

נְתַתַּנִי — id. pret. 2 pers. sing. masc., suff. 1 pers. sing. [for תַּנִי § 2. rem. 1] . . נתן

ס

ס

סְאָה — וְ fem. pl. סְאִים, du. סָאתַיִם (for סָאתַיִם) *a seah,* a measure of capacity for dry things, containing the third part of an ephah. Arab. סאא *to extend, expand.*

סֵאסֵאָה — fem. contr. from סְאָה סְאָה *measure* (and) *measure,* Is. 27. 8.

סָאוֹן — noun masc. sing. . . . . סאן

סְאִים — noun fem. with pl. masc. term. fr. סְאָה (q v.) סאה

Je. 51. 22.   2 Ch. 33. 3.   Eze. 16. 39.   Is. 5. 27.   Pr. 25. 20.   Je. 12. 15.   2 Ch. 7. 20.   Eze. 16. 18, 36.   2 Ki. 7. 1, 18.
2 Ki. 7. 12.   Ju. 6. 28.   De. 12. 3.   Ju. 20. 32.   1 Ki. 14. 15.   Je. 12. 14.   Eze. 16. 33.   Le. 26. 25.   2 Ki. 7. 18.
Je. 50. 14.   Je. 39. 8.   Le. 13. 30.   Je. 3. 20.   Je. 45. 4.   Ps. 9. 7.   Eze. 17. 22.   Ju. 4. 7.   Is. 9. 4.

סֹאֵן part. only Is. 9. 4, *one shod with a warrior's shoe* or *greaves*. i. e. a warrior, soldier. Syr. סאן *to shoe.*

סְאוֹן masc. *a warrior's shoe* or *greaves*, an armour for the legs, ibid.

סְאתַים‎ ‎*a* [ו] noun fem. du. by Syriasm [for סְאָתַיִם] from סְאָה (q. v.) . . . . . סאה

סֹב Kal imp. sing. m.; or (De. 2. 3) inf. constr. סבב

[סָבָא] *to drink to excess,* Is. 56. 13; part. סֹבֵא *a drunkard;* pass. סָבוּא *drunken,* Na. 1. 10, *for as thorns folden together* וּכְסָבְאָם סְבוּאִים, *the drunken, like their wine, shall be consumed.*

סֹבֵא masc. *drunkard,* Eze. 23. 42 Keri.

סֹבֶא masc. dec. 6 c.—I. *wine,* or perhaps any other *strong, inebriating drink.*—II. *carouse, drinking bout,* Ho. 4. 18.

סְבָא‎ ‎*b* pr. name—I. of a son of Cush, Ge. 10. 7. —II. of a people descended from him; pl. סְבָאִים *Sabeans.*

סֹבֵא‎ ‎*c* [ו] Kal part. act. sing. masc. dec. 7 b . סבא

סְבָאִים‎ ‎*d* gent. noun pl. from סְבָא q. v. . . סבא

סְבָאֶךָ‎ ‎*e* noun m. s., suff. 2 pers. s. f. fr. [סֹבֶא] d. 6 c סבא

סְבָאָם‎ ‎*f* id., suff. 3 pers. pl. masc. . . . סבא

[סָבַב] pl. סַבּוֹתֶם, סַבּוּ, סְבִיבֹת; inf. סֹב, סְבֹב (§ 18. r. 13); imp. סֹב (§18.r.3); fut. יָסֹב, יִסֹּב (r. 14).—I. *to turn oneself, to turn,* with עַל, אֶל, לְ *to any one,* and מִן, מֵעַל, מִפְּנֵי *from any one;* with אֶל־אַחֲרֵי *after any one, to follow him;* absol. *to return;* also absol. *to turn to, set about doing any thing,* as 1 Sa. 22. 17, 18; of things, *to be turned, brought to, conferred upon.* —II. *to turn, go about* in a place, *to go over, go round* a place, with בְּ, אֵת.—III. *to surround, encompass,* with acc., also עַל, אֶל; absol. *to surround, sit round* a table, 1 Sa. 16. 11.—IV. *to be turned, changed,* with כְּ Zec. 14. 10.—V. *to be the cause* or *occasion* of anything, with בְּ 1 Sa. 22. 22. Niph. נָסַב, נָסֵב (§18.r.7), fut. יִסַּב.—I. *to turn oneself, to turn,* hence *to be turned, transferred,* with לְ Je. 6. 12.—II. *to surround,* with עַל. Pi. סִבֵּב *to change,* 2 Sa. 14. 20. Po. סוֹבֵב—I. *to go about,* with בְּ *in* a place, with acc. *over* a place, with עַל *to go round* a place.—II. *to surround, encompass.* Hiph. הֵסֵב, fut. יָסֵב, יָסֹב (§ 18. r. 3).—I. *to cause to turn;* trans. *to turn;* hence *to transfer.*—II. *to cause to go about, to lead about, around;* hence, *to carry*

round a wall, 2 Ch. 14. 6.—III. *to surround, encompass.*—IV. *to change, alter.*—V. intrans. 2 Sa 5. 23. Hoph. הוּסַב, fut. יוּסַב (§ 18. r. 3).—I. *to turn,* intrans.; also *to roll.*—II. *to be surrounded.* —III. *to be changed,* Nu. 32. 38.

סִבָּה fem. *a turn of events, a change,* 1 Ki. 12. 15.

סָבִיב masc. dec. 3 a.—I. *a circuit;* מִסָּבִיב, *from around, around, round about;* סָבִיב סָבִיב, סָבִיב; לְ סָבִיב adv. and prep. *round about, around.*—II. pl. סְבִיבִים *round about,* of persons, *neighbours·* of place, *places round about* or *circumjacent, environs.* With suff. as a prep. סְבִיבָיו, סְבִיבֶיךָ *round about thee, him,* Je. 46. 14; Ps. 50. 3.—III. pl. סְבִיבוֹת (a) *circuits, orbits,* Ec. 1. 6; (b) i. q. סְבִיבִים *places round about, environs;* prep. *round about, around.*

מֵסַב masc. with suff. מְסִבּוֹ dec. 8 d.—I. *couches ranged round* for reclining on, Ca. 1. 12.—II. *environs,* 2 Ki. 23. 5.—III. adv. *round about,* 1 Ki. 6. 29.

מְסִבָּה fem. dec. 10, *revolution,* Job 37. 12.

מוּסַב masc. *circuit* of a house, Eze. 41. 7.

נְסִבָּה f. *a turn of events, a change,* 2 Ch. 10. 15.

סַבֵּב‎ ‎*g* Piel inf. constr. . . . . . סבב

סֹבֵב‎ ‎*h* Kal part. act. sing. masc. dec. 7 b . . סבב

סְבָבֻהוּ id. pret. 3 pers. pl., suff. 3 pers. sing. masc. סבב

סְבָבוּ‎ ‎*i* [ו] id. pret. 3 pers. pl. . . . . סבב

סְבָבוּם‎ ‎*m* id. id., suff. 3 pers. pl. masc. . . סבב

סְבָבוּנִי‎ ‎*n* id. id., suff., Kh. 'ני 1 pers. s., K. 'נו 1 p. pl. סבב

סְבָבוּנִי id. id., suff. 1 pers. sing. . . . . סבב

סֹבְבִים‎ ‎*o* id. part. act. masc., pl. of סֹבֵב dec. 7 b . סבב

סְבָבֻנִי‎ ‎*p* id. pret. 3 pers. pl., suff. 1 pers. sing. . סבב

סִבָּה‎ ‎*q* noun fem. sing. . . . . . . סבב

סֹבּוּ‎ ‎*r* [ו] Kal imp. pl. masc. . . . . . סבב

סְבוּאִים Kal part. pass. masc. pl. [of סָבוּא] dec. 3 a סבא

סַבּוּנִי Kal pret. 3 pers. pl., suff. 1 pers. sing. . סבב

סַבּוֹתִי‎ ‎*s* [ו] id. pret. 1 pers. sing. . . . . סבב

סֹבִּי‎ ‎*t* id. imp. sing. fem. . . . . . . סבב

סָבִיב‎ ‎*u* [ו] (prop., noun m. s. d. 3 a) as an adv. & prep. סבב

סְבִיב‎ ‎*v* id. constr. st. (subst.); ו bef. (:) . . סבב

סְבִיבוֹת‎ ‎*w* id. pl. fem. as a prep.; ו id. . . . סבב

סְבִיבוֹתַי id. pl. fem., suff. 1 pers. sing., prep. . . סבב

סְבִיבוֹתֶיהָ‎ ‎*x* id. pl. f., suff. 3 p. s. f., prep.; ו bef. (:) סבב

סְבִיבוֹתֵיהֶם id. pl. fem., suff. 3 pers. pl. masc., subst. (Ezr. 1. 6) and prep. . . . . . . סבב

סְבִיבוֹתָיו id. pl. fem., suff. 3 pers. sing. masc., subst. (Je. 50. 32) and prep. . . . . . . סבב

a 2 Ki. 7. 1, 16.   *b* Is. 1. 22.   *c* 2 Sa. 14. 20.   *d* Jos. 6. 15.   *e* Ps. 17. 11.   *f* Ho. 12. 1.   *g* Jos. 6. 7.   *h* Ec. 2. 20; 7. 25.   *i* Am. 3. 11.
Pr. 23. 21.   Ho. 4. 18.   Ec. 1. 6.   Ec. 12. 5.   1 Ki. 7. 24.   1 Ki. 12. 15.   Na. 1. 10.   Is. 23. 16.   Eze. 5. 5.
De. 21. 20.   Ese. 42. 19.   1 Ki. 5. 17.   Ho. 7. 2.

סְבִיבוֹתֶיךָ id. pl. fem., suff. 3 pers. sing. fem., *prep.*   סבב

סְבִיבוֹתֶיךָ id. pl. fem., suff. 2 pers. sing. masc., *prep.*   סבב

סְבִיבוֹתֵיכֶם id. pl. fem., suff. 2 pers. pl. masc., *prep.*   סבב

סְבִיבֶיהָ id. pl. masc., suff. 3 pers. sing. fem., *subst.*   סבב

סְבִיבָיו id. pl. masc., suff. 3 pers. sing. masc., *subst. and prep.*; ו bef. (:) .   סבב

סְבִיבֶיךָ id. pl. masc., suff. 2 pers. sing. masc., *subst.*   סבב

סְבִיבֶיךָ id. pl. masc., suff. 2 pers. sing. masc., *subst.*   סבב

סְבִיבֹת id. pl. fem., *prep.*   סבב

סְבִיבֹתוֹ id. pl. f., suff. 3 pers. s. m. (§ 4. r. 1), *prep.*   סבב

סְבִיבֹתַי id. pl. fem., suff. 1 pers. sing. for תַי', *prep.*   סבב

סְבִיבֹתֶיהָ id. pl. fem., suff. 3 pers. sing. fem., *prep.*   סבב

סְבִיבֹתֵיהֶם id. pl. fem., suff. 3 pers. pl. masc., *prep.*   סבב

סְבִיבֹתָיו id. pl. fem., suff. 3 pers. sing. masc., *subst.* (Ecc. 1. 6) and *prep.*   סבב

סְבִיבֹתֵיכֶם id. pl. fem., suff. 2 pers. pl. masc., *prep.*   סבב

סְבִיבֹתֵינוּ id. pl. fem., suff. 1 pers. pl., *subst.* (Nu. 22. 4; Da. 9. 16) and *prep.*   סבב

סְבִיבֹתָם id. pl. f., suff. 3 p. pl. (§ 4. r. 2) *subst.* and *prep.*   סבב

סָבַךְ *to interweave, entwine, fold together,* Na. 1. 10. Pu. pass. Job 8. 17.

סְבַךְ masc. *thicket,* Ge. 22. 13.

סְבָךְ masc. id. Ps. 74. 5.

סֹבֶךְ or סֹבֶךְ masc. dec. 6 b (§ 35. rem. 10, but comp. rem. 9, note) id. Is. 9. 17 ; 10. 34.

סֹבֶךְ masc. dec. 6 c, id. Je. 4. 7.

סִבְכַי (for סָבָךְ יָהּ *perplexity, confusion from the Lord*) pr. name of one of David's chiefs, for which מְבֻנַּי 2 Sa. 23. 27, comp. 2 Sa. 21. 18.

סַבְּכָא Chald. fem. the name of a certain *stringed instrument,* Da. 3. 5, elsewhere שַׂבְּכָא.

סַבְכַי pr. name masc.   סבב

סַבְכֵי noun m. pl. constr. [for סִבְכֵי without Meth. from סְבָךְ dec. 6 b, or סֹבֶךְ § 35. rem. 10]   סבב

סְבֻכִים Kal part. pass. masc. pl. [of סָבוּךְ] dec. 3 a   סבב

[סָבַל] fut. יִסְבֹּל *to bear, carry,* as a heavy load ; metaph. of sin. Pu. part. *laden,* i. e. big with young, Ps. 144. 14. Hithp. הִסְתַּבֵּל *to become a burden,* Ecc. 12. 5.

סְבַל Chald. in the Targums, *to lift up, erect ;* in the Bible only Poal part. *erected, built,* Ezr. 6. 3; Prof. Lee, *brought.*

סֵבֶל masc. *a burden.*

סֻבָּל masc. with suff. סֻבְּלוֹ (with dag. forte euphonic) *burden,* Is. 9. 3; 10. 27; 14. 25.

סַבָּל masc. dec. 1 b. *porter.*

סִבְלוֹת fem. pl. c. (from סִבְלָה or סְבָלָה) *burdens, labours, tasks.*

סֵבֶל noun masc. sing. (pl. סַבָּלִים') dec. 1 b   סבל

סִבְלִי noun masc. sing.   סבל

סֻבְּלוֹ (וֹ) noun masc. sing., suff. 3 pers. sing. masc., dag. euph. [from סֵבֶל § 35. rem. 17]   סבל

סִבְלוֹת noun fem. pl. constr. [from סִבְלָה or סְבָלָה]   סבל

סְבָלָם Kal pret. 3 pers. sing. m., suff. 3 pers. pl. m.   סבל

סְבָלָנוּ id. pret. 1 pers. pl. [for סְבָלֵנוּ § 8. rem. 7]   סבל

סִבְלֹת defect. for סִבְלוֹת (q. v.)   סבל

סִבֹּלֶת in the dialect of the Ephraimites for שִׁבֹּלֶת (q. v.)

סַבֵּנִי defect. for סַבּוּנִי (q. v.) .   סבב

[סְבַר] Chald. *to hope, purpose,* Da. 7. 25. Hence

סְבָרַיִם pr. name of a city in Syria, Eze. 47. 16 .   סבר

סַבְתָּא pr. name of a son of Cush and the people descended from him.

סַבְתָּה

סַבֹתִי Kal pret. 1 pers. sing. .   סבב

סַבְתְּכָא pr. name of a son of Cush, Ge. 10. 7.

סַבֹּתֶם Kal pret. 2 pers. pl. masc. .   סבב

סַג Kal pret. 3 pers. sing. masc. .   סוג

[סָגַד] fut. יִסְגֹּד *to fall down, to worship,* with לְ, used in reference to idols only. Hence

סְגִד Chald. Peal pret. 3 pers. sing. masc. (§ 47. rem. 6) fut. יִסְגֻּד, id. .   סגד

סָגְדִין Chald. id. part. act. masc. pl. of [סָגֵד] d. 2 b   סגד

סָגוּר Kal part. pass. sing. masc.   סגר

סְגוֹר noun masc. sing., comp. סֹגֵר   סגר

סֻגָּיִךְ [for סֻגָּיִךְ] the foll. with suff. 2 pers. sing. fem.   סוג

סִגִּים noun masc. pl. [as if fr. סֵג R. סגג], see 'סִין   סוג

סְגַל Root not used ; Chald. סְגַל *to gain, acquire.* Hence

סְגֻלָּה fem. dec. 10, *peculiar property* or *treasure* .   סגל

סְגֻלַּת id., constr. st. ; ו bef. (:)   סגל

[סָגָן] or [סֶגֶן] masc. dec. 6 (§ 35. rem. 10) only pl. סְגָנִים *chiefs* or *prefects* among the Babylonians and Persians, and among the Jews after the return from Babylon.

סְגַן Chald. masc. dec. 3 b, idem.

סִגְנַיָּא Chald. noun masc. pl. emph. from [סָגָן] d. 3 b   סגן

סְגָנֶיהָ (וּ) the foll. with suff. 3 pers. sing. f. ; ו bef. (:)   סגן

a Eze. 5, 12, 14, 15.   *d* Je. 49. 5.   *g* Ki. 17. 15;   *k* Na. 1. 10.   = Ex. 6. 7.   *p* Ex. 6. 6.   *t* 1 Sa. 22. 2.   *x* Da. 2. 46.   *a* Eze. 22. 18.
b Je. 21. 14.   *e* 1 Sa. 26. 5, 7.   Eze. 28. 24.   *l* 1 Ki. 11. 28.   *o* Is. 53. 4.   *r* Ju. 12. 6.   *u* Jos. 6. 3.   *y* Da. 3. 7, 12, 14.   *b* Ec. 2. 8.
Ps. 50. 3.   De. 17. 14.   *h* Is. 10. 34.   *i* Is. 14. 25.   La. 5. 7.   *s* 2 Sa. 22. 6.   *w* Ps. 53. 4.   *z* Is. 1. 25.   *c* Je. 51. 28. 32
c Je. 46. 14.

סְגָנִים [*a*] noun masc. pl. [of סֶגֶן or סָגֶן § 35. r. 10] סגן

סִגְנִין [*b*] Chald. noun masc. pl. of [סְגַן] dec. 3 b . סגן

סָגַר [*c*] [ו'] fut. יִסְגֹּר.—I. *to shut* a door.—II. *to shut up*, const. with בְּעַד, עַל; Ps. 35. 3, וּסְגֹר לִקְרַאת רֹדְפָי *and shut up* (the way) *against my persecutors.* III.—*to close* a breach, 1 Ki. 11. 27. Part. pass. סָגוּר *shut up*; hence *precious*; זָהָב סָגוּר *precious gold*, i. e. pure, unadulterated. Niph. pass. of Kal Nos. I & II; also *to shut up* oneself. Pi. סִגֵּר *to deliver up*, with בְּיַד. Pu. *to be shut up.* Hiph. I. *to shut up.*—II. *to deliver up*, with בְּיַד, לְ, אֶל.

סְגַר Chald. *to shut, close*, Da. 6. 23.

סְגֹר masc.—I. *enclosure*, Ho. 13. 8.—II. *precious, fine gold*, Job 28. 15, comp. the verb.

סוּגַר masc. *close confinement*; perhaps *a cage*, only Eze. 19. 9.

מַסְגֵּר masc. prop. part. Hiph. I. *a locksmith*; Prof. Lee, *joiner*.—II. that which *shuts up*, a *prison.*

מִסְגֶּרֶת fem. dec. 13 a (with suff. 'נַרְתּוֹ).—I. *close, confined place.*—II. *border, ridge*, as an enclosure.

סַגְרִיר masc. *rain*, Pr. 27. 15. Syr. סנרא id. Arab. שָׂגַר *to fill with water.*

סְגַר [*d*] [ו'] Ch. Peal pret. 3 pers. sing. masc.; [ו] bef. (־ַ) סגר

סִגֵּר [*e*] Piel pret. 3 pers. sing. masc. (§ 10. rem. 1) סגר

סֹגֵר [*f*] Kal part. act. sing. masc. . . סגר

סְגֹר [*g*] [ו] id. imp. sing. masc. (Is. 26. 20); Ps. 35. 3, perh. subst. defect. for סָגוֹר (q.v.); [ו] bef. (־ְ) סגר

סֻגַּר [*h*] Pual pret. 3 pers. sing. masc. . . סגר

סָגְרוּ / סָגְרוּ } Kal pret. 3 pers. pl. (§ 8. rem. 7) סגר

סִגְרוּ [*i*] [ו'] id. imp. pl. masc. . . . סגר

סֻגְּרוּ [*k*] [ו'] Pual pret. 3 pers. pl. . . . סגר

סַגְרִיר [*l*] noun masc. sing. . . . . סגר

סִגְּרַנִי [*m*] Piel pret. 3 pers. sing. masc., suff. 1 pers. sing. סגר

סָגַרְתְּ [*n*] [ו] Kal pret. 2 pers. sing. fem. . . סגר

סֹגֶרֶת [*kk*] id. part. act. sing. fem. of סֹגֵר masc. סגר

סָדַד Root not used; Arab. *to shut, stop up.*

סַד masc. *stocks*, a wooden frame or block in which the feet of prisoners were *inserted*, Job 13. 27; 33. 11. Prof. Lee, *fetters.*

סָדִין [*o*] noun masc. sing. dec. 3 a . . . סדן

סְדִינִים [*p*] id. pl., abs. st. . . . . סדן

סְדֹם pr. name, *Sodom*, one of the four cities in the vale of Siddim, which were destroyed for their wickedness in the time of Abraham

and Lot. Signification uncertain. Simonis, *dew*, or *plentiful waters*. Arab. סדא *rore aspersa fuit, maduit terra.* Gesenius, *conflagration.*

סְדֹמָה id. with parag. ה.

סָדַן Root not used; Arab. *to loosen, to let a garment hang loose.*

סָדִין masc. dec. 3 a, *a wide linen under-garment, worn next to the body.*

שָׂדַר , סָדַר Root not used; i. q. Syr. & Chald. סדר *to set in order.*

סֵדֶר masc. dec. 6 b, *order, orderly arrangement*, Job 10. 22.

שְׂדֵרָה fem. dec. 10, *order, row of soldiers, suite of chambers.*

מִסְדְּרוֹן masc. *porch, portico*, Ju. 3. 23.

סְדָרִים [*mm*] noun masc. pl. of [סֵדֶר] dec. 6 b . סדר

שָׂהַר , סָהַר Root not used; i. q. Samar. סחר *to surround, to be round.*

סַהַר masc. *roundness*, Ca. 7. 2.

סֹהַר masc. only בֵּית הַסֹּהַר *a prison*, from the round form of the building, q. d. *a round-house*, Gesenius, *house of the round-tower.*

שַׂהֲרֹנִים masc. pl. (of שַׂהֲרוֹן) *little moons*, as an ornament.

סוֹא pr. name of an Egyptian king, 2 Ki. 17. 4.

סוֹבָאִים [*q*] Kh. סוֹבָאִים, pl. of סֹבֵא q. v.; K. סָבָאִים noun masc. pl. [of סָבָא] . . . סבא

סוֹבֵב [*r*] [ו'] Kal part. act. sing. masc. dec. 7 b . סבב

סוֹבְבִים [*s*] id. pl., abs. st. . . . . . סבב

I. [סוּג] *to slide back, depart*, espec. from God; part. pass. Pr. 14. 14. סוּג לֵב *backslider in heart.* Niph. נָשׂוֹג, נָסוֹג.—I. *to be turned, driven back.*—II. *to decline, fall away*, espec. from God.

סוּג masc. *dross*, Eze. 22. 18. Kheth.

סִיג masc. pl. סִינִים, סִגִים, *that which goes off from metal, dross.*

שִׂיג masc. *retirement*, 1 Ki. 18. 27.

II. [סוּג] *to fence, hedge about*, Ca. 7. 3.

סוּג [*t*] Kal part. pass. sing. masc. . . . סוג

סוּגָה [*u*] id. part. pass. sing. fem. . . . סוג

סוֹד [*v*] [ו'] noun masc. sing. dec. 1 a [for יְסוֹד] . יסד

a Is. 41. 25.   *c* Da. 6. 23.   *g* Is. 24. 10.   *l* Je. 13. 19.   *i* 1 Sa. 24. 19.   *t* Pr. 31. 24.   *s* Eze. 23. 42.   *p* 2 Ch. 4. 3.   *r* Ca. 7. 3.
Da. 2. 48.   *d* Is. 22. 22.   *f* 2 Ki. 6. 32.   *k* Pr. 27. 15.   *2* 2 Ki. 4. 4.   *u* Ju. 14. 12, 13.   *v* Ec. 1. 6.   *q* Pr. 14. 14.   *x* Pr. 25. 9.
                                            kk Jos. 6. 1   *mm* Job 10. 22

סֹודוּ	id., suff. 3 pers. sing. masc. . . . יסר
סֹודִי	pr. name masc. . . . . . יסר
סֹודִי	noun masc. sing., suff. 1 pers. sing. from
	סוד dec. 1 a [for יְסֹוד] . . יסר

סָוָה Root not used; prob. *to cover*, cogn. צָפָה, זָוָה.

מַסְוֶה masc. *covering, veil*, Ex. 34. 33, 34, 35.

סוּת fem. *a garment*, Ge. 49. 11; but see
כָּסָה Root כְּסוּת.

סוּחַ Root not used; i. q. סָחָה *to sweep away*.

סוּחָה fem. *sweepings, filth*, Is. 5. 25.

סִיחֹון (*sweeping away*) pr. name of a king of
the Amorites.

סוּחַ pr. name masc. 1 Ch. 7. 36.

סֹוחֵר Kal part. act. sing. masc. dec. 7 b . סחר

סֹוטַי (*departing* סוט i. q. שׂוט) pr. name of a
man, Ezr. 2. 55; Ne. 7. 57.

[סוּךְ] I. *to anoint.*—II. *to anoint oneself.* **Hiph.** *to
anoint oneself*, 2 Sa. 12. 20.

אָסוּךְ masc. *oil-flask*, 2 Ki. 4. 2.

סֹוךְ	Kal inf. abs. . . . . סוך
סֹולְלָה	noun fem. sing. dec. 10 . . . סלל
סֹומֵךְ	Kal part. act. sing. dec. 7 b . . סמך

סוּמְפֹּנְיָה, סוּמְפֹנְיָה Chald. fem. Da. 3. 5, 15; but in
ver. 10 סִיפֹנְיָה συμφωνία, a musical instrument, supposed to be *a bagpipe*.

סְוֵנֵה pr. name of a city in Egypt, Eze. 29. 10; 30. 6.

סוּס וְ, י masc. dec. 1 a.—I. *a horse.*—II. *a swallow*,
Is 38. 14, & Je. 8. 7, where the Khethib has סִים.

סוּסָה fem. dec. 10, *a mare*, Ca. 1. 9. Others,
after the Sept. & Vulg. in a collective sense, *horses*.

סוּסִי (*horseman*) pr. name masc. Nu. 13. 11.

סוּם	Kh. סוּם q. v.; K. סִים noun masc. sing. סוס
סוּסָה	pr. name in compos. חֲצַר סוּסָה see חצר סוס
סוּסִי	pr. name masc. . . . . סוס
סוּסַי	noun masc. pl. constr. from סוּם dec. 1 a סוס
סוּסֵיהֶם	id. pl., suff. 3 pers. pl. masc. . . סוס
סוּסָיו	id. pl., suff. 3 pers. sing. masc. . . סוס
סוּסֶיךָ	id. pl., suff. 2 pers. sing. masc. . . סוס
סוּסֵיכֶם	id. pl., suff. 2 pers. pl. masc. . . סוס
סוּסִים	id. pl., abs. st. . . . . סוס

[סוּף] *to come to an end, to cease, perish.* **Hiph.** *to make
an end of, destroy.*

סוּף Chald. id. of prophecy, *to be accomplished*,

fulfilled, Da. 4. 30. **Aph.** *to make an end of, destroy*,
Da. 2. 44.

סֹוף masc. d. 1 a.—I. *end, extremity*, 2 Ch. 20. 16.
—II. *the rear* of an army.—III. *end, termination.*
—IV. *end, completion*, Ec. 3. 11.

סֹוף Chald. m. d. 1 a, i. q. Heb. Nos. I, III & IV.

סֹופָה fem. dec. 10, *whirlwind, hurricane.*

סוּף וְ, י masc.—I. *sea-weed, sedge*, Jon. 2. 6; יַם־סוּף *the
sea of weed, Red Sea.*—II. *reed, rush, bulrush.*—III.
pr. name of a place, De. 1. 1.

סוּף	noun masc. sing. dec. 1 a . . . סוף
סוּפָא	Chald. noun masc. sing., emph. of סוּף dec. 1 a סוף
סוּפָה	noun fem. sing. dec. 10 . . . סוף
סֹופֵר	וְ, י Kal part. act. sing. masc. dec. 7 b . ספר
סֹופְרִים	id. pl., abs. st. . . . . ספר
סוּפָתָה	וְ noun fem. sing. (סוּפָה q. v.) with parag. ה סוף

סוּר fut. יָסוּר, ap. וַיָּסַר (§ 21. rem. 9).—I. *to turn aside
or away, to depart*, e. g. from a way; const. with
בְּ, מֵאַחֲרֵי, מֵעַל; espec. *to turn away* from
God and His laws, *to apostatize, degenerate.* Part.
Pr. 11. 22, סָרַת טַעַם *deviating as to* (i. e. *lacking*
understanding.—II. *to be removed*; also *to pass
away.*—III. *to turn aside* to any person or thing,
to approach, draw near, with עַל; with אֶל *to turn
in* to any one, *to lodge with him.* **Hiph.** הֵסִיר,
fut. יָסִיר ap. וַיָּסַר (§ 21. rem. 19).—I. *to remove,
put away.*—II. *to take off*, e. g. a ring from the
finger, the head from any one.—III. *to lay, set, put
aside*; hence, *to omit, neglect.*—IV. *to turn, lead
away* any one, with מֵאַחֲרֵי De. 7. 4.—V. *to let
any thing be brought*, with אֵלָיו *to oneself*, 2 Sa. 6. 10.
Hoph. *to be removed.* **Pil.** *to turn aside, cause to
deflect*, spoken of a way, La. 3. 11.

סוּר masc. dec. 1 a, properly part. pass.—I. adj
removed, driven out.—II. Je. 2. 21, סוּרֵי הַגֶּפֶן *degenerate* (shoots) *of the vine.*—III. pr. name of
one of the gates of the temple, 2 Ki. 11. 6; called
יְסֹוד in 2 Ch. 23. 5.

סָרָה fem.—I. *a turning, departing* from God
apostasy.—II. *falsehood*, De. 19. 16.

סֵרָה (*recession*) pr. name of a cistern, 2 Sa. 3. 26.

יָסֹור masc. *one departing*, Je. 17. 13. Kheth.

סוּר	pr. name of a gate . . . . סור
סוּרִי	וְ Kal inf. constr. . . . . סור
סֻר	וְ id. inf. constr., or imp. sing. masc. . סור
סוּרָה	id. imp. with parag. ה (§ 8. rem. 11) סור

a Job 19. 19.   c Da. 10. 3.   e Ps. 37. 17.   g Je. 8. 7.   i Is. 31. 3.   Is. 19. 6.   m 2 Ch. 34. 13.   o Ho. 8. 7.   p Da. 9. 5, 1.

b Pr. 31. 14.   d Da. 11. 15.   f Da. 3. 5, 15.   h 2 Ki. 2. 11.   k Am. 4. 10.   l 1 Ch. 22. 23.   n Ru. 4. 1.   Je. 4. 18.

סוּרָה ‹ Kal part. pass. or adj. fem. from סוּר masc.   סור

סוּרוּ id. imp. pl. masc.   .   .   .   .   כור

סוּרֵי adj. pl. masc. from [סוּר] dec. 1 a   .   סור

סוֹרֵר Pilel pret. 3 pers. sing. masc.   .   .   סור

סוֹרֵד Kal part. act. sing. masc. dec. 7 b   .   סרד

סוֹרְרִים id. pl., abs. st.   .   .   .   .   סרד

סוֹרֶרֶת id. part. sing. fem.   .   .   .   סרד

סוּת Hiph. הֵסִית, הֵסִית; fut. יָסִית (§ 21. r. 24) to urge, excite, induce, persuade.

סוּתֹה noun fem. sing., suff. 3 pers. sing. masc. [from סוּת R. סָוָה, or by aphaeresis for כְּסוּת R. כסה]

[סָחַב] to draw or drag along the ground. סְחָבָה fem. only pl. הַסְּחָבוֹת בְּלוֹיֵ old torn clothes, rags.

סָחַבְנוּ ‹ Kal pret. 1 pers. sing.   .   .   סחב

סָחָה Pi. to sweep away, Eze. 26. 4. סְחִי masc. sweepings, offscouring, La. 3. 45.

סָחוֹב Kal inf. abs.   .   .   .   .   סחב

סָחוּ noun masc. sing.   .   .   .   סחה

סָחִישׁ 2 Ki. 19. 29, & שָׁחִיס Is. 37. 30, that which grows of itself the third year after sowing. Etymology uncertain .   .   .   סחש

סָחַבְנוּ ‹ Kal pret. 1 pers. pl.   .   .   סחב

סִחִיתִי ‹ Piel pret. 1 pers. sing. (§ 14. rem. 1); acc. shifted by conv. ו (comp. § 8. rem. 7)   סחה

סֹחֵף Kal part. sweeping, driving, as a violent shower of rain, Pr. 28. 3.   Niph. נִסְחַף to be swept away, destroyed, Je. 46. 15.

סָחַר I. to go, travel about, Je. 14. 18.—II. with אֶת to go round or over, traverse a country for the sake of traffic, Ge. 34. 21; 42. 34; סֹחֵר a travelling merchant or trader.   Pilp. (§ 6. No. 3) to go about in quick motion, of the heart, to palpitate, Ps. 38. 11.
סַחַר masc. dec. 4 a.—I. seat of commerce, mart, Is. 23. 3.—II. wealth, profit acquired by commerce.
סַחַר masc. (with suff. סַחְרָה § 35. rem. 5) profit, gain, either as acquired by trading, or in general.
סְחֹרָה fem. dec. 10, traffic, trade.
סֹחֵרָה fem. shield, Ps. 91. 4.   Others, a tower; Syr. סחרתא id.
סֹחֶרֶת fem. Est. 1. 6, a kind of valuable stone.

According to some, black marble; according to others, tortoise-shell.

מִסְחָר masc. dec. 2 a, traffic, trade, 1 Ki. 10. 15.

סָחַר ‹ noun masc. sing., constr. of [סַחַר] dec. 4 a   סחר

סֹחֵר • Kal part. act. sing. masc. dec. 7 b   סחר

סַחְרָה noun masc. sing., suff. 3 pers. sing. fem. [for סַחֲרָה § 35. rem. 5] from סַחַר dec. 6 d   סחר

סְחֹרָה ‹ noun fem. sing.   .   .   .   סחר

סְחָרוּ ‹ Kal pret. 3 pers. pl.   .   .   סחר

סְחָרוּהָ ‹ id. with suff. 3 pers. sing. fem.; ו for וּ, conv.   סחר

סְחַרְחַר Pilp. pret. 3 pers. sing. masc. (§ 6. No. 3)   סחר

סֹחֲרֵי ‹ו Kal part. act. pl. constr. m. from סֹחֵר d. 7 b   סחר

סֹחֲרֶיהָ id. pl., suff. 3 pers. sing. fem.   סחר

סֹחֲרַיִךְ   } id. pl., suff. 2 pers. sing. fem.   סחר
סֹחֲרָיִךְ

סֹחֲרִים id. pl., abs. st.   .   .   .   סחר

סֹחֶרֶת ‹ noun fem. sing. [for סַחֶרֶת comp. § 35. r. 2]   סחר

סֹחֶרֶת • noun fem. sing., constr. of [סֹחֵרָה] dec. 10   סחר

סֹחַרְתֵּךְ ‹ Kal part. act. sing. fem. [סֹחֶרֶת], suff. 2 pers. sing. fem. dec. 13 a, from סֹחֵר masc.   סחר

סָטַי pr. name masc. for סוֹטַי q. v.

סַטִּים noun masc. pl. for שִׁטִּים (q. v.)   .   שוט

סִינִים noun masc. pl. of סִין dec. 1 a   סין

סִיוָן (prob. bright, splendid סוֹי i. q. זיו) name of the third month of the Jewish year, Est. 8. 9.

סִיחוֹן   } pr. name masc.   .   .   סוח
סִיחֹן

סִין (mire, סֵין Chald., סִינָא Syr. id.) pr. name Sin.—I. a city in the north-eastern extremity of Egypt, according to Jerome, Pelusium. Eze. 30. 15, 16.—II. a desert westward of Mount Sinai.

סִינַי   (miry; others, thorn-bush, i. q. סְנֶה) pr. name, Sinai, a mountain in Arabia De-
סִינָי   serta, where the Mosaic law was given.

[סִינִי] pr. name, Sinite, a people of Canaan, Ge. 10. 17; 1 Ch. 1. 15.

סִינִים pr. name of a people, Is. 49. 12. According to some, the inhabitants of Pelusium, see סִין; according to Gesenius, the Chinese.

סִיסְרָא ‹ו (battle-array; Syr. סיסרתא id.) pr. name, Sisera.—I. a general under Jabin, king of the Canaanites, comp. Ju. 4. 2.—II. of a Jew, Ezr. 25. 53; Ne. 7. 55.

סִיעָא סִיעֲהָא pr. name masc. Ne. 7. 47; Ezr. 2. 44.

סִיפְנִיא ‹ו Kh. for סֻמְפֹּנְיָא q. v.

Is. 49. 21.   ᵃ Ge. 49. 11.   ⁱ 2 Ki. 19. 29.   ᵐ Pr. 28. 3.   ᵖ Ps. 91. 4.   ᵗ Ps. 38. 11.   ˣ Eze. 27. 21.   ᵃ Eze. 27. 15.   ᵉ Ps. 101. 2.
Je. 2. 21.   ᵇ 2 Sa. 17. 13.   ᵏ 2 Ki. 17. 13.   ⁿ Is. 23. 3; 45. 14.   ᵠ Je. 14. 18.   ᵘ Eze. 30. 15.   ʸ Is. 47. 15.   ᵇ Eze. 27. 12,   ᵈ Da. 3. 10.
ᶜ La. 3. 1.   ʰ Je. 22. 19.   ˡ Eze. 26. 4.   ° Is. 23. 2.   ʳ Ge. 34. 10.   ⁱ Is. 23. 3.   ᶻ Est. 1. 6.   16, 18.
ᵈ Ne. 9. 29.   ⁱ La. 3. 45.

סִיר com. dec. 1 a (pl. ־ים, ־ות).—I. *a pot, vessel.*—II. *thorn.*—III. *hook, fishhook.* Gesenius compares the Root סִיר with the Arab. שאר *to spring up, boil up; to rage* as a fever.

סִירִים   סיר   id. pl. masc., abs. st.

סִירֹתָיו   סיר   id. pl. fem., suff. 3 pers. sing. masc.

סִירֹתֵיכֶם   סיר   id. pl. fem., suff. 2 pers. pl. masc.

סֻכָּה   סכך   noun fem. sing. dec. 10

סֻכּוֹ   סכך   noun m. s., suff. 3 pers. s. m. fr. [סֹךְ] d. 8 c

סְכֻּת   סכך   noun fem. sing.

סֻכּוֹת   סכך   noun fem., pl. of סֻכָּה dec. 10, also pr. name, and in compos. סֻכּוֹת בְּנוֹת

סֻכּוֹתָה   סכך   full form for סֻכֹּת (q. v.)

סֻכִּיִּים   סכך   pr. name of a people

[שׂכך, **סָכַךְ**] I. *to cover,* with acc., עַל of the object covered; intrans. *to cover, conceal oneself,* La. 3. 43, 44.—II. *to protect,* with לְ; part. סוֹכֵךְ *that which protects, defends, a defence.*—III. *to place as a covering,* with עַל Ex. 33. 22; 40. 3.—IV. Ps. 139. 13, *to interweave, weave.* Prof. Lee, *to compact, put together.* Hiph. הֵסֵךְ.—I. *to cover, protect,* with עַל.—II. *to hedge in* (comp. Kal No. IV), or *to shut in, confine,* with בְּעַד Job 3. 23; 38. 8. Hoph. pass. see נָסַךְ. Pilp. סִכְסֵךְ (§ 6. No. 3) *to cover with arms,* Is. 9. 10; 19. 2. Others, *to mingle together,* comp. Kal No. IV.

סְכָכָה (*enclosure*) pr. name of a town in Judah, Jos. 15. 61.

סָךְ masc. *crowd, multitude,* Ps. 42. 5.

שֹׂךְ, סֹךְ masc. dec. 8 c.—I. *booth, hut.*—II. *thicket,* as the *covert* of wild beasts.

סֻכָּה fem. dec. 10.—I. *booth, tent, tabernacle,* made of boughs and branches.—II. *thicket,* Job 38. 40.—III. *a dwelling.*

סֻכּוֹת (*booths*) pr. name—I. of a station of the Israelites in the desert.—II. of a town in the tribe of Gad.—III. סֻכּוֹת בְּנוֹת 2 Ki. 17. 30, *booths of the daughters,* supposed to be *booths* made by the Babylonian colonists for the idolatrous worship of their *daughters.*

סַכּוּת fem. *shrine,* Am. 5. 26.

סֻכִּיִּים (*tent-dwellers*) pr. name of a people, 2 Ch. 12. 3.

מָסָךְ masc. constr. מְסַךְ, *a covering,* used espec. of the *curtain* in the tabernacle.

מְסֻכָּה fem. dec. 10 *a covering,* Eze. 28. 13.

מוּסָךְ masc. *a covering, porch,* 2 Ki. 16. 18, Kh. מֵיסָךְ.

סְכָכָה   סכך   pr. name of a place; ‖ bef.

סֹכְכִים   סכך   Kal part. act. masc. pl. of סֹכֵךְ

וַיְסֹכְכִים   סכך   dec. 7 b

סָכַל Kal not used; Syr. *to be foolish.* Niph. *to act foolishly, wickedly.* Pi. *to render foolish, to frustrate.* Hiph. *to act foolishly.*

סָכָל masc. dec. 4 a, *fool, foolish.*

סֶכֶל masc. *folly,* Ecc. 10. 6.

שִׂכְלוּת, סִכְלוּת fem. *folly.*

סֵכֶל   סכל   noun masc. sing. dec. 4 a

סַכֶּל־   סכל   Piel imp. sing. masc. [for סַכֵּל § 10. rem. 4]

סִכְלוּת   סכל   noun fem. sing.

סְכָלִים   סכל   noun masc. pl. of סֵכֶל dec. 4 a

[**סָכַן**] fut. יִסְכֹּן. Arab. שׁכן *to sit still; to dwell* with any one. Hence in the Heb.—I. Job 34. 9, *to be prosperous* (Lee); but see No. III.—II. part. סֹכֵן *associate, companion,* e. g. of a king, Is. 22. 15; fem. סֹכֶנֶת *a female companion, attendant,* 1 Ki. 1. 2, 4. Others, *steward,* fem. *nurse,* from the following signification.—III. *to be beneficial, profitable* to any one, with לְ, עַל, Job 22. 2; 35. 3; abs. Job 15. 3. Perh. intrans. *to profit,* Job 34. 9; but comp. No. I. Niph. Ecc. 10. 9, *to be endangered;* so in the Chald. Pu. part. מְסֻכָּן, Is. 40. 20, *brought down, reduced, poor,* from the primary idea of *sitting;* or perh. as *being benefitted by receiving the bounty* of others. Hiph. I. *to become familiar, acquainted with,* const. with עִם, Job 22. 21; with acc. *to know,* Ps. 139. 3.—II. *to be accustomed, be wont,* Nu. 22. 30.

מִסְכֵּן masc. *poor.*

מִסְכֵּנֻת fem. *poverty,* De. 8. 9.

מִסְכְּנוֹת fem. pl. (of מִסְכֶּנֶת) *stores, treasuries,* transp. for מִכְנְסוֹת from כָּנַס q. v.

סֹכֶנֶת   סכן   Kal part. act. sing. fem. of סֹכֵן

סִכְסַכְתִּי   סכך   Pilp. pret. 1 pers. sing. (§ 6. rem. 4); acc. shifted by conv. וְ (comp. § 8. rem. 7)

סָכַר Niph. *to be shut, stopped.* Pi. *to deliver up,* Is. 19. 4, comp. סָגַר.

סֹכְרִים   סכר   Kal part. act. pl. masc. for שֹׂכְרִים (q. v.)

סִכַּרְתִּי   סכר   Piel pret. 1 pers. sing.; acc. shifted by conv. וְ (comp. § 8. rem. 7)

ᵃ Ex. 27. 3.   ᶜ Jon. 4. 5.   ᵉ Am. 5. 26.   ᵍ Ex. 25. 20,   ⁱ 2 Sa. 15. 31.   ˡ Je. 4. 22.   ⁿ Is. 19. 2.   ᵒ Ezr. 4. 5.   ᵖ Is. 19 4.

ᵇ Ps. 68. 10.   ᵈ Is. 4. 6.   ᶠ Ex. 37. 9.   ʰ 1 Ch. 28. 18.   ᵏ Ec. 2. 12; 10. 1, 13.   ᵐ 1 Ki. 1. 2, 4.

סָכַת. Hiph. *to be silent,* De. 27. 9.

סָכְתְּ וְ Kal pret. 2 pers. sing. fem.; for וְ see lett. ו   סוך

סַכֹּתָ וְ Kal pret. 2 pers. sing. masc.; acc. shifted by conv. וְ (comp. § 8. rem. 7) . סכך

סֵכַת noun fem. sing., constr. of סֻכָּה dec. 10   סכך

סֻכַּת id. pl. defect. for סֻכּוֹת . . . סכך

סַכֹּתָה Kal pret. 2 pers. sing. masc. (§ 8. rem. 5) סכך

סֻכָּתָה pr. name of a place (סֻכּוֹת) with parag. ה   סכך

סֻכָּתוֹ noun fem. s., suff. 3 pers. s. m. fr. סֻכָּה d. 10 סכך

סַכֹּתִי Kal pret. 1 p. s. [for סַכֹּתִּי comp. § 8. r. 15] סוך

סַל [ן] noun masc. sing. dec. 8 d . . . סלל

סָלָא. Pu. *to be weighed,* La. 4. 2. Cogn. סָלָה, *to lift up.*

סְלוּא (*weighed*) pr. name masc. Nu. 25. 14.

סַלָּא, סַלּוּא (id.) pr. name masc. 1 Ch. 9. 7; Ne. 11. 7.

סַלּוּ (id.) pr. name masc. Ne. 12. 7, for which סַלַּי ver. 20.

סַלָּא, סַלָּא pr. names of a man and a place . סלל

סָלַד Kal not used; Arab. *to leap* (whence prob. Rabbin. *to praise*); also *to be hard;* Chald. סְלַד *to burn.* Hence Pi. only Job 6. 10, וַאֲסַלְּדָה בְחִילָה לֹא יַחְמוֹל כִּי וגו is variously rendered : (*a*) *and I will exult even under pain* which *does not spare, that,* &c. (*b*) *and I will praise under pain* Him who *spares not,* &c. (*c*) *and I will harden myself in pain,* &c. (*d*) *though I burn* or *be consumed with pain,* &c. Hence

סֶלֶד pr. name of a place . . . . סלד

[סָלָה] prop. *to lift up, raise;* hence—I. *to bear, carry away,* Ps. 119. 118. Others, as in the Syr. and Chald. *to reject, despise.* Pi. id. La. 1. 15 —II. Pu. *to be weighed,* Job 28. 16, 19. Hence

סֶלָה a musical note or term in the Psalms and Hab. and everywhere in pause for סֶלָה (comp. § 35. rem. 14) imp. with ה parag. from סָלָה *raise!* sc. the voice in response to the instrument; or, according to others who take שֶׁלָה=סֶלָה, *to rest:* hence, *rest! pause!*

סִלָּה Piel pret. 3 pers. sing. masc. . . סלה

סַלּוּ pr. name masc. . . . . סלא

סַלּוּ Kal imp. pl. masc. . . . . סלל

סַלֻּא pr. name masc. . . . . . סלא

סַלָּא pr. name masc. . . . . . סלא

סָלֻּהָ Kal imp. pl. masc. (סֹלּוּ), suff. 3 pers. sing. masc. (§ 18. rem. 4)   סלל

סְלֻלָה id. part. pass. sing. fem. [from סָלוּל] masc. סלל

סִלּוֹן noun masc. sing. . . . . . סלל

סַלּוֹנִים וְ noun masc. pl. of [סַלּוֹן] dec. 1 b . סלל

[סָלַח] fut. יִסְלָח (once אֶסְלֹחַ Je. 5. 7, Kh) *to forgive, pardon,* with ל of the person. Niph. *to be forgiven.* סַלָּח masc. *forgiving, placable,* Ps. 86. 5. סְלִיחָה fem. dec. 10, *forgiveness.*

סֶלַח וְ noun masc. sing. . . . . סלח

סְלַח Kal imp. sing. masc. . . . סלח

סְלֹחַ id. inf. constr. . . . . סלח

סְלָחָה id. imp. sing. masc. (סְלַח) with parag. ה (§ 8. rem. 11 & 12) . . . סלח

סָלַחְתָּ / וְסָלַחְתָּ } Kal pret. 2 pers. sing. masc.; acc. shifted by conv. וְ (§ 8. rem. 7) } סלח

סָלַחְתִּי / וְסָלַחְתִּי } id. pret. 1 pers. sing. (v. id.) . ולח

סַלַּי pr. name masc. for סַלָּי . . . . סלל

סַלֵּי noun masc. pl. constr. from סַל dec. 8 d . סלל

סְלִיחוֹת noun fem. pl. of סְלִיחָה dec. 10   סלח

סְלִיקוּ accord. to some copies, סָלִקוּ (q. v.) . סלק

סַלִּיתָ Kal pret. 2 pers. sing. masc. . . . סלה

סַלְכָה pr. name of a city in the kingdom of Bashan.

[סָלַל] fut. יָסֹל.—I. *to raise, cast up* into a heap or mound, Je. 50. 26; specially *to cast up, prepare, make a way.*—II. in the Arab. *to connect, knit, link together,* comp. derivv. סַל, סַלְסַלּוֹת. Pilp. (§ 6. No. 3) *to raise, exalt,* Pr. 4. 8. Hithpo. הִסְתּוֹלֵל *to oppose oneself, to resist,* with בְּ Ex. 9. 17.

סֹלְלָה fem. dec. 10, *a mound, rampart.*

סַל masc. dec. 8 d, *basket.*

סֶלָא (*elevation* or *way*) pr. name of a town near Jerusalem, 2 Ki. 12. 21.

סִלּוֹן, סַלּוֹן masc. dec. 1 b, *thorn,* Eze. 28. 24, metaph. *a wicked man,* Eze. 2. 6.

סַלֻּי (*elevated, exalted*) pr. name masc. Ne. 11. 8; see also סַלּוּ R. סָלָה.

סֻלָּם masc. *a ladder,* Ge. 28. 12.

סַלְסִלּוֹת fem. pl. *baskets,* Je. 6. 9.

מְסִלָּה fem. dec. 10.—I. *a raised way, highway*

a Ru. 3. 3.   d La. 3. 44.   g La. 1. 15.   i Je. 18. 15.   l Eze. 2. 6.   m De. 29. 19.   p La. 3. 42.   r Ge. 40. 16.   t Ezr. 4. 12.
b Ex. 40. 3.   e Da. 10. 3.   h Je. 50. 26.   k Eze. 28. 24.   n Da. 9. 19.   q Nu. 14. 20.   s Ne. 9. 17.   u Ps. 119. 118.
Am. 9. 11.   f Nu. 6. 15.

38

trop. *manner of life.*—II. *steps, stairs,* 2 Ch. 9. 11. Prof. Lee, *terraces.*

מַסְלוּל masc. *highway,* Is. 35. 8.

סְלֻלָּה defect. for סְלוּלָה (q. v.) . . . סלל

סְלֻלָּה noun sing. fem. dec. 10 . . . סלל

סֻלָּם noun masc. sing. [סֹל] with the term. ־ָם. סלל

סַלְסְלָה Pilp. imp. sing. masc. (§ 6. No. 4) . סלל

סַלְסִלּוֹת noun fem. pl. of סַלְסִלָּה סלל

סֶלַע masc. dec. 6 (with suff. סַלְעִי § 35. rem. 5).—I. *a rock.*—II. pr. name, *Sela,* i. e. Petra, in Edom.

סָלַע id. in pause (§ 35. rem. 2) . . סלע

סַלְעוֹ id. with suff. 3 pers. sing. masc. . סלע

סַלְעִי id., suff. 1 pers. sing. . . . סלע

סְלָעִים id. pl., abs. st. . . . . סלע

[סָלְעָם] masc. a species of *locust,* Le. 11. 22

סָלַף Pi.—I. *to subvert, overthrow.*—II. *to pervert.* Hence

סֶלֶף masc. *perverseness,* Pr. 11. 3 ; 15. 4 . סלף

[סְלִק] Chald. *to go* or *come up.*

סְלִקוּ Chald. Peal pret. 3 pers. pl. masc. (§ 47. r. 6) סלק

סָלְקָן Chald. id. part. act. fem. pl. [of סָלְקָה] d. 8a סלק

סִלְקַת / סְלֵקַת } Chald. Peal pret. 3 pers. sing. fem. . סלק

וְסֹלֶת com. *fine meal, flour.*

סַמְגַּר נְבוּ pr. name of a Babylonian general, Je. 39. 3.

סְמָדַר masc. *a vine blossom.*

סָמוּךְ Kal part. pass. sing. masc. dec. 3a . . סמך

סְמוּכִים id. pl., abs. st. . . . . סמך

סַמִּים noun masc. pl. of [סַם] dec. 8d . . סמם

סָמַךְ וְ fut. יִסְמֹךְ.—I. *to lean* or *lay, to impose,* as the hand, with עַל *upon* any thing.—II. intrans. *to lean, rest heavily upon,* with עַל Ps. 88. 8.—III. *to uphold, support.*—IV. *to advance, draw near,* with אֶל Eze. 24. 2. Niph.—I. *to lean upon.*—II. metaph. *to trust in.* Pi. *to stay, refresh,* Ca. 2. 5.

סְמַכְיָהוּ (whom *the Lord upholds*) pr. name masc. 1 Ch. 26. 7.

יִסְמַכְיָהוּ (*the Lord uphold* him) pr. name masc. 2 Ch. 31. 13.

שְׂמִיכָה fem. *mattress, covering,* Ju. 4. 18 (some MSS. read סְמִיכָה).

סָמְכָה Kal pret. 3 pers. sing. fem. . סמך

סָמְכוּ וְ id. pret. 3 pers. pl. . . סמך

סְמָכוּנִי Piel pl. with suff. 1 pers. sing. סמך

סֹמְכֵי Kal part. act. pl. constr. m. from סוֹמֵךְ d. 7b סמך

סָמְכֵהוּ וְ pr. name masc.; וְ bef. (1) סמך

סָמְכֵנִי id. inf., suff. 1 pers. sing. . . סמך

סְמַכְתָּ וְ id. pret. 2 pers. sing. masc.; acc. shifted by conv. וְ (§ 8. rem. 7) . . . סמך

סְמָכַתְהוּ id. pret. 3 pers. sing. fem., suff. 3 pers. sing. masc. [for כַּתְהוּ] . . . . סמך

סְמַכְתִּיו id. pret. 1 pers. sing., suff. 3 pers. sing. masc. סמך

סְמָכַתְנִי id. pret. 3 pers. sing. fem., suff. 1 pers. sing. סמך

סֶמֶל masc. *a figure, image,* with the art. הַסֶּמֶל.

סָמֶל in pause for סֶמֶל (§ 35. rem. 2) . . סמל

סָמַם Root not used; Arab. *to smell.* סַמִּים masc. pl. (of סַם) *sweet spices, aromatics.*

סָמַן Niph. *to be marked off, appointed,* Is. 28. 25.

סָמַר *to shudder,* Ps. 119. 120. Pi. *to bristle up, stand on end,* of the hair, Job 4. 15. סָמָר masc. *bristly, having bristly hairs,* Je. 51. 27. מִסְמְרִים, מַשְׂמֵר, מַסְמֵר masc. only pl. מַסְמְרוֹת *nails.*

סָמָר noun masc. sing. . . . . סמר

סָנָא Root not used; prob. i. q. סָנָה (whence סְנֶה) *to be thorny, prickly,* cogn. Syr. סָנָא, Heb. שָׂנֵא *to hate.* סְנָאָה (*thorny*) pr. name of a town in Judah. סְנֻאָה (*hated*) pr. name probably of a woman, Ne. 11. 9.

סְנָאָה pr. name of a place . . . סנא

סַנְבַלַּט וְ (*hatred in secret;* comp. סָנֵא) pr. name, *Sanballat,* a Persian governor in Samaria.

סְנֶה masc. *a bush, thorn-bush.* For the Root see סָנָא.

סֶנֶה (for סְנֶה § 35. rem. 14) pr. name of a rock, 1 Sa. 14. 4.

סַנָּה pr. name, see קִרְיַת סַנָּה . . . תרה

סָנַוֵר Root not used; Chald. *to blind, dazzle.* סַנְוֵרִים m. pl. *blindness,* Ge. 19. 11; 2 Ki. 6. 18.

סַנְחֵרִב
סַנְחֵרִיב } pr. name, *Sennacherib*, king of Assyria.

סָנָן Root not used; signification uncertain.

סַנְסַנָּה (*palm-branch*; others, *full of thorns*, comp. סְנֶה) pr. name of a town in the tribe of Judah, Jos. 15. 31.

סַנְסִנִּים masc. pl. (of סַנְסָן) *palm-branches*, Ca. 7. 8, according to the Sept. *tops*.

סַנְסַנָּה } pr. name of a place . . . סנן

סְנַפִּיר masc. *fin* of a fish, Le. 11. 9, 10; De. 14. 9, 10.

סָס masc. *a moth*, an insect that eats cloth, Is. 51. 8.

סָסִים } defect. for סוּסִים q. v. . . . סוס

סִסְמַי } pr. name masc. 1 Ch. 2. 40.

סָעַד } fut. יִסְעַד.—I. *to support, uphold.*—II. *to stay, aid.*—III. *to stay, refresh*, the heart.

סְעַד Ch. Pa. *to assist, aid*, with לְ, Ezr. 5. 2.

מִסְעָד masc. prop, *support*, 1 Ki. 10. 12.

סְעַד Kal imp. sing. masc. . . . סעד

סְעָד־ id. id. bef. Mak. [for סְעַד § 8. rem. 18] סעד

סַעֲדָה id. id. with parag. ה [for סַעֲדָה, for סֶעֱיָדָה, fr. סְעַד comp. § 8. r. 11]; the (ּ) under ס seems to result from the influence of the following guttural, and the preceding u sound, comp. לְקָחָה, וַיִּצְקִי. סעד

סַעֲדוּ } id. imp. pl. masc. . . . סעד

סְעָדֵנִי id. imp. s. m. (סְעַד), suff. 1 p. s. (§ 16. r. 11) סעד

סָעָה } *to run, rush*, Ps. 55. 9.

סֹעָה Kal part. act. sing. fem. [of סֹעֶה] . סעה

סְעוּ } Kal imp. pl. masc.; } bef. (ּ) נסע

סָעִיף noun masc. sing. dec. 1 a . . . סעף

שָׂעַף סָעַף Kal not used; prob. i. q. Arab. שׁאב *to divide*. Pi. (denom. fr. סָעִיף) *to cut off branches*, Is. 10. 33.

סָעֵף adj. masc. dec. 7 b, *divided*, i. e. as to mind, *doubting*, only Ps. 119. 113.

סְעַפָּה fem. dec. 10, *branch*, Eze. 31. 6, 8.

סַרְעַפָּה fem. id. (with ר inserted) Eze. 31. 5.

סְעִפָּה fem. *division, party*, 1 Ki. 18. 21, *how long will ye halt* עַל־שְׁתֵּי הַסְּעִפִּים *between two parties*; others, *upon two boughs*, like a bird *hopping* backwards and forwards.

סָעִיף masc. dec. 1 a.—I. *cleft, fissure.*—II. *branch, bough.*

שְׂעַפִּים masc. pl. (of שָׂעֵף) *thoughts*, prob. *distracting thoughts*, Job 4. 13; 20. 2.

שַׂרְעַפִּים m. pl. (of שַׂרְעַף) id. Ps. 94. 19; 139. 23.

סַעְפֵּי n. m. pl. constr. [for סְעִיפֵי] from סָעִיף dec. 1 a סעף

סְעִפֶּיהָ id. pl., suff. 3 pers. sing. fem. [for סְעִיפֶיהָ] סעף

סְעַפִּים noun masc. pl. of [סָעֵף] dec. 7 b . סעף

סְעַפֹּתָיו noun fem. pl., suff. 3 pers. sing. masc. from [סְעַפָּה] dec. 10 . . . סעף

סָעַר I. *to be tempestuous, tossed* by a tempest, as the sea, Jon. 1. 11, 13; metaph. *to be agitated* by adversity, Is. 54. 11.—II. *to rage*, as a foe, Hab. 3. 14. Niph. *to be agitated, disquieted*, 2 Ki. 6. 11. Pi. *to scatter*, Zec. 7. 14. Po. *to be scattered*, Hos. 13. 3.

סַעַר masc. dec. 6 d, *storm, tempest*.

סְעָרָה f. d. 11 c (constr. סַעֲרַת § 42. r. 1) id.

סַעַר } noun masc. sing. dec. 6 d . . . סער

סֹעֵר } Kal part. act. sing. masc. . . . סער

סְעָרָה } noun f. s. d. 11 c (constr. סַעֲרַת § 42. r. 1) סער

סֹעֲרָה Kal part. act. sing. fem. of סֹעֵר סער

סְעָרוֹת noun fem. pl. abs. from סְעָרָה dec. 11 c סער

סַעֲרַת id. sing., constr. st. (§ 42. rem. 1) . סער

סַף n. m. s. (suff. סִפּוֹ) d. 8 e, also pr. name סף

סְפָא Root not used; Arab. *to satiate*; Chald. *to feed*.

מִסְפּוֹא masc. *provender, fodder*.

סָפַד fut. יִסְפֹּד *to mourn, lament, bewail*, const. with לִפְנֵי, עַל, לְ. Niph. *to be lamented*.

מִסְפֵּד m. d. 7 c (comp. § 36. r. 1) *lamentation*.

סָפְדָה } Kal pret. 3 pers. sing. fem. . . . ספד

סָפְדוּ } id. pret. 3 pers. pl. . . . ספד

סִפְדוּ } id. imp. pl. masc. . . . ספד

סֹפְדִים id. part. masc. pl. [of סֹפֵד] dec. 7 b . ספד

סְפֹדְנָה id. imp. pl. fem. . . . ספד

סָפָה I. *to take off*, as the beard; *to take away*, as life; hence, *to destroy.*—II. intrans. *to be taken away, to perish.*—III. i. q. יָסַף *to add*; *to increase*. Niph. I. *to betake, withdraw oneself*, Is. 13. 15.—II. *to be taken away, destroyed, to perish*. Hiph. *to heap up, accumulate*, De. 32. 23.

סָפוּ } Kal pret. 3 pers. pl.; acc. shifted by } סוף

סָפוּ } conv. וְ (comp. § 8. rem. 7) .

ᵃ 2 Sa. 15. 1.   ᵈ 1 Ki. 13. 7.   ᵍ Ps. 55. 9.   ᵏ Is. 57. 5.   ⁿ Eze. 31. 8.   ᵖ Eze. 13. 11, 13.   ˢ Zec. 12. 12.   ᵘ Is. 32. 12.   ʸ Ps. 73 12.
ᵇ Pr. 20. 28.   ᵉ Ge. 18. 5.   ʰ De. 2. 24.   ˡ Is. 27. 10.   ° Jon. 1. 11, 13.   ᵠ Eze. 40. 7.   ᵗ Je. 4. 8.   ˣ Je. 49. 3.   ᶻ Am. 3. 15.
ᶜ Ju. 19. 5.   ᶠ Ps. 119. 117.   ⁱ Ju. 15. 11.   ᵐ Ps. 119. 113.   ʳ Is. 54. 11.   ʳʳ Ju. 19. 8.

38*

סְפוּ׳	ן noun m. s., suff. 3 pers. s. m. fr. סוּף d. 1 a
סְפוּ	Kal imp. pl. masc.
סָפוֹד׳	ן Kal inf. abs.
סָפוֹד׳	id. inf. constr. (§ 8. rem. 18)
סָפוּן	׳ן Kal part. pass. sing. masc. dec. 3 a
סְפוּנִים׳	id. pl., abs. st.
סְפוֹת	Kal inf. constr.
סָפוֹת׳	ו n. m. with pl. f. term. fr. סַף d. 8 e

[סָפַח] to join, or admit, 1 Sa. 2. 36. Niph. to be joined, Is. 14. 1. Pi. to pour out, Hab. 2. 15. Pu. to be scattered, Job 30. 7; others, to be joined, gathered together. Hithpa. to join oneself, with בְּ 1 Sa. 26. 19.

סָפִיחַ masc. dec. 3 a.—I. an overflowing, Job 14. 19.—II. produce of grain accidentally spilt, instead of being sown, self-sown grain (Prof. Lee).

סַפַּחַת fem. scurf, scab, Le. 13. 2; 14. 56.

מִסְפַּחַת fem. id. Le. 13. 6, 7, 8.

מִסְפָּחָה fem. dec. 11 a, cushion, quilt, coverlet, from the idea of spreading, Eze. 13. 18, 21.

סְפָחֵנִי	Kal imp. s. m. [סָפַח], suff. 1 p. s. (§ 16. r. 11)
סִפַּחַת׳	noun fem. sing.
סַפִּי׳	pr. name masc., see סַף
סִפִּי׳	noun masc. sing., suff. 1 pers. s. fr. סַף d. 8 e
סִפִּיחָ	noun masc. sing. dec. 3 a
סְפִיחַ׳	id., constr. st.
סְפִיחֶיהָ	id. pl., suff. 3 pers. sing. fem.
סַפִּיר	׳ן noun masc. sing. dec. 1 b
סַפִּירִים׳	id. pl., abs. st.

[סֵפֶל] masc. dish, bowl, Ju. 5. 25 ; 6. 38.

סִפָּם׳	noun masc. sing., suff. 3 pers. pl. masc. from סַף dec. 8 e

[סָפַן] fut. יִסְפֹּן.—I. to cover, spec. with boards or planks.—II. to hide, preserve, De. 33. 21.

סָפֻן masc. ceiling, 1 Ki. 6. 15.

סְפִינָה fem. ship, Jon. 1. 5.

סָפֻן׳	ן defect. for סָפוּן (q. v.)

סָפַף Kal not used; Ethiop. to extend, expand. Hithpo. הִסְתּוֹפֵף (denom. from סַף q. v.) to stand at the threshold, as a door-keeper, Ps. 84. 11. סַף masc. dec. 8 e (pl. סִפִּים, סָפּוֹת).—I. dish, basin.—II. threshold.—III. pr. name masc. 2 Sa. 21. 18, for which סִפַּי in 1 Ch. 20. 4.

סָפַק ן fut. יִסְפֹּק.—I. to strike, smite or clap, as the hands together, whether in anger, exultation, insolence or derision ; סַ׳ עַל or סַ׳ אֶל יָרֵךְ to smite oneself on the thigh, sc. in indignation or mourning.—II. to smite, chastise, Job 34. 26.—III. Je. 48. 26, to throw oneself about, as a drunken man (Eng. vers. wallow). So Kimchi. Rabbin. סָפַק in Pu. and Ithp. to waver, doubt.

סֵפֶק masc. dec. 6 b, abundance, sufficiency, Job 20. 22. Syr. ספק to suffice.

סְפֹק׳	Kal imp. sing. masc.
סָפְקוּ׳	id. pret. 3 pers. pl
סִפְקוֹ׳	noun m. s., suff. 3 p. s. m. fr. [סֵפֶק] d. 6 b
סְפָקָם׳	Kal pret. 3 pers. sing. m., suff. 3 pers. pl. m.
סָפַקְתִּי׳	id. pret. 1 pers. sing.

סָפַר ׳ן fut. יִסְפֹּר.—I. to write, only in part. סֹפֵר a writer, scribe.—II. to number, count. Niph. to be numbered. Pi.—I. to number, count.—II. to recount, relate, tell.—III. to speak, talk. Pu. to be related, told.

סָפַר Chald. masc. dec. 2 a (prop. part. act.) a scribe.

סֵפֶר masc. dec. 6 b.—I. writing, art of writing, comp. Is. 29. 11.—II. a writing, something written, letter, epistle.—III. a book.—IV. enumeration, Ge. 5. 1 (Lee).

סְפַר Chald. masc. dec. 3 b, a book.

סְפָר masc.—I. a numbering, 2 Ch. 2. 16.—II. pr. name of a city, Ge. 10. 30.

סִפְרָה fem. a book, Ps. 56. 9.

סְפֹרָה׳ fem. dec. 10, number, Ps. 71. 15.

סְפֶרֶת (scribe) pr. name masc. Ezr. 2. 55 ; Ne. 7. 57.

מִסְפָּר masc. dec. 2 b.—I. number ; אֵין מִ׳ without number, innumerable ; מְתֵי מִ׳ or אַנְשֵׁי מִ׳ men of number, i. e. who can be numbered, a few.—II. relation, narration, Ju. 7. 15.—III. pr. name masc. Ezr. 2. 2, for which מִסְפֶּרֶת in Ne. 7. 7.

סַפִּיר masc. dec. 1 b, a sapphire. Etymology uncertain.

סָפַר׳	Chald. noun masc. sing. dec. 2 a
סַפֵּר	Piel imp. sing. m. (Is. 43. 26), inf. Ex. a. 16
סָפֵר׳	Ch. noun masc. sing. dec. 3 b
סְפֹר׳	ן Kal imp. sing. masc. ; ו bef. (:)
סֵפֶר	׳ן noun masc. sing. dec. 6 b
סֹפֵר	Kal part. act. sing. masc. dec. 7 b

a Joel 2. 20.   e Je. 22. 14.   h 2 Sa. 17. 28.   k Eze. 43. 8.   o Ca. 5. 14.   r Je. 48. 26.   u Job 20. 22.   x 2 Sa. 24. 10.   Ezr. 6. 18.
b Zec. 7. 5.   f Hag. 1. 4.   i 1 Sa. 2. 36.   l Le. 25. 5.   p Eze. 43. 8.   s Eze. 21. 17.   v Job 34. 26.   y Le. 15. 13.   Ge. 5. 5.
Ec. 3. 4.   g 2 Ki. 12. 14.   k Le. 13. 2.   m Job 28. 16.   q 1 Ki. 7. 3, 7.   t La. 2. 15.   w Je. 31. 19.   z Ezr. 7. 12, 21.   Job 31. 38
d De. 33. 21

כֻּפַּר	Pual pre 3 pers sing. masc.	ספר
סִפְרָא	Ch. noun masc. sing., emph. of [סְפָר] d. 2 a	ספר
סְפָרָד	pr. name of a region, Ob. 20.	
סָפְרָה	ı Kal pret. 3 pers. sing. fem.	ספר
סַפְּרָה	Piel imp. sing. masc. (סַפֵּר) with parag ה (comp. § 8. rem. 11)	ספר
סְפָרָה	pr. name of a place (סְפָר) with parag. ה	ספר
סַפְּרוּ	} Piel imp. pl. masc. (comp. § 8. rem. 7, 12, 15)	ספר
סִפְרוּ	Kal imp. pl. masc.	ספר
סִפְּרוּ	Piel pret. 3 pers. pl.	ספר
סְפַרְוַיִם	ı pr. name of a city in Assyria. Gent. n. סְפַרְוִים 2 Ki. 17. 31 ; ı bef.	
סְפָרוֹת	noun fem. pl. of [סְפָרָה] dec. 10	ספר
סֹפְרֵי	Kal part. act. pl. constr. masc. fr. סֹפֵר d. 7 b	ספר
סָפְרַיָּא	Ch. noun masc. pl. emph. from סְפָר dec. 3 b	ספר
סְפָרִים	ı noun masc., pl. of סֵפֶר d. 6 b ; ı bef.	ספר
סְפָרִים	Kh. סְפָרִים, K. סְפָרַיִם q. v.	
סֹפְרִים	Kal part. act. masc. pl. of סֹפֵר dec. 7 b	ספר
סָפְרִין	ı Chald. noun masc., pl. of סְפָר dec. 3 b	ספר
סִפְרְךָ	noun m. s., suff. 2 pers. s. m. fr. סֵפֶר d. 6 b	ספר
סְפָרָם	Kal pret. 3 pers. sing. m., suff. 3 pers. pl. m.	ספר
סְפַרְתָּם	ı id. pret. 2 pers. sing. masc.; acc. shifted by conv. ı (§ 8. rem. 7)	ספר
סֹפֶרֶת	pr. name masc.	ספר
סְפַרְתָּה	Kal pret. 2 pers. sing. masc. (§ 8. rem. 5)	ספר
סִפַּרְתִּי	Piel pret. 1 pers. sing.	ספר
סְפַרְתֶּם	ı Kal pret. 2 pers. pl. masc.; ı for ı conv.	ספר
סָפַת	Chald. Peal pret. 3 pers. sing. fem.	סוף
סִפְתָה	Kal pret. 3 pers. sing. fem.	ספה
סָקוֹל	Kal inf. abs.	סקל
[סָקַל]	to stone. Niph. to be stoned. Pi. I. to stone, 2 Sa. 16. 6, 13.—II. to clear of stones. Pu. to be stoned, 1 Ki. 21. 14, 15.	
סֻקְּלִי	Pual pret. 3 pers. sing. masc.	סקל
סִקְלֻהוּ	ı Kal imp. pl. masc., suff. 3 pers. sing. masc.	סקל
סַקְּלוּ	Piel imp. pl. masc.	סקל
סְקָלֻהָ	ı Kal pret. 3 p. pl. m., suff. 3 p. s. f.; ı bef.	סקל
סְקָלֻנִי	ı id. id., suff. 1 pers. sing.; ı id.	סקל
סְקַלְתֻּהוּ	ı id. pret. 2 pers. s. m., suff. 3 p. s. m.; ı id.	סקל
סְקַלְתָּם	ı id. id., suff. 3 pers. pl. masc.; ı id.	סקל
סְקַלְתֶּם	ı id. pret. 2 pers. pl. masc.; ı id.	סקל
סָר	ı Kal pret. 3 p. s., or part. act. s. m. d. 1 a	סור
סַר	adj. masc. sing. fem. סָרָה	סור

סָרַב	Root not used ; Chald. to be refractory. Hence	
סָרָבִים	m. pl. [of סָרָב for סָרָב] rebellious, Eze. 2. 6	
סַרְבָּל	Root not used ; Chald. to cover, clothe. סַרְבָּלִין masc. pl. trowsers, Da. 3. 21, 27.	
סרבל	ı Ch. noun m. pl. [סַרְבָּלִין], suff. 3 p. pl. m.	
סַרְגּוֹן	pr. name of a king of Assyria, Is. 20. 1.	
סֶרֶד	(fear) pr. name masc. Ge. 46. 14. Patronym. סַרְדִּי Nu. 26. 26.	
סָרָה	ı Kal pret. 3 pers. sing. fem.	סור
סָרָה	adj. fem. [for סָרָה] from סָר masc.	סרר
סָרָה	ı noun fem. sing.	סור
סָרוּ	ı Kal pret. 3 pers. pl.	סור
סָרוּ	defect. for סוּרוּ (q. v.)	סור
סָרוּחַ	Kal part. pass. sing. masc. dec. 3 a	סרח
סְרוּחֵי	} id. pl., constr. and abs.	סרח
סְרוּחִים		
[סָרַח]	I. to be stretched out, Am. 6. 4, 7.—II. to spread forth, of a luxuriant vine, Eze. 17. 6.—III. to be redundant, to hang over or loose, Ex. 26. 12, 13; Eze. 23. 15 : סְרוּחֵי טְבוּלִים redundant as to turbans, i. e. wearing turbans long and hanging down. Niph. to be poured out, spilt, trop. of wisdom, Je 49. 7 ; or, as in the Syr. and Chald. to have an ill savour. Hence	
סֶרַח	ı m. superfluous part, remainder, Ex. 26. 12	
סֶרַח	pr. name, see תִּמְנַת סָ.	
סְרֻחִים	ı defect. for סְרוּחִים (q. v.) ; ı bef.	סרח
סֹרַחַת	Kal part. act. sing. fem. [of סֹרַחַת]	סרח
סָרֵי	Kal part. act. pl. constr. masc. from סָר dec. 1 a (§ 30. No. 3)	סור
סָרִים	noun masc. s. d. 1 b, or 3 a (comp. the foll.)	סרס
סָרִים	id., constr. st.	סרס
סָרִיסֵי	} id. pl., constr. st.	סרס
סָרִיסֵי		
סָרִיסֶיהָ	ı id. pl., suff. 3 pers. sing. fem.	סרס
סָרִיסָיו	ı id. pl., suff. 3 pers. sing. masc.	סרס
סָרִיסִים	id. pl., abs. st.	סרס
[סָרֵךְ]	Chald. masc. dec. 2 b, only in the pl., superin- tendents, Da. 6. 3—8.	
סָרְכֵי	Chald. noun masc. pl. constr. fr. [סָרֵךְ] d. 2 b	סרך
סָרְכַיָּא	Chald. id. pl., emph. st.	סרך
סָרְכִין	Chald. id. pl., abs. st.	סרך

ª Is. 52. 15.	ᵇ Ezr. 6. 1.	ˡ Le. 25. 8.	ᵍ Da. 4. 30.	ᵖ De. 22. 21.	ª Da. 3. 27.	ª¹ Sa. 15. 6.	ᵐ Eze. 17. 6.	ᵛ 2 Ki. 24. 12.
ᵇ Le. 15. 28.	ᶜ 2 Ch. 32. 17.	ʰ Ps. 56. 9.	ʳ Je. 12. 4.	ᵗ Ex. 17. 4.	ᵇ 1 Sa. 16. 14.	ᵍ Ex. 26. 13.	ⁿ Je. 6. 28.	ʷ Da. 6. 8.
ᶜ 2 Ki. 8. 4.	ᵈ Da. 7. 10.	ⁱ Ps. 119. 13, 26.	ˢ 1 Ki 21.14,15.	ᵘ De. 13. 11.	ᶜ 1 Ki. 21. 5.	ʰ Ese. 23. 15.	ᵒ Est. 6. 14.	ˣ Da. 6. 4, 5, 7.
ᵈ Joel 1. 3.	ᵉ Ps. 139. 16.	ᵏ Is. 22. 10.	ᵗ 1 Ki. 21. 10.	ᵛ De. 17. 5.	ᵈ Is. 59. 13.	ⁱ Am. 6. 7.	ᵖ Ge. 40. 7.	ʸ Da. 6. 3.
ᵉ Ps. 71. 15.	ᶠ 2 Ch. 2. 16.	ˡ Le. 23. 15.	ᵘ Is. 62. 10.	ʷ De. 22. 24.	ᵉ Ex. 8. 7.	ᵏ Am. 6. 4.	ᵠ Est. 4. 4.	

[סֶרֶן] masc. dec. 6a (pl. c. סַרְנֵי) only in the pl.—I. *axles*, 1 Ki. 7. 30.—II. *princes, lords*.

סרן סַרְנֵי id. pl., constr. st. . . .

סָרַס Root not used; Syr. and Chald. *to castrate*.
סָרִיס masc. constr. סְרִיס, pl. סָרִיסִים, constr. סָרִיסֵי, סְרִיסֵי (§ 32. rem. 2).—I. *an eunuch*, one castrated.—II. *courtier, chamberlain*, or *any chief officer*, as eunuchs were commonly entrusted with the most important offices at court; hence the Syriac everywhere renders this word by מְהַימְנָא *faithful*.

סרס וְ סָרִסִים defect. for סָרִיסִים (q. v.)
סעף סַרְעַפֹּתָיו n. f. pl., suff. 3 p. s. m. fr. [סַרְעַפָּה] d. 10

סָרַף Kal not used; i. q. שָׂרַף *to burn*. Pi. id. Am. 6. 10.
[סַרְפָּד] masc. Is. 55. 13, the name of a plant; species uncertain; Eng. vers. *brier*; most of the old versions, *nettle*.

סָרַר to be *refractory, rebellious, perverse*. Arab. *bad, evil*. סַר masc. סָרָה fem. (§ 37. rem. 7) adj. *sad, sullen, angry*.

סרר סֹרְרָה / סֹרֶרֶת } Kal part. act. sing. fem. of סֹרֵר
סור סָרָה } Kal part. f. constr. [of סָרָה d. 10] fr. סָר m.
סור סַרְתִּי Kal pret. 1 pers. s. [for סָרֹתִי comp. § 8. r. 7]
סור סַרְתֶּם } id. pret. 2 pers. pl. masc. . .

סָתָה Root not used; Arab. שתא *to winter*.
סָתָו masc. *winter*, Ca. 2. 11, Kh., סִתָיו Keri.
סתם סָתוּם Kal part. pass. sing. masc.
סתור pr. name masc. . . .

סָתַם I. *to stop up, obstruct*.—II. *to shut up, conceal*. Niph. *to close, repair a breach*, Ne. 4. 1. Pi. *to stop up*, Ge. 26. 15, 18.

סתם Kal imp. sing. masc. . . .
סָתְמוּם Piel pret. 3 pers. pl., suff. 3 pers. pl. masc. (for † fem. § 2. rem. 5) . . .
סתם סְתֻמִים Kal part. pass. pl. masc. from סָתוּם dec. 3a

[סָתַר] *to hide, conceal oneself*, Pr. 22. 3. Niph. I. *to be hid, to lie hidden* or *concealed, secreted*; hence *to be unknown*; part. נִסְתָּרוֹת *hidden, secret things*.—II. *to hide oneself*. Pi. *to hide, conceal*, Is. 16. 3. Pu. *to be hid, secret*, Pr. 27. 5. Hiph. הִסְתִּיר.—I. *to hide, cover*, as the face; hence, *to hide one's face*, i. e. *to disregard*.—II. *to hide, conceal*, with מִפְּנֵי, מִן *from any one*.—III. *to protect, defend* Hithp. הִסְתַּתֵּר (for הִתְסַתֵּר) *to hide oneself*.

סְתַר Chald. Pa. id.—I. part. pass. pl. *hidden, secret things*, Da. 2. 22.—II. *to destroy*, prop. *to put out of sight*, Ezr. 5. 12.

סֵתֶר masc. dec. 6b.—I. prop. *a hiding*, hence *secrecy*; בַּסֵּתֶר *secretly*.—II. *a covering, hiding place, secret place*.—III. *shelter, protection*.

סִתְרָה fem. *shelter, protection*, De. 32. 38.

סִתְרִי (for סִתְרְיָה *protection of the Lord*) pr name masc. Ex. 6. 22.

סְתוּר (*hidden, protected*) pr. name m. Nu. 13. 13
מִסְתּוֹר masc. *hiding place*, Is. 4. 6.
מִסְתָּר m. dec. 2b.—I. *secret place*.—II. *lurking place, an ambush*.

סָתֶר in pause [for סֵתֶר § 35. rem. 2] Seg. noun masc. see סֵתֶר . . .
סתר סֵתֶר } noun masc. sing. dec. 6b .
סתר סִתְרֵהּ Chald. Peal pret. 3 p. s. m., suff. 3 p. s. m.
סתר סִתְרָה noun fem. sing. . . .
סתר סִתְרוֹ noun m. s., suff. 3 pers s m. fr. סֵתֶר d. 6b
סתר סִתְרִי Piel imp. sing. fem.
סתר סִתְרִי } pr. name masc.
סתר סִתְרִי noun masc. s., suff. 1 pers. s. fr. סֵתֶר d. 6b
סתר סְתָרִים id. pl. abs. st

ע

עוב עָב } n. m. s. d. 1 (§ 30. No. 3, yet once עַב constr.)
עבב עָב } noun masc. sing. comp. עָבִים

עבב Root not used; Chald. *to cover, hide*.
עָב masc. a term in architecture, *a covering* of planks. Vulg. *epistylium*, a roof supported on

columns so as to form a portico. Gesenius, *thresholds steps*. 1 Ki. 7. 6; Eze. 41. 25; pl. עָבִים (from עָב) ver. 26.

עבד וְ יַעֲבֹד } fut. —I. *to work, labour*, variously; when spoken of the ground, *to till, cultivate*; of a vine-

a Je. 41. 16. d Ho. 4. 16. g Pr. 11. 22. i 2 Ch. 32. 30. m Pr. 25. 23. p Ps. 18. 12. s Ps. 119. 114. v 1 Ki. 7. 6;
b Eze. 31. 5. e Zec. 7. 11. f Ps. 119. 102. k Ge. 26. 15. n Ezr. 5. 12. r Is. 16. 3. t Pr. 9. 17. Eze. 41. 25.
c Ho. 4. 16. f Pr. 7. 11. f Eze. 28. 3. l Da. 12. 9. o De. 32. 38. w Nu. 18. 23

yard, *to dress it,* De. 28. 39.—II. *to serve, work for*
another, const. with acc., לְ, עִם of the person
served; *to serve God,* or idols, i. e. *to worship*
them.—III. with בְּ *to impose servitude upon, make*
to serve. Niph. I. *to be cultivated, tilled.*—II. *to*
be served, Ec. 5. 8. Pu. with בְּ *labour to be im-*
posed upon. Hiph. I. *to cause* or *compel to work*
or *labour.*—II. *to cause to serve;* also, *to reduce to*
servitude.—III. *to weary,* Is. 43. 23, 24. Hoph.
הָעֳבַד *to be made to serve.*

עֲבַד Chald. *to make* or *do.* Ithpe. pass.

עֶבֶד masc. dec. 6 a (with suff. עַבְדִּי).—I. *a*
servant, slave; also applied to *a vassal,* and any
one employed in the service of a king; frequently
used as a submissive epithet in addressing a
superior; עֶבֶד יְהוָה *servant of the Lord,* one *doing*
the will of God, as a true worshipper; or one
executing the purpose of God, as a mere instrument, comp. Je. 25. 9.—II. pr. name masc. of two
different persons.

עֶבֶד־מֶלֶךְ (*servant of the king*) pr. name of an
Ethiopian in the service of Zedekiah. Je. 38. 7;
39. 16.

עֶבֶד נְגוֹ, עֶבֶד נְגוֹא (*servant of Nego,* i. e. *of ex-*
pedition; Simonis, coll. Arab.) pr. name given in
Babylon to Azariah one of Daniel's companions.

עֲבֵד Chald. masc. dec. 3 a, i. q. עֶבֶד, *servant.*

עֹבֵד masc. dec. 1 a, *work, deed,* Ec. 9. 1.

עֹבֵד (*serving*) pr. name masc. of several persons.

עֹבֵד אֱדֹם (*serving Edom*) pr. name of a Levite.

עַבְדָּא (*servant*) pr. name masc.—I. 1 Ki. 4. 6.
—II. Ne. 11. 17, for which עֹבַדְיָה in 1 Ch. 9. 16.

עַבְדְּאֵל (*servant of God*) pr. name masc. Je. 36. 26.

עֲבוֹדָה, עֲבֹדָה fem. dec. 10.—I. *work, labour.*
—II. *tillage, agriculture.*—III. *work, employment,*
business.—IV. *service;* also *religious service.*—V.
service, use, benefit.

עֲבֻדָּה fem. coll. *body of servants, domestics.*

עַבְדּוֹן (*servile*) pr. name of a city of the Levites
in the tribe of Asher.

עֲבֻדוּת fem. dec. 10, *servitude, bondage.*

עַבְדִּי (for עֲבַדְיָה *servant of the Lord*) pr. name
masc. of three different persons.

עַבְדִּיאֵל (*servant of God*) pr. name m. 1 Ch. 5. 15.

עֲבַדְיָהוּ, עֹבַדְיָה (*servant of the Lord*) pr. name
masc. of several persons, especially of a prophet
at the time of Jeremiah.

עֲבִידָא Chald. fem. dec. 8 a.—I. *work, labour.*—

II. *business, public business.*—III. *service, worship,*
Ezr. 6. 18.

מַעֲבָד masc. dec. 1 b (Heb. & Chald.) *work,*
doing, Job 34. 25; Da. 4. 34.

עֲבָד	in pause for עֶבֶד (q. v. and § 35. rem. 2)	עבד
עָבֵד	]'[Chald. Peal part. act. sing. masc.	עבד
עֲבַד	Chald. Peal pret. 3 pers. sing. masc.; or (Da. 6. 21) noun masc. dec. 3 a	עבד
עֶבֶד	]'נ[pr. name in compos. עֶבֶד נְגוֹ;]ו[bef. (-:)	עבד
עֲבֹד	Kal imp. s. m. (1 Sa. 26. 19); or inf. constr.	עבד
עֲבָד־	id. inf. with Mak. (§ 8. rem. 18)	עבד
עַבְדְּ	]'ו[noun masc. sing. (suff. עַבְדְּךָ) dec. 6 a, also pr. name, and in compos. עֶבֶד מֶלֶךְ	עבד
עֹבֵד	]'ו[Kal part. act. sing. masc.; also pr. name in compos. עֹבֵד אֱדֹם	עבד
עֻבַּד	Pual pret. 3 pers. sing. masc.	עבד
עָבְדָא	Chald. Peal part. act. sing. fem. of עֲבַד	עבד
עַבְדְּאֵל	]'ו[pr. names masc.	עבד
עֲבָדַהּ	]נ[Kal pret. 3 pers. sing. masc., suff. 3 pers. sing. fem.;]ו[bef. (-:)	עבד
עֲבֹדָה	]'נ[noun fem. sing. dec. 10;]ו[id.	עבד
עֲבֻדָּה	]נ[noun fem. sing.;]ו[id.	עבד
עֲבָדוּהִ	]ו[defect. for עֲבָדוּהוּ (q. v.)	עבד
עָבְדֵהוּ	]ו[Kal imp. sing. masc., suff. 3 pers. sing. m.	עבד
עֲבָדֵהוּ	]ו[id. imp. pl. m. (עִבְדוּ), suff. 3 pers. s. m.	עבד
עֲבָדָו	]'נ[Kh. for עֲבָדָיו (q. v.)	עבד
עָבְדוּ	]'ו[}Kal pret. 3 pers. pl. (§ 8. rem. 7)	עבד
עָבְדֻ	}	עבד
עֲבָדוֹ	]'נ[id. pret. 3 p. s. m., suff. 3 p. s. m.;]ו[bef. (-:)	עבד
עֲבַדוּ	]נ'[Chald. Peal pret. 3 pers. pl. masc.;]ו[id.	עבד
עַבְדּוֹ	]'ו[noun m. s., suff. 3 p. s. m. fr. עֶבֶד d. 6 a	עבד
עַבְדֵּן	Kh. עַבְדּוֹ q. v., K. עַבְדְּךָ (q. v.)	עבד
עִבְדוּ	}Kal imp. pl. masc. (§ 8. rem. 12)	עבד
עִבְדוּ	}	עבד
עֲבָדוּהִג	id. pret. 3 pers. pl., suff. 3 pers. sing. masc.	עבד
עֲבָדוֹהִי	Chald. noun masc. pl., suff. 3 pers. sing. masc. from עֲבַד dec. 3 a	עבד
עֲבָדוּךָ	]'ו[Kal pret. 3 p. pl., suff. 2 p. s. m.;]ו[bef. (-:)	עבד
עֲבָדוּם	]'ו[id., suff. 3 pers. pl. masc.;]ו[id.	עבד
עַבְדּוֹן	pr. name of a man or place	עבד
עַבְדִּי	]'ו[the foll. with suff. 1 pers. sing.;]ו[bef. (-:)	עבד
עַבְדֵי	]'ו[noun masc. pl. constr. from עֶבֶד dec. 6 a	עבד
עַבְדִּי	]'ו[pr. name masc.	עבד
עַבְדִּי	]'ו[noun m. s., suff. 1 pers. s. fr. עֶבֶד d. 6 a	עבד
עֹבְדֵי	Kal part. act. pl. constr. masc. fr. עֶבֶד d. 7 b	עבד
עֲבַדְיָהוּ, עֹבַדְיָה, עַבְדִּיאֵל	]'ו[pr. names masc.	עבד
עֲבָדֶיהָ	]נ[noun masc. pl., suff. 3 pers. sing. fem. from עֶבֶד dec. 6 a;]ו[bef. (-:)	עבד

עַבְדֵיהֶם	id. pl., suff. 3 pers. pl. masc.	עבד
עַבְדֵיהֶם׳	וְ noun masc. pl. with suff. 3 pers. sing.	עבד
	m. fr. [עֶבֶד] d. 1 a (§ 30. No. 3); וְ bef. (־ִ)	
עֲבָדָיו	וְ noun masc. pl., suff. 3 pers. sing. masc.	עבד
	from עֶבֶד dec. 6 a; וְ id.	
עֹבְדָיו׳	Kal part. act. pl. masc., suff. 3 pers. sing.	עבד
	masc. from עָבַד dec. 7 b	
עֲבָדֶיךָ	וְ noun masc. pl., suff. 2 pers. sing. masc.	עבד
	from עֶבֶד dec. 6 a; וְ bef. (־ִ)	
עַבְדָּיִךְ׳	Chald. noun masc. pl., suff. 2 pers. sing.	עבה
	masc. from עֲבַד dec. 3 a	
עַבְדֵיכֶם	וְ noun masc. pl., suff. 2 pers. pl. masc.	עבד
	from עֶבֶד dec. 6 a	
עֲבָדִים	וְ id. pl., abs. st.; וְ bef. (־ִ)	עבד
עֹבְדִים	וְ Kal part. act. masc., pl. of עָבַד dec. 7 b	עבד
עָבְדִין׳	Chald. Peal part. m., pl. of עֲבַד d. 2 b	עבד
עֲבָדְךָ	וְ Kal pret. 3 pers. sing. masc., suff. 2 pers.	עבד
	sing. masc.; וְ bef. (־ִ)	
עַבְדְּךָ	} noun masc. sing., suff. 2 pers. sing. masc. }	עבד
עַבְדֶּךָ	} from עֶבֶד dec. 6 a }	
עָבְדְךָ	Kal inf. [for עֲבֹד], suff. 2 pers. sing. masc.	עבד
עַבְדְּכֶם	noun m. s., suff. 2 pers. pl. m. fr. עֶבֶד d. 6 a	עבד
עֲבָדֶם׳	וְ defect. for עֲבָדִים (q. v.)	עבד
עָבַדְתָּ	וְ	עבד
עָבַדְתָּ	} Kal pret. 2 pers. sing. masc. (§ 8. r. 7)	עבד
עֲבַדְתְּ	וְ	
עֲבַדְתְּ	Chald. Peal pret. 2 pers. sing. masc.	עבד
עֲבַדֵּת	Chald. id. pret. 1 pers. sing.	עבד
עֲבֹדַת	וְ noun f. s., constr. of עֲבוֹדָה d. 10; וְ bef. (־ִ)	עבד
עֲבֹדָתוֹ	id., suff. 3 pers. sing. masc.	עבד
עֲבַדְתִּי	} Kal pret. 1 pers. sing.; acc. shifted by }	עבד
עֲבַדְתִּי׳	} conv. וְ (§ 8. rem. 7) }	
עֲבֹדָתִי	noun f. sing., suff. 1 pers. s. fr. עֲבוֹדָה d. 10	עבד
עֲבַדְתִּיךָ	Kal pret. 1 pers. sing., suff. 2 pers. sing. m.	עבד
עֲבֹדַתְכֶם	noun f. s., suff. 2 pers. pl. fr. עֲבוֹדָה d. 10	עבד
עֲבַדְתֶּם	וְ Kal pret. 2 pers. sing. masc., suff. 3 pers.	עבד
	pl. masc.; וְ for וְ, conv.	
עֲבַדְתֶּם	וְ id. pret. 2 pers. pl. masc.; וְ id.	עבד
עֲבֹדָתִי	noun masc. sing., suff. 3 pers. pl. masc.	עבד
	from עֲבוֹדָה dec. 10	
עֲבַדְתָּנוּ	id., suff. 1 pers. pl.	עבד
עֲבַדְתָּנִי	וְ Kal pret. 2 pers. sing. masc., suff. 1 pers.	עבד
	sing.; וְ for וְ, conv.	

עָבָה   to be thick, gross.

עֳבִי masc. density, compactness.

עֳבִי masc. dec. 6 k, thickness.

מַעֲבֶה	masc. dec. 9 a, density, compactness 1 Ki. 7. 46.	
עֲבוֹדָה׳	וְ noun fem. sing. dec. 10; וְ bef. (־ִ)	עבד
עֲבֹדַת׳	וְ PP id., constr. st.; וְ id.	עבד
עֲבוֹדָתִי׳	id., suff. 1 pers. sing.	עבד
עֲבוֹדָתָם׳	id., suff. 3 pers. pl. masc.	עבד
עָבוֹד׳	Kal inf. abs.	עבד
עֲבוֹר	id. inf. constr. (§ 8. rem. 18)	עבד
עָבוֹת	noun com., pl. of עָב dec. 1 (§ 30. No. 3, yet once, constr. עֲבֹת)	עבה
עָבֹת׳	adj. masc. sing. comp. עָבֵת	עבת
עֲבוֹת׳	noun com. sing. dec. 1 a	עבת
עֲבוֹתִים	id. pl., abs. st.	עבת

[עָבַט]   fut. יַעֲבֹט to give a pledge, De. 24. 10; hence, to borrow upon a pledge, De. 15. 6. Pi. to change, alter, a course, Joel 2. 7. Prof. Lee, to break the ranks. Hiph. to lend upon a pledge, De. 15. 6, 8.

עֲבֹט masc. dec. 1 a, a pledge, De. 24. 10, 11, 12.

עֲבָטִים masc. an accumulation of debts, Hab. 2. 6. Eng. vers. "thick clay."

עֲבֹטוֹ	noun m. s., suff. 3 pers. s. m. fr. עֲבוֹט d. 1 a	עבט
עֲבָטִיט׳	noun masc. sing.	עבט
עֲבֵי	noun masc. pl. constr. fr. עָב d. 1 a (§ 30. No. 3)	עוב
עֲבִידַת	Ch. noun fem. sing., constr. of [עֲבִידָא] d. 8 a	עבד
עֲבִידְתָּא׳	וְ Chald. id., emph. st.; וְ bef. (־ִ)	עבד
עֲבָיו׳	noun masc. pl., suff. 3 pers. sing. masc. from	
	עָב dec. 1 a (§ 30. No. 3)	עוב
עָבְיוֹ	וְ noun masc. sing., suff. 3 pers. sing. masc.	
	[from עֳבִי] dec. 6 k	עבה
עָבִים	noun masc. pl. of עָב dec. 1 a (§ 30. No. 3)	עוב
עָבִיתָ׳	Kal pret. 2 pers. sing. masc.	עבה

עָבָל   Root not used; Arab. (conj. IV) to be leafless, stripped of leaves.

עוּבָל (stripped of foliage) pr. name of a region, and a people descended from Joktan.

עֵיבָל (id.) pr. name of a rock in the northern part of mount Ephraim.

עָבַר   וְ fut. יַעֲבֹר —I. to pass over, as a river, a sea, const. with acc., or בְּ; and with אֶל of the place to which; to pass over any thing, and hence to transgress; spoken of water, to overflow; of an army, to overwhelm; to pass over to the side or cause of any one, with עַל, Is. 45. 14.—II. to pass through a place, country, &c. with acc., בְּ,

a Ec. 9. 1.   e 1 Ki. 5. 1.   i Ge. 24. 35.   n Nu. 4. 47; Is. 32. 17.   r Nu. 18. 31.   v 1 Ch. 28. 14, 21.   y 2 Sa. 17. 16.   b De. 24. 10.   e Ezr. 5. 8.
b 2 Ki. 10. 19.   f Ezr. 4. 15.   k De. 28. 39.   o 2 Sa. 15. 8.   s Ne. 10. 38.   w 2 Ch. 12. 8.   z Eze. 20. 28.   c Hab. 2. 6.   f Ps. 18. 12.
c Ezr. 4. 11.   g De. 15. 18.   l De. 28. 47.   p Ge. 30. 26.   t Ge. 30. 15.   x 1 Ch. 6. 17.   a Ps. 129. 4.   d Da. 2. 49.   g De. 32. 15.
   De. 12. 12.   h Job 39. 9.   m Da. 4. 32.   q 2 Ch. 31. 21.

כֶּסֶף עֹבֵר בֵּין, also absolutely; Ge. 23. 16, *money passing, current.*—III. *to pass by, along a place or person,* with עַל פְּנֵי, מֵעַל, עַל, לִפְנֵי; metaph. *to pass by,* i. e. *forgive transgression.*—IV. *to pass away,* of time; *to pass away, vanish; to pass away, perish.*—V. *to pass, pass on, move on, go further,* with אַחֲרֵי, לִפְנֵי, מִן *from, before, after any one;* עָבֹר וָשׁוֹב *to pass on and return;* עָבַר בַּבְּרִית *to enter into a covenant.*—VI. const. with עַל (rarely acc.) *to pass, go or come upon any one, to overwhelm, overcome, assail.*—VII. *to drop as a liquid,* Ca. 5. 5, 13. Niph. *to be passed,* Eze. 47. 5. Pi. I. *to cause to pass, as a bar, bolt;* hence *to bar, bolt,* 1 Ki. 6. 21.—II. *to conceive, become pregnant,* Job 21. 10. Hiph. הֶעֱבִיר.—I. *to cause to pass over, send or conduct over,* e. g. *a river; to transfer from place to place; to cause to transgress a law,* 1 Sa. 2. 24; הֶעֱבִיר עַל הֲ' *to cause a razor to pass upon, to shave,* Nu. 8. 7.—II. *to cause to pass through;* הֶעֱבִיר קוֹל בְּ *to cause to proclaim throughout.*—III. *to cause to pass by;* trop. of sin, *to remit, forgive.*—IV. *to cause to pass, go or come, to bring, offer.*—V. *to lead, take or put away, to remove;* hence *to avert evil, reproach.* Hithpa. *to be angry,* prop. *to allow oneself to go beyond proper limits, to give way to one's feelings;* with acc., בְּ, עַל, עִם; also *to be proud,* Pr. 14. 16.

עֵבֶר masc. dec. 6 b (with suff. עֶבְרוֹ § 35. rem. 6).—I. *passage of a river, a ford.*—II. *a mountain pass,* 1 Sa. 26. 13.—III. *a region or country near a river or sea on either side.*—IV. *a side;* אֶל־עֵבֶר *beyond, over,* De. 30. 13; *over against,* Jos. 22. 11; *towards,* Ex. 28. 26; אֶל־עֵבֶר פְּנֵי *in front of,* Ex. 25. 37; אֶל־עֵבֶר פָּנָיו *forwards, straight forwards;* לְעֶבְרוֹ *straight forwards;* מֵעֵבֶר *from the other side; on the other side; beyond.*—V. pr. name, *Eber;* (a) *the grandson of Shem, and progenitor of Abraham;* (b) Ne. 12. 20; (c) 1 Ch. 8. 12; (d) 1 Ch. 8. 22; (e) 1 Ch. 5. 13.

עֲבַר Chald. i. q. עֵבֶר No. III.

עֶבְרָה fem. dec. 11 c (§ 42. rem. 1).—I. *a ferryboat,* 2 Sa. 19. 19.—II. עֲבָרוֹת 2 Sa. 15. 28, Kh. for עֲבֻרוֹת Keri q. v.

עֶבְרָה fem. dec. 12 b (pl. c. עֶבְרוֹת, עֲבָרוֹת).—I. *anger,* comp. Hithpa.—II. *pride, haughtiness.*

עִבְרִי noun gent. masc. *a Hebrew,* pl. עִבְרִים; fem. עִבְרִיָּה, pl. עִבְרִיּוֹת, עִבְרִיֹּת.

עֲבָרִים (*regions beyond*) pr. name, *Abarim,* Je. 22. 20; fully הָרֵי הָעֲ or הַרְהָעֲבָרִים *a range of hills beyond Jordan over against Jericho.*

עֶבְרוֹנָה (*passage*) pr. name of a station of the Israelites, Nu. 33. 34.

עָבוּר masc. only constr. עֲבוּר *produce of the ground,* Jos. 5. 11, 12.

עֲבוּר prop. subs. *transition;* always with בְּ pref. בַּעֲבוּר.—I. prep. *because of; for, in return for.*—II. conj. *because; that, for the purpose that; while,* 2 Sa. 12. 21; בַּעֲבוּר אֲשֶׁר, לְבַעֲבוּר *for the purpose that.*

מַעֲבָר masc. dec. 2 b.—I. *place of passing,* Is. 30. 32.—II. *ford,* Ge. 32. 23.—III. *mountain pass,* 1 Sa. 13. 23.

מַעֲבָרָה fem. dec. 11 a.—I. *ford.*—II. *mountain pass.* Pl. abs. מַעֲבָרוֹת prop. from מַעֲבֶרֶת.

וְ Kal pret. 3 p. s. m. for עָבַר (comp. § 8. r. 7)	.	עבר
Chald. noun masc. sing.	.	עבר
וְ Kal inf., or imp. sing. masc.	.	עבר
Kh. עָבַר q. v., K. יַעֲבֹר (q. v.)	.	עבר
וְ noun masc. sing. dec. 6 (§ 35. rem. 6), also pr. name	.	עבר
Piel pret. 3 pers. sing. masc. (§ 10. rem. 1)	.	עבר
וְ Kal part. sing. masc. dec. 7 b	.	עבר
id. pret. 3 pers. sing. fem.	.	עבר
וְ noun fem. sing. dec. 12 b	.	עבר
} Kal pret. 3 pers. pl. (§ 8. rem. 7)	.	עבר
וְ }		
id. inf., suff. 3 pers. sing. masc.	.	עבר
id. pret. 3 pers. sing. m., suff. 3 pers. s. m.		עבר
וְ id. imp. pl. masc.	.	עבר
noun fem. pl. abs. from עֶבְרָה dec. 12 b (comp. § 35. rem. 6)		עבר
id. pl., constr. st.	.	עבר
Kal inf., suff. 1 pers. sing.	.	עבר
} id. imp. sing. fem. (§ 8. rem. 12)	.	עבר
וְ gent. noun from עֵבֶר (q. v.)	.	עבר
Kal part. act. pl. constr. masc. fr. עוֹבֵר d. 7 b		עבר
noun masc. pl., suff. 3 pers. pl. masc. from עֵבֶר dec. 6 d (§ 35. rem. 6)		עבר
id. pl. with suff. 3 pers. sing. masc.		עבר
וְ gent. noun, pl. of עִבְרִי from	.	עבר
Kal part. act. masc., pl. of עוֹבֵר dec. 7 b		עבר
id. inf., suff. 2 pers. pl. masc.	.	עבר
וְ pr. name of a place, see עַבְדּוֹן. R		עבר
וְ Kal pret. 1 pers. pl.	.	עבר
id. inf., with suff. 3 pers. pl. masc.	.	עבר

עַבְרֵנוּ   id. with suff. 1 pers. pl., Kh. עֲבָרֵנוּ, or suff.
3 pers. pl. masc., K. עֲבָרָם   .   עבר

עֲבַרְףָ   id. pret. 2 pers. sing. masc.; acc. shifted
וַעֲבַרְףָ   by conv. ו (§ 8. rem. 7)   עבר

עֶבְרַת   noun fem. sing., constr. of עֶבְרָה dec. 12b
(comp. § 35. rem. 6)   .   .   עבר

עֲבָרְתוֹ   id., suff. 3 pers. sing. masc.   .   עבר

עָבַרְתִּי   Kal pret. 1 pers. sing.; acc. shifted by
וְעָבַרְתִּי   conv. ו (§ 8. rem. 7)   עבר

עֶבְרָתִי   noun fem. sing., suff. 1 pers. sing. from עֶבְרָה
dec. 12b (comp. § 35. rem. 6) .   עבר

עֲבַרְתְּךָ   id., suff. 2 pers. sing. masc. [for עֲבָרָתְךָ]   עבר

עֲבַרְתֶּם   Kal pret. 2 pers. pl. masc.; וַ for וְ, conv.   עבר

עֶבְרָתָם   noun fem. sing., suff. 3 pers. pl. masc. from
עֶבְרָה dec. 12b (comp. § 35. rem. 6) .   עבר

[עָבַשׁ]   to dry up, Joel 1. 17; others, to rot.

עָבְשׁוּ[f]   Kal pret. 3 pers. pl.   .   .   עבש

עָבַת   Kal not used; prob. to be twisted or interwoven,
cogn. עוּת, עָבַט.   Pi. to perplex, complicate, sc.
oppression, Mi. 7. 3; others, to pervert, sc. the
cause in judgment.   Hence the two following.

עָבֹת   adj., f. עֲבֻתָּה interwoven, thick, bushy, of trees.

עֲבֹת   com. dec. 1a (pl. ־ים, ־וֹת).—I. wreathen
work, Ex. 28. 14, 24.—II. a cord, line,
Ju. 15. 13, 14; hence pl. bands.—III.
branches with thick, entangled foliage.

עֲבֻתָּה[g]   adj. fem. sing. from עָבֹת masc.   .   עבת

עֲבֹתוֹ[h]   noun com. sing., suff. 3 p. s. m. fr. עֲבֹת d. 1a   עבת

עֲבֹתִים   id. pl., abs. st.   .   .   .   עבת

עֲבֹתֵימוֹ[i]   id. pl., suff. 3 pers. pl. masc.   .   עבת

עֲבֹתֹת[k]   id. with pl. fem. term.   .   .   עבת

עֹג   pr. name masc., see עוֹג   .   .   עוג

[עָגַב]   fut. יַעְגַּב (§ 13. rem. 5) to love, espec. in a bad
sense, const. with acc., עַל.

עֲגָבִים   masc. pl. (of עֶגֶב) love, Eze. 33. 31, 32.

עֲגָבָה   fem. dec. 11c (§ 42. rem. 1) inordinate
love, Eze. 23. 11.

עֻגָב   (עֻגָב, עוּגָב masc. (once with suff. עֻגָבִי) a
kind of musical instrument supposed to be a flute
or organ.

עֵגֶב   or accord. to some עָנָב see עוּנָב   .   ענב

עָגְבָה[m]   Kal pret. 3 pers. sing. fem. (§ 8. rem. 7)   ענב
עָגְבָה[n]

עֲגָבִים[o]   noun masc. pl. [of עֶגֶב] dec. 6a   .   ענב

עִנְבִי[oo]   noun masc. s., suff. 1 pers. s. fr. עוּנָב d. 2b   ענב

עֹנְבִים[p]   Kal part. act. masc. pl. [of עָנַב] dec. 7b   ענב

עֲנָבָתָהּ[q]   noun fem. sing., suff. 3 pers. sing. fem. from
[עֲנָבָה] dec. 11c (§ 42. rem. 1)   .   ענב

עֹנָה   noun fem. sing. dec. 10 [for עוּנָה, עָנָה]   עון

עָגֹל   in full for עָגֹל (q. v.)   .   .   ענל

עֹנֵר   noun masc. sing.   .   .   ענר

עֹנוֹת   noun fem., pl. of עָנָה (q. v.)   .   עון

עָגִיל   noun masc. sing. dec. 3a   .   .   ענל

עֲגִילִים   id. pl. abs.; ו bef. (־:)   .   ענל

עָגַל   Root not used; Syr. to roll, revolve.

עָגֹל   masc. עֲגֻלָּה fem. round, circular.

עָגִיל   masc. dec. 3a, earring.

עֵגֶל   masc. dec. 6b (with suff. עֶגְלִי) § 35. rem. 6)
—I. a calf, young bullock; עֵ מַסֵּכָה a molten calf
—II. metaph. prince, leader, Ps. 68. 31.

עֶגְלָה   fem. dec. 12b.—I. cow-calf, heifer; more
fully עֶגְלַת בָּקָר prop. a calf of the beeves, in con-
tradistinction to neat cattle; עֶגְלַת שְׁלִישִׁיָּה a heifer
three years old.—II. pr. name of a wife of David.

עֲגָלָה   fem. dec. 11c (with suff. עֲגָלָתוֹ) § 42
rem. 1).—I. cart or waggon.—II. threshing-dray
Is. 28. 27, 28.—III. war-chariot, Ps. 46. 10.

עֶגְלוֹן   (vitulinus) pr. name—I. of a king of
Moab, Ju. 3. 12.—II. of a city in the tribe of
Judah.

מַעְגָּל   masc. dec. 2b.—I. a track, in which
wheels roll.—II. way, path; hence, way, manner
of life.—III. a barricade of waggons, 1 Sa. 26. 5, 7.

מַעְגָּלָה   fem. dec. 11a, i. q. מַעְגָּל Nos. II & III.

עָגֹל   adj. masc. sing., pl. fem. עֲגֻלּוֹת   .   ענל

עֵגֶל   noun masc. sing. dec. 6 (§ 35. rem. 6) .   ענל

עֶגְלָה   noun fem. sing. dec. 11c (§ 42. rem. 1)   ענל

עֶגְלָה   noun fem. sing. (no pl. abs.)   .   ענל

עֶגְלוֹן   pr. name of a man and a place   .   ענל

עֲגָלוֹת   noun fem. pl. abs. from עֲגָלָה dec. 11c   ענל

עֲגֻלּוֹת[r]   adj. fem. pl. [of עֲגֻלָּה] from עָגֹל masc.   ענל

עֲגִילֵי   constr. of the foll.   .   .   ענל

עֲגָלִים   noun masc., pl. of עֵגֶל dec. 6 (§ 35. rem.
6); ו bef. (־:)   .   .   .   ענל

עֶגְלַיִם   id. du., pr. name in compos. עֵין עֶנ'   צין

עֶגְלָתֵךְ[y]   id. sing. with suff. 2 pers. sing. fem.   ענל

עֶגְלֹנָה   pr. name of a place (עֶגְלוֹן) with parag. ה   ענל

עֶגְלַת   noun fem. sing., constr. of עֶגְלָה (no pl. abs.)   ענל

---

[a] Jos. 5. 1.	[d] De. 12. 10.	[g] Eze. 6. 13.	[k] Ex. 28. 24.	[n] Eze. 23. 7, 9.	[p] Je. 4. 30.	[r] Je. 8. 7; Is. 38. 14.	[w] Eze. 16. 12.	[y] Am. 6. 4.
[b] 1 Ki. 2. 37.	[e] Ge. 49. 7.	[h] Job 39. 10.	Ps. 150. 4.	[o] Eze. 33. 31, 32.	[q] Eze. 23. 11.	[s] Nu. 31. 50.	[x] 1 Ki. 7. 31.	[z] Ho. 8. 5.
[c] Ex. 12. 12.	[f] Joel 1. 17.	Ps. 2. 3.	[i] Eze. 23. 12.	[m] Job 30. 31.				

עֶגְלַת noun fem. pl. constr. from עֶגְלָה dec. 11 c (§ 42. rem. 1) . . . . עגל

עֶגְלָתוֹ id. sing. with suff. 3 pers. sing. masc. עגל

[עָגַם] to be sad, to grieve for any one, with לְ only in the following form.

עָגְמָה Kal pret. 3 pers. sing. fem. . . . עגם

עָגַן Niph. to be shut up, prevented from marrying, Ru. 1. 13.

עָגַר Root not used; perh. i. q. גָּעַר, as in the Ethiop., to cry out; Arab. flexit, inflexit.

עָגוּר masc. the crane, Is. 38. 14; Je. 8. 7. Gesenius takes it as an epithet of the swallow, signifying turning round, flying in a circle.

עֲגַּת ['וְ] noun fem. sing., constr. of עֵגָה (q. v.) עוג

עֻגֹּת pl. of the preced. . . . . עוג

עַד ['וְ] noun m. s.; also a prep., pl. c. עָדֵי, suff.
עַד עָדֶיךָ (§ 31. rem. 5); for וְ see lett. 1) עדה
עַד ['וְ, 'וֵ] noun masc. sing. dec. 1a (§ 30. No. 3); וְ id. . . . . עוד

עַד defect. for עוֹד (q. v.) . . . . עוד

עַדָּא pr. name masc., see עִדּוֹ עדד

עָדַד Root not used; Arab. to number, compute, espec. time.

עֵד masc. dec. 8 b, only pl. עִדִּים Is. 64. 5, stated times, of the monthly courses of women, Arab. עָדָה.

עִדּוֹ, עִדּוֹא (timely) pr. name masc.—I. of a prophet, 2 Ch. 12. 15; 13. 22.—II. of the grandfather of the prophet Zechariah.

עִדָּן Chald. masc. dec. 1 a, time, used also of a prophetic period.

עֲדָעֲדָה (festival; Syr. id.) pr. name of a town in the tribe of Judah, Jos. 15. 22.

עָדָד pr. name masc. . . . . עוד

עָדָה I. to go or pass by, with עַל, Job 28. 8.—II. to put on, sc. an ornament; also to deck, adorn oneself. Hiph. I. to remove, put away, a garment, Pr. 25. 20.

עֲדָא, עֲדָה Chald.—I. to pass upon any one, with בְּ, Da. 3. 27.—II. to pass away, depart, with מִ, Da. 4. 28; hence, to be abolished. Aph. to take away, remove.

עָדָה (ornament) pr. name—I. of a wife of Lamech.—II. of a wife of Esau, Ge. 36. 4, 12.

עַד masc.—I. prey, spoil, from the idea of rushing upon, Ge. 49. 27; Is. 33. 23; Zep. 3. 8.—II. perpetuity, eternity; וָעֶד, לָעַד, לְעוֹלָם (for עֲדֵי עַד ,וְלָעֶד ,לְעַד) for ever, for ever and ever.—III. (pl. עֲדֵי, with suff. עָדֶיךָ § 31. rem. 5) prep. (a) while, as long as; (b) to, unto, as far as; (c) until; עַד כֹּה, עַד עַתָּה, עַד הֵנָּה hitherto; עַד־אָנָה, עַד־מָה, עַד־מָתַי until when? how long?—IV. conj. (a) while, during, with the pret. and participle; עַד שֶׁ, עַד־אֲשֶׁר while; עַד לֹא, עַד שֶׁ while not, while as yet not, before; (b) until עַד אֲשֶׁר, עַד כִּי, עַד אִם, עַד אֲשֶׁר until that (c) so that, even so that.

עַד Chald.—I. prep. (a) during, within, Da. 6. 8, 13; (b) until; עַד כְּעַן until now; (c) to, for, of purpose; עַד דִּבְרַת דִּי to the intent that, Da. 4. 14.—II. conj. עַד דִּי; (a) while, when, meantime, Da. 6. 25; (b) until.

עַד־הֵנָּה ,עֲדֶנָּה contr. from עֲדֶה hitherto, as yet עֲדִי masc. dec. 6 i (with suff. עֶדְיִי § 35. rem. 14). —I. age, Ps. 103, 5.—II. ornaments.—III. trappings of a horse, Ps. 32. 9.

עֲדִיאֵל (ornament of God) pr. name masc. of three different persons.

עֲדָיָה, עֲדָיָהוּ (whom the Lord adorns) pr. name masc. of several persons.

עֲדִיתָיִם (double ornament) pr. name of a town in the tribe of Judah, Jos. 15. 36.

עֵת com. dec. 8 b (contr. from עֶדֶת) time, season; adv. a long time; כָּעֵת at this time, now; כָּעֵת מָחָר about this time to-morrow; pl. עִתִּים, עִתּוֹת times, vicissitudes; עִתִּים רַבּוֹת many times, repeatedly, Ne. 9. 28.

עֵת קָצִין (time of the prince) pr. name of a town in Zebulon, with ה local עִתָּה קָצִין, Jos. 19. 13.

עַתָּה adv.—I. at this time, now; עַד־עַתָּה until now מֵעַתָּה from this time.—II. soon, shortly, presently.

עַתַּי (opportune) pr. name masc. of three different persons.

עִתִּי masc. adj. fit, opportune, Le. 16. 21.

עַתְּדוֹ pr. name masc. 2 Ch. 9. 26, Keri.

מַעֲדָיָה (ornament of the Lord) pr. name masc. Ne. 12. 5, for which מוֹעַדְיָה ver. 17.

מַעֲדַי (for מַעַדְיָה) pr. name masc. Ezr. 10. 34.

עָדָה pr. name fem. . . . . עדה

עֶדָה ['וְ] noun fem. sing. dec. 11 b . . . יעד

עֵדָה ['וְ] noun fem. sing. dec. 10 (comp. § 30. No. 3) עוד

עֲדֵה Kal imp. sing. masc. . . . . עדה

עָדוֹ עִדּוֹא	} pr. name masc.	עדד
עֵדוּת	n. f. s. [pl. עֵדְוֹת comp. Ch. d.8], see the foll.	עוד
עֵדְוֹתָיו	id. pl., suff. 3 pers. sing. masc.	עוד
וְעֵדְוֹתָיו	noun fem. pl., suff. 3 p. s. m. fr. עֵדָה d. 10	עוד
עֵדְוֹתֶיךָ	noun f. s., suff. 2 pers. s. m. fr. עֵדוּת (q. v.)	עוד
עָדַי	prep. (עַד) pl. with suff. 1 p. s. (§ 31. r. 5)	עדה
עָדֵי	id. pl., constr. st.	עדה
עֶדְיִי	noun masc. s. (suff. עֶדְיוֹ) d. 6i (§ 35. r. 14)	עדה
עֶדְיִי עֶדְיִי	} the foll. with suff. 1 pers. sing.	עוד
עֵדַי	noun m. pl. constr. fr. עֵד d. 1a (§ 30. No. 3)	עוד
עֵדִי	id. sing., suff. 1 pers. sing.	עוד
עֵדִי	in pause for עֶדְיִי q. v. (§ 35. rem. 14)	עדה
עֲדִיאֵל	'ן, עֲדָיָה, pr. names masc.; ן bef. (-)	עדה
עֶדְיָהּ	prep. (עַד) pl. with suff. 3 p. s. f. (§ 31. r. 5)	עדה
עֶדְיָהּ	n. m. s., suff. 3 p. s. f. fr. עֲדִי d.6i (§ 35. r. 14)	עדה
עֲדָיָהוּ	pr. name masc., see עֲדָיָה	עדה
עֲדֵיהֶם	noun masc. pl., suff. 3 pers. pl. masc. from עֵד dec. 1a (§ 30. No. 3)	עוד
עָדָיו	prep. (עַד) pl. with suff. 3 p. s. m. (§ 31. r. 5)	עדה
עֶדְיוֹ	n. m. s., suff. 3 p. s. m. fr. עֲדִי d. 6i (§ 35. r.14)	עדה
עֲדָיִים	id. pl., abs. st.	עדה
עֶדְיֵךְ	'ן prep. (עַד) pl. with suff. 2 p. s. m. (§ 31. r. 5)	עדה
עֵדַיִךְ	n. m. pl., suff. 2 p. s. m. fr. עֵד d. 1a (§ 30. No. 3)	עוד
עֶדְיֵךְ	n. m. s., suff. 2 p. s. f. fr. עֲדִי d. 6i (§ 35. r. 14)	עדה
עֶדְיֵךְ	id. with suff. 2 pers. sing. masc.	עדה
עֲדֵיכֶם	ן prep. (עַד) with suff. 2 pers. pl. masc. re- taining (-) against anal. (§ 31. rem. 5)	עדה
עֶדְיָם	n. m. s., suff. 3 p. pl. m. fr. עֲדִי d. 6i (§ 35. r.14)	עדה
עֵדִים	noun masc., pl. of עֵד dec. 1a (§ 30. rem. 3)	עוד
עֵדִים	noun masc., pl. of עֵד dec. 8b	עדד
עֶדֶן	pr. name masc.	עדן
עַדְנָא	pr. name masc.	עדן
עֲדִינָה	adj. fem. sing. [from עָדִין masc.]	עדן
עֲדִינוֹ	pr. name masc.; see this form under the R.	עדן
עָדִית	ן Kal pret. 2 pers. sing. fem.	עדה
עֲדִיתַיִם	ן pr. name of a place; ן bef. (-)	עדה
עֶדְךָ	defect. for עוֹדְךָ (q. v.)	עוד
עָדַל	Root not used; Arab. *to be just.* Hence	
עֲדְלַי	(for עֲדַלְיָה=עֲדַלְיָה *justice of God*) pr. name masc. 1 Ch. 27. 29	עדל
עֲדֻלָּם	ן (*justice of the people*) pr. name of a city in Judah, in the vicinity of which was the *cave of Adullam.* Hence the foll.	עדל
עֲדֻלָּמִי	gent. noun from the preced.	

עָדַן	Kal not used; Arab. *to be soft, lax, pliant.* Hithp. *to live luxuriously*, Ne. 9. 25.	
עָדִין	masc. — I. adj. *luxurious, delicate,* fem. עֲדִינָה Is. 47.8.—II. pr. name masc. Ezr. 2. 15; Ne. 7. 20.	
עֲדִינָא	(*pliability,* or *voluptuousness*) pr. name masc. 1 Ch. 11.42.	
עֲדִינוֹ	(for עֲדִינוֹ *pliant,* or *voluptuous*) pr. name masc. 2 Sa. 23. 8. According to Gesenius, as an appellative, *his vibration,* i. e. *brandishing* of the spear, comp. the Root. Simonis, *his smiting,* from עָדַן Arab. *to smite with a pointed weapon.*	
עֵדֶן	masc. dec. 6b.—I. *delight, pleasure.*—II. pr. name, *Eden,* the pleasant region in which the garden, גַּן עֵדֶן, the abode of our first parents, was placed.	
עֵדֶן	(*pleasantness*) pr. name of a region in Me- sopotamia.	
עַדְנָא	(*pleasure*) pr. name masc. Ezr. 10. 30.	
עַדְנָה	(id.) pr. name masc.—I. 1 Ch. 12. 20.— II. 2 Ch. 17. 14.	
עֶדְנָה	fem. *pleasure,* Ge. 18. 12.	
מַעֲדָן	מַעֲדָן masc. only pl. מַעֲדַנּוֹת, מַעֲדַנִּים.—I. *de- lights, pleasure,* Pr. 29. 17; adv. *cheerfully, wil- lingly,* 1 Sa. 15. 32.—II. *delicacies, dainties.*	
עֲדֶן	contr. from עַד־הֵנָּה	עדה
עֵדֶן	ן pr. name masc. (and in compos. see בֵּית)	עדן
עֵדֶן	ן pr. name masc.; for ן see lett. ו.	עדן
עִדָּן	ן Chald. noun masc. sing. dec. 1a	עדד
עֶדְנָא	pr. name masc.	עדן
עִדָּנָא	Chald. noun masc. sing., emph. of עִדָּן d. 1a	עדד
עַדְנָה	pr. name masc.	עדן
עֲדֶנָּה	contr. from עַד־הֵנָּה	עדה
עֶדְנָה	noun fem. sing.	עדן
עֹדֶנּוּ	ן defect. for עוֹדֶנּוּ (q. v.)	עוד
עִדָּנַיָּא	Chald. noun masc. pl. emph. from עִדָּן d. 1a	עדד
עֲדָנֶיךָ	the foll. with suff. 2 pers. sing. masc.	עדן
עֲדָנִים	noun masc., pl. of עֵדֶן dec. 6b	עדן
עִדָּנִין	'ן Chald. noun masc. pl. of עִדָּן dec. 1a	עדד
וַעֲדָעָה	ן pr. name of a place	עדד
[עָדַף]	I. *to be over, superabundant,* or *superfluous.*—II. *to exceed,* Nu. 3. 46, 48, 49. Hiph. *to cause to super- abound, to have over,* Ex. 16. 18.	
[עָדַר]	*to set in order, arrange, array.* Niph. I. *to be cleansed* or *cleared,* as a vineyard, by hoeing or	

a Ps. 78. 56.   d Job 6. 20.   h Eze. 26. 7.   m Ps. 103. 5.   p Ex. 33. 6.   t Eze. 23. 40.   x Da. 7. 12, 25.   b Ge. 18. 12.   f Ps. 36. 9.
b Is. 44. 8.   e Je. 2. 32.   i Mi. 7. 12.   n Ex. 33. 5.   q Is. 64. 5.   u Job 2. 9.   y Da. 2. 8, 9.   c Job 2. 3; 8. 12.   g 2 Sa. 1. 24.
c Is. 43. 10, 12.   g Is. 43. 9; 44. 9.   k Job 10. 17.   o Is. 47. 8.   r Ec. 4. 3.   v Ec.   z Da. 2. 21.   d Da. 7. 25.
l Job 16. 19.   h Is. 45. 24.   Job 32. 12.

raking, Is. 5. 6; 7. 25.—II. *to be missing* in a mustering, comp. פָּקַד.—III. *to be left behind.* Pi. *to omit, neglect,* 1 Ki. 5. 7.

עֵדֶר masc. dec. 6b (with suff. עֶדְרוֹ § 35. rem. 6).—I. *flock, herd.*—II. pr. name of a town in the tribe of Judah, Jos. 15. 21.—III. pr. name of a man.

עֶדֶר (*flock*) pr. name masc. 1 Ch. 8. 15.

עַדְרִיאֵל (*flock of God*) pr. name of a son-in-law of king Saul.

מַעְדֵּר masc. *a rake,* Is. 7. 25.

עֵדֶר וְ pr. name m. for עֶדֶר (§ 35. r. 2); for וְ see ו עדר

עֵדֶר וְ, ' noun m. s. d 6 (§ 35. r. 6), also pr. n. עדר

עֶדְרוֹ וְ id. with suff. 3 pers. sing. masc. עדר

עֹדְרֵי Kal part. act. pl. constr. masc. [fr. עָדַר] d. 7 b עדר

עֶדְרֵי noun m. pl. constr. fr. עֵדֶר d. 6 (§ 35. r. 6) עדר

עֶדְרֵיהֶם id. with suff. 3 p. pl. m. עדר

עֲדָרִים וְ', ' id. pl., abs. st.; וְ bef. (-:) עדר

עֲדָשִׁים pl. m. *lentils.* In the Talm. the sing. is עֲדָשָׁה

עֲדָת Chald. Peal pret. 3 pers. sing. fem. עדה

עֲדַת וְ', ' noun f. s., constr. of עֵדָה d. 11 b; וְ bef. (-:) יעד

עֲדָתוֹ וְ' id., suff. 3 pers. sing. masc.; וְ id. יעד

עֲדָתִי id., suff. 1 pers. sing. יעד

עֶדְוֹתַי וְ noun fem. pl., suff. 1 pers. sing. [for עֵדְוֹתַי] (§ 4. r. 2) fr. עֵדָה d. 10 (comp. § 30. No.3) עוד

עֵדְוֹתָיו וְ' id. pl., suff. 3 pers. sing. masc. עוד

עֵדְוֹתֶיךָ וְ' id. pl., suff. 2 pers. sing. masc. עוד

עֵדָתְךָ noun fem. sing., suff. 2 pers. sing. masc. from עֵדָה dec. 11b יעד

עוּב . Hiph. *to cover with darkness, darken* (Syr. Aph. *to obscure*), La. 2. 1.

עָב masc. dec. 1 a (pl. עָבִים, עָבוֹת).—I. *darkness,* chiefly of clouds.—II. *thick cloud.*—III. *a thicket,* Je. 4. 29.

עוֹבֵד ,' וְ עוֹבַדְיָה pr. names masc. עבד

עוֹבָל pr. name masc. עבל

עוֹבֵר Kal part. act. sing. masc. dec. 7 b. עבר

עוֹבְרֵי id. pl., constr. st. עבר

עוּג *to bake cakes,* Eze. 4. 12.

עֻגָּה ,עֻגָה fem. *cake, bread-cake.* מָעוֹג masc. id. 1 Ki. 17. 12; Ps. 35. 16.

עוֹג וְ' pr. name of a king of Bashan, famous for his gigantic stature. עוֹג supposed to stand for עָנֹק, עֶנֶק *long-necked, gigantic.*

עוּגָב וְ'- noun masc. sing. dec. 2b ענב

עוּד in Kal only, La. 2. 13 Kethib, *to say again and again, to testify.* Pi. *to surround,* Ps. 119. 61 Hiph. הֵעִיד.—I. *to call* or *take as a witness,* with בְּ *against* any one.—II. *to testify, bear witness,* with acc. *against* or *for* any one.—III. *to protest, affirm solemnly,* with בְּ of the person.—IV. *to exhort, admonish,* with בְּ, עַל.—V. *to enjoin, command.* Hoph. הוּעַד *to be testified, warning be given to,* with בְּ, Ex. 21. 29. Pil. *to set up, confirm.* Hithpal. *to keep oneself erect, upright,* Ps. 20. 9.

עוֹד, עֹד adv.—I. *again.*—II. *again and again, repeatedly.*—III. *further, besides.*—IV. *yet, as yet, still;* עוֹדֶנִּי, עוֹדְךָ, עוֹדֶנּוּ, עוֹדֶנָּה *I am, thou art, he, she is as yet* or *still.*—V. with prefixes; (a) בְּעֹד, בְּעוֹד *while, while yet;* בְּעֹדִי *while yet I am, while I yet have being; within yet;* (b) מֵעוֹד *since;* מֵעוֹדִי *since, ever since, I am.*

עוֹד Chald. *while,* Da. 4. 23.

עוֹדֵד (*setting up;* for מְעוֹדֵד) pr. name masc —I. 2 Ch. 15. 1, 8.—II. 2 Ch. 28. 9.

עֵד masc. dec. 1 a (comp. § 30. rem. 3).—I. *a witness.*—II. *testimony.*—III. *proof.*

עֵדָה fem. dec. 10 (comp. עֵד).—I. *a witness* (fêm.) Ge. 31. 52.—II. *testimony;* frequently of *the precepts* of God.

עֵדוּת fem. dec. 1 b, pl. עֵדְוֹת (comp. Chald. d. 8, pl. עֵדְוָן, מַלְכוּ).—I. *testimony* or *witness,* i. e. that which *testifies* or *witnesses* to the will and requirements of God; it is applied to the law, the decalogue, and the sacred rites; אֲרוֹן הָעֵדוּת *the ark of testimony,* as containing the tables of stone on which the decalogue was written; אֹהֶל הָעֵדֻת *the tabernacle of testimony,* where the sacred rites were performed.—II. the titles of Psalms 60 and 80.

תְּעוּדָה fem. *testimony* (comp. עֵדָה No. 1) applied to the law or precepts of God, Is. 8. 16, 20; and *to custom,* Ru. 4. 7.

עוֹד וְ' (prop., inf. abs.) only as an *adv.* עוד

עוֹדֵד pr. name masc. עוד

עוֹדִי וְ adv. (עוֹד) with suff. 1 pers. sing. עוד

עוֹדֵינָה id. pl., suff., Kh. נָה 3 p. pl. f., K. נוּ 1 p. pl. עוד

עוֹדֵךְ id. sing., suff. 2 pers. sing. fem. עוד

עוֹדְךָ וְ' id. sing., suff. 2 pers. sing. masc. עוד

עוֹדָם id. sing., suff. 3 pers. pl. masc. עוד

עוֹדֶנָּה id. sing., suff. 3 pers. sing. fem. עוד

עוֹדֶנּוּ ,' וְ id. sing., suff. 3 pers. sing. masc. עוד

עוֹרְדֵנִי Piel pret. 3 pers. pl., suff. 1 pers. sing. — עור

עוֹרְדֵנִּי adv. (עוֹד) with suff. 1 pers. sing. — עור

[עָוָה] to deal perversely, to sin. Niph. I. to be bent with pain, Is. 21. 3.—II. to be bowed down with sorrow, Ps. 38. 7.—III. to be perverse. Pi. עִוָּה. —I. to make crooked, La. 3. 9.—II. to overturn, turn upside down, Is. 24. 1. Hiph. הֶעֱוָה.—I. to make crooked, pervert one's way.—II. to act perversely.

עַוָּה, עַוָּה (overturning, ruin) pr. name, Ivvah or Avvah, an Assyrian city.

עַוָּה fem. overturning, overthrow, Eze. 21. 32.

עַוִּי, pl. עַוִּים.—I. gent. noun, Avites the earliest inhabitants of Philistia.—II. the inhabitants of the city עַוָּא or עַוָּה q. v. 2 Ki. 17. 31.—III. הָעַוִּים a city in the tribe of Benjamin, Jos. 18. 23.

עָוֹן, עָווֹן masc. dec. 3 a (pl. עֲווֹנִים, עֲוֹנוֹת).—I. iniquity, sin.—II. guilt.—III. punishment for sin.

עֲוָיָא Chald. fem. dec. 8 a, iniquity, sin, Da. 4. 24.

עֲוִית (ruins) pr. name of a town in Edom, Ge. 36. 35.

עַוְעֶה masc. dec. 9 a, perversity, Is. 19. 14.

עִי masc. (for עֱוִי; pl. עִיִּים § 37. No. 4).—I. ruin, heap of ruins.—II. עִיִּים pr. name of a part of mount Abarim.—III. עִיִּים pr. name of a city in Judah, Jos. 15. 29.

עַי (for עֱוִי, heap of ruins) pr. name of a Canaanitish city in the northern part of the tribe of Benjamin; called also עַיָּא, עַיָּה, עַיַּת.

עִיּוֹן (a ruin) pr. name of a city in the tribe of Naphtali.

מְעִי (for מַעֲוִי) masc. a heap of ruins, Is. 17. 1.

עָוָה noun fem. sing. — עוה

עַוָּה pr. name of a place — עוה

עִוָּה Piel pret. 3 pers. sing. masc. — עוה

עָווֹן noun masc. sing. dec. 3 a, comp. עָוֹן — עוה

עֲווֹן id., constr. st. — עוה

עֲווֹנֹתָיו id. pl. fem., suff. 3 pers. sing. masc. — עוה

[עוּז] or [עוֹז] to flee for refuge, with בְּ to any one, Is. 30. 2. Arab. عاذ id. Hiph. to cause to flee for refuge, safety, with acc. Ex. 9. 19; acc. implied, to save by flight, sc. one's effects.

עֹז noun masc. sing. for עֹז, (suff. עֻזִּי & עָזִּי) d. 8 c — עזז

עוּזָּה Kal imp. sing. masc. [עוּז] with parag. ה, — עזז

עֻזֵּנוּ n. m. s. with suff. 1 pers. pl. fr. עֹז d. 8 c [for עֻזֵּנוּ] — עזז

עוֹזֵר Kal part. act. sing. masc. dec. 7 b — עזר

עוּט Root not used; Arab. to impress, dig in

עֵט masc.—I. style, graver.—II. pen.

עֲוִיל noun masc. sing. — עול

עֲוִילֵיהֶם noun m. pl., suff. 3 p. pl. m. fr. [עֲוִיל] d. 3 a — עול

עֲוִילִים id. pl., abs. st. — עול

עָוִינוּ Kal pret. 1 pers. pl. — עוה

עֲוִית pr. name of a place — עוה

עֲוָיָתְךָ Ch. noun fem. pl., suff. 2 pers. sing. masc. from [עֲוָיָא] dec. 8 a; ן bef. (-ָ) — עוה

עוֹכֵר Kal part. act. sing. masc. dec. 7 b — עכר

עָוַל Kal not used; Arab. to decline, turn aside. Pi. to deal unrighteously, unjustly.

עַוָּל masc. unjust, wicked.

עָוֶל masc. (constr. עֶוֶל, with suff. עַוְלוֹ § 35. rem. 11) iniquity, injustice.

עַוְלָה fem. (with ה parag. עַוְלָתָה, contr. עוֹלָת pl. עוֹלוֹת) iniquity, wickedness.

עֹלָה fem. id. Ho. 10. 9, transp. for עַוְלָה.

עַלְוָן (unjust) pr. name masc. Ge. 36. 23, for which עַלְיָן 1 Ch. 1. 40.

עַוִּיל m. wicked, Job 16. 11; another under עוּל.

עוּל only in part. pl. fem. עָלוֹת.—I. being with young. —II. milk-giving, milch.

עוּל masc. (prop., part. pass. suckled) suckling, child, Is. 49. 15; 65. 20.

עוֹלֵל masc. dec. 3 a (pass. § 26. No. 5; and comp. עוּל subst.) id. Job 21. 11; 19. 18.

עֹל noun masc. sing. with suff. עֻלּוֹ (§ 35. r. 11) — עול

עֹל noun masc. sing. — עול

עֹל noun masc. sing., for עַל dec. 8 c — עלל

עוּל noun masc. sing. dec. 1 a — עול

עוֹלָה noun fem. sing. (§ 43. rem.) — עול

עֹלָה noun fem. sing. dec. 10 — צלה

עֹלָה Kal part. act. sing. masc. dec. 9 a — צלה

עֻלָּה noun m. s., suff. 3 pers. s. f. fr. עֹל d. 1 a — צול

עֹלוֹת noun fem. pl. of עֹלָה dec. 10 — עלה

עֹלוֹתֵיכֶם id. with suff. 2 pers. pl. masc. — עלה

עוֹלֵל noun masc. sing. dec. 2 b — עלל

עוֹלֵל Poal (pass.) pret. 3 pers. sing. masc. — עלל

עוֹלֵל Poel inf. (Je. 6. 9; La. 1. 22); or n. m. s. d. 7 b — עלל

---

a Ps. 119. 61.   d Is. 24. 1.   g Pr. 5. 22.   k Ps. 81. 2.   l Job 21. 11.   n Da. 9. 5.   p 1 Ch. 2. 7.   s Is. 49. 15.   t La. 1. 12.
b Eze. 21. 32.   e 2 Ki. 7. 9.   h Ps. 68. 29.   i Job 16. 11.   m Da. 4. 24.   o Job 19. 18.   q Is. 65. 20.   r Am. 5. 22.   u La. 1. 22.
c La. 3. 9.   f 1 Ch. 21. 8.   AA Eze. 43. 27.

עֹלְלָה	id. pret. 3 pers. sing. masc.	עלל
עֹלֵלוֹת	noun fem. pl., comp. עֹלֵלוֹת	עלל
עֹלְלֵי	noun masc. pl. constr. fr. עוֹלֵל dec. 7 b	עלל
עֹלְלֶיהָ	noun masc. pl., suff. 3 pers. sing. fem. from עוֹלֵל dec. 2 b	עלל
עֹלָלַיִךְ	id. pl., suff. 2 pers. sing. fem.	עלל
עֹלְלִים	id. pl., abs. st.	עלל
עֹלְלִים	noun masc. pl. of עוֹלֵל dec. 7 b	עלל
עֹלֵלְתָּ	Poel pret. 3 pers. sing. masc.	עלל
עוֹלָם	Kh. עוֹלָם, K. עֵילָם, pr name of a man and a province	עלם
עוֹלָם	noun masc. sing. dec. 2 b	עלם
עוֹלָמֵי	id. pl., constr. st.	עלם
עוֹלָמִים	id. pl., abs. st.	עלם
עוֹלַת	noun fem. sing., constr. of עוֹלָה dec. 10	עלה
עוֹלֹת	id. pl. comp. עֹלֹת & עוֹלוֹת	עלה
עוֹלֹת	noun fem., pl. of עֹלָה (§ 43. rem.)	עול
עוֹלָתָה	id. sing. with parag. ה	עול
עוֹלָתוֹ	noun fem. sing., suff. 3 pers. sing. masc. from עוֹלָה dec. 10	עלה
עוֹלֹתֵיהֶם	id. pl., suff. 3 pers. pl. masc.	עלה
עוֹלֹתֶיךָ	id. pl., suff. 2 pers. sing. masc.	עלה
עוֹלֹתֵיכֶם	id. pl., suff. 2 pers. pl. masc.	עלה
עוֹלָתְךָ	id. sing., suff. 2 pers. sing. masc.	עלה
עוֹמֵד	Kal part. act. sing. masc. dec. 7 b	עמד
עוֹמֶדֶת	id. part. sing. fem. dec. 13	עמד

עוֹן Root not used; *to dwell.* Arab. עני *to stay;* also *to take a wife;* עאן *to be married.*

עוֹנָה fem. dec. 10, *cohabitation, conjugal rights,* Ex. 21. 10.

מָעוֹן masc. dec. 3 a (pl. מְעוֹנִים § 32. rem. 5) —I. *habitation, dwelling.*—II. *refuge,* Ps. 71. 3; 90. 1; 91. 9.—III. pr. name (a) of a town in the tribe of Judah; (b) of a people, Ju. 10. 12; pl. מְעוֹנִים, 2 Ch. 26. 7; (c) of a man, 1 Ch. 2. 45.

מְעוֹנָה מָעֹנָה fem. d.10.—I. *habitation, dwelling.*—II. *den* of wild beasts.—III. *refuge,* De. 33. 27.

מְעוֹנִים pr. name—I. see מָעוֹן No. III (b).—II. of a man, Ezr. 2. 50; Ne. 7. 52.

מְעוֹנֹתַי (*my habitations*) pr. name m. 1 Ch. 4. 14.

מְעוֹנִים pr. name, 1 Ch. 4. 41, Kheth. i. q. מְעוּנִים No. I.

עוֹן noun masc. sing. dec. 3 a   עוה

עוֹן	id., constr. st.	עוה
עֹוֵן	K. עֹוֵן, Kal part. act. sing. masc.	עין
עֹנָה	noun masc. sing., suff. 3 pers. sing. fem.	עוה
עֹנֹה	(§ 3. rem. 3) from עוֹן dec. 3 a	
עֹנֶה	Kal part. act. sing. masc. dec. 9 a	ענה
עוֹנוֹ	noun masc. sing., suff. 3 pers. sing. masc. from עוֹן dec. 3 a	עוה
עוֹנוֹת	נ׳ id. pl. fem.; ו bef. (-:)	עוה
עוֹנֹתֵיהֶם	id. pl. fem., suff. 3 pers. pl. masc.	עוה
עוֹנֹתָיו	id. pl. fem., suff. 3 pers. sing. masc.	עוה
עוֹנֹתֵיכֶם	id. pl. fem., suff. 2 pers. pl. masc.	עוה
עוֹנֹתָם	id. pl. fem., suff. 3 pers. pl. masc. (§ 4. r. 2)	עוה
עֹנִי	נ׳ id. sing., suff. 1 pers. sing.; ו bef. (-:)	עוה
עֹנֶיךָ	id. pl. masc., suff. 2 pers. sing. masc.	עוה
עוֹנֵינוּ	id. pl. masc., suff. 1 pers. pl.	עוה
עוֹנְךָ עֹנְךָ	id. sing., suff. 2 pers. sing. masc.	עוה
עֹנֵךְ	id. sing., suff. 2 pers. sing. fem.	עוה
עֹנֵךְ	Kal part. act. sing. masc., suff. 2 pers. sing. masc. from עֹנָה dec. 9 a	ענה
עֹנְכִי	noun masc. sing., suff. 2 pers. sing. fem (§ 4. rem. 2) from עוֹן dec. 3 a	עוה
עֹנְכֶם	id., suff. 2 pers. pl. masc.	עוה
עֹנָם	id., suff. 3 pers. pl. masc.	עוה
עֹנֵן	ו Kal part. act. sing. masc. dec. 7 b	ענן
עֹנֵנוּ	ן׳ noun masc. sing., or pl. (for עֹנֵינוּ), suff. 1 pers. pl. from עוֹן dec 3 a; ו bef. (-:)	עוה
עֹנֹת	נ׳ id. pl. fem.; ו id.	עוה
עֹנֹתַי	id. pl. fem., suff. 1 pers. sing.	עוה
עֹנֹתֵיהֶם	id. pl. fem., suff. 3 pers. pl. masc.	עוה
עֹנֹתֵיכֶם	id. pl. fem., suff. 2 pers. pl. masc.	עוה
עֹנֹתֵינוּ	נ׳ id. pl. fem., suff. 1 pers. pl.; ו bef. (-:)	עוה
עֹנֹתָם	נ׳ id. pl. fem., suff. 3 pers. pl. m. (§ 4. r. 2)	עוה
עֹעִים	noun masc. pl. of [עֹעֶה] dec. 9 a	עוה

עוּף cogn. עוּב q. v. fut. יָעוּף, ap. וַיָּעַף.—I. *to cover with the wings,* as a bird its young, Is. 31. 5; *to cover with darkness* (Syr. id.), but only intrans. and trop. of calamity, Job 11. 17.—II. *to fly, fly away,* of birds; trop. of ships, of an army; with בְּ perh. *to fly upon, attack,* Is. 11. 14 (Prof. Lee).—III. *to fly away, vanish,* of a dream, of human life.—IV. fut. ap. וַיָּעַף (§ 21. rem. 9) *to be faint, weary* cogn. עָיֵף, יָעַף, comp. עָטַף. Pil. עוֹפֵף.—I. *to fly.*—II. *to cause to fly, brandish,* a sword, Eze. 32. 10. Hiph. *to make fly, turn quickly* the eyes, Pr. 23. 5. Hithpal. *to fly away, vanish,* Ho. 9. 11.

* La. 3. 51.   Je. 49. 9.   La. 2. 20.   La. 1. 5.
Ps. 8. 3.   Is. 45. 17.   Nu. 28. 24.   De. 27. 6.
Eze. 46. 2.   Is. 56. 7.   Ps. 50. 8.   Ps. 89. 8.
Ps. 19. 10.   1 Sa. 18. 9.   Nu. 15. 31.   Is. 66. 4.
Ne. 9. 2.   Je. 33. 8.   Ps. 130. 8.   Eze. 32. 27.
Ps. 32. 5.   Eze. 28. 18.   Job 5. 1.   Ps. 103. 3.
Eze. 21. 29.   Je. 16. 10.   Is. 64. 5.   Is. 65. 7.
La. 5. 7.   Is. 59. 12.   Le. 16. 22.
Is. 53. 11.   Is. 19. 14.   Job 5. 7.

עוֹף masc. collect *birds, fowls.*

עוֹף Chald. masc. 1. Da. 2. 38 ; 7. 6.

עֵיפָה fem.—I. *darkness.*—II. pr. name (a) of a son of Midian and the tribe descended from him ; (b) of a man, 1 Ch. 2. 47; (c) of a woman, 1 Ch. 2. 46.

עַפְעַפַּיִם masc. du. (of עַפְעַף dec. 8 d) *eyelids* ; poet. for *the eyes.*

מָעוּף masc. dec. 3 a, *darkness,* Is. 8. 22.

מוּעָף masc. id. Is. 8. 23.

עוֹף . ךָ ,יְ"ָ noun masc. sing. ; ךָ see lett. ו .

עוֹף . Kh. עוֹפַי, K. עֵיפַי pr. name masc.

עפר . עֹפֶרֶת noun fem. sing., comp. וְ

[עוּץ] *to consult, take counsel,* Ju. 19. 30 ; Is. 8. 10.

יָעוּץ (*counsellor*) pr. name masc. 1 Ch. 8. 10.

עוּץ וְ pr. name—I. of a son of Aram, Ge. 10. 23. —II. of a son of Nahor, Ge. 22. 21, from whom the land of *Uz* is supposed to derive its name, viz. *Ausitis,* a district of Arabia. —III. masc. Ge. 36. 28.

עוּק . Hiph. *to press, press down.*

עָקָה fem. dec. 10, *oppression,* Ps. 55. 4.

מוּעָקָה fem. *oppressive burden, affliction* or *pain,* Ps. 66. 11.

עוּר Kal not used ; *to dig, dig out,* i. q. חוּר . Pi. עוֵּר *to blind, make blind.*

עִוֵּר adj. masc. d. 7 b, *blind* ; also, *mentally blind.*

עִוָּרוֹן masc. *blindness,* De. 28. 28 ; Zec. 12. 4.

עַוֶּרֶת fem. idem. Le. 22. 22.

מְעָרָה fem. dec. 10, *cave, cavern.*

I. עוּר (inf. does not occur) *to awake, rouse oneself, rise* ; part. עֵר (§ 21. rem. 2) *waking, watching.* Niph. נֵעוֹר (§ 21. rem. 11).—I. *to be awakened, roused.* —II. *to be stirred* or *raised up, to arise.* Pil. עוֹרֵר—I. *to awaken, rouse.*—II. *to stir up, excite.* —III. *to raise, lift up* a sword, a scourge. Pilp. (§ 6. No. 4) *to excite* a cry, Is. 15. 5. Hiph. הֵעִיר. —I. *to awaken, rouse.*—II. *to stir up, excite.*—III. intrans. *to awake, bestir oneself,* with עַל *for* any one. Hithpal. I. *to raise* or *rouse oneself.*—II. perh. *to be elated,* Job 31. 29.

עָר masc. (*city* ; whence properly pl. עָרִים , see עִיר) pr. name of the metropolis of Moab, עָר־מוֹאָב *Ar of Moab,* otherwise called רַבָּה .

עֵר (*waking, watchful*) pr. name—I. of a son of Judah.—II. 1 Ch. 4. 21.

עֵרִי (for עֶרְיָה *watching,* i. e. serving *the Lord*) pr. name of a son of Gad, Ge. 46. 16. Patronym. עֵרִי (for עֵרִי) Nu. 26. 16.

עֵרָן (*watchful*) pr. name masc. Nu. 26. 36. Patronym. עֵרָנִי ibid.

עִיר fem. irr. (§ 45).—I. *a city, town,* prop. *a watching,* a place fortified and watched.—II. in composition with pr. names : עִיר הַמֶּלַח (*city of salt*) in the desert of Judah, near the Salt Sea, Jos. 15. 62 ;— עִיר נָחָשׁ (*city of serpents*) 1 Ch. 4. 12; — עִיר שֶׁמֶשׁ (*city of the sun*) in the tribe of Dan, Jos. 19. 41 ;— עִיר הַתְּמָרִים (*city of palm-trees*) for Jericho, abounding with palm-trees.—III. pr. name of a man, 1 Ch. 7. 12, for which עִירִי ver. 7.

עִיר Ch. m. d. 1 a, *a watcher,* Da. 4. 10, 14, 20

עִירָא (*watch*) pr. name masc.—I. 2 Sa. 20. 26 —II. 2 Sa. 23. 26.—III. 2 Sa. 23. 28.

עִירוּ (*a watching*) pr. name masc. 1 Ch. 4. 15.

עִירָם (*citizen* or *watchman*) pr. n. m. Ge. 36. 43.

יָעִיר (*whom He stirs up*) pr. name masc. 1 Ch 20. 5, Keri ; Kh. יָעוּר .

II עוּר Kal not used ; i. q. עָרָה , עָרַר . Niph. *to be made bare,* Hab. 3. 9.

עוֹר masc. dec. 1 a (pl. עוֹרוֹת), *skin* of man or of animals, prob. so called from the idea of *nakedness* ; Job 19. 20, עוֹר שִׁנָּי *skin of the teeth,* i. e. the gums.

מְעוֹרִים m. pl. (of מָעוֹר) *nakedness,* Hab. 2. 15.

עוּר Chald. masc. *chaff,* only כְּעוּר , Da. 2. 35.

עוּר . וְ b Piel pret. 3 pers. sing. m. ; or adj. m. d. 7 b

עוּר . עוֹר noun masc. sing. dec. 1 a .

ערב . עוֹרֵב pr. name of a man and a rock .

עוּר . עוּרָה c וְ Kal imp. sing. masc. with parag. ה (§ 21. rem. 5, comp. § 8. rem. 11) .

עוֹר . עוֹרוֹ noun masc. sing., suff. 3 p. s. m. fr. עוֹר d. 1 a

עוּר . עוֹרֹת adj. fem. pl. [of עַוֶּרֶת dec. 13], fr. עִוֵּר masc.

עוֹר . עוֹרִי e וְ noun masc. sing., suff. 1 pers. sing. from עוֹר dec. 1 a .

עוּר . עוֹרִי Kal imp. sing. fem. .

עיר . עֹרִים Kh. for עָרִים K. (q. v.) .

עוּר . עֹרִים adj. masc. pl. of עִוֵּר dec. 7 b .

עוֹר . עֹרָם g וְ noun masc. sing., suff. 3 pers. pl. masc. from עוֹר dec. 1 a .

עוֹר . עוֹרֵנוּ id. sing., suff. 1 pers. pl. .

עוּר . עוֹרֵר וְ Pilel pret. 3 pers. sing. masc. .

עֽוֹרֲרָה֒	id. imp. sing. masc. with parag. ה (comp. § 21. rem. 5, & § 8. rem. 11) .	עור
עֽוֹרְרוּ֖	Poel pret. 3 pers. pl. . . .	ערר
עֽוֹרַרְתִּי֗	וֹ Pilel pret. 1 pers. sing.; acc. shifted by conv. וֹ (comp. § 8. rem. 7) . .	עור
עֽוֹרַרְתִּ֫יךָ	id. with suff. 2 pers. sing. masc. .	עור
עֶ֫רֶת	noun fem. sing.	עור
עֹרֹת֗	noun masc. with pl. fem. term. fr. עוֹר d. 1 a	עור

[עוּשׁ]   i. q. חוּשׁ to hasten, make haste, Joel 4. 11.

עוּשׁ (hastener) pr. name m. of several persons.

עֹשֶׂה	Kal part. act. sing. masc. dec. 9a . .	עשה
עֹשֵׂה	וֹ id., constr. st. . . .	עשה
עֹשׂוּ֫	Kal imp. pl. masc. . . .	עוש
עֹשֵׂי֗	Kal part. act. pl. c. from עֹשֶׂה dec. 9a.	עשה
עֹשֵׁק	Kal part. act. sing. masc. dec. 7 b	עשק

עָוַת . Pi. עִוֵּת.—I. to make crooked, Ec. 7. 13.—II. to pervert, subvert; of judgment, to wrest. Pu. part. crooked, Ec. 1. 15. Hithpa. to bend oneself, bow down, Ec. 12. 3.

עַוָּתָה fem. dec. 10, oppression, La. 3. 59.

עוּת to aid, help, with acc. of the pers. and thing, only לָעוּת Is. 50. 4.

עֹתִי (for עֲתָיָה succoured of the Lord) pr. name masc. of two persons, 1 Ch. 9. 4; Ezr. 8. 14.

עָוָ֫תָה	Kal pret. 3 pers. sing. fem. . .	עוה
עִוְּתִי֗	Piel pret. 3 p. s. m. [עִוֵּת], suff. 3 p. s. m.	עות
עִוְּתוּ֫נִי	id. pret. 3 pers. pl., suff. 1 pers. sing. .	עות
עוּתִי	pr. name masc. . . .	עות
עִוְּתַ֫נִי	Piel pret. 3 pers. sing. m. [עִוֵּת], suff. 1 p. s.	עות
עַוָּתִי֗	noun fem. sing., suff. 1 pers. sing. [fr. עַוָּתָה]	עות
עָז	} adj. masc. sing. dec. 8a; subst. Ge. 49. 3	עזז
עֹז		
עֵז	וֹ, עֹ׳ noun f. sing. d. 8b; for וֹ see lett. וֹ	עזז
עֹז	וֹ, עָ׳ noun masc. sing. dec. 8c (§ 37. rem. 2); וֹ id. . .	עזז
עֹזִי֗	}	עזז
עִזָּא	וֹ pr. name masc. . . .	עזז
[עֲזָאזֵל]	masc. the scape-goat, Le. 16. 8, 10, 26, lit. goat of departure, comp. of עֵז & אָזַל q. v. Hengstenberg, who with some of the Jews, takes this word to signify a demon or devil, supposes the act of sending the goat to have been a symbol by which the kingdom of darkness and its prince were renounced,

and the sins sent back to him by which he had sought to enslave the people.

עָזַב (וֹ) fut. יַעֲזֹב.—I. to leave, forsake, desert.—II. to leave, leave behind.—III. to leave, commit to any one, with לְ, אֶל, עַל; intrans. Ps. 10. 14.—IV. to leave off, cease from, give up.—V. to set free or loose, Ex. 23. 5; part. עָזוּב set free. Niph. v: be left, forsaken, deserted; with לְ to be left, given over to, Is. 18. 6. Pu. id. Is. 32. 14.

עֲזוּבָה fem. dec. 10.—I. a forsaking, Is. 6. 12.—II. ruins.—III. pr. name (a) of the mother of Jehoshaphat, 1 Ki. 22. 42; (b) of the wife of Caleb, 1 Ch. 2. 18, 19.

עִזָּבוֹן masc. dec. 3c.—I. a market, market-place, Eze. 27. 12, 14, 16, 19, 22.—II. merchandise, Eze. 27. 27, 33.

עָזֹב֗	Kal pret. 3 pers. s. m. for עָזַב (comp. § 8. r. 7)	עזב
עָזֹב֗	id. inf. abs. (§ 8. rem. 8) . .	עזב
עֲזֹב֗	וֹ id. imp. sing. masc.; וֹ bef. (−ׄ) .	עזב
עֹזֵב	וֹ id. part. act. sing. masc. dec. 7 b .	עזב
עֻזַּב֗	Pual pret. 3 p. s. m. [for עֻזַּב comp. § 8. r. 7]	עזב
עָזְבָה֗	Kal pret. 3 pers. sing. f. [for עָזְבָה § 8. r. 7]	עזב
עָזְבָה֗	id. imp. sing. masc. with parag. ה (§ 8. r. 11)	עזב
עָזְבָהּ֗	id. inf. with suff. 3 pers. sing. fem. .	עזב
עֻזְּבָה֗	Pual pret. 3 pers. sing. fem. . .	עזב
עָזְבוּ֗	} Kal pret. 3 pers. pl. (§ 8. rem. 7) .	עזב
עָֽזְבוּ֗		
עֲזָבֽוֹ	id. pret. 3 pers. sing. masc., suff. 3 pers. s. m.	עזב
עִזְבוּ֗	id. imp. pl. masc. . . .	עזב
עֲזָבֽוּהָ	id. id., suff. 3 pers. sing. fem. .	עזב
עֲזָבֽוּךְ	וֹ id. pret. 3 p. pl., suff. 2 p. s. f.; וֹ bef. (−ׄ)	עזב
עֲזָבֽוּנִי	id. id., suff. 1 pers. sing. . .	עזב
עִזְּבוֹנַ֫יִךְ	} noun masc. pl., suff. 2 pers. sing. fem.	עזב
עִזְּבוֹנַ֫יִךְ	וֹ } from [עִזָּבוֹן] dec. 3c .	
עַזְבּוּק	pr. name masc. . . .	עזז
עֲזֻבוֹת	Kal part. pass. fem. pl. of עֲזוּבָה dec. 10, from עָזוּב masc. . .	עזב
עֹזְבֵי֗	וֹ id. part. act. pl. constr. m. fr. עֹזֵב d. 7 b	עזב
עֹזְבִי֗	id. sing., suff. 1 pers. sing. .	עזב
עֹזְבָיו֗	id. pl., suff. 3 pers. sing. masc. .	עזב
עֹזְבֶ֫יךָ	id. pl., suff. 2 pers. sing. masc. .	עזב
עָזְבֵךְ	id. inf., suff. 2 pers. sing. fem. .	עזב
עֲזָבָ֫ם	id. id., suff. 3 pers. pl. masc. .	עזב
עֲזַבְנֻ֫הוּ	id. pret. 1 pers. pl. (עֲזַבְנוּ), suff. 3 p. s. m.	עזב
עֲזָבַ֫נִי	id. pret. 3 pers. sing. masc., suff. 1 pers. pl.	עזב
עֲזַבְנוּ	id. pret. 1 pers. pl. . . .	עזב

a Ps. 80. 3.   f Ex. 39. 34.   k Ps. 119. 78.   q Le. 7. 23.   v Ex. 23. 5.   y Je. 49. 11.   d Je. 51. 9.   g Is. 1. 28.   l Je. 2. 17, 19.
b Is. 23. 13.   g Joel 4. 11.   l Job 19. 6.   r Is. 26. 1.   P Ps. 37. 8.   z 2 Ki. 8. 6.   e Eze. 23. 29.   h Zec. 11. 17.   m Je. 9. 12.
c Zec. 9. 13.   h Est. 1 16.   m La. 3. 59.   s Ge. 44. 22.   q Is. 32. 14.   a Je. 49. 25.   f Eze.27.12,14,22.   i Ezr. 8. 22.   n 2 Ch. 13. 10.
d Ca. 8. 5.   i Ec. 7. 13.   n Ge. 15. 9.   t Is. 58. 2.   b Ps. 19. 11.   c Eze. 27. 27, 33.   k Je. 17. 13.   o Ezr. 9. 9.
e Le. 23. 22.

39

עֲזָבַ֫נִי } id. pret. 3 pers. sing. masc., suff. 1 pers. sing.; } bef. (‑ָ) . . עזב
עֲזָבֻ֫נִי id. pret. 3 pers. pl. (עָֽזְבוּ), suff. 1 pers. sing. . עזב
עָזַ֫בְתְּ id. pret. 2 pers. sing. masc. . . עזב
עָזַ֫בְתִּי id. pret. 1 pers. sing. . . . עזב
עֲזַבְתִּ֫יךָ id. id., suff. 2 pers. sing. fem. . עזב
עֲזַבְתִּ֫ים id. id., suff. 3 pers. pl. m.; } for } conv. עזב
עֲזַבְתָּ֫ם id. pret. 2 pers. sing. m., suff. 3 pers. pl. m. עזב
עֲזַבְתֶּם } id. pret. 2 pers. pl. masc.; } for } conv. עזב
עֲזַבְתֶּ֫ן id. pret. 2 pers. pl. fem. . . עזב
עֲזַבְתַּ֫נִי id. pret. 2 pers. sing. masc., suff. 1 pers. sing. (for תַּ֫נִי § 2. rem. 1) . . . עזב
עַזְגָּד pr. name masc. . . . עזג

עָזָה Root not used; Arab. עזי to console.
יַעֲזִיאֵל (whom God consoles) pr. name masc. 1 Ch. 15. 18; for which עֲזִיאֵל ver. 20.
יַעֲזִיָה (whom the Lord consoles) pr. name masc. 1 Ch. 24. 26, 27.
מַעֲזְיָהוּ, מַעֲזְיָה (consolation of the Lord) pr. name masc. 1 Ch. 24. 18; Ne. 10. 9

עַזָּה } adj. fem. s. d. 10, fr. עַז m.; also pr. name עזז
עַזָּה pr. name masc. . . . עזז
עֻזָּה noun masc. sing., suff. 3 pers. sing. fem. from עֹז dec. 8 c . . . עזז
עֻזֹּה } id., suff. 3 pers. sing. masc. . . עזז
עֻזּוֹ }
עָזוֹב } Kal inf. abs. . . . עזב
עָזוּב } id. part. pass. sing. masc. . עזב
עֲזוּבָה id. id. fem.; also pr. name . עזב
עִזּוּז } adj. masc. sing. . . . עזז
עֵזוּז } noun masc. sing. dec. 1 a; } bef. (‑ֵ) עזז
עֱזוּזוֹ } id. with suff. 3 pers. sing. masc.; } id. עזז
עָזוּר pr. name masc. . . . עזר
עַזּוֹת adj. fem., pl. of עַזָּה from עַז masc. עזז

[עָזַז] fut. יָעֹז, inf. עֲזוֹז.—I. to make strong, to strengthen, const. with לְ Ec. 7. 19.—II. to be or wax strong; hence, to prevail.—III. to be, or show oneself strong, powerful, mighty. Hiph. הֵעֵז to make bold, with פָּנִים בְּפָנִים Pr. 7. 13; 21. 29.
עַזָּז (strong) pr. name masc. 1 Ch. 5. 8.
עִזּוּז masc. strong, mighty, Ps. 24. 8; collect. strong men, Is. 43. 7.
עִזּוּז masc. dec. 1 a, strength, might.
עַזִּיזָא (strength) pr. name masc., Ezr. 10. 27.
עַז masc. dec. 8 d, עַזָּה fem. dec. 10, adj.—I.

strong, vehement, fierce.—II. strong, fortified, Nu. 21. 24.—III. harsh, cruel, hardened, Is. 19. 4; עַד־פָּנִים bold, impudent.
עֵז fem. dec. 8 b.—I. goat; גְּדִי עִזִּים a kid of the goats; שֶׂה עִזִּים an animal of the goat kind.—II. pl. goat's-hair.
עֵז Chald. id., Ezr. 6. 17.
עֹז, עוֹז masc. dec. 8 c (§ 37. rem. 2).—I. strength, might, power; concr. strong ones, Ju. 5. 21.—II refuge, defence.—III. ascription of power, praise.
עֻזָּא, עֻזָּה (strength) pr. name m. of several men.
עַזָּה (strong, fortified) pr. name, Gaza, a city of the Philistines. Gent. noun עַזָּתִי.
מָעוֹז, מָעֹז masc. dec. 8 c (with suff. מָעֻזִּי, מְעֻזּוֹ § 37. rem. 2 & 4).—I. place of strength, stronghold, fortress.—II. refuge, asylum.
עֲזַזְיָהוּ (whom the Lord strengthens) pr. name masc. of several persons.
עֻזִּי (for עֻזִּיָּה q. v.) pr. name masc. of several persons.
עֻזִּיאֵל (strength of God) pr. name masc. of several persons. Patronym.—
עֻזִּיאֵלִי Nu. 3. 27.
עֻזִּיָּהוּ, עֻזִּיָּה pr. name, Uzziah, king of Judah, called also עֲזַרְיָהוּ, עֲזַרְיָה; also the name of several other persons.
עַזְבּוּק (strength exhausted) pr. name masc., Ne. 3. 16
עַזְגָּד (strength of fortune) pr. name masc.
עַזְמָ֫וֶת (strength of death) pr. name masc.—I. 2 Sa. 23. 31.—II. 1 Ch. 27. 25; see also בֵּית.
עֲזַזְיָהוּ ,עֲזָז } pr. names masc.; } bef. (‑ָ) . עזז
עָנִי noun masc. sing., suff. 1 pers. sing. from עֹז dec. 8 c (§ 37. rem. 2) . . עזז
עַזֵּי adj. pl. constr. masc. from עַז dec. 8 d עזז
עֻזִּי noun masc. sing., suff. 1 pers. sing. fr. עֹז d. 8 c עזז
עֻזִּיָּא, עֻזִּיָּה (for עֻזִּיָּה) pr. names masc. עזז
עֲזִיאֵל } pr name masc.; } bef. (‑ָ) . עזה
וַעֲזִיזָא, עֲזִיזָה } pr. names masc. עזז
עֻזֵּיִךְ } noun fem. pl., suff. 2 pers. s. m. fr. עֹז dec.8 b עזז
עַזִּים adj. pl. abs. masc. from עַז dec. 8 d עזז
עִזִּים } noun fem., pl. of עֵז dec. 8 b עזז
עִזִּין Chald. id. pl. abs. dec. 5 b עזז
עֻזֵּךְ noun masc. s., suff. 2 pers. s. m. fr. עֹז d. 8 c עזז
עֻזָּ֫ךְ } id., suff. 2 pers sing. masc. . . עזז
עֻזֶּ֫ךָ }

a Ps. 40. 13.   d Ps. 9. 11.   f Is. 42. 16.   h Ne.9.17,19,31.   k Hab. 3. 4.   m 2 Ki. 14. 26.   o Is. 43. 17.   r Pr. 18. 23.   s Ge. 31. 38.
b De. 31. 16.   e Is. 54. 7.   g De. 31. 17.   i Ex. 2. 20.   l Je. 14. 5.   n Ps. 24. 8.   p Ps. 78. 4.   q Is. 56. 11.   t Ezr. 6. 17.
c Je. 19. 4.

עֻזְּכֶם	id., suff. 2 pers. pl. masc. . . .	עזז
עֻזָּמוֹ	id., suff. 3 pers. pl. masc. . . .	עזז
עַזְמָוֶת ('וְ)	pr. name masc. (in compos. see בֵּית)	עזז
עַזָּן	pr. name masc. Nu. 34. 26.	

עָזְנִיָּה   fem. a species of *eagle*, according to the Sept. and Jerome, *the ospray*, or *the sea-eagle*, Le. 11. 13; De. 14. 12.

עָזַק   Pi. עִזֵּק *to dig*, Is. 5. 2.

עִזְקָא   Chald. fem. dec. 8 a, *engraved ring, seal*, Da. 6. 18.

עֲזֵקָה   (*dug up* or *over*) pr. name of a city in the plain of Judah.

עָזְקָה ('וְ)   pr. name of a place; וְ bef. (-:)

[עָזַר]   fut. יַעֲזֹר pl. יַעְזְרוּ (§ 13. rem. 5) *to help, assist, aid*, const. with acc., לְ, עִם, אַחֲרֵי; part. עֹזֵר *helper*; in war, *an ally*. Niph. *to be helped, to obtain help*. Hiph. i. q. Kal.

עֵזֶר   masc. dec. 6 b (with suff. עֶזְרִי § 35. rem. 6).—I. *help*; also as a concr. *helper*.—II. pr. name m.—(a) 1 Ch. 4. 4, for which עֶזְרָה ver. 17; (b) 1 Ch. 12. 9; (c) Ne. 3. 19.

עֵזֶר   (*help*) pr. name masc.—I. Ne. 12. 42.—II. 1 Ch. 7. 21.

עֶזֶר, עָזוּר   (*helper*) pr. name masc.—I. Je. 28. 1. —II. Eze. 11. 1.—III. Ne. 10. 18.

עֶזְרָא   (*help*) pr. name, *Ezra*.—I. a priest and scribe, who led up a colony of Jews from Babylon to Jerusalem.—II. Ne. 12. 1, 13.

עֶזְרָה   fem. (with suff. עֶזְרָתִי; no pl.).—I. *help*. —II. pr. name masc.; see עֵזֶר.

עֲזָרָה   fem.—I. *a court* of the temple.—II. *a settle* or *inbenching* in the altar of *burnt-offerings*, Eze. 43. 14, 17, 20; עָזַר i. q. חָצַר *to enclose*.

עֶזְרָת   fem. with ה parag. עֶזְרָתָה, *help*.

עֲזַרְאֵל   (whom *God helps*) pr. name masc. of several persons.

עַזְרִי   (for עֲזַרְיָה *help of the Lord*) pr. name masc., 1 Ch. 27. 26.

עֲזְרִיאֵל   (*help of God*) pr. name masc.—I. 1 Ch. 5. 24.—II. 1 Ch. 27. 19.—III. Je. 36. 26.

עֲזַרְיָהוּ, עֲזַרְיָה   (whom *the Lord helps*) pr. name masc. of several persons; it stands also for עֻזִּיָּה king of Judah, q. v.

עַזְרִיקָם   (*help against the enemy*) pr. name masc.

—I. 1 Ch. 3. 23.—II. 1 Ch. 8. 38; 9. 44.—III 1 Ch. 9. 14.—IV. 2 Ch. 28. 7.

יַעְזֵר, יַעֲזֵר   (*He will help*) pr. name of a city in the tribe of Gad.

עֶזֶר ('וְ)	for עֵזֶר (§ 35. rem. 2) pr. name masc. (see also רֹמַמְתִּי־עֶזֶר R. רום).	עזר
עָזוּר	Kal part. pass. sing. masc. [for עָזוּר] .	עזר
עָזּוּר	pr. name masc.	עזר
עֶזֶר ('וְ)	pr. name m. (see also רֹמַמְתִּי־עֶזֶר R. רום).	עזר
עֵזֶר ('וֹ)	noun m. s. d. 6 (§ 35. r. 6), also pr. name	עזר
עֹזֵר	Kal part. act. sing. masc. dec. 7 b .	עזר
עֶזְרָא ('וְ), עֶזְרָה, נַ, עֲזַרְאֵל	(see עֵזֶר) pr. names masc.	עזר
עֶזְרָה	noun fem. sing. (no pl.) . .	עזר
עֶזְרֹה	noun masc. sing., suff. 3 pers. sing. masc. (K. עֶזְרֹו) from עֵזֶר dec. 6 (§ 35. rem. 5) .	עזר
עֲזָרֹו	Kal pret. 3 pers. sing. m., suff. 3 pers. sing. m.	עזר
עֲזָרוּ	id. pret. 3 pers. pl. . . .	עיר
עֶזְרִי	pr. name masc. . . .	עזר
עֶזְרִי	noun masc. sing., suff. 1 pers. sing from עֵזֶר dec. 6 (§ 35. rem. 6) .	עזר
עֹזְרֵי	Kal part. act. pl. constr. masc. fr. עֹזֵר d. 7 b	עזר
עֲזַרְיָה, נַ, עֲזַרְיָהוּ	pr. names masc.; וַ bef. (-:)	עזר
עֹזְרֶיהָ	Kal part. act. pl., suff. 3 pers. sing. fem. from עֹזֵר dec. 7 b	עזר
עֲזַרְיָהוּ ('וַ)	pr. name masc., see עֲזַרְיָה . .	עזר
עֹזְרָיו	Kal part. act. pl., suff. 3 pers. sing. masc. from עֹזֵר dec. 7 b	עזר
עַזְרִיקָם ('וְ)	pr. name masc. . .	עזר
עֲזָרְךָ	Kal pret. 3 pers. sing. m., suff. 2 pers. sing. m.	עזר
עֶזְרְךָ, עֶזְרֶךָ	noun masc. sing., suff. 2 pers. sing. masc. from עֵזֶר dec. 6 (§ 35. rem. 6) .	עזר
עֲזָרָם	Kal pret. 3 pers. pl. (עָזְרוּ), suff. 3 pers. p. m.	עזר
עֶזְרָם	noun masc. sing., suff. 3 pers. pl. masc. from עֵזֶר dec. 6 (§ 35. rem. 6) .	עזר
עֲזָרֻנוּ	Kal pret. 3 pers. sing. masc., suff. 1 pers. pl.	עזר
עֶזְרֵנוּ	noun masc. sing., suff. 1 pers. pl. fr. עֵזֶר dec. 6 (§ 35. rem. 6)	עזר
עָזְרֵנִי ('וְ)	Kal imp. sing. masc. with suff. 1 pers. pl.	עזר
עִזְרוּנִי ('וְ)	id. imp. pl. masc. [עִזְרוּ], suff. 1 pers. sing.	עזר
עֲזָרֻנִי	id. imp. sing. masc., suff. 1 pers. sing.	עזר
עֲזָרַנִי	id. pret. 3 pers. sing. masc., suff. 1 pers. sing. (§ 2. rem. 1) . . .	עזר
עֶזְרָת	noun fem. sing. . .	עזר
עֶזְרַת	noun fem. sing., constr. of עֶזְרָה (no pl.)	עזר
עֲזַרְתָּ	Kal pret. 2 pers. sing. masc.	עזר
עֶזְרָתָה	noun fem. sing. (עֶזְרָת) with parag. ה	עזר
עֶזְרָתִי	noun fem. s., suff. 1 pers. s. fr. עֶזְרָה (no pl.)	עזר
עֲזַרְתִּיךָ	Kal pret. 1 pers. sing., suff. 2 pers. sing. masc.	עזר

a Ps. 89. 18.   c De. 33. 7.   e Eze. 12. 14.   g Eze. 30. 8.   i 1 Ch. 12. 18.   l Ps. 20. 3.   n Jos. 10. 6.   p Ps. 118. 13.   r Job 26. 2.
b Is. 31. 3.   d Ps. 46. 2.   f 2 Ch. 18. 31.   h Eze. 32. 21.   k De. 33. 29.   m 1 Sa. 7. 12.   o Jos. 10. 4.   q Is. 31. 2.

39*

עֲזַרְתִּיךָ id. id., suff. 2 pers. sing. fem. . . עזר

עֲזַרְתֶּם ׳וְ id. pret. 2 pers. pl. masc.; ׳וְ for ׳וָ, conv. עזר

עֶזְרָתֵנוּ noun fem. s., suff. 1 pers. pl. fr. עֶזְרָה (no pl.) עזר

עֲזַרְתַּנִי Kal pret. 2 pers. sing. masc., suff. 1 pers. s. עזר

עַזָּתָה pr. name of a place (עַזָּה) with parag. ה . עזז

עֵט noun masc. sing. . . . עוט

עֵטָא Chald. noun fem. sing. . . . יעט

עָטָה ׳וַ fut. יַעֲטֶה, ap. יַעַט (§ 24. rem. 3).—I. to cover, with עַל, to cover over.—II. to cover oneself, put on.—III. to wrap or roll up, Is. 22.17; intrans. to wrap oneself up in any thing, Je. 43.12.—IV. to become languid, to faint (comp. עָטַף) Ca. 1.7. Hiph. הֶעֱטָה to cover, with acc., עַל.

מַעֲטֶה masc. dec. 9a, covering, garment, Is. 61.3.

עֹטֶה Kal inf. abs. עטה

עֹטֶה id. part. act. sing. masc. dec. 9a . עטה

עָטוּ id. pret. 3 pers. pl. עטה

עֲטִינָיו noun masc. pl., suff. 3 p. s. m. fr. [עָטִין] d. 3a עטן

עֲטִישֹׁתָיו noun f. pl., suff. 3 p. s. m. fr. [עֲטִישָׁה] d. 10 עטש

עֹטְךָ ׳וְ Kal part. act. sing., suff. 2 pers. sing. masc. from עָטָה dec. 9a . . . עטה

[עֲטַלֵּף] masc. dec. 1b, bat.

עָטַן Root not used; Arab. to dress skins.

עָטִין masc. dec. 3a, skin-bottle for holding milk or water, Job 21.24.

[עָטַף] fut. יַעֲטֹף יַעַטָף (§ 13. rem. 5).—I. to cover, to clothe.—II. to cover oneself, to be covered.—III. to languish, faint, comp. עָטָה; part. עָטוּף languid, faint; weak, feeble. Niph. to languish, faint, La. 2.11. Hiph. to be weak, feeble, Ge. 30.42. Hithpa. to faint, of the mind.

מַעֲטָפָה fem. mantle, Is. 3.22.

[עָטַר] to surround, encompass, with acc., לְ. Pi. עִטֵּר to crown, with acc., לְ. Hiph. to crown, distribute crowns, Is. 23.8.

עֲטָרָה fem. constr. עֲטֶרֶת pl. עֲטָרוֹת (§ 42. r. 5). —I. crown, diadem.—II. pr. name fem. 1 Ch. 2.26.

עֲטָרוֹת (crowns) pr. name—I. of a city in the tribe of Gad, Nu. 32.3, 34.—II. of a city in Ephraim, Jos. 16.7, called also עֲטָרוֹת אַדָּר (crowns of Addar).—III. עֲ בֵּית יוֹאָב (crowns of the house of Joab) a city in the tribe of Judah, 1 Ch. 2.54.— IV. עֲ שׁוֹפָן a city in Gad, Nu. 32.35.

עֲטָרָה pr. name fem. . . . עטר

עֲטָרוֹת noun fem. pl. abs., from עֲטָרָה constr. (§ 42. rem. 5); also pr. name עטר

עֲטָרוֹת pr. name in compos. as עֲטְ אַדָּר &c. עטר

עֹטְרִים Kal part. act. masc., pl. of עֹטֵר dec. 7b עטר

עֲטֶרֶת ׳וְ noun fem. sing., used as the constr. of עֲטָרָה (§ 42. rem. 5); ׳וְ bef. (־) . עטר

עֲטֶרֶת שׁוֹפָן pr. name in compos. עטר

עֲטַרְתְּ Piel pret. 2 pers. sing. masc. . עטר

עָטַשׁ Root not used; Arab. to sneeze.

עֲטִישָׁה fem. dec. 10, a sneezing, Job 41.10.

עִי וְעַיָּא (see עִי) pr. name of place . עוה

עֵיבָל ׳וְ pr. name of a man and a mount עבל

עִירַי in some copies for עֲרִי (q. v.) . עוד

עִיּוֹן pr. name of a place . . עוה

עַוִּית Kh. עִיּוּת, K. עַיִּת pr. name of a place עוה

עִיט or עוֹט only fut. ap. וַיַּעַט, also וַתַּעַט (§ 22. rem. 3, & § 21. rem. 8).—I. to be angry with, with בְּ 1 Sa. 25.14.—II. to rush, fall upon with fury. Hence

עַיִט masc. dec. 6 h, rapacious bird or beast. עֵיט Coll. birds of prey . . . עיט עֵיטָם (place of rapacious beasts) pr. name of a town and hill in the tribe of Judah . עיט

עֵינִים ׳וְ noun masc. pl. of עִי dec. 8 (§ 8. No. עֵינוֹ 4), also pr. name עוה

עֵילִי pr. name masc. . . . עלה

עֵילָם ׳וְ pr. name—I. of a son of Shem, Ge. 10. 22, and a Persian province called after him Elam, i. e. Elymaïs. Gent. noun Chald. עֵלְמָיֵא Elamites.—II. Ezr. 2.7; 8.7; 10.2. —III. Ezr. 2.31.

[עַיִם] m. ardour, violence, Is. 11.15. Prof. Lee, drought.

עַיִן ׳וְ com. dec. 6h (du. עֵינַיִם).—I. eye; לְעֵינֵי פֹּ before the eyes of any one, in his presence; בְּעֵינֵי פֹּ in the eyes of any one, in his opinion, judgment; hence טוֹב בְּעֵינַי it seemeth good to me, i. e. it pleases me; חָכָם בְּעֵינָיו wise in his own estimation, conceited; מֵעֵינֵי פֹּ away from the eyes of any one, i. e. behind his back; בֵּין עֵינַיִם between the eyes, i. e. on the forehead; הָיָה לְעֵינַיִם לְ to be for eyes to any one, i. e. to lead him the right way; עַיִן בְּעַיִן eye with eye, with both eyes, plainly; עֵינַיִם רָמוֹת lofty eyes, i. e. pride.—

II. *face, surface.*—III. *face, appearance.*—IV. *fountain;* pl. עֲיָנוֹת, constr. עֵינוֹת (§ 35. rem. 12).— V. pr. name of a city of the Levites in the tribe of Simeon.—VI. pr. name of a place in the north of Palestine, Nu. 34. 11.—VII. עֵין גֶּדִי (*fountain of the kid*) a city in the desert of Judah.— עֵין גַּנִּים (*fountain of gardens*) a city of Judah, Jos. 15. 34 ; also a city of the Levites in Issachar.—עֵין דֹּאר, עֵין דֹּר (*fountain of the dwelling*) a city in the tribe of Manasseh.—עֵין חַדָּה (*sharp or swift fountain*) a city of Issachar, Jos. 19. 21.—עֵין חָצוֹר (*fountain of the court or village*) a city in Naphtali, Jos. 19. 37.—עֵין מִשְׁפָּט (*fountain of judgment*) i. q. קָדֵשׁ Ge. 14. 7 ; comp. Nu. 20. 13.— עֵין עֶגְלַיִם (*fountain of the two calves*) a city in Moab, Eze. 47. 10.—עֵין רֹגֵל (*fountain of the fuller*) a fountain in the confines of Judah and Benjamin. —עֵין רִמּוֹן (*fountain of pomegranates*) a city of Judah, Ne. 11. 28.—עֵין שֶׁמֶשׁ (*fountain of the sun*) a city on the confines of Judah and Benjamin, Jos. 15. 7.—עֵין תַּנִּים (*fountain of dragons*) a fountain near Jerusalem, Ne. 2. 13.—עֵין תַּפּוּחַ (*fountain of the city* תַּפּוּחַ) in the tribe of Manasseh, Jos. 17. 7.

עֵין Chald. dec. 3 d, id.

עַיִן part. (denom. of עַיִן) *to eye, view with envy,* 1 Sa. 18. 9, Kh. עוֹן.

עֵינַיִם (*two fountains*) pr. name of a town in the tribe of Judah, Ge. 38. 21 ; contr. עֵינָם Jos. 15. 34.

עֵינָן (*having eyes*) pr. name of a man.

עֵינָם (contr. from עֵינָיִם *fountains*) pr. name of a town in Judah, Jos. 15. 50.

עֵנָם (contr. for עֵינַיִם *two fountains*) pr. name of a city in Issachar, 1 Ch. 6. 58, elsewhere called עֵין גַּנִּים.

מַעְיָן masc. dec. 2 b (with ו parag. מַעְיְנוֹ ; pl. מַעְיְנוֹת, מַעְיָנִים) *fountain, well of water.*

עֵן noun fem. sing. dec. 6 h, for עֵין (§ 35. rem. 2) ; also pr. name ; for ן see lett. ו . עין

עֵן id., constr. st., also in compos. with pr. name, as עֵין גֶּדִי &c. . עין

עֵינָהּ id., suff. 3 pers. sing. fem. עין

עֵינָו id. du., suff. 3 pers. sing. masc. (§ 4. r. 1) עין

עֵינוֹ id. sing., suff. 3 pers. sing. masc. עין

עֵינֹן pr. name, see חֲצַר עֵינוֹן under . חצר

עֵינוֹת noun fem. pl., constr. of עֵינֹת, from עֵין dec. 6 h (§ 35. rem. 12) . עין

עֵינַי Chald. id. pl. (עֵינִין), suff. 1 pers. sing. d. 3 d עין

—

עֵינַי, עֵינָי } id. du., suff. 1 pers. sing. . עין

עֵינֵי ן id. du., constr. st. עין

עֵינִי ן id. sing., suff. 1 pers. sing. עין

עֵינֶיהָ id. du., suff. 3 pers. sing. fem. עין

עֵינֶיהוּ } id. du., suff. 3 pers. sing. masc. (§ 4. r. 5) עין

עֵינֵיהֶם id. du., suff. 3 pers. pl. masc. עין

עֵינָיו ן id. du., suff. 3 pers. sing. masc. עין

עֵינָו id. du. (Kh. עֵינָיו q. v.), or sing. (K. עֵינוֹ), suff. 3 pers. sing. masc. עין

עֵינַיִךְ ן id. du., suff. 2 pers. sing. fem. עין

עֵינֶיךָ ן id. du., suff. 2 pers. sing. masc. . עין

עֵינֵיכֶם id. du. (Kh. עֵינְכֶם), or sing. (K. עֵינְכֶם), suff. 2 pers. pl. masc. עין

עֵינֵיכֶם ן id. du., suff. 2 pers. pl. masc. . עין

עֵינַיִם, עֵינָיִם } id. du., abs. st. ; also pr. name עין

עַיְנִין ן Chald. id. pl., abs. st. dec. 3 d עין

עֵינֵינוּ ן id. du., suff. 1 pers. pl. עין

עֵינֶךָ, עֵינְךָ } id. sing., suff. 2 pers. sing. masc.; the first form also def. for עֵינֶיךָ } עין

עֵינֵךְ id. sing., suff. 2 pers. sing. fem. עין

עֵינְכֶם, עֵנָם } id. sing., suff. 2 pers. pl. masc. עין

עֵינָמוֹ } id. sing., suff. 3 pers. pl. masc. עין

עֵינָן pr. name masc. (see also חֲצַר עֵ. R. חצר) עין

עֵינֵנוּ noun fem. sing., suff. 1 pers. pl. fr. עֵין d. 6 h עין

עֵינֹת id. pl. abs. fem. (§ 35. rem. 12) עין

עֵינֹת id. pl. constr. fem. . עין

עֵינֹתָם Kh. עֵינֹתָם noun fem. pl. with suff. from עֵין q. v.; K. עֹנֹתָם [from עֹנָה] see . עון

[עָיֵף] *to be weary,* Je. 4. 31.

עָיֵף masc. dec. 5 c, עֲיֵפָה fem. adj. *weary, exhausted,* of fatigue, hunger, thirst ; trop. of a land.

עֵיפִי (*weary*) pr. name m. Je. 40. 8 ; Kh. עוֹפַי .

עָיֵף ן adj. masc. sing. dec. 5 c עיף

עָיְפָה Kal pret. 3 pers. sing. fem. עיף

עֲיֵפָה adj. fem. sing. from עָיֵף masc. . עיף

עֵיפָה ן noun fem. sing., also pr. name masc. . עוף

עֲיֵפִים adj. masc., pl. of עָיֵף dec. 5 c . עיף

[עִיר] *to heat* an oven, Ho. 7. 4. Arab. עאר *to be hot, ardent.*

עִיר masc.—I. *heat, anger,* Ho. 11. 9, perh. also Ps. 73. 20.—II. *fear, terror,* Je. 15. 8 ; perh. also, with the Syr., Job 24. 12, מֵעִיר מְתִים

יְנָאֵקוּ *from terror* (agony of death) *the dying groan*, reading מְתִים for מְתִים.

עָר masc. dec. 1 a, *an enemy*, 1 Sa. 28. 16; Is. 14. 21; Ps. 139. 20.

עָר Chald. masc. id. Da. 4. 16.

עַיִר "וְ] masc. dec. 6 h (pl. עֲיָרִים § 35. rem. 12) *a young ass, an ass colt;* also *a full grown ass.*

עִיר noun masc. sing. · עור

עִיר Chald. noun masc. sing. dec. 1 a · עור

עִיר וְ] noun fem. sing. irr., pl. עָרִים, once עֲיָרִים (§ 45); also pr. name · עור

עִירָא pr. name masc. · עור

עִירָד וְ] pr. name masc. · ערד

עִירָהּ noun masc. sing., suff. 3 pers. sing. fem. from עִיר irr. (§ 45) · עור

עִירֹה noun masc. sing., suff. 3 p. s. m. fr. עִיר d. 6 h · עיר

עִירוֹ noun fem. sing., suff. 3 pers. sing. masc. from עִיר irr. (§ 45) · עור

עִירוּ pr. name masc. · עור

עִירִי וְ] pr. name masc., see עִיר · עור

עִירִי noun m. s., suff. 1 pers. s. fr. עִיר irr. (§ 45) · עור

עֲיָרִים id. pl., abs. st. · עור

עֲיָרִים noun masc. pl. of עַיִר dec. 6 h (§ 35. r. 12) · עיר

עִירִין Chald. noun masc. pl. of עִיר dec. 1 a · עור

עִירְךָ noun f. s., suff. 2 p. s. m. fr. עִיר irr. (§ 45) · עור

עָרֵם נ] defect. for עֲיָרִים ; ו bef. (-:) · עיר

עֵירֹם וְ] adj. masc. sing., pl. עֵירֻמָּם, dec. 8 c · ערב

עֵירָם pr. name masc. · עור

עִירָם noun f. s., suff. 3 p. pl. m. fr. עִיר irr. (§ 45) · עור

עֵירֻמָּם adj. masc. pl. of עֵירֹם dec. 8 c · ערם

עַיִשׁ וְ] the name of a constellation, Job 38. 32, supposed to be *the Great Bear, Arcturus,* בָּנֶיהָ (her sons) being the three stars in its tail. It is also called עָשׁ q. v.

עָיַת pr. name of a place, see עַי · עוה

עַכְבּוֹר וְ] pr. name masc. · עכבר

עַכָּבִישׁ masc. *a spider,* Job 8. 14; Is. 59. 5.

[עַכְבָּר] masc. dec. 2 b, *mouse*; Prof. Lee, *jerboa.*

עַכְבּוֹר (*mouse*) pr. name masc. of two different persons.

עַכְבְּרֵי וְ] noun masc. pl. constr. from עַכְבָּר dec. 2 b · עכבר

עַכְבְּרֵיכֶם id. pl., suff. 2 pers. pl. masc. · עכבר

עַכּוֹ pr. n. of a city in the tribe of Asher, Ju. 1. 31.

עָכוֹר pr. name of a valley · עכר

עָכָן (*troubler,* i. q. עָכָר, comp. 1 Ch. 2. 7) pr. name masc. comp. Jos. 7. 1.

יַעְכָּן (id.) pr. name masc. 1 Ch. 5. 13.

עָכַס Kal not used; Arab. *to bind.* Pi. (denom. עֶכֶס q. v.) *to wear anklets,* or *to make a tinkling with them.*

עֶכֶס masc. dec. 6 a.—I. *fetter,* Pr. 7. 22.—II. pl. *anklets, ornamental foot-rings* or *chains,* Is. 3. 18. Hence

עַכְסָה (*anklet*) pr. name of the daughter of Caleb, Jos. 15. 16; Ju. 1. 12; 1 Ch. 2. 49.

עָכַר *to trouble, cause sorrow.* Niph. *to be irritated, excited,* Ps. 39. 3; part. fem. *confusion,* Pr. 15. 6.

עָכוֹר (*causing sorrow*) pr. name of a valley near Jericho.

עָכָר (*troubler*) pr. name m., elsewhere עָכָן q. v.

עָכְרָן (*troubled*) pr. name m. Nu. 1. 13; 2. 27.

עָכָר pr. name masc. · עכר

עֹכֵר וְ] Kal part. act. sing. masc. dec. 7 b · עכר

עָכְרָן pr. name masc. · עכר

עֲכַרְתִּי Kal pret. 1 pers. sing. · עכר

עֲכַרְתֶּם וְ] id. pret. 2 pers. pl. masc.; וַ for וְ, conv. · עכר

עֲכַרְתָּנוּ id. pret. 2 pers. sing. masc., suff. 1 pers. pl. · עכר

עַכְשׁוּב masc. *an asp,* Ps. 140. 4.

עַל noun m. s. (Ho. 7. 16); or *adv.* (2 Sa. 23. 1) · עלה

עַל noun masc. sing. · עלה

עַל וְ] prep., pl. c. עֲלֵי, with suff. עָלַי (§ 31. r. 5) · עלה

עַל Chald. Peal pret. 3 pers. sing. masc. · עלל

עַל־ Kh. עַל prep. q. v., K. עֲלֵי (q. v.) · עלה

אֶל־ Kh. עַל prep. R. עלה, K. אֶל (q. v.) ₪. · אלה

עֹל noun masc. sing. dec. 8 c · עלל

עֵלָא pr. name masc. · עלל

עֵלָּא וְ] Ch. עַל with parag. א, comp. [מַעְלָה] *adv.* · עלה

עֶלְבוֹן pr. name, see אֲבִי עַל · אב

עָלַג Root not used; i. q. לָעַג q. v. Hence

עִלְּגִים masc. pl. [of עִלֵּג d. 7 b] *stammerers,* Is. 32. 4 · עלג

עָלָה וְ] fut. יַעֲלֶה, ap. יַעַל (§ 24. rem. 3).—I. *to go* or *come up, to ascend, mount up,* with בְּ, לְ, אֶל, עַל also acc. of the place.—II. *to arise,* of the dawn. —III. *to spring* or *grow up;* Ge. 40. 10, עָלְתָה נִצָּהּ *it* (the vine) *sprang up into its blossom,* i. e. put

a Je. 15. 8.   d Ge. 49. 11.   g Da. 9. 19.   k Ge. 3. 7.   o 1 Sa. 6. 5.   t 1 Ki. 18. 18.   y Jos. 7. 25.   * Ho. 11. 7.   d 1 Ki. 1. 33.
b Da. 4. 10. 20.   e Ju. 10. 4.   h Ge. 32. 16.   l Job 38. 32.   p 1 Sa. 14. 29.   u Ge. 34. 30.   z 2 Sa. 23. 1;   b Da. 2. 16, 24.   e Da. 6. 3.
c De. 22. 21.   f Da. 4. 14.   i Eze. 18. 7, 16.   1 Sa. 6. 4, 11, 18.   r Pr. 11. 17.   x Jos. 6. 18.   Ho. 7. 16.   c Job 7. 1.   f Is. 32. 4.
* יעל 11. 12.

forth blossoms, comp. Pr. 24. 31; hence part. עֹלֶה Job 36. 33, *the rising*, sc. plant.—IV. *to rise, increase*. Niph. נַעֲלָה (§ 13. rem. 7, note).—I. *to be brought up*, Ezr. 1. 11.—II. *to be led* or *driven away*.—III. *to be exalted*. Hiph. הֶעֱלָה; fut. יַעֲלָה, ap. יַעַל (§ 24. rem. 16).—I. *to cause to go up, to lead, bring* or *carry up*.—II. *to put* or *set up*.—III. *to bring, offer*, or *present* an offering upon the altar.—IV. *to bring* into an account, *to enrol*, 1 Ki. 9. 21. Hoph. pass. of Hiph. Nos. I, III & IV. Hithp. *to exalt oneself*, Je. 51. 3.

עָלֶה masc. dec. 9 b, *a leaf*; collect. *foliage*.

עַל masc.—I. *high, the Most High*, Ho. 7. 16; 11. 7.—II. adv. *on high*, 2 Sa. 23. 1; מֵעַל *from above*, Ge. 27. 39; 49. 25; *above*, Ps. 50. 4.

עַל (prop. constr. of עַל dec. 2 a) pl. c. עֲלֵי, with suff. עָלַי, עָלֶיךָ, עָלָיו, &c. prep.—I. noting a state of rest, of one thing *upon, on, over, above* another, to the question *where?* as he sits עַל הַמִּטָּה *upon the bed*; espec. (a) with words which imply clothing, covering, protecting; and intellectually, trusting, sparing, pitying, pleasing; (b) with the idea of burden, trouble, and hence, duty or obligation; הָיוּ עָלַי לְטֹרַח *they are a burden upon me*; עָלַי לָתֵת *it lay on me to give*; then of hostility, as קוּם עַל *to rise against*; חָרָה עַל, קָצַף עַל *to be wrath against*; moreover with verbs of commissioning, ruling, commanding, as פָּקַד עַל, מָלַךְ עַל; (c) of the objects, means, instruments by which any thing is effected; as, to live עַל הַחֶרֶב *by the sword*; עַל הַלֶּחֶם *by bread*; frequently in the titles of the Psalms, e. g. עַל הַגִּתִּית *upon Gittith*; (d) of norm, rule, standard and cause, עַל דִּבְרָתִי כְּ *after the manner of Melchizedek*; עַל כָּכָה *in this manner*; עַל דְּבַר *because of, on account of*; עַל מָה *wherefore?* with inf. *because that*.—II. noting contiguity, (a) *at, by, near*; (b) *with*; e. g. flesh עַל הַדָּם *with the blood*; (c) as a periphrase for adverbs, עַל יֶתֶר *with abundance, abundantly*; עַל נְקַלָּה *lightly*.—III. with idea of motion, to the question *whither?* *upon, down upon, to, towards*, after verbs of laying, casting, raining; hence—IV. frequently i. q. אֶל, לְ marking the dative, *to, for*.—V. conj. (a) *though, although*, i. q. עַל אֲשֶׁר; (b) *because that, because*; more fully עַל אֲשֶׁר, עַל כִּי.—VI. with other particles. כְּעַל *according to*; as a conj. *accordingly*, Is. 59. 18. מֵעַל *from upon, from above*; also *from* (being) *near, at*, hence simply *away from, from*, after verbs of passing,

moving, turning. מֵעַל לְ *above, over*; also, *at, by, near, by the side of*.

עֲלֵיהוֹן, עֲלֵינָא, עֲלוֹהִי.—Chald. with suff. I. *upon, above, over*; עַל דְּנָה *therefore*.—II. i. q. אֶל *to*; and for לְ marking the dative.

עוֹלָה, עֹלָה fem. dec. 10.—I. *a step*, Eze. 40. 26. —II. *a burnt-offering*, a sacrifice which is wholly consumed.

עֵלָּא Chald. with מִן *above*, Da. 6. 3.

עֲלָוָ Chald. fem. *burnt-offering*, only pl. עֲלָוָן (comp. dec. 8 c) Ezr. 6. 9.

עֱלִי masc. *pestle*, Pr. 27. 22.

עֵלִי (*exalted*) pr. name, *Eli*, the high-priest.

עִלָּי Chald. masc. *the Supreme, Most High*, only emph. st. עִלָּיָא Kh. עִלָּאָה K.

עִלִּי adj. only fem. עִלִּית *upper*, Ju. 1. 15; pl. עִלִּיוֹת Jos. 15. 19.

עִלִּי Chald. fem. dec. 8 c, *upper chamber*, Da. 6. 11

עִילַי (*supreme*, i. q. Chald. עֶלְי) pr. name masc. 1 Ch. 11. 29, called צָלְמוֹן in 2 Sa. 23. 28.

עֲלִיָּה fem. dec. 10.—I. *upper room, chamber.*—II. *ascent, staircase*, 2 Ch. 9. 4.

עֶלְיוֹן masc. עֶלְיוֹנָה fem. adj.—I. *very high, lofty*, 1 Ki. 9. 8; 2 Ch. 7. 21.—II. *higher, upper.*—III. *high, exalted.*—IV. *the Supreme, Most High.*

עֶלְיוֹן Chald. masc. only pl. עֶלְיוֹנִין prob. *high places*, comp. מְרוֹמִים; others, *the Most High*, Da. 7. 18, 22, 25, 27.

מַעֲלֶה masc. dec. 9 a.—I. *ascent, place of ascent.* —II. *stage, platform*, Ne. 9. 4.—III. *ascent, acclivity, hill*; מַעֲלֵה אֲדֻמִּים *hill of the red ones*, on the confines of Judah and Benjamin; מ' עֲקְרַבִּים *hill of scorpions*, in the south of Palestine.

מַעַל adv. *above*; but only in composition.—I. מִמַּעַל *from above*, Is. 45. 8; also simply *above*; מִמַּעַל לְ *above, upon.*—II. מַעְלָה (with parag. ה) *upwards*; מַעְלָה מַעְלָה *higher and higher*; also *upward, above*, mostly of time; also *forward, onward*, 1 Sa. 16. 13.—III. לְמַעְלָה *upwards*; also *upward, above*; עַד לְמַעְלָה *to a high degree, exceedingly.*—IV. מִלְמַעְלָה *from above.*

מֹעַל *a lifting up, elevating*, Ne. 8. 6.

מַעֲלָה fem. dec. 10.—I. *ascent, going up*, Ezr. 7. 9; metaph. *suggestion*, Eze. 11. 5.—II. *step of a stair.*—III. *degree* of a sundial.—IV. שִׁיר הַמַּעֲלוֹת *song of degrees* in the title of fifteen psalms, prob. so called from having been sung upon the *steps* of the temple.

תְּעָלָה fem. dec. 10.—I. *channel for water, a*

conduit.—II. *plaster, bandage*, something *placed upon* a wound, Je. 30. 13; 46. 11. Others, *a recovery, a getting up* from illness.

עֹלֶה	noun masc. sing. dec. 9 b .	עלה
עֹלֵה	id. constr. st.; or Kal imp. s. m., וְ bef. (–ְ)	עלה
עֹלֶהָ	id. with suff. 3 pers. sing. fem.	עלה
עָלֹה	Kal inf. abs.	עלה
עָלֹה	Kh. עָלָה q. v.; K. עָלוּ (q. v.)	עלה
עֲלָה	Chald. noun fem. sing.	עלל
עֹלָה	וְ noun fem. sing.; or fem. of the foll.	עלה
עֹלֶה	Kal part. act. sing. masc. dec. 9 a	עלה
עֹלֵהוּ	וְ noun masc. sing., suff. 3 pers. sing. masc from עֹלֶה dec. 9 b	עלה
עֲלֹהִי	Chald. prep. (עַל) with suff. 3 pers. sing. m.	עלה
עֲלֵהֶם	defect. for עֲלֵיהֶם (q. v.)	עלה
עֲלֵהֶן	defect. for עֲלֵיהֶן (q. v.)	עלה
עֲלוֹ	וְ Kh. for עָלָיו K. (q. v.)	עלה
עָלוּ	וְ Kal pret. 3 pers. pl.	עלה
עֲלוּ	וְ id. imp. pl. masc., וּ bef. (–ְ)	עלה
עֻלּוֹ	וְ noun masc. sing., suff. 3 pers. sing. masc. from עֹל dec. 8 e	עלל
עֻלָּה	noun f. s. by transp. for עַוְלָה ; also pr. n. m.	עול
עֲלֹהִי	Chald. prep. (עַל) with suff. 3 pers. sing. masc.	עלה
עֲלוּמֵימוֹ / עֲלוּמָיו	noun masc. pl. [עֲלוּמִים], suff. 3 pers. sing. masc. (§ 4. rem. 1)	עלם
עֲלוּמָיִךְ	id. with suff. 2 pers. sing. fem.	עלם
עֲלוֹן	pr. name masc. [for עֵילוֹן]	עול
עֹלוֹת	Kal part. act. fem. pl. [of עָלָה fr. עַל masc.]	עול
עֲלוֹת	Kal inf. constr.	עלה
עֹלוֹת	id. part. act. f., pl. of עָלָה d. 10, fr. עָלָה m.	עלה
עֹלוֹת	וְ noun fem. pl. of עֹלָה dec. 10	עלה
עֲלוֹתָהּ	Kal inf. (עֲלוֹת), suff. 3 pers. sing. fem. dec. 1 a	עלה
עֲלוֹתוֹ	noun fem. pl., suff. 3 pers. sing. masc. from עֹלָה dec. 10	עלה
עֲלוֹתֵיכֶם	id. with suff. 2 pers. pl. masc.	עלה

[עָלַז] fut. יַעֲלֹז to *exult, rejoice*, with בְּ of the object of joy.

עָלֵז masc. dec. 1 b, one *rejoicing, expressing joy*. And the following.

עָלֵז	וְ adj. masc. one *exulting, rejoicing*	עלז
עִלְזוּ	וְ Kal imp. pl. masc.	עלז
עֲלֹזִי	וְ id. imp. sing. fem. (§ 8. rem. 12)	עלז

עֶלֶט	Root not used; Arab. *to be dense*, and transp. עטל *to be dark.* Hence	עטל
עֲלָטָה	וְ fem. *thick darkness*; וְ bef. (–ְ)	עלט
עָלַי / עֲלֵי	prep. (עַל) pl. with suff. 1 pers. sing. (§ 31. rem. 5)	עלה
עֲלַי	Ch. id. with suff. 1 pers. sing.	עלה
עֲלֵי	וְ id. pl. constr.; or noun masc. pl. c. fr. עָלֶה dec. 9 b; וְ bef. (–ְ)	עלה
עֲלִי	Kal imp. sing. fem.	עלה
עֵלִי	וְ pr. name masc.	עלה
עִלָּיָא	Chald. Kh. עִלָּיָא by Syriasm, K. עִלָּאָה adj. masc. sing. emph. [of עִלַּי comp. § 63]	עלה
עָלֶיהָ	וְ prep. (עַל) pl. with suff. 3 pers. sing. fem. (§ 31. rem. 5)	עלה
עַלְיָה	Kh., עַלְוָה K. pr. name masc.	עלה
עֲלֵיהּ	Ch. prep. (עַל) pl. with suff. 3 pers. sing. fem.	עלה
עֲלֵיהוֹן	Ch. id. with suff. 3 pers. pl. masc.	עלה
עֲלֵיהֶם	וְ id. with suff. 3 pers. pl. masc.; וַ bef. (–ְ)	עלה
עֲלֵיהֹם	Ch. id. with suff. 3 pers. pl. masc.	עלה
עֲלֵיהֶן	id. with suff. 3 pers. pl. fem.	עלה
עָלָיו	וְ id. with suff. 3 pers. sing. masc. (§ 31. r. 5)	עלה
עֶלְיוֹן	וְ adj. masc. sing.	עלה
עֶלְיוֹנִין	Ch. id. pl. abs. dec. 1 a	עלה
עֶלְיֹנוֹת	adj. fem., pl. of עִלִּי [from עֶלְיֹן masc.]	עלה
עֲלִיּוֹת	וְ noun fem., pl. of עֲלִיָּה dec. 10; וְ bef. (–ְ)	עלה
עֲלִיֹּתָיו	וְ id., suff. 3 pers. sing. masc.; וְ id.	עלה
עֶלְיֹנָה	adj. fem. sing. [from עֶלְיוֹן masc.]	עלז
עֶלְיֹנֵי / עֶלְיֹנִים	id. pl., constr. and abs. masc.	עלז
עֲלָיִךְ	Ch. prep. (עַל) pl. with suff. 2 pers. sing. masc.	עלה
עָלַיִךְ / וְעָלַיִךְ	id. with suff. 2 pers. sing. f. (§ 31. r. 5)	עלה
עָלֶיךָ	id. with suff. 2 pers. sing. masc.	עלה
עָלַיִכִי	id. with suff. 2 pers. sing. f. [עָלַיִךְ § 4. r. 4]	עלה
עֲלֵיכֶם	id. with suff. 2 pers. pl. masc.	עלה
עֲלִילָה	noun fem. sing. dec. 10	עלל
עֲלִילוֹתַי	id. pl., suff. 3 pers. sing. masc.	עלל
עֲלִילוֹתַיִךְ	id. pl., suff. 2 pers. sing. fem.	עלל
עֲלִילוֹתֵיכֶם	id. pl., suff. 2 pers. pl. masc.	עלל
עֲלִילוֹתָם	id. pl., suff. 3 pers. pl. (§ 4. rem. 2)	עלל
עֲלִילֹת	id. pl., comp. עֲלֹלוֹת	עלל
עֲלִילֹתָיו	id. pl., suff. 3 pers. sing. masc.	עלל

a De. 10.1.   b 1 Sa. 2.10.   i Job 20.11.   m Is. 5.14.   q Ge. 15.17.   t Da. 7.18, 22, 25, 27.   x Je. 22.14.   aa Is. 24.8.   ee Zep. 3.11.
c Is. 1.30.   e 2 Sa. 20.8.   k Is. 54.4.   n Ps. 68.5.   r Ezr. 5.1, 3.   y Ps. 104.3.   bb Is. 60.2.   ff De. 22.14, 17.
d 2 Ki. 24.10.   f Is. 10.27.   l Ho. 2.17.   o Zep. 3.14.   s Ezr. 7.24.   u Jos. 15.19.   z Je. 22.13.   cc Ps. 116.7.   gg 1 Ch.16.8; Is.12.4.
g Ezr. 6.11.   h Ho. 10.9.   Eze. 40.26.   pp Ge. 41.3, 5.

עֹלִים	Kal part. act. masc., pl. of עָלָה dec. 9a	עלה
עָלֵימוֹ	'ו prep. (עַל) pl. with suff. 3 p. pl. m. (§ 31. r. 5)	עלה
עֵלְיוֹן	pr. name masc., see עֶלְיוֹן	עול
עֲלֵינָא	Chald. prep. (עַל) pl. with suff. 1 pers. pl.	עלה
עֲלֶינָא		
עָלֵינוּ	Heb. id. with suff. 1 pers. pl. (§ 31. rem. 5)	עלה
עָלִינוּ	'ו Kal pret. 1 pers. pl.	עלה
עֲלִיצֻתָם	noun f. s., suff. 3 p. pl. m. fr. [עֲלִיצוּת] d. 10	עלץ
עָלִיתָ	'ו Kal pret. 2 pers. sing. masc.	עלה
עָלִית	id. pret. 2 pers. sing. fem.	עלה
עֲלִיַּת	noun fem. sing., constr. of עֲלִיָּה dec. 10	עלה
עֶלְיַת	adj. fem. sing. [from עֶלִי masc.]	עלה
עֲלִיָּתוֹ	ו noun fem. sing., suff. 3 pers. sing. masc. from עֲלִיָּה dec. 10 ; ו bef. (־ְ)	עלה
עָלִיתִי	'ו Kal pret. 1 pers. sing.	עלה
עֲלִיתָיו	ו id. pl. with suff. 3 pers. sing. m.; ו bef. (־ְ)	עלה
עֲלִיתֶם	ו Kal pret. 2 pers. pl. masc.; ו for ו conv.	עלה
עֻלְּךָ	noun masc. s., suff. 2 pers. s. f. fr. עֹל d. 8c	עלל
עֻלְּכֶם	id. with suff. 2 pers. pl. masc.	עלל

עָלַל Kal not used; i. q. גָּלַל to roll (comp. Fürst in concord.), hence to repeat an action, to do habitually or effectually (comp. Prof. Lee s. v.). Po. עוֹלֵל. —I. to roll any thing in the dust, Job 16. 15.—II. to glean, prop. to repeat an action, to go over again.—III. with לְ, to treat, to act towards, espec. to maltreat; hence to affect painfully, La. 3. 51. —IV. to act as a child, only part. מְעוֹלֵל a child, Is. 3. 12. Hithpa. with בְּ.—I. to exert oneself against any one.—II. to abuse, insult. Hithpo. to practise, Ps. 141. 4.

עֲלַל Chald. to go in, to enter. Aph. הַנְעֵל (§ 47. rem. 4, comp. § 52. rem. 2) to bring in. Hoph. to be brought in, Da. 5. 13, 15.

עוֹלֵל, עוֹלָל masc. dec. 7b & 2b, a child, boy, comp. Poel No. IV.

עוֹלֵלוֹת, עֹלֵלוֹת fem. pl. dec. 11b, gleanings.

עֹל masc. dec. 8c, a yoke; trop. servitude.

עַלָּא (yoke) pr. name masc. 1 Ch. 7. 39.

עִלָּה Chald. fem. pretext, pretence, Da. 6. 5, 6.

עָלִיל masc. crucible, Ps. 12. 7.

עֲלִילָה fem. work, deed, action.

עֲלִילִיָּה fem. id. Je. 32. 19.

מֶעָל Ch. pl. מֶעָלִין a setting of the sun, Da. 6. 15.

מַעֲלָל masc. dec. 2b, only pl. works, deeds.

מַעֲלִיל	masc. id. Zec. 1. 4, Kh.	
תַּעֲלוּל	masc. dec. 1b, only pl.—I. children, boys Is. 3. 4, comp. Poel No. IV, and עוֹלָל.—II. vexations, adversities, Is. 66. 4.	
עֹלֹלוֹת	defect. for עוֹלֵלוֹת (q. v.)	עלל
עֹלֵלוֹת	noun fem. pl. abs. dec. 11b	עלל
עֹלֵלוֹת	id. pl., constr. state	עלל
עֹלְלֵי	noun masc. pl. constr. from עוֹלָל dec. 7b	עלל
עֹלָלֶיהָ	noun masc. pl., suff. 3 p. s. f. fr. עוֹלָל d. 2b	עלל
עֹלְלֵיהֶם	'ו id. pl., suff. 3 pers. pl. masc.	עלל
עָלֲלִין	Chald., Kh. עָלְלִין Peal part. act. masc. pl. [of עֲלַל] dec. 2b ; K. עָלִּין contr.	עלל
עַלְּלַת	Ch., Kh. עַלֲלַת id. pret. 3 p. s. f.; K. עַלַּת contr.	עלל
עוֹלַלְתִּי	ו Poel pret. 1 pers. sing.	עלל

[עָלַם] I. to hide, conceal, only part. pass. עֲלֻמִים hidden, secret, sc. sins.—II. Arab. to grow ripe of age and desirous of marriage; hence derivv. עֶלֶם, עַלְמָה, עֲלוּמִים. Niph. נֶעְלַם to be hidden; part. נֶעְלָמִים hidden, i. e. crafty dissemblers, Ps. 26. 4. Hiph. הֶעְלִים to hide, conceal, with מִן (once בְּ) from any one, with עֵינַיִם, אֹזֶן to turn one's eyes or ears from any one, so as not to see or hear. Hithp. to hide oneself, to be hidden.

עֹלָם, עוֹלָם masc. dec. 2b, a time hidden, indefinite or unlimited.—I. of the past; (a) antiquity, ancient times; מֵעוֹלָם of ~, from ancient times; (b) time everlasting, u~~ut beginning; מֵעוֹלָם from everlasting, comp. Ps. 90. 2; 93. 2; Pr. 8. 23.—II. of the future; (a) very long, indefinite duration to come; לְעוֹלָם for ever, not endless, comp. Ex. 21. 6; 1 Ki. 1. 31; (b) eternity, everlasting duration; לְעוֹלָם for ever; עַד עוֹלָם id comp. Ps. 90. 2; 103. 17; Ps. 10. 16, מֶלֶךְ עוֹלָם וָעֶד king of eternity and perpetuity, i. e. king for ever and ever.—III. pl. עוֹלָמִים i. q. sing. Nos. I & II, comp. Ps. 77. 6; 145. 13; Is. 26. 4; —adv. for ever.

עֵילוֹם masc. i. q. עוֹלָם 2 Ch. 33. 7.

עָלַם Chald. masc. dec. 2a, id.

עֶלֶם m. a youth, young man, 1 Sa. 17. 56; 20. 22.

עַלְמָה fem. dec. 12a.—I. a maiden, virgin, marriageable but not married (comp. the Root No. II), so in the seven passages of its occurrence, viz. Ge. 24. 43; Ex. 2. 8; Is. 7. 14; Ps. 68. 26; Pr. 30. 19; Ca. 1. 3; 6. 8.—II. pl. עַל עֲלָמוֹת in the title of

Ps. 46, upon *Alamoth*, prob. the name of a musical instrument; others, with *female voices*.

עֲלוּמִים masc. pl. (of עָלוּם dec. 1 a) *youth, youthful age*; trop. for *vigour*, Job 20. 11.

עַלְמוֹן (*concealment*) pr. name—I. of a town in the tribe of Benjamin, Jos. 21. 18, for which עַלֶּמֶת in 1 Ch. 6. 45.—II. עֲ דִּבְלָתָיְמָה a station of the Israelites in the desert, Nu. 33. 46.

עֶלֶמֶת (*covering*) pr. name masc. of two different persons.

יַעְלָם (whom *He hides, protects*) pr. name masc. Ge. 36. 5, 14.

תַּעֲלֻמָה fem. dec. 10, *hidden thing, secret*.

עָלֵם   Chald. noun masc. sing. dec. 2 a   עלם

עֲלֵם•   noun masc. s., suff. 3 p. pl. m. fr. עַל d. 8 c   עלל

עָלְמָא   Chald. noun masc. sing., emph. of עָלַם d. 2 a   עלם

עֲלוּמוֹ•   noun masc. s., suff. 3 p. s. m. fr. עוֹלָם d. 2 b   עלם

עַלְמוֹן   pr. name of a place   .   עלם

עֲלָמוֹת ◌ֵן׳   noun f. pl. abs. fr. עַלְמָה d. 12 a; ◌ַ◌ bef. (◌ֵ)   עלם

עַלְמַיָּא•   Chald. noun masc. pl. emph. from עָלַם d. 2 a   עלם

עֵלְמָיֵא   Chald. gent. noun masc. pl. from עֵילָם q. v.

עֹלָמִים   defect. for עוֹלָמִים (q. v.)   .   עלם

עֲלֻמֵּנוּ   Kal part. pass. pl. masc., suff. 1 pers. pl. [from עָלַם] dec. 3 a   .   עלם

עָלֶמֶת עָלָמֶת ◌ְ׳ } pr. name masc. (comp. § 35. r. 2)   עלם

עַלֶּמֶת   pr. name of a place, see עַלְמוֹן   עלם

עֲלֵנוּ   noun masc. sing., suff. 1 pers. pl. fr. עַל d. 8 c   עלל

[עָלַס]   to *exult, rejoice*, Job 20. 18. Niph. id. Job 39. 13. Hithp. to *delight oneself*, Pr. 7. 18.

עָלַע   Pi. to *sip, suck up*, Job 39. 30.

עֲלַע   Chald. masc. *a rib*, only in the following form.

עִלְעִין׳   Chald. noun masc. pl. of [עֲלַע] dec. 3 b   עלע

עָלַף   Pu. I. to *be covered over*, Ca. 5. 14.—II. to *be languid, faint*, Is. 51. 20. Hithp. I. to *veil oneself*, Ge. 38. 14.—II. to *become languid, faint*. Hence

עֻלְפֶּה   masc. *languor, fainting*, Eze. 31. 15   עלף

עֻלְּפוּ‹   Pual pret. 3 pers. pl.   .   עלף

עָלַץ‹   fut. יַעְלֹץ to *exult, rejoice*, with בְּ in one, with לְ over one, to *triumph* over him.

עֲלִיצוּת   fem. *exultation, rejoicing*, Hab. 3. 14.

עֲלַק   Root not used; Arab. to *adhere*.

עֲלוּקָה fem. *leech*, Pr. 30. 15.

עָלֹת׳   defect. for עֲלוֹת (q. v.)   .   עלה

עֹלַת ◌ַ◌׳   noun fem. sing., constr. of עֹלָה dec. 10   עלה

עֹלֹת ◌ַ◌׳ᵏ   id. pl.; or (Ge. 41. 2, 22) part. comp.   עלה

עָלְתָה עָלָתָה ◌ַ◌׳ } Kal pret. 3 pers. sing. fem. (comp. § 8. rem. 7) עלה

עֹלָתָה׳   ◌ַ◌ noun fem. sing. (עוֹלָה) with parag. ה (§. 43. rem.)   עול

עֲלָתָהּ•   defect. for עֲלוֹתָהּ (q. v.)   עלה

עֲלָתָה•   Kh. עַלָתָה q. v.; K. עַוְלָתָה (q. v.)   עול

עֲלֹתוֹ•   Kal inf. (עֲלוֹת), suff. 3 pers. sing. masc. dec. 1 a   .   עלה

עֹלָתוֹ ◌ִ׳•   noun fem. sing., suff. 3 pers. sing. masc. from עֹלָה dec. 10   עלה

עֹלֹתֶיךָ   id. pl., suff. 2 pers. sing. masc.   עלה

עֹלֹתֵיכֶם   id. pl., suff. 2 pers. pl. masc.   עלה

עֹלָתְךָ   id. sing., suff. 2 pers. sing. masc.   עלה

עֹלָתָם•   id. sing., suff. 3 pers. pl. masc.   עלה

עַם ◌ַ◌׳, עָם ◌ְ׳, ◌ָ◌, (with distinct. acc.) noun com. sing., pl. עַמִּים dec. 8 d, also pl. עֲמָמִים (§ 45)   .   עמם

עִם ◌ְ׳   prep. with suff. עִמִּי, עִמְּךָ (§ 5)   עמם

עַמָּא•   Chald. noun com. sing., emph. of עַם dec. 5 a, but pl. עַמְמַיָּא (§ 68)   עמם

I. עָמַד ◌ַ◌׳ fut. יַעֲמֹד .—I. to *stand*, spoken of animate and inanimate things; with לִפְנֵי to *stand before* any one, to *serve, minister* to him; with עַל to *stand, be set over*; to *stand upon, confide in*, Eze. 33. 26; to *stand by* or *for*, i. e. to *defend*.—II. to *stand, stand firm, endure*; with בְּ, בִּפְנֵי, נֶגֶד, לִפְנֵי before or against any one.—III. to *stay, remain*; hence, to *remain alive*, Ex. 21. 21.—IV. to *stand still, stop*; hence, to *desist, leave off*; with מִן from any thing. —V. to *stand up, arise*; with עַל against any one. Hiph. הֶעֱמִיד .—I. to *cause to stand*.—II. to *set up, erect*.—III. to *set, place*.—IV. to *set, establish, appoint*, e. g. an ordinance, with לְ, עַל for any one also to *appoint, constitute* to an office.—V. to *confirm, accomplish*.—VI. intrans. to *stand still*, 2 Ch. 18. 34. Hoph. הָעֳמַד .—I. to *be set, placed*, Le. 16. 10.—II. to *remain*, 1 Ki. 22. 35.

II. עָמַד   once by transp. for מָעַד in Hiph. Eze. 29. 7, to *make to tremble*.

עֹמֶד prop. *standing being*; hence, with the suff. of 1 pers. (only) עָמְדִי *with me*.

עֹמֶד masc. dec. 6 c, *a standing place, station*.

עֶמְדָּה fem *a place for stopping*, only sing. Mi. 1. 11.

עַמּוּד masc. dec. 1 b.—I. *column, pillar*.—II. *stage, scaffold*

מַעֲמָד masc. dec. 2 b.—I. *standing, order*, 1 Ki. 10. 5.—II. *station, place of standing*.

מָעֳמָד masc. *place for standing, bottom*, Ps. 69. 3.

עָמַד *a*וְ) Kal pret. 3 pers. s. masc. for עָמַד (§ 8. r. 7) עמד
עֲמֹד *b*וְ) id. inf. abs. עמד
עֲמֹד *c*וְ) id. imp. s. masc.; or inf. constr.; וְ bef. (־) עמד
עֲמָד־ *d* id. imp. (§ 8. rem. 18) עמד
עֹמֵד *a* id. part. act. sing. masc. dec. 7 b עמד
עָמְדָה *e*וְ) id. pret. 3 pers. sing. fem. עמד
עָמְדוֹ *f*וְ) defect. for עַמּוּדָיו (q. v.) עמד
עָמְדוּ
עָמְדוּ } Kal pret. 3 pers. pl. (§ 8. rem. 7) עמד
עָמְדוֹ id. inf or, 2 Ch. 34. 31, subst. [עֹמֶד dec. 6 c], suff. 3 pers. sing. masc. עמד
עִמְדוּ *g*
עִמְדוּ *h* } id. imp. pl. masc. (§ 8. rem. 12) עמד
עֹמְדוֹת *i* id. part. act. fem., pl. of עֹמֶדֶת dec. 13, from עוֹמֵד masc. עמד
עָמְדִי noun m. s., suff. 1 pers. sing. fr. [עֹמֶד] d. 6 c עמד
עָמְדִי *k*וְ) defect. for עַמּוּדִי (q. v.) עמד
עִמְדִי *m*וְ) prep. [עֹמֶד] with suff. 1 pers. sing. עמד
עִמְדִי Kal imp. sing. fem. עמד
עֲמֻדָיהָ *n* noun masc. pl., suff. 3 pers. sing. masc. from עַמּוּד dec. 1 b עמד
עַמּוּדֵיהֶם *o*וְ) id. pl., suff. 3 pers. pl. masc.; id. עמד
עַמּוּדָיו וְ) id. pl., suff. 3 pers. sing. masc.; id. עמד
עַמּוּדִים *p*וְ) id. pl., abs. st. עמד
עֹמְדִים Kal part. act. masc., pl. of עוֹמֵד dec. 7 b עמד
עָמְדְךָ id. inf., suff. 2 pers. sing. masc. עמד
עָמְדְךָ noun masc. sing., suff. 2 pers. sing. masc. from [עֹמֶד] dec. 6 c עמד
עָמְדָם id. id., suff. 3 pers. pl. masc. עמד
עָמַדְנוּ *u*וְ) id. pret. 1 pers. pl. עמד
עָמַדְתָּ
עָמַדְתְּ } id. pret. 2 pers. sing. masc.; acc. shifted by conv. וְ . עמד
עֹמֶדֶת } id. part. act. sing. fem. dec. 13, from עוֹמֵד masc. (§ 8. rem. 19) עמד
עֲמָדָתוֹ *v* noun. fem. s., suff. 3 pers. s. m. [from עֶמְדָּה] עמד
עָמַדְתִּי
עָמַדְתִּי } Kal pret. 1 pers. sing.; acc. shifted by conv. עמד

עֲמַדְתֶּם *n*וְ) id. pret. 2 pers. pl. masc.; וְ for וְ, conv. עמד

עָמָה Root not used; cogn. עָמַם q. v.

עָמִית fem. dec. 3 a, *society, fellowship*, Zec. 13. ; then for the concr. *fellow-man, neighbour*.

עַמָּה *a*וְ Chald. emph. of עַם irr. (§ 68) עמם
עַמָּהּ *b*וְ) noun com. sing., suff. 3 pers. sing. fem. from עַם dec. 8 d (exc. pl. עֲמָמִים § 45) עמם
עִמָּהּ prep. (עַם) with suff. 3 pers. sing. fem. (§ 5) עמם
עִמֵּהּ Chald. id. with suff. 3 pers. sing. masc. עמם
עָמָּה וְ pr. name of a place עמם
עִמְּהוֹן *c*וְ Ch. prep. (עַם) with suff. 3 pers. pl. masc. עמם
עִמְּהֶם וְ) Heb. id. with suff. 3 pers. pl. masc. עמם
עַמּוֹ וְ) noun com. sing., suff. 3 pers. sing. masc. from עַם dec. 8 d (exc. pl. עֲמָמִים § 45) עמם
עִמּוֹ וְ) prep. (עַם) with suff. 3 pers. sing. m. (§ 5) עמם
עַמּוּד *c*וְ) noun masc. sing. dec. 1 b עמד
עַמּוּדוֹ id., suff. 3 pers. sing. masc. עמד
עַמּוּדֵי וְ) id. pl., constr. st. עמד
עַמּוּדֶיהָ *g*וְ) id. pl., suff. 3 pers. sing. fem. עמד
עַמּוּדֵיהֶם *h* id. pl., suff. 3 pers. pl. masc. עמד
עַמּוּדָיו וְ) id. pl., with suff. 3 pers. sing. masc. עמד
עַמּוּדִים id. pl., abs. st. עמד
עַמּוֹן וְ) pr. name of a people עמם
עַמּוֹנִי gent. noun from עַמּוֹן עמם
עַמּוֹנִיּוֹת } id. fem., pl. of עַמּוֹנִית (§ 39, 4, rem. 1, note), K. עַמֳּנִיּוֹת עמם
עָמוֹס pr. name masc. עמם
עֲמוּסוֹת *i* Kal part. pass. f. pl. [of עֲמוּסָה fr. עָמוּס m.] עמם
עָמוֹק pr. name masc. עמק
עֲמֻקָּה *k* adj. fem. sing. fr. עָמֹק masc. (§ 39, 3. r. 1) עמק
עַמֵּי *l*וְ) noun com. pl. constr. from עַם dec. 8 d (exc. עֲמָמִים § 45) עמם
עַמַּי וְ) id. sing. with suff. 1 pers. sing. עמם
עִמִּי prep. (עַם) with suff. 1 pers. sing. עמם
עַמִּיאֵל pr. name masc. עמם
עַמֶּיהָ *m* noun com. pl., suff. 3 pers. sing. fem. fr. עַם dec. 8 d (exc. עֲמָמִים § 45) עמם
עַמִּיהוּד pr. name masc. עמם
עַמַּי noun com. pl., suff. 3 pers. sing. masc. fr. עַם dec. 8 d (exc. עֲמָמִים § 45) עמם
עַמִּיזָבָד pr. name masc. עמם
עַמִּיחוּר Kh., עַמִּיהוּד K. q. v. עמם
עַמִּיךָ noun com. pl., suff. 2 pers. s. m. fr. עַם d. 8 d עמם
עַמִּים וְ) id. pl., abs. st., comp. עֲמָמִים (§ 45) עמם
עַמִּינָדָב וְ) pr. name masc. עמם
עֲמִיקְתָא Ch. adj. f. s. emph. [of עֲמִיקָא fr. עָמִיק m.] עמק

a 2 Sa. 20. 12.   *f* Ex. 27. 11.   *k* Ex. 38. 17.   *s* Ex. 38. 19.   *x* De. 4. 10.   *y* Eze. 33. 26.   *d* Da. 2. 22.   *g* Job 9. 6.   *h* Pr. 23. 27.
b Est. 9. 16.   *g* Na. 2. 9.   *l* Nu. 3. 37.   *p* 1 Ki. 7. 41.   *t* Ec. 1. 4.   *z* Je. 7. 10.   *e* Ezr. 5. 2.   *h* Ex. 38. 10, 11,   *l* Ne. 10. 32.
c Da. 10. 11.   *h* 2 Ch. 35. 5.   *m* Ru. 1. 8.   *q* Ob. 11.   *u* Mi. 1. 11.   *a* Ezr. 5. 12.   *f* Ex. 13. 22.   12, 14.   *m* Ex. 31. 14.
d 2 Sa. 1. 9.   *i* Ps. 122. 2.   *n* Ex. 39. 40.   *r* Da. 10. 11.   *v* 1 Sa. 19. 3.   *b* Is. 65. 18.   *g* 2 Ch. 23. 13.   *i* Is. 46. 1.   *n* Da. 2. 22.
e Ki. 1. 2.   *k* Sa. 14. 9.

עָמִיר^a noun masc. sing. . . . עמר

עֲמִישַׁדַּי pr. name masc. . . . עמם

עֲמִיתוֹ noun fem. sing., suff. 3 pers. sing. masc. from [עָמִית] dec. 3 a . . עמה

עֲמִיתִי^b id., suff. 1 pers. sing. . . עמה

עֲמִיתֶךָ } id., suff. 2 pers. sing. masc. עמה
עֲמִיתֶךָ^c }

עַמֶּךָ (וֹ) } noun com. sing., suff. 2 pers. sing. m. } עמם
עַמָּךְ (וֹ) } from עַם dec. 8 a (exc. עֲמָמִים § 45) }
עַמֵּךְ^d } id. with suff. 2 pers. sing. fem. . עמם
עַמֵּךְ prep. (עֵם) with suff. 2 pers. sing. fem. עמם
(Chald. masc.), or in pause for the foll.

עַמְּךָ (וֹ) } id. with suff. 2 pers. sing. masc. (§ 3. } עמם
עַמְּכָה^e } rem. 2) . . . . }
עַמְּכֶם (וֹ) id. with suff. 2 pers. pl. masc. (§ 5) . עמם

עָמַל^f fut. יַעֲמֹל to toil, labour, travail. Hence the two following.

עָמָל (וֹ) masc. dec. 4 c.—I. labour, toil.—II. travail, vexation, sorrow.—III. fruit of labour.— IV. mischief, iniquity, sin, Nu. 23. 1, perh. also Is. 10. 1.—V. pr. name m. 1 Ch. 7. 35 עמל

עָמֵל adj. masc. dec. 5 c.—I. labouring, toiling; pl. labourers, workmen, Ju. 5. 26.—II. weary, wretched עמל

עֲמַל^g (וַ) n. m. s., constr. of עָמָל d. 4 c; וֹ bef. (–ֹ) עמל

עָמְלָה^h Kal pret. 3 pers. sing. fem. . . עמל

עֲמָלוֹ (וֹ) n. m. s., suff. 3 p. s. m. fr. עָמָל d. 4 c; וֹ bef. (–ֹ) עמל

עָמְלוּⁱ Kal pret. 3 pers. pl. . . . עמל

עֲמָלִי (חֲ) n. m. s., suff. 1 p. s. fr. עָמָל d. 4 c; וֹ bef. (–ֹ) עמל

עֲמֵלִים^k adj. masc., pl. of עָמֵל dec. 5 c עמל

עֲמָלֵנוּ^l noun masc. s., suff. 1 pers. pl. fr. עָמָל d. 4 c עמל

עֲמָלֵק (וַ) pr. name—I. of a grandson of Esau, Ge. 36. 12, 16.—II. of a people who inhabited the south of Palestine, and the borders of the desert of Sinai. Hence

עֲמָלֵקִי (וַ) gent. noun from the preceding, Amalekite.

עָמַלְתָּ^m Kal pret. 2 pers. sing. masc. . . עמל

עָמַם I. to hide, conceal, Eze. 31. 8; intrans. to be hidden, Eze. 28. 3.—II. as in the Arab. to be common, in common, whence derivv. עַם, עָם, עַמָּה. Hoph. הוּעַם to become obscured, dim, La. 4. 1.

עַם, עָם com. dec. 8 a or d (pl. עַמִּים, עֲמָמִים § 45).—I. people, nation; most frequently of Israel opposed to גּוֹיִם gentiles; pl. עַמִּים is also used for other nations; בְּנֵי עַמִּי the children of my people,

i. e. my countrymen; בַּת עַמִּי the daughter of my people, i. e. my people or country; it is applied to a tribe, comp. Ju. 5. 18; also to family, kindred, relatives, comp. Le. 21. 1, 4; 19. 16.—II. of animals, a swarm or flock.

עַם Chald. id. pl. עַמְמִין (§ 68).

עִם prep. (with suff. עִמִּי, עִמְּךָ &c. § 5).—I. with, along with; Ne. 5. 18, עִם־זֶה with this, notwithstanding; Ps. 72. 5, עִם־שָׁמֶשׁ with the sun, i. e. as long as the sun endures; עָשָׂה חֶסֶד עִם to do kindness with any one, i. e. to show him kindness—II. at, by, near.—III. like as, comp. Ec. 2. 16; Ps. 72. 5.—IV. with, amid.—V. מֵעִם prop. from (being) with, at, by; hence (a) simply from; Job 34. 33 מֵעִמְּךָ from with thee, i. e. according as it proceeds from thy mind or judgment; (b) from among, Ru. 4. 10.

עִם Chald. i. q. Heb. with, along with; עִם־לֵילְיָא in the night; עִם־דָּר וְדָר during generation and generation, as long as the generations of men endure.

עֻמָּה fem. dec. 10.—I. prop. union, connexion; as a prep. לְעֻמַּת, עֻמַּת, לְעֻמּוֹת, (a) by, at, near, (b) against, Eze. 3. 8; (c) opposite to, 1 Ch. 26. 16; like, even as; כָּל־עֻמַּת wholly as, Ec. 5. 15; מִלְּעֻמַּת near by.—II. pr. name of a town in the tribe of Asher, Jos. 19. 30.

עַמּוֹן (of or from the people or kindred, i. e. בֶּן־עַמּוֹן Ge. 19. 38) pr. name of the son of Lot' daughter and his descendants. Gent. noun עַמּוֹנִי fem. עַמּוֹנִית Ammonite, pl. fem. עַמּוֹנִיּוֹת.

עַמְעָד (people of duration) pr. name of a town of Asher, Jos. 19. 26.

עַמְרָם (the people is exalted) pr. name—I. of the father of Moses. Patronym. עַמְרָמִי.—II. Ezr. 10. 34.

עַמִּיאֵל (kindred of God) pr. name masc. of several persons.

עַמִּיהוּד (kindred of Judah, for עַמִּי יְהוּד) pr. name masc. of several persons.

עַמִּיזָבָד (kindred of the Giver) pr. name masc. 1 Ch. 27. 6.

עַמִּיהוּר (kindred of nobility) pr. name masc. 2 Sa. 13. 37, Kh.

עַמִּינָדָב (kindred of the prince) pr. name masc. of several persons.

עַמִּישַׁדַּי (kindred of the Almighty) pr. name masc. Nu. 1. 12; 2. 25.

עִמָּנוּאֵל (*God with us*) a prophetic title of the Messiah, Is. 7. 14; 8. 8.

עִמָּם noun com. sing. with suff. 3 pers. pl. masc. from עַם dec. 8d (exc. עֲמָמִים § 45) .

עִמָּם prep. (עִם) with suff. 3 pers. pl. masc. (§ 5)

עֲמָמֻהוּ Kal pret. 3 pers. pl. [עָמְמוּ], suff. 3 p. s. m.

עֲמָמוּךָ id., suff. 2 pers. sing. masc. .

עַמְמֵי constr. of עֲמָמִים (q. v.) .

עַמְמַיָּא Ch. noun com. pl. emph., irr. of עַם (§ 68)

עֲמָמִים וְ noun com. pl., irr. of עַם (§ 45); וְ bef. (ָ)

עֲמָמֵנוּ id. sing. with suff. 1 pers. pl. dec. 8d

עִמָּנוּ וְ prep. (עִם) with suff. 1 pers. pl. (§ 5)

עַמֹּנִים prophetic name

עַמֹּנִים gent. noun, pl. of עַמֹּנִי from עַמֹּון .

[עָמַשׂ , עָמֵם] fut. יַעֲמֹס—I. *to take* or *lift up*, Zec. 12. 3.—II. *to bear, carry*, Is. 46. 3.—III. *to load, lay a burden upon*, with עַל, לְ. Hiph. *to load, burden*, with עַל.

עָמֹוס (*bearer* of burden) pr. name, *Amos*, the prophet.

עֲמָשָׂא (*burden*) pr. name masc. of two different persons.

עֲמָשַׂי (*burdensome*) pr. name of three different persons.

עֲמַסְיָה (*the Lord bears* him *up*) pr. name masc. 2 Ch. 17. 16.

מַעֲמָסָה fem. *burden*, Zec. 12. 3.

עֲמַסְיָה pr. name masc. . . .

עֲמַסְיָהֿ the foll. with suff. 3 pers. sing. fem.

עֹמְסִים וְ Kal part. act. masc. pl. [of עֹמֵס] dec. 7 b

עַמְעָד וְ pr. name masc. . . .

[עָמֵק] *to be deep, unsearchable*, Ps. 92. 6. Hiph. *to make deep*; Je. 49. 8, 30 הֶעֱמִיקוּ לָשֶׁבֶת *make deep to dwell*, i. e. make your dwellings deep in the earth; metaph. *to act deeply, lay deep designs*.

עָמֵק adj. masc. dec. 5, *deep, profound*, only pl. c. עִמְקֵי שָׂפָה *of unintelligible speech*.

עֹמֶק masc. pl. עֲמָקִים, fem. עֲמֻקָּה.—I. *deep*.—II. metaph. *unsearchable*.

עָמֹוק (*deep*) pr. name masc. Ne. 12. 7, 20.

עַמִּיק Chald. only fem. עַמִּיקָא (dec. 8a) adj. *deep, profound, unsearchable*, Da. 2. 22.

עֵמֶק masc. dec. 6b.—I. *deep place*, Pr. 9. 18.—II. *valley* or *vale*.—III. עֵ הָאֵלָה *valley of terebinths*, near Bethlehem; עֵ בְּרָכָה *valley of blessing*, 2 Ch. 20. 26; עֵ הַמֶּלֶךְ *the king's valley*, not far

from the Dead Sea; עֵ רְפָאִים *valley of the Rephaim*, south-west of Jerusalem.—IV. עֵ קָצִיץ (*valley of cutting*) pr. name of a town in Benjamin, Jos. 18. 21.

עֹמֶק fem. *depth*, Pr. 25. 3

מַעֲמַק masc. dec. 8a, only pl., *depths*.

עָמֹק וְ adj. m. s., pl. עֲמֻקִים d. 8c (§ 37. No. 3c)

עֹמֶק וְ noun masc. sing. dec. 6b . .

עֲמֻקָּה adj. fem. sing. dec. 10, from עָמֹק masc. (q. v.)

עָמְקוּ Kal pret. 3 pers. pl. .

עֲמֻקֹּות adj. fem., pl. of עֲמֻקָּה fr. עָמֹק masc. (q. v.)

עִמְקֵי adj. pl. constr. masc. from [עָמֹק] dec. 5 .

עֲמָקֵךְ the foll. with suff. 2 pers. sing. fem. .

עֲמָקִים וְ noun masc.,pl. of עֵמֶק dec. 6b; וְ bef. (ָ)

עֲמֻקִּים adj. masc., pl. of עָמֹק dec. 6c (§ 37. No. 3c)

עֻמְקֵךְ noun masc. sing., suff. 2 pers. s. f. עֹמֶק d. 6b

עֻמְקָם id., suff. 3 pers. pl. masc.

עָמַר Pi. *to bind* sheaves, Ps. 129. 7. Hithp. with בְּ *to serve oneself with* any one, *treat* him *as a slave*.

עֲמַר Chald. *wool*, i. q. Heb. צֶמֶר Da. 7. 9.

עָמִיר masc. *a sheaf*. See also the three following.

עֹמֶר masc. dec. 6c.—I. *sheaf*.—II. *Omer*, a measure of things dry, tenth part of an ephah .

עֲמֹרָה וְ pr. name, *Gomorrah*, one of the four cities of the valley of Siddim, destroyed in the time of Lot and Abraham .

עָמְרִי וְ (for עָמַרְיָה *servant of the Lord*) pr. name —I. *Omri*, king of Israel.—II. of three other men . .

עַמְרָם pr. name masc. . . .

עֲמָשָׂא pr. name masc. . . .

עֲמָשַׂי
עֲמָשַׂי } pr. name masc.; וְ bef. (ָ)

עֹמְשִׂים Kal part. act. pl. masc. for עֹמְסִים .

עֲמַשְׂסַי וְ pr. name masc. Ne. 11. 13.

עֻמַּת (prop. noun fem. sing., constr. of עֻמָּה) adv.

עֲנָב Root not used; Chald. *to bind together*.

עֲנוּב (*bound together*) pr. name masc. 1 Ch. 4. 8. Also the two following.

עֲנָב וְ (i. q. עֵנָב *cluster*) pr. name of a town in Judah, Jos. 11. 21; 15. 50 .

עֵנָב masc. dec. 4b, *clusters of grapes* .

עִנְּבֵי id. pl. constr. with dag. euph. (§ 33. rem. 1

עֲנָבִים וְ id. pl. abs.; וְ bef. (ָ)

עֲנָבֵמֹו id. pl., suff. 3 pers. pl. masc.

עֵנֶג. Pu. part. *delicately brought up*, Je. 6. 2. Hithp.
I. *to be delicate*, De. 28. 56.—II. *to delight oneself,
to rejoice in any thing*, with עַל, also כְּמֶן—III. *to
sport oneself against any*, with עַל Is. 57. 4.

עָנֹג masc. עֲנֻגָּה fem. adj. *delicate, tender.*

עֹנֶג masc. *delight, pleasure*, Is. 13. 22; 58. 13.

תַּעֲנוּג masc. dec. 1 b (pl. ־ים, ־וֹת) *delight,
pleasure, enjoyment, luxury.*

עֶנֶג noun masc. sing. · · · · ענג

עֲנֻגָּה‎ f adj. fem. sing. from עָנֹג masc. (§ 37.
No. 3 c); וַ bef. · · · ענג

[עָנַד] *to bind on.*

מַעֲדַנּוֹת (for מַעֲדֻנוֹת) fem. pl. *bands*, Job 38. 31.

עָנְדֵם‎ Kal imp. sing. masc., suff. 3 pers. pl. masc.
(ם for ן fem. § 2. rem. 5) · · ענד

I. עָנָה‎ וְ‎ fut. יַעֲנֶה, ap. וַיַּעַן (§ 24. rem. 3).—I. *to answer*,
const. with acc. of the thing answered, also with
acc. of the person; *to answer God*, is to dispute
with him; it is spec. spoken (a) of judges, Ex. 23. 2;
(b) of those who *answer* to inquiries of the judge,
to give testimony, to testify, with בְּ *for*, but more
frequently *against* any one; (c) frequently of God,
to answer prayer; hence *to impart* or *grant* any
thing; Ec. 10. 19, הַכֶּסֶף יַעֲנֶה אֶת־הַכֹּל *money
answers (serves)* all sc. purposes.—II. *to answer in
singing, sing alternately, in response*; hence *to sing
to any one*, with לְ *to celebrate* him; also *to cry,
call, shout*, as soldiers in battle, or the jackals in
the desert, Is. 13. 22.—III. *to speak, begin to speak*;
of God, *to announce, declare* an oracle. Niph.
I. *to be answered.*—II. *to be induced to answer*,
Eze. 14. 4, 7. Pi. *to sing.* Hiph. *to answer favourably, grant, impart.*

עָנָה, עֲנָא Chald. *to answer, speak, begin to speak.*

II. [עָנָה]‎ I. *to bestow labour upon, to exercise oneself*, with
בְּ, Ec. 1. 13; 3. 10.—II. *to be afflicted, depressed,
humbled.* Niph. *to be afflicted, humbled*, with
מִפְּנֵי *to humble oneself before* any one, Ex. 10. 3.
Pi. *to oppress, subdue, afflict, humble*; with אִשָּׁה
to ravish a woman; with נֶפֶשׁ *to fast.* Pu. *to be
afflicted, humbled.* Hiph. *to oppress, afflict.* Hithp.
I. *to humble, submit oneself.*—II. *to be afflicted*,
1 Ki. 2. 26.

עֲנָה Chald. *to be afflicted.*

עֲנָה (*answer* sc. to prayer) pr. name—I. of a

son of Seir, and his descendants.—II. of a son of
Zibeon, grandson of Seir.

עָנָו masc. dec. 4 c, *humble, meek, poor, afflicted.*

עֲנָוָה fem. dec. 11 c (§ 42. r. 1) *humility, meekness.*

עֲנָוָה fem. id. Ps. 45. 5.

עֱנוּת fem. *affliction*, Ps. 22. 25; others, *cry.*

עָנִי masc. dec. 8 f. עֲנִיָּה fem. adj. *afflicted, distressed, poor, needy.*

עֳנִי masc. dec. 6 k, *affliction, misery.*

עֻנִּי (*depressed*) pr. name of a man.

עֲנָיָה (*whom the Lord answers*) pr. name masc.
Ne. 8. 4; 10. 23.

עֵינָיו masc. frequently in Keri for עֵנָו in Khethib.

עִנְיָן masc. dec. 2 b, *business, affair, matter, thing.*

עֲנָת (*answer*) pr. name masc. Ju. 3. 31; 5. 6.

עֲנָתוֹת (*answers*) pr. name—I. of a city of the
Levites in the tribe of Benjamin. Gent. noun
עֲנְתֹתִי.—II. of two men, 1 Ch. 7. 8; Ne. 10. 20.

עֲנְתֹתִיָּה (*answer from the Lord*) pr. name masc.
1 Ch. 8. 23.

יַעַן I. prep. *on account of, because of.*—II. conj.
because that, because; יַעַן אֲשֶׁר (a) *because that*,
(b) *to the intent that*, Eze. 12. 12; יַעַן כִּי *because
that*; יַעַן בְּיַעַן, וּבְיַעַן *because, even because.*

יַעֲנַי (for יַעֲנְיָה *the Lord answers*) pr. name masc.
1 Ch. 5. 12.

מַעֲנֶה masc. dec. 9 a.—I. *answer.*—II. *intent, end,
purpose*, Pr. 16. 4.

מַעַן prop. for מַעֲנֶה *intent, purpose*, only in the
combination לְמַעַן, with suff. לְמַעֲנָה, לְמַעֲנִי, &c.
(comp. dec. 6 d).—I. prep. *on account of, because
of, for the sake of.*—II. conj. *in order that, so that*;
לְמַעַן אֲשֶׁר *to the end that, in order that*; also
because that.

מַעֲנָה fem. *furrow*, 1 Sa. 14. 14.

מַעֲנִית fem. dec. 1 b, id. Ps. 129. 3. Keri.

תַּעֲנִית f. d. 1 b, *self-humiliation, fasting*, Ezr. 9. 5.

עֲנֹה‎ וַ pr. name masc.; וַ bef. · · ענה

עָנֵה Chald. Peal part. act. s. m. d. 6 a (§ 55, note) ענה

עַנֵּה‎ Piel inf. abs. · · · · ענה

עֲנֵה Kal imp. sing. masc. · · · ענה

עִנָּה Piel pret. 3 pers. sing. masc. · · ענה

עֹנֶה‎ וְ Kal part. act. sing. masc. dec. 9 a · ענה

עָנָהוּ id. pret. 3 p. s. m., suff. 3 p. s. m. (§ 24. r. 21) ענה

עֹנֵהוּ‎ id. part. act. s. m., suff. 3 p. s. m. fr. עֹנֶה d. 9 a ענה

עָנָו adj. masc. sing. dec. 4 c; Cheth. עָנָיו. ענה

עֲנוֹ Chald. Peal pret. 3 pers. pl. masc. · ענה

עֲנוּ‎ וַ Kal pret. 3 pers. pl. · · · ענה

עֲנוּ *gg* id. imp. pl. masc. · · · ענה

עַנּוּ	/'| Piel imp. pl. masc.	ענה
עָנוּ	Kal imp. pl. masc.	ענה
עִנּוּ	/'| Piel pret. 3 pers. pl.	ענה
עַנּוּ	Kh. עָנוּ, K. עַנִּי pr. name masc.	ענה
עָנוּב	pr. name masc.	ענב
עֲנָוָה	noun fem. sing. dec. 11 c (§ 42. rem. 1)	ענה
עַנְוָה	ו noun fem. sing.	ענה
עֲנָוֵי	noun masc. pl. constr. from עָנָו dec. 4 c	ענה
עֲנָוִי	Kh. עֲנָוִי q. v., K. עַנְוֵי (q. v.)	ענה
עֲנָוִים	/'| adj. masc., pl. of עָנָו dec. 4 c; ו bef. (־ֵ)	ענה
עֲנָוִים	Kh. עֲנָוִים q. v., K. עֲנָיִים (q. v.)	ענה
עָנוֹשׁ	Kal inf. abs.	ענש
עֲנוֹשׁ	id. inf. constr.	ענש
עֲנוּשִׁים	id. part. pass. masc. pl. [of עָנוּשׁ] dec. 3 a	ענש
עֲנוֹת	Kal inf. constr. (and pr. name in compos. see בֵּית)	ענה
עַנּוֹת	Piel inf. constr.	ענה
עֱנוּת	noun fem. sing.	ענה
עֻנּוֹתוֹ	Pual inf. (עֻנּוֹת), suff. 3 pers. sing. m. d. 1 b	ענה
עֲנוּתֵךְ	ו noun fem. sing. with suff. 2 pers. sing. masc. from עֲנָוָה dec. 11 c (§ 42. rem. 1)	ענה
עָנִי	/'| adj. masc. sing., pl. עֲנִיִּים d. 8 (§ 37. No. 4)	ענה
עָנִי	Kh.; עֵינִי K. (q. v.)	עין
עֳנִי		
עֹנִי	noun masc. sing. dec. 6 k (§ 35. rem. 14)	ענה
עֻנִּי	ו pr. name masc.	ענה
עֲנָיָה	ו pr. name masc.; ו bef. (־ֲ)	ענה
עָנְיָהּ	noun masc. sing., suff. 3 pers. sing. fem. from עֳנִי dec. 6 k	ענה
עֲנִיָּה	adj. fem. sing. from עָנִי masc.	ענה
עֲנִיָּו	ו adj. pl. masc., suff. 3 pers. sing. masc. from עָנִי dec. 8 (§ 37. No. 4); ו bef. (־ֲ)	ענה
עָנְיִי	noun masc. s., suff. 1 pers. sing. fr. עֳנִי d. 6 k	ענה
עֲנִיֵּי	adj. pl. constr. masc. fr. עָנִי d. 8 (§ 37. No. 4)	ענה
עֲנִיֵּיךְ	ו id. pl. with suff. 2 pers. sing. m.; ו bef. (־ֲ)	ענה
עֲנִיִּים	id. pl., abs. st. Kh. עֲנִיִּים, but עֲנָוִים K. (q. v.)	ענה
עֲנִיִּים	id. pl., abs. st.; ו bef. (־ֲ)	ענה
עָנְיֵךְ	noun masc. sing., suff. 2 pers. s.m. fr. עֳנִי d. 6 k	ענה
עָנְיָם	id. with suff. 3 pers. pl. masc.	ענה
עָנִים	ו pr. name of a place	עין
עָנַיִן	Chald. Peal part. act. masc., pl. of עֲנָה [for עֲנָא] dec. 6 a	ענה
עֲנַיִן	Ch. id. part. pass. m. pl. [of עֲנָה for עֲנָא] d. 6 a	ענה
עִנְיָן	noun masc. sing. dec. 2 b	ענה
עִנְיַן	ו id., constr. st.	ענה
עָנְיֵנוּ	noun masc. sing., suff. 1 pers. pl. fr. עֳנִי d. 6 k	ענה

עֱנְיָנוֹ	noun masc. s., suff. 3 pers. sing. m. fr. עִנְיָן d. 2 b	ענה
עִנִּינוּ	Piel pret. 1 pers. pl.	ענה
עָנִיתָ	ו Kal pret. 2 pers. sing. masc.	ענה
עִנִּיתָ	Piel pret. 2 pers. sing. masc.	ענה
עִנִּיתָהּ	id. with suff. 3 pers. sing. fem.	ענה
עָנִיתִי	Kal pret. 1 pers. sing.	ענה
עִנִּיתִי	Piel pret. 1 pers. sing. (§ 24. rem. 11)	ענה
עֻנֵּיתִי	Pual pret. 1 pers. sing.	ענה
עֲנִיתִיךָ	Kal pret. 1 pers. sing. (עֲנִיתִי), suff. 2 pers. s.m.	ענה
עֲנִיתָם	ו id. pret. 2 pers. sing. masc. (עָנִית), suff. 3 pers. pl. masc.; ו for ו, conv.	ענה
עֲנִיתֶם	id. pret. 2 pers. pl. masc.	ענה
עִנִּיתֶם	ו Piel pret. 2 pers. pl. masc.	ענה
עִנִּיתֻנִי	id. pret. 2 pers. sing. masc., suff. 1 pers. pl.	ענה
עֲנִיתֻנִי	Kal pret. 2 pers. s. m. (עָנִית), suff. 1 pers. s.	ענה
עִנִּיתֻנִי	Piel pret. 2 pers. sing. masc., suff. 1 pers. sing.	ענה
עֲנִיתָךְ	Kal pret. 2 pers. sing. masc. (עָנָה), suff. 2 p. s.m. (§ 2 rem. 2 and 24. rem. 21)	ענה
עֲנָם	id., suff. 3 pers. pl. masc.	ענה
עָנֵם	pr. name of a place	עין
עֲנָמִים	pr. name of a people, not definitely known, Ge. 10. 13.	
עֲנַמֶּלֶךְ	ו pr. name of an idol of the Sepharvites, 2 Ki. 17. 31.	

עָנָן ו masc. dec. 4 c.—I. a cloud.—II. pr. name masc. Ne. 10. 27.

עִנֵּן Pi. to cloud, bring a cloud, Ge. 9. 14. Poel. עוֹנֵן to divine, by the clouds or perh. the sky generally; part. מְעוֹנֵן, a diviner, meteorologist; fem. עוֹנְנָה for מְעוֹנְנָה.

עֲנָן Chald. masc. dec. 1 a, cloud, Da. 7. 13.

עֲנָנָה fem. id. Job 3. 5.

עֲנָנִי (for עֲנַנְיָה, q. v.) pr. name masc. 1 Ch. 3. 24.

עֲנַנְיָה (whom the Lord covers, protects) pr. name —I. of a man, Ne. 3. 23.—II. of a town in the tribe of Benjamin, Ne. 11. 32.

עֲנַן	/ו id., constr. st.; ו bef. (־ֲ)	ענן
עֲנָנָה	noun fem. sing.	ענן
עֹנְנָה	Kal part. act. fem. from עוֹנֵן masc.	ענן
עֲנָנוֹ	noun masc. sing., suff. 3 pers. sing. masc. from עָנָן dec. 4 c	ענן
עֲנֵנוּ	/ו Kh. עֲנֵנוּ q. v., K. עֲנֵנִי (q. v.)	ענה
עֲנֵנִי	Kal imp. sing. masc. (עֲנֵה), suff. 1 pers. pl. (§ 24. rem. 21)	ענה
עָנֵנִי	/ו id. pret. 3 p. s.m. (עָנָה), suff. 1 p. s. (§ 24. r. 2)	ענה

ᵃ Is. 27. 2.   ᶠ Pr. 17. 26.   ⁱ Ps. 18. 36.   ᵖ Ps. 72. 2; 74. 19.   ᵗ Da. 3. 24.   ˣ Is. 58. 3.   ᵇ Ps. 35. 13.   ⁱ 1 Ki. 12. 7.   ᵐ Job 3. 5.
ᵇ Ju. 19. 24.   ᵍ Am. 2. 8.   ᵏ Is. 3. 8.   ᵠ Is. 58. 7.   ᵘ Da. 4. 24.   ʸ De. 26. 5.   ˢ Ps. 119. 71.   ᵏ Ps. 90. 15.   ⁿ Is. 57. 3.
ᶜ Ps. 45. 5.   ʰ Ex. 32. 18.   ˡ La. 1. 7.   ʳ Ge. 16. 11.   ᵛ Ec. 1. 13; 4. 8.   ᶻ Is. 49. 8.   ᵗ Ps. 119. 75.   ⁱ 1 Ki. 18. 26.
ᵈ Ps. 37. 11.   ʰ Ps. 22. 25.   ⁱ Is. 49. 13.   ˢ Ex. 4. 31.   ʷ Ec. 2. 9.   ᵉ De. 21. 14.   ᵘ Ps. 99. 8.   ᵘ Nu. 10. 34.   ᵖ Ps. 34. 5.
ᵉ Ex. 21. 22.   ⁱ Ps. 132. 1.

עֲנִי   בְ׳ pr. name masc.; וְ bef.   .   .   עון

עֲנָנֵי   Chald. noun masc. pl. constr. fr. [עֲנָן] dec. 1 a   עננה

עֲנֵנִי   בְ׳ Kal imp. sing. masc. (עֲנֵה), suff. 1 pers. sing. (§ 24. rem. 21); וְ bef. (-ַ)   .   ענה

עֲנָיָה   pr. name of a man and a place   .   .   ענן

עֲנָנֵיכֶם   the foll. with suff. 2 pers. pl. masc.   .   ענן

עֲנָנִים   וְ Kal part. act. masc. pl. of עוֹנֵן dec. 7 b   ענן

עֲנָנְךָ   noun masc. sing., suff. 2 pers. sing. masc. from עָנָן q. v.; וְ bef. (-ַ)   .   .   ענן

עָנָף   וְ׳ masc. dec. 4 a, *branch, bough.*

עֲנֵפָה   fem., עֲנֵפָה adj., *full of branches,* Eze. 19. 10.

עֲנַף   Chald. masc. dec. 3 a, *branch, bough,* Da. 4. 9, 11, 18.

עֲנַף   וְ id., constr. st.; וְ bef.   .   ענף

עֲנֵפָה   וְ adj. fem. sing. [from עָנָף masc.]; וְ id.   ענף

עַנְפּוֹהִי   Chald. noun masc. pl., suff. 3 pers. sing. masc. from [עֲנַף] dec. 3 a   ענף

עֲנָפֶיהָ   וְ noun masc. pl., suff. 3 pers. sing. fem. from עָנָף dec. 4 c; וְ bef. (-ַ)   ענף

עַנְפְּכֶם   id. sing., suff. 2 pers. pl. masc.   .   ענף

עֲנָק   masc. dec. 1 a (pl. ־ים, ־וֹת).—I. *a necklace, neck-chain* or *collar.*—II. (*long-necked;* Arab. id.) pr. name, *Anak,* the father of the *Anakim* (בְּנֵי עֲנָק, עֲנָקִים, or בְּנֵי הָעֲנָק ,יְלִידֵי הָעֲנָ), a Canaanitish people, who were giants.

עָנַק (denom. of עֲנָק) *to adorn with a necklace,* Ps. 73. 6, *pride surrounds them, like a necklace.* הִעֲנִיק niph. *to lay upon the neck* of any one, *to lade him liberally,* De. 15. 14.

עָנוֹק i. q. עֲנָק No. II, Jos. 21. 11.

עֲנָקִים   וְ׳ id. pl., also pr. name; וְ bef. (-ַ)   ענק

עֲנָת קְתּוֹ   Kal pret. 3 pers. s. fem. with suff. 3 pers. pl. m.

עֲנֵר   pr. name—I. of a Canaanite, Ge. 14. 13, 24.—II. of a city, 1 Ch. 6. 55; elsewhere תַּעֲנָךְ q. v.

[עָנַשׁ]   fut. יַעֲנֹשׁ.—I. *to tax.*—II. *to fine in money,* with לְ. Niph. *to be fined, mulcted.*

עֲנַשׁ   Chald. masc. *fine, mulct,* Ezr. 7. 26. Also the following.

עֹנֶשׁ   masc. *fine, mulct,* 2 Ki. 23. 33; Pr. 19. 19

עָנְשׁוּ   וְ Kal pret. 3 pers. pl.   .   ענש

עֲנָת   pr. name masc. (and in compos. see בֵּית עֲנָת)   ענה

עֲנָת   Chald. Peal pret. 3 pers. sing. fem.   ענה

עָנְתָה   וְ Kal pret. 3 pers. sing. fem.   ענה

עָנְתָהּ   וְ noun fem. sing., suff. 3 pers. sing. fem. from [עוֹנָה] dec. 10   .   עון

עַנּוֹתוֹ   Piel inf. (עַנּוֹת), suff. 3 pers. s. masc. dec. 1 b   ענה

עֲנָתוֹת   וְ pr. name of a man and a place; וְ bef. (-ַ)   ענה

עַנֹּתְךָ   Piel inf. (עַנּוֹת), suff. 2 pers. s. masc. dec. 1 b   ענה

עֲנָתְךָ   וְ contr. from עֲנָוְתְךָ (q. v.)   .   ענה

עֲנִיתִךְ   וְ Piel pret. 1 pers. s. (עִנִּיתִי), suff. 2 pers. s. f.   ענה

עֲנָתֹת   pr. name of a place   .   .   ענה

עֲנַתֹתִיָּה   וְ pr. name masc.   .   .   ענה

עֲסוֹתֶם   וְ Kal pret. 2 pers. pl. masc.   .   עסס

עָסִים   noun masc. sing. dec. 3 a   .   עסס

[עָסַס]   *to tread down,* Mal. 3. 21.

עָסִים   masc. dec. 3 a, *must, new wine.*

עֳפָאִים   noun masc. pl. of [עֳפִי] dec. 6 k   .   עפה

עָפָה   Root not used; Syr. *to flourish.*

עֳפִי   masc. only pl. עֳפָאִים (§ 35. rem. 15) *branches, boughs.*

עֳפִי   Chald. *branch, bough,* with suff. עָפְיֵהּ (comp. dec. 6 k) Da. 4. 9, 11, 18.

עֹפָה   Kal part. act. fem. [of עָף masc.]   .   עוף

עָפוּ   וְ id. pret. 3 pers. pl.; acc. shifted by conv. וְ (comp. § 8. rem. 7)   .   .   עוף

עָפוֹת   id. part. act. fem., pl. of עָפָה [fr. עָף masc.]   עוף

עָפְיֵהּ   וְ Chald. noun masc. sing., suff. 3 pers. sing. masc. [from עֳפִי comp. Heb. dec. 6 k]   עפה

עָפַל   Pu. *to be swollen,* metaph. *elated, proud,* Hab. 2. 4 Hiph. *to act arrogantly, presumptuously,* Nu. 14. 44. Hence

עֹפֶל   masc. dec. 6 c.—I. *swelling, tumour.*—II. *mount, hill*   .   .   .   עפל

עָפְלָה   Pual pret. 3 pers. sing. fem.   .   עפל

עֲפֹלֵי   Kh. עֳפֹלֵי n. m. pl. c. fr. עֹפֶל d. 6 c (K. טְחֹרֵי q.v.)   עפל

עֳפֹלֵיכֶם   Kh. עֳפֹלֵיכֶם id. pl. with suff. 2 pers. pl. masc. (K. טְחֹרֵיכֶם)   .   .   עפל

עֳפֹלִים   Kh. עֳפֹלִים id. pl., abs. st. (K. טְחֹרִים)   עפל

[עֳפְנִי]   only in the form הָעֲפְנִי (כְּפַר) *village of the Ophnite,* pr. name of a town in Benjamin, Jos. 18. 24.

עַפְעַפָּי   noun du. [עַפְעַפַּיִם], suff. 1 pers. sing. [from עַפְעָף dec. 8 d]   .   .   עוף

עַפְעַפָּיו   וְ׳ id. du., suff. 3 pers. sing. masc.   עוף

עַפְעַפֶּיךָ   וְ id. du., suff. 2 pers. sing. masc.   עוף

עַפְעַפֵּינוּ   וְ id. du., suff. 1 pers. pl.   עוף

---

a Da. 7. 13.   e Mal. 3. 19.   i Ps. 80. 11.   m De. 22. 19.   r 2 Sa. 22. 36.   Zec. 5. 1, 2.   b Hab. 2. 4.   e 1 Sa. 5. 9.   h Pr. 30. 13.
b Je. 27. 9.   f Le. 23. 40.   k Eze. 36. 8.   n Na. 5. 10.   Na. 1. 12.   Is. 11. 14.   c 1 Sa. 6. 4.   f Job 16. 16.   Pr. 4. 25.
c Is. 2. 6.   g Eze. 19. 10.   l Pr. 1. 9.   o Ex. 21. 10.   Mal. 3. 21.   Is. 31. 5.   d 1 Sa. 6. 5.   g Ps. 11. 4.   Je. 9. 17.
d Nu. 14. 14.   h Da. 4. 11.   Ps. 73. 6.   De. 8. 2, 16.   Ps. 104. 12.   Da. 4. 9, 11, 18.

עָפָר '}ן masc. dec. 4 c (pl. c. עַפְרוֹת).—I. *dust, dry earth.*—II. *earth, mould, clay.*—III. *the earth.*—IV. pl. *clods, lumps.*

עִפֵּר Pi. (denom. of עָפָר) *to dust, throw dust at* any one, 2 Sa. 16. 13.

עֵפֶר (i. q. עֹפֶר) pr. name masc.—I. Ge. 25. 4.—II. 1 Ch. 4. 17.—III. 1 Ch. 5. 24.

עֹפֶר masc. dec. 6 c, *fawn,* i. e. young deer, roe, gazelle.

עָפְרָה (*female fawn*) pr. name—I. of a city in the tribe of Benjamin, called also בֵּית לְעַפְרָה (*house of the fawn*) Mi. 1. 10.—II. of another in Manasseh.—III. of a man, 1 Ch. 4. 14.

עֶפְרוֹן (*vitulinus*) pr. name—I. of a city on the borders of Ephraim, 2 Ch. 13. 19, in Keri עֶפְרַיִן.—II. of a mountain on the confines of Judah and Benjamin, Jos. 15. 9.—III. of a Hittite, comp. Ge. 23. 8.

עֹפֶרֶת, עוֹפֶרֶת fem. *lead;* אֶבֶן הָעֹ a stone, i. e. weight, of lead.

עָפָר	'}ן noun m. s., constr. of עָפָר d. 4 c; ן bef. (-:)	עפר [a]
עִפֵּר	ן Piel pret. 3 pers. sing. masc.	עפר [b]
עֵפֶר	,ן '}ן pr. name masc.; for ן see letter ו	עפר
עָפְרָה	'}ן pr. name of a man and a place	עפר
עֲפָרֶהָ	'}ן n. m. s., suff. 3 p. s. f.fr. עָפָר d. 4 c; ן bef.(-:)	עפר [c]
עֲפָרוֹ	id. with suff. 3 pers. sing. masc.	עפר
עֶפְרוֹן	'}ן pr. name of a man and a place	עפר
עֶפְרָיִן	Kh. עֶפְרוֹן, K. עֶפְרַיִן pr. name of a place	עפר
עַפְרוֹת	'}ן noun m. with pl. constr. fem. fr. עָפָר d. 4 c	עפר [f]
עֳפָרִים	noun masc. pl. of עֹפֶר dec. 6 c	עפר
עֲפָרְךָ	,ן n. m. s., suff. 2 p.s.m.fr. עָפָר d.4c; ן bef. (-:)	עפר [g]
עֲפָרָם	'}ן id., suff. 3 pers. pl. masc.	עפר [h]
עֶפְרוֹן	pr. name masc.	עפר
עָפְרָתִי עֶפְרָתִי	}noun fem. sing. (comp. § 35. rem. 2)	עפר
עֶפְרָתָה	pr. name (עֶפְרָה) with parag. ה	עפר
עֶפְתָה	noun fem. sing. (עֵפָה) with parag. ה	עוף
עֵץ	,ן "ן noun masc. sing. d. 7 a (§ 36. r. 2 & 4)	עצה

[עָצַב] I. *to travail, suffer pain.*—II. *to pain, grieve.* Niph. *to be pained, grieved,* with בְּ, אֶל, עַל with any thing. Pi. I. *to form, fashion,* Job 10. 8.—II. *to pain, grieve.* Hiph. I. *to serve, worship,* Je. 44. 19.—II. *to grieve, provoke,* Ps. 78. 40. Hithp. *to grieve oneself, be grieved.*

עֲצַב Chald. part. pass. *grieved, afflicted,* Da. 6. 21.

עָצָב masc. dec. 8 a (pl. עֲצַבִּים) *images, idols.*

עֶצֶב, עֶצֶב masc. dec. 6 b.—I. *earthen vessel,* Je. 22. 28 ; Prof. Lee, *tendon, sinew;* Eng. vers. "idol."—II. *labour, travail.*—III. *pain;* also *grief.*

עֹצֶב masc. dec. 6 c.—I. *image, idol.*—II. *pain, grief.*

עִצָּבוֹן masc. dec. 3 c.—I. *labour, toil, travail.*—II. *pain, sorrow,* Ge. 3. 16.

עַצֶּבֶת fem. dec. 13 a (constr. עַצֶּבַת prop. from עֲצֵבָה or עָצְבָה) *pain, grief, sorrow.*

מַעֲצֵבָה fem. *labour, affliction,* Is. 50. 11.

עֶצֶב	noun masc. sing. dec. 6 a	עצב
עֹצֶב	noun masc. sing. dec. 6 c	עצב
עֲצָבוֹ	Kal pret. 3 pers. sing. m., suff. 3 pers. s. m.	עצב [p]
עִצְּבוּ	ן Piel pret. 3 pers. pl.	עצב [q]
עִצְּבוּנִי	id., suff. 1 pers. sing.	עצב
עִצְּבוֹנְךָ	noun masc. s., suff. 2 p. s. f. fr. עִצָּבוֹן d. 3 c	עצב
עַצְּבוֹתָם	noun f. pl., suff. 3 p. pl. m. fr. עַצֶּבֶת (q. v.)	עצב
עֲצַבֵּי	n. m. pl. constr.fr. [עָצָב] d. 8 a (§ 37. No.3 c)	עצב
עָצְבִּי	Kal inf., or noun masc. sing., suff. 1 pers. sing. from עֶצֶב dec. 6 c	עצב
עַצְּבֶיהָ	noun masc. pl., suff. 3 pers. sing. fem. from [עָצָב] dec. 8 a (§ 37. No. 3 c)	עצב
עַצְּבֵיהֶם	id., suff. 3 pers. pl. masc.	עצב
עַצְּבֶיךָ	,ן noun masc. pl., suff. 2 pers. sing. masc. from עֶצֶב dec. 6 a; ן bef. (-:)	עצב
עַצְּבֵיכֶם	id., suff. 2 pers. pl. masc. and dag. euph.	עצב
עֲצַבִּים	noun m. pl. [of עָצָב] d. 8 a (§ 37. No.3 c)	עצב
עַצֶּבֶת	[for עֲצֶבֶת] noun fem. sing., constr., pl. עֲצָבוֹת	עצב
עַצַּבְתִּי	id. pl., suff. 1 pers. sing. [for עַצְבֹתִי]	עצב

עָצַד Root not used ; Arab. *to cut with an axe.*

מַעֲצָד masc. *an axe,* Is. 44. 12 ; Je. 10. 3.

עָצָה *to close* the eyes, Pr. 16. 30. Arab. also *to be hard, firm,* hence עֵץ, עֵצָה.

עָצֶה masc. *back-bone, spine.*

עֵץ masc. dec. 7 a (with suff. עֵצִי, pl. עֵצִים, c. עֲצֵי § 26. rem. 2 & 4).—I. *tree;* עֵץ פְּרִי *fruit trees.*—II. *wood;* pl. עֵצִים *wood,* i. e. sticks for fuel, or *timber for building.*—III. *stake, gibbet, gallows.*

עֵצָה fem. *wood, timber,* Je. 6. 6; according to Gesenius also Pr. 27. 9, עֲצַת נָפֶשׁ *fragrant wood*(?).

עֶצְיוֹן גֶּבֶר (*back-bone of a man*) pr. name of a seaport in the Red Sea.

עֵצָה noun fem. sing. (comp. מֹעֵצָת) . . . עצה

[a] Is. 49. 23.   [c] Pr. 8. 26.   [h] Is. 34. 7.   [i] Zec. 5. 7.   [k] Ps. 139. 24.   [l] Job 10. 8.   [m] Ps. 135. 15.   [y] Je.50.2; Mi.1.7.   [p] Pr. 10. 10.

2 Sa. 16. 13.   [d] Job 28. 6.   Je. 6. 29.   Job 10. 22.   [p1] Ki. 1. 6.   Ge. 3. 16.   [*] 1 Ch. 4. 10 ;   [q] Pr. 5. 10.   Job 9. 28.

[b] Is. 34. 9.   [e] Eze. 26. 12.   Job 19. 24.   1 Ch. 22. 15.   Is. 63. 10.   Ps. 16. 4.   Is. 48. 5.   Is. 58. 3.   Je. 6. 6.

[d] Da. 9. 21.

40

וְ] עֵצָה	noun fem. sing. dec. 11 b . . .	יעץ
עֶצְהּ•	noun masc. sing., suff. 3 pers. sing. fem. from עֵץ (§ 36. rem. 2)	עצה
עֹצֶהּ•	Kal part. act. sing. masc. . . .	עצה
עֹצוּ	Kal imp. pl. masc. . . .	עוץ
עֲצוּבַת•	וַ] Kal part. pass. sing. masc. constr. [of עֲצוּבָה from עָצוּב masc.] ; וְ] bef. (-)	עצב
עָצוּם	וְ] adj. masc. sing. dec. 3 a . .	עצם
עֲצוּמִים	id. pl. abs. ; וְ] bef. (-) . .	עצם
עָצוּר	וְ] Kal part. pass. sing. masc. .	עצר
עֵצוֹת	noun fem. pl. abs. from עֵצָה dec. 11 b	יעץ
עֲצֵי•	וְ] noun m. pl. constr. fr. עֵץ d. 7 a ; וְ] bef. (-)	עצה
עֲצִיב	Chald. Peal part. pass. sing. masc.	עצב
עֲצֵיהָ	noun masc. pl., suff. 3 pers. sing. fem. from עֵץ (§ 36. rem. 2 & 4) .	עצה
עֲצָיו	id. pl., suff. 3 pers. sing. masc.	עצה
עֲצַיִךְ•	וְ] id. pl., suff. 2 pers. sing. fem.	עצה
עֲצַיִךְ•	id. pl., suff. 2 pers. sing. masc.	עצה
עֲצִים	וְ] id. pl., abs. st. . .	עצה
עֲצֵינוּ•	id. pl., suff. 1 pers. pl. . .	עצה
עֵצְךָ•	id. sing., suff. 2 pers. sing. masc.	עצה

עָצֵל Niph. to be sluggish, slothful, Ju. 18. 9. Hence

עָצֵל	וְ] adj. masc. sluggard, slothful man	עצל
עַצְלָה•	fem. sloth, indolence ; du. עַצְלְתַּיִם [fr. great slothfulness	עצל
עַצְלוּת	idem, Pr 31. 27 . . .	עצל

עָצַם I. to close the eyes (prop., as in the Arab., to tie or bind up), Is. 33. 15.—II. intrans. [עָצֵם] to be or become strong, mighty, powerful, great.—III. to be strong in number, be numerous, many. Pi. I. to close or bind up the eyes, Is. 29. 10.—II. (denom. of עֶצֶם) to break the bones, Je. 50. 17 ; others, to gnaw the bones. Hiph. to make strong, Ps. 105. 24.

עָצוּם adj. masc. dec. 3 a.—I. strong, mighty, great.—II. strong, numerous.

עֲצוּמִים masc. pl. (of עָצוּם) strength, power, Ps. 10. 10.

עֲצֻמוֹת fem. pl. strong defence, trop. of arguments, Is. 41. 21.

עֶצֶם fem. dec. 6 a (pl. עֲצָמִים, עֲצָמַי, also עֲצָמוֹת).—I. bone.—II. body, La. 4. 7.—III. self, self-same.—IV. pr. name of a city in the tribe of Simeon.

עֹצֶם masc. dec. 6 c.—I. strength.—II. body, substance, Ps. 139. 15.

עָצְמָה	fem. (constr. עָצְמַת).—I. strength.—II number, multitude, Na. 3. 9.	
עַצְמוֹן	(strong) pr. name of a town in the south of Canaan.	
תַּעֲצֻמוֹת	f. pl. (of תַּעֲצוּמָה) strength, Ps. 68. 36.	
עֶצֶם•	וְ] noun fem. sing. dec. 6 a (§ 35. rem. 2), also pr. name	עצם
עֶצֶם	וְ]	עצם
עֹצֵם•	וְ] Kal part. act. sing. masc. . .	עצם
עֹצֶם•	וְ] noun masc. sing. dec. 6 c . .	עצם
עָצְמָה	noun fem. sing. (no pl.) . .	עצם
עָצְמוּ•	} Kal pret. 3 pers. pl. (§ 8. rem. 1 a)	עצם
עָצְמוּ		עצם
עָצְמוֹ	noun fem. sing., suff. 3 pers. sing. masc. from עֶצֶם dec. 6 a . .	עצם
עִצְּמוֹ•	Piel pret. 3 pers. sing. masc. [עָצַם], suff. 3 pers. sing. masc. . . .	עצם
עַצְמוֹנָה	pr. name of a place (עַצְמוֹן), with parag. ה	עצם
עֲצָמוֹת	noun fem. pl. abs. from עֶצֶם dec. 6 a	עצם
עַצְמוֹת	וְ] id. pl., constr. st. . .	עצם
עַצְמֹתַי	} id. pl. with suff. 1 pers. sing	עצם
עַצְמוֹתַי	וְ]	עצם
עַצְמֹתֵיהֶם•	id. pl., suff. 3 pers. pl. masc. .	עצם
עַצְמוֹתָיו	id. pl., suff. 3 pers. sing. masc. .	עצם
עַצְמוֹתֵיכֶם•	וְ] id. pl., suff. 2 pers. pl. masc. .	עצם
עַצְמוֹתֵיכֶם•	noun fem. pl. [עֲצָמוֹת], suff. 2 pers. pl. m.	עצם
עַצְמוֹתֵינוּ•	noun fem. pl., suff. 1 pers. pl. from עֶצֶם d. 6 a	עצם
עַצְמוֹתָם•	id. pl., suff. 3 pers. pl. masc. (§ 4. rem. 2)	עצם
עֲצָמַי•	} id. pl. m., suff. 1 pers. sing. ; וְ] bef. (-)	עצם
עֲצָמַי•	וְ]	עצם
עָצְמִי•	noun masc. sing., suff. 1 pers. s. fr. עֹצֶם d. 6 c	עצם
עָצְמִי•	וְ] noun fem. sing., suff. 1 pers. s. fr. עָצְמָה d. 6 a	עצם
עֲצָמֶיהָ	id. pl., suff. 3 pers. sing. fem. .	עצם
עֲצָמָיו	id. pl., suff. 3 pers. sing. masc. .	עצם
עֲצָמִים	id. pl., abs. st. . .	עצם
עֲצֻמִים•	וְ] defect. for עֲצוּמִים (q. v.) .	עצם
עֲצָמֵינוּ•	noun fem. pl., suff. 1 pers. pl. from עֶצֶם d. 6 a	עצם
עַצְמְךָ•	id. sing., suff. 2 pers. sing. masc. .	עצם
עַצְמְכֶם•	id. sing., suff. 2 pers. pl. masc. .	עצם
עַצְמָם•	id. sing., suff. 3 pers. pl. masc. .	עצם
עָצְמֹנָה	pr. name of a place (עַצְמוֹן) with local ה	עצם
עָצַמְתָּ•	Kal pret. 2 pers. sing. masc. . .	עצם
עַצְמֹתַי•	} noun fem. pl., suff. 1 pers. sing. from עֶצֶם dec. 6	עצם
עַצְמֹתַי		עצם
וְ]עַצְמֹתֵיהֶם•	id. pl., suff. 3 pers. sing. masc. .	עצם
עַצְמֹתָיו•	id. pl., suff. 3 pers. sing. masc. .	עצם
עַצְמֹתֶיךָ•	וְ] id. pl., suff. 2 pers. sing. masc. .	עצם
עַצְמֹתָם•	id. pl., suff. 3 pers. pl. masc. (§ 4. rem. 2)	עצם

De. 20. 19.   ⸏ De. 29. 10.   ⸹ Pr. 19. 15.   ⸸ De. 8. 17.   ¹ 1 Ch. 10. 12.   ⸲ Eze. 37. 11.   ⸱ Ps. 139. 15.   ⸳ Ps. 141. 7.   ⸴ 1 Ki. 13. 31.
Pr. 16. 30.   ⸺ La. 5. 4.   ⸹ Da. 8. 24; 11. 23.   ⸵ Ps. 38. 20.   ⸶ Eze. 6. 5.   ⸷ Mi. 3. 2.   ⸸ Job 30. 30.   ⸹ Ju. 9. 2.   ⸺ Nu. 24. 8.
Is. 54. 6.   ⸏ De. 28. 42.   ⸹ Pr. 15. 30.   ⸸ Je. 50. 17.   ⸹ Is. 66. 14.   ⸹ Job 30. 17.   ⸸ Eze. 24. 5.   ⸹ La. 4. 8.   ⸺ Is. 58. 11.
Da. 6. 21.   ⸏ Pr. 26. 14.   ⸹ Is. 33. 15.   ⸸ Ps. 103. 4.   ⸹ Is. 41. 21.   ⸹ Ps. 31. 11.   ⸸ Mi. 4. 3.   ⸹ Ge. 26. 16.   ⸺ Eze. 32. 27.
Eze. 26. 12.

עֵצֶן Root not used; whence

עֲצִנוֹ 2 Sa. 23.8 (Keri עֶצְנִי, *Eznite*, one of David's heroes. According to Simonis and Gesenius, an appellative, *spear* (Arab. עצן *branch*), hence *his spear*, according to Khethib. Comp. עֵדֶן.

עָצַר ‛וְ fut. יַעֲצֹר, יֶעְצֹר (§ 13. rem. 5).—I. *to shut, close up.*—II. *to hold back, restrain, detain.*—III. *to retain* strength.—IV. *to rule, reign*, with בְּ 1 Sa. 9.17. Niph. I. *to be shut up.*—II. *to be restrained, detained, stayed.*—III. *to be assembled*, 1 Sa. 21.8.

עֶצֶר masc. *rule, dominion*, Ju. 18. 7.

עֹצֶר masc.—I. *a shutting up, restraining* the womb from childbearing, Pr. 30. 16.—II. *oppression, vexation*, Ps. 107. 39; perh. *prison*, Is. 53. 8.

עֲצָרָה fem. dec. 11 c (§ 42. rem. 1) and עֲצֶרֶת, *assembly*; frequently of the *solemn assemblies* when the people came together for the celebrating of festivals.

מַעְצוֹר masc. *restraint, hinderance*, 1 Sa. 14. 6.

מַעְצָר m. *restraint, power of restraint*, Pr. 25. 28.

עָצֹר Kal inf. abs. . . . . . עצר
עָצֹר defect. for עָצוֹר (q. v.) . . . עצר
עֶצֶר noun masc. sing. . . . . עצר
עֹצֶר ‛וְ noun masc. sing. . . . עצר
עֲצֹר ‛וְ Kal inf.constr. [for וַיַּעֲצֹר comp.§ 13.r.1&2] עצר
עֲצָרָה s‛וְ noun fem. s. d. 11 c (§ 24. r. 1); וְ bef. (‑ָ) עצר
עֲצוּרָה Kal part. pass. sing.,fem. of עָצוּר עצר
עָצְרוּ id. pret. 3 pers. pl. . . . עצר
עֲצָרָנִי id. pret. 3 pers. sing. masc., suff. 1 pers. sing. עצר
עֲצֶרֶת } noun fem. sing., see under עֲצָרָה עצר
עֲצַרְתִּי ‛וְ Kal pret. 1 pers. sing. . . עצר
עֲצַת ‛וְ noun fem. s. constr. of עֵצָה d.11b; וְ bef. (‑ָ) יעץ
עֲצָתוֹ ‛וְ id., suff. 3 pers. sing. masc.; וְ id. יעץ
עֲצָתוֹ id., suff., Kh. תוֹ‛ 3 pers. sing. masc., K. תִי‛ 1 pers. sing. . . . . יעץ
עֲצָתִי id., suff. 1 pers. sing. . . . יעץ
עֲצַתָךְ id. pl., suff. 2 pers. sing. fem. . יעץ
עֲצָתֵךְ id. sing., suff. 2 pers. sing. masc. . יעץ
עֲצָתָם id. sing., suff. 3 pers. pl. masc. . יעץ

עָקַב ‛וְ fut. יַעֲקֹב.—I. *to take by the heel*, Ho. 12. 4.—II. *to supplant, circumvent, defraud*. Pi. *to hold back, retard*, Job 37. 4; Prof. Lee, *to trace*, comp. עָקֵב. עָקֵב masc. dec. 5c (pl. עֲקֵבִים, constr. עִקְּבֵי, עָקְבוֹת, § 34. rem. 4, comp. § 33. rem. 1).—I. *heel.*—II. *hoof* of a horse.—III. *rear* of an army.—IV. *impression of the heel, trace, track, footstep.*—V. *a supplanter, insidiator*, Ps. 49. 6.

עָקֹב masc.—I. *crooked place*, Is. 40. 4; Gesenius, *steep place.*—II. adj. *fraudulent, deceitful*, Je. 17. 9.—III. fem. עֲקֻבָּה (denom. of עָקֵב) *traced, marked*, Ho. 6. 8.

עַקּוּב (*insidious*) pr. name masc. of three different persons.

עֵקֶב masc.—I. *end*, only as an adv. *to the end*, Ps. 119. 33, 112.—II. *recompense, reward.*—III. עֵקֶב, עַל עֵקֶב (a) adv. *on account of, because*; (b) conj. *because*; עֵ אֲשֶׁר ‛פִי idem.

יַעֲקֹב (*taking by the heel, supplanter*) pr. name, *Jacob*, son of Isaac, called also *Israel*; hence the Israelites, his descendants, are called בֵּית יַעֲקֹב; it is likewise simply applied to them and their land.

יַעֲקֹבָה (id.) pr. name masc. 1 Ch. 4. 36.

עָקֵב noun masc. sing. dec. 5 (§ 34. rem. 4) . עקב
עָקֹב adj. masc. sing., comp. עֲקֻבָּה . עקב
עֵקֶב noun masc. sing., also as an adv. . עקב
עֲקֻבָּה adj. fem. s. fr. עָקֹב m. (comp. § 37. No. 3) עקב
עֲקֵבוֹ noun masc. sing., suff. 3 pers. sing. masc. from עָקֵב dec. 5 . . . . עקב
עָקְבוֹת id. pl. constr. fem., dag. euph. (§ 34. rem 4) עקב
עִקְּבוֹתֶיךָ ‛וְ id. pl. fem., suff. 2 pers. s. masc., dag. euph. עקב
עֲקֵבַי id. pl. masc., suff. 1 pers. sing. . עקב
עִקְּבֵי id. pl., constr. masc., dag. euph. (§ 34. rem. 4) עקב
עֲקֵבַיִךְ id. pl. masc., suff. 2 pers. sing. fem. . עקב

[עָקַד] *to bind*, Ge. 22. 9. Hence

עָקֹד adj. m. *striped, ring-streaked*; pl. עֲקֻדִּים (q.v.) עקד
עָקָר pr. name, see בֵּית עֵקֶר הָרֹעִים under בֵּית
עֲקֻדִּים adj. masc., pl. of עָקֹד (§ 37. No. 3c) עקד

עָקָה Root not used; Arab. *to retain, detain*.

מַעֲקֶה masc. *parapet, battlement*, De. 22. 8.

עָקוֹב Kal inf. abs. . . . . עקב
עַקּוּב ‛וְ pr. name masc. . . . עקב

עָקַל only Pu. part. *perverted*, Hab. 1. 4.

עֲקַלְקַל adj. only pl. f. עֲקַלְקַלּוֹת *crooked, perverted*.
עֲקַלָּתוֹן masc. *crooked*, Is. 27. 1.

עֲקַלְקַלּוֹת adj. pl. fem. [from עֲקַלְקַל dec. 8] עקל
עֲקַלְקַלּוֹתָם id. pl., suff. 3 pers. pl. masc. . עקל

a De. 11. 17.	f Ju. 18. 7.	g Is. 1. 13.	k 2 Ch. 7. 9.	m Is. 19. 3.	P Ps. 20. 5.	t Ho. 6. 8.	y Ps. 77. 20.	f Je. 9. 3.
Ge. 20. 18.	b Pr. 30. 16.	h 1 Sa. 21. 6.	l Da. 10. 8, 16.	n Is. 46. 11.	q Ho. 12. 5.	u Jos. 8. 13.	z Je. 13. 22.	g Ju. 5. 6.
c Je. 20. 9.	f Job 4. 2.	i Ge. 16. 2.	Is. 66. 9.	o Is. 47. 13.	Je. 17. 9.	x Ps. 89. 52.	a Ge. 30. 40.	d Ps. 125. 5.

40*

עקל   יַעֲקַלְתֹן • noun masc. sing.

עָקָן   וֹ pr. name m. Ge. 36. 27, elsewhere called יַעֲקָן.

[עָקַר]   to root out, pluck up, Ec. 3. 2. Niph. *to be rooted up, destroyed*, Zep. 2. 4. Pi. *to hough or hamstring horse.*

עקר   עֲקַר Chald. Ithpe. *to be rooted out*, Da. 7. 8.

עקר   עָקָר masc., עֲקָרָה fem. *barren, sterile.*

עקר   עֵקֶר masc.—I. *root*, only trop. for *stock, family*, Le. 25. 47.—II. pr. name masc. 1 Ch. 2. 27.

עקר   עִקַּר Chald. masc. dec. 1 b, *stump, trunk*, Da. 4. 12, 20.

עקר   עֶקְרוֹן (*eradication*) pr. name of one of the principal cities of the Philistines. Gent. noun עֶקְרֹנִי.

עקר   עָקָר • adj. masc. sing., fem. עֲקָרָה

עקר   עֲקַר • Chald. noun masc. sing. constr. [of עִקַּר]

עקר   עִקֵּר • Piel pret. 3 pers. sing. masc.

עקר   וְ pr. name masc.; for וְ see lett. ו.

עקרב   עַקְרָב • masc. dec. 8 a.—I. *scorpion.*—II. *a kind of scourge*, armed with knots and thorns.

עקרב   עַקְרַבִּים id. pl., abs. st., (Eze. 2. 7.); also pr. name

עקר   וַ • adj. fem. sing. from עָקָר masc.

עקר   עִקְּרוּ • Piel pret. 3 pers. pl.

עקר   וְ • pr. name of a place

עקר   עֲקֶרֶת • adj. fem. sing. from עָקָר masc.

עָקַשׁ   to convict of perverseness, Job 9. 20. Niph. *to be perverse*, Pr. 28. 18. Pi. *to pervert.*

עִקֵּשׁ adj. masc. dec. 7 b.—I. *perverse, false, deceitful.*—II. pr. name masc. 2 Sa. 23. 26.

עִקְּשׁוּת fem. *perverseness*, Pr. 4. 24; 6. 12.

מַעֲקַשִּׁים masc. pl. (of מַעֲקָשׁ), *crooked ways*, Is. 42. 16.

עקשׁ   עִקֵּשׁ • pr. name masc.

עקשׁ   וְ • adj. masc. sing. dec. 7 b (§ 36. rem. 3)

עקשׁ   עִקְּשׁוּ • Piel pret. 3 pers. pl.

עקשׁ   עִקְּשׁוּת • noun fem. sing.

עקשׁ   עִקְּשֵׁי adj. masc. pl. constr. and abs. from עִקֵּשׁ dec. 7 b

עקשׁ   עִקְּשִׁים •

עוק   עָקַת • noun fem. sing., constr. of [עָקָה] dec. 10 (comp. § 30. No. 3)

עור   עָר • pr. name of a place

עור   עֵר • Kal part. act. s. m. (§ 21. r. 2); also pr. name

I. עָרַב   inf. עָרֹב.—I. *to exchange, barter*, Eze. 27. 9, 27.—II. *to become surety, to pledge oneself* for another,

const. with acc. of pers.—III. *to pledge, give as a pledge.*—IV. [עָרֵב] intrans. fut. יֶעֱרַב *to be agreeable, pleasant, sweet*, with לְ, עַל of pers. Hithp. I. *to intermix, intermeddle, interfere*, Pr. 14. 10.—II. *to have intercourse, be familiar with* any one, with בְּ, לְ, עִם.—III. *to enter into a negociation*, with אֵת.

עָרַב Chald. Pa. *to mix*, only part. pass. Da. 2. 43. Ithpa. *to be mixed*, ibid.

עָרֵב adj. masc. *agreeable, sweet.*

עָרֹב masc. *gadfly.* Sept. κυνόμυια.

עֵרֶב masc.—I. *woof*, Le. 13. 48—59.—II. collect *foreigners, strangers* (Arab. ערב *to travel in foreign lands*), Ex. 12. 38; Ne. 13. 3; with the art. הָעֵרֶב 1 Ki. 10. 15; Je. 25. 20, 24; 50. 37; Eze. 30. 5.

עֲרֻבָּה fem. dec. 10.—I. *surety, security*, Pr. 17. 18.—II. *pledge*, 1 Sa. 17. 18.

עֵרָבוֹן masc. *pledge*, Ge. 38. 17, 18, 20.

מַעֲרָב masc. dec. 2 b, *wares, merchandise*, Eze. 27, 19, &c. Another under No. II.

תַּעֲרֻבָה fem. dec. 10, *suretyship*; בְּנֵי תַּ hostages.

II. עָרַב   (Arab. *to be black*) *to become dark, drawing towards evening*, inf. Ju. 19. 9, and 3 pers. fem. metaph. Is. 24. 11. Hiph. inf. הַעֲרִב adv. *at evening*, 1 Sa. 17. 16, comp. Hiph. of שָׁכַם.

עֹרֵב masc. dec. 7 b.—I. *a raven.*—II. pr. name (a) of a prince of Midian; (b) of a rock beyond Jordan.

עֶרֶב com. d. 6 a.—I. *evening*; בָּעֶרֶב, לָעֶרֶב, also עֶרֶב *in the evening, at evening*; du. בֵּין הָעַרְבַּיִם *between the two evenings*, the time between the declining and the setting of the sun.—II. pl. עֲרָבִים, c. עַרְבֵי, *oziers, willows*; נַחַל הָעֲ *brook of willows.*—III. see עֶרֶב under R. No. I.

מַעֲרָב masc. *the west.* Another under No. I.

מַעֲרָבָה fem. id. Is. 45. 6.

III. עָרַב   Root not used; i. q. חָרַב *arid, sterile.*

עֲרָב, עָרָב pr. name, *Arabia.* Gent. noun עַרְבִי *Arab, Arabian*; pl. עַרְבִיאִים, עַרְבִים, *Arabs, Arabians.*

עֲרָבָה fem. dec. 11 c (§ 42. rem. 1).—I. *arid tract, desert.*—II. *plain, open country*; in Ps. 68. 5 perh. metaph. for *the heavens*, see Buxtorf on this word.—III. הָעֲרָבָה the country between the Dead Sea and the Elantic Gulf; יָם הָעֲ *the sea of the desert* or *plain*, the Dead Sea; נַחַל הָעֲ *the brook* of Kedron; עֲרָבוֹת יְרֵחוֹ, עֲ מוֹאָב the plains of Jericho, Moab.—IV. pr. name of a town in Benjamin; gent noun עַרְבָתִי, see under בֵּית.

עֶרֶב עֲרָב }	pr. name of a country	עֶרֶב
עָרֵב	adj masc. sing.	ערב
עָרֶב	in pause for עֶרֶב (q. v. & § 35. rem. 2)	ערב
עֶרֶב	noun masc. sing.	ערב
עֲרֹב	Kal imp. sing. masc.	ערב
עֵרֶב	noun masc. sing.	ערב
עֹרֵב	לׂ noun masc. sing. (pl. c. עֹרְבֵי) dec. 6 a; for ן see lett. ו	ערב
עֹרֵב	pr. name masc.	ערב
עֹרֵב	ן noun masc.; or (Pr. 17. 18) Kal part. act. sing. masc. dec. 7 b	ערב
עֲרָבָה	ן noun fem. s. d. 11 c (§ 42. r. 1); ן bef. (-)	ערב
עָרְבָה	ן Kal pret. 3 pers. sing. fem.	ערב
עֲרֻבָּה	noun fem. sing. dec. 10	ערב
עָרְבוּ	Kal pret. 3 pers. sing.	ערב
עֵרָבוֹן	noun masc. sing.	ערב
עֲרָבוֹת	noun m. with pl f. term., abs. fr. עֶרֶב d. 6 a	ערב
עַרְבוֹת	noun f. pl. constr. fr. עֲרָבָה d. 11 c (§ 42. r. 1)	ערב
עַרְבִי	gent. noun from עֲרָב	ערב
עֹרְבֵי	ן noun masc. pl. constr. from עֶרֶב dec. 6 a	ערב
עֹרְבֵי	ן Kal part. act., or noun masc. pl. c. from עֹרֵב dec. 7 b	ערג
עֹרְבִים	noun masc., pl. of עֶרֶב dec. 6 a	ערב
עֹרְבִים	Kal part. act. masc., pl. of עֹרֵב dec. 7 b	ערב
עָרְבֵנִי	id. imp. sing. masc., suff. 1 pers. sing.	ערב
עָרַבְתָּ	id. pret. 2 pers. sing. masc.	ערב
עָרַבְתְּ	id. pret. 2 pers. sing. fem.	ערב
עַרְבֹת	defect. for עֲרָבוֹת (q. v.)	ערב
עֲרֻבָּתָהּ	ן noun fem. sing., suff. 3 pers. sing. fem. from עֲרֻבָּה dec. 11 c (§ 42. rem. 1)	ערב
עַרְבָתָם	noun fem. sing., suff. 3 pers. pl. masc. from עֲרָבָה dec. 10	ערב

[עָרַג] fut. תַּעְרֹג.—I. to low, bleat, as an animal from desire, longing, Joel 1. 20.—II. to desire, to long for, with עַל, אֶל Ps. 42. 2.
    עֲרוּגָה fem. dec. 10, a raised bed in a garden. Arab. ערג to rise, ascend.

עֲרֻגֹת noun fem. pl. of [עֲרוּגָה] dec. 10   ערג

עָרֹד Root not used; Arab. to flee; Syr. to be wild.
    עָרוֹד masc. wild ass, Job 39. 5.
    עֵירָד (wild ass) pr. name masc. Ge. 4. 18.

עֲרָד masc. dec. 1 a, wild ass, Da. 5. 21. Also the following.

עַרְד ן (wild ass) pr. name.—I. of a man, 1 Ch. 8. 15.
    —II. of a town in the southern part of Palestine . . . . . ערד

עֲרָדַיָּא Chald. noun masc. pl. emph. of [עֲרָד] d. 1 a   ערד

עָרָה Pi. עֵרָה, inf. עָרוֹת, fut. ap. וַתְּעַר.—I. to make naked or bare, to uncover.—II. to empty, pour out. Hiph. הֶעֱרָה.—I. to make bare, to expose, uncover, Le. 20. 18, 19.—II. to pour out, Is. 53. 12. Niph. to be poured, Is. 32. 15. Hithp. I. to make oneself naked, La. 4. 21.—II. to spread oneself abroad, Ps. 37. 35.
    עָרָה fem. only pl. עָרוֹת, bare places, pastures, Is. 19. 7.
    עֶרְוָה fem. dec. 10.—I. nakedness, Hos. 2. 11; metaph. of an unfortified part of a country, Ge. 42. 9, 12.—II. nudity of a person, male or female. —III. offensiveness, shamefulness; disgrace.
    עַרְוָא Chald. fem. dec. 8 a, damage, detriment, Ezr. 4. 14.
    עֶרְיָה fem. nakedness, need, destitution.
    מַעֲרֶה masc. dec. 9 a, a bare place, a plain or moor, Ju. 20. 33.
    מַעַר masc.—I. nudity, Na. 3. 5.—II. naked, empty space, 1 Ki. 7. 36.
    מַעֲרָת (naked, bare place) pr. name of a town in the tribe of Judah, Jos. 15. 59.
    תַּעַר masc. (with suff. תַּעְרָהּ).—I. razor.—II. penknife, Je. 36. 23.—III. scabbard, sheath of a sword.

עֵרָה	Piel pret. 3 pers. sing. masc.	ערה
עֹרָהּ	noun masc. s., suff. 3 pers. s. fem. fr. עוֹר d. 1 a	עור
עֹרָה	ן Kal imp. sing. masc. with parag. ה (comp. § 8. rem. 11, & § 18. rem. 4)	ערר
עָרוּ	Piel imp. pl. masc.	ערה
עֹרוֹ	noun masc. s., suff. 3 pers. s. m. fr. עוֹר d. 1 a	עור
עָרוֹד	noun masc. sing.	ערד
עֶרְוָה	noun fem. sing. (no pl.)	ערה
עָרוּךְ	Kal part. pass. sing. masc. dec. 3 a	ערך
עֲרוּךְ	id., constr. st.	ערך
עֲרוּכָה	id. part. sing. fem. dec. 10	ערך
עָרוֹם	ן adj. m. sing., pl. עֲרוּמִים (§ 37. rem. 2)	ערם
עָרֻם	ן adj. masc. sing. dec. 3 a	ערם
עֲרוּמִּים	adj. masc. pl. of עָרוֹם (§ 37. rem. 2)	ערם
עֲרוּמִים	ן adj. masc. pl. of עָרֻם dec. 3 a; ן bef. (-)	ערם

ᵃ Ps. 119. 122.   ᵉ Ge. 38. 17.   ⁱ Le. 23. 40.   ᵐ Ps. 137. 2.   ᵖ Eze. 16. 37.   ˢ 1 Sa. 17. 18.   ʷ Nu. 19. 5.   ᵃ Job 39. 5.   ᵉ Mi. 1. 8.
ᵇ Ps. 65. 9.   ᶠ Je. 5. 6.   ᵏ Pr. 30. 17.   ⁿ Ne. 5. 3.   ᵠ Nu. 31. 12.   ᵗ Eze. 17. 10.   ˣ Is. 32. 11.   ᵇ Joel 2. 5.   ᶠ Pr. 14. 15.
ᶜ Pr. 17. 18.   ᵍ Jos. 4. 13.   ˡ Eze. 27. 27.   ᵒ Pr. 6. 1.   ʳ Is. 51. 3.   ᵘ Da. 5. 21.   ʸ Ps. 137. 7.   ᶜ 2 Sa. 23. 5.   ᵍ Pr. 14. 18.
ᵈ Je. 6. 20.   ʰ Job 40. 22.

עֲרוֹעֵר	pr. name of a place	ערר
עֵרוֹת	noun fem. pl. abs. [from עָרָה]	ערה
עֵרוֹת	Piel inf. constr.	ערה
עֶרְוַת	Chald. noun fem. sing. constr. of [עֶרְוָא] d. 8 a	ערה
עֶרְוַת	noun fem. sing. constr. of עֶרְוָה (no pl.)	ערה
עֶרְוָתָהּ	id., suff. 3 pers. sing. fem.	ערה
עֶרְוָתוֹ	id., suff. 3 pers. sing. masc.	ערה
עֶרְוָתְךָ	id., suff. 2 pers. sing. masc.	ערה
עֶרְוָתֵךְ	id., suff. 2 pers. sing. fem.	ערה
עֶרְוָתָן	id., suff. 3 pers. pl. fem.	ערה
עָרַי	n. f., pl. (עָרִים), suff. 1 p. s., irr. of עִיר (§ 45)	עור
עָרֵי	id. pl., constr. st.	עור
עֵרִי	pr. name masc.	עור
עָרֶיהָ	noun fem. pl., (עָרִים), suff. 3 pers. sing. fem., irr. of עִיר (§ 45)	עור
עָרָה	noun fem. sing.	ערה
עֲרֵיהֶם	noun fem. pl., (עָרִים), suff. 3 pers. pl. masc., irr. of עִיר (§ 45)	עור
עָרָיו	id. pl., suff. 3 pers. sing. masc.	עיר
עָרַיִךְ	id. pl., suff. 2 pers. sing. fem.	עור
עָרֶיךָ	id. pl., suff. 2 pers. sing. masc.	עור
עָרֶיךָ	noun masc. pl., suff. 2 pers. s. m. fr. [עַר] d. 1 a	עיר
עָרֵיכֶם	the foll. with suff. 2 pers. pl. masc.	עור
עָרִים	noun fem. pl. properly of עַר see עִיר (§ 45)	עיר
עָרִים	noun masc. pl. of [עַר] dec. 1 a	עיר
עֲרִיסֹתֵכֶם	noun f. pl., suff. 2 p. pl. m. fr. עֲרִיסָה d. 10	ערס
עֲרִיסֹתֵינוּ	id. pl., suff. 1 pers. pl.	ערס
עָרִיץ	noun masc. sing. [for עָרִיץ] dec. 1 b	ערץ
עָרִיצֵי	id. pl., constr. st.	ערץ
עָרִיצִים	id. pl., abs. st.	ערץ
עֲרִירִי	adj. masc. sing. dec. 1 b	ערר
עֲרִירִים	id. pl., abs. st.	ערר

עָרַךְ fut. יַעֲרֹךְ.—I. *to set in order, to arrange, dispose*; hence, *to prepare* a table; *to array* a battle, with אֵת, לִקְרַאת *against* any one; part. עֹרְכֵי מִלְחָמָה, or simply עָרוּךְ *arrayed for battle*; עָרַךְ מִלִּין, and simply עָרַךְ *to set in order, prepare* or *utter* a speech, with לְ *to*, with אֶל *against* any one; עֵ' מִשְׁפָּט *to prepare a cause for judgment.*—II. *to place together, to compare,* with לְ, אֶל.—III. *to estimate, value,* Job 36. 19. Hiph. *to estimate, value.*

עֵרֶךְ masc. dec. 6 (with suff. עֶרְכִּי § 35. rem. 6).—I. *row, pile,* of the shew-bread, Ex. 40. 23.—II. *a preparation,* i. e. *suit of clothes.*—III. *valuation, estimation.*

מַעֲרָךְ masc. dec. 2 b, *arrangement, disposing,* only pl. c. מַעַרְכֵי Pr. 16. 1.

מַעֲרָכָה, מַעֲרֶכֶת fem. (pl. מַעֲרָכוֹת, constr. מַעַרְכוֹת).—I. *arrangement, disposition, order.*—II. *row, pile, heap.*—III. *array of battle.*

עֶרְךָ	noun masc. sing., suff. 2 pers. sing. masc. from [עַר] dec. 1 a (§ 30. No. 3)	עיר
עָרֹךְ	Kal inf. abs.	ערך
עֲרֹךְ	id. inf. constr.	ערך
עֶרְכְּךָ / עֶרְכֶּךָ	} noun masc. sing. dec. 6 (§ 35. rem. 6)	ערך
עָרְכָה	Kal pret. 3 pers. sing. fem.	ערך
עֶרְכָּהּ	n. m. s., suff. 3 p. s. f. fr. עֵרֶךְ d. 6 (§ 35. r. 6)	ערך
עָרְכָה	Kal imp. sing. m. with parag. ה (§ 8. r. 11)	ערך
עָרְכוּ	id. pret. 3 pers. pl.	ערך
עֶרְכּוֹ	noun masc. sing., suff. 3 pers. sing. masc. from עֵרֶךְ dec. 6 (§ 35. rem. 6)	ערך
עִרְכוּ	Kal imp. pl. masc.	ערך
עֹרְכֵי	id. part. act. pl. constr. m. [fr. עוֹרֵךְ] d. 7 b	ערך
עֶרְכְּךָ / עֶרְכְּךָ	} noun masc. sing., suff. 2 pers. sing. masc. from עֵרֶךְ dec. 6 (§ 35. rem. 6)	ערך
עָרַכְתָּ	Kal pret. 2 pers. sing. masc.; acc. shifted by conv. וְ (§ 8. rem. 7)	ערך
עָרַכְתִּי	id. pret. 1 pers. sing.	ערך

עָרֵל adj. masc. dec. 5 c (constr. עֲרַל, עֲרֵל § 34. No. 2) *uncircumcised*; עֲרַל שְׂפָתַיִם *uncircumcised,* i. e. *dull of speech,* hesitating or stammering; used also of the ear, the heart.

עָרֵל (denom.) *to regard as uncircumcised, profane,* Le. 19. 23. Niph. *to show oneself uncircumcised,* Hab. 2. 16.

עָרְלָה fem. dec. 12 c.—I. *foreskin*; עָרְלַת לֵב *uncircumcision of the heart.*—II. applied to the fruit of the three first years, Le. 19. 23.—III. pl. עֲרָלוֹת pr. name of a place near Gilgal, Jos. 5. 3.

עֲרֵל / עֲרַל	} adj. masc. sing., constr. of עָרֵל dec. 5 c (§ 34. No. 2)	ערל
עֲרֵלָה	noun fem. sing., pl. abs. עֲרֵלוֹת dec. 12 c	ערל
עֲרֵלָה	adj. fem. sing. from עָרֵל masc.	ערל
עַרְלוֹת	noun fem. pl. constr. from עָרְלָה dec. 12 c	ערל
עֲרֵלֵי / עֲרֵלִים	} adj. masc. pl. constr. & abs. from עָרֵל dec. 5 c	ערל
עָרְלַת	noun fem. sing. constr. of עָרְלָה dec. 12 c	ערל
עָרְלָתוֹ	id., suff. 3 pers. sing. masc.	ערל
עָרְלָתֵיהֶם	id. pl., suff. 3 pers. pl. masc.	ערל

a Is. 19. 7.   b Hab. 3. 13.   c Ezr. 4. 14.   d Le. 20. 17.   e Le. 18. 9, 10.   f Zec. 1. 17.   g Ps. 35. 9.   h Ps. 139. 20.   i Le. 26. 33.   k Is. 14. 21.   l Eze. 44. 30.   m Ne. 10. 38.   n Le. 20. 20, 21.   o Job 32. 14.   p 1 Sa. 28. 16.   q Is. 21. 5.   r Ps. 40. 6.   s Ex. 40. 23.   t Ju. 17. 10.   u Pr. 9. 2.   x Job 28. 13.   y Job 33. 5.   z Ju. 20. 22.   a Ex. 40. 4.   b Ge. 17. 14.   c Le. 27. 13.   d Le. 27. 3, 7, 15, 16, 19, 25.   e Eze. 44. 9, 9.   f Ge. 34. 14.   g Je. 6. 10.   h Eze. 44. 7.   i 1 Sa. 18. 27.

ᵃ עָרֹלְתְכֶם id. sing., suff. 2 pers. pl. masc. . . . . עֲרֵל

ᵇ עָרֹלְתָם id. pl., suff. 3 pers. pl. masc. . . . . עֲרֵל

ᶜ וַעֲרַלְתֶּם וְ Kal pret. 2 pers. pl. masc.; וְ for וְ conv.

עָרֹם I. *to be cunning, subtle, only inf.* עָרֹם 1 Sa. 23. 22.—II. Arab. *to make bare, see derivv.* Hiph. I. *to make crafty, with* סוֹד *to devise crafty counsel,* Ps. 83. 4.—II. *to act cunningly, craftily,* 1 Sa. 23. 22.—III. *to act prudently, wisely.*

עָרוֹם עָרֹם masc. pl. עֲרוּמִים, fem. עֲרֻמָּה (§ 37. No. 3 c) adj. *naked, stripped.*

עָרוּם adj. masc. dec. 3 a.—I. *crafty, cunning, subtle.*—II. *prudent, cautious.*

עָרֹם עֵירֹם masc. pl. עֵירֻמִּים (§ 37. No. 3 c).—I. adj. *naked,* Ge. 3. 7, 10, 11.—II. subst. *nakedness.*

עֹרֶם masc. dec. 6 c, *craftiness, cunning,* Job 5. 13.

עָרְמָה f.—I. *craftiness, cunning.*—II. *prudence.*

עַרְמוֹן masc. dec. 1 b, *plane tree.*

מַעֲרֻמִּים masc. pl. (of מַעֲרֹם § 37. No. 3 c) *nakedness,* 2 Ch. 28. 15.

II. עָרַם *to become heaped up,* Ex. 15. 8.

עֲרֵמָה fem. dec. 10 (pl. וֹת, ־ים), *a heap,* e. g. of rubbish, of grain.

ᵈ עָרֹם וְ Kal inf. abs. (1 Sa. 23. **22**); or defect. for עָרוֹם (q. v.) . . . . עָרַם

עֵרֹם וְ defect. for עֵירֹם (q. v.) . . . עָרַם

עָרְמָה noun fem. sing. . . . . עָרַם

עֲרֻמָּה adj. fem. sing. from עָרֹם masc. (§ 37. No. 3 c) עָרַם

עַרְמוֹן וְ noun masc. sing. dec. 1 b . . . עָרַם

עֲרֵמוֹת עֲרֵמִים } noun fem., pl. of עֲרֵמָה dec. 10 . . עָרַם

עַרְמֹנִים וְ noun masc., pl. of עַרְמוֹן dec. 1 b . עָרַם

עֲרֵמַת noun fem. sing., constr. of עֲרֵמָה dec. 10 . עָרַם

עָרַם Root not used; prob. *to break, pound,* comp. גָּרַם.

עֲרִיסָה fem. dec. 10, only pl. *groats, grits.* Others, *dough,* coll. with Chald. עֲרַם *to mix.*

ᵉ עֲרִסֹתֵכֶם עֲרִסֹתֵכֶם } noun fem. pl. with suff. 2 pers. pl. masc. [from עֲרִיסָה] dec. 10 . . . עָרַם

עַרְעֵר Pilp. (§ 6. No. 4) inf. abs. (Je. 51. 58) עָרַר

עָרֵר pr. n. of a place (Is. 17. 2), defect. for עֲרוֹעֵר עָרַר

עָרַף only fut. יַעֲרֹף *to drop, distil,* De. 32. 2; 33. 28.

עֲרִיפִים m. pl. (of עָרִיף) *clouds, for the skies,* Is. 5. 30.

עֲרָפֶל masc. *thick clouds, darkness, gloom.*

עֹרֶף masc. d. 6 c, *neck;* נָתַן ע' פָּנָה ע' *to turn the back,* with אֶל *to any,* i. e. *to turn away from him;* הָפַךְ ע', פָּנָה ע' *to turn the back,* i. e. *flee.*

עָרַף (denom.) *to break the neck* of an animal; metaph. *to throw down, destroy* an altar, Ho. 10. 2.

עֹרֵף Kal part. act. sing. masc. . . . עָרַף

עָרְפָּה (for עָפְרָה *fawn*) pr. name fem. Ru. 1. 4, 14.

ᶠ וְעָרְפוּ וְ Kal pret. 3 pers. pl. . . . . עָרַף

עָרְפּוֹ noun m. s., suff. 3 pers. s. m. fr. עֹרֶף d. 6 c עָרַף

עָרְפֶּךָ עָרְפְּךָ } id., suff. 2 pers. sing. masc. . . עָרַף

ᵍ וְעָרְפְּכֶם וְ id., suff. 2 pers. pl. masc. . . . עָרַף

ʰ עָרְפֶּל וְ noun masc. sing.; וְ bef. (ֶ) . . עָרַף

ⁱ וְעָרְפָּם וְ noun masc. sing., suff. 3 pers. pl. masc. from עֹרֶף dec. 6 c . . . . עָרַף

וְעָרַפְתּוֹ וְ Kal pret. 2 pers. sing. masc., suff. 3 pers. sing. masc.; וְ for וְ conv.

[עָרַץ] fut. יַעֲרֹץ.—I. *to terrify, make afraid.*—II. intrans. *to tremble, fear, be afraid,* with מִפְּנֵי *before or of* any one. Niph. part. נַעֲרָץ *terrible.* Hiph. I. *to make afraid,* Is. 8. 13.—II. *to fear,* with acc.

עֲרוּץ masc. *horror,* Job 30. 6.

עָרִיץ masc. dec. 1 b.—I. *strong, mighty.*—II. *violent, fierce, a tyrant.*

מַעֲרָצָה fem. *terror,* Is. 10. 33.

[עָרַק] I. *to flee,* Job 30. 3.—II. (as in Syr.) *to gnaw,* Job 30. 7, part. עֹרְקַי *my gnawers,* i. e. *my gnawing pains; others, my nerves.*

עַרְקִי gent. noun, *an Arkite,* an inhabitant of the city *Arca* or *Arce,* in Syria, Ge. 10. 17.

[עָרַר] *to be naked,* Is. 32. 11. Po. עוֹרֵר *to make naked, bare,* of a foundation, *to demolish,* Is. 23. 13. Pilp. עַרְעֵר and Hithpalp. הִתְעַרְעֵר (§ 6. No. 4) *to be laid bare, exposed, demolished.*

עֲרִירִי adj. masc. dec. 1 b, *solitary, forsaken,* hence *childless.*

עָרָר adj. *naked, destitute, poor.*

עַרְעָר, עֲרוֹעֵר masc.—I. *naked, bare,* prob. of a leafless tree, Je. 48. 6. Gesenius, *needy, outcast.* Eng. vers. "heath."—II. pr. name, *Aroer,* a city on the banks of Arnon, called also עֲרוֹעֵר, comp. Jos. 12. 2 with Ju. 11. 26.—III. pr. name, *Aroer,* a city near Rabbath-Ammon, on the brook of Jabbok.—IV. pr. name, *Aroer,* a city in the tribe of Judah, 1 Sa. 30. 28. Gent. noun עֲרֹעֵרִי, 1 Ch. 11. 44.

ᵃ Ge. 17. 11.   ᵉ Le. 19. 23.   ⁱ Eze. 18. 7, 16.   ᵐ Ge. 30. 37.   ᵍ Je. 50. 36.   ᵘ Is. 66. 3.   ᵘ Is. 48. 4.   ᵖ 2 Ch. 30. 8.   ˢ Job 22. 13.
ᵇ Ge. 17. 25.   ᵈ Job 1. 21.   ᶠ Ho. 2. 5.   ᵏ 2 Ch. 31. 6.   ᵏ Eze. 31. 3.   ᵑ De. 21. 4.   ⁿ De. 31. 27.   ʳ De. 10. 16.   ᵗ Ne. 9. 29.
ᶜ Nu. 15. 21.   ᵈᵈ Nu. 15. 20.

וְ עֹרְקִי Kal part. act. pl., suff. 1 pers. sing. [from עֹרֵק] dec. 7 b . . . . . . ערק

עֹרֵר Pilel inf. constr. . . . . . . עור

עֶרֶשׂ fem. dec. 6 a (pl. עֲרָשׂוֹת) *couch, bed.*

עָרֶשׂ id. in pause (§ 35. rem. 2) . . . ערשׂ

עַרְשׂוֹ id. with suff. 3 pers. sing. masc. . . ערשׂ

עַרְשִׂי id., suff. 1 pers. sing. . . . . . ערשׂ

עַרְשֵׂנוּ id., suff. 1 pers. pl. . . . . ערשׂ

עַרְשֹׂתָם id. pl. fem., suff. 3 pers. pl. masc. (§ 4. r. 2) ערשׂ

וְ עֹרֶת noun masc. with pl. f. term. fr. עוֹר d. 1 a עור

עֹרֹתָם id. with suff. 3 pers. pl. masc. (§ 4. rem. 2) עור

עָשׁ the name of a constellation, Job 9. 9, supposed to be the *Great Bear, Arcturus,* called also עַיִשׁ (q. v.)

עָשׁ noun masc. sing. . . . . . עָשֵׁשׁ

וְ עֵשֶׂב masc. dec. 6 (suff. עֶשְׂבָּם § 35. rem. 6; pl. c. עֶשְׂבוֹת) *green herb;* collect. *herbs, vegetables.*

עֲשַׂב Chald. dec. 3 b, idem. Da. 4. 12, 21, 22, 29, 30; 5, 21.

וְ עִשְׂבָּא Chald. noun m. s., emph. of עֲשַׂב d. 3 b עשׂב

עֶשְׂבוֹת noun fem. pl. constr. dag. euph. from עֵשֶׂב dec. 6 (§ 35. rem. 17) . . . . עשׂב

עֶשְׂבָּם id. sing., suff. 3 pers. pl. masc. (§ 35. rem 6) עשׂב

וְ עָשָׂה fut. יַעֲשֶׂה, ap. יַעַשׂ (§ 24. rem. 3).—I. *to work, labour,* with בְּ.—II. *to make, fabricate,* with acc.; *into* anything, with לְ & acc.; *to make* a thing into something, with double acc.; spoken of God, *to create:* hence part. עֹשֶׂה *maker, creator,* עֹשִׂי, עֹשֵׂהוּ *my, his maker, creator.*—III. *to produce, yield,* as fruit, flour, milk.—IV. *to make, get, acquire;* עָ חַיִל, עָ שֵׁם *to get riches, a name.*—V. *to make ready, prepare, dress,* as a meal, feast, the beard, a sacrifice.—VI. *execute, accomplish, perform,* a command, order; עָ שַׁבָּת, עָ פֶּסַח *to keep* or *celebrate* the Sabbath, Passover, with לְ to the Lord.—VII. *to make, do, act,* with לְ, בְּ, also acc.; עָ רָעָה, עָ חֶסֶד with לְ, עִם, אֶת, בְּ *to show kindness* or *unkindness* to any one; עָ מִלְחָמָה *to make war.* Niph. נַעֲשָׂה *to be made, be done.* Pi. *to press, squeeze,* Eze. 23. 3, 8. Pu. *to be made, created,* Ps. 139. 15.

עֲשָׂהאֵל (whom *God made, constituted*) pr. name masc. of three different persons.

עֲשִׂיאֵל (*made, constituted of God*) pr. name masc. 1 Ch. 4. 35.

עֲשָׂיָה (whom *God made, constituted*) pr. name masc. of several persons.

יַעֲשַׂי (for יַעֲשָׂיָה *may the Lord constitute* him) pr. name masc. Ezr. 10. 37 Kheth.

יַעֲשִׂיאֵל (*may God constitute* him) pr. name masc. 1 Ch. 11. 47.

מַעֲשֶׂה masc. dec. 9 a.—I. *work* of an artificer.—II. *labour, business, occupation.*—III. *deed, act.*—IV. *work,* the fruit of one's labour, *goods, property* also *fruits, produce.*

מַעֲשַׂי (for מַעֲשִׂיָה) pr. name masc. 1 Ch. 9. 12.

מַעֲשִׂיָה, מַעֲשֵׂיָהוּ (*work of the Lord*) pr. name of several men.

וְ עֲשׂה pr. name in compos. עֲשָׂהאֵל see עֲשָׂה אֵל עשׂה

וְ עֲשׂה id. inf. abs. . . . . . עשׂה

עֲשׂה id. inf. constr. . . . . עשׂה

וְ עֲשֵׂה id. imp. sing. masc.; בֵ bef. (־:) עשׂה

עֲשָׂה id. part. act. fem. from עָשָׂה masc. עשׂה

וְ עֹשֵׂהוּ id. part. act. masc. (עֹשֶׂה), suff. 3 pers. sing. fem. dec. 9 a . . . עשׂה

וְ עֹשֵׂה id. id., constr. st. . . . . עשׂה

וְ עֹשֶׂה id. id., abs. st. . . . . עשׂה

וְ עֲשָׂהאֵל pr. name masc.; וְ bef. (־:) עשׂה

וְ עֲשָׂהוּ Kal pret. 3 pers. sing. m., suff. 3 pers. s. m. עשׂה

עֲשֹׂהוּ id. inf. constr. (עֲשֹׂה), suff. 3 pers. sing. masc. (§ 24. rem. 2) . . . עשׂה

עֹשֵׂהוּ id. part. act. sing. masc. (עֹשֶׂה), suff. 3 pers. sing. masc. dec. 9 a . . עשׂה

וְ עֵשָׂו (*hairy;* coll. Arab.) pr. name, *Esau,* the son of Isaac; בֵּית עֵשָׂו, בְּנֵי עֵשָׂו, and simply עֵשָׂו the Esauites, i. e. the Edomites, הַר עֵשָׂו *mountain of Esau* or *Edom.*

עָשׂוֹ Kal inf. abs. (§ 24. rem. 2) . . . עשׂה

וְ עָשׂוּ id. pret. 3 pers. pl. . . . . עשׂה

עָשׂוֹ Kh. q. v., K. עֲשִׂי (q. v.) . . . עשׂה

עֲשׂוֹ Kal inf. constr. (§ 24. rem. 2) . . עשׂה

וְ עֲשׂוּ id. imp. pl. masc.; וַ bef. (־:) עשׂה

וְ עָשׂוּ Kh. וְעָשׂוּ q. v.; K. יַעֲשׂוּ Kal fut. 3 p. pl. m. עשׂה

עִשׂוּ Piel pret. 3 pers. pl. . . . . עשׂה

עֲשׂוּהוּ Kal pret. 3 pers. pl., suff. 3 pers. sing. masc. עשׂה

עֲשׂוֹוֹת id. part. pass. pl. fem. from עָשׂוּי masc. (§ 24. rem. 4); K. עֲשִׂיוֹת from . . עשׂה

וְ עָשׂוּי id. id. masc. dec. 3 a . . . עשׂה

וְ עֲשׂוּיָה id. id. fem. dec. 10, וַ bef. (־:) עשׂה

עֲשׂוּיִם id. id. pl. masc. from עָשׂוּי dec. 3 a עשׂה

עֲשׂוּנִי id. pret. 3 pers. pl., suff. 1 pers. sing. עשׂה

עָשׁוֹק noun masc. sing. . . . . . עשׁק

עָשׁוּק Kal part. pass. sing. masc. dec. 3 a עשׁק

a Job 30. 17.   d De. 3. 11.   g Le. 16. 27.   k Is. 42. 15.   n Is. 64. 4.   q Is. 16. 3.   t Eze. 23. 3, 8.   y Eze. 41. 18.   b Ps. 119. 73.

b Job 3. 8.   e Ca. 1. 16.   h Da. 4. 22, 30.   l Je. 33. 2.   Ge. 31. 29.   u Ec. 2. 12.   z Eze. 21. 20.   c Je. 22. 3.

c Am. 3. 12.   f Am. 6. 4.   Pr. 27. 25.   m Is. 45. 18.   p Ex. 18. 18.   s Eze. 46.   r 1 Sa. 25. 18.   x Eze. 41. 25.

עֲשׁוּקִים	בְּ id. pl. (Je. 50. 33; Ps. 103. 6); or noun m. pl.	עשׁק
עָשׁוֹר	noun masc. sing.	עשׁר
עֲשׂוֹת	adj. masc. sing.	עשׁת
עֲשֶׂוֹת	וְ pr. name masc. 1 Ch. 7. 33.	
עֲשׂוֹת	Kal. inf. constr.	עשׂה
עֹשׂוֹת	וְ id. part. act. fem., pl. of עֹשֶׂה d. 10, fr. עָשָׂה m.	עשׂה
עֲשֹׂתָהּ	id. inf. (עֲשׂוֹת), suff. 3 pers. sing. fem. dec. 1 a	עשׂה
עֲשׂוֹתְכֶם	id. id., suff. 2 pers. pl. masc.	עשׂה
עֲשִׂי	וְ id. imp. sing. fem.; וְ bef. (־ְ)	עשׂה
עֹשַׂי	id. part. act. pl. masc., suff. 1 pers. sing. from	
	עָשָׂה dec. 9 a	עשׂה
עֹשֵׂי	וְ id. id., constr. st.	עשׂה
עֲשִׂיאֵל	וַ וְ עֲשָׂיָה pr. names masc.; וְ bef. (־ְ)	עשׂה
עֹשֶׂיהָ	Kal part. act. pl., suff. 3 p. s. fem. fr. עֹשֶׂה d. 9 a	עשׂה
עֹשֵׂיהֶם	id. pl., suff. 3 pers. pl. masc.	עשׂה
עֹשַׂיִךְ	id. pl., suff. 2 pers. sing. fem.	עשׂה
עֹשִׂים	וְ id. pl., abs. st.	עשׂה
עָשִׂינוּ	וְ id. pret. 3 pers. pl.	עשׂה
עָשִׂיר	וְ noun masc. sing. dec. 3 a	עשׁר
עֲשִׂירֵי	id. pl., constr. st.	עשׁר
עֲשִׂירִי	adj. ord. masc. from עֶשֶׂר	עשׁר
עֲשִׂירִיָּה	noun masc. pl., suff. 3 pers. sing. fem. from	
	עָשִׂיר dec. 3 a	עשׁר
עֲשִׂירִיָּה	adj. ord. fem. from עֲשִׂירִי masc.	עשׁר
עֲשִׂירִים	וְ noun masc., pl. of עָשִׁיר dec. 3 a; וְ bef. (־ְ)	עשׁר
עֲשִׂירִית / עֲשִׂירִת	adj. ord. fem., from עֲשִׂירִי masc.; וְ id.	עשׁר
עָשִׂיתָ	וְ Kal pret. 2 pers. sing. masc.	עשׂה
עָשִׂית	וְ Kh. עָשִׂיתָ q. v., K. עָשִׂיתִי (q. v.)	עשׂה
עָשִׂית	Kal pret. 2 pers. sing. fem.	עשׂה
עֲשִׂית	Chald. Peal pret. 3 pers. sing. masc. (§ 47. r. 6)	עשׁת
עָשִׂיתָה	Kal pret. 2 pers. sing. masc. (§ 8. rem. 5)	עשׂה
עֲשִׂיתָהּ	id. id., suff. 3 pers. sing. fem.	עשׂה
עָשִׂיתִי	וְ id. pret. 1 pers. sing.	עשׂה
עָשִׂיתִי	Kh. עָשִׂיתִי, K. עָשִׂית Kal pret. 2 pers. sing.	
	fem. (comp. § 8. rem. 5)	עשׂה
עָשִׂיתְ	Kh. עָשִׂיתִי q. v., K. עָשִׂת (q. v.)	עשׂה
עֻשֵּׂיתִי	Pual part. 1 pers. sing.	עשׂה
עֲשִׂיתִיהוּ	וְ Kal pret. 1 pers. sing., suff. 3 pers. sing.	
	masc.; וְ for וָ, conv.	עשׂה
עֲשִׂיתִיו	וַ id. id., suff. 3 pers. sing.; וְ id.	עשׂה
עֲשִׂיתֶם	וַ id. pret. 2 p. s. m., suff. 2 pers. pl. m.; וְ id.	עשׂה
עֲשִׂיתֶם	וַ id. pret. 2 pers. pl. masc.; וְ id.	עשׂה
עֲשִׂיתֶם	וַ id. pret. 1 pers. sing., suff. 3 pers. pl.; וְ id.	עשׂה
עֲשִׂיתֶן	id. pret. 2 pers. pl. fem.	עשׂה
עֲשִׂיתַנִי	id. pret. 2 pers. s. m., suff. 1 pers. s. (§ 2. r. 1)	עשׂה

עֲשִׂיתַנִי	id. pret. 1 pers. sing., suff. 1 pers. sing.	עשׂה
עֲשִׂיתְךָ	id. pret. 3 pers. sing. masc. (עָשָׂה), suff.	
	2 pers. sing. masc. (§ 24. ren. 21)	עשׂה
עֹשֵׂךְ	id. part. act. sing. masc., suff. 2 pers. sing.	
	masc. from עָשָׂה dec. 9 a	עשׂה
עֲשָׂם	id. pret. 3 pers. sing. masc. (עָשָׂה), suff.	
	3 pers. pl. masc. (§ 24. rem. 21)	עשׂה
עָשַׁן	fut. יֶעְשַׁן (§ 13. rem. 5) to smoke. Hence the	
	two foll.	
עָשָׁן	וְ masc. dec. 4 c (constr. עֲשַׁן, עֶשֶׁן § 33. r. 3),	
	a smoke; metaph. of anger, of a cloud	עשׁן
עָשֵׁן	adj. masc. dec. 5 c, smoking	עשׁן
עֲשַׁן	noun masc. sing. constr. of עָשָׁן dec. 4 c	עשׁן
עֲשָׁנָהּ	id. with suff. 3 pers. sing. fem.	עשׁן
עֲשָׁנוֹ	id. with suff. 3 pers. sing. masc.	עשׁן
עֲשָׂנוּ	Kal pret. 3 pers. sing. masc. (עָשָׂה), suff.	
	1 pers. pl. (§ 24. rem. 21)	עשׂה
עֹשֵׂנוּ	id. part. act. s. m., suff. 1 p. pl. fr. עֹשֶׂה d. 9 a	עשׂה
עָשַׂנִי	id. pret. 3 p. s. m. (עָשָׂה), suff. 1 p. s. (§ 24. r. 21)	עשׂה
עֹשֵׂנִי	id. part. act. sing. masc., suff. 1 pers. sing.	
	(§ 2. rem. 7) from עֹשֶׂה dec. 9 a	עשׂה
עָשִׂנְתָּ	Kal pret. 2 pers. sing. masc.	עשׁן
עָשַׂק	Hithp. to strive, contend, Ge. 26. 20. Hence	
עֵשֶׂק	(strife) pr. name of a well near Gerar, Ge. 26. 20	עשׂק
עָשַׁק	fut. יַעְשֹׁק.—I. to oppress, treat with violence and	
	injustice.—II. to defraud, extort by fraud.—III. to	
	press upon.	
	עָשׁוּק masc. oppressor, Je. 22. 3.	
	עֲשׁוּקִים masc. pl. oppressions, acts of violence,	
	Job 35. 9; Am. 3. 9.	
	עֵשֶׁק (oppression) pr. name masc. 1 Ch. 8. 39.	
	עֹשֶׁק masc.—I. violence, oppression, injury.—II	
	something extorted by fraud and violence, unjust gain.	
	עָשְׁקָה fem. pressure, distress, anguish, Is. 38. 14.	
	מַעֲשַׁקּוֹת fem. pl. oppressions, exactions, Pr. 28. 16.	
עָשַׁק	Kal pret. 3 pers. sing. masc. for עָשַׁק (§ 8. r. 7)	עשׁק
עָשֵׁק	defect. for עָשׁוּק (q. v.)	עשׁק
עֶשֶׁק	pr. name masc.	עשׁק
עֹשֵׁק	וְ Kal part. sing. masc. dec. 7 b	עשׁק
עֹשֶׁק	noun masc. sing.	עשׁק
עָשְׁקָה	noun fem. sing.	עשׁק
עֲשָׁקוֹ	Kal pret. 3 pers. sing. m., suff. 3 pers. sing. m.	עשׁק
עֲשָׁקוּ	וְ id. pret. 3 pers. pl.	עשׁק

a Job 35. 9.   g Is. 22. 11.   l Is. 6. 13.   q Da. 6. 4.   y Ps. 139. 15.   e Eze. 37. 19.   i Ex. 19. 18.   s Ps. 100. 3.   v Pr. 28. 3.
b Am. 3. 9.   h Is. 54. 5.   Ec. 10. 6.   r 1 Ki. 17. 12.   Job 10. 9.   Is. 4. 5.   Ps. 95. 6.   Is. 38. 14.
c Eze. 13. 18.   Eze. 33. 32.   m Nu. 28. 5.   Eze. 16. 31, 43,   Eze. 12. 25.   Eze. 29. 3.   Is. 29. 16.   Is. 52. 4.
d Je. 11. 15.   Pr. 18. 23.   Eze. 45. 11.   47, 51.   Ne. 9. 31.   De. 32. 6.   Ex. 20. 18.   Ps. 80. 5.   y Eze. 22. 29.
Je. 7. 13.   Ps. 45. 13.   Eze. 16. 59.   2 Sa. 14. 21.   Ex. 4. 21.   Is. 48. 5.   Is. 34. 10.   Pr. 28. 17.   Mi. 2. 2.
Job 35. 10.   Mi. 6. 12.   Eze. 27. 19.   Le. 5. 23.   Ex. 19. 18.

עשׁק   id. part. pl., suff. 3 pers. pl. masc. fr. עשׁק d. 7 b   עֲשֹׁקֵיהֶם [a]

עשׁק   id. pret. 1 pers. sing.   עֲשַׁקְתִּי

עשׁק   id. pret. 2 pers. sing. masc., suff. 1 pers. pl.   עֲשַׁקְתָּנוּ

עֶשֶׂר, וַ֫, fem. עֲשָׂרָה, עֶ֫שְׂרַת maso ten; pl. עֲשָׂרוֹת tens, decades.

עֶ֫שֶׂר masc. עֲשָׂרָה fem ten, used only in composition with other numbers, as אַחַד־עָשָׂר eleven, אַרְבָּעָה עָשָׂר fourteen; שִׁשָּׁה עָשָׂר sixteen; also as ordinals, eleventh, fourteenth, sixteenth; fem. אַרְבַּע עֶשְׂרֵה, אַחַת עֶשְׂרֵה, &c. Pl. עֶשְׂרִים (of עֶ֫שֶׂר § 35. rem. 16) com. twenty; also twentieth.

עֲשַׂר Ch. fem. עֲשָׂרָה m. ten. Pl. עֶשְׂרִין twenty.

עָשַׂר fut. יַעֲשֹׂר (§ 13. rem. 5) to tithe, take the tenth part, 1 Sa. 8. 15, 17. Pi. to give the tenth part, pay tithe. Hiph. id.

עָשׂוֹר masc. ten, בֶּעָשׂוֹר לַחֹ֫דֶשׁ in the tenth [day] of the month; נֵ֫בֶל עָ, and simply עָשׂוֹר a lyre of ten strings.

עֲשִׂירִי adj. ordinal, tenth; fem. עֲשִׂירִיָּה, עֲשִׂירִית the tenth, sc. part.

עִשָּׂרוֹן masc. dec. 3 c (pl. עִשְׂרֹנִים) a measure of things dry, the tenth part of an ephah.

מַעֲשֵׂר, מַעֲשֵׂר masc. dec. 7 c (constr. מַעֲשַׂר; pl. מַעְשְׂרוֹת) tithe.

עֶ֫שֶׂר num. card. masc.   עשׂר

עֲשַׂר Chald. num. card. masc.   עשׂר

עָ֫שַׂר in pause for עֶ֫שֶׂר (q. v. § 35. rem. 2)   עשׂר

עַשֵּׂר Piel inf. constr. used as an abs.   עשׂר

[עָשַׁר] fut. יֶעְשַׁר (§ 13. rem. 5) to be rich. Pi. I. to make rich, to enrich.—II. to be or become rich. Hithp. to feign oneself rich, Pr. 13. 7.

עָשִׁיר masc. d. 3 a.—I. rich.—II. proud, arrogant.

Also

עֹ֫שֶׁר, וַ֫, masc. dec. 6 c, riches; for וַ see lett. וַ [d]

עֲשָׂרָה, וַ֫ num. card. masc. from עֶ֫שֶׂר fem.; וַ bef. (ַ.)   עשׂר

עֲשַׂרְתָּ Chald. num. card. masc. from עֲשַׂר fem.   עשׂר [e]

עֲשָׂרָה num. card., fem. of עֶ֫שֶׂר masc.   עשׂר

עֶשְׂרוֹ noun masc. sing., suff. 3 pers. sing. masc. from עֶ֫שֶׂר dec. 6 c   עשׂר

עִשָּׂרוֹן, וַ֫ noun m. sing., pl. עִשְׂרֹנִים d. 3 c (§ 32. r. 3)   עשׂר

עֶשְׂרִים, וַ֫ num. card. com. gend., pl. of עֶ֫שֶׂר (§ 35. r. 16)   עשׂר

עֶשְׂרִין, וַ Chald. num. card. com. pl.   עשׂר

עֲשִׂירִת defect. for עֲשִׂירִית (q. v.)   עשׂר [g]

עֶשְׂרָם noun masc. sing. with suff. 3 pers. pl. masc. from עֶ֫שֶׂר dec. 6 c   עשׂר

עֶשְׂרֹנִי, וַ defect. for עִשָּׂרוֹן noun masc. sing. dec. 3 c   עשׂר

עֶשְׂרֹנִים id. pl. abs. et.   עשׂר

עֲשֶׂ֫רֶת num. card. masc. pl. of עֲשָׂרָה   עשׂר

עֲשֶׂ֫רֶת, וַ id. constr. (§ 42. rem. 5); וַ bef. (ַ.)   עשׂר

עָשַׂ֫רְתִּי Kal pret. 1 pers. sing.   עשׂר

[עָשֵׁשׁ] to waste away, become old. עָשׁ masc. moth.

עָשְׁשָׁה Kal pret. 3 pers. sing. fem.   עשׁשׁ

עָשֵׁ֫שׁוּ id. pret. 3 pers. pl. [for עָֽשְׁשׁוּ § 8. rem. 1]   עשׁשׁ [i]

[עָשַׁת] to be made smooth, bright, polished, hence, metaph. of the skin, to shine, Je. 5. 28. Hithp. to think of, remember, Jon. 1. 6, see Chald. עֲשַׁת.

עֲשַׁת, עֲשִׁית Chald. (§ 47. rem. 6) to think, intend, purpose, Da. 6. 4.

עָשׁוּת adj. m. shining, bright, of iron, Eze. 27. 19; others, forged, wrought.

עֶ֫שֶׁת fem. dec. 6 a.—I. something wrought, artificial work.—II. thought, opinion, only pl. עֶשְׁתּוֹת Job 12. 5, where many MSS. read עַשְׁתּוּת.—III. pl. c. עַשְׁתֵּי only in combination with the number ten, as עַשְׁתֵּי עֶשְׂרֵה, עַשְׁתֵּי עָשָׂר to express the number eleven, also eleventh. Etymology uncertain.

עֶשְׁתֹּנוֹת fem. pl. thoughts, devices, Ps. 146. 4.

עֶ֫שֶׁת noun fem. sing. [for עֶשְׁתָּת]   עשׂת

עָשְׂתָה, וַ Kal pret. 3 pers. sing. fem. (§ 24. rem. 1)   עשׂה

עָשָׂ֫תָה id. pret. 3 pers. sing. fem. (comp. § 8. rem. 7)   עשׂה

עֲשׂ֫תָהּ id. inf. (עֲשׂוֹת), suff. 3 pers. sing. fem. dec. 1 a   עשׂה [m]

עָשׂוּ Kal pret. 3 pers. pl.   עשׂה

עֲשׂתוֹ Kal inf. (עֲשׂוֹת), suff. 3 pers. sing. m. d. 1 a   עשׂה

עֶשְׁתֵּי noun masc. pl. constr. from עֶ֫שֶׁת dec. 6 a   עשׂת

עֲשָׂתְנִי Kal pret. 3 pers. sing. fem. (עָשְׂתָה), suff. 1 pers. sing.   עשׂה [pp]

עֶשְׁתֹּנֹתָיו noun f. pl., suff. 3 pers. s. m. [fr. עֶשְׁתֹּנֶת]   עשׂת [qq]

עַשְׁתָּרֹת, וַ noun fem. pl. abs. & constr. from עֲשָׁתֶּרֶת q. v. (§ 44. rem. 5).

עַשְׁתָּ֫רֶת fem.—I. Gr. Ἀστάρτη, Astarte, perhaps the deified planet Venus, worshipped by the Phœnicians and Philistines.—II. pl. עַשְׁתָּרוֹת (§ 44. rem. 5) images or statues of Astarte. —III. עַשְׁתְּרוֹת צֹאן (amours) offspring or increase of the flock.—IV. Ashtaroth, pi name of a city of Bashan, De. 1. 4; Jos. 13. 12; called עַשְׁתְּרֹת קַרְנַ֫יִם (Astarte with horns) Ge. 14. 5, and בְּעַשְׁתְּרָה q. v. Gent. noun עַשְׁתְּרָתִי 1 Ch. 11. 44.

עַתָּ, וַ Kh., עַתָּה K., adv.   עדה [r]

עֵת
עֶת־ } noun com. sing. dec. 8 b   עדה

עָתַד . Pi. *to make ready, prepare,* Pr. 24. 27. Hithp. *to be ready, destined,* Job 15. 28.
עָתֻד i. q. עָתִיד Is. 10. 13 ; Est. 8. 13 Kheth.
עָתִיד m. l. 3 a, adj. *ready, prepared.* Pl. עֲתִידוֹת —I. *things ready, destined to take place,* De. 32. 35. —II. *things prepared, acquired,* i. e. *riches,* Is. 10. 13.
עָתִיד Chald. dec. 1 a, *ready,* Da. 3. 15.
עָתּוּד masc. dec. 1 b.—I. *he-goat.*—II. metaph. *leader, prince.*

עֶתְרָה ‹ Piel imp. sing. m. [עֲתֹד], suff. 3 pers. s. f. עתד
עַתְרִים defect. for עֲתוּדִים (q. v.) . . . עתד
עֲתֶרֹת adj. fem. pl. [of עֲתִידָה from עָתִיד masc. עתד
עַתָּה
עַתָּה } adv. . . . . עדה
עִתָּהּ noun com. s., suff. 3 pers. s. f. fr. עֵת d. 8 b עדה
עִתּוֹ noun com. s., suff. 3 pers. s. m. fr. עֵת d.8b עדה
עַתּוּדִי noun masc. pl. constr. from [עָתּוּד] dec. 1 b עתד
עַתּוּדִים Kh. עֲתוּדִים adj. masc., pl. of [עָתּוּד] dec. 3 a; K. עֲתִידִים (q. v.) . . עתד
עַתּוּדִים ‹ noun masc. pl. [of עָתּוּד] dec. 1 b . עתד
עַתַּי
עַתָּי } pr. name masc. . . . עדה
עַתִּי adj. masc. sing. . . . עדה
עָתִיד adj. masc. sing. dec. 3 a . עתד
עֲתִידִים id. pl., abs. st. . . עתד
עֲתִידִין Chald., adj. masc., pl. of [עָתִיד] dec. 1 a . עתד
עַתִּדוֹתֵיהֶם Kh. עַתִּי, K. עֲתִי adj. pl. fem., suff. 3 pers. pl. masc. fr. עָתִיד [or עָתּוּד] d. 3 a עתד
עֲתָיָה pr. name masc. Ne. 11. 4.
עִתֶּיךָ n. com. pl. with suff. 2 p. s. m. fr. עֵת d. 8 b עדה
עִתִּים id. pl., abs. st. . . עדה
עָתִיק adj. masc. sing. . . עתק
עַתִּיק ‹ Chald., adj. masc. sing. . עתק
עַתִּיקִי } adj. masc. pl. abs. & constr. from [עַתִּיק] עתק
עַתִּיקִים } dec. 1 b
[עֶתֶר] pr. name of a town in the tribe of Judah, 1 Sa. 30. 30.
עִתֶּךָ noun com. s., suff. 2 pers. s. f. fr. עֵת d. 8 b עדה
עִתְּךָ id., suff. 2 pers. sing. masc. עדה
עֲתַלְיָ [for עֲתַלְיָה, ap. fr. עֲתַלְיָהוּ] pr. n. m. Ezr. 10. 28.
עֲתַלְיָה
עֲתַלְיָהוּ } (whom *the Lord has afflicted;* coll. Arab.) pr. name—I. of a man, 1 Ch. 8. 26.—II. of a man, Ezr. 8. 7.—III. of a queen of Judah.

עָתַם . Niph. *to be burned, consumed,* Is. 9. 18. Others, *to be darkened.*
עֲתָמוֹ noun com. sing., 3 pers. pl. masc. fr. עֵת d. 8 b עדה
עָתְנִי (for עָתְנִיָּה *lion of the Lord;* Arab. עתון *lion*) pr. name masc. 1 Ch. 26. 7.
עַתְנִיאֵל (*lion of God*) pr. name of a judge of Israel.

[עָתַק] fut. יֶעְתַּק (§ 13. rem. 3).—I. *to be removed, transferred* from place to place.—II. *to advance in age, grow old.* Hiph. הֶעְתִּיק (§ 13. rem. 9).—I. *to remove, take away.*—II. *to remove, break up* a camp.—III. *to transfer, transcribe,* Pr. 25. 1.
עָתָק adj. masc. *bold, insolent, wicked.*
עָתֵק adj. m. *beautiful, shining,* Pr. 8. 18. Vulg. *opes superbæ.* Prof. Lee, subst. *freedom, liberty.*
עָתִיק adj. masc. *neat, elegant, splendid,* Is. 23. 18.
עַתִּיק adj. masc. dec. 1 b.—I. *removed, taken away,* sc. *from the mother's breast, weaned,* Is. 28. 9.—II. *ancient,* 1 Ch. 4. 22.
עַתִּיק Ch. *ancient,* Da. 7. 9, 13, 22.
עֶתֶק noun masc. sing. . . . עתק
עָתֵק adj. masc. sing. . . עתק
עָתְקָה Kal pret. 3 pers. sing. fem. . עתק
עָתְקוּ id. pret. 3 pers. pl. . . עתק

I. עָתַר only fut. יֶעְתַּר *to entreat, supplicate,* with אֶל, לְ . Niph. *to be prevailed upon by entreaty, to become propitious;* part. pl. fem. נַעְתָּרוֹת *seemingly propitious, false,* Pr. 27. 6 (Prof. Lee), see No. II. Hiph. *to entreat, supplicate,* with בְּעַד, לְ *for any one.*

II. עָתַר . Niph. *to be rich, abundant,* only part., Pr. 27. 6, comp. Niph. of No. I. Hiph. *to make abundant, to multiply,* Eze. 35. 13.
עָתָר masc. dec. 4 c.—I. *suppliant,* Zep. 3. 10.—II. *abundance,* Eze. 8. 11. Gesenius, *incense, perfumed smoke, fragrant vapour.*
עֶתֶר (*abundance*) pr. name of a town in the tribe of Simeon.
עֲתֶרֶת fem. *abundance, riches,* Je. 33. 6.
עֲתַר ‹ noun m. s. constr. [of עָתָר] d. 4 c; ‹ bef. (–) עתר
עֶתֶר ‹ pr. name of a place עתר
עֲתָרִי noun masc. pl. with suff. 1 pers. sing. from [עָתָר] dec. 4 c . . . עתר
עֲתֶרֶת noun fem. sing. . . . עתר
עֲתֹתַי noun com. pl. with suff. 1 pers. sing. from עֵת dec. 8 b . . . עדה

פ

פָא ¹ adv. i. q. פֹּה *here*, Job 38. 11; ¹ bef. lab.

פָּאָה Kal not used; "to which I do not hesitate to assign the signification of *breathing, blowing*, like the cogn. פָּעָה (פָּהָה), also פּוּחַ, פּוּגַ, פּוּחַ" (Gesenius). Hiph. *to blow away*, i. e. scatter like the wind, De. 32. 26.

פֵּאָה fem. dec. 11 b.—I. *side, quarter* of the heavens (prop. wind, comp. רוּחַ).—II. *side, district, region*.—III. *corner*, e. g. of a field; פְּאַת זָקָן *corner* or *extremity of the beard*, i. e. *whiskers*; קְצוּצֵי פֵאָה *men having their whiskers clipped.*

פֶּה masc. (for פֵּאָה, § 45).—I. *mouth*; פֶּה אֶל־פֶּה *mouth to mouth*, i. e. without the intervention of any one; פֶּה אֶחָד *with one mouth*, i. e. *unanimously*.—II. *mouth, aperture, entrance.*—III. *edge* of a sword.—IV. *edge, border, side*; פֶּה לָפֶה *from one side* or *end to the other.*—V. *part, portion*; פִּי שְׁנַיִם *portion of two*, i. e. *two parts.*—VI. *word, command; expression, tenor*; כְּפִי *according to the word* or *command of*, also, *in proportion, according to*; Job 33. 6 כְּפִיךָ *as thou art*; כְּפִי אֲשֶׁר *according as, even as* (and אֲשֶׁר omitted), *so as, so that*; לְפִי *in proportion, according to*; עַל פִּי *according to the word* or *command; also according to.*

פִּיָּה fem. (for פֵּאָה) *edge* of a sword, only pl. פִּיּוֹת Ju. 3. 16.

פִּיפִיּוֹת fem. pl. *edges, two edges*; בַּעַל פִּ' *having many edges.*

פִּי־בֶסֶת pr. name of a city in Egypt, Eze. 30. 17.

פִּי־הַחִירֹת (*mouth of the caverns*) pr. name of a place on the Red Sea.

פִּיכֹל (*all-commanding*) pr. name of the chief of Abimelech's troops.

פִּינְחָס (*mouth of brass*) pr. name, *Phinehas*.—I. a son of Eleazar, son of Aaron.—II. son of the high priest, Eli.—III. Ezr. 8. 33.

פֵּאָה noun fem. sing. dec. 11 b . . . פאה

I פָּאַר Pi. פֵּאֵר.—I. *to adorn, beautify, honour.*—II. *to glean*, comp. פֹּארָה, De. 24. 20. Hithp. I. *to be adorned, honoured, glorified*, with בְּ in any one.— II. *to vaunt, boast oneself*, with עַל *against any one.*

פְּאֵר masc. dec. 1 a (but pl. c. פַּאֲרֵי, § 35 rem. 10), *ornamental headdress, turban.*

פֹּארָה fem. dec. 10, *a green bough; branch.*

פֻּארָה fem. idem. Is. 10. 33.

פֻּרָה (for פֹּארָה *bough*) pr. name masc. Ju 7. 10, 11.

פָּארוּר masc. *beauty, brightness*; קִבֵּץ פ' *to gather in*, i. e. *lose one's brightness, to grow pale.*

פָּרוּר masc. (פָּארוּר) *pot for boiling*; Arab. פאר *to be hot, to boil.*

תִּפְאָרָה, תִּפְאֶרֶת fem. dec. 13 a (with suff. תִּפְאַרְתִּי).—I. *ornament, beauty, splendour.*—II. *glory, honour.*—III. *glorying, boasting; also the object of glorying.*

II פָּאַר Kal not used; Arab. *to dig down*, cogn. בָּאַר. Hithp. *to explain, declare oneself*, Ex. 8. 5.

פְּאֵרֹת (for פְּאָרֹת) *holes*, see under R. חָפַר.

פָּארָן (*abounding in caverns*) pr. name of a desert and somewhat mountainous tract between Egypt and Palestine.

פְּאֵר noun masc. sing.	.	פאר
פֹּארָה noun fem. sing.	.	פאר
פָּארוּר noun masc. sing.	.	פאר
פַּאֲרֵי noun masc. pl. constr. from פְּאֵר (§ 35. r. 10)		פאר
פֵּאַרְתְּ Piel pret. 3 pers. sing. masc. [פֵּאֵר], suff. 2 pers. sing. fem.		פאר
פְּאֵרְךָ noun masc. sing., suff. 2 pers. sing. masc. from פְּאֵר (§ 35. rem. 10)		פאר
פַּאֲרֵכֶם ¹ id. pl., suff. 2 pers. pl. masc. [for פְּאֵרֵיכֶם]; ¹ bef. lab.		פאר
פָּארָן pr. name of a region	.	פאר
פֹּארֹת noun fem. pl. of [פֹּארָה] dec. 10		פאר
פֹּארֹתָיו id. pl., suff. 3 pers. sing. masc.		פאר
פְּאַת ¹ noun fem. sing., constr. of פֵּאָה dec. 11 b; ¹ bef. lab.		פאה
פַּאֲתֵי id. du. constr. [of פַּאֲתַיִם]		פאה

פָּגַג Root not used; Arab. *to be unripe*.

פַּג masc. dec. 8 d, *unripe fig*, Ca. 2. 13.

פַּגּוּל noun masc. sing. dec. 1 b . . . פגל

פָּגֹשׁ Kal inf. abs. . . . פגש

פַּגִּיָּה ² noun masc. pl., suff. 3 pers. sing. fem. from [פַּג] dec. 8 d . . . . . פגג

פָּגַל Root not used; Eth. *to be impure.*

פִּגּוּל masc. dec. 1 b, *something impure, abominable.*

פְּגֻלִים noun masc., pl. of פִּגּוּל dec. 2 b . . . . . . פגל

פָּגַע *'ז* I. *to meet, meet with, light upon,* with acc., בְּ.
—II. *to fall upon* any one, in a hostile sense.—
III. *to reach unto, border upon,* with בְּ, אֶל.—
IV. *to assail* with petitions, *to urge, entreat, supplicate,* with בְּ, לְ.—V. *to meet, regard with favour,* Is. 47. 3; 64. 4. Hiph. I. *to cause to fall upon, to lay upon,* Is. 53. 6.—II. *to cause to entreat, supplicate,* Je. 15. 11.—III. intrans. *to fall upon,* only Job 36. 32 מַפְגִּיעַ *assailant, enemy.*—IV. *to entreat, supplicate,* with בְּ, לְ.

פֶּגַע masc. *occurrence, incident, event.*

פַּגְעִיאֵל (*event of God*) pr. n. of a prince of Asher.

מִפְגָּע masc. *attack, object of attack,* Job 7. 20.

פָּנֹט *[לֹ]* noun masc. sing.; for וֹ see lett. ו . . פנע

פָּנַע *ו'* Kal imp. sing. masc.; ו bef. lab. . . פנע

פָּנְעוֹ *ו'* id. pret. 3 pers. sing. masc., suff. 3 pers. sing. masc.; ו id. . . . . . פנע

פָּנְעוּ *ו'* id. imp. pl. masc.; ו id. . . . פנע

פַּנְעִיאֵל pr. name masc. . . . . . פנע

פְּנַעְתָּ } Kal pret. 2 pers. sing. masc.; acc. shifted
פְּנַעְתָּ *ו* } by conv. ו bef. lab. (§ 8. rem. 7) } פנע

פָּגַר Pi. *to become weary, exhausted,* 1 Sa. 30. 10, 21. Hence

פֶּגֶר } masc. dec. 6 a (pl. com. פְּגָרִי), *corpse,*
פֶּגֶר } *carcase,* of man or beast } פגר

פִּגְּרוּ *ו* Piel pret. 3 pers. pl. . . . . פגר

פִּגְרֵי *ו'* n. m. pl. constr. fr. פֶּגֶר d. 6 a; ו bef. lab. פגר

פִּגְרֵיהֶם *ו* id. pl., suff. 3 pers. pl.; ו id. . . פגר

פִּגְרֵיכֶם *'ו* id. pl., suff. 2 pers. pl. masc.; ו id. . . פגר

פְּגָרִים *ו'* id. pl., abs. st.; ו id. . . . . פגר

[פָּגַשׁ] fut. יִפְגֹּשׁ.—I. *to meet, fall in with,* with acc., בְּ.—II. *to fall upon,* in a hostile sense. Niph. *to meet each other.* Pi. *to light upon, meet with,* Job 5. 14.

פָּגְשׁוּ *ו* Kal pret. 3 pers. pl.; ו bef. lab. . . פגשׁ

פְּגַשְׁתִּי id. pret. 1 pers. sing. [for פָּגַשְׁתִּי] . . פגשׁ

פָּדָה *'ז ו* t. *to redeem, ransom.*—II. *to set free, let go.*—III. *to deliver, preserve.* Niph. *to be redeemed.* Hiph. *to cause to be redeemed,* Ex. 21. 8. Hoph. *to be redeemed,* Le. 19. 20.

פְּדוּי masc. only pl. פְּדוּיִים *price of redemption, ransom,* Nu. 3. 46, 48, 49, 51; 18. 16.

פָּדוֹן (*deliverance*) pr. name masc. Ezr. 2. 44; Ne. 7. 47.

פְּדוּת fem.—I. *deliverance.*—II. *distinction,* Ex 8. 19, Sept. διαστολή.

פִּדְיוֹן, פִּדְיֹם masc. *price of redemption, ransom.*

פְּדַהְאֵל (*whom God has delivered*) pr. name masc. Nu. 34. 28.

פְּדָהצוּר (*whom the Rock has delivered*) pr. name masc. Nu. 1. 10; 2. 20.

פְּדָיָהוּ, פְּדָיָה (*whom the Lord has delivered*) pr. name masc. of several persons.

יִפְדְּיָה (*whom the Lord delivers*) pr. name masc. 1 Ch. 8. 25.

פָּדֹה Kal inf. abs. . . . . פדה

פְּדֵה id. imp. sing. masc. . . . . . פדה

פְּדַהְאֵל, פְּדָהצוּר pr. names masc. . . . . פדה

פְּדוּיָן *ו* noun masc. pl., suff. 3 pers. sing. masc. from פְּדוּי] dec. 1 a; ו bef. lab. . . פדה

פְּדוּיֵי id. pl., constr. st. . . . . . פדה

פְּדוּיֵי *ו* Kal part. pass. pl. constr. [from פָּדוּי] dec. 3 a; ו bef. lab. . . . . פדה

פָּדוֹן pr. name masc. . . . . . . פדה

פְּדוּת noun fem. sing. . . . . . . פדה

פְּדָיָה *ו', פְּדָיָהוּ* pr. names masc. . . . . פדה

פִּדְיוֹן }
פִּדְיֹם } noun masc. sing. . . . . . פדה

פָּדִיתָ }
פְּדִיתָה *ו* } Kal pret. 2 pers. sing. masc. (§ 8. r. 5) פדה

פְּדִיתִיךָ *ו* id. pret. 1 pers. sing., suff. 2 pers. sing. masc. פדה

פְּדִיתִים *ו* id., suff. 3 pers. pl. masc. . . פדה

פְּדָךָ id. pret. 3 pers. sing. masc. (פָּדָה), suff. 2 pers. sing. masc. (§ 24. rem. 21) . . פדה

פָּדָם *ו* id. id., suff. 3 pers. pl. masc. . . פדה

[פַּדָּן] masc. *field, plain;* פַּדַּן־אֲרָם *Padan-aram,* the plain of Syria, i. e. Mesopotamia.

אַפֶּדֶן masc. dec. 6 a, *palace,* Da. 11. 45.

פְּדֶנָה pr. name [פַּדָּן] with parag. ה . . פדן

פְּדֵנוּ *ו* Kal imp. sing. masc. (פְּדֵה), suff. 1 pers. pl. (§ 24. rem. 21); ו bef. lab. . פדה

פְּדֵנִי id. id., suff. 1 pers. sing. . . . פדה

[פָּדַע] *to redeem, deliver,* Job 33. 24.

פְּדָעֵהוּ *ו* Kal imp. sing. masc. [פְּדַע], suff. 3 pers. sing. masc. (§ 16. rem. 12) . . פדע

ᵃ Is. 65. 4.   ᶜ Ge. 23. 8.   ᵉ 1 Sa. 17. 46.   ᵍ Is. 34. 3.   ⁱ Is. 34. 14.   ᵏ Ps. 25. 22.   ᵐ Ps. 49. 9.   ᵒ Mi. 6. 4.   ᵠ Ps. 78. 42.
ᵇ 1 Ki. 5. 13.   Is. 64. 4.   1 Sa. 30. 10, 21.   Nu. 16. 32.   Ge. 33. 8.   Nu. 18. 16.   Ex. 21. 30.   Zec. 10. 8.   Ps. 44. 27.
Ec. 9. 11.   Ge. 10. 5.   Ese. 43. 9.   2 Ch. 20. 25.   Le. 27. 27.   Nu. 3. 46,48,49.   Ps. 31. 6.   Job 5. 22.   Job 33. 24.
Am. 5. 19.   Na. 3. 3.

[פֶּדֶר] masc. dec. 6 a (with suff. פִּדְרוֹ), *fat, grease*.

פִּדְרוֹ id. with suff. 3 pers. sing. masc. . . פדר

פֶּדְת defect. for פְּדוּת (q. v.) . . . פדה

פְּדִתִיךָ defect. for פְּדִיתִיךָ q. v.; ו bef. lab. פדה

פֹה ו adv.—I. *here, in this place*.—II. *hither*; מִפֹּו מִפֹּה *from here, hence*.

פֵּה ו noun masc. sing. irr. (§ 45); ו bef. lab. פאה

פּוּאָה ו pr. name masc.—I. 1 Ch. 7. 1, elsewhere פֻּנָה.—II. Ju. 10. 1.

[פּוּג] *to become chilled, languid; to cease to act.* Niph. *to be languid,* Ps. 38. 9.

פּוּגָה fem. dec. 10, *intermission, rest,* La. 2. 18.

הַפֻּגָה fem. dec. 10, idem, La. 3. 49.

פּוּגַת noun fem. sing. constr. [of פּוּגָה] dec. 10 פוג

פּוֹדֶה Kal part. act. sing. masc. dec. 9a . . פדה

[פּוּחַ] *to blow, breathe,* Ca. 2. 17; 4. 6, *the day blows,* i. e. *grows cool by the evening breeze.* Hiph. I. *to blow upon,* with acc. Ca. 4. 16.—II. *to blow, kindle a fire,* with בְּ, Eze. 21. 36; metaph. *to inflame, excite,* Pr. 29. 8.—III. *to puff at, rail at,* with בְּ, לְ.—IV. *to breathe out, utter, speak.*

פִּיחַ masc. *dust, ashes,* Ex. 9. 8, 10.

פּוֹחֲזִים Kal part. act. masc. pl. [of פּוֹחֵז] dec. 7 b. פחז

פֻּוָה ו pr. name masc. Ge. 46. 13; Nu. 26. 23, see פּוּאָה.

פּוּט ו (*afflicted*) pr. name of one of the sons of Ham and his descendants, according to the Sept. & Vulg. *the Libyans.*

פּוֹטִי פֶרַע pr. n., *Potipherah,* the father-in-law of Joseph.

פּוּטִיאֵל (*afflicted of God*) pr. name masc. Ex. 6. 25.

פּוֹטִיפַר pr. name, *Potiphar,* a chief of Pharaoh's guard, Ge. 39. 1.

פּוֹטֵר Kal part. act. sing. masc. . . . פטר

[פּוּךְ] masc.—I *eye-paint, stibium,* prepared from antimony; see also קֶרֶן.—II. אַבְנֵי פוּךְ a kind of costly stone or species of marble, 1 Ch. 29. 2.

[פּוֹל] ו masc. *beans,* 2 Sa. 17. 28; Eze. 4. 9.

פּוּל pr. name—I. of a people and region in Africa, Is. 66. 19.—II. of a king of Assyria, 2 Ki. 15. 19; 1 Ch. 5. 26.

פּוּם only defect. פֻּם Chald. dec. 1 a.—I. *mouth.*—II. *aperture,* Da. 6. 18.

[פּוּן] *to be perplexed, distracted,* Ps. 88. 16.

פּוּנִי patronym. from an unknown person פּוּן (*distracted*) Nu. 26. 23.

פִּינוֹן (*perplexed*; Gesenius, *darkness*) pr. name of a city of Idumea, Nu. 33. 42.

פִּינֹן (id.) pr. n. of an Idumean prince, Ge. 36. 41.

פּוּעָה pr. name of a woman . . . יפט

[פּוּץ] I. *to disperse themselves, be scattered;* part. pass. פוּץ *dispersed,* Zep. 3. 10.—II. *to overflow,* Pr. 5. 16; metaph. Zec. 1. 17. Niph. *to be scattered.* Pil. פּוֹצֵץ *to break, shatter in pieces,* Je. 23. 29. Pilp. פִּצְפֵּץ (§ 6. No. 4) id. Job 16. 12. Hiph. I. *to disperse, scatter, confuse.*—II. *to pour abroad,* Job 40. 11.—III. intrans. *to spread abroad, be scattered* Hithpal. (§ 6. No. 4) *to be scattered,* Hab. 3. 6.

מֵפִיץ masc. *battle-hammer, maul,* Pr. 25. 18.

פּוּצַי Kal part. pass. pl., suff. 1 p. s. fr. [פּוּץ] d. 1 a פוץ

[פּוּק] I. *to move to and fro, to waver, be unsteady,* Is. 28. 7 —II. i. q. Chald. נְפַק *to go out,* see Hiph. Hiph I. *to move, be moved,* Je. 10. 4.—II. causat. (comp Kal No. II.) (a) *to give out, furnish, supply;* (b *to get, obtain* from any one; (c) *to further, le succeed,* Ps. 140. 9.

פּוּקָה fem. *stumblingblock,* 1 Sa. 25. 31.

פִּיק masc. *tottering,* Na. 2. 11.

פּוֹקֵד Kal part. act. sing. masc. . . . פקד

פֻּקוּ Chald. Peal imp. pl. masc. . . . נפק

[פּוּר] *to break in pieces,* Is. 24. 19. Hiph. הָפִיר —I. *to break, violate,* Eze. 17. 19.—II. *to frustrate,* 2 Sa. 15. 34; Ps. 33. 10.

פּוּרָה fem. *wine-press,* Is. 63. 3; Hag. 2. 16.

פּוּר masc. dec. 1a, *lot;* pl. פּוּרִים (a) *lots;* (b) *th feast of Purim.*

פּוֹר Kal inf. abs. R. פּוּר, or [for פֹּר] R. . פרר

פֻּרָה noun fem. sing. . . . . פור

פּוּרִים noun masc., pl. of פּוּר dec. 1 a . . פור

פּוֹרֵעַ Kal part. act. sing. masc. . . . פרע

פּוֹרַדְתָּ Poel pret. 2 pers. sing. masc. . . פרר

פּוֹרֵשׁ Kal part. act. sing. masc. dec. 7 b . פרש

פּוֹרָתָא pr. name of one of the sons of Haman, Est. 9. 8.

[פּוּשׁ] I. *to spread, thrive, grow fat.*—II. *to spread themselves,* Hab. 1. 8. Niph. *to be scattered,* Na. 3. 18.

a Le. 1. 12.   c Je. 15. 21.   e Pr. 26. 28.   g Ps. 34. 23.   i Pr. 17. 14.   l Zep. 3. 10.   n Est. 3. 7.   p Est. 9. 26.   Pr. 29. 5.
b Ex. 8. 12.   d Jos. 18. 8.   f La. 2. 18.   h Zep. 3. 4.   k 1 Ch. 29. 2.   m Da. 3. 26.   - Is. 24. 19.   Ps. 74. 13.

פֵּשׁ masc. Job 35. 15, perh. *excess*; others, *multitude*; Gesenius, *arrogance, wickedness*, or, as apoc. from פֶּשַׁע פֶּשַׁע *transgression*.

פִּישׁוֹן (*spreading, overflowing*) pr. name, *Pishon*, one of the rivers issuing from the garden of Eden, Ge. 2. 11.

פֹּשְׁעִים Kal part. act. masc., pl. of פֹּשֵׁעַ dec. 7 b . פשע

פּוּת Root not used; prob. *to be spread open*, cogn. פָּתַח, פָּתָה, פּוּשׁ.

פֹּת masc.—I. *nakedness, pudendum muliebre*, with suff. פָּתְהֶן, Is. 3. 17.—II. pl. פֹּתוֹת *hinges*, 1 Ki. 7. 50.

פּוּתִי patronym. 1 Ch. 2. 53.

פִּיתוֹן pr. name masc. 1 Ch. 8. 35; 9. 41.

פֹּתָה Kal part. act. sing., fem. of פֹּתֶה masc. . פתה

פֹּתֵחַ Kal part. act. sing. masc. dec. 7 b . . פתח

פֹּתֵרִי Kal part. act. sing. masc. . . . פתר

פָּז noun masc. sing. . . . . פזז

[פָּזַז] I. *to be light, active, agile*, Ge. 49. 24. Pi. *to leap*, 2 Sa. 6. 16.—II. i. q. Arab. פצץ *to purify* metals, Heb. only Hoph. part. זָהָב מוּפָז *purified, pure gold*, 1 Ki. 10. 18, for which 2 Ch. 9. 17, זָהָב טָהוֹר.

פָּז adj. masc. *purified, pure*, an epithet of gold, Ca. 5. 11; then for *refined, pure gold*.

פְּזוּרָה Kal part. pass. sing. fem. [of פָּזוּר masc.] פזר

[פָּזַר] *to disperse, scatter*, Je. 50. 17. Pi. I. *to disperse, scatter*.—II. *to distribute liberally*. Niph. & Pu. *to be scattered*.

פִּזֵּר Piel pret. 3 pers. sing. masc. (§ 10. rem. 1) פזר

פִּזְּרוּ id. pret. 3 pers. pl. . . . פזר

פִּזַּרְתָּ id. pret. 2 pers. sing. masc. . . . פזר

פָּח } (וֹ) noun masc. sing., pl. פַּחִים (§ 37. פחח
פַּח } rem. 7); for וֹ see lett. וֹ . . }

פָּחַד (וֹ) fut. יִפְחַד.—I. *to tremble, fear, be afraid*, with מִפְּנֵי *before* any one.—II. *to be agitated* with wonder and joy, Is. 60. 5; Je. 33. 9.—III. *to hasten, make haste*, Ho. 3. 5. Pi. *to fear greatly, continually*, Is. 51. 13; hence, *to be very careful, solicitous*, Pr. 28. 14. Hiph. *to cause to tremble, to terrify*, Job 4. 14.

פַּחַד masc. dec. 6 d (with suff. פַּחְדּוֹ § 35. r. 5). —I. *fear, dread*.—II. *fear, reverence*, Ps. 36. 2.—

III. *object of fear or reverence*.—IV. *thigh*, Job 40. 17, so Schultens and Prof. Lee, coll. with the Arab. פַּחְדָּה f. *fear, terror*, only פַּחְדָּתִי Je. 2. 19

פָּחָד Kal pret. 3 pers. sing. m. for פָּחַד (§ 8. r. 7) פחד

פָּחַד (וֹ, וֹ) n. m. s. d. 6 d; וֹ bef. lab., for וֹ see lett. וֹ פחד

פָּחֲדוּ } Kal pret. 3 pers. pl. (§ 8. rem. 7); } פחד
פָּחָדוּ } וֹ bef. lab. . . . . }

פַּחְדוֹ noun masc. pl., suff. 3 pers. sing. masc. from פחד
     פַּחַד dec. 6 d . . . .

פַּחְדּוֹ (וֹ) id. sing., suff. 3 pers. sing. masc. (§ 35. פחד
     rem. 5); וֹ bef. lab. . . .

פַּחְדִּים id. pl., abs. st. . . . . פחד

פַּחְדְּךָ id. sing., suff. 2 pers. sing. masc. (§ 35. r. 5) פחד

פַּחְדְּכֶם id. sing., suff. 2 pers. pl. masc. . פחד

פַּחְדָּם id. sing., suff. 3 pers. pl. masc. . פחד

פָּחַדְתָּ וֹ Kal pret. 2 pers. sing. masc.; acc. shifted פחד
     by וֹ, for וֹ, conv. (§ 8. rem. 7) .

פָּחַדְתִּי id. pret. 1 pers. sing. . . . פחד

פַּחְדָּתִי noun fem. sing., suff. [from פַּחְדָּה no pl.] פחד

פֶּחָה Heb. & Chald. masc. irr. (§ 45) *governor, deputy* of a province.

פֶּחַ masc. idem, Ne. 5. 14, see § 45.

פַּחַת־מוֹאָב (*governor of Moab*) pr. name of a man.

פַּחֲווֹת (וֹ) noun masc. with pl. fem. term. from }
פַּחֹת (וֹ) פֶּחָה irr. (§ 45); וֹ bef. lab. . } פחה

פַּחֲוָתָא וֹ Ch. id. pl., emph. st.; וֹ id. . פחה

פַּחֲוֹתֶיהָ id. pl., suff. 3 pers. sing. fem. . פחה

[פָּחַז] in the Chald. *to boil up or over*, hence—I. *to be wanton, rash*, Ju. 9. 4.—II. *to be proud, vainglorious*, Zep. 3. 4.

פַּחַז masc. *wantonness, arrogance*, Ge. 49. 4.

פַּחֲזוּת f. d. 10, *boasting, vain-glory*, Je. 23. 32.

פַּחַז noun masc. sing. . . . . פחז

פֹּחֲזִים וֹ Kal part. act. m. pl. [of פוֹחֵז] d. 7 b; וֹ bef. lab. פחז

פָּחַח Hiph. הֵפַח (denom. from פַּח) *to spread a net, ensnare*, Is. 42. 22.

פַּח masc. pl. פַּחִים (dag. forte impl. § 37. r. 7). —I. *snare, gin*; metaph. *cause of ruin, destruction*; hence, *ruin, destruction*.—II. pl. פַּחִים *plates of metal*.—III. Ps. 11. 6, פַּחִים *snares*, for *crooked lightnings*; others take it as a sing. i. q. פֶּחָם *coal, coals*.

פַּחֵי noun masc. pl. constr. from פַּח (§ 37. r. 7) פחח

ᵃ Is. 46. 8.	ᵉ Ge. 41. 8.	ᶠ Ps. 89. 11.	ⁱ Job 40. 17.	ᵏ Job 15. 21.	ᵗ Job 3. 25.	ᵘ Ne. 2. 7, 9.	ʸ Je. 51. 23, 57.	ᶻ Ju. 9. 4.
ᵇ Ho. 7. 11.	ᶜ Je. 50. 17.	ᵍ Ps. 119. 161.	ʲ 1 Ch. 14. 17.	ˡ De. 2. 25.	ᵐ Je. 2. 19.	ᵛ Esr. 8. 36.	ʳ Ge. 49. 4.	ˢ Ex. 39. 2.
ᵈ Ps. 145. 16.	Joel 4. 2.	Ps. 78. 53.	ʰ Job 13. 11.	ⁿ De. 28. 66.	Esr. 5. 14.			

פְּחִי ¹ Kal imp. sing. fem. ; ¹ bef. lab. .   נפח

פָּחִים ¹ʲ noun masc. pl. of פַּח (§ 37. r. 7) ; ¹ id.   פחח

פֶּחָם masc. *coal, charcoal*, Pr. 26. 21 ; also *burning coal*, Is. 44. 12 ; 54. 16.

     פֶּחָם masc. id. so according to some in Ps. 11. 6, see פַּח.

פֶּחָם ¹ noun masc. sing., suff. 3 pers. pl. masc. [as if from פַּח], see פֶּחָה irr. (§ 45)   פחה

פֶּחָר Ch. masc. *potter*, Da. 2. 41.   Syr. פחרא id.

פָּחַת Root not used ; Syr. *to dig, excavate.*

     פַּחַת m. d. 6 d, *pit* ; metaph. *ruin destruction.*

     פְּחֶתֶת fem. *corrosion, inward fretting* of the leprosy in a garment, Le. 13. 55.

פַּחַת ⎫ noun masc. sing. dec. 6 d ; for וַ see ⎫
פַּחַת ⎬ lett. ו . . . . . ⎬ פחת
פֶּחַת ⎭   ⎭

noun masc. with fem. term., constr. of פֶּחָה irr. (§ 45), and pr. n. in compos. פֶּחַ' מוֹאָב   פחה

פְּחֶתֶת noun fem. sing., from פַּחַת masc.   פחת

פִּטְדָּה fem. a precious stone, according to most of the ancient versions the *topaz.*

פִּטְדַת id., constr. st. . . . . פטדה

פְּטוּרֵי ¹ Kal part. pass. pl. constr. [from פָּטוּר dec. 3 a ; ¹ bef. lab. . . . פטר

פְּטִירִים Kh. פְּטִרִים adj. masc. pl. of [פָּטִיר] ; K. פְּטוּ' part. pass. pl. masc., dec. 3 a   פטר

פַּטִּישׁ noun masc. sing. . . . . פטש

פַּטִּישֵׁיהוֹן Ch. noun masc. pl., suff. 3 pers. pl. masc. Keth. פַּטִּישֵׁיהוֹן [from פַּטִּישׁ dec. 1] ; K. פַּטְשֵׁיהוֹן [from פְּטַשׁ dec. 3 a] . פטש

פָּטַר fut. יִפְטַר.—I. *to burst open,* only part. pass. פְּטֻרֵי צִצִּים *bursted ones of the flowers,* i. e. *open flowers.*—II. *to let out* water, Pr. 17. 14.—III. *to let go, dismiss, exempt from duty.*—IV. *to slip away,* 1 Sa. 19. 10.

     פָּטִיר masc. *free, exempt from duty,* 1 Ch. 9. 33, Kheth.

     פֶּטֶר masc. *a breaking forth, opening,* פֶּטֶר רֶחֶם *firstborn,* so also without רֶחֶם.

     פִּטְרָה fem. dec. 10, idem, Nu. 8. 16.

פֶּטֶר ¹ʲ noun masc. sing. ; ¹ bef. lab. . . פטר

פְּטֻרֵי ¹ defect. for פְּטוּרֵי (q. v.) . פטר

פִּטְרַת noun fem. sing. constr. [of פִּטְרָה no pl.] פטר

פָּטַשׁ Root not used ; Arab. *to hammer,* also *to spread out.*

     פַּטִּישׁ masc. *a hammer.*

     פַּטִּישׁ Chald. masc. dec. 1 a, *a tunic,* Da. 3. 21.

פִּי ¹ noun masc. sing. constr. st. or with suff. 1 pers. sing. from פֶּה irr. (§ 45) ; also pr. name in compos., as פִּי־בֶסֶת, &c. ; ¹ bef. lab. פאה

פִּיד Root not used ; Arab. *to disappear, die.* Hence

פִּיד ¹ masc. sing. dec. 1 a, *calamity* ; ¹ bef. lab. . פיד

פִּיהָ ¹ʲ noun masc. sing., suff. 3 pers. sing. fem. from פֶּה irr. (§ 45) ; ¹ id. . . . פאה

פִּיהוּ ¹ʲ id., suff. 3 pers. sing. masc. ; ¹ id. . פאה

פִּיהֶם ¹ id., suff. 3 pers. pl. masc. ; ¹ id. . פאה

פִּיו ¹ʲ id., suff. 3 pers. sing. masc. ; ¹ id. . פאה

פֵּיוֹת ¹ noun fem. pl. of [פִּיָּה] dec. 10 . פאה

פִּיּוֹת ¹ noun m. with pl. f. term. fr. פֶּה irr. (¹ 45) פאה

פִּיחַ ¹ noun masc. sing. . . . . פוח

פִּיךָ ¹ noun masc. s., suff. 2 p. s. m. fr. פֶּה (§ 45) פאה

פִּיכֹל ¹ pr. name masc. ; ¹ bef. lab. . פאה

פִּילֶגֶשׁ (for פַּלֶּגֶשׁ dag. forte resolved in ') noun fem. sing. dec. 6 a (§ 35. rem. 16) . פלגש

פִּילַגְשֵׁהוּ ¹ id., suff. 3 pers. sing. masc. ; ¹ bef. lab. פלגש

פִּילַגְשׁוֹ ¹ id., suff. 3 pers. sing. masc. ; ¹ id. . פלגש

פִּילַגְשִׁי ¹ id., suff. 1 pers. sing. ; ¹ id. . פלגש

פִּילַגְשָׁיו ¹ id. pl., suff. 3 pers. sing. masc. ; ¹ id. . פלגש

פִּילַגְשִׁים ¹ id. pl., abs. st. ; ¹ id. . . פלגש

פִּים Root not used ; Arab. *to be fat.*

     פִּימָה fem. *fat, fatness,* Job 15. 27.

פִּים noun masc. pl. of פֶּה irr. (§ 45) . פאה

פִּימָה noun fem. sing. . . . . פים

פִּימוֹ noun masc. sing., suff. 3 pers. sing. masc. from פֶּה irr. (§ 45) . . . . פאה

פִּינוּ id. with suff. 1 pers. pl. . . . פאה

פִּינְחָס ¹ pr. name masc. ; ¹ bef. lab. . פאה

פִּינֹן pr. name of a place, see פּוּנֹן . פון

פִּיפִיּוֹת noun masc. with pl. fem. term. [from פִּיפָה] comp. פִּיּוֹת . . . . . פאה

פִּיק ¹ noun masc. sing. ; ¹ bef. lab. . פוק

פִּישׁוֹן pr. name of a river . . . פוש

פִּיתוֹן ⎫ pr. name of a place . . . פות
פִּיתֹן ⎭

פַּךְ noun masc. sing. . . . . פכה

פָּכָה Pi. *to flow out,* Eze. 47. 2.

     פַּךְ masc. *flask, cruse.*

a Eze. 37. 9.   d Je. 48. 28.   g 1 Ki. 6. 18, 29, 32.   i 2 Ch. 23. 8.   n Nu. 8. 16.   r Job 29. 23.   v Pr. 5. 4.   y Ju. 20. 4, 5.   b Job 15. 27.
b Je. 18. 22.   e Le. 13. 55.   h 1 Ch. 9. 33.   k Ex. 34. 20.   o Pr. 24. 22.   s Pr. 18. 6.   w Ex. 9. 8, 10.   z 2 Ch. 11. 21.   c Ps. 126. 2.
c Ne. 5. 14.   f Job 28. 19.   i Da. 3. 21.   m 1 Ki. 6. 35.   p 1 Ki. 7. 31.   t Ju. 3. 16.   x Ju. 19. 24.   a 1 Sa. 13. 21.   d Na. 2. 11.

פֹּכֶרֶת הַצְּבָיִים (*snaring the gazelles*) pr. name m. Ezr. 2. 57; Ne. 7. 59.

פָּלָא Kal not used; i. q. פָּלָה *to separate, distinguish.* Niph. I. *to be extraordinary, great,* 2 Sa. 1. 26, part. נִפְלָאוֹת *great things,* Da. 11. 36.—II. *to be* or *appear hard, difficult,* with בְּעֵינֵי *in the eyes of any one.*—III. *to be wonderful, marvellous;* part. נִפְלָאוֹת *wonderful, marvellous things* or *deeds,* also adv. *wonderfully, marvellously.* Pi. *to set apart, dedicate,* with נֶדֶר *a thing vowed.* Hiph. I. i. q. Pi.—II. *to make extraordinary, great,* e. g. kindness, *to show great kindness;* inf. הַפְלֵא adv. *exceedingly, very.*—III. *to make wonderful, admirable;* with אֶת *to act wonderfully;* inf. לְהַפְלִיא adv. *wonderfully.* Hithp. *to show oneself wonderful,* Job 10. 16.

פַּלּוּא (*distinguished*) pr. name of a son of Reuben. Patronym. פַּלֻּאִי, Nu. 26. 5.

פָּלִיא, fem. פְּלִיאָה adj. *wonderful,* only Ps. 139. 6, Keri.

פֶּלֶא masc. dec. 6a (with suff. פִּלְאֲךָ).—I. *something wonderful, a miracle;* pl. פְּלָאִים adv. *wonderfully;* פְּלָאוֹת *wonderful things.*—II. *the wonderful,* Is. 9. 5.

פִּלְאִי, fem. פִּלְאִיָה adj. *wonderful,* only in Kheth. Ju. 13. 18; Ps. 139. 6.

פְּלָאיָה (*whom the Lord separated*) pr. name of a man.

פְּלָיָה (id.) pr. name masc. 1 Ch. 3. 24.

מִפְלָאָה fem. dec. 11a, *miracle,* Job 37. 16.

פֶּלֶא ⟨ן⟩ noun masc. sing. (suff. פִּלְאֲךָ) dec. 6a; for ן see lett. ן . . . פלא

פִּלְאוֹתִי id. with pl. fem. term., abs st. . פלא

פִּלְאִי Kh. פֶּלְאִי adj. from פֶּלֶא with the adj. term. י◌, K. פֶּלִי by contraction . . פלא

פְּלָאיָה pr. name masc. . . . . . . פלא

פְּלִיאָה Kh. פְּלָאיָה adj., fem. of פִּלְאִי; K. פְּלִיאָה fem. of an obsol. פִּלְיא . . . פלא

פְּלָאִים noun masc., pl. of פֶּלֶא dec. 6a . . פלא

פִּלְאֲךָ
פִּלְאֲךָ id. sing., suff. 2 pers. sing. masc. . פלא

פִּלְאָסֶר see תִּגְלַת פִּלֶ .

פָּלַג Niph. *to be divided.* Pi. I. *to cut out, form,* Job 38. 25.—II. *to divide,* Ps. 55. 10.

פְּלַג Chald. *to divide,* Da. 2. 41.

פְּלַג Chald. masc. *half,* Da. 7. 25.

פֶּלֶג masc. dec. 6a (pl. c. פַּלְגֵי).—I. *brook, stream.*—II. pr. name of a son of Eber.

פְּלַגָּה fem. dec. 10, *brook.*

פְּלֻגָּה fem. dec. 10, *division,* 2 Ch. 35. 5.

פְּלֻגָּא Chald. fem. dec. 8a, idem, Ezr. 6. 18.

מִפְלַגָּה fem. dec. 10, idem, 2 Ch. 35. 12.

פַּלֵּג Piel imp. sing. masc. (§ 10. rem. 3) . פלג

פֶּלֶג
פֶּלֶג } pr. name masc. (§ 35. rem. 2) . פלג

פֶּלֶג noun masc. sing. (pl. c. פַּלְגֵי) dec. 6a . פלג

פִּלַּג Piel pret. 3 pers. sing. masc. (§ 10. rem. 1) פלג

פְּלַג ⟨י⟩ Chald. noun masc. sing.; ⟨ב⟩ bef. lab. . פלג

פַּלְגֵי noun masc. pl. constr. from פֶּלֶג dec. 6a פלג

פְּלָגָיו id. pl., suff. 3 pers. sing. masc. . . פלג

פְּלָגִים id. pl., abs. st. . . . . . . פלג

פִּילֶגֶשׁ, פִּלֶגֶשׁ fem. d. 6a (with suff. פִּילַגְשׁוֹ § 35. r. 16), *concubine.*

פִּלַגְשֵׁי id. pl., constr. st. . . . . . פלגש

פִּלַגְשֵׁיהֶם id. pl., suff. 3 pers. pl. masc. . פלגש

פִּלַגְשֶׁךָ id. pl., suff. 2 pers. sing. masc. . פלגש

פִּילַגְשִׁים id. pl., abs. st. . . . . . . פלגש

פָּלַד Root not used; Arab. *to cut up.*

פְּלָדָה fem. dec. 12a, *iron, steel,* Na. 2. 4.

פִּלְדָּשׁ pr. name masc. Ge. 22. 22.

פְּלָדֹת noun fem. pl. abs. from [פְּלָדָה] dec. 12a פלד

פָּלָה Niph. I. *to be separated, distinguished,* Ex. 33. 16.—II. *to be made wonderful,* i. e. *wonderfully made,* Ps. 139. 14. Hiph. I. *to set apart.*—II. *to separate, distinguish.*

פְּלֹנִי masc.—I. *a certain one,* always followed by אַלְמֹנִי, *such an one, such and such place.*—II. gent. noun, *Pelonite,* 1 Ch. 11. 27, 36.

פְּלֹנִי masc. id. by contr. for פְּלָנִי אַלְמֹנִי.

פַּלּוּא ⟨ב⟩ pr. name masc.; ⟨ב⟩ bef. lab. . . פלא

[פָּלַח] *to cut, cleave,* Ps. 141. 7. Pi. I. *to cut in pieces,* 2 Ki. 4. 39.—II. *to cleave.*—III. *to let break forth, to bring forth,* Job 39. 3.

פְּלַח Chald. *to serve, worship.*

פֶּלַח masc.—I. *slice, piece.*—II. *millstone;* פֶּ׳ רֶכֶב *upper millstone;* פֶּ׳ תַּחְתִּית *nether millstone.*

פִּלְחָא (*slice*) pr. name masc. Ne. 10. 25.

פָּלְחָן Chald. m. d. 1b, *service, worship,* Ezr. 7. 19.

פָּלַח Ch. Peal part. act. s. m. (§ 49. rem. 4) d. 2a   פלח

פֶּלַח noun fem. sing.   .   .   .   פלח

פֹּלֵחַ Kal part. act. sing. masc.   .   פלח

פִּלְחָא pr. name masc.   .   .   .   פלח

פָלְחֵי } Chald. Peal part. act. masc. pl. constr. &
פָלְחִין }   abs. from פְּלַח (§ 49. rem. 4) dec. 2a }   פלח

[פָּלַט] to slip away, escape, Eze. 7. 16. Pi. I. to escape, be delivered, Job 23. 7.—II. to let escape, deliver; hence—III. to bring forth, Job 21. 10. Hiph. I. to deliver, Mi. 6. 14.—II. to carry away safely, Is. 5. 29.

פָּלֵט adj. masc. dec. 5, escaped by flight.

פָלִיט adj. masc. dec. 3a, idem.

פְּלֵטָה, פְּלֵיטָה fem. dec. 10.—I. escape, deliverance.—II. that which escapes; collect. those escaped, remnant.

פָּלִיט adj. masc. dec. 3a, one escaped by flight.

פֶּלֶט masc. deliverance, Ps. 32. 7.

פֶּלֶט (deliverance) pr. name masc.—I. 1 Ch. 2. 47.—II. 1 Ch. 12. 3.

פַּלְטִי (for פְּלַטְיָה deliverance of the Lord) pr. name masc.—I. Nu. 13. 9.—II. 1 Sa. 25. 44, called פַּלְטִיאֵל 2 Sa. 3. 15.

פַּלְטִי (for פְּלַטְיָה) pr. name masc. Ne. 12. 17.

פְּלַטְיָהוּ, פְּלַטְיָה (whom the Lord delivers) pr. name masc. of several persons.

מִפְלָט masc. escape, safety, Ps. 55. 9.

פָּלֵט pr. name, see בֵּי־ פָּלֶט   .   בית

פַּלֵּט (prop. Piel inf.) as a subst.   .   פלט

פַּלֵּט Piel imp. sing. masc. [for פַּלְּט § 10. rem. 4]   פלט

פָלֵט וְ pr. name masc.; for וְ see lett. ו   פלט

פַּלְּטָה Piel imp. s. m. with parag ה (comp. § 8. r. 11) פלט

פְּלֵטָה noun fem. sing. dec. 10   .   פלט

פָּלְטוּ וְ Kal pret. 3 pers. pl.; וְ, for וְ, conv.   פלט

פַּלְּטוּ Piel imp. pl. masc.   .   .   פלט

פְּלַטְיָהוּ וְ, פְּלַטְיָה וְ, פַּלְטִיאֵל, פַּלְטִי (for מְטִי) pr. names masc.; וְ bef. lab.   פלט

פְּלֵטִים וְ adj. masc. pl. of פָּלֵט dec. 5a; וְ bef. lab. פלט

פַּלְּטֵנִי Piel imp. sing. masc., suff. 1 pers. sing.   פלט

פְּלִיגָה Chald. Peal part. pass. sing. fem. [of פְּלִיג] פלג

פְּלָיָה וְ pr. name masc.; וְ bef. lab.   פלא

פָּלִיט וְ adj. masc. sing. dec. 3a; וְ id.   פלט

פְּלֵיטָה וְ noun fem. sing. dec. 10; וְ id.   פלט

פְּלִיטֵי adj. pl. constr. masc. from פָּלִיט dec. 3a   פלט

פְּלֵיטֵיהֶם id. pl., suff. 3 pers. pl. masc. .   .   פלט

פְּלֵיטָיו id. pl., suff. 3 pers. sing. masc. .   .   פלט

פְּלֵיטְכֶם id. pl., suff. 2 pers. pl. masc. .   .   פלט

פְּלֵיטִים־ } adj. masc., pl. of [פָּלִיט] dec. 3 a .   פלט
פְּלֵיטִם }

פְּלֵיטַת n. f. s., constr. of פְּלֵיטָה d. 10; וְ bef. lab. פלט

פְּלִילָה noun fem. sing.   .   .   .   פלל

פְּלִילִי } adj. masc. and fem. sing.   פלל
פְּלִילִיָּה }

פְּלִילִים noun masc., pl. of [פָּלִיל] dec. 3a   .   פלל

פֶּלֶךְ Root not used; Arab. to be round. Hence

פֶּלֶךְ־ } masc. d. 6a (but with suff. פִּלְכוֹ § 35.
פֶּלֶךְ } r. 2 & 3).—I. circuit, district.—II. distaff, Pr. 31. 19.—III. staff, 2 Sa. 3. 29; according to others, distaff } פלך

פָּלַל Pi. פִּלֵּל.—I. to judge, 1 Sa. 2. 25.—II. to adjudge, with לְ, Eze. 16. 52.—III. to execute judgment, inflict judicial punishment, Ps. 106. 30.—IV. to judge, suppose, Ge. 48. 11. Hithp. I. to intercede, supplicate, pray for any one, with לְ, עַל, בְּעַד, for whom, with אֶל with whom one intercedes.—II. generally to supplicate, pray, with אֶל, לְ, לִפְנֵי to whom, with אֶל for which one prays.

פָּלָל (judge) pr. name masc. Ne. 3. 25.

פָּלִיל masc. dec. 3a, a judge.

פְּלִילָה fem. justice, Is. 16. 3.

פְּלִילִי masc. adj. judicial, Job 31. 28; fem פְּלִילִיָּה what is judicial, for judgment, Is. 28. 7 (Gesenius, judgment-seat, tribunal).

פְּלַלְיָה (whom the Lord judges) pr. n. m. Ne. 11. 12

אֶפְלָל (judgment) pr. name masc. 1 Ch. 2. 37.

תְּפִלָּה fem. dec. 10.—I. intercession.—II. supplication, prayer.

פָּלָל pr. name masc.   .   .   .   פלל

פִּלְלוֹ וְ Piel pret. 3 pers. ... . [פָּלַל], suff. 3 pers. sing. m. (comp. § 10. r. 7); וְ, for וְ, conv. פלל

פְּלַלְיָה pr. name masc.   .   .   .   פלל

פִּלַלְתְּ id. pret. 2 pers. sing. fem.   .   פלל

פִּלַּלְתִּי id. pret. 1 pers. sing. [for פִּלַּלְתִּי] .   פלל

פְּלֹנִי adj. masc. sing.   .   .   .   פלה

פִּלְנְאֶסֶר } pr. name, see תִּגְלַת פַּל.
פִּלְאֶסֶר }

a Da. 6. 17, 21.   d Ps. 32. 7.   g Eze. 14. 22.   l Je. 50. 28.   n Je. 44. 28.   r Eze. 6. 9.   t Is. 10. 20.   y Is. 28. 7.   z Eze. 16. 52.
b Ps. 141. 7.   e Ps. 56. 8.   h Eze. 7. 16.   m Ps. 31. 2; 71. 4.   o Eze. 7. 16.   s Is. 66. 19.   u Is. 16. 3.   v Pr. 31. 19.   w Ge. 48. 11.
c Exr. 7. 24.   f Ps. 17. 13.   i Ps 82. 4.   k Da. 2. 41.   p Ob. 14.   q Nu. 21. 29.   x Job 31. 28.   1 Sa. 2. 25.

פָּלַס. Pi. I. *to make level, plain,* a way.—II. *to weigh,* trop. Ps 58. 3; hence *to ponder, consider,* Pr. 5. 21.

פֶּלֶס m. *balance, steelyard,* Pr. 16. 11; Is. 40. 12.

מִפְלָשׂ m. d. 2 b, *a poising, balancing,* Job 37. 16.

פלם Piel imp. sing. masc. . . . . פַּלֵּס[a]

פלם noun masc. sing. . . . . פֶּלֶס[a]

פלסר pr. name, see תִּגְלַת פְּלֶ׳.

פָּלַץ Hithp. *to shake, tremble,* Job 9. 6.

פַּלָּצוּת fem. *trembling, fear.*

מִפְלֶצֶת fem. dec. 13 a (with suff. מִפְלַצְתָּהּ), *fear, object of fear,* used of *images, idols.*

תִּפְלֶצֶת fem. dec. 13 a, *fear, terror,* Je. 49. 16.

פלץ noun fem. sing. . . . . פַּלָּצוּת

פָּלַשׁ. Hithp. *to roll oneself, to wallow* sc. in the dust.

פלש { פְּלֶשֶׁת pr. name, Philistia, a country west and south-west of Palestine. Gent. n. פְּלֶשֶׁת

פְּלִשְׁתִּי Philistine .

פלש פְּלִשְׁתִּיִּים Philistines, pl. of פְּלִשְׁתִּי see the preceding . . . . } פְּלִשְׁתִּיִּים

פָּלַת Root not used; Arab. *to escape, flee,* comp. פָּלַט.

פְּלָתִי masc. collect. *public runners, couriers.* According to others, one of the tribes of the Philistines, *Pelethites,* employed as mercenary soldiers, which is very improbable. Hence also

פֶּלֶת (*swiftness*) pr. name masc.—I. Nu. 16. 1.— פלת II. 1 Ch. 2. 33

פֻּם[b] פֻּם Chald. noun masc. sing. d. 1 a; ו bef. lab.

פֶּן־ פֶּן only with Mak.; conj.; ו id. . . . פנה

פַּנַּג masc. Eze. 27. 17, prob. *some delicate spice* or *gum;* Chald. פְּנַק *to be delicate.* Sept. μύρων, or κασίας. Vulg. *balsamum.* Gesenius, *pastry* or *sweet cake.*

פָּנָה fut. יִפְנֶה.—I. *to turn, turn oneself,* in order to go or look away; with אֶל, לְ, בְּ, ל, *to turn to* or *towards;* with אַחֲרֵי *to follow* any one; with מֵעַם *to turn away from* any one.—II. of time, *to turn, decline;* לִפְנוֹת בֹּקֶר *at the turning,* i. e. *approach* of the morning; לִפְנוֹת עֶרֶב *at the approach of evening.*—III. trans. *to turn,* only in the phrase פָּנָה עֹרֶף *to turn the neck.* Pi. I. *to remove.*—II. *to clear,* a house or a road, i. e. *to prepare it.* Hiph. I. *to turn.*—II. intrans. *to turn oneself.* Hoph. *to be turned, to turn oneself.*

פָּנֶה masc. dec. 9 b, only pl. פָּנִים.—I. *face, countenance;* also pl. *faces;* בְּפָנִים, פָּנִים אֶל־פָּנִים *face to face;* עַל־פְּנֵי פ׳ or אֶל־פְּנֵי *to the face of* any one, i. e. freely, frankly, or insolently, so also שׁוּם פָּנִים with לְ, עַל, אֶל, בְּפָנָיו *to set one's face towards* any quarter, or, followed by an inf., *to intend* to do any thing; id. with בְּ *to set one's face in anger against* any one, and so נָתַן פָּנִים בְּ.— II. *person, presence;* פָּנַי *my person, myself.*—III. *face, surface,* hence *appearance.*—IV. *fore part, front;* of a sword, *the edge,* Ec. 10. 10; Eze. 21. 21. Adv. פָּנִים *in front;* לְפָנִים (a) *forwards;* (b) *before, of old;* מִלְּפָנִים *from of old, from ancient times;* מִפָּנִים *in front, before.*—V. with prepositions: אֶל־פְּנֵי (a) *in presence of, before,* implying either motion or rest; (b) *upon the surface of;* אֶת־פְּנֵי *before;* מֵאֵת פְּנֵי *from before;* בִּפְנֵי *in front of, before;* לִפְנֵי *before;* with suff. לְפָנֶיךָ, לְפָנַי, &c. (a) *in the presence of;* (b) *in the presence,* as long as endures, Ps. 72. 5, 17; (c) *in front of, before;* (d) *before, preceding,* of time; מִלִּפְנֵי (a) *from before, from the presence of;* (b) *because of,* 1 Ch. 16. 33; מִפְּנֵי (a) *from the face, presence, front of,* hence *from, away from;* (b) *before;* (c) *because of, on account of,* and with אֲשֶׁר *because that;* (d) *towards,* Je. 1. 13; עַל פְּנֵי (a) *upon* or *above, the surface,* implying either motion or rest; hence *along, towards, against,* but also *at, before;* (b) *above, besides,* Ex. 20. 3.

פְּנוּאֵל, פְּנִיאֵל (*face of God*) pr. name.—I. of a place beyond Jordan.—II. of two men.

פֵּן prop. *a turning to, regarding, considering,* hence פֶּן as a conj. *lest, lest perhaps, for fear that, beware, lest.*

יִפְנֶה (*turned, removed*) pr. name.—I. of the father of Caleb.—II. 1 Ch. 7. 38.

לִפְנַי adj. *anterior, front, in front,* 1 Ki. 6. 17.

פנה פָּנֹה Kal inf. abs.

פנה[bb] פִּנָּה Piel pret. 3 p. s. m. R. פנה; also subs. f. R.

פנה[h] פִּנָּה noun m. s., suff. 3 pers. s. fem. fr. [פֵּן] d. 8 b

פנה פְּנֵה Kal imp. sing. masc.

פנה פֹּנֶה id. part. sing. masc. dec. 9 a

פנה פָּנוּ id. pret. 3 pers. pl.

פנה פַּנּוּ Piel imp. pl. masc.

פנה פִּנּוּ id. pret. 3 pers. pl.; ו, for וַ, conv.

פנה פְּנוּ Kal imp. pl. masc.; ו bef. lab.

פנה פְּנוּאֵל pr. name masc.; ו id.

פנה פְּנוֹת Kal inf. constr.

Hebrew	Definition	Root
פְּנוֹת	noun fem. pl. of פִּנָּה dec. 10	פנן
פְּנוֹתָם	id. pl., suff. 3 pers. pl. masc. (§ 4. rem. 2)	פנן
פְּנֻחָם	pr. name masc., see פִּינְחָס; bef. lab.	פאה
פָּנַי / פָּנָי	the foll. with suff. 1 pers. sing.; id.	פנה
פָּנַי	noun masc. pl.,constr. of פָּנִים [fr. פָּנָה] dec. 9 b; id.	פנה
פָּנָיו	Kh. פָּנָי q. v., K. פִּי noun masc. sing. constr. of פֶּה irr. (§ 45)	פאה
פְּנִיאֵל	pr. name masc., see פְּנוּאֵל	פנה
פָּנֶיהָ	noun masc. pl., (פָּנִים), suff. 3 pers. sing. fem. [from פָּנָה] dec. 9 b; bef. lab.	פנה
פְּנֵיהֶם	id. pl., suff. 3 pers. pl. masc.; id.	פנה
פָּנָיו	id. pl., suff. 3 pers. sing. masc.; id.	פנה
פָּנֶיךָ / פָּנַיִךְ	id. pl., suff. 3 pers. sing. fem.	
פָּנֶיךָ	id. pl., suff. 2 pers. sing. masc.; bef. lab.	פנה
פְּנֵיכֶם	id. pl., suff. 2 pers. pl. masc.	פנה
פָּנִים	id. pl., abs. st.; bef. lab.	פנה
פֹּנִים	Kal part act. masc., pl. of פָּנָה dec. 9 a	פנה
פְּנִימָה	noun masc. sing. [פָּנִים] with loc. ה	פנם
פְּנִימוֹ	noun masc. pl., (פָּנִים), suff. 3 pers. pl. masc. from [פָּנָה] dec. 9 b	פנה
פָּנֵינוּ	id. pl. with suff. 1 pers. pl.	פנה
פָּנִינוּ	Kal pret. 1 pers. pl.	פנה
פְּנִינִים	noun masc. pl. [from פָּנִין]	פנן
פָּנִיתָ	Kal pret. 2 pers. sing. masc.; , for , conv.	פנה
פִּנִּיתָ	Piel pret. 2 pers. sing. masc.	פנה
פָּנִיתִי	Kal pret. 1 pers. sing.; bef. lab.	פנה
פִּנִּיתִי	Piel pret. 1 pers. sing.	פנה

פָּנַם doubtful Root; according to Fürst (in concord.), to hide, conceal.

פָּנִים masc. prop. *interior, inner part*, only as an adv. מִלְּפָנִים *within*, 1 Ki. 6. 29; with ה parag. פְּנִימָה; (a) *to the inside, inward*; (b) *within, inside* a house or palace; (c) *within, on the inside*. לִפְנִימָה *to the inside, inward*, Eze. 41. 3; also *within, on the inside*; מִפְּנִימָה *on the inside, within*. פְּנִימִי fem. פְּנִימִית (pl. פְּנִימִיּוֹת) adj. *inner*.

פָּנַן Root not used; Arab. *to divide*.
פֵּן masc. dec. 8 b, *corner*, Pr. 7. 8; Zec. 14. 10.
פִּנָּה f. d.10.—I. *corner*; אֶבֶן פִּ׳, רֹאשׁ פִּ׳ *corner-stone.*—II. *battlement, parapet.*—III. *chief, prince*. פָּנִינִים m. pl. *pearls*; others, *red corals*. Hence also
פְּנִנָּה (*pearl*) pr. name fem. 1 Sa. 1. 2, 4 | פנן

פָּנַק Pi. *to bring up, train delicately*, Pr. 29. 21.

פִּנַּת	noun fem. sing., constr. of פִּנָּה dec 10	פנן
פִּנָּתָהּ	id., suff. 3 pers. sing. fem.	פנן
פִּנֹּתָיו	id. pl., suff. 3 pers. sing. masc.	פנן
פַּס	Chald. noun masc. sing. dec. 5 a	פסס
פַּסָּא	Chald. id., emph. st.	פסס

פָּסַג Pi. prop. *to divide*, hence *to distinguish, view or consider*, Ps. 48. 14.
פִּסְגָּה (*part, piece*) pr. name of a mountain ridge in the territory of Moab.

פַּסְּגוּ	Piel imp. pl. masc.	פסג
פִּסְּגוּ	Piel pret. 3 pers. pl.	פסס
פָּסֹחַ	Kal inf. abs.	פסח

פָּסַח I. *to leap* or *pass over* or *by, to spare*, with עַל. —II. *to halt, limp*, 1 Ki. 18. 21. Niph. *to become lame*, 2 Sa. 4. 4. Pi. *to leap about*, 1 Ki. 18. 26.
פֶּסַח (*lame*) pr. name masc. of three different persons.
פֶּסַח masc. dec. 6 (§ 35. rem. 5) *the passover*; (a) *the paschal lamb*; (b) *the festival of the passover*.
פִּסֵּחַ masc. dec. 7 b, adj. *lame*.
תִּפְסַח (*passage*) pr. name of a city on the Euphrates, *Thapsacus*.

פָּסֵחַ	pr. name masc.	פסח
פֶּסַח	noun masc. sing. dec. 6 a	פסח
פִּסֵּחַ	adj. masc. sing. dec. 7 b; bef. lab.	פסח
פִּסְחִים	id. pl., abs. st.	פסח
פֹּסְחִים	Kal part. act. masc. pl. [of פּוֹסֵחַ] dec. 7 b	פסח
פָּסַחְתִּי	id. pret. 1 pers. sing.; acc. shifted by , for , conv. (§ 8. rem. 7)	פסח
פָּסִי	pr. name, see וָפְסִי under lett.	
פְּסִילֵי	n. m. pl. constr. fr. [פָּסִיל] d. 3 a; bef. lab.	פסל
פְּסִילֶיהָ	id. pl., suff. 3 pers. sing. fem.	פסל
פְּסִילֵיהֶם	id. pl., suff. 3 pers. pl. masc.; bef. lab.	פסל
פְּסִילֵיכֶם	id. pl., suff. 2 pers. sing. masc.	פסל
פְּסִילִים	id. pl., abs. st.	פסל
פַּסִּים	noun masc. pl. of פַּס dec. 8 d	פסס
פָּסֵךְ	pr. name masc. 1 Ch. 7. 33.	

[פָּסַל] fut. יִפְסֹל *to cut* or *hew*, espec. stones; *to carve* wood.
פָּסִיל masc. dec. 3 a.—I. *a carved image.*—II. *quarry*, Ju. 3. 19, 26, and the following.

פֶסֶל ‎ ‎ masc. dec. 6a (suff. פִּסְלִי), *carved image* or *idol*; also for *a molten image*; ‎ bef. lab. פסל

פְּסָל־ Kal imp. sing. masc. [for פְּסָל § 8. rem. 18] פסל

פְּסָלוֹ id. pret. 3 pers. sing. m., suff. 3 pers. s. m. פסל

פִּסְלִי ‎ n. m. s., suff. 1 p. s. fr. פֶסֶל d. 6a; ‎ bef. lab. פסל

פִּסְלָם id. with suff. 3 pers. pl. masc. . . פסל

פְּסַנְתֵּרִין
פְּסַנְתֵּרִין } Chald. a musical instrument, ψαλτήριον,
פְּסַנְתֵּרִין   *psaltery*, Da. 3. 5, 7, 10, 15.

[פָּסַם] to *cease, fail, have an end*, Ps. 12. 2.

פַּס masc. *extremity*; only in the phrase כְּתֹנֶת פַּסִּים a long dress with sleeves covering the hands.

פַּס Chald. dec. 5a, *extremity* of the hand, Da. 5. 5, 24.

פִּסָּה fem. dec. 10, *abundance*, Ps. 72. 16.

פִּסְפָּה ‎ pr. name masc. 1 Ch. 7. 38.

פִּסַּת noun fem. sing., constr. of [פִּסָּה] dec. 10 פסם

[פָּעָה] to *cry out*, only Is. 42. 14. Syr. to *bleat, low*; Arab. to *hiss*, of a serpent (Gesenius). Hence

פָּעוּ (*a bleating*) pr. name of a place in Edom, Ge. 36. 39, called פָּעִי 1 Ch. 1. 50.

אֶפְעֶה com. *adder, viper*.

אֶפַע masc. id. Is. 41. 24, מֵאֶפַע (*worse*) *than vipers*. Others regard it as a corrupt reading for מֵאֶפֶס *than nothing*.

פְּעוֹר pr. name (see בֵּית & בַּעַל פְּעוֹר) . פער

פָּעִי pr. name of a place, see פָּעוּ פעה

פָּעַל ‎ fut. יִפְעָל, יִפְעַל (Job 35. 6).—I. to *work*.—II. to *make, form*.—III. to *do, perform*.—IV. to *practise*.

פֹּעַל masc. dec. 6f.—I. *work, a thing made*.—II. *deed, action*.—III. *acquisition*, Pr. 21. 6.—IV. *wages*.

פְּעֻלָּה fem. dec. 10.—I. *work, employment, business*.—II. *reward, wages*.

פְּעֻלְּתַי (for פְּעֻלָּתְיָה *reward of the Lord*) pr. name masc. 1 Ch. 26. 5.

מִפְעָל masc. dec. 2b, & מִפְעָלָה fem. dec. 11a, *work, doing* of God.

פָּעַל Kal pret. 3 rs. sing. masc. for פָּעַל (§ 8. rem. 7) פעל

פֹּעַל ‎ noun masc. s. d. 6f (§ 35. r. 8); ‎ bef. lab. פעל
פֹּעֵל ‎ Kal part. act. sing. masc. dec. 7b; ‎ id. פעל

פָּעֲלָה
פָּעֲלוּ } id. pret. 3 pers. pl. (§ 8. rem. 7) . פעל

פָּעֳלוֹ
פָּעֳלוֹ } noun masc. sing., suff. 3 pers. sing. masc.
פָּעֳלוֹ   fr. פֹּעַל d. 6 f (§ 35. rem. 8); ‎ bef. lab. פעל

פֹּעֲלֵי ‎ Kal part. act. pl. constr. masc. from פֹּעַל dec. 7 b; ‎ id. . . . . פעל

פָּעֳלִי noun masc. sing., suff. 1 pers. s. fr. פֹּעַל d. 6 f פעל

פָּעֳלָיִם id. pl., abs. st. פעל

פָּעָלְךָ
פָּעָלֶךָ } id. sing., suff. 2 pers. sing. masc.;
  ‎ bef. lab. . . } פעל

פָּעֳלֵךְ id. sing., suff. 2 pers. sing. fem. . . פעל

פָּעָלְכֶם ‎ id. sing., suff. 2 pers. pl. masc.; ‎ bef. lab. פעל

פָּעֳלָם id. sing., suff. 3 pers. pl. masc. פעל

פָּעַלְתָּ Kal pret. 2 pers. sing. masc. פעל

פְּעֻלַּת noun fem. sing., constr. of [פְּעֻלָּה] dec. 10 פעל

פְּעֻלֹּת ‎ id. pl. . . . . . . פעל

פָּעֳלָתוֹ ‎ id. sing., suff. 3 pers. sing. masc.; ‎ bef. lab. פעל

פָּעַלְתִּי Kal pret. 1 pers. sing. פעל

פְּעֻלָּתִי ‎ noun fem. sing., suff. 1 pers. sing. from [פְּעֻלָּה] dec. 10; ‎ bef. lab. פעל

פָּעַלְתִּי pr. name masc. פעל

פָּעֳלָתָם noun fem. sing., suff. 3 pers. pl. masc. from פְּעֻלָּה dec. 10 פעל

[פָּעַם] to *impel, urge, move*, Ju. 13. 25. Niph. *to be moved, disturbed*. Hithp. id. Da. 2. 1.

פַּעַם fem. (masc. Ju. 16. 28) dec. 6 d, prop. *a striking* or *stamping*, hence—I. *an anvil*, Is. 41. 7; others, *hammer*.—II. *step, footstep*; metaph. of the *progress* of a chariot, Ju. 5. 28; hence *foot, pedestal*, Ex. 25. 12.—III. אַחַת פַּעַם, פַּ' *once*, פַּעֲמַיִם *twice*, שָׁלֹשׁ פְּעָמִים *three times*; הַפַּעַם *this time, now*; כְּפַעַם בְּפַעַם *as at other times*; פַּעַם–פַּעַם *at one time—at another*, Pr. 7. 12.

פַּעֲמֹן masc. dec. 1 b, *a bell*.

פַּעַם
פַּעַם } noun fem. sing. dec. 6 d (§ 35. rem. 2) פעם

פַּעֲמֵי id. pl., constr. st. . . . . . פעם

פְּעָמַי
פְּעָמַי } id. pl., suff. 1 pers. sing. פעם

פְּעָמָיו id. pl., suff. 3 pers. sing. masc. פעם

פְּעָמֶיךָ id. pl., suff. 2 pers. sing. fem. פעם

פְּעָמַיִךְ id. pl., suff. 2 pers. sing. fem. פעם

פַּעֲמַיִם
פַּעֲמָיִם } id. du., abs. st. . . . . פעם

פְּעָמִים id. pl., abs. st. . . . . . פעם

פַּעֲמֹן noun masc. sing. dec. 1 b פעם

* Hab. 2. 18.   ᵈ Ps. 72. 16.   ᵍ Ps. 15. 2.   ʲ Ps. 95. 9.   ᵐ Is. 45. 9.   ᵖ Is. 41. 24.   ˢ Ps. 28. 5.   ᵛ Is. 49. 4.   ʸ Ca. 7. 2.
ᵇ Is. 48. 5.   ᵉ Is. 44. 12.   ʰ Zep. 2. 3.   ᵏ Hab. 3. 2.   ⁿ Ru. 2. 12.   ᵠ Job 36. 9.   ᵗ Eze. 29. 20.   Is. 41. 7.   ᶻ Ps. 74. 3.
ᶜ Is. 45. 20.   Ps. 11. 3.   ⁱ Mi. 2. 1.

פַּעֲמֹנֵי 'ŋ id. pl., constr. st.; ŋ bef. lab. . . פעם

פַּעֲמֹתָיו noun fem. pl., suff. 3 pers. sing. masc. from פַּעַם dec. 6 d . . פעם

פַּעְנֵחַ pr. name, see צָפְנַת פַּעְנֵחַ.

[פָּעַר] to open wide the mouth, to gape.

פְּעוֹר (a gap) pr. name of a mountain in Moab. בַּעַל פְּעוֹר, also simply פְּעוֹר, an idol of the Moabites.

פַּעֲרִי pr. name masc. 2 Sa. 23. 35, for which נַעֲרַי 1 Ch. 11. 37.

פָּעֲרָה 'ŋ Kal pret. 3 pers. sing. fem.; ŋ, for ŋ, conv. . . פער

פָּעֲרוּ id. pret. 3 pers. pl. . . פער

פַּעֲרִי pr. name masc. . . פער

פָּעַרְתִּי id. pret. 1 pers. pl. . . פער

[פָּצָה] I. to open the mouth; with עַל to gape upon.—II. to tear away, save, deliver.

פְּצֵה Kal imp. sing. masc. . . פצה

פֹּצֶה 'ŋ id. part. act. sing. masc.; ŋ bef. lab. . . פצה

פָּצוּ id. pret. 3 pers. pl. . . פצה

פָּצֵגוּ Kal imp. pl. masc. [for פוצו] . . פוץ

פְּצוּעַ Kal part. pass. s. m. constr. [of פָּצוּעַ] dec. 3 a פצע

[פָּצַח] to break forth into singing, rejoicing. Pi. to break in pieces, Mi. 3. 3.

פָּצְחוּ Kal pret. 3 pers. pl. . . פצח

פִּצְּחוּ Piel pret. 3 p. pl. [for פִּצְּחוּ, comp. § 8. r. 7] פצח

פִּצְחוּ Kal imp. pl. masc. . . פצח

פִּצְחִי id. imp. sing. fem. . . פצח

פָּצַחְתָּה Kal pret. 2 pers. sing. masc. (comp. § 8. r. 5) פצח

פָּצַחְתִּי id. pret. 1 pers. sing. . . פצח

פַּצֵּל- Pi. to peel, Ge. 30. 37, 38. פָּצַל i. q. Hence

פְּצָלוֹת fem. pl. parts peeled or stripped of the bark, Ge. 30. 37 . . פצל

פָּצַם to break, rend, only in the foll. form.

פְּצַמְתָּהּ Kal pret. 3 pers. s. masc., suff. 3 pers. s. fem. פצם

פְּצֵנִי Kal imp. sing. masc., (פְּצֵה), suff. 1 pers. sing. (§ 24. rem. 21) . . . . פצה

[פָּצַע] to wound; פְּצוּעַ דַּכָּה eunuch, see דָּכָה. Hence

פֶּצַע } masc. dec. 6 a (with suff. פִּצְעִי, § 35. r. 5), a wound . . . . פצע

פָּצֹעַ 'ŋ Kal inf. abs.; ŋ bef. lab. . . פצע

פְּצָעוּנִי id. pret. 3 pers. pl., suff. 1 pers. sing. . . פצע

פְּצָעַי noun masc. pl., suff. 1 pers. sing. from פֶּצַע dec. 6 a (§ 35. rem. 5) . . . פצע

פִּצְעֵי id. pl., constr. st. . . פצע

פְּצָעִים id. pl., abs. st. . . פצע

פָּצַץ Root not used; i. q. פוץ to disperse.

פִּצֵּץ (dispersion) pr. name masc. 1 Ch. 24. 15.

פֶּצֶץ pr. name, see בֵּית פ׳ . . . בית

[פָּצַר] fut. יִפְצַר.—I. to press upon, with בְּ Ge. 19. 3.—II. to press, urge. Hiph. to be stubborn, wilful, 1 Sa. 15. 23.

פְּצִירָה פִים fem. pressed, 1 Sa. 13. 21, pressed or rubbed (upon) edges, i. e. a file for sharpening or setting edges

פָּצְתָה 'ŋ Kal pret. 3 pers. sing. fem.; ŋ, for ŋ, conv. פצה

פָּקַד fut. יִפְקֹד.—I. to visit, go or come to see.—II. to examine, prove.—III. to visit, punish, with עַל also אֶל, בְּ, acc. of the person.—IV. to review, muster, number.—V. to miss, sc. in reviewing.—VI. to look after, to take care of.—VII. to set over, appoint, with עַל, אֶת part. pass. פְּקוּדִים officers.—VIII. to charge with, enjoin upon the care of any one, with עַל.—IX. to deposit, lay up, 2 Ki. 5. 24 Niph. I. to be missed.—II. to be visited, punished.—III. to be set over, appointed. Pi. to muster, Is. 13. 4. Pu. I. to be mustered, numbered, Ex. 38. 21.—II. to be missed, Is. 38. 10; Eng. vers. "deprived." Hiph. I. to set over, appoint, with בְּ, לְ, עַל.—II. to charge with, to commit to the care of any one, with בְּיַד, עַל יְדֵי.—III. to deposit, lay. Hoph. I. to be set over, have the oversight of.—II. to be visited, punished, Je. 6. 6.—III. to be deposited, Le. 5. 23. Hothpa. (§ 6. No. 10, note) to be mustered, numbered.

פָּקוֹד masc.—I. visitation, punishment, allegorically for Babylon, Je. 50. 21.—II. dominion, Eze. 23. 23.

פְּקֻדָּה fem. dec. 10.—I. care, providence.—II. visitation, punishment.—III. oversight, office, charge.—IV. custody; בֵּית הַפְּקֻדוֹת prison.—V. store treasure, Is. 15. 7.

פָּקִיד masc. dec. 3 a, overseer, chief officer.

פְּקִדֻת fem. oversight, office, Je. 37. 13.

פִּקּוּדִים masc. pl. (of פִּקּוּד dec. 1 b) commands, precepts.

a Ex. 28.33; 39.25.   d Eze. 2.8.   g De. 23.2.   i Ju. 11.36.   m Ge. 30.38.   p Ps. 144.7,11.   s 1 Ki. 20.37.   u Job 9.17.   x Pr. 23.29.
b Is. 5. 14.   e Is. 10.14.   h Is. 14.7.   k Ju. 11.35.   n Ps. 60 4.   q Ex. 21.25.   t Ca. 5.2.   v Pr. 27.6.   y Nu.16.30.
c Ps. 119.131.   f 1 Sa. 14.34.   i Is. 54.1.

פִּקָּדוֹן masc. *what is laid up, a deposit.*

מִפְקָד masc. dec. 2 b.—I. *a numbering, census,* 2 Sa. 24. 9.—II. *appointment, arrangement,* 2 Ch. 31. 13.—III. *appointed place,* Eze. 43. 21.—IV. שַׁעַר הַמִּפְקָד name of a gate in Jerusalem, Ne. 3. 31.

פָּקֹד	Kal inf. abs.	פקד
פְּקֹד־	ᵇ⁄ id. imp. sing. masc.; ⁴ bef. lab.	פקד
פֹּקֵד	id. part. act. sing. masc. dec. 7 b	פקד
פֻּקַד	Pual pret. 3 pers. sing. masc.	פקד
פְּקֻדָּה׳	noun fem. sing. dec. 10	פקד
פָּקְדוּ⁴	Kal pret. 3 pers. pl. (§ 8. rem. 7);	פקד
פָּקָדוּ ᵍ⁄	⁴ bef. lab.	
פִּקְדוּ ʰ⁄	id. imp. pl. masc.; ⁴ id.	פקד
פְּקָדוּךָ	id. pret. 3 pers. pl., suff. 2 pers. sing. masc.	פקד
פְּקֻדּוֹת	noun fem., pl. of פְּקֻדָּה dec. 10	פקד
פָּקְדִי	Kal inf., suff. 1 pers. sing.	פקד
פְּקֻדֵי⁴	id. part. pass. pl. constr. m. [fr. פָּקוּד] dec. 3 a	פקד
פְּקֻדֵיהֶם	ᵍ⁄ id. pl., suff. 3 pers. pl. masc.; ⁴ bef. lab.	פקד
פְּקֻדָיו	ᵍ⁄ id. pl., suff. 3 pers. sing. masc.; ⁴ id.	פקד
פִּקּוּדָיו⁴	noun masc. pl., suff. 3 pers. sing. masc. from [פִּקּוּד] dec. 1 b	פקד
פְּקֻדֶיךָ⁴	id. pl., suff. 2 pers. sing. masc.	פקד
פְּקֻדֵיכֶם"	Kal part. pass. pl. masc., suff. 2 pers. pl. masc. [from פָּקוּד] dec. 3 a	פקד
פְּקִדִים	noun masc., pl. of פָּקִיד dec. 3 a	פקד
פְּקַדְנוּ	Kal pret. 1 pers. pl.	פקד
פָּקְדֵנִי׳	⁴⁄ id. imp. s. m., suff. 1 pers. s.; ⁴ bef. lab.	פקד
פָּקַדְתָּ	id. pret. 2 pers. sing. masc.; acc. shifted	פקד
פָּקַדְתָּ⁴	by ⁴, for ⁴, conv. (§ 8. rem. 7)	
פְּקֻדַּת	⁴⁄ noun fem. sing., constr. of פְּקֻדָּה dec. 10; ⁴ bef. lab.	פקד
פִּקֻדַת׳	noun fem. sing. [defect. for פְּקִידֻת]	פקד
פְּקֻדֹת׳	noun fem., pl. of פְּקֻדָּה dec. 10	פקד
פְּקַדְתּוּ	id. sing., suff. 3 pers. sing. masc.	פקד
פָּקַדְתִּי	Kal pret. 1 pers. sing.; acc. shifted by ⁴,	פקד
פָּקַדְתִּי⁴	for ⁴, conv. (§ 8. rem. 7)	
פֻּקַּדְתִּי׳	Pual pret. 1 pers. sing.	פקד
פְּקַדְתִּיו	Kal pret. 1 pers. sing., suff. 3 pers. sing. m.	פקד
פְּקַדְתִּיךָ⁴	id. id., suff. 2 pers. sing. masc.	פקד
פְּקַדְתִּים	id. id., suff. 3 pers. pl. masc.	פקד
פְּקֻדָּתֵךְ⁴	noun fem. s., suff. 2 p. s. f. fr. פְּקֻדָּה d. 10	פקד
פְּקַדְתִּךָ⁴	⁴⁄ id., suff. 2 pers. sing. masc.; ⁴ bef. lab.	פקד
פְּקַדְתָּם	⁴⁄ id., suff. 3 pers. pl. masc.; ⁴ id.	פקד
פְּקַדְתֶּם	ᵍ⁄ Kal pret. 2 pers. pl. masc.; ⁴ id.	פקד
פָּקְדוּ⁴	Kal pret. 3 pers. pl.	פוק
פָּקוּד	noun masc. sing.	פקד

פְּקוּדֵי | noun masc. pl. constr. from [פָּקוּד] dec. 1 b | פקד
פְּקוּדֵי | ᵍ⁄ Kal part. pass. pl. constr. masc. [from פָּקוּד] dec. 3 a; ⁴ bef. lab. | פקד
פְּקוּדָיו | noun masc. pl., suff. 3 pers. sing. masc. from [פָּקוּד] dec. 1 b | פקד
פְּקוּדֶיךָ⁴ | id., suff. 2 pers. sing. masc. | פקד

פָּקַח'. fut. יִפְקַח *to open,* espec. the eyes, also the ears. Niph. *to be opened.*

פֶּקַח (*opening,* sc. of the eyes) pr. name of a king of Israel.

פִּקֵּחַ masc. dec. 7 b, *seeing, having the eyes open.*

פְּקַחְיָה (*the Lord has opened,* sc. his eyes) pr. name of a king of Israel.

פְּקַח־קוֹחַ masc. *opening,* sc. of the prison, *deliverance,* Is. 61. 1

פָּקֹחַ"	Kal inf. abs.	פקח
פְּקַח	id. imp. sing. masc. (see also פְּקַח־קוֹחַ)	פקח
פֶּקַח⁴	pr. name masc.; ⁴ bef. lab.	פקח
פִּקֵּחַ"	adj. masc. sing. dec. 7 b	פקח
פֹּקֵחַ°	Kal part. act. sing. masc.	פקח
פְּקַחְהֶּ	Kh. פְּקַחַ, K. פָּקַח, Kal imp. sing. masc. (§ 8. rem. 11)	קח
פְּקֻחוֹת"	Kal part. pass. fem. pl. [of פְּקֻחָה for פָּקוּחַ]	פקח
פְּקַחְיָה	pr. name masc.	פקח
פִּקְחִים׳	adj. masc., pl. of פִּקֵּחַ dec. 7 b	פקח
פָּקַחְתָּ׳	Kal pret. 2 pers. sing. masc.	פקח
פָּקִיד	⁴⁄ noun masc. sing. dec. 3 a; ⁴ bef. lab.	פקד
פְּקִיד	⁴⁄ id., constr. st.; ⁴ id.	פקד
פְּקִידוֹ⁴	id., suff. 3 pers. sing. masc.	פקד
פְּקִידִים	id. pl., abs. st.	פקד

פָּקַע Root not used; Syr. *to split,* i. q. בָּקַע. Hence

פְּקָעִים ⁴⁄ masc. pl. [of פֶּקַע § 35. r. 5] *wild cucumbers;* others, *mushrooms,* as an architectural ornament, 1 Ki. 6. 18; 7. 24 | פקע
פַּקֻּעֹת fem. pl. id. 2 Ki. 4. 39 | פקע

פַּר noun masc. sing., pl. פָּרִים, dec. 8 (§ 37. rem. 7); ⁴ bef. lab. | פר

פָּרָא. Hiph. *to be fruitful,* Ho. 13. 15.

פָּרֶה, פֶּרֶא masc. dec. 6 a, *wild ass.*

פִּרְאָם (*like a wild ass*) pr. name of a king of Canaan, Jos. 10. 3.

פְּרָאִים ᵍ⁄ id. pl., abs. st.; ⁴ bef. lab. | פרא

ᵃ Nu. 3, 15, 40.   ᵍ De. 20. 9.   ᵐ Ps.119.4,45,56,   ʳ Jo b 5. 24.   ˢ Je. 49. 8.   ᵈ Job 10. 12.   ˡ Ps. 111. 7.   ᵐ Is. 42. 20.   ᵗ Ex. 23. 8.
ᵇ Ps. 80. 15.   ʰ 2 Sa. 24. 2.   87,93,100,141.   ⁱ Je. 37. 13.   ᵗ Je. 50. 31.   ᵉ Is. 15. 7.   ᵏ Ps. 119. 27, 63,   ⁿ Ex. 4. 11.   ᵘ Job 14. 3.
ᶜ Ex. 38. 21.   ⁱ Is. 26. 16.   ⁿ Nu. 14. 29.   ᵘ 2 Ki. 11. 18   ᵘ Je. 6. 15.   ᶠ Je. 23. 2.   69, 94, 134, 159,   ᵖ Ps. 146. 8.   ᵛ Ne. 11. 14.
ᵈ Is. 10. 3.   ᵏ 2 Ki. 11. 15.   ᵒ 1 Sa. 25. 15.   ᵛ Ps. 109. 8.   ᵛ Is. 60. 17.   ᵍ Nu. 4. 27.   168, 173.   ᵠ Da. 9. 18.   ʷ Ju. 9. 28.
Is. 34. 16.   ˡ Ps. 103. 18.   ᵖ Ps. 106. 4.   ᵠ Is. 38. 10.   ʷ Mi. 7. 4.   ʰ Is. 28. 7.   ᵛ Job 27. 19.   ʳ Je. 32. 19.   ˣ Je. 14. 6.
Nu. 26. 63, 64.   ᵠ Je. 15. 15.

פִּרְאָם pr. name masc. . . . . פרא

פָּארָתִי transp. for פָּארָתִי (q. v.) . . פאר

[פַּרְוָר, פַּרְבָּר] masc. *suburb*, 2 Ki. 23. 11; 1 Ch. 26. 18.

[פָּרַד] *to separate, spread* the wing, Eze. 1. 11. Niph. *to be separated, divided*; also *to separate oneself*, with מִן, מֵעַל *from any one.* Pi. *to go aside*, Ho. 4. 14. Pu. part. *separated, singular*, Est. 3. 8; others, *dispersed*. Hiph. I. *to separate.*—II. *to scatter, disperse*, De. 32. 8; others, *to separate, divide*. Hithp. I. *to separate oneself, to be sundered.*—II. *to be dispersed, scattered*, Job 4. 11.

פֶּרֶד masc. dec. 6 a (with suff. פִּרְדּוֹ), *a mule.*

פִּרְדָּה fem. *she-mule*, 1 Ki. 1. 33, 38, 44.

פְּרוּדָא (*seed*) pr. name masc. Ezr. 2. 54, for which פְּרִידָא Ne. 7. 57.

פְּרֻדוֹת f. pl. *seeds scattered, corn sown*, Joel 1. 17.

פֶּרֶד noun masc. sing. dec. 6 a; for ו see lett. ו פרד

פְּרָדוֹ id. with suff. 3 pers. sing. masc. . פרד

פְּרֻדוֹת Kal part. pass. or (Joel 1. 17) subst. fem. pl. [of פְּרֻדָה from פָּרוּד masc.] פרד

פִּרְדֵיהֶם the foll. with suff. 3 pers. pl. masc. פרד

פְּרָדִים noun masc., pl. of פֶּרֶד dec. 6 a; ו bef. lab. פרד

פַּרְדֵּס masc. dec. 1 b, *garden, park.*

פַּרְדְּסִים id. pl. abs.; ו bef. lab. פרדס

פַּרְדָּת noun fem. sing., constr. of פִּרְדָּה (no pl.) פרד

[פָּרָה] fut. יִפְרֶה *to be fruitful, to bear fruit*; part. fem. פֹּרָת, פֹּרִיָּה *fruit-bearing*, fruitful, sc. tree. Hiph. *to make fruitful.*

פְּרִי masc. d. 6 i (with suff. 3 pers. pl. פִּרְיָם). —I. *fruit, produce*; עֵץ פְּרִי *fruit-tree.*—II. *fruit* of the body, *offspring.*—III. metaph. *result, consequence, reward.*

אַפִּרְיוֹן masc. *sedan, litter*, Ca. 3. 9.

פָּרָה noun fem. sing. dec. 10 [for פָּרָה comp. § 37. rem. 7] from פַּר masc.; ו bef. lab. פרר

פָּרָה for פָּרָא (q. v.) . . . . פרא

פְּרֵה Kal imp. sing. masc. . . . פרה

פֹּרֶה id. part. sing. masc. . . . פרה

פָּרָה pr. name masc., see פָּארָה; ו bef. lab. פאר

פָּרוּ id. pret. 3 pers. pl.; ו, for ו, conv. פרה

פְּרוּ id. imp. pl. masc. . . . פרה

פְּרוּדָא pr. name masc. . . . . פרד

פָּרוֹחַ Kal inf. abs. . . . . . פרח

פֶּרַח pr. name masc. . . . . פרח

פַּרְוַיִם pr. name of a country, 2 Ch. 3. 6.

פָּרוּעַ Kal part. pass. sing. masc. . . פרע

פְּרוּצָה Kal part. pass. sing. fem. [of פָּרוּץ] פרץ

פְּרוּצִים id. part. pass. masc. pl. [of פָּרוּץ] dec. 3 a פרץ

פְּרוּשָׁה Kal part. pass. sing. fem. from פָּרוּשׁ masc. פרש

פָּרוֹת noun fem., pl. of פָּרָה d. 10, from פַּר masc. פרר

פָּרוֹת see חֲפַר־פָּרוֹת חפר

פָּרַן Root not used; Arab. *to separate*, i. q. פָּרַד, פָּרַשׁ; hence perh. *to scatter*, see פְּרָזָה.

פְּרָז masc. dec. 4 a, *ruler, leader*, Hab. 3. 14.

פְּרָזוֹן masc. d. 3 c (§ 32. r. 2) id., Ju. 5. 7, 11.

פְּרָזָה f. *a scattered place, unwalled town, village.*

פְּרָזִי masc. *one living in an unwalled town or village.*

פְּרִזּוֹי masc. id. Est. 9. 19, Kheth.

פְּרִזִּי pr. name collect. *Perizzites*, a people of Canaan.

פְּרָזָיו noun m. pl., suff. 3 p. s. m. fr. [פֶּרֶז] d. 4 a פרז

פְּרָזוֹן noun masc. sing., comp. dec. 3 c פרז

פְּרָזוֹנוֹ id. with suff. 3 pers. sing. masc. . פרז

פְּרָזוֹת noun fem. pl. abs. [from פְּרָזָה] פרז

פַּרְזֶל Chald. masc. i. q. Heb. בַּרְזֶל *iron.*

פַּרְזְלָא Chald. id., emph. st. . . . פרזל

פָּרַח fut. יִפְרַח.—I. *to sprout, flourish, blossom.*—II. *to break out*, as ulcers, leprosy.—III. *to fly*, only part. Eze. 13. 20 לְפֹרְחוֹת *that they fly away* (for לִהְיוֹת פֹּרְחוֹת lit. *that they become flying ones*); Gesenius, *as flying ones*, i. e. *birds.* Hiph. I. *to cause to flourish.*—II. intrans. *to flourish, blossom.*

פֶּרַח masc. dec. 6 a (with suff. פִּרְחוֹ § 35. r. 5). —I. *young shoot*, Na. 1. 4.—II. *flower, blossom.*— III. as an artificial ornament, Ex. 25. 33.

פִּרְחָה fem. *brood*, Job 30. 12; comp. אֶפְרֹחַ.

פָּרֻחַ (*flourishing*) pr. name masc. 1 Ki. 4. 17.

אֶפְרֹחַ masc. dec. 1 b, *the young* of birds, *a brood.*

פָרַח in pause for פֶּרַח (q. v.) . . . פרח

פָּרֹחַ Kal inf. abs. . . . . . . פרח

פֶּרַח noun masc. sing. (suff. פִּרְחָהּ) dec. 6 a (§ 35. rem. 5); ו bef. lab., for ו see lett. ו פרח

פֹּרֵחַ Kal part. act. sing. masc. . . . פרח

פָּרְחָה
פָּרֵחָה } id. pret. 3 pers. sing. fem. (§ 8. rem. 7) פרח

• Eze. 31. 12, 13.   ² 2 Ki. 5. 17.   ¹ 1 Ki. 1. 38, 44.   ᵏ Je. 2. 24.   • Ex. 1. 7.   ᵖ Pr. 25. 28.   ᵗ Is. 2. 20.   ʸ Ju. 5. 11.   ᶜ Ex. 9. 9, 10.
ᵇ 1 Ki. 18. 5.   ᶠ Ca. 4. 13.   ᵍ Nu. 19. 2;   ˡ Ge. 35. 11.   ᵖ Le. 13. 12.   ᵠ Ne. 2. 13.   ᵘ Hab. 3. 14.   ᶻ Is. 35. 2.   ᵈ Le. 13. 20, 25.
ᶜ 2 Sa. 13. 29.   ᵍ Ec. 2. 5.   Is. 11. 7.   ᵐ De. 29. 17.   ᵖ Le. 13. 45.   Ho. 5. 1.   Ju. 5. 7.   ᵃ Na. 1. 4.   ᵘ Ca. 7. 13.
ᵈ Eze. 1. 11.

פִּרְחָח   noun masc. sing., suff. 3 pers. sing. fem. from פֶּרַח dec. 6a (§ 35. rem. 5) .   פרח

פִּרְחָה   noun fem. sing.   פרח

פְּרָחֶיהָ   ⁱ noun masc. pl., suff. 3 pers. sing. fem. from פֶּרַח dec. 6a (§ 35. rem. 5) ; ⁱ bef. lab.   פרח

פְּרָחָם   ⁱ id. sing., suff. 3 pers. pl. masc. ; ⁱ id. .   פרח

פֹּרַחַת   Kal part. act. sing. fem. from פָּרַח masc.   פרח

[פָּרַט]   prob. *to cut, divide*, cogn. פָּרַד ; hence *to sing* (comp. Pi. of זָמַר) Am. 6. 5.   Hence

פֶּרֶט   ⁱ grapes fallen off of themselves and lying about *scattered* or *strewed*, Le. 19. 10 .   פרט

פְּרִי   ⁱ } noun masc. sing. dec. 6 i (§ 35. rem. 14) ; פרה

פְּרִי   ⁱ } ⁱ bef. lab. .   פרה

פְּרִידָא   pr. name masc.   פרד

פִּרְיָה   n. m. pl., suff. 3 p. s. f. fr. פַּר d. 8 (§ 37. r. 7)   פרר

פִּרְיֹה   noun masc. sing., suff. 3 p. s. f. fr. פְּרִי d. 6 0   פרה

פֹּרִיָּה   Kal part. act. s. f. [as if fr. פּוֹרִי § 24. r. 4]   פרה

פִּרְיָהֶם   noun masc. s., suff. 3 p. pl. m. fr. פְּרִי d. 6i   פרה

פִּרְיָהֶן   id., suff. 3 pers. pl. fem.   פרה

פִּרְיוֹ   ⁱ id., suff. 3 pers. sing. masc. ; ⁱ bef. lab.   פרה

פִּרְיִי   id., suff. 1 pers. sing.   פרה

פִּרְיְךָ   id., suff. 2 pers. sing. masc.   פרה

פִּרְיֵךְ   id., suff. 2 pers. sing. fem.   פרה

פִּרְיְכֶם   ⁱ id., suff. 2 pers. pl. masc. ; ⁱ bef. lab.   פרה

פָּרִים   ⁱ noun masc. pl. of פַּר d. 8 (§ 37. r. 7) ; ⁱ id.   פרר

פִּרְיָם   noun masc. s., suff. 3 p. pl. m. fr. פְּרִי d. 6i   פרה

פִּרְיָמוֹ   id., suff. 3 pers. pl. masc.   פרה

פִּרְיָן   id., suff. 3 pers. pl. fem.   פרה

פְּרִינוּ   ⁱ Kal pret. 1 pers. pl. ; ⁱ, for ⁱ, conv.   פרה

פְּרִיסַת   Ch. Peal part. pass. 3 pers. s. f. (§ 47. r. 11)   פרס

פָּרִיץ   noun masc. sing. [for פָּרִיי] dec. 1 b   פרץ

פְּרִיץ   ⁱ id. constr. st. (accord. to dec. 3a, § 32. rem. 2) ; ⁱ bef. lab.   פרץ

פְּרִיצֵי   id. pl., constr. st.   פרץ

פְּרִיצִים   id. pl., abs. st.   פרץ

פְּרִיתֶם   ⁱ Kal pret. 2 pers. pl. masc. ; ⁱ, for ⁱ, conv.   פרה

פֶּרֶךְ   Root not used ; i. q. פָּרַק *to break*.

פֶּרֶךְ m. *oppression, rigour*. Also the following.

פָּרֹכֶת   fem. *the vail* or *curtain* which *separated* the holy place from the holy of holies .   פרך

פָּרַם   fut. יִפְרֹם *to rend, tear*, as a garment.   פרם

פְּרוּמִים   Kal part. pass. masc. pl. [of פָּרוּם] dec. 3 a   פרם

פַּרְמַשְׁתָּא   pr. name of a son of Haman, Est. 9. 9.

פַּרְנָךְ   pr. name masc. Nu. 34. 25.

[פָּרַם]   *to break* bread, *to any one*, *to give* or *distribute to* Hiph. *to cleave, divide* the hoof.

פְּרַס   Chald. *to divide*, Da. 5. 25, 28.

פֶּרֶס   masc. a species of eagle, the osprey.

פַּרְסָה   fem. dec. 12a (pl. ־וֹת, ־ים,), *hoof*.

פָּרַס   ⁱ } Heb. & Chald. pr. name, *Persia, Persians.*

פָּרַס   ⁱ } Gent. noun פַּרְסִי *Persian.*

אֲפַרְסָיֵא   pr. name of an unknown tribe, Ezr. 4. 9.

אֲפַרְסַתְכָיֵא, אֲפַרְסְכָיֵא   pr. name of two Syrian tribes, Ezr. 4. 9 ; 5. 6.

פָּרֹס   Kal inf. abs.   פרס

פָּרֻס   Peal part. pass. sing. masc. (§ 47. rem. 1)   פרס

פַּרְסָה   ⁱ noun fem. sing. dec. 12a ; ⁱ bef. lab. .   פרס

פַּרְסוֹת   ⁱⁱ id. pl., constr. st. ; ⁱ id.   פרס

פְּרָסוֹת   id. pl., abs. st.   פרס

פַּרְסָיֵא   Ch. K. פַּרְסָאָה gent. n., emph. of פָּרַס d. 7, fr.   פרס

פַּרְסֵיהֶן   ⁱ noun f. with pl. m. term. [פַּרְסִים], and suff. 3 p. pl. fem. from פַּרְסָה d. 12a ; ⁱ bef. lab.   פרס

פָּרְסִין   ⁱⁱ Ch. Peal part. act. m. pl. [for פָּרְסִים § 58. r. 1] ; ⁱ id.   פרס

פְּרָסֹת   noun fem., pl. of פַּרְסָה dec. 12a .   פרס

פַּרְסֹתֶיךָ   ⁱ id. pl. fem., suff. 2 pers. s. fem. ; ⁱ bef. lab.   פרס

פָּרַע   ⁱ fut. יִפְרַע.—I. *to free, exempt* from punishment, Eze. 24. 14.—II. *to free, deliver*, Ju. 5. 2, בִּפְרֹעַ פְּרָעוֹת *for working deliverance* ; Gesenius, *in lead ing on the leaders*, and so the LXX. Eng. Vers. " for avenging," from the Chald. פְּרַע *to retribute.*—III. *to let go loose, in a state of disorder*, Ex. 32. 25. —IV. *to neglect, reject*, e. g. counsel.—V. *to make bare* the head, espec. by cutting off the hair. Niph. *to become lawless*, Pr. 29. 18. Hiph. I. *to set loose, disengage*, Ex. 5. 4.—II. *to cause disorder, lawlessness*, 2 Ch. 28. 19.

פֶּרַע   masc. dec. 6 (§ 35. rem. 5).—I. *the hair* or *locks* as growing *loose and free*.—II. pl. fem. פְּרָעוֹת Ju. 5. 2, *deliverance* ; others, *leaders, princes* ; or *revenges*, see the Root No. II ; constr. פַּרְעוֹת De. 32. 42.

פִּרְעָתוֹן   (perh. *principal*, or *free-town*) pr. name of a city of Ephraim, Ju. 12. 13. Gent. noun פִּרְעָתֹנִי.

פָּרֹעַ   defect. for פָּרוֹעַ (q. v.) .   פרע

פֶּרַע   ⁱ noun masc. sing. ; ⁱ bef. lab. .   פרע

פַּרְעֹה   ⁱ (*king*) the title of all monarchs of Egypt down to the time of the Persian invasion.

פָּרְעָה   ⁱ Kal pret. 3 pers. sing. m., suff. 3 pers. sing. m.   פרע

פְּרָעֵהוּ   ⁱ id. imp. s. m., suff. 3 p. s. m. (§ 16. r. 12)   פרע

ᵃ Nu. 8. 4.   ᵉ Le. 19. 10.   ⁱ Pr. 8. 19.   ᵐ Ps. 21. 11.   ᵍ Is. 35. 9.   ᵘ Le. 13. 45.   ᵉ De. 14. 6.   ᵈ Nu. 5. 18.   ⁱ Eze. 44. 20.

ᵇ Job 30. 12.   ᶠ Le. 50. 27.   ᵏ Ho. 14. 9.   ⁿ Je. 29. 5.   ʳ Da. 11. 17.   ᵛ Is. 58. 7.   ᶻ Zec. 11. 16.   ᵏ Ex. 32. 25.   ⁱ Ex. 32. 25.

ᶜ Is. 5. 24.   ᵍ Am. 9. 14.   ˡ Eze. 25. 4.   ᵖ Ge. 26. 22.   ᵗ Eze. 7. 22.   ʷ Da. 5. 28.   ᵃ Le. 11. 3.   ᵐ Nu. 6. 5.   ⁱ Pr. 4. 15.

ᵈ Le. 13. 42, 57.   ʰ Je. 29. 23.   ᵐ Eze. 36. 8.   ᵠ Da. 5. 28.   ᵘ Je. 3. 16.   ˣ Eze. 32. 12.   ᵇ Mi. 4. 13.   ˢᵖ Nu. 5. 25.

פְּרָעוֹת
פְּרָעֹת } noun masc. with pl. fem. term., constr. and abs., from פֶּרַע d. 6 (§ 35. rem. 5) } פרע

פַּרְעֹשׁ masc.—I. *a flea*, 1 Sa. 24. 15; 26. 20.—II. pr. name of a man.

פַּרְעָתֹנִי gent. noun from פִּרְעָתוֹן פרע
פַּרְפַּר pr. name of a river; bef. lab. פרר

פָּרַץ fut. יִפְרֹץ.—I. *to break* or *tear down, demolish,* e. g. a wall.—II. *to break asunder,* i. e. *to disperse, scatter.*—III. *to break, afflict,* Job 16. 14.—IV. *to break forth,* as a child from the womb, Ge. 38. 29; of water, *to burst forth,* Job 28. 4, נַחַל פ' *a torrent bursts forth* (but according to Gesenius, *he breaks a mine through, sinks a shaft*); also *to break out, act with violence,* Ho. 4. 2; with בְּ *to break forth upon, break in upon, cause an overthrow among;* hence *to press upon, urge.*—V. *to spread abroad, to increase;* also *to overflow, abound with,* Pr. 3. 10. Niph. part. *spread abroad, common,* 1 Sa. 3. 1. Pu. *to be broken down,* Ne. 1. 3. Hithp. *to break away, loose,* 1 Sa. 25. 10.

פָּרִיץ masc. constr. פְּרִיץ, pl. פְּרִיצִים, constr. פְּרִיצֵי.—I. *violent, rapacious.*—II. *ravenous, wild, wild beast,* Is. 35. 9.

פֶּרֶץ masc. dec. 6a (pl. with suff. פְּרָצֵיהֶן).—I. *a breaking forth,* Ge. 38. 29; of water, *a bursting forth,* 2 Sa. 5. 20.—III. *a breach of a wall.*—IV. *overthrow, calamity, affliction.*—V. pr. name masc. Patronym. פַּרְצִי.—VI. פֶּרֶץ עֻזָּא pr. name of a place, 2 Sa. 6. 8; 1 Ch. 13. 11.

מִפְרָץ masc. dec. 2b, *creek* or *haven,* Ju. 5. 17.

פָּרֹץ Kal inf. abs. פרץ
פֶּרֶץ
פָּ֫רֶץ } noun masc. sing. (pl. & suff. פְּרָצֵיהֶם) d. 6a; also pr. name; for see lett. פרץ
פֹּרֵץ Kal part. act. sing. masc.; bef. lab. פרץ
פָּרְצוּ
פָּרָ֫צוּ } Kal pret. 3 pers. pl. (§ 8. rem. 7) פרץ
פְּרָצֵיהֶן noun m. pl., suff. 3 pers. s. fem. fr. פֶּרֶץ d. 6a פרץ
פְּרָצִים defect. for פְּרִיצִים (q. v.) פרץ
פְּרָצִים noun masc., pl. of פֶּרֶץ dec. 6a; also pr. name; bef. lab. פרץ
פָּרַצְתָּ
פָּרַ֫צְתָּ } Kal pret. 3 pers. sing. masc.; acc. shifted by , for , conv. (§ 8. rem. 7). פרץ
פְּרַצְתָּ֫נוּ id. id. with suff. 1 pers. pl. פרץ

[פָּרַק] I. *to break off,* Ge. 27. 40.—II. *to break, crush,* as a wild beast the limbs, Ps. 7. 3.—III. *to tear away,*

rescue, deliver. Pi. I. *to break* or *tear off.*—II. *to break* or *rend in pieces,* 1 Ki. 19. 11. Hithp. I. *to break* or *tear off from oneself,* Ex. 32. 3, 24.—II. *to be broken in pieces,* Eze. 19. 12.

פְּרַק Chald. *to break off, expiate,* Da. 4. 24.

פָּרָק masc. dec. 4a, *broth,* from the *fragments* it contains, Is. 65. 4, Kh.

פֶּרֶק masc.—I. *violence, rapine,* Na. 3. 1.—II. *cross-way,* Ob. 14.

מַפְרֶקֶת fem. dec. 13a, *the vertebra of the neck,* 1 Sa. 4. 18.

פְּרָק noun masc. sing. פרק
פֶּרֶק noun masc. sing., constr. of [פָּרָק] dec. 4a; bef. lab. פרק
פְּרֻק Chald. Peal imp. sing. masc. פרק
פֹּרֵק Kal part. act. sing. masc. פרק
פָּרְקוּ Piel imp. pl. masc. פרק
פָּרַקְתָּ id. pret. 2 pers. sing. masc.; acc. shifted by , for , conv. (§ 8. rem. 7) פרק

[פָּרַר] I. *to break in pieces,* Is. 24. 19; but see פּוּר.—II. Arab. *to be borne swiftly, to run,* see derivv. Hiph. הֵפַר, הֵפֵר (§ 18. r. 10).—I. *to break, violate.*—II. *to frustrate* a counsel; *to declare void* a vow, Nu. 30. 9, 13.—III. *to annul, abolish.*—IV. intrans. *to fail,* Ec. 12. 5. Hoph. *to come to nought, be frustrated.* Po. פּוֹרֵר *to cleave, rend,* Ps. 74. 13 Hithpo. *to be broken, rent,* Is. 24. 19. Pilp. (§ 6 No. 4) *to shake, agitate violently.*

פַּר masc. with the art. הַפָּר (pl. פָּרִים § 37 rem. 7) *a young bull, bullock.*

פָּרָה fem. (for פָּרַה § 37. rem. 7) dec. 10.—I. *young cow, heifer.*—II. הַפָּרָה pr. name of a town in the tribe of Benjamin, Jos. 18. 23.

פַּרְפַּר (*swift*) pr. name of a small stream which flows into the Amana near Damascus, 2 Ki. 5. 12.

פָּרַשׂ fut. יִפְרֹשׂ.—I. i. q. פָּרַס *to break* bread, with לְ *to give* or *distribute* (it) to.—II. *to spread,* e. g. a garment; metaph. Pr. 13. 16.—III. *to stretch out* the hands. Niph. *to be scattered,* Eze. 17. 21. Pi. I. *to spread out* the hands.—II. *to disperse, scatter.*

מִפְרָשׂ masc. dec. 2b.—I. *a spreading out, expansion,* Job 36. 29.—II. *sail of a ship,* Eze. 27. 7.

[פָּרַשׁ] prop. *to divide;* hence, *to decide, determine, declare,* Le. 24. 12. Niph. *to be dispersed, scattered,* Eze.

34. 12. Pu. *to be made clear, declared,* Nu. 15. 24; part. מְפֹרָשׁ *distinctly,* Ne. 8. 8. Hiph. *to sting, wound,* Pr. 23. 32.

פְּרַשׁ Chald. Pa. part. pass. מְפָרַשׁ *distinctly, accurately,* Ezr. 4. 18

פֶּרֶשׁ masc. dec. 6a (with suff. פִּרְשׁוֹ).—I. *dung.* —II. pr. name masc. 1 Ch. 7. 16.

פָּרָשָׁה fem. (for פַּרְשָׁה) dec. 10, *distinct declaration, specification,* Est. 4. 7; 10. 2.

פָּרָשׁ masc. (for פָּרַשׁ) dec. 1b (but constr. פָּרַשׁ § 30. rem. 1).—I. *horseman, rider.*—II. *horse for riding.*

פָּרַשׁ id., constr. st. . . . . . . פרש

פָּרוּשׁ Kal part. pass. sing. masc. [for פָּרוּשׁ] . פרש

פֵּרֵשׁ Piel pret. 3 pers. sing. masc. (comp. § 10. rem. 1); וַ, for וְ, conv. . . . פרש

פֶּרֶשׁ noun m. s. (suff. פִּרְשׁוֹ) d. 6a, also pr. name פרש

פֹּרַשׁ Pual pret. 3 pers. sing. masc. . . פרש

פֹּרֵשׁ Kal part. act. sing. masc. dec. 7b . פרש

פַּרְשֶׁגֶן, פַּתְשֶׁגֶן masc. Heb. & Chald. *transcript, copy of a writing.*

פָּרְשֵׁד Root not used; Arab. *to separate or spread out the feet.*

פַּרְשְׁדֹן masc. *the interstice of the legs,* Ju. 3. 22.

פָּרְשָׁה Kal pret. 3 pers. sing. fem. . . פרש

פֵּרְשָׁה Piel pret. 3 pers. sing. fem. . . פרש

פִּרְשָׁהּ noun masc. s., suff. 3 p. s. f. fr. פֶּרֶשׁ d. 6a פרש

פָּרְשׂוּ Kal pret. 3 pers. pl.; וַ bef. lab.   פרש

פִּרְשׁוֹ noun masc. sing., suff. 3 pers. sing. masc. from פֶּרֶשׁ dec. 6a; וְ id. . . פרש

פְּרֻשׂוֹת Kal part. pass. fem., pl. of פְּרֻשָׂה [from פָּרוּשׂ masc.] . . . . . פרש

פָּרְשֵׂז *to spread out, expand,* Job 26. 9.

פֹּרְשֵׂי Kal part. act. pl. constr. masc. from פָּרַשׂ dec. 7b; וְ bef. lab. . . פרש

פֹּרְשָׂיו the foll. with suff. 3 pers. sing. m.; וְ id. . . פרש

פָּרָשִׁים noun masc., pl. of פָּרַשׁ dec. 1b . פרש

פֹּרְשִׂים Kal part. act. pl. masc. from פָּרַשׂ dec. 7b . . פרש

פִּרְשָׂם noun masc. s., suff. 3 p. pl. m. fr. פֶּרֶשׂ d. 6a . פרש

פַּרְשַׁנְדָּתָא pr. name of one of Haman's sons, Est. 9. 7.

פָּרְשַׁת noun fem. sing., constr. of [פָּרָשָׁה] dec. 10 פרש

פָּרַשְׂתָּ Kal pret. 1 & 2 pers. sing. masc.; acc.

פָּרַשְׂתִּי shifted by וַ, for וְ, conv. (§ 8. rem. 7)

פֵּרַשְׂתִּי Piel pret. 1 pers. sing. . . פרש

פָּרֹת defect. for פָּרוֹת (q. v.) . . . פרר

פְּרָת (*sweet water*) pr. name, the river *Euphrates.*

פֹּרָת Kal part. act. sing. fem. [for פֹּרָה comp. § 24. rem. 1] from פָּרָה masc. . פרה

פְּרָתָה pr. name of a river (פְּרָת) with parag. ה פרת

פִּרְתוֹ noun fem. sing., suff. 3 pers. sing. masc. from פָּרָה dec. 10, from פָּר masc. . . פֹּ

פַּרְתְּמִים masc. only pl. פַּרְתְּמִים *nobles, princes,* Est. 1. 3; 6. 9; Da. 1. 3.

פָּשָׂה fut. יִפְשֶׂה *to spread,* as the leprosy.

פָּשֹׂה Kal inf. abs. . . . . . . פשה

פָּשׂוּ Kal pret. 3 pers. pl.; וַ, for וְ, conv.   פוש

פִּשַּׁח Pi. *to tear in pieces,* La. 3. 11.

פַּשְׁחוּר pr. name masc. of several persons, espec. a priest contemporary with Jeremiah, Je. 20. 3; 38. 1.

פָּשַׁט fut. יִפְשֹׁט.—I. *to strip or put off* a garment.— II. *to spread oneself out,* of a hostile troop, with בְּ, אֶל, עַל, *to invade.* Pi. *to strip, pillage, plunder.* Hiph. I. *to strip* a person.—II. *to strip off* a garment.—III. *to flay, skin.* Hithp. *to strip oneself,* 1 Sa. 18. 4.

פִּשְׁטָה Kal imp. s.m. [פְּשֹׁט] with parag. ה (§ 8. r. 12) פשט

פָּשְׁטוּ id. pret. 3 pers. pl. . . פשט

פֹּשְׁטִים id. part. act. masc. pl. [of פֹּשֵׁט] dec. 7b פשט

פָּשַׁטְנוּ id. pret. 1 pers. pl. . . פשט

פָּשַׁטְתָּ id. pret. 2 pers. sing. masc., acc. shifted by וַ, for וְ, conv. (§ 8. rem. 7) . פשט

פָּשַׁטְתִּי id. pret. 1 pers. sing. . . פשט

פְּשַׁטְתֶּם id. pret. 2 pers. pl. masc. . . פשט

פָּשַׂע only fut. יִפְשַׂע, *to step, pass through,* with בְּ, Is. 27. 4.

פֶּשַׂע masc. *step, stride,* 1 Sa. 20. 3.

מִפְשָׂעָה fem. *the buttocks,* 1 Ch. 19. 4.

פָּשַׁע fut. יִפְשַׁע.—I. *to revolt, rebel,* with מִתַּחַת בְּ.— II. *to transgress, sin,* with עַל *against* any one. Niph. part. *transgressed against, offended,* Pr. 18. 19.

פֶּשַׁע masc. dec. 6 (with suff. פִּשְׁעִי § 35. rem. 5). —I. *rebellion, defection.*—II. *trespass, fault.*—III. *transgression, sin.*—IV. perh. *offering for sin,* Mi. 6. 7.

פֶּשַׁע for פֶּשַׁע (q. v. § 35. rem. 2) . פשע

פָּשֹׁעַ Kal inf. abs. . . . . . . פשע

פֶּשַׁע noun masc. sing. (suff. פִּשְׁעִי) dec. 6a (§ 35. rem. 5); for וְ see lett. וְ . . פשע

a Eze. 26. 10.	e Nu. 15. 34.	i La. 1. 17.	l 1 Ki. 8. 54.	o Est. 4. 7; 10. 2.	r Job 21. 10.	t Hab. 1. 8.	x 1 Sa. 30. 14.	b 1 Sa. 27. 10.
a Joel 2. 2.	f La. 4. 4.	k Nu. 19. 5.	m Is. 19. 8.	p Ge. 41. 26.	s Le. 13. 7, 22,	u Is. 32. 11.	y Ju. 9. 33.	c Nu. 14. 18.
b Is. 25. 11.	g Pr. 31. 20.		n Le. 4. 11.	q Ge. 49. 22.	27, 35.	v Ne. 4. 17.	z Ca. 5. 3.	d Is. 59. 13.
d Mal. 2. 3, 3.								

פֹּשֵׁעַ Kal part. act. sing. masc. d. 7 b; בְ bef. lab.   פשע

פִּשְׁעָה noun masc. sing., suff. 3 pers. sing. fem. from פֶּשַׁע dec. 6a (§ 35. rem. 5;   פשע

פָּשְׁעוּ
פָשְׁעוּ } Kal pret. 3 pers. pl. (§ 8. rem. 7)   פשע

פִּשְׁעוֹ noun masc. sing., suff. 3 pers. sing. masc. from פֶּשַׁע dec. 6a (§ 35. rem. 5)   פשע

פִּשְׁעוּ וְ Kal imp. pl. masc.; בְ bef. lab.   פשע

פִּשְׁעִי
פְשָׁעִי } the foll. with suff. 1 pers. sing.; בְ id.   פשע

פִּשְׁעֵי noun m. pl. constr. from פֶּשַׁע d. 6a (§ 35.r.5)   פשע

פְּשָׁעַי id. sing., suff. 1 pers. sing.   פשע

פְּשָׁעֶיהָ id. pl., suff. 3 pers. sing. fem.   פשע

פִּשְׁעֵיהֶם id. pl., suff. 3 pers. pl. masc.; בְ bef. lab.   פשע

פְּשָׁעָיו id. pl., suff. 3 pers. sing. masc.   פשע

פְּשָׁעֶיךָ id. pl., suff. 2 pers. sing. masc.   פשע

פִּשְׁעֵיכֶם id. pl., suff. 2 pers. pl. masc.   פשע

פְּשָׁעִים id. pl., abs. st.   פשע

פֹּשְׁעִים וְ Kal part. act. m. pl. of פֹּשֵׁעַ d. 7b; בְ bef. lab.   פשע

פְּשָׁעֵינוּ n. m. pl., suff. 1 p. pl. fr. פֶּשַׁע d. 6a (§ 35.r.5)   פשע

פִּשְׁעָם id. sing., suff. 3 pers. pl. masc.   פשע

פָּשַׁעְנוּ Kal pret. 1 pers. pl.   פשע

פָּשַׁעְתְּ
פָּשָׁעַתְּ } id. pret. 2 pers. sing. fem. (§ 8. rem. 7)   פשע

פְּשַׁעְתֶּם id. pret. 2 pers. pl. masc.   פשע

[פָּשַׂק] to distend, open wide the lips, Pr. 13. 3. Pi. id. of the feet, Eze. 16. 25.

פֹּשֵׂק Kal part. act. sing. masc.   פשׂק

[פְּשַׁר] Chald. i.q. Heb. פָּתַר to interpret, explain, Da. 5. 16. Hence the two foll.

פְּשַׁר Chald. m. d. 3b, interpretation, explanation   פשר

פֵּשֶׁר masc. id. Ec. 8. 1   פשר

פִּשְׁרָא Ch. n. m. s., emph. of פְּשַׁר d. 3b; בְ bef. lab.   פשר

פִּשְׁרֵא Chald. id. with suff. 3 pers. sing. masc. for פִּשְׁרֵהּ; בְ id.   פשר

פִּשְׁרָה Chald. id. emph. st. for פִּשְׁרָא; בְ id.   פשר

פִּשְׁרֵהּ id. with suff. 3 pers. sing. masc.; בְ id.   פשר

פִּשְׁרִין id. pl., abs. st.   פשר

פֶּשֶׁת obsolete and doubtful Root, whence

פִּשְׁתָּה fem. with suff. פִּשְׁתָּהּ, pl. פִּשְׁתִּים, constr. פִּשְׁתֵּי.—I. flax; Jos. 2. 6 פִּשְׁתֵּי הָעֵץ flax of the tree, i. e. cotton.—II. linen.—III. wick of a lamp, Is. 42. 3; 43. 17.

פָּשְׁתָה
פָּשָׁתָה } Kal pret. 3 pers. sing. fem. (comp. § 8. rem. 7) } פשה

פִּשְׁתָּה noun fem. sing.; בְ bef. lab.   פשת

פִּשְׁתִּי id. with suff. 1 pers. sing.; בְ id.   פשת

פִּשְׁתִּים id. pl., abs. st.; בְ id.   פשת

פְּשַׁתֶּם־ וְ Kal pret. 2 pers. pl. masc. [for פְּשַׁתֶּם § 21. rem. 2]; בְ, for וְ, conv.   פוש

פַּת noun fem. sing. (suff. פִּתִּי) dec. 8e   פתת

פִּתְאֹם adv. [for פִּתְעֹם] see   פתע

פְּתָאִים noun masc., pl. of [פֶּתִי] d. 6i (§ 35. r. 15)   פתה

פִּתְאֹם וְ adv. [for פִּתְעֹם]; בְ bef. lab.   פתע

פַּתְבַּג masc. [constr. of פַּתְבָּג dec. 2b] delicate food, dainties; prob. compounded of פַּת (R. פָּתַת) & בַּג (q. v.); but modern interpreters assign to it a Persian origin.

פַּתְבַּגְנוֹ id. with suff. 3 pers. sing. masc.

פַּתְבַּגְנָם id. with suff. 3 pers. pl. masc.

פִּתְגָּם masc.—I. Chald. & Heb. word, sentence, decree.—II. Chald. epistle, letter, Ezr. 5. 7.—III. Chald. thing, matter, Ezr. 6. 11.

פִּתְגָּמָא Chald. id. emph. st.   פתגם

[פָּתָה] fut. יִפְתֶּה.—I. to open wide, Pr. 20. 19 פֹתֶה שְׂפָתָיו babbler.—II. prop. to be open, ingenuous; hence to be (easily) persuaded, enticed, De. 11. 16; part. act. simple, silly. Pi. I. to persuade, entice.—II. to deceive, seduce. Pu. pass. of Piel. Hiph. to make wide, to enlarge, with לְ, Ge. 9. 27.

פְּתָי Chald. masc. dec. 1a, breadth.

פֶּתִי masc. dec. 6i (pl. פְּתָאִים, פְּתָיִם § 35. rem. 15).—I. simplicity, folly, Pr. 1. 22.—II. simple, inexperienced, ignorant.

פְּתַיּוּת fem. folly, for concr. foolish, Pr. 9. 13.

פְּתוּאֵל (enlarged of God) pr. name m. Joel 1. 11.

יֶפֶת (enlargement) pr. n. Japheth, son of Noah.

פֹּתֶה וְ Kal part. act. sing. masc.; בְ bef. lab.   פתה

פִּתְהֹן noun m. s., suff. 3 pers. s. f. [§ 3. r. 5; fr. פַּת, like בְּשִׁתִּי fr. בֹּשֶׁת, comp. § 39. No. 4d]   פות

פְּתוּאֵל pr. name masc.   פתה

פָּתוֹחַ Kal inf. abs.   פתח

פָּתוּחַ id. part. pass. sing. masc.   פתח

פִּתּוּחַ noun masc. sing. dec. 1b   פתח

פְּתוּחָה Kal part. pass. sing. fem. from פָּתוּחַ masc.   פתח

פִּתּוּחֹת id. pl., comp. פְּתֻחֹת & פִּתֻחֹת   פתח

פִּתּוּחֵי noun masc. pl. constr. from פִּתּוּחַ dec. 1b   פתח

פִּתּוּחֶיהָ id. pl., suff. 3 pers. sing. fem.   פתח

a Is. 48. 8.   b Ps. 25. 7.   c La. 3. 42.   d Da. 7. 16.   e Da. 5. 16.   f Is. 42. 3.   g Mal. 3. 1.   h Da. 1. 16.   i Na. 3. 13.
b Is. 24. 20.   f La. 1. 5.   k Je. 3. 13.   n Da. 4. 15.   o Le. 13. 23.   p Ho. 2. 7, 11.   q Da. 1. 13, 15.   r Job 5. 2.   s 2 Ch. 2. 13.
c Ho. 8. 1.   g Job 36. 9.   l Zep. 3. 11.   o Da. 2. 9, 45.   p Le. 13. 8, 28.   q Mal. 3. 20.   r Da. 11. 26.   s Is. 3. 17.   t Ps. 74. 6.
d Am. 4. 4.   h Pr. 10. 12.   m Pr. 13. 3.

פְּתוּחִים   id. pl., abs. st. . . . . .   פתח

פְּתוֹרָה   pr. name of a place (פְּתוֹר) with parag. ה   פתר

פָּתוֹת   Kal inf. abs. . . . . .   פתח

פָּתַח ' fut. יִפְתַּח.—I. *to open*, as a door, window, the womb, sack, roll, &c.; יָד פָּ' *to open the hand*, with לְ, *to act liberally to any one*; אָזְנֵי פּ' to *open the ears* of any one, i. e. *to reveal anything to him*.—II. *to cleave* a rock, Ps. 105. 41.—III. *to loosen, untie*.—IV. *to draw, unsheath* a sword.—V. *to open, begin*, Ps. 49. 5. Niph. pass. of Kal Nos. I & II. Pi I. *to open*; intrans. *to open itself, to be open*.—II. *to loosen, untie*.—III. *to plough*, Is. 28. 24.—IV. *to engrave, carve, sculpture*. Pu. *to be engraved*, Ex. 39. 6. Hithp. *to loose oneself*, Is. 52. 2.

פְּתַח Chald. *to open*, Da. 6. 11; 7. 10.

פֶּתַח masc. dec. 6 (with suff. פִּתְחִי § 35. rem. 5). —I *opening, entrance*.—II. *door, gate*.

פֵּתַח masc. *opening, laying open*, Ps. 119. 130.

פִּתְחוֹן masc. dec. 3c, *an opening* of the mouth, Eze. 16. 63; 29. 21.

פִּתּוּחַ masc. dec. 1b, *engraving, carving*.

פְּתִיחָה f. d. 10, only pl. *drawn swords*, Ps. 55. 22.

פְּתַחְיָה (whom *the Lord liberates*) pr. name masc. of several persons.

יִפְתָּח (*opening*) pr. name—I. of a place in the tribe of Judah, Jos. 15. 43.—II. of a judge in Israel, *Jephtha*.

מַפְתֵּחַ masc. *key*.

מִפְתָּח masc. dec. 2b, *an opening*, Pr. 8. 6.

פָּתַח in pause for פֶּתַח (q. v. § 8. rem. 7) .   פתח

פָּתַח Kal pret. 3 pers. sing. masc. for פָּתַח (§ 8. rem. 7)   פתח

פָּתֹחַ id. inf. abs. . . . . .   פתח

פַּתֵּחַ Piel inf. constr. . . . . .   פתח

פֶּתַח noun masc. sing. . . . .   פתח

פֶּתַח ' noun masc. s. (suff. פִּתְחִי) d. 6a (§ 35. r. 5)   פתח

פְּתַח Kal imp. sing. masc. . . . .   פתח

פִּתַּח } Piel pret. 3 pers. sing. masc. (§ 15.
פִּתֵּחַ } rem. 1); ו bef. lab.   פתח

פֹּתֵחַ Kal part. act. sing. masc. dec. 7b .   פתח

פָּתְחָה ' id. pret. 3 pers. sing. fem.; ו, for וְ, conv.   פתח

פִּתְּחָה Piel pret. 3 pers. sing. fem. . .   פתח

פְּתָחָהּ ' noun masc. sing., suff. 3 pers. sing. fem. from פֶּתַח (§ 35. rem. 5) d. 6a; ו bef. lab.   פתח

פְּתָחָיו " noun masc. s., suff. 3 p. s. f. fr. פֶּתַח d. 1b   פתח

פָּתְחוּ
פָּתְחוּ } Kal pret. 3 pers. pl. (§ 8. rem. 7)   פתח

פִּתְחוֹ n.m.s.,suff. 3 p. s. m. fr. פֶּתַח (§35. r. 5) d. 6a   פתח

פִּתְחוּ Kal imp. pl. masc. . . . .   פתח

פַּתְּחוּ ' Piel imp. pl. masc.; ו bef. lab. .   פתח

פִּתְחוֹן noun masc. sing., constr. of [פִּתָּחוֹן] dec. 3c   פתח

פְּתִיחוֹת ' noun fem., pl. of [פְּתִיחָה] dec. 10   פתח

פְּתֻחוֹת defect. of פְּתוּחוֹת (q. v.) . .   פתח

פְּתָחַי " the fol'. with suff. 1 pers. sing. . .   פתח

פִּתְחֵי noun m. pl. constr. fr. פֶּתַח d. 6a (§ 35. r. 5)   פתח

פִּתְחִי Kal imp. sing. fem. . . . .   פתח

פְּתָחֶיהָ ' noun masc. pl., suff. 3 pers. sing. fem. from פֶּתַח dec. 6a (§ 35. rem. 5)   פתח

פְּתַחְיָה ' pr. name masc.; ו bef. lab. . .   פתח

פִּתְחֵיהֶם ' noun masc. pl., suff. 3 pers. pl. masc. from פֶּתַח dec. 6a (§ 35. rem. 5); ו id.   פתח

פְּתָחִים " id. pl., abs. st. . . . . .   פתח

פְּתָחֵינוּ ' id. pl., suff. 1 pers. sing. . .   פתח

פְּתֻחֹת defect. for פְּתוּחוֹת (q. v.) . .   פתח

פָּתַחְתָּ ' Kal pret. 2 p. s. m.; ו, for וְ, conv. (§ 8. r. 7)   פתח

פִּתַּחְתָּ ' Piel pret. 2 pers. sing. masc.; ו id.   פתח

פָּתַחְתִּי Kal pret. 1 pers. sing. . . .   פתח

פִּתַּחְתִּיךָ ' Piel pret. 1 pers. sing., suff. 2 pers. sing. m.   פתח

פִּתְחִי Piel imp. sing. fem. . . . .   פתח

פֶּתִי ' n.m.s. [for פֶּתִי §35. r. 14] d. 6i; ו bef. lab.   פתח

פַּתִּי noun fem., suff. 1 pers. s. fr. פַּת d. 8e   פתח

פְּתִיגִיל ' masc. Is. 3. 24, Eng. vers. " stomacher;" according to others, *a wide mantle*. Etymology obscure.

פִּתְיֵהּ Ch. noun m. s., suff. 3 p. s. m. fr. [פְּתִי] d. 1a   פתה

פְּתִיחַן Ch. Peal part. pass. 3 p. pl. m. (§ 47. r. 11)   פתה

פְּתִיחוּת ' noun fem. sing. . . . .   פתה

פְּתִיחָן Ch. Peal part. pass. fem. pl. [of פְּתִיחָא from פְּתִיחַ masc.] . . . .   פתה

פְּתָיִים " noun masc., pl. of [פֶּתִי] d. 6i; ו bef. lab.   פתה

פָּתִיל noun masc. sing. dec. 3a . .   פתל

פְּתִיל ' id., constr. st.; ו bef. lab. . .   פתל

פְּתִילֶךָ ' id., suff. 2 pers. s. m. [for פְּתִילְךָ]; ו id.   פתל

פְּתִילִם id. pl., abs. st. . . . .   פתל

פְּתִים defect. for פְּתָיִים (q. v.) . .   פתה

פִּתִּים noun fem., pl. of פַּת dec. 8e . .   פתת

פִּתִּיתִי Piel pret. 1 pers. sing. (§ 24. rem. 11)   פתה

פִּתִּיתַנִי " id. pret. 2 pers. sing. masc., suff. 1 pers. s.   פתה

פִּתֵּךְ ' noun fem. sing., suff. 2 pers. sing. masc. from פַּת dec. 8e . . . .   פתת

פַּתֵּךְ id. with suff. 2 pers. sing. fem.   פתת

* 2 Ch. 2. 6.   / Is. 58. 6.   * Is. 48. 8.   ¶ Pr. 17. 19.   * Ca. 5. 2.   ª 1 Ki. 8. 29, 52.   ² Is. 3. 24.   ª Pr. 22. 3.   * Pr. 1. 22, 32.
* Le. 2. 6.   g Ps. 119. 130.   ' Ez. 40. 38.   * Is. 60. 11.   y Is. 3. 26.   ª 2 Ki. 9. 3.   ² Da. 7. 10.   ª Nu. 19. 15.   ' Eze. 14. 9.
* Ps. 78. 23.   * 2 Ch. 3. 7.   ' Zec. 3. 9.   * Ps. 55. 22.   * Eze. 42. 4.   ª Je. 40. 4.   ² Pr. 9. 13.   ³ Eze. 40. 3.   * Je. 20. 7.
De. 15. 8, 11   ' Pr. 31. 26.   * Ps. 109. 2.   ' 2 Ch. 6. 40; 7. 15.   * Pr. 8. 3.   ' Pr. 19. 25.   ² Da. 6. 11.   ' Ge. 38. 18.   * Pr. 23. 8.
  * De. 20. 11.   * Ps. 37. 14.   ᵖ Pr. 8. 34.   ' Ca. 7. 14.   ' Job 31. 17.   * Ps. 119. 130.   * Ex. 39. 3.   y Ru. 2. 14.

פָּתַל Niph. I. prop. *to be twisted*, only metaph. *to be perverse, false, deceitful.*—II. *to wrestle, struggle*, Ge. 30. 8. Hithp. *to show oneself false*, Ps. 18. 27; 2 Sa. 22. 27; Prof. Lee, *to struggle*.

פָּתִיל masc. dec. 3a, *thread, string, cord*; also *a string for a signet-ring*, Ge. 38. 18, 25.

פְּתַלְתֹּל masc. *crooked, perverse*, De. 32. 5.

נַפְתּוּל masc. dec. 1 b, only pl. *wrestlings, struggles*, De. 32. 5.

נַפְתָּלִי (*my wrestling*, Ge. 30. 8) pr. name, *Naphtali*, son of Jacob by Bilhah.

פְּתַלְתֹּל• adj. masc. sing.; ו bef. lab. . . פתל
פִּתֹם pr. name, *Pithom*, a city in Egypt, on the eastern bank of the Nile, Ex. 1. 11.

פֶּתֶן ,ֶ[וֹ']masc. dec. 6 a, *asp*. פֶּתַן prob. i. q. פָּתַל *to twist*; מִפְתָּן masc. dec. 2 b, *threshold*. Arab. פתן *to be strong, firm* (Gesenius).

פֶּתֶן′ noun masc. sing. dec. 6, for פֶּתֶן (§ 35. rem. 2); for ו see lett. ו . . . . פתן

פְּתָנִים id. pl., abs. st . . . . . פתן

פֶּתַע masc. *suddenness*, hence—I. פֶּתַע ,בְּפֶתַע adv. *sud-*

denly.—II. בְּפֶתַע, *accidentally, undesignedly*, Nu. 35. 22.

פִּתְאֹם (for פִּתְעֹם) adv. *suddenly*; בְּפִתְאֹם id ′פּ ,לְפֶתַע פִּ′ ,בְּפֶתַע פֶּ′ ,פֶתַע פּ′ *very suddenly*.

פָּתַר fut. יִפְתֹּר *to interpret, explain.*

פְּתוֹר (*interpretation*) pr. name of the residence of Balaam.

פִּתְרוֹן masc. dec. 1 b, *interpretation*.

פָּתַר Kal pret. 3 pers. sing. m. for פָּתַר (§ 8. r. 7) פתר
פֹּתֵר ,ֶ id. part. act. sing. masc.; ו bef. lab. . . פתר
פַּתְרוֹס pr. name of a country in Egypt; according to some, *Upper Egypt*. Gent. n. פַּתְרֻסִים.

פִּתְרֹנוֹ′ noun m. s., suff. 3 p. s. m. fr. פִּתָרוֹן′ d. 1 b פתר
פִּתְרֹנִים′ id. pl., abs. st. . . . . . פתר

פַּתְרֻס pr. name of a region, see פַּתְרוֹס.

פַּתְרֻסִים gent. noun, pl. from the preced.

פַּתְשֶׁגֶן noun masc. i. q. פַּרְשֶׁגֶן (q. v.).

[פָּתַת] *to break*, Le. 2. 6.

פַּת fem. d. 8 e, *piece, crumb, morsel*, sc. of bread
פִּתּוֹת masc. dec. 1 a, id. Eze. 13. 19.

צ

צֵא ,ֶ[וֹ']Kal imp. sing. masc. . . . יצא
צֵאָה id. with parag. ה [for צֵאָה]; for ו see let. ו יצא
צֵאָה noun fem. sing. dec. 10 . . . . יצא
צְאוּ
ו,ֶ } Kal imp. pl. masc.; ו bef. (ְ) . . . יצא
צְאוֹנֵנוּ Kh. צְאוֹנֵנוּ noun com. sing., suff. 1 pers. pl.
[from צָאוֹן]; K. צֹאנֵנוּ (q. v.) . . צאן
צְאִי Kal imp. sing. fem. . . . . יצא
צֶאינָה id. imp. pl. fem. (§ 23. rem. 3) . . יצא
צֶאֱלִים m. pl. Job 40. 21, 22, *lotus bushes*, coll. with the Arab. צאל, so Schultens; others, *shades*, i. e. *shady trees* [for צְלָלִים].

צֹאן ,ֶ[וֹ'] (for צָאן) com. dec. 1 a, collect.—I. *small cattle, sheep and goats.*—II. *flock, flocks of sheep and goats*; metaph. of a people.
צֹאון idem, Ps. 144. 13, Khethib.
צַאֲנָן (*place of flocks*; others, *fertile*) pr. name of a place in the tribe of Judah, Mi. 1. 11.

צֹאנוֹ id. with suff. 3 pers. sing. masc. . . צאן

צֹאנִי ,ֶ[וֹ″] id., suff. 1 pers. sing. . . . צאן
צֹאנֵינוּ′ ,ֶ id. pl. or sing. (for צֹאנֵנוּ), suff. 1 pers. pl. צאן
צֹאנֶךָ′ ,ֶ
ו,ֶ } id., suff. 2 pers. sing. masc. . . צאן
צֹאנֶךָ
צֹאנְכֶם′ ,ֶ[וֹ″] id., suff. 2 pers. pl. masc. . . צאן
צֹאנָם ,ֶ[וֹ'] id., suff. 3 pers. pl. masc. . . צאן
צַאֲנָן′ pr. name of a place . . . . צאן
צֶאֱצָאַי′ the coll. with suff. 1 pers. sing. . . יצא
צֶאֱצָאִים′ noun masc. pl. constr. fr. [צֶאֱצָא] dec. 1 b יצא
צֶאֱצָאֶיהָ′ id. pl., suff. 3 pers. sing. fem. . יצא
צֶאֱצָאֵיהֶם id. pl., suff. 3 pers. pl. masc. . יצא
צֶאֱצָאָיו′ id. pl., suff. 3 pers. sing. masc. . יצא
צֶאֱצָאֶיךָ′ ,ֶ id. pl., suff. 2 pers. sing. masc. . יצא
צֵאת″ noun fem. sing., constr. of [צֵאָה] dec. 10 יצא
צֵאת Kal inf. constr. [for צֵאֶת § 25. No. 2 d] יצא
צֵאת′ ,ֶ noun fem. sing., constr. of צֵאָה dec. 10 יצא
צֵאתוֹ Kal inf. [for צֵאֶת § 25. No. 2 d], suff. 3 pers. sing. masc. . . . . . יצא
צֵאתֵךְ′ noun fem sing., suff. 2 pers. sing. masc. [for צֵאָתֵךְ from צֵאָה dec. 10 יצא

• De. 32. 5.   ⁴ Is. 11. 8.   ⁴ Ju. 9. 29.   ᵏ Ca. 1. 8.   ⁿ Ne. 10. 37.   ᵖ Is. 48. 19.   ʳ Job 27. 14.   ᵗ Job 5. 25.   ⁴ Is. 4. 4.
Ps. 58. 5.   ᵉ Ge. 40. 12, 18.   ⁱ Is. 28. 8.   ⁱ Ca. 3. 11.   Job 31. 8.   ᵠ Is. 34. 1; 42. 5.   ˢ Is. 44. 3.   ᵘ Eze. 4. 12.   ʸ De. 23. 14.
Ps. 91. 13.   ᶠ Ge. 40. 8.   Ps. 144. 13.   ᵐ Eze. 34. 19.   ∞ De. 12. 6.

צֵאתְךָ '1 Kal inf. (צֵאת for צֵאָת § 25. No. 2 d), suff. 2 pers. sing. masc. . . . . . יצא

צֵאתָם id., suff. 3 pers. pl. masc. . . . . יצא

צֵאתֵנוּ id., suff. 1 pers. pl. . . . . . יצא

צָב noun masc. sing. dec. 8 a . . . . . צבב

[צָבָא] I. *to go forth to war*, *to carry on war*, with עַל against any one.—II. *to go forth to service, to serve in the temple.* Hence

צָבָא '1 masc. (fem. Is. 40. 2; Da. 8. 12) dec. 4 a, constr. צְבָא (§ 33. rem. 2), pl. צְבָאִים, צְבָאוֹת (Ps. 103. 21; 148. 2).—I. *army, host*; אַנְשֵׁי צָ' *warriors, soldiers;* שַׂר הַצָּ' *captain of the host, commander in chief;* צְבָא הַשָּׁמַיִם *host of heaven,* 1. e. *the angels,* sometimes also *the sun, moon and stars* ; hence the epithet אֱלֹהֵי צָ', יְהֹוָה צְבָאוֹת —II. *warfare, military service;* trop. *struggle, trial, affliction.*

[צְבָא] Chald. *to will, please, choose.*

צְבוּ Chald. fem. *determination, resolution, purpose,* Da. 6. 18.

צָבֵא Chald. Peal part. act. sing. masc. . . . צבא

צְבָא '1 noun masc. sing., constr. of צָבָא dec. 4 a (§ 33. rem. 2) ; 1 bef. (:) . . . . . צבא

צְבָאָהּ id. with suff. 3 pers. sing. fem. . . . צבא

צָבְאוּ Kal pret. 3 pers. pl. . . . . . צבא

צְבָאָיו n. m. pl. with suff. 3 p. s. m. from צָבָא dec. 4 a צבא

צְבָאוֹ '1 id. sing., suff. 3 pers. sing. masc.; 1 bef. (:) צבא

צְבָאוֹת id. pl. abs. fem. . . . . . צבא

צִבְאוֹת id. pl. constr. fem. . . . . . צבא

צִבְאוֹתֵיכֶם id. pl. fem., suff. 2 pers. pl. masc. . . צבא

צְבָאִי id. sing., suff. 1 pers. sing. . . . . צבא

צְבָאָיו id. pl. masc., suff. 3 pers. sing. masc. . צבא

צְבָאֶךָ id. sing., suff. 2 pers. sing. masc. . . צבא

צְבָאָם id. sing., suff. 3 pers. pl. masc. . . . צבא

צִבְאֹתַי id. pl. fem., suff. 1 pers. sing. . . . . צבא

צִבְאֹתָם id. pl. fem., suff. 3 pers. pl. masc. (§ 4. rem. 1) צבא

צָבַב Root not used; Arab. *to cover.*

צָב עֶגְלַת masc. dec. 8 a.—I. *covering,* covered waggon, Nu. 7. 3, and (without עֶגְלָה) Is. 66. 20, id.—II. a species of *lizard,* Le. 11. 29.

צֹבֵבָה (*stout, fat,* Simonis) pr. name f. 1 Ch. 4. 8.

[צָבָה] *to swell,* Nu. 5. 27. Arab. *to shine,* comp. צְבִי, perh. prim. *to be prominent.*

צָבָה, fem. צָבֶה adj. *swelling,* Nu. 5. 21.

צְבִי masc. dec. 6 i.—I. *splendour, beauty, glory.*—II. *gazelle;* pl. צְבָיִים, צְבָאִים, צְבָאוֹת (§ 35. r. 15).

צִבְיָא (*gazelle*) pr. name masc. 1 Ch. 8. 9.

צְבִיָּה (id.) pr. name of the mother of king Josiah.

צְבִיָּה fem. *female gazelle,* Ca. 4. 5 ; 7. 4.

צְבֹיִם, צְבֹיִים, צְבֹיִם (*gazelles*) pr. name of one of the cities destroyed with Sodom.

צָבָה adj. fem. sing. [from צָבֶה masc.] . . . צבה

צְבוּ Ch. noun fem. sing. . . . . . צבה

צָבוּעַ noun masc. sing. . . . . . צבע

[צָבַט] *to reach* or *hold out,* Ru. 2. 14.

צְבִי '1 noun masc. sing. dec. 6 i ; 1 bef. (:) . צבה

צִבְיָא pr. name masc. . . . . . צבה

צְבִיָּה noun fem. sing. from צְבִי masc. . . צבה

צְבִיָּה pr. name fem. . . . . . צבה

צֹבְיָה Kal part. act. pl. masc., suff. 3 pers. sing fem. [for צֹבְאֶיהָ from צָבָא] . . . צבא

צְבֹיִים, צְבֹיִם '1 pr. name of a place ; 1 bef. (:) . צבה

צְבִית Chald. Peal pret. 1 pers. sing. . . . צבא

צָבַע Root not used; Arab. *to dip in, to tinge, dye.*

צְבַע Chald. Aph. *to wet, moisten,* Da. 4. 22. Ithp. אִצְטַבַּע pass.

צֶבַע masc. *dyed garments,* Ju. 5. 30; pl. צְבָעִים

צָבוּעַ masc. *hyena,* Je. 12. 9. Arab. צבע id.

צְבֹעִים (*hyenas*) pr. name, *Zeboim,* a valley and town in the tribe of Benjamin.

צִבְעוֹן (*coloured*) pr. name of a son of Seir.

אֶצְבַּע fem. dec. 2 b (pl. אֶצְבָּעוֹת § 31. rem. 5). —I. *finger,* espec. *forefinger;* pl. *fingers,* poet. for *hand,* Ps. 8. 4 ; 144. 1.—II. *a digit,* a measure, Je. 52. 21.—III. with רַגְלַיִם *a toe.*

אֶצְבַּע Chald. dec. 2 a, only אֶצְבְּעָן *fingers,* Da. 5. 5 ; *toes,* Da. 2. 41, 42.

צֶבַע noun masc. sing. dec. 6 (§ 35. rem. 5) . צבע

צִבְעוֹן '1 pr. name masc. . . . . . צבע

צְבָעִים noun masc., pl. of צֶבַע dec. 6 (§ 35. rem. 5) צבע

צְבֹעִים pr. name of a valley . . . . . צבע

צָבַר only fut. יִצְבֹּר.—I. *to heap up.*—II. *to lay, treasure up.* Hence

צִבֻּרִים noun masc. pl. [of צִבּוּר] *heaps,* 2 Ki. 10. 8 צבר

צָבַת Root not used; Arab. *to bind,* also *to take in the hand.*

צֶבֶת m. *bundle, sheaf,* Ru. 2. 16 ; others, *handful*

צבה   צָבְתָה ‖ Kal pret. 3 pers. sing. fem.

צדד   צַד noun masc. sing. (suff. צִדּוֹ) dec. 8 e

צָדַד Root not used; Arab. *to turn away*; Talm. צָדַד *to turn one's side* to any one.

צַד masc. dec. 8 e.—I. *side*; with ה parag. צָדָה *to* or *at the side*, 1 Sa. 20. 20; מִצַּד *at the side of*; עַל צַד *on the side*, i. e. where a child is carried upon the arm, comp. Is. 60. 4.—II. *adversary*, Ju. 2. 3.

צַד Chald. *side*; מִצַּד *on the side of*, in reference to Da. 6. 5; לְצַד *against*, Da. 7. 25.

צָדִים (*sides*) pr. name of a town in Naphtali, Jos. 19. 35. Also

צְדָדָה pr. name [צְדָד] with local ה, a place in the north of Palestine, Nu. 34. 8; Eze. 47. 15   צדד

צָדָה *to lie in wait for*. Niph. *to be destroyed, desolated*, Zep. 3. 6.

צְדָא Chald. *purpose, intention*, Da. 3. 14, הַצְדָא *was it on purpose?* According to Fürst, *it is derision, mockery*, for אַצְדָא (§ 47. rem. 4) Targ. אַצְדֵּי Aph. *to deride*, R. צְדָה.

צְדִיָּה fem. *purpose, design*, Nu. 35. 20, 22.

צוד   צֵדָה defect. for צֵידָה (q. v.)

צדד   צֵדֹה noun masc. sing. (צַד) with parag. ה dec. 8 e

צדה   צֹדֶה Kal part. act. sing. masc.

צוד   צָדוּ Kal pret. 3 pers. pl.

צוד   צָדוּם ‖ id., suff. 3 pers. pl. masc.

צוד   צָדוּנִי id., suff. 1 pers. sing.

צדק   צָדוֹק ‖ pr. name masc.

צדד   צָדֵי noun masc. pl. constr. from צַד dec. 8 e

צדה   צְדִיָּה noun fem. sing.

צדד   צָדָיו noun m. pl., suff. 3 pers. s. m. fr. צַד d. 8 e

צדק   צַדִּיק ‖ adj. masc. sing. dec. 1 b

צדק   צַדִּיקִים / צַדִּיקֵם ‖ id. pl., abs. st.

צדד   צִדְּךָ / צִדֶּךָ ‖ noun masc. sing., suff. 2 pers. sing. masc. from צַד dec. 8 e

צוד   צִדֹנִי gent. noun from צִידוֹן

צוד   צִדֹנִים / צִדֹנִין ‖ id. pl. masc.

צוד   צִדֹנִית id. pl. fem.

[צָדַק] fut. יִצְדַּק.—I. *to be just, righteous, equitable.*—II. *to be in the right, to have a just cause.*—III. *to be right, correct*, Job 33. 12.—IV. *to be declared righteous, be justified.* Niph. Da. 8. 14, *to be puri-*

fied, so the Sept. and Vulg. Others, *to be justified, vindicated*, sc. from injury. Pi. *to justify.* Hiph. I. *to make righteous, lead to righteousness or justification*, Da. 12. 3.—II. *to do justice to*, 2 Sa. 15. 4—III. *to pronounce just, righteous, to justify*, with acc. לְ. Hithp. *to justify oneself*, Ge. 44. 16.

צָדוֹק (*just*) pr. name of the father-in-law of king Josiah and several other men.

צַדִּיק adj. masc. dec. 1 b.—I. *just, equitable* in the administration of justice.—II. *just, righteous* in character and general conduct.—III. *having a just cause.*—IV. *blameless, innocent.*—V. *true*, Is. 41. 26.

צֶדֶק masc. dec. 6 a (with suff. צִדְקִי), & צְדָקָה dec. 11 c.—I. *justice, equity* in the administration of justice.—II. *righteousness, justice* of character and conduct.—III. *right, what is right, fair.*—IV. *truth*, comp. Ps. 52. 5.—V. *justification, acquittal*, Job 6. 29; Da. 9. 24.—VI. pl. צְדָקוֹת *righteous acts, righteousness.*

צִדְקָה Chald. fem. *equity, righteousness*, Da. 4. 24

צִדְקִיָּהוּ (*justice of the Lord*) pr. name—I. of a king of Judah.—II. of a false prophet under Ahab, called also צִדְקִיָּה, 1 Ki. 22. 11.—III. of three other men.

צדק   צֶדֶק /צֶ׳/ noun masc. sing. (suff. צִדְקִי) dec. 6 a; for וְ see lett. ו

צדק   צָדְקָה Kal pret. 3 pers. sing. fem.

צדק   צְדָקָה /צְ׳/ noun fem. sing. dec. 11 c; וְ bef. (:)

צדק   צִדְּקָה Piel pret. 3 pers. sing. fem.

צדק   צִדְקָתֹה noun masc. sing., suff. 3 pers. sing. fem. from צֶדֶק dec. 6 a

צדק   צָדְקוּ Kal pret. 3 pers. pl.

צדק   צַדְּקוֹ Piel inf. (צַדֵּק), suff. 3 pers. sing. m. d. 7 b

צדק   צִדְקוֹ noun m. s., suff. 3 pers. s. m. fr. צֶדֶק d. 6 a

צדק   צְדָקוֹת noun fem. pl. abs. from צְדָקָה dec. 11 c

צדק   צִדְקוֹת id. pl., constr. st.

צדק   צִדְקִי noun m. sing., suff. 1 pers. sing. fr. צֶדֶק d. 6 a

צדק   צִדְקִיָּה / צִדְקִיָּהוּ /צִ׳/ pr. name masc.

צדק   צַדִּקִים /צַ׳/ defect. for צַדִּיקִים (q. v.)

צדק   צַדֶּקְךָ Piel inf. (צַדֵּק), suff. 2 pers. sing. masc. [for צַדֶּקְךָ dec. 7 b. § 16. rem. 15]

צדק   צִדְקָתֵךְ noun m. s., suff. 2 pers. s. fem. fr. צֶדֶק d. 6 a

צדק   צִדְקָתְךָ id., suff. 2 pers. sing. masc. for צִדְקָתְךָ

צדק   צִדְקֵנוּ id., suff. 1 pers. pl.

צדק   צָדַקְתִּי Kal pret. 1 pers. sing.

צדק   צִדְקַת /צִ׳/ noun fem. sing., constr. of צְדָקָה dec. 11 c

● Nu. 5. 27.   ¹ 1 Sa. 24. 12.   ᵍ La. 3. 52.   ᵏ Eze. 4. 8.   ⁿ Ps. 85. 12.   • Je. 3. 11.   ᵗ Ps. 19. 10.   ᵘ Ho. 14. 10.   ᵉ Is. 62. 1.
Ex. 21. 13.   ᵈ La. 4. 18.   ʰ Ex. 26. 13.   Eze. 4. 4, 6, 9.   ᵖ Ge. 38. 26.   ᵖ Is. 62. 1.   ʳ Job 32. 2.   ᵗ Job 33. 32.   ᶻ Is. 5. 28.
● 1 Sa. 20. 20.   ● Je. 16. 16.   ᶜ Nu. 35. 22.

וְצִדְקָתוֹ	id., suff. 3 pers. sing. masc.	צדק
צִדְקֹתָיו	id. pl., suff. 3 pers. sing. masc.	צדק
וְצִדְקָתִי	Kal pret. 1 pers. sing.	צדק
וְצִדְקָתִי	noun fem. s., suff. 1 pers. s. fr. צְדָקָה d. 11c	צדק
צִדְקֹתֶיךָ	id. pl., suff. 2 pers. sing. masc.	צדק
צִדְקֹתֵינוּ	id. pl., suff. 1 pers. pl.	צדק
צִדְקָתֵךְ	id. sing., suff. 2 pers. sing. fem.	צדק
צִדְקָתֶךָ / וְצִדְקָתְךָ	id. sing., suff. 2 pers. sing. masc.	צדק
וְצִדְקָתָם	id. sing., suff. 3 pers. pl. masc.	צדק

צָהֹב , only Hoph. part. *shining like gold,* or perh. *gold-coloured,* Ezr. 8.27. Hence

צָהֹב adj. *gold-coloured, yellow,* Le. 13.30, 32 . צהב

[צָהַל] I. *to neigh,* of a horse, Je. 5.8; of persons, *to shout for joy;* also *for fear,* Is. 10.30.—II. i.q. זָהַר *to shine,* only Hiph. *to cause to shine,* Ps. 104.15.

מִצְהָלָה fem. d. 11a, *a neighing,* Je. 8.16; 13.27.

צָהֲלָה	Kal pret. 3 pers. sing. fem.	צהל
צָהֲלוּ	id. pret. 3 pers. pl.	צהל
וְצַהֲלוּ	id. imp. pl. masc.	צהל
וְצַהֲלִי	id. imp. sing. fem.	צהל

צָהַר Kal not used; i.q. זָהַר *to shine.* Hiph. (denom. from יִצְהָר) *to make* or *press out oil,* Job 24.11.

צֹהַר masc. dec. 6f.—I. *a light, window,* Ge. 6.16.—II. du. צָהֳרַיִם (§ 35. rem. 9 & 16) *noon,* metaph. of great prosperity.

יִצְהָר masc. dec. 2b.—I. *oil,* espec. *new oil.*—II. pr. name of a son of Kohath. Patronym. יִצְהָרִי.

צַר masc. (for צָהָר, צֹהַר *splendour*) *the moon,* so according to some, in Is. 5.30.

צֶרֶת (for צֶהֶרֶת *splendour*) pr. name—I. of a man, 1 Ch. 4.7.—II. צֶרֶת הַשַּׁחַר (*splendour of the dawn*) of a city in Reuben, Jos. 13.19.

צֹהַר	noun fem. sing. dec. 6f	צהר
צָהֳרַיִם / וְצָהֳרָיִם	id. du., abs. st.	צהר
צָו	noun masc. sing. for צַו	צוה
וְצָו	ap. for צַוָּה q. v.; or (Is. 28. 10, 13) n. m.	צוה
צֹאִים	adj. masc., pl. of [צֹא] dec. 1a	יצא
צַוָּאר	noun masc. sing. dec. 2b	צור
צַוַּאר	id., constr. st.	צור
צַוָּארָהּ	id., suff. 3 pers. sing. fem.	צור
צַוְּארֵהּ	Ch. id., suff. 3 pers. sing. masc.	צור
צַוָּארוֹ	id. pl., suff. 3 p. s. m. for צַוָּארָיו (§ 4. rem. 1)	צור

צַוָּארוֹ	id. sing., suff. 3 pers. sing. masc.	צור
צַוָּארִי	id. sing., suff. 1 pers. sing.	צור
צַוְּארֵי	id. pl., constr. st.	צור
צַוְּארֵיהֶם	id. pl., suff. 3 pers. pl. masc.	צור
צַוָּארָיו	id. pl., suff. 3 pers. sing. masc.	צור
צַוְּארֵיכֶם	id. pl., suff. 2 pers. pl. masc.	צור
צַוָּארֵךְ	id. sing., suff. 2 pers. sing. fem.	צור
צַוְּארָךְ	Ch. id. sing., suff. 2 pers. sing. masc.	צור
צַוָּארֶךָ [for צַוָּארְךָ]	id. sing., suff. 2 pers. sing. m.	צור
צַוָּארֵנוּ	id. sing., suff. 1 pers. pl.	צור
צַוְּארֹתֵיכֶם	id. pl. fem., suff. 2 pers. pl. masc.	צור
צוֹבָא / צוֹבָה	pr. name of a place	נצב

[צוּד] *to hunt* wild beasts; *to lay snares* for birds; metaph. *to hunt, pursue* men. Pil. *to ensnare, beguile,* Eze 13.18, 20. Hithp. הִצְטַיָּר (denom. from צַיִד) *to furnish oneself with provision,* Jos. 9.12.

צַיִד masc. dec. 6h.—I. *a hunting,* Ge. 10.9.—II. *game, venison,* Ge. 25.28.—III. *provision, food.*

צֵדָה , צֵידָה fem. *provision, food.*

צַיָּד masc. dec. 1b, *hunter,* Je. 16.16.

צִידוֹן , צִידֹן (*fishery*) pr. name, *Zidon,* an ancient city of Phœnicia.—Gent. noun צִידֹנִי, pl. f. צִידֹנִית, strong place, citadel, fortress.

מָצֹד masc. dec. 1a (pl. מְצֹדוֹת abs. & constr.) *strong place, citadel, fortress.*

מָצוֹד masc. dec. 3a (with suff. מְצוֹדִי § 32. rem. 5).—I. *capture, prey,* Pr. 12.12.—II. *net of hunters.*—III. *fortress,* Ec. 9.14.

מְצוֹדָה fem. d. 10.—I. *net,* Ec. 9.12.—II. *citadel, fortress.*

מְצוּדָה f. d. 10.—I. *capture, prey,* Eze. 13.21.—II. *net of a hunter,* Eze. 12.13.—III. *citadel, fortress.*

צוּד	Kal inf. abs.	צוד
וְצוּדָה	id. imp. sing. masc. with parag. ה	צוד

צִוָּה Kal not used; Syr. *to set up, erect.* Pi. צִוָּה.—I. *to set over, appoint, constitute,* with acc. of the person and עַל of the thing.—II. *to appoint, determine, decree.*—III. *to charge, command,* with acc., also עַל, אֶל, לְ.—IV. *to send with orders, to commission,* with לְ, אֶל, עַל, *to* or *concerning* whom; צִוָּה לְבֵיתוֹ *to give one's last orders to his family.* Pu. *to be commanded, charged.*

צַו masc. *command, precept.*

צִיּוּן masc. dec. 1b.—I. *pillar, monument.*—II. *way-mark,* Je. 31.21.

מִצְוָה fem. dec. 10, *commandment, precept.*

a Job 10.15.	d Is. 54.17.	g Je. 31.7.	k Ps. 55.18.	m Zec. 3.3.	q Ge. 33.4.	t Je. 27.12.	x La. 5.5.	z La. 3. 52
b Da. 9.16.	e Est. 8.15.	h Is. 54.1.	l Ho. 5.11.	n Ho. 10.11.	r La. 1.14.	u Da. 5.16.	y Mi. 2.3.	Ge. 27.9
Is. 57.12.	Is. 24.14.	Ge. 6.16.	De. 3.28.	Da. 5.7, 29.	Jos. 10.24.			

42

צַוֵּה	Piel imp. sing. masc. . .	צוה
צִוָּה	ן id. pret. 3 pers. sing. masc. . .	צוה
צֻוָּה	Pual pret. 3 pers. sing. masc.	צוה
צִוָּהוּ	Piel pret. 3 pers. sing. m., suff. 3 pers. s. m.	צוה
צַוּוּ	ן id. imp. pl. masc. . .	צוה

[צָנַח] to cry, shout for joy, Is. 42. 11.   Hence

צְוָחָה	fem. dec. 11c, a cry for joy or sorrow .	צוח
צִוְחַת	ן id., constr. st. . . .	צוח
צִוְחָתֵךְ	ן id., suff. 2 pers. sing. fem.	צוח
צִוִּיתָ	}	
צִוִּיתִי	} Piel pret. 2 pers. sing. masc. (comp. § 8.	
צִוִּיתָה	} rem. 5 & 7) . . .	צוה
צֻוֵּיתָה	Pual pret. 2 pers. sing. masc. (comp. § 8. r. 5)	צוה
צִוֵּיתִי	} Piel pret. 1 pers. sing (§ 24. rem. 11)	צוה
צֻוֵּיתִי	Pual pret. 1 pers. sing. . .	צוה
צִוִּיתִיהָ	Piel pret. 1 pers. sing., suff. 3 pers. sing. fem.	צוה
צִוִּיתִיו	id. id., suff. 3 pers. sing. masc.	צוה
צִוִּיתִיךָ	id. id., suff. 2 pers. sing. masc.	צוה
צִוִּיתִים	id. id., suff. 3 pers. pl. masc.	צוה
צִוִּיתְךָ	defect. for צִוִּיתִיךָ (q. v.) .	צוה
צִוִּיתָם	defect. for צִוִּיתִים (q. v.) .	צוה
צִוִּיתָנוּ	Piel pret. 2 pers. sing. masc., suff. 1 pers. pl.	צוה
צִוִּיתַנִי	id. id., suff. 1 pers. sing. [for תַנִי' § 2. r. 1]	צוה
צִוָּךְ	} id. pret. 3 pers. sing. masc. (צִוָּה), suff.	
צִוְּךָ	} ן 2 pers. sing. masc. (§ 24. rem. 21) }	צוה

צוּל Root not used; prob. i. q. צָלַל to sink.

צוּלָה fem. the deep, Is. 44. 27.

מְצוֹלָה, מְצוּלָה fem. dec. 10, depth, deep place.

[צוּם] to fast.   Hence

צוֹם	ן masc. dec. 1 a (pl. צוֹמוֹת), a fast, fasting	צום
צָמוּ	Piel pret. 3 pers. sing. masc. (צִוָּה), suff.	
	3 pers. pl. masc. (§ 24. rem. 21)	צוה
צוּמוּ	ן Kal imp. pl. masc. . .	צום
צוֹמֵחַ	Kal part. act. sing. masc. . .	צמח
צִוָּנוּ	Piel pret. 3 pers. sing. masc., (צִוָּה), suff.	
	1 pers. pl. (§ 24. rem. 21) .	צוה
צַוֵּנִי	} id. id. with suff. 1 pers. sing. .	צוה
צִוַּנִי	}	

צוּע Root not used; to form, design.

צַעֲצֻעִים masc. pl. carved work, 2 Ch. 3. 10.

צוֹעֵר	pr. name of a place . . .	צער
צוֹעָר	pr. name masc. . . .	צער

[צוּף] to overflow, overwhelm, La. 3. 54. Hiph. I. to cause to overflow, De. 11. 4.—II. to cause to swim, 2 Ki. 6. 6.

צוּף masc. dec. 1 a.—I. honeycomb.—II. pr. name masc. 1 Sa. 1. 1; also 1 Ch. 6. 20, Kh. for which צוֹפַי, 1 Ch. 6. 11.

צָפָה fem. dec. 10, an overflowing, Eze. 32. 6

צַפְצָפָה fem. a willow, Eze. 17. 5.

צוֹף	noun masc. sing. dec. 1 a, also pr. name .	צוף
צֹפֶה	Kal part. act. sing. masc. dec. 9 a, comp. צָפָה	צפה
צוֹפוֹת	id. pl. fem. [from צֹפֶה] dec. 10 .	צפה
צוֹפָח	} pr. name masc. . . .	צפח
צוֹפַח	}	
צוֹפַי	pr. name masc., see צוּף . .	צוף
צוֹפִיָּה	Kal part. act. sing. fem. [as if from a masc.	
	צוֹפִי § 24. rem. 4] . . .	צפה
צוֹפִים	pr. name in compos., רָמָתַיִם צוֹפִים, see under	רום
צוּפִים	noun masc., pl. of צוּף dec. 1 a	צוף
צוֹפָר	ן pr. name masc. . . .	צפר

[צוּץ] to flower, flourish, Eze. 7. 10. Hiph. I. to glitter, shine.—II. to flower, blossom.

צִיץ masc.—I. a shining plate of gold on the forehead of the high priest.—II. flower; pl. צִצִּים.—III. plumage, wing, Je. 48. 9.—IV. pr. name of a place, 2 Ch. 20. 16.

צִיצָה fem. dec. 10, a flower, Is. 28. 4.

צִיצִת fem.—I. a lock of hair, Eze. 8. 3.—II. fringe, Nu. 15. 38, 39.

I. צוּק Hiph. הֵצִיק.—I. to straiten, distress; part. oppressor, Is. 51. 13.—II. to press, urge, with acc. לְ.

צוֹק masc. distress, oppression, trouble, Da. 9. 25.

צוּקָה fem. id. Pr. 1. 27; 30. 6.

מָצוֹק masc. and מְצוּקָה fem. dec. 10, idem.

מוּצָק masc.—I. something narrow, scanty, Job 36. 16; 37. 10.—II. straitness, distress, Is. 8. 23.

II. צוּק to pour out, only צָקוּן (for צָקוּ) Is. 26. 16; fut. יָצוּק Job 28. 2; 29. 6.

מֻצָק masc. dec. 3 a.—I. pillar, column, 1 Sa. 2. 8 (צוּק i. q. הֵצִיק to set up, R. יָצַק).—II metaph. a precipitous rock, 1 Sa. 14. 5.

צוּקָה ן noun fem. sing. . . . | צוק

[צוּר] fut. יָצוּר, ap. וַיָּצַר (see analyt. order).—I. to bind up.—II. to press, besiege, with acc. עַל, אֶל.—III. to press upon, beset, assail.—IV. with acc. and עַל to press or thrust forward, to cause to advance, as

troops against a city, Is. 29. 3 ; or, *to stir* a city,
i. e. *to urge* it to sedition, Ju. 9. 31.—V. *to form,
fashion.*

צַוָּאר, צַוָּר (Ne. 3. 5) masc. dec. 2 b (constr.
צַוַּאר ; pl. צַוָּארִים, constr. צַוְּארֵי, צַוְּארֹת), *the
neck* ; sometimes also for the *back* ; pl. *necks*, but
more frequently in the sense of the singular, *neck.*
Chald. id.

צַוְּרֹן masc. dec. 3 c, only pl. Ca. 4. 9, *the neck.*

צוּר masc. dec. 1 a (pl. ־ים, ־ֹת).—I. *a rock* ;
metaph. of God, *strength* or *refuge.*—II. *a stone.*
—III. *sharp stone* used as a knife, Jos. 5. 2, 3 ;
hence, *an edge* of a sword, Ps. 89. 44.—IV. *form,
shape*, Ps. 49. 15.—V. pr. name m. of two persons.

צֹר, צוּר masc.—I. *a rock*, Eze. 3. 9.—II. *a
sharp stone*, Ex. 4. 25.—III. pr. name, *Tyre*, the
capital of Phœnicia. Gent. noun, צֹרִי *a Tyrian.*

צוּרָה fem. dec. 10, *form*, Eze. 43. 11.

צוּרִיאֵל (*my rock is God*) pr. name masc. Nu. 3. 35.

צוּרִישַׁדָּי (*my rock is the Almighty*) pr. name of
a man, comp. Nu. 1. 6 ; 2. 12.

צִיר masc. dec. 1 a.—I. *figure, image*, Is. 45. 16.
—II. *form, shape*, Ps. 49. 15.

מָצוֹר masc. dec. 3 a (with suff. מְצוּרֶךָ § 32.
rem. 5).—I. *straitness, distress.*—II. *siege.*—III.
mound, bulwark.—IV. *fortification, fortress.*

מְצוּרָה fem. dec. 10.—I. *mound, entrenchment,*
Is. 29. 3.—II. *fortress, fortified city.*

צוּר	noun masc. sing. dec. 1 a, also pr. name in compos. (see בֵּית) . . .	
צוֹר	pr. name of a place . . .	צור
צוּרֵ־	[for צֹר] Kal imp. sing. masc. . .	צרר
צוּרֵי	noun masc. pl. constr. from צוּר dec. 1 a	צור
צוּרִי	id. sing. with suff. 1 pers. sing. .	צור
צוּרִי	Kal imp. sing. masc. . . .	צור
צוּרִישַׁדָּי צוּרִיאֵל	pr. names masc. . . .	צור
צוּרָם	defect. for צַוָּארָם (q. v.) . .	צור
צוּרָם	noun masc. sing., suff. 3 pers. pl. masc. from צוּר dec. 1 a . . .	צור
צֹרֵף	Kal part. act. sing. masc. dec. 7 b	צרף
צֹרְפִים	id. pl., abs. st. . . .	צרף
צֹרְפָם	id. sing., suff. 3 pers. pl. masc.	צ ךף
צֹרְרִי צֹרְרַי	} Kal part. act. pl. masc., suff. 1 pers. sing. from צֹרֵר dec. 7 b	} צור
צֹרְרִי	id. sing., suff. 1 pers. sing. .	צרר
צוֹרְרָיו	id. pl., suff. 3 pers. sing. masc.	צרר
צוֹרְרֶיךָ	id. pl., suff. 2 pers. sing. masc.	צרר

צָרַת	noun fem. sing., constr. of [צָרָה] dec. 10	צור
צָרָתוֹ	id., suff. 3 pers. sing. masc.	צור
צָרֹתָיו	id. pl., suff. 3 pers. sing. masc., K. תָיו' .	צור

צוּת . Hiph. הִצִּית *to set on fire, kindle*, Is. 27. 4.

צִוַּתָּה	the foll. with suff. 3 pers. sing. f. (§ 24. r. 21)	צוה
צִוְּתָה	Piel pret. 3 pers. sing. fem. . .	צוה
צַוֹּתוֹ	id. inf. (צַוֹּת), suff. 3 pers. sing. masc. d. 1 b	צוה
צַח	adj. masc. sing. . . .	צחח
צָחָא	pr. name masc.	צחח

צָחָה Root not used ; Chald. *to thirst, be dry.*

צָחָא (*dryness*) pr. name of a man. Also

צָחֶה adj. masc. [constr. of צָחֶה dec. 9 a] *dry*, sc.
from thirst, Is. 5. 13 . . . צחה

צָחוּ	Kal pret. 3 pers. pl. (dag. forte impl. in ח)	צחה
צְחֹת	adj. pl. fem. from צַח masc. (§ 37. rem. 7)	צחה

[צָחַח] *to be bright, white*, La. 4. 7.

צַח masc. adj.—I. *bright, white*, Ca. 5. 10.—II.
bright, serene ; metaph. *clear, plain*, Is. 32. 4.

צָחִיחַ masc. *dry, parched.*

צְחִיחָה fem. *dry, parched land*, Ps. 68. 7.

צָחִיחִי masc. pl. צְחִיחִים *dry places*, Ne. 4. 7.

צְחִיחֹת fem. pl. id. Is. 58. 11.

צָחִיחַ	noun masc. sing. . . .	צחח
צְחִיחָה	noun fem. sing. . . .	צחח

צָחַן Root not used ; prob. *to be foul, stinking* (cogn.
זָנַח). Syr. *to be filthy.*

צַחֲנָה fem. dec. 10, *stench*, Joel 2. 20.

צַחֲנָתוֹ noun fem. s., suff. 3 pers. s. m. [fr. צַחֲנָה] | צחן

[צָחַק] fut. יִצְחַק *to laugh*, with לְ at any one. Pi. I.
to play, sport, jest.—II. *to laugh, mock at, insult,*
with בְּ Ge. 39. 14, 17.

צְחֹק m. *laughter, ridicule*, Ge. 21. 6 ; Eze. 23. 32.

יִצְחָק (*laughter*, or *he laughs*) pr. name, *Isaac,*
the patriarch, son of Abraham and Sarah ; sometimes written יִשְׂחָק.

צְחֹק	noun masc. sing. . . .	צחק
צָחֲקָה	Kal pret. 3 pers. sing. fem. .	צחק
צָחַקְתְּ	id. pret. 2 pers. sing. f. [for צָחַקְתְּ § 8. r. 7]	צחק
צָחַקְתִּי	id. pret. 1 pers. sing. .	צחק

צֹחַר [for צָהַר] masc. *whiteness*, Eze. 27. 18. Hence
the two following.

a Is. 8. 16.   d Ne. 3. 5.   f Ps. 31. 12.   k Eze. 43. 11.   n Ru. 3. 6.   q La. 4. 7.   s Ps. 68. 7.   u Ge. 21. 6.   x Ge. 18. 15.
b 1 Sa. 24. 3.   e Ne. 3. 8.   g Ps. 7. 5.   l Eze. 43. 11.   o Est. 4. 17.   r Is. 32. 4.   t Joel 2. 20.   y Ge. 18. 13.   z Ge. 18. 15.
c Is. 29. 3.   f Je. 9. 6.   h Ps. 10. 5.   m Eze. 43. 11.   p Le. 7. 38.   s Eze. 24 7. 8.

42*

צֹחַר	ן (whiteness) pr. name masc. of several persons, espec. of a son of Simeon, called also זֶרַח comp. Nu. 26. 13, with Ge. 46. 12	צחר
צְחֹרוֹת	adj. fem. pl. [of צְחֹרָה from צָחֹר masc.] white, Ju. 5. 10	צחר
צִי	ן noun masc. sing., pl. צִיִּים & צִים	ציה
צִיבָא	ן pr. name masc.	נצב
צַיִד	ר noun masc. sing. dec. 6h (comp. § 35. rem. 2)	צוד
צֵיד	}	צוד
צֵיד	id., constr. st.	צוד
צֵידָה	Kh. צֵידָה q. v., K. צַיִד (q. v.)	צוד
צֵידָה	ן noun fem. sing.	צוד
צֵידָהּ	noun masc. s., suff. 3 pers. s. f. fr. צַיִד d. 6h	צוד
צֵידוֹ	id. with suff. 3 pers. sing. masc.	צוד
צִידוֹן	ן pr. name of a place	צוד
צִידֹנִים	ן gent. noun pl. from the preced.	צוד
צַיָּדִים	noun masc., pl. of [צַיָּד] dec. 1b	צוד
צֵידָם	noun masc. s., suff. 3 p. pl. m. fr. צַיִד d. 6h	צוד
צִידֹן	pr. name of a man and a place	צוד
צִידֹנִים	gent. noun pl. from the preced.	צוד
צָיָה	Root not used; i. q. Arab. צוה Chald. & Syr. צוא to dry up.	

צִי masc. (for צֵיִי) pl. צִיִּים & צִים, a ship.

צִיָּה fem. dec. 10, drought; אֶרֶץ צִיָּה land of drought, i. e. dry land, a desert.

צָיוֹן masc. dry, parched land, Is. 25. 5; 32. 2.

צִיּוֹן (parched place; others citadel) pr. name, Zion, the most southern and highest of the hills on which Jerusalem was built, often put for Jerusalem itself.

צִיִּי masc. (denom. from צִי, צִיָּה desert) only pl. צִיִּים inhabitants of the desert, men or beasts.

צִיחַ	ן noun fem. sing. dec. 10	ציה
צִיּוֹן	pr. name of a place	ציה
צִיּוֹן	noun masc. sing. dec. 1b	צוה
צִיֹּנָה	pr. name of a place (צִיּוֹן) with parag. ה	ציה
צִיחָא	ן pr. name masc., see צָחָא	צחח
צִיִּים	noun masc., pl. of צִיִּי, or (Da. 11. 30) of צִי	ציה
צִים	ן noun masc., pl. of צִי	ציה
צִיֹּנִים	ן noun masc., pl. of צִיּוֹן dec. 1b	צוה
צִעֹר	ן pr. name of a place	צער
צוּף	Kh. צִיף, K. צוּף, pr. name masc.	צוף
צִיץ	ר ן noun masc. sing. dec. 1a	צוץ
צִיצַת	noun fem. sing., constr. of [צִיצָה] dec. 10	צוץ
צִיצַת	noun fem. sing.	צוץ
צִיקְלַג	pr. name of a place, see צָקְלַג.	

צִיר	Kal not used;—I. Arab. to go. Hithp. הִצְטַיָּר prepare for a journey, Jos. 9. 4.—II. to go round, revolve; Arab. צאר to writhe with pain (Gesenius), only in the following deriv.	
צִיר	ן masc. dec. 1 a.—I. hinge of a door, Pr. 26. 14.—II. pl. writhings, pains, pangs.—III. messenger	ציר
צִירָהּ	id., suff. 3 pers. sing. fem.	ציר
צִירַי	id. pl., suff. 1 pers. sing.	ציר
צִירַיִךְ	id. pl., suff. 2 pers. sing. fem.	ציר
צִירִים	id. pl., abs. st.	ציר
צִירִים	noun masc., pl. of [צִיר] dec. 1 a	צור
צִירָם	ן id. sing., suff. 3 pers. pl. masc. (Kh. צִירָם); K. צוּרָם (q. v.)	צור
צֵל	noun masc. sing. dec. 8 b	צלל
צְלָא	Ch. only Pa. to pray, Da. 6. 11; Ezr. 6. 10.	
[צָלָה]	to roast.	
צָלִי	masc. dec. 3 a, roasted, a roast.	
צִלָּה	ן pr. name fem.	צלל
צִלָּהּ	noun masc. sing., suff. 3 pers. sing fem. from צֵל dec. 8 b	צלל
צְלוּל	Kh. צלול, K. צָלִיל noun masc. sing.	צלל
[צָלַח]	fut. יִצְלָח—I. to pass over or cross a river, 2 Sa. 19. 18.—II. to come, fall or descend upon, with עַל, אֶל.—III. to advance, flourish, prosper.—IV. to be fit for any thing, with לְ. Hiph. I. to cause or make to prosper.—II. to accomplish prosperously, successfully.—III. to have success, be prosperous.	

צְלַח Ch. Aph. I. to prosper, promote, Da. 3. 30 to accomplish prosperously, Ezr. 6. 14.—II. to prosper, be promoted, Da. 6. 29; to be prosperous, successful, Ezr. 5. 8.

צַלַּחַת, צְלֹחִית, צְלֹחָה fem. dish, bowl.

צְלַח	Kal imp. sing. masc.	צלח
צָלְחָה	} Kal pret. 3 pers. sing. fem. (§ 8. rem. 1 & 7)	צלח
צָלֵחָה	}	צלח
צָלְחוּ	ן id. pret. 3 pers. pl.	צלח
צְלֹחִית	noun fem. sing.	צלח
צָלֵחַ	adj. masc. sing. (comp. § 37. No. 4) dec. 3a	צלח
צְלִי	id., constr. st.	צלה
צִלְּךָ	noun masc. sing., suff. 2 pers. sing. fem. from צֵל dec. 8 b	צלל
צִלְּךָ	id. with suff. 2 pers. sing. masc.	צלל

a Is. 33. 21.   e Ps. 132. 15.   i Eze. 39. 15.   m Is. 28. 4.   q Pr. 26. 14.   u Is. 45. 16.   y Ps. 45. 5.   z 2 Sa. 19. 18.   c Ex. 12. 8, 9.
b Le. 17. 13.   f Je. 16. 16.   k Nu. 24. 24.   n Nu. 15. 38.   r Da. 10. 16.   v Ps. 49. 15.   z Je. 12. 1.   a 2 Ki. 2. 20.   d Is. 16. 3.
c Ge. 27. 5.   g Jos. 9. 5.   l Je. 31. 21.   o Pr. 25. 13.   s Is. 57. 9.   w Ju. 7. 13.   b 1 Sa. 10. 6.   c Is. 44. 16.   e Ps. 121. 5.
d 1 Sa. 22. 10.   h Is. 35. 1.   Is. 28. 1.

צָלַל [I. *to tingle*, of the ears; trop. of the lips, *to quiver*, Hab. 3. 16. Hiph. *to tingle*, 1 Sa. 3. 11.—II. Kal *to roll* or *tumble down*, i. e. *sink*, Ex. 15. 10. —III. Kal *to be shaded, dark*, Ne. 13. 19. Hiph. *to shadow*, Eze. 31. 3.

צָלוּל masc. *a cake*, Ju. 7. 13 (Keri צְלִיל) from its *roundness*, comp. R. No. II.

צֵלֶל masc. dec. 6 b, *shade, shadow*.

צֵל m. d. 8 b, *shade, shadow*; metaph. *covering, shelter*; hence *protection, defence*.

צִלָּה (*shade*) pr. name of a wife of Lamech, Ge. 4. 19, 22, 23.

צִלְּתַי (for צֵלַת יָהּ *shadow of the Lord*) pr. name of two men, 1 Ch. 8. 20; 12. 20.

צֶלְצַל m. (constr. צִלְצַל).—I. *rattling, rustling*, Is. 18. 1.—II. *fishing instrument, harpoon*, Job 40. 31. —III. pl. צִלְצָלִים, constr. צִלְצְלֵי (comp. dec. 8, § 36. rem. 5, & dec. 4) *cymbals*.—IV. a species of *locust*, De. 28. 42; others, *crickets*.

מְצִלָּה fem. only pl. מְצִלּוֹת *bells*, Zec. 14. 20.

מְצֻלָּה fem. *a shady place*, Zec. 1. 8.

מְצִלְתַּיִם fem. (§ 39. No. 4. rem. 1) dual מְצִלְתַּיִם dec. 13 b, *cymbals*.

צַלְמָוֶת masc. *shadow of death*, poet. for *thick darkness*.

צַלְמֻנָּע (*shade withheld from him*) pr. name of a prince of Midian.

צֶלַח (*shade from the sun*) pr. name of a place in Benjamin, 1 Sa. 10. 2.

צִלְּפוֹנִי (*shade turned towards me*) pr. name masc. 1 Ch. 4. 3.

בְּצַלְאֵל (*in the shadow of God*) pr. name masc. Bezaleel.—I. a famous artificer appointed by God to the work of the tabernacle.—II. Ezr. 10. 30.

צָלְלוּ
צָלֲלוּ } Kal pret. 3 pers. pl.   . . .   צלל

צִלְלוֹ noun masc. sing., suff. 3 pers. sing. masc. from [צֵלֶל] dec. 6 b   . .   צלל

צִלְלֵי id. pl., constr. st.   . .   צלל

צֶלֶם Root not used; Arab. *to be obscure, dark*; Syr. *to figure, delineate*.

צֶלֶם masc. dec. 6 a (with suff. צַלְמִי).—I. *shade, shadow*, Ps. 39. 7; metaph. *shadow, illusion*, Ps. 73. 20.—II. *image, likeness*.

צְלֵם, צֶלֶם Ch. masc. dec. 3 a, *image, idol*.

צַלְמוֹן (*shady*) pr. name, Salmon—I. of a

---

mountain of Ephraim near Shechem.—II. of a man, 2 Sa. 23. 28.—III. *shade, gloom, darkness*, so, according to Kimchi, in Ps. 68. 15, *it shone like snow in darkness*, comp. שֶׁלֶג.

צַלְמוֹנָה (*shady*) pr. name of a station of the Israelites in the desert, Nu. 33. 41.

צֶלֶם וּ Ch. noun masc. sing. dec. 3 a; ‍וּ bef. (:)   צלם

צַלְמָם noun masc. sing., suff. 3 pers. pl. masc. from צֵל dec. 8 b   . .   צלל

צַלְמָא Ch. noun masc. sing., emph. of צֶלֶם dec. 3 a   צלם

צַלְמוֹן pr. name of a man and a place   צלם

צַלְמָוֶת וּ noun m. s., compnd. of צֵל & מָוֶת, see under   צלם

צַלְמֵי וּ noun masc. pl. constr. from צֶלֶם dec. 6 a   צלם

צְלָמָיו id. pl., suff. 3 pers. sing. masc.   .   צלם

צַלְמֵיכֶם id. pl., suff. 2 pers. pl. masc.   .   צלם

צַלְמָם id. sing., suff. 3 pers. pl. masc.   .   צלם

צַלְמֻנָּע וּ pr. name of a man   .   צלל

צֵלָע וּ fem. constr. צֶלַע, צֶלֶע with suff. צַלְעִי (§ 33. rem. 3).—I. *rib*; pl. צְלָעוֹת *ribs of a building, planks for wainscotting*, 1 Ki. 6. 15; 7. 3.—II. *side of a man*, also of inanimate things; pl. צְלָעוֹת constr. צַלְעוֹת *sides*; pl. צְלָעִים *sides* or *leaves of a double door*.—III. *a side-chamber*; also *a series of side-chambers*.—IV. pr. name of a city in Benjamin where Saul was buried.

צָלַע (denom. from צֵלָע) *to lean on one side*, q. d. *to halt, limp*.

צֶלַע masc. dec. 6 (with suff. צַלְעִי § 35. rem. 5), *a halting, falling*, Ps. 35. 15; 38. 18, and perh Je. 20. 10.

צֶלַע noun fem., constr. of צֵלָע (q. v.)   .   צלע

צֹלֵעַ Kal part. act. sing. masc.   . .   צלע

צַלְעוֹ noun fem. sing., suff. 3 pers. sing. masc. from צֵלָע dec. 4 (§ 33. rem. 2)   .   צלע

צְלָעוֹת id. pl. fem., abs. st.   . .   צלע

צַלְעוֹת ‍ id. pl. fem., constr. st.   . .   צלע

צַלְעִי id. sing. with suff. 1 pers. sing.   .   צלע

צְלָעִים id. (masc. gen.) with pl. masc. term.   .   צלע

צַלְעֹת id. pl. fem., constr. st., comp. צְלָעוֹת   .   צלע

צַלְעֹתָיו id. pl. fem., suff. 3 pers. sing. masc.   צלע

צָלָף (*fracture, wound*) pr. name of a man, Ne. 3. 30.

צְלָפְחָד וּ (*first rupture*) pr. name of a man; ‍וּ bef. (:)

צִלְצַל noun m. s., constr. of צֶלְצַל (comp. d. 4 & 11 c)   צלל

צָלָק (*fissure*) pr. n. of one of David's military chiefs.

צְלָתִּי	וְ pr. name masc. for צְלָתִי	צלל
צָם	Kal part. act. sing. masc.	צום

[צָמֵא] fut. יִצְמָא to thirst; metaph. to desire earnestly.

צָמָא masc. dec. 4 a (§ 33. rem. 2), thirst.

צָמֵא masc. dec. 5 a, fem. צְמֵאָה adj. thirsty.

צִמְאָה fem. thirst, Je. 2. 25.

צִמָּאוֹן masc. thirsty land.

צָמָא[a]	וְ noun masc. sing. dec. 4 a (§ 33. rem. 2)	צמא
צָמֵא[b]	וְ adj. masc. sing. dec. 5 a	צמא
צָמְאָה	Kal pret. 3 pers. sing. fem.	צמא
צָמְאוּ[d]	id. pret. 3 pers. pl.	צמא
צִמָּאוֹן	וְ noun masc. sing.	צמא
צְמֵאִים[c]	adj. masc., pl. of צָמֵא dec. 5 a	צמא
צְמָאָם[f]	noun masc. sing., suff. 3 pers. pl. masc. from צָמָא dec. 4 a	צמא

צָמַד Niph. to be bound to, joined to, with לְ. Pu. to be bound, fastened, 2 Sa. 20. 8. Hiph. to contrive, frame, Ps. 50. 19.

צָמִיד masc. dec. 3 a.—I. band, bracelet.—II. lid or cover of a vessel, Nu. 19. 15. Also the one following.

צֶמֶד	וְ masc. sing. dec. 6 a.—I. pair, couple, yoke of oxen, mules, horsemen.—II. a quantity of land ploughed in a day by a pair of oxen, an acre	צמד
צִמְדּוֹ[g]	וְ id., suff. 3 pers. sing. masc.	צמד
צִמְדֵּי[h]	id. pl., constr. st.	צמד
צְמָדִים	id. pl., abst. st.	צמד
צְמֻקִּים[i]	noun masc., pl. of [צָמוּק] dec. 1 b	צמק

צָמַח[k] fut. יִצְמַח to shoot, spring, grow up; metaph. to spring up, arise, begin, of events. Pi. to grow, of hair. Hiph. to cause to spring up, make to grow. Hence

צֶמַח	וְ noun masc. sing. (suff. צִמְחָה) dec. 6 a, a shooting, springing up.—I. shoot.—II. plant.—III. branch	צמח
צָמַח[m]	Piel pret. 3 pers. sing. [for צִמַּח § 15. rem. 1]	צמח
צִמְחָה	noun masc. sing., suff. 3 pers. sing. fem. from צֶמַח dec. 6 a (§ 35. rem. 5)	צמח
צָמְחוּ[n]	וְ Kal pret. 3 pers. pl.	צמח
צֹמְחוֹת[o]	id. part. act. fem. pl. [of צֹמַחַת dec. 13] from צֹמֵחַ masc.	צמח
צָמִיד[p]	וְ noun masc. sing. dec. 3 a	צמד
צְמִידִים	id. pl., abst. st.	צמד

צָמִים[q]	noun masc. sing.	צמם
צַמְּכֶם[r]	noun m. s., suff. 2 pers. pl. m. fr. צוֹם d. 1a	צום

צָמַם Root not used; Arab. طمم צמם, טמם to braid, plait, bind.

צַמָּה fem. dec. 10, a veil.

צַמִּים masc. a noose, snare, Job 18. 9; metaph. destruction, Job 5. 5.

צַמְנוּ	Kal pret. 1 pers. pl.	צום

[צָמַק] to be dried up, Ho. 9. 14.

צִמּוּק masc. dec. 1 b, dried grapes or raisins.

צְמֻקִים[s]	וְ defect. for צְמוּקִים (q. v.)	צמק
צֹמְקִים[t]	Kal part. act. masc. pl. [of צָמַק] dec. 7 b	צמק

צֶמֶר וְ masc. dec. 6 a (with suff. צַמְרִי), wool; also woollen garments, Eze. 34. 3; 44. 17. R. צָמַר perh. i. q. סָמַר to stand out, bristle up.

צַמֶּרֶת fem. dec. 13 a (with suff. צַמַּרְתּוֹ), foliage.

צִמְרִי pr. name of a Canaanitish tribe, Ge. 10. 18.

צְמָרַיִם (two hills?) pr. name of a city in the tribe of Benjamin, Jos. 18. 22; hence הַר צ' in the mountains of Ephraim, 2 Ch. 13. 4.

צֶמֶר[u]	noun masc. sing. dec. 6 a (for צֶמֶר § 35. r. 2)	צמר
צַמְרִי[v]	id. with suff. 1 pers. sing.	צמר
צְמָרַיִם	וְ pr. name of a place; וְ bef. (:)	צמר
צַמֶּרֶת[w]	noun fem. sing. dec. 13 a	צמר
צַמַּרְתּוֹ[x]	id., suff. 3 pers. sing. masc.	צמר
צַמְרָתָם[y]	id., suff. 3 pers. pl. masc.	צמר

[צָמַת] to cut off, destroy, La. 3. 53. Niph. to be cut off, to perish. Pi. Ps. 119. 139. Hiph., & Pilp. Ps. 88. 17, to cut off, destroy.

לִצְמִיתֻת fem. cutting off, extinction, hence until extinction, i. e. so long as the thing lasts, i. e. for ever, Le. 25. 23, 30 (Gesenius). Others, absolutely, entirely.

צָמַתָּ	וְ Kal pret. 2 pers. sing. fem. (§ 23. rem. 11)	צמא
צַמְתָּ[z]	Kal pret. 2 pers. sing. masc.	צום
צָמְתוּ[aa]	Kal pret. 3 pers. pl.	צמת
צָמַתִּי[bb]	Kal pret. 1 pers. sing. (§ 23. rem. 10)	צמא
צַמְתִּי[cc]	Kal pret. 1 pers. sing.	צום
צֻמָּתֵךְ[dd]	noun fem. s., suff. 2 p. s. fem. fr. [צַמָּה] d. 10	צמם
צַמְתֶּם[ee]	Kal pret. 2 pers. pl. masc.	צום
צַמְתֻּנִי[ff]	id. id. with suff. 1 pers. sing.	צום
צִמְּתַתְנִי	[reduplicated for צִמְּתֻנִי] Piel pret. 3 pers. pl., suff. 1 pers. sing.	צמת
צִמְּתַתְנִי	Piel pret. 3 pers. s. fem. [צִמְּתָה], suff. 1 p. s.	צמת

* Am. 8. 11.   ° Ps. 107. 5.   ' 2 Sa. 16. 1.   " Is. 44. 4.   ° Is. 58. 3.   ° Eze. 27. 18.   ° Eze. 31. 3, 10.   ' La. 3. 53.   * Zec. 7. 5.
* Eze. 19. 13.   ' Ps. 104. 11.   * Le. 13. 37.   ° Ge. 41. 6, 23.   ' Is. 58. 3.   ° 2 Ki. 7. 4.   ° Eze. 31. 14.   ° Ju. 4. 19.   ' Zec. 7. 5.
* 2 Sa. 17. 29.   ' Je. 51. 23.   ' Ge. 19. 25.   ° Nu.19.15;31,50.   ' 1 Ch. 12. 40.   ° Ho. 2. 7, 11.   ° Ru. 2. 9.   ° 2 Sa. 12. 22.   ' Ps. 88. 17.
* Is. 48. 21.   ' Is. 5. 10.   " Eze. 16. 7.   ' Job 5. 5; 18. 9.   " Ho. 9. 14.   ° Eze. 17. 3.   ' 2 Sa. 12. 21.   ' Is. 47. 2.   ° Ps. 119. 139.

צֵן pr. name of the desert between Palestine and Idumea, with ה parag. צֵנָה.

[צֹנֶא] com.d.7b, & צֹנֶה i.q. צֹאן flocks, Nu.32.24; Ps.8.8.

צֵנָה pr. name (צֵן q. v.) with parag. ה.

צִנָּה ' noun fem. sing. dec. 10   צנן

צֹנֶה noun com. sing., see   צנא

צְנוּעִים[c] Kal part. pass. masc. pl. [of צָנוּעַ] dec. 3a   צנע

צָנוֹף[c] Kal inf. abs.   צנף

צְנוּף[d] ¹ Kh. צְנוּף, K. צְנִיף, noun masc. sing. constr. [of צָנוּף or צְנִיף dec. 3a] .   צנף

צַנּוֹרֶיךָ[a] noun m. pl., suff. 2 pers. s. m. fr. צִנּוֹר d. 1b   צנר

צַנּוֹת[a] noun fem., pl. of צָנָה dec. 10 .   צנן

[צָנַח] I. to alight, Jos. 15.18; Ju. 1.14.—II. to go down, i. e. penetrate, Ju. 4.21.

צִנִּים[e] noun masc., pl. of [צֵן] dec. 8b .   צנן

צָנִיף[a] 'ב noun masc. sing. dec. 3a .   צנף

צָנַם prob. to be hard, dry, only in the foll. form.

צְנֻמוֹת[a] Kal part. pass. fem. pl. [of צְנוּמָה fr. צָנֻם m.] צנם

צָנַן Root not used; prob.—I. i.q. שָׁנַן to be sharp; Chald. צְנַן to be cold.—II. i.q. Arab. צאן to keep, also to lay up, Heb. גָּנַן to protect.

צְנִין masc. only pl. צְנִינִים thorns.

צֵן masc. only pl. צִנִּים id. Pr. 22.5; Job 5.5.

צִנָּה fem. dec. 10.—I. thorn; trop. צִנּוֹת hooks, fish-hooks.—II. a cooling, refreshing, Pr. 25.13; Prof. Lee, a vesse. for containing snow, comp. צִנְצֶנֶת.—III. a shield.

צִנְצֶנֶת fem. urn, vase, Ex. 16.33; others, basket.

צָנָן pr. name of a place, see צַאֲנָן .   צאן

[צָנַע] i.q. כָּנַע to be bowed down, humble, lowly, cogn. צָנַח, Pr. 11.2. Hiph. to act humbly, Mi. 6.8.

[צָנַף] to wind or wrap round.

צְנֵפָה fem. a winding or wrapping round, Is. 22.18; Gesenius, a ball.

צָנִיף masc. dec. 3a (pl. צְנִיפוֹת), turban.

צְנוּף masc. id. Is. 62. 3, Kh.

מִצְנֶפֶת fem. turban, espec. of the high priest.

צְנֵפָה[i] noun fem. sing. .   צנף

צְנֶפֶת[a] noun fem. sing. .   צנן

צָנַק Root not used · Samar. to shut up.

צִינֹק masc. fetters, Arab. זנאק compedes, Je. 29.2[c] (Prof. Lee); others, a prison.

צָנַר Root not used; meaning uncertain.

צִנּוֹר masc. dec. 1b, waterfall, cataract.

צַנְתָּרוֹת pl. fem. [constr. of צַנְתָּרוֹת] pipes, tubes, Zec. 4.12. Etymology uncertain.

[צָעַד] fut. יִצְעַד.—I. to step, walk, advance; poet. for to shoot, Ge. 49.22.—II. to pass through, with acc. Hab.3.12. Hiph. to cause to march, to chase, Job 18.14.

צַעַד masc. d. 6d.—I. a stepping, going, Pr. 30.29 —II. step, pace; metaph. conduct.

צְעָדָה fem.—I. a going, marching.—II. pl. צְעָדוֹת ornamental chains worn at the ankles, ankle chains, Is. 3. 20.

אֶצְעָדָה fem. bracelet; pl. אֶצְעָדוֹת.

מִצְעָד masc. dec. 2b, step, walk.

צַעַד[e] noun masc. sing. dec. 6d [for צַעַד § 35. r. 2] צעד

צָעֲדָה[a] Kal pret. 3 pers. sing. fem. .   צעד

צְעָדָה[a] noun fem. sing. .   צעד

צָעֲדוּ[g] Kal pret. 3 pers. pl. .   צעד

צַעֲדוֹ noun m. sing., suff. 3 pers. s. m. fr. צַעַד d. 6d צעד

צְעָדֵי[i] id. pl., constr. st. .   צעד

צְעָדִי[i] id. sing., suff. 1 pers. sing. .   צעד

צְעָדַי id. pl., suff. 1 pers. sing. .   צעד

צְעָדֶיהָ id. pl., suff. 3 pers. sing. fem. .   צעד

צְעָדָיו[a] id. pl., suff. 3 pers. sing. masc. .   צעד

צְעָדִים[a] id. pl., abs. st. .   צעד

צְעָדֵינוּ[a] id. pl., suff. 1 pers. pl. .   צעד

צַעַדְךָ[p] id. sing., suff. 2 pers. sing. masc. [for צַעַדְךָ] צעד

[צָעָה] cogn. סָעָה, צָעַן, צָעַד.—I. to step, stride, Is.63.1. —II. to wander, to emigrate; part. צֹעֶה (a) an exile: (b) wanderer, stranger, Je. 2. 20; 48. 12. Pi. to make or induce to wander, emigrate, Je. 48. 12.

צֹעָה[c] } Kal part. act. sing. fem. and masc.   צעה
צֹעֶה

צֵעֹהוּ[f] ¹ Piel pret. 3 pers. pl. [צֵעוּ], suff. 3 pers. s. m. צעה

צְעוּרֶיהָ[b] Kh. צעו', K. צְעִי', adj. pl. masc., suff. 3 pers. sing. fem. from צָעוּר or צָעִיר dec. 3a . צער

צְעוּרֵיהֶם[c] Kh. צעו', K. צְעִי', id. pl., with suff. 3 p. m. pl. צער

צֹעִים[a] Kal part. act. masc., pl. of צֹעֶה dec. 9a . צעה

צָעִיפָה[c] noun m. s., suff. 3 pers. s. fem. fr. צָעִיף d. 3a צעף

צָעִיר adj. masc. sing. dec. 3a .   צער

צְעִירָה pr. name of a place (צָעִיר) with parag. ה צער

צְעִירוֹ[i] adj. m. s., suff. 3 pers. sing. m. fr. צָעִיר d. 3a צער

• Ps. 8.8.   ◦ Ps. 42.8.   i Job 29.14.   ■ Ex. 16.33.   p 2 Sa. 5.24.   ♦ Pr. 5.5.   ♦ La. 4.18.   ♦ Je. 48.12.   d Je. 48.12.
• Pr. 11.2.   ◦ 2 Ch. 11.12.   ♦ Ge. 41.23.   ■ Pr. 30.29.   q 2 Sa. 6.13.   ♦ Job 34.21.   ♦ Pr. 4.12.   ♦ Je. 48.4.   ♦ Ge. 38.19.
• Is. 22.18.   g Pr. 22.5.   l Is. 22.18.   ■ Ge. 49.22.   r Job 18.7.   ■ 2 Sa. 6.13.   ♦ Je. 2.20.   • Je. 14.3.   l 1 Ki. 16.24.
• Is. 62.3.   ♦ Zec. 3.5.

צֵעִירֵי   id. pl., constr. st.   צער

צְעִירִים‎   id. pl., abs. st.   צער

[צָעַן]   to wander, remove, Is. 33. 20.

צַעֲנַנִּים (wanderings) pr. name of a city of the Kenites, in the tribe of Naphtali.

צֹעַן   pr. name, Zoan, an ancient city in Lower Egypt.

צָעַף   Root not used; Arab. to double.

צָעִיף masc. dec. 3 a, a veil.

צֶאֱצָעִים   noun masc. pl. [of צֶאֱצָע] dec. 1 b   צוע

צָעַק   fut. יִצְעַק to cry out, espec. for help. Pi. to cry out, exclaim, 2 Ki. 2. 12. Hiph. to call together, convoke. Niph. to be called, or to come, together.

צְעָקָה fem. dec. 11 c (constr. צַעֲקַת § 42. rem. 1), a cry for help.

צָעֹק Kal inf. abs.   צעק

צָעֲקָה id. pret. 3 pers. sing. fem.   צעק

צְעָקָה noun fem. sing. dec. 11 c (§ 42. rem. 1)   צעק

צָעֲקוּ / צָעָקוּ   Kal pret. 3 pers. pl. (§ 8. rem. 7)   צעק

צַעֲקִי / וּצְעָקִי   id. imp. fem. sing. for the latter form comp. וּצְעָדָה   צעק

צֹעֲקִים id. part. act. masc. pl. [of צֹעֵק] dec. 7 b   צעק

צְעַקְנָה id. imp. pl. fem.   צעק

וְצַעֲקַת n.fem.s., constr. of צְעָקָה d. 11 a (§ 42.r.1)   צעק

צֹעֲקַת Kal part. act. sing. fem. [of צֹעֵק]   צעק

צַעֲקָתוֹ noun fem. sing., suff. 3 pers. sing. masc. from צְעָקָה dec. 11 c (§ 42. rem. 1)   צעק

צָעַקְתִּי Kal pret. 1 pers. sing.   צעק

צַעֲקָתָם noun fem. sing., suff. 3 pers. pl. masc. from צְעָקָה dec. 11 c (§ 42. rem. 1)   צעק

[צָעַר]   to be small; metaph. to be brought low.

צָעִיר masc. dec. 3 a, fem. צְעִירָה.—I. small.—II. young.—III. pr. name of a place, 2 Ki. 8. 21.

צְעִירָה fem. dec. 10, smallness, sc. in age, youth.

צֹעַר i. q. צָעִיר Je. 14. 3; 48. 4, Kh.

צֹעַר (smallness) pr. name, Zoar, a town near the Dead Sea.

צֹעֵר (reduced) pr. name of a man.

צָעִיר (smallness) pr. name of a place of Judah, Jos. 15. 54.

מִצְעָר masc. dec. 2 b, smallness, hence—I. small, little.—II. few, 2 Ch. 24. 24.—III. short time, Is. 63. 18.

מִצְעִירָה fem. very small, Da. 8. 9.

צֹעַר   pr. name of a place   צער

צֹעֲרָה   id. with parag. ה   צער

צָפַד   to adhere, cleave, La. 4. 8.

I. [צָפָה]   I. to look about, keep watch; part. צֹפֶה a watchman.—II. to look out for, await; hence with לְ to lie in wait for, Ps. 37. 32.—III. to watch, observe closely, with acc., בְּ, בֵּין.—IV. to look out, select, Job 15. 22. Pi. I. i. q. Kal No. I.—II. to look out for, expect help, with אֶל, בְּ, and abs. Ps. 5. 4.

צְפוֹ (watch-tower) pr. name m. Ge. 36. 11, 15, called צְפִי 1 Ch. 1. 36.

צִפִּיָּה fem. dec. 10, watch-tower, La. 4. 17.

צִפְיוֹן (expectation) pr. name m. Ge. 46. 16, for which צָפוֹן Nu. 26. 15, and patronym. צְפוֹנִי ibid.

צְפִית fem. a watching, watch, Is. 21. 5.

צְפַת (watch-tower) pr. name of a city of Canaan, Ju. 1. 17.

צְפָתָה (id.) pr. name of a valley near Maresha in Judah, 2 Ch. 14. 9.

מִצְפֶּה masc. dec. 9 a.—I. watch-tower, Is. 21. 8; 2 Ch. 20. 24.—II. pr. name (a) of a town in Judah, Jos. 15. 38; (b) in Moab; (c) in Gad, Ju. 11. 29; (d) in Benjamin, Jos. 18. 26; (e) a valley in the region of Lebanon, Jos. 11. 8.

מִצְפָּה (watch-tower) pr. name—I. of a town in Gilead, the same as מִצְפֵּה־גִלְעָד.—II. of a town in Benjamin, called מִצְפָּה Jos. 18. 26.

II. [צָפָה]   Pi. צִפָּה to cover, overlay, as with wood, metal. Pu. pass.

צִפּוּי masc. a covering or overlaying of metal.

צֶפֶת fem. a chapiter, capital of a column, 2 Ch. 3. 15.

צָפֹה Kal inf. abs.   צפה

צִפָּה Piel imp. sing. masc.   צפה

צָפָה id. pret. 3 pers. sing. masc.   צפה

צֹפֶה Kal part. act. sing. masc. dec. 9 a   צפה

צָפוּ Kal pret. 3 pers. pl.   צוף

צָפוּי Kal part. pass. sing. masc. (§ 24. rem. 4)   צפה

צְפוֹ pr. name masc.   צפה

צֹפִים Kal part. act. pl. masc., suff. 3 pers. sing. masc. from צָפָה dec. 10   צפה

צִפּוּי noun masc. sing.   צפה

צָפוֹן noun masc. sing. dec. 3 a, also pr. name   צפן

צָפוֹן pr. name, see בַּעַל צָפוֹן, & צָפָה R. צפה & בעל R.

צָפוּן	וְ Kal part. pass. sing. masc. dec. 3 a .	
צָפֹנָה	וְ noun masc. sing. (צָפוֹן) with parag. ה	
צְפוּנָה	Kal part. pass. sing., fem. of צָפוּן	
צְפוּנִי	id. m. with suff. 1 pers. sing. fr. צָפוּן d. 3 a	
צְפוּנֶיךָ	id. pl. masc. with suff. 2 pers. sing. masc.	
צְפוּעֵי	Kh. צָפוּעֵי, K. צָפִיעֵי, noun masc. pl. constr. [fr. צָפִיעַ or צָפוּעַ] dec. 3 a	צפע
צִפּוֹר	וְ noun com. sing., pl. צִפֳּרִים (§ 30. rem. 1); also pr. name .	צפר

צָפַח Root not used; Arab. *to be spread out*.
   צוֹפַח (*cruse*) pr. name masc. 1 Ch. 7. 35, 36.
   צַפִּיחִת fem. *a flat cake*, Ex. 16. 31.   Also

צַפַּחַת	וְ noun fem. *a cruse* or *flask* .	צפח
צַפִּי	וְ Piel imp. sing. fem. .	צפה
צְפִי / צִפְיוֹן	pr. names masc. .	צפה
צַפְּךָ	the foll. with suff. 2 pers. sing. masc.	צפה
צֹפִים	Kal part. act. masc., pl. of צָפָה dec. 9 a	צפה
צִפִּינוּ	Piel pret. 1 pers. pl.	צפה
צְפוּנְךָ	וְ Kh. צָפוּי, K. צָפוּן adj. or Kal part. p.m., with suff. 2 pers. s. m. [fr. צָפִין] or צָפוּן d. 3 a	צפן
צָפִיר	וְ noun m. s., constr. of צָפִיר d. 3 a; וְ bef. (:)	צפר
צְפִירֵי	וְ id. pl., constr. st.; once Chald. Ezr. 6. 17, [from צָפִיר]; וְ id.	צפר
צָפִיתָ	וְ Kal pret. 2 pers. sing. masc.; acc. shifted by conv. וְ (comp. § 8. rem. 7) .	צפה

צָפַן fut. יִצְפֹן.—I. *to hide, conceal.*—II. *to lay, treasure up*; part. pass. *a treasure.*—III. *to keep back, restrain.*—IV. *to lie hid, lurk* in ambush, with ל. Niph. I. *to be hidden*, with מִן.—II. *to be laid up, destined*, with ל, Job 15. 20. Hiph. *to hide.*
   צָפוֹן com. dec. 3 a.—I. *the north*, prop. *hidden, dark quarter*; מִצָּפוֹן לְ, צָפוֹן לְ *on the north of*; צָפֹנָה, לְצָפוֹנָה *northward, towards the north*; מִצְּפוֹנָה לְ *on the north side*; מִצָּפוֹנָה *on the north side of* any place.—II. pr. name of a town in Gad, Jos. 13. 27.
   צְפוֹנִי adj. masc. *northern*, Joel 2. 20.
   צָפִין masc. dec. 3 a, *a treasure*, Ps. 17. 14, Kh.
   צְפַנְיָה (*whom the Lord has hidden*) pr. name masc.—I. the prophet *Zephaniah.*—II. a priest in the time of Jeremiah, called also צְפַנְיָהוּ.—III. Zec. 6. 10, 14.—IV. 1 Ch. 6. 21, called also אוּרִיאֵל comp. ver. 9.
   מַצְפּוּן masc. d. 1 b, only pl. *hidden places*, Ob. 6.

צָפֹן	pr. name in compos. בַּעַל צָפוֹן see under	בעל
צָפֹן	וְ Kheth. וְצָפֹן q. v., K. יִצְפֹּן Kal fut. 3 p. s. m.	צפן
צָפֹנָה	וְ defect. for צָפוֹנָה (q. v.) .	צפן
צְפַנְיָה	pr. name masc. .	צפן
צֹפֶנְיָה	Kal part. act. pl. masc., suff. 3 pers. sing. [from צָפַן] dec. 7 b .	צפן
צְפַנְיָהוּ	pr. name masc., see צְפַנְיָה	צפן
צָפַנְתָּ	Kal pret. 2 pers. sing. masc.	צפן

צָפְנַת פַּעְנֵחַ an Egyptian title given to Joseph, Ge. 41. 45, according to Jablonsky and others, *Saviour of the age.*

צָפַנְתִּי	Kal pret. 1 pers. sing. .	צפן

צָפַע Root not used; Arab. דפע *to emit, thrust out.*
   צָפוּעַ or צְפִיעַ m. d. 3 a, *excrement, dung*, Eze. 4. 15.
   צְפִיעָה fem. dec. 10, pl. *shoots*, trop. for *lower offspring*, Is. 22. 24.

צֶפַע masc. *basilisk*, Is. 14. 29.   Also

צִפְעוֹנִי	masc. i. q. צֶפַע *a basilisk* .	צפע
צִפְעֹנִים	id. pl., abs. st. .	צפע

צָפַף only Pilp. (§ 6. rem. 4).—I. *to pip, chirp.*—II. *to speak in a low, whispering voice.*

צַפְצָפָה	noun fem. sing. .	צוף

צָפַר only fut. יִצְפֹּר *to turn, return*, Ju. 7. 3. For the derivv. comp. the Arab. I. *to dance, leap, spring.*—II. *to chirp.*—III. i. q. ספר *to scratch* (Gesenius).
   צָפִיר masc. dec 3 a, *goat, he-goat.*
   צְפִיר Chald. masc. dec. 1 a, idem. Ezr. 6. 17.
   צְפִירָה fem. dec. 10.—I. *crown*, Is. 28. 5.—II. *circle, turn*, Eze. 7. 7, 10; Eng. vers. "*morning.*"
   צִפּוֹר com. (pl. צִפֳּרִים § 30. rem. 2).—I. *bird*; espec. *a sparrow.*—II. pr. name of the father of Balak, king of Moab.
   צִפַּר Chald. com. dec. 2 a, *bird*; pl. צִפֳּרִין, c. צִפֳּרֵי, Da. 4. 9, 11, 18, 30.
   צִפֹּרָה (*bird*) pr. name of the wife of Moses.
   צוֹפַר pr. name of one of Job's friends.
   צִפֹּרֶן masc. dec. 6 c.—I. *nail* of the finger, De. 21. 12.—II. *point* of a graver, Je. 17. 1.

צָפֹר	pr. name masc., see צִפּוֹר .	צפר
צֹפַר	pr. name masc., see צוֹפַר .	צפר
צְפַרְדֵּעַ	וְ masc. dec. 7 b, *frog*; collect. *frogs.*	
צְפַרְדְּעִים	id. pl., abs. st. .	צפרדע

a Pr. 13. 22.   d Ps. 83. 4.   g Je. 48. 19.   k La. 4. 17.   n Da. 8. 5, 8.   q 2 Ch. 29. 21.   t Pr. 2. 7.   w Pr. 27. 16.   z Eze. 17. 5.
b Ho. 13. 12.   e Eze. 4. 15.   h Is. 52. 8.   l Ps. 17. 14.   o Ezr. 8. 35.   p Pr. 27. 16.   s Ge. 28. 14.   Je. 8. 17.   Ps. 78. 45.
c Eze. 7. 22.   f Ps. 142. 19.

צִפֹּרָה	pr. name fem. . . . . צפר
צִפְּרֵי	Chald. noun com. pl. constr. fr. [צָפַּר] d. 1 b . צפר
צִפֲּרַיָּא	] Chald. id., pl. emph. st. . . צפר
צִפֳּרִים	'] noun com., pl. of צִפּוֹר (§ 30. rem. 1) . צפר
צִפֳּרֶנֶיהָ	noun masc. pl., suff. 3 pers. sing. fem. from צָפֹרֶן dec. 6c (§ 35. rem. 16) . . צפר

צֶפֶת Root not used; Syr. צֶפְתָּא *ornament.*
צֶפֶת masc. *chapiter, capital* of a column, 2 Ch. 3. 15.

צֶפֶת	pr. name of a place . . . צפה
צְפָתָה	pr. name of a valley . . . צפה
צְפָתֵךְ	noun fem. sing., suff. 2 pers. sing. masc. [from צָפָה dec. 10, comp. § 30. No. 3] . צוף
צָץ	Kal pret. 3 pers. sing. masc. . . ציץ
צִצִים	[for צִיצִים] noun masc., pl. of צִיץ dec. 1a ציץ
צָק	Kal imp. sing. masc. . . . יצק
צָקוּן	Kal pret. 3 p. pl. [צָקוּ] with parag. ן (§ 8. r. 4) יצק

צְקל Root not used; meaning uncertain.
צִקְלוֹן masc. dec. 1b, *bag, scrip,* 2 Ki. 4. 42; others, *husk.*

צִקְלַג / צִקְלָג	] pr. name of a city of the Philistines in the territory of Simeon; written also צִיקְלַג.
צַר / צָר	] adj. or subst. masc. sing. dec. 8. § 37. r. 7 (for this form in Is. 5. 30, see R. צָהַר) צרר
צָר	pr. name of a place . . . צרר
צֹר	noun masc. sing. (Ex. 4. 25); also pr. name צור

צָרַב Niph. *to be scorched,* Eze. 21. 3. Hence the two following.

צָרֶבֶת	[for צָרְבָת from צָרַב masc.] adj. *scorching, burning,* Pr. 16. 27 . . צרב
צָרֶבֶת	fem. *inflammation,* Le. 13. 23, 28 צרב

צָרַד Root not used; Arab. *to cool.*
צְרֵדָה (*cooling*) pr. name of a town in the tribe of Manasseh, prob. the same with צָרְתָן, צְרֵדָה.

צְרֵדָתָה	id. with parag. ה . . . צרד

צָרָה Root not used; Arab. צְרִי *to flow.*
צֳרִי, צְרִי masc.—I. *balsam,* distilling from a tree or shrub growing in Gilead.—II. pr. name, 1 Ch. 25. 3, for יִצְרִי, see יֵצֶר.
צְרוּיָה, צְרוּיָה (*fragrant*) pr. name of the mother of Joab.

צָרָה	Kal pret. 3 pers. sing. fem. [for צָרְרָה] צרר
צָרָה	] adj. or subst. fem. sing. dec. 10 [for צָרְרָה] from צַר masc. . . . צרר
צְרוּיָה	pr. name fem. . . . צרה
צָרוּעַ	Kal part. pass. sing. masc. . . צרע
צְרוּעָה	pr. name fem. . . . צרע
צָרוֹף	Kal inf. abs. . . . . צרף
צָרוּף	id. part. sing. masc. . . . צרף
צְרוֹפָה,	id. imp. sing. masc. with parag. ה, K. צָרְפָה (§ 8. rem. 11) . . צרף
צְרוּפָה	id. part. pass. sing. fem. from צָרוּף masc. צרף
צָרוֹר	Kal inf. abs. . . . . צרר
צָרוּר	id. part. pass. sing. masc. . . צרר
צְרוֹר	noun masc. sing. dec. 1 a; also pr. name צרר
צְרוּרָה	Kal part. pass. sing. fem. from צָרוּר masc. צרר
צָרוֹת	'] noun fem., pl. of צָרָה dec. 10, from צַר masc. (comp. § 30. No. 3) . . . צרר
צָרוֹתַי	id. pl., suff. 3 pers. sing. masc. . . צרר
צָרוֹתָם	id. pl., suff. 3 pers. pl. masc. (§ 4. rem. 2) צרר

[צָרַח] *to cry aloud,* Zep. 1. 14. Hiph. *to shout,* Is. 42. 13
צָרִיחַ masc. dec. 1 a, *tower, watch-tower.*

צֹרֵחַ	Kal part. act. sing. masc. . . צרח
צָרִי / צָרִי	] the foll. with suff. 1 pers. sing. . צרר
צָרֵי	noun m. pl. constr. from צַר d. 8 (§ 37. r. 7) צרר
צָרִי	id. sing. with suff. 1 pers. sing. . צרר
צֹרִי	gent. noun from צוֹר . . . צור
צְרִי / צְרִי	] noun masc. sing. (§ 35. rem. 14); for ן see lett. ן צרה
צֳרִי	] noun m. s., or pr. name (1 Ch. 25. 3); ן bef. (:) צרה
צָרֶיהָ	noun masc. pl., suff. 3 pers. sing. fem. from צַר dec. 8 (§ 37. rem. 7) . . צרר
צִרֶיהָ	noun masc. pl., suff. 3 pers. sing. masc. from צִיר dec. 1 a . . . . ציר
צָרֵיהֶם	] noun masc. pl., suff. 3 pers. pl. masc. from צַר dec. 8 (§ 37. rem. 7) . . צרר
צָרָיו	id. pl. with suff. 3 pers. sing. masc. . צרר
צְרִיחַ	noun masc. sing. dec. 1 a . . . צרר
צָרַיִךְ / צָרָיִךְ	] noun masc. pl., suff. 2 pers. sing. fem. from צַר dec. 8 (§ 37. rem. 7) . . צרר
צָרַיִךְ	id. pl. with suff. 2 pers. sing. masc. . צרר
צָרִים	id. pl., abs. st. . . . . צרר
צִרִים	noun masc. pl., of צִיר dec. 1 a . . ציר
צָרִימוֹ	noun masc. pl., suff. 3 pers. pl. masc. from צַר dec. 8 (§ 37. rem. 7) . . צרר
צָרֵינוּ	id. pl. with suff. 1 pers. pl. . . צרר

a Da. 4. 9, 18. | e Eze. 32. 6. | i Is. 23. 20. | m Ps. 26. 2. | q 1 Sa. 25. 29. | u Ps. 119. 157. | y Ge. 37. 25. | A Je. 50. 7. | E Je. 30. 16.
b Da. 4. 11. | f Eze. 7. 10. | k Ps. 78. 49. | n Nu. 25. 17. | r 1 Sa. 34. 18. | v Job 16. 9. | z La. 1. 5. | B Ju. 9. 45. | F La. 1. 7.
c Ne. 5. 19. | g 2 Ki. 4. 41. | l Je. 6. 29. | o Ho. 13. 12. | s Zep. 1. 14. | w Eze. 27. 17. | C 1 Sa. 4. 19. | D La. 2. 17. | G De. 32. 27.
d De. 21. 12. | h Is. 26. 16. | m Ps. 12. 7. | nn De.30.17,21.

צֹרֶךְ — masc. *need, necessity*, only in the following form.

צָרְכֶּֽךָ — noun masc. sing., suff. 2 pers. sing. masc. from [צֹרֶךְ] dec. 6 c . . . צרך

צָרַע — only part. pass. צָרוּעַ, and Pu. part. מְצֹרָע *struck with leprosy, leprous.*

צְרוּעָה (*leprous*) pr. name of the mother of Jeroboam, 1 Ki. 11. 26.

צִרְעָה fem. collect. *wasps* or *hornets.* Also the two following.

צָרְעָה (?) (*smiting, defeat*; Geser.ius, *place of hornets*) pr. name of a town of the Danites in Judah. Gent. noun צָרְעָתִי, צָרְעִי . צרע

צָרַעַת / צָרַעַת (?) — {fem. dec. 13 a [for צַרְעַת, hence with suff. צָרַעְתּוֹ] *leprosy*, of men, houses, garments}   צרע

צָרַף — fut. יִצְרֹף.—I. *to refine* metals; part. צֹרֵף *refiner*; also *goldsmith, silversmith.*—II. metaph. *to purify*, Da. 11. 35; part. pass. צָרוּף *purified, pure.*—III. metaph. *to try, prove.*

צָרְפִי (*goldsmith*) pr. name masc. Ne. 3. 31.

צָרְפַת (*fusion*) pr. name of a town between Tyre and Zidon.

וְיִּצְרֹף (??) Kal part. act. sing. masc. dec. 7 b . צרף
צָרְפַת pr. name of a place . . . צרף
צָרְפָתָה id. with parag. ה . . . צרף
צְרָפַתְהוּ Kal pret. 3 pers. sing. fem., suff. 3 pers. s. m.   צרף
צְרַפְתִּיךָ id. pret. 1 pers. sing., suff. 2 pers. sing. masc.   צרף
צְרָפִים id. id., suff. 3 pers. pl. masc.; וֹ, for וְ, conv.   צרף
צְרַפְתָּנוּ id. pret. 2 pers. sing. masc., suff. 1 pers. pl.   צרף
צְרַפְתָּנִי id. id., suff. 1 pers. sing. . . צרף

צָרַר — I. *to tie* or *bind up*; metaph. of the wind, Ho. 4. 19.—II. *to shut up*, 2 Sa. 20. 3.—III. *to be hostile to*; part. צֹרֵר *adversary.*—IV. intrans. *to be straitened, distressed*, only impers. צַר לִי *I am distressed, in a strait; I grieve*; fut. וַיֵּצֶר לִי (§ 18. rem. 6) id. Pu. part. *bound up.* Hiph. הָצֵר, inf. הָצֵר.—I. *to straiten, distress, vex.*—II. *to be distressed, in pains, pangs*, Je. 48. 41; 49. 22.

צַר masc. dec. 8 (§ 37. rem. 7).—I. adj. *strait, narrow*; fem. צָרָה Pr. 23. 27.—II. subst. *adversary, enemy.*—III. subst. *distress, adversity.*—IV. *stone, flint*, Is. 5. 28.

צֵר (*flint*) pr. name of a place in Naphtali, Jos. 19. 35.

צָרָה fem. dec. 10 (for צַרָּה, comp. צַר).—I. *female adversary, a rival*, 1 Sa. 1. 6.—II. *distress, adversity*; with ה parag. צָרָתָה.—III. *anguish.*

צְרוֹר masc. (pl. צְרֹרוֹת).—I. *bundle.*—II. *bag, purse.*—III. *a small stone, a grain, kernel*, 2 Sa. 17. 13; Am. 9. 9.—IV. pr. name masc. 1 Sa. 9. 1.

מֵצַר masc. dec. 8 (§ 37. rem. 7; pl. מְצָרִים), *straitness, distress.*

צֹרֵר Kal part. act. sing. masc. dec. 7 b . . צרר
צָרְרוּ id. pret. 3 pers. pl.   צרר
צְרָרוּנִי id. id., suff. 1 pers. sing. . . צרר
צְרֹרוֹת noun m. with pl. fem. term. fr. צְרוֹר dec. 1 a   צרר
צְרֹרִי the foll. with suff. 1 pers. sing.   צרר
צֹרְרֵי Kal part. act. pl. constr. masc. from צוֹרֵר dec. 7 b . . צרר
צֹרְרֶיךָ id. pl., suff. 2 pers. sing. masc.   צרר
צֹרְרִים id. pl., abs. st. . . צרר
צְרֻרֹת id. part. pass. fem. pl. of צְרוּדָה fr. צָרוּר masc.   צרר
צַרְתָּ Kal pret. 2 pers. sing. masc.; acc. shifted by conv. וְ (comp. § 8. rem. 7) . צור
צָרַת noun fem. sing., constr. of צָרָה dec. 10, from צַר masc.   צרר
צָרֶת pr. name [for צֹהֶרֶת] . . צהר
צָרָתָהּ adj. fem. sing., suff. 3 pers. sing. fem. from צָרָה dec. 10, from צַר masc. (§ 30. No. 3)   צרר
צָרָתִי noun fem. sing., suff. 1 pers. s. fr. צָרָה d. 10   צרר
צַרְתִּי Kal pret. 1 pers. sing.; acc. shifted by conv. וְ (comp. § 8. rem. 7) . צור
צָרַתְכֶם noun fem. pl., suff. 2 pers. pl. masc. from צָרָה dec. 10, from צַר masc. (§ 30. No. 3)   צרר
צָרַתְכֶם id. sing., suff. 2 pers. pl. masc.   צרר
צָרַתָם id. sing., suff. 3 pers. pl. masc.   צרר
צָרְתָן pr. name of a place, see צְרֵדָה under . צרד
צָרְתָנָה id. with parag. ה.
צַרְתָּנִי Kal pret. 2 pers. sing. masc., suff. 1 pers. sing.   צור

ק

קָאָה Kal pret. 3 pers. sing. fem. . קוא
קָאוֹ noun masc. s., suff. 3 p. s. m. fr. [קֵא] d. 1 a   קוא
קָאֵם Chald. Peal part. act. sing. masc. dec. 2 b   קום

קָאם Kal pret. 3 pers. s. m. for קָם (§ 21. r. 1)   קום
קָאֲמַיָּא Ch. Peal part. act. pl. emph. m. fr. קָאֵם d. 2 b   קום
קָאֲמִין Chald. id. pl. abs.; K. קָיְמִין from קָאֵם . קום

a 2 Ch. 2. 15.   b Ps. 105. 19.   c Ps. 66. 10.   d Ps. 129. 1, 2.   e Is. 11. 13.   f 1 Sa. 1. 6.   g Ps. 139. 5.   h Da. 2. 31.   i Da. 7. 16
k 2 Ki. 5. 27.   l Is. 48. 10.   m Ps. 17. 3.   n Ge. 42. 35.   o Nu. 25. 18.   p 1 Sa. 10. 19.   q Le. 18. 28.   r Ho. 10. 14.   s Da. 3. 3
t Je. 6. 29.   u Zec. 13. 9.   v Nu. 33. 55.   w Ps. 23. 5.   x Ge. 42. 21.   y Ju. 10. 14.   z Pr. 26. 11.   aa Is. 40. 19.

קוֹא   קָאת noun fem. sing. (constr. קָאת) .

קבב   קָב‏ֹ Kal inf. abs. . . .

[קָבַב] *to curse.* According to the derivv. *to hollow out; to arch, vault,* Arab. id.

קַב masc. *a cab,* a measure containing the sixth part of a סְאָה, 2 Ki. 6. 25.

קֻבָּה fem. dec. 10, *alcove, tent,* Nu. 25. 8.

קבב   קָבֳּה‏ֹ id. imp. sing. masc. [קֹב] with parag. ה

קבב   קָבֳּה id. pret. 3 pers. s. m. [קַב], suff. 3 p. s. m.

קבץ   קִבּוּצֶיִ‏ךָ noun m. pl., suff. 2 pers. s. f. fr. [קִבּוּץ] d. 1 b

קבץ   קְבוּצִים Kal part. pass. masc. pl. [of קָבוּץ] dec. 3 a .

קבר   קָבוֹר‏ֹ id. inf. abs.

קבר   קָבוּר‏ֹ id. part. pass. sing. masc. dec. 3 a

קבר   קְבוּרָה‏ֹ noun fem. sing. dec. 10 . .

קבר   קְבֻרַת id., constr. st. . .

קָבַל Kal not used; prob. *to be before, in front;* Arab. *to meet.* Pi. קִבֵּל.—I. *to receive,* sc. a person who comes to meet one, 1 Ch. 12. 18; hence *to receive, accept* instruction, Pr. 19. 20.—II. *to take.*—III. *to undertake,* Est. 9. 23; with עַל *to take upon* oneself, ver. 27. Hiph. *to stand over against each other.*

קְבַל Chald. Pa. *to receive.*

קֹבֶל masc. (prop. *something opposed*) poet. for *battering-ram,* Eze. 26. 9. And the foll.

קֳבֵל Heb. (only 2 Ki. 15. 10) יִקָבֵל, קֳבֵל Chald. —I. prep. לְקֳבֵל, לָקֳבֵל (a) *over against,* Da. 5. 5; (b) *before,* with suff. לְקָבְלָךְ; and without לְ 2 Ki. 15. 10, *in the presence of;* (c) *on account, because of,* Da. 5. 1; Ezr. 4. 16; (d) with דִּי, conj. *because that,* Ezr. 6. 13.—II. כָּל־קֳבֵל־דְּנָה conj. lit. *wholly on account of this,* i. e. *for this cause;* כָּל־קֳבֵל דִּי, *because that, since.*

קבל   וַ‏ֹקַבֵּל Chald. Peal 3 p. s. m.; Heb. Piel imp. s. m.

קבל   קַבֵּל‏ֹ Piel imp. sing. masc. for קַבֵּל (§ 10. rem. 4)

קבל   קִבֵּל‏ֹ id. pret. 3 pers. sing. masc. . .

קבל   וַ‏ֹקְבְּלוּ id. pret. 3 pers. pl. . .

קבל   קַבְּלוֹ‏ֹ noun masc. sing., suff. 3 pers. s. m. [fr. קֹבֶל]. A composite sheva to be followed by dag. forte, as is the case in this word and in קְטַנִּי, is contrary to the principles of Heb. syllabication; and since the copies vary in both these instances, the forms קַבֵּלוֹ

קבל   קְטַנִּי or קָטְנִי‏ֹ, קַבְּלוּ, קַטְנִי are to be preferred, comp. § 35. rem. 8, & § 37. No. 3

קבב   וַ‏ֹקָבְנוּ‏ֹ Kal imp. sing. masc. [קֹב] with epenth. נ and suff. 3 pers. sing. masc. (§ 16. r. 13)

קבע   וַ‏ֹקָבַע‏ֹ fut. יִקְבַּע (Arab. *to cover, hide;* hence) *to defraud, rob.*

קוֹבַע m. (constr. קוֹבַע, comp. § 31. r. 5) *helmet.* קֻבַּעַת fem. *cup, goblet,* Is. 51. 17, 22.

קבע   קֻבְעֵיהֶם‏ֹ the foll. with suff. 3 pers. pl. masc. .

קבע   קֹבְעִים‏ֹ Kal part. act. masc. pl. [of קֹבֵעַ] dec. 7 b

קבע   קְבַעֲנוּ‏ֹ id. pret. 1 pers. pl., with suff. 1 pers. pl.

קבע   קֻבַּעַת‏ֹ noun fem. sing. . .

קָבַץ fut. יִקְבּ‏ֹץ.—I. *to collect, gather.*—II. *to gather together, assemble.* Niph. pass. Pi. I. *to take into one's arms,* Is. 40. 11.—II. *to collect, gather.*—III. *to gather together, assemble.*—IV. *to gather to oneself, draw in,* Joel 2. 6; Na. 2. 11. Pu. pass. Hithp. reflex.

קִבּוּץ masc. dec. 1 b, *company, troop,* Is. 57. 13. קְבֻצָה fem. dec. 10, *collection, heap,* Eze. 22. 20. קְבָצַיִם (*two heaps*) pr. n. of a town in Ephraim Jos. 21. 22.

קַבְצְאֵל, יְקַבְצְאֵל (*which God shall gather*) pr name of a town in Judea.

קבץ   קַבֵּץ‏ֹ Piel inf. constr. for abs. . .

קבץ   קְבֹץ‏ֹ Kal imp. sing. masc. . .

קבץ   וַ‏ֹקְבֵּץ‏ֹ id. part. act. sing. masc. . .

קבץ   קַבְצְאֵל pr. name masc., see יְקַבְצְאֵל (q. v.) .

קבץ   קִבְּצָה‏ֹ Piel pret. 3 pers. s. f. [for קִבְּצָה as if fr. a s. קָבַץ comp. § 10. r. 1, & § 8. r. 1 & 7]

קבץ   קִבְּצוּ‏ֹ id. pret. 3 pers. pl.

קבץ   קִבְצוּ‏ֹ וַ‏ֹ Kal imp. pl. masc.

קבץ   קַבְצִי‏ֹ Piel inf. (קְבֹץ), suff. 1 pers. sing. dec. 7 b

קבץ   קִבְצַיִם pr. name of a place

קבץ   קִבֶּצְךָ‏ֹ Piel pret. 3 p. s. m. [קִבֵּץ], suff. 2 p. s. m.

קבץ   קִבְּצָם‏ֹ, קִבְּצָן‏ֹ id. id., suff. 3 pers. pl. masc. & fem. .

קבץ   קִבְּצֵנוּ‏ֹ id. imp. sing. masc. [קְבֹץ], suff. 1 pers. pl.

קבץ   קְבֻצַת‏ֹ noun fem. sing., constr. of [קְבוּצָה] dec. 10

קבץ   קִבַּצְתִּי‏ֹ Piel pret. 1 p.s.; acc. shifted by conv. וַ(§ 8.r.7)

קבץ   קִבַּצְתִּים‏ֹ id. id., suff. 3 pers. pl. masc. . .

קָבַר‏ֹ fut. יִקְבּ‏ֹר *to bury.* Niph. pass. Pi. *to bury.* Pu. pass. Ge. 25. 10.

קְבוּרָה‏ֹ f. d.10.—I. *burial.*—II. *burial-place.* Also

a Nu. 23. 25.   e Ne. 5. 16.   Da. 6. 1.   m Est. 9. 27.   Pr. 22. 23.   s Is. 51. 17, 22.   b Eze. 22. 19.   z 2 Ch. 24. 5.   i Is. 34. 16.
b Nu. 22. 11, 17.   f Dc. 21. 23.   k Da. 5. 5.   o Ezr. 8. 30.   q Pr. 22. 23.   t 1 Ki. 20. 1.   c Zep. 3. 20.   Eze. 22. 20.
c Nu. 23. 8.   g 1 Ki. 18. 31.   l 1 Ch. 21. 11.   p Eze. 26. 9.   r Mal. 3. 8, 9.   u Mi. 2. 12.   d De. 30. 3.   k Ge. 23. 19.
d Is. 57. 13.   h Ec. 6. 3.   m Est. 4. 4; 9. 23.   w Nu. 23. 13.   Mal. 3. 8.   g 1 Ki. 18. 19.   e Mi. 1. 7.

קָבַר
קֶבֶר — m. d. 6 a (with suff. קִבְרִי, though in pause קָבֶר § 35. rem. 2, & pl. קְבָרִים, קְבָרוֹת).—I. *sepulchre.*—II. קִבְרוֹת הַתַּאֲוָה (*sepulchres of lust*) pr. name of a place in the desert of Sinai

קְבֹר — Kal imp. sing. masc.; בef.   קבר
קִבְרִי — id. part. act. sing. masc. dec. 7 b   קבר
קֻבַּר — Pual pret. 3 pers. sing. masc.   קבר
קְבָרֻהוּ — Kal pret. 3 pers. pl. (קָבְרוּ), suff. 3 pers. s. m.   קבר
קָבְרוֹ — id. inf., suff. 3 pers. sing. masc.   קבר
קָבְרוּ — id. pret. 3 pers. pl.   קבר
קִבְרוֹ — noun m. s., suff. 3 pers. sing. m. fr. קֶבֶר d. 6 a   קבר
קִבְרוּ — Kal imp. pl. masc.   קבר
קָבְרוּהָ — id. id., suff. 3 pers. sing fem.   קבר
קְבָרוּם — id. pret. 3 p. pl., suff. 3 p. pl. m.; בef.   קבר
קִבְרוֹת — noun masc. with pl. fem. term., constr. st. fr. קֶבֶר d. 6 a, & pr. name in compos. קִ׳ הַתַּאֲוָה   קבר
קִבְרוֹתֶיהָ — id. pl., suff. 3 pers. sing. fem.   קבר
קִבְרוֹתֶיךָ — id. pl., suff. 2 pers. sing. masc.   קבר
קִבְרוֹתֵיכֶם — id. pl., suff. 2 pers. pl. masc.   קבר
קִבְרֵי — id. pl., constr. masc.   קבר
קִבְרִי — id. sing., suff. 1 pers. sing.   קבר
קְבָרִים — id. pl., abs. masc.   קבר
קְבֻרִים — Kal part. pass. masc., pl. of קָבוּר dec. 3 a   קבר
קֹבְרִים — id. part. act. masc pl. of קֹבֵר dec. 7 b   קבר
קִבְרֵינוּ — noun masc. pl., suff. 1 pers. pl. from קֶבֶר d. 6 a   קבר
קִבְרְךָ — id. sing., suff. 2 pers. sing. masc.   קבר
קְבֻרַת — n. f. s., constr. of קְבוּרָה d. 10, comp.   קבר
קְבֻרָתָהּ — id. with suff. 3 pers. sing. fem.   קבר
קְבֻרֹתָהּ — defect. for קִבְרוֹתֶיהָ (q. v.)   קבר
קְבֻרָתוֹ — noun fem. s., suff. 3 pers. s. m. fr. קְבוּרָה d. 10   קבר
קְבַרְתּוֹ — Kal pret. 2 pers. sing. masc., suff. 3 pers. sing. masc.; וֹ, for וֹ, conv.   קבר
קָבַרְתִּי — id. pret. 1 pers. sing.   קבר
קְבָרֹתֶיהָ — noun masc., with pl. fem. term. & suff. 3 pers. sing. fem. from קֶבֶר dec. 6 a   קבר
קִבְרֹתָיו — id. pl. with suff. 3 pers. sing. masc.   קבר
קִבְרֹתֶיךָ — id. pl. with suff. 2 pers. sing. masc.   קבר
קְבַרְתֶּם — Kal pret. 2 pers. pl. masc.; וֹ, for וֹ, conv.   קבר
קְבַרְתַּנִי — id. pret. 2 pers. s. m. with suff. 1 p. s.; וֹ id.   קבר
קֻבָּתָהּ — noun fem. s., suff. 3 p. s. f. [fr. קֻבָּה for נְקֻבָּה]   נקב
קַבֹּתוֹ — Kal pret. 2 p. s. m. [קַבֹּתָ], suff. 3 pers. sing. masc.   קבב

קָדַד — only fut. יִקֹּד (§ 18. rem. 14) *to bow the head*, demon. of

קָדְקֹד — masc. (with suff. קָדְקֳדוֹ § 36. rem. 6) *crown of the head.*

קִדָּה — fem. *cassia*, Ex. 30. 24 ; Eze. 27. 19.   קדה
קַדּוּמִים — noun masc. p.   קדם
קָדוֹשׁ — adj. masc. sing. dec. 3 a   קדש
קְדוֹשׁ — id., constr. st.; בef. (:)   קדש
קְדוֹשׁוֹ — id., suff. 3 pers. sing. masc.; id.   קדש
קְדוֹשִׁים — id. pl., abs. st.   קדש
קְדוֹשְׁכֶם — id. sing., suff. 2 pers. pl. masc.   קדש

[קָדַח] — I. *to kindle.*—II. *to be kindled, to burn.*
קַדַּחַת — fem. *burning fever.*
אֶקְדָּח — masc. prob. *the carbuncle*, Is. 54. 12

קָדְחָה — Kal pret. 3 pers. sing. fem.   קדח
קֹדְחֵי — id. part. act. pl. c. masc. [from קֹדַח] dec. 7 b   קדח
קְדַחְתֶּם — id. pret. 2 pers. pl. masc.   קדח
קָדִים — noun masc. sing.   קדם
קָדִימָה — id. with loc. ה   קדם
קַדִּישׁ — Chald. adj. masc. sing. dec. 1 a   קדש
קַדִּישֵׁי — Chald. id. pl., constr. st.   קדש
קַדִּישִׁין — Chald. id. pl., abs. st.   קדש

קָדַם — Pi. קִדֵּם.—I. *to go before, precede.*—II. *to be beforehand, prevent, anticipate*; hence *to be early*, Ps. 119. 147.—III. *to meet any one with an offering, for succour, also in a hostile manner.* Hiph. I. *to come before, anticipate*, Job 41. 3.—II. *to come upon*, as calamity, Am. 9. 10.

קֶדֶם — masc. dec. 6 a, strictly *what is before, in front.*—I. adv. *before*, Ps. 139. 5.—II. *the east*; מִקֶּדֶם *on the east*; מִקֶּדֶם לְ *on the east of.*—III. *olden time*; מִקֶּדֶם *of old*; adv. *formerly.*—IV. *beginning*, Pr. 8. 23.

קֵדְמָה — masc. only with ה loc. קֵדְמָה *eastward.*
קָדִים — masc.—I. *the front*, only קָדִימָה *forwards*, Hab. 1. 9.—II. *the east.*—III. *east wind.*
קַדְמוֹנִים — masc. pl. *ancients*, Ju. 5. 21.
קֳדָם — Chald. *before*; מִן־קֳדָם *from before, from the presence of, by order of*; with suff. קָדָמֵיהוֹן, קָדָמוֹהִי, קָדָמָיִךְ
קַדְמָה — fem. (constr. קַדְמַת, pl. קַדְמוֹת, no pl. abs.)—I. *beginning, origin.*—II. *former state.*
קַדְמָה — Chald. *former time*; מִן־קַדְמַת דְּנָה *aforetime, formerly.*
קֵדְמָה — (*eastward*) pr. name masc. Ge. 25. 15.
קֵדְמָה — fem. only constr. קִדְמַת *eastward of.*
קַדְמוֹן — adj. masc. *eastern*, Eze. 47. 8.
קְדֵמוֹת — (*origin*) pr. name of a city of Reuben and an adjacent desert.

Ge. 23. 11, 15; 50. 6.   2 Ki. 9. 10. Ge. 25. 10.   2 Ch. 24. 25.   Ge. 49. 29.   2 Ki. 9. 34.   Eze. 39. 12.   Eze. 32. 26.   2 Ch. 34. 28.   Eze. 37. 12. 13.   Je. 20. 17.   Ec. 8. 10.   2 Ki. 13. 21.   Ge. 23. 6.   Na. 1. 14.   Ge. 35. 20.   Eze. 32. 25.   De. 34. 6.   1 Ki. 2. 31.   Eze. 32. 23.   Eze. 32. 22.   2 Ki. 22. 20.   1 Ki. 13. 31.   Ge. 47. 30.   Nu. 25. 8.   Nu. 23. 27.   Ju. 5. 21.   Is. 10. 17; 49. 7.   Is. 43. 15.   Is. 50. 11.   Is. 17. 4.   Da. 4. 10, 20.   Da. 7. 18, 27.

קַדְמֹנִי masc. adj.—I. *front, anterior,* Eze. 10. 19; 11. 1. — II. *eastern.* — III. *former, ancient*; pl. קַדְמֹנִים *ancients*; fem. קַדְמֹנִיֹּות *former things.*— IV. pr. name of a Canaanitish tribe, Ge. 15. 19.

קַדְמַי Chald. masc. dec. 7, *first, former.*

קַדְמִיאֵל (*one in the presence of God*) pr. name of a man.

קֳדָם Chald. (prop. subs. masc.) as a *prep.* dec. 1a   קדם

וְקֳדָם ᶜᶜ noun masc. & prep. d. 6a; for ו see lett. ו   קדם

קָדְמָה • defect. for קְדִימָה (q.v.) . . . קדם

קַדְּמֵה ᵍ Piel imp. sing. masc. [קַדַּם] with parag. ה   קדם

וְקֵדְמָה ᵍ noun masc. sing. [קֶדֶם] with loc. ה, also pr. name; for ו see lett. ו . . . קדם

קִדְּמוּ Piel pret. 3 pers. pl. . . . קדם

קָדְמֹוהִי } Chald. prep. (קֳדָם, קֳדָם) pl. with suff.
קָדָמֹוהִי } 3 pers. sing. masc. dec. 1a; ו bef. ‿ } קדם

קִדְּמוּנִי Piel pret. 3 pers. pl., suff. 1 pers. sing.   קדם

קַדְמֹונִים • adj. masc. pl. [of קַדְמֹונִי] . . . קדם

קִדְמֹות ᶦ pr. name of a place; ו bef. ‿   קדם

קָדָמַי } Chald. prep. (קֳדָם) pl. with suff. 1 pers.
קָדָמָי } sing. dec. 1 } קדם

קַדְמָיָא Chald. adj. pl. emph. masc. [fr. קַדְמַי comp. dec. 7 & § 63] . . . .   קדם

קַדְמִיאֵל pr. name masc.   קדם

קָדָמֹיהּ } Chald. prep. (קֳדָם) pl. with suff. 3 pers.
קָדָמַיהּ ᵍ } sing. fem. dec. 1a } קדם

קָדָמֵיהֹון Chald. id. pl., suff. 3 pers. pl. masc. .   קדם

קָדָמָיךְ ᶦ Chald. id. pl., suff. 2 pers. sing. masc. .   קדם

קַדְמָיְתָא Chald. adj. pl. fem. emph. [of קַדְמָאָה dec. 11, from קַדְמַי masc.] .   קדם

קַדְמָיְתָא Chald. id. sing., emph. st. . . . קדם

קָדָמָךְ Chald. prep. (קֳדָם) pl. with suff. 2 p. s. m.   קדם

קָדְמֵנִי • defect. for קְדִימֹנִי (q.v.) . . . קדם

וְקַדְמֹנִיֹּות adj. fem. pl. [of נִיָה, from קַדְמֹנִי masc.]   קדם

וְקַדְמֹנִים • defect. for קַדְמֹונִים (q.v.) . . . קדם

קַדְמַת ᶦ Chald. noun f. s. constr. [of קַדְמָה, no pl.]   קדם

קִדְמַת noun fem. sing. constr. [of קִדְמָה] as a *prep.*   קדם

קַדְמָתֵהּ ᵍ noun fem. sing., suff. 3 pers. sing. fem. [from קַדְמָה, no pl.]   קדם

קִדַּמְתִּי Piel pret. 1 pers. sing. . . . קדם

וְקָדְקֹד noun masc. sing. (§ 36. r. 6, & § 30. r. 2)   קדד

קָדְקֳדֹו } id., suff. 3 pers. sing. masc. . . . קדד
קָדְקֳדֹו }

קָדְקֳדֶךָ • id., suff. 2 pers. sing. masc. . . . קדד

קָדַר I. *to be turbid,* Job 6. 16.—II. *to be black, dark.* — III. part. act. *mourning.* Hiph. I. *to darken,*

---

obscure, Eze. 32. 7, 8.—II. *to cause to mourn,* Eze. 31. 15. Hithp. *to become darkened,* 1 Ki. 18. 45.

קֵדָר (*dark-skinned*) pr. name of a son of Ishmael; also a tribe descended from him, more fully בְּנֵי קֵדָר.

קִדְרֹון (*turbid*) pr. name, *Kedron,* a brook between Jerusalem and the mount of Olives.

קַדְרוּת fem. *darkness,* Is. 50. 3.

קְדֹרַנִּית adv. *mournfully,* Mal. 3. 14.

וְקֵדָר ᵖ pr. name of a tribe . . . קדר

קֹדֵר Kal part. act. sing. masc. dec. 7b . . קדר

קָדְרוּ } Kal pret. 3 pers. pl. (§ 8. rem. 7) . . קדר
וְ᾿ ᵍ }

קִדְרֹון pr. name of a brook . . . . קדר

קַדְרוּת noun fem. sing. . . . . קדר

וְקֹדְרִים ᵏ Kal part. act. masc., pl. of קֹדֵר dec. 7b   קדר

קְדֹרַנִּית adv. after the form אַחֲרַנִּית . . קדר

קָדַרְתִּי Kal pret. 1 pers. sing. . . . קדר

קָדֵשׁ וְ, also קָדַשׁ (Nu. 17. 2) fut. יִקְדַּשׁ.—I. *to be holy,* spoken of a man who devotes himself to God, and thus *separates* himself from the rest of the people, comp. Is. 65. 5; Syr. ܩܕܫ *to separate, devote, consecrate.*—II. *to be sacred,* of things *set apart* for God; also *to be consecrated, rendered sacred,* either by touching sacred things, or by being destined for the sacred worship. Niph. I. *to be rendered holy, consecrated,* Ex. 29. 43.—II. *to be regarded as holy, to be sanctified, reverenced.* Pi. I. *to set apart for sacred use, to consecrate, hallow, sanctify.* —II. *to regard as sacred, to keep holy.*—III. *to hallow, sanctify, reverence,* sc. God.—IV. *to render sacred,* by contact.—V. *to appoint a fast or religious festival.*—VI. *to prepare by sacred rites;* hence, *to purify.* Pu. pass. of Pi. No. I, also II, Is. 13. 3. Hiph. i. q. Pi. Nos. I, II & III. Hithp. I. *to consecrate oneself;* espec. *to prepare oneself before approaching something sacred;* hence, *to purify oneself.*—II. *to sanctify oneself, cause to be reverenced,* Eze. 38. 23 — III. *to be celebrated, kept holy,* Is. 30. 29.

קָדֵשׁ masc.—I. *a male prostitute, sodomite;* fem. קְדֵשָׁה *prostitute, harlot;* prop. one *devoted to prostitution in honour of idols.*—II. קָדֵשׁ בַּרְנֵעַ pr. name of a city in the desert, south of Palestine, between Idumea and Egypt.

קָדֹושׁ adj. masc. dec. 3a.—I. *holy,* of God.—II.

ᵃ Ez. 48. 4, 5, 23.   ᵈ Eze. 38. 17.   ᵍ Da. 7. 20.   ᵏ Da. 7. 8.   ⁿ Mal. 3. 4.   ᵖ Da. 6. 11.   ᵗ Job 2. 7.   ʸ Je. 14. 2.   ᵇ Job 5. 11.
ᵇ Ps. 17. 13.   ᵉ Da. 7. 24.   ʰ Da. 4. 4.   ˡ Da. 7. 4.   ᵒ Is. 43. 18.   ᵠ Is. 23. 7.   ᵘ De. 28. 35.   ᶻ Je. 4. 28.   ᶜ Je. 8. 21.
ᶜ Da. 7. 13.   ᶠ Da. 7. 7, 8.   ᶦ Da. 6. 23.   ᵐ Da. 5. 23.   ᵖ Job 18. 20.   ʳ Je. 48. 45.   ˣ Mi. 3. 6.   ᵃ Is. 50. 3.   ᵈ Ex. 29. 21.

set apart, sacred, holy to God; pl. קְדֹשִׁים (*a*) of God; (*b*) of angels; (*c*) of men, *saints*.

קַדִּישׁ Chald. masc. dec. 1 a, *holy*, of God; of angels; of men, *saints*.

קֶדֶשׁ (*sanctuary*) pr. name—I. of a town in Judah, Jos. 15. 23.—II. of another in Naphtali.—III. of a third in Issachar, 1 Ch. 6. 57, called also קִשְׁיוֹן Jos. 19. 20; 21. 28.

קֹדֶשׁ (once קוֹדֶשׁ) masc. dec. 6 c (comp. § 35. rem. 8).—I. *holiness.*—II. *that which is holy, sacred, consecrated* to God.—III. *holy place*; קֹדֶשׁ קָדָשִׁים (*a*) *something most holy*; (*b*) *Holy of Holies*, the place within the vail of the tabernacle.

מִקְדָּשׁ masc. dec. 2 b.—I. *any thing sacred*, Nu. 18. 29.—II. *holy place, sanctuary.*—III. *asylum, place of refuge.*

קָדַשׁ	noun masc. sing. dec. 4 a	קדש
קָדֵשׁ	pr. name of a place, and in compos. קָ׳ בַּרְנֵעַ	קדש
קָדֹשׁ	adj. masc. sing. dec. 3 a	קדש
קַדֵּשׁ־	} Piel imp. sing. masc. (§ 10. rem. 4)	קדש
קַדֵּשׁ	}	
קָדֵשׁ	} pr. name of a place	קדש
קְדוֹשׁ	adj. masc. sing., constr. of קָדֹשׁ dec. 3 a	קדש
קִדֵּשׁ	} Piel pret. 3 pers. sing. masc. (§ 10. r. 1)	קדש
קָדְשׁוֹ	} noun masc. sing. dec. 6 c	קדש
קָדֵשָׁה	pr. name of a place (קָדֵשׁ) with loc. ה	קדש
קֵדְשָׁה	} pr. name of a place (קֶדֶשׁ) with loc. ה	קדש
קַדְשָׁה	}	
קְדֵשָׁה	noun fem. sing., pl. קְדֵשׁוֹת, from קָדֵשׁ masc.	קדש
קָדְשׁוּ	Kal pret. 3 pers. pl. [for קָדְשׁוּ § 8. r. 1 & 7]	קדש
קַדְּשׁוּ	} Piel imp. pl. masc. (v. id.)	קדש
קַדְּשׁוֹ	}	
קִדְּשׁוֹ	} id. pret. 3 pers. sing. masc., suff. 3 p. s. m.	קדש
קִדְּשׁוּ	} id. pret. 3 pers. pl.	קדש
קָדְשׁוֹ	noun m. s., suff. 3 pers. s. m. fr. קֹדֶשׁ d. 6 c	קדש
קָדְשׁוֹ	} Kh. קָדְשׁוֹ q. v., K. קָדְשֵׁי (q. v.)	קדש
קִדְּשׁוֹהוּ	Piel pret. 3 pers. pl., suff. 3 pers. sing. masc.	קדש
קָדְשִׁי	} noun masc. pl., suff. 1 pers. sing. from	קדש
קָדְשֵׁי	} קֹדֶשׁ dec. 6 c	
קָדְשֵׁי	} id. pl., constr. st.	קדש
	id. sing., suff. 1 pers. sing.	
קְדֹשִׁי	adj. masc. s., suff. 1 pers. s. fr. קָדֹשׁ d. 3 a	קדש
קָדְשֵׁיהֶם	noun m. pl., suff. 3 p. pl. m. fr. קֹדֶשׁ d. 6 c	קדש
קָדְשָׁיו	} id. pl. suff. 3 pers. sing. masc. (§ 35.	קדש
קֳדָשָׁיו	} rem. 8)	
קְדֹשָׁיו	adj. pl. masc., suff. 3 pers. sing. masc. from	קדש
	קָדֹשׁ dec. 3 a	

קְדֹשֶׁיךָ	noun masc. pl., suff. 2 pers. sing. masc. from קֹדֶשׁ dec. 6 c (§ 35. rem. 8)	קדש
קָדְשֵׁיכֶם	id. pl., suff. 2 pers. pl. masc.	קדש
קֳדָשִׁים	id. pl., abs. st. (§ 35. rem. 8)	קדש
קְדֹשִׁים	adj. masc., pl. of קָדֹשׁ dec. 3 a	קדש
קָדְשְׁךָ	} noun masc. sing., suff. 2 pers. sing. masc.	קדש
קָדְשֶׁךָ	} from קֹדֶשׁ dec. 6 c	
קָדְשֵׁנִי	id. with suff. 1 pers. pl.	קדש
קִדַּשְׁתָּ	Piel pret. 2 pers. sing. masc.; acc. shifted by conv. וְ (comp. § 8. rem. 7)	קדש
קִדְּשׁוּתוֹ	id. id., suff. 3 pers. sing. masc.	קדש
קִדַּשְׁתִּי	} id. pret. 1 pers. sing.; acc. shifted by conv. וְ (comp. § 8. rem. 7)	קדש
קְדַשְׁתִּיךָ	Kal pret. 1 pers. sing., suff. 2 pers. sing. m.	קדש
קִדַּשְׁתָּם	} id. Piel pret. 2 pers. s. m., suff. 3 pers. pl. m.	קדש
קִדַּשְׁתֶּם	} id. pret. 2 pers. pl. masc.	קדש

[קָהָה] *to be blunt*, of the teeth, *to be set on edge*. Pi. *to be blunt*, only in the foll. form.

קֵהָה	Piel pret. 3 pers. sing. masc.	קהה

קָהַל. Hiph. הִקְהִיל *to call together, assemble.* Niph. *to assemble, come together.*

קָהָל masc. dec. 4 a.—I. *a meeting.*—II. *congregation, assemblage of persons.*—III. *multitude.*

קְהֵלָתָה (*convocation*) pr. name of a station of the Israelites in the wilderness, Nu. 33. 22.

קְהִלָּה fem. dec. 10, *assembly, congregation.*

קֹהֶלֶת masc. (fem. Ec. 7. 27) *preacher*, properly *convoker*; pr. name applied to Solomon in the book of Ecclesiastes.

מַקְהֵלִים pl. masc. *congregations*, Ps. 26. 12.

מַקְהֵלוֹת pl. fem.—I. *congregations*, Ps. 68. 27. —II. pr. name of a station of the Israelites in the desert, Nu. 33. 25.

וְקָהָל	} noun masc. sing. dec. 4 a	קהל
קְהַל	} id., constr. st.; וְ bef. (:)	קהל
קְהָלָהּ	id. with suff. 3 pers. sing. fem.	קהל
קְהִלָּה	noun fem. sing. dec. 10	קהל
קְהָלֶיךָ	noun masc. pl., suff. 2 p. s. m. fr. קָהָל d. 4 a	קהל
קְהָלֶךָ	id. sing., suff. 2 pers. sing. masc. [for קְהָלְךָ	קהל
קְהָלֵךְ	id. sing., suff. 2 pers. sing. fem.	קהל
קְהַלְכֶם	id. sing., suff. 2 pers. pl. masc.	קהל
קְהִלַּת	noun fem. sing., constr. of קְהִלָּה dec. 10	קהל
קֹהֶלֶת	noun fem. sing.	קהל

* Jos. 7. 13.   Da. 8. 13.   Le. 16. 19.   Ne. 3. 1.   2 Ch. 15. 18.   Is. 65. 5.   Eze. 26. 7.   Ne. 5. 7.   Eze. 27. 27 34.
Ex. 13. 2.   Nu. 17. 2.   Eze. 44. 8.   De. 12. 26.   Ex. 19. 10.   Ge. 35. 11.   Eze. 38. 7.   De. 5. 19.
1 Ki. 8. 64.   Eze. 20. 20.   Mi. 3. 5.   2 Ch. 31. 14.   Eze. 20. 40.   Eze. 38. 22, 23.   Eze. 38. 13.   De. 33. 4.
Nu. 6. 11.   2 Ch. 29. 5.   1 Ki. 15. 15.   Hab. 1. 12.   Is. 64. 10.   Ec. 10. 10.

קְהָת
גּ קְהָת
(assembly ; קָהַת i. q. Chald. קְהָא to assemble, to which Root יִקְּהַת Ge. 49. 10, has been referred by some) pr. name of a son of Levi. Patronym. קְהָתִי .

קְהָתָה (assembly) pr. n. m. 2 Ch. 34. 22, Keri.

ק֫ו
קָו
} noun masc. sing. dec. 8 (§ 37. No. 4) . קוה

[קוֹא] to spew out, vomit, only metaph. for, to reject, Le. 18. 28. Hiph. id.

קֵא masc. dec. 1 a, vomit, Pr. 26. 11.
קִיא masc. dec. 1 a, idem.
קָאָה (secondary Root) to vomit, only Je. 25. 27.
קָאַת fem. with the art. הַקָּאַת, constr. קָאַת (contrary to the analogy of derivv. from עו § 30. No. 2) the pelican, so called from its vomiting the things which it has too voraciously swallowed (Gesenius).

קוּבֵעִי
קוּבָּעַ
} noun masc. sing. (comp. § 31. rem. 5) קבע
קוֹבֵר Kal part. act. sing. masc. dec. 7 b . קבר
קוֹדֶשׁ fully for קֹדֶשׁ (q. v.) . . קדש

[קָוָה] I. to wait for, hope in.—II. Arab. to twist, wind, bind ; hence, to be strong, comp. derivv. תִּקְוָה, קָו. Pi. I. to wait for, confide in, with אֶל, לְ.—II. to wait, lie in wait for, with לְ, acc. Niph. to gather themselves together.
קֹוֶה or קָוֶה masc. a cord, only in Kheth. 1 Ki. 7. 23 ; Je. 31. 39 ; Zec. 1. 16.
קָו, ק֫ו masc. with suff. קַוָּם (dec. 8).—I. cord, line, 1 Ki. 7. 23.—II. measuring line.—III. cord, string, Ps. 19. 5.—IV. rule, direction, Is. 28. 10.—V. strength, might, Is. 18. 2, 7, גּוֹי קַו־קָו, a nation most mighty, so, those who refer this prophecy to Egypt ; others, a land of rule upon rule, meaning Judah ; Eng. vers. "meted out," comp. No. II.
מִקְוֶה masc. dec. 9 a.—I. expectation, hope, confidence.—II. collection of waters, of men, or animals, company, band, 1 Ki. 10. 28.
מִקְוֶה fem. place of collecting, reservoir, Is. 22. 11.
תִּקְוָה fem. dec. 10.—I. cord, line, Jos. 2. 18, 21.—II. expectation, hope.—III. pr. name masc. 2 Ki. 22. 14, for which תָּקְהַת in 2 Ch. 34. 22.
קַוֹּה ן Piel inf. constr. or imp. sing. masc. . קוה
קֹוֹה id. inf. abs. . . . . קוה

קֻוָּה ן Kh. קֻוֶּה noun masc. sing., K. קָו (q. v.) קוה
קֻוּוּ Piel pret. 3 pers. pl. . . . קוה
קוֹט see פַּקַח־קוֹחַ . . . . פקח

[קוּט] to loath, abhor, be grieved with, with בְּ. Niph. and Hithpal. id.

קֹוַי [for קֹוְיַ] the foll. with suff. 1 pers. sing. קוה
קֹוֵי ן Kal part. act. pl. c. masc. [fr. קֹוֶה] d. 9 a קוה
קֹוֶיךָ id. pl., suff. 2 pers. sing. masc. . קוה
קִוִּינוּ Piel pret. 1 pers. pl. . . . קוה
קִוִּינֻךָ id. id., suff. 2 pers. sing. masc. . קוה
קִוֵּיתִי
קִוִּיתִי
} id. pret. 1 pers. sing. (§ 24. rem. 11) קוה
קִוִּיתִ֫יךָ id. id., suff. 2 pers. sing. masc. . קוה
קִוִּיתֶם ן id. pret. 2 pers. pl. masc. . . קוה

קוֹל ן, ק֫ל masc. dec. 1 a (pl. וֹת).—I. voice.—II. cry of animals.—III. sound, noise.—IV. thunder.—V. rumour, report.
קָל Ch. masc. a voice.
קוֹלָיָה (voice of the Lord) pr. name masc.—I. Je. 29. 21.—II. Ne. 11. 7.
קוֹלָהּ ן id., suff. 3 pers. sing. fem. . . קול
קוֹלוֹ ן id., suff. 3 pers. sing. masc. . . קול
קוֹלוֹת id. pl. fem. . . . . . קול
קוֹלִי ן id. sing., suff. 1 pers. sing. ; or (Ps. 116. 1) with י parag. . . . . קול
קוֹלָיָה pr. name masc. . . . . קול
קוֹלֶךָ noun masc. sing., suff. 2 p. s. f. fr. קוֹל d. 1 a
קוֹלֵךְ
קוֹלֵךְ
} id. sing., suff. 2 pers. sing. masc. . קול
קוֹלְכֶם id. sing., suff. 2 pers. pl. masc. . קול
קוֹלָם id. sing., suff. 3 pers. pl. masc. . קול
קוֹלָן id. sing., suff. 3 pers. pl. fem. . קול
קוֹלֵעַ Kal part. act. sing. masc. . . קלע

קוּם ן (inf. & imp.) fut. יָקוּם, יָקֻם, ap. יָקֹם ; once pret. קָאם.—I. to rise, arise, e. g. from bed, a seat ; frequently pleonastically וַיָּקָם וַיֵּלֶךְ and he arose and went.—II. with עַל, אֶל, בְּ to rise up against any one ; part. קָמַי those that rise up against me, him.—III. to rise, appear, e. g. light.—IV. to rise, flourish, prosper, Pr. 28. 12.—V. to stand, stand firm ; also, to be fixed, of the eyes.—VI. to remain, endure, be established ; hence to stand good, be valid. Pi. קִיֵּם.—I. to strengthen,

Ps. 119. 28; hence *to confirm.*—II. *to enjoin,* with
עַל a thing upon any one; קִים עָלָיו *to take upon
oneself.*—III. *to keep, fulfil, perform,* Ps. 119. 106.
Pil. קוֹמֵם.—I. *to raise up, restore.*—II. *to rise up,*
Mi. 2. 8. Hiph. הֵקִים.—I. *to cause to rise up.*—
II. *to raise, lift up.*—III. *to raise, set or rear up.*
—IV. *to raise up, constitute, appoint.*—V. *to raise
up, bring into existence.*—VI. *to cause or make to
stand.*—VII. *to make to stand still,* Ps. 107. 29.—
VIII. *to confirm, establish.*—IX. *to fulfil, perform.*
Hoph. pass. of Hiph. Nos. III, IV & VIII. Hithpal.
הִתְקוֹמֵם with לְ *to rise up against;* part. *adversary.*
קוּם Chald.—I. *to arise.*—II. *to stand up.*—III.
to stand; hence *to remain, endure.* Pa. קַיֵּם *to confirm, establish,* Da. 6. 8. Aph. הֲקֵים, אֲקִים; fut.
יְהָקִים, יְקִים.—I. *to set up, erect.*—II. *to constitute,
appoint.* Hoph. *to be made to stand,* Da. 7. 4.
קָמָה fem. dec. 10, *standing corn.*
קָמוֹן *(standing firm)* pr. name of a town in
Gilead, Ju. 10. 5.
קוֹמָה fem. dec. 10, *stature, height.*
קוֹמְמִיּוּת adv. *upright, erect,* Le. 26. 13.
קִים masc. dec. 1a, *adversary,* Job 22. 20.
קִימָה fem. dec. 10, *a rising up,* La. 3. 62.
קְיָם Chald. masc. *statute, edict,* Da. 6. 8, 16.
קַיָּם Chald. masc. adj. *enduring, sure.*
יָקִים *(He will establish* him) pr. name masc. of
two persons, 1 Ch. 8. 19; 24. 12.
יְקוּם masc. *whatever exists, lives; a being.*
מָקוֹם com. dec. 3a (pl. מְקוֹמוֹת).—I. *place,
room, space.*—II. *habitation, abode, home.*—III.
place, town.
תְּקוּמָה f. *power of standing, resisting,* Le. 26. 37.
תְּקוֹמֵם masc. dec. 7b, *adversary,* Ps. 139. 21.

קָמַם noun masc. sing., suff. 3 pers. pl. masc. from
קֵי dec. 8 (§ 37. No. 4) . . . קוה
קוֹם Kal inf. abs. . . . . קום
קוֹמָה ’ן noun fem. sing. dec. 10 . . קום
קוֹמָה Kh. קוֹמָה q. v., K. קוֹמַת (q. v.) . קום
קוּמָה וְ’ן, קוֹמָה Kal imp. s. m. (קוּם) with parag. ה קום
קוּמוּ ’ן id. imp. pl. masc. . . . קום
קוּמִי id. imp. sing. fem. & Chald. Da. 7. 5 קום
קוּמִי ’ן id. inf. constr., suff. 1 p. s. fr. קוּם d. 1a קום
קוֹמְמִיּוּת (prop. noun fem. sing.) adv. . קום
קוֹמַת ’ן noun fem. sing., constr. of קוֹמָה dec. 10 . קום
קוֹמָתָהּ id., suff. 3 pers. sing. fem. . . קום
קוֹמָתוֹ id., suff. 3 pers. sing. masc. . . קום
קוֹמָתֵךְ id., suff. 2 pers. sing. fem. . קום

I. קִין. Pil. קוֹנֵן *to utter a lamentation, to lament,* with עַל,
אֶל *over a person or thing.*
קִינָה fem. dec. 10 (pl. ־ים, ־וֹת).—I. *lamentation.*—II. pr. name of a town in Judah, Jos. 15. 22.

II. קִין. Root not used; Arab. קאן *to form, forge;* Heb. also
i. q. קנה, whence pr. n. קַיִן *(acquisition)* Ge. 4. 1
קַיִן masc. dec. 6h.—I. *lance, spear,* 2 Sa. 21. 16.
—II. pr. name, *Cain,* the son of Adam.—III. pr.
name of the tribe of the Kenites.—IV. הַקַּיִן pr.
name of a town in Judah, Jos. 15. 57.
קֵינִי, קֵנִי gent. noun, *Kenite, Kenites,* one
of the tribes of Canaan.
קֵינָן *(smith)* pr. name masc. Ge. 5. 9; 1 Ch. 1. 2.
קוֹנֶה Kal part. act. sing. masc. dec. 9a . . קנה
קוֹנֵנּוּ וְ Pilel pret. 3 pers. pl. . . . קון
קוֹנְנוּהָ וְ id., with suff. 3 pers. sing. fem. . . קון

קוֹעַ Root not used; prob. i. q. קוּר *to dig,* cogn. Arab.
וקע *to wound, mark, brand;* Talm. קַעֲקַע *to cau-
terize.*
קַעֲקַע masc. *a mark cut into the skin,* Le. 19. 28.
קוֹעַ וְ masc. *prince;* Eze. 23. 23; so Vulg. and
others; others again take it as a pr. name.

קוֹף Root not used; i. q. נָקַף *to go round.*
קוֹף dec. 1a, *an ape.*
תְּקוּפָה fem. dec. 10.—I. *circuit, orbit* of the sun,
Ps. 19. 7.—II. *revolution of time*
קוֹפִים וְ noun masc., pl. of קוֹף dec. 1a . . קוף

I. קוּץ (inf. does not occur).—I. *to loathe, abhor,* with בְּ.
—II. *to fear,* with מִפְּנֵי. Hiph. הֵקִיץ *to put in
fear,* i. e. *besiege,* Is. 7. 6.

II. קוּץ i. q. יָקַץ only Hiph. הֵקִיץ.—I. *to awake* from
sleep, death.—II. *to awake, arise.*

III. קוּץ Root not used; perh. i. q. קָצַץ *to cut, cut off.*
קוֹץ masc. dec. 1a.—I. *thorn, thorn-bush.*—II. pr.
name masc. of several persons.
קְוֻצּוֹת fem. pl. *locks of hair,* so called from being
cut (Gesenius).
קַיִץ masc. dec. 6h.—I. *fruit-harvest,* q. d. the
time for cutting and gathering the fruits, Is. 16. 9;
28. 4.—II. *summer-fruit.*—III. *summer.*
קוּץ *(denom. fr.* קַיִץ) *to pass the summer,* Is. 18. 6.
קוֹץ ’ן noun masc. sing. dec. 1a, also pr. name . קוץ

---

a Ps. 19. 5.   c Je. 52. 21.   e Zep. 3. 8.   g Le. 26. 13.   Pr. 15. 32.   k Eze. 27. 32.   · Eze. 32. 16.   = 2 Ch. 9. 21.   n Is. 32. 13, etc.
Je. 44. 29.   d Ps. 35. 2.   f Ps. 139. 2.   h Ca. 7. 8.

קוֹצּוֹתַי	noun fem. pl., suff. 1 pers. s. fr. [קְוֻצָּה] d. 10 קוץ
קוֹצּוֹתָיו	id. pl., suff. 3 pers. sing. masc. . קוץ
קוֹצֵי	constr. of the foll. קוץ
קוֹצִים	noun masc. pl. constr.&abs. fr. קוֹץ dec. 1 a
קוֹצֵר	Kal part. act. sing. masc. dec. 7 b . קצר

[קוּר] to dig a well, 2 Ki. 19.24; Is. 37.25; Hiph. to let spring up water, Je. 6.7. Pilp. קִרְקֵר (§ 6. No. 4).—I. to dig under a wall, Is. 22.5.—II. to destroy, Nu. 24.17.

מָקוֹר masc. dec. 3 a, spring, fountain.

קַרְקֹר (foundation) pr. name of a place beyond Jordan, Ju. 8.10.

[קוּר] m. dec. 1 a, thin thread of a spider's web, Is. 59.5,6.

קוֹרָא	Pual pret. 3 pers. masc. sing. for קָרָא . קרא
קוֹרֵא	' Kal part. act. sing. m. d. 7 b, also pr. name קרא
קוֹרָה	noun fem. sing. dec. 10 . קרה
קוֹרֵי	' noun masc. pl. constr. from [קוּר] dec. 1 a קור
קוֹרֵיהֶם	id. pl., suff. 3 pers. pl. masc. . . קור
קוֹרֵץ	Kal part. act. sing. masc. . . קרץ

[קוֹש] to lay snares, Is. 29.21. Arab. to be curved, bent.

קוּשָׁיָה (bow of the Lord) pr. name masc. 1 Ch. 15.17; called קִישִׁי in 1 Ch. 6.29.

קִישׁ (bow) pr. name of the father of Saul, and of several other men.

קִישׁוֹן (winding) pr. name of a stream near mount Tabor.

קֶשֶׁת com. (with suff. קַשְׁתִּי dec. 13 a; but pl. קְשָׁתוֹת c. ת treated as if radical).—I. a bow for shooting arrows; meton. for archer.—II. rainbow.

קַשָּׁת masc. archer, Ge. 21.20.

קוֹשּׁוּ	' Kal imp. pl. masc.; for ' see lett. ו . קשש
קוּשָׁיָהוּ	pr. name masc. . . . קוש
קִוְּתָה	Piel pret. 3 pers. sing. fem. . . קוה
קַח	Kal pret. 3 p. s. m. for לָקַח (comp. § 17. r. 8) לקח
קַח	id. imp. sing. masc. לקח
קָחָה	id. id. with parag. ה . . לקח
קָחֵהוּ	id. imp. pl. masc. (קְחוּ), suff. 3 pers. sing. masc. (§ 16. rem. 11) לקח
קְחוּ	id. imp. pl. masc.; ו bef. (:) . . לקח
קְחִי	' id. imp. sing. fem.; ו id. . לקח
קָחָם	id. inf., or perh. pret. 3 pers. sing. masc. (comp. קַח), suff. 3 pers. pl. masc. לקח

קָחָם־	id. imp. sing. masc. (קַח), suff. 3 pers. pl. masc. [for קְחָם; § 16. rem. 11] . לקח
קָחֶנָּה	id. id., suff. 3 pers. sing. fem. . . לקח
קָחֶנּוּ	' id. id., suff. 3 pers. sing. masc. . . לקח
קַחַת / קַחַת־	id. inf. constr. לקח
קַחְתִּי	id. id. with suff. 1 pers. sing. dec. 13 a . לקח
קַחְתֵּךְ	id. id. with suff. 2 pers. sing. fem. . לקח
קְטֹל	Kal pret. 3 pers. sing. masc. . . קום

קָטַב Root not used; Arab. & Chald. to cut, hence, to cut off.

קֶטֶב masc. dec. 6 c, destruction, Ho. 13.14. Also

קָטֶב / קֶטֶב	(§ 35. rem. 2) masc.—I. destruction, Is. 28.2.—II. contagion, pestilence קטב
קִטְבְּךָ	noun masc. sing. with suff. 2 pers. sing. masc. from [קֶטֶב] dec. 6 c (§ 35. rem. 8) קטב
קְטוֹרָה	noun fem. sing. . . . קטר
קְטוּרָה	pr. name fem. . . . . קטר

[קָטַט] to be cut off, Job 8.14. Arab. trans.

| קְטִיל | Chald. Peal part. pass. sing. masc. . קטל |
| קְטִילַת | Chald. id. id. with afformative 2 pers. sing. fem. (§ 47. rem. 11) קטל |

[קָטַל] fut. יִקְטֹל to kill, slay.

קְטַל Chald. id. Pa. id. intens. to slay many. Ithpe. & Ithpa. to be slain.

קֶטֶל masc. slaughter, Ob. 9.

| קָטֵל | Chald. Peal part. act. sing. masc. . קטל |
| קַטֵּל | Chald. Pael pret. 3 pers. s. masc. (§ 47. r. 1) קטל |

[קָטֹן] (§ 8. rem. 1) fut. יִקְטַן.—I. to be little, small.—II. trop. to be of no account, unworthy.

קָטָן masc. dec. 8 a (with suff. קְטַנִּי), קְטַנָּה fem. dec. 10, adj.—I. little, small.—II. young, younger.—III. trop. small, least, unimportant.—IV. הַקָּטָן pr. name masc. Ezr. 8.12.

קָטֹן masc. dec. 3 a, idem.

קֹטֶן masc. the little finger, 1 Ki. 12 10; 2 Ch. 10.10.

קַטָּת (for קְטַנַּת small) pr. name of a town in Zebulon, Jos. 19.15.

יָקְטָן (diminished) pr. name of a son of Eber progenitor of several Arabian tribes.

| קָטֹן | adj. m. s. with suff. קְטַנָּם d. 8a (§ 3'' No. 2) קטן |
| קָטֹן | adj. masc. sing. dec. 3 a . . . קטן |

a Ca. 5.2.   e Ps. 129.7.   i Pr. 6.13.   m 1 Sa. 21.10.   r Je. 46.11.   w 1 Sa. 16.11.   z Eze. 16.47.   e Ho. 13.14.   a Da. 7.11.
b Ca. 5.11.   f 2 Ki. 6.2.   k Zep. 2.1.   n Ge. 15.9.   s Ho. 11.3.   x 2 Ki. 12.9.   a Is. 28.2.   f De. 33.10.   b Da. 5.19.
c Ju. 8.7, 16.   g Is. 59.5.   l Ps. 130.5.   o 1 Ki. 20.33.   t Ge. 48.9.   y Eze. 24.25.   c De. 32.24.   g Da. 5.30.   k Da. 3.22.
d Is. 59.6.   h Eze. 17.5.   v Ge. 43.13.   u Je. 36.14.   y Ge. 30.15.   dd Eze. 10.13.

קָטֹן id., constr. st.

קְטַנָּה } adj. fem. sing. & pl. dec. 10, from קָטָן } קטן

קְטַנּוֹת masc.; ו bef. (:)

קָטְנִי noun m. s., suff. 1 p. s. [fr. קֹטֶן comp. קָבְּלוֹ] קטן

קְטַנַּי } adj. masc. pl. constr. & abs. from קָטָן } קטן

קְטַנִּים dec. 8a (§ 37. No. 2); ו bef. (:)

קְטַנָּם id. sing., suff. 3 pers. pl. masc. קטן

קָטֹנְתִּי Kal pret. 1 pers. sing. (§ 8. rem. 1) קטן

[קָטַף] fut. יִקְטֹף *to pluck off.* Niph. pass. Job 8. 12.

קָטַף Kal pret. 3 pers. sing. m. [for קָטַף § 8. r. 7] קטף

קְטַפְתָּ id. pret. 2 pers. sing. masc.; acc. shifted by conv. ו (§ 8. rem. 7) קטף

I. קָטַר Pi. קִטֵּר *to raise an odour by burning, to burn incense,* also *fat;* part. מְקַטְּרוֹת *altars of incense.* Pu. *to be perfumed,* Ca. 3. 6. Hiph. *to burn incense,* also *sacrifices.* Hoph. pass. Le. 6. 15; part. מֻקְטָר *incense,* Mal. 1. 11.

קְטוֹרָה fem. *incense,* De. 33. 10.

קְטֹרֶת fem. dec. 13c, *incense;* also *the fat of a* victim burned as incense, Ps. 66. 15.

קְטוּרָה (*incense*) pr. name of a wife of Abraham.

קִטֵּר masc. *a burning of incense,* Je. 44. 21.

קִיטוֹר masc.—I. *smoke.*—II. *vapour,* Ps. 148. 8.

מִקְטָר masc. dec. 2b, *incense,* Ex. 30. 1.

מְקַטֶּרֶת fem. dec. 13 (with suff. טַרְתִּי), *a censer.*

II. קָטַר *to bind,* only part. קְטֻרוֹת *bound, joined,* Eze. 46. 22.

קְטַר Chald. masc. dec. 3b, only pl.—I. *joints, ligatures,* Da. 5. 6.—II. *knots, difficult questions,* Da. 5. 12, 16.

קִטְרוֹן (*knotty*) pr. name of a town in Zebulun, Ju. 1. 30.

קַטֵּר Piel inf. abs., used also as an abs. קטר

קִטְּרוּ id. pret. 3 pers. pl. קטר

קִטְרוֹן pr. name of a place קטר

קְטֻרוֹת Kal part. pass. pl. fem. [from קָטוּר masc.] קטר

קִטְרֵי } Chald. noun masc. pl. constr. & abs. } קטר

קִטְרִין from [קְטַר] dec. 3 b

קְטֹרֶת noun fem. sing. dec. 13d; ו bef. (:) קטר

קְטָרְתִּי id. with suff. 1 pers. s.; ו id. קטר

קִטַּרְתֶּם Piel pret. 2 pers. pl. masc. קטר

קַטָּת pr. name of a place קטן

קֵיא noun masc. sing. dec. 1a קוא

קִיא Kal imp. pl. masc.; ו bef. (:) comp. R. קיא

קַיָּם Chald. noun masc. sing. קום

קִיטוֹר } noun masc. sing. סטר

קִיטֹר

קְיָם Chald. noun masc. sing.; ו bef. (:) קום

קַיָּם Chald. adj. masc. sing. קום

קִיֵּם Piel pret. 3 pers. sing. masc. (§ 10. rem. 1) קום

קַיָּמָא Chald. adj. fem. sing., from קַיָּם masc. קום

קִיְּמוּ Piel pret. 3 pers. pl. קום

קִימוֹשׁ noun masc. sing., for קִמּוֹשׁ (q. v.) קמש

קִימָנוּ n.m.s.,suff. 1 p.pl. [for קִימֵנוּ, fr. קִים, § 3. r.4] קום

קִימֵנִי Piel imp. sing. masc. [קַיֵּם], suff. 1 pers. s. קום

קִימָתָם noun f. s., suff. 3 p. pl. m. fr. [קִימָה] d. 10 קום

קִין } pr. name of a man and a people קין

קַיִן

קִינָה noun fem. sing. dec. 10, also pr. name קין

קִינִי noun m. s., suff. 3 pers. s. m. fr. [קַיִן] d. 6h קין

קֵינִי pr. name of a people קין

קִינִים noun fem. with pl. masc. term. fr. קִינָה d. 10 קין

קֵינָן pr. name masc. קון

קַיִץ } noun masc. sing. dec. 6h; for ו }

קַיִץ, קֵץ see lett. ו } קיץ

קֵיצֵךְ id. with suff. 2 pers. sing. fem. קיץ

קִיקָיוֹן masc. Jon. 4. 6, 7, 9, 10, the name of a plant, according to the Syr. and Jerome, the *palma Christi, ricinus communis,* called in Egypt KIKI; Sept. κολόκυνθα *gourd.*

קִיקָלוֹן } noun masc. sing. קלל

קִיר } masc. dec. 1a (pl. קִירוֹת).—I. *a wall,* of a city, of a house.—II. *side of an altar;* applied to the *sides* of the heart, Je. 4. 19.—III. pr. name קִיר חֲרָשֶׂת, קִיר חֶרֶשׂ a city in the territory of Moab.—IV. pr. name of a people and region of Assyria.

קִירָה pr. name of a place (קִיר) with loc. ה קיר

קִירוֹת noun masc. with pl. fem. term. from קִיר d. 1a קיר

קִירֹמֶתָה id. pl., suff. 3 pers. sing. fem. קיר

קִירוֹתָיו id. pl., suff. 3 pers. sing. masc. קיר

קִירֵם pr. name masc. see קֶרֶם קרם

קִירֹתִי defect. for קִירוֹתִי (q. v.) קיר

קִישׁ pr. name masc. קוש

קִישׁוֹן pr. name of a stream קוש

קִישִׁי pr. name masc., see קוּשָׁיָהוּ קוש

קַתְרֹם Chald. masc. Kheth. קִיתְרֹם, Keri קַתְרֹם, *harp, lyre,* Gr. κίθαρις *cithara.* Da. 3. 5, 7, 10, 15.

קֹל Chald. noun masc. sing. קול

קַל adj. masc. sing. dec. 8d קלל

קֹל defect. for קוֹל (q. v.) קול

a 2 Ch. 21. 17.   e Ge. 32. 11.   i Da. 5. 6.   n Da. 2. 35.   r Da. 6. 27.   v Ho. 9. 6.   z 2 Sa. 21. 16.   d Hab. 2. 16.   h Eze. 41. 22.

b Pr. 30. 24.   f Exe. 17. 4.   k Da. 5. 12, 16.   o Ps. 148. 8.   s Est. 9, 31, 32.   w Job 22. 20.   a Eze. 2. 10.   e Eze. 41. 12, 20.   i Da.3.5,7,10,15.

c Je. 16. 6.   g De. 23. 26.   l Is. 28. 8.   p Ge. 19. 28.   t Da. 4. 25.   x Ps. 119. 28.   b Eze. 41. 13.   f Eze. 41. 13.   k Am. 2. 15.

d Jon. 3. 5.   h Eze. 46. 22.   m Je. 25. 27.   q Da. 6. 8, 16.   u Est. 9, 27, 31.   y La. 3. 63.   c Jon. 4. 6.   g 2 Ch. 3. 7.   l Ex. 19. 16.

קָלָה perh. i. q. קָהַל, **only Niph.** *to be assembled,* 2 Sa. 20. 14, Kheth.

I. [קָלָה] I. *to roast, parch,* e. g. corn.—II. *to burn,* Je. 29. 22. Niph. part. *burning disease,* Ps. 38. 8.

קָלִי, קָלְיָא m. *corn roasted or parched in the ear.*

II. [קָלָה] Kal not used; i. q. קָלַל. Niph. *to be made light of, to be despised;* part. *despised, mean.* Hiph. *to make light of, to despise,* De. 27. 16.

קָלוֹן masc. dec. 3 a.—I. *shame, contempt.*—II. *shameful deed.*—III. *shame, pudenda.*

קָלָה᷎ adj. fem. sing. from קַל masc. . . קלל

קָלֹה᷎ defect. for קוֹלֹה (q. v.) . . . קול

קָלּוּ᷎וְ Kal pret. 3 pers. pl. . . . קלל

קֹלוֹ noun masc. sing., suff. 3 pers. sing. masc.
from קוֹל dec. 1 a . . . . . קול

קָלוּט᷎וְ Kal part. pass. sing. masc. . . קלט

קָלוּי᷎וְ Kal part. pass. sing. . . . קלה

קָלוֹן᷎וְ noun masc. sing. dec. 3 a . . קלה

קְלוֹן᷎ id., constr. st. . . . . . קלה

קְלוֹנֵךְ᷎ id., suff. 2 pers. sing. fem. . . קלה

קַלּוֹתָ᷎ Kal pret. 2 pers. sing. masc. . . קלל

קָלוֹת noun masc. with pl. fem. term. from קוֹל d. 1 a

קָלַח Root not used; Talm. *to flow.*

קַלַּחַת᷎ [for קַלַּחַת] fem. *pot, kettle* . קלח

קָלַט (Arab. קלט *to contract*) only part.; קָלוּט *contracted, dwarfish,* Le. 22. 23.

קְלִיטָא (*dwarfish*) pr. name masc., called also קֵלָיָה, comp. Ezr. 10. 23.

מִקְלָט masc. dec. 2 b, *refuge, asylum.* Chald. קְלַט *to receive to oneself.*

קָלִי᷎וְ noun masc. sing. . . . . . קלה

קַלַּי pr. name masc. . . . . . קלל

קֵלָיָה᷎וְ pr. name masc., see קְלִיטָא . . קלט

קְלִיטָא pr. name masc. . . . . . קלט

קַלִּים adj. masc. pl. of קַל dec. 8 d . . קלל

קֹלִי᷎ noun m. sing., suff. 1 pers. sing. m. fr. קוֹל d. 1 a

[קָלַל] fut. יֵקַל (§ 18. rem. 6) *to be light,* i. e. not heavy, hence—I. *to be swift.*—II. *to be lessened, diminished, abated,* Ge. 8. 8, 11.—III. *to be lightly esteemed, be despised, mean.* Niph. נָקַל (§ 18. rem. 7). —I. *to be light, slight;* עַל נְקַלָּה *slightly;* hence,

to be easy.—II. *to be swift,* Is. 30. 16.—III. *to be small, unimportant.*—IV. *to be despised,* 2 Sa. 6. 22. Pi. קִלֵּל *to revile, curse,* with בְּ, with לְ *to bring a curse upon oneself,* 1 Sa. 3. 13. Pu. *to be cursed, accursed.* Hiph. הֵקַל.—I. *to lighten, remove,* a burden, מֵעַל מִן *from any one.*—II. *to make light of, to despise; to bring into contempt,* Is. 8. 23. Pilp. (§ 6. No. 4).—I. *to shake together,* sc. arrows in divination, Eze. 21. 26.—II. *to polish, sharpen,* Ec. 10. 10. Hithpalp. *to be shaken,* Je. 4. 24.

קָלָל adj. masc. *polished, shining.*

קְלָלָה fem. dec. 11 c.—I. *a reviling, cursing.*—II. *curse, imprecation;* an object *of curse.*

קַל masc. dec. 8 d, קַלָּה fem. adj.—I. *light, swift.* —II. adv. *swiftly.*

קָלָי (*swift*) pr. name masc. Ne. 12. 20.

קַלְקַל masc. *light, mean, vile,* Nu. 21. 5.

קִיקָלוֹן (for קַלְקָלוֹן) masc. *ignominy, shame,* Hab. 2. 16. Eng. vers. after the Vulg. " shameful spewing," as compnd. of קָלוֹן & קִי.

קַלָּל adj. sing. masc. . . . . . קלל

קַלֵּל᷎ Piel imp. sing. masc. . . . . קלל

קִלֵּל᷎וְ id. pret. 3 pers. sing. masc. . . קלל

קְלָלָה᷎וְ noun fem. sing. dec. 11 c; וְ bef. (:) קלל

קִלְלַנִי᷎ Piel pret. 3 p.s.m. (קִלֵּל), suff. 1 p.s. (§ 10. r. 7) קלל

קִלַּלְתָּ᷎פ id. pret. 2 pers. sing. masc. . . . קלל

קִלְלַת noun fem. sing., constr. of קְלָלָה dec. 11 c קלל

קִלְלָתוֹ᷎ id., suff. 3 pers. sing. masc. . . . קלל

קִלְלָתְךָ᷎ id., suff. 2 pers. sing. masc. . . . קלל

קָלֻם᷎וְ Kal pret. 3 pers. sing. masc. [קָלָה], suff. 3 pers. pl. masc. (§ 24. rem. 21) . . קלה

קֹלֵנוּ᷎וְ noun masc. s., suff. 1 pers. pl. fr. קוֹל dec. 1 a קול

קָלַס Pi. *to mock, scorn,* Eze. 16. 31. Hithp. id. with בְּ. Hence

קֶלֶס᷎וְ masc. *scorn, derision.*

קַלָּסָה᷎ fem. id.

קָלַע וְ᷎ I. *to sling, throw with a sling;* trop. *to cast out, reject,* Je. 10. 18.—II. *to cut out, carve.* Pi. i. q. Kal No. I.

קֶלַע masc. dec. 6 a (with suff. קַלְעִי § 35. rem. 5). —I. *a sling.*—II. *curtain, hanging.*

קַלָּע masc. dec. 1 b, *slinger,* 2 Ki. 3. 25.

מִקְלַעַת fem. dec. 13 a, *carving, sculpture.*

קֶלַע noun masc. sing., suff. קַלְעוֹ dec. 6 a (§ 35. r. 5) קלע

Je. 2. 23.   Le. 22. 23.   Is. 22. 18.   Ge. 3. 10.   De. 11. 26.   Ec. 7. 22.   Ge. 27. 13.   Ps. 44. 14.   1 Ki. 6. 29,
Ge. 21. 16.   Le. 2. 14.   Na. 1. 14.   2 Sa. 16. 10.   1 Ki. 2. 8.   2 Sa. 16. 12.   Je. 29. 22.   Eze. 22. 4.   32, 35.
Hab. 1. 8.   Jos. 5. 11.   Mi. 3. 3.   Is. 8. 21.

קלֵעַ   Kal part. act. sing. masc. . . . קלע

קַלְעוֹᵇ   ן noun masc. sing., suff. 3 pers. sing. masc. from קֶלַע dec. 6 a (§ 35. rem. 5) . . קלע

קַלְעֵי   וֹ'ו id. pl., constr. st. . . . . קלע

קְלָעִים   id. pl., abs. st. . . . . . קלע

קִלְקֵל   Pilp. pret. 3 pers. sing. masc. (§ 6. rem. 4)

קָלַשׁ   Root not used ; meaning uncertain. Hence

קִלְּשׁוֹןᵃ   masc. שָׁלֹשׁ קִ *a three-pronged pitchfork.*

קֹלָת   noun masc. with pl. fem. term. fr. קוֹל dec. 1 a קול

קַלֹּתִיⁱ   Kal pret. 1 pers. sing. . . . . קלל

קָם   ן, וֹ'ו Kal pret. 3 pers. sing. masc., Chald. Da. 3. 24; for ן see lett. ו . . קום

קֻם   id. imp. s. masc. for קוּם (but comp. § 21. r. 5)ᵍ קום

קָמָה   Root not used ; Arab. קמא *to heap together, to collect.*

קְמוּאֵל   (*assembly of God*) pr. name masc.—I. Ge. 22. 21.—II. Nu. 34. 24.—III. 1 Ch. 27. 17.

יְקַמְיָה   (*the Lord shall gather together*) pr. name masc.—I. 1 Ch. 2. 41.—II. 1 Ch. 3. 18.

יָקְמְעָם   (*he shall gather the people*) pr. name masc. 1 Ch. 23. 19; 24. 23.

יָקְמְעָם   (*the people shall be gathered*) pr. name of a city in Ephraim.

קָמָה   ᵏ'ו Kal pret. 3 pers. sing. fem . . קום

קָמָהⁱ   id. part. sing. fem. . . . . קום

קָמָה   noun fem. s. dec. 10 (constr. קָמַת § 30. No. 3) קום

קָמֹהᵏ   ן defect. for קוֹמָה (q. v.) . . . קום

קָמוּ   ו', וֹ'ו Kal pret. 3 pers. pl., Chald. Ezr. 5. 2 ; ן bef. pause   הום

קֻמוֹᵍ   id. imp. pl. masc. (for קוּמוּ) . . קום

קְמוּאֵל   pr. name masc.   קמה

קִמּוֹשׁᵐ   noun masc. sing., comp. קִימוֹשׁ . קמש

קֶמַח   ו'ו masc. *flour.* Talm. קמח *to grind.*

קָמַח   id. in pause (§ 35. rem. 2)   קמח

[קָמַט]   *to bind,* Job 16. 8 ; so according to the Arab. ; others, *to seize firmly,* cogn. קָפַץ, קָבַץ, קָמַץ. Pu. *to be taken away,* Job 22. 16.

קֻמְּטוּᵖ   Pual pret. 3 pers. pl. . . . . קמט

קָמַי   ᵍ'ו Kal part. act. pl. masc., suff. 1 pers. sing. [from קָם] dec. 1 a (§ 30. No. 3) . .

קָמַיו   id. pl., suff. 3 pers. sing. masc. . . קום

קָמֶיךָ   id. pl., suff. 2 pers. sing. masc. . . קום

קָמִיםⁱ   id. pl., abs. st. . . . . . קום

קָמֵינוּᵈᵈ   id. pl., suff. 1 pers. pl. . . . . קום

קָמֵל   *to wither,* Is. 33. 9, and the foll. form.

קָמֵלוּʳ   Kal pret. 3 pers. pl. for קָמְלוּ [§ 8. r. 1 & 7] קמל

קָמְנָהˢ   Kal pret. 3 pers. pl. fem. . . . קום

קַמְנוּᵗ   id. pret. 1 pers. pl. . . . . קום

קָמַץ   ן *to grasp, take a grasp.*

קֹמֶץ   masc. dec. 6 c, *a handful* ; לִקְמָצִיםᵇ *by handfuls,* i. e. abundance.

קֻמְצוֹ   noun masc. sing., suff. 3 pers. sing. masc. from [קֹמֶץ] dec. 6 c (§ 35. rem. 8) . קמץ

קָמַשׁ   Root not used ; Arab. *to heap together.*

קִמּוֹשׁ   קִימּוֹשׁ m. *nettles,* Is. 34. 13; Ho. 9. 6.

קִמְּשׂוֹן   masc. dec. 3 c, idem, Pr. 24. 31.

קִמְּשֹׂנִיםᵛ   noun masc. pl. of [קִמְּשׂוֹן] dec. 3 c   קמש

קָמַתⁱ   noun fem. sing., constr. of קָמָה dec. 10 (comp. § 30. No. 3) . . . . קום

קַמְתָּ   Kal pret. 2 pers. sing. masc.; acc. shifted

קָמְתָּ   by conv. ו (comp. § 8. rem. 7) . . קום

קָמְתוּ   noun fem. s., suff. 3 pers. s. m. fr. קוֹמָה d. 10 קום

קַמְתִּי

קַמְתִּי   Kal pret. 1 pers. sing.; acc. shifted by

קָמְתִּי   conv. ו (comp. § 8. rem. 7) . . קום

קַמְתֶּם   id. pret. 2 pers. pl. masc. . . . קום

קֵן   noun masc. sing., constr. & abs. dec. 8 b

קֵן   (§ 37. rem. 1) . . . . . . קנן

קָנָא   ן'ו Pi. I. *to be jealous,* with acc., בְּ, of a wife, rival.—II. *to provoke to jealousy, anger,* with בְּ by or with.—III. *to envy,* with בְּ, acc., לְ of the person.—IV. *to be jealous* or *zealous for,* with לְ. —V. *to emulate,* with בְּ Pr. 3. 31. Hiph. *to provoke to jealousy.*

קַנָּא   adj. masc. *jealous,* of God.

קַנּוֹא   id. Jos. 24. 19 ; Na. 1. 2.

קִנְאָה   fem. dec. 12 b.—I. *jealousy.*—II. *envy* ; also *object of envy,* Ec. 4. 4.—III. *zeal, ardour.*— IV. *ardour, anger.*

קַנָּא   noun masc. sing. . . . . . קנא

קַנֹּאʄ   Piel inf. abs. . . . . . . קנא

קִנֵּאᵍ   ן'ו id. pret. 3 pers. sing. masc. . . קנא

קִנְאָה   ʰ'ו noun fem. sing. dec. 12 b . . . קנא

קִנְאוּנִי   Piel pret. 3 pers. pl., suff. 1 pers. s. (§ 10. r. 7) קנא

קִנְאֹתᵏ   noun fem. pl. abs. from קִנְאָה dec. 12 b קנא

ᵃ Ju. 20. 16.   ᵇ Job 40. 4.   ⁱ Mi. 7. 6.   ᵏ Is. 34. 13.   ᵖ De. 33. 11.   ʳ Ps. 20. 9.   ˢ Mi. 7. 8.   ᵗ Nu. 5. 14.   ᵛ Eze. 16. 38.

¹ Sa. 17. 40.   ʲ Pr. 24. 16.   ᵏ Ex. 27. 18.   ² Sa. 17. 28.   Pr. 24. 31.   ʳ Pr. 24. 31.   ᵈ De. 22. 6.   ᶠ 1 Ki. 19. 10, 14.   ³ De. 32. 21.

ᶜ Nu. 3. 26.   ᵍ Jos. 7. 10, 13.   ˡ Is. 49. 7.   ᵐ Job 22. 16.   ⁱ Is. 19. 6.   De. 23. 26.   ᶜ Nu. 25. 13.   ᵍ Nu.5.14; 25.13.   ᵏ Nu. 5. 15, 18.

ᵈ 1 Sa. 13. 21.   ¹ Sa. 24. 21.   ᵐ De. 2. 13.   ⁿ Je. 51. 1.   ᵒ Is. 32. 9.   ² Sa. 12. 21.   ᵈᵈ Ps. 44. 6.

קְנָאַת	id. sing., constr. st. . . .	קנא
וְקִנְאָתוֹ	id. sing., suff. 3 pers. sing. masc.	קנא
קִנְאָתִי	id. sing., suff. 1 pers. sing. .	קנא
קִנֵּאתִי	Piel pret. 1 pers. sing.; acc. shifted by	
וְקִנֵּאתִי	conv. } (comp. § 8. rem. 7) }	קנא
קִנְאָתְךָ	} noun fem. sing., suff. 2 pers. sing. masc. }	
קִנְאָתְךָ	} from קִנְאָה dec. 12 b . }	קנא
קִנְאָתָם	id., suff. 3 pers. pl. masc. . .	קנא

קָנָה fut. יִקְנֶה.—I. *to form, create.*—II. *to get, acquire;* also *to obtain,* Ge. 4. 1.—III. *to buy, purchase;* hence *to redeem.*—IV. *to possess.* Niph. *to be acquired, purchased.* Hiph. *to buy,* Zec. 13. 5.

קְנָא Ch. *to buy,* Ezr. 7. 17.

קִנְיָן masc. dec. 2 b.—I. *creature,* Ps. 104. 24.—II. *acquisition, purchase.*—III. *possession, wealth.*

קְנָת (*possession*) pr. name of a city in the country of Gilead.

יָקְנְעָם (*gotten by the people*) pr. name of a town in the tribe of Zebulun.

מִקְנֶה masc. dec. 9 a (comp. § 38. rem. 1).—I. *purchase,* Ge. 49. 32.—II. *possession, riches, wealth,* but chiefly consisting in *cattle;* אַנְשֵׁי מִ men of (i. e. possessing) *cattle;* אֶרֶץ מִ *a place for cattle,* adapted for pasturage.

מִקְנָה fem. dec. 10.—I. *purchase.*—II. *thing purchased,* Ge. 17. 12, 13, 23.—III. *price of purchase.* —IV. *possession,* Ge. 23. 18.

מִקְנֵיָהוּ (*possession of the Lord*) pr. name masc. 1 Ch. 15. 18, 21.

וְקָנֶה masc. dec. 9 b (pl. קָנִים, קָנוֹת).—I. *reed, cane.* —II. *sweet cane.*—III. *stalk of wheat,* Ge. 41. 5, 22. —IV. *a measuring reed.*—V. *beam of a balance,* Is. 46. 6.—VI. *branch of a candlestick.*—VII. *arm-bone* above the elbow, Job 31. 22. Hence

וְקָנָה (*place of reeds*) pr. name—I. of a stream on the borders of Ephraim and Manasseh.— II. of a town in Asher, Jos. 19. 28.

קָנָהּ	} noun masc. sing. with suff. 3 pers. sing. fem. from קָנֶה dec. 9 b	קנה
קָנֹה	Kal inf. abs.	קנה
קְנֵה	id. imp. sing. masc. . .	קנה
קְנֵה	} noun masc. sing., constr. of קָנֶה d. 9 b; } bef. (:)	קנה
קְנֹה	Kal inf. constr. (§ 24. rem. 2)	קנה
קָנָהּ	noun masc. s., suff. 3 pers. s. fem. fr. קֵן d. 8 b	קנן

קֹנֶה	} Kal part. act. sing. masc. constr. & abs. }	
קֹנֶה	} dec. 9 a . . . . . }	קנה
קָנָהוּ	id. pret. 3 pers. sing. m., suff. 3 pers. sing. m.	קנה
קֹנֵהוּ	id. part. sing. masc., suff. 3 pers. sing. masc.	
	from קֹנֶה dec. 9 a . . .	קנה
קָנֹה	id. inf. abs. (§ 24. rem. 2) .	קנה
קִנּוֹ	noun m. sing., suff. 3 pers. sing. m. fr. קֵן d. 8 b	קנן
קַנּוֹא	noun masc. sing. . . .	קנא
קְנֹת	} Kal inf. constr. dec. 1; } bef. (:) .	קנה
קְנֹתְךָ	id., suff. 2 pers. sing. masc. .	קנה

קְנַז } pr. name—I. of a descendant of Esau, from whom an Arabian country derived its name, Ge. 36. 11, 15.—II. the father of Othniel the judge. Patronym. קְנִזִּי.—III. of a grandson of Caleb, 1 Ch. 4. 15.

קְנִזִּי pr. name, *Kenizzite,* a people of Canaan. For another, see קְנַז.

קְנֵי	noun masc. pl. constr. from קָנֶה dec. 9 b	קנה
קָנִי	noun m. sing., suff. 1 pers. sing. fr. קֵן d. 8 b	קנן
קֹנֵיהֶן	Kal part. act. pl. masc., suff. 3 pers. pl.	
	fem. from קֹנֶה dec. 9 a	קנה
קָנִים	noun masc. pl. of קָנֶה dec. 9 b	קנה
קִנִּים	noun masc., pl. of קֵן dec. 8 b	קנן
קִנְיָן	} noun masc. sing. dec. 2 b	קנה
קִנְיַן	id., constr. st. . . .	קנה
קָנִינוּ	Kal pret. 1 pers. pl. . .	קנה
קִנְיָנֵנוּ	noun m. sing., suff. 3 pers. s. m. fr. קִנְיָן d. 2 b	קנה
קִנְיָנֶךָ	} id., pl. and sing. suff. 2 pers. sing. masc.	
קִנְיָנְךָ	}	קנה
קִנְיָנָם	} id., suff. 3 pers. pl. masc. .	קנה
קָנִיתָ	} Kal pret. 2 pers. sing. masc.; acc. shifted }	
קָנִיתָ	} by conv. } (comp. § 8. rem. 7) }	קנה
קָנִיתִי	Kh. קָנִיתִי q. v. K. קָנִיתְ (q. v.) .	קנה
קָנִיתִי	Kal pret. 1 pers. sing. . .	קנה
קְנָךָ	id. pret. 3 pers. sing. masc. (קָנָה), suff. 2 pers. sing. masc. (§ 24. rem. 21) .	קנה
קִנֶּךָ	noun m. sing., suff. 2 pers. sing. m. fr. קֵן d. 8 b	קנן

וְקִנָּמוֹן m. d. 3 c, *cinnamon,* only Ca. 4. 14, and the foll.

וְקִנְּמָן } id. constr. st. with mak. [for קִנָּמוֹן § 32. r. 7].

קָנֵן Pi. קִנֵּן *to nest, build a nest.* Pu. *to have one's nest built,* Je. 22. 23.

קֵן masc. dec. 8 b (constr. קַן § 37. rem. 1).—I. *a nest;* meton. *young birds of a nest,* Is. 16. 2; metaph. (a) *a dwelling;* (b) meton. *family,* Job 29. 18. —II. pl. קִנִּים *cells, chambers,* Ge. 6. 14.

a Zep. 1. 18.   f Ps. 79. 5.   k Pr. 16. 16.   l Le. 27. 24.   n Ru. 4. 5.   s Ge. 6. 14.   t Ne. 5. 8, 16.   v Pr. 4. 7.   x De. 32. 6.
b De. 29. 19.   c Is. 63. 15.   d Pr. 27. 8.   2 Sa. 24. 24.   o Job 29. 18.   p Eze. 38. 12, 13.   u Ps. 104. 24.   w Ge. 34. 23.   z Ex. 30. 23.
c Eze. 39. 25.   f Ec. 9. 6.   i Ge. 14. 19, 22.   m Pr. 16. 16.   Zec. 11. 5.   q Le. 22. 11.   yy Pr. 7. 17.

קִנְּנָה Piel pret. 3 pers. sing. fem. .   קנן

קִנְּנוּ id. pret. 3 pers. pl. (§ 10. rem. 7) . קנן

קָנָנִי Kal pret. 3 pers. sing. masc. (קָנָה), suff. 1 pers. sing. (§ 24. rem. 21) .   קנה

קְנָצֵי noun masc. pl. c. [for קְצֵי dag. forte resolved in נ] from קֵץ dec. 8b . . קצץ

קְנָת } pr. name of a place . . קנה
קְנָת }

קָנְתָה Kal oret. 3 pers. sing. fem. . . קנה

קִנֹתָם noun masc. with pl. fem. term. and suff. 3 pers. pl. masc. from קֵן d. 9b ; וּ bef. (:)   קנה

קְסוֹמִי Kh. קְסֹמִי, K. קְסָמִי Kal imp. sing. fem. (§ 8. rem. 2 & 14) . . קסם

[קָסַם] fut. יִקְסֹם to divine, spoken espec. of false prophets. קֶסֶם masc. dec. 6a.—I. divination ; trop. decision, certainty, Pr. 16. 10.—II. meton. reward of divination, Nu. 22. 7.

מִקְסָם masc. d. 2b, divination, Eze. 12. 24 ; 13. 7.

קָסֶם , קָסֵם } noun masc. sing. dec. 6a (§ 35. rem. 2)   קסם

קֹסֵם Kal part. act. sing. masc. dec. 7b . קסם

קֹסְמֵיכֶם id. pl., suff. 2 pers. pl. masc. . קסם

קְסָמִים noun masc., pl. of קֶסֶם dec. 6a ; וּ bef. (:)   קסם

קֹסְמִים Kal part. act. masc., pl. of קֹסֵם dec. 7b . קסם

קֶסֶם only Po. קוֹסֵם to cut off, comp. קָצַץ, Eze. 17. 9.

קֶשֶׂת noun masc. sing. . . קשׁה

קְעִלָה } pr. name of a city in the tribe of Judah.
קְעִלָה }

מְקַעְקֵעַ noun masc. sing. . . קוע

קָעַר Root not used ; Arab. to be deep ; cogn. קוּר. קְעָרָה fem. (§ 42. rem. 1 & 3) a dish, charger.

קַעֲרַת noun f. s., constr. of קְעָרָה d. 11c (§ 42. r. 1)   קער

קַעֲרֹת id. pl., constr. st. . . קער

קְעָרֹתָיו id. pl., suff. 3 pers. sing. masc. (§ 42. rem. 3)   קער

[קָפָא] to congeal, become condensed, Ex. 15. 8 ; perh. also Zec. 14. 6, Kheth. יִקְרוֹת יְקֻפָּאוֹן the splendid ones, i. e. stars, shall become condensed, shall contract their light. Metaph. Zep. 1. 12, to be congealed upon the lees, i. e. to sit quiet, indifferent. Hiph. to make to curdle, Job 10. 10.

קִפָּאוֹן masc. a congealing, denseness, Zec. 14. 6, Keri, see the verb.

קָפְאוּ Kal pret. 3 pers. pl. . . קפא

קָפַד Kal not used ; Ch. קְפַד to cut off. Pi. id. Is. 38. 12. קֶפֶד masc. destruction, Eze. 7. 25.

קִפֹּד , קִפּוֹד masc. hedgehog. (Arab. קנפד id.)

קֹפֶד noun masc. sing. . . קפד

קִפְּדָה noun masc. sing. [קָפַד or קָפַד] with parag. ה   קפד

קִפַּדְתִּי Piel pret. 1 pers. sing. . . קפד

קִפּוֹד וּ noun masc. sing. . . קפד

קִפּוֹז noun masc. sing. . . קפז

קָפַז Root not used ; Arab. to leap, spring, comp. Pi. of קָפַץ. קִפּוֹז masc. the arrow-snake, Is. 34. 15.

קִפִּים וּ noun masc., pl. of קוֹף dec. 1a . קוף

קָפַץ fut. יִקְפֹּץ to contract, close, shut, as the mouth, hand. Niph. to be shut up, sc. in the grave, Job 24. 24. Others, to be contracted, to die. Pi. to leap, spring, Ca. 2. 8.

קָפְצָה Kal pret. 3 pers. sing. fem. . קפץ

קָץ וּ Kal pret. 3 p. s. m. (see קוּץ), or part. m.   קוץ

קֵץ noun masc. sing. dec. 8b . . קצץ

[קָצַב] fut. יִקְצֹב.—I. to cut off or down, e. g. wood or a tree, 2 Ki. 6. 6.—II. to shear sheep, Ca. 4. 2. Hence

קֶצֶב וּ masc. dec. 6a (pl. c. קִצְבֵי).—I. form, shape.—II. end, extremity, Jon. 2. 7 ; Prof. Lee, cleft . . קצב

[קָצָה] to cut off, destroy, Hab. 2. 10. Pi. to cut off. Hiph. to scrape off, Le. 14. 41, 43.

קָצֶה masc. dec. 9b.—I. end, limit, of space or time ; Ge. 19. 4, מִקָּצֶה from every end, i. e. from all parts, מִקְצֵה שְׁלֹשֶׁת יָמִים at the end of three days.—II. the whole, the sum.

קָצָה fem. dec. 11a.—I. end, extremity of space מִקְצֵה at the extreme part.—II. the whole, the sum, mass, e. g. of people.

קֵצֶה masc. end, limit.

קָצֶו masc. dec. 6a, קַצְוֵי אֶרֶץ ends of the earth. קָצָת fem. i. q. קָצֶה, קָצָה ; pl. קָצָוֹת with suff. קְצָוֹתַי (comp. כְּנַת § 45).

קְצָת Chald. fem. constr. of קְצָת, idem.

קָצִין masc. dec. 3a.—I. a judge.—II. leader, chief.—III. prince.

קָצַה Kal pret. 3 pers. sing. fem. . קוץ

קָצָה noun masc. sing. . . קצה

קְצֵה noun masc. sing., constr. of קָצֶה dec. 9b   קצה

Is. 34. 15.   d Job 18. 2.   g Eze. 21. 26.   k Je. 29. 8, 9.   n Eze. 9. 2, 3.   r Nu. 7. 84.   t Is. 38. 12.   y 1 Ki. 10. 22.   b 1 Ki. 6. 25 ;
Eze. 31. 6.   e Ps. 78. 54.   h De. 18. 10.   l Nu. 22. 7.   o Le. 19. 28.   p Ex. 15. 8.   u Is. 34. 11.   z Ps. 77. 10.   7. 37.
Pr. 8 22.   f 1 Sa. 28. 8.   i Is. 3. 2.   m De. 18. 14.   p Nu. 7. 13, 19, &c.   q Eze. 7. 25.   w Is. 34. 15.   a Is. 18. 6 ; 7. 16.   c Nu. 21. 5.

קָצֶה˝ Kh. for קָצוּ (q. v.) . . . .   קצץ

קָצֵהוּ noun masc. sing., suff. 3 pers. sing. masc. from קָצֶה dec. 9 b . . .   קצה

קָצוּ *וְ' noun masc. sing., suff. 3 pers. sing. masc. from קֵץ dec. 8 b . .   קצץ

קְצוֹתֵי Kh. קְצוֹתָיו noun fem. pl. with suff., see ; קָצוֹת K. קְצוֹתָי (q. v.) .   קצה

קַצְוֵי noun masc. pl. constr. from [קָצָו] dec. 6 a   קצה

קְצוּצֵי Kal part. pass. pl. c. masc. [fr. קָצוּץ] d. 3 a   קצץ

קְצָוֹת noun fem. pl. abs., fr. קָצָה (comp. מָנָת § 45)   קצה

קְצוֹת noun fem. pl. constr. from קָצֶה' dec. 11 a; or (Hab. 2. 10) inf. constr.   קצה

קְצוֹתָיו id. pl., suff. 3 pers. sing. masc.   קצה

קְצוֹתָם* id. pl., suff. 3 pers. pl. masc. (§ 4. rem. 2)   קצה

קֶצַח masc. *black cummin,* Is. 28. 25, 27.

קִצִּי noun masc. sing., suff. 1 pers. s. fr. קֵץ d. 8 b   קצה

קֵצִים *וְ'* noun masc., pl. of קוֹץ dec. 1 a   קוץ

קָצִין noun masc. sing. dec. 3 a   קצה

קְצִין id., constr. st.   קצה

קְצִינֵי *ε'* id. pl., constr. st.; וּ bef. (:)   קצה

קְצִינַיִךְ^ id. pl., suff. 2 pers. sing. fem.   קצה

קְצִיעָה pr. name masc.   קצע

קְצִיעוֹת noun fem., pl. of קְצִיעָה dec. 10   קצע

קָצִיץ pr. name in compos. עֵמֶק קְ   עמק

קָצִיר *וְ'* noun masc. sing. dec. 3 a   קצר

קְצִיר *וְ'* id., constr. st.; וּ bef. (:)   קצר

קְצִירָהּ id., suff. 3 pers. sing. fem.   קצר

קְצִירוֹ id., suff. 3 pers. sing. masc.   קצר

קְצִירֶיהָ id. pl., suff. 3 pers. sing. fem.   קצר

קְצִירְךָ id. sing., suff. 2 pers. sing. masc.   קצר

קְצִירֵךְ id. sing., suff. 2 pers. sing. fem.   קצר

קְצִירְכֶם id. sing., suff. 2 pers. pl. masc.   קצר

קִצְּךָ* noun masc. s., suff. 2 pers. s. f. fr. קֵץ d. 8 b   קצץ

קָצֵנוּ* id. with suff. 1 pers. pl. . .   קצץ

קָצַע Kal not used; i. q. קָצָה, קָצַץ *to cut;* also *to break,* comp. derivv. Hiph. *to scrape off.* Pu. and Hoph. part. מְהֻקְצָעוֹת, מָקְצָעוֹת *angles, corners.*

קְצִיעָה fem. dec. 10.—I. *cassia,* Ps. 45. 9.—II. pr. name of one of Job's daughters, Job 42. 14.

מִקְצוֹעַ masc. dec. 1 b (pl. ־ים) *angle, corner.* מַקְצֻעָה fem. dec. 10, *a plane,* Is. 44. 13.

קָצַף fut. יִקְצֹף *to be angry, wroth,* with עַל, אֶל of the person. Hiph. *to provoke to anger.* Hithp. *to become angry.*

קְצַף Chald. *to be angry,* Da. 2. 12.

קֶצֶף masc. dec. 6 a (with קִצְפִּי, קֶצְפְּךָ).—I. *chip, splinter,* Hos. 10. 7.—II. *anger, wrath.*—III. *strife,* Est. 1. 18.

קְצַף Chald. masc. *anger,* Ezr. 7. 23.

קְצָפָה f. *a breaking,* Joel 1. 7. Sept. συγκλασμός; *splinter;* comp. κλασμός, *fragment.*

קֶצֶף *וְ'* noun masc. sing. (suff. קִצְפִּי) dec. 6 a   קצף
קֶצֶף *וְ'* (§ 35. rem. 2)

קְצַף *וְ'* Ch. Peal pret. 3 p. s. m. or n. m.; וּ bef. (:)   קצף

קֹצֵף *וְ'* Kal part. act. sing. masc.   קצף

קִצְפְּךָ* וְ noun m. s., suff. 2 pers. s. m. fr. קֶצֶף d. 6 a   קצף

קָצַפְתָּ Kal pret. 2 pers. sing. masc.   קצף

קָצַפְתִּי id. pret. 1 pers. sing. . .   קצף

[קָצַץ] *to cut off.* Pi. קִצֵּץ, קָצַץ (§ 10. rem. 1).—I. *to cut off;* also *to cut asunder* or *in pieces.*—II. *to cut up,* as plates *into* wires, Ex. 39. 3. Pu. pass Ju. 1. 7.

קְצַץ Chald. Pa. *to cut off,* Da. 4. 11.

קֵץ masc. dec. 8 b.—I. *end, limit,* of space, time, condition, or circumstances , לְקֵץ, מִקֵּץ *at the end of, after.*—II. *end, termination, destruction.*

קִיצוֹן (for קָצוֹן) only fem. קִיצוֹנָה *the last, extreme.*

מָקֵץ (*end*) pr. name of a place, 1 Ki. 4. 9.

קִצֵּץ *וְ'*
קִצֵּץ *וְ'* } Piel pret. 3 pers. sing. masc. (§ 10. r. 1)   קצץ

קַצִּצוּ* וְ Ch. Pael pret. 3 pers. pl. masc. (§ 47. r. 1 c)   קצץ

קָצַר *וְ'* I. fut. יִקְצֹר, *to cut down, reap;* part. קוֹצֵר *reaper.* —II. fut. יִקְצַר (once יְקֹצַר Pr. 10. 27) *to be shortened, short;* trop. of one's hand, *to be shortened,* i. e. *to be deficient, unable;* and so of one's spirit, soul, *to be impatient, grieved, vexed.* Pi. *to shorten,* Ps. 102. 24. Hiph. I. *to reap,* Job 24. 6, Kh.— II. *to shorten,* Ps. 89. 46.

קָצֵר adj. m. dec. 5 a, *short,* Eze. 42. 5 ; קְצַר יָד *short of hand,* i. e. *weak, feeble,* Is. 37. 27 ; קְ רוּחַ אַפַּיִם *impatient, passionate;* Pr. 14. 17, 29; קְ יָמִים *short-lived,* Job 14. 1.

קֹצֶר masc. *shortness* of spirit, i. e. *impatience,* Ex. 6. 9.

קָצִיר masc. dec. 3 a.—I. *fruits cut down, harvest;* hence *time of harvest;* meton. for *harvest-men,* Is. 17. 5.—II. *branch, bough.*

קְצַר *וְ'* adj. m. s., constr. of [קָצֵר] d. 5 a; וּ bef. (:)   קצר

---

a Da. 9. 26.   d Ps. 19. 7.   g Mi. 3. 1. 9.   k Ru. 2. 23.   o Le. 23. 10.   r Zec. 1. 15.   u Zec. 1. 15.   y Ps. 129. 4.   a Is. 28. 20.
Ex. 37. 8; 39. 4.   e Je. 12. 13.   h Is. 22. 3.   l Ps. 80. 12.   p Je. 51. 13.   s Ezr. 7. 23.   x Ps. 102. 11.   z Da. 4. 11.   b Pr. 14. 29.
Ps. 65. 9.   c Is. 3. 7.   i Ps. 45. 9.   m Is. 16. 9.   q La. 4. 18.   t Da. 2. 12.   2 Ki. 18. 16.

קְצֵר֫	Piel pret. 3 pers. sing. masc. (§ 10. rem. 1) קצר
קָצְרָה	Kal pret. 3 pers. sing. fem. . . קצר
קָצְר֫וּ	id. pret. 3 pers. pl. [for קָצְר֫וּ § 8. rem. 7] קצר
וְ׳	id. imp. pl. masc. . . . קצר
קְצֻר֫וֹת	id. part. pass. f. pl. [of קְצוּרָה fr. קָצוּר m.] קצר
קִצְרֵי	adj. pl. constr. masc. from [קָצֵר] dec. 5 a קצר
קוֹצְרִים	Kal part. act. masc., pl. of קוֹצֵר dec. 7 b קצר
וַ׳	id. pret. 2 pers. pl. masc.; וַ, for וְ, conv. קצר
קְצָת	Chald. noun fem. sing. (constr. קְצָת) קצה
קַצֹּתָה	וַ׳ Kal pret. 2 pers. sing. masc. (§ 8. rem. 5); acc. shifted by conv. וַ (§ 8. rem. 7) . קצץ
קַצֹּ֫תִי	Kal pret. 1 pers. sing. . . . קוץ
וַ׳ קֵר	Kh. adj. masc., pl. קָרִים, q. v.; K. יָקָר, constr. of יָקָר (q. v.) . . . יקר
קִר֫	defect. for קִיר (q. v.) . . . קיר
וַ׳ קָר	noun masc. sing. . . . . קרר

I. קָרָא וַ׳ fut. יִקְרָא.—I. *to cry, call out, shout*, with אֶל, עַל *to, after* any one.—II. *to cry for help, to call upon, invoke*, with בְּשֵׁם, אֶל.—III. *to cry, proclaim, publish*; Ex. 33. 19, קְ׳ בְּשֵׁם *to proclaim the name of*; hence *to praise, celebrate.*—IV. *to call, call for*, either *summon* or *invite*; hence *to call together, convoke*; also *to call to an office*, with acc. קְ׳ בְּשֵׁם פּ׳ *to call one by his name*, i. e. *to nominate, constitute him*, Is. 43. 1; 45. 3, 4.—V. *to call, to name*, with acc. of the name, and לְ of the person or thing named, also both in the acc.—VI. *to read aloud, recite.* Niph. I. *to be called for, summoned; to be called together, convoked.*—II. *to be called, named*, const. i. q. Kal No. V.—III. *to be read aloud.* Pu. I. *to be called, chosen*, Is. 48. 12.—II. *to be called, named.*

קְרָא Chald.—I. *to call out, proclaim.*—II. *to read aloud.* Ithpe. *to be called*, Da. 5. 12.

קֹרֵא masc.—I. *partridge.*—II. pr. name of a man.

קָרִיא masc. dec. 3 a, *called, selected.*

קְרִיאָה fem. *proclamation*, Jon. 3. 2

מִקְרָא masc. d. 1 b.—I. *a calling together, convocation.*—II. *convocation, assembly.*—III. *a reading, reciting*, Ne. 8. 8.

II. קָרָא *to meet, befall, happen.* Niph. I. *to meet, happen to meet*, with לִפְנֵי, עַל.—II. *to happen.* Hiph. *to cause to happen or befall*, Je. 32. 23.

קֹרְאָה fem. *a meeting*, everywhere with לְ pref.

לִקְרַאת (constr. st. for לְקָרַאת § 23. rem. 2, comp.

(מְלָאכֶת for מְלֶאכֶת, מְלָאכָה for מְלָאכָה for *meeting, to meet* (with suff. לִקְרָאתִי, לִקְרַאתְכֶם), as a prep.—I. *towards*; in a hostile sense *against.*—II. *over against.*	
קָרֵא	Chald. Peal part. act. sing. masc. . קרא
קְרָא וּ	Kal imp. sing. masc.; וּ bef. (:) קרא
קְרֹא	id. inf. constr. . . . קרא
קֹרָא וְ׳	Pual pret. 3 pers. sing. masc. . קרא
קֹרֵא	Kal part. act., or (Je. 17. 11) subst. masc. dec. 7 b; also pr. name . . קרא
קָרְאָה	id. pret. 3 pers. sing. fem. . . קרא
קְרָא֫הוּ וַ׳	id. pret. 3 pers. sing. masc., suff. 3 pers. sing. masc.; וַ, for וְ, conv. . קרא
קְרָא֫הוּ	id. imp. pl. masc., suff. 3 pers. sing. masc. (§ 16. rem. 11) . . . קרא
קָרְא֫וּ / קָרָא֫וּ	} id. pret. 3 pers. pl. . . . קרא
קִרְא֫וּ וַ׳ / קְרָא֫וּ וַ׳	} id. imp. pl. masc. (§ 8. rem. 12); וַ bef. . . } קרא
קְרֹאות	id. inf. constr. (§ 23. rem. 2, comp. rem. 9) קרא
קְרוּאֵי	adj. pl. constr. masc. [from קָרִיא] dec. 3 a קרא
קְרֻאֶי֫הָ	Kal part. pass. pl., suff. 3 pers. sing. fem. from קָרוּא dec. 3 a קרא
קְרֻאָיו	id. id. pl., suff. 3 pers. sing. masc. קרא
קֹרְאָיו	id. part. act. pl. masc., suff. 3 pers. sing. masc. from קֹרֵא dec. 7 b . . קרא
קֹרְאֶ֫יךָ	id. id., suff. 2 pers. sing. masc. . קרא
קְרֻאִים	id. part. pass. masc., pl. of קָרוּא dec. 3 a קרא
קֹרְאִים	id. part. act. pl. masc. from קֹרֵא dec. 7 b קרא
קְרָאֵךְ	id. pret. 3 pers. sing. m., suff. 2 pers. sing. fem. קרא
קָרְאָם	id. inf., suff. 3 pers. pl. masc. . . קרא
קְרֶאןָ / קְרֶ֫אןָ	} id. imp. pl. fem. (comp. § 8. rem. 16) } קרא
קְרָאֶ֫נָּה וַ׳	id. imp. sing. masc. (קְרָא), suff. 3 pers. sing. fem. (§ 16. rem. 11); וַ bef. (:) קרא
קְרָאֵ֫נִי וַ׳	id. id., suff. 1 pers. sing.; וַ id. קרא
קָרְאֵ֫נוּ	id. inf., suff. 1 pers. pl. . . קרא
קְרָאַ֫נִי וְ׳ / קְרָאַ֫נִי	} id. pret. 3 pers. sing. masc., suff. 1 pers. sing. (§ 2. rem. 1) } קרא
קְרָא֫וּנִי	id. pret. 3 pers. pl. masc. (קָרְאוּ), suff. 1 pers. sing. קרא
קָרָ֫אתָ וְ׳	id. pret. 2 pers. sing. masc. . קרא
קָרָ֫את וְ׳	id. pret. 2 pers. sing. fem., or 3 pers. sing. fem. [for קָרְאַת § 23. rem. 1] . . קרא
קְרָאתִי K	K קָרָאתִי q. v., K. קָרָאת (q. v.) קרא
קָרָ֫אתִי וְ׳	Kal pret. 1 pers. sing. . . קרא
קְרָאתִיו	id. id., suff. 3 pers. sing. masc. . קרא
קְרָאתִ֫יךָ	id. id., suff. 2 pers. sing. masc. . קרא

---

a Ps. 102. 24.   b Ho. 10. 13.   c Ge. 27. 46.   d Ge. 42. 38.   e Nu. 16. 2.   f Ps. 86. 5.   g Is. 54. 6.   h Je. 36. 15.   i Job 4. 14.
b Ho. 10. 12.   k Le. 23. 10.   l Pr. 17. 27.   m Pr. 9. 18.   n Is. 55. 6.   o 2 Sa. 15. 16.   p Ru. 1. 20.   q Je. 13. 22.
c Ese. 42. 5.   d Da. 2. 42.   e Is. 22. 5.   f Is. 34. 16.   g Zep. 1. 7.   h Ps. 99. 6.   i Ex. 2. 20.   k Je. 3. 4.
d 1 Sa. 6. 13.   e De. 25. 12.   f Ge. 8. 22.   g Ju. 8. 1.   h Ps. 145. 18.   i Je. 12. 13.   k Is. 49. 1.

קְרָאתִיךְ id. part. act. pl. fem., suff. 2 pers. sing. fem.
[fr. קָרָא or קָרָאת sing. § 8. rem. 19] קרה

קְרָאתֶם id. pret. 2 pers. pl. masc.; וֹ, for וֹ, conv. קרא

קָרַב [also קְרֵב according to Zep. 3. 2] fut. יִקְרַב; inf. קְרֹב, imp. קְרַב.—I. *to draw* or *come near, approach*, with בְּ, אֶל, לְ.—II. *to advance* in order to attack, with עַל, אֶל.—III. *to keep by oneself*, with אֶל, Is. 65. 5, comp. גֶּשׁ־הָלְאָה. Niph. *to draw near, approach.* Pi. קֵרַב.—I. *to bring near, cause to approach or advance.*—II. intrans. *to be near*, Eze. 36. 8. Hiph. I. *to cause to come near, to allow or let approach.*—II. *to bring* or *join together*, Is. 5. 8.—III *to bring, offer* or *present a gift, offering.*—IV. *to remove*, with מִן, 2 Ki. 16. 14.—V. intrans. *to draw near, approach.*

קְרֵב Chald. *to come near.* Pa. *to bring, offer*, Ezr. 7. 17. Aph. I. *to bring near*, Da. 7. 17.—II. *to bring, offer*, Ezr. 6. 10, 17.

קָרֵב masc. dec. 5 a, *drawing near, approaching.*
קָרוֹב masc. dec. 3 a, קְרוֹבָה fem. dec. 10, adj.—I. *near*, of place or time; De. 32. 17, מִקָּרוֹב *from near, from the vicinity.*—II. *kindred.*—III. *short*, of short continuance, Job 17. 12; מִקָּרוֹב adv. (*a*) *for a short time*, Job 20. 5; (*b*) *shortly, soon*, Eze. 7. 8.

קְרָב masc. (pl. קְרָבוֹת) *encounter, battle, war.*
קְרָב Chald. id. Da. 7. 21.
קִרְבָה fem. dec. 11 c, *approach, access.*
קָרְבָּן masc. dec. 2 b, and קֻרְבָּן (Eze. 40. 43), *an offering, oblation, sacrifice.*
קֻרְבָּן masc. dec. 2 b, id. Ne. 10. 35; 13. 31.

קֶרֶב וֹ masc. dec. 6 a (with suff. קִרְבִּי).—I. *inward part, inwards, bowels*; hence *the heart.*—II. *the inner part, middle, midst*; בְּקֶרֶב *in the midst, middle, among*; and of time, *within*, Hab. 3. 2.

קָרֵב וֹ Piel imp. sing. masc. (§ 10. rem. 1) . . . קרב
קָרֵב וֹ adj. masc. sing. dec. 5 a . . . קרב
קֶרֶב וֹ noun masc. s. d 1 a (§ 30. No. 3); וֹ bef. (:) קרב
קְרַב Kal imp. sing. masc. . . . . קרב
קְרֵב Chald. Peal pret. 3 pers. sing. m. (§ 47. r. 6) קרב
קָרְבָה } Kal pret. 3 pers. sing. fem. (§ 8. rem. 1 & 7) . . . . . . } קרב
קָרְבָה id. imp. 2 pers. s. m. parag. ה (§ 8. rem. 11) קרב
קְרֵבָה adj. fem. sing. dec. 10, from קָרוֹב masc. קרב
קָרְבוּ Kal pret. 3 pers. pl. . . . קרב
קָרְבוּ Piel imp. pl. masc. . . . קרב

קָרְבוּ id. pret. 3 pers. pl. . . . קרב
קְרִבוּ Chald. Peal pret. 3 pers. pl. masc. (§ 47. r. 6) קרב
קְרֵבוֹ adj. masc. sing., suff. 3 pers. sing. masc. from קָרֵב dec. 3 a . . . . קרב
וְקָרְבוֹ noun masc. sing., suff. 3 pers. sing. masc from קֶרֶב dec. 6 a . . . . קרב
קִרְבוּ Kal imp. pl. masc. . . . . קרב
קְרָבוֹת noun masc. with pl. **fem.** term. from קְרָב dec. 1 a (§ 30. No. 3) . . . . קרב
קִרְבִּי noun masc. sing., suff. 1 pers. sing. from קֶרֶב dec. 6 a . . . . קרב
קְרָבַי id. pl. with suff. 1 pers. sing. . . . קרב
קְרֵבִים adj. masc., pl. of קָרֵב dec. 5 a . . קרב
קְרֹבִים adj. masc., pl. of קָרוֹב dec. 3 a . . קרב
קִרְבָּם noun masc. sing., suff. 3 pers. pl. **masc.** from קֶרֶב dec. 6 a . . . . קרב
קָרְבָּן noun masc. sing. dec. 2 b (but comp. §30. r. 3) קרב
קָרְבַּן id., constr. st. . . . . . . קרב
קֻרְבָּן Chald. noun masc. sing. . . . . קרב
קָרְבָּנָהּ noun masc. sing., suff. 3 pers. sing. fem. from קָרְבָּן dec. 2 b . . . . . . קרב
קָרְבָּנֶיהָ noun masc. sing., suff. 3 pers. sing. fem. (§ 3. rem. 5) from קֶרֶב dec. 6 a . . . . קרב
וְקָרְבָּנוֹ noun masc. sing., suff. 3 pers. sing. masc. from קָרְבָּן dec. 2 b . . . . קרב
קָרְבָּנִי id., suff. 1 pers. sing. . . . . קרב
קַרְבְּנֵיהֶם id. pl., suff. 3 pers. pl. masc. (others read קָרְבְּנֵיהֶם) . . . . . . קרב
קָרְבָּנְךָ } id. sing., suff. 2 pers. sing. **masc.** . . . } קרב
קָרְבַּנְךָ
קָרְבַּנְכֶם id. sing., suff. 2 pers. pl. masc. . . . קרב
קָרְבָּנָם id. sing., suff. 3 pers. pl. masc. . . . קרב
קָרַבְתָּ } Kal pret. 2 pers. sing. **masc.**; **acc.** shifted by conv. וֹ (§ 8. rem. 7) . . . . } קרב
קָרָבְתָּ
וְקָרַבְתָּ
קָרְבַת noun fem. sing., constr. of [קָרְבָה] dec. 11 c קרב
קִרְבֵת Chald. Peal pret. 1 pers. sing. . . . קרב
וְקָרַבְתִּי Kal pret. 1 pers. sing.; **acc.** shifted by conv. וֹ (§ 8. rem. 7) . . . . . . קרב
קֵרַבְתִּי Piel pret. 1 pers. sing. . . . . קרב

[קַרְדֹּם] masc. dec. 8 c (pl. דֻּמִּים, דֻּמוֹת), *an axe.*
קַרְדֻּמּוֹ id. with suff. 3 pers. sing. masc.
קַרְדֻּמּוֹת id. with pl. fem. term.

[קָרָה] fut. יִקְרֶה.—I. *to meet, to go* or *come to meet.*—II. *to befall, happen* to any one, with acc., לְ, of

---

a Is. 51. 19.　e Ps. 55. 22.　i Ps. 69. 19.　m Is. 16. 11.　r Nu. 5. 15.　v Le. 7. 38.　z Le. 1. 2.　d De. 2. 19.　i Is. 46. 13.
b Ju. 14. 15.　f Da. 3. 26.　k Eze. 42. 14.　n Ps. 103. 1.　s Ge. 41. 21.　w Le. 2. 5, 7.　a De. 2. 37.　k Da. 7. 16.　l 1 Sa. 18. 20.
c Ps. 64. 7.　g Zep. 3. 2.　l Is. 41. 21.　o De. 20. 3.　t Nu. 7. 13.　x Le. 2. 13.　b La. 3. 57.　e Mal. 3. 5.　Ps. 74. 5.
d Eze. 37. 17.　h De.15.9; 25.11.　Ps. 68. 31.　p Ne. 10. 35.　q Nu. 28. 2.

the person. Niph. I. *to meet, fall in with*, with
עַל.—II. *to happen, chance*, 2 Sa. 1. 6. Pi.
קֵרָה *to join* or *lay beams* or *rafter*; hence *to frame,
build*, Ps. 104. 3. Hiph. I. *to cause to meet, to let
occur.*—II. *to make suitable, convenient*, Nu. 35. 11.

קָרֶה masc. dec. 9 b, *accident*, De. 23. 11.

קוֹרָה fem. dec. 10.—I. *a beam.*—II. *a roof*,
Ge. 19. 8.

קְרִי masc. only in pause קֶרִי (§ 35. rem. 14),
contrariness, opposition, with הָלַךְ *to walk contrary,
in opposition*.

קִרְיָה fem. (no pl.).—I. *city, town.*—II. combined
in pr. names of cities or towns. קִרְיַת אַרְבַּע (*city
of Arba*) the ancient Hebron in Judah, comp. Ge.
23. 2.—ק׳ בַּעַל (*city of Baal*) i. q. ק׳ יְעָרִים.—
ק׳ חֻצוֹת (*city of streets*) in Moab, Nu. 22. 39.—
ק׳ עָרִים, ק׳ יְעָרִים (*city of forests*) in the confines
of Judah and Benjamin.—ק׳ סַנָּה (*city of palms*)
& ק׳ סֵפֶר (*city of the book*) in Judah, also called
דְּבִיר.—קִרְיָתַיִם (*double-city*) one in the tribe of
Reuben; and another in Naphtali, 1 Ch. 6. 61,
also called קַרְתָּן.

קִרְיָא, קִרְיָה Chald. fem. dec. 8 a, idem, Ezr.
4. 10, 12, 13, 15.

קְרִיּוֹת (*cities*) pr. name—I. of a city in Judah,
Jos. 15. 25.—II. of another in Moab.

קֶרֶת fem. poet. i. q. קִרְיָה *a city*.

קַרְתָּה (*city*) pr. name of a town in Zebulun,
Jos. 21. 34.

קַרְתָּן pr. name of a town, Jos. 21. 32, the same
as קִרְיָתַיִם see קִרְיָה.

מִקְרֶה masc. dec. 9 a.—I. *chance, accident.*—II.
event, result.

מִקְרֶה masc. *building, edifice*, Ec. 10. 18.

קָרָה noun fem. sing. dec. 10 [for קָרַּה fr. קַר m.]
קָרָהוּ ו׳ Kal pret. 3 pers. sing. masc. [קָרָה], suff.
   3 pers. sing. masc. (§ 24. rem. 21)
קָרוּא Kal part. pass. sing. masc. dec. 3 a
קְרוּאֵי Kh. קְרוּאֵי constr. of the foll.; K. קְרוּאֵי adj.
   pl. constr. masc. [from קָרִיא] dec. 3 a
קְרֻאִים ו׳ Kal part. pass. pl. m. fr. קָרוּא d. 3 a; ו׳ bef. (:)
קָרוֹב ו׳ adj. masc. sing. dec. 3 a
קְרֹב Kal inf. constr.
קְרוֹבָה adj. fem. sing. dec. 10, from קָרוֹב masc.
קְרוֹבֵי
קְרוֹבַי } id. pl. masc., suff. 1 pers. pl.; ו׳ bef. (:)
קְרוֹבִים id. pl. masc., abs. st.

קְרוּגֶהָ Piel pret. 3 pers. pl., suff. 3 pers. sing. masc.
קָרוּעַ Kal part. pass. sing. masc. dec. 3 f
קְרוּעֵי id. pl., constr. st.
קֹרוֹת noun fem., pl. of קוֹרָה dec. 10

[קָרַח] *to make* (smooth) *bald*. Niph. *to be made bald*,
Je. 16. 6. Hiph. i. q. Kal, Eze. 27. 31. Hoph.
pass. Eze. 29. 18. Hence the following.

קֶרַח } masc. (§ 35. rem. 2).—I. *ice.*—II. *cold.*
וְקֶרַח } —III. *crystal*, Eze. 1. 22
קָרֵחַ (*bald-head*) pr. name m. 2 Ki. 25. 23; Je. 40. 8
קֵרֵחַ masc. [for קָרֵחַ § 26. No. 9] one *bald* on the
   crown of the head
קֹרַח וְ masc. dec. 6 c (§ 35. rem. 5).—I. *ice*, Ps.
   147. 17.—II. pr. name, *Korah*, a son of
   Esau, Ge. 36. 5, 14.—III. a son of Eliphaz,
   and a tribe descended from him.—IV. a
   Levite who conspired against Moses. Patronym. קָרְחִי

קָרְחָא
קָרְחָה } fem. dec. 10, & קָרַחַת dec. 13 a (with suff.
   קָרַחְתּוֹ).—I. *baldness, bald part* on the
   crown or front part of the head.—II. trop.
   bareness, threadbare spot, only Le. 13. 55

קָרְחוֹ noun m. s., suff. 3 p. s. m. fr. [קֶרַח] d. 6 c
קְרָחִי Kal imp. sing. fem. (§ 8. rem. 12)
קָרַחְתֵּךְ noun fem. sing., suff. 2 pers. sing. fem. from
   קָרְחָה (no pl.)
קֶרִי noun masc. sing. [for קְרִי § 35. rem. 14]
קְרִי Chald. Peal part. pass. sing. masc. (§ 35. r. 4)
קִרְיָא Chald. noun fem. sing. dec. 8 a
קִרְיָאֵי Kh. קִרְיָאֵי adj. pl. constr. masc. [from קָרִיא]
   dec. 3 a, K. קְרֻאֵי (q. v.)
קִרְיָה noun fem. sing. (no pl.)
קְרִיּוֹת ו׳ pr. name of a place; ו׳ bef. (:)
קָרִים adj. masc. pl., of קַר dec. 8 (§ 37. rem. 7)
קִרְיַת ו׳ noun fem. s., constr. of קִרְיָה (no pl.); also
   pr. name, and in compos. as ק׳ אַרְבַּע &c.
קִרְיְתָא ו׳ Chald. noun fem. s., emph. of קִרְיָא d. 8 a
קִרְיָתַיִם
קִרְיָתָיִם } ו׳ pr. name of a place, see קִרְיָה
קִרְיָתְמָה ו׳ id. with parag. ה, K. תֵּימָה
קָרֶךָ Kal pret. 3 pers. sing. masc. (קָרָה), suff.
   2 pers. sing. masc. (§ 24. rem. 21)

[קָרַם] *to cover*, with עַל, Eze. 37. 6; intrans. ver. 8.
קָרַמְתִּי וְ Kal pret. 1 pers. sing.; acc. shifted by
   conv. ו׳ (§ 8. rem. 7)

a Ge. 44. 29.   d Ps. 32. 9.   g Ne. 3, 3, 6.   k Ge. 31. 40.   n Mi. 1. 16.   p Le. 26. 21, 23, 28.   r Ezr. 4. 15.   t Ezr. 4. 12, 13,   w De. 25. 18.
b Est. 5. 12.   e Job 19. 14.   h 2 Sa. 15. 32.   l Eze. 27. 31.   o Mi. 1. 16.   q Ezr. 4. 18, 23.   s Nu. 1. 16.   15, 16, 19, 21.   x Eze. 37. 6.
c Eze. 23. 23.   f Ps. 38. 12.   i Ca. 1. 17.   m Ps. 147. 17.

קֶרֶן וְ‎ fem. dec. 6a (du. קַרְנַיִם, קְרָנַיִם; pl. קְרָנוֹת, c. קַרְנוֹת).—I. *horn* of an animal.—II. *horn*, as a vessel for oil.—III. *horn, wind instrument*, Jos. 6. 5.—IV. *horn*, as a symbol of *strength, power* in men or state; הֵרִים קֶרֶן *to lift up, exalt the horn*, i.e. *to strengthen.*—V. *peak, summit* of a mountain, Is. 5. 1.—VI. pl. *horns* or the projecting points on the four corners of an altar.—VII. du. *beams, rays* of light, Hab. 3. 4.—VIII. קֶרֶן הַפּוּךְ (*paint-horn*), pr. name fem. Job 42. 14.

    קֶרֶן Chald. d. 3a (du. קַרְנַיִן § 59), idem. Hence

קָרַן *to emit rays, to shine*, Ex. 34. 29, 30, 35. Hiph. *to have horns*, Ps. 69. 32.

קָרֶן	in pause for קֶרֶן (§ 35. rem. 2)	קרן
קַרְנָא וְ‎	Ch. noun f. s., emph. of קֶרֶן dec. 3a (§ 59)	קרן
קַרְנִ	Heb. id., suff. 3 pers. sing. masc. dec. 6a	קרן
קַרְנוֹת	id. pl., constr. st.	קרן
קְרָנוֹת‎	id. pl. fem., abs. st.	קרן
קַרְנוֹתָיו‎	id. pl. fem., suff. 3 pers. sing. masc.	קרן
קַרְנֵי וְ‎	id. du., constr. of קְרָנַיִם	קרן
קַרְנֵי	id. sing., suff. 1 pers. sing.	קרן
קַרְנַיָּא וְ‎	Ch. id. du., emph. of קַרְנַיִן	קרן
קַרְנָיו‎	Heb. id. du., suff. 3 pers. sing. masc.	קרן
קַרְנֵיהֶ‎	id. du. (קְרָנַיִם q. v.), suff. 3 pers. sing. masc.	קרן
קְרָנַיִם‎ קַרְנַיִם	} id. du., abs. st.	קרן
קַרְנַיִם	id. du. [for קְרָנַיִם as if from קֶרֶן]	קרן
קַרְנַיִן וְ‎	Chald. id. du., abs. st.	קרן
קַרְנְךָ	Heb. id. sing., suff. 2 pers. sing. masc.	קרן
קַרְנֵךְ‎	id. sing., suff. 2 pers. sing. fem.	קרן
קַרְנְכֶם‎	id. sing., suff. 2 pers. pl. masc.	קרן
קַרְנֵנוּ‎	id. sing., suff. 1 pers. pl.	קרן
קַרְנֹת	id. pl. fem., constr. st.	קרן
קַרְנֹתָיו‎	id. pl. fem., suff. 3 pers. sing. masc.	קרן

[קָרַם] *to bend, stoop.*

    קֶרֶם masc. dec. 6a (pl. c. קַרְסֵי), *hook, tache.*

    קֵירֹס קֶרֶם (*weaver's comb*; from the Chald.) pr. name masc. Ezr. 2. 44; Ne. 7. 47.

    קַרְסֹל masc. du. קַרְסֻלַּיִם *ankles*, 2 Sa. 22. 37; Ps. 18. 37.

קֶרֶם	pr. name masc.	קרם
קֹרֵם‎	Kal part. act. sing. masc.	קרם
קָרְסוּ‎	id. pret. 3 pers. pl.	קרם
קַרְסֵי‎	noun masc. pl., constr. from [קֶרֶם] dec. 6a	קרם
קְרָסָיו‎	id. pl., suff. 3 pers. sing. masc.	קרם

קַרְסֻלַּי‎ noun du., suff. 1 pers. sing. fr. [קַרְסֹל] dec. 8c

קָרַע וְ‎ I. *to tear, rend*—II. *to tear off* or *away.*—III. *to cut in pieces*, Je. 36. 23.—IV. *to cut out.* Niph *to be rent, torn.*

    קֶרַע masc. only pl. קְרָעִים *rendings, rags.*

קָרֹעַ	Kal inf. abs.	קרע
קֹרֵעַ‎	id. part. act. sing. masc.	קרע
קָרְעָה‎	id. pret. 3 pers. sing. fem. [for קָרְעָה § 8. r. 7]	קרע
קָרְעוּ‎	id. pret. 3 pers. pl.	קרע
קִרְעוּ וְ‎	id. imp. pl. masc.	קרע
קְרֻעֵי‎	defect. for קְרוּעֵי (q. v.)	קרע
קְרָעִים‎	noun masc., pl. of [קֶרַע] dec. 6 (§ 35. rem. 5); בֶּ bef. (..)	קרע
קְרֻעִים‎	Kal part. pass. pl. masc. from קָרוּעַ dec. 3a	קרע
קָרַעְתָּ‎	id. pret. 2 pers. sing. masc.	קרע
קָרַעְתִּי‎ קָרַעְתִּי	} id. pret. 1 pers. sing.; acc. shifted by conv. וְ (§ 8. rem. 7) }	קרע

[קָרַץ] *to close, press together*, as the lips or eyes, denoting *fraud, cunning, &c.* (Prof. Lee). Others, *to cut, bite* the lips; this is however unsuitable of the eyes. Pu. *to be cut out*, Job 33. 6.

    קְרָץ Chald. masc. dec. 3a, *a piece*; only in the phrase אֲכַל קַרְצֵי דִי *to eat the pieces* of any one, q. d. *to eat him up in piece-meal*, metaph. for *to slander.* The figure is taken from various dogs devouring a corpse; comp. the English *backbite* Also

קֶרֶץ	masc. *destruction*, Je. 46. 20	קרץ
קֹרֵץ‎	Kal part. act. sing. masc.	קרץ
קַרְצוֹהִי‎	Chald. noun masc. pl., suff. 3 pers. sing. masc. from [קְרָץ] dec. 3a	קרץ
קַרְצֵיהוֹן‎	Chald. id. pl., suff. 3 pers. pl. masc.	קרץ
קֹרַצְתִּי‎	Pual pret. 1 pers. sing.	קרץ

קַרְקַע‎ masc.—I. *floor, bottom.*—II. *bottom* of the sea, Am. 9. 3.—III. pr. n. of a town in Judah, Jos. 15. 3

קַרְקָרִ וְ‎ Piel inf. abs. (§ 6. No. 4)   קור

קָרַר‎ Root not used; Syr. *to be cold*; Arab. *to be cool, quiet.*

    קַר masc. (pl. קָרִים § 37. rem. 7) adj.—I. *cold, cool.*—II. *cool, quiet*, Pr. 17. 27.

    קֹר masc. *cold*, Ge. 8. 22.

    קָרָה fem. dec. 10, idem.

    מְקֵרָה fem. *a cooling, refreshing*, Ju. 3. 20, 24.

a Da. 7. 20, 21.   d Da. 7. 8, 20, 24.   i Hab. 3. 4.   m Mi. 4. 13.   r Is. 46. 2.   v Joel 2. 13.   a Pr. 23. 21.   d Je. 46. 20.   g Job 33. 6.
Zec. 2. 1.   e De. 33. 17.   k De. 8. 3.   n Ps. 75. 6.   s 1 Ki. 11. 11.   w 2 Sa. 13. 31.   b Exr. 9. 3.   e Da. 6. 25.   h 1 Ki. 6. 15, 38
Eze. 43. 20.   f Da. 8. 7.   l Da. 7. 7.   o Ps. 89. 18.   t 2 Sa. 13. 19.   x Je. 41. 5.   c Eze. 13. 20, 21.   f Da. 3. 8.   i Nu. 24. 17.
De. 33. 17.   h Am. 6. 13.   =1 Sa. 16. 1.   q Is. 46. 1.   u 2 Sa. 3. 31.

קָרַשׁ Root not used; Arab. *to cut.* Hence

קֶרֶשׁ
קָרֶשׁ } masc. dec. 6 & (with suff. קַרְשׁוֹ).—I. *board,* *plank.*—II. *bench* of a ship.   קרשׁ

קַרְשֵׁי id. pl., constr. st. . . . . קרשׁ

קְרָשָׁיו id. pl., suff. 3 pers. sing. masc. . קרשׁ

קְרָשִׁים id. pl., abs. st. . . . . קרשׁ

קְרָשֵׁךְ id. sing., suff. 2 pers. sing. fem. . קרשׁ

קֶרֶת noun fem. sing. [for קִרְיָה comp. § 35. r. 2] קרה

קַרְתָּה pr. name of a place . . . קרה

קַרְתוֹ noun fem. sing., suff. 3 pers. sing. masc. from

    קָרָה [for קִרְיָה] dec. 10 . . . קרר

קָרָתִי Kal pret. 1 pers. sing. . . . קור

קֵרָתִי noun fem. sing., suff. 1 pers. s. fr. קוֹרָה d. 10 קרה

קַרְתָּן pr. name of a place . . . קרה

קַשׁ
קָשׁ } noun masc. sing. . . . . קשׁשׁ

קִשֻּׁא Root not used; prob. i. q. קָשָׁה *to be hard.*

קִשֻּׁא masc. d. 1 a, *cucumber* or *melon,* Nu. 11. 5.

מִקְשָׁה fem. (for מִקְשָׁאָה) *field* or *garden* of *cucumbers,* Is. 1. 8.

[קָשַׁב] fut. יִקְשֹׁב *to attend, listen,* Is. 32. 3. Hiph. *to attend to, hearken,* with בְּ, עַל, אֶל, לְ.

קַשֶּׁבֶת fem. קַשֶּׁבֶת adj. *attentive,* Ne. 1. 6, 11.

קַשָּׁב adj. id. Ps. 130. 2. Also

קֶשֶׁב
קָשֶׁב } masc. (§ 35. rem. 2) *attention* . . קשׁב

קַשֻּׁבוֹת adj. pl. fem. [from קָשֻׁב masc.] . קשׁב

קַשֶּׁבֶת adj. fem. sing. from קַשֻׁב masc. (§ 39. No. 4) קשׁב

[קְשָׂה] fem. dec. 11 a, *dish, bowl.*

קַשְׂוָה fem. dec. 12 a, id.

קֶסֶת fem. *a vessel for ink, inkhorn,* Eze. 9. 2, 3, 11.

קַשְׂקֶשֶׂת fem. (pl. קַשְׂקַשִּׂים § 39. No. 4. rem. 1).—I. *scales* of a fish.—II. *scale armour,* 1 Sa. 17. 5.

[קָשָׁה] I. *to be hard, harsh, severe.*—II. *to be hard, difficult.* Niph. part. נִקְשָׁה *subject to hardships,* Is. 8. 21. Pi. *to labour hard, have hard labour,* of a parturient woman, Ge. 35. 16. Hiph. הִקְשָׁה.—I. *to harden* sc. the neck, the heart, make stubborn, obdurate. —II. *to make hard, grievous,* a yoke.—III. *to make hard, difficult.*—IV. i. q. Pi. Ge. 35. 17.

קָשֶׁה masc. dec. 9 b, קָשָׁה fem. dec. 11 a; adj.— I. *hard, firm, unyielding;* with עֹרֶף לֵב *stiff-necked, hard-hearted, stubborn, obstinate;* with פָּנִים *im-*

pudent.—II. *hard, vehement, strong.*—III. *hard, severe, grievous.*—IV. *hard, difficult,* Ex. 18. 26.— V. *heavy, depressed,* 1 Sa. 1. 15.

קְשִׁי masc. *stubbornness,* De. 9. 27.

קִשְׁיוֹן (*hardness*) pr. name of a place in Issachar, Jos. 19. 20; 21. 28; called also קֶדֶשׁ, 1 Ch. 6. 57.

מִקְשֶׁה masc. *a wreathing, plaiting* of the hair, Is. 3. 24 (Prof. Lee), comp. the following.

מִקְשָׁה fem. *turned work, opus turnatum.* Arab. קשׁא *to take off the bark,* espec. by *turning* (Gesenius); *opere tornatili elaboravit* (Prof. Lee).

קָשָׁה h'ו fem. of the foll., dec. 10 . . . קשׁה

קָשֶׁה adj. masc. sing. dec. 9 b . . קשׁה

קְשֵׁה id., constr. st. . . . . . קשׁה

קְשׁוֹט Chald. noun masc. sing. . . . קשׁט

קְשֻׁרָה Kal part. pass. sing. fem. [of קָשׁוּר masc.] קסר

קָשׁוֹת adj. fem. pl. abs. of קָשָׁה d. 11 a, fr. קָשֶׁה m. קשׁה

קְשׁוֹת noun fem. pl. constr. from [קְשָׂה] dec. 11 a קשׂה

קְשׂוֹתָיו ו id., suff. 3 pers. sing. masc.; ו bef. (:) קשׂה

קָשַׁח Hiph. I. *to harden, make obdurate* the heart, Is. 63. 17.—II. *to treat harshly,* Job 39. 16.

קָשַׁט Root not used; Arab. *to divide,* whence, keston, *pair of scales.*

קְשִׂיטָה fem. *something weighed,* a certain coin or weight of this name.

קָשַׁט Root not used; Arab. *to divide out equally; to be equal, right.* Hence

קֹשְׁט
קֹשֶׁט } masc. *truth,* Ps. 60. 6; Pr. 22. 21 . קישׁט

קְשֹׁט Chald. m. id. Da. 2. 47, and קְשׁוֹט Da. 4. 34 קשׁט

קָשֹׁים י adj. pl. constr. masc. from קָשֶׁה dec. 9 b קשׁה

קְשִׁי noun masc. sing. . . . . קשׁה

קִשְׁיוֹן י pr. name of a place . . . קשׁה

קְשִׂיטָה noun fem. sing. . . . . קשׁט

קָשִׁים adj. masc., pl. of קָשֶׁה dec. 9 b . קשׁה

קַשְׂקַשִּׂים י noun fem. with pl. masc. term. from the foll. קשׁה

קַשְׂקֶשֶׂת ו noun fem. sing. (§ 39. No. 4. rem. 1) קשׁה

קָשַׁר fut. יִקְשֹׁר.—I. *to bind, tie.*—II. *to conspire against,* with עַל.—III. part. pass. קָשׁוּר *bound, firm, strong,* Ge. 30. 42. Niph. I. *to be bound,* metaph. 1 Sa. 18. 1 —II. *to be joined, closed,* Ne. 3. 38. Pi. *to bind,* Job 38. 31; *to bind on* oneself, Is. 49. 18. Pu. part. *strong,* Ge. 30. 41. Hithp. i. q. Kal No. II.

קֶשֶׁר masc. dec. 6 a (with suff. קִשְׁרוֹ), *conspiracy*

קִשֻּׁר masc. dec. 1 b, *band, girdle.*

קָשַׁר   Kal pret. 3 pers. sing. masc. for קָשֵׁר (§ 8. r. 7)   קשר

קֶשֶׁר   } noun masc. sing. dec. 6a (§ 35. rem. 2),   קשר
קֶשֶׁר   } yet see the foll.

קִשְׁרוֹ   } id. with suff. 3 pers. sing. masc.   קשר

קְשָׁרֶיהָ   noun masc. pl., suff. 3 pers. sing. fem. from [קֶשֶׁר] dec. 1 b   קשר

קָשְׁרֵם   Kal imp. sing. masc., suff. 3 pers. pl. masc. (□ for ן fem. in Pr. 6. 21; 7. 3, § 2. rem. 5)   קשר

קְשַׁרְתִּי   id. pret. 1 pers. sing.   קשר

קְשַׁרְתָּם   } id. pret. 2 pers. sing. masc., suff. 3 pers. pl. masc.; ן, for ו, conv.   קשר

קְשַׁרְתֶּם   } id. pret. 2 pers. pl. masc.; ו id.   קשר

[קָשַׁשׁ]   to collect, assemble together, Zep. 2. 1. Po. to collect, gather, as stubble, wood. Hithpo. to assemble themselves, Zep. 2. 1.

קַשׁ masc.—I. stubble.—II. chaff.

וַ קֹשְׁשׁוּ   } Poel pret. 3 pers. pl.   קשש

קֹשֶׁת   in pause for קֶשֶׁת (q. v. comp. § 35. rem. 2)   קוש

קַשְׁתְּ◌   noun fem. sing.   קוש

קָשָׁה   adj. fem. s., constr. of קָשָׁה d. 11 a, fr. קָשֶׁה m.   קשה

וַ קֶשֶׁת   noun com. sing., suff. קַשְׁתִּי, pl. קְשָׁתוֹת, c. קַשְׁתוֹת, ת treated as if radical, comp. d. 6 a   קוש

קָשְׁתָה   } Kal pret. 3 pers. sing. fem. (comp.
קָשְׁתָה   } § 8. rem. 7)   קשה

קַשְׁתּוֹ   noun com. s., suff. 3 pers. s. m. fr. קֶשֶׁת (q.v.)   קוש

וַ קְשָׁתוֹת   id. pl., abs. st.; ו bef. (:)   קוש

וַ קַשְׁתוֹתָם   id. pl., suff. 3 pers. sing. masc.   קוש

קַשְׁתִּי   וַ id. sing., suff. 1 pers. sing.   קוש

קַשְׁתֶּךָ   } וַ
קַשְׁתֵּךְ   } id. sing., suff. 2 pers. sing. masc.   קוש

קַשְׁתָּם   id. sing., suff. 3 pers. pl. masc.   קוש

וַ קַשְׁתוֹתֵיהֶם   id. pl., suff. 3 pers. pl. masc.   קוש

קַשְׁתוֹתָיו   id. pl., suff. 3 pers. sing. masc.   קוש

ר

רָאָה   וַ fut. יִרְאֶה, ap. יֵרֶא, וַיֵּרֶא, וַתֵּרֶא (§ 24. rem. 3).—I. to see, generally, const. with acc., once לְ (Ps. 64. 6); espec. to see the sun, to live, Ec. 7. 11; and simply, to see, exist, live, Ge. 16. 13; to see a vision, hence part. רֹאֶה a seer, prophet.—II. to see, look at, view, regard, observe; hence to see either with delight, to rejoice in, or with grief, usually with בְּ; also to care for.—III. to visit.—IV. to look out, provide, choose, with לְ for oneself.—V. to have in view, Ge. 20. 10.—VI. to perceive, experience; hence to perceive, understand.—VII. to discern, discriminate. Niph. נִרְאָה.—I. to be seen.—II. to appear, with אֶת־פְּנֵי, לְ, אֶל.—III. to be provided, Ge. 22. 14. Pu. to be seen, Job 33. 21. Hiph. הִרְאָה, הֶרְאָה, fut. יַרְאֶה, ap. וַיַּרְא (§ 11. rem. 1; § 24. rem. 16).—I. to cause to see, to show.—II. to cause to see or experience, with בְּ. Hoph. I. to be shown.—II. to be shown, be made to see. Hithp. to look at each other.

רָאֶה   adj. masc. dec. 9 b, seeing, Job 10. 15.

רָאָה   fem. the name of an unclean bird, De. 14. 13, for which in the parallel passage, Le. 11. 14, it is דָּאָה a kite.

רֹאֶה   masc. dec. 9.—I. part. act. seer, prophet.—II. vision, Is. 28. 7, comp. חֹזֶה.

רָאוּת   fem. a seeing, viewing, Ec. 5. 10, Keri.

רְאִי   masc. mirror, Job 37. 18.

רֳאִי   masc. (in pause רֹאִי, § 35. rem. 14).—I. vision, revelation, Ge. 16. 13.—II. sight, view.—III. spectacle, gazing-stock, Ne. 3. 6.

רְאִית   fem. a seeing, Ec. 5. 10, Kheth.

רֵו   Chald. masc. dec. 1 a (for רְאוֹ), aspect, appearance, Da. 2. 31; 3. 25.

רְאוּבֵן   (behold a son!) pr. name, Reuben, the eldest son of Jacob, and head of the tribe which was named from him. Patronym. רְאוּבֵנִי.

רְאָיָה   (the Lord looks upon him) pr. name masc. of three different men, for which also הָרָאָה comp. 1 Ch. 4. 2, with 1 Ch. 2. 52.

יְרִאיָּה   (the Lord shall look upon him) pr. name masc. Je. 37. 13, 14.

מַרְאֶה   masc. dec. 9 a.—I. a seeing, looking.—II. sight, vision.—III. appearance, form.

מַרְאָה   fem. dec. 10.—I. vision.—II. mirror, Ex. 38. 8.

רָאָה   Kal pret. 3 pers. sing. masc., suff. 3 pers. sing. fem. (§ 24. rem. 21).   ראה

רָאֹה   וַ id. inf. abs.   ראה

רְאֵה   ו id. imp. sing. masc.; ו bef. (:)   ראה

רֹאֶה   ו adj. m. s., constr. of [רָאֶה] dec. 9 b; ו id.   ראה

---

a Je. 2. 32.   d 1 Sa. 22. 8, 13.   g Ge. 21. 20.   k Ge. 49. 7.   n Ps. 37. 15.   r Hab. 3. 9.   u Eze. 39. 3.   x Is. 5. 28.   y Ex. 9. 11.
b 2 Ki. 10. 9.   e De. 11. 18.   h 1 Sa. 1. 15.   l 1 Sa. 5. 7.   o Ge. 9. 13.   s Ge. 27. 3.   v Ne 4. 7.   z Job 28. 27.   a Job 10. 15.
c De. 6. 8.   f Ex. 5. 7.   i Ho. 2. 20.   m Je. 51. 52.   p Job 22. 20.

רְאֹה	Kal inf. constr. . . . . ראה
רֹאָה[b]	id. part. act. sing. fem. dec. 10, fr. רֹאֶה masc. ראה
רֹאֶה[c]	{id. part. act. sing. masc. constr. & abs.}
רֹאֶה[d]	{dec. 9 a . . . . .} ראה
רָאָהוּ[e]	id. pret. 3 pers. sing. masc., suff. 3 pers.
	sing. masc. (§ 24. rem. 21) . הה
רָאֹו	id. inf. abs. for רָאֹה (§ 24. rem. 2) . הה
רָאוּ	id. pret. 3 pers. pl. . . . . הה
רְאוּ[f]	id. imp. pl. masc.; וּ bef. (;) . . הה
רֻאּוּ	Pual pret. 3 pers. pl. (note א with dag.) . הה
רְאוּבֵן[g]	pr. name of a man and a tribe; וּ bef. (;) . ראה
רְאוּהָ	Kal pret. 3 pers. pl., suff. 3 pers. sing. fem. ראה
רְאוּךָ	id. id., suff. 2 pers. sing. masc. . . ראה
רְאוּמָה	pr. name fem. . . . . . ראם
רְאוּנִי[h]	Kal pret. 3 pers. pl., suff. 1 pers. sing. . ראה
רְאוֹת	id. inf. constr. . . . . . ראה
רֹאוֹת	id. part. act. fem. pl. of רֹאֶה d. 10, fr. רֹאֶה m. ראה
רְאוֹתִי[i]	id. inf. (רְאוֹת), suff. 1 pers. sing. dec. 1 a ראה
רְאִי[k]	id. imp. sing. fem.; וּ bef. (;) . . ראה
רֹאִי	id. part. act. pl. masc., suff. 1 pers. sing from
	רֹאֶה dec. 9 a . . . . . הה
רֹאַי[l]	id. id. pl., constr. st. . . . . ראה
רְאִי	} noun masc. sing. (§ 35. rem. 14) . . ראה
רְאָיָה	}
רְאָיָה	id. pr. name masc.; וּ bef. (;) . . ראה
רֹאִיָה[m]	Kal part. act. pl. masc., suff. 3 pers. sing.
	fem. from רֹאֶה dec. 9 a . . . ראה
רְאִיהֶם	id. pl., suff. 3 pers. pl. masc. . . ראה
רְאִיו[n]	id. pl., suff. 3 pers. sing. masc. . . ראה
רְאִיךְ[o]	id. pl., suff. 2 pers. sing. fem. . . ראה
רְאִיךָ	id. pl., suff. 2 pers. sing. masc. . . ראה
רְאִים	id. pl., abs. st. . . . . . ראה
רְאֶינָה[p]	id. imp. pl. fem. (§ 23. rem. 3) ; וּ bef. (;) ראה
רְאִינוּ	id. pret. 1 pers. pl. . . . . ראה
רִאשֹׁנָה	Kh. רִאשֹׁנָה adj. fem.; K. רִאשֹׁנָה (q. v.) ראש
רְאִיתָ	וּ Kal pret. 2 pers. sing. masc. . . ראה
רְאִיתְ[q]	id. pret. 2 pers. sing. fem. . . . ראה
רָאִית[r]	Kh. רָאִית q. v., K. רָאוֹת Kal inf. abs.
	(§ 24. rem. 2) . . . . . ראה
רְאִית[s]	Kh. רְאִית, K. רָאוֹת noun fem. sing. . ראה
רְאִיתָה	וּ Kal pret. 3 pers. sing. masc. (§ 8. rem. 5) ראה
רְאִיתִי	וּ id. pret. 1 pers. sing. . . . ראה
רְאִיתִיהָ[t]	וּ id. id., suff. 3 pers. sing. f.; וּ for וְ, conv. ראה
רְאִיתִיו[u]	וּ id. id., suff. 3 pers. sing. masc.; וּ bei. (;) ראה
רְאִיתִיךָ	id. id., suff. 2 pers. sing. masc. . . ראה
רְאִיתֶם	וּ id. pret. 2 pers. pl. masc.; וּ for וְ, conv. ראה
רְאִיתֶן	וּ id. pret. 2 pers. pl. fem.; וּ id. ראה

רְאִיתַנִי	וּ id. pret. 2 pers. sing. masc., suff. 1 pers.
	sing.; וּ, for וְ, conv. . . . ראה
וָרָאךָ[f]	וּ id. pret. 3 pers. sing. masc. (רָאָה), suff.
	2 pers. sing. masc. (§ 24. rem. 21) . ראה

[רָאֵם] *to be high*, Zec. 14. 10.

רֵים, רְאֵים, רֵים masc. dec. 1 a, *according to* Bochart, *oryx*. A. Schultens, *buffalo* (and so Gesenius and Prof. Lee). Sept. μονόκερως, *unicorn*.

רָאמוֹת fem. pl.—I. *high, sublime things*, Pr. 24. 7.—II. *precious things.*—III. pr. name (*a*) of a town in Gilead, the same as רָמוֹת, רָמֹת מִצְפֶּה; (*b*) of another in Issachar, 1 Ch. 6. 58.

רָאמַת נֶגֶב (*height of the south*) pr. name of a town in Simeon, Jos. 20. 8, for which רָמוֹת נֶגֶב 1 Sa. 30. 27.

רְאוּמָה (*high*) pr. name fem. Ge. 22. 24.

רָאַם	Kal pret. 3 pers. sing. masc. (רָאָה), suff.
	3 pers. pl. masc. (§ 24. rem. 21) . ראה
רְאֵם	noun masc. sing., pl. רְאֵמִים . . ראם
רָאֲמָה	וּ Kal pret. 3 pers. sing. fem. . . ראם
רָאמוֹת[d]	וּ noun f. pl. of [רָאֵמָה] d. 10; also pr. name ראם
רְאֵמִים	noun masc. pl. of רְאֵם . . . ראם
רָאמֹת	pr. name of a place, see רָאמוֹת . ראם
רֹאֲנוּ	Kal part. act. sing. masc., suff. 1 pers. pl.
	from רֹאֶה dec. 9 a . . . . . ראה
רֹאֵנִי[g]	id. with suff. 1 pers. sing. (§ 2. rem. 1 & 7) ראה

רֹאשׁ[h] וָ[וּ] m. irr. (§ 45).—I. *head* of men and animals. —II. *head, chief, leader*; רֹ בֵּית אָבוֹת *chief of a family*; כֹּהֵן הָרֹאשׁ *chief priest, high priest.*—III. *chief city metropolis.*—IV. *chief, top, summit*, of a mountain, column.—V. *first, chief, principal* of anything; רֹ פִּנָּה *head-stone of the corner*; רֹ שְׂמָחִים *chief, highest joy*; רָאשֵׁי בְשָׂמִים *most precious spices.*—I. *head, first, foremost, beginning*; Ge. 2. 10, רָאשִׁים *beginnings of streams*; רֹ דֶּרֶךְ *beginning of the ways, cross-ways*; of time, רֹ חֳדָשִׁים *first of the months*; מֵרֹאשׁ *from the beginning.*—VI. *whole number, capital, amount, sum*, נָשָׂא רֹ *to take the sum*, to number.—VII. *body, band, company.*—VIII. *a poisonous plant*; according to some, *hemlock*; others, *colocynth.* Gesenius, *the poppy*, whence מֵי רֹ *opium*; and then for poison in general.

רֵאשׁ Chald. masc. dec. 1 a (pl. once רֵאשִׁין § 68) —I. *head.*—II. *sum, amount*, Da. 7. 1.

[a] Ge 48. 11.	[e] Job 33. 21.	[i] Ge. 16. 13.	[m] Job 20. 7.	[p] Jos. 21. 10.	[s] Ec. 5. 10.	[v] Da. 8. 7.	[d] 1 Ch. 17. 17.	[g] Eze. 27. 16.

(Footnote references:)
Ge 48. 11. — Job 33. 21. — Ge. 16. 13. — Job 20. 7. — Jos. 21. 10. — Ec. 5. 10. — Da. 8. 7. — 1 Ch. 17. 17. — Eze. 27. 16.
Pr. 20. 12. — Job 29. 8. — Est. 2. 15. — Na. 3. 7. — 1 Sa. 28. 13. — Nu. 27. 13. — Job 8. 18. — Ex. 4. 14. — Is. 29. 15.
Ps. 64. 9. — Ge. 46. 30. — Is. 61. 9. — Ca. 3. 11. — Is. 42. 20. — Ex. 1. 16. — Ex. 4. 14. — Zec. 14. 1. — Is. 47. 10.
Ec. 11. 4. — Est. 1. 14. — La. 3. 19. — Ge. 9. 16.

רֵאשָׁה f. d. 10 (for רֵאשָׁה), *beginning*, Eze. 36. 11.

רֹאשָׁה fem. הָאֶבֶן הָרֹאשָׁה *the head-stone*, Zec. 4. 7.

רִאשׁוֹן (for רֵאשׁוֹן), רִישׁוֹן masc. d. 1 b, רִאשֹׁנָה fem. dec. 10.—I. adj. *first*, in time, order or dignity, pl. רִאשֹׁנִים *ancestors*; הָרִאשֹׁנוֹת *the former things.*—II. רִאשֹׁנָה adv. *first, foremost*; of time, *at first, before*; בָּרִאשֹׁנָה *first*, in order and time; *aforetime, formerly*; לָרִאשֹׁנָה *at the first.*

רִאשֹׁנִי fem. ־ית *first*, Je. 25. 1.

רֵאשִׁית, רֵשִׁית fem. dec. 1 b.—I. *a beginning; former time, former state.*—II. *the first* of its kind, in respect to time, rank and worth, hence *firstling.*

רֵאשֹׁת fem. pl., only constr. רַאֲשֹׁתֵי (with double plural, comp. § 37. rem. 5, & § 4. rem. 2) *the part about the head*, 1 Sa. 26. 12.

מַרְאֵשָׁה, מָרֵשָׁה (*what is at the head*) pr. name—I. of a city in the plains of Judah.—II. of a man, 1 Ch. 2. 42.

מְרַאֲשׁוֹת fem. pl. *place of* or *about the head*, hence מְרַאֲשֹׁתָיו *at his head.*

מַרְאָשׁוֹת fem. pl. (dec. 11 a) idem, Je. 13. 18.

רֹאשׁ ׳נ pr. name of a northern nation, supposed to be the *Russians*, Eze. 38. 2, 3; 39. 1.

רֹאֵשׁ Kal part. act. sing. masc. dec. 1 a (§ 21. r. 1) רוּשׁ

רֵאשׁ Kh. ראשׁ q. v. K. רֵאשׁ (q. v.) . ראשׁ

רֵאשׁ Chald. noun masc. sing. irr. (§ 68) . ראשׁ

רֵישׁ noun masc. sing. dec. 1 (for רֵישׁ) . רושׁ

רֵאשָׁא Ch. noun masc. sing. emph. of רֵאשׁ irr. (§ 68) ראשׁ

רֵאשֵׁהּ Chald. id., suff. 3 pers. sing. masc. ראשׁ

רֹאשָׁהּ noun masc. sing., suff. 3 pers. sing. fem. from ראשׁ irr. (§ 45) . . ראשׁ

רֵאשְׁהוֹן Chald. noun masc. sing., suff. 3 pers. pl. masc. from רֵאשׁ irr. (§ 68) ראשׁ

רֹאשׁוֹ ׳נ noun masc. sing., suff. 3 pers. sing. masc. from רֹאשׁ irr. (§ 45) . . ראשׁ

רִאשׁוֹן adj. masc. sing. dec. 1 a . . ראשׁ

רִאשׁוֹנָה id. fem. as an *adv.* . . ראשׁ

רָאשֵׁי ׳נ noun masc. pl. constr. fr. רֹאשׁ irr. (§ 45) ראשׁ

רֵאשֵׁי Ch. noun m. s., suff. 1 p. s. fr. רֵאשׁ irr. (§ 68) ראשׁ

רֹאשִׁי noun m. s., suff. 1 p. s. fr. רֹאשׁ irr. (§ 45) ראשׁ

רָאשֶׁיהָ id. pl., suff. 3 pers. sing. fem. ראשׁ

רָאשֵׁיהֶם id. pl., suff. 3. pers. pl. masc. ראשׁ

רָאשֵׁיהֶן id. pl., suff. 3 pers. pl. fem. ראשׁ

רָאשָׁיו id. pl., suff. 3 pers. sing. masc. ראשׁ

רָאשֵׁיכֶם id. pl., suff. 2 pers. plur. masc. ראשׁ

רָאשִׁים id. pl., abs. st. . . ראשׁ

רֹאשִׁים Kal part. act. m. pl. of רֹאשׁ d. 1 a (§ 21. r. 1) רושׁ

רֵאשִׁין Ch. noun masc. pl. of רֵאשׁ irr. (§ 68) . ראשׁ

רֵאשִׁית ׳נ noun fem. sing. dec. 1 a . . ראשׁ

רֵאשִׁיתְךָ id., suff. 2 pers. sing. masc. ראשׁ

רֵאשִׁיתָם id., suff. 3 pers. pl. masc. ראשׁ

רֵאשְׁךָ Ch. n. m. s., suff. 2 p. s. m. fr. רֵאשׁ irr. (§ 68) ראשׁ

רֹאשְׁךָ noun masc. s., suff. 2 p. s. m. fr. רֹאשׁ d. 1 a ראשׁ

רֹאשֶׁךָ } noun masc. sing., suff. 2 pers. sing. masc.

רֹאשֵׁךְ } from רֹאשׁ irr. (§ 45) . . ראשׁ

רֹאשֵׁךְ id., suff. 2 pers. sing. fem. ראשׁ

רֹאשְׁכֶם id., suff. 2 pers. pl. masc. ראשׁ

רֹאשָׁם ׳נ id., suff. 3 pers. pl. masc. ראשׁ

רֹאשָׁן id., suff. 3 pers. pl. fem. ראשׁ

רִאשֹׁנָה adj. fem., as an *adv.* from רִאשׁוֹן m. ראשׁ

רֹאשֵׁנוּ noun m. s., suff. 1 p. pl. fr. רֹאשׁ irr. (§ 45) ראשׁ

רִאשֹׁנוֹת ׳נ } adj. pl. fem. & masc. from רִאשׁוֹן . ראשׁ

רִאשֹׁנִים }

רָאֲתָה } Kal pret. 3 pers. sing. fem. (comp. § 8.

רָאָתָה ׳נ } rem. 7) . . . . } ראה

רָאֲתָה defect. for רָאֲתָה (q. v.) . . ראה

רָאַתְךָ Kal pret. 3 p. s. f., suff. 2 p. s. m. (§ 24. r. 21) ראה

רְאֹתְךָ id. inf. (רְאוֹת), suff. 2 pers. sing. masc. d. 1 a ראה

רָב ׳נ Kal pret. 3 pers. sing. masc., or part. act. masc.; for ן see lett. ו . . ריב

רַב Kal pret. 3 pers. sing. masc. [for רָבַב] רבב

רַב ׳נ } adj. & subst. (also *adv.*) masc. sing.

רָב, רַב ׳נ } d. 8 d (Ch. d. 5); for ן see lett. ו } רבב

רָב ׳נ defect. for ריב (q. v.) . . ריב

רַב ן K. יֶרֶב q. v. R. רבה; Kh. וְרֹב (q. v.) . רבב

רֹב ׳נ } noun masc. sing. dec. 8 c (§ 37. rem. 2) } רבב

רֹב ׳נ }

רַבָּא Ch. adj. & subst. masc. s. emph. of רַב d. 5 a רבב

רִבֹּאות } noun fem. pl. of רִבּוֹ see רִבּוֹ . . רבב

רִבֹּאות }

I. [רָבַב] *to be* or *become many, numerous.* Pu. (denom. from רְבָבָה) *to increase to myriads*, Ps. 144. 13.

רַב masc. dec. 8 d, רַבָּה fem. dec. 10, adj.—I. *much, many, numerous*; adv. *much, abundantly, enough.*—II. *great, vast.*—III. *mighty, powerful.*—IV. *elder*, Ge. 25. 23; *aged*, Job 32. 9.—V. *chief, captain, leader*; hence, *a master*, one skilled in any art, Pr. 26. 10.—VI. neut. & subst. *greatness*, Ps. 145. 7; Is. 63. 7.

רַב Chald. masc. dec. 5 a, רַבָּא fem. dec. 8 a (only Da. 4. 27), adj.—I. *great, large.*—II. subst. *chief, head, prince.*

ᵃ Ne. 12. 46.   ᵇ Da. 3. 27.   ᶜ Pr. 13. 23.   ᵈ Da. 2. 28.   ᵉ La. 5. 16.   ᶠ 2 Ki. 11. 1.   ᵍ Ex. 10. 28.   ʰ De. 2. 10, 21.   ⁱ 2 Ch. 24. 27.
Da. 7. 1.   Mi. 3. 11.   Pr. 6. 11.   Da. 7. 6.   Is. 43. 9.   Ps. 10. 14.   Is. 19. 20.   Ex. 23. 2.   Da. 11. 12.
Pr. 30. 8.   Eze. 23. 42.   Job 8. 7.   Eze. 44. 20.   Is. 64. 3.   Job 42. 5.   Ps. 18. 15.   Job 29. 16.   Ezr. 2. 69.
Da. 2. 38.   Is. 15. 2.   Nu. 18. 12.   La. 2. 10.   Le. 19. 27.

רֹב masc. dec. 8 c (also רוֹב).—I. *multitude, abundance.*—II. *greatness.*

רַבָּה (*metropolis*) pr. name—I. of the capital of the Ammonites, fully רַבַּת בְּנֵי עַמּוֹן.—II. of a city in Judah, Jos. 15. 60.

רְבָבָה fem. dec. 11 c, *myriad, ten thousand*; pl. רְבָבוֹת *myriads.*

רִבְּוָא Chald. fem. dec. 8 a, id. Da. 7. 10, Keri.

רִבּוֹ fem. id. du. רִבּוֹתַיִם *two myriads*; pl. רִבּוֹת, רִבֹּאוֹת *myriads.*

רִבּוֹ Chald. fem. id. pl. רִבְבָן (dec. 8 c) Da. 7. 10, Khethib.

רַבִּית (*multitude*) pr. name of a city in Issachar, Jos. 19. 20.

רְבִיבִים masc. pl. *showers of rain.*

רַבְרַב Chald. masc. dec. 2 b, רַבְרְבָא fem. dec. 8 a, adj. *great*, Da. 2. 48; 3. 33; 7. 3, 7, 11, 17, pl. fem. רַבְרְבָן *great* (boasting) *things*, Da. 7. 8, 20.

רַבְרְבָן Chald. masc. dec. 1 a, *great, noble, prince.*

רַבְשָׁקֵה (*chief cup-bearer*) pr. name of a military chief of the Assyrians.

יָרָבְעָם (whose *people is numerous*, for יָרֹב עָם) pr. name, *Jarobeam*, commonly, *Jeroboam*, two kings of Israel, one, the son of Nebat, the other, the son of Joash.

מֵרַב (*increase*) pr. name of a daughter of Saul.

II. [רָבַב] *to shoot arrows*, Ge. 49. 23 ; Ps. 18. 15 ; unless the latter passage be rendered וּבְרָקִים רַב *and lightnings in abundance*, see רַב No. I, R. *I.*

רָב masc. dec. 8 d, *arrow*, Job 16. 13.

רְבָבָה [a] noun fem. sing. dec. 11 c; וּ bef. (ː)

רְבָבוֹת id. pl., abs. st. . . .

רִבְבוֹת } id. pl., constr. st. . . .
רְבֹבוֹת }

רְבִבִים [b] defect. for רְבִיבִים (q. v.) . .

[רָבַד] *to spread, strew, make up* a bed, Pr. 7. 16. Arab. *to bind.*

רָבִיד masc. dec. 3 a, *collar, neck-chain.*

מַרְבַדִּים masc. pl. (of מַרְבָד) *coverlets*, Pr. 7. 16 ; 31. 22.

רְבִד [c] [for רָבִיד] noun m. s., constr. of רָבִיד d. 3 a

רָבַדְתִּי [d] Kal pret. 1 pers. sing. . .

[רָבָה] fut. יִרְבֶּה, ap. יֵרֶב, יֶרֶב (§ 24. rem. 3).—I. *to be* or *become many, numerous, to multiply.*—II. *to be* or *become great*, or *greater*; hence *to grow up*;

also *to be mighty, powerful.* Pi. רִבָּה.—I. *to make much, to increase, multiply.*—II. *to let grow up, bring up.* Hiph. הִרְבָּה; fut. יַרְבֶּה, ap. יֶרֶב; inf. abs. הַרְבָּה, הַרְבֵּה, constr. הַרְבּוֹת.—I. *to make* or *do much, to increase*; הִרְבָּה לַעֲשׂוֹת *to increase doing*, i. e. *to do much*; לְהָבִיא ל' [e] *to bring much*; inf. הַרְבֵּה, rarely הַרְבּוֹת adv. *much*; לְהַרְבֵּה *plentifully.*—II. *to increase, multiply.*—III. *to have much* or *many.*—IV. *to give much*, Ex. 30. 15.—V. *to make great, enlarge.*

רְבָה Ch. *to become great, to grow*, Da. 4. 8, 19. Pa. *to make great, exalt*, Da. 2. 48.

רְבוּ Chald. fem. dec. 9 b, *greatness.*

אַרְבֶּה masc. a species of *locust.*

מַרְבֶּה masc. dec. 9 a, *increase, abundance.*

מַרְבֶּה fem. *largeness, amplitude*, Eze. 23. 32.

מַרְבִּית fem. dec. 1 b.—I. *multitude*, 2 Ch. 30. 18. —II. *greatness*, 2 Ch. 9. 6.—III. *the greater part*, 1 Ch. 12. 29.—IV. *increase, offspring*, 1 Sa. 2. 33 —V. *increase, interest, usury*, Le. 25. 37.

תַּרְבּוּת fem. *progeny*, Nu. 32. 14.

תַּרְבִּית fem. *interest, usury.*

רבב	Kal pret. 3 pers. sing. fem. [for רַבָּה]	רַבָּה [h]
רבב	adj. fem. s. d. 10, fr. רַב m. (also pr. name)	רַבָּה
רבה	Piel inf. abs. [for רַבֵּה]	רַבֹּה [i]
רבה	Chald. Peal pret. 3 pers. sing. masc.	רְבָה [k]
רבה	Kal imp. sing. masc. ; וּ bef. (ː)	רְבֵה וּ
רבה	id. part. act. sing. masc.	רֹבֶה [m]
ריב	Kal pret. 3 pers. pl.	רָבוּ
רבה	Kal pret. 3 pers. pl.	רָבוּ וּ
רבב	Kal pret. 3 pers. pl.	רָבּוּ ; רַבּוּ וּ
רבה	noun fem. sing. dec. 1 b (Chald. dec. 8 c)	רִבּוֹ וּ [o]
רבה	Kal pret. 3 pers. pl. ; for וּ see lett. ו .	רְבוּ נָ [o]
רבב	Kh. רְבוֹ q. v., K. רְבֵי n. m. pl. c. fr. רֹב d. 8 c	רִבֵּי [o]
רבה	Kal imp. pl. masc. ; וּ bef. (ː)	רְבוּ וּ
רבה	Chald. noun fem. sing. dec. 8 c ; וּ id.	רִבּוּ וּ
רבב	noun fem. sing. dec. 1 b	רִבּוֹא
רבב	Ch. Kh., pl. of רִבּוֹ ; K. רִבְבָן, pl. of רְבָבָה	רִבְוָן [q]
רבע	Kal part. pass. sing. masc. dec. 3 a	רְבֻעַ
רבה	adj. fem. pl. of רַבָּה dec. 10, fr. רַב masc.	רַבּוֹת [rrr]
רבה	Kal inf. constr.	רְבוֹת [r]
רבב	noun fem. pl. of רִבּוֹ dec. 1 b	רִבּוֹת [r]
ריב	noun masc. with pl. f. term. fr. רִיב dec. 1 a	רִבוֹת וּ
רבה	Ch. noun f. s., emph. of רְבוּ d. 8 c ; וּ bef. (ː)	רְבוּתָא [pp]
רבה	Chald. noun fem. sing., suff. 2 pers. sing. masc. from רְבוּ dec. 9 b ; וּ id.	רְבוּתָךְ וּ
רבב	noun masc. pl. constr. from רַב dec. 8 d	רַבֵּי וּ [r]

---

a Ps. 91. 7.   d De. 33. 17.   g Pr. 7. 16.   k Da. 4. 8, 17, 30.   m Ge. 21. 20.   o Ho. 8. 12.   r Da. 7. 10.   u Ne. 7. 71.   w Da. 4. 19.
b 1 Sa. 18. 8.   e Je. 3. 3.   h Ge. 18. 20.   l Ge. 35. 11.   p Da. 4. 33.   s Ex. 11. 9.   x Je. 39. 13 ; 41. 1.
c Nu. 10. 36.   f Ge. 41. 42.   i Ju. 9. 29.   n Da. 7. 10.   q Da. 11. 41.   t Job 13. 6.   pp Da. 5. 19.

44

רַבִּי Chald. Pael pret. 3 pers. sing. masc.   רבה

רְבִיבִים noun masc. pl. abs.   רבב

רְבִיד noun masc. sing. dec. 3 a   רבד

רְבִיו noun masc. pl., suff. 3 pers. sing. masc. from רַב dec. 8 d   רבב

רַבִּים adj. & subst. masc. pl. of רַב dec. 8 d   רבב

רְבִיעִי adj. ord. masc. from אַרְבַּע   רבע

רְבִיעָא Chald. Kh. רְבִיעַי, K. רְבִיעָאָה adj. ord. sing. masc., emph. [of רְבִיעִי dec. 7. § 63]   רבע

רְבִיעָאָה Chald. Kh. רְבִיעָיָא, K. רְבִיעָאָה id. fem. abs. dec. 11 [from רְבִיעִי masc.]   רבע

רְבִיעִים adj. ord. masc., pl. of רְבִיעִי   רבע

רְבִיעִית id. sing. fem. from רְבִיעִי masc.; וַ bef. (:)   רבע

רְבִיעָיְתָא Chald. adj. ord. sing. fem., emph. of רְבִיאָעָה dec. 11 [from רְבִיעִי masc.]   רבע

רְבִעָת defect. for רְבִיעִית (q. v.)   רבע

רַבִּית Chald. Kh. רְבַית, K. contr. רְבַת Peal pret. 2 pers. sing. masc.   רבה

רָבִיתָ Kal pret. 2 pers. sing. masc.   רבה

רִבִּיתָ Piel pret. 2 pers. sing. masc.   רבה

רָבִיתִי id. pret. 1 pers. sing.   רבה

רְבִיתֶם Kal pret. 2 pers. pl. masc.; וַ, for וְ, conv.   רבה

רָבַךְ Kal not used; Arab. *to mix.* Hoph. part. מָרְבֶּכֶת *mixed, saturated.*

רָבַל Root not used. Arab. *to be much, fertile, abundant.* רִבְלָה (*fertility*) pr. name of a city on the northern borders of Palestine. רִבְלָתָה id. with parag. ה.

I. [רָבַע] *to lie with,* carnally. Hiph. *to copulate,* Le. 19. 19. רֶבַע masc. *a lying down,* only רִבְעִי, Ps. 139. 3.

II. [רָבַע] Kal only in part. pass. רָבוּע (denom. from אַרְבַּע *four) four-sided, four-square.* Pu. part. מְרֻבָּע idem. אַרְבַּע fem. אַרְבָּעָה, constr. אַרְבַּעַת masc.—I. num. card. *four;* rarely for the ordinal, *fourth;* with suff. אַרְבַּעְתָּם *they four;* du. אַרְבַּעְתַּיִם *fourfold;* pl. אַרְבָּעִים com. *forty.*—II. *Arba,* pr. name of a giant. אַרְבַּע Chald. fem. אַרְבְּעָה masc. *four.* רֶבַע masc. dec. 6 a (pl. with suff. רִבְעָהֶן § 35. rem. 5).—I. *a fourth part.*—II. *a side,* i. e. one side of four.—III. pr. name of a king of the Midianites. רֹבַע masc. *the fourth part.*

רִבֵּעַ masc. only pl. רִבֵּעִים *posterity in the fourth generation.*

רְבִיעִי masc. רְבִיעִית fem. adj. ordinal, *fourth;* בְּנֵי רְבִיעִים *children of the fourth generation;* fem. רְבִיעִית *the fourth part.* רְבִיעַי Chald. id. רְבִיעָיָא Kh., רְבִיעָאָה K. emph. or fem. abs., רְבִיעָיְתָא pl. fem. emph.   רבע

רֶבַע noun masc. sing. (suff. רִבְעִי) dec. 6 a (§ 35. rem. 5); also pr. name   רבע

רֹבַע noun masc. sing.   רבע

רֹבְעָה Kal part. act. sing. fem., of רָבוּעַ masc.   רבע

רִבְעִי noun masc. sing., suff. 1 pers. sing. from רֶבַע dec. 6 a (§ 35. rem. 5)   רבע

רִבְעָתָה id. pl., suff. 3 pers. sing. fem.   רבע

רִבְעֵיהֶם id. pl., suff. 3 pers. pl. masc.   רבע

רִבְעֵיהֶן id. pl., suff. 3 pers. pl. fem.   רבע

רִבְעָיו id. pl., suff. 3 pers. sing. masc.   רבע

רִבְעִים defect. for רְבִיעִים (q. v.)   רבע

רְבֻעִים Kal part. pass. masc., pl. of רָבוּעַ dec. 3 a   רבע

רְבָעִים noun masc., pl. of רֶבַע dec. 1 b   רבע

רְבָעִית defect. of רְבִיעִית (q. v.)   רבע

רָבַץ fut. יִרְבַּץ *to lie down* for repose, spoken of quadrupeds; metaph. of men, waters, a curse. Hiph. I. *to cause to lie down.*—II. *to set,* of precious stones, Is. 54. 11. רֵבֶץ masc. dec. 6 b.—I. *place of lying down* for animals.—II. *resting place* for man, Pr. 24. 15. מַרְבֵּץ masc. *a place for lying down, couching place,* Zep. 2. 15; constr. מִרְבַּץ (§ 36. rem. 1) Eze. 25. 5.

רֹבֵץ Kal part. act. sing. masc. dec. 7 b   רבץ

רָבְצָה } id. pret. 3 pers. sing. fem. (§ 8. rem. 7)   רבץ
רִבְצָה

רִבְצָה noun masc. sing., suff. 3 pers. sing. fem. from רֶבֶץ dec. 6 b   רבץ

רָבְצוּ Kal pret. 3 pers. pl.   רבץ

רִבְצוֹ noun masc. sing., suff. 3 p. s. m. fr. רֶבֶץ d. 6 b   רבץ

רֹבְצִים Kal part. act. masc., pl. of רֹבֵץ dec. 7 b   רבץ

רִבְצָם noun masc. sing., suff. 3 p. pl. m. fr. רֶבֶץ d. 6 b   רבץ

רֹבֶצֶת Kal part. act. s., fem. of רֹבֵץ m. (§ 8. r. 19)   רבץ

רָבַצְתָּ id. pret. 2 pers. sing. masc., acc. shifted by conv. וַ (§ 8. rem. 7)   רבץ

רָבַק Root not used; Arab. *to tie, fasten,* espec. an animal. רִבְקָה (*binding,* i. e. *engaging, captivating*) pr. name, *Rebecca,* the wife of Isaac.

a Da. 2. 48.   b Da. 3. 25.   c Ne. 9. 3.   d De. 30. 16.   e Nu. 23. 10.   f Eze. 43. 17.   g 2 Ki. 10. 30.   h Eze. 19. 2.   i Ge. 29. 2.
j Je. 14. 22.   k Da. 2. 40;   l Da. 7. 19, 23.   m Ps. 44. 13.   n 2 Ki. 6. 25.   o Eze.1.3;10.11.   p 1 Ki. 7. 5.   q De. 29. 19.   r Je. 50. 6.
s Ese. 16. 11.   7. 7, 23.   t Nu. 28. 14.   u Lu. 2. 22.   v Eze. 41. 21.   w Eze. 1. 17.   x 1 Ki. 6. 32.   y Is. 35. 7.   z Job 11. 19.
a Job 16. 12.   b 2 Ki. 15. 12.   c Da. 4. 19.   d De. 8. 1.   e Ps. 139. 3.   f Eze. 43. 16.   g Ge. 49. 2.   h Pr. 24. 15.

מַרְבֵּק masc. *a stall*, in which cattle are *tied* for fattening ; עֵגֶל מ׳ *a calf of the stall*, i. e. a fatted calf.

רִבְקָה ן׳ pr. name fem. .   רבק

רַבְרְבִין Chald. adj. masc. pl. [of רַבְרַב] dec. 2 a   רבב

רַבְרְבָן Chald. id. fem. pl. [of רַבְרְבָא] dec. 9 a   רבב

רַבְרְבָנוֹהִי ן׳ Chald. noun masc. pl., suff. 3 pers. sing. masc. from [רַבְרְבָן] dec. l.a . רבב

רַבְרְבָנַי ן׳ Chald. id. pl., suff. 1 pers. sing. . רבב

רַבְרְבָנָךְ ן׳ Chald. id. pl., suff. 2 pers. s. masc., Keri נָךְ רבב

רַבְרְבָתָא Chald. adj. pl. emph. fem. [from רַבְרְבָא dec. 9 a, from רַבְרַב masc.]   רבב

רַבְשָׁקֵה pr. name masc. . רבב

רַבְתָּ Kal pret. 2 pers. sing. masc.   רוב

רַבַּת pr. name, constr. of רַבָּה   רבב

רַבַּת s׳ן adj. (also as an *adv.*) fem. sing., constr. of רַבָּה dec. 10, from רַב masc.   רבב

רַבְתָא Chald. Peal pret. 3 pers. sing. fem.   רבה

רַבְתָא Ch. adj. f. s. emph. [of רַבָּא d. 8 a] fr. רַב m.   רבב

רַבָּתָה pr. name of a place (רַבָּה) with parag. ה   רבב

רִבְתָה Kal pret. 3 pers. sing. fem. . רבה

רִבְתָה Piel pret. 3 pers. sing. fem. . רבה

רַבָּתִי adj. רַבָּה (q. v.) with parag. י   רבב

רִבֹּתַיִם noun fem. du. of רִבּוֹ dec. 1 b . רבב

רָגַב Root not used ; cogn. רָגַם *to heap together* stones, lumps, clods, &c.

    רֶגֶב masc. dec. 6 b, *a clod of earth.*

    אַרְגֹּב (*heap of stones*) pr. name—I. of a region beyond Jordan subject to Og, king of Bashan.— II. of a man, 2 Ki. 15. 25.

רִגְבֵי constr. of the foll.   רגב

רְגָבִים ו׳ noun masc. pl. of [רֶגֶב] dec. 6 b ; ו bef. (ׁ)   רגב

רָגֹם Kal inf. abs. : רגם

רָגַז ן׳ fut. יִרְגַּז.—I. *to shake, tremble.*—II. *to be moved, agitated,* with anger, grief. Hiph. I. *to make tremble, shake.*—II. *to move, disquiet,* with acc. לְ. —III. *to agitate, excite to anger,* Job 12. 6. Hithp. *to rage, rave against,* with אֶל.

    רְגַז Chald. Aph. *to excite to anger,* Ezr. 5. 12.

    רְגַז Chald. masc. *anger,* Da. 3. 13.

    רֹגֶז masc. *trembling,* De. 28. 65.

    רֹגֶז masc. dec. 6 c.—I. *disquiet, perturbation, trouble.*—II. *a raging,* of thunder, of a horse.—III. *anger, fury,* Hab. 3. 2.

    רָגְזָה fem. *trembling, perturbation,* Eze. 12. 18.

אַרְגָּז masc. *box, chest, coffer,* hanging from the side of a cart or waggon, 1 Sa. 6. 8, 11, 15.

רַגֶז noun masc. sing.   רגז

רֹגֶז ן׳ noun masc. sing. dec. 6 c   רגז

רָגְזָה Kal pret. 3 pers. sing. fem.   רגז

רָגְזָה id. imp. s. m. (רְגַז) with parag. ה (§ 8. r. 12)   רגז

רָגְזוּ ן׳ id. pret. 3 pers. pl.   רגז

רִגְזוּ id. imp. pl. masc. . רגז

רֶגֶל ן׳ fem. dec. 6 a (with suff. רַגְלִי).—I. *foot,* of man or beast ; בְּרֶגֶל *on foot* ; לְרַגְלֵי פ׳, בְּרַגְלֵי פ׳ *at the foot* or *in the track of any,* i. e. behind or after him ; הִשְׁקָה בְּרֶגֶל *to water* (sc. land) *with the foot,* by means of a machine trodden with the feet, De. 11. 10 ; מֵימֵי רַגְלַיִם *water of the feet,* urine. —II. *step, pace,* Ge. 33. 14 ; לְרַגְלִי Ge. 30. 30, *at my proceeding, as I proceeded,* sc. in the service pl. רְגָלִים (*steps*) *times,* comp. פַּעַם.

    רְגַל Chald. fem. dec. 3 a, *foot.* Also

רָגַל (denom. fr. רֶגֶל) *to go about slandering, back- biting,* Ps. 15. 3. Pi. I. i. q. Kal, with בְּ, 2 Sa. 19. 28.—II. *to explore, spy out* ; part. מְרַגֵּל *a spy.* Tiph. (§ 6. No. 5) *to teach to walk, to lead by the hand* (a child), Ho. 11. 3.

    רֹגֵל (*fuller*) pr. name—I. see under עֵין.—II רֹגְלִים (*fullers' place*) a town in Gilead.

    רַגְלִי masc. (pl. רַגְלִים) *footman, foot soldier.*

    מַרְגְּלוֹת fem. pl. (of מַרְגֶּלֶת) *what is at the fe* of any one ; adv. *at the feet,* Ru. 3. 8.

רֵגֶל noun fem. sing. dec. 6 a, for רֶגֶל (§ 35. r. 2)   רגל

רֹגֵל pr. name, see עֵין רֹגֵל under   עין

רַגְלָהּ noun fem. sing., suff. 3 pers. s. f. fr. רֶגֶל d. 6 a   רגל

רַגְלָו id. du., suff. 3 pers. s. m. ; K. לָיו   רגל

רַגְלוֹ id. sing., suff. 3 pers. sing. masc. . רגל

רַגְלוּ ן׳ Piel imp. pl. masc. . רגל

רַגְלוֹהִי Chald. noun fem. du., suff. 3 pers. sing masc. from [רְגַל] dec. 3 a   רגל

רַגְלַי ן׳ן noun fem. du., suff. 1 pers. sing. from } רַגְלֵי } רֶגֶל dec. 6 a }   רגל

רַגְלֵי ן׳ id. du., constr. st. . רגל

id. s., suff. 1 p. s. ; or noun m. (pl. רַגְלִים)   רגל

רַגְלַיָּא Chald. noun fem. du. emph. from רְגַל d. 3 a   רגל

רַגְלֶיהָ noun fem. du. (רַגְלַיִם), suff. 3 pers. sing. fem. from רֶגֶל dec. 6 a   רגל

רַגְלֵיהֶם ן׳ id. du., suff. 3 pers. pl. masc.   רגל

רַגְלָיו ן׳ id. du., suff. 3 pers. sing. masc.   רגל

a Da. 3. 33.   c Da. 4. 33.   f La. 3. 58.   i Da. 4. 27.   m La. 1. 1.   p Job 38. 38.   s De. 28. 65.   u Ps. 4. 5.   x Da. 2. 33, 34.
b Da. 5. 2, 3, 9,   d Da. 5. 23.   g 1 Sa. 2. 5.   k 1 Sa. 14. 30.   n Ps. 68. 18.   q Le. 24. 16.   t Job 39. 24.   v 1 Ki. 5. 17.   y Ps. 22. 17.
10; 6. 18.   e Da. 7. 11, 17.   h Da. 4. 19.   l Eze. 19. 2.   o Job 21. 33.   r Pr. 29. 9.   s Is. 32. 11.   w Jos. 7. 2.   z Da. 5. 41, 42.

44*

רַגְלָיו id. du., suff. 3 p.s.m (read לָיו K. רַגְלֵי q.v.)   רגל

רַגְלָיו id. du., suff. 3 pers. sing. masc. (Kh. לָיו but K. רַגְלוֹ q.v.)   רגל

רַגְלֵךְ id. du., suff. 2 pers. sing. fem.   רגל

רַגְלֶיךָ id. du., suff. 2 pers. sing. masc.   רגל

רַגְלֶיךְ id. du., suff. 2 pers sing. masc. (Kh. לָיִךְ but K. רַגְלֶךְ q.v.)   רגל

רַגְלֵיכֶם id. du., suff. 2 pers. pl. masc.   רגל

רַגְלַיִם id. du., abs. st.   רגל

רַגְלֵי noun masc., pl. of רֶגֶל   רגל

רְגָלִים noun fem., pl. of רֶגֶל dec. 6a   רגל

רַגְלִין Chald. noun fem., du. of רְגַל dec. 3a   רגל

רַגְלֵינוּ noun fem. du. (רַגְלַיִם), suff. 1 p.pl. fr. רֶגֶל d.6a

רַגְלְךָ id. sing., suff. 2 pers. sing. masc.   רגל

רַגְלֵךְ id. sing., suff. 2 pers. sing. fem.   רגל

רַגְלְכֶם id. sing., suff. 2 pers. pl. masc.   רגל

רַגְלָם id. sing., suff. 3 pers. sing. masc.   רגל

רַגְלֵנוּ id. sing., suff. 1 pers. pl.   רגל

[רָגַם] to stone to death, const. with בְּ, עַל.

רִגְמָה fem. crowd, throng, band, Ps. 68. 28.

מַרְגֵּמָה fem. heap of stones, Pr. 26. 8.

רֶגֶם (friend; Arab. id.) pr. name m. 1 Ch. 2. 47.

רֶגֶם מֶלֶךְ (friend of the king) pr. name masc. Zec. 7. 2   רגם

רָגֹם Kal inf. abs.   רגם

רְגָמֻהוּ id. pret. 3 pers. pl. (רָגְמוּ), suff. 3 pers. sing. masc.; וּ, for וְ, conv.   רגם

וְרָגְמוּ id. pret. 3 pers. pl.   רגם

רְגָמָתָם noun fem. s., suff. 3 p. pl. m. [fr. רִגְמָה no pl.]   רגם

[רָגַן] to murmur, rebel, Is. 29. 24. Niph. id. De. 1. 27; Ps. 106. 25.

רָגַע cogn. רָעַשׁ, רָעַע, רָגַשׁ, רָגַז.—I. to be in a commotion, make a noise, spoken of the sea, Job 26. 12; Is. 51. 15; Je. 31. 35.—II. to tremble, or perh. shrink (Ethiop. to contract, curdle), Job 7. 5.

רֶגַע masc. dec. 6a (§ 35. rem. 5), a moment (prop. a twinkling, sc. of the eye, comp. moment for movement; בְּרֶגַע, כְּרֶגַע in a moment, suddenly; לִרְגָעִים every moment, repeatedly; also suddenly, Eze. 26. 16.

רָגַע Kal not used; to rest, be quiet, comp. adj. רָגֵעַ. Niph. id. Je. 47. 6. Hiph. I. to cause to rest, give or restore rest, quiet; Je. 49. 19, אַרְגִּיעָה אֲרִיצֶנּוּ will restore rest, I will cause him to run; which Gesenius renders, I will wink, &c.—II. intrans. to have rest, dwell quietly, De. 28. 65; Is. 34. 14.

רָגֵעַ adj. masc. dec. 5a, still, quiet, Ps. 35. 20

מַרְגּוֹעַ masc. a rest, Je. 6. 16.

מַרְגֵּעָה fem. id. Is. 28. 12.

רֶגַע noun masc. sing. dec. 6 (§ 35. rem. 5)   רגע

רֹגַע Kal part. act. sing. (§ 36. rem. 1)   רגע

רְגֵעִי adj. pl. constr. masc. [from רָגֵעַ] dec. 5a   רגע

[רָגַשׁ] to rage, make a noise, tumult, Ps. 2. 1.

רְגַשׁ Ch. to run together in a tumult, Da. 6. 7, 12, 16.

רֶגֶשׁ masc. a bustling crowd, multitude, Ps. 55. 15.

רִגְשָׁה fem. id. only constr. רִגְשַׁת Ps. 64. 3.

רָגְשׁוּ Kal pret. 3 pers. pl.   רגש

רָדוּ Kal pret. 3 pers. sing. masc.   דוד

רַד Kal pret. 3 pers. sing. masc. by aphaer. for יָרַד   ירד

רַד id. imp. sing. masc.; for וְ see lett. ו   רד

[רָדַד] (prop. to spread out) to prostrate, subdue, Ps. 144. 2 Is. 45. 1. Hiph. to overlay with metal, 1 Ki. 6. 31

רָדִיד masc. dec. 3a, a wide mantle.

רַדַּי (subduing) pr. name masc. 1 Ch. 2. 14.

רָדָה fut. יִרְדֶּה, ap. וַיֵּרֶדְ (§ 24. rem. 3).—I. to tread a winepress, Joel 4. 13; with בְּ upon any one, Ps. 49. 15; with acc. Is. 14. 6; perh. also to tread, walk, Je. 5. 31, and the priests יִרְדּוּ עַל־יְדֵיהֶם walk at their side, i.e. assist them; this is usually referred either to No. II or III.—II. to subdue, rule over; poet. of a spreading fire, La. 1. 13.—III. to take, Ju. 14. 9; others, to break. Pi. to tread under foot, break, or subdue, only fut. ap. יֵרְדְ Ju. 5. 13, 13; according to others imp. of יָרַד. Hiph. to cause to rule, Is. 41. 2.

רְדֵה Kal imp. sing. masc. (רַד) with parag. ה (§ 20. rem. 3)   ירד

רְדֵה id. imp. sing. masc.   רדה

רֹדֶה id. part. act. sing. masc. dec. 9a   רדה

וְרָדוּ id. pret. 3 pers. pl.   רדה

רְדוּ Kal imp. pl. masc.; וּ bef.   ירד

רְדוּ Kal imp. pl. masc.; וּ id.   רדה

רָדֻפִי Kal inf., suff. 1 pers. sing. Kh. רְדוּפִי, K. רָדְפִי (§ 8. rem. 12) acc. retracted bef. monos.   רדף

a 2 Sa. 22. 34.   c Ec. 4. 17.   e Da. 7. 4.   h Nu. 15. 35.   m Je. 18. 2.   o Ho. 12. 1.   t Ju. 14. 9.   v Am. 6. 2.   z Ge. 1. 28.
b Ps. 105. 18.   d Job 29. 15.   f Je. 2. 25.   i De. 21. 21.   n Ps. 35. 20.   p Ju. 19. 11.   u 2 Ki. 1. 9, 11.   y Joel 4. 13.   a Ps. 38. 21.
g 2 Sa. 3. 34.   f Je. 12. 5.   g Ps. 66. 9.   k Ps. 68. 28.   s Ps. 2. 1.   r 1 Ki. 18. 44.   x Ps. 110. 2.

רְדוֹת	Kal inf. constr.	רדה
רַדַּי	pr. name masc.	רדד
רְדִי	Kal imp. sing. fem.	ירד
רְדִידִי	noun m. s., suff. 1 pers. s. fr. [רָדִיד] d. 3 a	רדד
רְדִיתֶם	Kal pret. 2 pers. pl. masc.	רדה

רָדַם Niph.—נִרְדַּם—I. *to lie in a deep sleep.*—II. *to sink down stupified* or *senseless.*

תַּרְדֵּמָה fem. dec. 10.—I. *deep sleep.*—II. *slug-gishness, inactivity.*

רֹדֵם Kal part. act. sing. masc., suff. 3 pers. pl. masc. from רָדָה dec. 9 a . . רדה

רַדְנוּ Kal pret. 1 pers. pl. . . רוד

רָדַף וְ fut. יִרְדֹּף.—I. *to follow after.*—II. *to pursue, persecute,* with acc., אַחֲרֵי, אֶל, לְ,—III. *to put to flight, to chase,* Le. 26. 36. Niph. *to be pursued;* part. נִרְדָּף *that which is past,* Ec. 3. 15. Pi. i. q. Kal Nos. I & II. Pu. *to be chased, driven away,* Is. 17. 13. Hiph. *to persecute,* Ju. 20. 43. Hoph. part. מֻרְדָּף *persecuted,* Is. 14. 6, according to Gesenius, as a subst. *persecution.*

רְדֹף	Kal imp. sing. masc.; וְ bef. (:)	רדף
רֹדֵף	id. part. act. sing. masc. dec. 7 b	רדף
רֻדַּף	Pual pret. 3 pers. sing. masc.	רדף
רָדְפָה	Piel pret. 3 pers. sing. fem.	רדף
רָדְפֵהוּ	Kal imp. sing. masc., suff. 3 pers. sing. m.	רדף
רָדְפוּ	id. pret. 3 pers. pl. (§ 8. rem. 7)	רדף
רִדְפוּ	id. imp. pl. masc.	רדף
רָדְפוֹ	id. inf. with suff. 3 pers. sing. masc.	רדף
רְדָפוּךָ	id. pret. 3 pers. pl., suff. 2 pers. sing. masc.; וְ, for וַ, conv.	רדף
רְדָפוּם	id. id., suff. 3 pers. pl. masc.	רדף
רְדָפוּנִי	id. id., suff. 1 pers. sing.	רדף
רֹדְפִי	id. part. act. pl. masc., suff. 1 pers. sing. from רֹדֵף dec. 7 b	רדף
רֹדְפֵי	id. pl., constr. st.	רדף
רְדָפָהּ	id. id. with suff. 3 pers. sing. fem.	רדף
רְדָפִיהֶם	id. id., suff. 3 pers. pl. masc.	רדף
רֹדְפֵיכֶם	id. id., suff. 2 pers. pl. masc.	רדף
רֹדְפִים	id. id., abs. st.	רדף
רֹדְפֵינוּ	id. id. with suff. 1 pers. pl.	רדף
רֹדְפֶךָ	id. id. sing. with suff. 2 pers. sing. masc.	רדף
רֹדְפָם	id. id. sing., suff. 3 pers. pl. masc.	רדף
רָדַפְתִּי	id. pret. 1 pers. sing.; acc. shifted by conv. (§ 8. rem. 7)	רדף

רְדַפְתֶּם	id. pret. 2 pers. pl. masc.; וְ, for וַ, conv.	רדף
רֶדֶת	Kal inf. constr. dec. 13 (§ 44. rem. 1)	ירד
רִדְתָּהּ	id., suff. 3 pers. sing. fem.	ירד
רִדְתּוֹ	id., suff. 3 pers. sing. masc.	ירד

[רָהַב] I. *to act insolently* (Syr. *to make a noise*), with בְּ, *against,* Is. 3. 5.—II. *to urge, press upon,* Pr. 6. 3. Hiph. I. *to embolden,* Ps. 138. 3.—II. *to overcome,* trop. Ca. 6. 5.

רָהָב masc. dec. 4 a, *insolent, proud,* Ps. 40. 5.

רַהַב masc.—I. *insolence, pride.*—II. *Rahab* a poetic name for Egypt.

רֹהַב masc. dec. 6 f, *pride,* Ps. 90. 10.

רָהַב } noun masc. sing. . . . רהב
רַהַב }

רְהַב Kal imp. sing. masc.; וְ bef. (:) . רהב

רְהָבִים adj. masc. pl. of [רָהָב] dec. 4 a . רהב

רַהְבָּם וְ noun masc. sing., suff. 3 pers. pl. masc. from רֹהַב dec. 6 (§ 35. rem. 5) רהב

רָהָה a spurious Root, to which is ascribed the signification of *to fear,* on account of תִּרְהוּ Is. 44. 8; but see יָרֵא.

רָהַט Root not used; Syr. *to run, flow.*

רַהַט masc. d. 6 d, only pl.—I. *watering-troughs.* —II. *locks, curls,* so called from their *flowing* down the neck, Ca. 7. 6.

רָהִיט masc. dec. 1 b, *a ceiling done with fret-work,* resembling little channels or troughs, Ca. 1. 17. Vulg. laquearia. Sept. φατνώματα. The Khethib has רַחִיטִים; but a Root רָחַט is not extant.

רֹגְנִים וְ Kal part. act. masc. pl. [of רֹגֵן dec. 7 b] רגן

[רוּד] I. *to wander, rove,* Je. 2. 31; Arab. راد *to run about.*—II. in a good sense, *to walk,* sc. עִם־אֵל with God, Ho. 12. 1. Hiph. *to wander,* as non ades, Ge. 27. 40; *to wander, go about,* of one in afflic-tion, Ps. 55. 3.

אַרְוַד (*a wandering*) pr. name of a Phœnician city, Eze. 27. 8, 11. Gent. noun אַרְוָדִי.

מָרוּד masc. dec. 3 a, *a wandering, erring about,* pl. מְרוּדִים Is. 58. 7, for concr. *wanderers.*

רוֹדָנִים וְ pr. name of a people, 1 Ch. 1. 7, supposed to be the *Rhodians;* elsewhere it is דֹּדָנִים.

רוֹדֵף Kal part. act. sing. masc. dec. 7 b רדף

a Eze. 29. 15. c Je. 2. 31. f Ps. 34. 15. h De. 28. 22, 45; q Ps. 35. 3. u Ju. 8. 4. x Je. 29. 18. k Eze. 31. 15. b Ps. 90. 10.
b Eze. 34. 4. g Is. 17. 13. Le. 26. 8. 30. 7. r La. 1. 3. v Le. 26. 7. y 2 Sa. 24. 13. c De. 28. 52. g Pr. 6. 3. i Is. 29. 24.
c Ps. 68. 28. Ho. 2. 9. m Am. 1. 11. p Jos. 8. 24. s Ne. 9. 11. w Ps. 35. 6. z De. 20. 20. e Eze. 40. 5.
 p Ps. 119. 86, 161. t Is. 30. 16.

[רָוָה] *to be* or *become satiated with drink* (Syr. *to be drunken*), also *with fat*; metaph. *with unlawful love*; const. with acc., מִן. Pi. I. *to be satiated, filled, soaked.*—II. *to cause to drink in*, i. e. *to water.*—III. *to satiate*, with fatness; metaph. *to satisfy, delight*, Pr. 5. 19. Hiph. I. *to give to drink, to water.*—II. *to satiate*, with fatness, Is. 43. 24.

רָוֶה masc. רָוָה fem. adj. *satiated with drink*, De. 29. 18; also *soaked, well watered*, of gardens.

רְוָיָה fem. *abundance, plenty of drink.*

רִי m. (for רְוִי) *a watering, irrigation*, Job 37. 11.

רָוֵהַ adj. masc. sing. · · · רוה

רַוֵּה‹ Piel imp. sing. masc. · · רוה

וְ רְוֵה‹ m. sing., suff. 3 pers. sing. masc.
[from רְאוּ for רְאִי] · · ראה

וְ רַהֲבָהּ Kh., רוֹהֲבָה K., רַהֲבָה K. pr. n. m. 1 Ch. 7. 34.

רוּן Root not used; Syr. רון, רן *to hide, keep secret.*
רָז Chald. masc. dec. 1 a, *a secret.*

וְ רוֹזְנִים‹ Kal part. act. masc. pl. [of רֹזֵן] dec. 7 b רזן

רָוַח‹ ‹ cogn. רוּחַ (prop. *to be airy, spacious, wide*); only impers. יָרְוַח לִי *I am relieved.* Pu. part. *spacious, wide*, Je. 22. 14.

רֶוַח masc.—I. *relief, enlargement*, Est. 4. 14.—II. *space, distance*, Ge. 32. 17.

רְוָחָה fem. dec. 11 c, *relief, enlargement.*

רוּחַ Kal not used. Hiph. הֵרִיחַ.—I. *to smell*; metaph. *to smell, touch fire*, Ju. 16. 9; also *to scent, perceive*, as a horse the battle, Job 39. 25.—II. const. with בְּ *to smell with pleasure*; hence generally, *to enjoy, delight in.*

רוּחַ com. dec. 1 a (pl. רוּחוֹת, רְחוֹת).—I. *air, breeze*; רוּחַ הַיּוֹם *cool air of the day*, i. e. *evening.* —II. *breath*; metaph. *vanity, folly.*—III. *spirit, soul.*—IV. *mind, spirit, disposition*; אֶרֶךְ רוּחַ *patience*; קֹצֶר רוּחַ *impatience*; גְּבַהּ רוּחַ *proud of spirit*; קְשֵׁה רוּחַ *sorrowful of spirit.*—V. *the spirit of God.*—VI. *wind*; also *tempest, hurricane.*—VII. *wind, side, quarter of the heavens.*—VIII. *anger, wrath*, from the idea of breathing, snuffing.

רוּחַ Chald. com. dec. 1 a.—I. *wind.*—II. *spirit, mind.*—III. *spirit of God.*

רֵיחַ masc. dec. 1 a, *odour, scent, smell.*

רֵיחַ Chald. masc. id. Da. 3. 27.

רַחַת fem. *winnowing fan*, Is. 30. 24.

יְרִיחָה, יְרֵחוֹ, יְרִיחוֹ (*place of fragrance*) pr. name,

Jericho, a city in Palestine, in the territory of Benjamin.

רוּחַ‹ וְ‹ noun masc. sing. · · רוח

רוּחַ‹ וְ‹ noun com. sing. dec. 1 a · רוח

רוּחָא‹ Ch. id., emph. st. · · רוח

רוּחָה‹ Heb. id. with parag. ה · רוח

רוּחֵהּ‹ וְ Ch. id. with suff. 3 pers. sing. masc.   רוח

רוּחוֹ‹ וְ‹ id. with suff. 3 pers. sing. masc.   רוח

רוּחוֹת id. pl. with fem. term. · · רוח

רוּחֵי‹ Ch. id. pl. constr. masc. · רוח

רוּחִי‹ וְ‹ id. sing. with suff. 1 pers. sing.   רוח

רוּחֲךָ‹
רוּחֵךְ‹ } id. sing. with suff. 2 pers. sing. masc.   רוח

רוּחֲכֶם id. sing. with suff. 2 pers. pl. masc.   רוח

רוּחָם id. sing. with suff. 3 pers. pl. masc.   רוח

רְוָיָה‹ noun fem. sing. · · רוח

וְ רִוֵּיתִי‹ Piel pret. 1 pers. sing.; acc. shifted by conv. וְ (comp. § 8. rem. 7) · רוח

רוֹכֵל‹ Kal part. act. sing. masc. dec. 7 b   רכל

רוּם‹ fut. יָרוּם, ap. יָרֹם, וַיָּרָם.—I. *to be high, lofty.* —II. *to raise oneself, to rise, be lifted up*, Job 22. 12; hence *to rise, grow*, of worms, Ex. 16. 20.—III. *to be raised, made high*, Is. 49. 11.—IV. metaph. *to be high, exalted*, in power or rank; *to be lifted up, elated with pride.* Part. רָם, fem. רָמָה (a) *high, lofty, tall*; (b) *lifted up*; of the voice, *loud*; (c) metaph. *high, powerful, mighty*; *elated with pride, haughty*; *high, difficult*, Pr. 24. 7; pl. רָמִים *heights of heaven*, Ps. 78. 69. Pil. רוֹמֵם.—I. *to raise a building*, Ezr. 9. 9; a plant, *to make to grow*, Eze. 31. 4; children, *to bring up.*—II. *to lift up, set on a high place.*—III. metaph. *to exalt*; with praises *to extol.* Pul. רוֹמַם pass. Hiph. הֵרִים.—I. *to lift up, raise.* —II. *to set up, erect.*—III. *to take away.*—IV. *to take up for an offering, to offer.* Hoph. הוּרַם pass. of Hiph. Nos. III & IV. Hithpal. *to exalt oneself.*

רוּם Chald. *to be lifted up*, Da. 5. 20. Pal. *to exalt, extol*, Da. 4. 34. Aph. *to exalt in dignity*, Da. 5. 19. Ithpal. *to lift up oneself, rise up against*, with עַל, Da. 5. 23.

רוּם masc.—I. *height, elevation*, Pr. 25. 3.—II. *a lifting up of the eyes, the heart*, i. e. *haughtiness, pride.*

רוּם Chald. masc. dec. 1 a, *height.*

רוֹם masc. *height*, Hab. 3. 10; which others take as an adv. *on high.*

רוֹמָה f. *haughtiness*, as an adv. *haughtily*, Mi. 2. 3.

רוּמָה (*lofty*) pr. name ot a place, 2 Ki. 23. 36.

רוֹמֵם masc. *exaltation, praise,* Ps. 66. 17; pl. constr. רוֹמְמוֹת Ps. 149. 6.

רוֹמְמֻת fem. dec. 3 b, *a lifting up,* Is. 33. 3.

רָם I. part. *high,* see the verb.—II. pr. name masc. of several persons.

רָמָה fem. dec. 10.—I. *high place,* 1 Sa. 22. 6; espec. for the worship of idols, Eze. 16. 24, 25, 39. —II. pr. name, *Ramah,* (*a*) a city in Benjamin; (*b*) a city in the mountains of Ephraim, called also רָמָתַיִם צוֹפִים; (*c*) a city in the tribe of Naphtali, Jos. 19. 36; (*d*) a city in Gilead, 2 Ki. 8. 29, called also רָמַת הַמִּצְפֶּה Jos. 13. 26, and רָמוֹת, רָאמוֹת; (*e*) i. q. רָמַת לֶחִי q. v. Gent. n. רָמָתִי 1 Ch. 27. 27.

רָמוֹת (*heights*) pr. name—I. of a city in Gilead, called also רָאמוֹת.—II. i. q. רָמוֹת נֶגֶב רָאמוֹת נֶגֶב (q. v.) 1 Sa. 30. 27.

רָמֻת fem. dec. 1 b, *heap, pile,* Eze. 32. 5.

רֶמֶת (*height*) pr. name of a city in Issachar, Jos. 19. 21.

רֹמַמְתִּי עֶזֶר (*I have raised help*) pr. name masc. 1 Ch. 25. 4, 31.

מָרוֹם masc. dec. 3 a.—I. *height, altitude;* בַּמָּרוֹם, מָרוֹם *on high;* concr. *the Most High,* Ps. 92. 9; also collect. *high ones, princes,* Is. 24. 4.—II. *height, high place.*—III. *haughtiness,* only as an adv. *haughtily,* Ps. 56. 3.

מָרוֹם (*height*) pr. name מֵי מֵרוֹם *the waters of Merom,* a lake at the foot of Mount Lebanon. Gr. Σαμοχωνίτις.

מְרֹמוֹת (*elevations*) pr. name m. of two persons.

תְּרוּמָה fem. dec. 10.—I. *an offering, present, gift;* espec. an *oblation* to the temple and the priests; 2 Sa. 1. 21 שְׂדֵי תְרוּמֹת *a field of oblation,* i. e. fertile and producing fruits fit for oblations.— II. *heave-offering,* a sacrifice consecrated by *elevating* it; שׁוֹק הַתְּרוּמָה *heave-shoulder.*

תְּרוּמִיָּה fem. *an offering,* Eze. 48. 12.

רוֹם (prop. subst.) as an adv. · · · רום

רוּם Kal inf. constr. (De. 17. 20) or subst. · רום

רוֹמָה• (prop. subst.) as an adv. · · רום

רוּמָה pr. name of a place · · · רום

רוּמָה Kal imp. sing. masc. with parag. ה · רום

רוּמֵהּ וְ] Chald. noun masc. sing., suff. 3 pers. sing. masc. from רום dec. 1 a · · רום

רוֹמֵי• Kal part. act. pl. constr. m. [fr. רֹמֵה] d. 9a רמה

רוֹמֵם• וְ] noun masc. sing. dec. 2 b · רום

רֹמֵמָה/ Kal part. act. sing. fem. · · · רמם

רוֹמְמוּ· Pilel imp. pl. masc. · · · רום

רוֹמְמוֹת• noun pl. constr. fem. from רֹמֵם dec. 2 b   רום

רוֹמַמְתִּי וְ] Pilel pret. 1 pers. sing. · · רום

רוֹמֵשׂ Kal part. act. sing. masc. · · רמשׂ

רוּן Kal not used; Arab. *to conquer.* Hithp. *to be overcome* of wine, Ps. 78. 65.

רוֹעַ Kal not used; (cogn. Arab. רעא) *to make a loud noise.* Niph. fut. יֵרוֹעַ.—I. *to become evil, be made worse,* Pr. 13. 20.—II. *to suffer evil, injury,* Pr. 11. 15. Hiph. הֵרִיעַ.—I. *to cry aloud,* Job 30. 5.—II. *to shout,* in joy, alarm, or war.—III. *to sound a trumpet,* with בְּ; espec. *to sound an alarm.* Pul. fut. יֻרַע *there shall be shouting,* for joy, Is. 16. 10. Hithpal. הִתְרוֹעֵעַ *to shout* for joy.

רֵעַ masc. dec. 1 a, *noise, outcry;* perh. of *the noise of thunder,* Job 36. 33.

תְּרוּעָה fem. dec. 10.—I. *a shout,* of joy, or of battle.—II. *a sound* of a trumpet.

רֹעֶה• וְ] Kal part. act. sing. masc. d. 10, comp. רֹעֶה רעה

רֹעִי• id. pl., constr. st. comp. רֹעֵי · רעה

I. רוּף Pul. *to be agitated, shaken,* Job 26. 11.

II. רוּף Root not used; cogn. Arab. רפת *to bruise, pound,* Eng. *rub;* perh. also i. q. רָפָא *to heal.*

רִיפוֹת pl. fem. *bruised corn, grits.*

תְּרוּפָה fem. *medicine,* or *healing, cure,* Eze. 47. 12.

[רוּץ] *to run;* with בְּ *into,* for refuge; with אֶל, עַל *to run, rush upon, assail.* Part. pl. *runners, couriers.* Pil. רוֹצֵץ *to run swiftly,* Na. 2. 5. Hiph. I. *to cause to run.*—II. *to bring quickly.*—III. *to let make haste,* sc. the hands in work, service, Ps. 68. 32.

מֵרוֹץ masc. *a running, race,* Ec. 9. 11.

מְרוּצָה fem. d. 10, idem. Another under רָצַץ.

רוּץ Kal imp. sing. masc. · · רוץ

רוֹצֶה Kal part. act. sing. masc. dec. 9a רצה

רוֹצֵחַ Kal part. act. sing. masc., comp. רֹצֵחַ רצח

רוּק Hiph. I. *to empty,* e. g. a vessel, sack.—II. *to pour out.*—III. *to draw out,* a sword, spear.—IV. *to draw, lead out,* sc. troops, Ge. 14. 14. Hoph. *to be poured out,* Ca. 1. 3.

רֵיק masc.—I. adj. *empty,* Je. 51. 34: hence *vain,*

vain thing.—II. **adv.** *in vain*, more fully רָרִיק,
בדי רִיק, לָרִיק

רֵיק masc. dec. 1 a, רֵיקָה fem. dec. 10, adj.—
I. *empty*; hence *vain*, De. 32. 47.—II. *emptied,
impoverished, poor*, Ne. 5. 13.—III. *worthless,
wicked.*

רֵיקָם adv.—I. *emptily*, Je. 14. 3.—II. *empty
handed.*—III. *without effect, in vain.*—IV. *without
a cause.*

רוֹקֵחַ רקח Kal part. act. sing. masc. dec. 7 b, comp. רֹקַח

[רוּר] *to flow*, with an acc. *to emit*, Le. 15. 3.

רִיר masc. dec. 1 a, *saliva, spittle*, 1 Sa. 21. 14;
poet. *slaver* or *slime* of a yolk, i. e. the white of
an egg, Job 6. 6 Prof. Lee, *whey*, comp. חֶלְמוּת

[רוּשׁ] *to be poor, in want*; part. רָשׁ, *poor, needy.*
Hithpal. *to feign oneself poor*, Pr. 13. 7.

רֵאשׁ, רֵישׁ, רִישׁ masc. dec. 1 a, *poverty.*

רֹאשׁ • noun masc. sing. for רֹאשׁ . . . ראשׁ

רוּת וְ (contr. for רְעוּת *friend*, R. רָעָה; or for
רְאוּת *appearance*, R. רָאָה) pr. name *Ruth*,
the wife of Chilion, afterwards of Boaz,
whose history is contained in the book
of *Ruth.*

רָוְתָה וְ Kal pret. 3 pers. sing. fem. . . . רוה
רִוְּתָה וְ Piel pret. 3 pers. sing. fem. . . . רוה
רָז Chald. noun masc. sing. dec. 1 a . . . רוה
רָזָא Chald. id., emph. st. . . . . רוה

רָזָה *to attenuate, cause to waste away*, Zep. 2. 11.
Niph. *to become lean, to waste away.*

רָזֶה, fem. רָזָה.—I. *lean*, Eze. 34. 20.—II. *barren*
of land, Nu. 13. 20.

רָזוֹן masc.—I. *a wasting, consumption.*—II.
diminution, scantiness, Mi. 6. 10.

רָזִי masc. *destruction, woe*, only Is. 24. 16, רָזִי לִי
woe unto me!

רָזָה adj. fem. sing. [from רָזֶה masc.] . . . רזה
רָזוֹן noun masc. sing. . . . . . . רזה
רָזוֹן noun masc. sing. . . . . . . רזן
רָזוֹן pr. name masc. . . . . רזן

רָזַח Root not used; Arab. *to raise the voice.*

מַרְזֵחַ masc. *outcry*, either for joy or sorrow,
Je. 16. 5; constr. מִרְזַח (§ 36. rem. 1), Am. 6. 7.

רָזִיא noun masc. sing. . . . . . . רזה

רְנֵיא
רָנַוֹ } Chald. noun masc. pl, emph. & abs.,
from רָז dec. 1 a . . . . רוז

[רָזַם] *to wink* with the eyes; Job 15. 12 (i. q. Aram.
רְמַז); Prof. Lee, *to be fixed, fastened.*

רָזַן (Arab. *to be weighty*) only part. רוֹזֵן *chief, prince.*
רָזוֹן masc. *prince*, Pr. 14. 28.
רְזוֹן (*prince*) pr. name masc. 1 Ki. 11. 23.

רָזַן וְ רוֹזְנִים ' Kal part. act. pl. masc. [from רוֹזֵן] dec. 7 b

רֵחָה or רֵחֶה masc. only du. רֵחַיִם (*a pair of millstones*)
a hand-mill. R. uncertain.

רָחַב וְ ' ' *to be* or *become wide, large, spacious.* Niph.
part. *large, extended*, Is. 30. 23. Hiph.—
I. *to make wide, broad, enlarge*, with נֶפֶשׁ *to enlarge
oneself.*—II. with לְ *to make room for.*—III. *to open
wide*, as the mouth; trop. the heart, for instruction.—IV. intrans. *to be enlarged, great*, Ps. 25. 17;
except we render הִרְחִיבוּ *they enlarged*, sc. the
ensnaring enemies.

רָחָב masc. dec. 4 a, רְחָבָה fem. dec. 11 c.—I.
adj. *wide, broad, large, spacious*; רְחַב יָדַיִם
large on both sides, very large; רַחֲבַת יָדַיִם
רְחַב נֶפֶשׁ, רְחַב לֵב *puffed up, proud, arrogant*; also
as a subst. *arrogance*, Pr. 21. 4.—II. רָחָב pr.
name, *Rahab*, a harlot of Jericho.

רָחָב masc. dec. 6 d, *wide place*, Job 36. 16; 38. 18.

רֹחַב masc. dec. 6 c (§ 35. rem. 5).—I. *width,
breadth.*—II. *largeness*, with לֵב *largeness of understanding, comprehensive understanding*, 1 Ki. 5. 9.

רְחוֹב, רְחֹב fem. dec. 1 a (pl. רְחֹבוֹת).—I. *a
wide open place, a street, square, market-place.*—II.
pr. name, see בֵּית.

רְחֹבוֹת (*wide, open places*) pr. name—I. of a
well, Ge. 26. 22.—II. רְ עִיר, a city in Assyria,
Ge. 10. 11.—III. רְ הַנָּהָר, a city on the Euphrates,
Ge. 36. 37.

רְחַבְיָהוּ, רְחַבְיָה (*enlargement of* [from] *the
Lord*) pr. name of a man.

רְחַבְעָם (*enlargement of the people*) pr. name,
Rehoboam, son and successor of king Solomon.

מֶרְחָב masc. dec. 2 b, *wide place*; metaph. of
freedom, deliverance.

רָחָב adj. masc. sing. dec. 4 c; also pr. name . רחב
רֹחַב noun masc. sing. dec. 6 g . . . . רחב
רְחַב ' adj. m. sing., constr. of רָחָב d. 4 c; וּ bef. (ְ רחב

רָחֹב	i pr. name of a man and a place (see also בֵּית‎); i bef. (:) . . .	רחב
רָחָב	i noun m. s. with suff. רָחְבּוֹ d. 6 (§ 35. r. 5)	רחב
רָחֲבָה	i Kal pret. 3 pers. sing. masc.	רחב
רְחָבָה	i adj. fem. sing. (constr. רַחֲבַת) dec. 11 c, from רָחָב masc.; i bef. (:)	רחב
רָחְבָּהּ	noun fem. sing. with suff. 3 pers. sing. fem. from רְחוֹב dec. 1 a	רחב
רָחְבָּהּ	i noun masc. sing. with suff. 3 pers. sing. fem. from רֹחַב dec. 6 (§ 35. rem. 5)	רחב
רָחְבּוֹ	i id. with suff. 3 pers. sing. masc. .	רחב
רְחֹבוֹת	i noun fem., pl. of רְחוֹב dec. 1 a; i bef. (:)	רחב
רַחֲבֵי	adj. (Is. 33. 21), or subst. (Job 38. 18) pl. c. fr. רָחָב or רַחַב (q. v.) . .	רחב
רַחַבְיָה רַחַבְיָהוּ	} pr. name masc. . . .	רחב
רָחְבָּן	noun masc. sing. with suff. 3 pers. pl. fem. from רֹחַב dec. 6 (§ 35. rem. 5) .	רחב
רְחַבְעָם	i pr. name masc.; i bef. (:) . .	רחב
רַחֲבַת	adj. fem. sing., constr. of רְחָבָה, dec. 11 c (§ 42. rem. 1), from רָחָב masc.	רחב
רְחֹבֹת	pr. name of a place . . .	רחב
רְחוֹב	i noun fem. sing., pl. רְחֹבוֹת dec. 1 a, also pr. name; i bef. (:) . .	רחב
רָחוּם	i adj. masc. sing. . . .	רחב
רְחוּם	pr. name masc. . . .	רחב
רָחוֹק	i adj. or subst. (Jos. 3. 4) masc. dec. 3 a	רחק
רְחוֹקָה רְחוֹקוֹת	} adj. fem. sing. & pl. dec. 10, from רָחוֹק masc. . . .	רחק
רְחוֹקִים	i adj. masc. pl. of רָחוֹק dec. 3 a; i bef. (:)	רחק
רְחִיטֵנוּ	K. רָהִיטֵנוּ noun masc. sing., suff. 1 pers. pl. [from רָחִיט or רָהִיט] see .	רהט
רֵחַיִם	noun masc. du. of [רֵחֶה] dec. 9 a .	רח
רְחִיקִין	Chald. adj. masc. pl. of [רַחִיק] dec. 1 a .	רחק
[רָחֵל]	fem. dec. 5 a, a ewe; then a sheep generally.	
רָחֵל	i (ewe) pr. name, Rachel, wife of Jacob.	רחל
רְחֵלֶיךָ	the foll. with suff. 2 pers. sing. masc.	רחל
רְחֵלִים	noun fem. pl. of רָחֵל dec. 5 a .	רחל
[רָחַם]	to love, Ps. 18. 2. Pi. רִחַם (§ 14. rem. 1) to love tenderly, to pity, to have compassion or mercy upon any one, with acc., עַל of pers. Pu. רֻחַם to obtain mercy.	
	רָחָם, רְחָמָה masc. a small species of vulture, the aquiline vulture, Le. 11. 18; De. 14. 17.	

רֶחֶם	com. dec. 6 a (with suff. רַחְמִי), the womb.	
רַחַם	fem. dec. 6 d.—I. the womb.—II. a maiden, Ju. 5. 30.—III. pr. name masc. 1 Ch. 2. 44.—IV. pl. רַחֲמִים (§ 35. rem. 16); (a) the intestines, Pr. 12. 10; (b) tender affection, love; (c) compassion, pity, mercy.	
רַחֲמִין	Ch. masc. pl. compassion, mercy, Da. 2. 18.	
רַחֲמָה	fem. a maiden, only du. רַחֲמָתַיִם Ju. 5. 30.	
רַחֲמָנִי	adj. masc. merciful, compassionate, La. 4. 10.	
רַחוּם	adj. id. used only of God.	
רְחוּם	(merciful) pr. name of a Persian governor in Samaria, Ezr. 4. 8; also of several other persons.	
יְרֻחָם	(he shall obtain mercy) pr. name masc. of several persons.	
יְרַחְמְאֵל	(whom the Lord will pity) pr. name masc. of several persons. Patronym. יְרַחְמְאֵלִי.	
רַחַם רֶחֶם	} i noun masc. sing., pl. רַחֲמִים [for § 35. r. 16]; for i see lett. i }	רחם
רֶחֶם	pr. name masc.	רחם
רַחֵם	Piel inf. constr. (§ 14. rem. 1)	רחם
רֶחֶם	noun masc. sing. (suff. רַחְמָה) dec. 6 a	רחם
רֵחֶם	pr. name masc., see רְחוּם	רחם
רִחַם	i Piel pret. 3 pers. sing. (§ 14. rem. 1) .	רחם
רַחְמָה	i noun masc. (fem. Je. 20. 17), suff. 3 pers. sing. fem. from רֶחֶם dec. 6 a	רחם
רֻחָמָה	Pual (§ 14. r. 1) pret. 3 pers. f. s. [for רֻחֲמָה]	רחם
רַחֲמוֹ	Kh. רַחֲמָיו K. (q. v.) . .	רחם
רִחֲמוּם	i Piel (§ 14. r. 1) pret. 3 p. pl., suff. 3 p. pl. m.	רחם
רַחֲמֵי	i noun m. pl., constr. of רַחֲמִים [for § 36. rem. 16] from רֶחֶם	רחם
רַחֲמֶיהָ	id. pl., suff. 3 pers. sing. fem.	רחם
רַחֲמָיו	i id. pl., 3 pers. sing. masc.	רחם
רַחֲמֶיךָ	i id. pl, 2 pers. sing. masc.	רחם
רַחֲמִים	i id. pl. abs. [for רַחֲמִים § 36. rem. 16]	רחם
רַחֲמִין	i Chald. id. pl. abs.	רחם
רַחֲמָנִיּוֹת	adj. pl. fem. [from רַחֲמָנִי masc.]	רחם
רִחַמְךָ רִחַמְךָ	} i Piel (§ 14. rem. 1) pret. 3 pers. sing. masc., suff. 2 pers. sing. masc. }	רחם
רִחַמְתִּי	i id. pret. 1 pers. sing.; acc. shifted by conv. i (comp. § 8. rem. 7)	רחם
רִחַמְתִּיךְ	id. id., with suff. 2 pers. sing. fem.	רחם
רַחֲמָתַיִם	noun fem. dual of [רַחֲמָה] dec. 10 .	רחם
רִחַמְתִּים	i Piel (§ 14. r. 1) pret. 1 p. s. with suff. 3 p. pl. m.	רחם
[רָחַף]	to shake, tremble, Je. 23. 9. Pi. רִחֵף (§ 14. rem. 1) to flutter, hover, brood.	
רָחֲפוּ	Kal pret. 3 pers. pl. . . .	רחף

a Eze. 41. 7.	e Zec. 8. 5.	k Eze. 12. 27.	o Ge. 31. 38.
b Ps. 119. 96.	f Eze. 42. 11.	l Ca. 1. 17.	p Ge. 32. 15.
c De. 13. 17.	g Je. 12. 2.	m Ezr. 6. 6.	q Ge. 49. 25.
d Zec. 5. 2.			r 1 Ki. 8. 50.

רָחַץ [וְ'] fut. יִרְחַץ, inf. רְחֹץ.—I. *to wash*, in reference to the body or other flesh.—II. *to wash away*, Is. 4. 4.—III. *to wash oneself, to bathe.* Pu. רֻחַץ (§ 14. rem. 1) *to be washed*, Pr. 30. 12. Hithp. *to wash oneself, to bathe*, Job 9. 30.

רַחַץ masc. dec. 6 d, *a washing*.

רַחְצָה f. *a washing-place* for sheep, Ca. 4. 2; 6. 6.

רְחִץ Chald. only Ithpa. *to trust on* or *in* any one, with עַל Da. 3. 28.

רְחַץ [וּ'] Kal imp. sing. masc.; וּ bef. (:) .
רֻחַץ Pual pret. 3 p. s. m. in pause (§ 14. rem. 1)
רַחֲצוּ } Kal pret. 3 pers. pl. (§ 8. rem. 7)
רַחֲצוּ
רַחֲצוּ [וְ'] id. imp. pl. masc.
רֹחֲצוֹת id. part. act. f., pl. of רֹחֶצֶת d. 13 [fr. רֹחֵץ m.]
רַחְצִי noun masc. sing., suff. 1 pers. sing. from [רַחַץ] dec. 6 d (§ 35. rem. 5)
רָחַצְתָּ [וְ'] Kal pret. 2 pers. sing. masc.; acc. shifted by conv. וְ (§ 8. rem. 7)
רָחַצְתְּ [וְ'] id. pret. 2 pers. sing. fem.
רֹחַצְתְּ id. part. sing. fem. dec. 13
רֻחַצְתְּ Pual pret. 2 pers. sing. fem. (§ 14. rem. 1)
רָחַצְתִּי Kal pret. 1 pers. sing.

רָחַק fut. יִרְחַק.—I. *to go far away, to recede*, with מִן.—II. *to be far off, distant, remote*, with מִן, מֵעַל. Niph. *to be removed*, Ec. 12. 6, Kheth. Pi. רִחַק (§ 14. rem. 4) *to put far away, to remove.* Hiph. I. *to put far away, to remove*; הַרְחִיק לָלֶכֶת *to go far away*, Ex. 8. 24; inf. הַרְחֵק adv. *afar off*, Ge. 21. 16.—II. *to go far away.*

רָחֵק adj. masc. dec. 5 a, *going far away, departing*, Ps. 73. 27.

רָחוֹק masc. dec. 3 a, רְחוֹקָה fem. dec. 10.—I. *far off, remote, distant*, of space and time; neut. *remoteness, distance*, Jos. 3. 4; בְּרָחוֹק *at a distance*; מֵרָחוֹק *from a distance, from afar*; also *afar off*, and of time, *long ago*; לְמֵרָחוֹק, עַד מֵרָחוֹק *far off; from afar*, and of time *long ago.*—II. *far above*, sc. in value, Pr. 31. 10.

רַחִיק Chald. masc. dec. 1 a, *distant*, Ezr. 6. 6.

מֶרְחָק masc. pl. מַר', מֶרְחַקִּים, *distance, distant part*; מִמֶּרְחָק *from afar*, also Is. 17. 13, *while yet far off*; אֶרֶץ מֶרְחָק *a distant land*; pl. מֶרְחַקִּים, מֶרְחַקֵּי אֶרֶץ, אֶרֶץ מַר' *distant lands.*

רָחוֹק [וּ'] defect. for רָחוֹק (q. v) . . . רחק [m]

רִמַּק [וּ'] Piel pret. 3 pers. sing. masc. (§ 14. r. 1) רחק [*]
רָחֲקָה Kal pret. 3 pers. sing. fem. רחק
רָחֲקָה defect. for רְחוֹקָה (q. v.) רחק
רָחֲקוּ } Kal pret. 3 pers. pl. (§ 8. rem. 7) . רחק
רָחֲקוּ [וִ']
רַחֲקוּ id. imp. pl. masc. . . . רחק
רַחֲקִי id. imp. sing. fem. . . . רחק
רְחֵקֶיךָ adj. pl. masc., suff. 2 pers. sing. masc. from [רָחֵק] dec. 5 a רחק
רְחֵקִים defect. for רְחוֹקִים (q. v.) . רחק
רִחַקְתָּ Piel pret. 2 pers. sing. masc. (§ 14. rem. 1) רחק

רָחַשׁ *to boil up, throw up* as a fountain, metaph. Ps. 45. 2.
מַרְחֶשֶׁת fem. *pot, kettle* for boiling, Le. 2. 7; 7. 9.

[רָטֹב] *to be wet*, Job 24. 8. Hence
רָטֹב adj. masc. *moist, fresh*, Job 8. 16 . . . רטב

רָטָה perh. i. q. Arab. رطا *to throw*, hence יִרְטֵנִי Job 16. 11, *they give me over*; but see יָרַט.

רֶטֶט [וְ'] masc. *trembling, fear*, Je. 49. 24. Syr. & Chald רְטַט *to tremble, be terrified.*

רֻטֲפַשׁ *to grow moist, fresh, to revive*, Job 33. 25.

רָטַשׁ Pi. I. *to dash in pieces* against a rock.—II. *to strike to the ground* with arrows, Is. 13. 18. Pu. pass. of Piel, No. I.

רֻטָּשָׁה Pual pret. 3 pers. sing. fem. [for רֻטְּשָׁה, comp. § 8. rem. 7] . . . רטש

רִיב [also רוּב, comp. יָרוּב, Pr. 3. 30, Kh. and pr. names יְרֻבַּעַל, נַרְבֶּשֶׁת pret. רָב, רַבְתָּ, רִיבֹתָ; inf. abs. רֹב, constr. and imp. רִיב; fut. יָרִיב, ap יָרֶב (§ 22. rem. 1, sq.).—I. *to contend, strive, quarrel*, with בְּ, אֶל, אֵת, עִם, rarely acc. *with whom*, with לְ, עַל *for what* one contends.—II. *to plead* or *defend a cause*, with acc. of the person whose cause is sustained, also acc. of the cause; part. רָב *defender*, Is. 19. 20.—III. *to decide a cause favourably.* Hiph. part. מֵרִיב *contending*, hence *adversary.*

רִיב masc. dec. 1 a (pl. ־ים, ־וֹת).—I. *contention, strife, quarrel*; אִישׁ רִיב *an adversary.*—II. *controversy, suit, cause*; אִישׁ רִיב *one who has a cause* (perh. for יְרִיבִי q. v.) pr. name of a man

a 2 Ki. 5. 13.   d 1 Ki. 22. 38.   g Eze. 23. 40.   k Eze. 16. 4.   m Pr. 31. 10.   o Ps. 119. 150.   r Eze. 11. 15.   s Ps. 73. 27.   u Ho. 10. 14.
b 2 Sa. 11. 8.   e Is. 1. 16.   h Ru. 3. 3.   i Ca. 5. 3.   n Is. 6. 12; 26. 15.   p Is. 49. 19.   r Is. 54. 14.   t Is. 26. 15.   x Je. 50. 34.
c Pr. 30. 12.   f Ca. 5. 12.   2 Sa. 11. 2.

יָרִיב masc. dec. 3 a.—I. *adversary.*—II. pr. name masc. Ezr. 8. 16; see also יָכִין. R. רִיב.

יְרִיבַי (for יְרִיבְיָה whom *the Lord defends*) pr. name masc. 1 Ch. 11. 46.

יְרֻבַּעַל (for יָרֹב בַּעַל *let Baal contend*) a surname of Gideon, the judge of Israel, comp. Ju. 6. 32. Called also

יְרֻבֶּשֶׁת (*let the idol contend*) in 2 Sa. 11. 21, comp. the preced.

יָרָבְעָם (who *contends with the people*) pr. name of two kings of the ten tribes, Jeroboam, son of Nebat, and Jeroboam, son of Joash.

מְרִיבָה fem. dec. 10.—I. *contention, strife.*—II. pr. name, *Meribah,* a fountain in the desert of Sin. —III. מֵי מְרִיבָה (*waters of strife*) pr. name of a fountain at Kadesh in the desert of Zin; fully מֵי מְרִיבוֹת קָדֵשׁ, Eze. 47. 19.

רִיב	רִיב' Kal imp.; or subst. masc. sing. dec. 1 a.
רִיב	רִיבָה' [a] id. imp. sing. masc. with parag. ה.
רִיב	רִיבוּ id. imp. pl. masc.
רִיב	רִיבוֹתָ' id. pret. 3 pers. sing. masc.
רִיב	רִיבִי' pr. name masc.
רִיב	רִיבֵי' noun masc. pl. constr. from רִיב dec. 1 a.
רִיב	רִיבִי' id. sing., suff. 1 pers. sing.
רִיב	רִיבְךָ רִיבְךָ' } id. sing., suff. 2 pers. sing. masc.
רִיב	רִיבֵךְ' id. sing., suff. 2 pers. sing. fem.
רִיב	רִיבְכֶם' [g] id. sing., suff. 2 pers. pl. masc.
רִיב	רִיבָם' id. sing., suff. 3 pers. pl. masc.
רִיב	רִיבֹת' [h] id. with pl. fem. term.
רוּח	רֵיחַ' noun masc. sing. dec. 1 a
רוּח	רֵיחוֹ' [k] id., suff. 3 pers. sing. masc.
רוּח	רֵיחֵנוּ' id., suff. 1 pers. pl.
ראם	רֵים noun masc. sing. dec. 1 a, for רְאֵם
רעה	רֵיעֲכֶם [for רֵעֲכֶם] noun masc. sing., suff. 2 pers. pl. masc. from רֵעַ dec. 1 a
	רִיפַת' pr. name of a son of Gomer, and of a people descended from him, Ge. 10. 3.
רוק	רֵיק' [n] noun masc. sing., used also as an *adv.*; for ן see lett. ן
רוק	רֵיקָה' [m] adj. fem. sing. dec. 10, from רֵיק masc.
ריק	רֵיקִים' id. pl. masc. from רֵיק dec. 1 a
ריק	רֵיקָם' [p] *adv.* from רֵיק with the term. ָ–ם
רור	רִירֹו' noun masc. s., suff. 3 p. s. m. fr. רִיר d. 1 a
רוש	רֵישׁ' noun masc. sing. dec. 1 a
רוש	רֵישִׁי' noun masc. sing. dec. 1 a
רוש	רֵישׁוֹ' id. with suff. 3 pers. sing. masc.

ראש	רִאשׁוֹן' adj. masc. sing. [for רָאִישׁוֹן]
רוש	רֵישְׁךָ' noun m. s., suff. 2 pers. s. m. fr. רֵישׁ d. 1 a
רוש	רֵישָׁם' id., suff. 3 pers. pl. masc.
יכך	וָרֵךְ' Kal pret. 3 p. s. m. 2 Ki. 22.19; 2 Ch. 34.27, וָרַךְ' or adj. masc. s. dec. 8 d; for ן see lett. ן }

רָכַב' fut. יִרְכַּב, inf. רְכֹב *to ride* either on the back of an animal or in a chariot, const. with עַל, בְּ, also acc.; part. רֹכֵב *a rider, horseman;* metaph. of God *riding,* being borne upon the clouds, &c. Hiph. I. *to cause* or *make to ride* upon an animal, also *to carry* in a chariot.—II. *to place, put,* or *lay upon,* 2 Ki. 13. 16.—III. *to cause to be ridden,* Ho. 10. 10.

רֶכֶב masc. dec. 6 a (with suff. רִכְבִּי).—I. *a rider,* perh. so 2 Ki. 7. 14; collect. *riders, cavalry,* Is. 21. 7.—II. *chariot,* collect. *chariots.*—III. also *chariot horses,* 2 Sa. 8. 4.—IV. *the upper millstone,* lit. *the rider.*

רַכָּב masc. dec. 1 b.—I. *a horseman,* 2 Ki. 9. 17. —II. *charioteer.*

רֵכָב (*rider*) pr. name—I. of the father of Jonadab, the progenitor of a wandering tribe called after him רֵכָבִים *Rechabites,* comp. Je. 35. 24, seq. —II. of two other men, 2 Sa. 4. 2; Ne. 3. 14.

רִכְבָּה fem. *a riding,* Eze. 27. 20.

רְכוּב masc. dec. 1 a, *vehicle, chariot,* Ps. 104. 3.

מֶרְכָּב masc. dec. 2 b.—I. *a chariot.*—II. *the seat of a chariot.*

מֶרְכָּבָה fem. constr. מֶרְכֶּבֶת, with suff. מֶרְכַּבְתּוֹ (§ 42. rem. 5) pl. abs. מַרְכָּבוֹת, constr. מַרְכְּבוֹת, *a chariot.*

רְכַב Root not used; prob. i. q. בֶּרֶךְ *to bend* (comp. Fürst. in concord.)

אַרְכֻּבָּה Chald. fem. dec. 8 a, *a knee,* Da. 5. 6. Targ. רְכוּב id.

רכב	רַכָּב' noun masc. sing. dec. 1 b (§ 37. No. 3)
רכב	רֶכֶב', וָ' noun masc. sing. dec. 6 a (§ 35. r. 2, רֶכֶב, וָ', but with suff. רִכְבּוֹ); for ן see lett. ן }
רכב	רֵכָב' pr. name masc.
רכב	רְכַב' Kal imp. sing. masc.
רכב	רֹכֵב' id. part. act. sing. masc. dec. 7 b
רכב	רִכְבָּהּ' noun masc. sing., suff. 3 p. s. f. fr. רֶכֶב d. 6 a
רכב	רִכְבוּ' [d] Kal pret. 3 pers. pl.
רכב	רִכְבּוֹ' noun masc. sing., suff. 3 pers. sing. masc. from רֶכֶב dec. 6 a

a Ps. 43. 1.   d Pr. 25. 9.   g De. 1. 12.   k Je. 48. 11.   m Is. 30. 7.   l 1 Sa. 21. 14.   t Pr. 31. 7.   y Pr. 10. 15.   b Ps. 45. 5.
b Job 33. 13.   e Je. 51. 36.   h De. 17. 8.   l Ex. 5. 21.   o Is. 29. 8.   p 1 Pr. 13. 18.   u Job 8. 8.   x Est. 6. 8.   c Na. 2. 14.
c La. 3. 58.   f Is. 41. 21.   i Ca. 1. 12.   =Job 6. 27.   p Ru. 1. 21.   s Pr. 28. 19.   w Pr. 24. 34.   a 2 Ki. 9. 17.   d 1 Sa. 30 17.

רְכֻבוֹ וְ Kal part. act. sing. masc., suff. 3 pers. sing. masc. from רֹכֵב dec. 7b . רכב

רִכְבִּי noun masc. sing., suff. 1 pers. sing. from רֶכֶב dec. 6a . רכב

רֹכְבֵי Kal part. act. pl. constr. masc. fr. רֹכֵב d. 7b רכב

רֹכְבֶיהָ וְ id. pl., suff. 3 pers. sing. fem. . רכב

רֹכְבֵיהֶם וְ id. pl., suff. 3 pers. pl. masc. . רכב

רֹכְבִים id. pl., abs. st. . . . . רכב

רָכַבְתָּ id. pret. 2 pers. sing. masc. . רכב

רֹכַבְתְּ id. part. act., fem. of רֹכֵב (§ 8. rem. 19) רכב

רַכָּה adj. fem. sing. from רַךְ masc. . רכך

רַכָּה pr. name masc. 1 Ch. 4. 12.

רָכְבוּ Kal pret. 3 pers. pl. . . . רכך

רִכֻבּוֹ noun masc. sing., suff. 3 pers. sing. masc. from רָכוּב dec. 1a . . רכב

רְכוּשׁ י noun masc. sing. dec. 1a; וּ bef. (1) רכש

רְכוּשׁוֹ id., suff. 3 pers. sing. masc. . רכש

רְכוּשֶׁךָ id., suff. 2 pers. sing. masc. [for רְכוּשְׁךָ] רכש

רְכוּשָׁם id., suff. 3 pers. pl. masc. . רכש

רְכוּשֵׁנוּ id., suff. 1 pers. pl. . . . רכש

רַכּוֹת adj. fem., pl. of רַכָּה dec. 10, from רַךְ masc. רכך

רָכִיל noun masc. sing. . . . רכל

רַכִּים adj. pl. masc. from רַךְ dec. 8d רכך

[רָכַךְ] fut. יֵרַךְ (§ 18. rem. 6).—I. to be tender, of the heart, contrite, 2 Ki. 22. 19; hence, to be timid, faint.—II. to be soft, of words, Ps. 55. 22. Pu. to be softened, Is. 1. 6. Hiph. to make timid, the heart, Job 23. 16.

רַךְ masc. dec. 8d, רַכָּה fem. dec. 10.—I. tender, young.—II. tender, delicate, effeminate.—III. soft, gentle, of words.—IV. tender, weak, sore, of the eyes.—V. faint, timid, of the heart.

רֹךְ masc. delicateness, effeminacy, De. 28. 56.

מֹרֶךְ m. softness, timidity, cowardice, Le. 26. 36.

רֻכְּכָה Pual pret. 3 pers. sing. fem. . . רכך

[רָכַל] to go about, particularly as a trader for traffic, hence (and only) part. רֹכֵל, fem. רֹכֶלֶת trader, merchant.

רָכָל (traffic) pr. name of a town in Judah, 1 Sa. 30. 29.

רְכֻלָּה fem. dec. 10, trade, traffic.

רָכִיל masc. talebearing, slandering; אַנְשֵׁי רָ tale-bearers, slanderers; הָלַךְ רָ to go about talebearing.

מַרְכֹּלֶת fem. dec. 13c, market, mart, Eze. 27. 24.

רֹכְלַיִךְ Kal part. act. pl. constr. masc. from רֹכֵל d. 7b רכל

רֹכְלַיִךְ / רֹכְלָיִךְ } id. pl., suff. 2 pers. sing. fem. . רכל

רֹכְלִים id. pl., abs. st. . . . . רכל

רֹכֶלֶת id. sing. fem. (§ 8. rem. 19) dec. 13a רכל

רְכֻלָּתֵךְ noun fem. s., suff. 2 pers. s. fem. [רְכֻלָּה] d. 10 רכל

רְכֻלָּתֵךְ id. with suff. 2 pers. sing. masc. . רכל

רֹכַלְתֵּךְ Kal part. act. sing. fem., suff. 2 pers. sing. fem. from רֹכֶלֶת (q. v.) . . רכל

[רָכַם] to bind on or to any thing.

רֶכֶם masc. only pl. רְכָסִים difficult, rugged places, Is. 40. 4.

רֶכֶם masc. dec. 6c, conspiracy, plot, Ps. 31. 21.

רָכַשׁ to get, gain, acquire.

רֶכֶשׁ, רְכוּשׁ m. d. 1a, substance, property, wealth.

[רֶכֶשׁ] masc. a species of swift horse. Syr. רכשא a horse, espec. a stallion.

רָכַשׁ / רָכַשׁ } Kal pret. 3 pers. sing. masc. (§ 8. rem. 7) רכש

רָכַשׁ defect. for רָכוּשׁ (q. v.) . . רכש

רָכְשׁוּ / רָכָשׁוּ } Kal pret. 3 pers. pl. (§ 8. rem. 7) . רכש

רְכֻשׁוֹ defect. for רְכוּשׁוֹ (q. v.) . רכש

רָם pr. name masc. רום

רָם וְ, וָ Kal pret. 3 pers. sing. masc.; or part. dec. 1a (§ 30. No. 3); for וָ see lett. וָ . רום

רָם Chald. part. Peil pret. 3 pers. s. m. (§ 54. r. 6) רום

רָם וְ defect. for רוּם subst. (q. v.) . . רום

רָמָה I. to cast, throw.—II. to shoot with a bow. Pi. רִמָּה to deceive (prop. to make fall).

רָמָא, רְמָה Chald.—I. to cast, throw.—II. to set, place, Da. 7. 9.—III. to impose tribute, Ezr. 7. 24. Ithpe. to be cast, thrown, Da. 3. 6, 15.

רְמִיָה (whom the Lord has set, appointed) pr. name masc. Ezr. 10. 25.

רְמִיָה fem.—I. slackness, remissness (prop. a letting fall of the hands); adv. remissly, Je. 48. 10. —II. deceit.

יִרְמְיָהוּ, יִרְמְיָה (whom the Lord sets, appoints) pr. name, Jeremiah.—I. the prophet, son of Hilkiah a priest.—II. pr. name of several other men.

מִרְמָה fem. dec. 10.—I. deceit, fraud; אִישׁ מִ fraudulent man; אַבְנֵי מִ false weights; meton. goods obtained by fraud.—II. pr. name m. 1 Ch. 8. 10

• Ge. 49. 17.   ᵈ Hag. 2. 22.   ᵍ Ps. 55. 23.   ᵏ Ezr. 8. 21.   ⁿ Eze. 27. 22, 23.   ᵖ Eze. 27. 3.   ᵗ Eze. 27. 20, 23.   ʸ Ge. 12. 5.   ᵇ Da. 5. 20.
• 2 Ki. 19. 23;   ᵉ Nu. 22. 30.   ʰ Ps. 104. 3.   ˡ Ge. 33. 13.   Eze. 27. 13, 17, 22.   Eze. 26. 12.   ᵘ Ge. 31. 18.   ᶻ Ge. 46. 6.   ᶜ Je. 48. 29.
Is. 37. 24.   ᶠ 1 Sa. 25. 20.   2 Ch. 21. 14.   ᵐ Is. 1. 6.   ᵖ Eze. 17. 4.   ˢ Eze. 28. 16, 18.   ˣ Ge. 14. 11.   ᵃ Ge. 14. 16.   ᵈ Ex. 15. 1, 21.
Hag. 2. 22.

תָּרְמָה fem. *deceit, craft,* Ju. 9. 31.

תַּרְמוּת fem. Je. 14. 14 Kh., and

תַּרְמִית fem. dec. 1 b, *deceit, craft.*

רָמָה רום Kal pret. 3 pers. sing. fem.

רָמָה רום id. part. s. fem. or subst. f., d. 10; also pr. name

רָמָה רמה Kal pret. 3 pers. sing. masc.

רָמָה וְ noun fem. sing. . . רמם

רִמָּה רמה Piel pret. 3 pers. sing. masc.

רֹמֵה וְ Kal part. act. sing. masc.,constr. of רָמֵה d. 9 a רמה

רָמוּ רום Kal pret. 3 pers. pl., and in pause רָמוּ

רְמוֹ הּ Peal pret. 3 pers. pl. masc.; וּ bef. (:) רמה

רָמוּ רמם Kal pret. 3 pers. pl.

רִמּוֹן וְ noun masc. sing. dec. 1 b; also pr. name רמם

רִמּוֹנוֹ pr. name of a place, see רִמּוֹן . . רמם

רִמּוֹנֵי noun masc. pl. constr. from רִמּוֹן dec. 2 b רמם

רִמּוּנִי Piel pret. 3 pers. pl. with suff. 1 pers. sing. רמה

רִמּוֹנִים וְ noun masc.,pl. of רִמּוֹן dec. 1 b . רמם

רָמוֹת Kal part. act. fem.,pl. of רָמֵה, dec. 10, from

   masc. (§ 30. No. 3) . . רום

רְמוּתְךָ noun fem. sing., suff. 2 pers. sing. masc.

   from [רָמוּת, comp. § 30. No. 3] dec. 1 b רום

רֹמַח וְ masc. dec. 6 c (§ 35. rem. 5), *lance, spear.*

רָמְחֵיהֶם id. pl. with suff. 3 pers. pl. masc. . רמח

רְמָחִים וּ id. pl., abs. st. (§ 35. rem. 9); וּ bef. (:) רמח

רָמֵי וְ Kal part. act. pl. c. masc. from רָם dec. 1 a רום

   (§ 30. No. 3) . . . . .

רַמְיָה pr. name masc. . . . . רמה

רִמְיָה וּ noun fem. sing.; וּ bef. (:) . רמה

רְמִיו וּ Chald. Peal pret. 3 pers. pl. masc. (§ 55.

   rem. 1); וּ id. . . . . רמה

רָמִים Kal part. act. m.,pl. of רָם d. 1 a (§ 30. No. 3) רום

רֵמִים for רְאֵמִים noun masc., pl. of רְאֵם dec. 1 a ראם

רְמֵינָא Chald. Peal pret. 1 pers. pl. . רמה

רִמִּיתֶם Piel pret. 2 pers. pl. masc. . רמה

רִמִּיתַנִי id. pret. 2 pers. sing. masc., suff. 1 pers. sing. רמה

רִמִּיתִנִי id. pret. 2 pers. sing. fem., suff. 1 pers. sing. רמה

[רָמָךְ] fem. dec. 1 b, *a mare,* Est. 8. 10.

רְמַלְיָהוּ (whom *the Lord* has *adorned,* coll. with the

   Arab.) pr. name of the father of Pekah,

   king of Israel.

[רָמַם] I. i. q. רום *to be high, lofty.*—II. Arab. *to rot,* hence

   deriv. רִמָּה. Niph. *to lift oneself up, to rise up.*

     רִמָּה fem. *worm,* collect. *worms.*

     רִמּוֹן masc. dec. 1 b.—I. *pomegranate;* also as

---

an artificial ornament.—II. *pomegranate tree.*—III.

pr. name (*a*) of a city in the tribe of Simeon ·

(*b*) of another in the tribe of Zebulun, Jos. 19. 13,

called רִמּוֹנוֹ 1 Ch. 6. 62; (*c*) of a rock near

Gibeah; (*d*) of a Syrian idol, 2 Ki. 5. 18; (*e*) of

a man, 2 Sa. 4. 2; (*f*) רִמּוֹן פֶּרֶץ of a station of

the Israelites in the desert, Nu. 33. 19.

רֹמַמְתָּהֻגּ Pilel pret. 3 pers. sing. fem. [רוֹמְמָה] with

   suff. 3 pers. sing. masc. . . רום

רִמּוֹן וְ noun masc. sing., also pr. name, see רִמּוֹן רמם

רִמַּנִי Piel pret. 3 pers. sing. masc. (רִמָּה), suff.

   1 pers. sing. (§ 24. rem. 21) . רמה

רִמֹּנֵי noun masc. pl. constr. masc. fr. רִמּוֹן dec. 1 b רמם

רִמֹּנַי id. sing., suff. 1 pers. sing. . רמם

רִמֹּנִים וְ id. pl., abs. st. . . רמם

רָמַס וְ fut. יִרְמֹס.—I. *to tread* with the feet, e. g. as

   the potter the clay, with acc. בְּ.—II. with עַל *to*

   tread upon, walk over any thing, Ps. 91. 13.—III.

   to tread down, trample under foot; part. רֹמֵס *a*

   treader down, oppressor, Is. 16. 4. Niph. *to be*

   trodden down, Is. 28. 3.

     מִרְמָס masc. dec. 2 b, *a treading down, something*

   trodden under foot.

רְמֹס Kal inf. constr. . . . רמס

רֹמֵס id. part. act. sing. masc. . רמס

רִמְסִי וְ id. imp. sing. fem. . . רמס

[רָמַשׂ] fut. יִרְמֹשׂ.—I. *to creep,* of reptiles.—II. *to move,* of

   any living creature; Ge. 9. 2, אֲשֶׁר תִּרְמֹשׂ הָאֲדָמָה

   with which the earth moves, for, *which moves upon*

   the earth. Hence

רֶמֶשׂ וְ, וְ masc.—I. *reptile,* collect. *reptiles.*—

   II. *that which moves* (on the earth), *any*

   land animal, in opposition to *fowls;* once

   of *water animals,* Ps. 104. 25 . רמשׂ

רֹמֵשׂ Kal part. act. sing. masc. . רמשׂ

רָמַת pr. name in compos. as רָ לֶחִי &c. . רום

וְרָמֹת, רָמֹת pr. names of places . רום

רָמֹתֶיךָ noun fem. pl., suff. 2 pers. sing. fem. from

   רָמָה dec. 10 (comp. § 30. No. 3) . רום

רָמָתֵךְ וְ id. sing., suff. 2 pers. sing. fem. . רום

[רָנַח] *to rattle,* Job 39. 23.

רִנָּה וְ noun fem. sing. dec. 10, also pr. name רנן

רַנּוּ Kal imp. pl. masc. (§ 18. rem. 14) . רנן

* Ex. 15. 1. 21.   * Job 24. 24.   * Eze. 32. 5.   * Da. 3. 21; 7. 9.   * 1 Sa. 19. 17.   * Ca. 8. 2.   * Mi. 5. 7.   * Na. 3. 14.   * Eze. 16. 39.
* Pr. 26. 19.   * Ex. 39. 24.   * Ne. 4. 7.   * Ps. 22. 22.   * Ex. 39. 26.   * 1 Ki. 7. 42.   * Is. 1. 13.   * Ho. 2. 20.   * Eze. 16. 25,
* Je. 4. 29.   * La. 1. 19.   * Is. 10. 33.   * Da. 3. 24.   * 2 Sa. 19. 27.   * Is. 16. 4.   * Ge. 1. 24.   31.
* Da. 6. 17, 25.   * Je. 52. 22.   * Pr. 13. 24.   * Jos. 9. 23   * Ex. 28. 33.   * Eze. 31. 4.

רַנִּי   Kal imp. sing. fem. (§ 18. rem. 4) ;   רנן
רֹנִּי   for וָ see lett. ו .
רֵעַי   noun masc. pl. constr. from [רֹן] dec. 8 c (comp.   רנן
    § 37. rem. 2)

[רָנַן]   fut. יָרֹן, also יָרוּן (§ 18. rem. 12).—I. *to shout
for joy*, and hence frequently *to sing*.—II. *to call
out* in invitation, Pr. 1. 20; 8. 3.—III. *to cry out
for help*, La. 2. 19; Gesenius, *to wail*. Piel רִגֵּן.
—I. *to shout, sing, rejoice*, with בְּ, עַל *over*.—II. *to
sing, celebrate, praise*, with acc. אֶל, לְ of the person
or thing. Hiph. I. *to cause to sing or rejoice*.—II.
to shout for joy.

    רִנָּה fem. dec. 11 c.—I. *singing, rejoicing*.—II.
pl. רְנָנִים *ostriches*, Job 39. 13.
    רֹן masc. dec. 8 c, *a shouting, rejoicing*, Ps. 32. 7.
    רִנָּה fem. dec. 10.—I. *shouting, singing, rejoicing*.
—II. *outcry, cry for help*.—III. pr. name masc.
1 Ch. 4. 20.
    אַרְנוֹן (*rushing, roaring*) pr. name, *Arnon*, a tor-
rent flowing from the eastward into the Dead Sea.

רַנֵּן   Piel inf. constr.   רנן
רְנָנָה   noun fem. sing. dec. 11 c   רנן
רַנְּנוּ   Piel imp. pl. masc.   רנן
וַיְרַנְּנוּ   id. pret. 3 pers. pl.   רנן
רְנָנוֹת
רְנָנִים   noun fem. pl. abs. from רְנָנָה dec. 11 a   רנן
רִנְנַת   id. sing., constr. st.   רנן
רִנָּתִי   noun fem. sing., suff. 1 pers. s. fr. רִנָּה d. 10   רנן
רִנָּתָם   id., suff. 3 pers. pl. masc.   רנן
רְסִיסֵי   noun masc. pl. constr. & abs. [from רָסִים   רסם
רְסִיסִים   or [רְסִים]

רָסַן   Root not used; Arab. رسن *to bind*. Hence
רֶסֶן   וָ, רֶ' masc. dec. 6 a.—I. *bridle, halter*.—II.
the inner part of the mouth, the jaws, Job
41. 5, בְּכֶפֶל רִסְנוֹ *into the jaws*, the double
row of the teeth of the crocodile (Gesenius,
and so most of the modern interpreters).

רִסְנוֹ   id. with suff. 3 pers. sing. masc.   רסן

[רָסַם]   I. *to moisten, sprinkle*, Eze. 46. 14.—II. in the
deriv. i. q. רָצַץ *to break in pieces*.
    רְסִיסִים masc. pl. (of רָסִים or [רְסִים]).—I. *dew-
drops*, Ca. 5. 2.—II. *fractures*, Am. 6. 11.
    רִסָּה (*fracture, ruins*) pr. name of a station of
the Israelites in the desert, Nu. 33. 21, 22.

רַע   Kal pret. 3 pers. s. m. ; & adj. or subst.   רעע
רַע   m. d. 8 (§ 37. r. 7); for וָ see lett. ו .
רֵעַ, רֵ'   noun masc. s. d. 1 a (§ 36. r. 2); וָ id.   רעה
רֵעַ   noun masc. sing. dec. 1 a (§ 30. No. 3)   רוע
רֵעַ   noun masc. sing.   רעע

[רָעֵב]   I. *to be hungry*.—II. *to suffer from famine, to
famish*.—III. with לְ *to hunger after*, Je. 42. 14.
Hiph. *to cause to hunger*.
    רָעָב masc. dec. 4 a.—I. *hunger*.—II. *famine*.
    רָעֵב masc. dec. 5 a, רְעֵבָה fem. adj.—I. *hungry*.
—II. *famishing*, Job 18. 12.
    רְעָבוֹן masc. dec. 3 c (§ 32. No. 3), *famine*.

רָעָב   וָ noun masc. sing. dec. 4 a   רעב
רָעֵב   וָ adj. masc. sing. dec. 5 a   רעב
רְעֵבָה   fem. of the preced.   רעב
רָעֵבוּ   Kal pret. 3 pers. pl. [for רָעֲבוּ § 8. rem. 1]   רעב
רְעָבוֹן
רְעָבוֹן   noun masc. sing., constr. & abs. dec. 3 c   רעב
    (§ 32. No. 2)
רְעֵבִים   adj. masc. pl. of רָעֵב dec. 5 a ; וָ bef. (:)   רעב

[רָעַד]   *to tremble, quake*, Ps. 104. 32. Hiph. *to tremble,
shake*. Hence
רַעַד
רַעַד   masc. *a trembling, awe*; for וָ see lett. ו .
רְעָדָה   fem. *a trembling, awe*; וָ bef. (:).

רָעָה   וָ fut. יִרְעֶה, ap. יֵרַע (§ 24. rem. 3).—I. *to feed,
pasture* a flock, with acc., בְּ; part. רֹעֶה *a shepherd,
herdsman*, fem. רֹעָה *shepherdess*.—II. trop. *to lead,
rule, govern*; also *to feed, nourish*.—III. intrans.
to feed, pasture, graze, as does a flock.—IV. *to
feed down, consume, devastate*.—V. *to feed upon,
i. e. to delight, take pleasure in*.—VI. *to associate
with*. Pi. רֵעָה *to treat as a friend, make a companion of*, Ju. 14. 20. Hithp. *to make friendship,
hold intercourse with*, Pr. 22. 24.
    רֵעֶה masc. dec. 9 a (Tseri unchangeable), *acquaint-
ance, companion, friend*.
    רֵעַ masc. dec. 1 a (for רֵעֶה).—I. *acquaintance,
companion, friend*.—II. *one beloved, lover*.—III.
neighbour, fellow; אִישׁ אֶל־רֵעֵהוּ *one to another*;
used also of inanimate things.—IV. *thought, will*,
Ps. 139. 2, 17; Chald. רְעָה *to will*, Syr. רעא *to
think*.
    רֵעָה fem. dec. 10, *a female companion*.
    רְעוּ (*friendship, friend*) pr. name masc. Ge. 11. 18.

Is. 12. 6; La. 2. 19. b Is. 35. 2. g Ps. 63. 6. k Ca. 5. 2. m Ps. 32. 9. p Ps. 88. 19. t Ps. 34. 11. x Ps. 37. 19. z Ps. 55. 6.
Ps. 32. 7. c Job 3. 7. h Job 39. 13. l Am. 6. 11. n Job 30. 29. q Mi. 4. 9. u Ge. 42. 19, 33. v Ez. 15. 15. a Job 4. 14.
Ps. 132. 16. f Je. 31. 12; 51. 48. i Job 20. 5. u Job 41. 5.

רְעוּאֵל (*friend of God*) pr. name—I. of a son of Esau, Ge. 36. 4, 10.—II. of the father of Jethro.—III. 1 Ch. 9. 8.—IV. Nu. 2. 14, elsewhere דְּעוּאֵל comp. Nu. 1. 14.

רְעוּת fem. dec. 1 a.—I. prop. *friendship*, used for *female friend* or *companion*, אִשָּׁה־רְעוּתָהּ *one another*.—II. רְעוּת רוּחַ *a feeding upon the wind*; others, *desire after the wind*, i. e. something vain, comp. רַע No. IV.

רְעוּת Chald. fem. (prop. constr. of רְעוּ dec. 8 c) *will, wish*, Ezr. 5. 17 ; 7. 18, comp. רַע No. IV.

רְעִי masc. *pasture*, 1 Ki. 5. 3.

רֵעִי (*social*) pr. name masc. 1 Ki. 1. 8.

רֹעִי masc.—I. adj. (denom. of רֹעֶה) *of a shepherd, pastoral*, Is. 38. 12.—II. subst. *shepherd*, Zec. 11. 17.

רַעְיוֹן m. *desire, pursuit, striving*, comp. רַע No. IV.

רַעְיוֹן Chald. masc. dec. 1 a, *thought*.

מִרְעֶה masc. dec. 9 a, *pasture* for cattle.

מַרְעִית fem. dec. 1 b.—I. *a pasturing, feeding*.—II. *flock*, Je. 10. 21.

מֵרֵעַ masc. dec. 1 b (Tseri unchangeable), *companion, friend*.

רָעָה וְ Kal pret. 3 pers. sing. fem. ; adj. or subst. fem. dec. 10 [for רָעָה], from רַע masc.   רעע

רָעָה Kh. רָעָה q. v., K. רֵעַ (q. v.)   רעע

רֵעָה Piel pret. 3 pers. sing. masc.   רעה

רֵעֶה וְ Kh. רָעָה q. v., K. רַע (q. v.)   רעה

רֹעֶה } noun masc. sing. constr. & abs. dec. 9 a .   רעה
רְעֵה

רְעֵה וֹ Kal imp. sing. masc. ; וֹ bef. (:)   רעה

רֹעָה id. part. sing. fem. dec. 10, from רֹעֶה masc.   רעה

רֹעֶה n. f. s., & רֹעָה (Is. 24. 19) Kal inf. with parag. ה   רעע
רֹעֶה
רֹעֶה } Kal part. sing. masc. constr. & abs. d. 9 a   רעה
רֹעֵה

רְעֵהוּ וֹ noun masc. sing., or (Job 42. 10) pl., for רֵעֵיהוּ suff. 3 p. s. m. fr. רֵעַ d. 1 a (§ 36. r. 2)   רעה

רָעוּ וֹ Kal pret. 3 pers. pl. .   רעה

רָעוּ וֹ Kal pret. 3 pers. pl., for רָעוּ=רָעְיוּ acc. shifted by conv. וְ (comp. § 8. rem. 7)   רעע

רֵעוֹ וֹ noun masc. sing., suff. 3 pers. sing. masc. from רֵעַ dec. 1 (§ 36. rem. 2)   רעה

רֵעוֹ noun masc. sing. with suff. 3 pers. sing. masc. from רֵעַ dec. 1 a (§ 30. No. 3)   רוע

רְעוּ pr. name masc.   רעה

רְעוּ Kal imp. pl. masc.   רעה

רֹעוּ Kal imp. pl. masc.   רעע

רְעוּאֵל pr. name masc.   רעה

רָעוּם וְ Kal pret. 3 pers. pl., suff. 3 pers. pl. masc.   רעה

רָעוֹת וְ adj. or subst. fem., pl. of רָעָה dec. 10 [for רָעֹת], from רַע masc.   רעע

רֹעוֹת Kal part act. fem. pl. of רֹעֶה d. 10, fr. רַע m.   רעה

רְעוּת וֹ noun fem. sing. dec. 1 a ; וֹ bef. (:)   רעה

רְעוּתָהּ id., suff. 3 pers. sing. fem.   רעה

רֵעוֹתֶיהָ וְ noun fem. pl., suff. 3 pers. sing. fem. from [רֵעָה] dec. 10 (comp. § 36. rem. 2)   רעה

רֵעוֹתֵיכֶם noun fem. pl., suff. 2 pers. pl. masc. from רֵעָה dec. 10 [for רָעֹת], from רַע masc. .   רעע

רָעֵי adj. pl. constr. masc. fr. רַע d. 8 e (§ 37. r. 7)   רעע

רֵעִי
רֵעַי } the foll. with suff. 1 pers. sing. .   רעה

רֵעַי noun m. pl. constr. fr. רֵעַ d. 1 a (§ 36. r. 2)   רעה

רֵעַי id. sing. with suff. 1 pers. s. ; also pr. name   רעה

רְעִי וֹ Kal imp. sing. fem., or subst. ; וֹ bef. (:)   רעה

רֹעִי the foll. with suff. 1 pers. sing.   רעה

רֹעֵי Kal part. act. pl. constr. masc. fr. רֹעֶה d. 9 a   רעה

רֹעִי id. sing., suff. 1 pers. sing. ; or רֹעִי adj. (Is. 38. 12) and subst. (Zec. 11. 17) .   יעה

רֵעֶיהָ noun masc. pl., suff. 3 pers. sing. fem. from רֵעַ dec. 1 a (§ 36. rem. 2) .   רעה

רֵעֵיהֶם id. pl., suff. 3 pers. pl. masc. .   רעה

רֹעֵיהֶם וְ Kal part. act. pl. masc., suff. 3 pers. pl. masc. from רֹעֶה dec. 9 a .   רעה

רֵעָיו noun masc. pl., suff. 3 pers. sing. masc. from רֵעַ dec. 1 a (§ 36. rem. 2) .   רעה

רַעְיוֹן וְ noun masc. sing. dec. 1 a   רעה

רַעְיוֹנַי Chald. id. pl., suff. 1 pers. sing.   רעה

רַעְיוֹנֵי וְ Chald. id. pl., constr. st.   רעה

רַעְיוֹנָךְ וְ Chald. id. pl., suff. 2 pers. sing. masc.   רעה

רֵעַיִךְ noun masc. pl., suff. 2 pers. sing. fem. from רֵעַ dec. 1 a (§ 36. rem. 2) .   רעה

רֵעַיִךְ וְ id. pl., suff. 2 pers. sing. masc. ; Pr. 6. 3, sing. with suff. from רֵעֶה (§ 38. rem. 1)   רעה

רֹעַיִךְ Kal part. act. pl. masc., suff. 2 pers. sing. fem. from רֹעֶה dec. 9 a .   רעה

רֹעַיִךְ id. pl. with suff. 2 pers. sing. masc. . .   רעה

רָעִים וְ adj. or subst. (Ps. 78. 49) masc., pl. of רַע dec. 8 (§ 37. rem. 7) .   רעע

רֵעִים noun masc., pl. of רֵעַ dec. 1 a (§ 36. rem. 2)   רעה

רֹעִים וְ Kal part. act. masc., pl. of רֹעֶה dec. 9 a   רעה

רַעְיֹנֹהִי וְ Chald. noun masc. pl., suff. 3 pers. sing. masc. from רַעְיוֹן dec. 1 a .   רעה

רַעְיָתִי וְ noun fem. sing., suff. 1 pers. sing. from [רַעְיָה] dec. 10   רעה

a Mi. 3. 2.   e Ps. 37. 3.   i Je. 11. 16.   m Is. 3. 9.   r Ju. 11. 33.   Job 2. 11.   Je. 50. 6.   f Da. 7. 28.   k Zec. 3. 8.
b Ju. 14. 20.   f Ge. 29. 9.   k Je. 6. 21.   n Is. 25. 4.   Ese. 7. 24.   1 Ki. 5. 3.   Zec. 11. 5.   g Da. 2. 30.   l Je. 22. 22.
c Pr. 27. 10.   g Pr. 25. 19.   l Job 36. 33.   o Job 1. 14.   Ps. 122. 8.   Ca. 1. 8.   Job 32. 3.   h Da. 2. 29 ; 5. 10.   = Is. 13. 20.
d 2 Sa. 16. 16.   h 1 Ki. 16. 11.   = Ge. 29. 7.   q Ps. 45. 15.   Ps. 38. 12.   La. 1. 2.   Eze. 1. 17 ; 4. 16.   i Eze. 22. 12.

רָעַת	• noun fem. sing., constr. of רָעָה dec. 10	רעע
	[for רָעַה], from רַע masc. . .	
רָעֹת	id. pl. constr.	רעע
רָעָתָהּ	id. sing., suff. 3 pers. sing. fem. .	רעע
רָעָתוֹ	• id. sing., suff. 3 pers. sing. masc.	רעע
רָעָתִי	id. sing., suff. 1 pers. sing. .	רעע
רָעֹתֵיכֶם	id. pl., suff. 2 pers. pl. masc. .	רעע
רָעָתְךָ רָעָתֶךָ	} id. sing., suff. 2 pers. sing. masc.	רעע
רָעָתֵךְ	id. sing., suff. 2 pers. sing. fem.	רעע
רָעָתֵכִי	id. sing., suff. 2 pers. sing. fem. (§ 3. rem. 2)	רעע
רָעַתְכֶם	id. sing., suff. 2 pers. pl. masc. .	רעע
רָעָתָם	id. sing., suff. 3 pers. pl masc. .	רעע

רָפָא (Milêl bef. monos.).—I. *to heal, cure*; part. רֹפֵא *a physician.*—II. metaph. (*a*) *to restore to prosperity*; (*b*) *to restore* in a spiritual sense, from a state of habitual neglect of God's commandments, for, *to pardon, forgive*; (*c*) for, *to restore, to comfort, console,* Job 13. 4. Niph. I. *to be repaired,* Je. 19. 11.—II. *to be healed, cured*; of waters, *to be made wholesome*; metaph. *to be restored* to prosperity, Is. 53. 5. Pi. I. *to repair,* 1 Ki. 18. 30.—II. *to heal, cure*; of waters, *to render wholesome,* 2 Ki. 2. 21; metaph. *to comfort, console,* Je. 8. 11. —III. *to cause to be healed,* Ex. 21. 19. Hithp. *to get oneself cured,* 2 Ki. 8. 29.

רָפָא masc.—I. only in the pl. רְפָאִים *the quiet,* comp. the verb No. II. (*c*); or רָפָה=רָפֶה, *the languid, feeble,* poet. for *the dead, the departed.*—II. pr. name, *Rapha,* (*a*) the progenitor of the tribe Rephaim, comp. 1 Ch. 20. 4, also רָפָה; (*b*) two other persons, 1 Ch. 4. 12; 8. 2.

רְפָאִ, only pl. רְפָאִים pr. name of a people beyond Jordan, celebrated for their gigantic stature, the descendants of רָפָא, רָפָה.

רְפוּא (*healed*) pr. name masc. Nu. 13. 9.

רְפֻאָה fem. only pl. רְפֻאוֹת *medicines.*

רִפְאוּת fem. *healing, health,* Pr. 3. 8.

רְפָאֵל (whom *God healed*) pr. name m. 1 Ch. 26. 7.

רְפָיָה (whom *the Lord healed*) pr. name masc. of several persons.

יִרְפְּאֵל (which *God heals*) pr. name of a place in Benjamin, Jos. 18. 27.

מַרְפֵּא masc. — I. *healing, cure.*—II. *remedy,* means of cure, Je. 33. 6.—III. trop. *refreshment, recreation*: also *relief* from calamity.—IV.

calmness, tranquillity (comp. verb No. II. (*c*)), Pr. 14. 30; 15. 4; Ec. 10. 4.

רְפָא	pr. name masc. . . .	רפא
רְפָא	Kal imp. sing. masc. . . .	רפא
רַפֹּא	Piel inf. abs. . . .	רפא
רֹפֵא	Kal part. act. sing. masc. dec. 7b .	רפא
רְפָאָה	id. imp. s. m., with parag. ה (§ 8. rem. 12)	רפא
רְפָאוֹת	noun fem., pl. of (רְפָאָה) dec. 10 .	רפא
רִפְאוּת	noun fem. sing. . .	רפא
רֹפְאֵי	Kal part. act. pl. constr. masc. from רֹפֵא d. 7b	רפא
רֹפְאִים	noun masc. pl., also pr. name .	רפא
רֹפְאֶךָ	Kal part. act. sing. masc., suff. 2 pers. sing.	רפא
	[for רֹפְאֲךָ] from רֹפֵא dec. 7b .	
רְפָאֵל	pr. name masc.; bef. (:)	רפא
רְפָאָם	Kal pret. 3 pers. sing. masc., suff. 3 pers.	
	pl. masc.; ו, for וְ, conv. .	רפא
רְפָאנוּ	Piel pret. 1 pers. pl. (§ 23. rem. 9)	רפא
רְפָאֵנִי	Kal imp. sing. masc., suff. 1 pers. sing.	רפא
רִפֵּאתִי	Piel pret. 1 pers. sing. (§ 23. rem. 9) .	רפא
רְפָאתִיו	Kal pret. 1 pers. sing., suff. 3 pers. sing.	
	masc.; ו, for וְ, conv. . .	פא
רְפָאתִים רְפָאתָם	} id., suff. 3 pers. pl. masc.; id.	רפא
רְפָאתֶם	Piel pret. 2 pers. pl. masc. . .	רפא

[רָפַד] *to strew, spread,* Job 41. 22. Pi. I. *to spread* a bed, Job 17. 13.—II. *to stay, refresh,* Ca. 2. 5.

רְפִידָה fem. dec. 10, *support,* prob. *the sides and back* of a portable couch, Ca. 3. 10.

רְפִידִים (*couches*) pr. name of a station of the Israelites in the desert.

אַרְפַּד (*support*) pr. name of a city of Syria.

רַפְּדוּנִי	Piel imp. pl. masc., suff. 1 pers. sing. .	רפד
רִפַּדְתִּי	id. pret. 1 pers. sing. . . .	רפד

רָפָה fut. יִרְפֶּה, ap. יֶרֶף.—I. *to hang down* the hands, *to become relaxed, feeble.*—II. *to decline,* of the day, Ju. 19. 9.—III. *to sink down,* of straw in the fire, Is. 5. 24.—IV. *to relax, abate, to desist* from a person or thing, with מִן. Niph. *to be remiss, idle, lazy,* Ex. 5. 8, 17. Pi. I. *to let down* the wings, Eze. 1. 24, 25.—II. *to relax, loosen,* Job 12. 21.—III. *to relax, weaken.* Hiph. הִרְפָּה.—I. *to slacken* the hand, *to desist* from smiting, 2 Sa. 24. 16; with מִן *from* any one, i. e. *to desert* him, Jos. 10. 6.—II. (*without* יָד) *to let alone, cease from,* with מִן.—III. *to leave off, cease.*—IV. *to*

a Zec. 7. 10.	d Je. 48. 16.	g Is. 6. 10.	k Ps. 41. 5.	o Ex. 15. 26.	p Je. 51. 9.	r Is. 57. 19.	t Eze. 34. 4.	x Job 17. 13.
b Je. 44. 9.	e Je. 44. 9.	h Nu. 12. 13.	l Pr. 3. 8.	m Is. 19. 22.	q 2 Ki. 2. 21.	s Je. 33. 6.	v Ca. 2. 5.	y Ju. 19. 9.
c Je. 3. 7.	f Je. 11. 15.	i Ex. 21. 19.	=Job 13. 4.					

45

give up, forsake.—V. *to let go, dismiss.* Hithp. *to relax oneself, be slothful.*

רָפָה pr. name—I. of a giant, whose descendants are called רְפָאִים; also יְלִידֵי הָרָפָה, see רָפָא.—II. 1 Ch. 8. 37, for which רָפָה 1 Ch. 9. 43.

רָפֶה masc. dec. 9 b, pl. fem. רָפוֹת, adj. *relaxed, weak, feeble.*

רִפְיוֹן masc. *weakness,* Je. 47. 3.

רָפָה	pr. name masc.	.	.	.	רפה
רְפֵה [a]	Kal imp. sing. masc. for רְפָא (§ 23. rem. 10)				רפא
רְפֵה [b]	וּ adj. masc. sing., constr. of רָפֶה dec. 9 b ; וּ bef. (:)			.	רפה
רִפָּה [c]	Piel pret. 3 pers. sing. masc.		.	.	רפה
רָפוּ [d]	וְ Kal pret. 3 pers. pl.			.	רפה
רָפוּא	pr. name masc.		.	.	רפא
רָפוֹא [e]	וְ Kal inf. abs.			.	רפא
רְפוֹת	adj. fem. pl. [of רָפֶה from רָפָה] masc.			.	רפה
רֶפַח	וְ (*riches*) pr. name masc. 1 Ch. 7. 25.				
רְפִידָתוֹ [f]	noun fem. s., suff. 3 p. s. from [רְפִידָה] d. 10			.	רפד
רְפָיָה	וּ pr. name masc. ; וּ bef. (:)		.	.	רפא

[רָפַשׂ, רָפַס] *to tread, trample upon,* espec. of water, *troubled, made turbid,* Eze. 34. 18 ; 32. 2. Niph. part. נִרְפָּשׂ *troubled, made turbid by trampling,* Pr. 25, 26. Hithpa. הִתְרַפֵּס *to humble, submit oneself.* רְפַס Chald. *to trample down, stamp upon,* Da. 7. 7. מִרְפָּשׂ masc. dec. 2 b, *water made turbid by trampling,* Eze. 34. 19.

רַפְסֹדוֹת fem. pl. *floats, rafts,* 2 Ch. 2. 15. Etymology uncertain.

רָפְסָה Chald. Peal part. sing. fem. [of רְפַס masc.] רפס

רָפַק Hithp. *to support oneself, to lean,* Ca. 8. 5.

רֶפֶשׁ masc. *mud, mire,* Is. 57. 20.

[רֶפֶת] masc. dec. 6 a, *a stall for cattle,* Hab. 3. 17.

רָפְתָה	Kal pret. 3 pers. sing. fem.		.	.	רפה
רָץ	Kal pret. 3 pers. sing. masc.; or part. act. dec. 1 a (§ 30. No. 3)		.	.	רוץ
רָץ	id. imp. sing. masc. (§ 21. rem. 5)				רוץ

[רָצָא] i. q. רוּץ *to run,* Eze. 1. 14.

רָצָאתִי [g] וְ Kal pret. 1 pers. s. [for רָצִיתִי § 24. r. 19] רצה

רָצַד Kal not used; Arab. *to observe, watch narrowly.* Pi. id. Ps. 68. 17. Others, after the Targ. (מְפַזֵּ), i. q. רָקַד *to leap, spring.*

רָצָה fut. יִרְצֶה.—I. *to delight, take pleasure in, to be well pleased with,* const. with בְּ, acc.—II. *to accept kindly* or *graciously;* part. pass. רָצוּי *accepted, acceptable.*—III. *to associate, be in friendship with,* const. with עִם.—IV. *to be pleased to do any thing,* followed by an inf.—V. *to satisfy, discharge, make compensation for.* Niph. I. *to be graciously received.*—II. *to be paid off, compensation made for* Is. 40. 2. Pi. *to satisfy, conciliate,* Job 20. 10. Hiph. *to satisfy, make compensation for,* Le. 26. 34 Hithp. *to make oneself acceptable, pleasing,* 1 Sa. 29. 4.

רָצוֹן masc. dec. 3 a.—I. *delight, satisfaction, acceptance;* עַל־רָצוֹן, לְרָצוֹן *acceptable, well pleasing* —II. *object of delight, acceptance.*—III. *will, pleasure;* hence *wantonness,* Ge. 49. 6.—IV. *good-will, favour, grace;* meton. *favours, benefits.*

רְצִיָא (*delight*) pr. name masc. 1 Ch. 7. 39.

רְצִין (*accepted, beloved;* or i. q. רָזוֹן *prince,* Arab *stable, firm*) pr. name—I. of a king of Damascus.— II. Ezr. 2. 48 ; Ne. 7. 50.

תִּרְצָה (*delight*) pr. name—I. of a royal city in the kingdom of Israel.—II. of a daughter of Zelophehad.

רְצֵה	Kal imp. sing. masc.	.	.	.	רצה
רָצוּ [h]	id. pret. 3 pers. pl.	.	.	.	רצה
רָצוּ [i]	} Kal pret. 3 pers. pl.; acc. shifted by conv. וְ (comp. § 8. rem. 7)			}	רוץ
וַ רָצוּ [j]					
רָצוֹא [k]	Kal inf. abs.	.	.	.	רצא
רָצוּי [l]	וְ Kal part. pass. sing. masc. dec. 3 a		.	.	רצה
רְצוּי [m]	id., constr. st.	.	.	.	רצה
רָצוֹן	noun masc. sing. dec. 3 a	.	.	.	רצה
רְצוֹן [n]	וּ id., constr. st.; וּ bef. (:)	.	.	.	רצה
רְצוֹנוֹ	וּ id., suff. 3 pers. sing. masc.; וּ id.			.	רצה
רְצוֹנֶךָ [o]	} id., suff. 2 pers. sing. masc.				רצה
רְצוֹנֶךָ [p]					
רְצוֹנָם [q]	id., suff. 3 pers. pl. masc.		.	.	רצה
רָצוּף [r]	Kal part. pass. sing. masc.	.	.	.	רצף
רָצוּץ [s]	וְ Kal part. pass. sing. masc. dec. 3 a		.	.	רצץ
רְצוּץ [t]	id. id., constr. st.	.	.	.	רצץ
רְצוּצִים [u]	id. id. pl., abs. st.	.	.	.	רצץ
רַצּוֹתִי [v]	id. pret. 1 pers. sing.	.	.	.	רצץ
רַצּוֹתָנוּ [w]	id. pret. 2 pers. sing. masc., suff. 1 pers. pl.			.	רצץ

רָצַח [x] וְ *to kill, slay;* רָ נֶפֶשׁ *to smite dead;* part. רֹצֵחַ *manslayer, homicide.* Niph. pass. Ju. 20. 4. Pi. I. *to dash in pieces.*—II. *to murder, be a murderer.*

רֶצַח masc.—I. *a crushing,* Ps. 42. 11.—II. *killing, slaughter,* Eze. 21. 27.

a Ps. 60. 4.   d Je. 6. 24.   g Da. 7. 7, 19.   k Je. 23. 21.   o Est. 10. 3.   r Ps. 143. 10.   u Ca. 3. 10.   x Ho. 5. 11.   ¹ 1 Sa. 12. 3.
b 1 Sa. 17. 2.   e Is. 19. 22.   h Eze. 43. 27.   l 1 Sa. 8. 11.   p De. 33. 24.   s Ps. 40. 9.   v Is. 42. 3.   y Is. 58. 6.   ² Nu. 35. 27.
c Job 12. 21.   f Ca. 3. 10.   i Ps. 102. 15.   m Eze. 1. 14.   q De. 33. 16.   t 2 Ch. 15. 15.   w De. 28. 33.   ¹ 1 Sa. 12. 4.

וְֽרָצֹחַ׳ Kal inf. abs. . . . . . רצח

רֹצֵחַ id. part. act. sing. masc. . . רצח

רְצָחוּ׳ id. pret. 3 pers. sing. masc., suff. 3 pers. sing. masc.; ּ bef. (:) . . רצח

רְצָא׳ pr. name masc. . . . . רצה

רָצִים Kal part. act. masc. pl. of רָץ d. 1 a (§ 30. No. 3) רוץ

רְצִין pr. name masc. . . . . רצה

רָצִיתָ׳ Kal pret. 2 pers. sing. masc. . רצה

רְצִיתָם׳ id. id., suff. 3 pers. pl. m.; ּ, for ּ, conv. רצה

רָצָם id. pret. 3 pers. sing. masc. (רָצָה), suff. 3 pers. pl. masc. (§ 24. rem. 21) . רצה

רֹצָם׳ id. part. act. sing. masc., suff. 3 p. pl. m. from רוֹצֶה dec. 9 a . . רצה

רָצַע ׀ to pierce, bore through, Ex. 21. 6.
מַרְצֵעַ masc. an awl.

[רָצַף] to range stones artificially, e. g. in a pavement or inlaid work, to checker; only part. pass. checkered, tesselated, Ca. 3. 10 (Gesenius). Some regard רָצַף=צָרַף to burn.

רֶצֶף masc. dec. 6 a.—I. hot stone, 1 Ki. 19. 6; others, coals.—II. pr. name of a city subject to the Assyrians, Is. 37. 12.

רִצְפָּה fem.—I. hot stone or coal, Is. 6. 6.—II. tesselated pavement.—III. pr. name of a woman.

מַרְצֶפֶת fem. pavement, 2 Ki. 16. 17.

רֶצֶף ׀ pr. name of a place . . רצף

רִצְפָּה׳ noun fem. sing. (no pl.); also pr. name רצף

רְצָפִים׳ noun masc. pl. of [רֶצֶף] dec. 6 a . רצף

רִצְפַּת׳ noun fem. sing., constr. of רִצְפָּה (no pl.) רצף

[רָצַץ] fut. יָרוּץ (§ 18. rem. 12).—I. to break, bruise, crush.—II. trop. to treat with violence, to oppress.—III. intrans. to be broken, Ec. 12. 6. Niph. נָרוֹץ to be broken, bruised. Pi. רִצֵּץ intens. of Kal Nos. I & II. Po. רוֹצֵץ to oppress, Ju. 10. 8. Hiph. to break in pieces, Ju. 9. 53. Hithpo. to struggle together, Ge. 25. 22.

רָץ masc. dec. 8 d, a fragment, piece, Ps. 68. 31.

מְרוּצָה fem. (for מְרָצָה) oppression, Je. 22. 17.

רִצֵּץ׳ Piel pret. 3 pers. sing. masc. (§ 10. rem. 1) רצץ

רִצַּצְתָּ׳ id. pret. 2 pers. sing. masc. רצץ

רָצְצָה Kal pret. 3 pers. sing. fem. . רצה

רַצְתָה׳ id. pret. 2 pers. sing. masc. (comp. § 8. r. 5) רוץ

רַצְתִּי׳ id. pret. 1 pers. sing. . . . רוץ

וְֽרַק׳ adv. . . . . . . רקק

וְֽרָק׳gg adj. masc. sing. dec. 1 a; for ּ see lett. ו רוק

וְרֹק׳ noun masc. sing. dec. 8 c; ּ id. . . רקק

[רָקַב] fut. יִרְקַב to rot, decay. Hence

רָקָב׳ masc. dec. 4 a, and רִקָּבוֹן (Job 41. 19) decay, rottenness . . . . . רקב

רָקָב׳ id., constr. st.; ּ bef. (:) . . רקב

רִקָּבוֹן׳ noun masc. sing. . . . רקב

[רָקַד] to leap, skip, dance. Pi. id.; also trop. of the jolting of a chariot. Hiph. to cause to leap, Ps. 29. 6.

רָקְדוּ׳ Kal pret. 3 pers. pl. . . . רקד

רַקָּה׳ adj. fem. sing. dec. 10, from רַק masc. . רוק

רְקוֹד׳ Kal inf. constr. . . . . רקד

וְֽרַקּוֹת׳ adj. fem. pl. of רַקָּה from רַק masc. רקק

[רָקַח] to compound or prepare ointment, Ex. 30. 33; part. רֹקֵחַ perfumer or apothecary. Pu. pass. 2 Ch. 16. 14. Hiph. to spice, season, Eze. 24. 10.

רֶקַח masc. a spicing, Ca. 8. 2.

רֹקַח masc. ointment, perfume, Ex. 30. 25.

רַקָּח masc. dec. 1 b, perfumer or apothecary. Fem. רַקָּחָה, 1 Sa. 8. 13.

רִקֻּחַ masc. dec. 1 b, ointment, perfume, Is. 57. 9.

מֶרְקָח masc. only pl. מֶרְקָחִים aromatic herbs, Ca. 5. 13.

מֶרְקָחָה fem.—I. ointment, Eze. 24. 10.—II. pot of ointment, Job 41. 23.

מִרְקַחַת fem.—I. preparation of ointments.—II. ointment, 1 Ch. 9. 30.

רֹקַח׳kk noun masc. sing. . . . . רקח

רֹקֵחַ׳ Kal part. act. sing. masc. dec. 7 b . רקח

רֹקְחֵי׳a id. pl., constr. st. . . . רקח

רַקֻּחָיִךְ׳b noun masc. pl., suff. 2 pers. sing. fem. from [רִקֻּחַ] dec. 1 b . . . . רקח

רַקִּי׳c noun masc. s., suff. 1 pers. s. fr. רַק d. 8 c רקק

רַקִּים׳ adj. masc., pl. of רַק dec. 1 a . רוק

רָקִיעַ׳ noun masc. sing. dec. 3 a . . רקע

רְקִיעַ׳ id., constr. . . . . רקע

וְֽרָקִיק׳ noun masc. sing. dec. 3 a . רקק

רְקִיקִים׳ id., constr. st.; ּ bef. (:) . רקק

רְקִיקֵי׳ ּ id. pl., constr. st.; ּ id. . . רקק

[רָקַם] to embroider, or to weave with threads of different colours, only part. רֹקֵם an embroiderer, or a weaver

---

• Je. 7. 9.   ‖ Ps. 44. 4.   ♦ Eze. 40. 17.   ℓ Job 20. 19.   ª 2 Ki. 5. 20.   ʰ Hab. 3. 16.   ■ Ps. 114. 4.   ● Ge. 41. 19.   ᵏ Job 7. 19.
ᵇ Ho. 4. 2.   ∫ 2 Ch. 10. 7.   ¹ 1 Ki. 19. 6.   ═ Ps. 74. 14.   ᵖ Job 30. 10.   ͥ Pr. 14. 30.   ᶻ Eze. 24. 11.   ♦ 1 Ch. 9. 30.   ᵈ Ge. 1. 20.
ᶜ De. 22. 26.   ᵉ Je. 14. 12.   ♭ Est. 1. 6.   ■ Je. 12. 5.   ͭ Is. 50. 6.   ᵗ Job 41. 19.   ♭ Ec. 3. 4.   ♭ Is. 57. 9.   ᵉ Nu. 6. 19.
ᵈ Ps. 85. 2.   gg Ne. 5. 13.

45.*

in colours. **Pu.** *to be curiously wrought* or *woven,* metaph. Ps. 139. 15.

רֶקֶם (*variegated*) pr. name—I. of a city in Benjamin, Jos. 18. 27.—II. of a king of the Midianites.—III. of two men, 1 Ch. 2. 43; 7. 16.

רִקְמָה fem. d. 12 b.—I. *a variegation* or *variety of colour.*—II. *variegated work,* or *embroidery;* du. רִקְמָתַיִם prob. *stuff worked on both sides,* Ju. 5. 30.

רֶקֶם	וְ‎ pr. name of a man and a place; for וְ‎
רֶקֶה	וְ‎ see lett. ו‎ . . . . .
רֹקֵם	וְ‎ Kal part. act. sing. masc. . . . רקם
רִקְמָה	וְ‎ noun fem. sing. dec. 12 b . . . רקם
רֻקַּמְתִּי	Pual pret. 1 pers. sing. . . . רקם
רִקְמָתַיִם	noun fem., du. of רִקְמָה dec. 12 b . רקם
רִקְמָתֵךְ	id. sing., suff. 2 pers. sing. fem. . . רקם
רִקְמָתָם	id. sing., suff. 3 pers. pl. masc. . . רקם

[רָקַע] I. *to stamp* with the feet.—II. *to stamp, tread down,* 2 Sa. 22. 43.—III. *to stretch, spread out, expand.* **Pi.** I. *to beat into thin plates.*—II. *to cover with metallic plates,* Is. 40. 19. **Pu.** part. *beaten* or *spread into plates,* Je. 10. 9. **Hiph.** *to stretch out, expand,* Job 37. 18.

רָקִיעַ m. d. 3 a, *the expanse.* Vulg. *firmamentum.*

רִקֻּעִים m. pl. (of רָקָע) *plates of metal,* Nu. 17. 3.

יָרְקְעָם (for יָרְקַע עָם *the people is spread abroad*) pr. name of a town in Judea, 1 Ch. 2. 44.

רֹקֵעַ	Kal part. act. sing. masc. (§ 36. rem. 1) רקע
רְקַע	וְ‎ id. imp. sing. masc.; וְ‎ bef. (:) רקע
רִקְעֵי	noun masc. pl. constr. from [רָקָע] dec. 1 b רקע
רְקָעֲךָ	וְ‎ Kal inf. [רָקַע], suff. 2 pers. s. m. (§16. r.10) רקע

I. רָקַק *Root not used;* Arab. *to be thin.*

רַק masc.—I. adj. *thin, lean,* Ge. 41. 19, 20, 27.—II. adv. (*a*) *only, alone;* (*b*) *surely, certainly;* (*c*) *save, except.*

רַקָּה fem. dec. 10.—I. *the temple of the head.*—II. poet. for *the cheek,* Ca. 4. 3; 6. 7.

רַקַּת (*thinness;* Chald. רַקְתָּא *shore*) pr. name of a city in the tribe of Naphtali, Jos. 19. 35.

רַקּוֹן (id.) pr. name of a city in Dan, Jos. 19. 46.

רָקִיק masc. dec. 3 a, *a thin cake.*

II. רָקַק i. q. יָרַק *to spit,* only fut. יָרֹק Le. 15. 8.

רֹק masc. dec. 8 c *spittle.*

רַקַּת pr. name of a place . . . . רקק

רֻקָּתוֹ	noun f. s., suff. 3 pers. s. m. fr. [רַקָּה] d. 10 רקק
רֻקָּתֵךְ	id., suff. 2 pers. sing. fem. . . . רקק
רָר	Kal pret. 3 pers. sing. masc. . . . רור
רָשׁ, וְ‎	Kal part. act. sing. masc. dec. 1 a רוש
	(§ 30. rem. 3); for וְ‎ see lett. ו‎ . .
רֵשׁ f.‎	}
רַשׁ‎	} Kal imp. sing. masc. (§ 20. rem. 2) ירשׁ

רָשָׁה *Root not used;* Chald. רְשָׁא *to be able, have permission.*

רִשְׁיוֹן masc. *grant, permission,* Ezr. 3. 7.

רָשׁוּ	Kal pret. 3 pers. pl. . . . רוש
רְשׁוּ	וְ‎ Kal imp. pl. masc.; וְ‎ bef. (:) ירשׁ
רְשִׁים	Ch. Peal part. pass. sing. masc. רשׁם

[רְשַׁם] *to write down, record,* Da. 10. 21. Hence

יִרְשָׁם	Ch. fut. יִרְשָׁם idem. רשׁם
רִשַׁמְתָּ	Ch. Peal pret. 2 pers. sing. masc. . . רשׁם

[רָשַׁע] fut. יִרְשַׁע.—I. *to be wicked, to act wickedly, unjustly, impiously.*—II. *to be guilty, have an unjust cause,* Job 9. 29; 10. 7, 15. **Hiph.** הִרְשִׁיעַ.—I. *to declare guilty, to condemn.*—II. *to cause mischief, disquiet* (Syr. רתע *to be restless, to disturb*), 1 Sa. 14. 47.—III. *to be wicked, act wickedly.*

רָשָׁע masc. d. 4 a, רְשָׁעָה fem. adj.—I. *wicked, ungodly, impious.*—II. *having an unjust cause.*—III. *guilty, punishable.*

רֶשַׁע masc. dec. 6 a (with suff. רִשְׁעוֹ § 35. r. 5)—I. *wickedness, ungodliness.*—II. *injustice,* מֹאזְנֵי רֶ׳ *unjust, i. e. false balances.*—III. perh. pl. רְשָׁעִים *wicked deeds,* Job 34. 26.

רִשְׁעָה fem. (constr. רִשְׁעַת, no pl.)—I. *wickedness, ungodliness.*—II. *guilt, fault,* De. 25. 2.

מִרְשַׁעַת fem. *wickedness,* for concr. *wicked person,* 2 Ch. 24. 7.

רָשָׁע	וְ‎ adj. masc. sing. dec. 4 a . . . . רשׁע
רֶשַׁע	noun masc. sing. (suff. רִשְׁעוֹ) d. 6 (§ 35. r. 5) רשׁע
רִשְׁעָה	וְ‎ noun fem. sing. (no pl.) . . . . רשׁע
רִשְׁעוֹ	noun masc. sing., suff. 3 pers. sing. masc.
	from רֶשַׁע dec. 6 (§ 35. rem. 5) רשׁע
רִשְׁעֵי	constr. of the foll. . . . . . רשׁע
רְשָׁעִים	וְ‎ adj. masc., pl. of רָשָׁע dec. 4 a; or perh.
	(Job 34. 26) pl. of רֶשַׁע q. v.; וְ‎ bef. (:) רשׁע
רִשְׁעֶךָ	noun masc. sing., suff. 2 pers. sing. masc. from
	רֶשַׁע dec. 6 (§ 35. rem. 5) . . . רשׁע
רְשַׁעְנוּ	וְ‎ Kal pret. 1 pers. pl. [for רָשַׁעְנוּ] רשׁע

Ps. 139. 15.   ᶜ Eze. 16. 18.   ᵉ Eze. 6. 11.   ᵍ Eze. 25. 6.   ⁱ Le. 15. 3.   ˡ De. 2. 24, 31.   ⁿ Da. 6. 10.   ᵖ Pr. 13. 6.   ʳ Job 35. 8.
Ju. 5. 30.   ᵈ Eze. 26. 16.   ᶠ Nu. 17. 3.   ʰ Ju. 5. 26.   ᵏ Pr. 13. 8   ᵐ Ps. 34. 11.   ᵒ Da. 6. 13, 14.   �q De. 9. 27.   ˢ 2 Ch. 6. 37.

רִשַׁעֲנוּ noun masc. sing., suff. 1 pers. sing. from רָשַׁע dec. 6 (§ 35. rem. 5) . . . רשע

רִשְׁעַת וְ noun fem. sing., constr. of רִשְׁעָה (no pl.) רשע

רִשְׁעָתוֹ id. with suff. 3 pers. sing. masc. . . רשע

רָשַׁעְתִּי Kal pret. 1 pers. sing. . . . רשע

רְשַׁעְתַּיִם רְשַׁעְתָּיִם } pr. name masc., see גֻּשָׁן ר׳.

רֶשֶׁף וְ masc. dec. 6a (pl. c. רִשְׁפֵי).—I. a flame, Ca. 8. 6; others, burning coal.—II. lightning, Ps. 78. 48; metaph. Ps. 76. 4 רִשְׁפֵי קֶשֶׁת lightnings of the bow, for arrows; Job 5. 7 בְּנֵי רֶ׳ sons of lightning, i. e. arrows, or (according to Gesenius) birds of prey which fly swift as the lightning; others, sons of the flame, i. e. sparks.—III. burning disease.—IV. pr. name masc. 1 Ch. 7. 25.

רִשְׁפֵי noun masc. pl., constr. st. . . . רשף

רִשְׁפֶיהָ id. pl., suff. 3 pers. sing. fem. . . רשף

רָשַׁשׁ Kal not used; cogn. רָצַץ. Po. to break in pieces, to destroy, Je. 5. 17. Pu. pass. Mal. 1. 4.

תַּרְשִׁישׁ—I. pr. name, Tarshish, supposed to be a city and kingdom in Spain; אֳנִיּוֹת תַּ׳ Tarshish ships, prop. ships employed by the Tyrians in voyages to and from Tarshish; but also generally for all large merchant ships bound on long voyages, though to other countries.—II. a precious stone brought from Tarshish, according to some the chrysolite, others amber.—III. pr. name of a Persian king, Est. 1. 14, and another person, 1 Ch. 7. 10.

רֻשַּׁשְׁנוּ Pual pret. 1 pers. pl. . . רשש

רֶשֶׁת וְ׳ noun fem. sing. dec. 13 (§ 44. rem. 1 & 2) רש

רִשְׁתּוֹ וְ id., suff. 3 pers. sing. masc. . . ירש

רִשְׁתִּי id., suff. 1 pers. sing. . . ירש

רִשְׁתָּם id., suff. 3 pers. pl. masc. . . ירש

רָתַח Pi. to make boil, Eze. 24. 5. Pu. to boil, metaph. fo. to be agitated, Job 30. 27. Hiph. i. q. Pi. Job 41. 23. רֶתַח masc. d. 6 (§ 35. r. 5), a boiling, Eze. 24. 5.

רַתַּח Piel imp. sing. masc. . . . רתח

רֻתְּחוּ Pual pret. 3 pers. pl. . . . רתח

רְתִיחֹתֶיהָ noun masc. pl., suff. 3 pers. sing. fem. from רָתַח § 35. rem. 5] dec. 6 . . רתח

[רָתַם] to bind, yoke, or harness, Mi. 1. 13. רֹתֶם masc. (pl. רְתָמִים) the broom, Spanish retama. Jerome the juniper. רִתְמָה (broom) pr. name of a station of the Israelites in the desert, Nu. 33. 18, 19.

רְתֹם Kal imp. sing. masc. . . תם

רֹתֶם noun masc. sing. dec. 6c . . רתם

רְתָמִים id. pl., abs. st. (§ 35. rem. 9) . . רתם

רָתַק Niph. to be bound, Ec. 12. 6, Keri. Pu. id. Na. 3. 10 רָתוּק masc. a chain, Eze. 7. 23. רַתּוּקָה fem. id. 1 Ki. 6. 21, K., in Kh. רַתִּיקָה. רְתֻקוֹת fem. pl. chains, Is. 40. 19.

רֻתְּקוּ Pual pret. 3 pers. pl. . . רתק

רַתֻּקוֹת וְ noun fem. pl. of [רַתָּקָה] dec. 10; וְ bef. (:) רתק

רְתֵת masc. i. q. רָטֵט trembling, terror, Ho. 13. 1.

שׁ

שֶׁ less frequently שַׁ (before gutturals dag. forte is omitted, once שָׁ) and rarely שְׁ, a pref. i. q. אֲשֶׁר fr. which it is abbreviated, אֲ being dropped by aphaeresis and ר assimilated to the next letter.—I. a relative pronoun (a) who, which, what; (b) as a mere sign of relation, as שָׁם שֶׁ whither, comp. Ec. 1. 7; (c) followed by לְ שֶׁל equivalent to the genitive, Ca. 1. 6; 3. 7.—II. as a relative conj. (a) that; עַד שֶׁ till that; כִּמְעַט שֶׁ scarcely that; (b) so that, Ec. 3. 14; (c) because that, for; שַׁלָּמָה for why?—III. with prefixes, בְּשֶׁ because that; כְּשֶׁ as, also as, when.

שֶׁל, a particle made up of שֶׁ q. v. & לְ, occurs only with prefix.—I. בְּשֶׁל on account of, because; בְּשֶׁלְמִי on whose account; בְּשֶׁלִּי on my account.—II. בְּשֶׁל אֲשֶׁר in whatsoever, or how much soever, Ec. 8. 17.

שָׂא וְ׳ Kal imp. sing. masc. . . . נשא

שָׂא Chald. Peal imp. sing. masc. . . נשא

[שָׁאַב] fut. יִשְׁאָב to draw water. מַשְׁאָב masc. only pl. מַשְׁאַבִּים watering-troughs, or watering places, Ju. 5. 11.

שֹׁאֵב Kal part. act. sing. masc. dec. 7b . . שאב

שאב   id. imp. sing. fem. . . . . שָׁאֲבִי

שאב d. 7 b   } id. part. act. pl. constr. masc. fr. שָׁאַב   שֹׁאֲבֵי

שאב   } id. pret. 2 pers. pl. masc.; ࡳ, for ࡳ, conv.   שְׁאַבְתֶּם

שָׁאַג   (§ 8. rem. 2) fut. יִשְׁאַג.—I. *to roar, as a* lion, thunder, &c.—II. *to groan,* Ps. 38. 9.

שְׁאָגָה   fem. dec. 11 c (§ 42. rem. 1).—I. *a roaring,* of a lion, Is. 5. 29.—II. *a groaning, groan.*

שאג   Kal inf. abs. . . . . שְׁאֹג

שאג   } Kh. יִשְׁאַג, Kal fut., K. וְשָׁאַג pret. 3 p s. m.   שֹׁאֵג

שאג   } Kal part. act. sing. masc. dec. 7 b   שֹׁאֵג

שאג   noun fem. sing. dec. 11 c (§ 42. rem. 1)   שְׁאָגָה

שאג   Kal pret. 3 pers. pl.   שָׁאֲגוּ

שאג   id. part. act. masc. pl. of שֹׁאֵג dec. 7 b   שֹׁאֲגִים

שאג   noun fem. sing., constr. of שְׁאָגָה dec. 11 c (§ 42. rem. 1) . . . . שַׁאֲגַת

שאג   id. with suff. 3 pers. sing. masc. . . שַׁאֲגָתוֹ

שאג   Kal pret. 1 pers. sing. . . . שָׁאַגְתִּי

שאג   noun fem. sing., suff. 1 pers. sing. from שְׁאָגָה dec. 11 c (§ 42. rem. 1) . . שַׁאֲגָתִי

שאג   id. pl., suff. 1 pers. sing. . . . שַׁאֲגֹתַי

[שָׁאָה]   *to be desolate* (prob. *to fall with a crash*), Is. 6. 11. Niph. I. *to make a noise, rushing,* Is. 17. 12, 13; Prof. Lee, *to be dashed together.*—II. *to be laid waste,* Is. 6. 11. Hiph. *to lay waste.* Hithp. הִשְׁתָּאָה *to be confused, astonished,* Ge. 24. 21; others, *to gaze at;* Sept. καταμανθάνω, Vulg. *contemplor,* as synonymous with הִשְׁתָּעָה R. שָׁעָה.

שְׁאָוָה   fem. *tempest,* Pr. 1. 27, Kh.

שָׁאוֹן   masc. dec. 3 a.—I. *a noise, tumult, bustle, shouting,* Je. 48. 45; בְּנֵי שׁ *tumultuous warriors.*—II. *destruction,* Ps. 40. 3.

שְׁאִיָּה   fem. *a crash or destruction,* Is. 24. 12.

שְׁאֵת   fem. *desolation,* La. 3. 47.

שֵׁת   fem. (for שְׁאֵת) *noise, tumult,* Nu. 24. 17; according to others, *a pr. name.*

שוא   defect. for שׁוֹאָה (q. v.) . . . שֹׁאָה

אהב   pref. שְׁ (q. v.))(Kal pret. 3 pers. sing. fem.   שֶׁהֲבָה

נשא   Kal imp. sing. masc. (שָׂא), suff. 3 pers. sing. masc. (§ 25. No. 2 a) . . שָׂאֵהוּ

שאה   Kal pret. 3 pers. pl.   שָׁאוּ

נשא   } Kal imp. pl. masc.; ࡳ bef. (:)   שְׂאוּ

שאל   } Kal inf. abs.   שָׁאוֹל

שאל   } id. part. pass. sing. masc.; also pr. name   שָׁאוּל

שאל   noun masc. sing. dec. 1 a   שְׁאוֹל

שאל   id. with parag. ה   שְׁאוֹלָה

שאה   noun masc. sing. dec. 3 a   שָׁאוֹן

שאה   } id. constr. st.; ࡳ bef. (:)   שְׁאוֹן

שאה   } id., suff. 3 pers. sing. fem.; ࡳ id.   שְׁאוֹנָהּ

נשא   Kal imp. pl. masc. (שְׂאוּ), suff. 1 pers. sing. (comp. § 16. rem. 11) . . שָׂאוּנִי

שָׁאַט   Root not used; prob. i. q. שׁוּט *to contemn, despise.* שְׁאָט masc. *contempt* (for another); with suff. see the following.

שאט   noun masc. sing., suff. 2 pers. sing. masc. [for שְׁאָטְךָ] from שְׁאָט . . שָׁאטְךָ

נשא   } Kal imp. sing. fem.; ࡳ bef. (:) . . שְׂאִי

שאה   } noun fem. sing.; ࡳ id.   שְׁאִיָּה

אין   pref. שְׁ (q. v.))(adv., constr. of אַיִן dec. 6 b   שְׁאֵין

שָׁאַל   } [also שָׁאֵל, comp. Ge. 32. 18; 1 Sa. 12. 13] fut. יִשְׁאַל.—I. *to ask, inquire of, interrogate,* with לְ, עַל *concerning* any one, with בְּ *to inquire of, consult,* e. g. God; שׁ לְרֵעֵהוּ לְשָׁלוֹם *to ask after the welfare of any one, to salute him.*—II. *to ask, demand, require,* with מִן, מֵאֵת *of* any one.—III. *to request, petition,* with מִן, מֵאֵת, מֵעִם; abs. *to beg,* Pr. 20. 4.—IV. *to ask as a loan, to borrow;* with לְ *to lend,* 1 Sa. 2. 20. Niph. *to ask for oneself, to ask leave.* Pi. שִׁאֵל (§ 14. rem. 1).—I. *to beg,* Ps. 109. 10.—II. *to ask, inquire,* 2 Sa. 20. 18. Hiph. *to lend.*

שאל   Chald.—I. *to ask, interrogate,* with לְ, acc. of pers. Ezr. 5. 9, 10.—II. *to ask, demand.*

שאל   (*petition*) pr. name masc. Ezr. 10. 29.

שְׁאֵלָה, שְׁאֵלָה   fem. (§ 42. rem. 4).—I. *request, petition.*—II. *thing lent, a loan,* 1 Sa. 2. 20.

שְׁאֵלָא   Chald. fem. dec. 8 a, *subject of inquiry, matter, affair,* Da. 4. 14.

שְׁאוֹל, שְׁאוֹל   masc.—I. *grave;* hence—II. *the abode of the departed souls;* Sept. mostly Ἄδης, *Hades.* It is so called either from its devouring and ever craving character, Pr. 15. 11, or the Root שָׁאַל may be in signification i. q. שָׁעַל *to be hollow.*

שָׁאוּל   (*asked for* or *lent*) pr. name, *Saul.*—I. the first king of the Israelites, from the tribe of Benjamin.—II. a king of Edom, Ge. 36. 37.—III. Ge. 46. 10, patronym. שָׁאוּלִי Nu. 26. 13.—IV. 1 Ch. 6. 9.

שְׁאַלְתִּיאֵל, שַׁלְתִּיאֵל   (*I have asked* him *of God*) pr. name of a man.

אֶשְׁתָּאוֹל   (*petition*) pr. name of a city in Dan. Gent. noun אֶשְׁתָּאֻלִי.

Na. 3. 14.   Am. 3. 8.   Ju. 14. 5.   Ps. 74. 4.   Ps. 22. 2.   Is. 6. 11.   Ge. 42. 38.   Is. 5. 14.   Is. 24. 12.
Jos. 9. 21, 23, 27.   Je. 25. 30.   Ps. 22. 14.   Eze. 19. 7.   Job 3. 24.   1 Sa. 22. 13.   Is. 17. 12.   Eze. 25. 6.   Ps. 146. 3.
Is. 12. 3.   Is. 5. 29.   Is. 5. 29.   Ps. 38. 9.

מְשָׁאָל (*petition*) pr. name of a city in the tribe of Asher.

מִשְׁאָלָה fem. dec. 12 a, *petition, request*, Ps. 20. 6 ; 37. 4.

אֹשֶׁל Kal pret. 3 pers. s. m. for שָׁאַל (§ 8. rem. 7)   שָׁאֵל

שָׁאֵל Chald. Peal part. act. sing. masc.   שאל

שָׁאֵל 'ו pr. name masc. ; ו bef. (:)   שאל

שְׁאַל Kal imp. sing. masc.   שאל

שְׁאֵל Chald. Peal pret. 3 pers. sing. masc.   שאל

שְׁאֹל pref. שְׁ (q. v.) χ noun masc. sing. dec. 1 a (§ 30. No. 3)   אול

שְׁאֹל defect. for שְׁאוֹל (q. v.)   שאל

שֹׁאֵל 'ו Kal part. act. sing. masc. dec. 7 b   שאל

שָׁאֲלָה }
שָׁאֲלָי 'ו } id. pret. 3 pers sing. fem. (§ 8. rem. 7)   שאל

שַׁאֲלָה id. imp. sing. masc. (שְׁאַל) with parag. ה (§ 8. rem. 12)   שאל

שְׁאֵלָה noun fem. sing. dec. 10 & 11 c (§ 42. rem. 4)   שאל

שְׁאֹלָה defect. for שְׁאוֹלָה (q. v.)   שאל

שָׁאֲלוּ
שָׁאֲלוּ 'ו } Kal pret. 3 pers. pl. (§ 8. rem. 7)   שאל

שַׁאֲלוּ 'ו id. imp. pl. masc.   שאל

שֵׁאֵלוּ ו Piel pret. 3 pers. pl. [for שָׁאֲלוּ § 14. rem. 1, comp. § 8. rem. 7]   שאל

שָׁאֲלוּנוּ Kal pret. 3 pers. pl., suff. 1 pers. pl. (§ 16. r. 1)   שאל

שָׁאֲלוּנִי id. id. with suff. 1 pers. sing.   שאל

שַׁאֲלִי 'ו id. imp. sing. fem.   שאל

שְׁאֵלְךָ ו id. pret. 3 pers. sing. m. [שָׁאַל], suff. 2 pers. sing. masc. (§ 16. rem. 1) ; ו bef. (:)   שאל

שְׁאֵלֵךְ ו id. id., suff. 2 pers. sing. fem. ; ו id.   שאל

שְׁאֶלְנָא Chald. Peal pret. 1 pers. pl.   שאל

שָׁאַלְתָּ
שָׁאַלְתְּ } Kal pret. 2 pers. sing. masc. (§ 8. rem. 7)   שאל

שָׁאֲלְתָּ ו
שָׁאֲלְתִּ ו } id. id.; acc. shifted by conv. ו, retained bef. monos. (§ 8. rem. 7)   שאל

שָׁאַלְתְּ id. pret. 2 pers. sing. fem.   שאל

שֹׁאֶלֶת id. part. act. sing., fem. of שֹׁאֵל (§ 8. rem. 19)   שאל

שְׁאֵלְתָּא Chald. noun fem. sing., emph. of [שְׁאֵלָא] d. 8 a   שאל

שָׁאַלְתִּי Kal pret. 1 pers. sing.   שאל

שְׁאֵלָתִי noun fem. sing., suff. 1 pers. sing. from שְׁאֵלָה (§ 42. rem. 4) }   שאל

שְׁאַלְתִּיאֵל pr. name masc.   שאל

שְׁאִלְתִּיהוּ Kal pret. 1 pers. s., suff. 3 p. s. m. (§ 8. r. 1 b)   שאל

שְׁאִלְתִּיו id. id., suff. 3 pers. sing. masc.   שאל

שְׁאֵלָתֶךָ noun fem. s., suff. 2 p. s. fem. fr. שְׁאֵלָה d. 10   שאל

שְׁאֵלָתָם id. with suff. 3 pers. pl. dec. 11 c (§ 42. r. 4)   שאל

שְׁאֶלְתֶּם ו'ב Kal pret. 2 pers. pl. masc. (§ 8. rem. 1 b); ו, for ו, conv.   שאל

שָׁאַן Kal not used ; i. q. שָׁעַן *to lean, rest.* Pil. (§ 6. No. 2), *to be quiet, live quietly.*

שַׁאֲן (*quiet*) pr. name, see בֵּית שׁ.

שׁוּנִי (for שַׁאֲנִי *quiet*) pr. name masc. Ge. 46.16; also patronym. (for שׁוּנִיּ) Nu. 26. 15.

שׁוּנֵם (perh. *two resting places*, comp. עֵינָם for עֵינַיִם Gesen.) pr. name of a city in the tribe of Issachar. Gent. noun fem. שׁוּנַמִּית.

שַׁאֲנָן שָׁאֵן masc. שַׁאֲנָה fem. adj.—I. *quiet, living in quiet, peace.*—II. *at ease, careless, proud.*—III. subst *wantonness, pride.*

שַׁלְאֲנָן (with ל inserted) *at ease*, Job 21. 23.

בֵּית pr. name, see בֵּית שָׁאָן   בית

שָׁאֲנִי pref. שְׁ (q. v.) χ pron. pers. com. sing.   אני

שְׁאֲנִיחֶנּוּ pref. id. χ Hiph. fut. 1 pers. sing. [אַנִּיחַ § 21. rem. 24], suff. 3 pers. sing. masc.   נוח

שָׁאֵן adj. masc. sing. (pl. שַׁאֲנַנִּים) dec. 8 a   שאן

שַׁאֲנַן 'ו Pilel pret. 3 pers. sing. masc. (§ 6. No. 2)   שאן

שַׁאֲנַנּוּ id. pret. 3 pers. pl. [for שַׁאֲנְנוּ comp. § 8. r. 7]   שאן

שַׁאֲנַנּוֹת adj. pl. fem. from שַׁאֲנָן masc.   שאן

שַׁאֲנַנְךָ ו id. masc. sing., suff. 2 pers. sing. masc. [for נַנְךָ] from שַׁאֲנָן dec. 8 a   שאן

שֹׁאסַיִךְ Kal part. act. pl. masc., suff. 2 pers. sing. fem. [by Syr. for שֹׁסַיִךְ § 18. rem. 17]   שסס

שָׁאַף ו *to draw in*, sc. the air, wind, cogn. שָׁאַב ; hence —I. abs. *to pant, gasp*, Ps. 119. 131 ; of one in anger, *to breathe hard, puff*, Is. 42. 14 ; hence *to hasten*, Ec. 1. 5.—II. *to breathe in, snap, snuff up*, the air, wind, with acc. ; trop. *to pant for, desire eagerly* ; once with עַל Am. 2. 7 ; metaph. of savage enemies, *to swallow up, destroy.*

שָׁאֹף ו Kal inf. abs.   שאף

שָׁאֲפָה id. pret. 3 pers. sing. fem.   שאף

שָׁאֲפוּ id. pret. 3 pers. pl.   שאף

שֹׁאֲפִי id. part. act. s. m., suff. 1 p. s. fr. שׁוֹאֵף d. 7 b   שאף

שְׁאָפַנִי id. pret. 3 pers. sing. masc., suff. 1 pers. sing.   שאף

שְׂאֹר , שָׂאַר Roots not used ; Arab. תאר, שׁאר *to be hot, to boil up* (Gesenius).

שְׂאֹר masc. *leaven.*

מִשְׁאֶרֶת fem. dec. 13 a, *a kneading-trough.*

a Da. 2. 11, 27.	e Ex. 3. 22.	i Ps. 109. 10.	m Ge. 32. 18.	q 1 Ki. 3. 11.	u Job 6. 8.	z 1 Sa. 25. 5.	*e Je. 48. 11.	i Eze. 36. 3.
b Da. 2. 10.	f Is. 7. 11.	k Ps. 137. 3.	n Ju. 4. 20.	r 1 Sa. 1. 17.	v Ju. 13. 6.	a Ca. 1. 6;	f Job 3. 18.	k Je. 2. 24.
Ps. 146. 5.	g 1 Sa. 10. 4.	l Is. 45. 11.	o Ezr. 5. 9, 10.	s 1 Ki. 2. 20, 22.	w 1 Sa. 1. 20.	Ec. 2. 18.	g Je. 30. 16.	l Ps. 57. 4.
De. 18. 11.	h Je. 6. 16.		p 1 Ki. 9. 22.	t De. 13. 15.	x Da. 4. 14.	d Ps. 106. 15.	h Job 5. 5.	m Ps. 56. 2.
					y 1 Sa. 1. 20.	c Eze. 2. 18.		

שָׁאַר *to remain,* 1 Sa. 16. 11. Niph. I. *to remain, be left over.*—II. *to remain, be left behind.* Hiph. I. *to let remain, to leave.*—II. *to leave behind,* Joel 2. 14. —III. *to have left, to retain.*

שְׁאָר masc. *remainder, remnant.*

שְׁאָר Chald. masc. dec. 1 b, idem.

שְׁאָר יָשׁוּב (*a remnant shall return*) pr. name of a son of Isaiah, Is. 7. 3.

שְׁאֵרִית, contr. שֵׁרִית fem. dec. 1 b, *remainder, remnant.*

שְׁאֵר masc. dec. 1 a.—I. *flesh.*—II. *blood-relation, kindred.* —III. *food, aliment,* Ex. 21. 10 ; Prof. Lee, *a right arising from marriage.*

שַׁאֲרָה fem. *blood-relationship,* concr. *near relative,* Le. 18. 17.

שֶׁאֱרָה (id.) pr. name fem. 1 Ch. 7. 24.

שְׁאָר ׀ n. m. s., constr. שְׁאָר Ezr. 7. 20. ; ׀ bef. (ː)   שאר

שְׁאָר noun masc. sing. . . .   שאר

שְׁאָר יָשׁוּב ׀ pr. name masc.; ׀ bef. (ː)   שאר

שְׁאָרָא ׀ Ch. noun m. sing., emph. of שְׁאָר d. 1 b; ׀ id.   שאר

שְׁאֵרָה noun fem. sing. . .   שאר

שְׁאֵרָה ׀ noun m. s., suff. 3 pers. s. fem. fr. שְׁאֵר d. 1 a   שאר

שֶׁאֱרָה pr. name fem. . .   שאר

שְׁאֵרוֹ noun m. sing., suff. 3 pers. s. m. fr. שְׁאֵר d. 1 a   שאר

שְׁאֵרִי ׀ id., suff. 1 pers. sing. ; ׀ bef. (ː)   שאר

שְׁאֵרִית ׀ noun fem. sing. dec. 1 b ; ׀ id.   שאר

שְׁאֵרִיתוֹ ׀ id., suff. 3 pers. sing. masc ; ׀ id.   שאר

שְׁאֵרִיתֵךְ ׀ id., suff. 2 pers. sing. fem. ; ׀ id.   שאר

שְׁאֵרִיתָם ׀ id., suff. 3 pers. pl. masc. ; ׀ id.   שאר

שְׁאֵרְךָ ׀ noun masc. sing., suff. 2 pers. sing. masc. from שְׁאֵר dec 1 ; ׀ id.   שאר

שְׁאֵרָם ׀ id., suff. 3 pers. pl. masc. ; ׀ id.   שאר

שְׂאֵת Kal inf. constr., or subst. fem. dec. 1 [for שְׂאֵת § 25, No. 2 a]   נשא

שְׂאֵתְךָ pref. שֶׁ (q. v.) ✕ pron. pers. masc. sing.   אנת

שְׂאֵתוֹ ׀ Kal inf. (De. 14. 24), or subst. fem., suff. 3 pers. sing. masc. fr. שְׂאֵת (q.v.); ׀ bef. (ː)   נשא

שְׂאֵתִי id. inf. with suff. 1 pers. sing.   נשא

שָׁב Kal part. sing. masc. . .   שוב

שָׁב ׀ Kal pret. 3 pers. sing. masc.   שוב

שָׁב ׀ id. part. act. sing. masc. dec. 1 a (§ 30. No. ○); for ׀ see lett. ׀   שוב

שֵׁב ׀ Kal imp. sing. masc.   ישב

שֻׁב defect. for שׁוּב (q. v.) .   שוב

שֵׁב Kal imp. sing. masc. (§ 21. rem. 5)   שוב

שְׁבָא pr. name—I. of a son of Raamah, grandson of Cush, comp. Ge. 10. 7.—II. of a son of Joktan, Ge. 10. 28.—III. of a grandson of Abraham by Keturah.—IV. of a people and a country in Arabia Felix.

שְׁבָא pref. שֶׁ ✕ (Kal pret. 3 pers. sing. masc.   בוא

שְׁבָאֵל ׀ pr. name masc., see שְׁבוּאֵל   שבה

שְׁבָכִים noun masc. pl. . . .   שבב

שָׁבַב Root not used.—I. Arab. *to kindle.*—II. Chald שְׁבַב, *to break.*

שָׁבִיב masc. dec. 3 a, *a flame,* Job 18. 5.

שְׁבִיב Chald. masc. dec. 1 a, idem, Da. 3. 22 ; 7. 9.

שְׁבָבִים masc. pl. *fragments,* Ho. 8. 6.

שַׁבְּתִּי ׀ Pilel pret. 1 pers. sing. ; acc. shifted by conv. ׀ (§ 8. rem. 7) . .   שוב

שַׁבְּתִּיךָ ׀ id. id., suff. 2 pers. sing. masc.   שוב

שָׁבָה fut. apoc. יִשְׁבְּ (§ 24. rem. 3), *to take prisoner, to carry away captive, to carry off* ; part. pass. שְׁבִים, שְׁבִיוֹת *captives.* Niph. pass.

שְׁבוּאֵל (*captive of God*) pr. name masc. of two persons, also written שׁוּבָאֵל.

שְׁבוּת fem. dec. 1 a.—I. *captivity* ; meton. *captives.*—II. trop. *a state of great affliction and misery,* Job 42. 10.

שְׁבִי masc. dec. 6 i (§ 35. rem. 14).—I. *captivity* ; meton. *captives.*—II. *a captive,* Ex. 12. 29 ; fem. שִׁבְיָה, Is. 52. 2.

שֹׁבִי (*one who takes captive*) pr. name of a man.

שֹׁבִי (id.) pr. name of a man, 2 Sa. 17. 27.

שִׁבְיָה fem. *captivity* ; meton. *captives.*

שְׁבִית fem. dec. 1 a, *captivity.*

תִּשְׁבִּי gentile noun of the prophet Elijah, *Tisbite,* from a city of Naphtali, called תִּשְׁבֶּה or תִּשְׁבָּה (*captivity*).

שָׁבָה Kal part. act. sing., fem. of שָׁב   שוב

שָׁבָה ׀ id. pret. 3 pers. sing. fem. ; acc. shifted by conv. ׀   שוב

שְׁבָה Kal imp. sing. masc. (שֵׁב) with parag. ה (§ 20. rem. 3)   ישב

שָׁבָה ׀ defect. for שׁוּבָה (q. v.)   שוב

שְׁבֶה ׀ Kal imp. sing. m.; (comp. the form זָהָב (וְזָהָב)   שבה

שְׁבוֹ masc. *an agate* ; Sept. ἀχάτης, Ex. 28. 19 ; 39. 12.

שָׁבוּ ׀, ׀ Kal pret. 3 pers. pl. ; for ׀ see lett. ׀   שוב

שָׁבוּ Kal pret. 3 pers. pl. . .   שבה

ᵃ 1 Sa. 16. 7.   ᵉ Ps. 73. 26.   ⁱ Eze. 5. 10.   ᵐ Pr. 5. 11.   ᵖ Hab. 1. 7   ᵗ Ge. 35. 1.   ˣ Ho. 8. 6.   ᵇᵇ Je. 41. 14.   ᶠᶠ Je. 40. 5.
ᵇ Da. 7. 7, 19.   ᶠ Je. 51. 35.   ᵏ Is. 14. 30.   ⁿ Mi. 3. 2.   ᵍ Job 15. 10.   ᵘ Jos. 2. 16.   ʸ Je. 50. 19.   ᶜᶜ Est. 2. 14.   ᵍᵍ Ju. 5. 12.
ᶜ Le. 18. 17.   ᵍ Is. 44. 17.   ˡ Je. 15. 9.   ᵒ Ju. 6. 17.   ʳ Je. 30. 18.   ᵛ Ec. 5. 15 ; 11. 8.   ᶻ Eze. 39. 2.   ᵈᵈ 2 Sa. 15. 27.   ʰʰ Zec. 10. 9.
   Ex. 21. 10.

שְׁבוּ ^{וּ} Kal imp. pl. masc.; וּ bef. (:) .   ישב

שֵׁבוּ defect. for שׁוּבוּ (q. v.) .   שוב

שְׁבוּאֵל pr. name masc. .   שבה

שִׁבֻּלֵי Kh. שִׁבּוּלֵי, K. שְׁבִילֵי, noun masc. pl. constr. [from שְׁבִיל or שְׁבוּל] .   שבל

שָׁבוּם וּ Kal pret. 3 pers. pl., suff. 3 pers. pl. masc. .   שבה

שָׁבוֹעַ וּ Kal inf. abs. .   שבע

שָׁבוּעַ noun masc. sing., constr. שְׁבֻעַ pl. שְׁבֻעִים, dec. 3a & 1b (§ 32. rem. 1) .   שבע

שְׁבוּעָה noun fem. sing. dec. 10 .   שבע

שְׁבֻעַת id., constr. st. .   שבע

שְׁבוּעָתוֹ וּ id., suff. 3 pers. sing. masc.; וּ bef. (:) .   שבע

שָׁבוּר Kal part. act. sing. masc. .   שבר

שְׁבוֹר id. inf. const .   שבר

שְׁבוּת Kh. שבות; K. שְׁבִית noun fem. sing. d. 1 a .   שבה

שְׁבוֹת Kal inf. constr. .   שבה

שְׁבוּת noun fem. sing. dec. 1 a .   שבה

שְׁבוּתְהֶן id., suff. 3 pers. pl. fem. (Kh. שְׁבוּתְהֶן), K. שְׁבִיתְהֶן from שְׁבִית .   שבה

שְׁבוּתֵיכֶם id. pl., suff. 2 pers. pl. masc. .   שבה

שְׁבוּתְךָ id. sing., suff. 2 pers. sing. masc. .   שבה

שְׁבוּתָם id. sing., suff. 3 pers. pl. masc., K. שְׁבוּתָם from שְׁבִיתָם .   שבה

שְׁבוּתֵנוּ id. sing., suff. 1 pers. pl. (Kh. שְׁבוּתֵנוּ), K. שְׁבִיתֵנוּ from שְׁבִית .   שבה

שָׁבַח Pi. שִׁבַּח.—I. to soothe, calm, quiet, Ps. 89. 10; Pr. 29. 11.—II. to praise, laud.—III. to pronounce happy, Ec. 4. 2. Hiph. to still, calm, Ps 65. 8. Hithp. to praise oneself, to boast of, with בְ.

שְׁבַח Ch. Pa. to praise, laud.

יִשְׁבָּח (soothing) pr. name masc. 1 Ch. 4. 17.

מְשַׁבֵּחַ וּ Piel part. sing. masc. [for מְשַׁבֵּחַ comp. § 10. rem. 6] .   שבח

שַׁבַּחוּ וּ Ch. Pael pret. 3 pers. pl. masc. .   שבח

שַׁבְּחֻהוּ Piel imp. pl. masc., suff. 3 pers. sing. masc. .   שבח

שַׁבְּחִי id. imp. sing. fem. .   שבח

שַׁבַּחְתָּ Ch. Pael pret. 2 pers. sing. masc. .   שבח

שַׁבַּחְתֵּ Ch. id. pret. 1 pers. sing. .   שבח

שִׁבַּחְתִּי וּ Piel pret. 1 pers. sing. .   שבח

שֵׁבֶט וּ m. dec. 6 b (in pause שָׁבֶט, from שֵׁבֶט=שִׁבְט § 35. rem. 2).—I. staff.—II. rod, for punishment; also as a measure, and meton. a portion measured

off.—III. a sceptre, of a leader, chief, king.—IV. a tribe.—V. a spear, lance, 2 Sa. 18. 14.

שְׁבַט Ch. 3 b, tribe.

שַׁרְבִּיט masc. i. q. שֵׁבֶט (with ר inserted) a sceptre.

שְׁבָט the eleventh month of the Hebrew year, corresponding to February and March, Zec. 1. 7.

שֵׁבֶט [for שֵׁבֶט § 35. r. 2] Seg. noun, see שֵׁבֶט שבט

שִׁבְטוֹ noun masc. sing., suff. 3 pers. sing. masc. from שֵׁבֶט dec. 6 b .   שבט

שִׁבְטֵי וּ id. pl., constr. st. [Chald. Ezr. 6. 17] .   שבט

שִׁבְטֶיהָ id. pl., suff. 3 pers. sing. fem. .   שבט

שִׁבְטֶיךָ id. pl., suff. 2 pers. sing. masc. .   שבט

שִׁבְטֵיכֶם id. pl., suff. 2 pers. pl. masc. .   שבט

שְׁבָטִים id. pl., abs. st. .   שבט

שִׁבְטְךָ id. sing., suff. 2 pers. sing. masc. .   שבט

שָׁבַי וּ Ch. Peal part. act. pl. c. from שְׁבָ dec. 1 a (comp. § 30. No. 3) .   שיב

שְׁבִי וּ Kal imp. sing. fem.; וּ bef. (:) .   ישב

שְׁבִי noun masc. sing. dec. 6 i (§ 35. rem. 14) .   שבה

שֶׁבִי pr. name masc. for שׁוֹבִי .   שבה

שֹׁבִי וּ pr. name masc. .   שבה

שֵׁבִי defect. for שׁוֹבִי (q. v.) .   שוב

שְׁבִיא וּ for Keri שְׁבִי (q. v.) .   שוב

שְׁבִיב noun masc. sing., constr. of [שָׁבִיב] dec. 3 a .   שבב

שְׁבִיבָא Ch. noun masc. sing., emph. of [שְׁבִיב] d. 1 a .   שבב

שְׁבִיבִין Ch. id. pl., abs. st. .   שבב

שָׁבֶיהָ וּ Kal part. act. pl. masc., suff. 3 pers. sing. fem. from שָׁבָ dec. 1 a (§ 30. No. 3) .   שוב

שִׁבְיָה noun fem. sing. .   שבה

שִׁבְיָה וּ noun fem. sing. .   שבה

שִׁבְיָהּ noun masc. sing., suff. 3 pers. sing. fem. from שְׁבִי dec. 6 i .   שבה

שֹׁבֶיהֶם Kal part. act. pl. masc., suff. 3 pers. pl. masc. from שָׁבָה dec. 9a .   שבה

שִׁבְיוֹ noun m. s., suff. 3 pers. s. m. fr. שְׁבִי d. 6 i .   שבה

שִׁבְיְךָ id. with suff. 2 pers. sing. masc. .   שבה

שִׁבְיְכֶם וּ id., suff. 2 p. pl. m. (§ 35. r. 14); וּ bef. (:) .   שבה

שְׁבִילְךָ וּ Kh. לָךְ, K. לְךָ noun masc. pl. or sing., suff. 2 pers. sing. m. fr. [שְׁבִיל] d. 1 a; וּ id. .   שבל

שָׁבִים Kal part. act. m., pl. of שָׁבָ d. 1 a (§ 30. No. 3) .   שוב

שְׁבִים noun m. s., suff. 3 pers. pl. m. fr. שְׁבִי d. 6 i .   שבה

שֹׁבִים Kal part. act. masc. pl. [of שָׁבָה] dec. 9a .   שבה

שָׁבִיתָ וּ id. pret. 2 pers. sing. masc. .   שבה

שְׁבִית וּ n. f. s. d. 1 a; Kh. שבית, K. שְׁבוּת; וּ bef. (:) .   שבה

Footnotes

a Je. 13. 18; 29. 5, 28.   b Je. 18. 15.   c Da. 9. 27.   d Ec. 8. 2.

e Le. 22. 22.   f Je. 28. 12.   g Ps. 85. 2.   h Ob. 11.   i Eze. 16. 53.

k Zep. 3. 20.   l De. 30. 3.   m Zep. 2. 7.   n Ps. 126. 4.   o Ec. 4. 2.

p Da. 5. 4.   q Ps. 117. 1.   r Ps. 147. 12.   s Da. 5. 23.   t Da. 4. 31.

u Ec. 8. 15.   v Eze. 37. 19.   w Is. 19. 13.   x Ps. 23. 4.   y Ezr. 6. 14.

z Is. 47. 1.   a Je. 31. 21.   b Job 6. 20.   c Job 18. 5.   d Nu. 31. 19.

e Da. 3. 23.   f Da. 7. 9.   g Is. 1. 27.   h Is. 52. 2.

i De. 32. 42.   k De. 21. 13.   l De. 21. 10.   m Ju. 5. 12.

n Ps. 77. 20.   o Is. 14. 2.   p De. 21. 10.   q Eze. 16. 53.

שָׁבָה   id. pl., suff. 2 pers. sing. fem. . . .   שְׁבִיתֲיִךְ•

שָׁבָה   id. sing., suff. 2 p. s. f. Kh. שְׁבִיתֵךְ K.   שְׁבִיתָֽךְ

שָׁבָה   id. sing., suff. 2 p. pl. m., Kh. שְׁבִי K. שְׁבוּ   שְׁבִיתְכֶם•

שָׁבָה   Kal pret. 2 pers. pl. masc. . .   שְׁבִיתֶם•

שָׁבַךְ

Root not used; i. q. סָבַךְ to interweave.

שָׂבָךְ masc. only pl. שְׂבָכִים ornaments of network, 1 Ki. 7. 17.

שְׂבָכָה fem.—I. a net, Job 18. 8.—II. network, ornamenting the capitals of pillars.—III. lattice of a window, 2 Ki. 1. 2.

שֹׂבֶךְ masc. thick branches, thicket, 2 Sa. 18. 9.ᵃ

שַׂבְּכָא Chald. noun fem. sing. see סַבְּכָא.

שׂבך   noun fem. sing., pl. שְׂבָכוֹת & bef. (:)   שְׂבָכָה

שׂבך   noun masc., pl. of [שָׂבָךְ] d. 6 (§ 35. r. 10)   שְׂבָכִים•

כרם   preff. שְׁ, & בְ for בְּהַ)(n. m. pl. of כֶּרֶם d. 6a   שְׁבַּכְּרְמִים•

שָׁבַל

Root not used; according to Gesenius, coll. with the Arab., (a) to go: (b) to rise, grow; (c) to flow copiously.

שֹׁבֶל masc. a train of a robe, Is. 47. 2,ᵇ Eng. vers. "locks" of hair, both from the idea of flowing.

שַׁבְּלוּל masc. a snail, so called from the slimy trail it leaves as it goes along, Ps. 58. 9.ᵈ

שִׁבֹּלֶת fem. (pl. שִׁבֳּלִים § 44. No. 2; constr. שִׁבֳּלֵי Zec. 4. 12,ᶜ where most codices read שִׁבֳּלֵי, from a form שִׁבֶּלֶת).—I. an ear of corn.—II. a branch, Zec. 4. 12.—III. stream, flood.

שׁוֹבָל (shoot) pr. name m. of two different persons.

שׁבל   שְׁבִיל Kh. שְׁבִיל K. masc. dec. 1 a, way, path

שׁבל   noun masc. sing.   שְׁבִיל

שׁבל   noun masc. sing. . .   שַׁבְּלוּל

שׁבל   or שִׁבֳּלֵי noun fem. pl. constr. see שִׁבֹּלֶת under the R.   שִׁבֳּלֵי•

שׁבל   noun fem., pl. of the foll. .   שִׁבֳּלִיʼᵐ

שׁבל   noun fem. sing. dec. 13 c (§ 44. No. 2)   שִׁבֹּלֶת

שָׁבָה   Kal pret. 3 pers. sing. masc. (שָׁבָה), suff. 3 pers. pl. masc. (§ 24. rem. 21)   שָׁבָם

  pr. name of a city in the tribe of Reuben;   שְׂבָם

  & bef. (:)ʼ   שְׂבָמָה

שָׁבַן

Root not used; Arab. to be tender, delicate.

שֶׁבְנָה, שֶׁבְנָא (tenderness, tender) pr. name of a scribe or secretary of king Hezekiah.

שְׁבַנְיָה (tender one of the Lord) pr. name masc. of several persons; the one of Ne. 10. 5; 12. 14, is written שְׁבַנְיָה in Ne. 12. 3.

בנה   pref. שְׁ)(noun m. s., constr. of בֵּן irr. (§ 15)   שְׁבֶּן•

שֶׁבְנָא }

שֶׁבְנָה } pr. name masc. . .   שבן

ישׁב   Kal imp. pl. fem. . . .   שֵׁבְנָה•

שׁוב   id. pret. 1 pers. pl. . . .   שַׁבְנוּ

שְׁבַנְיָה }

שְׁבַנְיָהוּ } pr. name masc.; & bef. (:)   שבן

שָׁבַם

Root not used; perh. i. q. שָׁבַץ to mingle, interweave.

שְׁבִיסִים masc. pl. (of שָׁבִים) cap of network, cauls, Is. 3. 18; others (i. q. Arab. שְׁבִישָׁא), little suns, as an ornament, comp. שַׂהֲרֹנִים.

שָׂבַע

[also שָׂבֵעַ, comp. Is. 9. 19; De. 14. 29; 26. 12] fut. יִשְׂבַּע to be or become satiated, satisfied, filled, espec. with food, less frequently with drink; with acc., מִן, בְּ, of the thing with which; metaph. to be satisfied with any thing, to have enough. Pi. to satisfy, satiate. Hiph. to satisfy, satiate, with acc., מִן, בְּ, of the thing, acc., לְ, of the person; metaph. Ps. 91. 16.ⁿ

שֹׂבַע masc. abundance, plenty.

שָׂבֵעַ masc. d. 5 a, satiated, satisfied, full; metaph. enough, abounding, rich.

שֹׂבַע masc. dec. 6 c (§ 35. rem. 5), satiety, fulness, abundance; לְשֹׂבַע to the full.

שָׂבְעָה, שׇׂבְעָה fem. (no pl.) idem.

שֶׁבַע

שֶׁבַע ו, רֵ (constr. שְׁבַע § 35. rem. 7) fem. שִׁבְעָה masc. (constr. שִׁבְעַת).—I. num. card. seven; שֶׁבַע שָׁנִים seven years, and with the constr. שִׁבְעַת יָמִים seven days; less frequently preceded by the noun, as אֵילִים שִׁבְעָה seven rams; also as an ordinal when preceded by a noun in the construct state, as שְׁנַת שֶׁבַע seventh year; שִׁבְעָה שִׁבְעָה by sevens; שִׁבְעָה עָשָׂר masc. & שְׁבַע עֶשְׂרֵה fem. seventeen.— II. (שֶׁבַע) adv. seven times, Ps. 119. 164; Pr. 24. 16. Du. שִׁבְעָתַיִם sevenfold. Pl. שִׁבְעִים (§ 35. rem. 16) seventy. For another שֶׁבַע (& שִׁבְעָה see) below.

שִׁבְעָה Chald. masc. seven.

שִׁבְעָנָה masc. seven, Job 42. 13.

שָׁבוּעַ masc. (constr. שְׁבוּעַ, pl. c. שְׁבֻעוֹת, du. שְׁבֻעַיִם d. 3 a; but also pl. (abs.) שְׁבֻעוֹת, שְׁבֻעִים with suff. שְׁבֻעוֹתֵיכֶם § 32. rem. 1).—I. a week, seven days; חַג שָׁבֻעוֹת the feast of weeks, pentecost. —II. a week of years, comp. Da. 9. 24, seq.

שְׁבִיעִי masc. שְׁבִיעִית fem. adj. ordin. from שֶׁבַע, *seventh.*

שָׁבַע *to swear* (since oaths were usually confirmed by seven victims), Eze. 21. 28. Niph. נִשְׁבַּע *to swear*, with בְּ *by*, לְ *to*, any thing or any one; with acc. *to promise with an oath*, comp. Ge. 50. 24. Hiph. I. *to cause to swear.*—II. *to adjure, charge solemnly.*

שֶׁבַע (*oath*) pr. name—I. of two men, 2 Sa. 20. 1; 1 Ch. 5. 13.—II. of a town in the tribe of Simeon, Jos. 19. 2.—III. see under בְּאֵר.—IV. בְּאֵר שֶׁבַע Ge. 26. 33, i. q. בְּאֵר שֶׁבַע.

שְׁבוּעָה, שְׁבֻעָה fem. dec. 10.—I. *an oath.*—II. *oath of imprecation, curse.*

אֱלִישֶׁבַע (*adjuration*) pr. name masc. 1 Ch. 4. 21.

שֶׁבַע noun masc. sing. . . . שבע
שֶׁבַע for בְּאֵר שֶׁבַע (§ 35. r. 2) pr. n. in compos. באר
שֶׁבַע adj. masc. sing. dec. 5 a . . שבע
שֶׁבַע, שֶׁבַע num. card., constr. of שֶׁבַע (§ 35. rem. 7); בֶּ bef. (:), for the form וּשְׁבַע comp. שָׂדֶה, זָהָב . . שבע
שֶׁבַע Kal imp. or adj. m. s., con. of שֶׁבַע d. 5 a; id. שבע
שֶׁבַע noun masc. sing., constr. of שָׂבוּעַ dec. 3 a שבע
שֶׁבַע noun masc. sing. dec. 6 c (§ 35. rem. 5) . שבע
שָׁבְעָה Kal pret. 3 pers. sing. fem. . . שבע
שִׁבְעָה noun fem. sing. (no pl.) . . . שבע
שְׁבֻעָה adj. fem. sing., from שָׂבַע masc. . שבע
שְׁבֻעָה defect. for שְׁבוּעָה (q. v.) . . . שבע
שִׁבְעָה num. card. masc., from שֶׁבַע fem. שבע
שָׁבְעוּ, שָׁבְעוּ Kal pret. 3 pers. pl. (§ 8. rem. 7) . שבע
שְׁבֻעוֹת noun masc. pl. abs. from שָׂבוּעַ (§ 32. rem. 1) שבע
שְׁבֻעוֹת id. constr. st. (Eze. 45. 21); or pl. of שְׁבוּעָה שבע
שְׁבֻעֵי Kal part. pass. pl. constr. masc. [from שָׂבוּעַ] dec. 3 a . . . שבע
שָׁבֻעִים noun masc., pl. of שָׂבוּעַ (§ 32. rem. 1) שבע
שִׁבְעִים adj. masc., pl. of שֶׁבַע dec. 5 a . שבע
שִׁבְעַיִם noun masc., du. of שָׂבוּעַ dec. 3 a שבע
שִׁבְעִים num. card. com., pl. of שֶׁבַע fem. שבע
שִׁבְעֲךָ noun masc. sing., suff. 2 pers. sing. masc. from שֶׁבַע dec. 6 c (§ 35. rem. 5) . שבע
שִׁבְעָנָה num. i. q. שִׁבְעָה . . . שבע
שְׁבַעֲנֶנוּ Kal pret. 1 pers. pl. . . . שבע
שַׁבְּעֵנוּ Piel imp. sing. masc. [שַׁבֵּעַ], suff. 1 pers. pl. שבע
שָׁבַעְתָּ, שָׁבַעְתָּ Kal pret. 2 pers. sing. masc. (§ 8. rem. 7) . . . שבע
שָׁבַעַתְּ id. pret. 2 pers. sing. fem. . . שבע

שְׁבֻעֹת defect. for שְׁבֻעוֹת (q. v.) . . שבע
שְׁבֻעַת defect. for שְׁבֻעוֹת (q. v.) . . שבע
שְׁבֻעֹת pl. c. of שָׂבוּעַ, see שְׁבֻעוֹת . . שבע
שִׁבְעַת num. card. masc., constr. of שִׁבְעָה from שֶׁבַע fem. . . . שבע
שִׁבְעַת noun fem. sing., constr. of שִׁבְעָה שבע
שָׁבַעְתִּי Kal pret. 1 pers. sing. . . שבע
שִׁבְעָתַיִם Kh. q. v.; K. שִׁבְעָתַיִם, num. [prop. fr. שִׁבְעָה i. q. שִׁבְעָה] with suff. 3 pers. pl. m. שבע
שִׁבְעָתַיִם du. of שִׁבְעָה num. . . שבע
שָׁבְעָתֵךְ noun fem. s., suff. 2 p. s. fem. fr. שָׁבְעָה (no pl.) שבע
שְׁבַעְתֶּם Kal pret. 2 pers. pl. masc.; וּ, for וְ, conv. שבע

שָׁבַץ Root not used; Syr. *to mingle, interweave*; Arab. (conj. V) *to be interwoven, intricate* (Gesenius, Winer, and others), only Pi. *to work* or *weave in checker-work*, Ex. 28. 39; Eng. vers. "embroider." Pu. *to be set, enchased*, of precious stones, Ex. 28. 20.

שָׁבָץ masc. *perplexity, terror*, 2 Sa. 1. 9; others, *giddiness;* according to the Rabbins, *the cramp.*

מִשְׁבְּצֹת fem. only pl. מִשְׁבְּצוֹת—I. *textures, cloth interwoven* or *embroidered* with gold threads, Ps. 45. 14.—II. *settings* or *bezels* for precious stones.

תַּשְׁבֵּץ masc. *checker-work* or *embroidery*, Ex. 28. 4.

שִׁבַּצְתָּ Piel pret. 2 pers. sing. masc. . . שבץ

[שְׁבַק] *to leave.* Ithpe. *to be left*, Da. 2. 44.

שׁוֹבֵק (*forsaking*) pr. name masc. Ne. 10. 21.

יִשְׁבָּק (id.) pr. name of a son of Abraham by Keturah.

שְׁבֻקוּ Chald. Peal imp. pl. masc. . שבק

[שָׁבַר] *to view, examine*, with בְּ, Ne. 2. 13, 15. Pi. *to look, wait for, hope*, with לְ, אֶל.

שֵׂבֶר masc. dec. 6 b, *hope*, Ps. 119. 116; 146. 5.

שָׁבַר fut. יִשְׁבֹּר.—I. *to break, break in pieces;* metaph. *to break, quench* the thirst, Ps. 104. 11; *to break, afflict the heart.*—II. *to tear*, as a wild beast.—III. *to break down, destroy.*—IV. *to define, assign*, with עַל *to* or *for*, Job 38. 10.—V. (denom. from שֶׁבֶר q. v.) *to buy* or *sell corn.* Niph. pass. of Kal, Nos. I, II & III. Pi. שִׁבַּר (§ 10. rem. 1) *to break, shiver in pieces.* Hiph. I. *to cause to break through*, of the fœtus, Is. 66. 9.—II. *to sell corn.* Hoph. *to be broken, afflicted, distressed*, Je. 8. 21.

a 1 Ki. 14. 21.   c Is. 56. 11.   f Ho. 13. 6.   m Da. 9. 25.   p De. 23. 25.   r Ps. 90. 14.   x Zec. 8. 17.   z Is. 1. 11.   d Eze. 16. 28.
b Ge. 29. 27, 28.   d Pr. 27. 7.   h De. 16. 9, 10.   n 1 Sa. 2. 5.   q Job 42. 18.   s Hab. 2. 16.   y Je. 5. 24.   b Job 7. 4.   e Ex. 28. 39.
c Ps. 16. 11.   e Nu. 30. 3.   i Eze. 21. 28.   o Le. 12. 5.   r Ps. 123. 3.   t Eze. 16. 28, 29.   z Eze. 16. 49.   c 2 Sa. 21. 9.   f Da. 12. 20.
d Jer. 46. 10.   k Is. 9. 19.   l Pr. 20. 13.   oo Ex. 34. 22.

שֶׁבֶר =שָׁבַר masc. dec. 6 b (in pause שָׁבֶר, from שָׁבַר § 35. rem. 2).—I. *a breaking, breach, fracture*; metaph. *sorrow, vexation, calamity.*—II. (prop. *definition,* comp. Kal. No. IV) *solution, interpretation,* Ju. 7. 15.—III. *destruction, ruin.*—IV. *terror,* Job 41. 17.

שֶׁבֶר masc. dec. 6 a (with suff. שִׁבְרוֹ), *grain, corn.* Etym. uncertain.

שִׁבָּרוֹן masc. dec. 3 c.—I. *breaking, pain,* Eze. 21. 11.—II. *destruction, ruin,* Je. 17. 18.

מִשְׁבָּר masc. *matrix;* constr. מִשְׁבַּר (§ 36. r. 1).

מִשְׁבָּר masc. dec. 2 b, *waves, breakers.*

שֻׁבַּר שבר Kal pret. 3 pers. s. masc. for שֻׁבַּר (§ 8. r. 7)

שֶׁבֶר שבר for שֶׁבֶר (q. v.) Seg. noun masc., see under the R.

שַׁבֵּר שבר ְ Piel inf. constr.

שֶׁבֶר שבר noun masc. sing. dec. 6 b

שֶׁבֶר שבר ְ, ְ noun masc. sing. (suff. שִׁבְרִי) d. 6 a; also pr. name; for ְ see lett. ְ

שְׁבֹר שבר Kal imp. sing. masc.

שִׁבֵּר שבר ְ Piel pret. 3 pers. sing. masc. (§ 15. rem. 1)

שֹׁבֵר שבר Kal part. act. sing. masc. dec. 7 b

שֹׁבֵר שבר Kal part. act. sing. masc.

שָׁבְרָה שבר id. pret. 3 pers. sing. fem.

שְׁבָרָהּ שבר ְ id. pret. 3 pers. sing. masc., suff. 3 pers. sing. fem.; ְ, for ְ, conv.

שִׁבְרָהּ שבר noun masc. sing., suff. 3 pers. sing. fem. from שֶׁבֶר dec. 6 b

שָׁבְרוּ שבר Kal pret. 3 pers. pl.

שִׁבְרוֹ שבר noun masc. sing., suff. 3 pers. sing. masc. from שֶׁבֶר or שֶׁבֶר dec. 6 b

שִׁבְרוֹ שבר noun masc. sing., suff. 3 pers. sing. masc. from [שֶׁבֶר] dec. 6 b

שִׁבְּרוּ שבר Piel pret. 3 pers. pl. (comp. § 8. rem. 7)

שִׁבְּרוּ שבר Piel pret. 3 pers. pl.

שִׁבְרוּ שבר ְ Kal imp. pl. masc.

שִׁבָּרוֹן שבר noun masc. sing. dec. 3 c

שִׁבְרִי שבר noun masc. sing., suff. 1 pers. sing. from שֶׁבֶר dec. 6 b

שְׁבָרֶיהָ שבר id. pl., suff. 3 pers. sing. fem.

שֹׁבְרִים שבר Kal part. act. masc., pl. of שֹׁבֵר dec. 7 b

שְׁבַרְךָ שבר id. pret. 3 pers. s. masc., suff. 2 pers. s. fem.

שִׁבְרֵךְ שבר noun masc. sing., suff. 2 pers. sing. fem. from שֶׁבֶר dec. 6 b

שִׁבְרְךָ שבר id., suff. 2 pers. sing. masc.

שְׁבָרָם שבר d. 6 a noun masc. s., suff. 3 pers. pl. m. fr. שֶׁבֶר

שְׁבֹרֵם שבר Kal imp. sing. masc., suff. 3 pers. pl. masc.

שָׁבַרְתְּ שבר id. pret. 3 pers. s. m., acc. shifted by conv. ְ (§ 8. rem. 7)

שָׁבַרְתָּ שבר

שִׁבַּרְתָּ שבר Piel pret. 2 pers. sing. masc.

שָׁבַרְתִּי שבר Kal pret. 1 pers. sing., acc. shifted by conv. ְ (§ 8. rem. 7)

שָׁבַרְתִּי שבר

שִׁבַּרְתִּי שבר Piel pret. 1 pers. sing.

שְׁבַרְתֶּם שבר ְ Piel pret. 2 pers. pl. masc.

שְׁבֵשׁ . Chald. Ithpa. *to be perplexed,* Da. 5. 9.

שֶׁבְּשִׁפְלֵנוּ שפל preff. שֶׁ & בְּ) noun masc. sing., suff. 1 pers. pl. from שֵׁפֶל dec. 6 b

שָׁבַת fut. יִשְׁבֹּת, יֵשֵׁב.—I. *to rest* from labour, with מִן; of land, *to lie uncultivated.*—II. *to cease, desist* with מִן & inf., from doing any thing.—III. *to cease, be interrupted,* Ne. 6. 3.—IV. *to cease to be, have an end.*—V. with שַׁבָּת *to keep the sabbath,* Le. 23. 32. Niph. *to cease, have an end.* Hiph. I. *to make* or *let rest* from labour; of work, *to intermit.*—II. *to restrain, still,* Ps. 8. 3.—III. *to cause to cease* from doing any thing, with לְבִלְתִּי, מִן & inf.—IV. *to make to cease, to interrupt, put an end to.*—V. *to put away, remove.*

שֶׁבֶת masc. dec. 6 a (with suff. שִׁבְתּוֹ).—I. *a ceasing, cessation.*—II. *interruption, loss of time,* Ex. 21. 19.

שַׁבָּת com. (constr. שַׁבַּת, with suff. שַׁבַּתּוֹ; pl. שַׁבָּתוֹת, constr. שַׁבְּתוֹת) *day of rest, sabbath;* שַׁבַּת שָׁנִים *a sabbath of years,* every seventh year. שַׁבָּתוֹן masc. id.; שַׁבַּת שַׁבָּתוֹן *a great sabbath.* שַׁבְּתַי (*sabbath-born*) pr. name of a man. מִשְׁבָּת m. pl. מִשְׁבַּתִּים *destruction, ruin,* La. 1. 7.

שָׁבַת שוב ְ Kal pret. 3 pers. sing. fem. for שָׁבָה, (comp. § 8. rem. 3 & § 24. rem. 1)

שֶׁבֶת שבת for שֶׁבֶת Seg. n. [as if from שָׁבַת § 35. rem. 2 & 3, but see under the R.]

שַׁבָּת שבת ְ noun com. sing. (see the inflexion of this word in its place under the R.)

שַׁבַּת שבת id., constr. st.

שַׁבַּתָּ שוב Kal pret. 2 pers. sing. masc.; acc. shifted by conv. ְ (comp. § 8. rem. 7)

שֶׁבֶת שוב

שֶׁבֶת שוב Kal inf. constr. (suff. שִׁבְתִּי) § 35. rem. 3) d. 13

שִׁבְתּוֹ שבת noun masc. sing. (suff. שִׁבְתּוֹ) dec. 6 a

ᵃ Ps. 105. 16. ᵍ Ps. 10. 15. ᵐ Is. 30. 13. ᵗ Est. 9. 1. ᵛ Ps. 60. 4. ᵉ Ge. 42. 26. ᵏ Je. 19. 10. ᵈ De. 12. 3. ᵗ Is. 30. 7.
ᵇ Pr. 17. 19. ᶠ Ex. 9. 25. ʰ Je. 5. 5. ᵘ Ge. 42. 2. ᵒ Ge. 47. 14. ʳ Je. 17. 18. ˢ Eze. 30. 21. ˣ Ps. 136. 23. ᵏ Ps. 85. 2.
ᶜ Ex. 23. 24. ᵍ Ge. 29. 21. ᵖ Ps. 146. 5. ᵛ Je. 17. 18. ᵂ Eze. 27. 26. ᵗ Je. 28. 13. ʸ Ps. 119. 165. ᶻ Eze. 46. 17. ˡ Pr. 20. 3.
ᵈ Am. 6. 6. ʰ Is. 30. 14. ⁿ 2 Ch. 28. 17. ⁿ Je. 15. 15. ᵉ Eze. 124. 9.

שָׁבְתָה־
וַתִּשְׁבֹּת } Kal pret. 3 pers. sing. fem. (§ 8 rem. 7) שבת

שַׁבְתָּהּ־ } noun com. sing., suff. 3 pers. sing. fem. from שַׁבָּת (q. v.) . . . שבת

שִׁבְתָּהּ־ Kal inf. (שֶׁבֶת), suff. 3 pers. sing. fem. dec. 13 (§ 35. rem. 3) . . . ישב

שָׁבְתוּ־ Kal pret. 3 pers. pl. [for שָׁבֲבוּ § 8. rem. 7] שבת

שִׁבְתּוֹ noun masc. sing., suff. 3 pers. sing. masc. from שֶׁבֶת dec. 6a . . . שבת

שִׁבְתּוֹ Kal inf. (שֶׁבֶת), suff. 3 pers. sing. masc. dec. 13 (§ 35. rem. 3) } . . ישב

שַׁבָּתוֹן noun masc. sing. . . . שבת

שַׁבְּתוֹת noun com. pl. abs. from שַׁבָּת (q. v.) . שבת

שַׁבְּתוֹתַי id. pl., suff. 1 pers. sing. . . . שבת

שַׁבְּתוֹתֶיהָ id. pl., suff. 3 pers. sing. fem. . שבת

שְׁבַתְיָ־ pr. name masc. . . . שבת

שַׁבְתִּי
וָ } Kal pret. 1 pers. sing.; acc. shifted by conv. וָ (§ 8. rem. 7) } שוב

שַׁבְתִּי for יָשַׁבְתִּי Kal pret. 1 pers. sing. (comp. יָרַד for רַד) ישב

שַׁבְתִּי־ Kal pret. 1 pers. sing.; for וָ see lett. וָ שיב

שִׁבְתִּי Kal inf. (שֶׁבֶת), suff. 1 p. s. d. 13 (§ 35. r. 3) ישב

שִׁבְתְּךָ
וָ } id. with suff. 2 pers. sing. masc. . ישב

שַׁבַּתְּכֶם־ noun com. sing., suff. 2 pers. pl. masc. from שַׁבָּת (q. v.) . . . . שבת

שַׁבְתֶּם־ } Kal pret. 2 pers. pl. masc. . . שוב

שִׁבְתְּכֶם Kal inf. (שֶׁבֶת), suff. 3 pers. pl. masc. dec. 13 (§ 35. rem. 3) ישב

שַׁבָּתֹת n. com. pl., constr. of שַׁבָּתוֹת, fr. שַׁבָּת (q. v.) שבת

שַׁבְּתֹתַי id. pl., suff. 1 pers. sing. . . . שבת

שַׁבְּתֹתֶיהָ id. pl., suff. 3 pers. sing. fem. . שבת

[שָׂגָא] Kal not used; i. q. שָׂגָה to be or become great. Hiph. I. to make great, with לְ, Job 12. 23.—II. to magnify, laud, Job 36. 24.

שְׂגָא Chald. to become great, to increase.

שַׂגִּיא masc. great.

שַׂגִּיא Chald. masc., שַׂגִּיאָה fem. dec. 8a, adj.—I. great.—II. much, many.—III. adv. greatly.

שָׁגָא Root not used; i. q. שָׁגָה to err.

שְׁגִיאָה fem. dec. 10, error, sin through ignorance, Ps. 19. 13. Also

שָׁגֵא (erring) pr. name masc. 1 Ch. 11. 34.

[שָׂגֵב] I. to be lifted, raised up, Job 5. 11.—II. to be high, inaccessible, De. 2. 36. Niph. I. to be high, Pr.

18. 11.—II. to be exalted.—III. to be high, secure, safe, Pr. 18. 10.—IV. to be high, difficult to comprehend, Ps. 139. 6. Pi. I. to raise, set in security.—II. to make powerful, to strengthen, Is. 9. 10. Pu. pass. of Pi. No. I, Pr. 29. 25. Hiph. to be exalted, Job 36. 22.

שְׂגוּב (elevated) pr. name masc.—I. 1 Ch. 2. 21, 22.—II. 1 Ki. 16. 34, K., שְׂגִיב Kh.

מִשְׂגָּב masc. dec. 8a.—I. hill, rock, strong place.—II. refuge.—III. pr. name of a town in Moab, Je. 48. 1.

שָׂגְבָה־ Kal pret. 3 pers. sing. fem. . . שגב

שָׂגְבוּ־ id. pret. 3 pers. pl. . . . . שגב

שָׁגַג (§ 8. rem. 7) to err, commit an error; inf. שֵׁג, Ge. 6. 3.

שְׁגָגָה fem. d. 11c, error, sin through ignorance.

שֹׁגֵג Kal part. act. sing. masc. . . . שגג

שְׁגָגָה noun fem. sing. dec. 11c . . . שגג

שִׁגְגָתוֹ id., suff. 3 pers. sing. masc. . . שגג

שִׁגְגָתָם id., suff. 3 pers. pl. masc. . . שגג

[שָׂגָה] to become great. Hiph. to increase, Ps. 73. 12.

[שָׁגָה] I. to wander, go astray.—II. to err, sin through ignorance. Hiph. I. to cause to go astray.—II. to let err, Ps. 119. 10.

שִׁגָּיוֹן masc. dec. 3c, a psalm, perh. composed on an occasion of wandering and persecution, or apostacy from God, Ps. 7. 1; Hab. 3. 1.

מִשְׁגֶּה masc. error, mistake, Ge. 43. 12.

שֹׁגֶה Kal part. act. sing. masc. dec. 9a . שנה

שָׁגוּ Kal pret. 3 pers. pl. . . . . שנה

שְׂגוּב pr. name masc.; וָ bef. (:) . . שגב

שָׁגַח Hiph. to look.

שַׂגִּיא Heb. & Chald. adj. masc. sing. . . שגא

שִׂגְאוֹת־ noun fem., pl. of שִׂגְיָאָה dec. 10 שנא

שַׂגִּיאָן Ch. adj. f. pl. [of שַׂגִּיאָה or שַׂגִּיָּא fr. שַׂגִּיא m.] שנא

שִׁגָּיוֹן noun masc. sing. dec. 3c . . . שנה

שִׁגְיֹנוֹת־ pl. of the preced. . . . . שנה

שָׁגִיתִי Kal pret. 1 pers. sing. . . . שנה

[שָׁגַל] to lie with a woman. Niph. & Pu. pass. Hence שגל

שֵׁגַל Heb. & Chald. fem. a queen . . שגל

שֻׁגְּלוּ pref. שְׁ)(Kal pret. 3 pers. pl. נלש

שֻׁגַּלְתְּ Pual pret. 2 pers. sing. fem. (K. שֻׁכַּבְתְּ) שגל

• 2 Ch. 36. 21.   d Ru. 2. 7.   g Le. 23. 15.   k 1 Sa. 12. 2.   • Job 5. 11.   p Le. 5. 18.   r Is. 28. 7.   t Ps. 7. 1.   x Ps. 45. 10.
• Le. 25. 2.   • La. 5. 14.   2 Ch. 36. 21.   i Le. 23. 32.   • Le. 5. 18.   • Nu. 15. 25.   • Ps. 19. 13   • Hab. 3. 1.   x Je. 3. 9.
• Ho. 2. 13.   • Ex. 21. 19.   f Ps. 23. 6.   m De. 2. 36.

שׁנל · שְׁגַלְתֵּהּ Ch. noun fem. pl., suff. 3 pers. sing. m. fr. שְׁגַל

שׁנל · שְׁגַלְתָּךְ Ch. id. pl., suff. 2 pers. sing. fem.

נמם · שֶׁגַּם pref. שֶׁ ✕ conj.

נמל · שֶׁנָּמַלְתְּ pref. id. ✕ Kal pret. 2 pers. sing. fem.

שָׁגַע · Pu. part. מְשֻׁגָּע maddened, mad; also applied contemptuously to prophets. Hithp. to act, behave like a madman, 1 Sa. 21. 15, 16.

שִׁגָּעוֹן masc. madness; impetuosity, 2 Ki. 9. 20.

שֶׁגֶר, שְׁגַר (constr. § 35. rem. 7) masc. the young, offspring. Chald. שְׁגַר to cast forth, eject.

שׁדה · שַׁד noun m. s., du. שָׁדַיִם, c. שְׁדֵי d. 2 (§ 31. r. 5)

שׁדד · שָׁד noun masc. sing.; for וְ see lett. ו.

שׁדה · שָׂד noun masc. sing. (i. q. שָׂר)

שָׂדַד Kal not used; coll. with the Arab. to be straight, even. Pi. to harrow.

שִׂדִּים (plains) pr. name, עֵמֶק הַשִּׂדִּים, the plain of the cities, Sodom and Gomorrah.

[שָׁדַד] pl. שָׁדָּדוּ, שַׁדּוּ, fut. with suff. יְשָׁדְּדֵם (§ 18. rem. 13 & 15).—I. to treat with violence, to oppress.—II. to attack, invade.—III. to plunder; part. שֹׁדֵד a plunderer.—IV. to lay waste, destroy, e. g. a land; part. pass. שָׁדוּד destroyed, dead, of a person, Ju. 5. 27. Niph. to be laid waste. Pi. to spoil, waste, ruin. Pu. pass. Po. i. q. Pi. Ho. 10. 2. Hoph. to be spoiled, laid waste.

שֹׁד, שׁוֹד masc.—I. violence, oppression.—II. wealth obtained by violence, extortion, Am. 3. 10.—III. devastation, ruin, destruction.

שִׁדָּה fem. dec. 10, prop. mistress, lady, hence, a wife, Ec. 2. 8 (Arab. שׁידה mistress); others female cupbearers (comp. Chald. שְׁדָא to pour out). Eng. vers. " musical instruments " (Arab. שׁדא שׁדו to sing).

שַׁדַּי masc. pl. The Almighty; Omnipotent (Arab. שׁדיד strong, vehement).

אַשְׁדּוֹד (strong-hold) pr. name, Ashdod, one of the principal cities of the Philistines. Gent. n. אַשְׁדּוֹדִי Ashdodite, fem. ־ית women of Ashdod; the latter also as an adv., in the language of Ashdod, Ne. 13. 23.

שׁדד · שֹׁדֵד Kal part. act. sing. masc. dec. 7 b.

שׁדד · שֻׁדַּד, שֹׁדַּד Pual pret. 3 pers. sing. masc.

שׁדד · שָׁדְּדָה, שָׁדְּדָה id. pret. 3 pers. sing. fem. (§ 10. rem. 5, comp. § 8. rem. 7)

שׁדד · שָׁדְדוּ Kal pret. 3 pers. pl.

שׁדד · שָׁדְדוּ id. imp. pl. masc. [for שָׁדּוּ § 18. rem. 13]

שׁדד · שֻׁדְּדוּ Pual pret. 3 pers. pl. (comp. § 8. rem. 7)

שׁדד · שֹׁדְדֵי, שֹׁדְדִים Kal part. act. pl. masc., constr. and abs. from שֹׁדֵד dec. 7 b.

שׁדד · שֻׁדַּדְנוּ Pual pret. 1 pers. pl. [for שֻׁדַּדְנוּ]

שָׂדֶה, וְ (שָׂדֶה) masc. dec. 9 b (pl. שָׂדוֹת, constr. שְׂדֵי, שְׂדוֹת).—I. plain, level tract of country; שְׂדֵה אֲרָם the plain of Syria, i. e. Mesopotamia.—II. field, piece of cultivated ground.—III. collect. the fields, the country.—IV. country, territory.

שָׂדַי masc. poet. for שָׂדֶה plain, field.

שָׁדָה Root not used; Arab. שׁרא to moisten, irrigate; Chald. to cast, shoot, pour out.

שַׁד masc. (du. שָׁדַיִם, constr. שְׁדֵי § 35. rem. 1), the breast, teat, spoken of men and animals.

שֹׁד masc. idem. Job 24. 9; Is. 60. 16.

שְׁדֵיאוּר (shedding or darting light) pr. name masc. Nu. 1. 5; 2. 10.

שׁדה · שָׂדֶהָ id. with suff. 3 pers. sing. fem.

שׁדה · שְׂדֵה, שָׂדֵה id. constr. st. (for the first form comp. וּשְׁבַע, וְזָהָב)

שׁדד · שָׂדֶהָ noun fem. sing. dec. 10

שׁדה · שָׂדֵהוּ noun m. s., suff. 3 pers. sing. m. fr. שָׂדֶה d. 9 b

שׁדד · שָׂדוֹד Kal inf. constr.

שׁדד · שָׂדוּד id. part. pass. sing. masc.

שׁדד · שְׁדָּדוּנִי id. pret. 3 pers. pl., suff. 1 pers. sing.

שׁרף · שְׂדֻפֹת Kal part. pass. pl. fem. [from שָׂדֻף masc.]

שׁדה · שָׂדוֹת noun masc. with pl. fem. term., abs. st., from שָׂדֶה dec. 9 b

שׁדד · שָׂדוֹת noun fem., pl. of שָׂדֶה dec. 10

שׁדה · שְׂדוֹתֵיהֶם noun masc. with pl. fem. term. and suff. 3 pers. pl. masc. from שָׂדֶה dec. 9 b

שׁדד · שְׂדוֹתֵיכֶם id. pl. fem., suff. 2 pers. pl. masc.

שׁדה · שָׂדַי, שָׂדָי noun masc. sing., poet. for שָׂדֶה

שׁדד · שָׁדַי n. m. pl., suff. 1 p. s. fr. שַׁד d. 2 (§ 31. r. 5)

שׁדד · שָׁדַי noun masc. [שַׁד] with the pl. term. ־ָי

שׁדה · שָׂדִי noun masc. s., suff. 1 pers. s. fr. שָׂדֶה d. 9 b

שׁדה · שְׂדֵי id. pl. constr. [of שָׂדִים] ccmp. שָׂדוֹת

שׁדד · שְׁדֵי n. m. du., constr. of שָׁדַיִם, fr. שַׁד d. 2 (§ 31. r. 5)

a Da. 5. 2, 3.   d Ps. 137. 8.   h Je. 10. 20.   l Eze. 32. 12.   p Je. 4. 20.   r Le. 25. 34.   s Ps. 17. 9.   u Ec. 2. 8.   c Ca. 1. 13; 8. 10.
b Da. 5. 23.   e Ex. 13. 12.   Na. 3. 7.   Je. 49. 28.   o Ob. 5.   f Ec. 2. 8.   g Ge. 41. 6.   t Je. 8. 10.   d Je. 32. 7, 8.
c Ec. 1. 17; 2. 15; f La. 4. 3.   Je. 48. 1.   Zec. 11. 2.   Mi. 2. 4.   2 Ki. 8. 3, 5.   Je. 32. 15.   1 Sa. 8. 14.   e 2 Sa. 1. 21.
8. 14.   g Is. 60. 16.

שְׁדֵיאוּר pr. name masc. . . . שׁדה

שָׁדֶיהָ n. m. du., suff. 3 p. s. f. fr. שַׁד d. 2 (§ 31. r. 5) שׁדה

שָׁדֵיהֶן id. du., suff. 3 pers. pl. fem. . שׁדה

שָׁדַיִך 'ו id. du., suff. 2 pers. sing. fem. . שׁדה

שָׁדֶיךָ noun m. pl., suff. 2 p. s. m. fr. שָׂדֶה d. 9b שׁדה

שַׁדַּיִם } noun masc., du. of שַׁד dec. 2 (§ 31. שׁדה
שָׁדַיִם 'ו } rem. 5) . . .

שָׁדִין pref. שַׁ ✗ Kh. דִּין q. v.; K. דֻּן n. m. s., see דון

שָׁדִינוּ noun masc. pl., suff. 1 pers. pl. fr. שָׂדֶה d. 9b שׁדה

שָׁדֶךָ } id. sing., suff. 2 pers. sing. masc. שׁדה
שָׂדְךָ }

שָׁדֵם Root not used; signification uncertain. Hence

שְׁדֵמָה fem. dec. 11c (§ 42. rem. 4).—I. *blasted corn*, i. q. שְׁדֵפָה Is. 37. 27.—II. pl. שְׁדֵמוֹת *fields*; espec. *corn fields*; also *vineyards*, De. 32. 32.

שָׁדַם וְ Kh. וְשַׁדָּם Kal pret. 3 pers. sing. masc. [שַׁד] with suff.: K. יְשָׁדֵם fut. 3 pers. sing. masc. [יָשֹׁד], suff. 3 pers. pl. masc. (§ 18. r. 5) שׁדד

שַׁדְמָה ו noun fem. sing. dec. 11c (§ 42. rem. 4); ו bef. (:) . . . שׁדם

שַׁדְמוֹת id. pl., constr. st. . . שׁדם

שַׁדְמוֹת ו id. pl., abs. st.; ו bef. (:) שׁדם

שָׁדַף [ ] *to blight*, as the east wind corn, Ge. 41. 6, 23, 27. Hence the two following.

שְׁדֵפָה ו fem. *blight* in corn, 2 Ki. 19. 26; ו bef. (:) שׁדף

שִׁדָּפוֹן masc. the same . . . שׁדף

שְׁדֻפוֹת Kal part. pass. pl. fem. [from שָׁדֻף masc.] שׁדף

שַׁדַּר Chald. Ithpa. *to exert oneself*, Da. 6. 15.
אֶשְׁתַּדּוּר Chald. masc. *rebellion*, Ezr. 4. 15, 19.

שַׁדְרַך Chald. pr. name, *Shadrach*, given to Hananiah, one of Daniel's companions at the court of Babylon.

שְׂדֵרֹת ו noun f. pl. abs. [fr. שְׂדֵרָה]; ו bef. (:) see סדר

שַׂדְתָּ ו Kal pret. 2 pers. sing. masc.; acc. shifted by conv. ו (§ 8. rem. 7) שׂיד

שָׂדֵהָתִיהָ ו noun masc. with pl. fem. term. & suff. 3 pers. sing. fem. from שָׂדֶה dec. 9; ו bef. (:) שׁדה

שְׂדֹתֵיהֶם id. pl., suff. 3 pers. sing. masc. שׁדה

שְׂדֹתֵינוּ 'ו id. pl., suff. 1 pers. pl.; ו bef. (:) שׁדה

שֶׂה 'ו } noun masc. s. constr. & abs. (§ 45); שׂיה
שֶׂה 'ו , ו for ו se lett. ו }

שֶׁהֱבֵאתִי K. ref. שַׁ ✗ Hiph. pret. 1 pers. sing., בוא
שֶׁהֲבֵאתִי Kh. } suff. 3 p. s. m. (§ 21. r. 13 & 14)

שְׁהַד Root not used; Syr. & Chald. סְהַד *to testify, bear witness.*
שָׂהֵד masc. dec. 5a, *a witness.*
שָׂהֲדוּ fem. (a Chald. & Syr. word, dec. 9b) *testimony*, Ge. 31. 47.

שָׁהָה [ ] prob. i. q. Arab. سها *to forget, neglect*, De. 32. 18, but comp. שָׁיָה.

שָׂהֲדוּתָא noun f. s. emph. [of שָׂהֲד] comp. Ch. d. 9b שׁהד

שָׂהֲדִי ו better שָׂהֲדִי n. m. s., suff. 1 p. s. [fr. שָׂהֵד] שׁהד

שֶׁהוּא pref. שֶׁ ✗ pron. pers. 3 pers. sing. masc. . הוא

שֶׁהָיָה pref. id. ✗ Kal pret. 3 pers. sing. masc. . היה

שֶׁהָיוּ pref. id. ✗ id. pret. 3 pers. pl. . היה

שֶׁהַיָּמִים preff. שֶׁ & הַ ✗ noun m. pl., irr. of יוֹם (§ 45) יום

שֶׁהִכָּה pref. שֶׁ ✗ Hiph. pret. 3 pers. sing. masc. נכה

שֹׁהַם 'ו masc.—I. *the onyx*, or *sardonyx*.—II. pr. name masc. 1 Ch. 24. 27.

שֶׁהֵם 'ו } pref. שֶׁ שֵׁ or ✗ pron. pers. masc. pl. הם
שֶׁהֵם 'ו }
שֶׁהֵם-ו }

שֶׁהַמֶּלֶך preff. שֶׁ & הַ ✗ noun masc. sing. dec. 6a מלך

שֶׁהַנְּחָלִים preff. id. ✗ noun masc., pl. of נַחַל dec. 6d נחל

שֶׁהַתַּקִּיף preff. id. (Kh. שֶׁהֶ) ✗ adj. masc. sing. . תקף

שָׁוָא Root not used; i. q. שָׁאָה, *to make a noise, crashing*; Arab. سوا *to be evil*, comp. רָעַע רוּעַ.
שֹׁוָא masc. dec. 1a, *destruction*, Ps. 35. 17; Prof. Lee, *mischievous design*, or *raging*.
שׁוֹאָה fem. dec. 10.—I. *storm, tempest*.—II. *destruction, ruin*.—III. *ruins, desolate places*.
שָׁוְא masc.—I. *evil, iniquity, wickedness*.—II. *evil, calamity, destruction*.—III. *worthlessness, vanity*; לַשָּׁוְא *in vain*.—IV. *falsehood, lie*; שֵׁמַע שָׁוְא *false report*; לַשָּׁוְא *in vain*.
שְׁוָא (*vanity*) pr. name masc.—I. 1 Ch. 2. 49.—II. 2 Sa. 20. 25, see שְׂרָיָה.
שֵׁו masc. i. q. שָׁוְא, Job 15. 31, Kheth.
שִׁיאוֹן (*desolation, ruins*) pr. name of a city in Issachar, Jos. 19. 19.
מְשׁוֹאָה fem. *desolation*, Zep. 1. 15; also *desolate places, ruins*.
מַשּׁוּאוֹת fem. pl. *desolations*, Ps. 73. 18; 74. 3.
תְּשׁוּאָה fem. *noise, tumult, clamour*.

שׁוּא 'ו noun masc. sing. . . . שׁוא

שׁוּעָ pr. name masc. . . . שׁוא

^a Ho. 2. 4.   ^f Job 19. 29.   ^k Is. 37. 27.   ^p 1 Ki. 6. 9.   ^u Ne. 5. 3, 4, 5.   ^z Job 16. 19.   ^e Ec. 7. 10.   ^j Ca. 6. 5.   ^o Ca. 1. 12.
^b Ese. 23. 3.   ^g Mi. 2. 4.   ^l Is. 16. 8.   ^q De. 27. 2, 4.   ^v De. 14. 4.   ^a Ec. 2. 22.   ^f Ps. 135. 8, 10.   ^k La. 4. 9.   ^p Ec. 1. 7.
^c 1 Ki. 2. 26.   ^h Le. 25. 3.   ^m Hab. 3. 17.   ^r Ne. 11. 30.   ^w Ca. 3. 4.   ^b Ec. 2. 7.   ^g Ex. 28. 20.   ^l Ec. 3. 18.   ^q Ec. 6. 5.
^d Joel 2. 16.   ⁱ 11. 3.   ⁿ Ge. 41. 23, 27.   ^s Ne. 5. 11.   ^y Ge. 31. 47.

שׁוֹא noun fem. sing. dec. 10 . . שׁוא

שׁוֹאֵנ Kal part. act. sing. masc. dec. 7 b   שׁאנ

שׁוֹאֵלֹ Kal part. act. sing. masc. dec. 7 b   שׁאל

שׁוֹאֵף Kal part. act. sing. masc. dec. 7 b   שׁאף

שׁוּב fut. יָשׁוּב, יָשֵׁב, ap. יָשֵׁב, וַיָּשָׁב.—I. *to turn, turn back, return*, const. with מִן *from*, מֵאַחֲרֵי *from following*, אֶל *to*, any one; with ה, לְ (local) *to a place. Trop. to return, to God,* withᵃ עַד, אֶל, לְ, בְּ, *and without addition, to be converted.*—II. *to return, go back, be restored*, as a field to the former possessor; a thing to its former state.—III. *to turn away, cease, desist*, with מֵעַל מֵאַחֲרֵי *from any one.*—IV. *to return to the doing of* any thing, joined with another verb, e. g. אָשׁוּבָה אֶרְעֶה *I will feed again*, Ge. 30. 31; comp. 2 Ki. 1. 11; Job 7. 7.—V. *to lead or bring back.* Pil. שׁוֹבֵב.—I. *to cause to return, bring back*, Je. 50. 19; trop. *to convert*, Is. 49. 5.—II. *to restore, renew;* with נֶפֶשׁ *to refresh*, Ps. 23. 3.—III. *to turn, take away,* Mi. 2. 4; trop. Is. 47. 10. Pul. part. *brought back,* Eze. 38. 8. Hiph. הֵשִׁיב.—I. *to cause to return, to bring or lead back;* hence *to drive back, repulse;* הֵ' חֵמָה *to turn away, avert anger,* also *to withdraw, appease anger;* הֵ' יָד *to withdraw the hand;* הֵ' פְּנֵי פּ' *to turn away the face* of any one, *to repulse him, deny his request;* הֵ' נֶפֶשׁ *to restore life, to revive, refresh;* הֵ' רוּחַ *to draw breath.*—II. *to return, give back, restore;* hence *to requite;* הֵ' דָּבָר *to return word, to answer,* and so with מִלִּין, אֲמָרִים, and simply הֵשִׁיב *to answer.*—III. *to recall, revoke* a declaration.—IV. *to bring, pay* tribute, offering.—V. *to turn, direct, apply;* with הֵ' יָדוֹ עַל or עַל־לֵב אֶל־לֵב *to lay to heart, to consider;* מֵעַל *to turn one's hand against* any one; with מֵעַל, *to turn away from.* Hoph. הוּשַׁב *to be brought, led, given back.*

שׁוּבָה fem. *returning,* sc. to God, Is. 30. 15.

שִׁיבָה fem. dec. 10, *a return*, concr. *those that return*, Ps. 126. 1.

שׁוֹבָב masc.—I. adj. *turning away, rebellious.*—II. pr. name (a) of a son of David; (b) 1 Ch. 2. 18ᵇ, שׁוֹבֵב, f. שׁוֹבֵבָה adj. *rebellious,* Je. 31. 22; 49. 4. יָשׁוּב (*turning himself*) pr. name masc.—I. Nu. 26. 24; patronym. יָשֻׁבִי.—II. Ezr. 10. 29.

יָשָׁבְעָם (*the people shall return*) pr. name of a man.

מְשׁוֹבָב (*restored*) pr. name masc. 1 Ch. 4. 34.

מְשׁוּבָה fem. dec. 10, *a returning, defection, apostacy;* as a concr. *rebellious, apostate,* Je. 3. 6, 8, 11, 12.

תְּשׁוּבָה fem. d. 10.—I. *a return.*—II. *an answer.*

שׁוֹב ᵈ'ַ, וַ Kal inf. abs.; for וַ see lett. ו . .

יָשֹׁב Kal inf. abs. for יָשׁוֹב

שׁוֹב ', וַ Kal imp. s.m.; or inf. d. 1 a; forוַ see lett. ו

שְׁבָה pr. name masc., see שְׁבוּאֵל . .

שׁוֹב וַ adj. masc. sing. dec. 2 b, also pr. name ᵍ

שׁוֹבְבָהᵏ Pilel pret. 3 pers. sing. fem. . .

שׁוֹבְבִים adj. masc., pl. of שׁוֹבֵב dec. 2 b

שׁוֹבְבִיםˣ K. שׁוֹבְבִים Pil. pret. 3 pers. pl., suff. 3 pers. pl. masc., Kh. שׁוֹבְבִים (q. v.) . .

שׁוֹבַבְתִּיךָⁱ וַ id. pret. 1 pers. s. with suff. 2 pers. s. m.

שׁוֹבַבְתֵּךְᵐ id. pret. 3 pers. sing. fem. (שׁוֹבְבָה), suff 2 pers. sing. fem. (§ 16. rem. 2)

שׁוּבָה Kal imp. sing. masc. (שׁוּב) with parag. ה

שׁוּבֵנוּ id. inf. (שׁוּב), suff. 3 pers. sing. masc. d. 1 a

שׁוּבוּ ', וַ id. imp. pl. masc.; for וַ see lett. ו

שׁוּבֵי id. part. pass. pl. constr. m. [fr. שׁוּב] d. 1 a

שׁוּבִי id. imp. sing. fem.

שׁוּבִי id. inf. (שׁוּב), suff. 1 pers. sing. dec. 1 a

שׁוֹבֵיהֶם Kal part. act. pl. m., suff. 3 p. pl. m. fr. שָׁבָה d. 9 a

שׁוֹבֵינוּ id. pl. with suff. 1 pers. pl. . .

שׁוֹבָךְ } pr. name masc., see שׁוֹפָךְ under שׁפך
שׁוֹבָךְ }

שׁוֹבָךְⁱ noun masc. sing. . . .

שׁוֹבְךָ } Kal inf. (שׁוּב), suff. 2 pers sing. masc.
שׁוֹבְךָⁱ } dec. 1 a }

שׁוֹבָל וַ pr. name masc.

שׁוֹבָל pr. name masc.

שׁוֹבֵנוּⁱ Kal imp. sing. masc., suff. 1 pers. pl.

שׁוֹבֵק pr. name masc.

שׁוּג Kal not used; i. q. סוּג *to hedge about.* Pilp. שֹׂגְשַׂג (§ 6. No. 4) *to hedge about*, Is. 17. 11; others *to cause to grow*, from שָׁנָה, שָׁנָא=שָׂנָה.

שׁוּג Root not used; i. q. שָׁנָה, שָׁנַג. מִשְׁגּוּגָה fem. dec. 10, *error*, Job 19. 4.

שׁנה שׁוֹנִיםⁿ Kal part. act. masc., pl. of שָׁנָה dec. 9 a

[שׁוּד] i. q. שָׁדַד *to lay waste*, Ps. 91. 6. שֵׁד masc. dec. 1 a, *demon*. Syr. שׁאדא id.

שׁוֹדֵד Kal part. act. sing. masc. dec. 7 b . שׁדד

שָׁוָה (Milêl bef. monos.).—I. *to be equal* in value, with —II. *to countervail, be sufficient* for a damage, sc.

ᵃ Eze. 22. 25.   ᵈ Je. 3. 1.   ᵍ Is. 57. 17.   ᵏ Le. 50. 6.   ⁿ Is. 47. 10.   ᵖ Mi. 2. 8.   ᵗ 2 Sa. 18. 9.   ᵛ Ge. 3. 19.   ᵞ Ps. 119. 118.
ᵇ Mi. 7. 3.   ᵉ Je. 42. 10.   ʰ Je. 8. 5.   ˡ Eze. 38. 4.   ᵐ Ex. 32. 27.   ᵠ Ps. 137. 3.   ᵘ Ju. 6. 18.   ˣ Ps. 85. 5.   ᵛ Job 23. 27.
ᶜ Ec. 1. 5.   ᶠ Pr. 3. 28.   ⁱ Je. 3. 14. 22.

to make it good, Est. 7. 4; hence, *to be sufficient,
enough*, Est. 5. 13; impers. שָׁוֶה לִי *it satisfied me,*
Job 33. 27; which latter Prof. Lee regards as a
subst. *equity*.—III. *to be fitting, proper*, with לְ,
Est. 3. 8.—IV. *to be like, to resemble*, with לְ. Pi.
שִׁוָּה.—I. *to make level, even*, Is. 28. 25.—II. *to
make similar, like*, Ps. 18. 34; 131. 2; also *to make
oneself like*, Is. 38. 13, unless שִׁוִּיתִי, in this passage,
stands for שִׁוַּעְתִּי (Prof. Lee).—III. *to put, set,
place*, with עַל *to bestow upon*.—IV. *to put forth,
yield*, fruit, Ho. 10. 1.—V. see Nithpa. Hiph.
to liken, compare, La. 2. 13. Nithpa. נִשְׁתַּוָּה (§ 6.
No. 10) *to be compared, considered like*, Pr. 27. 15;
others, *to be feared*, as the Ithp. signifies in the
Chald.; and hence render the Pi. Job 30. 22,
Kheth. *to terrify*.

שְׁוָה or שְׁוָא Ch. Pa. *to set, place*, with עִם *to
place with, make equal with*, Da. 5. 21. Ithpa.
to be made into, Da. 3. 29.

שָׁוֵה (*plain*) pr. name—I. of a valley north of
Jerusalem.—II. שָׁוֵה קִרְיָתַיִם a plain near Kiriathaim
in the tribe of Reuben, Ge. 14. 5.

יִשְׁוָה (*likeness, similarity*) pr. name m. Ge. 46. 17.

יִשְׁוִי (*like, similar*) pr name masc.—I. Ge. 46. 17.
—II. 1 Sa. 14. 49.

שָׁוֵה	pr. name of a valley . . . . שׁוה
שִׁוָּה[b]	Piel pret. 3 pers. sing. masc. . . שׁוה
שֹׁוֶה	Kal part. act. sing. masc. . . . שׁוה

[שׂוּחַ] *to meditate*, i. q. שִׂיחַ, Ge. 24. 63; others, *to walk,*
or *to converse*.

[שׁוּחַ] I. *to sink down*, Pr. 2. 18.—II. *to be bowed down,
depressed*.

שׁוּחַ (*pit*) pr. name of a son of Abraham by
Keturah, Ge. 25. 2; 1 Ch. 1. 32. Patronym. שׁוּחִי,
comp. Job 2. 11; 8. 1, &c.

שׁוּחָה fem.—I. *a pit*.—II. pr. name masc. 1 Ch.
4. 11, for which חוּשָׁה ver. 4.

שׁוּחָם (*pit-digger*; Simonis, *haste*, for חוּשָׁם)
pr. name masc. Nu. 26. 24, called חֻשִׁים Ge. 46. 23.

שִׁיחָה fem. dec. 10, *a pit*.

שַׁחַת fem. (once with suff. שַׁחְתָּם).—I. *pit*;
also a *pitfall*, metaph. for plot, treachery, destruction.—II. *dungeon*, Is. 51. 14.—III. *grave, sepulchre*. See also שְׁחָת.

יְשׁוֹחָיָה (*whom the Lord bows down*) pr. name
masc. 1 Ch. 4. 36.

שׁוּט	רְ pr. name masc. . . . שׁוח
שׁוּחָה	רְ[b] noun fem. sing., also pr. name . שׁוח
שֹׂחֵט[c]	Kh. שׁוֹחֵט q. v., K. שָׁחוּט (q. v.) . שׁחט
שֹׁחֵט	Kal part. act. sing. masc. dec. 7 b . שׁחט

[שׂוּט] *to go* or *turn aside*, Ps. 40. 5.

שֵׂט, סֵט masc. dec. 1 a, *one who turns aside*,
Ho. 5. 2; Ps. 101. 3.

I. [שׁוּט] I. *to row* (prop. *to lash* the water with oars, Arab.
שׁאט *to whip*) only part. *rower*, Eze. 27. 8, 26.
—II. *to go, run to and fro*. Pil. שׁוֹטֵט i. q. Kal
No. II; metaph. *to run through* or over a book, i. e.
to examine it thoroughly, Da. 12. 4; so most of
the moderns, but not necessarily so. Hithpal.
i. q. Pil. Je. 49. 3.

II. [שׁוּט] i. q. שׁאַט *to contemn, despise*, Eze. 16. 57;
28. 24, 26.

שׁוֹט masc. d. 1 a, *a whip, scourge*; trop. *scourge,
calamity*.

שִׁיט masc.—I. *scourge*, Is. 28. 15, Kheth.—II.
oar, oars, Is. 33. 21.

שֵׁטֶט masc. *scourge*, Jos. 23. 13.

מָשׁוֹט masc. *an oar*, Eze. 27. 29.

מִשְׁוֹט masc. dec. 1 b, id. Eze. 27. 6.

שׁוֹט	noun masc. sing. dec. 1 a . . . שׁוט
שׁוּט[d]	Kal imp. sing. masc. . . . . שׁוט
שׁוֹטְטוּ[e]	Pilel imp. pl. masc. . . . . שׁוט
שֹׁוּטְמֵנוּ	Kal part. act. pl. m., suff. 1 p. s. fr. שׂטן d. 7 b
שׁוֹטֵף	Kal part. act. sing. masc. dec. 7 b . שׁטף
שַׁוִּי[g]	Ch. Pael pret. 3 pers. sing. masc. שׁוה
שִׁוִּיתִי	Piel pret. 1 pers. sing. . . . שׁוה

[שׂוּךְ, סוּךְ] *to hedge in, to fence* (prop. with a thorn
hedge), Job 1. 10; Ho. 2. 8. Pil. id. Job 10. 11;
others, *to twist, weave*, comp. Ps. 139. 13.

שׂוֹךְ m. d. 1 a, *a bough*, Ju. 9. 49. (Syr. & Ch. id.)

שׂוֹכָה fem. dec. 10, id. Ju. 9. 48.

שׂוֹכוֹ, שׂוֹכֹה (*hedge, fence*) pr. name of a town
in Judah.

שׂוּכָתִי gent. noun, *Suchathite*, of an unknown
place שׂוֹכָה, 1 Ch. 2. 55.

מְסוּכָה, מְשׂוּכָה fem. d. 10, *hedge, thorn-hedge*.

שׁוֹכֵב[h]	Kal part. act. sing. masc. dec. 7 b שׁכב
שׂוֹכֹה	רְ pr. name of a place . . . שׂוך
שׂוֹכוֹ	
שׂוֹכֹה[i]	noun m sing., suff. 3 pers. s. m. fr. [שׂוך] d. 1 a שׂוך

a Is. 28. 25.   *b* Je. 2. 6   *c* Je. 9. 7.   *d* 2 Sa. 24. 2.   *e* Je. 5. 1.   *f* Ps. 109. 29.   *g* Da. 5. 21.   *h* Eze. 4. 9.   *i* Ju. 9. 49.

46

שׁוֹכַת noun fem. sing., constr. of [שׁוֹכָה] dec. 10   שׂוֹךְ
שׁוּכָתִים gent. noun pl. [from שׁוֹכָה] . . . שׂוֹךְ

שׁוּל masc. dec. 1 a, only found in the pl.—I. *train* of a robe.—II. *hem* of a garment, Ex. 28. 33, 34.

שׁוֹלֵחַ Kal part. act. sing. masc. dec. 7 b . שׁלח
שׁוּלֵי noun masc. pl. constr. from [שׁוּל] dec. 1 a שׁוּל
שׁוּלָיו id. pl., suff. 3 pers. sing. masc. . שׁוּל
שׁוּלַיִךְ id. pl., suff. 2 pers. sing. fem. . שׁוּל
שׁוֹלָל adj. masc. sing. . . . . . שׁלל

שׂוּם, שִׂים fut. יָשִׂים (only Ex. 4. 11), יָשֵׂם, ap. יָשֵׂם, וַיָּשֶׂם; inf. abs. שׂוֹם; imp. שִׂים.—I. *to put, set, place*, of persons and things made to *stand erect*; hence—II. *to set* a plant.—III. with בָּנִים *to set children*, sc. into the world, i. e. *to beget* them, Ezr. 10. 44.—IV. *to set in array* an army.—V. *to set, constitute, appoint*, with acc., ל; with עַל *to set over*.—VI. *to set up*, e. g. a pillar; hence, *to found, establish*; with שְׁמוֹ, of God, *to establish* his name, the true worship; and, *to set, fix* a law, a place.—VII. *to put, set, lay*, of inanimate things; e. g. שׂוֹם יָד עַל פֶּה *to lay* the hand upon the mouth; אֵשׁ שׂ׳ *to set* or *lay* a fire; with שֵׁם לְ *to set a name*, i. e. give a name to any one; trop. שׂ׳ בְּאָזְנֵי פ׳ *to put into the ear*, i.e. to recite to or tell any one; שׂ׳ עַל לֵב, or בְּלֵב, אֶל לֵב *to lay to heart*, also *to purpose*; שׂ׳ לֵב לְ *to set the heart upon, to attend, consider*; with פָּנִים *to set* or *direct* the face, eye, with עַל, לְ, בְּ.—VIII. *to lay up, preserve*, Job 36. 13.—IX. with עַל *to lay* or *put on* a garment.—X. *to put, lay, impose upon*; hence *to impute*, e. g. guilt; const. with עַל, לְ, בְּ.—XI. *to set* in a position or state, hence *to make*, espec. into any thing; rarely *to do, perform*, as שׂ׳ אֹתוֹת *to perform miracles*.—XII. with לְ *to render, give, bestow*; with רַחֲמִים *to show mercy*. Hiph. *to mark, attend, notice* (לֵב implied), Job 34. 23; Eze. 21. 21. Hoph. *to be set*, Ge. 24. 33.

שׂוּם Ch. *to put, set, place*; hence the phrases שֵׁם שׂ׳ *to name*; שׂ׳ בָּל לְ *to set the heart upon, to purpose*, comp. Heb. No. VII; שׂ׳ טְעֵם *to put forth, give out a decree*; שׂ׳ טְעֵם עַל *to regard*, Da. 3. 12. Ithpe. I. *to be put, placed*, Ezr. 5. 8; of a decree, *to be put forth* or *given*, Ezr. 4. 21.—II. *to be made*, Da. 2. 5.

יְשִׂימָאֵל (*whom God constitutes*) pr. name masc. 1 Ch. 4. 36.

תְּשׂוּמֶת fem. with יָד *a deposit*, Le. 5. 21.

[שׁוּם] masc. *garlic*, Nu. 11. 5.
שׁוּמָתִי patronym. *Shumathite*, 1 Ch. 2. 53, from an unknown שׁוּמָה (*garlic*).

שׁוֹם Kh. שׁוֹם, K. שִׂים (q. v.) . . . שׂום
שׂוֹם וְ Kal inf. abs., or (Ne. 8. 8) constr. . שׂום
שׂוֹם id. inf. constr. . . . . שׂום
שׁוֹמֵם Kal part. act. sing. m., pl. שׁוֹמְמִים (q. v.) שׁמם
שׁוֹמֵמָה id. fem. dec. 11 b . שׁמם
שׁוֹמְמִים שׁוֹמְמִין } id. masc., pl. of שׁוֹמֵם comp. dec. 7 a . שׁמם
שׁוֹמֵעַ Kh. שׁוֹמֵעַ s. K. שׁמֵעַ (q.v.) Kal part. masc. שׁמע
שׁוֹמֵר Kal part. act. sing. m. d. 7 b, also pr. name שׁמר

שׁוּן Root not used; Syr. תון *mingere*.
שַׁיִן masc. dec. 6 h, only pl. *urine*, 2 Ki. 18. 27; Is. 36. 12, Kheth.

שׂוֹנֵא וְ Kal part. act. sing. masc. dec. 7 b . שׂנא
שׂוֹנֶה Kal part. act. sing. masc. dec. 9 a . שׂנה
שׁוּנִי pr. name masc. [for שָׁאנִי] . . שׁאן
שׁוֹנִים Kal part. act. masc., pl. of שׁוֹנֶה dec. 9 a שׁנה
שׁוּנֵם pr. name of a place [for שָׁאנֵם] . שׁאן
שׁוֹסֵינוּ Kal part. act. pl. masc., suff. 1 pers. pl. [from שָׁסָה] dec. 9 a . . . שׁסה

שָׁוַע only Pi. שִׁוַּע *to cry for help*.
שֶׁוַע masc. dec. 6 a (§ 35. rem. 5), *a cry for help*, Ps. 5. 3.
שׁוֹעַ masc. id. Is. 22. 5.
שׁוֹעַ masc. id. Job 30. 24.
שַׁוְעָה fem. (constr. שַׁוְעַת; no pl.) id.

שׁוֹעַ Root not used; i. q. יָשַׁע q. v.
שׁוֹעַ masc.—I. *rich, opulent*.—II. *liberal, noble*, Is. 32. 5.
שׁוֹעַ m. d. 1 a.—I. *riches, wealth*, Job 36. 19.—II. pr. name masc. 1 Ch. 7. 32.
שׁוּעָא (*riches*) pr. name masc. 1 Ch. 7. 32.
תְּשׁוּעָה fem. dec. 10, *salvation, deliverance*.
שׁוּעַ וְ noun masc. sing. . . . . שׁוע
שׁוּעָא noun masc. sing. dec. 1 a, also pr. name . שׁוע
שׁוּעָא pr. name masc. . . . . שׁוע
שׁוּעִי noun masc. sing., suff. 1 pers. sing. [from שֶׁוַע § 35. rem. 5] dec. 6a . . שׁוע

שׁוּעֶךָ	noun masc. sing., suff. 2 pers. sing. masc. from שׁוּעַ dec. 1 a . . .	שׁוע
שׁוּעָלִי	ן' noun m. s. (no vowel change); also pr. name	שׁעל
שׁוּעָלִים	id. pl., abs. st. . . .	שׁעל
שׁוֹעֲרִים	ן' noun masc., pl. of שֹׁעֵר dec. 7 b .	שׁער
שׁוְעַת	noun fem. sing. constr. [of שַׁוְעָה, no pl.]	שׁוע
שַׁוְעָתִי	ן' id. with suff. 1 pers. sing. .	שׁוע
שִׁוַּעְתִּי	Piel pret. 1 pers. sing. . .	שׁוע
שַׁוְעָתָם	noun masc. sing., suff. 3 pers. pl. masc. [from שַׁוְעָה, no pl.] . .	שׁוע

שׁוּף I. *to bruise, wound,* Ge. 3. 15; Job 9. 17.—II. *to cover with darkness* (comp. נֶשֶׁף), Ps. 139. 11.

שׁוֹפֵט	Kal part. act. sing. masc. dec. 7 b	שׁפט
שׁוֹפָךְ	ן' pr. name masc. . . .	שׁפך
שׁוֹפֵךְ	Kal part. act. sing. masc. dec. 7 b	שׁפך
שׁוֹפָן	pr. name, see עַטְרֹת שׁוֹ.	
שׁוֹפָר	noun masc. sing. dec. 2 b .	שׁפר
שׁוֹפַר	id., constr. st. . . .	שׁפר
שׁוֹפָרוֹת	id. pl., abs. st. . . .	שׁפר
שׁוֹפְרוֹת	id. pl., constr. st. . . .	שׁפר
שׁוֹפְרֹתֵיהֶם	id. pl., suff. 3 pers. pl. masc.	שׁפר

שׁוּק Kal not used; cogn. שָׁקַק *to run;* hence *to run after, to desire.* Hiph. *to run over, to overflow,* Joel 2.24; 4.13. Pil. שׁוֹקֵק *to cause to overflow,* Ps. 65. 10.
שׁוֹק com. dec. 1 a, *a leg* of a man or animal.
שׁוּק masc. (pl. שְׁוָקִים § 35. rem. 13) *a street.*
שָׁק Chald. masc. dec. 1 a, *leg.*
תְּשׁוּקָה fem. dec. 10, *desire, longing.*

שׁוֹק	noun fem. sing. dec. 1 a .	שׁוק
שׁוֹקָיו	id. pl., suff. 3 pers. sing. masc.	שׁוק
שׁוֹקֵק	Kal part. act. sing. masc. .	שׁקק
שׁוֹקֵקָה	id. part. act. sing. fem. (§ 39. No. 3. rem. 4)	שׁקק

שׂוּר [שׂוּר] fut. וַיָּשַׂר (§ 21. rem. 9). I. i. q. שָׂרָה, שָׂרַר, (1) *to contend, strive,* Ho. 12. 5; (2) *to be prince, to have dominion,* Ju. 9. 22. Hiph. *to appoint princes,* Ho. 8. 4. II. *to saw,* 1 Ch. 20. 3. III. i. q. סוּר *to go away, depart.*

I. [שׁוּר] I. *to see, view, behold.*—II. *to watch for.*
שׁוּר m. d. 1 a, *a lyer-in-wait, enemy,* Ps. 92. 12.

II. [שׁוּר] *to go, travel,* espec. for traffic, Is. 57. 9; part. fem.
שָׁרָה *a travelling company, caravan,* Eze. 27. 25.
תְּשׁוּרָה fem. *gift, present,* 1 Sa. 9. 7.

III. שׁוּר masc. dec. 1 a (pl. שׁוּרוֹת).—I. *wall* (perh. from שׁוּר, No. II, *to go round,* comp. תּוּר).—II. pr. name of a place in the desert between Egypt and Palestine; מִדְבַּר שׁוּר the desert extending from the borders of Palestine to Shur.
שׁוּר Chald. m. d. 1 a, *a wall,* Ezr. 4. 12, 13, 6.
שׁוּרָה fem. dec. 10, id. Je. 5. 10.

שׁוֹר וָ', וְ' masc. dec. 1 a (pl. שְׁוָרִים § 35. rem. 13).—I. *an ox.*—II. *herd of oxen.*

שׁוֹר	noun masc. sing. dec. 1 b, also pr. name	שׁור
שׁוּרָ	ן' Kal imp. sing. masc. .	שׁור
שׁוֹרָה	noun fem. sing. . . .	שׁור
שׁוֹרָה	pr. name of a place (שׁוּר) with parag. ה	שׁור
שׁוֹרוֹ	וְ' noun masc. sing., suff. 3 pers. sing. masc. from שׁוֹר (q. v.) . . .	שׁור
שְׁוּרִי	וְ' Kh. for שׁוּרַיָּא K. (q. v.) .	שׁור
שׁוּרַיָּא	וְ' Chald. noun masc. pl. emph. from שׁוּר	שׁור
שׁוּרַיָּה	וְ' dec. 1 . . .	שׁור
שְׁוָרִים	noun masc., pl. of שׁוֹר (q. v.) .	שׁור
שׁוּרֵךְ	וְ' id. sing., suff. 2 pers. sing. masc.	שׁור
שׁוּרֵק	noun masc. sing.; also pr. name .	שׁרק
שֹׁרְרַי	Kal part. act. pl. masc., suff. 1 pers. sing.	שׁרר
שׁוֹרְרָי	from שֹׁרֵר dec. 7 b . .	שׁור
שׁוֹרֹתָם	noun masc. with pl. fem. term. & suff. 3 pers. pl. masc. from שׁוּר dec. 1 a .	שׁור

[שׂישׂ, שׂוּשׂ] fut. יָשׂוּשׂ (only Is. 35. 1) יָשִׂישׂ; inf. abs. שׂושׂ; imp. שִׂישׂ *to exult, be glad, rejoice,* with בְ, עַל.
שָׂשׂוֹן masc. dec. 3 a (§ 32. rem. 5), *joy, gladness.*
מָשׂושׂ m. d. 3 a, *joy, rejoicing;* also, *object of joy.*

שׁוּשׁ Root not used; prob. *to be white.*
שַׁיִשׁ masc. *white marble,* 1 Ch. 29. 2.
שֵׁשׁ masc.—I. *white marble.*—II. *fine linen, byssus.*
שֵׁשַׁי (*white*) pr. name of an Anakite, comp. Nu. 13. 22.
שֵׁשִׁי (id.) pr. name masc. Ezr. 10. 40.
שֵׁשָׁן (id., or i. q. שׁוּשָׁן) pr. name masc. 1 Ch 2. 31, 34, 35.
שׁוּשַׁן masc.—I. *a lily, artificial lily,* 1 Ki. 7. 19 —II. שׁוּשָׁן עֵדֻת prob. the name of a musical instrument, resembling a lily, Ps. 60. 1.—III. pr. name, *Susa,* the capital of Persia.
שׁושָׁן masc.—I. *a lily.*—II. *an artificial lily*

a Job 36. 19.   d Ps. 40. 2.   g Ju. 7. 16.   k Ca. 5. 15.   o Ju. 6. 4.   r Ex. 20. 17.   t Ezr. 4. 16.   y Je. 2. 21.   z Ps. 56. 3.
b Ne. 3. 35.   e Job 12. 21.   h Jos. 6.4,6,8,13.   l Pr. 28. 15.   p Job 35. 5.   s Ezr. 4. 12.   u Ho. 12. 12.   z Ps. 5. 9.   aa De. 15. 19.
c 2 Ch. 34. 13   f Ps. 95. 9.   Ju. 7. 8.   m Is. 29. 8.   Is. 28, 25.   q Ezr. 4. 13.   x De. 5. 14.

1 Ki. 7. 22, 26.—III. pl. שׁוֹשַׁנִּים the name of a musical instrument, Ps. 45. 1; 69. 1; 80. 1, comp. שׁוּשָׁן.

שׁוֹשַׁנָּה fem. dec. 10, *a lily.*

שׁוּשַׁנְכָיֵא Chald. gent. noun pl. *inhabitants of Susa,* Ezr. 4. 9.

שׁוֹשׁ Kal inf. abs. . . . . שׁוֹשׁ

שׁוֹשָׁא pr. name masc., see שְׂרָיָה under שׂרה

שׁוֹשָׁן noun masc. sing., pl. שׁוֹשַׁנִּים dec. 8a שׁוֹשׁ

שׁוּשָׁן
שׁוּשָׁן } pr. name of a place . . . שׁוֹשׁ
שׁוּשָׁן

שׁוּשָׁן noun masc. sing. . . . . שׁוֹשׁ

שׁוֹשַׁנָּה noun fem. sing. dec. 10 שׁוֹשׁ

שׁוֹשַׁנִּים noun masc., pl. of שׁוֹשָׁן dec. 8a שׁוֹשׁ

שׁוּשַׁנְכָיֵא Chald. gent. noun pl. from שׁוּשָׁן (q. v.) שׁוֹשׁ

שׁוֹשַׁנַּת noun fem. sing., constr. of שׁוֹשַׁנָּה dec. 10 שׁוֹשׁ

שׁוֹשָׁק Kh. שׁוּשַׁק, K. שִׁישַׁק q. v.

שׁוֹשַׁתִּי Poel (§ 6. No. 1) pret. 1 p. s. [for שׁוֹשַׂתִּי] שׁסה

שׁוֹתִי } Kal part. act. masc., pl. constr. & abs. שׁתה
שׁוֹתִים } from שָׁתָה dec. 9a . . .
וְ

שׁוּתֶלַח } pr. name—I. Nu. 26. 35. Patronym.
שׁוּתַלְחִי } ibid.—II. 1 Ch. 7. 20, 21.
וְ

שֵׁזֵב Chald. only Peil שֵׁיזֵיב; fut. יְשֵׁיזֵיב; inf. שֵׁיזָבוּת (§ 68 d) *to deliver, rescue.*

מְשֵׁיזַבְאֵל (whom *God delivers*) pr. name masc. Ne. 3. 4; 10. 22; 11. 24.

שֵׁיזֵיב Ch. Peil pret. 3 pers. sing. masc. (§ 48) . שׁזב
וְ

[שָׁזַף] *to see, look upon, behold;* metaph. of the sun, Ca. 1. 6, which some render *the sun has scorched me;* regarding שָׁזַף i. q. שָׂרַף Chald. *to scorch, burn;* and thence derive the signification of *looking, casting a glance.*

שְׁזָפַתּוּ Kal pret. 3 pers. fem. with suff. 3 pers. s. m. שׁזף

שָׁזַר Kal not used; Arab. *to twist;* hence Hoph. part. שֵׁשׁ מָשְׁזָר *twined linen.*

שָׁח Kal pret. 3 p. s. m.; or (Job 22. 29) adj. m. שׁחח
וְ

שֶׁחְבְּרָה pref. שֶׁ)(Pual pret. 3 pers. sing. fem. . חבר

[שָׁחַד] *to give presents, to bribe.* Hence

שֹׁחַד masc.—I. *gift, present.*—II. *a bribe.*—III. *bribery,* Job 15. 34 שׁחד
וְ

שַׁחֲדוּ Kal imp. pl. masc. [for שַׁחֲדוּ or שְׁחֲדוּ] שׁחד

[שָׂחָה] *to swim,* Is. 25. 11. Hiph. *to make to swim, overflow,* Ps. 6. 7.

שָׂחוּ fem. *a swimming,* Ezr. 47. 5.

[שָׁחָה] *to bow, stoop down,* Is. 51. 23. Hiph. הִשְׁחָה *to bow down, depress,* Pr. 12. 25. Hithpal. הִשְׁתַּחֲוָה (§ 6. No. 2, & § 24. rem. 25).—I. *to bow down, prostrate oneself,* with לִפְנֵי, לְ, before any one, once עַל Le. 26. 1.—II. *to worship.*

שָׁחוּת fem. dec. 1a, *a pit,* Pr. 28. 10.

שָׁחִית fem. dec. 1a (pl. שְׁחִיתוֹת), id.

שָׁחָה Kal pret. 3 pers. sing. fem. . שׁוח

שָׁחוּ noun fem. sing. (after the form אָחוּ) שׁחה

שָׁחוּ Kal pret. 3 pers. pl. [for שָׁחוּ dag. f. impl.] שׁחח

שְׁחוֹ noun m. s., suff. 3 pers. s. m. fr. [שַׁח] d. 1a שׁיח

שְׁחוֹחַ Kal inf. constr., others, subst. masc. שׁחח

שָׁחוּט Kal part. pass. sing. masc. . . שׁחט

שְׁחוֹלַת pref. שֶׁ)(Kal part. act. sing. fem., constr. of חָלָה dec. 10, from חָלָה masc. . חלה

שְׂחוֹק noun masc. sing. . . . . שׂחק

שִׁחוֹר pr. name of a river . . . . שׁחר

שְׁחוֹרָה adj. fem. sing. dec. 10, from שָׁחֹר masc. שׁחר

שַׁחוֹתִי Kal pret. 1 pers. sing. (dag. forte impl. in ח) שׁחח

[שָׁחַח] pl. שָׁחֲחוּ, שַׁחוּ (§ 18. rem. 13).—I. *to bow, stoop down.*—II. *to be bowed down, brought low, be depressed.*—III. *to humble oneself, to submit.* Niph. *to be bowed down, brought low, be depressed.* Hiph. הֵשַׁח *to bring low, cast down.* Hithpo. הִשְׁתּוֹחַח *to be brought low, be cast down,* of the soul.

שַׁח adj. masc. *cast down,* with עֵינַיִם *cast down as to the eyes,* i. e. *with cast down eyes,* Job 22. 29.

שְׁחוֹחַ masc. *a bowing down, submission,* Is. 60. 14, others regard it as an inf. and render it: **they shall come** *to submit themselves.*

שָׁחֲחוּ Kal pret. 3 pers. pl. (also שַׁחוּ § 18. rem. 13) שׁחח

[שָׁחַט] *to squeeze, press out,* Ge. 40. 11.

שָׁחַט fut. יִשְׁחַט.—I. *to slaughter, kill* animals.—II. *to kill, slay* persons.—III. part. זָהָב שָׁחוּט *alloyed gold* (Arab. שׁחט *to dilute wine*). Niph. *to be slaughtered.*

שְׁחִיטָה fem. dec. 10, *a slaughtering* of victims, 2 Ch. 30. 17.

שָׁחֹט Kal inf. abs. . . . . שׁחט
וְ

שָׁחֲטָה id. inf. constr. (§ 8. rem. 10) . שׁחט
וְ

Is. 61. 10.   Ca. 2. 1.   1 Ch. 12. 39.   Is. 2. 11, 17.   Job 6. 22.   Am. 4. 13.   2 Ch. 9. 15, 16.   Ca. 1. 5.   Is. 22. 13.
1 Ki. 7. 22, 26.   Is. 10. 13.   Da. 3. 28; 6. 28.   Ps. 122. 3.   Is. 60. 14.   Ca. 5. 8.   Job 9. 13.   Ho. 5. 2.
2 Ch. 4. 5.   Ps. 69. 13.   Eze. 47. 5.

שְׁחֲטוּ ׀ וְ id. pret. **3 pers. pl.** . . . שחט

שְׁחֲטוּ ׀ id. imp. pl. masc. . . . שחט

שְׁחֲטוּ ׀ id. pret. 3 pers. sing. masc., suff. **3 pers.** sing. masc.; ׀, for ׀, conv. . . . שחט

שְׁחֲטֵי id. part. act. pl. c. masc. from שָׁחַט dec. 7 b שחט

שְׁחַטְתָּ ׀ id. pret. 2 pers. sing. masc.; acc. shifted by conv. ׀ (§ 8. rem. 7) . . . שחט

שְׁחַטְתֶּם ׀ id. pret. 2 pers. pl. masc.; ׀, for ׀, conv. שחט

שְׁחִי Kal imp. sing. fem. . . . שחה

שְׁחִי defect. for שִׂיחִי (q. v.) . . . שיח

שְׁחִיטַת noun fem. sing., constr. of [שְׁחִיטָה] dec. 10 שחט

שְׁחִין noun masc. sing. . . . שחן

שְׁחִיס noun masc. sing. see סָחִישׁ.

שְׁחִיף noun masc. sing. constr. [from שָׁחִיף or שְׂחִיף] שחף

שְׁחִיתָה ׀ Ch. Peal part. pass. s. f. [of שְׁחִית]; ׀ bef. (:) שחת

שְׁחַכְמְתִּי ׀ pref. שְׁ X Kal pret. 1 pers. sing. . . חכם

שַׁחַל, שָׁחַל (§ 35. rem. 2) masc. *lion.*

שְׁחֵלֶת ׀ fem. *onyx, an odoriferous shell,* Ex. 30. 34. Arab. שחל *to peel, shell.*

שָׁחַן Root not used; Arab. *to be hot, inflamed.* שְׁחִין masc. *boil, sore, ulcer.*

שָׁחַף Root not used; Arab. *to be thin.* שָׁחִיף or שְׂחִיף masc. *thin board,* Eze. 41. 16. שַׁחַף masc. *the seagull,* Le. 11. 16; De. 14. 15. שַׁחֶפֶת fem. *consumption,* Le. 26. 16; De. 28. 22.

שָׁחַץ Root not used; Arab. *to lift up oneself.* שַׁחַץ masc. *elation, pride,* hence בְּנֵי שַׁ *sons of pride,* for the larger and stronger kind of wild beasts, Job 28. 8; 41. 26. שַׁחֲצִים (*heights*) pr. name of a place in Issachar, Jos. 19. 22.

שַׁחַץ noun masc. sing. [for שַׁחַץ § 35. rem. 2] שחץ שַׁחֲצוֹמָה ׀ Kh. שַׁחֲצוֹמָה K. שַׁחֲצִים pr. name שִׁחְצוֹם or שַׁחֲצִים with parag. ה . . . שחץ

שָׂחַק ׀ I. *to laugh,* abs.—II. with אֶל *to smile upon, approve,* Job 29. 24.—III. with עַל, לְ *to laugh at, deride, scorn.*—IV. *to make sport,* Ju. 16. 27. Pi. שִׂחֵק (§ 14. rem. 1).—I. *to rejoice,* Je. 15. 17; Pr. 8. 30, 31.—II. *to sport, play.*—III. *to make sport;* hence *to skirmish,* 2 Sa. 2. 14.—IV. *to play* on a musical instrument. Hiph. *to laugh at, to scorn* with עַל 2 Ch. 30. 10.

שְׂחֹק, שְׂחוֹק masc.—I. *laughter.*—II. *object of laughter, scorn.*—III. *jest, sport,* Pr. 10. 23. יִשְׂחָק put poetically for יִצְחָק *Isaac,* q. v. מִשְׂחָק m. *object of laughter, derision,* Hab. 1. 10.

[שָׁחַק] I. *to bruise, pound, reduce to dust.*—II. *to wear away,* Job 14. 19. שַׁחַק masc. dec. 6 d.—I. *dust,* Is. 40. 15.—II. *cloud;* pl. שְׁחָקִים *clouds.*—III. *the sky.*

שָׁחַק noun masc. sing., comp. שְׂחוֹק . שחק שָׁחֲקוּ Kal pret. 3 pers. pl. . . שחק שָׁחֲקוּ Kal pret. 3 pers. pl. . . שחק שְׁחָקִים ׀ noun masc., pl. of שַׁחַק dec. 6 d; ׀ bef. (:) שחק שְׁחַקְתָּ ׀ Kal pret. 2 pers. sing. masc.; acc. shifted by conv. ׀ (§ 8. rem. 7) . . . שחק שִׁחַקְתִּי ׀ Piel (§ 14. rem. 1) pret. 1 pers. sing.; acc. shifted by conv. ׀ (comp. § 8. rem. 7) . שחק

שָׁחַר I. *to be black,* Job 30. 30.—II. (denom. from q. v.) prop. *to do early,* comp. הַשְׁכִּים, hence *to seek early, diligently,* Pr. 11. 27. Pi. שִׁחֵר (§ 14 rem. 1) *to seek early,* also *diligently,* const. with acc., לְ, אֶל, with inf. שַׁחַר masc. d. 3 a, שְׁחֹרָה fem. d. 10, adj. *black.* שְׁחוֹר masc. *blackness,* La. 4. 8. שַׁחַר masc. dec. 6 d (with suff. שַׁחְרָהּ § 35. r. 5). —I. *the dusk* of the morning; hence *dawn, morning;* בֶּן־שַׁחַר *son of the dawn,* i. e. *the Morning Star, Lucifer.*—II. adv. *at dawn, early.*—III. *rise, origin,* Is. 47. 11.—IV. perh. *dawn* for *light,* and metaph. for *sense, reason,* Is. 8. 20, which passage may be rendered: *by the law and the testimony* (I declare) *that they shall say* (comp. אִם) *such a thing as this* (see the preceding ver. 19) *in which there is no light.* שַׁחֲרוּת fem. *dawn of life,* i. e. *youth,* Ec. 11. 10 שְׁחַרְחֹר, only fem. שְׁחַרְחֹרֶת adj. *blackish, swarthy* (§ 26. Nos. 21, 22, 23), Ca. 1. 6. שְׁחַרְיָה (*whom the Lord seeks*) pr. name masc. 1 Ch. 8. 26. שַׁחֲרַיִם (*two dawns, twilights*) pr. name masc. 1 Ch. 8. 8. שִׁיחוֹר, שְׁחוֹר, שִׁחֹר (*black, turbid*) pr. name— I. the Hebrew appellation for the *Nile.*—II. שִׁיחוֹר לִבְנָת *a small river* in the tribe of Asher, Jos. 19. 26. אֲשְׁחוּר (*blackness*) pr. name m. 1 Ch. 2. 24; 4. 5 מִשְׁחָר masc. *the dawn, morning,* Ps. 110. 3.

שַׁחַר
שָׁחַר } noun masc. sing. dec. 6d (§ 35. rem. 2)

שָׁחֹר adj. masc. sing. dec. 3a . . . שחר

שִׁחֹר pr. name of a river . . . . שחר

שֹׁחֵר Kal part. act. sing. masc. . . . שחר

שַׁחֲרָהּ noun masc. sing., suff. 3 pers. sing. fem. from
שַׁחַר dec. 6d [for שַׁחֲרָהּ § 35. rem. 5] שחר

שִׁחֲרוֹ Piel (§ 14. rem. 1) pret. 3 pers. sing. masc.
[שִׁחֵר], suff. 3 pers. sing. masc. . שחר

שִׁחֲרֻ וְ id. pret. 3 pers. pl. . . . שחר

שְׁחֹרוֹת adj. fem., pl. of שְׁחוֹרָה d. 10, from שָׁחֹר masc. שחר

שְׁחַרְחֹרֶת adj. fem. sing. from שְׁחַרְחֹר masc. שחר

שַׁחֲרָיָה ,וְ שַׁחֲרַיִם וְ pr. names masc.; וְ bef. (:) שחר

שְׁחֹרִים adj. masc., pl. of שָׁחֹר dec. 3a שחר

וְשִׁחַרְתַּנִי Piel pret. 2 pers. s. m., suff. 1 p. s. (§ 14. r. 1) שחר

שָׁחַת. Niph. I. *to be marred* or *spoiled by rotting*, Je. 13. 7.
—II. *to be corrupted*, morally, Ge. 6. 11, 12.—III.
to be laid waste, Ex. 8. 20. Pi. שִׁחֵת (§ 14. rem. 1).
—I. *to destroy, ruin*, e. g. land, persons; metaph.
of compassion, Am. 1. 11, of wisdom, Eze. 28. 17,
of a covenant, prob. *to corrupt, pervert*, Mal. 2. 8.—
II. *to act corruptly, wickedly*. Hiph. I. i. q. Pi.
No. I.—II. *to corrupt, pervert*, as one's way, actions.
Hoph. *to be corrupted, spoiled*.

שָׁחַת Chald. part. pass. fem. שְׁחִיתָה *corrupt*, of
words, Da. 2. 9; neut. *corrupt deed, crime*, Da. 6. 5.
שַׁחַת masc. *corruption, putridity*, Job 17. 14;
Ps. 16. 10.
מַשְׁחִית masc. dec. 1b.—I. *destruction, ruin*.—
II. *snare, trap*, Je. 5. 26.
מַשְׁחֵת masc. dec. 1 b, *destruction*, Eze. 9. 1.
מָשְׁחָת m. d. 2 b, *corruption, defilement*, Le. 22. 25.

שַׁחַת noun masc. sing. [for שַׁחַת § 35. rem. 2] . שחת

שַׁחַת
שַׁחַת } noun fem. sing. dec. 13 a (comp. § 35. r. 2) שוח

שַׁחֵת Piel inf. constr. (§ 14. rem. 1) . . שחת

שִׁחַתָּ וְ id. pret. 2 pers. sing. m. [for שִׁחַתָּ § 25. r.] שחת

שִׁחֵת וְ id. pret. 3 pers. sing. masc. . . שחת

שַׁחֲתָהּ id. inf. (שַׁחֵת), suff. 3 pers. sing. fem. dec. 7 b שחת

שִׁחֲתָהּ וְ id. pret. 3 pers. sing. masc. (שִׁחֵת), suff.
3 pers. sing. fem. . . . . שחת

שַׁחֲתוּ וְ id. imp. pl. masc. [for שַׁחֲתוּ comp. § 8. r. 7] שחת

שִׁחֲתוּ
שִׁחֲתוּ וְ } id. pret. 3 pers. pl. (comp. id.) . . שחת

שִׁחַתְךָ id. pret. 3 pers. sing. masc. (שִׁחֵת § 14.
r. 1), suff. 2 pers. sing. masc. (§ 16. r. 15) שחת

שְׁחַתֶּם וְ id. pret. 2 p. pl. m. [for שְׁחַתְּתֶּם § 25. r.] שחת

[שָׂטָה] fut. יִשְׂטֶה, ap. יֵשְׂטְ (§ 24. rem. 3), *to turn aside,
go astray*.

שִׁטָּה fem.—I. *acacia*, Is. 41. 19; pl. שִׁטִּים *acacia wood*.
—II. שִׁטִּים pr. name of a valley in Moab on the
borders of Palestine.

שְׂטֵה Kal imp. sing. masc. . . . . שׂטה

שָׂטוּ Kal pret. 3 pers. pl. . . . . שׂוט

שֶׁטּוֹב pref. שֶׁ)(adj. masc. sing. dec. 1 a . טוב

שָׂטוֹחַ Kal inf. abs. . . . . . שׂטח

[שָׂטַח] I. *to spread abroad, expand, enlarge*.—II. *to strew,
scatter*.

מִשְׁטָח m. d. 2 b, *a place for spreading*, Eze. 26. 5, 14.
מִשְׁטוֹחַ masc. id. Eze. 47. 10.

שֹׁטֵחַ Kal part. act. sing. masc. . . . שׂטח

שְׁטָחוּם וְ id. pret. 3 pers. pl. masc., suff. 3 pers. pl.
masc.; וְ, for וְ, conv. . . . שׂטח

שָׁטַחְתִּי Piel pret. 1 pers. sing. . . . שׂטח

שֹׁטֵי וְ Kal part. act. pl. constr. masc. [from שָׂט
dec. 1 a, § 30. No. 3] . . . שׂוט

שָׂטִים Kal part. act. pl. m. [fr. שָׂט d. 1 a, §30. No.3] שׂוט

שִׁטִּים noun masc. pl. [of שֵׁט] . . . שׂוט

שִׁטִּים noun fem., pl. of שִׁטָּה dec. 10 . . שׂטה

שָׂטִית Kal pret. 2 pers. sing. fem. . . שׂטה

[שָׂטַם] fut. יִשְׂטֹם *to hate, persecute*; others, coll. with the
Syr., *to lay snares for*.

מַשְׂטֵמָה fem. *hatred, persecution*, Ho. 9. 7, 8;
others, *snares, destruction*.

[שָׂטַן] *to be hostile, to oppose*; part. שֹׂטֵן *adversary*. Hence
the two following.

הַשָּׂטָן וְ masc.—I. *adversary, opponent*.—II.
the adversary, the devil, Satan . . שׂטן

שִׂטְנָה fem.—I. *accusation*, Ezr. 4. 6.—II. pr name
of a well, Ge. 26. 21 . . . . שׂטן

שֹׂטְנִי the foll. with suff. 1 pers. sing. . . שׂטן

שֹׂטְנֵי Kal part. act. pl. constr. m. [fr. שָׂטַן] d. 7 b שׂטן

שָׁטַף וְ I. *to wash away*, Eze. 16. 9.—II. *to wash,
rinse, cleanse by washing*, Le. 15. 11; . Ki. 22. 38.
—III. *to overflow, inundate, overwhelm*; hence
metaph. *to sweep away as with a flood*. Niph.

Le. 13. 31, 37.   Ps. 78. 34.   Job 7. 21.   Eze. 22. 30.   Ho. 13. 9.   Pr. 4. 15.   Job 12. 23.   Eze. 27. 8.   Ps. 109. 20.
Pr. 11. 27.   Ca. 5. 11.   Ps. 16. 10.   Ex. 21. 26.   Mal. 2. 8.   Nu. 11. 8.   Je. 8. 2.   Ho. 5. 2.   Ps. 71. 13.
Is. 47. 11.   Ca. 1. 6.   Ge. 13. 10.   Nu. 32. 15.   Ec. 2. 26.   Nu. 11. 32.   Ps. 88. 10.   Nu. 5. 19, 20.   Da. 11. 10.
Is. 13. 34.   Zec. 6. 2.   Pr. 23. 8.   Eze. 26. 4.   Is. 41. 19.   Nu. 11. 32.   Ps. 40. 5.   Ps. 109. 6.

pass. of Kal Nos. II & III. Pu. *to be washed, rinsed*, Le. 6. 21. Hence

שֶׁטֶף, וְ'שֶׁטֶף masc.—I. *an overflowing* of water, metaph. of an effusion of anger, of the devastation of an army.—II. *flood, inundation.*

שֹׁטֵף Kal part. act. sing. masc. dec. 7 b   שטף
שֹׁטְפּוּ וְ Pual pret. 3 pers. sing. masc.   שטף
שְׁטָפֻנוּ Kal pret. 3 pers. pl. with suff. 1 pers. pl.   שטף
שֹׁטְפִים id. part. act. masc., pl. of שֹׁטֵף dec. 7 b   שטף
שְׁטָפַתְנִי id. pret. 3 pers. sing. fem., suff. 1 pers. sing.   שטף

[שָׁטַר] Arab. (שטר) *to write*; whence part. שֹׁטֵר *officer, overseer* or *magistrate.*

שְׁטַר Ch. m. *a side*, Da. 7. 5. Targ. סְטַר id.
שִׁטְרִי (*writer*) pr. name m. 1 Ch. 27. 29, Kh.
מִשְׁטָר masc. dec. 2 a, *dominion*, Job 38. 33.

שֹׁטֵר Kal part. act. sing. masc. dec. 7 b   שטר
שֹׁטְרֵי pr. name masc.   שטר
שֹׁטְרֵי Kal part. act. pl. c. masc. from שֹׁטֵר d. 7 b   שטר
שֹׁטְרֵיהֶם id. pl., suff. 3 pers. pl. masc.   שטר
שֹׁטְרָיו id. pl., suff. 3 pers. sing. masc.   שטר
שֹׁטְרֵיכֶם id. pl., suff. 2 pers. pl. masc.   שטר
שֹׁטְרִים id. pl., abs. st.   שטר

שַׁי } masc. *present, gift.* Etym. uncertain.

שַׁיָּא pr. name, see שְׁרָיָה, under   שרה
שִׁיאוֹ noun masc. sing., suff. 3 pers. sing. masc.
[from שִׂיא for נְשִׂיא]   נשא
שִׁיאוֹן וְ pr. name of a place   שוא
שִׁיאַחֵז pref. שְׁ X Kal fut. 3 pers. sing. masc.   אחז
שִׁיאכַל pref. id. X Kal fut. 3 pers. sing. masc.   אכל
שִׁיאמַר pref. id. X Kal fut. 3 pers. sing. masc.   אמר
שִׁיאמְרוּ pref. id. X id. fut. 3 pers. pl. masc.   אמר
שִׁיאֹן pr. name of a mountain   נשא

[שִׂיב] *to be grey-headed*, 1 Sa. 12. 2; part. שָׂב *grey-headed, old man.*
שִׂיב Chald. id. only in the participle, Ezr. 5. 5, 8, 9; 6. 7, 14.
שֵׂיב masc. dec. 1 a, *grey hairs, old age*, 1 Ki. 14. 4. Also
שֵׂיבָה וְ fem. dec. 10, *grey hair*   שׂיב
שֵׁיבוֹא pref. שְׁ X Kal fut. 3 pers. sing. masc.   בוא
שֵׂיבַת noun fem. sing., constr. of שֵׂיבָה dec. 10   שׂיב
שֵׁיבַת noun fem. sing., constr. of [שֵׁיבָה] dec. 10   שוב
שֵׂיבָתוֹ noun fem. sing., suff. 3 pers. sing. masc.
from שֵׂיבָה dec. 10   שׂיב

שִׁיבְתִּי id., suff. 1 pers. sing.   שׁיב
שִׁיבְתֵּךְ id., suff. 2 pers. sing. fem.   שׁיב
שִׂיג noun masc. sing., see   סוג

שִׂיד masc. *lime, plaster.*
שִׂיד *to cover with lime, to plaster*, De. 27. 2, 4.
שִׂידְבַּר pref. שְׁ X Pual fut. 3 pers. sing. masc.   דבר

[שָׁיָה] (cogn. שָׁהָה, Arab. שהא) *to forget, neglect*, De. 32. 18, but comp. שָׁהָה

[שֶׂיָה] De. 22. 1; 1 Sa. 14. 34, elsewhere by cont. com., constr. שֶׂה (comp. § 45) *one of the flock, a sheep* or *goat.*
שֵׂיָהוּ id. with suff. 3 pers. sing. masc.   שׂיה
שְׁיֶהֹוָה pref. שְׁ X the most sacred name of God, יהוה with the vowels of אֲדֹנָי   הוה
שְׁיִהְיֶה pref. שְׁ X Kal fut. 3 pers. sing. masc.   היה
שְׁיִהְיוּ pref. id. X id. fut. 3 pers. pl. masc.   היה
שְׂיוֹ noun masc. sing., suff. 3 pers. sing. masc. from שֶׂה irr. (§ 45)   שׂיה
שִׁיזָא pr. name of a man, 1 Ch. 11. 42
שְׁיִזְעַק pref. שְׁ X Kal fut. 3 pers. pl. masc.   זעק

[שִׂיחַ] I. *to speak*, const. with לְ, acc. (Pr. 6. 22) *with*, with בְּ *of any one.*—II. *to complain, lament.*—III. *to meditate*, with בְּ. Pil. שׂוֹחֵחַ.—I. *to tell, declare*, Is. 53. 8.—II. *to meditate*, Ps. 143. 5.
שִׂיחַ masc. dec. 1 a.—I. *speech, discourse*, 2 Ki. 9. 11.—II. *complaint.*—III. *meditation* or *talk*, 1 Ki. 18. 27.
שֶׂחַ masc. dec. 1 a, *thought, purpose*, Am. 4. 13.
שִׂיחָה fem. dec. 10, *meditation*, espec. *pious meditation.*

שִׂיחַ masc. dec. 1 a, *plant, shrub, bush.*
שִׂיחַ Kal imp. sing. masc.   שׂיח
שִׂיחָה } noun fem. sing. dec. 10 (K. שׂוּחָה)   שׂוח
שִׂיחָה noun fem. sing. dec. 10   שׂיח
שִׂיחִי noun masc. sing., suff. 3 pers. sing. masc. from שִׂיחַ dec. 1 a   שׂיח
שִׂיחוּ Kal imp. pl. masc.   שׂיח
שִׁיחוֹר pr. name of a river   שׁחר
שִׂיחֹת noun fem., pl. of שׂיחָה dec. 10   שׂוח
שִׂיחִי noun masc. sing., suff. 1 pers. sing. from שִׂיחַ dec. 1 a   שׂיח

שְׂחִים id. pl., abs. st. . . . . שׂיח

שְׁחָנֵּגּוּ pref. שְׁ)(Kal fut. 3 pers. sing. masc. (יָחֹן), suff. 1 pers. pl. (§ 18. rem. 5) . חנן

שִׂיחָתִי noun fem. s., suff. 1 pers. s. fr. שִׂיחָה dec. 10   שׂיח

שׁוֹט noun masc. sing. . . . שוט

שׁוֹט Kh. שַׁיְט q. v., K. שׁוֹט (q. v.) . שוט

שְׁיִרְאוּ pref. שְׁ)(Kal fut. 3 pers. pl. masc. . ירא

שִׁילֹה noun masc. sing. (or it is to be read (שִׁלֹה=שִׁילוֹ), see R. . . שלה

שַׁילֵךְ pref. שְׁ)(Hiph. fut. 3 pers. sing. masc., ap. & defect. for יוֹלִיךְ . . ילך

שׁוֹלָל Kh. שׁוֹלָל, Keri שׁלָל adj. masc. sing.   שלל

שִׂים ׀וְ Kal inf. c. (Job 20. 4), or imp. sing. masc. R. שִׂים, see . שום

שִׂים Chald. Peal part. pass. sing. masc. R. שִׂים (§ 54. rem. 6), see . . שום

שִׂימָה Kal imp. sing. masc. (שִׂים) with parag. ה, see שום

שִׂימָה id. id. with suff. 3 pers. sing. fem.   שום

שִׂימָה id. part. pass. sing. fem., Kh. שִׂימָה from שִׂים, K. שׂוּמָה from שׂום . שום

שִׂימוּ ׀וְ id. imp. pl. masc.; Chald. Ezr. 4. 21   שום

שִׁימוֹן pr. name masc. . . . ישם

שִׂימֵנִי Kal imp. sing. masc. (שִׂים), suff. 1 p. s., see   שום

שְׁיָמֻתוּ pref. שְׁ)(Kal fut. 3 pers. pl. masc.   מות

שִׁנֵּיהֶם Kh. שִׁנֵּיהֶם n. m. pl. with suff. from an obsol. (מֵימֵי רַגְלַיִם K.) שָׁיִן 2 Ki. 18. 27; Is. 36. 12.   שון

שֶׁיַּעֲמֹל pref. שְׁ)(Kal fut. 3 pers. sing. masc.   עמל

שֶׁיֵּעָשֶׂה pref. id.)(Niph. fut. 3 pers. sing. masc.   עשה

שֶׁיָּפוּחַ pref. id.)(Kal fut. 3 pers. sing. masc.   פוח

שֶׁיִּפוֹל ׀ שֶׁיִּפֹּל ׀ pref. id.)(Kal fut. 3 pers. sing. masc.   נפל

שֶׁיֵּצֵא pref. id.)(Kal part. act. sing. fem. [for יֹצֵא] contr. for יֹצְאָה (comp. § 23. rem. 11)   יצא

שֵׁיצִיא ׀ וְ Chald. Shaph. pret. 3 pers. sing. masc. (§ 48)   יצא

שִׁיר [שׁוּר] fut. יָשִׁיר, ap. וַיָּשַׁר (§ 22. rem. 3) once Job 33. 27 (?), to sing, with לְ to or concerning, with בְּ of any one; part. שָׁר, pl. שָׁרִים, fem. שָׁרוֹת singers. Pil. שׁוֹרֵר to sing; part. מְשֹׁרֵר a singer. Hoph. הוּשַׁר to be sung, Is. 26. 1.   שִׁיר masc. dec. 1 a.—I. a singing, song; musical instruments.—II. sacred song, hymn. שִׁירָה fem. dec. 10, a song.

שִׁיר ׀ (Ne. 12. 46) noun masc. sing. dec. 1 a .   שיר

שִׁירֶךָ pref. שְׁ)(Kal part. act. sing. masc. dec. 7 b   ירד

שִׁירָה ׀ שִׁירוֹ ׀ noun masc. sing., suff. 3 pers. sing. masc. from שִׁיר dec. 1 a   שיר

שִׁירוּ Kal imp. pl. masc. . . . שיר

שִׁירוֹת noun fem., pl. of שִׁירָה dec. 10   שיר

שִׁירַיִךְ noun masc. pl., suff. 2 pers. sing. fem. from שִׁיר dec. 1 a   שיר

שִׁירֵיכֶם id. pl., suff. 2 pers. pl. masc.   שיר

שִׁירַת noun fem. sing., constr. of שִׁירָה dec. 10   שיר

שַׁיִשׁ noun masc. sing. . . . שוש

שֶׁיֵּשׁ pref. שְׁ)(adv. . . . ישה

שִׁישָׁא pr. name, see שְׂרָיָה, under . שרה

שִׁישׂוּ Kal imp. pl. masc., R. שִׂישׂ, see   שוש

שִׂישִׂי id. imp. sing. fem., R. שִׂישׂ, see   שוש

שֶׁיְּשַׁלֶּם־ pref. שְׁ)(Piel fut. 3 pers. sing. masc. for יְשַׁלֵּם (§ 10. rem. 4) . שלם

שִׁישַׁק ׀ שׁוּשַׁק ׀ pr. name of a king of Egypt, contemporary with Jeroboam.

שִׁית [also שׁוּת, Is. 22. 7] fut. יָשִׁית, ap. וַיָּשֶׁת.—I. to put, set, place, of persons or things made to stand or regarded as erect.—II. to set in array, מַחֲנֶה implied; i. e. to set oneself in array.—III. to constitute, appoint, with acc., לְ; with עַל to set over.—IV to set a limit, a term; ellipt. & impers. Job 38. 11.—V. to put, set, lay; שִׁ יָד עַל to lay the hand upon any, in protection; שִׁ יָד עִם to join hands.—VI. to set, direct, turn; שִׁ פָּנִים אֶל to set or turn the face towards, Nu. 24. 1; שִׁ עֵינַיִם to set or turn the eyes, i. e. to intend doing any thing, Ps. 17. 11; שִׁ לֵב to lay to heart, to regard. —VII. to put or lay on an ornament, Ex. 33. 4.— VIII. perh. to cast, throw, Job 22. 24; others, to lay up.—IX. to set in a position or state, hence to make, with לְ into, with כְּ as any thing; rarely to do, perform.—X. to render, give. Hoph. הוּשַׁת, with עַל to be laid, imposed upon, Ex. 21. 30.

    שִׁית masc. attire, dress, Pr. 7. 10; Ps. 73. 6.

    שֵׁת masc. dec. 1 a (pl. שָׁתוֹת), foundation; others, pillars.

    שֵׁת masc. dec. 7 a (pl שָׁתוֹת).—I. buttock.—II. (gift, or compensation, Ge. 4. 25) pr. name of the third son of Adam.

שַׁיִת ׀ וְ in pause שָׁיִת masc. (with suff. שִׁיתוֹ) thorn, collect. thorns, everywhere coupled with שָׁמִיר. Etym. doubtful.

שִׁית ׀ וְ noun masc. sing. dec. 6 h; for וְ see lett. ו

שִׁית ׀ וְ Kal inf. (Job 22. 24), or imp. sing. masc. (Pr. 27. 23), or subst. m., Ps. 73. 6; Pr. 7, 10.   שית

• Job 30. 7.   • Is. 28. 15.   • Mi. 1. 8.   • Ec. 9. 5.   • Ec. 10. 5.   • Ps. 42. 9.   • Eze. 26. 13.   • 1 Ch. 29. 2.   • Ps. 137. 8.
• Ps. 123. 2.   • Ec. 3. 14.   • De. 31. 19.   • Ec. 1. 9.   • Ezr. 6. 15.   • 1 Ki. 5. 12.   • Am. 8. 3.   • Ec. 2. 13.   • Is. 27. 4.
• Ps. 119. 97.   • Ge. 49. 10.   • 2 Sa. 13. 32.   • Ec. 11. 3.   • Ps. 133. 2, 3.   • Am. 8. 3.   • Is. 5. 1.   • La. 4. 21.   • Job 22. 24.
• Is. 33. 21.   • Ec. 5. 14.   • Ca. 8. 6.   • Ec. 4. 10.

שִׁיתָה id. imp. sing. masc. (שִׁית) with parag ה   שית

שִׁיתוֹ noun masc. sing., suff. 3 pers. sing. masc.

from שִׁית dec 6h . . . שית

שִׁיתוּ Kal imp. pl. masc. . . . שית

שִׁיתִי id. imp. sing. fem. . . . שית

שִׁיתֵמוֹ id. imp. sing. masc. (שִׁית), suff. 3 pers. pl. m. שית

שׁוֹר Kal part. act. sing. masc. . . שור

שָׁכַב וְ' fut. יִשְׁכַּב.—I. to lie down; espec. to lie down to sleep or to rest oneself.—II. to lie, keep one's bed.—III. to lie, of one slain; שָׁ׳ עִם אֲבֹתָיו to lie or sleep with his fathers, i. e. to die.—IV. to lie with carnally, with עִם, אֶת. Niph. to be lain with, ravished, Is. 13. 16; 7 c. 14. 2. Pu. id. Je. 3. 2. Hiph. הִשְׁכִּיב.—I. to cause to lie, to lay down.—II. to stop, Job 38. 37; others, to pour out (Arab. שכב id.). Hoph. to be laid, to lie.

שִׁכְבָה fem. dec. 11 c.—I. the act of lying with.—II. a layer of dew.

שְׁכֹבֶת fem. dec. 13 c, the act of lying with.

מִשְׁכָּב masc. dec. 2 b (pl. ־ים, ־וֹת).—I. a lying down.—II. a lying with.—III. couch, bed, 2 Sa. 17. 28.—IV. a bier.

מִשְׁכָּב Chald. masc. dec. 2 a, couch, bed.

שָׁכַב׳ Kal pret. 3 pers. sing. m. for שָׁכַב (§ 8. r. 7) שכב

שָׁכֹב᷄ id. inf. abs. . . . שכב

שְׁכֹב

שְׁכַב } id. inf. constr.; or imp. sing. masc. שכב

שֹׁכֵב id. part. act. sing. masc. dec. 7 b . שכב

שָׁכְבָה וְ' id. pret. 3 pers. sing. fem. . . שכב

שִׁכְבָה id. imp. s. m. (שְׁכַב) with parag. ה (§ 8. r. 11) שכב

שָׁכְבוּ id. pret. 3 pers. pl. . . . שכב

שִׁכְבִי id. imp. sing. fem. . . . שכב

שֹׁכְבֵי᷄ id. part. act. pl. constr. masc. from שֹׁכֵב d. 7 b שכב

שֹׁכְבִים id. pl., abs. st. . . . שכב

שְׁכְבָר׳ pref. שֶׁ)(adv. . . . כבר

שָׁכַבְתָּ᷄

שָׁכָבְתָּ } Kal pret. 2 pers. sing. masc.; acc. shifted by conv. וְ (§ 8. rem. 7) . } שכב

שֹׁכַבְתְּ noun fem. sing., constr. of [שִׁכְבָה] dec. 11 c שכב

שֹׁכַבְתְּ᷄ Kal part. act. sing., fem. of שֹׁכֵב . שכב

שָׁכַבְתּוֹ᷄ noun fem. s., suff. 3 p. s. m. fr. [שְׁכֹבֶת] d. 13 c שכב

שָׁכַבְתְּ׳ וְ Kal pret. 2 pers. sing. fem. (§ 8. r. 5) Kh. תִּי שכב

שָׁכַבְתִּי׳

שָׁכַבְתִּי וְ } id. pret. 1 pers. sing.; acc. shifted by conv. וְ (§ 8. rem. 7) } שכב

שְׁכָבְתְּךָ᷄ noun fem. s., suff. 2 pers. sing. masc. from [שְׁכֹבֶת] dec. 13 c . . שכב

שְׁכַבְתֶּם᷄ וְ Kal pret. 2 pers. pl. masc.; וְ, for וֹ, conv. שכב

שָׁכָה Root not used; סְכָא Syr to look for; Chald. to view, regard.

שֶׂכוּ (watch-tower; Chald. סָבוּת id.) pr. name of a place near Ramah, 1 Sa. 19. 22.

שֶׂכְוִי masc. intelligence, only meton. the seat of it, the heart, mind; Targ. לִבָּא, Job 38. 36; some Jewish commentators regard it as an epithet for the cock.

שְׂכִיָּה fem. dec. 10, a sight, an object gazed upon, Is. 2. 16.

מַשְׂכִּית fem. (מַשְׂכִּיּוֹת).—I. image, figure.—II. imagination, idea, thought.

שָׂכָה Kal not used; perh. i. q. שָׁנָה (Ethiop. שׂכי) to wander, rove. Hiph. to wander about lasciviously, Je. 5. 8.

שָׂכְיָה (wandering) pr. name masc. 1 Ch. 8. 10.

שֹׁכָה pr. name of a place, see שׂוֹכֹה שׂוֹכ

שְׁכוֹ noun masc. sing., suff. 3 pers. sing. masc.

from [שֶׂךְ] dec. 8 c, see סֹךְ סכך

שָׁכוּל adj. masc. sing. . . . שכל

שִׁכּוּל noun masc. sing. . . . שכל

שְׁכוּלָה Kal part. pass. sing. fem. [of שָׁכוּל masc.] שכל

שִׁכּוֹר᷄ Kal part. pass. sing. masc. . . שכר

שִׁכּוֹר adj. masc. sing. dec. 1 b . . שכר

שִׁכּוֹרֵי᷄ id. pl., constr. st. . . . שכר

שִׁכּוֹרִים᷄ id. pl., abs. st. . . . שכר

שָׁכַח וְ' [also שְׁכֵחַ, comp. Pr. 2. 17; Is. 49. 14] fut. יִשְׁכַּח.—I. to forget.—II. to leave from forgetfulness, De. 24. 19.—III. to forget, disregard, neglect. Niph. I. to be forgotten.—II. to be forgotten, neglected, Job 28. 4. Pi. & Hiph. causative. Hithp. הִשְׁתַּכַּח to be forgotten, Ec. 8. 10.

שָׁכֵחַ masc. dec. 5 a (but pl. c. שְׁכֵחֵי § 34. rem. 2), forgetting, neglecting.

שְׁכַח Chald. Ithpe. הִשְׁתְּכַח (§ 47. rem. 4) to be found. Aph. הַשְׁכַּח (§ 47. rem. 4).—I. to find.—II. to get, obtain, Ezr. 7. 16.

שְׁכֹחַ᷄ Kal inf. abs. . . . . שכח

שִׁכַּח᷄ Piel pret. 3 pers. sing. masc. . . שכח

שָׁכְחָה׳

שְׁכֵחָה᷄ } Kal pret. 3 pers. sing. fem. (§ 8. rem. 1 & 7) שכח

שָׁכְחוּ᷄ id. pret. 3 pers. pl. . . . שכח

שְׁכֵחֶךְ᷄᷄ id. id., suff. 2 pers. sing. fem. (§ 16. rem. 1) שכח

שְׁכֵחֵנִי᷄ id. id., suff. 1 pers. sing. . . . שכח

ᵃ Is. 10. 17.   ᵉ Ps. 83. 12, 14.   ⁱ Le. 15. 24.   ᵐ Ps. 88. 6.   ᵖ Ru. 3. 8.   ᵗ Le. 18. 20, 23.   ˣ Is. 49. 21.   ʸ Joel 1. 5.   ᵇ La. 2. 6.
ᵇ Ps. 48. 14.   ᶠ Ho. 2. 8.   ᵏ 1 Ki. 1. 2; 3, 19.   ⁿ Ec. 4. 2.   ᵠ Ru. 3. 4.   ᵘ Le. 26. 6.   ʸ Ne. 6. 13.   ᶻ Ge. 27. 45.   ᵈ Pr. 2. 17.
ᶜ Is. 16. 3.   ᵍ Ju. 5. 27.   Ge. 39. 7, 12.   ᵒ Is. 14. 8.   ʳ Ge. 47. 30.   ᵛ La. 2. 6.   ʷ Is. 28. 3.   ᵃ De. 8. 19.   ᵉ Ho. 2. 15.
ᵈᵈ Je. 30. 14.

שִׁבְחֵי adj. pl. constr. masc. [from שֶׁבַח] dec. 5a . שבח

שִׁבְחִי } Kal imp. sing. fem. . . . שבח

שֹׁבְחֵי id. part. act. pl. constr. masc. [fr. שֹׁבֵחַ] d. 7b שבח

שְׁבַחְנוּ id. pret. 1 pers. pl. . . . שבח

שְׁבַחֲנוּךָ id. id., suff. 2 pers. sing. masc. . שבח

שְׁבֵחַנִי id. pret. 3 pers. sing. masc. [שָׁבַח], suff. 1 pers. sing. (§ 16. rem. 1) . . . שבח

שְׁבֵחֻנִי id. pret. 3 pers. pl., suff. 1 pers. sing. (v. id.) שבח

שָׁבַחַתְּ id. pret. 2 pers. sing. fem. . . שבח

שָׁבַחְתָּ } id. pret. 2 pers. sing. masc.; acc. shifted by conv. } (§ 8. rem. 7) . . . שבח

שָׁבַחְתִּי } id. pret. 1 pers. sing. (§ 8. rem. 7) שבח
שִׁבַּחְתִּי }

שִׁבַּחְתַּנִי id. pret. 2 pers. sing. masc., suff. 1 pers. sing. שבח

שֶׁבַחְיָה pr. name masc. . . . . שבח

שְׁבִיּוֹת noun fem., pl. of (שְׁבִיָּה) dec. 10 . שבה

שַׂכִּין masc. a knife, Pr. 23. 2 ; Chald. סַכִּין. Etym. doubtful, comp. however שָׂכַךְ.

שָׂכִיר } noun masc. sing. dec. 3a . . . שכר

[שָׂכַךְ] to cover, Ex. 33. 22. In the derivv. i. q. סוּךְ to weave, to hedge ; but perh. also to cut (comp. Lat. secare), whence שָׂכִין, and then to be sharp, pointed.

שֵׂךְ masc. dec. 8b, thorn, Nu. 33. 55.

שָׂךְ masc. dec. 8c, hedge, fence, La. 2. 6.

שֻׂכָּה fem. dec. 10, a spear, Job 40. 31.

מְשׂוּכָה fem. dec. 10, hedge, fence, Is. 5. 5.

[שָׁכַךְ] I. to bow, stoop down, Je. 5. 26.—II. to lower itself, abate. Hiph. to cause to abate, to quiet, still, Nu. 17. 20.

שֵׁשַׁךְ Sheshach, a name for Babylon, Je. 25. 26 ; 51. 41. According to C. B. Michaelis for שֵׁשְׁבָּךְ (comp. שָׁשַׁק, בָּבֶל,) χαλκόπυλος having brazen gates, from שַׁךְ Arab. to overlay a gate with iron or brass ; according to Hengstenberg, a sinking down, with reference to its future destiny.

שָׁכְכָה Kal pret. 3 pers. sing. fem. [for שָׁכְכָה § 8. r. 7]
שָׁכְכָה pref. יְ- (adv. see כָּכָה.

שָׂכַל to act wisely, prudently, 1 Sa. 18. 30. Pi. to act wisely, wittingly, Ge. 48. 14. Hiph. I. to look at, Ge. 3. 6.—II. to consider, attend to, with בְּ, עַל, אֶל (Da. 9. 13).—III. to be or become intelligent, wise, or prudent ; also to act wisely, prudently ; part. מַשְׂכִּיל wise, prudent, godly, pious ; as a title of several Psalms (besides Ps. 47. 8) prob. a devout poem, which others render a didatic poem (comp. No V),

not alike suitable to all those Psalms ; inf. הַשְׂכִּיל הַשְׂכֵּל as a subst. intelligence, wisdom, prudence.— IV. to prosper, have success.—V. to make wise, teach, instruct.—VI. to cause to prosper, 1 Ki. 2. 3.

שְׂכַל Chald. Ithpa. אִשְׂתַּכַּל to consider, Da. 7. 8.

שֵׂכֶל masc. & שֶׂכֶל (in pause שָׂכֶל § 35. rem. 2). —I. regard, estimation, Pr. 3. 4.—II. intelligence, understanding.—III. signification, Ne. 8. 8.—IV craft, cunning, Da. 8. 25.

שָׂכְלְתָנוּ Chald. fem. intelligence, understanding, Da. 5. 11, 12, 14.

[שָׁכֹל] § 8. rem. 1] fut. יִשְׁכַּל to lose children, to become childless ; part. pass. שְׁכוּלָה childless, Is. 49. 21. Pi. שִׁכֵּל.—I. to make childless, to bereave.—II. to cause abortion, 2 Ki. 2. 19.—III. to produce an abortion, to miscarry ; part. מְשַׁכֵּלֶת as a subst. abortion, 2 Ki. 2. 21.—IV. metaph. of a vine, to be unfruitful. Hiph. i. q. Pi. Nos. I & III, Je. 50. 9 ; Ho. 9. 14.

שְׁכוֹל masc.—I. loss of children, bereavement.— II. destitution, Ps. 35. 12.

שַׁכּוּל adj. masc.—I. bereaved of children, deprived of the young.—II. without young, Ca. 4. 2 ; 6. 6.

שְׁכֻלִים m.pl. bereavement, childless state, Is. 49. 20

אֶשְׁכֹּל masc. (pl. אֶשְׁכְּלוֹת, אַשְׁכְּלוֹת § 36. rem. 6 & § 44. rem. 5).—I. a cluster, bunch of grapes or flowers (Ca. 1. 14 ; 7. 8). Arab. שׁכל to bind.— II. pr. name of a valley in the south of Palestine. —III. pr. name masc. Ge. 14. 13, 24.

שֵׂכֶל } noun masc. sing. dec. 6b & a . . שׂכל
שֶׂכֶל }

שִׂכֵּל Piel pret. 3 pers. sing. masc. . . שׂכל

שְׁכֻלָה } adj. fem. sing. dec. 10, from שַׁכּוּל masc. שׁכל

שִׂכְּלָה } Piel pret. 3 pers. sing. fem. . שׂכל

שִׂכְּלוּ id. pret. 3 pers. pl. [for שִׂכְּלוּ comp. § 8. r. 7] שׂכל

שִׂכְלוֹ noun m. sing., suff. 3 pers. s. m. fr. שֵׂכֶל d. 6b שׂכל

אֶשְׁכְּלוֹת adj. fem.,pl. of שַׁכּוּל d. 10, from שַׁכּוּל masc. שׁכל

שִׂכְלוּת } noun fem. sing., see . . . . סכל

שְׁכֻלַיִךְ noun m. pl. [שְׁכֻלִים], suff. 2 pers. sing. fem. שׁכל

שִׁכְּלֻךְ Piel pret. 3 pers. pl., suff. 2 pers. sing. fem. שׂכל

שַׁכְלְלֵהּ Chald. Shaph. pret. 3 pers. sing. masc., suff. 3 pers. sing. masc. (§ 48) . . . כלל

שַׁכְלִלוּ } Chald. id. pret. 3 pers. pl. masc. כלל

שִׁכְּלַתָּה Piel pret. 3 pers. s. fem., suff. 3 pers. s. fem. שׂכל

---

a Ps. 9. 18.   d Ps. 44. 18.   g Ps. 102. 5.   k Est. 7. 10.   m Ge. 48. 14.   o Ge. 31. 38.   r Ec. 1. 17.   t Eze. 5. 17.   w Ezr. 6. 14.
b Ps. 45. 11.   e Is. 49. 14.   h Ps. 42. 10.   i Pr. 3. 4.   n Le. 26. 22.   p Je. 18. 21.   s Is. 49. 20.   u Ezr. 5. 11.   x Eze. 14. 15.
c Ps. 44. 21.   f Je. 18. 15.   i Is. 2. 16.

שְׁכָלְם pref. שְׁ (noun masc. sing., suff. 3 pers. pl. masc. from כֹּל dec. 8 c . . . כלל

שָׁכַלְתִּי Kal pret. 1 pers. sing. for שָׁכֹלְתִּי R. . שׁכל

שִׁכַּלְתִּי id. pret. 1 pers. sing. (§ 8. rem. 1) R. שׁכל

שִׁכַּלְתִּי Piel pret. 1 pers. sing. . . שׁכל

שִׁכַּלְתִּים id. id., suff. 3 pers. pl. masc. . שׁכל

שְׁכֻלְתֶּם id. pret. 2 pers. pl. masc. . . שׁכל

וְשִׁכֻלְתְּנוּ Chald. noun fem. sing. . . שׁכל

שָׁכַם Hiph. הִשְׁכִּים.—I. to rise early in the morning, with or without בַּבֹּקֶר.—II. to get early to a place, with לְ, comp. Ge. 19. 27, or perh. וַיֵּלֶךְ is to be implied.—III. inf. הַשְׁכֵּם adv. in the morning, 1 Sa. 17. 16; hence, early, without delay; part. מַשְׁכִּים early, Ho. 6. 4.

שְׁכֶם ' ו masc. dec. 6 b (§ 35. rem. 10).—I. shoulder, shoulders.—II. part, portion, Ge. 48. 22.—III. pr. name, Shechem, a city in the mountains of Ephraim, pertaining to the Levites; with ה parag. שְׁכְמָה. —IV. pr. name of a Canaanite, comp. Ge. 33. 19.

שֶׁכֶם (portion) pr. name masc.—I. Nu. 26. 31; Jos. 17. 2, where his brother's name is said to be חֵלֶק; patronym. שִׁכְמִי, Nu. 26. 31.—II. 1 Ch. 7. 19. שְׁכְמָה fem. shoulder, Job 31. 22.

שֶׁכֶם (' ו, ') noun masc. sing., suff. שִׁכְמִי dec. 6 } שֶׁכֶם (§ 35. rem. 10), also pr. name } שׁכם
שִׁכְמָה } id. (pr. name) with parag. ה . . שׁכם
שְׁכְמָה }
שִׁכְמָהּ id., suff. 3 pers. sing. fem. . . שׁכם
שִׁכְמוֹ id., suff. 3 pers. sing. masc. . . שׁכם
שִׁכְמִי id., suff. 1 pers. sing. . . . שׁכם
שִׁכְמְךָ id., suff. 2 pers. sing. masc. . . שׁכם
שִׁכְמָם id. suff. 3 pers. pl. masc. . . שׁכם

שָׁכַן ,שָׁכֵן (' ו fut. יִשְׁכֹּן.—I. to lie down, to rest.—II. to rest, abide, continue.—III. to dwell; part. שׁוֹכֵן settled, dwelling.—IV. to inhabit. Pi. שִׁכֵּן.—I. to cause to dwell.—II. to place, fix. Hiph. i. q. Pi.

שָׁכֵן Chald. id. Da. 4. 18. Pa. to cause to dwell, Ezr. 6. 12.

שָׁכֵן masc. dec. 5 a, fem. שְׁכֶנֶת (§ 44. rem. 3), pl. שְׁכֵנוֹת.—I. inhabitant.—II. neighbour.

שֶׁכֶן masc. dec. 6 a, a dwelling, De. 12. 5.

שְׁכַנְיָה (dweller with the Lord) pr. name masc. of several persons.

שְׁכַנְיָהוּ (id.) pr. name masc. 2 Ch. 31. 15.

מִשְׁכָּן masc. dec. 2 b (pl. ־ים, ־וֹת).—I. habitation, dwelling; also habitation of God, the temple.—II. tent, Ca. 1. 8.—III. the sacred tabernacle of the Israelites.—IV. lair of beasts, Job 39. 6.

מִשְׁכַּן Chald. masc. dec. 2 a, habitation, Ezr. 7. 15.

שֹׁכֵן adj. masc. sing. dec. 5 a . . שׁכן

שַׁכֵּן Chald. Pael pret. 3 pers. sing. masc. (§ 47. r. 1) שׁכן

שֹׁכֵן adj. masc., constr. of שֹׁכֵן dec. 5 a . שׁכן

שְׁכֹן (' ו) Kal imp. sing. masc. (§ 8. rem. 18) ; } שׁכן
שְׁכָן־ ' } bef. (:) }

שִׁכֵּן Piel pret. 3 pers. sing. masc. . . שׁכן

שָׁכַן Kal pret. 3 pers. sing. masc. . . שׁכן

שֹׁכֵן id. pret. 3 pers. sing. masc. dec. 7 b שׁכן

שָׁכְנָה id. pret. 3 pers. sing. fem. . . שׁכן

שָׁכְנוּ (' ו) id. pret. 3 pers. pl. . . שׁכן

שְׁכֹנוּ (' ו) id. imp. pl. masc. . . שׁכן

שְׁכֵנוֹ (') adj. masc. sing., suff. 3 pers. sing. masc. from שֵׁכֵן dec. 5 a; ' ו bef. (:) שׁכן

שְׁכֵנִי id. pl. with suff. 1 pers. sing. . שׁכן

שֹׁכְנֵי (') Kal part. act. pl. c. masc. from שֹׁכֵן dec. 7 b שׁכן

שֹׁכְנִי id. sing., with parag. ' (§ 8. rem. 19) שׁכן

שְׁכֵנֶיהָ (') adj. pl. masc., suff. 3 pers. sing. fem. from שֵׁכֵן dec. 5 a; ' ו bef. (:) שׁכן

שְׁכַנְיָה } pr. name masc.; ' ו id. . . שׁכן
שְׁכַנְיָהוּ (' ו }

שֹׁכְנֵיהֶם (') Kal part. act. pl., suff. 3 pers. pl. masc. from שֹׁכֵן dec. 7 b . . שׁכן

שְׁכֵנָיו (') adj. pl. m., suff. 3 pers. s. m. fr. שֵׁכֵן d. 5 a שׁכן

שְׁכֵנַיִךְ id. pl., suff. 2 pers. sing. fem. . . שׁכן

שְׁכֵנַיְכִי id. pl., suff. 2 p. s. f., Kh. ־יְכִי, K. ־יִךְ (§ 4. r. 4) שׁכן

שָׁכַנְתְּ Kal pret. 2 pers. sing. masc. . . שׁכן

שָׁכַנְתָּ (') id. pret 2 pers. sing. fem. . . שׁכן

שָׁכַנְתִּי } id. pret. 1 pers. sing.; acc. shifted by }
וְשָׁכַנְתִּי conv. ' ו (§ 8. rem. 7) . . } שׁכן

שִׁכַּנְתִּי (') Piel pret. 1 pers. sing. . . שׁכן

שָׁכַנְתִּי Kh. שְׁכַנְתְּ, K. שָׁכַנְתְּ Kal part. act. sing. fem. (§ 39. No. 4. rem. 3, also § 8. rem. 5) שׁכן

שָׁכַר fut. יִשְׂכֹּר.—I. to hire.—II. to bribe. Niph. to hire out oneself, 1 Sa. 2. 5. Hithp. הִשְׂתַּכֵּר id. Hag. 1. 6.

שֵׂכָר masc. dec. 4 a.—I. hire, wages, reward.—II. pr. name of two men, 1 Ch. 11. 35 (for which שָׂרָר 2 Sa. 23. 33), & 26. 4.

שָׂכָר masc. hire, wages.

שָׂכִיר masc. dec. 3 a, hired labourer, hireling.

שְׂכִירָה fem. a hiring, Is. 7. 20.

יִשָּׂשכָר (Kh. יִשְׁשָׂכָר for יִשְׂשָׂכָר he brings

a Ca. 4. 2; 6. 6.   h Ho. 9. 12.   i Job 31. 36.   n Ho. 10. 5.   r Ps. 78. 60.   u Je. 12. 14.   x Job 26. 5.   d Eze. 16. 26.   g Mi. 4. 10.
b Ge. 43. 14.   c Ge. 41. 36.   k Is. 10. 27.   o Ge. 26. 2.   s Ps. 68. 7.   v Is. 18. 3.   y De. 1. 7.   e 2 Ki. 4. 3.   h Je. 7. 7, 12.
c Ge. 48. 14.   d Da. 5. 11, 12, 14.   l Ex. 12. 34.   p Je. 48. 28.   t Ps. 37. 27.   w Je. 49. 18;   z Je. 49. 10.   f Ps. 74. 2.   i Je. 51. 13.
Je 15. 7.   g Ps. 21. 13.   m Ezr. 6. 12.   q Ps. 37. 3.   Ex. 12. 4.   50. 40.

reward; invariably in Keri יִשָּׂכָר *gotten by hire*, comp. Ge. 30. 16) pr. name of the fifth son of Jacob and the tribe descended from him.

מַשְׂכֹּרֶת fem. dec. 13 c, *wages*.

[שָׁכַר] fut. יִשְׁכַּר.—I. *to drink to the full, drink to hilarity.* —II. *to be intoxicated*; metaph. *to be giddy.* Pi. & Hiph. *to make drunken.* Hithp. *to act like one drunken*, 1 Sa. 1. 14.

שֵׁכָר masc. *strong, intoxicating drink.*

שִׁכֹּר, שִׁכּוֹר masc. dec. 1 b, *drunken, intoxicated*; fem. שִׁכֹּרָה 1 Sa. 1. 13.

שִׁכָּרוֹן masc. *drunkenness*, Eze. 23. 33; 39. 19.

שִׁכָּרוֹן (*drunkenness*) pr. name of a place in Judah, Jos. 15. 11.

אֶשְׁכָּר masc. *gift, present.* Arab. שכר *to give a reward, a present.*

שָׂכָר noun masc. sing. dec. 4 a; also pr. name וְ

שַׂכֵּר Piel inf. constr.

שָׂכֹר Kal inf. abs.

שֶׂכֶר noun masc. sing. וְ

שֵׂכֶר noun m. s., constr. of שָׂכָר d. 4 a; וְ bef. (:)

שָׂכָר noun masc. sing.

שֹׂכֵר Kal part. act. sing. masc. dec. 7 b וְ

שִׁכֹּר defect. for שִׁכּוֹר (q. v.)

שְׂכָרָהּ noun masc. sing., suff. 3 pers. sing. fem. from שָׂכָר dec. 4 a

שְׂכָרוּ Kal pret. 3 pers. pl.

שְׂכָרוֹ id. pret. 3 pers. s. masc., suff. 3 pers. s. masc.

שְׂכָרוֹ noun masc. sing., suff. 3 pers. sing. masc. from שָׂכָר dec. 4 a

שִׂכְרוּ Kal imp. pl. masc. וְ

שִׁכָּרוֹן noun masc. sing.

שִׁכְּרוֹנָה pr. name of a place [שִׁכְּרוֹן] with parag. ה

שְׂכָרִי noun masc. s., suff. 1 pers. s. fr. שָׂכָר dec. 4 a

שְׂכֻּרִי defect. for שְׂכוֹרִי (q. v.)

שְׂכִירֶיהָ noun m. pl., suff. 3 pers. s. fem. fr. שָׂכִיר d. 3 a

שֹׂכְרִים Kal part. act. masc., pl. of שֹׂכֵר dec. 7 b

שְׂכָרֵךְ noun masc. sing., suff. 2 pers. sing. fem. from שָׂכָר dec. 4 a

שְׂכָרֶךָ } id., suff. 2 pers. sing. masc.
שְׂכָרְךָ }

שְׂכֻרַת Kal part. pass. constr. [of שְׂכוּרָה from masc.]; וְ bef. (:)

שְׂכַרְתִּיךָ id. pret. 1 pers. sing., suff. 2 pers. sing. masc.

שָׂכַרְתָּ Kal pret. 2 pers. sing. masc.

שָׂכַרְתִּי Kal pret. 1 pers. sing.; acc. shifted by conv. וְ (comp. § 8. rem. 7)

שַׁל Kal imp. sing. masc.

שָׁלֹל Kal inf. abs.

שְׁלֹא pref. שֶׁ χ adv.

שַׁלְאֲנָן adj. masc. sing., שַׁאֲנָן with ל inserted

שָׁלַב Kal not used; Chald. שְׁלַב Pa. *to join together.* Pu. part. מְשֻׁלָּבוֹת *joined together*, Ex. 26. 17; 36. 22 שְׁלַבִּים masc. pl. *joinings, edges, borders*, 1 Ki 7. 28, 29.

שֶׁלֶג, שָׁלָג (§ 35. r. 2) masc. *snow*. הִשְׁלִיג Hiph. *to be white as snow*, of the bones of the slain, only Ps. 68. 15; or perh. causative like הִמְטִיר, *to cause to snow* (תַּשְׁלֵג 2 pers.), in allusion to some destructive snowfall; see also צַלְמוֹן.

[שָׁלוּ, שָׁלָה] pret. 1 pers. שָׁלַוְתִּי, 3 pers. pl. שָׁלוּ; ap. יֵשֶׁל —I. *to be quiet, at ease, to enjoy prosperity.* —II. *to make prosperous*, Job 27. 8; others, *to draw out*, i. q. שָׁלַל; נָשַׁל, or the form יֵשֶׁל 1. c. is supposed to stand for יִשְׁאַל *he shall require.* Niph. *to become negligent*, 2 Ch. 29. 11; others, *to go astray, err*, i. q. Chald. שְׁלָה. Hiph. 2 Ki. 4. 28, *to deceive*, either from the idea of *quieting, flattering*, by promise of happiness, or *leading astray*, comp. Niph

שְׁלָה Chald. *to be at ease*, Da. 4. 1.

שַׁל masc. *fault, error*, 2 Sa. 6. 7, comp. Niph.

שָׁלֵיו, שָׁלֵו, שָׁלֵו (pl. c. שַׁלְוֵי dec. 5, comp. § 33. rem. 1), fem. שְׁלֵוָה.—I. adj. *at ease, prosperous.* —II. *careless, unmindful* of God, Eze. 23. 42.—III. subst. *quiet, prosperity*, Job 20. 20.

שֶׁלֶו masc. dec. 6 a (with suff. שַׁלְוִי), *quiet, prosperity*, Ps. 30. 7.

שָׁלוּ Chald. fem. *failure, negligence*, or *error, fault* (comp. Niph.), Da. 6. 5; Ezr. 4. 22; 6. 9; & Da. 3. 29, where Khethib has שָׁלָה.

שַׁלְוָה fem. (constr. שַׁלְוַת; no pl. abs.).—I. *quiet, prosperity.*—II. *carelessness, negligence* of God, Pr. 1. 32.

שְׁלֵוָא Chald. fem. d. 8 a, *quiet, prosperity*, Da. 4. 24

שֶׁלִי masc. *quiet, stillness*, 2 Sa. 3. 27.

שִׁלְיָה fem. *the after-birth.*

שִׁילֹה I. *Shiloh*, Ge. 49. 10, *pacificator*, or *bringer of peace*, i. e. the Messiah; but the ancient versions have evidently read here שֶׁלֹּה (שֶׁלּוֹ) *whose it is*, שֶׁ, i. q. אֲשֶׁר, & לֹה לוֹ *to him*, comp. Eze. 21. 32. —II. שָׁלֹה, שִׁילוֹ, שִׁלֹה pr. name of a city

Eze. 29. 18.   Pr. 26. 10.   Is. 29. 9.   Je. 13. 13; Eze. 23. 33.   Je. 46. 21.
Hab. 2. 15.   1 Sa. 25. 36.   Ne. 6. 12.   Is. 28. 1.   2 Ch. 24. 12.
Ge. 30. 16.   Jon. 1. 3.   Ex. 2. 9.   Ge. 31. 8, 8.   Ge. 30. 16.   Ex. 33. 22.
  Is. 51. 21.   Job 1. 10.   Ru. 2. 16.   Job 21. 23.

in tbe tribe of Ephraim, north of Bethel, where the tabernacle remained for a long time. Gent. noun שִׁילֹנִי *Shilonite*.

שָׁלָה Chald. Kh. שָׁלָה, K. שְׁלוּ noun fem. sing.

שָׁלָה׳ pr. name masc. (for שְׁאָלָה)

שְׁלֵה Chald. Peal part. pass. sing. masc. (§ 55, note)

שִׁלֹה pr. name, see תַּאֲנַת שִׁ.

שַׁלְהֶבֶת
שַׁלְהֶבֶת׳ } noun fem. sing. . . . . . להב

שְׂלָו masc. (pl. שַׂלְוִים § 35. rem. 10) *quails*. In the sing. the Keri has everywhere שְׂלָיו.

שָׁלֵו adj. m. sing., pl. c. שַׁלְוֵי d.5 (comp. § 35. r. 1) שלה

שָׁלוּ Kal pret. 3 pers. pl., or Chald. noun fem. sing. שלה

שִׁלוּ pr. name of a place, see שִׁילֹה

שַׁלְוָה׳ 's׳ noun fem. sing. (no pl.) שלה

שְׁלֵוָה ו adj. fem. sing. from שָׁלֵו masc., ו bef. (:) שלה

שָׁלוֹחַ׳ ו׳ Kal inf. abs. שלה

שָׁלוּחַ׳ id. part. pass. sing. masc. . . שלה

שְׁלוּחָה id. part. pass. sing. fem. . . שלה

שְׁלוּחֶיהָ the foll. with suff. 3 pers. sing. fem. שלה

שִׁלּוּחִים noun masc., pl. of [שִׁלּוּחַ] dec. 1 b שלה

שְׁלוּחֵי׳ ו adj. pl. constr. masc. see שָׁלֵו dec. 5 (comp. § 33. rem. 1) . . . . שלה

שַׁלְוִים noun masc., pl. of שָׁלֵו dec. 6 (§ 35. rem. 16, comp. rem. 10) . . . שלו

שָׁלוֹם׳ ו adj. or subst. masc. dec. 3 a . . שלם

שָׁלוֹם׳ ו pr. name masc. . . . . שלם

שְׁלוֹם noun masc. sing., constr. of שָׁלוֹם dec. 3 a שלם

שְׁלוֹמִי id. with suff. 1 pers. sing. . . שלם

שְׁלוֹמִים adj. masc., pl. of שָׁלוֹם dec. 3 a שלם

שִׁלּוּמִים noun masc., pl. of שִׁלּוּם dec. 1 b שלם

שְׁלוֹמִית pr. name masc. . . . . שלם

שְׁלוֹמְךָ noun masc. sing., suff. 2 pers. sing. masc. from שָׁלוֹם dec. 3 a . . . שלם

שְׁלוֹמֵנוּ id. with suff. 1 pers. pl. . . שלם

שַׁלְוֹן pr. name masc. . . . . שלל

שְׁלוּפָה Kal part. pass. sing. fem. [of שָׁלוּף] . שלף

שָׁלוֹשׁ׳ ו׳ num. card. fem. sing. . . שלש

שְׁלוֹשׁ׳ id. constr. st. . . . . שלש

שְׁלוֹשָׁה (2 Ch. 4. 4.) id. masc.; ו bef. (:) שלש

שָׁלוֹשׁ id. com. gen. pl. . . . . שלש

שְׁלוֹשֶׁת׳ ו un fem. sing., constr. of שָׁלֹשָׁה (no pl.) שלה

שָׁלֹתִי׳ Kal pret. 2 pers. sing. masc. . . שלל

שָׁלַוְתִּי׳ Kal pret. 1 pers. sing. R. שָׁלָה see . . שלה

שָׁלַח׳ ו׳ fut. יִשְׁלַח; inf. c. שְׁלֹחַ, שְׁלַח.—I. *to send* a person or thing, with אֶל, עַל of the person to whom; with לְ and inf. *to send to do any thing*; with בְּיַד *by whom*; שְׁלַח לְךָ *send for thyself*, Nu. 13. 2.—II. *to send word, a message, a charge.*—III. *to send, commission*, comp. 2 Sa. 11. 22.—IV. *to send away*, i. e. *to let loose, let go*, Ps. 50. 19; שָׁלַח יַד מִן *to let go the hand from* any thing, i. e. *to withdraw it*, 1 Ki. 13. 4, Ca. 5. 4.—V. *to put forth, stretch out, extend*, שֶׁ יָד בְּ *to lay hand on* a person or thing, i. e. *to injure*, or on a thing, *to take it unjustly*, and is const. also with אֶל, עַל; part. שָׁלוּחַ *stretched out, slim, slender*, Ge. 49. 21. Niph. *to be sent*, Est. 3. 13. Pi. שִׁלַּח.—I. *to send*, with עַל *to whom*; espec. in reference to calamities which God sends, with בְּ, אֶל, עַל *on whom.*—II. *to send away, let go, dismiss*; e. g. one on his way, *to accompany him*; a husband his wife, *to divorce*.—III. *to let loose, set free, set at liberty*, שֶׁ מָדוֹן *to let loose, occasion strife.*—IV. *to give up, deliver up*, with בְּ, בְּיַד, Job 8. 4; Ps. 81. 13.—V. *to let down* by a cord, Je. 38. 6, 11; *to let hang down* the hair, Eze. 44. 20.—VI. *to cast, throw, shoot*; also *to cast down, cast off, cast forth.*—VII. שֶׁ בָּאֵשׁ *to set on fire.*—VIII. *to put forth, stretch out, extend*, espec. the hand. Pu. I. *to be sent.*—II. *to be sent away, let go, dismissed*; of a woman, *to be divorced*; hence *to be left, forsaken.*—III. *to be cast out, driven out.* Hiph. *to send*, e. g. plagues, &c. with בְּ *on* any one.

שְׁלַח Chald. fut. יִשְׁלַח.—I. *to send.*—II. *to put forth* the hand.

שֶׁלַח masc. dec. 6 (with suff. שִׁלְחוֹ, but in pause שָׁלַח § 35. rem. 2 & 5).—I. a *missile, weapon*, as a dart, javelin, spear.—II. *shoot, sprout.*—III. pr. name masc. Ge. 10. 24; 11. 12.—IV. pr. name of a pool near mount Zion, called also שִׁלֹחַ Ne. 3. 15.

שִׁלֹחַ (*a sending forth*, sc. of water) pr. name, *Siloah*, a spring and conduit on the south-east of Jerusalem.

שִׁלּוּחִים masc. pl. (of שִׁלּוּחַ dec. 1 b) prop. a *sending away.*—I. *divorce*, Ex. 18. 2; *bill of divorce*, Mi. 1. 14.—II. *presents, dowry.*

שַׁלְּחוֹת f. pl. (of שְׁלוּחָה dec. 10) *shoots*, Is. 16. 8

שְׁלֻחִי (*armed*, comp. שֶׁלַח) pr. name of a man.

* Da. 3. 29.   ° Ca. 8. 6;   ° Ps. 122. 7.   ' Mi. 1. 14.   ° Nu. 11. 31.   ° Is. 34. 8.   ° Is. 53. 5.   ° Est. 4. 11;   ° Hab. 2. 8.
° Da. 4. 1.   Eze. 21. 3.   ° Pr. 17. 1.   ° Ps. 73. 12.   ° Je. 13. 19.   Is. 48. 18.   ° Eze. 40. 11.   2 Ch. 16. 12.
° Job 15. 30.   ° Ps. 105. 40.   ° Ex. 18. 2.   ° Job 3. 26.

שְׁלָחִים (*armed men*) pr. name of a city in the tribe of Judah, Jos. 15. 32.

שֻׁלְחָן masc. dec. 2b (pl. שֻׁלְחָנוֹת), *a table*; עָרַךְ שֻׁ to spread, prepare a table; שֻׁלְחַן הַפָּנִים, שֻׁ הַמַּעֲרֶכֶת *table of shewbread.*

מִשְׁלָח masc. dec. 2b.—I. *a sending forth* of cattle for grazing, Is. 7. 25.—II. *a putting forth* of the hand, i.e. *that to which the hand is put, business.*

מִשְׁלוֹחַ masc. *a sending*, Est. 9. 19, 22; with יָד *that on which the hand is laid, prey, booty.*

מִשְׁלַחַת fem.—I. *a sending*, Ps. 78. 49.—II. *a dismission, discharge,* Ec. 8. 8.

שֶׁלַח	pr. name masc. for שֶׁלַח (§ 35. rem. 2) . . . שלח
שָׁלֹחַ	וֹ Kal inf. abs. . . . . שלח
שַׁלַּח	וֹ Piel inf. constr. or imp. sing. masc. . . שלח
שַׁלֵּחַ	id. inf. abs. . . . . שלח
שֶׁלַח	וֹ noun masc. sing. (suff. שִׁלְחוֹ) dec. 6 (§ 35. rem. 5), also pr. name . . שלח
שְׁלַח	וֹ Kal imp. s. m. or (Is. 58. 9) inf.; וֹ bef. (:) שלח
שְׁלַח	Chald. Peal pret. 3 pers. sing. masc. . שלח
שְׁלֹחַ	Kal inf. constr. . . . . שלח
שִׁלַּח	וֹ Piel pret. 3 pers. sing. masc. . . שלח
שֹׁלֵחַ	וֹ Kal part. act. sing. masc. dec. 7b . . שלח
שֻׁלַּח	} Pual pret. 3 pers. sing. masc. . . שלח
שֻׁלָּח	
שָׁלְחָה	וֹ Kal pret. 3 pers. sing. fem. . . שלח
שַׁלְּחָה	Piel inf. (שַׁלֵּחַ), suff. 3 pers. sing. fem. d. 7b שלח
שִׁלְחָה	defect. for שְׁלוּחָה (q. v.) . . . שלח
שִׁלְחָה	Kal imp. s. m. (שְׁלַח) with parag. ה (§ 8. r. 11) שלח
שַׁלְּחָה	Piel pret. 3 pers. sing. fem. for which שָׁלְחָה Eze. 17. 7; 34. 4 (§ 10. rem. 7) . שלח
שִׁלְּחָהּ	וֹ id. pret. 3 p. s. m. (שִׁלַּח), suff. 3 p. s. f. שלח
שֻׁלְּחָה	Pual pret. 3 pers. sing. fem. . . שלח
שִׁלְּחוּהָ	Piel pret. 3 pers. pl. (שִׁלְּחוּ), saff. 3 p. s. m. שלח
שָׁלְחוּ	וֹ Kal pret. 3 pers. pl. . . . שלח
שַׁלְּחוּ	Piel imp. pl. masc. . . . שלח
שְׁלָחוֹ	Kal pret. 3 pers. sing. m., suff. 3 pers. s. m. שלח
שְׁלָחוּ	in pause for שְׁלָחוּ (§ 8. rem. 12) . . שלח
שְׁלַחוּ	Chald. Peal pret. 3 pers. pl. masc. . שלח
שְׁלָחוּ	in pause for שְׁלָחוּ (§ 8. rem. 12) . שלח
שִׁלְחוֹ	n. m. s., suff. 3 p. s. m. fr. שֶׁלַח d. 6 (§ 35. r. 5) שלח
שִׁלְּחוֹ	וֹ Piel pret. 3 p. s. m. (שִׁלַּח), suff. 3 p. s. m. שלח
שַׁלְּחוּ	וֹ Kal imp. pl. masc. . . . שלח

שִׁלְּחוּ	Piel pret. 3 pers. pl. (§ 10. rem. 7) שלח
שֻׁלְּחוּ	Pual pret. 3 pers. pl. . . . שלח
שִׁלַּחֲךָ	Piel pret. 3 pers. pl., suff. 2 pers. sing. masc. שלח
שַׁלְּחוּנִי	id. imp. pl. masc., suff. 1 pers. sing. שלח
שִׁלְחִי	pr. name masc. . . . . שלח
שֹׁלְחִי	Kal part. act. s. m., suff. 1 p. s. fr. שֹׁלֵחַ d. 7b שלח
שְׁלָחַיִךְ	n. m. pl., suff. 2 p. s. f. fr. שֶׁלַח d. 6 (§ 35. r. 5) שלח
שִׁלְחִים	defect. for שְׁלוּחִים (q. v.) . . . שלח
שִׁלְחִים	וֹ pr. name of a place . . . שלח
שֹׁלְחִים	Kal part. act. masc., pl. of שֹׁלֵחַ dec. 7b שלח
שָׁלְחֲךָ	id. inf., suff. 2 pers. sing. masc. . שלח
שְׁלָחֲךָ	id. pret. 3 pers. sing. m., suff. 2 pers. s. m. שלח
שְׁלָחֵךְ	id. id., suff. 2 pers. sing. fem. . . שלח
שִׁלֵּחֲךָ	Piel pret. 3 pers. sing. m., suff. 2 pers. s. m. שלח
שֹׁלֵחֲךָ	Kal part. act. sing. masc., suff. 2 **pers. sing.** masc. from שֹׁלֵחַ dec. 7b (§ 36. rem. 3) שלח
שַׁלְּחָם	Piel inf. (שַׁלֵּחַ), suff. 3 pers. pl. masc. d. 7b שלח
שְׁלָחָם	Kal pret. 3 pers. sing. m., suff. 3 pers. pl. m. שלח
שִׁלְּחָם	Piel pret. 3 p. pl. m. (שִׁלַּח), suff. 3 p. pl. m. שלח
שֻׁלְחָן	וֹ noun masc. sing. dec. 2b שלח
שֻׁלְחַן	id., constr. st. שלח
שְׁלַחְנָא	Chald. Peal pret. 1 pers. pl. שלח
שֻׁלְחָנָהּ	noun m. s., suff. 3 pers. s. f. fr. שֻׁלְחָן d. 2b שלח
שְׁלַחְנוּ	Kal pret. 1 pers. pl. [for שְׁלַחְנוּ] . שלח
שְׁלָחַנוּ	id. pret. 3 pers. sing. masc., suff. 1 pers. pl. שלח
שִׁלַּחְנוּ	Piel pret. 1 pers. pl. . . . שלח
שֻׁלְחָנוֹ	noun m. s., suff. 3 pers. s. m. fr. שֻׁלְחָן d. 2b שלח
שֻׁלְחָנוֹת	id. with pl. fem. term., abs. st. שלח
שַׁלְּחֵנִי	Piel imp. sing. masc. (שַׁלֵּחַ), suff. 1 pers. s. שלח
שִׁלְחֵנִי	defect. for שִׁלְּחוּנִי (q. v.) . . שלח
שְׁלָחַנִי	} Kal pret. 3 pers. sing. masc. with suff. } שלח
שְׁלָחָנִי	1 pers. sing. . . .
שַׁלְּחֵנִי	id. imp. sing. masc. (שַׁלֵּחַ), suff. 1 pers. s. שלח
שֻׁלְחָנִי	noun m. s., suff. 1 pers. s. fr. שֻׁלְחָן d. 2b שלח
שְׁלָחֲךָ	} id with suff. 2 pers. sing. masc. . שלח
שֻׁלְחָנְךָ	
שְׁלָחָם	id. with suff. 3 pers. pl. masc. שלח
שִׁלַּחְתָּ	} Kal pret. 2 pers. sing. masc. (§ 8. } שלח
שָׁלַחְתָּ	rem. 7) . . . .
שִׁלַּחְתָּ	Piel pret. 2 pers. sing. masc. שלח
שְׁלַחְתָּהּ	וֹ id. id., suff. 3 pers. sing. fem. שלח
שְׁלַחְתּוֹ	וֹ id. id., suff. 3 pers. sing. masc. שלח

a Nu. 22. 37.   d De. 22. 29.   l 1 Sa. 5. 11.   q Ge. 44. 3.   x 1 Ki. 9. 16.   a 1 Sa. 21. 3.   f Pr. 9. 2.   t Ge. 24. 54.   n 1 Sa. 25. 25.
b 2 Ch. 32. 5.   e Ge. 49. 21.   m 2 Ki. 2. 17.   r Ob. 7.   y Ge. 38. 17.   b Eze. 13. 6.   h Jos. 6. 17.   k Is. 6. 8.   o De. 21. 14.
c Job 5. 10.   f De. 24. 1, 3, 4.   n 1 Sa. 24. 20.   s Ge. 24. 56.   z 1 Sa. 25. 32.   c Jos. 22. 7.   i 1 Sa. 25. 40.   l Job 36. 16.   p 2 Sa. 3. 24.
d Ob. 1.   g Is. 50. 1.   o Ne. 8. 10.   t Ca. 4. 13.   a 1 Sa. 20. 22.   d Exr. 4. 14.   k Ex. 14. 5.   m Ps. 69. 23.   q Je. 34. 14.
e De. 25. 11.   h 1 Ch. 12. 19.   p Ps. 74. 7.

שְׁלַחְתּוּן	Ch. Peal pret. 2 pers. pl. masc. . שלח
שָׁלַחְתִּי	Kal pret. 1 pers. sing.; acc. shifted by conv. וְ (§ 8. rem. 7) . } שלח
וָשָׁלַחְתִּי	
שִׁלַּחְתִּי	Piel pret. 1 pers. sing.; acc. shifted (v. i.) . . . } שלח
וְשִׁלַּחְתִּי	
שֻׁלַּחְתִּי	Pual pret. 1 pers. sing. . . שלח
שִׁלְחֹתֶיהָ	noun f. pl., suff. 3 pers. s. f. fr. [שִׁלְחָה] d. 10 שלח
שִׁלַּחְתִּיהָ	Piel pret. 1 pers. sing., suff. 3 pers. sing. fem. שלח
שְׁלַחְתִּיו	Kal pret. 1 pers. sing., suff. 3 pers. sing. m. שלח
שְׁלַחְתִּיךָ	id. id., suff. 2 pers. sing. masc. . שלח
וְשִׁלַּחְתִּיךָ	וְ Piel pret. 1 pers. sing., suff. 2 pers. sing. m. שלח
שְׁלַחְתִּים	Kal pret. 1 pers. sing., suff. 3 pers. pl masc. שלח
שִׁלַּחְתָּם	וְ Piel pret. 2 pers. s. m., suff. 3 pers. pl. m. שלח
שְׁלַחְתֶּם	וּ Kal pret. 2 pers. pl. masc.; וּ, for וְ, conv. שלח
שִׁלַּחְתֶּם	וְ Piel pret. 2 pers. pl. masc. . שלח
שְׁלַחְתָּנוּ	Kal pret. 2 pers. sing. masc., suff. 1 pers. pl. שלח
שְׁלַחְתַּנִי	id. id., suff. 1 pers. sing. [for תַּנִי] שלח
שִׁלַּחְתַּנִי	Piel pret. 2 pers. sing. masc., suff. 1 pers. sing. . . . } שלח
וְשִׁלַּחְתַּנִי	

שָׁלַט fut. יִשְׁלָט to rule, have dominion or power over, with בְּ, עַל. Hiph. I. to let rule, let have dominion, Ps. 119. 133.—II. to give permission, to permit, Ec. 5. 18; 6. 2.

שְׁלֵט Ch.—I. to rule, have dominion or power over, with בְּ.—II. to get the mastery of, to seize, Da. 6. 25. Aph. to cause to rule, appoint ruler, with בְּ, Da. 2. 38, 48.

שֶׁלֶט masc. dec. 6 a (pl. c. שִׁלְטֵי), a shield.

שַׁלִּיט masc. dec. 1 b, שַׁלֶּטֶת fem. adj.—I. imperious, impudent, Eze. 16. 30.—II. having power, bearing rule, Ec. 8. 8.—III. subst. ruler, magistrate.

שַׁלִּיט Ch. masc. dec. 1 a.—I. powerful, mighty, having power.—II. being permitted, lawful, לָא שַׁ it is not lawful, Ec. 7. 24.—III. ruler, prince.

שִׁלְטוֹן m. power, authority, Ec. 8. 4, 8; others, adj. powerful, potent.

שִׁלְטוֹן Ch. m. d. 1 a, ruler, magistrate, Da. 3. 2, 3.

שָׁלְטָן Ch. masc. d. 1 b, dominion, power, empire.

שְׁלֵט	Ch. Peal pret. 3 pers. sing. masc. . שלט
שְׁלִטוּ	Kal pret. 3 pers. pl. . . שלט
שְׁלִטוּ	Ch. Peal pret. 3 pers. pl. masc. . שלט
שִׁלְטוֹן	noun masc. sing. . . . שלט

שָׁלְטוֹנִי	Ch. id. pl., constr. st. dec. 1 a . שלט
שַׁלְמֵי	noun masc. pl. constr. fr. [שֶׁלֶם] dec. 6 a שלם
שַׁלְמֵיהֶם	id. pl., suff. 3 pers. pl. masc. . שלם
שָׁלְטָן	וְ Chald. noun masc. sing. dec. 1 b . שלט
שָׁלְטָן	Chald. id., constr. st. . . שלט
שָׁלְטָנָא	וְ Chald. id., emph. st. . . שלט
שָׁלְטָנֵהּ	וְ Chald. id., suff. 3 pers. sing. masc. . שלט
שָׁלְטָנְהוֹן	Chald. id., suff. 3 pers. pl. masc. . שלט
שָׁלְטֹנִי	defect. for שָׁלְטוֹנִי (q. v.) . שלט
שָׁלְטָנַיָּא	Chald. noun masc. pl., emph. st. fr. שָׁלְטָן d. 1 b שלט
שָׁלְטָנָךְ	וְ Chald. id. sing., suff. 2 pers. sing. masc. . שלט
שַׁלֶּטֶת	adj. fem. sing. [for שָׁלֶטֶת] from שַׁלִּיט masc. (§ 39. No. 4 d) . . . שלט
שֶׁלִּי	pref. שֶׁ & pref. prep. לְ with suff. 1 pers. sing. לי
שֶׁלָּיו	וְ in full for שֶׁלּוֹ (q. v.) . . שלה
שָׁלֵיו	adj. masc. sing., see שָׁלֵו under שלה
שְׁלִיחַ	Chald. Peal part. pass. sing. masc. . שלח
שַׁלִּיט	וְ adj. or subst. masc. dec. 1 b . שלט
שַׁלִּיטָא	Chald. id., emph. st. . . שלט
שַׁלִּיטִים	id. pl., abs. st. . . . שלט
שַׁלִּיטִין	וְ Ch. id. pl., abs. st. . . שלט
שַׁלִּיטִם	Chald. Peal part. pass. sing. masc. . שלט
שָׁלִישׁ	noun masc. sing. (§ 32. rem. 1) . שלש
שָׁלִישׁוֹ	id. with suff. 3 pers. sing. masc. . שלש
שְׁלִישִׁי	adj. ord. masc. & fem. sing. from שָׁלִישׁ שלש
שְׁלִישִׁיָּה	
שְׁלִישִׁיּוֹ	the foll. with suff. 3 pers. sing. masc. . שלש
שְׁלִישִׁים	noun masc. pl. of שָׁלִישׁ dec. 1 b (§ 32. r. 1) שלש
שְׁלִישִׁית	adj. ord. fem. from שְׁלִישִׁי masc.; וּ bef. (:) } שלש
וּשְׁלִישִׁת	
שְׁלִישִׁתָה	id. with parag. ה, adv. . . שלש

שָׁלַךְ Hiph. הִשְׁלִיךְ—I. to throw, cast, with אֶל into, בְּ upon, מִן from; הַ אַחֲרָיו to cast behind him, i. e. to despise.—II. to cast off, as a plant its flowers, Job 15. 33.—III. to cast out, expel, banish.—IV. to cast down, overthrow, destroy. Hoph. הָשְׁלַךְ, הֻשְׁלַךְ (§ 11. rem. 10).—I. to be thrown, cast.—II. to cast forth.—III. to be cast down, overthrown, Da. 8. 11

שָׁלָךְ masc. the gannet, a sea-fowl, Le. 11. 17; De. 14. 17. Also

שַׁלֶּכֶת fem.—I. a felling of a tree, Is. 6. 13.—II. pr. name of a gate of the temple, 1 Ch. 26. 16 שלך

a Ezr. 4. 18.   f Je. 34. 16.   k 1 Sa. 20. 5.   p Da. 3. 3.   u Da. 4. 31; 7. 14.   z Eze. 16. 30.   g Da. 2. 10.   l Ezr. 4. 20.   p 2 Ch. 8. 9.
b Da. 10. 11.   g 1 Sa. 6. 8.   m Ec. 8. 9.   q Eze. 27. 11.   v Da. 7. 12.   a Ca. 1. 6; 8. 12.   h Da. 2. 15.   m Ezr. 5. 16.   q Eze. 23. 15, 23.
c Is. 16. 8.   h Nu. 13. 27.   n Da. 3. 27.   r Da. 7. 6.   w Da. 4. 31; 7. 14.   b Job 21. 23.   i Ec. 7. 19.   n Ps. 80. 6.   r Nu. 25. 14.
d Je. 27. 3.   i Ex. 5. 22.   Ne. 5. 15.   s Da. 7. 27.   x Je. 49. 31.   o Da. 2. 15.   s 2 Ki. 15. 25.   s Eze. 21. 20.
e 2 Sa. 15. 36.   j Ge. 31. 42.   Da. 6. 25.   t Da. 7. 27.   y Da. 4. 19.

שָׁלַל] pret. שָׁלַל, שָׁלוֹתִי; inf. שָׁל, שְׁלֹל (§ 18. rem. 13).
—I. *to draw out,* Ru. 2. 16; Arab. id.—II. *to plunder, spoil.*—III. *to carry off spoil,* Is. 10. 6; Eze. 29. 19. Hithpo. אֶשְׁתּוֹלֵל (Chald. form for הִשְׁתּוֹלֵל) *to be spoiled, become a prey,* Ps. 76. 6; Is. 59. 15.

שָׁלָל masc. dec. 4 a.—I. *spoil, plunder, booty.*—II. *gain, profit,* Pr. 31. 11.

שׁוֹלָל m.—I. *stripped, naked,* Mi. 1. 8; Sept. & Syr. *barefoot.*—II. *captive, prisoner,* Job 12. 17, 19.

שִׁלָּן (*spoil*) pr. name masc. Ne. 3. 15.

שְׁלָל] noun masc. sing. dec. 4 a	שלל
שְׁלַל 'ד id., constr. st.; ד bef. (:)	שלל
שְׁלָלָהּ id. with suff. 3 pers. sing. fem.	שלל
שָׁלְלוּ] Kal pret. 3 pers. pl.	שלל
שְׁלָלוֹ noun m. s., suff. 3 pers. s. m. fr. שְׁלָל dec. 4 a	שלל
שֹׁלְלֶיהָ Kal part. act. pl. masc., suff. 3 pers. sing. fem. from שָׁלַל dec. 7 b	שלל
שֹׁלְלֵיהֶם' id. pl., suff. 3 pers. pl. masc.	שלל
שְׁלָלֵךְ' noun masc. s., suff. 2 pers. s. fem. fr. שָׁלָל d. 4 a	שלל
שְׁלַלְכֶם' 'ד id., suff. 2 pers. pl. masc.; ד bef. (:)	שלל
שְׁלָלָם 'ד id., suff. 3 pers. pl. masc.; ד id.	שלל

שָׁלֵם a Root which does not exist, the following being a mere transposition of letters.

שַׂלְמָה fem. dec. 12 a (transp. for שִׂמְלָה, see שָׂמַל).—I. *a garment.*—II. pr. name of the father of Boaz, called also שַׂלְמוֹן, comp. Ru. 4. 20, 21, & שַׂלְמָא 1 Ch. 2. 11.

שַׂלְמָא (*garment*) pr. name of a son of Caleb, 1 Ch. 2. 51, 54, see also the preced.

וְשָׁלֵם] fut. יִשְׁלַם.—I. *to be entire,* i. e. *sound, safe,* Job 9. 4; 22. 21.—II. *to be completed, finished.*—III. *to be at peace,* only part. Ps. 7. 5, שׁוֹלְמִי *one at peace with me, my friend;* pass. שָׁלֵם *peaceable,* 2 Sa. 20. 19. Pi. שִׁלֵּם, שַׁלֵּם (§ 10. rem. 1).—I. *to preserve, keep uninjured,* Job 8. 6.—II. *to complete, finish,* 1 Ki. 9. 25.—III. *to restore, make good.*—IV. *to repay, pay a debt.*—V. *to pay, perform,* as a vow.—VI. *to requite, recompense,* with acc. of the thing, and with ל, also acc. of person. Pu. I. *to be perfected,* only part. *perfect,* Is. 42. 19, of the servant of God, comp. ver. 1.—II. *to be paid, performed,* as a vow, Ps. 65. 2.—III. *to be requited, recompensed.* Hiph. I. *to complete, execute, perform.* —II. *to make peace with* any one, with אֵת, עִם;

with אֵל *to submit oneself in peace to any one,* Jos. 11. 19.—III. *to cause to be at peace with,* with עִם Pr. 16. 7. Hoph. *to be at peace with,* with ל, Job 5. 23.

שְׁלֵם Ch. *to complete, finish,* Ezr. 5. 16. Aph. I. *to make an end of,* Da. 5. 26.—II. *to restore,* Ezr. 7. 19.

שָׁלֵם masc. dec. 5 a, fem. שְׁלֵמָה adj.—I. *whole;* אֲבָנִים שְׁלֵמוֹת *whole, unhewn stones.*—II *perfect, complete, full,* e. g. אֶבֶן שְׁלֵמָה *full weight;* גֹּלוֹת שְׁלֵמָה *captives in full number,* Am. 1. 6, 9. —III. *complete, finished,* 2 Ch. 8. 16.—IV. *safe, uninjured,* Ge. 33. 18.—V. *peaceable, at peace with,* with אֵת, Ge. 34. 21, לֵב שָׁלֵם עִם יְהֹוָה *a heart at peace with God;* better with others, *whole, perfect, sincere with God.*—VI. pr. name, *Salem,* i. q. Jerusalem.

שָׁלוֹם masc. dec. 3 a.—I. adj. *sound, well in health.*—II. *the whole,* only pl. adverbially, *wholly,* Je. 13. 19.—III. *safe, secure, enjoying peace.*—IV. *peaceably, friendlily disposed,* Ps. 55. 21.—V. subst. *health, welfare, prosperity, peace;* הֲשָׁלוֹם לוֹ *is it well with him?* שָׁאַל לוֹ לְשָׁלוֹם *to inquire after the welfare of any one;* שָׁלוֹם לָךְ *peace be to thee;* or affirmatively, *it is well with thee;* לֵךְ לְשָׁלוֹם *go in peace.*—VI. *peace,* as opposed to war; קָרָא לְשָׁלוֹם *to offer peace,* or *make peaceable proposals;* עָנָה שָׁלוֹם אֵת *to give a peaceable answer,* i. e. *to accept peace offered;* עָשָׂה שָׁלוֹם לְ *to make peace with any one.*—VII. *friendship;* אִישׁ שְׁלֹמִי *my friend.*

שְׁלָם Chald. masc. dec. 1 a, *peace, prosperity.*

שֶׁלֶם masc. dec. 6 a (pl. with suff. שַׁלְמֵיכֶם), *peace-offering;* perh. also *thank-offering.*

שִׁלֵּם masc.—I. *retribution,* De. 32. 35.—II. pr. name masc. Ge. 46. 24, for which שַׁלּוּם 1 Ch. 7. 13. Patronym. שִׁלֵּמִי Nu. 26. 49.

שִׁלּוּם, שָׁלוּם masc. dec. 1 b, *retribution.*

שַׁלּוּם, שַׁלֻּם (*retribution*) pr. name—I. of a king of Israel.—II. of a king of Judah, son of Josiah, Je. 22. 11.—III. of several other men.

שִׁלֻּמָה fem. d. 10, *retribution, punishment,* Ps. 91. 8.

שְׁלֹמֹה (*peaceable*) pr. name, *Solomon,* son of David and king of Israel.

שְׁלֻמִי (*peaceable*) pr. name masc. Nu. 34. 27.

שֶׁלֶמִי (for שְׁלֶמְיָה q. v.) pr. name masc. Ne. 7. 48; Ezr. 2. 46, where Khethib has שַׁמְלַי.

שְׁלֻמִיאֵל (*at peace with God,* or *friend of God*) pr. name masc. Nu. 1. 6; 2. 12.

שְׁלֶמְיָה, שְׁלֶמְיָהוּ (*retribution of the Lord*) pr. name masc. of several men.

שְׁלֹמִית (*peaceable*) pr. name—I. of two women, Le. 24. 11 & 1 Ch. 3. 19.—II. of several men, called also שְׁלֹמוֹת 1 Ch. 24. 22, and so in Khethib, 1 Ch. 23. 9; 26. 25.

שׁוּלַמִּית (*peaceable*) pr. name of a maiden celebrated in the book of Canticles.

שִׁלְמוֹן masc. dec. 1 b, *reward, gift*, Is. 1. 23.

מְשֻׁלָּם (*rewarded*, i. e. *given as a reward*) pr. name masc. of several persons.

מְשֻׁלֶּמוֹת (*retributions*) pr. name masc.—I. 2 Ch. 28. 12.—II. Ne. 11. 13, for which מְשִׁלֵּמִית 1 Ch. 9. 12.

מְשֶׁלֶמְיָה, מְשֶׁלֶמְיָהוּ (for מְשַׁלֶּמְיָה whom *the Lord* repays, or *gives as a reward*) pr. name masc. 1 Ch. 9. 21; 26. 1, 9, called שֶׁלֶמְיָהוּ 1 Ch. 26. 14.

מְשֻׁלֶּמֶת (fem. of מְשֻׁלָּם q. v.) pr. name of the wife of king Manasseh, 2 Ki. 21. 19.

שָׁלֵם adj. masc. sing. dec. 5 a, also pr. name

שָׁלֵם defect. for שָׁלוֹם (q. v.) . . .

שַׁלֵּם *'ו* Piel imp. s. masc.; or inf. constr. as an abs.

שֶׁלֶם *ו* noun masc. sing. (pl. c. שַׁלְמֵי) dec. 6 a

שֶׁלֶם pr. name masc. . . .

שִׁלֵּם *'ו* Piel pret. 3 pers. sing. masc. (§ 10 r. 1)

שָׁלָם *ו* noun masc. sing., also pr. name

שְׁלָם Chald. noun masc. sing. dec. 1 a

שְׁלֹם *ו* [for שָׁלֹם] Kal imp. sing. masc.; *ו* bef. (:)

שַׁלְמָא *ו* pr. name masc.

שְׁלָמָא Chald. noun masc. sing., emph. of שְׁלָם d. 1 a

שַׁלְמָה pref. שֶׁ אֲ adv. . . .

שַׁלְמָה noun fem. sing. dec. 12 a, also pr. name

שְׁלֵמָה adj. fem. sing. from שָׁלֵם masc. .

שִׁלֵּם *ו* pr. name masc.; *ו* bef. (:)

שִׁלְמוּ *ו* Kal pret. 3 pers. pl.

שַׁלְּמוּ *'ו* Piel imp. pl. masc.

שִׁלֵּמוּ *ו* id. pret. 3 pers. pl. [for שִׁלְּמוּ comp. § 8. r. 7]

שִׁלְמוֹן *ו* pr. name masc.

שְׁלָמוֹת *ו* noun f. pl. abs. fr. שַׁלְמָה d. 12 a; *ו* bef. (:)

שְׁלֵמוֹת adj. fem., pl. of שְׁלֵמָה, from שָׁלֵם masc.

שְׁלֹמוֹת pr. name masc.

שְׁלֹמוֹת *ו* Kh. שְׁלֹמוֹת q. v., K. שְׁלֹמִית (q. v.)

שַׁלְמֹתִי noun fem. pl., suff. 1 pers. s. fr. שַׁלְמָה d. 12 a

שַׁלְמֹתֵינוּ id. with suff. 1 pers. pl.

שִׁלְמַי pr. name masc. . . .

שַׁלְמֵי noun masc. pl. constr. from שֶׁלֶם dec. 6 a

שַׁלְמִי *'ו* Piel imp. sing. fem. . . .

שַׁלְמַי pr. name masc. . . .

שִׁלֹמִי defect. for שִׁלוֹמִי (q. v.)

שַׁלְּמֵי Kal part. p. pl. constr. m. [fr. שָׁלוּם] d. 3 a

שַׁלְּמֵי id. part. act. s. m., suff. 1 p. s. [fr. שַׁלֵּם] d. 7 b

שֶׁלֶמְיָה *ו*, שֶׁלֶמְיָהוּ *ו*, שֶׁלֶמְיָאֵל, pr. names masc.

שַׁלְמֵיהֶם noun m. pl., suff. 3 p. pl. m. fr. שֶׁלֶם d. 6 a

שַׁלְמָיו id. pl., suff. 3 pers. sing. masc. . .

שַׁלְמֶיךָ id. pl., suff. 2 pers. sing. masc. . .

שַׁלְמֵיכֶם id. pl., suff. 2 pers. pl. masc. .

שְׁלָמִים *'ו* id. pl., abs. st.; *ו* bef. (:)

שְׁלֵמִים adj. masc. pl. of שָׁלֵם dec. 5 a .

שְׁלֹמִית *'ו* pr. name masc. & fem.; *ו* bef. (:)

שְׁלֹמֶךָ *ע* defect. for שְׁלוֹמֶךָ (q. v.)

שְׁלָמְכוֹן Ch. n. m. s., suff. 2 p. pl. m. fr. שְׁלָם d. 1 a

שְׁלָמָם noun m. s., suff. 3 p. pl. m. fr. שָׁלוֹם d. 3 a

שַׁלְמָן Ho. 10. 14, elsewhere שַׁלְמַנְאֶסֶר pr. name of a king of Assyria, who carried away the ten tribes into captivity.

שַׁלְמֹנִים noun masc., pl. of [שַׁלְמֹן] dec. 1 b .

שִׁלְמַת noun fem. sing., constr. of שַׁלְמָה dec. 12 a

שִׂמְלַת *ו* noun fem. sing., constr. of [שִׂמְלָה] dec. 10

שַׁלְמֹתַי noun fem. pl., suff. 1 pers. s. fr. שַׁלְמָה d. 12 a

שִׁלַּמְתִּי } Piel pret. 1 pers. sing.; acc. shifted by
שִׁלַּמְתִּי *ו* } conv. *ו* (comp. § 8. rem. 7) }

שַׁלְמֹתֵיהֶם noun fem. pl., suff. 3 pers. pl. masc. from שַׁלְמָה dec. 12 a

שַׁלְמֹתַיִךְ id. pl., suff. 2 pers. sing. fem. . .

שַׁלְמֹתֵיכֶם id. pl., suff. 2 pers. pl. masc. .

שִׁלַּמְתֶּם Piel pret. 2 pers. pl. masc. . .

שָׁלַף fut. יִשְׁלֹף—I. *to draw* a sword; שֹׁלֵף חֶרֶב *one drawing the sword*, i. e. *armed man*.—II. *to pull off* a shoe, Ru. 4. 7, 8.—III. *to pluck up* grass, Ps. 129. 6.

שֶׁלֶף [for שֶׁלֶף] pr. name of an Arabian tribe, Ge. 10. 26; 1 Ch. 1. 20

שְׁלֹף Kal imp. sing. masc. . . .

שֹׁלֵף id. part. act. sing. masc. dec. 7 b

שִׁלְפָה defect. for שִׁלוּפָה (q. v.)

שֹׁלְפֵי Kal part. act. pl. c. masc. from שָׁלַף dec. 7 b

ᵃ Ps. 50. 14.   *ᵉ* Ezr. 4. 17.   *ⁱ* Is. 60. 20.   *ᵐ* Job 9. 31.   *ᵍ* 2 Ki. 4. 7.   *ᵘ* Ex. 20. 24.   *ᵃ* Ex. 22. 25.   *ᵈ* Ne. 9. 21.   *ᵍ* Ge. 44. 4.
ᵇ Am. 5. 22.   *ᶠ* Job 22. 21.   *ᵏ* Je. 50. 29.   *ⁿ* Jos. 9. 13.   *ʳ* Je. 20. 10.   *ᵛ* Je. 38. 22; Ob. 7.   *ᵇ* Ca. 4. 11.   *ʰ* Nu. 22. 31.
ᶜ Ju. 1. 7.   *ᵍ* Ezr. 5. 7.   *ˡ* Ps. 76. 12.   *ᵒ* Le. 10. 14.   *ˢ* 2 Sa. 20. 19.   *ᶜ* Is. 1. 23.   De. 29. 4.   *ᶜ* Job 9. 31.
De. 32. 35.   *ᵈ* Ca. 1. 7.   *ˡ* Is. 19. 21.   *ᵗ* Na. 2. 1.   *ᵗ* Ps. 7. 5.

47

שָׁלֹשׁ, שָׁלוֹשׁ ('ו) (שָׁלֹשׁ־, שְׁלשׁ־) fem.; שְׁלֹשָׁה (constr. שְׁלֹשֶׁת § 42. rem. 5) masc.—I. num. card. *three*; שָׁנִים שָׁלֹשׁ *three years*; rarely preceded by the noun, עָרִים שָׁלֹשׁ *three cities*; as an ordinal when preceded by a noun in the constr. st. בִּשְׁנַת שָׁלֹשׁ *in the third year*, prop. *in the year three*; שְׁלֹשָׁה עֶשְׂרֵה fem., שְׁלֹשָׁה עָשָׂר masc. *thirteen*; שְׁלָשְׁתְּכֶם *ye three*; שְׁלָשְׁתָּם *they three*.—II. *thrice*, Job 33. 29. Pl. שְׁלֹשִׁים *thirty*.

שִׁלֵּשׁ Pi. I. *to divide into three parts*, De. 19. 3.—II. *to do a third time*, 1 Ki. 18. 34.—III. *to do on the third day*, 1 Sa. 20. 19. Pu. part. מְשֻׁלָּשׁ —I. *threefold*.—II. *three years old*, Ge. 15. 9.

שֶׁלֶשׁ (*triad*) pr. name masc. 1 Ch. 7. 35.

שְׁלִישִׁי masc., שְׁלִישִׁיָּה fem., pl. שְׁלִישִׁים —1. adj. ord. *third*.—II. pl. *chambers of the third story*, Ge. 6. 16.—III. fem. (a) *third, third part*; (b) adv. *third time*, Eze. 21. 19; (c) *third year*, Is. 15. 5; 48. 34, see עֶגְלָה.

שָׁלִישׁ, שָׁלֹשׁ masc. (§ 32. rem. 1).—I. *a measure*, prob. *the third part of an Ephah*.—II. *a musical instrument*, either *a triangle*, or *a harp with three strings*, pl. 1 Sa. 18. 6.—III. *an officer of high* (prob. *the third*) *rank*.—IV. *a peculiar class of soldiers*, supposed to have been *chariot-warriors*, three of whom were contained in one chariot.

שִׁלֵּשִׁים masc. pl. *descendants of the third generation*, *great-grandchildren*; בְּנֵי שׁ' *children of great-grandchildren*.

שְׁלִשָׁה (*in a triangle*) pr. name of a district in Palestine, 1 Sa. 9. 4.

שְׁלֹשָׁה (*triad*) pr. name masc. 1 Ch. 7. 37.

שִׁלְשׁם, שִׁלְשׁוֹם adv. *three days ago, the day before yesterday*; תְּמוֹל שׁ' *yesterday and the day before*; כִּתְמוֹל שׁ' *heretofore, formerly*; גַּם אֶתְמוֹל גַּם שׁ' *as before*; מִתְּמוֹל שׁ' *before, in time past*.

מְשֻׁלָּשׁ masc. *a triad*, כְּמִשְׁלֹשׁ חֳדָשִׁים *about three months after*, Ge. 38. 24.

שֵׁלֵשׁ ('ו) id., constr. st. (§ 32. rem. 7); וּ bef. (:) — שְׁלֹשָׁה ('ו) pr. name of a region —

שָׁלִשָׁה Kh., but K. שָׁלִישׁוֹ (q. v.).

שֶׁלֶשׁ ('ו) pr. name masc.

שֵׁשֶׁת ('ו) num. card. masc., constr. שֵׁשֶׁת from שְׁלֹשָׁה masc.; וּ bef. (:) —

שַׁלְּשׁוּ Piel imp. pl. masc. [for שַׁלִּשׁוּ comp. § 8. r. 7]

שְׁלֹשׁוֹם Kh. שְׁלֹשׁוֹם q. v., K. שָׁלֹשִׁים (q. v.).

שָׁלֹשָׁה adv. [from שָׁלֹשׁ] with term. ־ֹם—

שְׁלֹשִׁיָה defect. for שְׁלִישִׁיָּה (q. v.).

שְׁלֹשׁוֹ ('ו) defect. for שְׁלִישׁוֹ (q. v.).

שָׁלֹשִׁים defect. for שְׁלֹשִׁים (q. v.).

שְׁלֹשָׁם Kh. שְׁלֹשָׁם q. v., K. שָׁלֹשִׁים (q. v.).

שְׁלֹשִׁים ('ו) adj. ord. masc., pl. of שְׁלִישִׁי; וּ bef. (:)

שְׁלֹשִׁים num. card. com., pl. of שָׁלֹשׁ; וּ id.

שְׁלֹשִׁים noun masc., pl. of [שֶׁלֶשׁ] dec. 1 b

שָׁלֹשִׁית defect. for שְׁלִישִׁית (q. v.).

שְׁלִשֹׁלֹמֹה preff. שְׁ, & לְ bef. (:) χ pr. name masc.

שְׁלֹשִׁים ('ו) defect. for שְׁלֹשִׁים (q. v.).

שְׁלֹשָׁם adv., defect. for שִׁלְשׁוֹם (q. v.).

שִׁלַּשְׁתָּ ('ו) Piel pret. 2 pers. sing. masc.; acc. shifted by conv. וּ (comp. § 8. rem. 7)

שְׁלֹשֶׁת ('ו) num. card. masc., constr. of שְׁלֹשָׁה (§ 42 rem. 5) from שָׁלֹשׁ masc.; וּ bef. (:)

שְׁלִשְׁתֵּךְ adj. ord. fem. sing., suff. 2 pers. sing. fem. (§ 3. rem. 2) from שְׁלִישִׁית (q. v.)

שְׁלָשְׁתְּכֶם num. card. (שְׁלֹשֶׁת q. v.), suff. 2 pers. pl., comp. dec. 13 c

שְׁלָשְׁתָּם id. with suff. 3 pers. pl. masc.

שַׁלְתִּיאֵל pr. name, see שְׁאַלְתִּיאֵל

שֶׁלְתֶּךָ contr. for שְׁאֵלָתֶךָ (q. v.)

שָׁם ('ו) adv.—I. *there, in that place*; אֲשֶׁר שָׁם *where*; שָׁם–שָׁם *here—there*; מִשָּׁם *thence*; אֲשֶׁר מִשָּׁם *whence*.—II. *thither*, after verbs of motion; אֲשֶׁר שָׁם *whither*.—III. *then, at that time*.—IV. with ה parag. שָׁמָּה *thither*; rarely i. q. שָׁם *there*; שָׁמָּה *whither*,—rarely *where*.

שֵׁם ('י, 'ו) masc. dec. 7a (pl. שֵׁמוֹת).—I. *a name*.—II. *fame, renown, reputation*; אַנְשֵׁי שֵׁם *men of renown*; שֵׁם רַע *ill report*.—III. *a name after death, memory*.—IV. perh. *a monument*, 2 Sa. 8. 13; Is. 55. 13.—V. שֵׁם יְהֹוָה, and by way of eminence הַשֵּׁם *the name of the Lord*.—VI. pr. name *Shem*, the eldest son of Noah.

שֻׁם Chald. masc. irr. (§ 68) *a name*.

שְׁמִידָע (*fame of knowledge*) pr name masc. Patronym. שְׁמִידָעִי, Nu. 26. 32.

שְׁמִירָמוֹת (*name of exaltation*; others, *a watching of the heights*, for שִׁמְרְמוֹת) pr. name of two Levites.

שָׁם ׀] Kal (Chald. Peal) pret. 3 pers. sing. masc.; or part. act. dec. 1a (§ 30. No. 3) . שׂום

שָׁם Kh. שָׁם q. v., K. שָׁמָּה (q. v.) . שם

שָׁם־ with Makkeph for שָׁם q. v. (§ 36. rem. 3) שם

שֵּׁם Chald. noun masc. sing. irr. (§ 68) . שם

שִׁמְאָ ׀ pr. name masc. שמם

שִׁמְאָבֶר ׀ pr. name masc. שמה

שִׁמְאָה (perh. for שִׁמְעָא fame) pr. name m. 1 Ch. 8. 32, called שִׁמְאָם 1 Ch. 9. 38.

שְׂמֹאול ׀ noun masc. sing. dec. 1a; ׀ bef. (:) שׂמאל

שְׂמֹאולָה id., suff. 3 pers. sing. fem. . שׂמאל

שְׂמֹאולֵךְ id., suff. 2 pers. sing. fem. . שׂמאל

שְׂמֹאולָם id., suff. 3 pers. pl. masc. . שׂמאל

שְׂמֹאול, שְׂמֹאל ׀ masc. dec. 1a.—I. the left, left side; מִשְּׂמֹאל on the left; עַל שְׂ׳, שְׂ׳ to the left; יַד שְׂ׳ the left hand.—II. (without יָד) the left hand. —III. the north, Job 23. 9; Ge. 14. 15. הִשְׂמִיל, הִשְׂמְאִיל, הַשְׂמְאִיל Hiph. I. to turn or go to the left.—II. to use the left hand, 1 Ch. 12. 2. שְׂמָלִי, שְׂמָלִי masc. שְׂמָאלִית fem. adj. left, on the left.

שְׂמֹאלָהּ id. with suff. 3 pers. sing. fem. . שׂמאל

שְׂמֹאלֹו ׀ id., suff. 3 pers. sing. masc.; ׀ bef. (:) שׂמאל

שְׂמֹאלֶךָ id., suff. 2 pers. sing. masc. . שׂמאל

שִׁמְאָם pr. name masc., see שִׁמְאָה.

שַׁמְגִּיעַ׳ pref. שֶׁ׳ ∫ Hiph. part. sing. masc. dec. 1b נגע

שַׁמְגַּר pr. name of a judge of Israel, Ju. 3. 31; 5. 6.

שָׁמֵד Hiph. I. to destroy, lay waste.—II. to destroy, cut off persons, nations. Inf. הַשְׁמֵד destruction. Niph. pass. of Hiph. שְׁמַד Chald. Aph. to destroy, Da. 7. 26.

שָׁמָה Root not used; Arab. שׂמא to be high. שָׁמַי masc. only pl. שָׁמַיִם (constr. שְׁמֵי, with suff. שָׁמָיו § 38. rem. 2) heaven, the heavens; הַשָּׁמַיְמָה, הַשָּׁמַיִם שְׁמַיִם towards heaven, heavenward. שְׁמַי Chald. masc. only pl. emph. שְׁמַיָּא heaven. שְׁמֵאָבֶר (soaring on high, for שְׂמֵאָבֶר from שֵׁם=שָׂמָה height, and אָבֶר) pr. name of a king of Zeboim, Ge. 14. 2.

שָׂמָה Kal pret. 3 pers. sing. fem. . שׂום

שָׂמָהּ ׀ id. pret. 3 pers. s. m. (שָׂם), suff. 3 p. s. fem. שׂום

שָׁמָּה ׀ adv. (שָׁם) with parag. ה . שם

שַׁמָּה noun fem. sing. dec. 10, also pr. name . שׁמם

שָׂמֵהּ׳ Ch. Peal pret. 3 pers. s. m. (שָׂם), suff. 3 p.s.m. שׂום

שְׁמָהּ ׀ noun masc. sing., suff. 3 pers. sing. fem. from שֵׁם dec. 7; ׀ bef. (:) שם

שְׁמֵהּ׳ Chald. noun masc. sing., suff. 3 pers. sing. masc. (prop. from שֵׁם, see שֵׁם § 68) . שם

שָׂמָהוּ׳ Kal pret. 3 pers. sing. m. (שָׂם), suff. 3 pers. s.m. שׂום

שַׁמָּהוּת pr. name masc., see שַׁמָּה . שׁמם

שְׁמָהָת׳ Chald. noun masc. pl. constr., irr. of שֵׁם (§ 68) שם

שְׁמָהָתְהֹם׳ Chald. id. pl., suff. 3 pers. pl. masc. שם

שָׂמֹו ׀° Kal pret. 3 pers. sing. m., suff. 3 pers. s. m. שׂום

שָׂמוּ ׀ id. pret. 3 pers. pl.; acc. shifted by } שׂום

שָׂמוּ conv. ׀ (comp. § 8. rem. 7) . }

שָׂמוּ׳ ׀ defect. for שִׂימוּ (q. v.) . שׂום

שְׁמֹו ׀ noun masc. sing., suff. 3 pers. sing. masc. from שֵׁם dec. 7a; ׀ bef. (:) שם

שִׁמּוּ׳ Kal imp. pl. masc. . שׁמם

שְׁמוּאֵל ׀ pr. name masc.; ׀ bef. (:) שׁמע

שָׁמֹוט׳ Kal inf. abs. . שׁמט

שָׁמֹורִי׳ Kal pret. 3 pers. pl., suff. 2 pers. sing. masc. שׂום

שְׁמֹונֶה ׀ } num. card. fem. & masc.; ׀ bef. (:) שׁמן

שְׁמֹנֶה ׀ }

שְׁמֹונִים ׀ id. com. gen. pl.; ׀ id. שׁמן

שְׁמֹונַת׳ ׀ id. fem. sing., constr. of שְׁמֹונָה; ׀ id. שׁמן

שָׁמֹועַ Kal inf. abs. . שׁמע

שַׁמּוּעַ pr. name masc. see שְׁמֵעָא . שׁמע

שָׁמֹועַ Kal inf. constr. . שׁמע

שְׁמוּעָה׳ ׀ noun fem. sing. dec. 10; ׀ bef. (:) שׁמע

שָׁמֹור Kal inf. abs. . שׁמר

שָׁמוּר id. part. pass. sing. masc. . שׁמר

שָׁמוּר pr. name masc. Kh. שָׁמִיר, K. שָׁמִיר (q. v.) שׁמר

שְׁמֹר׳ Kal imp. sing. masc. . שׁמר

שַׁמֹּות׳ Kal inf. (§ 18. rem. 3), or noun fem. pl. of שַׁמָּה dec. 10; also pr. name (see שַׁמָּה) שׁמם

שֵׁמֹות noun m. with pl. fem. term., abs. st. fr. שֵׁם d. 7a שם

שְׁמֹות id. pl., constr. st. . שם

שְׁמֹותָם id. pl., suff. 3 pers. pl. masc. (§ 4. rem. 2) שם

שְׁמֹותָן׳ ׀ id. pl., suff. 3 pers. pl. fem.; ׀ bef. (:) שם

שָׂמַח ׀ [also שָׂמֵחַ comp. Ne. 12. 43] fut. יִשְׂמַח.—I. to shine cheerfully, of a candle, Pr. 13. 9.—II. to be joyful, glad.—III. to express joy, const. with בְּ, עַל, לְ. Pi. שִׂמַּח to cheer, gladden, cause to rejoice, with מִן, לְ, עַל. Hiph. id. Pr. 89. 43. שָׂמֵחַ masc. dec. 5a, שִׂמְחָה fem. adj. joyful, glad, rejoicing. שִׂמְחָה fem. dec. 12b.—I. joy, rejoicing.—II loud expressions of joy, festivity, mirth.

שָׂמֵחַ ׀° adj. masc. sing. dec. 5a (§ 34. rem. 2) שׂמח

שַׂמֵּחַ ׀ Piel imp. sing. masc. . שׂמח

▪ 2 Sa. 21. 12.   ▪ Ju. 7. 20.   g 1 Sa. 19. 13.   ◦ Da. 2. 20, etc.   ◦ Ezr. 5. 10.   ◦ Je. 2. 12.   ◦ 1 Ch. 29. 7.   y Ps. 46. 9;   ◦ Eze. 23. 4.
▪ Zec. 4. 11.   ▪ Zec. 4. 3.   ▪ Je. 13. 16.   ◦ Eze. 7. 20.   ◦ Le. 6. 3.   ▪ De. 15. 2.   ▪ Pr. 25. 25.   Eze. 36. 3.   ◦ Pr. 29. 6.
Ere. 16. 46.   ◦ Ec. 8. 14.   ◦ Ezr. 5. 14.   ▪ Ezr. 5. 4.   y Je. 40. 10.   ◦ Ps. 85. 14.   ◦ Eze. 12. 13.   yy Ezr. 5. 10

רז.*

שִׂמַּח   id. id. (Ps. 86. 4) ; or inf. abs. (Je. 20. 15)

שָׂמֵחַ   ! id. pret. 3 pers. sing. masc. .

שְׂמַח   Kal imp. sing. masc. ; ו bef. (:)

שָׂמְחָה   id. pret. 3 p. s. fem. [for שָׂמְחָה § 8. r. 1 & 7]

שְׂמֵחָה   adj. fem. sing. from שָׂמֵחַ masc.

שִׂמְחָה   noun fem. sing. dec. 12 b

שִׂמְּחֵהוּ   Piel pret. 3 pers. s. m. (שִׂמַּח), suff. 3 pers. s. m.

שָׂמְחוּ / שָׂמֵחוּ   Kal pret. 3 pers. pl. (§ 8. rem. 1 & 7)

שִׂמְחוּ   id. imp. pl. masc. .

שִׂמְּחוּךָ   Piel pret. 3 pers. pl., suff. 2 pers. sing. masc.

שְׂמָחוֹת   noun fem. pl. abs. for שִׂמְחָה dec. 12 b .

שִׂמְחִי   in pause for שִׂמְחִי (§ 8. rem. 12) ; ו bef. (:)

שִׂמְחֵי / שִׂמְחֵי   adj. pl. constr. masc. from שָׂמֵחַ (§ 34. r. 2)

שִׂמְחִי   Kal imp. sing. fem.

שְׂמֵחִים   adj. masc., pl. of שָׂמֵחַ dec. 5 a ; ו bef. (:)

שִׂמְּחָם   Piel pret. 3 pers. s. m. (שִׂמַּח), suff. 3 p. pl. m.

שַׂמְּחֵנוּ   id. imp. sing. masc. (שַׂמַּח), suff. 1 pers. pl.

שָׂמַחְתָּ   Kal pret. 2 pers. sing. masc. ; acc. shifted by conv. ו (§ 8. rem. 7)

שִׂמַּחְתָּ   Piel pret. 2 pers. sing. masc.

שִׂמְחַת   noun fem. sing., constr. of שִׂמְחָה d. 12 b

שָׂמַחְתִּי   Kal pret. 1 pers. sing. .

שִׂמְחָתִי   noun f. s., suff. 1 pers. s. fr. שִׂמְחָה d. 12 b

שִׂמַּחְתִּים   ! Piel pret. 1 pers. sing., suff. 3 pers. pl. m.

שִׂמְחַתְכֶם   noun f. s., suff. 2 pers. pl. m. fr. שִׂמְחָה d. 12 b

שְׂמַחְתֶּם   ו Kal pret. 2 pers. pl. masc. ; ו, for ו, conv.

שִׂמַּחְתָּנִי   Piel pret. 2 pers. sing. masc., suff. 1 pers. s.

[שָׁמַט]   I. to let go, release, remit, a debt, De. 15. 2.—II. to let lie uncultivated, Ex. 23. 11.—III. to cease from, with מִן Je. 17. 4.—IV. to throw down, 2 Ki. 9. 33.—V. intrans. to set oneself free, to break loose, 2 Sa. 6. 6; others, to kick (Arab. שמט to strike, smite); or, to stick fast; others again, to drop, slip, stumble. Niph. to be thrown down, Ps. 141. 6. Hiph. to release, remit, De. 15. 3. Hence

שְׁמִטָּה   fem. a remission, release, De. 15. 1, 2; שְׁנַת הַשְּׁמִטָּה the year of release, De. 15. 9 ; 31. 10

שָׁמְטוּ   Kal pret. 3 pers. pl.

שְׁמָטֻהוּ   id. imp. pl. m., suff. 'הוּ or 'הָ 3 pers. s. m. or f.

שְׁמַטְתָּה   ! Kal pret. 2 pers. sing. masc. ; acc. shifted by conv. ו (§ 8. rem. 7)

שַׁמַּי / שַׁמָּי   pr. name masc.

שְׁמֵי   noun masc. pl., constr. of שָׁמַיִם [fr. שָׁמֶה § 38. rem. 2] ; ו bef. (:)   שׁמה

שְׁמִי   noun masc. sing. with suff. 1 pers. sing. from שֵׁם dec. 7 a ; ו id.   שׁם

שִׂימִי   Kal imp. sing. fem. R. שִׂים see   שׂום

שְׁמַיָּא   Ch. noun masc. pl. emph. [of שְׁמַיִן fr. sing. comp. § 38. rem. 2]   שׁמה

שְׁמִידָע   pr. name masc. ; ו bef. (:)   שׁם

שְׁמֵימוֹ   noun masc. pl. (שָׁמַיִם) with suff. 3 pers. sing. masc. [from שְׁמֵי § 38. rem. 2]   שׁמה

שָׁמֶיךָ   id. pl., suff. 2 pers. sing. masc.   שׁמה

שְׁמֵיכֶם   id. pl., suff. 2 pers. pl. masc.   שׁמה

שָׁמַיִם / שָׁמַיִם   id. pl., abs. st.   שׁמה

שָׂמִים   Kal part. act. m., pl. of שָׂם d. 1 a (§ 30. No. 3)   שׂום

שָׁמִיר   noun masc. sing. dec. 3 a, also pr. name   שׁמר

שְׁמִירוֹ   id., suff. 3 pers. sing. masc. ; ו bef. (:)   שׁמר

שְׁמִירָמוֹת   pr. name masc. ; ו id.   שׁם

שָׂמְךָ   Kal pret. 3 pers. sing. m., suff. 2 pers. s. m.   שׂום

שִׁמְךָ   noun m. s., suff. 2 pers. s. f. fr. שֵׁם d. 7 a   שׁם

שְׁמֶךָ / שְׁמֶךָ   id., suff. 2 pers. sing. masc.   שׁם

שִׁמְכֶם   id., suff. 2 pers. pl. masc.   שׁם

שָׂמַל   Root not used ; Arab. to cover with a garment, conj. IV to wrap oneself in a garment (Gesenius) Hence the two following.

שַׂלְמָה   ! fem. dec. 12 b, a garment ; espec. a wide outer garment or mantle ; frequently by transposition שַׂלְמָה q. v.

שַׂמְלָה   (garment) pr. name of a king of Edom, Ge. 36. 36 ; 1 Ch. 1. 47 ; see a similar form under שַׂלְמָה

שַׂלְמַי   Kh. for שַׂלְמַי (q. v.)   שׁלם

שֶׁמַּלְכְּךָ   pref. שֶׁ X noun masc. sing., suff. 2 pers. sing. masc. from מֶלֶךְ dec. 6 a   מלך

שִׂמְלַת   noun fem. sing., constr. of שִׂמְלָה dec. 12 b   שׂמל

שְׂמָלֹת   ! id. pl., abs. st. ; ו bef. (:)   שׂמל

שִׂמְלָתוֹ   id. sing., suff. 3 pers. sing. masc.   שׂמל

שִׂמְלֹתָו / שִׂמְלֹתֵימוֹ   id. pl., suff. 3 pers. sing. masc. (§ 4. r. 1)   שׂמל

שִׂמְלֹתַיִךְ   id. pl., suff. 2 pers. sing. fem.   שׂמל

שִׂמְלֹתֵיכֶם   id. pl., suff. 2 pers. pl. masc.   שׂמל

שִׂמְלָתְךָ   id. sing., suff. 2 pers. sing. masc.   שׂמל

שִׂמְלֹתָם   id. pl., suff. 3 pers. pl. masc. (§ 4. rem. 2) .   שׂמל

שִׂמְלָתֵנוּ   ו id. sing., suff. 1 pers. pl.   שׂמל

---

a De. 24. 5.   f Je. 20. 15.   l Ps. 45. 9.   q Is. 24. 7.   v Ps. 137. 6.   aa Je. 17. 4.   ff Is. 65. 15 ; 66. 22.   z Ex. 22. 26.   hh Ge. 35. 2.
b Pr. 5 18.   g Zec. 4. 10.   m Ps. 16. 11.   r Zep. 3. 14.   w Je. 31. 21.   bb Ec. 10. 16, 17.   gg 2 Sa. 12. 20.   ii De. 8. 4.
c Est. 8. 15.   h Zec. 10. 7 ; Ne. 12. 43.   i Joel 2. 21.   s Ps. 90. 15.   x Nu. 10. 10.   cc Ge. 45. 22.   g Ru. 3. 3.   jj Is. 4. 1.
d Ps. 113. 9.   k Joel 2. 23.   p Ps. 35. 26.   t Ps 30. 2.   y Ps. 92. 5.   dd Is. 10. 17.
    u De. 33. 28.   z 2 Ki. 9. 33.   ee Le. 26. 19.

שָׁמַם Root not used ; Arab. *to poison.*

שְׂמָמִית fem. **a species** of *poisonous lizard,* Pr. 30. 28 (Bochart).

[שָׁמֵם] fut. יִשֹׁם, pl. יִשֹׁמּוּ (perh. also תֵּשַׁם q. v.).—I. *to be desolate, laid waste;* part. שׁוֹמֵם *desolate,* and of persons, (a) *wasted, perishing,* La. 1. 13, 16 ; (b) *solitary.*—II. less frequently trans. *to lay waste, make desolate ;* part. שׁוֹמֵם *desolator.*—III. *to be astonished, amazed,* with עַל, לְ. Niph. נָשַׁם, i. q. Kal Nos. I & III. Po. I. part. מְשׁוֹמֵם *desolator.* —II. *to be astonished,* Ezr. 9. 3. Hiph. הֵשַׁם (fut. יָשֵׁים ; inf. הַשֵּׁם § 18. rem. 13 & 14).—I. *to make desolate, to lay waste.*—II. *to astonish,* Eze. 32. 10 ; also intrans. *to be astonished.* Hoph. הֻשַּׁם (for הָשַּׁם, הֻשַּׁם § 8. rem. 13).—I. *to be laid waste.*—II. *to be astonished,* Job 21. 5. Hithpo. הִשְׁתּוֹמֵם.—I. *to destroy oneself,* Ec. 7. 16.—II. *to be astonished, amazed, confounded.*

שְׁמַם Chald. Ithpo. *to be astonished,* Da. 4. 16.

שָׁמֵם masc., שְׁמֵמָה fem. adj. *laid waste, desolate.*

שְׁמָמָה fem. dec. 11c.—I. *desolation, waste, desert.* —II. *astonishment,* Eze. 7. 27.

שִׁמָמָה fem. *desolation,* Eze. 35. 7, 9.

שִׁמָּמוֹן masc. *astonishment, amazement,* Eze. 4. 16; 12. 19.

שַׁמָּה fem. dec. 10.—I. *desolation.*—II. *astonishment,* Je. 8. 21 ; meton. *object of astonishment.*— III. pr. name masc. (a) Ge. 36. 13, 17 ; (b) of a brother of David, 1 Sa. 16. 9 ; 17. 13, called also שַׁמָּעָה 2 Sa. 13. 3, & שִׁמְעָא 1 Ch. 2. 13 ; (c) 2 Sa. 23. 25, for which שַׁמּוֹת 1 Ch. 11. 27, & שַׁמְהוּת 1 Ch. 27. 8 ; (d) of two other persons, 2 Sa. 23. 11, 33.

שַׁמָּא (*desert*) pr. name masc. 1 Ch. 7. 37.

שַׁמַּי (*desolated*) pr. name of three men, 1 Ch. 2. 28, 44 ; 4. 17.

מְשַׁמָּה fem. dec. 10.—I. *desolation.*—II. *astonishment, amazement.*

שְׁמַם noun m. s., suff. 3 pers. pl. m. fr. שֵׁם d. 7a . שם
שֹׁמֵם Kal part. act. sing. masc. dec. 7b . . שמם
שָׁמֵמָה id. pret. 3 p. s. f. [for שֵׁמֵמָה § 8. r. 1 & 7] שמם
שָׁמֵמָה Kh. שֵׁמֵמָה q. v., K. שֵׁמֵמוּ for שֵׁמֵמוּ (q. v.) שמם
שֹׁמֵמָה Kal part. act. s. f. fr. שׁוֹמֵם m. (§ 39. No. 3. r. 4) שמם
שְׁמֵמָה noun fem. sing. dec. 11c ; ¹ bef. (:) . שמם
שְׁמֵמָה adj. fem. sing. from שָׁמֵם masc. . שמם
שָׁמֵמוּ Kal pret. 3 pers. pl. . . שמם
שְׁמֵמוֹת }
שִׁמְמוֹת } noun fem. pl. constr. from שְׁמָמָה dec. 11c שמם

<hr/>

שִׁמְמוֹת constr. of the foll. . . . . שמם
שֹׁמֵמוֹת Kal part. act. fem., pl. of שֹׁמֵמָה fr. שׁוֹמֵם m. שמם
שְׁמִיר noun fem. sing. . . . . שמם
שְׁמַמְתִּיךְ } Kal part. act. pl. fem., suff. 2 pers. sing. fem. from שְׁמָמָה (q. v.) . . . . שמם
שְׁמַמְתִּינוּ id. pl. with suff. 1 pers. pl. . . שמם

[שָׁמֵן] or [שָׁמַן] fut. יִשְׁמַן, *to be* or *become fat.* Hiph. I. *to make fat,* metaph. Is. 6. 10.—II. *to become fat,* Ne. 9. 25.

שָׁמֵן masc. שְׁמֵנָה fem. *fat ;* spoken of persons, *stout, robust ;* of land, *fertile ;* of food, *nourishing.*

שֶׁמֶן masc. dec. 6a (with suff. שַׁמְנִי).—I. *fatness ·* spoken of food, *richness, delicacy ;* of land, *fertility ;* metaph. *prosperity,* Is. 10. 27.—II. *oil ;* עֵץ שֶׁמֶן *wild olive tree.*—III. *ointment.*

שְׁמָנִים masc. pl. *fatness, rich production* of the earth, Ge. 27. 28.

אַשְׁמַנִּים masc. pl. *fatness, fertile fields,* Is. 59. 10 ; others, *darkness* (Syr. אותמניא id.). Eng. vers. *"desolate places"* (Syr. אשימון *desert,* Heb. יְשִׁימוֹן).

מִשְׁמָן masc. dec. 8a.—I. *fatness,* Is. 17. 4.— II. pl. מִשְׁמַנִּים *fat, fertile places,* Da. 11. 24.— III. pl. concr. *fat, stout,* of warriors.

מִשְׁמַנָּה (*fatness*) pr. name masc. 1 Ch. 12. 10.

מַשְׁמַנִּים masc. pl. *rich, delicate food,* Ne. 8. 10.

שְׁמֹנָה fem. שְׁמֹנָה masc. constr שְׁמֹנַת, *eight.* P. שְׁמֹנִים *eighty.*

שְׁמִינִי masc. שְׁמִינִית fem. adj. ord. *eighth.* Fem. שְׁמִינִית prob. *a musical instrument* with *eight strings* ; others, *the octave* in music.

שָׁמֵן adj. masc. sing. from שְׁמֵנָה . שמן
שֶׁמֶן noun masc. sing. dec. 6a (§ 35. r. 2) ; שמן
שֶׁמֶן for וְ see lett. ו . . שמן
שַׁמְנָהּ id. with suff. 3 pers. sing. fem. שמן
שְׁמֵנָה adj. fem. sing. from שָׁמֵן masc. שמן
שְׁמֹנָה }
שְׁמֹנָה } num. card. masc. & fem. ; וְ bef. (:) שמן
שָׁמַנּוּ pp Kal pret. 1 pers. pl. [for שָׁמַנּוּ] שום
שָׁמְנוּ Kal pret. 3 pers. pl. שמן
שְׁמֵנִי noun masc. s., suff. 1 pers. pl. fr. שֵׁם d. 7a שם
שָׂמֵנִי Kal pret. 3 pers. s. m. (שָׂם), suff. 1 pers. s. שום
שָׂמוּנִי id. pret. 3 pers. pl. (שָׂמוּ), suff. 1 pers. sing. שום
שַׁמְנִי noun masc. s., suff. 1 pers. s. fr. שֶׁמֶן d. 6a שמן
שְׁמָנֵךְ id. pl., suff. 2 pers. sing. fem. שמן
שְׁמָנֶיךָ id. pl., suff. 2 pers. sing. masc. שמן
שְׁמָנִים id. pl., abs. st. שמן

שׁמן   שְׁמֹנִים num. card. com., pl. of שְׁמֹנֶה ; ‎ bef. (:)

שׁמן   שָׁמַנְתָּ Kal pret. 2 pers. sing. masc.

שׁמן   שְׁמֹנַת num. card. m., constr. of שְׁמֹנֶה fr. שְׁמֹנָה f.

שָׁמַע

שָׁמַע in pause שָׁמֵעַ Ps. 22. 25 (comp. also Ju. 2. 17; Je. 13. 11, &c.) fut. יִשְׁמַע.—I. *to hear.*—II. *to listen, give attention,* with acc. אֶל, לְ, בְּ to any one.—III. *to hear, accept prayer,* of God.—IV. *to hearken, obey.*—V. *to understand;* לֵב שֹׁמֵעַ *an understanding heart.* Niph. I. *to be heard.*—II. *to show oneself obedient or submissive,* Ps. 18. 45.—III. *to be understood,* Ps. 19. 4. Pi. *to cause to hear, to summon.* Hiph. I. *to cause to hear* or *be heard.*—II. *to proclaim.*—III. *to call, summon.*—IV. *to sing* or *play aloud.*

שְׁמַע Chald. *to hear,* Da. 5. 14, 16. Ithpe. *to show oneself obedient, to obey,* Da. 7. 27.

שֶׁמַע (*hearing*) pr. name masc. 1 Ch. 11. 44.

שֵׁמַע masc. dec. 6 e.—I. *the act of hearing.*—II. *report, rumour.*—III. *sound, music,* Ps. 150. 5.

שֶׁמַע (*report*) pr. name masc.—I. 1 Ch. 2. 43, 44. —II. 1 Ch. 5. 8.—III. Ne. 8. 4.—IV. 1 Ch. 8. 13.

שְׁמַע (*fame*) pr. name of a city in the tribe of Judah, Jos. 15. 26.

שֹׁמַע masc. dec. 6 c (§ 35. rem. 5), *fame.*

שִׁמְעָא (*report*) pr. name—I. of a son of David, 1 Ch. 3. 5, elsewhere called שַׁמּוּעַ.—II. 1 Ch. 6. 15. —III. 1 Ch. 6. 24.—IV. of a son of Jesse, 1 Ch. 2. 13, elsewhere שִׁמְאָה (q. v.) & שִׁמְעָה 2 Sa. 13. 3, 32; patronym. שִׁמְעָתִי 1 Ch. 2. 55.

שְׁמָעָה (*obedience*) pr. name masc. 1 Ch. 12. 3.

שִׁמְעוֹן (*a hearing, accepting*) pr. name, *Simeon.* —I. a son of Jacob by Leah's handmaid, and of the tribe descended from him. Patronym. שִׁמְעֹנִי.—II. Ezr. 10. 31.

שִׁמְעִי (*renowned*) pr. name masc. of several persons. Patronym. שִׁמְעִי for שִׁמְעָי.

שְׁמַעְיָהוּ, שְׁמַעְיָה (*the Lord has heard,* i. e. answered prayer) pr. name, *Shemaiah.*—I. a prophet, 1 Ki. 12. 22.—II. another, Je. 29. 31.—III. of several other men.

שְׁמֻעָה (*report*) pr. n. f. 2 Ki. 12. 22; 2 Ch. 24. 26.

שְׁמוּעָה, שְׁמֻעָה fem. dec. 10.—I. *news, tidings.* —II. *information, report,* 2 Ch. 9. 6.—III. *information, teaching, doctrine,* Is. 28. 9.

שְׁמוּאֵל (for שֶׁמַעֵאל *heard of God,* comp. 1 Sa. 1. 20) pr. name, *Samuel.*—I. the judge and prophet of the Israelites.—II. three other persons; (*a*) 1 Ch. 6. 13, 18; (*b*) Nu. 34. 20; (*c*) 1 Ch. 7. 2.

אֶשְׁתְּמֹעַ (*obedience*) pr. name of a city of the Levites in the tribe of Judah; once written אֶשְׁתְּמֹה Jos. 15. 50.

הַשְׁמָעוּת fem. *a causing to hear, information,* Eze. 24. 26.

יִשְׁמָעֵאל (*God hears*) pr. name, *Ishmael.*—I. son of Abraham by Hagar, the progenitor of several Arabian tribes. Patronym. יִשְׁמְעֵאלִי *Ishmaelite.*— II. the murderer of Gedaliah, comp. Je. 40. 8, and several other persons.

יִשְׁמַעְיָה (*the Lord hears*) pr. name m. 1 Ch. 12. 4.

יִשְׁמַעְיָהוּ (*id.*) pr. name masc. 1 Ch. 27. 19.

מִשְׁמָע masc. dec. 2 b.—I. *a hearing,* Is. 11. 3.— II. pr. name of two men, Ge. 25. 14 ; 1 Ch. 4. 25

מִשְׁמַעַת fem. dec. 13 a (with suff. מִשְׁמַעְתּוֹ comp. § 35. rem. 5).—I. *a hearing, audience.*— II. *obedience,* as a concr. & collect. *subjects,* Is. 11. 14.

שֶׁמַע pr. name masc.	שמע
שָׁמֵעַ in pause for שָׁמַע (§ 35. r. 2 & 5) see שָׁמַע	שמע
שָׁמֹעַ Kal inf. abs.	שמע
שָׁמֵעַ in pause for שָׁמַע q. v. (comp. וַיֵּהַב,	שמע
שָׁמֵעַ (וַיֵּשְׁב, וִישְׂדֵה) ; ‎ bef. (:)	
שָׁמַע pr. name of a place; ‎ id.	שמע
שְׁמַע Chald. Peal pret. 3 pers. sing. masc.	שמע
שְׁמַע Kal imp. sing. masc.; ‎ bef. (:)	שמע
שֵׁמַע noun masc. sing. dec. 6 e	שמע
שֶׁמַע pr. name masc.	שמע
שְׁמֹעַ Kal inf. constr.	שמע
שֹׁמֵעַ id. part. act. sing. masc. dec. 7 b	שמע
שִׁמְעָא pr. name masc.	שמע
שָׁמְעָה Kal pret. 3 pers. sing. fem.	שמע
שָׁמְעָה in pause for שָׁמְעָה q. v. (§ 8. rem. 12)	שמע
שִׁמְעָה defect. for שְׁמוּעָה (q. v.)	שמע
שִׁמְעָה pr. name masc.	שמע
שִׁמְעָה Kal imp. s. m. (שְׁמַע) with parag. ה (§ 8. r. 11)	שמע
שֻׁמְעוֹ noun masc. sing., suff. 3 pers. s. f. שֵׁמַע d. 6 e	שמע
שֹׁמְעָהּ Kal part. act. sing. masc., suff. 3 pers. sing. fem. from שֹׁמֵעַ dec. 7 b	שמע
שִׁמְעוֹ id. inf. (Nu. 30. 6, 8, 13, 15), or subst. masc. [שֵׁמַע], with suff. 3 pers. sing. masc.	שמע
שָׁמְעוּ id. pret. 3 pers. pl. (§ 8. rem. 1 & 7)	שמע
שִׁמְעוּ	
שִׁמְעִי id. imp. pl. masc. (§ 8. r. 12); ‎ bef. (:)	שמע
שִׁמְעוּ	
שֹׁמְעוֹ id. part. a. s. m., suff. 3 p. s. m. fr. שֹׁמֵעַ d. 7 b	שמע
שִׁמְעוֹן pr. name of a man and a tribe	שמע
שִׁמְעוּנִי Kal imp. pl. m. (שִׁמְעוּ), suff. 1 p. s. (§ 16. r. 11)	שמע

שְׁמָעוֹת	¹ noun fem.,pl. of שְׁמוּעָה dec. 10 ; ¹ bef. (:) . . שמע
שִׁמְעָה	Kh. שִׁמְעָה, K. שִׁמְעָה pr. name masc. . שמע
שִׁמְעִי	¹ פ׳ pr. name masc. . . . . שמע
שִׁמְעִי	Kal imp. fem. sing.; or (Is. 66. 19) noun masc. with suff. from שֵׁמַע dec. 6 e . שמע
שִׁמְעִי	id. part. act. pl. c. masc. from שֹׁמֵעַ dec. 7 b . שמע
שִׁמְעָה	} pr. name masc.; ¹ bef. (:) . . שמע
שְׁמַעְיָהוּ	
שִׁמְעוֹ	the foll. with suff. 3 p. s. m. K. שִׁמְעָה (q. v.) שמע
שֹׁמְעִים	¹ פ׳ Kal part. act. masc., pl. of שֹׁמֵעַ dec. 7 b . שמע
שָׁמְעִין	Chald. Peal part. act. pl. m. [fr. שְׁמַע] d. 2 b . שמע
שָׁמְעֲךָ	noun masc. sing. with suff. 2 pers. sing. masc. from שֵׁמַע dec. 6 e . . . שמע
שָׁמְעָם	id. with suff. 3 pers. pl. masc. . . שמע
שִׁמְעָן	Kal imp. pl. fem. for שְׁמַעְנָה (comp. § 8. r.16) שמע
שְׁמָעֶנָּה	id. imp. sing. masc. (שְׁמַע), suff. 3 pers. sing. fem. (§ 16. rem. 11) . . . שמע
שְׁמַעְנָה	id. imp. pl. fem. . . . . . שמע
שָׁמַעְנוּ	} id. pret. 1 pers. pl. (§ 8. rem. 7) . שמע
שְׁמַעְנוּ	
שְׁמָעֵנוּ	id. imp. s. m. (שְׁמַע), suff. 1 p. pl. (§ 16. r. 11) שמע
שְׁמַעֲנוּהָ	id. pret. 1 pers. pl. (שְׁמַעֲנוּ),suff. 3 pers. s.fem. שמע
שְׁמָעֵנִי	id. imp. s. m. (שְׁמַע), suff. 1 p. s. (§ 16. r. 11) שמע
שְׁמַעְתָּ	} id. pret. 2 pers. sing.masc.; acc.shifted by conv. ו (§ 8. rem. 7) . . שמע
שָׁמַעְתָּ	
שְׁמַעַתְּ	id. pret. 2 pers. sing. fem. . . שמע
שְׁמַעַת	noun fem. sing., constr. of שְׁמוּעָה dec. 10 שמע
שִׁמְעָת	pr. name masc. . . . . . שמע
שִׁמְעֵת	¹ פ׳ Chald. Peal pret. 1 pers. sing. . שמע
שֹׁמַעַת	} Kal part. act. sing.,fem. of שֹׁמֵעַ (§ 8. r. 19) שמע
שֹׁמָעַת	
שָׁמַעְתְּ	id. pret. 2 p. s. f., Kh. תִּי׳, K. שָׁמַעַתְּ (§ 8. r. 5) שמע
שָׁמַעְתִּי	} id. pret. 1 pers. sing.; acc. shifted by conv. ו (§ 8. rem. 7) . . שמע
שְׁמַעְתִּי	
שְׁמַעְתִּיו	¹ id. id., suff. 3 pers.sing.masc.; ו, for ו, conv. שמע
שְׁמַעְתִּיךָ	id. id., suff. 2 pers. sing. masc. . שמע
שִׁמְעָתִים	patronym. pl. from שִׁמְעָה . . שמע
שְׁמַעְתָּם	Kal pret. 2 pers. sing. masc., suff. 3 pers. pl. m. שמע
שְׁמַעְתֶּם	¹ id. pret. 2 pers. pl. masc.; ו, for ו, conv. שמע

שָׁמַן   Root not used; Arab. *to impel, drive, thrust*; also *to speak rapidly*. Hence the two foll.

שֶׁמֶץ   masc. *a short, gentle sound, a whispering,* Job 4. 12; 26. 14; Prof. Lee, *a hint*; others regard it i. q. שֵׁמַע *report.* And

שִׁמְצָה	fem. Ex. 32. 25, *a whispering muttering;* others, *rout, overthrow;* or *ill fame, reproach,* i. q. שֶׁמֶץ.
שְׁמַצְאָתִי	pref. שֶׁ)(Kal pret. 1 pers. sing. . מצא
שֶׁמִּקָּרֶהָ	pref. id.)(noun masc. sing. dec. 9 a . קרה

שָׁמַר   פ׳ fut. יִשְׁמֹר.—I. *to keep, watch, guard;* part שֹׁמֵר *a watchman.*—II. *to keep safe, preserve, protect,* with acc., בְּ, אֶל, עַל of the object, with מִן *from* or *against* anything.—III. *to keep, retain, reserve.*—IV. *to keep, observe, mark,* with acc., עַל, אֶל.—V. *to keep, observe,* as the commandments of God.—VI. *to take heed,* with לְ and inf. *to do anything.*—VII. *to regard, reverence.*—VIII. *to keep oneself from,* with מִן, Jos. 6. 18. Niph. I. *to be kept, preserved,* Ps. 37. 28.—II. *to keep oneself from,* with מִן.—III. *to take heed, beware,* with בְּ, לְ, מִן. Pi. *to regard,* Jon. 2. 9. Hithpa. הִשְׁתַּמֵּר.—I. *to be kept, observed,* Mi. 6. 16.—II. *to take heed to oneself, to beware,* Ps. 18. 24.

שָׁמִיר   masc. dec. 3 a.—I. *thorn;* collect. *thorns.*—II. *diamond.*—III. pr. name (*a*) of a city in Judah, Jos. 15. 48; (*b*) of a city in Ephraim, Ju. 10. 1, 2; (*c*) of a man, 1 Ch. 24. 24 Keri, שָׁמוּר Kh.

שֶׁמֶר   masc. dec. 6 a (pl. with suff. שְׁמָרֶיהֶם).—I. pl. *sediment, lees* of wine.—II. pr. name of several men.

שֶׁמֶר   (*keeper*) pr. name.—I. masc. 1 Ch. 7. 32, for which שֶׁמֶר ver. 34.—II. fem. 2 Ki. 12. 22, for which שִׁמְרִית 2 Ch. 24. 26.

שִׁמְרָה   fem. *a watching,* poet. for *eyelid,* Ps. 77. 5.

שְׁמֻרָה   fem. *watch, guard,* Ps. 141. 3.

שִׁמֻּרִים   masc. pl. *observance, keeping* of a festival, Ex. 12. 42.

שִׁמְרוֹן   (*watch, guard*) pr. name—I. of a son of Issachar, Ge. 46. 13. Patronym. שִׁמְרֹנִי Nu. 26. 24. —II. pr. name of a town of Zebulun, Jos. 11. 1; 19. 15, called שְׁ מְראוֹן Jos. 12. 20.

שֹׁמְרוֹן   (*watch-hill* or *height*) pr. name, *Samaria.* —I. the capital of the kingdom of Israel.—II. the kingdom of Israel or the ten tribes. Gent. n שֹׁמְרֹנִי 2 Ki. 17. 29.

שִׁמְרִי   (*watchful*) pr. name masc. of several men.

שְׁמַרְיָה   (*whom the Lord keeps*) pr. name—I. of a son of Rehoboam, 2 Ch. 11. 19.—II. of two other men, Ezr. 10. 32, 41.

שְׁמַרְיָהוּ   (id.) pr. name masc. 1 Ch. 12. 5.

שִׁמְרַיִן   Ch. i. q. Heb. שֹׁמְרוֹן, Ezr. 4. 10, 17.

שְׁמֶרֶת (watch, guard) pr. name m. 1 Ch. 8. 21.

אַשְׁמֹרֶת, אַשְׁמוּרָה fem. (§ 39. No. 4 d), pl. אַשְׁמֻרוֹת night-watch.

יִשְׁמְרַי (for יִשְׁמַרְיָה whom the Lord keeps) pr. name masc. 1 Ch. 8. 18.

מִשְׁמָר masc. dec. 2 b.—I. a watching, guarding, Pr. 4. 23.—II. a watch, i. e. place of watching ; also a watch, persons watching, guards.—III. custody, prison.—IV. observance, rite, Ne. 13. 14.

מִשְׁמֶרֶת fem. dec. 13 a (with מַרְתִּי ';, pl. מִשְׁמָרוֹת § 44. r. 5).—I. a watching, guarding, 2 Ki. 11. 5, 6, meton. an object guarded, 1 Sa. 22. 23.—II. place of watching, post, station ; also a watch, persons keeping watch.—III. a keeping, preservation.—IV. observance or performance.—V. what is to be observed, a charge, law, usage, rite.—VI. adherence to any one, 1 Ch. 12. 29.

שְׁמַר Kal pret. 3 pers. sing. m. for שָׁמַר (§ 8. r. 7) | שמר

שְׁמֵר ן pr. n. m. for שָׁמֵר (§35. r. 2) ; for ן see lett. ו | שמר

שָׁמֹר Kal inf. abs. | שמר

שֶׁמֶר pr. name masc. | שמר

שְׁמֹר ן } Kal imp. sing. masc., or (De. 8. 11) | שמר

שְׁמָר ן } inf. constr. (§ 8. r. 18) ; ן bef. (:) | שמר

שֹׁמֵר ן id. part. act. sing. m. d. 7 b, also pr. name | שמר

שָׁמְרָה id. pret. 3 pers. sing. fem. | שמר

שָׁמְרָה id. imp. (§ 8. rem. 11), or (Ps. 141. 3) n. f. s. | שמר

שְׁמָרָהּ • id. pret. 3 pers. sing. masc. (שָׁמַר), suff. 3 pers. sing. fem., acc. drawn back before penacute (נְצֶה) for שְׁמָרָהּ (§ 2. rem. 3) | שמר

שְׁמוּרָה ' id. part pass., fem. of שָׁמוּר ; ן bef. (:) | שמר

שָׁמְרוּ ן } id. pret. 3 pers. pl. (§ 8. rem. 7) . | שמר

שָׁמְרוּ ' } | שמר

שָׁמְרוּהוּ ' id. pret. 3 p. s. m., suff. 3 p. s. m. ; ן bef. | שמר

שִׁמְרוֹן ן pr. name of a place, also in compos. שֵׁ מְרָאוֹן | שמר

שֹׁמְרוֹן ' pr. name of a place | שמר

שֹׁמְרוֹנָה • id. with parag. ה | שמר

שְׁמֻרוֹת • noun fem., pl. of [שְׁמֻרָה] dec. 10 | שמר

שִׁמְרִי pr. name masc. | שמר

שֹׁמְרִי ' ן Kal part. act. pl. c. masc. fr. שֹׁמֵר d. 7 b | שמר

שְׁמַרְיָה pr. name masc. | שמר

שִׁמְרָיו ' noun m. pl., suff. 3 pers. s. f. fr. שֶׁמֶר d. 6 a | שמר

שְׁמַרְיָהוּ ' ן pr. name masc. see שְׁמַרְיָה ; ן bef. (:) | שמר

שִׁמְרֵיהֶם • noun m. pl., suff. 3 pers. pl. m, fr. שֶׁמֶר d. 6 a | שמר

שְׁמָרָיו • id. pl., suff. 3 pers. sing. masc. | שמר

שְׁמָרִים • id. pl., abs. st. | שמר

שְׁמָרִים • noun masc. pl. | שמר

שֹׁמְרִים Kal part. act. masc., pl. of שֹׁמֵר dec. 7 b | שמר

שְׁמָרִימוֹת ' Kh. for שְׁמִירָמוֹת (q. v.) | שם

שִׁמְרָיִן Ch. pr. name of a place | שמר

שְׁמָרִית pr. name masc. see שָׁמֵר | שמר

שְׁמָרְךָ Kal part. act. sing. masc., suff. 2 pers. sing. masc. from שֹׁמֵר dec. 7 b | שמר

שָׁמְרֵם ™ id. imp. sing. masc., suff. 3 pers. pl. masc. | שמר

שִׁמְרֹן ן pr. name masc. | שמר

שִׁמְרֹנָה pr. name of a place (שִׁמְרֹון) with parag. ה | שמר

שְׁמַרְנוּ Kal pret. 1 pers. pl. | שמר

שְׁמָרַנִי " ן id. pret. 3 pers. sing. masc., suff. 1 pers. sing. ; ן, for ן, conv. | שמר

שָׁמְרֵנִי id. imp. sing. masc., suff. 1 pers. sing. | שמר

שְׁמַרְתָּ } id. pret. 2 pers. sing. masc. ; acc. shifted | שמר

שָׁמַרְתָּ } by conv. ן (§ 8. rem. 7) | שמר

שְׁמֶרֶת ן pr. name masc. | שמר

שְׁמַרְתִּי } Kal pret. 1 pers. sing. (§ 8. rem. 7) . | שמר

שָׁמַרְתִּי } | שמר

שְׁמַרְתִּיךָ ' id. id., suff. 2 pers. sing. masc. ; ן, for ן, conv. | שמר

שְׁמַרְתֶּם ' id. pret. 2 pers. pl. masc. ; ן id. | שמר

שְׁמַרְתֻּנִי ' id. pret. 2 pers. sing. masc., suff. 1 pers. sing. for תֶּנִי ; ן id. | שמר

[שְׁמַשׁ] Ch. to attend, serve, Da. 7. 10.

שֶׁמֶשׁ com. dec. 6 a (with suff. שִׁמְשֶׁךָ).—I. the sun.—II. pl. שְׁמָשׁוֹת windows, Is. 54. 12; others, notched battlements.

שִׁמְשׁוֹן (sun-like) pr. name, Samson, a judge of Israel, celebrated for his strength.

שִׁמְשַׁי (id.) pr. name masc. Ezr. 6. 8, 17.

שֶׁמֶשׁ ' ן id. in pause (§ 35. rem. 2); for ן see lett. ו | שמש

שִׁמְשָׁא Ch. id. emph. st. dec. 3 b | שמש

שִׁמְשָׁהּ id., suff. 3 pers. sing. fem. | שמש

שִׁמְשׁוֹן pr. name masc. | שמש

שִׁמְשַׁי ן pr. name masc. | שמש

שִׁמְשֵׁךְ noun com. sing., suff. 2 pers. sing. fem. from שֶׁמֶשׁ dec. 6 a | שמש

שַׁמְשְׁרַי ן pr. name masc. 1 Ch. 8. 26. | שמש

שִׁמְשׁתַיִךְ id. noun c. with pl. fem. & suff. 2 pers. s. fem. | שמש

שָׁמְתְּ • Ch. Peal pret. 2 pers. sing. masc. | שום

שָׂמֵת • Ch. id. pret. 1 pers. sing. | שום

שַׂמְתָּ } Kal pret. 2 pers. sing. masc. ; acc. | שום

שַׂמְתָּה } shifted by conv. ן (comp. § 8. rem. 7) | שום

שַׂמְתְּ id. pret. 2 pers. sing. fem. | שום

שִׂמַת • ן Ch. part. pass. with afform. 3 pers. sing. fem. (§ 54. rem. 2) | שום

a Am. 1. 11.   d Je. 31. 10.   g Zep. 1. 12.   k Ex. 12. 42.   n Ge. 28. 20.   p Job 10. 14.   s Je. 15. 9.   u Is. 54. 12.   y Ezr. 6. 12.
b 2 Sa. 23. 5.   e Ps. 77. 5.   h Je. 48. 11.   l Ps. 121. 3, 5.   o Ps. 119. 67.   q Da. 6. 15.   t Is. 60. 20.   x Da. 3. 10.   z Da. 6. 18.
c Ge. 41. 35.   f Ps. 75. 9.   i Is. 25. 6.   m Pr. 4. 21.   r Ge. 28. 15.

שֶׁמֶת	noun masc. with pl. fem. term. abs. fr. שֵׁם d. 7 a	שם
שְׁמֹת	id., constr. st. comp. שְׁמֹת, שְׁמוֹת	שם
שָׂמַתְהוּ	Kal pret. 3 pers. s. f. (שָׂמָה), suff. 3 pers. s. m.	שום
שַׂמְתּוֹ•	id. pret. 2 pers. s. masc., suff. 3 pers. s. m.	שום
שַׂמְתִּי	} id. pret. 1 pers. sing.; acc. shifted by conv. וֹ (comp. § 8. rem. 7)	שום
וָשִׂם•		
שַׂמְתְּ•	} id. pret. 2 pers. sing. fem., Kh. שַׂמְתִּי, K. שַׂמְתְּ (§ 8. rem. 5)	שום
שַׂמְתִּיהָ•	} id. pret. 1 pers. sing., suff. 3 pers. sing. masc.	שום
שַׂמְתִּיו•	id. id., suff. 3 pers. sing. masc.	שום
שַׂמְתִּיךָ	} id. id., suff. 2 pers. sing. m.	שום
שַׂמְתִּיךְ•	} id. id., suff. 2 pers. sing. fem.	שום
שַׂמְתִּים	} id. id., suff. 3 pers. pl. masc. (ם for ן fem. in Ho. 2. 14, § 2. rem. 5)	שום
שְׂמֹתָם	defect. for שְׂמוֹתָם (q. v.)	שם
שַׂמְתָּם	} Kal pret. 2 pers. s. masc., suff. 3 pers. pl. m.	שום
שַׂמְתֶּם•	} id. pret. 2 pers. pl. masc.	שום
שְׂמַתְנִי	id. pret. 3 pers. s. fem. (שָׂמָה), suff. 1 pers. s.	שום
שַׂמְתַּנִי•	id. pret. 2 pers. sing. masc., suff. 1 pers. sing.	שום
שָׁן	pr. name, see בֵּית שָׁאָן.	
שֵׁן	} noun com. sing. dec. 8 b (§ 36. rem. 3)	שנן
וְשֵׁן•		

שָׂנֵא fut. יִשְׂנָא to hate; part. שֹׂנֵא, hater, enemy. Niph. to be hated, Pr. 14. 17, 20. Pi. part. מְשַׂנֵּא hater, enemy.

שָׂנֵא Chald. only part. hater, Da. 4. 16.

שִׂנְאָה fem. (constr. שִׂנְאַת; no pl.) hatred.

שָׂנִיא only fem. שְׂנִיאָה adj. hated, De. 21. 15.

שָׂנֹא•	Kal inf. abs.	שנא
שֵׁנָא•	noun fem. sing. for שֵׁנָה (q. v.)	ישן
שַׁנָּא•	} Piel pret. 3 pers. s. masc. for שָׁנָה (§ 24. r. 19)	שנה
שְׂנֹא•	Kal inf. constr.	שנא
שֹׂנֵא•	id. part. act. sing. masc. dec. 7 b	שנא
שֶׁנְאָב	pr. name masc.	שנן
שָׂנְאָה	Kal pret. 3 pers. sing. fem.	שנא
שְׂנֵאָה•	} id. pret. 3 pers. sing. masc. (שָׂנֵא), suff. 3 pers. s. fem. (§ 16. r. 1); וֹ, for וֹ, conv.	שנא
וְשָׂנְאָה•	} noun fem. sing. (no pl. abs.)	שנא
שְׂנֵאָהוּ•	the foll. with suff. 3 pers. s. masc. (§ 16. r. 1)	שנא
שָׂנְאוּ•	Kal pret. 3 pers. pl.	שנא
שְׂנוּאִי•	Kh. שְׂנֻאַי q. v.; K. שְׂנוּאַי; Kal part. pass. pl. c. from שָׂנוּא dec. 3 a	שנא
שִׂנְאוּ•	Kal imp. pl. masc.	שנא
שְׂנֵאוּנִי•	id. pret. 3 p. pl. (שָׂנְאוּ), suff. 1 p. s. (§ 16. r. 1)	שנא

שְׂנֵאֲחָזִים•	pref. שֶׁ)(Niph. part. pl. m. [fr. נֶאֱחָז § 13. r. 7]	אחז
שְׂנֵאַי	} the foll. with suff. 1 pers. sing.	שנא
שֹׂנְאַי		
שֹׂנְאֵי•	} וֹ Kal part. act. pl. c. masc. from שָׂנֵא d. 7 b	שנא
שֹׂנְאִי•	id. sing., with parag. י (Kh. שֹׂנְאִי § 8. r. 19); K. שֹׂנֵא (q. v.)	שנא
שֹׂנְאֵיהֶם•	id. pl., suff. 3 pers. pl. masc.	שנא
שֹׂנְאָיו	id. pl., suff. 3 pers. sing. masc.	שנא
שֹׂנְאֶיךָ	id. pl., suff. 2 pers. sing. masc.	שנא
שֹׂנְאֵיכֶם•	id. pl., suff. 2 pers. pl. masc.	שנא
שֹׂנְאֵינוּ•	id. pl., suff. 1 pers. pl.	שנא
שֹׂנַאֲךָ	id. sing., suff. 2 pers. sing. masc.	שנא
שְׂנֵאֲךָ•	} וֹ id. pret. 3 pers. sing. masc. (שָׂנֵא), suff. 2 pers. sing. masc. (§ 16. rem. 1); וֹ bef. (:)	שנא
שָׁנָאן•	noun masc. sing.	שנה
שֶׁנְאַצַּר	} pr. name masc. 1 Ch. 3. 18.	
שָׂנֵאתָ•	Kal pret. 2 pers. sing. masc. (§ 23. rem. 1)	שנא
שָׂנֵאת	id. pret. 2 pers. sing. fem.	שנא
שְׂנֹאת•	id. inf. constr. (§ 23. rem. 2)	שנא
שִׂנְאַת•	} noun fem. sing., constr. of שִׂנְאָה (no pl. abs.)	שנא
שְׂנֵאתָהּ•	Kal pret. 2 pers. sing. masc., suff. 3 pers. sing. fem. (§ 23. rem. 1)	שנא
שְׂנֵאתִי	} id. pret. 1 pers. sing.; acc. shifted by conv. וֹ (§ 8. rem. 7)	שנא
וְשָׂנֵאתִי•		
שְׂנֵאתִיהָ•	id. id., suff. 3 pers. sing. fem.	שנא
שְׂנֵאתִיהוּ•	id. id., suff. 3 pers. sing. masc.	שנא
שְׂנֵאתִיו•	id. id., suff. 3 pers. sing. masc.	שנא
שֹׂנְאֹתַיִךְ•	id. part. act. fem. pl., suff. 2 pers. sing. fem. [from שֹׂנְאֹת or שִׂנְאָה]	שנא
שְׂנֵאתִים•	id. pret. 1 pers. s., suff. 3 pers. pl. m. (§ 23. r. 1)	שנא
שִׂנְאָתָם•	noun fem. sing., suff. 3 pers. pl. masc. from שִׂנְאָה (no pl. abs.)	שנא
שְׂנֵאתֶם	Kal pret. 2 pers. pl. masc. (§ 23. rem. 1)	שנא
שְׂנֵאתַנִי	id. pret. 2 pers. sing. masc., suff. 1 pers. sing.	שנא

שָׁנָב Root not used; Arab. to be cool.

אֶשְׁנָב masc. dec. 8a, a latticed window.

שָׁנָה (Milêl bef. monos.) fut. יִשְׁנֶה.—I. to repeat, to do the second time or again.—II. to be different from, with מִן, Est. 1. 7 ; 3. 8.—III. to alter, change, be changed ; part. שֹׁנִים changeable, given to change unsteady, Pr. 24. 21. Niph. to be repeated, Ge. 41. 32 Pi. שִׁנָּה.—I. to change, e. g. a garment.—II. to change, alter a promise, one's way.—III. to change, disfigure the countenance, Job 14. 20 ; with טַעֲמוֹ one's (own) understanding, i. e. to feign oneself mad.

ᵃ Hab. 1. 12.   ᵍ Ge. 27. 37.   ˡ Job 39. 28.   ᵗ Ge. 37. 5, 8.   ᶻ Ec. 9. 12.   ᵇ Ps. 106. 41.   ᶠ Ps. 68. 18.   ᵏ Ec. 2. 17, 18.   Eze. 16. 27.

ᵇ Je. 13. 1.   ʰ Is. 41. 15.   ᵐ De. 32. 24.   ᵘ 2 Sa. 13. 15.   ʸ Ps. 41. 8.   ᵍ Ge. 24. 60.   ᵍ Pr. 8. 13.   Je. 12. 8.   ᵖ Ec. 9. 6.

ᶜ Je. 33. 25.   ⁱ Ca. 6. 12.   ⁿ Ju. 15. 2.   ᵛ Pr. 19. 7.   ˣ Ps. 34. 22.   ʰ Ex. 1. 10.   ʰ Ps. 25. 19.   ᵐ 2 Ch. 18. 7.   ᵍ Ju. 14. 16.

ᵈ Ru. 3. 3.   ʲ Job 7. 20.   ᵒ Ps. 127. 2.   ʷ 2 Sa. 5. 8.   ᵈ Pr. 28. 16.   ⁱ Pr. 25. 17.   ⁱ Ju. 15. 2.   ⁿ 1 Ki. 22. 8.   ʳ 2 Sa. 20. 10.

ᵉ Eze. 5. 5.   ᵏ 1 Sa. 14. 4.   ᵖ 2 Ki. 25. 29.   ˣ Ps. 25. 19.

IV. *to transfer* or remove to another place, Est. 2. 9. Pu. *to be changed, altered*, Ec. 8. 1. Hithpa. *to change, disguise oneself*, 1 Ki. 14. 2.

שְׁנָא Chald.—I. *to be changed, altered.*—II. *to be different from*, with מִן. Pa. I. *to change, make different to*, with מִן, Da. 4. 13; part. passive, *different*, Da. 7. 7.—II. *to change, violate*, Da. 3. 28. Ithpa. *to be changed, altered.* Aph. I. *to change, alter.*—II. *to transgress*, Ezr. 6. 11, 12.

שָׁנָה fem. dec. 11a (pl. שָׁנוֹת, שָׁנִים).—I. *a year*; מִדֵּי שׁ׳ בְּשָׁנָה שׁ׳, שָׁנָה שָׁנָה *every year, from year to year*; pl. שָׁנִים *years*, also indef. *some years*; dual שְׁנָתַיִם *two years.*—II. trop. *the produce of a year*, Joel 2. 25.

שְׁנָה or שְׁנָא Chald. fem. (constr. שְׁנַת; pl. שְׁנִין) *year.*

שָׁנִי masc. (constr. שְׁנִי, pl. שָׁנִים) *bright, scarlet colour* (Arab. שנא *to shine, be bright*) obtained from the coccus; תּוֹלַעַת; pl. *scarlet clothes, or garments.*

שְׁנַיִם masc. du. constr. שְׁנֵי; fem. שְׁתַּיִם (prob. for שְׁנְתַּיִם, to distinguish it from the du. of שָׁנָה *a year*), constr. שְׁתֵּי.—I. num. card. *two*; שְׁנַיִם שְׁנַיִם *two and two, by pairs*; שְׁתֵּיהֶם, שְׁנֵיהֶם *they two, both of them.*—II. fem. *a second time, again,* Ne. 13. 20; בִּשְׁתַּיִם id. Job 33. 14.—III. masc. שְׁנֵים עָשָׂר שְׁתֵּים עָשָׂר fem. *twelve*; also *twelfth.*

שֵׁנִי masc. שֵׁנִית fem —I. adj. ord. *second.*—II. pl. שְׁנִיִּם *chambers of the second story*, Ge. 6. 16; but in Nu. 2. 16, *the second.*—III. fem. also as an adv. *the second time, again.*

שִׁנְאָן m. Ps. 68. 18, Eng. vers. "angels;" perh. *changed, glorified ones*; others, אַלְפֵי שׁ׳ *thousand of repetition*, i. e. thousands upon thousands.

מִשְׁנֶה masc. dec. 9a.—I. *second rank*, in order or dignity; כֹּהֵן הַמִּשְׁנֶה *the priest next* to the high priest.—II. *second in rank*, in succession, dignity or quality, *second, next, the next*; אֲחֵיהֶם הַמִּשְׁנִים *their younger brethren*, 1 Ch. 15. 18; מִשְׁנֶה הַמֶּלֶךְ *the one next to the king*; 1 Ch. 15. 18 silver cups of (מִשְׁנִים) *second quality*, 1 Sa. 15. 9.—III. *a doubling, double.*—IV. *a duplicate, copy.*—V. *a division of Jerusalem*, so called 2 Ki. 22. 14; 2 Ch. 34. 22; Zep. 1. 10.

שָׁנָה	ı noun fem. sing. dec. 11a . . .	שנה
שָׁנָה	Kh. שָׁנָה subst. q. v., K. שָׁנִים (q. v.,	ישן
	noun fem. sing. dec. 11b [for וִישֵׁנָה]	ישן
שִׁנָּה	ı Piel pret. 3 pers. sing. masc. . . .	שנה
שֹׁנֶה	ı Kal part. act. sing. masc. dec. 9a .	שנה

שְׁנַהֲבִּים	noun masc. pl.	שנן
שְׁנוֹ	Ch. Peal pret. 3 pers. pl. masc. . .	שנה
שְׁנוּ	Kal imp. pl. masc.	שנה
שִׁנּוּ	noun com. sing., suff. 3 pers. s. m. fr. שֵׁן d. 8b	שנן
שְׁנוּאָה	Kal part. pass. fem. sing. [from שָׂנֵא m.]	שׂנא
שַׁנּוֹהִי	Ch. Peal pret. 3 pers. pl. m., suff. 3 pers. s. m.	שנה
שָׁנוּן	Kal part. pass. sing. masc. dec. 3a	שנן
שְׁנוּנִים	id. pl., abs. st.	שנן
שָׁנוֹת	noun fem. pl. abs. from שֵׁנָה dec. 11 b .	ישן
שְׁנוֹת	noun f. pl., constr. of שָׁנָה fr. שָׁנָה d. 11 a	שנה
שֹׁנוֹת	Kal part. act. pl. fem. [fr. שָׁנָה] fr. שָׁנָה m.	שנה
שָׁנוֹתִי	Kal pret. 1 pers. sing. . . .	שנה
שְׁנוֹתַי שְׁנוֹתָי	} noun fem. pl., suff. 1 pers. sing. from שָׁנָה dec. 11 a; ı bef. (:)	שנה
שְׁנוֹתָיו	id. pl., suff. 3 pers. sing. masc. . .	שנה
שְׁנוֹתַיִךְ	id. pl., suff. 2 pers. sing. fem. [for תַיִךְ]	שנה
שְׁנוֹתֶיךָ	id. pl., suff. 2 pers. sing. masc.; ı bef. (:)	שנה
שְׁנוֹתֵינוּ	id. pl., suff. 1 pers. pl. . . .	שנה
שְׁנוֹתָם	id. pl., suff. 3 p. pl. m. (§ 4. r. 2); ı bef. (:)	שנה
שְׁנִי	noun masc. sing., constr. of שֵׁן; pl. שָׁנִים	שנן
שְׁנֵי	noun f. with pl. m. term., constr. of שָׁנִים, fr. שָׁנָה d. 11a; or constr. of שְׁנַיִם (q. v.)	שנה
שֵׁנִי	adj. ord. m. s. (pl. שְׁנִים d. 8 f) fr. שָׁנָה card.	שנה
שְׁנִי	noun masc., constr. of שֵׁן; ı bef. (:)	שנה
שְׁנִי	ı see וְשֵׁנִי under lett. ı.	
שְׁנִי	[for שֶׁנִּי] the foll. with suff. 1 pers. sing. .	שנן
שְׁנַּי	ı noun com. du., constr. of שְׁנַיִם fr. שֵׁן d. 8 b	שנן
שְׁנִיָּה	Ch. Peal part. act. f. [fr. שָׂנֵא m.] R. שׂנא under	שׂנא
שִׁנַּיָּה	Ch. noun com. du. (שִׁנַּיִן), suff. 3 pers. sing. fem. from שֵׁן dec. 5 b . .	שנן
שְׁנֵיהֶם	ı num. card. masc. (שְׁנַיִם) with suff. 3 pers. pl. masc.; ı bef. (:)	שנה
שְׁנֵיהֶם	ı noun fem. pl. (שָׁנִים) with suff. 3 pers. pl. masc. from שָׁנָה dec. 11 a; ı id.	שנה
שִׁנֵּיהֶם	noun com. pl., suff. 3 pers. pl. m. fr. שֵׁן d. 8 b	שנן
שָׁנָיו	noun f. pl. (שָׁנִים), suff. 3 p. s. m. fr. שָׁנָה d. 11a	שנה
שַׁנִּיו	Ch. Pael pret. 3 pers. masc. . . .	שנה
שִׁנָּיו	noun com. pl., suff. 3 pers. s. m. fr. שֵׁן d. 8 b	שנן
שִׁנַּיִךְ	id. pl., suff. 2 pers. sing. fem. . .	שנן
שְׁנֵיכֶם	num. card. m. (שְׁנַיִם) with suff. 2 pers. pl. m.	שנה
שְׁנִים	noun masc., pl. of שָׁנִי (q. v.) . .	שנה
שָׁנִים	ı noun f. with pl. m. term. fr. שָׁנָה d. 11 a	שנה
שְׁנַיִם שְׁתַּיִם	} num. card. masc. du., constr. of שְׁנֵי & fem., שְׁתֵּים, ı bef. (:)	שנה
שִׁנַּיִם	noun com., dual of שֵׁן dec. 8 b . .	שנן
שְׁנִים	ord. num. masc., constr. of שְׁנַיִם (q. v.)	שנה
שְׁנִיִּים	adj. ord. masc., pl. of שֵׁנִי dec. 8f; ı bef. (:)	שנה

a 2 Ki. 8. 17. e 1 Ki. 18. 34. i Da. 5. 6. l De. 32. 41. o Ps. 31. 11. r Ps. 102. 28. u Le. 14. 6, 51. x Job 36. 11. z Pr. 31. 21.
b Je. 52. 33. f Ex. 21. 27. k Pr. 25. 18. m Is. 38. 10. p Ps. 61. 7. s Ps. 90. 10. v Da. 7. 19. a Ge. 6. 16.
c Pr. 17. 9. g Is. 60. 15. h Est. 3. 8. n Is. 38. 15. q Eze. 22. 4. t Ps. 78. 33. y Da. 7. 5, 19. b Ge. 27. 45. Nu. 2. 16.
d Da. 3 27.

שְׁנֵימוֹ	noun com. dual, suff. 3 pers. pl. m. fr. שֵׁן d. 8 b	שׁן
שָׁנְיָא	Ch. Peal part. act. pl. m. [fr. שְׁנָא] d. 6 a	שנה
שָׁנְיָן	Ch. id. part. a. f.,pl. of שְׁנְיָה [for שָׁנְיָא] d. 10	שנה
שְׁנָיִן	ו Ch. noun com., dual of שֵׁן dec. 5 b	שׁן
שָׁנִין	Ch. noun f. with pl. m. term. fr. [שְׁנָה] d. 9 a	שנה
שָׁנֵינוּ	noun f. pl. (שָׁנִים), suff. 1 p. pl. fr. שָׁנָה d. 11 a	שנה
שְׁנֵינוּ	num. card m. du. (שְׁנַיִם) with suff. 1 pers. pl.	שנה
שְׂנִיר	ו pr. name of mount Hermon among the Amorites.	
שֵׁנִית	adj. ord., fem. of שֵׁנִי, as an adv. .	שנה
שָׁנִיתִי	Kal pret. 1 pers. sing. . . .	שנה

[שָׁנַן] I. *to sharpen*, e. g. a sword; part. שָׁנוּן *sharp*.— II. metaph. *to sharpen* the tongue, to utter sharp and insulting words. Pi. *to inculcate, teach diligently*, De. 6. 7. Hithpo. הִשְׁתּוֹנָן *to be pricked, pierced with pain*, Ps. 73. 21.

שֵׁן com. dec. 8 b.—I. *a tooth.*—II. *ivory.*—III. *tooth* or *prong* of a fork, 1 Sa. 2. 13.—IV. *a sharp cliff.*—V. pr. name of a place, 1 Sa. 7. 12.

שִׁנְאָב (*father's tooth*) pr. name of a Canaanitish king, Ge. 14. 2.

שֶׁנְהַבִּים masc. pl. *ivory*, 1 Ki. 10. 22, 2 Ch. 9. 21. הַבִּים is supposed to be a contraction for הָאִבִּים *the elephants*. Sansc. *ibha*, id.

שְׁנִינָה fem. *sharp* or *pointed saying, a taunt*.

שָׁנְנוּ	Kal pret. 3 pers. pl. . . .	שׁנן
שִׁנַּנְתָּם	ו Piel pret. 2 pers. s. masc., suff. 3 pers. pl. m.	שׁנן

שָׁנַס Pi. *to gird up* the loins, 1 Ki. 18. 46.

שִׁנְעָר	pr. name, *Shinar*, the country round Babylon.	
שֶׁנַּעֲשָׂה	pref. שֶׁ)(Niph. pret. 3 pers. sing. masc.	עשׂה
שֶׁנַּעֲשׂוּ	pref. id.)(id. pret. 3 pers. pl.	עשׂה
שְׁנָת	noun fem. sing. Ps. 132. 4.	ישׁן
שְׁנַת	noun fem. sing., constr. of שָׁנָה dec. 11 b	ישׁן
שְׁנַת	ו noun f. s., constr. of שָׁנָה d. 11 a; ו bef. (:)	ישׁן
שְׁנָתָהּ	id. with suff. 3 pers. sing. fem. . .	שנה
שְׁנָתֵהּ	ו Ch. noun fem. sing., suff. 3 pers. sing. masc. from [שְׁנָא] dec. 9 a . . .	ישׁן
שְׁנָתוֹ	noun fem. sing., suff. 3 pers. sing. masc. from שָׁנָה dec. 11 a . . .	שנה
שְׁנָתוֹ	ו noun fem. sing., suff. 3 pers. sing. masc. from שָׁנָה dec. 11 b; ו bef. (:)	ישׁן
שְׁנָתִי	וׁ id., suff. 1 pers. sing.; ו id. .	ישׁן
שְׁנָתַיִם שְׁנָתַיִם	} noun fem., du. of שָׁנָה dec. 11 a	שנה
שְׁנֹתֶךָ	וׁ id. pl., suff. 2 p. s. m. שְׁנוֹתֶיךָ; ו bef. (:)	שנה

שְׁנָתְךָ	noun fem. s., suff. 2 pers. s. m. fr. שָׁנָה d. 11 b	ישׁן
שְׁנָתָם	id., suff. 3 pers. pl. masc. . . .	ישׁן
שֶׁנָּתַן	pref. שֶׁ)(Kal pret. 3 pers. sing. masc.	נתן

[שָׁסָה] *to plunder, spoil*; part. שֹׁסִים *spoilers*. Po. שׁוֹשָׂה (for שׁוֹסָה) id. Is. 10. 13.

שָׁסָהוּ	Kal pret. 3 pers. pl. [שָׁסוּ], suff. 3 pers. s. m.	שסה
שֹׁסֵהוּ	Kal part. act. sing. masc., suff. 3 pers. sing. masc. [from שֹׁסֶה] dec. 9 a .	שסה
שָׁסּוּ	id. pret. 3 pers. pl. . . .	שסה
שָׁסוּי	ו id. part. pass. sing. masc.	שסה
שֹׁסֵי	id. part. act. pl. constr. masc. fr. שֹׁסֶה dec. 9 a	שסה
שֹׁסֵיהֶם	ו id. id., suff. 3 pers. pl. masc.	שסה
שֹׁסִים	id. id. pl., abs. st. . . .	שסה

[שָׁסַם] fut. יָשֹׁם *to plunder, spoil*. Niph. נָשַׁם *to be plundered, spoiled*.

מְשִׁסָּה fem. dec. 10, *prey, booty*.

[שָׁסַע] *to cleave, divide*; שֹׁסַע שֶׁסַע פַּרְסָה *cleaving the cleft of the hoof*, i. e. *having a divided hoof*. Pi. I. *to cleave*, Le. 1. 17.—II. *to rend, tear asunder*, Ju. 14. 6.—III. *to chide, rebuke*, 1 Sa. 24. 8; others, *to keep off, withhold, stay*. Hence

שֶׁסַע	ו masc. *cleft, division* in a hoof .	שסע
שִׁסַּע	ו Piel pret. 3 pers. sing. masc. . .	שסע
שֹׁסֵעַ שֹׁסַעַת	} Kal part. act. sing. masc. & fem. } (§ 36. rem. 1) . . .	שסע

שָׁסַף Pi. *to cut* or *hew in pieces*, 1 Sa. 15. 33.

שֶׁעֲבַרְתִּי	pref. שֶׁ)(Kal pret. 1 pers. sing. .	עבר

שָׁעָה I. *to look at, regard with attention*, with בְּ, Ex. 5. 9; Ps. 119. 117.—II. *to look at with favour, regard graciously*, with אֶל.—III. *to look out* or *about* for help, 2 Sa. 22. 42; and perh. also Is. 32. 3 (to which is assigned the sense of שָׁעַע; Syr. שׁעא *to be blinded*), with אֶל, עַל *to look to any one, expecting help.*—IV. *to look away from, allow respite to*, with מִן, מֵעַל. Hiph. *to look away from*, with מִן, Ps. 39. 14. Hithpa. הִשְׁתָּעָה. —I. *to look about with alarm*, Is. 41. 10.—II. *to be dismayed*, Is. 41. 23; others, *to look at* or *face one another*.

שָׁעָה or שָׁעָא Chald. (only emph. שַׁעְתָּא, שַׁעֲתָא) *a moment of time*; whence in the Targums and elsewhere, *an hour*.

a Da. 5. 9.	e Mal. 3. 6.	i Ec. 1. 14.	l Da. 2. 1.	o Pr. 5. 9.	r Ps. 89. 42.	s Is. 42. 22.	x Le. 11. 26.	y Le. 11. 26.
b Da. 7. 3.	f De. 6. 7.	k Ec. 1. 63. 4.	m Ge. 31. 40.	p Pr. 3. 24.	q 1 Sa. 14. 48.	t Je. 50. 11.	v Le. 11. 17.	z Ca. 3. 4.
c Da. 7. 7.	g Ec. 1. 9; 2. 17.		n Da. 6. 19.		Je. 31. 26.	u Esr. 8. 20.	Ps. 44. 11.	v Ju. 2. 16.	Le. 11. 7.	Ge. 4. 5.
d Ps. 90. 9.								

שְׁעֵה‎ Kal imp. sing. masc. . . . שעה
שָׁעוּ‎ id. pret. 3 pers. pl. . . . שעה
שְׁעוּ‎ id. imp. pl. masc. . . . שעה
שְׁעוּ‎ וֹ Kal imp. pl. masc.; for וֹ see lett. ו . שעע
שְׂעוֹרָה‎ noun fem. sing. dec. 10 . . שער
שְׂעוֹרִים‎ וֹ (2 Ch. 27. 5) id. pl., abs. st.; וֹ bef. (:) שער

שָׁעַט‎ Root not used; Arab. תעם *to stamp, pound in pieces.*
   שַׁעֲטָה‎ fem. dec. 11 c (§ 42. rem. 1), *a stamping* of the horse hoofs, Je. 47. 3.

שַׁעַטְנֵז‎ *a cloth made of different threads,* Le. 19. 19; De. 22. 11, in which latter passage the word is explained by a mixture *of wool and flax together.* According to Bochart it is compounded of שָׁעַם i. q. Arab. שׁאם *to mix,* and the Chald. נוז *to twist threads together.* Others compare it with the Egyptian שֶׁנְטְנָז a kind of linen.

שֶׁעָטְרָה‎ pref. שֶׁ ꓹ Piel pret. 3 pers. sing. fem. עטר
שֶׁעָטַת‎ noun fem. sing., constr. of [שָׁעֲטָה] dec. 11 c שׁעט
שְׂעָר‎ וֹ noun masc. sing. dec. 3 a . . שׁער
שְׂעָר‎ וֹ id., constr. st.; וֹ bef. (:) . שׁער
שֵׂעִיר‎ וֹ pr. name of a man and a country . שׁער
שֵׂעִירָה‎ id. with parag. ה . . . שׁער
שְׂעִירֵי‎ וֹ noun masc. pl. constr. fr. שָׂעִיר dec. 3 a שׁער
שְׂעִירִים‎ וֹ id. pl., abs. st.; וֹ bef. (:) . שׁער
שְׂעִירַת‎ noun fem. sing., constr. of [שְׂעִירָה] dec. 10 שׁער

שָׁעָל‎ Root not used; to which the idea of *hollowness* is ascribed, as it appears from some of the derivatives.
   שֹׁעַל‎ m. d. 6 f, *the hollow hand, palm,* Is. 40. 12.
   שֹׁעַל‎ masc. dec. 6 d, *a handful.*
   שַׁעַלִים‎ (*foxes;* שַׁעַל i. q. שׁוּעָל) pr. name of a district, 1 Sa. 9. 4.
   שׁוּעָל‎ masc. (pl. שׁוּעָלִים).—I. *a fox.*—II. pr. name, (1) of a man, 1 Ch. 7. 36; (2) of a district in Benjamin, 1 Sa. 13. 17.
   שַׁעַלְבִּין, שַׁעַלְבִים‎ (*foxes;* Arab. תעלב *fox*) pr. name of a city in the tribe of Dan. Gent. noun שַׁעַלְבֹנִי.
   מִשְׁעוֹל‎ m. *a narrow path, a hollow way,* Nu. 22. 24.

שֶׁעָלַי‎ pref. שֶׁ ꓹ prep., with suff. עָלַי (§ 31. rem. 5) עלה
שֶׁעַלְבִּים‎ וֹ pr. name of a place . . שׁעל
שֶׁעָלוּ‎ וֹ pref. id. ꓹ Kal pret. 3 pers. pl. עלה
שַׁעֲלִים‎ pr. name of a district . . שׁעל
שַׁעֲלִים‎ defect. for שׁוּעָלִים (q. v.) . . שׁעל
שֶׁעֹמְדִים‎ pref. שֶׁ ꓹ Kal part. act., pl. of עָמַד dec. 7 b עמד

שֶׁעִמָּהֶם‎ pref. id. ꓹ prep. (עִם) with suff. 3 pers. pl. masc. (§ 5) . . עמם
שֶׁעֲמָלוֹ‎ pref. id. ꓹ noun masc. sing. suff. 3 pers. sing. masc. from עָמָל dec. 4 c . . עמל
שֶׁעָמַלְתִּי‎ pref. id. ꓹ Kal pret. 1 pers. sing. עמל

שָׁעַן‎ Niph. נִשְׁעַן.—I. *to lean, rest upon,* with עַל.—II. metaph. *to rely upon, to trust in,* with בְּ, אֶל, עַל.—III. *to touch, border upon, be adjacent to,* with עַל, לְ.—IV. *to recline,* abs. Ge. 18. 4.
   אֶשְׁעָן‎ (*support*) pr. name of a city in the tribe of Judah, Jos. 15. 52.
   מִשְׁעָן‎ masc. dec. 2 b, *a stay, support.*
   מַשְׁעֵן‎ masc., מַשְׁעֵנָה fem. id. Is. 3. 1.
   מִשְׁעֶנֶת‎ fem. dec. 13 a (with suff. מִשְׁעַנְתּוֹ), *a staff*

[שָׁעַע]‎ *to be overspread, to be closed* (Syr. & Chald. שָׁעַע, שׁוּעַ trans. *to spread over;* also, *to stroke, caress, flatter*); of the eyes, *to be blinded,* Is. 29. 9. Hiph. *to cover, blind* the eyes, Is. 6. 10. Pilp. שִׁעֲשַׁע (§ 6. No. 4).—I. *to delight, rejoice,* Ps. 94. 19.—II. *to delight oneself, be delighted.* Pulp. שֻׁעֲשַׁע *to be fondled, caressed,* Is. 66. 12. Hithpalp. הִשְׁתַּעֲשַׁע *to delight oneself,* with בְּ in any one, Ps. 119. 16, 47; abs. i. q. *to indulge oneself,* Is. 29. 9; others, *to be dazzled or blinded.*
   שַׁעֲשֻׁעִים‎ masc. pl. (of שַׁעֲשׁוּעַ dec. 1 b) *delight pleasure.*

שָׁעָף‎ וֹ pr. name masc. of two persons, 1 Ch.
שֶׁעַף‎ 2. 47, 49; for וֹ see lett. ו.
שְׂעִפַּי‎ וֹ noun masc. pl., suff. 1 pers. sing. from [שָׂעֵף] dec. 8 b (§ 37. No. 2), see . . . סעף

[שָׂעַר]‎ I. *to shudder.*—II. *to fear, reverence,* De. 32. 17.—III. *to sweep, tear away with a tempest,* Ps. 58. 10. Niph. impers. *it is tempestuous,* Ps. 50. 3. Pi. *to sweep away with a tempest,* Job 27. 21. Hithpa. *to rage against, or rush upon like a tempest,* with עַל, Da. 11. 40.
   שַׂעַר‎ masc.—I. *a storm, tempest,* Is. 28. 2.—II. *a shuddering, horror.* See also under the foll. R.
   שְׂעָרָה‎ fem. id. Job 9. 17; Na. 1. 3.
   שְׂעִירִים‎ masc. pl. *showers,* De. 32. 2.

שֵׂעָר‎ וֹ masc. dec. 4 b, *a hair;* collect. *hair.*
   שֵׂעָר‎ masc. dec. 6 d, *the hair,* Ca. 4. 1; 6. 5; Is. 7. 20. For another, see above.
   שְׂעַר‎ Chald. id. Da. 3. 27; 7. 9.

a Job 14. 6.   c Is. 22. 4.   e Ca. 3. 11.   g Is. 34. 14.   i Nu. 7. 87.   k Ju. 7. 12; 8. 26.   l 1 Ch. 5. 20.   p Ec. 2. 11, 19, 20.   r Le. 13. 3, 31, 27.
b Is. 31. 1.   d Is. 29. 9.   f Je. 47. 3.   h Le 16. 5; 2 Ch. 29. 23.   k Is. 13. 21.   m Ps. 135. 2.   n Ec. 2. 21.   t Job 20. 2.   w Joel 1. 11.

שַׂעֲרָה fem. dec. 12 d, *a hair*; collect. *the hair*.

שְׂעֹרָה, שְׂעוֹרָה fem. *barley*, the plant as it grows; pl. שְׂעֹרִים *barley*, of the grain.

שְׂעֹרִים (*barley*) pr. name masc. 1 Ch. 24. 8.

שָׂעִיר masc. dec. 3 a.—I. adj. *hairy*, Ge. 27. 11, fem. שְׂעִירָה ver. 23.—II. *he-goat*; שְׂעִיר עִזִּים *a buck of the goats*.—III. pl. *demons*, prob. worshipped under the figure of *goats*, Le. 17. 7; 2 Ch. 11. 15.

שֵׂעִיר (*hairy*) pr. name, *Seir*.—I. a chief of the Horites, comp. Ge. 36. 20, 30.—II. a mountainous country east and south of the Dead Sea, inhabited first by the Horites, and afterwards by the posterity of Esau, comp. De. 2. 12.—III. a mountain in Judah, Jos. 15. 10.

שְׂעִירָה fem. dec. 10.—I. *she-goat*.—II pr. name of a place in Ephraim, Ju. 3. 26.

I. שָׁעַר *to estimate the value*, abs. Pr. 23. 7; prob. from the primary signification *to cleave, divide* (whence *to decide, determine*, &c.), Arab. תער intrans. *to be cleft*; Chald. תִּרְעָא by transp. *an aperture*, and then *a gate*.

שַׁעַר com. dec. 6 d.—I. *gate* of a camp, a palace, a temple, but espec. of a city; meton. for the *city* itself, comp. De. 12. 17; 17. 2.—II. *gate*, as the place for administering justice, and for any public business; meton. for *the people assembled at the gate*, Ru. 3. 11.—III. *a measure*, Ge. 26. 12.

שַׁעֲרַיִם (*two gates*) pr. name of a city in the tribe of Judah.

שׁוֹעֵר masc. dec. 7 b, *gate-keeper, porter*.

שְׁעַרְיָה (*whom the Lord values*) pr. name masc. 1 Ch. 8. 38; 9. 44.

II. שָׁעַר Root not used; prob. i. q. שָׂעַר *to shudder*.

שֹׁעָר adj. *horrid, bad*, of figs, Je. 29. 17; Prof. Lee, *blighted figs* (Arab. שׁער *to infect with a contagion*).

שַׁעֲרוּר, fem. שַׁעֲרוּרָה adj. *horrible*, Je. 5. 30; 23. 14.

שַׁעֲרוּרִי, fem. רִית', רִיָּה' adj. Ho. 6. 10; neut. *a horrible thing*, Je. 18. 13.

שָׁעֶר in pause for שַׁעַר (q. v. & § 35. rem. 2)

שַׂעֲר, שַׂעַר } noun fem. sing. dec. 6 d (§ 35. rem. 2)

שֵׂעָר noun masc. sing. dec. 6 d

שֵׂעִר adj. masc. sing., defect. for שָׂעִיר

שֵׁעָר noun masc. sing. dec. 4 d

שְׁעָר id., constr. st.; or Chald. noun masc. dec. 3 a; bef. (:)

שֶׁעַר noun masc. sing. dec. 7 b

שַׁעְרָה noun fem. s. (שַׁעַר) with loc. ה [for שַׁעֲרָה]

שַׂעֲרֵהּ Ch. n. m. s., suff. 3 p. s. m. from שְׂעַר dec. 3 a

שַׂעֲרָהּ, שַׂעֲרָהּ } noun masc. sing., suff. 3 pers. sing. fem. from שֵׂעָר dec. 3 d (§ 3. r. 3); bef. (:)

שַׂעֲרָה noun fem. sing., pl. שְׂעָרִים; id.

שָׁעֲרוּ Kal pret. 3 pers. pl.

שַׂעֲרוּ id. imp. pl. masc.

שְׂעָרוֹ Kh. for שְׂעָרָיו K. (q. v.)

שַׂעֲרוֹ noun masc. sing., suff. 3 pers. sing. masc. from שֵׂעָר dec. 4 d

שְׂעָרוּם Kal pret. 3 pers. pl. with suff. 3 pers. pl. masc.

שַׁעֲרוּרָה וְ adj. fem. sing. [from שַׁעֲרוּר masc.]

שַׂעֲרֵי וְ noun fem. pl., constr. from שֵׂעָר dec. 6 d

שַׂעֲרֶיהָ id. pl., suff. 3 pers. sing. fem.; bef. (:)

שְׁעַרְיָה pr. name masc.; id.

שַׂעֲרֵיהֶם noun fem. pl., suff. 3 pers. pl. masc. from שֵׂעָר dec. 6 d

שַׂעֲרָיו id. pl., suff. 3 pers. sing. masc.

שַׂעֲרֵיִךְ, שַׂעֲרֵךְ } id. pl., suff. 2 pers. sing. fem.; bef. (:)

שַׂעֲרֵךְ id. pl., suff. 2 pers. sing. masc.

שַׁעֲרַיִם id. du. as a pr. name

שְׁעָרִים id. pl., abs. st.; bef. (:)

שְׁעָרִים noun fem. with pl. m. term. from שַׁעְרָה d. 10

שֹׁעֲרִים noun masc., pl. of שֹׁעֵר dec. 7 b

שַׁעֲרִירִיָה Kh. שַׁעֲרוּרִיָה K., adj. fem. from שַׁעֲרוּרִי or שַׁעֲרִירִי

שַׂעֲרֵךְ, שַׂעֲרֵךְ } noun masc. sing., suff. 2 pers. sing. fem. from שֵׂעָר dec. 6 d (§ 35. rem. 5)

שַׂעֲרֵךְ noun masc. sing., suff. 2 pers. sing. fem. from שֵׂעָר dec. 3 d; bef. (:)

שַׁעֲרוּרֵת adj. fem. sing. [from שַׁעֲרוּרִי masc.]

שַׂעֲרַת noun fem. sing., constr. of שַׂעֲרָה (no pl. abs.)

שְׂעִירֹת adj. fem., pl. of שְׂעִירָה, from שָׂעִיר masc.

שַׁעֲשְׁגַז pr. name of a Persian eunuch, Est. 2. 14.

שֶׁעָשׂוּ pref. שֶׁ X Kal pret. 3 pers. pl.

שִׁעֲשַׁע Pilp. pret. 3 pers. sing. masc. (§ 6. No. 4)

שַׁעֲשָׁעָיו the foll. with suff. 3 pers. sing. masc.

שַׁעֲשׁוּעִים noun masc., pl. of [שַׁעֲשׁוּעַ] dec. 1 b

שַׁעֲשָׁעַי, שַׁעֲשֻׁעָי } id. pl. with suff. 1 pers. sing.

שִׁעֲשַׁעְתִּי Pilp. pret. 1 pers. sing.

שַׁעֲתָא, שַׁעֲתָּא } Chald. noun fem., emph. of שָׁעָה

Footnotes

a Job 18. 20.   d Da. 4. 30.   i Eze. 27. 35.   m De. 32. 17.   r 1 Ch. 23. 5.   u Ca. 4. 1.   y Job 4. 15.   c Is. 11. 8.   g Pr. 8. 31.
b Is. 7. 20.   e Le. 13. 4.   k Je. 2. 12.   n Ob. 11.   s Ho. 6. 10.   v Ge. 27. 23.   a Is. 5. 7.   d Ps. 119. 70.
c Ge. 27. 11.   f Le. 13. 30.   l Ps. 147. 18.   o Ca. 6. 5.   w Je. 18. 13.   b Ec. 2. 11.   e Ps. 119. 24.   Da. 4.
f Is. 28. 6.   h Job 31. 40.   Le. 14. 8, 9.   Is. 60. 11.

שָׂפָה ו' fem. dec. 11a (du. שְׂפָתַיִם, pl. c. שִׂפְתוֹת).—
I. *lip*; אִישׁ שְׂפָתַיִם *a loquacious man*; דְּבַר שׂ' *talk of the lips*, i. e. *vain words, idle talk*.—II. *speech, words*.—III. *language, dialect*; עִמְקֵי שָׂפָה *men of unintelligible language, barbarians*.—IV. *brim of a vessel*.—V. *shore of the sea*; *bank of a river*.—VI. *edge, edging, border*.—VII. *border, boundary*, Ju. 7. 22.

שָׂפָם masc. dec. 4a, *the lower part of the face, the chin, the beard*; עָשָׂה שְׂפָמוֹ *to trim one's beard*.

שָׁפָה Kal not used; Arab. שׁפא *to appear, become visible*. Niph. part. *conspicuous, lofty*, Is. 13. 2. Pu. *to become prominent, to stand out*, of the bones, Job 33. 21.

שְׁפָה or שָׁפָה fem. dec. 11, *cheese*, 2 Sa. 17. 29 (Syr. שפא *to cleanse from the dregs*).

שְׁפוֹ (*eminent, excellent*) pr. name masc. Ge. 36. 23, for which שְׁפִי 1 Ch. 1. 40.

שְׁפִי masc. dec. 6i.—I. *eminence, elevated place*.—II. pr. name, see שְׁפוֹ.

שָׁפָם (*eminent, excellent*) pr. name m. 1 Ch. 5. 12.

שָׁפָם (*elevated place*) pr. name of a town in Judah, Nu. 34. 10, 11; called שְׁפָמוֹת 1 Sa. 30. 28. Gent. n. שָׁפְמִי 1 Ch. 27. 27.

יִשְׁפָּה (*eminent*) pr. name masc. 1 Ch. 8. 16.

יִשְׁפָּן (prob. id.) pr. name masc. 1 Ch. 8. 22.

שְׁפוֹ | pr. name masc. . . . שפה

שָׁפוֹט | Kal inf. abs. . . . שפט

שְׁפוֹט |
שְׁפוּטִים | } noun masc. sing., & pl. abs. (§ 30. rem. 4); ו bef. (:) } שפט

שְׁפוֹךְ | Kal imp. sing. masc. . . . שפך

שְׁפוּכָה | id. part. pass., fem. of שָׁפוּךְ . . . שפך

שְׁפוּפָן | ו pr. name masc.; ו bef. (:) . שפף

שְׁפוֹת | ו noun f. pl. constr. [fr. שָׁפָה or שָׁפָה; ו id. שפה

שָׁפַח Kal not used; *to pour out*, comp. סָפַח. Pi. *to make to fall off*, sc. the hair by disease, scab, &c. hence, *to make bald*, Is. 3. 17.

מִשְׂפָּח masc. *a shedding of blood*, Arab. שׁפח *to shed blood*, Is. 5. 7; Prof. Lee, *violence*, Arab. שׁפע *to strike*, and then *to propel, drive away*. It may be worth inquiry, whether *confusion*, so closely allied to the signification of *pouring* (comp. נָסַךְ I & II), may not be intended in this passage?

שָׁפַח Root not used; perh. *to join, associate*, cogn. סָפַח (comp. Fürst in conc.)

שִׁפְחָה fem. dec. 12b, *female servant, handmaid*; Lat. *famula*, "as if, one of the family." (Gesen.)

מִשְׁפָּחָה fem. (constr. מִשְׁפַּחַת, with suff. 'פַּחְתִּי; pl. 'פָּחוֹת § 42. rem. 5).—I. *family, household*, comp. Ex. 12. 21.—II. *family, clan*, comp. Jos. 7. 14.—III. *tribe*, comp. Ju. 18. 2; also for a whole *nation*.—IV. *race, kind*, of animals.

שִׁפַּח ו Piel pret. 3 pers. sing. masc. . . שפה

שִׁפְחָה ו noun fem. sing. dec. 12b . . שפה

שְׁפָחוֹת ו id. pl., abs. st.; ו bef. (:) . . שפה

שִׁפְחוֹתֵיכֶם ו id. pl., suff. 2 pers. pl. masc. . . שפה

שְׁפָחֹת ו id. pl., abs. st.; ו bef. (:) . . שפה

שִׁפְחַת id. sing., constr. st. . . . שפה

שִׁפְחָתָהּ id. sing., suff. 3 pers. sing. fem. . . שפה

שִׁפְחָתוֹ id. sing., suff. 3 pers. sing. masc. . . שפה

שִׁפְחָתִי id. sing., suff. 1 pers. sing. . . שפה

שִׁפְחֹתָיו id. pl., suff. 3 pers. sing. masc. . . שפה

שִׁפְחָתְךָ |
שִׁפְחָתֶךָ | } id. sing., suff. 2 pers. sing. masc. . . שפה

שִׁפְחָתֵךְ id. sing., suff. 2 pers. sing. fem. . . שפה

שִׁפְחֹתֶךָ id. pl., suff. 2 pers. sing. masc. (§ 4. rem. 2) שפה

שָׁפַט ו fut. יִשְׁפֹּט.—I. *to judge, administer justice*; with בֵּין–לְ, בֵּין–וּבֵין *to decide between*; part. שׁוֹפֵט *a judge*.—II. *to judge, do justice to, to defend or vindicate the cause* of any one.—III. *to condemn, punish*.—IV. *to rule*; שֹׁפֵט *a judge, ruler*. Niph. נִשְׁפַּט.—I. *to be judged*.—II. *to litigate, contend before a judge*, with אֶת, עִם, לְ, of the person *with* whom, with acc., עַל of the thing *about which*. Po. part. *a judge*, Job 9. 15.

שָׁפֵט Chald. part. שָׁפֵט *a judge*, Ezr. 7. 25.

שָׁפָט (*judge*) pr. name masc. of several persons.

שֶׁפֶט masc. dec. 6a, only pl. שְׁפָטִים *judgments, punishments*.

שְׁפוֹט masc. *judgment, punishment*, 2 Ch. 20. 9; pl. שְׁפוּטִים (§ 30. rem. 4) Eze. 23. 10.

שִׁפְטָן (*judicial*) pr. name masc. Nu. 34. 24.

שְׁפַטְיָה (*whom the Lord judges, defends*) pr. name —I. of a son of David, 2 Sa. 3. 4.—II. of several other men.

שְׁפַטְיָהוּ (id.) pr. name—I. of a son of Jehoshaphat, 2 Ch. 21. 2.—II. of two other men, 1 Ch. 12. 5; 27. 16.

מִשְׁפָּט masc. dec. 2b.—I. *judgment, the act of judging*.—II. *judgment, sentence, decision*.—III. *punishment*.—IV. *place of judgment, court of justice* —V. *cause, suit*; בַּעַל מִ' *opponent, adversary*; דִּבֶּר מִשְׁפָּטִים אֶת *to litigate, contend with* any one, also (comp. No. II.) *to pronounce severe judg-*

ments *upon* any one.—VI. *justice, equity, right.*—VII. *right, privilege.*—VIII. *law, institution.*—IX. *custom, usage.*—X. *mode, manner.*

שָׁפָט   '1 pr. name masc. . . .   שׁפט
שָׁפַט   Kal pret. 3 pers. sing. masc. (§ 8. rem. 2)   שׁפט
שְׁפֹט   id. inf. constr. . . .   שׁפט
שְׁפֹט־   id. imp. sing. masc. (for שְׁפֹט § 8. rem. 18)   שׁפט
שְׁפָט   '1 id. part. act. sing. masc. dec. 7 b   שׁפט
שָׁפְטָה   id. imp. s. m. [שְׁפֹט] with parag. ה (§ 8. r. 11)   שׁפט
שֹׁפְטָה   id. part. act. sing., fem. of שֹׁפֵט (§ 8. r. 19)   שׁפט
שְׁפָטָהוּ   id. pret. (Kh. וּשְׁפָטָהוּ), or fut. (K. יִשְׁפָטֵהוּ), 3 pers. pl. masc. suff. 3 pers. sing. masc. .   שׁפט
שָׁפְטוּ } id. pret. 3 pers. pl. (§ 8. rem. 7) .   שׁפט
'1 }
שְׁפָטוּ   id. pret. 3 pers. sing. m., suff. 3 pers. sing. m.   שׁפט
שְׁפָטוּ } id. pret. 3 pers. pl. (§ 8. rem. 12) .   שׁפט
שְׁפָטוּךָ   id. pret. 3 p. pl., suff. 2 p. s. f.; '1, for 1, conv.   שׁפט
שְׁפָטוּם   id. id., suff. 3 pers. pl. masc.; 1 id.   שׁפט
שְׁפָטוּנוּ   id. id., suff. 1 pers. pl. . .   שׁפט
שֹׁפְטַי   noun m. pl., suff. 1 pers. s. from [שֶׁפֶט] d. 6 a   שׁפט
שֹׁפְטֵי   Kal part. act. pl. c. masc. from שֹׁפֵט dec. 7 b   שׁפט
שְׁפַטְיָה   pr. name masc. . . .   שׁפט
שֹׁפְטֶיהָ   '1 Kal part. act. pl., suff. 3 pers. sing. fem. from שֹׁפֵט dec. 7 b . .   שׁפט
שְׁפַטְיָהוּ   pr. name masc. . . .   שׁפט
שֹׁפְטֵיהֶם   Kal part. act. pl., suff. 3 p. pl. m. fr. שֹׁפֵט d. 7 b   שׁפט
שֹׁפְטָיו   1 id. pl., suff. 3 pers. sing. masc.   שׁפט
שֹׁפְטַיִךְ   id. pl., suff. 2 pers. sing. fem.   שׁפט
שֹׁפְטֶיךָ   1 id. pl., suff. 2 pers. sing. masc.   שׁפט
שֹׁפְטֵיכֶם   id. pl., suff. 2 pers. pl. masc.   שׁפט
שְׁפָטִים   noun masc., pl. of [שֶׁפֶט] dec. 6 a .   שׁפט
שֹׁפְטִים   '1 Kal part. act. masc., pl. of שֹׁפֵט dec. 7 b   שׁפט
שָׁפְטִין   Ch. Peal part. act. pl. masc. [from שְׁפַט] d. 2 b   שׁפט
שֹׁפְטֵינוּ   Kal part. act. pl. m., suff. 1 p. pl. fr. שֹׁפֵט d. 7 b   שׁפט
שְׁפָטְךָ   id. pret. 3 pers. sing. m., suff. 2 pers. sing. m.   שׁפט
שָׁפְטָן   pr. name masc. . . .   שׁפט
שְׁפָטָנוּ   1 Kal pret. 3 pers. sing. masc., suff. 1 pers. pl.; '1, for 1, conv.   שׁפט
שֹׁפְטֵנוּ   id. part. act. s. m., suff. 1 p. pl. fr. שֹׁפֵט d. 7 b   שׁפט
שָׁפְטֵנִי   id. imp. sing. masc., suff. 1 pers. sing.   שׁפט
שָׁפַטְתָּ   1 id. pret. 2 pers. sing. masc.; acc. shifted by conv. 1 (§ 8. rem. 7) .   שׁפט
שָׁפַטְתִּי   1 id. pret. 1 pers. sing.; acc. id. .   שׁפט
שְׁפַטְתִּיךְ   1 id. id., suff. 2 pers. sing. fem.; '1, for 1, conv.   שׁפט
שְׁפַטְתִּים   id. id., suff. 3 pers. pl. masc. .   שׁפט

שְׁפַטְתֶּם   1 id. pret. 2 pers. pl. masc.; '1, for 1, conv.   שׁפט
שֶׁפִי } noun masc. sing., pl. שְׁפָיִים dec. 6 i (§ 35.) rem. 14), also pr. name . }   שׁפה
שְׁפִי
שְׁפֹה   Kh. שְׁפִי q. v.; K. שֻׁפּוּ Pual pret. 3 pers. pl.   שׁפה
שְׁפָיִים } noun masc., pl. of שְׁפִי dec. 6 i .   שׁפה
שְׁפָיִם
שִׁפְעָן   noun masc. sing. . . .   שׁפף
שַׁפִּיר   pr. name of a place . . .   שׁפר
שַׁפִּיר   Ch. adj. masc. sing. 1 suff. 3 pers. sing. m.   שׁפר

שָׁפַךְ '1 fut. יִשְׁפֹּךְ.—I. *to pour out*; metaph. *to pour out* one's prayer, soul, heart, before the Lord; also *to pour out* one's anger upon any one; moreover, God is said *to pour out, bestow in profusion*, the Spirit.—II. *to shed* blood.—III. *to throw up a mound*, Eze. 26. 8. Niph. I. *to be poured out, shed*; metaph. of a person in extreme weakness, Ps. 22. 15.—II. *to be profusely expended*, of money, Eze. 16. 36. Pu. I. *to be shed*.—II. of steps, *to slip*, Ps. 73. 2. Hithpa. הִשְׁתַּפֵּךְ *to be poured out*, La. 4. 1; metaph. of the soul, life

שֶׁפֶךְ   masc. *place of pouring out*, Le. 4. 12.
שָׁפְכָה   fem. *membrum virile*, De. 23. 2.
שׁוֹפָךְ   (*effusion, increase*) pr. name masc. 1 Ch. 19. 16, 18, for which שׁוֹבַךְ 2 Sa. 10. 16, 18 (Arab. שׁבך *to pour out*).

שָׁפַךְ   Kal pret. 3 pers. sing. m. for שָׁפַךְ (§ 8. r. 7)   שׁפך
שֶׁפֶךְ   '1 noun masc. sing. . . .   שׁפך
שֹׁפֵךְ   Kal part. act. sing. masc. dec. 7 b .   שׁפך
שְׁפֹךְ   id. imp. sing. masc. . . .   שׁפך
שְׁפָךְ־   id. id. (Ps. 69. 25), or inf. constr.   שׁפך
שֻׁפַּךְ   '1 Pual pret. 3 pers. sing. masc.   שׁפך
שִׁפְכָה   noun fem. sing. . . .   שׁפך
שָׁפְכָה   Kh. שָׁפְכָה, K. שָׁפְכוּ, Kal pret. 3 pers. sing. fem., or 3 pers. pl.   שׁפך
שֻׁפְּכָה   Kh. שֻׁפְּכָה, K. שֻׁפְּכוּ, Pual pret. 3 pers. sing. fem., or 3 pers. pl.   שׁפך
שָׁפְכוּ   '1 Kal pret. 3 pers. pl.   שׁפך
שִׁפְכוּ   '1 id. imp. pl. masc.   שׁפך
שֹׁפְכוֹ   id. part. act. sing. masc., suff. 3 pers. sing. masc. from שֹׁפֵךְ dec. 7 b   שׁפך
שֹׁפְכוֹת   id. part. act. s. f. fr. שֹׁפֶכֶת (§ 8. r. 19) d. 13 a   שׁפך
שִׁפְכִי   id. imp. sing. masc. . . .   שׁפך
שָׁפַכְתָּ } id. pret. 2 pers. sing. masc.; acc. shifted by conv. 1 (§ 8. rem. 7) }   שׁפך
שָׁפַכְתְּ
וְ

a 1 Sa. 7. 17.   c Eze. 44. 24.   i Eze. 23. 24; 24. 14.   p Ezr. 10. 14.   u Da. 9. 12.   b De. 1. 16.   h Nu. 35. 33.   l Ps. 73. 2.   r Nu. 35. 33.
b Ru. 1. 1.   e Je. 5. 28.   z 2 Sa. 18. 31.   b Nu. 23. 3.   i Zep. 1. 17.   m La. 2. 19.
Pr. 31. 9.   d 2 Ki. 23. 22.   k Jos. 8. 33.   q Is. 1. 26.   o Job 33. 22.   k Le. 14. 41.
Ex. 2. 14.   2 2 Sa. 18. 19.   = Da 9. 12.   s De. 1. 16.   s Ps. 62. 9.   l 1 Ch. 22. 3.
Ju. 4. 4.   f Zec. 7. 9.   n Eze. 14. 21.   t Ezr. 7. 25.   Eze. 36. 19.   De. 21. 7.   Je. 6. 6.   1 Cu. 22. 3.
Le. 4. 12.

שְׁפַכְתְּ   id. pret. 2 pers. sing. fem.   .   .   שׁפך

שֹׁפֶכֶת   id. part. act. sing. fem. (§ 8. r. 19) fr. שָׁפַךְ m. שׁפך

שֹׁפְכֹת   id. id. pl. dec. 13a   .   .   .   שׁפך

שְׁפָכַתְהוּ   id. pret. 3 pers. sing. fem., suff. 3 pers. sing. m. שׁפך

שָׁפַכְתִּי   } id. pret. 1 pers. sing. ; acc. shifted by } שׁפך
וָשָׁפַכְתִּי   } conv. וְ (§ 8. rem. 7)   .   .   }

שָׁפֵל   וְ fut. יִשָּׁפֵל.—I. *to be made low, to be lowered.*—II. *to be depressed,* of the voice, Ec. 12. 4.—III. *to be humbled*; inf. שְׁפַל רוּחַ *to be humble* in spirit, Pr. 16. 19. Hiph. I. *to bring low, throw down.*—II. *to humble.*—III. intrans. *to humble oneself,* Job 22. 29; Is. 57. 9 (trans. according to Prof. Lee, rendering the latter passage, *to send down*); with other verbs adverbially, Je. 13. 18; הַשְׁפִּילוּ שֵׁבוּ *sit down low,* Ps. 113. 6.

שְׁפַל   Chald. Aph. *to bring down, to humble.*

שָׁפָל   m. d. 4 a, שְׁפָלָה fem. d. 11 c, adj.—I. *low.*—II. *low, mean, contemptible.*—III. *humble, lowly.*

שְׁפַל   Chald. *low, humble,* Da. 4. 14.

שֵׁפֶל   masc. d. 6 b, *lowness, low place or condition.*

שִׁפְלָה   fem. id. Is. 32. 19.

שְׁפֵלָה   f. d. 10, *low country;* הַשְּׁפֵלָה *the low country* or *plain* along the Mediterranean from Joppa to Gaza.

שִׁפְלוּת   fem. *lowness* of the hands, *remissness, idleness,* Ec. 10. 18.

שָׁפָל   וְ adj. masc. sing. dec. 4 a   .   . שׁפל

שְׁפַל   וְ adj. masc. sing., constr. of שָׁפָל   dec. 4 a (perh. inf. Pr. 16. 19) ; וְ bef. (:)   .   שׁפל

שְׁפַל   וְ Chald. adj. sing. masc. ; וְ id.   .   שׁפל

שְׁפֵלָה   וְ adj. sing. fem. d. 11 c, from שָׁפָל m. ; וְ id. שׁפל

שְׁפֵלִים   וְ id. masc., pl. of שָׁפָל dec. 4 a ; וְ id. שׁפל

שָׁפַלְתְּ   וְ Kal pret. 2 pers. sing. fem.   .   . שׁפל

שִׁפְלַת   adj. fem. s., constr. of שְׁפֵלָה d. 11 c, fr. שָׁפָל m. שׁפל

שִׁפְלָתֹה   וְ noun fem. sing., suff. 3 pers. sing. masc. from שְׁפֵלָה dec. 10 ; וְ bef. (:)   שׁפל

שָׁפָם   noun masc. sing. dec. 4 a   .   . שׂפה

שָׁפָם   וְ pr. name masc.   .   .   .   . שׁפה

שָׂפָם   וְ pr. name masc., for שָׂפִים   .   . שׁפך

שִׁפְמָה   pr. name (שְׂפָם) with parag. ה   . שׂפה

שְׂפָמֹו   noun m. sing., suff. 3 pers. s. m. fr. שָׂפָם d. 4 a שׂפה

[שָׁפַן]   *to cover, hide,* De. 33. 19.

שָׁפָן   וְ masc. dec. 8 a.—I. *the jerboa*; Sept. χοιρογρύλλιος; Rabbins, *the coney.*—II. pr. name of the scribe or secretary of king Josiah ; also of another man.

שָׁפֻנִי   וְ Kal part. p. pl. c. m. [fr. שָׁפֹון] d. 3 a ; וְ bef. שׁפן

שְׁפַנִּים   noun masc., pl. of שָׁפָן dec. 8 a (§ 37. No. 2) שׁפן

שֶׁפַע   masc. *an overflowing, abundance,* De. 33. 19.

שִׁפְעָה   fem. (only constr. שִׁפְעַת).—I. *overflowing, abundance* of water.—II. *multitude* of camels. Also

שֶׁפַע   (*abundant*) pr. name masc. 1 Ch. 4. 37 . שׁפע

שִׁפְעַת   וְ noun fem. sing. constr. [of שִׁפְעָה no pl.] שׁפע

שָׁפַף   Root not used ; Syr. *to reep.*

שְׁפִיפֹן   masc. *a species of serpent,* Ge. 49. 17 (Arab. شَفّ *a speckled serpent*).

שְׁפוּפָם   (perh. *serpent*) pr. name masc. Nu. 26. 39. Patronym. שׁוּפָמִי ibid.

שְׁפוּפָן   (id.) pr. name masc. 1 Ch. 8. 5.

שֻׁפִּים   (*serpents*) pr. name of two men, 1 Ch. 7. 12. 15, & 26. 16.

[שָׁפַק]   I. *to smite, clap the hands,* Job 27. 23.—II. *to suffice,* 1 Ki. 20. 10, comp. סָפַק. Hiph. *to strike,* or *make a league with,* with בְּ Is. 2. 6; better perh. *to applaud,* or *to abound with.*

שֶׁפֶק   masc. *a smiting, chastisement,* Job 36. 18. Prof. Lee, *contempt.*

[שָׁפַר]   prop. *to be bright,* see Pi.; hence, *to be pleasant, acceptable to,* with עַל Ps. 16. 6. Pi. *to make bright, beautiful,* Job 26. 13 ; but the word שִׁפְרָה is best taken as a subst., *brightness, beauty.*

שְׁפַר   Chald. (*to be fair*) *to please, be acceptable to,* with קֳדָם, עַל.

שֶׁפֶר   masc.—I. *beauty, pleasantness,* Ge. 49. 21.—II. pr. name of a mountain in the Arabian desert, Nu. 33. 23, 24.

שִׁפְרָה   fem.—I. *brightness, beauty,* see Pi.—II. pr. name fem. Ex. 1. 15.

שֹׁופָר   m. d. 2 b (pl. שֹׁופָרֹות), *trumpet, curved horn.*

שָׁפִיר   (*fair*) pr. name of a place, Mi. 1. 11.

שַׁפִּיר   Ch. masc. *beautiful, pleasing,* Da. 4. 9, 18.

שְׁפָרוּר   or שַׁפְרִיר   masc. *royal canopy,* Je. 43. 10.

שַׁפַּרְפָּר   Chald. masc. d. 2 a, *the dawn,* Da. 6. 20.

אֶשְׁפָּר   masc. *a measure*; etym. uncertain.

שַׁפֵּר   noun m. s. [for שֶׁפֶר § 35. r. 2], also pr. name שׁפר

שְׁפַר   Chald. Peal pret. 3 pers. sing. masc.   .   שׁפר

שֹׁפָר   defect. for שֹׁופָר (q. v.)   .   .   . שׁפר

שָׁפְרָה   Kal pret. 3 pers. sing. fem.   .   . שׁפר

שִׁפְרָה   pr. name fem.   .   .   .   .   . שׁפר

שִׁפְרָה   subst. f. or Piel pret. 3 p. s. f. [for שִׁפְרָה § 10. r. 7] שׁפר

שַׁפְרוּרוֹ Kh. שַׁפְרִירוֹ, K. שַׁפְרִירוּ noun masc. with suff. [from שַׁפְרִיר or שַׁפְרוּר] . . שפר

[שָׁפַת] fut. יִשְׁפֹּת.—I. *to set, put, place.*—II. *to give*, Is. 26. 12.

שְׁפַתַּיִם masc. du. *stalls, folds for cattle*, Ps. 68. 14; Eze. 40, 43, others, *pots, cooking vessels.*

מִשְׁפְּתַיִם masc. du. *folds, enclosures for cattle*, Ge. 49. 14; Ju. 5. 16.

שְׂפַת noun fem. sing., constr. of שָׂפָה dec. 11 a . שפה

שְׁפֹת Kal imp. sing. masc. . . . שפת

שְׂפָתָהּ noun fem. sing., suff. 3 pers. sing. fem. from שָׂפָה dec. 11 a . . . . שפה

שְׂפָתוֹ id., suff. 3 pers. sing. masc.; ו bef. (:) שפה

שִׂפְתוֹת id. pl. constr. [of שָׂפָתוֹת] . . שפה

שִׂפְתוֹתָיו id. pl., suff. 3 pers. sing. masc. שפה

שִׂפְתוֹתַיִךְ id. pl., suff. 2 pers. sing. fem. . שפה

שִׂפְתוֹתֵיכֶם id. pl., suff. 2 pers. pl. masc. . שפה

שְׂפָתַי } id. du. (שְׂפָתַיִם), suff. 1 pers. sing. שפה
שְׂפָתָי }

שְׂפָתָי וְ id. du., constr. st. . . . שפה

שְׂפָתֶיהָ id. du., suff. 3 pers. sing. fem. . שפה

שִׂפְתֵיהֶם id. du., suff. 3 pers. pl. masc. . שפה

שְׂפָתָיו id. du., suff. 3 pers. sing. masc.; ו bef. (:) שפה

שְׂפָתָיו id. id. Kh. שְׂפָתָי, K. שְׂפָתוֹ (q. v.) . שפה

שְׂפָתֶיךָ id. du., suff. 2 pers. sing. masc.; ו bef. (:) שפה

שְׂפָתַיִם } id. du., abs. st. . . . שפה
שְׂפָתָיִם }

שְׂפָתַיִם noun m., du. of שָׂפָת [§ 37. Nos. 2 & 3) d. 8 שפת

שִׂפְתֵימוֹ noun fem. du. (שְׂפָתַיִם), suff. 3 pers. pl. masc. from שָׂפָה dec. 11 a . . שפה

שְׂפָתֵינוּ id. du., suff. 1 pers. pl. . . . שפה

שְׂפָתָם id. sing., suff. 3 pers. pl. masc. . שפה

[שֶׁצֶף] masc. i. q. שֶׁטֶף *an overflowing*, Is. 45. 8.

שַׂק } noun masc. sing. dec. 8 d . . . שׂקק
שָׂק וְ }

שָׁקַד. Niph. *to be bound, fastened*, La. 1. 14.

שָׁקַד fut. יִשְׁקֹד.—I. *to wake, be sleepless.*—II. *to watch*, with עַל *over any thing*, or *for any thing, to lie in wait for*, Je. 5. 6.

שָׁקֵד masc. dec. 5 a.—I. *almond tree*, Je. 1. 11, 12.
—II. *almond.* Pu. part. מְשֻׁקָּדִים *formed like almonds*, Ex. 25. 33, 34 . . שקד

שֹׁקֵד Kal part. act. sing. masc. dec. 7 b . שקד

שִׁקְדוּ id. imp. pl. masc. . . . . שקד

שֹׁקְדֵי id. part. act. pl. c. masc. from שָׁקַד dec. 7 b שקד

שְׁקֵדִים noun masc., pl. of שָׁקֵד dec. 5 a; ו bef. (:) שקד

שִׁקְדֻמַת pref. שֶׁ X noun f. s. constr. [of קַדְמָה, no pl.] קדם

שָׁקַדְתִּי Kal pret. 1 pers. sing. . . . שקד

שָׁקָה. Hiph. הִשְׁקָה.—I. *to give to drink, to let drink*, with double acc. of pers. and thing; with בְּ, מִן *out of* anything; מַשְׁקֶה *cupbearer, butler.*—II. *to water* cattle.—III. *to water, irrigate* the ground. Niph. *to be overflown*, Am. 8. 8, Kh. Pu. *to be moistened, refreshed*, Job 21. 24.

שֹׁקֶת f. *drinking-trough*, Ge. 24. 20; pl. שְׁקָתוֹת (as if from שָׁקַת § 35. rem. 9, note) Ge. 30. 38.

שִׁקּוּי masc. dec. 1 b.—I. *drink*, Ho. 2. 7.—II. *moistening, refreshment*, Pr. 3. 8.

שִׁקֻּיִים masc. pl. (of שִׁקּוּי) *drink*, Ps. 102. 10.

מַשְׁקֶה masc. d. 9 a.—I. *drink.*—II. *a well-watered country.*

שְׁקֵה וְ Kal imp. sing. masc. with parag. ה, comp. נשק
שְׁקֵה וְ וּשְׁבַע, וּשְׁבָה, וְזָהָב; ו bef. (:)

שׁוֹקוֹ noun m. s., suff. 3 pers. s. m. fr. שָׁק d. 8 d שׁוק

שֹׁקֵיהוֹ Ch. n. m. pl., suff. 3 p. s. m. fr. [שָׁק] d. 1 a שׁוק

שִׁקּוּי וְ noun masc. sing. dec. 1 b . . . שקה

שִׁקּוּיַי וְ noun masc. pl., suff. 1 pers. sing. [fr. שִׁקּוּי] שקה

שִׁקּוּיָי וְ noun m. pl., suff. 1 pers. s. fr. שִׁקּוּי d. 1 b שקה

שִׁקּוּיְנָהֻ pref. שֶׁ X Piel pret. 1 p. pl. with suff. 3 p. s. m. קוה

שָׁקוֹל Kal inf. abs. . . . . שקל

שִׁקּוּץ noun masc. sing. dec. 1 b . . . שקץ

שִׁקּוּצֵי id. pl., constr. st. . . . שקץ

שִׁקּוּצֶיהָ id. pl., suff. 3 pers. sing. fem. . שקץ

שִׁקּוּצֵיהֶם id. pl., suff. 3 pers. pl. masc. . שקץ

שִׁקּוּצַיִךְ }
שִׁקּוּצָיִךְ } id. pl., suff. 2 pers. sing. fem. שקץ

שִׁקּוּצֶיךָ id. pl., suff. 2 pers. sing. masc. . שקץ

שִׁקּוּצִים id. pl., abs. st. . . . שקץ

שָׁקַט fut. יִשְׁקֹט.—I. *to rest, be quiet, undisturbed.*—II. *to rest, be free from*, with מִן.—III. *to be inactive.*—IV. *to be silent*, Ps. 76. 9. Hiph. I. *to give rest.*—II. *to quiet, still*, Pr. 15. 18.—III. *to keep quiet, be quiet*; inf. הַשְׁקֵט *rest, quiet.* Hence.

שֶׁקֶט masc. *rest, quiet*, 1 Ch. 22. 9. שקט

שֹׁקֵט וְ Kal part. act. sing. masc. dec. 7 b . שקט

a Je. 43. 10.   c Ca. 4. 3, 11.   e Ps. 68. 14.   h Ezr. 8. 29.   l Ps. 129. 6.   o Ps. 102. 10.   s Da. 12. 11.   x Je. 13. 27.   aa 1 Ch. 22. 9.
b Eze. 43. 13.   d Is. 59. 3.   f Ge. 11. 7.   i Is. 29. 20.   m Ge. 27. 26.   p Ho. 2. 7.   t Eze. 20. 7, 8.   y Eze. 5. 11.   bb Ju. 18. 7, 27.
c Ec. 10. 12.   e Pr. 18. 7.   g Ps. 127. 1.   k Nu. 17. 23.   n Da. 2. 33.   q La. 2. 16.   u Eze. 11. 18.   z Je. 4. 1.   cc Je. 48. 11.
d Ca. 5. 13.   f Pr. 16. 27.   = Je. 1. 11.   Ge. 43. 11.   Pr. 3. 8.   r Job 6. 2.   w Je. 4. 1.   dd Pr. 24. 2.
48

וְ} שָׁקְטָה שׁקט
שָׁקְטָה} id. pret. 3 pers. sing. fem. (§ 8. rem. 7) שׁקט

שָׁקְטֶת
שָׁקְטֶת} id. par act. sing., fem. of שָׁקֵט (§ 8. r. 19) שׁקט

שָׁקַטְתִּי
שָׁקַטְתִּי} id. pret. 1 pers. sing.; acc. shifted by
conv. וְ } שׁקט

שִׁקִּי noun masc. sing., suff. 1 pers. s. fr. שֵׁק d. 8d שׁקק
שָׁקֵיהֶם id. pl., suff. 3 pers. pl. masc. . . . שׁקק
שָׁקִים id. pl., abs. st. . . . . שׁקק
שׁוֹקֵים noun fem., du. of שׁוֹק dec. 1a שׁוק

שָׁקַל { fut. יִשְׁקֹל.—I. to weigh.—II. to weigh out, to pay, with לְ, עַל to any one.—III. trop. to examine, try, Job 6. 2; 31. 6. Niph. pass. of Kal Nos. II & III.

שֶׁקֶל masc. dec. 6a (pl. c. שִׁקְלֵי), a shekel, a standard weight for weighing gold or silver. Two kinds of shekels are distinguished in Ex. 30. 13, & 2 Sa. 14. 26.

אַשְׁקְלוֹן (migration, Syr. שְׁקַל to migrate, Simonis) pr. name, Askelon, a city of the Philistines. Gent. noun אֶשְׁקְלוֹנִי Jos. 13. 3.

מִשְׁקָל masc. dec. 2b.—I. the act of weighing.—II. weight.

מִשְׁקוֹל masc. weight, Eze. 4. 10.

מִשְׁקֹלֶת, מִשְׁקָלֶת plummet; Sept. στάθμιον, balance. Is. 28. 17; 2 Ki. 21. 13.

שֶׁקֶל
שֶׁקֶל
שֶׁקֶל} noun masc. sing (pl. c. שִׁקְלֵי §35. rem. 2)} dec. 6a . . . . שׁקל
Kal part. act. sing. masc. . . שׁקל

שִׁקְלֵי
שְׁקָלִים} noun masc. pl. constr. & abs. from שֶׁקֶל} dec. 6a . . . . שׁקל

שִׁקְמָה f. only in the pl. שִׁקְמִים, שִׁקְמוֹת sycamore trees.

שִׁקְמוֹתָם } noun f. pl., suff. 3 p. pl. m. fr. [שִׁקְמָה] d. 10 שׁקם
שִׁקְמִים id. with pl. masc. term. abs. st. שׁקם
שַׁקְמֹתִי pref. שַׁ)(Kal pret. 1 pers. sing. . . קום

[שָׁקַע] I. to sink in water, Je. 51. 64.—II. to be overflown, Am. 9. 5.—III. to subside, abate, of fire, Nu. 11. 2. Niph. to be submerged, overflown, Am. 8. 8, K. Hiph. I. to cause to sink, depress, Job 40. 25.—II. to cause to subside, Eze. 32. 14.

מִשְׁקָע masc. dec. 2b, a pool, pond, Eze. 34. 18.

שָׁקְעָה } Kal pret. 3 pers. sing. fem. . שׁקע
שְׁקַעֲרוּרֹת fem. pl. hollow places in a wall, Le. 14. 37, compounded of שָׁקַע & קָעַר q. v.

שָׁקַף Kal not used; Arab. שקף to cover (Gr. σκεπάω), also to be long and bending from length (Gesen.). Niph. (prop. to bend forward in order to see).—I. to look out abroad, e. g. through a window, with בְּעַד.—II. of a mountain, to overhang, to look towards, with עַל פְּנֵי.—III. metaph. to impend, threaten, Je. 6. 1. Hiph. id. to look, La. 3. 50; with בְּעַד through, עַל, אֶל towards, מִן from.

שֶׁקֶף masc. covering, coping, 1 Ki. 7. 5.
שְׁקֻפִים m. pl. coped, having copings, 1 Ki. 7. 4; 6. 4.
מַשְׁקוֹף masc. lintel, the timber over the door-posts, Ex. 12. 7, 22, 23.

שֶׁקֶף noun masc. sing. [for שֶׁקֶף § 35. rem. 2] שׁקף
שְׁקֻפִים noun masc., pl. of [שָׁקוּף] d. 3a; וְ bef. (:) שׁקף

שָׁקַץ Pi. I. to contaminate, pollute.—II. to loathe, abominate, abhor.

שֶׁקֶץ masc. abominable thing.
שִׁקּוּץ m. dec. 1b, abomination, abominable thing.

שַׁקֵּץ Piel inf. constr. as an abs. . . שׁקץ
שֶׁקֶץ וְ (Le. 11. 11.) noun masc. sing. . שׁקץ
שִׁקַּץ Piel pret. 3 pers. sing. masc. (§ 10. rem. 1) שׁקץ
שִׁקּוּץ noun masc. sing. dec. 1b, comp. שׁקץ
שִׁקּוּצָיו id. pl., suff. 3 pers. sing. masc. . שׁקץ
שִׁקֻּצִים id. pl., abs. st. . . . . שׁקץ

שָׂקַק Root not used; prob. i. q. זָקַק q. v. Gr. σακκίζω, Lat. saccavit, i. e. to strain (Gese.). Ethiop. סקסם lattice (Fürst in conc.).

שַׂק m. d. 8d.—I. sackcloth.—II. a sack for grain.

[שָׁקַק] fut. יָשֹׁק.—I. to run to and fro.—II. to be eager, greedy. Hithpalp. הִשְׁתַּקְשֵׁק (§ 6. No. 4) to run to and fro, Na. 2. 5.

שֵׁשַׁק (שָׁשַׁק for שַׁקְשַׁק eagerness, comp. בָּבֶל) pr. name. masc. 1 Ch. 8. 14, 25.

מַשָּׁק masc. d. 2b; a running to and fro, Is. 33. 4.

שֹׁקֵק Kal part. act. sing. masc. . . שׁקק
שׁוֹקְקָה id. fem. comp. שׁוֹקְקָה . . . שׁוק

שָׁקַר Kal not used; Chald. סְקַר to look; also, to stain, paint. Pi. to wink with the eyes, or, to paint the eyes, Is. 3. 16.

שֶׁקֶר (only fut. יְשַׁקֵּר) to act falsely towards, with לְ Ge. 21. 23. Pi. I. to lie, speak falsehood, 1 Sa. 15. 29.—II. with בְּ to deceive.—III. with בְּ to act falsely to, to violate a covenant. Hence

a Ps. 76. 9.   d Job 3. 26.   f Ps. 30. 12.   h Pr. 26. 7.   k Ps. 78. 47.   m Am. 9. 5.   o De. 7. 26.   q Zec. 9. 7.   s Is. 33. 4.
b Zec. 1. 11.   e Eze. 16. 42.   g Ge. 42. 25.   i 1 Ch. 21. 25.   Ju. 5. 7.   1 Ki. 6. 4; 7. 4.   p Ps. 22. 25.   r Na. 3. 6.   t Ps. 107. 9.
c 1 Ch. 4. 40.   1 Ki. 7. 5.

שֶׁקֶר / וְ masc. dec. 6 a (§ 35. rem. 2; but pl. with suff. שִׁקְרֵיהֶם).—I. *lie, falsehood*; אִישׁ שֶׁקֶר *a liar*; עֵד שֶׁ *a false witness*; בַּשֶּׁקֶר, לַשֶּׁקֶר *falsely.*—II. *deceitful, vain thing*; לַשֶּׁקֶר, & שֶׁקֶר *adv. in vain.*

שְׁקָרִים id. pl., abs. st.	שקר
שִׁקַּרְנוּ Piel pret. 1 pers. pl. . . .	שקר
שָׁר וְ Kal pret. 3 pers. sing. masc., or part. act. dec. 1 a . . .	שיר
שָׂר וְ / שַׂר noun masc. sing., pl. שָׂרִים dec. 8 (§ 37. rem. 7)	שרר
שְׁרָא Ch. Peal pret. 3 pers. sing. masc. (§ 47. r. 6)	שרה

שַׁרְאֶצֶר וְ pr. name—I. of a son of Sennacherib.—II. Zec. 7. 2.

שְׁרָאשִׁי pref. שְׁ (noun masc. sing. רֹאשׁ irr. (§ 45) ראש

שָׁרָב masc.—I. *heat* of the sun, or *drought*, Is. 49. 10. Syr. & Chald. שְׁרַב *to be hot, dry.*—II. *the mirage*, a phenomenon frequent in Arabia and Egypt, when the desert presents the appearance of a sea or a lake (Arab. שראב), Is. 35. 7.
שְׁרֶבְיָה (*heat of the Lord*) pr. name of a man.

שַׁרְבָט defect. for שַׁרְבִיט (q. v.) . . .	שבט
שֵׁרֵבְיָה וְ pr. name masc. . . .	שרב
שַׁרְבִיט noun masc. sing. . . .	שבט

שָׂרַג Pu. *to be interwoven*, Job 40. 17. Hithpa. הִשְׂתָּרֵג id. La. 1. 14.
שֵׂרֻג (*branch*, i. q. שָׂרִיג) pr. name m. Ge. 11. 20.
שָׂרִיג masc. dec. 1 b, only pl. *branches* of a vine.

[שָׂרַד] *to flee, escape*, Jos. 10. 20.
שָׂרִיד masc. dec. 3 a.—I. *one left, escaped.*—II. *remnant.*

שְׂרָד masc. prob. *colour*; בִּגְדֵי שְׂ *coloured garments.* Samar. שרדה *varie picta, et colorata vestis* (Prof. Lee). Sept. στολαί λειτουργικαί, *ministering apparel*, i. q. שָׂרָת.
שֶׂרֶד masc. *red chalk* or *ochre*, Is. 44. 33; Gesenius (Coll. Arab.), *style, graver.*
שָׂרְדוּ Kal pret. 3 pers. pl. . . . שרד

שָׂרָה *to contend, wrestle*, with עִם, אֵת, Ge. 32. 29; Ho. 12. 4. Others, *to be a prince with, to prevail*; but against the context, on account of וַתּוּכָל in Gen. l. c.

שׁוּרָה fem. *row*, adverbially *in a row*, Is. 28. 25 (Arab. id.)

שָׂרַי (*contentious?*) pr. name, *Sarai*, the wife of Abraham, afterwards called שָׂרָה q. v. R. שָׂרַר.

שְׂרָיָה, שְׂרָיָהוּ pr. name, *Seraiah.*—I. of the scribe or secretary of David, 2 Sa. 8. 17; for which שְׁיָא (Kh. שֵׁיָא) 2 Sa. 20. 25, שַׁוְשָׁא 1 Ch. 18. 16, שִׁישָׁא 1 Ki. 4. 3. Simonis compares, for these three variations, the Arab. שׁוי and the Syr. ܫܘܫ *to dwell*, and assigns to them the signification of *habitation*; for שְׂרָיָה he reads with the Syr. שְׂרָיָה *habitation of God*, comp. R. שָׂרָה.—II. of the father of Ezra, Ezr. 7. 1.—III. of several other men.

יִשְׂרָאֵל (*wrestler with God*; others, *prince with God*) pr. name, *Israel*, the new name given to Jacob, Ge. 32. 29, afterwards employed as the name of his descendants, and after the division of the kingdom under Rehoboam, to *the kingdom of the ten tribes* in opposition to that of Judah.

מִשְׂרָה fem. *government*, Is. 9. 5, 6.

שָׂרָה Pi. שֵׂרָה *to loose, set free*, Je. 15. 11.

שְׁרָא Ch.—I. *to loose, untie, solve.*—II. *to lodge, dwell* (comp. Gr. καταλύω, *to unloose*, whence κατάλυμα, *a lodging*), Da. 2. 22. Pa. I. *to solve*, Da. 5. 12.—II. *to begin*, Ezr. 5. 2. Ithpa. אִשְׁתָּרִיא *to be loosened*, Da. 5. 6.

שֵׁרוּת fem. dec. 1 b, *beginning*, Je. 15. 11, Kh.

שָׂרוּחֶן (for שְׂרוּת חֵן *pleasant lodging*) pr. name of a town in Simeon, Jos. 19. 6.

שֵׁרִי (*beginning*) pr. name masc. Ezr. 10. 40.

שִׁרְיָה fem. *coat of mail*, Job 41. 18 (Arab. שׂרי *to glitter*).

שִׁרְיוֹן m., also סִרְיֹן Je. 46. 4, d 1 b.—I. *coat of mail*, see שִׁרְיָה.—II. pr. name, *Sirion*, the name of mount Hermon among the Sidonians, De. 3. 9.

שִׁרְיָן masc. i. q. שִׁרְיוֹן No. I.

מִשְׂרָה fem. dec. 10, *solution, maceration*, Nu. 6. 3, מִשְׂרַת עֲנָבִים *maceration of grapes*, a drink prepared from macerated grapes.

שָׂרָה וְ pr. name fem. . . .	שרר
שֵׂרוּג pr. name masc. . . .	שרג
שָׂרוּחֶן וְ pr. name of a place . . .	שרה
שָׂרוֹט Kal inf. abs. . . .	שרט
שָׂרוֹךְ noun masc. sing. . . .	שרך
שָׁרוֹן pr. name of a region . . .	ישר
שָׂרוּעַ Kal part. pass. sing. masc. . . .	שרע

---

a Mi. 2. 11.   c Ps. 7. 1.   e Ho. 3. 4.   g Da. 2. 22.   h Ca. 5. 2.   Est. 8. 4.   k Ex. 39. 1.   l Jos. 10. 20.   m Zec. 13. 3.
b Ps. 44. 18.   d Pr. 25. 20.   f 2 Ch. 32. 21.

שָׂרוּף   Kal inf. abs. . . . .

שְׂרוּפָה‎ id. part. pass. sing. fem. from שָׂרוּף masc.

שְׂרוּפוֹת‎ id. id. pl. dec. 10 . . . .

שְׂרוּקִים‎ noun masc. pl. [שְׂרוּקִים], suff. 3 pers. s. f.

שְׂרוּקֹת‎ Kh. שְׂרוּקֹת noun fem. pl. [of שְׂרוּקָה], K. שְׂרֻקוֹת (q. v.)

שָׂרוֹת‎ Kal part. act. f. pl. [of שָׂרָה], fr. שַׂר m.

שָׂרוֹת‎ noun f. pl. of [שָׂרָה] d. 10 [for שָׂרֹה], fr. שַׂר m.

שָׂרוֹתֶיהָ‎ id. pl., suff. 3 pers. sing. fem.

שָׂרוֹתֵיהֶם‎ id. pl., suff. 3 pers. pl. masc.

שָׂרוֹתַיִךְ‎ Kal part. fem. pl., suff. 2 pers. sing. fem. [fr. שָׂרָה d. 10, fr. שַׂר masc. §30. No. 3]

שְׂרֻתְךָ‎ Kh. שְׂרֻתְךָ noun fem. sing. with suff. [fr. שְׂרֻת]; K. שְׂרִיתָךְ Piel pret. 1 pers. sing., suff. 2 pers. sing. masc. . .   שאר

שֶׂרַח‎ (abundance, comp. סֶרַח) pr. name masc. Ge. 46. 17; 1 Ch. 7. 30.

[שָׂרַט] to cut, make incisions in the body. Niph. to tear or hurt oneself by lifting, Zec. 12. 3. Hence

שֶׂרֶט‎ masc. שָׂרֶטֶת fem. an incision in the body.

שָׂרֶטֶת‎ noun fem. sing. [for שֶׂרֶטֶת]   שרט

שָׂרַי‎ pr. name masc. for שָׂרָה   שרה

שָׂרַי‎ }
שָׂרָי‎ } pr. name fem. . . .   שרה

שָׂרִי‎ the foll. with suff. 1 pers. sing. . .

שָׂרֵי‎ noun m. pl. constr. fr. שַׂר m. d. 8 (§ 37. r. 7)

שָׂרֶיהָ‎ the foll. with suff. 3 pers. sing. fem.

שָׂרֵינָם‎ noun masc., pl. of [שָׂרִין] dec. 1 b

שָׂרִיד‎ noun masc. sing. dec. 3 a, also pr. name

שְׂרִידֵי‎ id. pl., constr. st.

שְׂרִידָיו‎ id. pl., suff. 3 pers. sing. masc.

שָׂרֶיהָ‎ noun masc., pl., suff. 3 pers. sing. fem. from שַׂר dec. 8 (§ 37. rem. 7)

שְׂרָיָה‎ }
שְׂרָיָהוּ‎ } pr. name masc.; וּ bef. (:)

שְׂרִיָּה‎ noun fem. sing. . . .   שרה

שָׂרֵיהֶם‎ noun masc. pl., suff. 3 pers. pl. masc. from שַׂר dec. 8 (§ 37. rem. 7)

שָׂרָיו‎ id. pl., suff. 3 pers. sing. masc.

שָׂרָיוּ‎ Chald. Pael pret. 3 pers. pl. m. (§ 49. No. 3)   שרא

שִׂרְיוֹן‎ noun masc. sing. dec. 1 b   שרה

שָׂרַיִךְ‎ noun masc. pl., suff. 2 pers. sing. fem. from שַׂר dec. 8 (§ 37. rem. 7)

שָׂרַיִךְ‎ noun masc. pl., suff. 2 pers. sing. masc. from שַׂר dec. 1 a   שיר

שָׂרֵיכֶם‎ the foll. with suff. 2 pers. pl. masc.   שרר

שָׂרִים‎ noun masc., pl. of שַׂר dec. 8 (§ 37. rem. 7)   שרר

שָׁרִים‎ Kal part. act. masc., pl. of שָׁר dec. 1 a   שיר

שָׁרַיִן‎ Chald. Peal part. pass. pl. m. [fr. שְׁרָא] d. 6 a   שרה

שִׂרְיוֹן‎ pr. name of a mount . .   שרה

שָׂרֵינוּ‎ noun masc. pl., suff. 1 pers. pl. from שַׂר dec. 8 (§ 37. rem. 7) . .   שור

שִׂרְיֹנוֹת‎ noun m. with pl. fem. term. fr. שִׂרְיוֹן d. 1 b   שרה

שְׂרִיקוֹת‎ adj. fem. pl. [of שְׂרִיקָה from שָׂרִיק masc.]   שרק

שָׂרִיתָ‎ Kal pret. 2 pers. sing. masc.   שרה

שְׂרִית‎ noun fem. sing., contr. for שְׁאֵרִית   שאר

שָׂרַךְ Pi. part. מְשָׂרֶכֶת twisting, winding her course, Je 2. 23, cog. שָׂרַג.

שְׂרוֹךְ masc. a shoe-latchet.

שְׂרוֹכְךָ noun masc. sing., suff. 2 pers. sing. masc. from [שְׂרוֹךְ] dec. 8 c (§ 37. rem. 7)   שרר

שְׂרֹכְכֶם noun masc. sing., suff. 2 pers. pl. masc. from שַׂר dec. 8 (§ 37. rem. 7) . .   שרר

שַׂרְסְכִים pr. name of a chief of the eunuchs, in the army of Nebuchadnezzar, Je. 39. 3.

שָׂרַע only part. שָׂרוּעַ stretched out, prolonged, i. e. having any member too long, unnaturally grown out, Le. 21. 18; 22. 23. Hithpa. הִשְׂתָּרַע to stretch oneself out, Is. 28. 20.

שַׂרְעַפַּי }
שַׂרְעַפָּי } noun masc. pl., suff. 1 pers. sing. from [שַׂרְעַף] dec. 8 d, see } סעף

שָׂרַף I. to burn, consume.—II. to burn lamps or torches for the dead, a rite still existing among the Jews, with לְ, 2 Ch. 16. 14; Je. 34. 5.—III. to burn or bake bricks, Ge. 11. 3. Niph. to be burned. Pi. id. Le. 10. 16.

שָׂרָף masc. dec. 4 a.—I. a species of venomous serpent.—II. pl. שְׂרָפִים seraphim, an order of angelic beings attending upon the divine majesty, represented in the vision, Is. 6. 2, 6, as having six wings.—III. pr. name masc. 1 Ch. 4. 22.

שְׂרֵפָה fem. dec. 10.—I. a burning, conflagration. —II. a funeral-burning, a burning for the dead, comp. שָׂרַף, No. II.

מִשְׂרָפָה fem. dec. 11 a.—I. a burning of lime, Is. 33. 12; a funeral-burning, Je. 34. 5.—II. מִשְׂרְפוֹת מַיִם (flowings of water; Chald. שָׂרַף Ithpe. to drop), pr. name of a town near Sidon.

a 2 Sa. 23. 7.   f Je. 18. 16.   k Le. 19. 28.   p Joel 1. 7.   u Job 41. 18.   z Is. 1. 23.   e Ps. 87. 7.   i Is. 19. 9.   h Da. 10. 21.
b 1 Sa. 30. 3.   g Ju. 5. 29.   l Le. 21. 5.   q Ge. 40. 10.   v Je. 17. 25.   a Ec. 10. 16, 17.   f Ge. 32. 29.   ll Ps. 139. 23.
c Ne. 3. 34.   h Eze. 27. 25.   m Is. 10. 8.   r Je. 31. 2.   w Ezr. 5. 2.   b Da. 3. 35.   g 1 Ch. 12. 38.   mm Ps. 94. 19.
d Is. 16. 8.   e Je. 15. 11.   n Ju. 5. 15.   s La. 2, 2, 9.   t 1 Sa. 17. 5, 38.   c Je. 44. 21.   d Je. 44. 17.   mm Is. 49. 23.
                                            y Am. 5. 23.   d 2 Ch. 26. 14.   e Eze. 16. 4.

שְׂרָף [ן'] noun masc. sing. dec. 4 a   שרף

שְׂרֹף Kal inf. constr.   שרף

שֹׁרַף Pual pret. 3 pers. sing. masc. [for שֹׂרַף]   שרף

שְׂרָפָהּ id Kal pret. 3 pers. sing. masc., suff. 3 pers. sing. fem.; ו, for ן, conv.   שרף

שְׂרָפָה id. pret. 3 pers. pl. (שָׂרְפוּ), suff. 3 pers. sing. fem.; ו id.   שרף

שְׂרֵפָה noun fem. sing. (constr. שְׂרֵפַת) dec. 10   שרף

שְׂרֵפָה defect. for שְׂרוּפָה (q. v.)   שרף

שָׂרְפוֹ Kal inf., suff. 3 pers. sing. masc.   שרף

שְׂרָפוּ id. pret. 3 pers. pl.   שרף

שְׂרָפוֹ id. pret. 3 pers. sing. masc., suff. 3 pers. sing. masc.; ו, for ן, conv.   שרף

שְׂרָפוּהָ id. pret. 3 pers. pl., suff. 3 pers. sing. fem.; ו id.   שרף

שְׂרֻפוֹת defect. for שְׂרוּפוֹת (q. v.)   שרף

שְׂרָפִים noun masc. pl. of שָׂרָף dec. 4 a   שרף

שֹׂרְפִים Kal part. act. masc. pl. of שׂוֹרֵף dec. 7 b   שרף

שְׂרָפָם id. pret. 3 pers. sing. masc., suff. 3 pers. pl. masc.; ו, for ן, conv.   שרף

שְׂרָפָנוּ id. pret. 1 pers. pl.   שרף

שְׂרָפְתָּ / שְׂרָפְתָּ וְ } id. pret. 2 pers. sing. masc.; acc. shifted by conv. ו   שרף

שְׂרֵפַת noun fem. sing., constr. of שְׂרֵפָה dec. 10   שרף

שְׂרַפְתִּי Kal pret. 1 pers. sing.   שרף

שְׂרָפָתַם id. pret. 3 pers. sing. fem., suff. 3 pers. pl. m.   שרף

שָׁרַץ [ן'] I. to creep, of reptiles and smaller aquatic animals.—II. to abound, swarm with.—III. to produce abundantly, to multiply. Hence

שֶׁרֶץ masc. collect.—I. reptiles, creeping things.— II. the smaller aquatic animals, Ge. 1. 20; Le. 11. 10   שרץ

שָׁרְצוּ [ן'] Kal pret. 3 pers. pl.   שרץ

שִׁרְצוּ id. imp. pl. masc.   שרץ

שָׂרַק Root not used; i. q. שָׂבַךְ שָׂרַךְ to interweave; Syr. סְרַק to comb flax, prop. to disentangle.

שֹׂרֵק masc. שֹׂרֵקָה fem.—I. a vine of a choice quality.—II. pr. name, Sorek, a valley between Askelon and Gaza, Ju. 16. 4.

שֹׂרוּקִים m. pl. shoots, tendrils of a vine, Is. 16. 8.

שָׂרִיק, שְׂרֵקָה fem. adj. combed, Is. 19. 9.

מַשְׂרֵקָה (vineyard) pr. name of a place in Edom, Ge. 36. 36; 1 Ch. 1. 47.

שָׂרֹק adj. bay, of horses, only pl. שְׂרֻקִים, Zec. 1. 8.

שָׁרַק [ן'] fut. יִשְׁרֹק.—I. to hiss, to lure by hissing or whistling, with לְ.—II. to hiss at in contempt, with עַל.

שְׁרֵקָה fem. a hissing, derision; object of contempt

שְׁרִיקָה fem. dec. 10.—I. a hissing, derision, Je. 18. 16.—II. whistling, piping, Ju. 5. 16.

מַשְׁרוֹקִי Chald. masc. dec. 8 b, pipe, flute, Da. 3. 5, 7, 10, 15.

שָׁרֵק id Kal pret. 3 pers. sing. m. for שָׁרַק (§ 8. r. 7)   שרק

שֶׁרֶק noun masc. sing.   שרק

שְׁרֵקָה id noun fem. sing.; ו bef. (:)   שרק

שָׁרְקוּ Kal pret. 3 pers. pl.   שרק

שְׁרֵקוֹת noun fem. pl. of [שְׁרִיקָה] dec. 10   שרק

שְׂרֻקִים adj. masc. pl. [of שָׂרֹק dec. 8 c, § 37. No. 3 c]   שרק

[שָׂרַר] to have dominion, to rule, be a prince. Hithpa. הִשְׂתָּרֵר to make oneself a ruler, prince, Nu. 16. 13. שַׂר masc. dec. 8 (pl. שָׂרִים § 37. rem. 7).— I. commander, chief.—II. noble, prince.

שָׂרָה fem. dec. 10 (for שַׂרָה).—I. princess, noble lady.—II. pr. name, Sarah, the wife of Abraham, see שָׂרַי R. שָׂרָה.

שָׁרַר only part. שֹׁרֵר adversary, enemy. Syr. to be firm. Pa. to make firm. Gesenius supposes the primary meaning to be, to twist, press together, comp. צָרַר, hence to oppress. Here may suitably be referred Job 33. 27, יָשֹׁר עַל־אֲנָשִׁים if he acts as an enemy or oppressor towards men.

שַׁמָּר (firm) pr. name masc. 2 Sa. 23. 33, for which שָׁכָר 1 Ch. 11. 35.

שֹׁר masc. d. 6 c, navel (prop. navel-cord, Gesen.), Ca. 7. 3.

שֹׁר masc. dec. 8 c (with suff. שָׁרֶּךָ).—I. sinew, muscle, collect. Pr. 3. 8.—II. navel, Eze. 16. 4.

שָׁרִיר masc. dec. 3 a, firm part, Job 40. 16.

שְׁרִירוּת fem. firmness, everywhere with לֵב stubbornness, obstinacy of heart.

שֵׁרָה fem. dec. 10 (for שְׁרָה), a chain, Is. 3. 19.

שַׁרְשְׁרָה fem. dec. 10, id., and by contraction שַׁרְשָׁה Ex. 28. 22.

שָׁרָר pr. name masc.   שרר

שֹׁרֵר Kal part. act. sing. masc.   שרר

שֹׁרְרוּ Pilel pret. 3 pers. pl.   שרר

שְׁרִירוּת noun fem. sing.   שרר

שֹׁרְרִי defect. for שׁוֹרְרִי (q. v.)   שרר

שָׁרְרֵךְ noun m. s., suff. 2 pers. s. f. fr. [שֹׁר] d. 6 c   שרר

a Is. 30. 6.   d Am. 2. 1.   f 2 Ki. 17. 31.   i 1 Sa. 30. 14.   p Is. 47. 14.   c Ge. 1. 21; 8. 17.   t 1 Ki. 9. 8.   x Ju. 5. 16.   β Job 36. 24.
b Je. 36. 25, 27.   e Eze. 43. 21.   h Jos. 11. 13.   m Je. 36. 29.   q Ps. 105. 30.   n Ge. 9. 7.   u Is. 5. 2.   y Zec. 1. 8.   γ Ps. 27. 11.
c Le. 10. 16.   f Is. 1. 7.   · Je. 43. 12.   n Is. 44. 19.   r Ex. 7. 28.   s Is. 5. 26.   w Je. 51. 37.   z Est. 1. 22.   δ Ca. 7. 3.
d Ps. 80. 17.   g Is. 6. 2.   u Nu. 19. 6, 17.

שֶׁרֶשׁ (וְ) masc. dec. 6c (pl. שָׁרָשִׁים § 35. rem. 9).—I. *root.*—II. *what springs up from the root, shoot, sprout,* Is. 53. 2 ; 11. 10.—III. *foot of a mountain,* Job 28. 9.—IV. *the bottom of the sea,* Job 36. 30. —V. *the sole of the foot,* Job 13. 27.—VI. *origin, source, cause.*

שְׁרֵשׁ Chald. masc. dec. 3e, *root,* Da. 4. 12, 20, 23. Hence the three foll.

שֶׁרֶשׁ [for שֶׁרֶשׁ *root*] pr. name masc. 1 Ch. 7. 16.

שָׁרֵשׁ Po. *to take root,* Is. 40. 24. Poal id. Je. 12. 3. Pi. שָׁרֵשׁ *to root out, extirpate.* Pu. pass. Job 31. 8. Hiph. הִשְׁרִישׁ *to strike, take root.*

שָׁרְשׁוּ or שָׁרֵשׁוּ Ch. fem. *a rooting out,* Ezr. 7. 26.

שָׁרְשׁוֹ noun m. s., suff. 3 pers. s. m. from שֶׁרֶשׁ d.6c

שָׁרְשׁוּ Poal (pass.) pret. 3 p. pl. [for שֹׁרְשׁוּ, s. שָׁרֵשׁ]

שָׁרְשׁוֹהִי Ch. noun masc. pl., suff. 3 pers. sing. masc. from שֹׁרֶשׁ (§ 59b)

שָׁרְשֵׁי (וְ) noun masc. pl. constr. from שֶׁרֶשׁ dec. 6c

שָׁרְשִׁי id. sing., suff. 1 pers. sing.

שָׁרָשֶׁיהָ id. pl., suff. 3 pers. sing. fem. (§ 35. rem. 9)

שָׁרָשָׁיו (וְ) id. pl., suff. 3 pers. sing. masc.

שָׁרָשֶׁךָ id. sing., suff. 2 pers. sing. fem.

שֵׁרֵשְׁךָ (וְ) Piel pret. 3 p. s. m. [שֵׁרֵשׁ], suff. 2 p. s. m.

שָׁרְשָׁם noun masc. sing., suff. 3 pers. pl. masc. from שֶׁרֶשׁ dec. 6c

שַׁרְשְׁרוֹת
שַׁרְשְׁרָת (וְ) noun fem., pl. of [שַׁרְשְׁרָה] dec. 10

שַׁרְשְׁרֹת noun fem. pl. [of שַׁרְשְׁרָה for שַׁרְשָׁרָה]

שָׂרֵת a doubtful Root ; whence appears to be derived מַשְׂרֵת masc. *a frying-pan,* 2 Sa. 13. 9 ; Chald. מַסְרִיתָא, מַסְרֵת id.

שָׁרֵת Pi. שָׁרֵת.—I. *to wait upon, to serve, minister,* with לְ, אֶת.—II. *to minister, perform the service of the sanctuary.*—III. *to worship,* Eze. 20. 32. Part. מְשָׁרֵת *minister, attendant.* Hence

שָׁרֵת masc. *service, ministry*

שָׁרֵת (וְ) Piel pret. 3 pers. sing. masc.

שֵׁרְתוּ id. pret. 3 pers. pl.

שָׁרַתִּי noun fem. sing. [שָׁרָה] with parag. י

שֵׁשׁ (וְ) (נָ) fem. שִׁשָּׁה masc. (constr. שֵׁשֶׁת § 39. No. 4, rem. 1) *six.* Pl. שִׁשִּׁים *sixty.*

שִׁשָּׁה Pi. *to give the sixth part,* Eze. 45. 13.

שִׁשִּׁי masc. שִׁשִּׁית adj. ord. *sixth;* fem. *sixth part.*

שָׁשׁ (וְ) Kal pret. 3 pers. sing. masc. or part.

שֵׁשׁ (וְ), (וְ) noun masc. sing.

שֶׁשׁ־ with Mak. for שֵׁשׁ (§ 36. rem. 3)

שֵׁשָׁא Pi. *to lead,* only in the following form.

שֵׁשֵׁאתִיךָ (וְ) Piel pret. 1 pers. sing., suff. 2 pers. sing. m.

שֵׁשְׁבַּצַּר pr. name masc. Ezr. 1. 8 ; 5. 14.

שֵׁשָׁה (וְ) num. card. m., constr. שֵׁשֶׁת from שֵׁשׁ fem.

שָׁשׁוּ Kal pret. 3 pers. pl.

שָׂשׂוֹן (וְ) noun masc. sing. dec. 3a (§ 32. rem. 6)

שְׂשׂוֹן id. constr. st.

שְׁשַׁזְפָתְנִי pref. שְׁ (וְ) Kal pret. 3 p. s. f. [שְׁזָפָה], suff. 1 p. s.

שֵׁשַׁי pr. names masc.

שֵׁשִׁי Kh. for שֵׁשׁ subst.

שִׁשִּׁי adj. ord. masc. sing., fem. שִׁשִּׁית, from שֵׁשׁ

שִׁשִּׁים (וְ) num. card. com. gen., pl. of שֵׁשׁ

שִׁשִּׁית adj. ord. fem. sing. from שִׁשִּׁי masc.

שִׁשִּׂיתֶם (וְ) Piel pret. 2 pers. pl. masc. [from שָׁשָׂה] R.

שֵׁשַׁךְ a name of Babylon

שָׁשָׁם pref. שְׁ (וְ) adv.

שָׁשָׂמָם pref. id. (וְ) Kal pret. 3 pers. sing. masc.

שָׁשׁוֹן defect. for שִׁשּׁוֹן q. v.

שִׁשָׁן pr. name masc.

שֹׁשַׁנִּים defect. for שׁוֹשַׁנִּים (q. v.)

שֵׁשַׁק
שָׁשַׁק } pr. name masc.

[שָׁשַׁר] masc. *red colour, red ochre,* Je. 22. 14; Eze. 23. 14.

שֵׁשֶׁת (וְ) num. card. masc., constr. of שִׁשָּׁה (§ 39. No. 4, rem. 1) from שֵׁשׁ fem.

שַׁשְׁתִּי
שָׁשִׁתִּי } Kal pret. 1 pers. sing. ; acc. shifted by conv. וְ (comp. § 8. rem. 7)

שֵׁת, שֵׁת Chald. i. q. Heb. שֵׁשׁ *six,* Da. 3. 1 ; Ezr. 6. 15. Pl. שִׁתִּין *sixty.*

שָׁת Kal pret. 3 pers. sing. masc.

שַׁתָּ id. pret. 2 pers. sing. masc. [for שַׁתָּה § 25. r.]

שֵׁת noun fem. sing. contr. for שְׁאֵת

שֵׁת noun masc. sing., pl. with suff. שְׁתוֹתֵיהֶם ; also pr. name

שֵׁת Kal inf. abs. (§ 22. rem. 2)

שָׁתָה (וְ) fut. יִשְׁתֶּה, ap. יֵשְׁתְּ (§ 24. rem. 3).—I. *to drink,* with acc. of the drink, with מִן, בְּ of the vessel ; metaph. Job 15. 16.—II. *to banquet,* Est. 7. 1. Niph. *to be drunk,* Le. 11. 34.

שְׁתָה, שְׁתָא Chald. *to drink,* Da. 5. 1—4, 23.

a Je. 12. 2.   d Job 29. 19.   g Ex. 28. 22.   m Is. 66. 14.   t La. 1. 21.   Eze. 16. 13.   p Ps. 122. 4.   h Ps. 45. 1.   n Nu. 24. 17.

b Da. 4. 12, 20, 23.   e Is. 14. 30.   h 2 Ch. 24. 14.   n Est. 1. 6.   u Est. 8. 17.   Ge. 30. 19.   q La. 5. 18.   Ps. 119. 14.   Is. 20. 4.

c Job 13. 27;   f Ps. 52. 7.   i Nu. 3. 6.   o Pr. 6. 16.   Ca. 1. 6.   Eze. 45. 13.   Est. 8. 16.   Ps. 90. 8.   Is. 22. 7.

36. 30.   g 2 Ch. 3. 5.   l La. 1. 1.   p Eze. 39. 2.

שְׁתִי *masc.*—I. *a drinking*, Ec. 10. 17.—II. *the warp* of a web, Le. 13. 48, 49, sq.; שׁתִי Arab. *to fix the warp to the loom*; Syr. *to weare.*

שְׁתִיָּה *fem. a drinking*, Est. 1. 8.

מִשְׁתֶּה *masc.* dec. 9 a.—I. *a drinking.*—II. *drink.*—III. *banquet, feast.*

מִשְׁתֵּא Chald. *masc.* dec. 6 b, *id.* Da. 5. 10.

שׁית . . Kal pret. 3 pers. sing. fem.   שָׁתָה

שׁתה (§ 62) Chald. Peal part. act. sing. masc. d. 6 a   שָׁתֵה•

שׁית Kal pret. 2 pers. s. m. [for שָׁתִיתָ § 25. rem.]   שַׁתָּה•

שׁית *id.* pret. 1 pers. sing., suff. 3 pers. sing. fem. [for שְׁתִיתִיהָ] . . שְׁתִיתָּ•

שׁתה . . . Kal inf. abs. . . שָׁתֹה

שׁתה *id.* imp. sing. masc.; וּ bef. (:)   שְׁתֵה•

שׁתה *id.* part. act. sing., fem. of שֹׁתֶה   שֹׁתָה•

שׁתה *id.* part. act. sing. masc. dec. 9 a   שֹׁתֶה

שׁתה *id.* inf. abs. for שָׁתֹה (§ 24. rem. 2)   שָׁתוֹ•

שׁתה   *id.* pret. 3 pers. pl.   שָׁתוּ•

שׁית   Kal pret. 3 pers. pl.   שָׁתוּ

שׁתת   Kal pret. 3 pers. pl.   שַׁתּוּ

שׁתה Kal inf. constr., comp. שְׁתוֹ (§ 24. rem. 2)   שְׁתוֹ•

שׁתה *id.* imp. pl. masc.; וּ bef. (:)   שְׁתוּ•

שׁתל Kal part. pass. sing. masc. dec. 3 a   שָׁתוּל

שׁתל *id.* part. pass. sing. fem.   שְׁתוּלָה

שׁתל *id.* part. pass. masc., pl. of שָׁתוּל dec. 3 a   שְׁתוּלִים•

שׁתה   Kal inf. abs. (§ 24. rem. 2)   שָׁתוֹת§

שׁתה . *id.* inf. constr. dec. 1 a   שְׁתוֹת¶¶

שׁתה *id. id.*, suff. 3 pers. sing. masc.   שְׁתוֹתוֹ•

שׁית noun pl. fem., suff. 3 pers. pl. masc. from שֵׁת   שָׁתוֹתֵיהֶם

חפץ pref. שֶׁ) (Kal fut. 3 pers. s. fem. [for תַּחְפֹּץ]   שֶׁתֶּחְפָּץ•

שׁית •וְ) Kal pret. 1 pers. s. [for שָׁתִיתִי § 25. rem.]   שַׁתִּי

שׁתי וְ) pr. name, see וָשְׁתִּי under lett. ו.   שְׁתִּי

שׁנה *id.* num. card. f., constr. of שְׁתַּיִם q.v.; וּ bef.   שְׁתֵּי•

שׁית Kal inf. (שִׁית), suff. 1 pers. s., or imp. s. fem.   שְׁתִי••

שׁתה Kal part. act. pl. c. masc. from שֹׁתֶה dec. 9 a   שֹׁתֵי•

שׁנה num. card. fem. (שְׁתַּיִם q. v.), suff. 3 pers. pl. masc. from שְׁנַיִם masc.   שְׁתֵּיהֶם

שׁנה *id. id.*, suff. 3 pers. pl. fem.   שְׁתֵּיהֶן•

שׁתה •וְ) Kal part. act. masc., pl. of שֹׁתֶה dec. 9 a   שֹׁתִים

שׁנה { num. card. du. [for שְׁנַתַיִם], fem. of   שְׁתַּיִם•

שׁנה } •) *id.*; וּ bef. (:)   שְׁתַּיִם

שׁנה •) *id.*, constr. st., followed by עֶשֵׂר, otherwise שְׁתֵּי; וּ *id.*   שְׁתֵּים

שׁתה (§ 62) Ch. Peal part. act. m., pl. of שָׁתֵה d. 6 a •)   שָׁתַיִן•

שׁת Chald. num. card. com. gen., pl. of שֵׁת •)   שִׁתִּין

שׁתה   Kal pret. 1 pers. pl. •)   שָׁתִינוּ•

שׁתה   *id.* pret. 2 pers. sing. fem. •וְ)   שָׁתִית•

שׁתה   *id.* pret. 1 pers. sing. •וְ)   שָׁתִיתִי•

שׁתה *id.* pret. 2 pers. pl. masc.; וּ bef. (:) •)   שְׁתִיתֶם•

שׁתל *fut.* יִשְׁתֹּל *to plant.*   [שָׁתַל]

שׁתל *masc.* dec. 3 a, *shoot, branch,* Ps. 128. 3.   שָׁתִיל

שׁתל   Kal pret. 1 pers. sing. וְ   שָׁתַלְתִּי•

שׁתם (comp. § 8. rem. 7) *to stop, shut out,* La. 3. 8.   שָׁתַם

שׁתם *to open,* only part. שְׁתֻם הָעַיִן *having his eyes opened,* Nu. 24. 3, 15; Chald. *to bore through.*   שָׁתַם

שׁית Kal pret. 3 pers. s. m. (שָׁת), suff. 3 pers. pl. m.   שָׁתָם•

שׁתם Kal part. pass. sing. masc. constr. [fr. שָׁתוּם] dec. 3 a . שְׁתֻם••

שׁתן Hiph. *to make water,* only part. מַשְׁתִּין *mingen* against the wall, i. e. *a male child;* according to others, *a dog.*   שָׁתַן•

שׁית Kal pret. 2 pers. s. m. (שָׁתָ q. v.), suff. 1 p. s.   שַׁתָּנִי•

שׁתק *fut.* יִשְׁתֹּק *to be still, to rest, to abate,* of waves, of strife.   [שָׁתַק]

שׁתר Niph. *to break forth,* 1 Sa. 5. 9. Arab. שׁתר *to split, burst* (Gesen.).   שָׁתַר•

שׁתר *(star)* pr. name of a Persian prince, Est. 1. 14.   שָׁתָר

שׁתר וּ) *(shining star)* pr. name of a Persian governor, Ezr. 5. 3; 6. 6.   שְׁתַר בּוֹזְנַי

שׁית i. q. שִׁית *to set, place, put.*   [שָׁתַת]

שׁית noun pl. fem., suff. 3 pers. sing. fem. from [שֵׁת] dec. 1 a (§ 30. No. 3) . שָׁתֹתֶיהָ•

ת

תוה . . noun masc. sing. dec. 1 a   תָּא

אבד i. q. תָּעַב only Pi. part. מְתָאֵב *abhorring,* Am. 6. 8.   II. [תָּאַב]

אבד Piel fut. 2 pers. sing. masc., or (2 Ki. 11. 1) 3 pers. sing. fem.; וְ conv.   תְּאַבֵּד•וַ

ז'. [תָּאַב] i. q. אָוָה *to desire, long for,* with לְ Ps. 119. 40, 174.   תַּאֲבָה *fem. desire,* Ps. 119. 20.

• Da. 5. 1.   ᵈ Job 6. 4.   ᵍ Is. 22. 13.   ᵏ Ps. 73. 28.   Je. 31. 21.   ᵖ Da. 5. 23.   ʳ Is. 51. 17.   ᵗ Ge. 30. 40.   ˣ Ps. 88. 7, 9.

ᵇ Ps. 8. 7.   ᵉ Pr. 31. 4.   ʰ 1 Ki. 13. 23.   ⁱ Ex. 23. 31.   1 Sa. 25. 43.   ᵠ La. 5. 4.   ˢ Eze. 17. 22.   ᵘ Nu. 24. 3, 15.   ʸ Is. 19. 10.

ᶜ Ho. 2. 5.   ᶠ Ps. 92. 14.   ⁱ 2 Sa. 10. 4.   ᵐ Ex. 10. 1.   Ne. 13. 20.   ¶¶ Je. 35. 8, 14.

תֵּאָבֵד }
תֹּאבַד } Kal fut. 3 pers. sing. fem. (§ 19. rem. 1)   אבד

תְּאַבְּדוּ· Piel fut. 2 p. pl. m. [for תְּאַבְּדוּ comp. § 8. r. 15]   אבד

תֹּאבְדוּ·
וַתֹּאבְדוּ· } Kal fut. 2 pers. pl. masc. (§ 8. rem. 15)   אבד

תְּאַבְּדוּן Piel fut. 2 pers. pl. masc. with parag. ן   אבד

תֹּאבֵדוּן Kal fut. 2 pers. pl. masc. with parag. ן [for

    תֹּאבְדוּן comp. § 8. rem. 7] . .   אבד

תְּאַבְּדֵם Piel fut. 3 pers. sing. fem., suff. 3 pers. pl. m.   אבד

וַתֹּאבַדְנָה· וַ Kal fut. 3 pers. pl. fem.; וַ conv. .   אבד

תֹּאבֶה Kal fut. 2 pers. sing. masc., or (Ge. 24. 5, 8)

    3 pers. sing. fem. . . . .   אבה

תֹּאבוּ· id. fut. 2 pers. pl. masc. (§ 25. No. 2c)   אבה

תֹּאבַל·
תֹּאבֵל· } Kal fut. 3 pers. sing. fem. (§ 8. rem. 15)   אבל

תָּאַבְתִּי· Kal pret. 1 pers. sing.   תאב

תֶּאְגֹּר· Kal fut. 2 pers. sing. masc. (§ 13. rem. 4)   אגר

תָּאָה· Pi. *to mark out*, Nu. 34. 7, 8.

   תֹּוא, תְּאֹו masc. a species of *gazelle*, De. 14. 5;

   Is. 51. 20 (Arab. تَأَى *to outrun*); Vulg. *oryx*.

תֶּאֱהַב·
תֶּאֱהֲבִי· } Kal fut. 2 pers. sing. masc. (§ 8. rem. 15, & § 13. rem. 5)

וַתֶּאֱהַב·] id. fut. 3 pers. sing. fem.; וַ conv.   אהב

תֶּאֱהָבוּ· id. fut. 2 pers. pl. masc. [for תֶּאֱהֲבוּ § 8. r. 15]   אהב

תֶּאֱהָבוּ· id. id., Aram. form [for תֶּאֱהָבוּ] .   אהב

תֶּאֱהָבוּן id. id. with parag. ן (§ 8. rem. 17)   אהב

תְּאֹו· ן noun m. pl., suff. 3 pers. s. m. fr. תָּא d. 1a   תוה

תְּאֹו· ן noun masc. sing.; וֹ bef. (:)   תאה

תֹּאֲוָה noun fem. sing. dec. 10 . .   אוה

תְּאַוֶּה Piel fut. 3 pers. sing. fem.   אוה

תְּאֹומִי·
תְּאֹומִים· } noun masc. pl. constr. & abs. from

    [תָּאֹם] dec. 3a . . .   תאם

תַּאֲוַת· noun fem. sing., constr. of תַּאֲוָה dec. 10   אוה

תַּאֲוָתִי· id., suff. 1 pers. sing. .   אוה

תַּאֲוָתָם· id., suff. 3 pers. pl. masc.   אוה

תֶּאְזֹור· Kal fut. 2 pers. sing. masc. (§ 13. rem. 4)   אזר

תְּאַזְּרֵנִי·] Piel fut. 2 pers. s. m., suff. 1 pers. s.; וַ conv.   אזר

תֶּאֱחֹז· Kal fut. 2 pers. sing. masc. (§ 13. rem. 4)   אחז

תֹּאחֵז·
תֹּאחֲזֵ· } id. fut. 3 pers. s. fem. (§ 19. r. 4); וַ conv.   אחז

תֹּאחֲזֵנִי·] id. id. with suff. 1 pers. sing.   אחז

תְּאַחַר·
תְּאַחֵר· } Piel fut. 2 pers. sing. masc., or (Is. 46. 13) 3 pers. sing. fem. (§ 14. rem. 1)

תְּאַחֲרוּ· id. fut. 2 pers. pl. masc.   אחר

תֶּאֱטֹר/ Kal fut. 3 pers. sing. fem. (§ 13. rem. 5)   אטר

תָּאֵי· ן noun masc. pl. constr. from תָּא dec. 1a   תוה

תָּאִיצוּ· Hiph. fut. 2 pers. pl. masc.   אוץ

תָּאִירוּ· Hiph. fut. 2 pers. sing. m., or 3 pers. sing. fem.   אור

תָּאִירוּ· id. fut. 2 pers. pl. masc.   אור

תַּאֲכִל· Hiph. fut. 2 pers. sing. masc. ap. [from תַּאֲכִיל]   אכל

תֵּאָכֵל· Niph. fut. 3 pers. sing. fem.   אכל

תֹּאכַל·
תֹּאכֵל· } וַ Kal fut. 2 pers. sing. masc., or 3 pers. sing. fem. (§ 10. rem. 1); וַ conv.   אכל

תֵּאכֻל·] Chald. Peal fut. 3 pers. sing. fem. .   אכל

תְּאַכְּלֵהוּ· Piel fut. 3 pers. sing. fem. with suff. 3 pers. sing. masc. [for תְּאַכְּלֵהוּ § 10. rem. 7]   אכל

תֹּאכְלֻהוּ· Kal fut. 2 pers. pl. masc., suff. 3 pers. sing. m.   אכל

תְּאֻכְּלוּ· Pual fut. 2 pers. pl. masc.   אכל

תֹּאכֵלוּ·
תֹּאכְלוּ· } Kal fut. 2 pers. pl. masc. (§ 19. rem. 1)   אכל

תֹּאכְלוּם· id. id., suff. 3 pers. pl. masc. .   אכל

תֹּאכְלוּן· id. id. with parag. ן .   אכל

תֹּאכְלִי· id. fut. 2 pers. sing. fem.   אכל

תֹּאכְלֵךְ· id. fut. 3 pers. sing. fem., suff. 2 pers. sing. fem.   אכל

תֹּאכְלְכֶם· id. id., suff. 2 pers. pl. masc.   אכל

תֹּאכְלֵם· וַ, וַתֹּ· id. id., suff. 3 pers. pl. masc.; וַ conv.   אכל

תֵּאָכַלְנָה· Niph. fut. 3 pers. pl. fem.   אכל

תֹּאכַלְנָה· וַ Kal fut. 3 pers. pl. fem.; וַ conv.   אכל

תֹּאכְלֶנָּה· id. fut. 2 pers. sing. m., suff. 3 pers. sing. fem.   אכל

תֹּאכְלֶנּוּ· id. id., suff. 3 pers. sing. masc.   אכל

תֹּאכְלֶנּוּ· id. fut. 3 pers. sing. fem., suff. 1 pers. pl.   אכל

תֹּאכְלֶנּוּ· id. fut. 2 p. s. m., or 3 p. s. f., suff. 3 p. s. m.   אכל

תֵּאָלֵם· Niph. fut. 2 pers. sing. masc.   אלם

תֵּאָלַמְנָה· id. fut. 3 pers. pl. fem.   אלם

תֶּאֱלֹף· Kal fut. 2 pers. sing. masc. (§ 13. rem. 5)   אלה

תְּאַלְּצֵהוּ· וַ Piel fut. 3 pers. sing. fem. [תְּאַלְּץ], suff. 3 pers. sing. masc. (§ 10. rem. 7); וַ conv.   אלץ

תָּאֲלָתְךָ· noun f. s., suff. 2 p. s. m. fr. [תָּאֲלָה] d. 10   אלה

תָּאַם· to b: *double*, only part. תְּאוֹמִים *doubled, coupled*. Hiph. *to bear twins*.

   תֹּאַם masc. dec. 6f, *twin*, Ca. 7. 4.

   תָּאֹם masc. dec. 3a, id., pl. תְּאוֹמִים, תֹּמִים.

תֹּאֲמֵי· noun masc. pl. constr. from [תֹּאַם] dec. 6f   תאם

תַּאֲמִין· Hiph. fut. 2 pers. sing. masc.   אמן

תַּאֲמִינוּ· id. fut. 2 pers. pl. masc. .   אמן

תֵּימִינוּ· Hiph. fut. 2 pers. pl. masc. [for תֵּימִינוּ]   ימן

a Nu. 33. 52.   h Ps. 119. 40, 174.   o Ps. 4. 3.   u Ps. 38. 10.   α Ge. 24. 56.   e Eze. 3. 3.   r Nu. 11. 19.   ′ Ge. 41. 4, 20.   ″ Ju. 16. 16.
b Est. 4. 14.   i De. 28. 39.   p Eze. 40. 21, 29,   v Ps. 78. 29.   β Ps. 69. 16.   f Da. 7. 23.   s Na. 3. 15.   k Eze. 4. 9, 10.   La. 3. 65.
c Ps. 2. 12.   k 2 Ch. 19. 2.   33, 36.   w Je. 1. 17.   γ Job 20. 26.   g Is. 33. 11.   t Ps. 21. 10.   l De. 5. 25.   Ca. 7. 4.
d De. 12. 2.   l Pr. 20. 13.   q De. 14. 5.   x Ec. 7. 18.   δ Is. 22. 4.   h Le. 7. 24.   u Job 1. 16.   m Eze. 24. 27.   De. 28. 66.
e Pr. 1. 32.   m 1 Sa. 18. 20.   r Ca. 4. 5.   y De. 32. 41.   ε Is. 1. 20.   i Job 1. 16.   v Ps. 31. 19.   n Is. 43. 10.
f 1 Sa. 9. 3.   n Zec. 8. 17.   s Ge. 38. 27.   z Ru. 3. 15.   ζ Ec. 8. 1.   k Le. 11. 42.   w Je. 24. 2.   o Pr. 22. 25.   Is. 30. 21.
g Job 14. 22.   g Pr. 1. 22.   t Pr. 10. 24.   t Ps. 139. 10.   h Mal. 1. 10.

תָּאֵם defect. for תּוֹאֲמִים (q. v.) . . . תאם

תָּאֵמִין }
תָּאֵמֵן { Hiph. fut. 2 pers. sing. masc., ap. from } אמן

תָּאֲמַנָּה Niph. fut. 3 pers. pl. fem. [for תֵּאָמַנָּה, § 9. rem. 4, comp. § 25. rem.] אמן

תָּאֲמֵנוּ 'ן id. fut. 2 pers. pl. masc. . אמן

תָּאַמֵּץ 'ן Piel fut. 2 pers. sing. masc., or (Pr. 31. 17) 3 pers. fem. sing.; וַ conv. . אמץ

תָּאַמְּצֶנּוּ id. fut. 3 pers. sing. fem., suff. 3 pers. s. m. אמץ

תֹּאמַר }
תֹּאמַר { Kal fut. 2 pers. sing. masc., or 3 pers. sing. fem. (§ 19. rem. 1) . . } אמר

תֹּאמַר }
תֹּאמַר { 'ן id. id. with conv. וַ (§ 19. rem. 2) } אמר

תֹּאמְרוּ }
תֹּאמְרוּ { 'ן id. fut. 2 pers. pl. masc.; וַ conv. } אמר

תֵּאמְרוּן Chald. Peal fut. 2 pers. pl. masc. (§ 53) אמר

תֹּאמְרוּן Kal fut. 2 pers. pl. masc. with parag. ן אמר

תֹּאמְרִי 'ן id. fut. 2 pers. sing. fem.; וַ conv. אמר

תֹּאמְרֻן id. fut. 2 pers. pl. masc. for תֹּאמְרוּן . אמר

תֹּאמַרְן }
תֹּאמַרְנָה { 'ן id. fut. 3 pers. pl. fem. (§ 8. rem. 16); וַ conv. } אמר

תְּאֵנָה 'ן f. (pl. תְּאֵנִים) fig tree; also fig. R. doubtful.

תְּאֻנֶּה Pual fut. 3 pers. sing. fem. . אנה

תְּאֵנָה noun fem. sing. . . . אנה

תֵּאָנַח Niph. fut. 2 pers. sing. masc. . אנה

תְּאֵנִיָּה noun fem. sing. . . . אנה

תֹּאנֵיכֶם ן the foll. with suff. 2 pers. pl. m.; ו bef. (:) תאן

תֹּאנִים 'ן noun fem. with pl. masc. term. from תֹּאנָה dec. 10; ן id. . . תאן

תְּאֵנִים noun masc. pl. . . . און

תֶּאֱנַף Kal fut. 2 pers. sing. masc. . אנף

תַּאֲנַת pr. name in compos. תַּאֲנַת שִׁלֹה . אנה

תַּאֲנָתָהּ noun f. s., suff. 3 pers. s. f. fr. [תְּאֵנָה] d. 10 אנה

תַּאֲנָתָהּ ן noun fem. sing., suff. 3 pers. sing. fem. from תֹּאנָה dec. 10; ן bef. (:) תאן

תֹּאנָתוֹ id., suff. 3 pers. sing. masc. . תאן

תֹּאנָתִי ן id., suff. 1 pers. sing.; ן bef. (:) תאן

תֹּאנָתְךָ ן id., suff. 2 pers. sing. masc.; ן id. תאן

תֹּאנָתָם ן id., suff. 3 pers. pl. masc.; ן id. תאן

תֵּאָסֵף Niph. fut. 3 pers. sing. fem. . אסף

תֶּאֱסֹף Kal fut. 2 p. s. m., or 3 p. s. f. (§ 13. r. 4.) אסף

תַּאַסְפוּן Hiph. fut. 2 p. pl. m. [for תּוֹסִיפוּן]; ן parag. יסף

תֶּאֱסְפִי Kal fut. 2 pers. sing. fem. (§ 13. rem. 6) אסף

תֵּאָסֵר Niph. fut. 2 pers. sing. masc. . אסר

תַּאַסְרֶהוּ ן Kal fut. 3 pers. sing. fem. [תֶּאֱסֹר], suff. 3 pers. sing. masc. (§ 13. rem. 6); וַ conv. אסר

תֵּאָפֶה Niph. fut. 3 pers. sing. fem. . אפה

תֵּאָפוּ Kal fut. 2 pers. pl. masc. (§ 25. No. 2c) . אפה

תֵּאָפֶינָה Niph. fut. 3 pers. pl. fem. . . אפה

תָּאַר ן to be drawn, marked out. Pi. to mark out, delineate, Is. 44. 13. Pu. part. מְתֹאָר marked off, Jos. 19. 13 render, which is marked off (i. e.) pertains) to Neah; others take it as a proper name. Hence

תֹּאַר masc. d. 6f (§ 35. r. 8).—I. form, personal appearance.—II. handsome form, beauty.

תָּאֹר Kal fut. 2 pers. sing. masc. . אר

תֶּאֱרֹב Kal fut. 2 p. s. m. or (Pr. 7. 12; 23. 28) 3 p. s. f. ארב

תַּאַרְגִּי Kal fut. 2 pers. sing. fem. (§ 13. rem. 6) ארג

תָּאֲרוּ }
תֹּאֲרוֹ { noun masc. sing., suff. 3 pers. sing. masc. from תֹּאַר dec. 6 (§ 35. rem. 8) } תאר

תַּאֲרִיךְ Hiph. fut. 2 pers. sing. masc. . ארך

תַּאֲרִיכוּ id. fut. 2 pers. pl. masc. . ארך

תַּאֲרִיכֻן id. id. with parag. ן . ארך

תַּאֲרַכְנָה ן Kal fut. 3 pers. pl. f. (§ 13. r. 4); וַ conv. ארך

תָּאֳרָם noun masc. sing., suff. 3 pers. pl. masc. from תֹּאַר dec. 6f . תאר

תַּאְרֵעַ ן pr. name masc. 1 Ch. 8. 35, called תַּחְרֵעַ in 1 Ch. 9. 41.

תָּאַרֵשׁ Piel fut. 2 pers. sing. masc. . . ארש

תָּאֲשׁוּר ן noun masc. sing.; ו bef. (:) אשר

תֶּאְשַׁם Kal fut. 3 pers. sing. fem. (§ 13. rem. 5) אשם

תֶּאְשְׁמוּ id. fut. 2 pers. pl. masc. [for תֶּאֱשְׁמוּ v. id. & § 8. rem. 15] אשם

תְּאַשֵּׁר Piel fut. 2 pers. sing. masc. . . אשר

תְּאַשְּׁרֵנִי ן id. fut. 3 pers. sing. fem., suff. 1 pers. sing.; וַ conv. . . אשר

תֶּאֱתֶה Kal fut. 3 pers. sing. fem. [for תֶּאֱתֶה § 13, rem. 4, § 19. rem. 3, & § 25. No. 2c] אתה

תָּבֵא ן Hiph. fut. 3 p. s. f., ap. fr. תָּבִיא; וַ conv. בוא

תָּבֹא וַ, וַתָּ id. fut. 2 pers. sing. masc., or 3 pers. sing. fem. (§ 25. No. 2b); וַ id. בוא

תֵּבֵא Kal fut. 2 pers. sing. masc. Chaldaism for תֹּבֶה (§ 24. r. 19), for תֹּאבֶה (§ 19. r. 5) אבה

תְּבִאֶהָ ן Hiph. fut. 2 pers. s. m. (Je. 13. 1), or 3 pers. sing. fem. (תָּבִיא), suff. 3 p. s. m.; וַ conv. בוא

תָּבֹאוּ וַ Kal fut. 2 pers. pl. masc.; וַ id. . בוא

תָּבֹאִי ן id. fut. 2 pers. sing. fem.; וַ id. . בוא

תְּבֹאינָה }
תְּבֹאֶינָה { id. fut. 3 pers. pl. fem., Kh. תָּבֹאנָה (§ 21. rem. 10, & § 25. No. 2f) } בוא

תְּבִיאֵמוֹ Hiph. fut. 2 p. s. m. (תָּבִיא), suff. 3 p. pl. m. בוא

a Ex. 26. 24.   f Pr. 31. 17.   m Je. 21. 3.   r Eze. 24. 12.   x Nu. 12. 14.   d Le. 23. 17.   m Is. 52. 14.   s Pr. 4. 14.   x Je. 13. 1.
b Je. 12. 6.   g Ps. 89. 22.   n Ps. 91. 10.   s Je. 2. 24.   y Ex. 5. 7.   e Jos. 15. 9, 11;   n De. 4. 40.   t Job 29. 11.   y Ex. 16. 7.
c Pr. 26. 25.   h 1 Ki. 5. 20;   o Ju. 14. 4.   t Ho. 2. 14.   z Jos. 2. 18.   18. 14, 17.   o Eze. 31. 5.   u Mi. 4. 8.   z 1 Sa. 10. 7.
d Is. 60. 4.   Pr. 1. 21.   p Eze. 21. 11.   u Joel 1. 7.   a Ju. 16. 6, 10, 13.   f Pr. 24. 15.   p La. 4. 8.   v Is. 47. 11.   a Ps. 45. 16.
Is. 7. 9.   i Je. 23. 38.   q Am. 4. 9.   v Je. 5. 17.   b Ju. 16. 8, 12.   g Ju. 16. 13.   q De. 28. 30.   w Pr. 1. 10.   b Ex. 15. 17.
2 Ch. 20. 20.   k Je. 10. 11.   l Ne. 13. 15.   w Ps. 105. 33.   c Ex. 16. 23.   h 1 Sa. 28. 14.   r Ho. 14. 1.

תָּבֹאןָ תָּבֹאנָה	Kal fut. 3 pers. pl. fem. (§ 21. rem. 10, & § 25. No. 2f); וַתָּ׳, וְ׳, ו conv.	בוא
תְּבֹאֵנּוּ	id. fut. 3 pers. s. m. (תָּבֹא), suff. 3 p. s. m.	בוא
תְּבִיאֵנִי	Hiph. fut. 3 pers. sing. fem. (תָּבִיא), suff. 1 pers. sing.; וְ׳ conv.	בוא
תָּבֹאשׁ	וְ׳ Kal fut. 3 pers. sing. fem.; וְ׳ id.	באש
תָּבֹאתִי	וְ Kal fut. 2 pers. sing. fem., Kh. תָּבֹאתִי, K. תָּבֹאת for תָּבֹאִי, an anom. form, perhaps a fut. with both the preformative and aformative of the fem., comp. pret. בָּאת; for תִי comp. § 8. rem. 5	בוא
תִּבָּגְדוּ	Kal fut. 2 pers. pl. m. [for תִּבְגְּדוּ § 8. r. 15]	בגד
תִּבְגּוֹד	id. fut. 2 pers. sing. masc. (§ 8. rem. 18)	בגד
תַּבְדִּיל	Hiph. fut. 2 pers. sing. masc.	בדל
[תֵּבָה]	fem. dec. 10, strictly a chest, box; it is used for— I. the ark of Noah, built in the form of a chest. —II. the ark in which Moses was exposed, Ex. 2. 5.	
תְּבַהֵל	Piel fut. 2 pers. sing. masc. (§ 14. rem. 1)	בהל
תִּבָּהֵל	וְ׳ Niph. fut. 2 pers. sing. masc.; וְ׳ conv.	בהל
תְּבַהֲלֵם	Piel fut. 2 pers. sing. masc. (תְּבַהֵל § 14. rem. 1), suff. 3 pers. pl. masc.	בהל
תְּבַהֵלְנָה	Niph. fut. 3 pers. pl. fem.	בהל
תָּבֹוא תָּבֹואָה	וְ׳ Kal fut. 2 pers. sing. masc., or 3 pers. sing. fem. (§ 8. rem. 13); וְ׳ conv.	בוא
תְּבוּאָה	noun fem. sing. dec. 10	בוא
תְּבוֹאֵהוּ	וְ׳ Kal fut. 3 pers. sing. fem. (תָּבֹוא), suff. 3 pers. sing. masc.; וְ׳ conv.	בוא
תְּבוּאוֹת	noun fem., pl. of תְּבוּאָה dec. 10	בוא
תָּבֹואִי	Kal fut. 2 pers. sing. fem. (§ 25. No. 2f)	בוא
תְּבֹואֶינָה תְּבֹואֶנָה	וְ׳ id. fut. 3 pers. pl. fem., K. תְּבֹואֶנָה (§ 21. rem. 10); וְ׳ conv., ו bef. (:)	בוא
תְּבֹואֵךְ	id. fut. 3 pers. s. f. (תָּבֹוא), suff. 2 p. s. m.	בוא
תָּבֹואֶנָה	וְ׳ id. fut. 3 pers. pl. fem. (§ 21. rem. 10)	בוא
תְּבֹואֶנּוּ	id. fut. 3 p. s. f. (תָּבֹוא), suff. 3 p. s. m.	בוא
תְּבֹואֵנִי	id. id. with suff. 1 pers. sing.	בוא
תְּבוּאַת	וְ׳ noun f. s., constr. of תְּבוּאָה d. 10; ו bef. (:)	בוא
תְּבוּאֹת	id. pl., comp. תְּבוּאוֹת	בוא
תְּבֹואָתָה	Kal fut. 3 pers. sing. fem. for תָּבֹא, an anom. form with the parag. syllable תָה, perh. intended for an aform. of the fem., comp. תְּבֹואָתֵךְ & תָּבֹאתִי	בוא
תְּבוּאָתָה	וְ׳ n.f.s., suff. 3 p.s.f. fr. תְּבוּאָה d.10; ו bef. (:)	בוא
תְּבוּאָתֹה	id., suff. 3 pers. sing. masc., K. אָתוֹ׳	בוא
תְּבוּאָתֹו	id., suff. 3 pers. sing. masc.	בוא
תְּבוּאָתִי	וְ׳ id., suff. 1 pers. sing.; ו bef. (:)	בוא

תְּבֹואָתְךָ	made up from the form תְּבוּאָתָה (q. v.) & suff. 2 pers. sing. masc.	בוא
תְּבוּאָתְךָ תְּבוּאָתֶךָ	noun fem. sing., suff. 2 pers. sing. masc. from תְּבוּאָה dec. 10	בוא
תְּבוּאָתֵנוּ	id., suff. 1 pers. pl.	בוא
תָּבוּז	Kal fut. 2 pers. sing. masc.	בוז
תִּבֹּוז	Niph. fut. 3 pers. sing. fem. (§ 18. rem. 7)	בזז
תְּבוּנָה	וְ׳ noun fem. sing. dec. 10; ו bef. (:)	בין
תְּבוּנֹות	id., pl. of the preced.	בין
תְּבוּנֹתֵיכֶם	id. pl., suff. 2 pers. pl. masc.	בין
תָּבוּס	Kal fut. 3 pers. sing. fem.	בוס
תְּבוּסַת	noun fem. sing., constr. of תְּבוּסָה dec. 10	בוס
תִּבֹּוק	Niph. fut. 3 pers. sing. fem. (§ 18. rem. 7)	בקק
תָּבֹור	pr. name of a place	תבר
תֵּבֹושׁ	Kal fut. 3 pers. sing. fem. (§ 21. rem. 6)	בוש
תֵּבֹושִׁי	id. fut. 2 pers. sing. fem.	בוש
תָּבֹוז	Kal fut. 2 pers. sing. masc.	בזז
תִּבֶן	וְ Kal fut. 3 pers. s. fem., ap. fr. תִּבְזֶה; וְ׳ conv.	בזה
תָּבֹז	וְ Kal fut. 3 pers. sing. fem. (§ 21. rem. 7)	בזז
תִּבְזֶה	Kal fut. 2 pers. sing. masc.	בזה
תִּבְזּוּ	Kal fut. 2 pers. pl. masc.	בזז
תִּבְחַן	Kal fut. 3 pers. s. fem. [for תִּבְחַן § 8. r. 15]	בחן
תִּבָּחֲנוּ	Niph. fut. 2 p. pl. m. [for תִּבָּחֲנוּ comp. § 8.r.15]	בחן
תִּבְחָנֶנּוּ	Kal fut. 2 pers. sing. masc. (תִּבְחַן), suff. 3 pers. sing. masc. (§ 16. rem. 12)	בחן
תִּבְחַר	וְ׳, וַתִּ׳ Kal fut. 2 pers. sing. masc., or (Job 7. 15) 3 pers. sing. fem.; וְ׳ conv.	בחר
תַּבֵּט	וְ׳ Hiph. fut. 2 pers. sing. masc., or 3 pers. sing. fem., ap. from נַבִּיט; תַּבֵּט; וְ׳ id.	נבט
תִּבְטַח	וְ Kal fut. 2 pers. sing. masc.; וְ׳ id.	בטח
תִּבְטְחוּ תִּבְטָחוּ	id. fut. 2 pers. pl. masc. (§ 8. rem. 15); וְ׳ id.	בטח
תִּבְטְחִי	וְ id. fut. 2 pers. sing. fem.; וְ׳ id.	בטח
תָּבִיא	Hiph. fut. 2 pers. sing. masc., or 3 pers.s. fem.	בוא
תְּבִיאֶהָ	וְ id. fut. 3 pers. sing. fem., suff. 3 pers. sing. masc.; וְ׳ conv.	בוא
תָּבִיאוּ	id. fut. 2 pers. pl. masc.	בוא
תְּבִיאֶינָה	id. fut. 3 pers. pl. fem.	בוא
תְּבִיאֵם	וְ id. fut. 2 pers. sing. masc., suff. 3 pers. pl. masc.; וְ׳ conv.	בוא
תְּבִיאֶנָה	id. id., suff. 3 pers. sing. fem.	בוא
תְּבִיאֶנּוּ	id. id., suff. 3 pers. sing. masc.	בוא
תְּבִיאֵנִי	id. id., suff. 1 pers. sing.	בוא
תַּבִּיט	Hiph. fut. 2 pers. sing. masc.	נבט
תָּבִין	Kal fut. 2 pers. sing. masc.	בין
תָּבִינוּ	וְ id. fut. 2 pers. pl. masc.	בין

a Ge. 30. 38.   d Mal. 2. 16.   g Eze. 7. 27.   k Eze. 32. 11.   n Ne. 9. 37.   q Le. 25. 20.   t Is. 24. 3.   w Job 7. 18.   z Le. 7. 30.
b Is. 47. 9.   e Is. 48. 8.   h De. 19. 27.   l Is. 5. 19.   o 2 Ch. 9. 21.   r Pr. 23. 22.   u Is. 51. 47.   x Job 15. 5.   a Ne. 9. 23.
c Job 20. 22.   f De. 19. 27.   i Ps. 35. 8;   m Je. 9. 16.   p Job 31. 12.   s Is. 24. 3.   v De. 20. 14.   y Job 7. 15.   b Le. 6. 14.
d Is. 50. 2.   Ec. 8. 3.   109. 17.   Ps. 76. 12.   Job 32. 11.   Pr. 30. 17.   1 Sa. 16. 7.   De. 33. 7.
Ex. 8. 10.   Job 4. 5.   Est. 4. 4.   De. 22. 9.   Job 22. 21.   Pr. 27. 7.   Jos. 8. 2.   Is. 30. 12.   1 Sa. 20. 8.
1 Sa. 25. 34.   Ps. 83. 16.   Je. 9. 16.   De. 33. 16.   Pr. 3. 9.   2 Ch. 22. 7.   Ge. 42. 15.   Ju. 19. 3.   Is. 43. 10.

תְּבִינֵם	Hiph. fut. 3 pers. s. fem., suff. 3 pers. pl. masc.	בין
תְּבִירָה	Ch. Peal part. pass. sing. fem. [of תְּבִיר masc.]	תבר
תְּבִישׁוּ	Hiph. fut. 2 pers. pl. masc.	בוש
תְּבִישֵׁנִי	id. fut. 2 pers. sing. masc., suff. 1 pers. sing.	בוש
תֵּבְךְ	ן ap. from the foll. (§ 24. rem. 3)	בכה
תִּבְכֶּה	וְ Kal fut. 3 pers. sing. masc., or 3 pers. sing. fem.; וְ conv.	בכה
תִּבְכּוּ	וְ id. fut. 2 pers. pl. masc.; וְ id.	בכה
תִּבְכִּי	id. fut. 2 pers. sing. fem.	בכה
תִּבְכֶּינָה / תִּבְנֶנָה	וַ id. fut. 3 pers. pl. fem.; וַ conv.	בכה
תֵּבֵל	וְ noun fem. sing.	יבל
תֶּבֶל	noun masc. sing.	בלל
תִּבֹּל	Kal fut. 2 pers. sing. masc. (§ 17. rem. 3)	נבל
תֵבֵל	וְ pr. name of a people, see תּוּבַל	יבל
תִּבְלֶה	Kal fut. 3 pers. sing. fem.	בלה
תַּבְלִיתָם	noun fem. sing., suff. 3 pers. pl. masc. from [תַּבְלִית] dec. 1 b	בלה
תְּבַלֻּל	noun masc. sing.	בלל
תְּבַלַּע	Piel fut. 2 pers. sing. masc.	בלע
תִּבְלַע	וְ Kal fut. 3 pers. sing. fem.; וְ conv.	בלע
תִּבְלָעֵם	id., suff. 3 pers. pl. masc. (§ 16. r. 12); וְ id.	בלע
תִּבְלָעֵמוֹ	id., suff. 3 pers. pl. masc.	בלע
תִּבְלַעְןָ / תִּבְלַעְנָה	וַ Kal fut. 3 pers. pl. fem. (§ 8. rem. 16); וַ conv.	בלע
תְּבַלְּעֵנּוּ	Piel fut. 3 pers. sing. masc., suff. 3 pers. sing. m.	בלע
תִּבְלָעֵנוּ	Kal fut. 3 pers. sing. fem. (תִּבְלַע), suff. 1 pers. pl. (§ 16. rem. 12)	בלע
תִּבְלָעֵנִי	id. with suff. 1 pers. sing.	בלע
תִּבְלָעֵנִי	וְ Piel fut. 2 pers. s. m., suff. 1 pers. s.; וְ conv.	בלע

תֶּבֶן וְ masc. *straw.*
מַתְבֵּן masc. *straw, heap of straw,* Is. 25. 10.

תִּבֶן	וְ Kal fut. 3 pers. sing. fem. ap. and conv. from תָּבִין	בין
תָּבֵן	וְ Kal fut. 3 pers. s. fem., ap. fr. תִּבְנֶה; וְ conv.	בנה
תִּבָּנֶה	Niph. fut. 2 pers. sing. masc. (Job 22. 23), or 3 pers. sing. fem.	בנה
תִּבְנֶה	Kal fut. 2 pers. sing. masc.	בנה
תִּבְנוּ	id. fut. 2 pers. pl. masc.	בנה
תִּבְנִי	pr. name masc.	בנה
תִּבְנִי	וְ Kal fut. 2 pers. sing. fem.; וְ conv.	בנה
תִּבָּנֶינָה	Niph. fut. 3 pers. pl. fem.	בנה
תַּבְנִית	וְ noun fem. sing. dec. 10	בנה

תַּבְנִיתוֹ	id., suff. 3 pers. sing. masc.	בנה
תִּבְעֶה	Kal fut. 3 pers. sing. fem.	בעה
תִּבְעֲטוּ	Kal fut. 2 pers. pl. masc.	בעט
תִּבְעָיוּן	Kal fut. 2 pers. pl. m. with parag. ן (§ 24. r. 5)	בעה
תַּבְעִיר	Hiph. fut. 2 pers. sing. masc.	בער
תִּבָּעֵל	Niph. fut. 3 pers. sing. fem.	בעל
תַּבְעֶנָה	Hiph. fut. 3 pers. pl. fem.	נבע
תְּבַעֵר	Piel fut. 2 pers. sing. masc. (§ 14. rem. 1)	בער
תִּבְעַר	וַ Kal fut. 3 pers. sing. fem.; וַ conv.	בער
תַּבְעֵרָה	pr. name of a place	בער
תְּבַעֲרוּ	Piel fut. 2 pers. pl. masc. (§ 14. rem. 1)	בער
תְּבַעֵת	Piel fut. 3 pers. sing. fem. (§ 14. rem. 1)	בעת
תְּבַעֲתֶךָ	id., suff. 2 pers. sing. masc. [for עָתְךָ § 2. r. 3]	בעת
תְּבַעֲתַנִּי	id. fut. 2 pers. sing. masc. (Job 7. 14), or 3 pers. sing. fem., suff. 1 pers. sing.	בעת
תֵּבֵץ	pr. name of a place near Shechem, Ju. 9. 50; 2 Sa. 11. 21.	
תִּבְצְעִי	וְ Piel fut. 2 pers. sing. fem.; וְ conv.	בצע
תִּבְצַעְנָה	id. fut. 3 pers. pl. fem.	בצע
תְּבַצְּרֶהָ	Piel fut. 2 pers. sing. masc.	בצר
תִּבְצֹר	Kal fut. 2 pers. sing. masc.	בצר
תִּבְצְרוּ	id. fut. 2 pers. pl. masc.	בצר
תְּבַקֵּעַ / תִּבָּקֵעַ	Piel fut. 2 pers. sing. masc., or 3 pers. sing. fem. (§ 15. rem. 1)	בקע
תִּבָּקַע	וְ Niph. fut. 2 pers. sing. fem.; וְ conv.	בקע
תְּבַקְּעֵם	Piel fut. 3 pers. sing. fem., suff. 3 pers. pl. masc.	בקע
תִּבְקַעְנָה	וְ id. fut. 3 pers. pl. fem.; וְ conv.	בקע
תְּבַקֵּשׁ	Piel fut. 2 pers. sing. masc.	בקש
תְּבַקֶּשׁ	id., id., or (Pr. 18. 15) fut. 3 p. s. f. (§ 10. r. 4)	בקש
תְּבַקְּשׁוּ	id. fut. 2 pers. pl. masc. (§ 10. rem. 7)	בקש
תְּבַקְשׁוּן	id. id. with parag. ן [for תְּבַקְשׁוּן § 10. r. 4]	בקש
תְּבַקְשִׁי	id. fut. 2 pers. sing. fem. (§ 10. rem. 7)	בקש
תְּבֻקְשִׁי	וְ Pual fut. 2 pers. sing. fem. (§ 10. rem. 7); וְ bef. (:), comp. וְשָׁבַע	בקש
תְּבַקְשֵׁם	Piel fut. 2 pers. sing. masc. (תְּבַקֵּשׁ), suff. 3 pers. pl. masc. (§ 10. rem. 7)	בקש
תְּבַקְשֶׁנָּה	id. id., suff. 3 pers. sing. fem.	בקש
תְּבַקְשֶׁנּוּ	id. id., suff. 3 pers. sing. masc.	בקש

תָּבַר Ch. i. q. Heb. שָׁבַר *to break,* only part. pass. תְּבִיר *fragile, brittle,* Da. 2. 42.

תָּבוֹר (*quarry*; or i. q. טַבּוּר *height*) pr. name, *Tabor.*—I. a mountain in Galilee, on the confines of Zebulun and Naphtali.—II. a grove of oaks, in Benjamin, 1 Sa. 10. 3.—III. a city of the Levites, in Benjamin, 1 Ch. 6. 62.

- Job 32. 8.
- Da. 2. 42.
- Ps. 14. 6.
- Ps. 119. 31, 116.
- 1 Sa. 1. 8.
- Ps. 78. 64.
- Ru. 1. 9, 14.
- Job 27. 15.
- Ex. 18. 18.
- Is. 51. 6.
- Is. 10. 25.
- Le. 21. 20.
- 2 Sa. 20. 19.
- De. 11. 6.
- Ex. 15. 12.
- Ge. 41. 24.
- Ge. 41. 7.
- Ec. 10. 12.
- Nu. 16. 34.
- Is. 64. 1.
- Job 10. 8.
- Job 13. 1.
- Is. 21. 12.
- Eze. 16. 24.
- 1 Ch. 28. 12.
- 2 Ki. 16. 10.
- Is. 64. 1.
- 1 Sa. 2. 29.
- Is. 21. 12.
- Eze. 5. 2.
- Ps. 119. 171.
- De. 21. 9.
- Ex. 35. 3.
- Le. 25. 11.
- Job 33. 7.
- Job 9. 34; 13. 21.
- Eze. 22. 12.
- Zec. 4. 9.
- Je. 51. 53.
- Le. 25. 11.
- Ho. 13. 8.
- Hab. 3. 9.
- 2 Ki. 8. 12; Eze. 13. 11.
- Is. 59. 5.
- Ho. 13. 8.
- 2 Ki. 2. 24.
- 2 Ki. 6. 19.
- Na. 3. 11.
- Eze. 26. 21.
- Ge. 43. 9.

Word	Description	Root
תָּבֹר	pr. name, כְּסֻלוֹת תָּ׳ under	כסל
וַתְּבָרַח	Kal fut. 3 pers. sing. fem.; וַ conv.	ברח
תְּבָרֵךְ	Piel fut. 2 pers. sing. masc.	ברך
תְּבֹרָךְ	Pual fut. 3 pers. sing. fem.	ברך
תְּבָרְכוּ	Piel fut. 2 pers. pl. masc.	ברך
תְּבָרֲכֶךָ	id. fut. 3 pers. sing. fem., suff. 2 pers. s. m.	ברך
תְּבָרְכֶנּוּ	id. id., suff. 3 pers. sing. masc.	ברך
תְּבָרֲכֵנּוּ	id. id., suff. 3 pers. sing. masc.	ברך
תְּבָרֲכֵן	id., suff. 1 pers. sing.	ברך
תְּבָרֲכֵנִי	id. fut. 2 pers. sing. masc., suff. 1 pers. sing.	ברך
וַתְּבָרֵנִי	Hiph. fut. 3 pers. sing. fem. [תַּבְרֶה], suff. 1 pers. sing. (§ 24. rem. 21)	ברה
תֵּבֹשׁוּ	Kal fut. 2 pers. pl. masc. (§ 21. rem. 6)	בוש
תֵּבֹשִׁי	id. fut. 2 pers. sing. fem.	בוש
וַתְּבַשֵּׁל	Piel fut. 2 pers. sing. masc., or (2 Sa. 13. 8) 3 pers. sing. fem.	בשל
תְּבֻשַּׁל	Pual fut. 3 pers. sing. fem.	בשל
תְּבַשְּׁלוּ	Piel fut. 2 pers. pl. masc.	בשל
תְּבַשֵּׂר	Piel fut. 2 pers. sing. fem.	בשר
תְּבַשְּׂרוּ	id. fut. 2 pers. pl. masc.	בשר
תֵּבַת	noun fem. sing., constr. of תֵּבָה dec. 10	תבה
תִּגְאַל	Kal fut. 2 pers. sing. masc.	גאל
תִּגָּאֵלוּ	Niph. fut. 2 pers. pl. masc. [for תִּגָּאֲלוּ comp. § 8. rem. 15]	גאל
וַתִּגְבַּהּ	Kal fut. 3 pers. sing. fem.; וַ conv.	גבה
תִּגְבְּהוּ	id. fut. 2 pers. pl. m. [for תִּגְבְּהוּ § 8. r. 15]	גבה
תִּגְבַּהְנָה	id. fut. 3 pers. pl. f. (§ 8. r. 16); וַ conv.	גבה
תַּגְבִּיהַּ	Hiph. fut. 2 pers. sing. masc.	גבה
תִּגָּבֵל	Kal fut. 3 pers. s. f. [for תִּגָּבֵל § 8. r. 18]	נבל
וַתַּגֵּד	Hiph. fut. 3 pers. sing. fem. ap. from תַּגִּיד (§ 11. rem. 4); וַ conv.	נגד
תַּגִּידֵלוּ	Hiph. fut. 2 pers. pl. masc.; וַ id.	נדל
תַּגְדֵּל	id. fut. 2 pers. s. m. ap. [fr. תַּגְדִּיל]; וַ id.	גדל
וַתִּגְדַּל	Kal fut. 3 pers. sing. fem.; וַ id.	גדל
וַתִּגְדְּלִי	id. fut. 2 pers. sing. fem.; וַ id.	גדל
תְּגַדֶּלְךָ	Piel fut. 2 pers. sing. m., suff. 3 pers. s. m.	גדל
תְּנַדְּעוּן	Piel fut. 2 pers. pl. masc. with parag. ן [for תְּנַדְּעוּן § 10. rem. 4]	נדע
וַתִּגְדְּרוּ	Kal fut. 2 pers. pl. masc.; וַ conv.	נדר
תִּגֹּף	Kal fut. 2 pers. sing. masc. (§ 17. rem. 3)	ננף
תָּגוּר	Kal fut. 2 pers. sing. masc.	נור
תָּגוּרוּ	id. fut. 2 pers. pl. masc.	נור
תָּגוּרִי	id. fut. 2 pers. sing. fem.	נור
תִּגֹּז	Kal fut. 2 pers. sing. masc.	נזז

Word	Description	Root
תִּגֹּל / תִּגֹּל	Kal fut. 2 pers. sing. masc. (§ 8. rem. 18)	נזל
וַתִּגֹּר	Kal fut. 2 pers. sing. masc.	נזר
וַתָּגַח	Kal fut. 2 p. s. m., ap. & conv. (§ 22. r. 3)	ניח
תַּגִּיד / וַתַּגֵּד	Hiph. fut. 2 p. s. m., or (Est. 2. 10) 3 p. sing. f.; second form plene for תַּגֵּד ap.	נגד
תַּגִּידוּ	id. fut. 2 pers. pl. masc.	נגד
תַּגִּידִי	id. fut. 2 pers. sing. fem.	נגד
תַּגִּיל	Kal fut. 2 pers. sing. masc., or 3 pers. s. f.	ניל
תַּגִּיעַ	Hiph. fut. 2 pers. sing. fem.	נגע
תַּגִּישׁ	Hiph. fut. 2 pers. sing. fem.	נגש
תַּגִּישְׁנָה / וַ	id. fut. 2 pers. pl. masc.	נגש
וְתָגֵל	Hiph. fut. 3 pers. sing. fem., ap. fr. נִיל	ניל
תְּגַל / וַתְּגַל	Piel fut. 2 pers. sing. masc., or 3 pers. sing. fem. ap. from תְּגַלֶּה	נלה
תִּגָּל	Niph. fut. 3 pers. sing. fem., ap. from תִּגָּלֶה	נלה
תְּגַלֶּה	Piel fut. 2 pers. sing. masc. (comp. § 24. rem. 20)	נלה
וַתִּגָּל	Niph. fut. 3 pers. sing. fem.; וַ conv.	נלה
וַתְּגַלַּח	Piel fut. 3 pers. sing. fem.; וַ id.	נלח
תְּגַלִּי	Piel fut. 2 pers. sing. fem.	נלה
וַתָּגֵלְנָה	Kal fut. 3 pers. pl. fem.; וַ conv.	ניל
תִּגְלַת פִּלְאֶסֶר also written תִּ׳ פִּלְנְאֶסֶר and פִּלְנֶסֶר pr. n. Tiglath-pileser, a king of Assyria.		
תַּגְמוּלוֹהִי	noun m. pl., suff. 3 p. s. m. (§ 4. r. 5), fr.	נמל
וַתִּגְמֹל	Kal fut. 2 p. s. m., or 3 p. s. f.; וַ conv.	נמל
וַתִּגְמְלֵהוּ	id. fut. 3 pers. s. f., suff. 3 p. s. m.; וַ id.	נמל
תִּגְמְלוּ	id. fut. 2 pers. pl. masc.	נמל
וַתִּגְנֹב	Kal fut. 2 pers. sing. masc.; וַ conv.	ננב
וַתִּגְנֹב	id. fut. 3 pers. sing. fem.; וַ id.	ננב
תִּגָּנֵבוּ	id. fut. 2 pers. pl. m. [for תִּגָּנֵבוּ § 8. r. 15]	ננב
וַתַּגַּע	Hiph. fut. 3 p. s. f., ap. fr. תַּגִּיעַ; וַ conv.	נגע
תִּגַּע / תִּ׳	Kal fut. 3 pers. sing. fem. (§ 8. rem. 15); וַ conv.	נגע
תִּגְּעוּ / תִּגְּעוּ	id. fut. 2 pers. pl. masc.	נגע
תִּגְעַל	Kal fut. 3 pers. sing. fem.	נעל
תִּגְעֲרוּ	Kal fut. 2 pers. pl. masc.	נער
וַתִּגְעַשׁ	Kal fut. 3 pers. sing. fem.; וַ conv.	נעש
וַתִּגְעַשׁ	Kh. תִּגְעַשׁ q. v., K. וַיִּתְגָּעַשׁ Hithp. fut. 3 pers. sing. masc.; וַ conv.	נעש
וַתָּגָר	Kal fut. 3 pers. sing. f., ap. & conv. fr. תָּגוּר	נור
וַתַּגֵּר	Hiph. fut. 2 pers. sing. masc. ap. [from תַּגִּיר]; וַ conv.	נור

a Ge. 16. 6.   b Ju. 5. 24.   c Nu. 6. 23.   d Ge. 27. 4, 25.   e Nu. 23. 20.   f 2 Ki. 4. 29.   g Ge. 27. 19, 31.
h 1 Ch. 4. 10.   i 2 Sa. 13. 5.   j 2 Sa. 13. 8.   k Le. 6. 21.   l Ex. 16. 23.   m 2 Sa. 1. 20.   Ru. 4. 4.
o Is. 52. 3.   p Eze. 19. 11.   q Eze. 16. 50.   r Zec. 9. 2.   s Job 19. 5.   t Eze. 35. 13.   u Ob. 12.
v Ge. 19. 19.   w Eze. 16. 7.   x Job 7. 17.   y Eze. 13. 5.   z De. 18. 6.   a De. 1. 17.   b 2 Ki. 8. 1.
c De. 15. 19.   d Pr. 22. 22.   e Job 22. 28.   f Ex. 19. 3.   g Jos. 2. 20.   h Je. 13. 15.
i Is. 41. 16; Ps. 35. 9.   j Le. 5. 7.   k Am. 9. 10.   l Ju. 16. 19.   m Is. 16. 3.   n Am. 6. 3.
o Pr. 25. 9.   p Is. 47. 3.   q Le. 18. 7, 8, 11, 15.   r Eze. 16. 36.   s De. 32. 6.   t Mal. 1. 8.   u Ps. 97. 8.   v Ex. 4. 25.
w Ps. 116. 12.   x Ps. 142. 8.   y Ho. 1. 8.   z 1 Ki. 11. 20.   a Ge. 31. 26, 27.   b Le. 19. 11.
Le. 12. 4.   Le. 26. 11, 15.   Ru. 2. 1.   Ps. 18. 8.   2 Sa. 22. 8.   2 Ki. 8. 2.   Eze. 35. 5.

תֹּגַרְמָה וְ Ge. 10. 3; elsewhere תּוֹגַרְמָה pr. name of a son of Gomer, Ge. 10. 3; 1 Ch. 1. 6, and his descendants inhabiting a region north of Palestine, Eze. 38. 6; 27. 14.

תְּגָרְמִי Piel fut. 2 p. s. f. [for תְּגָרְמִי comp. § 8. r.15]   נרם

תִּגְרַע וְ Kal fut. 2 pers. sing. masc.   נרע

תִּגְרְעוּ id. fut. 2 pers. pl. masc.   נרע

תְּגָרֵשׁ Piel fut. 2 pers. sing. masc.; וַ conv. (§ 10. rem. 4)   נרשׁ
תְּגָרְשֵׁן

תְּגָרְשׁוּן id. fut. 2 pers. pl. masc. with parag.   נרשׁ

תְּגָרְשׁוּנִי וַ id. id., suff. 1 pers. sing.; וַ conv.   נרשׁ

תַּגֵּשׁ וַ Hiph. fut. 3 pers. s f., ap. fr. תַּגִּישׁ; וַ id.   נגשׁ

תִּגַּשׁ וַ Kal fut. 2 pers. s. m., or 3 p. s. f.; וַ id.   נגשׁ

תִּגַּשׁ Kal fut. 2 pers. sing. masc. (§ 17. rem. 3)   נגשׁ

תִּגְּשׁוּ Kal fut. 2 pers. pl. masc. (§ 8. rem. 15)   נגשׁ
תִּגְּשׁוּ־

תִּגַּשְׁןָ וַ id. fut. 3 pers. pl. fem. (§ 8. r. 16); וַ conv.   נגשׁ

תִּדְבַּק Kal fut. 2 pers. sing. masc., or 3 pers. sing. f.   דבק

תִּדְבַּק וַ id. fut. 3 pers. sing. fem.; וַ conv.   דבק

תִּדְבָּקוּ id. fut. 2 pers. pl. masc. [for תִּדְבְּקוּ § 8. r.15]   דבק

תִּדְבָּקוּן id. id. with parag. [for תִּדְבְּקוּן § 8. r. 17]   דבק

תִּדְבָּקִין id. fut. 2 p. s. f. with parag. [for תִּדְבְּקִין]   דבק

תִּדְבָּקֵנִי id.fut. 3 p. s. f. (תִּדְבַּק), suff.l p. s. (§ 16. r.12)   דבק

תְּדַבֵּר וַ Piel fut. 3 pers. sing. fem.; וַ conv.   דבר

תְּדַבֵּר וַתְּ, id. fut. 2 p. s. m.; וְ bef. (ּ); וַ id.   דבר

תְּדַבֵּר־ id. fut. 3 pers. s. f.for תְּדַבֵּר (§ 10. r.4); וַ id.   דבר

תְּדַבְּרוּ id. fut. 2 pers. pl. masc.   דבר

תְּדַבְּרוּן id. id., parag. (§ 10. rem. 4)   דבר
תְּדַבֵּרוּן

תְּדַבְּרִי id. fut. 2 p. s. f. [for תְּדַבְּרִי comp. § 8. r.15]   דבר

תְּדַבֵּרְנָה id.fut.2 p.pl.f.(Je.44.25),or 3 p.pl.f.; וַ conv.   דבר

תִּדֹּד וַ Kal fut. 3 pers. sing. fem.; וַ id.   נדד

תִּדְהַר noun masc. sing.   דהר

תְּדִיּוּן Kal fut. 3 pers. sing. fem.   דוץ

תְּדוּרִי Chald. Peal fut. 3 pers. sing. fem.   דור

תָּדוּשׁ Kal fut. 2 pers. sing. masc.   דושׁ

תְּדוּשֶׁהָ id. fut. 3 pers. sing. fem., suff. 3 pers. s. f.   דושׁ

תְּדוּשַׁנָּה Ch. Peal fut. 3 p. s. f., suff. 3 p. s. f.; וְ bef. (ּ)   דושׁ

תַּדִּיחוּם וַ Hiph. fut. 2 p. pl. m., suff. 3 p. pl. m.; וַ conv.   נדח

תַּדִּיחֶנּוּ id. fut. 3 pers. sing. f. with suff. 3 pers. s. m.   נדח

תָּדִין Kal fut. 2 pers. sing. masc. R. דִּין see   דון

תְּדִינֵנִי id. with suff. 1 pers. sing. R. דִּין see   דון

תְּדַכֵּא Piel fut. 2 pers. sing. masc.   דכא

תְּדַכְּאוּ id. fut. 2 pers. pl. masc.   דכא

תְּדַכְּאוּנַּנִי id. id., suff. 1 pers. sing.; וְ bef. (ּ)   דכא

תִּדְלַח וַ Kal fut. 2 pers. sing. masc.; וַ conv.   דלח

תִּדְלָחֵם id. fut. 3 p. s. f., suff. 3 p. pl. m. (§ 16. r. 12)   דלח

תִּדְלַחְנָה וַ Kal fut. 3 pers. pl. f. (§ 24. r. 7); וַ conv.   דלה

תִּדֹּם Kal fut. 3 pers. s. fem. [for תִּדֹּם § 18. r. 14]   דמם

תִּדְמֶה Kal fut. 3 pers. sing. fem.   דמה

תִּדַּמּוּ Niph. fut. 2 pers. pl. masc.   דמם

תְּדַמִּי Piel fut. 2 pers. sing. fem.   דמה

תִּדַּמִּי Niph. fut. 2 pers. sing. fem. (§ 18. rem. 7)   דמם

תְּדַמְּיוּן Piel fut. 2 pers. pl. masc., parag. (§ 24. r. 13)   דמה

תְּדַמְּיוּנִי id. with suff. 1 pers. sing.   דמה

תִּדְמֶינָה Kal fut. 3 pers. pl. fem.   דמה

תִּדְמַע Kal fut. 3 pers. sing. fem.   דמע

תַּדְמֹר (city of palm trees) pr. name, Tadmor, a city in the Syrian desert between Damascus and the Euphrates, founded by Solomon, 2 Ch. 8. 4; Gr. Palmyra. The same is called תָּמָר (palm) in 1 Ki. 9. 18, Khethib.

תֵּדַע וַ Kal fut. 2 pers. sing. masc. (§ 20. rem. 1); וַ conv.   ידע
תֵּדַע וַ

תֵּדָעֵהוּ וַ id. id., suff. 3 pers. s. m. (§ 16. r. 12); וַ id.   ידע

תֵּדְעוּ id. fut. 2 pers. pl. masc. (§ 8. rem. 15)   דע
תֵּדְעוּ

תֵּדָעֶהָ id. id., suff. 3 pers. sing. fem. (§ 16. r. 12)   ידע

תֵּדְעוּן id. id. with parag.   ידע

תֵּדְעִי id. fut. 2 pers. sing. fem. (§ 8. rem. 15)   ידע

תֵּדְעִין id. with parag.   ידע

תִּדְעָל (fear; from דְּעַל Samar. & Syr. to fear) pr. name masc. Ge. 14. 1.

תִּדְפֶּנּוּ Kal fut. 3 pers. s. fem. [תִּדֹּף], suff. 3 p. s. m.   נדף

תִּדְק וְ Kal fut. 2 pers. sing. masc.   דקק

תַּדֵּק Ch. Aph. fut. 3 pers. sing. fem.   דקק

תַּדְקִנַּהּ id., suff. 3 pers. sing. fem.   דקק

תִּדֹּר וְ Kal fut. 2 p. s. m., or 3 p. s. f. (§ 17. r. 3); וַ conv.   נדר

תִּדְּרוּ id. fut. 2 p. pl. m. [for תִּדֹּרוּ, comp. § 10. r. 1]   נדר

תִּדְרוֹשׁ Kal fut. 2 pers. sing. masc.   דרשׁ

תִּדְרֹךְ Kal fut. 2 pers. sing. masc., or 3 pers. s. fem.   דרך

תִּדְרְכוּ id. fut. 2 pers. pl. masc.   דרך

תִּדְרְכִי id. fut. 2 pers. sing. fem.   דרך

תִּדְרֹשׁ Kal fut. 2 pers. sing. masc.   דרשׁ

תִּדְרְשֵׁהֲגוּ id. fut. 2 pers. pl. masc., suff. 3 pers. s. masc.   דרשׁ

תִּדְרְשֵׁנּוּ id. fut. 2 pers. s. masc., suff. 3 pers. s. masc.   דרשׁ

תִּדְרְשֵׁנִּי id. fut. 2 pers. pl. m. (תִּדְרְשׁוּ), suff. 1 pers. s.   דרשׁ

תַּדְשֵׁא Hiph. fut. 3 pers. sing. fem., ap. [fr. תַּדְשִׁיא]   דשא

תְּדַשֵּׁן Piel fut. 3 pers. s. fem. [for תְּדַשֵּׁן § 10. r. 4]   דשׁן

תְּדֻשַּׁן Pual fut. 3 pers. s. f. [for תְּדֻשַּׁן comp. § 8. r.15]   דשׁן

ᵃ Eze. 23. 34.   ᵍ De. 15. 3.   ˡ De. 13. 5.   ʳ Ge. 32. 20.   ᶻ Zec. 3. 7.   ᵉ Ex. 2. 16.   ᵏ Je. 14. 17.   ᵗ Ru. 3. 18.   ᵛ Job 10. 6.
ᵇ Job 15. 4, 8.   ʰ Eze. 9. 6.   ᵐ Ru. 2. 8, 21.   ˢ Ge. 31. 40.   ᵃ Ps. 54. 3.   ᵖ La. 2. 18.   ᵘ Je. 13. 17.   ᵃ Ps. 1. 4.   ᵂ De. 11. 25.
ᶜ Ps. 80. 9.   ⁱ Ex. 19. 15.   ⁿ Ge. 19. 19.   ᵗ Job 41. 14.   ᵇ Pr. 22. 22.   ᵠ Ju. 3. 49.   ᵛ Ps. 139. 1.   ᵇ Is. 41. 15.   ˣ Ju. 5. 21.
ᵈ Jos. 24. 12.   ᵏ Ge. 33. 6.   ᵒ De. 10. 20;   ᵘ Is. 3. 15.   ᶜ Da. 4. 18.   ʳ Is. 51. 6.   ʷ Ps. 144. 3.   ᶜ Da. 2. 40, 44.   ʸ 2 Ch. 15. 2.
ᵉ Mi. 2. 9.   ˡ De. 10. 20;   ᵖ 2 Sa. 14. 12   ᵛ Job 39. 15.   ᵈ Job 19. 2.   ˢ Est. 4. 13.   ˣ Je. 48. 2.   ᵈ Je. 29. 13.
ᶠ Ju. 11. 7.   ᵐ Eze 29. 4.   ᵠ 1 Sa. 25. 24.   ʷ Da. 7. 23.   ᵉ Eze. 32. 2.   ᵗ Je. 43. 19.   ʸ 1 Sa. 1. 11.   ᵉ Ge. 1. 11.
ᵍ Ju. 65. 3.   ᵖ Jos. 23. 5.   ʳ Ps. 58. 2.   ˣ Je. 23. 2.   ᶠ Is. 40. 18.   ᵘ Je. 47. 11.   ᶻ De. 12. 11.   ᶠ Pr. 15. 30
ʰ Ge. 33. 7.   ᵖᵖ Pr. 7. 21-

תְּהַבְּלוּ   Kal fut. 2 pers. pl. masc. [for תְּהַבְּלוּ § 8. rem. 15, & § 13. rem. 5 & 6]   הבל

תֶּהְגֶּה   Kal fut. 3 pers. sing. fem. (§ 13. rem. 5)   הגה

תֶּהְגּוּ   id. fut. 2 pers. pl. masc.   הגה

תֶּהְדְּפוּ   Kal fut. 2 pers. pl. masc. [for תֶּהְדְּפוּ § 8. rem. 15, & § 13. rem. 5]   הדף

תֶּהְדָּר   Kal fut. 2 pers. sing. masc. (§ 13. rem. 5)   הדר

תָּהָה   Root not used; Chald. תְּהָא *to be waste, desolate,* whence תְּהִי, תֶּהְוָא *waste, desert,* Arab. tahiy-you, *empty, chaos.* Hence

תֹּהוּ   masc. (Seg. n. for תֹּהֶו).—I. *desolation.*—II. *a desert.*—III. *emptiness,* Ge. 1. 2.—IV. *vanity, a vain, worthless thing.*—V. לְתֹהוּ, תֹהוּ adv. *in vain.*

תֶּהֱוֵא   Chald. Peal fut. 3 pers. sing. fem.   הוה

תְּהוֹבֵד   Chald. Aph. fut. 2 pers. sing. masc. (§ 52. r. 2)   אבד

תְּהוֹדְעוּן   Chald. Aph. fut. 2 pers. pl. masc. (§ 47. r. 4)   ידע

תְּהוֹדְעוּנַּנִי   }   Chald. id. with suff. 1 pers. sing.   ידע
תְּהוֹדְעֻנַּנִי

תֶּהֱוֶה   Chald. Peal fut. 3 pers. sing. masc. for תֶּהֱוֵא   הוה

תְּהוֹם   noun com. sing. dec. 1 a   הום

תְּהוֹמוֹת   id. with pl. fem. term.   תהם

תְּהוֹתְתוּ   Pilel fut. 2 pers. pl. masc.   הות

תְּהַחֲוֻן   Chald. Pael (dag. forte impl.) fut. 2 pers. pl. m.   חוה

תְּהַחֲוֻנַּנִי   Chald. id. with suff. 1 pers. sing.   חוה

תְּהִי   }   Kal fut. 2 p m. or, 3 p. s. f. ap. fr. תִּהְיֶה (§ 24. r. 3 e); conv. bef.   היה
תְּהִי

תְּהִיֶה־   }   id. fut. 2 pers. sing. masc., or 3 pers. sing. fem. (§ 14. rem. 13, & § 24. rem. 20)   היה
תִּהְיֶה

תִּהְיוּ   }   id. fut. 2 pers. pl. masc.; conv.   היה
תִּהְיוּן

תִּהְיִי   id. fut. 2 pers. sing. fem.; id.   היה

תִּהְיֶין   }   id. fut. 3 pers. pl. fem. (comp. § 8. rem. 16); id.   היה
תִּהְיֶינָה

תְּהִימֶנָּה   Hiph. fut. 3 pers. pl. fem. (§ 21. rem. 13)   הום

תְּהִינָה   defect. for תִּהְיֶינָה (q. v.)   היה

תְּהִינוּ   Hiph. fut. 2 pers. pl. masc.; conv.   הון

תַּהְכִּרוּ   Kal or Hiph. fut. 2 pers. pl. masc. [for תַּהְכִּירוּ § 11. rem. 7]   הכר

תָּהֶל   Hiph. fut. 3 pers. sing. fem. bef. monos. [for תָּהֵל § 18. rem. 11]   הלל

תְּהִלָּה   noun fem. sing.   הלל

תְּהִלָּה   noun fem. sing. dec. 10; bef.   הלל

תְּהַלְּלוּ   Kal fut. 2 pers. pl. masc.   הלל

תְּהִלּוֹת   noun fem., pl. of תְּהִלָּה dec. 10; bef.   הלל

תַּהֲלֹךְ   Kal fut. 3 pers. sing. masc. for תֵּהֵלֵךְ (§ 13. rem. 12); conv.   הלך

תַּהֲלֻכוֹת   noun fem., pl. of [תַּהֲלוּכָה] dec. 10   הלך

תְּהַלֵּל   Piel fut. 3 pers. sing. fem.   הלל

תְּהַלֶּלֶךְ   id., suff. 2 pers. sing. masc. for תְּהַלֶּלְךָ (§ 10. rem. 7, & § 2. rem. 2); for conv.   הלל

תְּהִלַּת   noun fem. sing., constr. of תְּהִלָּה dec. 10   הלל

תְּהִלֹּת   id. pl., comp. תְּהִלּוֹת   הלל

תְּהִלָּתוֹ   id. sing., suff. 3 pers. sing. masc.; bef.   הלל

תְּהִלָּתִי   id. sing., suff. 1 pers. sing.; id.   הלל

תְּהִלֹּתֶיךָ   id. pl., suff. 2 pers. sing. masc., but see § 4. r. 4   הלל

תְּהִלָּתֶךָ   }   id. sing., suff. 2 pers. sing. masc.   הלל
תְּהִלָּתֶךָ

תְּהֹם   Kal fut. 3 pers. sing. fem. [for תֶּהֱהֹם; § 18. rem. 7]; conv.   המם

תְּהֹמוֹת   noun com., pl. of תְּהוֹם dec. 10   תהם

תֶּהֱמִי   Kal fut. 2 pers. sing. fem.; conv.   המה

תְּהֻמֵּם   Kal fut. 2 pers. sing. masc. [תָּהֹם], suff. 3 pers. pl. masc. (§ 18. rem. 5); bef.   המם

תְּהֹמֹת   defect. comp. תְּהוֹמוֹת   תהם

תְּהַנְזִק   Ch. Pael fut. 2 pers. sing. m. (§ 47. r. 1 & 4)   נזק

תַּהְפֹּךְ   Kal fut. 3 pers. sing. fem.; conv.   הפך

תֵּהָפֵךְ   Niph. fut. 2 pers. sing. masc.   הפך

תַּהְפֻּכוֹת   }   noun fem., pl. of [תַּהְפּוּכָה] dec. 10   הפך
תַּהְפֻּכֹת

תַּהַר   Kal fut. 3 pers. sing. fem. ap. [for תַּהֲרֶה § 24. rem. 3]; conv.   הרה

תַּהֲרֹג   Kal fut. 2 pers. sing. masc.   הרג

תַּהַרְגֶנְהוּ   id. fut. 3 pers. sing. fem., suff. 3 pers. sing. m.   הרג

תַּהַרְגוּ   }   id. fut. 2 pers. pl. masc. (§ 8. rem. 15); conv.   הרג
תַּהַרְגוּ

תַּהַרְגֵם   id. fut. 2 pers. sing. masc., or (Pr. 1. 32) 3 pers. sing. fem., suff. 3 pers. pl. masc.   הרג

תְּהָרַנֶּנָּה   Niph. fut. 3 pers. pl. fem. (§ 9. rem. 4)   הרג

תַּהַרְגֵנִּי   Kal fut. 2 pers. s. m. (תַּהֲרֹג), suff. 3 pers. s. m.   הרג

תַּהֲרוּ   Kal fut. 2 pers. pl. masc.   הרה

תַּהֲרִין   id. fut. 3 p. pl. fem. (comp. § 8. r. 16); conv.   הרה

תַּהֲרֹס   Kal fut. 2 pers. sing. masc.   הרס

תֵּהָרֵס   Niph. fut. 3 pers. sing. fem.   הרס

תַּהַרְסֵם   Piel fut. 2 pers. s. m. [תְּהָרֵס], suff. 3 p. pl. m.   הרס

תַּהַרְסֵנּוּ   Kal fut. 3 pers. sing. fem. (תַּהֲרֹס), suff. 3 pers. sing. masc. (contrary to § 13. rem. 6)   הרס

תְּהַשְׁכַּח   Chald. Aph. fut. 2 pers. sing. masc. (§ 47. rem. 4); bef.   שכח

a Is. 16. 7.   g Da. 2. 9.   m Am. 4. 11.   t De. 1. 41.   b Ps. 73. 9.   h De. 10. 21.   z 2 Ch. 9. 12.   p Ps. 59. 12.   Ex. 15. 7.
Eze. 34. 21.   Ps. 62. 4.   Ex. 22. 30.   Job 19. 3.   Ex. 9. 23.   Ps. 42. 6.   De. 32. 20.   Eze. 26. 6.   Pr. 11. 11.
Is. 40. 17; 41 29.   c Da. 2. 6.   n Ho. 3. 3.   Ne. 12. 31.   Ps. 14. 6.   Job 20. 16.   De. 13. 10.   Ex. 23. 24.
b Da. 2. 24.   Eze. 16. 8.   Job 4. 18.   Ps. 150. 6.   Ese. 9. 6.   Is. 33. 11.   Pr. 14. 5.
c Ezr. 7. 25.   La. 3. 37.   Mi. 2. 12.   Ps. 75. 5.   De. 8.   Ps. 119. 175.   Le. 20. 15.   Ge. 19. 36.   Ezr. 4. 15; 7. 16
d Da. 2. 5.   Je. 12. 17.   l Ch. 7. 15.   Is. 60. 14.   Ps. 9. 15.   Ezr. 4. 13.

תְּהָתֵלּוּ • Piel fut. 2 pers. pl. masc. R. התל see תלל.

תֵּו pp • noun masc. sing. [for תָּוֶה] . . . תוה

תּוֹאֲמָם • Kal part. act. masc. pl. [of תּוֹאָם] dec. 7 b תאם

תּוּב • Chald. only fut. יְתוּב, i. q. Heb. שׁוּב to return, Da. 4. 31, 33. Aph. הָתִיב (§ 47. rem. 4) to return, give or send back: הָתִיב פִּתְגָם to return an answer, to answer.

תּוּבַל • pr. name masc., and in compos. תּוּ קָיִן יבל

תּוּבַל • Hoph. fut. 3 pers. sing. fem. . . יבל

תּוּבָלוּן • id. fut. 2 pers. pl. masc., ן parag. [for תּוּבָלוּ § 8. rem. 17] . . . . יבל

תּוּבַלְנָה • id. fut. 3 pers. pl. fem. . . . יבל

תּוּגָה • noun fem. sing. dec. 10 . . . . ינה

תּוֹגְיוּן • Kal fut. 2 pers. pl. masc., ן parag. (§ 24. r. 5) ינה

תּוֹגַרְמָה • pr. name, see תֹּגַרְמָה.

תּוּגַת • noun fem. sing., constr. of תּוּגָה dec. 10 ינה

תּוֹדָה • noun fem. sing. dec. 10 . . . . ידה

תּוֹדֹת • id. pl., comp. תֹּדֹת . . . ידה

תּוֹדִיעַ • Hiph. fut. 2 pers. sing. masc. . . ידע

תּוֹדִיעֵנִי • id. with suff. 1 pers. sing. . . ידע

תּוֹדֵךְ • Hiph. fut. 3 pers. sing. fem. [תּוֹדֶה], suff. 2 pers. sing. masc. (§ 24. rem. 20) ידה

תִּוָּדַע • Niph. fut. 3 pers. s. f. [for תִּוָּדַע § 15. r. 1] ידע

תִּוָּדְעִי • id. fut. 2 pers. sing. fem. . . ידע

תּוֹדַת • noun fem. sing., constr. of תּוֹדָה dec. 10 ידה

תּוֹדֹת • id. pl. comp. תֹּדֹת . . . ידה

תְּוַהּ • Ch. to be astonished, amazed, Da. 3. 24.

I. תָּוָה • Pi. תִּוָּה to make marks, to scribble, 1 Sa. 21. 14, cog. תָּאַר. Hiph. I. to mark, set a mark upon, with עַל Eze. 9. 4.—II. to limit, Ps. 78. 41, comp. תָּאַר; others, to grieve (Syr. to repent, be grieved).
תָּו masc.—I. a mark, sign, Eze. 9. 4.—II. signature, subscription, Job 31. 35, תָּוִי my subscription, q. d. affixed to my pleadings. Others take תָּוִי as a contraction תַּאֲוִי my desire, R. אָוָה.

II. תָּוָה • Root not used; i. q. Arab. תוי to abide, dwell. תָּא masc. dec. 1a (for תָּוָא, תָּוֶה), pl. ־ים, ־וֹת, a chamber, Ch. תָּוָא.

תּוּחַ • Root not used; Arab. תאח to descend, sink down. תּוּחַ (lowness, low) pr. name masc. 1 Ch. 6. 19, for which נַחַת ver. 11, & תֹּחוּ 1 Sa. 1. 1.

תַּחַת • fem. (with suff. chiefly attached to the plural, תַּחְתֵּינוּ, תַּחְתֶּיהָ, תַּחְתָּיו, תַּחְתֶּיךָ, תַּחְתָּי, תַּחְתֵּיהֶם, with the singular only, תַּחְתֶּנִי, תַּחְתָּם, תַּחְתֶּנָּה) prop. what is below, underneath, hence a place.—I. adv. below, beneath.—II. prep. under. —III. in place of, instead of.—IV. in return for.— V. on account of.—VI. תַּחַת אֲשֶׁר (a) instead that; (b) because that, because.—VII. with prefixes, (a) מִתַּחַת from under, from beneath; also simply, under; (b) מִתַּחַת לְ below, under anything; (c) לְמִתַּחַת לְ under, after a verb of motion, 1 Ki. 7. 32; (d) אֶל־תַּחַת under of the place whither; also of the place where, 1 Sa. 21. 4.—VIII. (place, station) pr. name (a) of a station of the Israelites in the desert, Nu. 33. 26; (b) of two men, 1 Ch. 6. 9, 22; 7. 20.

תְּחֹת • Da. 4. 11, elsewhere תְּחוֹת Ch. prep. under. תַּחְתִּי masc., תַּחְתִּית fem. adj. lower, lowest; pl. תַּחְתִּיִּים, תַּחְתִּיּוֹת lowest parts or places. תַּחְתּוֹן masc. תַּחְתּוֹנָה fem. adj. lower, lowest.

תּוֹחַ • pr. name masc. . . . . תוח

תּוֹחֵל • Hiph. fut. 2 pers. sing. masc. ap. [fr. תּוֹחִיל] יחל

תּוֹחֶלֶת • noun fem. sing. dec. 13a . . יחל

תּוֹחַלְתּוֹ • id., suff. 3 pers. sing. masc. . יחל

תּוֹחַלְתִּי • id., suff. 1 pers. sing. . . יחל

תָּוִי • noun masc. sing., suff. 1 pers. sing. from תָּו [for תָּוֶה] תוה

תָּוֶךְ • (in this form only with pref.) masc dec. 6g, the middle, midst; בְּתוֹךְ (a) in the midst of; (b) in, within; (c) among; מִתּוֹךְ from the midst of, also simply out of, from; אֶל־תּוֹךְ into the midst of. תִּיכוֹן masc. תִּיכוֹנָה fem. adj. middle.

תּוֹךְ • noun masc. sing., constr. of תָּוֶךְ dec. 6g תוך

תּוֹכוֹ • id., suff. 3 pers. sing. masc. . . תוך

תּוֹכִיחַ • Hiph. fut. 2 pers. sing. masc., ap. fr. יכח

תּוֹכֵחָה • noun fem. sing. dec. 10 (§ 39. No. 3. r. 4) יכח

תּוֹכָחֹת • noun fem. pl. abs., from תּוֹכַחַת (§ 44. r. 5) יכח

תּוֹכֵחוֹת • noun f., pl. of תּוֹכֵחָה d. 10 (§ 39. No. 3. r. 4) יכח

תּוֹכְחוֹת • noun fem. pl., constr. of תּוֹכָחֹת (q. v.) . יכח

תּוֹכַחֵךְ • Hiph. fut. 3 pers. sing. fem. (תּוֹכִיחַ for תּוֹכַחְנָה), suff. 2 pers. sing. fem. . . יכח

תּוֹכַחַת • noun fem. sing. dec. 13a, but pl. תּוֹכָחוֹת (§ 44. rem. 5) יכח

תּוֹכַחְתִּי • id. with suff. 1 pers. sing. . . יכח

תּוֹכִיחַ • Hiph. fut. 2 pers. sing. masc. . . יכח

תּוֹכִיחוּ • id. fut. 2 pers. pl. masc. . . יכח

ᵃ Job 13. 9.   ᵉ Ps. 45. 16.   ⁱ Ps. 56. 13.   ᵐ Ru. 3. 3.   ᵍ 1 Sa. 10. 8.   ᵘ Ps. 39. 8.   ᵍ Jos. 12. 2.   ᵇ Ho. 5. 9.   ᵉ Je. 2. 19.
ᵇ Ex. 36. 29.   ᶠ Pr. 14. 13.   ᵏ 2 Ch. 29. 31.   ⁿ Le. 7. 13, 15.   ʳ Pr. 11. 7.   ᵗ La. 3. 18.   ʰ Eze. 15. 4.   ᵖ Ps. 149. 7.   ᶠ Le. 19. 17.
ᶜ Ps. 45. 15.   ᵍ Job 19. 2.   ˡ Hab. 3. 2.   ᵒ Ne. 12. 31.   ˢ Job 41. 1.   ᵛ Job 31. 35.   ᶜ Pr. 9. 8.   ᵍ Pr. 6. 23.   ᵍ Job 19. 5.
ᵈ Is. 55. 12.   ʰ Pr. 10. 3.   ᵐ Jᵣ. 14. 33.   ᵖᵖ Eze. 9. 4.

תּוֹכִיחֵֽנִי	id. fut. 2 pers. s. m. (תּוֹכִיחַ), suff. 1 pers. s.	יכח
וְתֻכְיִים׳	noun masc. pl. see	תכי
תּוֹכְךָ׳	noun masc. sing., suff. 2 pers. sing. masc. from תָּוֶךְ dec. 6g	תוך
תּוּכַֽל׳	Kh. תּוֹכַל Hoph., K. תַּכֻּל Peal, fut. 2 pers. sing. masc. (§ 52. rem. 2)	יכל
תּוּכַל / תּוֹכַל	Hoph. fut. 2 pers. sing. masc., or 3 pers. sing. fem.; וְ conv.	יכל
תּוּכְלוּ׳	id. fut. 2 pers. pl. masc.	יכל
תּוּכְלִי׳	id. fut. 2 pers. sing. fem.	יכל
תּוֹכְכֶם׳	noun masc. sing., suff. 3 pers. pl. masc. from תָּוֶךְ dec. 6g	תוך
תִּוָּלֵד׳	Niph. fut. 2 pers. sing. masc.	ילד
תּוֹלְדוֹת / תּוֹלְדֹת	noun fem. pl. constr. [from תּוֹלְדָה or תּוֹלֶדֶת	ילד
תּוֹלְדֹתָם׳	id. pl., suff. 3 pers. pl. masc.	ילד
תּוֹלִיד׳	Hiph. fut. 2 pers. sing. masc.	ילד
וְתִלּוֹן׳	Kh. תּלּוֹן, K. תִּילוֹן pr. name masc. 1 Ch. 4. 20.	
תּוֹלֵלֵינוּ׳	noun masc. pl. suff. 1 pers. pl. [fr. תּוֹלָל]	ילל
תּוֹלָע	pr. name masc.	תלע
תּוֹלָע׳	noun masc. sing. (pl. תּוֹלָעִים)	תלע
תּוֹלֵעָה	noun fem. sing.	תלע
תּוֹלָעִים׳	noun masc. pl. of תּוֹלָע	תלע
תּוֹלַעַת׳ / וְתֹלַעַת׳	} noun fem. sing. dec. 13 a	תלע
תּוֹלַעְתָּם׳	id., suff. 3 pers. pl. masc. (§ 35. rem. 5)	תלע
תּוֹמְכִי׳	Kal part. act. sing. masc. for תֹּמֵךְ (§ 8. r. 19)	תמך
וְתוֹמֵךְ׳	Kal part. act. sing. masc. dec. 7b	תמך
תוֹמִם׳	by contr. for תְּאוֹמִים (q. v.) . .	תאם
תּוֹמָן׳	Kh. תּוֹמָן, K. תֵּימָן pr. name masc.	ימן
וַתּוּמַת׳	Hoph. fut. 3 pers. sing. fem.; וַ conv.	מות
תּוֹנֶה׳	Hiph. fut. 2 pers. sing. masc. (§ 25. No. 2 e)	ינה
תּוֹנוּ׳	id. fut. 2 pers. pl. masc.	ינה
תּוֹנֶֽנּוּ׳	id. fut. 2 pers. sing. masc. (תּוֹנֶה), suff. 3 pers. sing. masc. (§ 24. rem. 21)	ינה
תִּוָּסֵד׳	Niph. fut. 2 pers. sing. masc.	יסד
תּוֹסִיף׳	Hiph. fut. 2 pers. sing. masc., or 3 pers. s. fem.	יסף
תּוֹסִיפוּ׳	id. fut. 2 pers. pl. masc.	יסף
תּוֹסִיפִי׳	id. fut. 2 pers. sing. fem.	יסף
תּוֹסֵף׳ / תּוֹסֵף׳	} id. fut. 2 pers. sing. masc., ap. from תּוֹסִיף (comp. § 19. rem. 2)	יסף
וְתֹסֵף׳	id. fut. 3 pers. sing. fem. ap.; וְ conv.	יסף
תּוֹסֵף׳	id. fut. 3 pers. sing. masc. ap. (§ 20. rem. 9)	יסף

תּוֹסֵף	id. fut. 2 pers. sing. masc., or 3 pers. sing. fem., defect. for תּוֹסִיף	סף
תּוֹסְפִי׳	defect. for תּוֹסִיפִי (q. v.)	סף
תִּוָּסְרוּ׳	Niph. fut. 2 pers. pl. masc.	יסר
וְתוֹעֵבָה	noun fem. sing. dec. 11 b	תעב
תּוֹעֲבוֹת	id. pl., constr. st.	תעב
תּוֹעֵבוֹת	id. pl., abs. st.	תעב
תּוֹעֲבוֹתֶיהָ	id. pl., suff. 3 pers. sing. fem.	תעב
וְתוֹעֲבוֹתֵיהֶם׳	id. pl., suff. 3 pers. pl. masc.	תעב
תּוֹעֲבוֹתֵיהֶן׳	id. pl., suff. 3 pers. pl. fem.	תעב
וְתוֹעֲבֹתָיו׳	id. pl., suff. 3 pers. sing. masc.	תעב
תּוֹעֲבוֹתַיִךְ׳ / וְתוֹעֲבֹתַיִךְ׳	} id. pl., suff. 2 pers. sing. fem.	תעב
וְתוֹעֲבוֹתָם׳	id. pl., suff. 3 pers. pl. masc. (§ 4. rem 2)	תעב
תּוֹעֲבַת׳	id. sing., constr. st.	תעב
תּוֹעֲבָתָהּ׳	id. sing., suff. 3 pers. sing. fem.	תעב
תּוֹעֲבָתִיהֶם׳	id. sing., suff. 3 pers. pl. masc.	תעב
תּוֹעֲבָתֵךְ׳ / תּוֹעֲבָתֵךְ׳	} id. sing., suff. 2 pers. sing. fem.	תעב
תּוֹעֲבָתִיכֶם׳	id. sing., suff. 2 pers. pl. masc.	תעב
תּוֹעֲבָתָם׳	id. sing., suff. 3 pers. pl. masc. (§ 4. rem. 2)	תעב
תּוֹעָה׳	noun fem. sing.	תעה
תּוֹעֶה׳	Kal part. act. sing. masc. dec. 9a	תעה
תּוֹעֲפוֹת׳	noun fem. pl. abs. from [תּוֹעָפָה] dec. 11 a	יעף
וְתוֹעֲפֹת׳	id. pl., constr. st.	יף

תּוּף Root not used; Arab. *to spit out with contempt.*

תֹּפֶת f.—I. *a spitting*, Job 17.6, לְפָנִים אֶהְיֶה *I am become a spitting in the face*, i. e. as one before whose face men spit.—II. pr. name of a place in the valley of the sons of Hinnom, near Jerusalem, noted for the abominations committed there in the service of Moloch; with ה parag. תָּפְתֶּה Is. 30. 33 (§ 39. No. 4 d).

תּוֹפִיעַ׳	Hiph. fut. 3 pers. sing. fem. ap. [fr. תּוֹפִיעַ]	יפע
תּוֹפְפוֹת׳	Kal part. act. f. pl. [of תּוֹפֵפָה fr. תּוֹפֵף m.]	תפף
וַתּוֹצֵא׳	וַ Hiph. fut. 3 pers. sing. fem., ap. fr. תּוֹצִיא	יצא
תּוֹצָאוֹת׳	noun fem. pl. abs. from תּוֹצָאָה dec. 11a	יצא
תּוֹצְאוֹת	id. pl., constr. st.	יצא
תּוֹצְאוֹתָיו׳	id. pl., suff. 3 pers. sing. masc. (read. תָּיו), K. תּוֹצָאוֹת (q. v.)	יצא
תּוֹצְאוֹתָם׳	id. pl., suff. 3 pers. pl. masc. (§ 4. rem. 2)	יצא
תּוֹצְאֹת׳	id. pl., constr. st.	יצא
תּוֹצְאֹתָיו׳	id. pl., suff. 3 pers. sing. masc.	יצא
תּוֹצִיא׳	Hiph. fut. 2 pers. sing. masc., or 3 pers. s. f.	יצא
תּוֹצִיאוּ׳	id. fut. 2 pers. pl. masc.	יצא

ᵃ 2 Ch. 9. 21.	ᵍ Ps. 137. 3.	ᵐ Ps. 16. 5.	ˢ De. 23. 17.	ʸ Pr. 30. 6.	ᵉ Eze. 23. 36.	ᵍ Eze.7.20; 44.13.	ⁱ Pr. 21. 16.	ᵒ Ge. 1. 24.
ᵇ Eze. 28. 16.	ʰ La. 4. 5.	ⁿ Am. 1. 5, 8.	ᵗ Is. 44. 28.	ᶻ Zep. 3. 11.	ᶠ 2 Ch. 36. 8.	ʰ Eze. 11. 18.	ᵏ Job 22. 25.	ᵖ Ps. 98. 21.
ᶜ Da. 5. 16.	ⁱ Ex. 16. 20.	ᵒ Ge. 25. 24.	ᵘ 2 Ki. 11. 15, 16.	ᵃ Le. 26. 23.	ᵍ Mal. 2. 11.	ⁱ Eze. 7. 4; 16.	ˡ Job 3. 4.	ᵈ Is. 18. 19.
ᵈ Is. 47. 11, 12.	ᵏ Nu. 19. 6.	ᵖ 2 Ki. 11. 15, 16.	ᵛ Job 40. 32.	ᵇ Eze. 7. 4; 16.	ʰ Eze. 7. 9; 16.	ᵐ Ps. 68. 35.		ᵈ 1 Ch. 5. 14.
Ne. 4. 5.	Is. 66. 24.	ᵠ Ex. 23. 29.	ˣ De. 3. 26.	Eze. 12. 16.	36, 51, 58.	22, 51.		

תּוֹצִיאֵנוּ   וַ id. fut. 2 pers. s. m., suff. 1 p. pl.; וַ conv.   יצא

תּוֹצִיאֵנִי   id. id., suff. 1 pers. sing.   יצא

תּוּקַד / תּוּקָד   } Hoph. fut. 3 pers. sing. fem. (comp. § 8. rem. 15)   יקד

תּוֹקַהַת Kh. תּוֹקַהַת, K. תָּקְהַת   pr. name masc.   קהת

תּוֹקֵעַ   וַ Kal part. act. sing. masc. dec. 7 b   תקע

תּוֹקְעִים   id. pl., abs. st.   תקע

תִּנָּקֵשׁ   Niph. fut. 2 pers. sing. masc.   יקשׁ

[תּוּר] to go round, or about, cogn. דּוּר, hence—I. to go or travel about, as a merchant, 1 Ki. 10. 15.—II. to go about as a spy, to spy out.—III. to search out, explore, investigate.—IV. to think of, to purpose, Ec. 2. 3.—V. to go astray, metaph. Nu. 15. 39. Hiph. I. to send spies, to spy out, Ju. 1. 23.—II. to lead or direct aright, Pr. 12. 26; 2 Sa. 22. 33.

תּוּר masc. dec. 1 a.—I. turn, order, Est. 2. 12, 15. —II. row or string of beads, Ca. 1. 10, 11.

יְתוּר masc. (after the form יָקוּם) a searching out, meton. that which is sought, found by search, Job 39. 8; others, abundance, from יָתַר.

תּוֹר   וַ masc. dec. 1 a, a turtle-dove.

תּוֹר Chald. masc. only pl. תּוֹרִין oxen, i. q. Heb. שׁוֹר.

תִּוָּרֵא   Niph. fut. 2 pers. sing. masc.   ירא

תּוֹרֵד   Hiph. fut. 2 pers. sing. masc. ap. [fr. תּוֹרִיד]   ירד

תּוֹרֶד   וַ id. fut. 3 pers. sing. fem., ap. & conv.   ירד

תּוּרַד   Hoph. fut. 2 pers. sing. masc.   ירד

תּוֹרֵדֵם   וַ Hiph. fut. 2 p. s. m., or 3 p. s. f., suff. 3 p. pl. m.   ירד

תּוֹרָה   וַ noun fem. sing. dec. 10   ירה

תּוֹרֹת   וַ id. pl., comp. תּוֹרֹת   ירה

תּוֹרֵי   noun masc. pl. constr. from תּוֹר dec. 1 a   תור

תּוֹרִין   Chald. noun masc., pl. of [תּוֹר] dec. 1 a   תור

תּוֹרִישׁ   Hiph. fut. 2 pers. sing. masc.   ירשׁ

תּוֹרִישׁוּ   id. fut. 2 pers. pl. masc.   ירשׁ

תּוֹרִישֵׁמוֹ   id. fut. 3 pers. sing. fem., suff. 3 pers. pl. m.   ירשׁ

תּוֹרִישֵׁנִי   וַ id. fut. 2 pers. sing. masc., suff. 1 pers. s.   ירשׁ

תּוֹרְךָ   noun m. s., suff. 2 p. s. m. fr. תּוֹר d. 1 a   תור

תּוֹרְךָ   וְ Hiph. fut. 3 pers. sing. fem. [תּוֹרֶה], suff. 2 pers. sing. masc. (§ 25. No. 2 e)   ירה

תּוֹרֵם   id. fut. 2 pers. sing. masc., suff. 3 p. pl. m.   ירה

תּוּרַק   Hoph. fut. 3 pers. sing. fem.   רוק

תִּוָּרֵשׁ   Niph. fut. 2 pers. sing. masc.   ירשׁ

תּוֹרַת   וְ noun fem. sing., constr. of תּוֹרָה dec. 10   ירה

תּוֹרֹת   id. pl., comp. תּוֹרֹת   ירה

תּוֹרָתֵנוּ   id. pl., suff. 3 pers. sing. masc.   ירה

תּוֹרֹתַי   וְ id. sing., suff. 1 pers. sing.   ירה

תּוֹרֹתִי / תּוֹרֹתַי   } id. pl., suff. 1 pers. sing.   ירה

תּוֹרֹתָיו   וְ id. pl., suff. 3 pers. sing. masc.   ירה

תּוֹרָתֶךָ / תּוֹרָתְךָ   וְ } id. sing., suff. 2 pers. sing. masc.   ירה

תּוֹשָׁב   וְ noun masc. sing. dec. 2 b   ישׁב

תּוֹשַׁב   id., constr. st.   ישׁב

תּוֹשֵׁב   וַ Hiph. fut. 2 pers. sing. masc., ap. & conv. [from תּוֹשִׁיב]   ישׁב

תּוּשַׁב   Hoph. fut. 3 pers. sing. fem. [for תּוּשָׁב]   ישׁב

תּוֹשָׁבִים   וְ noun masc., pl. of תּוֹשָׁב, q. v.   ישׁב

תּוּשַׁד   Hoph. fut. 2 pers. sing. masc.   שׁדד

תּוֹשִׁיבֵנִי   Hiph. fut. 2 pers. sing. masc., suff. 1 pers. sing.   ישׁב

תּוּשִׁיָּה   וְ noun fem. sing.   ישׁה

תּוֹשִׁיעַ   וְ Hiph. fut. 2 pers. sing. masc., or (Job 40. 14) 3 pers. sing. fem.   ישׁע

תּוֹשִׁיעוּן   id. fut. 2 pers. pl. masc. with parag. ן   ישׁע

תּוֹשִׁיעֵנוּ   id. fut. 2 pers. sing. masc., suff. 1 pers. pl.   ישׁע

תּוֹשִׁיעֵנִי   וְ id. fut. 3 pers. sing. fem., suff. 1 pers. sing.   ישׁע

תִּוָּשַׁע   Niph. fut. 3 pers. sing. fem.   ישׁע

תּוֹשַׁע   וַ Hiph. fut. 3 pers. sing. fem., ap. from תּוֹשִׁיעַ   ישׁע

תִּוָּשֵׁעוּן   Niph. fut. 2 pers. pl. masc., ן parag. [for תִּוָּשֵׁעוּן, comp. § 10. rem. 4]   ישׁע

תּוּשָׁעִי   id. fut. 2 pers. s. f. [for תִּוָּשַׁע, comp. § 8. r. 7]   ישׁע

תּוֹתַח   noun masc. sing.   יתח

תּוֹתִירוּ   Hiph. fut. 2 pers. pl. masc.   יתר

תּוֹתַר   Hiph. fut. 2 pers. sing. masc. ap. [for תּוֹתִיר] comp. § 19. rem. 2, from תּוֹתִיר   יתר

תִּזְבַּח   Kal fut. 2 pers. sing. masc.   זבח

תִּזְבָּחֶהָ   וַ id. fut. 3 pers. sing. fem., suff. 3 pers. sing. masc. (§ 16. rem. 12); וַ conv.   זבח

תִּזְבָּחֶהָ   id. fut. 2 pers. pl. masc., suff. 3 pers. s. masc.   זבח

תִּזְבָּחוּ   } id. fut. 2 pers. pl. masc. (§ 8. rem. 15)   זבח

תִּזְבָּחִים   וַ id. fut. 2 pers. sing. fem. [תִּזְבְּחִי], suff. 3 pers. pl. masc. (§ 16. rem. 12); וַ conv.   זבח

תִּזְבָּחֵנוּ   id. fut. 2 pers. s. masc., suff. 3 pers. s. masc.   זבח

תָּזֹרִי   וַ Hiph. fut. 2 pers. pl. masc.; וַ conv.   זור

תָּזוּב   Kal fut. 3 pers. sing. fem.   זוב

תִּזֹּרֶהָ   Kal fut. 3 pers. s. fem. [תָּזוּר], suff. 3 p. s. fem.   זור

תִּזְכֶּה   Kal fut. 2 pers. sing. masc.   זכה

תִּזְכּוֹר   Kal fut. 2 pers. sing. masc. (§ 8. rem. 18)   זכר

תַּזְכִּירוּ   Hiph. fut. 2 pers. pl. masc.   זכר

תִּזָּכֵר   Niph. fut. 3 pers. sing. fem. (denom. of זָכָר)   זכר

a Ps. 66.12.   f Le. 12.6.   t Jos. 2.15.   x Ex. 15.9.   a Is. 24.5.   c 2 Ki. 17.26.   h Ju. 6.31.   n Ge. 49.4.   s De. 1.43.
b Ps. 31.5.   g Ps. 130.4.   m Ne. 9.13.   y Job 1..26.   y Eze. 44.24.   d Is. 44.26.   i Jos. 22.22.   o 1 Sa. 28.24.   t Le. 15.25.
c 2 Ch. 23.13.   h 1 Ki. 2.6.   n Ca. 1.11.   x Is. 74.19.   z Ex. 18.16.   e Is. 33.1.   k Ps.44.7;138.7.   p Le. 19.5.   u De. 39.15.
d Pr. 11.15.   i Is. 14.15.   o Jos. 17.18.   P Ps. 45.5.   a Ps. 105.45.   f Ps. 4.9.   l Is. 30.15.   q Eze. 16.20.   x Ps. 51.6.
e De. 7.25.   k Ps. 55.24.   P Le. 22.10.   q Ca. 1.3.   b Nu. 33.55.   g 2 Ch. 20.9.   m Je. 4.14.   De. 15.21.   y Ex. 34.19
f Ge. 24.46.   kk Job 41.21.

49

תִּזָּכֵר	id. fut. 3 pers. sing. fem.	זכר
תִּזְכֹּר		זכר
תִּזְכְּרֵ֫	id. fut. 2 pers. sing. masc. (§ 8. rem. 18)	זכר
תִּזְכְּר֫וּ	id. fut. 2 pers. pl. masc.	זכר
תִּזָּכֵ֫רִי	Niph. fut. 2 p. s. f. [for תִּזָּכְרִי comp. § 8. r. 15]	זכר
תִּזְכְּרִי	Kal fut. 2 pers. sing. fem.	זכר
תִּזָּכַ֫רְן	Niph. fut. 3 pers. pl. fem. (comp. § 8.	זכר
תִּזָּכַ֫רְנָה	rem. 16, & § 9. rem. 4)	
תִּזְכְּרֶ֫נּוּ	Kal fut. 2 pers. sing. masc., suff. 3 pers. s. m.	זכר
תִּזְכְּרֵ֫נִי	id. with suff. 1 pers. sing.	זכר
תִּזַּל	Kal fut. 3 pers. sing. fem.	נזל
תֵּזְלִי	Kal fut. 2 pers. s. f. [for תֵּאזְלִי § 19. r. 3]	אזל
תִּזְמֹר	Kal fut. 2 pers. sing. masc.	זמר
תֵּזֶן	Kal fut. 3 pers. sing. fem., ap. from תִּזְנֶה	זנה
תַּזְנֶה	Hiph. fut. 3 pers. sing. fem.; וְ conv.	זנה
תִּזְנֶה	Kal fut. 3 pers. sing. fem.; וַ id.	זנה
תַּזְנוּתֶ֫יהָ	noun fem. pl., suff. 3 p. s. f. fr. [תַּזְנוּת] d. 1 b	זנה
תַּזְנוּתַ֫יִךְ	id. pl., suff. 2 pers. sing. fem.	זנה
תַּזְנוּתֵ֫יִךְ		
תַּזְנוּתֵ֫ךְ	id. sing., suff. 2 pers. sing. fem. (read תַּזְנוּתֵךְ);	זנה
	K. תַּזְנוּתָ֫יִךְ (q. v.)	
תַּזְנוּתֵ֫ךְ	id. sing., suff. 2 pers. sing. fem.	זנה
תַּזְנוּתָ֫ם	id. sing., suff. 3 pers. pl. masc. (§ 4. rem. 2)	זנה
תִּזְנֶ֫ח	וַ Kal fut. 2 pers. sing. masc.; וְ conv.	זנח
תִּזְנִי	וְ Kal fut. 2 pers. sing. fem.; or (Je. 3. 6)	זנה
	3 pers. s. f. for תִּזְנֶה (§ 24. rem. 18); וְ id.	
תִּזְנִים	וַ id. fut. 2 pers. s. f., suff. 3 p. pl. m.; וְ id.	זנה
תִּזְנֶ֫ינָה	וַ id. fut. 3 pers. pl. fem.; וַ id.	זנה
תַּזְנוּתֵ֫ךְ	defect. for תַּזְנוּתַיִךְ (q. v.)	זנה
תַּזְנוּתֵ֫ךְ	defect. for תַּזְנוּתֵךְ (q. v.)	זנה
תִּזְעַק	sing. fem., or (Je. 30. 15)	זעק
תִּזְעָ֫ק	2 pers. sing. masc. (§ 8. r. 15); וַ conv.	
תִּזְרֶה	Kal fut. 2 pers. sing. masc.	זרה
תִּזְרַ֫ח	Kal fut. 3 pers. sing. fem.	זרח
תַּזְרִ֫יעַ	Hiph. fut. 3 pers. sing. fem.	זרע
תִּזְרֵם	Kal fut. 2 pers. sing. masc. (תִּזְרֶה), suff.	זרה
	3 pers. pl. masc. (§ 24. rem. 21)	
תִּזְרֵ֫נִי	וַ Piel fut. 2 pers. sing. masc., suff. 1 pers.	אזר
	sing. for תְּאַזְּרֵנִי (§ 19. rem. 10); וַ conv.	
תִּזָּרֵ֫עַ	Niph. fut. 3 pers. sing. fem.	זרע
תִּזְרַע		זרע
תִּזְרָ֫ע	Kal fut. 2 pers. sing. masc. (§ 8. rem. 15)	
תִּזְרְעוּ		זרע
תִּזְרָ֫עוּ	id. fut. 2 pers. pl. masc.	
תִּזְרָעֶ֫נּוּ	id. fut. 3 p. s. f., suff. 3 p. s. m. (§ 16. r. 12)	זרע

תִּזְרֹק	Kal fut. 2 pers. sing. masc.	זרק
תֵּחָבֵא	וְ Hiph. fut. 3 pers. sing. fem.; וְ conv.	חבא
תֵּחָבֵא	Niph. fut. 2 pers. sing. masc.	חבא
תַּחְבֹּ֫ט	וְ Kal fut. 2 pers. sing. masc., or 3 pers. sing.	חבט
	fem. (§ 13. rem. 5); וְ conv.	
תַּחְבֹּל	Kal fut. 2 pers. sing. masc. (§ 13. rem. 5)	חבל
תַּחְבֹּל		
תְּחַבֵּל	Piel fut. 3 pers. sing. fem.	חבל
תַּחְבֻּלֹות	noun fem., pl. of [תַּחְבּוּלָה] dec. 10	חבל
תַּחְבֹּק	וְ Piel fut. 2 pers. sing. masc.; וְ bef. (:)	חבק
תְּחַבְּקֶ֫נָּה	id. id., suff. 3 pers. sing. fem.	חבק
תְּחַבְּקֵ֫נִי	id. fut. 3 pers. sing. fem., suff. 1 pers. sing.	חבק
תַּחְבֹּ֫שׁ	וְ Kal fut. 3 pers. sing. fem.; וְ conv.	חבשׁ
תַּחֲנֹג	Kal fut. 2 pers. sing. masc.	חנג
תַּחְגְּרֵ֫הוּ	the foll. with suff. 3 pers. sing. masc.	חגר
תַּחְגֹּ֫רוּ	Kal fut. 2 pers. pl. masc. (§ 18. rem. 5)	חגר
תַּחְגֹּר	Kal fut. 2 pers. sing. masc. (§ 13. rem. 5)	חגר
תַּחְגְּרוּ	וְ id. fut. 2 pers. pl. masc. (§ 13. r. 6); וְ conv.	חגר
תַּחְגֹּ֫רְנָה	id. fut. 3 pers. pl. fem.	חגר
תֵּחַד	Kal fut. 2 pers. sing. masc., or 3 pers. s. fem.	יחד
תֶּחְדֵּ֫הוּ	Piel fut. 2 pers. sing. masc., suff. 3 pers. s. m.	חדה
תֶּחְדַּל	id. fut. 2 pers. sing. masc., or 3 pers.	חדל
תֶּחְדְּלִי	s. f. (§ 8. r. 15, & § 13. r. 5); וְ conv.	
תְּחַדֵּ֫שׁ	וְ Piel fut. 2 pers. sing. mas. וְ bef. (:)	חדשׁ
תְּחוּ	pr. name masc., see תּוּחַ	תוח
תְּחוֹלֵל	וְ, וַתְּ Pilel fut. 2 pers. sing. masc., or	חול
	3 pers. sing. fem.; וְ bef. (:); וַ conv.	
תְּחוֹלֶלְכֶ֫ם	id. fut. 3 pers. s. fem. with suff. 2 pers. pl. m.	חול
תָּחֹום	Kal fut. 3 pers. sing. fem. (§ 21.	חום
תָּחֹ֫וּס	rem. 3 & 7)	
תַּ֫חַת	Chald. prep., with suff. תְּחֹתֹ֫והִי	תחת
תֹּחֵז	וְ Kal fut. 3 p. s. f. for תֹּאחֵז (§19.r.5); וְ conv.	אחז
תַּ֫חַז	וְ Kal fut. 3 p. s. f., ap. for the foll. (§ 24. r. 3)	חזה
תֶּחֱזֶה	id. fut. 2 pers. sing. masc.	חזה
תֶּחֱז֫וּ	id. fut. 2 pers. pl. masc.	חזה
תֶּחֱזֶ֫ינָה	id. fut. 3 pers. pl. fem.	חזה
תַּחֲזֵק	וְ Hiph. fut. 3 pers. sing. fem. ap. [for	חזק
תַּחֲזֵ֫ק	וְ תַּחֲזִיק § 11. rem. 7]; וְ conv.	
תְּחַזֵּק	Piel fut. 2 pers. sing. masc.	חזק
תֶּחֱזַק	וְ Kal fut. 3 pers. sing. fem.; וְ conv.	חזק
תֶּחֱזְקוּ	id. fut. 2 pers. pl. masc.	חזק
תֶּחֱזַ֫קְנָה	id. fut. 3 pers. pl. fem.	חזק
תֶּחֱטָא	וְ defect. for תַּחֲטִיא q. v.; וְ conv.	חטא
תֶּחֱטָא	Kal fut. 3 pers. sing. fem.	חטא
תֶּחֱטָא	וְ id. fut. 2 pers. sing. masc.; וְ conv.	חטא

a Eze. 25. 10.   i Eze. 23, 29, 35.   q Eze. 16. 15, 16,   x Ps. 104. 22.   A De. 24. 20.   p Ex. 12. 14.   u Ps. 21. 7.   e Job 35. 14.   m 2 Ki. 4. 27.
b Ps. 79. 8.   k Eze. 16. 15.   17, 26, 28.   y Ps. 90. 2.   B Ru. 2. 12.   q Job 14. 7.   v Ps. 90. 2.   f 2 Ki. 4. 8.
c Ps. 8. 5.   l Eze. 16. 25.   r Eze. 16. 28.   z 2 Sa. 22. 40.   C De. 24. 17.   r Ps. 76. 11.   w De. 23. 23.   g Is. 51. 2.   o Job 4. 3.
d Job 14. 13.   m Eze. 16. 29.   s Ho. 4. 13, 14.   a De. 29. 22.   D Mi. 2. 10.   s De. 1. 41.   x Is. 13. 18.   h Ex. 12. 35.   p 2 Ki. 4. 3.
e De. 32. 2.   n Eze. 23. 8.   t Eze. 23. 3.   b Je. 4. 3.   E Pr. 5. 20.   t Ps. 65. 13.   y Job 10. 17.   i 2 Sa. 20. 9.   q 1 Sa. 19. 5;
f Je. 2. 36.   o Job 3. 17.   u Eze. 16. 22.   c Is. 17. 10.   F Pr. 4. 8.   t Ge. 49. 6;   z Ps. 104. 30.   k Mi. 4. 1.   Job 5. 24.
g Le. 25. 3, 4.   p Ho. 3. 3.   v Eze. 16. 26.   d 2 Ki. 6. 29.   Is. 14. 20.   G Pr. 25. 22.   l Ex. 18. 21.   r Eze. 28. 16
h 2 Ch. 21. 13.   w Eze. 5. 2.   e Job 5. 21.

תֶּחֱטָאוּ / תֶּחֱטָּאוּ }	id. fut. 2 pers. pl. masc. (§ 8. rem. 15)	חטא
תֶּחֱטָאֵנִי	Piel fut. 2 pers. sing. masc., suff. 1 pers. sing.	חטא
תַּחֲטִיא	Hiph. fut. 2 pers. sing. masc. .	חטא
תְּחִי	'י, וַתְּחִ Kal fut. 3 pers. sing. fem., ap. for תִּחְיֶה (§ 24. rem. 3 e); וּ bef. (ִ;); וַ conv.	חיה
תְּחַיֶּה	Piel fut. 2 pers. sing. masc., or (Ec. 7. 12) 3 pers. sing. fem.	חיה
תִּחְיֶה	Kal fut. 2 pers. sing. masc., or (Jos. 6. 17) 3 pers. sing. fem. (§ 13. rem. 13)	חיה
תִּחְיוּ	id. fut. 2 pers. pl. masc. . .	חיה
תְּחַיּוּן	Piel fut. 2 pers. pl. masc. with parag. ן	חיה
תִּחְיוּן	Kal fut. 2 p. pl. m. with parag. ן (§ 13. r. 13)	חיה
תִּחְיִי	id. fut. 2 pers. sing. fem. .	חיה
תְּחַיֶּינָה	Piel fut. 2 pers. pl. fem., or 3 pers. pl. fem. (§ 8. rem. 16); וַ conv. .	חיה
תִּחְיֶינָה	id. fut. 2 pers. pl. fem.	חיה
תִּחְיֶינָה	Kal fut. 3 pers. pl. fem. (§ 13. rem. 13)	חיה
תְּחַיֵּינוּ	Piel fut. 2 pers. sing. masc., suff. 1 pers. pl.	חיה
תְּחַיֵּנוּ	id. with suff. (Kh. וּ) 1 p. pl. (K. נִי) 1 p. s.	חיה
תָּחֵל	וְ Hiph. fut. 3 pers. sing. fem. .	חול
תָּחֵלִי	Kh. תָּחֵל, K. תָּחֵל Hiph. or Kal fut. 3 p. s. f.	חול
תָּחֵלוּ	Hiph. fut. 2 pers. pl. masc. .	חול
תָּחֵלִין	id. fut. 2 pers. s. f. with parag. ן (§ 8. r. 17)	חול
תְּחַנִּי	Piel fut. 2 pers. s. m., or (Job 33. 4) 3 pers. s. f. (תְּחַיֶּה) with suff. 1 p. s. (§ 24. r. 21)	חיה
תְּחַכֶּה	Piel fut. 2 pers. sing. masc. .	חכה
תַּחְכֶּם	Kal fut. 2 pers. sing. masc. (§ 13. rem. 5)	חכם
תַּחְכְּמֹנִי	pr. name masc. . . .	חכם
תְּחַכְּמֵנִי	Piel fut. 2 pers. s. m. [תְּחַכֶּם], suff. 1 pers. s.	חכם
תָּחֵל	Hiph. fut. 2 pers. sing. masc. .	חלל
תָּחֵל	וְ Hiph. fut. 3 pers. s. f., ap. fr. תָּחִיל; וַ conv.	חול
תָּחֵל	וְ Hiph. fut. 3 pers. sing. fem., acc. drawn back by conv. וַ for תָּחֵל	חלל
תָּחֶל	וְ Kal fut. 3 pers. s. f. ap. [fr. תָּחֹל]; וַ conv.	חול
תֵּחֵל	Niph. fut. 3 pers. s. f. [for תֵּחֵל § 18. r. 7]	חלל
תַּחְלְאֶיהָ	the foll. with suff. 3 pers. sing. fem.	חלא
תַּחֲלֻאִים	noun masc., pl. of [תַּחֲלוּא] dec. 1 b	חלא
תִּחְלוּ	Kal fut. 2 pers. pl. masc. .	חלל
תַּחֲלוּאֵי	noun masc. pl. constr. from [תַּחֲלוּא] d. 1 b	חלא
תַּחֲלֻאָיְכִי	id. pl., suff. 2 pers. sing. fem. (§ 4. rem. 4)	חלא
תַּחֲלִימֵנִי	וְ Hiph. fut. 2 pers. sing. m., suff. 1 pers. s.	חלם
תְּחַלֶּינָה	וְ Hiph. fut. 3 pers. pl. fem.; וַ conv. .	חלל
תַּחֲלִיף	Hiph. fut. 3 pers. sing. fem. .	חלף
תַּחֲלִיפָם	id. fut. 2 pers. sing. masc., suff. 3 pers. pl. m.	חלף
תְּחַלֵּל	Piel fut. 2 pers. sing. masc.	חלל
תְּחַלְּלֶהָ	וְ id. id., suff. 3 pers. s. f. (§ 10. r. 7); וַ conv.	חלל
תְּחַלֶּלְנָה	וְ id. fut. 2 pers. pl. fem.; וַ id.	חלל
תְּחַלְּלוּ	וְ id. fut. 2 pers. pl. masc.; וַ id. .	חלל
תְּחַלְּלֶנּוּ	id. fut. 2 pers. sing. masc., suff. 3 pers. s. m.	חלל
תַּחֲלֵף	וְ Hiph. fut. 2 pers. sing. masc. ap. [from תַּחֲלִיף]; וַ conv.	חלף
תַּחְלְפֵהוּ	Kal fut. 3 pers. sing. fem. [תַּחֲלֹף], suff. 3 pers. sing. masc. (§ 13. rem. 5)	חלף
תַּחֲלֹץ	Kal fut. 2 pers. sing. masc. .	חלץ
תֵּחָלְצוּ	Niph. fut. 2 pers. pl. masc. .	חלץ
תֵּחָלֵק	Niph. fut. 3 pers. sing. fem.	חלק
תְּחַלֵּק	Piel fut. 2 pers. sing. masc. .	חלק
תְּחֻלַּק	Pual fut. 3 pers. sing. fem. .	חלק
תַּחְלְקוּ	Kal fut. 2 pers. pl. masc. (§ 13. rem. 5 & 6)	חלק
תַּחְלְקֵם	וְ id. fut. 2 p. s. m., suff. 3 p. pl. m.; וַ conv.	חלק
תֶּחְלַת	noun fem. sing., constr. of תְּחִלָּה dec. 10	חלל
תֵּחַם	Kal fut. 3 pers. sing. fem. (§ 18. rem. 6)	חמם
תַּחְמֹד	Kal fut. 2 pers. sing. masc. (§ 13. rem. 5)	חמד
תַּחְמֹל	וְ Kal fut. 2 pers. sing. masc., or (Ex. 2. 6) 3 pers. sing. fem. (§ 13. rem. 5); וַ conv.	חמל
תַּחְמְלוּ / תַּחְמֹלוּ }	id. fut. 2 pers. pl. masc. (§ 8. rem. 15)	חמל
תְּחַמֵּם	Piel fut. 3 pers. sing. fem. .	חמם
תַּחְמֹסוּ	Kal fut. 2 pers. pl. m. [for תַּחְמְסוּ § 8. rem. 15, & § 13. rem. 5] . .	חמס
תַּחְמְרָה	וְ Kal fut. 3 pers. sing. fem. with parag. ה (§ 8. rem. 13, & § 13. rem. 5); וַ conv.	חמר
תָּחֹן	Kal fut. 2 pers. sing. masc. .	חנן
תַּחֲנֶה	Kal fut. 3 pers. sing. fem. .	חנה
תַּחֲנָה	noun fem. sing. dec. 10, pr. name	חנה
תַּחֲנוּ	Kal fut. 2 pers. pl. masc. .	חנה
תַּחֲנוּנֹתַי	noun masc. with pl. fem. term. & suff. 1 pers. sing. from [תַּחֲנוּן] dec. 1 b	חנן
תַּחֲנוּנַי / תַּחֲנוּנָי }	id. pl. masc. with suff. 1 pers. sing.	חנן
תַּחֲנוּנֵי	id. pl. masc., constr. st. . .	חנן
תַּחֲנוּנָיו	id. pl. masc. with suff. 3 pers. sing. masc.	חנן
תַּחֲנוּנֶיךָ	id. pl. masc. with suff. 2 pers. sing. masc.	חנן
תַּחֲנוּנִים	וְ id. pl. masc., abs. st. .	חנן
תַּחֲנוּנֵנוּ	id. pl. masc. with suff. 1 pers. pl.	חנן
תַּחֲנִפוּ	Hiph. fut. 2 pers. pl. masc. .	חנף
תַּחֲנִיפִי	וְ id. fut. 2 pers. sing. fem.; וַ conv.	חנף

a Ps. 51. 9.   d Eze. 13. 19.   o 2 Ki. 9. 3.   u Le. 21. 9.   a Is. 38. 16.   i Je. 34. 16.   p Nu. 26. 53, 56.   s Ex. 2. 6.   d Ex. 14. 2.
b De. 24. 4.   i Ps. 71. 20.   p Pr. 19. 20.   v De. 29. 21.   a Ge. 41. 54.   k De. 28. 30.   y Ps. 68. 13.   y Eze. 9. 5.   e Da. 9. 17.
c Ge. 45. 27.   k Zec. 9. 5.   q Ps. 119. 98.   y Eze. 9. 6.   b Ex. 31. 41.   l Am. 7. 17.   z Job 39. 14.   z Ex. 2. 3.   f Da. 9. 23.
d Ex. 1. 22.   l Eze. 30. 16.   r De. 16. 9.   x Je. 14. 18.   c Ex. 20. 25.   h Is. 20. 2.   a 2 Sa. 19. 30.   c Ps. 59. 6.   g Da. 9. 18.
2 Ki. 4. 7.   m Je. 5. 22.   s Ps. 97. 4.   y Ps. 103. 3.   Ex. 20. 25.   i Ne. 9. 22.   h Nu. 33. 38.
f Ex. 1. 17, 18.   n Is. 45. 10.   t Je. 51. 29.   k Eze. 13. 19   Nu. 32. 20   Ex. 24. 1.   b Ps. 27. 3.   i Je. 3. 2.
g Eze. 13. 18.   nn Ps. 86. 6.

תְּחֻנֵּם Kal fut. 2 pers. sing. masc. (תְּחֹן), suff. 3 pers. pl. masc. (§ 18. rem. 5) . חנן

תְּחַנֵּף } Kal fut. 3 pers. sing. fem. (§ 8. rem. 15); חנף
תַּחֲנֵף } וַ conv.

תִּחְנַּת noun fem. sing., constr. of תְּחִנָּה dec. 10 . חנן

תְּחִנָּתוֹ id. with suff. 3 pers. sing. masc. . חנן

תְּחִנֹּתַי noun fem. pl., suff. 1 pers. sing. [fr. תַּחֲנָה; for תְּחִנֹּתַי § 4. rem. 2] חנה

תְּחִנָּתִי noun fem. sing., suff. 1 p. s. fr. תְּחִנָּה d. 10 . חנן

תְּחִנָּתֵיהֶם id. pl., suff. 3 pers. pl. masc. . חנן

תְּחִנָּתְךָ id. sing., suff. 2 pers. sing. masc. . חנן

תְּחִנַּתְכֶם id. sing., suff. 2 pers. pl. masc. . חנן

תְּחִנָּתָם id. sing., suff. 3 pers. pl. masc. . חנן

תְּחִנָּתֵנוּ id. sing., suff. 1 pers. pl. . חנן

תָּחֹס / **תָּחָס** } Kal fut. 3 pers. s. f., ap. & conv. fr. תָּחוּס } the acc. drawn back by conv. וַ } חוס

תְּחַסֶּה Kal fut. 2 pers. sing. masc. (§ 13. rem. 5) חסה

תְּחַסֵּם Kal fut. 2 pers. sing. masc. (§ 13. rem. 5) חסם

תַּחְסֵר / **תֶחְסָר** } Kal fut. 3 pers. sing. fem. (§ 8. rem. 5), 1 Ki.17.14; Pr.13.25; or 2 p.m.De.8.9 } חסר

וַתְּחַסְּרֵהוּ } Piel fut. 2 pers. sing. masc. [תְּחַסֵּר], suff. 3 pers. sing. masc.; וַ conv. חסר

תַּחְפְּזוּ Kal fut. 2 pers. pl. masc. (§ 13. rem. 5 & 6) חפז

תַּחְפְּרִי Kal fut. 2 pers. sing. fem. (§ 13. rem. 5) חפר

תַּחְפְּנֵחֵס, **תַּחְפַּנְחֵס**, **תַּחְפְּנֵס** pr. name of a city in Egypt, *Daphne*, near Pelusium.

תַּחְפְּנֵיס pr. name of an Egyptian queen, 1 Ki.11.19, 20.

תַּחְפֹּץ Kal fut. 2 pers. sing. masc. (§ 13. rem. 5) חפץ

וַתַּחְפְּרוּ } Kal fut. 2 pers. pl. masc. (§ 13. rem. 5 & 6) חפר

תַּחְפְּשֶׂנָּה } Kal fut. 2 pers. sing. fem., suff. 3 pers. sing. fem. (§ 13. rem. 5) חפש

תַּחֲצֵץ } Niph. fut. 3 pers. sing. fem., ap. [fr. תֶּחָצֶה] חצה

תַּחְצֹב Kal fut. 2 pers. sing. masc. (§ 13. rem. 5) חצב

תַּחְקְרוּן } Kal fut. 2 pers. pl. masc., } parag. (§ 13. rem. 5 & 6, & § 8. rem. 17) חקר

תַּחְרָא noun masc. sing. . חרה

תֶּחֱרַב / **תֶּחְרַב** } Kal fut. 3 pers. sing. fem. (§ 8. rem. 15) חרב

תֶּחֱרַבְנָה id. fut. 3 pers. pl. fem. . חרב

תַּחֲרִים Hiph. fut. 2 pers. sing. masc. . חרם

תַּחֲרִימוּ id. fut. 2 pers. pl. masc. . חרם

תַּחֲרִימֵם id. fut. 2 pers. s. masc., suff. 3 pers. pl. masc. . חרם

תַּחֲרִישׁ Hiph. fut. 2 pers. sing. masc. . חרש

תַּחֲרִישׁוּן id. fut. 2 pers. pl. masc. with parag. } חרש

תַּחֲרִישִׁי id. fut. 2 pers. sing. fem. . חרש

תִּחְרַע } וַ pr. name masc., see תֶּאָרַע.

תֶּחֱרַף Kal fut. 3 pers. sing. fem. [for תֶּחְרַף § 8. r. 15] חרף

תֶּחֱרַץ Kal fut. 2 pers. s. masc. [for תֶּחְרַץ § 8. r. 15] חרץ

תַּחֲרִישׁ Hiph. fut. 2 pers. sing. masc. ap. [fr. תַּחֲרִישׁ] חרש

תַּחֲרֵשׁ Kal fut. 2 pers. sing. masc. . חרש

תֵּחָרֵשׁ Niph. fut. 3 pers. sing. fem. . חרש

תַּחֲרֵשׁ / **תַּחֲרִישׁ** } Kal fut. 2 pers. sing. masc. (§ 8. rem. 15) חרש

תַּחֲרִשׁוּן defect. for תַּחֲרִישׁוּן (q. v.) . חרש

תֶּחֱרַשְׁנָה Kal fut. 3 pers. pl. fem. . חרש

תַּחַשׁ , תָּחָשׁ masc. dec. 6 d.—I. *badger;* עוֹרֹת תְּחָשִׁים *badgers' skins.*—II. pr. name masc. Ge. 22. 24.

וַתָּחָשׁ Kal fut. 3 pers. sing. fem., dag. forte impl. [for תָּחֻשׁ § 21. rem. 24] . חוש

תֵּחָשֵׁב / **וַ** } Niph. fut. 3 pers. sing. fem. (§ 9. rem. 3) חשב

תַּחְשֹׁב Kal fut. 3 pers. sing. fem. (§ 13. rem. 5 & 6) חשב

תַּחְשְׁבוּ / **תַּחְשְׁבוּ** } id. fut. 2 pers. pl. masc. (v. 1. & § 8. rem. 15) חשב

וַתְּחַשְּׁבֶהָ } Piel fut. 2 p. s. m., suff. 3 p. s. m.; וַ conv. חשב

תְּחַשְּׁבוּן id. fut. 2 p. pl. m. with parag. } (§ 10. r. 4) חשב

וַתְּחַשְּׁבֵנִי } Kal fut. 2 pers. sing. masc., suff. 1 pers. sing. (§ 13. rem. 5 & 6); וַ conv. חשב

תַּחְשְׁבֵנִי id. fut. 2 pers. pl. masc., suff. 1 pers. sing. חשב

תַּחְשֶׂה Kal fut. 2 pers. sing. masc. . חשה

תַּחְשׂוֹךְ Kal fut. 2 pers. s. masc. (§ 8. r.18, & § 13. r. 5) חשך

תַּחְשִׁים noun masc., pl. of תַּחַשׁ dec. 6d תחש

תַּחְשֹׁךְ Kal fut. 2 pers. sing. masc. (§ 13. rem. 5) חשך

וַתַּחְשֵׁךְ Kal fut. 3 pers. sing. f. (§ 13. r. 5); וַ conv. חשך

תַּחְשְׂכִי Kal fut. 2 p. s. f. (§ 8. r. 15, comp. § 13. r. 6) חשך

תַּחְשַׁכְנָה Kal fut. 3 pers. sing. fem. (§ 13. rem. 5) חשך

תַּחַת / **וַ** } adv. & prep., also pr. name . תוח

תֵּחֹת } Chald. Aph. fut. 2 pers. s. m. (§ 51. r. 1) נחת

תַּחַת / **תֵּחַת** } Kal fut. 2 pers. sing. masc., or (Is. 51. 6) 3 pers. sing. fem. (§ 18. rem. 6) חתת

תַּחַת Kal fut. 3 pers. sing. fem. (for תִּנְחַת) נחת

תַּחְתּוּ Kh. for תַּחְתָּיו Keri (q. v.) תוח

תֵּחַתּוּ / **תֵּחַתּוּ** } Kal fut. 2 pers. pl. masc. (§ 18. rem. 6) חתת

תַּחְתּוֹהִי Ch. prep. (תְּחוֹת) pl. with suff. 3 pers. s. m. תוח

תְּחוֹתֵיהִי Ch. prep. (תְּחוֹת) pl. with suff. 3 pers. s. m. תוח

תַּחְתּוֹן adj. masc. sing. . תוח

תַּחְתַּי / **וַ** } adv. or prep. (תַּחַת) pl. with suff. 1 pers. sing. תוח

a De. 7.2.   g Je. 42.9.   m De. 20.3.   r Job 32.11.   v Job 13.5.   x Mi. 7.16.   Job 6.26.   Is. 58.1.   Ezr. 6.5.
b Mi. 4.11.   h Je. 42.2.   n Is. 54.4.   s Est. 4.11.   w Nu. 4.6.14.   y Ps. 144.3.   Ec. 12.2.   Pr. 17.10.
c Je. 3.1.   i Ge. 45.20.   o Is. 1.29.   t Is. 18.6.   Job 31.5.   z Na. 1.9.   Da. 4.11.
d 2 Ki. 6.8.   k Ps. 91.4.   p Je. 26.9.   u Pr. 2.4.   2 Sa. 5.24.   Pr. 27.14.   Job 13.24.   Is. 54.2.   Ex. 10.15.   Da. 4.11.
e 2 Ch. 6.39.   l De. 25.4.   De. 7.2.   Da. 11.4.   1 Sa. 7.8.   Ps. 106.31.   Job 19.15.   Ps. 69.24.   Jos. 18.13.
f 1 Ki. 9.3.   Ps. 8.6.   De. 8.9.   Hab. 1.13.   Ex. 14.14.   Ps. 52.4.   Pr. 24.11.   Ge.49.25; De.33.13.   Hab.3.16,etc.

תַּחְתִּיָּה‎	‪*‬‫ו‬' id. with suff. 3 pers. sing. fem.	תוח
תַּחְתִּיָה‎	adj. fem. sing. [from תַּחְתִּי‎ masc.]	תוח
תַּחְתִּיֶהֶם‎	prep. (תַּחַת‎) pl. with suff. 3 pers. pl. masc.	תוח
תַּחְתִּיֶהֶן‎	id. with suff. 3 pers. pl. fem.	תוח
תַּחְתָּיו‎	id. (adv. & prep.), suff. 3 pers. sing. masc.	תוח
תַּחְתִּיּוֹת‎	adj. fem., pl. of תַּחְתִּיָה‎ [from תַּחְתִּי‎ masc.]	תוח
תַּחְתֶּיךָ‎	prep. (תַּחַת‎) pl. with suff. 2 pers. sing. m.	תוח
תַּחְתֵּיכֶם‎	id. with suff. 2 pers. pl. masc.	תוח

תַּחְתִּים חׇדְשִׁי‎ pr. name of an unknown region, mentioned only in 2 Sa. 24. 6.

תַּחְתִּים‎‪*‬	adj. masc. pl. [of תַּחְתִּי‎] dec. 8f	תוח
תַּחְתֵּינוּ‎‪*‬	adv. (תַּחַת‎), pl. with suff. 1 pers. pl	תוח
תַּחְתִּית‎	adj. fem. sing. [from תַּחְתִּי‎ masc.]	תוח
תַּחְתָּם‎	adv. or prep. (תַּחַת‎) with suff. 3 pers. pl. m.	תוח
תַּחְתֹּם‎‪*‬	‫ו‬ Kal fut. 3 pers. s. fem. (§ 13. r. 5); ‫ו‬' conv.	חתם
תַּחְתֶּנָּה‎‪*‬	(prep. תַּחַת‎) with suff. 3 pers. sing. fem.	תוח
תַּחְתֵּנִי‎‪*‬	id. with suff. 1 pers. sing.	תוח
תֵּט‎	Hiph. fut. 2 pers. sing. masc., ap. from תַּטֶּה‎ (§ 25. No. 2b)	נטה
תֵּט‎	‫ו‬' Kal fut. 2 pers. sing. masc., or 3 pers. sing. fem., ap. from תִּטֶּה‎ (§ 25. No. 2b); ‫ו‬' conv	נטה
תִּטְבְּלֵנִי‎‪*‬	Kal fut. 2 pers. sing. m. (תִּטְבֹּל‎), suff. 1 pers. s.	טבל
תִּטְבַּע‎‪*‬	‫ו‬ Kal fut. 3 pers. sing. fem.; ‫ו‬' conv.	טבע
תַּטֶּה‎	Hiph. fut. 2 pers. sing. masc. (§ 25. No. 2b)	נטה
תִּטֶּה‎‪*‬	Kal fut. 3 pers. sing. fem. (§ 25. No. 2b)	נטה
תַּטֵּהוּ‎‪*‬	‫ו‬ Hiph. fut. 3 pers. sing. fem., suff. 3 pers. sing. masc. (§ 24. r. 21, & § 25. No. 2b); ‫ו‬' conv.	נטה
תִּטְהָר‎‪*‬	Kal fut. 3 pers. sing. m. [for תִּטְהַר‎ § 8. r. 15]	טהר
תִּטְהָרוּ‎‪*‬	id. fut. 2 pers. pl. masc. [for תִּטְהֲרוּ‎]	טהר
תִּטְהָרִי‎	id. fut. 2 pers. sing. fem.	טהר
תְּטַהֲרֵם‎‪*‬	‫ו‬ Piel (§ 14. rem. 1) fut. 3 pers. sing. fem., suff. 3 pers. pl. masc.; ‫ו‬' conv.	טהר
תִּטְחַן‎‪*‬	Kal fut. 3 pers. sing. fem.	טחן
תִּטְחָנוּ‎‪*‬	id. fut. 2 pers. pl. masc. [for תִּטְחֲנוּ‎ § 8. r. 15]	טחן
תֵּטִיב‎‪*‬	Hiph. fut. 2 pers. s. m. (better תֵּיטִיב‎ q.v.)	יטב
תַּטִּיפִי‎‪*‬	Hiph. fut. 2 pers. sing. masc.	נטף
תַּטִּיפוּ‎‪*‬	id. fut. 2 pers. sing. masc.	נטף
תִּטַּל‎‪*‬	Chald. Aph. fut. 3 pers. sing. fem.	טלל
תְּטַמֵּא‎	Piel fut. 2 pers. sing. masc.	טמא
תִּטְמָא‎‪*‬	‫ו‬' Kal fut. 3 pers. sing. fem.; ‫ו‬' conv.	טמא
תְּטַמְּאוּ‎‪*‬	‫ו‬' Piel fut. 2 pers. pl. masc.; ‫ו‬' id.	טמא
תִּטַּמְּאוּ‎ תִּטַּמָּאוּ‎	} Hithpa. fut. 2 pers. pl. m. [for תִּתְטַמְּאוּ‎ § 12. rem. 2, comp. § 8. rem. 15]	טמא
תִּטְמְנֵם‎‪*‬	‫ו‬ Kal fut. 3 pers. sing. fem. [תִּטְמֹן‎], suff. 3 pers. pl. masc.; ‫ו‬' conv.	טמן
תִּטַּע‎	Kal fut. 2 pers. sing. masc.	נטע

תִּטָּעֶהָ‎‪*‬	‫ו‬ the foll. with suff. 3 pers. sing. fem. (§ 16. rem. 12); ‫ו‬' conv.	נטע
תִּטְּעוּ‎‪*‬	id. fut. 2 pers. pl. masc. [for תִּטָּעוּ‎ § 8. r. 15]	נטע
תִּטְּעִי‎	id. fut. 2 pers. sing. fem.	נטע
תִּטָּעֵם‎‪*‬	‫ו‬ id. fut. 2 pers. sing. masc., suff. 3 pers. pl. masc. (§ 16. rem. 12); ‫ו‬' conv.	נטע
תִּטָּעֵמוֹ‎‪*‬	‫ו‬ id. id., suff. 3 pers. pl. masc.	נטע
תִּטֹּף‎‪*‬	Kal fut. 3 pers. sing. fem.	נטף
תִּטְפֹּל‎‪*‬	‫ו‬ Kal fut. 2 pers. sing. masc.; ‫ו‬' conv.	טפל
תִּטֹּפְנָה‎	Kal fut. 3 pers. pl. fem.	נטף
תִּטֹּר‎‪*‬	Kal fut. 2 pers. sing. masc. (§ 17. rem. 3)	נטר
תִּטֹּשׁ‎‪*‬	‫ו‬' Kal fut. 2 pers. sing. masc., or (1 Sa. 4. 2) 3 pers. sing. fem.; ‫ו‬' conv.	נטש
תִּטְּשֵׁנִי‎‪*‬	id. fut. 2 pers. sing. masc., suff. 1 pers. sing.	נטש
תְּיַבֵּב‎‪*‬	‫ו‬ Piel fut. 3 pers. sing. fem.; ‫ו‬' conv.	יבב
תְּיַבֵּשׁ‎‪*‬ תְּיַבֶּשׁ־‎	} Piel fut. 3 pers. sing. fem. (§ 10. rem. 4)	יבש
תִּיבַשׁ‎ תִּיבָשׁ‎ ‫ו‬'	} Kal fut. 3 pers. sing. fem. (§ 8. rem. 16); ‫ו‬' conv.	יבש
תְּיַגַּע‎‪*‬	Piel fut. 3 pers. sing. masc.	יגע
תִּיגַע‎‪*‬	Kal fut. 2 pers. sing. masc.	יגע
תְּיַגְּעֶנּוּ‎‪*‬	Piel fut. 3 pers. s. fem. (תְּיַגֵּעַ‎), suff. 3 p. s. m.	יגע

תִּין‎‪*‬. Hiph. to cut off, Is. 18. 5.

תִּיטַב‎‪*‬	‫ו‬', וַתִּ‎ Kal fut. 3 pers. sing. fem.; ‫ו‬' conv.	יטב
תֵּיטֵב‎‪*‬	‫ו‬ Hiph. fut. 3 pers. sing. fem., ap. and conv. from תֵּיטִיב‎	יטב
תֵּיטְבִי‎	id. fut. 2 pers. sing. masc.	יטב
תֵּיטִיב‎‪*‬	id. fut. 2 p. s. m., or 3 p. s. f. (see also תֵּטִיב‎)	יטב
תֵּיטִיבוּ‎	id. fut. 2 pers. pl. masc.	יטב
תְּיֵלִילוּ‎‪*‬	Hiph. fut. 2 p. pl. m. [for תְּהֵילִילוּ‎ § 20. r. 15]	ילל
תֵּימָא‎	‫ו‬' pr. name of a son of Ishmael, Ge. 25. 15, and of his posterity called *Tema* after him.	
תֵּימָן‎	noun masc. sing., also pr. name	ימן
תֵּימָנָה‎	‫ו‬' id. with loc. ‫ה‬	ימן
תֵּימָנִי‎	patronym., see תֵּימָן‎	ימן
תֵּינַק‎‪*‬	‫ו‬ Hiph. fut. 3 pers. sing. fem.	ינק
תֵּינֵק‎‪*‬	‫ו‬ id. ap. and conv.	ינק
תֵּינְקוּ‎‪*‬	Kal fut. 2 pers. pl. masc.	ינק
תֵּינְקִי‎‪*‬	id. fut. 2 pers. sing. fem. [for תִּינַקִי‎ § 8. r. 15]	ינק
תְּיַסְּרֶךָּ‎‪*‬	Piel fut. 3 pers. sing. fem. [תְּיַסֵּר‎], suff. 2 pers. sing. fem.	יסר
תְּיַסְּרֶנּוּ‎‪*‬	id. fut. 3 pers. sing. m., suff. 3 pers. sing. m.	יסר
תְּיַסְּרֵנִי‎‪*‬	id. id., suff. 1 pers. sing.	יסר
תֵּיעָשֶׂה‎‪*‬	Niph. fut. 3 pers. s. fem. (for תֵּעָשֶׂה‎ § 13. r. 8)	עשה
תִּיפִי‎‪*‬	‫ו‬ Kal fut. 2 p. s. fem. (§ 25. No. 2e); ‫ו‬' conv.	יפה

‪a‬ Job 28. 5.   ‪b‬ Job 9. 31.   ‪c‬ Job 37. 21.   ‪d‬ Da. 4. 9.   ‪e‬ Ps. 44. 3.   Ps. 27. 9.   ‪f‬ Pr. 23. 4.   ‪u‬ Ps. 49. 19;   ‪l‬ Is. 66. 11.
‪‬ Ps. 86. 13.   ‪f‬ 1 Sa. 17. 49.   ‪‬ Job 31. 10.   ‪d‬ Le. 11. 44.   ‪‬ Ju. 5. 28.   ‪g‬ Ec. 10. 15.   Pr. 15. 2.   ‪c‬ Is. 60. 16.
‪‬ Je. 28. 13.   ‪i‬ Job 31. 7.   ‪‬ Is. 3. 15.   ‪‬ Je. 2. 7.   ‪‬ Job 29. 22.   ‪‬ Est. 2. 4, 9;   ‪‬ Is. 65. 14.   ‪d‬ Je. 2. 19.
‪‬ Ge. 6. 16.   ‪k‬ 2 Sa. 21. 10.   ‪‬ Ge. 4. 7.   ‪‬ Jos. 2. 6.   ‪f‬ Job 14. 17.   ‪‬ Pr. 17. 22.   ‪y‬ De. 3. 27.   ‪‬ Ps. 94. 12.
‪‬ 1Sa.14.9;Ps.47.4.   ‪m‬ Le. 15. 28.   ‪‬ Am. 7. 16.   ‪‬ Ps. 80. 9.   ‪‬ Le. 19. 18.   ‪k‬ 1 Ki. 13. 4.   ‪z‬ 2 Ki. 9. 30.   ‪‬ Ex. 2. 7.   ‪f‬ Ex. 25. 31.
   ‪n‬ Le. 16. 30.   ‪i‬ Mi. 2. 6.   ‪‬ Je. 55. 7.   ‪h‬ 1 Sa. 4. 2.   ‪‬ Jos. 7. 3.   ‪‬ Je. 2. 33.   ‪‬ 1 Sa. 1. 23.   ‪g‬ Eze. 16. 13.

Hebrew	Description	Root
[תִּיצִי]	gent. noun 1 Ch. 11. 45, from a place תִּיץ otherwise unknown.	
תִּיקַד	וְ Kal fut. 3 pers. sing. fem.; וַ conv.	יקד
תִּיקַר	Kal fut. 3 pers. sing. fem.	יקר
תִּירָא	וְ Kal fut. 2 pers. sing. masc., or (Zec. 9. 5) 3 pers. sing. fem.	ירא
תִּירְאוּ	וַ Kal fut. 2 pers. pl. masc. (§ 8. rem. 15);	ירא
תִּירְאוּ	וְ conv.	ירא
תִּירָאוּם	id. id., with suff. 3 p. pl. m. (comp. § 16. r. 12)	ירא
תִּירָאוּן	id. id. with parag. ן.	ירא
תִּירְאִי	id. fut. 2 pers. sing. fem.; וַ conv.	ירא
תִּירְאִי		
תִּירֶאם	defect. for תִּירָאוּם (q. v.)	ירא
תִּירְאָן	וַ Kal fut. 3 pers. pl. fem. (§ 8. r. 16); וַ conv.	ירא
תִּירוֹשׁ	וְ noun masc. sing. dec. 1 b	ירש
תִּירוֹשִׁי	וְ id., suff. 1 pers. sing.	ירש
תִּירוֹשֶׁךָ	id., suff. 2 pers. sing. fem.	ירש
תִּירוֹשָׁם	וְ id., suff. 3 pers. pl. masc.	ירש
תִּירְיָא	pr. name masc.	ירא
תִּירָם	וְ pr. name of a son of Japhet, Ge. 10. 2; 1 Ch. 1. 5.	
תִּירַשׁ	Kal fut. 2 pers. sing. masc. (§ 8. rem. 15)	ירש
תִּירַשׁ	id. fut. 3 pers. sing. fem.	ירש
תִּירֹשׁ	וְ defect. for תִּירוֹשׁ (q. v.)	ירש
תִּירְשׁוּ	Kal fut. 2 pers. pl. masc. (§ 8. rem. 15);	ירש
תִּירְשׁוּ	וַ conv.	ירש
תִּירָשׁוּן	id. id. with parag. ן [for תִּירְשׁוּן § 8. rem. 17]	ירש
תִּירָשְׁךָ	וְ noun masc. sing., suff. 2 pers. sing. fem. from תִּירוֹשׁ dec. 1 b	ירש
תִּירָשֶׁנּוּ	Kal fut. 2 pers. sing. masc. (תִּירַשׁ), suff. 3 pers. sing. masc. (§ 16. rem. 12)	ירש
תַּיִשׁ	[for תַּיִשׁ] masc., pl. תְּיָשִׁים (§ 35. rem. 12) a he-goat or ram.	
תִּשְׁבְּנָה	Kh. תִּישְׁבְּנָה, K. תְּשֻׁבְנָה Kal fut. 3 pers. pl. fem. R. יָשַׁב or	שוב
תְּיָשִׁים	וּ noun masc., pl. of תַּיִשׁ dec. 6 h, וּ bef.	תיש
תִּישַׁמְנָה	Kal fut. 3 pers. pl. fem. [for תִּשַׁמְנָה]	ישם
תִּישַׁן	Kal fut. 2 pers. sing. masc.	ישן
תִּישְׁנֶהוּ	וְ Piel fut. 3 pers. sing. fem. [תְּיַשֵּׁן], suff. 3 pers. sing. masc.; וַ conv.	ישן
תִּישַׁר	Piel fut. 2 pers. sing. masc.	ישר
תִּישַׁר	וְ Kal fut. 3 pers. sing. fem.; וַ conv.	ישר
תַּךְ	וְ Hiph. fut. 3 pers. sing. fem., ap. from תָּכָּה (§ 25. No. 2 b); וְ id.	נכה

Hebrew	Description	Root
תָּךְ	noun masc. sing.; for וְ see lett. וְ	תכך
תָּכְאָבוּ	Hiph. fut. 2 pers. pl. masc.	כאב
תְּכַבֵּד	וְ Piel fut. 2 pers. sing. masc.; וַ conv.	כבד
תִּכְבַּד	וַ Kal fut. 3 pers. sing. fem.; וַ id.	כבד
תְּכַבְּדוּ	Piel fut. 2 pers. pl. masc.	כבד
תְּכַבְּדִי	וְ Kal fut. 2 pers. sing. fem.; וַ conv.	כבד
תְּכַבֶּדְךָ	id. fut. 3 pers. sing. fem., suff. 2 pers. s. m.	כבד
תְּכַבְּדֵנִי	id. fut. 2 pers. sing. masc., or (Is. 43. 20) 3 pers. s. f., suff. 1 pers. s.; וְ, for וַ, conv.	כבד
תְּכַבֶּה	Piel fut. 2 pers. sing. masc.	כבה
תִּכְבֶּה	Kal fut. 2 pers. sing. masc.	כבה
תְּכַבֵּס	Piel fut. 2 pers. sing. masc.	כבס
תְּכַבְּסִי	id. fut. 2 pers. sing. fem.	כבס
תְּכַבְּסֵנִי	id. fut. 2 pers. sing. masc., suff. 1 pers. sing.	כבס
תִּכְבְּשׁוּ	וַ Kal fut. 2 pers. pl. masc.; וְ conv.	כבש
תָּכָה	Kal not used; Arab. תכא to lean upon. Pu. to be laid down, De. 33. 3.	
תְּכַהֶּה	Piel fut. 2 pers. sing. masc. (§ 25. No. 2 b)	נכה
תֵּכַהּ	וְ ap. & conv. from the foll. (§ 24. rem. 3)	כהה
תִּכְהֶה	Kal fut. 3 pers. sing. fem.	כהה
תִּכְהֶיןָ	וְ id. fut. 3 pers. pl. fem. (§ 8. r. 16); וַ conv.	כהה
תֻּכּוּ	Pual pret. 3 pers. pl.	תכה
תֻּכֶּה	Hoph. fut. 2 pers. pl. masc. (§ 25. No. 2 b)	נכה
תִּכּוֹנֶה	Niph. fut. 2 pers. sing. masc.	כוה
תִּכּוֹנֶינָה	id. fut. 3 pers. pl. fem.	כוה
תִּכּוֹן	וַ Niph. fut. 2 pers. sing. masc. (1 Sa. 20. 31), or 3 pers. sing. fem.; וַ conv.	כון
תְּכוֹנֵן	וַ, וַתְּ Pilel fut. 2 p. s. m.; וְ for וַ; וְ id.	כון
תִּכּוֹנֵן	וְ Hithpal fut. 3 pers. sing. fem. [for תִּתְכּוֹנֵן § 12. rem. 3]	כון
תְּכוֹנְנִי	id. fut. 2 pers. s. f. [for תְּכוֹנְנִי § 21. r. 21]	כון
תְּכוּנָתוֹ	noun 'em. sing., suff. 3 pers. sing. masc. from [תְּכוּנָה] dec. 10	כון
תְּכוּנָתוֹ	וּ noun fem. sing., suff. 3 pers. sing. masc. from תְּכוּנָה dec. 10; וּ bef.	תכן
תְּכַזֵּב	וְ Piel fut. 2 pers. sing. masc.	כזב
תְּכַזְּבִי	id. fut. 2 p. s. f. [for תְּכַזְּבִי comp. § 8. r. 15]	כזב
תְּכַחֵד	Piel (§ 14. rem. 1) fut. 2 pers. sing. masc.	כחד
תִּכָּחֵד	וְ Niph. fut. 2 pers. sing. masc., or (Zec. 11. 9) 3 pers. sing. fem.; וַ conv.	כחד
תְּכַחֲדוּ	Piel (§ 14. rem. 1) fut. 2 pers. pl. masc. [for תְּכַחֵדוּ comp. § 8. rem. 15]	כחד
תְּכַחֲדִי	id. fut. 2 pers. sing. fem.	כחד
תְּכַחֵשׁ	וְ Piel fut. 3 pers. s. f. (§ 14. r. 1); וַ conv.	כחש
תְּכַחֲשׁוּ	id. fut. 2 pers. pl. masc.	כחש

a De. 32. 22.   h Ju. 9. 13.   o Ge. 27. 28, 37.   y Eze. 6. 6.   f 2 Ki. 3. 19.   n 2 Sa. 21. 17.   u De. 33. 3.   c Nu. 21. 27.   i Zec. 11. 9.
b Zec. 9. 5.   i Ho. 2. 11.   p Eze. 33. 25, 26.   z Ps. 44. 24.   g 1 Sa. 2. 29.   o Je. 2. 22.   v Is. 1. 5.   d Is. 54. 14.   k Ex. 9. 15.
c Job 6. 21.   k Is. 62. 8.   q Jos. 24. 8.   a Ju. 16. 19.   h 1 Sa. 3. 6.   p Ps. 51. 9.   w Is. 43. 2.   e Job 23. 3.   l Je. 50. 2.
d Je. 51. 46.   l Ps. 4. 8.   r De. 5. 33.   b Pr. 11. 5.   i Eze. 27. 25.   q Je. 34. 16.   x Pr. 6. 28.   f Eze. 43. 11.   m 2 Sa. 14. 18.
e De. 2. 22.   m Ju. 11. 24.   s Ju. 11. 23.   c Ju. 14. 7.   k Is. 43. 20.   r Job 17. 7.   y Ps. 7. 10; 21. 13.   g 2 Ki. 4. 16.   n Ge. 18. 15.
f Nu. 14. 9.   n Pr. 30. 23.   t Pr. 30. 31.   d Jon. 4. 7, 8.   l Is. 43. 20.   s Zec. 11. 17.   z 2 Sa. 7. 24.   h Is. 57 11.   o Le. 19. 11.
g Ex. 1. 17.   o Je. 31. 12.   u Eze. 35. 9.   e Ps. 10. 7. 55. 12.   m Ps. 50. 15.   Ge. 27. 1.

תְּכַחֲשׁוּן id. id. with parag. ן (§ 10. rem. 4) . כחש

תֻּכִּי masc. only pl. תֻּכִּיִּים, תֻּכִּיִּם, *peacocks*, 1 Ki. 10. 22; 2 Ch. 9. 21.

תָּכִין Hiph. fut. 2 pers. sing. masc., or 3 pers. s. f. כון

תְּכִינֶהָ id. fut. 2 pers. sing. masc., suff. 3 pers. s. f. כון

תַּכִּיר Hiph. fut. 2 pers. sing. masc. . . נכר

תַּכִּירוּ id. fut. 2 pers. pl. masc. . . . נכר

תָּכַךְ Root not used; Arab. *to cut, cut off*; Ch. תּוּךְ *to injure.*

תּוֹךְ, תֹּךְ masc. *violence, oppression.* Also, תְּכָכִים masc. pl. *oppressions, injuries*, Pr. 29. 13.

תָּכַל Root not used; prob. *to peel, shell*, comp. שַׁחֶלֶת. תְּכֵלֶת fem. a colour obtained from a mussel (helix janthina) *cerulean purple*, and hence any material dyed of this colour.

וַתֵּכַל, וַתְּ Piel fut. 2 pers. sing. masc., or 3 pers. sing. fem., ap. from תְּכַלֶּה; ו, for ן, וֹ conv. .

תֵּכַל ן Kal fut. 3 pers. sing. fem., ap. fr. תִּכְלֶה (§ 24. rem. 3); וֹ id. . .

תִּכְלָא Kal fut. 2 pers. sing. masc.

תִּכְלָאִי id. fut. 2 pers. s. f. [for תִּכְלְאִי § 8. r. 15]

תְּכַלֶּה Piel fut. 2 pers. sing. masc. . . כלה

תִּכְלֶה Kal fut. 3 pers. sing. fem. (§ 24. r. 19); or (Ps. 119. 96) noun fem. sing.

תַּכְלִימֵזָה Hiph. fut. 2 pers. pl. masc., suff. 3 pers. s. f. כלם

תַּכְלִימוּנִי id. id., suff. 1 pers. sing.

תַּכְלִימֵנוּ ן id. fut. 2 p. s. m., suff. 1 pers. pl.; וֹ conv. כלם

תִּכְלֶינָה וַ Kal fut. 3 pers. pl. fem.; וֹ id. כלה

תַּכְלִית noun fem. sing. כלה

תִּכָּלֵם Niph. fut. 3 pers. sing. fem. כלם

תִּכָּלְמוּ id. fut. 2 pers. pl. masc. כלם

תִּכָּלְמִי id. fut. 2 pers. sing. fem. כלם

תְּכַלֶּנָה Piel fut. 2 pers. sing. masc. (תְּכַלֶּה), suff. 3 pers. sing. fem. (§ 24. rem. 21) כלה

תְּכַלֶּינָה defect. for תְּכַלֶּינָה (q. v.) כלה

תֵּכֵלֶת וֹ noun fem. sing.; וֹ bef. (:) תכל

[תָּכַן] *to weigh*, metaph. *to ponder, examine, try.* Niph. I. *to be weighed, examined*, 1 Sa. 2. 3.—II. *to be equal, fair, just.* Pi. תִּכֵּן.—I. *to weigh*, Job 28. 25.

—II. *to measure*, Is. 40. 12.—III. *to fix*, Ps. 75. 4.—IV. *to direct*, Is. 40. 13. Pu. *to weigh out money*, 2 Ki. 12. 12.

תֹּכֶן masc.—I. *a fixed quantity*, Ex. 5. 18.—II. *measure*, Eze. 45. 11.—III. pr. name of a place, in the tribe of Simeon, 1 Ch. 4. 32.

תְּכוּנָה fem. dec. 10.—I. *arrangement, structure*, Eze. 43. 11.—II. *proportion, measure*, Na. 2. 10; others, *costly furniture.*

תָּכְנִית fem.—I. *arrangement, structure*, Eze. 43. 10.—II. *perfect form, perfection of beauty*, Eze. 28. 12.

מַתְכֹּנֶת fem. dec. 13 c, *measure, proportion.*

תָּכֵן Hiph. fut. 2 pers. sing. m., defect. for תָּכִין כון

תִּכֵּן Piel pret. 3 pers. sing. masc. . . תכן

תִּכֹּן ן Niph. fut. 3 pers. sing. fem., defect. for וֹ; תִּכּוֹן conv. . . כון

תֹכֵן וֹ Kal part. act. sing. masc. . . תכן

תֹּכֶן וֹ noun masc. sing., also pr. name . תכן

תַּכֵּנוּ Hiph. fut. 2 pers. sing. masc. (תַּכֶּה), suff. 3 pers. sing. masc. (§ 25. No. 2 b) נכה

תַּכְנִיעַ Hiph. fut. 2 pers. sing. masc. כנע

תָּכְנִית noun fem. sing. תכן

תַּכְנִיעַ ו ap. & conv. from תַּכְנִיעַ q. v. כנע

תִּכָּנַע ן Niph. fut. 2 pers. sing. masc., or (Ju. 3. 30) 3 pers. sing. fem.; וֹ conv. כנע

תִּכַּנְתִּי Piel pret. 1 pers. sing. תכן

תְּכַס וֹ ap. from the foll.; וֹ conv. . כסה

תְּכַסֶּה Piel fut. 2 pers. sing. masc., or 3 pers. sing. f. כסה

תְּכַסֶּהָ וֹ id. fut. 3 p. s. f., suff. 3 p. s. f.; וֹ bef. (:) כסה

תִּתְכַּסֶּה Hithpa. fut. 3 p. s. f. [for תִּתְכַּסֶּה § 12. r. 3] כסה

תְּכַסֵּהוּ ו Piel fut. 3 p. s. f., suff. 3 p. s. m.; וֹ conv. כסה

תְּכַסּוּ Kal fut. 2 pers. pl. masc. כסס

תְּכַסִּי Piel fut. 2 pers. sing. fem. . כסה

תְּכַסִּים ו id. id., suff. 3 pers. pl. masc.; וֹ conv. כסה

תְּכַסֶּךָ id. fut. 3 pers. sing. fem. (תְּכַסֶּה) with תְּכַסֶּךָ suff. 2 pers. sing. masc. כסה

תְּכַסֵּךְ id. id., suff. 2 pers. sing. fem. כסה

תְּכַסֵּנוּ ו id. id., suff. 1 pers. pl.; ו bef. (:) כסה

תְּכַסֵּנִי ו id. id., suff. 1 pers. sing.; וֹ conv. כסה

תִּכְסֹף Kal fut. 2 pers. sing. masc. . q. v. כסף

תַּכְעִיסוּ Hiph. fut. 2 pers. pl. masc. רעס

תַּכְעִסֶנָּה id. fut. 3 pers. s. f. [תַּכְעִים], suff. 3 p. s. fem. כעס

תִּכָּפֵל ן Niph. fut. 3 pers. sing. fem. כפל

תְּכַפֵּר Piel fut. 2 pers. sing. masc. . כפר

תְּכֻפַּר Pual fut. 3 pers. sing. fem. [for תִּכֻפַּר] . כפר

a Jos. 24. 27. — b Ps. 65. 10. — c De. 16. 19. — d De. 1. 17. — e Nu. 17. 25. — f Ex. 39. 32. — g Ps. 40. 12. — h Is. 43. 6. — i 1 Ki. 17. 14. — k Ru. 2. 15. — l Job 19. 3. — m Ps. 44. 10. — n Ge. 6. 16. — o Ge. 41. 53. — p Nu. 12. 14. — q Ps. 89. 3. — r Is. 45. 17. — s Is. 54. 4. — t Ge. 6. 16. — u Job 17. 3. — v Is. 25. 5. — w Pr. 24. 12. — x Eze. 45. 11. — y Ex. 5. 18. — z Pr. 23. 13, 14. — a Ne. 9. 24. — b Ps. 75. 4. — c Ne. 3. 37. — d Mi. 7. 10. — e Pr. 26. 26. — f Ju. 4. 18, 19. — g Ex. 12. 4. — h Job 16. 18. — i Eze. 16. 18. — k Ob. 10. — l Is. 60. 6. — m Je. 3. 25. — n Ps. 55. 6. — o Job 14. 15. — p Je. 25. 6. — q 1 Sa. 1. 7. — r Eze. 21. 19. — s Is. 6. 7.

תִּכְפְּרֵם- Piel fut. 2 pers. s. m. (תְּכַפֵּר), suff. 3 p. pl. m.   כפר

תִּכְרוּ 'וֹ Kal fut. 2 pers. pl. masc.   .   כרה

תַּכְרִיךְ- noun masc. sing.   .   .   כרך

תַּכְרִיעַ Hiph. fut. 2 pers. sing. masc.   .   כרע

תַּכְרִית Hiph. fut. 2 pers. sing. masc.   .   כרת

תַּכְרִיתוּ id. fut. 2 pers. pl. masc.   .   כרת

תַּכְרִיתֵךְ id. fut. 3 pers. sing. fem., suff. 2 pers. s. fem.   כרת

תִּכְרַע 'וַ Kal fut. 3 pers. sing. fem.; 'וַ conv.   כרע

תִּכְרְעוּ id. fut. 2 pers. pl. masc. [for תִּכְרָעוּ § 8. r.15]   כרע

תִּכְרַעְנָה id. fut. 3 pers. pl. fem.   .   כרע

תִּכָּרֵת Niph. fut. 3 pers. sing. fem.   .   כרת

תִּכְרֹת 'וַ Kal fut. 2 pers. sing. masc., or (Ex. 4. 25) 3 pers. sing. fem.; 'וַ conv.   כרת

תִּכְרָת- 'וַ id. fut. 2 pers. sing. masc. with Mak. (§ 8. rem. 18); 'וַ id.   כרת

תִּכְרְתוּ 'וַ id. fut. 2 pers. pl. masc.; 'וַ id.   כרת

תִּכְרֵתוּן id. id., 'ן parag. [for תִּכְרָתוּן § 8. rem. 17]   כרת

תִּכָּשֵׁל Niph. fut. 3 pers. sing. masc.   כשל

תַּכְשִׁלִי Hiph. fut. 2 pers. sing. fem.   כשל

תְּכַשֵּׁלִי Piel fut. 2 pers. s. f., R. כָּשֵׁל K. תִּשְׁכַּלִי R.   שכל

תִּכָּתֵב Niph. fut. 3 pers. sing. masc., bef. a monos. [for תִּכָּתֵב § 9. rem. 3]   .   .   כתב

תִּכְתֹּב 'וַ Kal fut. 2 pers. sing. masc., or 3 pers. sing. fem.; 'וַ conv.   כתב

תִּכְתְּבוּ id. fut. 2 pers. pl. masc.   כתב

תִּכְתּוֹשׁ Kal fut. 2 pers. sing. masc. (§ 8. rem. 18)   כתש

תֵּל noun masc. sing. dec. 8 b, and pr. name in compos. as תֵּל אָבִיב, &c.   .   תלל

תָּלָא only part. תְּלוּאִים.—I. suspended, placed in suspense or uncertainty, De. 28. 66.—II. hanging after, i. e. bent upon, addicted to, with לְ, Ho. 11. 7.

תִּלְאֶ 'וַ ap. fr. תִּלְאֶה q. v. (§ 24. rem. 3); 'וַ conv.   לאה

תִּלְאָה- 'וֹ noun fem. sing.; 'וֹ bef. (:)   .   לאה

תִּלְאֶה Kal fut. 2 pers. sing. masc. .   .   לאה

תִּלְאוּ Hiph. fut. 2 pers. pl. masc.   .   לאה

תְּלָאֹת noun fem., pl. of (תְּלָאוּבָה) dec. 10   לאב

תְּלָאִים- defect. for תְּלוּאִים (q. v.)   .   תלא

תְּלַאשַּׂר [תְּלַאשַּׂר] pr. name of a region in Syria or Mesopotamia, 2 Ki. 19. 12; Is. 37. 12.

תְּלַבֵּב- 'וֹ, 'וַתְּ Piel fut. 3 pers. s. fem.; 'וֹ, for 'וֹ; 'וַ conv.   לבב

תִּלְבַּשׁ Hiph. fut. 3 pers. sing. fem.   .   לבש

תַּלְבִּישֵׁנִי id. fut. 2 pers. sing. masc., suff. 1 pers. sing.   לבש

תִּלְבַּשׁ- 'וַ ap. from תַּלְבִּישׁ q. v.; 'וַ conv.   לבש

תִּלְבַּשׁ Kal (Ch. Da. 5. 16) fut. 2 p. s. m., or 3 pers. s. fem. (§ 8. r. 15); 'וַ conv.   לבש

תִּלְבְּשׁוּ id. fut. 2 pers. pl. m. [for תִּלְבָּשׁוּ § 8. r. 15]   לבש

תִּלְבְּשִׁי- / תִּלְבָּשִׁי- id. fut. 2 pers. sing. fem.   .   .   לבש

תִּלְבַּשְׁנָה id. fut. 3 pers. pl. fem.   .   לבש

תִּלְבֹּשֶׁת noun fem. sing.   .   .   לבש

[תְּלַג] Chald. i. q. Heb. שֶׁלֶג snow.

תִּלְנַת pr. name in compos. see תִּגְלַת.

תֵּלֵד / תֵּלֶד 'וַ Kal fut. 3 pers. sing. fem. (§ 20. rem. 4); 'וַ conv.   ילד

תֵּלְדוּ id. fut. 2 pers. pl. masc.   .   ילד

תֵּלְדוֹת defect. for תּוֹלְדוֹת (q. v.)   .   ילד

תֵּלְדִי Kal fut. 2 pers. sing. fem.   .   ילד

תֵּלַדְןָ / תֵּלַדְנָה 'וַתֵּ Kal fut. 3 pers. pl. fem. (§ 8. rem. 16); 'וַ conv.   ילד

תֹּלְדֹת defect. for תּוֹלְדוֹת (q. v.)   .   ילד

תָּלָה 'וַ I. to hang, suspend.—II. to hang, execute. Niph. pass. La. 5. 12. Pi. to hang, suspend, Eze. 27. 10, 11.

תְּלִי masc. dec. 6i, a quiver, as being suspended, Ge. 27. 3.

יִתְלָה (hanging, lofty) pr. name of a place in the tribe of Dan, Jos. 19. 42.

תַּלְפִּיּוֹת fem. pl. armoury, a place where weapons were hung up, from תֵּל, & פִּיּוֹת edges, sc. of swords, Ca. 4. 4; others, deadly things, i. e. weapons (Arab. תלף to perish; conj. IV. to destroy).

תִּלְהֶ 'וַ Kal fut. 3 pers. sing. fem., ap. [fr. תִּלְהֶה § 24. rem. 3]; 'וַ conv.   להה

תִּלְהֶ noun masc. s., suff. 3 pers. s. f. fr. תֵּל d. 8 b   תלל

תֹּלֶה Kal part. act. s. m., bef. penacute [for תֹּלֶה]   תלה

תְּלֻהוּ id. imp. pl. masc., suff. 3 pers. sing. masc.   תלה

תִּלְהַט 'וֹ, 'וַתְּ Piel fut. 3 pers. sing. fem. (§ 14 rem. 1); 'וֹ bef. (:) for 'ן, 'וַ conv.   להט

תְּלַהֲטֵהוּ 'וֹ id. with suff. 3 pers. sing. masc.; 'וַ id   להט

תָּלוּ 'וַ Kal pret. 3 pers. pl.   .   תלה

תְּלוּ id. Piel fut. 3 pers. pl.   .   תלה

תְּלוּאִים Kal part. pass. masc. pl. [of תָּלוּא] dec. 3 a   תלא

תִּלְוֶה Hiph. fut. 2 pers. sing. masc.   .   לוה

* Ps. 65. 4.   ᵏ 1 Sa. 4. 19.   ᵖ Ex. 34. 13.   ᵗ Pr. 27. 22.   ᵈ De. 28. 66.   ᵏ De. 22. 11.   ᵉ Ge. 30. 3.   ʸ Ge. 25. 12.   ᵗ Ps. 97. 3.
ᵇ De. 2. 6.   ⁱ Is. 65. 12.   ᵍ Pr. 4. 12.   ᵉ Job 4. 5.   Eze. 34. 3.   ᶠ Is. 33. 11.   ᶻ Ge. 40. 19.   ᵘ De. 32. 22.
ᶜ Job 6. 27.   ᵏ Job 39. 3.   ʳ Eze. 36. 15.   ᶻ La. 3. 5.   2 Sa. 13. 6, 8.   ᵐ Is. 49. 18.   ᵉ Ge. 3. 16.   ᵃ Ge. 47. 13.   ᵍ Is. 42. 25.
ᵈ Est. 8. 15.   ˡ Ex. 4. 25.   ˢ Eze. 36. 14.   ᵃ Job 4. 2.   ᶠ Pr. 23. 21.   ⁿ Je. 4. 30.   ᵈ Ge. 30. 39.   ᵇ Je. 30. 18.   ᵘ Eze. 27. 10 u
ᵉ Nu. 4. 18.   ᵐ Is. 57. 8.   ᵗ Ps. 102. 19.   ᵇ Is. 7. 13.   ᵍ Job 10. 11.   ᵒ Ge. 27. 15.   ᵉ 2 Sa. 13. 18.   ᶜ Job 26. 7.   ᵏ Ho. 11. 7.
ᶠ Na. 3. 15.   ⁿ Ju. 2. 2.   ᵘ Jos. 18. 6.   ᶜ Ho. 13. 5.   ʰ Job 40. 10.   ᵖ Is. 59. 17.   ᵉ Eze. 23. 4.   ᵈ Est. 7. 9.   ˡ Ex. 22. 24.
ᵍ Is. 45. 23.   ᵒ Je. 34. 15.

תִּלְוֶה	Kal fut. 2 pers. sing. masc.	לוה
תָּלֻי	Kal part. pass. sing. masc. dec. 3a	תלה
תְּלוּיִם	id. pl., abs. st.	תלה
וְתָלוּל	Kal part. pass. sing. masc.	תלל
תְּלָאֻם	Kh. תְּלָאֻם Kal pret. 3 pers. pl., suff. 3 pers. pl. masc., R. תלה K. תְּלָאוּם R.	תלא
תַּלְוֵנוּ	Hiph. fut 2 pers. sing. masc. (תַּלְוֶה), suff. 3 pers. sing. masc. (§ 24. rem. 21)	לוה
תִּלּוֹנוּ	Kh. תִּלּוֹנוּ Niph., K. תַּלִּינוּ Hiph. fut. 2 pers. pl. masc. (§ 21. rem. 24)	לון
תְּלוּנֹת	noun fem.,pl. of (תְּלוּנָּה) dec. 10	לון
תְּלֻנֹּתָם	id., suff. 3 pers. pl. masc. (§ 4. rem. 2)	לון
וַתִּלּוֹשׁ	Kh. וַתָּלוֹשׁ Kal fut. 3 pers. sing. fem. K. תָּלָשׁ ap. (§ 21. rem. 7); וַ conv.	לושׁ
תֶּלַח	(breach) pr. name masc. 1 Ch. 7. 25.	
תִּלָּחֵם	Niph. fut. 3 pers. sing. fem.	לחם
תִּלָּחֵם	Kal fut. 2 pers. sing. masc.	לחם
תִּלָּחֲמוּ	Niph. fut. 2 pers. pl. masc.	לחם
תִּלָּחֵמוּן	id. with parag. ן	לחם
וַתִּלָּחֵץ	Niph. fut. 3 pers. sing. fem.; וַ conv.	לחץ
תִּלְחַץ / וַתִּלְחַץ	Kal fut. 2 pers. sing. masc., or 3 pers. sing. fem. (§ 8. rem. 15); וַ id.	לחץ
תִּלְחָצֶנּוּ	id. fut. 2 p. s. m., suff. 3 p. s. m. (§ 16. r. 12)	לחץ
תֶּלְיְךָ	noun m. s., suff. 2 pers. s. m. fr. (תְּלִי) d. 6i	תלה
תָּלִין	Kal fut. 3 pers. sing. fem., R. לין see	לון
תָּלִינוּ	id. fut. 2 pers. pl. masc.	לון
תָּלִינוּ	Kal pret. 1 pers. pl.	תלה
תְּלִינִי	Kal fut. 2 pers. sing. fem., R. לין see	לון
וְתָלִיתָ	Kal pret. 2 pers. sing. masc.	תלה
תְּלִיתָאָה	Ch. adj. ord. fem. [of תְּלִיתָי masc. comp. d. 7]	תלת
תֵּלֶךְ / וַתֵּלֶךְ	Kal fut. 2 pers. sing. masc., or 3 pers. sing. fem. (§ 20. rem. 4); וַ conv.	ילד
וַתֵּלֶד	Niph. fut. 3 pers. sing. fem.; וַ id.	לכד
תִּלְכְּדוֹ	Kal fut. 3 pers. s. f. [תִּלְכֹּד], suff. 3 p. s. m.	לכד
תִּלָּכְדִי	Niph. fut. 2 pers. sing. fem. [for תִּלָּכְדִי comp. § 8. rem. 15]	לכד
תֵּלְכוּ / וַתֵּלְכוּ	Kal fut. 2 pers. pl. masc. (comp. id.); וַ conv.	ילד
תֵּלְכוּן / תֵּלֵכוּן	id. id. with parag. ן (comp. § 8. rem. 17)	ילד
תֵּלְכִי	Kh. תֵּלְכִי q. v., K. תֵּלְכוּ (q. v.).	ילד
תֵּלְכִי / וַתֵּלְכִי	Kal fut. 2 pers. sing. fem. (comp. § 8. rem. 15); וַ conv.	ילד

תֵּלַכְנָה	וַ id. fut. 2 pers. pl. fem. (Ru. 1. 11), or 3 pers. pl. fem.; וַ conv.	לך

[תָּלַל] I. to raise or heap up, as a mound, only part. pass. raised, lofty, Eze. 17. 22.—II. in the derivv. to vibrate, wave, Arab. id., cogn. תָּלָה, סָלָה, סָלַל. Hiph. הֵתַל (inf. הָתֵל; fut. יְהָתֵל, יַהֲתֵל, q. v.)—I. to mock, deride, 1 Ki. 18. 27, comp. זָלַל.—II. to deceive, delude, with בְּ. Hoph. הוּתַל to be deceived, Is. 44. 20.

תֵּל masc. dec. 8b.—I. heap of ruins.—II. hill, mound, Jos. 11. 13.—III. pr. name תֵּל אָבִיב (hill of corn-ears) a city in Mesopotamia, Eze. 3. 15.— תֵּל חַרְשָׁא (hill of the forest) a city in Babylonia. —תֵּל מֶלַח (hill of salt) another city in Babylonia. תַּלְתַּלִּים masc. pl. waving palm-branches, comp. זַלְזַלִּים, Ca. 5. 11. Sept. ἐλάται. Vulg. elatæ palmarum (the clusters or strings of embryo fruits after they have burst the sheaths of the female palm-tree, and which then hang down and resemble locks of flowing hair).

הֲתֻלִים masc. pl. mockings, poet. for mockers, Job 17. 2.

מַהֲתֻלּוֹת fem. pl. delusions, Is. 30. 10.

תֶּלֶם Root not used; Arab. to break, break open. תֶּלֶם masc. dec. 6a (pl. c. תַּלְמֵי), a furrow. תַּלְמַי (full of furrows?) pr. name—I. of a king of Geshur, father-in-law of David, 2 Sa. 3. 3; 13. 37.—II. of an Anakite, comp. Nu. 13. 22.

תְּלָמוֹ	noun m. s., suff. 3 pers. pl. m. fr. תֶּל d. 8b	תלל
תִּלְמַד	Kal fut. 2 pers. sing. masc.	למד
תִּלְמְדוּ	id. fut. 2 pers. pl. m. [for תִּלְמְדוּ § 8. r. 15]	למד
תְּלַמְּדֵם	Piel fut. 2 pers. s. m. [תְּלַמֵּד], suff. 3 p. pl. m.	למד
תְּלַמְּדֶנּוּ	id., suff. 3 pers. sing. masc.	למד
תְּלַמְּדֵנִי	id., suff. 1 pers. sing.	למד
תַּלְמַי / תַּלְמָי	pr. name masc.	תלם
תַּלְמֵי	noun masc. pl. constr. from תֶּלֶם dec. 6a	תלם
תַּלְמִיד	noun masc. sing.	למד
תַּלְמֶיהָ	noun m. pl., suff. 3 pers. s. f. fr. תֶּלֶם d. 6a	תלם
תָּלַן / תָּלֶן	Kal fut. 3 pers. sing. fem., or 2 pers. sing. masc.,ap.fr. תָּלִין (§ 22. r. 3) R. לין see	לון
תְּלֻנּוֹת	noun fem.,pl. of [תְּלוּנָּה] dec. 10	לון
תְּלֻנֹּתֵיכֶם	id. pl., suff. 2 pers. pl. masc.	לון

a De. 28. 12.   b Jos. 10. 26.   c Eze. 17. 22.   d 2 Sa. 21. 12.   e De. 28. 44.   f Ex. 16. 12.   g Nu. 17. 25.   h 2 Sa. 13. 8.   i Zec. 14. 14.   k Pr. 23. 6.   l 1 Ki. 12. 24.   m Nu. 22. 25.   n Ex. 23. 9.   o Nu. 22. 25.   p Ex. 22. 20.   q Ge. 27. 3.   r Ps. 137. 2.   s Ru. 1. 16.   t De. 21. 22.   u Da. 2. 39.   v Je. 50. 9.   w 1 Sa. 10. 21.   x Ps. 35. 8.   y Ru. 2. 11.   z Je. 48. 7.   a De. 6. 14.   b Je. 6. 25.   c De. 5. 28.   d Ps. 94. 12.   e Jos. 11. 13.   f Je. 10. 2.   g Ge. 28. 12.   h Job 17. 2.   i 1 Ch. 25. 8.   k Ju. 19. 20; Is. 48. 7.   l 2 Sa. 17. 16.   m Ez. 16. 7, 8, 9.   n Je. 48. 1.

תֻּלַּע Pu. part. *clothed in scarlet*, denom. of תּוֹלָע q. v. Na. 2. 4.

תּוֹלָע masc. (pl. תּוֹלָעִים).—I. *a worm.*—II. espec. *the worm used in dying scarlet, the coccus*; hence *scarlet colour*, also *scarlet cloths or garments.*—III. pr. name (a) of a son of Issachar; Patronym. תּוֹלָעִי; (b) of a judge in Israel, Ju. 10. 1.

תּוֹלֵעָה fem. *a worm*, Job 25. 6; Is. 14. 11.

תּוֹלַעַת fem. dec. 13a (with תּוֹלַעְתָּם) i. q. תּוֹלָע q. v. & שָׁנִי.

תִּלַּעְ וְ Kal fut. 2 p. s. m., or (Pr. 30. 17) 3 p. s. f.   לען

תִּלְעִינִי Hiph. fut. 2 pers. sing. masc.   לען

תִּלַּעַת וְ defect. for תּוֹלַעַת (q. v.)   תלע

תִּלָּקַח וְ Niph. fut. 3 pers. sing. fem.; וְ conv.   לקח

תְּלַקֵּט וְ Piel fut. 2 pers. s. m., or 3 pers. s. fem.; וְ id.   לקט

תִּלְקְטֵהוּ Kal fut. 3 pers. pl. masc., suff. 3 pers. s. masc.   לקט

תִּלְקְטוּ Pual fut. 2 pers. pl. masc.   לקט

תֵּלַשׁ וְ Kal fut. 3 p. s. fem. [for תָּלוֹשׁ], ap. & conv.   לושׁ

תַּלְשִׁין Hiph. fut. 2 pers. sing. masc. ap. [fr. תַּלְשִׁין]   לושׁ

תְּלָת וְ Ch. fem. תְּלָתָא, תְּלָתָה masc. i. q. Heb. שָׁלֹשׁ *three*; pl. תְּלָתִין *thirty.*

תְּלָת Ch. adj. masc. dec. 3 a, ord. *third in rank*, Da. 5. 16, 29.

תַּלְתִּי Ch. *third*, Da. 5. 7.

תְּלִיתִי Ch. masc. dec. 7, *third*, Da. 2. 39.

תַּלְתָּא וְ Ch. adj. ord. emph. masc. [from תְּלַת], comp. dec. 3 a   תלת

תְּלָתָא תְּלָתָה Ch. num. card. masc. from תְּלַת fem.; וְ bef.   תלת

תְּלָתְהוֹן Ch. id. fem. (תְּלָת) with suff. 3 pers. pl. masc.   תלת

תַּלְתֵּי וְ Ch. adj. ord. masc.   תלת

תְּלָתִין Ch. num. card. com. gen., pl. of תְּלַת fem.   תלת

תַּלְתַּלִּים noun masc., pl. of תַּלְתַּל dec. 8 a   תלל

תָּם Ch. i. q. Heb. שָׁם *there*, only with ה parag. תַּמָּה   תמם

תָּם adj. masc. sing.   תמם

תַּם וְ Kal pret. 3 pers. sing. masc.   תמם

תֹּם תָּם־ Kal inf., or subst. masc. dec. 8 c   תמם

תֵּמָא pr. name, see תֵּימָא.

תְּמָאֵן וְ Piel fut. 2 p. s. m. or 3 pers. s. fem.; וְ conv.   מאן

תְּמָאֲנוּ id. fut. 2 pers. pl. masc. (comp. § 8. rem. 15); וְ id.   מאן

תְּמָאֵן וְ

תִּמָּאֵס Niph. fut. 3 pers. sing. fem.   מאס

תִּמְאַס וְ Kal fut. 2 pers. sing. masc. (§ 8. rem. 15); וְ conv.   מאס

תִּמְאָסוּ id. fut. 2 pers. pl. masc. [for תִּמְאֲסוּ]   מאס

תְּמָגְנֵנִי וְ Pilel fut. 2 pers. sing. masc., suff. 1 pers. sing.; וְ bef.   מוג

תְּמַגְּנֶךָ Piel fut. 3 pers. s. fem. [תְּמַגֵּן], suff. 2 pers. s. masc. [for תְּמַגְּנֶךָ § 2. r. 2, & § 16. r. 15]   מגן

תִּמְדּוּ Kal fut. 2 pers. pl. masc.   מדד

[תָּמַהּ] I. *to wonder, be astonished, be amazed.*—II. *to look with astonishment or surprise.* Hithp. הִתַּמַּהּ (for הִתְתַּמַּהּ), i. q. Kal No. I, Hab. 1. 5.

תְּמַהּ Ch. masc. dec. 3 b, *wonder, miracle.*

תִּמָּהוֹן masc. dec. 3 c, *astonishment, consternation.*

תָּמַהּ Ch. adv. [תַּם] with loc. ה.   תם

תָּמְהוּ Kal pret. 3 pers pl. [for תָּמְהוּ § 8. rem. 7]   תמה

תִּמְהוּ id. imp. pl. masc. [for תִּמְהוּ, from sing. תְּמַהּ § 8. rem. 11]; וְ bef.   תמה

תִּמְהוֹהִי וְ Ch. noun masc. pl., suff. 3 pers. sing. masc. from [תְּמַהּ] dec. 3 b   תמה

תִּמְהַיָּא וְ Ch. id. pl., emph. st.   תמה

תִּמְהִין וְ Ch. id. pl., abs. st.   תמה

תְּמַהֵר וְ Piel fut. 3 pers. s. fem. (§ 14. r. 1); וְ conv.   מהר

תְּמַהֲרוּ id. fut. 2 pers. pl. masc.   מהר

תְּמַהֵרְנָה id. fut. 3 pers. pl. fem.; וְ bef.   מהר

תַּמּוּ וְ Kal pret. 3 pers. pl.   תמם

תֻּמּוֹ Kal inf., or subst. masc., suff. 3 pers. sing. masc. from תֹּם dec. 8 c.   תמם

תָּמוּג וְ Kal fut. 3 pers. sing. fem.; וְ conv. (§ 21. rem. 7)   מוג

תְּמוֹגְגֶנָּה Pilel fut. 2 pers. sing. masc. [תְּמוֹגֵג], suff. 3 pers. sing. fem. (§ 2. rem. 2)   מוג

תָּמוּגֵנוּ וְ Kal fut. 2 pers. sing. masc. (תָּמוּג), suff. 1 pers. pl.; וְ conv.   מוג

תָּמוּד Kal fut. 2 pers. s. masc. [for תָּמֹד § 18. r. 2]   מדד

[תַּמּוּז] pr. name, *Tammuz*, an Assyrian idol, Eze. 8. 14.

תָּמוּט Kal fut. 3 pers. sing. fem.   מוט

תִּמּוֹט Niph. fut. 3 pers. sing. fem.   מוט

תִּמּוֹטֶינָה Kal fut. 3 pers. pl. fem.   מוט

תָּמוּל adv.   מול

תְּמוּנָה noun fem. sing. dec. 10; וְ bef.   מון

תְּמוּנַת id., constr. st.   מון

תְּמוּנָתְךָ id., suff. 2 pers. sing. masc. [for תְּמוּנָתְךָ]   מון

תְּמוּרָתָהּ noun fem. sing., suff. 3 pers. sing. fem. from תְּמוּרָה dec. 10; וְ bef.   מור

---

a Job 11.3.   b Job 21.3.   Ex. 26.1.   Est. 2.8,16.   Ex. 16.26.   Is. 27.12.

g 1 Sa. 25.24.   h Pr. 30.10.   Da. 7.5,8,20.   l Le. 16.29.   l Ezr. 6.4.   Da. 3.23.

m Da. 5.7.   n Da. 6.8,13.   o Ca. 5.11.   p Le. 26.20.   q Job 4.6.   r Pr. 13.6.

s Ex. 4.23; Est. 1.12.   t Pr. 1.24.   u Ps. 89.39.   v Job 10.3.

w Le. 26.15.   x Job 30.22.   y Pr. 4.9.   z Eze. 47.18.   Ps. 48.6.   Da. 7.24.

Hab. 1.5.   Is. 29.9.   Da. 3.33.   Da. 3.32.   Da. 6.28.

Is. 32.4.   2 Ch. 24.5.   Je. 9.17.   2 Ki. 7.13.   Je. 44.12,27.   Eze. 45.3.

Am. 9.5.   Ps. 46.7.   Ps. 65.11.   Is. 64.6.   Ps. 17.15.

Is. 54.10.   De. 4.12.   De. 4.16,23,25.   Ps. 17.15.   Job 28.17.

תְּמוּרָתוֹ	id., suff. 3 pers. sing. masc.; ‌ bef. (:)	מור
תְּמוֹשׁ	Kal fut. 3 pers. sing. fem.	מוש
תָּמוּת	Kal fut. 2 pers. sing. masc., or **3 pers. sing. fem.**	מות
תְּמוּתָה	noun fem. sing.	מות
תְּמוּתוּ	Kal fut. 2 pers. pl. masc.	מות
תְּמוּתוּן	id. id. with parag. ‌	מות
תְּמוּתִי	id. fut. 2 pers. sing. fem.	מות
תְּמוּתֶנָה	id. fut. 3 pers. pl. fem., defect. for תֶּינָה	מות
תְּמוֹתֵת	Pilel fut. **3 pers. sing. fem.**	מות
תֶּמַח	[for תֶּמַח] pr. name m. Ezr. 2. 53; Ne. 7. 55.	
תִּמַח	Hiph. fut. 2 p. s. m., ap. [fr. תִּמְחֶה § 24. r.16]	מחה
תֶּמַח	ap. from the foll.	מחה
תִּמָּחֶה	Niph. fut. 3 pers. sing. fem.	מחה
תִּמְחֶה	Kal fut. 2 pers. sing. masc.	מחה
תַּמְחִי	Hiph. fut. 2 pers. sing. masc. (§ 24. r. 18)	מחה
תִּמְחַץ	Kal fut. 2 pers. sing. masc.	מחץ
תַּמְטִיר	Hiph. fut. 2 pers. sing. m.	מטר
תַּמְטֵרִי	Niph. fut. 3 pers. sing. fem.	מטר
תֻּמִּי	Kal inf. (תֹּם), suff. 1 pers. sing. dec. 8 c	תמם
תָּמִיד	‌ noun masc. sing., also as an *adv.*	מוד
תְּמִידֶךָ	noun m. pl., suff. 2 pers. sing. m. fr. תֹּם d. 8 c	תמם
תָּמִים	adj. masc. sing. dec. 3 a	תמם
תָּמִים	adj. pl. [for תְּאָמִים] *joined, coupled*, comp.	תאם
תֻּמִּים	‌ noun masc., pl. of תֹּם dec. 8 c	תמם
תְּמִים	adj. masc. sing., constr. of תָּמִים dec. 3 a	תמם
תְּמִימָה	id. fem. sing. dec. 10	תמם
תְּמִימֵי	id. masc., pl. constr. from תָּמִים dec. 3 a	תמם
תְּמִימִם / תְּמִימִים	id. masc. pl. abs.; ‌ bef. (:)	תמם
תְּמִימֹת	id. fem., pl. of תְּמִימָה dec. 10	תמם
תָּמִישׁ	Kh. תָּמִישׁ Hiph., K. תָּמוּשׁ Kal, fut. 3 p. s. fem.	מוש
תְּמִישׁוּ	Hiph. fut. 2 pers. pl. masc.	מוש
תְּמִית	Hiph. fut. 2 pers. sing. m., or **3 pers. sing. fem.**	מות
תְּמִיתֻהוּ	id. fut. 2 pers. pl. masc., suff. 3 pers. sing. m.	מות
תְּמִיתֶהָ	id. id., suff. 3 pers. sing. fem.	מות
תְּמִיתֶנּוּ	id. fut. 3 pers. sing. fem., suff. 3 pers. sing. m.	מות
תְּמִיתֵנִי	id. fut. 2 pers. sing. masc., suff. 1 pers. sing.	מות

תָּמַךְ fut. יִתְמֹךְ.—I. *to take hold of*, with acc., בְּ.—II. *to obtain, acquire.*—III. *to hold fast*, with acc.; metaph. *to retain*, Pr. 4. 4.—IV. *to hold up, support*, with בְּ.—V. recipr. *to hold together, follow each other*, Job 36. 17. Niph. *to be holden*, Pr. 5. 22.

תְּמֹךְ	Kal inf. abs.	תמך
תָּמְכָה	id. pret. **3 pers. sing. fem.**	תמך
תָּמְכוּ	id. pret. 3 pers. pl.	תמך

תֹּמְכֶיהָ	‌ id. part. act. pl. masc., **suff. 3 pers. sing. fem.** from תֹּמֵךְ dec. 7 b	תמך
תִּמָּכֵר	Niph. fut. 3 pers. sing. fem.	מכר
תִּמָּכֵר	Kal fut. 2 p. s. m., or (Pr. 31.24) 3 p. s. fem.	מכר
תִּמְכְּרוּ	id. fut. 2 pers. pl. masc.	מכר
תִּמְכְּרֶנָּה	id. fut. 2 pers. sing. m., suff. 3 pers. sing. fem.	מכר
תָּמַכְתָּ	Kal pret. 2 pers. sing. masc.	תמך
תְּמַכְתִּיךָ	id. pret. 1 pers. sing., suff. 2 pers. sing. masc.	תמך
תְּמַלֵּא	‌ Piel fut. 2 p. s. m., or 3 p. s. fem.; ‌ conv.	מלא
תִּמָּלֵא	‌ Niph. fut. 3 pers. sing. fem.; ‌ id.	מלא
תִּמָּלְאִי / תִּמָּלֵאִי	Niph. fut. 2 pers. sing. fem. (comp. § 8. rem. 15); ‌ id.	מלא
תִּמְלָאֵמוֹ	Kal fut. 3 pers. sing. fem., suff. 3 pers. pl. m.	מלא
תְּמַלֶּאנָה	‌ Piel fut. 3 pers. pl. fem.; ‌ conv.	מלא
תִּמְלוֹךְ	Kal fut. 2 pers. sing. masc. (§ 8. rem. 18)	מלך
תִּמְלְחָ	Kal fut. 2 pers. sing. m. [for תִּמְלַח § 8. r. 15]	מלח
תִּמָּלֵט	Niph. fut. 2 p. s. m., or (Je.48.8) 3 p. s. fem.	מלט
תְּמַלֵּט	‌ Piel fut. 3 pers. sing. fem.; ‌ conv.	מלט
תַּמְלִיכוּ	‌ Hiph. fut. 2 pers. pl. masc.; ‌ id.	מלך
תִּמְלֹךְ	Kal fut. 2 pers. sing. masc., or 3 pers. sing. fem.	מלך
תְּמַלֵּל	Piel fut. 2 pers. sing. m. [for תְּמַלֵּל § 10. r. 4]	מלל

[**תָּמַם**] fut. יִתֹּם, יָתֹם, pl. יִתַּמּוּ.—I. *to be completed, ended;* also trans. *to complete, finish,* Ps.64.7; with לְ and inf. *to cease doing.*—II. *to be complete, whole,* in number.—III. *to be perfect, upright,* (integer), Ps. 19. 14.—IV. *to cease, be ended, come to an end* —V. *to be consumed, exhausted, spent;* עַד תֹּם *until they were consumed, destroyed.* Niph. (fut. pl. יִתַּמּוּ).—I. *to be ended, come to an end,* Ps. 102. 28.—II. *to be consumed.* Hiph. הֵתֵם (fut. יָתֵם § 18. rem. 14).—I. *to complete, make ready,* Eze. 24. 10.—II. *to complete, make perfect, upright,* Job 23. 3.—III. *to complete, execute, finish,* 2 Sa. 20. 18.—IV. *to finish, cease,* Is. 33. 1; causat. *to cause to cease, to remove,* with מִן, Eze. 22. 15.—V. *to take the sum, count,* 2 Ki. 22. 4; others, *pay out,* i. q. שָׁלַם.—VI. intrans. *to be consumed,* Da. 8. 23; or perh. *be made* or *declared perfect* (?). Hithp. הִתַּמֵּם (for הִתְתַּמֵּם) *to show oneself perfect, upright,* Ps. 18. 26.

תָּמִים masc. dec. 3 a, תְּמִימָה fem. dec. 10, adj.—I. *complete, perfect.*—II. *whole, entire.*—III. *sound, without blemish, defect.*—IV. *perfect, upright, sincere,* (integer).—V. subst. *integrity.*

---

a Le. 27. 10, 33.   f Ps. 109. 14.   l Am. 4. 7.   q Pr. 17. 13.   v 2 Ch. 23. 14.   a Le. 25. 23.   f Eze. 23. 33.   l Ex. 2. 16.   p Ju. 9. 16, 18.
b Is. 22. 25.   g De. 25. 19.   m Je. 27. 8.   r Mi. 2. 3.   w Pr. 21. 25.   b Pr. 31. 24.   g Eze. 27. 25.   m 1 Sa. 24. 21.   q Ge.37.8; 1Sa.
c Ru. 1. 17.   h Je. 18. 23.   n De. 33. 8.   s Ge. 42. 37.   x 1Sa.30.15; Je.38.15.   c De. 21. 14.   h Ex. 15. 9.   n Is. 34. 15.   23.17; Est.2.4.
d Ps. 34. 22.   i Ps. 68. 24.   o Ne. 7. 65.   t Job 5. 2.   y Ps. 17. 5.   d Ps. 41. 13.   i Job 39. 2.   o Eze. 18. 19.   r Job 8. 2.
e Ne. 13. 14.   k Am. 4. 7.   p Le. 23. 15.   u Ki. 3. 26, 27.   z Ps. 63. 9.   e Is. 41. 10.   k Ps. 82. 7.   s Pr. 3. 18.
x Ex.26.24; 36.29.

תָּם masc. תַּמָּה fem. dec. 10, adj.—I. *whole, perfect, sincere, honest.*—II. subst. *integrity*, Ps. 37. 37.

תֹּם masc. dec. 8 c.—I. *completeness, fulness in number*, Is. 47. 9.—II. *welfare, prosperity.*—III. *integrity, uprightness, sincerity.*—IV. pl. תֻּמִּים *truth.*

תֻּמָּה fem. dec. 10, *integrity, sincerity, innocence.*

מְתֹם masc. *soundness*, Ps. 38. 4, 8 ; Is. 1. 6.

תֹּם	Kal inf. (תֹּם), suff. 3 pers. pl. masc. dec. 8 c	תמם
תֵּימָן	defect. for תֵּימָן (q. v.) . . .	ימן
תִּמְנָה	pr. name of a place . . .	מנה
תִּמְנָה	Kal fut. 2 pers. sing. masc. . .	מנה
תִּמֹּנוּ / תִּמֹּנוּ	} Kal pret. 1 pers. pl. [for תָּמֹונוּ § 18. r. 16]	תמם
תִּמָּנַע	Niph. fut. 2 pers. sing. masc. . .	מנע
תִּמְנַע	pr. name masc. and fem. . .	מנע
תִּמְנַע	Kal fut. 2 pers. sing. masc. . .	מנע
תִּמְנַת	pr. name in compos. תִּ סֶרַח . .	מנה
תְּמֻנָה	noun f. s., constr. of תְּמוּנָה d.10 ; bef. (:)	מון
תִּמְנָתָה	pr. name (תִּמְנָה) with parag. ה .	מנה
תְּמַסֵּם	noun masc. sing. . . .	מסס
תִּמַס	Hiph. fut. 2 p. s. m. ap. [fr. תִּמְסֶה] ; נַ conv.	מסה
תִּמְעַד	Kal fut. 3 pers. sing. fem. . .	מעד
תִּמְעֲטוּ	Kal fut. 2 p. pl. m. [for § 8. r. 15]	מעט
תִּמְעֲטֵנִי	the foll. with suff. 1 pers. sing.	מעט
תַּמְעִיט	Hiph. fut. 2 pers. sing. masc.	מעט
תִּמְעֲטוּ	id. fut. 2 pers. pl. masc.	מעט
תִּמְעֲטִי	id. fut. 2 pers. sing. fem. . .	מעט
תִּמְעַל	נַ Kal fut. 3 pers. sing. fem.; נַ conv.	מעל
תִּמְעֲלוּ	id. fut. 2 pers. pl. m. [for תִּמְעֲלוּ § 8. r. 15]	מעל
תִּמָּצֵא	נַ Niph. fut. 3 pers. sing. fem.; נַ conv.	מצא
תִּמְצָא	נַ Kal fut. 2 pers. sing. masc., or 3 pers. sing. masc.; נַ id.	מצא
תִּמְצָאֶהָ	id. fut. 2 p. pl. m., suff. 3 p. s. m. (§ 16. r. 12)	מצא
תִּמְצְאוּ / תִּמְצָאוּ	} id. fut. 2 pers. pl. masc. (§ 8. rem. 15)	מצא
תִּמְצָאוּן	id. with parag. ן (§ 8. rem. 17)	מצא
תִּמְצְאִי	Niph. fut. 2 pers. sing. fem.	מצא
תִּמְצֶאינָה	id. fut. 3 pers. pl. fem. (comp. § 23. rem. 3)	מצא
תִּמְצָאֵךְ	Kal fut. 3 pers. sing. fem., suff. 2 pers. sing. masc. (§ 16. rem. 12)	מצא
תִּמְצָאֵם	id. fut. 2 pers. sing. m., suff. 3 pers. pl. m.	מצא
תִּמְצָאן	id. fut. 3 pers. pl. fem. (§ 8. rem. 16)	מצא
תִּמְצָאֻנוּ	id. fut. 2 p. s. m., suff. 3 p. s. m. (§ 16. r. 12)	מצא
תִּמְצוּ	Kal fut. 2 pers. pl. masc. . .	מצץ
תִּמָּק	Niph. fut. 3 pers. sing. fem. .	מקק
תִּמַּקְנָה	id. fut. 3 pers. pl. fem. (§ 18. rem. 16)	מקק

תָּמָר וְ m. d. 4 a.—I. *palm-tree.*—II. pr. name of a town in the south of Palestine.—III. pr. name of another town, 1 Ki. 9. 18, i. q. תַּדְמֹר q. v.—IV. pr. name fem. (*a*) of a daughter-in-law of Judah; (*b*) of a daughter of David, 2 Sa. 13. 1; (*c*) of a daughter of Absalom, 2 Sa. 14. 27

תֹּמֶר masc. *palm-tree*, Ju. 4. 5; Je. 10. 5.

תִּמֹּרָה fem. dec. 10 (pl. תִּמֹּרִים, תִּמֹּרוֹת) *artificial palm-trees.*

תִּימָרָה fem. dec. 11 a, *pillar* of smoke.

תַּמְרוּר masc. dec. 1 b, *column, pillar*, Je. 31. 21

תַּ . כֹּר Kh. תָּמֹר, see תַּדְמֹר.

תַּמֵּר	Hiph. fut. 2 p. s. m. [for תָּמֵר § 18. r. 14]	מרר
תַּמֵּר	וַ Hiph. fut. 3 p. s. f., ap. [for תַּמְרֶה]; וַ conv.	מרה
תֹּמֶר	noun masc. sing. . .	מרר
תִּמְרְדוּ / תִּמְרֹדוּ	} Kal fut. 2 pers. pl. masc. (§ 8. rem. 15)	מרד
תְּמוֹרָה	וְ noun fem. sing. dec. 10 . .	תמר
תִּמְרוּ	וַ Hiph. fut. 2 pers. pl. masc.; וַ conv.	מרה
תְּמֹרוּ	n. f. with pl. m. term., suff. 3 p.s.m. fr. תְּמוֹרָה d. 10 (others read תִּמֹרוֹ, as if from תִּימֹרָה	תמר
תֹּמְרוּ	Kal fut. 2 pers. pl. m. for תֹּאמְרוּ (§ 19. r. ε)	אמר
תַּמְרוּקֶיהָ	n. m. pl., suff. 3 p. pl. f. fr. תַּמְרוּק d. 1 b	מרק
תַּמְרוּרִים	noun masc., pl. of תַּמְרוּר dec. 1 b	מרר
תַּמְרוּרִים	noun masc., pl. of תַּמְרוּר dec. 1 b	תמר
תִּימֲרוֹת	noun fem. pl. constr. of תִּימָרָה dec. 12 a	תמר
תִּמֹרוֹת	וְ noun fem., pl. of תִּמֹרָה dec. 10	תמר
תַּמְרִיא	Hiph. fut. 3 pers. sing. fem.	מרא
תְּמָרִים	noun masc., pl. of תָּמָר dec. 4 a	תמר
תִּמֹרִים	וְ noun fem. with pl. m. term. fr. תִּמֹרָה d. 10	תמר
תַּמְרִיק	Kh. תַּמְרִיק, K. תַּמְרֻק noun masc. sing. d. 1 b	מרק
תַּמְרֻקֵיהֶן	noun m. pl., suff. 3 p. pl. f. fr. תַּמְרֻק d. 1 b	מרק
תְּמֹרֹת	וְ noun fem., pl. of תְּמוֹרָה dec. 10	תמר
תִּמֹשׁ	Kal fut. 2 pers. sing. masc. (§ 21. rem. 7)	מוש
תִּמְשֹׁל	Kal fut. 3 pers. sing. fem. (§ 8. rem. 18)	משל
תִּמְשְׁחָה / תִּמְשַׁח	} Kal fut. 2 pers. sing. masc. (§ 8. rem. 15)	משח
תַּמְשִׁילֵהוּ	Hiph. fut. 2 pers. sing. m., suff. 3 pers. s. m.	משל
תִּמָּשֵׁךְ	Niph. fut. 3 pers. sing. fem.	משך
תִּמְשֹׁךְ	וַ Kal fut. 2 pers. sing. masc.; וַ conv.	משך
תִּמְשְׁכֵנִי	id. fut. 2 pers. sing. masc., suff. 1 pers. sing.	משך
תִּמְשְׁלוּ / תִּמְשֹׁלוּ	} Kal fut. 2 pers. pl. masc. (§ 8. rem. 18)	משל
תַּמְשִׁלֵנִי	וַ Hiph. fut. 2 p. pl. m. [תַּמְשִׁלוּ], suff. 1 p. s.	משל
תָּמֹת / תָּמָת	} (וַתָּ h, גַ') Kal fut. 3 pers. sing. fem., ap. & conv. fr. תָּמוּת (§ 21. r. 7 & 8)	מות
תֻּמַּת	noun fem. sing., constr. of תֻּמָּה dec. 10	תמם

a Job 9. 9.   h Je. 10. 24.   o 1 Sa. 13. 22.   x Je. 50. 20.   c Zec. 14. 12.   i Jos. 22. 18.   p Je. 31. 21.   x Pr. 12. 24.   e Ge. 37. 8.
b Nu. 22. 16.   i Nu. 35. 8.   p Is. 10. 14.   l 1 Sa. 23. 17.   d Zec. 14. 12.   k Eze. 41. 18.   y 1 Ki. 6. 35.   s Ex. 30. 30.   f Ge. 4. 7.
c Nu. 12. 8.   k 2 Ki. 4. 3.   r Ex. 16. 25.   l Is. 41. 12.   e Joel 1. 12.   l 1 Sa. 12. 14.   z Job 39. 18.   t Ps. 8. 7.   g Is. 46. 4.
d Ps. 58. 9.   l Le. 5. 15.   s Ex. 5. 11.   m De. 31. 12.   f Ex. 23. 21.   m Eze. 40. 22.   a Pr. 20. 30.   u Eze. 12. 25, 28.   h Is. 50. 2.
e Ps. 39. 12.   m Nu. 5. 27.   t 1 Sa. 9. 13.   n Ec. 11. 1.   g Eze. 5. 6.   n Est. 2. 3.   b 2 Sa. 19. 14.   v Est. 2. 9.   i Ju. 20. 5.
f Ps. 37. 31.   n Ne. 1. 8.   u Eze. 26. 21.   o Is. 66. 11.   h Ju. 4. 5.   o Est. 2. 12.   c Ju. 6. 18.   w Ps. 28. 3.   k Pr. 11. 3.
g Je. 29. 6.   mm 1 Ki. 20. 25.   tt Joel 3. 3.

תְּמֻתוּ — defect. for תָּמוּתוּ (q. v.) . . . מות

תְּמֻתוּן — defect. for תָּמוּתוּן (q. v.) . . . מות

תַּמָּתִי — adj. fem. sing., suff. 1 pers. sing. [from תַּמָּה dec. 10] from תָּם masc. . . . תמם

תַּמָּתִי — noun fem. sing., suff. 1 pers. s. fr. [תַּמָּה] d. 10 . . . תמם

תַּמְתִּיק — Hiph. fut. 3 pers. sing. fem. . . . מתק

תְּמִתֻנַּגוּ — Hiph. fut. 2 pers. s. m. (תָּמִית), suff. 1 p. pl. . . . מות

תֵּן / תֶּן־ — } Kal imp. sing. masc. (§ 17. rem. 2) . . . נתן

תְּנָא — Ch. Root not used; i. q. Heb. שָׁנָה *to repeat.*

    תִּנְיָן Ch. *second,* Da. 7. 5.

    תִּנְיָנוּת Ch. *a second time,* Da. 2. 7.

תִּנְאַף / וַתִּנְאַף — } Kal fut. 2 pers. sing. masc., or 3 pers. sing. fem.; וַ conv. . . . נאף

תִּנְאַפְנָה — Piel fut. 3 pers. pl. fem. . . . נאף

תִּנְאַץ — Kal fut. 2 pers. sing. masc. . . . נאץ

תִּנָּבֵא — Niph. fut. 2 pers. sing. masc. . . . נבא

תִּנָּבְאוּ — id. fut. 2 pers. pl. masc. . . . נבא

תְּנַבֵּל — Piel fut. 2 pers. sing. masc. . . . נבל

תְּנַגַּח — Piel fut. 2 pers. sing. masc. . . . נגח

תִּנָּגְחוּ — id. fut. 2 pers. pl. masc. . . . נגח

תִּנָּגְפוּ — Niph. fut. 2 pers. pl. masc. . . . נגף

תִּנָּגְשׁוּ — Kal fut. 2 pers. pl. m. [for תִּנָּגְשׁוּ § 8. r. 15] . . . נגש

תָּנֹד — Kal fut. 2 pers. sing. masc., ap. from תָּנוּד . . . נוד

תְּנֻד — Ch. Peal fut. 3 pers. sing. fem. . . . נוד

תָּנֻדוּ — Kal fut. 2 pers. pl. masc. [for תָּנוּדוּ] . . . נוד

תְּנִדֵנִי — Hiph. fut. 2 pers. s. m. [תָּנִיד], suff. 1 p. s. . . . נוד

תִּנְדַּע — } Ch. Peal fut. 2 pers. sing. m., dag. forte resolved in נ [for תֵּדַּע § 52. r. 2] . . . ידע

תִּנְדֹּף — Kal fut. 2 pers. sing. masc. . . . נדף

[תָּנָה] — *to give presents, distribute gifts* in order *to hire* any one, Ho. 8. 10. Pi. *to praise, celebrate,* with acc., לְ. Hiph. *to hire,* Ho. 8. 9.

    אֶתְנָה fem. *gift, wages* of prostitution, Ho. 2. 14.

    אֶתְנִי (*giving, munificent*) pr. name m. 1 Ch. 6. 26.

    אֶתְנַן masc. dec. 8 a.—I. *gift, wages* of prostitution.—II. pr. name masc. 1 Ch. 4. 7.

    יְתַנְאֵל (*whom God bestows,* i. e. given of God) pr. name masc. 1 Ch. 26. 2.

    יִתְנָן (*gift*) pr. name of a city in Judah, Jos. 15. 23.

תְּנָה — Kal imp. s. m. (תֵּן), with parag. ה (§ 17. r. 2) . . . נתן

תְּנַהֵג / וַ — Piel fut. 2 pers. s. m. (§ 14. r. 1); וַ conv. . . . נהג

תְּנֵהוּ / וּ — Kal imp. sing. masc. (תֵּן), suff. 3 pers. sing. masc.; וּ bef. (:) . . . נתן

תְּנַהֲלֵנִי — וּ Piel (§ 14. rem. 1) fut. 2 pers. sing. masc., suff. 1 pers. sing.; וּ bef. (:) . . . נהל

תְּנוּ — וַ Kal imp. pl. masc.; וּ id. . . . נתן

תְּנוּאוּן — Kh. תְּנוּאוּן Kal, K. תְּנִיאוּן Hiph. fut. 2 pers. pl. masc.; ן parag. . . . נוא

תְּנוּאוֹת — noun fem., pl. of [תְּנוּאָה] dec. 10 . . . נוא

תְּנוּאָתִי — id. sing., suff. 1 pers. sing. . . . נוא

תְּנוּבָה — noun masc. sing. dec. 10 . . . נוב

תְּנוּבַת — id., constr. st.; וּ bef. (:) . . . נוב

תְּנוּבֹת — id. pl. . . . נוב

תְּנוּבֹתַי — id. sing., suff. 1 pers. sing. . . . נוב

תָּנוּד — Kal fut. 2 pers. sing. masc. . . . נוד

תָּנוּחַ — Kal fut. 2 p. s. m. (Da. 12. 13), or 3 p. s. f. . . . נוח

תָּנוּט — Kal fut. 2 pers. sing. fem. . . . נוט

תָּנוּךְ — noun masc. sing. . . . תנך

תְּנוּמָה — noun fem. sing. dec. 10; וּ bef. (:) . . . נום

תְּנוּמוֹת — id. pl. . . . נום

תָּנוּם — Kal fut. 2 pers. sing. masc. . . . נום

תְּנוּסוּ / תְּנוּסוּן — } id. fut. 2 pers. pl. masc.; ן parag. . . . נום

תָּנוּעַ — Kal fut. 3 pers. sing. fem. . . . נוע

תְּנוּפָה — noun fem. sing. dec. 10 . . . נוף

תְּנוּפַת — id., constr. st. . . . נוף

תְּנוּפֹת — id. pl. . . . נוף

תַּנּוּר — וּ noun masc. sing. dec. 1 b . . . תנר

תָּנַח — וַ Kal fut. 3 pers. sing. fem., ap. and conv. from תָּנוּחַ (§ 21. rem. 9); וַ conv. . . . נוח

תַּנַּח — וַ Hiph. fut. 2 p. s. m., or (Ge. 39. 16) 3 p. s. f., ap. & conv. [fr. תָּנִיחַ=תַּנְיִחַ § 21. r. 24] . . . נוח

תַּנְחֶה — Hiph. fut. 3 pers. sing. fem. . . . נחה

תַּנְחוּמוֹת — noun pl. fem. from [תַּנְחוּם] dec. 1 a . . . נחם

תַּנְחוּמֶיךָ — id. pl. masc., suff. 2 pers. sing. masc. . . . נחם

תַּנְחוּמִים — id. id., abs. st. . . . נחם

תַּנְחוּמֹתֵיכֶם — id. pl. fem., suff. 2 pers. pl. masc. . . . נחם

תַּנְחִיל — Hiph. fut. 2 pers. sing. masc. . . . נחל

תַּנְחִילֶנָּה — id., suff. 3 pers. sing. fem. . . . נחל

תִּנְחַל / תִּנְחָל — } Kal fut. 2 pers. sing. masc. (§ 8. r. 15) . . . נחל

תַּנְחֵם — Hiph. fut. 2 pers. sing. masc., or (Pr. 11. 3) 3 pers. sing. fem. [תַּנְחֶה], suff. 3 pers. pl. masc. (§ 24. rem. 21) . . . נחה

תְּנֻחָמוּ — Pual (§ 14. rem. 1) fut. 2 pers. pl. masc. [for תְּנֻחֲמוּ comp. § 8. rem. 15] . . . נחם

תְּנַחֲמוּנִי — Piel (§ 14. rem. 1) fut. 2 pers. pl. masc., suff. 1 pers. sing. . . . נחם

תַּנְחֻמֶיהָ — noun m. pl., suff. 3 p. s. f. fr. [תַּנְחֻם] d. 1 b . . . נחם

° Job 20. 12.   g Je. 14. 21.   n Ps. 36. 12.   l 1 Ch. 21. 22.   t Is. 27. 6.   k Ps. 99. 1.   m Is. 24. 20.   f Job 15. 11.   e De. 31. 7.

Je. 41. 8.   i Eze. 34. 21.   v Da. 2. 30.   q Ne. 1. 11.   u Eze. 36. 30.   i Ps. 132. 4.   n Nu. 18. 11.   b Ps. 94. 19.   b Is. 18. 20.

Je. 3. 9.   k Is. 58. 3.   w Da. 4. 22,23,29.   r Ps. 31. 4.   v De. 32. 13.   k Pr. 6. 4.   o Is. 31. 9.   e Je. 16. 7.   c Is. 66. 13.

Ho. 4. 13, 14.   l Is. 16. 5.   x Ezr. 4. 15.   s Nu. 32. 7.   w Ju. 9. 11.   l Jo. 10; 24. 33.   p Ge. 39. 16.   r Job 21. 1.   d Job 21. 34.

Je. 14. 21.   l Da. 4. 11.   y Ps. 68. 3.   t Jos 33. 10.   x Je. 4. 1.   m Is. 10. 3.   q Pr. 6. 22.   s Jos. 1. 6.   t Is. 66. 11.

Am. 2. 12.   m Je. 22. 10.   z Ge. 31. 26.   u Nu. 14. 34.   d Da. 12. 13.   n Is. 30. 15.

תְּנַחֲמֵנּוּ Piel fut. 3 pers. sing. masc. [תְּנַחֵם § 14. rem. 1], suff. 3 pers. sing. masc. . . נחם

תְּנַחֲמֵנִי id. fut. 2 pers. sing. masc., or (Job 7. 13) 3 pers. sing. f., suff. 1 pers. s.; ו bef. (:) . נחם

תַּנְחֻמֶת pr. name masc. . . . . . נחם

תַּנִּחֵנוּ Hiph. fut. 2 pers. sing. masc. [תַּנִּיחַ § 21. rem. 24], suff. 1 pers. pl. . . . נוח

תַּנְחֵנִי Hiph. fut. 2 pers. sing. masc., or (Ps. 139. 10) 3 pers. sing. fem. [תַּנְחֶה], suff. 1 pers. sing. (§ 24. rem. 21) . . . נחה

תְּנַחֲשׁוּ Piel fut. 2 pers. pl. masc. (§ 14. rem. 1) . נחש

תִּנְחַת ו Kal fut. 3 pers. sing. fem.; ו conv. . נחת

תְּנִי / תְּנִי } Kal imp. sing. fem. (comp. § 8. rem. 12) . נתן

תְּנִיחֶנּוּ Hiph. fut. 3 pers. sing. fem. [תָּנִיחַ], suff. 3 pers. sing. masc. . . . . נוח

תַּנִּיחֵנִי id. fut. 2 pers. sing. masc. תַּנִּיחַ § 21. rem. 24], suff. 1 pers. sing. . . ינח

תַּנִּים noun m. s. for תַּנִּין by interch. of the liquids תנן

תַּנִּים ו noun masc., pl. of [תַּן] dec. 8 d . תנן

תַּנִּין id. pl. with Chald. term. . . . תנן

תַּנִּין ו noun masc. sing., pl. תַּנִּינִים dec. 1 b . תנן

תִּנְיָנָה Ch. adj. ord. fem. sing [from תִּנְיָן masc.] תנא

תִּנְיָנוּת Ch. noun fem. sing. . . . תנא

תַּנִּינִים / תַּנִּינִם } noun masc., pl. of תַּנִּין dec. 1 b . תנן

תְּנִיעֵנִי ו Hiph. fut. 3 pers. sing. fem. (תָּנִיעַ), suff. 1 pers. sing.; ו conv. . . . נוע

תָּנִיף Hiph. fut. 2 pers. sing. masc. . . נוף

תְּנִיקֵהוּ ו Hiph. fut. 3 pers. sing. fem. [תָּנִיק], suff. 3 pers. sing. masc.; ו conv. . . . נוק

תָּנֵךְ Root not used; Syr. Ethpe. to come to an end. תְּנוּךְ masc. extremity, tip of the ear.

תְּנַכְּרוּ Piel fut. 2 p. pl. m. [for תְּנַכֵּרוּ comp. § 8. r. 15] . . נכר

תְּנֵם ו Kal imp. sing. masc. (תֵּן), suff. 3 pers. pl. masc.; ו bef. (:) . . . נתן

תָּנַן Root not used; to which is ascribed the sense of stretching out, extending.

תַּן or תָּן masc. only pl. תַּנִּים huge serpents; others, jackals.

תַּנִּים masc. for תַּנִּין a great serpent, sea monster, Eze. 29. 3.

תַּנָּה fem. dec. 10, serpent, Mal. 1. 3; others, dwelling, habitation. (Arab. תנא to abide, dwell.)

תַּנִּין masc. (pl. תַּנִּינִים (תַּנִּינִים).—I. serpent.—II. a large fish, sea monster.—III. crocodile.

אַתּוּן Ch. masc. dec. 1 a, furnace, for אַתְּנוּן, Ch. תְּנַן to smoke. According to some also תַּנּוּר q. v. R. תָּנַר.

תְּנֵהוּ Kal imp. s. masc. with suff. 3 pers. sing. fem. . נתן

תָּנֹם ו Kal fut. 3 pers. sing. fem., ap. & conv. [from תָּנוּם § 21. rem. 7 & 8] . . נום

תְּנוּסוּ id. fut. 2 pers. pl. masc. defect. for תְּנוּסוּ . נום

תְּנַסֶּף / תְּנַסּוּן } Piel fut. 2 pers. pl. masc., ו parag. . נסה

תְּנַפְּצֵם Piel fut. 2 pers. sing. masc. [תְּנַפֵּץ], suff. 3 pers. pl. masc. . . . . נפץ

תִּנָּצֵל ו Niph. fut. 2 pers. sing. fem., or (Ge. 32. 31) 3 pers. sing. fem.; ו conv. . צנל

תִּנָּצְלִי id. fut. 2 pers. s. f. [for תִּנָּצֵלִי comp. § 8. r. 15] . נצל

תִּנְצָרֶכָּה Kal fut. 3 pers. sing. fem. [תִּנְצֹר], suff. 2 pers. sing. masc. [for תִּנְצָרְךָ § 2. r. 2] נצר

תִּנְצְרֵנִי id. fut. 2 pers. sing. masc., suff. 1 pers. sing. נצר

תִּנָּקֶה Niph. fut. 2 pers. sing. masc. . . נקה

תְּנַקֵּהוּ Piel fut. 2 pers. s. masc., suff. 3 pers. s. masc. נקה

תִּנָּקוּ Niph. fut. 2 pers. pl. masc. . . . נקה

תְּנַקֵּנִי Piel fut. 2 pers. sing. masc. [תְּנַקֶּה], suff. 1 pers. sing. (§ 24. rem. 21) . . נקה

תְּנַקֵּר Piel fut. 2 pers. sing. masc. . . . נקר

תִּנָּקֵשׁ Niph. fut. 2 pers. sing. masc. . . . נקש

תָּנַר Root not used; whence apparently

תַּנּוּר masc. dec. 1 b, oven, furnace. Some derive it from נוּר to shine, Chald. subst. fire; others regard it as a compounded word from תָּן, Chald. תָּנַן to smoke, & נוּר; comp. אַתּוּן, R. תָּנַן.

תִּתְנַשֵּׂא ו Hithpa. fut. 3 pers. sing. fem. [for תִּתְנַשֵּׂא § 12. rem. 3] . . . . נשא

תִּנָּשְׂאוּ Niph. fut. 2 pers. pl. masc. [for תִּנָּשְׂאוּ, comp. § 8. rem. 15] . . . . נשא

תִּנָּשֶׂאנָה id. fut. 3 pers. pl. fem. . . . נשא

תִּנָּשֵׂנִי Niph. fut. 2 pers. sing. masc. [תִּנָּשֶׂה], suff. 1 pers. sing. (§ 24. rem. 21) . . נשה

תְּנַתֵּחַ Piel fut. 2 pers. s. masc. [for תְּנַתַּח § 15. r. 1] נתח

תִּנָּתֵן ו תַּתֵּן Niph. fut. 2 pers. sing. masc., or 3 pers. sing. fem.; ו conv. . . . נתן

תִּנָּתָן id. fut. 3 pers. s. fem. (bef. monos. § 9. r. 3) נתן

תִּנְתֵּן Chald. Peal fut. 2 pers. sing. masc. . נתן

תְּנַתְּקוּ Piel fut. 2 pers. pl. masc. [for תְּנַתֵּקוּ, comp. § 8. rem. 15] . . . . . נתק

Is. 66. 13.   ⸍ Is. 43. 6.   La. 4. 3.   ♭ Da. 10. 10.   ₰ 2 Sa. 4. 4.   ◁ Ge. 32. 31.   ʰ Nu. 16. 14.   ▬ Is. 49. 22.   ⸱ Est. 9. 14.
Is. 12. 1.   ᵍ Is. 63. 14.   ⸗ Ps. 91. 13.   ▪ Ex. 2. 9.   ʸ Is. 30. 17.   ◁ Mi. 4. 10.   ⸍ De. 12. 30.   ⸱ Is. 44. 21.   ⸱ Est. 7. 2, 3.
Je. 14. 9.   ʰ Ps. 119. 121.   ᵇ Da. 7. 5.   ♭ Job 21. 29.   ⸍ Pr. 2. 11.   ⸱ Nu. 24. 7.   ⸱ Ex. 29. 17.   ⸱ Ezr. 7. 20.
Le. 19. 26.   ⸱ Eze. 29. 3.   ᵉ Da. 2. 7.   ⸱ Ne. 3. 36.   ⸱ Ex. 17. 2.   ⸱ Is. 66. 12.   ᵖ Da. 11. 6.   ⸱ Eze. 23. 34.
Ps. 38. 3.   ᵏ Is. 13. 22.   ᵐ De. 32. 33.   ⸱ 1 Sa. 21. 10.   ⸱ Ps. 2. 9.   ⸱ 1 Ki. 2. 9.   u Je. 25. 29.

תְּנַתְּקִי	id. fut. 2 pers. s. f. [for תְּנַתְּקִי comp. § 8. r.15]	נתק
תְּנָתֵשׁ	Niph fut. 3 pers. sing. fem.	נתש
תָּסֹב	וַתָּ, ן Kal fut. 2 pers. sing. masc., or 3 pers. sing. fem. [for תָּסֹב § 18. rem. 14]; ן conv.	סבב
תְּסֻבּוּ	id. fut. 2 pers. pl. masc.	סבב
תְּסֻבֶּינָה	id. fut. 3 pers. pl. fem.	סבב
תַּסֵּג	ן ap. from תַּסִּיג (q. v.)	נסג
תִּסְגְּדוּן	ן Chald. Peal fut. 2 pers. pl. masc.	סגד
תַּסְגִּיר / תַּסְגֵּר	Hiph. fut. 2 pers. sing. masc.	סגר
תִּסָּגֵר	ן Niph. fut. 3 pers. sing. fem.; ן conv.	סגר
תִּסָּגֵר	ן Kal fut. 3 pers. sing. fem.; ן id.	סגר
תַּסְגִּרֵנִי	Hiph. fut. 2 pers. s. m. (תַּסְגִּיר), suff. 1 pers. s.	סגר
תָּסוֹב	Kal fut. 3 pers. sing. fem., comp. תָּסֹב	סבב
תְּסוֹבֵב	Pilel fut. 3 pers. sing. fem.	סבב
תְּסוֹבְבֶךָ	id. id., suff. 2 pers. sing. masc. [for תְּסוֹבְבֶךָ § 2. rem. 2, comp. § 16. rem. 15]	סבב
תְּסוֹבְבֵנִי	id. fut. 2 pers. sing. with suff. 1 pers. sing.	סבב
תָּסוּג	Kal fut. 2 pers. sing. masc.	סוג
תְּסוּגִי	id. fut. 2 pers. sing. fem.	סוג
תָּסוּר	Kal fut. 2 pers. sing. masc., or 3 pers. s. fem.	סור
תָּסוּרוּ	id. fut. 2 pers. pl. masc.	סור
תִּסְחָרוּ	Kal fut. 2 pers. pl. m. [for תִּסְחֲרוּ § 8. rem. 15]	סחר
תַּסִּיג	Hiph. fut. 2 pers. sing. masc.	נסג
תַּסִּיעַ	Hiph. fut. 2 pers. sing. masc.	נסע
תַּסִּיעִי	id. fut. 2 pers. sing. fem.	נסע
תֹּסִף	Hiph. fut. 2 pers. sing. masc. defect. for תּוֹסִיף	יסף
תָּסִיר	Hiph. fut. 2 pers. sing. masc.	סור
תְּסִיתֵהוּ	ן Hiph. fut. 3 pers. sing. fem. [תָּסִית], suff. 3 pers. sing. masc.; ן conv.	סות
תְּסִיתֵנִי	ן id. fut. 2 pers. s. masc., suff. 1 pers. s.; ן id.	סות
תָּסֵךְ	ן Hiph. fut. 2 pers. sing. masc.	סכך
תִּסְכּוּ	Kal fut. 2 pers. pl. masc.	נסך
תִּסְכְּנִי	Kal fut. 2 pers. sing. masc. [תָּסֹךְ], suff. 1 pers. sing. (§ 18. rem. 5)	סכך
תְּסֻלֶּה	Pual fut. 3 pers. sing. fem.	סלה
תְּסַלֵּף	Piel fut. 3 pers. sing. fem.	סלף
תִּסְמְכֵנִי	Kal fut. 2 pers. sing. masc., or 3 pers. sing. fem., suff. 1 pers. sing.	סמד
תְּסַמֵּר	Piel fut. 3 pers. sing. fem.	סמר
תִּסְעָדֵנִי	Kal fut. 3 pers. sing. fem. [תִּסְעַד], suff. 1 pers. sing. (§ 16. rem. 12)	סעד
תִּסְעוּ	Kal fut. 2 p. pl. m. [for תִּסְעֲוּ, comp. § 10. r.7]	נסע
תָּסֵף	ן Chald. Aph. fut. 3 pers. sing. fem.	סוף
תֹּסֵף	Kal fut. 2 pers. s. m. [for תֹּאסֵף § 19. r. 4 & 5]	אסף

תֹּסֵף / וַ‹ן תֹּסֵף	Hiph. fut. 2 pers. sing. masc., or 2 pers. sing. fem., ap. conv. & defect. for תּוֹסִיף	יסף
תֹּסִיף	id. fut. 3 pers. sing. fem. defect. for תּוֹסִיף	יסף
תִּסְפֹּד	וַ‹ן Kal fut. 2 pers. s. m., or 3 p. s. f.; ן conv.	ספד
תִּסְפְּדוּ	id. fut. 2 pers. pl. masc.	ספד
תִּסָּפֶה	Niph. fut. 2 pers. sing. masc.	ספה
תִּסְפֶּה	Kal fut. 2 pers. s. m., or (Is. 7. 20) 3 p. s. fem.	ספה
תִּסָּפוּ	Niph. fut. 2 pers. pl. masc.	ספה
תִּסְפוּ	Hiph. fut. 2 pers. pl. masc. defect. for תּוֹסִיפוּ; ן parag.	יסף
תִּסְפּוֹר	Kal fut. 2 pers. sing. masc. (§ 8. r. 18)	ספר
תְּסַפֵּר	Piel fut. 2 pers. sing. masc.	ספר
תְּסַפֵּר	ן id. fut. 3 pers. s. fem. (§ 10. r. 4); ן conv.	ספר
תִּסְפֹּר / תִּסְפְּרִי	Kal fut. 2 pers. sing. masc. (§ 8. rem. 18)	ספר
תְּסַפְּרוּ	Piel fut. 2 pers. pl. masc.	ספר
תִּסְפְּרוּ	Kal fut. 2 pers. pl. masc.	ספר
תָּסַ‹ן	Hiph. fut. 3 pers. sing. fem., ap. & conv. [from תָּסִיר § 21. rem. 9]	סור
תָּסֵר	ן id. fut. 3 pers. sing. fem. ap. [from תָּסִיר]	סור
תָּסֵרוּ	defect. for תָּסוּרוּ (q. v.)	סור
תִּסְרַח	Kal fut. 2 pers. sing. masc.	סרח
תַּסְתִּיר	Hiph. fut. 2 pers. sing. masc.	סתר
תַּסְתִּירֶהָ / תַּסְתִּירֵהוּ	ן id. fut. 3 pers. s. fem., suff. 3 p. s. m.; ן conv.	סתר
תַּסְתִּירֵם	id. fut. 2 pers. s. masc., suff. 3 pers. pl. masc.	סתר
תַּסְתִּירֵנִי	id. id. with suff. 1 pers. sing.	סתר
תַּסְתִּמוּ	Kal fut. 2 pers. pl. m. [for תִּסְתְּמוּ § 8. r. 15]	סתם
תַּסְתֵּר	Hiph. fut. 2 pers. sing. masc., ap. from תַּסְתִּיר	סתר
תִּסָּתֵר	Niph. fut. 2 pers. sing. masc.	סתר
תִּסָּתְרוּ	id. fut. 2 pers. pl. masc.	סתר
תִּסְתַּתֵּר	Hithpa. fut. 3 p. s. f. [for תִּתְסַתֵּר § 12. r. 1 & 3]	סתר

תָּעַב. Pi. תִּעֵב (§ 14. rem. 1).—I. *to abhor.*—II. *to render abominable, cause to be abhorred,* Eze. 16. 25.—III. *to excite abhorrence, be an object of abhorrence,* Is. 49. 7. Hiph. *to make abominable, to act abominably.* Niph. *to be abhorred, detested.*

תּוֹעֵבָה fem. dec. 11 b.—I. *abomination, abominable thing, object of abomination.*—II. *abominable act or practice.*

תָּעֵב	ן Piel inf. abs. (§ 14. rem. 1)	תעב
תַּעֲבֹד	Kal fut. 2 pers. sing. masc.	עבד
תֵּעָבֵד	Niph. fut. 3 pers. sing. fem.	עבד
תַּעַבְדוּ / תַּעַבְדוּ	וַ‹ן Kal fut. 2 pers. pl. masc. (§ 8. rem. 15); ן conv.	עבד

a Eze. 23. 34   b Da. 11. 4.   c Ps. 71. 21.   d 1 Ki. 2. 15.   e Jos. 6. 4.   f Ge. 37. 7.   g Mi. 6. 14.

h Da. 3. 5, 15.   i De. 23. 16.   k Ob. 14.   l Nu. 12. 14, 15.   m 1 Ki. 4. 5, 21.   n 2 Ki. 4. 4.   o Je. 31. 72.

p Ps. 7. 8.   q Ps. 32. 7.   r Ps. 139. 13.   s Ge. 42. 34.   t De. 19. 14.   u Job 28. 16, 19.   v 2 Ki. 4. 4.

w Job 2. 3.   x Ps. 5. 12.   y Ex. 30. 9.   z Ps. 139. 13.   a' Ps. 104. 29.   b' Ge. 4. 12.   c' De. 13. 1.

d' Ps. 18. 36.   e' Jos. 3. 3.   f' Da. 2. 44.   g' Ge. 19. 15, 17.   h' Ge. 18. 23, 24.   i' Job 14. 16.

k' Eze. 24. 16.   l' 2 Sa. 11. 26.   m' Eze. 24. 23.

n' Ex. 10. 2.   o' 2 Ki. 8. 6.   p' Job 39. 2.   q' De. 5. 29.   r' Ex. 36. 13.   s' 2 Ch. 22. 11.   t' Ps. 31. 21.

u' Ge. 38. 14, 19.   v' Ho. 2. 4.   w' De. 5. 29.   x' Ex. 26. 13.   y' Le. 23. 16.

z' 2 Ki. 8. 19.   a" Ps. 89. 47.   b" Zep. 2. 3.   c" Is. 29. 14.   d" De. 7. 26.   e" Eze. 36. 34.

תַּעַבְדוּם	id. id., suff. 3 pers. pl. **masc.**	עבד
תַּעַבְדוּן	id. id. with parag. ן (§ 4. rem. 17); Chald. Ezr. 6. 8; 7. 18	עבד
תַּעַבְדֵם	Hoph. fut. 2 pers. sing. m., suff. 3 pers. pl. m.	עבד
תַּעַבְדוּנִי	Piel (§ 14. r. 1) pret. 3 pers. pl., suff. 1 p. s.	תעב
תַּעֲבוֹר	Kal fut. 2 pers. sing. masc. (§ 8. rem. 18)	עבר
תַּעֲבוּרִי	id. fut. 2 pers. sing. fem. (§ 8. rem. 14)	עבר
תַּעֲבוֹת	defect. for תּוֹעֵבוֹת (q. v.)	תעב
תַּעְבֵּט	Kal fut. 2 pers. sing. masc.	עבט
תַּעֲבִיטֶנּוּ	Hiph. fut. 2 pers. sing. m., suff. 3 pers. sing. m.	עבט
תַּעֲבִיר	Hiph. fut. 2 pers. sing. masc.	עבר
תַּעֲבִירוּ	id. fut. 2 pers. pl. masc.	עבר
תַּעֲבֹר וַ'	Kal fut. 2 pers. sing. masc., or 3 pers. sing. fem. (§ 8. rem. 18); וַ' conv.	עבר
תַּעַבְרוּ וַ'	id. fut. 2 pers. pl. masc. (§ 8. rem. 15); וַ' id.	עבר
תַּעֲבֹרְנָה	id. fut. 3 pers. pl. fem.	עבר
תַּעֲבִרֶנּוּ	Hiph. fut. 2 pers. s. m. [תַּעֲבִיר], suff. 1 pers. pl.	עבר
תַּעֲנֹב וַ	Kh. תַּעֲנֹב q. v., K. תַּעֲנְבָה (q. v.)	ענב
תַּעֲנֹב וַ	Kal fut. 3 pers. s. fem. (§ 13. r. 5); וַ conv.	ענב
תַּעַנְבָה וַ	id. fut. 3 pers. sing. fem. with parag. ה (§ 8. rem. 13); וַ' id.	ענב
תַּעֲגֶנָה	Niph. fut. 3 pers. pl. fem. (§ 8. rem. 13, note)	ענן
תַּעֲנֶּנָה	Kal fut. 2 p. s. m., suff. 3 p. s. f., denom. fr. עֹנָה	עונ
תָּעַד	Hiph. fut. 2 pers. sing. masc. ap. & conv. for תָּעִיד (§ 21. rem. 9)	עוד
תָּעַד וַ	Kal fut. 3 pers. sing. fem. ap. from תַּעֲדֶה (§ 24. rem. 3); וַ' conv.	עדה
תַּעְדֵּא	Chald. Peal fut. 3 pers. sing. fem. (§ 49. r. 2)	עדה
תַּעֲדֶה	Kal fut. 3 pers. sing. fem. (§ 13. rem. 5)	עדה
תַּעֲדִי וַ'	id. fut. 2 pers. sing. fem.; וַ' conv.	עדה
תָּעָה	fut. יִתְעַע, ap. יֵתַע (§ 24. rem. 3).—I. *to wander, go astray*.—II. *to stagger* through drunkenness, Is. 28. 7.—III. trop. *to stray, err*, with מֵעַל *away from*, מֵאַחֲרֵי *from following*.—IV. perh. *to perish*, Pr. 14. 22, comp. אָבַד. Niph. I. *to stagger*, Is. 19. 14. —II. *to be led astray, to be deceived*, Job 15. 31. Hiph. הִתְעָה—I. *to cause to wander*, or *go astray*.—II. *to lead astray, to seduce*.—III. *to commit error, to err*. תּוֹעָה fem.—I. *error*, or *apostacy*, Is. 32. 6.—II. *hurt, injury*, Ne. 4. 2. תֹּעוּ (*error*) pr. name of a king of Hamath, 1 Ch. 18. 9, 10; called תֹּעִי 2 Sa. 8. 9, 10.	תעה
תֹּעֶה	Kal part. act. sing. masc. dec. 9a	תעה
תָּעוּ	id. pret. 3 pers. pl.	תעה

תֹּעוּ	pr. name masc.	תעה
תְּעוּדָה	noun fem. sing.	עוד
תְּעוֹלֵל	Poel fut. 2 pers. sing. masc.	עלל
תְּעוֹנְנֵנוּ	Poel fut. 2 pers. pl. masc. [for תְּעוֹנְנֵנוּ comp. § 8. rem. 15]	ענן
תָּעוּף	Kal fut. 3 pers. sing. fem.	עוף
תְּעוּפֶינָה	id. fut. 3 pers. pl. fem.	עוף
תֵּעוֹר	Niph. fut. 3 pers. sing. fem.	עור
תְּעוֹרְרוּ	Pilel fut. 2 pers. pl. masc.	עור
תָּעֹז / תָּעֹז וַ'	Kal fut. 2 pers. sing. fem. (§ 18. rem. 5); וַ' conv.	עזז
תַּעֲזֹב וַ'	Kal fut. 2 pers. sing. masc., or (Job 39. 14) 3 pers. sing. fem.	עזב
תֵּעָזֵב / תֵּעָזֵב	Niph. fut. 3 pers. sing. fem. (§ 9. rem. 4)	עזב
תַּעַזְבָה	Kal fut. 2 pers. s. m. (תַּעֲזֹב), suff. 3 p. s. fem.	עזב
תַּעַזְבֻהוּ	id. fut. 2 pers. pl. masc., suff. 3 pers. sing. m.	עזב
תַּעַזְבוּ / תַּעֲזֹבוּ	id. fut. 2 pers. pl. masc. (§ 8. rem. 15)	עזב
תַּעַזְבִי וַ	id. fut. 2 pers. sing. fem.; וַ' conv.	עזב
תַּעַזְבֵם וַ	id. fut. 2 pers. sing. masc. (תַּעֲזֹב), suff. 3 pers. pl. masc.; וַ' id.	עזב
תַּעַזְבֵנוּ	id. id., suff. 1 pers. pl.	עזב
תַּעַזְבֵנוּ	id. id., suff. 3 pers. sing. **masc.**	עזב
תַּעַזְבֵנִי	id. id., suff. 1 pers. sing.	עזב
תַּעַט וַ	Hiph. fut. 3 p. s. f. ap. & conv. (§ 21. r. 24)	עיט
תַּעֲטֶה	Kal fut. 2 pers. sing. masc.	עטה
תַּעֲטוּ	id. fut. 2 pers. pl. masc. (§ 13. rem. 5 & 6)	עטה
תַּעַטְרֵהוּ	Piel fut. 3 p. s. fem. [תַּעֲטֵר], suff. 3 p. s. m.	עטר
תַּעַטְרֵנוּ	Kal fut. 2 pers. sing. masc. [תַּעֲטֹר], suff. 3 pers. sing. masc. [for תַּעַטְרֵנּוּ § 13. rem. 5]	עטר
תֹּעֵי	Kal part. act. pl. constr. masc. from תֹּעֶה d. 9a	תעה
תֹּעִי	[for תֹּעוּ] pr. name masc., see תֹּעוּ	תעה
תָּעִיד	Hiph. fut. 2 pers. sing. masc.	עוד
תְּעִידֵנִי וַ	id. fut. 3 pers. s. fem., suff. 1 p. s.; וַ' conv.	עוד
תָּעִינוּ	Kal fut. 1 pers. pl.	תעה
תָּעִיק	Hiph. fut. 3 pers. sing. fem.	עוק
תָּעִירוּ	Hiph. fut. 2 pers. pl. masc.	עור
תָּעִיתִי	Kal pret. 1 pers. sing.	תעה
תְּעֻבַּסְנָה	Piel fut. 3 pers. pl. f. [for תְּעֻבַּסְנָה § 10. r. 4]	עכס
תַּעַל וַ / תַּעַל וַ', וַ'	Kal fut. 3 pers. sing. fem., ap. from תַּעֲלֶה (§ 24. r. 3 & 16); וַ' conv.	עלה
תַּעַל וַ	Hiph. fut. 2 pers. sing. masc., or 3 pers. sing. fem., ap. from תַּעֲלֶה (§ 24. r. 3 & 16); וַ' id.	עלה
תַּעֲלֶה וַ'	Kal fut. 2 pers. sing. masc., or 3 pers. sing. fem.; or Hiph. fut. 2 pers. sing. m.; וַ' id.	עלה

Ex. 3. 12.   De. 15. 6.   Eze. 23. 5.   Is. 61. 10.   De. 4. 17.   2 Ch. 15. 2.   1 Sa. 15. 19.   1 Sa. 8. 9.   Is. 3. 16.
Jos. 24. 15.   De. 15. 8.   Eze. 23. 20.   Hab. 3. 9.   Pr. 4. 2.   Eze. 24. 17.   Job 29. 11.   Ge. 24. 16.
Job 9. 31.   Job 7. 21.   Ru. 1. 13.   Is. 21. 4.   Ru. 2. 11.   Eze. 24. 22.   Is. 53. 6.   Joel 2. 20.
2 Sa. 17. 16.   Jos. 24. 11.   Eze. 4. 12.   Is. 8. 16.   Ne. 9. 28.   Ps. 8. 6.   Am. 2. 13.   Eze. 19. 3
Ru. 2. 8.   Nu. 32. 5.   Ho. 2. 16.   Le. 19. 26.   Pr. 4. 6.   Ps. 5. 13.   Ps.119.110,176.   Jon. 2. 7.
Ch. 36. 14.   Eze. 23. 16.   Da. 6. 9, 13.   Ne. 9. 29, 30.   La. 5. 20.   Is. 60. 8.

תְּעָלָה — noun fem. sing., constr. תְּעָלַת, dec. 10 . עלה

תַּעֲלֵהוּ —] Hiph. fut. 3 pers. sing. fem., suff. 3 pers. sing. masc.; וְ conv. . עלה

תַּעֲלוּ — וְ/ Kal or Hiph. fut. 2 pers. pl. masc.; וַ id. . עלה

תֵּעָלוּ —] Niph. fut. 2 pers. pl. masc.; וַ id. . עלה

תַּעֲלוּלִים —] noun masc., pl. of תַּעֲלוּל dec. 1 b . עלל

תַּעֲלִי — Kal fut. 2 pers. sing. fem. for תַּעֲלִי (§ 8. r. 15) . עלה

תַּעַלְזִי — id. id. (Kh.); K. תַּעֲלֹזוּ fut. 2 pers. pl.m. עלז

תַּעֲלֹזְנָה — וְ/ id. fut. 3 pers. sing. fem. . עלז

תַּעֲלִי —] Kal fut. 2 pers. sing. fem.; וַ conv. . עלה

תַּעֲלִים — Hiph. fut. 2 pers. sing. masc. (§ 13. rem. 5) עלם

תַּעֲלֹמְנָה — וַ Kal fut. 3 pers. pl. fem.; וַ conv. . עלה

תַּעֲלֵם — ap. from תַּעֲלִים q. v. (§ 13. rem. 5) . עלם

תַּעֲלֻמָה תַּעֲלֻמוֹת — } noun fem. sing. and pl. dec. 10 . עלם

תַּעֲלֶנָּה — Hiph. fut. 2 pers. sing. masc. (תַּעֲלֶה) with suff. 3 pers. sing. fem. (§ 24. rem. 21) עלה

תַּעֲלֵנוּ — id. with suff., Kh. נוּ 1 pers. pl., K. נִי 1pers. s. עלה

תַּעֲלֵנוּ — id., suff. 1 pers. pl. עלה

תַּעֲלֵנִי — id., suff. 1 pers. sing. עלה

תַּעֲלֹץ — Kal fut. 3 pers. sing. fem. עלץ

תַּעֲלַת — noun fem. sing., constr. of תְּעָלָה dec. 10 עלה

תַּעֲלֹתֶיהָ — id. pl., suff. 3 pers. sing. fem. . עלה

תַּעֲמֹד — וַתַּ/ וַ Kal fut. 2 pers. sing. masc., or 3 pers. sing. fem.; וַ conv. . עמד

תַּעַמְדוּ — id. fut. 2 pers. pl. masc. [for תַּעַמְדוּ § 8. r. 15] עמד

תַּעֲמֹדוּן —] id. id. with parag.; וַ conv. עמד

תַּעֲמֹדְנָה —] id. fut. 3 pers. pl. fem.; וַ id. עמד

תַּעֲמִידֵנִי —] Hiph. fut. 3 pers. sing. fem. [תַּעֲמִיד], suff. 1 pers. sing.; וַ id. עמד

תַּעֲמֹדְנָה —] Kal fut. 3 pers. sing. fem. (§ 8. r. 18); וַ id. עמד

תַּעַן — וַ ap. from תַּעֲנֶה q. v.; וַ id. ענה

תַּעֲנֻגֹת —] noun fem. pl. [of תַּעֲנֻגָה] ענג

תַּעֲנֻגֶיהָ — noun m. pl., suff. 3 pers. s. f. fr. תַּעֲנוּג d. 1 b ענג

תַּעֲנֶה — Kal fut. 2 pers. s. m., or (Ho. 2. 24) 3 p. s. f. ענה

תַּעֲנֶהָ —] Piel fut. 3 pers. s. f., suff. 3 p. s. f.; וַ conv. ענה

תַּעַנֶּה — id. fut. 2 pers. sing. masc. . ענה

תֵּעָנֶה — Pual fut. 3 pers. sing. fem. . ענה

תַּעֲנֶהָ — the foll. with suff. 3 pers. sing. masc. ענה

תַּעֲנוּ —] Kal fut. 2 pers. pl. masc.; וַ conv. ענה

תַּעֲנוּ — Piel fut. 2 pers. pl. masc. ענה

תַּעֲנוּג — noun masc. sing. dec. 1 b ענג

תַּעֲנוּגֶיךָ — id. pl., suff. 2 pers. sing. fem. ענג

תַּעֲנוּן — Piel fut. 2 pers. pl. masc. with parag.] ענה

תַּעֲנֶינָה —] Kal fut. 3 pers. pl. fem.; וַ conv. ענה

תַּעֲנִיק — Hiph. fut. 2 pers. sing. masc. . ענק

תַּעֲנָךְ תַּעֲנָךְ — } pr. name of a city of the Manassites in the territory of Issachar.

תַּעֲנֶךָ — Kal fut. 3 pers. sing. fem. (תַּעֲנֶה), suff. 2 pers. sing. masc. (§ 24. rem. 21) . ענה

תַּעֲנֵם — id. fut. 2 pers. sing. masc., suff. 3 pers. pl. m. ענה

תַּעֲנֶנָּה — id. fut. 3 pers. pl. fem. (§ 24. rem. 6) ענה

תַּעֲנֵנוּ — id. fut. 2 pers. sing. masc., suff. 1 pers. pl. ענה

תַּעֲנֵנוּ — id. id., suff. 3 pers. sing. masc. . ענה

תַעֲנֵנוּ —] Piel fut. 2 pers. sing. masc. (תְּעַנֶּה), suff. 1 pers. pl. (§ 24. rem. 21);] bef. (:) . ענה

תַּעֲנֵנִי —] Kal fut. 2 pers. sing. masc. (תַּעֲנֶה), suff. 1 pers. sing. (§ 24. rem. 21); וַ conv. ענה

תְּעַנֵּנִי — Piel fut. 2 pers. sing. masc. (תְּעַנֶּה), suff. 1 pers. sing. (§ 24. rem. 21) . ענה

תָּעַע — Pil. תִּעְתַּע (§ 6. rem. 4) to mock, scoff, Ge. 27. 12. Hithpal הִתְעַתַּע (for הִתְתַּעְתַּע) to mock, scoff at, with בְּ 2 Ch. 36. 16.
  תַּעְתֻּעִים masc. pl. mockeries, delusions, Je. 10. 15; 51. 18.

תָּעֻפָה — Kal fut. 2 pers. sing. masc. [תָּעוּף] with parag. ה (comp. § 8. rem. 13) . עוף

תֵּעָצְבוּ תֵּעָצֵבוּ — } Niph. fut. 2 pers. pl. masc. (comp. § 8. rem. 15) . עצב

תֵּעָצְלוּ — Niph. fut. 2 pers. pl. masc. עצל

תַּעֲצֻמוֹת —] noun fem. pl. [of תַּעֲצֻמָה] עצם

תֵּעָצֵר — Kal fut. 3 pers. sing. fem. (§ 13. rem. 5) עצר

תֵּעָצֵר — id. fut. 2 pers. s. m. (§ 8. r. 18, & § 13. r. 5) עצר

תֵּעָצֵר — וַתֵּ/ וַ Niph. fut. 3 p. s. f. (§ 9. r. 4); וַ conv. עצר

תַּעַצְרֵנִי — Kal fut. 2 pers. s. m., suff. 1 p. s. (§ 13. r. 5) עצר

תֵּעָקֵר — Niph. fut. 3 pers. sing. fem. עקר

תַּעֲקֹר — Piel fut. 2 pers. sing. fem. עקר

תַּעַר — noun masc. sing. [for תַּעֲרָה] ערה

תָּעַר — וַ/ Piel fut. 2 pers. sing. masc., or 3 pers. sing. fem. ap. [from תְּעָרֶה]; וַ conv. ערה

תַּעֲרֹב — Kal fut. 3 pers. sing. fem. ערב

תַּעֲרֹג — Kal fut. 3 pers. sing. fem. . ערג

תַּעְרָהּ — noun masc. sing., suff. 3 pers. sing. fem. from תַּעַר [for תַּעֲרָהּ comp. § 35 r. 5] . ערה

תַּעֲרֹג — Kal fut. 3 pers. sing. fem. (§ 8. rem. 18) ערג

תַּעֲרֹץ — Kal fut. 2 pers. sing. masc. (§ 8. rem. 18) ערץ

תַּעַרְצִי — id. fut. 2 pers. s. f. [for תַּעַרְצִי § 8. r. 18] ערץ

1 Sa. 1. 24. — De. 1. 43. — Eze. 36. 3. — Is. 3. 4. — Je. 11. 15. — Je. 50. 11. — 2 Sa. 1. 20. | Pr. 23. 16. — Is. 57. 8. — Ps. 10. 1. — Is. 65. 17. — Pr. 11. 10. — La. 3. 56. — Job 28. 11. | Ju. 13. 16. — De. 4. 11. — Ex. 33. 15. — Ps. 102. 25. — Is. 7. 3. — Eze. 31. 4. | Da. 12. 13. — De. 4. 11. — Ru. 2. 7. — Ec. 2. 8. — Ge. 16. 6. — Le. 23. 29. | De. 1. 14, 41. — Le. 16. 29. — Pr. 19. 10. — Mi. 1. 16. — Ex. 22. 21. — De. 15. 14. | De. 20. 11. — Ju. 5. 29. — Ps. 65. 5. — 2 Ki. 4. 29. — Is. 54. 11. — 2 Sa. 13. 12. | Job 11. 17. — Ne. 8. 10, 11. — Ge. 45. 5. — Ju. 18. 9. — Ps. 68. 36. — Ps. 141. 8. — Da. 11. 6. | 2 Ki. 4. 24. — Ju. 13. 16. — Zep. 2. 4. — Jos. 11. 6. — Ps. 141. 8. — Ge. 24. 20. | Pr. 13. 19. — Ps. 42. 2. — Eze. 21. 35. — Joel 1. 20. — Job 13. 25. — Is. 47. 12.
50

תַּעֲרִיצוּ⁎	Hiph. fut. 2 pers. pl. masc.	ערץ
תַּעֶרְךָּ	noun masc. sing., suff. 2 pers. sing. masc. from עֶר [for תַּעֲרֵךָ comp. § 35 r. 5]	ערה
תַּעֲרֹךְ⁎	וַ] Kal fut. 2 pers. sing. masc., or 3 pers. sing. fem.; וְ] conv.	ערך
תַּעַרְכוּ⁎	id. fut. 2 pers. pl. masc.	ערך
תַּעֲרֹץ	Kal fut. 2 pers. sing. masc.	ערץ
תַּעַרְצוּ תַּעַרְצוּן⁎	} id. fut. 2 pers. pl. masc., ‖ parag.	ערץ
תְּעֹרֵר⁎	Pilel fut. 3 pers. sing. fem.	עור
תְּעֹרְרוּ⁎	id. fut. 2 pers. pl. masc.	עור
תַּעַשׂ	וַ] ap. from תַּעֲשֶׂה (q. v.)	עשה
תַּעַשׂ⁎	Kh. תַּעַשׂ q. v., K. תַּעֲשֶׂה (q. v.)	עשה
תֵעַשׂ	וְ] ap. from תַּעֲשֶׂה (q. v.)	עשה
תַּעֲשֵׂהָ	Kal fut. 2 pers. sing. masc. (תַּעֲשֶׂה), suff. 3 pers. sing. fem. (§ 24. rem. 21)	עשה
תַּעֲשֶׂה	id. fut. 2 pers. sing. masc. (§ 24. rem. 20)	עשה
תַּעֲשֶׂה	וְ] id. fut. 2 pers. s. m., or 3 p. s. f.; וְ] conv.	עשה
תֵּעָשֶׂה	Niph. fut. 3 pers. sing. fem.	עשה
תַּעֲשׂוּ תַּעֲשׂוּן	} Kal fut. 2 pers. pl. masc., ‖ parag.; וְ] conv.	עשה
תַּעֲשִׂי תַּעֲשִׂין⁎	} id. fut. 2 pers. sing. fem., ‖ parag.; וְ] id.	עשה
תַּעֲשֶׂינָה	וְ] id. fut. 2 p. (Je. 44. 25) or 3 p. pl. f.; וְ] id.	עשה
תֵּעָשֶׂינָה	Niph. fut. 3 pers. pl. fem.	עשה
תַּעֲשִׂיר⁎	Hiph. fut. 3 pers. sing. fem.	עשר
תַּעֲשֶׂנָה	defect. for תַּעֲשֶׂינָה (q. v.)	עשה
תַּעֲשֵׂנוּ⁎	Kal fut. 2 pers. sing. masc. (תַּעֲשֶׂה), suff. 3 pers. sing. masc. (§ 24. rem. 21)	עשה
תַּעֲשֹׁק	Kal fut. 2 pers. sing. masc.	עשק
תַּעַשְׁקוּ⁎	id. fut. 2 pers. pl. m. [for תַּעֲשֹׁקוּ § 8. r. 15]	עשק
תַּעֲשֵׂר⁎	Piel fut. 2 pers. sing. masc.	עשר
תַּעַשְׂרֶנָּה	[for תַּעֲשִׂירֶנָּה] Hiph. fut. 2 pers. sing. masc. (תַּעֲשֵׂר], suff. 3 pers. sing. f. (§ 16. r. 16)	עשר
תַּעְתִּיר⁎	Hiph. fut. 2 pers. sing. masc. (§ 13. rem. 9)	עתר
תַּעְתְּעִים	noun masc. pl. [of תַּעְתֻּעַ]	תעע
תֹּף	וְ] noun masc. sing. dec. 8 c	תפף
תְּפָאֵר⁎	Piel fut. 2 pers. sing. masc.	פאר
תִּפְאָרָה	noun fem. sing. (§ 42. rem. 5)	פאר
תִּפְאֶרֶת תִּפְאֶרֶת	וְ] id., constr. st.	פאר
תִּפְאַרְתּוֹ	וְ] id., suff. 3 pers. sing. masc	פאר
תִּפְאַרְתִּי	id., suff. 1 pers. sing.	פאר
תִּפְאַרְתֶּךָ תְּפָאַרְתְּךָ	(וְ]} id., suff. 2 pers. sing. masc.	פאר
תִּפְאַרְתֵּךְ	id., suff. 2 pers. sing. fem.	פאר

תִּפְאַרְתְּכֶם	id., suff. 2 pers. pl. masc.	פאר
תִּפְאַרְתָּם	id., suff. 3 pers. pl. masc.	פאר
תִפְאַרְתֵּנוּ	id., suff. 1 pers. pl.	פאר
תִּפְגַּע	Kal fut. 2 pers. sing. masc.	פגע
תִּפְגְּעוּן⁎	id. fut. 2 pers. pl. masc. with parag.	פגע
תִּפְגְּעִי⁎	id. fut. 2 pers. sing. fem.	פגע
תִּפְגֹּשׁ⁎	וְ] Kal fut. 3 pers. sing. fem.; וְ] conv.	פגשׁ
תִּפָּדֶה	Niph. fut. 3 pers. sing. fem.	פדה
תִּפְדֶּה	Kal fut. 2 pers. sing. masc.	פדה
תִּפְדֶּהוּ	וְ] Kal fut. 3 pers. sing. fem., suff. 3 pers. sing. masc. [for תִּפְדֶּהוּ § 19. rem. 5]; וְ] conv.	אפה
תִּפְדּוּנִי⁎	Kal fut. 2 pers. pl. masc., suff. 1 pers. sing.	פדה
תָּפוּג	Kal fut. 3 pers. sing. fem.	פוג
תַּפּוּחַ⁎	וְ] noun masc. sing., also pr. name (& in compos. see בֵּית)	נפח
תַּפּוּחֵי	id. pl., constr. st.	נפח
תִּפּוֹל	Kal fut. 2 pers. s. m., or 3 p. s. fem. (§ 17. r. 3)	נפל
תְּפוֹצוֹתִיכֶם	noun fem. pl., suff. 2 pers. pl. masc. [from תְּפוֹצָה]; וְ] bef. (:)	פוץ
תָּפוּצֶין⁎ תְּפוּצֶינָה⁎	} Kal fut. 3 pers. pl. fem. (comp. § 8. rem. 16, & § 24. rem. 6); וְ, for וְ]; וְ] conv.	פוץ
תָּפוּשׂ⁎	Kal part. pass. sing. masc.	תפשׂ
תְּפוּשׂוּ⁎	Kh. תְּפוּשׂוּ, K. תָּפֹשׂוּ, Kal fut. 2 pers. sing. fem., or 2 pers. pl. masc.	פושׂ
תְּפֹרִי⁎	וְ] Piel fut. 2 pers. sing. fem.; וְ] conv.	פזר
תֹּפַח	וְ] pr. name masc., see תַּפּוּחַ	נפח
תִּפְחָד⁎	וְ] Piel fut. 2 pers. s. masc. (§14. r.1); וְ] conv.	פחד
תִּפְחָד	Kal fut. 2 pers. s. masc. [for תִּפְחַד § 8. r. 15]	פחד
תִּפְחֲדוּ⁎	id. fut. 2 pers. pl. masc.	פחד
תְּפִיךָ⁎	noun m. pl., suff. 2 pers. s. fem. fr. תֹּף dec. 4 c	תפף
תֻּפֶּיךָ⁎	id. pl., suff. 2 pers. sing. masc.	תפף
תַּפִּיל	Hiph. fut. 2 p. s. m., or (Pr. 19.15) 3 p. s. fem.	נפל
תַּפִּילוּ	id. fut. 2 pers. pl. masc.	נפל
תֻּפִּים⁎	noun masc., pl. of תֹּף dec. 8 c	תפף
תְּפִינֵי⁎	noun masc. pl. constr. [from תֻּפִּין]	אפה
תָּפִין⁎	Hiph. fut. 3 pers. sing. fem.	פון
תְּפִיצֵם⁎	וְ] id. fut. 2 pers. s. m., suff. 3 p. pl. m.; וְ] bef. (:)	פוץ

תָּפֵל וְ] masc.—I. *any thing unseasoned, unsavoury*, Job 6. 6.—II. metaph. *insipid, foolish*, La. 2. 14.—III. *lime, mortar*.

תֹּפֶל (*lime*) pr. name of a place in the desert of Sinai, De. 1. 1.

תִּפְלָה fem. *insipidity, folly, impiety*.

ᵃ Is. 8. 12.	ᵍ Pr. 10. 12.	ᵐ Pr. 10. 4, 22.	ᵗ 1 Sa. 10. 5.	ᵃ Is. 64. 10.
ᵇ Je. 47. 6.	ʰ Ca. 4. 4.	ⁿ Job 5. 12.	ᵘ De. 24. 20.	ᵇ Ju. 15. 12.
ᶜ Ps. 23. 5.	ⁱ Je. 40. 16.	ᵒ Ex. 28. 15.	ᵛ Is. 63. 15.	ᶜ Ru. 1. 16.
ᵈ 1 Sa. 17. 21.	ᵏ Ge. 6. 16.	ᵖ De. 14. 22.	ʷ Ju. 4. 9.	ᵈ 1 Sa. 25. 20.
ᵉ Is. 40. 18.	ˡ Ru. 3. 4.	ᵠ Ps. 65. 10.	ˣ Je. 13. 18.	Is. 1. 27.
ᶠ De. 1. 29.	ᵐ Eze. 16. 50.	ʳ Job 22. 27.		
			ᶻ 1 Sa. 28. 24.	ᶻ Zec. 13. 7.	ᵗ Je. 3. 13.	ᵃ Is. 24. 8.
			ᵍ Job 6. 23.	ᵃ Eze. 34. 5.	ᵘ Is. 51. 13.	ᵛ Le. 6. 14.
				ᵇ Zec. 1. 17.	ᵛ Is. 44. 8.	ˣ Is. 41. 15.
				ᶜ Pr. 25. 11.	ᵂ Hab. 2. 19.	ᶻ Je. 31. 4.	ᵇ Ps. 144. 6.
				ᵈ Je. 25. 34.	ᵉ Je. 50. 11.	ᵈ Eze. 28. 18.	ᵉ La. 2. 14.

תַּפְלִי '֗וּ	Hiph. fut. 2 pers. sing. masc., or 3 pers. sing. fem., ap. from תַּפִּיל ; וַ֗' conv.	נפל
וַתֵּ֗'ל "תָפֵל	Kal fut. 2 pers. sing. masc. (Je. 39. 18), or 3 pers. s. f. (§ 17. r. 3); וַ֗' id.	נפל
תָּפֵל	id. fut. 3 p. s. fem. with Mak. (comp. § 8. r. 18)	נפל
תֹּפֶל	pr. name of a place . . .	תפל
תְּפִלָּה '֗וּ	noun fem. sing. dec. 10; ֗וּ bef. (֗:)	פלל
תִּפְלָה	noun fem. sing. . . .	תפל
תַּפְלִי '֗וּ	defect. for תַּפִּילִי (q. v.)	נפל
תַּפְלוּ	Kal fut. 2 pers. pl. masc. [for תַּפְלוּ § 8. r. 15]	נפל
תִּפְלוּן	Chald. Peal fut. 2 pers. pl. masc.	נפל
תְּפִלּוֹת '֗וּ	noun fem., pl. of תְּפִלָּה dec. 10	פלל
תִּפְלַחְנָה	Piel fut. 3 pers. pl. fem.	פלח
תְּפַלֵּט	Piel fut. 2 pers. sing. masc., or 3 pers. s. fem.	פלט
תְּפַלְּטֵמוֹ '֗וּ	id. fut. 2 pers. s. m., suff. 3 p. pl. m.; וּ conv.	פלט
תְּפַלְּטֵנִי '֗וּ, וַתְּ'	id. id., suff. 1 pers. s.; ֗וּ for וָ, ֗וּ id.	פלט
תְּפַלֵּט	Hiph. fut. 2 pers. sing. masc.	פלט
תִּפֹּלְנָה	Kal fut. 3 pers. pl. fem.	נפל
תְּפַלֵּס	Piel fut. 2 pers. sing. masc.	פלס
תְּפַלְּסוּן	id. fut. 2 pers. pl. masc., ֗וּ parag. [for תְּפַלְּסוּ § 8. rem. 17]	פלס
תִּפְלַצְתָּ֑ךְ	noun fem. sing., suff. 2 pers. sing. masc. from [תִּפְלֶצֶת] dec. 13 a	פלץ
תְּפִלַּת	noun fem. s., constr. of תְּפִלָּה d. 10; ֗וּ bef. (֗:)	פלל
תְּפִלָּתוֹ '֗וּ	id., suff. 3 pers. sing. masc.; ֗וּ id.	פלל
תְּפִלָּתִי '֗וּ	id., suff. 1 pers. sing.; ֗וּ id.	פלל
תְּפִלָּתֶךָ תְּפִלָּתֶ֑ךָ	id., suff. 2 pers. sing. masc.	פלל
תְּפִלָּתָם	id., suff. 3 pers. pl. masc.	פלל
תֵּפֶן	'֗וּ ap. from the foll. (§ 24. rem. 3); ֗וּ conv.	פנה
תִּפְנֶה	Kal fut. 2 pers. s. m., or (Le. 20. 6) 3 p. s. fem.	פנה
תִּפְנוּ '֗וּ	id. fut. 2 pers. pl. masc.	פנה
תִּפְסַח	pr. name of a place . . .	פסח
תֹּפִעַ '֗וּ	Hiph. fut. 3 p. s. fem., ap. & conv. [fr. תּוֹפִיעַ]	יפע
תִּפְעַל	Kal fut. 2 pers. s. masc. [for תִּפְעַל § 8. r. 15]	פעל
תִּפְעָל־	id. with Mak. [for תִּפְעַל § 8. rem. 18]	פעל
תִּפְעֲלוּן	id. fut. 2 pers. pl. masc., ֗וּ parag. [for תִּפְעֲלוּ § 8. rem. 17]	פעל
תִּפָּעֵם	'֗וּ Niph. fut. 3 pers. sing. fem.; (§ 9. rem. 3) ֗וּ conv.	פעם
[תָּפַף]	to beat the tabret, Ps. 68. 26. Pu. to smite upon the breast, with עַל, Na. 2. 8.	
	תֹּף masc. dec. 8 c, drum, tabret.	

תָּפֵק '֗וּ	Hiph. fut. 2 pers. s. masc. ap. [fr. תָּפִיק] פוק	פוק
תִּפָּקֵד	Niph. fut. 2 pers. sing. masc., or 3 pers. s. fem.	פקד
תִּפְקֹד '֗וּ	Kal fut. 2 pers. sing. masc.; ֗וּ conv.	פקד
תִּפְקְדוּ	id. fut. 2 pers. pl. masc. . .	פקד
תִּפְקְדִי '֗וּ	id. fut. 2 pers. sing. fem.; ֗וּ conv.	פקד
תִּפְקְדֵם	id. fut. 2 pers. sing. m., suff. 3 pers. pl. m.	פקד
תִּפְקְדֶנּוּ '֗וּ	id. id., suff. 3 pers. sing. masc.; ֗וּ conv.	פקד
תִּפָּקַחְנָה '֗וּ	Niph. fut. 3 pers. pl. fem.; ֗וּ id.	פקח
[תָּפַר]	to sew, join together. Pi. id. Eze. 13. 18.	
תָּפֵר '֗וּ	Hiph. fut. 2 pers sing. masc., or (Ec. 12. 5) 3 pers. sing. fem. . .	פרר
תֻּפַר '֗וּ תֻּפָר֗' וַ֗'	Hoph. fut. 3 pers. sing. fem. [defect. for תּוּפַר]; ֗וּ conv.	פרר
תִּפְרֶה	Kal fut. 2 pers. sing. masc.	פרה
תִּפְרוּ '֗וּ	Hiph. fut. 2 p. pl. masc.	פרר
תִּפְרַח '֗וּ	Kal fut. 3 pers. sing. fem. (§ 8. rem. 15)	פרח
תִּפְרַחְנָה '֗וּ	id. fut. 3 pers. pl. fem. . .	פרח
תַּפְרִיחִי	Hiph. fut. 2 pers. sing. masc.	פרח
תַּפְרִיעוּ '֗וּ	Hiph. fut. 2 pers. pl. masc.	פרע
תִּפְרְמוּ '֗וּ	Kal fut. 2 pers. s. m. [for תִּפְרְמוּ § 8. r. 15]	פרם
תִּפְרָעוּ '֗וּ תִּפְרָ֗עוּ	Kal fut. 2 pers. pl. masc. (§ 8. rem. 15); ֗וּ conv.	פרע
תִּפְרֹץ '֗וּ	Kal fut. 3 pers. sing. fem. [for תִּפְרֹץ § 8. rem. 18]; ֗וּ id.	פרץ
תִּפְרְצִי '֗וּ	id. fut. 2 pers. s. f. [for תִּפְרְצִי § 8. rem. 15]	פרץ
תְּפָרֵשׂ '֗וּ	Piel fut. 3 pers. sing. fem.	פרשׂ
תִּפְרֹשׂ '֗וּ	Kal fut. 3 pers. sing. fem.; ֗וּ conv.	פרשׂ
תָּפַרְתִּי	Kal pret. 1 pers. sing.	תפר
תָּפַשׂ '֗וּ	fut. יִתְפֹּשׂ—I. to lay hold of, to seize, with acc., בְּ.—II. to take, capture.—III. to handle, e. g. a bow, harp, &c.; metaph. to handle, administer the law, Je. 2. 8; of the name of God, to use irreverently, Pr. 30. 9.—IV. part. pass. held, set in gold, Hab. 2. 19. Niph. to be taken, caught, captured. Pi. to take hold, Pr. 30. 28.	
תָּפֹשׂ '֗וּ	Kal inf. abs. . .	תפשׂ
תְּפֹשׂ '֗וּ	id. inf. constr. . .	תפשׂ
תֹּפֵשׂ '֗וּ	id. part. act. sing. masc. dec. 7 b	תפשׂ
תְּפָשָׂהּ '֗וּ	id. pret. 3 pers. sing. masc., suff. 3 pers. sing. fem.; ֗וּ, for וָ, conv.	תפשׂ
תִּפְשָׂה	Kal fut. 3 pers. sing. fem.	פשׂה
תְּפַשְׂהוּ '֗וּ	defect. for תְּפָשׂוּהוּ (q. v.)	תפשׂ
תְּפָשׂוּ '֗וּ	Kal pret. 3 pers. pl.	תפשׂ

ᵃ Est. 6. 10.	ᵈ Mi. 6. 14;	ᵉ Je. 49. 16.	Ps. 58. 3.	ʰ Ps. 8. 5.	ˡ Zec. 11. 11.	ᵍ Ex. 5. 4.	ʲ Je. 4. 31.	ᵍ Ge. 4. 21.
ᵇ Da. 8. 10.	Job 21. 10.	ᶠ Pr. 28. 9.	Ps. 140. 9.	Job 7. 18.	Ex. 23. 30.	ʷ Le. 10. 6.	ᵛ 2 Sa. 17. 19.	ʰ Da. 22. 28.
ᶜ Eze. 47. 22.	Ps. 22. 5.	ᵍ 1 Ki. 9. 3.	Is. 58. 10.	Is. 35. 5.	ᵐ Je. 33. 20.	Le. 10. 6; Pr. 8. 33.	ᵡ Job 16. 15.	ⁱ Le. 13. 7, 22, 27
Da. 3. 5, 15.	Ps. 7. 2.	ˡ Le. 19. 4, 31.	Is. 29. 6;	Hab. 3. 11.	Pr. 1. 25.	ᵗ 2 Ki. 14. 7.	ᵏ 1 Ki. 13. 4.
ᵉ Ps. 72. 20.	ᶠ 2 Sa. 22. 44.	ᵐ Job 10. 22.	Eze. 38. 8.	Is. 35. 1.	ʸ Ps. 106. 29.	ᵘ Je. 34. 3.	ˡ Jos. 8. 23.
ᶠ Job 39. 3.	ᵐ Mi. 6. 14.	Job 11. 8.	ⁿ 2 Sa. 3. 8.	Is. 8. 10.	Is. 54. 3.	ᶻ Eze. 14. 5.	ᵐ De. 21. 19
	Ps. 58. 3.	Job 35. 6.	Eze. 23. 21.	Je. 33. 21.	ᵏ Is. 47. 11.		

50*

תְּפֹשׂוּ	id. imp. pl. masc.	תפש
תִּפְשׂוּהוּ	} id. id., suff. 3 pers. sing. masc.	תפש
תִּפְשׂוּם	id. id., suff. 3 pers. pl. masc.	תפש
תִּפְשְׂטוּן	Hiph. fut. 2 pers. pl. masc. with parag. ן	פשט
תֹּפְשֵׂי	} Kal part. act. pl. constr. m. fr. תֹּפֵשׂ d. 7 b	תפש
תֹּפְשִׂי	id. sing. with parag. י (§ 8. rem. 19)	תפש
תַּפְשִׁיט	Hiph. fut. 2 pers. sing. masc.	פשט
תִּפְשַׁע	Kal fut. 3 pers. sing. fem.	פשע
תִּפְשְׂקִי	} Piel fut. 2 pers. sing. fem.; ו conv.	פשק
תָּפַשְׂתִּי	} Kal pret. 1 pers. sing.	תפש
תְּפַשְׂתֶּם	id. pret. 2 pers. pl. masc.	תפש
תֹּף	} noun fem. sing.	תוף
תֻּפֶּה	noun masc. sing.	תוף
תְּפַתֶּה	Piel fut. 2 pers. sing. masc.	פתה
תִּפְתַּח	} Piel fut. 2 pers. sing. masc. (§ 15. rem. 1)	פתח
תִּפָּתֵחַ	Niph. fut. 3 pers. sing. fem.	פתח
תִּפְתַּח	} Kal fut. 2 pers. sing. masc., or 3 pers. sing. fem. (§ 8. rem. 15); ו conv.	פתח
תִּפְתַּחְנָה	Niph. fut. 3 pers. pl. fem. (§ 10. rem. 4)	פתח
תִּפְתָּאֵי	Chald. masc. pl. emph. [of תִּפְתָּי § 63] *lawyers* or *judges*, Da. 3. 2, 3. Etymology doubtful.	
תֵּצֵא	} וְ, תֵּ, וַתֵּ Kal fut. 2 pers. sing. masc., or 3 pers. sing. fem.; ו conv.	יצא
תּוֹצֵא	} Hiph. fut. 2 pers. sing. masc., ap. & defect. for תּוֹצִיא; ו id.	יצא
תֵּצְאוּ	} Kal fut. 2 pers. pl. masc. (comp. § 8. rem. 15)	יצא
תֵּצְאוֹת	defect. for תּוֹצָאוֹת (q. v.)	יצא
תֵּצְאִי	Kh. תֵּצְאִי q. v., K. תֵּצְאִי (q. v.)	יצא
תֵּצְאִי	Kal fut. 2 pers. sing. fem.	יצא
תֵּצֶאןָ	} id. fut. 3 pers. pl. fem.; ו conv.	יצא
תֵּצֶאנָה	} id. fut. 2 pers. pl. fem. (Am. 4. 3), or 3 pers. pl. fem. (§ 25. No. 2 d); ו id.	יצא
תּוֹצְאֹתָו	} noun fem. pl., suff. 3 pers. sing. masc. (§ 3. rem. 1) from תּוֹצָאָה dec. 11 a	יצא
תּוֹצְאֹתָיו		
תִּצְבֹּר	} Kal fut. 3 pers. sing. fem. [for תִּצְבֹּר § 8. rem. 18]; ו conv.	צבר
תִּצְדַּק	} Kal fut. 2 pers. sing. masc. (§ 8. r. 15)	צדק
תִּצְדַּקִּי	} Piel fut. 2 pers. sing. fem.; ו conv.	צדק
תִּצְדַּקְנָה	Kal fut. 3 pers. pl. fem.	צדק
תִּצְהֲלִי	} Kh. תִּצְהֲלִי Kal fut. 2 pers. sing. fem., K. 2 pers. pl. masc.; ו conv.	צהל

תָּצוּרִי	Kal fut. 3 pers. sing. fem.	צור
תְּצוֹרַדְנָה	Pilel fut. 2 pers. pl. fem.	צור
תְּצוּרֵנִי	Kal fut. 2 pers. s. m. [תָּצוּר], suff. 1 pers. s.	צור
תְּצַוֶּה	Piel fut. 2 pers. sing. masc.	צוה
תְּצַוֵּהוּ	} id. fut. 3 pers. sing. fem. with suff. 3 pers. sing. masc.; ו conv.	צוה
תְּצַוֵּם	id. fut. 2 pers. pl. masc., suff. 3 pers. pl. masc. (§ 24. rem. 21)	צוה
תָּצוּמוּ	Kal fut. 2 pers. pl. masc.	צום
תְּצַוֶּנּוּ	} Piel fut. 2 pers. sing. masc. (תְּצַוֶּה), suff. 3 pers. sing. masc. (§ 24. rem. 21)	צוה
תְּצַוֻּנִי	id. fut. 2 pers. pl. m. [תָּצוּר], suff. 1 pers. s.	צוה
תָּצוּרֵ	Kal fut. 2 pers. sing. masc.	צור
תִּצְחַק	} Kal fut. 3 pers. sing. fem.; ו conv.	צחק
תַּצִּיבֵנִי	} Hiph. fut. 2 p. s. m., suff. 1 p. s.; ו id.	יצב
תַּצִּיג	Hiph. fut. 2 pers. sing. masc. (§ 20. r. 16)	יצג
תַּצִּיל	Hiph. fut. 2 pers. sing. masc., or 3 pers. s. f.	נצל
תַּצִּילֵם	} id. id., suff. 3 pers. pl. masc.	נצל
תַּצִּילֵנּוּ	id. id., suff. 3 pers. s. m.	נצל
תַּצִּילֵנִי	id. id., suff. 1 pers. sing.	נצל
תִּצֶּינָה	Kal fut. 3 pers. pl. fem. (§ 25. No. 2 b)	נצה
תַּצִּיתוּ	Hiph. fut. 2 pers. pl. masc. (§ 20. rem. 16)	יצת
תַּצֵּל	Hiph. fut. 2 pers. sing. masc., ap. from תַּצִּיל	נצל
תִּצְלַח	} Kal fut. 3 pers. sing. fem. (§ 8. rem. 15); ו conv.	צלח
תִּצְלָח		
תִּצְלְחָי	} id. fut. 3 pers. sing. fem.; ו id.	צלח
תַּצְלִיחַ	Hiph. fut. 2 pers. sing. masc.	צלח
תַּצְלִיחוּ	id. fut. 2 pers. pl. masc.	צלח
תַּצְלִיחִי	id. fut. 2 pers. sing. fem.	צלח
תַּצְלֵחְנָה	Hiph. fut. 3 pers. pl. fem.	צלל
תִּצְלֶלְנָה	Kal fut. 3 pers. pl. fem. (§ 18. rem. 16)	צלל
תִּצְמָאוּ	Kal fut. 2 pers. pl. m. [for תִּצְמָאוּ] § 8. r. 15]	צמא
תַּצְמִחַ	defect. for תַּצְמִיחַ (q. v.)	צמח
תִּצְמַר	Kal fut. 3 pers. s. fem. [for תִּצְמָר § 8. r. 15]	צמח
תִּצְמַחְנָה	id. fut. 3 pers. pl. fem.	צמח
תַּצְמִיד	Hiph. fut. 3 pers. sing. fem.	צמד
תַּצְמִיחַ	Hiph. fut. 3 pers. sing. fem.	צמח
תַּצְמִית	Hiph. fut. 2 pers. sing. masc.	צמת
תִּצְנַה	} Kal fut. 3 pers. sing. fem.; ו conv.	צנח
תִּצְעַד	Kal fut. 3 pers. sing. fem.	צעד
תַּצְעִידֵהוּ	} Hiph. fut. 3 pers. s. f. with suff. 3 p. s m.	צעד
תִּצְעַק	Kal fut. 2 pers. sing. masc.	צעק
תִּצְעֲקוּ	} id. fut. 2 pers. pl. masc.; ו conv.	צעק
תְּצַפֶּה	Piel fut. 2 pers. sing. masc.	צפה

a 1 Ki. 18. 40.   b Ps. 71. 11.   c Mi. 2. 8.   d Je. 2. 8.   e Je. 49. 16.   f Job 22. 6.   g Eze. 16. 25.

h Pr. 30. 9.   i Je. 40. 10.   k Job 17. 6.   l Is. 30. 33.   m Job 38. 31.   n Ex. 28. 11.   o Je. 1. 14.

p Ps. 51. 17.   q Is. 35. 5.   r Da. 3. 2, 3.   s Ju. 9. 20.   t Je. 32. 21.   u Je. 6. 25.   v Ex. 15. 20.

w Am. 4. 3.   x Jos. 16. 3.   y Zec. 9. 3.   z Ps. 51. 6.   aa De. 32. 46.   bb Eze. 16. 52.   cc Je. 50. 11.

dd Pr. 6. 26.   ee De. 20. 19.   ff Ge. 18. 12.   gg Est. 4. 5, 10.   hh Ju. 7. 5.   ii Pr. 11. 6.   kk Is. 58. 4.   ll Ne. 9. 28.

mm Is. 45. 11.   nn Eze. 13. 18.   oo De. 8. 12.   pp Ps. 41. 13.   qq De. 28. 29.   rr Je. 2. 37.

ss Eze. 33. 12.   tt Je. 4. 7   uu Ps. 119. 43.   vv Eze. 16. 13.   ww Ps. 50. 19.   xx Ps. 143. 12.

1 Sa. 3. 11.   Is. 65. 13.   De. 29. 22.   Is. 42. 9.   bb Jos. 8. 8.

Hab. 3. 12.   Job 18. 14.   Ex. 14. 15.   Is. 65. 14.   Ju. 10. 12.   Ex. 26. 29.

תִּצְפֶּינָה*	Kal fut. 3 pers. pl. fem. . . .	צפה
תִּצְפֹּן	Kal fut. 2 pers. sing. masc. . .	צפן
תִּצְפְּנֵהוּ]	ו id. fut. 3 pers. sing. fem., suff. 3 pers. sing. masc.; ו conv. . .	צפן
תִּצְפְּנֵנּוּ	Piel fut. 2 pers. sing. masc. (תְּצַפֶּה), suff. 3 pers. sing. masc. (§ 24. rem. 21) .	צפה
תִּצְפְּנוֹ]	ו Kal fut. 3 p. s. fem., suff. 3 p. s. m.; ו conv.	צפן
תִּצְפְּנֶךָ	id. fut. 3 pers. sing. fem., suff. 3 pers. pl. m.	צפן
תַּצְפִּנֵנִי	Hiph. fut. 2 pers. s. m. [תַּצְפִּין], suff. 1 p. s.	צפן
תְּצַפְצֵף	Pilp. fut. 3 pers. sing. fem. (§ 6. No. 4) .	צפף
תָּצֹק] h	ו Kal fut. 3 p. s. fem. (§ 20. r. 16); ו conv.	יצק
תָּצֻרִי	Kal fut. 2 pers. sing. masc. ap. (§ 21. rem. 9)	צור
תָּצַר]	ו Kal fut. 3 pers. sing. fem.; ו conv. .	יצר
תָּצַר	Kal fut. 2 p. s. m., or (Pr. 13.6) 3 p. s. fem.	נצר
תִּצְרִי	Kal fut. 2 pers. sing. fem. .	יצר
תָּצְרֵם]	Kal fut. 2 pers. sing. masc. (תָּצוּר) with suff. 3 pers. pl. masc. .	צור
תִּצְרָךְ]	ו Kal fut. 3 pers. sing. fem. (תָּצֹר), suff. 2 pers. sing. masc. [for תִּצָּרְךָ § 2. rem. 2] .	נצר
תִּצְּרֶנּוּ	id. fut. 2 pers. sing. masc., suff. 3 pers. sing. m.	נצר
תִּצְּרֵנִי	id. id., suff. 1 pers. sing. . .	נצר
תִּצַּת]	ו Kal fut. 3 pers. s. fem. (§ 20. r. 16); ו conv.	יצת
תִּצַּתְנָה	id. fut. 3 pers. pl. fem. .	יצת
תָּקִא]	ו defect. for תָּקִיא q. v.; ו conv.	קוא
תָּקֹב dd	Kal fut. 2 pers. sing. masc. . .	נקב
תְּקַבְּלוּן	Chald. Pael fut. 2 pers. pl. masc. .	קבל
תִּקְבְּנֶנּוּ	Kal fut. 2 pers. sing. masc. (תִּקֹּב), suff. 3 pers. sing. masc. (§ 8. rem. 14) . .	נקב
תִּקָּבֵץ]	Niph. fut. 2 pers. sing. masc. .	קבץ
תִּקְבְּצִי	Kal fut. 2 pers. sing. masc. .	קבץ
תִּקְבְּצוּ	Kal fut. 2 pers. pl. masc. .	קבץ
תִּקְבְּצוּ]	ו Piel fut. 2 pers. pl. masc.; ו conv.	קבץ
תְּקַבְּצֵם]	id. fut. 3 pers. s. f. [תְּקַבֵּץ], suff. 3 pers. pl. m.	קבץ
תִּקָּבֵר]	ו Niph. fut. 2 p. s. m., or 3 pers. s. f.; ו conv.	קבר
תִּקְבְּרוּ]	ו Kal fut. 2 pers. pl. masc.; ו id.	קבר
תְּקַבְּרֵם]	Piel fut. 3 pers. s. f. [תְּקַבֵּר], suff. 3 pers. pl. m.	קבר
תִּקְבְּרֶנּוּ	Kal fut. 2 pers. sing. masc. [תִּקְבֹּר], suff. 3 pers. sing. masc.	קבר
תִּקְבְּרֵנִי	id. with suff. 1 pers. sing. .	קבר
תִּקֹּד] kk	ו Kal fut. 3 pers. sing. fem.; ו conv.	קדד
תַּקְדִּים]	ו Hiph. fut. 3 pers. sing. fem.; ו id.	קדם
תַּקְדִּישׁ	Hiph. fut. 2 pers. sing. masc. .	קדש
תַּקְדִּישׁוּ	id. fut. 2 pers. pl. masc. .	קדש
תְּקַדְּמֶךָ	Piel fut. 3 pers. s. f. [תְּקַדֵּם], suff. 2 pers. s. m. [fr. תְּקַדְּמְךָ § 2. r. 2, & § 16 r. 15]	קדם
תְּקַדְּמֶנּוּ	id. fut. 2 pers. sing. masc., suff. 3 pers. s. m.	קדם
תַּקְדֵּשׁ h	Kal fut. 3 pers. sing. fem. . .	קדש
תִּקְהֶינָה	Kal fut. 3 pers. pl. fem. . .	קהה
תִּקָּהֵל]	ו Niph. fut. 3 pers. sing. fem.; ו conv.	קהל
תִּקְוָה] i	ו noun fem. sing. dec. 10, pr. name	קוה
תָּקוּם	Kal fut. 2 pers. sing. masc., or 3 pers. s. f.	קום
תְּקוּם m	Chald. Peal fut. 3 pers. sing. fem.	קום
תְּקוּמָה n	noun fem. sing. . . .	קום
תָּקוּמוּ o	Kal fut. 2 pers. pl. masc. . .	קום
תְּקוֹמֵם p	Pilel fut. 2 pers. sing. masc. . .	קום
תְּקוֹמֵנָה	Pilel fut. 3 pers. pl. fem. (§ 18. r. 15, note)	קון
תָּקוֹעַ]	ו Kal inf. abs. . . .	תקע
תָּקוֹעַ	pr. name of a place . . .	תקע
תְּקוֹעָה	id. with parag. ה . . .	תקע
תְּקוּפַת]	noun fem. sing., constr. of [תְּקוּפָה] dec. 10	קוף
תְּקוּפָתוֹ	id., suff. 3 pers. sing. masc.; ו bef. (ִ)	קוף
תִּקְוַת]	ו noun fem. sing., constr. of תִּקְוָה dec. 10	קוה
תִּקְוָתָהּ]	id., suff. 3 pers. sing. fem. .	קוה
תִּקְוָתִי]	id., suff. 1 pers. sing. .	קוה
תִּקְוָתֶךָ]	ו id., suff. 2 pers. sing. masc.	קוה
תִּקְוָתָם]	ו id., suff. 3 pers. pl. masc.	קוה
תִּקְוָתֵנוּ v	id., suff. 1 pers. pl. .	קוה
תִּקַּח	Kal fut. 2 pers. s. m., or 3 pers.	לקח
תִּקַּח] ו/, וַ	s. f. (§ 17. rem. 8); ו conv.	לקח
תֻּקַּח a	ו Hoph. fut. 3 pers. s. f. (§ 17. r. 8); ו id.	לקח
תִּקָּחֵהוּ	ו Kal fut. 3 pers. sing. fem. (תִּקַּח), suff. 3 pers. sing. masc. (§ 16. r. 12, & § 17. r. 8); ו id.	לקח
תִּקָּחֶהָ qq	ו id., suff. 3 pers. sing. fem.; ו id. .	לקח
תִּקְחוּ	ו id. fut. 2 pers. pl. masc. (§ 8. rem. 15, comp. § 10. rem. 7)	לקח
תִּקָּחוּ		
תִּקְחִי b	ו/ id. fut. 2 p. s. m. (comp. § 10. r. 7); ו conv.	לקח
תִּקָּחֵךְ	id. fut. 3 pers. sing. fem., suff. 2 pers. sing. masc. (§ 16. rem. 12)	לקח
תִּקָּחֵם d	ו/ id. id., suff. 3 pers. pl. masc.; ו conv.	לקח
תִּקָּחֶנָּה	id. fut. 2 pers. sing. masc., suff. 3 pers. s. f.	לקח
תִּקָּחֶנּוּ	id. id., suff. 3 pers. sing. masc.	לקח
תִּקָּחֵנִי g	ו/ id. fut. 2 pers. sing. masc., or (Eze. 3.14) 3 pers. sing. fem.; ו conv.	לקה
תַּקְטִיר	Hiph. fut. 2 p. s. m. (Nu. 18.17) or 3 p. f. s. yy	קטר
תַּקְטִירוּ	id. fut. 2 pers. pl. masc. . .	קטר
תִּקְטֹל h	Kal fut. 2 pers. sing. masc. . .	קטל
תִּקְטֹן]	ו Kal fut. 3 pers. sing. fem.; ו conv.	קטן
תֻּקְטַר] i	Hoph. fut. 3 pers. sing. fem. [for תֻּקְטָר comp. § 8. rem. 15]	קטר
תָּקִיא	Hiph. fut. 3 pers. sing. fem. . .	קוא
תְּקִיאֶנָּה	id. fut. 2 pers. sing. masc., suff. 3 pers. s. f.	קוא
תְּקִילְתָּא]	Chald. Peil pass. 2 pers. s. m. (§ 47. r. 11)	תקל

---

a Ps. 66.7.   b 2 Sa. 13.9.   p Is. 9.17.   s Ne. 4.14.   e Am. 9.10.   l Je. 29.11.   r Ex. 34.22.   u Je. 9.19.   f Eze. 5.1.

Ex. 2.2.   f De. 2.19.   q Je. 49.2.   t Is. 22.9.   m De. 15.19.   Da. 2.39,44.   s Ps. 19.7.   v Ge. 12.15.   g Eze. 3.14.

Ex. 25.11.   k Is. 49.19.   r Le. 18.25.   u Ho. 9.6.   n Is. 8.13.   o Le. 26.37.   t Eze. 19.5.   w Zep. 3.7.   h Ps. 139.19.

Jos. 2.4.   l De. 2.19.   Da. 2.6.   2 Sa. 2.5.   o Ps. 88.14.   p Is. 25.27.   Job 4.6.   x Pr. 6.5.   i Le. 6.15.

Ps. 31.21.   m Pr. 4.6.   Nu. 23.25.   Ho. 9.6.   p Ps. 21.4.   q Is. 58.12.   v Job 11.20.   y Am. 9.2.   k Pr. 23.8.

j Job 14.13.   Ps. 12.8.   Eze. 29.5.   De. 21.23.   De. 32.19.   Jos. 6.13.   Eze. 37.11.   Job 1.15.   l Da. 5.27

k Is. 29.4.   Ps. 32.7.   De. 18.17.   dd Job 40.26.   kk 1 Ki. 1.16,31.   qq Ex. 2.5.   yy Ho. 2.15.

תָּקִים	Hiph. fut. 2 pers. sing. masc. .	קום
•תָּקִים	Chald. Aph. fut. 2 pers. sing. masc. .	קום
תָּקִימוּ	Hiph. fut. 2 pers. pl. masc. .	קום
תְּקִימֶנָה	id. fut. 2 pers. pl. fem. (for תָּקִמְנָה)	קום
תַּקִּיפָא• / תַּקִּיפָה	} Chald. adj. fem. sing. from תַּקִּיף masc.	תקף
תַּקִּיפִין	Chald. id. masc., pl. of תַּקִּיף dec. 1a .	תקף

[תְּקַל] Chald. *to weigh*, Da. 5. 25, 27. Peil pret. *to be weighed*, Da. 5. 27.

תִּקְל/	] Kal fut. 3 pers. s. f. (§ 18. r. 6); •וַ conv.	קלל
תְּקִיל s	Ch. Peal part. pass. s. m. [for תְּקִיל § 47. r. 1]	תקל
תְּקַלֵּל	Piel fut. 2 pers. sing. masc. .	קלל
תְּקֻלַּל	Pual fut. 3 pers. sing. fem. .	קלל
תָּקֵם	] Hiph. fut. 2 p. s. m. ap. & conv. from תָּקִים	קום
תָּקָם	] Kal fut. 3 pers. s. f. ap. & conv. from תָּקוּם	קום
תִּקֹּם•	Kal fut. 2 pers. sing. masc. .	נקם
תְּקֻמֻ	defect. for תָּקוּמוּ (q. v.) .	קום
תְּקֻמְמֵנִי	] Kal fut. 2 pers. s. m., suff. 1 p. s.; •וַ conv.	קמט

[תָּקַן] *to be arranged, straight*, Ec. 1. 15. Pi. I. *to make straight*, Ec. 7. 13.—II. *to set in order, compose*, Ec. 12. 9.

תְּקֵן Chald. Hoph. *to be established*, Da. 4. 33.

תִּקֵּן	Piel pret. 3 pers. sing. masc. .	תקן
תְּקַנֵּא	] Piel fut. 2 pers. sing. masc., or (Ge. 30. 1) 3 pers. sing. fem.; •וַ conv. .	קנא
תְּקַנֵּא•	Chald. Peal fut. 2 pers. sing. m. R. קנא see	קנה
תִּקְנֶה	Kal fut. 2 pers. sing. masc. .	קנה
תִּקְנוּ•	id. fut. 2 pers. pl. masc. .	קנה
תְּקַנֵּן	Piel fut. 3 pers. sing. fem. .	קנן
תְּקַסַּמְנָה	Kal fut. 2 pers. pl. fem. .	קסם

תָּקַע •וְ I. *to smite, clap* the hands, as a sign of joy.—II. *to strike hands*, as a sign of surety.—III. *to strike, drive, fix in*, as a nail.—IV. *to fasten with nails.*—V. *to pitch* a tent.—VI. *to thrust in*, e. g. a spear.—VII. *to cast, throw in*, Ex. 10. 19.—VIII. with בְּשׁוֹפָר, שׁוֹפָר *to strike* for *to blow the trumpet*; with תְּרוּעָה *to sound an alarm.* Niph. I. *to strike hands, become surety*, with לְיַד of the person with whom, Job 17. 3.—II. with שׁוֹפָר *to be blown.*

תְּקוֹעַ masc. *a blast with the trumpet*, Eze. 7. 14.

תְּקוֹעַ pr. name of a city in the tribe of Judah. Gent. noun תְּקֹעִי, fem. תְּקֹעִית.

תֶּקַע masc. *blast of the trumpet*, Ps. 150. 3.

תִּקַע/	] Kal fut. 3 pers. sing. fem.; •וַ conv. .	יקע
וַתֵּקַע• •וְ	defect. for תּוֹקַע (q. v.) .	תקע
תִּקְעוּ/	] Kal pret. 3 pers. pl. .	תקע
תִּקְעוּ •וְ	id. imp. pl. masc. .	תקע
תָּקְעוּ•	id. pret. 3 pers. pl. (Kh. תְּקָעוּ); K. תְּקֹעֵי part. act. pl. constr. m. from תּוֹקֵע dec. 7b	תקע
תִּקְעַתְּ•	id. fut. 2 pers. sing. masc. .	תקע
תָּקַעְתִּי•	] id. fut. 1 pers. sing.; acc. shifted by conv. וַ (§ 8. rem. 7) .	תקע
תָּקַעְתִּיו	] id. id., suff. 3 pers. sing. m.; וַ, for וְ, conv.	תקע
תְּקַעְתֶּם	] id. fut. 2 pers. pl. masc.; וַ id. .	תקע

[תָּקַף] *to overpower, prevail over, oppress.*

תְּקֵף Chald.—I. *to be* or *become great, strong, powerful.*—II. *to become firm, obstinate*, Da. 5. 20. Pa. *to make strong*, Da. 6. 8.

תְּקָף masc. dec. 6 c, *might, power, authority.*

תְּקָף Chald. m. (emph. תָּקְפָּא) id. Da. 2. 37; 4. 27

תַּקִּיף adj. masc. *strong, mighty*, Ec. 6. 10.

תַּקִּיף Chald. masc. dec. 1 a, adj.—I. *strong, hard*, Da. 2. 40, 42.—II. *mighty, powerful*, Da. 3. 33.

תֹּקֶף•	noun masc. sing. dec. 6 c .	תקף
תְּקֵף•	] Chald. Peal pret. 3 pers. sing. masc. (§ 47. rem. 6); וַ bef. (:) .	תקף
תָּקְפָּא/	] Chald. noun masc. s., emph. of תְּקָף (§ 59)	תקף
תָּקְפּוֹ s	noun masc. s., suff. 3 pers. s. m. fr. תֹּקֶף dec. 6c	תקף
תִּקְפּוּ h	Hiph. fut. 2 pers. pl. masc. .	נקף
תַּקְפִיאֵנִי	Hiph. fut. 2 pers. sing. masc., suff. 1 pers. s.	קפא
תִּקְפֹּץ•	Kal fut. 2 pers. sing. masc. .	קפץ
תָּקְפַּת•	Ch. Peal pret. 3 pers. sing. fem. .	תקף
תָּקְפְתָּ m	] Ch. id. pret. 2 pers. sing. masc.; וַ bef. (:)	תקף
תָּקִץ kk	Kal fut. 2 pers. sing. masc. ap. [from תָּקִיץ]	קוץ
תִּקְצוֹר	Kal fut. 2 pers. sing. masc. (§ 8. rem. 18)	קצר
תִּקְצֹף	Kal fut. 2 pers. sing. masc. .	קצף
תִּקְצַר/ תִּקְצָר־	} Kal fut. 3 pers. sing. masc. (§ 8. rem. 15); וַ conv. }	קצר
תִּקְצָר p	id. fut. 2 pers. sing. m. .	קצר
תִּקְצְרוּ q	id. fut. 2 pers. pl. masc. .	קצר
תִּקְצֹרְנָה	id. fut. 3 pers. pl. fem. .	קצר
תַּקְרִא•	] Hiph. fut. 2 pers. sing. masc. ap. [from תַּקְרִיא]; וַ conv.	קרא
תִּקְרָא•	] Kal fut. 2 pers. sing. masc., or 3 pers. sing. fem.; •וַ id. .	קרא
תִּקְרְאוּ•	id. fut. 2 pers. pl. masc. .	קרא
תִּקְרָאוּ ∞	Niph. fut. 2 pers. pl. masc. [for תִּקָּרְאוּ, comp. § 8. rem. 15] .	קרא

•a Da. 6. 9.   ƒ Ge. 16. 4.   i Job 16. 8.   ᵐ Je. 48. 28.   z 2 Ki. 11. 14.   c Is. 22. 23.   g Est. 10. 2.   t Da. 5. 20.   p De. 24. 19
b Je. 44. 25,   g Da. 5. 25, 27.   = Ec. 12. 9.   r Eze. 13. 23.   y Je. 4. 5. (Kh.)   d Est. 9. 29.   h Le. 19. 27.   q Le. 25. 11,
c Da. 2. 42; 7. 7.   h Job 24. 18.   n Ge. 30. 1.   s Eze. 33. 3.   k Jos. 6. 9.   h Da. 4. 8, 17.   h Nu. 11. 23.   r Pr. 10. 27
d Da. 2. 40.   i Le. 19. 18.   o Ezr. 7. 17.   t Je. 6. 8.   e Pr. 6. 1.   j Da. 2. 37.   i De. 15. 7.   Job 21. 4.   s Je. 32. 22.
e Da. 3. 33,   k Jos. 8. 7.   v Le. 25. 44, 45.   p Pr. 17. 18.   k Ju. 7. 18.   ⱱ Ne. 9. 8.   kk Pr. 3. 11.   ∞ Is. 61. 6.

תִּקְרְאִי	Kal fut. 2 pers. sing. fem. . .	קרא
תִּקְרָאֵם	id. fut. 2 pers. sing. masc., suff. 3 pers. pl. masc. (comp. § 16. rem. 12) . .	קרא
תִּקְרֶאןָ	id. fut. 3 p. pl. fem. (comp. § 8. r. 16); וַ conv.	קרא
תִּקְרֶאנָֽה	' id. fut. 2 or 3 pers. pl. fem. (for Ex. 1. 10, see § 2. rem. 4); וַ id. . .	קרא
תַּקְרִיב	Hiph. fut. 2 pers. s. masc., defect. for תַּקְרִיב	קרב
תִּקְרַב	} Kal fut. 2 pers. s. masc., or 3 pers.	קרב
תִּקְרַב	} וַ', וַ', sing. fem. (§ 8. r. 15); וַ conv. }	קרב
תְּקָרֵב	' Piel (Chald. Pael.) fut. 2 pers. s. m.; וַ bef. (:)	קרב
תִּקְרְבוּ	וַ Kal fut. 2 pers. pl. masc.; וַ conv.	קרב
תַּקְרִיבוּן	Hiph. fut. 2 pers. pl. masc. (תַּקְרִיב), וַ parag. (comp. § 8. rem. 17)	קרב
תִּקְרְבוּן	וַ Kal fut. 2 pers. pl. masc., וַ parag. (§ 8. rem. 17); וַ conv.	קרב
תִּקְרְבֶנָה	וַ id. fut. 3 pers. pl. fem.; וַ id. .	קרב
תַּקְרִיב	Hiph. fut. 2 pers. sing. masc., or 3 pers. s. fem.	קרב
תַּקְרִיבוּ	id. fut. 2 pers. pl. masc.	קרב
תַּקְרִיבִי	' id. fut. 2 pers. sing. fem.; וַ conv.	קרב
תִּקְרֶינָה	Kal fut. 3 pers. pl. fem. . .	קרה
תִּקְרַע	וַ Kal fut. 2 pers. s. m., or 3 p. s. fem.; וַ conv.	קרע
תִּקְרְעִי	id. fut. 2 pers. sing. fem. . .	קרע
תְּקַשֵּׁשׁ	' Piel fut. 3 p. s. fem. ap. [fr. קָשַׁשׁ]; conv. וַ	קשה
תִּקְשַׁבְנָה	Kal fut. 3 pers. pl. fem. .	קשב
תַּקְשִׁיבוּ	Hiph. fut. 2 pers. pl. masc.	קשה
תַּקְשִׁיב	Hiph. fut. 3 pers. sing. fem.	קשב
תַּקְשִׁיחַ	Hiph. fut. 2 pers. sing. masc.	קשח
תִּקָּשֵׁר	וַ Niph. fut. 3 pers. sing. fem.; וַ conv.	קשר
תִּקְשָׁר	וַ Kal fut. 2 pers. sing. masc. (Je. 51. 63), or 3 pers. sing. fem.; וַ id.	קשר
תִּקְשְׁרִי	id. fut. 2 pers. sing. fem.	קשר
תְּקַשְּׁרִים	' Piel fut. 2 p. s. f., suff. 3 p. pl. m.; וַ bef. (:)	קשר
תִּקְשְׁרֶנּוּ	וַ Kal fut. 2 p. s. m. (תִּקְשֹׁר), suff. 3 p. s. m.	קשר
תָּתֻר	וַ defect. for תּוּר (q. v.) . .	תור
תֵּרֶא	וַ', וַ', ap. fr. תִּרְאֶה q. v. (§ 24. r. 3); וַ conv.	ראה
תֵּרָאֶה	וַ Niph. fut. 3 pers. sing. fem.	ראה
תֵּרָאֶה	Kh. תֵּרָאֶה q. v. K. תֵּרֵא (q. v.)	ראה
תִּרְאֶה	Kal fut. 2 pers. sing. masc. (§ 24. rem. 20)	ראה
תִּרְאֶה	id. fut. 2 pers. sing. masc., or 3 pers. sing. f.	ראה
תִּרְאֶהוּ	וַ id. fut. 3 pers. sing. fem., suff. 3 pers. sing. masc. (§ 24. rem. 21); וַ conv.	ראה
תִּרְאוּ	וַ' id. fut. 2 pers. pl. masc.; וַ id.	ראה
תִּרְאִי	Kal fut. 2 p. s. m. for תִּרְאֶה R., or for תֵּרֶא R.	ראה
תִּרְאִי	id. fut. 2 pers. sing. fem.	ראה
תִּרְאֶינָה	וַ' id. fut. 3 pers. pl. fem.; וַ conv.	ראה
תִּרְאֲלָה	וַ pr. name of a town in Benjamin, Jos. 18. 27.	

תִּרְאֶנָה	וַ Kal fut. 3 pers. pl. f. (Kh. תֵּרֶאנָה R. ראה),	אור
	K. תֵּרֶאנָה Root . . .	
תִּרְאֶנּוּ	Kal fut. 2 pers. sing. masc. (תִּרְאֶה), suff. 3 pers. sing. masc. (§ 24. rem. 21) . .	ראה
תִּרְאֵנִי	Hiph. fut. 2 pers. sing. masc. [תַּרְאֶה], suff. 1 pers. sing. (§ 24. rem. 21)	ראה
תִּרְאֵנִי	וַ Kal fut. 3 pers. sing. fem. (תִּרְאֶה), suff. 1 pers. sing. (§ 24. rem. 21); וַ conv.	ראה
תִּרְאֵנִי	id. fut. 2 pers. s. m., or 3 pers. s. f., suff. 1 p. s.	ראה
תִּרְאֵנִי	id. fut. 2 pers. pl. m. (תִּרְאוּ), suff. 1 pers. s.	ראה
תֵּרֶב	וַ Kal fut. 3 pers. sing. fem., ap. fr. תִּרְבֶּה (§ 24. rem. 3); וַ conv.	רבה
תֶּרֶב	וַ' Hiph. fut. 2 pers. sing. m., ap. fr. תַּרְבֶּה	רבה
תַּרְבֶּה	וַ' id. fut. 2 pers. sing. masc., or (Eze. 23. 19) 3 pers. sing. fem.; וַ conv.	רבה
תִּרְבֶּה	וַ' Kal fut. 3 pers. sing. fem.	רבה
תַּרְבּוּ	Hiph. fut. 2 pers. pl. masc.	רבה
תִּרְבּוּ	Kal fut. 2 pers. pl. masc.	רבה
תִּרְבּוּן	id. with parag. וַ (comp. § 8. rem. 17)	רבה
תַּרְבּוּת	noun fem. sing. . . .	רבה
תַּרְבִּי	וַ', וַתַּ Hiph. fut. 2 pers. sing. fem.; וַ conv.	רבה
תִּרְבִּי	וַ Kal fut. 2 pers. sing. fem.; וַ id.	רבה
תִּרְבֶּינָה	וַ' id. fut. 3 pers. pl. fem.; וַ id.	רבה
תַּרְבִּיעַ	Hiph. fut. 2 pers. sing. masc.	רבע
תַּרְבִּיץ	Hiph. fut. 2 pers. sing. masc.	רבץ
תַּרְבִּית	וַ noun fem. sing. . .	רבה
תַּרְבֵּנִי	Hiph. fut. 3 p. s. f. (תַּרְבֶּה), suff. 1 p. s. (§ 24. r. 21)	רבה
תִּרְבַּץ	וַ Kal fut. 2 pers. sing. masc.	רבץ
תִּרְבַּצְנָה	id. fut. 3 pers. pl. fem.	רבץ
תִּרְגַּז	וַ' Kal fut. 3 pers. sing. fem.; וַ conv.	רגז
תִּרְגָּזוּ	id. fut. 2 pers. pl. masc.	רגז
תִּרְגָּזִי	וַ' id. fut. 2 pers. sing. fem.; וַ conv.	רגז
תִּרְגַּזְנָה	id. fut. 3 pers. pl. fem.	רגז
תַּרְגִּיעַ	Hiph. fut. 2 pers. sing. masc.	רגע
תִּרְגַּלְתִּי	Tiph. pret. 1 pers. sing. (§ 6. No. 5)	רגל

תַּרְגֵּם Chald. *to interpret, translate,* only part. pass. מְתַרְגַּם Ezr. 4. 7.

תִּרְגַּנְנוּ	וַ Niph. fut. 2 pers. pl. masc.; וַ conv.	רגן
תֵּרֵד	וַ' } Kal fut. 2 pers. sing. masc., or 3 pers.	ירד
תֵּרֵד	} sing. fem. (§ 20. rem. 2) . . }	ירד
תֵּרֶד	וַ id. fut. 3 pers. sing. fem. bef. monos. or conv. וַ (§ 20. rem. 4) . . .	ירד
תֹּרֶד	וַ Hiph. fut. 3 pers. sing. fem., ap. & defect. for תּוֹרֵד; וַ conv.	ירד
תִּרְדֶּה	Kal fut. 2 pers. sing. masc. . .	רדה

• Je. 36. 6.   ᵍ Eze. 37. 7.   ᵖ Ps. 10. 17.   ᵗ Ge. 15. 9.   ᶻ Zep. 3. 15   ᵐ Ca. 1. 6.   ʰ De. 6. 3.   ᵉ Eze. 34. 14.   ᵏ De. 1. 27.
Nu. 25. 2.   ʰ De. 1. 17.   ᵍ Is. 63. 17.   ʸ Mi. 7. 10.   ᵃ 1 Sa. 14. 27.   ⁿ Nu. 32. 14.   ⁱ Am. 8. 8.   ᶠ Ge. 45. 24.   ᵐ Je. 13. 17.
Le. 2. 4.   ⁱ Eze. 22. 4.   ᵠ Ne. 3. 38.   ᶻ Ge. 1. 9.   ᵇ Nu. 23. 13.   ᵒ Je. 2. 22.   ᵍ Eze. 16. 43.   ⁿ Is. 14. 5.
ᵉ Le. 18. 14.   ⁱ Is. 41. 22.   ʳ Je. 51. 63.   ᵃ Je. 3. 7.   ᶜ Hab. 1. 3.   ᵖ Eze. 23. 19.   ᵏ Is. 32. 10.   ᵒ 2 Ki. 1. 10, 12.
Is. 5. 19.   ᵏ Je. 4. 30.   ᵐ Jos. 2. 18.   ᵘ Da. 1. 13.   ᵈ Nu. 22. 33.   ᵈ De. 7. 22.   ⁿ Eze. 31. 5.   ᵉ Le. 25. 43, 46.
ᶠ Ps. 85. 5.   ᵐ Is. 35. 16.   ⁿ Is. 49. 18.   ᵉ Ex. 2. 6.   ᵉ Je. 2. 3;   ᵈ Da. 12. 4.   ˡ De. 28. 65.   ᵖᵖ Nu. 22. 27.
Ezr. 7. 17.   ⁿ Is. 32. 3.   ᵒ Job. 40. 29.   ⁱ Is. 60. 5.   Job 19. 18.   ᶠ Je. 3 16.   ᶜ Ca. 1. 7.   ᶠ Ho. 11. 3.

תַּרְדֵּמָ֫ה	['] noun fem. sing. dec. 10	רדם
תַּרְדֵּמַת	id., constr. st.	רדם
תֵּרַ֫דְנָה	['] Kal fut. 3 pers. pl. fem. (§ 2. r. 4, note)	ירד
תְּרַדֵּף	Piel fut. 3 pers. sing. fem.	רדף
תִּרְדֹּף	Kal fut. 2 p. s. m., or (Job 30.15) 3 p. s. f.	רדף
תִּרְדְּפֵם	id. fut. 2 pers. sing. m., suff. 3 pers. pl. m.	רדף
תִּרְדְּפֵ֫נוּ	id. id., suff. 1 pers. pl.; [ו] conv.	רדף
תִּרְדְּפֵ֫נִי	id. fut. 2 pers. pl. m. [תִּרְדְּפוּ], suff. 1 pers. s.	רדף
תַּרְהִבֵ֫נִי	Hiph. fut. 2 pers. s. m. [תַּרְהִיב], suff. 1 p. s.	רהב
תִּרְהוּ	Kal fut. 2 pers. pl. masc. R. רהה, or תִּירְהוּ, for תִּירְהוּ. R.	ירה
תִּרְהָ֫קָה	pr. name of a king of Egypt and Ethiopia, 2 Ki. 19.9; Is. 37.9.	
תָּ֫רוּ	Kal pret. 3 pers. pl.	תור
תָּר֫וֹב	Kal fut. 2 pers. sing. masc., Kh. תָּרוֹב, R. רוב. K. תָּרִיב ריב. R. see both under	ריב
תָּרוּם	Kal fut. 3 pers. sing. fem.	רום
תְּרוּמָה	[ומ'] noun fem. sing. and pl. dec. 10;	רום
תְּרוּמֹת	[ו] bef.	
תְּרוּמִיָּה	noun fem. sing.	רום
תְּרוֹמֵם	[ו'] Pilel fut. 2 pers. sing. masc. (Job 17.4), or 3 pers. sing. fem.; [ו] conv.	רום
תְּרוֹמְמֶ֫ךָ	[ו] id. fut. 3 pers. sing. fem., suff. 2 pers. sing. masc. [for תְּרוֹמְמֶ֫ךָ § 2. rem. 2]; [ו] bef.	רום
תְּרוֹמַמְנָה	Pilal (pass.) fut. 3 pers. pl. fem.	רום
תְּרוֹמְמֵ֫נִי	Pilel fut. 2 pers. sing. masc., suff. 1 pers. s.	רום
תְּרוּמַח	[ו'] noun f. s., constr. of תְּרוּמָה d. 10; [ו] bef.	רום
תְּרוּמֹת	id. pl.	רום
תְּרוּמֹתַי	id. sing., suff. 1 pers. sing.	רום
תְּרוּמֹתַי	id. pl., suff. 1 pers. sing.	רום
תְּרוּמֹתֵיכֶם	id. pl., suff. 2 pers. pl. masc.	רום
תְּרוּמֹתֵ֫ינוּ	[ו] id. pl., suff. 1 pers. pl.; [ו] bef.	רום
תְּרוּמַתְכֶם	id. sing., suff. 2 pers. pl. masc.	רום
תְּרוּמָתָם	id. sing., suff. 3 pers. pl. masc. (§ 4. rem. 2)	רום
תְּרוּעָה	[ו] noun fem. sing. dec. 10; [ו] bef.	רוע
תְּרוּעַת	[ו] id., constr. st.; [ו] id.	רוע
תָּרוּץ	Kal fut. 2 pers. sing. masc.	רוץ
תְּרוֹץ	Niph. fut. 2 pers. sing. masc. (§ 18. r. 7)	רצץ
תִּרְזָה	fem. a species of *hard tree*; Vulg. *ilex*, Is. 44.14.	
תֶּ֫רַח / תָּ֫רַח	pr. name—I. of a station of the Israelites in the desert, Nu. 33.27.—II. of the father of Abraham.	
תַּרְחִיב	Hiph. fut. 2 pers. sing. masc.	רחב
תַּרְחִ֫יבוּ	id. fut. 2 pers. pl. masc.	רחב

תַּרְחִיק	Hiph. fut. 2 pers. sing. masc.	רחק
תַּרְחִ֫יקוּ	id. fut. 2 pers. pl. masc.	רחק
תְּרַחֵם	Piel fut. 2 pers. sing. masc. (§ 14. rem. 1)	רחם
תְּרַחֲנָה	pr. name masc. 1 Ch. 2.48.	
תִּרְחַק / תִּרְחָק	Kal fut. 2 pers. sing. masc., or 3 pers. sing. fem. (§ 8. rem. 15); [ו] conv.	רחק
תְּרַטֵּשׁ	Piel fut. 2 pers. sing. masc.	רטש
תְּרֻטַּ֫שְׁנָה	id. fut. 3 pers. pl. fem. (§ 10. rem. 4)	רטש
תְּרֵי	Chald. num. card. masc., constr. of תְּרֵין q. v.	
תְּרִיבֵ֫הוּ	Kal fut. 2 pers. s. m. [תָּרִיב], suff. 3 pers. s. m.	ריב
תְּרִ֫יבוּ	id. fut. 2 pers. pl. masc.	ריב
תְּרִיב֫וּן	id. id. with parag. [ן] (comp. § 8. rem. 17)	ריב
תְּרִיבֶ֫נָּה	id. fut. 2 pers. sing. m., suff. 3 pers. sing. fem.	ריב
תְּרִיבֵ֫נִי	id. id., suff. 1 pers. sing.	ריב
תָּרִיד	Hiph. fut. 2 pers. sing. masc.	ירד
תָּרִים	Kh. תָּרִים Hiph. fut. 2 pers. sing. masc., K. תָּרוּם Kal fut. 3 pers. sing. fem.	רום
תָּרִים	noun masc., pl. of תּוֹר dec.	תור
תָּרִ֫ימוּ	Hiph. fut. 2 pers. pl. masc.	רום
תְּרֵין	Chald. only constr. תְּרֵי masc. and תַּרְתֵּין fem. *two*	
תָּרִ֫יעוּ	Hiph. fut. 2 pers. pl. masc.	רוע
תָּרִ֫יעִי	id. fut. 2 pers. sing. fem.	רוע
תָּרִיץ	Hiph. fut. 3 pers. sing. fem.	רוץ
תֵּרֵךְ	[ו] defect. and with epenth. [נ] for תֵּירֹךְ q. v. (§ 2. rem. 2)	ירה
תִּרְכַּב	[ו'] Kal fut. 2 pers. s. m., or 3 p. s. fem.; [ו] conv.	רכב
תִּרְכַּ֫בְנָה	id. fut. 3 pers. pl. fem.; [ו] id.	רכב
תַּרְכִּיבֵ֫נִי	Hiph. fut. 2 pers. sing. masc., suff. 1 pers. sing.	רכב
תָּרֵם	Hiph. fut. 3 pers. s. fem., ap. & conv. fr. תָּרִים	רום
תָּרֶם	Kal fut. 3 pers. sing. fem., ap. & conv. from תָּרוּם	רום
תַּרְמוֹת	[ו] noun fem. sing., Kh. תַּרְמוּת K. תַּרְמִית q. v.	רמה
תַּרְמִית	noun fem. sing. dec. 1 b	רמה
תַּרְמִיתָם	id., suff. 3 pers. pl. masc.	רמה
תִּרְמֹס	[ו'] Kal fut. 2 pers. sing. masc. (Ps. 91.13), or 3 pers. sing. fem.; [ו] conv.	רמס
תִּרְמְ֫סוּ	id. fut. 2 pers. pl. masc.	רמס
תִּרְמְסֵם	[ו] id. fut. 3 p. s. fem., suff. 3 p. pl. m.; [ו] con.	רמס
תֵּרָמַ֫סְנָה	Niph. fut. 3 p. pl. f. (§ 2. r. 4, note, & § 10 r.4)	רמס
תֵּרָמֶ֫סְנָה	Kal fut. 3 p. s. fem. [תִּרְמֹס], suff. 3 p. s. fem.	רמס
תִּרְמֹשׂ	Kal fut. 3 pers. sing. fem.	רמש
תַּרְמִת	defect. for תַּרְמִית (q. v.)	רמה
תָּרֻמַת	[ו] defect. for תְּרוּמַת (q. v.); [ו] bef.	רום
תָּרֹן	[ו] Kal fut. 3 pers. sing. fem.	רנן

---

a Ge. 15.12.   h Ps. 138.3.   p Pr. 4.8.   w Ex. 29.2.   c Ps. 106.17.   i Job 10.2.   p Hab. 3.8.   v Ge. 7.17.   Da. 8.10
1 Sa. 26.12.   i Is. 44.8.   q Ps. 75.11.   x Nu. 23.21.   d 2 Ki. 8.12.   k Ge. 27.40.   q 1 Sa. 25.42.   w Je. 14.14.   b Is. 28.3.
Je. 9.17.   k Nu. 13.32.   r Nu. 18.19.   y Pr. 4.12.   e Is. 13.18.   l Ps. 89.18.   r Ge. 24.61.   x Zep. 3.13.   c Is. 26.6.
Pr. 13.21.   l Pr. 3.30.   s Ex. 25.2.   z Eze. 29.7.   f De. 33.8.   m Mi. 4.9.   s Job 30.22.   y Ps. 119.118.   d Je. 23.26.
Ps. 83.16.   m Ex. 29.28.   t Nu. 18.8.   a Is. 57.4.   g Je. 2.29.   n Ps. 68.32.   t Ps. 92.11.   z Ps. 91.13.   e De. 12.11.
La. 3.43.   n Eze. 48.12.   u Ne. 10.38.   b Job 22.23.   h Is. 27.5.   o Job 12.7,8.   u Mi. 5.8.   a Eze. 34.18.   f Is. 35.6.
Job 19.22.   o Ps. 107.25.   Nu. 18.27.

תְּרָן֖ masc. dec. 6 c.—I. *mast.*—II. *banner,* Is. 30. 17.

תְּרָנָּה Kal fut. 3 pers. pl. fem. with parag. ה (comp. § 8. rem. 13) .   רנן

תְּרָנֶּה Kal fut. 3 pers. sing. fem. .   רנה

תַּרְנִין Hiph. fut. 2 pers. sing. masc.   רנן

תְּרָנֵם noun m. sing., suff. 3 pers. pl. m. fr. תְּרָן d. 6 c   תרן

תְּרַנֵּן Piel 3 pers. sing. fem.   רנן

תְּרַנֵּנָה id. fut. 3 pers. pl. fem. [for תְּרַנֵּנָנָה § 18. rem. 15, note] .   רנן

תְּרַע Chald. masc.—I. *a door,* Da. 3. 26.—II. *gate* of the king, for royal palace, Da. 2. 49.

    תְּרָע Ch. m. d. 1 a, *doorkeeper, porter,* Ezr. 7. 24.

    תִּרְעָתִי gent. noun, 1 Ch. 2. 55, from a place תִּרְעָה (*gate*) otherwise unknown.

תְּרַע / תְּרַע Hiph. fut. 2 pers. sing. masc. ap. & conv. (§ 18. rem. 11) .   רעע

תָּרֵעַ Kal fut. 3 pers. sing. fem. (§ 18. rem. 6)   רעע

תְּרֹעַ Chald. Peal fut. 3 pers. sing. fem. .   רעע

תִּרְעַב / תִּרְעָב Kal fut. 3 pers. sing. fem. (§ 8. rem. 15); וְ conv. .   רעב

תִּרְעָבוּ id. fut. 2 pers. pl. masc. [for תִּרְעֲבוּ v. id.]   רעב

תִּרְעַד Kal fut. 3 pers. sing. fem. [for תִּרְעָד § 8. rem. 15] ; וְ conv. .   רעד

תִּרְעֶה Kal fut. 2 pers. s. m., or (Je. 22. 22) 3 p. s. fem.   רעה

תָּרֵעוּ Hiph. fut. 2 pers. pl. masc.   רעע

תִּרְעוּ Kal fut. 2 pers. pl. masc.   רעה

תַּרְעֵא noun masc. pl. emph. from תְּרַע dec. 1   תרע

תִּרְעֶינָה Kal fut. 3 pers. pl. fem.; וְ conv.   רעה

תַּרְעֵלָה noun fem. sing.   רעל

תַּרְעֵם Hiph. fut. 2 pers. sing. masc. ap. [fr. תַּרְעֵים]   רעם

תַּרְעֵם Kal fut. 2 pers. s. m., suff. 3 pers. pl. m.   רעע

תִּרְעֵץ Kal fut. 3 pers. sing. fem.   רעץ

תִּרְעַשׁ / וַתִּ Kal fut. 3 pers. sing. fem.; וְ conv.   רעש

תִּרְעַשְׁנָה id. fut. 3 pers. pl. fem.   רעש

תִּרְעָתִים gent. noun pl. from תְּרַעַת   תרע

תַּרְף Hiph. fut. 2 pers. sing. masc. ap. [fr. תַּרְפֶּה]   רפה

תֵּרָפֵא Niph. fut. 2 pers. sing. masc.   רפא

תֵּרָפְאוּ id. fut. 2 pers. pl. masc.   רפא

תִּרְפָּאֵנִי Kal fut. 2 pers. sing. masc., suff. 1 pers. sing. (comp. § 16. rem. 12); וְ conv.   רפא

תְּרָפִים masc. pl. *Teraphim,* a kind of penates or household gods.

תְּרַפֶּינָה Piel fut. 3 pers. pl. fem.   רפה

תִּרְפֶּינָה Kal fut. 3 pers. pl. fem.   רפה

תִּרְפֶּינָה Kal fut. 3 pers. pl. fem. (§ 23. rem. 1) .   רפא

תִּרְפֵּנִי Hiph. fut. 2 pers. sing. masc. [תַּרְפֶּה], suff. 1 pers. sing. (§ 24. rem. 21) .   רפה

תִּרְפֹּשׂ Kal fut. 2 pers. sing. masc.; וְ conv. see   רפס

תִּרְפְּשׂוּן id. fut. 2 pers. pl. masc., וְ parag. [for § 8. rem. 17] .   רפס

תָּרֶץ Hiph. fut. 3 p. s. fem. (§ 18. r. 12); וְ conv.   רצץ

תָּרָץ Kal fut. 3 pers. s. fem. ap. & conv. fr. תָּרוּץ   רוץ

תִּרַץ Kal fut. 3 pers. sing. fem. (§ 18. rem. 12)   רצץ

תֵּרֶץ / וְ, וַתֵּ ap. from תִּרְצֶה q.v.; וְ conv. .   רצה

תִּרְצְדוּן Piel fut. 2 pers. pl. masc. with parag. וְ   רצד

תִּרְצָה pr. name fem., also of a place   רצה

תִּרְצֶה Kal fut. 2 pers. s. m., or (Le. 26. 34) 3 p. s. fem.   רצה

תִּרְצַח / תִּרְצָח Kal fut. 2 pers. sing. masc. (§ 8. rem. 15)   רצח

תִּרְצָחוּ Piel fut. 2 pers. pl. masc. [for תִּרְצָחוּ § 10. r. 7]   רצח

תִּרְצֶנָה Kal fut. 3 pers. pl. fem., Kh. תִּרְצֶנָה (§ 24. rem. 7) R. רצה, K. תִּצֹּרֶנָה R.   נצר

תִּרְצֵנִי Kal fut. 2 pers. sing. masc. (תִּרְצֶה), suff. 1 pers. sing. (§ 24. rem. 21); וְ conv.   רצה

תִּרְצָתָה pr. name (תִּרְצָה) with parag. ה .   רצה

תִּרְקְדוּ Kal fut. 2 pers. pl. masc.   רקד

תִּרְקִיעַ Hiph. fut. 2 pers. sing. masc.   רקע

תֶּרֶשׁ pr. name of a eunuch at the court of Ahasuerus, Est. 2. 21; 6. 2.

תַּרְשִׁיעַ Hiph. fut. 2 pers. sing. masc.   רשע

תַּרְשִׁיעִי id. fut. 2 pers. sing. fem.   רשע

תַּרְשִׁיעֵנִי id. fut. 2 pers. sing. masc. suff. 1 pers. sing.   רשע

תַּרְשִׁישׁ pr. name of a place   רשׁשׁ

תַּרְשִׁישׁ noun masc. sing.   רשׁשׁ

תַּרְשִׁישָׁה pr. name (תַּרְשִׁישׁ) with parag. ה   רשׁשׁ

תִּרְשֵׁם Ch. Peal fut. 2 pers. sing. masc.   רשם

תִּרְשַׁע Kal fut. 2 pers. sing. masc.   רשע

תַּרְתִּי Kal pret. 1 pers. sing.   תור

תַּרְתֵּין Ch. num. card. fem., from תְּרֵין masc. q.v.   תור

תַּרְתֶּם Kal pret. 2 pers. pl. masc.   תור

תַּרְתָּן pr. name of an Assyrian general.

תַּרְתָּק pr. name of an idol of the Arvadites, 2 Ki. 17. 31.

תִּשָּׁא / וְ, וַתִּ Kal fut. 2 pers. sing. masc., or 3 pers. sing. fem.; וְ conv. .   נשא

תִּשְׁאַב / וְ Kal fut. 3 pers. sing. fem. (§ 8. rem. 15); וְ conv. .   שאב

תִּשְׁאֶה Niph. fut. 3 pers. sing. fem.   שאה

תִּשָּׁאֵהוּ Kal fut. 3 pers. sing. fem., suff. 3 pers. sing. masc. (§ 16. rem. 12); וְ conv.   נשא

תִּשְׂאוּ Hiph. fut. 2 pers. pl. masc.   נשא

ᵃ Eze. 27. 5.   ᵉ 1 Ki. 14. 9.   ᵖ Is. 41. 23.   ᵗ Ex. 15. 6.   Eze. 1. 24, 25.   ᵐ Ec. 12. 6.   ʳ Ps. 62. 4.   Is. 54. 17.   Job 22. 26.

ᵇ Job 39. 23.   De. 28. 54, 56.   Eze. 34. 3, 18.   ᵘ Job 5. 18.   Le. 26. 43.   Pr. 23. 26.   Da. 6. 9.   Ge. 24. 45.

ᶜ Ps. 65. 9.   Da. 2. 40.   Ezr. 7. 24.   Job 7. 19.   Ps. 50. 18.   Ge. 33. 10.   Ec. 7. 17.   Ge. 24. 20.

ᵈ Is. 33. 23.   Pr. 19. 15.   Ge. 41. 2, 18.   Eze. 26. 10.   Eze. 32. 2.   Ps. 114. 6.   Ezr. 4. 24.   Is. 6. 11.

ᵉ Ps. 51. 16.   Ge. 41. 55.   Ps. 60. 5.   Je. 51. 8.   Eze. 34. 18.   Ex. 20. 13;   Job 37. 18.   2 Sa. 4. 4.

ᶠ Ps. 71. 23.   Is. 65. 13.   Job 40. 9.   1 Sa. 6. 3.   Ju. 9. 53.   De. 5. 17.   y Job 34. 17.   Nu. 14. 34.

ᵍ Ps. 44. 3.   Ps. 104. 32.   Ps. 2. 9.   Ps. 39. 3.   Je. 37. 9.

תִּשָּׂאוּ	} Kal fut. 2 pers. pl. masc. (§ 8. rem. 15,	נשא
תִּשָּׂאוּ	} comp. § 10. rem. 7)	
תִּשָּׂאוּן	id. with parag. ן [for תִּשָּׂאוּ § 8. rem. 17]	נשא
תְּשֻׁאוֹת	noun fem., pl. of [תְּשֻׁאָה] dec. 10	שוא
תִּשְׂאִי	Kal fut. 2 pers. sing. fem.	נשא
תִּשֶּׂאינָה	id. fut. 2 pers. pl. fem. (§ 23. rem. 3)	נשא
תַּשְׁאִיר	Hiph. fut. 3 pers. sing. fem.	שאר
תִּשְׁאַל	וַ' Kal fut. 2 pers. sing. masc.; וַ' conv.	שאל
תִּשְׁאָלֵךְ	Kal fut. 3 pers. sing. fem. (תִּשְׁאַל), suff. 2	שאל
	pers. sing. masc. (§ 16. rem. 12)	
תִּשְׁאָלֵנִי	id. fut. 2 pers. sing. masc., suff. 1 pers. sing.	שאל
תִּשָּׂאֵם	Kal fut. 3 pers. sing. fem., suff. 3 pers. pl.	
	masc. (comp. § 16. rem. 12)	נשא
תִּשֶּׂאנָה	וַ id. fut. 3 pers. pl. fem.; וַ' conv.	נשא
תִּשָּׂאֵנִי	וַ' id. fut. 2 pers. sing. masc. (Job 30. 22),	
	or 3 pers. sing. fem., suff. 1 pers. sing.	
	(comp. § 16. rem. 12); וַ' id.	נשא
תִּשְׁאַף	Kal fut. 2 pers. sing. masc.	שאף
תִּשָּׁאֵר	וַ' Niph. fut. 3 pers. sing. fem.; וַ' conv.	שאר
תִּשָּׁאַרְנָה	id. fut. 3 pers. pl. fem.	שאר
תָּשֵׁב	} Hiph. fut. 2 pers. sing. masc., ap. fr.	
תָּשֶׁב	} תָּשִׁיב (§ 21. rem. 18)	שוב
תָּשָׁב	וַ } Kal fut. 2 pers. sing. masc., or 3 pers.	
תָּשָׁב	וַ } sing. fem., ap. & conv. from תָּשׁוּב	שוב
תֵּשֵׁב	} Kal fut. 2 pers. sing. masc., or 3 pers.	
תֵּשֶׁב	וַ } sing. fem.; וַ' conv.	ישב
תָּשֻׁבוּ	וַ defect. for תָּשִׁיבוּ q. v.; וַ' id.	שוב
תָּשֻׁבוּ	וַ defect. for תָּשׁוּבוּ q. v.; וַ' id.	שוב
תֵּשְׁבוּ	} Kal fut. 2 pers. pl. masc. (comp. § 8.	
תֵּשְׁבוּ	וַ } rem. 15); וַ' id.	ישב
תְּשֻׁבוּן	defect. for תְּשׁוּבוּן (q. v.)	שוב
תְּשַׁבְּחֵם	Piel fut. 2 pers. s. m. [תְּשַׁבַּח], suff. 3 p. pl. m.	שבח
תַּשְׁבִּי	Hiph. fut. 2 pers. sing. fem.	שוב
תֵּשְׁבִי	} Kal fut. 2 pers. sing. fem. (comp. § 8.	
תֵּשְׁבִי	} rem. 15)	ישב
תָּשֹׁבְנָה	Kal fut. 3 pers. pl. fem.	שוב
תַּשְׁבִּיעַ	Hiph. fut. 2 pers. sing. masc.	שבע
תַּשְׁבִּיעוּ	Hiph. fut. 2 pers. pl. masc.	שבע
תַּשְׁבִּיתָ	Hiph. fut. 2 pers. sing. masc.	שבת
תַּשְׁבִּיתוּ	id. fut. 2 pers. pl. masc.	שבת
תְּשַׁבֵּךְ	Kal fut. 3 pers. sing. fem. [תִּשְׁבֶּה], suff.	
	2 pers. sing. masc. (§ 24. rem. 21)	שבה
תָּשֹׁבְן	Kal fut. 3 pers. pl. fem. (§ 21. rem. 10)	שוב
תְּשַׁבֵּנָה	Hiph. fut. 3 pers. pl. fem.	שוב
תְּשַׁבֵּנָה	וַ Kal fut. 3 pers. pl. fem. (§ 21. r.10); וַ' conv.	שוב
תְּשִׁבֵנִי	defect. for תְּשִׁיבֵנִי (q. v.)	שוב

תִּשָּׁבַע	} Niph. fut. ? pers. sing. masc., or 3 pers.	שבע
תִּשָּׁבַע	} sing. fem. (§ 15. rem. 1)	
תִּשְׁבַּע	} Kal fut. 2 pers. sing. masc., or 3 pers.	שבע
תִּשְׁבַּע	וַ' } sing. fem. (§ 8. rem. 15); וַ' conv.	
תִּשְׁבְּעוּ	Niph. fut. 2 pers. pl. masc.	שבע
תִּשְׁבְּעוּ	} Kal fut. 2 pers. pl. masc. (§ 8. rem. 15)	שבע
תִּשְׁבְּעוּ	}	
תִּשְׁבַּעְנָה	id. fut. 3 pers. pl. fem.	שבע
תִּשְׁבָּעֶנּוּ	id. fut. 2 pers. s. m., suff. 3 p. s. m. (§ 16. r.12)	שבע
תִּשְׁבָּץ	noun masc. sing.	שבץ
תְּשַׁבֵּר	Piel fut. 2 pers. sing. masc.	שבר
תִּשָּׁבֵר	Niph. fut. 2 pers. sing. masc. (§ 10. rem. 4)	שבר
תִּשְׁבֹּר	וַ' id. fut. 2 pers. sing. masc. (Eze. 29. 7), or	
	3 pers. sing. fem.; וַ' conv.	שבר
תִּשְׁבֹּרְנָה	ן id. fut. 3 pers. s. fem. bef. monos. (§ 9. r. 3)	שבר
תִּשְׁבֹּר	Kal fut. 3 pers. s. fem. [for תִּשְׁבֹּר § 8. r.18]	שבר
תְּשַׁבְּרוּן	Piel fut. 2 pers. pl. masc. [for תְּשַׁבְּרוּ,	
	comp. § 8. r. 15]	שבר
תִּשָּׁבְרוּ	} Kal fut. 2 pers. pl. masc. (§ 8. rem. 15)	שבר
תִּשָּׁבְרוּ	}	
תִּשְׁבְּרוּן	Piel fut. 2 pers. pl. masc., ן parag. [for	
	תְּשַׁבְּרוּ § 10. rem. 4]	שבר
תְּשַׁבֵּרְנָה	Piel fut. 2 pers. pl. fem.	שבר
תִּשָּׁבַרְנָה	וַ Niph. fut. 3 pers. pl. fem.; וַ' conv.	שבר
תְּשַׁבְּרֵנִי	Hiph. fut. 2 pers. sing. masc., suff. 1 pers. s.	שבר
תְּשׁוּבֹת	noun fem., pl. of [תְּשׁוּבָה] dec. 10	שוב
תִּשְׁבֹּת	Kal fut. 3 pers. sing. fem. (§ 8. rem. 13)	שבת
תִּשְׁבֹּת	id. fut. 2 pers. sing. masc., or (Le. 26. 35)	
	3 pers. sing. fem. (§ 8. rem. 13)	שבת
תִּשְׁבְּתוּ	id. fut. 2 pers. pl. masc.	שבת
תְּשׁוּבָתוֹ	ן noun fem. sing., suff. 3 pers. sing. masc.	
	from [תְּשׁוּבָה] dec. 10; ן bef. (:)	שוב
תְּשַׂגְּבֵנִי	Piel fut. 2 pers. sing. masc., or 3 pers. sing.	
	fem. [תְּשַׂגֵּב], suff. 1 pers. sing. (§ 10. r. 7)	שגב
תִּשְׁגֶּה	Kal fut. 2 pers. sing. masc.	שגה
תִּשְׁגּוּ	id. fut. 2 pers. pl. masc.	שגה
תַּשְׂגִּיא	Hiph. fut. 2 pers. sing. masc.	שגא
תִּשָּׁגַלְנָה	Niph. fut. 3 pers. pl. fem. (K. תִּשָּׁכַבְנָה q. v.)	שגל
תַּשְׂגֵּנִי	Hiph. fut. 2 pers. sing. masc. [תַּשְׂגֶּה], suff.	
	1 pers. sing. (§ 24. rem. 21)	שגה
תְּשַׂגְשְׂנִי	Pilpel fut. 2 pers. sing. fem. (§ 6. No. 4)	שוג
תְּשַׁדֵּד	Piel fut. 2 pers. sing. masc.	שדד
תַּשְׁדֶּה	Hiph. fut. 2 pers. sing. masc.	נשה
תָּשׁוּב	Kal fut. 2 pers. sing. masc., or 3 pers. sing. f.	שוב
תְּשׁוֹבֵב	Pilel fut. 2 pers. sing. masc.	שוב
תָּשׁוּבוּ	Kal fut. 2 pers. pl. masc.	שוב

Mi. 6.16.   Ru. 1.9.   1 Ki. 13. 6;   1 Ki. 2. 16.   Ex. 12. 15.   Ru. 2. 14.   Pr. 25. 15.   De. 2. 28.   Job 36. 24.
Job 13. 8, 10.   Job 30. 22.   Job 10. 16.   Nu. 24. 22.   Ex. 16. 12.   De. 7. 5.   Job 34. 36.   Ps. 119. 10.
Eze. 23. 49.   Job 36. 20.   1 Ki. 17. 21.   Ho. 3. 3.   Eze. 16. 55.   Le. 11. 33.   Le. 23. 32.   Is. 17. 11.
Am. 5. 3.   Ex. 10. 26.   Je. 34. 16.   Is. 58. 10.   Job 20. 10.   Pr. 25. 16.   1 Sa. 7. 17.   Pr. 24. 15.
2 Ch. 1. 11.   Ru. 1. 3, 5.   Ge. 34. 10.   Is. 58. 10.   1 Sa. 7. 14.   Eze. 32. 28.   Pr. 5. 19, 20.   De. 24. 10.
De. 14. 26.   Ex. 8. 5, 7.   1 Ki. 9. 6.   Jos. 23. 7.   Je. 37. 20.   Ru. 1. 13.   Nu. 15. 22.   Ps. 60. 3.
1 Sa. 28. 16.   1 Ki. 2. 20.   Ps. 89. 10.   Le. 2. 13.   Ec. 12. 6.   Mi. 6. 14.

תְּשׁוּבוּ Kh. תְּשֻׁבִי q. v. K. תְּשֻׁבִי Kal fut. 2 p. s. f. — שוב

תְּשׁוּבוּן } Kal fut. 2 pers. pl. masc. with parag. } — שוב

תְּשֻׁבֻן } (comp. § 8. rem. 17) } — שוב

תְּשׁוּבַת noun fem. sing., constr. of [תְּשׁוּבָה] dec. 10 — שוב

תְּשׁוּבֹתֵיכֶם id. pl., suff. 2 pers. pl. masc.; ו bef. (:) — שוב

תְּשַׁוֶּה Piel fut. 2 pers. sing. masc. — שוה

תְּשֻׁוֶּה Kh. תְּשֻׁוֶּה q. v., K. תֻּשִׁיָּה for תּוּשִׁיָּה (q. v.) — ישה

תִּשְׁוֶה Kal fut. 2 pers. sing. masc. — שוה

תַּשְׁווּ Hiph. fut. 2 pers. pl. masc. — שוה

תְּשׁוֹמֵם Hithpoel fut. 2 p. s. m. [for תִּתְשׁוֹמֵם § 12. r. 3] — שמם

תְּשַׁוַּע } Piel fut. 2 pers. sing. masc., or 3 pers. — שוע

תְּשַׁוֵּעַ } sing. fem. (§ 15. rem. 1) } — שוע

תְּשׁוּעָה noun fem. sing. dec. 10; ו bef. (:) — שוע

תְּשׁוּעַת id. constr. st.; ו id. — שוע

תְּשׁוּעָתִי id., suff. 1 pers. sing.; ו id. — שוע

תְּשׁוּעָתְךָ } id. with suff. 2 pers. sing. masc.; — שוע

תְּשׁוּעָתֶךָ } ו id. — שוע

תְּשׁוּפֶנּוּ Kal fut. 2 p. s. m. [תָּשׁוּף], suff. 3 p. s. m. — שוף

תְּשׁוּקָתוֹ noun f. s., suff. 3 p. s. m. fr. [תְּשׁוּקָה] d. 10 — שוק

תְּשׁוּקָתֵךְ id., suff. 2 pers. sing. fem. — שוק

תְּשׁוּרָה noun fem. sing.; ו bef. (:) — שור

תְּשׁוּרִי id. fut. 2 pers. sing. fem. — שור

תְּשׁוּרֶנּוּ id. fut. 2 p. s. m., or 3 p. s. f., suff. 3 p. s. m. — שור

תְּשׁוּרֵנִי id. fut. 2 pers. sing. masc., or 3 pers. sing. fem., suff. 1 pers. sing. —

תֵּשַׁח Niph. fut. 3 pers. sing. fem. — שחח

תִּשְׁחֲדִי Kal fut. 2 pers. s. f. (§ 8. r. 14); וַ conv. — שחד

תִּשְׁחַט Niph. fut. 3 pers. sing. fem. — שחט

תִּשְׁחַט Kal fut. 2 pers. sing. masc. — שחט

תִּשְׁחֲטוּ id. fut. 2 pers. pl. masc. — שחט

תִּשְׁחֲטִי id. fut. 2 pers. sing. fem.; וַ conv. — שחט

תַּשְׁחִית Hiph. fut. 2 pers. sing. masc. — שחת

תַּשְׁחִיתֵהוּ id., suff. 3 pers. sing. masc. — שחת

תַּשְׁחִיתֵם id., suff. 3 pers. pl. masc.; וַ conv. — שחת

תִּשְׂחָק Kal fut. 2 pers. sing. masc. (§ 8. rem. 15) — שחק

תִּשְׂחָק וַ id. fut. 2 pers. sing. masc. (Ps. 59. 9), or 3 pers. sing. fem.; וַ conv. — שחק

תְּשַׁחֵר Piel fut. 2 pers. sing. masc. (§ 14. rem. 1) — שחר

תַּשְׁחֵת Hiph. fut. 2 pers. sing. masc., or (Eze. 23. 11) 3 pers. sing. fem.; וַ conv. — שחת

תִּשָּׁחֵת וַ Niph. fut. 3 pers. sing. fem.; וַ id. — שחת

תַּשְׁחִיתוּ Hiph. fut. 2 pers. pl. masc. [תַּשְׁחִיתוּ], parag. (comp. § 8. rem. 17) — שחת

תַּשְׁחִיתִי id. fut. 2 pers. sing. fem.; וַ conv. — שחת

תִּשְׁטֶה Kal fut. 3 pers. sing. fem. — שטה

תִּשְׂטֶח וַ Kal fut. 3 pers. sing. fem.; וַ conv. — שטח

תְּשַׁטְּמֵנִי Kal fut. 2 pers. s. m. [תִּשְׂטֹם], suff. 1 pers. s. — שטם

תִּשְׂטֹף Kal fut. 2 pers. sing. masc. — שטף

תִּשְׂטְפֵנִי id. fut. 3 pers. sing. fem., suff. 1 pers. sing. — שטף

תְּשִׁי Kal fut. 2 pers. sing. masc. ap. for תְּשִׁי R.

שָׁיָה (§ 24. r. 3e, comp. § 35. r. 14), or תְּשִׁי

may be contracted fr. תִּשְׁהֶה, תִּשְׁהֶי (after

the analogy of וַן for וַן, נִי for נְהִי,) R. שהה

תָּשִׁיב Hiph. fut. 2 p. s. m., or (Ju. 5. 29) 3 p. s. f. — שוב

תָּשִׁיבוּ וַ Hiph. fut. 2 pers. pl. masc.; וַ conv. — שוב

תָּשִׁיבוּ Hiph. fut. 2 p. pl. masc. — שוב

תְּשִׁיבֵם id. fut. 2 pers. sing. masc., suff. 3 pers. pl. m. — שוב

תְּשִׁיבֵנּוּ id. id., suff. 3 pers. sing. masc. — שוב

תְּשִׁיבֵנוּ id. id., suff. 1 pers. pl. — שוב

תְּשִׁיבֵנִי id. id., suff. 1 pers. sing. — שוב

תַּשִּׂיג Hiph. fut. 2 p. s. m. (1 Sa. 30. 8), or 3 p. s. fem. — נשג

תַּשִּׂיגֵהוּ id. fut. 3 pers. sing. fem., suff. 3 pers. sing. m. — נשג

תַּשִּׂיגוּם id. fut. 2 pers. pl. masc., suff. 3 pers. pl. masc. — נשג

תַּשִּׂיגֵם id. fut. 3 pers. sing. fem., suff. 3 pers. pl. masc. — נשג

תַּשִּׂיגֵנוּ id. id., suff. 1 pers. pl. — נשג

תָּשִׂיחַ Kh. תָּשִׂיחַ, K. תָּשׂוּחַ Hiph. or Kal fut. 3 p. s. f. — שוח

תְּשִׂיחֶךָ Kal fut. 3 pers. s. fem. [תָּשִׂיחַ], suff. 2 p. s. m. — שיח

תַּשִּׁיךְ Hiph. fut. 2 pers. sing. masc. — נשך

תָּשִׂים Kal fut. 2 pers. sing. masc. R. שׂים see — שום

תָּשִׂימוּ id. fut. 2 pers. pl. masc. — שום

תְּשִׂימוּן וַ id. id. with parag. — שום

תְּשִׂימִי וַ id. fut. 2 pers. sing. fem.; וַ conv. — שום

תְּשִׂימֵנוּ id. id. fut. 2 pers. sing. masc., suff. 1 pers. pl. — שום

תְּשִׂימֵנִי id. id., suff. 1 pers. sing. — שום

תְּשִׂימֵנִי id. fut. 2 pers. pl. masc., suff. 1 pers. sing. — שום

תָּשִׁישׂ Kal fut. 3 pers. sing. fem., R. שִׂישׂ, see — שושׂ

תָּשִׁית Kal fut. 2 pers. sing. masc. — שית

תְּשִׁיתֵהוּ id. id., suff. 3 pers. sing. masc. — שית

תְּשִׁיתֵמוּ id. fut. 2 pers. pl. masc. — שית

תְּשִׁיתִי id. fut. 2 pers. sing. fem. — שית

תְּשִׁיתֵמוֹ id. fut. 2 pers. s. masc., suff. 3 pers. pl. masc. — שית

תִּשְׁכַּב וַ } Kal fut. 2 pers. s. masc., or 3 pers. — שכב

תִּשְׁכַּב וַתֵּ, וַ } sing. fem. (§ 8. r. 15); וַ conv. } — שכב

תִּשְׁכַּבְהֵגוּ defect. for תִּשְׁכְּבֶיהָ q. v. — שכב

תִּשְׁכְּבוּן } Kal fut. 2 pers. pl. masc., parag. — שכב

תִּשְׁכְּבוּן } (§ 8. rem. 17) } — שכב

תִּשְׁכַּבְנָה Keri, Niph. fut. 3 pers. pl. fem. (§ 10. r. 4) — שכב

תִּשְׁכֹּן id. fut. 2 pers. s. m. (Is. 13. 20), or 3 p. s. fem. — שכב

תִּשָּׁכַח } Niph. fut. 3 pers. sing. fem. (§ 15. — שכח

תִּשָּׁכַח } rem. 1) } — שכח

תִּשְׁכַּח } Kal fut. 2 pers. sing. masc., or 3 pers. — שכח

תִּשְׁכַּח וַ } sing. fem. (§ 8. rem. 15); וַ conv. } — שכח

---

a Je. 3. 19.   k Pr. 26. 4.   p Ps. 40. 11;119. 41.   u Eze. 16. 33.   ƒ Pr. 31. 25.   2 Sa. 17. 19.   Ps. 44. 11.   De. 23, 20, 21.   l 2 Sa. 13. 20.

b 2 Ch. 7. 19.   l Is. 46. 5.   q Ge. 3. 15.   v Le. 6. 18.   g Job 8. 5.   a Job 30. 21.   z Job 27. 20.   Eze. 44. 8.   m Ru. 3. 7.

c Nu. 32. 15.   m Ec. 7. 16.   r Ge. 3. 16.   w Ex. 34. 25.   h Job 14. 19.   b Jos. 2. 5.   Is. 51. 23.   n Eze. 32. 28.

d 1 Ch. 20. 1.   n Is. 58. 9.   s 1 Sa. 9. 7.   x Le. 22. 28.   i Ps. 69. 16.   c Ho. 10. 9.   a Is. 3. 7.   o 2 Ki. 4. 21.

e Job 21. 34.   o Job 24. 12.   t Ca. 4. 8.   y Ge. 6. 11.   k De. 32. 18.   d Is. 59. 9.   b Is. 50. 11.

f Ps. 21. 6.   p Ps. 37. 39.   u Job 29, 9; 35. 14.   z Ps. 78. 45.   l Ezr. 10. 10.   e La. 3. 20.   c Ps. 68. 14.

g Job 30. 22.   q Is. 46. 13.   Is. 29. 4.   Job 5. 22.   m Nu. 5. 12, 29.   f De. 22. 1.   d Pr. 6. 22.   e Ps. 62. 11.   De. 31. 21.

תִּשְׁכָּחֻהוּ	id. fut. 2 pers. pl. masc.	שכח
תִּשְׁכָּחֻהוּ		
תִּשְׁכָּחִי	id. fut. 2 pers. sing. fem.	שכח
תִּשְׁכָּחִי		
תִּשְׁכַּחְנָה	id. fut. 3 pers. pl fem.	שכח
תִּשְׁכָּחֵנוּ	id. fut. 2 pers. s. m., suff. 1 p. pl. (§ 16. r. 12)	שכח
תִּשְׁכָּחֵנִי	id. id. with suff 1 pers. sing.	שכח
וַתַּשְׁכִּיבֵהוּ	וַ Hiph. fut. 3 pers. sing. fem., suff. 3 pers. sing. masc.; וַ conv.	שכב
תַּשְׂכִּיל	Hiph. fut. 2 pers. sing. masc.	שׂכל
תַּשְׂכִּילוּ	id. fut. 2 pers. pl. masc.	שׂכל
תַּשְׂכִּים	Hiph. fut. 2 pers. sing. masc.	שׁכם
תִּשְׂכְּבֵנִי	Pilel fut. 2 pers. sing. masc., suff. 1 pers. sing.	שׂוך
וַתַּשְׂכֵּל	וַ ap. from תַּשְׂכִּיל (q. v.)	שׂכל
תְּשַׁכֵּל	(De. 32. 25) Piel fut. 3 p. s. f.	שׂכל
תִּשְׁכַּל	Kal fut. 3 pers. sing. fem.	שׂכל
תַּשְׁכֵּן	Hiph. fut. 2 pers. sing. masc. ap. [תַּשְׁכִּין]	שכן
תִּשְׁכֹּן		
תִּשְׁכָּן	Kal fut. 3 pers. sing. fem. (§ 8. rem. 18)	שכן
תִּשְׁכֹּנָּה	id. fut. 3 pers. pl. fem. [for תִּשְׁכֹּנְנָה comp. § 18. rem. 15, note]	שכן
תִּשְׁכְּרִי	Kal fut. 2 pers. sing. fem.	שכר
תַּשְׁלֵגְ	Hiph. fut. 2 pers. sing. masc. ap. [fr. תַּשְׁלִיג]	שׁלג
תַּשְׁלֶה	Hiph. fut. 2 pers. sing. masc.	שׁלה
תִּשְׁלוּ	Kal fut. 2 pers. pl. masc.	שׁלל
תִּשָּׁלֶה	Niph. fut. 2 pers. pl. masc.	שׁלה
תְּשַׁלַּח	Piel fut. 2 pers. sing. masc.	שׁלח
וַתְּשַׁלַּח	וַ id. fut. 3 pers. sing. fem.; וַ conv.	שׁלח
תִּשְׁלַח	Kal fut. 2 pers. sing. masc. (§ 8. rem. 15)	שׁלח
תִּשְׁלַח	וַ id. id., or fut. 3 p. s. m.; וַ conv.	שׁלח
וַתְּשַׁלְּחֵהוּ	וַ Piel fut. 2 pers. sing. masc. (תְּשַׁלַּח), suff. 3 pers. sing. masc. (§ 10. rem. 7); וַ id.	שׁלח
תְּשַׁלְּחֻנוּ	id. fut. 2 pers. pl. masc. (comp. § 8. r. 15)	שׁלח
תְּשַׁלְּחֻנוּ		
תִּשְׁלְחוּ	Kal fut. 2 pers. pl. masc. (§ 8. rem. 15)	שׁלח
תִּשְׁלְחוּ		
תְּשַׁלְּחוּם	Piel fut. 2 pers. pl. m., suff. 3 pers. pl. m.	שׁלח
תְּשַׁלְּחֻנִי	וַ id. id., suff. 1 pers. sing.; וַ conv.	שׁלח
תְּשַׁלְּחִי	וַ id. fut. 2 pers. sing. fem.; וַ id.	שׁלח
תְּשַׁלְּחֵם	וַ id. fut. 2 pers. sing. masc., or 3 pers. sing. fem., suff. 3 pers. pl. masc.; וַ id.	שׁלח
תִּשְׁלָחֵם	Kal fut. 2 pers. sing. masc. (תִּשְׁלַח), suff 3 pers. pl. masc. (§ 16. rem. 12)	שׁלח

תְּשַׁלַּחְנָה	Piel fut. 3 pers. pl. fem.	שׁלח
תִּשְׁלַחְנָה	Kal fut. 3 or 2 pers. pl. fem. (§ 2. r. 4, note)	שׁלח
תְּשַׁלְּחֶנּוּ	Piel fut. 2 p. s. m. (תְּשַׁלַּח), suff. 3 p. s. m.	שׁלח
תִּשְׁלָחֵנוּ	Kal fut. 2 pers. sing. masc. (תִּשְׁלַח), suff. 1 pers. pl. (§ 16. rem. 12)	שׁלח
תְּשַׁלְּחֵנִי	Piel fut. 2 pers. s. m. (תְּשַׁלַּח), suff. 1 p. s.	שׁלח
תִּשְׁלָחֵנִי	Kal fut. 2 pers. sing. masc. (תִּשְׁלַח), suff. 1 pers. sing. (§ 16. rem. 12)	שׁלח
תַּשְׁלֵט	Hiph. fut. 2 p. s. m. ap. [for תַּשְׁלֵיט § 11. r. 7]	שׁלט
תַּשְׁלֵט	Chald. Peal fut. 2 pers. sing. masc., or 3 pers. sing. fem. (§ 8. rem. 15)	שׁלט
תַּשְׁלָט		
וַתַּשְׁלֵךְ	וַ Hiph. fut. 2 pers. sing. masc.	שׁלך
תַּשְׁלִיכֵהוּ	וַ id. fut. 3 pers. sing. f., suff. 3 pers. s. m.	שׁלך
תַּשְׁלִיכֵהוּ	id. fut. 2 pers. pl. masc., suff. 3 pers. s. m.	שׁלך
וַתַּשְׁלִיכִי	וַ id. fut. 2 pers. sing. fem.; וַ conv.	שׁלך
וַתַּשְׁלִיכֵנִי	וַ id. fut. 3 pers. sing. f., suff. 1 pers. s.; וַ id.	שׁלך
תַּשְׁלִים	Hiph. fut. 3 pers. sing. fem.	שׁלם
תַּשְׁלִימֵנִי	id. fut. 2 pers. sing. masc., suff. 1 pers. sing.	שׁלם
וַתַּשְׁלֵךְ	וַ וַתַּ Hiph. fut. 2 pers. sing. masc. (Ps. 50.17), or 3 p. s. f., ap. fr. תַּשְׁלִיךְ; וַ conv.	שׁלך
תַּשְׁלִכוּן	Hiph. fut. 2 pers. pl. masc. with parag. ן (comp. § 8. rem. 17)	שׁלך
וַתֻּשְׁלְכִי	וַ Hoph. fut. 2 p. s. f. (§ 11. r. 10); וַ conv.	שׁלך
תְּשַׁלֵּם	Piel fut. 2 pers. sing. masc.	שׁלם
וַתְּשַׁלֵּם	וַ Kal fut. 3 pers. sing. fem.; וַ conv.	שׁלם
וַתָּשֶׂם	וַ Kal fut. 2 p. s. m. ap. fr. תָּשִׂים R. שׂים see שׂום	שׂום
וַתָּשֶׂם	וַ id. fut. 2 pers. sing. masc. (1 Sa. 9. 20), or 3 pers. sing. fem.; וַ conv.	שׂום
תָּשֵׂם	Kal fut. 3 pers. sing. fem. R. שׁמם (§ 18. rem. 6) or	ישׁם
וַתָּשֹׁם		
תַּשְׂמְאִילוּ	Hiph. fut. 2 pers. pl. masc.	שׂמאל
תִּשָּׁמְדוּן	Niphal fut. 2 p. pl. masc. parag. ן [for תִּשָּׁמֵדְוּן comp. § 8. rem. 17]	שׁמד
תְּשִׂמוּן	defect. for תְּשִׂימוּן (q. v.)	שׂום
וַתִּשְׁמֹר	וַ id. fut. 2 pers. sing. masc. (§ 8. rem. 18)	שׁמר
תִּשְׁמְרֵם	id. fut. 3 p. s. f., suff. 3 p. pl. m. (§ 8. r. 14)	שׁמר
תִּשְׂמַח	וַ Kal fut. 2 pers. sing. masc., or 3 pers. sing. fem. (§ 8. rem. 15); וַ conv.	שׂמח
וַתִּשְׂמַח		
תִּשְׂמְחִי	id. fut. 2 pers. sing. fem.	שׂמח
תִּשְׂמְחִי	id. fut., Kh. מְחִי 2 pers. sing. fem., K. מְחִי 2 pers. pl. masc.	שׂמח
תִּשְׂמַחְנָה	id. fut. 3 pers. pl. fem.	שׂמח
תַּשְׁמֵט	Hiph. fut. 2 pers. sing. m. ap. [fr. תַּשְׁמִיט]	שׁמט
תִּשְׁמְטֶנָּה	Kal fut. 2 p. s. m. (תִּשְׁמֹט), suff. 3 p. s. f.	שׁמט

a 2 Ki. 17. 38.	h 1 Ki. 3. 20.	p Eze. 17. 23.	x Ex. 4. 13.	f Job 39. 3.	m Da. 2. 39.	t Da. 8. 12.	b Eze.12.19; 19.7.	p Pr. 24. 17.
b De. 4. 23.	i Ju. 9. 33.	q Ps. 68. 15.	y Job 14. 20.	g De. 15. 12, 13.	n Mi. 7. 19.	u Ex. 22. 30.	c Is. 30. 21.	q 1 Sa. 19. 5.
c Is. 54. 4.	k Job 10. 11.	r 2 Ki. 4. 28.	z Nu. 5. 3.	h Jos. 1. 16.	o Job 18. 7.	v Eze. 16. 5.	d De. 4. 26.	r Je. 50. 11.
d Ps. 103. 2.	l Da. 9. 25.	s Ru. 2. 16.	a Nu. 5. 3.	i 1 Ki. 11. 22.	p Ex. 1. 22.	w Je. 42. 15.	e Job 13. 27.	s 2 Sa. 1. 20.
e Is. 49. 15.	m 1 Sa. 15. 33.	t 2 Ch. 29. 11.	b Ge. 26. 27.	k Ne. 2. 5.	q Eze. 23. 35.	x 1 Sa. 9. 20.	f Ge. 47. 19.	t De. 15. 3
	n Job 11. 14.	u Ps. 80. 12.	c Jos. 2. 21;	l Ps. 119. 133.	r De. 20. 12.	y Ge. 47. 19.	g Pr. 14. 3.	u Ex. 23. 11.
	o Job 3. 5.	w Eze. 17. 6.	Ps. 44. 3.	m Da. 5. 16.	s Is. 38. 12, 13.			

Form	Description	Root
תַּשְׁמִיד	Hiph. fut. 2 pers. sing. masc.	שמד
תַּשְׁמִידוּ	id. fut. 2 pers. pl. masc.	שמד
תַּשְׁמִידֵם	וַתַּ׳ id. fut. 2 pers. sing. masc., suff. 3 pers. pl. masc.; וַ׳ conv.	שמד
תַּשְׁמִיעוּ	Hiph. fut. 2 pers. pl. masc.	שמע
תַּשְׁמִיעֵנִי	id. fut. 2 pers. sing. masc., suff. 1 pers. sing.	שמע
תָּשֵׁמֶן	וְ Kal fut. 3 pers. sing. fem. (תָּשֵׂם), suff. 3 pers. pl. masc. R. שִׂים see	שום
תַּשְׁמַע	Hiph. fut. 2 pers. sing. m. ap. [from תַּשְׁמִיעַ]	שמע
תִּשָּׁמַע	וַ׳ Niph. fut. 3 pers. sing. fem.; וַ׳ conv.	שמע
תִּשְׁמַע / וַתִּ׳	Kal fut. 2 pers. sing. masc., or 3 pers. s. f. (§ 8. r. 15); id.	שמע
תִּשְׁמְעוּ / וַ׳	Kal fut. 2 pers. pl. masc.; id.	שמע
תִּשְׁמָעוּהָ	id., suff. 3 pers. sing. fem. (§ 16. rem. 12)	שמע
תִּשְׁמְעוּן / תִּשְׁמָעוּן	id. fut. 2 pers. pl. masc., parag. (§ 8. rem. 17)	שמע
תִּשְׁמְעוּן	Peal fut. 2 pers. pl. masc.	שמע
תִּשְׁמַעְנָה	וַ׳ Kal fut. 3 pers. pl. fem.	שמע
תִּשָּׁמֵר	Niph. fut. 3 pers. sing. fem.	שמר
תִּשְׁמֹר / וַתִּשְׁמֹר	id. fut. 2 pers. sing. masc., or 3 pers. sing. fem. (§ 8. r. 18); וַ׳ conv.	שמר
תִּשְׁמְרוּ	Niph. fut. 2 pers. pl. masc. [for תִּשָּׁמְרוּ comp. § 8. rem. 1?]	שמר
תִּשְׁמְרוּ / וַ׳	Kal fut. 2 pers. pl. masc. (§ 8. r. 15); וַ׳ conv.	שמר
תִּשְׁמְרוּן	id. id. with parag. (§ 8. rem. 17)	שמר
תִּשְׁמְרֶךָ	id. fut. 3 pers. sing. fem. (תִּשְׁמֹר), suff. 2 pers. sing. masc. [for תִּשְׁמָרְךָ]	שמר
תִּשְׁמְרֵם	id. fut. 2 pers. sing. masc., suff. 3 pers. pl. m.	שמר
תִּשְׁמְרֵנִי	id. id., suff. 1 pers. sing.	שמר
תִּשְׂנָא	וַ׳ Kal fut. 2 pers. sing. masc.; וַ׳ conv.	שנא
תִּשְׁנֵא	Ch. Peal fut. 3 pers. sing. fem.	שנה
תִּשְׁנוּ	Kal fut. 2 pers. pl. masc.	שנה
תִּשֶּׁנָה / וַתִּ׳	Kal fut. 3 pers. pl. fem. for תִּשָּׂאנָה (§ 23. rem. 10); וַ׳ conv.	נשא

תֵּשַׁע וָ׳, constr. תְּשַׁע (§ 35. rem. 7) fem., constr. תִּשְׁעַת m. *nine*; also *ninth*, בְּתִשְׁעָה לַחֹדֶשׁ *on the ninth day of the month*. Pl. תִּשְׁעִים com. *ninety*.

תְּשִׁיעִי masc. תְּשִׁיעִית fem. *ninth*.

Form	Description	Root
תֵּשַׁע	id. constr. st. (§ 35. rem. 7); וּ bef. (:)	תשע
תִּשְׁעָה	וְ id. masc., abs.	תשע
תִּשְׁעֶה	Kal fut. 2 pers. sing. masc.	שעה
תִּשְׁעִים	וְ num. card. com. gen., pl. of תֵּשַׁע (§ 35. r. 16)	תשע

Form	Description	Root
תִּשְׁעֶינָה	Kal fut. 3 pers. pl. fem.	שעה
תִּשָּׁעֵן	Niph. fut. 2 pers. sing. masc.	שען
תִּשָּׁעֵנוּ	וַ׳ id. fut. 2 pers. pl. masc.; וַ׳ conv.	שען
תַּשְׁעֵנִי	Hiph. fut. 2 pers. s. m. (תַּשְׁעִי), suff. 1 pers. s.	ישע
תִּשְׁתַּעְשְׁעוּ	Pulpal (§ 6. No. 4) fut. 2 pers. pl. masc. [for תְּשַׁעְשְׁעוּ from שַׁעֲשַׁע]	שעע
תִּשְׁפּוֹט / תִּשְׁפֹּט / תִּשְׁפָּט־	Kal fut. 2 pers. sing. masc. (§ 8. r. 18)	שפט
תִּשְׁפְּטוּ	id. fut. 2 pers. pl. masc.	שפט
תַּשְׁפִּיל	Hiph. fut. 2 pers. sing. masc.	שפל
תַּשְׁפִּילִי	וַ׳ id. fut. 2 pers. sing. fem.; וַ׳ conv.	שפל
תַּשְׁפִּילֶנּוּ	id. fut. 3 pers. sing. fem., suff. 3 pers. s. m.	שפל
תִּשְׁפֹּךְ	Kal fut. 2 pers. sing. masc.	שפך
תִּשְׁפְּכוּ / תִּשְׁפְּכוּ	id. fut. 2 pers. pl. masc. (§ 8. rem. 15)	שפך
תִּשְׁפְּכִי	וַ׳ id. fut. 2 pers. sing. fem.; וַ׳ conv.	שפך
תִּשְׁפְּכֶנּוּ	id. fut. 2 pers. sing. masc., suff. 3 pers. s. m.	שפך
תִּשְׁפְּלִי	Kal fut. 3 pers. sing. fem.	שפל
תִּשְׁפַּלְנָה	id. fut. 3 pers. pl. fem.	שפל
תִּשְׁפֹּת	Kal fut. 2 pers. sing. masc.	שפת
תִּשְׁפְּתֵנִי	id. with suff. 1 pers. sing.	שפת
תַּשְׁקְ	וַ׳ Hiph. fut. 3 pers. sing. f. ap. [from תַּשְׁקֶה § 24. rem. 16]; וַ׳ conv.	שקה
תֵּשְׁקְ	וַ׳ Kal fut. 3 pers. sing. f.; וַ׳ id.	נשק
תַּשְׁקֶה	Hiph. fut. 2 pers. sing. masc.	שקה
תַּשְׁקֵהוּ	וַ׳ id. fut. 3 p. s. f., suff. 3 p. s. m.; וַ׳ conv.	שקה
תַּשְׁקוּ	וַ׳ id. fut. 2 pers. pl. masc.; וַ׳ id.	שקה
תִּשְׁקֹל	Kal fut. 2 pers. sing. masc. (§ 8. rem. 18)	שקל
תִּשְׁקֹט	וַ׳ Kal fut. 2 pers. sing. masc. (Ps. 83. 2), or 3 pers. sing. fem.; וַ׳ conv.	שקט
תִּשְׁקְטִי	id. fut. 2 pers. sing. f. [for תִּשְׁקֹטִי § 8. r. 15]	שקט
תִּשְׁקֹטְן	וַ׳ Hiph. fut. 3 pers. pl. fem. (comp. § 8. rem. 16); וַ׳ conv.	שקה
תַּשְׁקִיעַ	Hiph. fut. 2 pers. sing. masc.	שקע
תִּשְׁקְלוּ	Kal fut. 2 pers. pl. masc.	שקל
תַּשְׁקֵם	וַ׳ Hiph. fut. 2 pers. sing. masc. (תַּשְׁקֶה), suff. 3 pers. pl. masc. (§ 24. rem. 21)	שקה
תַּשְׁקֵמוֹ	וַ׳ id., suff. 3 pers. plur. masc.; וַ׳ conv.	שקה
תִּשְׁקַעְנָה	וַ׳ Kal fut. 3 pers. sing. fem.; וַ׳ id.	שקע
תַּשְׁקִף	וַ׳ Hiph. fut. 3 p. s. f. ap. [fr. תַּשְׁקִיף]; וַ׳ id.	שקף
תִּשְׁקְצוּ / תְּשַׁקְצוּ	Piel fut. 2 pers. pl. masc. (comp. § 8. r. 15)	שקץ
תְּשַׁקְצֶנּוּ	id. fut. 2 pers. sing. masc., suff. 3 pers. s. m.	שקץ
תְּשׁוֹקְקָה	וַ׳ Pilel fut. 2 pers. sing. masc. [תְּשֹׁקֵק], suff. 3 pers. sing. fem.; וַ׳ conv.	שוק

a 1 Sa. 24. 22.   h Je. 18. 22.   q Ps. 130. 3.   x Ps. 45. 8.   e Job 7. 19.   n 2 Ch. 20. 12.   u Is. 5. 15.   a Ps. 83. 2.   g Je. 51. 64.
b La. 3. 66.   i Ne. 12. 43.   r 1 Ki. 3. 6.   y Ne. 13. 21.   f Is. 32. 3.   o Is. 57. 9.   v Is. 26. 12.   b Je. 47. 6, 7.   h Nu. 11. 2.
c Is. 26. 14.   k Jos. 22. 2.   s Ex. 23. 13.   z Je. 9. 17.   g Pr. 3. 5.   p Pr. 29. 23.   w Ps. 22. 16.   c Ge. 19. 33, 35.   i Ki. 9. 30.
d Jos. 6. 10.   l Je. 13. 17.   t Je. 35. 18.   a Ru. 1. 14; Ze. 5. 9.   h Ru. 3. 5.   q Ex. 29. 12.   x Ge. 19. 33, 35.   d 2 Ki. 9. 30.   k Le. 11. 11.
e Ps. 51. 10.   m Da. 3. 5, 15.   u Ge. 5. 8, 11.   b Is. 30. 12.   i 1 Sa. 30. 12.   r Ge. 33. 25.   y Job 40. 25.   e Ps. 36. 9.   l De. 7. 26.
f Ge. 31. 34.   n Pr. 4. 6.   v 2 Sa. 22. 44.   c 14, 20, 27.   k 2 Sa. 22. 44.   s Eze. 16. 15.   z Am. 2. 12.   f Ps. 80. 6.   m Ps. 65. 10.
g Ju. 18. 25.   o Mi. 6. 1.   w Le. 19. 17.   d Ezr. 2. 42.   l Is. 66. 12.   t 2 Ch. 1. 11.
  p Ju. 13. 13.   m Is. 32. 19.   1 Ki. 20. 39.

תִּשְׁקֹר Kal fut. 2 pers. sing. masc. . . שקר	תִּתְאַבְּלוּ Hithpa. fut. 2 pers. pl. masc. . אבל
תִּשַׁקְּרוּ Piel fut. 2 pers. pl. masc. שקר	תִּתְאַוּוּ Piel fut. 2 pers. pl. masc. . תאה
תָּשַׁר ו Kal fut. 3 pers. s. f. ap. & conv. (§ 22. r. 3) שיר	תִּתְאָו ap. from the foll. (§ 24 rem. 12) . אוה
תָּשֻׁרִי ו defect. for (תָּשׁוּרִי) (q. v.) . שור	תִּתְאַוֶּה Hithpa. fut. 2 pers. sing. masc. . אוה
תִּשָּׂרֵף ו' Niph. fut. 3 pers. sing. fem. שרף	תִּתְאַפַּק Hithpa. fut. 2 pers. sing. masc. (§ 12. rem. 1) אפק
תִּשְׂרֹף Kal fut. 2 pers. sing. masc. שרף	תִּתְבֹּנָן ו Hithpal. fut. 2 pers. sing. masc. (§ 12. rem. 4); ו' conv. . בין
תִּשְׂרְפוּ id. fut. 2 pers. pl. m. [for תִּשְׂרְפוּ § 8. r. 15] שרף	תִּתְבּוֹנָנוּ id. fut. 2 pers. pl. masc. . בין
תִּשְׂרְפֻן id. id. with parag. (§ 8. rem. 17) שרף	תִּתְבַּלַּע Hithpa. fut. 3 pers. sing. fem. בלע
תִּשְׂרַפְנָה Niph. fut. 3 pers. pl. fem. שרף	תִּתְבְּנֵא Chald. Ithpe. fut. 3 pers. sing. fem. בנה
תִּשְׂרְפֶנּוּ Kal fut. 2 p s. m (תִּשְׂרֹף), suff. 3 p s. m. שרף	defect. & in pause for תִּתְבּוֹנָנוּ (q. v.) . בין
תַּשְׁרֵשׁ ו Hiph. fut. 3 p. s. f. ap. [fr. תַּשְׁרִישׁ]; ו' conv. שרש	תִּתְבָּרָךְ / תִּתְבָּרֵךְ } Hithpa. fut. 2 pers. sing. masc. (§ 18. rem. 18) ברד
תְּשָׁרֵשׁ Piel fut. 3 pers. sing. fem. שרש	תִּתְגֹּדְדוּ Hithpo. fut. 2 pers. pl. masc. נדד
תְּשָׁרְתֵהוּ ו Piel fut. 3 pers. sing. fem. [תְּשָׁרֵת], suff. 3 pers. sing. masc.; ו' conv. שרת	תִּתְגֹּדְדִי / תִּתְגּוֹדָדִי } id. fut. 2 pers. sing. fem. (comp. § 21. r. 20) נדד
תָּשֶׁת / תָּשֵׁת ו' } Kal fut. 2 pers. sing. masc. ap. & conv. for תָּשִׁית שית	תִּתְגָּר ap. from the foll. (§ 24. rem. 12) נרה
תָּשֶׁת ו' Kal fut. 2 pers. s. m., or (Nu. 20. 11) 3 pers. sing. fem. ap. fr. תָּשְׁתָה (§ 24. r. 3); ו' conv. שתה	תִּתְגָּרֶה Hithpa. fut. 2 pers. sing. masc. נרה
תִּשְׁתְּבֵק Ithpe. fut. 3 pers. sing. fem. Chald. [for תִּתְשְׁבֵק comp. § 12 rem. 3] שבק	תִּתְגָּרוּ id. fut. 2 pers. pl. masc. נרה
תִּשְׁתֶּה Kal fut. 2 pers. sing. masc. שתה	תַּתָּה Kal pret. 2 pers. sing. masc. for נָתַתָּה (comp. רד for יָרַד) see § 17 r. 9. נתן
תֵּשֶׁתְּהוּ ו Kal fut. 3 person. sing. fem. [תָּשִׁית], suff. 3 pers. sing. masc.; ו' conv. שית	תִּתְהַדַּר Hithpa. fut. 2 pers. sing. masc. הדר
תִּשְׁתּוּ Kal fut. 2 pers. pl. masc. שתה	תִּתְהַלַּכְנָה ו Hithpa. fut. 3 pers. pl. fem.; ו' conv. הלך
תִּשְׁתּוֹחָח Hithpo. fut. 3 pers. sing. fem. [for תִּתְשׁוֹחָח comp. § 12. rem. 3] שחח	תִּתְהַלָּךְ / תִּתְהַלָּל } Hithpa. fut. 2 pers. sing. masc., or (Ps. 34. 3) 3 pers. sing. fem. (§ 12. rem. 1) הלל
תִּשְׁתּוֹחֲחִי id. fut. 2 pers. sing. fem. שחח	תִּתְהַלְלִי id. fut. 2 pers. sing. fem. . הלל
תִּשְׁתַּחֲוֻ ו / תִּשְׁתַּחֲווּ ו 3 pers. sing. fem. ap. from the foll. שחה	תִּתְהַפֵּךְ Hithpa. fut. 3 pers. sing. fem. הפך
תִּשְׁתַּחֲוֶה [transp. for תִּתְשׁ § 12. rem. 3] Hithpalel fut. 2 pers. sing. masc., 3d rad. ה doubled [for תִּשְׁתַּחֲוָה § 6. No. 2, & § 24. rem. 22] שחה	תִּתּוֹ Kal inf. (תֵּת § 17. rem. 9), suff. 3 pers. sing. masc. dec. 13 (§ 44. rem. 1) נתן
תִּשְׁתַּחֲווּ id. fut. 2 pers. pl. masc. שחה	תָּתוּרוּ Kal fut. 2 pers. pl. masc. . תור
תִּשְׁתַּחֲוֶינָ ו id. fut. 3 p. pl. f. (comp. § 8. r. 16); ו' conv. שחה	תִּתְחַבַּל Chald. Ithpa. fut. 3 pers. sing. fem. חבל
תִּשְׁתִּי Kal fut. 2 pers. sing. fem. שתה	תִּתְחַדֵּשׁ Hithpa. fut. 3 pers. sing. fem. חרש
תִּשְׁתֶּינָה id. fut. 3 pers. pl. fem. שתה	תִּתְחַטָּאוּ / תִּתְחַטָּאוּ } Hithpa. fut. 2 pers. pl. masc. (comp. § 8. rem. 15) חטא
תִּשְׁתַּכָּרִין Hithpa. fut. 2 pers. sing. fem., parag. [for תִּתְשַׁכְּרִין § 12. rem. 3, & § 8. rem. 17] שכר	תִּתְחַכַּם Hithpa. fut. 2 pers. sing. masc. (§ 12. rem. 1) חכם
תִּשְׁתָּעַ [for תִּתְשָׁעַ § 12. rem. 3] Hithpa. fut. 2 pers. sing. masc. ap. [from תִּשְׁתָּעֶה § 24. r. 12] שעה	תִּתְחַלְחַל ו Hithpalp. fut. 3 pers. sing. fem.; ו' conv. חול
תִּשְׁתַּפֵּךְ Hithpa. fut. 3 p. s. f. [for תִּתְשַׁפֵּךְ § 12. r. 3] שפך	תִּתְחַמָּקִין Hithpa. fut. 2 pers. sing. fem., parag. [for תִּתְחַמְּקִין § 8. rem. 17] חמק
תִּשְׁתַּפֵּכְנָה id. fut. 3 pers. pl. masc. שפך	תִּתְחַנָּן Hithpa. fut. 2 pers. sing. masc. (§ 12. rem. 1) חנן
תִּשְׁתָּרֵר Hithpa. fut. 2 p. s. m. [for תִּתְשָׂרֵר § 12. r. 3] שרר	תִּתְחַנָּן ו id. fut. 3 pers. s. fem. (§ 12. r. 4); ו' conv. חנן
תֵּת Kal inf. constr. (suff. תִּתִּי) dec. 13 [for תֵּנְת=תֵּנֶת § 17. rem. 9, & § 44. rem. 1] נתן	תִּתְחַסָּד Hithpa. fut. 2 pers. sing. masc. (§ 12. rem. 1) חסד
	תִּתְחַקֶּה Hithpa. fut. 2 pers. sing. masc. חקה
	תִּתְחָר Hithpa. fut. 2 pers. sing. masc. ap. [from תִּתְחָרֶה § 24. rem. 12] חרה

a Ge. 21. 23.   g Le. 13. 55, 57.   p Ru. 4. 16.   t Job 30. 16.   b Is. 64. 11.   Ps. 18. 27.   Zec. 6. 7.   Nu. 15. 29.   Est. 4. 4.
Le. 19. 11.   Ps. 80. 10.   Ps. 42. 7.   La. 4. 1.   Job 30. 20.   De. 14. 1.   Is. 41. 16.   Ps. 103. 5.   Je. 31. 22.
Ju. 5. 1.   Job 31. 12.   2 Sa. 14. 4.   Nu. 16. 18.   Ps. 107. 27.   Mi. 4. 14.   Pr. 31. 30.   Nu. 31. 20.   Job 8. 5.
Is. 57. 9.   1 Ki. 1. 4.   Eze. 34. 19.   Ne. 8. 9.   Ezr. 4. 13, 21   Je. 49. 4.   Je. 47. 5.   Nu. 31. 19.   Est. 8. 3.
Ge. 38. 24.   Nu. 12. 11.   1 Sa. 1. 14.   Nu. 34. 7, 8.   Is. 43. 18.   De. 2. 5.   Job 38. 14.   Ec. 7. 16.   Job 13. 27.
Pr. 6. 27.   Da. 2. 44.   Is. 41. 10.   De. 5. 21.   2 Sa. 22. 27.   2 Sa. 22. 41.   De. 2. 9, 19.   Pr. 25. 6

תִּתְחֲרֶהֿ	Tiphal fut. 2 pers. sing. masc. (§ 6. No. 5) חרה
תִּתְחַחֵּן	Hithpa. fut. 2 pers. sing. masc. . חתן
תִּתִּי	Kal inf. (תֵּת § 17. rem. 9), suff. 1 pers. sing. dec. 13 (§ 44. rem. 1) נתן
תִּתְיְהִב	Chald. Ithpe. fut. 3 pers. sing. fem. . יהב
תַּתִּיכֵנִי	Hiph. fut. 2 pers. sing. masc., suff. 1 pers. sing. נתך
תִּתְיַמְּרוּ	Hithpa fut. 2 p. pl. m. [for תִּתְיַמְּרוּ § 12. r. 1] ימר
תִּתְיַפָּח	Hithpa. fut. 3 p. s. fem. [for תִּתְיַפַּח § 15. r. 1] יפח
תִּתְיַפִּי	Hithpa. fut. 2 pers. sing. fem. . יפה
תִּתְיַצֵּב	Hithpa. fut. 2 pers. sing. masc. יצב
תִּתֵּךְ	וֹ Kal fut. 3 pers. sing. fem.; וֹ conv. נתך
תִּתְּךָ	Kal inf. (תֵּת § 17. rem. 9), suff. 2 pers. sing. masc. dec. 13 (§ 44. rem. 1) נתן
תֻּתְּכוּ	Hoph. fut. 2 pers. pl. masc. נתך
תִּתְכַּם	וֹ Hithpa. fut. 3 pers. sing. fem. ap. [from תִּתְכַּסֶּה § 24. rem. 12]; וֹ conv. כסה
תִּתְלוֹצְצוּ	Hithpal. fut. 2 pers. pl. masc. [for תִּתְלוֹצְצוּ § 21. rem. 20] לוץ
תָּתֵם	Hiph. fut. 2 pers. s. m. [for תָּתֵם § 18. r. 14] תמם
תִּתֻּם	Kal inf. (תֵּת § 17. rem. 9), suff. 3 pers. pl. masc. dec. 13 (§ 44. rem. 1) נתן
תִּתֹּם / תָּתֹם	וֹ Kal fut. 3 pers. sing. fem. [for תָּתֹם § 18. rem. 14]; וֹ conv. תמם
תִּתְמַהּ	Kal fut. 2 pers. sing. masc. . תמה
תִּתְמוֹגָג	Hithpal. fut. 3 pers. sing. fem. (§ 21. rem. 20) מוג
תִּתְמוֹגַגְנָה	id. fut. 3 pers. pl. fem. מוג
תִּתְמֹד	Kal fut. 3 pers. sing. fem. תמד
תִּתְתַּמָּם	Hithpa. fut. 2 p. s. m. [for תִּתְתַּמָּם § 12. r. 1] תמם
תִּתִּי	Kh. תִּתֵּן for תִּנְתֵּן, inf. of a reduplicated form, K. תֵּן Kal inf. נתן
תִּתֵּן / תִּתֶּן	וֹ Kal fut. 3 pers. sing. masc., or 3 pers. sing. fem.; וֹ conv. נתן
תִּתְּנֶהָ	וֹ id. fut. 2 p. s. m., suff. 3 pers. s. fem.; וֹ id. נתן
תִּתְּנֶהוּ	וֹ id. fut. 2 pers. sing. masc., or 3 pers. sing. fem., suff. 3 pers. sing. masc.; וֹ id. נתן
תִּתְּנֻהָ	id. fut. 2 pers. pl. masc., suff. 3 sing. m. נתן
תִּתְּנוּהוּ	id. fut. 2 pers. sing. m., suff. 3 pers. sing. m. נתן
תִּתֵּנוּ	id. fut. 2 pers. pl. masc. (comp. § 8. r. 15) נתן
תִּתְנוֹדָד	Hithpal. fut. 2 pers. sing. masc. (§ 21. rem. 20) נוד
תִּתְּנוּם	Kal fut. 2 pers. pl. masc., suff. 3 pers. pl. m. נתן
תִּתְנַחֲלוּ / תִּתְנַחֲלוּ	Hithpa. fut. 2 pers. pl. masc. (§ 14. rem. 1, & § 12. rem. 1) נחל
תִּתְנַי	pr. name of a Persian noble, Ezr. 5. 3; 6. 6.
תִּתְּנִי	Kal fut. 2 pers. sing. fem. נתן

תִּתְּנֵם	וֹ id. id., suff. 3 pers. pl. masc.; וֹ conv. נתן
תִּתְּנֵם / תִּתֵּם	וֹ id. fut. 2 pers. sing. masc. (תִּתֵּן), suff. 3 pers. pl. masc.; וֹ id. . נתן
תִּתְּנֶנָּה	id. id., suff. 3 pers. sing. fem. נתן
תִּתְּנֶנּוּ	id. id., suff. 1 pers. pl. נתן
תִּתְּנֶנּוּ	id. id., suff. 3 pers. sing. masc. נתן
תִּתְּנֵנִי	id. id., suff. 1 pers. sing. נתן
תִּתְנַקֵּם	Hithpa. fut. 3 pers. sing. fem. נקם
תִּתְנַשֵּׂא	Hithpa. fut. 2 pers. sing. masc. . נשא
תִּתְנַשְּׂאוּ	id. fut. 2 pers. pl. masc. נשא
תֵּתַע	וֹ Kal fut. 2 pers. sing. masc., or 3 pers. sing. fem. ap. [fr. תִּתְעֶה § 24. rem. 3]; וֹ conv. תעה
תְּתַעֵב	Piel fut. 2 pers. sing. masc., or 3 pers. sing. fem. (§ 14. rem. 1) . תעב
תִּתְעַבְּדוּן	Chald. Ithpa. fut. 2 pers. pl. masc. עבד
תְּתַעֲבִי	וֹ Piel fut. 2 pers. s. fem. (§ 14. r. 1); וֹ conv. תעב
תְּתַעֲבֶנּוּ	id. fut. 2 pers. sing. m., suff. 3 pers. sing. m. תעב
תִּתְעַטֵּף / תִתְעַטֵּף	Hithpa. fut. 3 pers. sing. fem. (§ 12. rem. 1); וַתּ וֹ conv. עטף
תִּתְעַלֵּם / תִּתְעַלָּם	Hithpa. fut. 2 pers. sing. masc. (§ 12. r. 1) עלם
תִּתְעַלָּף	וֹ Hithpa. fut. 3 pers. s. f. (§ 12. r. 1); וֹ conv. עלף
תִּתְעַלַּפְנָה	id. fut. 3 pers. pl. fem. עלף
תַּתְעֵם	Hiph. fut. 3 pers. sing. fem. [תַּתְעֶה], suff. 3 pers. pl. masc. (§ 24. rem. 21) תעה
תִּתְעַמֵּר	Hithpa. fut. 2 pers. sing. masc. . עמר
תִּתְעַנֵּג / תִּתְעַנָּג	id. fut. 2 pers. sing. masc., or 3 pers. sing. fem. (§ 12. rem. 1) ענג
תִּתְעַנְּגוּ	id. fut. 2 pers. pl. masc. [for עַנְּגוּ] ענג
תַּתְעֵנוּ	Hiph. fut. 2 pers. sing. masc. [תַּתְעֶה], suff. 1 pers. pl. (§ 24. rem. 21) תעה
תִּתְעָרֵב	Hithpa. fut. 2 pers. sing. masc. (§ 12. r. 1) ערב
תִּתְעָרִי	וֹ Hithpa. fut. 2 pers. sing. fem. ערה
תִּתְעַרְעָר	Hithpalp. fut. 3 pers. sing. fem. (§ 6. No. 4) ערר
תִּתְפַּלִּי	by contr. and transp. for תִּתְפַּתֵּל Hithpa. fut. 2 pers. sing. masc. (§ 18. rem. 18) פתל
תִּתְפַּלָּא	Hithpa. fut. 2 pers. sing. masc. . פלא
תִּתְפַּלֵּל	וֹ Hithpa. fut. 2 pers. sing. masc., or 3 pers. sing. fem.; וֹ conv. פלל
תִּתְפַּעֵם	וֹ Hithpa. fut. 3 pers. sing. fem. (§ 12. rem. 4); וֹ id. פעם
תִּתָּפֵשׂ	וֹ Niph. fut. 2 pers. sing. masc., or (Je. 51. 41) 3 pers. sing. fem.; וֹ id. תפש
תְּתַפֵּשׂ	Piel fut. 3 pers. sing. fem. . תפש

a Je. 12. 5.   b Eze. 28. 6.   p Ec. 5. 7.   y Ju. 17. 4.   f Ne. 9. 24, 27, 30.   m Pr. 7. 25.   s Ps. 107. 5.   d De. 21. 14.   t Je. 51. 58.
c Ezr. 6. 4.   Eze. 22. 22.   q Ps. 107. 26.   z 2 Ki. 12. 8.   g De. 14. 21.   n Ps. 44. 12.   Ps. 77. 4; 143. 4.   e Job 22. 26.   u 2 Sa. 22. 27.
d Job 10. 10.   Ge. 24. 65.   r Am. 9. 13.   a Ex. 22. 29.   h Ps. 44. 12.   o De. 23. 8;   x Is. 52. 7.   f Is. 55. 2; 58. 14.   Da. 2. 1.
i Is. 61. 6.   Is. 28. 22.   Pr. 11. 16.   b 1 Ki. 17. 14.   Ps. 74. 14.   Ps. 107. 18.   Ps. 55. 2.   g Is. 57. 4.   Je. 51. 4.
k Je. 4. 31.   Job 22. 3.   c Jos. 10. 19.   Ps. 27. 12.   Da. 2. 5.   Ge. 38. 14.   h Is. 63. 17.   Pr. 30. 26.
l Je. 4. 30.   2 Ch. 25. 20.   d 2 Ch. 20. 7.   Nu. 33. 54.   Eze. 29. 15.   Eze. 16. 25.   Am. 8. 13.   La. 4. 21.
m Sa. 18. 13.   Eze. 24. 11.   Ps. 41. 3.   Eze. 16. 21.   Nu. 16. 3.   De. 7. 26.   Pr. 12. 26.

וְתִּתְפְּשֵׂהוּ	Kal fut. 3 p. s. f., suff. 3 p. s. m.; וְ conv.	תפש
תִּתָּפֵשׂוּ	Niph. fut. 2 pers. pl. masc. [for תִּתָּפֵשׂוּ, comp. § 8. rem. 15] .	תפש
תִּתְפַּתְּלִ	Hithp. fut. 2 pers. sing. masc. (§ 12. rem. 1)	פתל
וְתִּתְיַצֵּב	Hithpa. fut. 3 pers. sing. fem. (for תִּתְיַצֵּב § 20. rem. 13 and § 12 r. 1); וְ conv.	יצב
תִּתְּצוּ / וְ id.	Kal fut. 2 pers. pl. masc. (§ 8. r. 15);	נתץ
תִּתְּצוּן	id. with parag. ן [for תִּתְּצוּ § 8. rem. 17]	נתץ

וְ	Kal fut. 3 pers. sing. fem.; וְ conv. . .	תקע
תִּתְקְעוּ	id. fut. 2 pers. pl. masc. . . .	תקע
תִּתְקְפֵהוּ	Kal fut. 2 p. s. m., or 3 p. s. f., suff. 3 p. s. m.	תקף
וַתֹּתַר	Hiph. fut. 3 pers. sing. fem. ap. & conv. [for וַתֹּתֵר § 20. r. 9, comp. § 9. r. 3 & 4]	יתר
תִּתְרָאוּ	Hithpa. fut. 2 p. pl. m. [for תִּתְרָאוּ § 8. r. 15]	ראה
תִּתְרְמוּן	Ch. Ithpe. fut. 2 pers. pl. masc. R. רְמָא, see	רמה
תִּתְרָע [תִּתְרָעֶה]	Hithpa. fut. 2 pers. sing. m. ap. [fr. תִּתְרָעֶה]	רעה
וַתֻּתַּשׁ	Hoph. fut. 3 pers. sing. fem.; וְ conv.	נתש

a Ge. 39. 12.   c Ps. 18. 27   De. 7. 5.   f Nu. 10. 7.   h Ru. 2. 14.   i Ge. 42. 1.   k Da. 3. 15.   l Pr. 22. 24.   m Eze. 19. 12.
Eze. 21. 23.   d Ex. 2. 4.   Is. 22. 10.

Co. 54